# Standard & Poor's
# 500 Guide

# Standard & Poor's 500 Guide

### 2009 Edition

**Standard & Poor's**

New York   Chicago   San Francisco
Lisbon   London   Madrid   Mexico City
Milan   New Delhi   San Juan   Seoul
Singapore   Sydney   Toronto

**FOR STANDARD & POOR'S**
Managing Director, Equity Research Services: Robert Barriera
Publisher: Frank LoVaglio

*The McGraw-Hill Companies*

1 2 3 4 5 6 7 8 9 0    CUS/CUS    0 1 0 9

ISBN-    978-0-07-161515-0
MHID-    0-07-161515-6

This book is printed on acid-free paper.

This publication is designed to provide accurate and authoritative information in regard to the subject matter covered. It is sold with the understanding that the publisher is not engaged in rendering legal, accounting, or other professional service. If legal advice or other expert assistance is required, the services of a competent professional person should be sought.
—*From a declaration of principles jointly adopted by a committee of the American Bar Association and a committee of publishers*

The companies contained in this handbook represented the components of the S&P 500 Index as of November 17, 2008.
Additions to or deletions from the Index will cause its composition to change over time. Company additions and company deletions from the Standard & Poor's equity indexes do not in any way reflect an opinion on the investment merits of the company.

## ABOUT THE AUTHOR

Standard & Poor's, a division of The McGraw-Hill Companies, Inc., is the nation's leading securities information company. It provides a broad range of financial services, including the respected Standard & Poor's ratings and stock rankings, advisory services, data guides, and the most closely watched and widely reported gauges of stock market activity—the S&P 500, S&P MidCap 400, S&P SmallCap 600, and the S&P Composite 1500 stock price indexes. Standard & Poor's products are marketed around the world and used extensively by financial professionals and individual investors.

# Introduction

*by* David M. Blitzer, Ph. D.
      Managing Director & Chairman of the Index Committee
      Standard & Poor's

## The S&P 500

Any Web site, television news program, newspaper, or radio report covering the stock market gives the latest results of a handful of stock indices, including the Dow Industrials, the NASDAQ, and the S&P 500. The Dow is the oldest, extending back over 100 years, and has covered only 30 stocks since shortly before the crash of 1929. The NASDAQ came to fame in the tech boom but ignores all the companies listed on the New York Stock Exchange. The S&P 500 is the index used by market professionals and institutional investors when they need to know what the stock market is doing. While there are several thousand stocks traded in the U.S. market, the S&P 500 covers the most significant ones, representing some three-quarters of the total value of all U.S. equities. More than one trillion dollars invested through mutual funds, pensions, and exchange-traded funds track the S&P 500. These funds mimic what the index does—if the index rises, so do the funds. Further, when a stock is added to or dropped from the index, these trillions of dollars of funds buy, or sell, the stock. The S&P 500 is also the way the market and its condition is measured—for Wall Street, corporate earnings are the earnings per share calculated for the S&P 500, and the market's valuation is gauged by the price-earnings ratio on the S&P 500.

## The S&P 500 and You, the Investor

If you picked up this book, you are probably interested in the stock market or stocks you might invest in; you may be wondering why institutional investors and market professionals focus so much attention on the 500 or what you can learn from the index. So, what can the index do? It can:

- Give you a benchmark for investment performance
- Tell you what kinds of stocks performed well or poorly in the past
- Let you see if today's valuations are higher or lower than in the past
- Help you compare one company or industry to another

We will look at these in turn before describing what's inside the S&P 500 and how S&P maintains the index.

*Benchmarks*: Monitoring investment performance—keeping score—is what separates occasional stock pickers from serious investors. People who chat about stocks with fellow workers or around the backyard barbeque rarely maintain records beyond the minimum level required to file their taxes. For these investors, stocks that go up are good and stocks that go down are disappointing; there is no serious analysis of what makes stocks move. Serious investors, whether institutional investors or individuals committed to managing their investments, know that understanding whether your stock selections work out requires knowing what the market did and how your portfolio compares to the market. This is where an index benchmark is essential.

The first question most investors have about their success is whether they are beating the market. A rough and ready answer can be found by comparing your portfolio's results to the S&P 500. More in-depth answers would either include dividends as well as price changes or would adjust for investment risks, or both. All the necessary data are widely available for the S&P 500 as well as being included in some brokerage statements and most mutual fund reports.

*What went up and what went down*: Simply looking at whether the market—the index—gained or lost can tell you a lot about what happened to your portfolio. For most portfolios and most stocks, the largest factor in their movements is how the overall market did. The second largest factor is often how similar stocks—in the same economic sector or industry—behaved. Because the S&P 500 covers 75 percent of the total value of the U.S. equity market, it is a very good indication of what the market did. The stocks in the index are all classified into sectors and industries, so you can use these segments of the index to see if your stocks did better or worse than others in the same sector.

There are ten economic sectors that classify all the stocks in the S&P 500; the table following lists these sectors, the number of stocks in each, and the weight (based on market values) of each sector in the index. Simply watching how these sectors change and shift can tell you a lot about the market. Anyone who remembers the late 1990s won't be surprised to learn that the dominant sector was technology, which accounted for about one-third of the total market value of the index at its peak. In the bottom of the 2000–2002 bear market and in the rebound from 2002 to 2007, financials became the largest sector, though never by as much as technology had been. The credit crisis and recession of 2007–2009 (+?) has hit financials the hardest of all—their weight in the index has dropped from 22 percent at the end of 2006 to 13 percent as of November 30, 2008. One comment heard from time to time is that no sector holds the leadership in the S&P 500 forever, so be wary of anything that seems to overstay its welcome at the top of the list.

There are other classifications of stocks in the S&P 500. Not only are stocks assigned to an economic sector. They are also assigned to an industry group, an industry, and a subindustry, using a classification standard called GICS® or the Global Industry Classification Standard.[1] There are 10 sectors, about 25 industry groups, some 60 industries, and about 150 subindustries. Separately from GICS, stocks are classified as growth or value stocks. Traditionally, growth stocks are those with fast-growing earnings, which offer investors the promise of higher earnings in the future. Value stocks are stocks believed to offer unrecognized values that are not reflected in the stock price. The classification is based on a number of financial ratios and measures, including earnings growth, price/earnings ratios, dividend yields, and similar measures. Although most investors hunt for growth stocks, value stocks tend to perform better over the long run. During periods of a few years or less, either one can easily outperform the other. Investors aren't the only people seeking growth; few if any companies want to be known as value stocks, and all want to be called growth stocks.

*Market Valuations*: The past year proved that there are times when markets go down and down; those who remember the 1990s, or even the years 2003–2007, know that there are also times when the market goes up. We

---

[1]GICS® is maintained jointly by Standard & Poor's and MSCIBarra. Standard & Poor's is a division of the McGraw-Hill Companies, Inc.

would all like to know if stocks are really cheap and the market is likely to rise, or if stocks are overpriced and the market will tumble. So how can we tell if stocks cost too much or not enough?

Economics tells us that a stock's value lies in the future earnings and dividends. Two convenient measures of how stock prices compare to earnings and dividends are the ratio of the price to earnings (the P/E) and the dividend yield or percentage that the dividend is of the stock's price. Just as these are used for individual stocks, they are also used for the overall market by calculating these measures for the S&P 500. As of early December 2008, the figures for the index were a P/E of 13.3 and a dividend yield of 3 percent. These numbers change as the market rises or falls and as company earnings and dividends change. Up-to-date numbers are published by Standard & Poor's on the Web at www.indices.standardandpoors.com and by various newspapers, magazines, and financial and investing Web sites.

A P/E of 13.3 for the index is a bit lower than the average of the last 15 to 25 years. Broadly speaking, the P/E ranges from a low of about eight to a high in the low to mid thirties. Many investors see a P/E below average as a sign that stocks are undervalued and that there are buying opportunities. Earnings move up and down just as stock prices do, so both can affect the P/E ratio. Corporate earnings tend to fall in recessions and rise in good times, and these movements could distort P/E ratios. One idea to limit the distortion is compare prices to the average earnings over a long period, such as the last ten years. On this basis, the P/E is a bit less attractive than the simple one-year measure of 13.3.

Dividends have dropped out of fashion in the last two decades, and fewer investors seem to watch dividend yields. However, about 375 of the 500 stocks in the S&P 500 pay dividends, so the current dividend yield of 3 percent may tell us something about the market. Since the 1950s, the dividend yield on the S&P 500 has almost always been lower than the yield on U.S. treasury or high-grade corporate bonds. The bonds may be attractive for their safety, but they don't offer any opportunity for growth, although companies often raise their dividends as their earnings grow. As of late 2008, this pattern has changed; the dividend yield of 3 percent is higher than the yield on 10-year U.S. treasuries.

Both these measures may give some sense of whether the market is over or under prices. However, neither of these is even close to being a fail-safe guide to the stock market in any time period. Moreover, the wide price swings seen in 2007 and 2008 should remind all investors that the market constantly changes and evolves and must be approached with both care and respect.

*Comparing One Company to Another*: Suppose you neighbor or a coworker tells you about a stock you "have to own" because the P/E is only 10, a quarter less than the overall market. Is it a buy? Maybe, or maybe not. The index and its components can tell you a lot about the stocks in the index as well as about the market. Stocks in the same industry or industry group often rise and fall together because the economic events and factors that affect one stock in an industry will affect others as well. When oil prices rise, most oil company stocks tend to do well. Rumors of changes in Medicare and other health care programs may affect all pharmaceutical stocks at once. One can compare data about a stock to the same information for similar stocks, to the industry or economic sector, and to the whole market. The S&P 500 and information about the stocks in it make this possible.

How does this help decide if a stock is cheap? Suppose the market's P/E as measured by the S&P 500 is 14 and the stock's P/E is 18, so it looks to be overpriced. Before forgetting about it, compare the data on the stock—P/E ratios, dividend yields, or other statistics—to similar stocks. The easiest way to find similar stocks is to use the sector and industry classifications from the S&P 500, as shown on the stock reports. As you do this with various stocks, you will begin to see that some sectors or industries seem to always have P/E's higher than the market while other sectors have low P/Es. Some sectors focus on growth stocks, which have high P/Es, while others focus on value stocks. You will notice similar patterns if you compare dividend yields. In fact, even looking for stocks that pay dividends will reveal some patterns.

The stock market is shifting all the time, with some sectors becoming relatively more expensive and others fading from popularity. Within a sector there are similar movements among stocks as some move up faster while others may fade. It is useful to know how a stock compares to its peers in the same industry or sector as well as to understand how it compares to the entire market. Using the S&P 500 and the data shown on the stock reports, one can see these shifts and comparisons.

## What's in the S&P 500

The S&P 500 Index consists of 500 stocks selected by Standard & Poor's to represent the U.S. stock market and, through the market, the U.S. economy. It is not the 500 "largest" stocks in the market. Rather, it is sometimes described as containing the leading stocks in leading industries. The stocks are selected based on published guidelines; all members of the S&P 500 must be U.S. companies. When they join the index, they must have market values of at least $3 billion, trade with reasonable liquidity, be profitable, and have at least half their shares available to investors. The selection of companies also considers the balance of economic sectors in the market and the index so that the index is a fair representation of the market as a whole.

The S&P 500 index is reported on television, Web sites and newspapers very widely. Data are also published on the S&P Web site at www.indices.standardandpoors.com. Many investors and investment analysts use the S&P 500 to help choose stocks, as described above. However it has many other investment uses: index mutual funds, exchange-traded funds (ETFs), futures, and options. Index mutual funds are mutual funds that track an index. The first funds, and the largest index funds today, track the S&P 500. Exchange-traded funds have grown in popularity in recent years. These are similar to index mutual funds except that they trade on an exchange and can by bought and sold at any time of day whereas mutual funds are only sold at prices based on the market close. The first U.S. ETF was based on the S&P 500; there are two large ETFs based on the S&P 500. In addition, numerous pension funds, endowments, and other institutional investments track the S&P 500. As of the end of 2007, over $1.5 trillion was invested in various investments that track the S&P 500 as closely as possible. This means that the fund tries to mimic the index, adding stocks when they are added to the index and matching any other adjustments in the index.

There are relatively few changes in the index; most of these changes are caused by mergers, acquisitions, and other corporate actions that remove companies from the index. Over the last several years, the index has seen about 30 changes each year where a "change" is one company added and one dropped. If one thinks of the index as a portfolio, it is amazingly stable compared to most mutual funds—the turnover in the S&P 500 is about 5 to 10 percent of its value each year, whereas mutual funds can see a turnover of over 100 percent in a single year. A typical change in the index occurs when a company is acquired and is dropped from the index and replaced with another company. At times, especially recently with the turmoil in the markets, companies in the index are removed because of bankruptcy.

While changes to the index don't occur every day, they can be important to some traders. Because so much money tracks the index, about 10 percent of the outstanding stock of any company in the index is bought by index funds, ETFs, and other index investors when a stock is added to the index. Further, this buying occurs over a relatively short period of time—a few weeks or less. The result is that stocks added to the S&P 500 often see their prices rise when they go into the index.

The S&P 500 index was created and is maintained by S&P. There is an Index Committee of S&P professional staff who oversee the index and are responsible for making necessary changes to assure that the index will be an accurate reflection of the U.S. equity markets. Because changes in the index can move the market, all the work done by the Index Committee is confidential until any changes to the index are announced. Moreover, because the changes can move the market, the announcements are made available to the public, and no one gets any advance notice before the public announcements on S&P's Web site.

Beyond various kinds of index funds and ETFs, there are other investment uses of the index—futures and options. These are derivatives based on the value of the index that offer investors—mostly institutional investors, but some individuals as well—opportunities to either hedge their positions or to easily establish a leveraged position in the index. Futures and options are usually seen as more complex and often riskier than buying stocks. Just as successful stock investing requires research and understanding, successful use of futures and options demands a solid understanding of how the instruments work and what the risks are. At times these can magnify the impact of shifts in the index. Furthermore, unlike stocks, futures and options have firm expiration dates that must be considered in any investment plan.

## History

The S&P 500 celebrated its fiftieth anniversary in March 2007. However, its forebears go farther back. The S&P 500 is not the oldest index, an honor which goes to the Dow Jones Industrials. The 500 traces its lineage back to an index of 233 companies published weekly by The Standard Statistics Company beginning in 1923. That index was one of the first to have industry classifications to support investment analysis. In 1926 Standard Statistics began a daily index of 90 stocks. A decade and a half later, in 1941, Standard Statistics merged with Poor's Publishing to form S&P. In 1957 the indices were combined and gave us the S&P 500. A small number of companies in the current S&P 500 can trace their membership back to the

1920s, over 50 were members in 1957.

The index has seen various changes over the years as it kept up with the times and with developments in the market. Different industries have come and gone. Some of today's leading sectors were barely present or nonexistent in 1957. Technology is now a much bigger part of the index. Investment banks and brokerage houses were all private partnerships in 1957 and didn't begin to enter the index until the 1970s. In many ways the index's history is the history of the U.S. stock market.

Many investors, especially those who consider mutual funds, have seen data on the history of the U.S. stock market since 1926. That history is the S&P 500 and the 90 stock index that preceded the 500. Mutual funds and other investment products often compare their performance to the market; the market is the S&P 500. You might think that 500 stocks chosen simply to represent the market without any attempt to select "good" stocks that will beat the market might be an easy target to outperform. Actually, it is not; in fact, it is very difficult to consistently outperform the S&P 500 or most other broad-based indices. Research by Standard & Poor's and by various others shows that in a typical period of three or more years, fewer than one-third of mutual funds outperform the index. Further, a fund that managed to be in the lucky third that beat the index in the last three years has only a one-in-three chance of beating the index in the next three years. Why? First, index funds and ETFs are cheap, with very low expenses. Second, since it is very hard to know which stocks will go up first, it helps to own a lot of stocks.[2]

Today Standard & Poor's publishes literally hundreds of thousands of indices, each covering over 80 stock markets in almost every country where there is a stock market. The largest indices have several times more stocks than the 500, including a global equity index with over 11,000 securities. At the other extreme there are narrow indices focused on a small subindustry in one country. All these indices are used by investors, often in the same way the 500 can be used, as described here.

## In Conclusion

When you want to know how the market did, what went up or down, or whether your stock picks beat the market, the best place to look is the S&P 500.

### S&P 500 Global Industry Classification Standard (GICS) Sectors

*As of November 28, 2008*

| | Number of Cos. | % of Market Capitalization |
|---|---|---|
| Consumer Discretionary | 81 | 8.0 % |
| Consumer Staples | 41 | 13.1 % |
| Energy | 40 | 14.3 % |
| Financials | 84 | 13.4 % |
| Health Care | 55 | 14.0 % |
| Industrials | 57 | 11.0 % |
| Information Technology | 73 | 15.1 % |
| Materials | 28 | 3.0 % |
| Telecommunication Services | 9 | 3.8 % |
| Utilities | 32 | 4.2 % |

[2] On index results vs. mutual funds, see S&P's SPIVA reports on S&P's Web site or books by John Bogle or Burton Malkiel.

## What You'll Find in This Book

In the pages that follow you will find an array of text and statistical data on 500 different companies spanning 154 sub-industries. This information, dealing with everything from the nature of these companies' basic businesses, recent corporate developments, current outlooks, and select financial information relating to revenues, earnings, dividends, margins, capitalization, and so forth, might initially seem overwhelming. However, it's not that difficult. Just take a few moments to familiarize yourself with what you'll find on these pages.

Following is a glossary of terms and definitions used throughout this book. Please refer to this section as you encounter terms which need further clarification.

### Glossary

**S&P STARS** -Since January 1, 1987, Standard & Poor's Equity Research Services has ranked a universe of common stocks based on a given stock's potential for future performance. Under proprietary STARS (STock Appreciation Ranking System), S&P equity analysts rank stocks according to their individual forecast of a stock's future total return potential versus the expected total return of a relevant benchmark (e.g., a regional index (S&P Asia 50 Index, S&P Europe 350 Index or S&P 500 Index)), based on a 12-month time horizon. STARS was designed to meet the needs of investors looking to put their investment decisions in perspective.

**S&P 12-Month Target Price** -The S&P equity analyst's projection of the market price a given security will command 12 months hence, based on a combination of intrinsic, relative, and private market valuation metrics.

**Investment Style Classification** - Characterizes the stock as either a growth- or value-oriented investment, and, indicates the market value (size) of the company as large-cap, mid-cap or small-cap. Growth stocks typically have a higher price-to-earnings and price-to-cash flow ratio, that represents the premium that is being paid for the expected higher growth. Value stocks typically have higher dividends and more moderate price-to-earnings ratios consistent with their current return policies.

**Qualitative Risk Assessment** - The S&P equity analyst's view of a given company's operational risk, or the risk of a firm's ability to continue as an ongoing concern. The Qualitative Risk Assessment is a relative ranking to the S&P U.S. STARS universe, and should be reflective of risk factors related to a company's operations, as opposed to risk and volatility measures associated with share prices.

**Quantitative Evaluations** - In contrast to our qualitative STARS recommendations, which are assigned by S&P analysts, the quantitative evaluations described below are derived from proprietary arithmetic models. These computer-driven evaluations may at times contradict an analyst's qualitative assessment of a stock. One primary reason for this is that different measures are used to determine each. For instance, when designating STARS, S&P analysts assess many factors that cannot be reflected in a model, such as risks and opportunities, management changes, recent competitive shifts, patent expiration, litigation risk, etc.

**S&P Quality Rankings** (also known as **S&P Earnings & Dividend Rankings**) - Growth and stability of earnings and dividends are deemed key elements in establishing S&P's Quality Rankings for common stocks, which are designed to capsulize the nature of this record in a single symbol. It should be noted, however, that the process also takes into consideration certain adjustments and modifications deemed desirable in establishing such rankings. The final score for each stock is measured against a scoring matrix determined by analysis of the scores of a large and representative sample of stocks. The range of scores in the array of this sample has been aligned with the following ladder of rankings:

| A+ | Highest       | B-  | Lower             |
|----|---------------|-----|-------------------|
| A  | High          | C   | Lowest            |
| A- | Above Average | D   | In Reorganization |
| B+ | Average       | NR  | Not Ranked        |
| B  | Below Average |     |                   |

**S&P Fair Value Rank** - Using S&P's exclusive proprietary quantitative model, stocks are ranked in one of five groups, ranging from Group 5, listing the most undervalued stocks, to Group 1, the most overvalued issues. Group 5 stocks are expected to generally outperform all others. A positive (+) or negative (-) Timing Index is placed next to the Fair Value ranking to further aid the selection process. A stock with a (+) added to the Fair Value Rank simply means that this stock has a somewhat better chance to outperform other stocks with the same Fair Value Rank. A stock with a (-) has a somewhat lesser chance to outperform other stocks with the same Fair Value Rank. The Fair Value rankings imply the following: 5-Stock is significantly undervalued; 4-Stock is moderately undervalued; 3-Stock is fairly valued; 2-Stock is modestly overvalued; 1-Stock is significantly overvalued.

**S&P Fair Value Calculation** - The price at which a stock should trade at, according to S&P's proprietary quantitative model that incorporates both actual and estimated variables (as opposed to only actual variables in the case of S&P Quality Ranking). Relying heavily on a company's actual return on equity, the S&P Fair Value model places a value on a security based on placing a formula-derived price-to-book multiple on a company's consensus earnings per share estimate.

**Insider Activity** - Gives an insight as to insider sentiment by showing whether directors, officers and key employees who have proprietary information not available to the general public, are buying or selling the company's stock during the most recent six months.

**Investability Quotient (IQ)** - The IQ is a measure of investment desirability. It serves as an indicator of potential medium-to-long term return and as a caution against downside risk. The measure takes into account variables such as technical indicators, earnings estimates, liquidity, financial ratios and selected S&P proprietary measures.

**Volatility** - Rates the volatility of the stock's price over the past year.

**Technical Evaluation** - In researching the past market history of prices and trading volume for each company, S&P's computer models apply special technical methods and formulas to identify and project price trends for the stock.

**Relative Strength Rank** - Shows, on a scale of 1 to 99, how the stock has performed versus all other companies in S&P's universe on a rolling 13-week basis.

**Global Industry Classification Standard (GICS)** - An industry classification standard, developed by Standard & Poor's in collaboration with Morgan Stanley Capital International (MSCI). GICS is currently comprised of 10 Sectors, 24 Industry Groups, 68 Industries, and 154 Sub-Industries.

**S&P Core Earnings** - Standard & Poor's Core Earnings is a uniform methodology for adjusting operating earnings by focusing on a company's after-tax earnings generated from its principal businesses. Included in the Standard & Poor's definition are employee stock option grant expenses, pension costs, restructuring charges from ongoing operations, write-downs of depreciable or amortizable operating assets, purchased research and development, M&A related expenses and unrealized gains/losses from hedging activities. Excluded from the definition are pension gains, impairment of goodwill charges, gains or losses from asset sales, reversal of prior-year charges and provision from litigation or insurance settlements.

**S&P Issuer Credit Rating** - A Standard & Poor's Issuer Credit Rating is a current opinion of an obligor's overall financial capacity (its creditworthiness) to pay its financial obligations. This opinion focuses on the obligor's capacity and willingness to meet its financial commitments as they come due. It does not apply to any specific financial obligation, as it does not take into account the nature of and provisions of the obligation, its standing in bankruptcy or liquidation, statutory preferences, or the legality and enforceability of the obligation. In addition, it does not take into account the creditworthiness of the guarantors, insurers, or other forms of credit enhancement on the obligation. The Issuer Credit Rating is not a recommendation to purchase, sell, or hold a financial obligation issued by an obligor, as it does not comment on market price or suitability for a particular investor. Issuer Credit Ratings are based on current information furnished by obligors or obtained by Standard & Poor's from other sources it considers reliable. Standard & Poor's does not perform an audit in connection with any Issuer Credit Rating and may, on occasion, rely on unaudited financial information. Issuer Credit Ratings may be changed, suspended, or withdrawn as a result of changes in, or unavailability of, such information, or based on other circumstances.

Standard & Poor's Equity Research Services – Standard & Poor's Equity Research Services U.S. includes Standard & Poor's Investment Advisory Services LLC; Standard & Poor's Equity Research Services Europe includes Standard & Poor's LLC- London; Standard & Poor's Equity Research Services Asia includes Standard & Poor's LLC's offices in Hong Kong and Singapore, Standard & Poor's Malaysia Sdn Bhd, and Standard & Poor's Information Services (Australia) Pty Ltd.

<u>**Abbreviations Used in S&P Equity Research Reports**</u>
CAGR- Compound Annual Growth Rate
CAPEX- Capital Expenditures
CY- Calendar Year
DCF- Discounted Cash Flow
EBIT- Earnings Before Interest and Taxes
EBITDA- Earnings Before Interest, Taxes, Depreciation and Amortization
EPS- Earnings Per Share
EV- Enterprise Value
FCF- Free Cash Flow
FFO- Funds From Operations
FY- Fiscal Year
P/E- Price/Earnings
PEG Ratio- P/E-to-Growth Ratio
PV- Present Value
R&D- Research & Development
ROE- Return on Equity
ROI- Return on Investment
ROIC- Return on Invested Capital
ROA- Return on Assets
SG&A- Selling, General & Administrative Expenses
WACC- Weighted Average Cost of Capital

Dividends on American Depository Receipts (ADRs) and American Depository Shares (ADSs) are net of taxes (paid in the country of origin).

## REQUIRED DISCLOSURES

### S&P Global STARS Distribution

**In North America**
As of December 31, 2008, research analysts at Standard & Poor's Equity Research Services North America recommended 27.0% of issuers with buy recommendations, 61.2% with hold recommendations and 11.8% with sell recommendations.

**In Europe**
As of December 31, 2008, research analysts at Standard & Poor's Equity Research Services Europe recommended 30.4% of issuers with buy recommendations, 45.3% with hold recommendations and 24.3% with sell recommendations.

**In Asia**
As of December 31, 2008, research analysts at Standard & Poor's Equity Research Services Asia recommended 33.9% of issuers with buy recommendations, 54.4% with hold recommendations and 11.7% with sell recommendations.

Globally

As of September 30, 2008, research analysts at Standard & Poor's Equity Research Services globally recommended 28.1% of issuers with buy recommendations, 58.3% with hold recommendations and 13.6% with sell recommendations.

5-STARS (Strong Buy): Total return is expected to outperform the total return of a relevant benchmark, by a wide margin over the coming 12 months, with shares rising in price on an absolute basis.

4-STARS (Buy): Total return is expected to outperform the total return of a relevant benchmark over the coming 12 months, with shares rising in price on an absolute basis.

3-STARS (Hold): Total return is expected to closely approximate the total return of a relevant benchmark over the coming 12 months, with shares generally rising in price on an absolute basis.

2-STARS (Sell): Total return is expected to underperform the total return of a relevant benchmark over the coming 12 months, and the share price not anticipated to show a gain.

1-STAR (Strong Sell): Total return is expected to underperform the total return of a relevant benchmark by a wide margin over the coming 12 months, with shares falling in price on an absolute basis.

Relevant benchmarks: In the North America, the relevant benchmark is the S&P 500 Index, in Europe and in Asia, the relevant benchmarks are generally the S&P Europe 350 Index and the S&P Asia 50 Index.

For All Regions:

All of the views expressed in this research report accurately reflect the research analyst's personal views regarding any and all of the subject securities or issuers. No part of analyst compensation was, is, or will be directly or indirectly, related to the specific recommendations or views expressed in this research report.

Additional information is available upon request.
Other Disclosures

This report has been prepared and issued by Standard & Poor's and/or one of its affiliates. In the United States, research reports are prepared by Standard & Poor's Investment Advisory Services LLC ("SPIAS"). In the United States, research reports are issued by Standard & Poor's ("S&P"); in the United Kingdom by Standard & Poor's LLC ("S&P LLC"), which is authorized and regulated by the Financial Services Authority; in Hong Kong by Standard & Poor's LLC, which is regulated by the Hong Kong Securities Futures Commission; in Singapore by Standard & Poor's LLC, which is regulated by the Monetary Authority of Singapore; in Malaysia by Standard & Poor's Malaysia Sdn Bhd ("S&PM"), which is regulated by the Securities

Commission; in Australia by Standard & Poor's Information Services (Australia) Pty Ltd ("SPIS"), which is regulated by the Australian Securities & Investments Commission; and in Korea by SPIAS, which is also registered in Korea as a cross-border investment advisory company.

The research and analytical services performed by SPIAS, S&P LLC, S&PM, and SPIS are each conducted separately from any other analytical activity of Standard & Poor's.

Standard & Poor's or an affiliate may license certain intellectual property or provide pricing or other services to, or otherwise have a financial interest in, certain issuers of securities, including exchange-traded investments whose investment objective is to substantially replicate the returns of a proprietary Standard & Poor's index, such as the S&P 500. In cases where Standard & Poor's or an affiliate is paid fees that are tied to the amount of assets that are invested in the fund or the volume of trading activity in the fund, investment in the fund will generally result in Standard & Poor's or an affiliate earning compensation in addition to the subscription fees or other compensation for services rendered by Standard & Poor's. A reference to a particular investment or security by Standard & Poor's and/or one of its affiliates is not a recommendation to buy, sell, or hold such investment or security, nor is it considered to be investment advice.

Standard & Poor's and its affiliates provide a wide range of services to, or relating to, many organizations, including issuers of securities, investment advisers, broker-dealers, investment banks, other financial institutions and financial intermediaries, and accordingly may receive fees or other economic benefits from those organizations, including organizations whose securities or services they may recommend, rate, include in model portfolios, evaluate or otherwise address.

For a list of companies mentioned in this report with whom Standard & Poor's and/or one of its affiliates has had business relationships within the past year, please go to:
http://www2.standardandpoors.com/portal/site/sp/en/us/page.article/2,5,1,0,1145719622102.html

Disclaimers

This material is based upon information that we consider to be reliable, but neither S&P nor its affiliates warrant its completeness, accuracy or adequacy and it should not be relied upon as such. With respect to reports issued to clients in Japan and in the case of inconsistencies between the English and Japanese version of a report, the English version prevails. Neither S&P nor its affiliates guarantee the accuracy of the translation. Assumptions, opinions and estimates constitute our judgment as of the date of this material and are subject to change without notice. Neither S&P nor its affiliates are responsible for any errors or omissions or for results obtained from the use of this information. Past performance is not necessarily indicative of future results.

This material is not intended as an offer or solicitation for the purchase or sale of any security or other financial instrument. Securities, financial instruments or strategies mentioned herein may not be suitable for all investors. Any opinions expressed herein are given in good faith, are subject to change without notice, and are only correct as of the stated date of their issue. Prices, values, or income from any securities or investments mentioned in this report may fall against the interests of the investor and the investor may get back less than the amount invested. Where an investment is described as being likely to yield income, please note that the amount of income that the investor will receive from such an investment may fluctuate. Where an investment or security is denominated in a different currency to the investor's currency of reference, changes in rates of exchange may have an adverse effect on the value, price or income of or from that investment to the investor. The information contained in this report does not constitute advice on the tax consequences of making any particular investment decision. This material is not intended for any specific investor and does not take into account your particular investment objectives, financial situations or needs and is not intended as a recommendation of particular securities, financial instruments or strategies to you. Before acting on any recommendation in this material, you should consider whether it is suitable for your particular circumstances and, if necessary, seek professional advice.

For residents of the U.K. –this report is only directed at and should only be relied on by persons outside of the United Kingdom or persons who are inside the United Kingdom and who have professional experience in matters relating to investments or who are high net worth persons, as defined in Article 19(5) or Article 49(2) (a) to (d) of the Financial Services and Markets Act 2000 (Financial Promotion) Order 2005, respectively.

For residents of Singapore, anything herein that may be construed as a recommendation is intended for general circulation and does not take into account the specific investment objectives, financial situation or particular needs of any particular person. Advice should be sought from a financial adviser regarding the suitability of an investment, taking into account the specific investment objectives, financial situation or particular needs of any person in receipt of the recommendation, before the person makes a commitment to purchase the investment product.

For residents of Malaysia, all queries in relation to this report should be referred to Alexander Chia, Desmond Ch'ng, or Ching Wah Tam.

This investment analysis was prepared from the following sources: S&P MarketScope, S&P Compustat, S&P Industry Reports, I/B/E/S International, Inc.; Standard & Poor's, 55 Water St., New York, NY 10041.

*Key Stock Statistics*

**Market Cap.**—The stock price multiplied by number of shares outstanding, based on market value calculated at the issue level.

**Institutional Holdings**—Shows the percent of total common shares held by financial institutions. This information covers some 2,500 institutions and is compiled by Vickers Stock Research Corporation, 226 New York Avenue, Huntington, N.Y. 11743

**Value of $10,000 Invested 5 years ago**—The value today of a $10,000 investment in the stock made 5 years ago, assuming year-end reinvestment of dividends.

**Beta**—The beta coefficient is a measure of the volatility of a stock's price relative to the S&P 500 Index (a proxy for the overall market). An issue with a beta of 1.5 for example, tends to move 50% more than the overall market, in the same direction. An issue with a beta of 0.5 tends to move 50% less. If a stock moved exactly as the market moved, it would have a beta of 1.0. A stock with a negative beta tends to move in a direction opposite to that of the overall market.

### Per Share Data ($) Tables

**Cash Flow**—Net income plus depreciation, depletion, and amortization, divided by shares used to calculate earnings per common share. (See also: "Cash Flow" under Industrial Companies.)

**Earnings**—The amount a company reports as having been earned for the year on its common stock based on generally accepted accounting standards. Earnings per share are presented on a "diluted" basis pursuant to FASB 128, which became effective December 15, 1997, and are generally reported from continuing operations, before extraordinary items. This reflects a change from previously reported *primary earnings per share*. Insurance companies report *operating earnings* before gains/losses on security transactions and *earnings* after such transactions.

**Dividends**—Generally total cash payments per share based on the ex-dividend dates over a 12-month period. May also be reported on a declared basis where this has been established to be a company's payout policy.

**Net Asset Value**—Appears on investment company reports and reflects the market value of stocks, bonds, and net cash divided by outstanding shares. The % difference indicates the percentage premium or discount of the market price over the net asset value.

**Payout Ratio**—Indicates the percentage of earnings paid out in dividends. It is calculated by dividing the annual dividend by the earnings. For insurance companies, *earnings* after gains/losses on security transactions are used.

**P/E Ratio High/Low**—The ratio of market price to earnings—essentially indicates the valuation investors place on a company's earnings. Obtained by dividing the annual earnings into the high and low market price for the year. For insurance companies, *operating earnings* before gains/losses on security transactions are used.

**Portfolio Turnover**—Appears on investment company reports and indicates percentage of total security purchases and sales for the year to overall investment assets. Primarily mirrors trading aggressiveness.

**Prices High/Low**—Shows the calendar year high and low of a stock's market price.

**Tangible Book Value; Book Value** (See also: "Common Equity" under Industrial Companies)—Indicates the theoretical dollar amount per common share one might expect to receive from a company's tangible "book" assets should liquidation take place. Generally, book value is determined by adding the stated value of the common stock, paid-in capital and retained earnings and then subtracting intangible assets (excess cost over equity of acquired companies, goodwill, and patents), preferred stock at liquidating value and unamortized debt discount. Divide that amount by the outstanding shares to get book value per common share.

## Income/Balance Sheet Data Tables

*Banks*

**Cash**—Mainly vault cash, interest-bearing deposits placed with banks, reserves required by the Federal Reserve, and items in the process of collection—generally referred to as float.

**Commercial Loans**—Commercial, industrial, financial, agricultural loans and leases, gross.

**Common Equity**—Includes common/capital surplus, undivided profits, reserve for contingencies and other capital reserves.

**Deposits**—Primarily classified as either *demand* (payable at any time upon demand of depositor) or *time* (not payable within 30 days).

**Deposits/Capital Funds**—Average deposits divided by average capital funds. Capital funds include capital notes/debentures, other long-term debt, capital stock, surplus, and undivided profits. May be used as a "leverage" measure.

**Earning Assets**—Assets on which interest is earned.

**Effective Tax Rate**—Actual income tax expense divided by net before taxes.

**Gains/Losses on Securities Transactions**—Realized losses on sales of securities, usually bonds.

**Government Securities**—Includes United States Treasury securities and securities of other U.S. government agencies at book or carrying value. A bank's major "liquid asset."

**Investment Securities**—Federal, state, and local government bonds and other securities.

**Loan Loss Provision**—Amount charged to operating expenses to provide an adequate reserve to cover anticipated losses in the loan portfolio.

**Loans**—All domestic and foreign loans (excluding leases), less unearned discount and reserve for possible losses. Generally considered a bank's principal asset.

**Long-Term Debt**—Total borrowings for terms beyond one year including notes payable, mortgages, debentures, term loans, and capitalized lease obligations.

**Money Market Assets**—Interest-bearing interbank deposits, federal funds sold, trading account securities.

**Net Before Taxes**—Amount remaining after operating expenses are deducted from income, including gains or losses on security transactions.

**Net Income**—The final profit before dividends (common/preferred) from all sources after deduction of expenses, taxes, and fixed charges, but before any discontinued operations or extraordinary items.

**Net Interest Income**—Interest and dividend income, minus interest expense.

**Net Interest Margin**—A percentage computed by dividing net interest income, on a taxable equivalent basis, by average earning assets. Used as an analytical tool to measure profit margins from providing credit services.

**Noninterest Income**—Service fees, trading, and other income, excluding gains/losses on securities transactions.

**Other Loans**—Gross consumer, real estate and foreign loans.

**% Equity to Assets**—Average common equity divided by average total assets. Used as a measure of capital adequacy.

**% Equity to Loans**—Average common equity divided by average loans. Reflects the degree of equity coverage to loans outstanding.

**% Expenses/Op. Revenues**—Noninterest expense as a percentage of taxable equivalent net interest income plus noninterest income (before securities gains/losses). A measure of cost control.

**% Loan Loss Reserve**—Contra-account to loan assets, built through provisions for loan losses, which serves as a cushion for possible future loan charge-offs.

**% Loans/Deposits**—Proportion of loans funded by deposits. A measure of liquidity and an indication of bank's ability to write more loans.

**% Return on Assets**—Net income divided by average total assets. An analytical measure of asset-use efficiency and industry comparison.

**% Return on Equity**—Net income (minus preferred dividend requirements) divided by average common equity. Generally used to measure performance.

**% Return on Revenues**—Net income divided by gross revenues.

**State and Municipal Securities**—State and municipal securities owned at book value.

**Taxable Equivalent Adjustment**—Increase to render income from tax-exempt loans and securities comparable to fully taxed income.

**Total Assets**—Includes interest-earning financial instruments—principally commercial, real estate, consumer loans and leases; investment securities/trading accounts; cash/money market investments; other owned assets.

*Industrial Companies*

*Following data is based on Form 10K Annual Report data as filed with SEC.*

**Capital Expenditures**—The sum of additions at cost to property, plant and equipment, and leaseholds, generally excluding amounts arising from acquisitions.

**Cash**—Includes all cash and government and other marketable securities.

**Cash Flow**—Net income (before extraordinary items and discontinued operations, and after preferred dividends) plus depreciation, depletion, and amortization.

**Common Equity** [See also "Tangible Book Value" under Per Share Data($) Tables]—Common stock plus capital surplus and retained earnings, less any difference between the carrying value and liquidating value of preferred stock.

**Current Assets**—Those assets expected to be realized in cash or used up in the production of revenue within one year.

**Current Liabilities**—Generally includes all debts/obligations falling due within one year.

**Current Ratio**—Current assets divided by current liabilities. A measure of liquidity.

**Depreciation**—Includes noncash charges for obsolescence, wear on property, current portion of capitalized expenses (intangibles), and depletion charges.

**Effective Tax Rate**—Actual income tax charges divided by net before taxes.

**Interest Expense**—Includes all interest expense on short/long-term debt, amortization of debt discount/premium, and deferred expenses (e.g., financing costs).

**Long-Term Debt**—Debts/obligations due after one year. Includes bonds, notes payable, mortgages, lease obligations, and industrial revenue bonds. Other long-term debt, when reported as a separate account, is excluded. This account generally includes pension and retirement benefits.

**Net Before Taxes**—Includes operating and nonoperating revenues (including extraordinary items not net of taxes), less all operating and nonoperating expenses, except income taxes and minority interest, but including equity in nonconsolidated subsidiaries.

**Net Income**—Profits derived from all sources after deduction of expenses, taxes, and fixed charges, but before any discontinued operations, extraordinary items, and dividends (preferred/common).

**Operating Income**—Net sales and operating revenues less cost of goods sold and operating expenses (including research and development, profit sharing, exploration and bad debt, but excluding depreciation and amortization).

**% Long-Term Debt of Invested Capital**—Long-term debt divided by total invested capital. Indicates how highly "leveraged" a business might be.

**% Operating Income of Revenues**—Net sales and operating revenues divided into operating income. Used as a measure of operating profitability.

**% Net Income of Revenues**—Net income divided by sales/operating revenues.

**% Return on Assets**—Net income divided by average total assets on a per common share basis. Used in industry analysis and as a measure of asset-use efficiency.

**% Return on Equity**—Net income less preferred dividend requirements divided by average common shareholders' equity on a per common share basis. Generally used to measure performance and industry comparisons.

**Revenues**—Net sales and other operating revenues. Includes franchise/leased department income for retailers, and royalties for publishers and oil and mining companies. Excludes excise taxes for tobacco, liquor, and oil companies.

**Total Assets**—Current assets plus net plant and other noncurrent assets (intangibles and deferred items).

**Total Invested Capital**—The sum of stockholders' equity plus long-term debt, capital lease obligations, deferred income taxes, investment credits, and minority interest.

*Insurance Companies*

**Life Insurance In Force**—The total value of all life insurance policies including ordinary, group, industrial and credit. Generally the figure is reported before any amounts ceded, or the portions placed with other insurance companies.

**Premium Income**—The amount of premiums earned during the year is generally equal to the net premiums written plus any increase or decrease in earned premiums. The categories are divided into Life, Accident & Health, Annuity and Property & Casualty.

**Net Investment Income**—Income received from investment assets (before taxes) including bonds, stocks, loans and other investments (less related expenses).

**Total Revenues**—Includes premium income, net investment income and other income.

**Property & Casualty Underwriting Ratios**— Includes: Loss Ratio—losses and loss adjustment expenses divided by premiums earned; Expense Ratio—underwriting expenses divided by net premiums written; Combined Loss-Expense Ratio—Measures claims losses and operating expenses against premiums. The total of losses and loss expenses, before policyholders' dividends, to premiums earned. e.g. At 106.0%, equivalent to a loss of six cents of every premium dollar before investment income and taxes.

**Net Before Taxes**—Total operating income before income taxes and security gains or losses. Generally will include any equity in income of subsidiaries.

**Net Operating Income**—Includes income from operations, before security gains or losses, and before results of discontinued operations and special items.

**Net Income**—Includes income from operations, after security gains or losses, and before results of discontinued operations and special items.

**% Return On Revenues**—Is the net operating income divided by the total revenues.

**% Return On Assets**—Is the net operating income divided by the mean/average assets.

**% Return On Equity**—Is obtained by dividing the average common equity for the year into the net operating income, less any preferred stock dividend requirements.

**Cash & Equivalent**—Includes cash, accrued investment income and short term investments (except when classified as investments by the company).

**Premiums Due**—Generally includes premiums owed but uncollected, agent's balances receivable and earned and unbilled premiums receivable.

**Investment Assets**—Includes all investments shown under the company's investment account. Bonds, values at cost, includes bonds and notes, debt obligations and any short-term investments. Stocks, values at market, includes common and preferred stocks in the investment portfolio. Loans, includes mortgage, policy and other loans.

**% Investment Yield**—Is the return received on the company's investment assets, and is obtained by dividing the average investment assets into the net investment income, before applicable income taxes.

**Deferred Policy Costs**—Reflect certain costs of acquiring insurance business which have been deferred. These costs are primarily related to the production of business such as commissions, expenses in issuing policies and certain agency expenses.

**Total Assets**—Includes total investments, cash and cash items, accrued investment income, Premiums due, deferred policy acquisition costs, property and equipment separate accounts and other assets.

**Debt**—Includes bonds, debentures, notes, loans and mortgages payable.

**Common Equity**—Consists of common stock, additional paid in capital, net unrealized capital gains or losses on investments, retained earnings—less treasury stock at cost.

*Investment Companies*

**Total Investment Income**—The sum of income received from dividends and interest on portfolio holdings.

**Net Investment Income**—The amount of income remaining after operating expenses are deducted from total investment income. The per share figure is generally reported by the company, or may be obtained by dividing the net investment income by the shares outstanding. This amount is available for the payment of distributions.

**Realized Capital Gains**—Represents the net gain realized on the sale of investments, as reported by the company in the statement of changes in net assets. Divide amount by shares outstanding to obtain per share figure.

**% Net Investment Income/Net Assets**—Measures return on net assets. Percentage is obtained by dividing net investment income by average net assets.

**% Expenses/Net Assets**—Generally measures cost control. Percentage is obtained by dividing operating expenses by average net assets.

**% Expenses/Investment Income**—Indicates the amount of income absorbed by expenses. Percentage is obtained by dividing operating expenses by total investment income.

**Net Assets**—Represents the total market value of portfolio securities, including net cash, short-term investments, and stocks and bonds at market.

**% Change S&P ``500"**—Measures the percentage change in Standard & Poor's 500 stock price index, before reinvestment of dividends, and is a general indicator of overall stock market performance.

**% Change AAA Bonds**—Measures the percentage change in the Standard & Poor's high grade bond index, before reinvestment of interest, and is a measure of AAA bond price movements.

**% Net Asset Distribution**—Indicates the percentage breakdown of net assets in the following categories: a) net cash (cash receivables and other assets, less liabilities); b) short-term obligations (U.S. Government securities, commercial paper and certificates of deposit); c) bonds and preferred stocks; d) common stocks. To calculate the % net asset distribution, divide net assets into each of the above categories.

*Real Estate Investment Trusts and Savings & Loans*

**Rental Income**—Primarily income received from rental property.

**Mortgage Income**—Primarily income derived from mortgages.

**Total Income**—Includes rental and mortgage income, gains on sale of real estate and other.

**General Expenses**—Includes property operating expenses, real estate taxes, depreciation & amortization, administrative expenses and provision for losses.

**Interest Expense**—Includes interest paid on mortgage debt, convertible debentures, other debt obligations and short-term debt.

**% Expenses/Revenues**—Total expenses divided by revenues. The result represents the percentage of revenues (or the number of cents per dollar of income) absorbed by expenses.

**Provision for Losses**—Reserve charged to income for possible real estate losses.

**Net Income**—Profits for the year. This would include any gains/losses on the sale of real estate but exclude extraordinary items.

**% Earnings & Depreciation/Assets**—Obtained by dividing average assets into the sum of net income and depreciation expense (a measure of ``cash flow" for REITs).

**Total Assets**—The sum of net investments in real estate and other assets.

**Real Estate Investments**—The sum of gross investments in real estate, construction in process and mortgage loans and notes before allowances for losses and accumulated depreciation.

**Loss Reserve**—Reserves set aside for possible losses on real estate investments.

**Net Investment**—Real estate investments less accumulated depreciation and loss reserves.

**Cash**—Cash on hand, cash in escrow and short-term investments.

**S T Debt**—Short-term obligations due and payable within one year of balance sheet date. This would include the current portion of long-term debt, mortgages and notes, bank loans and commercial paper.

**Debt**—Includes debentures, mortgages and other long-term debt due after one year of balance sheet date.

**Equity**—Represents the sum of shares of beneficial interest or common stock, convertible preferred stock when included as equity, capital surplus and undistributed net income.

**Total Capitalization**—Is the sum of the stated values of a company's total shareholders' equity including preferred, common stock and debt obligations.

**Price Times Book Value Hi Lo**—Indicates the relationship of a stock's market price to book value. Obtained by dividing year end book values into yearly high/low range.

*Utilities*

**Capital Expenditures**—Represents the amounts spent on capital improvements to plant and funds for construction programs.

**Capitalization Ratios**—Reflect the percentage of each type of debt/equity issues outstanding to total capitalization. % DEBT is obtained by dividing total debt by the sum of debt, preferred, common, paid-in capital and retained earnings. % PREFERRED is obtained by dividing the preferred stocks outstanding by total capitalization. % COMMON, divide the sum of common stocks, paid-in capital and retained earnings by total capitalization.

**Construction Credits**—Credits for interest charged to the cost of constructing new plant. A combination of allowance for equity funds used during construction and allowance for borrowed funds used during construction—credit.

**Depreciation**—Amounts charged to income to compensate for the decline in useful value of plant and equipment.

**Effective Tax Rate**—Actual income tax expense divided by the total of net income and actual income tax expense.

**Fixed Charges Coverage**—The number of times income before interest charges (operating income plus other income) after taxes covers total interest charges and preferred dividend requirements.

**Gross Property**—Includes utility plant at cost, plant work in progress, and nuclear fuel.

**Long-Term Debt**—Debt obligations due beyond one year from balance sheet date.

**Maintenance**—Amounts spent to keep plants in good operating condition.

**Net Income**—Amount of earnings for the year which is available for preferred and common dividend payments.

**Net Property**—Includes items in gross property less provision for depreciation.

**Operating Revenues**—Represents the amount billed to customers by the utility.

**Operating Ratio**—Ratio of operating costs to operating revenues or the proportion of revenues absorbed by expenses. Obtained by dividing operating expenses including depreciation, maintenance, and taxes by revenues.

**% Earned on Net Property**—Percentage obtained by dividing operating income by average net property for the year. A measure of plant efficiency.

**% Return on Common Equity**—Percentage obtained by dividing income available for common stock (net income less preferred dividend requirements) by average common equity.

**% Return on Invested Capital**—Percentage obtained by dividing income available for fixed charges by average total invested capital.

**% Return on Revenues**—Obtained by dividing net income for the year by revenues.

**Total Capitalization**—Combined sum of total common equity, preferred stock and long-term debt.

**Total Invested Capital**—Sum of total capitalization (common-preferred-debt), accumulated deferred income taxes, accumulated investment tax credits, minority interest, contingency reserves, and contributions in aid of construction.

Finally, at the very bottom of the right-hand page, you'll find general information about the company: its address and telephone number, the names of its senior executive officers and directors (usually including the name of the investor contact), and the state in which the company is incorporated.

## How to Use This Book to Select Investments

And so, at last, we come to the $64,000 question: Given this vast array of data, how might a businesswoman seeking to find out about her competition, the marketing manager looking for clients, a job seeker, and the investor use it to best serve their respective purposes?

If you are like one of the first three of these individuals—a businesswoman, the marketing manager, or the job seeker—your task will be arduous, to be sure, but this book will provide you with an excellent starting point and your payoff can make it all worthwhile. You will have to go through this book page by page, looking for those companies that are in the industries in which you are interested, that are of the size and financial strength that appeal to you, that are located geographically in your territory or where you're willing to relocate, that have been profitable and growing, and so forth. And then you will have to read about just what's going on at those companies by referring to the appropriate "Highlights" and "Business Summary" comments in these reports.

Of course, this book won't do it *all* for you. It is, after all, just a starting point, not a conclusive summary of everything you might need to know. It is designed to educate, not to render advice or provide recommendations. But it will get you pointed in the right direction.

Finally, what about the investor who wants to use this book to find good individual investments from among the 500 stocks in the S&P 500 Index? If you fall into that category, what should you do?

Well, you can approach your quest the same way that the businesswoman looking for information about her competitors, the marketing manager, and the job seeker approached theirs—by thumbing through this book page by page, looking for companies with high historic growth rates, generous dividend payout policies, wide profit margins, A+ Standard & Poor's Quality Rankings, or whatever other characteristics you consider desirable in stocks in which you might invest. In this case, however, we have made your job just a little bit easier.

We have already prescreened the 500 companies in this book for several of the stock characteristics in which investors generally are most interested, including Standard & Poor's Quality Rankings, growth records, and dividend payment histories, and we're pleased to present on the next several pages lists of those companies which score highest on the bases of these criteria. So if you, like most investors, find these characteristics important in potential investments, you might want to turn first to the companies on these lists in your search for attractive investments.

Good luck and happy investment returns!

# Companies With Five Consecutive Years of Earnings Increases

This table, compiled from a computer screen of the stocks in this handbook, shows companies that have recorded rising per-share earnings for five consecutive years, have a minimum 10% five-year EPS growth rate based on trailing 12-month earnings, have estimated 2008 EPS at least 10% above those reported for 2007, pay dividends, and have Standard & Poor's Quality Rankings of A– or better.

| Company | Business | Fiscal Year End | 5 Yr EPS Growth Rate % | EPS $ 2007 Act. | EPS $ 2008 Est. | S&P Quality Rank | Price | P/E on 2008 Est. | % Yield |
|---|---|---|---|---|---|---|---|---|---|
| AFLAC Inc | Insurance & broadcasting | Dec | 12 | 3.31 | 3.99 | A | 44.13 | 11.1 | 2.5 |
| Brown-Forman'B' | Mkt whisky,wine prd/Lenox chin | Apr# | 11 | 2.50 | 2.85 | A | 45.92 | 16.1 | 2.3 |
| C.H. Robinson Worldwide | Motor freight transportat'n | Dec | 27 | 1.86 | 2.08 | A+ | 52.45 | 25.2 | 1.8 |
| CVS Caremark Corp | Oper drug/health stores | Dec | 16 | 1.92 | 2.44 | A | 28.87 | 11.8 | 0.9 |
| Caterpillar Inc | Earthmoving mchy: diesel eng | Dec | 28 | 5.37 | 5.99 | A | 36.87 | 6.2 | 4.5 |
| Chevron Corp | Major integrated int'l oil | Dec | 22 | 8.77 | 12.32 | A- | 73.54 | 6.0 | 3.5 |
| Costco Wholesale | Wholesale cash & carry mdsg | Aug# | 12 | 2.37 | 2.89 | A- | 52.28 | 18.1 | 1.2 |
| Deere & Co | Lgst mfr farm eq:constr mchy | Oct | 24 | 4.00 | 4.86 | A- | 35.12 | 7.2 | 3.1 |
| Devon Energy | Oil & gas devel prod'n | Dec | 25 | 7.99 | 11.70 | A- | 74.00 | 6.3 | 0.8 |
| Dover Corp | Elevators:petrol eq:ind'l pr | Dec | 18 | 3.26 | 3.69 | A- | 29.94 | 8.1 | 3.3 |
| Ecolab Inc | Comm'l cleaning&sanitizing | Dec | 12 | 1.70 | 1.87 | A | 31.78 | 17.0 | 1.6 |
| Emerson Electric | Mfr electric/electronic prdts | Sep# | 19 | 2.66 | 3.06 | A | 31.79 | 10.4 | 4.1 |
| Entergy Corp | Owns five operating utilities | Dec | 12 | 5.60 | 6.70 | A- | 77.91 | 11.6 | 3.8 |
| Expeditors Intl,Wash | Int'l air freight forward'g | Dec | 18 | 1.21 | 1.34 | A+ | 33.29 | 24.8 | 0.9 |
| Exxon Mobil | World's leading oil co | Dec | 23 | 7.28 | 9.03 | A+ | 72.65 | 8.0 | 2.2 |
| Fastenal Co | Fasteners/constrn supply strs | Dec | 25 | 1.55 | 1.95 | A | 35.98 | 18.5 | 1.5 |
| Genl Dynamics | Armored/space launch vehicles | Dec | 19 | 5.08 | 6.18 | A+ | 59.29 | 9.6 | 2.3 |
| Grainger (W.W.) | Nat'l dstr indus/comm'l prod | Dec | 18 | 4.94 | 6.10 | A | 70.07 | 11.5 | 2.2 |
| Hudson City Bancorp | Savings bank,New Jersey | Dec | 16 | 0.58 | 0.91 | A | 17.53 | 19.3 | 2.9 |
| L-3 Communications Hldgs | Communication systems/pds | Dec | 20 | 5.98 | 7.48 | A- | 73.68 | 9.9 | 1.6 |
| NIKE, Inc'B' | Athletic footwear | May# | 16 | 2.93 | 3.74 | A+ | 45.67 | 12.2 | 2.0 |
| Omnicom Group | Major int'l advertising co | Dec | 13 | 2.95 | 3.25 | A+ | 26.58 | 8.2 | 2.2 |
| Parker-Hannifin | Fluid pwr systems & comp | Jun# | 22 | 4.68 | 5.53 | A- | 36.61 | 6.6 | 2.7 |
| Paychex Inc | Computer payroll acctg svcs | May# | 15 | 1.35 | 1.56 | A+ | 26.09 | 16.7 | 4.7 |
| Praxair Inc | Ind'l gases/spcl coatings | Dec | 19 | 3.62 | 4.24 | A | 59.84 | 14.1 | 2.5 |
| Questar Corp | Nat'l gas dstr:oil/gas:mfg | Dec | 29 | 2.89 | 3.75 | A | 30.58 | 8.2 | 1.6 |
| Sigma-Aldrich | Specialty chem prod | Dec | 13 | 2.34 | 2.66 | A+ | 41.01 | 15.4 | 1.2 |
| State Street Corp | Banking/financial svcs | Dec | 15 | 3.45 | 5.17 | A | 42.17 | 8.2 | 2.2 |
| Stryker Corp | Specialty medical devices | Dec | 22 | 2.44 | 2.88 | A+ | 49.12 | 17.1 | 0.6 |
| United Technologies | Aerospace,climate ctrl sys | Dec | 15 | 4.27 | 4.93 | A+ | 51.80 | 10.5 | 2.9 |

#Actual 2008 EPS; P/E based on actual 2008 EPS.
Chart based on November 11, 2008 prices and data.
NOTE: All earnings estimates are Standard & Poor's projections.

# S&P 500 STOCK SCREENS

## Stocks With A+ Rankings

**Based on the issues in this handbook, this screen shows stocks of all companies with Standard & Poor's Quality Rankings of A+.**

| Company | Business | Company | Business |
|---|---|---|---|
| Air Products & Chem | Indust'l gases,eq,chemicals | Kimco Realty | Real estate investment trust |
| Anheuser-Busch Cos | Largest U.S. brewer:baking | Lowe's Cos | Dstr bldg mtls: consum'r gds |
| Archer-Daniels-Midland | Process soybeans:flour mill'r | McCormick & Co | Spices, flavoring, tea, mixes |
| Automatic Data Proc | Computer services | NIKE, Inc'B' | Athletic footwear |
| Carnival Corp | Cruise ships,hotel,casino | Omnicom Group | Major int'l advertising co |
| C.H. Robinson Worldwide | Motor freight transportat'n | Paychex Inc | Computer payroll acctg svcs |
| Cintas Corp | Sales & rental of uniforms | PepsiCo Inc | Soft drink:snack foods |
| Colgate-Palmolive | Household & personal care | Procter & Gamble | Hshld,personal care,food prod |
| Danaher Corp | Mfr hand tools,auto parts | Sigma-Aldrich | Specialty chem prod |
| Expeditors Intl,Wash | Int'l air freight forward'g | Smucker (J.M.) | Preserves: jellies & fillings |
| Exxon Mobil | World's leading oil co | Stryker Corp | Specialty medical devices |
| Family Dollar Stores | Self-service retail stores | Sysco Corp | Food distr & service systems |
| Genl Dynamics | Armored/space launch vehicles | Target Corp | Depart/disc/spec stores |
| Genl Electric | Consumer/ind'l prod,broad'cst | 3M Co | Scotch tapes: coated abrasives |
| Harley-Davidson | Manufactures motorcycles | TJX Companies | Off-price specialty stores |
| Home Depot | Bldg mtls,home improv strs | United Technologies | Aerospace,climate ctrl sys |
| Illinois Tool Works | Fasteners,tools, plastic items | UnitedHealth Group | Manages health maint svcs |
| Johnson Controls | Auto interior sys/bldg ctrls | Wal-Mart Stores | Operates discount stores |
| Johnson & Johnson | Health care products | Walgreen Co | Major retail drug chain |

Table based on November 11, 2008 prices and data.

## S&P 500 STOCK SCREENS

# Rapid Growth Stocks

The stocks listed below have shown strong and consistent earnings growth. Issues of rapidly growing companies tend to carry high price-earnings ratios and offer potential for substantial appreciation. At the same time, though, the stocks are subject to strong selling pressures should growth in earnings slow. Five-year earnings growth rates have been calculated for fiscal years 2003 through 2007 and the most current 12-month earnings.

| Company | Business | S&P Quality Ranking | Fiscal Year End | EPS $ — 2007 Act. | EPS $ — 2008 Est. | 5 Yr. EPS% Growth | Price | P/E on 2008 Est. | % Yield |
|---|---|---|---|---|---|---|---|---|---|
| CVS Caremark Corp | Oper drug/health stores | A | Dec | 1.92 | 2.44 | 16 | 28.87 | 11.8 | 0.9 |
| Cameron Intl | Oil & gas ind services/prod | B | Dec | 2.17 | 2.66 | 60 | 21.46 | 8.1 | 0.0 |
| Coach Inc | Design,mkt leather goods | NR | Jun# | 1.76 | 2.17 | 27 | 16.20 | 7.5 | 0.0 |
| Cognizant Tech Solutions'A' | Computer software & svcs | B+ | Dec | 1.15 | 1.45 | 46 | 18.09 | 12.5 | 0.0 |
| ENSCO Intl | Offshore contract drill'g | B+ | Dec | 6.74 | 8.36 | 75 | 33.31 | 4.0 | 0.3 |
| Express Scripts | Health care management svcs | B+ | Dec | 2.15 | 3.10 | 29 | 60.83 | 19.6 | 0.0 |
| Fastenal Co | Fasteners/constrn supply strs | A | Dec | 1.55 | 1.95 | 25 | 35.98 | 18.5 | 1.5 |
| Fiserv Inc | Data process'g services | B+ | Dec | 2.60 | 3.30 | 15 | 31.99 | 9.7 | 0.0 |
| Genl Dynamics | Armored/space launch vehicles | A+ | Dec | 5.08 | 6.18 | 19 | 59.29 | 9.6 | 2.3 |
| Grainger (W.W.) | Natl dstr indus/comm'l prod | A | Dec | 4.94 | 6.10 | 18 | 70.07 | 11.5 | 2.2 |
| L-3 Communications Hldgs | Communication systems/pds | A- | Dec | 5.98 | 7.48 | 20 | 73.68 | 9.9 | 1.6 |
| Manitowoc Company | Mfr heavy-lift cranes:shipyd | B | Dec | 2.64 | 2.95 | 122 | 8.19 | 2.8 | 0.9 |
| Natl Oilwell Varco | Oil & gas ind equip/repair svc | B+ | Dec | 3.76 | 4.88 | 65 | 25.98 | 5.3 | 0.0 |
| NIKE, Inc'B' | Athletic footwear | A+ | May# | 2.93 | 3.74 | 16 | 45.67 | 12.2 | 2.0 |
| Questar Corp | Nat'l gas dstr:oil/gas:mfg | A | Dec | 2.89 | 3.75 | 29 | 30.58 | 8.2 | 1.6 |
| Rockwell Collins | Aviation/communic elec tr'ns | NR | Sep# | 3.45 | 4.16 | 24 | 33.55 | 8.1 | 2.8 |
| St. Jude Medical | Heart valve:electro med dev | B+ | Dec | 1.59 | 2.30 | 16 | 34.93 | 15.2 | 0.0 |
| Smith Intl | Varied line drill,boring eq | B+ | Dec | 3.20 | 3.88 | 45 | 29.56 | 7.6 | 1.6 |
| Stryker Corp | Specialty medical devices | A+ | Dec | 2.44 | 2.88 | 22 | 49.12 | 17.1 | 0.6 |
| United Technologies | Aerospace,climate ctrl sys | A+ | Dec | 4.27 | 4.93 | 15 | 51.80 | 10.5 | 2.9 |
| Zimmer Holdings | Dvlp reconstruction implants | NR | Dec | 3.26 | 3.97 | 21 | 40.73 | 10.3 | 0.0 |

#Actual 2008 EPS; P/E based on actual 2008 EPS.
Chart based on November 11, 2008 prices and data.
NOTE: All earnings estimates are Standard & Poor's projections.

# S&P 500 STOCK SCREENS

# Fast-Rising Dividends

Based on the issues in this handbook, the companies below were chosen on the basis of their five-year annual growth rate in dividends to the current 12-month indicated rate. All have increased their dividend payments each calendar year from 2003 to their current 12-month indicated rate.

| Company | -- $ Divd. --<br>Paid 2003 | Paid 2007 | †Ind. Divd. Rate | * Divd. Growth Rate % | Price | % Yield |
|---|---|---|---|---|---|---|
| AFLAC Inc | 0.30 | 0.80 | 1.12 | 29.48 | 44.13 | 2.5 |
| Air Products & Chem | 0.88 | 1.48 | 1.76 | 14.03 | 54.37 | 3.2 |
| Allstate Corp | 0.91 | 1.49 | 1.64 | 12.14 | 25.73 | 6.4 |
| Anheuser-Busch Cos | 0.83 | 1.25 | 1.48 | 11.70 | 66.84 | 2.2 |
| Archer-Daniels-Midland | 0.24 | 0.46 | 0.52 | 16.39 | 24.16 | 2.2 |
| Automatic Data Proc | 0.48 | 1.10 | 1.32 | 23.10 | 34.99 | 3.8 |
| Avon Products | 0.42 | 0.74 | 0.80 | 12.48 | 23.78 | 3.4 |
| Becton, Dickinson | 0.40 | 0.98 | 1.14 | 21.74 | 68.27 | 1.7 |
| H & R Block | 0.37 | 0.55 | 0.60 | 10.20 | 18.01 | 3.3 |
| C.H. Robinson Worldwide | 0.16 | 0.59 | 0.96 | 40.47 | 52.45 | 1.8 |
| Cardinal Health | 0.11 | 0.42 | 0.56 | 42.54 | 39.30 | 1.4 |
| Caterpillar Inc | 0.71 | 1.32 | 1.68 | 18.95 | 36.87 | 4.6 |
| Century Tel Inc | 0.22 | 0.26 | 2.80 | 45.51 | 24.86 | 11.3 |
| Chevron Corp | 1.43 | 2.26 | 2.60 | 13.07 | 73.54 | 3.5 |
| Cincinnati Financial | 0.88 | 1.40 | 1.56 | 12.04 | 24.11 | 6.5 |
| Cintas Corp | 0.27 | 0.39 | 0.46 | 10.97 | 22.25 | 2.1 |
| Clorox Co | 0.98 | 1.42 | 1.84 | 12.13 | 58.59 | 3.1 |
| Coca-Cola Co | 0.88 | 1.36 | 1.52 | 11.33 | 44.44 | 3.4 |
| Colgate-Palmolive | 0.90 | 1.40 | 1.60 | 12.52 | 61.91 | 2.6 |
| Danaher Corp | 0.05 | 0.10 | 0.12 | 19.53 | 55.64 | 0.2 |
| Emerson Electric | 0.79 | 1.09 | 1.32 | 10.72 | 31.79 | 4.2 |
| Expeditors Intl, Wash | 0.08 | 0.28 | 0.32 | 33.52 | 33.29 | 1.0 |
| Exxon Mobil | 0.98 | 1.37 | 1.60 | 10.00 | 72.65 | 2.2 |
| Family Dollar Stores | 0.29 | 0.45 | 0.50 | 11.33 | 27.71 | 1.8 |
| Fastenal Co | 0.10 | 0.44 | 0.54 | 36.18 | 35.98 | 1.5 |
| Federated Investors 'B' | 0.30 | 0.81 | 0.96 | 25.90 | 22.99 | 4.2 |
| Gannett Co | 0.97 | 1.33 | 1.60 | 10.10 | 9.59 | 16.7 |
| Genl Dynamics | 0.63 | 1.10 | 1.40 | 16.95 | 59.29 | 2.4 |
| Genl Electric | 0.76 | 1.12 | 1.24 | 10.79 | 17.81 | 7.0 |
| Grainger (W.W.) | 0.73 | 1.34 | 1.60 | 17.62 | 70.07 | 2.3 |
| Harley-Davidson | 0.20 | 1.06 | 1.32 | 43.77 | 19.27 | 6.9 |
| Hershey Co | 0.72 | 1.14 | 1.19 | 10.57 | 35.68 | 3.3 |
| Home Depot | 0.26 | 0.90 | 0.90 | 32.27 | 20.51 | 4.4 |
| Hudson City Bancorp | 0.16 | 0.33 | 0.52 | 22.77 | 17.53 | 3.0 |
| Illinois Tool Works | 0.47 | 0.91 | 1.24 | 21.75 | 32.26 | 3.8 |
| Intl Bus. Machines | 0.63 | 1.50 | 2.00 | 27.15 | 82.74 | 2.4 |

| Company | -- $ Divd. --<br>Paid 2003 | Paid 2007 | †Ind. Divd. Rate | * Divd. Growth Rate % | Price | % Yield |
|---|---|---|---|---|---|---|
| Johnson & Johnson | 0.93 | 1.62 | 1.84 | 14.52 | 59.55 | 3.1 |
| Kimberly-Clark | 1.32 | 2.08 | 2.32 | 11.51 | 57.59 | 4.0 |
| Leggett & Platt | 0.53 | 0.70 | 1.00 | 11.64 | 15.32 | 6.5 |
| Linear Technology Corp | 0.23 | 0.72 | 0.84 | 30.49 | 21.32 | 3.9 |
| Lowe's Cos | 0.05 | 0.26 | 0.34 | 48.07 | 19.05 | 1.8 |
| M&T Bank | 1.20 | 2.60 | 2.80 | 18.51 | 68.64 | 4.1 |
| Marshall & Ilsley | 0.70 | 1.20 | 1.28 | 13.13 | 15.69 | 8.2 |
| Marriott Intl 'A' | 0.14 | 0.28 | 0.35 | 19.45 | 17.88 | 2.0 |
| Masco Corp | 0.58 | 0.91 | 0.94 | 10.44 | 8.20 | 11.5 |
| McCormick & Co | 0.46 | 0.80 | 0.88 | 13.50 | 30.09 | 2.9 |
| McDonald's Corp | 0.40 | 1.50 | 2.00 | 38.73 | 56.29 | 3.6 |
| McGraw-Hill Companies | 0.54 | 0.82 | 0.88 | 10.44 | 23.66 | 3.7 |
| Medtronic, Inc | 0.27 | 0.47 | 0.75 | 20.30 | 40.08 | 1.9 |
| New York Times 'A' | 0.57 | 0.86 | 0.92 | 10.52 | 8.38 | 11.0 |
| Nordstrom, Inc | 0.20 | 0.54 | 0.64 | 27.11 | 13.30 | 4.8 |
| Paychex Inc | 0.45 | 1.02 | 1.24 | 23.88 | 26.09 | 4.8 |
| PepsiCo Inc | 0.62 | 1.35 | 1.70 | 21.52 | 55.08 | 3.1 |
| Pfizer, Inc | 0.60 | 1.16 | 1.28 | 17.43 | 16.77 | 7.6 |
| Praxair Inc | 0.46 | 1.20 | 1.50 | 26.93 | 59.84 | 2.5 |
| T. Rowe Price Group | 0.34 | 0.68 | 0.96 | 22.60 | 33.06 | 2.9 |
| Procter & Gamble | 0.86 | 1.36 | 1.60 | 12.65 | 63.82 | 2.5 |
| Sherwin-Williams | 0.62 | 1.26 | 1.40 | 19.11 | 54.09 | 2.6 |
| Sigma-Aldrich | 0.29 | 0.46 | 0.52 | 11.60 | 41.01 | 1.3 |
| State Street Corp | 0.54 | 0.86 | 0.96 | 12.00 | 42.17 | 2.3 |
| Stryker Corp | 0.06 | 0.22 | 0.33 | 41.54 | 49.12 | 0.7 |
| SunTrust Banks | 1.80 | 2.92 | 3.08 | 11.87 | 36.16 | 8.5 |
| Sysco Corp | 0.44 | 0.76 | 0.88 | 14.47 | 24.05 | 3.7 |
| TJX Companies | 0.14 | 0.34 | 0.44 | 26.29 | 23.45 | 1.9 |
| Target Corp | 0.26 | 0.52 | 0.64 | 19.91 | 35.85 | 1.8 |
| United Technologies | 0.57 | 1.17 | 1.54 | 21.01 | 51.80 | 3.0 |
| VF Corp | 1.01 | 2.23 | 2.36 | 22.39 | 49.08 | 4.8 |
| Vulcan Materials | 0.98 | 1.84 | 1.96 | 16.75 | 54.15 | 3.6 |
| Wal-Mart Stores | 0.34 | 0.83 | 0.95 | 21.50 | 54.75 | 1.7 |
| Walgreen Co | 0.16 | 0.34 | 0.45 | 22.48 | 23.64 | 1.9 |
| Wells Fargo | 0.75 | 1.18 | 1.36 | 11.36 | 28.83 | 4.7 |

†12-month indicated rate.   *Five-year annual compounded growth rate.   Chart based on November 11, 2008 prices and data.

## S&P 500 STOCK SCREENS

# Stock Reports

In using the Stock Reports in this handbook, please pay particular attention to the dates attached to each evaluation, recommendation, or analysis section. Opinions rendered are as of that date and may change often. It is strongly suggested that before investing in any security you should obtain the current analysis on that issue.

To order the latest Standard & Poor's Stock Report on a company, for as little as $3.00 per report, please call:

**S&P Reports On-Demand at 1-800-292-0808.**

# Abbott Laboratories

| S&P Recommendation  **STRONG BUY** ★ ★ ★ ★ ★ | Price | 12-Mo. Target Price | Investment Style |
|---|---|---|---|
| | $55.06 (as of Nov 14, 2008) | $65.00 | Large-Cap Growth |

**GICS Sector** Health Care
**Sub-Industry** Pharmaceuticals

**Summary** This diversified life science company is a leading maker of drugs, nutritional products, diabetes monitoring devices, and diagnostics.

## Key Stock Statistics (Source S&P, Vickers, company reports)

| | | | | | | | |
|---|---|---|---|---|---|---|---|
| 52-Wk Range | $61.09– 45.75 | S&P Oper. EPS 2008E | 3.32 | Market Capitalization(B) | $85.430 | Beta | 0.14 |
| Trailing 12-Month EPS | $2.91 | S&P Oper. EPS 2009E | 3.65 | Yield (%) | 2.62 | S&P 3-Yr. Proj. EPS CAGR(%) | 13 |
| Trailing 12-Month P/E | 18.9 | P/E on S&P Oper. EPS 2008E | 16.6 | Dividend Rate/Share | $1.44 | S&P Credit Rating | AA |
| $10K Invested 5 Yrs Ago | NA | Common Shares Outstg. (M) | 1,551.6 | Institutional Ownership (%) | 68 | | |

## Price Performance

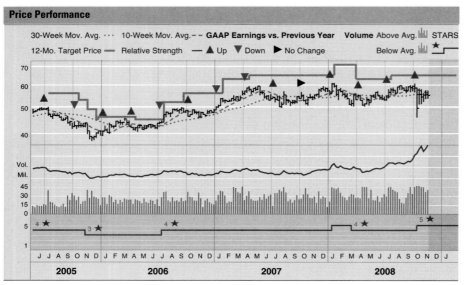

30-Week Mov. Avg. · · ·   10-Week Mov. Avg. - -   **GAAP Earnings vs. Previous Year**   Volume Above Avg. STARS
12-Mo. Target Price —   Relative Strength —   ▲ Up  ▼ Down  ► No Change   Below Avg. ★

Options: ASE, CBOE, P, Ph

Analysis prepared by **Herman B. Saftlas** on October 20, 2008, when the stock traded at **$ 57.55**.

## Highlights

➤ We see 2009 revenues rising 8%, to about $32 billion, supported by growth in all major business segments. Despite expected steep generic erosion the Depakote line, we see higher pharmaceutical sales, led by continued momentum in sales of Humira autoimmune agent, and by gains in Lupron, Tricor and Niaspan. Benefiting from impressive clinical data and new indications, Humira sales should climb 30%, to $6 billion, by our analysis. Vascular sales should be augmented by the recently launched Xience drug-eluting coronary stent, which has already become the leading stent in the U.S. market. We see single-digit gains for nutritional and diagnostic product sales.

➤ We expect modest expansion in gross margins, helped by higher projected volume and manufacturing efficiencies. SG&A and R&D spending as a percentage of total sales will likely decline somewhat from cost streamlining measures. However, the tax rate is likely to be slightly higher.

➤ We forecast operating EPS of $3.65 for 2009, up from an estimated $3.32 in 2008. Operating EPS were $2.84 in 2007.

## Investment Rationale/Risk

➤ Our strong buy recommendation reflects potential catalysts that we see on the horizon. We remain positive on both the short-term and long-term prospects for Humira, and we consider the drug to have an advantage over Enbrel in the dermatology space. We expect Humira sales to grow 30% in 2009, boosted by expanded uses. We think revenues will also benefit from increased sales in the vascular intervention area, supported by the recent launch Xience drug-eluting stent, as well as gains in diagnostics and nutritional products.

➤ Risks to our recommendation and target price include lower-than-expected product sales (notably for Humira), new generic competition to Synthroid and Biaxin, and pipeline disappointments.

➤ Our 12-month target price of $65 applies a premium-to-peers P/E of 17.8X to our 2009 EPS estimate. We think this valuation is justified, given ABT's rapidly growing franchises in diversified healthcare markets. Our DCF model, which assumes a WACC of 8.25% and terminal growth of 2%, also implies an intrinsic value of $65.

## Qualitative Risk Assessment

| LOW | MEDIUM | HIGH |
|---|---|---|

Our risk assessment reflects Abbott's operations in competitive markets and its exposure to the potential for generic competition. However, we believe the company has a relatively strong new product pipeline, with possible significant launches in both the medical device and pharmaceutical areas. In our opinion, the company is financially sound, with a strong balance sheet.

## Quantitative Evaluations

**S&P Quality Ranking**                    A-

| D | C | B- | B | B+ | A- | A | A+ |
|---|---|---|---|---|---|---|---|

**Relative Strength Rank**                STRONG

88

LOWEST = 1                          HIGHEST = 99

## Revenue/Earnings Data

**Revenue (Million $)**

| | 1Q | 2Q | 3Q | 4Q | Year |
|---|---|---|---|---|---|
| 2008 | 6,766 | 7,314 | 7,498 | -- | -- |
| 2007 | 5,290 | 6,371 | 6,377 | 7,221 | 25,914 |
| 2006 | 5,183 | 5,501 | 5,574 | 6,218 | 22,476 |
| 2005 | 5,383 | 5,524 | 5,384 | 6,047 | 22,338 |
| 2004 | 4,641 | 4,703 | 4,682 | 5,654 | 19,680 |
| 2003 | 4,580 | 4,724 | 4,846 | 5,531 | 19,681 |

**Earnings Per Share ($)**

| | | | | | |
|---|---|---|---|---|---|
| 2008 | 0.60 | 0.85 | 0.69 | E1.06 | E3.32 |
| 2007 | 0.41 | 0.63 | 0.46 | 0.77 | 2.31 |
| 2006 | 0.56 | 0.40 | 0.46 | -0.31 | 1.12 |
| 2005 | 0.53 | 0.56 | 0.44 | 0.63 | 2.16 |
| 2004 | 0.52 | 0.40 | 0.51 | 0.62 | 2.02 |
| 2003 | 0.51 | 0.16 | 0.48 | 0.60 | 1.75 |

Fiscal year ended Dec. 31. Next earnings report expected: Late January. EPS Estimates based on S&P Operating Earnings; historical GAAP earnings are as reported.

## Dividend Data (Dates: mm/dd Payment Date: mm/dd/yy)

| Amount ($) | Date Decl. | Ex-Div. Date | Stk. of Record | Payment Date |
|---|---|---|---|---|
| 0.325 | 12/14 | 01/11 | 01/15 | 02/15/08 |
| 0.360 | 02/15 | 04/11 | 04/15 | 05/15/08 |
| 0.360 | 06/06 | 07/11 | 07/15 | 08/15/08 |
| 0.360 | 09/12 | 10/10 | 10/15 | 11/15/08 |

Dividends have been paid since 1926. Source: Company reports.

# Abbott Laboratories

**STANDARD &POOR'S**

## Business Summary October 20, 2008

CORPORATE OVERVIEW. Abbott Laboratories (ABT) is a leading player in several growing health care markets. Through acquisitions, product diversification and R&D programs, ABT offers a wide range of prescription pharmaceuticals, infant and adult nutritionals, diagnostics, and medical devices.

During 2007, pharmaceuticals accounted for 57% of operating revenues, while nutritionals represented 17%, diagnostics contributed 12%, and vascular represented 6%. Sales of other products represented 8% of 2007 sales.

ABT's Pharmaceutical Products Group markets a wide array of human therapeutics. Major products include: Humira to treat rheumatoid arthritis and psoriatic arthritis ($3.0 billion in 2007 sales); Biaxin ($724 million), a major class of a broad-spectrum antibiotic used for a wide variety of infections, including h-pylori (associated with duodenal ulcers); Depakote ($1.6 billion), a leading anti-epileptic and bipolar disorder drug; Kaletra, an anti-HIV medication ($1.3 billion); and cholesterol treatment TriCor ($1.2 billion). In May 2005, the FDA approved oral Zemplar for secondary hyperparathyroidism in predialysis patients.

Nutritionals fall under U.S.-based Ross Products and Abbott Nutrition International. Products include leading infant formulas sold under the Similac and Isomil names, as well as adult nutritionals, such as Ensure and ProSure for patients with special dietary needs, including cancer and diabetes patients. ABT also markets enteral feeding items.

Abbott Diabetes Care markets the Precision and FreeStyle lines of hand-held glucose monitors for diabetes patients. This division also markets data management and point-of-care systems, insulin pumps and syringes, and Glucerna shakes and nutrition bars tailored for diabetics.

Abbott Vascular markets coronary and carotid stents, catheters and guide wires, and products used for surgical closure. In April 2006, Abbott acquired Guidant's vascular business from Boston Scientific for approximately $4.1 billion. Boston Scientific is also entitled to milestones if the Xience V stent is approved in the U.S. or Japan.

## Company Financials Fiscal Year Ended Dec. 31

| Per Share Data ($) | 2007 | 2006 | 2005 | 2004 | 2003 | 2002 | 2001 | 2000 | 1999 | 1998 |
|---|---|---|---|---|---|---|---|---|---|---|
| Tangible Book Value | 1.24 | NM | 2.89 | 2.22 | 2.90 | 1.93 | 1.14 | 4.54 | 3.78 | 2.88 |
| Cash Flow | 3.50 | 2.13 | 3.02 | 2.84 | 2.56 | 2.52 | 1.74 | 2.31 | 2.10 | 2.02 |
| Earnings | 2.31 | 1.12 | 2.16 | 2.02 | 1.75 | 1.78 | 0.99 | 1.78 | 1.57 | 1.51 |
| S&P Core Earnings | 2.31 | 1.16 | 2.01 | 1.90 | 1.95 | 1.62 | 0.77 | NA | NA | NA |
| Dividends | 1.27 | 1.16 | 1.09 | 1.03 | 0.97 | 0.92 | 0.82 | 0.74 | 0.66 | 0.58 |
| Payout Ratio | 55% | 104% | 50% | 51% | 55% | 51% | 83% | 42% | 42% | 39% |
| Prices:High | 59.50 | 49.87 | 50.00 | 47.63 | 47.15 | 58.00 | 57.17 | 56.25 | 53.31 | 50.06 |
| Prices:Low | 48.75 | 39.18 | 37.50 | 38.26 | 33.75 | 29.80 | 42.00 | 29.38 | 33.00 | 32.53 |
| P/E Ratio:High | 26 | 45 | 23 | 24 | 27 | 33 | 58 | 32 | 34 | 33 |
| P/E Ratio:Low | 21 | 35 | 17 | 19 | 19 | 17 | 42 | 16 | 21 | 22 |

| Income Statement Analysis (Million $) | 2007 | 2006 | 2005 | 2004 | 2003 | 2002 | 2001 | 2000 | 1999 | 1998 |
|---|---|---|---|---|---|---|---|---|---|---|
| Revenue | 25,914 | 22,476 | 22,338 | 19,680 | 19,681 | 17,685 | 16,285 | 13,746 | 13,178 | 12,478 |
| Operating Income | 7,378 | 6,419 | 5,738 | 5,187 | 4,597 | 4,815 | 3,062 | 4,228 | 3,977 | 3,902 |
| Depreciation | 1,855 | 1,559 | 1,359 | 1,289 | 1,274 | 1,177 | 1,168 | 827 | 828 | 784 |
| Interest Expense | 593 | 416 | 241 | 200 | 146 | 239 | 307 | 114 | 81.8 | 160 |
| Pretax Income | 4,479 | 2,276 | 4,620 | 4,126 | 3,734 | 3,673 | 1,883 | 3,816 | 3,397 | 3,241 |
| Effective Tax Rate | 19.3% | 24.6% | 27.0% | 23.0% | 26.3% | 23.9% | 17.7% | 27.0% | 28.0% | 28.0% |
| Net Income | 3,606 | 1,717 | 3,372 | 3,176 | 2,753 | 2,794 | 1,550 | 2,786 | 2,446 | 2,333 |
| S&P Core Earnings | 3,609 | 1,787 | 3,158 | 2,972 | 2,971 | 2,561 | 1,233 | NA | NA | NA |

| Balance Sheet & Other Financial Data (Million $) | 2007 | 2006 | 2005 | 2004 | 2003 | 2002 | 2001 | 2000 | 1999 | 1998 |
|---|---|---|---|---|---|---|---|---|---|---|
| Cash | 2,821 | 521 | 2,894 | 1,226 | 995 | 704 | 657 | 914 | 608 | 383 |
| Current Assets | 14,043 | 11,282 | 11,386 | 10,734 | 10,290 | 9,122 | 8,419 | 7,376 | 6,420 | 5,553 |
| Total Assets | 39,714 | 36,178 | 29,141 | 28,767 | 26,715 | 24,259 | 23,296 | 15,283 | 14,471 | 13,216 |
| Current Liabilities | 9,103 | 11,951 | 7,416 | 6,826 | 7,640 | 7,002 | 7,927 | 4,298 | 4,517 | 4,962 |
| Long Term Debt | 9,488 | 7,010 | 4,572 | 4,788 | 3,452 | 4,274 | 4,335 | 1,076 | 1,337 | 1,340 |
| Common Equity | 17,779 | 14,054 | 14,415 | 14,326 | 13,072 | 10,665 | 9,059 | 8,571 | 7,428 | 5,714 |
| Total Capital | 27,266 | 21,064 | 19,570 | 19,334 | 16,525 | 14,939 | 13,395 | 9,647 | 9,046 | 7,163 |
| Capital Expenditures | 1,656 | 1,338 | 1,207 | 1,292 | 1,247 | 1,296 | 1,164 | 1,036 | 217 | 991 |
| Cash Flow | 5,461 | 3,276 | 4,731 | 4,465 | 4,027 | 3,971 | 2,718 | 3,613 | 3,274 | 3,117 |
| Current Ratio | 1.5 | 0.9 | 1.5 | 1.6 | 1.3 | 1.3 | 1.1 | 1.7 | 1.4 | 1.1 |
| % Long Term Debt of Capitalization | 34.8 | 33.3 | 23.4 | 24.8 | 20.9 | 28.6 | 32.4 | 11.2 | 14.8 | 18.7 |
| % Net Income of Revenue | 13.9 | 7.6 | 15.1 | 16.1 | 14.0 | 15.8 | 9.5 | 20.3 | 18.6 | 18.7 |
| % Return on Assets | 9.5 | 5.3 | 11.6 | 11.6 | 10.8 | 11.7 | 8.0 | 18.7 | 17.6 | 18.5 |
| % Return on Equity | 22.7 | 12.1 | 23.5 | 23.2 | 23.2 | 28.3 | 17.6 | 34.8 | 37.2 | 43.6 |

Data as orig reptd.; bef. results of disc opers/spec. items. Per share data adj. for stk. divs.; EPS diluted. E-Estimated. NA-Not Available. NM-Not Meaningful. NR-Not Ranked. UR-Under Review.

**Office:** 100 Abbott Park Road, Abbott Park, IL 60064-6400.
**Telephone:** 847-937-6100.
**Website:** http://www.abbott.com
**Chrmn & CEO:** M.D. White

**COO:** O. Bohuon
**EVP & CFO:** T.C. Freyman
**EVP, Secy & General Counsel:** L.J. Schumacher
**Chief Acctg Officer & Cntlr:** G.W. Linder

**Investor Contact:** L. Peepo (847-935-6722)
**Board Members:** R. J. Alpern, R. S. Austin, W. M. Daley, W. Farrell, H. L. Fuller, A. J. Higgins, W. A. Osborn, D. Owen, B. Powell, Jr., W. A. Reynolds, R. S. Roberts, S. C. Scott, III, W. D. Smithburg, G. F. Tilton, M. D. White

**Founded:** 1888
**Domicile:** Illinois
**Employees:** 68,000

The McGraw-Hill Companies

# Abercrombie & Fitch Co.

**STANDARD &POOR'S**

| S&P Recommendation | HOLD ★★★☆☆ | Price | 12-Mo. Target Price | Investment Style |
|---|---|---|---|---|
| | | $17.79 (as of Nov 14, 2008) | $25.00 | Large-Cap Growth |

**GICS Sector** Consumer Discretionary
**Sub-Industry** Apparel Retail

**Summary** This apparel retailer, which specializes in lifestyle branding, operates about 1,000 retail apparel stores across five brands.

## Key Stock Statistics (Source S&P, Vickers, company reports)

| | | | | | | | |
|---|---|---|---|---|---|---|---|
| 52-Wk Range | $84.54– 17.73 | S&P Oper. EPS 2009E | 3.30 | Market Capitalization(B) | $1.548 | Beta | 1.48 |
| Trailing 12-Month EPS | $5.25 | S&P Oper. EPS 2010E | 2.90 | Yield (%) | 3.93 | S&P 3-Yr. Proj. EPS CAGR(%) | 8 |
| Trailing 12-Month P/E | 3.4 | P/E on S&P Oper. EPS 2009E | 5.4 | Dividend Rate/Share | $0.70 | S&P Credit Rating | NA |
| $10K Invested 5 Yrs Ago | $6,376 | Common Shares Outstg. (M) | 87.0 | Institutional Ownership (%) | 97 | | |

## Price Performance

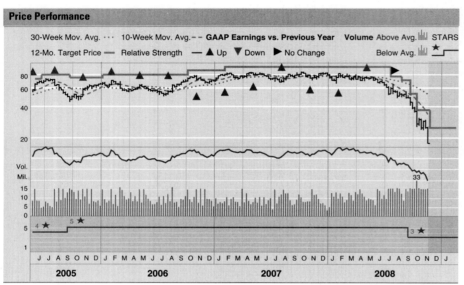

30-Week Mov. Avg. ··· 10-Week Mov. Avg. - - **GAAP Earnings vs. Previous Year** Volume Above Avg. STARS
12-Mo. Target Price — Relative Strength — ▲ Up ▼ Down ► No Change Below Avg. ★

Options: ASE, CBOE, P, Ph

## Qualitative Risk Assessment

| LOW | MEDIUM | HIGH |
|---|---|---|

Our risk assessment reflects our view of ANF's debt-free balance sheet and strong cash flow, offset by a consumer base whose tastes change constantly.

## Quantitative Evaluations

**S&P Quality Ranking**     A-

| D | C | B- | B | B+ | A- | A | A+ |
|---|---|---|---|---|---|---|---|

**Relative Strength Rank**     WEAK

13

LOWEST = 1     HIGHEST = 99

## Revenue/Earnings Data

**Revenue (Million $)**

| | 1Q | 2Q | 3Q | 4Q | Year |
|---|---|---|---|---|---|
| 2009 | 800.2 | 845.8 | -- | -- | -- |
| 2008 | 742.4 | 804.5 | 973.9 | 1,229 | 3,750 |
| 2007 | 657.3 | 658.7 | 863.5 | 1,139 | 3,318 |
| 2006 | 546.8 | 571.6 | 704.9 | 961.4 | 2,785 |
| 2005 | 411.9 | 401.4 | 520.7 | 687.3 | 2,021 |
| 2004 | 346.7 | 355.7 | 445.0 | 560.4 | 1,708 |

**Earnings Per Share ($)**

| | | | | | |
|---|---|---|---|---|---|
| 2009 | 0.69 | 0.87 | E0.75 | E1.00 | E3.30 |
| 2008 | 0.65 | 0.87 | 1.29 | 2.40 | 5.20 |
| 2007 | 0.62 | 0.72 | 1.11 | 2.14 | 4.59 |
| 2006 | 0.45 | 0.63 | 0.79 | 1.80 | 3.66 |
| 2005 | 0.30 | 0.44 | 0.42 | 1.15 | 2.28 |
| 2004 | 0.26 | 0.35 | 0.51 | 0.96 | 2.06 |

Fiscal year ended Jan. 31. Next earnings report expected: Late November. EPS Estimates based on S&P Operating Earnings; historical GAAP earnings are as reported.

## Highlights

➤ The 12-month target price for ANF has recently been changed to $25.00 from $37.00. The Highlights section of this Stock Report will be updated accordingly.

## Investment Rationale/Risk

➤ The Investment Rationale/Risk section of this Stock Report will be updated shortly. For the latest News story on ANF from MarketScope, see below.

➤ 11/14/08 10:00 am ET ... S&P MAINTAINS HOLD RECOMMENDATION ON SHARES OF ABERCROMBIE & FITCH (ANF 21.04***): Oct-Q EPS of $0.72 vs. $1.29 is below our $0.75 estimate as comps-store sales declined 14%, driving deleveraging of fixed store and distribution expenses, up 660 bps. CEO Mike Jeffries contract is up for renewal and it is not clear which way discussions are going. We believe Jeffries is driving force behind ANF brand and without his leadership in this environment, we see increased risk. We are reducing FY 09 (Jan.) and FY 10 EPS estimates to $3.30 and $2.90 from $4.00 and $4.05, and our 12-month target price to $25 from $37 based on a peer multiple and new FY 10 estimate. /M. Driscoll-CFA

## Dividend Data (Dates: mm/dd Payment Date: mm/dd/yy)

| Amount ($) | Date Decl. | Ex-Div. Date | Stk. of Record | Payment Date |
|---|---|---|---|---|
| 0.175 | 02/15 | 02/27 | 02/29 | 03/18/08 |
| 0.175 | 05/16 | 05/28 | 05/30 | 06/17/08 |
| 0.175 | 08/15 | 08/27 | 08/29 | 09/16/08 |
| 0.175 | 11/14 | 11/25 | 11/28 | 12/16/08 |

Dividends have been paid since 2004. Source: Company reports.

# Abercrombie & Fitch Co.

STANDARD
&POOR'S

## Business Summary October 10, 2008

CORPORATE OVERVIEW. Abercrombie & Fitch, established in 1892, operates four branded retail concepts: Abercrombie & Fitch (353 stores as of July 2008), abercrombie (209), Hollister (479) and RUEHL (25), and eight Gilly Hicks and e-commerce sites for the three larger retail concepts. Each targets a different age demographic and all employ casual luxury positioning. Hollister targets 14 to 17 year old high school boys and girls at lower price points than traditional A&F stores, thereby minimizing cannibalization between brands.

MARKET PROFILE. The company participates in the specialty apparel retail market targeted at youth, spanning the tween to young adult demographic. While the U.S. apparel market is considered mature, with demand mirroring population growth and a modicum related to fashion, the youth marketplace is generally considered attractive based on its spending clout. According to NPD consumer data, collectively, this group accounts for approximately 35% of total apparel spending, with the "sweet spot" being teenagers, who represent about 20%.

COMPETITIVE LANDSCAPE. The retail landscape is consolidating, with share accruing to the mass merchants and specialty chains while the traditional department store is losing ground. Specialty chains compete on customer

knowledge garnered from daily interactions, focus groups and marketing intelligence, and this knowledge is often combined with high customer service levels to result in an attractive price/value equation for the consumer. ANF's target demographic is attracted to strong brands, as well as fashion and value, when determining apparel selections. While the specialty channel holds the largest share of the apparel market, S&P estimates that the sub-segment serving the youth demographic represents about 3% of total retail sales. With barriers to entry minimal (capital investment in merchandise, rent and labor expense) and potential returns on investment high and quick (four wall return on investment exceed 40% in 12 months for many specialty retailers), there is a steady flow of new industry participants. In addition to competing with other apparel retailers, regardless of channel, for the youth's discretionary spending, ANF competes with merchandise and services, especially consumer electronics and entertainment services.

## Company Financials Fiscal Year Ended Jan. 31

| Per Share Data ($) | 2008 | 2007 | 2006 | 2005 | 2004 | 2003 | 2002 | 2001 | 2000 | 1999 |
|---|---|---|---|---|---|---|---|---|---|---|
| Tangible Book Value | 23.45 | 19.17 | 11.34 | 7.78 | 9.21 | 7.71 | 6.02 | 4.28 | 3.05 | 1.83 |
| Cash Flow | 7.21 | 6.18 | 5.02 | 3.39 | 2.73 | 2.50 | 2.05 | 1.85 | 1.65 | 1.16 |
| Earnings | 5.20 | 4.59 | 3.66 | 2.28 | 2.06 | 1.94 | 1.65 | 1.55 | 1.39 | 0.96 |
| S&P Core Earnings | 5.20 | 4.59 | 3.38 | 2.32 | 1.81 | 1.70 | 1.45 | 1.35 | NA | NA |
| Dividends | 0.70 | 0.60 | 0.50 | 0.50 | Nil | Nil | Nil | Nil | Nil | Nil |
| Payout Ratio | 13% | 13% | 14% | 22% | Nil | Nil | Nil | Nil | Nil | Nil |
| Calendar Year | 2007 | 2006 | 2005 | 2004 | 2003 | 2002 | 2001 | 2000 | 1999 | 1998 |
| Prices:High | 85.77 | 79.42 | 74.10 | 47.45 | 33.65 | 33.85 | 47.50 | 31.31 | 50.75 | 36.13 |
| Prices:Low | 67.72 | 49.98 | 44.17 | 23.07 | 20.65 | 14.97 | 16.21 | 8.00 | 21.00 | 14.44 |
| P/E Ratio:High | 16 | 17 | 20 | 21 | 16 | 17 | 29 | 20 | 37 | 38 |
| P/E Ratio:Low | 13 | 11 | 12 | 10 | 10 | 8 | 10 | 5 | 15 | 15 |

| Income Statement Analysis (Million $) | | | | | | | | | | |
|---|---|---|---|---|---|---|---|---|---|---|
| Revenue | 3,750 | 3,318 | 2,785 | 2,021 | 1,708 | 1,596 | 1,365 | 1,238 | 1,042 | 816 |
| Operating Income | 912 | 794 | 661 | 453 | 398 | 370 | 313 | 284 | 270 | 188 |
| Depreciation | 184 | 146 | 124 | 106 | 66.6 | 56.9 | 41.2 | 30.7 | 27.7 | 20.9 |
| Interest Expense | Nil | Nil | Nil | Nil | Nil | Nil | Nil | Nil | Nil | Nil |
| Pretax Income | 759 | 672 | 549 | 353 | 335 | 316 | 277 | 261 | 249 | 170 |
| Effective Tax Rate | 37.4% | 37.2% | 39.2% | 38.7% | 38.8% | 38.4% | 39.0% | 39.5% | 40.0% | 40.0% |
| Net Income | 476 | 422 | 334 | 216 | 205 | 195 | 169 | 158 | 150 | 102 |
| S&P Core Earnings | 476 | 422 | 312 | 220 | 180 | 170 | 148 | 138 | NA | NA |

| Balance Sheet & Other Financial Data (Million $) | | | | | | | | | | |
|---|---|---|---|---|---|---|---|---|---|---|
| Cash | 649 | 530 | 462 | 350 | 521 | 401 | 239 | 138 | 194 | 164 |
| Current Assets | 1,140 | 1,092 | 947 | 652 | 753 | 601 | 405 | 304 | 300 | 218 |
| Total Assets | 2,568 | 2,248 | 1,790 | 1,348 | 1,199 | 995 | 771 | 588 | 458 | 319 |
| Current Liabilities | 543 | 511 | 492 | 414 | 280 | 211 | 164 | 155 | 138 | 122 |
| Long Term Debt | Nil | Nil | Nil | Nil | Nil | Nil | Nil | Nil | Nil | Nil |
| Common Equity | 1,618 | 1,405 | 995 | 669 | 871 | 750 | 595 | 423 | 311 | 186 |
| Total Capital | 1,641 | 1,436 | 1,034 | 725 | 891 | 770 | 597 | 423 | 311 | 186 |
| Capital Expenditures | 403 | 403 | 256 | 185 | 99.1 | 93.0 | 127 | 153 | 83.8 | 41.9 |
| Cash Flow | 659 | 568 | 458 | 322 | 272 | 252 | 210 | 189 | 177 | 123 |
| Current Ratio | 2.1 | 2.1 | 1.9 | 1.6 | 2.7 | 2.8 | 2.5 | 2.0 | 2.2 | 1.8 |
| % Long Term Debt of Capitalization | Nil | Nil | Nil | Nil | Nil | Nil | Nil | Nil | Nil | Nil |
| % Net Income of Revenue | 12.7 | 12.7 | 12.0 | 10.7 | 12.0 | 12.2 | 12.4 | 12.8 | 14.4 | 12.5 |
| % Return on Assets | 19.8 | 20.9 | 21.0 | 15.8 | 18.5 | 22.1 | 24.8 | 30.2 | 38.5 | 40.6 |
| % Return on Equity | 31.5 | 35.2 | 40.1 | 28.3 | 25.3 | 29.0 | 33.1 | 43.1 | 60.2 | 83.4 |

Data as orig reptd.; bef. results of disc opers/spec. items. Per share data adj. for stk. divs.; EPS diluted. E-Estimated. NA-Not Available. NM-Not Meaningful. NR-Not Ranked. UR-Under Review.

**Office:** 6301 Fitch Path, New Albany, OH 43054.
**Telephone:** 614-283-6500.
**Email:** investor_relations@abercrombie.com
**Website:** http://www.abercrombie.com

**Chrmn & CEO:** M.S. Jeffries
**SVP, CFO & Chief Acctg Officer:** M.M. Nuzzo
**SVP, Secy & General Counsel:** D.S. Cupps
**Investor Contact:** T.D. Lennox (614-283-6751)

**Cntlr:** B. Logan
**Board Members:** J. B. Bachmann, L. J. Brisky, A. M. Griffin, M. S. Jeffries, J. W. Kessler, E. Limato

**Founded:** 1892
**Domicile:** Delaware
**Employees:** 99,000

# Adobe Systems Inc

**STANDARD &POOR'S**

**S&P Recommendation** HOLD ★★★☆☆

| Price | 12-Mo. Target Price | Investment Style |
|---|---|---|
| $22.34 (as of Nov 14, 2008) | $44.00 | Large-Cap Growth |

**GICS Sector** Information Technology
**Sub-Industry** Application Software

**Summary** This company provides software for multimedia content creation, distribution and management.

## Key Stock Statistics (Source S&P, Vickers, company reports)

| | | | | | | | | |
|---|---|---|---|---|---|---|---|---|
| 52-Wk Range | $46.44– 21.12 | S&P Oper. EPS 2008E | 1.70 | Market Capitalization(B) | $11.862 | Beta | 1.56 |
| Trailing 12-Month EPS | $1.51 | S&P Oper. EPS 2009E | 1.90 | Yield (%) | Nil | S&P 3-Yr. Proj. EPS CAGR(%) | 15 |
| Trailing 12-Month P/E | 14.8 | P/E on S&P Oper. EPS 2008E | 13.1 | Dividend Rate/Share | Nil | S&P Credit Rating | NA |
| $10K Invested 5 Yrs Ago | $10,891 | Common Shares Outstg. (M) | 531.0 | Institutional Ownership (%) | 87 | | |

## Price Performance

30-Week Mov. Avg. · · · 10-Week Mov. Avg. - - **GAAP Earnings vs. Previous Year** Volume Above Avg. STARS
12-Mo. Target Price — Relative Strength — ▲ Up ▼ Down ▶ No Change Below Avg.

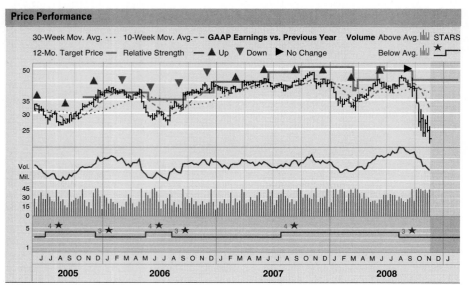

Options: ASE, CBOE, P, Ph

Analysis prepared by **Zaineb Bokhari** on September 26, 2008, when the stock traded at **$ 39.45**.

## Qualitative Risk Assessment

| LOW | MEDIUM | HIGH |
|---|---|---|

Our risk assessment reflects our view of ADBE's size and market leadership, consistent operating history, and strong balance sheet. This is offset by the regularly changing nature of the software industry.

## Quantitative Evaluations

**S&P Quality Ranking**     B+

| D | C | B- | B | B+ | A- | A | A+ |
|---|---|---|---|---|---|---|---|

**Relative Strength Rank**     MODERATE

35

LOWEST = 1       HIGHEST = 99

## Revenue/Earnings Data

**Revenue (Million $)**

| | 1Q | 2Q | 3Q | 4Q | Year |
|---|---|---|---|---|---|
| 2008 | 890.5 | 886.9 | 887.3 | -- | -- |
| 2007 | 649.4 | 745.6 | 851.7 | 911.2 | 3,158 |
| 2006 | 655.5 | 635.5 | 602.2 | 682.2 | 2,575 |
| 2005 | 472.9 | 496.0 | 487.0 | 510.4 | 1,966 |
| 2004 | 423.3 | 410.1 | 403.7 | 429.5 | 1,667 |
| 2003 | 296.9 | 320.2 | 319.1 | 358.6 | 1,295 |

**Earnings Per Share ($)**

| | | | | | |
|---|---|---|---|---|---|
| 2008 | 0.38 | 0.41 | 0.35 | E0.43 | E1.70 |
| 2007 | 0.24 | 0.25 | 0.35 | 0.38 | 1.21 |
| 2006 | 0.17 | 0.20 | 0.16 | 0.30 | 0.83 |
| 2005 | 0.30 | 0.29 | 0.29 | 0.31 | 1.19 |
| 2004 | 0.25 | 0.22 | 0.21 | 0.23 | 0.91 |
| 2003 | 0.12 | 0.14 | 0.14 | 0.17 | 0.55 |

Fiscal year ended Nov. 30. Next earnings report expected: NA. EPS Estimates based on S&P Operating Earnings; historical GAAP earnings are as reported.

## Dividend Data

No cash dividends have been paid since 2005.

## Highlights

➤ We expect sales to rise 15% in FY 08 (Nov.), with new products remaining a driver of sales growth. Year-to-year comparisons for Creative Suite 3 (CS3) sales turned negative in the August 2008 quarter, in anticipation, we think, of the launch of CS4, which we expect to ship in October 2008 (English). We expect CS4 to be feature rich, but note that CS3 benefited from several factors, including a longer time between releases, integration with acquired solutions from Macromedia, and pent-up demand for MacIntel users. We forecast 12% revenue growth in FY 09.

➤ We believe gross margins in FY 08 will widen slightly to about 90%, from 89% in FY 07, as we forecast modestly wider gross margins for products and services and support. We see FY 08 non-GAAP operating margins widening to almost 40%, from 38% in FY 07, based on our outlook for modestly lower R&D expenses and sales and marketing expenses as a percentage of sales. We think operating margins will widen slightly in FY 09 as sales growth moderates.

➤ Our estimates for operating EPS are $1.75 for FY 08 and $1.90 for FY 09, versus $1.46 in FY 07. We expect share repurchases to aid EPS.

## Investment Rationale/Risk

➤ We believe ADBE is well positioned to benefit from the continuing growth in rich Internet applications, web-based graphics and video creation and document processing. We expect new products including Acrobat 9, and the next version of Creative Suite (CS4) to help support growth in future periods. While ADBE shares generally rise in anticipation of new releases, we think that the impact on multiples may be muted because, in our view, the advantages that CS3 offered over CS2 were probably more significant to users than those offered by CS4 over CS3.

➤ Risks to our recommendation and target price include weaker demand than we expect for ADBE's CS4 and subsequent products, and increased competition for the Acrobat franchise from lower-cost PDF creation software.

➤ Our 12-month target price of $44 is based on an intrinsic value calculation using our discounted cash flow model, which assumes a weighted average cost of capital of 11.0% and 4% terminal growth. At this level, ADBE shares would trade at a P/E of about 23.2X our FY 09 operating EPS estimate, within the shares' historical trading range of 19.0X-29.3X.

---

**Please read the Required Disclosures and Analyst Certification on the last page of this report.**

*The McGraw-Hill Companies*

# Adobe Systems Inc

STANDARD &POOR'S

## Business Summary September 26, 2008

CORPORATE OVERVIEW. Adobe Systems (founded in 1982) is one of the world's largest software companies. It offers creative, business and mobile software and services used by consumers, artistic professionals, designers, knowledge workers, original equipment manufacturers, developers and enterprises for producing, managing, delivering and experiencing content across multiple operating systems, devices and media. Its cornerstone products include Acrobat (for document creation, distribution and management), Illustrator (to make graphic artwork), and Photoshop (for photo design, enhancement, and editing). In December 2005, ADBE acquired Macromedia, a leading developer of software that enables the creation and consumption of digital content, for $3.5 billion in stock and related costs. We believe this was an extremely important transaction for the company through which ADBE gained Macromedia's significant products included Dreamweaver (Web development) and Flash (which provides an environment to produce dynamic digital content). Subsequent acquisitions have been much smaller; during FY 07 (Nov.), ADBE acquired two businesses and completed one asset acquisition for about $80 million.

In FY 07, the company categorized its products in five segments: Creative Solutions, Knowledge Worker Solutions, Enterprise and Developer Solutions, Mobile and Device Solutions and Other. In the February 2008 quarter, ADBE combined Knowledge Worker Solutions and Enterprise and Developer Solutions into a new segment called Business Productivity Solutions.

CORPORATE STRATEGY. ADBE's indicated strategy is to address the needs of a variety of customers with offerings that support industry standards and can be deployed in a variety of contexts. We believe ADBE is focused on leveraging its market leading software franchises with bundles and enhancements. Selling multiple products together has enabled ADBE to gain market share, increase penetration with existing customers, and expand its overall customer base, in our view. The Creative Suite is the company's flagship bundled offering. Macromedia was acquired to further this strategy, and bundles of legacy Adobe and Macromedia software were released just days after their combination was completed.

We believe the purchase of Macromedia was an excellent strategic move for ADBE because it contributed technologies and products that have achieved notable adoption in the areas of dynamic digital content creation, and mobile platforms. In our opinion, ADBE's offerings in these segments were previously somewhat lacking, and Macromedia should bolster these businesses.

## Company Financials Fiscal Year Ended Nov. 30

| Per Share Data ($) | 2007 | 2006 | 2005 | 2004 | 2003 | 2002 | 2001 | 2000 | 1999 | 1998 |
|---|---|---|---|---|---|---|---|---|---|---|
| Tangible Book Value | 3.67 | 4.25 | 3.54 | 2.68 | 2.08 | 1.24 | 1.23 | 1.45 | 1.01 | 1.03 |
| Cash Flow | 1.74 | 1.33 | 1.31 | 1.03 | 0.65 | 0.52 | 0.53 | 0.65 | 0.56 | 0.30 |
| Earnings | 1.21 | 0.83 | 1.19 | 0.91 | 0.55 | 0.40 | 0.42 | 0.57 | 0.46 | 0.19 |
| S&P Core Earnings | 1.21 | 0.76 | 1.01 | 0.69 | 0.18 | 0.05 | 0.11 | NA | NA | NA |
| Dividends | Nil | Nil | 0.01 | 0.03 | 0.03 | 0.03 | 0.03 | 0.03 | 0.03 | 0.03 |
| Payout Ratio | Nil | Nil | 1% | 3% | 5% | 6% | 6% | 6% | 5% | 13% |
| Prices:High | 48.47 | 43.22 | 39.48 | 32.24 | 23.19 | 21.66 | 30.81 | 43.66 | 19.75 | 6.48 |
| Prices:Low | 37.20 | 25.98 | 25.80 | 17.15 | 12.29 | 8.25 | 11.10 | 13.36 | 4.71 | 2.95 |
| P/E Ratio:High | 40 | 52 | 33 | 35 | 42 | 55 | 74 | 77 | 43 | 33 |
| P/E Ratio:Low | 31 | 31 | 22 | 19 | 22 | 21 | 27 | 24 | 10 | 15 |

| Income Statement Analysis (Million $) | | | | | | | | | | |
|---|---|---|---|---|---|---|---|---|---|---|
| Revenue | 3,158 | 2,575 | 1,966 | 1,667 | 1,295 | 1,165 | 1,230 | 1,266 | 1,015 | 895 |
| Operating Income | 1,173 | 870 | 793 | 653 | 428 | 368 | 447 | 457 | 337 | 220 |
| Depreciation | 315 | 308 | 64.3 | 60.8 | 49.0 | 63.5 | 56.6 | 43.3 | 50.8 | 56.3 |
| Interest Expense | Nil | Nil | Nil | Nil | Nil | Nil | Nil | Nil | Nil | Nil |
| Pretax Income | 947 | 680 | 766 | 609 | 380 | 285 | 307 | 444 | 374 | 168 |
| Effective Tax Rate | 23.5% | 25.6% | 21.3% | 26.0% | 30.0% | 32.8% | 33.0% | 35.1% | 36.5% | 37.3% |
| Net Income | 724 | 506 | 603 | 450 | 266 | 191 | 206 | 288 | 238 | 105 |
| S&P Core Earnings | 721 | 466 | 515 | 343 | 86.7 | 20.6 | 51.7 | NA | NA | NA |

| Balance Sheet & Other Financial Data (Million $) | | | | | | | | | | |
|---|---|---|---|---|---|---|---|---|---|---|
| Cash | 946 | 772 | 421 | 376 | 190 | 184 | 219 | 237 | 171 | 111 |
| Current Assets | 2,573 | 2,884 | 2,009 | 1,551 | 1,329 | 814 | 767 | 878 | 623 | 456 |
| Total Assets | 5,714 | 5,963 | 2,440 | 1,959 | 1,555 | 1,052 | 931 | 1,069 | 804 | 767 |
| Current Liabilities | 852 | 677 | 480 | 451 | 437 | 377 | 314 | 315 | 268 | 251 |
| Long Term Debt | Nil | Nil | Nil | Nil | Nil | Nil | Nil | Nil | Nil | Nil |
| Common Equity | 4,650 | 5,152 | 1,864 | 1,423 | 1,101 | 674 | 617 | 753 | 512 | 516 |
| Total Capital | 4,799 | 5,223 | 1,943 | 1,502 | 1,119 | 674 | 617 | 755 | 536 | 516 |
| Capital Expenditures | 132 | 83.3 | 48.9 | 63.2 | 39.5 | 31.6 | 46.6 | 29.8 | 42.2 | 59.7 |
| Cash Flow | 1,039 | 814 | 667 | 511 | 315 | 255 | 262 | 331 | 289 | 161 |
| Current Ratio | 3.0 | 4.3 | 4.2 | 3.4 | 3.0 | 2.2 | 2.4 | 2.8 | 2.3 | 1.8 |
| % Long Term Debt of Capitalization | Nil | Nil | Nil | Nil | Nil | Nil | Nil | Nil | Nil | Nil |
| % Net Income of Revenue | 22.9 | 19.6 | 30.7 | 27.0 | 20.6 | 16.4 | 16.7 | 22.7 | 23.4 | 11.8 |
| % Return on Assets | 12.3 | 12.0 | 27.4 | 25.6 | 20.4 | 19.3 | 20.6 | 30.7 | 30.3 | 12.3 |
| % Return on Equity | 14.7 | 14.4 | 36.7 | 35.7 | 30.0 | 29.6 | 30.0 | 45.5 | 46.2 | 17.1 |

Data as orig reptd.; bef. results of disc opers/spec. items. Per share data adj. for stk. divs.; EPS diluted. E-Estimated. NA-Not Available. NM-Not Meaningful. NR-Not Ranked. UR-Under Review.

**Office:** 345 Park Avenue, San Jose, CA, USA 95110-2704.
**Telephone:** 408-536-6000.
**Email:** ir@adobe.com
**Website:** http://www.adobe.com

**Co-Chrmn:** J. Warnock
**Co-Chrmn:** C. Geschke
**Pres, CEO & COO:** S. Narayen
**EVP & CFO:** M. Garrett

**SVP, Secy & General Counsel:** K.O. Cottle
**Board Members:** C. M. Baldwin, E. W. Barnholt, R. K. Burgess, M. R. Cannon, B. R. Chizen, J. E. Daley, C. Geschke, S. Narayen, C. M. Pouliot, R. Sedgewick, J. Warnock, D. W. Yocam

**Founded:** 1983
**Domicile:** Delaware
**Employees:** 6,794

# Advanced Micro Devices Inc.

**STANDARD &POOR'S**

| S&P Recommendation **HOLD** ★★★☆☆ | Price<br>$2.43 (as of Nov 14, 2008) | 12-Mo. Target Price<br>$6.00 | Investment Style<br>Large-Cap Value |
|---|---|---|---|

**GICS Sector** Information Technology
**Sub-Industry** Semiconductors

**Summary** This company is a leading producer of semiconductors that are used principally in computers and related products.

## Key Stock Statistics (Source S&P, Vickers, company reports)

| | | | | | | | | |
|---|---|---|---|---|---|---|---|---|
| 52-Wk Range | $12.61–2.30 | S&P Oper. EPS 2008E | -0.98 | Market Capitalization(B) | $1.479 | Beta | 2.53 |
| Trailing 12-Month EPS | $-5.74 | S&P Oper. EPS 2009E | -0.79 | Yield (%) | Nil | S&P 3-Yr. Proj. EPS CAGR(%) | NM |
| Trailing 12-Month P/E | NM | P/E on S&P Oper. EPS 2008E | NM | Dividend Rate/Share | Nil | S&P Credit Rating | B |
| $10K Invested 5 Yrs Ago | $1,361 | Common Shares Outstg. (M) | 608.5 | Institutional Ownership (%) | 67 | | |

## Price Performance

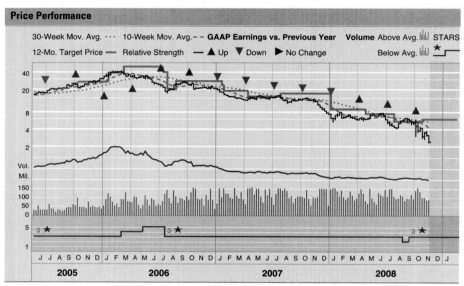

30-Week Mov. Avg. · · · 10-Week Mov. Avg. – · – **GAAP Earnings vs. Previous Year** Volume Above Avg. STARS
12-Mo. Target Price — Relative Strength — ▲ Up ▼ Down ▶ No Change Below Avg.

2005 2006 2007 2008

Options: ASE, CBOE, P, Ph

Analysis prepared by **Clyde Montevirgen** on October 21, 2008, when the stock traded at **$ 3.99**.

### Highlights

➤ We expect flat revenues in 2009, following a projected 5% increase in 2008 that includes license revenues. We see healthy computer shipments over the next two years, and think that AMD will be able to further penetrate lower-end markets, and improve sales of its quad-core and graphics chips. We believe PC makers prefer to have more than one microprocessor supplier, and will try to support AMD as long as it is financially feasible. However, AMD will likely lose market share to larger competitor Intel (INTC: buy, $16), in our view.

➤ We believe that AMD's non-GAAP gross margin will widen through 2009. We anticipate more modest price deterioration ahead as AMD looks to improve profitability. We also think that results will benefit from production shifts to smaller linewidths, unit shipment growth, traction of new chip offerings, and outsourcing. However, we believe higher R&D expenses will limit profitability, and see improving, yet still negative, operating margins ahead.

➤ We look for an operating loss per share of $0.79 for 2009, compared to a projected loss of $0.98 in 2008.

### Investment Rationale/Risk

➤ With global computer demand resiliently strong, AMD's new line of quad-core microprocessors has kept it in the microprocessor race against Intel. We think demand for these chips will aid near-term revenue growth and margins expansion. AMD's new graphics chips also appear to be gaining traction. Furthermore, AMD unveiled a new manufacturing strategy that we think will help to reduce business risk and strengthen its balance sheet. However, we believe that AMD has lost its technological edge and has become more vulnerable to share losses in lucrative higher-end markets, and expect Intel's upcoming chip launches to pose more challenges. We also see AMD's financial situation contributing to slower technological advances and limiting longer-term growth opportunities.

➤ Risks to our recommendation and target price include worse than anticipated demand for computers, greater market share losses, and an inability to pay off debt.

➤ Our 12-month target price of $6 is derived by applying a price-to-sales ratio of about 0.6X, at the low end of the historical average, to our forward 12-month sales per share estimate.

### Qualitative Risk Assessment

| LOW | MEDIUM | HIGH |
|---|---|---|

AMD is subject to the cyclical swings of the semiconductor industry, demand fluctuations for computer end-products, vacillation in average selling prices for chips, and strong competition from Intel, which is a much larger rival in microprocessors.

### Quantitative Evaluations

**S&P Quality Ranking** C

| D | C | B- | B | B+ | A- | A | A+ |
|---|---|---|---|---|---|---|---|

**Relative Strength Rank** WEAK

20

LOWEST = 1 HIGHEST = 99

### Revenue/Earnings Data

**Revenue (Million $)**

| | 1Q | 2Q | 3Q | 4Q | Year |
|---|---|---|---|---|---|
| 2008 | 1,505 | 1,349 | 1,776 | -- | -- |
| 2007 | 1,233 | 1,378 | 1,632 | 1,770 | 6,013 |
| 2006 | 1,332 | 1,216 | 1,328 | 1,773 | 5,649 |
| 2005 | 1,227 | 1,260 | 1,523 | 1,838 | 5,848 |
| 2004 | 1,236 | 1,262 | 1,239 | 1,264 | 5,001 |
| 2003 | 714.6 | 645.3 | 953.8 | 1,206 | 3,519 |

**Earnings Per Share ($)**

| | | | | | |
|---|---|---|---|---|---|
| 2008 | -0.59 | -0.44 | -0.05 | E-0.10 | E-0.98 |
| 2007 | -1.11 | -1.09 | -0.71 | -3.06 | -6.06 |
| 2006 | 0.38 | 0.18 | 0.27 | -1.08 | -0.34 |
| 2005 | -0.04 | 0.03 | 0.18 | 0.21 | 0.40 |
| 2004 | 0.12 | 0.09 | 0.12 | -0.08 | 0.25 |
| 2003 | -0.42 | -0.40 | -0.09 | 0.12 | -0.79 |

Fiscal year ended Dec. 31. Next earnings report expected: Mid January. EPS Estimates based on S&P Operating Earnings; historical GAAP earnings are as reported.

### Dividend Data

No cash dividends have been paid.

# Advanced Micro Devices Inc.

**STANDARD &POOR'S**

## Business Summary October 21, 2008

CORPORATE OVERVIEW. Advanced Micro Devices makes digital integrated circuits, including microprocessors for computers, embedded microprocessors for personal connectivity devices and, as a result of the company's acquisition of ATI Technologies in October 2006, 3D graphics, video, and multimedia products for various computing products. AMD also makes processors for consumer electronic devices such as mobile phones, digital televisions, and game consoles.

The company has three reportable segments: Computing Solutions, Graphics, and Consumer Electronics. The Computing Solutions segment (78% of 2007 total revenues) includes sales of microprocessors, chipsets, and embedded processors. The Graphics segment (15%) includes graphics, video and multimedia products. The Consumer Electronics segment (7%) includes products used in handheld devices, digital televisions and other consumer electronics products, as well as revenue from royalties received in connection with sales of game console systems that incorporate its technology. In addition to these three segments, the company also has another non-reportable All Other category, which includes expenses and credits that are not allocated to any of the operating segments.

COMPETITIVE LANDSCAPE. AMD generally competes in three main chip markets: microprocessor, graphics, and consumer electronics. The microprocessor is the central processing unit (CPU), or the "brains" of a computer. The microprocessor market is highly competitive, with competitors focusing on microprocessor performance as a way to gain market share, in our opinion. The company notes work-per-cycle, clock speed, power consumption, number of cores, bit ratings, memory size, and data access speed as key indicators or factors of processor performance. The semiconductor graphics market addresses the need for visual processing in various computing computers. The primary product in this space is the graphics processor unit (GPU), which offloads the burden of graphics processing from the CPU. More broadly characterized, the consumer electronics semiconductor market includes video, graphics and media processors in consumer electronics products that address the need for enhancing the visual experience. Similar to the microprocessor market, competitors in the GPU and consumer electronic chip markets focus on speed and performance as a means to improve multimedia functions in devices.

## Company Financials Fiscal Year Ended Dec. 31

| Per Share Data ($) | 2007 | 2006 | 2005 | 2004 | 2003 | 2002 | 2001 | 2000 | 1999 | 1998 |
|---|---|---|---|---|---|---|---|---|---|---|
| Tangible Book Value | 0.82 | 2.49 | 7.70 | 7.68 | 6.96 | 7.16 | 10.64 | 10.09 | 6.66 | 6.89 |
| Cash Flow | -3.72 | 1.36 | 3.14 | 3.54 | 2.08 | -1.60 | 1.69 | 4.53 | 1.45 | 1.27 |
| Earnings | -6.06 | -0.34 | 0.40 | 0.25 | -0.79 | -3.81 | -0.18 | 2.95 | -0.30 | -0.36 |
| S&P Core Earnings | -6.08 | -0.35 | 0.38 | -0.19 | -1.08 | -4.24 | -0.49 | NA | NA | NA |
| Dividends | Nil | Nil | Nil | Nil | Nil | Nil | Nil | Nil | Nil | Nil |
| Payout Ratio | Nil | Nil | Nil | Nil | Nil | Nil | Nil | Nil | Nil | Nil |
| Prices:High | 20.63 | 42.70 | 31.84 | 24.95 | 18.50 | 20.60 | 34.65 | 48.50 | 16.50 | 16.38 |
| Prices:Low | 7.26 | 16.90 | 14.08 | 10.76 | 4.78 | 3.10 | 7.69 | 13.56 | 7.28 | 6.38 |
| P/E Ratio:High | NM | NM | 80 | NM | NM | NM | NM | 16 | NM | NM |
| P/E Ratio:Low | NM | NM | 35 | NM | NM | NM | NM | 5 | NM | NM |

| Income Statement Analysis (Million $) | 2007 | 2006 | 2005 | 2004 | 2003 | 2002 | 2001 | 2000 | 1999 | 1998 |
|---|---|---|---|---|---|---|---|---|---|---|
| Revenue | 6,013 | 5,649 | 5,848 | 5,001 | 3,519 | 2,697 | 3,892 | 4,644 | 2,858 | 2,542 |
| Operating Income | 94.0 | 1,238 | 1,451 | 1,452 | 748 | -139 | 654 | 1,468 | 233 | 304 |
| Depreciation | 1,305 | 837 | 1,219 | 1,224 | 996 | 756 | 623 | 579 | 516 | 468 |
| Interest Expense | 390 | 126 | 105 | 112 | 110 | 71.3 | 61.4 | 60.0 | 69.3 | 66.5 |
| Pretax Income | -3,321 | -115 | 33.7 | 116 | -316 | -1,258 | -75.0 | 1,263 | 78.4 | -196 |
| Effective Tax Rate | NM | NM | NM | 5.05% | NM | NM | NM | 20.3% | NM | NM |
| Net Income | -3,379 | -166 | 165 | 91.2 | -274 | -1,303 | -60.6 | 1,006 | -88.9 | -104 |
| S&P Core Earnings | -3,391 | -170 | 155 | -68.2 | -373 | -1,450 | -161 | NA | NA | NA |

| Balance Sheet & Other Financial Data (Million $) | 2007 | 2006 | 2005 | 2004 | 2003 | 2002 | 2001 | 2000 | 1999 | 1998 |
|---|---|---|---|---|---|---|---|---|---|---|
| Cash | 1,889 | 1,380 | 633 | 918 | 968 | 429 | 427 | 591 | 294 | 362 |
| Current Assets | 3,816 | 3,963 | 3,559 | 3,228 | 2,900 | 2,020 | 2,353 | 2,658 | 1,410 | 1,562 |
| Total Assets | 11,550 | 13,147 | 7,288 | 7,844 | 7,094 | 5,619 | 5,647 | 5,768 | 4,378 | 4,253 |
| Current Liabilities | 2,625 | 2,852 | 1,822 | 1,846 | 1,452 | 1,372 | 1,314 | 1,224 | 911 | 841 |
| Long Term Debt | 5,031 | 3,672 | 1,327 | 1,628 | 1,900 | 1,780 | 673 | 1,168 | 1,427 | 1,372 |
| Common Equity | 2,990 | 5,785 | 3,352 | 3,010 | 2,438 | 2,467 | 3,555 | 3,172 | 1,979 | 2,005 |
| Total Capital | 8,292 | 9,778 | 5,006 | 5,583 | 5,213 | 4,247 | 4,333 | 4,544 | 3,467 | 3,412 |
| Capital Expenditures | 1,685 | 1,857 | 1,513 | 1,440 | 570 | 705 | 679 | 805 | 620 | 996 |
| Cash Flow | -2,074 | 671 | 1,385 | 1,315 | 721 | -547 | 562 | 1,585 | 427 | 364 |
| Current Ratio | 1.5 | 1.4 | 2.0 | 1.7 | 2.0 | 1.5 | 1.8 | 2.2 | 1.5 | 1.9 |
| % Long Term Debt of Capitalization | 60.7 | 37.6 | 26.5 | 29.2 | 36.4 | 41.9 | 15.5 | 25.7 | 41.2 | 40.2 |
| % Net Income of Revenue | NM | NM | 2.8 | 1.8 | NM | NM | NM | 21.7 | NM | NM |
| % Return on Assets | NM | NM | 2.2 | 1.2 | NM | NM | NM | 19.8 | NM | NM |
| % Return on Equity | NM | NM | 5.2 | 3.3 | NM | NM | NM | 39.1 | NM | NM |

Data as orig reptd.; bef. results of disc opers/spec. items. Per share data adj. for stk. divs.; EPS diluted. E-Estimated. NA-Not Available. NM-Not Meaningful. NR-Not Ranked. UR-Under Review.

**Office:** One AMD Place, Sunnyvale, CA 94088-3453.
**Telephone:** 408-749-4000.
**Email:** investor.relations@amd.com
**Website:** http://www.amd.com

**Chrmn:** H.D. Ruiz
**Pres & CEO:** D.R. Meyer
**Investor Contact:** R.J. Rivet (408-749-4000)
**COO, EVP & Chief Admin Officer:** R.J. Rivet

**SVP, Secy & General Counsel:** H.A. Wolin
**Board Members:** W. M. Barnes, J. E. Caldwell, B. L. Claflin, F. M. Clegg, H. P. Eberhart, D. R. Meyer, R. B. Palmer, H. D. Ruiz, M. L. Topfer

**Founded:** 1969
**Domicile:** Delaware
**Employees:** 16,420

*The McGraw-Hill Companies*

# AES Corporation (The)

**STANDARD &POOR'S**

| S&P Recommendation | BUY ★★★★☆ | Price $8.28 (as of Nov 14, 2008) | 12-Mo. Target Price $12.00 | Investment Style Large-Cap Growth |
|---|---|---|---|---|

**GICS Sector** Utilities
**Sub-Industry** Independent Power Producers & Energy Traders

**Summary** The world's largest independent power producer, AES produces and distributes electricity in international and domestic markets.

## Key Stock Statistics (Source S&P, Vickers, company reports)

| | | | | | | | | |
|---|---|---|---|---|---|---|---|---|
| 52-Wk Range | $22.54– 6.30 | S&P Oper. EPS 2008E | 1.08 | Market Capitalization(B) | $5.483 | Beta | 1.42 |
| Trailing 12-Month EPS | $1.89 | S&P Oper. EPS 2009E | 1.21 | Yield (%) | Nil | S&P 3-Yr. Proj. EPS CAGR(%) | 12 |
| Trailing 12-Month P/E | 4.4 | P/E on S&P Oper. EPS 2008E | 7.7 | Dividend Rate/Share | Nil | S&P Credit Rating | BB- |
| $10K Invested 5 Yrs Ago | $9,283 | Common Shares Outstg. (M) | 662.2 | Institutional Ownership (%) | 88 | | |

## Price Performance

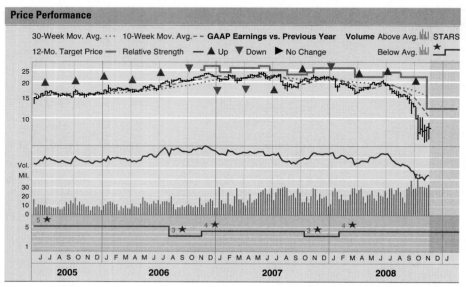

- 30-Week Mov. Avg. ···
- 10-Week Mov. Avg. – –
- **GAAP Earnings vs. Previous Year**
- Volume Above Avg.
- STARS
- 12-Mo. Target Price —
- Relative Strength —
- ▲ Up ▼ Down ► No Change
- Below Avg.

Options: ASE, CBOE, P, Ph

Analysis prepared by **Christopher B. Muir** on November 06, 2008, when the stock traded at **$ 6.67**.

### Highlights

► We see revenues rising 20% in 2008 and 9.5% in 2009. We project strong revenue growth in unregulated operations, supported by what we expect to be continued increases in demand for contract generation and strength in Latin American generation. We also see a rise in regulated revenues, aided by growth in customer demand overseas, partly offset by the absence of Venezuelan revenues.

► Our operating margin forecasts are 22.2% for 2008 and 22.4% for 2009, versus 22.2% in 2007. In 2008, we expect lower per-revenue selling and administrative expenses and unregulated cost of sales to be more than offset by higher per-revenue regulated cost of sales. Our pretax margin forecasts are 15.3% in 2008 and 16.3% in 2009, up from 13.1% in 2007. We see higher non-operating income and relatively flat net interest expense.

► Assuming an effective tax rate of 34.3% and a slight decrease in diluted shares outstanding, we estimate 2008 operating EPS of $1.16, up 16% from 2007. Our 2009 EPS forecast is $1.35, up an additional 16%.

### Investment Rationale/Risk

► We believe AES is a superior independent power producer. We think it should see above-average earnings growth and an improving balance sheet over the next couple of years, partly due to stronger economic growth in emerging markets. Results should also be helped by cost controls and strategic growth initiatives. Recent financial restatements have been relatively small and should not materially affect future results, in our view.

► Risks to our recommendation and target price include financial statement revisions, currency fluctuations, political and regulatory uncertainty regarding utility rates and U.S. power margins, and counterparty default risk.

► The stock recently traded at 5.8X our 2009 EPS estimate, or a 40% discount to independent power producer peers. Our 12-month target price of $12 is 8.9X our 2009 EPS estimate, or a 35% discount to our peer target, due to our view of AES's solid operations, offset by our view of risk created by recent financial reporting difficulties and volatility in exchange rates leading to earnings volatility.

### Qualitative Risk Assessment

| LOW | **MEDIUM** | HIGH |
|---|---|---|

Our risk assessment reflects the company's relatively large capitalization and mix of lower-risk regulated utility businesses in North America, offset by higher-risk merchant power operations and utility operations in emerging markets in South America, Eastern Europe, Central America and Asia.

### Quantitative Evaluations

**S&P Quality Ranking** B

| D | C | B- | **B** | B+ | A- | A | A+ |
|---|---|---|---|---|---|---|---|

**Relative Strength Rank** MODERATE

49

LOWEST = 1     HIGHEST = 99

### Revenue/Earnings Data

**Revenue (Million $)**

| | 1Q | 2Q | 3Q | 4Q | Year |
|---|---|---|---|---|---|
| 2008 | 4,104 | 4,146 | 4,345 | -- | -- |
| 2007 | 3,121 | 3,344 | 3,471 | 3,673 | 13,588 |
| 2006 | 2,973 | 3,044 | 3,135 | 3,147 | 12,299 |
| 2005 | 2,663 | 2,668 | 2,782 | 2,973 | 11,086 |
| 2004 | 2,257 | 2,263 | 2,423 | 2,543 | 9,486 |
| 2003 | 1,911 | 1,992 | 2,231 | 2,281 | 8,415 |

**Earnings Per Share ($)**

| | | | | | |
|---|---|---|---|---|---|
| 2008 | 0.35 | 1.31 | 0.22 | E0.26 | E1.08 |
| 2007 | 0.18 | 0.41 | 0.14 | 0.01 | 0.73 |
| 2006 | 0.53 | 0.33 | -0.51 | 0.07 | 0.43 |
| 2005 | 0.19 | 0.13 | 0.37 | 0.27 | 0.95 |
| 2004 | 0.12 | 0.10 | 0.20 | 0.14 | 0.57 |
| 2003 | 0.23 | 0.24 | 0.10 | 0.01 | 0.56 |

Fiscal year ended Dec. 31. Next earnings report expected: Mid March. EPS Estimates based on S&P Operating Earnings; historical GAAP earnings are as reported.

### Dividend Data

No cash dividends have been paid.

# AES Corporation (The)

**STANDARD &POOR'S**

## Business Summary November 06, 2008

CORPORATE OVERVIEW. AES Corporation (AES) owns and operates a portfolio of electricity generation and distribution business in 28 countries through its subsidiaries and affiliates. The company has two principal businesses: generation and regulated utilities.

The generation business provides power for sale to utilities and other wholesale customers while the regulated utilities business distributes power to retail, commercial, industrial, and governmental customers. In 2007, the generation unit contributed 49% of total revenues. It primarily sells electricity to utilities or other wholesale customers under power purchase agreements that are generally for five years or longer. We are positive on AES usually retaining 75% or more of a given customer's total capacity needs. The generation business also sells electricity to wholesale customers through competitive markets.

The remaining 51% of total revenues in 2007 came from the regulated utilities business. It markets electricity to residential, business, and government customers through integrated transmission and distribution systems.

The company also reports results geographically by segment. Latin American

operations accounted for 64% of revenues, North American operations for 24%, European and African operations for 12%, Middle Eastern and Asian operations for 6% and corporate activities for -6%. The company's largest exposure geographically is to Brazil (35%), the U.S. (19%), Chile (7%) and Argentina (5%).

CORPORATE STRATEGY. AES pursues both a global and a local growth strategy to increase its business. The company's global strategy focuses on large-scale projects and pursues strategic initiatives. It concentrates on mergers and acquisitions, exploring opportunities in the climate change business such as the production of greenhouse gas reduction activities and related industries that involve environmental issues. The company also aims to mitigate exposure to price swings. In 2007, 62% of the revenues from its generation business was from plants that operate under PPAs of five years or longer for at least 75% of their output capacity.

## Company Financials Fiscal Year Ended Dec. 31

| Per Share Data ($) | 2007 | 2006 | 2005 | 2004 | 2003 | 2002 | 2001 | 2000 | 1999 | 1998 |
|---|---|---|---|---|---|---|---|---|---|---|
| Tangible Book Value | 1.91 | 1.97 | NM | NM | NM | NM | 2.87 | 5.21 | 3.88 | 4.79 |
| Earnings | 0.73 | 0.43 | 0.95 | 0.57 | 0.56 | -4.81 | 0.87 | 1.42 | 0.63 | 0.84 |
| S&P Core Earnings | 0.65 | 0.78 | 1.04 | 0.51 | 0.94 | -3.66 | 0.74 | NA | NA | NA |
| Dividends | Nil | Nil | Nil | Nil | Nil | Nil | Nil | Nil | Nil | Nil |
| Payout Ratio | Nil | Nil | Nil | Nil | Nil | Nil | Nil | Nil | Nil | Nil |
| Prices:High | 24.24 | 23.85 | 18.13 | 13.71 | 9.50 | 17.92 | 60.15 | 72.81 | 38.19 | 29.00 |
| Prices:Low | 16.69 | 15.63 | 12.53 | 7.56 | 2.63 | 0.92 | 11.60 | 34.25 | 16.41 | 11.50 |
| P/E Ratio:High | 33 | 55 | 19 | 24 | 17 | NM | 69 | 51 | 61 | 35 |
| P/E Ratio:Low | 23 | 36 | 13 | 13 | 5 | NM | 13 | 24 | 26 | 14 |
| **Income Statement Analysis (Million $)** | | | | | | | | | | |
| Revenue | 13,588 | 12,299 | 11,086 | 9,486 | 8,415 | 8,632 | 9,327 | 6,691 | 3,253 | 2,398 |
| Depreciation | 942 | 933 | 889 | 841 | 781 | 837 | 859 | 582 | 278 | 196 |
| Maintenance | NA | NA | NA | NA | NA | NA | NA | NA | NA | NA |
| Fixed Charges Coverage | 1.90 | 1.94 | 1.73 | 1.30 | 1.38 | 0.34 | 1.42 | 1.80 | NA | NA |
| Construction Credits | NA | NA | NA | NA | NA | NA | NA | NA | NA | NA |
| Effective Tax Rate | 42.4% | 31.0% | 31.9% | 28.2% | 30.3% | NM | 28.7% | 24.7% | 26.4% | 26.6% |
| Net Income | 495 | 286 | 632 | 366 | 336 | -2,590 | 467 | 648 | 245 | 307 |
| S&P Core Earnings | 447 | 526 | 693 | 332 | 564 | -1,970 | 394 | NA | NA | NA |
| **Balance Sheet & Other Financial Data (Million $)** | | | | | | | | | | |
| Gross Property | 27,522 | 26,053 | 24,741 | 24,141 | 23,098 | 23,050 | 26,748 | 19,150 | NA | NA |
| Capital Expenditures | 2,425 | 1,460 | 1,143 | 892 | 1,228 | 2,116 | 3,173 | 2,150 | 918 | 574 |
| Net Property | 20,020 | 19,074 | 18,654 | 18,788 | 18,505 | 18,846 | 23,434 | 17,846 | NA | NA |
| Capitalization:Long Term Debt | 16,629 | 14,892 | 36,674 | 16,823 | 16,792 | 17,684 | 20,564 | 16,927 | NA | NA |
| Capitalization:% Long Term Debt | 84.0 | 83.1 | 95.7 | 91.1 | 96.3 | 102.0 | 78.8 | 77.9 | 75.9 | 64.4 |
| Capitalization:Preferred | Nil | Nil | Nil | Nil | Nil | Nil | Nil | NA | NA | NA |
| Capitalization:% Preferred | Nil | Nil | Nil | Nil | Nil | Nil | Nil | NA | NA | NA |
| Capitalization:Common | 3,164 | 3,036 | 1,649 | 1,645 | 645 | -341 | 5,539 | 4,811 | 2,637 | 1,794 |
| Capitalization:% Common | 16.0 | 16.9 | 4.30 | 8.91 | 3.70 | -1.97 | 21.2 | 22.1 | NA | NA |
| Total Capital | 24,282 | 21,818 | 40,655 | 20,758 | 19,293 | 19,142 | 29,537 | 24,752 | 17,708 | 8,585 |
| % Operating Ratio | 83.7 | 83.8 | 85.5 | 84.2 | 84.5 | 88.5 | 89.7 | 88.3 | NA | NA |
| % Earned on Net Property | 15.5 | 23.0 | 20.9 | 18.5 | 17.0 | 14.3 | 13.6 | 14.0 | NA | NA |
| % Return on Revenue | 3.6 | 2.3 | 5.7 | 3.9 | 4.0 | NM | 5.0 | 9.7 | 7.5 | 12.8 |
| % Return on Invested Capital | 16.7 | 16.3 | 7.0 | 13.6 | 13.6 | 21.6 | 7.3 | 9.8 | NA | NA |
| % Return on Common Equity | 15.9 | 12.3 | 48.5 | 33.4 | 221.1 | NM | 8.4 | 17.4 | 11.1 | 18.8 |

Data as orig reptd.; bef. results of disc opers/spec. items. Per share data adj. for stk. divs.; EPS diluted. E-Estimated. NA-Not Available. NM-Not Meaningful. NR-Not Ranked. UR-Under Review.

**Office:** 4300 Wilson Blvd., Arlington, VA 22203-4167.
**Telephone:** 703-522-1315.
**Email:** invest@aes.com
**Website:** http://www.aes.com

**Chrmn:** P. Odeen
**Pres & CEO:** P. Hanrahan
**COO & EVP:** A.R. Weilert
**EVP & CFO:** V.D. Harker

**EVP, Secy & General Counsel:** B.A. Miller
**Investor Contact:** A. Pasha (703-682-6552)
**Board Members:** P. Hanrahan, K. M. Johnson, J. A. Koskinen, P. Lader, J. H. McArthur, S. O. Moose, P. Odeen, C. O. Rossotti, S. Sandstrom

**Founded:** 1981
**Domicile:** Delaware
**Employees:** 28,000

**The McGraw-Hill Companies**

# Aetna Inc.

STANDARD
&POOR'S

| S&P Recommendation | BUY ★★★★☆ | Price $23.33 (as of Nov 14, 2008) | 12-Mo. Target Price $36.00 | Investment Style Large-Cap Blend |
|---|---|---|---|---|

**GICS Sector** Health Care
**Sub-Industry** Managed Health Care

**Summary** This company is a leading U.S. provider of health care, dental, pharmacy, group life, disability and long-term care benefits.

## Key Stock Statistics (Source S&P, Vickers, company reports)

| | | | | | | | |
|---|---|---|---|---|---|---|---|
| 52-Wk Range | $60.00– 20.41 | S&P Oper. EPS 2008E | 3.92 | Market Capitalization(B) | $10.757 | Beta | 1.61 |
| Trailing 12-Month EPS | $3.27 | S&P Oper. EPS 2009E | 4.08 | Yield (%) | 0.17 | S&P 3-Yr. Proj. EPS CAGR(%) | 12 |
| Trailing 12-Month P/E | 7.1 | P/E on S&P Oper. EPS 2008E | 6.0 | Dividend Rate/Share | $0.04 | S&P Credit Rating | A- |
| $10K Invested 5 Yrs Ago | $15,656 | Common Shares Outstg. (M) | 461.1 | Institutional Ownership (%) | 95 | | |

## Price Performance

30-Week Mov. Avg. · · · 10-Week Mov. Avg. - - **GAAP Earnings vs. Previous Year**   Volume Above Avg. ||||   STARS
12-Mo. Target Price — Relative Strength — ▲ Up ▼ Down ▶ No Change   Below Avg. ||||   ★⌐

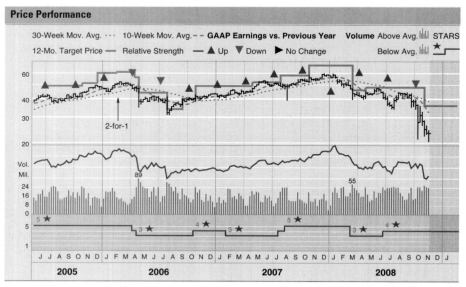

Options: ASE, CBOE, P, Ph

Analysis prepared by **Phillip M. Seligman** on November 04, 2008, when the stock traded at **$ 24.75**.

### Highlights

➤ We forecast health care operating revenues to grow by over 6% in 2009, to $30.5 billion, from the $28.7 billion we expect in 2008. Drivers we see include 100,000 Connecticut Medicaid members whose contract was delayed until 2009 and AET's anticipated first quarter net membership growth of 800,000 commercial (predominantly ASC) members, partly offset by fewer risk-based commercial members amid continued economic softness. Such growth is below the 17.5% we project for 2008, given 800,000 fully insured and ASC members added so far this year and 2007 acquisitions.

➤ Assuming pricing is in line with the 7.5% to 8.5% medical cost trends it projects, about 50 basis points above its 2008 levels, we expect the commercial medical benefit ratio (MBR) to be flat to modestly higher. Still, we expect the firmwide MBR to rise on higher Medicare and Medicaid revenue in the mix. The SG&A cost ratio rises on higher pension expense.

➤ We project operating EPS of $3.92 in 2008, reflecting lower investment income, and $4.08 in 2009, after an incremental $0.35 in amortized (non-cash) pension expense, due to 2008 equity market performance.

### Investment Rationale/Risk

➤ We believe AET's reduced 2008 EPS target and incremental 2009 pension expense reflect deterioration in the capital markets, not in its core business. While AET views the second quarter claims spike that caused the third quarter's unfavorable prior period reserve development as aberrant, we think the company was prudent to update its pricing model and reserves assuming a sustained uptick in costs. We believe AET exhibits above-peer execution, with its focus on new markets and products helping it attain its 2008 member growth target as of September 30, the Connecticut Medicaid contract, and expanded Bank of America, Citigroup, and Home Depot contracts and the new Progressive contract that starts in 2009. Despite capital losses recognized in the third quarter, we view AET's financial position as healthy.

➤ Risks to our recommendation and target price include intensified competition, a weak economy, and adverse medical cost trends.

➤ We apply a forward P/E of about 9X to our 2009 EPS estimate to derive our 12-month target price of $36. This multiple reflects groupwide valuation contraction, but is above peers on our view of superior management execution.

## Qualitative Risk Assessment

| LOW | MEDIUM | HIGH |
|---|---|---|

Our risk assessment reflects AET's leadership in the highly fragmented managed care market. We see competition intensifying in the managed care sub-industry, as consolidation has led the largest companies, AET included, to bump up against one another in more market sectors and geographies. However, we believe AET's expanding product, market and geographic diversity will permit stable operational performance over the longer term.

## Quantitative Evaluations

**S&P Quality Ranking** NR

| D | C | B- | B | B+ | A- | A | A+ |
|---|---|---|---|---|---|---|---|

**Relative Strength Rank** MODERATE

39

LOWEST = 1     HIGHEST = 99

## Revenue/Earnings Data

**Revenue (Million $)**

| | 1Q | 2Q | 3Q | 4Q | Year |
|---|---|---|---|---|---|
| 2008 | 7,739 | 7,828 | 7,625 | | |
| 2007 | 6,700 | 6,794 | 6,961 | 7,144 | 27,600 |
| 2006 | 6,235 | 6,252 | 6,300 | 6,360 | 25,146 |
| 2005 | 5,427 | 5,497 | 5,701 | 5,867 | 22,492 |
| 2004 | 4,821 | 4,875 | 5,040 | 5,168 | 19,904 |
| 2003 | 4,467 | 4,466 | 4,469 | 4,575 | 17,976 |

**Earnings Per Share ($)**

| | | | | | |
|---|---|---|---|---|---|
| 2008 | 0.85 | 0.97 | 0.58 | E0.94 | E3.92 |
| 2007 | 0.81 | 0.85 | 0.95 | 0.87 | 3.47 |
| 2006 | 0.65 | 0.67 | 0.85 | 0.80 | 2.96 |
| 2005 | 0.70 | 0.68 | 0.63 | 0.71 | 2.70 |
| 2004 | 0.51 | 0.45 | 0.48 | 0.49 | 1.94 |
| 2003 | 0.53 | 0.22 | 0.34 | 0.39 | 1.48 |

Fiscal year ended Dec. 31. Next earnings report expected: Early February. EPS Estimates based on S&P Operating Earnings; historical GAAP earnings are as reported.

## Dividend Data (Dates: mm/dd Payment Date: mm/dd/yy)

| Amount ($) | Date Decl. | Ex-Div. Date | Stk. of Record | Payment Date |
|---|---|---|---|---|
| 0.040 | 09/28 | 11/13 | 11/15 | 11/30/07 |
| 0.040 | 09/26 | 11/10 | 11/13 | 11/28/08 |

Dividends have been paid since 2001. Source: Company reports.

---

**Please read the Required Disclosures and Analyst Certification on the last page of this report.**

# Aetna Inc.

## Business Summary November 04, 2008

CORPORATE OVERVIEW. In December 2000, Aetna sold its financial services and international operations for $5 billion ($35.33 a share, not adjusted) and the assumption of $2.7 billion of debt. AET shareholders received $35.33 a share in cash, plus one share of a new health care company named Aetna. Revenue contributions (excluding net investment and other income) from the company's business operations in 2007 were: Health Care 90%; Group Insurance 8%; and Large Case Pensions 2%.

The Health Care segment offers health maintenance organization (HMO), point-of-service (POS), preferred provider organization (PPO) and indemnity benefit products. The company had total health plan enrollment of 17,668,000 lives at September 30, 2008, up from 16,853,000 at December 31, 2007. Commercial risk enrollment was 5,525,000 lives, versus 5,390,000, while commercial administrative services (ASC; fee-based, self-funded accounts) was 10,931,000 lives, versus 10,453,000. Medicare enrollment was 365,000 lives, versus 207,000, while Medicaid enrollment was 845,000 lives, versus 803,000. The company also provided dental benefits to 14,117,000 members, versus

13,832,000, and pharmacy benefits to 11,054,000 members, versus 10,732,000.

Group Insurance provides group life, disability and long-term care products; group life contracts and group conversion policies totaled 42,402,000 at December 31, 2007, up from 41,218,000 at December 31, 2006.

Large Case Pensions manages various retirement products, including pension and annuity products, for defined benefit and defined contribution plans. Aetna has not marketed its Large Case Pensions products since 1993, but continues to manage the run-off of existing business. At December 31, 2007, assets under management totaled $24.2 billion, up from $24.0 billion at December 31, 2006.

## Company Financials Fiscal Year Ended Dec. 31

| Per Share Data ($) | 2007 | 2006 | 2005 | 2004 | 2003 | 2002 | 2001 | 2000 | 1999 | 1998 |
|---|---|---|---|---|---|---|---|---|---|---|
| Tangible Book Value | 8.46 | 7.46 | 8.57 | 8.42 | 6.15 | 4.69 | 4.51 | 4.25 | NA | NA |
| Cash Flow | 4.08 | 2.96 | 3.04 | 2.22 | 1.79 | 1.14 | 0.54 | 0.82 | NA | NA |
| Earnings | 3.47 | 2.96 | 2.70 | 1.94 | 1.48 | 0.64 | -0.51 | -0.23 | 0.84 | NA |
| S&P Core Earnings | 3.39 | 2.96 | 2.55 | 1.71 | 1.51 | 0.19 | -1.12 | NA | NA | NA |
| Dividends | 0.04 | 0.04 | 0.02 | 0.01 | 0.01 | 0.01 | 0.01 | Nil | NA | NA |
| Payout Ratio | 1% | 1% | NM | NM | 1% | 2% | NM | Nil | NA | NA |
| Prices:High | 60.00 | 52.48 | 49.68 | 31.89 | 17.56 | 12.98 | 10.67 | 10.59 | NA | NA |
| Prices:Low | 39.02 | 30.94 | 29.93 | 16.41 | 9.98 | 7.48 | 5.75 | 8.23 | NA | NA |
| P/E Ratio:High | 17 | 18 | 18 | 16 | 12 | 20 | NM | NM | NA | NA |
| P/E Ratio:Low | 11 | 10 | 11 | 8 | 7 | 12 | NM | NM | NA | NA |

| Income Statement Analysis (Million $) | 2007 | 2006 | 2005 | 2004 | 2003 | 2002 | 2001 | 2000 | 1999 | 1998 |
|---|---|---|---|---|---|---|---|---|---|---|
| Revenue | 27,600 | 25,146 | 22,492 | 19,904 | 17,976 | 19,879 | 25,191 | 26,819 | 22,110 | 16,589 |
| Operating Income | 3,234 | 2,983 | 2,807 | 2,184 | 1,596 | 1,119 | 460 | 1,104 | NA | NA |
| Depreciation | 322 | 270 | 204 | 182 | 200 | 302 | 598 | 588 | NA | NA |
| Interest Expense | 181 | 148 | 123 | 105 | 103 | 120 | 143 | 248 | NA | NA |
| Pretax Income | 2,796 | 2,587 | 2,547 | 1,899 | 1,442 | 545 | -379 | -39.0 | 745 | 842 |
| Effective Tax Rate | 34.5% | 34.8% | 35.8% | 36.0% | 35.2% | 27.8% | NM | NM | 46.4% | 46.5% |
| Net Income | 1,831 | 1,686 | 1,635 | 1,215 | 934 | 393 | -292 | -127 | 399 | 450 |
| S&P Core Earnings | 1,792 | 1,682 | 1,542 | 1,072 | 957 | 140 | -639 | NA | NA | NA |

| Balance Sheet & Other Financial Data (Million $) | 2007 | 2006 | 2005 | 2004 | 2003 | 2002 | 2001 | 2000 | 1999 | 1998 |
|---|---|---|---|---|---|---|---|---|---|---|
| Cash | 2,078 | 880 | 1,378 | 1,595 | 1,655 | 2,017 | 1,631 | 2,204 | 1,629 | 1,101 |
| Current Assets | 5,288 | 18,304 | 18,235 | 19,516 | 19,557 | 19,349 | 18,751 | 19,768 | NA | NA |
| Total Assets | 50,725 | 47,626 | 44,365 | 42,134 | 40,950 | 40,048 | 43,255 | 47,446 | 52,422 | 53,355 |
| Current Liabilities | 7,675 | 7,103 | 7,617 | 7,011 | 7,368 | 7,719 | 8,139 | 10,003 | NA | NA |
| Long Term Debt | 3,269 | 2,442 | 1,156 | 1,610 | 1,614 | 1,633 | 1,591 | Nil | NA | NA |
| Common Equity | 10,038 | 11,009 | 12,167 | 9,081 | 7,924 | 6,980 | 9,890 | 10,127 | 10,703 | 11,430 |
| Total Capital | 13,323 | 11,587 | 13,338 | 10,691 | 9,538 | 8,613 | 11,481 | 10,127 | NA | NA |
| Capital Expenditures | 400 | 291 | 272 | 190 | 211 | 156 | 143 | 36.9 | NA | NA |
| Cash Flow | 2,153 | 1,686 | 1,839 | 1,397 | 1,133 | 695 | 306 | 461 | NA | NA |
| Current Ratio | 0.7 | 2.6 | 2.4 | 2.8 | 2.7 | 2.5 | 2.3 | 2.0 | 2.0 | 2.4 |
| % Long Term Debt of Capitalization | 23.8 | 18.2 | 8.7 | 15.1 | 16.9 | 19.0 | 13.9 | Nil | 16.4 | 12.2 |
| % Net Income of Revenue | 6.6 | 6.7 | 7.6 | 6.4 | 5.2 | 2.0 | NM | NM | 1.8 | 2.7 |
| % Return on Assets | 3.7 | 3.7 | 3.8 | 2.9 | 2.3 | 0.9 | NM | NM | NA | NA |
| % Return on Equity | 19.1 | 14.5 | 14.0 | 14.3 | 12.5 | 4.7 | NM | NM | 3.6 | NA |

Data as orig reptd.; bef. results of disc opers/spec. items. Per share data adj. for stk. divs.; EPS diluted. E-Estimated. NA-Not Available. NM-Not Meaningful. NR-Not Ranked. UR-Under Review.

**Office:** 151 Farmington Avenue, Hartford, CT 06156-0002.
**Telephone:** 860-273-0123.
**Email:** investorrelations@aetna.com
**Website:** http://www.aetna.com

**Chrmn & CEO:** R.A. Williams
**Pres & COO:** M.T. Bertolini
**EVP & CFO:** J. Zubretsky
**SVP & General Counsel:** W.J. Casazza

**SVP & CIO:** M. McCarthy
**Investor Contact:** J. Chaffkin (860-273-7830)
**Board Members:** L. Abramson, F. M. Clark, Jr., B. Z. Cohen, M. J. Coye, R. N. Farah, B. H. Franklin, J. E. Garten, E. G. Graves, G. Greenwald, E. M. Hancock, R. J. Harrington, E. J. Ludwig, A. Misher, J. Newhouse, D. B. Soll, R. A. Williams

**Founded:** 1982
**Domicile:** Pennsylvania
**Employees:** 35,200

# Affiliated Computer Services Inc.

**STANDARD &POOR'S**

| S&P Recommendation **HOLD** ★★★☆☆ | Price $39.30 (as of Nov 14, 2008) | 12-Mo. Target Price $48.00 | Investment Style Large-Cap Growth |
|---|---|---|---|

**GICS Sector** Information Technology
**Sub-Industry** Data Processing & Outsourced Services

**Summary** This company provides a full range of information technology services, including technology outsourcing, business process outsourcing, and professional services.

## Key Stock Statistics (Source S&P, Vickers, company reports)

| | | | | | | | |
|---|---|---|---|---|---|---|---|
| 52-Wk Range | $57.40– 36.84 | S&P Oper. EPS 2009**E** | 3.72 | Market Capitalization(B) | $3.574 | Beta | 0.60 |
| Trailing 12-Month EPS | $3.53 | S&P Oper. EPS 2010**E** | 4.30 | Yield (%) | Nil | S&P 3-Yr. Proj. EPS CAGR(%) | 12 |
| Trailing 12-Month P/E | 11.1 | P/E on S&P Oper. EPS 2009**E** | 10.6 | Dividend Rate/Share | Nil | S&P Credit Rating | BB |
| $10K Invested 5 Yrs Ago | $8,387 | Common Shares Outstg. (M) | 97.6 | Institutional Ownership (%) | 96 | | |

## Price Performance

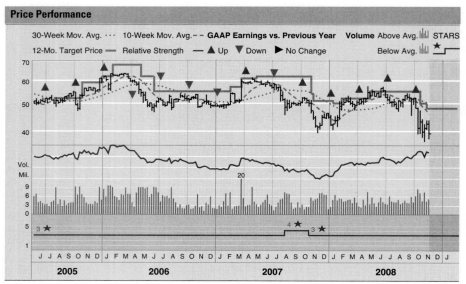

30-Week Mov. Avg. ···  10-Week Mov. Avg. - -  **GAAP Earnings vs. Previous Year**  Volume Above Avg. STARS
12-Mo. Target Price —  Relative Strength —  ▲ Up  ▼ Down  ▶ No Change  Below Avg.

Options: ASE, CBOE, P, Ph

Analysis prepared by **Dylan Cathers** on November 04, 2008, when the stock traded at **$ 42.15**.

### Highlights

➤ We expect revenues to advance 7% in FY 09 (Jun.) and 5% in FY 10, but we look for organic growth to be in the low to mid-single digits this fiscal year. In the commercial segment, we see faster growth, reflecting a high level of business process outsourcing signings, and gains in the communications and consumer goods verticals. Contract signings were solid in the September quarter, increasing 15%, year to year, which should help growth going forward. In the government segment, we look for low single digit growth, paced by electronic payment and child services verticals.

➤ We see operating margins widening in FY 09, as higher revenues, cost savings from last year's restructuring and improved contract terms outweigh start-up costs from recently signed contracts. Also aiding margins will be another round of restructuring, including an increased investment in sales personnel and the shifting of workers overseas; and lower levels of high-margin non-recurring revenues.

➤ Our FY 09 EPS estimate is $3.72. We view earnings quality as poor, reflecting numerous one-time items. For FY 10, we look for EPS of $4.30.

### Investment Rationale/Risk

➤ Our hold opinion is based on our concerns about ongoing expenses related to shareholder lawsuits and other charges, delays in recent contract signings, our view of modest internal growth in the commercial segment, and another restructuring program. These concerns are offset by our expectation of gains in the government business with its wider margins, given the improving pipeline.

➤ Risks to our recommendation and target price include competition in the IT services marketplace, particularly the business process outsourcing arena, which could cause pricing pressures, and ongoing expenses related to shareholder lawsuits. We also have corporate governance concerns, including a non-shareholder approved "poison pill" and an ongoing investigation of ACS's historical stock option pricing practices.

➤ Our 12-month target price of $48 is based on a peer-average P/E of 12.2X and a P/E-to-growth ratio of 1.02X, a slight premium versus more traditional outsourcers, based on estimated calendar 2009 EPS of $3.93 and assuming a three-year growth rate of 12%.

## Qualitative Risk Assessment

| LOW | MEDIUM | **HIGH** |
|---|---|---|

Our risk assessment reflects what we see as the highly competitive nature of the IT outsourcing and business process outsourcing markets, the company's recently increased debt load, and the SEC's informal investigation surrounding the timing of ACS's stock options.

## Quantitative Evaluations

**S&P Quality Ranking** B+

| D | C | B- | B | **B+** | A- | A | A+ |
|---|---|---|---|---|---|---|---|

**Relative Strength Rank** MODERATE

66

LOWEST = 1          HIGHEST = 99

## Revenue/Earnings Data

**Revenue (Million $)**

| | 1Q | 2Q | 3Q | 4Q | Year |
|---|---|---|---|---|---|
| 2009 | 1,604 | -- | -- | -- | -- |
| 2008 | 1,493 | 1,511 | 1,542 | 1,614 | 6,161 |
| 2007 | 1,385 | 1,427 | 1,441 | 1,520 | 5,772 |
| 2006 | 1,311 | 1,348 | 1,314 | 1,381 | 5,354 |
| 2005 | 1,046 | 1,027 | 1,063 | 1,214 | 4,351 |
| 2004 | 1,037 | 997.9 | 1,009 | 1,062 | 4,106 |

**Earnings Per Share ($)**

| | | | | | |
|---|---|---|---|---|---|
| 2009 | 0.85 | E0.90 | E0.92 | E1.01 | E3.72 |
| 2008 | 0.65 | 0.81 | 0.85 | 1.01 | 3.32 |
| 2007 | 0.59 | 0.72 | 0.82 | 0.37 | 2.49 |
| 2006 | 0.73 | 0.81 | 0.61 | 0.73 | 2.87 |
| 2005 | 0.72 | 0.73 | 0.88 | 0.87 | 3.19 |
| 2004 | 0.62 | 1.80 | 0.52 | 0.68 | 3.83 |

Fiscal year ended Jun. 30. Next earnings report expected: Early February. EPS Estimates based on S&P Operating Earnings; historical GAAP earnings are as reported.

## Dividend Data

No cash dividends have been paid.

# Affiliated Computer Services Inc.

**STANDARD & POOR'S**

## Business Summary November 04, 2008

CORPORATE OVERVIEW. ACS provides business process and information technology outsourcing solutions to commercial and government clients. In the commercial sector, the company provides business outsourcing, systems integration services and technology outsourcing to a variety of clients. The business process outsourcing division provides services such as claims processing, finance and accounting, and loan processing. The technology outsourcing division offers the delivery of information processing services on a remote basis from host data centers that provide processing capacity, network management, and desktop support. The systems integration services unit offers application development and implementation, applications outsourcing, technical support and training, network design and installation.

In the federal government sector, ACS offers business process outsourcing and systems integration services. The business process outsourcing unit consists primarily of loan servicing and human resource services for federal agencies. Within the state and local government sector, ACS designs, implements and operates large-scale health and human services programs and the supporting information technology solutions. ACS also provides child support and payment processing with high volume remittance processing and service center operations.

CORPORATE STRATEGY. Key elements of the company's business strategy include developing long-term relationships with new clients, expanding existing customer relationships, building recurring revenue streams, investing in technology, and completing strategic and tactical acquisitions. ACS provides a full range of information technology services to clients with time critical, transaction intensive business and information processing needs. Its services are designed to enable businesses and government agencies to focus on core operations, respond to rapidly changing technologies, and reduce expenses.

## Company Financials Fiscal Year Ended Jun. 30

| Per Share Data ($) | 2008 | 2007 | 2006 | 2005 | 2004 | 2003 | 2002 | 2001 | 2000 | 1999 |
|---|---|---|---|---|---|---|---|---|---|---|
| Tangible Book Value | NM | NM | NM | 0.30 | 2.64 | 1.94 | 0.11 | 0.90 | 0.44 | NM |
| Cash Flow | NA | 5.90 | 5.19 | 4.98 | 5.11 | 3.20 | 2.47 | 1.96 | 1.74 | 1.37 |
| Earnings | 3.32 | 2.49 | 2.87 | 3.19 | 3.83 | 2.20 | 1.76 | 1.23 | 1.04 | 0.83 |
| S&P Core Earnings | 3.31 | 2.45 | 2.70 | 3.03 | 2.48 | 2.11 | 1.73 | 1.11 | NA | NA |
| Dividends | Nil | Nil | Nil | Nil | Nil | Nil | Nil | Nil | Nil | Nil |
| Payout Ratio | Nil | Nil | Nil | Nil | Nil | Nil | Nil | Nil | Nil | Nil |
| Prices:High | 57.40 | 61.67 | 63.66 | 61.16 | 61.23 | 56.56 | 57.05 | 53.63 | 31.31 | 26.50 |
| Prices:Low | 36.84 | 39.46 | 46.50 | 45.81 | 46.01 | 40.01 | 32.70 | 26.81 | 15.50 | 15.88 |
| P/E Ratio:High | 17 | 25 | 22 | 19 | 16 | 26 | 32 | 44 | 30 | 32 |
| P/E Ratio:Low | 11 | 16 | 16 | 14 | 12 | 18 | 19 | 22 | 15 | 19 |

| Income Statement Analysis (Million $) | 2008 | 2007 | 2006 | 2005 | 2004 | 2003 | 2002 | 2001 | 2000 | 1999 |
|---|---|---|---|---|---|---|---|---|---|---|
| Revenue | 6,161 | 5,772 | 5,354 | 4,351 | 4,106 | 3,787 | 3,063 | 2,064 | 1,963 | 1,642 |
| Operating Income | NA | 960 | 926 | 887 | 742 | 671 | 511 | 317 | 265 | 225 |
| Depreciation | 381 | 346 | 290 | 233 | 184 | 152 | 110 | 93.6 | 84.8 | 66.7 |
| Interest Expense | NA | 183 | 68.4 | 18.6 | 17.0 | 25.2 | 30.6 | 23.7 | 24.0 | 17.6 |
| Pretax Income | 496 | 383 | 558 | 641 | 829 | 491 | 360 | 221 | 195 | 146 |
| Effective Tax Rate | 33.7% | 34.0% | 35.7% | 35.1% | 36.1% | 37.5% | 36.3% | 39.3% | 44.0% | 40.8% |
| Net Income | 329 | 253 | 359 | 416 | 530 | 307 | 230 | 134 | 109 | 86.2 |
| S&P Core Earnings | 328 | 249 | 337 | 393 | 339 | 291 | 225 | 119 | NA | NA |

| Balance Sheet & Other Financial Data (Million $) | 2008 | 2007 | 2006 | 2005 | 2004 | 2003 | 2002 | 2001 | 2000 | 1999 |
|---|---|---|---|---|---|---|---|---|---|---|
| Cash | 462 | 307 | 101 | 62.7 | 76.9 | 51.2 | 33.8 | 242 | 44.5 | 32.8 |
| Current Assets | NA | 1,811 | 1,529 | 1,244 | 1,044 | 979 | 874 | 810 | 772 | 416 |
| Total Assets | 6,469 | 5,982 | 5,502 | 4,851 | 3,907 | 3,699 | 3,404 | 1,892 | 1,656 | 1,224 |
| Current Liabilities | NA | 971 | 825 | 838 | 638 | 557 | 486 | 281 | 358 | 222 |
| Long Term Debt | NA | 2,342 | 1,614 | 750 | 372 | 498 | 708 | 649 | 526 | 382 |
| Common Equity | 2,308 | 2,066 | 2,456 | 2,838 | 2,590 | 2,429 | 2,095 | 886 | 711 | 607 |
| Total Capital | NA | 4,776 | 4,402 | 3,829 | 3,197 | 3,104 | 2,899 | 1,590 | 1,272 | 989 |
| Capital Expenditures | 268 | 317 | 394 | 253 | 225 | 206 | 144 | 99.1 | 71.5 | 61.1 |
| Cash Flow | NA | 599 | 649 | 649 | 714 | 459 | 340 | 228 | 194 | 153 |
| Current Ratio | 1.9 | 1.9 | 1.9 | 1.5 | 1.6 | 1.8 | 1.8 | 2.9 | 2.2 | 1.9 |
| % Long Term Debt of Capitalization | 50.0 | 49.0 | 36.7 | 19.6 | 11.6 | 16.1 | 24.4 | 40.8 | 41.3 | 38.6 |
| % Net Income of Revenue | 5.3 | 4.4 | 6.7 | 9.6 | 12.9 | 8.1 | 7.5 | 6.5 | 5.6 | 5.3 |
| % Return on Assets | 5.3 | 4.4 | 6.9 | 9.5 | 13.9 | 8.6 | 8.7 | 7.6 | 7.6 | 7.9 |
| % Return on Equity | 15.0 | 11.2 | 13.6 | 15.3 | 21.1 | 13.6 | 15.4 | 16.8 | 16.6 | 15.5 |

Data as orig reptd.; bef. results of disc opers/spec. items. Per share data adj. for stk. divs.; EPS diluted. E-Estimated. NA-Not Available. NM-Not Meaningful. NR-Not Ranked. UR-Under Review.

**Office:** 2828 North Haskell Avenue, Dallas, TX 75204-2988.
**Telephone:** 214-841-6111.
**Email:** info@acs-inc.com
**Website:** http://www.acs-inc.com

**Chrmn:** D. Deason
**Pres & CEO:** L. Blodgett
**COO & EVP:** T. Burlin
**EVP & CFO:** K. Kyser

**EVP, Secy & General Counsel:** T. Panos
**Investor Contact:** J. Puckett (214-841-8281)
**Board Members:** L. Blodgett, D. Deason, R. Druskin, K. Krauss, T. B. Miller, Jr., P. E. Sullivan, F. Varasano

**Founded:** 1971
**Domicile:** Pennsylvania
**Employees:** 65,000

# AFLAC Inc

**STANDARD &POOR'S**

| S&P Recommendation | STRONG BUY ★★★★★ | Price $41.77 (as of Nov 14, 2008) | 12-Mo. Target Price $55.00 | Investment Style Large-Cap Growth |
|---|---|---|---|---|

**GICS Sector** Financials
**Sub-Industry** Life & Health Insurance

**Summary** This company provides supplemental health and life insurance in the U.S. and Japan.

## Key Stock Statistics (Source S&P, Vickers, company reports)

| | | | | | | | |
|---|---|---|---|---|---|---|---|
| 52-Wk Range | $68.81–32.27 | S&P Oper. EPS 2008**E** | 3.99 | Market Capitalization(B) | $19.470 | Beta | 0.51 |
| Trailing 12-Month EPS | $2.97 | S&P Oper. EPS 2009**E** | 4.50 | Yield (%) | 2.68 | S&P 3-Yr. Proj. EPS CAGR(%) | 15 |
| Trailing 12-Month P/E | 14.1 | P/E on S&P Oper. EPS 2008**E** | 10.5 | Dividend Rate/Share | $1.12 | S&P Credit Rating | A |
| $10K Invested 5 Yrs Ago | $12,279 | Common Shares Outstg. (M) | 466.1 | Institutional Ownership (%) | 64 | | |

## Price Performance

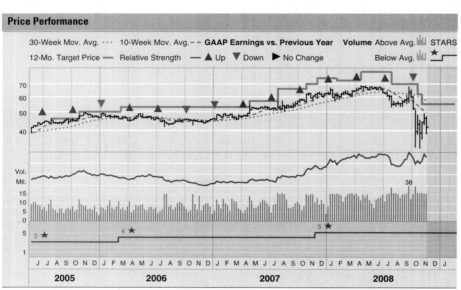

30-Week Mov. Avg. · · · 10-Week Mov. Avg. – – **GAAP Earnings vs. Previous Year** Volume Above Avg. STARS
12-Mo. Target Price — Relative Strength — ▲ Up ▼ Down ▶ No Change Below Avg. ★

2005 2006 2007 2008

Options: ASE, CBOE, Ph

Analysis prepared by **Bret Howlett** on October 28, 2008, when the stock traded at **$ 38.53**.

### Highlights

➤ We expect total revenues to rise in the single digits in 2008, driven by growth in premiums in both the U.S. and Japan. We believe AFL's focus on training and distribution in Japan should improve sales results for 2008, although the company is unlikely to hit its 3%-7% sales growth target despite a December sales push. AFL continues to ramp up sales through the bank channel, and we expect the company's partnership with Japan Post (started in October) to contribute to increased sales as well. We expect the benefit ratio in Japan to improve, as new sales of products such as EVER have a lower average benefit ratio.

➤ While we believe AFL will not reach its U.S. sales growth goal of 8%-12% in 2008, primarily due to the weak U.S. economy, we think the recent recruitment and training efforts for its sales force have been successful and should pave the way for future growth. We see the combined ratio remaining relatively flat for Aflac U.S., with increased ad spending limiting further improvements in the ratio.

➤ We forecast operating EPS growth of almost 22% in 2008, to $3.99, from $3.27 in 2007. Our 2009 operating EPS estimate is $4.50.

### Investment Rationale/Risk

➤ We believe that what we see as AFL's superior balance sheet and conservative investment approach relative to some peers, is a positive. AFL mainly invests in high quality corporate debt, and has no sub-prime holdings, and has low CMBS, RMBS, and equity exposure. We think AFL will improve Japanese sales over the next two years, as it focuses on strengthening its sales force and expands into the bank and Japan Post distribution channels. We expect its distribution partnership with Japan Post to lead to a meaningful increase in 2009 sales. We think the shares are compelling at current levels and believe AFL is poised to outperform peers due to its financial position and our view of its predictable earnings.

➤ Risks to our recommendation and target price include investment losses, unfavorable movements in the yen/dollar exchange rate, less organic premium growth than anticipated, particularly on new product sales, higher-than-projected underwriting and marketing expenses, and agent recruiting difficulties.

➤ Our 12-month target price is $55, or 3.0X our forecasted 2009 book value estimate, below historical multiples.

## Qualitative Risk Assessment

| LOW | MEDIUM | HIGH |
|---|---|---|

Our risk assessment for Aflac reflects its strong market share position and high risk-based capital ratio, and management's consistent track record for share repurchases and dividend increases. This is offset by potential investment losses given the turmoil in the financial markets.

## Quantitative Evaluations

**S&P Quality Ranking**      A

| D | C | B- | B | B+ | A- | A | A+ |
|---|---|---|---|---|---|---|---|

**Relative Strength Rank**      MODERATE

64

LOWEST = 1      HIGHEST = 99

## Revenue/Earnings Data

**Revenue (Million $)**

| | 1Q | 2Q | 3Q | 4Q | Year |
|---|---|---|---|---|---|
| 2008 | 4,267 | 4,336 | 3,691 | -- | -- |
| 2007 | 3,751 | 3,764 | 3,861 | 4,018 | 15,393 |
| 2006 | 3,559 | 3,697 | 3,672 | 3,687 | 14,616 |
| 2005 | 3,559 | 3,567 | 3,669 | 3,567 | 14,363 |
| 2004 | 3,280 | 3,233 | 3,321 | 3,448 | 13,281 |
| 2003 | 2,807 | 2,861 | 2,931 | 2,847 | 11,447 |

**Earnings Per Share ($)**

| | 1Q | 2Q | 3Q | 4Q | Year |
|---|---|---|---|---|---|
| 2008 | 0.98 | 1.01 | 0.21 | E1.00 | E3.99 |
| 2007 | 0.84 | 0.84 | 0.85 | 0.78 | 3.31 |
| 2006 | 0.74 | 0.81 | 0.73 | 0.67 | 2.95 |
| 2005 | 0.64 | 0.66 | 0.90 | 0.72 | 2.92 |
| 2004 | 0.61 | 0.51 | 0.58 | 0.81 | 2.52 |
| 2003 | 0.45 | 0.48 | 0.45 | 0.14 | 1.52 |

Fiscal year ended Dec. 31. Next earnings report expected: Late January. EPS Estimates based on S&P Operating Earnings; historical GAAP earnings are as reported.

## Dividend Data (Dates: mm/dd Payment Date: mm/dd/yy)

| Amount ($) | Date Decl. | Ex-Div. Date | Stk. of Record | Payment Date |
|---|---|---|---|---|
| 0.240 | 04/23 | 05/19 | 05/21 | 06/02/08 |
| 0.240 | 07/23 | 08/18 | 08/20 | 09/02/08 |
| 0.240 | 10/23 | 11/17 | 11/19 | 12/01/08 |
| 0.280 | 10/23 | 02/13 | 02/18 | 03/02/09 |

Dividends have been paid since 1973. Source: Company reports.

---

**Please read the Required Disclosures and Analyst Certification on the last page of this report.**

The **McGraw-Hill** Companies

# AFLAC Inc

**STANDARD &POOR'S**

## Business Summary October 28, 2008

CORPORATE OVERVIEW. Aflac provides supplemental health and life insurance in the U.S. and Japan. Most of Aflac's policies are individually underwritten and marketed at work sites through independent agents, with premiums paid by the employee. As of March 2007, Aflac believed it was the world's leading underwriter of individually issued policies marketed at work sites.

In 2007, Aflac Japan accounted for 71% of total revenues, compared to 72% in 2006. At December 31, 2007, Aflac Japan accounted for 82% of total company assets, the same as a year earlier. As of year-end 2005, Aflac Japan ranked first in terms of individual insurance policies in force, surpassing Nippon Life in March 2003.

Aflac Japan's insurance products are designed to help pay for costs that are not reimbursed under Japan's national health insurance system. Products include cancer life plans (33% of total Japanese sales in 2007; 28% in 2006); Rider MAX (7%; 10%), a rider for cancer life policies that provides accident and medical/sickness benefits; and EVER (33%; 33%), a stand-alone whole life

medical plan. Aflac Japan also offers ordinary life products (22%; 23%) and other products such as living benefit life plans and care products.

During 2007, the number of licensed sales associates rose to approximately 100,810 compared with 90,226 at December 31, 2006. The growth in licensed sales associates resulted primarily from individual agency recruitment.

Aflac U.S. sells cancer plans (18% of total U.S. sales in 2007; 18% in 2006) and various types of health insurance, including accident and disability (51%; 52%), fixed-benefit dental (6%; 7%), and hospital indemnity (14%; 12%). Other products include long-term care, short-term disability, and ordinary life policies (12%; 12%).

## Company Financials Fiscal Year Ended Dec. 31

| Per Share Data ($) | 2007 | 2006 | 2005 | 2004 | 2003 | 2002 | 2001 | 2000 | 1999 | 1998 |
|---|---|---|---|---|---|---|---|---|---|---|
| Tangible Book Value | 27.97 | 25.32 | 15.89 | 15.03 | 13.03 | 12.41 | 10.39 | 8.87 | 7.28 | 7.10 |
| Operating Earnings | NA | NA | NA | NA | NA | 1.56 | 1.34 | 1.21 | 1.00 | 0.78 |
| Earnings | 3.31 | 2.95 | 2.92 | 2.52 | 1.52 | 1.55 | 1.28 | 1.26 | 1.04 | 0.88 |
| S&P Core Earnings | 3.27 | 2.86 | 2.60 | 2.47 | 1.85 | 1.49 | 1.25 | NA | NA | NA |
| Dividends | 0.80 | 0.55 | 0.44 | 0.38 | 0.30 | 0.23 | 0.19 | 0.17 | 0.15 | 0.13 |
| Payout Ratio | 24% | 19% | 15% | 15% | 20% | 15% | 15% | 13% | 14% | 14% |
| Prices:High | 63.91 | 49.40 | 49.65 | 42.60 | 36.91 | 33.45 | 36.09 | 37.47 | 28.38 | 22.66 |
| Prices:Low | 45.18 | 41.63 | 35.50 | 33.85 | 28.00 | 23.10 | 23.00 | 16.78 | 19.50 | 11.34 |
| P/E Ratio:High | 19 | 17 | 17 | 17 | 24 | 22 | 28 | 30 | 27 | 26 |
| P/E Ratio:Low | 14 | 14 | 12 | 13 | 18 | 15 | 18 | 13 | 19 | 13 |

| Income Statement Analysis (Million $) | 2007 | 2006 | 2005 | 2004 | 2003 | 2002 | 2001 | 2000 | 1999 | 1998 |
|---|---|---|---|---|---|---|---|---|---|---|
| Life Insurance in Force | NA | NA | 80,610 | 80,496 | 69,582 | 56,680 | 46,610 | 51,496 | 44,993 | 28,182 |
| Premium Income:Life | NA | NA | 1,139 | 1,031 | 876 | 761 | 697 | 716 | 625 | 508 |
| Premium Income:A & H | NA | NA | 10,851 | 10,271 | 9,052 | 7,839 | 7,366 | 7,523 | 6,639 | 5,435 |
| Net Investment Income | 2,333 | 2,171 | 2,071 | 1,957 | 1,787 | 1,614 | 1,550 | 1,550 | 1,369 | 1,138 |
| Total Revenue | 15,393 | 14,616 | 14,363 | 13,281 | 11,447 | 10,257 | 9,598 | 9,720 | 8,640 | 7,104 |
| Pretax Income | 2,499 | 2,264 | 2,226 | 1,807 | 1,225 | 1,259 | 1,081 | 1,012 | 778 | 551 |
| Net Operating Income | NA | NA | NA | NA | NA | 825 | 720 | 657 | 550 | 429 |
| Net Income | 1,634 | 1,483 | 1,483 | 1,299 | 795 | 821 | 687 | 687 | 571 | 487 |
| S&P Core Earnings | 1,616 | 1,438 | 1,321 | 1,274 | 962 | 791 | 670 | NA | NA | NA |

| Balance Sheet & Other Financial Data (Million $) | 2007 | 2006 | 2005 | 2004 | 2003 | 2002 | 2001 | 2000 | 1999 | 1998 |
|---|---|---|---|---|---|---|---|---|---|---|
| Cash & Equivalent | 2,523 | 2,036 | 1,781 | 4,308 | 1,508 | 1,793 | 1,233 | 989 | 985 | 690 |
| Premiums Due | 732 | 535 | 479 | 417 | 547 | 435 | 347 | 301 | 270 | 229 |
| Investment Assets:Bonds | 55,410 | 50,686 | 47,551 | 48,024 | 42,893 | 37,483 | 31,677 | 31,305 | 31,175 | 26,424 |
| Investment Assets:Stocks | 22.0 | 25.0 | 84.0 | 77.0 | 73.0 | 258 | 245 | 236 | 215 | 177 |
| Investment Assets:Loans | Nil | Nil | Nil | Nil | Nil | Nil | Nil | Nil | Nil | 9.00 |
| Investment Assets:Total | 57,056 | 50,769 | 47,692 | 48,142 | 42,999 | 37,768 | 31,941 | 31,558 | 31,408 | 26,620 |
| Deferred Policy Costs | 6,654 | 6,025 | 5,590 | 5,595 | 5,044 | 4,277 | 3,645 | 3,685 | 3,692 | 3,067 |
| Total Assets | 65,805 | 59,805 | 56,361 | 59,326 | 50,964 | 45,058 | 37,860 | 37,232 | 37,041 | 31,183 |
| Debt | 1,465 | 1,420 | 1,050 | 1,141 | 1,409 | 1,312 | 1,000 | 956 | 931 | 596 |
| Common Equity | 8,795 | 8,341 | 7,927 | 7,573 | 6,646 | 6,394 | 5,425 | 4,694 | 3,868 | 3,770 |
| % Return on Revenue | 10.6 | 10.1 | 10.4 | 9.8 | 6.9 | 8.0 | 7.2 | 7.1 | 6.6 | 6.9 |
| % Return on Assets | 2.6 | 2.6 | 2.6 | 2.4 | 1.7 | 2.0 | 1.8 | 1.8 | 1.7 | 1.6 |
| % Return on Equity | 19.1 | 18.2 | 19.1 | 18.3 | 12.2 | 13.9 | 13.6 | 16.0 | 15.0 | 13.5 |
| % Investment Yield | 4.3 | 4.4 | 4.3 | 4.3 | 4.4 | 4.6 | 4.9 | 4.9 | 4.7 | 4.6 |

Data as orig reptd.; bef. results of disc opers/spec. items. Per share data adj. for stk. divs.; EPS diluted. E-Estimated. NA-Not Available. NM-Not Meaningful. NR-Not Ranked. UR-Under Review.

**Office:** 1932 Wynnton Road, Columbus, GA 31999.
**Telephone:** 706-323-3431.
**Email:** ir@aflac.com
**Website:** http://www.aflac.com

**Chrmn & CEO:** D.P. Amos
**Pres & COO:** P.S. Amos, II
**EVP, CFO & Treas:** K. Cloninger, III
**EVP & Chief Admin Officer:** R.C. Davis

**EVP, Secy & General Counsel:** J.M. Loudermilk
**Investor Contact:** K.S. Janke, Jr. (706-596-3264)
**Board Members:** D. P. Amos, J. S. Amos, II, P. S. Amos, II, Y. Aoki, M. H. Armacost, K. Cloninger, III, J. F. Harris, E. J. Hudson, K. S. Janke, D. W. Johnson, R. B. Johnson, C. B. Knapp, E. S. Purdom, B. K. Rimer, M. R. Schuster, D. G. Thompson, R. L. Wright

**Founded:** 1973
**Domicile:** Georgia
**Employees:** 8,048

# Agilent Technologies Inc.

**STANDARD &POOR'S**

| S&P Recommendation | HOLD ★★★☆☆ | Price $20.75 (as of Nov 14, 2008) | 12-Mo. Target Price $25.00 | Investment Style Large-Cap Blend |

**GICS Sector** Information Technology
**Sub-Industry** Electronic Equipment Manufacturers

**Summary** This Hewlett-Packard (HPQ) spin-off is a diversified global manufacturer of test and measurement instruments, and life sciences and chemical analysis instruments.

## Key Stock Statistics (Source S&P, Vickers, company reports)

| | | | | | | | |
|---|---|---|---|---|---|---|---|
| 52-Wk Range | $38.24 – 18.05 | S&P Oper. EPS 2008E | 1.90 | Market Capitalization(B) | $7.419 | Beta | 1.58 |
| Trailing 12-Month EPS | $1.70 | S&P Oper. EPS 2009E | 1.89 | Yield (%) | Nil | S&P 3-Yr. Proj. EPS CAGR(%) | 10 |
| Trailing 12-Month P/E | 12.2 | P/E on S&P Oper. EPS 2008E | 10.9 | Dividend Rate/Share | Nil | S&P Credit Rating | BBB- |
| $10K Invested 5 Yrs Ago | NA | Common Shares Outstg. (M) | 357.5 | Institutional Ownership (%) | 77 | | |

## Price Performance

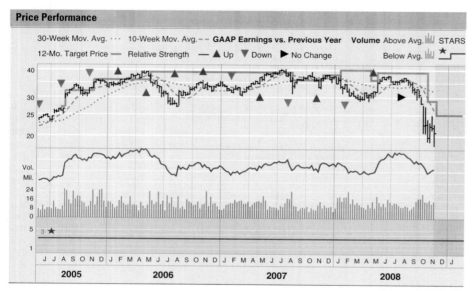

30-Week Mov. Avg. · · · 10-Week Mov. Avg. — GAAP Earnings vs. Previous Year Volume Above Avg. STARS
12-Mo. Target Price — Relative Strength — ▲ Up ▼ Down ► No Change Below Avg.

Options: ASE, CBOE, P, Ph

Analysis prepared by **Angelo Zino** on November 14, 2008, when the stock traded at **$ 21.08**.

## Highlights

➤ Following a 7% revenue increase in FY 08 (Oct.), we project that sales will decline 2% in FY 09, primarily reflecting weaker sales from A's electronic measurement markets. We project healthy demand and higher market share in both the chemical analysis and life science end markets. We anticipate mixed results for the electronic measurement unit. We remain cautious of its semiconductor line, which comprises 4% of sales, and expect calendar year 2009 to remain challenging for the business given the global economic conditions.

➤ We project the annual gross margin to remain relatively flat in FY 09, compared with a 55% margin posted in FY 08. We expect the product mix to be minimally impacted by higher sales from the slighter lower margin bio-analytical measurement market. We expect the operating margin to widen, reflecting cost savings from Agilent's multi-year restructuring efforts and limited headcount growth.

➤ The company has a $2 billion share buyback program, and we expect it to repurchase shares at a moderate pace in FY 09. Following operating EPS of $1.92 in FY 08, we see $1.89 for FY 09.

## Investment Rationale/Risk

➤ We expect Agilent to expand aggressively by introducing new products in high-growth industries such as broadband and wireless R&D, complemented by opportunistic acquisitions in the company's core markets. We see the potential for the company to increase share in its bio-analytical market, but think declining sales from its larger electronic measurement unit will limit near-term results. Agilent has made several divestitures over the past few years, which we believe has reduced the volatility of its quarterly results and improved the company's focus and predictability of results.

➤ Risks to our recommendation and target price include a weaker-than-expected global economy, narrower margins than we project, and weaker-than-anticipated traction for its new product introductions.

➤ Our 12-month target price of $25 is based on a peer-average price-to-earnings (P/E) multiple of 13.2X applied to our FY 09 operating EPS estimate of $1.89. We have a favorable view of the company's defensive revenue drivers, with its high exposure to the non-cyclical life sciences and chemical analysis markets.

## Qualitative Risk Assessment

| LOW | MEDIUM | HIGH |

Our risk assessment reflects the variability of Agilent's results in the past, offset by recent efforts to streamline its businesses and divest parts of its portfolio that contributed to this variability.

## Quantitative Evaluations

**S&P Quality Ranking** B-

| D | C | B- | B | B+ | A- | A | A+ |

**Relative Strength Rank** MODERATE

50

LOWEST = 1 HIGHEST = 99

## Revenue/Earnings Data

**Revenue (Million $)**

| | 1Q | 2Q | 3Q | 4Q | Year |
|---|---|---|---|---|---|
| 2008 | 1,393 | 1,456 | 1,444 | -- | -- |
| 2007 | 1,280 | 1,320 | 1,374 | 1,446 | 5,420 |
| 2006 | 1,167 | 1,239 | 1,239 | 1,328 | 4,973 |
| 2005 | 1,212 | 1,688 | 1,242 | 1,407 | 5,139 |
| 2004 | 1,643 | 1,831 | 1,885 | 1,822 | 7,181 |
| 2003 | 1,412 | 1,467 | 1,502 | 1,675 | 6,056 |

**Earnings Per Share ($)**

| | 1Q | 2Q | 3Q | 4Q | Year |
|---|---|---|---|---|---|
| 2008 | 0.31 | 0.47 | 0.45 | E0.60 | E1.90 |
| 2007 | 0.36 | 0.30 | 0.45 | 0.46 | 1.57 |
| 2006 | 2.03 | 0.28 | 0.51 | 0.31 | 3.26 |
| 2005 | 0.10 | 0.11 | 0.10 | -0.03 | 0.28 |
| 2004 | 0.14 | 0.21 | 0.20 | 0.15 | 0.71 |
| 2003 | -0.24 | -0.31 | -3.25 | 0.03 | -3.78 |

Fiscal year ended Oct. 31. Next earnings report expected: Mid November. EPS Estimates based on S&P Operating Earnings; historical GAAP earnings are as reported.

## Dividend Data

No cash dividends have been paid.

# Agilent Technologies Inc.

STANDARD &POOR'S

## Business Summary November 14, 2008

CORPORATE OVERVIEW. Agilent Technologies (A), which was spun off from Hewlett-Packard (HPQ) in 1999, provides investors with exposure to the communications, electronics, life sciences and chemical analysis industries. A's revenues during FY 07 (Oct.) came from two business segments: electronic measurement (63%) and bio-analytical measurement (37%).

A's electronic measurement products compete in the communications test market and the general test market, which represented 40% and 60% of FY 07 revenues, respectively. The communications test market includes handset manufacturers, network equipment manufacturers and communications service providers. A has a suite of fiber optic, broadband and data and wireless communications and microwave network products. General purpose test products and services are sold to the electronics industry and other industries with significant electronic content, such as the aerospace and defense, computer and semiconductor industries. A sells electronic measurement products that are used for electronics manufacturing testing, parametric testing, and flat panel display (FPD) markets.

Agilent's bio-analytical measurement business products include microarrays, microfluidics, gas chromatography, liquid chromatography, mass spectrometry, software and informatics, and related consumables and services used in pharmaceutical analysis, the proteomics and gene expression markets, as well as the petrochemical and environmental markets, among others. Applications include measuring octane levels in gasoline, and analyzing pesticide levels in drinking water. Customers span the hydrocarbon-processing, environmental, pharmaceutical and bioscience markets. In the pharmaceutical and biopharmaceutical markets, A's instruments help lower the cost of discovering and developing new drugs.

International revenues accounted for 66% of total sales in FY 07, compared with 66% in FY 06 and 64% in FY 05. Approximately 12% of annual sales in each of the past three years were derived from Japan.

## Company Financials Fiscal Year Ended Oct. 31

| Per Share Data ($) | 2007 | 2006 | 2005 | 2004 | 2003 | 2002 | 2001 | 2000 | 1999 | 1998 |
|---|---|---|---|---|---|---|---|---|---|---|
| Tangible Book Value | 6.75 | 7.79 | 7.39 | 6.42 | 5.09 | 8.44 | 9.95 | 10.37 | 8.90 | NM |
| Cash Flow | 2.04 | 3.64 | 0.65 | 1.31 | -3.02 | -0.62 | 0.72 | 2.75 | 2.60 | 1.93 |
| Earnings | 1.57 | 3.26 | 0.28 | 0.71 | -3.78 | -2.20 | -0.89 | 1.66 | 1.35 | 0.56 |
| S&P Core Earnings | 1.52 | 1.59 | -0.11 | 0.27 | -5.70 | -3.10 | -2.63 | NA | NA | NA |
| Dividends | Nil | Nil | Nil | Nil | Nil | Nil | Nil | Nil | Nil | NA |
| Payout Ratio | Nil | Nil | Nil | Nil | Nil | Nil | Nil | Nil | Nil | NA |
| Prices:High | 40.42 | 39.54 | 36.10 | 38.80 | 29.42 | 38.00 | 68.00 | 162.00 | 80.00 | NA |
| Prices:Low | 30.26 | 26.96 | 20.11 | 19.51 | 18.35 | 10.50 | 18.00 | 38.06 | 30.00 | NA |
| P/E Ratio:High | 26 | 12 | NM | 55 | NM | NM | NM | 98 | 59 | NA |
| P/E Ratio:Low | 19 | 8 | NM | 27 | NM | NM | NM | 23 | 22 | NA |

| Income Statement Analysis (Million $) | | | | | | | | | | |
|---|---|---|---|---|---|---|---|---|---|---|
| Revenue | 5,420 | 4,973 | 5,139 | 7,181 | 6,056 | 6,010 | 8,396 | 10,773 | 8,331 | 7,952 |
| Operating Income | 775 | 680 | 367 | 678 | -363 | -872 | -44.0 | 1,548 | 1,216 | 919 |
| Depreciation | 191 | 170 | 186 | 292 | 362 | 735 | 734 | 495 | 475 | 477 |
| Interest Expense | 91.0 | 69.0 | 27.0 | 36.0 | Nil | Nil | Nil | Nil | Nil | Nil |
| Pretax Income | 670 | 1,528 | 306 | 440 | -690 | -1,547 | -477 | 1,164 | 787 | 396 |
| Effective Tax Rate | 4.70% | 5.96% | 50.7% | 20.7% | NM | NM | NM | 35.0% | 34.9% | 35.1% |
| Net Income | 638 | 1,437 | 141 | 349 | -1,790 | -1,022 | -406 | 757 | 512 | 257 |
| S&P Core Earnings | 615 | 701 | -55.1 | 137 | -2,695 | -1,438 | -1,202 | NA | NA | NA |

| Balance Sheet & Other Financial Data (Million $) | | | | | | | | | | |
|---|---|---|---|---|---|---|---|---|---|---|
| Cash | 1,826 | 2,262 | 2,251 | 2,315 | 1,607 | 1,844 | 1,170 | 996 | Nil | Nil |
| Current Assets | 3,671 | 3,958 | 4,447 | 4,577 | 3,889 | 4,880 | 4,799 | 5,655 | 3,538 | 3,075 |
| Total Assets | 7,554 | 7,369 | 6,751 | 7,056 | 6,297 | 8,203 | 7,986 | 8,425 | 5,444 | 4,987 |
| Current Liabilities | 1,663 | 1,538 | 1,936 | 1,871 | 1,906 | 2,181 | 2,002 | 2,758 | 1,681 | 1,599 |
| Long Term Debt | 2,087 | 1,500 | Nil | 1,150 | 1,150 | 1,150 | Nil | Nil | Nil | Nil |
| Common Equity | 3,234 | 3,648 | 4,081 | 3,569 | 2,824 | 4,627 | 5,659 | 5,265 | 3,382 | 3,022 |
| Total Capital | 5,321 | 5,341 | 4,081 | 4,719 | 3,974 | 5,777 | 5,659 | 5,265 | 3,382 | 3,022 |
| Capital Expenditures | 154 | 185 | 139 | 118 | 205 | 301 | 881 | 824 | 434 | 410 |
| Cash Flow | 829 | 1,607 | 327 | 641 | -1,428 | -287 | 328 | 1,252 | 987 | 734 |
| Current Ratio | 2.2 | 2.6 | 2.3 | 2.4 | 2.0 | 2.2 | 2.4 | 2.1 | 2.1 | 1.9 |
| % Long Term Debt of Capitalization | 39.2 | 29.1 | Nil | 24.4 | 28.9 | 19.9 | Nil | Nil | Nil | Nil |
| % Net Income of Revenue | 11.7 | 28.9 | 2.7 | 4.9 | NM | NM | NM | 7.0 | 6.1 | 3.2 |
| % Return on Assets | 8.5 | 20.4 | 2.0 | 5.2 | NM | NM | NM | 10.9 | 9.8 | 5.1 |
| % Return on Equity | 18.5 | 37.2 | 3.7 | 10.9 | NM | NM | NM | 17.5 | 16.0 | 8.4 |

Data as orig reptd.; bef. results of disc opers/spec. items. Per share data adj. for stk. divs.; EPS diluted. E-Estimated. NA-Not Available. NM-Not Meaningful. NR-Not Ranked. UR-Under Review.

Office: 5301 Stevens Creek Blvd, Santa Clara, CA 95051-7201.
Telephone: 408-553-7777.
Email: investor_relations@agilent.com
Website: http://www.agilent.com

Chrmn: J.G. Cullen
Pres & CEO: W.P. Sullivan
EVP, CFO & Chief Admin Officer: A.T. Dillon
SVP & CTO: D.J. Solomon

SVP, Secy & General Counsel: D.C. Nordlund
Investor Contact: R. Gonsalves (408-345-8948)
Board Members: K. Boon Hwee, P. N. Clark, J. G. Cullen, R. J. Herbold, R. L. Joss, H. Kunz, D. M. Lawrence, A. B. Rand, W. P. Sullivan

Founded: 1999
Domicile: Delaware
Employees: 19,400

# Air Products and Chemicals Inc.

**STANDARD &POOR'S**

| S&P Recommendation | BUY ★★★★☆ | Price | 12-Mo. Target Price | Investment Style |
|---|---|---|---|---|
| | | $52.78 (as of Nov 14, 2008) | $68.00 | Large-Cap Blend |

**GICS Sector** Materials
**Sub-Industry** Industrial Gases

**Summary** This major producer of industrial gases and specialty and intermediate chemicals also has interests in environmental and energy-related businesses.

## Key Stock Statistics (Source S&P, Vickers, company reports)

| | | | | | | | |
|---|---|---|---|---|---|---|---|
| 52-Wk Range | $106.06– 46.33 | S&P Oper. EPS 2009E | 5.25 | Market Capitalization(B) | $11.181 | Beta | 1.03 |
| Trailing 12-Month EPS | $4.15 | S&P Oper. EPS 2010E | NA | Yield (%) | 3.33 | S&P 3-Yr. Proj. EPS CAGR(%) | 10 |
| Trailing 12-Month P/E | 12.7 | P/E on S&P Oper. EPS 2009E | 10.1 | Dividend Rate/Share | $1.76 | S&P Credit Rating | A |
| $10K Invested 5 Yrs Ago | $12,681 | Common Shares Outstg. (M) | 211.8 | Institutional Ownership (%) | 86 | | |

## Price Performance

30-Week Mov. Avg. · · ·   10-Week Mov. Avg. —   **GAAP Earnings vs. Previous Year**   Volume Above Avg. ||||   STARS
12-Mo. Target Price —   Relative Strength —   ▲ Up   ▼ Down   ► No Change   Below Avg. ||||   ★

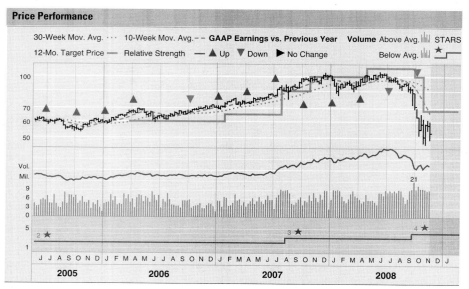

Options: CBOE, P, Ph

Analysis prepared by **Richard O'Reilly, CFA** on October 24, 2008, when the stock traded at **$ 52.86.**

## Highlights

➤ We expect sales to increase about 6% in FY 09 (Sep.), excluding currency exchange and the pass-through of changes in natural gas costs, with operating EPS rising to $5.25, from the $5.05 for FY 08. We believe underlying sales comparisons for industrial gases will remain upbeat, on continued favorable global volume growth for many key products. We expect continued positive volume comparisons for tonnage gases, driven by the growing use of hydrogen and pending start-up of new plants.

➤ We think U.S. merchant gases volumes should show low single digit percentage growth in FY 09 as APD operates at high rates while achieving continued good price hikes. Asian volumes will likely continue to increase at a solid rate, by our analysis. We see favorable volume growth for performance materials, but electronics products will likely struggle amid recent softening markets.

➤ We expect equipment unit profits in FY 09 to be about $25 million, down from $39 million for FY 08, reflecting reduced sales, and we see the tax rate at about 25.5%. Reported EPS will likely be hurt by unfavorable currency exchange rates.

## Investment Rationale/Risk

➤ The shares recently traded at a P/E of about 10.1X our FY 09 EPS estimate, below the level of the S&P 500 (12X). We think fundamentals overall remain sound despite challenging economic conditions, as APD holds strong positions in several growth products and markets for industrial gases and specialty chemicals. We also believe that the company has a strong backlog of gases projects, which should enhance long-term sales growth.

➤ Risks to our recommendation and target price include weaker-than-expected growth in U.S. industrial activity and in the global electronics materials industry, and higher-than-forecast raw material and energy prices.

➤ The dividend was raised in 2008 for the 26th consecutive year, a record that we see being extended. We believe the company has a relatively strong balance sheet. Based on a P/E of about 13X, similar to that of APD's industrial gases peer group, applied to our FY 09 EPS estimate, our 12-month target price is $68.

## Qualitative Risk Assessment

| LOW | MEDIUM | HIGH |
|---|---|---|

Our risk assessment reflects the stable growth of the industrial gases industry versus commodity chemicals, and what we see as the company's relatively strong balance sheet, offset by volatile raw material cost exposure in the chemical segment.

## Quantitative Evaluations

**S&P Quality Ranking**   A+

| D | C | B- | B | B+ | A- | A | A+ |
|---|---|---|---|---|---|---|---|

**Relative Strength Rank**   MODERATE

49

LOWEST = 1   HIGHEST = 99

## Revenue/Earnings Data

**Revenue (Million $)**

| | 1Q | 2Q | 3Q | 4Q | Year |
|---|---|---|---|---|---|
| 2008 | 2,474 | 2,605 | 2,808 | 2,715 | 10,415 |
| 2007 | 2,410 | 2,451 | 2,574 | 2,603 | 10,038 |
| 2006 | 2,016 | 2,230 | 2,246 | 2,359 | 8,850 |
| 2005 | 1,991 | 2,003 | 2,078 | 2,071 | 8,144 |
| 2004 | 1,685 | 1,857 | 1,893 | 1,978 | 7,411 |
| 2003 | 1,447 | 1,578 | 1,630 | 1,642 | 6,297 |

**Earnings Per Share ($)**

| | | | | | |
|---|---|---|---|---|---|
| 2008 | 1.16 | 1.16 | 0.23 | 1.26 | 4.98 |
| 2007 | 1.03 | 1.02 | 1.28 | 1.35 | 4.67 |
| 2006 | 0.80 | 0.89 | -- | 0.73 | 3.29 |
| 2005 | 0.72 | 0.75 | 0.82 | 0.79 | 3.08 |
| 2004 | 0.58 | 0.62 | 0.71 | 0.73 | 2.64 |
| 2003 | 0.58 | 0.51 | 0.12 | 0.58 | 1.79 |

Fiscal year ended Sep. 30. Next earnings report expected: Late January. EPS Estimates based on S&P Operating Earnings; historical GAAP earnings are as reported.

## Dividend Data (Dates: mm/dd Payment Date: mm/dd/yy)

| Amount ($) | Date Decl. | Ex-Div. Date | Stk. of Record | Payment Date |
|---|---|---|---|---|
| 0.380 | 11/15 | 12/28 | 01/02 | 02/11/08 |
| 0.440 | 03/20 | 03/28 | 04/01 | 05/12/08 |
| 0.440 | 05/15 | 06/27 | 07/01 | 08/11/08 |
| 0.440 | 09/18 | 09/29 | 10/01 | 11/10/08 |

Dividends have been paid since 1954. Source: Company reports.

---

**Please read the Required Disclosures and Analyst Certification on the last page of this report.**

*The McGraw·Hill Companies*

# Air Products and Chemicals Inc.

## Business Summary October 24, 2008

CORPORATE OVERVIEW. Air Products & Chemicals is one of the largest global producers of industrial gases, and has a large specialty chemicals business. APD focuses on several areas for growth in industrial gases, including electronics, hydrogen for petroleum refining, health care, and Asia. International operations accounted for 49% of FY 07 (Sep.) sales.

The industrial gases businesses consists of nitrogen, oxygen, argon, hydrogen, helium, carbon monoxide, synthesis gas, and fluorine compounds for both merchant (40% of sales and 51% of profits in FY 08) and on-site tonnage (35%, 31%) customers. Sales of atmospheric gases (oxygen, nitrogen and argon) accounted for 17% of the total in FY 07. APD is the world's leading supplier of hydrogen (15% of total sales) and carbon monoxide products (HYCO) and helium. Beginning with the fourth quarter of FY 08, the European healthcare business (sales of $360 million in FY 07) has been reported as part of the merchant gases segment. APD is the market leader in Spain, Portugal, and the U.K. The polyurethane intermediates business beginning in FY 08 was reported as part of the tonnage gases segment. The business had sales of $340 million in FY 07.

The electronics and performance materials segment (21%,16%) supplies specialty gases (nitrogen trifluoride, silane, phosphine), tonnage gases, specialty and bulk chemicals, services and equipment to makers of silicone and semi-conductors, displays and photovoltaic devices. Performance materials include epoxy and polyurethane additives, specialty amines, and surfactants for coatings, adhesives, personal care and cleaning products, and polyurethanes.

Equipment and energy (4%, 2%) includes cryogenic and process equipment for air separation, gas processing, natural gas liquefaction (LNG), and hydrogen purification. The segment also includes 50%-owned ventures in power cogeneration and flue gas desulfurization facilities.

In July 2008, APD decided to sell its U.S. healthcare business (sales of $240 million in FY 08; reported as discontinued operations beginning in FY 08). The company entered the U.S. home health care market in October 2002 by purchasing American Homecare Supply (AHS). The business had a net loss of $268 million in FY 08 with after-tax charges totaling $246.2 million ($1.12 a share), including $237.0 ($1.09) in the third quarter primarily for goodwill.

The water-based polymers emulsions was sold in February 2008 (sales of $619 million in FY 07; reported as discontinued operations beginning in FY 08).

## Company Financials Fiscal Year Ended Sep. 30

| Per Share Data ($) | 2008 | 2007 | 2006 | 2005 | 2004 | 2003 | 2002 | 2001 | 2000 | 1999 |
|---|---|---|---|---|---|---|---|---|---|---|
| Tangible Book Value | NA | 22.01 | 17.59 | 16.03 | 15.45 | 12.99 | 13.33 | 10.79 | 10.78 | 11.39 |
| Cash Flow | NA | 8.44 | 6.64 | 6.22 | 5.76 | 4.65 | 4.97 | 4.95 | 3.24 | 4.53 |
| Earnings | 4.98 | 4.67 | 3.29 | 3.08 | 2.64 | 1.79 | 2.36 | 2.12 | 0.57 | 2.09 |
| S&P Core Earnings | NA | 4.65 | 2.94 | 3.01 | 2.63 | 1.66 | 1.67 | 1.70 | NA | NA |
| Dividends | 1.70 | 1.48 | 1.34 | 1.25 | 1.04 | 0.88 | 0.82 | 0.78 | 0.74 | 0.70 |
| Payout Ratio | 34% | 32% | 41% | 41% | 39% | 49% | 35% | 37% | 130% | 33% |
| Prices:High | 106.06 | 105.02 | 72.45 | 65.81 | 59.18 | 53.07 | 53.52 | 49.00 | 42.25 | 49.25 |
| Prices:Low | 46.33 | 68.58 | 58.01 | 53.00 | 46.71 | 36.97 | 40.00 | 32.25 | 23.00 | 25.69 |
| P/E Ratio:High | 21 | 22 | 22 | 21 | 22 | 30 | 23 | 23 | 74 | 24 |
| P/E Ratio:Low | 9 | 15 | 18 | 17 | 18 | 21 | 17 | 15 | 40 | 12 |

| Income Statement Analysis (Million $) | | | | | | | | | | |
|---|---|---|---|---|---|---|---|---|---|---|
| Revenue | 10,415 | 10,038 | 8,850 | 8,144 | 7,411 | 6,297 | 5,401 | 5,717 | 5,496 | 5,020 |
| Operating Income | NA | 2,179 | 1,777 | 1,700 | 1,567 | 1,218 | 1,319 | 1,313 | 1,407 | 725 |
| Depreciation | 869 | 840 | 763 | 728 | 715 | 640 | 581 | 573 | 576 | 527 |
| Interest Expense | NA | 176 | 119 | 110 | 121 | 124 | 122 | 191 | 197 | 159 |
| Pretax Income | 1,479 | 1,376 | 1,049 | 998 | 851 | 565 | 784 | 737 | 118 | 669 |
| Effective Tax Rate | 24.7% | 21.9% | 25.8% | 26.4% | 26.6% | 26.0% | 30.7% | 29.7% | NM | 30.4% |
| Net Income | 1,091 | 1,043 | 748 | 712 | 604 | 400 | 525 | 513 | 124 | 451 |
| S&P Core Earnings | NA | 1,038 | 670 | 695 | 601 | 369 | 369 | 370 | NA | NA |

| Balance Sheet & Other Financial Data (Million $) | | | | | | | | | | |
|---|---|---|---|---|---|---|---|---|---|---|
| Cash | 104 | 42.3 | 35.2 | 55.8 | 146 | 76.2 | 254 | 66.2 | 94.1 | 61.6 |
| Current Assets | NA | 2,858 | 2,613 | 2,415 | 2,417 | 2,068 | 1,909 | 1,685 | 1,805 | 1,782 |
| Total Assets | 12,490 | 12,660 | 11,181 | 10,409 | 10,040 | 9,432 | 8,495 | 8,084 | 8,271 | 8,236 |
| Current Liabilities | NA | 2,423 | 2,323 | 1,943 | 1,706 | 1,581 | 1,256 | 1,352 | 1,375 | 1,858 |
| Long Term Debt | NA | 2,977 | 2,280 | 2,053 | Nil | 2,169 | 2,041 | 2,028 | 2,616 | 1,962 |
| Common Equity | 5,031 | 5,496 | 4,924 | 4,576 | 4,444 | 3,783 | 3,460 | 3,106 | 2,821 | 2,962 |
| Total Capital | NA | 9,362 | 8,215 | 7,644 | 5,401 | 6,845 | 6,411 | 6,030 | 6,334 | 5,782 |
| Capital Expenditures | 1,085 | 1,055 | 1,261 | 930 | 706 | 613 | 628 | 708 | 768 | 889 |
| Cash Flow | NA | 1,883 | 1,511 | 1,440 | 1,319 | 1,040 | 1,106 | 1,086 | 700 | 978 |
| Current Ratio | 1.3 | 1.2 | 1.1 | 1.2 | 1.4 | 1.3 | 1.5 | 1.2 | 1.3 | 1.0 |
| % Long Term Debt of Capitalization | 40.5 | 31.8 | 27.8 | 26.9 | Nil | 31.7 | 31.8 | 33.6 | 41.3 | 33.9 |
| % Net Income of Revenue | 10.5 | 10.4 | 8.5 | 8.7 | 8.2 | 6.4 | 9.7 | 9.0 | 2.3 | 9.0 |
| % Return on Assets | 8.7 | 8.8 | 6.9 | 7.0 | 6.2 | 4.5 | 6.3 | 6.3 | 1.5 | 5.7 |
| % Return on Equity | 20.7 | 20.0 | 15.8 | 15.8 | 14.7 | 11.1 | 16.0 | 17.3 | 4.3 | 16.0 |

Data as orig reptd.; bef. results of disc opers/spec. items. Per share data adj. for stk. divs.; EPS diluted. E-Estimated. NA-Not Available. NM-Not Meaningful. NR-Not Ranked. UR-Under Review.

**Office:** 7201 Hamilton Boulevard, Allentown, PA 18195-1501.
**Telephone:** 610-481-4911.
**Website:** http://www.airproducts.com
**Chrmn, Pres, CEO & COO:** J. McGlade

**SVP & CFO:** P.E. Huck
**SVP, Secy & General Counsel:** S.J. Jones
**CTO:** M. Alger
**Chief Acctg Officer & Cntlr:** M.S. Crocco

**Investor Contact:** N. Squires (610-481-7461)
**Board Members:** M. L. Baeza, W. L. Davis, III, M. J. Donahue, U. F. Fairbairn, W. D. Ford, E. E. Hagenlocker, E. Henkes, J. P. Jones, III, J. McGlade, M. G. McGlynn, C. H. Noski, L. S. Smith

**Founded:** 1940
**Domicile:** Delaware
**Employees:** 22,100

**STANDARD &POOR'S**

# Akamai Technologies Inc

| S&P Recommendation **BUY** ★★★★☆ | Price $12.76 (as of Nov 14, 2008) | 12-Mo. Target Price $17.00 | Investment Style Large-Cap Growth |
|---|---|---|---|

**GICS Sector** Information Technology
**Sub-Industry** Internet Software & Services

**Summary** This company develops and deploys solutions designed to accelerate and improve the delivery of Internet content and applications.

## Key Stock Statistics (Source S&P, Vickers, company reports)

| | | | | | | | | |
|---|---|---|---|---|---|---|---|---|
| 52-Wk Range | $40.90– 11.17 | S&P Oper. EPS 2008**E** | 0.72 | Market Capitalization(B) | $2.158 | Beta | 2.66 |
| Trailing 12-Month EPS | $0.77 | S&P Oper. EPS 2009**E** | 0.82 | Yield (%) | Nil | S&P 3-Yr. Proj. EPS CAGR(%) | 20 |
| Trailing 12-Month P/E | 16.6 | P/E on S&P Oper. EPS 2008**E** | 17.7 | Dividend Rate/Share | Nil | S&P Credit Rating | NR |
| $10K Invested 5 Yrs Ago | $11,632 | Common Shares Outstg. (M) | 169.1 | Institutional Ownership (%) | NM | | |

## Price Performance

30-Week Mov. Avg. · · · · 10-Week Mov. Avg. – – **GAAP Earnings vs. Previous Year** Volume Above Avg. STARS
12-Mo. Target Price — Relative Strength — ▲ Up ▼ Down ► No Change Below Avg. ★

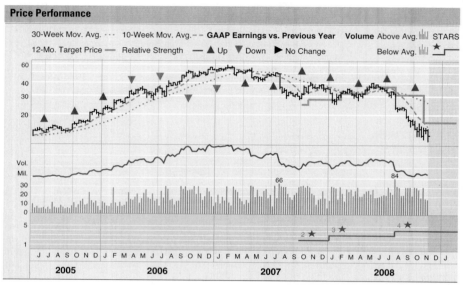

Options: ASE, CBOE, P, Ph

Analysis prepared by **Scott H. Kessler** on November 03, 2008, when the stock traded at **$ 13.60**.

## Highlights

➤ We project that revenues will rise 23% in 2008 and 15% in 2009, reflecting what we consider solid secular growth, driven by the increasing use and importance of the Internet to distribute content and applications, offset somewhat by a challenging global economic backdrop.

➤ We foresee annual gross margins declining through 2009, due to higher bandwidth costs and modest pricing pressures. However, we believe yearly operating and net margins will improve in 2008, reflecting scale and efficiency benefits, and moderate in 2009.

➤ AKAM has made some $335 million of technology-focused acquisitions since late 2006, enhancing its capabilities regarding content and application transmission speeds, rich-media distribution, and peer-to-peer networks. In December 2006, it purchased Nine Systems for some $158 million in cash and stock. In March 2007, AKAM bought Netli for $162 million in stock. In April 2007, the company acquired Red Swoosh for $15 million in stock. As of September 2008, AKAM had roughly $589 million of net cash and equivalents, including about $200 million of convertible debt.

## Investment Rationale/Risk

➤ AKAM is a pioneer in content and application distribution. However, we believe that even though this area will continue to grow rapidly, in part reflecting the growing demand for online video offerings, AKAM faces challenges related to macroeconomic weakness and companies providing less sophisticated products and services.

➤ Risks to our recommendation and target price include weaker demand for AKAM's solutions than we expect, more significant competition, and worse corporate execution than we foresee.

➤ Our discounted cash flow (DCF) analysis, with assumptions including a WACC of 13.5%, free cash flow growth averaging 20% from 2008 to 2012, and a terminal growth rate of 3%, leads to an intrinsic value calculation of $17, which is our 12-month target price. We think DCF considerations constitute the best way to value AKAM, because non-cash items, such as stock-based compensation, are very material to the company's GAAP results.

## Qualitative Risk Assessment

| LOW | MEDIUM | **HIGH** |
|---|---|---|

Our risk assessment reflects what we view as rapidly evolving technologies, and notable and increasing competition.

## Quantitative Evaluations

**S&P Quality Ranking** NR

| D | C | B- | B | B+ | A- | A | A+ |
|---|---|---|---|---|---|---|---|

**Relative Strength Rank** MODERATE

40

LOWEST = 1          HIGHEST = 99

## Revenue/Earnings Data

### Revenue (Million $)

| | 1Q | 2Q | 3Q | 4Q | Year |
|---|---|---|---|---|---|
| 2008 | 187.0 | 194.0 | 197.4 | -- | -- |
| 2007 | 139.3 | 152.7 | 161.2 | 183.2 | 636.4 |
| 2006 | 90.83 | 100.7 | 111.5 | 125.7 | 428.7 |
| 2005 | 60.10 | 64.65 | 75.71 | 82.66 | 283.1 |
| 2004 | 48.37 | 50.79 | 53.29 | 57.58 | 210.0 |
| 2003 | 36.56 | 37.76 | 41.77 | 45.17 | 161.3 |

### Earnings Per Share ($)

| | | | | | |
|---|---|---|---|---|---|
| 2008 | 0.20 | 0.19 | 0.18 | E0.18 | E0.72 |
| 2007 | 0.11 | 0.12 | 0.13 | 0.20 | 0.56 |
| 2006 | 0.07 | 0.07 | 0.08 | 0.12 | 0.34 |
| 2005 | 0.10 | 0.11 | 1.71 | 0.16 | 2.11 |
| 2004 | 0.02 | 0.05 | 0.08 | 0.10 | 0.25 |
| 2003 | -0.07 | -0.13 | -0.03 | -0.02 | -0.25 |

Fiscal year ended Dec. 31. Next earnings report expected: Early February. EPS Estimates based on S&P Operating Earnings; historical GAAP earnings are as reported.

## Dividend Data

No cash dividends have been paid.

# Akamai Technologies Inc

**STANDARD &POOR'S**

## Business Summary November 03, 2008

CORPORATE OVERVIEW. The Internet plays a crucial role in the way entities conduct business; however, it was not originally intended to accommodate the volume or complexity of today's demands. As a result, online information is often delayed or lost.

Akamai Technologies has developed solutions to accelerate and improve the delivery of Internet content and applications. Its solutions are designed to help customers enhance their revenues and reduce costs by maximizing the performance of their online businesses. Advancing website performance and reliability enable AKAM's customers to improve end-user experiences and promote more effective operations. Specifically, AKAM seeks to address issues related to performance, scalability and security. The company offers solutions focused on digital media distribution and storage, content and application delivery, application performance, on-demand managed services, and website intelligence.

CORPORATE STRATEGY. AKAM believes it has deployed the world's largest globally distributed computing platform, which includes more than 40,000 servers around the world. The company employs its proprietary solutions and specialized technologies such as advanced routing, load balancing, and data collection and monitoring to deliver customer content and applications. We perceive this platform and the related intellectual property as a notable competitive advantage the company will continue to leverage.

Although competition in this area has increased notably over the past few years, AKAM's focus on both dynamic (i.e., back and forth) distribution and segments beyond media and entertainment help insulate the company from substantial pricing pressures, in our view. Nonetheless, we believe lower-end business is more at risk given additional players entering the market.

We believe recent acquisitions have bolstered the company's base and breadth of technologies related to streaming rich media, enhancing distribution speeds, and peer-to-peer networks. We expect AKAM to continue pursuing transactions that are not transformational in nature.

## Company Financials  Fiscal Year Ended Dec. 31

| Per Share Data ($) | 2007 | 2006 | 2005 | 2004 | 2003 | 2002 | 2001 | 2000 | 1999 | 1998 |
|---|---|---|---|---|---|---|---|---|---|---|
| Tangible Book Value | 5.47 | 4.10 | 3.19 | NM | NM | NM | NM | 2.02 | 3.04 | NA |
| Cash Flow | 0.93 | 0.58 | 2.25 | 0.37 | 0.17 | -1.01 | -20.40 | -1.98 | -1.75 | NA |
| Earnings | 0.56 | 0.34 | 2.11 | 0.25 | -0.25 | -1.81 | -23.59 | -10.07 | -1.87 | -0.14 |
| S&P Core Earnings | 0.56 | 0.34 | 1.93 | -0.16 | -0.64 | -2.05 | -12.47 | NA | NA | NA |
| Dividends | Nil | Nil | Nil | Nil | Nil | Nil | Nil | Nil | Nil | NA |
| Payout Ratio | Nil | Nil | Nil | Nil | Nil | Nil | Nil | Nil | Nil | NA |
| Prices:High | 59.69 | 56.80 | 22.25 | 18.47 | 14.20 | 6.34 | 37.44 | 345.50 | 344.87 | NA |
| Prices:Low | 27.75 | 19.57 | 10.64 | 10.74 | 1.18 | 0.56 | 2.52 | 18.06 | 26.00 | NA |
| P/E Ratio:High | NM | NM | 11 | 74 | NM | NM | NM | NM | NM | NA |
| P/E Ratio:Low | NM | NM | 5 | 43 | NM | NM | NM | NM | NM | NA |

| Income Statement Analysis (Million $) | 2007 | 2006 | 2005 | 2004 | 2003 | 2002 | 2001 | 2000 | 1999 | 1998 |
|---|---|---|---|---|---|---|---|---|---|---|
| Revenue | 636 | 429 | 283 | 210 | 161 | 145 | 163 | 89.8 | 3.99 | NA |
| Operating Income | 217 | 124 | 98.5 | 69.2 | 30.1 | -46.3 | -131 | -187 | -53.0 | NA |
| Depreciation | 71.9 | 45.6 | 25.2 | 20.2 | 49.7 | 90.4 | 330 | 712 | 3.43 | 0.15 |
| Interest Expense | 3.09 | 3.17 | 5.33 | 10.2 | 18.3 | 18.4 | 18.9 | 8.93 | 2.15 | NA |
| Pretax Income | 168 | 98.5 | 70.4 | 35.1 | -28.7 | -204 | -2,434 | -886 | -54.2 | -2.67 |
| Effective Tax Rate | 40.0% | 41.7% | NM | 2.20% | NM | NM | NM | NM | NM | NA |
| Net Income | 101 | 57.4 | 328 | 34.4 | -29.3 | -204 | -2,436 | -886 | -54.2 | -2.67 |
| S&P Core Earnings | 101 | 57.2 | 300 | -19.9 | -75.6 | -231 | -1,286 | NA | NA | NA |

| Balance Sheet & Other Financial Data (Million $) | 2007 | 2006 | 2005 | 2004 | 2003 | 2002 | 2001 | 2000 | 1999 | 1998 |
|---|---|---|---|---|---|---|---|---|---|---|
| Cash | 546 | 270 | 292 | 70.6 | 165 | 115 | 211 | 310 | 270 | 6.80 |
| Current Assets | 695 | 375 | 355 | 109 | 202 | 142 | 228 | 355 | 274 | NA |
| Total Assets | 1,656 | 1,248 | 891 | 183 | 279 | 230 | 421 | 2,791 | 301 | 8.87 |
| Current Liabilities | 88.4 | 89.3 | 61.9 | 46.8 | 62.7 | 81.1 | 91.3 | 84.9 | 18.6 | NA |
| Long Term Debt | 200 | 200 | 200 | 257 | 386 | 301 | 300 | 300 | 0.73 | NA |
| Common Equity | 1,359 | 955 | 624 | -126 | -175 | -168 | 17.2 | 2,404 | 281 | -0.15 |
| Total Capital | 1,559 | 1,155 | 824 | 131 | 211 | 133 | 317 | 2,705 | 285 | NA |
| Capital Expenditures | 100 | 56.8 | 26.9 | 12.3 | 1.42 | 7.25 | 64.5 | 132 | 25.7 | 4.57 |
| Cash Flow | 173 | 103 | 353 | 54.6 | 20.5 | -114 | -2,106 | -174 | -53.0 | NA |
| Current Ratio | 7.9 | 4.2 | 5.7 | 2.3 | 3.2 | 1.7 | 2.5 | 4.2 | 14.7 | 9.7 |
| % Long Term Debt of Capitalization | 12.8 | 17.3 | 24.3 | 196.4 | 183.2 | 226.5 | 94.6 | 11.1 | 0.3 | Nil |
| % Net Income of Revenue | 15.9 | 13.4 | 115.9 | 16.4 | NM | NM | NM | NM | NM | NA |
| % Return on Assets | 7.0 | 5.4 | 61.1 | 14.9 | NM | NM | NM | NM | NM | NA |
| % Return on Equity | 8.7 | 7.3 | 131.7 | NM | NM | NM | NM | NM | NM | NA |

Data as orig reptd.; bef. results of disc opers/spec. items. Per share data adj. for stk. divs.; EPS diluted. E-Estimated. NA-Not Available. NM-Not Meaningful. NR-Not Ranked. UR-Under Review.

**Office:** 8 Cambridge Center, Cambridge, MA 02142-1413.
**Telephone:** 617-444-3000.
**Email:** ir@akamai.com
**Website:** http://www.akamai.com

**Chrmn:** G.H. Conrades
**Pres & CEO:** P.L. Sagan
**COO:** R. Blumofe
**SVP & CTO:** M.M. Afergan

**SVP, Secy & General Counsel:** M. Haratunian
**Investor Contact:** S. Smith (617-444-2804)
**Board Members:** G. H. Conrades, M. M. Coyne, II, C. K. Goodwin, R. L. Graham, J. A. Greenthal, D. Kenny, P. Kight, F. T. Leighton, G. A. Moore, P. L. Sagan, F. V. Salerno, N. Seligman

**Founded:** 1998
**Domicile:** Delaware
**Employees:** 1,300

# AK Steel Holding Corp

**STANDARD &POOR'S**

| S&P Recommendation | SELL ★ ★ ☆ ☆ ☆ | Price<br>$8.72 (as of Nov 14, 2008) | 12-Mo. Target Price<br>$9.00 | Investment Style<br>Large-Cap Blend |

**GICS Sector** Materials
**Sub-Industry** Steel

**Summary** This company produces carbon flat-rolled steel for the automotive, appliance, construction and manufacturing markets.

## Key Stock Statistics (Source S&P, Vickers, company reports)

| | | | | | | | | |
|---|---|---|---|---|---|---|---|---|
| 52-Wk Range | $73.07– 7.50 | S&P Oper. EPS 2008**E** | 4.14 | Market Capitalization(B) | $0.977 | Beta | 3.58 |
| Trailing 12-Month EPS | $4.82 | S&P Oper. EPS 2009**E** | 1.89 | Yield (%) | 2.29 | S&P 3-Yr. Proj. EPS CAGR(%) | 3 |
| Trailing 12-Month P/E | 1.8 | P/E on S&P Oper. EPS 2008**E** | 2.1 | Dividend Rate/Share | $0.20 | S&P Credit Rating | BB- |
| $10K Invested 5 Yrs Ago | $32,236 | Common Shares Outstg. (M) | 112.0 | Institutional Ownership (%) | 94 | | |

## Price Performance

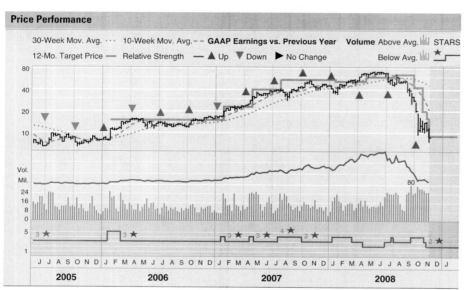

30-Week Mov. Avg. · · · ·  10-Week Mov. Avg. – –  **GAAP Earnings vs. Previous Year**  Volume Above Avg. STARS
12-Mo. Target Price —  Relative Strength —  ▲ Up  ▼ Down  ► No Change  Below Avg. ★

Options: ASE, CBOE, P, Ph

## Qualitative Risk Assessment

| LOW | MEDIUM | **HIGH** |

Our risk assessment reflects AKS's exposure to the auto industry and other cyclical markets, along with its highly leveraged balance sheet versus its peers. Partially offsetting these factors are AKS's debt reduction in recent years and success in reducing pension and health care costs.

## Quantitative Evaluations

**S&P Quality Ranking** B-

| D | C | **B-** | B | B+ | A- | A | A+ |

**Relative Strength Rank** WEAK

6

LOWEST = 1  HIGHEST = 99

## Revenue/Earnings Data

**Revenue (Million $)**

| | 1Q | 2Q | 3Q | 4Q | Year |
|---|---|---|---|---|---|
| 2008 | 1,791 | 2,237 | 2,158 | -- | -- |
| 2007 | 1,720 | 1,870 | 1,722 | 1,692 | 7,003 |
| 2006 | 1,436 | 1,497 | 1,554 | 1,582 | 6,069 |
| 2005 | 1,423 | 1,455 | 1,393 | 1,377 | 5,647 |
| 2004 | 1,134 | 1,312 | 1,337 | 1,434 | 5,217 |
| 2003 | 985.3 | 981.3 | 1,021 | 1,054 | 4,042 |

**Earnings Per Share ($)**

| | | | | | |
|---|---|---|---|---|---|
| 2008 | 0.90 | 1.29 | 1.67 | E0.28 | E4.14 |
| 2007 | 0.56 | 0.98 | 0.97 | 0.95 | 3.47 |
| 2006 | 0.06 | 0.26 | 0.23 | -0.45 | 0.11 |
| 2005 | 0.54 | 0.08 | -0.26 | 0.37 | 0.01 |
| 2004 | -0.15 | 0.18 | 1.09 | -0.84 | 0.28 |
| 2003 | -0.38 | -0.72 | -2.56 | -1.65 | -5.48 |

Fiscal year ended Dec. 31. Next earnings report expected: Late January. EPS Estimates based on S&P Operating Earnings; historical GAAP earnings are as reported.

## Dividend Data (Dates: mm/dd Payment Date: mm/dd/yy)

| Amount ($) | Date Decl. | Ex-Div. Date | Stk. of Record | Payment Date |
|---|---|---|---|---|
| 0.050 | 01/22 | 02/13 | 02/15 | 03/10/08 |
| 0.050 | 04/22 | 05/14 | 05/16 | 06/10/08 |
| 0.050 | 07/22 | 08/13 | 08/15 | 09/10/08 |
| 0.050 | 10/21 | 11/12 | 11/14 | 12/10/08 |

Dividends have been paid since 2008. Source: Company reports.

## Highlights

➤ The STARS recommendation for AKS has recently been changed to 2 (sell) from 3 (hold) and the 12-month target price has recently been changed to $9.00 from $16.00. The Highlights section of this Stock Report will be updated accordingly.

## Investment Rationale/Risk

➤ The Investment Rationale/Risk section of this Stock Report will be updated shortly. For the latest News story on AKS from MarketScope, see below.

➤ 11/12/08 09:41 am ET ... S&P DOWNGRADES RECOMMENDATION ON SHARES OF AK STEEL HOLDING TO SELL FROM HOLD (AKS 9.26**): Our opinion change is based on a more pessimistic outlook for EPS. The price of AKS shares is lower this morning after the company's announcement that it is idling two of its plants until early-to-mid-January '09 due to sharply lower demand for its products. On that basis, we are cutting our '08 EPS estimate to $4.14 from $4.27 and trimming our '09 forecast to $1.89 from $2.82. Based on our revised '09 EPS forecast, we are reducing our 12-month target price to $9 from $16, as we believe that AKS will carry a lower P/E than peers due to its greater exposure to the auto industry. /LLarkin

**STANDARD &POOR'S**

# AK Steel Holding Corp

## Business Summary November 04, 2008

AK Steel Holding, the third largest integrated U.S. steelmaker in terms of production, sells premium quality coated, cold rolled and hot rolled carbon steel to the automotive, appliance and manufacturing markets, as well as to the construction industry and to independent steel distributors and service centers.

Sales by market and other operating data in 2007 were: automotive 40% (41% in 2006), appliance, industrial machinery, construction and manufacturing 26% (29%), and distribution and service centers 34% (30%).

Shipments to GM accounted for 13% of sales in 2005 and less than 10% in 2006 and 2007.

Shipments in 2007 totaled 6,478,700 tons, versus shipments of 6,168,600 tons in 2006. There was an operating profit per ton of $103 in 2007, versus $35 in 2006.

In 2007, carbon steel products accounted for 52.6% of revenues, stainless and electrical steel comprised 43.9% and tubular products 3.5%.

AKS's chief U.S. competitors in high-margin products are Allegheny Technologies, Arcelor Mittal, North American Stainless, and U.S. Steel.

On March 14, 2007, AKS announced that members of the International Association of Machinists and Aerospace Workers (IAM), Local Lodge 1943, had ratified a 54-month, new-era labor agreement covering about 1,700 hourly production and maintenance employees at the company's Middletown (OH) Works. The ratification ended a strike that began on March 1, 2006. The new Middletown Works contract included, among numerous other provisions: a lock and freeze of the traditional defined-benefit pension plan, reduction of job classes to 7 from 1,000, a complete work force restructuring, the elimination of minimum base work force guarantee, and active employee and future retiree health care cost-sharing.

## Company Financials Fiscal Year Ended Dec. 31

| Per Share Data ($) | 2007 | 2006 | 2005 | 2004 | 2003 | 2002 | 2001 | 2000 | 1999 | 1998 |
|---|---|---|---|---|---|---|---|---|---|---|
| Tangible Book Value | 7.51 | 3.44 | 1.30 | 0.92 | NM | 3.02 | 7.40 | 11.03 | 10.42 | 15.75 |
| Cash Flow | 5.22 | 1.95 | 1.86 | 2.29 | -3.44 | -2.32 | 1.41 | 3.45 | 2.53 | 3.56 |
| Earnings | 3.46 | 0.11 | 0.01 | 0.28 | -5.48 | -4.42 | -0.87 | 1.20 | 0.62 | 1.92 |
| S&P Core Earnings | 3.43 | 1.00 | 0.84 | 2.70 | -2.71 | -1.06 | -1.89 | NA | NA | NA |
| Dividends | Nil | Nil | Nil | Nil | Nil | Nil | 0.13 | 0.50 | 0.50 | 0.50 |
| Payout Ratio | Nil | Nil | Nil | Nil | Nil | Nil | NM | 42% | 81% | 26% |
| Prices:High | 53.97 | 17.31 | 18.23 | 16.00 | 8.90 | 14.85 | 15.00 | 20.13 | 29.63 | 23.75 |
| Prices:Low | 16.13 | 7.58 | 6.23 | 3.65 | 1.74 | 6.45 | 7.50 | 7.50 | 13.75 | 13.63 |
| P/E Ratio:High | 16 | NM | NM | 57 | NM | NM | NM | 17 | 48 | 12 |
| P/E Ratio:Low | 5 | NM | NM | 13 | NM | NM | NM | 6 | 22 | 7 |

| Income Statement Analysis (Million $) | | | | | | | | | | |
|---|---|---|---|---|---|---|---|---|---|---|
| Revenue | 7,003 | 6,069 | 5,647 | 5,217 | 4,042 | 4,289 | 3,994 | 4,612 | 4,285 | 2,394 |
| Operating Income | 860 | 409 | 397 | 139 | 155 | 331 | 370 | 586 | 572 | 311 |
| Depreciation | 196 | 204 | 205 | 219 | 222 | 225 | 245 | 248 | 227 | 97.8 |
| Interest Expense | 68.3 | 89.1 | 86.8 | 110 | 118 | 128 | 133 | 136 | 124 | 56.0 |
| Pretax Income | 591 | -3.10 | 38.0 | -193 | -241 | -803 | -147 | 210 | 142 | 176 |
| Effective Tax Rate | 34.4% | NM | NM | NM | NM | NM | NM | 37.0% | 45.0% | 35.0% |
| Net Income | 388 | 12.0 | -0.80 | 30.5 | -594 | -476 | -92.4 | 132 | 71.3 | 115 |
| S&P Core Earnings | 385 | 110 | 92.4 | 295 | -326 | -125 | -204 | NA | NA | NA |

| Balance Sheet & Other Financial Data (Million $) | | | | | | | | | | |
|---|---|---|---|---|---|---|---|---|---|---|
| Cash | 714 | 519 | 520 | 377 | 54.7 | 283 | 101 | 86.8 | 54.4 | 83.0 |
| Current Assets | 2,427 | 2,548 | 2,246 | 2,107 | 1,358 | 1,700 | 1,548 | 1,522 | 1,433 | 808 |
| Total Assets | 5,197 | 5,518 | 5,488 | 5,453 | 5,026 | 5,400 | 5,226 | 5,240 | 5,202 | 3,306 |
| Current Liabilities | 973 | 932 | 903 | 747 | 779 | 860 | 954 | 890 | 868 | 531 |
| Long Term Debt | 653 | 1,115 | 1,115 | 1,110 | 1,198 | 1,260 | 1,325 | 1,388 | 1,451 | 1,145 |
| Common Equity | 875 | 417 | 220 | 197 | -52.8 | 529 | 1,021 | 1,307 | 1,263 | 930 |
| Total Capital | 1,527 | 1,532 | 1,335 | 1,307 | 1,145 | 1,789 | 2,358 | 2,707 | 2,929 | 2,143 |
| Capital Expenditures | 104 | 76.2 | 174 | 98.8 | 79.6 | 93.8 | 109 | 138 | 337 | 773 |
| Cash Flow | 584 | 216 | 204 | 250 | -373 | -250 | 152 | 379 | 278 | 212 |
| Current Ratio | 2.5 | 2.7 | 2.5 | 2.8 | 1.7 | 2.0 | 1.6 | 1.7 | 1.7 | 1.5 |
| % Long Term Debt of Capitalization | 42.7 | 72.8 | 83.5 | 84.9 | 104.6 | 70.4 | 56.2 | 51.3 | 53.1 | 53.4 |
| % Net Income of Revenue | 5.5 | NM | NM | NM | NM | NM | NM | 2.9 | 1.7 | 4.8 |
| % Return on Assets | 7.2 | NM | NM | NM | NM | NM | NM | 2.5 | 1.4 | 3.6 |
| % Return on Equity | 60.0 | NM | NM | NM | NM | NM | NM | 10.2 | 4.3 | 12.7 |

Data as orig reptd.; bef. results of disc opers/spec. items. Per share data adj. for stk. divs.; EPS diluted. E-Estimated. NA-Not Available. NM-Not Meaningful. NR-Not Ranked. UR-Under Review.

**Office:** 9227 Centre Pointe Dr, West Chester, OH 45069-4822.
**Telephone:** 513-425-5000.
**Website:** http://www.aksteel.com
**Chrmn, Pres & CEO:** J. Wainscott

**SVP, Secy & General Counsel:** D.C. Horn
**CFO:** A.E. Ferrara, Jr.
**Chief Acctg Officer & Cntlr:** R.K. Newport
**Investor Contact:** A.E. Ferrara, Jr. (513-425-2888)

**Board Members:** R. A. Abdoo, J. S. Brinzo, D. C. Cuneo, W. K. Gerber, B. Hill, R. H. Jenkins, D. J. Meyer, R. S. Michael, III, S. D. Peterson, J. A. Thomson, J. Wainscott

**Founded:** 1900
**Domicile:** Delaware
**Employees:** 6,900

# Alcoa Inc.

| S&P Recommendation SELL ★★☆☆☆ | Price $10.84 (as of Nov 14, 2008) | 12-Mo. Target Price $10.00 | Investment Style Large-Cap Value |
|---|---|---|---|

**GICS Sector** Materials
**Sub-Industry** Aluminum

**Summary** Alcoa is the third largest producer of aluminum and one of the world's largest producers of alumina.

## Key Stock Statistics (Source S&P, Vickers, company reports)

| | | | | | | | |
|---|---|---|---|---|---|---|---|
| 52-Wk Range | $44.77– 9.00 | S&P Oper. EPS 2008**E** | 1.52 | Market Capitalization(B) | $8.675 | Beta | 2.10 |
| Trailing 12-Month EPS | $2.11 | S&P Oper. EPS 2009**E** | 1.18 | Yield (%) | 6.27 | S&P 3-Yr. Proj. EPS CAGR(%) | -9 |
| Trailing 12-Month P/E | 5.1 | P/E on S&P Oper. EPS 2008**E** | 7.1 | Dividend Rate/Share | $0.68 | S&P Credit Rating | BBB+ |
| $10K Invested 5 Yrs Ago | $3,732 | Common Shares Outstg. (M) | 800.3 | Institutional Ownership (%) | 81 | | |

## Price Performance

30-Week Mov. Avg. · · · · 10-Week Mov. Avg. - - - **GAAP Earnings vs. Previous Year** Volume Above Avg. STARS
12-Mo. Target Price — Relative Strength — ▲ Up ▼ Down ► No Change Below Avg. ★

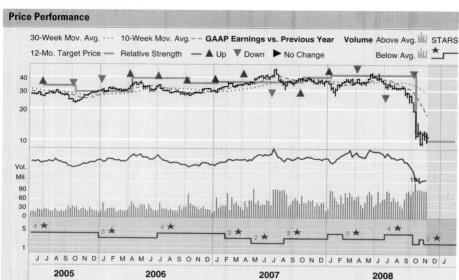

Options: ASE, CBOE, P, Ph

## Highlights

► The STARS recommendation for AA has recently been changed to 2 (sell) from 3 (hold) and the 12-month target price has recently been changed to $10.00 from $12.00. The Highlights section of this Stock Report will be updated accordingly.

## Investment Rationale/Risk

► The Investment Rationale/Risk section of this Stock Report will be updated shortly. For the latest News story on AA from MarketScope, see below.

► 11/11/08 09:26 am ET ... S&P DOWNGRADES RECOMMENDATION ON SHARES OF ALCOA INC TO SELL FROM HOLD (AA 11.78**): Our opinion change is based on valuation and a more pessimistic outlook for EPS. Shares of AA are down in premarket trading today after the company announced plans to reduce aluminum production by an additional 350,000 metric tons, bringing curtailed production to 15% of total capacity. On that basis, we are cutting our '08 EPS estimate to $1.52 from $1.70. Also, we trim '09's to $1.18 from $1.50, as we expect the production curtailment to extend into 2009. Based on our revised '09 estimate, we are reducing our 12-month target price to $10 from $12. /L.Larkin

## Qualitative Risk Assessment

| LOW | MEDIUM | HIGH |
|---|---|---|

Our risk assessment reflects our view that AA's sales and earnings are exposed to cyclical markets, such as autos and the home building sector of the construction market. Offsetting this is what we view as the company's moderate balance sheet leverage.

## Quantitative Evaluations

**S&P Quality Ranking** B+

| D | C | B- | B | B+ | A- | A | A+ |
|---|---|---|---|---|---|---|---|

**Relative Strength Rank** WEAK

21

LOWEST = 1   HIGHEST = 99

## Revenue/Earnings Data

**Revenue (Million $)**

| | 1Q | 2Q | 3Q | 4Q | Year |
|---|---|---|---|---|---|
| 2008 | 7,375 | 7,620 | 7,234 | -- | -- |
| 2007 | 7,908 | 8,066 | 7,387 | 7,387 | 30,748 |
| 2006 | 7,244 | 7,959 | 7,631 | 7,840 | 30,379 |
| 2005 | 6,226 | 6,698 | 6,566 | 6,669 | 26,159 |
| 2004 | 5,588 | 5,971 | 5,878 | 6,041 | 23,478 |
| 2003 | 5,140 | 5,497 | 5,335 | 5,532 | 21,504 |

**Earnings Per Share ($)**

| | 1Q | 2Q | 3Q | 4Q | Year |
|---|---|---|---|---|---|
| 2008 | 0.37 | 0.66 | 0.33 | E0.23 | E1.52 |
| 2007 | 0.77 | 0.81 | 0.64 | 0.74 | 2.95 |
| 2006 | 0.70 | 0.86 | 0.62 | 0.29 | 2.47 |
| 2005 | 0.30 | 0.53 | 0.33 | 0.24 | 1.40 |
| 2004 | 0.41 | 0.46 | 0.34 | 0.39 | 1.60 |
| 2003 | 0.23 | 0.26 | 0.32 | 0.39 | 1.20 |

Fiscal year ended Dec. 31. Next earnings report expected: Late January. EPS Estimates based on S&P Operating Earnings; historical GAAP earnings are as reported.

## Dividend Data (Dates: mm/dd Payment Date: mm/dd/yy)

| Amount ($) | Date Decl. | Ex-Div. Date | Stk. of Record | Payment Date |
|---|---|---|---|---|
| 0.170 | 01/18 | 02/06 | 02/08 | 02/25/08 |
| 0.170 | 03/14 | 04/30 | 05/02 | 05/25/08 |
| 0.170 | 07/18 | 08/06 | 08/08 | 08/25/08 |
| 0.170 | 09/19 | 11/05 | 11/07 | 11/25/08 |

Dividends have been paid since 1939. Source: Company reports.

---

**Please read the Required Disclosures and Analyst Certification on the last page of this report.**

# Alcoa Inc.

**STANDARD
&POOR'S**

## Business Summary October 30, 2008

CORPORATE OVERVIEW. Alcoa is the world's third largest producer of primary aluminum and is one of the world's largest supplier of alumina, an intermediate raw material used to make aluminum. In 2007, primary aluminum production totaled 3.7 million metric tons, versus 3.6 million tons in 2006; alumina production totaled 15.1 million metric tons, unchanged from 15.1 million metric tons in 2006.

MARKET PROFILE. The primary factor affecting demand for aluminum products is economic growth, in general, and growth in demand for durable goods, in particular. The three largest end markets for aluminum in North America are transportation, containers/packaging, and construction. In 2006 (latest available data), these markets accounted for 67% of revenues in North America. In terms of primary production, the size of the world market was 24.8 million metric tons in 2007. Alcoa's market share was 14.9%. From 1998 through 2007, global consumption rose at a compound annual growth rate (CAGR) of 6.2%.

COMPETITIVE LANDSCAPE. Alcoa's direct competitors in the aluminum market are Aleris International, Inc., Aluminum Corp. of China, Century Aluminum, Kaiser Aluminum, Norsk Hydro, United Company RUSAL and Quanex. Indirect competitors include mining companies that have aluminum and alumina operations, such as Vale, BHP Billiton and Rio Tinto. Led mostly by Alcoa and Al-

can (now a subsidiary of Rio Tinto), consolidation of the industry accelerated in the late 1990s and thereafter. As a result, the industry has become more concentrated, with Alcoa, Alcan and RUSAL accounting for some 39.2% of primary aluminum production in 2006. However, the price of aluminum in the recent economic expansion lagged the gains in other base metals such as carbon steel, copper and nickel by a wide margin. In our view, the reason for the less buoyant aluminum price is that exports from China have kept the aluminum market in overall surplus.

Beginning in 2003, China became a net exporter of aluminum, and we believe that its production has become a drag on the aluminum price. Aluminum faces competition from such materials as plastics, steel, glass, and ceramics. Plastic, in the form of polyethylene terephthalate (PET), provides strong competition in the container market. Steel competes with aluminum in automotive applications. After gaining substantial share in auto applications in the 1970s and 1980s, aluminum's rate of gain in market share slowed in the 1990s and thereafter.

## Company Financials Fiscal Year Ended Dec. 31

| Per Share Data ($) | 2007 | 2006 | 2005 | 2004 | 2003 | 2002 | 2001 | 2000 | 1999 | 1998 |
|---|---|---|---|---|---|---|---|---|---|---|
| Tangible Book Value | 12.75 | 8.53 | 6.96 | 6.72 | 5.36 | 3.27 | 4.96 | 6.19 | 6.62 | 6.08 |
| Cash Flow | 4.42 | 3.96 | 2.85 | 2.98 | 2.61 | 3.20 | 2.49 | 3.29 | 2.61 | 2.42 |
| Earnings | 2.95 | 2.47 | 1.40 | 1.60 | 1.20 | 0.58 | 1.05 | 1.81 | 1.41 | 1.21 |
| S&P Core Earnings | 1.74 | 2.46 | 1.05 | 1.52 | 0.92 | -0.17 | 0.17 | NA | NA | NA |
| Dividends | 0.68 | 0.60 | 0.60 | 0.60 | 0.60 | 0.60 | 0.60 | 0.50 | 0.40 | 0.38 |
| Payout Ratio | 23% | 24% | 43% | 38% | 50% | 103% | 57% | 28% | 29% | 31% |
| Prices:High | 48.77 | 36.96 | 32.29 | 39.44 | 38.92 | 39.75 | 45.71 | 43.63 | 41.69 | 20.31 |
| Prices:Low | 28.09 | 26.39 | 22.28 | 28.51 | 18.45 | 17.62 | 27.36 | 23.13 | 17.97 | 14.50 |
| P/E Ratio:High | 17 | 15 | 23 | 25 | 32 | 69 | 44 | 24 | 30 | 17 |
| P/E Ratio:Low | 10 | 11 | 16 | 18 | 15 | 30 | 26 | 13 | 13 | 12 |

| Income Statement Analysis (Million $) | | | | | | | | | | |
|---|---|---|---|---|---|---|---|---|---|---|
| Revenue | 30,748 | 30,379 | 26,159 | 23,478 | 21,504 | 20,263 | 22,859 | 22,936 | 16,323 | 15,340 |
| Operating Income | 4,779 | 5,410 | 3,398 | 3,397 | 2,885 | 2,663 | 3,523 | 4,304 | 2,821 | 2,509 |
| Depreciation | 1,268 | 1,280 | 1,267 | 1,212 | 1,202 | 2,224 | 1,253 | 1,219 | 901 | 856 |
| Interest Expense | 401 | 384 | 339 | 270 | 314 | 350 | 393 | 427 | 195 | 198 |
| Pretax Income | 4,491 | 3,432 | 1,933 | 2,204 | 1,669 | 925 | 1,641 | 2,812 | 1,849 | 1,605 |
| Effective Tax Rate | 34.6% | 24.3% | 22.8% | 25.3% | 24.2% | 31.6% | 32.0% | 33.5% | 29.9% | 32.0% |
| Net Income | 2,571 | 2,161 | 1,233 | 1,402 | 1,034 | 498 | 908 | 1,489 | 1,054 | 853 |
| S&P Core Earnings | 1,511 | 2,154 | 924 | 1,334 | 777 | -143 | 146 | NA | NA | NA |

| Balance Sheet & Other Financial Data (Million $) | | | | | | | | | | |
|---|---|---|---|---|---|---|---|---|---|---|
| Cash | 483 | 506 | 762 | 457 | 576 | 344 | 512 | 315 | 237 | 342 |
| Current Assets | 8,086 | 9,157 | 8,790 | 7,493 | 6,740 | 6,313 | 6,792 | 7,578 | 4,800 | 5,025 |
| Total Assets | 38,803 | 37,183 | 33,696 | 32,609 | 31,711 | 29,810 | 28,355 | 31,691 | 17,066 | 17,463 |
| Current Liabilities | 7,166 | 7,281 | 7,368 | 6,298 | 5,084 | 4,461 | 5,003 | 7,954 | 3,003 | 3,268 |
| Long Term Debt | 6,371 | 5,910 | 5,279 | 5,346 | 6,692 | 8,365 | 6,388 | 4,987 | 2,657 | 2,877 |
| Common Equity | 15,961 | 14,576 | 13,318 | 13,245 | 12,020 | 9,872 | 10,614 | 11,366 | 6,262 | 6,000 |
| Total Capital | 24,847 | 23,103 | 20,892 | 20,852 | 20,911 | 20,087 | 18,927 | 18,892 | 10,870 | 10,767 |
| Capital Expenditures | 3,636 | 3,201 | 2,124 | 1,142 | 863 | 1,263 | 1,177 | 1,121 | 920 | 932 |
| Cash Flow | 3,839 | 3,441 | 2,498 | 2,612 | 2,234 | 2,720 | 2,159 | 2,706 | 1,953 | 1,707 |
| Current Ratio | 1.1 | 1.3 | 1.2 | 1.2 | 1.3 | 1.4 | 1.4 | 1.0 | 1.6 | 1.5 |
| % Long Term Debt of Capitalization | 25.6 | 25.6 | 25.3 | 25.6 | 32.0 | 41.6 | 33.8 | 26.4 | 24.4 | 26.7 |
| % Net Income of Revenue | 8.3 | 7.1 | 4.7 | 6.0 | 4.8 | 2.5 | 4.0 | 6.5 | 6.5 | 5.6 |
| % Return on Assets | 6.7 | 6.1 | 3.7 | 4.4 | 3.4 | 1.7 | 3.0 | 6.1 | 6.1 | 5.6 |
| % Return on Equity | 10.2 | 15.5 | 9.3 | 11.1 | 9.4 | 4.9 | 8.2 | 16.9 | 17.2 | 16.4 |

Data as orig reptd.; bef. results of disc opers/spec. items. Per share data adj. for stk. divs.; EPS diluted. E-Estimated. NA-Not Available. NM-Not Meaningful. NR-Not Ranked. UR-Under Review.

**Office:** 390 Park Ave, New York, NY 10022-4608.
**Telephone:** 212-836-2674.
**Email:** investor.relations@alcoa.com
**Website:** http://www.alcoa.com

**Chrmn:** A.J. Belda
**Pres & CEO:** K. Kleinfeld
**EVP & CFO:** C.D. McLane, Jr.
**EVP & CTO:** M.A. Zaidi

**Chief Acctg Officer & Cntlr:** T.R. Thene
**Board Members:** A. J. Belda, K. S. Fuller, C. Ghosn, J. T. Gorman, J. M. Gueron, K. Kleinfeld, M. G. Morris, S. E. O'Neal, J. W. Owens, H. B. Schacht, R. N. Tata, F. A. Thomas, E. Zedillo

**Founded:** 1888
**Domicile:** Pennsylvania
**Employees:** 107,000

*The McGraw-Hill Companies*

# Allegheny Energy Inc.

**STANDARD &POOR'S**

| **S&P Recommendation** BUY ★★★★☆ | **Price** $28.70 (as of Nov 14, 2008) | **12-Mo. Target Price** $38.00 | **Investment Style** Large-Cap Blend |
|---|---|---|---|

**GICS Sector** Utilities
**Sub-Industry** Electric Utilities

**Summary** This diversified energy company engages in electric generation, transmission and delivery, and invests in and develops telecommunications and energy-related projects.

## Key Stock Statistics (Source S&P, Vickers, company reports)

| | | | | | | | |
|---|---|---|---|---|---|---|---|
| 52-Wk Range | $65.48– 23.86 | S&P Oper. EPS 2008E | 2.30 | Market Capitalization(B) | $4.852 | Beta | 1.35 |
| Trailing 12-Month EPS | $2.88 | S&P Oper. EPS 2009E | 3.00 | Yield (%) | 2.09 | S&P 3-Yr. Proj. EPS CAGR(%) | 15 |
| Trailing 12-Month P/E | 10.0 | P/E on S&P Oper. EPS 2008E | 12.5 | Dividend Rate/Share | $0.60 | S&P Credit Rating | BBB- |
| $10K Invested 5 Yrs Ago | $26,891 | Common Shares Outstg. (M) | 169.1 | Institutional Ownership (%) | 84 | | |

## Price Performance

30-Week Mov. Avg. · · · · 10-Week Mov. Avg. – – **GAAP Earnings vs. Previous Year** Volume Above Avg. STARS
12-Mo. Target Price — Relative Strength — ▲ Up ▼ Down ▶ No Change Below Avg. ★

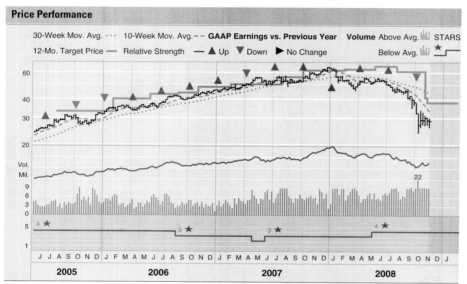

2005 2006 2007 2008

Options: ASE, CBOE, P

Analysis prepared by **Christopher B. Muir** on November 05, 2008, when the stock traded at **$29.56**.

## Highlights

➤ We see 2008 and 2009 revenues increasing 2.4% and 8.7%, respectively, aided by regulated operations. We expect regulated utility revenues to benefit from customer growth, a Virginia rate increase and expiration of rate caps in Maryland. We expect non-regulated revenues to rise due to higher power prices, increased generation capacity factors, rate increases for providers of last resort service in Pennsylvania, and the transitioning of some Virginia customers to market-based rates.

➤ We expect operating margins to fall to 23.2% in 2008, from 24.7% in 2007, as a result of higher per-revenue fuel costs, partly offset by slightly lower per-revenue depreciation and amortization charges, and operations and maintenance expense. We see operating margins rising to 26.9% in 2009. We see pretax profit margins falling to 17.2% in 2008, from 18.7% in 2007, despite lower interest expense. We see pretax margins rising to 21.8% in 2009.

➤ Assuming an effective tax rate of 32.8%, we forecast 2008 operating EPS of $2.30, up 2.6% from $2.24 in 2007. Our 2009 EPS estimate is $3.00, a 30% increase.

## Investment Rationale/Risk

➤ Operationally, we like AYE's focus on improving plant performance and controlling operational expenses. We also like the ending of distribution rate caps in Pennsylvania in 2007 and residential generation caps in Maryland in 2008. We note that AYE reduced its debt to total capitalization ratio to 58.0% as of June 30, 2008, from 61.5% at December 31, 2007, and 63.3% at the end of 2006.

➤ Risks to our recommendation and target price include lower than expected cash flows and a weaker than projected economy.

➤ The shares recently traded at 9.8X our 2009 EPS estimate, or a 13% discount to electric utility peers. Our 12-month target price of $38 values the stock at a P/E multiple of 12.7X our 2009 EPS estimate, a 24% discount to our peer target. We see this as merited by what we view as AYE's prospects for a continued recovery from near bankruptcy, which leads us to forecast double-digit earnings growth and significant strengthening of its balance sheet, offset by a lack of clarity surrounding its dividend policy and higher risk than peers.

## Qualitative Risk Assessment

| LOW | MEDIUM | HIGH |
|---|---|---|

Our risk assessment reflects the company's mid-level capitalization and balanced sources of earnings, which include both low-risk regulated electric utility and higher-risk unregulated power generation operations.

## Quantitative Evaluations

**S&P Quality Ranking** B

| D | C | B- | B | B+ | A- | A | A+ |
|---|---|---|---|---|---|---|---|

**Relative Strength Rank** MODERATE

60

LOWEST = 1 HIGHEST = 99

## Revenue/Earnings Data

### Revenue (Million $)

| | 1Q | 2Q | 3Q | 4Q | Year |
|---|---|---|---|---|---|
| 2008 | 875.0 | 953.5 | 849.6 | -- | -- |
| 2007 | 847.6 | 826.5 | 846.6 | 786.3 | 3,307 |
| 2006 | 845.6 | 722.2 | 816.6 | 737.0 | 3,121 |
| 2005 | 754.0 | 714.7 | 845.1 | 724.1 | 3,038 |
| 2004 | 735.4 | 608.9 | 723.3 | 688.5 | 2,756 |
| 2003 | 715.7 | 359.2 | 637.6 | 760.0 | 2,472 |

### Earnings Per Share ($)

| | | | | | |
|---|---|---|---|---|---|
| 2008 | 0.80 | 0.91 | 0.52 | E0.53 | E2.30 |
| 2007 | 0.65 | 0.45 | 0.67 | 0.65 | 2.43 |
| 2006 | 0.68 | 0.19 | 0.65 | 0.37 | 1.89 |
| 2005 | 0.24 | -0.04 | 0.26 | 0.02 | 0.47 |
| 2004 | 0.23 | -0.26 | 0.37 | 0.53 | 0.99 |
| 2003 | -0.30 | -1.82 | -0.40 | -0.11 | -2.64 |

Fiscal year ended Dec. 31. Next earnings report expected: Early February. EPS Estimates based on S&P Operating Earnings; historical GAAP earnings are as reported.

## Dividend Data (Dates: mm/dd Payment Date: mm/dd/yy)

| Amount ($) | Date Decl. | Ex-Div. Date | Stk. of Record | Payment Date |
|---|---|---|---|---|
| 0.150 | 02/22 | 03/06 | 03/10 | 03/24/08 |
| 0.150 | 05/15 | 06/05 | 06/09 | 06/23/08 |
| 0.150 | 07/10 | 09/11 | 09/15 | 09/29/08 |
| 0.150 | 10/02 | 12/11 | 12/15 | 12/29/08 |

Dividends have been paid since 2007. Source: Company reports.

# Allegheny Energy Inc.

**STANDARD &POOR'S**

## Business Summary November 05, 2008

CORPORATE OVERVIEW. AYE is an integrated electric distribution and generation company operating in the Mid-Atlantic region. The company has two operating segments: Delivery and Services, which includes AYE's electric transmission and distribution (T&D) operations, and Generation and Marketing, which includes the company's generation and unregulated businesses.

Its three distribution businesses operate under the trade name Allegheny Power. West Penn operates a T&D system in southwestern, northern and south central Pennsylvania, serving approximately 711,000 customers as of December 31, 2007. Potomac Edison operates a T&D system in portions of West Virginia, Maryland and Virginia. Potomac Edison serves approximately 475,000 electric customers. Monongahela conducts a T&D business that serves roughly 378,600 electric customers in northern West Virginia. The Delivery Services segment also includes investments in transmission line projects (TrAIL and PATH) and the unregulated Allegheny Ventures (includes communications and energy business).

Allegheny Energy Supply (AE Supply), AYE's primary unregulated generating division, ended 2007 with 6,899 megawatts (MW) of capacity. The division's capacity grew from 1999 to 2001 through the transfer of regulated power plants in Pennsylvania, Maryland, Virginia and Ohio from AYE's regulated utilities, acquisition of existing plants, and construction activities. AE Supply currently is contractually obligated to provide Potomac Edison and West Penn with the power that they need to meet a majority of their provider of last resort obligations, which represents a majority of AE Supply's operating capacity. In July 2005, Allegheny Energy Supply was awarded contracts to meet Allegheny Power's 2009 and 2010 generation supply needs in Pennsylvania.

Monongahela owns or controls about 2,806 MW of generating capacity, most of which is delivered to AYE's electric utilities. Additionally, AYE owns a 40% interest (or 1,059 MW) in the Bath County pumped-storage hydroelectric power station.

As of December 31, 2007, about 78.5% of AYE's 9,705 MW of owned and controlled capacity was coal-fired, 11.5% was gas-fired, 9.2% was hydroelectric, and 0.8% was oil-fired.

## Company Financials Fiscal Year Ended Dec. 31

| Per Share Data ($) | 2007 | 2006 | 2005 | 2004 | 2003 | 2002 | 2001 | 2000 | 1999 | 1998 |
|---|---|---|---|---|---|---|---|---|---|---|
| Tangible Book Value | 12.97 | 10.36 | 7.98 | 6.94 | 9.05 | 12.05 | 16.48 | 13.80 | 14.97 | 16.49 |
| Earnings | 2.43 | 1.89 | 0.47 | 0.99 | -2.64 | -4.00 | 3.73 | 2.84 | 2.45 | 2.15 |
| S&P Core Earnings | 2.23 | 1.90 | 0.45 | 0.56 | -2.60 | -4.22 | 3.24 | NA | NA | NA |
| Dividends | 0.15 | Nil | Nil | Nil | Nil | 1.29 | 1.72 | 1.72 | 1.72 | 1.72 |
| Payout Ratio | 6% | Nil | Nil | Nil | Nil | NM | 46% | 61% | 77% | 74% |
| Prices:High | 65.48 | 46.25 | 32.32 | 20.20 | 13.09 | 43.86 | 55.09 | 48.75 | 35.19 | 34.94 |
| Prices:Low | 44.28 | 31.33 | 18.25 | 11.75 | 4.70 | 2.95 | 32.99 | 23.63 | 26.19 | 26.63 |
| P/E Ratio:High | 27 | 24 | 69 | 20 | NM | NM | 15 | 17 | 14 | 15 |
| P/E Ratio:Low | 18 | 16 | 39 | 12 | NM | NM | 9 | 8 | 11 | 11 |

| Income Statement Analysis (Million $) | 2007 | 2006 | 2005 | 2004 | 2003 | 2002 | 2001 | 2000 | 1999 | 1998 |
|---|---|---|---|---|---|---|---|---|---|---|
| Revenue | 3,307 | 3,121 | 3,038 | 2,756 | 2,472 | 2,988 | 10,379 | 4,012 | 2,808 | 2,576 |
| Depreciation | 277 | 273 | 308 | 299 | 327 | 309 | 302 | 248 | 257 | 270 |
| Maintenance | NA | NA | NA | NA | NA | NA | 288 | 230 | 224 | 218 |
| Fixed Charges Coverage | 4.54 | 2.80 | 1.39 | 1.28 | -0.35 | -1.21 | 3.38 | 3.11 | 3.25 | 3.25 |
| Construction Credits | NA | NA | NA | NA | NA | 13.0 | 11.5 | 7.28 | 6.91 | 5.02 |
| Effective Tax Rate | 37.6% | 35.0% | 46.1% | NM | NM | NM | 35.2% | 37.1% | 36.6% | 39.0% |
| Net Income | 412 | 320 | 75.1 | 130 | -334 | -502 | 449 | 314 | 285 | 263 |
| S&P Core Earnings | 377 | 321 | 72.0 | 61.8 | -329 | -530 | 391 | NA | NA | NA |

| Balance Sheet & Other Financial Data (Million $) | 2007 | 2006 | 2005 | 2004 | 2003 | 2002 | 2001 | 2000 | 1999 | 1998 |
|---|---|---|---|---|---|---|---|---|---|---|
| Gross Property | 11,993 | 11,150 | 10,786 | 10,644 | 11,831 | 11,357 | 11,087 | 9,507 | 8,840 | 8,630 |
| Capital Expenditures | 848 | 447 | 306 | 266 | 254 | 403 | 463 | 402 | 467 | 234 |
| Net Property | 7,197 | 6,513 | 6,277 | 6,303 | 7,453 | 6,883 | 6,853 | 5,539 | 5,207 | 5,234 |
| Capitalization:Long Term Debt | 3,983 | 3,434 | 3,665 | 4,639 | 5,234 | 229 | 3,274 | 2,634 | 2,328 | 2,349 |
| Capitalization:% Long Term Debt | 61.1 | 62.3 | 58.8 | 77.4 | 77.5 | 10.6 | 54.7 | 60.2 | 57.9 | 53.6 |
| Capitalization:Preferred | Nil | Nil | Nil | Nil | Nil | Nil | Nil | Nil | Nil | Nil |
| Capitalization:% Preferred | Nil | Nil | Nil | Nil | Nil | Nil | Nil | Nil | Nil | Nil |
| Capitalization:Common | 2,535 | 2,080 | 1,695 | 1,354 | 1,516 | 1,932 | 2,710 | 1,741 | 1,695 | 2,034 |
| Capitalization:% Common | 38.9 | 37.7 | 98.6 | 22.6 | 22.5 | 89.4 | 45.3 | 39.8 | 42.1 | 46.4 |
| Total Capital | 7,877 | 6,462 | 6,228 | 6,733 | 7,713 | 3,358 | 7,090 | 5,372 | 5,062 | 5,351 |
| % Operating Ratio | 82.9 | 82.3 | 83.5 | 82.1 | 99.3 | 101.9 | 93.1 | 86.6 | 83.1 | 82.9 |
| % Earned on Net Property | 11.9 | 11.5 | 8.5 | 11.5 | NM | NM | 11.5 | 10.0 | 9.3 | 8.3 |
| % Return on Revenue | 12.5 | 10.2 | 2.5 | 4.7 | NM | NM | 4.3 | 7.8 | 10.2 | 10.2 |
| % Return on Invested Capital | 11.0 | 9.3 | 23.3 | 7.4 | 2.6 | 4.2 | 11.9 | 10.5 | 9.2 | 11.9 |
| % Return on Common Equity | 17.9 | 16.9 | 4.9 | 9.0 | NM | NM | 20.2 | 18.3 | 15.3 | 12.3 |

Data as orig reptd.; bef. results of disc opers/spec. items. Per share data adj. for stk. divs.; EPS diluted. E-Estimated. NA-Not Available. NM-Not Meaningful. NR-Not Ranked. UR-Under Review.

**Office:** 800 Cabin Hill Dr, Greensburg, PA 15601-1650.
**Telephone:** 724-837-3000.
**Email:** investorinfo@alleghenypower.com
**Website:** http://www.alleghenyenergy.com

**Chrmn, Pres & CEO:** P.J. Evanson
**SVP & CFO:** K.R. Oliver
**Chief Admin Officer:** P.E. Slobodian
**Chief Acctg Officer & Cntlr:** W.F. Wahl, III

**Treas:** B.E. Pakenham
**Investor Contact:** M. Kuniansky (724-838-6895)
**Board Members:** H. F. Baldwin, E. Baum, P. J. Evanson, C. F. Freidheim, Jr., J. L. Johnson, T. J. Kleisner, C. D. Pappas, S. H. Rice, G. E. Sarsten, M. H. Sutton

**Founded:** 1925
**Domicile:** Maryland
**Employees:** 4,355

**STANDARD &POOR'S**

# Allegheny Technologies Inc

| S&P Recommendation | STRONG BUY ★★★★★ | Price $21.20 (as of Nov 14, 2008) | 12-Mo. Target Price $34.00 | Investment Style Large-Cap Blend |
|---|---|---|---|---|

**GICS Sector** Materials
**Sub-Industry** Steel

**Summary** This company is a leading producer of specialty metals for a wide variety of end markets.

## Key Stock Statistics (Source S&P, Vickers, company reports)

| | | | | | | | |
|---|---|---|---|---|---|---|---|
| 52-Wk Range | $98.49–18.42 | S&P Oper. EPS 2008**E** | 5.47 | Market Capitalization(B) | $2.041 | Beta | 3.33 |
| Trailing 12-Month EPS | $5.96 | S&P Oper. EPS 2009**E** | 4.54 | Yield (%) | 3.40 | S&P 3-Yr. Proj. EPS CAGR(%) | -10 |
| Trailing 12-Month P/E | 3.6 | P/E on S&P Oper. EPS 2008**E** | 3.9 | Dividend Rate/Share | $0.72 | S&P Credit Rating | BBB- |
| $10K Invested 5 Yrs Ago | $28,037 | Common Shares Outstg. (M) | 96.3 | Institutional Ownership (%) | 79 | | |

## Price Performance

30-Week Mov. Avg. · · · · 10-Week Mov. Avg. ─ ─ **GAAP Earnings vs. Previous Year** Volume Above Avg. ▍▏▎ STARS
12-Mo. Target Price ─── Relative Strength ── ▲ Up ▼ Down ▶ No Change Below Avg. ▍▏▎ ★↗

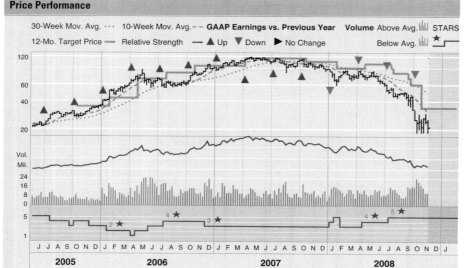

Options: ASE, CBOE, P, Ph

Analysis prepared by **Leo J. Larkin** on November 11, 2008, when the stock traded at **$23.85**.

## Highlights

➤ We project an 11% sales decline in 2009 following an estimated decrease of 3% in 2008. Our expectation for a more severe sales drop in 2009 is based on several assumptions. First, S&P estimates negative GDP of 0.1%, versus projected GDP growth of 1.6% this year. In our view, this will cut demand for durable goods and lead to reduced shipments and prices for stainless steel. Second, we think that distributors will cut their stainless inventories through at least the first half of 2009. Third, the recent strike at Boeing and the delay of the Boeing 787 will likely depress sales in the high performance metals.

➤ We look for another decline in operating profit in 2009, penalized mostly by margin contraction in stainless flat-rolled products and high performance metals. After flat interest expense and an unchanged tax rate, we project operating EPS of $4.54 in 2009, versus estimated EPS of $5.47 in 2008.

➤ We think that consolidation in the stainless steel industry and continuation of the current upturn in aerospace and other capital goods markets will bolster the long-term prospects for ATI's sales and earnings.

## Investment Rationale/Risk

➤ We view ATI as a vehicle for capitalizing on consolidation in the stainless steel industry and the ongoing upturn in the aerospace industry. While we look for another drop in sales and EPS in 2009, we think the long-term sales and earnings trend for the company is positive. We believe the concentration of stainless steel production in fewer hands will lead to better industry pricing discipline. We also expect ATI's results to be aided by increased demand for titanium from the aerospace industry. According to the Airline Monitor, an industry trade association, delivery of commercial aircraft will rise steadily through 2010. We believe that ATI, recently selling at a P/E of about 5.3X our 2009 estimate, is very attractively valued. On that basis, our recommendation is strong buy.

➤ Risks to our recommendation and target price include the possibility of further delays in airplane deliveries in 2009.

➤ We apply a P/E of 7.5X our 2009 EPS estimate, at the low end of ATI's P/E range for the past 10 years and a discount to the P/E we apply to its main peers. On that basis, our 12-month target price for these volatile shares is $34.

## Qualitative Risk Assessment

| LOW | MEDIUM | HIGH |
|---|---|---|

Our risk assessment reflects the exposure of ATI's sales and earnings to cyclical markets and our view of its comparatively high debt levels. Offsetting these factors are the company's improving free cash flow and its solid share of the markets it serves.

## Quantitative Evaluations

**S&P Quality Ranking**      B

| D | C | B- | B | B+ | A- | A | A+ |
|---|---|---|---|---|---|---|---|

**Relative Strength Rank**      WEAK

29

LOWEST = 1        HIGHEST = 99

## Revenue/Earnings Data

**Revenue (Million $)**

| | 1Q | 2Q | 3Q | 4Q | Year |
|---|---|---|---|---|---|
| 2008 | 1,343 | 1,461 | 1,392 | -- | -- |
| 2007 | 1,373 | 1,471 | 1,335 | 1,274 | 5,453 |
| 2006 | 1,041 | 1,211 | 1,288 | 1,397 | 4,937 |
| 2005 | 879.6 | 904.2 | 861.7 | 894.4 | 3,540 |
| 2004 | 577.8 | 646.5 | 730.6 | 778.1 | 2,733 |
| 2003 | 480.5 | 489.9 | 482.6 | 484.4 | 1,937 |

**Earnings Per Share ($)**

| | | | | | |
|---|---|---|---|---|---|
| 2008 | 1.40 | 1.66 | 1.45 | E0.96 | E5.47 |
| 2007 | 1.92 | 2.00 | 1.88 | 1.45 | 7.26 |
| 2006 | 1.00 | 1.37 | 1.58 | 1.63 | 5.59 |
| 2005 | 0.61 | 0.91 | 0.87 | 1.19 | 3.59 |
| 2004 | -0.63 | 0.31 | 0.09 | 0.35 | 0.22 |
| 2003 | -0.32 | -0.32 | -0.36 | -2.89 | -3.87 |

Fiscal year ended Dec. 31. Next earnings report expected: Late January. EPS Estimates based on S&P Operating Earnings; historical GAAP earnings are as reported.

## Dividend Data (Dates: mm/dd Payment Date: mm/dd/yy)

| Amount ($) | Date Decl. | Ex-Div. Date | Stk. of Record | Payment Date |
|---|---|---|---|---|
| 0.180 | 11/01 | 12/06 | 12/10 | 12/28/07 |
| 0.180 | 02/22 | 03/12 | 03/14 | 03/28/08 |
| 0.180 | 05/09 | 05/27 | 05/29 | 06/16/08 |
| 0.180 | 08/01 | 08/20 | 08/22 | 09/09/08 |

Dividends have been paid since 1996. Source: Company reports.

The **McGraw·Hill** Companies

# Allegheny Technologies Inc

STANDARD &POOR'S

## Business Summary November 11, 2008

In November 1999, Allegheny Technologies spun off all of the common stock of Teledyne Technologies Inc. (NYSE: TDY) and Water Pik Technologies, Inc. to ATI stockholders, and changed its name from Allegheny Teledyne Inc.

Following the spin-offs, ATI operates in three segments: Flat-Rolled Products, High Performance Metals, and Engineered Products. Markets for the three units include aerospace, oil and gas, transportation, food, chemical processing, consumer products, medical, and power generation.

The Flat-Rolled Products segment (54% of 2007 sales; 40% of operating profits) consists of Allegheny Ludlum Corp., Rodney Metals, the Allegheny Rodney Strip division of Allegheny Ludlum, and the company's interest in a Chinese joint venture, Shanghai STAL Precision Stainless Steel Ltd. The companies in this segment produce, convert and distribute stainless steel sheet, strip and plate, precision rolled strip products, flat-rolled nickel-based alloys and titanium, silicon electrical steels and tool steels. Shipments totaled 524,454 tons in 2007, versus 695,815 tons in 2006. The average realized price per ton was $5,628 in 2007, versus $3,876 in 2006. Operating profits totaled $505.2 million in 2007, versus $344.3 million in 2006.

Competitors in flat-rolled stainless include AK Steel Holding and North American Stainless.

The High Performance Metals segment (38%; 58%) consists of Allvac, Allvac Ltd., Oremet-Wah Chang, Titanium Industries, and Rome Metals. These companies produce, convert and distribute nickel- and cobalt-based alloys and superalloys, titanium and titanium-based alloys, zirconium and zirconium chemicals, hafnium and niobium, tantalum and other special metals, primarily in long-product form. The unit's titanium products are sold mostly to aircraft and jet engine manufacturers. Shipments of titanium mill products totaled 30,689 lbs. in 2007, versus 27,361 lbs. in 2006; shipments of nickel-based alloys were 44,688 lbs. in 2007, versus 42,873 lbs. in 2006; shipments of exotic alloys totaled 5,169 lbs. in 2007, versus 4,304 lbs. in 2006. Operating profits totaled $729.1 million in 2007, versus $657.5 million in 2006.

Competitors in high performance and exotic metals include Titanium Metals Corp., RTI International Metals, Verkhnaya Salda Metallurgical Production Organization and UNITI and certain Japanese producers in the industrial and emerging markets. According to the Airline Monitor, an industry trade association, delivery of commercial aircraft will rise steadily through 2010.

## Company Financials  Fiscal Year Ended Dec. 31

| Per Share Data ($) | 2007 | 2006 | 2005 | 2004 | 2003 | 2002 | 2001 | 2000 | 1999 | 1998 |
|---|---|---|---|---|---|---|---|---|---|---|
| Tangible Book Value | 19.82 | 12.71 | 6.11 | 2.30 | NM | 3.15 | 9.42 | 10.51 | 11.02 | 11.12 |
| Cash Flow | 8.26 | 6.48 | 4.47 | 1.00 | -2.96 | 0.30 | 0.91 | 2.80 | 2.15 | 3.53 |
| Earnings | 7.26 | 5.59 | 3.59 | 0.22 | -3.87 | -0.82 | -0.31 | 1.60 | 1.16 | 2.44 |
| S&P Core Earnings | 7.12 | 5.92 | 3.76 | 0.26 | -3.19 | -2.17 | -2.09 | NA | NA | NA |
| Dividends | 0.57 | 0.43 | 0.28 | 0.24 | 0.24 | 0.66 | 0.80 | 0.80 | 1.28 | 1.28 |
| Payout Ratio | 8% | 8% | 8% | 109% | NM | NM | NM | 50% | 110% | 52% |
| Prices:High | 119.70 | 98.72 | 36.66 | 23.48 | 14.00 | 19.10 | 21.07 | 26.81 | 48.37 | 59.12 |
| Prices:Low | 80.00 | 35.47 | 17.30 | 8.64 | 2.10 | 5.21 | 12.50 | 12.50 | 20.25 | 28.00 |
| P/E Ratio:High | 16 | 18 | 10 | NM | NM | NM | NM | 17 | 42 | 24 |
| P/E Ratio:Low | 11 | 6 | 5 | NM | NM | NM | NM | 8 | 17 | 11 |

| Income Statement Analysis (Million $) | | | | | | | | | | |
|---|---|---|---|---|---|---|---|---|---|---|
| Revenue | 5,453 | 4,937 | 3,540 | 2,733 | 1,937 | 1,908 | 2,128 | 2,460 | 2,296 | 3,923 |
| Operating Income | 1,256 | 970 | 452 | 87.7 | -110 | 65.0 | 166 | 358 | 284 | 579 |
| Depreciation | 103 | 84.2 | 77.3 | 76.1 | 74.6 | 90.0 | 98.6 | 99.7 | 95.3 | 109 |
| Interest Expense | 4.80 | 23.3 | 38.6 | 35.5 | 27.7 | 34.3 | 29.3 | 34.4 | 25.9 | 19.3 |
| Pretax Income | 1,147 | 869 | 307 | 19.8 | -280 | -104 | -36.4 | 209 | 174 | 391 |
| Effective Tax Rate | 34.9% | 34.2% | NM | NM | NM | NM | NM | 36.5% | 36.3% | 38.3% |
| Net Income | 747 | 572 | 362 | 19.8 | -313 | -65.8 | -25.2 | 133 | 111 | 241 |
| S&P Core Earnings | 733 | 605 | 378 | 23.3 | -258 | -176 | -168 | NA | NA | NA |

| Balance Sheet & Other Financial Data (Million $) | | | | | | | | | | |
|---|---|---|---|---|---|---|---|---|---|---|
| Cash | 623 | 502 | 363 | 251 | 79.6 | 59.4 | 33.7 | 26.2 | 50.7 | 74.8 |
| Current Assets | 2,249 | 1,988 | 1,484 | 1,160 | 743 | 812 | 926 | 1,023 | 1,034 | 1,365 |
| Total Assets | 4,096 | 3,282 | 2,732 | 2,316 | 1,885 | 2,093 | 2,643 | 2,776 | 2,751 | 3,176 |
| Current Liabilities | 704 | 646 | 561 | 493 | 395 | 342 | 333 | 414 | 540 | 622 |
| Long Term Debt | 507 | 530 | 547 | 553 | 504 | 509 | 573 | 491 | 200 | 447 |
| Common Equity | 2,224 | 1,493 | 800 | 426 | 175 | 449 | 945 | 1,039 | 1,200 | 1,340 |
| Total Capital | 2,731 | 2,023 | 1,347 | 979 | 679 | 958 | 1,671 | 1,689 | 1,401 | 1,787 |
| Capital Expenditures | 447 | 235 | 90.1 | 49.9 | 74.4 | 48.7 | 104 | 60.2 | 74.1 | 173 |
| Cash Flow | 850 | 656 | 439 | 95.9 | -239 | 24.2 | 73.4 | 232 | 206 | 350 |
| Current Ratio | 3.2 | 3.1 | 2.6 | 2.4 | 1.9 | 2.4 | 2.8 | 2.5 | 1.9 | 2.2 |
| % Long Term Debt of Capitalization | 18.6 | 26.2 | 40.6 | 56.5 | 74.3 | 53.2 | 34.3 | 29.1 | 14.3 | 25.0 |
| % Net Income of Revenue | 13.7 | 11.6 | 10.2 | 0.7 | NM | NM | NM | 5.4 | 4.8 | 6.1 |
| % Return on Assets | 20.3 | 19.0 | 14.3 | 0.9 | NM | NM | NM | 4.8 | 3.9 | 8.3 |
| % Return on Equity | 40.2 | 49.9 | 59.0 | 6.6 | NM | NM | NM | 11.8 | 8.7 | 20.6 |

Data as orig reptd.; bef. results of disc opers/spec. items. Per share data adj. for stk. divs.; EPS diluted. E-Estimated. NA-Not Available. NM-Not Meaningful. NR-Not Ranked. UR-Under Review.

**Office:** 1000 Six PPG Pl, Pittsburgh, PA 15222-5479.
**Telephone:** 412-394-2800.
**Website:** http://www.alleghenytechnologies.com
**Chrmn, Pres & CEO:** L.P. Hassey

**EVP & CFO:** R.J. Harshman
**EVP, Secy & General Counsel:** J.D. Walton
**Chief Acctg Officer, Treas & Cntlr:** D.G. Reid
**Investor Contact:** D.L. Greenfield (412-394-3004)

**Board Members:** D. C. Creel, J. C. Diggs, J. B. Harvey, L.
P. Hassey, B. S. Jeremiah, M. J. Joyce, J. E. Rohr, L. J.
Thomas, J. D. Turner

**Founded:** 1960
**Domicile:** Delaware
**Employees:** 9,700

# Allergan Inc.

**STANDARD &POOR'S**

| S&P Recommendation | HOLD ★★★☆☆ | Price $35.66 (as of Nov 14, 2008) | 12-Mo. Target Price $43.00 | Investment Style Large-Cap Growth |

**GICS Sector** Health Care
**Sub-Industry** Pharmaceuticals

**Summary** This technology-driven global health care company develops and commercializes products in the eye care, neuromodulator, skin care and other specialty markets.

## Key Stock Statistics (Source S&P, Vickers, company reports)

| | | | | | | | |
|---|---|---|---|---|---|---|---|
| 52-Wk Range | $70.40– 31.01 | S&P Oper. EPS 2008E | 2.57 | Market Capitalization(B) | $10.837 | Beta | 1.25 |
| Trailing 12-Month EPS | $1.91 | S&P Oper. EPS 2009E | 2.75 | Yield (%) | 0.56 | S&P 3-Yr. Proj. EPS CAGR(%) | 12 |
| Trailing 12-Month P/E | 18.7 | P/E on S&P Oper. EPS 2008E | 13.9 | Dividend Rate/Share | $0.20 | S&P Credit Rating | A |
| $10K Invested 5 Yrs Ago | $9,413 | Common Shares Outstg. (M) | 303.9 | Institutional Ownership (%) | 92 | | |

## Price Performance

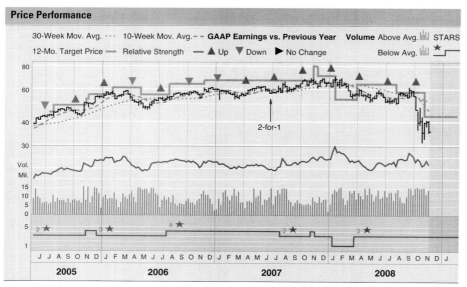

30-Week Mov. Avg. · · ·   10-Week Mov. Avg. – –   **GAAP Earnings vs. Previous Year**   Volume Above Avg. STARS
12-Mo. Target Price —   Relative Strength — ▲ Up ▼ Down ► No Change   Below Avg.

2-for-1

Options: ASE, CBOE, Ph

Analysis prepared by **Phillip M. Seligman** on November 04, 2008, when the stock traded at **$ 40.43**.

## Highlights

➤ We project that net product sales will rise at best about 1% in 2009 to $4.35 billion, from the $4.30 billion we see in 2008. The deceleration from 2008's 11% sales growth we see mainly reflects our expectation of lower aesthetics product sales amid U.S. economic softness, our forecast of slowing aesthetics market growth in Europe, and the stronger dollar. These products include Botox for cosmetic use, breast implants, obesity intervention devices, and dermal fillers, which we estimate normally account for 20% to 25% of revenue. Outweighing the decline, but not by much as we see U.S. pharmaceutical volumes slowing, are sales growth from new eyecare drugs and global penetration of existing drugs and Botox for therapeutic use.

➤ We expect gross margins to be flat in 2009, with the benefit from new products and improved manufacturing efficiencies offset by lower aesthetic sales. We look for the SG&A cost ratio to decline on revenue leverage, while R&D cost ratio expands on increased investment.

➤ Our outlook for operating EPS is $2.57 for 2008 and $2.75 for 2009, excluding goodwill amortization, versus 2007's $2.18.

## Investment Rationale/Risk

➤ We expect AGN's domestic aesthetics product sales to remain soft until the U.S. economy recovers, which we do not see in the near term. In addition, AGN has noticed a dropoff in breast implant sales in Europe, and we expect that financial and economic troubles that have spread to Europe will eventually hurt sales of AGN's other high-priced, discretionary aesthetic products. On a positive note, we are encouraged by AGN's focus on R&D and the many new products, product-line extensions, and new indications for existing products in the pipeline. Promising products include a pending eyelash-growth indication for bimatoprost (used in glaucoma drug Lumigan), an increasing number of Botox indications, and an experimental, improved version of Botox.

➤ Risks to our recommendation and target price include reduced discretionary consumer spending, a decline in elective medical procedures, and intensified competition.

➤ Our 12-month target price of $43 is derived by applying a 1.4X target P/E-to-growth (PEG) ratio, assuming three-year growth of almost 12%, to our 2008 EPS estimate. The PEG ratio assumes peerwide valuation contraction.

## Qualitative Risk Assessment

| LOW | MEDIUM | HIGH |

Our risk assessment reflects AGN's increased diversification of aesthetic products and markets via the acquisition of Inamed, our view of its strong focus on R&D, its leading market position in several ophthalmic drugs, and continued strong demand for Botox. However, we view the eye care and aesthetics markets as competitive, with the latter affected by the economic environment. We are also concerned that certain pipeline products may not be successful.

## Quantitative Evaluations

**S&P Quality Ranking**                    B

| D | C | B- | **B** | B+ | A- | A | A+ |

**Relative Strength Rank**         MODERATE

50

LOWEST = 1                            HIGHEST = 99

## Revenue/Earnings Data

**Revenue (Million $)**

| | 1Q | 2Q | 3Q | 4Q | Year |
|---|---|---|---|---|---|
| 2008 | 1,077 | 1,172 | 1,098 | -- | -- |
| 2007 | 886.5 | 988.1 | 993.7 | 1,091 | 3,939 |
| 2006 | 625.7 | 801.7 | 806.8 | 829.1 | 3,063 |
| 2005 | 527.2 | 591.0 | 606.1 | 594.9 | 2,319 |
| 2004 | 472.4 | 506.2 | 510.8 | 556.2 | 2,046 |
| 2003 | 391.2 | 447.7 | 443.3 | 479.4 | 1,771 |

**Earnings Per Share ($)**

| | | | | | |
|---|---|---|---|---|---|
| 2008 | 0.36 | 0.48 | 0.55 | E0.72 | E2.57 |
| 2007 | 0.14 | 0.45 | 0.50 | 0.52 | 1.62 |
| 2006 | -1.65 | 0.25 | 0.35 | 0.45 | -0.43 |
| 2005 | 0.30 | 0.13 | 0.56 | 0.52 | 1.50 |
| 2004 | 0.31 | 0.35 | 0.35 | 0.43 | 1.41 |
| 2003 | 0.26 | -0.42 | 0.29 | -0.35 | -0.20 |

Fiscal year ended Dec. 31. Next earnings report expected: Late January. EPS Estimates based on S&P Operating Earnings; historical GAAP earnings are as reported.

## Dividend Data (Dates: mm/dd Payment Date: mm/dd/yy)

| Amount ($) | Date Decl. | Ex-Div. Date | Stk. of Record | Payment Date |
|---|---|---|---|---|
| 0.050 | 01/30 | 02/13 | 02/15 | 03/07/08 |
| 0.050 | 05/07 | 05/21 | 05/23 | 06/13/08 |
| 0.050 | 07/30 | 08/13 | 08/15 | 09/05/08 |
| 0.050 | 10/29 | 11/06 | 11/10 | 12/01/08 |

Dividends have been paid since 1989. Source: Company reports.

# Allergan Inc.

**STANDARD &POOR'S**

## Business Summary November 04, 2008

CORPORATE OVERVIEW. Allergan is a leading producer of ophthalmic, neuro-muscular and skin care pharmaceuticals, and, with its March 2006 acquisition of Inamed Corp., aesthetic products. Eye care drugs accounted for 46% of 2007 sales from continuing operations, Botox/neuromodulator 31%, skin care treatments 3%, urologics 0.2%, breast implants 8%, devices for obesity treatment 7%, and dermal fillers 5%. About 34% of 2007 sales were derived from foreign markets.

Eye care drugs include prescription and nonprescription products to treat eye diseases and disorders, including glaucoma, inflammation, infection, allergy, and dry eye. Important products are Alphagan, Alphagan P, and Combigan (sales of $341 million in 2007, versus $296 million in 2006), Lumigan ($392 million versus $228 million) treatments, which are used to lower eye pressure in patients with open-angle glaucoma or ocular hypertension, and Restasis ($345 million, versus $270 million), for dry eye disease. Other eye care products include Acular, Alocril, and Elestat, for seasonal allergic conjunctivitis; and Zymar and Ocuflox, for bacterial conjunctivitis.

Originally used for ophthalmic movement disorders, AGN believes that Botox (botulinum toxin type A) is the widely accepted treatment for neuromuscular disorders and related pain. More recently, Botox garnered a rapidly growing market as a facial cosmetic agent. In April 2002, the FDA approved the injectable drug for removing brow furrows and other facial wrinkles. About 52% of Botox sales in 2006 (57% in 2005) were for therapeutic indications, with cosmetic uses comprising the balance. Botox is being studied for treating excessive sweating, post-stroke spasticity, back spasms, and migraines.

Skin care products include Zorac/Tazorac receptor-selective retinoids for acne and psoriasis; Prevage for fine lines and wrinkles; and Avage for facial fine wrinkling and blotchy skin discoloration.

Aesthetic products include breast implants for aesthetic augmentation and reconstructive surgery following a mastectomy, a range of dermal products to correct facial wrinkles, and the LAP-BAND and Intragastric Balloon (BIB) systems for obesity treatment.

## Company Financials Fiscal Year Ended Dec. 31

| Per Share Data ($) | 2007 | 2006 | 2005 | 2004 | 2003 | 2002 | 2001 | 2000 | 1999 | 1998 |
|---|---|---|---|---|---|---|---|---|---|---|
| Tangible Book Value | 0.72 | 0.88 | 5.34 | 3.99 | 2.47 | 3.02 | 3.24 | 2.82 | 1.87 | 1.99 |
| Cash Flow | 2.32 | 0.08 | 1.82 | 1.69 | 0.03 | 0.42 | 1.19 | 1.09 | 0.97 | -0.05 |
| Earnings | 1.62 | -0.44 | 1.51 | 1.41 | -0.20 | 0.25 | 0.85 | 0.81 | 0.70 | -0.35 |
| S&P Core Earnings | 1.64 | -0.42 | 1.36 | 1.26 | -0.33 | 0.45 | 0.70 | NA | NA | NA |
| Dividends | 0.20 | 0.20 | 0.20 | 0.18 | 0.18 | 0.18 | 0.18 | 0.16 | 0.14 | 0.13 |
| Payout Ratio | 12% | NM | 13% | 13% | NM | 73% | 21% | 20% | 20% | NM |
| Prices:High | 69.15 | 61.51 | 55.25 | 46.31 | 40.90 | 37.55 | 49.69 | 50.56 | 28.91 | 16.63 |
| Prices:Low | 52.50 | 46.29 | 34.51 | 33.39 | 35.83 | 24.53 | 29.50 | 22.25 | 15.84 | 7.94 |
| P/E Ratio:High | 43 | NM | 37 | 33 | NM | NM | 59 | 63 | 42 | NM |
| P/E Ratio:Low | 32 | NM | 23 | 24 | NM | NM | 35 | 28 | 23 | NM |

| Income Statement Analysis (Million $) | 2007 | 2006 | 2005 | 2004 | 2003 | 2002 | 2001 | 2000 | 1999 | 1998 |
|---|---|---|---|---|---|---|---|---|---|---|
| Revenue | 3,939 | 3,063 | 2,319 | 2,046 | 1,771 | 1,425 | 1,746 | 1,626 | 1,452 | 1,296 |
| Operating Income | 1,060 | 854 | 694 | 603 | 39.1 | 349 | 404 | 372 | 326 | 294 |
| Depreciation | 215 | 152 | 78.9 | 68.3 | 59.6 | 45.0 | 85.5 | 77.7 | 73.8 | 76.5 |
| Interest Expense | 72.7 | 60.2 | 12.4 | 18.1 | 15.6 | 17.4 | 21.4 | 19.8 | 15.1 | 16.4 |
| Pretax Income | 688 | -19.5 | 599 | 532 | -29.5 | 89.8 | 336 | 304 | 269 | -57.7 |
| Effective Tax Rate | 27.1% | NM | 32.1% | 28.9% | NM | 28.0% | 32.4% | 29.0% | 30.0% | NM |
| Net Income | 501 | -127 | 404 | 377 | -52.5 | 64.0 | 227 | 215 | 188 | -90.2 |
| S&P Core Earnings | 507 | -123 | 363 | 339 | -87.3 | 118 | 187 | NA | NA | NA |

| Balance Sheet & Other Financial Data (Million $) | 2007 | 2006 | 2005 | 2004 | 2003 | 2002 | 2001 | 2000 | 1999 | 1998 |
|---|---|---|---|---|---|---|---|---|---|---|
| Cash | 1,158 | 1,369 | 1,296 | 895 | 508 | 774 | 782 | 774 | 163 | 182 |
| Current Assets | 2,124 | 2,130 | 1,826 | 1,376 | 928 | 1,200 | 1,325 | 1,326 | 698 | 661 |
| Total Assets | 6,579 | 5,767 | 2,851 | 2,257 | 1,755 | 1,807 | 2,046 | 1,971 | 1,339 | 1,334 |
| Current Liabilities | 716 | 658 | 1,044 | 460 | 383 | 404 | 490 | 433 | 420 | 369 |
| Long Term Debt | 1,630 | 1,606 | 57.5 | 570 | 573 | 526 | 521 | 585 | 209 | 201 |
| Common Equity | 3,739 | 3,143 | 1,567 | 1,116 | 719 | 808 | 977 | 874 | 634 | 696 |
| Total Capital | 5,551 | 4,836 | 1,626 | 1,689 | 1,294 | 1,337 | 1,499 | 1,459 | 843 | 897 |
| Capital Expenditures | 142 | 131 | 78.5 | 96.4 | 110 | 78.8 | 89.9 | 66.9 | 63.3 | 50.6 |
| Cash Flow | 716 | 25.0 | 483 | 445 | 7.10 | 109 | 312 | 293 | 262 | -13.7 |
| Current Ratio | 3.0 | 3.2 | 1.7 | 3.0 | 2.4 | 3.0 | 2.7 | 3.1 | 1.7 | 1.8 |
| % Long Term Debt of Capitalization | 29.8 | 33.2 | 3.5 | 33.8 | 44.3 | 39.4 | 34.7 | 40.1 | 24.8 | 22.4 |
| % Net Income of Revenue | 12.7 | NM | 17.4 | 18.4 | NM | 4.5 | 13.0 | 13.2 | 13.0 | NM |
| % Return on Assets | 8.1 | NM | 15.8 | 18.8 | NM | 3.3 | 11.3 | 13.0 | 14.1 | NM |
| % Return on Equity | 14.6 | NM | 30.1 | 41.1 | NM | 7.2 | 24.5 | 28.5 | 28.3 | NM |

Data as orig reptd.; bef. results of disc opers/spec. items. Per share data adj. for stk. divs.; EPS diluted. E-Estimated. NA-Not Available. NM-Not Meaningful. NR-Not Ranked. UR-Under Review.

**Office:** 2525 Dupont Drive, Irvine, CA 92612.
**Telephone:** 714-246-4500.
**Email:** corpinfo@allergan.com
**Website:** http://www.alergan.com

**Chrmn & CEO:** D.E. Pyott
**Pres:** M. Ball
**Vice Chrmn:** H.W. Boyer
**EVP, Chief Admin Officer, Secy & General Counsel:** D.S. Ingram

**SVP, Chief Acctg Officer & Cntlr:** J.F. Barlow
**Investor Contact:** J. Hindman (714-246-4636)
**Board Members:** H. W. Boyer, D. Dunsire, M. R. Gallagher, G. S. Herbert, D. Hudson, R. A. Ingram, T. M. Jones, L. J. Lavigne, Jr., D. E. Pyott, R. T. Ray, S. J. Ryan, L. D. Schaeffer

**Founded:** 1948
**Domicile:** Delaware
**Employees:** 7,886

# Allied Waste Industries Inc.

STANDARD
&POOR'S

| S&P Recommendation HOLD ★★★☆☆ | Price $10.93 (as of Nov 14, 2008) | 12-Mo. Target Price $11.00 | Investment Style Large-Cap Value |
| --- | --- | --- | --- |

**GICS Sector** Industrials
**Sub-Industry** Environmental & Facilities Services

**Summary** This U.S. provider of collection, recycling and disposal services agreed in June 2008 to be acquired by Republic Services. Closing is expected in December 2008.

## Key Stock Statistics (Source S&P, Vickers, company reports)

| | | | | | | | |
| --- | --- | --- | --- | --- | --- | --- | --- |
| 52-Wk Range | $15.46– 7.77 | S&P Oper. EPS 2008**E** | 0.95 | Market Capitalization(B) | $4.751 | Beta | 1.65 |
| Trailing 12-Month EPS | $0.91 | S&P Oper. EPS 2009**E** | 1.10 | Yield (%) | Nil | S&P 3-Yr. Proj. EPS CAGR(%) | 12 |
| Trailing 12-Month P/E | 12.0 | P/E on S&P Oper. EPS 2008**E** | 11.5 | Dividend Rate/Share | Nil | S&P Credit Rating | BB |
| $10K Invested 5 Yrs Ago | $9,936 | Common Shares Outstg. (M) | 434.7 | Institutional Ownership (%) | 97 | | |

## Price Performance

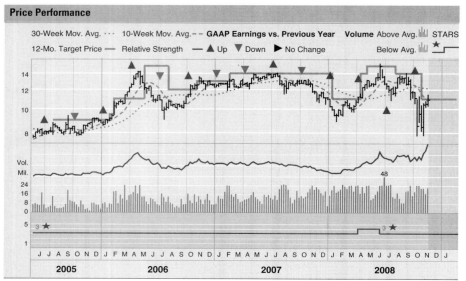

- 30-Week Mov. Avg. · · ·
- 10-Week Mov. Avg. - -
- **GAAP Earnings vs. Previous Year**
- Volume Above Avg. | Below Avg. |
- STARS
- 12-Mo. Target Price —
- Relative Strength —
- ▲ Up ▼ Down ► No Change

Options: ASE, CBOE, P, Ph

Analysis prepared by **Stewart Scharf** on October 30, 2008, when the stock traded at **$ 10.19.**

## Highlights

➤ We see organic revenue growth of 2%-3% in 2008, as price hikes offset 4% lower volume based on a soft housing market and economy. We expect AW to continue to sacrifice market share in favor of higher prices. Similar trends are likely in 2009, although AW will no longer be a publicly traded company, assuming shareholders and the Justice Department approve the proposed Republic Services takeover.

➤ Gross margins (before D&A) in 2008 should expand by at least 50 basis points, from 37.6% in 2007, driven by pricing and a better mix as AW rolls out a new national account, while a fuel recovery fee offsets higher diesel costs, which have been trending lower recently. We believe EBITDA margins will widen to about 29% (before merger-related costs of 0.5%), from 27.2% in 2007, reflecting lower repair, maintenance, disposal and labor costs, and new employee safety programs. We see SG&A expenses staying under 10% of revenues, with additional supply chain and procurement initiatives.

➤ We project a higher tax rate of 42.5% in 2008, and estimate EPS of $0.95, increasing 16% in 2009, to $1.10, before the pending merger with Republic Services.

## Investment Rationale/Risk

➤ Our hold opinion is based on our valuation models and AW's recent pact to be acquired by Republic Services (RSG: buy, $24), subject to necessary approvals, for 0.45 of an RSG share for each AW share. We believe the proposed merger will create long-term shareholder value.

➤ Risks to our opinion and target price include an inability to implement sustainable price hikes; a sizable market share loss based on price hikes; increased leverage; a further significant rise in fuel costs; and an inability to complete the merger with Republic Services.

➤ Correlating our relative metrics, we apply a P/E of 11X to our 2008 estimate, below AW's closest peers, and derive a value of $10.50. Our DCF model suggests that the shares were recently at an 11% discount to their intrinsic value of $11.50, assuming a terminal growth rate of 3.5% and a weighted average cost of capital (WACC) of 8%. Blending these measures, our 12-month target price is $11.

## Qualitative Risk Assessment

| LOW | MEDIUM | HIGH |
| --- | --- | --- |

Our risk assessment reflects the cyclical nature of the business, volatile energy costs, landfill overcapacity, a relatively high leverage ratio, and concerns related to corporate governance practices. This is offset by what we view as AW's positive cash generation and improving working capital.

## Quantitative Evaluations

**S&P Quality Ranking** — B-

| D | C | B- | B | B+ | A- | A | A+ |
| --- | --- | --- | --- | --- | --- | --- | --- |

**Relative Strength Rank** — STRONG — 93

LOWEST = 1    HIGHEST = 99

## Revenue/Earnings Data

**Revenue (Million $)**

| | 1Q | 2Q | 3Q | 4Q | Year |
| --- | --- | --- | --- | --- | --- |
| 2008 | 1,484 | 1,582 | 1,606 | -- | -- |
| 2007 | 1,457 | 1,560 | 1,556 | 1,520 | 6,069 |
| 2006 | 1,439 | 1,541 | 1,555 | 1,494 | 6,029 |
| 2005 | 1,341 | 1,449 | 1,477 | 1,468 | 5,735 |
| 2004 | 1,275 | 1,362 | 1,378 | 1,347 | 5,362 |
| 2003 | 1,231 | 1,343 | 1,362 | 1,313 | 5,248 |

**Earnings Per Share ($)**

| | 1Q | 2Q | 3Q | 4Q | Year |
| --- | --- | --- | --- | --- | --- |
| 2008 | 0.17 | 0.25 | 0.26 | E0.20 | E0.95 |
| 2007 | 0.07 | 0.21 | 0.15 | 0.33 | 0.71 |
| 2006 | 0.08 | 0.08 | 0.17 | Nil | 0.33 |
| 2005 | 0.05 | 0.12 | 0.10 | 0.15 | 0.43 |
| 2004 | Nil | -0.05 | 0.13 | 0.04 | 0.11 |
| 2003 | 0.07 | Nil | 0.12 | -2.29 | -2.36 |

Fiscal year ended Dec. 31. Next earnings report expected: Mid February. EPS Estimates based on S&P Operating Earnings; historical GAAP earnings are as reported.

## Dividend Data

No cash dividends have been paid.

# Allied Waste Industries Inc.

**STANDARD &POOR'S**

## Business Summary October 30, 2008

CORPORATE OVERVIEW. Allied Waste Industries provides non-hazardous waste collection, transfer, recycling and disposal services to more than eight million residential, municipal and commercial customers in 124 markets in 37 states and Puerto Rico. As of December 31, 2007, it had 291 collection companies, 161 transfer stations, 53 recycling facilities, and 161 active landfills. In 2007, revenues were derived from collection (70%, including 28% residential, 36% commercial, 30% roll-off and 5% recycling); disposal (21%, including 14% from landfill and 7% from transfer); recycling-commodity (4.2%); and other (5%). Collection operations involve collecting and transporting nonhazardous waste from the point of generation to the transfer station or the site of disposal. A transfer station receives solid waste from third-party and company-owned collection vehicles and then compacts and transfers the waste to specially constructed trailers for transportation to disposal facilities. As of late 2008, the customer retention rate was above 90%, well above AW's historical rate, while the commercial churn rate (spread between the price of new work and the price of business lost) remained positive.

We believe the company will continue to make progress with its strategic turnaround plan, divesting non-core assets and completing asset swaps with its closest competitors Waste Management and Republic Services. We think this plan will support AW's goal of improving margins, allocating capital more effectively, and improving return on invested capital (ROIC). In the third quarter of 2007, AW sold certain landfill and collection assets ($54 million in revenues) in Indiana, Illinois, Kentucky and Georgia for $90 million to Veolia ES Solid Waste. In March 2007, AW sold its South Florida operations ($64 million in revenues) to Waste Services, and acquired Waste Services' Phoenix, AZ, operations ($20 million in revenues).

In the third quarter of 2008, AW incurred a pretax charge of $12.5 million ($0.02 a share, after taxes), and in the second quarter $9 million ($0.02 per share) for merger-related costs. In the first quarter, AW incurred net charges of $0.03 a share, mainly due to an impairment charge related to a landfill closure in the Midwest.

## Company Financials Fiscal Year Ended Dec. 31

| Per Share Data ($) | 2007 | 2006 | 2005 | 2004 | 2003 | 2002 | 2001 | 2000 | 1999 | 1998 |
|---|---|---|---|---|---|---|---|---|---|---|
| Tangible Book Value | NM | NM | NM | NM | NM | NM | NM | NM | NM | NM |
| Cash Flow | 1.86 | 1.91 | 2.11 | 1.86 | 2.76 | 3.33 | 3.57 | 3.89 | 0.13 | 0.45 |
| Earnings | 0.71 | 0.33 | 0.43 | 0.11 | -2.36 | 0.76 | 0.01 | 0.36 | -1.33 | -0.54 |
| S&P Core Earnings | 0.69 | 0.33 | 0.37 | 0.07 | -2.43 | 0.53 | 0.13 | NA | NA | NA |
| Dividends | Nil | Nil | Nil | Nil | Nil | Nil | Nil | Nil | Nil | Nil |
| Payout Ratio | Nil | Nil | Nil | Nil | Nil | Nil | Nil | Nil | Nil | Nil |
| Prices:High | 14.10 | 14.38 | 9.46 | 14.44 | 14.05 | 14.55 | 19.90 | 14.75 | 24.06 | 31.63 |
| Prices:Low | 10.43 | 8.50 | 6.90 | 7.50 | 7.51 | 5.54 | 8.90 | 5.31 | 6.50 | 16.13 |
| P/E Ratio:High | 20 | 44 | 22 | NM | NM | 19 | NM | 41 | NM | NM |
| P/E Ratio:Low | 15 | 26 | 16 | NM | NM | 7 | NM | 15 | NM | NM |

| Income Statement Analysis (Million $) | | | | | | | | | | |
|---|---|---|---|---|---|---|---|---|---|---|
| Revenue | 6,069 | 6,029 | 5,735 | 5,362 | 5,248 | 5,517 | 5,565 | 5,707 | 3,341 | 1,576 |
| Operating Income | 1,650 | 1,559 | 1,470 | 1,446 | 1,581 | 1,743 | 1,931 | 2,010 | 1,161 | 528 |
| Depreciation | 554 | 569 | 554 | 559 | 546 | 496 | 693 | 674 | 273 | 180 |
| Interest Expense | 507 | 568 | 588 | 588 | 707 | 774 | 854 | 882 | 443 | 88.4 |
| Pretax Income | 517 | 400 | 328 | 128 | 202 | 411 | 270 | 381 | -227 | -54.5 |
| Effective Tax Rate | 40.0% | 59.7% | 40.9% | 56.6% | 44.0% | 44.7% | 70.7% | 62.3% | NM | NM |
| Net Income | 310 | 161 | 194 | 58.0 | 111 | 225 | 75.5 | 138 | -221 | -98.3 |
| S&P Core Earnings | 267 | 116 | 120 | 26.9 | -494 | 105 | 28.2 | NA | NA | NA |

| Balance Sheet & Other Financial Data (Million $) | | | | | | | | | | |
|---|---|---|---|---|---|---|---|---|---|---|
| Cash | 257 | 94.1 | 56.1 | 68.0 | 445 | 180 | 159 | 122 | 121 | 39.7 |
| Current Assets | 1,158 | 1,048 | 920 | 923 | 1,286 | 1,072 | 1,198 | 1,272 | 2,248 | 500 |
| Total Assets | 13,949 | 13,811 | 13,626 | 13,440 | 13,861 | 13,929 | 14,347 | 14,514 | 14,963 | 3,753 |
| Current Liabilities | 2,247 | 1,533 | 1,576 | 1,757 | 1,568 | 1,450 | 1,434 | 1,600 | 2,629 | 455 |
| Long Term Debt | 6,086 | 6,674 | 6,853 | 7,429 | 7,985 | 8,719 | 9,238 | 9,635 | 9,240 | 2,119 |
| Common Equity | 3,323 | 3,018 | 2,526 | 2,272 | 2,185 | 689 | 586 | 698 | 638 | 930 |
| Total Capital | 10,392 | 10,630 | 10,598 | 10,242 | 10,631 | 11,165 | 11,411 | 11,761 | 11,085 | 3,049 |
| Capital Expenditures | 670 | 669 | 696 | 583 | 492 | 542 | 501 | 390 | 339 | 302 |
| Cash Flow | 826 | 687 | 696 | 596 | 562 | 644 | 695 | 743 | 24.3 | 81.7 |
| Current Ratio | 0.5 | 0.7 | 0.6 | 0.5 | 0.8 | 0.7 | 0.8 | 0.8 | 0.9 | 1.1 |
| % Long Term Debt of Capitalization | 58.6 | 62.8 | 64.7 | 72.5 | 75.1 | 78.1 | 81.0 | 81.9 | 83.4 | 69.5 |
| % Net Income of Revenue | 5.1 | 2.7 | 3.4 | 1.1 | 2.1 | 4.1 | 1.4 | 2.4 | NM | NM |
| % Return on Assets | 2.0 | 1.2 | 1.4 | 0.4 | 0.8 | 1.6 | 0.5 | 0.9 | NM | NM |
| % Return on Equity | 8.6 | 4.3 | 5.9 | 1.6 | 1.1 | 23.1 | 0.4 | 10.4 | NM | NM |

Data as orig reptd.; bef. results of disc opers/spec. items. Per share data adj. for stk. divs.; EPS diluted. E-Estimated. NA-Not Available. NM-Not Meaningful. NR-Not Ranked. UR-Under Review.

**Office:** 18500 N Allied Way, Phoenix, AZ 85054-6164.
**Telephone:** 480-627-2700.
**Email:** info@awin.com
**Website:** http://www.alliedwaste.com

**Chrmn & CEO:** J.J. Zillmer
**Pres & COO:** D.W. Slager
**Investor Contact:** P.S. Hathaway (480-627-2700)
**EVP & CFO:** P.S. Hathaway

**EVP, Secy & General Counsel:** T. Donovan
**Board Members:** D. P. Abney, R. M. Agate, C. H. Cotros, J. W. Crownover, W. J. Flynn, D. I. Foley, D. B. Kaplan, N. Lehmann, L. J. Level, J. A. Quella, J. M. Trani, J. J. Zillmer

**Founded:** 1987
**Domicile:** Delaware
**Employees:** 23,300

The McGraw-Hill Companies

# Allstate Corp (The)

**STANDARD &POOR'S**

| S&P Recommendation | SELL ★ ★ ☆ ☆ ☆ | Price<br>$27.07 (as of Nov 14, 2008) | 12-Mo. Target Price<br>$23.00 | Investment Style<br>Large-Cap Blend |
|---|---|---|---|---|

**GICS Sector** Financials
**Sub-Industry** Property & Casualty Insurance

**Summary** Allstate, the second largest U.S. personal lines property-casualty insurer, has expanded into the life insurance and retirement savings arena.

## Key Stock Statistics (Source S&P, Vickers, company reports)

| | | | | | | | |
|---|---|---|---|---|---|---|---|
| 52-Wk Range | $55.50– 22.30 | S&P Oper. EPS 2008**E** | 3.60 | Market Capitalization(B) | $14.508 | Beta | 0.77 |
| Trailing 12-Month EPS | $0.38 | S&P Oper. EPS 2009**E** | 5.20 | Yield (%) | 6.06 | S&P 3-Yr. Proj. EPS CAGR(%) | 2 |
| Trailing 12-Month P/E | 71.2 | P/E on S&P Oper. EPS 2008**E** | 7.5 | Dividend Rate/Share | $1.64 | S&P Credit Rating | A+ |
| $10K Invested 5 Yrs Ago | $7,536 | Common Shares Outstg. (M) | 536.0 | Institutional Ownership (%) | 71 | | |

## Price Performance

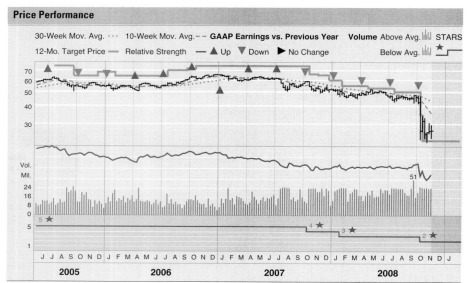

30-Week Mov. Avg. · · · 10-Week Mov. Avg. – – **GAAP Earnings vs. Previous Year** Volume Above Avg. STARS
12-Mo. Target Price — Relative Strength — ▲ Up ▼ Down ► No Change Below Avg. ★

Options: ASE, CBOE, P, Ph

Analysis prepared by **Cathy A. Seifert** on October 29, 2008, when the stock traded at **$ 25.13**.

### Highlights

➤ We expect operating revenues to be flat to down 2% in 2008, reflecting our forecast of flat to lower property-casualty earned premiums, flat to very little growth in financial services revenues, and a mid-single digit decrease in net investment income. This compares with revenue growth of 2.7% in 2007.

➤ We project underwriting results to remain modestly profitable in 2008, although we see margins contracting amid a deterioration in claim trends in a number of core lines. Underwriting results in 2007 deteriorated, and the combined loss/expense ratio increased to 89.8%, from 83.6% in 2006. Higher catastrophe losses of $3.1 billion in the first nine months of 2008 (versus $937 million in the year-ago period) offset stable claim trends and led to a combined ratio of 100.4%, versus 87.7%. The combined ratio excluding catastrophes increased to 85.2% in the 2008 interim, from 83.1% in the 2007 period.

➤ We estimate operating EPS of $3.60 in 2008 and $5.20 in 2009, versus the $6.47 reported for 2007. Our operating EPS estimates assume a "normal" level of catastrophe losses and the absence of any significant reserve increases, and exclude any asset writedowns.

### Investment Rationale/Risk

➤ Our sell recommendation reflects our view that a more competitive underwriting and investment environment that we anticipate for 2008 will continue to pressure the shares. Our outlook is also tempered by our disappointment that ALL has not made significant progress leveraging opportunities for growth at Allstate Financial. Also, we note that as of June 30, 2008 20% (or $22.7 billion) of ALL's $113.6 billion investment portfolio assets were classified as "level 3" under FAS fair value accounting rule 157. Level 3 assets are deemed the be the least liquid of a company's assets.

➤ Risks to our opinion and target price include a sharp rise in loss costs, greatly increased premium price competition, and further deterioration in the credit quality and liquidity of ALL's fixed-income investment portfolio.

➤ Our 12-month target price of $23 assumes that the shares will trade at 4.4X our $5.20 operating EPS estimate for 2009. This valuation represents a discount to most of ALL's peers and is at the low end of the stock's historical range, reflecting our view that concerns over ALL's balance sheet will continue to pressure the stock.

## Qualitative Risk Assessment

| LOW | MEDIUM | HIGH |
|---|---|---|

Our risk assessment reflects our view of ALL's potential to an outsize level of claims from catastrophes, partly offset by ALL's geographically diversified base of business. We also remain concerned over the level of illiquid assets in its investment portfolio.

## Quantitative Evaluations

**S&P Quality Ranking** B

| D | C | B- | B | B+ | A- | A | A+ |
|---|---|---|---|---|---|---|---|

**Relative Strength Rank** MODERATE

47

LOWEST = 1    HIGHEST = 99

## Revenue/Earnings Data

### Revenue (Million $)

| | 1Q | 2Q | 3Q | 4Q | Year |
|---|---|---|---|---|---|
| 2008 | 8,087 | 7,418 | 7,320 | -- | -- |
| 2007 | 9,331 | 9,455 | 8,992 | 8,991 | 36,769 |
| 2006 | 9,081 | 8,875 | 8,738 | 9,102 | 35,796 |
| 2005 | 8,705 | 8,791 | 8,942 | 8,945 | 35,383 |
| 2004 | 8,311 | 8,304 | 8,442 | 8,879 | 33,936 |
| 2003 | 7,861 | 7,899 | 8,127 | 8,262 | 32,149 |

### Earnings Per Share ($)

| | | | | | |
|---|---|---|---|---|---|
| 2008 | 0.62 | 0.05 | -1.71 | E1.38 | E3.60 |
| 2007 | 2.41 | 2.30 | 1.70 | 1.36 | 7.77 |
| 2006 | 2.19 | 1.89 | 1.83 | 1.93 | 7.84 |
| 2005 | 1.64 | 1.71 | -2.36 | 1.59 | 2.64 |
| 2004 | 1.59 | 1.47 | 0.09 | 1.64 | 4.79 |
| 2003 | 0.94 | 0.84 | 0.98 | 1.09 | 3.85 |

Fiscal year ended Dec. 31. Next earnings report expected: Late January. EPS Estimates based on S&P Operating Earnings; historical GAAP earnings are as reported.

## Dividend Data (Dates: mm/dd Payment Date: mm/dd/yy)

| Amount ($) | Date Decl. | Ex-Div. Date | Stk. of Record | Payment Date |
|---|---|---|---|---|
| 0.410 | 02/26 | 03/12 | 03/14 | 04/01/08 |
| 0.410 | 05/21 | 05/28 | 05/30 | 07/01/08 |
| 0.410 | 07/22 | 08/27 | 08/29 | 10/01/08 |
| 0.410 | 11/11 | 11/25 | 11/28 | 01/02/09 |

Dividends have been paid since 1993. Source: Company reports.

# Allstate Corp (The)

STANDARD
&POOR'S

## Business Summary October 29, 2008

CORPORATE OVERVIEW. Established in 1931 by Sears, Roebuck & Co., All-state is the second largest U.S. personal lines property-casualty insurer (based on earned premiums), and the 12th largest life insurer (based on life in-surance in force). It writes business mainly through 14,900 exclusive agen-cies. ALL has also implemented a multi-access distribution model designed to allow customers to purchase company products through agents, over the In-ternet, via telephone, and through The Good Hands Network. ALL became an independent company in June 1995, when Sears, Roebuck & Co. spun off its 80% interest in the company.

The company's primary business is the sale of private passenger automobile and homeowners insurance, and it maintains national market shares of 11% to 12% in each of these lines. ALL is licensed to write policies in all 50 states, the District of Columbia, Puerto Rico, and Canada. In 2007, property-liability net written premiums approached $27.2 billion, down from $27.5 billion in 2006. Of the 2007 total, standard automobile policies accounted for 63%, non-standard automobile policies 5%, homeowners' coverage 23%, commercial lines 3%, and other personal lines 6%. Property-liability premiums earned declined frac-tionally, to $27.2 billion in 2007, from $27.4 billion in 2006. Underwriting results

in 2007 deteriorated from the unusually favorable (in our view) results in 2006, reflecting a higher level of catastrophe losses and an erosion in underlying claim trends. As a result, pretax underwriting profits declined 38% in 2007, to $2.8 billion, from $4.5 billion in 2006. The combined loss and expense ratio de-teriorated to 89.8% in 2007, from 83.6% in 2006.

Allstate Financial (formerly Allstate Life) offers an array of life insurance, an-nuity, savings and investment and pension products through Allstate agents, financial institutions, independent agents and brokers, and direct marketing. Total premiums and deposits declined 18% in 2007, to $9.6 billion, from $11.7 billion in 2006. Of the 2007 total, interest-sensitive life insurance products ac-counted for 15%, traditional and other life insurance for 8%, fixed deferred an-nuities 28%, indexed annuities 6%, fixed immediate annuities 6%, institutional products 31%, and bank deposits 6%.

## Company Financials Fiscal Year Ended Dec. 31

| Per Share Data ($) | 2007 | 2006 | 2005 | 2004 | 2003 | 2002 | 2001 | 2000 | 1999 | 1998 |
|---|---|---|---|---|---|---|---|---|---|---|
| Tangible Book Value | 37.35 | 33.80 | 29.97 | 30.74 | 27.89 | 23.52 | 22.35 | 22.26 | 21.09 | 21.08 |
| Operating Earnings | NA | NA | NA | NA | 3.77 | 2.94 | 2.06 | 2.68 | 2.59 | 3.08 |
| Earnings | 7.77 | 7.84 | 2.64 | 4.79 | 3.85 | 1.13 | 1.61 | 2.95 | 3.38 | 3.94 |
| S&P Core Earnings | 6.56 | 7.91 | 2.21 | 4.33 | 3.82 | 2.64 | 1.66 | NA | NA | NA |
| Dividends | 1.52 | 1.40 | 1.28 | 1.12 | 0.92 | 0.84 | 0.76 | 0.68 | 0.58 | 0.52 |
| Relative Payout | 20% | 18% | 48% | 23% | 24% | 74% | 47% | 23% | 17% | 13% |
| Prices:High | 65.85 | 66.14 | 63.22 | 51.99 | 43.27 | 41.95 | 45.90 | 44.75 | 41.00 | 52.38 |
| Prices:Low | 48.90 | 50.22 | 49.66 | 42.55 | 30.05 | 31.03 | 30.00 | 17.19 | 22.88 | 36.06 |
| P/E Ratio:High | 8 | 8 | 24 | 11 | 11 | 37 | 29 | 15 | 12 | 13 |
| P/E Ratio:Low | 6 | 6 | 19 | 9 | 8 | 27 | 19 | 6 | 7 | 9 |

| Income Statement Analysis (Million $) | | | | | | | | | | |
|---|---|---|---|---|---|---|---|---|---|---|
| Life Insurance in Force | NA | NA | NA | NA | 409,068 | 396,943 | 387,039 | 367,914 | 334,895 | 276,032 |
| Premium Income:Life A & H | 27,233 | 27,369 | 27,039 | 25,989 | 24,677 | 23,361 | 2,230 | 2,205 | 1,623 | 1,519 |
| Premium Income:Casualty/Property. | 1,866 | 1,964 | 2,049 | 2,072 | 2,304 | 2,293 | 22,197 | 21,871 | 20,112 | 19,307 |
| Net Investment Income | 6,435 | 6,177 | 5,746 | 5,284 | 4,972 | 4,854 | 4,796 | 4,633 | 4,112 | 3,890 |
| Total Revenue | 36,769 | 35,796 | 35,383 | 33,936 | 32,149 | 29,579 | 28,865 | 29,134 | 26,959 | 25,879 |
| Pretax Income | 6,653 | 7,178 | 2,088 | 4,586 | 3,566 | 868 | 1,240 | 3,006 | 3,868 | 4,716 |
| Net Operating Income | NA | NA | NA | NA | 2,662 | 2,075 | 1,492 | 2,004 | 2,082 | 2,573 |
| Net Income | 4,636 | 4,993 | 1,765 | 3,356 | 2,720 | 803 | 1,167 | 2,211 | 2,720 | 3,294 |
| S&P Core Earnings | 3,915 | 5,040 | 1,487 | 3,028 | 2,692 | 1,879 | 1,201 | NA | NA | NA |

| Balance Sheet & Other Financial Data (Million $) | | | | | | | | | | |
|---|---|---|---|---|---|---|---|---|---|---|
| Cash & Equivalent | 6,113 | 4,935 | 1,387 | 1,428 | 1,434 | 1,408 | 1,146 | 1,164 | 1,066 | 1,009 |
| Premiums Due | 4,879 | 4,789 | 4,739 | 4,721 | 4,386 | 6,958 | 6,674 | 3,802 | 3,927 | 3,082 |
| Investment Assets:Bonds | 94,451 | 98,320 | 98,065 | 95,715 | 87,741 | 77,152 | 65,720 | 60,758 | 55,286 | 53,560 |
| Investment Assets:Stocks | 7,758 | 7,777 | 6,164 | 5,895 | 5,288 | 3,683 | 5,245 | 6,086 | 6,738 | 6,421 |
| Investment Assets:Loans | 10,830 | 9,467 | 8,748 | 7,856 | 6,539 | 6,092 | 5,710 | 4,599 | 4,068 | 3,458 |
| Investment Assets:Total | 118,980 | 119,757 | 118,297 | 115,530 | 103,081 | 90,650 | 79,876 | 74,483 | 69,645 | 66,525 |
| Deferred Policy Costs | 5,768 | 5,332 | 5,802 | 4,968 | 4,842 | 4,385 | 4,421 | 4,309 | 4,119 | 3,096 |
| Total Assets | 156,408 | 157,554 | 156,072 | 149,725 | 134,142 | 117,426 | 109,175 | 104,808 | 98,119 | 87,691 |
| Debt | 5,640 | 4,620 | 4,887 | 5,291 | 5,073 | 4,161 | 3,894 | 3,862 | 3,150 | 2,103 |
| Common Equity | 21,851 | 21,846 | 20,186 | 21,823 | 20,565 | 34,128 | 17,196 | 17,451 | 16,601 | 17,240 |
| Combined Loss-Expense Ratio | 89.6 | 83.6 | 102.4 | 93.0 | 94.6 | 98.9 | 102.9 | 99.2 | 97.4 | 93.2 |
| % Return on Revenue | 12.6 | 13.9 | 5.0 | 9.9 | 8.5 | 2.7 | 4.0 | 7.6 | 10.1 | 12.7 |
| % Return on Equity | 21.2 | 23.8 | 8.4 | 15.8 | 14.3 | 2.4 | 6.7 | 13.0 | 16.1 | 20.1 |
| % Investment Yield | 5.3 | 5.2 | 4.9 | 4.8 | 5.1 | 5.7 | 6.2 | 6.4 | 6.0 | 10.4 |

Data as orig reptd.; bef. results of disc opers/spec. items. Per share data adj. for stk. divs.; EPS diluted. E-Estimated. NA-Not Available. NM-Not Meaningful. NR-Not Ranked. UR-Under Review.

**Office:** 2775 Sanders Road, Northbrook, IL 60062-6127.
**Telephone:** 800-574-3553.
**Website:** http://www.allstate.com
**Chrmn, Pres & CEO:** T.J. Wilson, II

**SVP & CFO:** D. Civgin
**SVP & General Counsel:** M.C. Mayes
**Secy:** M.J. McGinn

**Board Members:** F. D. Ackerman, R. D. Beyer, W. Farrell, J. M. Greenberg, R. T. LeMay, H. J. Riley, Jr., J. I. Smith, J. A. Sprieser, M. A. Taylor, T. J. Wilson, II

**Founded:** 1953
**Domicile:** Delaware
**Employees:** 39,000

The McGraw-Hill Companies

# Altera Corp

**STANDARD &POOR'S**

| S&P Recommendation | HOLD ★★★☆☆ | | Price | 12-Mo. Target Price | Investment Style |
|---|---|---|---|---|---|
| | | | $15.02 (as of Nov 14, 2008) | $24.00 | Large-Cap Growth |

**GICS Sector** Information Technology
**Sub-Industry** Semiconductors

**Summary** ALTR is one of the largest makers of high-performance, high-density programmable logic devices (PLDs) and associated computer-aided engineering logic development tools.

## Key Stock Statistics (Source S&P, Vickers, company reports)

| | | | | | | | |
|---|---|---|---|---|---|---|---|
| 52-Wk Range | $24.19– 14.20 | S&P Oper. EPS 2008**E** | 1.19 | Market Capitalization(B) | $4.466 | Beta | 1.07 |
| Trailing 12-Month EPS | $1.09 | S&P Oper. EPS 2009**E** | 1.34 | Yield (%) | 1.33 | S&P 3-Yr. Proj. EPS CAGR(%) | 15 |
| Trailing 12-Month P/E | 13.8 | P/E on S&P Oper. EPS 2008**E** | 12.6 | Dividend Rate/Share | $0.20 | S&P Credit Rating | NA |
| $10K Invested 5 Yrs Ago | $6,719 | Common Shares Outstg. (M) | 297.4 | Institutional Ownership (%) | 96 | | |

## Price Performance

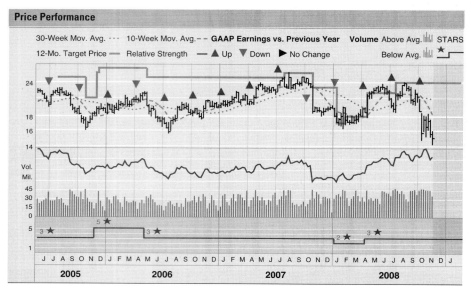

30-Week Mov. Avg. ···· 10-Week Mov. Avg. – – **GAAP Earnings vs. Previous Year** **Volume** Above Avg. STARS
12-Mo. Target Price — Relative Strength — ▲ Up ▼ Down ► No Change Below Avg.

Analysis prepared by **Clyde Montevirgen** on October 17, 2008, when the stock traded at **$ 17.21**.

### Highlights

➤ We expect revenues to increase 7% in 2009, following a projected 11% advance in 2008. We think that ALTR will benefit as customers launch products that use the company's chips, and we see new, competitive product offerings contributing to market share gains. We believe sales to the communication and computer markets will hold, but given macroeconomic pressures, we are growing more concerned about sales to the consumer and industrial markets, which is why we project decelerating growth ahead.

➤ We believe that the gross margin will remain around 67% for 2009, similar to expected 2008 results. ALTR outsources its manufacturing, which we see helping to limit gross margin variability. However, we think new products and further penetration of various markets will lead to better long term profitability. We anticipate that the adjusted operating margin will widen to around 31% for 2009, from an estimated 30% for 2008, reflecting leverage from higher sales.

➤ We estimate operating EPS of $1.34 in 2009, compared to a projected $1.19 in 2008.

### Investment Rationale/Risk

➤ Our hold recommendation reflects our view of solid fundamentals, which is balanced by what we see as lofty valuations. We expect past design wins to lead to sales momentum in multiple end markets. We think ALTR has done a good job taking market share and can continue to do so in higher-volume markets. Altera has effectively reduced operating costs, which should contribute to better profitability. However, we believe this growth is largely reflected in the shares, which trade at a premium to broader industry multiples, and we see risks related to the macroeconomic environment and formidable competition.

➤ Risks to our recommendation and target price include worse than expected economic conditions, market share losses to larger competitor Xilinx, and increases in costs to source semiconductors from the foundries.

➤ Our 12-month target price of $24 is based on our P/E analysis. We apply a P/E multiple of about 18X, above the peer average, but below the midpoint of ALTR's historical average, to our 2009 EPS estimate.

### Qualitative Risk Assessment

| LOW | MEDIUM | HIGH |
|---|---|---|

Our risk assessment reflects our view that Altera is subject to the sales swings of the semiconductor industry and competition from a larger rival. The shares have above-average price volatility, as indicated by a high beta. This is offset by the company's participation in a high-growth niche market.

### Quantitative Evaluations

**S&P Quality Ranking** B

| D | C | B- | **B** | B+ | A- | A | A+ |
|---|---|---|---|---|---|---|---|

**Relative Strength Rank** MODERATE

56

LOWEST = 1     HIGHEST = 99

### Revenue/Earnings Data

**Revenue (Million $)**

| | 1Q | 2Q | 3Q | 4Q | Year |
|---|---|---|---|---|---|
| 2008 | 336.1 | 359.9 | 356.8 | -- | -- |
| 2007 | 304.9 | 319.7 | 315.8 | 323.2 | 1,264 |
| 2006 | 292.8 | 334.1 | 341.2 | 317.4 | 1,286 |
| 2005 | 264.8 | 285.5 | 291.5 | 281.9 | 1,124 |
| 2004 | 242.9 | 269.0 | 264.6 | 239.9 | 1,016 |
| 2003 | 195.1 | 205.3 | 209.5 | 217.4 | 827.2 |

**Earnings Per Share ($)**

| | | | | | |
|---|---|---|---|---|---|
| 2008 | 0.27 | 0.32 | 0.31 | E0.30 | E1.19 |
| 2007 | 0.21 | 0.22 | 0.20 | 0.20 | 0.82 |
| 2006 | 0.16 | 0.21 | 0.24 | 0.27 | 0.88 |
| 2005 | 0.17 | 0.18 | 0.21 | 0.19 | 0.74 |
| 2004 | 0.15 | 0.20 | 0.22 | 0.15 | 0.72 |
| 2003 | 0.08 | 0.09 | 0.11 | 0.12 | 0.40 |

Fiscal year ended Dec. 31. Next earnings report expected: Early February. EPS Estimates based on S&P Operating Earnings; historical GAAP earnings are as reported.

### Dividend Data (Dates: mm/dd Payment Date: mm/dd/yy)

| Amount ($) | Date Decl. | Ex-Div. Date | Stk. of Record | Payment Date |
|---|---|---|---|---|
| 0.040 | 02/05 | 02/07 | 02/11 | 03/03/08 |
| 0.050 | 04/15 | 05/08 | 05/12 | 06/02/08 |
| 0.050 | 07/15 | 08/07 | 08/11 | 09/02/08 |
| 0.050 | 10/14 | 11/06 | 11/10 | 12/01/08 |

Dividends have been paid since 2007. Source: Company reports.

# Altera Corp

## Business Summary October 17, 2008

CORPORATE OVERVIEW. Altera Corp. is a worldwide supplier of programmable logic devices (PLDs), HardCopy brand structured application specific integrated circuits (ASICs), pre-defined design building blocks known as intellectual property cores, and associated software for logic development. PLDs are a high-growth category of semiconductors that address many applications in the communications, computer peripheral, consumer and industrial markets. PLDs offer high speed, high density, and low power characteristics.

The company's PLDs are standard products, shipped blank for user programming. They are programmed at the customer's PC or workstation, using ALTR's proprietary software. Since the company's chips are programmed at a desktop and not at a foundry, product time to market is dramatically shortened. In addition, because ALTR's integrated circuits are standard products, inventory risks are minimized for both the company and customers. The HardCopy product line assists customers who use PLDs for prototyping ASIC chips in converting the design for low cost production of non-programmable ASIC products.

Field Programmable Gate Arrays (FPGAs) include the Stratix lines, aimed at high performance applications, and the Cyclone product family, aimed at low-cost, high volume applications. General purpose Complex Programmable Logic Device (CPLD) product lines include the MAX family, which aims at low-cost, high volume markets. Sales of FPGA, CPLD and other products in 2007 were 71%, 19% and 10%, respectively, of the total. By end market, sales were as follows: communications 40% (42% in 2006), industrial 35% (34%), consumer 16% (14%), and computer and storage 9% (10%). International sales are significant, providing 78% of total sales in 2007, up from 76% in 2006 and 75% in 2005. About 94% of 2007 sales were handled by independent distributors, with about 45% by Arrow Electronics and 13% by Altima Corp., which serves the Japanese market. No single end customer accounted for over 10% of sales in 2007.

We believe competitive advantages offered to electronic system manufacturers by ALTR's products include enhanced design flexibility, shorter design cycles, lower up-front development costs, and the ability to get end-products to market faster, which can lead to significant cost savings for the customer. Drawbacks to PLDs compared to traditional ASICs include larger die size and higher cost per chip.

## Company Financials Fiscal Year Ended Dec. 31

| Per Share Data ($) | 2007 | 2006 | 2005 | 2004 | 2003 | 2002 | 2001 | 2000 | 1999 | 1998 |
|---|---|---|---|---|---|---|---|---|---|---|
| Tangible Book Value | 2.74 | 4.46 | 3.52 | 3.42 | 2.93 | 2.95 | 2.89 | 3.21 | 2.82 | 2.26 |
| Cash Flow | 0.91 | 0.96 | 0.82 | 0.80 | 0.51 | 0.36 | 0.04 | 1.29 | 0.61 | 0.45 |
| Earnings | 0.82 | 0.88 | 0.74 | 0.72 | 0.40 | 0.23 | -0.10 | 1.19 | 0.54 | 0.39 |
| S&P Core Earnings | 0.82 | 0.88 | 0.54 | 0.48 | 0.19 | -0.02 | -0.28 | NA | NA | NA |
| Dividends | 0.12 | Nil | Nil | Nil | Nil | Nil | Nil | Nil | Nil | Nil |
| Payout Ratio | 15% | Nil | Nil | Nil | Nil | Nil | Nil | Nil | Nil | Nil |
| Prices:High | 26.24 | 22.29 | 22.99 | 26.82 | 25.64 | 26.18 | 34.69 | 67.13 | 34.28 | 15.47 |
| Prices:Low | 18.00 | 15.54 | 15.96 | 17.50 | 10.30 | 8.32 | 14.66 | 19.63 | 11.97 | 7.06 |
| P/E Ratio:High | 32 | 25 | 31 | 37 | 64 | NM | NM | 56 | 63 | 40 |
| P/E Ratio:Low | 22 | 18 | 22 | 24 | 26 | NM | NM | 16 | 22 | 18 |

| Income Statement Analysis (Million $) | 2007 | 2006 | 2005 | 2004 | 2003 | 2002 | 2001 | 2000 | 1999 | 1998 |
|---|---|---|---|---|---|---|---|---|---|---|
| Revenue | 1,264 | 1,286 | 1,124 | 1,016 | 827 | 712 | 839 | 1,377 | 837 | 654 |
| Operating Income | 306 | 331 | 352 | 345 | 243 | 146 | 48.8 | 598 | 335 | 262 |
| Depreciation | 31.1 | 29.7 | 29.4 | 30.5 | 45.3 | 48.5 | 54.3 | 40.1 | 29.4 | 30.0 |
| Interest Expense | Nil | Nil | Nil | Nil | Nil | Nil | Nil | Nil | Nil | 6.36 |
| Pretax Income | 338 | 360 | 357 | 331 | 213 | 123 | -13.0 | 744 | 335 | 234 |
| Effective Tax Rate | 14.1% | 10.1% | 21.9% | 16.8% | 27.0% | 26.0% | NM | 33.2% | 33.2% | 34.0% |
| Net Income | 290 | 323 | 279 | 275 | 155 | 91.3 | -39.8 | 497 | 224 | 154 |
| S&P Core Earnings | 290 | 323 | 204 | 182 | 70.7 | -8.66 | -106 | NA | NA | NA |

| Balance Sheet & Other Financial Data (Million $) | 2007 | 2006 | 2005 | 2004 | 2003 | 2002 | 2001 | 2000 | 1999 | 1998 |
|---|---|---|---|---|---|---|---|---|---|---|
| Cash | 1,021 | 738 | 788 | 580 | 259 | 255 | 145 | 496 | 164 | 131 |
| Current Assets | 1,534 | 1,735 | 1,495 | 1,537 | 1,270 | 1,176 | 1,129 | 1,769 | 1,107 | 800 |
| Total Assets | 1,770 | 2,215 | 1,823 | 1,747 | 1,488 | 1,372 | 1,361 | 2,004 | 1,440 | 1,093 |
| Current Liabilities | 490 | 598 | 555 | 468 | 385 | 241 | 247 | 756 | 322 | 212 |
| Long Term Debt | 250 | 1.30 | 3.87 | Nil | Nil | Nil | Nil | Nil | Nil | Nil |
| Common Equity | 861 | 1,608 | 1,326 | 1,279 | 1,102 | 1,131 | 1,115 | 1,248 | 1,118 | 882 |
| Total Capital | 1,111 | 1,609 | 1,330 | 1,279 | 1,102 | 1,131 | 1,115 | 1,248 | 1,118 | 882 |
| Capital Expenditures | 31.2 | 36.5 | 25.9 | 24.7 | 13.9 | 9.87 | 65.8 | 87.5 | 29.8 | 24.0 |
| Cash Flow | 321 | 353 | 308 | 306 | 200 | 140 | 14.5 | 537 | 253 | 184 |
| Current Ratio | 3.1 | 2.9 | 2.7 | 3.3 | 3.3 | 4.9 | 4.6 | 2.3 | 3.4 | 3.8 |
| % Long Term Debt of Capitalization | 22.5 | 0.1 | 0.3 | Nil | Nil | Nil | Nil | Nil | Nil | Nil |
| % Net Income of Revenue | 23.0 | 25.1 | 24.8 | 27.1 | 18.8 | 12.8 | NM | 36.1 | 26.8 | 23.6 |
| % Return on Assets | 14.6 | 16.0 | 15.5 | 17.1 | 10.9 | 6.7 | NM | 28.9 | 17.7 | 15.1 |
| % Return on Equity | 23.5 | 22.5 | 21.0 | 23.1 | 13.9 | 8.1 | NM | 42.0 | 22.4 | 21.8 |

Data as orig reptd.; bef. results of disc opers/spec. items. Per share data adj. for stk. divs.; EPS diluted. E-Estimated. NA-Not Available. NM-Not Meaningful. NR-Not Ranked. UR-Under Review.

**Office:** 101 Innovation Drive, San Jose, CA 95134.
**Telephone:** 408-544-7000.
**Email:** inv_rel@altera.com
**Website:** http://www.altera.com

**Chrmn, Pres & CEO:** J.P. Daane
**COO:** W.Y. Hata
**SVP, CFO & Chief Acctg Officer:** T.R. Morse
**Secy & General Counsel:** K.E. Schuelke

**Cntlr:** J.W. Callas
**Board Members:** J. P. Daane, R. J. Finocchio, Jr., K. McGarity, G. Myers, K. A. Prabhu, J. C. Shoemaker, S. Wang

**Founded:** 1983
**Domicile:** Delaware
**Employees:** 2,651

# Altria Group Inc.

**STANDARD &POOR'S**

| S&P Recommendation **STRONG BUY** ★★★★★ | Price $16.26 (as of Nov 14, 2008) | 12-Mo. Target Price $24.00 | Investment Style Large-Cap Blend |
|---|---|---|---|

**GICS Sector** Consumer Staples
**Sub-Industry** Tobacco

**Summary** Altria Group (formerly Philip Morris Companies) is the largest U.S. cigarette producer. It spun off Kraft Foods in 2007 and its international cigarette operations in 2008.

## Key Stock Statistics (Source S&P, Vickers, company reports)

| | | | | | | | |
|---|---|---|---|---|---|---|---|
| 52-Wk Range | $79.59– 15.90 | S&P Oper. EPS 2008**E** | 1.67 | Market Capitalization(B) | $33.502 | Beta | 0.54 |
| Trailing 12-Month EPS | $3.07 | S&P Oper. EPS 2009**E** | 1.84 | Yield (%) | 7.87 | S&P 3-Yr. Proj. EPS CAGR(%) | 8 |
| Trailing 12-Month P/E | 5.3 | P/E on S&P Oper. EPS 2008**E** | 9.7 | Dividend Rate/Share | $1.28 | S&P Credit Rating | BBB+ |
| $10K Invested 5 Yrs Ago | NA | Common Shares Outstg. (M) | 2,060.4 | Institutional Ownership (%) | 71 | | |

## Price Performance

30-Week Mov. Avg. · · · ·  10-Week Mov. Avg. – – –  **GAAP Earnings vs. Previous Year**  Volume Above Avg.⊞ STARS
12-Mo. Target Price ——  Relative Strength — ▲ Up ▼ Down ▶ No Change  Below Avg.⊞ ★

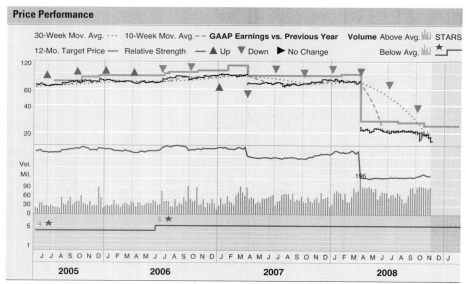

Options: ASE, CBOE, P, Ph

Analysis prepared by **Esther Y. Kwon, CFA** on October 24, 2008, when the stock traded at **$ 18.92**.

### Highlights

► On March 28, 2008, Altria completed the spinoff of Philip Morris International to shareholders with a share distribution ratio of one for one. The board of directors set Altria's initial dividend policy at a payout ratio of 75% for an annual rate of $1.16 per common share and announced a share repurchase program of $7.5 billion over two years.

► We expect sales volume to decline 4% to 5% in 2008, with brand investments, acquisitions, line extensions and new product introductions somewhat offsetting declining consumption trends. We see revenues rising about 5% on higher pricing. Over the next several years, we expect MO's margins to widen on restructuring actions, including the closure of its Cabarrus facility, consolidation of all manufacturing in Richmond, VA, and $300 million in new SG&A expense reductions. In 2008, we project that income growth will accelerate in the second half versus the first, as savings from restructuring actions begin to be realized.

► On fewer shares outstanding and an effective tax rate of 37.5%, up from a pro forma 33% before the spin-off, we project operating EPS of $1.67 for 2008 and $1.84 for 2009.

### Investment Rationale/Risk

► We see domestic litigation pressures continuing to ease. Following the dismissal of the Price and Engle class action cases, a Supreme Court review of the Williams case did not cap punitive damages, but it did result in the case being remanded to state court, with instructions to reduce the punitive damages award to a reasonable multiple of actual damages. We believe the rulings reduce Altria's cash flow risk considerably. We still await the appeal of the DOJ case, but the review of the Schwab class certification resulted in the removal of the certification earlier this April.

► Risks to our recommendation and target price include possible pressures on trading multiples as investors remain cautious about court trials, and potential increases in excise taxes and smoking bans at the state and local level.

► Our 12-month target price of $24 is based on historical and peer forward P/Es. We use a slightly below historical forward P/E of approximately 13.0X on our 2009 EPS estimate to calculate our target price. Reflecting high cash generation and the stock's indicated dividend yield of over 6.0%, we continue to find MO attractive.

### Qualitative Risk Assessment

| LOW | **MEDIUM** | HIGH |
|---|---|---|

MO is a large-cap company in an industry that is operationally very stable. However, the tobacco industry is beset by litigation. The company is subject to several ongoing legal actions, which could have a material impact on future cash flows.

### Quantitative Evaluations

**S&P Quality Ranking**  A

| D | C | B- | B | B+ | A- | **A** | A+ |
|---|---|---|---|---|---|---|---|

**Relative Strength Rank**  MODERATE

59

LOWEST = 1          HIGHEST = 99

### Revenue/Earnings Data

**Revenue (Million $)**

| | 1Q | 2Q | 3Q | 4Q | Year |
|---|---|---|---|---|---|
| 2008 | 3,604 | 4,179 | 4,341 | -- | -- |
| 2007 | 17,556 | 18,809 | 19,207 | 18,229 | 38,051 |
| 2006 | 24,355 | 25,769 | 25,885 | 25,398 | 101,407 |
| 2005 | 23,618 | 24,784 | 24,962 | 24,490 | 97,854 |
| 2004 | 21,721 | 22,894 | 22,615 | 22,380 | 89,610 |
| 2003 | 19,371 | 20,831 | 20,939 | 20,691 | 81,832 |

**Earnings Per Share ($)**

| | | | | | |
|---|---|---|---|---|---|
| 2008 | 0.29 | 0.43 | 0.42 | E0.38 | E1.67 |
| 2007 | 1.01 | 1.05 | 1.24 | 1.03 | 4.33 |
| 2006 | 1.65 | 1.29 | 1.36 | 1.40 | 5.71 |
| 2005 | 1.24 | 1.40 | 1.38 | 1.09 | 5.10 |
| 2004 | 1.06 | 1.26 | 1.28 | 0.96 | 4.57 |
| 2003 | 1.07 | 1.20 | 1.22 | 1.02 | 4.52 |

Fiscal year ended Dec. 31. Next earnings report expected: Late January. EPS Estimates based on S&P Operating Earnings; historical GAAP earnings are as reported.

### Dividend Data (Dates: mm/dd Payment Date: mm/dd/yy)

| Amount ($) | Date Decl. | Ex-Div. Date | Stk. of Record | Payment Date |
|---|---|---|---|---|
| 0.750 | 02/27 | 03/17 | 03/19 | 04/10/08 |
| Stk. | 01/30 | 03/31 | 03/19 | 03/28/08 |
| 0.290 | 05/28 | 06/11 | 06/13 | 07/10/08 |
| 0.320 | 08/28 | 09/11 | 09/15 | 10/10/08 |

Dividends have been paid since 1928. Source: Company reports.

# Altria Group Inc.

**STANDARD &POOR'S**

## Business Summary October 24, 2008

CORPORATE OVERVIEW. Altria Group (formerly Philip Morris Cos., Inc.) is a holding company for wholly owned and majority owned subsidiaries that make and market various consumer products, now primarily including cigarettes. Prior to the March 30, 2007, spinoff of Kraft Foods, Altria Group's reportable segments were domestic tobacco, international tobacco, North American food, international food and financial services. The spinoff of Philip Morris International was completed on March 28, 2008, at a one-for-one exchange rate.

Philip Morris U.S.A. (PM USA) is the largest U.S. tobacco company, with total U.S. cigarette shipments amounting to 175.1 billion units in 2007 (down 4.5% from 2006), accounting for 50.6% of total U.S. cigarette market shipments (up from 50.3% in 2006). Focus brands include Marlboro (the largest selling brand in the U.S.), Virginia Slims and Parliament in the premium category, and Basic in the discount category.

Kraft Foods, the largest packaged food company in North America and second largest in the world, was spun off on March 30, 2007, to MO shareholders as a tax-free stock dividend. MO shareholders received approximately 0.68 of a KFT share per MO share owned as a stock dividend at the end of March 2007, and cash in lieu of fractional shares.

In July 2002, MO sold its Miller Brewing Co. subsidiary to South African Brewers, plc., receiving $3.38 billion worth of shares in the newly formed company, SABMiller. As of December 31, 2007, this stake represented a 28.6% economic interest and voting interest.

CORPORATE STRATEGY. MO has recently considered a number of restructuring alternatives, including the possibility of separating Altria Group, Inc. into two, or potentially three, independent entities. In June 2007, it announced that cigarette production for international markets would be shifted from U.S. facilities to European plants, and subsequently decided to spin off its international tobacco operations, with an effective date of March 28, 2008.

## Company Financials Fiscal Year Ended Dec. 31

| Per Share Data ($) | 2007 | 2006 | 2005 | 2004 | 2003 | 2002 | 2001 | 2000 | 1999 | 1998 |
|---|---|---|---|---|---|---|---|---|---|---|
| Tangible Book Value | 3.97 | NM | NM | NM | NM | NM | NM | NM | NM | NM |
| Cash Flow | 4.79 | 6.57 | 5.92 | 5.35 | 5.22 | 6.10 | 4.93 | 4.50 | 3.90 | 2.89 |
| Earnings | 4.33 | 5.71 | 5.10 | 4.57 | 4.52 | 5.21 | 3.88 | 3.75 | 3.19 | 2.20 |
| S&P Core Earnings | 4.33 | 5.62 | 5.14 | 4.54 | 4.49 | 4.03 | 3.62 | NA | NA | NA |
| Dividends | 3.05 | 3.32 | 3.06 | 2.82 | 2.64 | 2.44 | 2.22 | 2.02 | 1.80 | 1.64 |
| Payout Ratio | 70% | 58% | 60% | 62% | 58% | 47% | 57% | 54% | 56% | 75% |
| Prices:High | 90.50 | 86.56 | 78.68 | 61.88 | 55.03 | 57.79 | 53.88 | 45.94 | 55.56 | 59.50 |
| Prices:Low | 63.13 | 68.36 | 60.40 | 44.50 | 27.70 | 35.40 | 38.75 | 18.69 | 21.25 | 34.75 |
| P/E Ratio:High | 21 | 15 | 15 | 14 | 12 | 11 | 14 | 12 | 17 | 27 |
| P/E Ratio:Low | 15 | 12 | 12 | 10 | 6 | 7 | 10 | 5 | 7 | 16 |

**Income Statement Analysis** (Million $)

| | 2007 | 2006 | 2005 | 2004 | 2003 | 2002 | 2001 | 2000 | 1999 | 1998 |
|---|---|---|---|---|---|---|---|---|---|---|
| Revenue | 73,801 | 101,407 | 97,854 | 89,610 | 81,832 | 80,408 | 89,924 | 80,356 | 78,596 | 74,391 |
| Operating Income | 14,892 | 19,705 | 19,004 | 17,929 | 17,663 | 18,476 | 18,039 | 16,396 | 15,192 | 15,048 |
| Depreciation | 980 | 1,804 | 1,675 | 1,607 | 1,440 | 1,331 | 2,337 | 1,717 | 1,702 | 1,690 |
| Interest Expense | 653 | 877 | 1,556 | 1,417 | 1,367 | 1,327 | 1,659 | 1,078 | 1,100 | 1,144 |
| Pretax Income | 13,257 | 16,536 | 15,435 | 14,004 | 14,760 | 18,098 | 14,284 | 13,960 | 12,695 | 9,087 |
| Effective Tax Rate | 30.9% | 26.3% | 29.9% | 32.4% | 34.9% | 35.5% | 37.9% | 39.0% | 39.5% | 40.9% |
| Net Income | 9,161 | 12,022 | 10,668 | 9,420 | 9,204 | 11,102 | 8,566 | 8,510 | 7,675 | 5,372 |
| S&P Core Earnings | 9,163 | 11,818 | 10,766 | 9,348 | 9,145 | 8,593 | 7,959 | NA | NA | NA |

**Balance Sheet & Other Financial Data** (Million $)

| | 2007 | 2006 | 2005 | 2004 | 2003 | 2002 | 2001 | 2000 | 1999 | 1998 |
|---|---|---|---|---|---|---|---|---|---|---|
| Cash | 6,498 | 5,020 | 6,258 | 5,744 | 3,777 | 565 | 453 | 937 | 5,100 | 4,081 |
| Current Assets | NA | 26,152 | 25,781 | 25,901 | 21,382 | 17,441 | 17,275 | 17,238 | 20,895 | 20,230 |
| Total Assets | 57,211 | 104,270 | 107,949 | 101,648 | 96,175 | 87,540 | 84,968 | 79,067 | 61,381 | 59,920 |
| Current Liabilities | NA | 25,427 | 26,158 | 23,574 | 21,393 | 19,082 | 20,141 | 25,949 | 18,017 | 16,379 |
| Long Term Debt | 11,046 | 14,498 | 17,868 | 18,683 | 21,163 | 21,355 | 18,651 | 19,154 | 12,226 | 12,615 |
| Common Equity | 18,554 | 39,619 | 35,707 | 30,714 | 25,077 | 19,478 | 19,620 | 15,005 | 15,305 | 16,197 |
| Total Capital | 33,610 | 68,496 | 71,945 | 67,714 | 64,110 | 56,832 | 52,768 | 40,824 | 33,211 | 33,892 |
| Capital Expenditures | 1,458 | 2,454 | 2,206 | 1,913 | 1,974 | 2,009 | 1,922 | 1,682 | 1,749 | 1,804 |
| Cash Flow | 10,141 | 13,826 | 12,343 | 11,027 | 10,644 | 12,433 | 10,903 | 10,227 | 9,377 | 7,062 |
| Current Ratio | 1.5 | 1.0 | 1.0 | 1.1 | 1.0 | 0.9 | 0.9 | 0.7 | 1.2 | 1.2 |
| % Long Term Debt of Capitalization | 30.0 | 21.2 | 24.8 | 27.6 | 33.0 | 37.6 | 35.3 | 46.9 | 36.8 | 37.2 |
| % Net Income of Revenue | 12.4 | 11.9 | 10.9 | 10.5 | 11.2 | 13.8 | 9.5 | 10.6 | 9.8 | 7.2 |
| % Return on Assets | 11.4 | 11.3 | 10.2 | 9.5 | 10.0 | 12.9 | 10.4 | 12.1 | 12.7 | 9.3 |
| % Return on Equity | 31.5 | 31.9 | 32.1 | 33.8 | 41.3 | 56.8 | 49.5 | 56.2 | 48.7 | 34.5 |

Data as orig reptd.; bef. results of disc opers/spec. items. Per share data adj. for stk. divs.; EPS diluted. E-Estimated. NA-Not Available. NM-Not Meaningful. NR-Not Ranked. UR-Under Review.

**Office:** 120 Park Avenue, New York, NY 10017-5577.
**Telephone:** 917-663-4000.
**Website:** http://www.altria.com
**Chrmn & CEO:** M. Szymanczyk

**EVP & CFO:** D.R. Beran
**EVP & Chief Admin Officer:** M.J. Barrington
**EVP & CTO:** J.R. Nelson
**EVP & General Counsel:** D.F. Keane

**Board Members:** E. E. Bailey, G. L. Baliles, D. S. Devitre, T. F. Farrell, II, M. M. Hart, R. E. Huntley, T. W. Jones, G. Munoz, N. Y. Sakkab, M. Szymanczyk

**Founded:** 1919
**Domicile:** Virginia
**Employees:** 84,000

The **McGraw·Hill** Companies

**STANDARD &POOR'S**

# Amazon.com Inc

| S&P Recommendation BUY ★★★★☆ | Price $41.75 (as of Nov 14, 2008) | 12-Mo. Target Price $62.00 | Investment Style Large-Cap Growth |
|---|---|---|---|

**GICS Sector** Consumer Discretionary
**Sub-Industry** Internet Retail

**Summary** This leading online retailer sells a broad range of items from books to consumer electronics to home and garden products.

## Key Stock Statistics (Source S&P, Vickers, company reports)

| | | | | | | | | |
|---|---|---|---|---|---|---|---|---|
| 52-Wk Range | $97.43–38.48 | S&P Oper. EPS 2008E | 1.35 | Market Capitalization(B) | $17.904 | Beta | 2.27 |
| Trailing 12-Month EPS | $1.46 | S&P Oper. EPS 2009E | 1.63 | Yield (%) | Nil | S&P 3-Yr. Proj. EPS CAGR(%) | 20 |
| Trailing 12-Month P/E | 28.6 | P/E on S&P Oper. EPS 2008E | 30.9 | Dividend Rate/Share | Nil | S&P Credit Rating | BB+ |
| $10K Invested 5 Yrs Ago | $7,960 | Common Shares Outstg. (M) | 428.8 | Institutional Ownership (%) | 76 | | |

## Price Performance

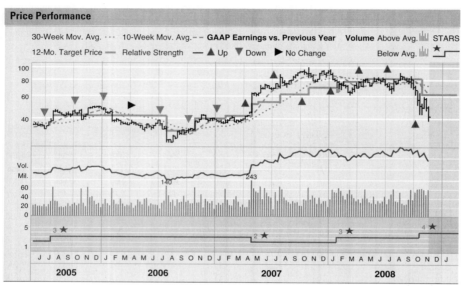

30-Week Mov. Avg. · · · · 10-Week Mov. Avg. - - GAAP Earnings vs. Previous Year  Volume Above Avg. STARS
12-Mo. Target Price — Relative Strength — ▲ Up ▼ Down ▶ No Change  Below Avg.

Options: ASE, CBOE, P, Ph

Analysis prepared by **Michael Souers** on October 27, 2008, when the stock traded at **$ 50.38.**

### Highlights

➤ We believe that AMZN has become a formidable online marketplace in the U.S. We estimate net sales will rise 17% in 2009, following our projection of a 30% advance in 2008. We expect this rapid growth to be driven by new product categories, international expansion, and an increase in third party sellers, partially offset by a modest headwind from foreign currency translation. The 2007 launch of Amazon Prime in the U.K., Germany and Japan should also continue to drive increased sales results and build customer loyalty.

➤ We expect gross margins will decline approximately 30 basis points due to shifts in product mix, the impact of free shipping offers, continued price reductions and other promotions. Due to slightly lower projected G&A and technology and content expenses, we look for only a slight decline in operating margins compared to last year.

➤ Factoring in a modest increase in interest income and a 30% effective tax rate, we expect 2009 EPS of $1.63, a 21% increase from the $1.35 we project the company to earn in 2008, excluding one-time items.

### Investment Rationale/Risk

➤ AMZN continues to demonstrate the strength and worldwide potential of its business model, in our view. Continued investments in long-term growth opportunities such as Amazon Prime, seller platforms and digital media stores should provide new sources of revenue over the next few years. Long term, we expect AMZN's initiatives to result in continued strong sales results and significant margin expansion, as it leverages its leading brand name and position as an Internet retailer. While the shares, at about 29X our 2009 EPS estimate, trade at a significant premium to peers and the S&P 500, we think this premium is warranted by recent execution and AMZN's growth potential.

➤ Risks to our recommendation and target price include the potential for lower-than-projected revenues should growth initiatives fail to live up to their potential, a severe decline in consumer discretionary spending, a lengthy recession and currency risk.

➤ Our 12-month target price of $62 is based on our discounted cash flow analysis, which assumes a weighted average cost of capital of 11.3% and a terminal growth rate of 4%.

### Qualitative Risk Assessment

| LOW | MEDIUM | HIGH |
|---|---|---|

Our risk assessment reflects AMZN's large market capitalization and leading position in the e-commerce industry, offset by increasing competition and the stock's high beta.

### Quantitative Evaluations

**S&P Quality Ranking**  B-

| D | C | B- | B | B+ | A- | A | A+ |
|---|---|---|---|---|---|---|---|

**Relative Strength Rank**  MODERATE

32

LOWEST = 1    HIGHEST = 99

### Revenue/Earnings Data

**Revenue (Million $)**

| | 1Q | 2Q | 3Q | 4Q | Year |
|---|---|---|---|---|---|
| 2008 | 4,135 | 4,063 | 4,264 | -- | -- |
| 2007 | 3,015 | 2,886 | 3,262 | 5,673 | 14,835 |
| 2006 | 2,279 | 2,139 | 2,307 | 3,986 | 10,711 |
| 2005 | 1,902 | 1,753 | 1,858 | 2,977 | 8,490 |
| 2004 | 1,530 | 1,387 | 1,462 | 2,541 | 6,921 |
| 2003 | 1,084 | 1,100 | 1,134 | 1,946 | 5,264 |

**Earnings Per Share ($)**

| | | | | | |
|---|---|---|---|---|---|
| 2008 | 0.34 | 0.37 | 0.27 | E0.51 | E1.35 |
| 2007 | 0.26 | 0.19 | 0.19 | 0.49 | 1.12 |
| 2006 | 0.12 | 0.05 | 0.05 | 0.23 | 0.45 |
| 2005 | 0.12 | 0.12 | 0.07 | 0.47 | 0.78 |
| 2004 | 0.26 | 0.18 | 0.13 | 0.82 | 1.39 |
| 2003 | -0.03 | -0.11 | 0.04 | 0.17 | 0.08 |

Fiscal year ended Dec. 31. Next earnings report expected: Late January. EPS Estimates based on S&P Operating Earnings; historical GAAP earnings are as reported.

### Dividend Data

No cash dividends have been paid.

# Amazon.com Inc

**STANDARD &POOR'S**

## Business Summary October 27, 2008

CORPORATE OVERVIEW. Since opening for business as "Earth's Biggest Bookstore" in July 1995, Amazon.com has expanded into a number of other product categories, such as: apparel, shoes and jewelry; electronics and computers; movies, music and games; toys, kids and baby; sports and outdoors; home and garden; tools, auto and industrial; grocery; health and beauty; and digital downloads.

AMZN has virtually unlimited online shelf space, and can offer customers a vast selection of products through an efficient search and retrieval interface. The company personalizes shopping by recommending items which, based on previous purchases, are likely to interest a particular customer. Key Web site features also include editorial and customer reviews, manufacturer product information, secure payment systems, wedding and baby registries, customer wish lists, and the ability to view selected interior pages and search the entire contents of many books (Look Inside the Book and Search Inside the Book).

The company operates the following retail Web sites: www.amazon.com (U.S.), www.amazon.co.uk (U.K.), www.amazon.de (Germany), www.amazon.fr (France), www.amazon.co.jp (Japan), www.amazon.ca (Canada), www.amazon.cn (China), www.joyo.cn, www.shopbop.com, and

www.endless.com. Amazon also designs, manufactures and sells a wireless e-reading device, the Amazon Kindle. It focuses first and foremost on the customer experience by offering a wide selection of merchandise, low prices and convenience.

In addition to being the seller of record for a broad range of new products, AMZN allows other businesses and individuals to sell new, used and collectible products on its Web sites through its Merchant and Amazon Marketplace programs. The company earns fixed fees, sales commissions, and/or per-unit activity fees under these programs.

Starting in 2003, the company began reporting results for two core segments: North America (55% of 2007 net sales) and International (45%). In 2007, media products accounted for 62% of net sales, electronics and other general merchandise 35%, and other 3%.

## Company Financials Fiscal Year Ended Dec. 31

| Per Share Data ($) | 2007 | 2006 | 2005 | 2004 | 2003 | 2002 | 2001 | 2000 | 1999 | 1998 |
|---|---|---|---|---|---|---|---|---|---|---|
| Tangible Book Value | 2.30 | 0.58 | 0.15 | NM | NM | NM | NM | NM | NM | NM |
| Cash Flow | 1.76 | 0.93 | 1.07 | 1.56 | 0.27 | -0.16 | -0.80 | -2.86 | -3.26 | -0.23 |
| Earnings | 1.12 | 0.45 | 0.78 | 1.39 | 0.08 | -0.40 | -1.53 | -4.02 | -2.20 | -0.42 |
| S&P Core Earnings | 1.12 | 0.48 | 0.83 | 1.27 | 0.02 | -0.64 | -2.49 | NA | NA | NA |
| Dividends | Nil | Nil | Nil | Nil | Nil | Nil | Nil | Nil | Nil | Nil |
| Payout Ratio | Nil | Nil | Nil | Nil | Nil | Nil | Nil | Nil | Nil | Nil |
| Prices:High | 101.09 | 48.58 | 50.00 | 57.82 | 61.15 | 25.00 | 22.38 | 91.50 | 113.00 | 60.31 |
| Prices:Low | 36.30 | 25.76 | 30.60 | 33.00 | 18.55 | 9.03 | 5.51 | 14.88 | 41.00 | 4.15 |
| P/E Ratio:High | 90 | NM | 64 | 42 | NM | NM | NM | NM | NM | NM |
| P/E Ratio:Low | 32 | NM | 39 | 24 | NM | NM | NM | NM | NM | NM |

### Income Statement Analysis (Million $)

| | 2007 | 2006 | 2005 | 2004 | 2003 | 2002 | 2001 | 2000 | 1999 | 1998 |
|---|---|---|---|---|---|---|---|---|---|---|
| Revenue | 14,835 | 10,711 | 8,490 | 6,921 | 5,264 | 3,933 | 3,122 | 2,762 | 1,640 | 610 |
| Operating Income | 926 | 629 | 553 | 508 | 349 | 193 | 35.1 | -257 | -346 | -55.2 |
| Depreciation | 271 | 205 | 121 | 75.7 | 78.3 | 87.8 | 266 | 406 | 253 | 56.8 |
| Interest Expense | 77.0 | 78.0 | 92.0 | 107 | 130 | 143 | 139 | 131 | 84.6 | 26.6 |
| Pretax Income | 660 | 377 | 428 | 356 | 35.3 | -150 | -557 | -1,411 | -720 | -125 |
| Effective Tax Rate | 27.9% | 49.6% | 22.2% | NM | NM | NM | NM | NM | NM | NM |
| Net Income | 476 | 190 | 333 | 588 | 35.3 | -150 | -557 | -1,411 | -720 | -125 |
| S&P Core Earnings | 476 | 203 | 354 | 539 | 10.3 | -242 | -910 | NA | NA | NA |

### Balance Sheet & Other Financial Data (Million $)

| | 2007 | 2006 | 2005 | 2004 | 2003 | 2002 | 2001 | 2000 | 1999 | 1998 |
|---|---|---|---|---|---|---|---|---|---|---|
| Cash | 3,112 | 2,019 | 2,000 | 1,779 | 1,395 | 1,301 | 997 | 1,101 | 706 | 373 |
| Current Assets | 5,164 | 3,373 | 2,929 | 2,539 | 1,821 | 1,616 | 1,208 | 1,361 | 1,012 | 424 |
| Total Assets | 6,485 | 4,363 | 3,696 | 3,249 | 2,162 | 1,990 | 1,638 | 2,135 | 2,472 | 648 |
| Current Liabilities | 3,714 | 2,532 | 1,929 | 1,620 | 1,253 | 1,066 | 921 | 975 | 739 | 162 |
| Long Term Debt | 1,282 | 1,247 | 1,521 | 1,855 | 1,945 | 2,277 | 2,156 | 2,127 | 1,466 | 348 |
| Common Equity | 1,197 | 431 | 246 | -227 | -1,036 | -1,353 | -1,440 | -967 | 266 | 139 |
| Total Capital | 2,479 | 1,678 | 1,767 | 1,628 | 909 | 924 | 716 | 1,160 | 1,733 | 487 |
| Capital Expenditures | 224 | 216 | 204 | 89.1 | 46.0 | 39.2 | 50.3 | 135 | 287 | 28.3 |
| Cash Flow | 747 | 395 | 454 | 664 | 114 | -62.2 | -291 | -1,005 | -1,015 | -67.7 |
| Current Ratio | 1.4 | 1.3 | 1.5 | 1.6 | 1.5 | 1.5 | 1.3 | 1.4 | 1.4 | 2.6 |
| % Long Term Debt of Capitalization | 51.7 | 74.3 | 86.1 | 113.9 | 213.9 | 246.3 | 301.1 | 183.4 | 84.6 | 71.5 |
| % Net Income of Revenue | 3.2 | 1.8 | 3.9 | 8.5 | 0.7 | NM | NM | NM | NM | NM |
| % Return on Assets | 8.8 | 4.7 | 9.6 | 21.8 | 1.7 | NM | NM | NM | NM | NM |
| % Return on Equity | 58.5 | 56.1 | NM | NM | NM | NM | NM | NM | NM | NM |

Data as orig reptd.; bef. results of disc opers/spec. items. Per share data adj. for stk. divs.; EPS diluted. E-Estimated. NA-Not Available. NM-Not Meaningful. NR-Not Ranked. UR-Under Review.

**Office:** 1200 12th Avenue South, Seattle, WA 98144-2734.
**Telephone:** 206-266-1000.
**Email:** ir@amazon.com
**Website:** http://www.amazon.com

**Chrmn, Pres & CEO:** J.P. Bezos
**COO:** M.A. Onetto
**SVP & CFO:** T.J. Szkutak
**SVP, Secy & General Counsel:** L.M. Wilson

**Chief Acctg Officer:** S.L. Reynolds
**Board Members:** T. A. Alberg, J. P. Bezos, J. S. Brown, J. Doerr, W. B. Gordon, M. S. Potter, T. O. Ryder, P. Q. Stonesifer

**Founded:** 1994
**Domicile:** Delaware
**Employees:** 17,000

# Ameren Corp

**STANDARD &POOR'S**

| **S&P Recommendation** BUY ★★★★☆ | **Price** $33.67 (as of Nov 14, 2008) | **12-Mo. Target Price** $39.00 | **Investment Style** Large-Cap Value |
|---|---|---|---|

**GICS Sector** Utilities
**Sub-Industry** Multi-Utilities

**Summary** Ameren is the holding company for the largest electric utility in the state of Missouri, and several utilities in Illinois.

## Key Stock Statistics (Source S&P, Vickers, company reports)

| | | | | | | | | |
|---|---|---|---|---|---|---|---|---|
| 52-Wk Range | $54.74–25.51 | S&P Oper. EPS 2008**E** | 2.90 | Market Capitalization(B) | $7.078 | Beta | 0.83 |
| Trailing 12-Month EPS | $3.14 | S&P Oper. EPS 2009**E** | 3.25 | Yield (%) | 7.54 | S&P 3-Yr. Proj. EPS CAGR(%) | 2 |
| Trailing 12-Month P/E | 10.7 | P/E on S&P Oper. EPS 2008**E** | 11.6 | Dividend Rate/Share | $2.54 | S&P Credit Rating | BBB- |
| $10K Invested 5 Yrs Ago | $9,891 | Common Shares Outstg. (M) | 210.2 | Institutional Ownership (%) | 60 | | |

## Price Performance

- 30-Week Mov. Avg. · · · 10-Week Mov. Avg. — **GAAP Earnings vs. Previous Year** Volume Above Avg. STARS
- 12-Mo. Target Price — Relative Strength — ▲ Up ▼ Down ► No Change Below Avg. ★

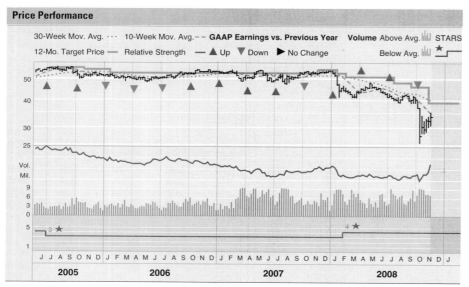

Options: P, Ph

Analysis prepared by **Justin McCann** on November 10, 2008, when the stock traded at **$ 32.56**.

## Highlights

► We expect EPS in 2008 to decline more than 13% from 2007 operating EPS of $3.34. Operating EPS in the first nine months of 2008 was down $0.20 from a year earlier, to $2.50, as higher generating margins were more than offset by milder weather and higher fuel prices for the utilities. We expect the Missouri utilities to earn about $1.21 a share in 2008, the Illinois utilities $0.23, and the generating segment $1.46.

► We believe earnings in 2009 will also be adversely affected by a weakening economy and rising operating costs related to AEE's regulated businesses. However we expect 2009 EPS to benefit from a recent rate increase in Illinois and one expected in early 2009 in Missouri. We see earnings from AEE's unregulated businesses remaining relatively flat through 2010.

► In August 2007, the governor of Illinois signed Senate Bill 1592, the electric rate compromise reached among state legislators, the attorney general, the state's utilities, and power marketers. Under the terms of the agreement, Ameren had to contribute $150 million to a $1 billion fund for rate relief programs aimed at mitigating the effect of the rate hikes that went into effect on January 2, 2007.

## Investment Rationale/Risk

► With the stock down about 40% year to date, and a well above peers yield from the dividend (recently at 7.8%), we believe the shares are attractive for above-average total return potential. In our view, the sharp drop reflects the crisis in the credit markets, an expected slowdown in the economy, the reduced earnings outlook, and the overall decline in the stock market. With the Illinois governor's signing of Senate Bill 1592, the uncertainties surrounding the electric rate settlement agreement were removed. Although Ameren's electric utility customers in Illinois were to receive benefits of $488 million, AEE only had to contribute about $150 million to the $1 billion rate relief fund.

► Risks to our recommendation and target price include a sharp decline in power supply margins, and a sharp drop in the average P/E ratio of AEE's peer group as a whole.

► While we do not expect Ameren's dividend to be increased (it has not been raised since 1997), we view it as stable, despite the above-average payout ratio of 88% of our EPS estimate for 2008. Our 12-month target price is $39, reflecting an approximate peer-level P/E of 12X our EPS forecast for 2009.

## Qualitative Risk Assessment

| LOW | MEDIUM | HIGH |
|---|---|---|

Our risk assessment reflects our expectation of steady cash flow from the company's regulated utilities, which have the benefit of fuel costs that, while rising, are still below the industry average. We believe that this, as well as the electric rate settlement agreement in Illinois, should help to offset the impact of the current crisis in the credit markets and an expected economic slowdown.

## Quantitative Evaluations

**S&P Quality Ranking** A-

| D | C | B- | B | B+ | A- | A | A+ |
|---|---|---|---|---|---|---|---|

**Relative Strength Rank** STRONG

83

LOWEST = 1    HIGHEST = 99

## Revenue/Earnings Data

**Revenue (Million $)**

| | 1Q | 2Q | 3Q | 4Q | Year |
|---|---|---|---|---|---|
| 2008 | 2,079 | 1,788 | 2,060 | -- | -- |
| 2007 | 2,019 | 1,723 | 1,997 | 1,807 | 7,380 |
| 2006 | 1,800 | 1,550 | 1,910 | 1,620 | 6,880 |
| 2005 | 1,626 | 1,586 | 1,868 | 1,701 | 6,780 |
| 2004 | 1,216 | 1,152 | 1,317 | 1,475 | 5,160 |
| 2003 | 1,108 | 1,088 | 1,350 | 1,047 | 4,593 |

**Earnings Per Share ($)**

| | | | | | |
|---|---|---|---|---|---|
| 2008 | 0.66 | 0.98 | 0.97 | E0.41 | E2.90 |
| 2007 | 0.59 | 0.69 | 1.18 | 0.52 | 2.98 |
| 2006 | 0.34 | 0.60 | 1.42 | 0.30 | 2.66 |
| 2005 | 0.62 | 0.93 | 1.37 | 0.21 | 3.13 |
| 2004 | 0.55 | 0.65 | 1.20 | 0.42 | 2.84 |
| 2003 | 0.52 | 0.68 | 1.70 | 0.24 | 3.14 |

Fiscal year ended Dec. 31. Next earnings report expected: Mid February. EPS Estimates based on S&P Operating Earnings; historical GAAP earnings are as reported.

## Dividend Data (Dates: mm/dd Payment Date: mm/dd/yy)

| Amount ($) | Date Decl. | Ex-Div. Date | Stk. of Record | Payment Date |
|---|---|---|---|---|
| 0.635 | 02/08 | 03/03 | 03/05 | 03/31/08 |
| 0.635 | 04/22 | 06/09 | 06/11 | 06/30/08 |
| 0.635 | 08/08 | 09/08 | 09/10 | 09/30/08 |
| 0.635 | 10/10 | 12/08 | 12/10 | 12/31/08 |

Dividends have been paid since 1906. Source: Company reports.

*The McGraw-Hill Companies*

# Ameren Corp

STANDARD
&POOR'S

## Business Summary November 10, 2008

CORPORATE OVERVIEW. Ameren Corporation (AEE) is a holding company that operates regulated electric and natural gas utilities and non-regulated operations, including energy marketing, trading and consulting services, in Missouri and Illinois. AEE's Utility Operations segment is comprised of its electric generation and electric and gas transmission and distribution operations. The company's subsidiaries include Union Electric Company (UE), Central Illinois Light Company (CILCO), Central Illinois Public Service Company (CIPS), Ameren Energy Generating Company (Genco), CILCORP Inc., and Illinois Power Company (IP). In 2007, electric services contributed 83.1% of total revenues while gas services contributed the rest.

CORPORATE STRATEGY. Although AEE has attempted to keep its rates low through disciplined cost control and efficient operations, the costs of nearly every aspect of its business have been rising at a rapid pace. Even after re-

cent rate increases, AmerenUE's electric rates are still about 40% below the national average. Since new customer rates are usually established on historical costs after an approximate one-year regulatory review, by the time they have been implemented they are already inadequate to fully recover the current costs and to earn a fair return on the company's investment. AEE has determined that in order to deal with this problem more effectively (and to avoid customer shock at a sudden sharp increase in rates), it intends to seek smaller and more frequent rate increases. It also plans to seek automatic cost recovery mechanisms for its most expensive items, such as its fuel costs and environmental investments.

## Company Financials Fiscal Year Ended Dec. 31

| Per Share Data ($) | 2007 | 2006 | 2005 | 2004 | 2003 | 2002 | 2001 | 2000 | 1999 | 1998 |
|---|---|---|---|---|---|---|---|---|---|---|
| Tangible Book Value | 27.48 | 26.80 | 25.08 | 24.92 | 23.19 | 24.95 | 24.26 | 23.34 | 22.55 | 22.27 |
| Earnings | 2.98 | 2.66 | 3.13 | 2.84 | 3.14 | 2.60 | 3.45 | 3.33 | 2.81 | 2.82 |
| S&P Core Earnings | 3.04 | 2.90 | 3.32 | 3.12 | 3.28 | 2.36 | 2.81 | NA | NA | NA |
| Dividends | 2.54 | 2.54 | 2.54 | 2.54 | 2.54 | 2.54 | 2.54 | 2.54 | 2.54 | 2.54 |
| Payout Ratio | 85% | 95% | 81% | 89% | 81% | 98% | 74% | 76% | 90% | 90% |
| Prices:High | 55.00 | 55.24 | 56.77 | 50.36 | 46.50 | 45.25 | 46.00 | 46.94 | 42.94 | 44.31 |
| Prices:Low | 47.10 | 47.96 | 47.51 | 40.55 | 42.55 | 34.72 | 36.53 | 27.56 | 32.00 | 35.56 |
| P/E Ratio:High | 18 | 21 | 18 | 18 | 15 | 17 | 13 | 14 | 15 | 16 |
| P/E Ratio:Low | 16 | 18 | 15 | 14 | 14 | 13 | 11 | 8 | 11 | 13 |
| **Income Statement Analysis** (Million $) | | | | | | | | | | |
| Revenue | 7,546 | 6,880 | 6,780 | 5,160 | 4,593 | 3,841 | 4,506 | 3,856 | 3,524 | 3,318 |
| Depreciation | 681 | 661 | 632 | 557 | 519 | 431 | 406 | 382 | 351 | 348 |
| Maintenance | NA | NA | NA | NA | NA | NA | 382 | 368 | 371 | 312 |
| Fixed Charges Coverage | 3.33 | 3.48 | 4.32 | 3.81 | 3.61 | 4.04 | 4.65 | 4.86 | 4.48 | NA |
| Construction Credits | NA | NA | NA | NA | 4.00 | 11.0 | 20.8 | 14.0 | 14.0 | 12.0 |
| Effective Tax Rate | 33.5% | 32.7% | 35.6% | 34.7% | 37.3% | 38.3% | 38.7% | 39.7% | 40.2% | 40.9% |
| Net Income | 629 | 558 | 628 | 530 | 506 | 382 | 475 | 457 | 385 | 386 |
| S&P Core Earnings | 632 | 597 | 666 | 582 | 530 | 347 | 387 | NA | NA | NA |
| **Balance Sheet & Other Financial Data** (Million $) | | | | | | | | | | |
| Gross Property | 23,484 | 22,013 | 20,800 | 20,291 | 17,511 | 15,745 | 14,962 | 13,910 | 13,056 | 12,531 |
| Capital Expenditures | 1,381 | 992 | 947 | 806 | 682 | 787 | 1,103 | 929 | 571 | 325 |
| Net Property | 15,069 | 14,286 | 13,572 | 13,297 | 10,917 | 8,914 | 8,427 | 7,706 | 7,165 | 6,928 |
| Capitalization:Long Term Debt | 5,902 | 5,498 | 5,568 | 5,236 | 4,273 | 3,626 | 3,071 | 2,980 | 2,683 | 2,525 |
| Capitalization:% Long Term Debt | 46.7 | 45.5 | 46.7 | 47.4 | 49.5 | 48.6 | 47.8 | 48.3 | 46.5 | 45.2 |
| Capitalization:Preferred | Nil | Nil | Nil | Nil | Nil | Nil | Nil | Nil | Nil | NA |
| Capitalization:% Preferred | Nil | Nil | Nil | Nil | Nil | Nil | Nil | Nil | Nil | NA |
| Capitalization:Common | 6,752 | 6,583 | 6,364 | 5,800 | 4,354 | 3,842 | 3,349 | 3,196 | 3,089 | 3,056 |
| Capitalization:% Common | 53.3 | 54.5 | 53.3 | 52.6 | 50.5 | 51.4 | 52.2 | 51.7 | 53.5 | 54.8 |
| Total Capital | 14,722 | 14,241 | 14,047 | 13,075 | 10,653 | 9,339 | 8,144 | 7,884 | 7,441 | 7,285 |
| % Operating Ratio | 86.6 | 87.1 | 86.3 | 84.6 | 83.9 | 81.0 | 85.2 | 83.4 | 84.1 | 82.8 |
| % Earned on Net Property | 9.1 | 8.4 | 9.6 | 8.9 | 10.7 | 7.2 | 8.2 | 8.6 | 8.0 | 8.2 |
| % Return on Revenue | 8.4 | 8.0 | 9.3 | 10.3 | 11.0 | 9.9 | 10.6 | 11.9 | 10.9 | 11.6 |
| % Return on Invested Capital | 7.5 | 6.6 | 7.0 | 6.9 | 7.4 | 8.1 | 8.6 | 8.5 | 7.7 | 11.3 |
| % Return on Common Equity | 9.3 | 8.4 | 10.3 | 10.4 | 12.3 | 10.6 | 14.5 | 14.5 | 12.5 | 12.7 |

Data as orig reptd.; bef. results of disc opers/spec. items. Per share data adj. for stk. divs.; EPS diluted. E-Estimated. NA-Not Available. NM-Not Meaningful. NR-Not Ranked. UR-Under Review.

**Office:** 1901 Chouteau Avenue, St. Louis, MO 63103.
**Telephone:** 314-621-3222.
**Email:** invest@ameren.com
**Website:** http://www.ameren.com

**Chrmn, Pres & CEO:** G.L. Rainwater
**COO & EVP:** T.R. Voss
**EVP & CFO:** W.L. Baxter
**SVP & Chief Admin Officer:** D.F. Cole

**SVP, Chief Acctg Officer & Cntlr:** M.J. Lyons
**Investor Contact:** B. Steinke (314-554-2574)
**Board Members:** S. F. Brauer, S. S. Elliott, W. J. Galvin, G. P. Jackson, J. C. Johnson, C. W. Mueller, D. R. Oberhelman, G. L. Rainwater, H. Saligman, P. T. Stokes, J. D. Woodard

**Founded:** 1881
**Domicile:** Missouri
**Employees:** 9,069

**STANDARD & POOR'S**

# American Capital Ltd

| S&P Recommendation | HOLD ★★★☆☆ | Price | 12-Mo. Target Price | Investment Style |
|---|---|---|---|---|
| | | $6.33 (as of Nov 14, 2008) | $12.00 | Large-Cap Growth |

**GICS Sector** Financials
**Sub-Industry** Asset Management & Custody Banks

**Summary** This buyout and mezzanine fund provides investment capital to middle-market companies.

## Key Stock Statistics (Source S&P, Vickers, company reports)

| | | | | | | | |
|---|---|---|---|---|---|---|---|
| 52-Wk Range | $39.06–5.53 | S&P Oper. EPS 2008E | 2.86 | Market Capitalization(B) | $1.310 | Beta | 0.92 |
| Trailing 12-Month EPS | $-8.39 | S&P Oper. EPS 2009E | 2.66 | Yield (%) | 64.61 | S&P 3-Yr. Proj. EPS CAGR(%) | -4 |
| Trailing 12-Month P/E | NM | P/E on S&P Oper. EPS 2008E | 2.2 | Dividend Rate/Share | $4.09 | S&P Credit Rating | NA |
| $10K Invested 5 Yrs Ago | $3,567 | Common Shares Outstg. (M) | 207.0 | Institutional Ownership (%) | 44 | | |

## Price Performance

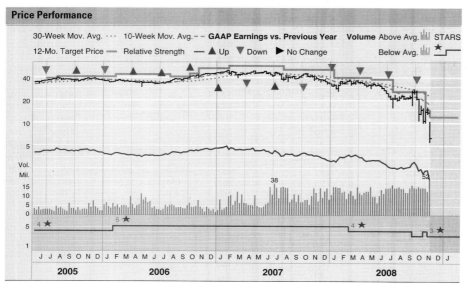

30-Week Mov. Avg. · · · 10-Week Mov. Avg. – – GAAP Earnings vs. Previous Year  Volume Above Avg. STARS
12-Mo. Target Price — Relative Strength — ▲ Up ▼ Down ► No Change  Below Avg. ★

Options: ASE, CBOE, P, Ph

Analysis prepared by **Matthew Albrecht** on November 14, 2008, when the stock traded at **$ 6.58**.

## Highlights

➤ We expect owned assets to decline during 2008, but we look for third-party assets under management to continue to grow through new fund introductions. Alternative assets managed through external funds totaled about $6.1 billion at the end of the third quarter, and have increased about 20% in the past year. Credit quality has deteriorated as the economy falters, and we expect the balance of loans on non-accrual and those past due to continue to increase into 2009. We expect portfolio income to remain at current levels, but a decrease in fee and other income should pressure the top line this year and next. We also anticipate continued pressure on ACAS's NAV due to realized and unrealized losses of the fair value of the portfolio.

➤ We think ACAS has done a good job controlling its operating costs base, and we think those expenses will decline in 2008 before advancing again in 2009, in line with business volume. Declining LIBOR rates should help keep interest costs down despite a rising debt balance.

➤ We forecast net operating EPS of $2.86 in 2008 and $2.66 in 2009.

## Investment Rationale/Risk

➤ We think the company has historically done well to provide value for shareholders, but current market conditions have caused it to rethink its dividend policy and preserve capital. ACAS will only pay a deemed dividend for the remainder of 2008, providing investors with an increased cost basis and a tax credit, and has only committed to pay its spillover 2008 taxable income in 2009, which we expect will amount to approximately $1.35 a share. We think the recent price accurately reflects a difficult operating environment and a decline in total return potential, and we would not add to positions.

➤ Risks to our recommendation and target price include potential credit deterioration, increased competition for new investments, the illiquid nature of ACAS's investments, and difficulty accurately valuing these investments.

➤ Our 12-month target price of $12 is equal to 0.5X our 12-month projected NAV per share. We think continued pressure on the shares is possible due to concerns in the market about the availability of funds amid a credit crunch for new investment activity.

## Qualitative Risk Assessment

| LOW | MEDIUM | HIGH |
|---|---|---|

Our risk assessment for ACAS reflects our view of the illiquid nature of many of the company's investments, the difficulty in placing an accurate value on these investments, and the uncertain timing around realized investment gains. We think this is offset by ACAS's diversified portfolio and track record of consistent dividend growth.

## Quantitative Evaluations

**S&P Quality Ranking**                    **B**

| D | C | B- | B | B+ | A- | A | A+ |
|---|---|---|---|---|---|---|---|

**Relative Strength Rank**                **WEAK**

6

LOWEST = 1                                  HIGHEST = 99

## Revenue/Earnings Data

**Revenue (Million $)**

| | 1Q | 2Q | 3Q | 4Q | Year |
|---|---|---|---|---|---|
| 2008 | 292.0 | 263.0 | 278.0 | -- | -- |
| 2007 | 250.0 | 326.0 | 310.0 | 354.0 | 1,240 |
| 2006 | 173.0 | 212.0 | 231.0 | 244.0 | 860.0 |
| 2005 | 100.9 | 131.7 | 148.8 | 173.2 | 554.5 |
| 2004 | 66.53 | 75.58 | 82.27 | 111.7 | 336.1 |
| 2003 | 43.06 | 43.21 | 53.32 | 66.69 | 206.3 |

**Earnings Per Share ($)**

| | 1Q | 2Q | 3Q | 4Q | Year |
|---|---|---|---|---|---|
| 2008 | -4.16 | -0.34 | -2.63 | E0.65 | E2.86 |
| 2007 | 0.86 | 4.68 | 0.11 | -1.27 | 3.96 |
| 2006 | 1.33 | 2.16 | 0.92 | 2.10 | 6.55 |
| 2005 | 1.22 | 0.82 | 0.90 | 0.71 | 3.60 |
| 2004 | 0.51 | 1.22 | 0.74 | 1.11 | 3.63 |
| 2003 | -0.02 | 0.48 | 0.48 | 1.07 | 2.15 |

Fiscal year ended Dec. 31. Next earnings report expected: Mid February. EPS Estimates based on S&P Operating Earnings; historical GAAP earnings are as reported.

## Dividend Data (Dates: mm/dd Payment Date: mm/dd/yy)

| Amount ($) | Date Decl. | Ex-Div. Date | Stk. of Record | Payment Date |
|---|---|---|---|---|
| 1.000 | 10/30 | 12/05 | 12/07 | 01/16/08 |
| 1.010 | 02/13 | 03/05 | 03/07 | 04/01/08 |
| 1.030 | 05/06 | 06/11 | 06/13 | 07/01/08 |
| 1.050 | 08/05 | 10/02 | 10/06 | 10/14/08 |

Dividends have been paid since 1997. Source: Company reports.

---

**Please read the Required Disclosures and Analyst Certification on the last page of this report.**

The McGraw-Hill Companies

# American Capital Ltd

STANDARD &POOR'S

## Business Summary November 14, 2008

CORPORATE OVERVIEW. American Capital Strategies Ltd. is a publicly traded buyout and mezzanine fund that provides investment capital to middle-market companies. American Capital is an equity partner in management and employee buyouts; provides mezzanine and senior debt financing for buyouts led by private equity firms; and supplies capital to private and small public companies to fund growth, acquisitions, and recapitalizations. ACAS's wholly owned operating subsidiary, American Capital Financial Services, Inc. (ACFS), provides financial advisory services to portfolio companies.

ACAS completed its IPO in August 1997, becoming a non-diversified, closed-end investment company; it elected to be regulated as a business development company, or BDC. ACAS began operations in October 1997 in order to qualify to be taxed as a regulated investment company (RIC). It is not subject to federal income tax on the portion of its taxable income and capital gains that it distributes to its stockholders.

Since its August 1997 IPO, ACAS has invested over $21 billion in debt and equity securities in middle-market companies. The company's portfolio includes services, transportation, construction, wholesale, retail, health care, and industrial, consumer, chemical and food products. At the end of 2007, ACAS's portfolio consisted of investments in 219 companies with an average investment size of $50 million. ACAS's largest concentration of investments was in the commercial services and supplies industry, making up 10% of the portfolio, followed by household durables and real estate, representing 8% and 7% of the portfolio, respectively. At the end of 2007, the company had about 684 employees, with 266 investment professionals actively engaged in the origination and approval process of its investing activities.

CORPORATE STRATEGY. ACAS generally focuses on middle-market companies that have been in business over 10 years, have positive cash flow, and have a significant market share in their products or services. As of December 31, 2007, the company's portfolio had an average age of 29 years, with sales in the most recent 12 months of $153 million and EBITDA of $30 million. ACAS generally invests between $5 million and $800 million in its North American targets and 55 million euros and 500 million euros in its European targets.

## Company Financials Fiscal Year Ended Dec. 31

| Per Share Data ($) | 2007 | 2006 | 2005 | 2004 | 2003 | 2002 | 2001 | 2000 | 1999 | 1998 |
|---|---|---|---|---|---|---|---|---|---|---|
| Tangible Book Value | 32.88 | 29.42 | 24.37 | 21.11 | 17.83 | 15.82 | 16.84 | 15.90 | 17.08 | 13.78 |
| Cash Flow | 3.96 | 6.54 | 3.60 | 3.63 | 2.15 | 0.50 | 0.58 | -0.19 | 5.33 | 1.53 |
| Earnings | 3.96 | 6.55 | 3.60 | 3.63 | 2.15 | 0.50 | 0.58 | -0.19 | 6.80 | 1.48 |
| S&P Core Earnings | 3.57 | 6.55 | 3.59 | 3.59 | 1.65 | 0.88 | 0.04 | NA | NA | NA |
| Dividends | 3.72 | 3.33 | 3.05 | 2.85 | 2.79 | 2.57 | 2.30 | 2.17 | 1.74 | 1.34 |
| Payout Ratio | 94% | 51% | 85% | 79% | 130% | NM | NM | NM | 27% | 88% |
| Prices:High | 49.96 | 46.45 | 39.61 | 34.91 | 30.00 | 32.98 | 29.89 | 27.75 | 23.13 | 24.63 |
| Prices:Low | 32.36 | 29.65 | 29.51 | 24.70 | 20.75 | 15.17 | 21.88 | 19.81 | 14.00 | 9.19 |
| P/E Ratio:High | 13 | 7 | 11 | 10 | 14 | 66 | 52 | NM | 3 | 17 |
| P/E Ratio:Low | 8 | 5 | 8 | 7 | 10 | 30 | 38 | NM | 2 | 6 |

| Income Statement Analysis (Million $) | 2007 | 2006 | 2005 | 2004 | 2003 | 2002 | 2001 | 2000 | 1999 | 1998 |
|---|---|---|---|---|---|---|---|---|---|---|
| Loan Fees | 241 | 191 | 129 | 64.9 | 47.0 | 25.0 | 15.6 | 11.3 | 2.57 | 2.55 |
| Interest Income | 999 | 669 | 426 | 271 | 159 | 122 | 88.3 | 58.0 | 30.8 | 14.4 |
| Total Revenue | 1,240 | 1,033 | 554 | 336 | 206 | 147 | 104 | 70.0 | 33.4 | 17.0 |
| Interest Expense | 287 | 190 | 101 | 36.9 | 18.5 | 14.3 | 10.3 | 9.69 | 4.72 | 0.06 |
| % Expense/Operating Revenue | 51.6% | 41.0% | 38.6% | 33.9% | 28.7% | 35.2% | 31.3% | 22.8% | 21.7% | 10.1% |
| Pretax Income | 706 | 906 | 377 | 284 | 118 | 20.1 | 18.6 | -4.37 | 97.2 | 16.9 |
| Effective Tax Rate | 0.85% | 1.21% | 3.31% | 0.75% | NM | NM | NM | NM | NM | NM |
| Net Income | 700 | 895 | 365 | 281 | 118 | 20.1 | 18.6 | -4.37 | 97.2 | 16.9 |
| S&P Core Earnings | 631 | 895 | 364 | 279 | 90.5 | 35.0 | 1.40 | NA | NA | NA |

| Balance Sheet & Other Financial Data (Million $) | 2007 | 2006 | 2005 | 2004 | 2003 | 2002 | 2001 | 2000 | 1999 | 1998 |
|---|---|---|---|---|---|---|---|---|---|---|
| Net Property | Nil | Nil | Nil | Nil | Nil | Nil | Nil | Nil | Nil | Nil |
| Cash & Securities | 143 | 77.0 | 5,216 | 3,280 | 1,920 | 1,262 | 877 | 594 | 384 | 96.1 |
| Loans | Nil | Nil | Nil | Nil | Nil | Nil | Nil | Nil | Nil | Nil |
| Total Assets | 11,732 | 8,609 | 5,449 | 3,491 | 2,042 | 1,319 | 904 | 615 | 395 | 270 |
| Capitalization:Debt | 4,557 | 3,573 | 2,286 | 1,430 | 772 | 323 | 103 | 87.2 | Nil | Nil |
| Capitalization:Equity | 6,441 | 4,342 | 2,957 | 1,872 | 1,176 | 688 | 640 | 445 | 312 | 153 |
| Capitalization:Total | 10,998 | 7,915 | 5,243 | 3,303 | 1,948 | 1,011 | 744 | 532 | 312 | 153 |
| Price Times Book Value:High | 1.5 | 1.6 | 1.6 | 1.7 | 1.7 | 2.1 | 1.8 | 1.7 | 1.4 | 1.8 |
| Price Times Book Value:Low | 0.9 | 1.0 | 1.2 | 1.2 | 1.2 | 1.0 | 1.3 | 1.2 | 0.8 | 0.7 |
| Cash Flow | 700 | 895 | 365 | 281 | 118 | 20.1 | 18.6 | -4.37 | 97.2 | 16.9 |
| % Return on Revenue | 56.5 | 86.6 | 65.8 | 83.7 | 57.3 | 15.9 | 17.8 | NM | 291.0 | 99.6 |
| % Return on Assets | 6.9 | 12.7 | 8.2 | 10.1 | 7.0 | 1.8 | 2.5 | NM | 29.2 | 8.0 |
| % Return on Equity | 13.0 | 24.7 | 15.0 | 18.5 | 12.6 | 3.0 | 3.4 | NM | 41.9 | 11.2 |

Data as orig reptd.; bef. results of disc opers/spec. items. Per share data adj. for stk. divs.; EPS diluted. E-Estimated. NA-Not Available. NM-Not Meaningful. NR-Not Ranked. UR-Under Review.

**Office:** 2 Bethesda Metro Ctr 14th Floor, Bethesda, MD 20814-6319.
**Telephone:** 301-951-6122.
**Email:** info@American-Capital.com
**Website:** http://www.americancapital.com

**Chrmn & CEO:** M. Wilkus
**COO:** G.J. O'Brien
**EVP, Secy & General Counsel:** S.A. Flax
**CFO, Chief Acctg Officer & Treas:** J.R. Erickson

**CTO:** M. Arnone
**Investor Contact:** A. Cuthbertson (301-951-5917)
**Board Members:** R. L. Albritton, M. C. Baskin, N. M. Hahl, P. R. Harper, J. A. Koskinen, S. Lundine, K. D. Peterson, Jr., E. L. Podsiadlo, A. N. Puryear, M. Wilkus

**Founded:** 1986
**Domicile:** Delaware
**Employees:** 619

# American Electric Power Co Inc

**STANDARD &POOR'S**

**S&P Recommendation** BUY ★★★★☆

| Price | 12-Mo. Target Price | Investment Style |
|---|---|---|
| $30.95 (as of Nov 14, 2008) | $38.00 | Large-Cap Value |

**GICS Sector** Utilities
**Sub-Industry** Electric Utilities

**Summary** This Ohio-based electric utility holding company has subsidiaries operating in 11 states in the U.S.

## Key Stock Statistics (Source S&P, Vickers, company reports)

| | | | | | | | |
|---|---|---|---|---|---|---|---|
| 52-Wk Range | $49.49– 25.54 | S&P Oper. EPS 2008E | 3.15 | Market Capitalization(B) | $12.490 | Beta | 0.76 |
| Trailing 12-Month EPS | $3.62 | S&P Oper. EPS 2009E | 3.25 | Yield (%) | 5.30 | S&P 3-Yr. Proj. EPS CAGR(%) | 6 |
| Trailing 12-Month P/E | 8.6 | P/E on S&P Oper. EPS 2008E | 9.8 | Dividend Rate/Share | $1.64 | S&P Credit Rating | BBB |
| $10K Invested 5 Yrs Ago | $13,810 | Common Shares Outstg. (M) | 403.6 | Institutional Ownership (%) | 73 | | |

## Price Performance

30-Week Mov. Avg. · · · 10-Week Mov. Avg. – – **GAAP Earnings vs. Previous Year** Volume Above Avg. STARS
12-Mo. Target Price — Relative Strength — ▲ Up ▼ Down ► No Change Below Avg. ★

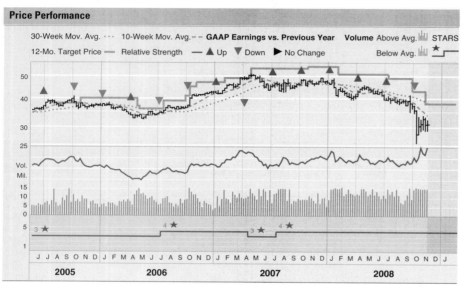

Options: ASE, CBOE, P, Ph

Analysis prepared by **Justin McCann** on November 04, 2008, when the stock traded at **$ 32.60**.

### Highlights

➤ We expect operating EPS in 2008 to increase about 5% from 2007 operating EPS of $3.00. Results in the first nine months of 2008 were aided by rate increases, higher net transmission revenues and offsystem sales, and the recovery of costs related to two ice storms in 2007. This was partially offset by mild summer weather, higher storm-related expenses, and the impact of an oil spill and floods on the barge business.

➤ For 2009, we expect operating EPS to increase about 3% from anticipated results in 2008. We believe the contraction in the economy and the capital markets will partially offset the benefit of higher net transmission revenues and expected base rate increases in Virginia, Oklahoma and Indiana. Rulings on the requested rate increases are expected by this December for Virginia, in the first quarter of 2009 for Oklahoma, and in June 2009 for Indiana.

➤ We expect AEP's longer-term annual EPS growth rate to range between 5% and 9%, with results driven by rate base investments in the company's generation and transmission operations. AEP plans to reduce greenhouse gas emissions to 6% below a baseline average of 1998 to 2001 emission levels by 2010.

### Investment Rationale/Risk

➤ Although the stock is down about 30% year-to-date, we believe it will recover and realize above-average total return. We believe the decline has reflected the crisis in the financial markets, an investor shift out of electric utilities and the potential impact of an economic slowdown. There have also been concerns over the potential impact of probable greenhouse gas legislation. However, we do not expect any significant financial impact until after 2020, and we believe AEP's substantial environmental investments will smooth the transition.

➤ Risks to our recommendation and target price include the potential for weaker than anticipated results from the wholesale operations, and a sharp decline in the average P/E multiple of the group as a whole.

➤ Reflecting its improved financial profile, AEP increased its quarterly dividend by $0.02 a share (5.1%) effective with the December 2007 payment. This helped to bring the current yield (recently at 5.1%) in line with the recent average for AEP's electric utility peers (5.1%). We expect the shares to trade at a discount-to-peers P/E of 11.7X our EPS estimate for 2009. Our 12-month target price is $38.

### Qualitative Risk Assessment

| LOW | MEDIUM | HIGH |
|---|---|---|

Our risk assessment reflects our view of the steady cash flow expected from the regulated utilities, with their low-cost fuel sources and generally supportive regulatory environments. The proceeds from the divestiture of most of AEP's high-risk unregulated energy businesses were used to enhance its balance sheet and financial strength.

### Quantitative Evaluations

**S&P Quality Ranking**    B

| D | C | B- | B | B+ | A- | A | A+ |
|---|---|---|---|---|---|---|---|

**Relative Strength Rank**    STRONG

74

LOWEST = 1      HIGHEST = 99

### Revenue/Earnings Data

**Revenue (Million $)**

| | 1Q | 2Q | 3Q | 4Q | Year |
|---|---|---|---|---|---|
| 2008 | 3,467 | 3,546 | 4,191 | -- | -- |
| 2007 | 3,169 | 3,146 | 3,789 | 3,276 | 13,380 |
| 2006 | 3,108 | 2,936 | 3,594 | 2,984 | 12,622 |
| 2005 | 3,065 | 2,819 | 3,328 | 2,899 | 12,111 |
| 2004 | 3,364 | 3,408 | 3,780 | 3,505 | 14,057 |
| 2003 | 3,834 | 3,451 | 3,940 | 3,320 | 14,545 |

**Earnings Per Share ($)**

| | | | | | |
|---|---|---|---|---|---|
| 2008 | 1.43 | 0.70 | 0.93 | E0.49 | E3.15 |
| 2007 | 0.68 | 0.64 | 1.02 | 0.52 | 2.86 |
| 2006 | 0.95 | 0.43 | 0.67 | 0.44 | 2.50 |
| 2005 | 0.90 | 0.57 | 0.94 | 0.23 | 2.63 |
| 2004 | 0.73 | 0.38 | 1.04 | 0.69 | 2.85 |
| 2003 | 0.83 | 0.47 | 0.75 | -0.65 | 1.35 |

Fiscal year ended Dec. 31. Next earnings report expected: Late January. EPS Estimates based on S&P Operating Earnings; historical GAAP earnings are as reported.

### Dividend Data (Dates: mm/dd Payment Date: mm/dd/yy)

| Amount ($) | Date Decl. | Ex-Div. Date | Stk. of Record | Payment Date |
|---|---|---|---|---|
| 0.410 | 01/23 | 02/06 | 02/08 | 03/10/08 |
| 0.410 | 04/22 | 05/07 | 05/09 | 06/10/08 |
| 0.410 | 07/23 | 08/06 | 08/08 | 09/10/08 |
| 0.410 | 10/28 | 11/06 | 11/10 | 12/10/08 |

Dividends have been paid since 1909. Source: Company reports.

---

**Please read the Required Disclosures and Analyst Certification on the last page of this report.**

*The McGraw-Hill Companies*

# American Electric Power Co Inc

**STANDARD &POOR'S**

## Business Summary November 04, 2008

CORPORATE OVERVIEW. AEP is a holding company that primarily operates electric utility services through its regulated subsidiaries. The utility services include the generation, transmission and distribution of electricity for sale to retail and wholesale customers in the U.S. AEP's non-regulated operations include the MEMCO Barge Line subsidiary, which is engaged in the transportation of coal and dry bulk commodities, mainly on the Ohio, Illinois and lower Mississippi rivers. In 2007, the utility segment accounted for 90.4% of total revenues.

CORPORATE STRATEGY. AEP's strategy is to focus on its core utility operations and to deliver low-cost electric power to the communities served. The company plans to improve its efficiency and to maximize the power that is delivered from its generation facilities. In order to provide safe and reliable power, AEP is making investments to upgrade its transmission and distribution in-

frastructure, as well as to be in compliance with the appropriate environmental standards. In January 2007, AEP signed a participation agreement with MidAmerican Energy Holdings to form a joint venture company, Electric Transmission Texas (ETT), to fund, own and operate electric transmission assets in Texas. On December 21, 2007, the Public Utility Commission of Texas (PUCT) approved the joint venture (which is 50%-owned by both AEP and MidAmerican) as a transmission-only utility within the Electric Reliability Council of Texas (ERCOT)

## Company Financials Fiscal Year Ended Dec. 31

| Per Share Data ($) | 2007 | 2006 | 2005 | 2004 | 2003 | 2002 | 2001 | 2000 | 1999 | 1998 |
|---|---|---|---|---|---|---|---|---|---|---|
| Tangible Book Value | 25.17 | 24.88 | 22.87 | 21.31 | 19.74 | 19.67 | 20.92 | 20.72 | 25.80 | 25.21 |
| Earnings | 2.86 | 2.50 | 2.63 | 2.85 | 1.35 | 0.06 | 3.11 | 0.94 | 2.69 | 2.81 |
| S&P Core Earnings | 2.77 | 2.35 | 2.26 | 2.58 | 1.47 | 0.07 | 2.17 | NA | NA | NA |
| Dividends | 1.58 | 1.50 | 1.42 | 1.40 | 1.65 | 2.40 | 2.40 | 2.40 | 2.40 | 2.40 |
| Payout Ratio | 58% | 60% | 54% | 49% | NM | NM | 77% | 255% | 89% | 85% |
| Prices:High | 51.24 | 43.13 | 40.80 | 35.53 | 31.51 | 48.80 | 51.20 | 48.94 | 48.19 | 53.31 |
| Prices:Low | 41.67 | 32.27 | 32.25 | 28.50 | 19.01 | 15.10 | 39.25 | 25.94 | 30.56 | 42.06 |
| P/E Ratio:High | 19 | 17 | 16 | 12 | 23 | NM | 16 | 52 | 18 | 19 |
| P/E Ratio:Low | 15 | 13 | 12 | 10 | 14 | NM | 13 | 28 | 11 | 15 |

| Income Statement Analysis (Million $) | 2007 | 2006 | 2005 | 2004 | 2003 | 2002 | 2001 | 2000 | 1999 | 1998 |
|---|---|---|---|---|---|---|---|---|---|---|
| Revenue | 13,380 | 12,622 | 12,111 | 14,057 | 14,545 | 14,555 | 61,257 | 13,694 | 6,916 | 6,346 |
| Depreciation | 1,513 | 1,467 | 1,318 | 1,300 | 1,299 | 1,377 | 1,383 | 1,062 | 600 | 580 |
| Maintenance | NA | NA | NA | NA | NA | NA | NA | NA | NA | 543 |
| Fixed Charges Coverage | 2.96 | 2.96 | 2.80 | 2.60 | 2.97 | 2.84 | 2.64 | 1.95 | 2.44 | 2.98 |
| Construction Credits | 33.0 | 30.0 | 21.0 | NA | NA | NA | NA | NA | NA | NA |
| Effective Tax Rate | 31.0% | 32.7% | 29.4% | 33.7% | 39.8% | 79.3% | 35.9% | 66.4% | 33.3% | 37.1% |
| Net Income | 1,147 | 995 | 1,029 | 1,127 | 522 | 21.0 | 1,003 | 302 | 520 | 536 |
| S&P Core Earnings | 1,107 | 934 | 883 | 1,021 | 573 | 21.1 | 698 | NA | NA | NA |

| Balance Sheet & Other Financial Data (Million $) | 2007 | 2006 | 2005 | 2004 | 2003 | 2002 | 2001 | 2000 | 1999 | 1998 |
|---|---|---|---|---|---|---|---|---|---|---|
| Gross Property | 46,145 | 42,021 | 39,121 | 37,286 | 36,033 | 37,857 | 40,709 | 38,088 | 22,205 | 20,146 |
| Capital Expenditures | 3,556 | 3,528 | 2,404 | 1,693 | 1,358 | 1,722 | 1,832 | 1,773 | 867 | 792 |
| Net Property | 29,870 | 26,781 | 24,284 | 22,801 | 22,029 | 21,684 | 24,543 | 22,393 | 13,055 | 11,730 |
| Capitalization:Long Term Debt | 14,263 | 12,490 | 11,073 | 11,069 | 12,459 | 9,329 | 10,230 | 10,097 | 6,500 | 6,974 |
| Capitalization:% Long Term Debt | 58.6 | 57.0 | 54.9 | 56.5 | 61.3 | 56.9 | 55.4 | 55.6 | 56.5 | 59.0 |
| Capitalization:Preferred | Nil | Nil | Nil | Nil | Nil | Nil | Nil | Nil | Nil | Nil |
| Capitalization:% Preferred | Nil | Nil | Nil | Nil | Nil | Nil | Nil | Nil | Nil | Nil |
| Capitalization:Common | 10,079 | 9,412 | 9,088 | 8,515 | 7,874 | 7,064 | 8,229 | 8,054 | 5,006 | 4,841 |
| Capitalization:% Common | 41.4 | 43.0 | 45.1 | 43.5 | 38.7 | 43.1 | 44.6 | 44.4 | 43.5 | 41.0 |
| Total Capital | 29,072 | 26,802 | 25,032 | 24,403 | 24,290 | 21,523 | 24,523 | 23,554 | 14,577 | 14,767 |
| % Operating Ratio | 86.5 | 87.2 | 84.1 | 85.8 | 88.8 | 91.3 | 96.1 | 85.2 | 81.1 | 84.9 |
| % Earned on Net Property | 8.2 | 7.7 | 8.2 | 8.9 | 7.7 | 5.8 | 10.2 | 9.2 | 10.1 | 8.2 |
| % Return on Revenue | 8.6 | 7.9 | 8.5 | 8.0 | 3.6 | 0.1 | 1.6 | 2.2 | 7.5 | 8.4 |
| % Return on Invested Capital | 7.1 | 7.5 | 6.2 | 6.1 | 9.4 | 8.8 | 8.4 | 6.8 | 7.2 | 7.0 |
| % Return on Common Equity | 1.0 | 10.7 | 11.7 | 13.8 | 7.0 | 0.3 | 12.3 | 3.6 | 10.6 | 11.3 |

Data as orig reptd.; bef. results of disc opers/spec. items. Per share data adj. for stk. divs.; EPS diluted. E-Estimated. NA-Not Available. NM-Not Meaningful. NR-Not Ranked. UR-Under Review.

**Office:** 1 Riverside Plz, Columbus , OH 43215-2373.
**Telephone:** 614-716-1000.
**Email:** corpcomm@aep.com
**Website:** http://www.aep.com

**Chrmn, Pres & CEO:** M.G. Morris
**COO:** C.L. English
**EVP & CFO:** H.K. Koeppel
**SVP, Chief Acctg Officer & Cntlr:** J.M. Buonaiuto

**SVP & Treas:** C.E. Zebula
**Investor Contact:** B. Rozsa (614-716-2840)
**Board Members:** E. R. Brooks, D. M. Carlton, R. D. Crosby, Jr., J. P. DesBarres, L. A. Goodspeed, T. E. Hoaglin, L. A. Hudson, Jr., M. G. Morris, L. L. Nowell, III, R. L. Sandor, K. D. Sullivan, J. F. Turner

**Founded:** 1906
**Domicile:** New York
**Employees:** 20,861

# American Express Co

STANDARD
&POOR'S

| S&P Recommendation | HOLD ★★★☆☆ | Price $19.99 (as of Nov 14, 2008) | 12-Mo. Target Price $30.00 | Investment Style Large-Cap Growth |
|---|---|---|---|---|

**GICS Sector** Financials
**Sub-Industry** Consumer Finance

**Summary** American Express is a leading global payments, network, and travel company.

## Key Stock Statistics (Source S&P, Vickers, company reports)

| | | | | | | | |
|---|---|---|---|---|---|---|---|
| 52-Wk Range | $59.79– 16.55 | S&P Oper. EPS 2008**E** | 2.74 | Market Capitalization(B) | $23.186 | Beta | 1.39 |
| Trailing 12-Month EPS | $2.82 | S&P Oper. EPS 2009**E** | 2.55 | Yield (%) | 3.60 | S&P 3-Yr. Proj. EPS CAGR(%) | 2 |
| Trailing 12-Month P/E | 7.1 | P/E on S&P Oper. EPS 2008**E** | 7.3 | Dividend Rate/Share | $0.72 | S&P Credit Rating | A+ |
| $10K Invested 5 Yrs Ago | NA | Common Shares Outstg. (M) | 1,159.9 | Institutional Ownership (%) | 81 | | |

## Price Performance

30-Week Mov. Avg. · · · 10-Week Mov. Avg. - - **GAAP Earnings vs. Previous Year** Volume Above Avg. ▌▍▎ STARS
12-Mo. Target Price — Relative Strength — ▲ Up ▼ Down ▶ No Change Below Avg. ▌▍▎ ★

Options: ASE, CBOE, P, Ph

Analysis prepared by **Stuart Plesser** on October 23, 2008, when the stock traded at **$ 23.53**.

## Highlights

➤ We expect 2009 revenue growth of roughly 5%, falling short of the company's long-term target of 8%, mainly from lower spending and a concerted effort by AXP to cutback on outstanding credit lines. We see sales slowing in the U.S and internationally, with growth coming largely from AXP's commercial and merchant servicer segments. We anticipate lower marketing and promotional expenses in 2009 to offset slower cardmember spending. Given U.S. credit deterioration, we think the Global Network & Merchant services division will be the most profitable business in 2009.

➤ We forecast an increase in interest expense and lower securitization volume that will likely crimp margins. We forecast an increase in the provision for losses, due largely to rising write-off and delinquency rates, exacerbated by what we believe will be higher unemployment rates. With reserves totaling 5.7% of owned loans in the second quarter, versus 5.2% in the previous quarter, we think AXP is adequately reserved.

➤ We see EPS of $2.74 in 2008, versus $3.39 in 2007. In 2009, we look for EPS of $2.55.

## Investment Rationale/Risk

➤ We view positively AXP's strong brand name, customer loyalty, and growth prospects. The company's closed loop network helps increase AXP's value to its merchant partners, in our view. However, we believe weakening international economies will dampen consumer spending and lead to rising chargeoffs in 2009. We also are concerned of higher funding costs and liquidity should the credit markets remain in turmoil for an extended period of time. As such, we believe AXP should trade at the low end of its historical multiple range.

➤ Risks to our recommendation and target price include an inability to secure funding, a larger-than-expected slowdown in consumer spending and business spending, and a rise in unemployment beyond our expectations that would pressure credit quality.

➤ Our 12-month target price of $30 values the stock at 11.8X our 2009 EPS estimate of $2.55, a discount to its historical P/E. We think this is an appropriate valuation multiple based on our view of deteriorating credit and possible liquidity issues.

## Qualitative Risk Assessment

| LOW | MEDIUM | HIGH |
|---|---|---|

Our risk assessment reflects what we see as solid business fundamentals and a strong customer base. We view AXP as able to withstand a major global or U.S. economic downturn, and we consider its credit quality to be solid.

## Quantitative Evaluations

**S&P Quality Ranking** A-

| D | C | B- | B | B+ | A- | A | A+ |
|---|---|---|---|---|---|---|---|

**Relative Strength Rank** WEAK

29

LOWEST = 1 HIGHEST = 99

## Revenue/Earnings Data

**Revenue (Million $)**

| | 1Q | 2Q | 3Q | 4Q | Year |
|---|---|---|---|---|---|
| 2008 | 8,105 | 8,340 | 8,007 | -- | -- |
| 2007 | 7,631 | 8,199 | 7,953 | 7,364 | 31,557 |
| 2006 | 6,319 | 6,850 | 6,759 | 7,208 | 27,136 |
| 2005 | 5,672 | 6,090 | 6,068 | 6,437 | 24,267 |
| 2004 | 6,910 | 7,232 | 7,202 | 7,771 | 29,115 |
| 2003 | 6,023 | 6,356 | 6,419 | 7,068 | 25,866 |

**Earnings Per Share ($)**

| | 1Q | 2Q | 3Q | 4Q | Year |
|---|---|---|---|---|---|
| 2008 | 0.84 | 0.56 | 0.74 | E0.58 | E2.74 |
| 2007 | 0.88 | 0.88 | 0.90 | 0.71 | 3.39 |
| 2006 | 0.70 | 0.78 | 0.78 | 0.76 | 3.01 |
| 2005 | 0.59 | 0.69 | 0.69 | 0.60 | 2.56 |
| 2004 | 0.66 | 0.68 | 0.69 | 0.71 | 2.74 |
| 2003 | 0.53 | 0.59 | 0.59 | 0.60 | 2.31 |

Fiscal year ended Dec. 31. Next earnings report expected: Late January. EPS Estimates based on S&P Operating Earnings; historical GAAP earnings are as reported.

## Dividend Data (Dates: mm/dd Payment Date: mm/dd/yy)

| Amount ($) | Date Decl. | Ex-Div. Date | Stk. of Record | Payment Date |
|---|---|---|---|---|
| 0.180 | 11/19 | 01/02 | 01/04 | 02/08/08 |
| 0.180 | 03/31 | 04/09 | 04/11 | 05/09/08 |
| 0.180 | 05/19 | 07/09 | 07/11 | 08/08/08 |
| 0.180 | 09/22 | 10/01 | 10/03 | 11/10/08 |

Dividends have been paid since 1870. Source: Company reports.

---

**Please read the Required Disclosures and Analyst Certification on the last page of this report.**

The McGraw-Hill Companies

# American Express Co

**STANDARD &POOR'S**

## Business Summary October 23, 2008

CORPORATE OVERVIEW. AXP is a leading global payments, network, and travel company. Its businesses are organized into two customer-focused groups, the global consumer group and the global business-to-business group. Accordingly, U.S. card services and international card services are aligned within the global consumer group and global commercial services and global network & merchant services are alligned within the global business-to-business group.

U.S. Card Services includes the U.S. proprietary consumer card business, OPEN from American Express, the global Travelers Cheques and Prepaid Services business, and the American Express U.S. Consumer Travel Network.

International Card Services issue proprietary consumer and small business cards outside the U.S.

Global Commercial Services offers global corporate payment and travel-related products and services to large and midsized companies. It offers four primary products and services: Corporate Card, issued to individuals through a corporate account established by their employer and designed primarily for travel and entertainment spending; Corporate Purchasing Solutions, an account established by corporations to pay for everyday business expenses

such as office and computer supplies; S2SSM suite of products, which include electronic solutions for companies looking to streamline their procurement processes; and American Express Business Travel, which helps businesses manage and optimize their travel expenses through a variety of travel-related products, services and solutions.

Global Network & Merchant Services consists of the merchant services businesses and global network services. Global Network Services develops and manages relationships with third parties that issue American Express branded cards. The Global Merchant Services businesses develop and manage relationships with merchants that accept American Express branded cards; authorize and record transactions; pay merchants; and provide a variety of value-added point of sale and back office services. In addition, in particular emerging markets, issuance of certain proprietary cards is managed within the Global Network Services business.

## Company Financials Fiscal Year Ended Dec. 31

| Per Share Data ($) | 2007 | 2006 | 2005 | 2004 | 2003 | 2002 | 2001 | 2000 | 1999 | 1998 |
|---|---|---|---|---|---|---|---|---|---|---|
| Tangible Book Value | 8.22 | 7.52 | 8.50 | 12.83 | 11.93 | 10.62 | 9.04 | 8.81 | 7.53 | 7.18 |
| Earnings | 3.39 | 3.01 | 2.56 | 2.74 | 2.31 | 2.01 | 0.98 | 2.07 | 1.81 | 1.54 |
| S&P Core Earnings | 2.87 | 2.85 | 2.49 | 2.53 | 2.09 | 1.68 | 0.73 | NA | NA | NA |
| Dividends | 0.60 | 0.54 | 0.48 | 0.32 | 0.38 | 0.32 | 0.32 | 0.32 | 0.30 | 0.30 |
| Payout Ratio | 18% | 18% | 19% | 12% | 16% | 16% | 33% | 15% | 17% | 19% |
| Prices:High | 65.89 | 62.50 | 59.50 | 57.05 | 49.11 | 44.91 | 57.06 | 63.00 | 56.29 | 39.54 |
| Prices:Low | 50.37 | 49.73 | 46.59 | 47.32 | 30.90 | 26.55 | 24.20 | 39.83 | 31.63 | 22.33 |
| P/E Ratio:High | 19 | 21 | 23 | 21 | 21 | 22 | 58 | 30 | 31 | 26 |
| P/E Ratio:Low | 15 | 17 | 18 | 17 | 13 | 13 | 25 | 19 | 18 | 14 |

| Income Statement Analysis (Million $) | 2007 | 2006 | 2005 | 2004 | 2003 | 2002 | 2001 | 2000 | 1999 | 1998 |
|---|---|---|---|---|---|---|---|---|---|---|
| Cards in Force | 86.4 | 78.0 | 71.0 | 65.4 | 60.5 | 57.3 | 55.2 | 51.7 | 46.0 | 42.7 |
| Card Charge Volume | NA | NA | 484,400 | 416,100 | 352,200 | 311,400 | 298,000 | 296,700 | 254,100 | 227,500 |
| Premium Income | Nil | Nil | Nil | 1,525 | 1,366 | 802 | 674 | 575 | 517 | 469 |
| Commissions | 4,343 | 4,333 | 4,236 | 4,079 | 3,484 | 3,521 | 3,969 | 4,165 | 3,626 | 3,304 |
| Interest & Dividends | 6,145 | 4,535 | 3,635 | 3,118 | 3,063 | 2,991 | 3,049 | 4,277 | 4,679 | 4,631 |
| Total Revenue | 31,557 | 27,136 | 24,267 | 29,115 | 25,866 | 23,807 | 22,582 | 23,675 | 16,599 | 14,501 |
| Net Before Taxes | 5,566 | 5,328 | 4,248 | 4,951 | 4,247 | 3,727 | 1,596 | 3,908 | 3,438 | 2,925 |
| Net Income | 4,048 | 3,729 | 3,221 | 3,516 | 3,000 | 2,671 | 1,311 | 2,810 | 2,475 | 2,141 |
| S&P Core Earnings | 3,426 | 3,531 | 3,144 | 3,244 | 2,723 | 2,245 | 986 | NA | NA | NA |

| Balance Sheet & Other Financial Data (Million $) | 2007 | 2006 | 2005 | 2004 | 2003 | 2002 | 2001 | 2000 | 1999 | 1998 |
|---|---|---|---|---|---|---|---|---|---|---|
| Total Assets | 149,830 | 127,853 | 113,960 | 192,638 | 175,001 | 157,253 | 151,100 | 154,423 | 148,517 | 126,933 |
| Cash Items | 14,036 | 11,270 | 7,126 | 9,907 | 5,726 | 10,288 | 7,222 | 8,487 | 7,471 | 4,092 |
| Investment Assets:Bonds | Nil | Nil | Nil | Nil | Nil | Nil | Nil | Nil | Nil | Nil |
| Investment Assets:Stocks | Nil | Nil | Nil | Nil | Nil | Nil | Nil | Nil | Nil | Nil |
| Investment Assets:Loans | 53,436 | 50,248 | 40,801 | 35,942 | 33,421 | 29,003 | 27,401 | 26,884 | 24,332 | 21,861 |
| Investment Assets:Total | 67,472 | 61,518 | 62,135 | 60,809 | 57,067 | 53,638 | 46,488 | 43,747 | 43,052 | 41,299 |
| Accounts Receivable | 95,441 | 89,099 | 35,497 | 34,650 | 31,269 | 29,087 | 29,498 | 30,543 | 26,467 | 22,224 |
| Customer Deposits | 15,397 | 24,656 | 24,579 | 21,091 | 21,250 | 18,317 | 14,557 | 13,870 | 12,197 | 10,398 |
| Travel Cheques Outstanding | 7,197 | 7,215 | 7,175 | 7,287 | 6,819 | 6,623 | 6,190 | 6,127 | 6,213 | 5,823 |
| Debt | 73,047 | 57,909 | 30,781 | 33,061 | 30,809 | 16,819 | 8,288 | 5,211 | 6,495 | 7,519 |
| Common Equity | 11,029 | 10,511 | 10,549 | 16,020 | 15,323 | 13,861 | 12,037 | 11,684 | 10,095 | 9,698 |
| % Return on Assets | 2.9 | 3.1 | 2.1 | 1.9 | 1.8 | 1.7 | 0.9 | 1.9 | 1.8 | 1.7 |
| % Return on Equity | 37.6 | 35.4 | 24.2 | 22.4 | 20.6 | 20.6 | 11.1 | 25.8 | 25.0 | 22.2 |

Data as orig reptd.; bef. results of disc opers/spec. items. Per share data adj. for stk. divs.; EPS diluted. E-Estimated. NA-Not Available. NM-Not Meaningful. NR-Not Ranked. UR-Under Review.

**Office:** World Financial Ctr, 200 Vesey Street, New York, NY 10285-4814.
**Telephone:** 212-640-2000.
**Website:** http://www.americanexpress.com
**Chrmn & CEO:** K.I. Chenault

**Pres:** A.F. Kelly, Jr.
**Vice Chrmn:** E. Gilligan
**EVP & CFO:** D.T. Henry
**EVP & General Counsel:** L.M. Parent

**Investor Contact:** R. Stovall (212-640-5574)
**Board Members:** D. F. Akerson, C. Barshefsky, U. M. Burns, K. I. Chenault, P. Chernin, E. Gilligan, J. Leschly, R. C. Levin, R. A. McGinn, E. D. Miller, S. S. Reinemund, R. D. Walter, R. A. Williams

**Founded:** 1868
**Domicile:** New York
**Employees:** 67,700

**The McGraw·Hill Companies**

# American International Group Inc

**STANDARD &POOR'S**

| **S&P Recommendation** HOLD ★★★☆☆ | **Price** $2.08 (as of Nov 14, 2008) | **12-Mo. Target Price** $3.50 |
|---|---|---|

**GICS Sector** Financials
**Sub-Industry** Multi-line Insurance

**Summary** One of the world's leading insurance organizations, AIG provides property, casualty and life insurance, as well as other financial services, in 130 countries.

## Key Stock Statistics (Source S&P, Vickers, company reports)

| | | | | | | | |
|---|---|---|---|---|---|---|---|
| 52-Wk Range | $62.30– 1.25 | S&P Oper. EPS 2008**E** | -7.15 | Market Capitalization(B) | $5.595 | Beta | 2.85 |
| Trailing 12-Month EPS | $-16.52 | S&P Oper. EPS 2009**E** | 0.40 | Yield (%) | Nil | S&P 3-Yr. Proj. EPS CAGR(%) | NM |
| Trailing 12-Month P/E | NM | P/E on S&P Oper. EPS 2008**E** | NM | Dividend Rate/Share | Nil | S&P Credit Rating | A- |
| $10K Invested 5 Yrs Ago | $377 | Common Shares Outstg. (M) | 2,689.9 | Institutional Ownership (%) | 71 | | |

## Price Performance

30-Week Mov. Avg. · · · · 10-Week Mov. Avg. – – **GAAP Earnings vs. Previous Year** Volume Above Avg. STARS
12-Mo. Target Price — Relative Strength — ▲ Up ▼ Down ▶ No Change Below Avg. ★

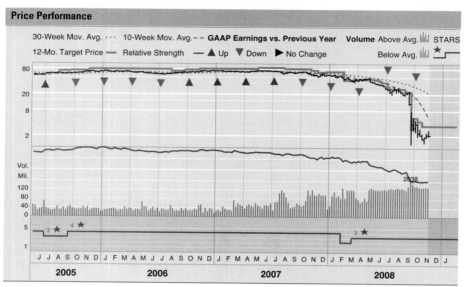

Options: ASE, CBOE, P, Ph

Analysis prepared by **Cathy A. Seifert** on October 24, 2008, when the stock traded at **$ 1.70**.

## Qualitative Risk Assessment

| LOW | MEDIUM | **HIGH** |
|---|---|---|

Our risk assessment remains high. AIG's outsized exposure (versus peers in the insurance industry) to the mortgage industry and to the credit default swap market recently led to an emergency bailout by the Federal Reserve. Going forward, we believe there remains a high degree of execution risk as AIG seeks to sell enough assets to pay off the Federal Reserve loan. Auditors have also claimed AIG has a "material weakness" in certain internal controls.

## Quantitative Evaluations

**S&P Quality Ranking** NR

| D | C | B- | B | B+ | A- | A | A+ |
|---|---|---|---|---|---|---|---|

**Relative Strength Rank** WEAK

3

LOWEST = 1    HIGHEST = 99

## Revenue/Earnings Data

**Revenue (Million $)**

| | 1Q | 2Q | 3Q | 4Q | Year |
|---|---|---|---|---|---|
| 2008 | 14,031 | 19,933 | 898.0 | -- | -- |
| 2007 | 30,645 | 31,150 | 29,836 | 18,433 | 110,064 |
| 2006 | 27,259 | 26,743 | 29,199 | 29,993 | 113,194 |
| 2005 | 27,202 | 27,903 | 26,408 | 27,392 | 108,905 |
| 2004 | 23,637 | 23,809 | 25,411 | 25,760 | 97,987 |
| 2003 | 18,927 | 19,891 | 20,306 | 22,179 | 81,303 |

**Earnings Per Share ($)**

| | | | | | |
|---|---|---|---|---|---|
| 2008 | -3.09 | -2.06 | -9.05 | E-1.75 | E-7.15 |
| 2007 | 1.58 | 1.64 | 1.19 | -2.07 | 2.39 |
| 2006 | 1.21 | 1.21 | 1.61 | 1.31 | 5.35 |
| 2005 | 1.45 | 1.71 | 0.66 | 0.17 | 3.99 |
| 2004 | 1.08 | 1.09 | 0.95 | 1.15 | 3.75 |
| 2003 | 0.74 | 0.87 | 0.89 | 1.03 | 3.53 |

Fiscal year ended Dec. 31. Next earnings report expected: Late February. EPS Estimates based on S&P Operating Earnings; historical GAAP earnings are as reported.

## Highlights

➤ AIG entered into an $85 billion revolving credit facility with the Federal Reserve Bank of New York on September 22, 2008. This action came after AIG's outsized exposure to mortgage and credit default swap losses threatened the firm and forced it to agree to the Fed's assistance. Terms of the $85 billion, two-year revolving credit facility include an interest rate of 3-month LIBOR plus 8.5%, plus commitment fees. The credit facility is secured by a pledge of AIG's assets, some of which are expected to be sold to repay the loan. AIG also entered a securities lending agreement with the Fed, to aid the liquidity in that program, which had $37.2 billion of securities subject to loans as of October 6.

➤ AIG is also required, under terms of the agreement, to issue a new series of convertible preferred stock, convertible at any time into 79.9% of the common stock of the company. The preferred stock is expected to remain outstanding, held in a trust for the benefit of the U.S. Treasury, even if the credit facility is repaid.

➤ We forecast an operating loss of $2.07 a share in 2008 and operating EPS of $0.40 in 2009, versus $3.31 of operating EPS reported for 2007.

## Investment Rationale/Risk

➤ At current levels, the shares are trading at a discount to our estimate of tangible book value (adjusted for the dilutive stock offering). Despite this discount to most peers and to historical levels, we would not add to positions until more detail emerges regarding AIG's future operating strategy.

➤ Risks to our recommendation and target price include the company's potential inability to sell enough assets in a timely manner to repay the Federal Reserve loan.

➤ Our 12-month target price of $3.50 assumes that the shares will trade at approximately 1X our very preliminary estimate of tangible book value, after giving effect to the above-mentioned Federal Reserve transaction and share issuance. Both of these metrics are discounted to AIG's historical and relative valuations. We view this discount as warranted in light of what we view as the above average risk embedded in the shares.

## Dividend Data (Dates: mm/dd Payment Date: mm/dd/yy)

| Amount ($) | Date Decl. | Ex-Div. Date | Stk. of Record | Payment Date |
|---|---|---|---|---|
| 0.200 | 09/04 | 12/05 | 12/07 | 12/21/07 |
| 0.200 | 11/14 | 03/05 | 03/07 | 03/21/08 |
| 0.200 | 03/12 | 06/04 | 06/06 | 06/20/08 |
| 0.220 | 05/08 | 09/03 | 09/05 | 09/19/08 |

Dividends have been paid since 1969. Source: Company reports.

---

**Please read the Required Disclosures and Analyst Certification on the last page of this report.**

*The McGraw-Hill Companies*

# American International Group Inc

**STANDARD &POOR'S**

## Business Summary October 24, 2008

One of the world's leading insurance organizations, American International Group provides property, casualty and life insurance, as well as other financial services, in 130 countries and territories.

Investigations by the New York Attorney General and the SEC into AIG's use of non-traditional insurance products and certain assumed reinsurance transactions (sometimes referred to as finite reinsurance) culminated in a number of events, including a management shake-up that led to: the resignation of AIG's long-time CEO, Maurice Greenberg; a write-down against earnings from 2000-2004 totaling nearly $4 billion; and a write-down of shareholders' equity of $2.26 billion. During 2005, AIG also incurred after-tax charges totaling $1.15 billion to settle its numerous regulatory issues and $1.19 billion to boost loss reserves. During 2007, AIG's management team was confronted with another significant issue: the downward spiral of the U.S. residential mortgage market and subsequent deterioration in broader credit market conditions. These conditions persisted into 2008. To help replenish its capital position in the wake of deteriorating mortgage-related conditions, AIG in late May 2008 raised $20 billion of new capital that included the sale of 196,710,525 common shares for $7.47 billion. These moves proved insufficient, and in late September 2008, AIG was forced to accept an emergency line of credit from the Federal Reserve.

Revenues totaled $110.1 billion in 2007 (versus $113.4 billion in 2006), with domestic general insurance accounting for 33%, foreign life and retirement services for 34%, domestic life and retirement services for 15%, foreign general insurance for 12%, and asset management for 6%. (Financial services revenues were less than 1% in 2007.) During 2007, activities in the United States and Canada accounted for 42% of revenues, while those in other foreign countries accounted for the remaining 58%.

## Company Financials Fiscal Year Ended Dec. 31

| Per Share Data ($) | 2007 | 2006 | 2005 | 2004 | 2003 | 2002 | 2001 | 2000 | 1999 | 1998 |
|---|---|---|---|---|---|---|---|---|---|---|
| Tangible Book Value | 34.15 | 37.96 | 30.13 | 27.73 | 24.39 | 20.32 | 19.94 | 16.98 | 14.33 | 13.78 |
| Operating Earnings | NA | NA | NA | NA | NA | NA | NA | 2.45 | 2.13 | 1.87 |
| Earnings | 2.39 | 5.35 | 3.99 | 3.75 | 3.53 | 2.10 | 2.07 | 2.41 | 2.15 | 1.91 |
| S&P Core Earnings | 3.29 | 5.36 | 4.35 | 3.77 | 3.89 | 2.63 | 2.06 | NA | NA | NA |
| Dividends | 0.73 | 0.63 | 0.55 | 0.28 | 0.22 | 0.18 | 0.16 | 0.14 | 0.13 | 0.11 |
| Relative Payout | 31% | 12% | 14% | 7% | 6% | 8% | 8% | 6% | 6% | 6% |
| Prices:High | 72.97 | 72.97 | 73.46 | 77.36 | 66.35 | 80.00 | 98.31 | 103.75 | 75.25 | 54.73 |
| Prices:Low | 50.86 | 57.52 | 49.91 | 54.28 | 42.92 | 47.61 | 66.00 | 52.38 | 51.00 | 34.60 |
| P/E Ratio:High | 31 | 14 | 18 | 21 | 19 | 38 | 47 | 43 | 35 | 29 |
| P/E Ratio:Low | 21 | 11 | 13 | 14 | 12 | 23 | 32 | 22 | 24 | 18 |

| Income Statement Analysis (Million $) | 2007 | 2006 | 2005 | 2004 | 2003 | 2002 | 2001 | 2000 | 1999 | 1998 |
|---|---|---|---|---|---|---|---|---|---|---|
| Life Insurance in Force | 2,312,045 | 2,070,600 | 1,852,833 | 1,858,094 | 1,596,626 | 1,324,451 | 1,228,501 | 583,059 | 584,959 | 499,167 |
| Premium Income:Life A & H | 33,627 | 30,636 | 29,400 | 28,082 | 22,879 | 20,320 | 19,243 | 13,610 | 11,942 | 10,247 |
| Premium Income:Casualty/Property. | 45,682 | 43,451 | 41,872 | 40,607 | 31,734 | 24,269 | 19,365 | 17,407 | 15,544 | 14,098 |
| Net Investment Income | 28,619 | 25,292 | 22,165 | 18,434 | 16,662 | 15,034 | 14,628 | 9,824 | 8,723 | 5,424 |
| Total Revenue | 110,064 | 113,194 | 108,905 | 97,987 | 81,303 | 67,482 | 52,852 | 40,717 | 36,356 | 29,939 |
| Pretax Income | 8,943 | 21,687 | 15,213 | 14,950 | 13,908 | 8,142 | 8,139 | 8,349 | 7,512 | 5,529 |
| Net Operating Income | NA | NA | 105 | NA | NA | NA | NA | 5,737 | 4,999 | 3,689 |
| Net Income | 6,200 | 14,014 | 10,477 | 9,875 | 9,265 | 5,519 | 5,499 | 5,636 | 5,055 | 3,766 |
| S&P Core Earnings | 8,534 | 14,018 | 11,396 | 9,928 | 10,208 | 6,931 | 5,476 | NA | NA | NA |

| Balance Sheet & Other Financial Data (Million $) | 2007 | 2006 | 2005 | 2004 | 2003 | 2002 | 2001 | 2000 | 1999 | 1998 |
|---|---|---|---|---|---|---|---|---|---|---|
| Cash & Equivalent | 8,871 | 7,681 | 7,624 | 7,597 | 5,881 | 1,165 | 698 | 256 | 132 | 1,874 |
| Premiums Due | 18,395 | 17,789 | 15,333 | 15,137 | 14,166 | 13,088 | 11,647 | 11,832 | 12,737 | 11,679 |
| Investment Assets:Bonds | 428,935 | 417,865 | 385,680 | 365,677 | 309,254 | 243,366 | 200,616 | 102,010 | 90,144 | 61,906 |
| Investment Assets:Stocks | 41,646 | 30,222 | 23,588 | 17,851 | 9,584 | 7,066 | 7,937 | 7,181 | 6,714 | 5,893 |
| Investment Assets:Loans | 33,727 | 28,418 | 24,909 | 22,463 | 21,249 | 19,928 | 18,092 | 12,243 | 12,134 | 8,247 |
| Investment Assets:Total | 755,596 | 719,685 | 614,759 | 494,592 | 449,657 | 339,320 | 357,602 | 140,910 | 185,882 | 141,923 |
| Deferred Policy Costs | 43,150 | 37,235 | 33,248 | 29,736 | 26,398 | 22,256 | 17,443 | 10,189 | 9,624 | 7,647 |
| Total Assets | 1,060,505 | 979,414 | 853,370 | 798,660 | 678,346 | 561,229 | 492,982 | 306,577 | 268,238 | 194,398 |
| Debt | 162,935 | 186,866 | 78,625 | 66,850 | 57,877 | 50,076 | 34,503 | 5,801 | 23,795 | 31,093 |
| Common Equity | 95,801 | 101,677 | 86,317 | 80,607 | 71,253 | 59,103 | 52,150 | 39,619 | 33,306 | 27,131 |
| Combined Loss-Expense Ratio | 90.3 | 89.1 | 104.7 | 100.1 | 92.4 | 106.0 | 100.7 | 96.7 | 96.4 | 96.4 |
| % Return on Revenue | 5.6 | 12.4 | 9.6 | 10.1 | 11.4 | 8.2 | 10.5 | 13.8 | 13.9 | 12.6 |
| % Return on Equity | 6.3 | 14.9 | 12.6 | 13.1 | 14.2 | 9.9 | 11.0 | 15.5 | 15.9 | 14.7 |
| % Investment Yield | 3.9 | 3.8 | 3.7 | 3.9 | 4.1 | 4.8 | 4.5 | 7.4 | 4.9 | 4.9 |

Data as orig reptd.; bef. results of disc opers/spec. items. Per share data adj. for stk. divs.; EPS diluted. E-Estimated. NA-Not Available. NM-Not Meaningful. NR-Not Ranked. UR-Under Review.

**Office:** 70 Pine Street, New York, NY 10270-0094.
**Telephone:** 212-770-7000.
**Website:** http://www.aigcorporate.com
**Chrmn & CEO:** E.M. Liddy

**Vice Chrmn:** P.R. Reynolds
**COO:** G. Flood
**EVP, CFO & Chief Acctg Officer:** D.L. Herzog
**EVP & General Counsel:** A.D. Kelly

**Investor Contact:** S.J. Bensinger
**Board Members:** S. F. Bollenbach, D. D. Dammerman, M. Feldstein, R. C. Holbrooke, S. N. Johnson, E. M. Liddy, G. L. Miles, Jr., M. W. Offit, J. F. Orr, III, P. R. Reynolds, J. J. Roberts, V. M. Rometty, M. H. Sutton, E. S. Tse

**Founded:** 1967
**Domicile:** Delaware
**Employees:** 116,000

*The McGraw-Hill Companies*

# American Tower Corp

**STANDARD &POOR'S**

| | | | | |
|---|---|---|---|---|
| **S&P Recommendation** | **STRONG BUY** ★★★★★ | **Price** $26.64 (as of Nov 14, 2008) | **12-Mo. Target Price** $51.00 | **Investment Style** Large-Cap Blend |

**GICS Sector** Telecommunication Services
**Sub-Industry** Wireless Telecommunication Services

**Summary** This company operates the largest independent portfolio of wireless communications and broadcast towers in North America.

## Key Stock Statistics (Source S&P, Vickers, company reports)

| | | | | | | | |
|---|---|---|---|---|---|---|---|
| 52-Wk Range | $46.20– 22.34 | S&P Oper. EPS 2008**E** | 0.52 | Market Capitalization(B) | $10.568 | Beta | 1.31 |
| Trailing 12-Month EPS | $0.61 | S&P Oper. EPS 2009**E** | 0.72 | Yield (%) | Nil | S&P 3-Yr. Proj. EPS CAGR(%) | 65 |
| Trailing 12-Month P/E | 43.7 | P/E on S&P Oper. EPS 2008**E** | 51.2 | Dividend Rate/Share | Nil | S&P Credit Rating | BB+ |
| $10K Invested 5 Yrs Ago | $25,014 | Common Shares Outstg. (M) | 396.7 | Institutional Ownership (%) | NM | | |

## Price Performance

30-Week Mov. Avg. · · · ·  10-Week Mov. Avg. – –  **GAAP Earnings vs. Previous Year**  Volume Above Avg. STARS
12-Mo. Target Price —  Relative Strength —  ▲ Up  ▼ Down  ► No Change  Below Avg. ★

Options: ASE, CBOE, P, Ph

Analysis prepared by **James Moorman, CFA** on November 03, 2008, when the stock traded at **$ 33.03**.

## Highlights

➤ Following a 10.6% revenue increase in 2007, we see growth of 9.7% in 2008 and 8.2% in 2009, reflecting increased lease activity per active tower and more new towers. We believe AMT will benefit from favorable tower industry trends such as wireless carriers' demands to improve their network quality and coverage both in the U.S. and internationally.

➤ We are positive on AMT's operating discipline, and look for operating expenses as a percentage of sales to continue to decline in 2008 and 2009. Driven by higher tower utilization, we forecast EBITDA margins widening by roughly 150 basis points, to 67.9%, in 2008, from 66.8% in 2007, and then to 69.1% in 2009, a level that is well above the peer average. We believe this efficiency will enable free cash flow to increase from $581 million in 2007 to $602 million in 2008 and $776 million in 2009.

➤ We estimate operating EPS of $0.52 for 2008 and $0.72 for 2009, including projected stock option expense of $0.14 per share in 2008 and 2009. The company repurchased roughly 8.3 million of its shares in the third quarter of 2008 for roughly $332 million.

## Investment Rationale/Risk

➤ As AMT is the market leader in the wireless tower industry, we believe its continued tower purchases will enable it to continue to achieve greater economies of scale through 2009. In our view, the recent spectrum auction will provide an additional revenue boost over the next several years. AMT has a 2008 net debt/EBITDA of 3.8X, well below its peers. We also expect AMT to continue to expand internationally in Mexico and Brazil, with additional expansion into India. We consider the shares highly attractive.

➤ Risks to our recommendation and target price include slower demand in the tower lease business; a negative outcome from the current internal review of past stock option granting practices; and an inability to meet $4.4 billion of debt obligations. CFO Brad Singer recently resigned, and failure to find a replacement could create instability in management.

➤ Our 12-month target price of $51 is largely based on 27X our free cash flow estimate for 2009, above the peer mean. Our target price also represents an enterprise value of 21.2X our 2009 EBITDA estimate, slightly above the industry average.

## Qualitative Risk Assessment

| LOW | MEDIUM | HIGH |
|---|---|---|

Our risk assessment reflects a possible negative outcome of the internal review of stock option practices. Despite the company's high 60% total debt to total capitalization, we believe AMT has steady cash flow and sufficient cash and investments to meet its working capital, capital expenditure and debt requirements.

## Quantitative Evaluations

**S&P Quality Ranking**   NR

| D | C | B- | B | B+ | A- | A | A+ |
|---|---|---|---|---|---|---|---|

**Relative Strength Rank**   MODERATE

51

LOWEST = 1          HIGHEST = 99

## Revenue/Earnings Data

**Revenue (Million $)**

| | 1Q | 2Q | 3Q | 4Q | Year |
|---|---|---|---|---|---|
| 2008 | 382.2 | 393.7 | 409.3 | -- | -- |
| 2007 | 352.5 | 358.4 | 367.6 | 378.1 | 1,457 |
| 2006 | 320.4 | 325.9 | 333.5 | 337.7 | 1,317 |
| 2005 | 184.4 | 188.1 | 264.8 | 307.6 | 944.8 |
| 2004 | 168.8 | 172.3 | 180.9 | 184.7 | 706.7 |
| 2003 | 161.5 | 175.3 | 186.9 | 191.5 | 715.1 |

**Earnings Per Share ($)**

| | 1Q | 2Q | 3Q | 4Q | Year |
|---|---|---|---|---|---|
| 2008 | 0.10 | 0.12 | 0.15 | E0.15 | E0.52 |
| 2007 | 0.05 | 0.03 | 0.14 | -0.01 | 0.22 |
| 2006 | -0.01 | 0.02 | 0.01 | 0.04 | 0.06 |
| 2005 | -0.14 | -0.14 | -0.06 | 0.13 | -0.44 |
| 2004 | -0.19 | -0.27 | -0.25 | -0.30 | -1.07 |
| 2003 | -0.41 | -0.40 | -0.18 | -0.20 | -1.17 |

Fiscal year ended Dec. 31. Next earnings report expected: NA. EPS Estimates based on S&P Operating Earnings; historical GAAP earnings are as reported.

## Dividend Data

No cash dividends have been paid.

---

**Please read the Required Disclosures and Analyst Certification on the last page of this report.**

# American Tower Corp

## Business Summary November 03, 2008

CORPORATE OVERVIEW. American Tower Corp. operates the largest independent portfolio of wireless communications and broadcast towers in North America, based on the number of towers and revenue. The company's primary business is leasing antenna space on multi-tenant communications towers to wireless service providers and radio and television broadcast companies. The tower portfolio provides AMT with a recurring base of leased revenues from its customers and growth potential to add more tenants and equipment to these towers from its unused capacity. The company also continues to expand its operations in Mexico and Brazil, and has started a controlled buildout in India.

IMPACT OF MAJOR DEVELOPMENTS. In August 2005, AMT issued approximately 181 million shares valued at $3.1 billion in a merger with SpectraSite. The transaction resulted in the combined company having a portfolio of 22,600 communications sites.

In May 2006, AMT announced it was conducting an internal review of its historical stock option granting practices. A securities class action lawsuit was filed in U.S. District Court (MA) against the company and its officers related to this matter. On December 13, 2007, AMT said it paid $14 million to settle the action, and all claims were dismissed.

In June 2008, CFO Brad Singer announced he was leaving the company to take the role of CFO with Discovery Communications, LLC. While AMT looks to replace the role both internally and externally, Jean Bua, EVP-Finance and Corporate Controller, will serve as interim CFO.

## Company Financials Fiscal Year Ended Dec. 31

| Per Share Data ($) | 2007 | 2006 | 2005 | 2004 | 2003 | 2002 | 2001 | 2000 | 1999 | 1998 |
|---|---|---|---|---|---|---|---|---|---|---|
| Tangible Book Value | 2.41 | 0.88 | 0.74 | NM | 0.28 | NM | 1.94 | 2.06 | 13.78 | 10.08 |
| Cash Flow | 1.41 | 1.28 | 0.92 | 0.40 | 0.34 | 0.01 | -0.05 | 0.55 | 0.53 | 0.13 |
| Earnings | 0.22 | 0.06 | -0.44 | -1.07 | -1.17 | -1.61 | -2.35 | -1.13 | -0.33 | -0.48 |
| S&P Core Earnings | 0.20 | 0.05 | -0.50 | -1.17 | -1.35 | -1.60 | -2.50 | NA | NA | NA |
| Dividends | Nil | Nil | Nil | Nil | Nil | Nil | Nil | Nil | Nil | Nil |
| Payout Ratio | Nil | Nil | Nil | Nil | Nil | Nil | Nil | Nil | Nil | Nil |
| Prices:High | 46.53 | 38.74 | 28.33 | 18.75 | 12.00 | 10.40 | 41.50 | 55.50 | 33.25 | 29.63 |
| Prices:Low | 36.34 | 26.66 | 16.28 | 9.89 | 3.55 | 0.60 | 5.25 | 27.63 | 17.13 | 13.25 |
| P/E Ratio:High | NM | NM | NM | NM | NM | NM | NM | NM | NM | NM |
| P/E Ratio:Low | NM | NM | NM | NM | NM | NM | NM | NM | NM | NM |

**Income Statement Analysis** (Million $)

| | 2007 | 2006 | 2005 | 2004 | 2003 | 2002 | 2001 | 2000 | 1999 | 1998 |
|---|---|---|---|---|---|---|---|---|---|---|
| Revenue | 1,457 | 1,317 | 945 | 707 | 715 | 788 | 1,134 | 735 | 258 | 104 |
| Operating Income | 898 | 803 | 589 | 423 | 377 | 312 | 251 | 196 | 91.5 | 36.7 |
| Depreciation | 510 | 528 | 411 | 329 | 313 | 317 | 440 | 283 | 133 | 52.1 |
| Interest Expense | 240 | 217 | 224 | 264 | 280 | 257 | 309 | 186 | 27.5 | 24.6 |
| Pretax Income | 153 | 70.9 | -130 | -317 | -305 | -248 | -567 | -250 | -49.0 | -42.2 |
| Effective Tax Rate | 39.1% | 58.9% | NM | NM | NM | NM | NM | NM | NM | NM |
| Net Income | 92.7 | 28.3 | -134 | -239 | -242 | -315 | -450 | -190 | -49.4 | -38.0 |
| S&P Core Earnings | 85.6 | 24.6 | -154 | -261 | -281 | -313 | -480 | NA | NA | NA |

**Balance Sheet & Other Financial Data** (Million $)

| | 2007 | 2006 | 2005 | 2004 | 2003 | 2002 | 2001 | 2000 | 1999 | 1998 |
|---|---|---|---|---|---|---|---|---|---|---|
| Cash | 94.0 | 281 | 113 | 216 | 105 | 127 | 130 | 128 | 25.2 | 186 |
| Current Assets | 246 | 486 | 226 | 309 | 412 | 536 | 522 | 471 | 139 | 208 |
| Total Assets | 8,130 | 8,613 | 8,768 | 5,086 | 5,332 | 5,662 | 6,830 | 5,661 | 3,019 | 1,502 |
| Current Liabilities | 317 | 570 | 453 | 332 | 295 | 670 | 343 | 298 | 125 | 116 |
| Long Term Debt | 4,240 | 3,289 | 3,451 | 3,155 | 3,284 | 3,195 | 3,549 | 2,457 | 736 | 279 |
| Common Equity | 3,022 | 4,382 | 4,527 | 1,464 | 1,706 | 1,740 | 2,869 | 2,877 | 2,145 | 1,092 |
| Total Capital | 7,309 | 7,678 | 7,988 | 4,626 | 5,008 | 4,950 | 6,433 | 5,350 | 2,890 | 1,385 |
| Capital Expenditures | 154 | 127 | 88.6 | 42.2 | 61.6 | 180 | 568 | 549 | 294 | 126 |
| Cash Flow | 603 | 556 | 277 | 90.2 | 71.0 | 2.11 | -9.72 | 93.1 | 83.2 | 14.1 |
| Current Ratio | 0.8 | 0.9 | 0.5 | 0.9 | 1.4 | 0.8 | 1.5 | 1.6 | 1.1 | 1.8 |
| % Long Term Debt of Capitalization | 58.6 | 42.9 | 43.2 | 68.2 | 65.6 | 64.5 | 55.2 | 45.9 | 25.5 | 20.2 |
| % Net Income of Revenue | 6.4 | 2.2 | NM | NM | NM | NM | NM | NM | NM | NM |
| % Return on Assets | 1.1 | 0.3 | NM | NM | NM | NM | NM | NM | NM | NM |
| % Return on Equity | 2.5 | 0.6 | NM | NM | NM | NM | NM | NM | NM | NM |

Data as orig reptd.; bef. results of disc opers/spec. items. Per share data adj. for stk. divs.; EPS diluted. E-Estimated. NA-Not Available. NM-Not Meaningful. NR-Not Ranked. UR-Under Review.

**Office:** 116 Huntington Avenue, Boston, MA 02116.
**Telephone:** 617-375-7500.
**Email:** ir@americantower.com
**Website:** http://www.americantower.com

**Chrmn, Pres & CEO:** J.D. Taiclet, Jr.
**Pres:** D. Carey
**COO:** W.H. Hess
**EVP, CFO, Chief Acctg Officer & Cntlr:** J.A. Bua

**EVP, Chief Admin Officer, Secy & General Counsel:** E. DiSanto
**Investor Contact:** M. Powell (617-375-7500)
**Board Members:** G. L. Cantu, R. P. Dolan, R. Dykes, C. F. Katz, J. A. Reed, P. D. Reeve, D. E. Sharbutt, J. D. Taiclet, Jr., S. L. Thompson

**Founded:** 1995
**Domicile:** Delaware
**Employees:** 1,124

# Ameriprise Financial Inc

**STANDARD &POOR'S**

| S&P Recommendation | HOLD ★★★☆☆ | Price<br>$18.00 (as of Nov 14, 2008) | 12-Mo. Target Price<br>$25.00 | Investment Style<br>Large-Cap Growth |
|---|---|---|---|---|

**GICS Sector** Financials
**Sub-Industry** Asset Management & Custody Banks

**Summary** This diversified financial services company, spun off from American Express in September 2005, provides insurance, investment and asset management services.

## Key Stock Statistics (Source S&P, Vickers, company reports)

| | | | | | | | | |
|---|---|---|---|---|---|---|---|---|
| 52-Wk Range | $61.58– 16.43 | S&P Oper. EPS 2008**E** | 1.77 | Market Capitalization(B) | $3.899 | Beta | 1.84 |
| Trailing 12-Month EPS | $2.56 | S&P Oper. EPS 2009**E** | 2.74 | Yield (%) | 3.78 | S&P 3-Yr. Proj. EPS CAGR(%) | -3 |
| Trailing 12-Month P/E | 7.0 | P/E on S&P Oper. EPS 2008**E** | 10.2 | Dividend Rate/Share | $0.68 | S&P Credit Rating | A |
| $10K Invested 5 Yrs Ago | NA | Common Shares Outstg. (M) | 216.6 | Institutional Ownership (%) | 87 | | |

## Price Performance

30-Week Mov. Avg. · · · · 10-Week Mov. Avg. – – **GAAP Earnings vs. Previous Year** Volume Above Avg. STARS
12-Mo. Target Price — Relative Strength — ▲ Up ▼ Down ► No Change Below Avg. ★

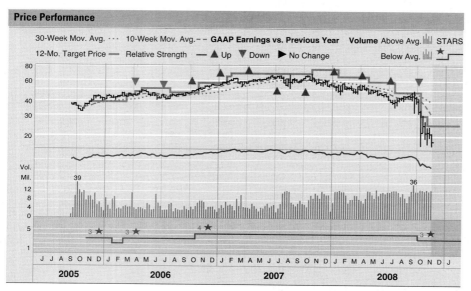

Options: ASE, CBOE, P, Ph

Analysis prepared by **Matthew Albrecht** on November 06, 2008, when the stock traded at **$ 20.35**.

## Highlights

➤ Falling client asset balances due to market declines, investment losses, and lower interest rates have pressured revenues, in our view. We expect continued outflows from Threadneedle institutional funds, while lagging performance at RiverSource funds may keep investors looking elsewhere. We expect wrap account sales to remain an area of relative strength, but variable annuity sales have slowed as the markets have fallen. The Protection segment continues to perform, though it too has seen investment losses. We expect investment losses and money market support costs to continue to weigh on results. We look for net revenues to decline 15% in 2008 before modest growth in 2009.

➤ We see distribution costs rising, but interest credited to fixed accounts should fall based on lower balances in fixed annuities and reduced interest rates. Cost controls related to G&A costs have helped reduce the fixed expense base, somewhat outweighing technology costs. We expect net revenue growth to lag expense growth in 2008, pressuring the pretax margin, before modest margin expansion in 2009.

➤ We see EPS of $1.77 in 2008 and $2.74 in 2009.

## Investment Rationale/Risk

➤ We think AMP has significant franchise value but will need to execute successfully as an independent company. We expect the company to improve its return on equity through capital redeployment, aided by common share repurchases, but recent market declines may make that more difficult. We believe AMP's focus on insurance products merits it a lower valuation than other asset managers. In our view, growing brand awareness will be offset in the near term by market uncertainty and expected writedowns, as well as declining asset balances.

➤ Risks to our recommendation and target price include potential market depreciation in client assets, and various regulatory issues.

➤ AMP recently traded at about 13.0X our 2008 EPS estimate, in line with its asset management peers. We expect these shares to trade at a discount to peers due to its revenue mix, with more reliance on insurance and annuity products, and uncertainty about the quality of its investment portfolio. Our 12-month target price of $25 is equal to 9.1X our 2009 EPS estimate, a discount to our coverage universe.

## Qualitative Risk Assessment

| LOW | MEDIUM | HIGH |
|---|---|---|

Our risk assessment reflects our view of the company's significant franchise value, offset by our concerns that the loss of the widely recognized American Express name could negatively affect AMP's ability to raise and retain client assets.

## Quantitative Evaluations

**S&P Quality Ranking** NR

| D | C | B- | B | B+ | A- | A | A+ |
|---|---|---|---|---|---|---|---|

**Relative Strength Rank** WEAK

22

LOWEST = 1     HIGHEST = 99

## Revenue/Earnings Data

**Revenue (Million $)**

| | 1Q | 2Q | 3Q | 4Q | Year |
|---|---|---|---|---|---|
| 2008 | 2,106 | 2,021 | 1,684 | -- | -- |
| 2007 | 2,063 | 2,182 | 2,202 | 2,319 | 8,654 |
| 2006 | 1,949 | 2,053 | 1,977 | 2,161 | 8,140 |
| 2005 | 1,847 | 1,895 | 1,873 | 1,869 | 7,484 |
| 2004 | -- | -- | -- | -- | 6,770 |
| 2003 | -- | -- | -- | -- | -- |

**Earnings Per Share ($)**

| | | | | | |
|---|---|---|---|---|---|
| 2008 | 0.83 | 0.93 | -0.32 | E0.33 | E1.77 |
| 2007 | 0.68 | 0.81 | 0.83 | 1.08 | 3.39 |
| 2006 | 0.57 | 0.57 | 0.71 | 0.69 | 2.54 |
| 2005 | 0.71 | 0.61 | 0.50 | 0.44 | 2.26 |
| 2004 | -- | -- | -- | -- | 2.80 |
| 2003 | -- | -- | -- | -- | -- |

Fiscal year ended Dec. 31. Next earnings report expected: Late January. EPS Estimates based on S&P Operating Earnings; historical GAAP earnings are as reported.

## Dividend Data (Dates: mm/dd Payment Date: mm/dd/yy)

| Amount<br>($) | Date<br>Decl. | Ex-Div.<br>Date | Stk. of<br>Record | Payment<br>Date |
|---|---|---|---|---|
| 0.150 | 01/24 | 01/31 | 02/04 | 02/15/08 |
| 0.150 | 04/22 | 04/30 | 05/02 | 05/16/08 |
| 0.170 | 07/23 | 08/06 | 08/08 | 08/22/08 |
| 0.170 | 10/22 | 11/05 | 11/07 | 11/21/08 |

Dividends have been paid since 2005. Source: Company reports.

---

**Please read the Required Disclosures and Analyst Certification on the last page of this report.**

The **McGraw·Hill** Companies

# Ameriprise Financial Inc

**STANDARD &POOR'S**

## Business Summary November 06, 2008

CORPORATE OVERVIEW. Ameriprise Financial completed its spinoff from American Express on September 30, 2005, and began trading on the New York Stock Exchange on October 3 under the symbol AMP. As of December 31, 2007, Ameriprise owned, managed and administered over $480 billion of client assets and operated a network of nearly 12,000 financial advisers. Ameriprise offers a broad assortment of products, including mutual funds, annuities and life insurance products. Ameriprise was originally named Investors Diversified Services before it was acquired by American Express in 1984. We think AMP will need to prove that it can grow and prosper without the benefits of its previous owner, American Express, which spun off the company in 2005. We believe the spinoff and new marketing campaign have raised AMP's visibility among prospective clients and may also help attract and retain financial advisers. In terms of corporate governance, we view favorably the high proportion of independent directors on the board, but would prefer that the company split the roles of chairman and CEO.

Ameriprise reorganized the company late in 2007, and now has five operating segments. Advice and Wealth Management accounted for about 44% of net revenues and 28% of pretax earnings in 2007, and provides financial advice and full service brokerage and banking services, primarily to retail clients, through its financial advisers. The Asset Management segment (20%, 30%) provides investment advice and investment products to retail and institutional clients. Threadneedle Investments predominantly provides international investment products and services, and RiverSource Investments predominantly provides products and services in the U.S. for domestic customers. Its domestic products are primarily distributed through the Advice and Wealth Management segment and third parties, while international products are mostly distributed through third parties. The Annuities segment (27%, 42%) provides RiverSource Life variable and fixed annuity products to retail clients, primarily through the Advice and Wealth Management segment. The Protection segment (23%, 48%) offers a variety of protection products to address the identified protection and risk management needs of retail clients including life, disability income and property-casualty insurance. The Corporate and Other segment consists of net investment income on corporate level assets, including unallocated equity and other revenues from various investments as well as unallocated corporate expenses. This segment, including intersegment eliminations, reduced net revenues by 14% and reduced pretax income by 48% in 2007.

## Company Financials Fiscal Year Ended Dec. 31

| Per Share Data ($) | 2007 | 2006 | 2005 | 2004 | 2003 | 2002 | 2001 | 2000 | 1999 | 1998 |
|---|---|---|---|---|---|---|---|---|---|---|
| Tangible Book Value | 34.81 | 31.10 | 30.75 | 6.45 | NA | NA | NA | NA | NA | NA |
| Cash Flow | 4.11 | 3.21 | 2.26 | NA | NA | NA | NA | NA | NA | NA |
| Earnings | 3.39 | 2.54 | 2.26 | 2.80 | NA | NA | NA | NA | NA | NA |
| S&P Core Earnings | 3.26 | 2.41 | 2.37 | 3.02 | 2.46 | NA | NA | NA | NA | NA |
| Dividends | 0.56 | 0.44 | 0.11 | NA | NA | NA | NA | NA | NA | NA |
| Payout Ratio | 17% | 17% | 5% | NA | NA | NA | NA | NA | NA | NA |
| Prices:High | 69.25 | 55.79 | 44.78 | NA | NA | NA | NA | NA | NA | NA |
| Prices:Low | 51.31 | 40.30 | 32.00 | NA | NA | NA | NA | NA | NA | NA |
| P/E Ratio:High | 20 | 22 | 20 | NA | NA | NA | NA | NA | NA | NA |
| P/E Ratio:Low | 15 | 16 | 14 | NA | NA | NA | NA | NA | NA | NA |

| Income Statement Analysis (Million $) | 2007 | 2006 | 2005 | 2004 | 2003 | 2002 | 2001 | 2000 | 1999 | 1998 |
|---|---|---|---|---|---|---|---|---|---|---|
| Income Interest | 3,238 | 2,204 | 2,241 | 2,125 | NA | NA | NA | NA | NA | NA |
| Income Other | 5,671 | 5,936 | 5,243 | 4,645 | NA | NA | NA | NA | NA | NA |
| Total Income | 8,909 | 8,140 | 7,484 | 6,770 | NA | NA | NA | NA | NA | NA |
| General Expenses | 7,353 | 7,343 | 6,739 | 5,756 | NA | NA | NA | NA | NA | NA |
| Interest Expense | 367 | 116 | 73.0 | 78.0 | NA | NA | NA | NA | NA | NA |
| Depreciation | 173 | 166 | 164 | NA | NA | NA | NA | NA | NA | NA |
| Net Income | 814 | 631 | 556 | 708 | NA | NA | NA | NA | NA | NA |
| S&P Core Earnings | 784 | 599 | 588 | 762 | 622 | NA | NA | NA | NA | NA |

| Balance Sheet & Other Financial Data (Million $) | 2007 | 2006 | 2005 | 2004 | 2003 | 2002 | 2001 | 2000 | 1999 | 1998 |
|---|---|---|---|---|---|---|---|---|---|---|
| Cash | 7,037 | 4,775 | 2,474 | 3,319 | NA | NA | NA | NA | NA | NA |
| Receivables | 7,244 | 6,668 | 2,172 | 2,526 | NA | NA | NA | NA | NA | NA |
| Cost of Investments | 30,625 | 35,553 | 39,100 | 40,157 | NA | NA | NA | NA | NA | NA |
| Total Assets | 109,230 | 104,172 | 93,121 | 90,934 | NA | NA | NA | NA | NA | NA |
| Loss Reserve | Nil | Nil | Nil | Nil | NA | NA | NA | NA | NA | NA |
| Short Term Debt | Nil | Nil | Nil | Nil | NA | NA | NA | NA | NA | NA |
| Capitalization:Debt | 2,018 | 2,225 | 1,833 | 1,878 | NA | NA | NA | NA | NA | NA |
| Capitalization:Equity | 7,810 | 7,925 | 7,687 | 8,058 | NA | NA | NA | NA | NA | NA |
| Capitalization:Total | 9,828 | 10,150 | 9,520 | 9,936 | NA | NA | NA | NA | NA | NA |
| Price Times Book Value:High | 2.0 | 1.7 | 1.5 | NA | NA | NA | NA | NA | NA | NA |
| Price Times Book Value:Low | 1.5 | 1.2 | 1.0 | NA | NA | NA | NA | NA | NA | NA |
| Cash Flow | 987 | 759 | 556 | NA | NA | NA | NA | NA | NA | NA |
| % Expense/Operating Revenue | 88.6 | 90.2 | 90.0 | 86.2 | NA | NA | NA | NA | NA | NA |
| % Earnings & Depreciation/Assets | 0.9 | 0.1 | 0.1 | NA | NA | NA | NA | NA | NA | NA |

Data as orig reptd.; bef. results of disc opers/spec. items. Per share data adj. for stk. divs.; EPS diluted. E-Estimated. NA-Not Available. NM-Not Meaningful. NR-Not Ranked. UR-Under Review.

**Office:** 1099 Ameriprise Financial Ctr, Minneapolis, MN 55474-0010.
**Telephone:** 612-671-3131.
**Website:** http://www.ameriprise.com
**Chrmn:** S.H. Davies

**CEO:** J. Cracchiolo
**EVP & CFO:** W.S. Berman
**EVP & General Counsel:** J.C. Junek
**SVP, Chief Acctg Officer & Cntlr:** D.K. Stewart

**Investor Contact:** L. Gagnon (612-671-2080)
**Board Members:** J. Cracchiolo, S. H. Davies, I. D. Hall, W. D. Knowlton, W. W. Lewis, S. S. Marshall, J. Noddle, R. F. Powers, III, H. J. Sarles, R. F. Sharpe, Jr., W. H. Turner

**Founded:** 1983
**Domicile:** Delaware
**Employees:** 8,750

# AmerisourceBergen Corp

**STANDARD &POOR'S**

| S&P Recommendation **BUY** ★★★★☆ | Price $29.98 (as of Nov 14, 2008) | 12-Mo. Target Price $42.00 | Investment Style Large-Cap Blend |
|---|---|---|---|

**GICS Sector** Health Care
**Sub-Industry** Health Care Distributors

**Summary** This distributor of pharmaceutical products and related health care services was formed via the August 2001 merger of Amerisource Health Corp. and Bergen Brunswig Corp.

## Key Stock Statistics (Source S&P, Vickers, company reports)

| | | | | | |
|---|---|---|---|---|---|
| 52-Wk Range | $48.60– 27.80 | S&P Oper. EPS 2009**E** | 3.15 | Market Capitalization(B) | $4.751 | Beta | 0.47 |
| Trailing 12-Month EPS | $1.54 | S&P Oper. EPS 2010**E** | 3.50 | Yield (%) | 1.33 | S&P 3-Yr. Proj. EPS CAGR(%) | 10 |
| Trailing 12-Month P/E | 19.5 | P/E on S&P Oper. EPS 2009**E** | 9.5 | Dividend Rate/Share | $0.40 | S&P Credit Rating | BBB |
| $10K Invested 5 Yrs Ago | NA | Common Shares Outstg. (M) | 158.5 | Institutional Ownership (%) | 100 | | |

## Price Performance

30-Week Mov. Avg. · · · 10-Week Mov. Avg. – – GAAP Earnings vs. Previous Year   Volume Above Avg. STARS
12-Mo. Target Price — Relative Strength — ▲ Up ▼ Down ► No Change   Below Avg.

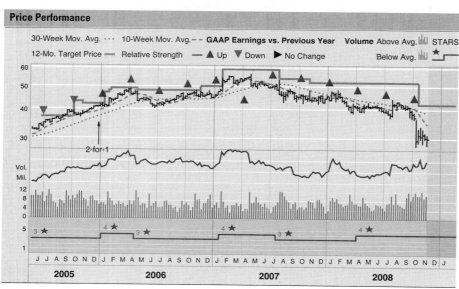

Options: ASE, CBOE, P

Analysis prepared by **Phillip M. Seligman** on November 07, 2008, when the stock traded at **$ 30.22**.

## Highlights

➤ We project FY 09 (Sep.) revenue to increase 2%, to $71.7 billion, reflecting slower market growth partly due to the soft economy and bulk deliveries to customer warehouses down on the loss of a large client. We expect growth to decelerate from FY 08's 6.9% advance, which benefited from the October 2007 acquisition of Bellco Health. We look for ABC's specialty drug revenue growth of 5% to 7%, despite the continued decline of oncology-related anemia drug sales we see due to the FDA label change in July. We also forecast generic drug volumes, which carry above-average margins, to continue to rise faster than overall volumes, but we expect those gains to be partly offset by the lower average prices commanded by such drugs.

➤ We forecast distribution operating margins to widen on an organic basis by a low to mid-single digit basis point amount, as benefits from generic drug and specialty drug penetration and lower SG&A expenses outweigh sell-side pricing pressure and IT spending.

➤ We expect FY 09 operating EPS of $3.15, versus FY 08's $2.86, and see $3.50 in FY 10, aided also by share buybacks.

## Investment Rationale/Risk

➤ We believe ABC has the wherewithal to manage through this period of sluggish pharmaceutical volume growth. The company controls costs tightly, in our view; it has no scheduled debt repayments for several years; and we expect its cash flow to remain healthy, albeit slightly below FY 08 levels, providing financial flexibility. Meanwhile, we see generic drug penetration rising faster, spurred by the soft economy, which we view as a positive for earnings. We expect ABC's specialty sales to grow significantly faster than the market as a whole. Also, we believe its contract with Longs Drug Stores will remain intact through FY 09, despite the latter's acquisition. Elsewhere, we like ABC's recent sale of its underperforming workers' compensation business, as it will no longer be a distraction.

➤ Risks to our opinion and target price include intensified competition and a major client loss.

➤ Our 12-month target price of $42 is based on our calendar 2009 EPS estimate of $3.25 and our P/E target multiple of 13X, reflecting groupwide valuation compression. This multiple is below the peer average, to reflect ABC's being less diversified.

## Qualitative Risk Assessment

| LOW | MEDIUM | HIGH |
|---|---|---|

Our risk assessment reflects what we view as ABC's improving financial performance, its ability to attract new accounts to more than compensate for account losses, and its healthy operating cash flow. However, the drug distribution arena is highly competitive, and ABC is less diversified than many of its large health care distribution peers.

## Quantitative Evaluations

**S&P Quality Ranking** A-

| D | C | B- | B | B+ | A- | A | A+ |
|---|---|---|---|---|---|---|---|

**Relative Strength Rank** MODERATE

67

LOWEST = 1    HIGHEST = 99

## Revenue/Earnings Data

**Revenue (Million $)**

| | 1Q | 2Q | 3Q | 4Q | Year |
|---|---|---|---|---|---|
| 2008 | 17,373 | 17,846 | 17,997 | 17,158 | 70,190 |
| 2007 | 16,725 | 16,513 | 16,446 | 16,390 | 66,074 |
| 2006 | 14,653 | 15,221 | 15,686 | 15,643 | 61,203 |
| 2005 | 13,639 | 13,192 | 13,832 | 13,918 | 54,577 |
| 2004 | 13,355 | 13,364 | 13,072 | 13,389 | 53,179 |
| 2003 | 12,435 | 12,163 | 12,421 | 12,640 | 49,657 |

**Earnings Per Share ($)**

| | | | | | |
|---|---|---|---|---|---|
| 2008 | 0.66 | 0.82 | 0.70 | 0.73 | 2.89 |
| 2007 | 0.63 | 0.68 | 0.69 | 0.63 | 2.63 |
| 2006 | 0.47 | 0.61 | 0.58 | 0.61 | 2.26 |
| 2005 | 0.33 | 0.46 | 0.48 | 0.10 | 1.37 |
| 2004 | 0.47 | 0.62 | 0.55 | 0.41 | 2.03 |
| 2003 | 0.42 | 0.52 | 0.50 | 0.52 | 1.95 |

Fiscal year ended Sep. 30. Next earnings report expected: Late January. EPS Estimates based on S&P Operating Earnings; historical GAAP earnings are as reported.

## Dividend Data (Dates: mm/dd Payment Date: mm/dd/yy)

| Amount ($) | Date Decl. | Ex-Div. Date | Stk. of Record | Payment Date |
|---|---|---|---|---|
| 0.075 | 02/05 | 02/13 | 02/18 | 03/03/08 |
| 0.075 | 05/08 | 05/15 | 05/19 | 06/02/08 |
| 0.075 | 08/07 | 08/14 | 08/18 | 09/02/08 |
| 0.100 | 11/13 | 11/20 | 11/24 | 12/08/08 |

Dividends have been paid since 2001. Source: Company reports.

# AmerisourceBergen Corp

STANDARD
&POOR'S

## Business Summary November 07, 2008

CORPORATE OVERVIEW. AmerisourceBergen Corp., one of the largest U.S. pharmaceutical distributors, began operation in August 2001, following the merger of Amerisource Health Corp. and Bergen Brunswig Corp. ABC accounted for the merger as an acquisition by Amerisource of Bergen.

The pharmaceutical distribution segment includes the AmerisourceBergen Drug Corporation (ABDC), AmerisourceBergen Specialty Group (ABSG) and the AmerisourceBergen Packaging Group (ABPG). ABDC distributes branded and generic pharmaceuticals, over-the-counter health care products, and home health care supplies and equipment to hospitals, pharmacies, mail order facilities, clinics, and alternate site facilities. ABSG ($12.2 billion of operating revenue in FY 07 (Sep.), versus $9.9 billion in FY 06) supplies goods and services to physicians and alternate care providers that specialize in disease states, such as oncology. ABPG repackages drugs from bulk to unit dose, unit of use, blister pack and standard bottle sizes.

National and retail drugstore chains, independent community drugstores, and pharmacy departments of supermarkets and mass merchandisers account for its retail market segment (38% of FY 07 operating revenue, which excludes

bulk deliveries to customer warehouses, of $61.7 billion), while the hospital/acute care, mail order and specialty pharmaceuticals markets together comprise its institutional market segment (62%). Revenues generated from sales to pharmacy benefit manager Medco Health Solutions (MHS) accounted for 90% of bulk deliveries and 8% of operating revenue in FY 07. With a contract signed in early FY 08, a majority of MHS's bulk delivery business is now being treated on an operating basis.

The "Other" segment is PharMerica's workers' compensation-related business, which provides pharmacy services to chronically and catastrophically ill patients under workers' comp programs, and provides pharmaceutical claims administration services for payors. On July 31, 2007, ABC spun off the PharMerica segment's long-term care business, a national dispenser of pharmaceutical products and services to patients in long-term care facilities.

## Company Financials Fiscal Year Ended Sep. 30

| Per Share Data ($) | 2008 | 2007 | 2006 | 2005 | 2004 | 2003 | 2002 | 2001 | 2000 | 1999 |
|---|---|---|---|---|---|---|---|---|---|---|
| Tangible Book Value | NA | 0.05 | 7.91 | 7.38 | 8.62 | 7.21 | 5.22 | 1.80 | 2.41 | 1.44 |
| Cash Flow | NA | 3.18 | 2.72 | 1.73 | 2.36 | 2.21 | 1.81 | 1.16 | 1.11 | 0.86 |
| Earnings | 2.89 | 2.63 | 2.26 | 1.37 | 2.03 | 1.95 | 1.58 | 1.05 | 0.95 | 0.69 |
| S&P Core Earnings | NA | 2.46 | 2.07 | 1.24 | 1.55 | 1.86 | 1.53 | 0.85 | NA | NA |
| Dividends | 0.30 | 0.20 | 0.10 | 0.05 | 0.05 | 0.05 | 0.05 | Nil | Nil | Nil |
| Payout Ratio | 10% | 8% | 4% | 4% | 2% | 3% | 3% | Nil | Nil | Nil |
| Prices:High | 48.60 | 56.56 | 48.96 | 42.18 | 32.01 | 36.72 | 41.43 | 36.00 | 26.84 | 20.69 |
| Prices:Low | 27.80 | 42.21 | 40.15 | 26.48 | 24.87 | 22.83 | 25.10 | 20.06 | 6.00 | 5.50 |
| P/E Ratio:High | 17 | 22 | 22 | 31 | 16 | 19 | 26 | 34 | 28 | 30 |
| P/E Ratio:Low | 10 | 16 | 18 | 19 | 12 | 12 | 16 | 19 | 6 | 8 |

| Income Statement Analysis (Million $) | | | | | | | | | | |
|---|---|---|---|---|---|---|---|---|---|---|
| Revenue | 70,190 | 66,074 | 61,203 | 54,577 | 53,179 | 49,657 | 45,235 | 16,191 | 11,645 | 9,760 |
| Operating Income | NA | 912 | 814 | 723 | 978 | 963 | 804 | 302 | 217 | 191 |
| Depreciation | 82.1 | 104 | 96.9 | 81.2 | 87.1 | 71.0 | 61.2 | 21.6 | 16.1 | 17.4 |
| Interest Expense | NA | 32.0 | 12.5 | 57.2 | 113 | 145 | 141 | 45.7 | 41.9 | 39.0 |
| Pretax Income | 761 | 7.85 | 741 | 469 | 760 | 726 | 572 | 202 | 160 | 119 |
| Effective Tax Rate | 38.4% | 37.1% | 36.8% | 37.7% | 38.4% | 39.2% | 39.7% | 38.6% | 38.0% | 40.6% |
| Net Income | 469 | 494 | 468 | 292 | 468 | 441 | 345 | 124 | 99.0 | 70.9 |
| S&P Core Earnings | NA | 462 | 429 | 264 | 356 | 421 | 333 | 99.8 | NA | NA |

| Balance Sheet & Other Financial Data (Million $) | | | | | | | | | | |
|---|---|---|---|---|---|---|---|---|---|---|
| Cash | 878 | 640 | 1,261 | 1,316 | 871 | 800 | 663 | 298 | 121 | 59.5 |
| Current Assets | NA | 8,714 | 9,210 | 7,988 | 8,295 | 8,859 | 8,350 | 7,513 | 2,321 | 1,920 |
| Total Assets | 12,153 | 12,310 | 12,784 | 11,381 | 11,654 | 12,040 | 11,213 | 10,291 | 2,459 | 2,061 |
| Current Liabilities | NA | 7,857 | 7,459 | 6,052 | 6,104 | 6,256 | 6,100 | 5,532 | 1,751 | 1,327 |
| Long Term Debt | NA | 1,227 | 1,094 | 951 | 1,157 | 1,723 | 1,756 | 1,872 | 413 | 559 |
| Common Equity | 2,710 | 3,100 | 4,141 | 4,280 | 4,339 | 4,005 | 3,316 | 5,677 | 565 | 166 |
| Total Capital | NA | 4,327 | 5,235 | 5,232 | 5,496 | 5,728 | 5,073 | 7,549 | 978 | 725 |
| Capital Expenditures | 137 | 118,051 | 113 | 203 | 189 | 90.6 | 64.2 | 23.4 | 16.6 | 15.8 |
| Cash Flow | NA | 598 | 565 | 373 | 555 | 512 | 406 | 145 | 115 | 88.3 |
| Current Ratio | 1.1 | 1.1 | 1.2 | 1.3 | 1.4 | 1.4 | 1.4 | 1.4 | 1.3 | 1.4 |
| % Long Term Debt of Capitalization | 30.5 | 28.3 | 20.9 | 18.2 | 21.1 | 30.1 | 34.6 | 24.8 | 42.3 | 77.1 |
| % Net Income of Revenue | 0.7 | 0.7 | 0.8 | 0.5 | 0.9 | 0.9 | 0.8 | 0.8 | 0.9 | 0.7 |
| % Return on Assets | 3.8 | 3.9 | 3.9 | 2.5 | 4.0 | 3.8 | 3.2 | 1.9 | 4.4 | 3.9 |
| % Return on Equity | 16.2 | 13.6 | 11.1 | 6.8 | 11.2 | 12.1 | 11.2 | 4.0 | 22.1 | 58.8 |

Data as orig reptd.; bef. results of disc opers/spec. items. Per share data adj. for stk. divs.; EPS diluted. E-Estimated. NA-Not Available. NM-Not Meaningful. NR-Not Ranked. UR-Under Review.

**Office:** 1300 Morris Drive, Chesterbrook, PA 19087-5594.
**Telephone:** 610-727-7000.
**Email:** investorrelations@amerisourcebergen.com
**Website:** http://www.amerisourcebergen.com

**Chrmn:** R.C. Gozon
**Pres & CEO:** R.D. Yost
**COO:** D. Shane
**EVP, CFO & Chief Acctg Officer:** M.D. Dicandilo

**SVP, Secy & General Counsel:** J.G. Chou
**Board Members:** C. H. Cotros, M. A. Delaney, R. W. Gochnauer, R. C. Gozon, E. E. Hagenlocker, J. E. Henney, M. J. Long, H. W. McGee, J. Wilson, R. D. Yost

**Founded:** 1985
**Domicile:** Delaware
**Employees:** 11,300

The McGraw-Hill Companies

# Amgen Inc

**STANDARD &POOR'S**

| S&P Recommendation | BUY ★★★★☆ | Price | 12-Mo. Target Price | Investment Style |
|---|---|---|---|---|
| | | $58.23 (as of Nov 14, 2008) | $69.00 | Large-Cap Growth |

**GICS Sector** Health Care
**Sub-Industry** Biotechnology

**Summary** Amgen, among the world's leading biotech companies, has major treatments for anemia, neutropenia, rheumatoid arthritis, psoriatic arthritis, psoriasis and cancer.

## Key Stock Statistics (Source S&P, Vickers, company reports)

| | | | | | | | | |
|---|---|---|---|---|---|---|---|---|
| 52-Wk Range | $66.51– 27.00 | S&P Oper. EPS 2008E | 4.50 | Market Capitalization(B) | $61.696 | Beta | | 0.62 |
| Trailing 12-Month EPS | $3.76 | S&P Oper. EPS 2009E | 4.62 | Yield (%) | Nil | S&P 3-Yr. Proj. EPS CAGR(%) | | 13 |
| Trailing 12-Month P/E | 15.5 | P/E on S&P Oper. EPS 2008E | 12.9 | Dividend Rate/Share | Nil | S&P Credit Rating | | A+ |
| $10K Invested 5 Yrs Ago | $9,997 | Common Shares Outstg. (M) | 1,059.5 | Institutional Ownership (%) | 80 | | | |

## Price Performance

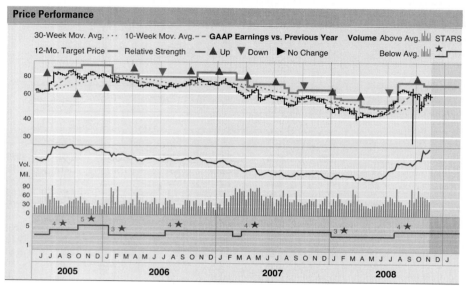

30-Week Mov. Avg. · · · · 10-Week Mov. Avg. – – GAAP Earnings vs. Previous Year Volume Above Avg. STARS
12-Mo. Target Price — Relative Strength — ▲ Up ▼ Down ► No Change Below Avg.

Options: ASE, CBOE, P, Ph

Analysis prepared by **Steven Silver** on October 29, 2008, when the stock traded at **$ 59.88**.

## Qualitative Risk Assessment

| LOW | MEDIUM | HIGH |
|---|---|---|

Our risk assessment reflects that the company's products are sold in highly competitive markets and are subject to government regulation. Changes to government reimbursement policies could significantly affect AMGN's revenues and profitability. Though adoption has been mild thus far, we believe that generics for Epogen could pose a long-term threat in Europe.

## Quantitative Evaluations

**S&P Quality Ranking** B+

| D | C | B- | B | B+ | A- | A | A+ |
|---|---|---|---|---|---|---|---|

**Relative Strength Rank** STRONG

94

LOWEST = 1    HIGHEST = 99

## Revenue/Earnings Data

**Revenue (Million $)**

| | 1Q | 2Q | 3Q | 4Q | Year |
|---|---|---|---|---|---|
| 2008 | 3,613 | 3,764 | 3,875 | -- | -- |
| 2007 | 3,687 | 3,728 | 3,611 | 3,745 | 14,771 |
| 2006 | 3,217 | 3,491 | 3,503 | 3,737 | 14,268 |
| 2005 | 2,833 | 3,172 | 3,154 | 3,271 | 12,430 |
| 2004 | 2,343 | 2,585 | 2,713 | 2,909 | 10,550 |
| 2003 | 1,761 | 2,041 | 2,207 | 2,346 | 8,356 |

**Earnings Per Share ($)**

| | | | | | |
|---|---|---|---|---|---|
| 2008 | 1.04 | 0.87 | 1.09 | E1.06 | E4.50 |
| 2007 | 0.94 | 0.90 | 0.18 | 0.77 | 2.82 |
| 2006 | 0.82 | 0.01 | 0.94 | 0.71 | 2.48 |
| 2005 | 0.67 | 0.82 | 0.77 | 0.66 | 2.93 |
| 2004 | 0.52 | 0.57 | 0.18 | 0.53 | 1.81 |
| 2003 | 0.37 | 0.45 | 0.46 | 0.41 | 1.69 |

Fiscal year ended Dec. 31. Next earnings report expected: Late January. EPS Estimates based on S&P Operating Earnings; historical GAAP earnings are as reported.

## Dividend Data

No cash dividends have been paid.

## Highlights

➤ We see 2008 revenues of $15.0 billion, compared with 2007's $14.8 billion, and we forecast 2009 revenues of $15.3 billion, as AMGN manages challenges to its anemia franchise. U.S. Aranesp sales declined 12% year over year in the third quarter of 2008, excluding a one-time accounting adjustment, as demand stabilizes but remains soft, following recent FDA label restrictions over safety concerns at higher doses. We also see signs of slowing demand for Enbrel from increased competition, with slight market share declines thus far this year.

➤ We forecast 2008 gross margins near 85%, roughly in line with those in recent years. We expect 2008 adjusted R&D expenses to be flat compared with 2007's 21% of sales, down from 23% in 2006, but still healthy as a percentage of product sales, in our view. We project 2008 adjusted SG&A expenses of around 23% of sales, in line with recent years, with AMGN containing costs amid revenue instability.

➤ We estimate 2008 EPS of $4.50 and 2009 EPS of $4.62. As of September 30, 2008, AMGN had $9.8 billion in cash, and debt of $11.2 billion. We are encouraged by AMGN's $1.2 billion of free cash flow in the third quarter of 2008.

## Investment Rationale/Risk

➤ Our buy recommendation reflects our favorable view of recent denosumab data in a pivotal Phase III study that met all osteoporosis-related fracture prevention endpoints, and eased concerns over the drug's safety profile. We believe denosumab represents a significant growth opportunity for AMGN, with over $3 billion in sales possible. We see denosumab, with initial launch likely in 2010, and Nplate, approved by FDA in August 2008, shifting investor focus back to AMGN's pipeline, which we think is among the most promising in the biotech industry. Though we believe AMGN still faces pressures to its anemia drug franchise from FDA and Medicare restrictions, we are encouraged by recent court action blocking the launch of Roche's rival Mircera drug.

➤ Risks to our recommendation and target price include further FDA and Medicare restrictions on anemia drug sales, negative clinical trial results, competition to existing products, and challenges to AMGN's product patents.

➤ Our 12-month target price of $69 applies a 15X multiple to our 2009 EPS estimate, a discount to profitable peers on our view of above industry-average safety and competitive risk.

---

**Please read the Required Disclosures and Analyst Certification on the last page of this report.**

The McGraw-Hill Companies

# Amgen Inc

**STANDARD &POOR'S**

## Business Summary October 29, 2008

CORPORATE OVERVIEW. Amgen, among the world's largest biotech companies, makes and markets five of the world's best-selling biotech drugs.

Epogen is a genetically engineered version of human erythropoietin (EPO), a hormone that stimulates red blood cell production in bone marrow. Its primary market is dialysis patients suffering from chronic anemia. Epogen sales were $2.49 billion in 2007 ($2.51 billion in 2006). Aranesp, a recombinant protein that stimulates the production of red blood cells in pre-dialysis and dialysis patients, is approved to treat anemia associated with chronic renal failure and cancer patients with chemotherapy-induced anemia (CIA). Aranesp sales were $3.61 billion in 2007 ($4.12 billion in 2006). AMGN is developing AMG 114, a next-generation EPO drug. In 2007, Phase III trial data showed a higher rate of death when using Aranesp in treating anemia-of cancer (AoC) not associated with chemotherapy, an off-label prescribed use. Medicare removed AoC as a reimbursable use for Aranesp. During 2007, several studies emerged suggesting that Aranesp may foster tumor growth in several cancers when dosed

at or above 12 g/dl.

Neupogen stimulates neutrophils (white blood cells that defend against bacterial infection) production in cancer patients whose natural neutrophils were destroyed by chemotherapy. In 2002, the FDA approved Neulasta, a long-acting white blood cell stimulant protecting chemo patients from infection. Total Neupogen and Neulasta 2007 sales were $4.28 billion ($3.92 billion in 2006).

Enbrel, acquired through the purchase of Immunex, (co-marketed with Wyeth) had 2007 sales of $3.23 billion ($2.88 billion in 2006) and is approved to treat rheumatoid arthritis (RA), psoriatic arthritis, and adults with moderate to severe chronic plaque psoriasis.

## Company Financials Fiscal Year Ended Dec. 31

| Per Share Data ($) | 2007 | 2006 | 2005 | 2004 | 2003 | 2002 | 2001 | 2000 | 1999 | 1998 |
|---|---|---|---|---|---|---|---|---|---|---|
| Tangible Book Value | 3.03 | 3.36 | 5.08 | 4.08 | 4.06 | 2.80 | 4.99 | 4.16 | 2.97 | 2.52 |
| Cash Flow | 3.89 | 3.29 | 3.59 | 2.35 | 2.19 | -0.82 | 1.28 | 1.24 | 1.18 | 0.95 |
| Earnings | 2.82 | 2.48 | 2.93 | 1.81 | 1.69 | -1.21 | 1.03 | 1.05 | 1.02 | 0.82 |
| S&P Core Earnings | 2.74 | 2.48 | 2.77 | 1.58 | 1.50 | -1.46 | 0.87 | NA | NA | NA |
| Dividends | Nil | Nil | Nil | Nil | Nil | Nil | Nil | Nil | Nil | Nil |
| Payout Ratio | Nil | Nil | Nil | Nil | Nil | Nil | Nil | Nil | Nil | Nil |
| Prices:High | 76.95 | 81.24 | 86.92 | 66.88 | 72.37 | 62.94 | 75.06 | 80.44 | 66.44 | 27.25 |
| Prices:Low | 46.21 | 63.52 | 56.19 | 52.00 | 48.09 | 30.57 | 45.44 | 50.00 | 25.69 | 11.66 |
| P/E Ratio:High | 27 | 33 | 30 | 37 | 43 | NM | 73 | 77 | 65 | 33 |
| P/E Ratio:Low | 16 | 26 | 19 | 29 | 28 | NM | 44 | 48 | 25 | 14 |

| Income Statement Analysis (Million $) | 2007 | 2006 | 2005 | 2004 | 2003 | 2002 | 2001 | 2000 | 1999 | 1998 |
|---|---|---|---|---|---|---|---|---|---|---|
| Revenue | 14,771 | 14,268 | 12,430 | 10,550 | 8,356 | 5,523 | 4,016 | 3,629 | 3,340 | 2,718 |
| Operating Income | 6,631 | 6,022 | 5,689 | 4,636 | 3,758 | 2,501 | 2,003 | 1,761 | 1,638 | 1,338 |
| Depreciation | 1,202 | 963 | 841 | 734 | 686 | 447 | 266 | 212 | 177 | 144 |
| Interest Expense | 305 | 129 | 99.0 | 38.0 | 31.5 | 44.2 | 13.6 | 15.9 | 15.2 | 10.0 |
| Pretax Income | 3,961 | 4,020 | 4,868 | 3,395 | 3,173 | -684 | 1,686 | 1,674 | 1,566 | 1,224 |
| Effective Tax Rate | 20.1% | 26.6% | 24.5% | 30.4% | 28.8% | NM | 33.6% | 32.0% | 30.0% | 29.5% |
| Net Income | 3,166 | 2,950 | 3,674 | 2,363 | 2,260 | -1,392 | 1,120 | 1,139 | 1,096 | 863 |
| S&P Core Earnings | 3,072 | 2,951 | 3,470 | 2,074 | 2,006 | -1,683 | 936 | NA | NA | NA |

| Balance Sheet & Other Financial Data (Million $) | 2007 | 2006 | 2005 | 2004 | 2003 | 2002 | 2001 | 2000 | 1999 | 1998 |
|---|---|---|---|---|---|---|---|---|---|---|
| Cash | 7,151 | 6,277 | 5,255 | 5,808 | 5,123 | 4,664 | 2,662 | 2,028 | 1,333 | 1,276 |
| Current Assets | 13,041 | 11,712 | 9,235 | 9,170 | 7,402 | 6,404 | 3,859 | 2,937 | 2,065 | 1,863 |
| Total Assets | 34,639 | 33,788 | 29,297 | 29,221 | 26,177 | 24,456 | 6,443 | 5,400 | 4,078 | 3,672 |
| Current Liabilities | 6,179 | 7,022 | 3,595 | 4,157 | 2,246 | 1,529 | 1,003 | 862 | 831 | 887 |
| Long Term Debt | 11,177 | 7,134 | 3,957 | 3,937 | 3,080 | 3,048 | 223 | 223 | 223 | 223 |
| Common Equity | 17,869 | 18,964 | 20,451 | 19,705 | 19,389 | 18,286 | 5,217 | 4,315 | 3,024 | 2,562 |
| Total Capital | 27,526 | 26,465 | 25,571 | 24,936 | 23,930 | 22,927 | 5,440 | 4,538 | 3,247 | 2,785 |
| Capital Expenditures | 1,267 | 1,218 | 867 | 1,336 | 1,357 | 658 | 442 | 438 | 304 | 408 |
| Cash Flow | 4,368 | 3,913 | 4,515 | 3,097 | 2,946 | -945 | 1,386 | 1,350 | 1,273 | 1,007 |
| Current Ratio | 2.1 | 1.7 | 2.6 | 2.2 | 3.3 | 4.2 | 3.8 | 3.4 | 2.5 | 2.1 |
| % Long Term Debt of Capitalization | 33.9 | 27.0 | 15.5 | 15.8 | 12.9 | 13.3 | 4.1 | 4.9 | 6.9 | 8.0 |
| % Net Income of Revenue | 21.4 | 20.7 | 29.6 | 22.4 | 27.0 | NM | 27.9 | 31.4 | 32.8 | 31.8 |
| % Return on Assets | 9.3 | 9.4 | 12.6 | 8.5 | 8.9 | NM | 18.9 | 24.0 | 28.3 | 25.5 |
| % Return on Equity | 17.2 | 15.0 | 18.3 | 12.1 | 12.0 | NM | 23.5 | 31.0 | 39.3 | 36.7 |

Data as orig reptd.; bef. results of disc opers/spec. items. Per share data adj. for stk. divs.; EPS diluted. E-Estimated. NA-Not Available. NM-Not Meaningful. NR-Not Ranked. UR-Under Review.

**Office:** One Amgen Center Drive, Thousand Oaks, CA 91320-1799.
**Telephone:** 805-447-1000.
**Email:** investor.relations@amgen.com
**Website:** http://www.amgen.com

**Chrmn, Pres & CEO:** K.W. Sharer
**COO:** F.J. Bonanni
**EVP & CFO:** R.A. Bradway
**SVP, Secy & General Counsel:** D.J. Scott

**SVP & CIO:** T.J. Flanagan
**Investor Contact:** A. Sood (805-447-1060)
**Board Members:** D. Baltimore, F. J. Biondi, Jr., J. D. Choate, V. D. Coffman, F. W. Gluck, F. C. Herringer, G. S. Omenn, J. C. Pelham, J. P. Reason, L. D. Schaeffer, K. W. Sharer, F. de Carbonnel

**Founded:** 1980
**Domicile:** Delaware
**Employees:** 17,500

# Amphenol Corp

**STANDARD &POOR'S**

| S&P Recommendation | BUY ★★★★☆ | Price<br>$22.25 (as of Nov 14, 2008) | 12-Mo. Target Price<br>$35.00 | Investment Style<br>Large-Cap Growth |
|---|---|---|---|---|

**GICS Sector** Information Technology
**Sub-Industry** Electronic Components

**Summary** This company makes connectors, cable and interconnect systems for electronics, cable TV, telecommunications, aerospace, transportation and industrial applications.

## Key Stock Statistics (Source S&P, Vickers, company reports)

| | | | | | | | |
|---|---|---|---|---|---|---|---|
| 52-Wk Range | $52.28– 21.15 | S&P Oper. EPS 2008E | 2.38 | Market Capitalization(B) | $3.911 | Beta | 1.58 |
| Trailing 12-Month EPS | $2.33 | S&P Oper. EPS 2009E | 2.60 | Yield (%) | 0.27 | S&P 3-Yr. Proj. EPS CAGR(%) | 12 |
| Trailing 12-Month P/E | 9.6 | P/E on S&P Oper. EPS 2008E | 9.3 | Dividend Rate/Share | $0.06 | S&P Credit Rating | NA |
| $10K Invested 5 Yrs Ago | $14,973 | Common Shares Outstg. (M) | 175.8 | Institutional Ownership (%) | 96 | | |

## Price Performance

30-Week Mov. Avg. · · · 10-Week Mov. Avg. – – **GAAP Earnings vs. Previous Year** Volume Above Avg. STARS
12-Mo. Target Price — Relative Strength — ▲ Up ▼ Down ▶ No Change Below Avg. ★

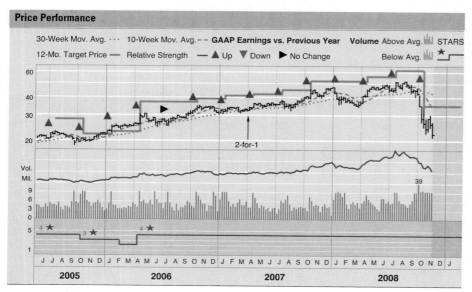

2-for-1

Options: ASE, P, Ph

Analysis prepared by **Michael W. Jaffe** on October 22, 2008, when the stock traded at **$ 26.10**.

## Highlights

➤ We see a 6% increase in sales in 2009, when we expect APH to benefit from the wide diversity of its customer base, and reflecting our outlook for ongoing economic strength in certain emerging markets. We see these factors outweighing challenging economies and credit markets in the U.S. and Western Europe, and their likely negative effect on demand for APH's products. We also expect the recent strengthening of the U.S. dollar against various foreign currencies to result in less favorable foreign exchange translation.

➤ We expect net margins to widen slightly in 2009, on APH's ongoing focus on cost controls, the better performance that we see in emerging markets, and the recent downturn in materials costs. We see these factors being largely offset by the impact of more challenging economic conditions in a large number of geographies.

➤ We believe Amphenol's strongest end markets in the coming year will be military/aerospace and mobile devices.

## Investment Rationale/Risk

➤ We think APH will post earnings gains through 2009, but that difficult economies in many of the company's primary geographic markets will limit its level of growth. We also see APH's long-term prospects aided by what we expect to be an ongoing expansion of the global communications infrastructure, a growing sophistication of military and space systems, and the use of more electronic devices in autos and other industrial products. Based on these factors and our relative P/E analysis, we view APH as undervalued.

➤ Risks to our recommendation and target price include even greater than expected weakness in the global economy and a major downturn in demand for APH's interconnect products.

➤ The shares recently traded at about 10X our 2009 EPS estimate, near the low end of APH's range for the past decade. Based on our belief that APH will manage to record modest EPS gains in the coming year, and in light of recent government efforts to stabilize financial markets, we think a higher valuation is merited. Our 12-month target price is $35, or 13.5X our 2009 estimate.

## Qualitative Risk Assessment

| LOW | MEDIUM | HIGH |
|---|---|---|

Our risk assessment for APH reflects what we view as the company's typically solid levels of cash flow and a strong business model. We see these factors being offset by the inherent cyclicality of APH's business. In addition, although long-term debt as a percentage of total capital has shrunk markedly since 1997, it still remained at what we see as a relatively high level of 34.5% at September 30, 2008.

## Quantitative Evaluations

**S&P Quality Ranking** B+

| D | C | B- | B | B+ | A- | A | A+ |
|---|---|---|---|---|---|---|---|

**Relative Strength Rank** WEAK

28

LOWEST = 1      HIGHEST = 99

## Revenue/Earnings Data

**Revenue (Million $)**

| | 1Q | 2Q | 3Q | 4Q | Year |
|---|---|---|---|---|---|
| 2008 | 770.7 | 846.8 | 863.7 | -- | -- |
| 2007 | 651.1 | 688.8 | 733.9 | 777.3 | 2,851 |
| 2006 | 569.0 | 606.6 | 636.4 | 659.4 | 2,471 |
| 2005 | 409.4 | 443.6 | 447.0 | 508.1 | 1,808 |
| 2004 | 355.3 | 387.1 | 384.1 | 404.0 | 1,530 |
| 2003 | 277.8 | 304.9 | 314.8 | 342.0 | 1,240 |

**Earnings Per Share ($)**

| | | | | | |
|---|---|---|---|---|---|
| 2008 | 0.54 | 0.61 | 0.63 | E0.60 | E2.38 |
| 2007 | 0.43 | 0.46 | 0.50 | 0.55 | 1.94 |
| 2006 | 0.32 | 0.29 | 0.37 | 0.43 | 1.40 |
| 2005 | 0.26 | 0.29 | 0.29 | 0.31 | 1.14 |
| 2004 | 0.20 | 0.23 | 0.24 | 0.26 | 0.91 |
| 2003 | 0.14 | 0.11 | 0.16 | 0.19 | 0.59 |

Fiscal year ended Dec. 31. Next earnings report expected: Mid January. EPS Estimates based on S&P Operating Earnings; historical GAAP earnings are as reported.

## Dividend Data (Dates: mm/dd Payment Date: mm/dd/yy)

| Amount ($) | Date Decl. | Ex-Div. Date | Stk. of Record | Payment Date |
|---|---|---|---|---|
| 0.015 | 01/25 | 03/10 | 03/12 | 04/02/08 |
| 0.015 | 04/25 | 06/09 | 06/11 | 07/02/08 |
| 0.015 | 07/25 | 09/08 | 09/10 | 10/01/08 |
| 0.015 | 10/24 | 12/15 | 12/17 | 01/07/09 |

Dividends have been paid since 2005. Source: Company reports.

---

**Please read the Required Disclosures and Analyst Certification on the last page of this report.**

# Amphenol Corp

STANDARD &POOR'S

## Business Summary October 22, 2008

CORPORATE OVERVIEW. Amphenol makes electrical, electronic and fiber optic connectors, interconnect systems, and coaxial and flat ribbon cable. In 2007, APH derived 60% of revenues from information technology and communications markets, 21% from industrial/automotive, and 19% from commercial aerospace and military. It derived 45% of sales in North America, 22% in Europe, and 33% in Asia and other countries.

APH makes a broad range of interconnect products and assemblies (90% of 2007 revenues) for voice, video and data communications systems, commercial aerospace and military systems, automotive and mass transportation applications, and industrial and factory automation equipment. Its connectors and interconnect systems are mostly used to conduct electrical and optical signals for sophisticated electronic applications.

In communications, the company supplies connector and cable assembly products used in base stations for wireless communication systems and Internet networking equipment; smart card acceptor devices used in mobile telephones, set top boxes and other applications to facilitate reading data from smart cards; fiber optic connectors used in fiber optic transmissions; backplane and input/output connectors for servers and data storage devices, and

for linking PCs and peripheral equipment; and sculptured flexible circuits for integrating circuit boards.

APH also makes radio frequency connector products and antennas used in telecommunications, computer and office equipment, instrumentation equipment, local area networks and automotive electronics. Radio frequency connectors are also used in base stations, mobile communications devices and other components of cellular and personal communication networks.

The company believes it is the largest supplier of high-performance, military-specification, circular environmental connectors, generally used in sophisticated aerospace, military, commercial and industrial equipment. APH also makes industrial interconnect products, used in applications such as factory automation equipment, mass transportation applications and automotive safety products.

## Company Financials Fiscal Year Ended Dec. 31

| Per Share Data ($) | 2007 | 2006 | 2005 | 2004 | 2003 | 2002 | 2001 | 2000 | 1999 | 1998 |
|---|---|---|---|---|---|---|---|---|---|---|
| Tangible Book Value | 1.00 | NM | NM | NM | NM | NM | NM | NM | NM | NM |
| Cash Flow | 2.38 | 1.79 | 1.42 | 1.13 | 0.80 | 0.66 | 0.76 | 0.88 | 0.49 | 0.50 |
| Earnings | 1.94 | 1.40 | 1.14 | 0.91 | 0.59 | 0.46 | 0.49 | 0.63 | 0.30 | 0.25 |
| S&P Core Earnings | 1.97 | 1.43 | 1.14 | 0.90 | 0.57 | 0.35 | 0.36 | NA | NA | NA |
| Dividends | 0.08 | 0.06 | 0.06 | Nil | Nil | Nil | Nil | Nil | Nil | Nil |
| Payout Ratio | 4% | 4% | 5% | Nil | Nil | Nil | Nil | Nil | Nil | Nil |
| Prices:High | 47.24 | 35.25 | 23.10 | 18.76 | 16.03 | 12.94 | 14.50 | 17.59 | 8.94 | 8.00 |
| Prices:Low | 30.61 | 21.94 | 16.62 | 13.95 | 9.25 | 6.87 | 7.08 | 7.58 | 3.68 | 3.38 |
| P/E Ratio:High | 24 | 25 | 20 | 21 | 27 | 28 | 30 | 28 | 30 | 32 |
| P/E Ratio:Low | 16 | 16 | 15 | 15 | 16 | 15 | 15 | 12 | 12 | 13 |

| Income Statement Analysis (Million $) | | | | | | | | | | |
|---|---|---|---|---|---|---|---|---|---|---|
| Revenue | 2,851 | 2,471 | 1,808 | 1,530 | 1,240 | 1,062 | 1,104 | 1,360 | 1,011 | 919 |
| Operating Income | 635 | 518 | 394 | 315 | 241 | 209 | 229 | 287 | 201 | 185 |
| Depreciation | 82.3 | 72.6 | 50.7 | 38.8 | 37.0 | 34.8 | 46.7 | 42.8 | 27.7 | 35.3 |
| Interest Expense | 36.9 | 38.8 | 24.1 | 22.5 | 29.5 | 45.9 | 56.1 | 61.7 | 79.3 | 81.2 |
| Pretax Income | 501 | 373 | 308 | 247 | 158 | 123 | 135 | 173 | 76.2 | 64.8 |
| Effective Tax Rate | 29.5% | 31.5% | 33.0% | 34.0% | 34.0% | 34.5% | 38.2% | 37.7% | 41.8% | 42.4% |
| Net Income | 353 | 256 | 206 | 163 | 104 | 80.3 | 83.7 | 108 | 44.3 | 36.5 |
| S&P Core Earnings | 359 | 261 | 206 | 161 | 99.8 | 60.0 | 62.0 | NA | NA | NA |

| Balance Sheet & Other Financial Data (Million $) | | | | | | | | | | |
|---|---|---|---|---|---|---|---|---|---|---|
| Cash | 184 | 74.1 | 38.7 | 30.2 | 23.5 | 20.7 | 28.0 | 24.6 | 12.9 | 3.10 |
| Current Assets | 1,224 | 935 | 710 | 529 | 451 | 389 | 370 | 413 | 335 | 288 |
| Total Assets | 2,676 | 2,195 | 1,933 | 1,307 | 1,181 | 1,079 | 1,027 | 1,004 | 836 | 807 |
| Current Liabilities | 520 | 448 | 336 | 278 | 218 | 236 | 203 | 243 | 146 | 124 |
| Long Term Debt | 722 | 677 | 766 | 432 | 532 | 566 | 661 | 700 | 746 | 952 |
| Common Equity | 1,265 | 903 | 689 | 482 | 323 | 167 | 104 | 29.2 | -81.2 | -292 |
| Total Capital | 1,986 | 1,580 | 1,455 | 914 | 856 | 733 | 765 | 729 | 664 | 660 |
| Capital Expenditures | 104 | 82.4 | 57.1 | 44.3 | 30.2 | 18.8 | 38.6 | 53.1 | 23.5 | 26.3 |
| Cash Flow | 435 | 328 | 257 | 202 | 141 | 115 | 130 | 151 | 72.0 | 71.8 |
| Current Ratio | 2.4 | 2.1 | 2.1 | 1.9 | 2.1 | 1.6 | 1.8 | 1.7 | 2.3 | 2.3 |
| % Long Term Debt of Capitalization | 36.4 | 42.9 | 52.6 | 47.3 | 62.2 | 77.2 | 86.4 | 96.0 | 112.2 | 144.3 |
| % Net Income of Revenue | 12.4 | 10.3 | 11.4 | 10.7 | 8.4 | 7.6 | 7.6 | 7.9 | 4.4 | 4.0 |
| % Return on Assets | 14.5 | 12.4 | 12.7 | 13.1 | 9.2 | 7.6 | 8.2 | 11.7 | 5.4 | 4.7 |
| % Return on Equity | 32.6 | 32.1 | 35.2 | 40.6 | 42.4 | 59.3 | 125.7 | NM | NM | NM |

Data as orig reptd.; bef. results of disc opers/spec. items. Per share data adj. for stk. divs.; EPS diluted. E-Estimated. NA-Not Available. NM-Not Meaningful. NR-Not Ranked. UR-Under Review.

**Office:** 358 Hall Avenue, Wallingford, CT 06492.
**Telephone:** 203-265-8900.
**Email:** aphinfo@amphenol.com
**Website:** http://www.amphenol.com

**Chrmn & CEO:** M.H. Loeffler
**Pres:** M.L. Schneider
**Pres & COO:** R.A. Norwitt
**SVP, CFO & Chief Acctg Officer:** D.G. Reardon

**Secy & General Counsel:** E.C. Wetmore
**Investor Contact:** D. Reardon (203-265-8630)
**Board Members:** R. P. Badie, S. L. Clark, E. G. Jepsen, A. E. Lietz, M. H. Loeffler, J. R. Lord, D. H. Secord

**Founded:** 1932
**Domicile:** Delaware
**Employees:** 32,000

# Anadarko Petroleum Corp

**STANDARD &POOR'S**

| S&P Recommendation **BUY** ★★★★☆ | Price $37.82 (as of Nov 14, 2008) | 12-Mo. Target Price $51.00 | Investment Style Large-Cap Blend |
|---|---|---|---|

**GICS Sector** Energy
**Sub-Industry** Oil & Gas Exploration & Production

**Summary** As one of the largest independent exploration and production companies in the world, this U.S. firm has associated businesses in marketing, trading and minerals. In 2006, the company acquired Kerr-McGee Corp. and Western Gas Resources, Inc.

## Key Stock Statistics (Source S&P, Vickers, company reports)

| | | | | | | | |
|---|---|---|---|---|---|---|---|
| 52-Wk Range | $81.36–24.57 | S&P Oper. EPS 2008E | 6.40 | Market Capitalization(B) | $17.361 | Beta | 1.23 |
| Trailing 12-Month EPS | $5.82 | S&P Oper. EPS 2009E | 3.85 | Yield (%) | 0.95 | S&P 3-Yr. Proj. EPS CAGR(%) | 9 |
| Trailing 12-Month P/E | 6.5 | P/E on S&P Oper. EPS 2008E | 5.9 | Dividend Rate/Share | $0.36 | S&P Credit Rating | BBB- |
| $10K Invested 5 Yrs Ago | $17,584 | Common Shares Outstg. (M) | 459.0 | Institutional Ownership (%) | 84 | | |

## Price Performance

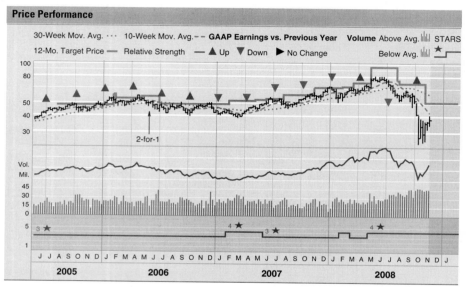

30-Week Mov. Avg. ···· 10-Week Mov. Avg. ─ ─ **GAAP Earnings vs. Previous Year** Volume Above Avg. STARS
12-Mo. Target Price ── Relative Strength ─ ▲ Up ▼ Down ▶ No Change Below Avg.

Options: ASE, CBOE, P, Ph

Analysis prepared by **Michael Kay** on November 06, 2008, when the stock traded at **$ 35.13**.

## Highlights

➤ Production fell 3% in the first nine months of 2008, reflecting asset sales, downtime at Independence Hub and the impact of hurricanes. We expect 2008 volumes down about 2%, but see second half production up 5% and 2009 up 7%. APC is seeing strong onshore growth in the Rockies, with production up about 50%, but given weaker prices, we see the possibility of shut-ins in the region. APC onshore programs at Haynesville and Marcellus shales are showing encouraging preliminary results. In the deepwater, APC recently announced a pre-salt discovery at the Wahoo prospect in Brazil.

➤ In May, APC's Mahogany-2 deepwater appraisal well offshore Ghana was successful at significant flow rates with estimated reserves for the field now between 500 million and 1.8 billion barrels and development slated for 2009.

➤ Operating earnings dropped 42% in 2007, mainly on lower realized natural gas prices and costs associated with acquisitions. We see a rise of 78% in 2008 before declining 40% in 2009 on lower prices. We see 2008 EPS of $6.40 (with $0.60 non-cash derivative gain in first nine months) and $3.85 in 2009.

## Investment Rationale/Risk

➤ While acquisitions have made APC larger with a focus shifted toward natural gas in the Rockies, the transformation originally weakened its balance sheet and led to increased costs. As a result, APC has raised cash through asset sales to repay debt incurred for the acquisitions. In recent months, APC has taken steps to lower its debt levels below $11 billion and improve its cash position to over $2 billion. We see APC being selective with its international exploration efforts going forward, and we expect the ongoing credit crisis and worsening economy to result in drilling capex cutbacks for 2009.

➤ Risks to our recommendation and target price include changes to economic, industrial or operating conditions, such as rising costs or difficulty in replacing reserves.

➤ A drop in oil and gas prices has led to a similar decline in E&P shares. On weaker economic forecasts, we see markets discounting probable reserves, and we now value APC on proven reserve NAV estimates. We blend our NAV of proven reserve estimate of $64 with DCF ($50; WACC of 8.7% and terminal growth of 3%), and relative metrics, to arrive at our 12-month target price of $51.

## Qualitative Risk Assessment

| LOW | MEDIUM | HIGH |
|---|---|---|

Our risk assessment reflects what we see as APC's solid business risk profile, as evidenced by its large undeveloped land base and significant long-life production assets, offset by an aggressive financial policy, as reflected in its two recent relatively high-priced leveraged acquisitions.

## Quantitative Evaluations

**S&P Quality Ranking** A-

| D | C | B- | B | B+ | A- | A | A+ |
|---|---|---|---|---|---|---|---|

**Relative Strength Rank** MODERATE

68

LOWEST = 1                    HIGHEST = 99

## Revenue/Earnings Data

**Revenue (Million $)**

| | 1Q | 2Q | 3Q | 4Q | Year |
|---|---|---|---|---|---|
| 2008 | 2,978 | 2,416 | 6,149 | -- | -- |
| 2007 | 2,683 | 3,313 | 3,030 | 3,062 | 11,232 |
| 2006 | 1,701 | 1,809 | 3,498 | 3,179 | 10,187 |
| 2005 | 1,526 | 1,592 | 1,737 | 2,245 | 7,100 |
| 2004 | 1,460 | 1,443 | 1,562 | 1,602 | 6,067 |
| 2003 | 1,255 | 1,249 | 1,340 | 1,278 | 5,122 |

**Earnings Per Share ($)**

| | | | | | |
|---|---|---|---|---|---|
| 2008 | 0.50 | 0.03 | 4.62 | E0.94 | E6.40 |
| 2007 | 0.17 | 1.38 | 1.10 | 0.35 | 8.05 |
| 2006 | 1.22 | 1.43 | 2.98 | 0.40 | 6.02 |
| 2005 | 1.03 | 1.06 | 1.26 | 1.87 | 5.20 |
| 2004 | 0.78 | 0.80 | 0.79 | 0.82 | 3.18 |
| 2003 | 0.73 | 0.60 | 0.55 | 0.58 | 2.46 |

Fiscal year ended Dec. 31. Next earnings report expected: Early February. EPS Estimates based on S&P Operating Earnings; historical GAAP earnings are as reported.

## Dividend Data (Dates: mm/dd Payment Date: mm/dd/yy)

| Amount ($) | Date Decl. | Ex-Div. Date | Stk. of Record | Payment Date |
|---|---|---|---|---|
| 0.090 | 02/12 | 03/10 | 03/12 | 03/26/08 |
| 0.090 | 05/20 | 06/09 | 06/11 | 06/25/08 |
| 0.090 | 08/07 | 09/08 | 09/10 | 09/24/08 |
| 0.090 | 11/05 | 12/08 | 12/10 | 12/24/08 |

Dividends have been paid since 1986. Source: Company reports.

---

**Please read the Required Disclosures and Analyst Certification on the last page of this report.**

*The McGraw-Hill Companies*

# Anadarko Petroleum Corp

**STANDARD &POOR'S**

## Business Summary November 06, 2008

CORPORATE OVERVIEW. As one of the largest independent exploration and production companies in the world, Anadarko Petroleum (APC) is engaged in the exploration, development, production, gathering, processing and marketing of natural gas, crude oil, condensate and natural gas liquids (NGLs).

The company's major areas of operations are located onshore in the U.S., the deepwater Gulf of Mexico, and Algeria. APC also has production in China and a development project in Brazil and is executing strategic exploration programs in other countries.

APC operations are conducted through three business segments: Oil and Gas Exploration & Production (49% of 2007 revenues, 90% of 2007 earnings before interest, tax, depreciation and exploration expenses), Midstream (2%, 8%), and Marketing (49%, 2%).

Proved oil and gas reserves dropped 19%, to 2.431 billion barrel oil equivalent (boe; 67% developed, 42% liquids, 85% located in the U.S.), in 2007, reflecting divestitures of non-core properties. However, oil and gas production rose

19%, to 211 million boe (45% liquids), in 2007. We estimate APC's organic reserve replacement at 118%. Using data from John S. Herold, we estimate APC's three-year (2004-06) finding and development costs at $38.37 per boe, above the peer average; its three-year proved acquisition costs at $14.01 per boe, above the peer average; its reserve replacement costs at $23.22 per boe, above the peer average; and its three-year reserve replacement at 308%, above the peer average.

APC invests in Midstream (gathering and processing) facilities in order to complement its oil and gas operations in regions where the company has natural gas production.

The company's Marketing segment manages the sales of APC's natural gas, crude oil and NGLs.

## Company Financials Fiscal Year Ended Dec. 31

| Per Share Data ($) | 2007 | 2006 | 2005 | 2004 | 2003 | 2002 | 2001 | 2000 | 1999 | 1998 |
|---|---|---|---|---|---|---|---|---|---|---|
| Tangible Book Value | 23.89 | 21.95 | 21.06 | 16.45 | 13.97 | 11.01 | 9.59 | 10.50 | 5.15 | 4.32 |
| Cash Flow | 14.23 | 10.28 | 8.04 | 6.05 | 5.01 | 3.74 | 2.09 | 3.64 | 1.00 | 0.65 |
| Earnings | 8.05 | 6.02 | 5.20 | 3.18 | 2.46 | 1.61 | -0.37 | 2.13 | 0.13 | -0.21 |
| S&P Core Earnings | 1.65 | 6.09 | 5.22 | 3.27 | 2.47 | 1.53 | -0.49 | NA | NA | NA |
| Dividends | 0.36 | 0.36 | 0.36 | 0.28 | 0.22 | 0.16 | 0.11 | 0.10 | 0.10 | 0.09 |
| Payout Ratio | 4% | 6% | 7% | 9% | 9% | 10% | NM | 5% | 80% | NM |
| Prices:High | 68.00 | 56.98 | 50.71 | 35.78 | 25.86 | 29.28 | 36.99 | 37.97 | 21.38 | 22.44 |
| Prices:Low | 38.40 | 39.51 | 30.01 | 24.00 | 20.14 | 18.39 | 21.50 | 13.78 | 13.13 | 12.38 |
| P/E Ratio:High | 8 | 9 | 10 | 11 | 11 | 18 | NM | 18 | NM | NM |
| P/E Ratio:Low | 5 | 7 | 6 | 8 | 8 | 11 | NM | 6 | NM | NM |

| Income Statement Analysis (Million $) | 2007 | 2006 | 2005 | 2004 | 2003 | 2002 | 2001 | 2000 | 1999 | 1998 |
|---|---|---|---|---|---|---|---|---|---|---|
| Revenue | 15,892 | 10,187 | 7,100 | 6,067 | 5,122 | 3,860 | 8,369 | 5,686 | 701 | 560 |
| Operating Income | 10,328 | 6,945 | 5,436 | 4,400 | 3,648 | 2,585 | 3,702 | 2,190 | 421 | 267 |
| Depreciation, Depletion and Amortization | 2,891 | 1,976 | 1,343 | 1,447 | 1,297 | 1,121 | 1,227 | 593 | 218 | 204 |
| Interest Expense | 1,214 | 655 | 201 | 352 | 253 | 203 | 92.0 | Nil | 74.1 | 57.7 |
| Pretax Income | 6,329 | 4,238 | 3,895 | 2,477 | 1,974 | 1,207 | -390 | 1,426 | 105 | -65.1 |
| Effective Tax Rate | 40.4% | 34.0% | 36.6% | 35.2% | 36.9% | 31.2% | NM | 42.2% | 59.4% | NM |
| Net Income | 3,770 | 2,796 | 2,471 | 1,606 | 1,245 | 831 | -176 | 824 | 42.6 | -42.2 |
| S&P Core Earnings | 773 | 2,826 | 2,478 | 1,646 | 1,248 | 785 | -243 | NA | NA | NA |

| Balance Sheet & Other Financial Data (Million $) | 2007 | 2006 | 2005 | 2004 | 2003 | 2002 | 2001 | 2000 | 1999 | 1998 |
|---|---|---|---|---|---|---|---|---|---|---|
| Cash | 1,268 | 491 | 739 | 874 | 62.0 | 34.0 | 37.0 | 199 | 44.8 | 17.0 |
| Current Assets | 4,516 | 4,614 | 2,916 | 2,502 | 1,324 | 1,280 | 1,201 | 1,894 | 356 | 230 |
| Total Assets | 48,481 | 58,844 | 22,588 | 20,192 | 20,546 | 18,248 | 16,771 | 16,590 | 4,098 | 3,633 |
| Current Liabilities | 5,257 | 16,758 | 2,403 | 1,993 | 1,715 | 1,861 | 1,801 | 1,676 | 387 | 289 |
| Long Term Debt | 14,747 | 11,520 | 3,555 | 3,671 | 5,058 | 5,171 | 4,638 | 3,984 | 1,443 | 1,425 |
| Common Equity | 16,319 | 15,201 | 10,967 | 9,219 | 8,510 | 6,673 | 6,262 | 6,586 | 1,335 | 1,059 |
| Total Capital | 39,929 | 39,673 | 19,330 | 17,393 | 17,909 | 15,578 | 14,454 | 10,770 | 3,555 | 3,208 |
| Capital Expenditures | 4,246 | 1,086 | 3,408 | 3,064 | 2,772 | 2,388 | 3,316 | 1,708 | 680 | 917 |
| Cash Flow | 6,658 | 4,769 | 3,809 | 3,048 | 2,537 | 1,946 | 1,044 | 1,406 | 250 | 155 |
| Current Ratio | 0.9 | 0.3 | 1.2 | 1.3 | 0.8 | 0.7 | 0.7 | 1.1 | 0.9 | 0.8 |
| % Long Term Debt of Capitalization | 44.9 | 28.8 | 18.4 | 21.1 | 28.2 | 33.2 | 32.1 | 37.0 | 40.6 | 44.4 |
| % Return on Assets | 7.0 | 6.9 | 11.5 | 7.9 | 6.4 | 4.7 | NM | 8.0 | 1.1 | NM |
| % Return on Equity | 24.2 | 21.3 | 24.4 | 17.9 | 16.1 | 12.8 | NM | 20.5 | 2.6 | NM |

Data as orig reptd.; bef. results of disc opers/spec. items. Per share data adj. for stk. divs.; EPS diluted. E-Estimated. NA-Not Available. NM-Not Meaningful. NR-Not Ranked. UR-Under Review.

**Office:** 1201 Lake Robbins Drive, The Woodlands, TX 77380-1124.
**Telephone:** 832-636-1000.
**Website:** http://www.anadarko.com
**Chrmn, Pres & CEO:** J.T. Hackett

**COO:** K.F. Kurz
**SVP & CFO:** R.A. Walker
**SVP, Chief Admin Officer & General Counsel:** R.K. Reeves
**Chief Acctg Officer & Cntlr:** M.C. Douglas

**Investor Contact:** J. Colglazier (832-636-2306)
**Board Members:** R. J. Allison, Jr., L. Barcus, J. L. Bryan, J. R. Butler, Jr., L. R. Corbett, H. P. Eberhart, P. J. Fluor, J. R. Gordon, J. T. Hackett, L. M. Jones, J. W. Poduska, P. R. Reynolds

**Founded:** 1985
**Domicile:** Delaware
**Employees:** 4,000

*The McGraw-Hill Companies*

# Analog Devices Inc.

**STANDARD &POOR'S**

| S&P Recommendation | **HOLD** ★★★☆☆ | Price $19.29 (as of Nov 14, 2008) | 12-Mo. Target Price $25.00 | Investment Style Large-Cap Growth |
|---|---|---|---|---|

**GICS Sector** Information Technology
**Sub-Industry** Semiconductors

**Summary** This company manufactures high-performance integrated circuits (ICs) used in analog and digital signal processing applications.

## Key Stock Statistics (Source S&P, Vickers, company reports)

| | | | | | | | |
|---|---|---|---|---|---|---|---|
| 52-Wk Range | $36.35 – 18.02 | S&P Oper. EPS 2008E | 1.65 | Market Capitalization(B) | $5.603 | Beta | 1.20 |
| Trailing 12-Month EPS | $2.45 | S&P Oper. EPS 2009E | 1.18 | Yield (%) | 4.15 | S&P 3-Yr. Proj. EPS CAGR(%) | 7 |
| Trailing 12-Month P/E | 7.9 | P/E on S&P Oper. EPS 2008E | 11.7 | Dividend Rate/Share | $0.80 | S&P Credit Rating | BBB+ |
| $10K Invested 5 Yrs Ago | $4,505 | Common Shares Outstg. (M) | 290.4 | Institutional Ownership (%) | 86 | | |

## Price Performance

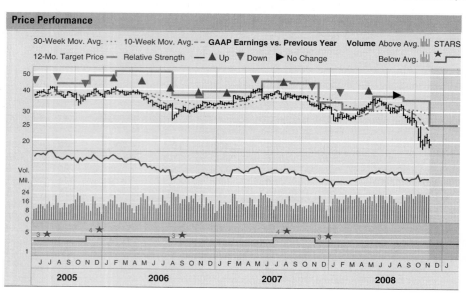

- 30-Week Mov. Avg. · · ·   10-Week Mov. Avg. – –   **GAAP Earnings vs. Previous Year**   Volume Above Avg. STARS
- 12-Mo. Target Price —   Relative Strength —   ▲ Up   ▼ Down   ► No Change   Below Avg. ★

Options: ASE, CBOE, P, Ph

Analysis prepared by **Clyde Montevirgen** on November 13, 2008, when the stock traded at **$ 19.87**.

### Qualitative Risk Assessment

| LOW | **MEDIUM** | HIGH |
|---|---|---|

Our risk assessment reflects that ADI is subject to the sales cycles of the semiconductor industry, offset by our view of relatively stable chip pricing owing to high proprietary design content, broad end-markets, a leading market share in key converter and amplifier product categories and what we consider a lack of debt.

### Quantitative Evaluations

**S&P Quality Ranking** B

| D | C | B- | **B** | B+ | A- | A | A+ |
|---|---|---|---|---|---|---|---|

**Relative Strength Rank** MODERATE

56

LOWEST = 1     HIGHEST = 99

### Revenue/Earnings Data

**Revenue (Million $)**

| | 1Q | 2Q | 3Q | 4Q | Year |
|---|---|---|---|---|---|
| 2008 | 613.9 | 649.3 | 659.0 | -- | -- |
| 2007 | 645.9 | 614.7 | 637.0 | 648.5 | 2,511 |
| 2006 | 621.3 | 643.9 | 663.7 | 644.3 | 2,573 |
| 2005 | 580.5 | 603.7 | 582.4 | 622.1 | 2,389 |
| 2004 | 605.4 | 678.5 | 717.8 | 632.1 | 2,634 |
| 2003 | 467.4 | 501.9 | 520.5 | 557.5 | 2,047 |

**Earnings Per Share ($)**

| | 1Q | 2Q | 3Q | 4Q | Year |
|---|---|---|---|---|---|
| 2008 | 0.40 | 0.44 | 0.44 | E0.38 | E1.65 |
| 2007 | 0.45 | 0.37 | 0.44 | 0.31 | 1.51 |
| 2006 | 0.32 | 0.39 | 0.39 | 0.39 | 1.48 |
| 2005 | 0.28 | 0.31 | 0.32 | 0.18 | 1.08 |
| 2004 | 0.30 | 0.39 | 0.43 | 0.34 | 1.45 |
| 2003 | 0.16 | 0.19 | 0.21 | 0.38 | 0.78 |

Fiscal year ended Oct. 31. Next earnings report expected: NA. EPS Estimates based on S&P Operating Earnings; historical GAAP earnings are as reported.

## Highlights

➤ We expect sales to fall about 7% in FY 09 (Oct.), compared to an estimated 5% advance in FY 08. We believe that orders will weaken as macro-economic headwinds hurt consumer end-markets. However, with its relatively large exposure to industrial and related end-markets, which are increasingly employing semiconductors in various applications, ADI should experience stable growth due to recent design wins, long product cycles, and its diversified customer base. Furthermore, we believe ADI will be able to protect its notable market share in the converter and amplifier markets.

➤ We are modeling a gross margin of 58% for FY 09, lower than the 61% we estimate for FY 08. We see a negative impact from rising sales of lower-margin consumer products and lower orders. However, ADI has divested less profitable product lines and consolidated manufacturing, which should aid longer-term profitability. We see the non-GAAP operating margin narrowing to 17% in FY 09, from a projected 24% in FY 08, as sales fall faster than expenses.

➤ We forecast operating EPS of $1.18 for FY 09, compared to an estimated $1.65 in FY 08.

## Investment Rationale/Risk

➤ We believe that ADI's analog portfolio is competitive and diversified compared to competitors, and should drive more stable revenue growth ahead. We also see better longer-term profitability from better cost containment, and think divestments of other lower-margin businesses should lead to wider margins. However, we think growth will largely come from operational efficiency and sales mix rather than through revenue increases, and we see macro-economic headwinds and formidable competition in certain businesses limiting revenue opportunities.

➤ Risks to our recommendation and target price include possible downward fluctuations in demand for semiconductors, steep market share declines, a worse than anticipated economic slowdown, and a less favorable sales mix.

➤ Our 12-month target price of $25 is based on a blend of relative metrics. We apply a P/E multiple of about 18X, above peers but below the historical average, to our FY 09 EPS estimate, implying a value of $21. We also apply a price-to-sales multiple of around 3.5X, below the historical average, to derive a value of $29.

### Dividend Data (Dates: mm/dd Payment Date: mm/dd/yy)

| Amount ($) | Date Decl. | Ex-Div. Date | Stk. of Record | Payment Date |
|---|---|---|---|---|
| 0.180 | 11/26 | 12/05 | 12/07 | 12/26/07 |
| 0.180 | 02/20 | 03/05 | 03/07 | 03/26/08 |
| 0.200 | 05/20 | 05/28 | 05/30 | 06/18/08 |
| 0.200 | 08/19 | 08/27 | 08/29 | 09/17/08 |

Dividends have been paid since 2003. Source: Company reports.

# Analog Devices Inc.

**STANDARD
&POOR'S**

## Business Summary November 13, 2008

CORPORATE OVERVIEW. Analog Devices designs, manufactures, and markets a broad line of high-performance analog, mixed-signal and digital signal processing (DSP) integrated circuits (ICs) that address a wide range of real-world signal processing applications. Real-world phenomena that these applications are designed for include temperature, pressure, sound, images, speed, acceleration, position and rotation. These phenomena are specifically analog in nature, consisting of continuously varying information. The expansion of broadband and wireless communications applications helps drive demand for analog and DSP chips. ADI's products are built into wireless telephones, base station equipment, and remote access servers, among others. The company's analog products are typically general purpose in nature and are used in a wide variety of equipment and systems. The company's chips are increasingly sold to PC and digital entertainment markets, as consumer equipment to handle voice, video and images becomes increasingly complex and sells to a wider audience.

ADI's products are sold both to OEMs and to customers building their own equipment. Key markets are industrial, which accounted for approximately 47% of sales in FY 07 (42% of FY 06 sales), communications 22% (29%), consumer 22% (17%), and computers 9% (12%). The customer base is fairly broad:

the 20 largest customers, excluding distributors, accounted for about 27% of sales in FY 07 (29% of sales in FY 06), and the largest customer, excluding distributors, accounted for approximately 3% (3%). About 53% of FY 07 sales (51% of FY 06 sales) were derived from sales made through distributors.

CORPORATE STRATEGY. Analog Devices is a leading provider of high-performance analog and mixed-signal, and DSP integrated circuits, two of the faster growing segments within the broader semiconductor industry. We believe that the higher-end analog space will continue to attract new entrants given its anticipated growth rate, relatively dispersed market share, stable pricing, higher-margin sales, and low capital expenditures. Lending to less risk, we think chipmakers in this segment generally post less variable operating results and more stable free cash flows than most semiconductor makers, which tend to experience volatile swings during various stages of the industry's business cycle.

## Company Financials Fiscal Year Ended Oct. 31

| Per Share Data ($) | 2007 | 2006 | 2005 | 2004 | 2003 | 2002 | 2001 | 2000 | 1999 | 1998 |
|---|---|---|---|---|---|---|---|---|---|---|
| Tangible Book Value | 6.71 | 9.17 | 9.61 | 9.66 | 8.42 | 7.50 | 7.20 | 5.90 | 4.54 | 3.47 |
| Cash Flow | 1.97 | 1.95 | 1.49 | 1.84 | 1.22 | 0.90 | 1.48 | 2.00 | 0.94 | 0.69 |
| Earnings | 1.51 | 1.48 | 1.08 | 1.45 | 0.78 | 0.28 | 0.93 | 1.59 | 0.55 | 0.36 |
| S&P Core Earnings | 1.45 | 1.46 | 0.29 | 0.91 | 0.20 | -0.32 | 0.44 | NA | NA | NA |
| Dividends | 0.70 | 0.56 | 0.32 | 0.20 | Nil | Nil | Nil | Nil | Nil | Nil |
| Payout Ratio | 46% | 38% | 30% | 14% | Nil | Nil | Nil | Nil | Nil | Nil |
| Prices:High | 41.10 | 41.48 | 41.40 | 52.37 | 50.35 | 48.84 | 64.00 | 103.00 | 47.25 | 19.81 |
| Prices:Low | 30.19 | 26.07 | 31.71 | 31.36 | 22.58 | 17.88 | 29.00 | 41.31 | 12.19 | 6.00 |
| P/E Ratio:High | 27 | 28 | 38 | 36 | 65 | NM | 69 | 65 | 86 | 56 |
| P/E Ratio:Low | 20 | 18 | 29 | 22 | 29 | NM | 31 | 26 | 22 | 17 |

| Income Statement Analysis (Million $) | | | | | | | | | | |
|---|---|---|---|---|---|---|---|---|---|---|
| Revenue | 2,546 | 2,573 | 2,389 | 2,634 | 2,047 | 1,708 | 2,277 | 2,578 | 1,450 | 1,231 |
| Operating Income | 916 | 771 | 703 | 852 | 552 | 405 | 675 | 924 | 391 | 289 |
| Depreciation | 155 | 172 | 156 | 153 | 168 | 238 | 210 | 157 | 143 | 128 |
| Interest Expense | Nil | 0.05 | 0.03 | 0.22 | 32.2 | 44.5 | 62.5 | 5.84 | 8.07 | 11.2 |
| Pretax Income | 659 | 664 | 588 | 733 | 382 | 140 | 507 | 866 | 258 | 150 |
| Effective Tax Rate | 24.0% | 17.1% | 29.4% | 22.1% | 21.9% | 25.0% | 29.7% | 29.9% | 23.6% | 20.6% |
| Net Income | 501 | 549 | 415 | 571 | 298 | 105 | 356 | 607 | 197 | 119 |
| S&P Core Earnings | 481 | 542 | 113 | 364 | 74.2 | -118 | 170 | NA | NA | NA |

| Balance Sheet & Other Financial Data (Million $) | | | | | | | | | | |
|---|---|---|---|---|---|---|---|---|---|---|
| Cash | 425 | 344 | 628 | 519 | 518 | 1,614 | 1,365 | 1,736 | 356 | 263 |
| Current Assets | 1,979 | 3,011 | 3,732 | 3,529 | 2,886 | 3,624 | 3,435 | 3,168 | 1,379 | 904 |
| Total Assets | 2,972 | 3,987 | 4,583 | 4,720 | 4,093 | 4,980 | 4,885 | 4,411 | 2,218 | 1,862 |
| Current Liabilities | 548 | 491 | 819 | 567 | 463 | 484 | 528 | 650 | 479 | 321 |
| Long Term Debt | Nil | Nil | Nil | Nil | Nil | 1,274 | 1,206 | 1,213 | 16.2 | 341 |
| Common Equity | 2,338 | 3,436 | 3,692 | 3,800 | 3,288 | 2,900 | 2,843 | 2,304 | 1,616 | 1,128 |
| Total Capital | 2,348 | 3,439 | 3,692 | 3,810 | 3,305 | 4,197 | 4,100 | 3,568 | 1,672 | 1,501 |
| Capital Expenditures | 142 | 129 | 85.5 | 146 | 67.7 | 57.4 | 297 | 275 | 77.5 | 167 |
| Cash Flow | 656 | 722 | 570 | 723 | 467 | 343 | 567 | 764 | 339 | 247 |
| Current Ratio | 3.6 | 6.1 | 4.6 | 6.2 | 6.2 | 7.5 | 6.5 | 4.9 | 2.9 | 2.8 |
| % Long Term Debt of Capitalization | Nil | Nil | Nil | Nil | Nil | 30.4 | 29.4 | 34.0 | 1.0 | 22.7 |
| % Net Income of Revenue | 19.6 | 21.4 | 17.4 | 21.7 | 14.6 | 6.2 | 15.7 | 23.6 | 13.6 | 9.7 |
| % Return on Assets | 14.3 | 12.8 | 8.9 | 13.0 | 6.6 | 2.1 | 7.7 | 18.3 | 9.6 | 6.6 |
| % Return on Equity | 17.3 | 15.4 | 11.1 | 16.1 | 9.6 | 3.7 | 13.8 | 31.0 | 14.3 | 10.5 |

Data as orig reptd.; bef. results of disc opers/spec. items. Per share data adj. for stk. divs.; EPS diluted. E-Estimated. NA-Not Available. NM-Not Meaningful. NR-Not Ranked. UR-Under Review.

**Office:** One Technology Way, Norwood, MA 02062-9106.
**Telephone:** 800-262-5643.
**Email:** investor.relations@analog.com
**Website:** http://www.analog.com

**Chrmn:** R. Stata
**Pres & CEO:** J.G. Fishman
**Treas:** W.A. Martin
**Secy & General Counsel:** M.K. Seif

**Investor Contact:** M. Kohl (781-461-3759)
**Board Members:** J. Champy, J. L. Doyle, J. G. Fishman, J. C. Hodgson, Y. Istel, N. Novich, F. G. Saviers, P. J. Severino, K. J. Sicchitano, R. Stata

**Founded:** 1965
**Domicile:** Massachusetts
**Employees:** 9,600

# Anheuser-Busch Companies Inc.

**STANDARD &POOR'S**

| S&P Recommendation | **HOLD** ★★★☆☆ | Price $68.50 (as of Nov 14, 2008) | 12-Mo. Target Price $70.00 | Investment Style Large-Cap Growth |
| --- | --- | --- | --- | --- |

**GICS Sector** Consumer Staples
**Sub-Industry** Brewers

**Summary** BUD, the parent company of the world's largest brewer, has agreed to be acquired by Belgium's InBev.

## Key Stock Statistics (Source S&P, Vickers, company reports)

| | | | | | | | |
| --- | --- | --- | --- | --- | --- | --- | --- |
| 52-Wk Range | $69.26– 45.55 | S&P Oper. EPS 2008**E** | 3.11 | Market Capitalization(B) | $49.528 | Beta | 0.31 |
| Trailing 12-Month EPS | $2.83 | S&P Oper. EPS 2009**E** | 3.30 | Yield (%) | 2.16 | S&P 3-Yr. Proj. EPS CAGR(%) | 9 |
| Trailing 12-Month P/E | 24.2 | P/E on S&P Oper. EPS 2008**E** | 22.0 | Dividend Rate/Share | $1.48 | S&P Credit Rating | BBB+ |
| $10K Invested 5 Yrs Ago | $14,665 | Common Shares Outstg. (M) | 723.0 | Institutional Ownership (%) | 61 | | |

## Price Performance

30-Week Mov. Avg. ···   10-Week Mov. Avg. —   **GAAP Earnings vs. Previous Year**   Volume Above Avg. ▮▮▮ STARS
12-Mo. Target Price —   Relative Strength — ▲ Up ▼ Down ▶ No Change   Below Avg. ▮▮▮ ★

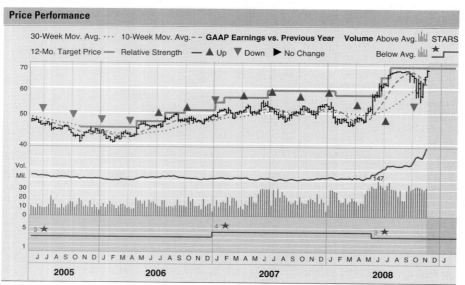

Options: ASE, CBOE, P, Ph

Analysis prepared by **Esther Y. Kwon, CFA** on October 16, 2008, when the stock traded at **$ 60.05**.

## Highlights

➤ We see net sales (after excise taxes) continuing to rise at a 4% pace, on improving domestic volume trends and strength in international sales. Pricing trends should also strengthen, and we expect net revenue per barrel to increase 4% with previous price increases supported by additional increases post-Labor Day. We look for worldwide shipment volumes to expand in the low single digits, reflecting acquisitions and growth in China and Canada.

➤ We project 2008 operating margins to remain about flat, as price increases, efficiency improvement and volume gains are offset by relatively high packaging and energy costs, increased marketing efforts and rising commodity costs. We estimate a 15% rise in advertising spending for the Budweiser family of products, including a $35 million initial campaign to launch Bud Light Lime, with the bulk of this increase seen spent in the second and third quarters.

➤ On about a 1% reduction in shares outstanding and a lower effective tax rate, partially offset by higher interest expense, we estimate a rise in 2008 operating EPS to $3.07, from $2.80 in 2007. For 2009, we see EPS rising further, to $3.30.

## Investment Rationale/Risk

➤ In June 2008, InBev, a Belgium-based brewer, submitted an offer to acquire BUD for $65 per share in cash, which was rejected by BUD's directors. In July, InBev raised its offer to $70, reflecting a price of 12.4X forward EV/EBITDA, which BUD's board accepted. We think the price is very attractive to shareholders, particularly in light of BUD's reliance on a slow growth domestic market, an inflationary input cost environment, and the potential strengthening competition from the SABMiller and Molson Coors joint venture. In October 2008, InBev postponed a $9.8 billion rights offering it was planning to use to finance its takeover due to global capital market turbulence, but stated it still expected to complete the deal by year end.

➤ Risks to our recommendation and target price include a withdrawal of InBev's bid and potential market share declines due to aggressive marketing by competitors, particularly in the wine and spirits categories, to first-time drinkers.

➤ Our 12-month target price of $70 is the price of InBev's offer. We expect the transaction to be completed near the end of the year, subject to necessary approvals.

## Qualitative Risk Assessment

| **LOW** | MEDIUM | HIGH |
| --- | --- | --- |

A large cap company, BUD has the biggest market share in an industry that has historically demonstrated stable revenue streams.

## Quantitative Evaluations

**S&P Quality Ranking**     A+

| D | C | B- | B | B+ | A- | A | **A+** |
| --- | --- | --- | --- | --- | --- | --- | --- |

**Relative Strength Rank**     **STRONG**

**97**

LOWEST = 1                                    HIGHEST = 99

## Revenue/Earnings Data

**Revenue (Million $)**

| | 1Q | 2Q | 3Q | 4Q | Year |
| --- | --- | --- | --- | --- | --- |
| 2008 | 4,099 | 4,721 | 4,917 | -- | -- |
| 2007 | 3,858 | 4,515 | 4,618 | 3,694 | 16,686 |
| 2006 | 3,756 | 4,256 | 4,281 | 3,425 | 15,717 |
| 2005 | 3,564 | 4,018 | 4,089 | 3,365 | 15,036 |
| 2004 | 3,477 | 4,010 | 4,080 | 3,367 | 14,934 |
| 2003 | 3,281 | 3,770 | 3,881 | 3,215 | 14,147 |

**Earnings Per Share ($)**

| | | | | | |
| --- | --- | --- | --- | --- | --- |
| 2008 | 0.71 | 0.95 | 0.90 | E0.40 | E3.11 |
| 2007 | 0.67 | 0.88 | 0.95 | 0.29 | 2.79 |
| 2006 | 0.64 | 0.82 | 0.82 | 0.25 | 2.53 |
| 2005 | 0.65 | 0.78 | 0.66 | 0.26 | 2.35 |
| 2004 | 0.67 | 0.83 | 0.85 | 0.42 | 2.77 |
| 2003 | 0.57 | 0.75 | 0.80 | 0.36 | 2.48 |

Fiscal year ended Dec. 31. Next earnings report expected: Early February. EPS Estimates based on S&P Operating Earnings; historical GAAP earnings are as reported.

## Dividend Data (Dates: mm/dd Payment Date: mm/dd/yy)

| Amount ($) | Date Decl. | Ex-Div. Date | Stk. of Record | Payment Date |
| --- | --- | --- | --- | --- |
| 0.330 | 01/10 | 02/07 | 02/11 | 03/10/08 |
| 0.330 | 04/23 | 05/07 | 05/09 | 06/09/08 |
| 0.370 | 07/23 | 08/07 | 08/11 | 09/09/08 |
| 0.370 | 10/22 | 11/06 | 11/10 | 12/09/08 |

Dividends have been paid since 1932. Source: Company reports.

# Anheuser-Busch Companies Inc.

**STANDARD
&POOR'S**

## Business Summary October 16, 2008

CORPORATE OVERVIEW. Anheuser-Busch Cos. is the holding company parent of the largest U.S. brewer, Anheuser-Busch, Inc. (ABI) -- which dates back to 1875, as Anheuser-Busch International, Inc. (ABII) -- and other subsidiaries that conduct various business operations.

BUD's beer products are sold in more than 90 countries and U.S. territories. Worldwide sales of the company's beer brands (including equity partners' volumes) in 2007 totaled 161.6 million barrels (up from 156.6 and 148.3 million barrels in 2006 and 2005, respectively). BUD operates 12 breweries, strategically located across the U.S., to serve its distribution system economically. U.S. sales totaled 104.4 million barrels in 2007 (up 2.1% from 2006), or about 48.5% of U.S. industry sales. International beer volume was 24.0 million barrels (up 5.7%). In 2007, domestic beer contributed 75.0% of net sales, and international beer 7.0%. Approximately 93% of BUD's net sales and 74% of net income is generated in the U.S.

Major beer brands include Budweiser, Bud Light, Budweiser Select, Michelob, Busch, Natural Light, King Cobra, Hurricane Malt Liquor, and in 2006, the company acquired Rolling Rock. BUD also imports and distributes Kirin, Tsing-

tao, Grolsch, Stella Artois, Beck's and Bass. Non-beer offerings include Bacardi branded malt beverages, Tilt, PEELS, and Tequiza. Non-alcoholic malt beverages include O'Doul's, and 180 energy drink.

Through various subsidiaries, the company is involved in a number of beer-related operations that help to insulate it from occasional rises in packaging and ingredient costs. These operations include can manufacturing, metalized paper printing, and barley malting. Packaging operations accounted for 10.0% of total net sales in 2007.

Through Busch Entertainment Corp., the company operates nine theme parks, including Busch Gardens in Florida and Virginia; Sea World parks in Florida, Texas and California; water parks in Florida and Virginia; and an educational play park in Pennsylvania. Busch Entertainment contributed 8.0% of total net sales in 2007.

## Company Financials Fiscal Year Ended Dec. 31

| Per Share Data ($) | 2007 | 2006 | 2005 | 2004 | 2003 | 2002 | 2001 | 2000 | 1999 | 1998 |
|---|---|---|---|---|---|---|---|---|---|---|
| Tangible Book Value | NM | 3.36 | 2.71 | 1.88 | 2.74 | 3.61 | 4.15 | 4.11 | 3.80 | 3.96 |
| Cash Flow | 4.11 | 3.80 | 3.60 | 4.04 | 3.53 | 3.16 | 2.82 | 2.56 | 1.47 | 2.02 |
| Earnings | 2.79 | 2.53 | 2.35 | 2.77 | 2.48 | 2.20 | 1.89 | 1.69 | 1.47 | 1.27 |
| S&P Core Earnings | 2.87 | 2.60 | 2.38 | 2.61 | 2.33 | 1.96 | 1.67 | NA | NA | NA |
| Dividends | 1.25 | 1.13 | 1.03 | 0.93 | 0.83 | 0.75 | 0.69 | 0.63 | 0.58 | 0.54 |
| Payout Ratio | 45% | 45% | 44% | 34% | 33% | 34% | 37% | 37% | 39% | 43% |
| Prices:High | 55.19 | 50.00 | 51.32 | 54.74 | 53.84 | 55.00 | 46.95 | 49.88 | 42.00 | 34.13 |
| Prices:Low | 46.74 | 40.17 | 40.15 | 49.42 | 45.30 | 43.65 | 36.75 | 27.31 | 32.22 | 21.47 |
| P/E Ratio:High | 20 | 20 | 22 | 20 | 22 | 25 | 25 | 30 | 29 | 27 |
| P/E Ratio:Low | 17 | 16 | 17 | 18 | 18 | 20 | 19 | 16 | 22 | 17 |

**Income Statement Analysis** (Million $)

| | 2007 | 2006 | 2005 | 2004 | 2003 | 2002 | 2001 | 2000 | 1999 | 1998 |
|---|---|---|---|---|---|---|---|---|---|---|
| Revenue | 16,686 | 15,717 | 15,036 | 14,934 | 14,147 | 13,566 | 12,911 | 12,262 | 11,704 | 11,245 |
| Operating Income | 3,864 | 3,708 | 3,705 | 4,294 | 4,077 | 3,827 | 3,540 | 3,299 | 3,080 | 2,862 |
| Depreciation | 996 | 989 | 979 | 933 | 877 | 847 | 834 | 804 | 777 | 738 |
| Interest Expense | 484 | 434 | 435 | 405 | 377 | 351 | 334 | 315 | 290 | 265 |
| Pretax Income | 3,085 | 2,866 | 2,690 | 2,999 | 3,169 | 2,975 | 2,618 | 2,380 | 2,165 | 1,937 |
| Effective Tax Rate | 31.4% | 31.4% | 31.6% | 38.7% | 34.5% | 35.0% | 34.9% | 34.8% | 35.2% | 36.3% |
| Net Income | 2,115 | 1,965 | 1,839 | 2,240 | 2,076 | 1,934 | 1,705 | 1,552 | 1,402 | 1,233 |
| S&P Core Earnings | 2,173 | 2,022 | 1,860 | 2,111 | 1,952 | 1,722 | 1,507 | NA | NA | NA |

**Balance Sheet & Other Financial Data** (Million $)

| | 2007 | 2006 | 2005 | 2004 | 2003 | 2002 | 2001 | 2000 | 1999 | 1998 |
|---|---|---|---|---|---|---|---|---|---|---|
| Cash | 283 | 219 | 226 | 228 | 191 | 189 | 163 | 160 | 152 | 225 |
| Current Assets | 2,025 | 1,830 | 1,759 | 1,818 | 1,630 | 1,505 | 1,550 | 1,548 | 1,601 | 1,640 |
| Total Assets | 17,155 | 16,377 | 16,555 | 16,173 | 14,690 | 14,120 | 13,862 | 13,085 | 12,640 | 12,484 |
| Current Liabilities | 2,304 | 2,246 | 1,983 | 1,969 | 1,857 | 1,788 | 1,732 | 1,676 | 1,987 | 1,730 |
| Long Term Debt | 9,140 | 7,654 | 1,682 | 8,279 | 7,285 | 6,603 | 5,984 | 5,375 | 4,881 | 4,719 |
| Common Equity | 3,152 | 3,939 | 3,343 | 2,668 | 2,712 | 3,052 | 4,062 | 4,128 | 3,921 | 4,216 |
| Total Capital | 13,607 | 12,787 | 6,708 | 12,674 | 11,459 | 11,962 | 11,334 | 10,876 | 10,147 | 10,238 |
| Capital Expenditures | 870 | 812 | 1,137 | 1,090 | 993 | 835 | 1,022 | 1,075 | 856 | 818 |
| Cash Flow | 3,112 | 2,954 | 2,818 | 3,173 | 2,953 | 2,781 | 2,539 | 2,356 | 1,402 | 1,971 |
| Current Ratio | 0.9 | 0.8 | 0.9 | 0.9 | 0.9 | 0.8 | 0.9 | 0.9 | 0.8 | 0.9 |
| % Long Term Debt of Capitalization | 74.4 | 59.9 | 25.1 | 65.3 | 63.6 | 55.2 | 52.8 | 49.4 | 48.1 | 46.1 |
| % Net Income of Revenue | 12.7 | 12.5 | 12.2 | 15.0 | 14.7 | 14.3 | 13.2 | 12.7 | 12.0 | 11.0 |
| % Return on Assets | 12.6 | 11.9 | 11.2 | 14.5 | 14.4 | 13.8 | 12.7 | 12.1 | 11.2 | 10.2 |
| % Return on Equity | 59.7 | 51.6 | 61.2 | 83.3 | 72.0 | 45.3 | 41.6 | 38.6 | 34.5 | 29.9 |

Data as orig reptd.; bef. results of disc opers/spec. items. Per share data adj. for stk. divs.; EPS diluted. E-Estimated. NA-Not Available. NM-Not Meaningful. NR-Not Ranked. UR-Under Review.

**Office:** 1 Busch Place, St. Louis, MO 63118.
**Telephone:** 314-577-2000.
**Website:** http://www.anheuser-busch.com
**Chrmn:** P.T. Stokes

**Pres:** D.A. Peacock
**CEO:** A.A. Busch, IV
**CFO:** W.R. Baker
**Chief Acctg Officer & Cntlr:** J.F. Kelly

**Board Members:** A. A. Busch, III, A. A. Busch, IV, J. J. Forese, J. R. Jones, V. R. Loucks, Jr., V. S. Martinez, W. B. Payne, J. M. Roche, H. H. Shelton, P. T. Stokes, A. C. Taylor, D. A. Warner, III, E. E. Whitacre, Jr.

**Founded:** 1852
**Domicile:** Delaware
**Employees:** 30,849

*The McGraw-Hill Companies*

# Aon Corp.

**STANDARD &POOR'S**

| S&P Recommendation | **BUY** ★★★★☆ | Price $42.16 (as of Nov 14, 2008) | 12-Mo. Target Price $55.00 | Investment Style Large-Cap Blend |
| --- | --- | --- | --- | --- |

**GICS Sector** Financials
**Sub-Industry** Insurance Brokers

**Summary** This Chicago-based holding company is comprised of a family of insurance brokerage, consulting and insurance underwriting subsidiaries.

## Key Stock Statistics (Source S&P, Vickers, company reports)

| | | | | | | | |
| --- | --- | --- | --- | --- | --- | --- | --- |
| 52-Wk Range | $51.32– 32.83 | S&P Oper. EPS 2008E | 2.82 | Market Capitalization(B) | $11.374 | Beta | 1.04 |
| Trailing 12-Month EPS | $5.40 | S&P Oper. EPS 2009E | 3.46 | Yield (%) | 1.42 | S&P 3-Yr. Proj. EPS CAGR(%) | 21 |
| Trailing 12-Month P/E | 7.8 | P/E on S&P Oper. EPS 2008E | 15.0 | Dividend Rate/Share | $0.60 | S&P Credit Rating | BBB+ |
| $10K Invested 5 Yrs Ago | $21,770 | Common Shares Outstg. (M) | 269.8 | Institutional Ownership (%) | 85 | | |

## Price Performance

30-Week Mov. Avg. · · · 10-Week Mov. Avg. - - GAAP Earnings vs. Previous Year Volume Above Avg. STARS
12-Mo. Target Price — Relative Strength — ▲ Up ▼ Down ► No Change Below Avg. ★

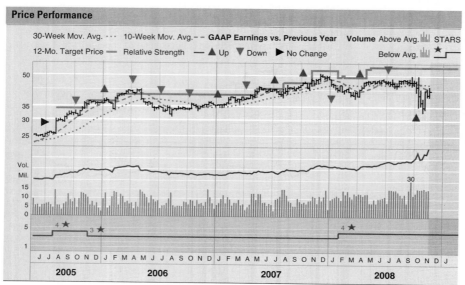

Options: ASE, CBOE, P, Ph

Analysis prepared by **Bret Howlett** on November 03, 2008, when the stock traded at **$ 41.73**.

## Highlights

➤ We expect single-digit revenue growth for AOC's risk and insurance brokerage segment this year as we see improved top-line gains in the Americas, reflecting modest growth in its U.S. retail sub-segment's middle market and large corporate accounts. We anticipate that the Asia-Pacific region will continue to experience solid new business growth and effective renewal book management. By our analysis, the pretax margin for risk and insurance brokerage should decrease slightly to 16% -17%, partially due to a decline in investment income. We believe that the company's ongoing restructuring program should result in $300 million in annualized savings by 2010.

➤ We see single-digit revenue growth for AOC's consulting segment this year, aided by its restructuring program and operational enhancement, partially offset by the weakening global economy. We believe AOC's recent acquisition of Benfield will increase its market share in reinsurance, and we believe that business will benefit from a firming of rates in 2009.

➤ We estimate EPS from continuing operations at $2.82 for 2008 and $3.46 for 2009.

## Investment Rationale/Risk

➤ Our buy recommendation reflects our belief that AOC possesses a business platform that can drive organic growth in a difficult environment and is well positioned for margin expansion and our expectations for an improved pricing environment in 2009. AOC has been gaining new businesses both in the U.S. and abroad, while maintaining a solid retention rate. We expect AOC to face headwinds in U.S. risk and brokerage services as the slowing economy pressures margins and volumes. However, we believe aggressive cost-cutting initiatives, a share buyback program, and earnings contributions from overseas will more than offset any impact from a slowdown in the U.S.

➤ Risks to our recommendation and target price include continuing pressure on operating results from the elimination of contingent commissions and from a soft property and casualty market; currency risks; and potential additional contingent commission probes by international authorities.

➤ Our 12-month target price of $55 is 15.9X our estimate of 2009 EPS from continuing operations, in line with historical multiples.

## Qualitative Risk Assessment

| LOW | **MEDIUM** | HIGH |
| --- | --- | --- |

Our risk assessment reflects what see as the company's well-diversified operations and solid balance sheet, with low debt, offset by the impact of the loss of contingent commissions and business restructuring.

## Quantitative Evaluations

**S&P Quality Ranking** B+

| D | C | B- | B | **B+** | A- | A | A+ |
| --- | --- | --- | --- | --- | --- | --- | --- |

**Relative Strength Rank** STRONG

93

LOWEST = 1          HIGHEST = 99

## Revenue/Earnings Data

### Revenue (Million $)

| | 1Q | 2Q | 3Q | 4Q | Year |
| --- | --- | --- | --- | --- | --- |
| 2008 | 1,932 | 1,980 | 1,847 | -- | -- |
| 2007 | 1,798 | 1,866 | 1,775 | 2,032 | 7,471 |
| 2006 | 2,165 | 2,208 | 2,168 | 2,413 | 8,954 |
| 2005 | 2,464 | 2,456 | 2,387 | 2,530 | 9,837 |
| 2004 | 2,564 | 2,544 | 2,402 | 2,662 | 10,172 |
| 2003 | 2,384 | 2,434 | 2,391 | 2,601 | 9,810 |

### Earnings Per Share ($)

| | | | | | |
| --- | --- | --- | --- | --- | --- |
| 2008 | 0.56 | 0.55 | 0.53 | E0.84 | E2.82 |
| 2007 | 0.51 | 0.57 | 0.42 | 0.11 | 2.10 |
| 2006 | 0.57 | 0.53 | 0.27 | 0.57 | 1.86 |
| 2005 | 0.58 | 0.54 | 0.35 | 0.42 | 1.89 |
| 2004 | 0.58 | 0.54 | 0.36 | 0.25 | 1.72 |
| 2003 | 0.49 | 0.48 | 0.44 | 0.67 | 2.08 |

Fiscal year ended Dec. 31. Next earnings report expected: Early February. EPS Estimates based on S&P Operating Earnings; historical GAAP earnings are as reported.

## Dividend Data (Dates: mm/dd Payment Date: mm/dd/yy)

| Amount ($) | Date Decl. | Ex-Div. Date | Stk. of Record | Payment Date |
| --- | --- | --- | --- | --- |
| 0.150 | 01/18 | 01/30 | 02/01 | 02/14/08 |
| 0.150 | 04/17 | 04/29 | 05/01 | 05/14/08 |
| 0.150 | 07/18 | 07/30 | 08/01 | 08/14/08 |
| 0.150 | 10/07 | 10/30 | 11/03 | 11/17/08 |

Dividends have been paid since 1950. Source: Company reports.

**Please read the Required Disclosures and Analyst Certification on the last page of this report.**

The McGraw-Hill Companies

# Aon Corp.

STANDARD
&POOR'S

## Business Summary November 03, 2008

CORPORATE OVERVIEW. Aon Corp. is a global provider of insurance broker-age services, insurance products, and risk and insurance advice, as well as other consulting services, conducting business in more than 120 countries and sovereignties. The company believes it is a leader in several sectors of the insurance industry.

AOC classifies its businesses into three operating segments: risk and insur-ance brokerage, consulting, and insurance underwriting. The risk and insur-ance brokerage segment accounted for 82% of total revenue from continuing operations in 2007, and the consulting segment 18%.

LEGAL/REGULATORY ISSUES. In March 2005, AOC reached a settlement with the New York, Illinois and Connecticut attorneys general and other regulators resolving all issues related to investigations conducted by these agencies. Under the settlement, AOC agreed to institute certain business reforms and pay $190 million into a fund to be distributed to eligible U.S. clients where AOC received certain related contingent commissions, with no portion of the pay-ments considered a fine or penalty.

CORPORATE STRATEGY. In December 2007, the company announced that it signed separate definitive agreements to sell its Combined Insurance Compa-

ny of America (CICA) and Sterling Life Insurance Company businesses. AOC agreed to sell its CICA business to ACE Limited for cash consideration of $2.4 billion, and its Sterling business to Munich Re Group for cash consideration of $352 million, subject to closing adjustments. Furthermore, AOC anticipates that it will receive a one-time cash dividend of $325 million from CICA prior to the close of the transaction. Total after-tax cash proceeds and dividends are expected to total $2.6 billion. The company expects the Sterling transaction to be completed by the end of the first quarter of 2008 and the CICA sale to be completed by the end of the second quarter of 2008. We are encouraged that the company plans to use the proceeds for share repurchases.

Due to the regulatory scrutiny regarding contingent commissions, AOC an-nounced in October 2004 that it was terminating its contingent commission arrangements with underwriters. We believe replacing this lost income will be a challenge for AOC, which earned about $132 million in contingent commis-sion revenue in 2004, versus $169 million in 2003.

## Company Financials Fiscal Year Ended Dec. 31

| Per Share Data ($) | 2007 | 2006 | 2005 | 2004 | 2003 | 2002 | 2001 | 2000 | 1999 | 1998 |
|---|---|---|---|---|---|---|---|---|---|---|
| Tangible Book Value | 4.37 | 2.14 | 2.48 | 0.76 | NM | NM | NM | NM | NM | NM |
| Cash Flow | 2.67 | NA | NA | NA | NA | NA | NA | NA | NA | NA |
| Earnings | 2.10 | 1.86 | 1.89 | 1.72 | 2.08 | 1.64 | 0.73 | 1.82 | 1.33 | 2.07 |
| S&P Core Earnings | 1.66 | 2.03 | 2.10 | 2.29 | 2.05 | 1.00 | -0.06 | NA | NA | NA |
| Dividends | 0.60 | 0.75 | 0.60 | 0.60 | 0.60 | 0.83 | 0.90 | 0.87 | 0.81 | 0.73 |
| Payout Ratio | 29% | 40% | 32% | 35% | 29% | 50% | 123% | 48% | 61% | 35% |
| Prices:High | 51.32 | 42.76 | 37.14 | 29.44 | 26.79 | 39.63 | 44.80 | 42.75 | 46.67 | 50.37 |
| Prices:Low | 34.30 | 31.01 | 20.64 | 18.15 | 17.41 | 13.30 | 29.75 | 20.69 | 26.06 | 32.17 |
| P/E Ratio:High | 24 | 23 | 20 | 17 | 13 | 24 | 61 | 23 | 35 | 24 |
| P/E Ratio:Low | 16 | 17 | 11 | 11 | 8 | 8 | 41 | 11 | 20 | 16 |

| Income Statement Analysis (Million $) | | | | | | | | | | |
|---|---|---|---|---|---|---|---|---|---|---|
| Revenue | 7,471 | 8,954 | 9,837 | 10,172 | 9,810 | 8,822 | 7,676 | 7,375 | 7,070 | 6,493 |
| Operating Income | 1,437 | 1,426 | NA | NA | NA | NA | NA | NA | NA | NA |
| Depreciation | 189 | 244 | 277 | 309 | 314 | 263 | 339 | 333 | 355 | 268 |
| Interest Expense | 138 | 129 | NA | NA | NA | NA | NA | NA | NA | NA |
| Pretax Income | 1,024 | 920 | 965 | 880 | 1,110 | 793 | 399 | 854 | 635 | 931 |
| Effective Tax Rate | 34.4% | 32.0% | 33.5% | 34.4% | 38.3% | 38.6% | 43.5% | 40.9% | 40.8% | 39.2% |
| Net Income | 672 | 626 | 642 | 577 | 663 | 466 | 203 | 481 | 352 | 541 |
| S&P Core Earnings | 531 | 683 | 709 | 765 | 652 | 281 | -19.4 | NA | NA | NA |

| Balance Sheet & Other Financial Data (Million $) | | | | | | | | | | |
|---|---|---|---|---|---|---|---|---|---|---|
| Cash | 4,915 | 4,726 | 476 | 570 | 540 | 506 | 439 | 1,118 | 837 | 786 |
| Current Assets | 17,973 | NA | NA | NA | NA | NA | NA | NA | NA | NA |
| Total Assets | 24,948 | 24,318 | 27,818 | 28,329 | 27,027 | 25,334 | 22,386 | 22,251 | 21,132 | 19,688 |
| Current Liabilities | 14,553 | NA | NA | NA | NA | NA | NA | NA | NA | NA |
| Long Term Debt | 2,145 | NA | NA | NA | NA | NA | NA | NA | NA | NA |
| Common Equity | 6,221 | 5,218 | 5,303 | 5,103 | 4,498 | 3,895 | 3,521 | 3,388 | 3,051 | 3,017 |
| Total Capital | 8,223 | 6,806 | NA | NA | NA | NA | NA | NA | NA | NA |
| Capital Expenditures | 170 | 152 | 126 | 80.0 | 185 | 278 | 281 | 179 | 271 | 300 |
| Cash Flow | 861 | 863 | NA | NA | NA | NA | NA | NA | NA | NA |
| Current Ratio | 1.2 | 1.1 | 1.0 | 1.0 | 1.0 | 0.9 | 0.9 | 1.0 | 0.9 | 0.9 |
| % Long Term Debt of Capitalization | 23.3 | 23.3 | 28.4 | 21.0 | 26.9 | 32.7 | 39.0 | 42.8 | 36.7 | 28.6 |
| % Net Income of Revenue | 9.0 | 7.0 | 6.5 | 5.7 | 6.8 | 5.3 | 2.6 | 6.5 | 5.0 | 8.3 |
| % Return on Assets | 2.7 | 2.4 | 2.3 | 2.1 | 2.5 | 2.0 | 0.9 | 2.2 | 1.7 | 2.8 |
| % Return on Equity | 11.8 | 11.9 | 12.3 | 12.0 | 15.8 | 12.6 | 5.9 | 14.9 | 11.6 | 18.5 |

Data as orig reptd.; bef. results of disc opers/spec. items. Per share data adj. for stk. divs.; EPS diluted. E-Estimated. NA-Not Available. NM-Not Meaningful. NR-Not Ranked. UR-Under Review.

**Office:** 200 E Randolph St Lowr, Chicago, IL 60601-6436.
**Telephone:** 312-381-1000.
**Website:** http://www.aon.com
**Chrmn:** L.B. Knight, III

**Pres & CEO:** G.C. Case
**EVP & CFO:** C. Davies
**EVP & Chief Admin Officer:** G.J. Besio
**EVP & General Counsel:** D.C. Findlay

**Investor Contact:** S. Malchow (312-381-3983)
**Board Members:** G. C. Case, F. Conti, E. D. Jannotta, P. J. Kalff, L. B. Knight, III, J. M. Losh, R. E. Martin, A. J. McKenna, R. S. Morrison, R. B. Myers, R. C. Notebaert, J. W. Rogers, Jr., G. Santona, C. Y. Woo

**Founded:** 1919
**Domicile:** Delaware
**Employees:** 42,500

# Apache Corp

**STANDARD &POOR'S**

| S&P Recommendation **BUY** ★★★★☆ | Price $76.04 (as of Nov 14, 2008) | 12-Mo. Target Price $91.00 | Investment Style Large-Cap Blend |
|---|---|---|---|

**GICS Sector** Energy
**Sub-Industry** Oil & Gas Exploration & Production

**Summary** One of the largest independent exploration and production companies in the U.S., Apache explores for, develops and produces natural gas, crude oil and natural gas liquids.

## Key Stock Statistics (Source S&P, Vickers, company reports)

| | | | | | | | | |
|---|---|---|---|---|---|---|---|---|
| 52-Wk Range | $149.23– 58.00 | S&P Oper. EPS 2008**E** | 13.24 | Market Capitalization(B) | $25.448 | Beta | 0.91 |
| Trailing 12-Month EPS | $14.02 | S&P Oper. EPS 2009**E** | 11.75 | Yield (%) | 0.79 | S&P 3-Yr. Proj. EPS CAGR(%) | 19 |
| Trailing 12-Month P/E | 5.4 | P/E on S&P Oper. EPS 2008**E** | 5.7 | Dividend Rate/Share | $0.60 | S&P Credit Rating | A- |
| $10K Invested 5 Yrs Ago | $21,718 | Common Shares Outstg. (M) | 334.7 | Institutional Ownership (%) | 86 | | |

## Price Performance

30-Week Mov. Avg. · · · · 10-Week Mov. Avg. — **GAAP Earnings vs. Previous Year** Volume Above Avg. ▮▮▮ STARS
12-Mo. Target Price — Relative Strength — ▲ Up ▼ Down ▶ No Change Below Avg. ▮▮▮ ★

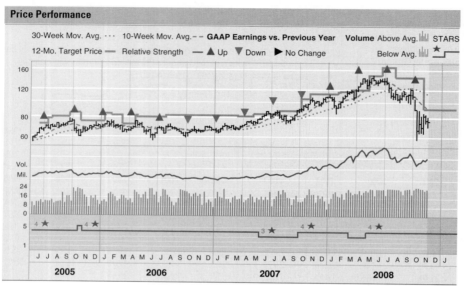

Options: ASE, CBOE, P, Ph

Analysis prepared by **Michael Kay** on November 03, 2008, when the stock traded at **$ 80.22**.

### Highlights

➤ Production declined 3% in the first nine months of 2008, as a pipeline rupture and fire at the Varanus Island gas plant in Australia, a strike in Scotland at the Forties Field and hurricane shut-ins in the U.S. hampered production. Despite disappointing production and our forecast for a 3.5% decline in 2008, APA has a pipeline of seven major projects scheduled to begin production between the latter half of 2008 and 2012, which should contribute about 135,000 boe/d of net new oil and gas production. For 2009, we see volume growth of 9%.

➤ Despite setbacks, APA sees growth resuming with the start-up of the Salam gas plant in Egypt, and restored production in Australia and Scotland. APA's 2008 budget is $6 billion, reflecting development spending at Geauxpher, its recent discovery in the deepwater Gulf of Mexico, and higher drilling activity.

➤ After-tax operating earnings rose 10% in 2007, and we expect growth of 67% in 2008 on higher oil and gas prices. We see 2008 EPS of $13.24, up from $7.99, and $11.75 in 2009 as production gains are offset by weakening prices. Third quarter lease operating expense was up 14% sequentially, an unexpected rise.

### Investment Rationale/Risk

➤ APA continues to exploit mature North American reserves and focus growth capital on international development projects (including Geauxpher in the Gulf of Mexico, the Van Gogh, Pyrenees, Julimar and Reindeer projects in Australia, and the Salam gas plant expansion in Egypt), which are expected to contribute to growth over the next four years. In addition, APA has added a new gas plant in Egypt, and the Ootla project in Canada has the potential to become another major development project. We remain positive on a pipeline of high-impact prospects, the main catalysts behind future production growth.

➤ Risks to our recommendation and target price include changes to economic, industrial and operating conditions, including increased costs, and difficulty replacing reserves.

➤ A drop in oil and gas prices has led to a similar decline in E&P shares. On weaker economic forecasts, we see markets discounting probable reserves and now value APA on proven reserve NAV estimates. We blend our NAV estimate ($96) with DCF ($101; WACC of 8.7%; terminal growth of 3%), and relative metrics to arrive at our 12-month target price of $91.

### Qualitative Risk Assessment

| LOW | MEDIUM | HIGH |
|---|---|---|

Our risk assessment for APA reflects our view of its position as a super-large exploration and production company diversified across major producing regions, focused on exploiting North American reserves and growing capital internationally. This is offset by moderate financial risk as the company uses its balance sheet to fund what we consider its aggressive acquisition strategy.

### Quantitative Evaluations

**S&P Quality Ranking** **A**

| D | C | B- | B | B+ | A- | A | A+ |
|---|---|---|---|---|---|---|---|

**Relative Strength Rank** **MODERATE**

62

LOWEST = 1     HIGHEST = 99

### Revenue/Earnings Data

**Revenue (Million $)**

| | 1Q | 2Q | 3Q | 4Q | Year |
|---|---|---|---|---|---|
| 2008 | 3,188 | 3,900 | 3,365 | -- | -- |
| 2007 | 1,997 | 2,468 | 2,499 | 3,014 | 9,969 |
| 2006 | 1,999 | 2,062 | 2,261 | 1,967 | 8,289 |
| 2005 | 1,662 | 1,759 | 2,061 | 2,102 | 7,584 |
| 2004 | 1,150 | 1,241 | 1,407 | 1,535 | 5,333 |
| 2003 | 966.6 | 1,054 | 1,105 | 1,065 | 4,190 |

**Earnings Per Share ($)**

| | | | | | |
|---|---|---|---|---|---|
| 2008 | 3.03 | 4.28 | 3.52 | E2.78 | E13.24 |
| 2007 | 1.47 | 1.89 | 1.83 | 3.19 | 8.39 |
| 2006 | 1.97 | 2.17 | 1.94 | 1.56 | 7.64 |
| 2005 | 1.67 | 1.76 | 2.05 | 2.35 | 7.84 |
| 2004 | 1.05 | 1.16 | 1.30 | 1.53 | 5.04 |
| 2003 | 0.97 | 0.75 | 0.85 | 0.80 | 3.35 |

Fiscal year ended Dec. 31. Next earnings report expected: Early February. EPS Estimates based on S&P Operating Earnings; historical GAAP earnings are as reported.

### Dividend Data (Dates: mm/dd Payment Date: mm/dd/yy)

| Amount ($) | Date Decl. | Ex-Div. Date | Stk. of Record | Payment Date |
|---|---|---|---|---|
| 0.100 | 02/15 | 02/22 | 02/26 | 03/18/08 |
| 0.150 | 02/15 | 04/18 | 04/22 | 05/22/08 |
| 0.150 | 05/13 | 07/18 | 07/22 | 08/22/08 |
| 0.150 | 09/16 | 10/20 | 10/22 | 11/21/08 |

Dividends have been paid since 1965. Source: Company reports.

**Please read the Required Disclosures and Analyst Certification on the last page of this report.**

# Apache Corp

**STANDARD &POOR'S**

## Business Summary November 03, 2008

CORPORATE OVERVIEW. As one of the largest independent exploration and production (E&P) companies in the U.S., Apache Corp. (APA) explores for, develops and produces natural gas, crude oil and natural gas liquids (NGLs).

In North America, APA's interests are focused in the Gulf of Mexico, the Gulf Coast, East Texas, the Permian Basin, the Anadarko Basin, and the Western Sedimentary Basin of Canada. Outside of North America, APA has interests in Egypt, offshore Western Australia, offshore the U.K. in the North Sea, and onshore Argentina. In November 2007, APA was a high bidder on two exploration blocks on the Chilean side of the island of Tierra del Fuego.

Proved oil and gas reserves rose 5.7%, to 2.445 billion barrel oil equivalent (boe; 69% developed; 46% liquids), in 2007. Oil and gas production rose 12%, to 561,239 boe per day (47% liquids). We estimate APA's 2007 organic reserve replacement at 132%. Using data from John S. Herold, we estimate APA's three-year (2004-2006) reserve replacement at 233%, in line with peers; three-year finding and development costs at $12.90 per boe, in line with peers; three-year

proved acquisition costs at $9.05 per boe, below the peer average; and three-year reserve replacement costs at $11.81 per boe, below the peer average.

MARKET PROFILE. APA has a large, geographically diversified reserve base with what we view as a good history of organic reserve replacement at an attractive cost. Nonetheless, the company has a history of supplementing its organic growth with acquisitions consistent with a strategy that emphasizes development over exploration. We expect mid-single digit production growth from 2007-2012 on exploration and development projects in the company's ACE (Australia, Canada, Egypt) core growth areas. In addition, APA has acquired over $1 billion of producing properties in the Permian Basin in west Texas (estimated 70 million boe, at year-end 2006).

## Company Financials Fiscal Year Ended Dec. 31

| Per Share Data ($) | 2007 | 2006 | 2005 | 2004 | 2003 | 2002 | 2001 | 2000 | 1999 | 1998 |
|---|---|---|---|---|---|---|---|---|---|---|
| Tangible Book Value | 46.49 | 39.30 | 31.06 | 24.18 | 19.25 | 15.33 | 14.69 | 12.07 | 8.97 | 7.54 |
| Cash Flow | 15.41 | 13.19 | 12.22 | 8.81 | 6.67 | 4.55 | 5.30 | 4.46 | 2.51 | 2.20 |
| Earnings | 8.39 | 7.64 | 7.84 | 5.04 | 3.35 | 1.80 | 2.37 | 2.48 | 0.74 | -0.58 |
| S&P Core Earnings | 8.38 | 7.30 | 7.60 | 5.19 | 3.29 | 1.73 | 2.28 | NA | NA | NA |
| Dividends | 0.60 | 0.60 | 0.34 | 0.32 | 0.21 | 0.19 | 0.12 | 0.09 | 0.12 | 0.12 |
| Payout Ratio | 7% | 8% | 4% | 6% | 6% | 11% | 5% | 4% | 16% | NM |
| Prices:High | 109.32 | 76.25 | 78.15 | 55.16 | 41.68 | 28.88 | 31.55 | 32.12 | 21.62 | 16.77 |
| Prices:Low | 63.01 | 56.50 | 47.45 | 36.79 | 26.26 | 21.12 | 16.56 | 13.91 | 7.63 | 9.12 |
| P/E Ratio:High | 13 | 10 | 10 | 11 | 12 | 16 | 13 | 13 | 29 | NM |
| P/E Ratio:Low | 8 | 7 | 6 | 7 | 8 | 12 | 7 | 6 | 10 | NM |

| Income Statement Analysis (Million $) | 2007 | 2006 | 2005 | 2004 | 2003 | 2002 | 2001 | 2000 | 1999 | 1998 |
|---|---|---|---|---|---|---|---|---|---|---|
| Revenue | 9,978 | 8,289 | 7,584 | 5,333 | 4,190 | 2,560 | 2,777 | 2,284 | 1,300 | 876 |
| Operating Income | 7,224 | 5,753 | 5,792 | 4,119 | 3,241 | 1,048 | 2,146 | 1,310 | 870 | 509 |
| Depreciation, Depletion and Amortization | 2,348 | 1,816 | 1,416 | 1,222 | 1,073 | 844 | 821 | 584 | 443 | 630 |
| Interest Expense | 312 | 158 | 122 | 120 | 127 | 133 | 132 | 109 | 84.6 | 70.4 |
| Pretax Income | 4,673 | 4,010 | 4,206 | 2,663 | 1,922 | 899 | 1,199 | 1,204 | 345 | -188 |
| Effective Tax Rate | 39.8% | 36.3% | 37.6% | 37.3% | 43.0% | 38.3% | 39.7% | 40.1% | 41.7% | NM |
| Net Income | 2,812 | 2,552 | 2,624 | 1,670 | 1,095 | 554 | 723 | 721 | 201 | -129 |
| S&P Core Earnings | 2,805 | 2,434 | 2,539 | 1,713 | 1,069 | 524 | 681 | NA | NA | NA |

| Balance Sheet & Other Financial Data (Million $) | 2007 | 2006 | 2005 | 2004 | 2003 | 2002 | 2001 | 2000 | 1999 | 1998 |
|---|---|---|---|---|---|---|---|---|---|---|
| Cash | 126 | 141 | 229 | 111 | 33.5 | 51.9 | 35.6 | 37.2 | 13.2 | 14.5 |
| Current Assets | 2,752 | 2,490 | 2,162 | 1,349 | 899 | 767 | 698 | 630 | 343 | 227 |
| Total Assets | 28,635 | 24,308 | 19,272 | 15,502 | 12,416 | 9,460 | 8,934 | 7,482 | 5,503 | 3,996 |
| Current Liabilities | 2,665 | 3,812 | 2,187 | 1,283 | 820 | 532 | 522 | 553 | 337 | 306 |
| Long Term Debt | 4,227 | 2,020 | 2,192 | 2,588 | 2,327 | 2,159 | 2,244 | 2,193 | 1,880 | 1,343 |
| Common Equity | 15,280 | 13,093 | 10,443 | 8,106 | 6,434 | 4,826 | 4,112 | 3,448 | 2,361 | 1,703 |
| Total Capital | 23,315 | 18,830 | 12,733 | 10,793 | 8,860 | 7,083 | 7,655 | 5,948 | 4,549 | 3,416 |
| Capital Expenditures | 5,807 | 3,892 | 3,716 | 2,456 | 1,595 | 1,037 | 1,525 | 1,011 | 591 | 700 |
| Cash Flow | 5,154 | 4,363 | 4,034 | 2,887 | 2,163 | 1,387 | 1,525 | 1,284 | 629 | 499 |
| Current Ratio | 1.0 | 0.7 | 1.0 | 1.1 | 1.1 | 1.4 | 1.3 | 1.1 | 1.0 | 0.7 |
| % Long Term Debt of Capitalization | 20.7 | 13.3 | 17.2 | 24.0 | 26.3 | 30.5 | 29.3 | 36.9 | 41.3 | 39.3 |
| % Return on Assets | 10.6 | 11.7 | 15.1 | 12.0 | 10.0 | 6.0 | 8.8 | 11.1 | 4.2 | NM |
| % Return on Equity | 19.8 | 21.6 | 28.2 | 22.9 | 19.4 | 12.2 | 18.6 | 24.1 | 9.2 | NM |

Data as orig reptd.; bef. results of disc opers/spec. items. Per share data adj. for stk. divs.; EPS diluted. E-Estimated. NA-Not Available. NM-Not Meaningful. NR-Not Ranked. UR-Under Review.

**Office:** 2000 Post Oak Blvd Ste 100, Houston, TX 77056-4400.
**Telephone:** 713-296-6000.
**Website:** http://www.apachecorp.com
**Chrmn:** R. Plank

**Pres, CEO & COO:** G.S. Farris
**EVP & CFO:** R.B. Plank
**SVP & General Counsel:** P.A. Lannie
**Chief Acctg Officer & Cntlr:** R.A. Hoyt

**Investor Contact:** R.J. Dye (713-296-6662)
**Board Members:** F. M. Bohen, G. S. Farris, R. M. Ferlic, E. C. Fiedorek, A. D. Frazier, Jr., P. A. Graham, J. A. Kocur, G. D. Lawrence, Jr., F. H. Merelli, R. D. Patton, C. Pitman, R. Plank

**Founded:** 1954
**Domicile:** Delaware
**Employees:** 3,521

# Apartment Investment and Management Co

**STANDARD &POOR'S**

| S&P Recommendation **HOLD** ★★★☆☆ | Price<br>$12.09 (as of Nov 14, 2008) | 12-Mo. Target Price<br>$15.00 | Investment Style<br>Large-Cap Value |
|---|---|---|---|

**GICS Sector** Financials
**Sub-Industry** Residential REITS

**Summary** This real estate investment trust is one of the largest U.S. owners and managers of multifamily apartment properties.

## Key Stock Statistics (Source S&P, Vickers, company reports)

| | | | | | | | |
|---|---|---|---|---|---|---|---|
| 52-Wk Range | **$43.67–10.00** | S&P FFO/Sh. 2008E | **3.18** | Market Capitalization(B) | **$1.072** | Beta | **0.95** |
| Trailing 12-Month FFO/Share | **NA** | S&P FFO/Sh. 2009E | **3.00** | Yield (%) | **19.85** | S&P 3-Yr. FFO/Sh. Proj. CAGR(%) | **3** |
| Trailing 12-Month P/FFO | **NA** | P/FFO on S&P FFO/Sh. 2008E | **3.8** | Dividend Rate/Share | **$2.40** | S&P Credit Rating | **BB+** |
| $10K Invested 5 Yrs Ago | **$5,877** | Common Shares Outstg. (M) | **88.7** | Institutional Ownership (%) | **NM** | | |

## Price Performance

Options: CBOE, P, Ph

Analysis prepared by **Royal F. Shepard, CFA** on November 12, 2008, when the stock traded at **$ 14.10**.

## Highlights

▶ We think rental rate increases will continue to moderate for the apartment sub-industry as it enters 2009, reflecting a slowing economy and excess supply in some markets. In our estimation, AIV's diversified portfolio should see an average rent hike of only about 1% in 2009, compared to 2.0% in 2008 and down from 4.4% in 2007. The trust's middle-market oriented apartments, however, could perform better than peers on average, in our opinion.

▶ Despite tight credit market conditions, AIV has had a measure of success in disposing of non-core properties in 2008. During the nine months, the trust recognized gross proceeds of $1.77 billion from the sale of about 90 properties. We think a portion of net proceeds will go toward an active property redevelopment program encompassing 61 properties, as of September 30, 2008.

▶ Our 2009 FFO estimate of $3.00, vs. $3.18 seen in 2008, reflects more shares outstanding and our expectation of lower incentive fees from the sale of joint ventured properties. AIV expects to declare a special dividend of $1.20 a share, including a combination of cash and stock, to cover taxable income generated by asset sales.

## Investment Rationale/Risk

▶ AIV holds a large and diversified portfolio of conventional and affordable residential properties, in our view. While we think challenging economic conditions will limit the ability of apartment owners to hike rents, we believe AIV's middle-market properties face minimal competition from excess housing supplies in some markets. Also, the trust is using recent asset dispositions to improve its financial position and renovate older properties. At a recent 4.7X estimated 2009 FFO, we think the shares trade at an appropriate discount to peers. Our hold opinion is based on total return potential.

▶ Risks to our opinion and target price include slower than expected employment growth in the trust's markets, higher borrowing rates on floating rate debt, and a significant increase in new construction that creates competitive supply.

▶ Our 12-month target price of $15 is based on a multiple of 5.0X our 2009 FFO estimate, a discount to peers, reflecting our view of AIV's below average financial position. Our net asset value model, based on recent transactions and a one-year cash return of 8.0%, leads to intrinsic value of $16.

## Qualitative Risk Assessment

| LOW | **MEDIUM** | HIGH |
|---|---|---|

Our risk assessment for AIV reflects its large, diversified operations and low stock volatility, offset by our view of recent weak operating performance and only modest coverage of the current common dividend.

## Quantitative Evaluations

**S&P Quality Ranking** **B-**

| D | C | **B-** | B | B+ | A- | A | A+ |
|---|---|---|---|---|---|---|---|

**Relative Strength Rank** **WEAK**

14

LOWEST = 1     HIGHEST = 99

## Revenue/FFO Data

**Revenue (Million $)**

| | 1Q | 2Q | 3Q | 4Q | Year |
|---|---|---|---|---|---|
| 2008 | 432.6 | 423.8 | 396.0 | -- | -- |
| 2007 | 413.1 | 426.4 | 426.7 | 455.0 | 1,721 |
| 2006 | 408.5 | 420.0 | 423.9 | 438.6 | 1,691 |
| 2005 | 361.6 | 372.3 | 386.8 | 400.9 | 1,522 |
| 2004 | 376.4 | 380.2 | 334.1 | 384.4 | 1,469 |
| 2003 | 397.5 | 378.4 | 377.4 | 381.9 | 1,516 |

**FFO Per Share ($)**

| | 1Q | 2Q | 3Q | 4Q | Year |
|---|---|---|---|---|---|
| 2008 | 0.79 | 0.83 | E0.84 | E0.72 | E3.18 |
| 2007 | 0.74 | 0.88 | 0.83 | 0.83 | 3.17 |
| 2006 | 0.68 | 0.73 | 0.74 | 0.91 | 3.07 |
| 2005 | 0.63 | 0.67 | 0.58 | 0.60 | 2.48 |
| 2004 | 0.67 | 0.63 | 0.78 | 0.72 | 2.79 |
| 2003 | 0.90 | 0.86 | 0.80 | 0.72 | 3.23 |

Fiscal year ended Dec. 31. Next earnings report expected: Mid February. FFO Estimates based on S&P Funds From Operations Est..

## Dividend Data (Dates: mm/dd Payment Date: mm/dd/yy)

| Amount ($) | Date Decl. | Ex-Div. Date | Stk. of Record | Payment Date |
|---|---|---|---|---|
| 2.4 Spl. | 07/18 | 07/24 | 07/28 | 08/29/08 |
| 0.600 | 07/18 | 07/24 | 07/28 | 08/29/08 |
| 1.20 Spl. | 10/16 | 10/23 | 10/27 | 12/01/08 |
| 0.600 | 10/16 | 10/23 | 10/27 | 12/01/08 |

Dividends have been paid since 1994. Source: Company reports.

---

**Please read the Required Disclosures and Analyst Certification on the last page of this report.**

*The McGraw-Hill Companies*

# Apartment Investment and Management Co

STANDARD
&POOR'S

## Business Summary November 12, 2008

CORPORATE OVERVIEW. Apartment Investment and Management Co. is one of the largest U.S. multifamily residential REITs in terms of units. At December 31, 2007, it owned, held an equity interest in, or managed a geographically diversified portfolio of 1,169 properties, including about 203,040 apartment units, located in 47 states, the District of Columbia and Puerto Rico.

The trust conducts substantially all its business, and owns all its assets, through AIMCO Properties, L.P., of which AIV owns approximately a 91% interest. AIV operates in two segments: the ownership, operation and management of apartment properties; and the management of apartment properties for third parties and affiliates.

MARKET PROFILE. The U.S. housing market is highly fragmented, and is characterized broadly by two types of housing units -- multifamily and single-family. At the end of 2007, the U.S. Census Bureau estimated that there were 128.65 million housing units in the country, an increase of 1.6% from 2006. Partially due to the high fragmentation since residents have the option of either being owners or tenants (renters), the housing market can be highly competitive. Main demand drivers for apartments are household formation and em-

ployment growth. We estimate that 1.1 million new households were formed in 2007, even with the estimated 1.1 million in 2006. Supply is created by new housing unit construction, which could consist of single-family homes, or multifamily apartment buildings or condominiums. We estimate 0.95 million total housing unit starts in 2008, down about 29% from 2007. Multifamily starts are expected to fall significantly less, approximately 6%.

With apartment tenants on relatively short leases compared to those of commercial and industrial properties, apartment REITs are generally more sensitive to changes in market conditions than REITs in other property categories. Results could be hurt by new construction that adds new space in excess of actual demand. Trends in home price affordability also affect both rent levels and the level of new construction, since the relative price attractiveness of owning versus renting is an important factor in consumer decision making.

## Company Financials Fiscal Year Ended Dec. 31

| Per Share Data ($) | 2007 | 2006 | 2005 | 2004 | 2003 | 2002 | 2001 | 2000 | 1999 | 1998 |
|---|---|---|---|---|---|---|---|---|---|---|
| Tangible Book Value | 9.82 | NA | NA | NA | NA | NA | 18.90 | 23.33 | 24.27 | 20.26 |
| Earnings | -1.14 | -1.29 | -1.25 | -0.39 | -0.25 | 0.94 | 0.23 | 0.52 | 0.38 | 0.80 |
| S&P Core Earnings | -1.12 | -1.29 | -1.25 | -0.39 | -0.32 | 0.89 | 0.19 | NA | NA | NA |
| Dividends | 2.40 | NA | NA | NA | NA | NA | 3.12 | 2.80 | 2.50 | 2.25 |
| Payout Ratio | NM | NM | NM | NM | NM | NM | NM | NM | NM | NM |
| Prices:High | 65.79 | 59.17 | 44.14 | 39.25 | 42.05 | 51.46 | 50.13 | 50.06 | 44.13 | 41.00 |
| Prices:Low | 33.97 | 37.76 | 34.17 | 26.45 | 33.00 | 33.90 | 39.25 | 36.31 | 34.06 | 30.00 |
| P/E Ratio:High | NM | NM | NM | NM | NM | 55 | NM | 96 | NM | 51 |
| P/E Ratio:Low | NM | NM | NM | NM | NM | 36 | NM | 70 | NM | 37 |

| Income Statement Analysis (Million $) | | | | | | | | | | |
|---|---|---|---|---|---|---|---|---|---|---|
| Rental Income | 1,641 | 1,630 | 1,460 | 1,402 | 1,446 | 1,292 | 1,298 | 1,051 | 534 | 377 |
| Mortgage Income | Nil | Nil | Nil | Nil | Nil | Nil | Nil | Nil | 43.5 | Nil |
| Total Income | 1,721 | 1,691 | 1,522 | 1,469 | 1,516 | 1,506 | 1,464 | 1,101 | 577 | 377 |
| General Expenses | 886 | 874 | 816 | 768 | 729 | 664 | 652 | 485 | 406 | 190 |
| Interest Expense | 422 | 408 | 368 | 367 | 373 | 340 | 316 | 270 | 140 | 89.4 |
| Provision for Losses | Nil | Nil | Nil | Nil | Nil | Nil | Nil | Nil | Nil | Nil |
| Depreciation | NA | 471 | 412 | 369 | 328 | 289 | 364 | 330 | 151 | 93.4 |
| Net Income | -48.1 | -42.7 | -27.9 | 55.7 | 70.7 | 175 | 107 | 99.2 | 83.7 | 64.5 |
| S&P Core Earnings | -112 | -124 | -117 | -35.5 | -29.2 | 77.1 | 13.8 | NA | NA | NA |

| Balance Sheet & Other Financial Data (Million $) | | | | | | | | | | |
|---|---|---|---|---|---|---|---|---|---|---|
| Cash | 210 | 230 | 330 | 293 | 98.0 | 97.0 | 820 | 1,068 | 1,123 | 127 |
| Total Assets | 10,607 | 10,290 | 10,017 | 10,072 | 10,113 | 10,317 | 8,323 | 7,700 | 5,685 | 4,268 |
| Real Estate Investment | 12,384 | 11,982 | 10,990 | 10,800 | 10,601 | 10,227 | 8,416 | 7,012 | 4,509 | 2,803 |
| Loss Reserve | Nil | Nil | Nil | Nil | Nil | Nil | Nil | Nil | Nil | Nil |
| Net Investment | 9,349 | 9,081 | 8,752 | 8,785 | 8,753 | 8,616 | 6,796 | 6,099 | 4,092 | 2,574 |
| Short Term Debt | Nil | Nil | Nil | Nil | Nil | Nil | 214 | 329 | 630 | 460 |
| Capitalization:Debt | 7,532 | 6,873 | 6,284 | 5,734 | 6,198 | 5,529 | 4,670 | 4,031 | 2,525 | 1,350 |
| Capitalization:Equity | 1,026 | 1,516 | 1,706 | 1,967 | 2,005 | 2,218 | 1,592 | 1,664 | 1,622 | 1,110 |
| Capitalization:Total | 9,838 | 9,165 | 9,436 | 9,246 | 9,580 | 9,180 | 7,904 | 7,037 | 5,181 | 2,795 |
| % Earnings & Depreciation/Assets | 4.2 | 4.2 | 3.8 | 4.2 | 3.9 | 5.0 | 5.9 | 1.5 | 4.7 | 4.7 |
| Price Times Book Value:High | 6.7 | 4.0 | 2.5 | 1.9 | 2.0 | 2.3 | 2.7 | 2.1 | 1.8 | 2.0 |
| Price Times Book Value:Low | 3.5 | 2.5 | 1.9 | 1.3 | 1.6 | 1.5 | 2.1 | 1.6 | 1.4 | 1.5 |

Data as orig reptd.; bef. results of disc opers/spec. items. Per share data adj. for stk. divs.; EPS diluted. E-Estimated. NA-Not Available. NM-Not Meaningful. NR-Not Ranked. UR-Under Review.

**Office:** 4582 S Ulster St Pkwy Ste 1100, Denver, CO 80237-2662.
**Telephone:** 303-757-8101.
**Email:** investor@aimco.com
**Website:** http://www.aimco.com

**Chrmn, Pres & CEO:** T. Considine
**COO:** T. Beaudin
**EVP & CFO:** T.M. Herzog
**EVP & Chief Admin Officer:** M. Cortez

**EVP & Treas:** P.K. Fielding
**Investor Contact:** J. Martin (303-691-4440)
**Board Members:** J. N. Bailey, T. Considine, R. S. Ellwood, T. L. Keltner, J. L. Martin, R. A. Miller, T. L. Rhodes, M. A. Stein

**Founded:** 1994
**Domicile:** Maryland
**Employees:** 5,900

# Apollo Group Inc

**STANDARD &POOR'S**

| S&P Recommendation | HOLD ★★★☆☆ | Price $68.11 (as of Nov 14, 2008) | 12-Mo. Target Price $72.00 | Investment Style Large-Cap Growth |
|---|---|---|---|---|

**GICS Sector** Consumer Discretionary
**Sub-Industry** Education Services

**Summary** This leading provider of higher education programs for working adults offers educational programs and services at a total of some 260 campuses and learning centers.

## Key Stock Statistics (Source S&P, Vickers, company reports)

| | | | | | | | |
|---|---|---|---|---|---|---|---|
| 52-Wk Range | $81.68–37.92 | S&P Oper. EPS 2009E | 3.25 | Market Capitalization(B) | $10.764 | Beta | 0.50 |
| Trailing 12-Month EPS | $2.87 | S&P Oper. EPS 2010E | 3.75 | Yield (%) | Nil | S&P 3-Yr. Proj. EPS CAGR(%) | 15 |
| Trailing 12-Month P/E | 23.7 | P/E on S&P Oper. EPS 2009E | 21.0 | Dividend Rate/Share | Nil | S&P Credit Rating | NA |
| $10K Invested 5 Yrs Ago | $10,236 | Common Shares Outstg. (M) | 158.5 | Institutional Ownership (%) | 85 | | |

## Price Performance

30-Week Mov. Avg. · · ·   10-Week Mov. Avg. – –   **GAAP Earnings vs. Previous Year**   Volume Above Avg. STARS
12-Mo. Target Price —   Relative Strength —   ▲ Up   ▼ Down   ► No Change   Below Avg.

Options: ASE, CBOE, P, Ph

### Qualitative Risk Assessment

| LOW | MEDIUM | HIGH |
|---|---|---|

Our risk assessment reflects a less vital for-profit education market, APOL's current transformation of its business model and recent executive changeover. In the corporate governance area, we have a negative view of the near 100% voting control held by insiders through separate voting shares. We believe these factors are offset by what we view as APOL's consistently solid levels of cash flow and a healthy balance sheet.

### Quantitative Evaluations

**S&P Quality Ranking** B+

| D | C | B- | B | B+ | A- | A | A+ |
|---|---|---|---|---|---|---|---|

**Relative Strength Rank** STRONG 97

LOWEST = 1     HIGHEST = 99

## Highlights

► The 12-month target price for APOL has recently been changed to $72.00 from $65.00. The Highlights section of this Stock Report will be updated accordingly.

## Investment Rationale/Risk

► The Investment Rationale/Risk section of this Stock Report will be updated shortly. For the latest News story on APOL from MarketScope, see below.

► 10/29/08 10:49 am ET ... S&P REITERATES HOLD RECOMMENDATION ON SHARES OF APOLLO GROUP (APOL 65.17***): Aug-Q EPS of $0.75 vs. $0.62, both before items, is $0.09 above our forecast. Revenues rose 17%, on what we view as impressive 15% and 19% gains in total and new enrollments. But much of the outperformance is from ex-president's forfeiture of stock options and from lower bad debt expense. Selling costs also rose 28%, as APOL continues extensive actions to build brand identity and support enrollments. We are raising our FY 09 (Aug.) EPS estimate by $0.10 to $3.25 and see $3.75 in FY 10. We also raise our target price by $7 to $72, a premium-to-peers 21X calendar '09 forecast. /M.Jaffe

## Revenue/Earnings Data

### Revenue (Million $)

| | 1Q | 2Q | 3Q | 4Q | Year |
|---|---|---|---|---|---|
| 2008 | 780.7 | 693.6 | 835.2 | 831.4 | 3,141 |
| 2007 | 668.3 | 608.7 | 733.4 | 713.9 | 2,724 |
| 2006 | 628.9 | 569.6 | 653.6 | 624.2 | 2,478 |
| 2005 | 534.9 | 505.7 | 619.0 | 591.8 | 2,251 |
| 2004 | 411.8 | 396.9 | 497.0 | 492.8 | 1,798 |
| 2003 | 308.9 | 295.2 | 364.2 | 371.3 | 1,340 |

### Earnings Per Share ($)

| | | | | | |
|---|---|---|---|---|---|
| 2008 | 0.83 | -0.19 | 0.85 | 1.43 | 2.87 |
| 2007 | 0.66 | 0.35 | 0.75 | 0.60 | 2.36 |
| 2006 | 0.73 | 0.46 | 0.77 | 0.54 | 2.35 |
| 2005 | 0.58 | 0.47 | 0.77 | 0.58 | 2.39 |
| 2004 | 0.44 | 0.35 | 0.56 | -0.59 | 0.77 |
| 2003 | 0.30 | 0.24 | 0.39 | 0.37 | 1.30 |

Fiscal year ended Aug. 31. Next earnings report expected: Early January. EPS Estimates based on S&P Operating Earnings; historical GAAP earnings are as reported.

## Dividend Data

No cash dividends have been paid.

# Apollo Group Inc

STANDARD
&POOR'S

## Business Summary October 20, 2008

CORPORATE OVERVIEW. Historically, Apollo Group has derived most of its revenues through the provision of higher education programs for working adults. It has several school units, but the large majority of its students have taken education programs at its University of Phoenix (UOP) unit. UOP offers its education programs at campuses, as well as through online programs. They consist mostly of associates, bachelors and masters degree programs in business, education, information technology, criminal justice and nursing. As of November 30, 2007 (latest available), APOL offered programs and services at 102 campuses and 154 learning centers in 40 states, the District of Columbia, Puerto Rico, Canada, the Netherlands and Mexico. Enrollment at UOP (including the Axia associates degree program, which became part of UOP in mid-calendar 2006) totaled 345,300 at May 31, 2008, up from 313,700 at August 31, 2007, and 282,300 at year-end FY 06 (Aug.).

CORPORATE STRATEGY. The level of Apollo's enrollment growth fell from 27.7% in FY 04's fourth quarter (under the old definition of enrollments), to 3.3% in FY 06's third quarter (under the new definition; it now reports only UOP and Axia), with sequential growth levels declining in all but one quarter. However, growth has since revived, and stood at 11.0% in FY 08's third quarter. We attribute the initial downturn to changing demographic trends, greater competition, more regulatory scrutiny and the law of big numbers. Until recently,

APOL focused almost entirely on students who were older than the traditional 18-to-22 year-old college student, particularly baby boomers. Yet, with the youngest baby boomers now over the age of 40, APOL has started to seek students in other demographic categories. As a result, it began to place much more concentration on its Axia College program, which offers associate degrees and targets younger students. We believe early results of its shift in focus have been encouraging.

In October 2007, Apollo formed a $1 billion joint venture with the Carlyle Group, a private equity firm, to make a range of investments in the foreign education services sector. APOL committed up to $801 million, and was to own 80.1% of the venture. We view this as an important step for APOL in preparing to expand its global footprint. In April 2008, the unit (Apollo Global) acquired Universidad de Artes, Ciencias y Comunicacion, an accredited, private arts and communications university in Chile, for a total of about $44 million in cash and assumed debt, and would also pay an earn-out in four years based on a multiple of earnings.

## Company Financials Fiscal Year Ended Aug. 31

| Per Share Data ($) | 2008 | 2007 | 2006 | 2005 | 2004 | 2003 | 2002 | 2001 | 2000 | 1999 |
|---|---|---|---|---|---|---|---|---|---|---|
| Tangible Book Value | 4.56 | 3.62 | 3.40 | 3.73 | 4.89 | 5.23 | 3.60 | 2.47 | 1.39 | 1.10 |
| Cash Flow | NA | 2.77 | 2.74 | 2.68 | 1.79 | 1.62 | 1.12 | 0.81 | 0.57 | 0.45 |
| Earnings | 2.87 | 2.35 | 2.35 | 2.39 | 0.77 | 1.30 | 0.87 | 0.60 | 0.41 | 0.33 |
| S&P Core Earnings | 2.87 | 2.35 | 2.42 | 2.30 | 0.72 | 1.22 | 0.79 | 0.52 | NA | NA |
| Dividends | NA | Nil | Nil | Nil | Nil | Nil | Nil | Nil | Nil | Nil |
| Payout Ratio | NA | Nil | Nil | Nil | Nil | Nil | Nil | Nil | Nil | Nil |
| Prices:High | NA | 80.75 | 63.26 | 84.20 | 98.01 | 73.09 | 46.15 | 33.31 | 22.64 | 15.22 |
| Prices:Low | NA | 39.02 | 33.33 | 57.40 | 62.55 | 40.72 | 28.13 | 19.33 | 8.17 | 7.81 |
| P/E Ratio:High | NA | 34 | 25 | 35 | NM | 56 | 53 | 56 | 55 | 46 |
| P/E Ratio:Low | NA | 17 | 13 | 24 | NM | 31 | 32 | 32 | 20 | 23 |

| Income Statement Analysis (Million $) | | | | | | | | | | |
|---|---|---|---|---|---|---|---|---|---|---|
| Revenue | 3,141 | 2,724 | 2,478 | 2,251 | 1,798 | 1,340 | 1,009 | 769 | 610 | 499 |
| Operating Income | NA | 697 | 738 | 767 | 481 | 428 | 293 | 194 | 141 | 113 |
| Depreciation | 79.7 | 71.1 | 67.3 | 54.5 | 43.2 | 40.3 | 35.2 | 32.7 | 27.4 | 20.6 |
| Interest Expense | NA | Nil | Nil | Nil | Nil | Nil | Nil | Nil | Nil | Nil |
| Pretax Income | 783 | 657 | 668 | 730 | 456 | 402 | 266 | 175 | 120 | 98.0 |
| Effective Tax Rate | 39.2% | 37.8% | 37.9% | 39.1% | 39.1% | 38.5% | 39.4% | 38.4% | 40.8% | 39.8% |
| Net Income | 477 | 409 | 415 | 445 | 278 | 247 | 161 | 108 | 71.2 | 59.0 |
| S&P Core Earnings | 477 | 409 | 428 | 427 | 131 | 218 | 140 | 90.1 | NA | NA |

| Balance Sheet & Other Financial Data (Million $) | | | | | | | | | | |
|---|---|---|---|---|---|---|---|---|---|---|
| Cash | 486 | 370 | 355 | 595 | 677 | 800 | 610 | 375 | 154 | 108 |
| Current Assets | NA | 925 | 803 | 835 | 855 | 950 | 730 | 487 | 247 | 198 |
| Total Assets | 1,860 | 1,450 | 1,283 | 1,303 | 1,452 | 1,378 | 980 | 680 | 405 | 348 |
| Current Liabilities | NA | 744 | 596 | 518 | 465 | 335 | 264 | 182 | 131 | 109 |
| Long Term Debt | NA | Nil | Nil | Nil | Nil | Nil | 15.5 | 14.8 | 9.97 | 4.22 |
| Common Equity | 834 | 634 | 604 | 707 | 957 | 1,027 | 699 | 482 | 261 | 231 |
| Total Capital | NA | 634 | 604 | 707 | 957 | 1,027 | 715 | 497 | 272 | 237 |
| Capital Expenditures | 105 | 61.2 | 44.6 | 104 | 80.3 | 55.8 | 36.7 | 44.4 | 34.8 | 44.7 |
| Cash Flow | NA | 480 | 482 | 499 | 321 | 287 | 196 | 141 | 98.6 | 79.6 |
| Current Ratio | 1.4 | 1.2 | 1.3 | 1.6 | 1.8 | 2.8 | 2.8 | 2.7 | 1.9 | 1.8 |
| % Long Term Debt of Capitalization | Nil | Nil | Nil | Nil | Nil | Nil | 2.2 | 3.0 | 3.7 | 1.8 |
| % Net Income of Revenue | 15.2 | 15.0 | 16.7 | 19.8 | 15.4 | 18.4 | 16.0 | 14.0 | 11.7 | 11.8 |
| % Return on Assets | 28.8 | 29.9 | 32.4 | 31.8 | 19.6 | 20.9 | 19.4 | 19.9 | 18.9 | 18.1 |
| % Return on Equity | 64.9 | 66.0 | 67.0 | 53.5 | 28.0 | 28.6 | 29.3 | 29.0 | 28.9 | 27.4 |

Data as orig reptd.; bef. results of disc opers/spec. items. Per share data adj. for stk. divs.; EPS diluted. E-Estimated. NA-Not Available. NM-Not Meaningful. NR-Not Ranked. UR-Under Review.

**Office:** 4615 East Elwood Street, Phoenix, AZ 85040-1958.
**Telephone:** 480-966-5394.
**Website:** http://www.apollogrp.edu
**Chrmn:** J. Sperling

**Pres, CFO & Treas:** J.L. D'Amico
**Vice Chrmn & SVP:** P.V. Sperling
**CEO:** C.B. Edelstein
**SVP & Chief Acctg Officer:** B.L. Swartz

**Investor Contact:** J. Pasinski (800-990-2765)
**Board Members:** G. W. Cappelli, D. J. Deconcini, C. B. Edelstein, R. A. Herberger, Jr., A. Kirschner, K. S. Redman, J. R. Reis, J. Sperling, P. V. Sperling, G. Zimmer

**Founded:** 1981
**Domicile:** Arizona
**Employees:** 44,647

The McGraw-Hill Companies

# Apple Inc

**STANDARD &POOR'S**

| **S&P Recommendation** | **BUY** ★★★★☆ | **Price** $90.24 (as of Nov 14, 2008) | **12-Mo. Target Price** $137.00 | **Investment Style** Large-Cap Growth |
|---|---|---|---|---|

**GICS Sector** Information Technology
**Sub-Industry** Computer Hardware

**Summary** This company is a leading provider of hardware and software, including the Macintosh (Mac) computer, the iPod digital media player, and the iPhone.

## Key Stock Statistics (Source S&P, Vickers, company reports)

| | | | | | | | |
|---|---|---|---|---|---|---|---|
| 52-Wk Range | $202.96– 85.00 | S&P Oper. EPS 2009**E** | 5.70 | Market Capitalization(B) | $80.218 | Beta | 2.62 |
| Trailing 12-Month EPS | $5.36 | S&P Oper. EPS 2010**E** | 7.30 | Yield (%) | Nil | S&P 3-Yr. Proj. EPS CAGR(%) | 19 |
| Trailing 12-Month P/E | 16.8 | P/E on S&P Oper. EPS 2009**E** | 15.8 | Dividend Rate/Share | Nil | S&P Credit Rating | NR |
| $10K Invested 5 Yrs Ago | $84,101 | Common Shares Outstg. (M) | 888.9 | Institutional Ownership (%) | 66 | | |

## Price Performance

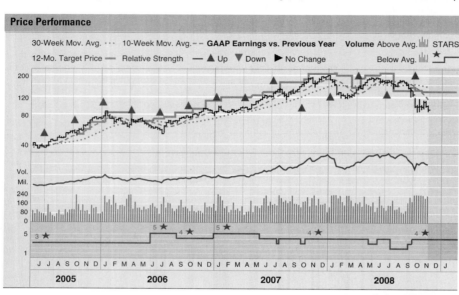

30-Week Mov. Avg. · · · 10-Week Mov. Avg. **GAAP Earnings vs. Previous Year** Volume Above Avg. STARS
12-Mo. Target Price — Relative Strength — ▲ Up ▼ Down ► No Change Below Avg. ★

Options: ASE, CBOE, P, Ph

Analysis prepared by **Thomas W. Smith, CFA** on October 23, 2008, when the stock traded at **$ 96.75**.

## Qualitative Risk Assessment

| LOW | MEDIUM | **HIGH** |
|---|---|---|

Our risk assessment reflects our view of a seemingly ever-evolving market for consumer-oriented technology products, potential challenges associated with the company's growing size and offerings, and the critical importance to the company of founder and CEO Steve Jobs.

## Quantitative Evaluations

**S&P Quality Ranking**      **B**

| D | C | B- | **B** | B+ | A- | A | A+ |
|---|---|---|---|---|---|---|---|

**Relative Strength Rank**     **MODERATE**

44

LOWEST = 1      HIGHEST = 99

## Revenue/Earnings Data

**Revenue (Million $)**

| | 1Q | 2Q | 3Q | 4Q | Year |
|---|---|---|---|---|---|
| 2008 | 9,608 | 7,512 | 7,464 | 7,895 | 32,479 |
| 2007 | 7,115 | 5,264 | 5,410 | 6,217 | 24,006 |
| 2006 | 5,749 | 4,359 | 4,370 | 4,837 | 19,315 |
| 2005 | 3,490 | 3,243 | 3,520 | 3,678 | 13,931 |
| 2004 | 2,006 | 1,909 | 2,014 | 2,350 | 8,279 |
| 2003 | 1,472 | 1,475 | 1,545 | 1,715 | 6,207 |

**Earnings Per Share ($)**

| | | | | | |
|---|---|---|---|---|---|
| 2008 | 1.76 | 1.16 | 1.19 | 1.26 | 5.36 |
| 2007 | 1.14 | 0.87 | 0.92 | 1.01 | 3.93 |
| 2006 | 0.65 | 0.47 | 0.54 | 0.62 | 2.27 |
| 2005 | 0.35 | 0.34 | 0.37 | 0.50 | 1.56 |
| 2004 | 0.09 | 0.06 | 0.08 | 0.13 | 0.36 |
| 2003 | -0.01 | 0.02 | 0.03 | 0.06 | 0.10 |

Fiscal year ended Sep. 30. Next earnings report expected: Late January. EPS Estimates based on S&P Operating Earnings; historical GAAP earnings are as reported.

## Dividend Data

No cash dividends have been paid since 1996.

## Highlights

➤ We project revenue growth of 15% for FY 09 (Sep.) and 22% for FY 10, driven by market share gains we expect for personal computers and smart phones. All major product lines have been refreshed ahead of the year-end selling season, with new iPhone models available since July 11, new iPods since September 9, and new MacBook PCs since October 14. We note that subscription accounting defers substantial iPhone revenue.

➤ We estimate the gross margin for FY 09 will narrow about 150 basis points to 32.8%, as expenses associated with new product launches outweigh advantages from higher volumes and modest costs for components. We expect R&D and SG&A costs to be slightly lower as a percentage of sales as volumes increase in FY 09.

➤ We forecast EPS of $5.70 for FY 09 and $7.30 for FY 10. We expect results to be aided by what we consider a healthy balance sheet, consisting of about $24.5 billion in net cash and investments as of September 27, 2008, and amounting to about $27.07 per diluted share. We see the potential for notable share repurchases at some point in the future.

## Investment Rationale/Risk

➤ Our buy opinion reflects the potential we see for new products to spur sales, tempered by our projection of a downward turn in gross margin trends and potential for consumer electronics demand to moderate with the U.S. economy. We also believe present valuation levels are attractive for the pace of EPS growth we anticipate. AAPL continues to provide what we view as simple, superior and differentiated products.

➤ Risks to our recommendation and target price include higher costs than we project for new product launches, more competitive threats to AAPL's digital media offerings, and slower sales than we forecast for the iPhone 3G and related application products.

➤ We apply a target P/E of 24X to our FY 09 EPS estimate of $5.70 to arrive at our 12-month target price of $137. Our target P/E is in the lower quartile of AAPL's historical range to reflect our projection of slowing near-term growth, but is still at a premium to large-cap peers to reflect AAPL's relatively fast growth, lack of debt, and ability to self-finance new products.

# Apple Inc

**STANDARD &POOR'S**

## Business Summary October 23, 2008

CORPORATE OVERVIEW. Apple Inc. (AAPL) may have a relatively small share of the worldwide market for computers (according to market research firm IDC), but in the rapidly expanding digital media player market, it has dominated with the success of the iPod. We believe the iPod has contributed to greater demand for AAPL computers. In fact, AAPL's share of the U.S. computer market has risen from about 3% to roughly 5% in recent years. We anticipate further growth in brand awareness from the introduction of the iPhone in late June 2007.

Personal computers was the largest product category ahead of iPod for FY 07 (Sep.). The company is ahead of an industry trend toward selling more laptop PCs than desktop models, with the crossover for AAPL occurring in FY 06, about a year earlier than for rival Dell. In FY 07, portable PCs represented 26% of net sales (21% of FY 06 sales), desktop PCs 17% (17%), iPod 35% (40%), music 10% (10%), iPhone 1% (0%), peripherals and other hardware 5% (6%), and software, service and other 6% (6%).

The company sourced about 60% of revenues from the U.S. in FY 07. Viewed according to the reporting segments, AAPL sourced 48% of net sales in FY 07 from the Americas (49% in FY 06), 23% from Europe (21%), 5% from Japan (6%), 17% from retail (17%), and 7% from other segments (7%).

In August 2006, as a result of an internal stock option investigation, AAPL announced it would likely need to restate its historical financial statements to record non-cash charges. In December 2006, AAPL confirmed that it was restating results for prior periods and recording non-cash charges totaling $84 million on an after-tax basis. While we view the news as disappointing, we believe it does not change AAPL's fundamental operating model. In April 2007, the SEC indicated it is not pursuing actions against AAPL or any of its current employees, including founder and CEO Steve Jobs.

## Company Financials Fiscal Year Ended Sep. 30

| Per Share Data ($) | 2008 | 2007 | 2006 | 2005 | 2004 | 2003 | 2002 | 2001 | 2000 | 1999 |
|---|---|---|---|---|---|---|---|---|---|---|
| Tangible Book Value | 23.04 | 16.27 | 11.47 | 8.83 | 6.36 | 5.61 | 5.54 | 5.59 | 6.00 | 4.59 |
| Cash Flow | NA | 4.29 | 2.52 | 1.77 | 0.55 | 0.50 | 0.25 | 0.09 | 1.21 | 0.99 |
| Earnings | 5.36 | 3.93 | 2.27 | 1.56 | 0.36 | 0.10 | 0.09 | -0.06 | 1.09 | 0.90 |
| S&P Core Earnings | 5.36 | 3.93 | 2.27 | 1.47 | 0.22 | -0.17 | -0.19 | -0.72 | NA | NA |
| Dividends | NA | Nil | Nil | Nil | Nil | Nil | Nil | Nil | Nil | Nil |
| Payout Ratio | NA | Nil | Nil | Nil | Nil | Nil | Nil | Nil | Nil | Nil |
| Prices:High | NA | 202.96 | 93.16 | 75.46 | 34.79 | 12.51 | 13.09 | 13.56 | 37.59 | 29.50 |
| Prices:Low | NA | 81.90 | 50.16 | 31.30 | 10.59 | 6.36 | 6.68 | 7.22 | 6.81 | 8.00 |
| P/E Ratio:High | NA | 52 | 41 | 48 | 98 | NM | NM | NM | 34 | 33 |
| P/E Ratio:Low | NA | 21 | 22 | 20 | 30 | NM | NM | NM | 6 | 9 |

| Income Statement Analysis (Million $) | 2008 | 2007 | 2006 | 2005 | 2004 | 2003 | 2002 | 2001 | 2000 | 1999 |
|---|---|---|---|---|---|---|---|---|---|---|
| Revenue | 32,479 | 24,006 | 19,315 | 13,931 | 8,279 | 6,207 | 5,742 | 5,363 | 7,983 | 6,134 |
| Operating Income | NA | 4,726 | 2,645 | 1,829 | 499 | 138 | 164 | -231 | 704 | 471 |
| Depreciation | 473 | 317 | 225 | 179 | 150 | 113 | 118 | 102 | 84.0 | 85.0 |
| Interest Expense | NA | Nil | Nil | Nil | 3.00 | 8.00 | 11.0 | 16.0 | 21.0 | 47.0 |
| Pretax Income | 6,895 | 5,008 | 2,818 | 1,815 | 383 | 92.0 | 87.0 | -52.0 | 1,092 | 676 |
| Effective Tax Rate | 29.9% | 30.2% | 29.4% | 26.4% | 27.9% | 26.1% | 25.3% | NM | 28.0% | 11.1% |
| Net Income | 4,834 | 3,496 | 1,989 | 1,335 | 276 | 68.0 | 65.0 | -37.0 | 786 | 601 |
| S&P Core Earnings | 4,834 | 3,496 | 1,989 | 1,259 | 164 | -119 | -137 | -465 | NA | NA |

| Balance Sheet & Other Financial Data (Million $) | 2008 | 2007 | 2006 | 2005 | 2004 | 2003 | 2002 | 2001 | 2000 | 1999 |
|---|---|---|---|---|---|---|---|---|---|---|
| Cash | 24,490 | 9,352 | 6,392 | 3,491 | 2,969 | 3,396 | 2,252 | 2,310 | 1,191 | 1,326 |
| Current Assets | NA | 21,956 | 14,509 | 10,300 | 7,055 | 5,887 | 5,388 | 5,143 | 5,427 | 4,285 |
| Total Assets | 39,572 | 25,347 | 17,205 | 11,551 | 8,050 | 6,815 | 6,298 | 6,021 | 6,803 | 5,161 |
| Current Liabilities | NA | 9,299 | 6,471 | 3,484 | 2,680 | 2,357 | 1,658 | 1,518 | 1,933 | 1,549 |
| Long Term Debt | NA | Nil | Nil | Nil | Nil | Nil | 316 | 317 | 300 | 300 |
| Common Equity | 21,030 | 14,532 | 9,984 | 7,466 | 5,076 | 4,223 | 4,095 | 3,920 | 4,031 | 2,954 |
| Total Capital | NA | 15,151 | 10,365 | 7,466 | 5,076 | 4,223 | 4,640 | 4,503 | 4,870 | 3,612 |
| Capital Expenditures | 1,091 | 735 | 657 | 260 | 176 | 164 | 174 | 735 | 107 | 47.0 |
| Cash Flow | NA | 3,813 | 2,214 | 1,514 | 426 | 181 | 183 | 65.0 | 870 | 686 |
| Current Ratio | 2.5 | 2.4 | 2.2 | 3.0 | 2.6 | 2.5 | 3.2 | 3.4 | 2.8 | 2.8 |
| % Long Term Debt of Capitalization | Nil | Nil | Nil | Nil | Nil | Nil | 6.8 | 7.0 | 6.2 | 8.3 |
| % Net Income of Revenue | 14.9 | 14.6 | 10.3 | 9.6 | 3.3 | 1.1 | 1.1 | NM | 9.8 | 9.8 |
| % Return on Assets | 14.9 | 16.4 | 13.9 | 13.6 | 3.7 | 1.0 | 1.1 | NM | 13.1 | 12.7 |
| % Return on Equity | 27.2 | 28.5 | 22.8 | 21.3 | 5.9 | 1.6 | 1.6 | NM | 22.5 | 27.0 |

Data as orig reptd.; bef. results of disc opers/spec. items. Per share data adj. for stk. divs.; EPS diluted. E-Estimated. NA-Not Available. NM-Not Meaningful. NR-Not Ranked. UR-Under Review.

**Office:** 1 Infinite Loop, Cupertino, CA 95014.
**Telephone:** 408-996-1010.
**Email:** investor_relations@apple.com
**Website:** http://www.apple.com

**CEO:** S.P. Jobs
**COO:** T.D. Cook
**SVP, CFO, Chief Acctg Officer & Cntlr:** P. Oppenheimer
**SVP, Secy & General Counsel:** D. Cooperman

**CTO:** R. LeFaivre
**Board Members:** W. V. Campbell, M. S. Drexler, A. A. Gore, Jr., S. P. Jobs, A. Jung, A. D. Levinson, E. E. Schmidt, J. B. York

**Founded:** 1977
**Domicile:** California
**Employees:** 35,100

The **McGraw·Hill** Companies

# Applied Biosystems Inc

STANDARD &POOR'S

| S&P Recommendation | HOLD ★★★☆☆ | Price $29.29 (as of Nov 14, 2008) | 12-Mo. Target Price $38.00 | Investment Style Large-Cap Growth |
|---|---|---|---|---|

**GICS Sector** Health Care
**Sub-Industry** Life Sciences Tools & Services

**Summary** ABI, which supplies instrument systems, reagents, software and related services for life science research, has agreed to be acquired by Invitrogen for cash and stock.

## Key Stock Statistics (Source S&P, Vickers, company reports)

| | | | | | |
|---|---|---|---|---|---|
| 52-Wk Range | $37.25– 25.85 | S&P Oper. EPS 2009E | 1.93 | Market Capitalization(B) | $4.987 | Beta | 0.77 |
| Trailing 12-Month EPS | $1.90 | S&P Oper. EPS 2010E | 2.20 | Yield (%) | 0.58 | S&P 3-Yr. Proj. EPS CAGR(%) | 14 |
| Trailing 12-Month P/E | 15.4 | P/E on S&P Oper. EPS 2009E | 15.2 | Dividend Rate/Share | $0.17 | S&P Credit Rating | NA |
| $10K Invested 5 Yrs Ago | $13,489 | Common Shares Outstg. (M) | 170.3 | Institutional Ownership (%) | 78 | | |

## Price Performance

Options: ASE, CBOE, P

Analysis prepared by **Jeffrey Loo, CFA** on November 04, 2008, when the stock traded at **$ 30.71**.

### Highlights

► In June 2008, Invitrogen (IVGN: strong buy, $28) agreed to acquire ABI in a cash and stock deal valued at $6.3 billion, subject to necessary approvals. ABI shareholders would receive $38 a share in cash and stock. The combined companies would be named Applied Biosystems and have sales of about $3.5 billion. The deal, approved by shareholders in October, is expected to close shortly after receipt of European antitrust clearance.

► As a stand-alone company, we see sales rising 7% in FY 09 (Jun.), to $2.38 billion, on mixed performances in ABI's five business units and the May 2008 rollout of ABI's next-generation sequencer, the SOLiD system. We expect low double digit growth in Real-time PCR, a decline in Other product lines, and low single digit growth in ABI's remaining three segments. We see gross margins improving 90 basis points (bps) despite the manufacturing ramp-up of SOLiD, and operating margins improving 120 bps on leverage.

► Our FY 09 EPS estimate is $1.93.

### Investment Rationale/Risk

► We view the pending deal positively, as we believe the combination of ABI's and IVGN's strengths and product portfolios would create a leading life science company offering an extensive array of instruments and consumables for genetic analysis. We believe the company would have a solid platform for expansion into high-growth markets within genomics, proteomics and cell biology, with about 70% of its sales from higher-margin consumables. We also think IVGN will benefit from ABI's years-long restructuring and product portfolio rebalancing with an increased focus on expanding consumable sales that will aid margin expansion. However, we see significant integration challenges, and believe the company would be highly leveraged, with debt of about $3.5 billion.

► Risks to our recommendation and target price include termination of the pending takeover and lower-than-expected sales.

► Our 12-month target price of $38 is based on IVGN's offer price.

## Qualitative Risk Assessment

| LOW | MEDIUM | HIGH |
|---|---|---|

Our risk assessment reflects ABI's diverse product portfolio and broad geographic client base, offset by its heavy dependence on academic clients that rely on government funding and the highly competitive industry in which it competes.

## Quantitative Evaluations

**S&P Quality Ranking** B+

| D | C | B- | B | B+ | A- | A | A+ |
|---|---|---|---|---|---|---|---|

**Relative Strength Rank** STRONG

76

LOWEST = 1     HIGHEST = 99

## Revenue/Earnings Data

**Revenue (Million $)**

| | 1Q | 2Q | 3Q | 4Q | Year |
|---|---|---|---|---|---|
| 2009 | 533.1 | -- | -- | -- | -- |
| 2008 | 501.2 | 561.9 | 552.6 | 609.0 | 2,225 |
| 2007 | 476.3 | 530.0 | 530.0 | 557.3 | 2,093 |
| 2006 | 415.5 | 481.9 | 490.7 | 523.1 | 1,911 |
| 2005 | 390.3 | 463.4 | 454.8 | 478.6 | 1,787 |
| 2004 | 382.7 | 458.4 | 439.6 | 460.4 | 1,741 |

**Earnings Per Share ($)**

| | 1Q | 2Q | 3Q | 4Q | Year |
|---|---|---|---|---|---|
| 2009 | 0.44 | E0.53 | E0.46 | E0.53 | E1.93 |
| 2008 | 0.32 | 0.49 | 0.48 | 0.50 | 1.78 |
| 2007 | -0.32 | 0.39 | 0.39 | 0.42 | 0.90 |
| 2006 | 0.21 | 0.17 | 0.65 | 0.41 | 1.43 |
| 2005 | 0.18 | 0.37 | 0.28 | 0.35 | 1.19 |
| 2004 | 0.16 | 0.25 | 0.22 | 0.20 | 0.83 |

Fiscal year ended Jun. 30. Next earnings report expected: Late January. EPS Estimates based on S&P Operating Earnings; historical GAAP earnings are as reported.

## Dividend Data (Dates: mm/dd Payment Date: mm/dd/yy)

| Amount ($) | Date Decl. | Ex-Div. Date | Stk. of Record | Payment Date |
|---|---|---|---|---|
| 0.043 | 11/15 | 11/29 | 12/03 | 01/02/08 |
| 0.043 | 01/17 | 02/28 | 03/03 | 04/01/08 |
| 0.043 | 05/05 | 05/29 | 06/02 | 07/01/08 |
| 0.043 | 08/21 | 08/28 | 09/02 | 10/01/08 |

Dividends have been paid since 1971. Source: Company reports.

# Applied Biosystems Inc

STANDARD &POOR'S

## Business Summary November 04, 2008

Applera Corp.-Applied Biosystems Group was formed in 1999 via a reorganization of Applera Corp. that created Applied Biosystems Group (ABI) and Celera Genomics Group (CRA). ABI serves the life science and research industry by developing and manufacturing instrument-based systems, consumables and reagents, software, and related services. Its instruments and tools are used in genomics to analyze nucleic acids (DNA and RNA), small molecule analysis and development, and proteomics to make scientific discoveries and develop new pharmaceuticals, and to conduct standardized testing.

ABI has developed technologies and products to support applications in genomics research such as sequencing, genotyping, and gene expression studies. Customers in the genomics market use ABI's instrument-based systems for the analysis of nucleic acids for basic research, pharmaceutical and diagnostic discovery and development, biosecurity, food and environmental testing, analysis of infectious diseases, and human identification and forensic analysis.

In the field of proteomics, the company has developed products for the identification, characterization, and measurement of expression of proteins and peptides. Gene codes for proteins in biological organisms and proteins are the key biological molecules that function in all aspects of living things such as

growth, development and reproduction. The proteomics research market uses the company's products for the analysis of proteins and peptides for the discovery of drug targets, protein therapeutics and diagnostics.

Products such as mass spectrometers are used by researchers to analyze small molecules (generally smaller than peptides), including metabolites, other small biological molecules found naturally in the body such as hormones, and trace contaminants in food, beverages, or environmental applications.

ABI also develops and manufactures informatics software and services used to integrate and automate life sciences research, development, and manufacturing laboratories, with the goal of increasing efficiency and effectiveness. Users are typically involved in gene mapping, drug discovery, drug development, and drug manufacturing. The company also offers software products for laboratory information management systems, to facilitate sample tracking, data collection, data analysis, and data mining to assist researchers in transforming data into useful information.

## Company Financials Fiscal Year Ended Jun. 30

| Per Share Data ($) | 2008 | 2007 | 2006 | 2005 | 2004 | 2003 | 2002 | 2001 | 2000 | 1999 |
|---|---|---|---|---|---|---|---|---|---|---|
| Tangible Book Value | NA | 6.04 | 6.40 | 7.68 | 6.36 | 6.63 | 5.38 | NM | NM | NM |
| Cash Flow | NA | 1.32 | 1.83 | 1.61 | 1.29 | 1.45 | 1.16 | 1.27 | 1.11 | 0.93 |
| Earnings | 1.78 | 0.90 | 1.43 | 1.19 | 0.83 | 0.95 | 0.78 | 0.96 | 0.86 | 0.72 |
| S&P Core Earnings | 1.65 | 0.89 | 1.46 | 0.36 | 0.30 | 0.31 | 0.34 | 0.32 | NA | NA |
| Dividends | 0.17 | 0.17 | 0.17 | 0.17 | 0.17 | 0.17 | 0.17 | 0.17 | 0.17 | 0.17 |
| Payout Ratio | 10% | 19% | 12% | 14% | 20% | 18% | 22% | 18% | 20% | 24% |
| Prices:High | 37.25 | 37.67 | 39.49 | 28.17 | 24.44 | 24.00 | 39.28 | 94.25 | 160.00 | 62.94 |
| Prices:Low | 25.85 | 27.79 | 26.13 | 19.20 | 17.76 | 14.90 | 13.00 | 18.49 | 42.81 | 21.97 |
| P/E Ratio:High | 21 | 42 | 28 | 24 | 29 | 25 | 50 | 98 | NM | 87 |
| P/E Ratio:Low | 15 | 31 | 18 | 16 | 21 | 16 | 17 | 19 | NM | 31 |

| Income Statement Analysis (Million $) | | | | | | | | | | |
|---|---|---|---|---|---|---|---|---|---|---|
| Revenue | 2,225 | 2,094 | 1,911 | 1,787 | 1,741 | 1,683 | 1,604 | 1,619 | 1,388 | 1,222 |
| Operating Income | NA | 429 | 388 | 357 | 330 | 324 | 318 | 347 | 270 | 234 |
| Depreciation | NA | 79.6 | 77.2 | 82.9 | 96.8 | 106 | 81.2 | 66.8 | 54.5 | 44.3 |
| Interest Expense | NA | NA | NA | Nil | Nil | Nil | 0.89 | 1.30 | 8.13 | 4.50 |
| Pretax Income | 446 | 259 | 317 | 297 | 240 | 239 | 238 | 304 | 276 | 192 |
| Effective Tax Rate | 29.0% | 34.0% | 13.3% | 20.3% | 28.2% | 19.6% | 29.1% | 30.2% | 32.5% | 15.9% |
| Net Income | 317 | 171 | 275 | 237 | 172 | 200 | 168 | 212 | 186 | 148 |
| S&P Core Earnings | 294 | 169 | 282 | 72.7 | 63.8 | 63.3 | 72.9 | 71.7 | NA | NA |

| Balance Sheet & Other Financial Data (Million $) | | | | | | | | | | |
|---|---|---|---|---|---|---|---|---|---|---|
| Cash | NA | 495 | 374 | 756 | 505 | 602 | 441 | 392 | 395 | 237 |
| Current Assets | NA | 1,234 | 1,013 | 1,391 | 1,110 | 1,232 | 1,072 | 1,014 | 998 | 918 |
| Total Assets | NA | 2,387 | 2,246 | 2,290 | 1,948 | 2,127 | 1,819 | 1,678 | 1,698 | 1,348 |
| Current Liabilities | NA | 588 | 573 | 547 | 518 | 541 | 522 | 508 | 603 | 644 |
| Long Term Debt | NA | Nil | Nil | Nil | Nil | Nil | Nil | Nil | 36.1 | 31.5 |
| Common Equity | NA | 1,590 | 1,477 | 1,523 | 1,244 | 1,388 | 1,125 | 1,041 | 934 | 534 |
| Total Capital | NA | 1,590 | 1,477 | 1,523 | 1,244 | 1,388 | 1,125 | 1,041 | 970 | 566 |
| Capital Expenditures | NA | 60.3 | 41.5 | 84.6 | 60.4 | 132 | 88.3 | 144 | 94.4 | 82.5 |
| Cash Flow | NA | 251 | 352 | 320 | 269 | 306 | 250 | 279 | 241 | 193 |
| Current Ratio | NA | 2.1 | 1.8 | 2.5 | 2.1 | 2.3 | 2.1 | 2.0 | 1.7 | 1.4 |
| % Long Term Debt of Capitalization | Nil | Nil | Nil | Nil | Nil | Nil | Nil | Nil | 3.7 | 5.6 |
| % Net Income of Revenue | 14.2 | 8.2 | 14.4 | 13.3 | 9.9 | 11.9 | 10.5 | 13.1 | 13.4 | 12.1 |
| % Return on Assets | NA | 7.4 | 12.1 | 11.2 | 8.5 | 10.1 | 9.6 | 12.6 | 12.2 | 12.0 |
| % Return on Equity | NA | 11.1 | 18.3 | 17.1 | 13.1 | 15.9 | 15.5 | 21.5 | 25.4 | 27.0 |

Data as orig reptd.; bef. results of disc opers/spec. items. Per share data adj. for stk. divs.; EPS diluted. E-Estimated. NA-Not Available. NM-Not Meaningful. NR-Not Ranked. UR-Under Review.

**Office:** 301 Merritt 7, Norwalk, CT 06856-5435.
**Telephone:** 203-840-2000.
**Website:** http://www.appliedbiosystems.com
**Chrmn & CEO:** T.L. White

**Pres & COO:** M.P. Stevenson
**SVP & CFO:** D.L. Winger
**SVP & General Counsel:** W.B. Sawch
**Investor Contact:** W. Craumer (650-638-6382)

**Board Members:** G. F. Adam, Jr., J. C. Blair, R. H. Hayes, A. J. Levine, W. H. Longfield, E. R. Mardis, T. E. Martin, C. W. Slayman, J. R. Tobin, T. L. White

**Founded:** 1937
**Domicile:** Delaware
**Employees:** 5,160

# Applied Materials Inc

**STANDARD &POOR'S**

| | | | |
|---|---|---|---|
| **S&P Recommendation** BUY ★★★★☆ | **Price** $10.23 (as of Nov 14, 2008) | **12-Mo. Target Price** $13.00 | **Investment Style** Large-Cap Blend |

**GICS Sector** Information Technology
**Sub-Industry** Semiconductor Equipment

**Summary** This company is the world's largest manufacturer of wafer fabrication equipment for the semiconductor industry.

## Key Stock Statistics (Source S&P, Vickers, company reports)

| | | | | | | | |
|---|---|---|---|---|---|---|---|
| 52-Wk Range | $21.75– 7.17 | S&P Oper. EPS 2008**E** | 0.71 | Market Capitalization(B) | $13.725 | Beta | 0.82 |
| Trailing 12-Month EPS | $0.82 | S&P Oper. EPS 2009**E** | 0.28 | Yield (%) | 2.35 | S&P 3-Yr. Proj. EPS CAGR(%) | 10 |
| Trailing 12-Month P/E | 12.5 | P/E on S&P Oper. EPS 2008**E** | 14.4 | Dividend Rate/Share | $0.24 | S&P Credit Rating | A- |
| $10K Invested 5 Yrs Ago | $4,546 | Common Shares Outstg. (M) | 1,341.7 | Institutional Ownership (%) | 81 | | |

## Price Performance

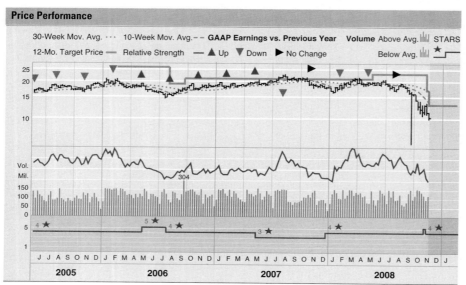

30-Week Mov. Avg. · · · 10-Week Mov. Avg. – – GAAP Earnings vs. Previous Year Volume Above Avg. STARS
12-Mo. Target Price — Relative Strength – – ▲ Up ▼ Down ▶ No Change Below Avg. ★

Options: ASE, CBOE, P, Ph

Analysis prepared by **Angelo Zino** on November 13, 2008, when the stock traded at **$ 10.55**.

## Qualitative Risk Assessment

| LOW | MEDIUM | HIGH |
|---|---|---|

Our risk assessment reflects the historical cyclicality of the semiconductor equipment industry, the lack of visibility in the intermediate term, the dynamic nature of the change in semiconductor technology, and intense competition. This is offset by AMAT's market leadership, size, and what we consider its solid balance sheet.

## Quantitative Evaluations

**S&P Quality Ranking** B

| D | C | B- | B | B+ | A- | A | A+ |
|---|---|---|---|---|---|---|---|

**Relative Strength Rank** MODERATE

40

LOWEST = 1     HIGHEST = 99

## Highlights

➤ We see revenues off 18% in FY 08 (Oct.), and falling an additional 16% in FY 09. While we expect flat panel and semiconductor equipment orders to remain muted amid a softening global economic landscape, we project healthy demand for AMAT's solar equipment over the next several quarters. We see AMAT's solar business reaching breakeven by the middle of FY 09, and we view positively its rising backlog. We think visibility for DRAM and NAND memory orders will remain weak until economic conditions improve.

➤ We project gross margins of 43% in FY 08 and 41% in FY 09. While we think margins will be pressured by higher spending to ramp up its solar business, we see AMAT reducing fixed costs in a difficult environment. Longer term, we see margins benefiting from AMAT's intent to move certain operations to lower cost regions.

➤ We expect AMAT to modestly repurchase shares, with an authorized buyback of $5 billion in place through March 2009. We think customers will be able to reduce their cost/watt to under $1 within the next 3-5 years, using AMAT's large-scale solar panels.

## Investment Rationale/Risk

➤ We have a favorable view of AMAT's end markets, and see potential for it to capture a significant share of the solar equipment market over the next 12 months. While we view semiconductor equipment industry conditions as weak, we think orders and revenues in its Silicon Systems Group are nearing trough levels. Considering our view of AMAT's diversified offerings, market share gains, aggressive share repurchases, and growth opportunities from new businesses, we think the company will fare better than most peers. We see potential for market share gains in both the etch and reticle inspection markets.

➤ Risks to our recommendation and target price include a greater than expected slowdown in the global economy, which could weaken demand for chips and increase pricing pressure.

➤ We derive our 12-month target price of $13 by applying a peer premium price/sales multiple of 2.6X to our FY 09 sales per share forecast, based on our expectation for AMAT to gain significant exposure in the high-growth solar industry. We see potential for multiple expansion, as solar accounts for an increasing percentage of sales (we project 20% by FY 10).

## Revenue/Earnings Data

**Revenue (Million $)**

| | 1Q | 2Q | 3Q | 4Q | Year |
|---|---|---|---|---|---|
| 2008 | 2,087 | 2,150 | 1,848 | -- | -- |
| 2007 | 2,277 | 2,530 | 2,561 | 2,367 | 9,735 |
| 2006 | 1,858 | 2,248 | 2,543 | 2,518 | 9,167 |
| 2005 | 1,781 | 1,861 | 1,632 | 1,718 | 6,992 |
| 2004 | 1,555 | 2,018 | 2,236 | 2,203 | 8,013 |
| 2003 | 1,054 | 1,107 | 1,095 | 1,221 | 4,477 |

**Earnings Per Share ($)**

| | 1Q | 2Q | 3Q | 4Q | Year |
|---|---|---|---|---|---|
| 2008 | 0.19 | 0.22 | 0.12 | E0.14 | E0.71 |
| 2007 | 0.29 | 0.29 | 0.12 | 0.30 | 1.20 |
| 2006 | 0.09 | 0.26 | 0.33 | 0.30 | 0.97 |
| 2005 | 0.17 | 0.18 | 0.23 | 0.15 | 0.73 |
| 2004 | 0.05 | 0.22 | 0.26 | 0.27 | 0.78 |
| 2003 | -0.04 | -0.04 | -0.02 | 0.01 | -0.09 |

Fiscal year ended Oct. 31. Next earnings report expected: NA. EPS Estimates based on S&P Operating Earnings; historical GAAP earnings are as reported.

## Dividend Data (Dates: mm/dd Payment Date: mm/dd/yy)

| Amount ($) | Date Decl. | Ex-Div. Date | Stk. of Record | Payment Date |
|---|---|---|---|---|
| 0.060 | 12/12 | 02/12 | 02/14 | 03/06/08 |
| 0.060 | 03/11 | 05/13 | 05/15 | 06/05/08 |
| 0.060 | 06/11 | 08/12 | 08/14 | 09/04/08 |
| 0.060 | 09/17 | 11/10 | 11/13 | 12/04/08 |

Dividends have been paid since 2005. Source: Company reports.

# Applied Materials Inc

**STANDARD &POOR'S**

## Business Summary November 13, 2008

CORPORATE OVERVIEW. At the end of FY 07 (Oct.), AMAT was the worldwide leader in the manufacturing of semiconductor capital equipment. AMAT divides its business into four segments. The Silicon segment, which accounted for 67% of FY 07 (65% in FY 06) sales, is focused on developing and selling equipment for use in the front end of the semiconductor fabrication process. The Applied Global Services segment, which accounted for 22% (24%) of FY 07 sales, provides solutions to optimize and increase productivity at customers fabs (semiconductor fabrication facilities). The Display segment, which accounted for 9% (10%) of FY 07 sales, develops equipment for the fabrication of flat panel displays. The Energy and Environmental Solutions segment, which is a new area for AMAT, accounted for 2% (less than 1%) of sales in FY 07, and involves products targeting the solar PV cell market and energy efficient glass. We expect significant growth in AMAT's solar business over the next several years.

AMAT's equipment in the silicon segment address most of the primary steps in chip fabrication. AMAT's deposition products are used to plant thin films of conductive or insulating material to form an integrated circuit (IC). AMAT deposition equipment use various technologies, including ALD (atomic layer de-

position), CVD (chemical vapor deposition), PVD (physical vapor deposition), and ECP (Electrochemical plating). AMAT's etch products selectively remove thin films of three different types of materials: metal, silicon, and dielectric thin films. Chemical-mechanical polishing products are used to smooth the surface of a wafer following deposition in order to facilitate subsequent processing steps. Metrology and inspection tools are used to measure critical parameters and find and classify defects.

Sales by geographic region in FY 07 were as follows: Taiwan 28%, Korea 19%, North America 16%, Japan 15%, Asia-Pacific 12%, and Europe 10%. While over 70% of sales were derived from Asia, the output of Asian chip manufacturers are exported widely across the globe, limiting the risk of economic weakness in that region. During FY 07, Samsung accounted for 12% of sales compared with 11% in FY 06 and 10% in FY 05, respectively.

## Company Financials Fiscal Year Ended Oct. 31

| Per Share Data ($) | 2007 | 2006 | 2005 | 2004 | 2003 | 2002 | 2001 | 2000 | 1999 | 1998 |
|---|---|---|---|---|---|---|---|---|---|---|
| Tangible Book Value | 4.65 | 5.80 | 5.30 | 5.33 | 4.62 | 4.67 | 4.51 | 4.20 | 2.59 | 2.05 |
| Cash Flow | 1.39 | 1.14 | 0.91 | 0.99 | 0.14 | 0.39 | 0.69 | 1.41 | 0.63 | 0.38 |
| Earnings | 1.20 | 0.97 | 0.73 | 0.78 | -0.09 | 0.16 | 0.46 | 1.20 | 0.46 | 0.19 |
| S&P Core Earnings | 1.20 | 0.97 | 0.54 | 0.59 | -0.33 | -0.04 | 0.33 | NA | NA | NA |
| Dividends | 0.22 | 0.16 | 0.06 | Nil | Nil | Nil | Nil | Nil | Nil | Nil |
| Payout Ratio | 18% | 16% | 8% | Nil | Nil | Nil | Nil | Nil | Nil | Nil |
| Prices:High | 23.00 | 21.06 | 19.47 | 24.75 | 25.94 | 27.95 | 29.55 | 57.50 | 32.25 | 11.75 |
| Prices:Low | 17.35 | 14.39 | 14.33 | 15.36 | 11.25 | 10.26 | 13.30 | 17.06 | 10.72 | 5.39 |
| P/E Ratio:High | 19 | 22 | 27 | 32 | NM | NM | 65 | 48 | 70 | 77 |
| P/E Ratio:Low | 14 | 15 | 20 | 20 | NM | NM | 29 | 14 | 23 | 35 |

### Income Statement Analysis (Million $)

| | 2007 | 2006 | 2005 | 2004 | 2003 | 2002 | 2001 | 2000 | 1999 | 1998 |
|---|---|---|---|---|---|---|---|---|---|---|
| Revenue | 9,735 | 9,167 | 6,992 | 8,013 | 4,477 | 5,062 | 7,343 | 9,564 | 4,859 | 4,042 |
| Operating Income | 2,665 | 2,517 | 1,748 | 2,313 | 440 | 683 | 1,538 | 3,149 | 1,257 | 910 |
| Depreciation | 268 | 270 | 300 | 356 | 382 | 388 | 387 | 362 | 275 | 285 |
| Interest Expense | 38.6 | 36.1 | 37.8 | 52.9 | 46.9 | 49.4 | 47.6 | 51.4 | 47.1 | 45.3 |
| Pretax Income | 2,440 | 2,167 | 1,582 | 1,829 | -212 | 341 | 1,104 | 2,948 | 1,056 | 438 |
| Effective Tax Rate | 29.9% | 30.0% | 23.5% | 26.1% | NM | 21.0% | 29.8% | 30.0% | 31.3% | 34.0% |
| Net Income | 1,710 | 1,517 | 1,210 | 1,351 | -149 | 269 | 775 | 2,064 | 726 | 289 |
| S&P Core Earnings | 1,710 | 1,511 | 905 | 1,017 | -562 | -65.2 | 558 | NA | NA | NA |

### Balance Sheet & Other Financial Data (Million $)

| | 2007 | 2006 | 2005 | 2004 | 2003 | 2002 | 2001 | 2000 | 1999 | 1998 |
|---|---|---|---|---|---|---|---|---|---|---|
| Cash | 1,203 | 861 | 990 | 2,282 | 1,365 | 1,285 | 1,356 | 1,648 | 823 | 575 |
| Current Assets | 6,606 | 6,081 | 9,449 | 10,282 | 8,371 | 8,073 | 7,782 | 8,839 | 5,060 | 3,519 |
| Total Assets | 10,654 | 9,481 | 11,269 | 12,093 | 10,312 | 10,225 | 9,829 | 10,546 | 6,707 | 4,930 |
| Current Liabilities | 2,373 | 2,436 | 1,765 | 2,288 | 1,641 | 1,501 | 1,533 | 2,760 | 1,669 | 1,118 |
| Long Term Debt | 202 | 205 | 407 | 410 | 456 | 574 | 565 | 573 | 584 | 617 |
| Common Equity | 7,821 | 6,651 | 8,929 | 9,262 | 8,068 | 8,020 | 7,607 | 7,104 | 4,337 | 3,121 |
| Total Capital | 8,023 | 6,856 | 9,336 | 9,672 | 8,524 | 8,594 | 8,172 | 7,677 | 4,954 | 3,749 |
| Capital Expenditures | 265 | 179 | 200 | 191 | 265 | 417 | 711 | 383 | 204 | 449 |
| Cash Flow | 1,978 | 1,787 | 1,510 | 1,707 | 233 | 657 | 1,162 | 2,426 | 1,001 | 573 |
| Current Ratio | 2.8 | 2.5 | 5.4 | 4.5 | 5.1 | 5.4 | 5.1 | 3.2 | 3.0 | 3.1 |
| % Long Term Debt of Capitalization | 2.5 | 3.0 | 4.4 | 4.2 | 5.4 | 6.7 | 6.9 | 7.5 | 11.8 | 16.4 |
| % Net Income of Revenue | 17.5 | 16.5 | 17.3 | 16.9 | NM | 5.3 | 10.5 | 21.6 | 14.9 | 7.1 |
| % Return on Assets | 16.9 | 14.6 | 10.4 | 12.1 | NM | 2.7 | 7.6 | 23.5 | 12.5 | 5.8 |
| % Return on Equity | 23.6 | 19.5 | 13.3 | 15.6 | NM | 3.4 | 10.5 | 35.3 | 19.5 | 9.5 |

Data as orig reptd.; bef. results of disc opers/spec. items. Per share data adj. for stk. divs.; EPS diluted. E-Estimated. NA-Not Available. NM-Not Meaningful. NR-Not Ranked. UR-Under Review.

**Office:** 3050 Bowers Avenue, Santa Clara, CA, United States 95054-3298.
**Telephone:** 408-727-5555.
**Email:** investor_relations@appliedmaterials.com
**Website:** http://www.appliedmaterials.com

**Chrmn:** J.C. Morgan
**Pres & CEO:** M.R. Splinter
**COO & SVP:** R. Thakur
**SVP & CFO:** G.S. Davis

**SVP & CTO:** M. Pinto
**Board Members:** D. A. Coleman, S. R. Forrest, P. V. Gerdine, T. J. Iannotti, A. Karsner, Y. S. Liu, J. C. Morgan, G. H. Parker, D. D. Powell, W. P. Roelandts, J. E. Rogers, M. R. Splinter, A. J. de Geus

**Founded:** 1967
**Domicile:** Delaware
**Employees:** 14,550

# Archer-Daniels-Midland Co

STANDARD
&POOR'S

| S&P Recommendation | HOLD ★★★☆☆ | Price $25.92 (as of Nov 14, 2008) | 12-Mo. Target Price $30.00 | Investment Style Large-Cap Blend |
|---|---|---|---|---|

**GICS Sector** Consumer Staples
**Sub-Industry** Agricultural Products

**Summary** This company is one of the world's leading agribusiness companies, with major market positions in agricultural processing and merchandising.

## Key Stock Statistics (Source S&P, Vickers, company reports)

| | | | | | | | |
|---|---|---|---|---|---|---|---|
| 52-Wk Range | $48.95– 13.53 | S&P Oper. EPS 2009E | 3.44 | Market Capitalization(B) | $16.699 | Beta | 1.00 |
| Trailing 12-Month EPS | $3.74 | S&P Oper. EPS 2010E | 2.99 | Yield (%) | 2.01 | S&P 3-Yr. Proj. EPS CAGR(%) | -13 |
| Trailing 12-Month P/E | 6.9 | P/E on S&P Oper. EPS 2009E | 7.5 | Dividend Rate/Share | $0.52 | S&P Credit Rating | A |
| $10K Invested 5 Yrs Ago | $19,556 | Common Shares Outstg. (M) | 644.3 | Institutional Ownership (%) | 73 | | |

## Price Performance

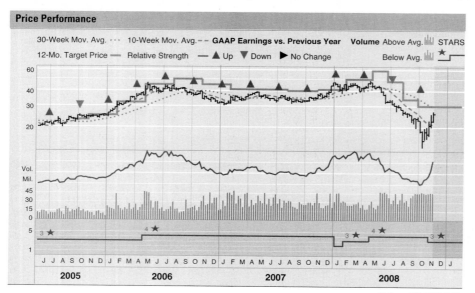

- 30-Week Mov. Avg. ····  10-Week Mov. Avg. —  **GAAP Earnings vs. Previous Year**  Volume Above Avg. STARS
- 12-Mo. Target Price —  Relative Strength —  ▲ Up  ▼ Down  ► No Change  Below Avg.

Options: ASE, CBOE, P, Ph

Analysis prepared by **Tina J. Vital** on November 05, 2008, when the stock traded at **$ 24.94**.

## Qualitative Risk Assessment

| LOW | MEDIUM | HIGH |
|---|---|---|

Our risk assessment reflects the company's exposure to volatile commodity industry conditions, and moderately aggressive financial policies and leverage levels given the inherent cyclicality of the company's agricultural operations.

## Quantitative Evaluations

**S&P Quality Ranking** A+

| D | C | B- | B | B+ | A- | A | A+ |
|---|---|---|---|---|---|---|---|

**Relative Strength Rank** STRONG

98

LOWEST = 1    HIGHEST = 99

## Revenue/Earnings Data

**Revenue (Million $)**

| | 1Q | 2Q | 3Q | 4Q | Year |
|---|---|---|---|---|---|
| 2009 | 21,160 | -- | -- | -- | -- |
| 2008 | 12,828 | 16,496 | 18,708 | 21,784 | 69,816 |
| 2007 | 9,447 | 10,976 | 11,381 | 12,214 | 44,018 |
| 2006 | 8,627 | 9,299 | 9,123 | 9,547 | 36,596 |
| 2005 | 8,972 | 9,064 | 8,484 | 9,424 | 35,944 |
| 2004 | 7,968 | 9,189 | 9,309 | 9,686 | 36,151 |

**Earnings Per Share ($)**

| | 1Q | 2Q | 3Q | 4Q | Year |
|---|---|---|---|---|---|
| 2009 | 1.63 | E0.70 | E0.78 | E0.79 | E3.44 |
| 2008 | 0.68 | 0.73 | 0.80 | 0.58 | 2.79 |
| 2007 | 0.61 | 0.67 | 0.56 | 1.47 | 3.30 |
| 2006 | 0.29 | 0.56 | 0.53 | 0.62 | 2.00 |
| 2005 | 0.41 | 0.48 | 0.41 | 0.30 | 1.59 |
| 2004 | 0.23 | 0.34 | 0.35 | -0.16 | 0.76 |

Fiscal year ended Jun. 30. Next earnings report expected: Early February. EPS Estimates based on S&P Operating Earnings; historical GAAP earnings are as reported.

## Highlights

- We believe ADM, as an internationally diversified agribusiness, is well positioned to outperform its peers based on scale and integration. We see increased feedstock and energy costs being partially offset by improved sales volumes and realized pricing on continued global demand, reflecting population growth and enhanced non-OECD economic growth.

- Oilseeds Processing operating profits rose in the September quarter on improved margins and increased equity earnings from Asian affiliates. Agricultural Services operating profits increased in the quarter, reflecting improved margins from opportunities created by market volatility. However, Corn Processing profits declined due to sharply higher net corn and energy costs, partially offset by increased sales volumes and average selling prices for sweeteners and starches, ethanol and lysine.

- We expect after-tax operating earnings to decline about 13% in FY 10 (Jun.) and about 38% in FY 11.

## Investment Rationale/Risk

- ADM has leading worldwide market positions in agricultural processing and merchandising, as well as ethanol production. During 2007, the company acquired seven businesses for $103 million, and we expect ADM to be acquisitive and to invest heavily in its own operations over the next five years. ADM expects its Columbus, NE, ethanol facility to start up in the FY 09 third quarter, and its Cedar Rapids, IA, ethanol facility is slated to start up in the FY 10 first quarter. These plants are expected to each produce about 275 million gallons of ethanol.

- Risks to our recommendation and target price include adverse changes in plantings, government farm programs and policies, and in economic, operational and industry conditions, such as fluctuations in commodity prices.

- Blending our discounted cash flow target price ($35 per share; assuming a WACC of 6.5% and terminal growth of 3%) and narrowed relative valuations, our 12-month target price is $30, representing an expected enterprise value of 7.4X our FY 10 EBITDA, a discount to U.S. ethanol peers.

## Dividend Data (Dates: mm/dd Payment Date: mm/dd/yy)

| Amount ($) | Date Decl. | Ex-Div. Date | Stk. of Record | Payment Date |
|---|---|---|---|---|
| 0.130 | 02/05 | 02/14 | 02/19 | 03/11/08 |
| 0.130 | 05/01 | 05/13 | 05/15 | 06/05/08 |
| 0.130 | 08/07 | 08/19 | 08/21 | 09/11/08 |
| 0.130 | 11/06 | 11/18 | 11/20 | 12/11/08 |

Dividends have been paid since 1927. Source: Company reports.

# Archer-Daniels-Midland Co

## Business Summary November 05, 2008

CORPORATE OVERVIEW. As successor to the Daniels Linseed Co., founded in 1902, Archer Daniels Midland (ADM) is one of the world's largest agricultural processors, with a global network of more than 240 processing plants in 60 countries. The company operates in four business segments: Oilseeds Processing (31% of FY 07 (Jun.) sales; 35% of FY 07 operating profit), Corn Processing (12%; 36%), Agricultural Services (46%; 16%), and Other (11%; 13%).

The Oilseeds Processing segment includes activities related to the processing of oilseeds such as soybeans, cottonseed, sunflower seeds, canola, peanuts, and flaxseed into vegetable oils and meals principally for the food and feed industries. In addition, oilseeds may be resold into the marketplace as a raw material for other processors. Golden Peanut Co. LLC, a joint venture between ADM (50%)and Alimenta (U.S.A.) Inc., is a major supplier of peanuts to domestic and international markets. Oilseeds Processing includes activities related to the company's interest in Wilmar International Ltd., the largest agricultural processing business in Asia.

The Corn Processing segment includes activities related to the production of sweeteners, starches, dextrose, and syrups for the food and beverage industry as well as activities related to the production, by fermentation, of bioprod-

ucts such as alcohol, amino acids, and other specialty food and feed ingredients. ADM owns a 50% interest in Almidones Mexicanos S.A., which operates a wet corn milling plant in Mexico, and a 50% interest in Eaststarch C.V. (Netherlands), which owns interests in companies that operate wet corn milling plants in Bulgaria, Hungary, Romania, Slovakia, and Turkey.

The Agricultural Services segment utilizes the company's extensive grain elevator and transportation network to buy, store, clean, and transport agricultural commodities, such as oilseeds, corn, wheat, milo, oats, and barley, and resells these commodities primarily as feed ingredients and as raw materials for the agricultural processing industry. Agricultural Services includes activities of A.C. Toepfer International (ADM has an 80% interest), a global merchandiser of agricultural commodities and processed products. ADM also has a 45% interest in Kalama Export Co., a grain export elevator in Washington.

Other includes the company's remaining operations, consisting principally of food, feed, and industrial businesses and financial activities.

## Company Financials Fiscal Year Ended Jun. 30

| Per Share Data ($) | 2008 | 2007 | 2006 | 2005 | 2004 | 2003 | 2002 | 2001 | 2000 | 1999 |
|---|---|---|---|---|---|---|---|---|---|---|
| Tangible Book Value | 20.16 | 17.01 | 14.47 | 12.47 | 11.31 | 10.43 | 10.39 | 9.56 | 9.21 | 9.23 |
| Cash Flow | NA | 4.36 | 3.00 | 2.60 | 1.82 | 1.69 | 1.64 | 1.44 | 1.35 | 1.26 |
| Earnings | 2.79 | 3.30 | 2.00 | 1.59 | 0.76 | 0.70 | 0.78 | 0.58 | 0.46 | 0.41 |
| S&P Core Earnings | 2.64 | 2.31 | 2.02 | 1.53 | 1.14 | 0.61 | 0.55 | 0.58 | NA | NA |
| Dividends | 0.49 | 0.43 | 0.37 | 0.32 | 0.27 | 0.24 | 0.20 | 0.19 | 0.14 | 0.13 |
| Payout Ratio | 18% | 13% | 19% | 20% | 36% | 34% | 25% | 32% | 30% | 32% |
| Prices:High | 48.95 | 47.33 | 46.71 | 25.55 | 22.55 | 15.24 | 14.85 | 15.80 | 14.46 | 14.74 |
| Prices:Low | 13.53 | 30.20 | 24.05 | 17.50 | 14.90 | 10.50 | 10.00 | 10.24 | 7.80 | 10.37 |
| P/E Ratio:High | 18 | 14 | 23 | 16 | 30 | 22 | 19 | 27 | 32 | 35 |
| P/E Ratio:Low | 5 | 9 | 12 | 11 | 20 | 15 | 13 | 18 | 17 | 25 |

| Income Statement Analysis (Million $) | | | | | | | | | | |
|---|---|---|---|---|---|---|---|---|---|---|
| Revenue | 69,816 | 44,018 | 36,596 | 35,944 | 36,151 | 30,708 | 23,454 | 20,051 | 12,877 | 14,283 |
| Operating Income | NA | 2,743 | 2,450 | 2,015 | 1,432 | 1,423 | 1,424 | 1,272 | 1,094 | 1,116 |
| Depreciation | 753 | 701 | 657 | 665 | 686 | 644 | 567 | 572 | 604 | 585 |
| Interest Expense | NA | Nil | 365 | Nil | Nil | Nil | 356 | 397 | 377 | 326 |
| Pretax Income | 2,624 | 3,154 | 1,855 | 1,516 | 718 | 631 | 719 | 522 | 353 | 420 |
| Effective Tax Rate | 31.3% | 31.5% | 29.3% | 31.1% | 31.1% | 28.5% | 28.9% | 26.6% | 14.7% | 33.1% |
| Net Income | 1,802 | 2,162 | 1,312 | 1,044 | 495 | 451 | 511 | 383 | 301 | 281 |
| S&P Core Earnings | 1,706 | 1,508 | 1,322 | 1,001 | 739 | 397 | 363 | 382 | NA | NA |

| Balance Sheet & Other Financial Data (Million $) | | | | | | | | | | |
|---|---|---|---|---|---|---|---|---|---|---|
| Cash | 1,265 | 2,087 | 2,334 | 1,430 | 1,412 | 765 | 844 | 676 | 477 | 1,461 |
| Current Assets | NA | 15,122 | 11,826 | 9,711 | 10,339 | 8,422 | 7,363 | 6,150 | 6,162 | 5,790 |
| Total Assets | 25,790 | 25,118 | 21,269 | 18,598 | 19,369 | 17,183 | 15,416 | 14,340 | 14,423 | 14,030 |
| Current Liabilities | NA | 7,868 | 6,165 | 5,367 | 6,750 | 5,147 | 4,719 | 3,867 | 4,333 | 3,840 |
| Long Term Debt | NA | 4,752 | 4,050 | 3,530 | 3,740 | 3,872 | 3,111 | 3,351 | 3,277 | 3,192 |
| Common Equity | 13,490 | 11,253 | 9,807 | 8,433 | 7,698 | 7,069 | 6,755 | 6,332 | 6,110 | 6,241 |
| Total Capital | NA | 16,537 | 14,614 | 12,743 | 12,092 | 11,485 | 10,498 | 10,327 | 9,948 | 10,053 |
| Capital Expenditures | 1,779 | 1,198 | 762 | 624 | 509 | 420 | 350 | 273 | 429 | 671 |
| Cash Flow | NA | 2,863 | 1,969 | 1,709 | 1,180 | 1,095 | 1,078 | 955 | 905 | 866 |
| Current Ratio | 4.5 | 1.9 | 1.9 | 1.8 | 1.5 | 1.6 | 1.6 | 1.6 | 1.4 | 1.5 |
| % Long Term Debt of Capitalization | 37.0 | 28.7 | 27.7 | 27.7 | 30.9 | 33.7 | 29.6 | 32.4 | 32.9 | 31.8 |
| % Net Income of Revenue | 2.6 | 4.9 | 3.6 | 2.9 | 1.4 | 1.5 | 2.2 | 1.9 | 2.3 | 2.0 |
| % Return on Assets | 7.1 | 9.3 | 6.6 | 5.5 | 2.7 | 2.8 | 3.4 | 2.7 | 2.1 | 2.0 |
| % Return on Equity | 14.6 | 20.5 | 14.4 | 12.9 | 6.7 | 6.5 | 7.8 | 6.2 | 4.9 | 4.4 |

Data as orig reptd.; bef. results of disc opers/spec. items. Per share data adj. for stk. divs.; EPS diluted. E-Estimated. NA-Not Available. NM-Not Meaningful. NR-Not Ranked. UR-Under Review.

**Office:** 4666 Faries Parkway, Decatur, IL 62525.
**Telephone:** 217-424-5200.
**Website:** http://www.admworld.com
**Chrmn, Pres & CEO:** P.A. Woertz

**EVP & CFO:** S.R. Mills
**EVP, Secy & General Counsel:** D.J. Smith
**CTO:** M.A. Pacheco
**Treas:** V. Luthar

**Investor Contact:** D. Grimestad (217-424-4586)
**Board Members:** G. W. Buckley, M. H. Carter, V. F. Haynes, P. Moore, B. Mulroney, A. M. Neto, T. F. O'Neill, K. R. Westbrook, P. A. Woertz

**Founded:** 1898
**Domicile:** Delaware
**Employees:** 27,600

# Assurant Inc.

**STANDARD &POOR'S**

| S&P Recommendation **HOLD** ★★★☆☆ | Price $19.98 (as of Nov 14, 2008) | 12-Mo. Target Price $35.00 | Investment Style Large-Cap Value |
|---|---|---|---|

**GICS Sector** Financials
**Sub-Industry** Multi-line Insurance

**Summary** This company pursues a differentiated strategy of building leading positions in niche insurance markets.

## Key Stock Statistics (Source S&P, Vickers, company reports)

| | | | | | | | | |
|---|---|---|---|---|---|---|---|---|
| 52-Wk Range | $71.31– 18.59 | S&P Oper. EPS 2008**E** | 5.50 | Market Capitalization(B) | $2.350 | Beta | 0.96 |
| Trailing 12-Month EPS | $3.24 | S&P Oper. EPS 2009**E** | 6.40 | Yield (%) | 2.80 | S&P 3-Yr. Proj. EPS CAGR(%) | 10 |
| Trailing 12-Month P/E | 6.2 | P/E on S&P Oper. EPS 2008**E** | 3.6 | Dividend Rate/Share | $0.56 | S&P Credit Rating | NA |
| $10K Invested 5 Yrs Ago | NA | Common Shares Outstg. (M) | 117.6 | Institutional Ownership (%) | 94 | | |

## Price Performance

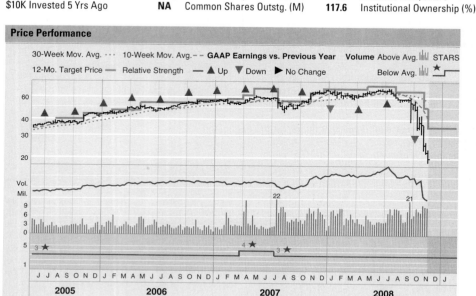

30-Week Mov. Avg. · · ·  10-Week Mov. Avg. - -  **GAAP Earnings vs. Previous Year**  Volume Above Avg. STARS
12-Mo. Target Price —  Relative Strength —  ▲ Up  ▼ Down  ▶ No Change  Below Avg. ★

2005  2006  2007  2008

Options: ASE, CBOE, P, Ph

Analysis prepared by **Bret Howlett** on November 14, 2008, when the stock traded at **$ 21.27**.

## Highlights

➤ We expect operating income for Assurant Solutions to decline in 2008, amid a slowdown in consumer spending. We expect the combined ratio for Solutions to deteriorate due in part to a less favorable domestic contract loss experience. Longer term, we believe that international earnings will act as a major contributor to the Solutions business as the company plans to step up its efforts in China. However, we anticipate that profitability will be hampered by a decline in operating income in Assurant Health, on a higher medical loss ratio, and contracting margins due to competitive pressures.

➤ We expect operating income in 2008 for the Specialty Property segment to increase slightly, driven by gains in creditor-placed homeowners insurance, acquisitions, and an improving combined ratio. However, we are concerned that premium growth in Specialty is losing momentum. We forecast a significant decline in operating earnings in 2008 for Assurant Employee Benefits, due to a less favorable loss ratio and a drop in investment income.

➤ We forecast 2008 operating EPS of $5.50, compared to 2007 operating EPS of $5.72. Our operating EPS estimate for 2009 is $6.40.

## Investment Rationale/Risk

➤ We believe that AIZ's underwriting remains strong, that it has a high level of expertise in the specialized lines it markets, and that it faces limited competition. AIZ has been successful in developing new specialty insurance segments. However, we believe AIZ faces a number of headwinds, which should act as a drag on earnings growth. We foresee a decline in earnings in Solutions due to a potential significant slowdown in the global economy. We still see growth opportunities in Specialty Property as we believe that its creditor-placed homeowners business will benefit from the decline in the housing market. However, we believe Health and Employee Benefits are becoming less profitable. We think concerns over capital and investment losses will weigh on the shares.

➤ Risks to our recommendation and target price include competitive pricing in the individual medical market, catastrophe risks,and the possibility that demand for homeowners coverage will slow. Future investment losses are also a risk.

➤ Our 12-month target price of $35 is 5.5X our 2009 operating EPS estimate, below the average historical multiple.

## Qualitative Risk Assessment

| LOW | MEDIUM | HIGH |
|---|---|---|

Our risk assessment for Assurant reflects the difficult operating environment for insurance companies and lack of transparency with future investment losses. Although AIZ has a solid track record of disciplined capital management, we remain concerned about the company's deteriorating capital levels amid the turbulent operating environment.

## Quantitative Evaluations

**S&P Quality Ranking**  NR

| D | C | B- | B | B+ | A- | A | A+ |
|---|---|---|---|---|---|---|---|

**Relative Strength Rank**  WEAK

12

LOWEST = 1  HIGHEST = 99

## Revenue/Earnings Data

**Revenue (Million $)**

| | 1Q | 2Q | 3Q | 4Q | Year |
|---|---|---|---|---|---|
| 2008 | 2,177 | 2,249 | 1,955 | -- | -- |
| 2007 | 2,057 | 2,065 | 2,148 | 2,183 | 8,454 |
| 2006 | 1,930 | 1,949 | 1,984 | 2,208 | 8,071 |
| 2005 | 1,862 | 1,874 | 1,879 | 1,882 | 7,498 |
| 2004 | 1,858 | 1,837 | 1,832 | 1,877 | 7,403 |
| 2003 | 1,732 | 1,723 | 1,776 | 1,836 | 7,066 |

**Earnings Per Share ($)**

| | | | | | |
|---|---|---|---|---|---|
| 2008 | 1.57 | 1.59 | -0.95 | E1.51 | E5.50 |
| 2007 | 1.45 | 1.36 | 1.56 | 1.01 | 5.38 |
| 2006 | 1.22 | 1.16 | 1.18 | 2.01 | 5.56 |
| 2005 | 0.82 | 0.92 | 0.74 | 1.03 | 3.50 |
| 2004 | 0.73 | 0.67 | 0.53 | 0.61 | 2.53 |
| 2003 | 0.67 | 0.83 | 0.91 | -0.71 | 1.70 |

Fiscal year ended Dec. 31. Next earnings report expected: Early February. EPS Estimates based on S&P Operating Earnings; historical GAAP earnings are as reported.

## Dividend Data (Dates: mm/dd Payment Date: mm/dd/yy)

| Amount ($) | Date Decl. | Ex-Div. Date | Stk. of Record | Payment Date |
|---|---|---|---|---|
| 0.120 | 01/25 | 02/21 | 02/25 | 03/10/08 |
| 0.140 | 05/16 | 05/22 | 05/27 | 06/10/08 |
| 0.140 | 08/12 | 08/21 | 08/25 | 09/09/08 |
| 0.140 | 11/14 | 11/20 | 11/24 | 12/10/08 |

Dividends have been paid since 2004. Source: Company reports.

---

The **McGraw-Hill** Companies

# Assurant Inc.

STANDARD
&POOR'S

## Business Summary November 14, 2008

CORPORATE OVERVIEW. Assurant Inc. provides specialized insurance products in North America and other selected markets. The company was indirectly wholly owned by Fortis N.V. until February 2004, when Fortis sold about 65% of its stake via an IPO. In January 2005, Fortis sold 27.2 million shares of AIZ in a secondary public offering at $30.60 per share. In conjunction with the offering, Fortis issued $774 million of 7.75% bonds that were mandatorily exchangeable for up to 23.0 million shares of AIZ, or the cash value thereof, by January 2008. Fortis distributed most of its remaining AIZ shares to the holders of these bonds in January 2008, leaving it with about a 3% interest in AIZ.

As of March 1, 2007, AIZ believed it was a leader or was aligned with clients who were leaders in creditor-placed homeowners insurance (based on servicing volume), manufactured housing homeowners insurance (based on the number of homes built), debt protection administration (based on credit card balances outstanding), group dental plans sponsored by employers (based on the number of subscribers and master contracts in force), and pre-funded fu-

neral insurance (based on the face amount of new policies sold).

On April 1, 2006, the company separated its Assurant Solutions unit into two business segments: Assurant Solutions and Assurant Specialty Property. In addition, with the creation of the new Assurant Solutions and Assurant Specialty Property segments, the company realigned the PreNeed segment under the new Assurant Solutions segment. In total, AIZ operates through four decentralized business segments: Assurant Solutions (34% of net earned premiums and other consideration in 2007); Assurant Specialty Property (23%); Assurant Health (28%); and Assurant Employee Benefits (16%). AIZ also reports a fifth segment, Corporate and Other.

## Company Financials Fiscal Year Ended Dec. 31

| Per Share Data ($) | 2007 | 2006 | 2005 | 2004 | 2003 | 2002 | 2001 | 2000 | 1999 | 1998 |
|---|---|---|---|---|---|---|---|---|---|---|
| Tangible Book Value | NM | 28.46 | 21.01 | 18.90 | 14.76 | NA | NA | NA | NA | NA |
| Operating Earnings | NA | NA | NA | NA | NA | NA | NA | NA | NA | NA |
| Earnings | 5.38 | 5.56 | 3.50 | 2.53 | 1.70 | NA | NA | NA | NA | NA |
| S&P Core Earnings | 5.60 | 4.77 | 3.49 | 2.50 | 1.72 | 38.61 | 15.43 | NA | NA | NA |
| Dividends | 0.46 | 0.38 | 0.31 | 0.21 | NA | NA | NA | NA | NA | NA |
| Relative Payout | 9% | 7% | 9% | 8% | NA | NA | NA | NA | NA | NA |
| Prices:High | 69.77 | 56.78 | 44.68 | 31.29 | NA | NA | NA | NA | NA | NA |
| Prices:Low | 45.27 | 42.72 | 29.70 | 22.00 | NA | NA | NA | NA | NA | NA |
| P/E Ratio:High | 13 | 10 | 13 | 12 | NA | NA | NA | NA | NA | NA |
| P/E Ratio:Low | 8 | 8 | 8 | 9 | NA | NA | NA | NA | NA | NA |

| Income Statement Analysis (Million $) | 2007 | 2006 | 2005 | 2004 | 2003 | 2002 | 2001 | 2000 | 1999 | 1998 |
|---|---|---|---|---|---|---|---|---|---|---|
| Life Insurance in Force | 94,087 | 99,645 | 111,186 | 166,452 | 169,787 | 192,984 | 203,660 | NA | NA | NA |
| Premium Income:Life A & H | 4,061 | 4,203 | 4,595 | 4,789 | 4,565 | 4,385 | 4,215 | NA | NA | NA |
| Premium Income:Casualty/Property. | 3,347 | 2,641 | 1,926 | 1,694 | 1,591 | 1,297 | 1,027 | NA | NA | NA |
| Net Investment Income | 799 | 737 | 687 | 635 | 607 | 632 | 712 | 691 | NA | NA |
| Total Revenue | 8,453 | 7,963 | 7,498 | 7,403 | 7,066 | 6,532 | 6,187 | 6,212 | NA | NA |
| Pretax Income | 1,011 | 1,096 | 656 | 536 | 259 | 370 | 206 | 194 | NA | NA |
| Net Operating Income | NA | NA | NA | NA | NA | NA | NA | NA | NA | NA |
| Net Income | 654 | 716 | 479 | 351 | 186 | 260 | 98.1 | 89.7 | NA | NA |
| S&P Core Earnings | 680 | 613 | 477 | 345 | 187 | 320 | 128 | NA | NA | NA |

| Balance Sheet & Other Financial Data (Million $) | 2007 | 2006 | 2005 | 2004 | 2003 | 2002 | 2001 | 2000 | 1999 | 1998 |
|---|---|---|---|---|---|---|---|---|---|---|
| Cash & Equivalent | 954 | 1,125 | NA | NA | NA | NA | NA | NA | NA | NA |
| Premiums Due | 580 | 612 | 455 | 435 | 368 | NA | NA | NA | NA | NA |
| Investment Assets:Bonds | 10,126 | 9,118 | 8,962 | 9,178 | 8,729 | NA | NA | NA | NA | NA |
| Investment Assets:Stocks | 636 | 742 | 693 | 527 | 456 | NA | NA | NA | NA | NA |
| Investment Assets:Loans | 1,491 | 1,325 | 1,273 | 1,119 | 1,001 | NA | NA | NA | NA | NA |
| Investment Assets:Total | 13,747 | 12,429 | 12,516 | 13,472 | 10,924 | NA | NA | NA | NA | NA |
| Deferred Policy Costs | 2,895 | 2,398 | 2,022 | 1,648 | 1,394 | NA | NA | NA | NA | NA |
| Total Assets | 26,750 | 25,165 | 25,365 | 24,504 | 23,728 | 22,924 | NA | NA | NA | NA |
| Debt | 972 | 972 | 972 | 972 | 1,946 | 975 | NA | NA | NA | NA |
| Common Equity | 4,089 | 3,833 | 3,778 | 3,768 | 2,832 | 3,346 | NA | NA | NA | NA |
| Combined Loss-Expense Ratio | 92.0 | 91.4 | 90.8 | 92.4 | 93.3 | NA | NA | NA | NA | NA |
| % Return on Revenue | 7.7 | 9.3 | 6.4 | 4.9 | 2.6 | 4.0 | 1.6 | 1.4 | NA | NA |
| % Return on Equity | 16.5 | 18.7 | 12.8 | 10.6 | 6.7 | NA | NA | NA | NA | NA |
| % Investment Yield | 6.1 | 5.7 | 5.2 | 5.2 | 5.8 | NA | NA | NA | NA | NA |

Data as orig reptd.; bef. results of disc opers/spec. items. Per share data adj. for stk. divs.; EPS diluted. E-Estimated. NA-Not Available. NM-Not Meaningful. NR-Not Ranked. UR-Under Review.

**Office:** One Chase Manhattan Plaza, New York, NY 10005.
**Telephone:** 212-859-7000.
**Website:** http://www.assurant.com
**Chrmn:** J.M. Palms

**Pres & CEO:** R.B. Pollock
**EVP & CFO:** M.J. Peninger
**EVP & Treas:** C.J. Pagano
**EVP, Secy & General Counsel:** B. Schwartz

**Investor Contact:** M. Kivett (212-859-7029)
**Board Members:** R. J. Blendon, B. L. Bronner, H. L. Carver, J. N. Cento, A. R. Freedman, D. B. Kelso, C. J. Koch, H. C. Mackin, J. M. Palms, R. B. Pollock

**Founded:** 1969
**Domicile:** Delaware
**Employees:** 14,000

The McGraw-Hill Companies

# AT&T Inc

**STANDARD &POOR'S**

| S&P Recommendation | STRONG BUY ★★★★☆ | Price $27.65 (as of Nov 14, 2008) | 12-Mo. Target Price $34.00 | Investment Style Large-Cap Value |
|---|---|---|---|---|

**GICS Sector** Telecommunication Services
**Sub-Industry** Integrated Telecommunication Services

**Summary** AT&T Inc. (formerly SBC Communications) provides telephone and broadband service, and the company holds full ownership of AT&T Mobility (formerly Cingular Wireless). AT&T Corp. was acquired in late 2005 and BellSouth in late 2006.

## Key Stock Statistics (Source S&P, Vickers, company reports)

| | | | | | | | |
|---|---|---|---|---|---|---|---|
| 52-Wk Range | $42.79–20.90 | S&P Oper. EPS 2008E | 2.87 | Market Capitalization(B) | $162.941 | Beta | 0.82 |
| Trailing 12-Month EPS | $2.27 | S&P Oper. EPS 2009E | 3.07 | Yield (%) | 5.79 | S&P 3-Yr. Proj. EPS CAGR(%) | 6 |
| Trailing 12-Month P/E | 12.2 | P/E on S&P Oper. EPS 2008E | 9.6 | Dividend Rate/Share | $1.60 | S&P Credit Rating | A |
| $10K Invested 5 Yrs Ago | $14,812 | Common Shares Outstg. (M) | 5,893.0 | Institutional Ownership (%) | 59 | | |

## Price Performance

30-Week Mov. Avg. ···  10-Week Mov. Avg. – –  **GAAP Earnings vs. Previous Year**  Volume  Above Avg. ▮▮▮  STARS
12-Mo. Target Price —  Relative Strength —  ▲ Up  ▼ Down  ► No Change  Below Avg. ▮▯▯  ★

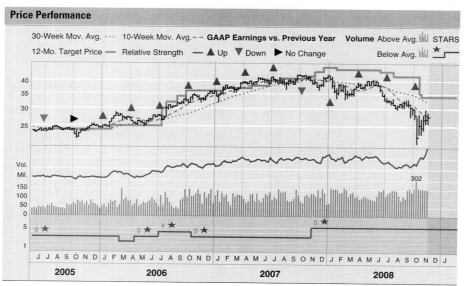

Options: ASE, CBOE, P, Ph

Analysis prepared by **Todd Rosenbluth** on October 23, 2008, when the stock traded at **$ 24.68**.

## Highlights

➤ We expect revenues to rise 4.7% in 2008 and 3.5% in 2009. We see wireless revenue growth of 13% in 2009 on customer additions and wireless data service, and smaller revenue gains in broadband and in regional business, helping outweigh competitive and economic pressure in consumer voice operations.

➤ Overall we see operating margins weakening to 22% in the second half of 2008, from 25% in the first half, on higher customer acquisition costs, before rebounding to 23% in 2009. We believe that wireline operating margins will be helped by work force reductions and network integrations that we see largely offsetting fiber-related buildout and marketing costs. On the wireless side, margin pressure from handset subsidies should offset higher revenue per user. Overall, depreciation costs should be up in 2009.

➤ We estimate operating EPS of $2.87 in 2008 and $3.07 in 2009, before one-time adjustments, with higher interest costs in late 2008 offset by a reduced share count. Results in 2007 included one-time charges related to merger activities.

## Investment Rationale/Risk

➤ We believe cost reductions and growth from wireless along with stability in enterprise will outweigh the pressure in consumer wireline and enable AT&T to generate relatively strong results into 2009. Despite a 40% decline in the shares since the end of May, we think the company's prospects will not be significantly impacted much by a slowing economy or tight credit markets in light of its strong brand loyalty and improved balance sheet. We believe the dividend is secure.

➤ Risks to our recommendation and target price include weakness in its balance sheet, increased pricing competition, weaker-than-projected wireless services execution, and a less successful rollout of new services.

➤ We view the shares as undervalued trading at a forward P/E of about 8X our 2009 estimate, relative to the 6% EPS growth we forecast. Our 12-month target price of $34 is based on our relative analysis, which assumes a P/E of about 11X our EPS estimate, in line with peers, and an enterprise value/EBITDA multiple of 5X. The stock is bolstered by its dividend, which recently yielded about 6.4%.

## Qualitative Risk Assessment

| LOW | MEDIUM | HIGH |
|---|---|---|

Our risk assessment reflects our view of the company's strong balance sheet and its power over suppliers, offset by the competitive nature of the telecom business and the integration challenges of numerous acquisitions.

## Quantitative Evaluations

### S&P Quality Ranking
B+

| D | C | B- | B | B+ | A- | A | A+ |
|---|---|---|---|---|---|---|---|

### Relative Strength Rank
STRONG
88
LOWEST = 1     HIGHEST = 99

## Revenue/Earnings Data

### Revenue (Million $)

| | 1Q | 2Q | 3Q | 4Q | Year |
|---|---|---|---|---|---|
| 2008 | 30,744 | 30,866 | 31,342 | -- | -- |
| 2007 | 28,969 | 29,478 | 30,132 | 30,349 | 118,928 |
| 2006 | 15,756 | 15,770 | 15,638 | 15,891 | 63,055 |
| 2005 | 10,248 | 10,328 | 10,320 | 12,966 | 43,862 |
| 2004 | 10,128 | 10,314 | 10,292 | 10,287 | 40,787 |
| 2003 | 10,333 | 10,204 | 10,239 | 10,067 | 40,843 |

### Earnings Per Share ($)

| | 1Q | 2Q | 3Q | 4Q | Year |
|---|---|---|---|---|---|
| 2008 | 0.57 | 0.63 | 0.55 | E0.68 | E2.87 |
| 2007 | 0.45 | 0.47 | 0.50 | 0.52 | 1.94 |
| 2006 | 0.37 | 0.46 | 0.56 | 0.50 | 1.89 |
| 2005 | 0.27 | 0.30 | 0.38 | 0.46 | 1.42 |
| 2004 | 0.59 | 0.35 | 0.38 | 0.21 | 1.50 |
| 2003 | 0.74 | 0.42 | 0.37 | 0.28 | 1.80 |

Fiscal year ended Dec. 31. Next earnings report expected: Late January. EPS Estimates based on S&P Operating Earnings; historical GAAP earnings are as reported.

## Dividend Data (Dates: mm/dd Payment Date: mm/dd/yy)

| Amount ($) | Date Decl. | Ex-Div. Date | Stk. of Record | Payment Date |
|---|---|---|---|---|
| 0.400 | 12/11 | 01/08 | 01/10 | 02/01/08 |
| 0.400 | 03/28 | 04/08 | 04/10 | 05/01/08 |
| 0.400 | 06/27 | 07/08 | 07/10 | 08/01/08 |
| 0.400 | 09/26 | 10/08 | 10/10 | 11/03/08 |

Dividends have been paid since 1984. Source: Company reports.

# AT&T Inc

STANDARD
&POOR'S

## Business Summary October 23, 2008

CORPORATE OVERVIEW. AT&T Inc. (T) combined SBC Communications with the acquired assets of AT&T Corp. following a November 2005 acquisition. At the end of 2006, T closed on its acquisition of BellSouth (BLS) for $86 billion in stock. As of September 2008, the company had 57 million in-region local phone lines (down 9% from a year earlier) and 12.7 million consumer broadband customers (up 9%). With the acquisition of BLS, T took full control of Cingular Wireless (32% of 2007 T revenues), the largest U.S. carrier now with 75 million subscribers (up 14% from a year earlier), and expanded its wireline presence into the Southeastern U.S. In early 2007, Cingular was renamed AT&T.

The inclusion of AT&T Corp. added voice, data, IP, and hosting services for enterprise customers as well as a national network. SBC expanded through a number of mergers of fellow Bell companies over the past 10 years. Reported results in 2006 largely exclude BLS operations, including its 40% stake in Cingular. Pro forma revenues in 2006 were $117 billion.

IMPACT OF MAJOR DEVELOPMENTS. In June 2006, T launched its new fiber-based network, which offers video and faster-speed broadband services. As of September 2008, the service, called U-verse, had been rolled out in part of T's operating territory with 781,000 customers, more than doubling the base in six months. AT&T plans to have 1 million subscribers to U-verse by the end of 2008 and expects to deploy it to 30 million households by 2010, up from 14 million households in September 2008.

At the end of June 2007, T became the exclusive provider of the iPhone, and by December, over 2 million customers had signed up for the service. In June 2008, the company announced an upgraded 3G version of the handset that T will subsidize (we estimate approximately $225 per unit) to drive customer demand and revenue per user. In the third quarter of 2008, T activated 2.4 million iPhones, above expectations. Even with higher revenue growth and supporting customer loyalty in a competitive market, we expect the iPhone to be earnings dilutive in 2008 and 2009.

In December 2007, T reported that it expects $5 billion in cost savings in 2008 from merger synergies such as network traffic integration and work force reductions. In late 2008, T announced plans to further integrate its wireline and wireless operations, which should lower its cost structure.

## Company Financials Fiscal Year Ended Dec. 31

| Per Share Data ($) | 2007 | 2006 | 2005 | 2004 | 2003 | 2002 | 2001 | 2000 | 1999 | 1998 |
|---|---|---|---|---|---|---|---|---|---|---|
| Tangible Book Value | NM | NM | 8.29 | 11.77 | 11.09 | 9.51 | 8.62 | 7.38 | 5.87 | 4.95 |
| Cash Flow | 5.43 | 2.77 | 3.68 | 3.80 | 4.16 | 4.79 | 2.25 | 5.16 | 4.37 | 4.66 |
| Earnings | 1.94 | 1.89 | 1.42 | 1.50 | 1.80 | 2.23 | 2.14 | 2.32 | 1.90 | 2.05 |
| S&P Core Earnings | 1.66 | 1.82 | 1.24 | 1.22 | 1.50 | 1.21 | 1.39 | NA | NA | NA |
| Dividends | 1.42 | 1.33 | 1.29 | 1.25 | 1.37 | 1.07 | 1.02 | 1.01 | 0.97 | 0.93 |
| Payout Ratio | 73% | 70% | 91% | 83% | 76% | 48% | 48% | 43% | 51% | 45% |
| Prices:High | 42.97 | 36.21 | 25.98 | 27.73 | 31.65 | 40.99 | 53.06 | 59.00 | 59.94 | 54.88 |
| Prices:Low | 31.94 | 24.24 | 21.75 | 22.98 | 18.85 | 19.57 | 36.50 | 34.81 | 44.06 | 35.00 |
| P/E Ratio:High | 22 | 19 | 18 | 18 | 18 | 18 | 25 | 25 | 32 | 27 |
| P/E Ratio:Low | 16 | 13 | 15 | 15 | 10 | 9 | 17 | 15 | 23 | 17 |

| Income Statement Analysis (Million $) | | | | | | | | | | |
|---|---|---|---|---|---|---|---|---|---|---|
| Revenue | 118,928 | 63,055 | 43,862 | 40,787 | 40,843 | 43,138 | 45,908 | 51,476 | 49,489 | 28,777 |
| Depreciation | 21,577 | 9,907 | 7,643 | 7,564 | 7,870 | 8,578 | 9,077 | 9,748 | 8,553 | 5,177 |
| Maintenance | NA | NA | NA | NA | NA | NA | NA | NA | NA | NA |
| Construction Credits | NA | NA | 36.0 | 31.0 | 37.0 | 58.0 | 119 | 81.0 | 81.0 | 59.0 |
| Effective Tax Rate | 34.0% | 32.4% | 16.3% | 30.5% | 32.9% | 28.5% | 36.1% | 38.2% | 39.4% | 36.2% |
| Net Income | 11,951 | 7,356 | 4,786 | 4,979 | 5,971 | 7,473 | 7,260 | 7,967 | 6,573 | 4,068 |
| S&P Core Earnings | 10,225 | 7,080 | 4,189 | 4,031 | 5,000 | 4,048 | 4,717 | NA | NA | NA |

| Balance Sheet & Other Financial Data (Million $) | | | | | | | | | | |
|---|---|---|---|---|---|---|---|---|---|---|
| Gross Property | 210,518 | 202,149 | 149,238 | 136,177 | 133,923 | 131,755 | 127,524 | 119,753 | 116,332 | 73,466 |
| Net Property | 95,890 | 94,596 | 58,727 | 50,046 | 52,128 | 48,490 | 49,827 | 47,195 | 46,571 | 29,920 |
| Capital Expenditures | 17,717 | 8,320 | 5,576 | 5,099 | 5,219 | 6,808 | 11,189 | 13,124 | 10,304 | 5,927 |
| Total Capital | 197,561 | 193,009 | 96,727 | 77,544 | 69,607 | 62,705 | 58,476 | 54,079 | 50,411 | 27,741 |
| Fixed Charges Coverage | 6.0 | 5.8 | 4.4 | 6.9 | 7.0 | 6.9 | 6.6 | 8.0 | 7.5 | 6.8 |
| Capitalization:Long Term Debt | 57,255 | 50,063 | 26,115 | 21,231 | 16,060 | 18,536 | 17,133 | 16,492 | 18,415 | 12,612 |
| Capitalization:Preferred | Nil | Nil | Nil | Nil | Nil | Nil | Nil | Nil | Nil | Nil |
| Capitalization:Common | 115,367 | 115,540 | 54,690 | 40,504 | 38,248 | 33,199 | 32,491 | 30,463 | 26,726 | 12,780 |
| % Return on Revenue | 10.0 | 11.7 | 10.9 | 12.2 | 14.6 | 17.3 | 15.8 | 15.5 | 13.3 | 14.1 |
| % Return on Invested Capital | 7.6 | 4.9 | 6.5 | 7.0 | 9.0 | 11.4 | 12.9 | 16.6 | 15.0 | 17.7 |
| % Return on Common Equity | 10.4 | 8.6 | 10.1 | 12.6 | 16.7 | 22.6 | 23.1 | 27.9 | 26.6 | 34.9 |
| % Earned on Net Property | 21.4 | 13.4 | 11.3 | 11.6 | 12.9 | 17.5 | 22.4 | 22.9 | 25.6 | 23.3 |
| % Long Term Debt of Capitalization | 33.2 | 30.3 | 32.3 | 34.4 | 29.6 | 35.8 | 34.5 | 35.1 | 40.9 | 49.7 |
| Capital % Preferred | Nil | Nil | Nil | Nil | Nil | Nil | Nil | Nil | Nil | Nil |
| Capitalization:% Common | 66.8 | 67.8 | 67.7 | 65.6 | 70.4 | 64.2 | 65.5 | 64.9 | 59.1 | 50.3 |

Data as orig reptd.; bef. results of disc opers/spec. items. Per share data adj. for stk. divs.; EPS diluted. E-Estimated. NA-Not Available. NM-Not Meaningful. NR-Not Ranked. UR-Under Review.

**Office:** 175 East Houston, San Antonio, TX 78205-2220.
**Telephone:** 210-821-4105.
**Website:** http://www.att.com
**Chrmn, Pres & CEO:** R.L. Stephenson

**EVP, CFO & Chief Acctg Officer:** R.G. Lindner
**EVP & General Counsel:** D.W. Watts
**SVP & Secy:** A.E. Meuleman
**SVP & Cntlr:** J.J. Stephens

**Investor Contact:** D. Cessac (210-351-2058)
**Board Members:** W. F. Aldinger, III, G. F. Amelio, R. V. Anderson, J. H. Blanchard, A. A. Busch, III, J. A. Harris, J. P. Kelly, J. C. Madonna, L. Martin, J. B. McCoy, M. S. Metz, J. C. Pardo, J. M. Roche, R. L. Stephenson, L. D. Tyson, P. P. Upton

**Founded:** 1983
**Domicile:** Delaware
**Employees:** 309,050

The McGraw-Hill Companies

**STANDARD &POOR'S**

# Autodesk Inc

| S&P Recommendation  HOLD ★★★☆☆ | Price $19.53 (as of Nov 14, 2008) | 12-Mo. Target Price $25.00 | Investment Style Large-Cap Growth |
|---|---|---|---|

**GICS Sector** Information Technology
**Sub-Industry** Application Software

**Summary** This company develops, markets and supports computer-aided design and drafting (CAD) software for use on desktop computers and workstations.

## Key Stock Statistics (Source S&P, Vickers, company reports)

| | | | | | | | |
|---|---|---|---|---|---|---|---|
| 52-Wk Range | $51.22– 15.06 | S&P Oper. EPS 2009E | 1.67 | Market Capitalization(B) | $4.393 | Beta | 2.15 |
| Trailing 12-Month EPS | $1.55 | S&P Oper. EPS 2010E | 1.61 | Yield (%) | Nil | S&P 3-Yr. Proj. EPS CAGR(%) | 8 |
| Trailing 12-Month P/E | 12.6 | P/E on S&P Oper. EPS 2009E | 11.7 | Dividend Rate/Share | Nil | S&P Credit Rating | NA |
| $10K Invested 5 Yrs Ago | $19,213 | Common Shares Outstg. (M) | 225.0 | Institutional Ownership (%) | 95 | | |

## Price Performance

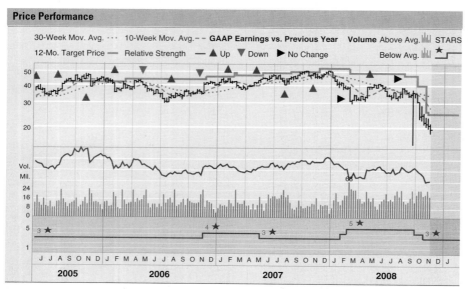

30-Week Mov. Avg. · · · 10-Week Mov. Avg. – – GAAP Earnings vs. Previous Year   Volume Above Avg. STARS
12-Mo. Target Price — Relative Strength — ▲ Up ▼ Down ► No Change   Below Avg. ★

Options: ASE, CBOE, P, Ph

Analysis prepared by **Jim Yin** on November 04, 2008, when the stock traded at **$ 22.50**.

## Highlights

➤ We project flat revenue in FY 10 (Jan.), compared to a 12% rise we expect in FY 09, reflecting our view of further deterioration in the global economy as the financial crisis in the U.S. likely spreads to the rest of the world. We forecast a 2.3% decline in license revenue in FY 10, as results should be hurt by unfavorable foreign currency exchange. These negative factors are somewhat mitigated by customer migration to 3D products, which we think are in the early stages of a long upgrade cycle.

➤ We see gross margins in FY 10 remaining at FY 09's projected 90%. We expect total operating expenses to increase modestly as a percentage of revenue due to higher head count and stock option expense. We estimate that operating margins will narrow to 20% in FY 10, from 21% seen in FY 09, as a result of higher wages and stock-based compensation and flat revenue growth.

➤ Our estimate for EPS is $1.61 for FY 10, versus our $1.67 forecast for FY 09. The projected decrease reflects narrower operating margins, partially offset by fewer shares outstanding due to ADSK's stock repurchase program.

## Investment Rationale/Risk

➤ We recently lowered our recommendation to hold, from buy, based on our concerns of a weaker global economy, which we think has worsened. We believe the decline in economic growth will be more severe outside the U.S., where ADSK derives more than 60% of its revenues. We also think operating results will be hurt by unfavorable foreign currency exchange. On the positive side, management has been focusing on controlling costs. We believe ADSK is fairly valued at recent levels following a steep decline in the share price.

➤ Risks to our opinion and target price include a loss of market share to competitors, poor sales execution, and further weakness in the global economy that causes a reduction in information technology spending.

➤ Our 12-month target price of $25 is based on a blend of our discounted cash flow (DCF) and P/E analyses. Our DCF model assumes a 13% weighted average cost of capital and 3% terminal growth, yielding intrinsic value of $27. For our P/E analysis, we derive a value of $22, based on an industry average P/E-to-growth ratio of 1.7X, or about 13.7X our FY 10 EPS estimate of $1.61.

## Qualitative Risk Assessment

| LOW | MEDIUM | HIGH |
|---|---|---|

Our risk assessment reflects ADSK's exposure to cyclical business spending and intense competition, partially offset by our view of the company's strong market position and size.

## Quantitative Evaluations

**S&P Quality Ranking**      B

| D | C | B- | B | B+ | A- | A | A+ |
|---|---|---|---|---|---|---|---|

**Relative Strength Rank**      MODERATE

37

LOWEST = 1      HIGHEST = 99

## Revenue/Earnings Data

**Revenue (Million $)**

| | 1Q | 2Q | 3Q | 4Q | Year |
|---|---|---|---|---|---|
| 2009 | 598.8 | 619.5 | -- | -- | -- |
| 2008 | 508.5 | 525.9 | 538.4 | 599.1 | 2,172 |
| 2007 | 436.0 | 449.6 | 456.8 | 497.4 | 1,840 |
| 2006 | 355.1 | 373.0 | 378.3 | 416.8 | 1,523 |
| 2005 | 297.9 | 279.6 | 300.2 | 356.2 | 1,234 |
| 2004 | 210.8 | 211.7 | 233.9 | 295.3 | 951.6 |

**Earnings Per Share ($)**

| | 1Q | 2Q | 3Q | 4Q | Year |
|---|---|---|---|---|---|
| 2009 | 0.41 | 0.39 | E0.42 | E0.46 | E1.67 |
| 2008 | 0.34 | 0.39 | 0.35 | 0.40 | 1.47 |
| 2007 | 0.20 | 0.36 | 0.24 | 0.40 | 1.19 |
| 2006 | 0.31 | 0.30 | 0.38 | 0.33 | 1.33 |
| 2005 | 0.18 | 0.16 | 0.30 | 0.26 | 0.90 |
| 2004 | 0.04 | 0.15 | 0.10 | 0.24 | 0.52 |

Fiscal year ended Jan. 31. Next earnings report expected: Mid November. EPS Estimates based on S&P Operating Earnings; historical GAAP earnings are as reported.

## Dividend Data

Quarterly cash dividends were discontinued after April 2005.

# Autodesk Inc

STANDARD
&POOR'S

## Business Summary November 04, 2008

CORPORATE OVERVIEW. Autodesk (ADSK) develops software solutions that enable customers in the architectural, engineering, construction, manufacturing, infrastructure, media and entertainment markets to create, manage and share their data and designs digitally. ADSK's software helps its customers to improve their designs before they actually begin the building process, thus saving time and money. The company is organized into two reportable operating segments: the Design Solutions segment, which accounted for 87% of net revenue in FY 08 (Jan.), and the Media and Entertainment segment, which accounted for 12%.

The Design Solutions segment sells design software for professionals and consumers who design, build and manage building and other infrastructure projects for both public and private users. The segment is comprised of three divisions: Platform Technology and Other, which accounted for 53% of the segment's revenues in FY 08; Architecture, Engineering and Construction, 25%; and Manufacturing Solutions, 22%.

Principal products sold by the Design Solutions segment include AutoCAD, a general-purpose computer aided design (CAD) tool for design, modeling, drafting, mapping, rendering and facility management tasks, AutoCAD LT, a

low-cost CAD package with 2D and basic 3D drafting capabilities, and Autodesk Buzzsaw, an online collaboration service that allows users to store, manage and share project documents from any Internet connection. Other products include Autodesk Mechanical Desktop, Autodesk Civil 3D, and Autodesk Revit products. The Design Solutions segment also offers a range of services including consulting, support and training.

The Media and Entertainment segment develops digital systems and software for creating 3D animation, color grading, visual effects compositing, editing and finishing. Its products are used for PC and console game development, animation, film, television, and design visualization. Products include Autodesk 3ds Max, a 3D modeling and animation software package; Autodesk Flame, a digital system used by professionals to create and edit special visual effects in real-time; and Autodesk Inferno, which provides all the features of flame with film tools, and increased image resolution and color control for digital film work.

## Company Financials  Fiscal Year Ended Jan. 31

| Per Share Data ($) | 2008 | 2007 | 2006 | 2005 | 2004 | 2003 | 2002 | 2001 | 2000 | 1999 |
|---|---|---|---|---|---|---|---|---|---|---|
| Tangible Book Value | 3.14 | 3.07 | 2.06 | 2.07 | 2.07 | 1.84 | 2.20 | 1.85 | 2.22 | 2.06 |
| Cash Flow | 1.68 | 1.37 | 1.51 | 1.11 | 0.74 | 0.35 | 0.68 | 0.69 | 0.36 | 0.79 |
| Earnings | 1.47 | 1.19 | 1.33 | 0.90 | 0.52 | 0.14 | 0.40 | 0.40 | 0.04 | 0.46 |
| S&P Core Earnings | 1.49 | 1.19 | 1.05 | 0.67 | 0.33 | -0.07 | 0.09 | 0.17 | NA | NA |
| Dividends | Nil | 0.02 | 0.06 | 0.06 | 0.06 | 0.06 | 0.06 | 0.06 | 0.06 | 0.06 |
| Payout Ratio | Nil | 2% | 5% | 7% | 12% | 43% | 15% | 15% | 150% | 13% |
| Calendar Year | 2007 | 2006 | 2005 | 2004 | 2003 | 2002 | 2001 | 2000 | 1999 | 1998 |
| Prices:High | 51.32 | 44.75 | 48.27 | 38.98 | 12.45 | 11.84 | 10.55 | 14.02 | 12.36 | 12.52 |
| Prices:Low | 36.74 | 29.56 | 26.20 | 12.10 | 6.41 | 5.09 | 6.05 | 4.86 | 4.25 | 5.41 |
| P/E Ratio:High | 35 | 38 | 36 | 43 | 24 | 85 | 26 | 35 | NM | 27 |
| P/E Ratio:Low | 25 | 25 | 20 | 13 | 12 | 36 | 15 | 12 | NM | 12 |

| Income Statement Analysis (Million $) | | | | | | | | | | |
|---|---|---|---|---|---|---|---|---|---|---|
| Revenue | 2,172 | 1,840 | 1,523 | 1,234 | 952 | 825 | 947 | 936 | 820 | 740 |
| Operating Income | 539 | 440 | 414 | 314 | 0.16 | 99.7 | 195 | 208 | 115 | 200 |
| Depreciation | 49.8 | 43.9 | 43.7 | 51.9 | 50.3 | 48.8 | 62.9 | 68.8 | 79.7 | 63.2 |
| Interest Expense | Nil | 2.10 | Nil | Nil | Nil | Nil | Nil | Nil | Nil | Nil |
| Pretax Income | 470 | 367 | 383 | 246 | 117 | 38.5 | 55.1 | 41.7 | 23.9 | 147 |
| Effective Tax Rate | 24.2% | 21.0% | 14.1% | 10.1% | NM | 17.1% | NM | NM | 59.0% | 38.2% |
| Net Income | 356 | 290 | 329 | 222 | 120 | 31.9 | 90.3 | 93.2 | 9.81 | 90.6 |
| S&P Core Earnings | 362 | 292 | 258 | 161 | 74.4 | -16.2 | 19.5 | 38.5 | NA | NA |

| Balance Sheet & Other Financial Data (Million $) | | | | | | | | | | |
|---|---|---|---|---|---|---|---|---|---|---|
| Cash | 949 | 778 | 369 | 533 | 364 | 247 | 505 | 423 | 359 | 378 |
| Current Assets | 1,482 | 1,190 | 739 | 782 | 597 | 450 | 564 | 491 | 545 | 450 |
| Total Assets | 2,209 | 1,798 | 1,361 | 1,142 | 1,017 | 884 | 902 | 808 | 907 | 694 |
| Current Liabilities | 746 | 574 | 507 | 477 | 385 | 310 | 371 | 334 | 299 | 232 |
| Long Term Debt | Nil | Nil | Nil | Nil | Nil | Nil | Nil | Nil | Nil | Nil |
| Common Equity | 1,231 | 1,115 | 791 | 648 | 622 | 569 | 529 | 460 | 602 | 460 |
| Total Capital | 1,231 | 1,115 | 791 | 648 | 629 | 571 | 529 | 473 | 607 | 461 |
| Capital Expenditures | 43.3 | 35.3 | 20.5 | 40.8 | 25.9 | 36.1 | 45.1 | 32.4 | 14.9 | 30.4 |
| Cash Flow | 406 | 334 | 373 | 273 | 171 | 80.7 | 153 | 162 | 89.6 | 154 |
| Current Ratio | 2.0 | 2.1 | 1.5 | 1.6 | 1.6 | 1.5 | 1.5 | 1.5 | 1.8 | 1.9 |
| % Long Term Debt of Capitalization | Nil | Nil | Nil | Nil | Nil | Nil | Nil | Nil | Nil | Nil |
| % Net Income of Revenue | 16.4 | 15.8 | 21.6 | 18.0 | 12.6 | 3.9 | 9.5 | 10.0 | 1.2 | 12.2 |
| % Return on Assets | 17.8 | 18.4 | 26.3 | 20.5 | 12.7 | 3.6 | 10.6 | 10.9 | 1.1 | 14.8 |
| % Return on Equity | 30.4 | 30.4 | 45.7 | 34.9 | 20.2 | 5.8 | 18.3 | 17.6 | 1.7 | 23.7 |

Data as orig reptd.; bef. results of disc opers/spec. items. Per share data adj. for stk. divs.; EPS diluted. E-Estimated. NA-Not Available. NM-Not Meaningful. NR-Not Ranked. UR-Under Review.

**Office:** 111 McInnis Parkway, San Rafael, CA 94903-2700.
**Telephone:** 415-507-5000.
**Email:** investor.relations@autodesk.com
**Website:** http://www.autodesk.com

**Chrmn:** C.A. Bartz
**Pres, CEO, CFO & Chief Acctg Officer:** C. Bass
**COO & SVP:** M. Chin
**SVP, Secy & General Counsel:** P.W. Di Fronzo

**CTO:** J.M. Kowalski
**Investor Contact:** S. Pirri (415-507-6467)
**Board Members:** C. A. Bartz, C. Bass, M. A. Bertelsen, C. W. Beveridge, J. H. Dawson, P. Halvorsen, S. M. Maloney, E. A. Nelson, C. J. Robel, S. M. West

**Founded:** 1982
**Domicile:** Delaware
**Employees:** 7,300

# Automatic Data Processing Inc.

**STANDARD &POOR'S**

| S&P Recommendation | BUY ★★★★☆ | Price | 12-Mo. Target Price | Investment Style |
|---|---|---|---|---|
| | | $35.12 (as of Nov 14, 2008) | $40.00 | Large-Cap Growth |

**GICS Sector** Information Technology
**Sub-Industry** Data Processing & Outsourced Services

**Summary** ADP, one of the world's largest independent computing services companies, provides a broad range of data processing services.

## Key Stock Statistics (Source S&P, Vickers, company reports)

| | | | | | | | |
|---|---|---|---|---|---|---|---|
| 52-Wk Range | $46.99– 30.83 | S&P Oper. EPS 2009E | 2.37 | Market Capitalization(B) | $17.837 | Beta | 0.51 |
| Trailing 12-Month EPS | $2.33 | S&P Oper. EPS 2010E | 2.63 | Yield (%) | 3.76 | S&P 3-Yr. Proj. EPS CAGR(%) | 12 |
| Trailing 12-Month P/E | 15.1 | P/E on S&P Oper. EPS 2009E | 14.8 | Dividend Rate/Share | $1.32 | S&P Credit Rating | AAA |
| $10K Invested 5 Yrs Ago | NA | Common Shares Outstg. (M) | 507.9 | Institutional Ownership (%) | 78 | | |

## Price Performance

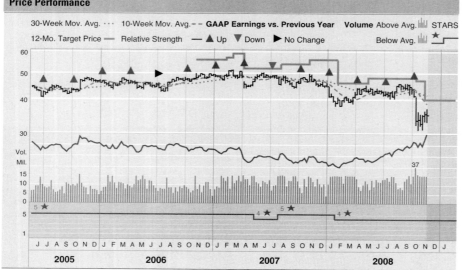

30-Week Mov. Avg. · · · ·  10-Week Mov. Avg. - - -  **GAAP Earnings vs. Previous Year**  Volume Above Avg. STARS
12-Mo. Target Price —  Relative Strength  — ▲ Up ▼ Down ► No Change  Below Avg.

Options: ASE, CBOE, P, Ph

Analysis prepared by **Dylan Cathers** on November 05, 2008, when the stock traded at **$ 34.66**.

### Highlights

➤ We see revenue growth slowing to 3.5% in FY 09 (Jun.), reflecting a strengthening U.S. dollar and slowing sales of the company's traditional payroll and tax filing business. We still foresee areas beyond payroll services -- such as benefits and retirement -- and the professional employer organization adding meaningfully to overall growth, but at a less robust pace than before. We note that customer retention rates remain high, which should help growth. Still, we think payroll data will continue to slow, given the ongoing weakness in the U.S. economy. Also, we see falling interest rates reducing income from funds held for clients, although we believe ADP is doing a good job of mitigating these declines through portfolio management. We believe Dealer Services will be a drag on results due to pricing pressures and lower volumes. We see revenue growth improving to 7% in FY 10.

➤ We look for modestly wider operating margins in FY 09, reflecting rising sales of higher-margin services, increased leverage, and cost containment measures.

➤ Our FY 09 EPS estimate is $2.37 and we look for EPS of $2.63 in FY 10.

### Investment Rationale/Risk

➤ We are seeing headwinds that will likely affect the company in the near term, namely slower employment growth, declining U.S. vehicle sales, and low interest rates. Over the longer term, we think the market for payroll outsourcing is relatively untapped, especially in the small and medium-sized business market and overseas, providing opportunities for future earnings growth. We view the company's balance sheet as strong, even after ADP repurchased 33 million of its shares in FY 08.

➤ Risks to our recommendation and target price stem from competition in the business process outsourcing market, an area into which ADP is venturing, which could lead to downward pressure on pricing and profit margins; a decrease in payrolls due to a slower economy; and failure of ADP to expand further into small and mid-sized business and international markets.

➤ Our 12-month target price of $40 is based on our relative valuation analysis, applying a peer-based P/E of 16.3X to our calendar 2009 EPS estimate of $2.45 and a P/E-to-growth ratio of 1.36X, assuming a three-year growth rate of 12%.

## Qualitative Risk Assessment

| LOW | MEDIUM | HIGH |
|---|---|---|

Our risk assessment reflects what we see as the company's strong balance sheet, steady cash inflow, and recurring revenue stream, offset by intense competition in payroll processing and the threat of new entrants into the marketplace.

## Quantitative Evaluations

**S&P Quality Ranking** A+

| D | C | B- | B | B+ | A- | A | A+ |
|---|---|---|---|---|---|---|---|

**Relative Strength Rank** STRONG

78

LOWEST = 1    HIGHEST = 99

## Revenue/Earnings Data

**Revenue (Million $)**

| | 1Q | 2Q | 3Q | 4Q | Year |
|---|---|---|---|---|---|
| 2009 | 2,182 | -- | -- | -- | -- |
| 2008 | 1,992 | 2,150 | 2,427 | 2,207 | 8,777 |
| 2007 | 1,755 | 1,874 | 2,171 | 2,000 | 7,800 |
| 2006 | 1,922 | 2,047 | 2,439 | 2,474 | 8,882 |
| 2005 | 1,855 | 1,994 | 2,349 | 2,302 | 8,499 |
| 2004 | 1,720 | 1,927 | 2,121 | 2,086 | 7,755 |

**Earnings Per Share ($)**

| | 1Q | 2Q | 3Q | 4Q | Year |
|---|---|---|---|---|---|
| 2009 | 0.54 | E0.56 | E0.80 | E0.47 | E2.37 |
| 2008 | 0.45 | 0.53 | 0.77 | 0.44 | 2.20 |
| 2007 | 0.39 | 0.45 | 0.65 | 0.35 | 1.83 |
| 2006 | 0.36 | 0.44 | 0.61 | 0.44 | 1.85 |
| 2005 | 0.35 | 0.42 | 0.57 | 0.44 | 1.79 |
| 2004 | 0.32 | 0.38 | 0.50 | 0.36 | 1.56 |

Fiscal year ended Jun. 30. Next earnings report expected: Early February. EPS Estimates based on S&P Operating Earnings; historical GAAP earnings are as reported.

## Dividend Data (Dates: mm/dd Payment Date: mm/dd/yy)

| Amount ($) | Date Decl. | Ex-Div. Date | Stk. of Record | Payment Date |
|---|---|---|---|---|
| 0.290 | 01/31 | 03/12 | 03/14 | 04/01/08 |
| 0.290 | 04/30 | 06/11 | 06/13 | 07/01/08 |
| 0.290 | 08/14 | 09/10 | 09/12 | 10/01/08 |
| 0.330 | 11/11 | 12/10 | 12/12 | 01/01/09 |

Dividends have been paid since 1974. Source: Company reports.

---

**Please read the Required Disclosures and Analyst Certification on the last page of this report.**

*The McGraw-Hill Companies*

# Automatic Data Processing Inc.

STANDARD
&POOR'S

## Business Summary November 05, 2008

CORPORATE OVERVIEW. Automatic Data Processing (ADP) is the largest global provider of payroll outsourcing services based on revenue. The company also offers human resources outsourcing, tax filing, and benefits administration, with a broad range of data processing services in two business segments: employer and dealer.

Employer Services provides payroll, human resource, benefits administration, time and attendance, and tax filing and reporting services to more than 570,000 clients in North America, Europe, Australia, Asia and Brazil. Dealer Services provides transaction systems, data products and professional services to automobile and truck dealers and manufacturers worldwide.

MARKET PROFILE. The market for HR management services, which is the largest segment of ADP's Employer Services division, totaled $98.4 billion worldwide in calendar 2007, according to market researcher IDC. Between 2007 and 2012, IDC expects this area to expand at a compound annual growth rate (CAGR) of 8.0%, with the market in the Americas increasing at a CAGR of 8.2%, from $53.3 billion in 2007. For the more narrow Payroll services market, where ADP is the dominant company, IDC sees a CAGR of 6.3% in the U.S. between 2007 and 2012. In contrast, in the market for business process outsourcing (BPO) services, an area in which we see ADP expanding further, IDC

expects a CAGR of 11.2% over the same time frame.

IMPACT OF MAJOR DEVELOPMENTS. In April 2006, ADP completed the sale of its Claims Services business for $975 million in cash, netting $480 million after taxes. In August 2006, ADP announced its intention to spin off its Brokerage Services business. The new public company, Broadridge Financial Services (BR: $12), which began trading on April 2, 2007, had sales of about $2 billion in FY 07 (Jun.), a high level of recurring revenues, and a revenue growth rate in the mid-single digits. This growth rate is below what we think the remaining Employer Services and Dealer Services units are capable of, especially given what we believe are strong overseas prospects. Further, the disposition of the Brokerage business (as well as the Claims sale) allows management to better concentrate on its two remaining businesses, in our opinion. With the Brokerage business spin-off complete, the new company distributed $690 million to ADP, which were used primarily for share buybacks, acquiring 40 million shares at a cost of about $2 billion in FY 07.

## Company Financials Fiscal Year Ended Jun. 30

| Per Share Data ($) | 2008 | 2007 | 2006 | 2005 | 2004 | 2003 | 2002 | 2001 | 2000 | 1999 |
|---|---|---|---|---|---|---|---|---|---|---|
| Tangible Book Value | 3.97 | 3.93 | 5.21 | 4.55 | 4.23 | 4.57 | 5.25 | 4.97 | 4.71 | 3.97 |
| Cash Flow | NA | 2.35 | 5.35 | 2.30 | 2.07 | 2.13 | 2.19 | 1.93 | 1.74 | 1.52 |
| Earnings | 2.20 | 1.83 | 1.85 | 1.79 | 1.56 | 1.68 | 1.75 | 1.44 | 1.31 | 1.10 |
| S&P Core Earnings | 2.11 | 1.78 | 1.85 | 1.60 | 1.38 | 1.42 | 1.49 | 1.31 | NA | NA |
| Dividends | 1.10 | 1.06 | 0.71 | 0.61 | 0.54 | 0.48 | 0.45 | 0.40 | 0.34 | 0.30 |
| Payout Ratio | 50% | 58% | 38% | 34% | 35% | 28% | 26% | 27% | 26% | 21% |
| Prices:High | 45.97 | 51.50 | 49.94 | 48.11 | 47.31 | 40.81 | 59.53 | 63.56 | 69.31 | 54.81 |
| Prices:Low | 30.83 | 43.89 | 42.50 | 40.37 | 38.60 | 27.24 | 31.15 | 41.00 | 40.00 | 36.25 |
| P/E Ratio:High | 21 | 28 | 27 | 27 | 30 | 24 | 34 | 44 | 53 | 50 |
| P/E Ratio:Low | 14 | 24 | 23 | 23 | 25 | 16 | 18 | 28 | 31 | 33 |

| Income Statement Analysis (Million $) | | | | | | | | | | |
|---|---|---|---|---|---|---|---|---|---|---|
| Revenue | 8,777 | 7,800 | 8,882 | 8,499 | 7,755 | 7,147 | 7,004 | 7,018 | 6,288 | 5,540 |
| Operating Income | NA | 1,795 | 1,967 | 1,948 | 1,745 | 1,793 | 1,952 | 1,938 | 1,904 | 1,376 |
| Depreciation | 319 | 289 | 289 | 304 | 307 | 275 | 279 | 321 | 284 | 273 |
| Interest Expense | NA | 94.9 | 72.8 | 32.3 | Nil | Nil | 21.2 | 14.3 | 13.1 | 19.1 |
| Pretax Income | 1,812 | 1,624 | 3,486 | 1,678 | 1,495 | 1,645 | 1,787 | 1,525 | 1,290 | 1,085 |
| Effective Tax Rate | 35.9% | 37.1% | 19.2% | 37.1% | 37.4% | 38.1% | 38.4% | 39.4% | 34.8% | 35.7% |
| Net Income | 1,162 | 1,021 | 2,815 | 1,055 | 936 | 1,018 | 1,101 | 925 | 841 | 697 |
| S&P Core Earnings | 1,115 | 992 | 1,077 | 940 | 824 | 857 | 940 | 842 | NA | NA |

| Balance Sheet & Other Financial Data (Million $) | | | | | | | | | | |
|---|---|---|---|---|---|---|---|---|---|---|
| Cash | 1,584 | 1,817 | 2,269 | 1,671 | 1,129 | 2,344 | 2,750 | 1,791 | 1,824 | 1,092 |
| Current Assets | NA | 3,364 | 4,760 | 4,441 | 2,762 | 3,676 | 2,817 | 3,083 | 3,064 | 2,194 |
| Total Assets | 23,734 | 26,649 | 27,490 | 27,615 | 21,121 | 19,834 | 18,277 | 17,889 | 16,851 | 5,825 |
| Current Liabilities | NA | 1,791 | 2,593 | 2,801 | 1,768 | 1,999 | 1,411 | 1,336 | 1,297 | 1,286 |
| Long Term Debt | NA | 43.5 | 74.3 | 75.8 | 76.2 | 84.7 | 90.6 | 110 | 132 | 146 |
| Common Equity | 5,087 | 5,148 | 6,012 | 5,784 | 5,418 | 5,371 | 5,114 | 4,701 | 4,583 | 4,062 |
| Total Capital | NA | 5,319 | 6,210 | 6,150 | 5,778 | 5,777 | 5,442 | 5,019 | 4,866 | 4,346 |
| Capital Expenditures | 181 | 173 | 292 | 196 | 196 | 134 | 146 | 185 | 166 | 178 |
| Cash Flow | NA | 1,310 | 3,104 | 1,360 | 1,242 | 1,293 | 1,380 | 1,246 | 1,125 | 970 |
| Current Ratio | 1.1 | 1.9 | 1.8 | 1.6 | 1.6 | 1.8 | 2.0 | 2.3 | 2.4 | 1.7 |
| % Long Term Debt of Capitalization | 1.0 | 0.8 | 1.2 | 1.2 | 1.3 | 1.5 | 1.7 | 2.2 | 2.7 | 3.4 |
| % Net Income of Revenue | 13.2 | 13.1 | 31.7 | 12.4 | 12.1 | 14.2 | 15.7 | 13.2 | 13.4 | 12.6 |
| % Return on Assets | 4.6 | 3.8 | 10.2 | 4.3 | 4.6 | 5.3 | 6.1 | 5.3 | 5.7 | 12.6 |
| % Return on Equity | 22.7 | 18.3 | 47.7 | 18.8 | 17.3 | 19.4 | 22.4 | 19.9 | 19.6 | 17.9 |

Data as orig reptd.; bef. results of disc opers/spec. items. Per share data adj. for stk. divs.; EPS diluted. E-Estimated. NA-Not Available. NM-Not Meaningful. NR-Not Ranked. UR-Under Review.

**Office:** 1 Adp Blvd, Roseland, NJ 07068-1728.
**Telephone:** 973-974-5000.
**Website:** http://www.adp.com
**Chrmn:** L.A. Brun

**Pres & CEO:** G.C. Butler
**COO:** S.M. Martone
**CFO:** F. Anderson, Jr.
**CFO:** C.R. Reidy

**Board Members:** G. D. Brenneman, L. A. Brun, G. C. Butler, L. G. Cooperman, E. C. Fast, R. G. Hubbard, J. P. Jones, III, F. V. Malek, C. H. Noski, S. Rowlands, G. L. Summe, H. Taub

**Founded:** 1949
**Domicile:** Delaware
**Employees:** 47,000

# AutoNation Inc

**STANDARD &POOR'S**

| **S&P Recommendation** HOLD ★★★☆☆ | **Price** $6.35 (as of Nov 14, 2008) | **12-Mo. Target Price** $7.50 | **Investment Style** Large-Cap Blend |
|---|---|---|---|

**GICS Sector** Consumer Discretionary
**Sub-Industry** Automotive Retail

**Summary** AutoNation, the largest U.S. retail auto dealer, owns and operates about 313 new vehicle franchises in 15 states.

## Key Stock Statistics (Source S&P, Vickers, company reports)

| | | | | | | | |
|---|---|---|---|---|---|---|---|
| 52-Wk Range | $19.59– 3.97 | S&P Oper. EPS 2008**E** | 1.03 | Market Capitalization(B) | $1.123 | Beta | 1.27 |
| Trailing 12-Month EPS | $-7.02 | S&P Oper. EPS 2009**E** | 0.92 | Yield (%) | Nil | S&P 3-Yr. Proj. EPS CAGR(%) | 6 |
| Trailing 12-Month P/E | NM | P/E on S&P Oper. EPS 2008**E** | 6.2 | Dividend Rate/Share | Nil | S&P Credit Rating | BBB- |
| $10K Invested 5 Yrs Ago | $3,536 | Common Shares Outstg. (M) | 176.9 | Institutional Ownership (%) | 98 | | |

## Price Performance

30-Week Mov. Avg. ···   10-Week Mov. Avg. - -   **GAAP Earnings vs. Previous Year**   Volume Above Avg. ⅊⅊⅊   STARS
12-Mo. Target Price —   Relative Strength —   ▲ Up ▼ Down ► No Change   Below Avg. ⅊⅊⅊   ★

Options: ASE, CBOE, P, Ph

## Highlights

► The 12-month target price for AN has recently been changed to $7.50 from $11.00. The Highlights section of this Stock Report will be updated accordingly.

## Investment Rationale/Risk

► The Investment Rationale/Risk section of this Stock Report will be updated shortly. For the latest News story on AN from MarketScope, see below.

► 11/06/08 01:09 pm ET ... S&P REITERATES HOLD OPINION ON SHARES OF AUTONATION (AN 5.62***): AN posts Q3 EPS from continuing operations of $0.25 vs. $0.39, in line with expectations, but aided by a lower tax rate. The company notes that it is in compliance with financial convenants. Following dismal October industry sales, we recently lowered our '08 industrywide light-vehicle sales forecast to 13.5M units, down 16% from '07, and '09's to 13.0M. We lower our '08 EPS estimate for AN by $0.07 to $1.03 and '09's by $0.08 to $0.92. We cut our target price by $3.50 to $7.50, blending DCF and P/E analyses. Lower earnings visibility limits our enthusiasm for the shares. /E.Levy-CFA

## Qualitative Risk Assessment

| LOW | MEDIUM | HIGH |
|---|---|---|

Our risk assessment reflects the cyclical nature of the automotive retailing industry, which is affected by interest rates, consumer confidence and personal discretionary spending, offset by the company's highly variable cost structure.

## Quantitative Evaluations

**S&P Quality Ranking** **B**

| D | C | B- | B | B+ | A- | A | A+ |
|---|---|---|---|---|---|---|---|

**Relative Strength Rank** **MODERATE**

39

LOWEST = 1   HIGHEST = 99

## Revenue/Earnings Data

**Revenue (Million $)**

| | 1Q | 2Q | 3Q | 4Q | Year |
|---|---|---|---|---|---|
| 2008 | 3,999 | 3,910 | 3,543 | -- | -- |
| 2007 | 4,395 | 4,559 | 4,602 | 4,214 | 17,692 |
| 2006 | 4,612 | 4,959 | 4,945 | 4,473 | 18,989 |
| 2005 | 4,561 | 5,019 | 5,188 | 4,485 | 19,253 |
| 2004 | 4,630 | 4,916 | 5,041 | 4,838 | 19,425 |
| 2003 | 4,459 | 5,069 | 5,257 | 4,596 | 19,381 |

**Earnings Per Share ($)**

| | | | | | |
|---|---|---|---|---|---|
| 2008 | 0.31 | 0.29 | -7.95 | E0.14 | E1.03 |
| 2007 | 0.39 | 0.38 | 0.39 | 0.27 | 1.44 |
| 2006 | 0.37 | 0.33 | 0.40 | 0.35 | 1.45 |
| 2005 | 0.33 | 0.40 | 0.45 | 0.30 | 1.48 |
| 2004 | 0.32 | 0.35 | 0.35 | 0.43 | 1.45 |
| 2003 | 0.72 | 0.37 | 0.38 | 0.28 | 1.76 |

Fiscal year ended Dec. 31. Next earnings report expected: Early February. EPS Estimates based on S&P Operating Earnings; historical GAAP earnings are as reported.

## Dividend Data

No cash dividends have been paid.

---

**Please read the Required Disclosures and Analyst Certification on the last page of this report.**

The McGraw-Hill Companies

# AutoNation Inc

STANDARD &POOR'S

## Business Summary November 05, 2008

CORPORATE OVERVIEW. AutoNation's vehicle retailing unit segment operates in saturated markets, in our view. Although the company is the largest U.S. auto retailer, it controls only about 2% of the $1 trillion U.S. new and used car market. About 75% of total U.S. vehicle sales are to replace existing autos. AN's new auto retailing operations (58% of 2007 revenues) consist of about 313 dealerships.

The sale of used vehicles accounted for nearly 24% of revenues in 2007. Fixed operations provided nearly 15% of sales, while finance and insurance and other accounted for the balance.

Investor Edward Lampert's ESL Investments Inc. owns about 40% of AutoNation's common shares.

MARKET PROFILE. The automotive retailing industry is the largest retail trade sector in the United States. It generates approximately $1.0 trillion in annual sales. The industry is highly fragmented, with the 100 largest automotive retailers generating approximately 15% of industry revenues.

Car retailing is a very competitive business. With razor-thin profit margins and highly leveraged inventories that depreciate rapidly, dealers must generate high volume and fast turnover. However, auto demand itself is driven by volatile factors such as the strength of the economy, interest rate levels, and consumer confidence. In addition, dealerships operate with high overhead costs, resulting in a high sales break-even point.

Consolidation is an important trend, as the number of franchised stores in the U.S. has declined in the past 20 years, from approximately 24,725 in 1983 to 21,522 in 2007. The large capital requirements necessary to operate and be competitive in today's retailing environment make it likely that consolidation will continue.

U.S. new vehicle sales totaled 16.1 million units in 2007 and more than 16.5 million units in 2006; we expect a drop to 13.5 million in 2008 and 13.0 in 2009.

## Company Financials Fiscal Year Ended Dec. 31

| Per Share Data ($) | 2007 | 2006 | 2005 | 2004 | 2003 | 2002 | 2001 | 2000 | 1999 | 1998 |
|---|---|---|---|---|---|---|---|---|---|---|
| Tangible Book Value | 2.37 | 2.66 | 6.53 | 4.53 | 3.91 | 3.14 | 2.99 | 2.64 | 4.72 | 11.84 |
| Cash Flow | 1.90 | 1.81 | 1.78 | 1.78 | 2.01 | 1.40 | 1.18 | 1.28 | 0.07 | 2.94 |
| Earnings | 1.44 | 1.45 | 1.48 | 1.45 | 1.76 | 1.19 | 0.73 | 0.91 | -0.07 | 0.71 |
| S&P Core Earnings | 1.44 | 1.45 | 1.44 | 1.41 | 1.69 | 1.12 | 0.57 | NA | NA | NA |
| Dividends | Nil | Nil | Nil | Nil | Nil | Nil | Nil | Nil | Nil | Nil |
| Payout Ratio | Nil | Nil | Nil | Nil | Nil | Nil | Nil | Nil | Nil | Nil |
| Prices:High | 23.19 | 22.94 | 22.84 | 19.33 | 19.19 | 18.73 | 13.07 | 10.75 | 18.38 | 30.00 |
| Prices:Low | 14.65 | 18.95 | 17.91 | 15.01 | 11.61 | 9.05 | 4.94 | 4.63 | 7.50 | 10.00 |
| P/E Ratio:High | 16 | 16 | 15 | 13 | 11 | 16 | 18 | 12 | NM | 42 |
| P/E Ratio:Low | 10 | 13 | 12 | 10 | 7 | 8 | 7 | 5 | NM | 14 |

| Income Statement Analysis (Million $) | 2007 | 2006 | 2005 | 2004 | 2003 | 2002 | 2001 | 2000 | 1999 | 1998 |
|---|---|---|---|---|---|---|---|---|---|---|
| Revenue | 17,692 | 18,989 | 19,253 | 19,425 | 19,381 | 19,479 | 19,989 | 20,610 | 20,112 | 16,118 |
| Operating Income | 798 | 879 | 888 | 861 | 805 | 786 | 667 | 855 | 461 | 1,588 |
| Depreciation | 91.7 | 82.9 | 80.7 | 89.7 | 71.0 | 69.7 | 152 | 134 | 60.0 | 1,052 |
| Interest Expense | 247 | 267 | 191 | 159 | 143 | 125 | 43.7 | 248 | 35.0 | 22.0 |
| Pretax Income | 459 | 542 | 623 | 607 | 591 | 618 | 401 | 525 | -27.0 | 523 |
| Effective Tax Rate | 37.3% | 38.9% | 36.5% | 34.7% | 14.4% | 38.3% | 38.9% | 37.5% | NM | 35.9% |
| Net Income | 288 | 331 | 396 | 396 | 506 | 382 | 245 | 328 | -31.0 | 335 |
| S&P Core Earnings | 288 | 331 | 385 | 385 | 486 | 359 | 192 | NA | NA | NA |

| Balance Sheet & Other Financial Data (Million $) | 2007 | 2006 | 2005 | 2004 | 2003 | 2002 | 2001 | 2000 | 1999 | 1998 |
|---|---|---|---|---|---|---|---|---|---|---|
| Cash | 32.8 | 52.2 | 244 | 107 | 171 | 176 | 128 | 82.2 | 369 | 217 |
| Current Assets | 3,238 | 3,386 | 3,880 | 3,678 | 3,990 | 3,629 | 3,153 | 4,176 | 4,301 | 8,406 |
| Total Assets | 8,480 | 8,607 | 8,825 | 8,699 | 8,823 | 8,585 | 8,065 | 8,830 | 9,613 | 13,926 |
| Current Liabilities | 2,902 | 3,031 | 3,412 | 3,411 | 3,810 | 2,981 | 2,578 | 3,141 | 3,165 | 5,540 |
| Long Term Debt | 3,917 | 1,558 | 484 | 798 | 808 | 643 | 647 | 850 | 836 | 2,316 |
| Common Equity | 3,474 | 3,713 | 4,670 | 4,263 | 3,950 | 3,910 | 3,828 | 3,843 | 4,601 | 5,425 |
| Total Capital | 5,446 | 5,496 | 5,340 | 5,218 | 4,935 | 5,500 | 5,329 | 5,570 | 6,241 | 9,968 |
| Capital Expenditures | 160 | 170 | 132 | 133 | 133 | 183 | 164 | 148 | 242 | 438 |
| Cash Flow | 380 | 414 | 476 | 486 | 577 | 451 | 397 | 462 | 29.0 | 1,387 |
| Current Ratio | 1.1 | 1.1 | 1.1 | 1.1 | 1.0 | 1.2 | 1.2 | 1.3 | 1.4 | 1.5 |
| % Long Term Debt of Capitalization | 33.5 | 28.3 | 9.1 | 15.3 | 16.4 | 11.7 | 12.1 | 15.3 | 13.4 | 29.1 |
| % Net Income of Revenue | 1.6 | 1.7 | 2.1 | 2.0 | 2.6 | 2.0 | 1.2 | 1.6 | NM | 2.1 |
| % Return on Assets | 3.4 | 3.8 | 4.5 | 4.5 | 5.8 | 4.6 | 2.9 | 3.6 | NM | 2.8 |
| % Return on Equity | 8.0 | 7.9 | 8.9 | 9.7 | 12.9 | 9.9 | 6.4 | 7.8 | NM | 7.5 |

Data as orig reptd.; bef. results of disc opers/spec. items. Per share data adj. for stk. divs.; EPS diluted. E-Estimated. NA-Not Available. NM-Not Meaningful. NR-Not Ranked. UR-Under Review.

**Office:** 110 SE 6th St, Ft. Lauderdale, FL 33301-5012.
**Telephone:** 954-769-6000.
**Website:** http://www.autonation.com
**Chrmn & CEO:** M. Jackson

**Pres & COO:** M.E. Maroone
**EVP & CFO:** M.J. Short
**EVP, Secy & General Counsel:** J.P. Ferrando
**Chief Acctg Officer & Cntlr:** M.J. Stephan

**Board Members:** R. L. Burdick, W. C. Crowley, D. B. Edelson, K. Goodman, R. R. Grusky, M. Jackson, M. E. Maroone, C. A. Migoya

**Founded:** 1991
**Domicile:** Delaware
**Employees:** 25,000

# AutoZone Inc

| S&P Recommendation | HOLD ★★★☆☆ | Price $105.76 (as of Nov 14, 2008) | 12-Mo. Target Price $145.00 | Investment Style Large-Cap Growth |
|---|---|---|---|---|

**GICS Sector** Consumer Discretionary
**Sub-Industry** Automotive Retail

**Summary** This retailer of automotive parts and accessories operates over 4,000 AutoZone stores throughout most of the U.S. and in Mexico.

## Key Stock Statistics (Source S&P, Vickers, company reports)

| | | | | | | | |
|---|---|---|---|---|---|---|---|
| 52-Wk Range | $143.80–93.55 | S&P Oper. EPS 2009E | 10.65 | Market Capitalization(B) | $6.131 | Beta | 0.94 |
| Trailing 12-Month EPS | $10.05 | S&P Oper. EPS 2010E | 11.58 | Yield (%) | Nil | S&P 3-Yr. Proj. EPS CAGR(%) | 9 |
| Trailing 12-Month P/E | 10.5 | P/E on S&P Oper. EPS 2009E | 9.9 | Dividend Rate/Share | Nil | S&P Credit Rating | BBB |
| $10K Invested 5 Yrs Ago | $11,556 | Common Shares Outstg. (M) | 58.0 | Institutional Ownership (%) | NM | | |

## Price Performance

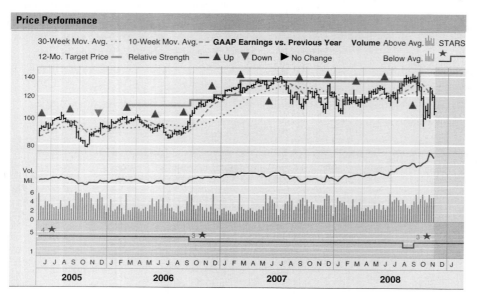

30-Week Mov. Avg. · · · 10-Week Mov. Avg. – – GAAP Earnings vs. Previous Year Volume Above Avg. STARS
12-Mo. Target Price — Relative Strength — ▲ Up ▼ Down ► No Change Below Avg. ★

Options: ASE, CBOE, P, Ph

Analysis prepared by **Michael Souers** on September 24, 2008, when the stock traded at **$ 125.70**.

## Highlights

➤ We see sales growth of 1.9% in FY 09 (Aug.), following a 5.7% advance in FY 08. This reflects our projections of approximately 200 new stores and flat to slightly higher same-store sales growth, offset by one fewer week of sales (52, versus 53 in FY 08). We think rising gasoline prices are posing a financial burden on consumers, inducing them to delay preventative maintenance on their vehicles.

➤ We look for operating margins to widen slightly, as supply chain efficiencies, direct importing initiatives, well-controlled store and payroll costs, and a greater share of wider-margin private label products in the retail segment outweigh an expected increased proportion of lower-margin commercial sales in the mix, greater occupancy costs and higher projected advertising and marketing spending.

➤ Reflecting our estimates of slightly lower interest expense, effective taxes at 37.0%, and about 3% fewer shares due to AZO's active share repurchase program, we forecast that FY 09 operating EPS will increase 6%, to $10.65, from the $10.04 earned in FY 08. We project FY 10 EPS of $11.58.

## Investment Rationale/Risk

➤ Following a nearly 10% decrease in the share price over the past few weeks, we now think AZO is fairly valued, and our recommendation is hold. The company maintains an industry-leading sales-to-square foot ratio, and sports higher gross, operating, and net margins than any of its peers. However, recent sales trends have been rather weak, in our opinion. Despite what we view as a rational pricing environment, we think margins will likely be pressured if same-store sales trends fail to improve from those in recent years. Longer term, we expect AZO to benefit from what we see as favorable vehicle demographic trends.

➤ Risks to our recommendation and target price include a significant decline in consumer spending; a rebound in oil prices; a decrease in auto usage and miles driven; and declines in same-store-sales, which would cause expense deleverage.

➤ Our 12-month target price of $145, based on our DCF analysis, is equal to about 14X our FY 09 EPS estimate. Our DCF model assumes a weighted average cost of capital of 9.3% and a terminal growth rate of 3.0%.

## Qualitative Risk Assessment

| LOW | MEDIUM | HIGH |
|---|---|---|

Our risk assessment for AutoZone reflects the cyclical and seasonal nature of the auto parts retailing industry, which is sensitive to various economic data points, offset by what we view as the company's strong financial metrics and margins.

## Quantitative Evaluations

**S&P Quality Ranking** B+

| D | C | B- | B | B+ | A- | A | A+ |
|---|---|---|---|---|---|---|---|

**Relative Strength Rank** STRONG

71

LOWEST = 1   HIGHEST = 99

## Revenue/Earnings Data

**Revenue (Million $)**

| | 1Q | 2Q | 3Q | 4Q | Year |
|---|---|---|---|---|---|
| 2008 | 1,456 | 1,339 | 1,517 | -2,211 | 6,523 |
| 2007 | 1,393 | 1,300 | 1,474 | 2,003 | 6,170 |
| 2006 | 1,338 | 1,254 | 1,417 | 1,939 | 5,948 |
| 2005 | 1,286 | 1,204 | 1,338 | 1,882 | 5,711 |
| 2004 | 1,282 | 1,159 | 1,360 | 1,836 | 5,637 |
| 2003 | 1,219 | 1,121 | 1,288 | 1,830 | 5,457 |

**Earnings Per Share ($)**

| | | | | | |
|---|---|---|---|---|---|
| 2008 | 2.02 | 1.67 | 2.49 | 3.88 | 10.05 |
| 2007 | 1.73 | 1.45 | 2.17 | 3.23 | 8.53 |
| 2006 | 1.48 | 1.25 | 1.89 | 2.92 | 7.50 |
| 2005 | 1.52 | 1.16 | 1.86 | 2.66 | 7.18 |
| 2004 | 1.35 | 1.04 | 1.68 | 2.53 | 6.56 |
| 2003 | 1.04 | 0.79 | 1.30 | 2.27 | 5.34 |

Fiscal year ended Aug. 31. Next earnings report expected: Early December. EPS Estimates based on S&P Operating Earnings; historical GAAP earnings are as reported.

## Dividend Data

No cash dividends have been paid.

# AutoZone Inc

**STANDARD &POOR'S**

## Business Summary September 24, 2008

CORPORATE OVERVIEW. AutoZone is the nation's leading specialty retailer and a leading distributor of automotive replacement parts and accessories, focusing primarily on do-it-yourself (DIY) consumers. As of August 25, 2007, the company operated 3,933 U.S. AutoZone stores, in 48 states, the District of Columbia and Puerto Rico, and 123 stores in Mexico. AZO also sells automotive diagnostic equipment and repair software through ALLDATA, and diagnostic and repair information, along with and parts and accessories, online at www.autozone.com.

The company's 3,933 U.S. stores represented 25.1 million sq. ft., up from 3,771 stores and 24.0 million sq. ft. a year earlier. Each store's product line includes new and remanufactured automotive hard parts, such as alternators, starters, water pumps, brake shoes and pads, carburetors, clutches and engines; maintenance items, such as oil, antifreeze, transmission, brake and power steering fluids, engine additives, protectants and waxes; and accessories, such as car stereos and floor mats. Parts are carried for domestic and foreign cars, sport utility vehicles, vans, and light trucks.

Stores, generally in high-visibility locations, range in size from about 4,000 sq. ft. to 8,100 sq. ft., with new stores increasingly using a larger format. As of August 25, 2007, AutoZone stores were principally in the following locations: 492 stores in Texas, 428 in California, 205 in Ohio, 192 in Illinois, 173 in Florida, 160 in Georgia, 145 in Tennessee, 145 in North Carolina, 133 in Michigan, 125 in Indiana, 112 in New York, 110 in Arizona, and 101 in Pennsylvania, with the rest in other states.

CORPORATE STRATEGY. AZO offers everyday low prices, and attempts to be the price leader in hard parts. Stores generally carry about 21,000 stock-keeping units. In addition to targeting the DIY customer, the company also has a commercial sales program in the U.S. (AZ Commercial), which provides commercial credit and delivery of parts and other products to local, regional and national repair garages, dealers and service stations. As of August 25, 2007, 2,182 stores had commercial sales programs. The hub stores provide fast replenishment of key merchandise to support the DIY and commercial sales businesses. AZO does not perform repairs or installations.

## Company Financials Fiscal Year Ended Aug. 31

| Per Share Data ($) | 2008 | 2007 | 2006 | 2005 | 2004 | 2003 | 2002 | 2001 | 2000 | 1999 |
|---|---|---|---|---|---|---|---|---|---|---|
| Tangible Book Value | NM | 1.52 | 2.35 | 1.15 | NM | 0.90 | 3.87 | 5.13 | 5.49 | 6.83 |
| Cash Flow | NA | 10.82 | 9.34 | 8.92 | 7.79 | 6.47 | 5.10 | 2.70 | 2.88 | 2.44 |
| Earnings | 10.05 | 8.53 | 7.50 | 7.18 | 6.56 | 5.34 | 4.00 | 1.54 | 2.00 | 1.63 |
| S&P Core Earnings | 9.91 | 8.53 | 7.50 | 7.03 | 6.40 | 5.09 | 3.87 | 1.45 | NA | NA |
| Dividends | NA | Nil | Nil | Nil | Nil | Nil | Nil | Nil | Nil | Nil |
| Payout Ratio | NA | Nil | Nil | Nil | Nil | Nil | Nil | Nil | Nil | Nil |
| Prices:High | NA | 140.29 | 120.37 | 103.94 | 92.35 | 103.53 | 89.34 | 80.00 | 32.50 | 37.31 |
| Prices:Low | NA | 103.40 | 83.81 | 77.76 | 70.35 | 58.21 | 59.20 | 24.37 | 21.00 | 22.56 |
| P/E Ratio:High | NA | 16 | 16 | 14 | 14 | 19 | 22 | 52 | 16 | 23 |
| P/E Ratio:Low | NA | 12 | 11 | 11 | 11 | 11 | 15 | 16 | 10 | 14 |

| Income Statement Analysis (Million $) | 2008 | 2007 | 2006 | 2005 | 2004 | 2003 | 2002 | 2001 | 2000 | 1999 |
|---|---|---|---|---|---|---|---|---|---|---|
| Revenue | 6,523 | 6,170 | 5,948 | 5,711 | 5,637 | 5,457 | 5,326 | 4,818 | 4,483 | 4,116 |
| Operating Income | NA | 1,215 | 1,239 | 1,114 | 1,106 | 1,028 | 889 | 646 | 630 | 555 |
| Depreciation | 170 | 159 | 139 | 138 | 107 | 110 | 118 | 131 | 118 | 122 |
| Interest Expense | NA | 119 | 110 | 104 | 93.0 | 84.8 | 79.9 | 101 | 76.8 | 45.3 |
| Pretax Income | 1,007 | 936 | 902 | 873 | 906 | 833 | 691 | 287 | 435 | 388 |
| Effective Tax Rate | 36.3% | 36.4% | 36.9% | 34.6% | 37.5% | 37.9% | 38.1% | 38.8% | 38.5% | 36.9% |
| Net Income | 642 | 596 | 569 | 571 | 566 | 518 | 428 | 176 | 268 | 245 |
| S&P Core Earnings | 633 | 596 | 569 | 560 | 553 | 492 | 415 | 165 | NA | NA |

| Balance Sheet & Other Financial Data (Million $) | 2008 | 2007 | 2006 | 2005 | 2004 | 2003 | 2002 | 2001 | 2000 | 1999 |
|---|---|---|---|---|---|---|---|---|---|---|
| Cash | 242 | 86.7 | 91.6 | 74.8 | 76.9 | 6.74 | 6.50 | 7.29 | 6.97 | 5.92 |
| Current Assets | NA | 2,270 | 2,119 | 1,929 | 1,756 | 1,585 | 1,450 | 1,329 | 1,187 | 1,225 |
| Total Assets | 5,257 | 4,805 | 4,526 | 4,245 | 3,913 | 3,680 | 3,478 | 3,433 | 3,333 | 3,285 |
| Current Liabilities | NA | 2,286 | 2,055 | 1,811 | 1,818 | 1,676 | 1,534 | 1,267 | 1,035 | 1,001 |
| Long Term Debt | NA | 1,936 | 1,857 | 1,862 | 1,869 | 1,547 | 1,195 | 1,225 | 1,250 | 888 |
| Common Equity | 230 | 403 | 470 | 391 | 171 | 374 | 1,378 | 866 | 997 | 1,324 |
| Total Capital | NA | 2,339 | 2,327 | 2,253 | 2,046 | 1,921 | 2,573 | 2,092 | 2,247 | 2,212 |
| Capital Expenditures | 244 | 224 | 264 | 283 | 185 | 182 | 117 | 169 | 250 | 428 |
| Cash Flow | NA | 755 | 709 | 709 | 673 | 627 | 546 | 307 | 386 | 367 |
| Current Ratio | 1.0 | 1.0 | 1.0 | 1.1 | 1.0 | 0.9 | 0.9 | 1.0 | 1.1 | 1.2 |
| % Long Term Debt of Capitalization | 90.7 | 82.8 | 79.8 | 82.6 | 91.3 | 80.5 | 46.4 | 58.6 | 55.6 | 40.2 |
| % Net Income of Revenue | 9.8 | 9.7 | 9.6 | 10.0 | 10.0 | 9.5 | 8.0 | 3.6 | 6.0 | 5.9 |
| % Return on Assets | 12.8 | 12.8 | 13.0 | 14.0 | 14.7 | 14.5 | 12.4 | 5.2 | 8.1 | 8.1 |
| % Return on Equity | 202.8 | 136.5 | 132.3 | 203.1 | 207.7 | 97.4 | 27.5 | 18.9 | 23.1 | 18.6 |

Data as orig reptd.; bef. results of disc opers/spec. items. Per share data adj. for stk. divs.; EPS diluted. E-Estimated. NA-Not Available. NM-Not Meaningful. NR-Not Ranked. UR-Under Review.

**Office:** 123 South Front Street, Memphis, TN 38103-3607.
**Telephone:** 901-495-6500.
**Email:** investor.relations@autozone.com
**Website:** http://www.autozone.com

**Chrmn, Pres & CEO:** W.C. Rhodes, III
**EVP & CFO:** W.T. Giles
**EVP, Secy & General Counsel:** H.L. Goldsmith
**SVP & Cntlr:** C. Pleas, III

**SVP & CIO:** J.A. Bascom
**Investor Contact:** B. Campbell (901-495-7005)
**Board Members:** W. C. Crowley, C. Elson, S. E. Gove, E. B. Graves, Jr., R. R. Grusky, N. G. House, J. R. Hyde, III, W. A. McKenna, G. R. Mrkonic, Jr., L. P. Nieto, Jr., W. C. Rhodes, III, T. W. Ullyot

**Founded:** 1979
**Domicile:** Nevada
**Employees:** 57,000

*The McGraw-Hill Companies*

# AvalonBay Communities Inc.

STANDARD
&POOR'S

| S&P Recommendation **HOLD** ★★★☆☆ | Price $55.46 (as of Nov 14, 2008) | 12-Mo. Target Price $67.00 | Investment Style Large-Cap Blend |
|---|---|---|---|

**GICS Sector** Financials
**Sub-Industry** Residential REITS

**Summary** This real estate investment trust, formed via the 1998 merger of Bay Apartment Communities and Avalon Properties, specializes in upscale apartment communities.

## Key Stock Statistics (Source S&P, Vickers, company reports)

| | | | | | | | |
|---|---|---|---|---|---|---|---|
| 52-Wk Range | $113.07– 52.48 | S&P FFO/Sh. 2008E | 5.05 | Market Capitalization(B) | $4.273 | Beta | 1.01 |
| Trailing 12-Month FFO/Share | NA | S&P FFO/Sh. 2009E | 5.15 | Yield (%) | 6.44 | S&P 3-Yr. FFO/Sh. Proj. CAGR(%) | 6 |
| Trailing 12-Month P/FFO | NA | P/FFO on S&P FFO/Sh. 2008E | 11.0 | Dividend Rate/Share | $3.57 | S&P Credit Rating | BBB+ |
| $10K Invested 5 Yrs Ago | $14,019 | Common Shares Outstg. (M) | 77.0 | Institutional Ownership (%) | NM | | |

## Price Performance

30-Week Mov. Avg. ···· 10-Week Mov. Avg. --- **GAAP Earnings vs. Previous Year** Volume Above Avg. STARS
12-Mo. Target Price — Relative Strength — ▲ Up ▼ Down ► No Change Below Avg. ★

Options: ASE, CBOE, P

## Qualitative Risk Assessment

| LOW | MEDIUM | HIGH |
|---|---|---|

Our risk assessment reflects AVB's geographically diverse asset base, strong dividend coverage ratio and low stock price volatility.

## Quantitative Evaluations

**S&P Quality Ranking** A

| D | C | B- | B | B+ | A- | A | A+ |
|---|---|---|---|---|---|---|---|

**Relative Strength Rank** MODERATE

35

LOWEST = 1    HIGHEST = 99

## Revenue/FFO Data

**Revenue (Million $)**

| | 1Q | 2Q | 3Q | 4Q | Year |
|---|---|---|---|---|---|
| 2008 | 211.8 | 217.9 | 219.7 | -- | -- |
| 2007 | 192.7 | 199.5 | 208.2 | 212.4 | 871.9 |
| 2006 | 175.2 | 180.7 | 187.7 | 193.8 | 737.3 |
| 2005 | 161.3 | 165.6 | 170.8 | 173.1 | 670.7 |
| 2004 | 154.8 | 160.0 | 165.2 | 168.4 | 648.5 |
| 2003 | 149.7 | 151.0 | 153.2 | 155.8 | 609.7 |

**FFO Per Share ($)**

| | 1Q | 2Q | 3Q | 4Q | Year |
|---|---|---|---|---|---|
| 2008 | 1.24 | 1.26 | E1.28 | E1.27 | E5.05 |
| 2007 | 1.11 | 1.17 | 1.19 | E1.18 | E4.65 |
| 2006 | 1.15 | 1.03 | 1.11 | 1.09 | 4.38 |
| 2005 | 0.96 | 0.97 | 0.91 | 0.93 | 3.77 |
| 2004 | 0.79 | 0.83 | 0.86 | 0.88 | 3.36 |
| 2003 | 0.83 | 0.83 | 0.80 | 0.81 | 3.27 |

Fiscal year ended Dec. 31. Next earnings report expected: Early February. FFO Estimates based on S&P Funds From Operations Est..

## Highlights

► The 12-month target price for AVB has recently been changed to $67.00 from $86.00. The Highlights section of this Stock Report will be updated accordingly.

## Investment Rationale/Risk

► The Investment Rationale/Risk section of this Stock Report will be updated shortly. For the latest News story on AVB from MarketScope, see below.

► 11/06/08 10:56 am ET ... S&P MAINTAINS HOLD OPINION ON SHARES OF AVALONBAY COMMUNITIES (AVB 61.5***): Q3 per-share funds from operations of $1.28 vs. $1.19, matches our estimate. On a same-property basis, income rises a moderate 2.0%, reflecting softer rental rates in the Mid-Atlantic and Southern California markets. Northern California and the Pacific Northwest markets remain strong. We keep our '08 FFO estimate of $5.05. However, we think AVB's high-end properties could meet resistance to monthly rental increases in 2009. We lower our '09 FFO estimate by $0.10 to $5.15. Our target price of $67, cut $19, is 13.0X our '09 FFO outlook, still a premium to peers. /R. Shepard

## Dividend Data (Dates: mm/dd Payment Date: mm/dd/yy)

| Amount ($) | Date Decl. | Ex-Div. Date | Stk. of Record | Payment Date |
|---|---|---|---|---|
| 0.850 | 12/14 | 12/27 | 12/31 | 01/15/08 |
| 0.893 | 02/05 | 03/28 | 04/01 | 04/15/08 |
| 0.893 | 06/16 | 06/26 | 06/30 | 07/15/08 |
| 0.893 | 09/18 | 10/01 | 10/03 | 10/15/08 |

Dividends have been paid since 1994. Source: Company reports.

# AvalonBay Communities Inc.

**STANDARD &POOR'S**

## Business Summary October 10, 2008

CORPORATE OVERVIEW. AvalonBay Communities (AVB) is a real estate investment trust (REIT) specializing in the ownership of multi-family apartment communities. At December 31, 2007, AVB owned or held an interest in 182 apartment communities containing 52,748 apartment homes in 10 states and the District of Columbia, of which 21 communities were under construction and nine communities were under reconstruction. AVB also owned a direct or indirect ownership interest in rights to develop an additional 48 communities; if developed in the manner expected, these would contain an estimated 13,656 apartment homes.

MARKET PROFILE. The housing market is highly fragmented and is broadly characterized by two types of housing units, multi-family and single-family. At the end of 2007, the U.S. Census Bureau estimated that there were 128.65 million housing units in the country, an increase of 1.6% from 2006. Partially on high fragmentation and the fact that residents have the option of either being owners or tenants (renters), the housing market can be highly competitive. Main demand drivers for apartments are household formation and employment growth. We estimate that 1.1 million new households were formed in

2007. Supply is created by new housing unit construction, which could consist of single-family homes, or multifamily apartment buildings or condominiums. We forecast 0.93 million housing unit starts in 2008, down about 31% from 2007. We expect multi-family starts to drop significantly less, falling approximately 6%.

With apartment tenants on relatively short leases compared to those of commercial and industrial properties, we believe apartment REITs are generally more sensitive to changes in market conditions than REITs in other property categories. Results could be hurt by new construction that adds new space in excess of actual demand. Trends in home price affordability also affect both rent levels and the level of new construction, since the relative price attractiveness of owning versus renting is an important factor in consumer decision making.

## Company Financials Fiscal Year Ended Dec. 31

| Per Share Data ($) | 2007 | 2006 | 2005 | 2004 | 2003 | 2002 | 2001 | 2000 | 1999 | 1998 |
|---|---|---|---|---|---|---|---|---|---|---|
| Tangible Book Value | 37.85 | NA | NA | NA | NA | 31.88 | NA | 29.31 | 36.04 | 36.42 |
| Earnings | 3.00 | 2.27 | 1.34 | 1.09 | 1.30 | 1.48 | 3.12 | 2.53 | 2.00 | 1.37 |
| S&P Core Earnings | 3.00 | 2.27 | 1.34 | 1.09 | 1.27 | 1.22 | 3.07 | NA | NA | NA |
| Dividends | 3.33 | NA | NA | NA | NA | NA | 2.56 | 2.24 | 2.05 | 1.86 |
| Payout Ratio | 111% | 137% | NM | NM | NM | 188% | 82% | 89% | 102% | 136% |
| Prices:High | 149.94 | 134.60 | 92.99 | 75.93 | 49.71 | 52.65 | 51.90 | 50.63 | 37.00 | 39.25 |
| Prices:Low | 88.94 | 88.95 | 64.98 | 46.72 | 35.24 | 36.38 | 42.45 | 32.63 | 30.81 | 30.50 |
| P/E Ratio:High | 50 | 59 | 69 | 65 | 38 | 35 | 17 | 20 | 18 | 29 |
| P/E Ratio:Low | 30 | 39 | 48 | 40 | 27 | 24 | 14 | 13 | 15 | 22 |

| Income Statement Analysis (Million $) | | | | | | | | | | |
|---|---|---|---|---|---|---|---|---|---|---|
| Rental Income | 807 | 731 | 666 | 648 | Nil | Nil | 637 | 572 | 503 | 352 |
| Mortgage Income | Nil | Nil | Nil | Nil | Nil | Nil | Nil | Nil | Nil | Nil |
| Total Income | 813 | 737 | 671 | 648 | 610 | 639 | 642 | 573 | 505 | 353 |
| General Expenses | 346 | 236 | 376 | 368 | 192 | 247 | 229 | 203 | 186 | 133 |
| Interest Expense | 97.5 | 111 | 127 | 131 | 135 | 121 | 103 | 83.6 | 74.7 | 54.0 |
| Provision for Losses | Nil | Nil | Nil | Nil | Nil | Nil | Nil | Nil | Nil | Nil |
| Depreciation | 180 | 163 | 159 | 152 | 151 | 144 | 130 | 123 | 110 | 78.4 |
| Net Income | 248 | 180 | 108 | 86.3 | 100 | 121 | 249 | 211 | 172 | 94.4 |
| S&P Core Earnings | 239 | 171 | 98.9 | 76.7 | 87.6 | 85.7 | 213 | NA | NA | NA |

| Balance Sheet & Other Financial Data (Million $) | | | | | | | | | | |
|---|---|---|---|---|---|---|---|---|---|---|
| Cash | 210 | 146 | 48.0 | 4,921 | 4,744 | 4,813 | 4,479 | 4,286 | 4,068 | 16.4 |
| Total Assets | 6,736 | 5,813 | 5,165 | 5,068 | 4,910 | 4,952 | 4,664 | 4,397 | 4,155 | 4,030 |
| Real Estate Investment | 5,038 | 5,662 | 5,874 | NA | 5,431 | 5,369 | 4,838 | 4,875 | 4,259 | 4,034 |
| Loss Reserve | Nil | Nil | Nil | NA | Nil | Nil | Nil | Nil | Nil | Nil |
| Net Investment | 6,297 | 4,562 | 4,946 | 4,919 | 4,736 | 4,800 | 4,391 | 4,212 | 4,052 | 3,891 |
| Short Term Debt | 514 | Nil | Nil | Nil | Nil | 165 | 101 | 14.1 | 3.60 | 4.50 |
| Capitalization:Debt | 2,694 | 2,705 | 2,177 | 2,335 | 2,337 | 2,307 | 1,983 | 1,716 | 1,411 | 1,480 |
| Capitalization:Equity | 3,027 | 2,631 | 2,542 | 2,385 | 2,311 | 2,194 | 2,314 | 2,442 | 2,370 | 2,339 |
| Capitalization:Total | 5,534 | 5,194 | 4,738 | 4,741 | 2,336 | 4,579 | 4,353 | 4,208 | 3,817 | 5.60 |
| % Earnings & Depreciation/Assets | 6.8 | 6.2 | 5.2 | NA | 5.1 | 5.5 | 8.4 | 7.8 | 6.8 | 6.5 |
| Price Times Book Value:High | 4.0 | 4.0 | 2.8 | NA | 1.5 | 1.7 | 1.6 | 1.7 | 1.0 | 1.1 |
| Price Times Book Value:Low | 2.3 | 2.7 | 2.0 | NA | 1.1 | 1.1 | 1.3 | 1.1 | 0.9 | 0.8 |

Data as orig reptd.; bef. results of disc opers/spec. items. Per share data adj. for stk. divs.; EPS diluted. E-Estimated. NA-Not Available. NM-Not Meaningful. NR-Not Ranked. UR-Under Review.

**Office:** 2900 Eisenhower Avenue, Alexandria, VA 22314.
**Telephone:** 703-329-6300.
**Email:** investments@avalonbay.com
**Website:** http://www.avalonbay.com

**Chrmn & CEO:** B. Blair
**Pres:** T.J. Naughton
**COO:** L.S. Horey
**EVP, CFO & Chief Acctg Officer:** T.J. Sargeant

**SVP, Secy & General Counsel:** E.M. Schulman
**Board Members:** B. Blair, B. A. Choate, J. J. Healy, Jr., G. M. Meyer, T. J. Naughton, L. R. Primis, P. S. Rummell, H. J. Sarles, W. E. Walter

**Founded:** 1978
**Domicile:** Maryland
**Employees:** 1,898

**The McGraw·Hill Companies**

# Avery Dennison Corp

**STANDARD &POOR'S**

| S&P Recommendation HOLD ★★★☆☆ | Price | 12-Mo. Target Price | Investment Style |
|---|---|---|---|
| | $30.63 (as of Nov 14, 2008) | $40.00 | Large-Cap Blend |

**GICS Sector** Industrials
**Sub-Industry** Office Services & Supplies

**Summary** This company is a leading worldwide manufacturer of pressure-sensitive adhesives and materials, office products, labels, retail systems and specialty chemicals.

## Key Stock Statistics (Source S&P, Vickers, company reports)

| | | | | | | | |
|---|---|---|---|---|---|---|---|
| 52-Wk Range | $55.00–28.74 | S&P Oper. EPS 2008**E** | 3.20 | Market Capitalization(B) | $3.256 | Beta | 0.92 |
| Trailing 12-Month EPS | $3.06 | S&P Oper. EPS 2009**E** | 3.80 | Yield (%) | 5.35 | S&P 3-Yr. Proj. EPS CAGR(%) | 10 |
| Trailing 12-Month P/E | 10.0 | P/E on S&P Oper. EPS 2008**E** | 9.6 | Dividend Rate/Share | $1.64 | S&P Credit Rating | BBB+ |
| $10K Invested 5 Yrs Ago | $6,843 | Common Shares Outstg. (M) | 106.3 | Institutional Ownership (%) | 90 | | |

## Price Performance

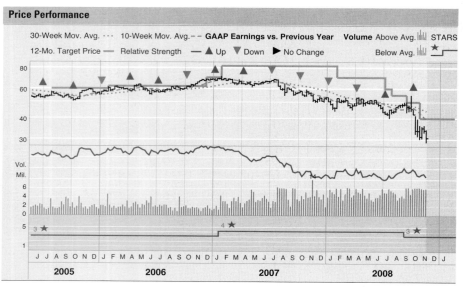

30-Week Mov. Avg. · · · 10-Week Mov. Avg. – – GAAP Earnings vs. Previous Year   Volume Above Avg. STARS
12-Mo. Target Price —  Relative Strength — ▲ Up ▼ Down ► No Change    Below Avg.

Options: CBOE, P, Ph

Analysis prepared by **Richard O'Reilly, CFA** on October 27, 2008, when the stock traded at **$ 30.88**.

## Highlights

➤ We expect sales in 2009 to decline modestly, on unfavorable currency exchange rates, after a rise for 2008 of about 8.5%, including a full-year contribution from the June 2007 purchase of Paxar Corp., which should account for about three-quarter of the increase, and favorable exchange rates. We see ongoing sales benefiting in 2009 amid continued good growth expected in Asia and Latin America businesses, offsetting consumer and retail markets softness in North America and Europe.

➤ The economically sensitive graphics and specialty tapes and films product lines will likely remain sluggish. Margins should be helped by additional price increases for the beginning of 2009 and a possible easing of raw material cost inflation.

➤ We expect accretion from Paxar of almost $0.45 a share in 2008 as AVY realizes nearly 100% of its projected $120 million in annual merger cost savings in early 2009. We also project additional restructuring savings, but a higher tax rate of about 18%, versus 9%. Our EPS estimate for 2008 excludes special charges of about $0.50, including $0.38 in the first nine months.

## Investment Rationale/Risk

➤ While organic growth in 2008 has again been slower than we had expected, we see stronger comparisons beginning in 2009. We believe fundamentals remain sound, with growth driven by the increasing use of non-impact printing systems for computers and for product tracking and information needs. We see a proliferation of high-quality graphics on packaging and consumer products spurring sales of pressure-sensitive labels. We view favorably the purchase in 2007 of Paxar, a major competitor in the product identification industry, and expect significant cost savings over the next two years.

➤ Risks to our recommendation and target price include the potentially adverse impact of remaining antitrust investigations and related civil suits involving AVY, an inability to introduce new products or raise selling prices in response to changes in raw material costs, and risks related to integration of the Paxar acquisition.

➤ Our 12-month target price is $40. We value AVY shares using a P/E of about 10.5X our 2009 EPS projection, below the stock's historical premium to the S&P 500 of almost 20% on a P/E basis.

## Qualitative Risk Assessment

| LOW | MEDIUM | HIGH |
|---|---|---|

Our risk assessment reflects the company's leading market shares in pressure-sensitive adhesives and office products, and our view of above-average growth rates in key end markets and a relatively strong balance sheet, offset by current sluggish domestic markets. The stock's S&P Quality Ranking is A-, the third highest possible, indicating a solid 10-year historical record of earnings and dividend growth.

## Quantitative Evaluations

**S&P Quality Ranking**  A-

| D | C | B- | B | B+ | A- | A | A+ |
|---|---|---|---|---|---|---|---|

**Relative Strength Rank**  MODERATE

51

LOWEST = 1     HIGHEST = 99

## Revenue/Earnings Data

**Revenue (Million $)**

| | 1Q | 2Q | 3Q | 4Q | Year |
|---|---|---|---|---|---|
| 2008 | 1,645 | 1,829 | 1,725 | -- | -- |
| 2007 | 1,390 | 1,524 | 1,680 | 1,714 | 6,308 |
| 2006 | 1,337 | 1,410 | 1,418 | 1,411 | 5,576 |
| 2005 | 1,346 | 1,419 | 1,363 | 1,364 | 5,474 |
| 2004 | 1,247 | 1,324 | 1,336 | 1,434 | 5,341 |
| 2003 | 1,135 | 1,192 | 1,204 | 1,231 | 4,763 |

**Earnings Per Share ($)**

| | 1Q | 2Q | 3Q | 4Q | Year |
|---|---|---|---|---|---|
| 2008 | 0.69 | 0.93 | 0.63 | E0.56 | E3.20 |
| 2007 | 0.80 | 0.87 | 0.59 | 0.81 | 3.07 |
| 2006 | 0.69 | 0.96 | 0.85 | 1.01 | 3.51 |
| 2005 | 0.58 | 0.89 | 0.86 | 0.57 | 2.90 |
| 2004 | 0.52 | 0.68 | 0.75 | 0.83 | 2.78 |
| 2003 | 0.71 | 0.70 | 0.65 | 0.40 | 2.43 |

Fiscal year ended Dec. 31. Next earnings report expected: Late January. EPS Estimates based on S&P Operating Earnings; historical GAAP earnings are as reported.

## Dividend Data (Dates: mm/dd Payment Date: mm/dd/yy)

| Amount ($) | Date Decl. | Ex-Div. Date | Stk. of Record | Payment Date |
|---|---|---|---|---|
| 0.410 | 01/24 | 03/03 | 03/05 | 03/19/08 |
| 0.410 | 04/24 | 06/02 | 06/04 | 06/18/08 |
| 0.410 | 07/23 | 08/29 | 09/03 | 09/17/08 |
| 0.410 | 10/23 | 12/01 | 12/03 | 12/17/08 |

Dividends have been paid since 1964. Source: Company reports.

**Please read the Required Disclosures and Analyst Certification on the last page of this report.**

*The McGraw-Hill Companies*

# Avery Dennison Corp

**STANDARD**
**&POOR'S**

## Business Summary October 27, 2008

CORPORATE OVERVIEW. Avery Dennison is the leading global manufacturer of pressure-sensitive technology and self-adhesive solutions for consumer products and label systems, including office products, product identification and control systems, and specialty tapes and chemicals.

Foreign operations accounted for 63% of sales in 2007.

The pressure-sensitive materials group (55% of sales and 62% of operating profits in 2007) includes Fasson- and JAC-brand pressure sensitive, self-adhesive coated papers, plastic films and metal foils in roll and sheet form; graphic and reflective decoration films and labels; and adhesives, protective coatings and electroconductive resins for industrial, automotive, aerospace, appliance, electronic, medical and consumer markets. The acquisition of Jackstadt in May 2002 was AVY's largest purchase in more than a decade, and, we believe, strengthened its business in many developing markets worldwide.

The office and consumer products group (16% and 34%) consists of consumer and office products such as pressure-sensitive labels; copier, laser and ink-jet print labels and template software; notebooks; presentation and organizing products (binders, sheet protectors, dividers); writing instruments; marking devices; security badge systems; and many other products sold under the Av-

ery, National, and Hi-Liter brands for office, home, and school uses.

Retail information services (19% and -1%) sell a variety of price marking and brand identification products for retailers, apparel manufacturers, distributors and industrial customers. Products include woven and printed labels; heat transfers; graphic and barcode tags; patches; integrated tags; price tickets; customer hard and soft good packaging; barcode printers; software; plastics fastening; and applications devices for use in identification, tracking and control applications.

Other businesses (10% and 5%) consists of industrial and automotive decoration films and graphics sold primarily to original equipment manufacturers; self-adhesive postal stamps and on-battery testing labels; and specialty fastening and bonding tapes sold in roll form. The radio frequency identification (RFID) business (inlays and labels) has been reported in this segment beginning in 2005. The RFID business had a net loss of about $30 million in each of 2005 and 2006, but the loss declined modestly in 2007 and we expect a further reduction in 2008.

## Company Financials Fiscal Year Ended Dec. 31

| Per Share Data ($) | 2007 | 2006 | 2005 | 2004 | 2003 | 2002 | 2001 | 2000 | 1999 | 1998 |
|---|---|---|---|---|---|---|---|---|---|---|
| Tangible Book Value | NM | 8.84 | 6.74 | 5.85 | 4.08 | 2.53 | 4.70 | 3.94 | 3.66 | 5.98 |
| Cash Flow | 5.13 | 5.50 | 4.95 | 4.66 | 4.22 | 4.12 | 4.05 | 4.41 | 3.61 | 3.37 |
| Earnings | 3.07 | 3.51 | 2.90 | 2.78 | 2.43 | 2.59 | 2.47 | 2.84 | 2.13 | 2.15 |
| S&P Core Earnings | 2.98 | 3.48 | 2.66 | 2.51 | 2.05 | 2.02 | 1.81 | NA | NA | NA |
| Dividends | 1.61 | 1.57 | 1.53 | 1.49 | 1.45 | 1.35 | 1.23 | 1.11 | 0.99 | 0.87 |
| Payout Ratio | 52% | 45% | 53% | 54% | 60% | 52% | 50% | 39% | 46% | 40% |
| Prices:High | 71.35 | 69.31 | 63.58 | 66.60 | 63.75 | 69.70 | 60.50 | 78.50 | 73.00 | 62.06 |
| Prices:Low | 49.69 | 54.95 | 49.60 | 53.50 | 46.25 | 52.06 | 43.25 | 41.13 | 39.38 | 39.44 |
| P/E Ratio:High | 23 | 20 | 22 | 24 | 26 | 27 | 24 | 28 | 34 | 29 |
| P/E Ratio:Low | 16 | 16 | 17 | 19 | 19 | 20 | 18 | 14 | 18 | 18 |

| Income Statement Analysis (Million $) | 2007 | 2006 | 2005 | 2004 | 2003 | 2002 | 2001 | 2000 | 1999 | 1998 |
|---|---|---|---|---|---|---|---|---|---|---|
| Revenue | 6,308 | 5,576 | 5,474 | 5,341 | 4,763 | 4,207 | 3,803 | 3,894 | 3,768 | 3,460 |
| Operating Income | 787 | 683 | 690 | 655 | 602 | 593 | 566 | 638 | 589 | 499 |
| Depreciation | 204 | 199 | 202 | 188 | 179 | 153 | 156 | 157 | 150 | 127 |
| Interest Expense | 111 | 55.5 | 57.9 | 58.5 | 57.7 | 43.7 | 50.2 | 54.6 | 43.4 | 34.6 |
| Pretax Income | 375 | 426 | 367 | 373 | 335 | 365 | 360 | 426 | 330 | 337 |
| Effective Tax Rate | 19.1% | 17.2% | 20.4% | 25.1% | 27.5% | 29.5% | 32.4% | 33.5% | 34.8% | 33.7% |
| Net Income | 304 | 353 | 292 | 280 | 243 | 257 | 243 | 284 | 215 | 223 |
| S&P Core Earnings | 294 | 348 | 269 | 251 | 205 | 201 | 179 | NA | NA | NA |

| Balance Sheet & Other Financial Data (Million $) | 2007 | 2006 | 2005 | 2004 | 2003 | 2002 | 2001 | 2000 | 1999 | 1998 |
|---|---|---|---|---|---|---|---|---|---|---|
| Cash | 71.5 | 58.5 | 98.5 | 84.8 | 29.5 | 22.8 | 19.1 | 11.4 | 6.90 | 18.5 |
| Current Assets | 2,058 | 1,655 | 1,558 | 1,542 | 1,441 | 1,216 | 982 | 982 | 956 | 802 |
| Total Assets | 6,245 | 4,294 | 4,204 | 4,399 | 4,105 | 3,652 | 2,819 | 2,699 | 2,593 | 2,143 |
| Current Liabilities | 2,478 | 1,699 | 1,526 | 1,387 | 1,496 | 1,296 | 951 | 801 | 850 | 664 |
| Long Term Debt | 1,145 | 502 | 723 | 1,007 | 888 | 837 | 627 | 773 | 701 | 466 |
| Common Equity | 1,989 | 1,681 | 1,512 | 1,549 | 1,319 | 1,056 | 929 | 828 | 810 | 833 |
| Total Capital | 3,376 | 2,261 | 2,235 | 2,647 | 2,274 | 1,968 | 1,647 | 1,695 | 1,610 | 1,363 |
| Capital Expenditures | 191 | 162 | 163 | 179 | 201 | 152 | 135 | 198 | 178 | 160 |
| Cash Flow | 508 | 552 | 493 | 468 | 422 | 410 | 399 | 440 | 366 | 351 |
| Current Ratio | 0.8 | 1.0 | 1.0 | 1.1 | 1.0 | 0.9 | 1.0 | 1.2 | 1.1 | 1.2 |
| % Long Term Debt of Capitalization | 33.9 | 22.2 | 32.4 | 38.1 | 39.0 | 42.5 | 38.0 | 45.6 | 43.5 | 34.2 |
| % Net Income of Revenue | 4.8 | 6.3 | 5.3 | 5.2 | 5.1 | 6.1 | 6.4 | 7.3 | 5.7 | 6.5 |
| % Return on Assets | 5.8 | 8.3 | 6.8 | 6.6 | 6.3 | 7.8 | 8.8 | 10.7 | 9.1 | 10.7 |
| % Return on Equity | 16.5 | 22.1 | 19.1 | 19.5 | 20.4 | 25.9 | 27.7 | 34.6 | 26.2 | 26.7 |

Data as orig reptd.; bef. results of disc opers/spec. items. Per share data adj. for stk. divs.; EPS diluted. E-Estimated. NA-Not Available. NM-Not Meaningful. NR-Not Ranked. UR-Under Review.

**Office:** 150 North Orange Grove Boulevard, Pasadena, CA 91103.
**Telephone:** 626-304-2000.
**Email:** investorcom@averydennison.com
**Website:** http://www.averydennison.com

**Chrmn:** K. Kresa
**Pres & CEO:** D.A. Scarborough
**EVP & CFO:** D.R. O'Bryant
**EVP, Secy & General Counsel:** R.G. van Schoonenberg

**SVP & CIO:** R.W. Hoffman
**Board Members:** P. K. Barker, R. Borjesson, J. T. Cardis, R. M. Ferry, K. C. Hicks, K. Kresa, P. W. Mullin, D. E. Pyott, D. A. Scarborough, P. T. Siewert, J. A. Stewart

**Founded:** 1935
**Domicile:** Delaware
**Employees:** 37,300

# Avon Products Inc.

**STANDARD
&POOR'S**

| S&P Recommendation | HOLD ★★★☆☆ | Price $22.53 (as of Nov 14, 2008) | 12-Mo. Target Price $26.00 | Investment Style Large-Cap Growth |
|---|---|---|---|---|

**GICS Sector** Consumer Staples
**Sub-Industry** Personal Products

**Summary** This company is the world's leading direct marketer of cosmetics, toiletries, fashion jewelry and fragrances, with more than 5 million sales representatives worldwide.

## Key Stock Statistics (Source S&P, Vickers, company reports)

| | | | | | | | |
|---|---|---|---|---|---|---|---|
| 52-Wk Range | $45.34– 19.85 | S&P Oper. EPS 2008**E** | 2.10 | Market Capitalization(B) | $9.604 | Beta | 0.29 |
| Trailing 12-Month EPS | $1.79 | S&P Oper. EPS 2009**E** | 2.35 | Yield (%) | 3.55 | S&P 3-Yr. Proj. EPS CAGR(%) | 11 |
| Trailing 12-Month P/E | 12.6 | P/E on S&P Oper. EPS 2008**E** | 10.7 | Dividend Rate/Share | $0.80 | S&P Credit Rating | NR |
| $10K Invested 5 Yrs Ago | $7,237 | Common Shares Outstg. (M) | 426.3 | Institutional Ownership (%) | 91 | | |

## Price Performance

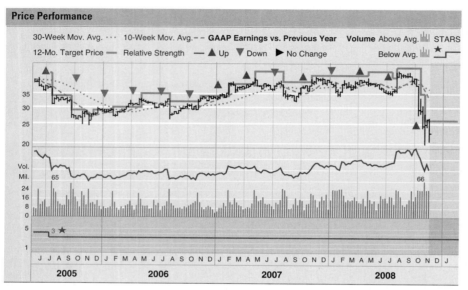

30-Week Mov. Avg. ···  10-Week Mov. Avg. - - **GAAP Earnings vs. Previous Year**  Volume Above Avg. STARS
12-Mo. Target Price —  Relative Strength — ▲ Up ▼ Down ► No Change  Below Avg. ★

Options: ASE, CBOE, P, Ph

Analysis prepared by **Loran Braverman, CFA** on November 03, 2008, when the stock traded at **$ 24.82**.

### Highlights

➤ In late 2005, AVP announced a multi-year restructuring plan in an effort to drive revenue and profit growth. The plan entails reorganizing and downsizing the organization, implementing global manufacturing, and increasing supply chain efficiencies. AVP plans to reinvest the savings from this plan in marketing, R&D, and incentivizing its sales force.

➤ Year-to-year sales comparisons started to pick up in mid-2006. For 2008, we forecast an 11% gain, assuming a 4% positive foreign currency effect, with the strongest growth expected from Latin America, China and Central & Eastern Europe, and slightly lower North American revenues. With a softening in sales late in the third quarter and a sharp rise in the U.S. dollar, we forecast 4.3% sales growth for 2009.

➤ We look for 250 basis points (bps) of operating margin improvement in 2008 (excluding restructuring and other charges from both years), still short of 2005's 14.1%. We see operating EPS rising to $2.10 in 2008, from $1.77 in 2007, with the latter figure excluding $0.56 in restructuring and other costs. For 2009, we project a 70 bps widening in the operating margin and EPS of $2.35.

### Investment Rationale/Risk

➤ We are encouraged by signs of stabilization in the Asia-Pacific region, an improvement in the active sales force base in North America following declines, and indications that the restructuring plan is helping to bring down costs. However, we are concerned that AVP's path to consistent, sustainable growth may be both prolonged and uneven. Also, recent strength in the U.S. dollar and a possible spreading of difficult economic conditions from developed to developing markets could impact AVP's results. Thus, we would not add to positions.

➤ Risks to our recommendation and target price include renewed weakness in the U.S. market, political and economic instability in international markets, competition from various sales channels, significant changes in foreign exchange rates and unfavorable consumer reception of new products.

➤ Our 12-month target price of $26 is a blend of our historical and relative analyses. Our historical analysis applies a P/E multiple of 12.9X, close to the 10-year historical low, to our 2009 estimate, implying a value of $30. Our peer analysis applies a discount to the peer average P/E, or 9.5X, for a value of $22.

## Qualitative Risk Assessment

| LOW | MEDIUM | HIGH |
|---|---|---|

Our risk assessment reflects that demand for personal care products is usually static and not generally affected by changes in the economy or geopolitical factors. However, certain product categories such as fragrances may be more susceptible to the aforementioned factors.

## Quantitative Evaluations

**S&P Quality Ranking**  A

| D | C | B- | B | B+ | A- | A | A+ |
|---|---|---|---|---|---|---|---|

**Relative Strength Rank**  MODERATE

34

LOWEST = 1          HIGHEST = 99

## Revenue/Earnings Data

**Revenue (Million $)**

| | 1Q | 2Q | 3Q | 4Q | Year |
|---|---|---|---|---|---|
| 2008 | 2,502 | 2,736 | 2,619 | -- | -- |
| 2007 | 2,185 | 2,329 | 2,349 | 3,076 | 9,939 |
| 2006 | 2,003 | 2,080 | 2,059 | 2,623 | 8,764 |
| 2005 | 1,881 | 1,984 | 1,886 | 2,398 | 8,150 |
| 2004 | 1,765 | 1,866 | 1,806 | 2,311 | 7,748 |
| 2003 | 1,481 | 1,656 | 1,629 | 2,109 | 6,876 |

**Earnings Per Share ($)**

| | | | | | |
|---|---|---|---|---|---|
| 2008 | 0.43 | 0.55 | 0.52 | E0.61 | E2.10 |
| 2007 | 0.34 | 0.26 | 0.32 | 0.30 | 1.22 |
| 2006 | 0.12 | 0.34 | 0.19 | 0.41 | 1.06 |
| 2005 | 0.36 | 0.69 | 0.35 | 0.40 | 1.81 |
| 2004 | 0.31 | 0.49 | 0.37 | 0.61 | 1.77 |
| 2003 | 0.21 | 0.36 | 0.28 | 0.55 | 1.39 |

Fiscal year ended Dec. 31. Next earnings report expected: Early February. EPS Estimates based on S&P Operating Earnings; historical GAAP earnings are as reported.

## Dividend Data (Dates: mm/dd Payment Date: mm/dd/yy)

| Amount ($) | Date Decl. | Ex-Div. Date | Stk. of Record | Payment Date |
|---|---|---|---|---|
| 0.200 | 02/07 | 02/19 | 02/21 | 03/03/08 |
| 0.200 | 05/01 | 05/13 | 05/15 | 06/02/08 |
| 0.200 | 08/01 | 08/13 | 08/15 | 09/02/08 |
| 0.200 | 11/06 | 11/19 | 11/21 | 12/01/08 |

Dividends have been paid since 1919. Source: Company reports.

---

**Please read the Required Disclosures and Analyst Certification on the last page of this report.**

*The McGraw-Hill Companies*

# Avon Products Inc.

**STANDARD &POOR'S**

## Business Summary November 03, 2008

CORPORATE OVERVIEW. Avon Products, which began operations in 1886, is a global manufacturer and marketer of beauty and related products. The company has three product categories: Beauty, Beauty Plus and Beyond Beauty. Beauty consists of cosmetics, fragrance and toiletries and accounted for 70% of sales in 2007. Beauty Plus (19%) consists of jewelry, watches and apparel and accessories. Beyond Beauty (11%) consists of home products, gift and decorative and candles. The company has operations in 66 countries and territories, including the U.S., and its products are distributed in 48 more, for coverage in 114 markets. Geographically, 26% of 2007 sales were derived from North America, while Latin America accounted for 33%, Western Europe, the Middle East & Africa 13%, Central & Eastern Europe 16%, Asia-Pacific 9%, and China 3%. Operations outside North America accounted for 81% of operating profits in 2007. Sales are made to the ultimate customer mainly through a combination of direct selling and marketing by about 5.4 million independent Avon representatives, around 459,000 of whom are in the U.S.

For 2007, the number of active representatives rose, year to year, 3% in North America, 8% in Latin America, 7% in Western Europe, Middle East & Africa, 13% in Central & Eastern Europe, 4% in Asia-Pacific, 145% in China (from a very low base) and 9% overall. The overall number of active representatives in

the first quarter of 2008 rose 14% versus the first quarter of 2007, with the biggest increases in Latin America, Central & Eastern Europe and China.

CORPORATE STRATEGY. AVP embarked on a multi-year restructuring plan in November 2005 in an effort to drive revenue and profit growth. The plan entails reorganizing and downsizing the organization, implementing global manufacturing, and increasing supply chain efficiencies. AVP expects restructuring benefits to help fund an increase in consumer research, marketing, and product development, which, in turn, is expected to enhance sales and ultimately profits. In fact, we have seen an improvement in the quarterly year-to-year sales growth rate starting in mid-2006, but, so far, savings from the plan have not been large enough to offset increases in the expenses mentioned above. Also in 2005, Avon started to implement a global supply chain strategy, which includes the development of a new common systems platform, known as enterprise resource planning (ERP).

## Company Financials Fiscal Year Ended Dec. 31

| Per Share Data ($) | 2007 | 2006 | 2005 | 2004 | 2003 | 2002 | 2001 | 2000 | 1999 | 1998 |
|---|---|---|---|---|---|---|---|---|---|---|
| Tangible Book Value | 1.66 | 1.79 | 1.68 | 2.02 | 0.79 | NM | NM | NM | NM | 0.55 |
| Cash Flow | 1.55 | 1.42 | 2.10 | 2.05 | 1.63 | 1.34 | 1.10 | 1.20 | 0.74 | 0.64 |
| Earnings | 1.22 | 1.06 | 1.81 | 1.77 | 1.39 | 1.11 | 0.90 | 1.01 | 0.58 | 0.51 |
| S&P Core Earnings | 1.25 | 1.16 | 1.80 | 1.80 | 1.37 | 0.95 | 0.77 | NA | NA | NA |
| Dividends | 0.74 | 0.70 | 0.66 | 0.70 | 0.42 | 0.40 | 0.38 | 0.37 | 0.36 | 0.34 |
| Payout Ratio | 61% | 66% | 36% | 40% | 30% | 36% | 42% | 37% | 62% | 67% |
| Prices:High | 42.51 | 34.25 | 45.66 | 46.65 | 34.88 | 28.55 | 25.06 | 24.88 | 29.56 | 23.13 |
| Prices:Low | 31.95 | 26.16 | 24.33 | 30.81 | 24.47 | 21.75 | 17.78 | 12.63 | 11.66 | 12.50 |
| P/E Ratio:High | 35 | 32 | 25 | 26 | 25 | 26 | 28 | 25 | 51 | 45 |
| P/E Ratio:Low | 26 | 25 | 13 | 17 | 18 | 20 | 20 | 12 | 20 | 25 |

| Income Statement Analysis (Million $) | | | | | | | | | | |
|---|---|---|---|---|---|---|---|---|---|---|
| Revenue | 9,939 | 8,764 | 8,150 | 7,748 | 6,876 | 6,228 | 5,995 | 5,715 | 5,289 | 5,213 |
| Operating Income | 1,176 | 1,146 | 1,289 | 1,361 | 1,162 | 1,029 | 951 | 886 | 762 | 706 |
| Depreciation | 145 | 160 | 140 | 135 | 124 | 125 | 109 | 97.1 | 83.0 | 72.0 |
| Interest Expense | 125 | 99.6 | 54.1 | 33.8 | 33.3 | 52.0 | 71.1 | 84.7 | 43.2 | 41.0 |
| Pretax Income | 796 | 704 | 1,124 | 1,188 | 994 | 836 | 666 | 691 | 507 | 456 |
| Effective Tax Rate | 33.0% | 31.8% | 24.0% | 27.8% | 32.1% | 35.0% | 34.7% | 29.2% | 40.3% | 41.9% |
| Net Income | 531 | 478 | 848 | 846 | 665 | 535 | 430 | 485 | 302 | 270 |
| S&P Core Earnings | 549 | 518 | 845 | 859 | 652 | 455 | 367 | NA | NA | NA |

| Balance Sheet & Other Financial Data (Million $) | | | | | | | | | | |
|---|---|---|---|---|---|---|---|---|---|---|
| Cash | 963 | 1,199 | 1,059 | 770 | 694 | 607 | 509 | 123 | 117 | 106 |
| Current Assets | 3,515 | 3,334 | 2,921 | 2,506 | 2,226 | 2,048 | 1,889 | 1,546 | 1,338 | 1,341 |
| Total Assets | 5,716 | 5,238 | 4,763 | 4,148 | 3,562 | 3,328 | 3,193 | 2,826 | 2,529 | 2,434 |
| Current Liabilities | 3,053 | 2,550 | 2,502 | 1,526 | 1,588 | 1,976 | 1,461 | 1,359 | 1,713 | 1,330 |
| Long Term Debt | 1,168 | 1,171 | 766 | 866 | 878 | 767 | 1,236 | 1,108 | 701 | 201 |
| Common Equity | 712 | 790 | 794 | 950 | 371 | -128 | -74.6 | -216 | -406 | 285 |
| Total Capital | 2,089 | 2,028 | 1,595 | 1,829 | 1,300 | 712 | 1,192 | 954 | 365 | 559 |
| Capital Expenditures | 279 | 175 | 207 | 250 | 163 | 127 | 155 | 194 | 203 | 190 |
| Cash Flow | 676 | 637 | 987 | 981 | 788 | 659 | 539 | 582 | 385 | 342 |
| Current Ratio | 1.2 | 1.3 | 1.2 | 1.6 | 1.4 | 1.0 | 1.3 | 1.1 | 0.8 | 1.0 |
| % Long Term Debt of Capitalization | 62.1 | 58.8 | 48.1 | 47.4 | 67.5 | 107.8 | 103.7 | 116.1 | 192.3 | 36.0 |
| % Net Income of Revenue | 5.3 | 5.4 | 10.4 | 10.9 | 9.7 | 8.6 | 7.2 | 8.5 | 5.7 | 5.2 |
| % Return on Assets | 9.7 | 9.6 | 19.0 | 21.9 | 19.3 | 16.4 | 14.3 | 18.1 | 12.2 | 11.5 |
| % Return on Equity | 70.7 | 60.3 | 97.2 | 128.0 | 545.8 | NM | NM | NM | NM | 94.7 |

Data as orig reptd.; bef. results of disc opers/spec. items. Per share data adj. for stk. divs.; EPS diluted. E-Estimated. NA-Not Available. NM-Not Meaningful. NR-Not Ranked. UR-Under Review.

**Office:** 1345 Avenue Of The Americas Bsmt, New York, NY 10105-0302.
**Telephone:** 212-282-5000.
**Email:** individual.investor@avon.com
**Website:** http://www.avoninvestor.com

**Chrmn & CEO:** A. Jung
**Pres:** E.A. Smith
**SVP & General Counsel:** K.K. Rucker
**SVP & CIO:** H. Edelman

**SVP & CIO:** D. Herlihy
**Investor Contact:** R. Johansen (212-282-5320)
**Board Members:** W. D. Cornwell, E. T. Fogarty, F. Hassan, A. Jung, M. E. Lagomasino, A. S. Moore, P. Pressler, G. M. Rodkin, P. Stern, L. A. Weinbach

**Founded:** 1886
**Domicile:** New York
**Employees:** 42,000

*The McGraw-Hill Companies*

# Baker Hughes Inc

**STANDARD &POOR'S**

| S&P Recommendation | HOLD ★★★☆☆ | Price $30.94 (as of Nov 14, 2008) | 12-Mo. Target Price $43.00 | Investment Style Large-Cap Growth |
|---|---|---|---|---|

**GICS Sector** Energy
**Sub-Industry** Oil & Gas Equipment & Services

**Summary** This company is one of the world's largest oilfield services companies, providing products and services to the energy industry.

## Key Stock Statistics (Source S&P, Vickers, company reports)

| | | | | | | | |
|---|---|---|---|---|---|---|---|
| 52-Wk Range | $90.81 – 27.59 | S&P Oper. EPS 2008**E** | 5.41 | Market Capitalization(B) | $9.515 | Beta | 1.53 |
| Trailing 12-Month EPS | $5.15 | S&P Oper. EPS 2009**E** | 5.68 | Yield (%) | 1.94 | S&P 3-Yr. Proj. EPS CAGR(%) | 11 |
| Trailing 12-Month P/E | 6.0 | P/E on S&P Oper. EPS 2008**E** | 5.7 | Dividend Rate/Share | $0.60 | S&P Credit Rating | A |
| $10K Invested 5 Yrs Ago | $10,913 | Common Shares Outstg. (M) | 307.5 | Institutional Ownership (%) | 91 | | |

## Price Performance

30-Week Mov. Avg. · · · · · 10-Week Mov. Avg. - - - **GAAP Earnings vs. Previous Year** Volume Above Avg. STARS
12-Mo. Target Price — Relative Strength — ▲ Up ▼ Down ► No Change    Below Avg. ★

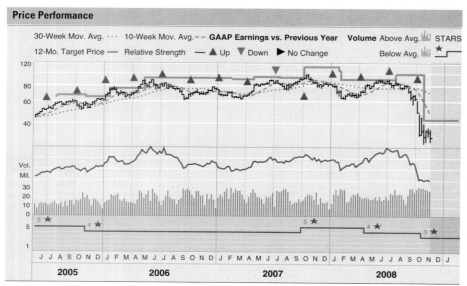

Options: ASE, CBOE, P, Ph

Analysis prepared by **Stewart Glickman, CFA** on October 22, 2008, when the stock traded at **$ 30.29**.

### Highlights

► Looking out over the next several years, we expect strong growth opportunities in the Eastern Hemisphere and view this as a primary catalyst for BHI; we see this region generating 54% of total revenues in 2009, versus 49% in 2007 and 48% in the first half of 2008. However, as the U.S. recession continues (with possible contagion to foreign markets), we expect that exploration drilling activity will temporarily subside, as upstream customers focus more on development activity.

► In October, BHI said that the current credit crunch and increased natural gas production (in excess of demand growth) should result in lower natural gas drilling activity in 2009. We expect upstream customers to pare back capital spending, particularly onshore North America, which should weigh on BHI's North American revenue growth, at least in the Drilling & Evaluation segment.

► We expect total revenues to increase about 13% this year, with greater gains in international markets than in North America, and 10% in 2009. Overall, we estimate EPS of $5.41 in 2008, rising to $5.68 in 2009.

### Investment Rationale/Risk

► We view the recent credit crisis and potentially global recession as unfortunate timing for BHI, as we expected the company to significantly accelerate its ramp-up in overseas markets during 2009. While such a ramp-up is still possible, we see higher likelihood of a scaling-back of BHI's capital spending, in accordance with an expected pullback in upstream capital spending. Looking out to 2010, we think BHI's growth prospects are still strong, mainly in the Eastern Hemisphere.

► Risks to our recommendation and target price include lower energy prices; reduced drilling activity in international markets; slower-than-planned infrastructure build; and higher than expected cost inflation.

► Our discounted cash flow model, which assumes a weighted average cost of capital of 11.7% and terminal growth of 3%, shows intrinsic value of about $41. Based on our view of below-average 2009 ROIC, we think a modest discount to peer valuations is warranted. Using multiples of 4.5X projected 2009 EBITDA and 5.5X estimated 2009 cash flow (slight discounts to peers), and blending with our DCF model, our 12-month target price is $43.

## Qualitative Risk Assessment

| LOW | MEDIUM | HIGH |
|---|---|---|

Our risk assessment reflects BHI's exposure to volatile crude oil and natural gas prices, capital spending decisions by its exploration and production customers, and political risk associated with operating in frontier regions. Offsetting these risks is BHI's strong position in drilling and completion products.

## Quantitative Evaluations

### S&P Quality Ranking    B

| D | C | B- | B | B+ | A- | A | A+ |
|---|---|---|---|---|---|---|---|

### Relative Strength Rank    WEAK

26

LOWEST = 1                    HIGHEST = 99

## Revenue/Earnings Data

### Revenue (Million $)

| | 1Q | 2Q | 3Q | 4Q | Year |
|---|---|---|---|---|---|
| 2008 | 2,670 | 2,998 | 3,010 | -- | -- |
| 2007 | 2,473 | 2,538 | 2,678 | 2,740 | 10,428 |
| 2006 | 2,062 | 2,203 | 2,309 | 2,453 | 9,027 |
| 2005 | 1,643 | 1,768 | 1,785 | 1,989 | 7,186 |
| 2004 | 1,388 | 1,499 | 1,538 | 1,679 | 6,104 |
| 2003 | 1,200 | 1,315 | 1,338 | 1,440 | 5,293 |

### Earnings Per Share ($)

| | 1Q | 2Q | 3Q | 4Q | Year |
|---|---|---|---|---|---|
| 2008 | 1.27 | 1.23 | 1.39 | E1.52 | E5.41 |
| 2007 | 1.17 | 1.09 | 1.22 | 1.26 | 4.73 |
| 2006 | 0.93 | 4.14 | 1.09 | 1.02 | 7.21 |
| 2005 | 0.53 | 0.64 | 0.64 | 0.76 | 2.56 |
| 2004 | 0.28 | 0.35 | 0.41 | 0.53 | 1.57 |
| 2003 | 0.15 | 0.24 | -0.29 | 0.30 | 0.40 |

Fiscal year ended Dec. 31. Next earnings report expected: Late January. EPS Estimates based on S&P Operating Earnings; historical GAAP earnings are as reported.

## Dividend Data (Dates: mm/dd Payment Date: mm/dd/yy)

| Amount ($) | Date Decl. | Ex-Div. Date | Stk. of Record | Payment Date |
|---|---|---|---|---|
| 0.130 | 01/24 | 01/31 | 02/04 | 02/15/08 |
| 0.130 | 04/24 | 05/01 | 05/05 | 05/16/08 |
| 0.150 | 07/24 | 07/31 | 08/04 | 08/15/08 |
| 0.150 | 10/23 | 10/30 | 11/03 | 11/14/08 |

Dividends have been paid since 1987. Source: Company reports.

# Baker Hughes Inc

**STANDARD &POOR'S**

## Business Summary October 22, 2008

CORPORATE OVERVIEW. Baker Hughes was formed through the 1987 merger of Baker International Corp. and Hughes Tool Co. In 1998, it acquired seismic and wireline logging company Western Atlas, creating the third largest oilfield services company. BHI has operations in over 90 countries. North America accounted for 42% of total revenues in 2007, followed by the Europe, CIS and Africa region (29%) and the Middle East and Asia-Pacific region (19%). In 2005, the company reorganized its seven product-line focused divisions into three operating segments: Drilling & Evaluation; Completion & Production; and Western Geco (which provides reservoir imaging, monitoring and development services). In April 2006, however, BHI sold its 30% minority stake in seismic company Western Geco to the majority joint venture partner, Schlumberger. We like the deal for BHI, as we think it should enable BHI to focus on its core oilfield operations of drilling, completion and production.

The Drilling & Evaluation segment (51% of 2007 total oilfield revenues and 56% of total oilfield segment income) consists of four operating divisions: Baker Hughes Drilling Fluids, Hughes Christensen, INTEQ, and Baker Atlas. The products and services in this segment are typically used in the drilling of crude oil and natural gas wells.

Baker Hughes Drilling Fluids provides drilling and completion fluids, and fluid

environmental services. Fluids are used in order to control downhole pressure, clean the bottom of the well, and to cool and lubricate the drill bit and drill string. Hughes Christensen manufactures drill bit products, primarily Tricone roller cone drill bits and polycrystalline diamond compact (PDC) fixed cutter bits. INTEQ supplies directional and horizontal drilling services, coring services, subsurface surveying, logging-while-drilling, and measurement-while-drilling services.

Baker Atlas provides formation evaluation and perforating services for oil and natural gas wells. Formation evaluation involves measuring and analyzing specific physical properties of the rock in the vicinity of the wellbore to determine a reservoir's boundaries, hydrocarbon volume, and ability to produce fluids to the surface. Perforating services involve puncturing a well's steel casing and cement sheath with explosive charges; this creates a fracture in the formation, and provides a path for the hydrocarbons in the formation to enter the wellbore.

## Company Financials Fiscal Year Ended Dec. 31

| Per Share Data ($) | 2007 | 2006 | 2005 | 2004 | 2003 | 2002 | 2001 | 2000 | 1999 | 1998 |
|---|---|---|---|---|---|---|---|---|---|---|
| Tangible Book Value | 15.14 | 11.58 | 9.42 | 7.35 | 5.87 | 6.05 | 5.69 | 4.64 | 4.17 | 3.98 |
| Cash Flow | 6.36 | 8.85 | 3.68 | 2.69 | 1.59 | 1.56 | 2.32 | 2.14 | 2.52 | 1.43 |
| Earnings | 4.73 | 7.21 | 2.56 | 1.57 | 0.40 | 0.66 | 1.31 | 0.31 | 0.16 | -0.92 |
| S&P Core Earnings | 4.70 | 4.24 | 2.47 | 1.50 | 0.62 | 0.55 | 1.17 | NA | NA | NA |
| Dividends | 0.52 | 0.52 | 0.48 | 0.46 | 0.46 | 0.46 | 0.46 | 0.46 | 0.46 | 0.46 |
| Payout Ratio | 11% | 7% | 19% | 29% | 115% | 70% | 35% | 148% | NM | NM |
| Prices:High | 100.29 | 89.30 | 63.13 | 45.30 | 36.15 | 39.95 | 45.29 | 43.38 | 36.25 | 44.13 |
| Prices:Low | 62.26 | 60.60 | 40.73 | 31.56 | 26.90 | 22.60 | 25.76 | 19.63 | 15.00 | 15.00 |
| P/E Ratio:High | 21 | 12 | 25 | 29 | 90 | 61 | 35 | NM | NM | NM |
| P/E Ratio:Low | 13 | 8 | 16 | 20 | 67 | 34 | 20 | NM | NM | NM |
| **Income Statement Analysis** (Million $) | | | | | | | | | | |
| Revenue | 10,428 | 9,027 | 7,186 | 6,104 | 5,293 | 5,020 | 5,382 | 5,234 | 4,547 | 6,312 |
| Operating Income | 2,799 | 2,417 | 1,616 | 1,195 | 957 | 856 | 1,077 | 1,076 | 992 | 1,058 |
| Depreciation, Depletion and Amortization | 521 | 434 | 382 | 374 | 349 | 302 | 345 | 612 | 778 | 758 |
| Interest Expense | 66.1 | 68.9 | 72.3 | 83.6 | 103 | 111 | 126 | 173 | 159 | 149 |
| Pretax Income | 2,257 | 3,737 | 1,279 | 780 | 328 | 380 | 662 | 236 | 85.0 | -281 |
| Effective Tax Rate | 32.9% | 35.8% | 31.6% | 32.3% | 45.1% | 41.2% | 33.7% | 56.7% | 37.6% | NM |
| Net Income | 1,514 | 2,399 | 874 | 528 | 180 | 224 | 439 | 102 | 53.0 | -297 |
| S&P Core Earnings | 1,504 | 1,393 | 842 | 506 | 209 | 186 | 393 | NA | NA | NA |
| **Balance Sheet & Other Financial Data** (Million $) | | | | | | | | | | |
| Cash | 1,054 | 750 | 697 | 319 | 98.4 | 144 | 45.4 | 34.6 | 18.0 | 16.6 |
| Current Assets | 5,456 | 4,968 | 3,840 | 2,967 | 2,524 | 2,556 | 2,697 | 2,487 | 2,330 | 2,725 |
| Total Assets | 9,857 | 8,706 | 7,807 | 6,821 | 6,302 | 6,401 | 6,676 | 6,453 | 7,040 | 7,811 |
| Current Liabilities | 1,618 | 1,622 | 1,361 | 1,236 | 1,302 | 1,080 | 1,212 | 988 | 1,000 | 1,310 |
| Long Term Debt | 1,069 | 1,074 | 1,078 | 1,086 | 1,133 | 1,424 | 1,682 | 2,050 | 2,706 | 2,726 |
| Common Equity | 6,306 | 5,243 | 4,698 | 3,895 | 3,350 | 3,397 | 3,328 | 3,047 | 3,072 | 3,199 |
| Total Capital | 7,791 | 6,617 | 6,004 | 5,214 | 4,611 | 4,988 | 5,221 | 5,255 | 5,813 | 6,082 |
| Capital Expenditures | 1,127 | 922 | 478 | 348 | 405 | 317 | 319 | 599 | 634 | 1,318 |
| Cash Flow | 2,035 | 2,832 | 1,257 | 902 | 529 | 525 | 783 | 714 | 831 | 461 |
| Current Ratio | 3.4 | 3.1 | 2.8 | 2.4 | 1.9 | 2.4 | 2.2 | 2.5 | 2.3 | 2.1 |
| % Long Term Debt of Capitalization | 13.7 | 16.2 | 18.0 | 20.8 | 24.6 | 28.6 | 32.2 | 39.0 | 46.6 | 44.8 |
| % Return on Assets | 16.3 | 29.1 | 12.0 | 8.0 | 2.8 | 3.4 | 6.7 | 1.5 | 0.7 | NM |
| % Return on Equity | 26.2 | 48.3 | 20.4 | 14.6 | 5.3 | 6.7 | 13.8 | 3.3 | 1.7 | NM |

Data as orig reptd.; bef. results of disc opers/spec. items. Per share data adj. for stk. divs.; EPS diluted. E-Estimated. NA-Not Available. NM-Not Meaningful. NR-Not Ranked. UR-Under Review.

**Office:** 2929 Allen Pkwy Ste 2100, Houston, TX 77019-7111.
**Telephone:** 713-439-8600.
**Website:** http://www.bakerhughes.com
**Chrmn, Pres & CEO:** C.C. Deaton

**SVP & CFO:** P.A. Ragauss
**SVP & General Counsel:** A.R. Crain, Jr.
**Chief Acctg Officer & Cntlr:** A.J. Keifer
**Treas:** J.K. Gaalen

**Board Members:** L. D. Brady, II, C. P. Cazalot, Jr., C. C. Deaton, E. P. Djerejian, A. G. Fernandes, C. W. Gargalli, P. Jungels, I, J. A. Lash, J. F. McCall, J. L. Nichols, H. J. Riley, Jr., C. L. Watson

**Founded:** 1972
**Domicile:** Delaware
**Employees:** 35,800

# Ball Corp

STANDARD
&POOR'S

**S&P Recommendation** HOLD ★★★☆☆

| Price | 12-Mo. Target Price | Investment Style |
|---|---|---|
| $32.77 (as of Nov 14, 2008) | $36.00 | Large-Cap Blend |

**GICS Sector** Materials
**Sub-Industry** Metal & Glass Containers

**Summary** Ball, one of the largest producers of metal beverage cans in the world, derives about 10% of its revenues from sales of hi-tech equipment to the aerospace industry.

## Key Stock Statistics (Source S&P, Vickers, company reports)

| | | | | | | | |
|---|---|---|---|---|---|---|---|
| 52-Wk Range | $56.20– 27.37 | S&P Oper. EPS 2008E | 3.65 | Market Capitalization(B) | $3.100 | Beta | 1.26 |
| Trailing 12-Month EPS | $3.24 | S&P Oper. EPS 2009E | 4.10 | Yield (%) | 1.22 | S&P 3-Yr. Proj. EPS CAGR(%) | 12 |
| Trailing 12-Month P/E | 10.1 | P/E on S&P Oper. EPS 2008E | 9.0 | Dividend Rate/Share | $0.40 | S&P Credit Rating | BB+ |
| $10K Invested 5 Yrs Ago | $12,438 | Common Shares Outstg. (M) | 94.6 | Institutional Ownership (%) | 76 | | |

## Price Performance

30-Week Mov. Avg. · · · · 10-Week Mov. Avg. – – **GAAP Earnings vs. Previous Year** Volume Above Avg. ▮▮▮ STARS
12-Mo. Target Price — Relative Strength — ▲ Up ▼ Down ▶ No Change Below Avg. ▮▮▮ ★

Options: ASE, CBOE, P, Ph

Analysis prepared by **Stewart Scharf** on November 11, 2008, when the stock traded at **$ 33.05**.

## Highlights

➤ We project low single digit organic revenue growth into 2009, as we think demand for metal beverage cans, especially in China and, to some extent, in Europe, will be partially offset by soft volume in North America. We see some recovery possible for plastic containers, while aerospace demand is hurt by new award delays. Metal food and household packaging should gradually rebound.

➤ In our view, gross margins (before D&A) will widen to about 16.5% in 2008, from 15.7% in 2007, with further expansion seen in 2009, reflecting pricing initiatives and stabilizing freight and energy costs. We look for EBITDA margins to widen from our near 13% projection for 2008 (11.4% in 2007), on improved productivity via plant consolidations, a better product mix in Europe and synergies from acquisitions. Interest expense should decline due to lower rates.

➤ We project a higher tax rate of about 32% for 2008, and estimate EPS of $3.65 (before $0.40 net charge), advancing to $4.10 in 2009. EPS will likely be negatively affected ($0.17 through the first nine months of 2008) by a weaker euro against the U.S. dollar.

## Investment Rationale/Risk

➤ Our hold recommendation is based on our valuation metrics, as well as our view of favorable trends for beverage cans and strong cash generation. We expect BLL to keep capacity in line with demand based on soft economic conditions.

➤ Risks to our recommendation and target price include negative exchange rate fluctuations; a decline in domestic soft drink sales, and in global beer sales in favor of wine and spirits; cost pressures in Europe and China; supply disruptions due to strikes in Europe; integration problems; and a further steep rise in raw material costs.

➤ We attribute the stock's recent P/E of 8.4X our 2009 estimate, a discount to the S&P Metal & Glass Containers group, to integration concerns regarding new businesses. Based on our relative metrics, including near peer price-to-sales and PEG (P/E-to-growth) ratios, we value the stock at $33. Our DCF model, which assumes a 3% perpetual growth rate and a WACC of 7%, derives an intrinsic value of $38. We blend these valuations, and apply a below historical P/E multiple of 8.8X to our 2009 estimate, to arrive at our 12-month target price of $36.

## Qualitative Risk Assessment

| LOW | MEDIUM | HIGH |
|---|---|---|

Our risk assessment reflects the seasonality inherent in the beverage can business, our view of BLL's high debt levels, our corporate governance concerns related to board and audit issues, and volatile raw material prices. These factors are offset by our expectations of lower interest expense due to debt refinancing and redemptions.

## Quantitative Evaluations

**S&P Quality Ranking**  B+

| D | C | B- | B | B+ | A- | A | A+ |
|---|---|---|---|---|---|---|---|

**Relative Strength Rank**  MODERATE

68

LOWEST = 1          HIGHEST = 99

## Revenue/Earnings Data

**Revenue (Million $)**

| | 1Q | 2Q | 3Q | 4Q | Year |
|---|---|---|---|---|---|
| 2008 | 1,740 | 2,080 | 2,008 | -- | -- |
| 2007 | 1,694 | 2,033 | 1,992 | 1,756 | 7,475 |
| 2006 | 1,365 | 1,843 | 1,822 | 1,592 | 6,622 |
| 2005 | 1,324 | 1,552 | 1,584 | 1,291 | 5,751 |
| 2004 | 1,232 | 1,467 | 1,479 | 1,263 | 5,440 |
| 2003 | 1,071 | 1,353 | 1,359 | 1,194 | 4,977 |

**Earnings Per Share ($)**

| | | | | | |
|---|---|---|---|---|---|
| 2008 | 0.85 | 1.02 | 1.05 | E0.61 | E3.65 |
| 2007 | 0.78 | 1.03 | 0.59 | 0.33 | 2.74 |
| 2006 | 0.43 | 1.23 | 1.02 | 0.46 | 3.14 |
| 2005 | 0.51 | 0.71 | 0.73 | 0.42 | 2.38 |
| 2004 | 0.41 | 0.80 | 0.90 | 0.50 | 2.60 |
| 2003 | 0.28 | 0.65 | 0.61 | 0.49 | 2.01 |

Fiscal year ended Dec. 31. Next earnings report expected: Late January. EPS Estimates based on S&P Operating Earnings; historical GAAP earnings are as reported.

## Dividend Data (Dates: mm/dd Payment Date: mm/dd/yy)

| Amount ($) | Date Decl. | Ex-Div. Date | Stk. of Record | Payment Date |
|---|---|---|---|---|
| 0.100 | 01/23 | 02/28 | 03/03 | 03/17/08 |
| 0.100 | 04/23 | 05/29 | 06/02 | 06/16/08 |
| 0.100 | 07/23 | 08/28 | 09/02 | 09/15/08 |
| 0.100 | 10/20 | 11/26 | 12/01 | 12/15/08 |

Dividends have been paid since 1958. Source: Company reports.

# Ball Corp

STANDARD &POOR'S

## Business Summary November 11, 2008

CORPORATE OVERVIEW. Ball Corp. primarily manufactures rigid packaging products for beverages and foods. Two beverage companies account for a substantial part of its packaging sales: SABMiller plc and PepsiCo. BLL is comprised of five segments: Metal Beverage Packaging (Americas/Asia); Metal Beverage Packaging (Europe); Metal Food & Household Packaging (Americas); Plastic Packaging (Americas); and Aerospace and Technologies. The Aerospace and Technologies segment provides products and services to the defense and commercial markets, with U.S. government agencies accounting for more than 80% of the segment's sales. In the first quarter of 2008, BLL's China operations were merged into the metal beverage packaging (Americas) segments due to management reporting changes.

The company's packaging products include aluminum and steel two-piece beverage cans, and two- and three-piece steel food cans. Metal Beverage Packaging (Americas) segment net sales represented 37% of the total in 2007 ($299 million in pretax earnings); Metal Beverage Packaging (Europe/Asia) 26% ($256 million); Metal Food and Household Packaging (Americas) 16% ($36 million); Plastic Packaging (Americas) 10% ($26 million); and Aerospace and Technologies 11% ($65 million). BLL entered the plastics business in 1995,

when it began to make polyethylene terephthalate (PET) bottles. Sales volumes of metal food containers in North America tend to be highest from June through October due to seasonal vegetable and salmon packs. BLL believes this accounts for more than 30% of all North American metal beverage can shipments. In 2007, sales to SABMiller plc and PepsiCo. accounted for 11% and 9% of net sales, respectively.

In the 2008 third quarter, BLL incurred a pretax charge of $9 million ($0.08 a share, after tax) related to three plant closures, including its aluminum beverage can manufacturing plant in Kent, WA, following $14.9 million in pretax charges ($0.10) in the second quarter. In the first quarter of 2008, it recorded a $0.05 a share gain on the sale of an aerospace engineering services business in Australia. In the fourth quarter of 2007, BLL recorded a $0.27 a share charge related to plant closures and equipment relocations.

## Company Financials Fiscal Year Ended Dec. 31

| Per Share Data ($) | 2007 | 2006 | 2005 | 2004 | 2003 | 2002 | 2001 | 2000 | 1999 | 1998 |
|---|---|---|---|---|---|---|---|---|---|---|
| Tangible Book Value | NM | NM | NM | NM | NM | NM | 1.27 | 1.81 | 1.27 | 0.32 |
| Cash Flow | 5.47 | 5.55 | 4.30 | 4.49 | 3.81 | 2.68 | 0.44 | 1.81 | 2.03 | 1.41 |
| Earnings | 2.74 | 3.14 | 2.38 | 2.60 | 2.01 | 1.38 | -0.93 | 0.54 | 0.79 | 0.23 |
| S&P Core Earnings | 3.31 | 2.30 | 2.54 | 2.67 | 2.12 | 1.10 | -0.88 | NA | NA | NA |
| Dividends | 0.40 | 0.40 | 0.40 | 0.35 | 0.24 | 0.18 | 0.15 | 0.15 | 0.15 | 0.15 |
| Payout Ratio | 15% | 13% | 17% | 13% | 12% | 13% | NM | 28% | 19% | 66% |
| Prices:High | 56.05 | 45.00 | 46.45 | 45.20 | 29.88 | 27.25 | 18.03 | 11.98 | 14.78 | 12.23 |
| Prices:Low | 43.51 | 34.16 | 35.06 | 28.26 | 21.15 | 16.30 | 9.52 | 6.50 | 8.84 | 7.16 |
| P/E Ratio:High | 20 | 14 | 20 | 17 | 15 | 20 | NM | 22 | 19 | 54 |
| P/E Ratio:Low | 16 | 11 | 15 | 11 | 11 | 12 | NM | 12 | 11 | 31 |

**Income Statement Analysis** (Million $)

| | 2007 | 2006 | 2005 | 2004 | 2003 | 2002 | 2001 | 2000 | 1999 | 1998 |
|---|---|---|---|---|---|---|---|---|---|---|
| Revenue | 7,475 | 6,622 | 5,751 | 5,440 | 4,977 | 3,859 | 3,686 | 3,665 | 3,584 | 2,896 |
| Operating Income | 914 | 729 | 697 | 739 | 663 | 458 | 127 | 445 | 442 | 334 |
| Depreciation | 281 | 253 | 214 | 215 | 206 | 149 | 153 | 159 | 163 | 155 |
| Interest Expense | 156 | 134 | 116 | 104 | 126 | 75.6 | 88.3 | 95.2 | 108 | 78.6 |
| Pretax Income | 377 | 462 | 362 | 436 | 331 | 245 | -110 | 110 | 171 | 32.9 |
| Effective Tax Rate | 25.4% | 28.5% | 27.5% | 31.9% | 30.2% | 34.3% | NM | 38.9% | 38.0% | 26.7% |
| Net Income | 281 | 330 | 262 | 296 | 230 | 159 | -99.2 | 68.2 | 104 | 32.0 |
| S&P Core Earnings | 340 | 242 | 280 | 304 | 242 | 127 | -96.0 | NA | NA | NA |

**Balance Sheet & Other Financial Data** (Million $)

| | 2007 | 2006 | 2005 | 2004 | 2003 | 2002 | 2001 | 2000 | 1999 | 1998 |
|---|---|---|---|---|---|---|---|---|---|---|
| Cash | 152 | 152 | 61.0 | 199 | 36.5 | 259 | 83.1 | 25.6 | 35.8 | 34.0 |
| Current Assets | 1,843 | 1,761 | 1,226 | 1,246 | 924 | 1,225 | 794 | 969 | 896 | 886 |
| Total Assets | 6,021 | 5,841 | 4,343 | 4,478 | 4,070 | 4,132 | 2,314 | 2,650 | 2,732 | 2,855 |
| Current Liabilities | 1,513 | 1,454 | 1,176 | 996 | 861 | 1,069 | 575 | 659 | 670 | 688 |
| Long Term Debt | 2,182 | 2,270 | 1,473 | 1,538 | 1,579 | 1,854 | 949 | 1,012 | 1,093 | 1,230 |
| Common Equity | 1,343 | 1,165 | 835 | 1,087 | 808 | 493 | 504 | 640 | 635 | 565 |
| Total Capital | 3,525 | 3,437 | 2,314 | 2,631 | 2,393 | 2,353 | 1,463 | 1,709 | 1,803 | 1,877 |
| Capital Expenditures | 309 | 280 | 292 | 196 | 137 | 158 | 68.5 | 98.7 | 107 | 84.2 |
| Cash Flow | 562 | 582 | 475 | 511 | 435 | 309 | 51.3 | 225 | 264 | 184 |
| Current Ratio | 1.2 | 1.2 | 1.0 | 1.3 | 1.1 | 1.1 | 1.4 | 1.5 | 1.3 | 1.3 |
| % Long Term Debt of Capitalization | 61.9 | 66.1 | 63.7 | 58.5 | 66.0 | 78.8 | 64.9 | 59.2 | 60.6 | 65.5 |
| % Net Income of Revenue | 3.8 | 5.0 | 4.5 | 5.4 | 4.6 | 4.1 | NM | 1.9 | 2.9 | 1.1 |
| % Return on Assets | 4.7 | 6.5 | 5.9 | 6.9 | 5.6 | 4.9 | NM | 2.5 | 3.7 | 1.3 |
| % Return on Equity | 22.4 | 32.7 | 27.2 | 31.2 | 35.4 | 32.0 | NM | 10.1 | 16.9 | 5.1 |

Data as orig reptd.; bef. results of disc opers/spec. items. Per share data adj. for stk. divs.; EPS diluted. E-Estimated. NA-Not Available. NM-Not Meaningful. NR-Not Ranked. UR-Under Review.

**Office:** 10 Longs Peak Dr, Broomfield, CO 80021-2510.
**Telephone:** 303-469-3131.
**Website:** http://www.ball.com
**Chrmn, Pres & CEO:** R.D. Hoover

**COO & EVP:** J.A. Hayes
**EVP, CFO & Chief Acctg Officer:** R.J. Seabrook
**Chief Admin Officer & Secy:** D.A. Westerlund
**Treas:** S.C. Morrison

**Investor Contact:** A.T. Scott (303-460-3537)
**Board Members:** R. W. Alspaugh, H. C. Fiedler, R. D. Hoover, J. F. Lehman, G. R. Nelson, J. Nicholson, G. M. Smart, T. M. Solso, S. A. Taylor, II, E. H. Van Der Kaay

**Founded:** 1880
**Domicile:** Indiana
**Employees:** 15,500

**STANDARD &POOR'S**

# Bank of America Corp

| S&P Recommendation | BUY ★★★★☆ | Price $16.42 (as of Nov 14, 2008) | 12-Mo. Target Price $31.00 | Investment Style Large-Cap Blend |
|---|---|---|---|---|

**GICS Sector** Financials
**Sub-Industry** Other Diversified Financial Services

**Summary** This banking company, with offices in 32 states and the District of Columbia, also provides international corporate financial services.

## Key Stock Statistics (Source S&P, Vickers, company reports)

| | | | | | | | |
|---|---|---|---|---|---|---|---|
| 52-Wk Range | $47.00– 14.88 | S&P Oper. EPS 2008E | 1.59 | Market Capitalization(B) | $82.389 | Beta | 0.40 |
| Trailing 12-Month EPS | $1.15 | S&P Oper. EPS 2009E | 2.56 | Yield (%) | 7.80 | S&P 3-Yr. Proj. EPS CAGR(%) | 6 |
| Trailing 12-Month P/E | 14.3 | P/E on S&P Oper. EPS 2008E | 10.3 | Dividend Rate/Share | $1.28 | S&P Credit Rating | AA- |
| $10K Invested 5 Yrs Ago | $5,577 | Common Shares Outstg. (M) | 5,017.6 | Institutional Ownership (%) | 59 | | |

## Price Performance

30-Week Mov. Avg. · · · 10-Week Mov. Avg. – – · **GAAP Earnings vs. Previous Year** Volume Above Avg. STARS
12-Mo. Target Price — Relative Strength — ▲ Up ▼ Down ► No Change Below Avg.

Options: ASE, CBOE, P, Ph

Analysis prepared by **Stuart Plesser** on October 20, 2008, when the stock traded at **$ 23.24**.

## Qualitative Risk Assessment

| LOW | MEDIUM | HIGH |
|---|---|---|

Our risk assessment reflects what we see as a strong U.S. presence with a robust customer base, offset by deteriorating U.S. consumer trends and exposure to residential lending and credit cards.

## Quantitative Evaluations

**S&P Quality Ranking** A-

| D | C | B- | B | B+ | A- | A | A+ |
|---|---|---|---|---|---|---|---|

**Relative Strength Rank** WEAK

26

LOWEST = 1          HIGHEST = 99

## Revenue/Earnings Data

**Revenue (Million $)**

| | 1Q | 2Q | 3Q | 4Q | Year |
|---|---|---|---|---|---|
| 2008 | 28,871 | 29,721 | 30,175 | -- | -- |
| 2007 | 30,447 | 32,409 | 29,347 | 26,987 | 119,190 |
| 2006 | 27,026 | 28,895 | 30,739 | 30,357 | 117,017 |
| 2005 | 19,168 | 21,222 | 21,621 | 22,280 | 83,980 |
| 2004 | 12,282 | 16,471 | 16,409 | 18,162 | 63,324 |
| 2003 | 11,410 | 12,250 | 12,294 | 12,111 | 48,065 |

**Earnings Per Share ($)**

| | | | | | |
|---|---|---|---|---|---|
| 2008 | 0.23 | 0.72 | 0.15 | E0.48 | E1.59 |
| 2007 | 1.16 | 1.28 | 0.82 | 0.05 | 3.30 |
| 2006 | 1.07 | 1.19 | 1.18 | 1.16 | 4.59 |
| 2005 | 1.07 | 1.17 | 0.95 | 0.88 | 4.04 |
| 2004 | 0.92 | 0.93 | 0.91 | 0.94 | 3.69 |
| 2003 | 0.80 | 0.90 | 0.96 | 0.92 | 3.57 |

Fiscal year ended Dec. 31. Next earnings report expected: Late January. EPS Estimates based on S&P Operating Earnings; historical GAAP earnings are as reported.

## Highlights

➤ We forecast total revenue growth of around 20% in 2009, and expect positive operating leverage to be driven by recent acquisitions and expense controls. BAC's net interest margin will likely stay flat at roughly 2.90% in 2009 vs. 2008, as we don't look for interest rates to be lowered significantly from today's levels. Still, we expect strong growth in net interest income growth in 2008 to continue in 2009 due to growth in earning assets. Specifically, BAC's average earning assets will likely increase in the high single-digits, after a projected double-digit increase in 2008. Deposit growth should continue to be strong reflecting a flight to higher quality banks.

➤ We look for additional securities writedowns but at a lower level than in the third-quarter of 2008. Based on further deterioration of U.S. credit quality, we look for chargeoff levels to accelerate through the first half of 2009, which should result in the need for continued elevated provisions. We think expenses will remain under tight control.

➤ Excluding merger-related expenses, we estimate operating EPS of $1.59 in 2008 and $2.56 in 2009.

## Investment Rationale/Risk

➤ Based on continued credit deterioration, particularly credit card loans, we think chargeoff levels will continue to rise, at least through the first half of 2009. BAC's reserves seem adequate for further writedowns, and with the recently raised capital position of $10 billion, plus a government injection of $25 billion, capital levels seem adequate to us. We are in favor of BAC recently halving its dividend, as we think funds can be better used to help integrate BAC's pending merger with Merrill Lynch (MER $18 ***). We view BAC's pending purchase of MER as a long-term positive, as we believe cross-selling opportunities will arise, although we have some concerns about near-term integration. Trading at 0.8X book value, we think BAC offers value.

➤ Risks to our recommendation and target price include worse-than-expected credit conditions brought about by a deterioration in housing prices.

➤ Our 12-month target price of $31 equates to about 1.03X current book value of $30, a discount to historical levels. We think BAC's book value has limited downside potential due to what we view as conservative writedowns.

## Dividend Data (Dates: mm/dd Payment Date: mm/dd/yy)

| Amount ($) | Date Decl. | Ex-Div. Date | Stk. of Record | Payment Date |
|---|---|---|---|---|
| 0.640 | 01/23 | 03/05 | 03/07 | 03/28/08 |
| 0.640 | 04/23 | 06/04 | 06/06 | 06/27/08 |
| 0.640 | 07/23 | 09/03 | 09/05 | 09/26/08 |
| 0.320 | 10/06 | 12/03 | 12/05 | 12/26/08 |

Dividends have been paid since 1903. Source: Company reports.

*The McGraw-Hill Companies*

# Bank of America Corp

**STANDARD &POOR'S**

## Business Summary October 20, 2008

CORPORATE OVERVIEW. Bank of America has operations in 32 states, the District of Columbia and 44 foreign countries. In the U.S., it has more than 6,100 retail banking centers and approximately 18,500 ATMs. BAC reports the results of its operations through three business segments: Global Consumer and Small Business Banking, Global Corporate and Investment Banking, and Global Wealth and Investment Management.

Global Consumer and Small Business Banking has about 59 million consumer and mass-market small business relationships and provides a diversified range of products and services to individuals and small businesses through multiple delivery channels. Global Corporate and Investment Banking provides comprehensive financial solutions. Services include: bank deposit and credit products; risk management, cash management and payment services; equity and debt capital raising; and advisory services. Global Wealth and Investment Management offers comprehensive banking and investment services to more than three million individual and institutional customers. Clients have access to services from three primary businesses: U.S. Trust, Bank of America Private Wealth Management; Columbia Management; and Premier Banking & Investments. Services include investment services, estate management, financial planning services, fiduciary management, credit and banking expertise, and diversified asset management products to institutional clients as well as high-net-worth individuals.

IMPACT OF MAJOR DEVELOPMENTS. On September 15, 2008, BAC announced it had agreed to acquire Merrill Lynch & Co., Inc. in a $50 billion all-stock transaction, pending the necessary approvals. We think the deal is a good fit for BAC, particularly as it adds 20,000 financial advisors and creates cross-selling oppurtunities. On July 1, 2008, BAC acquired Countrywide Financial in a stock deal valued at $2.5 billion. Although the deal makes BAC a top U.S. mortgage originator, we believe it increases BAC's risk profile due to Countrywide's loan portfolio, which has a high proportion of Option Arm loans. On October 1, 2007, BAC acquired LaSalle Bank from ABN AMRO for $21 billion in cash, with a $5 billion rebate of excess capital to BAC. The deal was expected to be immediately accretive to EPS, and BAC sees $400 million in annual after-tax cost savings in 2008, and $800 million in 2009. We believe the deal will provide BAC with a strong presence in the attractive Chicago market, and we expect BAC's experience in similar transactions, such as the acquisition of Fleet Financial, to add to the likelihood of a successful integration.

## Company Financials Fiscal Year Ended Dec. 31

| Per Share Data ($) | 2007 | 2006 | 2005 | 2004 | 2003 | 2002 | 2001 | 2000 | 1999 | 1998 |
|---|---|---|---|---|---|---|---|---|---|---|
| Tangible Book Value | 11.54 | 12.18 | 13.18 | 12.41 | 12.34 | 12.59 | 11.65 | 10.66 | 9.06 | 9.01 |
| Earnings | 3.30 | 4.59 | 4.04 | 3.69 | 3.57 | 2.96 | 2.09 | 2.26 | 2.24 | 1.45 |
| S&P Core Earnings | 3.26 | 4.47 | 4.06 | 3.75 | 3.54 | 2.70 | 1.96 | NA | NA | NA |
| Dividends | 2.40 | 2.12 | 1.90 | 1.70 | 1.44 | 1.22 | 1.14 | 1.03 | 0.93 | 0.80 |
| Payout Ratio | 73% | 46% | 47% | 46% | 40% | 41% | 55% | 46% | 41% | 55% |
| Prices:High | 54.21 | 55.08 | 47.44 | 47.47 | 42.45 | 38.54 | 32.77 | 30.50 | 38.19 | 44.22 |
| Prices:Low | 40.61 | 40.93 | 41.13 | 38.51 | 32.13 | 26.98 | 22.50 | 18.16 | 23.81 | 22.00 |
| P/E Ratio:High | 16 | 12 | 12 | 13 | 12 | 13 | 16 | 13 | 17 | 30 |
| P/E Ratio:Low | 12 | 9 | 10 | 10 | 9 | 9 | 11 | 8 | 11 | 15 |

| Income Statement Analysis (Million $) | | | | | | | | | | |
|---|---|---|---|---|---|---|---|---|---|---|
| Net Interest Income | 34,433 | 34,591 | 30,737 | 28,797 | 21,464 | 20,923 | 20,290 | 18,442 | 18,237 | 18,298 |
| Tax Equivalent Adjustment | 1,749 | 1,224 | 832 | 716 | 643 | 588 | 343 | 322 | 215 | 128 |
| Non Interest Income | 31,706 | 38,432 | 26,438 | 20,097 | 16,422 | 13,571 | 14,348 | 14,489 | 14,069 | 12,189 |
| Loan Loss Provision | 8,385 | 5,010 | 4,014 | 2,769 | 2,839 | 3,697 | 4,287 | 2,535 | 182 | 2,920 |
| % Expense/Operating Revenue | 56.0% | 47.9% | 50.4% | 54.5% | 52.2% | 63.1% | 59.8% | 63.7% | 56.9% | 67.4% |
| Pretax Income | 20,924 | 31,973 | 24,480 | 21,221 | 15,861 | 12,991 | 10,117 | 11,788 | 12,215 | 8,048 |
| Effective Tax Rate | 28.4% | 33.9% | 32.7% | 33.4% | 31.8% | 28.8% | 32.9% | 36.2% | 35.5% | 35.8% |
| Net Income | 14,982 | 21,133 | 16,465 | 14,143 | 10,810 | 9,249 | 6,792 | 7,517 | 7,882 | 5,165 |
| % Net Interest Margin | 2.60 | 2.82 | 2.84 | 3.26 | 3.36 | 3.75 | 3.68 | 3.22 | 3.47 | 3.69 |
| S&P Core Earnings | 14,615 | 20,568 | 16,499 | 14,308 | 10,708 | 8,452 | 6,384 | NA | NA | NA |

| Balance Sheet & Other Financial Data (Million $) | | | | | | | | | | |
|---|---|---|---|---|---|---|---|---|---|---|
| Money Market Assets | 303,389 | 302,482 | 294,292 | 197,308 | 153,090 | 115,687 | 81,384 | 76,544 | 81,226 | 73,498 |
| Investment Securities | 214,056 | 192,846 | 221,603 | 195,073 | 68,240 | 69,148 | 85,499 | 65,838 | 83,069 | 80,587 |
| Commercial Loans | 325,143 | 240,785 | 218,334 | 193,930 | 131,304 | 145,170 | 163,898 | 203,542 | 195,779 | 196,130 |
| Other Loans | 551,201 | 465,705 | 355,457 | 327,907 | 240,159 | 197,585 | 165,255 | 188,651 | 174,883 | 161,198 |
| Total Assets | 1,715,746 | 1,459,737 | 1,291,803 | 1,110,457 | 736,445 | 660,458 | 621,764 | 642,191 | 632,574 | 617,679 |
| Demand Deposits | 192,227 | 184,808 | 186,736 | 169,899 | 121,530 | 124,359 | 113,934 | 100,645 | 95,469 | 94,336 |
| Time Deposits | 612,950 | 508,689 | 447,934 | 448,671 | 292,583 | 262,099 | 259,561 | 263,599 | 251,804 | 262,974 |
| Long Term Debt | 197,508 | 146,000 | 100,848 | 98,078 | 75,343 | 67,176 | 68,026 | 72,502 | 60,441 | 50,842 |
| Common Equity | 142,394 | 132,421 | 101,262 | 99,374 | 47,926 | 50,261 | 48,455 | 47,556 | 44,355 | 45,855 |
| % Return on Assets | 0.9 | 1.5 | 1.4 | 1.5 | 1.5 | 1.4 | 1.1 | 1.2 | 1.3 | 0.9 |
| % Return on Equity | 10.8 | 18.1 | 16.3 | 19.2 | 22.0 | 18.7 | 14.1 | 16.3 | 17.5 | 11.5 |
| % Loan Loss Reserve | 1.3 | 0.4 | 1.4 | 1.7 | 1.7 | 2.0 | 2.1 | 1.7 | 1.8 | 2.0 |
| % Loans/Deposits | 105.5 | 304.3 | 87.4 | 84.4 | 89.7 | 88.4 | 97.8 | 107.7 | 106.7 | 99.4 |
| % Equity to Assets | 8.7 | 8.5 | 8.4 | 8.0 | 7.0 | 7.7 | 7.6 | 7.2 | 7.2 | 7.6 |

Data as orig reptd.; bef. results of disc opers/spec. items. Per share data adj. for stk. divs.; EPS diluted. E-Estimated. NA-Not Available. NM-Not Meaningful. NR-Not Ranked. UR-Under Review.

**Office:** 100 N Tryon St, Charlotte, NC 28255.
**Telephone:** 704-386-8486.
**Website:** http://www.bankofamerica.com
**Chrmn, Pres & CEO:** K.D. Lewis

**Vice Chrmn:** G.L. Curl
**EVP & General Counsel:** T.J. Mayopoulos
**SVP & Chief Acctg Officer:** N.A. Cotty
**CFO:** J.L. Price

**Investor Contact:** K. Stitt (704-386-5667)
**Board Members:** W. Barnet, III, F. P. Bramble, J. T. Collins, G. L. Countryman, G. L. Curl, T. Franks, C. K. Gifford, K. D. Lewis, M. Lozano, W. E. Massey, T. J. May, P. E. Mitchell, T. M. Ryan, O. T. Sloan, III, M. R. Spangler, A. Spence, R. L. Tillman, J. M. Ward

**Founded:** 1874
**Domicile:** Delaware
**Employees:** 210,000

*The McGraw-Hill Companies*

# Bank of New York Mellon Corp (The)

**STANDARD &POOR'S**

| **S&P Recommendation** HOLD ★★★☆☆ | **Price** $30.24 (as of Nov 14, 2008) | **12-Mo. Target Price** $36.00 | **Investment Style** Large-Cap Blend |
|---|---|---|---|

**GICS Sector** Financials
**Sub-Industry** Asset Management & Custody Banks

**Summary** This company is a leader in securities processing, and also provides a complete range of banking, asset management, and other financial services.

## Key Stock Statistics (Source S&P, Vickers, company reports)

| | | | | | | | |
|---|---|---|---|---|---|---|---|
| 52-Wk Range | $50.26– 20.49 | S&P Oper. EPS 2008**E** | 2.10 | Market Capitalization(B) | $34.702 | Beta | 0.65 |
| Trailing 12-Month EPS | $1.63 | S&P Oper. EPS 2009**E** | 3.12 | Yield (%) | 3.17 | S&P 3-Yr. Proj. EPS CAGR(%) | 9 |
| Trailing 12-Month P/E | 18.6 | P/E on S&P Oper. EPS 2008**E** | 14.4 | Dividend Rate/Share | $0.96 | S&P Credit Rating | A+ |
| $10K Invested 5 Yrs Ago | $10,783 | Common Shares Outstg. (M) | 1,147.6 | Institutional Ownership (%) | 78 | | |

## Price Performance

30-Week Mov. Avg. · · · ·  10-Week Mov. Avg. – –  **GAAP Earnings vs. Previous Year**  Volume Above Avg. STARS
12-Mo. Target Price —  Relative Strength —  ▲ Up ▼ Down ► No Change  Below Avg.  ★

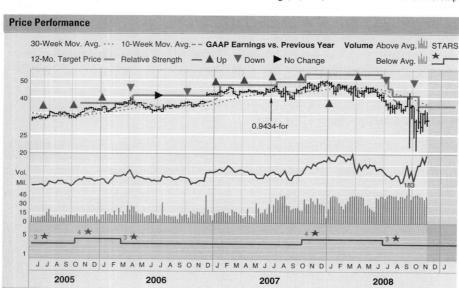

0.9434-for

Options: ASE, CBOE, P, Ph

Analysis prepared by **Stuart Plesser** on October 23, 2008, when the stock traded at **$ 28.73**.

## Highlights

➤ We expect total revenues to rise to $16.0 billion in 2009, 9.5% higher than our forecast for 2008, driven by fee growth and net interest income growth reflecting higher earnings assets. Although fees from its asset management business may come under pressure due to weakness in the equity markets, high volatility should favor its services business. We forecast a stable net interest margin of roughly 2.25%. We see BK continuing to restrict non-merger related expense growth. We expect much of the benefits of scale from the merger with Mellon Financial to help international growth, which currently totals 34% of revenue vs. 30% last year.

➤ We expect new business wins to continue as clients will likely move toward a flight to quality in light of turmoil in the credit markets. We are encouraged by BK's business strategy and see continued expense discipline and expansion through smaller acquisitions and international alliances ahead. That said, further impairment charges on BK's $41.5 billion investment portfolio may weigh on earnings in the coming quarters.

➤ We forecast operating EPS of $2.10 in 2008 and $3.12 in 2009.

## Investment Rationale/Risk

➤ We believe BK has taken the right steps to become a major global player in custody banking and corporate trust. We see execution and clearing services, foreign exchange and trading as areas for growth in 2009. We are encouraged by the strong performance of future growth drivers for BK, including new business wins, and expense savings. We further think BK could benefit as its competitors struggle with credit and subprime related issues. But in the near term, we are concerned of additional client support agreements and losses from BK's investment portfolio. We are also concerned regarding the outcome of $22.5 billion lawsuit by the Russian government for money laundering.

➤ Risks to our recommendation and target price include a significant decline in capital markets activity, credit losses and/or loan loss reserve provisions that are greater than our expectations, execution risks, litigation risk, and the need to support client funds.

➤ Our 12-month target price of $36 equates to a P/E of 11.6X our 2009 EPS estimate of $3.11, a discount to its historical average, justified by turmoil in the credit markets.

## Qualitative Risk Assessment

| LOW | **MEDIUM** | HIGH |
|---|---|---|

Our risk assessment reflects what we view as solid fundamentals and diverse business lines offset by an ongoing $22.5 billion lawsuit by the Russian government for money laundering and disruption in the credit markets. BK has provided stable earnings over the long term, and we believe it would be able to sustain a prolonged economic downturn.

## Quantitative Evaluations

**S&P Quality Ranking** A-

| D | C | B- | B | B+ | **A-** | A | A+ |
|---|---|---|---|---|---|---|---|

**Relative Strength Rank** **STRONG**

80

LOWEST = 1   HIGHEST = 99

## Revenue/Earnings Data

**Revenue (Million $)**

| | 1Q | 2Q | 3Q | 4Q | Year |
|---|---|---|---|---|---|
| 2008 | 3,745 | -- | -- | -- | -- |
| 2007 | 2,496 | 2,893 | 3,600 | 3,044 | 9,031 |
| 2006 | 2,074 | 2,276 | 2,219 | 2,493 | 9,062 |
| 2005 | 1,917 | 2,077 | 2,126 | 2,230 | 8,312 |
| 2004 | 1,671 | 1,767 | 1,739 | 1,968 | 7,144 |
| 2003 | 1,420 | 1,591 | 1,638 | 1,686 | 6,336 |

**Earnings Per Share ($)**

| | 1Q | 2Q | 3Q | 4Q | Year |
|---|---|---|---|---|---|
| 2008 | 0.65 | 0.26 | 0.27 | E0.72 | E2.10 |
| 2007 | 0.60 | 0.59 | 0.56 | 0.61 | 2.38 |
| 2006 | 0.50 | 0.55 | 0.41 | 0.59 | 2.05 |
| 2005 | 0.52 | 0.55 | 0.54 | 0.56 | 2.15 |
| 2004 | 0.50 | 0.51 | 0.49 | 0.48 | 1.96 |
| 2003 | 0.43 | 0.41 | 0.36 | 0.42 | 1.61 |

Fiscal year ended Dec. 31. Next earnings report expected: NA. EPS Estimates based on S&P Operating Earnings; historical GAAP earnings are as reported.

## Dividend Data (Dates: mm/dd Payment Date: mm/dd/yy)

| Amount ($) | Date Decl. | Ex-Div. Date | Stk. of Record | Payment Date |
|---|---|---|---|---|
| 0.240 | 01/08 | 01/18 | 01/23 | 02/01/08 |
| 0.240 | 04/08 | 04/21 | 04/23 | 05/02/08 |
| 0.240 | 07/08 | 07/21 | 07/23 | 08/01/08 |
| 0.240 | 10/14 | 10/22 | 10/24 | 11/03/08 |

Dividends have been paid since 1785. Source: Company reports.

**Please read the Required Disclosures and Analyst Certification on the last page of this report.**

The **McGraw-Hill** Companies

# Bank of New York Mellon Corp (The)

**STANDARD**
**&POOR'S**

## Business Summary October 23, 2008

CORPORATE OVERVIEW. Bank of New York Mellon provides a comprehensive array of services that enable institutions and individuals to move and manage their financial assets in more than 100 markets worldwide. The company has several core competencies: institutional services, private banking, and asset management. Its global client base includes a broad range of leading financial institutions, corporations, government entities, endowments, and foundations.

Key products include advisory and asset management services to support the investment decision, trade execution, clearance and settlement capabilities, custody, securities lending, accounting, and administrative services for investment portfolios, sophisticated risk and performance measurement tools for analyzing portfolios, and services for issuers of both equity and debt securities.

CORPORATE STRATEGY. BK's strategy over the past decade has been to focus on scalable, fee-based securities servicing and fiduciary businesses, and it has achieved top three market share in most of its major product lines. The company attempts to distinguish itself competitively by offering products and services around the investment lifecycle.

By providing integrated solutions for clients' needs, BK strives to be the preferred partner in helping its clients succeed in the world's rapidly evolving financial markets. The company's key objectives include achieving positive operating leverage on an annual basis and sustaining top-line growth by expanding client relationships and winning new ones.

To achieve its top objectives, BK has grown both through internal reinvestments as well as the execution of strategic acquisitions to expand product offerings and increase market share in its scale businesses. Internal reinvestment occurs mainly through increased technology spending, staffing levels, marketing/branding initiatives, quality programs, and product development. The company invests in technology to improve the breadth and quality of its product offerings, and to increase economies of scale. BK has acquired over 90 businesses over the past 10 years, almost exclusively in its securities servicing and asset management areas.

## Company Financials Fiscal Year Ended Dec. 31

| Per Share Data ($) | 2007 | 2006 | 2005 | 2004 | 2003 | 2002 | 2001 | 2000 | 1999 | 1998 |
|---|---|---|---|---|---|---|---|---|---|---|
| Tangible Book Value | 5.83 | 11.50 | 7.48 | 6.84 | 5.93 | 6.00 | 6.14 | 8.80 | 7.37 | 7.47 |
| Earnings | 2.38 | 2.05 | 2.15 | 1.96 | 1.61 | 1.31 | 1.92 | 2.04 | 2.41 | 1.62 |
| S&P Core Earnings | 2.33 | 2.01 | 2.11 | 1.83 | 1.55 | 1.07 | 1.65 | NA | NA | NA |
| Dividends | 0.95 | 0.91 | 0.87 | 0.84 | 0.81 | 0.81 | 0.76 | 0.70 | 0.61 | 0.57 |
| Payout Ratio | 40% | 45% | 40% | 43% | 50% | 61% | 40% | 34% | 26% | 35% |
| Prices:High | 50.26 | 42.98 | 35.71 | 36.94 | 35.50 | 49.29 | 61.61 | 62.94 | 47.90 | 43.00 |
| Prices:Low | 38.30 | 32.66 | 28.55 | 28.88 | 20.40 | 22.10 | 31.53 | 31.53 | 33.72 | 25.44 |
| P/E Ratio:High | 21 | 21 | 17 | 19 | 22 | 37 | 32 | 31 | 20 | 27 |
| P/E Ratio:Low | 16 | 16 | 13 | 15 | 13 | 17 | 16 | 15 | 14 | 16 |

| Income Statement Analysis (Million $) | | | | | | | | | | |
|---|---|---|---|---|---|---|---|---|---|---|
| Net Interest Income | 2,300 | 1,499 | 1,909 | 1,645 | 1,609 | 1,665 | 1,681 | 1,870 | 1,701 | 1,651 |
| Tax Equivalent Adjustment | 12.0 | NA | 29.0 | 30.0 | 35.0 | 49.0 | 60.0 | 54.0 | 44.0 | 58.0 |
| Non Interest Income | 9,232 | 5,337 | 4,888 | 4,613 | 3,971 | 3,261 | 3,386 | 2,959 | 3,294 | 2,108 |
| Loan Loss Provision | -10.0 | 20.0 | 15.0 | 15.0 | 155 | 685 | 375 | 105 | 135 | 20.0 |
| % Expense/Operating Revenue | 70.4% | 68.6% | 65.7% | 65.6% | 65.9% | 55.3% | 54.4% | 51.4% | 44.0% | 50.5% |
| Pretax Income | 3,225 | 2,170 | 2,367 | 2,199 | 1,762 | 1,372 | 2,058 | 2,251 | 2,840 | 1,891 |
| Effective Tax Rate | 31.0% | 32.0% | 33.6% | 34.5% | 34.3% | 34.3% | 34.7% | 36.5% | 38.8% | 37.0% |
| Net Income | 2,227 | 1,476 | 1,571 | 1,440 | 1,157 | 902 | 1,343 | 1,429 | 1,739 | 1,192 |
| % Net Interest Margin | 2.08 | 2.01 | 2.36 | 2.07 | 2.22 | 2.62 | 2.57 | 2.96 | 3.11 | 3.24 |
| S&P Core Earnings | 2,179 | 1,452 | 1,536 | 1,350 | 1,097 | 728 | 1,159 | NA | NA | NA |

| Balance Sheet & Other Financial Data (Million $) | | | | | | | | | | |
|---|---|---|---|---|---|---|---|---|---|---|
| Money Market Assets | 49,840 | 23,830 | 16,999 | 18,527 | 18,521 | 13,798 | 19,684 | 23,178 | 20,948 | 9,422 |
| Investment Securities | 48,698 | 21,106 | 27,326 | 23,802 | 22,903 | 18,300 | 12,862 | 7,401 | 6,899 | 6,415 |
| Commercial Loans | 4,766 | 5,925 | 13,252 | 12,624 | 13,646 | 20,335 | 19,034 | 21,327 | 17,851 | 16,407 |
| Other Loans | 43,465 | 31,868 | 27,474 | 23,157 | 21,637 | 11,004 | 16,713 | 14,934 | 21,251 | 21,979 |
| Total Assets | 197,656 | 103,370 | 102,074 | 94,529 | 92,397 | 77,564 | 81,025 | 77,114 | 74,756 | 63,503 |
| Demand Deposits | 32,372 | 19,554 | 18,236 | 17,442 | 14,789 | 13,301 | 12,635 | 13,255 | 12,162 | 11,480 |
| Time Deposits | 85,753 | 45,992 | 46,188 | 41,279 | 41,617 | 42,086 | 43,076 | 43,121 | 43,589 | 33,152 |
| Long Term Debt | 16,873 | 8,773 | Nil | Nil | Nil | Nil | Nil | 4,536 | 4,311 | 3,386 |
| Common Equity | 29,403 | 11,593 | 9,876 | 9,290 | 8,428 | 6,684 | 6,317 | 6,151 | 5,142 | 5,447 |
| % Return on Assets | 1.5 | 1.4 | 1.6 | 1.5 | 1.4 | 1.1 | 1.7 | 1.9 | 2.5 | 1.9 |
| % Return on Equity | 10.9 | 13.7 | 16.4 | 16.3 | 15.3 | 13.9 | 21.5 | 25.3 | 32.8 | 22.8 |
| % Loan Loss Reserve | 0.6 | 0.8 | 1.0 | 1.7 | 1.9 | 2.7 | 1.7 | 1.7 | 1.6 | 1.7 |
| % Loans/Deposits | 49.3 | 60.8 | 63.2 | 60.9 | 62.6 | 56.6 | 64.2 | 64.3 | 67.3 | 86.0 |
| % Equity to Assets | 13.6 | 10.5 | 9.7 | 9.5 | 8.9 | 8.2 | 7.9 | 7.4 | 7.7 | 8.5 |

Data as orig reptd.; bef. results of disc opers/spec. items. Per share data adj. for stk. divs.; EPS diluted. E-Estimated. NA-Not Available. NM-Not Meaningful. NR-Not Ranked. UR-Under Review.

**Office:** One Wall Street, New York, NY 10286.
**Telephone:** 212-495-1784.
**Email:** shareowner-svcs@bankofny.com
**Website:** http://www.bankofny.com

**Chrmn & CEO:** R.P. Kelly
**Pres:** G.L. Hassell
**Vice Chrmn:** S.G. Elliott
**Vice Chrmn:** D.F. Lamere

**EVP & CFO:** T.P. Gibbons
**Board Members:** R. E. Bruch, N. M. Donofrio, S. G. Elliott, G. L. Hassell, E. F. Kelly, R. P. Kelly, R. J. Kogan, M. J. Kowalski, D. F. Lamere, J. A. Luke, Jr., R. Mehrabian, M. A. Nordenberg, C. A. Rein, W. C. Richardson, S. C. Scott, III, J. Surma, Jr., W. W. von Schack

**Founded:** 1784
**Domicile:** New York
**Employees:** 42,100

The McGraw·Hill Companies

# Bard (C.R.) Inc

STANDARD &POOR'S

| S&P Recommendation | BUY ★★★★☆ | Price $82.91 (as of Nov 14, 2008) | 12-Mo. Target Price $96.00 | Investment Style Large-Cap Growth |
|---|---|---|---|---|

**GICS Sector** Health Care
**Sub-Industry** Health Care Equipment

**Summary** This diversified maker of therapeutic and diagnostic medical devices has exposure to the vascular, urology, oncology, and specialty surgical markets.

## Key Stock Statistics (Source S&P, Vickers, company reports)

| | | | | | | | |
|---|---|---|---|---|---|---|---|
| 52-Wk Range | $101.61– 70.00 | S&P Oper. EPS 2008E | 4.44 | Market Capitalization(B) | $8.225 | Beta | 0.43 |
| Trailing 12-Month EPS | $3.61 | S&P Oper. EPS 2009E | 5.10 | Yield (%) | 0.77 | S&P 3-Yr. Proj. EPS CAGR(%) | 14 |
| Trailing 12-Month P/E | 23.0 | P/E on S&P Oper. EPS 2008E | 18.7 | Dividend Rate/Share | $0.64 | S&P Credit Rating | A |
| $10K Invested 5 Yrs Ago | $22,427 | Common Shares Outstg. (M) | 99.2 | Institutional Ownership (%) | 89 | | |

## Price Performance

30-Week Mov. Avg. ···  10-Week Mov. Avg. — **GAAP Earnings vs. Previous Year**  Volume Above Avg. STARS
12-Mo. Target Price —  Relative Strength — ▲ Up ▼ Down ▶ No Change  Below Avg. ★

Options: ASE, CBOE, P, Ph

Analysis prepared by **Robert M. Gold** on October 24, 2008, when the stock traded at **$ 83.63**.

## Highlights

➤ We believe that net sales in 2008 will modestly exceed $2.4 billion, up from $2.2 billion in 2007, as double-digit growth in the vascular, oncology and urology segments joins about 4% growth in the surgery segment. We think new product launches will provide incremental sales growth in coming quarters. Our 2009 revenue forecast is $2.7 billion.

➤ We forecast that gross margins will expand about 40 basis points to 61.0% in 2008, due to increased product manufacturing at a facility in Puerto Rico, new product introductions, and a recovery in the hernia repair product category, with modest improvement also envisioned in 2009. We forecast that SG&A costs will remain at about 29% to 30% of sales through 2009, with R&D costs absorbing approximately 6.0% to 7.0%. We see an effective tax rate of 29% in 2008 and 2009.

➤ Our 2008 EPS estimate is $4.44, up from the $3.80 in operating EPS from continuing operations generated in 2007, which assumes additional common share repurchases during the year. Our 2009 EPS estimate is $5.10.

## Investment Rationale/Risk

➤ We believe new products in the oncology, hernia repair, and urology segments, plus momentum in existing categories, will help drive low-double-digit constant currency sales growth over the coming three years. While we think the company will no longer generate meaningful upside to our EPS estimates from gross margin expansion, we believe new product launches, product acquisitions and tight operating cost controls will allow Bard to generate 2008 revenue and earnings growth in line with medical device peers. Looking into 2009, we think Bard is positioned for growth ahead of peers due to the non-discretionary profile of its product line.

➤ Risks to our recommendation and target price include unfavorable patent litigation outcomes, adverse reimbursement changes, and a failure to commercialize new products in a timely fashion.

➤ Our projected long-term earnings growth rate for BCR is now modestly above peers, and we therefore believe a premium valuation is appropriate. By applying a forward P/E to earnings ratio of 1.34X to our 2009 EPS estimate, and assuming three-year EPS growth of 14%, our 12-month target price is $96.

## Qualitative Risk Assessment

| LOW | MEDIUM | HIGH |
|---|---|---|

Our risk assessment reflects that BCR operates in a highly competitive environment. In addition, hospital customers generate a large portion of revenues from Medicare, and are therefore subject to reimbursement risks that could reduce prices paid to suppliers. However, we believe BCR's product line is largely focused on areas that have not been subject to intense pricing pressure, and we think management has a solid track record in terms of identifying and integrating acquisitions.

## Quantitative Evaluations

**S&P Quality Ranking**  A-

| D | C | B- | B | B+ | A- | A | A+ |
|---|---|---|---|---|---|---|---|

**Relative Strength Rank**  STRONG

LOWEST = 1    81    HIGHEST = 99

## Revenue/Earnings Data

**Revenue (Million $)**

| | 1Q | 2Q | 3Q | 4Q | Year |
|---|---|---|---|---|---|
| 2008 | 584.0 | 617.1 | 616.8 | -- | -- |
| 2007 | 528.2 | 545.7 | 544.8 | 583.3 | 2,202 |
| 2006 | 467.5 | 498.2 | 498.9 | 520.9 | 1,986 |
| 2005 | 428.6 | 447.4 | 443.3 | 452.0 | 1,771 |
| 2004 | 393.8 | 416.3 | 421.9 | 424.1 | 1,656 |
| 2003 | 335.9 | 354.2 | 361.8 | 381.2 | 1,433 |

**Earnings Per Share ($)**

| | | | | | |
|---|---|---|---|---|---|
| 2008 | 0.76 | 0.76 | 1.09 | E1.18 | E4.44 |
| 2007 | 0.95 | 0.91 | 0.96 | 1.01 | 3.84 |
| 2006 | 0.76 | 0.76 | 0.82 | 0.21 | 2.55 |
| 2005 | 0.75 | 0.79 | 0.83 | 0.75 | 3.12 |
| 2004 | 0.68 | 0.55 | 0.95 | 0.65 | 2.82 |
| 2003 | 0.45 | 0.47 | 0.49 | 0.20 | 1.60 |

Fiscal year ended Dec. 31. Next earnings report expected: Early February. EPS Estimates based on S&P Operating Earnings; historical GAAP earnings are as reported.

## Dividend Data (Dates: mm/dd Payment Date: mm/dd/yy)

| Amount ($) | Date Decl. | Ex-Div. Date | Stk. of Record | Payment Date |
|---|---|---|---|---|
| 0.150 | 12/12 | 01/16 | 01/21 | 02/01/08 |
| 0.160 | 06/11 | 07/17 | 07/21 | 08/01/08 |
| 0.160 | 10/08 | 10/16 | 10/20 | 10/31/08 |

Dividends have been paid since 1960. Source: Company reports.

---

**Please read the Required Disclosures and Analyst Certification on the last page of this report.**

# Bard (C.R.) Inc

**STANDARD &POOR'S**

## Business Summary October 24, 2008

CORPORATE OVERVIEW. This company offers a range of medical, surgical, diagnostic and patient care devices. Sales in 2007 came from urology (30%), vascular (25%), oncology (25%), surgical specialties (16%), and other (4%) products.

Bard's vascular products include percutaneous transluminal angioplasty catheters, guide wires, introducers and accessories, peripheral stents, vena cava filters and biopsy devices; electrophysiology products such as lab systems, and diagnostic therapeutic and temporary pacing electrode catheters; and fabrics, meshes and implantable vascular grafts.

Urological diagnosis and intervention products include Foley catheters, procedure kits and trays, and related urine monitoring and collection systems; urethral stents; and specialty devices for incontinence, endoscopic procedures, and stone removal. Newer products include the Infection Control Foley catheter that reduces the rate of urinary tract infections; a collagen implant and sling materials used to treat urinary incontinence; and brachytherapy services, devices, and radioactive seeds to treat prostate cancer.

Oncology products include specialty access catheters and ports; gastroenterological products (endoscopic accessories, percutaneous feeding devices and stents); biopsy devices; and a suturing system for gastroesophageal reflux disease.

Surgical specialties products include meshes for hernia and other soft tissue repairs; irrigation devices for orthopedic, laparoscopic and gynecological procedures; and topical hemostatic devices. In January 2003, Bard introduced the VentralexT hernia patch, a simplified intra-abdominal hernia repair technology characterized by minimal suturing, small incisions, and potentially shorter recovery times. To further expand its markets around the hernia repair call point, in June 2004, Bard acquired the Salute Fixation system and related technology from Onux Inc. The device is used to attach mesh to host tissue for laparoscopic hernia repair procedures. In December 2007, Bard entered into a license agreement with Genzyme Corp. to manufacture and market the Sepramesh IP hernia repair product line and incorporate the related Sepra coating technology into the development of future hernia repair applications.

## Company Financials Fiscal Year Ended Dec. 31

| Per Share Data ($) | 2007 | 2006 | 2005 | 2004 | 2003 | 2002 | 2001 | 2000 | 1999 | 1998 |
|---|---|---|---|---|---|---|---|---|---|---|
| Tangible Book Value | 10.73 | 9.46 | 10.39 | 7.26 | 5.35 | 4.84 | 3.97 | 2.53 | 2.34 | 2.03 |
| Cash Flow | 4.59 | 3.25 | 3.71 | 3.33 | 2.03 | 1.87 | 1.89 | 1.53 | 1.61 | 2.78 |
| Earnings | 3.84 | 2.55 | 3.12 | 2.82 | 1.60 | 1.47 | 1.38 | 1.04 | 1.14 | 2.26 |
| S&P Core Earnings | 3.86 | 2.96 | 2.86 | 2.29 | 1.73 | 1.27 | 1.21 | NA | NA | NA |
| Dividends | 0.58 | 0.54 | 0.50 | 0.47 | 0.45 | 0.43 | 0.42 | 0.41 | 0.39 | 0.37 |
| Payout Ratio | 15% | 21% | 16% | 17% | 28% | 29% | 31% | 39% | 34% | 16% |
| Prices:High | 95.33 | 85.72 | 72.79 | 65.13 | 40.80 | 31.97 | 32.47 | 27.47 | 29.94 | 25.13 |
| Prices:Low | 76.61 | 59.89 | 60.82 | 40.09 | 27.02 | 22.05 | 20.43 | 17.50 | 20.84 | 14.25 |
| P/E Ratio:High | 25 | 34 | 23 | 23 | 25 | 22 | 24 | 26 | 26 | 11 |
| P/E Ratio:Low | 20 | 23 | 19 | 14 | 17 | 15 | 15 | 17 | 18 | 6 |

| Income Statement Analysis (Million $) | 2007 | 2006 | 2005 | 2004 | 2003 | 2002 | 2001 | 2000 | 1999 | 1998 |
|---|---|---|---|---|---|---|---|---|---|---|
| Revenue | 2,202 | 1,986 | 1,771 | 1,656 | 1,433 | 1,274 | 1,181 | 1,099 | 1,037 | 1,165 |
| Operating Income | 638 | 550 | 503 | 418 | 333 | 295 | 266 | 244 | 239 | 217 |
| Depreciation | 79.8 | 74.9 | 63.8 | 54.7 | 44.7 | 42.3 | 53.2 | 49.6 | 49.1 | 58.7 |
| Interest Expense | 11.9 | 16.9 | 12.2 | 12.7 | 12.5 | 12.6 | 14.2 | 19.3 | 19.3 | 26.4 |
| Pretax Income | 577 | 348 | 450 | 414 | 223 | 211 | 205 | 154 | 173 | 464 |
| Effective Tax Rate | 29.6% | 21.7% | 25.0% | 26.9% | 24.5% | 26.5% | 30.1% | 30.6% | 31.9% | 45.7% |
| Net Income | 406 | 272 | 337 | 303 | 169 | 155 | 143 | 107 | 118 | 252 |
| S&P Core Earnings | 409 | 317 | 309 | 244 | 182 | 134 | 126 | NA | NA | NA |

| Balance Sheet & Other Financial Data (Million $) | 2007 | 2006 | 2005 | 2004 | 2003 | 2002 | 2001 | 2000 | 1999 | 1998 |
|---|---|---|---|---|---|---|---|---|---|---|
| Cash | 571 | 416 | 754 | 541 | 417 | 23.1 | 30.8 | 21.3 | 17.3 | 25.6 |
| Current Assets | 1,242 | 1,134 | 1,264 | 1,054 | 875 | 758 | 647 | 527 | 529 | 489 |
| Total Assets | 2,476 | 2,277 | 2,266 | 2,009 | 1,692 | 1,417 | 1,231 | 1,089 | 1,126 | 1,080 |
| Current Liabilities | 282 | 296 | 641 | 390 | 422 | 317 | 235 | 225 | 353 | 303 |
| Long Term Debt | 150 | 151 | 0.80 | 151 | 152 | 152 | 156 | 204 | 158 | 160 |
| Common Equity | 1,848 | 1,698 | 1,536 | 1,360 | 1,046 | 880 | 789 | 614 | 574 | 568 |
| Total Capital | 2,018 | 1,871 | 1,544 | 1,534 | 1,197 | 1,033 | 945 | 818 | 733 | 728 |
| Capital Expenditures | 50.7 | 70.4 | 97.2 | 74.0 | 72.1 | 41.0 | 27.4 | 19.4 | 26.1 | 43.8 |
| Cash Flow | 486 | 347 | 401 | 358 | 213 | 197 | 196 | 157 | 167 | 311 |
| Current Ratio | 4.4 | 3.8 | 2.0 | 2.7 | 2.1 | 2.4 | 2.8 | 2.3 | 1.5 | 1.6 |
| % Long Term Debt of Capitalization | 7.4 | 8.1 | 0.1 | 9.9 | 12.7 | 14.7 | 16.5 | 25.0 | 21.6 | 22.0 |
| % Net Income of Revenue | 18.5 | 13.7 | 19.0 | 18.3 | 11.8 | 12.2 | 12.1 | 9.7 | 11.4 | 21.7 |
| % Return on Assets | 17.1 | 12.0 | 15.8 | 16.4 | 10.8 | 11.5 | 12.3 | 9.6 | 10.7 | 21.4 |
| % Return on Equity | 22.9 | 16.8 | 23.3 | 25.2 | 17.5 | 18.6 | 20.4 | 18.0 | 20.7 | 44.2 |

Data as orig reptd.; bef. results of disc opers/spec. items. Per share data adj. for stk. divs.; EPS diluted. E-Estimated. NA-Not Available. NM-Not Meaningful. NR-Not Ranked. UR-Under Review.

**Office:** 730 Central Avenue, New Providence, NJ 07974.
**Telephone:** 908-277-8000.
**Website:** http://www.crbard.com
**Chrmn & CEO:** T.M. Ring

**Pres & COO:** J.H. Weiland
**SVP & CFO:** T.C. Schermerhorn
**CTO:** J.A. DeFord
**Chief Acctg Officer & Cntlr:** F. Lupisella, Jr.

**Investor Contact:** E.J. Shick (908-277-8413)
**Board Members:** M. C. Breslawsky, T. K. Dunnigan, H. L. Henkel, T. E. Martin, G. K. Naughton, T. M. Ring, T. G. Thompson, J. H. Weiland, A. Welters, T. L. White

**Founded:** 1907
**Domicile:** New Jersey
**Employees:** 10,200

The McGraw-Hill Companies

# Barr Pharmaceuticals Inc

**STANDARD &POOR'S**

| S&P Recommendation HOLD ★★★☆☆ | Price $64.63 (as of Nov 14, 2008) | 12-Mo. Target Price $67.00 | Investment Style Large-Cap Growth |
| --- | --- | --- | --- |

**GICS Sector** Health Care
**Sub-Industry** Pharmaceuticals

**Summary** In mid-July 2008, Barr agreed to be acquired by Israeli-based Teva Pharmaceutical Industries Ltd. Terms of the deal call for each BRL common share to be exchanged for $39.90 in cash, plus 0.6272 Teva shares.

## Key Stock Statistics (Source S&P, Vickers, company reports)

| | | | | | | | |
| --- | --- | --- | --- | --- | --- | --- | --- |
| 52-Wk Range | $68.35– 37.40 | S&P Oper. EPS 2008E | 2.85 | Market Capitalization(B) | $7.073 | Beta | 0.44 |
| Trailing 12-Month EPS | $1.31 | S&P Oper. EPS 2009E | 3.40 | Yield (%) | Nil | S&P 3-Yr. Proj. EPS CAGR(%) | 15 |
| Trailing 12-Month P/E | 49.3 | P/E on S&P Oper. EPS 2008E | 22.7 | Dividend Rate/Share | Nil | S&P Credit Rating | NA |
| $10K Invested 5 Yrs Ago | $12,170 | Common Shares Outstg. (M) | 109.4 | Institutional Ownership (%) | 80 | | |

## Price Performance

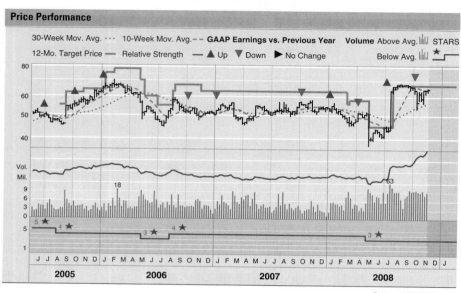

30-Week Mov. Avg. · · · 10-Week Mov. Avg. – – GAAP Earnings vs. Previous Year Volume Above Avg. STARS
12-Mo. Target Price — Relative Strength — ▲ Up ▼ Down ► No Change Below Avg.

Options: ASE, CBOE, P, Ph

Analysis prepared by **Herman B. Saftlas** on November 03, 2008, when the stock traded at **$ 63.87**.

## Highlights

► Based on Barr as an independent entity, we project revenue growth of about 10% in '08. Domestic generics sales should benefit from new generic versions of Fosamax, and Allegra D drugs, as well as generic forms of Orthro Tri-Cyclen Lo and Yasmin oral contraceptives (OCs). We also see growth in overseas generics sales. Projected gains in newer branded products such as Seasonique OC, ParaGard IUD, and Plan B emergency OC should more than offset expected declines in older lines.

► We expect gross margins to benefit from ongoing synergies accruing from the Pliva acquisition. We see SG&A expenses being well controlled, but R&D costs will likely account for a larger percentage of sales, reflecting stepped-up spending on new products. Interest expense will likely decline, but we expect the effective tax rate to be sharply higher.

► We project '08 operating EPS of $2.85, down from '07's $3.16. Results exclude amortization of acquired products and merger-related costs. However, we see EPS rising to $3.40 in 2009.

## Investment Rationale/Risk

► In July 2008, Barr and Israeli-based generic industry leader Teva Pharmaceutical Industries Ltd. (TEVA: strong buy, $43) signed a definitive agreement under which Barr would be acquired by Teva for cash and stock valued at about $7.5 billion, plus assumption of $1.5 billion of Barr's net debt. Terms of the deal call for each BRL share to be exchanged for $39.90 in cash plus 0.6272 TEVA ADRs. The combined firm would have $12 billion in pro forma sales, 500 marketed products, and a pipeline of 200 ANDAs. A recent debt amendment provides for BRL's debt facilities to remain in place after the merger. BRL holders are scheduled to vote on the deal on 11/21/08.

► Risks to our recommendation and target price include the failure to consummate the planned merger with Teva.

► Our 12-month target of $67 approximates the current value of the cash and stock that each BRL share would receive in the proposed merger, which we expect to be completed by the end of 2008. We believe the deal offers good value for Barr shareholders.

## Qualitative Risk Assessment

| LOW | MEDIUM | HIGH |
| --- | --- | --- |

Our risk assessment reflects risks inherent in the generic pharmaceutical business, which include the ability to develop generic products and legally challenge branded patents. However, we believe Barr's proven expertise in developing novel generic and proprietary drugs, and successful litigation of patent challenges, together with anticipated long-term benefits from the recent acquisition of Pliva, are offsetting factors.

## Quantitative Evaluations

**S&P Quality Ranking** B-

| D | C | B- | B | B+ | A- | A | A+ |
| --- | --- | --- | --- | --- | --- | --- | --- |

**Relative Strength Rank** STRONG

95

LOWEST = 1 HIGHEST = 99

## Revenue/Earnings Data

**Revenue (Million $)**

| | 1Q | 2Q | 3Q | 4Q | Year |
| --- | --- | --- | --- | --- | --- |
| 2008 | 608.0 | 779.0 | 737.0 | -- | -- |
| 2007 | 332.4 | 637.0 | 601.4 | 668.2 | 2,501 |
| 2006 | -- | -- | 332.4 | 548.0 | 916.4 |
| 2005 | 310.4 | 325.5 | 326.8 | 351.7 | 1,314 |
| 2004 | 244.5 | 257.4 | 265.0 | 280.5 | 1,047 |
| 2003 | 310.7 | 374.1 | 321.1 | 303.2 | 1,309 |

**Earnings Per Share ($)**

| | | | | | |
| --- | --- | --- | --- | --- | --- |
| 2008 | 0.21 | 0.52 | 0.31 | E0.93 | E2.85 |
| 2007 | 0.49 | -0.42 | 0.41 | 0.35 | 1.31 |
| 2006 | -- | -- | 0.49 | -3.67 | -3.18 |
| 2005 | 0.78 | 0.88 | 0.70 | 0.76 | 3.12 |
| 2004 | 0.49 | 0.56 | 0.58 | 0.40 | 2.03 |
| 2003 | 0.37 | 0.33 | 0.33 | 0.13 | 1.15 |

Fiscal year ended Dec. 31. Next earnings report expected: Late January. EPS Estimates based on S&P Operating Earnings; historical GAAP earnings are as reported.

## Dividend Data

No cash dividends have been paid.

# Barr Pharmaceuticals Inc

STANDARD
&POOR'S

## Business Summary November 03, 2008

CORPORATE OVERVIEW. Founded in 1970, Barr Pharmaceuticals (formerly Barr Laboratories) is a leading developer, producer and marketer of generic pharmaceuticals. BRL also sells a number of proprietary products. Much of Barr's growth has come from acquisitions such as Duramed, a maker of women's health and hormone replacement products, and Enhance Pharmaceuticals, an R&D company developing vaginal ring drug delivery systems. Pliva, a Croatia-based pharmaceutical company, was purchased on October 24, 2006, for $2.5 billion in cash.

With the acquisition of Pliva, Barr now ranks as the world's fourth largest generic drugmaker, with annual sales of about $2.5 billion in 2007. We believe Pliva has brought a number of positives to Barr, including entry into growing European markets, low-cost manufacturing, tax benefits, and new opportunities in the lucrative field of generic biologics.

Revenues in 2007 were divided as follows: generic drugs 76%, proprietary products 17%, and other revenues 7%. Oral contraceptives accounted for 31% of product sales in 2007, psychotherapeutics 11%, cardiovasculars 12%, antivirals and anti-infectives 10%, and all other 36%. Sales outside the U.S. represented 29% of product sales.

The company's generic division manufactures and distributes some 120 generic pharmaceuticals in the U.S. that are available in different dosage forms and strengths. During 2007, the company had worldwide generic sales of $1.9 billion. Barr is a leading supplier of oral contraceptives in the U.S., accounting for about 30% of the market. The company's oral contraceptives are sold under the Tri-Sprintec, Sprintec, Apri, Aviane, Kariva and other names. The company also sells generic versions of antidepressants Prozac and Remeron, Tamoxifen for breast cancer, anticoagulant Coumadin, and Adderall, a treatment for attention deficit hyperactivity disorder and other products.

Overseas, the company offers a portfolio of 1,025 generic and branded products that compete in Croatia, Poland, Germany, Spain, the U.K. and Russia. Barr also markets a large number of active pharmaceutical ingredients.

## Company Financials Fiscal Year Ended Dec. 31

| Per Share Data ($) | 2007 | 2006 | 2005 | 2004 | 2003 | 2002 | 2001 | 2000 | 1999 | 1998 |
|---|---|---|---|---|---|---|---|---|---|---|
| Tangible Book Value | 0.93 | NM | 11.54 | 10.81 | 9.18 | 8.07 | 6.80 | 4.59 | 3.60 | 2.78 |
| Cash Flow | 3.96 | -2.48 | 3.70 | 2.41 | 1.45 | 1.84 | 2.21 | 0.86 | 0.66 | 0.74 |
| Earnings | 1.31 | -3.18 | 3.12 | 2.03 | 1.15 | 1.62 | 2.08 | 0.74 | 0.53 | 0.62 |
| S&P Core Earnings | 1.37 | 3.20 | 2.20 | 1.49 | 2.03 | 2.43 | 0.97 | NA | NA | NA |
| Dividends | Nil | Nil | Nil | Nil | Nil | Nil | Nil | Nil | Nil | Nil |
| Payout Ratio | Nil | Nil | Nil | Nil | Nil | Nil | Nil | Nil | Nil | Nil |
| Prices:High | 58.38 | 70.25 | 70.25 | 63.60 | 53.99 | 56.91 | 35.56 | 40.27 | 35.61 | 14.39 |
| Prices:Low | 45.41 | 44.60 | 44.60 | 43.71 | 32.01 | 28.93 | 21.96 | 19.78 | 8.89 | 8.39 |
| P/E Ratio:High | 45 | NM | 23 | 31 | 47 | 35 | 17 | 55 | 67 | 23 |
| P/E Ratio:Low | 35 | NM | 14 | 22 | 28 | 18 | 11 | 27 | 17 | 14 |

| Income Statement Analysis (Million $) | 2007 | 2006 | 2005 | 2004 | 2003 | 2002 | 2001 | 2000 | 1999 | 1998 |
|---|---|---|---|---|---|---|---|---|---|---|
| Revenue | 2,501 | 916 | 1,314 | 1,047 | 1,309 | 903 | 1,189 | 510 | 482 | 444 |
| Operating Income | 686 | 240 | 549 | 357 | 225 | 249 | 341 | 72.4 | 75.2 | 88.9 |
| Depreciation | 288 | 74.4 | 62.0 | 40.8 | 32.1 | 22.7 | 15.3 | 10.8 | 10.4 | 9.31 |
| Interest Expense | 159 | 32.4 | 0.49 | 1.46 | 2.64 | 1.47 | 3.53 | 1.86 | 2.41 | 2.70 |
| Pretax Income | 208 | -303 | 524 | 330 | 194 | 263 | 338 | 101 | 67.8 | 8.13 |
| Effective Tax Rate | 31.1% | NM | 35.6% | 34.8% | 36.7% | 36.2% | 37.1% | 38.2% | 38.5% | NA |
| Net Income | 142 | -338 | 336 | 215 | 123 | 168 | 212 | 62.5 | 42.3 | 49.3 |
| S&P Core Earnings | 149 | 345 | 233 | 159 | 141 | 166 | 55.3 | NA | NA | NA |

| Balance Sheet & Other Financial Data (Million $) | 2007 | 2006 | 2005 | 2004 | 2003 | 2002 | 2001 | 2000 | 1999 | 1998 |
|---|---|---|---|---|---|---|---|---|---|---|
| Cash | 534 | 906 | 602 | 643 | 452 | 412 | 331 | 222 | 156 | 103 |
| Current Assets | 1,750 | 2,088 | 1,109 | 993 | 878 | 848 | 638 | 437 | 315 | 248 |
| Total Assets | 4,762 | 4,962 | 1,921 | 1,483 | 1,333 | 1,181 | 889 | 543 | 424 | 348 |
| Current Liabilities | 779 | 1,212 | 187 | 213 | 208 | 275 | 177 | 152 | 113 | 101 |
| Long Term Debt | 2,077 | 1,937 | 7.43 | 15.5 | 32.4 | 34.0 | 42.6 | 24.9 | 28.1 | 30.0 |
| Common Equity | 1,866 | 1,465 | 1,691 | 1,234 | 1,042 | 868 | 667 | 366 | 282 | 214 |
| Total Capital | 3,879 | 3,665 | 1,698 | 1,249 | 1,074 | 902 | 709 | 391 | 311 | 246 |
| Capital Expenditures | 123 | 33.7 | 61.0 | 55.2 | 46.9 | 80.6 | 47.2 | 17.7 | 12.1 | 12.3 |
| Cash Flow | 431 | 264 | 398 | 256 | 155 | 190 | 226 | 73.3 | 52.8 | 58.6 |
| Current Ratio | 2.3 | 1.7 | 5.9 | 4.7 | 4.2 | 3.1 | 3.6 | 2.9 | 2.8 | 2.5 |
| % Long Term Debt of Capitalization | 48.3 | 52.9 | 0.4 | 1.2 | 3.0 | 3.8 | 6.0 | 6.4 | 9.0 | 12.2 |
| % Net Income of Revenue | 5.7 | NM | 25.6 | 20.5 | 9.4 | 18.6 | 17.9 | 12.3 | 8.8 | 11.1 |
| % Return on Assets | 4.3 | NM | 19.7 | 15.3 | 9.8 | 16.2 | 27.3 | 12.9 | 11.0 | 15.0 |
| % Return on Equity | 8.0 | NM | 23.0 | 18.9 | 12.9 | 21.8 | 38.8 | 19.3 | 17.1 | 26.6 |

Data as orig reptd.; bef. results of disc opers/spec. items. Per share data adj. for stk. divs.; EPS diluted. Prior to 2006 (six months), fiscal year ended Jun. 30 of the fol. cal. yr. E-Estimated. NA-Not Available. NM-Not Meaningful. NR-Not Ranked. UR-Under Review.

**Office:** 225 Summit Ave, Montvale, NJ 07645-1523.
**Telephone:** 201-930-3300.
**Email:** ir@barrlabs.com
**Website:** http://www.barrlabs.com

**Chrmn, Pres, CEO & COO:** B.L. Downey
**EVP, CFO & Treas:** B. McKee
**EVP, Secy & General Counsel:** F.J. Killion
**SVP, Chief Acctg Officer & Cntlr:** S.C. Kirk

**SVP & CIO:** M. Kustoff
**Board Members:** H. Chefitz, B. L. Downey, R. R. Frankovic, J. S. Gilmore, III, P. R. Seaver, G. P. Stephan

**Founded:** 1970
**Domicile:** Delaware
**Employees:** 8,900

# Baxter International Inc

**STANDARD & POOR'S**

| **S&P Recommendation** 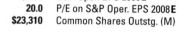 | **Price** | **12-Mo. Target Price** | **Investment Style** |
|---|---|---|---|
| | $60.00 (as of Nov 14, 2008) | $69.00 | Large-Cap Growth |

**GICS Sector** Health Care
**Sub-Industry** Health Care Equipment

**Summary** This global medical products and services company provides critical therapies for people with life-threatening conditions.

## Key Stock Statistics (Source S&P, Vickers, company reports)

| | | | | | | | |
|---|---|---|---|---|---|---|---|
| 52-Wk Range | $71.53–51.32 | S&P Oper. EPS 2008**E** | 3.36 | Market Capitalization(B) | $37.210 | Beta | 0.41 |
| Trailing 12-Month EPS | $3.00 | S&P Oper. EPS 2009**E** | 3.80 | Yield (%) | 1.73 | S&P 3-Yr. Proj. EPS CAGR(%) | 13 |
| Trailing 12-Month P/E | 20.0 | P/E on S&P Oper. EPS 2008**E** | 17.9 | Dividend Rate/Share | $1.04 | S&P Credit Rating | A+ |
| $10K Invested 5 Yrs Ago | $23,310 | Common Shares Outstg. (M) | 620.2 | Institutional Ownership (%) | 84 | | |

## Price Performance

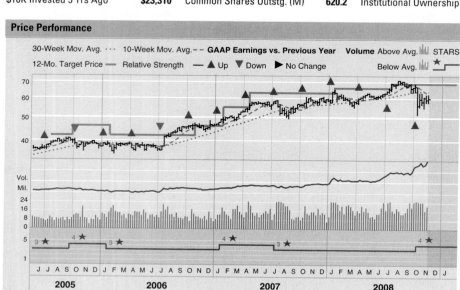

- 30-Week Mov. Avg. · · ·
- 10-Week Mov. Avg. – –
- **GAAP Earnings vs. Previous Year**
- Volume Above Avg. STARS
- 12-Mo. Target Price —
- Relative Strength —
- ▲ Up ▼ Down ► No Change
- Below Avg.

Options: ASE, CBOE, P, Ph

Analysis prepared by **Herman B. Saftlas** on October 13, 2008, when the stock traded at **$ 58.85.**

## Qualitative Risk Assessment

| LOW | MEDIUM | HIGH |
|---|---|---|

Our risk assessment reflects BAX's operations in a highly competitive business characterized by rapid technological change and new market entrants. In addition, the business entails regulatory and reimbursement risks, as well as liability risks from malfunctioning products. This is offset by our belief that health care products are immune to economic cycles, and that long-term demand should benefit from demographic growth in the elderly and a greater penetration of developing global markets.

## Quantitative Evaluations

**S&P Quality Ranking** B+

| D | C | B- | B | B+ | A- | A | A+ |
|---|---|---|---|---|---|---|---|

**Relative Strength Rank** **STRONG**

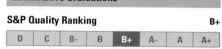

84

LOWEST = 1        HIGHEST = 99

## Highlights

▸ We project revenue growth of about 10% in 2008, with an estimated 5% coming from positive foreign exchange. Excluding currency gains, we see a low double-digit increase for BioScience sales, reflecting further growth in recombinants such as Advate factor VIII, plasma proteins, and antibody therapies. We expect sales of Advate to approach $1.4 billion. Volume in the Medication Delivery division will likely show only modest growth, in light of anticipated lower sales of the Colleague infusion pump, as well as declines in the global injectables business. Renal sales will likely be relatively flat.

▸ We see gross margins expanding to about 50.4%, from 2007's 49.4%, helped by stronger top-line growth, a more profitable sales mix, and ongoing productivity enhancements. We also forecast good control over SG&A costs. However, we see R&D spending ramping up to fund new products. The effective tax rate should be about 19%, versus 2007's 19.5%.

▸ We project operating EPS of $3.30 for 2008, up from $2.79 in 2007. We see further EPS progress to $3.70 in 2009.

## Investment Rationale/Risk

▸ We credit management with improving BAX's profitability by focusing on high-margin recombinants, plasma proteins, and antibody therapies, divesting low-margin businesses, and closing excess manufacturing capacity. Despite likely tougher near-term foreign currency exchange comparisons, we expect BAX to benefit from continued strong momentum in its principal recession-resistant, niche healthcare businesses, as well as from ongoing gross margin expansion. We also see interesting potential in using BAX's Gammagard immunodeficiency product to treat Alzheimer's disease.

▸ Risks to our recommendation and target price include lower-than-expected Advate sales, adverse adjustments to Medicare reimbursement rates, and an inability to further streamline operating costs.

▸ Our 12-month target price of $69 assumes a peer-level P/E of 18.6X our 2009 EPS forecast. Our target price also matches our intrinsic value estimate for BAX, derived from our discounted cash flow model, which assumes a weighted average cost of capital of 8.4%, and a terminal growth rate of 2%.

## Revenue/Earnings Data

**Revenue (Million $)**

| | 1Q | 2Q | 3Q | 4Q | Year |
|---|---|---|---|---|---|
| 2008 | 2,877 | 3,189 | 3,151 | -- | -- |
| 2007 | 2,675 | 2,829 | 2,750 | 3,009 | 11,263 |
| 2006 | 2,409 | 2,649 | 2,557 | 2,763 | 10,378 |
| 2005 | 2,383 | 2,577 | 2,398 | 2,491 | 9,849 |
| 2004 | 2,209 | 2,379 | 2,320 | 2,601 | 9,509 |
| 2003 | 1,997 | 2,163 | 2,219 | 2,537 | 8,916 |

**Earnings Per Share ($)**

| | | | | | |
|---|---|---|---|---|---|
| 2008 | 0.67 | 0.85 | 0.74 | E0.89 | E3.36 |
| 2007 | 0.61 | 0.65 | 0.61 | 0.74 | 2.61 |
| 2006 | 0.43 | 0.47 | 0.57 | 0.66 | 2.13 |
| 2005 | 0.36 | 0.51 | 0.18 | 0.46 | 1.52 |
| 2004 | 0.30 | -0.28 | 0.42 | 0.17 | 0.62 |
| 2003 | 0.36 | 0.08 | 0.47 | 0.62 | 1.52 |

Fiscal year ended Dec. 31. Next earnings report expected: Late January. EPS Estimates based on S&P Operating Earnings; historical GAAP earnings are as reported.

## Dividend Data (Dates: mm/dd Payment Date: mm/dd/yy)

| Amount ($) | Date Decl. | Ex-Div. Date | Stk. of Record | Payment Date |
|---|---|---|---|---|
| 0.218 | 02/12 | 03/06 | 03/10 | 04/01/08 |
| 0.218 | 05/06 | 06/06 | 06/10 | 07/01/08 |
| 0.218 | 07/29 | 09/08 | 09/10 | 10/01/08 |
| 0.260 | 11/11 | 12/08 | 12/10 | 01/06/09 |

Dividends have been paid since 1934. Source: Company reports.

**Please read the Required Disclosures and Analyst Certification on the last page of this report.**

*The McGraw-Hill Companies*

# Baxter International Inc

STANDARD
&POOR'S

## Business Summary October 13, 2008

CORPORATE OVERVIEW. Founded in 1931 as the first producer of commercially prepared intravenous (IV) solutions, Baxter International makes and distributes medical products and equipment, with a focus on the blood and circulatory system. In 2007, international sales accounted for 57% of the total. In March 2007, the company sold its Transfusion Therapies business to Texas Pacific Group and Maverick Capital for $540 million. Transfusion Therapies, a maker of manual and automated blood-collection products and storage equipment, had annual sales of about $500 million.

The BioSciences unit (42% of 2007 continuing sales) produces plasma-based and recombinant clotting factors for hemophilia, as well as biopharmaceuticals for immune deficiencies, cancer, and other disorders. It also offers biosurgery products for hemostasis, tissue sealing and tissue regeneration, vaccines, and blood processing and storage systems used by hospitals, blood banks and others. In addition, BAX sells a meningitis C vaccine, and is developing cell culture-derived vaccines for influenza, smallpox, Severe Acute Respiratory Syndrome and other diseases. Its most important Biosciences product is Advate, a recombinant blood-clotting agent produced without adding human or animal proteins in the cell culture, purification or final formulation process.

The Medication Delivery unit (38%) makes IV solutions and various specialty products such as critical-care generic injectable drugs, anesthetic agents, and nutrition and oncology products. The products work with devices such as drug-reconstitution systems, IV infusion pumps, nutritional compounding equipment, and medication management systems to provide fluid replenishment, general anesthesia, parenteral nutrition, pain management, antibiotic therapy, and chemotherapy.

Renal Care products (20%) comprise dialysis equipment and other products and services provided for kidney failure patients. BAX sells products for peritoneal dialysis (PD), including solutions, container systems and automated machines that cleanse patients' blood overnight while they sleep. The company also makes dialyzers and instrumentation for hemodialysis (HD). Another renal care product is Extraneal (icodextrin) solution, which facilitates increased fluid removal from the bloodstream during dialysis.

## Company Financials Fiscal Year Ended Dec. 31

| Per Share Data ($) | 2007 | 2006 | 2005 | 2004 | 2003 | 2002 | 2001 | 2000 | 1999 | 1998 |
|---|---|---|---|---|---|---|---|---|---|---|
| Tangible Book Value | 7.53 | 6.42 | 3.61 | 2.45 | 1.74 | 1.53 | 3.44 | 2.43 | 4.19 | 1.79 |
| Cash Flow | 3.46 | 3.01 | 2.45 | 1.59 | 2.42 | 2.38 | 1.81 | 1.91 | 1.95 | 1.28 |
| Earnings | 2.61 | 2.13 | 1.52 | 0.62 | 1.52 | 1.67 | 1.09 | 1.24 | 1.32 | 0.55 |
| S&P Core Earnings | 2.68 | 2.24 | 1.38 | 0.52 | 1.25 | 1.30 | 0.53 | NA | NA | NA |
| Dividends | 0.72 | 0.58 | 0.58 | 0.58 | 0.58 | 0.58 | 0.58 | 0.15 | 0.58 | 0.58 |
| Payout Ratio | 28% | 27% | 38% | 94% | 38% | 35% | 53% | 12% | 44% | 107% |
| Prices:High | 61.09 | 48.54 | 41.07 | 34.84 | 31.32 | 59.90 | 55.90 | 45.13 | 38.00 | 33.00 |
| Prices:Low | 46.07 | 35.12 | 33.08 | 27.10 | 18.18 | 24.07 | 40.06 | 25.88 | 28.41 | 24.25 |
| P/E Ratio:High | 23 | 23 | 27 | 56 | 21 | 36 | 51 | 37 | 29 | 61 |
| P/E Ratio:Low | 18 | 16 | 22 | 44 | 12 | 14 | 37 | 21 | 22 | 44 |

| Income Statement Analysis (Million $) | 2007 | 2006 | 2005 | 2004 | 2003 | 2002 | 2001 | 2000 | 1999 | 1998 |
|---|---|---|---|---|---|---|---|---|---|---|
| Revenue | 11,263 | 10,378 | 9,849 | 9,509 | 8,916 | 8,110 | 7,663 | 6,896 | 6,380 | 6,599 |
| Operating Income | 2,913 | 2,479 | 2,110 | 2,039 | 2,161 | 2,168 | 1,934 | 1,673 | 1,522 | 1,545 |
| Depreciation | 558 | 575 | 580 | 601 | 545 | 439 | 441 | 405 | 372 | 426 |
| Interest Expense | 136 | 101 | 166 | 99.0 | 118 | 71.0 | 108 | 124 | 152 | 193 |
| Pretax Income | 2,114 | 1,746 | 1,444 | 430 | 1,150 | 1,397 | 964 | 946 | 1,052 | 549 |
| Effective Tax Rate | 19.3% | 19.9% | 33.7% | 10.9% | 19.8% | 26.1% | 31.1% | 22.0% | 26.0% | 42.6% |
| Net Income | 1,707 | 1,398 | 958 | 383 | 922 | 1,033 | 664 | 738 | 779 | 315 |
| S&P Core Earnings | 1,757 | 1,467 | 864 | 323 | 756 | 794 | 313 | NA | NA | NA |

| Balance Sheet & Other Financial Data (Million $) | 2007 | 2006 | 2005 | 2004 | 2003 | 2002 | 2001 | 2000 | 1999 | 1998 |
|---|---|---|---|---|---|---|---|---|---|---|
| Cash | 2,539 | 2,485 | 841 | 1,109 | 927 | 1,169 | 582 | 579 | 606 | 709 |
| Current Assets | 7,555 | 6,970 | 5,116 | 6,019 | 5,437 | 5,160 | 3,977 | 3,651 | 3,819 | 4,651 |
| Total Assets | 15,294 | 14,686 | 12,727 | 14,147 | 13,779 | 12,478 | 10,343 | 8,733 | 9,644 | 10,085 |
| Current Liabilities | 3,812 | 3,610 | 4,165 | 4,286 | 3,819 | 3,851 | 3,294 | 3,372 | 2,700 | 2,988 |
| Long Term Debt | 2,664 | 2,567 | 2,414 | 3,933 | 4,421 | 4,398 | 2,486 | 1,726 | 2,601 | 3,096 |
| Common Equity | 6,916 | 6,272 | 4,299 | 3,705 | 3,323 | 2,939 | 3,757 | 2,659 | 3,348 | 2,839 |
| Total Capital | 9,580 | 8,839 | 6,713 | 7,638 | 7,744 | 7,366 | 6,461 | 4,545 | 6,260 | 6,440 |
| Capital Expenditures | 692 | 526 | 444 | 558 | 789 | 734 | 669 | 101 | 529 | 492 |
| Cash Flow | 2,265 | 1,973 | 1,538 | 984 | 1,467 | 1,472 | 1,105 | 1,143 | 1,151 | 741 |
| Current Ratio | 2.0 | 1.9 | 1.2 | 1.4 | 1.4 | 1.3 | 1.2 | 1.1 | 1.4 | 1.6 |
| % Long Term Debt of Capitalization | 27.8 | 29.0 | 36.0 | 51.5 | 57.1 | 59.7 | 38.5 | 38.0 | 41.5 | 48.1 |
| % Net Income of Revenue | 15.2 | 13.5 | 9.7 | 4.0 | 10.3 | 12.7 | 8.7 | 10.7 | 12.2 | 4.8 |
| % Return on Assets | 11.4 | 10.2 | 7.1 | 2.8 | 7.0 | 9.1 | 7.0 | 8.0 | 8.0 | 3.4 |
| % Return on Equity | 25.9 | 26.4 | 23.9 | 10.8 | 29.4 | 30.9 | 20.7 | 24.6 | 25.2 | 11.5 |

Data as orig reptd.; bef. results of disc opers/spec. items. Per share data adj. for stk. divs.; EPS diluted. E-Estimated. NA-Not Available. NM-Not Meaningful. NR-Not Ranked. UR-Under Review.

**Office:** One Baxter Parkway, Deerfield, IL 60015.
**Telephone:** 847-948-2000.
**Website:** http://www.baxter.com
**Chrmn, Pres & CEO:** R.L. Parkinson, Jr.

**CFO:** R.M. Davis
**CSO:** N.G. Riedel
**Chief Acctg Officer & Cntlr:** M.J. Baughman
**Treas:** R.J. Hombach

**Investor Contact:** M. Ladone (847-948-3371)
**Board Members:** W. E. Boomer, B. E. Devitt, P. C. Farrell, J. D. Forsyth, G. D. Fosler, J. R. Gavin, III, P. S. Hellman, W. T. Hockmeyer, J. B. Martin, R. L. Parkinson, Jr., C. J. Shapazian, T. T. Stallkamp, K. J. Storm, A. P. Stroucken.

**Founded:** 1931
**Domicile:** Delaware
**Employees:** 46,000

# BB&T Corp

**STANDARD &POOR'S**

| S&P Recommendation **BUY** ★★★★☆ | Price $28.05 (as of Nov 14, 2008) | 12-Mo. Target Price $42.00 | Investment Style Large-Cap Blend |
|---|---|---|---|

**GICS Sector** Financials
**Sub-Industry** Regional Banks

**Summary** This bank holding company has a large presence in its home state of North Carolina, as well as in Virginia, with additional offices in Georgia, South Carolina, the District of Columbia, and seven other states.

## Key Stock Statistics (Source S&P, Vickers, company reports)

| | | | | | | | |
|---|---|---|---|---|---|---|---|
| 52-Wk Range | $45.31– 18.71 | S&P Oper. EPS 2008**E** | 2.75 | Market Capitalization(B) | $15.497 | Beta | 0.17 |
| Trailing 12-Month EPS | $2.95 | S&P Oper. EPS 2009**E** | 3.10 | Yield (%) | 6.70 | S&P 3-Yr. Proj. EPS CAGR(%) | 8 |
| Trailing 12-Month P/E | 9.5 | P/E on S&P Oper. EPS 2008**E** | 10.2 | Dividend Rate/Share | $1.88 | S&P Credit Rating | A+ |
| $10K Invested 5 Yrs Ago | $8,935 | Common Shares Outstg. (M) | 552.5 | Institutional Ownership (%) | 43 | | |

## Price Performance

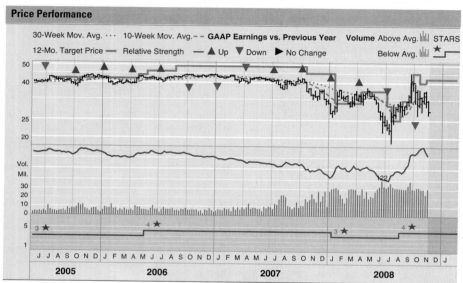

30-Week Mov. Avg. ··· 10-Week Mov. Avg. – – GAAP Earnings vs. Previous Year Volume Above Avg. STARS
12-Mo. Target Price — Relative Strength — ▲ Up ▼ Down ► No Change Below Avg. ★

Options: ASE, CBOE, P, Ph

## Qualitative Risk Assessment

| LOW | MEDIUM | HIGH |
|---|---|---|

Our risk assessment reflects the company's large-cap valuation, our view of the strong credit quality of its loan portfolio, and its history of profitability, offset by BBT's exposure to the banking industry's current issues with funding and credit quality.

## Quantitative Evaluations

**S&P Quality Ranking** A-

| D | C | B- | B | B+ | A- | A | A+ |
|---|---|---|---|---|---|---|---|

**Relative Strength Rank** MODERATE
66
LOWEST = 1    HIGHEST = 99

## Highlights

➤ The 12-month target price for BBT has recently been changed to $42.00 from $40.00. The Highlights section of this Stock Report will be updated accordingly.

## Investment Rationale/Risk

➤ The Investment Rationale/Risk section of this Stock Report will be updated shortly. For the latest News story on BBT from MarketScope, see below.

➤ 11/04/08 03:51 pm ET ... S&P MAINTAINS BUY RECOMMENDATION ON SHARES OF BB&T CORP (BBT 35.39****): We see the median multiple of U.S. regional banks on '09 expected EPS at 15.3X. Since we view this as high relative to the recent past, we think BBT should trade at a lower, mid-13's multiple on '09 EPS estimates, a multiple which we see as incorporating BBT's positives, such as maintainance of credit quality, high net interest margin and high loan loss reserves, as well as negatives, such as exposure to the southeastern housing construction market. We are raising our target price by $2 to $42, based on a 13.5X multiple on our unchanged '09 EPS estimate of $3.10. /E.Oja

## Revenue/Earnings Data

**Revenue (Million $)**

| | 1Q | 2Q | 3Q | 4Q | Year |
|---|---|---|---|---|---|
| 2008 | 2,655 | 2,617 | 2,585 | -- | -- |
| 2007 | 2,543 | 2,690 | 2,719 | 2,747 | 10,668 |
| 2006 | 2,165 | 2,319 | 2,463 | 2,468 | 9,414 |
| 2005 | 1,760 | 1,918 | 2,036 | 2,118 | 7,831 |
| 2004 | 1,559 | 1,693 | 1,698 | 1,736 | 6,666 |
| 2003 | 1,500 | 1,507 | 1,611 | 1,627 | 6,244 |

**Earnings Per Share ($)**

| | | | | | |
|---|---|---|---|---|---|
| 2008 | 0.78 | 0.78 | 0.65 | E0.78 | E2.75 |
| 2007 | 0.77 | 0.83 | 0.80 | 0.75 | 3.14 |
| 2006 | 0.79 | 0.79 | 0.77 | 0.46 | 2.81 |
| 2005 | 0.71 | 0.70 | 0.80 | 0.78 | 3.00 |
| 2004 | 0.60 | 0.72 | 0.74 | 0.75 | 2.80 |
| 2003 | 0.69 | 0.67 | 0.21 | 0.55 | 2.07 |

Fiscal year ended Dec. 31. Next earnings report expected: Mid January. EPS Estimates based on S&P Operating Earnings; historical GAAP earnings are as reported.

## Dividend Data (Dates: mm/dd Payment Date: mm/dd/yy)

| Amount ($) | Date Decl. | Ex-Div. Date | Stk. of Record | Payment Date |
|---|---|---|---|---|
| 0.460 | 12/12 | 01/09 | 01/11 | 02/01/08 |
| 0.460 | 02/26 | 04/10 | 04/14 | 05/01/08 |
| 0.470 | 06/24 | 07/09 | 07/11 | 08/01/08 |
| 0.470 | 08/26 | 10/15 | 10/17 | 11/03/08 |

Dividends have been paid since 1903. Source: Company reports.

# BB&T Corp

STANDARD
&POOR'S

## Business Summary September 30, 2008

CORPORATE OVERVIEW. BBT has bank operations providing loan, deposit and financial products primarily in the Southeast. BBT has seven reportable business segments: Banking Network, Mortgage Banking, Trust Services, Insurance Services, Investment Banking and Brokerage, Specialized Lending, and Treasury.

The Banking Network generated almost 72% of BBT's total revenues and more than 94% of segment net income in 2007. In addition to providing banking services, BBT's bank subsidiaries also offer brokerage, insurance and other financial services. The Insurance Services segment generated 12.8% of revenues and 7.8% of segment net profit in 2007, the Specialized Lending segment generated 8.2% and 4.7%, respectively, Financial Services generated 9.3% and 4.3%, and Residential Mortgage Banking 4.2% and 7.7%. The remaining revenues and segment net income were generated by other segments, offset by parent and reconciling items.

MARKET PROFILE. As of June 30, 2007, which is the latest available FDIC branch-level data, BBT had 1,474 branches and $84.7 billion in deposits, with about 56% of its deposits concentrated in North Carolina and Virginia, by our

calculations. The acquisition of Coastal Financial Corp., completed May 1, 2007, added 22 branches and $1.1 billion in deposits to BBT. In North Carolina, BBT had 343 branches, $27.7 billion of deposits, and a deposit market share of about 12%, which ranks third. In Virginia, BBT had 397 branches, $19.8 billion of deposits, and a deposit market share of about 8.6%, which ranks fifth. In Georgia, BBT had 151 branches, $8.1 billion of deposits, and a deposit market share of about 4.3%, which ranks fifth. In South Carolina, BBT had 119 branches, $7.0 billion of deposits, and a deposit market share of about 9.9%, which ranks third. In Maryland, BBT had 128 branches, $6.1 billion of deposits, and a deposit market share of about 5.7%, which ranks seventh. In addition, BBT had a number one market ranking in West Virginia, and was fourth in Kentucky, eighth in D.C., seventh in Tennessee, and 16th in Florida. Finally, BBT had a small presence in Alabama and Indiana.

## Company Financials Fiscal Year Ended Dec. 31

| Per Share Data ($) | 2007 | 2006 | 2005 | 2004 | 2003 | 2002 | 2001 | 2000 | 1999 | 1998 |
|---|---|---|---|---|---|---|---|---|---|---|
| Tangible Book Value | 12.73 | 11.04 | 11.76 | 12.26 | 11.66 | 12.04 | 13.50 | 11.91 | 9.66 | 9.95 |
| Earnings | 3.14 | 2.81 | 3.00 | 2.80 | 2.07 | 2.70 | 2.12 | 1.55 | 1.83 | 1.71 |
| S&P Core Earnings | 3.09 | 2.79 | 2.90 | 2.75 | 1.97 | 2.59 | 2.02 | NA | NA | NA |
| Dividends | 1.76 | 1.60 | 1.46 | 1.34 | 1.22 | 1.10 | 0.98 | 0.86 | 0.75 | 0.66 |
| Payout Ratio | 56% | 57% | 49% | 48% | 59% | 41% | 46% | 55% | 41% | 39% |
| Prices:High | 44.30 | 44.74 | 43.92 | 43.25 | 39.69 | 39.47 | 38.84 | 38.25 | 40.63 | 40.75 |
| Prices:Low | 30.36 | 38.24 | 37.04 | 33.02 | 30.66 | 31.03 | 30.24 | 21.69 | 27.19 | 26.25 |
| P/E Ratio:High | 14 | 16 | 15 | 15 | 19 | 15 | 18 | 25 | 22 | 24 |
| P/E Ratio:Low | 10 | 14 | 12 | 12 | 15 | 11 | 14 | 14 | 15 | 15 |

| Income Statement Analysis (Million $) | | | | | | | | | | |
|---|---|---|---|---|---|---|---|---|---|---|
| Net Interest Income | 3,880 | 3,708 | 3,525 | 3,348 | 3,082 | 2,747 | 2,434 | 2,018 | 1,582 | 1,247 |
| Tax Equivalent Adjustment | 68.0 | NA | 82.7 | NA | 21.2 | 151 | 19.1 | 130 | 86.7 | 64.8 |
| Non Interest Income | 2,777 | 2,594 | 2,326 | 2,113 | 1,782 | 1,522 | 1,256 | 996 | 639 | 520 |
| Loan Loss Provision | 448 | 240 | 217 | 249 | 248 | 264 | 224 | 127 | 92.1 | 80.3 |
| % Expense/Operating Revenue | 54.6% | 55.8% | 53.4% | 57.6% | 63.6% | 54.0% | 60.1% | 56.0% | 58.4% | 52.5% |
| Pretax Income | 2,570 | 2,473 | 2,467 | 2,322 | 1,617 | 1,791 | 1,360 | 906 | 904 | 734 |
| Effective Tax Rate | 32.5% | 38.2% | 33.0% | 32.9% | 34.1% | 27.8% | 28.4% | 30.8% | 32.2% | 31.6% |
| Net Income | 1,734 | 1,528 | 1,654 | 1,558 | 1,065 | 1,293 | 974 | 626 | 613 | 502 |
| % Net Interest Margin | 3.52 | 3.74 | 3.89 | 4.04 | 4.06 | 4.25 | 4.17 | 3.56 | 4.27 | 3.75 |
| S&P Core Earnings | 1,707 | 1,514 | 1,608 | 1,529 | 1,012 | 1,241 | 927 | NA | NA | NA |

| Balance Sheet & Other Financial Data (Million $) | | | | | | | | | | |
|---|---|---|---|---|---|---|---|---|---|---|
| Money Market Assets | 1,067 | 688 | 697 | 1,244 | 604 | 591 | 458 | 379 | 390 | 168 |
| Investment Securities | 23,428 | 22,868 | 20,489 | 19,173 | 16,317 | 17,655 | 16,662 | 13,851 | 10,579 | 8,099 |
| Commercial Loans | 44,870 | 41,300 | 37,655 | 34,321 | 12,429 | 7,061 | 6,551 | 5,894 | 4,593 | 3,444 |
| Other Loans | 46,037 | 41,611 | 36,739 | 33,228 | 49,151 | 44,079 | 38,985 | 33,561 | 24,320 | 19,932 |
| Total Assets | 132,618 | 121,351 | 109,170 | 100,509 | 90,467 | 80,217 | 70,870 | 59,340 | 43,481 | 34,427 |
| Demand Deposits | 14,260 | 14,726 | 13,477 | 12,246 | 11,098 | 7,864 | 6,940 | 5,064 | 3,908 | 3,247 |
| Time Deposits | 72,506 | 66,245 | 60,805 | 55,453 | 48,252 | 43,416 | 37,794 | 32,951 | 23,343 | 19,800 |
| Long Term Debt | 18,693 | 12,604 | 13,119 | 11,420 | 10,808 | 13,588 | 11,721 | 8,355 | 5,492 | 4,737 |
| Common Equity | 448 | 11,745 | 11,129 | 10,874 | 9,935 | 7,388 | 6,150 | 4,786 | 3,199 | 2,759 |
| % Return on Assets | 1.3 | 1.3 | 1.6 | 1.6 | 1.2 | 1.7 | 1.4 | 1.1 | 1.5 | 1.6 |
| % Return on Equity | 14.0 | 13.4 | 15.0 | 15.0 | 12.3 | 19.1 | 16.8 | 14.2 | 19.2 | 20.1 |
| % Loan Loss Reserve | 1.1 | 1.1 | 1.1 | 1.2 | 1.3 | 1.4 | 1.4 | 1.3 | 1.3 | 1.4 |
| % Loans/Deposits | 103.6 | 103.2 | 99.0 | 100.7 | 105.0 | 104.4 | 106.1 | 106.0 | 107.1 | 98.3 |
| % Equity to Assets | 9.6 | 9.9 | 10.5 | 10.9 | 10.1 | 9.0 | 8.4 | 7.9 | 7.7 | 7.9 |

Data as orig reptd.; bef. results of disc opers/spec. items. Per share data adj. for stk. divs.; EPS diluted. E-Estimated. NA-Not Available. NM-Not Meaningful. NR-Not Ranked. UR-Under Review.

**Office:** 200 West Second Street, Winston-Salem, NC 27101.
**Telephone:** 336-733-2000.
**Website:** http://www.bbandt.com
**Chrmn & CEO:** J.A. Allison, IV

**Pres:** R.E. Greene
**COO:** K.S. King
**EVP & CFO:** C.L. Henson
**EVP, Chief Acctg Officer & Cntlr:** E.D. Vest

**Investor Contact:** T. Gjesdal (336-733-3058)
**Board Members:** J. A. Allison, IV, J. S. Banner, A. R. Cablik, N. R. Chilton, R. E. Deal, T. D. Efird, B. J. Fitzpatrick, L. V. Hackley, J. P. Helm, E. M. Holland, J. P. Howe, III, A. O. Maccauley, J. H. Maynard, A. O. McCauley, J. H. Morrison, N. R. Qubein, T. N. Thompson, S. T. Williams

**Founded:** 1968
**Domicile:** North Carolina
**Employees:** 29,400

The McGraw-Hill Companies

# Becton, Dickinson and Co

STANDARD &POOR'S

| S&P Recommendation | **STRONG BUY** ★ ★ ★ ★ ★ | Price $67.69 (as of Nov 14, 2008) | 12-Mo. Target Price $85.00 | Investment Style Large-Cap Growth |
|---|---|---|---|---|

**GICS Sector** Health Care
**Sub-Industry** Health Care Equipment

**Summary** BDX provides a wide range of medical devices and diagnostic products used in hospitals, doctors' offices, research labs, and other settings.

## Key Stock Statistics (Source S&P, Vickers, company reports)

| | | | | | | | |
|---|---|---|---|---|---|---|---|
| 52-Wk Range | $93.24– 63.13 | S&P Oper. EPS 2009**E** | 4.90 | Market Capitalization(B) | $16.487 | Beta | 0.69 |
| Trailing 12-Month EPS | $4.46 | S&P Oper. EPS 2010**E** | 5.49 | Yield (%) | 1.68 | S&P 3-Yr. Proj. EPS CAGR(%) | 12 |
| Trailing 12-Month P/E | 15.2 | P/E on S&P Oper. EPS 2009**E** | 13.8 | Dividend Rate/Share | $1.14 | S&P Credit Rating | AA- |
| $10K Invested 5 Yrs Ago | $19,073 | Common Shares Outstg. (M) | 243.6 | Institutional Ownership (%) | 85 | | |

## Price Performance

30-Week Mov. Avg. · · · ·   10-Week Mov. Avg. - - -   **GAAP Earnings vs. Previous Year**   Volume Above Avg. STARS
12-Mo. Target Price —   Relative Strength —   ▲ Up   ▼ Down   ▶ No Change   Below Avg. ★

Options: CBOE, P, Ph

Analysis prepared by **Robert M. Gold** on November 06, 2008, when the stock traded at **$ 68.61**.

## Qualitative Risk Assessment

| LOW | MEDIUM | HIGH |
|---|---|---|

BDX's markets are competitive, and new product introductions by current and future competitors have the potential to significantly affect market dynamics. In addition, changes in domestic and foreign health care industry practices and regulations may result in increased pricing pressures and lower reimbursements for some of its products. However, we believe Becton's product line has more favorable demand and pricing characteristics than those in the medical equipment industry in general.

## Quantitative Evaluations

**S&P Quality Ranking** A

| D | C | B- | B | B+ | A- | A | A+ |
|---|---|---|---|---|---|---|---|

**Relative Strength Rank** STRONG

73

LOWEST = 1            HIGHEST = 99

## Highlights

➤ We look for FY 09 (Sep.) revenues of $7.3 billion, including an expected 5% reduction due to the recent rise in the U.S. dollar relative to several major currencies. By segment, we see 1% growth in the medical division, 2% to 3% in the diagnostics area, and biosciences up by an expected 4% to 5%. In our opinion, the company continues to have significant growth opportunities in the detection of bacterial (including drug-resistant) infections and cervical cancer.

➤ We see gross margins expanding by about 40 basis points in FY 09, due to a more favorable sales mix and manufacturing efficiencies, and believe the recent decline in resin prices will benefit margins in coming quarters. During FY 08, higher raw material costs reduced gross margins by about 50 basis points. We think R&D will absorb about 6% of sales through FY 10, while SG&A accounts for 24%-25%. Assuming capital expenditures of about $650 million, we look for FY 09 free cash flow of $1.1 billion. The company plans to spend about $450 million on common share buybacks in FY 09.

➤ Our FY 09 EPS estimate is $4.90, and we see FY 10 EPS rising 12%, to $5.49, in line with our projected three-year EPS growth rate.

## Investment Rationale/Risk

➤ We think BDX will continue to benefit from recovering end user demand in the life sciences industry, momentum in the diagnostics and diabetes management areas, and exposure to cancer diagnostics following the December purchase of TriPath. With a recent dividend yield of about 1.6%, BDX provides the highest yield in our medical equipment coverage universe, and the stock offers one of the highest S&P Quality Rankings in the health care sector, at A, reflecting its history of consistent stability and growth in earnings and dividends.

➤ Risks to our recommendation and target price include a slower than expected recovery in key life science markets, adverse patent litigation, and unfavorable foreign currency fluctuations.

➤ Recently at 14.5X our FY 09 EPS forecast and 2.4X estimated FY 09 sales per share, the stock was trading at a discount to our medical device coverage universe. In our opinion, a modest premium valuation is warranted by what we see as more consistent long-term fundamentals and superior dividend yield. Our 12-month target price of $85 is a P/E and PEG modestly above large cap health care equipment peers.

## Revenue/Earnings Data

### Revenue (Million $)

| | 1Q | 2Q | 3Q | 4Q | Year |
|---|---|---|---|---|---|
| 2008 | 1,706 | 1,747 | 1,868 | 1,836 | 7,156 |
| 2007 | 1,502 | 1,576 | 1,631 | 1,651 | 6,360 |
| 2006 | 1,414 | 1,449 | 1,484 | 1,488 | 5,835 |
| 2005 | 1,288 | 1,366 | 1,381 | 1,379 | 5,415 |
| 2004 | 1,185 | 1,254 | 1,243 | 1,253 | 4,935 |
| 2003 | 1,052 | 1,134 | 1,165 | 1,177 | 4,528 |

### Earnings Per Share ($)

| | | | | | |
|---|---|---|---|---|---|
| 2008 | 1.07 | 1.09 | 1.18 | 1.13 | 4.46 |
| 2007 | 0.51 | 0.92 | 0.95 | 0.98 | 3.36 |
| 2006 | 0.85 | 0.61 | 0.81 | 0.69 | 2.95 |
| 2005 | 0.74 | 0.71 | 0.73 | 0.47 | 2.66 |
| 2004 | 0.48 | 0.62 | 0.41 | 0.70 | 2.21 |
| 2003 | 0.43 | 0.54 | 0.49 | 0.61 | 2.07 |

Fiscal year ended Sep. 30. Next earnings report expected: Late January. EPS Estimates based on S&P Operating Earnings; historical GAAP earnings are as reported.

## Dividend Data (Dates: mm/dd Payment Date: mm/dd/yy)

| Amount ($) | Date Decl. | Ex-Div. Date | Stk. of Record | Payment Date |
|---|---|---|---|---|
| 0.285 | 11/20 | 12/10 | 12/12 | 01/02/08 |
| 0.285 | 01/29 | 03/06 | 03/10 | 03/31/08 |
| 0.285 | 05/20 | 06/05 | 06/09 | 06/30/08 |
| 0.285 | 07/22 | 09/05 | 09/09 | 09/30/08 |

Dividends have been paid since 1926. Source: Company reports.

# Becton, Dickinson and Co

STANDARD &POOR'S

## Business Summary November 06, 2008

Becton, Dickinson traces its roots to a concern started by Maxwell Becton and Fairleigh Dickinson in 1897. One of the first companies to sell U.S.-made glass syringes, BDX was also a pioneer in the production of hypodermic needles. The company now manufactures and sells medical supplies, devices, lab equipment and diagnostic products used by health care institutions, life science researchers, clinical laboratories, industry and the general public. In FY 08 (Sep.), more than half of the company's sales were generated from non-U.S. markets.

Major products in the core medical systems division (53% of FY 08 revenues) include hypodermic syringes and needles for injection, insulin syringes and pen needles for diabetes care, infusion therapy devices, prefillable drug delivery systems, and surgical blades and scalpels. The segment also markets specialty blades and cannulas for ophthalmic surgery procedures, anesthesia needles, critical care systems, elastic support products, and thermometers. The blood glucose monitoring and test strip business was sold in December 2006.

The diagnostics segment (30%) provides a range of products designed for the safe collection and transport of diagnostic specimens and instrumentation for analysis across a wide range of infectious disease testing, including health-care-associated infections (HAIs). Its principal products and services include integrated systems for specimen collection; an extensive line of safety-engineered blood collection products and systems; plated media; automated blood culturing systems; molecular testing systems for sexually-transmitted diseases and HAIs; microorganism identification and drug susceptibility systems; liquid-based cytology systems for cervical cancer screening; and rapid diagnostic assays. The segment also includes consulting services and customized, automated bar-code systems for patient identification and point-of-care data capture.

The biosciences unit (17%) provides research tools and reagents to clinicians and medical researchers studying genes, proteins and cells in order to better understand disease, improve diagnosis and disease management, and facilitate the discovery and development of novel therapeutics. Products include instrument systems for cell sorting and analysis, monoclonal antibody reagents and kits for diagnostic and research use, tools to aid in drug discovery and vaccine development, molecular biology products, fluid handling, cell growth and screening products.

## Company Financials  Fiscal Year Ended Sep. 30

| Per Share Data ($) | 2008 | 2007 | 2006 | 2005 | 2004 | 2003 | 2002 | 2001 | 2000 | 1999 |
|---|---|---|---|---|---|---|---|---|---|---|
| Tangible Book Value | NA | 13.41 | 11.96 | 10.28 | 9.28 | 8.82 | 6.06 | 5.35 | 3.80 | 2.74 |
| Cash Flow | NA | 5.09 | 4.52 | 4.36 | 3.57 | 3.54 | 2.92 | 2.76 | 2.58 | 2.01 |
| Earnings | 4.46 | 3.36 | 2.95 | 2.66 | 2.21 | 2.07 | 1.79 | 1.63 | 1.49 | 1.04 |
| S&P Core Earnings | NA | 3.38 | 2.99 | 2.75 | 2.39 | 2.01 | 1.57 | 1.38 | NA | NA |
| Dividends | NA | 0.98 | 0.86 | 0.72 | 0.60 | 0.40 | 0.39 | 0.38 | 0.37 | 0.34 |
| Payout Ratio | NA | 29% | 29% | 27% | 27% | 19% | 22% | 23% | 25% | 33% |
| Prices:High | NA | 85.89 | 74.25 | 61.17 | 58.18 | 41.82 | 38.60 | 39.25 | 35.31 | 44.19 |
| Prices:Low | NA | 69.30 | 58.08 | 49.71 | 40.90 | 28.82 | 24.70 | 29.96 | 23.75 | 22.38 |
| P/E Ratio:High | NA | 26 | 25 | 23 | 26 | 20 | 22 | 24 | 24 | 42 |
| P/E Ratio:Low | NA | 21 | 20 | 19 | 19 | 14 | 14 | 18 | 16 | 21 |
| **Income Statement Analysis (Million $)** | | | | | | | | | | |
| Revenue | 7,156 | 6,360 | 5,835 | 5,415 | 4,935 | 4,528 | 4,033 | 3,754 | 3,618 | 3,418 |
| Operating Income | NA | 1,644 | 1,456 | 1,419 | 1,244 | 1,094 | 1,002 | 952 | 861 | 780 |
| Depreciation | NA | 441 | 405 | 387 | 357 | 344 | 305 | 306 | 288 | 259 |
| Interest Expense | NA | 46.0 | 66.0 | 55.7 | 29.6 | 73.1 | 33.3 | 47.1 | 78.3 | 72.1 |
| Pretax Income | 1,554 | 1,204 | 1,035 | 1,005 | 753 | 710 | 629 | 577 | 520 | 373 |
| Effective Tax Rate | 27.4% | 28.8% | 27.0% | 31.1% | 22.6% | 22.9% | 23.6% | 24.0% | 24.4% | 26.0% |
| Net Income | 1,128 | 856 | 756 | 692 | 583 | 547 | 480 | 438 | 393 | 276 |
| S&P Core Earnings | NA | 863 | 766 | 714 | 628 | 523 | 417 | 364 | NA | NA |
| **Balance Sheet & Other Financial Data (Million $)** | | | | | | | | | | |
| Cash | NA | 511 | 1,000 | 1,043 | 719 | 520 | 243 | 82.1 | 49.2 | 59.9 |
| Current Assets | NA | 3,131 | 3,185 | 2,975 | 2,641 | 2,339 | 1,929 | 1,763 | 1,661 | 1,684 |
| Total Assets | NA | 7,329 | 6,825 | 6,072 | 5,753 | 5,572 | 5,040 | 4,802 | 4,505 | 4,437 |
| Current Liabilities | NA | 1,479 | 1,576 | 1,299 | 1,050 | 1,043 | 1,252 | 1,265 | 1,354 | 1,329 |
| Long Term Debt | NA | 956 | 957 | 1,061 | 1,172 | 1,184 | 803 | 1,902 | 780 | 954 |
| Common Equity | NA | 4,362 | 3,836 | 3,284 | 3,037 | 2,863 | 2,450 | 2,288 | 1,912 | 1,722 |
| Total Capital | NA | 5,318 | 4,793 | 4,345 | 4,328 | 4,200 | 3,396 | 4,321 | 2,823 | 2,764 |
| Capital Expenditures | NA | 556 | 459 | 318 | 266 | 261 | 260 | 371 | 376 | 312 |
| Cash Flow | NA | 1,297 | 1,161 | 1,080 | 940 | 889 | 783 | 742 | 679 | 532 |
| Current Ratio | NA | 2.1 | 2.0 | 2.3 | 2.5 | 2.2 | 1.5 | 1.4 | 1.2 | 1.3 |
| % Long Term Debt of Capitalization | Nil | 17.9 | 20.0 | 24.4 | 27.1 | 28.2 | 23.6 | 44.0 | 27.6 | 34.5 |
| % Net Income of Revenue | 15.8 | 13.4 | 12.9 | 12.8 | 11.8 | 12.1 | 11.9 | 11.7 | 10.9 | 8.1 |
| % Return on Assets | NA | 12.0 | 11.7 | 11.7 | 10.3 | 10.3 | 9.8 | 9.4 | 8.8 | 6.7 |
| % Return on Equity | NA | 20.8 | 21.2 | 21.9 | 19.7 | 20.5 | 20.2 | 20.8 | 21.5 | 16.6 |

Data as orig reptd.; bef. results of disc opers/spec. items. Per share data adj. for stk. divs.; EPS diluted. E-Estimated. NA-Not Available. NM-Not Meaningful. NR-Not Ranked. UR-Under Review.

**Office:** One Becton Drive, Franklin Lakes, NJ 07417-1880.
**Telephone:** 201-847-6800.
**Email:** investor_relations@bdhq.bd.com
**Website:** http://www.bd.com

**Chrmn, Pres & CEO:** E.J. Ludwig
**Vice Chrmn, EVP & CFO:** J.R. Considine
**SVP & CTO:** S.P. Bruder
**SVP & General Counsel:** J.S. Sherman

**Chief Acctg Officer & Cntlr:** W.A. Tozzi
**Investor Contact:** P.A. Spinella (201-847-5453)
**Board Members:** B. L. Anderson, H. P. Becton, Jr., J. R. Considine, E. F. DeGraan, C. M. Fraser-Liggett, M. O. Larsen, E. J. Ludwig, A. Mahmoud, G. A. Mecklenburg, C. E. Minehan, J. F. Orr, W. J. Overlock, Jr., B. L. Scott, A. Sommer

**Founded:** 1897
**Domicile:** New Jersey
**Employees:** 28,018

# Bed Bath & Beyond Inc

**STANDARD &POOR'S**

| S&P Recommendation | HOLD ★★★☆☆ | Price | 12-Mo. Target Price | Investment Style |
|---|---|---|---|---|
| | | $20.60 (as of Nov 14, 2008) | $36.00 | Large-Cap Growth |

**GICS Sector** Consumer Discretionary
**Sub-Industry** Homefurnishing Retail

**Summary** This company operates a nationwide chain of about 900 Bed Bath & Beyond superstores selling better-quality domestics merchandise and home furnishings; and additional retail stores under the names Christmas Tree Shops and Harmon.

## Key Stock Statistics (Source S&P, Vickers, company reports)

| | | | | | | | |
|---|---|---|---|---|---|---|---|
| 52-Wk Range | $34.73– 19.51 | S&P Oper. EPS 2009E | 1.83 | Market Capitalization(B) | $5.350 | Beta | 0.94 |
| Trailing 12-Month EPS | $1.94 | S&P Oper. EPS 2010E | 2.05 | Yield (%) | Nil | S&P 3-Yr. Proj. EPS CAGR(%) | 12 |
| Trailing 12-Month P/E | 10.6 | P/E on S&P Oper. EPS 2009E | 11.3 | Dividend Rate/Share | Nil | S&P Credit Rating | BBB |
| $10K Invested 5 Yrs Ago | $4,992 | Common Shares Outstg. (M) | 259.7 | Institutional Ownership (%) | NM | | |

## Price Performance

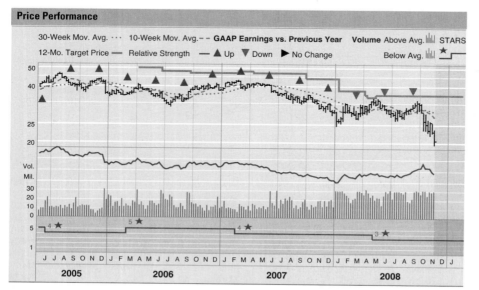

30-Week Mov. Avg. ··· 10-Week Mov. Avg. – – GAAP Earnings vs. Previous Year Volume Above Avg. STARS
12-Mo. Target Price — Relative Strength — ▲ Up ▼ Down ► No Change Below Avg.

Options: ASE, CBOE, Ph

Analysis prepared by **Michael Souers** on September 26, 2008, when the stock traded at **$ 31.67**.

## Highlights

➤ We expect sales to rise 5.6% in FY 09 (Feb.), following a 6.5% advance in FY 08. This reflects the projected addition of 50-55 new Bed Bath & Beyond stores and flat to slightly positive same-store sales results. We also anticipate the opening of 10-15 new Christmas Tree Shops, as well as a handful of new Harmon Stores and buybuy BABY stores. We see same-store sales being driven by an increase in the average ticket, offset by a decline in foot traffic.

➤ We expect gross margins to narrow modestly due to continued promotional activity, as BBBY attempts to gain market share from weaker competitors. We forecast a 200 basis point narrowing in operating margins on higher advertising spending and a modest deleveraging of expenses due to meager same-store sales results, partially offset by a decline in store opening costs.

➤ After slightly lower projected interest income, an anticipated effective tax rate of 36.9%, and approximately 4% fewer shares, we estimate FY 09 EPS of $1.83, a 12% decline from the $2.07 the company earned in FY 08, excluding one-time items. We see EPS of $2.05 in FY 10.

## Investment Rationale/Risk

➤ The shares recently traded at about 18X our FY 09 EPS estimate, a discount to BBBY's 20X average over the past three years, but a modest premium to the S&P 500. However, in our view, BBBY's normalized earnings power merits this premium, as we think the home furnishings industry is at a cyclical bottom -- plagued by cash-strapped consumers and a weak housing market. The company expects to grow to over 1,300 domestic stores, so we think BBBY is far from saturation. We expect BBBY to continue to gain market share in home furnishings, with better merchandising and execution than peers, and to also benefit from the recent bankruptcy of privately held Linens 'n Things.

➤ Risks to our recommendation and target price include a lengthy recession in the U.S., an unanticipated shift in consumer spending away from home-centered products, and possible miscues in BBBY's store expansion strategy.

➤ Our 12-month target price of $36, or about 18X our FY 10 EPS estimate, is based on our discounted cash flow analysis, which assumes a weighted average cost of capital of 10.8% and a terminal growth rate of 4.0%.

## Qualitative Risk Assessment

| LOW | MEDIUM | HIGH |
|---|---|---|

Our risk assessment reflects the cyclical nature of the home furnishing retail industry, which relies heavily on consumer spending, and, to a lesser extent, housing turnover, offset by significant growth areas we see in major domestic metro markets and Canada, and an S&P Quality Ranking of A-, which reflects above-average historical earnings growth.

## Quantitative Evaluations

**S&P Quality Ranking** A-

| D | C | B- | B | B+ | A- | A | A+ |
|---|---|---|---|---|---|---|---|

**Relative Strength Rank** MODERATE

47

LOWEST = 1 HIGHEST = 99

## Revenue/Earnings Data

**Revenue (Million $)**

| | 1Q | 2Q | 3Q | 4Q | Year |
|---|---|---|---|---|---|
| 2009 | 1,648 | 1,854 | -- | -- | -- |
| 2008 | 1,553 | 1,768 | 1,795 | 1,933 | 7,049 |
| 2007 | 1,396 | 1,607 | 1,619 | 1,995 | 6,617 |
| 2006 | 1,244 | 1,431 | 1,449 | 1,685 | 5,810 |
| 2005 | 1,101 | 1,274 | 1,305 | 1,468 | 5,148 |
| 2004 | 893.9 | 1,111 | 1,175 | 1,298 | 4,478 |

**Earnings Per Share ($)**

| | | | | | |
|---|---|---|---|---|---|
| 2009 | 0.30 | 0.46 | E0.44 | E0.63 | E1.83 |
| 2008 | 0.38 | 0.55 | 0.52 | 0.66 | 2.10 |
| 2007 | 0.35 | 0.51 | 0.50 | 0.72 | 2.09 |
| 2006 | 0.33 | 0.47 | 0.45 | 0.67 | 1.92 |
| 2005 | 0.27 | 0.39 | 0.40 | 0.59 | 1.65 |
| 2004 | 0.19 | 0.32 | 0.33 | 0.47 | 1.31 |

Fiscal year ended Feb. 29. Next earnings report expected: Early January. EPS Estimates based on S&P Operating Earnings; historical GAAP earnings are as reported.

## Dividend Data

No cash dividends have been paid.

---

**Please read the Required Disclosures and Analyst Certification on the last page of this report.**

The **McGraw·Hill** Companies

# Bed Bath & Beyond Inc

STANDARD
&POOR'S

## Business Summary September 26, 2008

CORPORATE OVERVIEW. Bed Bath & Beyond operates one of the largest U.S. chains of superstores selling domestics merchandise and home furnishings. BBBY stores predominantly range in size from 20,000 sq. ft. to 50,000 sq. ft., with some encompassing 100,000 sq. ft. The company has grown rapidly, from 34 stores at the end of FY 93 (Feb.) to 881 Bed Bath & Beyond stores in 49 states and Puerto Rico at year-end FY 08. BBBY opened 66 Bed Bath & Beyond Stores stores in FY 08, after opening 74 stores in FY 07; it expected to open 50-55 new stores in FY 09. During FY 08, total square footage of Bed Bath & Beyond stores grew 8.6%, to 30.2 million sq. ft., from 27.8 million sq. ft. Company stores are principally located in suburban areas of medium- and large-sized cities. These stores are situated in strip and power strip shopping centers, as well as in major off-price and conventional malls, and freestanding buildings.

In March 2002, the company acquired Harmon Stores, Inc., a health and beau-

ty care retailer. The Harmon chain had 40 stores in three states at March 1, 2008, ranging in size from approximately 5,000 to 9,000 sq. ft. In June 2003, BBBY acquired Christmas Tree Shops, a retailer of home decor, giftware, housewares, food, paper goods and seasonal products, for approximately $194.4 million, net of cash acquired. The company operated 41 Christmas Tree Shops in 10 states at year-end FY 08, ranging in size between 30,000 and 50,000 sq. ft. In March 2007, BBBY acquired buybuy BABY, a retailer of infant and toddler merchandise, for approximately $67 million, net of cash acquired. The company operated nine buybuy BABY stores at year-end FY 08, ranging in size from 28,000 to 60,000 square feet.

## Company Financials Fiscal Year Ended Feb. 29

| Per Share Data ($) | 2008 | 2007 | 2006 | 2005 | 2004 | 2003 | 2002 | 2001 | 2000 | 1999 |
|---|---|---|---|---|---|---|---|---|---|---|
| Tangible Book Value | 11.34 | 9.56 | 8.05 | 6.99 | 6.14 | 4.93 | 3.75 | 2.84 | 1.99 | 1.48 |
| Cash Flow | 2.69 | 2.56 | 2.29 | 1.96 | 1.59 | 1.25 | 0.94 | 0.75 | 0.57 | 0.42 |
| Earnings | 2.10 | 2.09 | 1.92 | 1.65 | 1.31 | 1.00 | 0.74 | 0.59 | 0.46 | 0.34 |
| S&P Core Earnings | 2.10 | 2.09 | 1.87 | 1.55 | 1.23 | 0.92 | 0.67 | 0.53 | NA | NA |
| Dividends | Nil | Nil | Nil | Nil | Nil | Nil | Nil | Nil | Nil | Nil |
| Payout Ratio | Nil | Nil | Nil | Nil | Nil | Nil | Nil | Nil | Nil | Nil |
| Calendar Year | 2007 | 2006 | 2005 | 2004 | 2003 | 2002 | 2001 | 2000 | 1999 | 1998 |
| Prices:High | 43.32 | 41.72 | 46.99 | 44.43 | 45.00 | 37.90 | 35.70 | 27.31 | 19.69 | 17.59 |
| Prices:Low | 27.96 | 30.92 | 35.50 | 33.88 | 30.18 | 26.70 | 18.70 | 11.00 | 12.75 | 8.56 |
| P/E Ratio:High | 21 | 20 | 24 | 27 | 34 | 38 | 48 | 46 | 43 | 52 |
| P/E Ratio:Low | 13 | 15 | 18 | 21 | 23 | 27 | 25 | 19 | 28 | 25 |

| Income Statement Analysis (Million $) | 2008 | 2007 | 2006 | 2005 | 2004 | 2003 | 2002 | 2001 | 2000 | 1999 |
|---|---|---|---|---|---|---|---|---|---|---|
| Revenue | 7,049 | 6,617 | 5,810 | 5,148 | 4,478 | 3,665 | 2,928 | 2,397 | 1,878 | 1,397 |
| Operating Income | 996 | 1,026 | 990 | 890 | 724 | 555 | 409 | 319 | 241 | 181 |
| Depreciation | 158 | 136 | 111 | 97.5 | 84.6 | 74.8 | 62.5 | 46.7 | 31.6 | 23.2 |
| Interest Expense | Nil | Nil | Nil | Nil | Nil | Nil | Nil | Nil | Nil | Nil |
| Pretax Income | 865 | 933 | 915 | 811 | 650 | 491 | 357 | 282 | 215 | 162 |
| Effective Tax Rate | 35.0% | 36.3% | 37.4% | 37.8% | 38.5% | 38.5% | 38.5% | 39.0% | 39.0% | 39.7% |
| Net Income | 563 | 594 | 573 | 505 | 399 | 302 | 220 | 172 | 131 | 97.3 |
| S&P Core Earnings | 563 | 594 | 557 | 470 | 370 | 277 | 200 | 155 | NA | NA |

| Balance Sheet & Other Financial Data (Million $) | 2008 | 2007 | 2006 | 2005 | 2004 | 2003 | 2002 | 2001 | 2000 | 1999 |
|---|---|---|---|---|---|---|---|---|---|---|
| Cash | 224 | 988 | 652 | 851 | 867 | 617 | 429 | 239 | 144 | 90.4 |
| Current Assets | 2,080 | 2,699 | 2,072 | 2,097 | 1,969 | 1,594 | 1,227 | 886 | 647 | 455 |
| Total Assets | 3,844 | 3,959 | 3,382 | 3,200 | 2,865 | 2,189 | 1,648 | 1,196 | 866 | 633 |
| Current Liabilities | 1,014 | 1,145 | 990 | 874 | 770 | 680 | 511 | 353 | 287 | 206 |
| Long Term Debt | Nil | Nil | Nil | Nil | Nil | Nil | Nil | Nil | Nil | Nil |
| Common Equity | 2,562 | 2,649 | 2,262 | 2,204 | 1,991 | 1,452 | 1,094 | 817 | 559 | 411 |
| Total Capital | 2,562 | 2,649 | 2,262 | 2,204 | 1,991 | 1,452 | 1,094 | 817 | 559 | 411 |
| Capital Expenditures | 358 | 318 | 220 | 191 | 113 | 135 | 121 | 140 | 90.1 | 62.3 |
| Cash Flow | 721 | 731 | 684 | 602 | 484 | 377 | 282 | 219 | 163 | 121 |
| Current Ratio | 2.1 | 2.4 | 2.1 | 2.4 | 2.6 | 2.3 | 2.4 | 2.5 | 2.3 | 2.2 |
| % Long Term Debt of Capitalization | Nil | Nil | Nil | Nil | Nil | Nil | Nil | Nil | Nil | Nil |
| % Net Income of Revenue | 8.0 | 9.0 | 9.9 | 9.8 | 8.9 | 8.2 | 7.5 | 7.2 | 7.0 | 7.0 |
| % Return on Assets | 14.4 | 16.2 | 17.4 | 16.7 | 15.8 | 15.8 | 15.4 | 16.7 | 17.5 | 17.8 |
| % Return on Equity | 21.6 | 24.2 | 25.7 | 24.1 | 23.2 | 23.7 | 23.0 | 25.0 | 27.1 | 27.6 |

Data as orig reptd.; bef. results of disc opers/spec. items. Per share data adj. for stk. divs.; EPS diluted. E-Estimated. NA-Not Available. NM-Not Meaningful. NR-Not Ranked. UR-Under Review.

**Office:** 650 Liberty Ave, Union, NJ 07083-8135.
**Telephone:** 908-688-0888.
**Website:** http://www.bedbathandbeyond.com
**Co-Chrmn:** L. Feinstein

**Co-Chrmn:** W. Eisenberg
**Pres:** A. Stark
**CEO:** S.H. Temares
**COO & CTO:** K. Wanner

**Investor Contact:** R. Curwin (908-688-0888)
**Board Members:** D. S. Adler, S. F. Barshay, W. Eisenberg, K. Eppler, L. Feinstein, P. R. Gaston, J. Heller, R. S. Kaplan, V. A. Morrison, F. Stoller, S. H. Temares

**Founded:** 1971
**Domicile:** New York
**Employees:** 39,000

# Bemis Co Inc

**STANDARD &POOR'S**

| S&P Recommendation **HOLD** ★★★☆☆ | Price $24.18 (as of Nov 14, 2008) | 12-Mo. Target Price $26.00 | Investment Style Large-Cap Blend |
|---|---|---|---|

**GICS Sector** Materials
**Sub-Industry** Paper Packaging

**Summary** This company is a leading maker of a broad range of flexible packaging and pressure-sensitive materials.

## Key Stock Statistics (Source S&P, Vickers, company reports)

| | | | | | | | |
|---|---|---|---|---|---|---|---|
| 52-Wk Range | $29.70 – 20.62 | S&P Oper. EPS 2009E | 1.90 | Market Capitalization(B) | $2.410 | Beta | 0.69 |
| Trailing 12-Month EPS | $1.74 | S&P Oper. EPS 2010E | NA | Yield (%) | 3.64 | S&P 3-Yr. Proj. EPS CAGR(%) | 9 |
| Trailing 12-Month P/E | 13.9 | P/E on S&P Oper. EPS 2009E | 12.7 | Dividend Rate/Share | $0.88 | S&P Credit Rating | A |
| $10K Invested 5 Yrs Ago | $12,101 | Common Shares Outstg. (M) | 99.7 | Institutional Ownership (%) | 78 | | |

## Price Performance

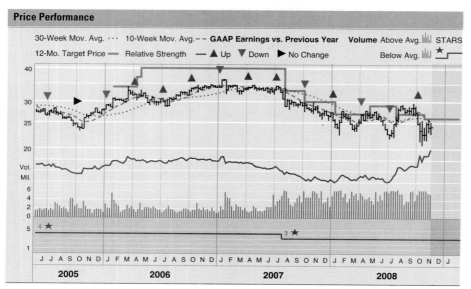

- 30-Week Mov. Avg. · · · ·   10-Week Mov. Avg. – – **GAAP Earnings vs. Previous Year**   **Volume** Above Avg. |||| STARS
- 12-Mo. Target Price —   Relative Strength —   ▲ Up   ▼ Down   ► No Change   Below Avg. |||| ★

Options: ASE, CBOE, P

Analysis prepared by **Stewart Scharf** on October 30, 2008, when the stock traded at **$ 23.45.**

### Highlights

➤ We expect organic sales growth (before a 2% to 3% positive foreign currency effect) to advance in the low-single digits in 2008, with similar growth likely in 2009, driven mainly by demand for flexible packaging products for food and medical devices. The more cyclical pressure-sensitive materials products segment, which is exposed to the economically sensitive label and promotional markets, should remain weak. We see the devaluation of the Brazilian real and the euro impacting total sales in early 2009.

➤ We think gross margins in 2008 will narrow to about 17%, from 18.5% in 2007, due to soft unit volume, a shift in the sales mix, customer delays in ramping up new business and a 90-day lag in price pass-throughs. We expect margins to improve during 2009 as resin and other raw material costs stabilize. In our view, operating margins (EBITDA) will expand sequentially, from below 12% projected for 2008 (12.7% in 2007), based on improved productivity and cost controls, as well as new products.

➤ We project an unchanged effective tax rate of 37% for 2008, and EPS of $1.73, advancing 10% to $1.90 in 2009.

### Investment Rationale/Risk

➤ We maintain our hold recommendation, based on our valuation metrics, along with our expectations of stabilizing oil prices. In our view, demand for certain food packaging products may pick up as more people choose to dine at home.

➤ Risks to our recommendation and target price include a change in customer order patterns due to a further rise in commodity prices, softer global demand, and negative foreign exchange rates. We have corporate governance concerns based on board and audit issues, including the CEO being a party to one or more related-party transactions.

➤ The shares recently traded at a premium to our projected 2009 P/E of 10.2X for S&P's Paper Packaging sub-industry group. With the stock's recent yield of about 3.8%, versus 3.1% for the S&P 500 Index, and BMS's solid earnings track record, we apply a near five-year historical forward P/E of 16X to derive a value of $30. Based on our DCF analysis, the stock has an intrinsic value of $23, assuming a 3% terminal growth rate and an 8.3% weighted average cost of capital. Blending these valuations, we arrive at our 12-month target price of $26.

### Qualitative Risk Assessment

| LOW | MEDIUM | HIGH |
|---|---|---|

Our risk assessment reflects the possibility of softer global economic conditions, higher raw material prices, and difficulty in integrating acquisitions. However, BMS has an S&P Quality Ranking of A, which indicates historically stable earnings and dividend growth.

### Quantitative Evaluations

**S&P Quality Ranking** A

| D | C | B- | B | B+ | A- | A | A+ |
|---|---|---|---|---|---|---|---|

**Relative Strength Rank** STRONG

86

LOWEST = 1     HIGHEST = 99

### Revenue/Earnings Data

**Revenue (Million $)**

| | 1Q | 2Q | 3Q | 4Q | Year |
|---|---|---|---|---|---|
| 2008 | 947.3 | 980.0 | 984.3 | -- | -- |
| 2007 | 909.1 | 921.8 | 905.7 | 912.7 | 3,649 |
| 2006 | 901.7 | 933.8 | 903.3 | 900.6 | 3,639 |
| 2005 | 831.9 | 879.9 | 870.1 | 892.1 | 3,474 |
| 2004 | 684.0 | 712.9 | 711.9 | 725.6 | 2,834 |
| 2003 | 638.6 | 670.2 | 662.0 | 664.3 | 2,635 |

**Earnings Per Share ($)**

| | | | | | |
|---|---|---|---|---|---|
| 2008 | 0.42 | 0.46 | 0.44 | E0.41 | E1.73 |
| 2007 | 0.45 | 0.47 | 0.40 | 0.42 | 1.74 |
| 2006 | 0.35 | 0.46 | 0.45 | 0.39 | 1.65 |
| 2005 | 0.30 | 0.38 | 0.41 | 0.42 | 1.51 |
| 2004 | 0.40 | 0.42 | 0.41 | 0.44 | 1.67 |
| 2003 | 0.33 | 0.36 | 0.32 | 0.35 | 1.37 |

Fiscal year ended Dec. 31. Next earnings report expected: Late January. EPS Estimates based on S&P Operating Earnings; historical GAAP earnings are as reported.

### Dividend Data (Dates: mm/dd Payment Date: mm/dd/yy)

| Amount ($) | Date Decl. | Ex-Div. Date | Stk. of Record | Payment Date |
|---|---|---|---|---|
| 0.220 | 01/31 | 02/13 | 02/15 | 03/03/08 |
| 0.220 | 05/01 | 05/14 | 05/16 | 06/02/08 |
| 0.220 | 08/01 | 08/13 | 08/15 | 09/02/08 |
| 0.220 | 10/30 | 11/12 | 11/14 | 12/01/08 |

Dividends have been paid since 1922. Source: Company reports.

---

**Please read the Required Disclosures and Analyst Certification on the last page of this report.**

The **McGraw-Hill** Companies

# Bemis Co Inc

**STANDARD &POOR'S**

## Business Summary October 30, 2008

CORPORATE OVERVIEW. Bemis Co., a leading North American producer of flexible packaging products, as well as pressure-sensitive materials, focuses primarily on the food industry (about 65% of sales). Markets also include the chemicals, agribusiness, pharmaceutical, personal care products, electronics, automotive and graphic industries. BMS has 56 manufacturing plants (four leased) in 10 countries.

Although BMS focuses on marketing its products in the U.S. (64% of 2007 net sales) and Europe (18%), it has broadened its reach to South America (15%), Southeast Asia and Mexico, due to strong demand for barrier films to extend the shelf life of perishable foods. Canada had sales of 0.4%, while 2.6% came from other regions.

The Flexible Packaging Products segment (82% of net sales in 2007; $347 million of operating profits) produces a wide range of consumer and industrial packaging products, including high barrier, polyethylene and paper products. High barrier products, which comprise more than 50% of net sales, include flexible polymer film structures and barrier laminates for food, medical and personal care products.

The Pressure Sensitive Materials segment (18%; $40 million in operating profits) produces printing products, decorative and sheet products, and technical products.

Flexible packaging competitors include Alcan Packaging, Sealed Air, Sonoco Products, Smurfit-Stone Container and Hood Packaging. Pressure-sensitive materials competitors include Avery Dennison, Minnesota Mining and Manufacturing (3M), Ricoh, Flexcon and Spinnaker Industries.

In January 2005, the company acquired majority ownership of Brazil-based Dixie Toga, a leading South American packaging company, for $250 million in cash (less than 6X Dixie's 2004 EBITDA). Dixie had annual sales of over $450 million in 2005. BMS controls 85% of Dixie's preferred shares.

## Company Financials  Fiscal Year Ended Dec. 31

| Per Share Data ($) | 2008 | 2007 | 2006 | 2005 | 2004 | 2003 | 2002 | 2001 | 2000 | 1999 |
|---|---|---|---|---|---|---|---|---|---|---|
| Tangible Book Value | NA | 9.70 | 7.31 | 6.29 | 7.48 | 5.81 | 4.11 | 4.39 | 4.76 | 5.52 |
| Cash Flow | NA | 3.28 | 3.08 | 2.98 | 2.88 | 2.56 | 2.65 | 2.49 | 2.24 | 2.02 |
| Earnings | 1.73 | 1.74 | 1.65 | 1.51 | 1.67 | 1.37 | 1.54 | 1.32 | 1.22 | 1.09 |
| S&P Core Earnings | NA | 1.67 | 1.64 | 1.48 | 1.65 | 1.32 | 1.28 | 1.02 | NA | NA |
| Dividends | 0.66 | 0.84 | 0.76 | 0.72 | 0.64 | 0.56 | 0.52 | 0.50 | 0.48 | 0.46 |
| Payout Ratio | 38% | 48% | 46% | 48% | 38% | 41% | 34% | 38% | 39% | 42% |
| Prices:High | 29.70 | 36.53 | 34.99 | 32.50 | 29.49 | 25.58 | 29.12 | 26.24 | 19.66 | 20.19 |
| Prices:Low | 20.62 | 25.53 | 27.86 | 23.20 | 23.24 | 19.67 | 19.70 | 14.34 | 11.47 | 15.09 |
| P/E Ratio:High | 17 | 21 | 21 | 22 | 18 | 19 | 19 | 20 | 16 | 19 |
| P/E Ratio:Low | 12 | 15 | 17 | 15 | 14 | 14 | 13 | 11 | 9 | 14 |
| **Income Statement Analysis** (Million $) | | | | | | | | | | |
| Revenue | NA | 3,649 | 3,639 | 3,474 | 2,834 | 2,635 | 2,369 | 2,293 | 2,165 | 1,918 |
| Operating Income | NA | 468 | 492 | 472 | 420 | 384 | 401 | 384 | 363 | 316 |
| Depreciation | NA | 159 | 152 | 151 | 131 | 128 | 119 | 124 | 108 | 97.7 |
| Interest Expense | NA | 54.5 | 49.3 | 38.7 | 15.5 | 12.6 | 15.4 | 30.3 | 31.6 | 21.2 |
| Pretax Income | NA | 290 | 289 | 282 | 294 | 240 | 268 | 228 | 212 | 190 |
| Effective Tax Rate | NA | 36.0% | 37.8% | 40.3% | 38.7% | 38.4% | 37.9% | 38.2% | 38.2% | 37.4% |
| Net Income | NA | 182 | 176 | 163 | 180 | 147 | 166 | 140 | 131 | 115 |
| S&P Core Earnings | NA | 174 | 176 | 160 | 179 | 142 | 137 | 108 | NA | NA |
| **Balance Sheet & Other Financial Data** (Million $) | | | | | | | | | | |
| Cash | NA | 147 | 112 | 91.1 | 93.9 | 76.5 | 56.4 | 35.1 | 28.9 | 18.2 |
| Current Assets | NA | 1,137 | 1,094 | 988 | 874 | 752 | 722 | 587 | 640 | 584 |
| Total Assets | NA | 3,191 | 3,039 | 2,965 | 2,487 | 2,293 | 2,257 | 1,923 | 1,889 | 1,532 |
| Current Liabilities | NA | 535 | 555 | 474 | 375 | 316 | 326 | 238 | 495 | 253 |
| Long Term Debt | NA | 843 | 722 | 790 | 534 | 583 | 718 | 595 | 438 | 372 |
| Common Equity | NA | 1,562 | 1,472 | 1,349 | 1,308 | 1,139 | 959 | 886 | 799 | 726 |
| Total Capital | NA | 2,533 | 2,358 | 2,336 | 2,019 | 1,878 | 1,788 | 1,606 | 1,342 | 1,227 |
| Capital Expenditures | NA | 179 | 159 | 187 | 135 | 106 | 91.0 | 117 | 100 | 137 |
| Cash Flow | NA | 341 | 329 | 313 | 311 | 275 | 285 | 264 | 239 | 212 |
| Current Ratio | NA | 2.1 | 2.0 | 2.1 | 2.3 | 2.4 | 2.2 | 2.5 | 1.3 | 2.3 |
| % Long Term Debt of Capitalization | NA | 32.6 | 30.6 | 33.8 | 26.4 | 31.1 | 40.2 | 37.1 | 32.6 | 30.3 |
| % Net Income of Revenue | NA | 5.0 | 4.8 | 4.7 | 6.3 | 5.6 | 7.0 | 6.1 | 6.0 | 6.0 |
| % Return on Assets | NA | 5.8 | 5.9 | 6.0 | 7.5 | 6.5 | 7.9 | 7.4 | 7.6 | 7.6 |
| % Return on Equity | NA | 12.0 | 12.5 | 12.2 | 14.7 | 14.0 | 17.9 | 16.7 | 17.1 | 16.2 |

Data as orig reptd.; bef. results of disc opers/spec. items. Per share data adj. for stk. divs.; EPS diluted. E-Estimated. NA-Not Available. NM-Not Meaningful. NR-Not Ranked. UR-Under Review.

**Office:** 1 Neenah Ctr 4th Fl, Neenah, WI 54956-3087.
**Telephone:** 920-727-4100.
**Website:** http://www.bemis.com
**Chrmn:** J.H. Curler

**Pres & CEO:** H.J. Theisen
**SVP & CFO:** G.C. Wulf
**CTO:** R. Germonprez
**Chief Acctg Officer & Cntlr:** S.A. Jaffy

**Investor Contact:** M.E. Miller (920-527-5045)
**Board Members:** W. Bolton, J. H. Curler, D. S. Haffner, B. L. Johnson, T. M. Manganello, R. D. O'Shaughnessy, P. S. Peercy, E. N. Perry, W. J. Scholle, H. J. Theisen, H. A. Van Deursen, P. G. Weaver, G. C. Wulf

**Founded:** 1858
**Domicile:** Missouri
**Employees:** 15,678

# Best Buy Co. Inc.

**STANDARD &POOR'S**

| S&P Recommendation | BUY ★★★★☆ | Price $22.06 (as of Nov 14, 2008) | 12-Mo. Target Price $32.00 | Investment Style Large-Cap Growth |
|---|---|---|---|---|

**GICS Sector** Consumer Discretionary
**Sub-Industry** Computer & Electronics Retail

**Summary** This leading retailer of consumer electronics and entertainment software operates nearly 1,300 stores in the U.S., Canada and China.

## Key Stock Statistics (Source S&P, Vickers, company reports)

| | | | | | | | |
|---|---|---|---|---|---|---|---|
| 52-Wk Range | $100.66–20.00 | S&P Oper. EPS 2009E | 2.62 | Market Capitalization(B) | $9.096 | Beta | 1.42 |
| Trailing 12-Month EPS | $3.16 | S&P Oper. EPS 2010E | 2.19 | Yield (%) | 2.54 | S&P 3-Yr. Proj. EPS CAGR(%) | 13 |
| Trailing 12-Month P/E | 7.0 | P/E on S&P Oper. EPS 2009E | 8.4 | Dividend Rate/Share | $0.56 | S&P Credit Rating | BBB |
| $10K Invested 5 Yrs Ago | $6,057 | Common Shares Outstg. (M) | 412.3 | Institutional Ownership (%) | 76 | | |

## Price Performance

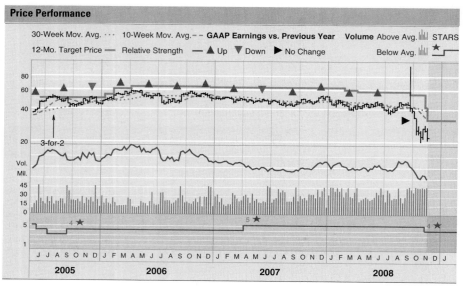

30-Week Mov. Avg. ···   10-Week Mov. Avg. --   **GAAP Earnings vs. Previous Year**   Volume Above Avg. STARS
12-Mo. Target Price —   Relative Strength   ▲ Up  ▼ Down  ► No Change   Below Avg.

3-for-2

Options: ASE, CBOE, P, Ph

Analysis prepared by **Michael Souers** on November 12, 2008, when the stock traded at **$ 22.12**.

## Qualitative Risk Assessment

| LOW | MEDIUM | HIGH |
|---|---|---|

Our risk assessment reflects what we view as BBY's strong balance sheet, sizable market share, numerous suppliers and buyers, and a history of profitability, offset by a highly competitive environment for consumer electronics retailing, with numerous rivals and strong price competition.

## Quantitative Evaluations

**S&P Quality Ranking**     B+

| D | C | B- | B | B+ | A- | A | A+ |
|---|---|---|---|---|---|---|---|

**Relative Strength Rank**     MODERATE

35

LOWEST = 1     HIGHEST = 99

## Revenue/Earnings Data

**Revenue (Million $)**

| | 1Q | 2Q | 3Q | 4Q | Year |
|---|---|---|---|---|---|
| 2009 | 8,990 | 9,801 | -- | -- | -- |
| 2008 | 7,927 | 8,750 | 9,928 | 13,418 | 40,023 |
| 2007 | 6,959 | 7,603 | 8,473 | 12,899 | 35,934 |
| 2006 | 6,118 | 6,702 | 7,335 | 10,693 | 30,848 |
| 2005 | 5,479 | 6,080 | 6,647 | 9,227 | 27,433 |
| 2004 | 4,668 | 5,396 | 6,034 | 8,449 | 24,547 |

**Earnings Per Share ($)**

| | | | | | |
|---|---|---|---|---|---|
| 2009 | 0.43 | 0.48 | E0.28 | E1.43 | E2.62 |
| 2008 | 0.39 | 0.48 | 0.53 | 1.71 | 3.12 |
| 2007 | 0.47 | 0.47 | 0.31 | 1.55 | 2.79 |
| 2006 | 0.34 | 0.37 | 0.28 | 1.29 | 2.27 |
| 2005 | 0.23 | 0.30 | 0.29 | 1.03 | 1.86 |
| 2004 | 0.14 | 0.28 | 0.25 | 0.95 | 1.63 |

Fiscal year ended Feb. 29. Next earnings report expected: Mid December. EPS Estimates based on S&P Operating Earnings; historical GAAP earnings are as reported.

## Highlights

➤ We view BBY as the best-of-class U.S. consumer electronics retailer, based on its digital product focus, knowledgeable sales staff, and effective advertising and marketing campaigns. We think BBY's focus on advanced TVs, notebook computers, video gaming devices, mobile phones and GPS devices will support strong revenue growth near term.

➤ We project a 12% increase in revenues for FY 09 (Feb.), following an 11% advance in FY 08. We expect this growth to be driven by the acquisition of Carphone Warehouse and approximately 125 net new stores worldwide, partially offset by a projected 2.5% decline in comparable-store sales, given our forecast of a modest decrease in consumer spending. We expect operating margins to narrow about 140 basis points, reflecting projected deleveraging of SG&A expenses due to weak same-store sales and investments to spur global growth.

➤ After slightly lower net interest income and about 6% fewer shares outstanding due to BBY's aggressive share repurchase plan, we project FY 09 EPS of $2.62, a 16% decline from the $3.12 the company earned in FY 08. We see FY 10 EPS of $2.19.

## Investment Rationale/Risk

➤ Despite the recent pressures facing consumers, we continue to have confidence in Best Buy's ability to execute on its growth strategy. In addition to capitalizing on the strength of the current consumer electronics product cycle, we believe BBY is positioned to grow its market share through initiatives such as Geek Squad, Best Buy Mobile and Apple store-within-a-store offerings. We think these initiatives, combined with BBY's customer focus, will enable the company to continue to differentiate itself in a competitive marketplace. We believe the shares are attractive, recently trading at under 9X our FY 09 EPS estimate, a significant discount to historical averages and the S&P 500.

➤ Risks to our recommendation and target price include a sharp deterioration in the economic climate and consumer confidence, and the risk that BBY will be unable to successfully execute its strategic objectives.

➤ Our 12-month target price of $32, about 15X our FY 10 EPS projection, is based on our DCF analysis, which assumes a weighted average cost of capital of 11.8% and a terminal growth rate of 4%.

## Dividend Data (Dates: mm/dd Payment Date: mm/dd/yy)

| Amount ($) | Date Decl. | Ex-Div. Date | Stk. of Record | Payment Date |
|---|---|---|---|---|
| 0.130 | 12/19 | 01/07 | 01/09 | 01/30/08 |
| 0.130 | 04/03 | 04/21 | 04/23 | 05/14/08 |
| 0.130 | 06/18 | 07/03 | 07/08 | 07/29/08 |
| 0.140 | 06/25 | 10/03 | 10/07 | 10/28/08 |

Dividends have been paid since 2003. Source: Company reports.

**Please read the Required Disclosures and Analyst Certification on the last page of this report.**

*The McGraw-Hill Companies*

# Best Buy Co. Inc.

**STANDARD
&POOR'S**

## Business Summary November 12, 2008

**CORPORATE OVERVIEW.** This leading consumer electronics retailer operated, as of March 3, 2008, 923 Best Buy stores, 19 Pacific Sales showrooms, 13 Magnolia Audio Video stores, nine Best Buy Mobile stand-alone stores and seven Geek Squad stand-alone stores in the U.S. The company also operated 51 Canada Best Buy stores, 131 Future Shop stores in Canada, 160 Five Star stores in China, and one Best Buy China store.

U.S. Best Buy stores average approximately 39,700 retail square feet, and offer products in six revenue categories: consumer electronics (41% of FY 08 (Feb.) revenues), home office (28%), entertainment software (19%), appliances (6%), services (6%), and other (0%). Best Buy's largest category, consumer electronics, includes products such as televisions, digital cameras and accessories, digital camcorders and accessories, DVD players, MP3 players and accessories, navigation products, home theater audio systems and components, and mobile electronics including car stereo and satellite radio products.

**CORPORATE STRATEGY.** BBY's business strategy centers on meeting individual consumer electronics needs with end-to-end solutions, which involves greater employee involvement and increased services. BBY is committed to scaling BBY customer-centricity across the organization, and completed the transition of all remaining stores to the customer-centricity operating model in FY 08. In FY 09, BBY plans to open 85-100 new stores in the U.S., 5-10 Pacific Sales stores, 6 Future Shop stores, 6 Best Buy Canada Stores, 8-16 Five Star stores and 1-3 Best Buy China stores. In addition, BBY will be extending the Best Buy Mobile experience from 181 Best Buy stores to the majority of stores over the next 18 months, and will expand its relationship with Apple by offering Apple computers and services to approximately 250 more stores in FY 09, from 357 as of March 3, 2008.

## Company Financials Fiscal Year Ended Feb. 29

| Per Share Data ($) | 2008 | 2007 | 2006 | 2005 | 2004 | 2003 | 2002 | 2001 | 2000 | 1999 |
|---|---|---|---|---|---|---|---|---|---|---|
| Tangible Book Value | 7.99 | 10.82 | 9.60 | 7.91 | 5.97 | 4.70 | 3.65 | 3.07 | 2.44 | 2.32 |
| Cash Flow | 4.40 | 3.80 | 3.16 | 2.76 | 2.41 | 1.91 | 1.91 | 1.18 | 0.95 | 0.64 |
| Earnings | 3.12 | 2.79 | 2.27 | 1.86 | 1.63 | 1.27 | 1.18 | 0.83 | 0.72 | 0.48 |
| S&P Core Earnings | 3.12 | 2.76 | 2.27 | 1.77 | 1.45 | 1.11 | 1.08 | 0.76 | NA | NA |
| Dividends | 0.36 | 0.36 | 0.31 | 0.50 | 0.27 | Nil | Nil | Nil | Nil | Nil |
| Payout Ratio | 12% | 13% | 14% | 38% | 17% | Nil | Nil | Nil | Nil | Nil |
| Calendar Year | 2007 | 2006 | 2005 | 2004 | 2003 | 2002 | 2001 | 2000 | 1999 | 1998 |
| Prices:High | 53.90 | 59.50 | 18.03 | 41.47 | 41.80 | 35.83 | 33.42 | 39.50 | 35.78 | 13.83 |
| Prices:Low | 41.85 | 43.32 | 14.84 | 29.25 | 15.77 | 11.33 | 12.36 | 9.33 | 13.72 | 4.00 |
| P/E Ratio:High | 17 | 21 | 14 | 22 | 26 | 28 | 28 | 48 | 49 | 29 |
| P/E Ratio:Low | 13 | 16 | 11 | 16 | 10 | 9 | 10 | 11 | 19 | 8 |

| Income Statement Analysis (Million $) | | | | | | | | | | |
|---|---|---|---|---|---|---|---|---|---|---|
| Revenue | 40,023 | 35,934 | 30,848 | 27,433 | 24,547 | 20,946 | 19,597 | 15,327 | 12,494 | 10,078 |
| Operating Income | 2,746 | 2,508 | 2,100 | 1,901 | 1,699 | 1,320 | 1,246 | 772 | 649 | 443 |
| Depreciation | 585 | 509 | 456 | 459 | 385 | 310 | 309 | 167 | 110 | 78.4 |
| Interest Expense | 62.0 | Nil | 30.0 | 44.0 | 31.0 | 25.0 | 2.00 | 6.90 | 5.10 | 23.8 |
| Pretax Income | 2,225 | 2,130 | 1,721 | 1,443 | 1,296 | 1,014 | 936 | 642 | 563 | 365 |
| Effective Tax Rate | 36.6% | 35.3% | 33.8% | 35.3% | 38.3% | 38.7% | 39.1% | 38.3% | 38.3% | 38.5% |
| Net Income | 1,407 | 1,377 | 1,140 | 934 | 800 | 622 | 570 | 396 | 347 | 224 |
| S&P Core Earnings | 1,407 | 1,364 | 1,140 | 873 | 704 | 538 | 512 | 361 | NA | NA |

| Balance Sheet & Other Financial Data (Million $) | | | | | | | | | | |
|---|---|---|---|---|---|---|---|---|---|---|
| Cash | 1,438 | 1,205 | 681 | 470 | 2,600 | 1,914 | 1,855 | 747 | 751 | 786 |
| Current Assets | 7,342 | 9,081 | 7,985 | 6,903 | 5,724 | 4,867 | 4,611 | 2,929 | 2,238 | 2,063 |
| Total Assets | 12,758 | 13,570 | 11,864 | 10,294 | 8,652 | 7,663 | 7,375 | 4,840 | 2,995 | 2,512 |
| Current Liabilities | 6,769 | 6,301 | 6,056 | 4,959 | 4,501 | 3,793 | 3,730 | 2,715 | 1,785 | 1,387 |
| Long Term Debt | 627 | 590 | 178 | 528 | 482 | 828 | 813 | 181 | 14.9 | 30.5 |
| Common Equity | 4,484 | 6,201 | 5,257 | 4,449 | 3,422 | 2,730 | 2,521 | 1,822 | 1,096 | 1,064 |
| Total Capital | 5,151 | 6,826 | 5,435 | 4,977 | 3,904 | 3,558 | 3,334 | 2,003 | 1,111 | 1,095 |
| Capital Expenditures | 797 | 733 | 648 | 502 | 545 | 725 | 627 | 658 | 361 | 166 |
| Cash Flow | 1,992 | 1,886 | 1,596 | 1,393 | 1,185 | 932 | 925 | 563 | 457 | 303 |
| Current Ratio | 1.1 | 1.4 | 1.3 | 1.4 | 1.3 | 1.3 | 1.2 | 1.1 | 1.3 | 1.5 |
| % Long Term Debt of Capitalization | 12.2 | 8.6 | 3.3 | 10.6 | 12.3 | 23.3 | 24.4 | 9.0 | 1.4 | 2.8 |
| % Net Income of Revenue | 3.5 | 3.8 | 3.7 | 3.4 | 3.3 | 3.0 | 2.9 | 2.6 | 2.8 | 2.2 |
| % Return on Assets | 10.7 | 10.8 | 10.3 | 9.9 | 9.8 | 8.3 | 9.3 | 10.1 | 12.6 | 9.8 |
| % Return on Equity | 26.3 | 24.0 | 23.5 | 23.7 | 26.0 | 23.8 | 26.2 | 27.1 | 32.6 | 27.7 |

Data as orig reptd.; bef. results of disc opers/spec. items. Per share data adj. for stk. divs.; EPS diluted. E-Estimated. NA-Not Available. NM-Not Meaningful. NR-Not Ranked. UR-Under Review.

**Office:** 7075 Flying Cloud Drive, Eden Prairie, MN 55344-3538.
**Telephone:** 952-947-2000.
**Email:** moneytalk@bestbuy.com
**Website:** http://www.bestbuy.com

**Chrmn:** R.M. Schulze
**Pres & COO:** B.J. Dunn
**Vice Chrmn:** A.U. Lenzmeier
**Vice Chrmn & CEO:** B.H. Anderson

**EVP & CFO:** J.L. Muehlbauer
**Investor Contact:** J. Driscoll (612-291-6110)
**Board Members:** B. H. Anderson, R. James, E. S. Kaplan, S. Khosla, A. U. Lenzmeier, G. L. Mikan, III, M. H. Paull, R. M. Rebolledo, R. M. Schulze, F. D. Trestman, H. Tyabji, K. J. Victor, G. R. Vittecoq

**Founded:** 1966
**Domicile:** Minnesota
**Employees:** 150,000

**STANDARD &POOR'S**

# Big Lots Inc

| S&P Recommendation | HOLD ★★★☆☆ | Price | 12-Mo. Target Price | Investment Style |
|---|---|---|---|---|
| | | $15.41 (as of Nov 14, 2008) | $35.00 | Large-Cap Blend |

**GICS Sector** Consumer Discretionary
**Sub-Industry** General Merchandise Stores

**Summary** This leading broadline closeout retailer has over 1,300 Big Lots stores in 47 states.

## Key Stock Statistics (Source S&P, Vickers, company reports)

| | | | | | | | |
|---|---|---|---|---|---|---|---|
| 52-Wk Range | $35.33– 12.40 | S&P Oper. EPS 2009E | 2.00 | Market Capitalization(B) | $1.264 | Beta | 0.97 |
| Trailing 12-Month EPS | $1.88 | S&P Oper. EPS 2010E | 2.15 | Yield (%) | Nil | S&P 3-Yr. Proj. EPS CAGR(%) | 20 |
| Trailing 12-Month P/E | 8.2 | P/E on S&P Oper. EPS 2009E | 7.7 | Dividend Rate/Share | Nil | S&P Credit Rating | NA |
| $10K Invested 5 Yrs Ago | $11,070 | Common Shares Outstg. (M) | 82.0 | Institutional Ownership (%) | NM | | |

## Price Performance

30-Week Mov. Avg. · · · 10-Week Mov. Avg. – – GAAP Earnings vs. Previous Year   Volume Above Avg. STARS
12-Mo. Target Price — Relative Strength — ▲ Up ▼ Down ▶ No Change   Below Avg. ★

Options: P, Ph

Analysis prepared by **Jason N. Asaeda** on August 26, 2008, when the stock traded at **$ 30.76**.

## Highlights

➤ We project net sales of $4.71 billion in FY 09 (Jan.) and $4.74 billion in FY 10. We anticipate an increased focus on traffic-driving brand-name closeouts and "treasure hunt" items, and improved product quality and in-stock levels, particularly on consumables. Balancing these positive factors against our expectation of a slowdown in consumer spending, we look for low single digit same-store sales growth annually. Based on BIG's plans to open new 20 stores and close approximately 45 underperforming units, we project about a 2% decline in selling square footage in FY 09. We believe the company will likely limit expansion in FY 10 to its most successful trade areas in an effort to achieve high sales productivity.

➤ Operating margins are likely to widen annually on: improving initial markups, supported in part by global sourcing; BIG's taking of markdowns more consistently in an effort to drive both same-store sales growth and higher inventory turns; a reduction in depreciation expense on disciplined capital allocation; and cost saving initiatives.

➤ We see operating EPS of $2.00 in FY 09 and $2.15 in FY 10.

## Investment Rationale/Risk

➤ Our hold recommendation is based on valuation. We look for BIG to weather a tough retail environment and to deliver strong earnings growth in FY 09, supported by the company's efforts to raise sales productivity and lower its cost structure by: better aligning products with customer preferences; moving to a new store layout that brings more merchandise to the selling floor and allocates more square footage to key categories; and accelerating the closure of underperforming units. Given what we see as its strong price-value proposition and attractive mix of everyday necessities and more discretionary-purchase items, we also see potential for BIG to gain incremental business from middle- and upper-income consumers trading down from national drugstore and supermarket chains and mass merchandisers.

➤ Risks to our recommendation and target price include sales shortfalls due to changes in consumer confidence and buying preferences, merchandise availability, and increased promotional activity by competitors.

➤ Our 12-month target price of $35 applies a premium-to-peers general merchandise company multiple of 16.1X to our FY 10 EPS estimate.

## Qualitative Risk Assessment

| LOW | MEDIUM | HIGH |
|---|---|---|

Our risk assessment reflects our expectation of improving company fundamentals, supported by BIG's new merchandising and cost reduction initiatives, offset by what we see as a challenging retail environment that could hinder a turnaround.

## Quantitative Evaluations

**S&P Quality Ranking**                                          B-

| D | C | B- | B | B+ | A- | A | A+ |
|---|---|---|---|---|---|---|---|

**Relative Strength Rank**                                   WEAK

25

LOWEST = 1                                          HIGHEST = 99

## Revenue/Earnings Data

**Revenue (Million $)**

| | 1Q | 2Q | 3Q | 4Q | Year |
|---|---|---|---|---|---|
| 2009 | 1,152 | 1,105 | -- | -- | -- |
| 2008 | 1,128 | 1,085 | 1,031 | 1,412 | 4,656 |
| 2007 | 1,092 | 1,057 | 1,050 | 1,545 | 4,743 |
| 2006 | 1,099 | 1,051 | 1,041 | 1,395 | 4,430 |
| 2005 | 1,019 | 995.0 | 980.0 | 1,381 | 4,375 |
| 2004 | 948.4 | 949.3 | 948.1 | 1,329 | 4,174 |

**Earnings Per Share ($)**

| | 1Q | 2Q | 3Q | 4Q | Year |
|---|---|---|---|---|---|
| 2009 | 0.42 | 0.32 | E0.19 | E1.07 | E2.00 |
| 2008 | 0.26 | 0.32 | 0.14 | 0.97 | 1.47 |
| 2007 | 0.13 | 0.04 | 0.02 | 0.83 | 1.01 |
| 2006 | 0.07 | -0.12 | -0.17 | 0.33 | 0.14 |
| 2005 | 0.05 | -0.07 | -0.23 | 0.51 | 0.27 |
| 2004 | 0.08 | -0.07 | -0.05 | 0.51 | 0.77 |

Fiscal year ended Jan. 31. Next earnings report expected: Early December. EPS Estimates based on S&P Operating Earnings; historical GAAP earnings are as reported.

## Dividend Data

Proceeds from the sale of rights amounting to $0.01 a share were distributed in 2001.

---

**Please read the Required Disclosures and Analyst Certification on the last page of this report.**

*The McGraw-Hill Companies*

# Big Lots Inc

**STANDARD &POOR'S**

## Business Summary August 26, 2008

CORPORATE OVERVIEW. BIG's strategy is to position itself as a preferred shopping destination for middle-income consumers seeking savings on brand-name closeouts and other value-priced merchandise. The company's product offerings range from everyday essentials such as food and other consumables, to more discretionary-purchase items, including furniture, holiday assortments, electronics, apparel, and small appliances. In our view, FY 07 (Jan.) was a transitional year for BIG, as the company slowed chain expansion in order to better focus on implementing operational changes to reverse a two-year trend of declining operating profits. Over the next few years, we look for BIG to apply successful merchandising and marketing strategies tested during FY 07 to further strengthen its financial performance.

CORPORATE STRATEGY. BIG's primary growth driver is expansion. The company seeks to build on its leadership position in broadline closeout retailing by expanding its market presence in both existing and new markets. From FY 00 through FY 05, the company increased its selling square footage at a compound annual growth rate (CAGR) of about 6% as it expanded its store count from 1,230 to 1,502. In FY 06, BIG continued to expand its store base, adding 73 new stores. However, the company also accelerated the closure of underperforming locations as part of its What's Important Now (WIN) turnaround strat-

egy, which was announced in November 2005. BIG closed 174 stores in FY 06. As a result, the company ended the fiscal year with 1,401 stores in 47 states, reflecting a 3.5% decline in selling square footage.

WIN is aimed at improving its financial performance via changes in the company's merchandising, cost structure, and real estate. As its first steps, BIG is attempting to raise productivity of its chain by closing low-volume stores located mainly in small, rural, or weaker performing markets, and by moving from an opportunistic real estate strategy to one focused on its most successful trade areas. These areas include California, Arizona, Washington, New York and New Jersey. During FY 07, the company scaled back new store openings to 11 and closed an additional 37 underperforming stores, ending the fiscal year with 1,375 stores. BIG remained committed to its market focused real estate strategy in FY 08, opening only seven new stores and closing 29 locations. The company ended FY 08 with 1,353 stores.

## Company Financials Fiscal Year Ended Jan. 31

| Per Share Data ($) | 2008 | 2007 | 2006 | 2005 | 2004 | 2003 | 2002 | 2001 | 2000 | 1999 |
|---|---|---|---|---|---|---|---|---|---|---|
| Tangible Book Value | 13.34 | 11.10 | 9.47 | 9.54 | 9.51 | 8.83 | 8.11 | 8.28 | 11.71 | 10.79 |
| Cash Flow | 2.34 | 1.91 | 1.15 | 1.17 | 1.56 | 1.38 | 0.37 | 1.44 | 1.74 | 1.71 |
| Earnings | 1.47 | 1.01 | 0.14 | 0.27 | 0.77 | 0.65 | -0.25 | 0.87 | 0.85 | 0.97 |
| S&P Core Earnings | 1.38 | 1.06 | 0.05 | 0.25 | 0.78 | 0.60 | -0.32 | 0.83 | NA | NA |
| Dividends | Nil | Nil | Nil | Nil | Nil | Nil | Nil | Nil | Nil | Nil |
| Payout Ratio | Nil | Nil | Nil | Nil | Nil | Nil | Nil | Nil | Nil | Nil |
| Calendar Year | 2007 | 2006 | 2005 | 2004 | 2003 | 2002 | 2001 | 2000 | 1999 | 1998 |
| Prices:High | 36.15 | 26.36 | 14.29 | 15.62 | 18.39 | 19.90 | 15.75 | 16.38 | 38.13 | 46.13 |
| Prices:Low | 15.35 | 11.83 | 10.06 | 11.05 | 9.92 | 9.75 | 7.15 | 8.25 | 13.69 | 15.50 |
| P/E Ratio:High | 25 | 26 | NM | 58 | 24 | 31 | NM | 19 | 45 | 48 |
| P/E Ratio:Low | 10 | 12 | NM | 41 | 13 | 15 | NM | 9 | 16 | 16 |

| Income Statement Analysis (Million $) | | | | | | | | | | |
|---|---|---|---|---|---|---|---|---|---|---|
| Revenue | 4,656 | 4,743 | 4,430 | 4,375 | 4,174 | 3,869 | 3,433 | 3,277 | 4,700 | 4,194 |
| Operating Income | 315 | 276 | 141 | 172 | 222 | 231 | 43.4 | 249 | 271 | 288 |
| Depreciation | 88.5 | 101 | 115 | 104 | 93.7 | 85.7 | 72.0 | 64.5 | 100 | 84.0 |
| Interest Expense | 2.51 | 0.68 | 6.27 | 24.8 | 16.4 | 21.0 | 20.5 | 23.6 | 25.3 | 24.3 |
| Pretax Income | 239 | 170 | 20.9 | 43.3 | 113 | 125 | -48.7 | 161 | 145 | 179 |
| Effective Tax Rate | 36.8% | 34.0% | 24.8% | 29.8% | 20.6% | 39.5% | NM | 39.5% | 39.5% | 39.0% |
| Net Income | 151 | 113 | 15.7 | 30.4 | 89.9 | 75.7 | -29.5 | 97.6 | 96.1 | 109 |
| S&P Core Earnings | 142 | 118 | 4.93 | 27.8 | 91.6 | 70.7 | -36.7 | 92.6 | NA | NA |

| Balance Sheet & Other Financial Data (Million $) | | | | | | | | | | |
|---|---|---|---|---|---|---|---|---|---|---|
| Cash | 37.1 | 282 | 1.71 | 2.52 | 174 | 160 | NA | NA | 96.3 | 75.9 |
| Current Assets | 891 | 1,149 | 994 | 1,035 | 1,134 | NA | NA | NA | 1,420 | 1,335 |
| Total Assets | 1,444 | 1,721 | 1,625 | 1,734 | 1,801 | 1,656 | 1,470 | 1,528 | 2,187 | 2,043 |
| Current Liabilities | 500 | 474 | 437 | 413 | 416 | NA | NA | NA | 711 | 460 |
| Long Term Debt | 165 | Nil | 5.50 | 159 | 204 | 204 | 204 | 268 | 60.5 | 296 |
| Common Equity | 638 | 1,130 | 1,167 | 1,075 | 1,109 | 1,020 | 923 | 924 | 1,300 | 1,182 |
| Total Capital | 804 | 1,130 | 1,173 | 1,235 | 1,313 | 1,224 | 1,127 | 1,192 | 1,468 | 1,583 |
| Capital Expenditures | 60.4 | 35.9 | 68.5 | 135 | 170 | 110 | NA | NA | 147 | 167 |
| Cash Flow | 240 | 214 | 130 | 135 | 184 | 161 | 42.5 | 162 | 197 | 193 |
| Current Ratio | 1.8 | 2.4 | 2.3 | 2.5 | 2.7 | NA | NA | NA | 2.0 | 2.9 |
| % Long Term Debt of Capitalization | 20.6 | Nil | 0.5 | 12.9 | 15.5 | 16.7 | 18.1 | 22.5 | 4.1 | 18.7 |
| % Net Income of Revenue | 3.3 | 2.4 | 0.4 | 0.7 | 2.2 | 2.0 | NM | 3.0 | 2.0 | 2.6 |
| % Return on Assets | 9.6 | 6.7 | 0.9 | 1.7 | 5.2 | 4.8 | NM | 5.3 | 4.5 | 5.8 |
| % Return on Equity | 17.1 | 10.2 | 1.4 | 2.8 | 8.4 | 7.8 | NM | 8.8 | 7.7 | 9.9 |

Data as orig reptd.; bef. results of disc opers/spec. items. Per share data adj. for stk. divs.; EPS diluted. E-Estimated. NA-Not Available. NM-Not Meaningful. NR-Not Ranked. UR-Under Review.

**Office:** 300 Phillipi Road, Columbus, OH 43228-1310.
**Telephone:** 614-278-6800.
**Website:** http://www.biglots.com
**Chrmn, Pres & CEO:** S.S. Fishman

**SVP, CFO, Chief Acctg Officer & Treas:** J.R. Cooper
**SVP, Secy & General Counsel:** C.W. Haubiel, II
**SVP & CIO:** L.M. Bachman
**Investor Contact:** T.A. Johnson (614-278-6622)

**Board Members:** J. Berger, S. M. Berman, S. S. Fishman, D. T. Kollat, B. J. Lauderback, P. E. Mallott, R. Solt, J. R. Tener, D. B. Tishkoff

**Founded:** 1983
**Domicile:** Ohio
**Employees:** 38,153

*The McGraw-Hill Companies*

# Biogen Idec Inc

**STANDARD &POOR'S**

| S&P Recommendation **HOLD** ★★★☆☆ | Price **$43.52** (as of Nov 14, 2008) | 12-Mo. Target Price **$49.00** | Investment Style **Large-Cap Growth** |

**GICS Sector** Health Care
**Sub-Industry** Biotechnology

**Summary** This major biopharmaceutical concern develops and markets targeted therapies for the treatment of multiple sclerosis, non-Hodgkin's lymphoma and rheumatoid arthritis.

## Key Stock Statistics (Source S&P, Vickers, company reports)

| | | | | | | | |
|---|---|---|---|---|---|---|---|
| 52-Wk Range | $78.57– 38.04 | S&P Oper. EPS 2008**E** | 3.56 | Market Capitalization(B) | $12.697 | Beta | 0.54 |
| Trailing 12-Month EPS | $2.62 | S&P Oper. EPS 2009**E** | 3.86 | Yield (%) | Nil | S&P 3-Yr. Proj. EPS CAGR(%) | 16 |
| Trailing 12-Month P/E | 16.6 | P/E on S&P Oper. EPS 2008**E** | 12.2 | Dividend Rate/Share | Nil | S&P Credit Rating | BBB |
| $10K Invested 5 Yrs Ago | $12,173 | Common Shares Outstg. (M) | 291.8 | Institutional Ownership (%) | 89 | | |

## Price Performance

30-Week Mov. Avg. · · · 10-Week Mov. Avg. – – **GAAP Earnings vs. Previous Year** Volume Above Avg. STARS
12-Mo. Target Price — Relative Strength — ▲ Up ▼ Down ► No Change Below Avg. ★

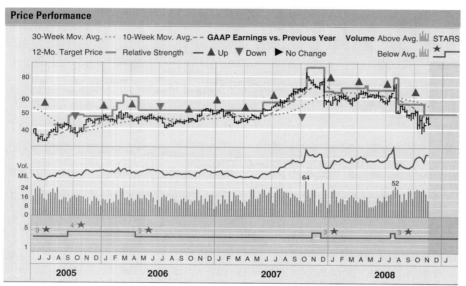

Options: ASE, CBOE, P, Ph

Analysis prepared by **Steven Silver** on October 30, 2008, when the stock traded at **$ 39.92**.

## Qualitative Risk Assessment

| LOW | MEDIUM | **HIGH** |

Our risk assessment reflects that Biogen Idec sells products in competitive markets, and its biggest near-term growth driver faces safety concerns, requiring a comprehensive risk minimization program. The company also is engaged in the development of new drugs in new markets, outside of its core multiple sclerosis area of expertise.

## Quantitative Evaluations

**S&P Quality Ranking** B

| D | C | B- | **B** | B+ | A- | A | A+ |

**Relative Strength Rank** STRONG

75

LOWEST = 1    HIGHEST = 99

## Revenue/Earnings Data

**Revenue (Million $)**

| | 1Q | 2Q | 3Q | 4Q | Year |
|---|---|---|---|---|---|
| 2008 | 942.2 | 993.4 | 1,093 | -- | -- |
| 2007 | 715.9 | 773.2 | 789.2 | 893.3 | 3,172 |
| 2006 | 611.2 | 660.0 | 703.5 | 708.3 | 2,683 |
| 2005 | 587.8 | 605.6 | 596.2 | 632.9 | 2,423 |
| 2004 | 541.7 | 538.8 | 543.3 | 587.8 | 2,212 |
| 2003 | 117.3 | 123.6 | 138.5 | 299.9 | 679.2 |

**Earnings Per Share ($)**

| | | | | | |
|---|---|---|---|---|---|
| 2008 | 0.54 | 0.70 | 0.70 | E0.89 | E3.56 |
| 2007 | 0.38 | 0.54 | 0.41 | 0.67 | 1.99 |
| 2006 | 0.35 | -0.50 | 0.45 | 0.32 | 0.62 |
| 2005 | 0.12 | 0.10 | 0.08 | 0.16 | 0.47 |
| 2004 | -0.12 | Nil | 0.10 | 0.08 | 0.07 |
| 2003 | 0.24 | 0.17 | 0.26 | -4.03 | -4.92 |

Fiscal year ended Dec. 31. Next earnings report expected: NA. EPS Estimates based on S&P Operating Earnings; historical GAAP earnings are as reported.

## Dividend Data

No cash dividends have been paid.

## Highlights

➤ We see revenues of $4.0 billion in 2008, 28% higher than 2007, and project 6% growth in 2009, to $4.3 billion. BIIB has set a goal of 15% compound annual revenue growth through 2010, which we view as challenging, given recent Tysabri safety concerns. As of September 30, 2008, BIIB cited 35,500 patients on Tysabri worldwide, with a 100,000 patient goal by year-end 2010. Avonex sales rose 26% in the third quarter of 2008, aided by price increases for the drug, but we see moderating unit and sales growth for this mature product.

➤ We expect operating expenses to amount to nearly 50% of total revenues in 2008 and 2009, down from 54% in 2007, and see cost controls aiding operating margin expansion to 38%-40%, from 2007's 36% level. We expect BIIB to remain opportunistic in terms of investing in R&D and acquiring new pipeline assets to meet its growth goals, with $2 billion in cash and securities as of September 2008.

➤ Our 2008 and 2009 EPS estimates are $3.56 and $3.86, respectively. In September 2007, BIIB set a goal of 20% compound annual adjusted EPS growth from 2007 through 2010.

## Investment Rationale/Risk

➤ Despite our view of strong performance thus far in 2008, we expect BIIB's valuation to be constrained by Tysabri safety concerns, after three cases of brain disease PML were confirmed in 2008, most recently in late October. As most current Tysabri patients near the two-year treatment mark, we believe sales growth of the drug will slow until longer-term use can validate BIIB's 1-in-1,000 PML risk estimate. Further, we also see long-term competition in BIIB's core multiple sclerosis (MS) program. We are encouraged, however, by BIIB's pipeline and expected robust clinical news flow through 2009. We expect aggressive R&D spending to ease, as its next wave of product candidates reaches the market in three to five years.

➤ Risks to our recommendation and target price include new safety concerns or weakening sales for Tysabri, increased MS market competition, and unfavorable Rituxan arbitration outcomes.

➤ Our 12-month target price of $49 applies a 12.8X multiple to our 2009 EPS estimate of $3.86, representing 0.8X (a discount to large-cap peers due to Tysabri safety concerns) our 16% long-term growth rate.

The McGraw-Hill Companies

# Biogen Idec Inc

## Business Summary October 30, 2008

CORPORATE OVERVIEW. Formed through the 2003 merger of IDEC Pharmaceuticals and Biogen, Biogen Idec researches, develops and markets therapeutics to treat cancer and autoimmune diseases.

BIIB's primary sources of revenue are Avonex and Rituxan. Avonex was approved by the FDA to treat relapsing forms of multiple sclerosis (MS) in 1996, and approved in Europe in 1997. Avonex sales were $1.87 billion in 2007, up 9% from $1.71 billion in 2006. The company estimates its U.S. MS market share at approximately 40% and growing as of year-end 2007.

Rituxan is a treatment for relapsed or refractory low-grade or follicular B-cell non-Hodgkin's lymphomas (NHL). There are over 300,000 U.S. patients with various forms of this disease. Rituxan is marketed and sold in the U.S. under a co-promotion agreement with Genentech; BIIB receives joint business revenues on a percentage of sales. Roche has marketing rights (under the name MabThera) outside the U.S., with BIIB receiving royalties. U.S. Rituxan sales generated revenues of $926 million for BIIB in 2007, 14% higher than $811 million in 2006. Rituxan is being explored for use in treating lupus and MS though it has failed in a study for progressive MS and one for systemic lupus erythematous (SLE) during 2008.

BIIB developed Tysabri with Elan Corp. Tysabri was approved for treating relapsing MS in late 2004. However, three adverse events related to progressive multifocal leukoencephalopathy (PML) -- a rare, fatal nervous system disorder -- were reported in 2005, causing the drug to be removed from the market. Following safety evaluations and an analysis of additional data, the FDA approved a U.S. re-launch in June 2006, contingent upon a restricted distribution program to limit risks. Tysabri is being launched across Europe in 2007 and 2008, with 15 EU countries expected by year-end 2008. As of September 2008, BIIB cited 35,500 patients on Tysabri worldwide. In July 2008, two new cases of PML were reported in Europe, and one U.S. case was confirmed in October 2008, which we expect will put the drug under renewed scrutiny.

Tysabri is also being developed for Crohn's disease, which afflicts nearly one million people worldwide. In July 2007, the European Medicines Agency (EMEA) issued a negative ruling that BIIB and Elan are appealing. However, the U.S. FDA approved Tysabri for moderate-to-severe Crohn's disease in January 2008, and the companies launched the drug for this indication in March 2008.

## Company Financials Fiscal Year Ended Dec. 31

| Per Share Data ($) | 2007 | 2006 | 2005 | 2004 | 2003 | 2002 | 2001 | 2000 | 1999 | 1998 |
|---|---|---|---|---|---|---|---|---|---|---|
| Tangible Book Value | 6.44 | 9.60 | 8.38 | 7.08 | 6.85 | 7.25 | 6.22 | 4.63 | 1.11 | 0.88 |
| Cash Flow | 3.18 | 1.71 | 1.63 | 1.35 | -4.57 | 0.88 | 0.62 | 0.39 | 0.31 | 0.18 |
| Earnings | 1.99 | 0.62 | 0.47 | 0.07 | -4.92 | 0.85 | 0.59 | 0.36 | 0.29 | 0.15 |
| S&P Core Earnings | 2.01 | 0.69 | 0.16 | -0.06 | -5.13 | 0.54 | 0.34 | NA | NA | NA |
| Dividends | Nil | Nil | Nil | Nil | Nil | Nil | Nil | Nil | Nil | Nil |
| Payout Ratio | Nil | Nil | Nil | Nil | Nil | Nil | Nil | Nil | Nil | Nil |
| Prices:High | 84.75 | 52.72 | 70.00 | 68.13 | 42.15 | 71.40 | 75.00 | 77.65 | 35.00 | 8.03 |
| Prices:Low | 42.86 | 40.24 | 33.18 | 36.60 | 27.80 | 20.76 | 32.63 | 18.54 | 6.60 | 2.88 |
| P/E Ratio:High | 43 | 85 | NM | NM | NM | 84 | NM | NM | NM | 52 |
| P/E Ratio:Low | 22 | 65 | NM | NM | NM | 24 | NM | NM | NM | 19 |

| Income Statement Analysis (Million $) | 2007 | 2006 | 2005 | 2004 | 2003 | 2002 | 2001 | 2000 | 1999 | 1998 |
|---|---|---|---|---|---|---|---|---|---|---|
| Revenue | 3,172 | 2,683 | 2,423 | 2,212 | 679 | 404 | 273 | 155 | 118 | 87.0 |
| Operating Income | 1,260 | 1,117 | 756 | 483 | 14.6 | 285 | 137 | 60.6 | 45.8 | 23.2 |
| Depreciation | 380 | 376 | 402 | 439 | 61.3 | 10.2 | 6.31 | 4.74 | 4.37 | 4.28 |
| Interest Expense | 50.6 | Nil | Nil | 18.9 | 15.2 | 16.1 | 7.30 | 7.05 | 6.06 | 0.63 |
| Pretax Income | 852 | 492 | 256 | 64.1 | -881 | 232 | 162 | 69.3 | 45.6 | 21.9 |
| Effective Tax Rate | 32.0% | 56.6% | 37.3% | 60.9% | NM | 36.0% | 37.1% | 17.2% | 5.37% | 1.93% |
| Net Income | 638 | 214 | 161 | 25.1 | -875 | 148 | 102 | 57.4 | 43.2 | 21.5 |
| S&P Core Earnings | 642 | 237 | 56.6 | -21.6 | -914 | 93.4 | 61.4 | NA | NA | NA |

| Balance Sheet & Other Financial Data (Million $) | 2007 | 2006 | 2005 | 2004 | 2003 | 2002 | 2001 | 2000 | 1999 | 1998 |
|---|---|---|---|---|---|---|---|---|---|---|
| Cash | 1,187 | 2,315 | 851 | 1,058 | 836 | 373 | 426 | 401 | 61.4 | 73.5 |
| Current Assets | 2,368 | 1,713 | 1,618 | 1,931 | 1,839 | 978 | 700 | 631 | 279 | 101 |
| Total Assets | 8,629 | 8,553 | 8,367 | 9,166 | 9,504 | 2,060 | 1,141 | 856 | 307 | 125 |
| Current Liabilities | 2,189 | 583 | 583 | 1,261 | 405 | 56.2 | 35.3 | 23.0 | 15.6 | 14.5 |
| Long Term Debt | 1,563 | 96.7 | 43.4 | 102 | 887 | 866 | 136 | 129 | 123 | 2.10 |
| Common Equity | 5,534 | 7,150 | 6,906 | 6,826 | 7,053 | 1,110 | 956 | 695 | 160 | 106 |
| Total Capital | 6,108 | 7,890 | 7,712 | 7,850 | 9,049 | 1,976 | 1,092 | 824 | 283 | 109 |
| Capital Expenditures | 284 | 198 | 318 | 361 | 301 | 166 | 0.07 | 31.4 | 4.29 | 1.72 |
| Cash Flow | 1,017 | 590 | 563 | 465 | -814 | 158 | 108 | 62.1 | 47.5 | 25.8 |
| Current Ratio | 1.1 | 2.9 | 2.8 | 1.5 | 4.5 | 17.4 | 19.8 | 27.4 | 17.8 | 7.0 |
| % Long Term Debt of Capitalization | 0.9 | 1.2 | 0.6 | 1.3 | 9.8 | 43.8 | 12.4 | 15.7 | 43.4 | 1.9 |
| % Net Income of Revenue | 20.1 | 8.0 | 6.6 | 1.1 | NM | 36.6 | 37.3 | 37.1 | 36.6 | 24.7 |
| % Return on Assets | 7.4 | 2.5 | 1.8 | 0.3 | NM | 9.3 | 10.2 | 9.9 | 20.0 | 18.6 |
| % Return on Equity | 10.1 | 3.0 | 2.3 | 0.4 | NM | 14.3 | 12.3 | 13.4 | 32.4 | 23.0 |

Data as orig reptd.; bef. results of disc opers/spec. items. Per share data adj. for stk. divs.; EPS diluted. E-Estimated. NA-Not Available. NM-Not Meaningful. NR-Not Ranked. UR-Under Review.

**Office:** 14 Cambridge Center, Cambridge, MA 02142.
**Telephone:** 617-679-2000.
**Website:** http://www.biogenidec.com
**Chrmn:** B.R. Ross

**Pres & CEO:** J.C. Mullen
**COO & EVP:** H.P. Hasler
**EVP & CFO:** P.J. Clancy
**EVP & Secy:** S.H. Alexander

**Investor Contact:** R. Jacobson (617-679-3710)
**Board Members:** L. C. Best, M. E. Dekkers, A. Denner, A. B. Glassberg, D. Gollerkeri, N. L. Leaming, J. C. Mullen, R. Mulligan, R. W. Pangia, S. Papadopoulos, C. B. Pickett, B. S. Posner, B. R. Ross, L. Schenk, P. Sharp, A. Young, W. D. Young

**Founded:** 1985
**Domicile:** Delaware
**Employees:** 4,300

# BJ Services Co

**STANDARD &POOR'S**

| S&P Recommendation **STRONG SELL** ★☆☆☆☆ | Price $10.93 (as of Nov 14, 2008) | 12-Mo. Target Price $10.00 | Investment Style Large-Cap Growth |

**GICS Sector** Energy
**Sub-Industry** Oil & Gas Equipment & Services

**Summary** This company provides pressure pumping and other oilfield services to the petroleum industry worldwide.

## Key Stock Statistics (Source S&P, Vickers, company reports)

| | | | | | | | |
|---|---|---|---|---|---|---|---|
| 52-Wk Range | $34.94– 8.93 | S&P Oper. EPS 2009**E** | 1.79 | Market Capitalization(B) | $3.215 | Beta | 0.79 |
| Trailing 12-Month EPS | $2.06 | S&P Oper. EPS 2010**E** | 2.03 | Yield (%) | 1.83 | S&P 3-Yr. Proj. EPS CAGR(%) | -7 |
| Trailing 12-Month P/E | 5.3 | P/E on S&P Oper. EPS 2009**E** | 6.1 | Dividend Rate/Share | $0.20 | S&P Credit Rating | BBB+ |
| $10K Invested 5 Yrs Ago | $6,668 | Common Shares Outstg. (M) | 294.2 | Institutional Ownership (%) | NM | | |

## Price Performance

30-Week Mov. Avg. · · · 10-Week Mov. Avg. – – **GAAP Earnings vs. Previous Year** Volume Above Avg. STARS
12-Mo. Target Price — Relative Strength — ▲ Up ▼ Down ► No Change Below Avg. ★

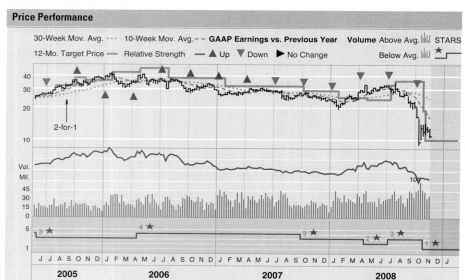

Options: ASE, CBOE, P, Ph

Analysis prepared by **Stewart Glickman, CFA** on November 11, 2008, when the stock traded at **$ 12.38**.

## Highlights

► Although BJS's main growth driver continues to be the U.S. market, which is relatively sensitive to natural gas price expectations, we see growing importance of overseas markets, which we view as less price sensitive. Based on data from Global Insight, we project natural gas prices of $9.16/MMBtu in 2008 (versus $6.87/MMBtu in 2007), $7.81/MMBtu in 2009, and $8.12/MMBtu in 2010.

► September quarter operating margins in the U.S./Mexico pressure pumping segment narrowed by 1,050 basis points, year to year, to 19.6%, from 30.1%. We believe industry capacity build helped weaken pricing, leading to the lower margins, and expect margins to remain challenged through FY 09 due to the financial crisis and expectations that upstream capital spending, particularly onshore North America, will be reduced. Long term, however, we think growing interest in Lower 48 unconventional gas plays should enable the incremental capacity to be absorbed.

► We project revenue growth of 4% in FY 09 and 5% in FY 10. We see EPS of $1.79 in FY 09, rising to $2.03 in FY 10.

## Investment Rationale/Risk

► In the short term, we see U.S. operating margins constrained by swelling industry capacity additions, and reduced pressure pumping demand due to the tight credit environment and high recent natural gas production. International demand should remain a bright spot, despite recent project delays. Longer-term, we see improving fundamentals for BJS, as we view growing interest in unconventional natural gas plays, such as the Barnett Shale and Haynesville Shale, as providing a strong secular growth catalyst.

► Risks to our recommendation and target price include higher demand for pressure pumping; lower-than-expected cost inflation; and higher-than-projected natural gas and oil prices.

► Our DCF model, which assumes free cash flow growth of about 14% for 10 years and 3% thereafter, discounted at a weighted average cost of capital of 13%, shows intrinsic value of about $10. In light of relatively weaker earnings visibility, we apply modest peer-discount multiples of 3.0X our calendar 2009 EBITDA projection and 3.5X our 2009 cash flow estimate. Blended with our DCF analysis, we arrive at our 12-month target price of $10.

## Qualitative Risk Assessment

| LOW | MEDIUM | **HIGH** |

Our risk assessment for BJS reflects its exposure to volatile hydrocarbon prices, particularly natural gas, the company's leverage to the North American market, and concerns over capacity additions for pressure pumping. Partly offsetting these risks is the company's strong position in pressure pumping services.

## Quantitative Evaluations

### S&P Quality Ranking — B+

| D | C | B- | B | **B+** | A- | A | A+ |

### Relative Strength Rank — WEAK

26
LOWEST = 1    HIGHEST = 99

## Revenue/Earnings Data

### Revenue (Million $)

| | 1Q | 2Q | 3Q | 4Q | Year |
|---|---|---|---|---|---|
| 2008 | 1,285 | 1,283 | 1,328 | 1,530 | 5,426 |
| 2007 | 1,184 | 1,187 | 1,153 | 1,279 | 4,802 |
| 2006 | 956.2 | 1,079 | 1,117 | 1,216 | 4,368 |
| 2005 | 737.8 | 795.9 | 817.3 | 892.3 | 3,243 |
| 2004 | 600.8 | 647.1 | 658.7 | 694.5 | 2,601 |
| 2003 | 473.1 | 534.6 | 546.6 | 588.6 | 2,143 |

### Earnings Per Share ($)

| | | | | | |
|---|---|---|---|---|---|
| 2008 | 0.58 | 0.43 | 0.48 | 0.57 | 2.06 |
| 2007 | 0.70 | 0.64 | 0.57 | 0.64 | 2.55 |
| 2006 | 0.48 | 0.62 | 0.67 | 0.76 | 2.52 |
| 2005 | 0.29 | 0.33 | 0.35 | 0.41 | 1.38 |
| 2004 | 0.19 | 0.23 | 0.40 | 0.29 | 1.11 |
| 2003 | 0.11 | 0.14 | 0.16 | 0.19 | 0.59 |

Fiscal year ended Sep. 30. Next earnings report expected: Late January. EPS Estimates based on S&P Operating Earnings; historical GAAP earnings are as reported.

## Dividend Data (Dates: mm/dd Payment Date: mm/dd/yy)

| Amount ($) | Date Decl. | Ex-Div. Date | Stk. of Record | Payment Date |
|---|---|---|---|---|
| 0.050 | 12/06 | 12/14 | 12/18 | 01/11/08 |
| 0.050 | 02/07 | 03/12 | 03/14 | 04/15/08 |
| 0.050 | 05/22 | 06/12 | 06/16 | 07/15/08 |
| 0.050 | 07/28 | 09/11 | 09/15 | 10/14/08 |

Dividends have been paid since 2004. Source: Company reports.

The McGraw-Hill Companies

# BJ Services Co

## Business Summary November 11, 2008

CORPORATE OVERVIEW. BJ Services is a leading provider of pressure pumping and other oilfield services to the petroleum industry worldwide. Demand for its services depends on the number of oil and natural gas wells being drilled, the depth and drilling conditions of the wells, the number of well completions, and the level of workover activity worldwide. BJS's principal customers consist of major and independent oil and natural gas producing companies. The company operates in 50 countries in the major international oil and natural gas producing areas of Canada, Latin America, Europe, Africa, Asia and the Middle East, including Russia and China. In FY 07 (Sep.), 53% of revenues were generated by U.S./Mexico pressure pumping; 8% by Canada pressure pumping; 22% by International pressure pumping; and 17% by other oilfield services. Other than Canada, the international market tends to be less volatile than the U.S. due to the size and complexity of investment, and projects tend to be managed with a longer-term perspective with regard to commodity prices. In addition, the international market is dominated by major oil and national oil companies, which tend to have different objectives and more operating stability than typical independent U.S. producers.

Pressure pumping services (84% of FY 07 revenues and 87% of segment operating profits) are used in the completion of oil and gas wells, both onshore and offshore. Customers are mainly served in the United States. Stimulation services (which accounted for 57% of this segment's revenues in FY 07) are designed to improve the flow of oil and natural gas from producing formations using fracturing, acidizing, sand control, nitrogen, coiled tubing and downhole tool services. Cementing (26%) is done between the casing pipe and the wellbore during the drilling and completion phase of a well. This is done to isolate fluids that could damage productivity, seal the casing from corrosive fluids, and provide structural support for the casing string. Cementing services are also used when recompleting wells from one producing zone to another, and when plugging and abandoning wells. The remaining 17% of segment revenues in FY 07 were derived from other activities.

## Company Financials Fiscal Year Ended Sep. 30

| Per Share Data ($) | 2008 | 2007 | 2006 | 2005 | 2004 | 2003 | 2002 | 2001 | 2000 | 1999 |
|---|---|---|---|---|---|---|---|---|---|---|
| Tangible Book Value | NA | 6.47 | 4.16 | 4.94 | 3.73 | 2.44 | 1.74 | 2.79 | 2.40 | 1.36 |
| Cash Flow | NA | 3.25 | 3.05 | 1.79 | 1.49 | 0.96 | 0.84 | 1.36 | 0.65 | 0.25 |
| Earnings | 1.99 | 2.55 | 2.52 | 1.38 | 1.11 | 0.59 | 0.52 | 1.04 | 0.35 | -0.11 |
| S&P Core Earnings | NA | 2.55 | 2.52 | 1.35 | 0.90 | 0.54 | 0.45 | 0.97 | NA | NA |
| Dividends | 0.20 | 0.20 | 0.20 | 0.12 | 0.04 | Nil | Nil | Nil | Nil | Nil |
| Payout Ratio | 10% | 8% | 8% | 9% | 4% | Nil | Nil | Nil | Nil | Nil |
| Prices:High | 34.94 | 31.26 | 42.85 | 39.78 | 27.33 | 21.20 | 19.75 | 21.55 | 19.19 | 10.86 |
| Prices:Low | 8.93 | 23.12 | 27.43 | 21.13 | 17.42 | 14.63 | 11.50 | 7.28 | 9.53 | 3.36 |
| P/E Ratio:High | 18 | 12 | 17 | 29 | 25 | 36 | 38 | 21 | 53 | NM |
| P/E Ratio:Low | 4 | 9 | 11 | 15 | 16 | 25 | 22 | 7 | 26 | NM |

| Income Statement Analysis (Million $) | | | | | | | | | | |
|---|---|---|---|---|---|---|---|---|---|---|
| Revenue | NA | 4,802 | 4,368 | 3,243 | 2,601 | 2,143 | 1,866 | 2,234 | 1,555 | 1,131 |
| Operating Income | NA | 1,360 | 1,340 | 788 | 567 | 414 | 368 | 641 | 297 | 125 |
| Depreciation, Depletion and Amortization | NA | 209 | 167 | 137 | 126 | 120 | 105 | 105 | 102 | 99.8 |
| Interest Expense | NA | 32.7 | 14.6 | 11.0 | 16.4 | 31.9 | 8.98 | 13.3 | 20.0 | 31.4 |
| Pretax Income | NA | 1,113 | 1,172 | 653 | 521 | 276 | 253 | 529 | 175 | -44.9 |
| Effective Tax Rate | NA | 32.3% | 31.4% | 30.7% | 30.7% | 31.7% | 34.1% | 34.0% | 32.7% | NM |
| Net Income | NA | 754 | 805 | 453 | 361 | 188 | 166 | 349 | 118 | -29.7 |
| S&P Core Earnings | NA | 754 | 805 | 447 | 295 | 174 | 142 | 324 | NA | NA |

| Balance Sheet & Other Financial Data (Million $) | | | | | | | | | | |
|---|---|---|---|---|---|---|---|---|---|---|
| Cash | NA | 58.2 | 92.4 | 357 | 425 | 278 | 84.7 | 84.1 | 6.47 | 3.92 |
| Current Assets | NA | 1,704 | 1,459 | 1,334 | 1,424 | 942 | 649 | 733 | 506 | 439 |
| Total Assets | NA | 4,715 | 3,862 | 3,396 | 3,331 | 2,786 | 2,442 | 1,985 | 1,785 | 1,825 |
| Current Liabilities | NA | 1,313 | 948 | 684 | 910 | 471 | 356 | 390 | 337 | 445 |
| Long Term Debt | NA | 250 | 500 | Nil | 78.9 | 494 | 489 | 79.4 | 142 | 423 |
| Common Equity | NA | 2,851 | 2,147 | 2,484 | 2,094 | 1,651 | 1,419 | 1,370 | 1,170 | 877 |
| Total Capital | NA | 3,197 | 2,713 | 2,548 | 2,262 | 2,152 | 1,917 | 1,460 | 1,320 | 1,306 |
| Capital Expenditures | NA | 752 | 460 | 324 | 201 | 167 | 179 | 183 | 80.5 | 111 |
| Cash Flow | NA | 963 | 971 | 590 | 487 | 308 | 271 | 454 | 220 | 70.1 |
| Current Ratio | NA | 1.3 | 1.5 | 2.0 | 1.6 | 2.0 | 1.8 | 1.9 | 1.5 | 1.0 |
| % Long Term Debt of Capitalization | NA | 7.8 | 18.4 | Nil | 3.5 | 22.9 | 25.5 | 5.4 | 10.8 | 32.4 |
| % Return on Assets | NA | 17.6 | 22.1 | 13.5 | 11.8 | 7.2 | 7.5 | 18.5 | 6.5 | NM |
| % Return on Equity | NA | 30.2 | 34.7 | 19.8 | 19.3 | 12.3 | 11.9 | 27.5 | 11.5 | NM |

Data as orig reptd.; bef. results of disc opers/spec. items. Per share data adj. for stk. divs.; EPS diluted. E-Estimated. NA-Not Available. NM-Not Meaningful. NR-Not Ranked. UR-Under Review.

**Office:** 4601 Westway Park Blvd, Houston, TX 77041-2037.
**Telephone:** 713-462-4239.
**Website:** http://www.bjservices.com
**Chrmn, Pres & CEO:** J.W. Stewart

**COO & EVP:** D.D. Dunlap
**SVP & CFO:** J.E. Smith
**CTO:** J. Hibbeler
**Treas:** D.B. Wells

**Investor Contact:** B. Wells (713-462-4239)
**Board Members:** L. W. Heiligbrodt, J. R. Huff, D. D. Jordan, M. E. Patrick, J. L. Payne, J. W. Stewart, W. H. White

**Founded:** 1872
**Domicile:** Delaware
**Employees:** 16,700

# Black & Decker Corp (The)

**STANDARD &POOR'S**

| S&P Recommendation | **HOLD** ★★★☆☆ | Price $39.48 (as of Nov 14, 2008) | 12-Mo. Target Price $59.00 | Investment Style Large-Cap Blend |
|---|---|---|---|---|

**GICS Sector** Consumer Discretionary
**Sub-Industry** Household Appliances

**Summary** This company is a leading global producer of power tools, hardware and home improvement products, and fastening systems.

## Key Stock Statistics (Source S&P, Vickers, company reports)

| | | | | | | | |
|---|---|---|---|---|---|---|---|
| 52-Wk Range | $84.76– 37.65 | S&P Oper. EPS 2008**E** | 5.45 | Market Capitalization(B) | $2.372 | Beta | 0.97 |
| Trailing 12-Month EPS | $7.08 | S&P Oper. EPS 2009**E** | 5.10 | Yield (%) | 4.26 | S&P 3-Yr. Proj. EPS CAGR(%) | 5 |
| Trailing 12-Month P/E | 5.6 | P/E on S&P Oper. EPS 2008**E** | 7.2 | Dividend Rate/Share | $1.68 | S&P Credit Rating | BBB |
| $10K Invested 5 Yrs Ago | $9,415 | Common Shares Outstg. (M) | 60.1 | Institutional Ownership (%) | NM | | |

## Price Performance

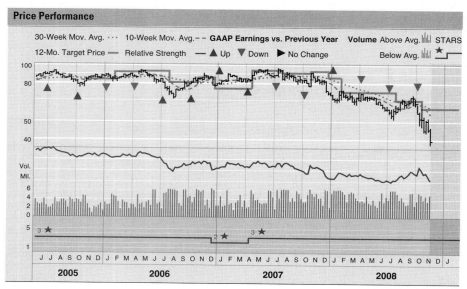

30-Week Mov. Avg. ···· 10-Week Mov. Avg. - - **GAAP Earnings vs. Previous Year** Volume Above Avg. STARS
12-Mo. Target Price — Relative Strength — ▲ Up ▼ Down ► No Change Below Avg.

Options: CBOE, P, Ph

Analysis prepared by **Kenneth M. Leon, CPA** on October 24, 2008, when the stock traded at **$ 45.27**.

## Highlights

➤ After a sales increase of 1.8% in 2007, we forecast a mid-single digit sales decline in both 2008 and 2009, excluding potential acquisitions, although we think BDK continues to seek bolt-on purchases. We expect U.S. and European housing and commercial construction markets to negatively impact BDK's 2009 sales outlook, especially in its Hardware and Home Improvement business units, offset by flat to low-single digit growth in the Fastening and Assembly Systems unit and Power Tools and Accessories units.

➤ We see operating margins of 8% to 9% both this year and next, down from 9.6% in 2007. Margins were as high as 13.5% in the 2006 second quarter, which we view as the end of the cycle-top year for BDK's addressable markets.

➤ We expect the company to seek more cost reductions in its businesses, after completing its last major program in 2005. In our opinion, widening margins may be challenging with slackening demand and commodity inflation driving higher raw material costs. We project EPS of $5.45 in 2008 and $5.10 in 2009.

## Investment Rationale/Risk

➤ We believe recent progress to improve operating margins through restructuring and productivity initiatives has been impaired by the more challenging customer markets related to housing and rising costs for raw materials. With only one third of its total sales coming from non-U.S. markets, we believe BDK will be challenged in driving better than low to mid-single digit revenue growth. While we view the company as well managed, we expect market conditions to be difficult throughout 2009 as construction declines and businesses likely defer spending.

➤ Risks to our recommendation and target price include a severe recession in the company's major markets, negative changes in BDK's relationships with leading customers, lack of market acceptance of new products, and unfavorable shifts in currency exchange rates or raw material prices.

➤ Our 12-month target price of $59 represents a target P/E of 11.6X our 2009 EPS estimate, which is at the low end of BDK's historical range but appropriate, we believe, given the strong headwinds in the commercial and residential construction markets.

## Qualitative Risk Assessment

| LOW | **MEDIUM** | HIGH |
|---|---|---|

Our risk assessment reflects our view of BDK's strong brand name and solid cash flow, offset by cyclicality related to homebuilding sales. Weak U.S. and European economies remains a drag on the company's sales outlook which shows positive sales growth in emerging markets.

## Quantitative Evaluations

**S&P Quality Ranking** B+

| D | C | B- | B | **B+** | A- | A | A+ |
|---|---|---|---|---|---|---|---|

**Relative Strength Rank** MODERATE

40

LOWEST = 1          HIGHEST = 99

## Revenue/Earnings Data

**Revenue (Million $)**

| | 1Q | 2Q | 3Q | 4Q | Year |
|---|---|---|---|---|---|
| 2008 | 1,496 | 1,642 | 1,571 | -- | -- |
| 2007 | 1,577 | 1,700 | 1,634 | 1,653 | 6,563 |
| 2006 | 1,529 | 1,697 | 1,610 | 1,611 | 6,447 |
| 2005 | 1,519 | 1,699 | 1,576 | 1,730 | 6,524 |
| 2004 | 1,093 | 1,298 | 1,283 | 1,725 | 5,398 |
| 2003 | 939.2 | 1,090 | 1,116 | 1,338 | 4,483 |

**Earnings Per Share ($)**

| | | | | | |
|---|---|---|---|---|---|
| 2008 | 1.09 | 1.58 | 1.42 | E-1.17 | E5.45 |
| 2007 | 1.61 | 1.75 | 1.59 | 2.94 | 7.85 |
| 2006 | 1.45 | 1.98 | 1.74 | 1.38 | 6.55 |
| 2005 | 1.79 | 1.88 | 1.73 | 1.28 | 6.69 |
| 2004 | 0.93 | 1.50 | 1.35 | 1.60 | 5.40 |
| 2003 | 0.55 | 0.94 | 0.95 | 1.23 | 3.68 |

Fiscal year ended Dec. 31. Next earnings report expected: Late January. EPS Estimates based on S&P Operating Earnings; historical GAAP earnings are as reported.

## Dividend Data (Dates: mm/dd Payment Date: mm/dd/yy)

| Amount ($) | Date Decl. | Ex-Div. Date | Stk. of Record | Payment Date |
|---|---|---|---|---|
| 0.420 | 02/14 | 03/12 | 03/14 | 03/28/08 |
| 0.420 | 04/24 | 06/11 | 06/13 | 06/27/08 |
| 0.420 | 07/25 | 09/10 | 09/12 | 09/26/08 |
| 0.420 | 10/23 | 12/15 | 12/17 | 12/30/08 |

Dividends have been paid since 1937. Source: Company reports.

# Black & Decker Corp (The)

## Business Summary October 24, 2008

CORPORATE OVERVIEW: Black & Decker, incorporated in 1910, is a global manufacturer and marketer of power tools and accessories, hardware and home improvement products, and technology-based fastening systems. Its products are sold under a number of well known brand names in more than 100 countries. The company has 44 manufacturing facilities, including 24 located outside the U.S. in 10 foreign countries.

MARKET PROFILE: BDK is one of the world's leading producers of portable electric power tools and electric lawn and garden tools, as well as one of the largest suppliers of power tool accessories and specialized, engineered fastening and assembly systems in the markets it serves. Its plumbing products business is one of the largest North American faucet makers. Operations consist of three segments: Power Tools and Accessories (72% of 2007 sales), Hardware and Home Improvement (15%), and Fastening and Assembly Systems (11%). The U.S. accounted for two thirds of sales in 2007, Europe 20%, and other countries 15%.

The Power Tools and Accessories segment manufactures and sells consumer and professional power tools (such as drills, screwdrivers and saws) and accessories, outdoor products (electric lawn and garden tools), cleaning and lighting products and product services. Products are sold mainly to retailers, wholesalers, jobbers, and distributors, although some discontinued or recon-

ditioned products are sold through company-operated service centers and factory outlets directly to end users. Principal materials used to manufacture products in this segment include plastics, aluminum, copper, steel, certain electronic components, and batteries.

The Hardware and Home Improvement segment (formerly building products) makes and sells security hardware (locksets and deadbolts) and plumbing products (faucets, shower heads and bath accessories). Products are sold primarily to retailers, wholesalers, distributors, and jobbers. Certain security hardware products are sold to commercial, institutional, and industrial customers. The principal materials used in the manufacture of products in this segment are plastics, aluminum, steel, brass, zamak (zinc alloy), and ceramics.

BDK's Fastening and Assembly Systems segment includes a line of metal and plastic fasteners and engineered fastening systems for commercial applications. Products are marketed directly to customers and also through distributors and representatives.

## Company Financials Fiscal Year Ended Dec. 31

| Per Share Data ($) | 2007 | 2006 | 2005 | 2004 | 2003 | 2002 | 2001 | 2000 | 1999 | 1998 |
|---|---|---|---|---|---|---|---|---|---|---|
| Tangible Book Value | 3.91 | NM | 5.27 | 4.57 | 0.96 | NM | NM | NM | 0.66 | NM |
| Cash Flow | 9.09 | 9.61 | 8.97 | 7.12 | 5.40 | 4.49 | 3.30 | 5.28 | 5.21 | -6.52 |
| Earnings | 7.85 | 6.55 | 6.69 | 5.40 | 3.68 | 2.84 | 1.33 | 3.34 | 3.40 | -8.22 |
| S&P Core Earnings | 8.08 | 6.79 | 6.22 | 4.93 | 3.23 | 1.56 | 0.11 | NA | NA | NA |
| Dividends | 1.68 | 1.52 | 1.12 | 0.84 | 0.57 | 0.48 | 0.48 | 0.48 | 0.48 | 0.48 |
| Payout Ratio | 21% | 23% | 17% | 16% | 15% | 17% | 36% | 14% | 14% | NM |
| Prices:High | 97.01 | 94.90 | 93.71 | 89.64 | 49.90 | 50.50 | 46.95 | 52.38 | 64.63 | 65.50 |
| Prices:Low | 69.15 | 66.04 | 75.70 | 48.07 | 33.20 | 35.00 | 28.26 | 27.56 | 41.00 | 37.94 |
| P/E Ratio:High | 12 | 14 | 14 | 17 | 14 | 18 | 35 | 16 | 19 | NM |
| P/E Ratio:Low | 9 | 10 | 11 | 9 | 9 | 12 | 21 | 8 | 12 | NM |

| Income Statement Analysis (Million $) | 2007 | 2006 | 2005 | 2004 | 2003 | 2002 | 2001 | 2000 | 1999 | 1998 |
|---|---|---|---|---|---|---|---|---|---|---|
| Revenue | 6,563 | 6,447 | 6,524 | 5,398 | 4,483 | 4,394 | 4,333 | 4,561 | 4,521 | 4,560 |
| Operating Income | 785 | 894 | 964 | 772 | 594 | 549 | 407 | 686 | 696 | 639 |
| Depreciation | 82.0 | 155 | 151 | 143 | 133 | 128 | 159 | 163 | 160 | 155 |
| Interest Expense | 102 | 103 | 81.9 | 57.9 | 60.7 | 84.3 | 84.3 | 104 | 126 | 145 |
| Pretax Income | 498 | 664 | 819 | 604 | 391 | 307 | 155 | 405 | 441 | -589 |
| Effective Tax Rate | NM | 26.8% | 33.6% | 27.0% | 26.5% | 25.3% | 30.5% | 30.3% | 32.0% | NM |
| Net Income | 518 | 486 | 544 | 441 | 287 | 230 | 108 | 282 | 300 | -755 |
| S&P Core Earnings | 533 | 505 | 506 | 401 | 251 | 126 | 9.48 | NA | NA | NA |

| Balance Sheet & Other Financial Data (Million $) | 2007 | 2006 | 2005 | 2004 | 2003 | 2002 | 2001 | 2000 | 1999 | 1998 |
|---|---|---|---|---|---|---|---|---|---|---|
| Cash | 255 | 233 | 968 | 514 | 308 | 517 | 245 | 135 | 147 | 88.0 |
| Current Assets | 2,840 | 2,703 | 3,347 | 2,927 | 2,203 | 2,194 | 1,892 | 1,962 | 1,911 | 1,752 |
| Total Assets | 5,411 | 5,248 | 5,817 | 5,531 | 4,223 | 4,131 | 4,014 | 4,090 | 4,013 | 3,853 |
| Current Liabilities | 1,881 | 1,780 | 2,264 | 1,793 | 1,312 | 1,453 | 1,071 | 1,632 | 1,573 | 1,375 |
| Long Term Debt | 1,179 | 1,170 | 1,030 | 1,201 | 916 | 928 | 1,191 | 798 | 847 | 1,149 |
| Common Equity | 1,459 | 1,164 | 1,524 | 1,559 | 846 | 600 | 751 | 692 | 801 | 573 |
| Total Capital | 2,638 | 2,532 | 2,742 | 2,930 | 1,942 | 1,739 | 2,204 | 1,712 | 1,892 | 2,002 |
| Capital Expenditures | 116 | 105 | 111 | 118 | 103 | 96.6 | 135 | 200 | 171 | 146 |
| Cash Flow | 600 | 641 | 695 | 584 | 421 | 358 | 267 | 445 | 460 | -600 |
| Current Ratio | 1.5 | 1.5 | 1.5 | 1.6 | 1.7 | 1.5 | 1.8 | 1.2 | 1.2 | 1.3 |
| % Long Term Debt of Capitalization | 55.3 | 46.2 | 37.6 | 41.0 | 47.1 | 53.4 | 54.1 | 46.6 | 44.8 | 57.4 |
| % Net Income of Revenue | 7.8 | 7.5 | 8.3 | 8.2 | 6.4 | 5.2 | 2.5 | 6.2 | 6.6 | NM |
| % Return on Assets | 9.7 | 8.8 | 9.6 | 9.0 | 6.9 | 5.6 | 2.7 | 7.0 | 7.6 | NM |
| % Return on Equity | 39.4 | 35.7 | 35.3 | 36.7 | 39.7 | 34.0 | 15.0 | 37.8 | 43.7 | NM |

Data as orig reptd.; bef. results of disc opers/spec. items. Per share data adj. for stk. divs.; EPS diluted. E-Estimated. NA-Not Available. NM-Not Meaningful. NR-Not Ranked. UR-Under Review.

**Office:** 701 East Joppa Road, Towson, MD 21286.
**Telephone:** 410-716-3900.
**Email:** investor.relations@bdk.com
**Website:** http://www.bdk.com

**Chrmn, Pres & CEO:** N.D. Archibald
**SVP & CFO:** S.F. Reeves
**SVP & General Counsel:** C.E. Fenton
**Chief Acctg Officer & Cntlr:** C.M. McMullen

**Investor Contact:** M.M. Rothleitner (410-716-3979)
**Board Members:** N. D. Archibald, N. R. Augustine, B. L. Bowles, G. W. Buckley, M. A. Burns, K. B. Clark, M. A. Fernandez, B. H. Griswold, IV, A. Luiso, R. L. Ryan, M. H. Willes

**Founded:** 1910
**Domicile:** Maryland
**Employees:** 25,000

# BMC Software Inc

**STANDARD &POOR'S**

| S&P Recommendation HOLD ★★★☆☆ | Price $25.02 (as of Nov 14, 2008) | 12-Mo. Target Price $29.00 | Investment Style Large-Cap Blend |
|---|---|---|---|

**GICS Sector** Information Technology
**Sub-Industry** Systems Software

**Summary** This company provides systems management software that improves the availability, performance and recovery of applications and data.

## Key Stock Statistics (Source S&P, Vickers, company reports)

| | | | | | | | |
|---|---|---|---|---|---|---|---|
| 52-Wk Range | $40.87–20.58 | S&P Oper. EPS 2009**E** | 1.29 | Market Capitalization(B) | $4.691 | Beta | 1.70 |
| Trailing 12-Month EPS | $1.29 | S&P Oper. EPS 2010**E** | 1.65 | Yield (%) | Nil | S&P 3-Yr. Proj. EPS CAGR(%) | 10 |
| Trailing 12-Month P/E | 19.4 | P/E on S&P Oper. EPS 2009**E** | 19.4 | Dividend Rate/Share | Nil | S&P Credit Rating | NA |
| $10K Invested 5 Yrs Ago | $15,321 | Common Shares Outstg. (M) | 187.5 | Institutional Ownership (%) | 98 | | |

## Price Performance

- 30-Week Mov. Avg.
- 10-Week Mov. Avg.
- GAAP Earnings vs. Previous Year
- Volume Above Avg.
- STARS
- 12-Mo. Target Price
- Relative Strength
- ▲ Up ▼ Down ► No Change
- Below Avg.

Options: ASE, CBOE, P, Ph

Analysis prepared by **Jim Yin** on October 20, 2008, when the stock traded at **$ 26.58**.

## Highlights

➤ We expect revenues to increase 5.2% in FY 10 (Mar.), after our projected 10% advance in FY 09. Our forecast includes revenue contributions from the acquisition of BladeLogic and reflects our view of a worsening global economy for the next several quarters. We project high-single digits growth in the Enterprise Service Management business segment and flat revenues in the Mainframe Service Management segment. We believe that total bookings will increase about 7% in FY 10, with ratable revenue rising to 55% of total revenue, compared to 54% in FY 09.

➤ We forecast FY 10 gross margins of 77%, the same percentage we see in FY 09. We expect operating expenses to decline to 59% as a percentage of revenue, from 62% projected in FY 09, due to cost saving initiatives and lower acquisition-related expenses. We believe operating margins in FY 10 will increase to 18% from 15% seen in FY 09.

➤ Our estimate of FY 10 EPS is $1.60, up from $1.18 seen in FY 09, as a result of higher revenues, improved operating margins, lower acquisition-related charges, and fewer shares outstanding as a result of the company's share repurchase program.

## Investment Rationale/Risk

➤ Our hold recommendation reflects our concerns about a slowing global economy, which should retard BMC's growth rate. We believe the acquisition of BladeLogic will dilute earnings in FY 09. On the positive side, we think BMC is executing well, demonstrated by revenue growth in the mid-single digits, which is slightly above the industry average in a challenging economic environment. We expect BMC to utilize cash flows from operations to repurchase shares and seek growth via acquisitions, integrating companies that will be complementary to its newer service management business. We view the shares as fairly valued at current levels.

➤ Risks to our recommendation and target price include further weakness in the global economy, increased competition from large platform vendors, a significant decline in corporate spending on information technology, and greater pricing pressures.

➤ Our 12-month target price of $29 is based on an industry average P/E-to-growth ratio of 1.8X, or 18.1X our FY 10 EPS estimate of $1.60. We believe that three year earnings growth of 10% is achievable by the company.

## Qualitative Risk Assessment

| LOW | MEDIUM | HIGH |
|---|---|---|

Our risk assessment for BMC Software reflects our concern that the company's legacy mainframe business remains vulnerable to competition from hardware vendors, notably IBM. Despite this competitive pressure, we see the company's newer product initiatives gaining traction in the marketplace and look for strong earnings gains supported by cost-cutting measures.

## Quantitative Evaluations

**S&P Quality Ranking** C

| D | C | B- | B | B+ | A- | A | A+ |
|---|---|---|---|---|---|---|---|

**Relative Strength Rank** STRONG

72

LOWEST = 1     HIGHEST = 99

## Revenue/Earnings Data

**Revenue (Million $)**

| | 1Q | 2Q | 3Q | 4Q | Year |
|---|---|---|---|---|---|
| 2009 | 437.5 | 466.7 | -- | -- | -- |
| 2008 | 385.0 | 420.7 | 459.0 | 466.9 | 1,732 |
| 2007 | 361.4 | 386.7 | 412.9 | 419.4 | 1,580 |
| 2006 | 348.3 | 361.8 | 380.3 | 407.9 | 1,498 |
| 2005 | 326.0 | 355.1 | 386.8 | 395.1 | 1,463 |
| 2004 | 309.9 | 333.8 | 374.8 | 400.2 | 1,419 |

**Earnings Per Share ($)**

| | | | | | |
|---|---|---|---|---|---|
| 2009 | 0.01 | 0.36 | E0.46 | E0.47 | E1.29 |
| 2008 | 0.27 | 0.38 | 0.45 | 0.46 | 1.57 |
| 2007 | 0.15 | 0.28 | 0.30 | 0.30 | 1.03 |
| 2006 | -0.19 | 0.19 | 0.22 | 0.31 | 0.47 |
| 2005 | 0.05 | 0.06 | 0.16 | 0.07 | 0.34 |
| 2004 | -0.03 | -0.06 | -0.20 | 0.16 | -0.12 |

Fiscal year ended Mar. 31. Next earnings report expected: Mid February. EPS Estimates based on S&P Operating Earnings; historical GAAP earnings are as reported.

## Dividend Data

No cash dividends have been paid.

---

**Please read the Required Disclosures and Analyst Certification on the last page of this report.**

# BMC Software Inc

STANDARD
&POOR'S

## Business Summary October 20, 2008

CORPORATE OVERVIEW. BMC Software is a leading independent software vendor. The company's software, called Business Service Management (BSM), helps customers increase productivity and reduce costs by automating IT processes and improving how IT responds to business decisions and challenges. BMC focuses on eight areas of BSM: Incident and Problem Management, Asset Management and Discovery, Identity Management, Service Impact and Event Management, Service Level Management, Capacity Management and Provisioning, Infrastructure and Application Management and Change and Configuration Management. These solutions are supported by a family of enabling technologies called BMC Atrium that provide a shared view of how IT supports business priorities.

BMC sells its software directly through its sales force and indirectly through resellers, distributors and systems integrators. The company also provides maintenance and support, which give customers the right to receive product upgrades. Product license and maintenance revenues accounted for 94% of total revenues in FY 06 and FY 07 (Mar.). BMC also provides professional services, which include implementation, integration and education services and contributed 6% of total revenues in FY 06 and FY 07.

In FY 07, BMC reorganized its software business into two segments. The Enterprise Service Management (ESM) business segment targets non-mainframe computing and addresses broad categories of IT management issues including Application Management, Database Management, Security Management, and Transaction Management. ESM license revenue accounted for 58%, 54% and 53% of total license revenue for FY 07, FY 06 and FY 05, respectively.

The Mainframe Service Management (MSM) segment includes automated tools that enhance the performance and availability of database management systems on mainframe platforms. This segment includes BMC's mainframe performance monitoring and management product line, MAINVIEW. It also includes the management and recovery of IBM's DB2 and IMS databases. MSM license revenue accounted for 42%, 46% and 47% of total license revenue in FY 07, FY 06 and FY 05, respectively.

## Company Financials Fiscal Year Ended Mar. 31

| Per Share Data ($) | 2008 | 2007 | 2006 | 2005 | 2004 | 2003 | 2002 | 2001 | 2000 | 1999 |
|---|---|---|---|---|---|---|---|---|---|---|
| Tangible Book Value | 0.41 | 1.66 | 2.31 | 2.60 | 3.11 | 3.70 | 5.49 | 5.67 | 5.67 | 5.64 |
| Cash Flow | NA | 1.79 | 1.40 | 1.33 | 1.03 | 1.25 | 0.78 | 1.42 | 1.89 | 1.77 |
| Earnings | 1.57 | 1.03 | 0.47 | 0.34 | -0.12 | 0.20 | -0.75 | 0.17 | 0.96 | 1.47 |
| S&P Core Earnings | 1.54 | 1.00 | 0.29 | -0.03 | -0.56 | -0.01 | -0.94 | -0.19 | NA | NA |
| Dividends | Nil | Nil | Nil | Nil | Nil | Nil | Nil | Nil | Nil | Nil |
| Payout Ratio | Nil | Nil | Nil | Nil | Nil | Nil | Nil | Nil | Nil | Nil |
| Calendar Year | 2007 | 2006 | 2005 | 2004 | 2003 | 2002 | 2001 | 2000 | 1999 | 1998 |
| Prices:High | 37.05 | 33.67 | 21.68 | 21.87 | 19.84 | 23.00 | 33.00 | 86.63 | 84.06 | 60.25 |
| Prices:Low | 24.77 | 19.90 | 14.44 | 13.70 | 13.18 | 10.85 | 11.50 | 13.00 | 30.00 | 29.25 |
| P/E Ratio:High | 24 | 33 | 41 | 64 | NM | NM | NM | NM | 88 | 41 |
| P/E Ratio:Low | 16 | 19 | 27 | 40 | NM | NM | NM | NM | 31 | 20 |

| Income Statement Analysis (Million $) | | | | | | | | | | |
|---|---|---|---|---|---|---|---|---|---|---|
| Revenue | 1,732 | 1,580 | 1,498 | 1,463 | 1,419 | 1,327 | 1,289 | 1,504 | 1,719 | 1,304 |
| Operating Income | NA | 413 | 334 | 264 | 162 | 349 | 400 | 336 | 656 | 548 |
| Depreciation | 152 | 161 | 205 | 222 | 259 | 248 | 376 | 315 | 236 | 76.8 |
| Interest Expense | NA | 1.50 | 1.70 | 2.00 | 1.10 | Nil | 0.40 | 11.3 | 23.4 | Nil |
| Pretax Income | 434 | 301 | 204 | 98.2 | -29.4 | 69.3 | -231 | 60.4 | 311 | 478 |
| Effective Tax Rate | 27.8% | 28.2% | 50.0% | 23.3% | NM | 30.7% | NM | 29.8% | 22.1% | 23.8% |
| Net Income | 314 | 216 | 102 | 75.3 | -26.8 | 48.0 | -184 | 42.4 | 243 | 364 |
| S&P Core Earnings | 308 | 211 | 63.9 | -5.94 | -128 | -3.42 | -232 | -46.6 | NA | NA |

| Balance Sheet & Other Financial Data (Million $) | | | | | | | | | | |
|---|---|---|---|---|---|---|---|---|---|---|
| Cash | 1,351 | 1,296 | 1,063 | 929 | 909 | 1,015 | 546 | 146 | 152 | 1,205 |
| Current Assets | NA | 1,790 | 1,506 | 1,440 | 1,425 | 1,098 | 997 | 903 | 896 | 873 |
| Total Assets | 3,346 | 3,260 | 3,211 | 3,298 | 3,045 | 2,846 | 2,676 | 3,034 | 2,962 | 2,283 |
| Current Liabilities | NA | 1,233 | 1,202 | 1,085 | 987 | 839 | 681 | 829 | 884 | 651 |
| Long Term Debt | NA | Nil | Nil | Nil | Nil | Nil | Nil | Nil | Nil | Nil |
| Common Equity | 994 | 1,049 | 1,099 | 1,262 | 1,215 | 1,383 | 1,507 | 1,815 | 1,781 | 1,334 |
| Total Capital | NA | 1,049 | 1,099 | 1,262 | 1,215 | 1,383 | 1,507 | 1,815 | 1,781 | 1,334 |
| Capital Expenditures | 38.4 | 33.7 | 24.1 | 57.7 | 50.4 | 23.6 | 64.3 | 183 | 148 | 116 |
| Cash Flow | NA | 377 | 307 | 297 | 233 | 296 | 192 | 357 | 478 | 441 |
| Current Ratio | 1.4 | 1.5 | 1.3 | 1.3 | 1.4 | 1.3 | 1.5 | 1.1 | 1.0 | 1.3 |
| % Long Term Debt of Capitalization | Nil | Nil | Nil | Nil | Nil | Nil | Nil | Nil | Nil | Nil |
| % Net Income of Revenue | 18.1 | 13.7 | 6.8 | 5.1 | NM | 3.6 | NM | 2.8 | 14.1 | 27.9 |
| % Return on Assets | 9.5 | 6.7 | 3.1 | 2.4 | NM | 1.7 | NM | 1.4 | 9.2 | 20.6 |
| % Return on Equity | 30.7 | 20.1 | 8.6 | 6.1 | NM | 3.3 | NM | 2.4 | 15.6 | 34.8 |

Data as orig reptd.; bef. results of disc opers/spec. items. Per share data adj. for stk. divs.; EPS diluted. E-Estimated. NA-Not Available. NM-Not Meaningful. NR-Not Ranked. UR-Under Review.

**Office:** 2101 Citywest Boulevard, Houston, TX 77042-2827.
**Telephone:** 713-918-8800.
**Email:** investor@bmc.com
**Website:** http://www.bmc.com

**Chrmn & CEO:** R.E. Beauchamp
**Pres:** D. Ittycheria
**Investor Contact:** S.B. Solcher
**SVP & CFO:** S.B. Solcher

**SVP, Secy & General Counsel:** D.M. Clolery
**Board Members:** J. E. Barfield, R. E. Beauchamp, G. L. Bloom, B. G. Cupp, M. K. Gafner, P. T. Jenkins, L. J. Lavigne, Jr., K. K. O'Neil, T. C. Tinsley

**Founded:** 1980
**Domicile:** Delaware
**Employees:** 5,800

# Boeing Co (The)

**STANDARD &POOR'S**

| S&P Recommendation **BUY** ★★★★☆ | Price $41.04 (as of Nov 14, 2008) | 12-Mo. Target Price $53.00 | Investment Style Large-Cap Growth |
|---|---|---|---|

**GICS Sector** Industrials
**Sub-Industry** Aerospace & Defense

**Summary** This company is the world's second largest commercial jet and military weapons manufacturer.

## Key Stock Statistics (Source S&P, Vickers, company reports)

| | | | | | | | |
|---|---|---|---|---|---|---|---|
| 52-Wk Range | $94.60– 39.07 | S&P Oper. EPS 2008**E** | 4.72 | Market Capitalization(B) | $30.076 | Beta | 1.05 |
| Trailing 12-Month EPS | $5.12 | S&P Oper. EPS 2009**E** | 5.85 | Yield (%) | 3.90 | S&P 3-Yr. Proj. EPS CAGR(%) | 8 |
| Trailing 12-Month P/E | 8.0 | P/E on S&P Oper. EPS 2008**E** | 8.7 | Dividend Rate/Share | $1.60 | S&P Credit Rating | A+ |
| $10K Invested 5 Yrs Ago | $11,395 | Common Shares Outstg. (M) | 732.8 | Institutional Ownership (%) | 68 | | |

## Price Performance

30-Week Mov. Avg. ···· 10-Week Mov. Avg. – – **GAAP Earnings vs. Previous Year** Volume Above Avg. ▮▮ STARS
12-Mo. Target Price — Relative Strength — ▲ Up ▼ Down ► No Change Below Avg. ▮▮ ★

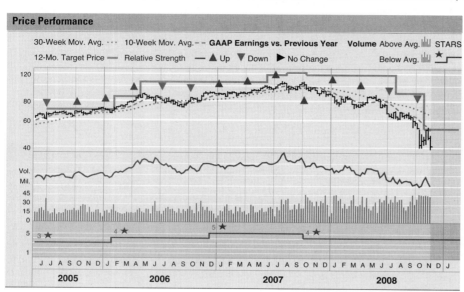

Options: ASE, CBOE, P, Ph

Analysis prepared by **Richard Tortoriello** on October 29, 2008, when the stock traded at **$ 49.72**.

## Highlights

➤ We project an 8% sales decline in 2008, due to an extended machinists' union strike. On October 28, 2008, Boeing and the union agreed to a new contract, but the contract must be ratified by members. In 2009, we project a 6% revenue increase, with 10% growth in commercial airplane sales and 3% growth in integrated defense systems. As of September 2008, Boeing's commercial airplane backlog totaled $276 billion, or over seven years of sales at pre-strike levels, and its defense backlog totaled $41 billion, or five quarters of sales.

➤ We see operating margins declining to 8.6% in 2008, from 8.8% in 2007, due to the machinists' strike, but see margins recovering to over 9% in 2009, on increased volume, better commercial airplane pricing, and productivity improvements.

➤ For 2008, we estimate EPS of $4.72 and free cash flow (cash from operating activities less capital expenditures) of about $0.05 per share, down from $10.00 per share in 2007, due to the strike and delays on the 787. We project EPS of $5.85 in 2009, with strongly improved cash flow.

## Investment Rationale/Risk

➤ Although we see the risk of cancellations and deferrals of orders due to declining air traffic growth amid a global economic slowdown, we continue to expect Boeing's order book to support strong production in 2009 and 2010. We believe that a resolution of the machinists' strike will enable BA to get the 787 into the air in 2009 and commence strong production in 2010, and note that BA has over 900 orders for the plane. At the same time we see valuations near historical lows.

➤ Risks to our recommendation and target price include the potential for government cuts in defense programs, slowing global economic growth, and aircraft development and production problems, particularly with the 787.

➤ Our 12-month target price of $53 is based on an enterprise value to 2008 estimated EBITDA multiple of 6.0X. This compares with a 10-year historical low EV-to-EBITDA multiple of 5.6X. We note that the shares recently sold at a forward P/E multiple of 8X our 2009 estimate, below a 10-year low of 9X.

## Qualitative Risk Assessment

| LOW | MEDIUM | HIGH |
|---|---|---|

Our risk assessment reflects BA's participation in highly cyclical, very competitive and capital-intensive businesses. This is offset by what we see as its strong cash position and strong free cash flow generation, along with a healthy and rising backlog of business.

## Quantitative Evaluations

**S&P Quality Ranking** B+

| D | C | B- | B | B+ | A- | A | A+ |
|---|---|---|---|---|---|---|---|

**Relative Strength Rank** MODERATE

47

LOWEST = 1     HIGHEST = 99

## Revenue/Earnings Data

**Revenue (Million $)**

| | 1Q | 2Q | 3Q | 4Q | Year |
|---|---|---|---|---|---|
| 2008 | 15,990 | 16,962 | 15,293 | -- | -- |
| 2007 | 15,365 | 17,028 | 16,517 | 17,477 | 66,387 |
| 2006 | 14,264 | 14,986 | 14,739 | 17,541 | 61,530 |
| 2005 | 12,987 | 15,025 | 12,629 | 14,204 | 54,845 |
| 2004 | 12,903 | 13,088 | 13,152 | 13,314 | 52,457 |
| 2003 | 12,258 | 12,772 | 12,241 | 13,214 | 50,485 |

**Earnings Per Share ($)**

| | | | | | |
|---|---|---|---|---|---|
| 2008 | 1.61 | 1.16 | 0.94 | E0.98 | E4.72 |
| 2007 | 1.12 | 1.35 | 1.43 | 1.35 | 5.26 |
| 2006 | 0.88 | -0.21 | 0.89 | 1.28 | 2.84 |
| 2005 | 0.64 | 0.70 | 1.26 | 0.59 | 3.19 |
| 2004 | 0.76 | 0.72 | 0.54 | 0.23 | 2.24 |
| 2003 | -0.60 | -0.24 | 0.32 | 1.40 | 0.89 |

Fiscal year ended Dec. 31. Next earnings report expected: Late January. EPS Estimates based on S&P Operating Earnings; historical GAAP earnings are as reported.

## Dividend Data (Dates: mm/dd Payment Date: mm/dd/yy)

| Amount ($) | Date Decl. | Ex-Div. Date | Stk. of Record | Payment Date |
|---|---|---|---|---|
| 0.400 | 12/10 | 02/06 | 02/08 | 03/07/08 |
| 0.400 | 04/29 | 05/07 | 05/09 | 06/06/08 |
| 0.400 | 06/23 | 08/06 | 08/08 | 09/05/08 |
| 0.400 | 10/27 | 11/05 | 11/07 | 12/05/08 |

Dividends have been paid since 1942. Source: Company reports.

---

*The McGraw-Hill Companies*

# Boeing Co (The)

## Business Summary October 29, 2008

CORPORATE OVERVIEW. This $66 billion in revenues global aerospace and defense giant conducts business through three operating segments. Boeing Commercial Aircraft (BCA; 50% of revenues and 49% of operating profits in 2007) and EADS's 80%-owned Airbus division are the world's only makers of 130-plus seat passenger jets. Integrated Defense Systems (IDS; 48%, 48%) is the world's second largest military contractor behind Lockheed Martin Corp. Boeing Capital Corp. (2%, 3%) primarily finances commercial aircraft for airlines.

BCA's commercial jet aircraft family includes the 737 Next-Generation narrow body model and the 747, 767, 777 and 787 wide body models. The 787 (Dreamliner) is Boeing's newest model, and is scheduled for first delivery, following over a year's delay, in the third quarter of 2009. BCA also offers aviation support, aircraft modifications, spare parts, training, maintenance documents, and technical advice. A new, larger 747 model is also under development, the 747-8 Intercontinental, as is a freighter version of the 747-8. Boeing had a commercial aircraft backlog at year-end 2007 of $255 billion. Dreamliner delays are expected to result in some penalty payments to customers.

IDS designs, develops and supports military aircraft, including fighters, transports, tankers, intelligence surveillance and reconnaissance aircraft, and helicopters; missiles; space systems; missile defense systems; satellites and satellite launch vehicles; and communication, information, and battle manage-ment systems. IDS's primary customer is the U.S. Department of Defense (84% of 2007 sales), but it also sells to NASA, international defense customers, civilian markets, and commercial satellite markets. Major programs include the AH-64 Apache and CH-47 Chinook helicopters, the C-17 Globemaster military transport, F/A-18E/F Super Hornet fighter jets, as well as commercial and military satellites.

MARKET PROFILE. Based on total unit orders of 100-plus seat jetliners in 2007, BCA and Airbus each control about half of the global commercial jetliner market. Demand for jetliners is driven primarily by growth in international air travel. Independent research firm Avitas Inc. projects that the global fleet of 100-plus seat jetliners will grow at a 4.3% compound annual rate over the next 20 years, due to its projection of 5.9% compound annual growth in passenger traffic over the same period. Although S&P believes that current very high jet fuel prices are going to result in a slowing in orders in 2008 and 2009, we think that given the economic development of many former third world countries in Asia, Eastern Europe and the Middle East, long-term fleet growth should continue at an above average rate for the foreseeable future.

## Company Financials Fiscal Year Ended Dec. 31

| Per Share Data ($) | 2007 | 2006 | 2005 | 2004 | 2003 | 2002 | 2001 | 2000 | 1999 | 1998 |
|---|---|---|---|---|---|---|---|---|---|---|
| Tangible Book Value | 3.78 | NM | 10.33 | 10.08 | 6.17 | 4.53 | 5.23 | 6.63 | 10.14 | 10.25 |
| Cash Flow | 7.18 | 4.76 | 5.08 | 4.00 | 2.68 | 2.46 | 5.52 | 4.14 | 4.27 | 2.84 |
| Earnings | 5.26 | 2.84 | 3.19 | 2.24 | 0.89 | 2.87 | 3.41 | 2.44 | 2.49 | 1.15 |
| S&P Core Earnings | 5.41 | 3.90 | 3.05 | 1.99 | 1.33 | 0.26 | -0.06 | NA | NA | NA |
| Dividends | 1.40 | 1.20 | 1.00 | 0.77 | 0.68 | 0.68 | 0.68 | 0.56 | 0.56 | 0.56 |
| Payout Ratio | 27% | 42% | 31% | 34% | 76% | 24% | 20% | 23% | 22% | 49% |
| Prices:High | 107.83 | 92.05 | 72.40 | 55.48 | 43.37 | 51.07 | 69.85 | 70.94 | 48.50 | 56.25 |
| Prices:Low | 84.60 | 65.90 | 49.52 | 38.04 | 24.73 | 28.53 | 27.60 | 32.00 | 32.56 | 29.00 |
| P/E Ratio:High | 20 | 32 | 23 | 25 | 49 | 18 | 20 | 29 | 19 | 49 |
| P/E Ratio:Low | 16 | 23 | 16 | 17 | 28 | 10 | 8 | 13 | 13 | 25 |

| Income Statement Analysis (Million $) | | | | | | | | | | |
|---|---|---|---|---|---|---|---|---|---|---|
| Revenue | 66,387 | 61,530 | 54,845 | 52,457 | 50,485 | 54,069 | 58,198 | 51,321 | 57,993 | 56,154 |
| Operating Income | 7,090 | 5,176 | 3,707 | 3,405 | 3,198 | 5,447 | 6,467 | 4,996 | 4,724 | 3,189 |
| Depreciation | 1,486 | 1,545 | 1,503 | 1,509 | 1,450 | 1,497 | 1,750 | 1,479 | 1,645 | 1,622 |
| Interest Expense | 196 | 593 | 653 | 685 | 800 | 730 | 650 | 445 | 431 | 453 |
| Pretax Income | 6,118 | 1,218 | 2,819 | 1,960 | 550 | 1,353 | 3,565 | 2,999 | 3,324 | 1,397 |
| Effective Tax Rate | 33.6% | NM | 9.12% | 7.14% | NM | 63.6% | 20.7% | 29.0% | 30.5% | 19.8% |
| Net Income | 4,058 | 2,206 | 2,562 | 1,820 | 718 | 492 | 2,827 | 2,128 | 2,309 | 1,120 |
| S&P Core Earnings | 4,177 | 3,042 | 2,450 | 1,616 | 1,074 | 203 | 284 | NA | NA | NA |

| Balance Sheet & Other Financial Data (Million $) | | | | | | | | | | |
|---|---|---|---|---|---|---|---|---|---|---|
| Cash | 7,042 | 6,118 | 5,412 | 3,204 | 4,633 | 2,333 | 633 | 1,010 | 3,354 | 2,462 |
| Current Assets | 27,280 | 22,983 | 21,968 | 15,100 | 17,258 | 16,855 | 16,206 | 15,864 | 15,712 | 16,375 |
| Total Assets | 58,986 | 51,794 | 60,058 | 53,963 | 53,035 | 52,342 | 48,343 | 42,028 | 36,147 | 36,672 |
| Current Liabilities | 31,538 | 29,701 | 28,188 | 20,835 | 18,448 | 19,810 | 20,486 | 18,289 | 13,656 | 13,422 |
| Long Term Debt | 7,455 | 8,157 | 9,538 | 10,879 | 13,299 | 12,589 | 10,866 | 7,567 | 5,980 | 6,103 |
| Common Equity | 9,004 | 4,739 | 11,059 | 11,286 | 8,139 | 7,696 | 10,825 | 11,020 | 11,462 | 12,316 |
| Total Capital | 17,649 | 12,896 | 22,664 | 23,255 | 21,438 | 20,285 | 21,868 | 18,587 | 17,614 | 18,419 |
| Capital Expenditures | 1,731 | 1,681 | 1,547 | 978 | 741 | 1,001 | 1,068 | 932 | 1,236 | 1,584 |
| Cash Flow | 5,544 | 3,751 | 4,065 | 3,329 | 2,168 | 1,989 | 4,577 | 3,607 | 3,954 | 2,742 |
| Current Ratio | 0.9 | 0.8 | 0.8 | 0.7 | 0.9 | 0.9 | 0.8 | 0.9 | 1.2 | 1.2 |
| % Long Term Debt of Capitalization | 42.2 | 63.3 | 42.1 | 46.8 | 62.0 | 62.1 | 49.7 | 40.7 | 34.0 | 33.1 |
| % Net Income of Revenue | 6.1 | 3.6 | 4.7 | 3.5 | 1.4 | 0.9 | 4.9 | 4.1 | 4.0 | 2.0 |
| % Return on Assets | 7.3 | 3.9 | 4.4 | 3.4 | 1.4 | 1.0 | 6.2 | 5.4 | 6.3 | 3.0 |
| % Return on Equity | 59.0 | 27.9 | 22.9 | 18.7 | 9.1 | 5.3 | 25.9 | 18.9 | 19.4 | 8.9 |

Data as orig reptd.; bef. results of disc opers/spec. items. Per share data adj. for stk. divs.; EPS diluted. E-Estimated. NA-Not Available. NM-Not Meaningful. NR-Not Ranked. UR-Under Review.

**Office:** 100 N. Riverside, Chicago, IL 60606.
**Telephone:** 312-544-2000 .
**Website:** http://www.boeing.com
**Chrmn, Pres & CEO:** W.J. McNerney, Jr.

**COO, SVP & CTO:** J.J. Tracy
**EVP & CFO:** J.A. Bell
**SVP & General Counsel:** J.M. Luttig
**Treas:** D. Dohnalek

**Board Members:** J. H. Biggs, J. E. Bryson, A. D. Collins, Jr., L. Cook, W. M. Daley, K. M. Duberstein, J. L. Jones, J. F. McDonnell, W. J. McNerney, Jr., M. S. Zafirovski
**Founded:** 1934
**Domicile:** Delaware
**Employees:** 159,300

# Boston Properties Inc

STANDARD &POOR'S

**S&P Recommendation** HOLD ★★★☆☆

| Price | 12-Mo. Target Price | Investment Style |
|---|---|---|
| $52.40 (as of Nov 14, 2008) | $69.00 | Large-Cap Blend |

**GICS Sector** Financials
**Sub-Industry** Office REITS

**Summary** This real estate investment trust primarily owns office buildings in the Boston, Washington, DC, New York City, San Francisco and Princeton markets.

## Key Stock Statistics (Source S&P, Vickers, company reports)

| | | | | | | | |
|---|---|---|---|---|---|---|---|
| 52-Wk Range | $132.00–51.14 | S&P FFO/Sh. 2008E | 4.75 | Market Capitalization(B) | $6.278 | Beta | 1.06 |
| Trailing 12-Month FFO/Share | NA | S&P FFO/Sh. 2009E | 4.80 | Yield (%) | 5.19 | S&P 3-Yr. FFO/Sh. Proj. CAGR(%) | 3 |
| Trailing 12-Month P/FFO | NA | P/FFO on S&P FFO/Sh. 2008E | 11.0 | Dividend Rate/Share | $2.72 | S&P Credit Rating | A- |
| $10K Invested 5 Yrs Ago | $15,515 | Common Shares Outstg. (M) | 119.8 | Institutional Ownership (%) | NM | | |

## Price Performance

30-Week Mov. Avg. · · · · 10-Week Mov. Avg. – – GAAP Earnings vs. Previous Year   Volume Above Avg. ▂▆▃ STARS
12-Mo. Target Price — Relative Strength — ▲ Up ▼ Down ▶ No Change        Below Avg. ▁▁▂ ★

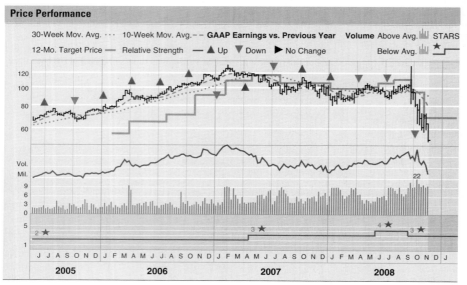

Options: ASE, CBOE, P

Analysis prepared by **Royal F. Shepard, CFA** on November 03, 2008, when the stock traded at **$ 66.11**.

## Highlights

➤ BXP's office portfolio, focused on urban markets, is operating close to full capacity, and we think rents on renewing leases are still trending above those previously in place. During 2009, only 6.8% of total space comes up for renewal. However, in the trust's New York City market, we think the risk of tenant defaults has risen with turmoil in the financial markets. During the third quarter, BXP took reserves against the possible loss of two troubled tenants, including Lehman Brothers.

➤ We expect a gradually increasing contribution from new development as projects are placed into service. During 2008, about $320 million in projects have been completed, and the trust expects another $250 million in completions for 2009.

➤ We expect the June 2008 purchase of a 60% interest in the General Motors Building in Manhattan is providing an immediate benefit to reported cash flow. In our estimation, the transaction will add about $0.30 to 2008 per share funds from operations. Our 2008 FFO estimate is $4.75 a share. For 2009, we expect a challenging economic environment to allow FFO to expand only modestly, to $4.80.

## Investment Rationale/Risk

➤ We think BXP's high-quality portfolio will hold up reasonably well, and the trust has minimal exposure to lease expirations. We expect average rents to increase as leases eventually renew. Also, a $2.5 billion pipeline of construction projects holds strong long-term potential, in our view. Even so, BXP's office markets are vulnerable to increased levels of space sublet by tenants facing financial challenges. With the shares recently selling at about 14.2X our 2009 FFO per share outlook, a premium to peers, we believe BXP's long-term growth potential is reflected in its price.

➤ Risks to our recommendation and target price include national employment growth lagging our expectations, and lower-than-anticipated regional economic strength in BXP's markets.

➤ Our 12-month target price of $69 is based primarily on applying a multiple of 14.5X our 2009 FFO per share estimate, a premium to office REITs serving less attractive suburban markets. We blend in our net asset value (NAV) model, which yields an intrinsic value of $65 based on recent market conditions and a one-year cash yield of 7.0%.

## Qualitative Risk Assessment

| LOW | MEDIUM | HIGH |
|---|---|---|

Our risk assessment reflects what we see as BXP's large and diverse asset portfolio, relatively unleveraged balance sheet, and consistent cash distribution.

## Quantitative Evaluations

**S&P Quality Ranking**   A-

| D | C | B- | B | B+ | A- | A | A+ |
|---|---|---|---|---|---|---|---|

**Relative Strength Rank**   MODERATE

31

LOWEST = 1                            HIGHEST = 99

## Revenue/FFO Data

**Revenue (Million $)**

| | 1Q | 2Q | 3Q | 4Q | Year |
|---|---|---|---|---|---|
| 2008 | 370.6 | 366.3 | 359.5 | -- | -- |
| 2007 | 363.7 | 392.4 | 371.5 | 380.8 | 1,413 |
| 2006 | 356.1 | 370.4 | 372.5 | 378.7 | 1,502 |
| 2005 | 356.2 | 360.6 | 361.8 | 366.3 | 1,438 |
| 2004 | 333.3 | 344.9 | 359.7 | 362.6 | 1,400 |
| 2003 | 319.7 | 323.4 | 331.2 | 336.2 | 1,310 |

**FFO Per Share ($)**

| | | | | | |
|---|---|---|---|---|---|
| 2008 | 1.18 | 1.19 | E1.13 | E1.32 | E4.75 |
| 2007 | 0.42 | 0.32 | 0.32 | E1.22 | E4.64 |
| 2006 | 0.27 | 0.39 | 0.32 | 0.32 | 4.17 |
| 2005 | 0.23 | 0.16 | 0.16 | 0.24 | 4.31 |
| 2004 | -1.16 | 0.11 | 0.22 | 0.22 | 4.16 |
| 2003 | 0.25 | 0.15 | 0.20 | 0.20 | 4.08 |

Fiscal year ended Dec. 31. Next earnings report expected: Late January. FFO Estimates based on S&P Funds From Operations Est..

## Dividend Data (Dates: mm/dd Payment Date: mm/dd/yy)

| Amount ($) | Date Decl. | Ex-Div. Date | Stk. of Record | Payment Date |
|---|---|---|---|---|
| 5.98 Spl. | 12/18 | 12/27 | 12/31 | 01/30/08 |
| 0.680 | 03/17 | 03/27 | 03/31 | 04/30/08 |
| 0.680 | 06/17 | 06/26 | 06/30 | 07/31/08 |
| 0.680 | 09/17 | 09/26 | 09/30 | 10/31/08 |

Dividends have been paid since 1997. Source: Company reports.

# Boston Properties Inc

## Business Summary November 03, 2008

CORPORATE OVERVIEW. Boston Properties, founded in 1970, is a real estate investment trust (REIT) that develops, acquires, manages, operates, and is one of the largest U.S. owners of, Class A office properties. BXP conducts substantially all of its business through its limited partnership, of which it is the sole general partner, and holds an 84% economic interest.

At December 31, 2007, the property portfolio consisted of 139 properties, totaling 43.8 million net rentable sq. ft. and structured parking facilities for vehicles containing approximately 9.9 million sq. ft. The properties included 125 in-service office buildings and one hotel in Cambridge, Massachusetts. In addition, BXP had 13 properties under construction totaling 3.9 million sq. ft.

MARKET PROFILE The market for office leases is inherently cyclical. Local economic conditions, particularly the employment level, play an important role in determining competitive dynamics. Standard & Poor's estimates that non-farm monthly payrolls will increase little, if any, on average through 2009, compared to growth of about 120,000 per month in 2007.

The U.S. office market tends to track the overall economy on a lagged basis. At the end of December 2007, we believe the national vacancy rate was about 12.5%, reflecting an improvement since cyclical lows in 2002-2003. Going for-

ward, we believe vacancy levels have stabilized and may increase modestly in 2008 due to a slowing economy. In our opinion, BXP's Washington, DC, and midtown Manhattan markets are among the nation's strongest. The metropolitan Boston, San Francisco and Princeton, NJ, markets have trailed the current recovery. In total, on December 31, 2007, BXP had an office vacancy rate of 5.1%, much better than the national averages. Leases will expire on only about 5.2% of existing office space in 2008, limiting opportunities for taking advantage of more favorable market rents. Moreover, only 252,000 square feet roll over in the particularly strong midtown Manhattan market.

Competition for leasing real estate is high. In addition, we believe that competition for the acquisition of new properties is intensifying from other REITs, private real estate funds, financial institutions, insurance companies and others. As a result, we think BXP could have difficulty finding new assets at attractive prices.

## Company Financials Fiscal Year Ended Dec. 31

| Per Share Data ($) | 2007 | 2006 | 2005 | 2004 | 2003 | 2002 | 2001 | 2000 | 1999 | 1998 |
|---|---|---|---|---|---|---|---|---|---|---|
| Tangible Book Value | 30.72 | 27.45 | 25.92 | 26.61 | 22.51 | 20.79 | 19.34 | 19.02 | 15.57 | 14.93 |
| Earnings | 9.06 | 7.46 | 3.46 | 2.35 | 2.94 | 4.40 | 2.26 | 2.01 | 1.71 | 1.61 |
| S&P Core Earnings | 9.06 | 7.46 | 3.46 | 2.34 | 2.88 | 4.37 | 2.20 | NA | NA | NA |
| Dividends | 2.72 | 2.72 | 5.19 | 2.58 | 2.50 | 2.41 | 2.27 | 1.96 | 1.73 | 1.64 |
| Payout Ratio | 30% | 36% | 150% | 110% | 85% | 55% | 100% | 96% | 101% | 101% |
| Prices:High | 133.02 | 118.22 | 76.67 | 64.90 | 48.47 | 41.55 | 43.88 | 44.88 | 37.50 | 36.06 |
| Prices:Low | 87.78 | 72.98 | 56.66 | 42.99 | 34.80 | 32.95 | 34.00 | 29.00 | 27.25 | 23.44 |
| P/E Ratio:High | 15 | 16 | 22 | 28 | 16 | 9 | 19 | 22 | 22 | 22 |
| P/E Ratio:Low | 10 | 10 | 16 | 18 | 12 | 7 | 15 | 14 | 16 | 14 |
| **Income Statement Analysis** (Million $) | | | | | | | | | | |
| Rental Income | 1,334 | 1,344 | 1,339 | 1,293 | 1,219 | 1,174 | 1,008 | 859 | 765 | 488 |
| Mortgage Income | Nil | Nil | Nil | Nil | Nil | Nil | Nil | Nil | Nil | Nil |
| Total Income | 1,482 | 1,502 | 1,438 | 1,400 | 1,310 | 1,235 | 1,033 | 879 | 787 | 514 |
| General Expenses | 554 | 557 | 545 | 528 | 498 | 464 | 351 | 300 | 279 | 173 |
| Interest Expense | 286 | 298 | 308 | 306 | 299 | 272 | 223 | 217 | 205 | 125 |
| Provision for Losses | Nil | Nil | Nil | Nil | Nil | Nil | Nil | Nil | Nil | Nil |
| Depreciation | 286 | 277 | 267 | 252 | 210 | 186 | 150 | 133 | 120 | 75.4 |
| Net Income | 1,098 | 874 | 393 | 255 | 290 | 420 | 215 | 153 | 120 | 98.6 |
| S&P Core Earnings | 1,094 | 874 | 393 | 254 | 284 | 413 | 203 | NA | NA | NA |
| **Balance Sheet & Other Financial Data** (Million $) | | | | | | | | | | |
| Cash | 1,716 | 752 | 377 | 345 | 133 | 199 | 201 | 378 | 88.7 | 78.0 |
| Total Assets | 11,193 | 9,695 | 8,902 | 9,063 | 8,551 | 8,427 | 7,254 | 6,226 | 5,435 | 5,235 |
| Real Estate Investment | 10,250 | 9,552 | 9,151 | 9,291 | 8,983 | 8,671 | 7,458 | 6,113 | 5,612 | 4,917 |
| Loss Reserve | Nil | Nil | Nil | Nil | Nil | Nil | Nil | Nil | Nil | Nil |
| Net Investment | 8,718 | 8,160 | 7,886 | 8,148 | 7,981 | 7,848 | 6,738 | 5,526 | 5,142 | 4,560 |
| Short Term Debt | Nil | Nil | Nil | Nil | Nil | Nil | 282 | 194 | 680 | 26.9 |
| Capitalization:Debt | 5,492 | 4,559 | 4,679 | 4,733 | 5,005 | 3,336 | 4,033 | 3,415 | 2,642 | 3,062 |
| Capitalization:Equity | 3,669 | 3,223 | 2,917 | 2,936 | 2,400 | 2,160 | 1,754 | 1,648 | 1,058 | 948 |
| Capitalization:Total | 9,216 | 8,406 | 8,335 | 8,455 | 8,235 | 6,340 | 6,732 | 6,040 | 4,582 | 5,089 |
| % Earnings & Depreciation/Assets | 13.3 | 12.3 | 7.3 | 5.8 | 5.9 | 7.7 | 5.4 | 4.9 | 4.5 | 5.0 |
| Price Times Book Value:High | 4.3 | 4.3 | 3.0 | 2.4 | 2.1 | 2.0 | 2.3 | 2.4 | 2.4 | 2.4 |
| Price Times Book Value:Low | 2.9 | 2.7 | 2.2 | 1.6 | 1.5 | 1.6 | 1.8 | 1.5 | 1.8 | 1.6 |

Data as orig reptd.; bef. results of disc opers/spec. items. Per share data adj. for stk. divs.; EPS diluted. E-Estimated. NA-Not Available. NM-Not Meaningful. NR-Not Ranked. UR-Under Review.

**Office:** 800 Boylston St Ste 1900, Boston, MA 02199-8103.
**Telephone:** 617-236-3300.
**Email:** investor_relations@bostonproperties.com
**Website:** http://www.bostonproperties.com

**Chrmn:** M.B. Zuckerman
**Pres:** D.T. Linde
**CEO:** E.H. Linde
**COO & EVP:** E.M. Norville

**SVP, CFO & Treas:** M.E. LaBelle
**Investor Contact:** M. Walsh (617-236-3300)
**Board Members:** L. S. Bacow, Z. Baird, C. B. Einiger, E. H. Linde, A. J. Patricof, R. E. Salomon, M. Turchin, D. A. Twardock, M. B. Zuckerman

**Founded:** 1970
**Domicile:** Delaware
**Employees:** 660

# Boston Scientific Corp

**STANDARD &POOR'S**

| S&P Recommendation | HOLD ★★★☆☆ | Price | 12-Mo. Target Price | Investment Style |
|---|---|---|---|---|
| | | $7.39 (as of Nov 14, 2008) | $10.00 | Large-Cap Growth |

**GICS Sector** Health Care
**Sub-Industry** Health Care Equipment

**Summary** This manufacturer of minimally invasive medical devices acquired device rival Guidant Corp. in April 2006 for $27 billion in cash and stock.

## Key Stock Statistics (Source S&P, Vickers, company reports)

| | | | | | | | |
|---|---|---|---|---|---|---|---|
| 52-Wk Range | $14.22– 6.34 | S&P Oper. EPS 2008**E** | 0.60 | Market Capitalization(B) | $11.096 | Beta | 0.80 |
| Trailing 12-Month EPS | $-0.07 | S&P Oper. EPS 2009**E** | 0.65 | Yield (%) | Nil | S&P 3-Yr. Proj. EPS CAGR(%) | 8 |
| Trailing 12-Month P/E | NM | P/E on S&P Oper. EPS 2008**E** | 12.3 | Dividend Rate/Share | Nil | S&P Credit Rating | BB+ |
| $10K Invested 5 Yrs Ago | $2,133 | Common Shares Outstg. (M) | 1,501.5 | Institutional Ownership (%) | 76 | | |

## Price Performance

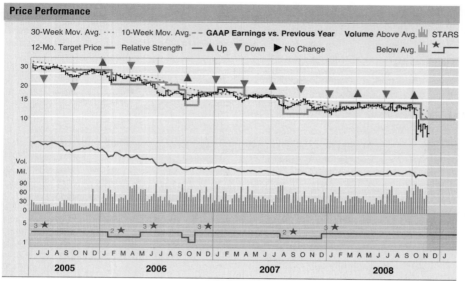

30-Week Mov. Avg. · · · ·  10-Week Mov. Avg. – –  **GAAP Earnings vs. Previous Year**  Volume Above Avg. STARS
12-Mo. Target Price —  Relative Strength  — ▲ Up ▼ Down ► No Change  Below Avg.  ★

2005  2006  2007  2008

Options: ASE, CBOE, P, Ph

Analysis prepared by **Robert M. Gold** on October 22, 2008, when the stock traded at **$ 8.44**.

## Qualitative Risk Assessment

| LOW | MEDIUM | **HIGH** |
|---|---|---|

Our risk assessment reflects the company's operations within intensely competitive areas of the health care industry, and its dependence for growth on the development and commercialization of new products. In addition, a large percentage of customers are reimbursed by the federal Medicare program, and we believe the government is likely to reduce the pace of expenditure growth by lowering reimbursement rates for expensive medical devices such as defibrillators and cardiac stents.

## Quantitative Evaluations

**S&P Quality Ranking**  C

| D | **C** | B- | B | B+ | A- | A | A+ |
|---|---|---|---|---|---|---|---|

**Relative Strength Rank**  MODERATE

40

LOWEST = 1    HIGHEST = 99

## Highlights

➤ We expect that difficult conditions in the defibrillator and stent markets will persist through 2008. Our sales forecast of $8.0 billion represents an approximate 4% decline from 2007. We see cardiac rhythm management revenues of $2.2 billion in 2008 (up from $2.1 billion in 2007), interventional cardiology of $2.8 billion ($3.1 billion), endosurgery of $1.5 billion ($1.5 billion), neuromodulation of $400 million ($317 million) and other product sales of $1.1 billion ($1.3 billion). Our 2009 revenue estimate is $8.3 billion.

➤ We believe the Guidant merger will be dilutive to EPS through at least 2009, and although we think asset sales and restructuring actions will help reduce debt and realign the operating cost structure amid decelerating revenue growth, we continue to have concerns about BSX's ability to generate sufficient excess cash flow and believe it may be forced to divest some important product lines in order to raise capital.

➤ We estimate 2008 operating EPS of $0.60, assuming higher operating margins than we had earlier forecast, and look for 2009 EPS of $0.65.

## Investment Rationale/Risk

➤ We are concerned about increasing levels of competition and declining unit prices in the drug coated stent markets, and slowing growth in the defibrillator segment. Pressures in these core businesses are particularly troublesome for BSX, in our view, due to the company's highly leveraged balance sheet following the 2006 acquisition of Guidant. To date, the company has targeted assets viewed as nonstrategic for divestiture in order to retire debt, but we believe protracted weakness in its core markets could force the sale of assets we view as more critical to its long term growth rate.

➤ Risks to our recommendation and target price include unfavorable litigation outcomes, intensified competition in key markets, and delays in commercializing key products in the pipeline.

➤ Our 12-month target price is $10, or about 15X our 2009 EPS estimate and in line with our sum-of-the-parts analysis. Although a modest P/E premium to peers, we think this is warranted by the benefits stemming from cost reductions and debt paydowns, and the prospect of industry-wide consolidation amid more challenging market conditions. In our view, BSX could attract suitors despite its high debt load.

## Revenue/Earnings Data

**Revenue (Million $)**

| | 1Q | 2Q | 3Q | 4Q | Year |
|---|---|---|---|---|---|
| 2008 | 2,046 | 2,024 | 1,978 | -- | -- |
| 2007 | 2,086 | 2,071 | 2,048 | 2,152 | 8,357 |
| 2006 | 1,620 | 2,110 | 2,206 | 2,065 | 7,821 |
| 2005 | 1,615 | 1,617 | 1,511 | 1,540 | 6,283 |
| 2004 | 1,082 | 1,460 | 1,482 | 1,600 | 5,624 |
| 2003 | 807.0 | 854.0 | 876.0 | 939.0 | 3,476 |

**Earnings Per Share ($)**

| | | | | | |
|---|---|---|---|---|---|
| 2008 | 0.22 | 0.07 | -0.04 | E0.19 | E0.60 |
| 2007 | 0.08 | 0.08 | -0.18 | -0.31 | -0.33 |
| 2006 | 0.40 | -3.21 | 0.05 | 0.19 | -2.81 |
| 2005 | 0.42 | 0.24 | -0.33 | 0.40 | 0.75 |
| 2004 | 0.23 | 0.36 | 0.30 | 0.35 | 1.24 |
| 2003 | 0.12 | 0.14 | 0.15 | 0.16 | 0.56 |

Fiscal year ended Dec. 31. Next earnings report expected: Early February. EPS Estimates based on S&P Operating Earnings; historical GAAP earnings are as reported.

## Dividend Data

No cash dividends have been paid.

---

**Please read the Required Disclosures and Analyst Certification on the last page of this report.**

The **McGraw·Hill** Companies

# Boston Scientific Corp

STANDARD
&POOR'S

## Business Summary October 22, 2008

CORPORATE OVERVIEW. Boston Scientific develops and markets minimally invasive medical devices that are used in a broad range of interventional medical specialties, including interventional cardiology, cardiac rhythm management, peripheral intervention, electrophysiology, gynecology, oncology, urology and neuromodulation.

Within the cardiovascular market, the company sells products used to treat coronary vessel disease known as arteriosclerosis. The majority of BSX's cardiovascular products are used in percutaneous transluminal coronary angioplasty (PTCA) and percutaneous transluminal coronary rotational atherectomy. These products include PTCA balloon catheters, rotational atherectomy systems, guide wires, guide catheters, diagnostic catheters, and, more recently, a cutting balloon catheter. Other products include thrombectomy catheters, peripheral vascular stents, embolic protection filters, blood clot fil-

ter systems, and electrophysiology products.

BSX also sells balloon-expandable and self-expanding coronary stent systems. In 2002, the company launched its Express 2 coronary stent system, featuring both the Express stent and the Maverick balloon dilation catheter. In early 2004, BSX launched Taxus, an Express stent coated with a polymer embedded with the anticancer compound paclitaxel. In January 2005, BSX launched its next-generation Taxus Liberte paclitaxel-eluting coronary stent in 18 Inter-Continental countries and in Europe. During 2007, drug coated coronary stents accounted for 21% of total revenues.

## Company Financials Fiscal Year Ended Dec. 31

| Per Share Data ($) | 2007 | 2006 | 2005 | 2004 | 2003 | 2002 | 2001 | 2000 | 1999 | 1998 |
|---|---|---|---|---|---|---|---|---|---|---|
| Tangible Book Value | NM | NM | 0.67 | 0.82 | 0.49 | 0.12 | NM | 0.33 | NM | NM |
| Cash Flow | 0.30 | -1.90 | 1.12 | 1.60 | 0.79 | 0.64 | 0.22 | 0.68 | 0.67 | -0.18 |
| Earnings | -0.33 | -2.81 | 0.75 | 1.24 | 0.56 | 0.45 | -0.07 | 0.46 | 0.45 | -0.34 |
| S&P Core Earnings | 0.16 | -2.75 | 1.39 | 1.27 | 0.50 | 0.33 | -0.10 | NA | NA | NA |
| Dividends | Nil | Nil | Nil | Nil | Nil | Nil | Nil | Nil | Nil | Nil |
| Payout Ratio | Nil | Nil | Nil | Nil | Nil | Nil | Nil | Nil | Nil | Nil |
| Prices:High | 18.69 | 26.56 | 35.50 | 46.10 | 36.85 | 22.15 | 13.95 | 14.59 | 23.53 | 20.42 |
| Prices:Low | 11.27 | 14.43 | 22.80 | 31.25 | 19.10 | 10.24 | 6.63 | 6.09 | 8.78 | 10.06 |
| P/E Ratio:High | NM | NM | 47 | 37 | 66 | 49 | NM | 32 | 52 | NM |
| P/E Ratio:Low | NM | NM | 30 | 25 | 34 | 23 | NM | 13 | 20 | NM |

| Income Statement Analysis (Million $) | 2007 | 2006 | 2005 | 2004 | 2003 | 2002 | 2001 | 2000 | 1999 | 1998 |
|---|---|---|---|---|---|---|---|---|---|---|
| Revenue | 8,357 | 7,821 | 6,283 | 5,624 | 3,476 | 2,919 | 2,673 | 2,664 | 2,842 | 2,234 |
| Operating Income | 2,158 | -2,383 | 2,338 | 1,989 | 945 | 757 | 614 | 819 | 857 | -93.8 |
| Depreciation | 939 | 781 | 314 | 275 | 196 | 161 | 232 | 181 | 178 | 129 |
| Interest Expense | 570 | 435 | 90.0 | 64.0 | 46.0 | 43.0 | 59.0 | 70.0 | 118 | 67.6 |
| Pretax Income | -569 | -3,535 | 891 | 1,494 | 643 | 549 | 44.0 | 527 | 562 | -274 |
| Effective Tax Rate | NM | NM | 29.5% | 28.9% | 26.6% | 32.1% | NM | 29.2% | 34.0% | NM |
| Net Income | -495 | -3,577 | 628 | 1,062 | 472 | 373 | -54.0 | 373 | 371 | -263 |
| S&P Core Earnings | 240 | -3,498 | 1,162 | 1,082 | 423 | 269 | -77.0 | NA | NA | NA |

| Balance Sheet & Other Financial Data (Million $) | 2007 | 2006 | 2005 | 2004 | 2003 | 2002 | 2001 | 2000 | 1999 | 1998 |
|---|---|---|---|---|---|---|---|---|---|---|
| Cash | 1,452 | 1,688 | 848 | 1,640 | 671 | 277 | 180 | 54.0 | 64.0 | 70.3 |
| Current Assets | 5,921 | 4,901 | 2,631 | 3,289 | 1,880 | 1,208 | 1,106 | 992 | 1,055 | 1,267 |
| Total Assets | 31,197 | 31,096 | 8,196 | 8,170 | 5,699 | 4,450 | 3,974 | 3,427 | 3,572 | 3,893 |
| Current Liabilities | 3,250 | 2,630 | 1,479 | 2,605 | 1,393 | 923 | 831 | 819 | 1,055 | 1,620 |
| Long Term Debt | 8,161 | 8,895 | 1,864 | 1,139 | 1,172 | 847 | 973 | 562 | 678 | 1,364 |
| Common Equity | 15,097 | 15,298 | 4,282 | 4,025 | 2,862 | 2,467 | 2,015 | 1,935 | 1,724 | 821 |
| Total Capital | 25,314 | 26,977 | 6,408 | 5,423 | 4,185 | 3,414 | 2,988 | 2,497 | 2,402 | 2,185 |
| Capital Expenditures | 363 | 341 | 341 | 274 | 188 | 112 | 121 | 76.0 | 80.0 | 174 |
| Cash Flow | 444 | -2,796 | 942 | 1,337 | 668 | 534 | 178 | 554 | 549 | -135 |
| Current Ratio | 1.8 | 1.9 | 1.8 | 1.3 | 1.3 | 1.3 | 1.3 | 1.2 | 1.0 | 0.8 |
| % Long Term Debt of Capitalization | 34.5 | 33.0 | 29.1 | 21.0 | 28.0 | 24.8 | 32.6 | 22.5 | 28.2 | 62.4 |
| % Net Income of Revenue | NM | NM | 10.0 | 18.9 | 13.6 | 12.8 | NM | 14.0 | 13.1 | 9.6 |
| % Return on Assets | NM | NM | 7.7 | 15.3 | 9.3 | 8.9 | NM | 10.7 | 9.9 | NM |
| % Return on Equity | NM | NM | 15.1 | 30.8 | 17.7 | 16.6 | NM | 20.4 | 29.2 | NM |

Data as orig reptd.; bef. results of disc opers/spec. items. Per share data adj. for stk. divs.; EPS diluted. E-Estimated. NA-Not Available. NM-Not Meaningful. NR-Not Ranked. UR-Under Review.

**Office:** One Boston Scientific Pl, Natick, MA 01760-1537.
**Telephone:** 508-650-8000.
**Email:** investor_relations@bsci.com
**Website:** http://www.bostonscientific.com

**Chrmn:** P.M. Nicholas, Jr.
**Pres & CEO:** J.R. Tobin
**COO:** K.J. Pucel
**EVP & CFO:** S.R. Leno

**EVP & CSO:** D.S. Baim
**Board Members:** J. E. Abele, U. M. Burns, N. M. DeParle, J. R. Elliott, J. L. Fleishman, M. A. Fox, R. J. Groves, K. M. Johnson, E. Mario, N. J. Nicholas, Jr., P. M. Nicholas, Jr., J. E. Pepper, Jr., U. E. Reinhardt, W. Rudman, J. R. Tobin

**Founded:** 1979
**Domicile:** Delaware
**Employees:** 27,500

The McGraw-Hill Companies

# Bristol-Myers Squibb Co

**STANDARD &POOR'S**

| S&P Recommendation **BUY** ★★★★☆ | Price $19.58 (as of Nov 14, 2008) | 12-Mo. Target Price $23.00 | Investment Style Large-Cap Value |
|---|---|---|---|

**GICS Sector** Health Care
**Sub-Industry** Pharmaceuticals

**Summary** This leading global drugmaker is strong in both prescription and nonprescription products.

## Key Stock Statistics (Source S&P, Vickers, company reports)

| | | | | | | | |
|---|---|---|---|---|---|---|---|
| 52-Wk Range | $29.76– 16.00 | S&P Oper. EPS 2008**E** | 1.70 | Market Capitalization(B) | $38.761 | Beta | 0.69 |
| Trailing 12-Month EPS | $1.97 | S&P Oper. EPS 2009**E** | 1.90 | Yield (%) | 6.33 | S&P 3-Yr. Proj. EPS CAGR(%) | 12 |
| Trailing 12-Month P/E | 9.9 | P/E on S&P Oper. EPS 2008**E** | 11.5 | Dividend Rate/Share | $1.24 | S&P Credit Rating | A+ |
| $10K Invested 5 Yrs Ago | $9,105 | Common Shares Outstg. (M) | 1,979.6 | Institutional Ownership (%) | 73 | | |

## Price Performance

30-Week Mov. Avg. ···· 10-Week Mov. Avg. – – **GAAP Earnings vs. Previous Year** Volume Above Avg. |ılıl STARS
12-Mo. Target Price — Relative Strength —— ▲ Up ▼ Down ▶ No Change   Below Avg. |ılıl ★

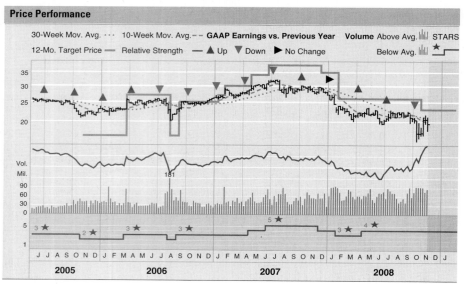

Options: ASE, CBOE, P, Ph

Analysis prepared by **Herman B. Saftlas** on November 03, 2008, when the stock traded at **$ 20.78**.

## Highlights

➤ We see sales from continuing operations rising 9% in 2009, from an estimated $20.8 billion in 2008, which excludes the sold medical imaging and ConvaTec businesses. The gain should be led by a strong rise in Plavix blood thinning agent. We also see higher volume in Abilify antipsychotic and Reyataz HIV/AIDS therapies. In addition, contributions from new drugs such as Orencia for rheumatoid arthritis and Sprycel for leukemia will likely augment volume. We look for these gains to more than offset lower sales of off-patent products. Sales of nutritional and other health care products should also experience growth.

➤ We see gross margins in 2009 comparing favorably with the 69.7% that we project for 2008, helped by a better sales mix. We also see operating margins benefiting from restrained spending growth in both SG&A and R&D expenses. Non-operating income is also expected to increase.

➤ After an estimated tax rate in the 24% area, we forecast EPS of $1.90 in 2009, up from an indicated $1.70 in 2008. Results exclude gains from asset sales, milestones and other special items.

## Investment Rationale/Risk

➤ Along with several other big pharma companies, BMY faces a fairly large patent cliff over 2011-2012, with patent expirations expected on Plavix and Avapro, whose combined sales we estimate will account for about one-third of BMY's total sales in 2008. Addressing this issue, BMY has become more aggressive in new product development in recent years, launching new anticancer drugs such as Sprycel and Ixempra, Orencia treatment for rheumatoid arthritis, and Sustiva and Reyataz for HIV/AIDS. BMY is also implementing productivity initiatives that are expected to yield cost savings of $1.5 billion by 2010. We also think BMY has a strong balance sheet, with $7.2 billion in cash.

➤ Risks to our recommendation and target price include increased competitive pressures in key product lines, and possible pipeline setbacks.

➤ Our 12-month target price of $23 applies a parity-to-peers P/E of 12.1X to our 2009 EPS estimate. Our DCF model, which assumes a WACC of 7.5% and terminal growth of 1%, also indicates intrinsic value of $23. The dividend recently yielded 6.0%.

## Qualitative Risk Assessment

| LOW | MEDIUM | HIGH |
|---|---|---|

In common with other large capitalization drugmakers, BMY is subject to the threat of generic challenges to its branded drugs, as well as risks associated with new drug development and regulatory approval. Although BMY faces the loss of patent protection on several key drugs over the 2011-2012 period, we believe these losses will be offset by new products and significant cost savings.

## Quantitative Evaluations

**S&P Quality Ranking** B+

| D | C | B- | B | B+ | A- | A | A+ |
|---|---|---|---|---|---|---|---|

**Relative Strength Rank** STRONG

86

LOWEST = 1     HIGHEST = 99

## Revenue/Earnings Data

**Revenue (Million $)**

| | 1Q | 2Q | 3Q | 4Q | Year |
|---|---|---|---|---|---|
| 2008 | 5,181 | 5,203 | 5,254 | -- | -- |
| 2007 | 4,317 | 4,757 | 4,893 | 5,381 | 19,348 |
| 2006 | 4,676 | 4,871 | 4,154 | 4,213 | 17,914 |
| 2005 | 4,532 | 4,889 | 4,767 | 5,019 | 19,207 |
| 2004 | 4,626 | 4,819 | 4,778 | 5,157 | 19,380 |
| 2003 | 4,728 | 5,129 | 5,372 | 5,665 | 20,894 |

**Earnings Per Share ($)**

| | | | | | |
|---|---|---|---|---|---|
| 2008 | 0.35 | 0.36 | 0.30 | E0.45 | E1.70 |
| 2007 | 0.33 | 0.33 | 0.41 | -0.07 | 0.99 |
| 2006 | 0.36 | 0.34 | 0.17 | -0.07 | 0.81 |
| 2005 | 0.27 | 0.50 | 0.49 | 0.26 | 1.52 |
| 2004 | 0.49 | 0.27 | 0.38 | 0.07 | 1.21 |
| 2003 | 0.41 | 0.46 | 0.47 | 0.26 | 1.59 |

Fiscal year ended Dec. 31. Next earnings report expected: Early February. EPS Estimates based on S&P Operating Earnings; historical GAAP earnings are as reported.

## Dividend Data (Dates: mm/dd Payment Date: mm/dd/yy)

| Amount ($) | Date Decl. | Ex-Div. Date | Stk. of Record | Payment Date |
|---|---|---|---|---|
| 0.310 | 03/04 | 04/02 | 04/04 | 05/01/08 |
| 0.310 | 06/10 | 07/02 | 07/07 | 08/01/08 |
| 0.310 | 09/09 | 10/01 | 10/03 | 11/03/08 |

Dividends have been paid since 1900. Source: Company reports.

*The McGraw·Hill Companies*

# Bristol-Myers Squibb Co

**STANDARD &POOR'S**

## Business Summary November 03, 2008

CORPORATE OVERVIEW. Bristol-Myers Squibb is a major global drugmaker, offering a wide range of prescription drugs. In recent years, BMY divested non-core beauty care, orthopedic devices, imaging products and cancer drug distribution businesses. Prescription drugs accounted for 81% of sales in 2007, nutritionals 13%, and medical devices 6%. Foreign sales accounted for 44% of total sales in 2007.

The company's largest selling drug is Plavix (sales of $4.8 billion in 2007), a platelet aggregation inhibitor for the prevention of stroke, heart attack and vascular disease. Plavix is produced through a joint venture with French drugmaker Sanofi-Aventis SA. Other cardiovasculars include Avapro/Avalide ($1.2 billion), an angiotensin II receptor blocker for hypertension; Pravachol anticholesterol ($443 million); and Coumadin blood thinning agent ($201 million). Principal anticancer drugs are Erbitux ($692 million), Taxol ($422 million) and Sprycel ($158 million).

The company's principal anti-infective drugs are HIV/AIDS treatments such as

Reyataz ($1.1 billion), Sustiva ($956 million), and Baraclude ($275 million). BMY also offers Cefzil, Tequin, Maxipime, and other antibiotics. Central nervous system agents include Abilify, an antipsychotic ($1.7 billion), Sinemet for Parkinson's disease, and various other drugs. Orencia, a new treatment for rheumatoid arthritis ($231 million), was approved in December 2005.

The Mead Johnson division offers nutritionals, consisting of infant formulas such as Enfamil and ProSobee, as well as other related items. BMY plans to sell a 10%-20% interest in Mead Johnson to the public through an IPO.

In early August 2008, BMY sold its ConvaTec ostomy and wound care business to a group of private equity funds for $4.1 billion in cash. In January 2008, the company sold its medical imaging business.

## Company Financials Fiscal Year Ended Dec. 31

| Per Share Data ($) | 2007 | 2006 | 2005 | 2004 | 2003 | 2002 | 2001 | 2000 | 1999 | 1998 |
|---|---|---|---|---|---|---|---|---|---|---|
| Tangible Book Value | 2.14 | 1.68 | 2.28 | 1.76 | 1.62 | 0.88 | 1.70 | 3.96 | 3.61 | 3.01 |
| Cash Flow | 1.39 | 1.28 | 1.98 | 1.66 | 1.99 | 1.43 | 1.68 | 2.42 | 2.39 | 1.85 |
| Earnings | 0.99 | 0.81 | 1.52 | 1.21 | 1.59 | 1.05 | 1.29 | 2.36 | 2.06 | 1.55 |
| S&P Core Earnings | 1.02 | 0.88 | 1.43 | 1.24 | 1.57 | 1.07 | 0.67 | NA | NA | NA |
| Dividends | 1.12 | 1.12 | 1.12 | 1.12 | 1.12 | 1.12 | 1.10 | 0.98 | 0.86 | 0.78 |
| Payout Ratio | 113% | 138% | 74% | 93% | 70% | 107% | 85% | 42% | 42% | 50% |
| Prices:High | 32.35 | 26.41 | 26.60 | 31.30 | 29.21 | 51.95 | 73.50 | 74.88 | 79.25 | 67.63 |
| Prices:Low | 25.73 | 20.08 | 20.70 | 22.22 | 21.00 | 19.49 | 48.50 | 42.44 | 57.25 | 44.16 |
| P/E Ratio:High | 33 | 33 | 17 | 26 | 18 | 49 | 57 | 32 | 38 | 44 |
| P/E Ratio:Low | 26 | 25 | 14 | 18 | 13 | 19 | 38 | 18 | 28 | 29 |

| Income Statement Analysis (Million $) | 2007 | 2006 | 2005 | 2004 | 2003 | 2002 | 2001 | 2000 | 1999 | 1998 |
|---|---|---|---|---|---|---|---|---|---|---|
| Revenue | 19,348 | 17,914 | 19,207 | 19,380 | 20,894 | 18,119 | 19,423 | 18,216 | 20,222 | 18,284 |
| Operating Income | 4,309 | 3,483 | 4,880 | 5,373 | 5,726 | 4,851 | 7,034 | 6,732 | 6,531 | 5,746 |
| Depreciation | 776 | 927 | 929 | 909 | 779 | 735 | 781 | 746 | 678 | 625 |
| Interest Expense | 457 | 498 | 349 | 310 | 277 | 410 | 182 | 108 | 130 | 154 |
| Pretax Income | 3,534 | 2,635 | 4,516 | 4,418 | 4,694 | 2,647 | 2,986 | 5,478 | 5,767 | 4,268 |
| Effective Tax Rate | 22.7% | 23.1% | 20.6% | 34.4% | 25.9% | 16.4% | 15.4% | 25.2% | 27.7% | 26.4% |
| Net Income | 1,968 | 1,585 | 2,992 | 2,378 | 3,106 | 2,034 | 2,527 | 4,096 | 4,167 | 3,141 |
| S&P Core Earnings | 2,024 | 1,727 | 2,808 | 2,448 | 3,043 | 2,076 | 1,321 | NA | NA | NA |

| Balance Sheet & Other Financial Data (Million $) | 2007 | 2006 | 2005 | 2004 | 2003 | 2002 | 2001 | 2000 | 1999 | 1998 |
|---|---|---|---|---|---|---|---|---|---|---|
| Cash | 2,225 | 4,013 | 5,799 | 7,474 | 5,457 | 3,989 | 5,654 | 3,385 | 2,957 | 2,529 |
| Current Assets | 10,348 | 10,302 | 12,283 | 14,801 | 11,918 | 9,975 | 12,349 | 9,824 | 9,267 | 8,782 |
| Total Assets | 26,172 | 25,575 | 28,138 | 30,435 | 27,471 | 24,874 | 27,057 | 17,578 | 17,114 | 16,272 |
| Current Liabilities | 8,644 | 6,496 | 6,890 | 9,843 | 7,530 | 8,220 | 8,826 | 5,632 | 5,537 | 5,791 |
| Long Term Debt | 4,381 | 7,248 | 8,364 | 8,463 | 8,522 | 6,261 | 6,237 | 1,336 | 1,342 | 1,364 |
| Common Equity | 10,562 | 9,991 | 11,208 | 10,202 | 19,572 | 8,967 | 10,736 | 9,180 | 8,645 | 7,576 |
| Total Capital | 14,943 | 17,307 | 19,572 | 18,665 | 28,094 | 15,228 | 16,973 | 10,516 | 9,987 | 8,940 |
| Capital Expenditures | 843 | 762 | 738 | 676 | 937 | 997 | 1,023 | 589 | 709 | 788 |
| Cash Flow | 2,744 | 2,512 | 3,921 | 3,287 | 3,885 | 2,769 | 3,308 | 4,842 | 4,845 | 3,766 |
| Current Ratio | 1.2 | 1.6 | 1.8 | 1.5 | 1.6 | 1.2 | 1.4 | 1.7 | 1.7 | 1.5 |
| % Long Term Debt of Capitalization | 29.3 | 42.0 | 42.7 | 45.3 | 30.3 | 41.1 | 36.7 | 12.7 | 13.4 | 15.3 |
| % Net Income of Revenue | 10.2 | 8.8 | 15.6 | 12.3 | 14.9 | 11.2 | 13.0 | 22.5 | 20.6 | 17.2 |
| % Return on Assets | 7.6 | 5.9 | 10.2 | 8.2 | 11.8 | 7.7 | 11.3 | 23.6 | 25.0 | 20.1 |
| % Return on Equity | 19.2 | 15.0 | 27.9 | 23.8 | 16.8 | 22.5 | 25.4 | 46.0 | 51.4 | 42.5 |

Data as orig reptd.; bef. results of disc opers/spec. items. Per share data adj. for stk. divs.; EPS diluted. E-Estimated. NA-Not Available. NM-Not Meaningful. NR-Not Ranked. UR-Under Review.

**Office:** 345 Park Ave, New York, NY 10154-0004.
**Telephone:** 212-546-4000.
**Website:** http://www.bms.com
**Chrmn & CEO:** J.M. Cornelius

**Pres & CSO:** E. Sigal
**COO & EVP:** L. Andreotti
**SVP & CFO:** J. Huet
**SVP, Secy & General Counsel:** S. Leung

**Investor Contact:** J. Elicker (212-546-3775)
**Board Members:** L. B. Campbell, J. M. Cornelius, L. J. Freeh, L. H. Glimcher, M. Grobstein, L. Johansson, A. J. Lacy, V. L. Sato, T. D. West, Jr., R. S. Williams

**Founded:** 1887
**Domicile:** Delaware
**Employees:** 42,000

# Broadcom Corp

STANDARD
&POOR'S

| S&P Recommendation **HOLD** ★★★☆☆ | Price $15.38 (as of Nov 14, 2008) | 12-Mo. Target Price $20.00 | Investment Style Large-Cap Blend |
|---|---|---|---|

**GICS Sector** Information Technology
**Sub-Industry** Semiconductors

**Summary** This company provides semiconductors for broadband communications markets, including cable set-top boxes, cable modems, office networks and home networking.

## Key Stock Statistics (Source S&P, Vickers, company reports)

| | | | | | |
|---|---|---|---|---|---|
| 52-Wk Range | $29.91–12.98 | S&P Oper. EPS 2008**E** | 0.89 | Market Capitalization(B) | $6.870 |
| Trailing 12-Month EPS | $0.86 | S&P Oper. EPS 2009**E** | 0.94 | Yield (%) | Nil |
| Trailing 12-Month P/E | 17.9 | P/E on S&P Oper. EPS 2008**E** | 17.3 | Dividend Rate/Share | Nil |
| $10K Invested 5 Yrs Ago | $6,466 | Common Shares Outstg. (M) | 510.5 | Institutional Ownership (%) | 88 |

| | |
|---|---|
| Beta | 2.50 |
| S&P 3-Yr. Proj. EPS CAGR(%) | 15 |
| S&P Credit Rating | NA |

## Price Performance

30-Week Mov. Avg. · · ·   10-Week Mov. Avg. – –   GAAP Earnings vs. Previous Year   Volume Above Avg. STARS
12-Mo. Target Price —   Relative Strength —   ▲ Up   ▼ Down   ► No Change   Below Avg. ★

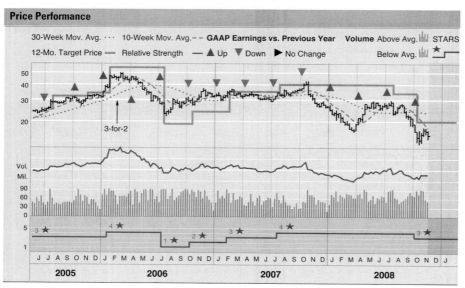

Options: ASE, CBOE, P, Ph

Analysis prepared by **Clyde Montevirgen** on October 22, 2008, when the stock traded at **$ 14.69.**

## Highlights

➤ We see revenues rising 10% in 2009, after a projected 26% jump in 2008, reflecting robust end-market demand and share gains for BRCM's well-diversified communications offerings. BRCM has invested in a wide range of new products that we think are well designed and should compete favorably against competitors' offerings. We see sales supported by growth for DTV, Bluetooth, Wireless LAN, and FM products, and we believe longer-term growth will be bolstered by BRCM's mobile handset and related chip sales.

➤ We forecast gross margins will narrow to around 51% in 2009, from an anticipated 53% in 2008, as sales mix shifts to lower-margin products. We see operating margins of around 9% in 2009, around expected 2008 results, reflecting continuing investments in developing and supporting new projects. BRCM's fabless manufacturing model and rising operating expenses will likely balance the positive impact from sales growth over the near term, in our view. Also, low effective taxes should aid profitability, in our view.

➤ We see EPS of $0.94 in 2009, compared to a projected $0.89 in 2008.

## Investment Rationale/Risk

➤ We believe that new mobile and wireless products, as well as anticipated growth for certain broadband communications products, will provide notable growth in the long term. We view favorably BRCM's migration to 65nm, and we think new designs, such as its latest 3G chip offering, will lead to market share gains. Although we anticipate improving growth in late 2009 as the company executes on supply agreements with large handset providers, we see the near-term risk of its relatively expensive operations hurting profitability if sales from its other segments show weakness.

➤ Risks to our recommendation and target price include a weaker than anticipated downturn, slower-than-anticipated orders for handset chips, and rising operating expenses.

➤ Our 12-month target price of $20 is based on a weighted blend of relative metrics. We apply a price-to-sales multiple of about 2.3X, above the peer average, to our forward 12-month sales per share estimate to derive a value of $22. We apply a 20X P/E multiple, also above peers but below the historical average, to our 2009 EPS estimate, implying a value of $18.

## Qualitative Risk Assessment

| LOW | MEDIUM | **HIGH** |
|---|---|---|

Our risk assessment reflects Broadcom's exposure to the sales cycles of the semiconductor industry, dependence on foundry partners for production, and greater reliance than most companies on stock-based compensation. This is partially offset by our view of a lack of debt and a broadening base of end users.

## Quantitative Evaluations

**S&P Quality Ranking**   B-

| D | C | **B-** | B | B+ | A- | A | A+ |
|---|---|---|---|---|---|---|---|

**Relative Strength Rank**   **MODERATE**

59

LOWEST = 1    HIGHEST = 99

## Revenue/Earnings Data

**Revenue (Million $)**

| | 1Q | 2Q | 3Q | 4Q | Year |
|---|---|---|---|---|---|
| 2008 | 1,032 | 1,201 | 1,298 | -- | -- |
| 2007 | 901.5 | 897.9 | 950.0 | 1,027 | 3,776 |
| 2006 | 900.7 | 941.1 | 902.6 | 923.5 | 3,668 |
| 2005 | 550.3 | 604.9 | 695.0 | 820.6 | 2,671 |
| 2004 | 573.4 | 641.3 | 646.5 | 539.4 | 2,401 |
| 2003 | 327.5 | 377.9 | 425.6 | 479.1 | 1,610 |

**Earnings Per Share ($)**

| | | | | | |
|---|---|---|---|---|---|
| 2008 | 0.14 | 0.25 | 0.31 | E0.19 | E0.89 |
| 2007 | 0.10 | 0.06 | 0.05 | 0.16 | 0.37 |
| 2006 | 0.20 | 0.18 | 0.19 | 0.08 | 0.64 |
| 2005 | 0.13 | 0.03 | 0.23 | 0.33 | 0.73 |
| 2004 | 0.08 | 0.12 | 0.09 | 0.13 | 0.42 |
| 2003 | -0.17 | -2.05 | -0.01 | 0.01 | -2.19 |

Fiscal year ended Dec. 31. Next earnings report expected: Late January. EPS Estimates based on S&P Operating Earnings; historical GAAP earnings are as reported.

## Dividend Data

No cash dividends have been paid.

---

The **McGraw·Hill** Companies

# Broadcom Corp

STANDARD
&POOR'S

## Business Summary October 22, 2008

CORPORATE OVERVIEW. Founded in 1991, Broadcom is a global provider in semiconductors for wired and wireless communications. The company's products enable the delivery of voice, video, data and multimedia to and throughout the home, the office and the mobile environment. Broadcom's diverse product portfolio includes solutions for digital cable, satellite and Internet Protocol (IP) set-top boxes and media servers; high definition television (HDTV); high definition DVD players and personal video recording (PVR) devices; cable and DSL modems and residential gateways; high-speed transmission and switching for local, metropolitan, wide area and storage networking; SystemI/O server solutions; broadband network and security processors; wireless and personal area networking; cellular communications; global positioning system (GPS) applications; mobile multimedia and applications processors; mobile power management; and Voice over Internet Protocol (VoIP) gateway and telephony systems.

The company has one reportable segment, but we believe that sales can be separated into three main target markets: Broadband Communications, Enterprise Networking, and Mobile and Wireless Networking. Broadband Commu-

nication products offer manufacturers a range of broadband communications and consumer electronics systems-on-a-chip (SoCs) that enable voice, video and data services over residential wired and wireless networks. Enterprise Networking enable a robust, scalable, secure and easy-to-manage network infrastructure for the carrier/service provider, data center, enterprise and small-to-medium-sized business, or SMB, markets. Its solutions aim to enable these networks to offer higher capacities and faster, more cost-efficient transport and management of voice, data and video traffic across wired and wireless networks. Mobile and Wireless Networking allow manufacturers to develop leading-edge mobile devices, enabling end-to-end wireless opportunities for the home, business and mobile markets. In 2007, net revenue by major target market was 30% (32% in 2006) enterprise networking; 37% (38%) broadband communications; and 32% (30%) mobile and wireless.

## Company Financials Fiscal Year Ended Dec. 31

| Per Share Data ($) | 2007 | 2006 | 2005 | 2004 | 2003 | 2002 | 2001 | 2000 | 1999 | 1998 |
|---|---|---|---|---|---|---|---|---|---|---|
| Tangible Book Value | 4.86 | 5.43 | 3.79 | 2.59 | 1.43 | 0.94 | 2.19 | 3.31 | 1.59 | 0.78 |
| Cash Flow | 0.48 | 0.73 | 0.85 | 0.59 | -1.98 | -5.20 | -4.87 | -1.59 | 0.28 | 0.16 |
| Earnings | 0.37 | 0.64 | 0.73 | 0.42 | -2.19 | -5.57 | -7.19 | -2.09 | 0.24 | 0.13 |
| S&P Core Earnings | 0.37 | 0.64 | -0.04 | -0.70 | -2.31 | -5.07 | -6.87 | NA | NA | NA |
| Dividends | Nil | Nil | Nil | Nil | Nil | Nil | Nil | Nil | Nil | Nil |
| Payout Ratio | Nil | Nil | Nil | Nil | Nil | Nil | Nil | Nil | Nil | Nil |
| Prices:High | 43.07 | 50.00 | 33.28 | 31.37 | 25.10 | 35.57 | 93.00 | 183.17 | 96.33 | 22.50 |
| Prices:Low | 25.70 | 21.98 | 18.25 | 16.83 | 7.91 | 6.35 | 12.27 | 49.83 | 15.42 | 4.00 |
| P/E Ratio:High | NM | 78 | 46 | 75 | NM | NM | NM | NM | NM | NM |
| P/E Ratio:Low | NM | 34 | 25 | 40 | NM | NM | NM | NM | NM | NM |

| Income Statement Analysis (Million $) | | | | | | | | | | |
|---|---|---|---|---|---|---|---|---|---|---|
| Revenue | 3,776 | 3,668 | 2,671 | 2,401 | 1,610 | 1,083 | 962 | 1,096 | 518 | 203 |
| Operating Income | 148 | 309 | 557 | 450 | -30.4 | -442 | -573 | -169 | 157 | 59.7 |
| Depreciation | 62.0 | 47.6 | 68.5 | 91.7 | 90.9 | 147 | 889 | 165 | 14.0 | 7.50 |
| Interest Expense | Nil | Nil | Nil | Nil | Nil | 3.60 | 5.00 | 0.33 | 0.55 | 0.47 |
| Pretax Income | 219 | 367 | 392 | 294 | -935 | -1,939 | -2,799 | -692 | 119 | 56.0 |
| Effective Tax Rate | 2.70% | NM | NM | 25.7% | NM | NM | NM | NM | 30.2% | 35.0% |
| Net Income | 213 | 379 | 412 | 219 | -960 | -2,237 | -2,742 | -688 | 83.3 | 36.4 |
| S&P Core Earnings | 215 | 379 | -25.7 | -330 | -1,011 | -2,039 | -2,617 | NA | NA | NA |

| Balance Sheet & Other Financial Data (Million $) | | | | | | | | | | |
|---|---|---|---|---|---|---|---|---|---|---|
| Cash | 2,329 | 2,680 | 1,733 | 1,183 | 606 | 503 | 540 | 524 | 174 | 62.6 |
| Current Assets | 3,054 | 3,352 | 2,336 | 1,584 | 996 | 722 | 674 | 876 | 391 | 157 |
| Total Assets | 4,838 | 4,877 | 3,752 | 2,886 | 2,018 | 2,216 | 3,623 | 4,678 | 585 | 237 |
| Current Liabilities | 758 | 679 | 595 | 497 | 504 | 534 | 412 | 203 | 86.1 | 27.1 |
| Long Term Debt | Nil | Nil | Nil | Nil | Nil | 1.21 | 4.01 | Nil | 0.55 | Nil |
| Common Equity | 4,036 | 4,192 | 3,145 | 2,366 | 1,490 | 1,645 | 3,207 | 4,475 | 499 | 210 |
| Total Capital | 4,036 | 4,192 | 3,145 | 2,366 | 1,490 | 1,646 | 3,211 | 4,475 | 499 | 210 |
| Capital Expenditures | 160 | 92.5 | 41.8 | 49.9 | 47.9 | 75.2 | 71.4 | 80.7 | 29.2 | 27.3 |
| Cash Flow | 275 | 427 | 480 | 310 | -869 | -2,090 | -1,853 | -523 | 97.3 | 43.9 |
| Current Ratio | 4.0 | 4.9 | 3.9 | 3.2 | 2.0 | 1.4 | 1.6 | 4.3 | 4.5 | 5.8 |
| % Long Term Debt of Capitalization | Nil | Nil | Nil | Nil | Nil | 0.1 | 0.1 | Nil | 0.1 | Nil |
| % Net Income of Revenue | 5.6 | 10.3 | 15.4 | 9.1 | NM | NM | NM | NM | 16.1 | 17.9 |
| % Return on Assets | 4.3 | 8.8 | 12.4 | 8.9 | NM | NM | NM | NM | 19.7 | 25.8 |
| % Return on Equity | 5.1 | 10.3 | 14.9 | 11.3 | NM | NM | NM | NM | 23.3 | 33.8 |

Data as orig reptd.; bef. results of disc opers/spec. items. Per share data adj. for stk. divs.; EPS diluted. E-Estimated. NA-Not Available. NM-Not Meaningful. NR-Not Ranked. UR-Under Review.

**Office:** 5300 California Ave, Irvine, CA 92617-3038.
**Telephone:** 949-926-5000.
**Email:** investorinfo@broadcom.com
**Website:** http://www.broadcom.com

**Chrmn:** J. Major
**Pres & CEO:** S.A. McGregor
**SVP & CFO:** E.K. Brandt
**SVP, Secy & General Counsel:** A. Chong

**SVP & CIO:** K.E. Venner
**Investor Contact:** P. Andrew (949-926-5663)
**Board Members:** G. L. Farinsky, N. H. Handel, E. W. Hartenstein, J. Major, S. A. McGregor, W. T. Morrow, A. E. Ross, R. E. Switz

**Founded:** 1991
**Domicile:** California
**Employees:** 4,676

# Brown-Forman Corp

STANDARD &POOR'S

| S&P Recommendation | BUY ★★★★☆ | Price $47.22 (as of Nov 14, 2008) | 12-Mo. Target Price $68.00 | Investment Style Large-Cap Growth |
|---|---|---|---|---|

**GICS Sector** Consumer Staples
**Sub-Industry** Distillers & Vintners

**Summary** This leading distiller and importer of alcoholic beverages, based in Kentucky, markets Jack Daniel's, Southern Comfort, Finlandia, Korbel and Bolla brands.

## Key Stock Statistics (Source S&P, Vickers, company reports)

| | | | | | | | |
|---|---|---|---|---|---|---|---|
| 52-Wk Range | $63.02– 41.94 | S&P Oper. EPS 2009E | 3.13 | Market Capitalization(B) | $4.451 | Beta | 0.54 |
| Trailing 12-Month EPS | $2.82 | S&P Oper. EPS 2010E | 3.41 | Yield (%) | 2.30 | S&P 3-Yr. Proj. EPS CAGR(%) | 10 |
| Trailing 12-Month P/E | 16.7 | P/E on S&P Oper. EPS 2009E | 15.1 | Dividend Rate/Share | $1.09 | S&P Credit Rating | A |
| $10K Invested 5 Yrs Ago | $15,325 | Common Shares Outstg. (M) | 150.9 | Institutional Ownership (%) | 74 | | |

## Price Performance

30-Week Mov. Avg. ···    10-Week Mov. Avg. --    **GAAP Earnings vs. Previous Year**    Volume Above Avg. ||| STARS
12-Mo. Target Price —    Relative Strength —    ▲ Up ▼ Down ► No Change    Below Avg. ||| ★

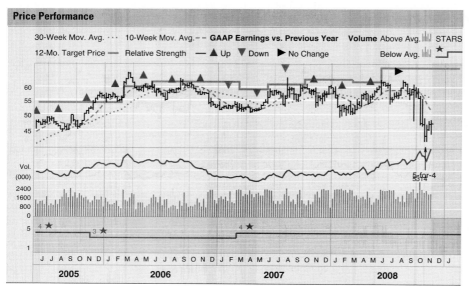

Analysis prepared by **Esther Y. Kwon, CFA** on September 08, 2008, when the stock traded at **$ 72.58**.

## Highlights

➤ We forecast about 6% wine and spirits sales growth in FY 09 (Apr.) on organic growth, international expansion, and development of the Casa Herradura brand. Along with price increases, our FY 09 growth projection reflects continued momentum in top spirits brands Jack Daniel's and Finlandia. While we expect a softer environment in the U.S., we think recent moves to improve off-premise sales of Jack Daniel's will pay dividends as on-premise consumption declines. In addition, with 52% of FY 08 net sales from outside the U.S., we see Finlandia and secondarily Jack Daniel's driving more than 50% of net sales growth.

➤ We look for gross margin contraction on higher raw material costs, offset somewhat by better integration of recent acquisitions into operations, likely improvement in the product mix, and a declining dollar. We think operating margins will benefit from prior years' investments in global distribution arrangements, partly offset by increased marketing support.

➤ On about a 2% reduction in diluted shares outstanding and a higher effective tax rate, we estimate FY 09 EPS of $3.91, up approximately 10% from continuing operations reported for FY 08.

## Investment Rationale/Risk

➤ Longer term, we look for continued strength in the global market, and think that spirits will continue to make successful inroads in the 21- to 27-year old demographic. BF should continue to capitalize on what we see as positive industry trends with its strong portfolio of spirits and international reach, particularly with its Jack Daniel's brand. In addition, we believe BF's commitment to improving distribution and brand building will support outperformance.

➤ Risks to our recommendation and target price include an unexpected slowdown in the growth of top-performing brands. Also, BF's dual-class structure and the majority representation of insiders on its board of directors pose corporate governance concerns to us.

➤ Our 12-month target price of $85 is supported by our DCF and P/E analyses. Based on our DCF model, assuming an 8.5% cost of capital and a 2.5% terminal growth rate, we estimate intrinsic value of $83. We apply a P/E of about 22X, in line with the stock's historical average, to our FY 09 EPS estimate, which leads to a value of $87. With a recent dividend yield of about 2%, we recommend the shares for total return potential.

## Qualitative Risk Assessment

| LOW | MEDIUM | HIGH |
|---|---|---|

Brown-Forman is a large-cap competitor in an industry that has historically demonstrated relative stability. However, we believe the company's dual-class structure and the majority representation of insiders on its board of directors pose corporate governance concerns.

## Quantitative Evaluations

**S&P Quality Ranking**    A

| D | C | B- | B | B+ | A- | A | A+ |
|---|---|---|---|---|---|---|---|

**Relative Strength Rank**    STRONG

76

LOWEST = 1    HIGHEST = 99

## Revenue/Earnings Data

**Revenue (Million $)**

| | 1Q | 2Q | 3Q | 4Q | Year |
|---|---|---|---|---|---|
| 2009 | 790.0 | -- | -- | -- | -- |
| 2008 | 739.0 | 893.0 | 877.0 | 772.0 | 3,282 |
| 2007 | 633.0 | 727.0 | 754.8 | 690.8 | 2,218 |
| 2006 | 547.0 | 666.0 | 637.0 | 594.0 | 2,444 |
| 2005 | 578.0 | 780.0 | 758.0 | 613.0 | 2,729 |
| 2004 | 532.6 | 725.2 | 697.0 | 625.0 | 2,577 |

**Earnings Per Share ($)**

| | | | | | |
|---|---|---|---|---|---|
| 2009 | 0.58 | E0.92 | E0.86 | E0.66 | E3.13 |
| 2008 | 0.58 | 0.83 | 0.74 | 0.65 | 2.85 |
| 2007 | 0.61 | 0.80 | 0.72 | 0.45 | 2.58 |
| 2006 | 0.57 | 0.73 | 0.78 | 0.49 | 2.56 |
| 2005 | 0.34 | 0.66 | 0.62 | 0.39 | 2.02 |
| 2004 | 0.20 | 0.58 | 0.53 | 0.38 | 1.69 |

Fiscal year ended Apr. 30. Next earnings report expected: Late November. EPS Estimates based on S&P Operating Earnings; historical GAAP earnings are as reported.

## Dividend Data (Dates: mm/dd Payment Date: mm/dd/yy)

| Amount ($) | Date Decl. | Ex-Div. Date | Stk. of Record | Payment Date |
|---|---|---|---|---|
| 0.340 | 01/22 | 03/03 | 03/05 | 04/01/08 |
| 0.340 | 05/22 | 06/02 | 06/04 | 07/01/08 |
| 0.340 | 07/24 | 09/04 | 09/08 | 10/01/08 |
| 5-for-4 | 09/29 | 10/28 | 10/06 | 10/27/08 |

Dividends have been paid since 1960. Source: Company reports.

---

**Please read the Required Disclosures and Analyst Certification on the last page of this report.**

# Brown-Forman Corp

**STANDARD &POOR'S**

## Business Summary September 08, 2008

CORPORATE OVERVIEW. Brown-Forman Corp.'s origins date back to 1870. It is the world's fourth largest producer of distilled spirits. With a portfolio of well known brands, the company is best known for its popular Jack Daniel's Tennessee Whiskey, which continues to be its largest sales and profit producer.

Although many alcoholic beverage companies have moved in recent years to reduce their dependence on the highly mature brown spirits market, BF has remained whiskey-oriented. Its product line is stocked with well known whiskies, bourbons, vodkas, tequilas, rums, and liqueurs. Brands include Jack Daniel's, Southern Comfort, Tequila Herradura, el Jimador Tequila, and Canadian Mist. Global depletions of Jack Daniel's in FY 08 (Apr.) increased 4%, compared to 6% in FY 07, and approached the 9.5 million nine-liter case mark. Statistics based on case sales rank Jack Daniel's as the largest selling American whiskey in the world, Canadian Mist as the second largest selling Canadian whiskey in the U.S. and third largest in the world, and Southern Comfort as the largest selling domestic proprietary liqueur in the U.S. Other major alcoholic beverage lines include Fetzer and Bolla wines, Finlandia vodka, Chambord liqueur, and Korbel Champagnes.

International sales, consisting principally of exports of wines and spirits, in-

creased to over $1.7 billion in FY 08, accounting for 52% of total net revenues. Beverage growth in recent years has come primarily from international markets for the company's spirits brands. The key export markets for brands include the U.K., Australia, Poland, Germany, Mexico, South Africa, Spain, France, Canada and Japan.

Until year-end FY 05, the consumer durables segment consisted of the Lenox Inc. subsidiary, which produced and marketed china, crystal and giftware under the Lenox and Gorham trademarks. The segment also included Dansk, a producer of tableware and giftware, Gorham, Kirk Steiff, and Hartmann Luggage. In July 2005, following a strategic review, the company agreed to sell Lenox to Department 56, Inc. for $190 million. On September 1, 2005, BF consummated the sale of substantially all of Lenox to Department 56 for $196 million. Consumer durables was eliminated as a segment, and in May 2007, the sale of substantially all of the assets of Hartmann to Clarion Capital Partners was completed.

## Company Financials Fiscal Year Ended Apr. 30

| Per Share Data ($) | 2008 | 2007 | 2006 | 2005 | 2004 | 2003 | 2002 | 2001 | 2000 | 1999 |
|---|---|---|---|---|---|---|---|---|---|---|
| Tangible Book Value | 2.24 | 1.42 | 6.79 | 4.55 | 3.43 | 1.93 | 6.17 | 5.40 | 4.54 | 3.81 |
| Cash Flow | 3.18 | 2.89 | 2.88 | 2.38 | 1.83 | 1.76 | 1.64 | 1.72 | 1.62 | 1.50 |
| Earnings | 2.85 | 2.58 | 2.56 | 2.02 | 1.69 | 1.45 | 1.33 | 1.36 | 1.27 | 1.17 |
| S&P Core Earnings | 2.82 | 2.54 | 2.52 | 1.90 | 1.66 | 1.24 | 1.11 | 1.22 | NA | NA |
| Dividends | 2.25 | 0.62 | 0.73 | 0.64 | 0.58 | 0.58 | 0.54 | 0.51 | 0.48 | 0.46 |
| Payout Ratio | 79% | 24% | 29% | 32% | 34% | 40% | 41% | 38% | 38% | 39% |
| Calendar Year | 2007 | 2006 | 2005 | 2004 | 2003 | 2002 | 2001 | 2000 | 1999 | 1998 |
| Prices:High | 63.90 | 66.04 | 57.92 | 40.07 | 38.05 | 32.22 | 28.80 | 27.70 | 30.90 | 30.75 |
| Prices:Low | 50.54 | 52.22 | 37.30 | 34.24 | 24.10 | 23.48 | 23.06 | 16.75 | 21.97 | 20.70 |
| P/E Ratio:High | 22 | 26 | 23 | 20 | 23 | 22 | 22 | 20 | 24 | 26 |
| P/E Ratio:Low | 18 | 20 | 15 | 17 | 14 | 16 | 17 | 12 | 17 | 18 |
| **Income Statement Analysis** (Million $) | | | | | | | | | | |
| Revenue | 3,282 | 2,806 | 2,444 | 2,729 | 2,577 | 2,378 | 1,958 | 1,924 | 1,877 | 1,776 |
| Operating Income | 735 | 627 | 560 | 513 | 473 | 429 | 408 | 438 | 410 | 377 |
| Depreciation | 52.0 | 44.0 | 44.0 | 58.0 | 56.0 | 55.0 | 55.0 | 64.0 | 62.0 | 55.0 |
| Interest Expense | 49.0 | 34.0 | 18.0 | 21.0 | 21.0 | 8.00 | 8.00 | 16.0 | 15.0 | 10.0 |
| Pretax Income | 644 | 586 | 559 | 476 | 388 | 373 | 348 | 366 | 343 | 318 |
| Effective Tax Rate | 31.7% | 31.7% | 29.3% | 35.3% | 33.5% | 34.3% | 34.5% | 36.3% | 36.4% | 36.5% |
| Net Income | 440 | 400 | 395 | 308 | 258 | 245 | 228 | 233 | 218 | 202 |
| S&P Core Earnings | 438 | 393 | 389 | 289 | 252 | 209 | 190 | 208 | NA | NA |
| **Balance Sheet & Other Financial Data** (Million $) | | | | | | | | | | |
| Cash | 119 | 283 | 475 | 295 | 68.0 | 72.0 | 116 | 86.0 | 180 | 171 |
| Current Assets | 1,456 | 1,635 | 1,610 | 1,317 | 1,083 | 1,068 | 1,029 | 994 | 1,020 | 999 |
| Total Assets | 3,405 | 3,551 | 2,728 | 2,624 | 2,376 | 2,264 | 2,016 | 1,939 | 1,802 | 1,735 |
| Current Liabilities | 984 | 1,347 | 569 | 638 | 369 | 548 | 495 | 538 | 522 | 517 |
| Long Term Debt | 417 | 422 | 351 | 352 | 630 | 629 | 40.0 | 40.0 | 41.0 | 53.0 |
| Common Equity | 1,725 | 1,672 | 1,563 | 1,310 | 1,085 | 840 | 1,311 | 1,187 | 1,048 | 917 |
| Total Capital | 2,231 | 2,150 | 2,047 | 1,794 | 1,837 | 1,547 | 1,409 | 1,289 | 1,184 | 1,107 |
| Capital Expenditures | 41.0 | 58.0 | 52.0 | 49.0 | 56.0 | 119 | 71.0 | 96.0 | 78.0 | 46.0 |
| Cash Flow | 492 | 444 | 439 | 366 | 314 | 300 | 283 | 297 | 280 | 257 |
| Current Ratio | 1.5 | 1.2 | 2.8 | 2.1 | 2.9 | 1.9 | 2.1 | 1.8 | 2.0 | 1.9 |
| % Long Term Debt of Capitalization | 18.7 | 19.6 | 17.1 | 19.6 | 34.3 | 40.7 | 2.8 | 3.1 | 3.5 | 4.8 |
| % Net Income of Revenue | 13.4 | 14.3 | 16.2 | 11.3 | 10.0 | 10.3 | 11.6 | 12.1 | 11.6 | 11.4 |
| % Return on Assets | 12.7 | 12.7 | 14.7 | 12.3 | 11.1 | 11.4 | 11.5 | 12.5 | 12.3 | 12.3 |
| % Return on Equity | 26.7 | 24.7 | 27.5 | 25.6 | 26.8 | 22.8 | 18.3 | 20.9 | 22.2 | 23.5 |

Data as orig reptd.; bef. results of disc opers/spec. items. Per share data adj. for stk. divs.; EPS diluted. E-Estimated. NA-Not Available. NM-Not Meaningful. NR-Not Ranked. UR-Under Review.

**Office:** 850 Dixie Highway, Louisville, KY 40210-1038.
**Telephone:** 502-585-1100.
**Website:** http://www.brown-forman.com
**Co-Chrmn:** G.G. Brown, IV

**Co-Chrmn & CEO:** P.C. Varga
**Vice Chrmn:** J.S. Welch, Jr.
**COO & EVP:** J.L. Bareuther
**EVP & CFO:** D.C. Berg

**Investor Contact:** T. Graven (502-774-7442)
**Board Members:** P. Bousquet-Chavanne, G. G. Brown, IV, M. S. Brown, Jr., D. G. Calder, J. D. Cook, S. A. Frazier, R. P. Mayer, W. E. Mitchell, M. R. Simmons, W. M. Street, D. B. Stubbs, P. C. Varga, J. S. Welch, Jr.

**Founded:** 1870
**Domicile:** Delaware
**Employees:** 4,466

The McGraw-Hill Companies

# Burlington Northern Santa Fe Corp

## STANDARD &POOR'S

| S&P Recommendation HOLD ★★★☆☆ | Price $79.63 (as of Nov 14, 2008) | 12-Mo. Target Price $92.00 | Investment Style Large-Cap Growth |
|---|---|---|---|

**GICS Sector** Industrials
**Sub-Industry** Railroads

**Summary** Through BNSF Railway Co. (formerly The Burlington Northern and Santa Fe Railway Co.), BNI owns one of the largest railroad networks in the U.S.

### Key Stock Statistics (Source S&P, Vickers, company reports)

| | | | | | | | |
|---|---|---|---|---|---|---|---|
| 52-Wk Range | $114.58– 74.20 | S&P Oper. EPS 2008E | 6.31 | Market Capitalization(B) | $27.259 | Beta | 1.20 |
| Trailing 12-Month EPS | $5.76 | S&P Oper. EPS 2009E | 6.93 | Yield (%) | 2.01 | S&P 3-Yr. Proj. EPS CAGR(%) | 12 |
| Trailing 12-Month P/E | 13.8 | P/E on S&P Oper. EPS 2008E | 12.6 | Dividend Rate/Share | $1.60 | S&P Credit Rating | BBB |
| $10K Invested 5 Yrs Ago | $28,704 | Common Shares Outstg. (M) | 342.3 | Institutional Ownership (%) | 80 | | |

### Price Performance

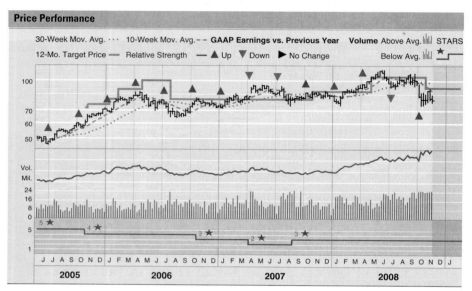

30-Week Mov. Avg. ···  10-Week Mov. Avg.- - GAAP Earnings vs. Previous Year   Volume Above Avg. STARS
12-Mo. Target Price — Relative Strength  — ▲ Up  ▼ Down  ► No Change   Below Avg.

Options: ASE, CBOE, P

Analysis prepared by **Kevin Kirkeby** on November 11, 2008, when the stock traded at **$ 82.75**.

### Qualitative Risk Assessment

| LOW | MEDIUM | HIGH |
|---|---|---|

Our risk assessment reflects what we believe is BNI's strong profitability, cash flow generation, and balance sheet, as well as a diverse customer base, offset somewhat by its exposure to economic cycles, freight demand, and regulations.

### Quantitative Evaluations

**S&P Quality Ranking**  A-

| D | C | B- | B | B+ | A- | A | A+ |
|---|---|---|---|---|---|---|---|

**Relative Strength Rank**  STRONG

72

LOWEST = 1          HIGHEST = 99

### Highlights

➤ We see revenue rising 16% in 2008, with two-thirds of that from fuel surcharges. We expect a 1.5% decline in volumes, but a 6% price gain. We anticipate that intermodal shipments will stay weak into 2009 due to shifts in ocean carrier routes and the weak outlook provided by various retailers. In our view, gains will mostly be achieved in non-cyclical segments like coal. We anticipate revenue growth will slow to about 8% in 2009, with 6% from pricing, 0.5% volume, and a flattening in fuel surcharges as diesel prices stabilize.

➤ We project that the operating margin in 2008 will narrow modestly to 22%, as we see the positive impact of higher pricing offset by the impact of severe weather and flooding in the first half of the year. We anticipate fuel will represent over 33% of BNI's total operating costs for 2008. For 2009, we see slightly wider margins on improved fuel recoveries and better asset utilization.

➤ We forecast EPS of $6.31 in 2008, excluding $0.26 in special charges, rising 10% to $6.93 in 2009. Our EPS estimate for 2008 factors in a 3% reduction in the average share count, based on BNI's buyback announcements.

### Investment Rationale/Risk

➤ Long-term, we think BNI will generate above-average revenue growth, driven by its exposure to the intermodal transport, long-haul coal and grain markets. For the 2008-2012 period, we see a compound annual growth rate in revenue of 8%, down from 17% over the prior three years. Reflecting continued gains in commodity shipments, but an apparent worsening in consumer spending, which will likely delay a turn in intermodal volumes, we think valuations near the middle of the 10-year range are warranted.

➤ Risks to our recommendation and target price include customer resistance to price increases, a greater role by regulators in setting rates, a reduction in long-haul grain exports, and a rerouting of containership cargoes away from West Coast ports.

➤ Our DCF model, which assumes an 8.9% weighted average cost of capital, 13% annual growth in free cash flow over the next five years, and 3.5% terminal growth, calculates an intrinsic value of $99. We believe an enterprise value to 12-month forward EBITDA ratio of 6.5X, which is near the 10-year average, is appropriate, leading to a value of $85. Combining these models, our 12-month target price is $92.

### Revenue/Earnings Data

**Revenue (Million $)**

| | 1Q | 2Q | 3Q | 4Q | Year |
|---|---|---|---|---|---|
| 2008 | 4,261 | 4,478 | 4,906 | -- | -- |
| 2007 | 3,645 | 3,843 | 4,069 | 4,245 | 15,802 |
| 2006 | 3,463 | 3,701 | 3,939 | 3,882 | 14,985 |
| 2005 | 2,982 | 3,138 | 3,317 | 3,550 | 12,987 |
| 2004 | 2,490 | 2,685 | 2,793 | 2,978 | 10,946 |
| 2003 | 2,232 | 2,294 | 2,395 | 2,492 | 9,413 |

**Earnings Per Share ($)**

| | 1Q | 2Q | 3Q | 4Q | Year |
|---|---|---|---|---|---|
| 2008 | 1.30 | 1.00 | 2.00 | E1.76 | E6.31 |
| 2007 | 0.96 | 1.20 | 1.48 | 1.46 | 5.10 |
| 2006 | 1.09 | 1.27 | 1.33 | 1.42 | 5.10 |
| 2005 | 0.83 | 0.96 | 1.09 | 1.13 | 4.01 |
| 2004 | 0.52 | 0.67 | 0.01 | 0.91 | 2.10 |
| 2003 | 0.40 | 0.54 | 0.55 | 0.61 | 2.09 |

Fiscal year ended Dec. 31. Next earnings report expected: Late January. EPS Estimates based on S&P Operating Earnings; historical GAAP earnings are as reported.

### Dividend Data (Dates: mm/dd Payment Date: mm/dd/yy)

| Amount ($) | Date Decl. | Ex-Div. Date | Stk. of Record | Payment Date |
|---|---|---|---|---|
| 0.320 | 02/13 | 03/07 | 03/11 | 04/01/08 |
| 0.320 | 04/24 | 06/06 | 06/10 | 07/01/08 |
| 0.400 | 07/24 | 09/08 | 09/10 | 10/01/08 |
| 0.400 | 10/23 | 12/10 | 12/12 | 01/02/09 |

Dividends have been paid since 1940. Source: Company reports.

# Burlington Northern Santa Fe Corp

**STANDARD & POOR'S**

## Business Summary November 11, 2008

CORPORATE OVERVIEW. Burlington Northern Santa Fe Corp., through its BNSF Railway Co. subsidiary, operates the second largest U.S. rail system, delivering about 49% of rail traffic in the West, and about 26% of U.S. rail traffic. BNSF operates a rail system of about 32,000 miles (23,000 owned, 9,000 trackage rights) that spans 28 western and midwestern states and two Canadian provinces.

MARKET PROFILE. We believe BNI's consumer/intermodal business, sensitive to U.S. import and consumption trends, is the industry volume leader, and is at the heart of its competitive strategy. Consumer freight provided 37% of freight revenues in 2007 and consisted primarily of intermodal service: international container traffic, services to United Parcel Service, less-than-truckload and truckload carriers, and automotive traffic. Industrial products, sensitive to U.S. GDP trends, provided 24% of freight revenues in 2007, and was comprised of construction and building products, chemicals, and petroleum. Coal accounted for 21% of 2007 freight revenues. A major transporter of low-sulfur coal, over 90% of BNI's coal traffic originates in the Powder River Basin of Wyoming and Montana, primarily delivered to power utilities. Agricultural products, sensitive to annual crop volumes, accounted for 18% of 2007 freight

revenues, including deliveries of grains, ethanol and fertilizer. We believe this has become BNI's most profitable segment due to a large spot market component, rather than long-term contracts, and large volume increases in the past two years.

COMPETITIVE LANDSCAPE. The U.S. rail industry has an oligopoly-like structure, with over 80% of revenues generated by the four largest railroads: BNI and Union Pacific Corp. operating on the West Coast, and CSX Corp. and Norfolk Southern Corp. operating on the East Coast. Railroads simultaneously compete for customers while cooperating by sharing assets, interfacing systems, and cooperatively fulfilling customer transports. Key suppliers include locomotive and rail equipment manufacturers, fuel suppliers, and labor. BNI's employees, about 85% of whom are unionized, enjoy above national average compensation due to their significant bargaining power.

## Company Financials Fiscal Year Ended Dec. 31

| Per Share Data ($) | 2007 | 2006 | 2005 | 2004 | 2003 | 2002 | 2001 | 2000 | 1999 | 1998 |
|---|---|---|---|---|---|---|---|---|---|---|
| Tangible Book Value | 70.50 | 29.04 | 25.57 | 24.71 | 22.84 | 21.10 | 20.33 | 19.08 | 17.96 | 16.53 |
| Cash Flow | 8.70 | 8.16 | 6.83 | 4.79 | 4.53 | 4.44 | 4.21 | 4.52 | 4.36 | 4.17 |
| Earnings | 5.10 | 5.10 | 4.01 | 2.10 | 2.09 | 2.00 | 1.89 | 2.36 | 2.45 | 2.43 |
| S&P Core Earnings | 5.15 | 5.13 | 4.10 | 2.03 | 2.01 | 1.75 | 1.73 | NA | NA | NA |
| Dividends | 1.14 | 0.90 | 0.74 | 0.64 | 0.54 | 0.48 | 0.49 | 0.48 | 0.48 | 0.42 |
| Payout Ratio | 22% | 18% | 18% | 30% | 26% | 24% | 26% | 20% | 20% | 17% |
| Prices:High | 95.47 | 87.99 | 72.00 | 49.25 | 32.50 | 31.75 | 34.00 | 29.56 | 37.94 | 35.71 |
| Prices:Low | 71.51 | 63.80 | 44.58 | 29.52 | 23.29 | 23.18 | 22.40 | 19.06 | 22.88 | 26.88 |
| P/E Ratio:High | 19 | 17 | 18 | 23 | 16 | 16 | 18 | 13 | 15 | 15 |
| P/E Ratio:Low | 14 | 13 | 11 | 14 | 11 | 12 | 12 | 8 | 9 | 11 |

| Income Statement Analysis (Million $) | | | | | | | | | | |
|---|---|---|---|---|---|---|---|---|---|---|
| Revenue | 15,802 | 14,985 | 12,987 | 10,946 | 9,413 | 8,979 | 9,208 | 9,205 | 9,100 | 8,941 |
| Operating Income | 4,860 | 4,625 | 3,997 | 2,698 | 2,575 | 2,587 | 2,664 | 3,003 | 3,096 | 2,990 |
| Depreciation | 1,293 | 1,130 | 1,075 | 1,012 | 910 | 931 | 909 | 895 | 897 | 832 |
| Interest Expense | 528 | 485 | 437 | 409 | 420 | 428 | 463 | 453 | 387 | 354 |
| Pretax Income | 2,957 | 2,992 | 2,448 | 1,273 | 1,231 | 1,216 | 1,182 | 1,585 | 1,819 | 1,849 |
| Effective Tax Rate | 38.2% | 36.9% | 37.5% | 37.9% | 36.9% | 37.5% | 37.6% | 38.2% | 37.5% | 37.5% |
| Net Income | 1,829 | 1,887 | 1,531 | 791 | 777 | 760 | 737 | 980 | 1,137 | 1,155 |
| S&P Core Earnings | 1,845 | 1,898 | 1,563 | 767 | 743 | 667 | 676 | NA | NA | NA |

| Balance Sheet & Other Financial Data (Million $) | | | | | | | | | | |
|---|---|---|---|---|---|---|---|---|---|---|
| Cash | 330 | 375 | 75.0 | 322 | 18.0 | 28.0 | 26.0 | 11.0 | 22.0 | 25.0 |
| Current Assets | 2,181 | 2,181 | 1,880 | 1,615 | 862 | 791 | 723 | 976 | 1,066 | 1,206 |
| Total Assets | 33,583 | 31,643 | 30,304 | 28,925 | 26,939 | 25,767 | 24,721 | 24,375 | 23,700 | 22,690 |
| Current Liabilities | 3,235 | 3,326 | 3,229 | 2,716 | 2,346 | 2,091 | 2,161 | 2,186 | 2,075 | 2,197 |
| Long Term Debt | 7,735 | 6,912 | 6,698 | 6,051 | 6,440 | 6,641 | 6,363 | 6,614 | 5,655 | 5,188 |
| Common Equity | 11,144 | 10,396 | 9,925 | 9,311 | 8,495 | 7,932 | 7,849 | 7,480 | 8,172 | 7,770 |
| Total Capital | 27,363 | 25,524 | 24,539 | 23,182 | 22,416 | 21,548 | 20,943 | 20,516 | 19,924 | 18,620 |
| Capital Expenditures | 2,248 | 2,014 | 1,750 | 1,527 | 1,726 | 1,358 | 1,459 | 1,399 | 1,788 | 2,147 |
| Cash Flow | 3,122 | 3,017 | 2,606 | 1,803 | 1,687 | 1,691 | 1,646 | 1,875 | 2,034 | 1,987 |
| Current Ratio | 0.7 | 0.7 | 0.6 | 0.6 | 0.4 | 0.4 | 0.3 | 0.4 | 0.5 | 0.5 |
| % Long Term Debt of Capitalization | 28.3 | 27.1 | 27.3 | 26.1 | 28.7 | 30.8 | 30.4 | 32.2 | 28.4 | 27.9 |
| % Net Income of Revenue | 11.6 | 12.6 | 11.8 | 7.2 | 8.3 | 8.5 | 8.0 | 10.6 | 12.5 | 12.9 |
| % Return on Assets | 5.6 | 6.1 | 5.2 | 2.8 | 2.9 | 3.0 | 3.0 | 4.1 | 4.9 | 5.2 |
| % Return on Equity | 17.0 | 18.9 | 15.6 | 8.9 | 9.5 | 9.6 | 9.6 | 12.5 | 14.3 | 15.8 |

Data as orig reptd.; bef. results of disc opers/spec. items. Per share data adj. for stk. divs.; EPS diluted. E-Estimated. NA-Not Available. NM-Not Meaningful. NR-Not Ranked. UR-Under Review.

**Office:** 2650 Lou Menk Dr, Fort Worth, TX 76131-2830.
**Telephone:** 800-795-2673.
**Email:** investor.relations@bnsf.com
**Website:** http://www.bnsf.com

**Chrmn, Pres & CEO:** M.K. Rose
**COO & EVP:** C.R. Ice
**EVP & CFO:** T.N. Hund
**EVP & Secy:** R. Nober

**CTO & CIO:** J.M. Olsovsky
**Investor Contact:** M. Bracker (817-352-4813)
**Board Members:** A. Boeckmann, D. G. Cook, V. S. Martinez, M. F. Racicot, R. S. Roberts, M. K. Rose, M. J. Shapiro, J. C. Watts, Jr., R. H. West, J. S. Whisler, E. E. Whitacre, Jr.

**Founded:** 1994
**Domicile:** Delaware
**Employees:** 40,000

# Cabot Oil & Gas Corp

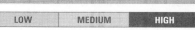

STANDARD
&POOR'S

| | | | |
|---|---|---|---|
| **S&P Recommendation** HOLD ★★★☆☆ | **Price** $26.54 (as of Nov 14, 2008) | **12-Mo. Target Price** $31.00 | **Investment Style** Large-Cap Growth |

**GICS Sector** Energy
**Sub-Industry** Oil & Gas Exploration & Production

**Summary** This company explores for, produces, purchases and markets natural gas, and, to a lesser extent, produces and sells crude oil.

## Key Stock Statistics (Source S&P, Vickers, company reports)

| | | | | | | | |
|---|---|---|---|---|---|---|---|
| 52-Wk Range | $72.92– 19.18 | S&P Oper. EPS 2008E | 2.31 | Market Capitalization(B) | $2.743 | Beta | 1.24 |
| Trailing 12-Month EPS | $2.09 | S&P Oper. EPS 2009E | 1.95 | Yield (%) | 0.45 | S&P 3-Yr. Proj. EPS CAGR(%) | 16 |
| Trailing 12-Month P/E | 12.7 | P/E on S&P Oper. EPS 2008E | 11.5 | Dividend Rate/Share | $0.12 | S&P Credit Rating | NA |
| $10K Invested 5 Yrs Ago | $30,340 | Common Shares Outstg. (M) | 103.4 | Institutional Ownership (%) | 91 | | |

## Price Performance

30-Week Mov. Avg. ··· · 10-Week Mov. Avg. – – **GAAP Earnings vs. Previous Year** Volume Above Avg. ▌▌▌ STARS
12-Mo. Target Price — Relative Strength — ▲ Up ▼ Down ▶ No Change Below Avg. ▌▌▌ ★

2-for-1

2005 | 2006 | 2007 | 2008

Options: ASE, CBOE, P, Ph

Analysis prepared by **Michael Kay** on November 03, 2008, when the stock traded at **$ 25.83**.

## Highlights

➤ Total volumes declined to 86 Bcfe in 2007 on the impact of sold assets; however, we believe COG met organic growth goals of 12%-18% via a successful drilling program. Continued drilling success, especially in the Gulf Coast at the County Line and Minden fields, as well as expected increases in Appalachia and Canada, have led to a 9% increase in volumes in the first nine months of 2008, and we see full year production growth of 13% and 2009's up 16% despite a lower drilling budget. Third quarter volumes were negatively impacted by hurricanes and missed estimates by 4%.

➤ In our view, asset sales have lowered the risk on COG's portfolio and will allow for continued drilling success. COG maintains a below-average cost profile, but we expect an 18% rise in 2008 lease operating expense, below peers.

➤ We see 2008 EBITDA rising 41% and EPS 31% on production gains and higher natural gas prices. We see exploration costs down 25%, after a similar decrease in 2007, and DD&A costs up 23% per Mcfe. COG's 2008 exploration and development budget is $750 million, and plans a 20% cut in 2009 to $600 million, with 90% allocated to the Marcellus Shale and East Texas.

## Investment Rationale/Risk

➤ We believe COG's core operating areas are performing well, with horizontal drilling programs in Appalachia and the County Line project in East Texas moving ahead nicely. We have greater confidence that COG can meet production goals and see strong potential for its large undeveloped acreage. COG plans five rigs to be redirected to the Marcellus shale in 2009, where it currently runs three rigs. In response to market conditions, COG has reduced leasing efforts in select areas and delayed wells, particularly in the West, and now sees a 2008 program of 450 wells.

➤ Risks to our recommendation and target price include declining oil and gas prices, difficulty replacing reserves, and production declines.

➤ A drop in oil and gas prices has caused a similar decline in E&P shares. On weakening economic forecasts, we see markets discounting most probable reserve estimates, and we value companies on our proven reserve NAV estimates. We blend our proven reserve NAV estimate of $40 with a target enterprise value to 2009 EBITDA of 4.5X and our DCF ($31; WACC 9.8%; terminal growth 3%), for a 12-month target price of $31.

## Qualitative Risk Assessment

| LOW | MEDIUM | HIGH |
|---|---|---|

Our risk assessment reflects that COG operates in a very capital-intensive industry that is cyclical and derives value from producing a commodity whose price is extremely volatile. In addition, we think the company struggles under a relatively uncompetitive cost structure. Partially offsetting this is its moderate use of debt and the primarily internal funding of its capital expenditures.

## Quantitative Evaluations

**S&P Quality Ranking** B+

| D | C | B- | B | B+ | A- | A | A+ |
|---|---|---|---|---|---|---|---|

**Relative Strength Rank** MODERATE

53

LOWEST = 1          HIGHEST = 99

## Revenue/Earnings Data

**Revenue (Million $)**

| | 1Q | 2Q | 3Q | 4Q | Year |
|---|---|---|---|---|---|
| 2008 | 219.7 | 248.9 | 244.8 | -- | -- |
| 2007 | 191.6 | 175.8 | 170.9 | 193.9 | 732.2 |
| 2006 | 214.8 | 190.8 | 184.7 | 171.7 | 762.0 |
| 2005 | 144.1 | 151.9 | 161.8 | 225.1 | 682.8 |
| 2004 | 136.6 | 119.7 | 119.4 | 154.6 | 530.4 |
| 2003 | 135.9 | 126.8 | 125.5 | 121.3 | 509.4 |

**Earnings Per Share ($)**

| | | | | | |
|---|---|---|---|---|---|
| 2008 | 0.47 | 0.55 | 0.64 | E0.45 | E2.31 |
| 2007 | 0.50 | 0.42 | 0.36 | 0.43 | 1.71 |
| 2006 | 0.55 | 0.47 | 1.92 | 0.33 | 3.32 |
| 2005 | 0.21 | 0.36 | 0.34 | 0.59 | 1.50 |
| 2004 | 0.19 | 0.20 | 0.18 | 0.33 | 0.90 |
| 2003 | -0.34 | 0.18 | 0.24 | 0.20 | 0.29 |

Fiscal year ended Dec. 31. Next earnings report expected: Mid February. EPS Estimates based on S&P Operating Earnings; historical GAAP earnings are as reported.

## Dividend Data (Dates: mm/dd Payment Date: mm/dd/yy)

| Amount ($) | Date Decl. | Ex-Div. Date | Stk. of Record | Payment Date |
|---|---|---|---|---|
| 0.030 | 01/23 | 02/05 | 02/07 | 02/21/08 |
| 0.030 | 04/30 | 05/09 | 05/13 | 05/27/08 |
| 0.030 | 07/24 | 08/06 | 08/08 | 08/22/08 |
| 0.030 | 10/29 | 11/07 | 11/12 | 11/26/08 |

Dividends have been paid since 1990. Source: Company reports.

**Please read the Required Disclosures and Analyst Certification on the last page of this report.**

The McGraw-Hill Companies

# Cabot Oil & Gas Corp

STANDARD
&POOR'S

## Business Summary November 03, 2008

CORPORATE OVERVIEW. Cabot Oil & Gas Corp. is an independent oil and gas company engaged in exploration, development, acquisition and exploitation of oil and gas properties located in five principal areas, including the Appalachian Basin, the Rocky Mountains, the Anadarko Basin, onshore and offshore the Texas and Louisiana Gulf Coast, and the gas basin of western Canada.

COG has funded most of its capital and exploration expenditures from operating cash flow. In 2007, it drilled 461 gross wells, with a success rate of 96%, compared to 387 gross wells, with a success rate of 96% in 2006. COG's proved reserves totaled 1,616 Bcfe at December 31, 2007, of which 97% was natural gas. This reserve level was up 14% from 1,416 Bcfe at December 31, 2006, on the strength of results from its drilling program and the increase in capital spending. In 2007, capital and exploration spending was $564.4 million, compared to $456.3 million of total capital and exploration spending in 2006. At the end of 2007, 73% of total proved reserves were developed and we estimate COG's reserve life to be 18.9 years, compared to 16.1 years at the end of 2006.

COG remains focused on its strategies of balancing its capital investments between acceptable risk and the strongest economics, along with balancing longer life investments that affect exploration opportunities. COG continues to use a portion of the cash flow from its long-lived natural gas reserves in the East and the Mid-Continent to fund exploration and development efforts in the Gulf Coast and Rocky Mountains areas.

MARKET PROFILE. COG's addressable market is the North American continent. As a relatively small onshore natural gas producer, COG competes in a fragmented market that is beginning to rationalize, in our view, with several large onshore players such as Devon Energy (DVN) and Chesapeake Energy (CHK) being the major agents of consolidation. We believe North America is a relatively mature supply source for hydrocarbons, and natural gas production has been relatively flat over the past seven years. COG has struggled to increase production and reserves organically, amid bureaucratic difficulties in the Rocky Mountain region, and increasing rates of decline in the Gulf region. We think that COG is beginning to create value in both the East and West regions employing so-called unconventional resource recovery techniques.

## Company Financials Fiscal Year Ended Dec. 31

| Per Share Data ($) | 2007 | 2006 | 2005 | 2004 | 2003 | 2002 | 2001 | 2000 | 1999 | 1998 |
|---|---|---|---|---|---|---|---|---|---|---|
| Tangible Book Value | 11.60 | 9.83 | 6.18 | 4.69 | 3.78 | 3.67 | 3.66 | 2.77 | 2.51 | 2.47 |
| Cash Flow | 3.36 | 4.57 | 2.58 | 1.94 | 1.27 | 1.18 | 1.41 | 0.93 | 0.79 | 0.58 |
| Earnings | 1.71 | 3.32 | 1.50 | 0.90 | 0.29 | 0.17 | 0.51 | 0.36 | 0.07 | 0.03 |
| S&P Core Earnings | 1.63 | 1.74 | 1.49 | 0.88 | 0.20 | 0.15 | 0.49 | NA | NA | NA |
| Dividends | 0.11 | 0.08 | 0.07 | 0.05 | 0.05 | 0.05 | 0.05 | 0.05 | 0.05 | 0.05 |
| Payout Ratio | 6% | 2% | 5% | 6% | 18% | 32% | 10% | 15% | 76% | NM |
| Prices:High | 42.50 | 33.26 | 26.75 | 16.30 | 10.17 | 8.85 | 11.45 | 10.67 | 6.67 | 8.00 |
| Prices:Low | 27.87 | 19.13 | 13.72 | 9.57 | 7.50 | 5.92 | 5.42 | 4.69 | 3.58 | 4.21 |
| P/E Ratio:High | 25 | 10 | 18 | 18 | 35 | 53 | 22 | 30 | 95 | NM |
| P/E Ratio:Low | 16 | 6 | 9 | 11 | 26 | 36 | 11 | 13 | 51 | NM |

| Income Statement Analysis (Million $) | | | | | | | | | | |
|---|---|---|---|---|---|---|---|---|---|---|
| Revenue | 732 | 762 | 683 | 530 | 509 | 354 | 447 | 369 | 182 | 160 |
| Operating Income | 423 | 436 | 380 | 278 | 252 | 182 | 191 | 132 | 35.5 | 26.9 |
| Depreciation, Depletion and Amortization | 162 | 129 | 108 | 103 | 94.9 | 96.5 | 80.6 | 53.4 | 53.4 | 41.2 |
| Interest Expense | 17.2 | 18.4 | 22.5 | 22.0 | 23.5 | 25.3 | 20.8 | 22.9 | 25.8 | 18.6 |
| Pretax Income | 258 | 511 | 236 | 139 | 43.0 | 23.8 | 74.5 | 41.9 | 13.7 | 8.81 |
| Effective Tax Rate | 35.0% | 37.1% | 37.2% | 36.2% | 35.0% | 32.3% | 36.8% | 39.3% | 37.7% | 39.8% |
| Net Income | 167 | 321 | 148 | 88.4 | 28.0 | 16.1 | 47.1 | 25.5 | 8.52 | 5.30 |
| S&P Core Earnings | 159 | 172 | 148 | 87.2 | 19.1 | 14.4 | 45.1 | NA | NA | NA |

| Balance Sheet & Other Financial Data (Million $) | | | | | | | | | | |
|---|---|---|---|---|---|---|---|---|---|---|
| Cash | 30.1 | 41.9 | 10.6 | 10.0 | 0.72 | 2.56 | 5.71 | 7.57 | 1.68 | 2.20 |
| Current Assets | 221 | 316 | 230 | 195 | 121 | 93.1 | 85.0 | 110 | 66.6 | 71.1 |
| Total Assets | 2,209 | 1,834 | 1,495 | 1,211 | 1,024 | 1,055 | 1,069 | 736 | 659 | 704 |
| Current Liabilities | 252 | 251 | 219 | 197 | 155 | 123 | 110 | 118 | 89.9 | 99.0 |
| Long Term Debt | 350 | 220 | 320 | 250 | 270 | 365 | 393 | 253 | 277 | 327 |
| Common Equity | 1,070 | 945 | 600 | 456 | 365 | 351 | 347 | 243 | 186 | 183 |
| Total Capital | 1,882 | 1,513 | 1,210 | 953 | 815 | 916 | 940 | 604 | 559 | 596 |
| Capital Expenditures | 557 | 467 | 351 | 207 | 122 | 103 | 127 | 99.4 | 82.2 | 204 |
| Cash Flow | 329 | 450 | 257 | 192 | 123 | 113 | 128 | 76.7 | 58.5 | 43.1 |
| Current Ratio | 0.9 | 1.3 | 1.1 | 1.0 | 0.8 | 0.8 | 0.8 | 0.9 | 0.7 | 0.7 |
| % Long Term Debt of Capitalization | 23.6 | 14.5 | 26.5 | 26.2 | 33.1 | 39.9 | 41.8 | 41.9 | 49.6 | 54.9 |
| % Return on Assets | 8.3 | 19.3 | 11.0 | 7.8 | 2.7 | 1.5 | 5.2 | 3.7 | 1.2 | 0.9 |
| % Return on Equity | 16.6 | 41.6 | 28.1 | 21.5 | 7.8 | 4.6 | 16.0 | 10.9 | 2.8 | 1.0 |

Data as orig reptd.; bef. results of disc opers/spec. items. Per share data adj. for stk. divs.; EPS diluted. E-Estimated. NA-Not Available. NM-Not Meaningful. NR-Not Ranked. UR-Under Review.

**Office:** 1200 Enclave Parkway, Houston, TX 77077.
**Telephone:** 281-589-4600.
**Website:** http://www.cabotog.com
**Chrmn, Pres & CEO:** D.O. Dinges

**COO & SVP:** M.B. Walen
**Investor Contact:** S.C. Schroeder (281-589-4993)
**Chief Acctg Officer, Treas & Cntlr:** H.C. Smyth
**Secy:** L.A. Machesney

**Board Members:** R. J. Best, J. G. Cabot, D. M. Carmichael, D. O. Dinges, R. L. Keiser, R. Kelley, P. D. Peacock, W. P. Vititoe

**Founded:** 1989
**Domicile:** Delaware
**Employees:** 404

# Cameron International Corp

**STANDARD &POOR'S**

| S&P Recommendation | HOLD ★★★☆☆ | Price<br>$20.62 (as of Nov 14, 2008) | 12-Mo. Target Price<br>$31.00 | Investment Style<br>Large-Cap Growth |
|---|---|---|---|---|

**GICS Sector** Energy
**Sub-Industry** Oil & Gas Equipment & Services

**Summary** This company is a leading international manufacturer of oil and gas blowout preventers, flow control valves, surface and subsea production systems, and related oilfield services products.

## Key Stock Statistics (Source S&P, Vickers, company reports)

| | | | | | | | | |
|---|---|---|---|---|---|---|---|---|
| 52-Wk Range | $58.53– 17.05 | S&P Oper. EPS 2008E | 2.66 | Market Capitalization(B) | $4.526 | Beta | 1.05 |
| Trailing 12-Month EPS | $2.46 | S&P Oper. EPS 2009E | 3.15 | Yield (%) | Nil | S&P 3-Yr. Proj. EPS CAGR(%) | 29 |
| Trailing 12-Month P/E | 8.4 | P/E on S&P Oper. EPS 2008E | 7.8 | Dividend Rate/Share | Nil | S&P Credit Rating | BBB+ |
| $10K Invested 5 Yrs Ago | $18,758 | Common Shares Outstg. (M) | 219.5 | Institutional Ownership (%) | 100 | | |

## Price Performance

30-Week Mov. Avg. ···  10-Week Mov. Avg. – –  **GAAP Earnings vs. Previous Year**  Volume Above Avg. ▌▍▌ STARS
12-Mo. Target Price ——  Relative Strength — — ▲ Up ▼ Down ► No Change  Below Avg. ▕▏▏ ★

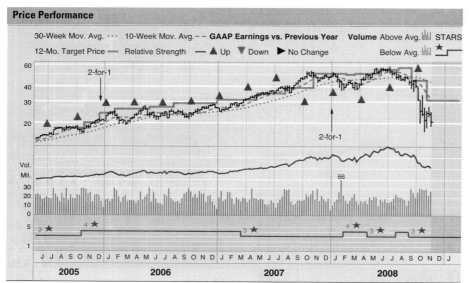

Options: ASE, CBOE, P, Ph

Analysis prepared by **Stewart Glickman, CFA** on November 12, 2008, when the stock traded at **$ 21.46.**

## Highlights

➤ In October, CAM said that approximately 70% of its $6.2 billion in backlog supports projects targeting deepwater subsea development, an area which we expect to maintain moderate growth in 2009 despite the recent drop in oil prices, given that such projects are typically pursued by deep-pocketed customers over a long time horizon. Also, CAM noted that 70% of its backlog was directed outside of North America, where we see the brunt of the expected 2009 pullback in upstream capital spending taking place.

➤ We see 2009 total revenue growth of about 12%, led by 12% growth in DPS. We see 2009 EBITDA margins of around 18.5%, versus a projected 17.9% in 2008. We believe that cost inflation pressures will abate somewhat in 2009, given an expected pullback in upstream capital spending. The total value of new orders was $2.61 billion in the third quarter of 2008, up about 96% from the $1.33 billion a year earlier. Total backlog rose about 18% sequentially, to $6.2 billion.

➤ We see EPS of $2.66 in 2008, rising to $3.15 in 2009.

## Investment Rationale/Risk

➤ Fundamentally, we view CAM as a play on expected growth in demand for oilfield capital equipment, where we see robust prospects in the long term, albeit with an expected deceleration in demand in 2009. As a major provider in the subsea completion market, CAM should benefit from expected gains in deepwater drilling. Long term, we think that North American demand for surface equipment, distributed valves and engineered valves will improve as a result of growing interest in unconventional natural gas plays.

➤ Risks to our recommendation and target price include less demand for pressure control equipment; lower than expected oil and natural gas prices; delays in completion of manufacturing facility expansions; and rising cost inflation.

➤ Our DCF model, assuming free cash flow growth of about 8% per year for 10 years, 3% thereafter, and a WACC of 12.9%, indicates intrinsic value of about $34. Using a 5.5X multiple of projected 2009 EBITDA and a 7.5X multiple on estimated 2009 operating cash flow (in line with peers), and blending with our DCF model, our 12-month target price is $31.

## Qualitative Risk Assessment

| LOW | MEDIUM | HIGH |
|---|---|---|

Our risk assessment reflects CAM's exposure to volatile crude oil and natural gas prices, capital spending decisions made by its oil and gas producing customers, and political risk associated with operating in frontier regions. Offsetting these risks is CAM's strength in deepwater-related applications.

## Quantitative Evaluations

**S&P Quality Ranking**     B

| D | C | B- | B | B+ | A- | A | A+ |
|---|---|---|---|---|---|---|---|

**Relative Strength Rank**     WEAK

27

LOWEST = 1     HIGHEST = 99

## Revenue/Earnings Data

**Revenue (Million $)**

| | 1Q | 2Q | 3Q | 4Q | Year |
|---|---|---|---|---|---|
| 2008 | 1,339 | 1,481 | 1,505 | -- | -- |
| 2007 | 997.0 | 1,139 | 1,186 | 1,344 | 4,666 |
| 2006 | 829.7 | 857.8 | 978.8 | 1,077 | 3,743 |
| 2005 | 547.9 | 594.8 | 636.6 | 738.6 | 2,518 |
| 2004 | 462.5 | 544.6 | 538.5 | 547.3 | 2,093 |
| 2003 | 361.1 | 400.9 | 429.1 | 443.2 | 1,634 |

**Earnings Per Share ($)**

| | 1Q | 2Q | 3Q | 4Q | Year |
|---|---|---|---|---|---|
| 2008 | 0.55 | 0.65 | 0.73 | E0.74 | E2.66 |
| 2007 | 0.44 | 0.54 | 0.66 | 0.54 | 2.17 |
| 2006 | 0.24 | 0.32 | 0.39 | 0.42 | 1.36 |
| 2005 | 0.13 | 0.18 | 0.22 | 0.24 | 0.76 |
| 2004 | 0.08 | 0.09 | 0.14 | 0.14 | 0.44 |
| 2003 | 0.04 | 0.09 | 0.11 | 0.02 | 0.26 |

Fiscal year ended Dec. 31. Next earnings report expected: Early February. EPS Estimates based on S&P Operating Earnings; historical GAAP earnings are as reported.

## Dividend Data (Dates: mm/dd Payment Date: mm/dd/yy)

| Amount<br>($) | Date<br>Decl. | Ex-Div.<br>Date | Stk. of<br>Record | Payment<br>Date |
|---|---|---|---|---|
| 2-for-1 | 12/07 | 12/31 | 12/17 | 12/28/07 |

Source: Company reports.

---

**Please read the Required Disclosures and Analyst Certification on the last page of this report.**

*The McGraw-Hill Companies*

# Cameron International Corp

STANDARD
&POOR'S

## Business Summary November 12, 2008

CORPORATE OVERVIEW. Cameron International, an international provider of oil and gas pressure control equipment, is organized into three business segments: Drilling & Production Systems (DPS), Valves & Measurement (V&M), and Compression. Primary customers of DPS, V&M and Compression are major and independent oil and gas exploration companies, foreign national oil and gas companies, drilling contractors, pipeline companies, refiners, and other industrial and petrochemical processing companies. The company serves customers in North America (37% of 2007 revenues), Asia/Middle East (21%), Europe (20%), Africa (13%), South America (7%), and Other (2%).

Drilling & Production Systems (62% of 2007 revenues and 59% of 2007 segment pretax income) manufactures pressure control equipment used at the wellhead in drilling, production and transmission of oil and gas, both onshore and offshore. Primary products include wellheads, drilling valves, blowout preventers, and control systems, marketed under the brand names Cameron, W-K-M, McEvoy, Willis, and Ingram Cactus. The segment also makes subsea production systems, which tend to be highly sophisticated technically. The company believes subsea capacity additions at manufacturing plants in Eng-

land, Brazil and Germany provide support for increased completions of subsea trees and associated manifolds, production controls and other equipment in the future.

Valves & Measurement (27%, 32%), split out from the DPS division as a separately managed business in 1995, provides a full range of ball valves, gate valves, butterfly valves, and accessories used primarily to control pressures and direct oil and gas as they are moved from individual wellheads through transmission systems to refineries, petrochemical plants, and other processing centers. In September 2005, CAM announced an agreement to acquire substantially all of the flow control businesses of Dresser Inc.; the acquisition was completed in January 2006. The acquisition, which expanded the company's valve product line, totaled $217.5 million in cash and assumed debt. The acquired businesses were added to the company's V&M segment.

## Company Financials Fiscal Year Ended Dec. 31

| Per Share Data ($) | 2007 | 2006 | 2005 | 2004 | 2003 | 2002 | 2001 | 2000 | 1999 | 1998 |
|---|---|---|---|---|---|---|---|---|---|---|
| Tangible Book Value | 6.67 | 5.11 | 4.40 | 3.83 | 3.81 | 3.39 | 2.92 | 2.69 | 2.14 | 2.29 |
| Cash Flow | 2.52 | 1.79 | 1.11 | 0.83 | 0.59 | 0.58 | 0.78 | 0.47 | 0.58 | 0.95 |
| Earnings | 2.17 | 1.36 | 0.76 | 0.44 | 0.26 | 0.28 | 0.44 | 0.13 | 0.20 | 0.62 |
| S&P Core Earnings | 2.27 | 1.43 | 0.73 | 0.34 | 0.17 | 0.12 | 0.21 | NA | NA | NA |
| Dividends | Nil | Nil | Nil | Nil | Nil | Nil | Nil | Nil | Nil | Nil |
| Payout Ratio | Nil | Nil | Nil | Nil | Nil | Nil | Nil | Nil | Nil | Nil |
| Prices:High | 53.83 | 28.91 | 21.55 | 14.19 | 13.90 | 14.90 | 18.25 | 20.97 | 12.50 | 17.75 |
| Prices:Low | 24.30 | 19.04 | 12.76 | 10.01 | 10.25 | 8.98 | 7.21 | 10.59 | 5.56 | 5.03 |
| P/E Ratio:High | 25 | 21 | 28 | 32 | 53 | 54 | 42 | NM | 64 | 29 |
| P/E Ratio:Low | 11 | 14 | 17 | 23 | 39 | 33 | 16 | NM | 29 | 8 |

| Income Statement Analysis (Million $) | | | | | | | | | | |
|---|---|---|---|---|---|---|---|---|---|---|
| Revenue | 4,666 | 3,743 | 2,518 | 2,093 | 1,634 | 1,538 | 1,564 | 1,387 | 1,465 | 1,882 |
| Operating Income | 814 | 605 | 340 | 232 | 164 | 196 | 251 | 215 | 193 | 323 |
| Depreciation, Depletion and Amortization | 81.5 | 101 | 78.4 | 82.8 | 83.6 | 77.9 | 83.1 | 75.3 | 83.7 | 72.5 |
| Interest Expense | 23.3 | 20.7 | 12.0 | 17.8 | 8.16 | 7.98 | 5.62 | 18.0 | 27.8 | 32.7 |
| Pretax Income | 708 | 489 | 263 | 133 | 77.6 | 85.1 | 143 | 43.8 | 70.9 | 196 |
| Effective Tax Rate | 29.3% | 35.0% | 34.9% | 29.0% | 26.2% | 29.0% | 31.0% | 36.8% | 39.4% | 30.4% |
| Net Income | 501 | 318 | 171 | 94.4 | 57.2 | 60.5 | 98.3 | 27.7 | 43.0 | 136 |
| S&P Core Earnings | 527 | 333 | 167 | 73.1 | 37.5 | 23.3 | 44.0 | NA | NA | NA |

| Balance Sheet & Other Financial Data (Million $) | | | | | | | | | | |
|---|---|---|---|---|---|---|---|---|---|---|
| Cash | 740 | 1,034 | 362 | 227 | 292 | 274 | 112 | 16.6 | 8.22 | 21.3 |
| Current Assets | 3,072 | 2,908 | 1,728 | 1,205 | 1,148 | 1,018 | 965 | 688 | 705 | 966 |
| Total Assets | 4,731 | 4,351 | 3,099 | 2,356 | 2,141 | 1,998 | 1,875 | 1,494 | 1,471 | 1,824 |
| Current Liabilities | 1,693 | 1,628 | 922 | 528 | 680 | 375 | 378 | 346 | 422 | 530 |
| Long Term Debt | 742 | 745 | 444 | 458 | 204 | 463 | 459 | 188 | 196 | 364 |
| Common Equity | 2,095 | 1,741 | 1,595 | 1,228 | 1,137 | 1,041 | 976 | 842 | 714 | 780 |
| Total Capital | 2,909 | 2,577 | 2,078 | 1,727 | 1,387 | 1,550 | 1,477 | 1,069 | 949 | 1,196 |
| Capital Expenditures | 246 | 185 | 77.5 | 53.5 | 64.7 | 82.1 | 125 | 66.6 | 55.7 | 108 |
| Cash Flow | 582 | 419 | 250 | 177 | 141 | 138 | 181 | 103 | 127 | 209 |
| Current Ratio | 1.8 | 1.8 | 1.9 | 2.3 | 1.7 | 2.7 | 2.6 | 2.0 | 1.7 | 1.8 |
| % Long Term Debt of Capitalization | 26.2 | 28.9 | 21.4 | 26.5 | 14.7 | 29.9 | 31.1 | 17.6 | 20.6 | 30.5 |
| % Return on Assets | 11.0 | 8.5 | 6.3 | 4.2 | 2.8 | 3.1 | 5.8 | 1.9 | 2.6 | 7.9 |
| % Return on Equity | 26.1 | 19.1 | 12.1 | 8.0 | 5.3 | 6.2 | 10.6 | 3.6 | 5.8 | 19.1 |

Data as orig reptd.; bef. results of disc opers/spec. items. Per share data adj. for stk. divs.; EPS diluted. E-Estimated. NA-Not Available. NM-Not Meaningful. NR-Not Ranked. UR-Under Review.

**Office:** 1333 West Loop South , Houston, TX 77027-9118.
**Telephone:** 713-513-3300.
**Website:** http://www.c-a-m.com
**Chrmn:** S.R. Erikson

**Pres & CEO:** J.B. Moore
**SVP, Secy & General Counsel:** W.C. Lemmer
**CFO:** C.M. Sledge
**CTO:** J.C. Bartos

**Investor Contact:** R.S. Amann (713-513-3344)
**Board Members:** N. M. Avery, C. B. Cunningham, S. R. Erikson, P. J. Fluor, D. L. Foshee, J. B. Moore, M. E. Patrick, D. W. Ross, III, B. W. Wilkinson

**Founded:** 1994
**Domicile:** Delaware
**Employees:** 15,400

# Campbell Soup Co

**STANDARD &POOR'S**

| S&P Recommendation | HOLD ★ ★ ★ ☆ ☆ | Price | 12-Mo. Target Price | Investment Style |
|---|---|---|---|---|
| | | $37.53 (as of Nov 14, 2008) | $38.00 | Large-Cap Growth |

**GICS Sector** Consumer Staples
**Sub-Industry** Packaged Foods & Meats

**Summary** Campbell Soup is a major producer of branded soups and other grocery food products.

## Key Stock Statistics (Source S&P, Vickers, company reports)

| | | | | | | | |
|---|---|---|---|---|---|---|---|
| 52-Wk Range | $40.85– 30.19 | S&P Oper. EPS 2009E | 2.22 | Market Capitalization(B) | $13.534 | Beta | 0.19 |
| Trailing 12-Month EPS | $3.06 | S&P Oper. EPS 2010E | NA | Yield (%) | 2.66 | S&P 3-Yr. Proj. EPS CAGR(%) | 7 |
| Trailing 12-Month P/E | 12.3 | P/E on S&P Oper. EPS 2009E | 16.9 | Dividend Rate/Share | $1.00 | S&P Credit Rating | A |
| $10K Invested 5 Yrs Ago | $16,213 | Common Shares Outstg. (M) | 360.6 | Institutional Ownership (%) | 41 | | |

## Price Performance

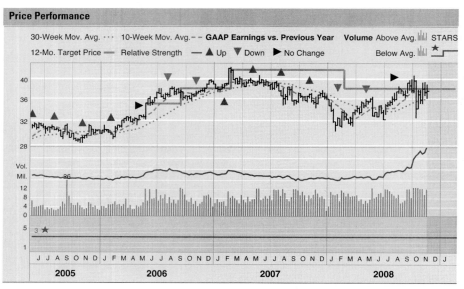

30-Week Mov. Avg. · · · 10-Week Mov. Avg. - - - **GAAP Earnings vs. Previous Year**   Volume Above Avg. STARS
12-Mo. Target Price —   Relative Strength — ▲ Up ▼ Down ► No Change   Below Avg.

Options: ASE, CBOE, P, Ph

Analysis prepared by **Tom Graves, CFA** on August 22, 2008, when the stock traded at **$ 37.34**.

## Highlights

➤ In FY 09 (Jul.), we look for net sales from continuing operations to rise about 4% from the $7.9 billion we project for FY 08, which has a 53rd week. These sales estimates exclude the Godiva chocolate business, which CPB sold to Yildiz Holding A.S. for $850 million in March 2008. Also, in FY 08, we see CPB's sales receiving a boost from currency translation. In FY 09, we do not anticipate currency fluctuation being as much of a favorable factor to sale growth.

➤ In FY 09, we expect CPB's sales to benefit from new or enhanced products. We anticipate that lower-salt and improved convenience products will help longer-term soup sales. We expect that profit margins will face pressure in FY 09 from cost inflation, at least partly offset by productivity gains and price increases.

➤ Excluding special items, we estimate FY 09 EPS from continuing operations of $2.15, up from the $2.00 projected for FY 08. Estimates for both years include some relatively modest EPS dilution from CPB's entry into the Russian and Chinese markets. We are encouraged by the news, in June 2008, that CPB directors have authorized a new program to repurchase up to $1.2 billion of the company's stock.

## Investment Rationale/Risk

➤ In FY 08's first nine months, CPB's gross profit margin from continuing operations narrowed to 39.9%, from 41.0% in the year-ago period, largely due to cost inflation and higher promotional spending. Longer term, we expect the company's revenue and profit growth prospects to be bolstered by new or enhanced products, increasingly portable packaging, and some expanded distribution, including overseas markets.

➤ Risks to our recommendation and target price include competitive pressures in CPB's businesses, consumer acceptance of new products, and the company's ability to achieve sales and earnings growth forecasts.

➤ The stock recently traded at about 17.7X our calendar 2008 EPS estimate from continuing operations of $2.10, which was a modest P/E discount to the average valuation of other packaged food stocks. Our 12-month target price of $38 is based on our expectation that the stock will trade at about a 5% P/E discount to other food stocks. The shares had a recent indicated dividend yield of about 2.4%.

## Qualitative Risk Assessment

| LOW | MEDIUM | HIGH |
|---|---|---|

Our risk assessment for Campbell Soup reflects the relatively stable nature of the company's end markets, our view that the company has strong cash flow, and corporate governance practices that we see as favorable relative to peers.

## Quantitative Evaluations

### S&P Quality Ranking
B+

| D | C | B- | B | B+ | A- | A | A+ |
|---|---|---|---|---|---|---|---|

### Relative Strength Rank
**STRONG**

93

LOWEST = 1                HIGHEST = 99

## Revenue/Earnings Data

### Revenue (Million $)

| | 1Q | 2Q | 3Q | 4Q | Year |
|---|---|---|---|---|---|
| 2008 | 2,185 | 2,218 | 1,880 | 1,715 | 7,998 |
| 2007 | 2,153 | 2,252 | 1,868 | 1,594 | 7,867 |
| 2006 | 2,002 | 2,159 | 1,728 | 1,454 | 7,343 |
| 2005 | 2,091 | 2,223 | 1,736 | 1,498 | 7,548 |
| 2004 | 1,909 | 2,100 | 1,667 | 1,433 | 7,109 |
| 2003 | 1,705 | 1,918 | 1,600 | 1,455 | 6,678 |

### Earnings Per Share ($)

| | | | | | |
|---|---|---|---|---|---|
| 2008 | 0.69 | 0.67 | 0.14 | 0.24 | 1.76 |
| 2007 | 0.66 | 0.72 | 0.55 | 0.24 | 2.08 |
| 2006 | 0.69 | 0.58 | 0.35 | 0.20 | 1.82 |
| 2005 | 0.56 | 0.57 | 0.35 | 0.23 | 1.71 |
| 2004 | 0.51 | 0.57 | 0.34 | 0.14 | 1.57 |
| 2003 | 0.47 | 0.56 | 0.31 | 0.18 | 1.52 |

Fiscal year ended Jul. 31. Next earnings report expected: Late November. EPS Estimates based on S&P Operating Earnings; historical GAAP earnings are as reported.

## Dividend Data (Dates: mm/dd Payment Date: mm/dd/yy)

| Amount ($) | Date Decl. | Ex-Div. Date | Stk. of Record | Payment Date |
|---|---|---|---|---|
| 0.220 | 11/15 | 12/27 | 12/31 | 01/28/08 |
| 0.220 | 03/27 | 04/03 | 04/07 | 04/28/08 |
| 0.220 | 06/26 | 07/02 | 07/07 | 08/04/08 |
| 0.250 | 09/25 | 10/02 | 10/06 | 11/03/08 |

Dividends have been paid since 1902. Source: Company reports.

---

**Please read the Required Disclosures and Analyst Certification on the last page of this report.**

# Campbell Soup Co

**STANDARD &POOR'S**

## Business Summary August 22, 2008

CORPORATE OVERVIEW. Probably known best for its ubiquitous red and white soup cans (elevated to icon status by Andy Warhol), Campbell Soup Co. is a major force in the U.S. packaged foods industry. The company, which traces its origins in the food business back to 1869, manufactures and markets a wide array of branded, prepared convenience food products worldwide.

In FY 07 (Jul.), operations outside the U.S. accounted for 30% of net sales and 20% of segment operating profits (before corporate expense), with much of the international sales and profits coming from Australia/Asia Pacific (13% of total net sales and 7% of segment profits) and Europe (9% and 4%).

The company reports results based on the following segments: U.S. Soup, Sauces and Beverages (44% of FY 07 sales, 62% of FY 07 segment profits); Baking and Snacking (24%, 17%), International Soup and Sauces (18%, 12%), and Other (14%, 9%).

Campbell's U.S. Soup, Sauces and Beverages segment includes major U.S. products such as both condensed and ready-to-serve soups (Campbell's, Home Cookin', Chunky, Healthy Request); broth (Swanson); chili (Campbell's Chunky); meal kits (Campbell's Supper Bakes); juices (Campbell's Tomato, V8,

V8 Splash); canned pasta, gravies and beans (Campbell's); spaghetti sauce (Prego); and Mexican sauces (Pace).

The company's Baking and Snacking division includes Pepperidge Farm cookies, crackers, breads and frozen products in the U.S.; Arnotts biscuits in Australia and Asia Pacific; and Arnotts salty snacks in Australia. The International Soup and Sauces segment includes the soup, sauces and beverage businesses outside of the United States, including Europe, Mexico, Latin America, the Asia Pacific region, and the retail business in Canada.

The balance of the portfolio reported in Other included Godiva Chocolatier (worldwide) and the company's Away From Home operations, which represent the distribution of products such as soup, specialty entrees, beverage products, other prepared foods and Pepperidge Farm products through various foodservice channels in the U.S. and Canada.

## Company Financials Fiscal Year Ended Jul. 31

| Per Share Data ($) | 2008 | 2007 | 2006 | 2005 | 2004 | 2003 | 2002 | 2001 | 2000 | 1999 |
|---|---|---|---|---|---|---|---|---|---|---|
| Tangible Book Value | NM | NM | NM | NM | NM | NM | NM | NM | NM | NM |
| Cash Flow | NA | 2.79 | 2.52 | 2.39 | 2.20 | 2.11 | 2.05 | 2.19 | 2.23 | 2.20 |
| Earnings | 1.76 | 2.08 | 1.82 | 1.71 | 1.57 | 1.52 | 1.28 | 1.55 | 1.65 | 1.63 |
| S&P Core Earnings | 1.52 | 1.95 | 1.81 | 1.63 | 1.47 | 1.46 | 1.00 | 1.28 | NA | NA |
| Dividends | 0.88 | 0.80 | 0.72 | 0.68 | 0.63 | 0.63 | 0.63 | 0.90 | 0.68 | 0.89 |
| Payout Ratio | 50% | 38% | 40% | 40% | 40% | 41% | 49% | 58% | 41% | 55% |
| Prices:High | 40.85 | 42.65 | 39.98 | 31.60 | 30.52 | 27.90 | 30.00 | 35.44 | 39.63 | 55.75 |
| Prices:Low | 30.19 | 34.17 | 28.88 | 27.35 | 25.03 | 19.95 | 19.65 | 25.52 | 23.75 | 37.44 |
| P/E Ratio:High | 23 | 21 | 22 | 18 | 19 | 18 | 23 | 23 | 24 | 34 |
| P/E Ratio:Low | 17 | 16 | 16 | 16 | 16 | 13 | 15 | 16 | 14 | 23 |

| Income Statement Analysis (Million $) | | | | | | | | | | |
|---|---|---|---|---|---|---|---|---|---|---|
| Revenue | 7,998 | 7,867 | 7,343 | 7,548 | 7,109 | 6,678 | 6,133 | 6,664 | 6,267 | 6,424 |
| Operating Income | NA | 1,541 | 1,445 | 1,483 | 1,394 | 1,376 | 1,442 | 1,470 | 1,516 | 1,625 |
| Depreciation | 271 | 23.0 | 289 | 279 | 260 | 243 | 319 | 266 | 251 | 255 |
| Interest Expense | NA | 163 | 165 | 184 | 174 | 186 | 190 | 216 | 192 | 184 |
| Pretax Income | 939 | 1,149 | 1,001 | 1,030 | 947 | 924 | 798 | 987 | 1,077 | 1,097 |
| Effective Tax Rate | 28.5% | 28.4% | 24.6% | 31.4% | 31.7% | 32.3% | 34.2% | 34.2% | 33.7% | 34.0% |
| Net Income | 671 | 823 | 755 | 707 | 647 | 626 | 525 | 649 | 714 | 724 |
| S&P Core Earnings | 579 | 772 | 751 | 675 | 603 | 604 | 413 | 536 | NA | NA |

| Balance Sheet & Other Financial Data (Million $) | | | | | | | | | | |
|---|---|---|---|---|---|---|---|---|---|---|
| Cash | 81.0 | 71.0 | 657 | 40.0 | 32.0 | 32.0 | 21.0 | 24.0 | 27.0 | 6.00 |
| Current Assets | NA | 1,578 | 2,112 | 1,512 | 1,481 | 1,290 | 1,199 | 1,221 | 1,168 | 1,294 |
| Total Assets | 6,474 | 6,445 | 7,870 | 6,776 | 6,675 | 6,205 | 5,721 | 5,927 | 5,196 | 5,522 |
| Current Liabilities | NA | 2,030 | 2,962 | 2,002 | 2,339 | 2,783 | 2,678 | 3,120 | 3,032 | 3,146 |
| Long Term Debt | NA | 2,074 | 2,116 | 2,542 | 2,543 | 2,249 | 2,449 | 2,243 | 1,218 | 1,330 |
| Common Equity | 1,318 | 1,295 | 1,768 | 1,270 | 874 | 387 | -114 | -247 | 137 | 275 |
| Total Capital | NA | 3,369 | 3,884 | 3,812 | 3,417 | 2,636 | 2,335 | 1,996 | 1,355 | 1,564 |
| Capital Expenditures | 298 | 334 | 309 | 332 | 288 | 283 | 269 | 200 | 200 | 297 |
| Cash Flow | NA | 1,106 | 1,044 | 986 | 907 | 869 | 844 | 915 | 965 | 979 |
| Current Ratio | 0.7 | 0.8 | 0.7 | 0.8 | 0.6 | 0.5 | 0.4 | 0.4 | 0.4 | 0.4 |
| % Long Term Debt of Capitalization | 55.3 | 61.6 | 54.5 | 66.7 | 74.4 | 85.3 | 104.9 | 112.4 | 89.9 | 85.0 |
| % Net Income of Revenue | 8.4 | 10.5 | 10.3 | 9.4 | 9.1 | 9.4 | 8.6 | 9.7 | 11.4 | 11.3 |
| % Return on Assets | 10.4 | 11.5 | 10.3 | 10.5 | 10.0 | 10.5 | 9.0 | 11.7 | 13.3 | 13.0 |
| % Return on Equity | 51.4 | 53.7 | 49.7 | 66.0 | 102.6 | 458.6 | NM | NM | 383.9 | 130.6 |

Data as orig reptd.; bef. results of disc opers/spec. items. Per share data adj. for stk. divs.; EPS diluted. E-Estimated. NA-Not Available. NM-Not Meaningful. NR-Not Ranked. UR-Under Review.

**Office:** 1 Campbell Pl, Camden, NJ 08103-1799.
**Telephone:** 856-342-4800.
**Website:** http://www.campbellsoup.com
**Chrmn:** H. Golub

**Pres & CEO:** D.R. Conant
**SVP, CFO & Chief Admin Officer:** B.C. Owens
**SVP & CIO:** J.C. Spagnoletti
**Secy:** J.J. Furey

**Investor Contact:** L.F. Griehs (856-342-6427)
**Board Members:** E. M. Carpenter, P. R. Charron, D. R. Conant, B. Dorrance, H. Golub, R. W. Larrimore, P. E. Lippincott, M. D. Malone, S. Mathew, D. C. Patterson, C. R. Perrin, A. B. Rand, G. W. Strawbridge, Jr., L. C. Vinney, C. C. Weber

**Founded:** 1869
**Domicile:** New Jersey
**Employees:** 19,400

The McGraw·Hill Companies

# CA Inc

**STANDARD &POOR'S**

| **S&P Recommendation** HOLD ★★★☆☆ | **Price** $17.02 (as of Nov 14, 2008) | **12-Mo. Target Price** $22.00 | **Investment Style** Large-Cap Blend |
| --- | --- | --- | --- |

**GICS Sector** Information Technology
**Sub-Industry** Systems Software

**Summary** This company (formerly Computer Associates International) develops systems software, database management systems and applications software.

## Key Stock Statistics (Source S&P, Vickers, company reports)

| | | | | | | | |
| --- | --- | --- | --- | --- | --- | --- | --- |
| 52-Wk Range | $26.87–12.00 | S&P Oper. EPS 2009E | 1.38 | Market Capitalization(B) | $8.821 | Beta | 1.20 |
| Trailing 12-Month EPS | $1.20 | S&P Oper. EPS 2010E | 1.40 | Yield (%) | 0.94 | S&P 3-Yr. Proj. EPS CAGR(%) | 8 |
| Trailing 12-Month P/E | 14.2 | P/E on S&P Oper. EPS 2009E | 12.3 | Dividend Rate/Share | $0.16 | S&P Credit Rating | BB+ |
| $10K Invested 5 Yrs Ago | $7,584 | Common Shares Outstg. (M) | 518.3 | Institutional Ownership (%) | 66 | | |

## Price Performance

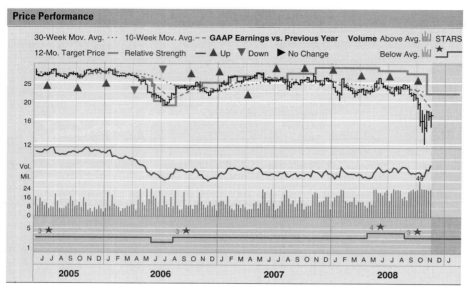

30-Week Mov. Avg. ··· 10-Week Mov. Avg. ─ ─ **GAAP Earnings vs. Previous Year** Volume Above Avg. STARS
12-Mo. Target Price ─ Relative Strength ─ ▲ Up ▼ Down ► No Change Below Avg.

Options: ASE, CBOE, P, Ph

Analysis prepared by **Jim Yin** on November 12, 2008, when the stock traded at **$ 16.05**.

## Highlights

➤ We estimate total revenues will increase 2.8% in FY 10 (Mar.), following projected 1.7% growth in FY 09. The revenue growth we see reflects our view of a slowing global economy and unfavorable currency exchange. We believe CA will be buffered to some extent from an economic slowdown by its ratable subscription revenue, which we forecast to rise 3.9% and to account for 86% of total revenues in FY 10. We also expect CA to gain market share through new product and service offerings.

➤ We expect gross margins in FY 10 to be flat with FY 09's expected 83%, as a larger revenue contribution from subscription revenue offsets higher amortization of capitalized software costs. We see operating expenses increasing as a percentage of revenues to 52% in FY 10, from 51% in FY 09, on higher wages and relatively flat revenues. We project that operating margins in FY 10 will remain at 27%.

➤ Our EPS estimate for FY 10 is $1.40, compared to our $1.38 estimate for FY 09. The projected slight increase in earnings reflects our forecast for only small changes in revenues and operating margins in a challenging sales environment.

## Investment Rationale/Risk

➤ Our hold recommendation reflects our concerns about a slowdown in the global economy, which we believe will last until the second half of 2009. Additionally, the company's financial results should be hurt by unfavorable currency exchange due to the recent strength in the U.S. dollar. Thus, we project revenue growth in FY 09 will come in at the low end of the company's guidance of 2%-8% growth. However, we expect CA to improve operating margins by streamlining operations and reducing employee headcount. We view CA shares as fairly valued following a significant price decline.

➤ Risks to our opinion and target price include significant declines in corporate spending on enterprise software from current levels, pricing pressure from increased competition, and further weakness in the global economy.

➤ Our 12-month target price of $22 is based on a blend of our discounted cash flow (DCF) and P/E analyses. Our DCF model assumes a 12% weighted average cost of capital and 3% terminal growth, yielding an intrinsic value of $25. For our P/E analysis, we derive a value of $19 based on an industry average P/E-to-growth ratio of 1.7X, or 13.6X our FY 10 EPS estimate.

## Qualitative Risk Assessment

| LOW | MEDIUM | HIGH |
| --- | --- | --- |

Our risk assessment for the company reflects our concerns regarding what we consider to be inconsistent financial results, modest underlying growth and a slowing global economy.

## Quantitative Evaluations

**S&P Quality Ranking** B-

| D | C | B- | B | B+ | A- | A | A+ |
| --- | --- | --- | --- | --- | --- | --- | --- |

**Relative Strength Rank** STRONG

75

LOWEST = 1          HIGHEST = 99

## Revenue/Earnings Data

**Revenue (Million $)**

| | 1Q | 2Q | 3Q | 4Q | Year |
| --- | --- | --- | --- | --- | --- |
| 2009 | 1,087 | 110.7 | -- | -- | -- |
| 2008 | 1,025 | 1,067 | 1,100 | 1,085 | 4,277 |
| 2007 | 949.0 | 987.0 | 1,002 | 1,005 | 3,943 |
| 2006 | 927.0 | 950.0 | 971.0 | 948.0 | 3,796 |
| 2005 | 850.0 | 858.0 | 910.0 | 912.0 | 3,530 |
| 2004 | 813.0 | 833.0 | 844.0 | 850.0 | 3,276 |

**Earnings Per Share ($)**

| | | | | | |
| --- | --- | --- | --- | --- | --- |
| 2009 | 0.37 | 0.39 | E0.33 | E0.29 | E1.38 |
| 2008 | 0.24 | 0.26 | 0.31 | 0.14 | 0.93 |
| 2007 | 0.06 | 0.09 | 0.10 | -0.04 | 0.22 |
| 2006 | 0.16 | 0.08 | 0.09 | -0.07 | 0.26 |
| 2005 | 0.08 | -0.16 | 0.06 | 0.04 | 0.02 |
| 2004 | 0.02 | -0.15 | 0.04 | 0.05 | -0.06 |

Fiscal year ended Mar. 31. Next earnings report expected: Early February. EPS Estimates based on S&P Operating Earnings; historical GAAP earnings are as reported.

## Dividend Data (Dates: mm/dd Payment Date: mm/dd/yy)

| Amount ($) | Date Decl. | Ex-Div. Date | Stk. of Record | Payment Date |
| --- | --- | --- | --- | --- |
| 0.040 | 02/26 | 03/12 | 03/14 | 03/28/08 |
| 0.040 | 06/11 | 06/11 | 06/13 | 06/27/08 |
| 0.040 | 06/11 | 06/13 | 06/17 | 06/27/08 |
| 0.040 | 09/10 | 09/18 | 09/22 | 09/30/08 |

Dividends have been paid since 1990. Source: Company reports.

---

**Please read the Required Disclosures and Analyst Certification on the last page of this report.**

The McGraw-Hill Companies

# CA Inc

STANDARD
&POOR'S

## Business Summary November 12, 2008

CORPORATE OVERVIEW. CA provides information technology (IT) management software, which helps customers better manage their IT infrastructure. The company has a broad portfolio of software products and services that span the areas of infrastructure management, IT security management, storage management, application performance management and business service optimization.

CORPORATE STRATEGY. In April 2007, CA announced a new strategy, Enterprise IT Management (EITM), for transforming the way companies manage their IT. The goal of EITM is to unify disparate elements of IT, including hardware, processes and people, so customers can have better control and manage these resources rather than replace existing IT investments. For example, CA's Unicenter Advanced Systems Management provides centralized management for virtualized and clustered server environments, enabling customers to assess and optimize network resources.

Key parts of CA's EITM strategy include:

Internal Product Development - CA plans to ship new versions of every major product, including those products obtained through acquisitions. The company has added headcount in India and Czech Republic research centers.

Strengthening Partner Relationships - CA intends to strengthen its global distribution by recruiting and educating channel partners on CA products and services. The company formed a Mid-Market and Storage organization that targets enterprises with 500-5,000 employees.

International Expansion - CA will invest in regions outside the U.S., especially in emerging markets such as China and India to increase the volume of enterprise sales. The company has also pursued small- and medium-sized customers in the Europe, Middle East and Africa (EMEA) region. International revenue comprised nearly 46% of total sales in FY 08, the same percentage in FY 07.

Strategic Acquisitions - CA has made several small acquisitions that the company considers strategic and complementary to its systems and security management offerings. In FY 07, the company completed the acquisitions of Cendura Corporation, XOsoft, Inc., MDY Group International, Inc. and Cybermation, Inc.

## Company Financials Fiscal Year Ended Mar. 31

| Per Share Data ($) | 2008 | 2007 | 2006 | 2005 | 2004 | 2003 | 2002 | 2001 | 2000 | 1999 |
|---|---|---|---|---|---|---|---|---|---|---|
| Tangible Book Value | NM | NM | NM | 0.50 | 8.09 | NM | NM | 0.66 | 1.71 | 2.06 |
| Cash Flow | NA | 0.47 | 1.22 | 0.24 | 0.17 | 0.60 | -0.01 | 0.89 | 2.32 | 1.69 |
| Earnings | 0.93 | 0.22 | 0.26 | 0.02 | -0.06 | -0.46 | -1.91 | -1.02 | 1.25 | 1.11 |
| S&P Core Earnings | 0.97 | 0.23 | 0.26 | 0.22 | 0.02 | -0.53 | -2.05 | -1.18 | NA | NA |
| Dividends | 0.16 | 0.16 | 0.08 | 0.08 | 0.08 | 0.08 | 0.08 | 0.08 | 0.08 | 0.08 |
| Payout Ratio | 17% | 73% | 31% | NM | NM | NM | NM | NM | 6% | 7% |
| Calendar Year | 2007 | 2006 | 2005 | 2004 | 2003 | 2002 | 2001 | 2000 | 1999 | 1998 |
| Prices:High | 28.46 | 29.50 | 31.35 | 31.71 | 29.29 | 38.74 | 39.03 | 79.44 | 70.63 | 61.94 |
| Prices:Low | 22.86 | 18.97 | 26.04 | 22.37 | 12.39 | 7.47 | 18.31 | 18.13 | 32.13 | 26.00 |
| P/E Ratio:High | 31 | NM | NM | NM | NM | NM | NM | NM | 56 | 56 |
| P/E Ratio:Low | 25 | NM | NM | NM | NM | NM | NM | NM | 26 | 23 |

| Income Statement Analysis (Million $) | | | | | | | | | | |
|---|---|---|---|---|---|---|---|---|---|---|
| Revenue | 4,277 | 3,943 | 3,796 | 3,530 | 3,276 | 3,116 | 2,964 | 4,198 | 6,766 | 5,253 |
| Operating Income | NA | 560 | 836 | 504 | 417 | 421 | -62.0 | 604 | 3,318 | 2,529 |
| Depreciation | 273 | 148 | 583 | 130 | 134 | 612 | 1,096 | 1,110 | 594 | 325 |
| Interest Expense | NA | 126 | 41.0 | 106 | Nil | 172 | 227 | 344 | 339 | 154 |
| Pretax Income | 808 | 154 | 121 | 11.0 | -54.0 | -363 | -1,385 | -666 | 1,590 | 1,010 |
| Effective Tax Rate | 38.1% | 21.4% | NM | NM | NM | NM | NM | NM | 56.2% | 38.0% |
| Net Income | 500 | 121 | 156 | 13.0 | -36.0 | -267 | -1,102 | -591 | 696 | 626 |
| S&P Core Earnings | 522 | 122 | 155 | 136 | 7.10 | -301 | -1,185 | -688 | NA | NA |

| Balance Sheet & Other Financial Data (Million $) | | | | | | | | | | |
|---|---|---|---|---|---|---|---|---|---|---|
| Cash | 2,796 | 2,280 | 1,865 | 3,125 | 1,902 | 1,512 | 1,180 | 850 | 1,387 | 536 |
| Current Assets | NA | 3,101 | 2,648 | 3,954 | 3,358 | 3,565 | 3,061 | 2,643 | 3,992 | 2,631 |
| Total Assets | 11,756 | 10,585 | 10,438 | 11,082 | 10,679 | 11,054 | 12,226 | 14,143 | 17,493 | 8,070 |
| Current Liabilities | NA | 3,714 | 3,377 | 3,664 | 2,455 | 2,974 | 2,321 | 2,286 | 3,004 | 1,863 |
| Long Term Debt | NA | 2,572 | 1,810 | 1,810 | 2,298 | 2,298 | 3,334 | 3,639 | 4,527 | 2,032 |
| Common Equity | 3,709 | 3,690 | 4,680 | 4,840 | 4,718 | 4,363 | 4,617 | 5,780 | 7,037 | 2,729 |
| Total Capital | NA | 6,282 | 6,536 | 6,822 | 7,634 | 7,525 | 9,218 | 11,319 | 13,929 | 5,795 |
| Capital Expenditures | 117 | 150 | 143 | 69.0 | 30.0 | 30.0 | 25.0 | 89.0 | 198 | 222 |
| Cash Flow | NA | 269 | 739 | 143 | 98.0 | 345 | -6.00 | 519 | 1,290 | 951 |
| Current Ratio | 1.0 | 0.8 | 0.8 | 1.1 | 1.4 | 1.2 | 1.3 | 1.2 | 1.3 | 1.4 |
| % Long Term Debt of Capitalization | 35.3 | 41.1 | 27.7 | 26.5 | 30.1 | 30.5 | 36.2 | 32.1 | 32.5 | 35.1 |
| % Net Income of Revenue | 11.7 | 3.1 | 4.1 | 0.4 | NM | NM | NM | NM | 10.2 | 11.9 |
| % Return on Assets | 4.5 | 1.2 | 1.4 | 0.1 | NM | NM | NM | NM | 5.4 | 8.5 |
| % Return on Equity | 13.5 | 2.9 | 3.2 | 0.3 | NM | NM | NM | NM | 14.3 | 24.0 |

Data as orig reptd.; bef. results of disc opers/spec. items. Per share data adj. for stk. divs.; EPS diluted. E-Estimated. NA-Not Available. NM-Not Meaningful. NR-Not Ranked. UR-Under Review.

**Office:** 1 Computer Associates Plz, Islandia, NY 11749-7000.
**Telephone:** 631-342-6000.
**Email:** cainvestor@ca.com
**Website:** http://www.ca.com

**Chrmn:** W.E. McCracken
**Pres & COO:** M.J. Christenson
**CEO:** J.A. Swainson
**EVP & CFO:** N.E. Cooper

**EVP & Chief Admin Officer:** J.E. Bryant
**Investor Contact:** R.G. Cirabisi (631-342-6000)
**Board Members:** R. E. Blanc, R. J. Bromark, A. M. D'Amato, G. J. Fernandes, C. B. Lofgren, W. E. McCracken, J. A. Swainson, L. S. Unger, A. Weinbach, R. Zambonini

**Founded:** 1974
**Domicile:** Delaware
**Employees:** 13,700

# Capital One Financial Corp.

**STANDARD &POOR'S**

**S&P Recommendation** HOLD ★★★☆☆

| Price | 12-Mo. Target Price | Investment Style |
|---|---|---|
| $31.19 (as of Nov 14, 2008) | $43.00 | Large-Cap Blend |

**GICS Sector** Financials
**Sub-Industry** Consumer Finance

**Summary** This diversified consumer finance company is one of the largest issuers of Visa and MasterCard credit cards in the world.

## Key Stock Statistics (Source S&P, Vickers, company reports)

| | | | | | | | |
|---|---|---|---|---|---|---|---|
| 52-Wk Range | $63.50– 28.98 | S&P Oper. EPS 2008**E** | 4.78 | Market Capitalization(B) | $12.216 | Beta | 0.98 |
| Trailing 12-Month EPS | $4.28 | S&P Oper. EPS 2009**E** | 4.29 | Yield (%) | 4.81 | S&P 3-Yr. Proj. EPS CAGR(%) | 7 |
| Trailing 12-Month P/E | 7.3 | P/E on S&P Oper. EPS 2008**E** | 6.5 | Dividend Rate/Share | $1.50 | S&P Credit Rating | BBB+ |
| $10K Invested 5 Yrs Ago | $5,515 | Common Shares Outstg. (M) | 391.7 | Institutional Ownership (%) | NM | | |

## Price Performance

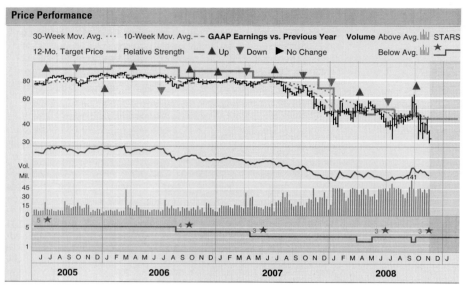

- 30-Week Mov. Avg. ··· 10-Week Mov. Avg. – – **GAAP Earnings vs. Previous Year** Volume Above Avg. STARS
- 12-Mo. Target Price — Relative Strength — ▲ Up ▼ Down ▶ No Change Below Avg.

Options: ASE, CBOE, P, Ph

Analysis prepared by **Stuart Plesser** on October 21, 2008, when the stock traded at **$ 39.45**.

### Highlights

➤ We anticipate revenues in 2009 will be up roughly 4.0% from projected 2008 levels despite a weakening economy and slowing consumer spending. We believe management is tightening its lending standards and we expect to see a slowdown in loan growth. However, due to a more favorable interest rate environment, we look for modest growth in net interest income. We forecast a continued rise in delinquencies and loan-loss provisions in all of COF's business lines. We also expect continued deterioration in its credit card portfolio and home equity lines of credit in 2009.

➤ Credit issues in the U.K. business will likely deteriorate, and we see a deterioration in consumer credit in the U.S. card business and expect COF to continue to build reserves in anticipation of rising chargeoffs. COF's U.S. card business should also experience higher chargeoffs in 2009 due to a mandated change in minimum payment policies. While we anticipate the continuation of solid expense management, we do not expect it to meaningfully offset credit pressures.

➤ Our operating EPS estimate for 2008 is $4.78, versus $6.48 in 2007. In 2009, we forecast $4.29.

### Investment Rationale/Risk

➤ We see a further pickup in delinquencies and chargeoffs, particularly as they relate to COF's prime, home equity and credit card loans. We are concerned regarding higher unemployment rates in the U.S. and the U.K., as we believe delinquencies and chargeoffs will rise as a result. We see COF significantly shrinking its U.K. portfolio business in the coming quarters. However, the company should benefit from a higher net interest margin, particularly in light of recent rate cuts, and the possibility we see that rates may be cut again. We also are encouraged by COF's strong liquidity and myriad of funding sources, particularly amid illiquidity in the securitization markets.

➤ Risks to our recommendation and target price include an increase in competition from larger credit card issuers; a decrease in consumer confidence; higher-than-expected deterioration from COF's remaining mortgage portfolio; and higher-than-expected unemployment rates that would hurt credit quality.

➤ Our 12-month target price of $43 is equal to about 10.0X our 2009 EPS estimate of $4.29. This valuation multiple is in line with COF's historical averages.

## Qualitative Risk Assessment

| LOW | MEDIUM | HIGH |
|---|---|---|

Our risk assessment reflects what we see as solid business fundamentals, diverse product offerings and a strong customer base, offset by what we perceive as the likelihood of a continued rise in consumer delinquency rates.

## Quantitative Evaluations

**S&P Quality Ranking** A

| D | C | B- | B | B+ | A- | A | A+ |
|---|---|---|---|---|---|---|---|

**Relative Strength Rank** MODERATE

47

LOWEST = 1 HIGHEST = 99

## Revenue/Earnings Data

**Revenue (Million $)**

| | 1Q | 2Q | 3Q | 4Q | Year |
|---|---|---|---|---|---|
| 2008 | 4,936 | 4,269 | 4,469 | -- | -- |
| 2007 | 4,598 | 4,719 | 4,917 | 5,119 | 19,132 |
| 2006 | 3,737 | 3,607 | 2,826 | 4,021 | 15,191 |
| 2005 | 2,852 | 2,934 | 2,999 | 3,300 | 12,085 |
| 2004 | 2,608 | 2,548 | 2,768 | 2,771 | 10,695 |
| 2003 | 2,411 | 2,381 | 2,466 | 2,525 | 9,784 |

**Earnings Per Share ($)**

| | | | | | |
|---|---|---|---|---|---|
| 2008 | 1.70 | 1.24 | 1.03 | E0.81 | E4.78 |
| 2007 | 1.62 | 1.89 | -2.09 | 0.85 | 6.55 |
| 2006 | 2.86 | 1.78 | 1.89 | 1.14 | 7.62 |
| 2005 | 1.99 | 2.03 | 1.81 | 0.97 | 6.73 |
| 2004 | 1.84 | 1.65 | 1.97 | 0.77 | 6.21 |
| 2003 | 1.35 | 1.23 | 1.23 | 1.11 | 4.92 |

Fiscal year ended Dec. 31. Next earnings report expected: Late January. EPS Estimates based on S&P Operating Earnings; historical GAAP earnings are as reported.

## Dividend Data (Dates: mm/dd Payment Date: mm/dd/yy)

| Amount ($) | Date Decl. | Ex-Div. Date | Stk. of Record | Payment Date |
|---|---|---|---|---|
| 0.375 | 01/31 | 02/07 | 02/11 | 02/20/08 |
| 0.375 | 04/24 | 05/08 | 05/12 | 05/21/08 |
| 0.375 | 07/24 | 08/07 | 08/11 | 08/20/08 |
| 0.375 | 10/30 | 11/06 | 11/10 | 11/20/08 |

Dividends have been paid since 1995. Source: Company reports.

# Capital One Financial Corp.

**STANDARD
&POOR'S**

## Business Summary October 21, 2008

CORPORATE OVERVIEW. Capital One Financial (COF) is one of the world's largest financial services franchises. It is a diversified financial services corporation focused primarily on consumer lending and deposits. The company's principal business segments are local banking and national lending. The national lending segment consists of three sub-segments: U.S. Card, Auto Finance and Global Financial Services.

U.S. Card Segment. COF offers a wide variety of credit card products throughout the U.S. It customizes products to appeal to different consumer preferences and needs by combining different product features, including annual percentage rates, fees and credit limits, rewards programs and other special features. COF's pricing strategies are risk-based; lower-risk customers may likely be offered products with more favorable pricing and we expect these products to yield lower delinquencies and credit losses. On products offered to higher-risk customers, however, COF is likely to experience higher delinquencies and losses, and it prices these products accordingly.

Auto Finance Segment. Through Capital One Auto Finance, Inc., the company

purchases retail installment contracts, secured by automobiles or other motor vehicles, through dealer networks throughout the U.S. In addition, COF utilizes direct marketing to offer automobile financing directly to consumers. Its direct marketed products include financing for the purchase of new and used vehicles, as well as refinancing of existing motor vehicle loans. As of December 31, 2007, COF was the third largest non-captive auto lender in the U.S. In January 2005, it acquired Onyx Acceptance Corporation, an auto finance company that provides financing to franchised and select independent dealerships throughout the U.S. The company also completed the acquisition of Key Bank's non-prime auto loan portfolio in 2005. Similar to its credit card strategy, COF customizes product features, such as interest rate, loan amount and loan terms, enabling it to lend to customers with a wide range of credit profiles.

## Company Financials Fiscal Year Ended Dec. 31

| Per Share Data ($) | 2007 | 2006 | 2005 | 2004 | 2003 | 2002 | 2001 | 2000 | 1999 | 1998 |
|---|---|---|---|---|---|---|---|---|---|---|
| Tangible Book Value | 31.86 | 25.37 | 33.99 | 33.98 | 25.75 | 20.44 | 15.33 | 9.94 | 7.69 | 6.45 |
| Earnings | 6.55 | 7.62 | 6.73 | 6.21 | 4.92 | 3.93 | 2.91 | 2.24 | 1.72 | 1.32 |
| S&P Core Earnings | 6.55 | 7.61 | 6.61 | 5.72 | 4.41 | 3.37 | 2.55 | NA | NA | NA |
| Dividends | 0.11 | 0.11 | 0.11 | 0.11 | 0.11 | 0.11 | 0.11 | 0.11 | 0.11 | 0.11 |
| Payout Ratio | 2% | 1% | 2% | 2% | 2% | 3% | 4% | 5% | 6% | 8% |
| Prices:High | 83.84 | 90.04 | 88.56 | 84.45 | 64.25 | 66.50 | 72.58 | 73.25 | 60.25 | 43.31 |
| Prices:Low | 44.40 | 69.30 | 69.09 | 60.04 | 24.91 | 24.05 | 36.40 | 32.06 | 35.81 | 16.85 |
| P/E Ratio:High | 13 | 12 | 13 | 14 | 13 | 17 | 25 | 33 | 35 | 33 |
| P/E Ratio:Low | 7 | 9 | 10 | 10 | 5 | 6 | 13 | 14 | 21 | 13 |

| Income Statement Analysis (Million $) | | | | | | | | | | |
|---|---|---|---|---|---|---|---|---|---|---|
| Net Interest Income | 6,530 | 5,100 | 3,680 | 3,003 | 2,785 | 2,719 | 1,663 | 1,589 | 1,053 | 695 |
| Non Interest Income | 8,054 | 6,997 | 6,358 | 5,900 | 5,416 | 5,467 | 4,420 | 3,034 | 2,372 | 1,488 |
| Loan Loss Provision | 2,637 | 1,476 | 1,491 | 1,221 | 1,517 | 2,149 | 990 | 718 | 383 | 267 |
| Non Interest Expenses | 8,078 | 6,967 | 5,718 | 5,322 | 4,857 | 4,586 | 4,058 | 3,148 | 2,465 | 1,472 |
| % Expense/Operating Revenue | 55.4% | 57.6% | 57.0% | 59.8% | 59.2% | 56.0% | 66.7% | 68.1% | 72.0% | 67.4% |
| Pretax Income | 3,870 | 3,653 | 2,829 | 2,360 | 1,827 | 1,451 | 1,035 | 757 | 577 | 444 |
| Effective Tax Rate | 33.0% | 33.9% | 36.1% | 34.6% | 37.0% | 38.0% | 38.0% | 38.0% | 37.1% | 38.0% |
| Net Income | 2,592 | 2,414 | 1,809 | 1,543 | 1,151 | 900 | 642 | 470 | 363 | 275 |
| % Net Interest Margin | 6.46 | 6.03 | 6.63 | 6.44 | 7.45 | 8.73 | 8.03 | 12.0 | 10.8 | 9.95 |
| S&P Core Earnings | 2,591 | 2,412 | 1,792 | 1,431 | 1,012 | 742 | 545 | NA | NA | NA |

| Balance Sheet & Other Financial Data (Million $) | | | | | | | | | | |
|---|---|---|---|---|---|---|---|---|---|---|
| Money Market Assets | 2,444 | 1,843 | 2,049 | 1,084 | 1,598 | 641 | 352 | 162 | 112 | 284 |
| Investment Securities | 19,782 | 15,452 | 14,350 | 9,300 | 5,867 | 4,424 | 3,116 | 1,697 | 1,856 | 1,797 |
| Earning Assets:Total Loans | 98,842 | 106,947 | 59,848 | 38,216 | 32,850 | 27,854 | 20,921 | 14,059 | 9,914 | 6,157 |
| Total Assets | 150,590 | 149,739 | 88,701 | 53,747 | 46,284 | 37,382 | 28,184 | 18,889 | 13,336 | 9,419 |
| Demand Deposits | 11,047 | 11,648 | NA | NA | Nil | Nil | Nil | Nil | Nil | Nil |
| Time Deposits | 71,944 | 74,123 | 43,092 | NA | 22,416 | 17,326 | 12,839 | 8,379 | 3,784 | 2,000 |
| Long Term Debt | 20,237 | 20,217 | 14,863 | Nil | 14,813 | 8,124 | Nil | 4,051 | 4,181 | 3,038 |
| Common Equity | 24,294 | 25,235 | 14,129 | 8,388 | 6,052 | 4,623 | 3,324 | 1,963 | 1,518 | 1,270 |
| % Return on Assets | 1.7 | 2.0 | 2.5 | 3.1 | 2.8 | 2.7 | 2.7 | 2.9 | 3.2 | 3.3 |
| % Return on Equity | 10.5 | 12.3 | 16.1 | 21.4 | 21.6 | 22.6 | 24.3 | 27.0 | 26.0 | 25.4 |
| % Loan Loss Reserve | 2.9 | 2.0 | 3.0 | 3.9 | 4.9 | 6.2 | 4.0 | 3.7 | 3.5 | 3.8 |
| % Loans/Deposits | 114.5 | 124.7 | 124.8 | 149.1 | 146.5 | 160.8 | 162.9 | 167.8 | 262.0 | 307.9 |
| % Loans/Assets | 64.2 | 70.0 | 68.8 | 71.0 | 71.9 | 74.4 | 74.3 | 72.3 | 70.6 | 66.8 |
| % Equity to Assets | 16.5 | 16.5 | 15.8 | 14.4 | 12.8 | 12.1 | 11.2 | 10.8 | 12.3 | 13.1 |

Data as orig reptd.; bef. results of disc opers/spec. items. Per share data adj. for stk. divs.; EPS diluted. E-Estimated. NA-Not Available. NM-Not Meaningful. NR-Not Ranked. UR-Under Review.

**Office:** 1680 Capital One Drive, McLean, VA 22102-3407.
**Telephone:** 703-720-1000.
**Email:** investor.relations@capitalone.com
**Website:** http://www.capitalone.com

**Chrmn, Pres & CEO:** R.D. Fairbank
**EVP, CFO & Chief Acctg Officer:** G.L. Perlin
**SVP & Treas:** S. Linehan
**Secy & General Counsel:** J.G. Finneran, Jr.

**Investor Contact:** M. Rowen (703-720-2455)
**Board Members:** E. R. Campbell, W. R. Dietz, R. D. Fairbank, P. W. Gross, A. F. Hackett, L. Hay, III, P. E. Leroy, M. A. Shattuck, III, B. H. Warner, S. I. Westreich

**Founded:** 1993
**Domicile:** Delaware
**Employees:** 27,000

*The McGraw-Hill Companies*

# Cardinal Health Inc

STANDARD
&POOR'S

| S&P Recommendation **BUY** ★★★★☆ | Price | 12-Mo. Target Price | Investment Style |
|---|---|---|---|
| | $36.09 (as of Nov 14, 2008) | $44.00 | Large-Cap Blend |

**GICS Sector** Health Care
**Sub-Industry** Health Care Distributors

**Summary** This company is one of the leading wholesale distributors of pharmaceuticals, medical/surgical supplies, and related products to a broad range of health care customers.

## Key Stock Statistics (Source S&P, Vickers, company reports)

| | | | | | | | |
|---|---|---|---|---|---|---|---|
| 52-Wk Range | $62.25– 34.50 | S&P Oper. EPS 2009E | 3.80 | Market Capitalization(B) | $12.978 | Beta | 1.01 |
| Trailing 12-Month EPS | $3.45 | S&P Oper. EPS 2010E | 4.15 | Yield (%) | 1.55 | S&P 3-Yr. Proj. EPS CAGR(%) | 10 |
| Trailing 12-Month P/E | 10.5 | P/E on S&P Oper. EPS 2009E | 9.5 | Dividend Rate/Share | $0.56 | S&P Credit Rating | BBB+ |
| $10K Invested 5 Yrs Ago | $6,071 | Common Shares Outstg. (M) | 359.6 | Institutional Ownership (%) | 85 | | |

## Price Performance

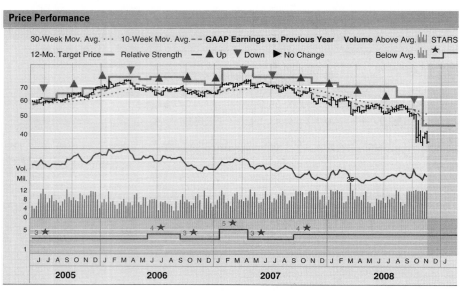

30-Week Mov. Avg. · · · 10-Week Mov. Avg. – – **GAAP Earnings vs. Previous Year** Volume Above Avg. STARS
12-Mo. Target Price — Relative Strength — ▲ Up ▼ Down ▶ No Change   Below Avg.  ★

Options: ASE, CBOE, P, Ph

Analysis prepared by **Phillip M. Seligman** on November 10, 2008, when the stock traded at **$ 39.88**.

## Highlights

➤ CAH plans to spin off its Clinical and Medical Products segment (CMP) in mid-calendar 2009. Until the transaction closes, we will continue to follow CAH in its current form. We expect total revenue to rise about 6.5% in FY 09 (Jun.) to $97 billion. We anticipate Healthcare Supply Chain Services (HSCS) segment revenue to grow 6%, driven mainly by growth in bulk sales to customer warehouses. We look for CMP's revenue to grow by 10% on new products and demand for infection prevention products, partly offset by delayed hospital purchase decisions.

➤ We project that FY 09 HSCS profit margins will narrow, with less profitable bulk sales continuing to outpace direct-store sales, and higher IT spending. However, we think the lapping of contract renewal repricing should benefit margin comps in the second half. Meanwhile, we expect CMP margins to narrow slightly on higher commodity costs and a planned hike in R&D spending.

➤ We look for operating EPS of $3.80 in FY 09, versus FY 08's $3.80, and $4.15 in FY 10, also impacted by a higher tax rate and fewer share buybacks.

## Investment Rationale/Risk

➤ We believe CAH's planned spin-off of CMP makes sense, as it would allow management to focus on turning HSCS around, while investors could possibly benefit from the traditionally faster-growing, more-profitable CMP business. Meanwhile, we are encouraged by the recent DEA resolution, but expect CAH to have difficulty regaining accounts once its closed distribution centers re-open. While CAH's planned incremental investments to strengthen R&D in CMP and improve IT in HSCS will impact FY 09 EPS, we see CMP growth dependent on a recovery of hospital capital spending and believe HSCS can strengthen competitively with improved service and a better generic drug strategy.

➤ Risks to our recommendation and target price include the loss of major accounts, unfavorable changes in contracts with drugmakers and/or retailers, and failure of the planned CMP spinoff.

➤ Our 12-month target price of $44 is based on a forward P/E of 11X, reflecting groupwide valuation compression and below-peer performance, applied to our calendar 2009 EPS estimate of $4.03.

## Qualitative Risk Assessment

| LOW | MEDIUM | HIGH |
|---|---|---|

Our risk assessment reflects CAH's diversified products and services and what we believe are good growth prospects for its contract drugmaking and its drug dispensing systems. However, we also see intense competition in the drug distribution market, and we believe that future drugmaker-distributor contract negotiations could be less favorable to distributors.

## Quantitative Evaluations

**S&P Quality Ranking**                                    A

| D | C | B- | B | B+ | A- | A | A+ |
|---|---|---|---|---|---|---|---|

**Relative Strength Rank**                          MODERATE

56

LOWEST = 1                                          HIGHEST = 99

## Revenue/Earnings Data

**Revenue (Million $)**

| | 1Q | 2Q | 3Q | 4Q | Year |
|---|---|---|---|---|---|
| 2009 | 24,347 | -- | -- | -- | -- |
| 2008 | 21,973 | 23,283 | 22,910 | 22,926 | 91,091 |
| 2007 | 20,938 | 21,785 | 21,867 | 22,263 | 86,852 |
| 2006 | 19,237 | 19,781 | 20,638 | 21,708 | 81,364 |
| 2005 | 17,796 | 18,555 | 19,103 | 19,457 | 74,911 |
| 2004 | 15,388 | 16,351 | 16,392 | 16,923 | 65,054 |

**Earnings Per Share ($)**

| | | | | | |
|---|---|---|---|---|---|
| 2009 | 0.69 | E0.90 | E1.10 | E1.06 | E3.80 |
| 2008 | 0.82 | 0.89 | 1.02 | 0.89 | 3.62 |
| 2007 | 0.71 | 0.77 | -0.01 | 0.61 | 2.08 |
| 2006 | 0.55 | 0.72 | 0.83 | 0.80 | 2.90 |
| 2005 | 0.50 | 0.47 | 0.84 | 0.59 | 2.40 |
| 2004 | 0.72 | 0.85 | 0.99 | 0.91 | 3.47 |

Fiscal year ended Jun. 30. Next earnings report expected: Late January. EPS Estimates based on S&P Operating Earnings; historical GAAP earnings are as reported.

## Dividend Data (Dates: mm/dd Payment Date: mm/dd/yy)

| Amount ($) | Date Decl. | Ex-Div. Date | Stk. of Record | Payment Date |
|---|---|---|---|---|
| 0.120 | 01/31 | 03/28 | 04/01 | 04/15/08 |
| 0.140 | 05/07 | 06/27 | 07/01 | 07/15/08 |
| 0.140 | 08/06 | 09/29 | 10/01 | 10/15/08 |
| 0.140 | 11/05 | 12/29 | 01/01 | 01/15/09 |

Dividends have been paid since 1983. Source: Company reports.

---

**Please read the Required Disclosures and Analyst Certification on the last page of this report.**

The McGraw-Hill Companies

# Cardinal Health Inc

STANDARD
&POOR'S

## Business Summary November 10, 2008

CORPORATE OVERVIEW. As of FY 08 (Jun.), Cardinal Health's reportable segments were realigned into two main segments, each comprised of two businesses:

Healthcare Supply Chain Services (HSCS):

Healthcare Supply Chain Services - Pharmaceutical (HSCS-Pharma: 85% of FY 08 operating revenue) distributes pharmaceutical and related health care products to independent and chain drug stores, hospitals, alternate care centers, and supermarket and mass merchandiser pharmacies. PDS operates a pharmaceutical repackaging and distribution program for retail and mail order customers.

Healthcare Supply Chain Services - Medical (HSCS-Medical; 9%) -- provides non-pharmaceutical health care products for hospitals and other health care providers.

Clinical and Medical Products (CMP):

Clinical Technologies and Services (CTS; 3%) provides automation and information products and services. One unit, Pyxis Corp., develops, manufactures and markets point-of-use pharmacy systems that automate the distribution

and management of medications and supplies in hospitals and other health care facilities.

Medical Products Manufacturing (MPM; 3%) -- manufactures sterile and non-sterile procedure kits, single-use surgical drapes, gowns and apparel, exam and surgical gloves, fluid suction and collection systems, respiratory therapy products, surgical instruments, special procedure products and other products.

As of FY 08, HSCS and CMP became operating and reportable segments. A third reporting segment consists of Medicine Shoppe International, Pharmacy services, Tecomet (orthopedic implants and instruments) and MedSystems (enteral devices and surgical protection products), and the company is conducting a review to evaluate their fit. On August 7, 2008, CAH announced it agreed to sell Tecomet, and on September 2, it announced the sale of MedSystems.

## Company Financials Fiscal Year Ended Jun. 30

| Per Share Data ($) | 2008 | 2007 | 2006 | 2005 | 2004 | 2003 | 2002 | 2001 | 2000 | 1999 |
|---|---|---|---|---|---|---|---|---|---|---|
| Tangible Book Value | 4.26 | 4.12 | 8.52 | 8.20 | 7.05 | 12.10 | 11.50 | 9.50 | 7.28 | 6.13 |
| Cash Flow | NA | 2.87 | 3.82 | 3.34 | 4.15 | 3.70 | 2.98 | 2.50 | 2.17 | 1.65 |
| Earnings | 3.62 | 2.07 | 2.90 | 2.40 | 3.47 | 3.12 | 2.45 | 1.88 | 1.59 | 1.09 |
| S&P Core Earnings | 3.64 | 3.08 | 2.88 | 2.16 | 3.14 | 2.78 | 2.26 | 1.69 | NA | NA |
| Dividends | 0.50 | 0.39 | 0.27 | 0.15 | 0.12 | 0.11 | 0.10 | 0.09 | 0.05 | 0.05 |
| Payout Ratio | 14% | 19% | 9% | 6% | 3% | 4% | 4% | 5% | 3% | 5% |
| Prices:High | 62.25 | 76.15 | 75.74 | 69.64 | 76.54 | 67.96 | 73.70 | 77.32 | 69.96 | 55.50 |
| Prices:Low | 34.50 | 56.41 | 61.15 | 52.85 | 36.08 | 50.00 | 46.60 | 56.67 | 24.67 | 24.67 |
| P/E Ratio:High | 17 | 37 | 26 | 29 | 22 | 22 | 30 | 41 | 44 | 51 |
| P/E Ratio:Low | 10 | 27 | 21 | 22 | 10 | 16 | 19 | 30 | 15 | 23 |

| Income Statement Analysis (Million $) | | | | | | | | | | |
|---|---|---|---|---|---|---|---|---|---|---|
| Revenue | 91,091 | 86,852 | 81,364 | 74,911 | 65,054 | 50,467 | 44,394 | 47,948 | 29,871 | 25,034 |
| Operating Income | NA | 2,485 | 2,474 | 2,555 | 2,694 | 3,723 | 2,216 | 1,893 | 1,377 | 1,257 |
| Depreciation | 381 | 322 | 393 | 410 | 299 | 266 | 244 | 281 | 246 | 234 |
| Interest Expense | NA | 121 | 132 | 134 | 98.9 | 115 | 133 | 155 | 117 | 99.4 |
| Pretax Income | 1,957 | 1,252 | 1,835 | 1,629 | 2,238 | 2,127 | 1,701 | 1,332 | 1,078 | 759 |
| Effective Tax Rate | 32.3% | 32.9% | 32.2% | 35.8% | 31.9% | 33.6% | 33.8% | 35.6% | 36.9% | 39.9% |
| Net Income | 1,325 | 840 | 1,245 | 1,047 | 1,525 | 1,412 | 1,126 | 857 | 680 | 456 |
| S&P Core Earnings | 1,326 | 1,247 | 1,236 | 936 | 1,369 | 1,266 | 1,045 | 771 | NA | NA |

| Balance Sheet & Other Financial Data (Million $) | | | | | | | | | | |
|---|---|---|---|---|---|---|---|---|---|---|
| Cash | 1,291 | 1,309 | 1,321 | 1,412 | 1,096 | 1,724 | 1,382 | 934 | 505 | 165 |
| Current Assets | NA | 14,545 | 14,777 | 13,443 | 13,058 | 13,250 | 11,907 | 10,716 | 6,871 | 5,147 |
| Total Assets | 23,448 | 23,154 | 23,374 | 22,059 | 21,369 | 18,521 | 16,438 | 14,642 | 10,265 | 8,289 |
| Current Liabilities | NA | 11,460 | 11,373 | 10,105 | 9,369 | 7,314 | 6,810 | 6,575 | 4,262 | 2,959 |
| Long Term Debt | NA | 3,457 | 2,600 | 2,320 | 2,835 | 2,472 | 2,207 | 1,871 | 1,486 | 1,224 |
| Common Equity | 7,756 | 7,377 | 8,491 | 8,593 | 7,976 | 7,758 | 6,393 | 5,437 | 3,981 | 3,463 |
| Total Capital | NA | 10,834 | 11,090 | 10,913 | 12,000 | 11,207 | 8,600 | 7,308 | 5,467 | 5,208 |
| Capital Expenditures | 376 | 1,630 | 443 | 572 | 410 | 423 | 285 | 341 | 308 | 320 |
| Cash Flow | NA | 1,162 | 1,637 | 1,456 | 1,824 | 1,678 | 1,370 | 1,138 | 926 | 690 |
| Current Ratio | 1.4 | 1.3 | 1.3 | 1.3 | 1.4 | 1.8 | 1.7 | 1.6 | 1.6 | 1.7 |
| % Long Term Debt of Capitalization | 31.8 | 31.9 | 23.4 | 21.3 | 23.6 | 22.1 | 25.7 | 25.6 | 27.2 | 23.5 |
| % Net Income of Revenue | 1.5 | 1.0 | 1.5 | 1.4 | 2.3 | 2.8 | 2.5 | 1.8 | 2.3 | 1.8 |
| % Return on Assets | 5.7 | 3.6 | 5.5 | 4.8 | 7.7 | 8.1 | 7.2 | 6.4 | 7.3 | 5.8 |
| % Return on Equity | 17.5 | 10.6 | 14.6 | 12.6 | 19.5 | 20.0 | 19.0 | 17.4 | 18.0 | 14.2 |

Data as orig reptd.; bef. results of disc opers/spec. items. Per share data adj. for stk. divs.; EPS diluted. E-Estimated. NA-Not Available. NM-Not Meaningful. NR-Not Ranked. UR-Under Review.

**Office:** 7000 Cardinal Place, Dublin, OH 43017.
**Telephone:** 614-757-5000.
**Website:** http://www.cardinal.com
**Chrmn & CEO:** R.K. Clark

**Vice Chrmn:** G.S. Barrett
**Vice Chrmn:** D.L. Schlotterbeck
**EVP & CFO:** J.W. Henderson
**EVP & Treas:** J.M. Gomez

**Board Members:** C. F. Arnold, G. S. Barrett, R. K. Clark, C. Darden, J. F. Finn, P. L. Francis, G. B. Kenny, J. M. Losh, J. B. McCoy, R. C. Notebaert, M. D. O'Halleran, D. W. Raisbeck, D. L. Schlotterbeck, J. G. Spaulding

**Founded:** 1979
**Domicile:** Ohio
**Employees:** 47,600

# Carnival Corp

**STANDARD**
**&POOR'S**

| S&P Recommendation SELL ★ ★ ☆ ☆ ☆ | Price<br>$18.97 (as of Nov 14, 2008) | 12-Mo. Target Price<br>$22.00 | Investment Style<br>Large-Cap Blend |
|---|---|---|---|

**GICS Sector** Consumer Discretionary
**Sub-Industry** Hotels, Resorts & Cruise Lines

**Summary** Carnival Corp. and Carnival plc own businesses that operate more than 80 cruise ships, as well as tour companies in Alaska and Canada.

## Key Stock Statistics (Source S&P, Vickers, company reports)

| | | | | | | | |
|---|---|---|---|---|---|---|---|
| 52-Wk Range | $46.20– 18.10 | S&P Oper. EPS 2008E | 2.79 | Market Capitalization(B) | $14.910 | Beta | 1.35 |
| Trailing 12-Month EPS | $2.87 | S&P Oper. EPS 2009E | 2.61 | Yield (%) | Nil | S&P 3-Yr. Proj. EPS CAGR(%) | -14 |
| Trailing 12-Month P/E | 6.6 | P/E on S&P Oper. EPS 2008E | 6.8 | Dividend Rate/Share | Nil | S&P Credit Rating | A- |
| $10K Invested 5 Yrs Ago | $6,043 | Common Shares Outstg. (M) | 786.0 | Institutional Ownership (%) | 60 | | |

## Price Performance

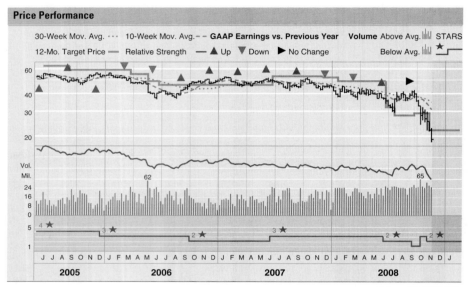

30-Week Mov. Avg. ··· 10-Week Mov. Avg. ─ ─ **GAAP Earnings vs. Previous Year** Volume Above Avg. ▎▎▎ STARS
12-Mo. Target Price ── Relative Strength ── ▲ Up ▼ Down ▶ No Change Below Avg. ▎▎▎ ★──

Options: ASE, CBOE, P, Ph

## Highlights

▶ The STARS recommendation for CCL has recently been changed to 2 (sell) from 3 (hold) and the 12-month target price has recently been changed to $22.00 from $29.00. The Highlights section of this Stock Report will be updated accordingly.

## Investment Rationale/Risk

▶ The Investment Rationale/Risk section of this Stock Report will be updated shortly. For the latest News story on CCL from MarketScope, see below.

▶ 10/31/08 01:10 pm ET ... S&P LOWERS OPINION ON SHARES OF CARNIVAL CORP TO SELL FROM HOLD (CCL 24.19**): CCL intends '09 dividend suspension to conserve cash, given tough financing environment and deteriorating operating conditions. In our view, this dividend suspension is a big negative for investors. CCL also lowered its constant dollar net yield expectations to a decline of 1% to 5%. On the other hand, lower fuel costs should help, as the company benefits from a non-hedging policy. We retain our strong belief that demand disappointment and a sharp slowdown scenario will be a key year-ahead theme. We are lowering our 12-month target price to $22 from $29. / P.Rambhiya

## Qualitative Risk Assessment

| LOW | MEDIUM | HIGH |
|---|---|---|

We believe that there are competitive advantages related to Carnival's industry leading position. However, the company's operations are subject to external factors, including economic conditions and hurricane activity.

## Quantitative Evaluations

**S&P Quality Ranking** A+

| D | C | B- | B | B+ | A- | A | A+ |
|---|---|---|---|---|---|---|---|

**Relative Strength Rank** WEAK

25

LOWEST = 1       HIGHEST = 99

## Revenue/Earnings Data

**Revenue (Million $)**

| | 1Q | 2Q | 3Q | 4Q | Year |
|---|---|---|---|---|---|
| 2008 | 3,152 | 3,378 | 4,814 | -- | -- |
| 2007 | 2,688 | 2,900 | 4,321 | 3,124 | 13,033 |
| 2006 | 2,463 | 2,662 | 3,905 | 2,809 | 11,839 |
| 2005 | 2,396 | 2,519 | 3,605 | 2,567 | 11,087 |
| 2004 | 1,980 | 2,256 | 3,245 | 2,243 | 9,727 |
| 2003 | 1,031 | 1,335 | 2,524 | 1,817 | 6,718 |

**Earnings Per Share ($)**

| | | | | | |
|---|---|---|---|---|---|
| 2008 | 0.30 | 0.49 | 1.64 | E0.39 | E2.79 |
| 2007 | 0.35 | 0.48 | 1.64 | 0.44 | 2.95 |
| 2006 | 0.31 | 0.46 | 1.49 | 0.51 | 2.77 |
| 2005 | 0.42 | 0.49 | 1.36 | 0.43 | 2.70 |
| 2004 | 0.25 | 0.41 | 1.23 | 0.36 | 2.24 |
| 2003 | 0.22 | 0.19 | 0.90 | 0.26 | 1.66 |

Fiscal year ended Nov. 30. Next earnings report expected: NA. EPS Estimates based on S&P Operating Earnings; historical GAAP earnings are as reported.

## Dividend Data (Dates: mm/dd Payment Date: mm/dd/yy)

| Amount ($) | Date Decl. | Ex-Div. Date | Stk. of Record | Payment Date |
|---|---|---|---|---|
| 0.400 | 04/24 | 05/21 | 05/23 | 06/13/08 |
| 0.400 | 07/14 | 08/20 | 08/22 | 09/12/08 |
| 0.400 | 10/31 | 11/19 | 11/21 | 12/12/08 |

Dividends have been paid since 1988. Source: Company reports.

# Carnival Corp

**STANDARD**
**&POOR'S**

## Business Summary October 24, 2008

CORPORATE OVERVIEW. Carnival Corp. is part of the world's largest cruise ship business, and has grown significantly through acquisitions and the addition of new ships. In 2003, Carnival merged with P&O Princess Cruises plc, which was renamed Carnival plc. As of September 2008, the combined Carnival operated 88 cruise ships with capacity for more than 167,000 passengers (based on two passengers per cabin, even though some cabins could accommodate more passengers). Also, Carnival has tour operations in Alaska and the Canadian Yukon.

With Carnival's dual listing company (DLC) format, there are separate stocks trading under the Carnival Corp. and Carnival plc names. Each company has retained its separate legal identity, but the two share a single senior executive management team, have identical boards of directors, and are run as if they were a single economic enterprise. In valuing the shares, we look at the combined financial results and equity base of the Carnival entities.

MARKET PROFILE. Looking ahead, we expect demand for cruise ship vacations to grow. In the U.S., we believe that most people have never taken a multi-night cruise ship vacation, and we expect that an aging U.S. population will lead to more interest in cruises. Also, we believe that a continued industry emphasis on providing ships with more features and the addition of more local ports will bolster passenger demand.

COMPETITIVE LANDSCAPE. We see Carnival enhancing its competitive position through the addition of new ships, which should encourage both returning and new customers. As of September 2008, there were 18 new Carnival ships scheduled to be delivered between October 2008 and June 2012. However, we expect that one or more ships will leave Carnival's fleet during this period, including the Queen Elizabeth 2 in the latter part of 2008. A new Queen Elizabeth ship is expected to be delivered in 2010.

In terms of capacity, Carnival was recently more than twice the size of its biggest competitor -- Royal Caribbean Cruises Ltd. (RCL, hold, $16.10).

## Company Financials Fiscal Year Ended Nov. 30

| Per Share Data ($) | 2007 | 2006 | 2005 | 2004 | 2003 | 2002 | 2001 | 2000 | 1999 | 1998 |
|---|---|---|---|---|---|---|---|---|---|---|
| Tangible Book Value | 19.01 | 17.10 | 15.47 | 13.96 | 11.83 | 11.48 | 10.13 | 8.84 | 8.86 | 6.46 |
| Cash Flow | 4.24 | 3.89 | 3.91 | 3.13 | 2.46 | 2.38 | 2.21 | 2.08 | 2.06 | 1.73 |
| Earnings | 2.95 | 2.77 | 2.70 | 2.24 | 1.66 | 1.73 | 1.58 | 1.60 | 1.66 | 1.40 |
| Dividends | 1.38 | 1.03 | 0.80 | 0.52 | 0.44 | 0.42 | 0.42 | 0.42 | 0.38 | 0.32 |
| Payout Ratio | 47% | 37% | 30% | 23% | 27% | 24% | 27% | 26% | 23% | 22% |
| Prices:High | 52.73 | 56.14 | 58.98 | 58.75 | 39.84 | 34.64 | 34.94 | 51.25 | 53.50 | 48.50 |
| Prices:Low | 41.70 | 36.40 | 45.78 | 39.75 | 20.34 | 22.07 | 16.95 | 18.31 | 38.13 | 19.00 |
| P/E Ratio:High | 18 | 20 | 22 | 26 | 24 | 20 | 22 | 32 | 32 | 35 |
| P/E Ratio:Low | 14 | 13 | 17 | 18 | 12 | 13 | 11 | 11 | 23 | 14 |

| Income Statement Analysis (Million $) | | | | | | | | | | |
|---|---|---|---|---|---|---|---|---|---|---|
| Revenue | 13,033 | 11,839 | 11,087 | 9,727 | 6,718 | 4,368 | 4,536 | 3,779 | 3,497 | 3,009 |
| Operating Income | 3,826 | 3,601 | 3,541 | 2,985 | 1,968 | 1,444 | 1,448 | 1,233 | 1,188 | 1,020 |
| Depreciation | 1,101 | 988 | 902 | 812 | 585 | 382 | 372 | 288 | 244 | 201 |
| Interest Expense | 367 | 312 | 330 | 284 | 195 | 111 | 121 | 41.4 | 47.0 | 57.8 |
| Pretax Income | 2,424 | 2,240 | 2,184 | 1,901 | 1,223 | 959 | 948 | 967 | 1,044 | 851 |
| Effective Tax Rate | 0.10% | NM | NM | 2.47% | 2.37% | NM | 2.34% | 0.11% | 0.27% | 0.45% |
| Net Income | 2,408 | 2,279 | 2,257 | 1,854 | 1,194 | 1,016 | 926 | 965 | 1,027 | 836 |

| Balance Sheet & Other Financial Data (Million $) | | | | | | | | | | |
|---|---|---|---|---|---|---|---|---|---|---|
| Cash | 943 | 1,163 | 1,178 | 643 | 1,070 | 667 | 1,421 | 189 | 522 | 137 |
| Current Assets | 1,976 | 1,995 | 2,215 | 1,728 | 2,132 | 1,132 | 1,959 | 549 | 792 | 370 |
| Total Assets | 34,181 | 30,552 | 28,432 | 27,636 | 24,491 | 12,335 | 11,564 | 9,831 | 8,286 | 7,179 |
| Current Liabilities | 7,260 | 5,415 | 5,192 | 5,034 | 3,315 | 1,620 | 1,480 | 1,715 | 1,405 | 1,135 |
| Long Term Debt | 6,313 | 6,355 | 5,727 | 6,291 | 6,918 | 3,012 | 2,955 | 2,099 | 868 | 1,563 |
| Common Equity | 19,963 | 18,210 | 16,972 | 15,760 | 13,793 | 7,418 | 6,591 | 5,871 | 5,931 | 4,285 |
| Total Capital | 26,276 | 24,565 | 22,699 | 22,051 | 20,711 | 10,430 | 9,546 | 7,970 | 6,799 | 5,981 |
| Capital Expenditures | 3,312 | 2,480 | 1,977 | 3,586 | 2,516 | 1,986 | 827 | 1,003 | 873 | 1,150 |
| Cash Flow | 3,509 | 3,267 | 3,159 | 2,666 | 1,779 | 1,398 | 1,298 | 1,253 | 1,271 | 1,037 |
| Current Ratio | 0.3 | 0.4 | 0.4 | 0.3 | 0.6 | 0.7 | 1.3 | 0.3 | 0.6 | 0.3 |
| % Long Term Debt of Capitalization | 24.0 | 25.9 | 25.2 | 28.5 | 33.4 | 28.9 | 31.0 | 26.3 | 12.8 | 26.1 |
| % Net Income of Revenue | 18.4 | 19.2 | 20.4 | 19.1 | 17.8 | 23.3 | 20.4 | 25.6 | 29.4 | 27.8 |
| % Return on Assets | 7.4 | 7.7 | 8.1 | 7.1 | 6.5 | 8.5 | 8.7 | 10.7 | 13.3 | 13.3 |
| % Return on Equity | 12.6 | 13.0 | 13.8 | 12.5 | 11.3 | 14.5 | 14.9 | 16.4 | 20.1 | 21.2 |

Data as orig reptd.; bef. results of disc opers/spec. items. Per share data adj. for stk. divs.; EPS diluted. E-Estimated. NA-Not Available. NM-Not Meaningful. NR-Not Ranked. UR-Under Review.

**Office:** 3655 NW 87th Avenue, Doral, FL 33178-2428.
**Telephone:** 305-599-2600.
**Website:** http://www.carnivalcorp.com
**Chrmn & CEO:** M.M. Arison

**Vice Chrmn & COO:** H.S. Frank
**SVP & CFO:** D. Bernstein
**SVP, Secy & General Counsel:** A. Perez
**Chief Acctg Officer & Cntlr:** L. Freedman

**Investor Contact:** B. Roberts (305-599-2600)
**Board Members:** M. M. Arison, R. G. Capen, Jr., R. H. Dickinson, A. W. Donald, P. L. Foschi, H. S. Frank, R. J. Glasier, M. A. Maidique, J. Parker, P. G. Ratcliffe, S. Subotnick, L. A. Weil, U. Zucker

**Founded:** 1974
**Domicile:** Panama
**Employees:** 81,200

*The McGraw·Hill Companies*

# Caterpillar Inc

**STANDARD &POOR'S**

| S&P Recommendation HOLD ★★★☆☆ | Price $36.96 (as of Nov 14, 2008) | 12-Mo. Target Price $50.00 | Investment Style Large-Cap Blend |
|---|---|---|---|

**GICS Sector** Industrials
**Sub-Industry** Construction & Farm Machinery & Heavy Trucks

**Summary** CAT, the world's largest producer of earthmoving equipment, is also a big maker of electric power generators and engines used in petroleum markets.

## Key Stock Statistics (Source S&P, Vickers, company reports)

| | | | | | | | |
|---|---|---|---|---|---|---|---|
| 52-Wk Range | $85.96– 31.95 | S&P Oper. EPS 2008**E** | 5.99 | Market Capitalization(B) | $22.296 | Beta | 1.34 |
| Trailing 12-Month EPS | $6.07 | S&P Oper. EPS 2009**E** | 5.90 | Yield (%) | 4.55 | S&P 3-Yr. Proj. EPS CAGR(%) | 7 |
| Trailing 12-Month P/E | 6.1 | P/E on S&P Oper. EPS 2008**E** | 6.2 | Dividend Rate/Share | $1.68 | S&P Credit Rating | A |
| $10K Invested 5 Yrs Ago | $11,225 | Common Shares Outstg. (M) | 603.2 | Institutional Ownership (%) | 72 | | |

## Price Performance

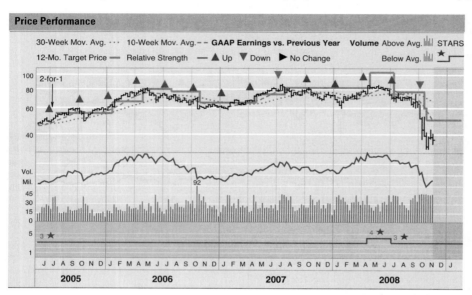

- 30-Week Mov. Avg. ···
- 10-Week Mov. Avg. ‑ ‑
- **GAAP Earnings vs. Previous Year**
- Volume Above Avg. STARS
- 12-Mo. Target Price —
- Relative Strength —
- ▲ Up ▼ Down ► No Change
- Below Avg.

Options: ASE, CBOE, P, Ph

Analysis prepared by **Adrian Compton** on October 22, 2008, when the stock traded at **$ 37.41**.

## Highlights

➤ We expect revenues to increase 12% in 2008, followed by a 4% gain in 2009. We see emerging markets continuing to grow through 2009, albeit at a slower rate, as need for infrastructure, construction, energy development, and mining continues. We see more modest sales gains in other foreign markets, notably weakness in Western European sales. We also expect relatively flat sales in North America, in light of the soft U.S. economy and the weak construction market.

➤ We project operating margins to widen in 2009, despite our forecast of less robust growth. We see the operating margin being aided by a pull back of historically high raw material costs given the global economic slowdown. However, we think this should be somewhat offset by our expectation for less favorable product mix.

➤ We see EPS continuing to decline through the first half of 2009, before a rebound to grow in the second half of 2009, our forecast for an economic recovery in Europe and North America. We project EPS of $5.99 for 2008 declining to $5.90 for 2009.

## Investment Rationale/Risk

➤ We expect CAT to post reduced EPS through 2009, based on our outlook for mixed trends in the wide variety of geographic markets that it serves. In light of our outlook for ongoing softness in the U.S. economy, Western Europe, and a reduced outlook in recently strong end market of China, Brazil and Australia, we think it will take some time before CAT's gains are able to grow more robust again.

➤ Risks to our opinion and target price include slower-than-expected economic growth, and a downturn in the infrastructure, non-residential construction and/or power markets. A delayed economic recovery in CAT's main end-markets.

➤ The shares recently traded at 7X our 2009 EPS forecast, which is the bottom of Caterpillar's valuation over the past decade. Applying a multiple of 8.5X to our 2009 EPS forecast, in line with peers, we arrive at a value of $50, which is our 12-month target price.

## Qualitative Risk Assessment

| LOW | MEDIUM | HIGH |
|---|---|---|

Our risk assessment for Caterpillar reflects its leading position in many of the end markets it serves, coupled with our reduced growth outlook for nonresidential construction activity, and the highly cyclical nature of the construction equipment and engine businesses.

## Quantitative Evaluations

**S&P Quality Ranking** A

| D | C | B- | B | B+ | A- | A | A+ |
|---|---|---|---|---|---|---|---|

**Relative Strength Rank** MODERATE

41

LOWEST = 1     HIGHEST = 99

## Revenue/Earnings Data

**Revenue (Million $)**

| | 1Q | 2Q | 3Q | 4Q | Year |
|---|---|---|---|---|---|
| 2008 | 11,796 | 13,624 | 12,981 | -- | -- |
| 2007 | 10,016 | 11,356 | 11,442 | 12,144 | 44,958 |
| 2006 | 9,392 | 10,605 | 10,517 | 11,003 | 41,517 |
| 2005 | 8,339 | 9,360 | 8,977 | 9,663 | 36,339 |
| 2004 | 6,467 | 7,564 | 7,649 | 8,571 | 30,251 |
| 2003 | 4,821 | 5,932 | 5,545 | 6,465 | 22,763 |

**Earnings Per Share ($)**

| | | | | | |
|---|---|---|---|---|---|
| 2008 | 1.45 | 1.74 | 1.39 | E1.38 | E5.99 |
| 2007 | 1.23 | 1.24 | 1.40 | 1.50 | 5.37 |
| 2006 | 1.20 | 1.52 | 1.14 | 1.32 | 5.17 |
| 2005 | 0.81 | 1.08 | 0.94 | 1.20 | 4.04 |
| 2004 | 0.60 | 0.80 | 0.71 | 0.78 | 2.88 |
| 2003 | 0.19 | 0.58 | 0.31 | 0.49 | 1.57 |

Fiscal year ended Dec. 31. Next earnings report expected: Late January. EPS Estimates based on S&P Operating Earnings; historical GAAP earnings are as reported.

## Dividend Data (Dates: mm/dd Payment Date: mm/dd/yy)

| Amount ($) | Date Decl. | Ex-Div. Date | Stk. of Record | Payment Date |
|---|---|---|---|---|
| 0.360 | 12/12 | 01/17 | 01/22 | 02/20/08 |
| 0.360 | 04/09 | 04/17 | 04/21 | 05/20/08 |
| 0.420 | 06/11 | 07/17 | 07/21 | 08/20/08 |
| 0.420 | 10/08 | 10/16 | 10/20 | 11/20/08 |

Dividends have been paid since 1914. Source: Company reports.

# Caterpillar Inc

**STANDARD**
**&POOR'S**

## Business Summary October 22, 2008

CORPORATE OVERVIEW. Caterpillar's distinctive yellow machines are in service in nearly every country in the world, with 62% of the company's revenues derived from foreign markets in 2007. As of 2007 year-end, 71% of CAT's independent dealers were located outside of the U.S.

CAT's largest operating segment, the Machinery unit (63% of revenues in 2007 and 9.7% operating margin), makes the company's well known earthmoving equipment. The division's products are used predominantly in heavy construction, general construction, mining, and quarry/aggregates markets. End markets are very cyclical and competitive; demand for CAT's earthmoving equipment is driven by many volatile factors, including the health of global economies, commodity prices, and interest rates, in our view. Principal competitors include Japan's Komatsu Ltd.; CNH Global NV (Case and NewHolland brands); Deere & Co.; and Sweden's Volvo.

For decades, the Engine segment (30% and 13.4%) made diesel engines solely for CAT's own earthmoving equipment. Currently, however, Engine derives the majority of its sales from third-party customers. Engine's major end markets

are petroleum, electric power generation, industrial, marine and on-highway vehicles. The division competes with a few global companies who are present in a variety of CAT's markets, and a larger set of companies who compete in a limited size range and/or application. Principal global competitors include Cummins, the MTU Friedrichshafen and MTU Detroit Diesel units of Tognum GmbH, and Wartsila.

The Financial Products segment (7% and 23.0%) primarily provides equipment financing to CAT dealers and customers. Financing plans include operating and finance leases, installment sales contracts, and retail and wholesale financing plans. Competitive sources that also fund CAT products include commercial banks and finance and leasing companies. At March 31, 2008, total long-term finance related receivables and long-term finance related debt stood at $14.1 billion and $14.0 billion, respectively.

## Company Financials Fiscal Year Ended Dec. 31

| Per Share Data ($) | 2007 | 2006 | 2005 | 2004 | 2003 | 2002 | 2001 | 2000 | 1999 | 1998 |
|---|---|---|---|---|---|---|---|---|---|---|
| Tangible Book Value | 14.88 | 7.07 | 9.77 | 8.34 | 6.48 | 5.51 | 5.75 | 5.97 | 5.56 | 5.45 |
| Cash Flow | 8.09 | 7.52 | 6.14 | 4.85 | 3.48 | 2.91 | 2.85 | 2.97 | 2.63 | 3.23 |
| Earnings | 5.37 | 5.17 | 4.04 | 2.88 | 1.57 | 1.15 | 1.16 | 1.51 | 1.32 | 2.06 |
| S&P Core Earnings | 5.46 | 5.48 | 4.05 | 2.76 | 1.50 | 0.20 | 0.16 | NA | NA | NA |
| Dividends | 1.32 | 1.10 | 0.91 | 0.78 | 0.71 | 0.70 | 0.69 | 0.67 | 0.63 | 0.55 |
| Payout Ratio | 25% | 21% | 23% | 27% | 45% | 61% | 59% | 44% | 48% | 27% |
| Prices:High | 87.00 | 82.03 | 59.88 | 49.36 | 42.48 | 30.00 | 28.42 | 27.56 | 33.22 | 30.38 |
| Prices:Low | 57.98 | 57.05 | 41.31 | 34.25 | 20.62 | 16.88 | 19.88 | 14.78 | 21.00 | 19.53 |
| P/E Ratio:High | 16 | 16 | 15 | 17 | 27 | 26 | 24 | 18 | 25 | 15 |
| P/E Ratio:Low | 11 | 11 | 10 | 12 | 13 | 15 | 17 | 10 | 16 | 10 |

| Income Statement Analysis (Million $) | 2007 | 2006 | 2005 | 2004 | 2003 | 2002 | 2001 | 2000 | 1999 | 1998 |
|---|---|---|---|---|---|---|---|---|---|---|
| Revenue | 44,958 | 41,517 | 36,339 | 30,251 | 22,763 | 20,152 | 20,450 | 20,175 | 19,702 | 20,977 |
| Operating Income | 7,850 | 7,634 | 6,029 | 4,650 | 3,505 | 3,060 | 3,137 | 3,447 | 2,999 | 3,607 |
| Depreciation | 1,797 | 1,602 | 1,477 | 1,397 | 1,347 | 1,220 | 1,169 | 1,022 | 945 | 865 |
| Interest Expense | 1,420 | 1,297 | 1,028 | 750 | 716 | 800 | 942 | 980 | 829 | 753 |
| Pretax Income | 5,026 | 4,942 | 3,974 | 2,766 | 1,497 | 1,110 | 1,172 | 1,500 | 1,401 | 2,178 |
| Effective Tax Rate | 29.6% | 28.4% | 28.2% | 26.4% | 26.6% | 28.1% | 31.3% | 29.8% | 32.5% | 30.5% |
| Net Income | 3,541 | 3,537 | 2,854 | 2,035 | 1,099 | 798 | 805 | 1,053 | 946 | 1,513 |
| S&P Core Earnings | 3,604 | 3,748 | 2,860 | 1,951 | 1,052 | 133 | 98.7 | NA | NA | NA |

| Balance Sheet & Other Financial Data (Million $) | 2007 | 2006 | 2005 | 2004 | 2003 | 2002 | 2001 | 2000 | 1999 | 1998 |
|---|---|---|---|---|---|---|---|---|---|---|
| Cash | 1,122 | 530 | 1,108 | 445 | 342 | 309 | 400 | 334 | 548 | 360 |
| Current Assets | 25,477 | 23,093 | 22,790 | 20,856 | 16,791 | 14,628 | 13,400 | 12,521 | 11,734 | 11,459 |
| Total Assets | 56,132 | 50,879 | 47,069 | 43,091 | 36,465 | 32,851 | 30,657 | 28,464 | 26,635 | 25,128 |
| Current Liabilities | 22,245 | 19,252 | 19,092 | 16,210 | 12,621 | 11,344 | 10,276 | 8,568 | 8,178 | 7,945 |
| Long Term Debt | 17,829 | 17,680 | 15,677 | 15,837 | 14,078 | 11,596 | 11,291 | 11,334 | 9,928 | 9,404 |
| Common Equity | 8,883 | 6,859 | 8,432 | 7,467 | 6,078 | 5,472 | 5,611 | 5,600 | 5,465 | 5,131 |
| Total Capital | 26,712 | 24,539 | 24,109 | 23,304 | 20,156 | 17,068 | 16,902 | 16,934 | 15,393 | 14,535 |
| Capital Expenditures | 3,040 | 2,675 | 2,415 | 2,114 | 1,765 | 1,773 | 1,968 | 1,388 | 1,280 | 1,269 |
| Cash Flow | 5,338 | 5,139 | 4,331 | 3,432 | 2,446 | 2,018 | 1,974 | 2,075 | 1,891 | 2,378 |
| Current Ratio | 1.2 | 1.2 | 1.2 | 1.3 | 1.3 | 1.3 | 1.3 | 1.5 | 1.4 | 1.4 |
| % Long Term Debt of Capitalization | 66.7 | 72.0 | 65.0 | 68.0 | 69.8 | 67.9 | 66.8 | 66.9 | 64.5 | 64.7 |
| % Net Income of Revenue | 7.9 | 8.5 | 7.9 | 6.7 | 4.8 | 4.0 | 3.9 | 5.2 | 4.8 | 7.2 |
| % Return on Assets | 6.6 | 7.2 | 6.3 | 5.1 | 3.2 | 2.5 | 2.7 | 3.8 | 3.7 | 6.6 |
| % Return on Equity | 45.0 | 46.3 | 35.9 | 30.0 | 19.0 | 14.4 | 14.4 | 19.0 | 17.9 | 30.8 |

Data as orig reptd.; bef. results of disc opers/spec. items. Per share data adj. for stk. divs.; EPS diluted. E-Estimated. NA-Not Available. NM-Not Meaningful. NR-Not Ranked. UR-Under Review.

**Office:** 100 N.E. Adams Street, Peoria, IL 61629.
**Telephone:** 309-675-1000.
**Email:** catir@cat.com
**Website:** http://www.cat.com

**Chrmn & CEO:** J.W. Owens
**Pres:** L.C. Calil
**Investor Contact:** D.B. Burritt
**CTO:** T.L. Utley

**Chief Acctg Officer:** J.A. Copeland
**Board Members:** W. Blount, J. R. Brazil, D. M. Dickinson, J. T. Dillon, E. V. Fife, G. D. Fosler, J. Gallardo, D. Goode, P. Magowan, W. A. Osborn, J. W. Owens, C. D. Powell, E. B. Rust, Jr., J. I. Smith

**Founded:** 1925
**Domicile:** Delaware
**Employees:** 102,623

The McGraw-Hill Companies

# CB Richard Ellis Group Inc

**STANDARD &POOR'S**

| **S&P Recommendation** SELL ★★☆☆☆ | **Price** $4.84 (as of Nov 14, 2008) | **12-Mo. Target Price** $4.00 | **Investment Style** Large-Cap Growth |
| --- | --- | --- | --- |

**GICS Sector** Financials
**Sub-Industry** Real Estate Services

**Summary** CB Richard Ellis Group is a global commercial real estate services company.

## Key Stock Statistics (Source S&P, Vickers, company reports)

| | | | | | | | |
| --- | --- | --- | --- | --- | --- | --- | --- |
| 52-Wk Range | $24.75– 3.54 | S&P Oper. EPS 2008E | 0.64 | Market Capitalization(B) | $0.979 | Beta | 1.41 |
| Trailing 12-Month EPS | $0.94 | S&P Oper. EPS 2009E | 0.75 | Yield (%) | Nil | S&P 3-Yr. Proj. EPS CAGR(%) | -17 |
| Trailing 12-Month P/E | 5.2 | P/E on S&P Oper. EPS 2008E | 7.6 | Dividend Rate/Share | Nil | S&P Credit Rating | NA |
| $10K Invested 5 Yrs Ago | NA | Common Shares Outstg. (M) | 202.4 | Institutional Ownership (%) | NM | | |

## Price Performance

30-Week Mov. Avg. ···· 10-Week Mov. Avg. – – **GAAP Earnings vs. Previous Year**   **Volume** Above Avg. |||| STARS
12-Mo. Target Price — Relative Strength   ▲ Up  ▼ Down  ▶ No Change   Below Avg. |||| ★

Options: ASE, CBOE, P, Ph

Analysis prepared by **Robert McMillan** on November 12, 2008, when the stock traded at **$ 4.68**.

## Highlights

➤ After a rise of 50% in 2007, we see revenues falling 15% in 2008 and about 4% in 2009 on lower sales activity on prolonged deterioration in the global credit markets, which has spread from the U.S. to the rest of the world. We also see the investment management business remaining under pressure. While we believe CBG will continue to benefit from the increasing trend of corporations to outsource the management of real estate properties, this will likely be insufficient to offset weakness elsewhere.

➤ Near term, the sharp decline in capital flows into the commercial real estate market combined with sizeable bid-ask spread between buyers and sellers for commercial properties suggests to us that CBG's business will remain under pressure for the rest of 2008 and well into 2009. Moreover, continued weak employment levels suggests that there will be less demand for office space as well, which should negatively impact leasing activity. During the third quarter, operating income fell 34% in the Americas, 72% in Europe, Middle East and Africa, and 72% in Asia Pacific.

➤ We see EPS of $0.64 in 2008 and $0.75 in 2009.

## Investment Rationale/Risk

➤ We see CBG suffering from a sharp downturn in commercial real estate activity and turmoil in the credit markets. However, long term, we see the company benefiting from its large size and its broad array of products and services relative to peers. We think the global reach of CBG's operations helps generate economies of scale that few other real estate firms can match, helping create sustainable barriers to entry. Nevertheless, we see the shares remaining under pressure until the turmoil in the financial markets abates.

➤ Risks to our recommendation and target price include higher than expected demand for office and industrial space, decreased competition, and a sharp increase in financing for commercial real estate transactions.

➤ The stock recently traded at a P/E of 6.6X our 2009 EPS estimate. Our 12-month target price of $4.00 reflects a P/E multiple of 6X our 2009 EPS forecast, on our assumption that the company's multiple will narrow until concerns about tight credit conditions and the state of CBG's business abate.

## Qualitative Risk Assessment

| LOW | MEDIUM | HIGH |
| --- | --- | --- |

Our risk assessment reflects CBG's position as one of the world's largest commercial real estate firms, with a diversified portfolio of operations and customers around the world.

## Quantitative Evaluations

**S&P Quality Ranking**                    NR

| D | C | B- | B | B+ | A- | A | A+ |
| --- | --- | --- | --- | --- | --- | --- | --- |

**Relative Strength Rank**              WEAK

13

LOWEST = 1                          HIGHEST = 99

## Revenue/Earnings Data

**Revenue (Million $)**

| | 1Q | 2Q | 3Q | 4Q | Year |
| --- | --- | --- | --- | --- | --- |
| 2008 | 1,231 | 1,315 | 1,300 | -- | -- |
| 2007 | 1,214 | 1,490 | 1,493 | 1,837 | 6,034 |
| 2006 | 903.5 | 751.3 | 967.9 | 1,409 | 4,032 |
| 2005 | 538.3 | 672.2 | 744.2 | 956.0 | 2,911 |
| 2004 | 441.0 | 550.9 | 575.0 | 798.2 | 2,365 |
| 2003 | 263.7 | 321.7 | 423.4 | 621.3 | 1,949 |

**Earnings Per Share ($)**

| | | | | | |
| --- | --- | --- | --- | --- | --- |
| 2008 | 0.10 | 0.08 | 0.15 | E0.32 | E0.64 |
| 2007 | 0.05 | 0.59 | 0.48 | 0.53 | 1.65 |
| 2006 | 0.16 | 0.27 | 0.39 | 0.53 | 1.35 |
| 2005 | 0.06 | 0.22 | 0.25 | 0.41 | 0.95 |
| 2004 | -0.09 | 0.01 | 0.05 | 0.29 | 0.30 |
| 2003 | -0.01 | 0.04 | -0.16 | -0.05 | -0.11 |

Fiscal year ended Dec. 31. Next earnings report expected: Early February. EPS Estimates based on S&P Operating Earnings; historical GAAP earnings are as reported.

## Dividend Data

No cash dividends have been paid.

---

# CB Richard Ellis Group Inc

**STANDARD &POOR'S**

## Business Summary November 12, 2008

CB Richard Ellis Group, Inc. is one of the largest global commercial real estate services companies in the world. The company's business is focused on several service competencies, including strategic advice and execution assistance for property leasing and sales, forecasting, valuations, origination and servicing of commercial mortgage loans, facilities and project management, and real estate investment management. The company generates revenues both on a per project or transaction basis and from annual management fees.

The company's primary business objective is to leverage its integrated global platform to garner an increasing share of industry revenues relative to competitors. CBG believes this will enable the company to maximize and sustain its long-term cash flow and increase long-term stockholder value. Management's strategy to achieve these business objectives consists of several elements: increasing revenues from large clients; capitalizing on cross-selling opportunities; continuing to grow the investment management business; ex-

panding through fill-in acquisitions; and focusing on improving operating efficiency.

CBG's Real Estate Services business offers a broad spectrum of services to occupiers/tenants and investors/owners. Real estate services include offering strategic advice and execution to owners, investors and occupiers of real estate in connection with the leasing, disposition and acquisition of property. During 2007, the company advised on over 31,000 lease transactions involving aggregate rents of approximately $48.3 billion and over 7,000 real estate sales transactions with an aggregate value of approximately $87.8 billion. This segment also provides investment sales property and valuation advice.

## Company Financials Fiscal Year Ended Dec. 31

| Per Share Data ($) | 2007 | 2006 | 2005 | 2004 | 2003 | 2002 | 2001 | 2000 | 1999 | 1998 |
|---|---|---|---|---|---|---|---|---|---|---|
| Tangible Book Value | NM | NM | NM | NM | NM | NA | NA | NA | NA | NA |
| Cash Flow | 2.09 | 1.64 | 1.14 | 0.56 | 0.38 | NA | NA | NA | NA | NA |
| Earnings | 1.65 | 1.35 | 0.95 | 0.30 | -0.11 | 0.15 | 0.32 | NA | NA | NA |
| S&P Core Earnings | 1.71 | 1.33 | 0.94 | 0.30 | NA | NA | NA | NA | NA | NA |
| Dividends | Nil | Nil | Nil | Nil | Nil | NA | NA | NA | NA | NA |
| Payout Ratio | Nil | Nil | Nil | Nil | Nil | NA | NA | NA | NA | NA |
| Prices:High | 42.74 | 34.26 | 19.92 | 11.36 | NA | NA | NA | NA | NA | NA |
| Prices:Low | 17.49 | 19.46 | 10.40 | 6.03 | NA | NA | NA | NA | NA | NA |
| P/E Ratio:High | 26 | 25 | 21 | 37 | NA | NA | NA | NA | NA | NA |
| P/E Ratio:Low | 11 | 14 | 11 | 20 | NA | NA | NA | NA | NA | NA |

| Income Statement Analysis (Million $) | | | | | | | | | | |
|---|---|---|---|---|---|---|---|---|---|---|
| Commissions | Nil | Nil | Nil | Nil | Nil | NA | NA | NA | NA | NA |
| Interest Income | 29.0 | 9.80 | 9.30 | 4.30 | 6.00 | NA | NA | NA | NA | NA |
| Total Revenue | 6,034 | 4,032 | 2,911 | 2,365 | 1,949 | 1,170 | 675 | NA | NA | NA |
| Interest Expense | 163 | 45.0 | 54.3 | 65.4 | 71.3 | NA | NA | NA | NA | NA |
| Pretax Income | 592 | 523 | 358 | 108 | -41.0 | 48.8 | 42.5 | NA | NA | NA |
| Effective Tax Rate | 32.5% | 37.9% | 38.8% | 40.2% | NM | 61.7% | 50.8% | NA | NA | NA |
| Net Income | 388 | 319 | 217 | 64.7 | -34.7 | 18.7 | 20.9 | NA | NA | NA |
| S&P Core Earnings | 403 | 314 | 216 | 64.0 | NA | NA | NA | NA | NA | NA |

| Balance Sheet & Other Financial Data (Million $) | | | | | | | | | | |
|---|---|---|---|---|---|---|---|---|---|---|
| Total Assets | 6,243 | 5,945 | 2,816 | 2,272 | 2,213 | 1,325 | 1,359 | NA | NA | NA |
| Cash Items | 392 | 244 | 449 | 257 | 164 | 79.7 | 57.5 | NA | NA | NA |
| Receivables | 1,337 | 985 | 739 | 532 | 553 | NA | NA | NA | NA | NA |
| Securities Owned | Nil | Nil | Nil | Nil | Nil | NA | NA | NA | NA | NA |
| Securities Borrowed | Nil | Nil | Nil | Nil | Nil | NA | NA | NA | NA | NA |
| Due Brokers & Customers | Nil | Nil | Nil | Nil | Nil | NA | NA | NA | NA | NA |
| Other Liabilities | 2,428 | 1,906 | 1,138 | 809 | 833 | NA | NA | NA | NA | NA |
| Capitalization:Debt | 1,992 | 2,193 | 821 | 761 | 1,061 | NA | NA | NA | NA | NA |
| Capitalization:Equity | 989 | 1,182 | 794 | 560 | 333 | 251 | 257 | NA | NA | NA |
| Capitalization:Total | 3,244 | 3,573 | 1,622 | 1,321 | 1,394 | NA | NA | NA | NA | NA |
| % Return on Revenue | 6.4 | 7.8 | 7.4 | 2.7 | NM | 1.6 | 3.1 | NA | NA | NA |
| % Return on Assets | 6.4 | 7.2 | 8.5 | 2.8 | NM | 1.4 | NA | NA | NA | NA |
| % Return on Equity | 35.8 | 32.2 | 32.0 | 14.4 | NM | 7.4 | NA | NA | NA | NA |

Data as orig reptd.; bef. results of disc opers/spec. items. Per share data adj. for stk. divs.; EPS diluted. E-Estimated. NA-Not Available. NM-Not Meaningful. NR-Not Ranked. UR-Under Review.

**Office:** 11150 Santa Monica Blvd Ste 1600, Los Angeles, CA 90025-3385.
**Telephone:** 310-405-8900.
**Website:** http://www.cbre.com
**Chrmn:** R.C. Blum

**Pres & CEO:** B. White
**Vice Chrmn:** R. Wirta
**Vice Chrmn:** P. Gunne
**COO:** W.M. Harris

**Investor Contact:** S. Young (212-984-8359)
**Board Members:** P. Aitken, R. C. Blum, P. M. Daniels, T. A. Daschle, N. Diment, C. F. Feeny, J. L. Fox, B. M. Freeman, P. Gunne, M. Kantor, F. V. Malek, C. P. Rullman, J. J. Su, R. E. Sulentic, B. White, G. L. Wilson, R. Wirta

**Founded:** 2001
**Domicile:** Delaware
**Employees:** 29,000

*The McGraw-Hill Companies*

# CBS Corp

**STANDARD &POOR'S**

| S&P Recommendation | STRONG SELL ★☆☆☆☆ | Price $6.62 (as of Nov 14, 2008) | 12-Mo. Target Price $5.00 | Investment Style Large-Cap Value |
|---|---|---|---|---|

**GICS Sector** Consumer Discretionary
**Sub-Industry** Broadcasting & Cable TV

**Summary** This major operator of TV, radio, and outdoor advertising properties is one of the two companies created after the separation of the "old" Viacom into two public entities.

## Key Stock Statistics (Source S&P, Vickers, company reports)

| | | | | | | | |
|---|---|---|---|---|---|---|---|
| 52-Wk Range | $28.00– 5.86 | S&P Oper. EPS 2008E | 1.56 | Market Capitalization(B) | $4.117 | Beta | 0.70 |
| Trailing 12-Month EPS | $-17.20 | S&P Oper. EPS 2009E | 1.32 | Yield (%) | 16.31 | S&P 3-Yr. Proj. EPS CAGR(%) | 3 |
| Trailing 12-Month P/E | NM | P/E on S&P Oper. EPS 2008E | 4.2 | Dividend Rate/Share | $1.08 | S&P Credit Rating | BBB |
| $10K Invested 5 Yrs Ago | NA | Common Shares Outstg. (M) | 679.6 | Institutional Ownership (%) | 87 | | |

## Price Performance

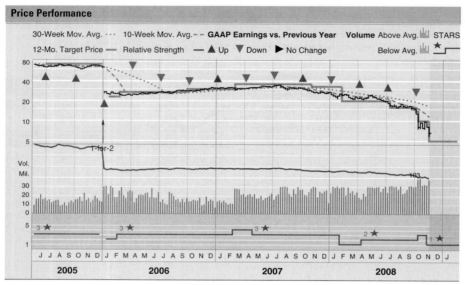

30-Week Mov. Avg. · · · 10-Week Mov. Avg. – – **GAAP Earnings vs. Previous Year** Volume Above Avg. STARS
12-Mo. Target Price — Relative Strength — ▲ Up ▼ Down ► No Change Below Avg. ★

Options: ASE, CBOE, P

## Highlights

► The STARS recommendation for CBS has recently been changed to 1 (strong sell) from 3 (hold) and the 12-month target price has recently been changed to $5.00 from $10.00. The Highlights section of this Stock Report will be updated accordingly.

## Investment Rationale/Risk

► The Investment Rationale/Risk section of this Stock Report will be updated shortly. For the latest News story on CBS from MarketScope, see below.

► 11/12/08 04:10 pm ET ... S&P REDUCES OPINION ON CLASS B SHARES OF CBS CORP TO STRONG SELL FROM SELL (CBS 6.14*): With '08 shaping as worst year yet, and doubtful of any appreciable improvement through at least '09 first half, we increasingly doubt CBS's ability to sustain (much less, hike) dividends now near 17% yield, as free cash stagnates. Also, ongoing debt refi talks between lenders and National Amusements, Chairman Sumner Redstone's control vehicle, amid resignation of daughter Shari as Chairman of affiliated Midway Games (MWY 0.25, NR), raises specter of further sales by Redstone, or key asset divestitures at fire-sale values. We cut PEG-based target price by $5 to $5. /T.Amobi-CPA,CFA

## Qualitative Risk Assessment

| LOW | MEDIUM | HIGH |
|---|---|---|

Our risk assessment reflects CBS's leading TV and outdoor properties and our view of the strong balance sheet and free cash flow generation. This is offset by continued challenges in the radio business and a soft advertising market.

## Quantitative Evaluations

**S&P Quality Ranking** B-

| D | C | B- | B | B+ | A- | A | A+ |
|---|---|---|---|---|---|---|---|

**Relative Strength Rank** WEAK

18

LOWEST = 1                 HIGHEST = 99

## Revenue/Earnings Data

**Revenue (Million $)**

| | 1Q | 2Q | 3Q | 4Q | Year |
|---|---|---|---|---|---|
| 2008 | 3,654 | 3,394 | 3,376 | -- | -- |
| 2007 | 3,658 | 3,375 | 3,281 | 3,759 | 14,073 |
| 2006 | 3,575 | 3,483 | 3,379 | 3,883 | 14,320 |
| 2005 | 5,577 | 5,876 | 5,943 | 3,828 | 14,536 |
| 2004 | 6,772 | 6,842 | 5,485 | 6,296 | 22,526 |
| 2003 | 6,051 | 6,418 | 6,600 | 7,516 | 26,585 |

**Earnings Per Share ($)**

| | 1Q | 2Q | 3Q | 4Q | Year |
|---|---|---|---|---|---|
| 2008 | 0.36 | 0.61 | -18.53 | E0.26 | E1.56 |
| 2007 | 0.28 | 0.55 | 0.48 | 0.40 | 1.70 |
| 2006 | 0.31 | 0.64 | 0.42 | 0.43 | 1.79 |
| 2005 | 0.72 | 0.94 | 0.94 | -6.07 | -5.27 |
| 2004 | 0.82 | 0.86 | 0.84 | -20.42 | -17.56 |
| 2003 | 0.52 | 0.74 | 0.80 | -0.44 | 1.62 |

Fiscal year ended Dec. 31. Next earnings report expected: Late February. EPS Estimates based on S&P Operating Earnings; historical GAAP earnings are as reported.

## Dividend Data (Dates: mm/dd Payment Date: mm/dd/yy)

| Amount ($) | Date Decl. | Ex-Div. Date | Stk. of Record | Payment Date |
|---|---|---|---|---|
| 0.250 | 02/21 | 02/29 | 03/04 | 04/01/08 |
| 0.270 | 04/29 | 05/30 | 06/03 | 07/01/08 |
| 0.270 | 08/11 | 08/29 | 09/03 | 10/01/08 |
| 0.270 | 11/13 | 12/02 | 12/04 | 01/01/09 |

Dividends have been paid since 2003. Source: Company reports.

---

**Please read the Required Disclosures and Analyst Certification on the last page of this report.**

**The McGraw-Hill Companies**

# CBS Corp

## Business Summary October 30, 2008

CORPORATE OVERVIEW. In its current form, the company is one of the two independent public entities created after the early 2006 separation of the "old" Viacom (which was renamed CBS Corp., while the other entity adopted the "Viacom" name). Pursuant to the separation, each Class A and B shareholder of the "old" Viacom received 0.5 of a share of corresponding A or B stock of each of the new entities. We believe that CBS Corp. was the lower-growth entity resulting from the separation, and that it was targeted to value-oriented investors. Nearly 70% of its revenues are generated from advertising-related businesses.

The television segment includes the CBS networks, CW network (a new joint venture with Time Warner's WB), 39 owned and operated (O&O) TV stations, Showtime cable networks and Paramount/King World TV production and syndication. In the 2008 first half, CBS sold a minority stake in the Sundance Channel. The radio division, CBS Radio, operates 178 radio stations in 40 U.S. markets (and owns interests of 18% in Westwood One and 10% in Spanish Broadcasting). The outdoor unit, Viacom Outdoor, operates billboards and out-of-home displays in the U.S. and abroad. The Publishing segment mainly includes book publishers Simon & Schuster. In 2006, the company sold its

Paramount Parks for $1.24 billion in cash. CBS is also launching a start-up movie studio to help provide some content to Showtime.

CORPORATE STRATEGY. In June 2008, aiming to bulk up its online businesses, CBS acquired CNET Networks for about $1.8 billion in cash. CNET became part of a new Interactive segment (including its online audience network), aligned into five new verticals: Technology, Entertainment, Sports, News and Business. CBS's online video syndication network has several distribution partners such as AOL, Microsoft, Comcast, Joost, Bebo, Brightcove, Netvibes, Sling Media, and Veoh. CBS is focused on a turnaround of its radio division, after recently divesting 39 radio stations and 11 TV stations; in July 2008, it set a plan to sell 50 other smaller-market radios. In May 2007, CBS acquired Last.fm, a music-based social network with nearly 20 million users in more than 200 countries, for $280 million in cash.

## Company Financials Fiscal Year Ended Dec. 31

| Per Share Data ($) | 2007 | 2006 | 2005 | 2004 | 2003 | 2002 | 2001 | 2000 | 1999 | 1998 |
|---|---|---|---|---|---|---|---|---|---|---|
| Tangible Book Value | NM | NM | NM | NM | NM | NM | NM | NM | NM | NM |
| Cash Flow | 2.34 | 2.36 | -9.91 | -16.62 | 2.77 | 3.55 | 3.31 | 3.04 | 3.43 | 1.90 |
| Earnings | 1.70 | 1.79 | -5.27 | -17.56 | 1.62 | 2.48 | -0.26 | -0.60 | 1.02 | -0.20 |
| S&P Core Earnings | 1.72 | 1.90 | 1.10 | 2.92 | 2.40 | 2.08 | -0.76 | NA | NA | NA |
| Dividends | 0.94 | 0.68 | 0.56 | 0.50 | 0.24 | Nil | Nil | Nil | Nil | Nil |
| Payout Ratio | 55% | NM | NM | NM | 15% | Nil | Nil | Nil | Nil | Nil |
| Prices:High | 35.75 | 32.04 | 77.98 | 90.10 | 99.50 | 103.78 | 119.00 | 151.75 | 120.87 | 74.25 |
| Prices:Low | 25.57 | 23.85 | 59.86 | 60.18 | 66.22 | 59.50 | 56.50 | 88.63 | 70.75 | 40.50 |
| P/E Ratio:High | 21 | 18 | NM | NM | 61 | 42 | NM | NM | NM | NM |
| P/E Ratio:Low | 15 | 13 | NM | NM | 41 | 24 | NM | NM | NM | NM |

| Income Statement Analysis (Million $) | | | | | | | | | | |
|---|---|---|---|---|---|---|---|---|---|---|
| Revenue | 14,073 | 14,320 | 14,536 | 22,526 | 26,585 | 24,606 | 23,223 | 20,044 | 12,859 | 12,096 |
| Operating Income | 3,078 | 3,135 | 3,165 | 5,838 | 5,957 | 5,542 | 4,667 | 4,243 | 2,162 | 1,529 |
| Depreciation | 456 | 440 | 499 | 810 | 1,000 | 946 | 3,087 | 2,224 | 845 | 777 |
| Interest Expense | 571 | 566 | 720 | 719 | 776 | 848 | 963 | 822 | 449 | 622 |
| Pretax Income | 2,052 | 2,036 | -7,513 | -13,676 | 2,861 | 3,695 | 656 | 436 | 783 | 96.0 |
| Effective Tax Rate | 40.0% | 32.0% | NM | NM | 55.9% | 39.2% | NM | NM | 52.5% | 145.0% |
| Net Income | 1,231 | 1,383 | -8,322 | -15,060 | 1,435 | 2,207 | -220 | -364 | 372 | -44.0 |
| S&P Core Earnings | 1,247 | 1,468 | 871 | 2,497 | 2,087 | 1,845 | -656 | NA | NA | NA |

| Balance Sheet & Other Financial Data (Million $) | | | | | | | | | | |
|---|---|---|---|---|---|---|---|---|---|---|
| Cash | 1,347 | 3,075 | 1,655 | 928 | 851 | 631 | 727 | 934 | 681 | 267 |
| Current Assets | 6,031 | 8,144 | 6,796 | 7,494 | 7,736 | 7,167 | 7,206 | 7,832 | 5,198 | 5,065 |
| Total Assets | 40,430 | 43,509 | 43,030 | 68,002 | 89,849 | 89,754 | 90,810 | 82,646 | 24,486 | 23,613 |
| Current Liabilities | 4,405 | 4,400 | 5,379 | 6,880 | 7,585 | 7,341 | 7,562 | 7,758 | 4,400 | 5,633 |
| Long Term Debt | 6,979 | 7,027 | 7,153 | 9,649 | 9,683 | 10,205 | 10,824 | 12,474 | Nil | 3,813 |
| Common Equity | 21,472 | 24,153 | 21,737 | 59,862 | 63,205 | 62,488 | 62,717 | 47,967 | 11,132 | 11,450 |
| Total Capital | 30,490 | 32,862 | 31,007 | 70,879 | 73,812 | 74,337 | 75,884 | 67,481 | 12,379 | 15,863 |
| Capital Expenditures | 469 | 394 | 376 | 415 | 534 | 537 | 515 | 659 | 706 | 604 |
| Cash Flow | 1,687 | 1,822 | -7,823 | -14,250 | 2,435 | 3,152 | 2,867 | 1,860 | 1,216 | 676 |
| Current Ratio | 1.4 | 1.9 | 1.3 | 1.1 | 1.0 | 1.0 | 1.0 | 1.0 | 1.2 | 0.9 |
| % Long Term Debt of Capitalization | 24.8 | 21.0 | 23.1 | 13.6 | 13.1 | 13.7 | 14.3 | 18.5 | Nil | 24.0 |
| % Net Income of Revenue | 8.8 | 9.7 | NM | NM | 5.4 | 9.0 | NM | NM | 2.9 | NM |
| % Return on Assets | 2.9 | 3.2 | NM | NM | 1.6 | 2.4 | NM | NM | 1.5 | NM |
| % Return on Equity | 5.5 | 5.9 | NM | NM | 2.3 | 3.5 | NM | NM | 3.3 | NM |

Data as orig reptd.; bef. results of disc opers/spec. items. Per share data adj. for stk. divs.; EPS diluted. Data as orig. reptd., for "old" Viacom through third qtr. 2005. E-Estimated. NA-Not Available. NM-Not Meaningful. NR-Not Ranked. UR-Under Review.

**Office:** 51 W 52nd St, New York, NY 10019-6188.
**Telephone:** 212-975-4321.
**Website:** http://www.cbscorporation.com
**Chrmn:** S.M. Redstone

**Pres & CEO:** L. Moonves
**Vice Chrmn:** S.E. Redstone
**EVP & CFO:** F.G. Reynolds
**EVP & General Counsel:** L.J. Briskman

**Investor Contact:** M.M. Shea
**Board Members:** D. R. Andelman, J. A. Califano, Jr., W. S. Cohen, G. L. Countryman, C. K. Gifford, L. Goldberg, B. S. Gordon, L. Griego, A. Kopelson, L. Moonves, D. P. Morris, S. E. Redstone, S. M. Redstone, F. V. Salerno

**Founded:** 1986
**Domicile:** Delaware
**Employees:** 23,970

STANDARD
&POOR'S

# Celgene Corp

| S&P Recommendation | STRONG BUY ★★★★★ | Price $58.86 (as of Nov 14, 2008) | 12-Mo. Target Price $81.00 | Investment Style Large-Cap Growth |
| --- | --- | --- | --- | --- |

**GICS Sector** Health Care
**Sub-Industry** Biotechnology

**Summary** This company primarily develops and commercializes small molecule drugs for the treatment of bloodborne and solid tumor cancers and inflammatory disease.

## Key Stock Statistics (Source S&P, Vickers, company reports)

| | | | | | | | |
| --- | --- | --- | --- | --- | --- | --- | --- |
| 52-Wk Range | $77.39– 41.26 | S&P Oper. EPS 2008E | 1.36 | Market Capitalization(B) | $26.969 | Beta | 0.07 |
| Trailing 12-Month EPS | $-3.07 | S&P Oper. EPS 2009E | 2.24 | Yield (%) | Nil | S&P 3-Yr. Proj. EPS CAGR(%) | 36 |
| Trailing 12-Month P/E | NM | P/E on S&P Oper. EPS 2008E | 43.3 | Dividend Rate/Share | Nil | S&P Credit Rating | NR |
| $10K Invested 5 Yrs Ago | $56,856 | Common Shares Outstg. (M) | 458.2 | Institutional Ownership (%) | 80 | | |

## Price Performance

30-Week Mov. Avg. · · · 10-Week Mov. Avg. − − GAAP Earnings vs. Previous Year   Volume Above Avg. STARS
12-Mo. Target Price — Relative Strength — ▲ Up ▼ Down ▶ No Change   Below Avg.

Options: ASE, CBOE, P, Ph

Analysis prepared by **Steven Silver** on October 24, 2008, when the stock traded at **$ 56.65**.

### Highlights

► We expect 2008 revenues of $2.25 billion, and 32% growth to $2.96 billion in 2009. We forecast 2008 Revlimid sales of $1.3 billion, roughly 58% of the total, and project 44% growth in 2009, to $1.89 billion. We see Revlimid's clinical program as a robust pipeline itself, with multiple new uses being explored in leading blood cancers, and view its worldwide expansion as CELG's key share catalyst. Still, we expect Vidaza, with a likely European launch for myelodysplastic syndrome in early 2009, to provide diversification.

► We forecast long-term gross margins in the 90%-91% range, as CELG focuses on enhancing manufacturing efficiencies. Further, we see the Pharmion acquisition enabling operating margin expansion, as CELG sells Revlimid, Thalomid and Vidaza within one infrastructure. We also view CELG's R&D investments favorably, as mid-stage pipeline candidates in psoriasis and small cell lung cancer near late-stage study.

► We project 2008 and 2009 EPS of $1.36 and $2.24, respectively, as we see CELG as well positioned (with solid cash flows and no debt) to repurchase shares and invest in growth initiatives.

### Investment Rationale/Risk

► We have a positive outlook for CELG, based on our view of its industry-leading growth prospects among large cap peers, supported by a strong financial position ($2.46 billion in cash at September 30, 2008) and a robust pipeline. We remain encouraged by Revlimid's European rollout and we expect continued off-label use in a first-line multiple myeloma setting while CELG pursues a formal filing for newly diagnosed patients and seeks to establish the drug as standard of care on the strength of its oral formulation and favorable survival data versus peers. We expect CELG's global footprint to expand rapidly, with strong growth seen for Revlimid and for Vidaza, following disappointing efficacy data reported by main rival Dacogen in mid-2008, supported by Pharmion's entrenched European sales force.

► Risks to our opinion and target price include slower-than-expected Revlimid sales growth, reimbursement issues for the drug, and clinical failure of CELG's other pipeline candidates.

► Our 12-month target price of $81 applies a 36X price-to-earnings multiple, a premium to profitable biotech peers given our view of a superior growth profile, to our 2009 estimate of $2.24.

## Qualitative Risk Assessment

| LOW | MEDIUM | HIGH |
| --- | --- | --- |

Our risk assessment reflects the strong competition we see in the blood cancer treatment markets, particularly from Velcade in multiple myeloma. Further, in Thalomid and Revlimid, the company currently depends on two products in the same markets for the majority of its revenues. We also see inherent risk in CELG's drugs maintaining a competitive safety profile versus peers.

## Quantitative Evaluations

**S&P Quality Ranking**                                    B-

| D | C | B- | B | B+ | A- | A | A+ |
| --- | --- | --- | --- | --- | --- | --- | --- |

**Relative Strength Rank**                          STRONG

81

LOWEST = 1                                      HIGHEST = 99

## Revenue/Earnings Data

**Revenue (Million $)**

| | 1Q | 2Q | 3Q | 4Q | Year |
| --- | --- | --- | --- | --- | --- |
| 2008 | 462.6 | 571.5 | 592.5 | -- | -- |
| 2007 | 293.4 | 347.9 | 349.9 | 414.6 | 1,406 |
| 2006 | 181.8 | 197.2 | 244.8 | 275.0 | 898.9 |
| 2005 | 112.4 | 145.7 | 129.5 | 149.3 | 536.9 |
| 2004 | 82.87 | 87.75 | 101.5 | 105.4 | 377.5 |
| 2003 | 49.09 | 67.29 | 74.33 | 80.77 | 271.5 |

**Earnings Per Share ($)**

| | | | | | |
| --- | --- | --- | --- | --- | --- |
| 2008 | -3.98 | 0.26 | 0.29 | E0.37 | E1.36 |
| 2007 | 0.14 | 0.13 | 0.09 | 0.18 | 0.54 |
| 2006 | 0.04 | 0.03 | 0.05 | 0.06 | 0.18 |
| 2005 | 0.13 | 0.03 | Nil | 0.01 | 0.18 |
| 2004 | 0.03 | 0.01 | 0.06 | 0.07 | 0.16 |
| 2003 | Nil | Nil | 0.01 | 0.01 | 0.04 |

Fiscal year ended Dec. 31. Next earnings report expected: Early February. EPS Estimates based on S&P Operating Earnings; historical GAAP earnings are as reported.

## Dividend Data

No cash dividends have been paid.

The McGraw-Hill Companies

# Celgene Corp

STANDARD
&POOR'S

## Business Summary October 24, 2008

CORPORATE OVERVIEW. Celgene develops and markets pharmaceuticals to treat cancer, immunological disorders, and other diseases. Its research focuses on small molecule compounds that inhibit Tumor Necrosis Factor alpha (TNFa) production or aberrant estrogen production, or may regulate kinases and ligases (enzymes involved in gene function that may contribute to disease when their proper function is altered).

The company is using its small molecule technology to develop Immunomodulatory Drugs (IMiDs) and Selective Cytokine Inhibitory Drugs (SelCIDs), an array of potent, orally available agents to fight acute and chronic diseases. The company's primary focus to date has been treating multiple myeloma (MM), the second most commonly diagnosed blood cancer. According to the International Myeloma Foundation, there are an estimated 750,000 people with MM worldwide. At any one time, there are more than 85,000 men and women in Europe undergoing treatment for multiple myeloma, and it is estimated that 25,000 people died from this blood cancer in 2007.

To date, Celgene's primary marketed products have been Thalomid and Revlimid. Thalomid is CELG's version of thalidomide, an antiangiogenic agent capable of inhibiting blood vessel growth and down-regulating TNFa. In 1998, Thalomid was approved by the FDA to treat leprosy-related conditions. In Feb-

ruary 2004, the company filed for FDA approval of Thalomid to treat multiple myeloma. The FDA approved Thalomid in May 2006. Thalomid is also being studied in numerous clinical trials for the treatment of myelodysplastic syndrome (MDS), prostate cancer, renal cell carcinoma, non-Hodgkin's and mantle cell lymphoma. European rights to Thalomid were re-acquired in the March 2008 acquisition of Pharmion, and the drug was approved in Europe for front-line multiple myeloma in April 2008.

On December 28, 2005, CELG announced FDA approval of Revlimid (the company's primary IMiD) to treat MDS patients with a rare chromosomal deletion (5q minus). On a monthly basis, the company estimates the cost of therapy to be between $4,500 and $4,700 per patient. Revlimid has received FDA approval to be used in combination with dexamethasone for the treatment of relapsed or refractory MM and, in June 2007, was approved in Europe for the same indications. The drug is also being tested in a number of earlier-stage trials including multiple myeloma in a first-line setting, amyloidosis, non-Hodgkin's lymphoma, and various solid tumor cancers.

## Company Financials Fiscal Year Ended Dec. 31

| Per Share Data ($) | 2007 | 2006 | 2005 | 2004 | 2003 | 2002 | 2001 | 2000 | 1999 | 1998 |
|---|---|---|---|---|---|---|---|---|---|---|
| Tangible Book Value | 6.80 | 4.83 | 1.48 | 1.06 | 0.93 | 0.85 | 1.03 | 1.00 | NM | 0.02 |
| Cash Flow | 0.60 | 0.23 | 0.23 | 0.18 | 0.06 | -0.31 | 0.01 | -0.05 | -0.31 | -0.16 |
| Earnings | 0.54 | 0.18 | 0.18 | 0.16 | 0.04 | -0.33 | -0.01 | -0.06 | -0.11 | -0.17 |
| S&P Core Earnings | 0.55 | 0.19 | 0.05 | 0.08 | -0.04 | -0.33 | -0.09 | NA | NA | NA |
| Dividends | Nil | Nil | Nil | Nil | Nil | Nil | Nil | Nil | Nil | Nil |
| Payout Ratio | Nil | Nil | Nil | Nil | Nil | Nil | Nil | Nil | Nil | Nil |
| Prices:High | 75.44 | 60.12 | 32.68 | 16.29 | 12.22 | 8.05 | 9.72 | 19.00 | 6.05 | 1.44 |
| Prices:Low | 41.26 | 31.51 | 12.35 | 9.37 | 5.04 | 2.83 | 3.60 | 4.58 | 0.94 | 0.34 |
| P/E Ratio:High | NM | NM | NM | NM | NM | NM | NM | NM | NM | NM |
| P/E Ratio:Low | NM | NM | NM | NM | NM | NM | NM | NM | NM | NM |

### Income Statement Analysis (Million $)

| | 2007 | 2006 | 2005 | 2004 | 2003 | 2002 | 2001 | 2000 | 1999 | 1998 |
|---|---|---|---|---|---|---|---|---|---|---|
| Revenue | 1,406 | 899 | 537 | 378 | 271 | 136 | 114 | 84.2 | 26.2 | 3.80 |
| Operating Income | 457 | 200 | 97.9 | 52.4 | 5.38 | -31.0 | -19.9 | -23.9 | -21.7 | -31.7 |
| Depreciation | 31.5 | 25.7 | 14.3 | 9.69 | 8.03 | 5.18 | 5.09 | 3.72 | 0.99 | 0.81 |
| Interest Expense | 11.1 | 9.42 | 9.50 | 9.55 | 5.67 | 0.03 | 0.08 | 2.08 | 2.84 | 0.26 |
| Pretax Income | 517 | 203 | 84.2 | 63.2 | 12.0 | -101 | -4.14 | -18.8 | -24.8 | -7.30 |
| Effective Tax Rate | 56.2% | 66.0% | 24.4% | 16.5% | NM | NM | NM | NM | NM | NM |
| Net Income | 226 | 69.0 | 63.7 | 52.8 | 12.8 | -101 | -2.90 | -17.0 | -21.8 | -32.0 |
| S&P Core Earnings | 230 | 71.5 | 10.8 | 25.0 | -13.0 | -88.6 | -26.5 | NA | NA | NA |

### Balance Sheet & Other Financial Data (Million $)

| | 2007 | 2006 | 2005 | 2004 | 2003 | 2002 | 2001 | 2000 | 1999 | 1998 |
|---|---|---|---|---|---|---|---|---|---|---|
| Cash | 2,739 | 1,982 | 724 | 749 | 667 | 261 | 310 | 161 | 15.3 | 5.12 |
| Current Assets | 3,084 | 2,311 | 973 | 850 | 730 | 296 | 336 | 332 | 27.8 | 9.59 |
| Total Assets | 3,611 | 2,736 | 1,247 | 1,107 | 791 | 327 | 354 | 347 | 32.3 | 11.9 |
| Current Liabilities | 433 | 240 | 136 | 141 | 71.8 | 44.3 | 30.0 | 33.8 | 9.30 | 7.12 |
| Long Term Debt | 22.6 | 400 | 400 | 400 | 400 | 0.04 | 11.8 | 12.3 | 38.5 | 8.55 |
| Common Equity | 2,844 | 1,976 | 636 | 477 | 310 | 277 | 310 | 296 | -15.7 | -3.73 |
| Total Capital | 2,877 | 2,376 | 1,036 | 877 | 710 | 277 | 322 | 308 | 22.8 | 4.81 |
| Capital Expenditures | 64.4 | 46.1 | 35.9 | 36.0 | 11.2 | 11.1 | 7.87 | 9.64 | 1.78 | 0.79 |
| Cash Flow | 258 | 94.7 | 77.9 | 62.4 | 20.8 | -95.8 | 2.18 | -13.3 | -20.8 | -31.2 |
| Current Ratio | 7.1 | 9.6 | 7.2 | 6.0 | 10.2 | 6.7 | 11.2 | 9.8 | 3.0 | 1.3 |
| % Long Term Debt of Capitalization | 0.8 | 16.8 | 38.6 | 45.6 | 56.3 | 0.0 | 3.7 | 4.0 | 168.9 | 177.6 |
| % Net Income of Revenue | 16.1 | 7.7 | 11.9 | 14.0 | 4.7 | NM | NM | NM | NM | NM |
| % Return on Assets | 7.1 | 3.5 | 5.4 | 5.5 | 2.3 | NM | NM | NM | NM | NM |
| % Return on Equity | 9.4 | 5.3 | 11.4 | 13.0 | 4.3 | NM | NM | NM | NM | NM |

Data as orig reptd.; bef. results of disc opers/spec. items. Per share data adj. for stk. divs.; EPS diluted. E-Estimated. NA-Not Available. NM-Not Meaningful. NR-Not Ranked. UR-Under Review.

**Office:** 86 Morris Ave, Summit, NJ 07901-3915.
**Telephone:** 908-673-9000.
**Email:** info@celgene.com
**Website:** http://www.celgene.com

**Chrmn & CEO:** S.J. Barer
**Pres, COO & Secy:** R.J. Hugin
**SVP & CFO:** D.W. Gryska
**Chief Acctg Officer & Cntlr:** A. Van Hoek

**Treas:** C.B. Elflein
**Investor Contact:** B.P. Gill (908-673-9530)
**Board Members:** S. J. Barer, M. D. Casey, R. L. Drake, A. H. Hayes, Jr., R. J. Hugin, G. Kaplan, J. J. Loughlin, E. Mario, W. L. Robb

**Founded:** 1986
**Domicile:** Delaware
**Employees:** 1,685

# CenterPoint Energy Inc.

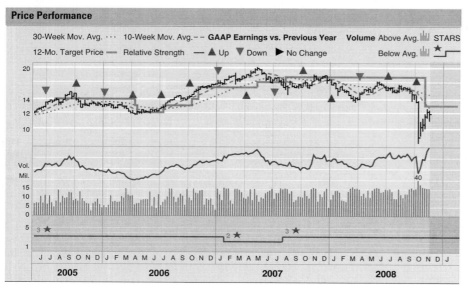

**STANDARD &POOR'S**

| S&P Recommendation | HOLD ★★★☆☆ | Price $11.85 (as of Nov 14, 2008) | 12-Mo. Target Price $13.00 | Investment Style Large-Cap Value |
|---|---|---|---|---|

**GICS Sector** Utilities
**Sub-Industry** Multi-Utilities

**Summary** This Houston-based energy company (formerly Reliant Energy) is one of the largest electric and natural gas delivery companies in the U.S.

## Key Stock Statistics (Source S&P, Vickers, company reports)

| | | | | | | | |
|---|---|---|---|---|---|---|---|
| 52-Wk Range | $18.45–8.48 | S&P Oper. EPS 2008E | 1.30 | Market Capitalization(B) | $4.078 | Beta | 0.97 |
| Trailing 12-Month EPS | $1.37 | S&P Oper. EPS 2009E | 1.27 | Yield (%) | 6.16 | S&P 3-Yr. Proj. EPS CAGR(%) | 6 |
| Trailing 12-Month P/E | 8.7 | P/E on S&P Oper. EPS 2008E | 9.1 | Dividend Rate/Share | $0.73 | S&P Credit Rating | BBB |
| $10K Invested 5 Yrs Ago | $14,985 | Common Shares Outstg. (M) | 344.2 | Institutional Ownership (%) | 71 | | |

## Price Performance

30-Week Mov. Avg. · · · · 10-Week Mov. Avg. – – GAAP Earnings vs. Previous Year  Volume Above Avg. |||| STARS
12-Mo. Target Price — Relative Strength — ▲ Up ▼ Down ► No Change  Below Avg. |||| ★

Options: ASE, CBOE, P, Ph

Analysis prepared by **Justin McCann** on October 31, 2008, when the stock traded at **$ 11.45**.

## Highlights

➤ We expect operating EPS in 2008 to remain flat with 2007 operating EPS of $1.17. While results should benefit from growth in the interstate pipelines segment and higher commodity prices in the field services segment, we expect this to be offset by the revenues lost due to Hurricane Ike. Results in the first half of 2008 were aided by the new pipeline that went into operation in May 2007 and more favorable weather.

➤ For 2009, we expect operating EPS to increase approximately 8% from anticipated results in 2008. We expect earnings growth to reflect the restoration of electric revenues lost due to the hurricane and more improvement in the natural gas distribution business. We also expect the expected weakening of the economy to result in a reduced level of growth at the interstate pipelines and field services operations.

➤ In May 2007, CNP's gas transmission unit placed into service the expanded capacity of a pipeline from Carthage, TX, to its Perryville hub in Northeast Louisiana. The expanded capacity was the primary driver in increasing the operating income of the interstate pipelines segment from $96 million in the first half of 2007 to $172 million in the first half of 2008.

## Investment Rationale/Risk

➤ The stock is down more than 30% year-to-date, hurt, in our view, by the impact of Hurricane Ike, the crisis in the credit markets and the anticipated slowdown in the economy. However, we expect the shares to be supported by a well-above peers yield from the dividend and, aided by CNP's improved financial strength and long-term earnings outlook, to recover and to perform roughly in line with electric and gas utility peers over the next 12 months.

➤ Risks to our recommendation and target price include the impact that would likely result from a potential weakening of CNP's financial strength, including a decreased ability to access capital markets on reasonable terms, as well as a sharp drop in the average P/E of the stock's industry peers.

➤ We expect CNP to use much of the proceeds from its "true-up" recovery to reduce its debt, which, as of June 30, 2008, was $9.35 billion. We expect CNP to emerge from this transitional period financially stronger. However, despite a recent above-peers dividend yield of around 6.5%, we see the stock trading at a discount-to-peers P/E of about 10.2X our 2009 EPS estimate. Our 12-month target price is $13.

## Qualitative Risk Assessment

| LOW | MEDIUM | HIGH |
|---|---|---|

Our risk assessment reflects the strong and steady cash flow that we expect from the Houston electric operations, which have a growing service territory; a low commodity risk profile; a generally supportive regulatory environment; and the gas purchase adjustment clauses that reduce the commodity risks related to the company's more diversified gas distribution operations.

## Quantitative Evaluations

**S&P Quality Ranking** — B

| D | C | B- | B | B+ | A- | A | A+ |
|---|---|---|---|---|---|---|---|

**Relative Strength Rank** — STRONG

78

LOWEST = 1                    HIGHEST = 99

## Revenue/Earnings Data

**Revenue (Million $)**

| | 1Q | 2Q | 3Q | 4Q | Year |
|---|---|---|---|---|---|
| 2008 | 3,363 | 2,670 | 2,515 | -- | -- |
| 2007 | 3,106 | 2,033 | 1,882 | 2,602 | 9,623 |
| 2006 | 3,077 | 1,843 | 1,935 | 2,464 | 9,319 |
| 2005 | 2,762 | 1,932 | 2,073 | 3,212 | 9,722 |
| 2004 | 2,959 | 2,241 | 1,667 | 2,618 | 8,510 |
| 2003 | 2,900 | 2,090 | 2,250 | 2,519 | 9,760 |

**Earnings Per Share ($)**

| | | | | | |
|---|---|---|---|---|---|
| 2008 | 0.36 | 0.30 | 0.39 | E0.29 | E1.30 |
| 2007 | 0.38 | 0.20 | 0.27 | 0.32 | 1.17 |
| 2006 | 0.28 | 0.61 | 0.26 | 0.20 | 1.33 |
| 2005 | 0.20 | 0.09 | 0.15 | 0.25 | 0.67 |
| 2004 | 0.24 | 0.19 | 0.05 | 0.46 | 0.61 |
| 2003 | 0.27 | 0.27 | 0.60 | 0.23 | 1.37 |

Fiscal year ended Dec. 31. Next earnings report expected: Late February. EPS Estimates based on S&P Operating Earnings; historical GAAP earnings are as reported.

## Dividend Data (Dates: mm/dd Payment Date: mm/dd/yy)

| Amount ($) | Date Decl. | Ex-Div. Date | Stk. of Record | Payment Date |
|---|---|---|---|---|
| 0.183 | 01/24 | 02/13 | 02/15 | 03/10/08 |
| 0.183 | 04/24 | 05/14 | 05/16 | 06/10/08 |
| 0.183 | 07/24 | 08/13 | 08/15 | 09/10/08 |
| 0.183 | 10/30 | 11/12 | 11/14 | 12/10/08 |

Dividends have been paid since 1922. Source: Company reports.

# CenterPoint Energy Inc.

STANDARD
&POOR'S

## Business Summary October 31, 2008

CORPORATE OVERVIEW. CenterPoint Energy (formerly Reliant Energy) is a Houston-based energy delivery company with operations that include electric transmission and distribution (50.9% of operating income in 2007), natural gas distribution (18.3%), interstate pipelines (17.2%), field services (7.3%), and competitive natural gas sales and services (6.3%).

MARKET PROFILE. The CenterPoint Energy Houston Electric (CEHE) utility serves approximately 2 million customers in a 5,000 square mile territory that includes the cities of Houston and Galveston, TX, and (with the exception of Texas City), nearly all of the Houston/Galveston metropolitan area. Following the deregulation of the industry in Texas, wholesale and retail suppliers pay the company to deliver the electricity over its transmission lines. The natural gas subsidiary, CenterPoint Energy Resources Corp. (CERC), serves about 3.2 million residential, commercial and industrial customers in Arkansas, Louisiana, Minnesota, Mississippi, Oklahoma and Texas. In 2007, approximately 43% of total demand was accounted for by residential customers, and about 57% was from commercial and industrial customers.

CERC's interstate pipeline business owns and operates about 8,100 miles of gas transmission lines primarily located in Arkansas, Illinois, Louisiana, Missouri, Oklahoma and Texas. It also owns and operates six natural gas storage fields with a combined daily volume of about 1.2 billion cubic feet per day. CERC's field services business owns and operates around 3,500 miles of gathering pipelines and processing plants, and about 151 natural gas gathering systems in Arkansas, Oklahoma, Louisiana, and Texas. On January 31, 2007, CNP agreed to discontinue the development of its proposed pipeline with Spectra Energy (the spun-off gas transmission unit of Duke Energy) due to market conditions. The proposed pipeline (announced on June 1, 2006) would have stretched from Texas to Pennsylvania.

## Company Financials Fiscal Year Ended Dec. 31

| Per Share Data ($) | 2007 | 2006 | 2005 | 2004 | 2003 | 2002 | 2001 | 2000 | 1999 | 1998 |
|---|---|---|---|---|---|---|---|---|---|---|
| Tangible Book Value | NM | NM | NM | NM | NM | NM | 13.05 | 8.11 | 7.69 | 6.77 |
| Earnings | 1.17 | 1.33 | 0.67 | 0.61 | 1.37 | 1.29 | 3.14 | 2.68 | 5.82 | -0.50 |
| S&P Core Earnings | 1.31 | 1.18 | 0.75 | 0.65 | 1.28 | 2.17 | 3.00 | NA | NA | NA |
| Dividends | 0.68 | 0.60 | 0.40 | 0.40 | 0.40 | 1.07 | 1.50 | 1.50 | 1.50 | 1.50 |
| Payout Ratio | 58% | 45% | 60% | 66% | 29% | 83% | 48% | 56% | 26% | NM |
| Prices:High | 20.20 | 16.87 | 15.14 | 12.32 | 10.49 | 27.10 | 50.45 | 49.00 | 32.50 | 33.38 |
| Prices:Low | 14.70 | 11.62 | 10.55 | 9.66 | 4.35 | 4.24 | 23.27 | 19.75 | 22.75 | 25.00 |
| P/E Ratio:High | 17 | 13 | 23 | 20 | 8 | 21 | 16 | 18 | 6 | NM |
| P/E Ratio:Low | 13 | 9 | 16 | 16 | 3 | 3 | 7 | 7 | 4 | NM |

| Income Statement Analysis (Million $) | 2007 | 2006 | 2005 | 2004 | 2003 | 2002 | 2001 | 2000 | 1999 | 1998 |
|---|---|---|---|---|---|---|---|---|---|---|
| Revenue | 9,623 | 9,319 | 9,722 | 8,510 | 9,760 | 7,923 | 46,226 | 29,339 | 15,303 | 11,488 |
| Depreciation | 631 | 599 | 541 | 490 | 625 | 616 | 911 | 906 | 911 | 857 |
| Maintenance | NA | NA | NA | NA | NA | NA | NA | NA | NA | NA |
| Fixed Charges Coverage | 1.95 | 1.80 | 1.35 | 1.15 | 1.37 | 1.80 | 3.33 | 2.60 | 2.32 | 1.64 |
| Construction Credits | NA | NA | NA | NA | NA | NA | NA | NA | Nil | 4.00 |
| Effective Tax Rate | 32.8% | 12.6% | 40.5% | NM | 35.6% | 35.0% | 33.3% | 32.9% | 35.0% | NM |
| Net Income | 399 | 432 | 225 | 206 | 420 | 386 | 919 | 771 | 1,666 | -141 |
| S&P Core Earnings | 444 | 384 | 254 | 224 | 390 | 642 | 868 | NA | NA | NA |

| Balance Sheet & Other Financial Data (Million $) | 2007 | 2006 | 2005 | 2004 | 2003 | 2002 | 2001 | 2000 | 1999 | 1998 |
|---|---|---|---|---|---|---|---|---|---|---|
| Gross Property | 13,250 | 12,567 | 11,558 | 10,963 | 11,812 | 11,409 | 24,214 | 15,260 | 20,133 | 17,030 |
| Capital Expenditures | 1,114 | 1,007 | 693 | 530 | 648 | 854 | 2,053 | 1,842 | 1,179 | 743 |
| Net Property | 9,740 | 9,204 | 8,492 | 8,186 | 11,812 | 11,409 | 15,857 | 15,260 | 13,267 | 11,531 |
| Capitalization:Long Term Debt | 8,364 | 7,802 | 8,568 | 7,193 | 10,783 | 9,194 | 6,448 | 5,701 | 5,666 | 7,153 |
| Capitalization:% Long Term Debt | 82.2 | 83.4 | 86.9 | 86.7 | 86.0 | 71.0 | 48.4 | 51.0 | 51.6 | 62.4 |
| Capitalization:Preferred | Nil | Nil | Nil | Nil | Nil | Nil | Nil | Nil | 10.0 | 10.0 |
| Capitalization:% Preferred | Nil | Nil | Nil | Nil | Nil | Nil | Nil | 0.09 | 0.09 | 0.01 |
| Capitalization:Common | 1,810 | 1,556 | 1,296 | 1,106 | 1,761 | 3,756 | 6,881 | 5,472 | 5,296 | 4,312 |
| Capitalization:% Common | 17.8 | 16.6 | 13.1 | 13.3 | 14.0 | 29.0 | 51.6 | 48.9 | 48.3 | 37.6 |
| Total Capital | 12,440 | 12,036 | 12,769 | 10,767 | 12,934 | 13,180 | 16,970 | 13,998 | 13,694 | 14,158 |
| % Operating Ratio | 87.7 | 88.8 | 90.3 | 88.2 | 85.8 | 85.8 | 96.6 | 94.9 | 97.8 | 86.9 |
| % Earned on Net Property | 12.5 | 11.8 | 11.3 | 10.6 | 21.8 | 17.2 | 12.8 | 13.2 | 10.0 | 13.0 |
| % Return on Revenue | 4.1 | 2.8 | 1.4 | 2.4 | 4.3 | 4.9 | 2.0 | 2.6 | 10.9 | NM |
| % Return on Invested Capital | 8.5 | 8.3 | 7.9 | 7.6 | 11.1 | 14.7 | 11.2 | 10.3 | 20.5 | 16.6 |
| % Return on Common Equity | 23.7 | 30.3 | 18.7 | 14.4 | 26.4 | 10.3 | 14.8 | 14.3 | 34.7 | NM |

Data as orig reptd.; bef. results of disc opers/spec. items. Per share data adj. for stk. divs.; EPS diluted. E-Estimated. NA-Not Available. NM-Not Meaningful. NR-Not Ranked. UR-Under Review.

**Office:** 1111 Louisiana Street, Houston, TX 77002-5230.
**Telephone:** 713-207-1111.
**Email:** info@reliantenergy.nl
**Website:** http://www.centerpointenergy.com

**Chrmn:** M. Carroll
**Pres & CEO:** D.M. McClanahan
**EVP & CFO:** G.L. Whitlock
**EVP, Secy & General Counsel:** S.E. Rozzell

**SVP, Chief Acctg Officer & Cntlr:** W.L. Fitzgerald
**Investor Contact:** M. Paulsen (713-207-6500)
**Board Members:** D. R. Campbell, M. Carroll, D. Cody, O. H. Crosswell, M. P. Johnson, J. M. Longoria, T. F. Madison, D. M. McClanahan, R. T. O'Connell, S. O. Rheney, M. E. Shannon, P. S. Wareing, S. M. Wolff

**Founded:** 1882
**Domicile:** Texas
**Employees:** 8,568

# Centex Corp.

STANDARD &POOR'S

| S&P Recommendation | HOLD ★★★☆☆ | Price $8.98 (as of Nov 14, 2008) | 12-Mo. Target Price $13.00 | Investment Style Large-Cap Blend |
|---|---|---|---|---|

**GICS Sector** Consumer Discretionary
**Sub-Industry** Homebuilding

**Summary** This major U.S. homebuilder sells homes in 22 states and engages in mortgage banking and title insurance sales.

## Key Stock Statistics (Source S&P, Vickers, company reports)

| | | | | | | | |
|---|---|---|---|---|---|---|---|
| 52-Wk Range | $30.29– 7.66 | S&P Oper. EPS 2009**E** | -4.55 | Market Capitalization(B) | $1.116 | Beta | 1.37 |
| Trailing 12-Month EPS | $-17.84 | S&P Oper. EPS 2010**E** | -1.60 | Yield (%) | Nil | S&P 3-Yr. Proj. EPS CAGR(%) | -5 |
| Trailing 12-Month P/E | NM | P/E on S&P Oper. EPS 2009**E** | NM | Dividend Rate/Share | Nil | S&P Credit Rating | BB |
| $10K Invested 5 Yrs Ago | $2,055 | Common Shares Outstg. (M) | 124.3 | Institutional Ownership (%) | NM | | |

## Price Performance

30-Week Mov. Avg. ···· 10-Week Mov. Avg. — **GAAP Earnings vs. Previous Year** Volume Above Avg. STARS
12-Mo. Target Price — Relative Strength — ▲ Up ▼ Down ► No Change Below Avg. ★

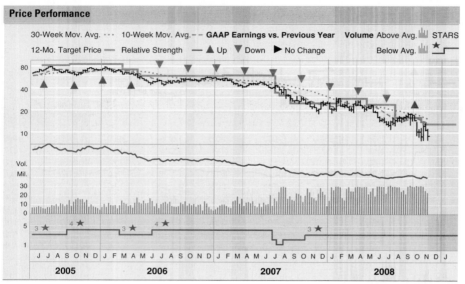

Options: ASE, CBOE, P, Ph

Analysis prepared by **Kenneth M. Leon, CPA** on October 30, 2008, when the stock traded at **$ 11.50.**

## Highlights

► Following a 36% revenue decrease in FY 08 (Mar.), we forecast a 51% decline for FY 09, reflecting continued weakness in the U.S. housing industry. With a backlog valued at $1.8 billion at September 30, 2008, we see flat revenue growth in FY 10, but the company has reduced its inventory of total owned lots by 31% to 63,311 units and 70% lower for lot option contracts to 11,866 units at the end of the second quarter.

► We believe FY 09 is seeing the same pressure on home prices and gross margins as the prior year. The company took writedowns in the September quarter of $102 million for impairments and other land charges, following writedowns of $80 million in the June quarter, and $3.1 billion cumulatively since the beginning of 2006. We view these inventory charges as large, but we see the size of writedowns declining further in the next six months.

► Acknowledging low earnings visibility, and given the potential we see for further inventory writedowns, we estimate a loss per share of $4.55 for FY 09, and a loss of $1.60 in FY 10.

## Investment Rationale/Risk

► We believe CTX will not reach profitability through any quarter in FY 10, as housing inventory remains too high, despite a major decline in mortgage rates in a weakening economy. In our opinion, asset impairments may be $75 million to $100 million in the third quarter of FY 09, after nearly $3.1 billion of writedowns since the beginning of 2006. We would hold CTX shares based on our view of the company's $1.3 billion of available cash and easing writedowns in FY 09.

► Risks to our recommendation and target price include any significant increase in mortgage rates or a weakening of job growth that deepens the US recession. These factors are key demand inputs for the highly cyclical homebuilding industry.

► We arrive at our 12-month target price of $13 by applying a target price-to-book ratio just under 0.8X, toward the low end of CTX's historical range and near peers based on the company's size, to our estimated book value per share of $15.90. Despite a weak housing market, we are confident in management's ability to operate effectively and position CTX to gain share when housing recovers.

## Qualitative Risk Assessment

| LOW | MEDIUM | HIGH |
|---|---|---|

Our high risk assessment reflects Centex's exposure to the sharp cyclicality of the housing industry and the company's liquidity should the current downturn extend into 2009. Partly offsetting these concerns are the company's national scope of operations and its large scale to gain volume discounts on material costs.

## Quantitative Evaluations

**S&P Quality Ranking** NR

| D | C | B- | B | B+ | A- | A | A+ |
|---|---|---|---|---|---|---|---|

**Relative Strength Rank** MODERATE

35

LOWEST = 1          HIGHEST = 99

## Revenue/Earnings Data

**Revenue (Million $)**

| | 1Q | 2Q | 3Q | 4Q | Year |
|---|---|---|---|---|---|
| 2009 | 1,126 | 1,005 | -- | -- | -- |
| 2008 | 1,902 | 2,186 | 1,873 | 2,314 | 8,276 |
| 2007 | 2,804 | 2,816 | 2,726 | 3,669 | 12,015 |
| 2006 | 3,222 | 3,630 | 3,738 | 4,550 | 14,400 |
| 2005 | 2,766 | 2,985 | 3,119 | 3,990 | 12,860 |
| 2004 | 2,173 | 2,428 | 2,570 | 3,193 | 10,363 |

**Earnings Per Share ($)**

| | 1Q | 2Q | 3Q | 4Q | Year |
|---|---|---|---|---|---|
| 2009 | -1.36 | -1.62 | E-0.84 | E-0.73 | E-4.55 |
| 2008 | -1.08 | -5.27 | -7.95 | -7.36 | -21.71 |
| 2007 | 1.37 | 0.65 | -2.02 | -0.18 | -0.10 |
| 2006 | 1.74 | 2.49 | 2.52 | 2.92 | 9.20 |
| 2005 | 1.35 | 1.61 | 1.91 | 2.75 | 7.64 |
| 2004 | 1.04 | 1.56 | 1.43 | 2.05 | 6.01 |

Fiscal year ended Mar. 31. Next earnings report expected: Late January. EPS Estimates based on S&P Operating Earnings; historical GAAP earnings are as reported.

## Dividend Data (Dates: mm/dd Payment Date: mm/dd/yy)

| Amount ($) | Date Decl. | Ex-Div. Date | Stk. of Record | Payment Date |
|---|---|---|---|---|
| 0.040 | 02/14 | 03/03 | 03/05 | 03/26/08 |
| 0.040 | 05/08 | 05/27 | 05/29 | 06/19/08 |
| 0.040 | 07/10 | 07/28 | 07/30 | 08/20/08 |

Dividends have been paid since 1973. Source: Company reports.

# Centex Corp.

STANDARD
&POOR'S

## Business Summary October 30, 2008

CORPORATE OVERVIEW. Centex Corp. constructs site-built homes in 74 markets in 22 states and the District of Columbia. CTX sells homes to first-time and move-up buyers, as well as active adult and second home buyers. It also has operations in real estate-related finance businesses. The company estimates that it accounted for about 4% of the new homes sold in the U.S. in FY 08 (Mar.).

CTX delivered 27,202 homes in FY 08, down from 35,785 homes in FY 07 and 39,232 homes in FY 06, reflecting the housing industry slowdown. Sales prices vary widely, with an average of about $276,788 for FY 08, down from $307,810 in FY 07. Average home prices dipped further, to $247,534, in the FY 09 second quarter. In the past fiscal year, 80% of the homes closed were single-family detached homes, which includes homes from resort and second homes, as well as on-your-lot operations.

IMPACT OF MAJOR DEVELOPMENTS. Relative to peers, Centex has historically relied less on acquisitions for its expansion. Its most recent acquisition occurred in January 2003, with the purchase of The Jones Company. Since that time, as the homebuilding upcycle entered its later stages, the company has become even more cautious about businesses that it considers non-core. As a result, Centex has been on the selling end of most strategic activity in the past few years.

In June 2003, CTX spun off its Cavco Industries manufactured home business to shareholders. Likewise, in January 2004, CTX spun off its 65% stake in Centex Construction Products, which was renamed Eagle Materials (EXP).

In September 2005, CTX sold Fairclough Homes, which operates in the U.K., generating cash proceeds of almost $320 million. In July 2006, the company sold its sub-prime lending operations for about $540 million, or a slight premium to the unit's book value. In April 2007, the company sold its commercial construction operations for about $362 million. In April 2008, CTX sold its home services operations for $135 million.

## Company Financials Fiscal Year Ended Mar. 31

| Per Share Data ($) | 2008 | 2007 | 2006 | 2005 | 2004 | 2003 | 2002 | 2001 | 2000 | 1999 |
|---|---|---|---|---|---|---|---|---|---|---|
| Tangible Book Value | 18.23 | 42.26 | 44.51 | 32.97 | 23.89 | 19.05 | 14.49 | 11.59 | 10.32 | 8.77 |
| Cash Flow | NA | 0.40 | 9.67 | 8.08 | 6.79 | 5.31 | 3.75 | 2.65 | 2.51 | 2.17 |
| Earnings | -21.71 | -0.10 | 9.20 | 7.64 | 6.01 | 4.41 | 3.06 | 2.33 | 2.11 | 1.88 |
| S&P Core Earnings | -21.37 | -0.10 | 9.20 | 7.64 | 5.90 | 4.25 | 2.86 | 2.17 | NA | NA |
| Dividends | 0.16 | 0.16 | 0.16 | 0.14 | 0.08 | 0.08 | 0.08 | 0.08 | 0.08 | 0.08 |
| Payout Ratio | NM | NM | 2% | 2% | 1% | 2% | 3% | 3% | 4% | 4% |
| Calendar Year | 2007 | 2006 | 2005 | 2004 | 2003 | 2002 | 2001 | 2000 | 1999 | 1998 |
| Prices:High | 56.45 | 79.40 | 79.66 | 59.98 | 56.54 | 31.55 | 29.40 | 20.00 | 22.88 | 22.88 |
| Prices:Low | 17.77 | 42.90 | 54.60 | 39.94 | 24.15 | 19.16 | 14.02 | 8.75 | 11.19 | 13.19 |
| P/E Ratio:High | NM | NM | 9 | 8 | 9 | 7 | 10 | 9 | 11 | 12 |
| P/E Ratio:Low | NM | NM | 6 | 5 | 4 | 4 | 5 | 4 | 5 | 7 |

### Income Statement Analysis (Million $)

| | 2008 | 2007 | 2006 | 2005 | 2004 | 2003 | 2002 | 2001 | 2000 | 1999 |
|---|---|---|---|---|---|---|---|---|---|---|
| Revenue | 8,276 | 12,015 | 14,400 | 12,860 | 10,363 | 9,117 | 7,748 | 6,711 | 5,956 | 5,155 |
| Operating Income | NA | 17.2 | 1,884 | 1,583 | 1,221 | 1,058 | 846 | 608 | 597 | 505 |
| Depreciation | 52.5 | 59.8 | 63.1 | 58.3 | 102 | 113 | 91.0 | 41.0 | 49.0 | 36.2 |
| Interest Expense | NA | Nil | 12.1 | 22.2 | 39.9 | 120 | 116 | 99.0 | 67.0 | 41.6 |
| Pretax Income | -2,875 | 103 | 1,895 | 1,574 | 1,149 | 825 | 640 | 468 | 481 | 427 |
| Effective Tax Rate | 7.45% | NM | 35.6% | 35.7% | 32.4% | 29.0% | 37.0% | 32.9% | 33.1% | 33.1% |
| Net Income | -2,661 | -11.8 | 1,221 | 1,011 | 777 | 556 | 382 | 282 | 257 | 232 |
| S&P Core Earnings | -2,619 | -11.8 | 1,221 | 1,011 | 765 | 536 | 358 | 264 | NA | NA |

### Balance Sheet & Other Financial Data (Million $)

| | 2008 | 2007 | 2006 | 2005 | 2004 | 2003 | 2002 | 2001 | 2000 | 1999 |
|---|---|---|---|---|---|---|---|---|---|---|
| Cash | 563 | 883 | 47.2 | 503 | 193 | 644 | 326 | 115 | 140 | 111 |
| Current Assets | NA | NA | NA | NA | NA | NA | NA | NA | NA | NA |
| Total Assets | 8,137 | 13,206 | 21,365 | 20,011 | 16,069 | 11,611 | 8,985 | 6,649 | 4,039 | 4,335 |
| Current Liabilities | NA | NA | NA | NA | NA | NA | NA | NA | NA | NA |
| Long Term Debt | NA | 3,963 | 6,059 | 12,968 | 8,616 | 6,237 | 4,944 | 3,041 | 751 | 284 |
| Common Equity | 2,299 | 5,112 | 5,012 | 4,281 | 3,050 | 2,459 | 2,116 | 1,714 | 1,420 | 1,198 |
| Total Capital | NA | 9,252 | 11,604 | 17,706 | 12,002 | 8,866 | 7,214 | 4,899 | 2,300 | 1,623 |
| Capital Expenditures | 6.64 | 40.6 | 92.2 | 43.3 | 53.8 | 63.0 | 60.0 | 52.0 | 88.0 | 52.5 |
| Cash Flow | NA | 48.0 | 1,284 | 1,070 | 879 | 669 | 473 | 323 | 306 | 268 |
| Current Ratio | 2.9 | 2.7 | 3.9 | 2.4 | 3.7 | 2.7 | 2.6 | 2.0 | 1.5 | 1.3 |
| % Long Term Debt of Capitalization | 55.6 | 42.8 | 52.2 | 73.2 | 71.8 | 70.3 | 68.5 | 62.1 | 32.7 | 17.5 |
| % Net Income of Revenue | NM | NM | 8.5 | 7.9 | 7.5 | 6.1 | 4.9 | 4.2 | 4.3 | 4.5 |
| % Return on Assets | NM | NM | 5.9 | 5.6 | 5.6 | 5.4 | 4.9 | 5.3 | 6.1 | 6.0 |
| % Return on Equity | NM | NM | 26.3 | 27.6 | 27.2 | 24.3 | 19.9 | 18.0 | 19.6 | 21.2 |

Data as orig reptd.; bef. results of disc opers/spec. items. Per share data adj. for stk. divs.; EPS diluted. E-Estimated. NA-Not Available. NM-Not Meaningful. NR-Not Ranked. UR-Under Review.

**Office:** 2728 N Harwood St, Dallas, TX, USA 75201-1516.
**Telephone:** 214-981-5000.
**Email:** ir@centex.com
**Website:** http://www.centex.com

**Chrmn, Pres, CEO & COO:** T. Eller
**SVP, Chief Acctg Officer & Cntlr:** M.D. Kemp
**SVP & Treas:** L. Angelilli
**SVP & General Counsel:** B.J. Woram

**CFO:** C.R. Smith
**Investor Contact:** M.G. Moyer (214-981-5000)
**Board Members:** B. T. Alexander, T. Eller, U. F. Fairbairn, T. J. Falk, C. W. Murchison, III, F. M. Poses, J. J. Postl, D. W. Quinn, M. K. Rose, T. M. Schoewe

**Founded:** 1950
**Domicile:** Nevada
**Employees:** 6,530

# CenturyTel Inc.

STANDARD &POOR'S

| S&P Recommendation | BUY ★★★★☆ | Price | 12-Mo. Target Price | Investment Style |
|---|---|---|---|---|
| | | $25.25 (as of Nov 14, 2008) | $36.00 | Large-Cap Blend |

**GICS Sector** Telecommunication Services
**Sub-Industry** Integrated Telecommunication Services

**Summary** This company provides wireline telecom services in 25 states, with operations concentrated in Alabama, Arkansas, Louisiana, Missouri and Wisconsin. In October, CTL agreed to acquire peer Embarq in a stock deal, pending necessary approvals.

## Key Stock Statistics (Source S&P, Vickers, company reports)

| | | | | | | | |
|---|---|---|---|---|---|---|---|
| 52-Wk Range | $43.02– 22.98 | S&P Oper. EPS 2008E | NA | Market Capitalization(B) | $2.528 | Beta | 0.61 |
| Trailing 12-Month EPS | $3.61 | S&P Oper. EPS 2009E | NA | Yield (%) | 11.09 | S&P 3-Yr. Proj. EPS CAGR(%) | 5 |
| Trailing 12-Month P/E | 7.0 | P/E on S&P Oper. EPS 2008E | null | Dividend Rate/Share | $2.80 | S&P Credit Rating | BBB- |
| $10K Invested 5 Yrs Ago | $8,103 | Common Shares Outstg. (M) | 100.1 | Institutional Ownership (%) | 92 | | |

## Price Performance

30-Week Mov. Avg. · · · ·   10-Week Mov. Avg. – – –   **GAAP Earnings vs. Previous Year**   **Volume** Above Avg. ⊪⊪⊪  STARS
12-Mo. Target Price —   Relative Strength —   ▲ Up  ▼ Down  ► No Change   Below Avg. ⊪⊪⊪  ★

Options: Cycle P, Ph

Analysis prepared by **Todd Rosenbluth** on October 27, 2008, when the stock traded at **$ 25.89**.

## Highlights

➤ We see revenues of $2.60 billion in 2008 and $2.57 billion in 2009, down slightly from recurring revenues in 2007, including assets that CTL acquired in mid-2007. On an organic basis, we foresee growth in DSL services offsetting the impact of weakness in voice services due to fewer access lines and lower universal service revenues. Our estimates exclude Embarq operations that CTL has agreed to acquire, subject to shareholder and regulatory approvals.

➤ Despite strong cost-cutting efforts, we look for EBITDA margins to narrow to 48.1% in 2008 and to 47.1% in 2009, from 49.5% in 2007, as benefits from system integrations are counterbalanced by increased selling and marketing costs and as demand for higher margin services declines. We believe the 2007 EBITDA margin was also aided by a revenue settlement.

➤ CTL reduced its share count by 7% in 2007 and 8% through the first nine months of 2008, helping boost EPS. With the pending acquisition, we expect no additional repurchases. We estimate EPS of $3.30 in 2008 and $3.24 in 2009. Second half 2007 results included $0.45 per share of one-time benefits.

## Investment Rationale/Risk

➤ CTL's pending stock-based acquisition of Embarq is a positive one, in our view. We believe CTL would be receiving a discounted price for assets that despite strong competitive pressure offer it sizable operating cost synergies. We believe the combined company will have credit access and provide ample dividend support. On a standalone basis, we see some gains through broadband, but we see revenue pressure and a need for cost savings. CTL's restriction from share buybacks limits the support for the stock, in our view.

➤ Risks to our recommendation and target price include adjustments to the universal service fund or access charges, from which CTL receives revenues; operating risk from its pending merger; and an increase in customer migration or line losses.

➤ Supported by a dividend yield of more than 10%, the shares appear attractive to us. Our 12-month target price of $36 is a blend of an 11X P/E applied to our 2009 EPS estimate and an enterprise value of 5.5X our 2009 EBITDA per share projection, slight discounts to multiples we expect for peers.

## Qualitative Risk Assessment

| LOW | MEDIUM | HIGH |
|---|---|---|

Our risk assessment reflects what we see as CTL's relatively strong balance sheet, the rural nature, less competitive nature of its markets relative to peers offset by its efforts to acquire a large company.

## Quantitative Evaluations

**S&P Quality Ranking**  A

| D | C | B- | B | B+ | A- | A | A+ |
|---|---|---|---|---|---|---|---|

**Relative Strength Rank**  MODERATE

50

LOWEST = 1     HIGHEST = 99

## Revenue/Earnings Data

**Revenue (Million $)**

| | 1Q | 2Q | 3Q | 4Q | Year |
|---|---|---|---|---|---|
| 2008 | 648.6 | 658.1 | 650.1 | -- | -- |
| 2007 | 600.9 | 690.0 | 708.8 | 656.6 | 2,656 |
| 2006 | 611.3 | 608.9 | 619.8 | 607.7 | 2,448 |
| 2005 | 595.3 | 606.4 | 657.1 | 620.5 | 2,479 |
| 2004 | 593.7 | 603.6 | 603.9 | 606.2 | 2,407 |
| 2003 | 580.5 | 590.2 | 603.8 | 606.3 | 2,381 |

**Earnings Per Share ($)**

| | | | | | |
|---|---|---|---|---|---|
| 2008 | 0.83 | 0.88 | 0.84 | E0.80 | E3.30 |
| 2007 | 0.68 | 1.00 | 1.01 | 1.05 | 3.72 |
| 2006 | 0.55 | 1.26 | 0.64 | 0.62 | 3.07 |
| 2005 | 0.59 | 0.64 | 0.68 | 0.59 | 2.49 |
| 2004 | 0.58 | 0.60 | 0.63 | 0.62 | 2.41 |
| 2003 | 0.58 | 0.60 | 0.63 | 0.57 | 2.38 |

Fiscal year ended Dec. 31. Next earnings report expected: Mid February. EPS Estimates based on S&P Operating Earnings; historical GAAP earnings are as reported.

## Dividend Data (Dates: mm/dd Payment Date: mm/dd/yy)

| Amount ($) | Date Decl. | Ex-Div. Date | Stk. of Record | Payment Date |
|---|---|---|---|---|
| 0.068 | 05/29 | 06/09 | 06/11 | 06/24/08 |
| .6325 Spl. | 06/24 | 07/02 | 07/07 | 07/21/08 |
| 0.700 | 08/25 | 09/05 | 09/09 | 09/22/08 |
| 0.070 | 08/25 | 09/05 | 09/09 | 09/22/08 |

Dividends have been paid since 1974. Source: Company reports.

# CenturyTel Inc.

**STANDARD &POOR'S**

## Business Summary October 27, 2008

CORPORATE OVERVIEW. As of September 2008, CTL operated 2.04 million telephone access lines, with about 85% penetration of households in its primarily rural and suburban markets. The company also generated revenues by providing long distance service to more than 60% of its customers, as well as by offering DSL broadband to 628,000 customers (31% penetrated), and dial-up Internet access to fewer than 100,000 customers. In addition, the company has partnered with EchoStar Communications to offer wholesale satellite services to customers through CTL's product bundles (6% penetrated). In the first nine months of 2008, 65% of revenues were from voice and network access services, with the remainder from data and fiber transport services.

COMPETITIVE LANDSCAPE. We believe CTL faces fewer challenges from technology substitution to cable telephony than metropolitan-based carriers such as AT&T. The penetration of the necessary broadband connection is smaller in the Tier II and Tier III markets in which CTL operates; as of mid 2008, more than 60% of its access line customers had the option of cable broadband, and 40% had the option of cable telephony from companies such as Charter and Comcast. Excluding acquisitions, CTL's local access lines declined 6.0% in the 12 months ended September 2008, up slightly from 5.7% at the end of 2007. CTL believes it has more than a 50% share of the broad-

band market in most territories. During the first nine months of 2008, we believe the slowing U.S. economy had a limited impact on CTL's access line count, and new customer additions picked up late in the first quarter.

CORPORATE STRATEGY. In October 2008, CTL agreed to acquire Embarq Corp (EQ) via a swap of 1.37 CTL shares per EQ share, equal to a purchase price of $11.6 billion that includes $6 billion in debt. EQ had 5.85 million access lines and 1.4 million DSL customers in 18 states including Florida, Nevada and Ohio. In the nine months ended September 2008, EQ had $4.65 billion in revenues, and $1.2 billion of operating income. The company sees $300 million in potential annual operating expense synergies, including from corporate and IT support, and an additional $30 million from capital expenditures.

In June 2008, CTL announced plans to increase its annual dividend to $2.80, from $0.27 beginning in July and to accelerate its share repurchase plans. We believe the dividend will use about 50% of CTL's free cash flow in 2008.

## Company Financials Fiscal Year Ended Dec. 31

| Per Share Data ($) | 2009 | 2008 | 2007 | 2006 | 2005 | 2004 | 2003 | 2002 | 2001 | 2000 |
|---|---|---|---|---|---|---|---|---|---|---|
| Tangible Book Value | NA | NA | NM | NM | 1.41 | NM | 0.37 | NM | NM | NM |
| Cash Flow | NA | NA | 8.44 | 7.31 | 6.37 | 5.90 | 5.63 | 4.21 | 5.73 | 4.36 |
| Earnings | 3.24 | 3.30 | 3.72 | 3.07 | 2.49 | 2.41 | 2.38 | 1.33 | 2.41 | 1.63 |
| S&P Core Earnings | NA | NA | 3.37 | 2.52 | 2.30 | 2.36 | 2.35 | 1.08 | 1.21 | NA |
| Dividends | NA | 0.91 | 0.26 | 0.25 | 0.24 | 0.23 | 0.22 | 0.21 | 0.20 | 0.19 |
| Payout Ratio | NA | 27% | 7% | 8% | 10% | 10% | 9% | 16% | 8% | 12% |
| Prices:High | NA | 42.00 | 49.94 | 44.11 | 36.50 | 35.54 | 36.76 | 35.50 | 39.88 | 47.31 |
| Prices:Low | NA | 28.50 | 39.91 | 32.54 | 29.55 | 26.20 | 25.25 | 21.13 | 25.45 | 24.44 |
| P/E Ratio:High | NA | 13 | 13 | 14 | 15 | 15 | 15 | 27 | 17 | 29 |
| P/E Ratio:Low | NA | 9 | 11 | 11 | 12 | 11 | 11 | 16 | 11 | 15 |

| Income Statement Analysis (Million $) | | | | | | | | | | |
|---|---|---|---|---|---|---|---|---|---|---|
| Revenue | NA | NA | 2,656 | 2,448 | 2,479 | 2,407 | 2,381 | 1,972 | 2,117 | 1,846 |
| Depreciation | NA | NA | 536 | 524 | 532 | 501 | 471 | 412 | 473 | 388 |
| Maintenance | NA | NA | NA | NA | NA | NA | NA | NA | NA | NA |
| Construction Credits | NA | NA | NA | NA | NA | NA | NA | NA | NA | NA |
| Effective Tax Rate | NA | NA | 32.4% | 37.4% | 37.8% | 38.4% | 35.2% | 35.3% | 37.2% | 39.0% |
| Net Income | NA | NA | 418 | 370 | 334 | 337 | 345 | 190 | 343 | 231 |
| S&P Core Earnings | NA | NA | 377 | 302 | 307 | 330 | 339 | 153 | 171 | NA |

| Balance Sheet & Other Financial Data (Million $) | | | | | | | | | | |
|---|---|---|---|---|---|---|---|---|---|---|
| Gross Property | NA | NA | 8,666 | 7,894 | 7,801 | 7,431 | 3,455 | 6,668 | 5,839 | 5,915 |
| Net Property | NA | NA | 3,108 | 3,109 | 3,304 | 3,341 | 3,455 | 3,532 | 3,000 | 2,959 |
| Capital Expenditures | NA | NA | 326 | 314 | 415 | 385 | 378 | 386 | 507 | 450 |
| Total Capital | NA | NA | 6,962 | 5,604 | 5,993 | 6,172 | 6,588 | 6,666 | 4,425 | 5,082 |
| Fixed Charges Coverage | NA | NA | 3.9 | 4.4 | 3.6 | 3.6 | 3.4 | 2.3 | 3.4 | 3.2 |
| Capitalization:Long Term Debt | NA | NA | 2,734 | 2,413 | 2,376 | 2,762 | 3,109 | 3,578 | 2,088 | 3,050 |
| Capitalization:Preferred | NA | NA | Nil | Nil | Nil | Nil | 7.98 | 7.98 | 7.98 | 7.98 |
| Capitalization:Common | NA | NA | 3,409 | 3,191 | 3,617 | 3,410 | 3,471 | 3,080 | 2,329 | 2,024 |
| % Return on Revenue | NA | NA | 15.8 | 15.1 | 13.5 | 14.0 | 14.5 | 9.6 | 16.2 | 12.5 |
| % Return on Invested Capital | NA | NA | 9.5 | 9.8 | 8.8 | 8.6 | 8.6 | 7.4 | 12.2 | 9.4 |
| % Return on Common Equity | NA | NA | 12.7 | 10.9 | 9.5 | 9.8 | 10.5 | 7.0 | 15.7 | 12.0 |
| % Earned on Net Property | NA | NA | 25.5 | 20.8 | 38.2 | 36.9 | 35.0 | 31.5 | 34.6 | 35.0 |
| % Long Term Debt of Capitalization | NA | NA | 44.5 | 43.1 | 39.6 | 44.8 | 47.2 | 53.7 | 47.2 | 60.0 |
| Capital % Preferred | NA | NA | Nil | Nil | Nil | Nil | 0.1 | 0.1 | 0.2 | 0.2 |
| Capitalization:% Common | NA | NA | 55.5 | 56.9 | 60.4 | 55.2 | 52.7 | 46.2 | 52.6 | 39.8 |

Data as orig reptd.; bef. results of disc opers/spec. items. Per share data adj. for stk. divs.; EPS diluted. E-Estimated. NA-Not Available. NM-Not Meaningful. NR-Not Ranked. UR-Under Review.

**Office:** 100 Centurytel Dr, Monroe, LA 71203.
**Telephone:** 318-388-9000.
**Website:** http://www.centurytel.com
**Chrmn & CEO:** G.F. Post, III

**Pres & COO:** K.A. Puckett
**Vice Chrmn:** H.P. Perry
**EVP & CFO:** R.S. Ewing, Jr.
**SVP, Secy & General Counsel:** S.W. Goff

**Investor Contact:** T. Davis (800-833-1188)
**Board Members:** W. R. Boles, Jr., V. Boulet, C. Czeschin, J. B. Gardner, W. B. Hanks, G. J. McCray, III, C. G. Melville, Jr., F. R. Nichols, H. P. Perry, G. F. Post, III, J. D. Reppond, J. R. Zimmel

**Founded:** 1968
**Domicile:** Louisiana
**Employees:** 6,600

**The McGraw-Hill Companies**

# Cephalon Inc

| | |
|---|---|
| **S&P Recommendation** BUY ★★★★☆ | **Price** $74.50 (as of Nov 14, 2008)    **12-Mo. Target Price** $90.00    **Investment Style** Mid-Cap Growth |

**GICS Sector** Health Care
**Sub-Industry** Biotechnology

**Summary** This biopharmaceutical company markets and develops human therapeutics for the treatment of neurological disorders, pain indications and most recently in oncology.

## Key Stock Statistics (Source S&P, Vickers, company reports)

| | | | | | | | |
|---|---|---|---|---|---|---|---|
| 52-Wk Range | $80.39– 56.20 | S&P Oper. EPS 2008**E** | 4.64 | Market Capitalization(B) | $5.099 | Beta | 0.79 |
| Trailing 12-Month EPS | $3.47 | S&P Oper. EPS 2009**E** | 5.63 | Yield (%) | Nil | S&P 3-Yr. Proj. EPS CAGR(%) | 16 |
| Trailing 12-Month P/E | 21.5 | P/E on S&P Oper. EPS 2008**E** | 16.1 | Dividend Rate/Share | Nil | S&P Credit Rating | NA |
| $10K Invested 5 Yrs Ago | $15,960 | Common Shares Outstg. (M) | 68.4 | Institutional Ownership (%) | NM | | |

## Price Performance

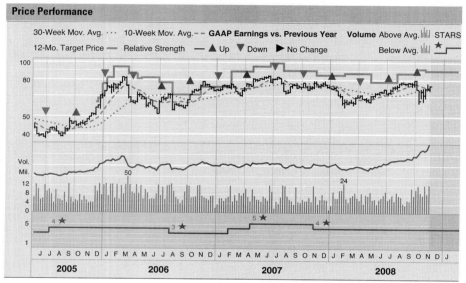

30-Week Mov. Avg. ... 10-Week Mov. Avg. — **GAAP Earnings vs. Previous Year** Volume Above Avg. STARS
12-Mo. Target Price — Relative Strength — ▲ Up ▼ Down ► No Change   Below Avg.

Options: ASE, CBOE, P, Ph

Analysis prepared by **Steven Silver** on November 04, 2008, when the stock traded at **$ 75.74**.

## Highlights

➤ We project 2008 sales of $1.95 billion, which represents 10% growth over 2007, and we forecast 13% sales growth in 2009, to $2.2 billion. We see CEPH's growth supported by the recent launches of Treanda and Amrix, helping to offset moderating trends of wakefulness drug Provigil, and its pain franchise with Fentora label expansion hampered by concerns over misuse, and Actiq sales eroded by generic competition. Despite approval challenges for non-cancer pain in the U.S., we see near-term Fentora sales benefiting from April 2008's Europe approval and rollout into 2009.

➤ We forecast an operating margin of 28% in 2008, in line with 2007 levels, and a rise to 30% in 2009, fueled by operating leverage from new product launches within an existing infrastructure, as in the current launch of Amrix within the Provigil-led central nervous system unit. While we expect CEPH to incur higher launch-related costs for Treanda and Amrix, we see cash flow supporting investment in research and commercialization initiatives.

➤ Our 2008 EPS estimate is $4.64. In 2009, we see earnings of $5.63 per share.

## Investment Rationale/Risk

➤ We have a positive outlook for CEPH's product portfolio, led by Treanda, which was approved for two indications in 2008, and Amrix, after the drug received a new formulation patent, extending the drug's patent protection until 2025. In our view, CEPH is well positioned to launch Nuvigil in late 2009, and to expand its indicated uses beyond its and predecessor Provigil's approved label. Though the FDA failed to approve expansion of Fentora use to non-cancer pain indications, consistent with a negative FDA advisory panel opinion earlier this year over misuse concerns, we see CEPH's new risk minimization program enhancing long-term approval prospects.

➤ Risks to our recommendation and target price include failure of Fentora sales growth to offset sales erosion of generic Actiq, further regulatory issues facing the company from product marketing or safety concerns, failure to successfully expand Nuvigil's product label, and clinical failure of CEPH's pipeline candidates.

➤ Our 12-month target price of $90 applies a 16X P/E multiple (1X our long-term growth rate for CEPH, in line with profitable sector peers) to our 2009 EPS estimate of $5.63.

## Qualitative Risk Assessment

| LOW | MEDIUM | HIGH |
|---|---|---|

Cephalon faces generic pressures in its pain franchise, has been subject to regulatory oversight of its marketing practices and drug safety, and is subject to changes in drug reimbursements. Also, the company is developing new drugs in competitive markets, which is a highly risky endeavor. Disappointing clinical results or sales trends of new products can negatively affect the stock price.

## Quantitative Evaluations

### S&P Quality Ranking    C

| D | C | B- | B | B+ | A- | A | A+ |
|---|---|---|---|---|---|---|---|

### Relative Strength Rank    STRONG

95
LOWEST = 1      HIGHEST = 99

## Revenue/Earnings Data

### Revenue (Million $)

| | 1Q | 2Q | 3Q | 4Q | Year |
|---|---|---|---|---|---|
| 2008 | 443.2 | 492.7 | 498.5 | -- | -- |
| 2007 | 437.0 | 447.2 | 438.4 | 450.0 | 1,773 |
| 2006 | 356.9 | 440.1 | 482.3 | 484.7 | 1,764 |
| 2005 | 280.0 | 286.0 | 309.5 | 336.4 | 1,212 |
| 2004 | 215.0 | 239.5 | 262.0 | 299.0 | 1,015 |
| 2003 | 137.6 | 160.3 | 184.9 | 202.5 | 714.8 |

### Earnings Per Share ($)

| | | | | | |
|---|---|---|---|---|---|
| 2008 | 0.52 | 0.80 | 1.42 | E1.31 | E4.64 |
| 2007 | 0.99 | -0.06 | -4.58 | 0.56 | -2.88 |
| 2006 | 0.05 | 0.76 | 1.43 | -0.08 | 2.08 |
| 2005 | 0.44 | -4.29 | 0.50 | 0.30 | -3.01 |
| 2004 | 0.37 | -0.15 | -2.94 | 1.23 | -1.31 |
| 2003 | 0.21 | 0.31 | 0.38 | 0.52 | 1.44 |

Fiscal year ended Dec. 31. Next earnings report expected: Mid February. EPS Estimates based on S&P Operating Earnings; historical GAAP earnings are as reported.

## Dividend Data

No cash dividends have been paid.

# Cephalon Inc

## Business Summary November 04, 2008

CORPORATE OVERVIEW. Cephalon develops, manufactures and markets therapeutics for the treatment of sleep disorders, neurodegenerative conditions, and cancer.

In 1998, the FDA approved Provigil (modafinil) tablets to treat excessive daytime sleepiness (EDS) due to narcolepsy, a chronic, lifelong sleep disorder. In January 2004, the FDA approved Provigil to treat EDS associated with obstructive sleep apnea/hypopnea syndrome and shift work sleep disorder (SWSD). In mid-2006, CEPH entered into an agreement with Takeda Pharmaceuticals to co-promote Provigil in the U.S, adding 750 Takeda sales reps to CEPH's 400 reps to co-promote the drug. Provigil has patent protection until 2012, by which time CEPH expects to transition users to Nuvigil. In February 2008, the U.S. Federal Trade Commission filed suit against CEPH, claiming the company illegally blocked generic competition to Provigil. CEPH denied any wrongdoing and plans to defend its agreements with generic drug makers. Provigil generated $852 million in 2007 sales, representing nearly half of CEPH's 2007 product sales.

Actiq (oral transmutes fontanel citrate), a cancer breakthrough pain control treatment approved by the FDA in 1998, saw 2007 sales fall by 41% in 2007 to $369 million due to generic competition which began in 2006. CEPH is receiv-

ing royalties on net profits from generic U.S. Actiq sales by Barr Labs. In August 2004, CEPH purchased CIA Labs for $515 million for rights to Coalescent fontanel (OF) tablet, marketed as Fentora, which CEPH launched in October 2006 for breakthrough cancer pain. In September 2007, CEPH warned of several deaths that occurred from inappropriate Fentora prescribing and dosing. In May 2008, an FDA advisory panel voted 17-3 against approving Fentora for non-cancer pain indications, despite positive Phase III study data, on concerns over patient misuse. CEPH unveiled a new risk minimization program which it plans to rollout for current Fentora users, while working with the FDA on an approval pathway. In September 2008, the FDA issued a complete response letter, delaying approval of the supplemental new drug application. Over the long-term, we believe label expansion represents a major opportunity, as we estimate 2 million to 3 million non-cancer pain sufferers who are potential users of Fentora. In April 2008, Fentora was approved in Europe for cancer breakthrough pain, and we expect product rollout into 2009.

## Company Financials Fiscal Year Ended Dec. 31

| Per Share Data ($) | 2007 | 2006 | 2005 | 2004 | 2003 | 2002 | 2001 | 2000 | 1999 | 1998 |
|---|---|---|---|---|---|---|---|---|---|---|
| Tangible Book Value | 0.11 | 5.93 | NM | NM | 1.98 | NM | NM | NM | 4.86 | 2.00 |
| Cash Flow | -1.02 | 3.75 | -1.56 | -0.37 | 2.01 | 3.12 | -1.03 | -2.42 | -1.75 | -1.87 |
| Earnings | -2.88 | 2.08 | -3.01 | -1.31 | 1.44 | 2.84 | -1.33 | -2.51 | -2.10 | -1.95 |
| S&P Core Earnings | 3.44 | 2.14 | -3.30 | -1.43 | 0.90 | 2.08 | -1.86 | NA | NA | NA |
| Dividends | Nil | Nil | Nil | Nil | Nil | Nil | Nil | Nil | Nil | Nil |
| Payout Ratio | Nil | Nil | Nil | Nil | Nil | Nil | Nil | Nil | Nil | Nil |
| Prices:High | 84.83 | 82.92 | 66.92 | 60.98 | 54.95 | 78.88 | 78.40 | 83.63 | 37.13 | 16.13 |
| Prices:Low | 64.65 | 51.58 | 37.35 | 41.58 | 36.92 | 35.82 | 36.38 | 29.88 | 7.25 | 3.88 |
| P/E Ratio:High | NM | 40 | NM | NM | 38 | 28 | NM | NM | NM | NM |
| P/E Ratio:Low | NM | 25 | NM | NM | 26 | 13 | NM | NM | NM | NM |

### Income Statement Analysis (Million $)

| | 2007 | 2006 | 2005 | 2004 | 2003 | 2002 | 2001 | 2000 | 1999 | 1998 |
|---|---|---|---|---|---|---|---|---|---|---|
| Revenue | 1,773 | 1,764 | 1,212 | 1,015 | 715 | 507 | 267 | 112 | 44.9 | 15.7 |
| Operating Income | 450 | 428 | 249 | 282 | 201 | 132 | 37.8 | -57.8 | -45.5 | -56.6 |
| Depreciation | 124 | 117 | 84.3 | 52.8 | 45.1 | 35.5 | 14.4 | 3.95 | 10.3 | 2.34 |
| Interest Expense | 19.8 | 67.0 | 25.2 | 50.4 | 28.9 | 38.2 | 73.1 | Nil | 8.25 | 1.87 |
| Pretax Income | -68.4 | 238 | -245 | -28.2 | 130 | 62.4 | -58.5 | -93.7 | -58.8 | -55.4 |
| Effective Tax Rate | NM | 39.2% | NM | NM | 35.6% | NM | NM | NM | NM | NM |
| Net Income | -192 | 145 | -175 | -73.8 | 83.9 | 175 | -58.5 | -93.7 | -58.8 | -55.4 |
| S&P Core Earnings | 230 | 149 | -191 | -80.6 | 51.1 | 140 | -89.9 | NA | NA | NA |

### Balance Sheet & Other Financial Data (Million $)

| | 2007 | 2006 | 2005 | 2004 | 2003 | 2002 | 2001 | 2000 | 1999 | 1998 |
|---|---|---|---|---|---|---|---|---|---|---|
| Cash | 826 | 497 | 205 | 574 | 1,116 | 486 | 549 | 36.6 | 13.2 | 3.98 |
| Current Assets | 1,422 | 1,198 | 1,049 | 1,180 | 1,370 | 786 | 734 | 141 | 212 | 72.6 |
| Total Assets | 3,506 | 3,045 | 2,819 | 2,440 | 2,382 | 1,689 | 1,389 | 308 | 234 | 94.7 |
| Current Liabilities | 2,006 | 1,377 | 1,279 | 216 | 138 | 120 | 107 | 80.8 | 57.5 | 18.5 |
| Long Term Debt | 3.79 | 225 | 763 | 1,284 | 1,409 | 861 | 867 | 55.1 | 14.0 | 15.1 |
| Common Equity | 1,302 | 1,309 | 612 | 830 | 770 | 643 | 399 | 165 | 317 | 57.6 |
| Total Capital | 1,362 | 1,607 | 1,486 | 2,209 | 2,225 | 1,556 | 1,265 | 220 | 331 | 72.7 |
| Capital Expenditures | 96.9 | 160 | 118 | 50.2 | 40.5 | 27.3 | 12.5 | 7.46 | 0.38 | 0.58 |
| Cash Flow | -67.9 | 261 | -90.6 | -21.0 | 129 | 211 | -49.7 | -98.9 | -51.9 | -53.1 |
| Current Ratio | 0.7 | 0.9 | 0.8 | 5.5 | 9.9 | 6.6 | 6.9 | 1.7 | 3.7 | 3.9 |
| % Long Term Debt of Capitalization | 0.3 | 14.0 | 51.4 | 58.2 | 63.3 | 55.3 | 68.5 | 25.0 | 4.2 | 20.8 |
| % Net Income of Revenue | NM | 8.2 | NM | NM | 11.7 | 34.5 | NM | NM | NM | NM |
| % Return on Assets | NM | 4.9 | NM | NM | 4.1 | 11.2 | NM | NM | NM | NM |
| % Return on Equity | NM | 15.1 | NM | NM | 11.9 | 33.6 | NM | NM | NM | NM |

Data as orig reptd.; bef. results of disc opers/spec. items. Per share data adj. for stk. divs.; EPS diluted. E-Estimated. NA-Not Available. NM-Not Meaningful. NR-Not Ranked. UR-Under Review.

**Office:** 41 Moores Rd, Frazer, PA 19355-1113.
**Telephone:** 610-344-0200.
**Email:** investorrelations@cephalon.com
**Website:** http://www.cephalon.com

**Chrmn, Pres & CEO:** F. Baldino, Jr.
**EVP, CFO & Chief Acctg Officer:** J.K. Buchi
**EVP & Chief Admin Officer:** C.A. Savini
**EVP & CSO:** J.L. Vaught

**EVP & General Counsel:** J. Pappert
**Board Members:** F. Baldino, Jr., W. P. Egan, M. D. Greenacre, V. M. Kailian, K. E. Moley, C. A. Sanders, G. R. Wilensky, D. L. Winger

**Founded:** 1987
**Domicile:** Delaware
**Employees:** 2,796

# CF Industries Holdings Inc

**STANDARD &POOR'S**

| S&P Recommendation HOLD ★★★☆☆ | Price $54.97 (as of Nov 14, 2008) | 12-Mo. Target Price $54.00 | Investment Style Large-Cap Value |
|---|---|---|---|

**GICS Sector** Materials
**Sub-Industry** Fertilizers & Agricultural Chemicals

**Summary** This company is a major manufacturer and distributor of nitrogen and phosphate fertilizer products in North America.

## Key Stock Statistics (Source S&P, Vickers, company reports)

| | | | | | | | |
|---|---|---|---|---|---|---|---|
| 52-Wk Range | $172.99–37.71 | S&P Oper. EPS 2008E | 13.02 | Market Capitalization(B) | $3.126 | Beta | 1.83 |
| Trailing 12-Month EPS | $10.98 | S&P Oper. EPS 2009E | 13.04 | Yield (%) | 0.73 | S&P 3-Yr. Proj. EPS CAGR(%) | 12 |
| Trailing 12-Month P/E | 5.0 | P/E on S&P Oper. EPS 2008E | 4.2 | Dividend Rate/Share | $0.40 | S&P Credit Rating | NA |
| $10K Invested 5 Yrs Ago | NA | Common Shares Outstg. (M) | 56.9 | Institutional Ownership (%) | 90 | | |

## Price Performance

30-Week Mov. Avg. ···  10-Week Mov. Avg. - - GAAP Earnings vs. Previous Year  Volume Above Avg. ⅊ STARS
12-Mo. Target Price — Relative Strength - ▲ Up ▼ Down ▶ No Change  Below Avg. ⅊ ★

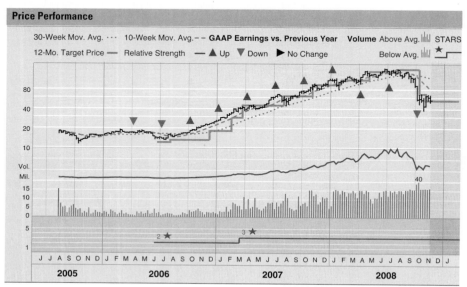

Options: ASE, CBOE, Ph

Analysis prepared by **Kevin Kirkeby** on October 30, 2008, when the stock traded at **$ 58.31**.

### Qualitative Risk Assessment

| LOW | MEDIUM | HIGH |
|---|---|---|

Our risk assessment reflects the cyclical and seasonal nature of the agriculture industry, the company's reliance on the volatile natural gas industry for much of its raw materials, and the competitive advantage of many overseas suppliers.

### Quantitative Evaluations

**S&P Quality Ranking**  NR

| D | C | B- | B | B+ | A- | A | A+ |
|---|---|---|---|---|---|---|---|

**Relative Strength Rank**  WEAK

29

LOWEST = 1                                      HIGHEST = 99

### Revenue/Earnings Data

**Revenue (Million $)**

| | 1Q | 2Q | 3Q | 4Q | Year |
|---|---|---|---|---|---|
| 2008 | 667.3 | 1,161 | 1,021 | -- | -- |
| 2007 | 447.7 | 848.9 | 582.9 | 852.5 | 2,757 |
| 2006 | 400.5 | 664.8 | 378.0 | 506.2 | 1,950 |
| 2005 | 459.3 | 626.7 | 359.4 | 463.0 | 1,908 |
| 2004 | 324.7 | 520.7 | 326.7 | 478.6 | 1,651 |
| 2003 | 229.6 | 405.0 | 313.6 | 421.7 | 1,370 |

**Earnings Per Share ($)**

| | | | | | |
|---|---|---|---|---|---|
| 2008 | 2.77 | 5.02 | 0.82 | E3.24 | E13.02 |
| 2007 | 1.02 | 1.65 | 1.52 | 2.38 | 6.57 |
| 2006 | -0.45 | 0.77 | 0.13 | 0.14 | 0.60 |
| 2005 | 0.41 | 0.78 | -1.81 | -0.18 | -0.66 |
| 2004 | -- | -- | -- | -- | 1.23 |
| 2003 | -- | -- | -- | -- | -0.33 |

Fiscal year ended Dec. 31. Next earnings report expected: Early February. EPS Estimates based on S&P Operating Earnings; historical GAAP earnings are as reported.

## Highlights

➤ Following an expected 45% rise in 2008, we forecast revenue growth will slow to 9% in 2009. Pricing, which rose sharply in 2008, reaching record highs, is expected to soften through 2009 as supply and demand come into balance. We believe CF is already producing near capacity, with little room to boost volumes near term. We expect planted acreage in 2009, particularly corn, to stabilize near 2008 levels. Fertilizer application rates will also remain near this year's levels, in our view, as the high cost encourages more selective usage.

➤ With less of a tailwind from pricing, we see margins narrowing in 2009 from 2008's projected record level. Natural gas, which is the primary input cost, has been quite volatile over the past twelve months, but we expect prices to average near 2008 levels. We also anticipate that transportation costs embedded in the price will be modestly higher.

➤ CF's earnings are subject to large fluctuations, depending on the size and direction of its hedge position relative to natural gas prices. We see EPS in 2009 of $13.04, versus $13.02 forecast for 2008, which excludes $1.17 of mark-to-market gains recorded in the first nine months.

## Investment Rationale/Risk

➤ CF Industries has a smaller geographic reach than most of its peers, and we consider its mix of products to be concentrated in more volatile market segments. However, we anticipate that CF will use its significant net cash position to reduce its dependence on high-cost feedstock sources and broaden its geographic coverage. Pricing risk has risen substantially since July 2008, in our opinion, due to economic and financial market concerns, as well as a sharp decline in grain prices. We believe CF should trade on a conservative valuation multiple, relative to historical averages for the fertilizer group.

➤ Risks to our recommendation and target price include increased import competition, global capacity additions, a resumption in Asian exports, a decline in grain prices, sharp increases in natural gas costs, and shifts in market sentiment toward investing in commodities.

➤ We apply a P/E multiple of 4.2X, representing a discount to peers with less volatile end markets, to our four-quarter forward EPS estimate to determine our 12-month target price of $54.

### Dividend Data (Dates: mm/dd Payment Date: mm/dd/yy)

| Amount ($) | Date Decl. | Ex-Div. Date | Stk. of Record | Payment Date |
|---|---|---|---|---|
| 0.100 | 02/07 | 02/20 | 02/22 | 02/29/08 |
| 0.100 | 04/23 | 05/13 | 05/15 | 06/02/08 |
| 0.100 | 07/23 | 08/13 | 08/15 | 09/02/08 |
| 0.100 | 10/27 | 11/12 | 11/14 | 12/01/08 |

Dividends have been paid since 2005. Source: Company reports.

---

**Please read the Required Disclosures and Analyst Certification on the last page of this report.**

The **McGraw-Hill** Companies

# CF Industries Holdings Inc

**STANDARD &POOR'S**

## Business Summary October 30, 2008

CORPORATE OVERVIEW. CF Industries is a major manufacturer and distributor of nitrogen and phosphate fertilizer products in North America. The company's principal products are ammonia, urea, urea ammonium nitrate solution (UAN), diammonium phosphate (DAP), and monoammonium phosphate (MAP). Its market share for the nitrogen segment is about 21%, and for phosphates, it is about 14% for agricultural fertilizer applications in the U.S. Core markets and distribution facilities for the company are concentrated in the midwestern U.S. grain-producing states. The company's primary competitors are Potash Corp., Agrium Inc., Terra Industries, The Mosaic Company, and Koch Nitrogen.

MARKET PROFILE. Potash, nitrogen and phosphates are the three primary plant nutrients that are essential for proper crop nutrition and maximum yields. They contribute to high-quality meat production as animal feed supplements and are also used as food-grade additives for human consumption and a wide range of industrial purposes. There are no substitutes for them and they are not substitutable for each other. Increases in world population, accelerated economic growth in many Asian and Latin American countries, and the rise and fall of commodity prices for both food crops and key raw material inputs all have an impact on production decisions and supply/demand fundamentals in the fertilizer industry. Nevertheless, growth in fertilizer volumes

has been fairly consistent and tends to rise at a little less than GDP growth. For instance, nitrogen demand has expanded at a 2.3% compound annual growth rate (CAGR) over the past decade, according to Fertecon, an industry research group. The global growth rate for the primary fertilizer nutrients is expected to be 2%-3% between 2005 and 2010, according to the International Fertilizer Association and Fertecon, yet most of this growth is forecast to come from outside of North America.

PRIMARY BUSINESS DYNAMICS. Energy costs are a major factor affecting the chemical industry in general and the fertilizer industry in particular, as the chemical industry accounts for 7% of the country's total energy consumption. Natural gas is the principal raw material, as well as the primary fuel source, used in the ammonia production process at both of the company's nitrogen fertilizer facilities. In 2007, natural gas purchases accounted for about 50% of CF's total cost of sales of nitrogen fertilizers and a substantially higher percentage of cash costs.

## Company Financials Fiscal Year Ended Dec. 31

| Per Share Data ($) | 2007 | 2006 | 2005 | 2004 | 2003 | 2002 | 2001 | 2000 | 1999 | 1998 |
|---|---|---|---|---|---|---|---|---|---|---|
| Tangible Book Value | 21.09 | 13.88 | 13.73 | 12.96 | NA | NA | NA | NA | NA | NA |
| Cash Flow | 8.06 | 2.32 | 1.11 | 3.21 | 1.57 | 2.14 | 0.77 | 1.57 | NA | NA |
| Earnings | 6.57 | 0.60 | -0.66 | 1.23 | -0.33 | -0.51 | -1.35 | -0.47 | NA | NA |
| S&P Core Earnings | 6.56 | 0.63 | -0.68 | 1.22 | -0.35 | NA | NA | NA | NA | NA |
| Dividends | 0.08 | 0.08 | 0.02 | NA | NA | NA | NA | NA | NA | NA |
| Payout Ratio | 1% | 13% | NM | NA | NA | NA | NA | NA | NA | NA |
| Prices:High | 118.88 | 26.60 | 18.00 | NA | NA | NA | NA | NA | NA | NA |
| Prices:Low | 25.70 | 12.91 | 11.19 | NA | NA | NA | NA | NA | NA | NA |
| P/E Ratio:High | 18 | 44 | NM | NA | NA | NA | NA | NA | NA | NA |
| P/E Ratio:Low | 4 | 22 | NM | NA | NA | NA | NA | NA | NA | NA |

| Income Statement Analysis (Million $) | 2007 | 2006 | 2005 | 2004 | 2003 | 2002 | 2001 | 2000 | 1999 | 1998 |
|---|---|---|---|---|---|---|---|---|---|---|
| Revenue | 2,757 | 1,950 | 1,908 | 1,651 | 1,370 | 1,014 | 1,160 | 1,160 | NA | NA |
| Operating Income | 686 | 166 | 236 | 258 | 99.4 | 89.6 | -32.1 | 97.6 | NA | NA |
| Depreciation | 84.5 | 94.6 | 97.5 | 109 | 105 | 108 | 102 | 112 | NA | NA |
| Interest Expense | 1.70 | 2.90 | 14.0 | 22.7 | 23.9 | 23.6 | 31.8 | 21.1 | NA | NA |
| Pretax Income | 627 | 81.8 | 110 | 132 | -25.0 | -38.3 | -151 | -40.1 | NA | NA |
| Effective Tax Rate | 31.8% | 24.1% | NM | 31.3% | NM | NM | NM | NM | NA | NA |
| Net Income | 373 | 33.3 | -36.2 | 67.7 | -18.4 | -28.1 | -59.7 | -25.8 | NA | NA |
| S&P Core Earnings | 372 | 34.9 | -37.1 | 67.5 | -19.7 | NA | NA | NA | NA | NA |

| Balance Sheet & Other Financial Data (Million $) | 2007 | 2006 | 2005 | 2004 | 2003 | 2002 | 2001 | 2000 | 1999 | 1998 |
|---|---|---|---|---|---|---|---|---|---|---|
| Cash | 861 | 25.4 | 37.4 | 72.8 | 169 | NA | NA | NA | NA | NA |
| Current Assets | 1,279 | 633 | 576 | NA | NA | NA | NA | NA | NA | NA |
| Total Assets | 2,013 | 1,290 | 1,228 | 1,149 | 1,405 | NA | NA | NA | NA | NA |
| Current Liabilities | 629 | 353 | 341 | NA | NA | NA | NA | NA | NA | NA |
| Long Term Debt | 4.90 | 4.20 | 4.20 | 4.01 | NA | NA | NA | NA | NA | NA |
| Common Equity | 1,187 | 767 | 756 | 720 | -0.79 | NA | NA | NA | NA | NA |
| Total Capital | 1,241 | 785 | 782 | 724 | NA | NA | NA | NA | NA | NA |
| Capital Expenditures | 105 | 59.3 | 69.4 | 33.7 | 28.7 | 26.3 | 41.7 | 52.3 | NA | NA |
| Cash Flow | 457 | 128 | 61.3 | 176 | 86.6 | 118 | 42.3 | 86.2 | NA | NA |
| Current Ratio | 2.0 | 1.8 | 1.7 | NA | 1.5 | NA | NA | NA | NA | NA |
| % Long Term Debt of Capitalization | 0.4 | 0.5 | 0.5 | 0.6 | 24.6 | Nil | NA | NA | NA | NA |
| % Net Income of Revenue | 13.5 | 1.7 | NM | 4.1 | NM | NM | NM | NM | NA | NA |
| % Return on Assets | 22.6 | 2.6 | NM | NA | NA | NA | NA | NA | NA | NA |
| % Return on Equity | 38.2 | 4.4 | NM | NA | NA | NA | NA | NA | NA | NA |

Data as orig reptd.; bef. results of disc opers/spec. items. Per share data adj. for stk. divs.; EPS diluted. 2004 pro forma as adjusted bal. sheet and book val. as of Jun. 30, 2005. Prior to 2005, per sh. data based on pro forma shs. E-Estimated. NA-Not Available. NM-Not Meaningful. NR-Not Ranked. UR-Under Review.

**Office:** 4 Parkway N Ste 400, Deerfield, IL 60015-2590.
**Telephone:** 847-405-2400.
**Website:** http://www.cfindustries.com
**Chrmn, Pres & CEO:** S.R. Wilson

**Pres & CEO:** R.C. Liuzzi
**COO:** D.J. Pruett
**SVP & CFO:** A.J. Nocchiero
**Chief Acctg Officer & Cntlr:** R.A. Hoker

**Investor Contact:** C. Nekvasil (847-307-2515)
**Board Members:** R. C. Arzbaecher, W. W. Creek, W. Davisson, S. A. Furbacher, D. R. Harvey, J. D. Johnson, E. A. Schmitt, S. R. Wilson

**Founded:** 1946
**Domicile:** Delaware
**Employees:** 1,500

The McGraw-Hill Companies

# Chesapeake Energy Corp

STANDARD &POOR'S

| S&P Recommendation | BUY ★★★★☆ | Price | $21.23 (as of Nov 14, 2008) | 12-Mo. Target Price | $32.00 | Investment Style | Large-Cap Blend |
|---|---|---|---|---|---|---|---|

**GICS Sector** Energy
**Sub-Industry** Oil & Gas Exploration & Production

**Summary** One of the largest independent exploration and production companies in the U.S., CHK focuses on U.S. onshore natural gas production east of the Rocky Mountains.

## Key Stock Statistics (Source S&P, Vickers, company reports)

| | | | | | | | |
|---|---|---|---|---|---|---|---|
| 52-Wk Range | $74.00–11.99 | S&P Oper. EPS 2008E | 3.32 | Market Capitalization(B) | $12.296 | Beta | 0.85 |
| Trailing 12-Month EPS | $3.27 | S&P Oper. EPS 2009E | 3.63 | Yield (%) | 1.41 | S&P 3-Yr. Proj. EPS CAGR(%) | 19 |
| Trailing 12-Month P/E | 6.5 | P/E on S&P Oper. EPS 2008E | 6.4 | Dividend Rate/Share | $0.30 | S&P Credit Rating | BB |
| $10K Invested 5 Yrs Ago | $17,629 | Common Shares Outstg. (M) | 579.2 | Institutional Ownership (%) | 75 | | |

## Price Performance

30-Week Mov. Avg. ···   10-Week Mov. Avg. - - -  **GAAP Earnings vs. Previous Year**   Volume Above Avg. STARS
12-Mo. Target Price —   Relative Strength — ▲ Up ▼ Down ► No Change   Below Avg.

Options: ASE, CBOE, P, Ph

Analysis prepared by **Michael Kay** on November 03, 2008, when the stock traded at **$ 20.27**.

## Highlights

➤ Production rose 24% in the first nine months of 2008 at CHK, the largest U.S. natural gas producer. Reflecting successful drilling, but also recent shut-ins, we expect volume growth of 19% in 2008 and 14% in 2009. In response to a major drop in natural gas prices, CHK has cut its drilling capex budget through 2010 by 25%, or $4.7 billion, and plans to reduce its rig count by 17, to 140 rigs by year end. Also, CHK has curtailed some unhedged Mid-Continent production. We believe recent JVs with Plains E&P (PXP) and BP plc (BP) will accelerate Haynesville and Fayetteville shale development.

➤ CHK recently closed on a $1.9 billion Fayetteville Shale 25% JV with BP, where CHK received $1.1 billion cash and another $800 million through 2009 for 100% of CHK's 75% share of drilling costs. CHK is in talks with several parties regarding a potential 25% Marcellus Shale JV and is looking to sell a minority interest in its midstream business for $1 billion.

➤ We see 2008 operating EPS of $3.32 a share (with a $0.38 non-cash derivative loss). CHK has 62% of fourth quarter expected natural gas production hedged at $9.15/Mcf, and 38% of 2009's at $9.33/Mcf.

## Investment Rationale/Risk

➤ We view CHK's business profile as solid, with an aggressive acquisition strategy that has seen it spend over $14 billion on acquisitions in the past 10 years, focused on unconventional natural gas plays. With the recent turmoil in credit markets, and CHK's highly leveraged balance sheet, CHK has plans to sell about $2.5-$3 billion of assets by year end, to add to its $1.5 billion cash position. With planned asset sales and lower drilling capex, CHK anticipates generating excess cash of $1-$1.5 billion in each of 2009 and 2010 for debt reduction.

➤ Risks to our recommendation and target price include changes in economic and operating conditions, a sustained decline in natural gas prices, and difficulty in replacing reserves.

➤ A drop in oil and gas prices, due to weaker economic forecasts resulting from the ongoing credit crisis, has caused a similar decline in E&P shares. Given uncertain debt and equity markets, we expect markets to discount unproven resource potential, and we now value CHK on our proved reserve NAV estimates. Our 12-month target price of $32 blends our proved NAV of $31 with our DCF ($31; WACC 6.6%; terminal growth 3%) and relative metrics.

## Qualitative Risk Assessment

| LOW | MEDIUM | HIGH |
|---|---|---|

Our risk assessment reflects CHK's business profile in a volatile, cyclical and capital-intensive segment of the energy industry. We believe CHK's financial strategy is aggressive, as the company has been one of the most active acquirers in exploration and production, and one of the most active users of commodity hedges. This is partly offset by strong volume growth and good drilling prospects.

## Quantitative Evaluations

**S&P Quality Ranking** B

| D | C | B- | B | B+ | A- | A | A+ |
|---|---|---|---|---|---|---|---|

**Relative Strength Rank** MODERATE

34

LOWEST = 1    HIGHEST = 99

## Revenue/Earnings Data

**Revenue (Million $)**

| | 1Q | 2Q | 3Q | 4Q | Year |
|---|---|---|---|---|---|
| 2008 | 1,611 | 3,372 | 7,491 | -- | -- |
| 2007 | 1,580 | 2,105 | 2,027 | 2,089 | 7,800 |
| 2006 | 1,945 | 1,584 | 1,929 | 1,868 | 7,326 |
| 2005 | 783.5 | 1,048 | 1,083 | 1,751 | 4,665 |
| 2004 | 563.1 | 574.3 | 629.8 | 942.1 | 2,709 |
| 2003 | 374.4 | 429.6 | 454.6 | 456.7 | 1,717 |

**Earnings Per Share ($)**

| | | | | | |
|---|---|---|---|---|---|
| 2008 | -0.29 | -3.16 | 5.58 | E0.82 | E3.32 |
| 2007 | 0.50 | 1.01 | 0.72 | 0.27 | 2.62 |
| 2006 | 1.44 | 0.82 | 1.13 | 0.96 | 4.35 |
| 2005 | 0.36 | 0.52 | 0.43 | 1.11 | 2.51 |
| 2004 | 0.38 | 0.30 | 0.29 | 0.52 | 1.53 |
| 2003 | 0.31 | 0.31 | 0.33 | 0.25 | 1.20 |

Fiscal year ended Dec. 31. Next earnings report expected: Late February. EPS Estimates based on S&P Operating Earnings; historical GAAP earnings are as reported.

## Dividend Data (Dates: mm/dd Payment Date: mm/dd/yy)

| Amount ($) | Date Decl. | Ex-Div. Date | Stk. of Record | Payment Date |
|---|---|---|---|---|
| 0.068 | 12/19 | 12/28 | 01/02 | 01/15/08 |
| 0.068 | 03/14 | 03/28 | 04/01 | 04/15/08 |
| 0.075 | 06/10 | 06/27 | 07/01 | 07/15/08 |
| 0.075 | 09/22 | 09/29 | 10/01 | 10/15/08 |

Dividends have been paid since 2002. Source: Company reports.

The McGraw-Hill Companies

# Chesapeake Energy Corp

## Business Summary November 03, 2008

CORPORATE OVERVIEW. As the third largest producer of natural gas in the U.S. (first among the independents), as of year-end 2007, Chesapeake Energy Corp. (CHK) is focused on discovering, acquiring, and developing conventional and unconventional natural gas reserves onshore in the U.S., east of the Rocky Mountains.

CHK operations are concentrated in six U.S. operating areas: Mid-Continent, Barnett Shale, Appalachian Basin, Permian and Delaware Basin, Ark-La-Tex, and South Texas and Texas Gulf Coast. Proved oil and gas reserves rose 22%, to 10.88 trillion cubic feet equivalent (Tcfe; 93% natural gas, 64% developed) in 2007. Oil and gas production rose 24%, to 714,261 million cubic feet equivalent (92% natural gas), in 2007. We estimate CHK's 2007 organic reserve replacement at 346%. Using data from John S. Herold, an oil industry analysis firm, we estimate CHK's three-year (2004-06) finding and development costs at $21.74 per boe, above the peer average, its three-year proved acquisition costs at $9.78 per boe, in line with the peer average, its three-year reserve replacement costs at $15.35 per boe, above the peer average, and its three-year reserve replacement at 511%, above the peer average.

As of year-end 2007, CHK owned interests in approximately 38,500 producing oil and gas wells. During 2007, CHK drilled 1,992 gross (1,695 net) operated wells and participated in another 1,679 gross (224 net) wells operated by other companies. The company's drilling success rate was 99% for company-operated wells and 97% for non-operated wells.

MARKET PROFILE. From 1998 to the present, CHK has integrated an aggressive and technologically advanced drilling program with an active property consolidation program focused on small to medium-sized corporate and property acquisitions. Beginning in 2006, CHK shifted its strategy from drilling inventory capture to drilling inventory conversion. In doing so, CHK has de-emphasized its acquisitions of proved properties while further emphasizing its drilling program and converting its substantial backlog of drilling opportunities into proved developed producing reserves.

CHK believes one of its most distinctive characteristics is its ability to increase its reserves and production through the drillbit. As of year-end 2007, CHK utilized 138 operated drilling rigs and 77 non-operated drilling rigs to conduct the most active drilling program in the U.S. CHK is active in most unconventional plays in the U.S. east of the Rockies, where the company drills more horizontal wells than any other company in the industry.

## Company Financials Fiscal Year Ended Dec. 31

| Per Share Data ($) | 2007 | 2006 | 2005 | 2004 | 2003 | 2002 | 2001 | 2000 | 1999 | 1998 |
|---|---|---|---|---|---|---|---|---|---|---|
| Tangible Book Value | 21.87 | 20.32 | 12.42 | 8.57 | 5.45 | 3.99 | 3.75 | 2.05 | NM | NM |
| Cash Flow | 6.87 | 7.36 | 5.05 | 3.56 | 2.61 | 1.54 | 2.52 | 3.67 | 1.30 | -8.18 |
| Earnings | 2.62 | 4.35 | 2.51 | 1.53 | 1.20 | 0.17 | 1.51 | 3.01 | 0.16 | -9.83 |
| S&P Core Earnings | 2.51 | 4.19 | 2.48 | 1.50 | 1.19 | 0.17 | 1.36 | NA | NA | NA |
| Dividends | 0.26 | 0.23 | 0.20 | 0.17 | 0.14 | 0.06 | Nil | Nil | Nil | 0.06 |
| Payout Ratio | 10% | 5% | 8% | 11% | 11% | 35% | Nil | Nil | Nil | NM |
| Prices:High | 41.19 | 35.57 | 40.20 | 18.31 | 14.00 | 8.55 | 11.06 | 10.50 | 4.13 | 7.75 |
| Prices:Low | 27.27 | 26.81 | 15.06 | 11.70 | 7.27 | 4.50 | 4.50 | 1.94 | 0.63 | 0.75 |
| P/E Ratio:High | 16 | 8 | 16 | 12 | 12 | 50 | 7 | 3 | 26 | NM |
| P/E Ratio:Low | 10 | 6 | 6 | 8 | 6 | 26 | 3 | 1 | 4 | NM |

| Income Statement Analysis (Million $) | | | | | | | | | | |
|---|---|---|---|---|---|---|---|---|---|---|
| Revenue | 7,800 | 7,326 | 4,665 | 2,709 | 1,717 | 738 | 969 | 628 | 355 | 378 |
| Operating Income | 4,638 | 3,413 | 1,773 | 992 | 675 | 191 | 597 | 384 | 207 | 177 |
| Depreciation, Depletion and Amortization | 1,989 | 1,463 | 945 | 611 | 386 | 235 | 178 | 105 | 99.5 | 152 |
| Interest Expense | 675 | 301 | 220 | 167 | 154 | 111 | 98.3 | 86.3 | 81.1 | 68.2 |
| Pretax Income | 2,341 | 3,255 | 1,493 | 805 | 501 | 67.1 | 438 | 196 | 35.0 | -921 |
| Effective Tax Rate | 38.0% | 38.5% | 36.5% | 36.0% | 38.0% | 40.0% | 39.9% | NM | 5.04% | NM |
| Net Income | 1,451 | 2,003 | 948 | 515 | 311 | 40.3 | 263 | 456 | 33.3 | -921 |
| S&P Core Earnings | 1,178 | 1,831 | 871 | 431 | 283 | 29.9 | 235 | NA | NA | NA |

| Balance Sheet & Other Financial Data (Million $) | | | | | | | | | | |
|---|---|---|---|---|---|---|---|---|---|---|
| Cash | 1.00 | 2.52 | 60.0 | 6.90 | 40.6 | 248 | 125 | 3.50 | 38.9 | 35.3 |
| Current Assets | 1,396 | 1,154 | 1,183 | 568 | 342 | 435 | 361 | 167 | 97.5 | 118 |
| Total Assets | 30,734 | 24,417 | 16,118 | 8,245 | 4,572 | 2,876 | 2,287 | 1,440 | 851 | 813 |
| Current Liabilities | 2,761 | 1,890 | 1,964 | 964 | 513 | 266 | 173 | 163 | 88.2 | 131 |
| Long Term Debt | 10,950 | 7,376 | 5,490 | 3,075 | 2,058 | 1,651 | 1,329 | 945 | 964 | 919 |
| Common Equity | 11,170 | 9,293 | 4,598 | 2,672 | 1,180 | 758 | 617 | 282 | -447 | -479 |
| Total Capital | 27,046 | 21,944 | 13,469 | 7,172 | 3,982 | 2,559 | 2,097 | 1,270 | 753 | 671 |
| Capital Expenditures | 9,705 | 986 | 484 | 127 | 71.5 | 33.6 | 24.9 | 78.9 | 49.9 | 271 |
| Cash Flow | 3,346 | 3,377 | 1,851 | 1,087 | 674 | 265 | 439 | 556 | 133 | -776 |
| Current Ratio | 0.5 | 0.6 | 0.6 | 0.6 | 0.7 | 1.6 | 2.1 | 1.0 | 1.1 | 0.9 |
| % Long Term Debt of Capitalization | 47.4 | 33.6 | 40.8 | 42.9 | 51.7 | 64.5 | 63.4 | 74.4 | 128.0 | 137.1 |
| % Return on Assets | 4.9 | 9.9 | 7.8 | 8.0 | 8.3 | 1.6 | 14.1 | 39.8 | 4.0 | NM |
| % Return on Equity | 13.3 | 27.6 | 24.9 | 24.7 | 29.7 | 4.4 | 58.1 | NM | NM | NM |

Data as orig reptd.; bef. results of disc opers/spec. items. Per share data adj. for stk. divs.; EPS diluted. E-Estimated. NA-Not Available. NM-Not Meaningful. NR-Not Ranked. UR-Under Review.

**Office:** 6100 North Western Avenue, Oklahoma City, OK 73118.
**Telephone:** 405-848-8000.
**Website:** http://www.chk.com
**Chrmn & CEO:** A.K. McClendon

**Pres:** J.M. Stice
**COO & EVP:** S.C. Dixon
**EVP & CFO:** M.C. Rowland
**SVP, Chief Acctg Officer & Cntlr:** M.A. Johnson

**Investor Contact:** J.L. Mobley (405-767-4763)
**Board Members:** R. K. Davidson, V. B. Hargis, F. Keating, B. M. Kerr, C. T. Maxwell, A. K. McClendon, M. A. Miller, Jr., D. L. Nickles, F. B. Whittemore

**Founded:** 1991
**Domicile:** Oklahoma
**Employees:** 6,200

# Chevron Corp

STANDARD
&POOR'S

| S&P Recommendation | STRONG BUY ★★★★★ | Price<br>$72.68 (as of Nov 14, 2008) | 12-Mo. Target Price<br>$113.00 | Investment Style<br>Large-Cap Blend |
|---|---|---|---|---|

**GICS Sector** Energy
**Sub-Industry** Integrated Oil & Gas

**Summary** This global integrated oil company (formerly ChevronTexaco) has interests in exploration, production, refining and marketing, and petrochemicals.

## Key Stock Statistics (Source S&P, Vickers, company reports)

| | | | | | | | |
|---|---|---|---|---|---|---|---|
| 52-Wk Range | $104.63– 55.50 | S&P Oper. EPS 2008E | 12.32 | Market Capitalization(B) | $147.671 | Beta | 0.91 |
| Trailing 12-Month EPS | $11.53 | S&P Oper. EPS 2009E | 11.73 | Yield (%) | 3.58 | S&P 3-Yr. Proj. EPS CAGR(%) | 12 |
| Trailing 12-Month P/E | 6.3 | P/E on S&P Oper. EPS 2008E | 5.9 | Dividend Rate/Share | $2.60 | S&P Credit Rating | AA |
| $10K Invested 5 Yrs Ago | $23,052 | Common Shares Outstg. (M) | 2,031.8 | Institutional Ownership (%) | 65 | | |

## Price Performance

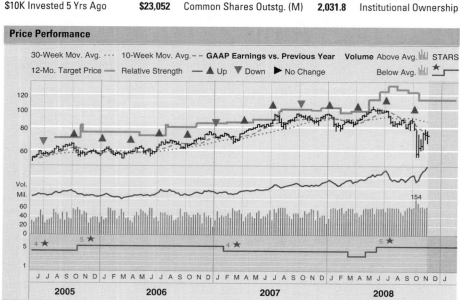

30-Week Mov. Avg. · · · · 10-Week Mov. Avg. – – **GAAP Earnings vs. Previous Year** Volume Above Avg. STARS
12-Mo. Target Price — Relative Strength — ▲ Up ▼ Down ► No Change Below Avg.

Options: ASE, CBOE, P, Ph

Analysis prepared by **Tina J. Vital** on November 05, 2008, when the stock traded at **$ 78.19**.

## Qualitative Risk Assessment

| LOW | MEDIUM | HIGH |
|---|---|---|

Our risk assessment reflects Chevron's diversified and strong business profile in volatile, cyclical and capital-intensive segments of the energy industry. With improved returns since the Texaco merger in 2001, we view its corporate governance practices as generally sound and its earnings stability as favorable.

## Quantitative Evaluations

**S&P Quality Ranking**     A-

| D | C | B- | B | B+ | A- | A | A+ |
|---|---|---|---|---|---|---|---|

**Relative Strength Rank**     STRONG

83

LOWEST = 1     HIGHEST = 99

## Revenue/Earnings Data

**Revenue (Million $)**

| | 1Q | 2Q | 3Q | 4Q | Year |
|---|---|---|---|---|---|
| 2008 | 65,903 | 78,310 | 73,615 | -- | -- |
| 2007 | 46,302 | 54,344 | 53,545 | 59,900 | 203,970 |
| 2006 | 54,624 | 53,536 | 54,212 | 47,746 | 210,118 |
| 2005 | 41,607 | 48,343 | 54,456 | 53,794 | 198,200 |
| 2004 | 33,063 | 36,579 | 39,611 | 41,612 | 155,300 |
| 2003 | 30,965 | 29,361 | 30,970 | 30,465 | 121,761 |

**Earnings Per Share ($)**

| | | | | | |
|---|---|---|---|---|---|
| 2008 | 2.48 | 2.89 | 3.86 | E2.81 | E12.32 |
| 2007 | 2.18 | 2.52 | 1.75 | 2.32 | 8.77 |
| 2006 | 1.80 | 1.97 | 2.29 | 1.74 | 7.80 |
| 2005 | 1.28 | 1.76 | 1.64 | 1.86 | 6.54 |
| 2004 | 1.20 | 1.93 | 1.38 | 1.63 | 6.14 |
| 2003 | 1.00 | 0.75 | 1.01 | 0.82 | 3.57 |

Fiscal year ended Dec. 31. Next earnings report expected: Early February. EPS Estimates based on S&P Operating Earnings; historical GAAP earnings are as reported.

## Dividend Data (Dates: mm/dd Payment Date: mm/dd/yy)

| Amount ($) | Date Decl. | Ex-Div. Date | Stk. of Record | Payment Date |
|---|---|---|---|---|
| 0.580 | 01/30 | 02/13 | 02/15 | 03/10/08 |
| 0.650 | 04/30 | 05/15 | 05/19 | 06/10/08 |
| 0.650 | 07/30 | 08/15 | 08/19 | 09/10/08 |
| 0.650 | 10/29 | 11/14 | 11/18 | 12/10/08 |

Dividends have been paid since 1912. Source: Company reports.

## Highlights

➤ In mid September 2008, CVX said that Saudi Arabia extended its existing exploration & production arrangement in the onshore area of the Partitioned Neutral Zone (PNZ, between the Kingdom and Kuwait) for another 30 years. The PNZ agreement grants CVX the right to operate on behalf of the Saudi government for its 50% undivided interest in the petroleum resources in the region.

➤ While projects have seen delays, CVX expects 2008 start-ups to include the Blind Faith deepwater project in the Gulf of Mexico, the Agbami deepwater project in Nigeria, and the Tengiz expansion in Kazakhstan. The Tahiti deepwater project in the Gulf of Mexico has been delayed until 2009. We expect 2008 oil and gas production will decline by about 3%, reflecting hurricane and entitlement impacts, before rebounding in 2009; overall, we expect annual growth between 2% to 3% in 2007-2012, at the lower end of CVX's target of more than 3% per annum during this period.

➤ After-tax operating earnings were about flat in 2007, but we expect increases of 45% in 2008 before declining 4.8% in 2009.

## Investment Rationale/Risk

➤ We have a positive outlook for CVX's upstream business, given its 2005 acquisition of Unocal and its ongoing international "Big Five" upstream development projects. We estimate CVX's three-year (2004-2006) reserve replacement rate as solid but below the peer average, and its three-year finding and development costs, proved acquisition costs and reserve replacement costs as above the peer average. However, we estimate CVX's 2007 reserve replacement at a sub-par 14%, which reflects the certification process of its large field developments.

➤ Risks to our recommendation and target price include declines in economic, industry and operating conditions, an inability to replace reserves, and geopolitical risks.

➤ Blending our DCF ($99 per share, assuming a WACC of 10.0% and terminal growth rate of 3%), net asset valuation ($132 per share; assuming a long term WTI oil price of $90 a barrel), and narrowed relative valuations leads to our 12-month target of $113 per share. This represents an expected enterprise value of 5.1X our 2009 EBITDA forecast, a slight discount to U.S. supermajor peers.

---

# Chevron Corp

**STANDARD &POOR'S**

## Business Summary November 05, 2008

CORPORATE OVERVIEW. In October 2001, Chevron Corp. (CHV) and Texaco Inc. (TX) merged, creating the second largest U.S.-based oil company at the time, ChevronTexaco Corp. (CVX). In May 2005, the company changed its name to Chevron Corp.

CVX separately manages its exploration and production (26% of 2007 revenues; 79% of 2007 segment income); refining, marketing and transportation (72%; 19%); chemicals (1%; 2%); and other businesses, includes its mining operations of coal and other minerals, power generation, insurance and real estate operations, and technical companies.

Net production of crude oil, natural gas liquids (NGLs) and natural gas rose 1.3%, to 3.272 million boe per day (68% liquids), including equity share in affiliates, in 2007. Net proved oil and gas reserves, excluding equity share in affiliates, declined 8.8%, to 7.86 million boe (59% liquids, 64% developed), as of December 31, 2007. We estimate its 2007 reserve replacement at a sub-par 14%. Using data from John S. Herold, we estimate CVX's three-year (2004-2006) re-

serve replacement rate at 103%, below the peer average; three-year finding and development costs at $29.49 per barrel of oil equivalent (boe), above the peer average; three-year proved acquisition costs at $8.02 per boe, above the peer average; and reserve replacement costs at $16.37 per boe, above the peer average.

As of December 31, 2007, CVX owned 10 refineries and two asphalt plants, and had interests in 12 international refineries, for a total production refining capacity of 2.115 million b/d (50% North America). As of year-end 2007, it had a network of 25,082 retail sites (including equity affiliates) worldwide. During 2007, CVX sold a number of refining and marketing interests in the Netherlands, Belgium, Luxembourg, and Uruguay, as well as its North American credit card operations.

## Company Financials Fiscal Year Ended Dec. 31

| Per Share Data ($) | 2007 | 2006 | 2005 | 2004 | 2003 | 2002 | 2001 | 2000 | 1999 | 1998 |
|---|---|---|---|---|---|---|---|---|---|---|
| Tangible Book Value | 41.68 | 29.71 | 25.99 | 21.47 | 16.98 | 14.80 | 15.92 | 15.54 | 13.53 | 13.05 |
| Cash Flow | 12.67 | 11.38 | 8.96 | 8.53 | 5.99 | 2.98 | 5.17 | 6.17 | 3.74 | 2.78 |
| Earnings | 8.77 | 7.80 | 6.54 | 6.14 | 3.57 | 0.54 | 1.85 | 3.99 | 1.57 | 1.02 |
| S&P Core Earnings | 8.34 | 7.88 | 6.62 | 5.88 | 3.50 | 1.22 | 1.66 | NA | NA | NA |
| Dividends | 2.26 | 2.01 | 1.75 | 1.53 | 1.43 | 1.40 | 1.33 | 1.30 | 1.24 | 1.22 |
| Payout Ratio | 26% | 26% | 27% | 25% | 40% | NM | 72% | 33% | 79% | 120% |
| Prices:High | 95.50 | 76.20 | 65.98 | 56.07 | 43.50 | 45.80 | 49.25 | 47.44 | 52.47 | 45.09 |
| Prices:Low | 64.99 | 53.76 | 49.81 | 42.00 | 30.66 | 32.71 | 39.22 | 34.97 | 36.56 | 33.88 |
| P/E Ratio:High | 11 | 10 | 10 | 9 | 12 | 86 | 27 | 12 | 33 | 44 |
| P/E Ratio:Low | 7 | 7 | 8 | 7 | 9 | 61 | 21 | 9 | 23 | 33 |

| Income Statement Analysis (Million $) | 2007 | 2006 | 2005 | 2004 | 2003 | 2002 | 2001 | 2000 | 1999 | 1998 |
|---|---|---|---|---|---|---|---|---|---|---|
| Revenue | 214,091 | 204,892 | 193,641 | 150,865 | 120,032 | 98,691 | 104,409 | 50,592 | 35,448 | 29,943 |
| Operating Income | 33,936 | 35,748 | 27,129 | 21,542 | 49,336 | 28,848 | 16,031 | 15,834 | 5,848 | 3,945 |
| Depreciation, Depletion and Amortization | 8,309 | 7,506 | 5,913 | 4,935 | 5,384 | 5,231 | 7,059 | 2,848 | 2,866 | 2,320 |
| Interest Expense | 468 | 451 | 482 | 406 | 474 | 565 | 833 | 460 | 463 | 405 |
| Pretax Income | 32,274 | 32,046 | 25,293 | 20,636 | 12,850 | 4,213 | 8,412 | 9,270 | 3,648 | 1,834 |
| Effective Tax Rate | 41.8% | 46.3% | 43.9% | 36.4% | 41.6% | 71.8% | 51.8% | 44.1% | 43.3% | 27.0% |
| Net Income | 18,688 | 17,138 | 14,099 | 13,034 | 7,426 | 1,132 | 3,931 | 5,185 | 2,070 | 1,339 |
| S&P Core Earnings | 17,772 | 17,310 | 14,277 | 12,471 | 7,454 | 2,590 | 3,518 | NA | NA | NA |

| Balance Sheet & Other Financial Data (Million $) | 2007 | 2006 | 2005 | 2004 | 2003 | 2002 | 2001 | 2000 | 1999 | 1998 |
|---|---|---|---|---|---|---|---|---|---|---|
| Cash | 8,094 | 11,446 | 11,144 | 10,742 | 5,267 | 3,781 | 3,150 | 2,630 | 2,032 | 1,413 |
| Current Assets | 39,377 | 36,304 | 34,336 | 28,503 | 19,426 | 17,776 | 18,327 | 8,213 | 8,297 | 6,297 |
| Total Assets | 148,786 | 132,628 | 125,833 | 93,208 | 81,470 | 77,359 | 77,572 | 41,264 | 40,668 | 36,540 |
| Current Liabilities | 33,798 | 28,409 | 25,011 | 18,795 | 16,111 | 19,876 | 20,654 | 7,674 | 8,889 | 7,166 |
| Long Term Debt | 6,753 | 7,679 | 12,131 | 10,456 | 10,894 | 10,911 | 8,989 | 5,153 | 5,485 | 4,393 |
| Common Equity | 77,088 | 73,684 | 66,722 | 48,575 | 40,022 | 36,176 | 37,120 | 21,761 | 17,749 | 17,034 |
| Total Capital | 95,532 | 93,219 | 90,315 | 66,471 | 57,601 | 53,009 | 52,524 | 31,822 | 28,244 | 25,072 |
| Capital Expenditures | 16,678 | 13,813 | 8,701 | 6,310 | 5,625 | 7,597 | 9,713 | 3,657 | 4,366 | 3,880 |
| Cash Flow | 26,997 | 24,644 | 20,012 | 17,969 | 12,810 | 6,363 | 10,990 | 8,033 | 4,936 | 3,659 |
| Current Ratio | 1.2 | 1.3 | 1.4 | 1.5 | 1.2 | 0.9 | 0.9 | 1.1 | 0.9 | 0.9 |
| % Long Term Debt of Capitalization | 7.3 | 8.2 | 13.4 | 15.7 | 18.9 | 20.6 | 17.1 | 16.2 | 19.4 | 17.5 |
| % Return on Assets | 13.3 | 13.3 | 12.9 | 14.9 | 9.4 | 1.5 | 5.1 | 12.7 | 5.4 | 3.7 |
| % Return on Equity | 25.6 | 24.4 | 24.5 | 29.4 | 19.5 | 3.1 | 10.7 | 25.1 | 11.9 | 7.8 |

Data as orig reptd.; bef. results of disc opers/spec. items. Per share data adj. for stk. divs.; EPS diluted. Quarterly revs. incl. other inc. E-Estimated. NA-Not Available. NM-Not Meaningful. NR-Not Ranked. UR-Under Review.

**Office:** 6001 Bollinger Canyon Road, San Ramon, CA 94583-2324.
**Telephone:** 925-842-1000.
**Email:** invest@chevrontexaco.com
**Website:** http://www.chevrontexaco.com

**Chrmn & CEO:** D. O'Reilly
**Vice Chrmn:** P. Robertson
**CFO:** S.J. Crowe
**CTO:** J.W. McDonald

**Chief Acctg Officer & Cntlr:** M.A. Humphrey
**Board Members:** S. H. Armacost, L. F. Deily, R. E. Denham, R. J. Eaton, S. L. Ginn, F. G. Jenifer, J. L. Jones, S. A. Nunn, D. O'Reilly, D. B. Rice, P. Robertson, K. W. Sharer, C. R. Shoemate, R. D. Sugar, C. Ware

**Founded:** 1901
**Domicile:** Delaware
**Employees:** 65,000

The McGraw-Hill Companies

# C.H. Robinson Worldwide Inc

STANDARD
&POOR'S

| S&P Recommendation **BUY** ★★★★☆ | Price $50.78 (as of Nov 14, 2008) | 12-Mo. Target Price $53.00 | Investment Style Large-Cap Growth |

**GICS Sector** Industrials
**Sub-Industry** Air Freight & Logistics

**Summary** This global provider of multimodal transportation services and logistics solutions has a network of over 200 offices in North America, South America, Europe and Asia.

## Key Stock Statistics (Source S&P, Vickers, company reports)

| | | | | | | | |
|---|---|---|---|---|---|---|---|
| 52-Wk Range | $67.36– 36.50 | S&P Oper. EPS 2008**E** | 2.08 | Market Capitalization(B) | $8.592 | Beta | 1.09 |
| Trailing 12-Month EPS | $2.05 | S&P Oper. EPS 2009**E** | 2.30 | Yield (%) | 1.89 | S&P 3-Yr. Proj. EPS CAGR(%) | 15 |
| Trailing 12-Month P/E | 24.8 | P/E on S&P Oper. EPS 2008**E** | 24.4 | Dividend Rate/Share | $0.96 | S&P Credit Rating | NA |
| $10K Invested 5 Yrs Ago | $26,906 | Common Shares Outstg. (M) | 169.2 | Institutional Ownership (%) | 77 | | |

## Price Performance

- 30-Week Mov. Avg. ····
- 10-Week Mov. Avg. ‑ ‑ ‑
- **GAAP Earnings vs. Previous Year**
- Volume Above Avg. ▐▌▌ STARS
- 12-Mo. Target Price —
- Relative Strength —
- ▲ Up ▼ Down ► No Change
- Below Avg. ▐▌▌ ★

Options: ASE, CBOE, P, Ph

Analysis prepared by **Jim Corridore** on October 23, 2008, when the stock traded at **$ 44.55**.

## Highlights

➤ We forecast 2009 gross revenue growth of 15%, versus the 20% growth we project for 2008. We believe CHRW will see decelerating growth in intermodal, ocean and air shipping services into the first half of 2009 due to a slower U.S. economy. We expect growth to come from market share gains as CHRW increases penetration into existing accounts and adds new accounts.

➤ We expect gross margins to narrow slightly, reflecting likely increased purchased transportation costs driven by higher fuel costs. In addition, truck capacity is likely to tighten as high fuel costs force some capacity providers out of business. This could put further pressure on what CHRW pays for truck capacity. We also see a higher percentage of business from slightly less profitable large customers. Partly offsetting this is likely to be fixed cost leverage on a higher revenue base and restrained operating costs.

➤ Our 2009 EPS estimate is $2.30, up 11% from our 2008 EPS estimate of $2.08. We believe the quality of CHRW's reported earnings is high relative to most other transportation companies that we cover.

## Investment Rationale/Risk

➤ After a recent price drop that has left CHRW well below our 12-month target price, we recommend buying the shares, despite a valuation premium to peers. This reflects our view of the company's history of strong returns on assets and equity relative to most other transportation companies. Also, CHRW has no long-term debt and has been a generator of cash over the past few years, and we think the quality of its reported earnings has been high relative to peers, as it has no defined benefit pension plan.

➤ Risks to our recommendation and target price include the possibility of investor rotation out of transportation stocks, a potential weakening of transport volumes if the U.S. economy slows sharply, and the possibility that tight industry capacity could lead to lost revenue opportunities, restricting earnings growth.

➤ Our 12-month target price of $53 values the stock at 23X our 2009 EPS estimate of $2.30. Our valuation is above peer levels, but at the low end of CHRW's historical P/E range over the past five years of 20.3X-36.1X earnings.

## Qualitative Risk Assessment

| LOW | MEDIUM | HIGH |

Our risk assessment reflects CHRW's lack of long-term debt, what we see as a high quality of earnings, and a non-asset-based structure. This is only partially offset, in our view, by its exposure to cyclical economic slowdowns and rising transportation costs.

## Quantitative Evaluations

**S&P Quality Ranking**  A+

| D | C | B- | B | B+ | A- | A | A+ |

**Relative Strength Rank**  STRONG

94

LOWEST = 1                    HIGHEST = 99

## Revenue/Earnings Data

**Revenue (Million $)**

| | 1Q | 2Q | 3Q | 4Q | Year |
|---|---|---|---|---|---|
| 2008 | 1,985 | 2,322 | 2,317 | -- | -- |
| 2007 | 1,619 | 1,880 | 1,865 | 1,952 | 7,316 |
| 2006 | 1,499 | 1,701 | 1,713 | 1,643 | 6,556 |
| 2005 | 1,215 | 1,405 | 1,485 | 1,584 | 5,689 |
| 2004 | 946.6 | 1,077 | 1,124 | 1,194 | 4,342 |
| 2003 | 816.7 | 935.2 | 919.3 | 942.4 | 3,614 |

**Earnings Per Share ($)**

| | | | | | |
|---|---|---|---|---|---|
| 2008 | 0.50 | 0.52 | 0.54 | E0.52 | E2.08 |
| 2007 | 0.42 | 0.47 | 0.48 | 0.49 | 1.86 |
| 2006 | 0.33 | 0.38 | 0.40 | 0.42 | 1.53 |
| 2005 | 0.24 | 0.29 | 0.31 | 0.33 | 1.16 |
| 2004 | 0.17 | 0.19 | 0.22 | 0.22 | 0.80 |
| 2003 | 0.16 | 0.17 | 0.17 | 0.17 | 0.67 |

Fiscal year ended Dec. 31. Next earnings report expected: Late January. EPS Estimates based on S&P Operating Earnings; historical GAAP earnings are as reported.

## Dividend Data (Dates: mm/dd Payment Date: mm/dd/yy)

| Amount ($) | Date Decl. | Ex-Div. Date | Stk. of Record | Payment Date |
|---|---|---|---|---|
| 0.240 | 05/17 | 12/03 | 12/05 | 01/02/09 |

Dividends have been paid since 1997. Source: Company reports.

# C.H. Robinson Worldwide Inc

STANDARD
&POOR'S

## Business Summary October 23, 2008

CORPORATE OVERVIEW. With 2007 revenues of about $7.3 billion, C.H. Robinson Worldwide is one of the largest third-party logistics companies in North America. At December 31, 2007, the company provided multimodal transportation services and logistics solutions through a network of 218 offices in North America, South America, Europe and Asia. In 2007, gross profits were divided as follows: 88% from transportation, 8% from sourcing, and 4% from information services. Within the transportation segment, CHRW offers several modes of service, including trucks (86% of gross profits in the transportation segment in 2007), intermodal (4%), ocean (4%), air (3%), and miscellaneous (3%).

Through contracts with about 48,000 transportation companies, including motor carriers, railroads, and air freight and ocean carriers, the company maintains the largest network of motor carrier capacity in North America. One of the largest third-party providers of intermodal services in the U.S., it also provides air, ocean and customs services. In addition, CHRW operates value-added logistics services, including fresh produce sourcing, freight consolidation and cross-docking. In 2007, the company handled more than 6.5 million shipments for more than 29,000 customers.

CORPORATE STRATEGY. CHRW has historically grown through internal growth, by expanding current offices, opening new branch offices and hiring additional sales people. Growth has also been augmented through selective acquisitions. In February 2005, the company acquired three produce sourcing and marketing companies: FoodSource Inc., FoodSource Procurement, LLC, and Epic Roots, Inc. The three companies had about $270 million in gross revenues in 2004. In the third quarter of 2005, CHRW purchased two freight forwarding businesses: Hirdes Group Worldwide and Bussini Transport S.r.l., with combined gross revenues of about $52 million in 2004. In May 2006, CHRW acquired certain assets of Paine Lynch and Associates, a third-party logistics company, for $30 million.

## Company Financials Fiscal Year Ended Dec. 31

| Per Share Data ($) | 2007 | 2006 | 2005 | 2004 | 2003 | 2002 | 2001 | 2000 | 1999 | 1998 |
|---|---|---|---|---|---|---|---|---|---|---|
| Tangible Book Value | 4.47 | 3.86 | 3.11 | 2.60 | 2.09 | 1.59 | 1.23 | 0.85 | 0.55 | 0.95 |
| Cash Flow | 2.00 | 1.66 | 1.27 | 0.86 | 0.73 | 0.64 | 0.60 | 0.52 | 0.38 | 0.31 |
| Earnings | 1.86 | 1.53 | 1.16 | 0.80 | 0.67 | 0.56 | 0.49 | 0.42 | 0.32 | 0.26 |
| S&P Core Earnings | 1.86 | 1.53 | 1.16 | 0.79 | 0.63 | 0.56 | 0.47 | NA | NA | NA |
| Dividends | 0.18 | 0.18 | 0.36 | 0.26 | 0.18 | 0.13 | 0.11 | 0.08 | 0.07 | 0.05 |
| Payout Ratio | 10% | 12% | 31% | 32% | 27% | 23% | 21% | 19% | 22% | 17% |
| Prices:High | 58.19 | 55.18 | 41.70 | 28.20 | 21.50 | 17.70 | 16.13 | 16.44 | 10.52 | 6.75 |
| Prices:Low | 42.11 | 35.55 | 23.60 | 18.30 | 13.50 | 12.92 | 11.41 | 8.58 | 6.00 | 3.59 |
| P/E Ratio:High | 31 | 36 | 36 | 35 | 32 | 32 | 33 | 40 | 33 | 26 |
| P/E Ratio:Low | 23 | 23 | 20 | 23 | 20 | 23 | 23 | 21 | 19 | 14 |

| Income Statement Analysis (Million $) | | | | | | | | | | |
|---|---|---|---|---|---|---|---|---|---|---|
| Revenue | 7,316 | 6,556 | 5,689 | 4,342 | 3,614 | 3,294 | 3,090 | 2,882 | 2,261 | 2,038 |
| Operating Income | 534 | 439 | 345 | 235 | 195 | 171 | 153 | 134 | 94.0 | 77.0 |
| Depreciation | 24.1 | 23.9 | 18.5 | 11.8 | 11.0 | 14.0 | 19.1 | 17.3 | 10.1 | 8.52 |
| Interest Expense | Nil | Nil | Nil | Nil | Nil | Nil | Nil | Nil | Nil | Nil |
| Pretax Income | 524 | 430 | 333 | 226 | 186 | 158 | 138 | 118 | 88.5 | 71.3 |
| Effective Tax Rate | 38.1% | 37.9% | 38.9% | 39.3% | 38.7% | 39.0% | 39.3% | 39.5% | 39.7% | 39.7% |
| Net Income | 324 | 267 | 203 | 137 | 114 | 96.3 | 84.0 | 71.2 | 53.3 | 43.0 |
| S&P Core Earnings | 324 | 267 | 203 | 136 | 107 | 94.9 | 79.8 | NA | NA | NA |

| Balance Sheet & Other Financial Data (Million $) | | | | | | | | | | |
|---|---|---|---|---|---|---|---|---|---|---|
| Cash | 455 | 349 | 231 | 166 | 199 | 133 | 116 | 79.9 | 49.6 | 130 |
| Current Assets | 1,389 | 1,256 | 1,085 | 846 | 717 | 589 | 503 | 460 | 343 | 375 |
| Total Assets | 1,811 | 1,632 | 1,395 | 1,081 | 908 | 778 | 683 | 644 | 523 | 409 |
| Current Liabilities | 758 | 687 | 612 | 453 | 381 | 343 | 324 | 346 | 276 | 240 |
| Long Term Debt | Nil | Nil | Nil | Nil | Nil | Nil | Nil | Nil | Nil | Nil |
| Common Equity | 1,042 | 944 | 780 | 621 | 517 | 426 | 356 | 297 | 247 | 170 |
| Total Capital | 1,042 | 944 | 782 | 621 | 524 | 432 | 359 | 298 | 247 | 170 |
| Capital Expenditures | 43.7 | 43.2 | 21.8 | 34.7 | 8.57 | 17.3 | 17.1 | 15.5 | 9.43 | 5.07 |
| Cash Flow | 348 | 291 | 222 | 149 | 125 | 110 | 103 | 88.6 | 63.5 | 51.5 |
| Current Ratio | 1.8 | 1.8 | 1.8 | 1.9 | 1.9 | 1.7 | 1.6 | 1.3 | 1.2 | 1.6 |
| % Long Term Debt of Capitalization | Nil | Nil | Nil | Nil | Nil | Nil | Nil | Nil | Nil | Nil |
| % Net Income of Revenue | 4.4 | 4.1 | 3.6 | 3.2 | 3.2 | 2.9 | 2.7 | 2.5 | 2.4 | 2.1 |
| % Return on Assets | 18.8 | 17.6 | 16.4 | 13.8 | 13.5 | 13.2 | 12.7 | 12.2 | 11.5 | 11.5 |
| % Return on Equity | 32.7 | 31.0 | 29.0 | 24.1 | 24.2 | 24.6 | 25.7 | 26.2 | 25.6 | 27.9 |

Data as orig reptd.; bef. results of disc opers/spec. items. Per share data adj. for stk. divs.; EPS diluted. E-Estimated. NA-Not Available. NM-Not Meaningful. NR-Not Ranked. UR-Under Review.

**Office:** 14701 Charlson Rd, Eden Prairie, MN 55347-5076.
**Telephone:** 952-937-8500.
**Website:** http://www.chrobinson.com
**Chrmn, Pres & CEO:** J.P. Wiehoff

**SVP, CFO & Chief Acctg Officer:** C.M. Lindbloom
**Treas:** T.A. Renner
**Secy & General Counsel:** L.U. Feuss
**Investor Contact:** A. Freeman (952-937-7847)

**Board Members:** R. Ezrilov, W. M. Fortun, K. E. Keiser, S. L. Polacek, R. K. Roloff, G. A. Schwalbach, B. Short, M. Wickham, J. P. Wiehoff

**Founded:** 1905
**Domicile:** Delaware
**Employees:** 7,332

# Chubb Corp (The)

STANDARD
&POOR'S

| S&P Recommendation | STRONG BUY ★★★★★ | Price $49.60 (as of Nov 14, 2008) | 12-Mo. Target Price $54.00 | Investment Style Large-Cap Blend |
|---|---|---|---|---|

**GICS Sector** Financials
**Sub-Industry** Property & Casualty Insurance

**Summary** One of the largest U.S. property-casualty insurers, Chubb has carved out a number of niches, including high-end personal lines and specialty liability lines coverage.

## Key Stock Statistics (Source S&P, Vickers, company reports)

| | | | | | | | |
|---|---|---|---|---|---|---|---|
| 52-Wk Range | $69.39–33.47 | S&P Oper. EPS 2008**E** | 5.50 | Market Capitalization(B) | $17.884 | Beta | 0.40 |
| Trailing 12-Month EPS | $5.48 | S&P Oper. EPS 2009**E** | 6.00 | Yield (%) | 2.66 | S&P 3-Yr. Proj. EPS CAGR(%) | 2 |
| Trailing 12-Month P/E | 9.1 | P/E on S&P Oper. EPS 2008**E** | 9.0 | Dividend Rate/Share | $1.32 | S&P Credit Rating | A |
| $10K Invested 5 Yrs Ago | $17,281 | Common Shares Outstg. (M) | 360.6 | Institutional Ownership (%) | 87 | | |

## Price Performance

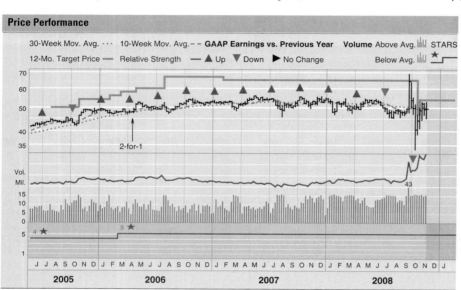

30-Week Mov. Avg. · · · 10-Week Mov. Avg. − − GAAP Earnings vs. Previous Year Volume Above Avg. STARS
12-Mo. Target Price — Relative Strength — ▲ Up ▼ Down ► No Change Below Avg.

2-for-1

Options: ASE, CBOE, P, Ph

Analysis prepared by **Cathy A. Seifert** on October 27, 2008, when the stock traded at **$ 45.05.**

## Qualitative Risk Assessment

| LOW | MEDIUM | HIGH |
|---|---|---|

Our risk assessment reflects our view that CB is a superior underwriter with sound capital and risk management practices and an attractive mix of business. This is offset by our concerns about the impact that a more competitive rate environment will have on CB's business, and by CB's exposure to catastrophe and professional liability claims.

## Quantitative Evaluations

**S&P Quality Ranking**                                        A-

| D | C | B- | B | B+ | A- | A | A+ |
|---|---|---|---|---|---|---|---|

**Relative Strength Rank**                                 STRONG
94

LOWEST = 1                                          HIGHEST = 99

## Revenue/Earnings Data

**Revenue (Million $)**

| | 1Q | 2Q | 3Q | 4Q | Year |
|---|---|---|---|---|---|
| 2008 | 3,489 | 3,354 | -- | -- | -- |
| 2007 | 3,519 | 3,521 | 3,549 | 3,518 | 14,107 |
| 2006 | 3,506 | 3,445 | 3,451 | 3,601 | 14,003 |
| 2005 | 3,449 | 3,451 | 3,479 | 3,703 | 14,082 |
| 2004 | 3,178 | 3,206 | 3,345 | 3,448 | 13,177 |
| 2003 | 2,616 | 2,839 | 2,947 | 2,992 | 11,394 |

**Earnings Per Share ($)**

| | | | | | |
|---|---|---|---|---|---|
| 2008 | 1.77 | 1.27 | 0.73 | E1.51 | E5.50 |
| 2007 | 1.71 | 1.75 | 1.87 | 1.68 | 7.01 |
| 2006 | 1.58 | 1.41 | 1.43 | 1.56 | 5.98 |
| 2005 | 1.18 | 1.23 | 0.60 | 1.46 | 4.47 |
| 2004 | 0.94 | 0.93 | 0.94 | 1.20 | 4.01 |
| 2003 | 0.66 | 0.73 | 0.69 | 0.19 | 2.23 |

Fiscal year ended Dec. 31. Next earnings report expected: Late January. EPS Estimates based on S&P Operating Earnings; historical GAAP earnings are as reported.

## Highlights

► We expect earned premium growth from ongoing operations to decline fractionally in 2008, as strength in some core lines (such as homeowners and surety) is offset by a competitive pricing environment for certain casualty lines of coverage. Earned premiums declined fractionally in 2007, in line with our forecast. We anticipate that underwriting margins will be buoyed by continued favorable claim trends in a number of core lines, although year-to-year comparisons could be difficult in 2008 amid higher third quarter catastrophe losses.

► We see investment income rising 5% to 6% in 2008, versus the 9.4% increase in 2007, as still relatively low investment yields are being offset by continued favorable cash flow trends. EPS results will likely be aided by share buybacks, such as the 41.7 million shares repurchased during 2007 at a cost of $2.2 billion.

► Our operating EPS estimates of $5.50 for 2008 and $6.00 for 2009 (versus the $6.41 reported for 2007) reflect our view that margins will narrow amid a more challenging underwriting and investment environment, but that CB will not incur any large one-time reserve boosts.

## Investment Rationale/Risk

► We view the shares of this property-casualty insurer as undervalued on both a relative and a historical basis. We believe the stock deserves premium-to-peers P/E and price/tangible book multiples, based on what we see as CB's superior personal lines franchise and its wider-margin mix of business. We also believe CB has a higher-quality balance sheet than some of its peers. Our outlook is tempered slightly by our concerns that claims in the professional liability line could trend upward, and that price competition in CB's commercial casualty line of business will heighten in coming periods.

► Risks to our recommendation and target price include a deterioration in claim trends and loss reserves, an escalation in premium price competition, and a significant terrorist attack or catastrophe in the U.S.

► Our 12-month target price of $54 assumes that the stock's forward P/E will increase to approximately 9X our operating EPS estimate for 2009, and its price to estimated 2009 tangible book value multiple to 1.3X. These multiples represent slight premiums to some of CB's peers, but are at the low end of CB's historical averages.

## Dividend Data (Dates: mm/dd Payment Date: mm/dd/yy)

| Amount ($) | Date Decl. | Ex-Div. Date | Stk. of Record | Payment Date |
|---|---|---|---|---|
| 0.290 | 12/13 | 12/14 | 12/18 | 01/15/08 |
| 0.330 | 03/13 | 03/26 | 03/28 | 04/15/08 |
| 0.330 | 06/12 | 06/25 | 06/27 | 07/15/08 |
| 0.330 | 09/04 | 09/17 | 09/19 | 10/07/08 |

Dividends have been paid since 1902. Source: Company reports.

# Chubb Corp (The)

**STANDARD &POOR'S**

## Business Summary October 27, 2008

CORPORATE OVERVIEW. CB's property-casualty operations are divided into three strategic business units: Personal Lines (31% of net written insurance premiums in 2007); Commercial Insurance (43%); and Specialty Insurance (26%). Net written premiums totaled $11.87 billion in 2007, down less than 1% from net written premiums of $11.97 billion recorded in 2006. During 2007, 78% of CB's written premiums originated in the United States, while 22% was derived from overseas.

The Personal Insurance division offers primarily automobile and homeowners' insurance coverage. The company's products are typically targeted to individuals with upscale homes and automobiles, requiring more coverage choices and higher policy limits than are offered under standard insurance policies. Net written premiums totaled $3.7 billion in 2007 (up 5.7% from $3.5 billion in 2006), and were divided as follows: homeowners' 65%, automobile 17%, and other (mainly personal article coverage) 18%.

Chubb Commercial Insurance underwrites an array of commercial insurance

policies, including those for multiple peril, casualty, workers' compensation, and property and marine coverage. Net written premiums totaled $5.08 billion in 2007 (down fractionally from $5.13 billion in 2006) and were divided as follows: commercial casualty 34%, commercial multi-peril 25%, property and marine 24%, and workers' compensation 17%.

Chubb Specialty Insurance offers a variety of specialized executive protection and professional liability products for privately and publicly owned companies, financial institutions, professional firms, and health care organizations. Net written premiums totaled $2.9 billion in 2007 (virtually unchanged from 2006 levels), and were divided as follows: professional liability 88% and surety 12%. Reinsurance assumed totaled $136 million in 2007, down from $390 million in 2006.

## Company Financials Fiscal Year Ended Dec. 31

| Per Share Data ($) | 2007 | 2006 | 2005 | 2004 | 2003 | 2002 | 2001 | 2000 | 1999 | 1998 |
|---|---|---|---|---|---|---|---|---|---|---|
| Tangible Book Value | 37.31 | 32.57 | 28.56 | 25.06 | 21.50 | 18.67 | 17.81 | 18.58 | 16.42 | 17.42 |
| Operating Earnings | NA | NA | NA | NA | NA | 0.58 | 0.31 | 1.91 | 1.67 | 1.83 |
| Earnings | 7.01 | 5.98 | 4.47 | 4.01 | 2.23 | 0.65 | 0.32 | 2.01 | 1.83 | 2.10 |
| S&P Core Earnings | 6.41 | 5.63 | 3.87 | 3.63 | 2.08 | 0.42 | 0.19 | NA | NA | NA |
| Dividends | 1.45 | 1.00 | 1.08 | 0.78 | 0.72 | 0.70 | 0.68 | 0.66 | 0.64 | 0.61 |
| Payout Ratio | 21% | 17% | 24% | 19% | 32% | 109% | NM | 33% | 35% | 29% |
| Prices:High | 55.99 | 54.73 | 49.73 | 38.73 | 34.65 | 39.32 | 43.31 | 45.13 | 38.19 | 44.41 |
| Prices:Low | 45.65 | 46.61 | 36.51 | 31.50 | 20.89 | 25.96 | 27.77 | 21.63 | 22.00 | 27.69 |
| P/E Ratio:High | 8 | 9 | 11 | 10 | 16 | 61 | NM | 23 | 21 | 21 |
| P/E Ratio:Low | 7 | 8 | 8 | 8 | 9 | 40 | NM | 11 | 12 | 13 |

| Income Statement Analysis (Million $) | | | | | | | | | | |
|---|---|---|---|---|---|---|---|---|---|---|
| Premium Income | 11,946 | 11,958 | 12,176 | 11,636 | 10,183 | 8,035 | 6,656 | 6,146 | 5,652 | 5,304 |
| Net Investment Income | 1,738 | 1,580 | 1,408 | 1,256 | 1,118 | 997 | 983 | 957 | 893 | 822 |
| Other Revenue | 423 | 465 | 12,675 | 286 | 93.2 | 57.7 | 115 | 6,294 | 184 | 224 |
| Total Revenue | 14,107 | 14,003 | 14,082 | 13,177 | 11,394 | 9,140 | 7,754 | 7,252 | 6,730 | 6,350 |
| Pretax Income | 3,937 | 3,525 | 2,447 | 2,068 | 934 | 168 | -66.0 | 851 | 710 | 850 |
| Net Operating Income | NA | NA | NA | NA | NA | 201 | 111 | 681 | 565 | 615 |
| Net Income | 2,807 | 2,528 | 1,826 | 1,548 | 809 | 223 | 112 | 715 | 621 | 707 |
| S&P Core Earnings | 2,564 | 2,378 | 1,578 | 1,402 | 754 | 146 | 65.2 | NA | NA | NA |

| Balance Sheet & Other Financial Data (Million $) | | | | | | | | | | |
|---|---|---|---|---|---|---|---|---|---|---|
| Cash & Equivalent | 2,953 | 449 | 427 | 392 | 1,044 | 1,644 | 691 | 720 | 735 | 229 |
| Premiums Due | 2,227 | 2,314 | 2,319 | 2,336 | 2,188 | 6,112 | 6,198 | 3,263 | 1,235 | 1,199 |
| Investment Assets:Bonds | 33,871 | 31,966 | 30,523 | 28,009 | 22,412 | 18,263 | 16,117 | 15,564 | 14,519 | 13,319 |
| Investment Assets:Stocks | 2,320 | 1,957 | 2,212 | 1,841 | 1,514 | 795 | 710 | 831 | 769 | 1,092 |
| Investment Assets:Loans | Nil | Nil | Nil | Nil | Nil | Nil | Nil | Nil | Nil | Nil |
| Investment Assets:Total | 40,081 | 37,693 | 34,893 | 31,504 | 26,934 | 21,279 | 17,784 | 17,001 | 16,019 | 14,755 |
| Deferred Policy Costs | 1,556 | 1,480 | 1,445 | 1,435 | 1,343 | 1,150 | 929 | 842 | 780 | 729 |
| Total Assets | 50,574 | 50,277 | 48,061 | 44,260 | 38,361 | 34,114 | 29,449 | 25,027 | 23,537 | 20,746 |
| Debt | 3,460 | 1,791 | 2,467 | 2,814 | 2,814 | 1,959 | 2,901 | 754 | 759 | 608 |
| Common Equity | 14,445 | 13,863 | 12,407 | 10,126 | 8,522 | 6,859 | 6,525 | 6,982 | 6,272 | 5,644 |
| Property & Casualty:Loss Ratio | 52.8 | 55.2 | 64.3 | 63.1 | 67.6 | 75.4 | 80.8 | 67.5 | 70.3 | 66.3 |
| Property & Casualty:Expense Ratio | 30.1 | 29.0 | 28.0 | 29.2 | 30.4 | 31.3 | 32.6 | 32.9 | 32.5 | 33.5 |
| Property & Casualty Combined Ratio | 82.9 | 84.2 | 92.3 | 92.3 | 98.0 | 106.7 | 113.4 | 100.4 | 102.8 | 99.8 |
| % Return on Revenue | 19.8 | 18.1 | 13.0 | 11.8 | 7.1 | 2.4 | 1.4 | 9.9 | 9.2 | 11.1 |
| % Return on Equity | 19.8 | 19.2 | 16.2 | 16.6 | 10.5 | 3.3 | 1.7 | 10.8 | 10.4 | 12.5 |

Data as orig reptd.; bef. results of disc opers/spec. items. Per share data adj. for stk. divs.; EPS diluted. E-Estimated. NA-Not Available. NM-Not Meaningful. NR-Not Ranked. UR-Under Review.

**Office:** 15 Mountain View Road, Warren, NJ 07061-1615.
**Telephone:** 908-903-2000.
**Email:** info@chubb.com
**Website:** http://www.chubb.com

**Chrmn, Pres & CEO:** J.D. Finnegan
**Vice Chrmn & COO:** J.J. Degnan
**EVP & CFO:** R.G. Spiro
**EVP & Chief Admin Officer:** D.E. Robusto

**EVP & General Counsel:** M.A. Brundage
**Investor Contact:** G.A. Montgomery (908-903-2365)
**Board Members:** Z. Baird, S. P. Burke, J. I. Cash, Jr., J. J. Cohen, J. J. Degnan, J. D. Finnegan, K. J. Mangold, M. G. McGuinn, L. M. Small, J. Soderberg, D. E. Somers, K. H. Williams, J. M. Zimmerman, A. W. Zollar

**Founded:** 1967
**Domicile:** New Jersey
**Employees:** 10,600

# CIENA Corp

| S&P Recommendation | HOLD ★★★☆☆ | Price $6.68 (as of Nov 14, 2008) | 12-Mo. Target Price $18.00 | Investment Style Large-Cap Blend |
| --- | --- | --- | --- | --- |

**GICS Sector** Information Technology
**Sub-Industry** Communications Equipment

**Summary** This company manufactures telecommunications equipment used to increase the capacity of fiber optic networks.

## Key Stock Statistics (Source S&P, Vickers, company reports)

| | | | | | | | |
| --- | --- | --- | --- | --- | --- | --- | --- |
| 52-Wk Range | $44.45– 5.81 | S&P Oper. EPS 2008**E** | 1.08 | Market Capitalization(B) | $0.603 | Beta | 2.56 |
| Trailing 12-Month EPS | $0.93 | S&P Oper. EPS 2009**E** | 1.25 | Yield (%) | Nil | S&P 3-Yr. Proj. EPS CAGR(%) | 20 |
| Trailing 12-Month P/E | 7.2 | P/E on S&P Oper. EPS 2008**E** | 6.2 | Dividend Rate/Share | Nil | S&P Credit Rating | B+ |
| $10K Invested 5 Yrs Ago | $1,484 | Common Shares Outstg. (M) | 90.3 | Institutional Ownership (%) | NM | | |

## Price Performance

30-Week Mov. Avg. · · · · 10-Week Mov. Avg. – – **GAAP Earnings vs. Previous Year** Volume Above Avg. ▮▮▮ STARS
12-Mo. Target Price — Relative Strength — ▲ Up ▼ Down ► No Change Below Avg. ▮▮▮ ★

Options: ASE, CBOE, P, Ph

Analysis prepared by **Ari Bensinger** on September 04, 2008, when the stock traded at **$ 13.22**.

## Highlights

➤ Following an estimated 22% increase in FY 08 (Oct.), we see sales advancing roughly 20% in FY 09, on increased demand for optical transport and switching products, as well as higher revenue contribution from World Wide Packets. We look for CIEN to benefit from new product introductions and penetration of new large customer accounts, although recent telecom spending patterns have softened amid a more difficult macroeconomic environment.

➤ We see FY 09 gross margins relatively flat with the prior period, at the 50% level. Long term, we foresee a more favorable product mix tilted towards software oriented solutions. Despite aggressive R&D investment, we look for FY 09 operating expenses as a percentage of sales to decline from FY 08.

➤ After reduced interest income on a lower cash balance reflecting the repayment of over $500 million of debt, and minimal taxes expected due to loss carryovers, we forecast FY 09 EPS of $1.25, up from $1.08 EPS that we estimate for FY 08. Projections for both years include $0.20 of projected stock option expense.

## Investment Rationale/Risk

➤ Aided by strong industry fundamentals as telecom operators accelerate spending on network infrastructure to support a material increase in bandwidth demand and new product traction, CIEN's sales growth profile is one of the best in the industry, by our analysis, evidenced by our forecast for 20% plus sales growth for both FY 08 and FY 09. Nevertheless, we see near-term operating margins being hampered by lower carrier spending and rising operating costs.

➤ Risks to our recommendation and target price include lower-than-expected sales growth for core optical products, poor execution in realizing higher sales from several recent acquisitions, and the loss of a major customer.

➤ Our 12-month target price of $18 is largely based on 17X our FY 08 EPS estimate of $1.08 and 2X our FY 08 sales per share forecast, in line with the industry average. While these multiples edge toward the low end of the company's historical valuation range, we believe sentiment related to optical equipment investments has dampened of late due to softening spending patterns among the telecom operators.

## Qualitative Risk Assessment

| LOW | MEDIUM | HIGH |
| --- | --- | --- |

Our risk assessment reflects the intense competitive environment in which the company operates and the increased buying power of customers. As CIEN competes against larger equipment companies with broader product offerings and larger service teams to meet customer needs, its profitability runs the risk of being pressured, in our view.

## Quantitative Evaluations

**S&P Quality Ranking** B

| D | C | B- | B | B+ | A- | A | A+ |
| --- | --- | --- | --- | --- | --- | --- | --- |

**Relative Strength Rank** WEAK

22

LOWEST = 1    HIGHEST = 99

## Revenue/Earnings Data

**Revenue (Million $)**

| | 1Q | 2Q | 3Q | 4Q | Year |
| --- | --- | --- | --- | --- | --- |
| 2008 | 227.4 | 242.2 | 253.2 | -- | -- |
| 2007 | 165.1 | 193.5 | 205.0 | 216.2 | 779.8 |
| 2006 | 120.4 | 131.2 | 152.5 | 160.0 | 564.1 |
| 2005 | 94.75 | 103.9 | 110.5 | 118.2 | 427.3 |
| 2004 | 66.41 | 74.70 | 75.59 | 82.01 | 298.7 |
| 2003 | 70.47 | 73.54 | 68.48 | 70.64 | 283.1 |

**Earnings Per Share ($)**

| | | | | | |
| --- | --- | --- | --- | --- | --- |
| 2008 | 0.28 | 0.23 | 0.12 | E0.06 | E1.08 |
| 2007 | 0.12 | 0.14 | 0.12 | 0.30 | 0.87 |
| 2006 | -0.08 | -0.02 | -0.05 | 0.14 | 0.01 |
| 2005 | -0.70 | -0.91 | -0.63 | -3.08 | -5.32 |
| 2004 | -1.12 | -1.12 | -1.75 | -6.09 | -10.57 |
| 2003 | -1.75 | -1.19 | -1.40 | -1.68 | -6.09 |

Fiscal year ended Oct. 31. Next earnings report expected: NA. EPS Estimates based on S&P Operating Earnings; historical GAAP earnings are as reported.

## Dividend Data

No cash dividends have been paid.

# CIENA Corp

STANDARD
&POOR'S

## Business Summary September 04, 2008

CORPORATE OVERVIEW. CIENA Corp. supplies application-focused communications networking equipment, software and services to communications service providers, cable operators, governments and enterprises. The company specializes in transitioning legacy communications networks to converged, next-generation architectures, capable of efficiently delivering a broader mix of high-bandwidth services. Customers AT&T and Sprint accounted for 25% and 13% of FY 07 (Oct.) sales, respectively. Product revenue is reported in four segments: converged Ethernet infrastructure, Ethernet access, and global network services.

PRIMARY BUSINESS DYNAMICS. Converged Ethernet infrastructure products account for the majority of company revenue (83% of FY 07 sales) and consist of metro and core transport and switching products, multiservice optical access solutions, and multiservice routing devices. These products enable service providers to increase the efficiency and bandwidth of their communications networks, allowing them to service more customers, more cost effectively. They also enable operators to transition their communications networks from legacy technologies, such as ATM and Frame Relay, to next-generation technologies, such as Ethernet and IP/MPLS. Flagship offerings in-

clude the CoreDirector optical switch and the CN 4200 FlexSelect advanced services platform.

Ethernet access products (6%) allow telecommunications service providers to transition their legacy voice networks to support next-generation services such as Internet-based (IP) telephony, video services and DSL. These products facilitate broader service offerings to compete with cable operators.

The global network services group (11%) includes revenue associated with the company's service, support and training activities.

We believe CIEN continues to focus on cost reductions across all product lines. It relies on electronic manufacturing service (EMS) providers to perform the majority of the manufacturing operations for its products and components, and is increasingly utilizing overseas suppliers in Asia.

## Company Financials Fiscal Year Ended Oct. 31

| Per Share Data ($) | 2007 | 2006 | 2005 | 2004 | 2003 | 2002 | 2001 | 2000 | 1999 | 1998 |
|---|---|---|---|---|---|---|---|---|---|---|
| Tangible Book Value | 6.37 | 5.19 | 0.66 | 6.58 | 13.10 | 20.24 | 40.62 | 19.54 | 26.19 | 15.55 |
| Cash Flow | 1.25 | 0.54 | -4.41 | -9.17 | -4.59 | -28.08 | -33.96 | 3.39 | 2.44 | 2.81 |
| Earnings | 0.87 | 0.01 | -5.32 | -10.57 | -6.09 | -30.60 | -40.27 | 1.89 | -0.11 | 1.72 |
| S&P Core Earnings | 0.92 | -0.05 | -4.48 | -7.70 | -6.09 | -23.52 | -22.47 | NA | NA | NA |
| Dividends | Nil | Nil | Nil | Nil | Nil | Nil | Nil | Nil | Nil | Nil |
| Payout Ratio | Nil | Nil | Nil | Nil | Nil | Nil | Nil | Nil | Nil | Nil |
| Prices:High | 49.55 | 39.36 | 24.02 | 57.00 | 54.20 | 121.15 | 756.30 | 1057 | 261.07 | 323.44 |
| Prices:Low | 24.75 | 20.38 | 11.51 | 11.69 | 29.35 | 16.88 | 64.43 | 158.88 | 47.71 | 28.45 |
| P/E Ratio:High | 57 | NM | NM | NM | NM | NM | NM | NM | NM | NM |
| P/E Ratio:Low | 28 | NM | NM | NM | NM | NM | NM | NM | NM | NM |

| Income Statement Analysis (Million $) | 2007 | 2006 | 2005 | 2004 | 2003 | 2002 | 2001 | 2000 | 1999 | 1998 |
|---|---|---|---|---|---|---|---|---|---|---|
| Revenue | 780 | 564 | 427 | 299 | 283 | 361 | 1,603 | 859 | 482 | 508 |
| Operating Income | 83.0 | 15.1 | -115 | -185 | -209 | -569 | 324 | 163 | 43.5 | 157 |
| Depreciation | 42.0 | 45.5 | 76.0 | 107 | 93.7 | 131 | 283 | 63.6 | 50.4 | 33.3 |
| Interest Expense | 27.0 | 24.2 | 25.4 | 26.8 | 36.3 | 45.3 | 30.6 | 0.34 | 0.50 | 0.26 |
| Pretax Income | 85.7 | 1.98 | -434 | -788 | -385 | -1,487 | -1,707 | 121 | -5.99 | 93.4 |
| Effective Tax Rate | 3.40% | 69.9% | NM | NM | NM | NM | NM | 32.5% | NM | 43.1% |
| Net Income | 82.8 | 0.60 | -436 | -789 | -387 | -1,597 | -1,794 | 81.4 | -3.92 | 53.2 |
| S&P Core Earnings | 87.6 | -3.97 | -367 | -573 | -386 | -1,225 | -1,001 | NA | NA | NA |

| Balance Sheet & Other Financial Data (Million $) | 2007 | 2006 | 2005 | 2004 | 2003 | 2002 | 2001 | 2000 | 1999 | 1998 |
|---|---|---|---|---|---|---|---|---|---|---|
| Cash | 892 | 220 | 373 | 203 | 310 | 377 | 398 | 238 | 262 | 243 |
| Current Assets | 1,969 | 1,098 | 1,102 | 1,079 | 1,229 | 1,638 | 2,191 | 813 | 533 | 428 |
| Total Assets | 2,416 | 1,840 | 1,675 | 2,137 | 2,378 | 2,751 | 3,317 | 1,027 | 678 | 572 |
| Current Liabilities | 730 | 162 | 178 | 159 | 186 | 224 | 254 | 173 | 106 | 61.9 |
| Long Term Debt | 802 | 844 | 650 | 692 | 794 | 919 | 870 | Nil | Nil | 1.41 |
| Common Equity | 850 | 754 | 735 | 1,154 | 1,331 | 1,527 | 2,129 | 810 | 530 | 475 |
| Total Capital | 1,652 | 1,598 | 1,385 | 1,846 | 2,125 | 2,246 | 3,063 | 849 | 567 | 510 |
| Capital Expenditures | 32.0 | 33.0 | 11.3 | 33.0 | 29.5 | 66.3 | 239 | 124 | 46.8 | 86.4 |
| Cash Flow | 125 | 46.0 | -360 | -682 | -293 | -1,466 | -1,511 | 145 | 46.5 | 86.5 |
| Current Ratio | 2.7 | 6.8 | 6.2 | 6.8 | 6.6 | 7.3 | 8.6 | 4.7 | 5.1 | 6.9 |
| % Long Term Debt of Capitalization | 48.5 | 52.8 | 46.9 | 37.5 | 37.4 | 37.6 | 28.4 | Nil | Nil | 2.8 |
| % Net Income of Revenue | 10.6 | 0.1 | NM | NM | NM | NM | NM | 9.5 | NM | 10.5 |
| % Return on Assets | 3.8 | 0.0 | NM | NM | NM | NM | NM | 9.5 | NM | 10.4 |
| % Return on Equity | 10.3 | 0.1 | NM | NM | NM | NM | NM | 12.1 | NM | 12.7 |

Data as orig reptd.; bef. results of disc opers/spec. items. Per share data adj. for stk. divs.; EPS diluted. E-Estimated. NA-Not Available. NM-Not Meaningful. NR-Not Ranked. UR-Under Review.

**Office:** 1201 Winterson Road, Linthicum, MD 21090-2205.
**Telephone:** 410-865-8500.
**Email:** ir@ciena.com
**Website:** http://www.ciena.com

**Chrmn:** P.H. Nettles
**Chrmn:** J.W. Bayless
**Pres & CEO:** G.B. Smith
**COO & SVP:** A.D. Smith

**SVP & CFO:** J.E. Moylan, Jr.
**Board Members:** J. W. Bayless, S. P. Bradley, H. B. Cash, B. L. Claflin, L. W. Fitt, P. H. Nettles, J. M. O'Brien, M. J. Rowny, G. B. Smith, G. H. Taylor

**Founded:** 1992
**Domicile:** Delaware
**Employees:** 1,797

# CIGNA Corp.

**STANDARD &POOR'S**

**S&P Recommendation** HOLD ★★★☆☆

| Price | 12-Mo. Target Price | Investment Style |
|---|---|---|
| $12.95 (as of Nov 14, 2008) | $21.00 | Large-Cap Growth |

**GICS Sector** Health Care
**Sub-Industry** Managed Health Care

**Summary** CIGNA is one of the largest investor-owned employee benefits organizations in the U.S. Its subsidiaries are major providers of employee benefits offered through the workplace.

## Key Stock Statistics (Source S&P, Vickers, company reports)

| | | | | | | | |
|---|---|---|---|---|---|---|---|
| 52-Wk Range | $56.98– 9.82 | S&P Oper. EPS 2008E | 4.10 | Market Capitalization(B) | $3.519 | Beta | 1.66 |
| Trailing 12-Month EPS | $2.73 | S&P Oper. EPS 2009E | 4.00 | Yield (%) | 0.31 | S&P 3-Yr. Proj. EPS CAGR(%) | 5 |
| Trailing 12-Month P/E | 4.7 | P/E on S&P Oper. EPS 2008E | 3.2 | Dividend Rate/Share | $0.04 | S&P Credit Rating | BBB+ |
| $10K Invested 5 Yrs Ago | $7,049 | Common Shares Outstg. (M) | 271.7 | Institutional Ownership (%) | 84 | | |

## Price Performance

30-Week Mov. Avg. · · · · 10-Week Mov. Avg. – – GAAP Earnings vs. Previous Year Volume Above Avg. STARS
12-Mo. Target Price — Relative Strength — ▲ Up ▼ Down ▶ No Change Below Avg. ★

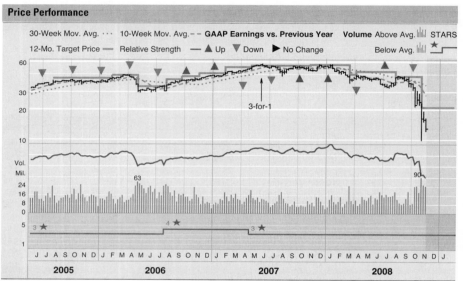

Options: ASE, CBOE, P, Ph

Analysis prepared by **Phillip M. Seligman** on November 06, 2008, when the stock traded at **$ 15.32**.

## Highlights

➤ We expect health plan premium and fee revenue to decline about 1% in 2009, as higher pricing is outweighed by CI's anticipated net 2% decline in overall medical membership, despite recent large account ASO wins. Revenue growth of about 9% we see for 2008 benefited from the April 1 acquisition of Great-West Healthcare (GWH), which has since lost members. Excluding GWH, we believe health plan enrollment will decline by 1% in 2008.

➤ Assuming pricing is above medical cost trend, which CI expects to rise 50 basis points (bps) in 2009 to 7%-8%, we estimate the guaranteed-cost and experience-rate books' medical loss ratios will decline. But CI sees an 8% enrollment decline in both groups, which suggests to us their earnings may be flat. We expect earnings from the GWH integration and non-health plan segments to be offset by higher operating expenses.

➤ We estimate operating EPS of $4.10 in 2008, excluding $0.70 in Variable Annuity Death Benefits (VADB) reserve charges in the run-off reinsurance segment that we view as one-time. We also project $4.00 in 2009.

## Investment Rationale/Risk

➤ CI, a one-time market-share gainer, is seeing commercial enrollment declines amid both intensified competition and the soft economy. Also, we see financial flexibility diminishing in 2009. CI said its capital position is strong, it has no need to issue equity, and does not expect to issue additional long-term debt until credit market conditions improve, but we think it will have to rely strongly on its cash flow and will likely re-enter the credit markets in 2009. It expects to have only $40 million in cash at the parent at year-end 2008, and plans to put up to $600 million in its now-underfunded pension plan. Also, it might have more VADB charges, depending on stock market performance. Meanwhile, it looks to improve its subsidiaries' capitalization by reducing their dividend payments to the parent.

➤ Risks to our recommendation and target price include intensified competition and higher-than-expected medical costs.

➤ Our 12-month target price of $21 assumes a below-peer P/E of 5.3X out 2008 estimate, reflecting groupwide valuation compression and our view of CI's sub-par performance.

## Qualitative Risk Assessment

| LOW | MEDIUM | HIGH |
|---|---|---|

Our risk assessment reflects our view of CI's improving cost structure, strong cash flow, diversity, and wide range of products. However, competition is intensifying in the managed care market, and CI's focus on maintaining pricing discipline amid a weak economy is contributing to declines in enrollment.

## Quantitative Evaluations

**S&P Quality Ranking** B

| D | C | B- | B | B+ | A- | A | A+ |
|---|---|---|---|---|---|---|---|

**Relative Strength Rank** WEAK

11

LOWEST = 1 HIGHEST = 99

## Revenue/Earnings Data

### Revenue (Million $)

| | 1Q | 2Q | 3Q | 4Q | Year |
|---|---|---|---|---|---|
| 2008 | 4,569 | 4,863 | 4,852 | -- | -- |
| 2007 | 4,374 | 4,381 | 4,413 | 4,455 | 17,623 |
| 2006 | 4,107 | 4,098 | 4,137 | 4,205 | 16,547 |
| 2005 | 4,345 | 4,107 | 4,022 | 4,210 | 16,684 |
| 2004 | 4,722 | 4,633 | 4,479 | 4,342 | 18,176 |
| 2003 | 4,900 | 4,634 | 4,773 | 4,501 | 18,808 |

### Earnings Per Share ($)

| | 1Q | 2Q | 3Q | 4Q | Year |
|---|---|---|---|---|---|
| 2008 | 0.20 | 0.98 | 0.62 | E0.94 | E4.10 |
| 2007 | 0.93 | 0.75 | 1.28 | 0.93 | 3.88 |
| 2006 | 0.96 | 0.78 | 0.93 | 0.76 | 3.44 |
| 2005 | 1.09 | 0.94 | 0.67 | 0.59 | 3.28 |
| 2004 | 0.49 | 1.20 | 0.75 | 1.39 | 3.81 |
| 2003 | 0.45 | -0.13 | 0.46 | 0.69 | 1.47 |

Fiscal year ended Dec. 31. Next earnings report expected: Early February. EPS Estimates based on S&P Operating Earnings; historical GAAP earnings are as reported.

## Dividend Data (Dates: mm/dd Payment Date: mm/dd/yy)

| Amount ($) | Date Decl. | Ex-Div. Date | Stk. of Record | Payment Date |
|---|---|---|---|---|
| 0.010 | 10/24 | 12/11 | 12/13 | 01/10/08 |
| 0.040 | 02/27 | 03/07 | 03/11 | 04/10/08 |

Dividends have been paid since 1867. Source: Company reports.

# CIGNA Corp.

## Business Summary November 06, 2008

CORPORATE OVERVIEW. CIGNA Corp., one of the largest U.S. employee benefits organizations, provides health care products and services and group life, accident and disability insurance.

Health Care offers group medical, dental, behavioral health and pharmacy services products. Medical products include consumer directed health plans (CDHPs), HMOs, network only, point-of-service (POS) plans, preferred provider organizations (PPOs), and traditional indemnity coverage. The health care products and services are offered through guaranteed cost, retrospectively experience-rated, administrative services only (ASO) and minimum premium funding arrangements. Under ASO, the employer or other plan sponsor self-funds all of its claims and assumes the risk for claim costs incurred. CI's CDHPs offer a modular product portfolio that provides a choice of benefits network and various funding, medical management, consumerism and health advocacy options for employers and consumers.

Medical covered lives at September 30, 2008, totaled 11,900,000 (versus

10,169,000 as of December 31, 2007): 1,108,000 (1,249,000) guaranteed cost (commercial HMO, Medicare, and voluntary/limited benefits); 901,000 (907,000) experience-related indemnity; 8,138,000 (8,013,000) ASO; and 1,708,000 (none) acquired business.

Disability and Life, which provides employer-paid and voluntary life, accident and disability products, held group life insurance policies covering 6.0 million lives at year-end 2007, up from 5.8 million at year-end 2006. International operates in selected markets outside the U.S., providing individual and group life, accident and health, health care and pension products. CI's invested assets under management at year-end 2007 totaled $17.5 billion, versus $18.3 billion at year-end 2006.

## Company Financials Fiscal Year Ended Dec. 31

| Per Share Data ($) | 2007 | 2006 | 2005 | 2004 | 2003 | 2002 | 2001 | 2000 | 1999 | 1998 |
|---|---|---|---|---|---|---|---|---|---|---|
| Tangible Book Value | 13.93 | 8.73 | 10.30 | 9.05 | 6.85 | 2.74 | 7.62 | 7.75 | 8.22 | 9.36 |
| Operating Earnings | NA | NA | NA | NA | NA | NA | 2.45 | 2.02 | 1.17 | 1.54 |
| Earnings | 3.88 | 3.44 | 3.28 | 3.81 | 1.47 | -0.94 | 2.20 | 2.03 | 1.18 | 2.02 |
| S&P Core Earnings | 4.10 | 3.34 | 2.80 | 2.62 | 1.21 | -0.24 | 1.77 | NA | NA | NA |
| Dividends | 0.04 | 0.03 | 0.03 | 0.14 | 0.44 | 0.44 | 0.43 | 0.41 | 0.40 | 0.38 |
| Relative Payout | 1% | 1% | 1% | 4% | 30% | NM | 19% | 20% | 34% | 19% |
| Prices:High | 57.61 | 44.59 | 39.94 | 27.76 | 19.53 | 37.00 | 44.98 | 45.58 | 32.88 | 27.46 |
| Prices:Low | 42.33 | 29.35 | 26.04 | 17.63 | 13.03 | 11.38 | 23.29 | 20.25 | 21.15 | 18.67 |
| P/E Ratio:High | 15 | 13 | 12 | 7 | 13 | NM | 20 | 22 | 28 | 14 |
| P/E Ratio:Low | 11 | 9 | 8 | 5 | 9 | NM | 11 | 10 | 18 | 9 |

| Income Statement Analysis (Million $) | 2007 | 2006 | 2005 | 2004 | 2003 | 2002 | 2001 | 2000 | 1999 | 1998 |
|---|---|---|---|---|---|---|---|---|---|---|
| Life Insurance in Force | NA | NA | NA | NA | 459,995 | 516,661 | 609,970 | 647,464 | 662,693 | 670,667 |
| Premium Income:Life A & H | 15,008 | 13,641 | 13,695 | 14,236 | 15,441 | 15,737 | 15,367 | 16,328 | 15,079 | 13,913 |
| Premium Income:Casualty/Property. | NA | NA | Nil | Nil | Nil | Nil | Nil | Nil | Nil | 2,500 |
| Net Investment Income | 1,114 | 1,195 | 1,359 | 1,643 | 2,594 | 2,716 | 2,843 | 2,942 | 2,959 | 3,705 |
| Total Revenue | 17,623 | 16,547 | 16,684 | 18,176 | 18,808 | 19,348 | 19,115 | 19,994 | 18,781 | 21,437 |
| Pretax Income | 1,631 | 1,731 | 1,793 | 2,375 | 903 | -569 | 1,497 | 1,497 | 1,219 | 2,010 |
| Net Operating Income | NA | NA | NA | NA | NA | NA | 1,101 | 983 | 695 | 1,190 |
| Net Income | 1,120 | 1,159 | 1,276 | 1,577 | 620 | -397 | 989 | 987 | 699 | 1,292 |
| S&P Core Earnings | 1,180 | 1,127 | 1,090 | 1,082 | 509 | -99.2 | 794 | NA | NA | NA |

| Balance Sheet & Other Financial Data (Million $) | 2007 | 2006 | 2005 | 2004 | 2003 | 2002 | 2001 | 2000 | 1999 | 1998 |
|---|---|---|---|---|---|---|---|---|---|---|
| Cash & Equivalent | 2,203 | 1,647 | 1,991 | 2,804 | 1,860 | 2,079 | 2,455 | 2,739 | 2,732 | 3,797 |
| Premiums Due | 8,736 | 9,501 | 8,616 | 16,223 | 9,421 | 9,981 | 2,832 | 2,814 | 2,475 | 4,469 |
| Investment Assets:Bonds | 12,081 | 12,155 | 14,947 | 16,136 | 17,121 | 27,803 | 23,401 | 24,776 | 22,944 | 32,634 |
| Investment Assets:Stocks | 132 | 131 | 135 | 33.0 | 11,300 | 295 | 404 | 569 | 585 | 1,043 |
| Investment Assets:Loans | 4,727 | 5,393 | 5,271 | 5,123 | 10,207 | 11,134 | 12,694 | 12,755 | 12,816 | 15,784 |
| Investment Assets:Total | 17,530 | 18,303 | 21,376 | 21,919 | 39,658 | 40,362 | 38,261 | 41,516 | 38,295 | 50,707 |
| Deferred Policy Costs | 816 | 707 | 618 | 544 | 580 | 494 | 448 | 1,052 | 927 | 1,069 |
| Total Assets | 40,065 | 42,399 | 44,863 | 81,059 | 90,953 | 88,950 | 91,589 | 95,088 | 95,333 | 114,612 |
| Debt | 1,790 | 1,294 | 1,338 | 1,438 | 1,500 | 1,500 | 1,627 | 1,163 | 1,359 | 1,431 |
| Common Equity | 4,748 | 4,330 | 5,360 | 5,203 | 4,465 | 3,665 | 5,055 | 5,634 | 6,149 | 8,277 |
| Combined Loss-Expense Ratio | NA | NA | NA | NA | NA | NA | NA | NA | NA | 107.1 |
| % Return on Revenue | 6.4 | 7.0 | 7.6 | 8.7 | 3.3 | NM | 5.2 | 4.9 | 3.7 | 6.0 |
| % Return on Equity | 24.7 | 23.9 | 24.2 | 32.2 | 15.3 | NM | 18.9 | 16.5 | 9.1 | 15.9 |
| % Investment Yield | 6.3 | 6.0 | 6.3 | 5.3 | 6.5 | 6.9 | 7.3 | 7.1 | 7.4 | 8.4 |

Data as orig reptd.; bef. results of disc opers/spec. items. Per share data adj. for stk. divs.; EPS diluted. E-Estimated. NA-Not Available. NM-Not Meaningful. NR-Not Ranked. UR-Under Review.

**Office:** 2 Liberty Pl, Philadelphia, PA 19192-0001.
**Telephone:** 215-761-1000.
**Website:** http://www.cigna.com
**Chrmn & CEO:** H.E. Hanway

**Pres & COO:** D.M. Cordani
**EVP & CFO:** M.W. Bell
**EVP & General Counsel:** C.A. Petren
**EVP & CIO:** M.D. Woeller

**Investor Contact:** T. Detrick (215-761-1414)
**Board Members:** R. H. Campbell, H. E. Hanway, I. Harris, Jr., J. E. Henney, P. Larson, R. Martinez, IV, J. E. Rogers, C. C. Wait, E. C. Wiseman, D. F. Zarcone, W. D. Zollars

**Founded:** 1792
**Domicile:** Delaware
**Employees:** 26,600

# Cincinnati Financial Corp

STANDARD &POOR'S

| S&P Recommendation | HOLD ★★★☆☆ | Price $26.23 (as of Nov 14, 2008) | 12-Mo. Target Price $28.00 | Investment Style Large-Cap Blend |
|---|---|---|---|---|

**GICS Sector** Financials
**Sub-Industry** Property & Casualty Insurance

**Summary** This insurance holding company markets primarily property and casualty coverage; it also conducts life insurance and asset management operations.

## Key Stock Statistics (Source S&P, Vickers, company reports)

| | | | | | | | |
|---|---|---|---|---|---|---|---|
| 52-Wk Range | $41.24–13.68 | S&P Oper. EPS 2008**E** | 2.20 | Market Capitalization(B) | $4.259 | Beta | 0.89 |
| Trailing 12-Month EPS | $2.75 | S&P Oper. EPS 2009**E** | 2.40 | Yield (%) | 5.95 | S&P 3-Yr. Proj. EPS CAGR(%) | -5 |
| Trailing 12-Month P/E | 9.5 | P/E on S&P Oper. EPS 2008**E** | 11.9 | Dividend Rate/Share | $1.56 | S&P Credit Rating | BBB+ |
| $10K Invested 5 Yrs Ago | $8,378 | Common Shares Outstg. (M) | 162.4 | Institutional Ownership (%) | 57 | | |

## Price Performance

30-Week Mov. Avg. · · · 10-Week Mov. Avg. – – **GAAP Earnings vs. Previous Year** Volume Above Avg. STARS
12-Mo. Target Price — Relative Strength — ▲ Up ▼ Down ▶ No Change Below Avg. ★

Options: CBOE, P

Analysis prepared by **Cathy A. Seifert** on November 06, 2008, when the stock traded at **$ 26.49**.

## Highlights

➤ We believe property-casualty earned premiums will decline by more than 5% in 2008, versus the fractional decline reported for 2007. We see the effects of CINF's expansion being offset by price competition, particularly in the commercial lines segment. We also believe that competition in many non-coastal regions (like those in which CINF operates) will remain intense. We anticipate that underwriting margins will contract in 2008, reflecting our expectation that certain claim trends will erode and catastrophe losses will return to more "normal" levels.

➤ We expect net investment income to decline more than 10% in 2008, versus a 6.6% rise in 2007. This rate of growth is below that of a number of CINF's peers, partly reflecting a different asset mix. As of June 30, 2008, nearly 43% of CINF's invested assets were in equity securities, versus an industry average that we estimate at less than 15%.

➤ We expect eroding premium volume and narrower underwriting margins, coupled with a more challenging investment environment, to produce operating EPS of $2.20 in 2008 and $2.40 in 2009, versus the $3.54 of operating EPS earned in 2007.

## Investment Rationale/Risk

➤ We recently lowered our opinion on the shares to hold from buy on our view that, at current levels, the shares are fairly valued relative to the company's peers and to historical valuation metrics. Our outlook remains tempered by what we see as the dual challenges of heightened price competition in many core lines of business and a more challenging investment environment. CINF has an outsized exposure to equity securities versus its peers, by our analysis. The company's equity securities portfolio has also been overweighted with financial services stocks, which have in recent periods underperformed the broader market.

➤ Risks to our opinion and target price include a lower-than-expected premium growth rate and a sharp deterioration in underwriting results and profitability.

➤ Our 12-month target price of $28 assumes the shares will trade at approximately 11.7X our 2009 operating EPS estimate, a premium of about 15% to 20% to most of the company's peers, but at the lower end of the company's historical range.

## Qualitative Risk Assessment

| LOW | MEDIUM | HIGH |
|---|---|---|

Our risk assessment reflects our view of the company as a fairly conservative underwriter with sound risk and capital management policies. However, CINF's investment allocation is more heavily weighted toward equity holdings than that of its peers.

## Quantitative Evaluations

**S&P Quality Ranking** A

| D | C | B- | B | B+ | A- | A | A+ |
|---|---|---|---|---|---|---|---|

**Relative Strength Rank** STRONG

93

LOWEST = 1 HIGHEST = 99

## Revenue/Earnings Data

### Revenue (Million $)

| | 1Q | 2Q | 3Q | 4Q | Year |
|---|---|---|---|---|---|
| 2008 | 704.0 | 917.0 | 1,186 | -- | -- |
| 2007 | 1,031 | 1,270 | 982.0 | 983.0 | 4,259 |
| 2006 | 1,607 | 981.0 | 967.0 | 995.0 | 4,550 |
| 2005 | 916.0 | 940.0 | 944.0 | 967.0 | 3,767 |
| 2004 | 870.0 | 923.0 | 879.0 | 942.0 | 3,614 |
| 2003 | 707.0 | 798.0 | 836.0 | 840.0 | 3,181 |

### Earnings Per Share ($)

| | 1Q | 2Q | 3Q | 4Q | Year |
|---|---|---|---|---|---|
| 2008 | -0.25 | 0.38 | 1.50 | E0.66 | E2.20 |
| 2007 | 1.11 | 2.02 | 0.72 | 1.11 | 4.97 |
| 2006 | 3.13 | 0.76 | 0.66 | 0.75 | 5.30 |
| 2005 | 0.81 | 0.89 | 0.66 | 1.03 | 3.40 |
| 2004 | 0.82 | 0.87 | 0.50 | 1.09 | 3.28 |
| 2003 | 0.31 | 0.48 | 0.58 | 0.72 | 2.10 |

Fiscal year ended Dec. 31. Next earnings report expected: Early February. EPS Estimates based on S&P Operating Earnings; historical GAAP earnings are as reported.

## Dividend Data (Dates: mm/dd Payment Date: mm/dd/yy)

| Amount ($) | Date Decl. | Ex-Div. Date | Stk. of Record | Payment Date |
|---|---|---|---|---|
| 0.355 | 11/19 | 12/19 | 12/21 | 01/15/08 |
| 0.390 | 02/01 | 03/18 | 03/21 | 04/15/08 |
| 0.390 | 05/23 | 06/18 | 06/20 | 07/15/08 |
| 0.390 | 08/18 | 09/17 | 09/19 | 10/15/08 |

Dividends have been paid since 1954. Source: Company reports.

---

**Please read the Required Disclosures and Analyst Certification on the last page of this report.**

# Cincinnati Financial Corp

STANDARD &POOR'S

## Business Summary November 06, 2008

CORPORATE OVERVIEW. Cincinnati Financial Corp. (CINF) underwrites and sells property-casualty insurance primarily in the Midwest and Southeast, through a network of independent agents. Operations as of 2007 year end were conducted in 34 states, through a network of 1,327 independent insurance agencies, many of which own stock in the company. The company is licensed in all 50 states, the District of Columbia, and Puerto Rico. An ongoing geographical expansion plan is being implemented. Ten states accounted for 69% of earned premium volume in 2007: Ohio (21%), Illinois (9%), Indiana (7%), Pennsylvania (6%), North Carolina (5%), Georgia (5%), Michigan (5%), Virginia (5%), Wisconsin (4%), and Tennessee (3%).

Property-casualty net earned premiums totaled $3.3 billion in 2007, with commercial lines accounting for 77% and personal lines for 23%. Commercial casualty lines of coverage accounted for 34% of commercial lines earned premiums in 2007, while commercial property lines coverage accounted for 21%, commercial auto for 18%, workers' compensation for 15%, special package coverages for 6%, surety and executive risk for 4% and other for 1%. Personal auto accounted for 48% of personal lines earned premiums in 2007, homeowners' coverage for 40%, and other personal lines for 12%.

Underwriting results improved in 2007, largely due to a lower level of catastrophe losses. The loss ratio in 2007 equaled 58.7% (including 0.9 points of catastrophe losses), versus 63.5% (including 5.5 points of catastrophe losses). The expense ratio inched upward, to 31.7%, from 30.4%. Taken together, the statutory combined ratio (before policyholder dividends) equaled 90.4% in 2007, an improvement from 2006's combined ratio of 93.9%. (A combined ratio of under 100% indicates an underwriting profit, while one in excess of 100% signals an underwriting loss.)

Life, accident and health insurance is marketed through property-casualty agents and independent life insurance agents. This unit has been expanding its work site marketing activities, introducing a new product line and exploring expansion opportunities. Term life insurance represents this unit's largest product line.

## Company Financials Fiscal Year Ended Dec. 31

| Per Share Data ($) | 2007 | 2006 | 2005 | 2004 | 2003 | 2002 | 2001 | 2000 | 1999 | 1998 |
|---|---|---|---|---|---|---|---|---|---|---|
| Tangible Book Value | 43.60 | 39.38 | 34.88 | 35.60 | 35.10 | 31.42 | 33.62 | 33.80 | 30.35 | 30.58 |
| Operating Earnings | NA | 2.82 | 3.02 | 2.93 | NA | 1.67 | 1.17 | 0.82 | 1.38 | 1.08 |
| Earnings | 4.97 | 5.30 | 3.40 | 3.28 | 2.10 | 1.32 | 1.08 | 0.66 | 1.38 | 1.28 |
| S&P Core Earnings | 3.49 | 2.78 | 3.10 | 2.87 | 2.09 | 1.55 | 1.06 | NA | NA | NA |
| Dividends | 1.42 | 1.34 | 1.21 | 1.04 | 0.91 | 0.81 | 0.76 | 0.69 | 0.60 | 0.54 |
| Relative Payout | 29% | 25% | 35% | 32% | 43% | 61% | 71% | 104% | 44% | 42% |
| Prices:High | 48.45 | 49.19 | 45.95 | 43.52 | 38.01 | 42.90 | 38.94 | 39.29 | 38.55 | 42.55 |
| Prices:Low | 36.00 | 41.21 | 38.38 | 36.57 | 30.00 | 29.42 | 30.84 | 23.75 | 27.32 | 27.66 |
| P/E Ratio:High | 10 | 9 | 14 | 13 | 18 | 32 | 36 | 59 | 28 | 33 |
| P/E Ratio:Low | 7 | 8 | 11 | 11 | 14 | 22 | 29 | 36 | 20 | 22 |

| Income Statement Analysis (Million $) | 2007 | 2006 | 2005 | 2004 | 2003 | 2002 | 2001 | 2000 | 1999 | 1998 |
|---|---|---|---|---|---|---|---|---|---|---|
| Life Insurance in Force | 61,873 | 56,971 | 51,493 | 44,921 | 48,492 | 32,486 | 27,534 | 23,525 | 17,890 | 13,048 |
| Premium Income:Life A & H | 125 | 115 | 106 | 101 | 95.0 | 87.0 | 81.0 | 79.3 | 75.0 | 70.1 |
| Premium Income:Casualty/Property. | 3,125 | 3,163 | 3,058 | 2,919 | 2,653 | 2,391 | 2,071 | 1,828 | 1,657 | 1,543 |
| Net Investment Income | 608 | 570 | 526 | 492 | 465 | 445 | 421 | 415 | 387 | 368 |
| Total Revenue | 4,259 | 4,550 | 3,767 | 3,614 | 3,181 | 2,843 | 2,561 | 2,331 | 2,128 | 2,054 |
| Pretax Income | 1,192 | 1,329 | 823 | 800 | 480 | 279 | 221 | 109 | 322 | 307 |
| Net Operating Income | NA | 496 | 562 | 524 | 286 | 300 | 210 | 120 | 255 | 199 |
| Net Income | 855 | 930 | 602 | 584 | 374 | 238 | 193 | 118 | 255 | 242 |
| S&P Core Earnings | 602 | 487 | 549 | 512 | 372 | 279 | 189 | NA | NA | NA |

| Balance Sheet & Other Financial Data (Million $) | 2007 | 2006 | 2005 | 2004 | 2003 | 2002 | 2001 | 2000 | 1999 | 1998 |
|---|---|---|---|---|---|---|---|---|---|---|
| Cash & Equivalent | 226 | 202 | 119 | 306 | 91.0 | 112 | 93.0 | 60.3 | 420 | 135 |
| Premiums Due | 1,861 | 1,811 | 1,797 | 1,799 | 1,677 | 1,483 | 732 | 652 | 192 | 164 |
| Investment Assets:Bonds | 5,848 | 5,805 | 5,476 | 5,141 | 3,925 | 3,305 | 3,010 | 2,721 | 2,617 | 2,812 |
| Investment Assets:Stocks | 6,249 | 7,799 | 7,106 | 7,498 | 8,524 | 7,884 | 8,495 | 8,526 | 7,511 | 7,455 |
| Investment Assets:Loans | Nil | Nil | Nil | Nil | Nil | Nil | Nil | Nil | Nil | Nil |
| Investment Assets:Total | 12,261 | 13,759 | 12,702 | 12,677 | 12,527 | 11,257 | 11,571 | 11,316 | 10,194 | 10,325 |
| Deferred Policy Costs | 461 | 453 | 429 | 400 | 372 | 343 | 286 | 259 | 154 | 143 |
| Total Assets | 16,637 | 17,222 | 16,003 | 16,107 | 15,509 | 14,059 | 13,959 | 13,287 | 11,380 | 11,087 |
| Debt | 860 | 840 | 791 | 791 | 603 | 420 | 609 | 449 | 457 | 472 |
| Common Equity | 5,929 | 6,808 | 4,145 | 6,249 | 6,204 | 5,998 | 5,998 | 5,995 | 5,420 | 5,621 |
| Combined Loss-Expense Ratio | 90.3 | 94.3 | 89.2 | 89.8 | 94.7 | 98.4 | 104.9 | 112.5 | 100.0 | 103.6 |
| % Return on Revenue | 20.1 | 23.4 | 16.0 | 16.2 | 11.8 | 8.4 | 7.5 | 5.1 | 12.0 | 11.8 |
| % Return on Equity | 13.4 | 14.4 | 15.4 | 8.0 | 5.4 | 3.6 | 3.2 | 1.0 | 4.6 | 4.7 |
| % Investment Yield | 4.7 | 4.3 | 4.1 | 3.9 | 3.9 | 3.9 | 3.7 | 3.9 | 3.8 | 3.8 |

Data as orig reptd.; bef. results of disc opers/spec. items. Per share data adj. for stk. divs.; EPS diluted. E-Estimated. NA-Not Available. NM-Not Meaningful. NR-Not Ranked. UR-Under Review.

**Office:** 6200 South Gilmore Road, Fairfield, OH 45014-5141.
**Telephone:** 513-870-2000.
**Email:** investor_inquiries@cinfin.com
**Website:** http://www.cinfin.com

**Chrmn:** J.J. Schiff, Jr.
**Pres & CEO:** K.W. Stecher
**Vice Chrmn:** J.E. Benoski
**SVP & Chief Acctg Officer:** E.N. Mathews

**CFO, Treas & Secy:** S.J. Johnston
**Investor Contact:** H.J. Wietzel (513-870-2768)
**Board Members:** W. F. Bahl, J. E. Benoski, G. T. Bier, K. C. Lichtendahl, W. R. McMullen, G. W. Price, T. R. Schiff, J. J. Schiff, Jr., D. S. Skidmore, K. W. Stecher, J. F. Steele, Jr., L. R. Webb, E. A. Woods

**Founded:** 1950
**Domicile:** Ohio
**Employees:** 4,087

**STANDARD &POOR'S**

# Cintas Corp

| S&P Recommendation | HOLD ★★★☆☆ | Price | 12-Mo. Target Price | Investment Style |
|---|---|---|---|---|
| | | $21.01 (as of Nov 14, 2008) | $33.00 | Large-Cap Growth |

**GICS Sector** Industrials
**Sub-Industry** Diversified Support Services

**Summary** A leader in the corporate identity uniform business, Cintas also provides entrance mats, sanitation supplies, and first aid and safety products.

## Key Stock Statistics (Source S&P, Vickers, company reports)

| | | | | | | | |
|---|---|---|---|---|---|---|---|
| 52-Wk Range | $35.61– 19.67 | S&P Oper. EPS 2009E | 2.23 | Market Capitalization(B) | $3.210 | Beta | 1.27 |
| Trailing 12-Month EPS | $2.15 | S&P Oper. EPS 2010E | 2.48 | Yield (%) | 2.19 | S&P 3-Yr. Proj. EPS CAGR(%) | 6 |
| Trailing 12-Month P/E | 9.8 | P/E on S&P Oper. EPS 2009E | 9.4 | Dividend Rate/Share | $0.46 | S&P Credit Rating | A |
| $10K Invested 5 Yrs Ago | $4,866 | Common Shares Outstg. (M) | 152.8 | Institutional Ownership (%) | 66 | | |

## Price Performance

30-Week Mov. Avg. · · · 10-Week Mov. Avg. - - - **GAAP Earnings vs. Previous Year** Volume Above Avg. STARS
12-Mo. Target Price — Relative Strength — ▲ Up ▼ Down ▶ No Change Below Avg.

Options: ASE, CBOE, P, Ph

Analysis prepared by **Kevin Kirkeby** on September 19, 2008, when the stock traded at **$ 29.97**.

## Highlights

► We forecast 5% revenue growth in FY 09 (May), largely on gains in CTAS's non-uniform segments. The uniform rental market is likely to remain challenging due to further plant closures, particularly in auto-related industries. Other services, including document management and first aid, should show a 9% gain in FY 09, compared to 14% in FY 08. We expect additional resources to be shifted away from fire suppression system installations, which is largely dependent upon new commercial construction, to other areas in the fire protection niche that we believe have a more favorable outlook.

► We see operating margins widening slightly in FY 09 as the expanded salesforce gains proficiency and focuses on cross-selling initiatives. We expect fuel costs to remain near an historically high 4% of revenues, but believe CTAS will increase its surcharge coverage. Legal and consulting fees should decline in FY 09.

► We forecast EPS of $2.23 in FY 09, up 3.7% over FY 08. Our estimate for FY 09 does not factor in any additional stock buybacks, despite about $228 million remaining in CTAS's authorization as of July 2008, as we believe acquisitions will take priority over buybacks.

## Investment Rationale/Risk

► Valuations have steadily compressed during the past three years and are in line with the S&P 500. We think this is partly due to a slowing in revenue growth as CTAS's traditional customer base in manufacturing has generally been reducing headcount. At the same time, CTAS has been investing heavily to achieve sufficient scale in its non-uniform service offerings. Until these businesses mature further and the economy begins to improve, we see muted free cash flow growth.

► Risks to our recommendation and target price include slower-than-expected growth in employment levels and uniform rentals, further hikes in fuel prices and labor costs, and a decline in the prices it receives for recycled paper.

► Applying a 13.5X multiple, at the low end of the historical range, to our four-quarter forward EPS estimate, we calculate a value of $31. Our DCF model yields an intrinsic value of $34, assuming a 10% weighted average cost of capital, 7% annual cash flow growth over the next five years, and 3.5% growth in perpetuity. Blending our valuation models results in our 12-month target price of $33.

## Qualitative Risk Assessment

| LOW | MEDIUM | HIGH |
|---|---|---|

Our risk assessment reflects the company's leading position in its core business, other related services that we believe are showing good growth, and what we view as a relatively strong balance sheet and cash flow.

## Quantitative Evaluations

**S&P Quality Ranking** A+

| D | C | B- | B | B+ | A- | A | A+ |
|---|---|---|---|---|---|---|---|

**Relative Strength Rank** MODERATE

60

LOWEST = 1                    HIGHEST = 99

## Revenue/Earnings Data

**Revenue (Million $)**

| | 1Q | 2Q | 3Q | 4Q | Year |
|---|---|---|---|---|---|
| 2009 | 1,002 | -- | -- | -- | -- |
| 2008 | 969.1 | 983.9 | 976.0 | 1,009 | 3,938 |
| 2007 | 914.2 | 923.3 | 905.4 | 964.1 | 3,707 |
| 2006 | 823.5 | 835.8 | 836.4 | 907.9 | 3,404 |
| 2005 | 746.0 | 756.8 | 755.2 | 809.3 | 3,067 |
| 2004 | 677.7 | 701.3 | 696.9 | 738.2 | 2,814 |

**Earnings Per Share ($)**

| | | | | | |
|---|---|---|---|---|---|
| 2009 | 0.51 | E0.54 | E0.57 | E0.61 | E2.23 |
| 2008 | 0.51 | 0.53 | 0.53 | 0.58 | 2.15 |
| 2007 | 0.53 | 0.51 | 0.48 | 0.57 | 2.09 |
| 2006 | 0.47 | 0.46 | 0.46 | 0.55 | 1.94 |
| 2005 | 0.42 | 0.43 | 0.41 | 0.48 | 1.74 |
| 2004 | 0.37 | 0.40 | 0.39 | 0.42 | 1.58 |

Fiscal year ended May 31. Next earnings report expected: Late December. EPS Estimates based on S&P Operating Earnings; historical GAAP earnings are as reported.

## Dividend Data (Dates: mm/dd Payment Date: mm/dd/yy)

| Amount ($) | Date Decl. | Ex-Div. Date | Stk. of Record | Payment Date |
|---|---|---|---|---|
| 0.460 | 01/16 | 02/04 | 02/06 | 03/12/08 |

Dividends have been paid since 1984. Source: Company reports.

---

**Please read the Required Disclosures and Analyst Certification on the last page of this report.**

*The McGraw-Hill Companies*

# Cintas Corp

## Business Summary September 19, 2008

CORPORATE OVERVIEW. Cintas Corp. is North America's leading supplier of corporate uniforms, as well as a significant provider of related services. FY 08 (May) marked Cintas Corp.'s 39th consecutive year of sales and profit growth. Starting with FY 08, the company began reporting financial results using four segments: Rental Uniforms and Ancillary Services, Uniform Direct Sales, Document Management, along with First Aid, Safety & Fire Protection.

The Rental operating segment (72% of total revenues in FY 08 and 74% of gross profits, with a 44.2% margin) designs and manufactures corporate uniforms that it rents to its customers. Services provided to the rental markets by the company also include the cleaning of uniforms, as well as the provision of ongoing replacements as required by each customer. The company also offers ancillary products, including the rental or sale of entrance and special purpose mats, towels, mops, and linen products, as well as sanitation supplies and services and cleanroom supplies. It operates through about 8,400 local delivery routes. We believe organic revenue growth has averaged about 5% over the past five years, but was 3.4% in FY 08.

The Uniform Direct Sales segment (13%, 10%, and 32.5% margin) includes the design, manufacture and direct sale of uniforms to CTAS's national account customers. In recent years, there has been an effort to offer more branded items in its catalogs alongside the traditional propriety uniform and apparel lines. This segment generally has less recurring business than the rental operations.

The First Aid, Safety and Fire Protection segment (10%, 10%, and 39.9% margin) provides inspection, repair and recharging of portable fire extinguishers, fire suppression systems, and emergency and exit lights. In a short period of time, CTAS believes it has become the second-largest fire protection services company in the U.S., with capabilities in at least 23 of the top 50 cities. The company estimates the market size for first aid and fire protection services to be about $4.5 billion a year.

The Document Management segment (5%, 6%, and 54.6% margin) provides on-site and off-site shredding of confidential documents. Document management services are now available in 85 of the 100 largest markets in the U.S. and Canada. The company estimates the potential annual market is $8 billion.

## Company Financials Fiscal Year Ended May 31

| Per Share Data ($) | 2008 | 2007 | 2006 | 2005 | 2004 | 2003 | 2002 | 2001 | 2000 | 1999 |
|---|---|---|---|---|---|---|---|---|---|---|
| Tangible Book Value | 4.92 | 4.73 | 4.73 | 6.15 | 6.32 | 5.42 | 4.39 | 6.42 | 5.42 | 4.54 |
| Cash Flow | NA | 2.96 | 2.78 | 2.43 | 2.26 | 2.12 | 1.95 | 1.82 | 1.60 | 1.23 |
| Earnings | 2.15 | 2.09 | 1.94 | 1.74 | 1.58 | 1.45 | 1.36 | 1.30 | 1.14 | 0.82 |
| S&P Core Earnings | 2.15 | 2.09 | 1.92 | 1.69 | 1.54 | 1.43 | 1.33 | 1.27 | NA | NA |
| Dividends | 0.39 | 0.35 | 0.32 | 0.32 | 0.29 | 0.27 | 0.25 | 0.22 | 0.19 | 0.15 |
| Payout Ratio | 18% | 17% | 16% | 18% | 18% | 19% | 18% | 17% | 17% | 18% |
| Calendar Year | 2007 | 2006 | 2005 | 2004 | 2003 | 2002 | 2001 | 2000 | 1999 | 1998 |
| Prices:High | 42.89 | 44.30 | 45.50 | 50.35 | 50.68 | 56.62 | 53.25 | 54.00 | 52.25 | 47.50 |
| Prices:Low | 31.14 | 34.57 | 37.51 | 39.51 | 30.60 | 39.15 | 33.75 | 23.17 | 26.00 | 26.00 |
| P/E Ratio:High | 20 | 21 | 23 | 29 | 32 | 42 | 39 | 42 | 46 | 58 |
| P/E Ratio:Low | 14 | 17 | 19 | 23 | 19 | 29 | 25 | 18 | 23 | 32 |

| Income Statement Analysis (Million $) | 2008 | 2007 | 2006 | 2005 | 2004 | 2003 | 2002 | 2001 | 2000 | 1999 |
|---|---|---|---|---|---|---|---|---|---|---|
| Revenue | 3,938 | 3,707 | 3,404 | 3,067 | 2,814 | 2,687 | 2,271 | 2,161 | 1,902 | 1,752 |
| Operating Income | NA | 713 | 674 | 614 | 602 | 539 | 478 | 459 | 423 | 338 |
| Depreciation | 149 | 135 | 127 | 120 | 117 | 115 | 101 | 90.2 | 78.5 | 68.8 |
| Interest Expense | NA | 50.3 | 31.8 | 24.4 | 25.1 | 30.9 | 11.0 | 15.1 | 15.9 | 16.4 |
| Pretax Income | 531 | 534 | 522 | 477 | 432 | 396 | 372 | 356 | 312 | 224 |
| Effective Tax Rate | 36.8% | 37.3% | 37.3% | 37.0% | 37.0% | 37.0% | 37.0% | 37.6% | 38.0% | 38.0% |
| Net Income | 335 | 335 | 327 | 301 | 272 | 249 | 234 | 222 | 193 | 139 |
| S&P Core Earnings | 335 | 335 | 324 | 293 | 265 | 245 | 229 | 219 | NA | NA |

| Balance Sheet & Other Financial Data (Million $) | 2008 | 2007 | 2006 | 2005 | 2004 | 2003 | 2002 | 2001 | 2000 | 1999 |
|---|---|---|---|---|---|---|---|---|---|---|
| Cash | 192 | 155 | 241 | 309 | 254 | 57.7 | 85.1 | 110 | 110 | 88.1 |
| Current Assets | NA | 1,157 | 1,178 | 1,167 | 1,034 | 878 | 853 | 820 | 721 | 634 |
| Total Assets | 3,809 | 3,570 | 3,425 | 3,060 | 2,810 | 2,583 | 2,519 | 1,752 | 1,581 | 1,408 |
| Current Liabilities | NA | 403 | 412 | 356 | 326 | 305 | 313 | 251 | 235 | 212 |
| Long Term Debt | NA | 877 | 794 | 465 | 474 | 535 | 703 | 221 | 254 | 284 |
| Common Equity | 2,254 | 2,168 | 2,088 | 2,104 | 1,888 | 1,646 | 1,424 | 1,231 | 1,043 | 871 |
| Total Capital | NA | 3,167 | 3,013 | 2,703 | 2,485 | 2,278 | 2,207 | 1,501 | 1,346 | 1,196 |
| Capital Expenditures | 190 | 181 | 157 | 141 | 113 | 115 | 170 | 147 | 161 | 171 |
| Cash Flow | NA | 470 | 454 | 420 | 389 | 365 | 335 | 313 | 272 | 208 |
| Current Ratio | 3.5 | 2.9 | 2.9 | 3.3 | 3.2 | 2.9 | 2.7 | 3.3 | 3.1 | 3.0 |
| % Long Term Debt of Capitalization | 29.5 | 27.7 | 26.4 | 17.2 | 19.1 | 23.5 | 31.9 | 14.7 | 18.9 | 23.7 |
| % Net Income of Revenue | 8.5 | 9.0 | 9.6 | 9.8 | 44.4 | 9.3 | 10.3 | 10.3 | 10.3 | 7.9 |
| % Return on Assets | 9.1 | 9.6 | 10.1 | 10.2 | 10.1 | 9.8 | 11.0 | 13.3 | 12.9 | 10.2 |
| % Return on Equity | 15.2 | 15.7 | 15.6 | 15.1 | 15.4 | 16.2 | 17.6 | 19.6 | 20.2 | 17.1 |

Data as orig reptd.; bef. results of disc opers/spec. items. Per share data adj. for stk. divs.; EPS diluted. E-Estimated. NA-Not Available. NM-Not Meaningful. NR-Not Ranked. UR-Under Review.

**Office:** 6800 Cintas Boulevard, Cincinnati, OH 45262-5737.
**Telephone:** 513-459-1200.
**Website:** http://www.cintas.com
**Chrmn:** R.T. Farmer

**Pres & COO:** J.P. Holloman
**Vice Chrmn:** R.J. Kohlhepp
**CEO:** S.D. Farmer
**Investor Contact:** W.C. Gale (513-459-1200)

**Board Members:** G. S. Adolph, P. R. Carter, G. V. Dirvin, J. Dirvin, R. T. Farmer, S. D. Farmer, J. Hergenhan, R. L. Howe, R. J. Kohlhepp, D. C. Phillips, R. W. Tysoe

**Founded:** 1968
**Domicile:** Washington
**Employees:** 34,000

# Cisco Systems Inc

**STANDARD &POOR'S**

| S&P Recommendation | **HOLD** ★★★☆☆ | Price<br>$16.62 (as of Nov 14, 2008) | 12-Mo. Target Price<br>$18.00 | Investment Style<br>Large-Cap Growth |
|---|---|---|---|---|

| | |
|---|---|
| **GICS Sector** Information Technology<br>**Sub-Industry** Communications Equipment | **Summary** This company offers a complete line of routers and switching products that connect and manage communications among local and wide area computer networks employing a variety of protocols. |

## Key Stock Statistics (Source S&P, Vickers, company reports)

| | | | | | | | |
|---|---|---|---|---|---|---|---|
| 52-Wk Range | **$29.99– 15.60** | S&P Oper. EPS 2009**E** | 1.25 | Market Capitalization(B) | **$97.776** | Beta | 1.39 |
| Trailing 12-Month EPS | **$1.33** | S&P Oper. EPS 2010**E** | 1.55 | Yield (%) | **Nil** | S&P 3-Yr. Proj. EPS CAGR(%) | 13 |
| Trailing 12-Month P/E | **12.5** | P/E on S&P Oper. EPS 2009**E** | 13.3 | Dividend Rate/Share | **Nil** | S&P Credit Rating | A+ |
| $10K Invested 5 Yrs Ago | **$7,466** | Common Shares Outstg. (M) | 5,883.0 | Institutional Ownership (%) | **72** | | |

## Price Performance

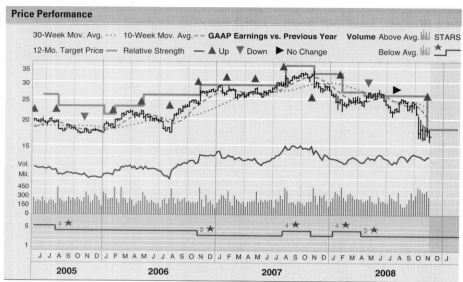

30-Week Mov. Avg. · · · 10-Week Mov. Avg. – – **GAAP Earnings vs. Previous Year** Volume Above Avg. STARS
12-Mo. Target Price — Relative Strength — ▲ Up ▼ Down ► No Change Below Avg. ★

Options: ASE, CBOE, P, Ph

Analysis prepared by **Ari Bensinger** on November 06, 2008, when the stock traded at **$ 16.98**.

## Highlights

➤ Following a 13% increase in FY 08 (Jul.), we project sales declining 3% in FY 09, reflecting lower routing and switching segment sales, owing to a decline in enterprise and telecom spending amid a weakening global economy. We expect revenues in the advanced technologies segment to increase in the mid-single digits, fueled by video systems and unified communications, which includes the recent major acquisitions of Scientific-Atlanta and WebEx.

➤ We look for the gross margin to narrow modestly, to slightly under 65%, in FY 09, primarily attributable to a less favorable sales mix that reflects strong advanced technology and emerging market growth, as well as intensifying product pricing pressure. In an effort to realign costs to the lower demand, CSCO plans to cut its operating expense rate by roughly $1 billion during FY 09.

➤ After lower interest income on reduced interest rate returns, a 23% tax rate, and continued share repurchases, we forecast FY 09 EPS of $1.25, down from the $1.39 posted in FY 08. Our estimate includes projected stock option expense of $0.12.

## Investment Rationale/Risk

➤ We expect the operating environment to remain challenging through 2009, with customers continuing to scrutinize spending budgets amid a softening economy. Still, we see CSCO taking advantage of its well-balanced portfolio and strong cash position to gain market share during the current weak climate. We are positive on the company's long-term growth due to its dominant market position in the large network routing and switching markets and successful positioning in attractive advanced technology segments.

➤ Risks to our recommendation and target price include a decline in enterprise spending, increased competition, and narrowing margins from intensifying pricing pressures.

➤ Our 12-month target price of $18 represents 14X our FY 09 EPS estimate, in line with peers. Using our three-year earnings growth rate projection of 13%, our target price represents a P/E-to-growth ratio of 1.1X, in line with the industry average. Our discounted cash flow model, assuming a weighted average cost of capital of 12.6% and terminal growth of 3%, indicates an intrinsic value of about $20.

## Qualitative Risk Assessment

| LOW | **MEDIUM** | HIGH |
|---|---|---|

Our risk assessment for CSCO reflects the highly competitive nature of the industry in which it operates, balanced by our view of its strong financials, including more than $26 billion in cash, and its dominant market position.

## Quantitative Evaluations

**S&P Quality Ranking** B+

| D | C | B- | B | **B+** | A- | A | A+ |
|---|---|---|---|---|---|---|---|

**Relative Strength Rank** MODERATE

61

LOWEST = 1 HIGHEST = 99

## Revenue/Earnings Data

### Revenue (Million $)

| | 1Q | 2Q | 3Q | 4Q | Year |
|---|---|---|---|---|---|
| 2009 | 10,331 | -- | -- | -- | -- |
| 2008 | 9,554 | 9,831 | 9,791 | 10,364 | 39,540 |
| 2007 | 8,184 | 8,439 | 8,866 | 9,433 | 34,922 |
| 2006 | 6,550 | 6,628 | 7,322 | 7,984 | 28,484 |
| 2005 | 5,971 | 6,062 | 6,187 | 6,581 | 24,801 |
| 2004 | 5,101 | 5,398 | 5,620 | 5,926 | 22,045 |

### Earnings Per Share ($)

| | | | | | |
|---|---|---|---|---|---|
| 2009 | 0.37 | E0.26 | E0.28 | E0.32 | E1.25 |
| 2008 | 0.35 | 0.33 | 0.29 | 0.33 | 1.31 |
| 2007 | 0.26 | 0.31 | 0.30 | 0.33 | 1.17 |
| 2006 | 0.20 | 0.22 | 0.22 | 0.25 | 0.89 |
| 2005 | 0.21 | 0.21 | 0.21 | 0.24 | 0.87 |
| 2004 | 0.15 | 0.18 | 0.17 | 0.20 | 0.70 |

Fiscal year ended Jul. 31. Next earnings report expected: Early February. EPS Estimates based on S&P Operating Earnings; historical GAAP earnings are as reported.

## Dividend Data

No cash dividends have been paid.

---

**Please read the Required Disclosures and Analyst Certification on the last page of this report.**

The **McGraw·Hill** Companies

# Cisco Systems Inc

STANDARD
&POOR'S

## Business Summary November 06, 2008

CORPORATE OVERVIEW. Cisco Systems, which supplies the majority of networking gear used for the Internet, is the world's largest supplier of high-performance computer internetworking systems. The company's sales strategy is primarily based on distribution channel partners, with over 40,000 reseller partner sales representatives around the world.

Product families are categorized into four segments: switches (42% of total FY 07 (Jul.) product sales), routers (23%), advanced technologies (27%), and other. There are currently eight primary advanced technology segments: home networking, unified communications, security, storage area networking, wireless technology, application networking services, hosted small business systems, and video systems (primarily digital set-top boxes and transport and access products via the acquisition of Scientific Atlanta). We estimate that the video systems, security, unified communications, home networking, and wireless sub-segments are all above or near the billion dollar level on an annual basis. Other products are comprised of primarily optical, access and network management software. The company also has a broad range of service offerings, including technical support services and advanced services.

In our view, the primary driver of company sales growth will be the advanced technologies segment. CSCO distinguishes its advanced technology sub-segments as industry segments with the potential to become billion dollar

businesses. We see the company continuing to identify additional advanced technology sub-segments.

MARKET PROFILE. With a dominant market share of approximately 70% of the overall Ethernet switching market, we believe CSCO has become the de facto choice for Ethernet switches. We view the company's large installed base as a significant competitive advantage over peers, especially in cases of modular switching solutions, where it is very difficult for competitors to displace the large modular chassis equipment. Because of its reputation and related large market share, in our opinion, Cisco products typically enjoy a price premium over the competition.

CSCO leads the overall routing market, with a more than 50% share. For core routers, which have speeds of more than 2.5 gigabits per second, CSCO and Juniper Networks dominate the market, with a combined market share of over 95%. In May 2004, Cisco introduced its new high-end core router, the Carrier Routing System-1 (CRS-1), with capacity for 1.2 terabits per second.

## Company Financials Fiscal Year Ended Jul. 31

| Per Share Data ($) | 2008 | 2007 | 2006 | 2005 | 2004 | 2003 | 2002 | 2001 | 2000 | 1999 |
|---|---|---|---|---|---|---|---|---|---|---|
| Tangible Book Value | NA | 2.76 | 2.07 | 2.74 | 3.16 | 3.35 | 3.33 | 3.07 | 3.14 | 3.57 |
| Cash Flow | NA | 1.40 | 1.10 | 1.02 | 0.91 | 0.72 | 0.52 | 0.17 | 0.47 | 0.76 |
| Earnings | 1.31 | 1.17 | 0.89 | 0.87 | 0.70 | 0.50 | 0.25 | -0.14 | 0.36 | 0.31 |
| S&P Core Earnings | 1.30 | 1.15 | 0.88 | 0.70 | 0.52 | 0.28 | 0.12 | -0.37 | NA | NA |
| Dividends | Nil | Nil | Nil | Nil | Nil | Nil | Nil | Nil | Nil | Nil |
| Payout Ratio | Nil | Nil | Nil | Nil | Nil | Nil | Nil | Nil | Nil | Nil |
| Prices:High | 27.72 | 34.24 | 27.96 | 20.25 | 29.39 | 24.60 | 21.84 | 44.50 | 82.00 | 53.59 |
| Prices:Low | 15.60 | 24.82 | 17.10 | 16.83 | 17.53 | 12.33 | 12.24 | 11.04 | 35.16 | 22.47 |
| P/E Ratio:High | 21 | 29 | 31 | 23 | 42 | 49 | 87 | NM | NM | NM |
| P/E Ratio:Low | 12 | 21 | 19 | 19 | 25 | 25 | 49 | NM | 98 | 72 |

### Income Statement Analysis (Million $)

| | 2008 | 2007 | 2006 | 2005 | 2004 | 2003 | 2002 | 2001 | 2000 | 1999 |
|---|---|---|---|---|---|---|---|---|---|---|
| Revenue | 39,540 | 34,922 | 28,484 | 24,801 | 22,045 | 18,878 | 18,915 | 22,293 | 18,928 | 12,154 |
| Operating Income | NA | 10,034 | 8,380 | 8,451 | 7,738 | 6,477 | 4,941 | 2,257 | 4,098 | 3,470 |
| Depreciation | 1,744 | 1,413 | 1,293 | 1,009 | 1,443 | 1,591 | 1,957 | 2,236 | 863 | 486 |
| Interest Expense | NA | Nil | Nil | Nil | Nil | Nil | Nil | Nil | Nil | Nil |
| Pretax Income | 10,255 | 9,461 | 7,633 | 8,036 | 6,992 | 5,013 | 2,710 | -874 | 4,343 | 3,316 |
| Effective Tax Rate | 21.5% | 22.5% | 26.9% | 28.6% | 28.9% | 28.6% | 30.1% | NM | 38.6% | 36.8% |
| Net Income | 8,052 | 7,333 | 5,580 | 5,741 | 4,968 | 3,578 | 1,893 | -1,014 | 2,668 | 2,096 |
| S&P Core Earnings | 7,985 | 7,197 | 5,499 | 4,645 | 3,652 | 2,051 | 931 | -2,641 | NA | NA |

### Balance Sheet & Other Financial Data (Million $)

| | 2008 | 2007 | 2006 | 2005 | 2004 | 2003 | 2002 | 2001 | 2000 | 1999 |
|---|---|---|---|---|---|---|---|---|---|---|
| Cash | 26,235 | 3,728 | 3,297 | 4,742 | 3,722 | 3,925 | 9,484 | 4,873 | 4,234 | 829 |
| Current Assets | NA | 31,574 | 25,676 | 13,031 | 14,343 | 13,415 | 17,433 | 12,835 | 11,110 | 4,615 |
| Total Assets | 58,734 | 53,340 | 43,315 | 33,883 | 35,594 | 37,107 | 37,795 | 35,238 | 32,870 | 14,725 |
| Current Liabilities | NA | 13,358 | 11,313 | 9,511 | 8,703 | 8,294 | 8,375 | 8,096 | 5,196 | 3,003 |
| Long Term Debt | NA | 6,408 | 6,332 | Nil | Nil | Nil | Nil | Nil | Nil | Nil |
| Common Equity | 34,353 | 31,480 | 23,912 | 23,174 | 25,826 | 28,029 | 28,656 | 27,120 | 26,497 | 11,678 |
| Total Capital | NA | 37,898 | 30,250 | 23,184 | 25,916 | 28,039 | 28,671 | 27,142 | 27,674 | 11,722 |
| Capital Expenditures | 1,268 | 1,251 | 772 | 692 | 613 | 717 | 2,641 | 2,271 | 1,086 | 584 |
| Cash Flow | NA | 8,746 | 6,873 | 6,750 | 6,411 | 5,169 | 3,850 | 1,222 | 3,531 | 2,582 |
| Current Ratio | 2.6 | 2.4 | 2.3 | 1.4 | 1.6 | 1.6 | 2.1 | 1.6 | 2.1 | 1.5 |
| % Long Term Debt of Capitalization | 15.5 | 16.9 | 20.9 | Nil | Nil | Nil | Nil | Nil | Nil | Nil |
| % Net Income of Revenue | 20.4 | 21.0 | 19.6 | 23.1 | 22.5 | 19.0 | 10.0 | NM | 14.1 | 17.2 |
| % Return on Assets | 14.4 | 15.2 | 14.5 | 16.5 | 13.7 | 9.6 | 5.2 | NM | 11.2 | 17.7 |
| % Return on Equity | 24.5 | 26.5 | 23.7 | 23.4 | 18.4 | 12.6 | 6.8 | NM | 13.9 | 22.3 |

Data as orig reptd.; bef. results of disc opers/spec. items. Per share data adj. for stk. divs.; EPS diluted. E-Estimated. NA-Not Available. NM-Not Meaningful. NR-Not Ranked. UR-Under Review.

**Office:** 170 West Tasman Drive, San Jose, CA 95134-1706.
**Telephone:** 408-526-4000.
**Email:** investor-relations@cisco.com
**Website:** http://www.cisco.com

**Chrmn, Pres & CEO:** J.T. Chambers
**COO:** R.J. Justice
**EVP & CFO:** F. Calderoni
**SVP, Chief Acctg Officer & Cntlr:** J. Chadwick

**SVP & Treas:** D.K. Holland
**Investor Contact:** L. Graves (408-526-6521)
**Board Members:** C. A. Bartz, M. M. Burns, M. D. Capellas, L. R. Carter, J. T. Chambers, M. A. Cirillo, B. L. Halla, J. L. Hennessy, R. M. Kovacevich, R. C. McGeary, M. K. Powell, A. S. Rachleff, S. M. West, J. Yang

**Founded:** 1984
**Domicile:** California
**Employees:** 66,129

# Citigroup Inc.

STANDARD &POOR'S

| S&P Recommendation | HOLD ★★★☆☆ | Price | 12-Mo. Target Price | Investment Style |
|---|---|---|---|---|
| | | $9.52 (as of Nov 14, 2008) | $15.00 | Large-Cap Blend |

**GICS Sector** Financials
**Sub-Industry** Other Diversified Financial Services

**Summary** This diversified financial services company provides a wide range of financial services to consumers and corporate customers in more than 100 countries and territories.

## Key Stock Statistics (Source S&P, Vickers, company reports)

| | | | | | | | |
|---|---|---|---|---|---|---|---|
| 52-Wk Range | $35.29–8.27 | S&P Oper. EPS 2008E | -2.50 | Market Capitalization(B) | $51.880 | Beta | 1.10 |
| Trailing 12-Month EPS | $-4.08 | S&P Oper. EPS 2009E | 0.72 | Yield (%) | 6.72 | S&P 3-Yr. Proj. EPS CAGR(%) | 9 |
| Trailing 12-Month P/E | NM | P/E on S&P Oper. EPS 2008E | NM | Dividend Rate/Share | $0.64 | S&P Credit Rating | AA- |
| $10K Invested 5 Yrs Ago | $2,532 | Common Shares Outstg. (M) | 5,449.5 | Institutional Ownership (%) | 62 | | |

## Price Performance

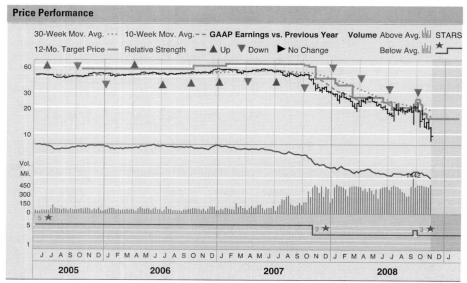

30-Week Mov. Avg. · · · 10-Week Mov. Avg. – – GAAP Earnings vs. Previous Year Volume Above Avg. ▌▌▌ STARS
12-Mo. Target Price — Relative Strength — ▲ Up ▼ Down ► No Change Below Avg. ▌▌▌ ★

Options: ASE, CBOE, P, Ph

Analysis prepared by **Stuart Plesser** on October 27, 2008, when the stock traded at **$ 12.14**.

## Highlights

➤ C's Tier 1 capital now stands at roughly 8.2%, versus 7.7% at the end of the first quarter. C is set to receive $25 billion from the government by issuing preferred shares with an attractively priced 5% yield, which should satisfy the need to raise additional capital. C's securities write-downs improved on a sequential basis in the first three quarters of 2008, as it took a roughly $4.0 billion writedown in the third quarter versus a $13 billion writedown in the first quarter. C will likely look to sell additional non-core as-sets to boost capital levels and focus its busi-ness efforts.

➤ We see continued rising credit losses in the U.S. and international consumer segments re-sulting in elevated provisions throughout 2008 and into 2009. We expect revenue to be bol-stered by international growth and expansion in the global wealth management business. We anticipate continuing job cut announcements as C seeks to enhance its cost savings plan, which gained traction in the second quarter and will likely result in expense reductions in coming quarters.

➤ We see a per share loss of $2.50 for 2008, fol-lowed by EPS of $0.72 in 2009.

## Investment Rationale/Risk

➤ We believe that continued divestitures of non-strategic assets, combined with C's participa-tion in the Trouble Asset Relief Program in which it's set to receive $25 billion by offering preferred shares with an attractively low 5.0% coupon yield, should stave off the need to re-turn to the market to raise capital. Expense sav-ing initiatives, which are gaining traction, are also a positive. However, we remain wary of the marks C has taken on its securities portfo-lio, and believe it may realize more significant marks in coming quarters. Also, deteriorating consumer credit -- both internationally and do-mestically -- will likely weigh on earnings through 2009.

➤ Risks to our recommendation and target price include a severe downturn in global economic conditions, higher-than-expected credit losses, and failure to implement announced cost re-duction initiatives.

➤ Our 12-month target price of $15 is equal to roughly 0.83X book value per share, below C's historical average, reflecting our view of a decline in investor confidence, uncertainty sur-rounding future writedowns, and weakening in-ternational consumer spending.

## Qualitative Risk Assessment

| LOW | MEDIUM | HIGH |
|---|---|---|

Our risk assessment reflects our view of C's large customer base and diversified business model, offset by its exposure to risky assets on its balance sheet and its exposure to deteriorating credit in both domestic and international markets.

## Quantitative Evaluations

**S&P Quality Ranking**     A

| D | C | B- | B | B+ | A- | A | A+ |
|---|---|---|---|---|---|---|---|

**Relative Strength Rank**     WEAK

24

LOWEST = 1     HIGHEST = 99

## Revenue/Earnings Data

### Revenue (Million $)

| | 1Q | 2Q | 3Q | 4Q | Year |
|---|---|---|---|---|---|
| 2008 | 29,696 | 32,392 | 29,456 | -- | -- |
| 2007 | 43,021 | 45,802 | 43,197 | 27,209 | 159,229 |
| 2006 | 34,290 | 35,899 | 36,323 | 40,046 | 146,558 |
| 2005 | 28,620 | 28,837 | 31,147 | 31,714 | 120,318 |
| 2004 | 25,976 | 27,287 | 26,408 | 28,605 | 108,276 |
| 2003 | 23,199 | 23,840 | 23,334 | 24,340 | 94,713 |

### Earnings Per Share ($)

| | | | | | |
|---|---|---|---|---|---|
| 2008 | -1.02 | -0.49 | -0.71 | E-0.28 | E-2.50 |
| 2007 | 1.01 | 1.24 | 0.44 | -1.99 | 0.72 |
| 2006 | 1.11 | 1.05 | 1.06 | 1.03 | 4.25 |
| 2005 | 0.98 | 0.91 | 0.97 | 0.98 | 3.82 |
| 2004 | 1.01 | 0.22 | 1.02 | 1.02 | 3.26 |
| 2003 | 0.79 | 0.83 | 0.90 | 0.91 | 3.42 |

Fiscal year ended Dec. 31. Next earnings report expected: Mid January. EPS Estimates based on S&P Operating Earnings; historical GAAP earnings are as reported.

## Dividend Data (Dates: mm/dd Payment Date: mm/dd/yy)

| Amount ($) | Date Decl. | Ex-Div. Date | Stk. of Record | Payment Date |
|---|---|---|---|---|
| 0.320 | 01/15 | 01/31 | 02/04 | 02/22/08 |
| 0.320 | 04/21 | 05/01 | 05/05 | 05/23/08 |
| 0.320 | 07/21 | 07/31 | 08/04 | 08/22/08 |
| 0.160 | 10/20 | 10/30 | 11/03 | 11/26/08 |

Dividends have been paid since 1986. Source: Company reports.

# Citigroup Inc.

**STANDARD &POOR'S**

## Business Summary October 27, 2008

CORPORATE OVERVIEW. Citigroup is organized into three major business groups: Global Consumer; Institutional Clients Group (comprised of Markets and Banking and Alternative Investments); and Global Wealth Management. The Citigroup Global Consumer business includes banking services, credit cards, loans and insurance. The Institutional Clients Group operates in about 100 countries and advises companies, governments and institutional investors on the best ways to realize their strategic objectives. The Global Wealth Management division at Citigroup is comprised of The Citigroup Private Bank, Smith Barney (private wealth management), and Citigroup Investment Research, and serves both private and institutional clients.

CORPORATE STRATEGY. Citigroup has five strategic initiatives: expand international distribution; increase U.S. distribution; transfer expertise; invest in technology and people; and allocate capital.

In our view, the large increase in international branches and consumer finance centers shows the growing importance C attaches to organic growth. Although we expect Citigroup to continue its international organic growth in 2008, we anticipate that the pace will slow significantly from 2006. We believe the increased pressure on C to cut expenses will lead to lower investment spending internationally.

UPCOMING CATALYSTS. A key catalyst for C, in our opinion, will be the execution of expense savings resulting from the company's structural expense review and the successful divestiture of non-core assets. Former CEO Charles Prince put Robert Druskin in charge of researching strategic cost-cutting initiatives to allow C to generate positive operating leverage. The results of the cost savings plan included projected expense savings of $2.1 billion in 2007, $3.7 billion in 2008, and $4.6 billion in 2009. The company took a pretax charge of $1.38 billion in the first quarter of 2007. Approximately $1.0 billion of the charge was related to severance packages for 17,900 job cuts. Most of the job eliminations were expected to come from back office, middle office and corporate functions, with approximately 57% from international operations. We believe management was careful not to hurt its ability to generate future revenue growth, and therefore limited the impact of the job cuts on client-facing functions.

## Company Financials Fiscal Year Ended Dec. 31

| Per Share Data ($) | 2007 | 2006 | 2005 | 2004 | 2003 | 2002 | 2001 | 2000 | 1999 | 1998 |
|---|---|---|---|---|---|---|---|---|---|---|
| Tangible Book Value | 9.95 | 14.14 | 12.76 | 11.72 | 10.75 | 9.70 | 15.49 | 12.84 | 10.64 | 8.95 |
| Earnings | 0.72 | 4.25 | 3.82 | 3.26 | 3.42 | 2.59 | 2.75 | 2.62 | 2.12 | 1.22 |
| S&P Core Earnings | 0.43 | 4.09 | 3.69 | 4.02 | 3.35 | 2.33 | 2.51 | NA | NA | NA |
| Dividends | 2.16 | 1.96 | 1.76 | 1.60 | 1.10 | 0.70 | 0.60 | 0.52 | 0.41 | 0.28 |
| Payout Ratio | NM | 46% | 46% | 49% | 32% | 27% | 22% | 20% | 19% | 23% |
| Prices:High | 56.28 | 57.00 | 49.99 | 52.88 | 49.15 | 52.20 | 57.38 | 59.13 | 43.69 | 36.75 |
| Prices:Low | 28.80 | 44.81 | 42.91 | 42.10 | 30.25 | 24.48 | 34.51 | 35.34 | 24.50 | 14.25 |
| P/E Ratio:High | 78 | 13 | 13 | 16 | 14 | 20 | 21 | 23 | 21 | 30 |
| P/E Ratio:Low | 40 | 11 | 11 | 13 | 9 | 9 | 13 | 13 | 12 | 12 |

| Income Statement Analysis (Million $) | 2007 | 2006 | 2005 | 2004 | 2003 | 2002 | 2001 | 2000 | 1999 | 1998 |
|---|---|---|---|---|---|---|---|---|---|---|
| Premium Income | 3,132 | 3,202 | 3,132 | 3,993 | 3,749 | 3,410 | 13,460 | 12,429 | 10,441 | 9,850 |
| Investment Income | 29,705 | 34,177 | 28,833 | 22,728 | 18,937 | 21,036 | 26,949 | 27,562 | 21,728 | 23,696 |
| Other Revenue | 126,392 | 109,179 | 88,353 | 81,555 | 72,027 | 68,110 | 71,613 | 71,835 | 49,836 | 42,885 |
| Total Revenue | 159,229 | 146,558 | 120,318 | 108,276 | 94,713 | 92,556 | 112,022 | 111,826 | 82,005 | 76,431 |
| Interest Expense | 48,790 | 56,943 | 36,676 | 22,086 | 17,271 | 21,248 | 31,965 | 36,638 | 24,768 | 27,495 |
| % Expense/Operating Revenue | 87.3% | 74.3% | 75.5% | 77.6% | 72.2% | 77.8% | 80.5% | 81.1% | 80.6% | 87.9% |
| Pretax Income | 1,701 | 29,639 | 29,433 | 24,182 | 26,333 | 20,537 | 21,897 | 21,143 | 15,948 | 9,269 |
| Effective Tax Rate | NM | 27.3% | 30.8% | 28.6% | 31.1% | 34.1% | 34.4% | 35.6% | 35.8% | 34.9% |
| Net Income | 3,617 | 21,249 | 19,806 | 17,046 | 17,853 | 13,448 | 14,284 | 13,519 | 9,994 | 5,807 |
| S&P Core Earnings | 2,154 | 20,311 | 19,114 | 20,934 | 17,424 | 12,000 | 12,943 | NA | NA | NA |

| Balance Sheet & Other Financial Data (Million $) | 2007 | 2006 | 2005 | 2004 | 2003 | 2002 | 2001 | 2000 | 1999 | 1998 |
|---|---|---|---|---|---|---|---|---|---|---|
| Receivables | 57,359 | 44,445 | 42,823 | 44,056 | 31,053 | 29,714 | 47,528 | 36,237 | 32,677 | 30,905 |
| Cash & Investment | 242,663 | 300,105 | 208,970 | 236,799 | 204,041 | 186,839 | 179,352 | 134,743 | 127,284 | 117,509 |
| Loans | 777,993 | 679,192 | 583,503 | 548,829 | 478,006 | 447,805 | 391,933 | 367,022 | 244,206 | 221,958 |
| Total Assets | 2,187,631 | 1,884,318 | 1,494,037 | 1,484,101 | 1,264,032 | 1,097,190 | 1,051,450 | 902,210 | 716,937 | 668,641 |
| Capitalization:Debt | 427,112 | 288,494 | 217,499 | 207,910 | 168,759 | 133,079 | 128,756 | 116,698 | 52,012 | 52,991 |
| Capitalization:Equity | 113,598 | 118,783 | 111,412 | 108,166 | 96,889 | 85,318 | 79,722 | 64,461 | 47,761 | 40,395 |
| Capitalization:Total | 540,710 | 408,277 | 330,036 | 317,201 | 284,251 | 219,797 | 210,003 | 182,904 | 101,698 | 95,839 |
| Price Times Book Value:High | 5.7 | 4.0 | 3.9 | 4.5 | 4.6 | 5.4 | 3.7 | 4.6 | 4.1 | 4.1 |
| Price Times Book Value:Low | 2.9 | 3.2 | 3.4 | 3.5 | 2.8 | 2.5 | 2.2 | 2.7 | 2.3 | 1.6 |
| % Return on Revenue | 2.3 | 22.0 | 16.5 | 15.7 | 18.8 | 14.5 | 12.8 | 12.9 | 12.2 | 7.6 |
| % Return on Assets | 0.2 | 1.3 | 1.3 | 1.2 | 1.5 | 1.3 | 1.5 | 1.6 | 1.4 | 1.1 |
| % Return on Equity | 3.1 | 18.5 | 18.0 | 16.6 | 19.5 | 11.6 | 19.7 | 22.2 | 22.3 | 14.2 |
| Loans/Equity | 6.3 | 5.5 | 5.2 | 5.1 | 5.1 | 3.6 | 5.3 | 5.6 | 5.3 | 516.9 |

Data as orig reptd.; bef. results of disc opers/spec. items. Per share data adj. for stk. divs.; EPS diluted. E-Estimated. NA-Not Available. NM-Not Meaningful. NR-Not Ranked. UR-Under Review.

**Office:** 399 Park Avenue, New York, NY, USA 10043.
**Telephone:** 212-559-1000.
**Website:** http://www.citigroup.com
**Chrmn:** W.W. Bischoff

**Pres:** W. McNamee
**Vice Chrmn:** J.B. Lane
**CEO:** V.S. Pandit
**COO & CTO:** K. Kessinger

**Board Members:** C. Armstrong, A. J. Belda, W. W. Bischoff, T. Browne, K. T. Derr, J. M. Deutch, A. Liveris, A. M. Mulcahy, V. S. Pandit, R. D. Parsons, R. H. Ramirez, L. Ricciardi, J. H. Rodin, R. E. Rubin, R. L. Ryan, F. A. Thomas

**Founded:** 1901
**Domicile:** Delaware
**Employees:** 387,000

# CIT Group Inc.

**STANDARD &POOR'S**

| S&P Recommendation | **HOLD** ★★★☆☆ | Price<br>$4.14 (as of Nov 14, 2008) | 12-Mo. Target Price<br>$5.00 | Investment Style<br>Large-Cap Value |
|---|---|---|---|---|

**GICS Sector** Financials
**Sub-Industry** Specialized Finance

**Summary** This diversified finance company engages in vendor, equipment, commercial, consumer and structured financing as well as leasing activities.

## Key Stock Statistics (Source S&P, Vickers, company reports)

| | | | | | | | |
|---|---|---|---|---|---|---|---|
| 52-Wk Range | $30.75– 2.65 | S&P Oper. EPS 2008**E** | -2.18 | Market Capitalization(B) | $1.181 | Beta | 2.26 |
| Trailing 12-Month EPS | $-11.98 | S&P Oper. EPS 2009**E** | 1.64 | Yield (%) | 9.66 | S&P 3-Yr. Proj. EPS CAGR(%) | NM |
| Trailing 12-Month P/E | NM | P/E on S&P Oper. EPS 2008**E** | NM | Dividend Rate/Share | $0.40 | S&P Credit Rating | A- |
| $10K Invested 5 Yrs Ago | $1,431 | Common Shares Outstg. (M) | 285.4 | Institutional Ownership (%) | NM | | |

## Price Performance

- 30-Week Mov. Avg. · · ·  10-Week Mov. Avg. - - **GAAP Earnings vs. Previous Year**  Volume Above Avg. STARS
- 12-Mo. Target Price —  Relative Strength — ▲ Up ▼ Down ► No Change  Below Avg.

Options: ASE, CBOE, P, Ph

## Qualitative Risk Assessment

| LOW | MEDIUM | **HIGH** |
|---|---|---|

Our risk assessment reflects declining net interest margins and a deteriorating credit environment, only partly offset by our view of the company's disciplined risk management policies and sound competitive position.

## Quantitative Evaluations

**S&P Quality Ranking** NR

| D | C | B- | B | B+ | A- | A | A+ |
|---|---|---|---|---|---|---|---|

**Relative Strength Rank** WEAK

29

LOWEST = 1    HIGHEST = 99

## Highlights

- ➤ The 12-month target price for CIT has recently been changed to $5.00 from $7.00. The Highlights section of this Stock Report will be updated accordingly.

## Investment Rationale/Risk

- ➤ The Investment Rationale/Risk section of this Stock Report will be updated shortly. For the latest News story on CIT from MarketScope, see below.

- ➤ 11/13/08 11:07 am ET ... S&P REITERATES HOLD OPINION ON SHARES OF CIT GROUP (CIT 3.81***): CIT has applied to become a bank holding company. It has also filed to change its Utah-based CIT Bank's charter to a Utah State Bank from an industrial bank classification. Concurrently, it has submitted an application to participate in the TARP Capital Purchase Program, contingent on the granting of a bank holding company charter by the U.S. Treasury. We think the status change and capital raise should help to diversify its funding base and improve its capital levels. Even so, we are lowering our target price by $2 to $5 to reflect falling peer multiples. /M.Albrecht

## Revenue/Earnings Data

**Revenue (Million $)**

| | 1Q | 2Q | 3Q | 4Q | Year |
|---|---|---|---|---|---|
| 2008 | 1,682 | 609.2 | 540.2 | -- | -- |
| 2007 | 1,946 | 1,758 | 1,810 | 1,840 | 8,605 |
| 2006 | 1,555 | 1,379 | 1,472 | 500.4 | 6,928 |
| 2005 | 1,261 | 1,387 | 1,408 | 1,522 | 5,653 |
| 2004 | 1,134 | 1,149 | 1,180 | 1,219 | 4,676 |
| 2003 | 1,175 | 1,161 | 1,142 | 1,172 | 4,678 |

**Earnings Per Share ($)**

| | | | | | |
|---|---|---|---|---|---|
| 2008 | -1.35 | 0.12 | -1.13 | E0.18 | E-2.18 |
| 2007 | 1.01 | -0.70 | -0.24 | -0.69 | -0.58 |
| 2006 | 1.12 | 1.16 | 1.44 | 1.28 | 5.00 |
| 2005 | 1.06 | 1.16 | 1.02 | 1.21 | 4.44 |
| 2004 | 0.88 | 0.82 | 0.86 | 0.95 | 3.50 |
| 2003 | 0.60 | 0.65 | 0.69 | 0.72 | 2.66 |

Fiscal year ended Dec. 31. Next earnings report expected: Mid January. EPS Estimates based on S&P Operating Earnings; historical GAAP earnings are as reported.

## Dividend Data (Dates: mm/dd Payment Date: mm/dd/yy)

| Amount<br>($) | Date<br>Decl. | Ex-Div.<br>Date | Stk. of<br>Record | Payment<br>Date |
|---|---|---|---|---|
| 0.250 | 01/15 | 02/13 | 02/15 | 02/29/08 |
| 0.100 | 04/17 | 05/13 | 05/15 | 05/30/08 |
| 0.100 | 07/14 | 08/13 | 08/15 | 08/29/08 |
| 0.100 | 10/14 | 11/12 | 11/14 | 11/28/08 |

Dividends have been paid since 2002. Source: Company reports.

---

**Please read the Required Disclosures and Analyst Certification on the last page of this report.**

The **McGraw·Hill** Companies

Stock Report | November 15, 2008 | NYS Symbol: **CIT**

# CIT Group Inc.

**STANDARD
&POOR'S**

## Business Summary October 22, 2008

CORPORATE OVERVIEW. CIT Group is a commercial and consumer finance company that has been providing financing and leasing products and services since 1908. The company seeks to mitigate losses and diversify risk by spreading its business around the globe, and it primarily focuses on firms in the middle market. It concentrates its business on the manufacturing, transportation, retailing, wholesaling healthcare, communications, energy and various service-related industries, as well as the education and home mortgage lending markets.

The company sources its loans through direct marketing efforts through referral sources and other channels to borrowers, lessees, manufacturers, vendors, distributors and end users. It also buys and sells participations in syndications of finance receivables and lines of credit and may buy or sell finance receivables on a whole-loan basis. In addition, it provides collection and servicing operations. Revenue is primarily generated through interest income from loans on the balance sheet, rental fees from the equipment it leases, and fee and other income for services. It may also syndicate and sell receivables and equipment to leverage its origination capabilities and manage its balance sheet.

CIT aims to meet customer needs through two groups of businesses, including five business segments. Its Commercial Finance Group includes corporate

and transportation finance operations, and its Specialty Finance Group offers trade and vendor finance, as well as consumer and small business lending. At December 31, 2007, the company had managed assets of $83.2 billion, comprised of a loan and lease portfolio of $76.9 billion and a securitized portfolio of $6.3 billion. It also serviced more than $6 billion in third-party assets under fee-based contracts at year end.

CORPORATE STRATEGY. The company has taken steps to increase its third-party assets under management and thereby increase fee-based revenues. Its goal is to leverage its origination capabilities and drive non-spread revenues. The first move in this initiative was its May 2007 CLO I origination, which includes middle-market loans originated by CIT as well as third parties. The company then closed the IPO of Care Investment Trust, a REIT formed to invest in health care-related commercial mortgage debt and real estate. It used the proceeds of its offering to purchase a portfolio of health care-related mortgage assets from a CIT subsidiary, and the portfolio is externally managed by CIT Healthcare LLC, a wholly owned subsidiary.

## Company Financials Fiscal Year Ended Dec. 31

| Per Share Data ($) | 2007 | 2006 | 2005 | 2004 | 2003 | 2002 | 2001 | 2000 | 1999 | 1998 |
|---|---|---|---|---|---|---|---|---|---|---|
| Tangible Book Value | 32.08 | 31.48 | 27.38 | 25.94 | 23.14 | 20.67 | NA | NA | NA | NA |
| Cash Flow | 5.55 | 10.19 | 9.10 | 7.95 | 7.61 | -25.75 | NA | NA | NA | NA |
| Earnings | -0.58 | 5.00 | 4.44 | 3.50 | 2.66 | -31.66 | NA | NA | NA | NA |
| S&P Core Earnings | -0.71 | 5.00 | 3.80 | 3.42 | 2.58 | -1.03 | NA | NA | NA | NA |
| Dividends | 1.00 | 0.80 | 0.61 | 0.52 | 0.48 | Nil | NA | NA | NA | NA |
| Payout Ratio | NM | 16% | 14% | 15% | 18% | Nil | NA | NA | NA | NA |
| Prices:High | 61.59 | 56.66 | 52.94 | 46.23 | 36.20 | 24.05 | NA | NA | NA | NA |
| Prices:Low | 21.80 | 41.91 | 35.41 | 32.65 | 16.08 | 13.80 | NA | NA | NA | NA |
| P/E Ratio:High | NM | 11 | 12 | 13 | 14 | NM | NA | NA | NA | NA |
| P/E Ratio:Low | NM | 8 | 8 | 9 | 6 | NM | NA | NA | NA | NA |
| **Income Statement Analysis (Million $)** | | | | | | | | | | |
| Revenue | 8,605 | 6,928 | 5,653 | 4,676 | 4,678 | 5,275 | 4,548 | NA | NA | NA |
| Operating Income | 4,789 | 4,089 | 3,410 | 3,481 | 3,270 | 2,299 | 2,394 | NA | NA | NA |
| Depreciation | 1,172 | 1,024 | 1,001 | 956 | 1,053 | 1,241 | 1,037 | NA | NA | NA |
| Interest Expense | 3,832 | 2,868 | 1,912 | 1,260 | 1,319 | 2,102 | 1,620 | NA | NA | NA |
| Pretax Income | -272 | 1,412 | 1,417 | 1,237 | 937 | -6,314 | 622 | NA | NA | NA |
| Effective Tax Rate | 71.4% | 25.7% | 32.8% | 39.1% | 38.9% | NM | 45.0% | NA | NA | NA |
| Net Income | -81.0 | 1,046 | 949 | 754 | 567 | -6,699 | 334 | NA | NA | NA |
| S&P Core Earnings | -135 | 1,017 | 802 | 735 | 549 | -200 | 379 | NA | NA | NA |
| **Balance Sheet & Other Financial Data (Million $)** | | | | | | | | | | |
| Cash | 6,792 | 4,458 | 4,811 | 3,438 | 1,974 | 2,274 | 808 | NA | NA | NA |
| Accounts Receivable | 61,705 | 54,405 | 45,293 | 36,072 | 31,575 | 27,681 | 31,387 | NA | NA | NA |
| Accounts Payable | 4,542 | 4,131 | 4,188 | 3,847 | 3,895 | 2,514 | 2,393 | NA | NA | NA |
| Total Assets | 90,248 | 77,068 | 63,387 | 51,111 | 46,343 | 42,710 | 51,090 | NA | NA | NA |
| Long Term Debt | 71,058 | 60,705 | 33,468 | 25,569 | 20,758 | 17,327 | 18,907 | NA | NA | NA |
| Lease Obligations | Nil | NA | NA | NA | NA | NA | NA | NA | NA | NA |
| Common Equity | 6,461 | 7,251 | 6,463 | 6,055 | 5,394 | 4,758 | 10,598 | NA | NA | NA |
| Total Capital | 78,077 | 68,496 | 40,480 | 31,665 | 26,191 | 22,085 | 29,505 | NA | NA | NA |
| Capital Expenditures | 2,865 | 2,860 | 2,359 | 1,489 | 2,096 | 1,877 | 1,451 | NA | NA | NA |
| Cash Flow | 1,061 | 2,070 | 1,950 | 1,710 | 1,620 | -5,458 | 1,371 | NA | NA | NA |
| % Long Term Debt of Capitalization | 91.0 | 88.6 | 82.6 | 80.7 | 79.3 | 78.5 | 64.1 | NA | NA | NA |
| % Net Income of Revenue | NM | 18.3 | 16.7 | 16.1 | 12.1 | NM | 7.3 | NA | NA | NA |
| % Return on Assets | NM | 1.4 | 1.6 | 1.6 | 1.3 | NM | NM | NA | NA | NA |
| % Return on Equity | NM | 15.2 | 15.1 | 13.1 | 11.2 | NM | NM | NA | NA | NA |

Data as orig reptd.; bef. results of disc opers/spec. items. Per share data adj. for stk. divs.; EPS diluted. E-Estimated. NA-Not Available. NM-Not Meaningful. NR-Not Ranked. UR-Under Review.

**Office:** 1 CIT Drive, Livingston, NJ 07039.
**Telephone:** 973-740-5000.
**Email:** investor.relations@cit.com
**Website:** http://www.citgroup.com

**Chrmn & CEO:** J.M. Peek
**Pres & COO:** A. Mason
**Vice Chrmn & CFO:** J.M. Leone
**EVP, Chief Acctg Officer & Cntlr:** W.J. Taylor

**EVP & Treas:** G.A. Votek
**Investor Contact:** S. Klimas (866-542-4847)
**Board Members:** G. C. Butler, W. M. Freeman, J. M. Leone, S. Lyne, J. S. McDonald, M. M. Parrs, J. M. Peek, T. M. Ring, J. R. Ryan, S. Sternberg, P. J. Tobin, L. M. Van Deusen

**Auditor:** Pricewaterhousecoopers
**Founded:** 1908
**Domicile:** Delaware
**Employees:** 6,700

*The McGraw-Hill Companies*

# Citrix Systems Inc

**STANDARD &POOR'S**

| S&P Recommendation **SELL** ★ ★ ☆ ☆ ☆ | Price<br>$22.95 (as of Nov 14, 2008) | 12-Mo. Target Price<br>$23.00 | Investment Style<br>Large-Cap Growth |
|---|---|---|---|

**GICS Sector** Information Technology
**Sub-Industry** Application Software

**Summary** This company is a leading developer and supplier of access infrastructure software and services.

## Key Stock Statistics (Source S&P, Vickers, company reports)

| | | | | | | | |
|---|---|---|---|---|---|---|---|
| 52-Wk Range | $39.20– 19.00 | S&P Oper. EPS 2008**E** | 0.91 | Market Capitalization(B) | $4.169 | Beta | 1.52 |
| Trailing 12-Month EPS | $0.96 | S&P Oper. EPS 2009**E** | 0.96 | Yield (%) | Nil | S&P 3-Yr. Proj. EPS CAGR(%) | 13 |
| Trailing 12-Month P/E | 23.9 | P/E on S&P Oper. EPS 2008**E** | 25.2 | Dividend Rate/Share | Nil | S&P Credit Rating | NR |
| $10K Invested 5 Yrs Ago | $9,107 | Common Shares Outstg. (M) | 181.7 | Institutional Ownership (%) | 88 | | |

## Price Performance

- 30-Week Mov. Avg. · · · · 10-Week Mov. Avg. - - **GAAP Earnings vs. Previous Year**   Volume Above Avg. STARS
- 12-Mo. Target Price —— Relative Strength — ▲ Up ▼ Down ► No Change   Below Avg.

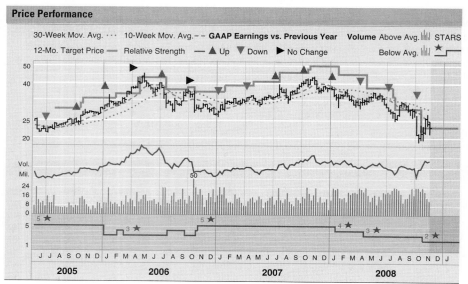

Options: ASE, CBOE, P, Ph

Analysis prepared by **Jim Yin** on November 12, 2008, when the stock traded at **$ 22.57**.

## Highlights

➤ We estimate that total revenue will increase 8.1% in 2009, down from our projection for 15% growth in 2008, reflecting our view of a worsening global economy and CTXS's reliance on the financial industry. We expect both online service and license update revenues to rise 12%. We see product license revenue growing 4.5%, reflecting the tail end of a major product upgrade cycle. We expect the acquisition of XenSource to add about $120 million of revenue in 2009, down from our prior estimate of $200 million, due to increased competition.

➤ We believe the gross margin in 2009 will remain steady at 89%. We project that operating expenses will decrease to 76% of revenue, from 77% in 2008, due to lower R&D expenses as a percentage of revenue following a significant increase seen in 2008. We expect operating margins in 2009 to widen to 12%, from an expected 10% in 2008.

➤ We estimate 2009 EPS of $0.96, versus $0.91 seen in 2008. The projected increase reflects higher revenues, and slower growth in research and development costs, partially offset by higher sales incentives, marketing expenses, and stock-based compensation.

## Investment Rationale/Risk

➤ Our sell recommendation is based on valuation following significant price appreciation. Even though CTXS reported better-than-expected third quarter results, we are concerned about a worsening global economy, hurt by financial uncertainty in the U.S. that has spread to the rest of the world. We are also wary of increased operating expenses as a result of the XenSource acquisition. We think the acquisition poses execution risks, because CTXS will enter a new market and trails the market leader, VMWare (VMW: NR, $22).

➤ Risks to our recommendation and target price include a recovery in the global economy, gain in market share for its server virtualization products, and higher revenue contribution from recent acquisitions.

➤ Our 12-month target price of $23 is based on a blend of our discounted cash flow (DCF) and P/E analyses. Our DCF model assumes a 12% weighted average cost of capital and 3% terminal growth, yielding an intrinsic value of $25. For our P/E analysis, we derive a value of $21, based on an industry average P/E-to-growth ratio of 1.7X, or 21.9X our 2009 operating EPS estimate of $0.96.

## Qualitative Risk Assessment

| LOW | MEDIUM | HIGH |
|---|---|---|

Our risk assessment reflects rapidly changing technology, the competitive nature of the enterprise software market, and a deteriorating global economy.

## Quantitative Evaluations

**S&P Quality Ranking**  B+

| D | C | B- | B | B+ | A- | A | A+ |
|---|---|---|---|---|---|---|---|

**Relative Strength Rank**  STRONG

76

LOWEST = 1          HIGHEST = 99

## Revenue/Earnings Data

**Revenue (Million $)**

| | 1Q | 2Q | 3Q | 4Q | Year |
|---|---|---|---|---|---|
| 2008 | 377.0 | 391.7 | 398.9 | -- | -- |
| 2007 | 308.1 | 334.4 | 349.9 | 399.6 | 1,392 |
| 2006 | 260.0 | 275.5 | 277.9 | 321.0 | 1,134 |
| 2005 | 201.9 | 211.2 | 227.0 | 268.7 | 908.7 |
| 2004 | 161.3 | 178.3 | 187.6 | 214.0 | 741.2 |
| 2003 | 143.5 | 143.1 | 144.3 | 157.7 | 588.6 |

**Earnings Per Share ($)**

| | | | | | |
|---|---|---|---|---|---|
| 2008 | 0.18 | 0.18 | 0.26 | E0.29 | E0.91 |
| 2007 | 0.20 | 0.29 | 0.33 | 0.33 | 1.14 |
| 2006 | 0.22 | 0.23 | 0.23 | 0.29 | 0.97 |
| 2005 | 0.22 | 0.16 | 0.23 | 0.32 | 0.93 |
| 2004 | 0.05 | 0.18 | 0.22 | 0.30 | 0.75 |
| 2003 | 0.18 | 0.17 | 0.18 | 0.21 | 0.74 |

Fiscal year ended Dec. 31. Next earnings report expected: Late January. EPS Estimates based on S&P Operating Earnings; historical GAAP earnings are as reported.

## Dividend Data

No cash dividends have been paid.

---

# Citrix Systems Inc

**STANDARD &POOR'S**

## Business Summary November 12, 2008

CORPORATE OVERVIEW. Citrix Systems designs, develops and markets technology solutions that enable users to access and share applications and files on-demand with a higher performance and level of security. CTXS's solutions help people conduct business in remote and mobile locations as they move from location to location, use multiple devices, and connect with a wide range of heterogeneous applications over wired, wireless and Internet networks.

CTXS organizes its products into four groups: Delivery Systems, Virtualization and Management Systems, Online Services and Technical Services.

Delivery Systems are focused on application virtualization, application networking and desktop virtualization. One key application is Citrix XenApp, previously called Citrix Presentation Server, which runs the business logic of applications on a central server and displays the video on the users' computers. By keeping applications under a centralized control, it improves data security and reduces the costs of managing many different applications on every user's desktop. Other key products include Citrix NetScaler and Citrix WAN-Scaler, which optimize the performance of a network by balancing the load and providing firewall protection.

Virtualization and Management Systems are focused on server virtualization, which allows servers to run multiple operating systems, thus enabling them to process multiple business applications. As a result, enterprises can reduce its infrastructure costs by aggregating servers and data storage into pools of shared resources. The key product is Citrix XenServer, which was obtained through the acquisition of XenSource. CTXS and Microsoft entered into patent cross license and source code licensing agreements related to Microsoft's operating systems. The technology collaboration agreement expires in December 2009.

Online Services are Web-based access and collaboration software and services. GoToMyPC allows users to remotely access PCs via the Internet. GoToMeeting enables online meetings, training sessions and collaborative gatherings. GoToAssist is an online solution that enables businesses to provide customer support over the Internet. GoToWebinar helps organizations conduct online events, such as large marketing events.

Technical Services include consulting, support, and training to help ensure that customers are achieving the maximum value of CTXS's products and services.

## Company Financials Fiscal Year Ended Dec. 31

| Per Share Data ($) | 2007 | 2006 | 2005 | 2004 | 2003 | 2002 | 2001 | 2000 | 1999 | 1998 |
|---|---|---|---|---|---|---|---|---|---|---|
| Tangible Book Value | 3.59 | 3.92 | 2.68 | 2.80 | 3.24 | 2.57 | 2.48 | 2.94 | 2.59 | 2.92 |
| Cash Flow | 1.60 | 1.32 | 1.06 | 0.95 | 0.94 | 0.75 | 0.95 | 0.72 | 0.75 | 0.84 |
| Earnings | 1.14 | 0.97 | 0.93 | 0.93 | 0.75 | 0.74 | 0.52 | 0.54 | 0.61 | 0.34 |
| S&P Core Earnings | 1.14 | 0.97 | 0.74 | 0.48 | 0.23 | -0.34 | -0.19 | NA | NA | NA |
| Dividends | Nil | Nil | Nil | Nil | Nil | Nil | Nil | Nil | Nil | Nil |
| Payout Ratio | Nil | Nil | Nil | Nil | Nil | Nil | Nil | Nil | Nil | Nil |
| Prices:High | 43.90 | 45.50 | 29.46 | 26.00 | 27.86 | 24.70 | 37.19 | 122.31 | 65.00 | 24.44 |
| Prices:Low | 26.10 | 26.62 | 20.70 | 15.02 | 10.48 | 4.70 | 16.88 | 14.25 | 13.25 | 9.09 |
| P/E Ratio:High | 39 | 47 | 32 | 35 | 38 | 47 | 69 | NM | NM | 73 |
| P/E Ratio:Low | 23 | 27 | 22 | 20 | 14 | 9 | 31 | NM | NM | 27 |

| Income Statement Analysis (Million $) | | | | | | | | | | |
|---|---|---|---|---|---|---|---|---|---|---|
| Revenue | 1,392 | 1,134 | 909 | 741 | 589 | 527 | 592 | 471 | 403 | 249 |
| Operating Income | 297 | 267 | 233 | 212 | 189 | 145 | 216 | 172 | 201 | 119 |
| Depreciation | 85.2 | 63.6 | 22.0 | 33.6 | 34.3 | 41.4 | 79.6 | 50.2 | 27.6 | 15.2 |
| Interest Expense | 0.74 | 0.93 | 2.23 | 4.37 | 18.3 | 18.2 | 20.6 | 17.0 | 12.6 | Nil |
| Pretax Income | 251 | 243 | 226 | 164 | 161 | 113 | 153 | 135 | 183 | 95.5 |
| Effective Tax Rate | 14.5% | 24.7% | 26.2% | 20.0% | 21.0% | 17.0% | 31.0% | 30.0% | 36.0% | 36.0% |
| Net Income | 214 | 183 | 166 | 132 | 127 | 93.9 | 105 | 94.5 | 117 | 61.1 |
| S&P Core Earnings | 214 | 183 | 131 | 83.5 | 39.3 | -60.5 | -36.2 | NA | NA | NA |

| Balance Sheet & Other Financial Data (Million $) | | | | | | | | | | |
|---|---|---|---|---|---|---|---|---|---|---|
| Cash | 580 | 349 | 484 | 73.5 | 359 | 143 | 140 | 375 | 216 | 128 |
| Current Assets | 934 | 812 | 726 | 427 | 809 | 375 | 346 | 587 | 570 | 244 |
| Total Assets | 2,535 | 2,024 | 1,682 | 1,286 | 1,345 | 1,162 | 1,208 | 1,113 | 1,038 | 431 |
| Current Liabilities | 654 | 536 | 426 | 342 | 626 | 189 | 193 | 159 | 137 | 85.1 |
| Long Term Debt | Nil | Nil | 31.0 | Nil | Nil | 334 | 346 | 330 | 314 | Nil |
| Common Equity | 1,838 | 1,464 | 1,203 | 925 | 707 | 622 | 647 | 593 | 533 | 297 |
| Total Capital | 1,838 | 1,464 | 1,234 | 925 | 707 | 955 | 994 | 923 | 847 | 297 |
| Capital Expenditures | 85.9 | 52.1 | 26.4 | 24.4 | 11.1 | 19.1 | 60.6 | 43.5 | 26.3 | 11.4 |
| Cash Flow | 300 | 247 | 188 | 165 | 161 | 135 | 185 | 145 | 145 | 76.3 |
| Current Ratio | 1.4 | 1.5 | 1.7 | 1.2 | 1.3 | 2.0 | 1.8 | 3.7 | 4.2 | 2.9 |
| % Long Term Debt of Capitalization | Nil | Nil | 2.5 | Nil | Nil | 34.9 | 34.8 | 35.8 | 37.1 | Nil |
| % Net Income of Revenue | 15.4 | 16.1 | 18.3 | 17.7 | 21.6 | 17.8 | 17.8 | 10.0 | 29.0 | 24.6 |
| % Return on Assets | 9.4 | 9.8 | 11.2 | 10.0 | 10.1 | 7.9 | 9.1 | 8.8 | 15.9 | 17.1 |
| % Return on Equity | 13.0 | 13.7 | 15.6 | 16.1 | 19.1 | 14.6 | 17.0 | 16.8 | 28.2 | 24.7 |

Data as orig reptd.; bef. results of disc opers/spec. items. Per share data adj. for stk. divs.; EPS diluted. E-Estimated. NA-Not Available. NM-Not Meaningful. NR-Not Ranked. UR-Under Review.

**Office:** 851 West Cypress Creek Road, Fort Lauderdale, FL 33309.
**Telephone:** 954-267-3000.
**Email:** investor@citrix.com
**Website:** http://www.citrix.com

**Chrmn:** T.F. Bogan
**Pres & CEO:** M.B. Templeton
**SVP, CFO & Chief Acctg Officer:** D.J. Henshall
**Secy:** A.G. Gomes

**General Counsel:** D.R. Friedman
**Investor Contact:** E. Fleites (954-267-3000)
**Board Members:** T. F. Bogan, N. Caldwell, M. Demo, S. M. Dow, A. Hirji, G. E. Morin, G. Sullivan, M. B. Templeton

**Founded:** 1989
**Domicile:** Delaware
**Employees:** 4,620

*The McGraw-Hill Companies*

# Clorox Co (The)

**STANDARD &POOR'S**

| S&P Recommendation | HOLD ★★★☆☆ | Price $59.30 (as of Nov 14, 2008) | 12-Mo. Target Price $64.00 | Investment Style Large-Cap Growth |

**GICS Sector** Consumer Staples
**Sub-Industry** Household Products

**Summary** This diversified producer of household cleaning, grocery and specialty food products is also a leading producer of natural personal care products.

## Key Stock Statistics (Source S&P, Vickers, company reports)

| | | | | | | | |
|---|---|---|---|---|---|---|---|
| 52-Wk Range | $66.90– 47.48 | S&P Oper. EPS 2009E | 3.60 | Market Capitalization(B) | $8.226 | Beta | 0.33 |
| Trailing 12-Month EPS | $3.40 | S&P Oper. EPS 2010E | NA | Yield (%) | 3.10 | S&P 3-Yr. Proj. EPS CAGR(%) | 8 |
| Trailing 12-Month P/E | 17.4 | P/E on S&P Oper. EPS 2009E | 16.5 | Dividend Rate/Share | $1.84 | S&P Credit Rating | BBB+ |
| $10K Invested 5 Yrs Ago | $14,049 | Common Shares Outstg. (M) | 138.7 | Institutional Ownership (%) | 76 | | |

## Price Performance

30-Week Mov. Avg. ···· 10-Week Mov. Avg. – – GAAP Earnings vs. Previous Year   Volume Above Avg. STARS
12-Mo. Target Price — Relative Strength — ▲ Up ▼ Down ► No Change   Below Avg. ★

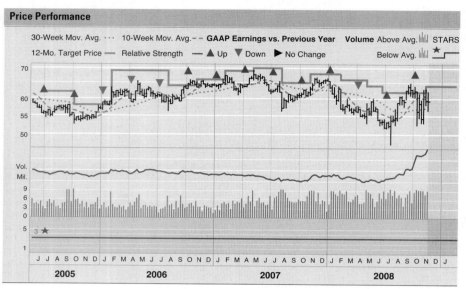

Options: ASE, CBOE, P, Ph

Analysis prepared by **Loran Braverman, CFA** on November 03, 2008, when the stock traded at **$ 61.93**.

## Highlights

➤ Sales increased 8.8% in FY 08 (Jun.), reflecting 4.7% in base sales growth (modest volume growth and price increases), 1.1% from foreign exchange, and 3.0% from acquisitions including Burt's Bees, a natural personal care products company, effective December 1, 2007. For FY 09, we forecast 5% sales growth, benefiting from price increases, inclusion of an extra five months of Burt's Bees and a full-year of Green Works cleaners, a line of natural cleaning products made from plant-based ingredients. We expect a 2% negative foreign currency impact.

➤ Operating margins fell 110 basis points in FY 08, with price hikes and cost saving programs more than offset by higher commodity (e.g., resin and agricultural commodities) and other costs and $19 million for the Burt's Bees purchase accounting step-up in inventory values. We see moderating commodity cost pressures in second half of FY 09 allowing for a modestly higher operating margin and further benefits from both lower restructuring charges and interest expense as a percentage of sales.

➤ Our FY 09 EPS estimate is $3.60, up from FY 08's $3.23.

## Investment Rationale/Risk

➤ In recent years, CLX's performance has been positive but erratic, in our view, due to the seasonal nature of some businesses, the diverse categories in which it operates, and the timing of new product introductions. However, we think its level of product innovation is respectable and bolsters the company's pricing power and competitive stance. We view positively CLX's increased presence in the fast-growing natural home/personal care products arena through Burt's Bees and Green Works.

➤ Risks to our recommendation and target price include increased competition and promotional activity that would affect profitability, poor consumer acceptance of new products, unfavorable foreign exchange, and potential challenges in the implementation of new enterprise resource planning system software.

➤ Our 12-month target price of $64 is a blend of our historical and relative analyses. Our historical analysis uses a modest discount to the 10-year historical median P/E applied to our pre-restructuring charge calendar 2009 EPS estimate of $3.76, implying a $70 value. Our relative analysis applies a slight discount to the average peer P/E multiple, for a value of $58.

## Qualitative Risk Assessment

| LOW | MEDIUM | HIGH |

Our risk assessment reflects our view of stable demand for household and personal care products, which is generally not affected by changes in the economy or by geopolitical factors.

## Quantitative Evaluations

**S&P Quality Ranking**   A

| D | C | B- | B | B+ | A- | A | A+ |

**Relative Strength Rank**   STRONG

92

LOWEST = 1          HIGHEST = 99

## Revenue/Earnings Data

**Revenue (Million $)**

| | 1Q | 2Q | 3Q | 4Q | Year |
|---|---|---|---|---|---|
| 2009 | 1,384 | -- | -- | -- | -- |
| 2008 | 1,239 | 1,186 | 1,353 | 1,495 | 5,273 |
| 2007 | 1,161 | 1,101 | 1,241 | 1,344 | 4,847 |
| 2006 | 1,104 | 1,064 | 1,157 | 1,319 | 4,644 |
| 2005 | 1,048 | 1,000 | 1,086 | 1,254 | 4,388 |
| 2004 | 1,048 | 947.0 | 1,086 | 1,243 | 4,324 |

**Earnings Per Share ($)**

| | | | | | |
|---|---|---|---|---|---|
| 2009 | 0.91 | E0.63 | E0.87 | E1.20 | E3.60 |
| 2008 | 0.76 | 0.65 | 0.71 | 1.13 | 3.25 |
| 2007 | 0.73 | 0.59 | 0.84 | 1.07 | 3.22 |
| 2006 | 0.70 | 0.55 | 0.72 | 0.92 | 2.89 |
| 2005 | 0.50 | 0.72 | 0.75 | 1.00 | 2.88 |
| 2004 | 0.60 | 0.52 | 0.59 | 0.83 | 2.55 |

Fiscal year ended Jun. 30. Next earnings report expected: Early February. EPS Estimates based on S&P Operating Earnings; historical GAAP earnings are as reported.

## Dividend Data (Dates: mm/dd Payment Date: mm/dd/yy)

| Amount ($) | Date Decl. | Ex-Div. Date | Stk. of Record | Payment Date |
|---|---|---|---|---|
| 0.400 | 11/13 | 01/24 | 01/28 | 02/15/08 |
| 0.400 | 02/07 | 04/23 | 04/25 | 05/15/08 |
| 0.460 | 05/13 | 07/24 | 07/28 | 08/15/08 |
| 0.460 | 09/16 | 10/24 | 10/28 | 11/14/08 |

Dividends have been paid since 1968. Source: Company reports.

The McGraw-Hill Companies

# Clorox Co (The)

## Business Summary November 03, 2008

CORPORATE OVERVIEW. From its divestiture from The Procter & Gamble Company in 1969 through its January 1999 acquisition of First Brands, Clorox expanded into a company with approximately $4.8 billion in annual sales, by focusing on building big-share brands in mid-sized categories. In November 2004, CLX completed the exchange of its ownership interest in a subsidiary for approximately 61.4 million of its shares held by Henkel KGaA, which represented about 29% of CLX's outstanding common stock prior to the exchange. The subsidiary transferred to Henkel contained CLX's existing insecticides and Soft Scrub cleaner businesses, its 20% interest in the Henkel Iberica, S.A. joint venture, and approximately $2.1 billion in cash.

Clorox has two segments for reporting purposes: North America (84% of FY 08 (Jun.) sales and 89% of segmental profits) and International (16% and 11%). In FY 08, Wal-Mart Stores and its affiliated companies accounted for 26% of consolidated net sales.

Clorox's products include: laundry additives, including bleaches, under the Clorox, Clorox 2 and Javex brands; cleaning products, primarily under the Clorox, Formula 409, Liquid-Plumr, Pine-Sol, S.O.S., and Tilex brands; natural

cleaning products under the Green Works brand (introduced in January 2008); water-filtration systems and filters under the Brita brand; professional cleaning products for institutional, janitorial, health care and food service markets; auto care products, primarily under the Armor All and STP brands; plastic bags, wraps and containers, under the Glad brand; cat litter products, primarily under the Fresh Step and Scoop Away brands; food products, primarily under the Hidden Valley and KC Masterpiece brands; charcoal products under the Kingsford and Match Light brands; and natural personal care products under the Burt's Bees brand. In FY 08, liquid bleach represented 14% of sales and trash bags 13%.

CLX owns and operates 26 manufacturing facilities in North America. The company also owns and operates 20 manufacturing facilities outside North America. CLX leases seven distribution centers located in North America and several other warehouse facilities.

## Company Financials Fiscal Year Ended Jun. 30

| Per Share Data ($) | 2008 | 2007 | 2006 | 2005 | 2004 | 2003 | 2002 | 2001 | 2000 | 1999 |
|---|---|---|---|---|---|---|---|---|---|---|
| Tangible Book Value | NM | NM | NM | NM | 0.77 | NM | 0.24 | 1.38 | 1.10 | 0.31 |
| Cash Flow | NA | 4.47 | 4.12 | 3.95 | 3.47 | 3.19 | 2.18 | 2.30 | 2.48 | 1.87 |
| Earnings | 3.25 | 3.22 | 2.89 | 2.88 | 2.55 | 2.33 | 1.37 | 1.36 | 1.64 | 1.03 |
| S&P Core Earnings | 3.15 | 3.26 | 2.94 | 2.73 | 2.43 | 2.26 | 1.63 | 1.11 | NA | NA |
| Dividends | 1.60 | 1.20 | 1.14 | 1.10 | 1.08 | 0.88 | 0.84 | 0.84 | 0.61 | 0.76 |
| Payout Ratio | 49% | 37% | 39% | 38% | 42% | 38% | 61% | 62% | 37% | 74% |
| Prices:High | 65.25 | 69.36 | 66.00 | 66.04 | 59.45 | 49.16 | 47.95 | 40.85 | 56.38 | 66.47 |
| Prices:Low | 47.48 | 56.22 | 56.17 | 52.50 | 46.50 | 37.40 | 31.92 | 29.95 | 28.38 | 37.50 |
| P/E Ratio:High | 20 | 22 | 23 | 23 | 23 | 21 | 35 | 30 | 34 | 65 |
| P/E Ratio:Low | 15 | 17 | 19 | 18 | 18 | 16 | 23 | 22 | 17 | 36 |

| Income Statement Analysis (Million $) | | | | | | | | | | |
|---|---|---|---|---|---|---|---|---|---|---|
| Revenue | 5,273 | 4,847 | 4,644 | 4,388 | 4,324 | 4,144 | 4,061 | 3,903 | 4,083 | 4,003 |
| Operating Income | NA | 1,059 | 967 | 1,011 | 1,069 | 1,046 | 942 | 895 | 981 | 933 |
| Depreciation | 205 | 192 | 188 | 190 | 197 | 191 | 190 | 225 | 201 | 202 |
| Interest Expense | NA | 113 | 127 | 79.0 | 30.0 | 28.0 | 39.0 | 88.0 | 98.0 | 97.0 |
| Pretax Income | 693 | 743 | 653 | 731 | 840 | 802 | 498 | 487 | 622 | 430 |
| Effective Tax Rate | 33.5% | 33.2% | 32.2% | 29.3% | 35.0% | 35.9% | 35.3% | 33.3% | 36.7% | 42.8% |
| Net Income | 461 | 496 | 443 | 517 | 546 | 514 | 322 | 325 | 394 | 246 |
| S&P Core Earnings | 448 | 501 | 450 | 489 | 521 | 496 | 383 | 266 | NA | NA |

| Balance Sheet & Other Financial Data (Million $) | | | | | | | | | | |
|---|---|---|---|---|---|---|---|---|---|---|
| Cash | 214 | 182 | 192 | 293 | 232 | 172 | 177 | 251 | 245 | 132 |
| Current Assets | NA | 1,032 | 1,007 | 1,090 | 1,043 | 951 | 1,002 | 1,103 | 1,454 | 1,116 |
| Total Assets | 4,708 | 3,666 | 3,616 | 3,617 | 3,834 | 3,652 | 3,630 | 3,995 | 4,353 | 4,132 |
| Current Liabilities | NA | 1,427 | 1,130 | 1,348 | 1,268 | 1,451 | 1,225 | 1,069 | 1,541 | 1,368 |
| Long Term Debt | NA | 1,462 | 1,966 | 2,122 | 475 | 495 | 678 | 685 | 590 | 702 |
| Common Equity | -370 | 171 | -156 | -553 | 1,540 | 1,215 | 1,354 | 1,900 | 1,794 | 1,178 |
| Total Capital | NA | 1,723 | 1,939 | 1,651 | 2,189 | 1,825 | 2,174 | 2,732 | 2,608 | 2,117 |
| Capital Expenditures | 170 | 147 | 180 | 151 | 172 | 205 | 177 | 192 | 158 | 176 |
| Cash Flow | NA | 688 | 631 | 707 | 743 | 705 | 512 | 550 | 595 | 448 |
| Current Ratio | 0.8 | 0.7 | 0.9 | 0.8 | 0.8 | 0.7 | 0.8 | 1.0 | 0.9 | 0.8 |
| % Long Term Debt of Capitalization | 115.7 | 84.9 | 101.4 | 128.5 | 21.7 | 27.1 | 31.2 | 25.1 | 22.6 | 33.2 |
| % Net Income of Revenue | 8.7 | 10.2 | 9.5 | 11.8 | 12.6 | 12.4 | 7.9 | 8.3 | 9.6 | 6.1 |
| % Return on Assets | 11.0 | 13.6 | 12.2 | 13.9 | 14.6 | 14.3 | 8.4 | 7.8 | 9.3 | 6.0 |
| % Return on Equity | NM | 6613.3 | NM | 104.8 | 39.6 | 39.8 | 19.8 | 17.6 | 23.4 | 19.6 |

Data as orig reptd.; bef. results of disc opers/spec. items. Per share data adj. for stk. divs.; EPS diluted. E-Estimated. NA-Not Available. NM-Not Meaningful. NR-Not Ranked. UR-Under Review.

**Office:** 1221 Broadway, Oakland, CA, USA 94612.
**Telephone:** 510-271-7000.
**Email:** investor_relations@clorox.com
**Website:** http://www.thecloroxcompany.com

**Chrmn & CEO:** D.R. Knauss
**COO:** F.A. Tataseo
**SVP & CFO:** D.J. Heinrich
**SVP & General Counsel:** L. Stein

**Chief Acctg Officer & Cntlr:** T.D. Johnson
**Investor Contact:** S. Austenfeld
**Board Members:** D. Boggan, Jr., R. H. Carmona, T. M. Friedman, G. J. Harad, D. R. Knauss, R. W. Matschullat, G. G. Michael, E. A. Mueller, J. L. Murley, P. Thomas-Graham, C. M. Ticknor

**Founded:** 1913
**Domicile:** Delaware
**Employees:** 8,300

# CME Group Inc

**STANDARD &POOR'S**

| S&P Recommendation | BUY ★★★★☆ | Price $209.03 (as of Nov 14, 2008) | 12-Mo. Target Price $350.00 | Investment Style Large-Cap Growth |
|---|---|---|---|---|

**GICS Sector** Financials
**Sub-Industry** Specialized Finance

**Summary** The CME Group, a combination of the Chicago Mercantile Exchange and CBOT Holdings, is the world's largest futures exchange.

## Key Stock Statistics (Source S&P, Vickers, company reports)

| | | | | | | | |
|---|---|---|---|---|---|---|---|
| 52-Wk Range | $714.48– 197.18 | S&P Oper. EPS 2008E | 16.62 | Market Capitalization(B) | $11.403 | Beta | 0.89 |
| Trailing 12-Month EPS | $15.36 | S&P Oper. EPS 2009E | 18.86 | Yield (%) | 2.20 | S&P 3-Yr. Proj. EPS CAGR(%) | 18 |
| Trailing 12-Month P/E | 13.6 | P/E on S&P Oper. EPS 2008E | 12.6 | Dividend Rate/Share | $4.60 | S&P Credit Rating | NA |
| $10K Invested 5 Yrs Ago | $31,671 | Common Shares Outstg. (M) | 54.6 | Institutional Ownership (%) | 75 | | |

## Price Performance

- 30-Week Mov. Avg. · · · · 10-Week Mov. Avg. - - - GAAP Earnings vs. Previous Year   Volume Above Avg. |||| STARS
- 12-Mo. Target Price — Relative Strength — ▲ Up ▼ Down ► No Change   Below Avg. |||| ★

Options: ASE, CBOE, P, Ph

Analysis prepared by **Rikin Pandya** on November 14, 2008, when the stock traded at **$ 225.20**.

## Highlights

➤ We believe CME's trading volumes will continue to benefit from increased investor sophistication, more active investment strategies, and growing demand for alternative investments. We view CME's market-leading position in key interest rate, agriculture and equity index futures as highly defensible, and we see ongoing uncertainty and volatility in interest rates, energy costs and equity markets benefiting CME's trading volumes and revenue.

➤ Third-quarter results saw interest-rate product trading down 25% due to continued credit market turmoil offset by an 18% increase in equity product volume. On a pro forma basis, revenues from CME's NYMEX acquisition, which closed in Q3 08, were 26% of total revenues. Management announced that they had achieved the planned $150 million in synergies from the CBOT acquisition. We forecast a 2008 operating margin of 63.9% versus 59.8% in 2007, and expect margins to improve even more in 2009 to 67.5% as CME continues to leverage its fixed cost structure.

➤ We expect EPS of $16.62 in 2008 and $18.86 in 2009, assuming roughly a 12% decline in trading volumes in 2009 on a comparable basis.

## Investment Rationale/Risk

➤ Following its combination with CBOT Holdings and NYMEX, we believe CME holds a dominant position in the futures markets for interest rates, agricultural commodities, and equities, and is expanding its presence in foreign exchange and energy. We also see central counterparty clearing for credit default swaps (CDS) as a significant opportunity for CME that should reap long-term rewards, and we will monitor developments in this area closely. We see CME, with what we view as broad product exposure, highly defensible positioning, and a low variable cost model, delivering sustained revenue growth and margin expansion. But we think a recent slowdown in trading volume warrants a lower valuation multiple than we previously used.

➤ Risks to our recommendation and target price include a significant decrease in trading volumes, a faster-than-expected mix shift to lower-margin member trading, stronger regulatory scrutiny, and integration risk relating to the combination with CBOT Holdings.

➤ Our 12-month target price of $350 is based on a P/E of 18.5X our 2009 EPS estimate, a premium to the current peer group multiple.

## Qualitative Risk Assessment

| LOW | MEDIUM | HIGH |
|---|---|---|

Our risk assessment reflects potential volatility in results due to changes in futures trading volumes, recent acquisition activity in the sector, and a changing regulatory environment.

## Quantitative Evaluations

**S&P Quality Ranking**  NR

| D | C | B- | B | B+ | A- | A | A+ |
|---|---|---|---|---|---|---|---|

**Relative Strength Rank**  WEAK

27

LOWEST = 1          HIGHEST = 99

## Revenue/Earnings Data

### Revenue (Million $)

| | 1Q | 2Q | 3Q | 4Q | Year |
|---|---|---|---|---|---|
| 2008 | 625.1 | 563.2 | 681.0 | -- | -- |
| 2007 | 332.3 | 329.0 | 565.2 | 529.5 | 1,756 |
| 2006 | 251.7 | 282.2 | 274.7 | 281.3 | 1,090 |
| 2005 | 223.9 | 252.2 | 249.6 | 251.6 | 977.3 |
| 2004 | 169.6 | 190.5 | 192.4 | 196.0 | 752.8 |
| 2003 | 128.6 | 142.4 | 135.0 | 134.6 | 544.8 |

### Earnings Per Share ($)

| | 1Q | 2Q | 3Q | 4Q | Year |
|---|---|---|---|---|---|
| 2008 | 5.25 | 3.67 | 2.81 | E4.89 | E16.62 |
| 2007 | 3.69 | 3.57 | 3.87 | 3.75 | 14.93 |
| 2006 | 2.61 | 3.12 | 2.95 | 2.91 | 11.60 |
| 2005 | 2.04 | 2.36 | 2.22 | 2.18 | 8.81 |
| 2004 | 1.35 | 1.66 | 1.72 | 1.64 | 6.38 |
| 2003 | 0.77 | 1.03 | 0.93 | 0.87 | 3.60 |

Fiscal year ended Dec. 31. Next earnings report expected: Early February. EPS Estimates based on S&P Operating Earnings; historical GAAP earnings are as reported.

## Dividend Data (Dates: mm/dd Payment Date: mm/dd/yy)

| Amount ($) | Date Decl. | Ex-Div. Date | Stk. of Record | Payment Date |
|---|---|---|---|---|
| 1.150 | 05/07 | 06/06 | 06/10 | 06/25/08 |
| 1.150 | 08/06 | 09/08 | 09/10 | 09/25/08 |
| 5.0 Spl. | 05/23 | 09/23 | 09/25 | 10/10/08 |
| 1.150 | 11/06 | 12/08 | 12/10 | 12/26/08 |

Dividends have been paid since 2003. Source: Company reports.

---

**Please read the Required Disclosures and Analyst Certification on the last page of this report.**

The McGraw-Hill Companies

**STANDARD &POOR'S**

# CME Group Inc

## Business Summary November 14, 2008

CORPORATE OVERVIEW. The largest futures exchange in the world, CME Group was formed in July 2007 from the merger of the Chicago Mercantile Exchange and CBOT Holdings. CME serves the risk management needs of clients worldwide through a diverse range of futures and options-on-futures products on its CME Globex electronic trading platform and on its trading floors. CME offers futures and options on futures primarily in four product areas: interest rates, stock indexes, foreign exchange, and commodities. CME is the leading exchange for trading Eurodollar futures, the world's most actively traded futures contract and a benchmark for measuring the relative value of U.S. dollar-denominated short-term fixed income securities.

CME operates its own clearing house, which clears, settles and guarantees every contract traded through its exchange. We view CME's internal clearing capabilities as a key competitive advantage as CME is able to capture the revenue associated with both the trading and clearing of its products. We expect CME to expand its clearing business by partnering with other exchanges, both domestically and abroad, and clearing over-the-counter (OTC) transactions.

In 2007, CME derived over 80% of its revenue from fees associated with trading and clearing its products. These fees include per contract charges for trade execution, clearing and CME Globex fees. Fees are charged at various rates based on the product traded, the method of trade, and the exchange trading privileges of the customer making the trade. Generally, members are charged lower fees than non-members. Certain customers benefit from volume discounts and limits on fees in order to encourage increased liquidity.

## Company Financials Fiscal Year Ended Dec. 31

| Per Share Data ($) | 2007 | 2006 | 2005 | 2004 | 2003 | 2002 | 2001 | 2000 | 1999 | 1998 |
|---|---|---|---|---|---|---|---|---|---|---|
| Tangible Book Value | NM | 42.91 | 32.38 | 23.83 | 17.10 | 13.71 | 12.39 | NA | NA | NA |
| Cash Flow | 18.00 | 13.67 | 10.71 | 7.93 | 5.16 | 4.76 | 3.61 | NA | NA | NA |
| Earnings | 14.93 | 11.60 | 8.81 | 6.38 | 3.60 | 3.13 | 2.33 | -0.21 | 0.10 | NA |
| S&P Core Earnings | 14.96 | 11.59 | 8.80 | 6.37 | 3.61 | 3.23 | NA | NA | NA | NA |
| Dividends | 3.44 | 2.52 | 1.84 | 1.04 | 0.63 | Nil | NA | NA | NA | NA |
| Payout Ratio | 23% | 22% | 21% | 16% | 18% | Nil | NA | NA | NA | NA |
| Prices:High | 714.48 | 557.97 | 396.90 | 229.80 | 79.30 | 45.50 | NA | NA | NA | NA |
| Prices:Low | 497.00 | 354.50 | 163.80 | 72.50 | 41.35 | 35.00 | NA | NA | NA | NA |
| P/E Ratio:High | 48 | 48 | 45 | 36 | 22 | 15 | NA | NA | NA | NA |
| P/E Ratio:Low | 33 | 31 | 19 | 11 | 11 | 11 | NA | NA | NA | NA |

| Income Statement Analysis (Million $) | | | | | | | | | | |
|---|---|---|---|---|---|---|---|---|---|---|
| Revenue | 1,756 | 1,090 | 977 | 753 | 545 | 469 | 397 | 227 | 211 | 197 |
| Operating Income | 1,258 | 694 | 631 | 464 | 290 | NA | NA | NA | NA | NA |
| Depreciation | 136 | 72.8 | 66.0 | 53.0 | 53.0 | 48.5 | 37.6 | 33.5 | 25.3 | 17.9 |
| Interest Expense | 115 | 92.1 | 57.0 | 19.0 | 8.74 | 15.9 | 9.48 | NA | NA | NA |
| Pretax Income | 1,096 | 672 | 508 | 368 | 206 | 154 | 114 | -8.08 | 6.64 | 14.2 |
| Effective Tax Rate | 39.9% | 39.4% | 39.6% | 40.2% | 40.7% | 39.0% | 40.3% | 41.3% | 27.9% | 30.4% |
| Net Income | 659 | 407 | 307 | 220 | 122 | 94.1 | 68.3 | -5.91 | 2.66 | 7.03 |
| S&P Core Earnings | 660 | 407 | 307 | 219 | 123 | 97.2 | NA | NA | NA | NA |

| Balance Sheet & Other Financial Data (Million $) | | | | | | | | | | |
|---|---|---|---|---|---|---|---|---|---|---|
| Cash | 4,744 | 3,872 | 904 | 660 | 442 | 339 | 292 | 75.0 | 74.4 | NA |
| Current Assets | 4,987 | 4,030 | 3,783 | 2,695 | 4,723 | 3,215 | 2,818 | NA | NA | NA |
| Total Assets | 20,306 | 4,307 | 3,969 | 2,857 | 4,873 | 3,355 | 2,958 | 381 | 303 | NA |
| Current Liabilities | 4,076 | 2,755 | 2,830 | 2,026 | 4,288 | 2,889 | 2,544 | NA | NA | NA |
| Long Term Debt | Nil | Nil | Nil | Nil | Nil | 2.33 | 8.22 | NA | NA | NA |
| Common Equity | 12,306 | 1,519 | 1,119 | 813 | 563 | 446 | 394 | 164 | 169 | NA |
| Total Capital | 16,154 | 1,519 | 1,119 | 813 | 563 | 448 | 402 | NA | NA | NA |
| Capital Expenditures | 164 | 87.8 | 85.6 | 67.0 | 63.0 | 56.3 | 16.3 | 11.2 | 37.5 | 18.8 |
| Cash Flow | 794 | 480 | 373 | 273 | 175 | 143 | 106 | NA | NA | NA |
| Current Ratio | 1.2 | 1.5 | 1.3 | 1.3 | 1.1 | 1.1 | 1.1 | 1.4 | 1.6 | NA |
| % Long Term Debt of Capitalization | Nil | Nil | Nil | Nil | Nil | 0.5 | 2.0 | Nil | Nil | Nil |
| % Net Income of Revenue | 37.5 | 37.4 | 31.4 | 29.2 | 22.5 | 20.1 | 17.2 | NM | 1.3 | 3.6 |
| % Return on Assets | 5.4 | 9.8 | 8.9 | 5.6 | 3.0 | 3.5 | 5.6 | NM | NA | NA |
| % Return on Equity | 9.5 | 30.9 | 31.7 | 31.9 | 24.2 | 27.1 | 33.0 | NM | NA | NA |

Data as orig reptd.; bef. results of disc opers/spec. items. Per share data adj. for stk. divs.; EPS diluted. E-Estimated. NA-Not Available. NM-Not Meaningful. NR-Not Ranked. UR-Under Review.

**Office:** 20 S Wacker Dr, Chicago, IL 60606-7408.
**Telephone:** 312-930-1000.
**Email:** info@cme.com
**Website:** http://www.cme.com

**Chrmn:** L. Rosenberg
**Chrmn:** T.A. Duffy
**Pres:** P.S. Gill
**Vice Chrmn:** C.P. Carey

**CEO:** C.S. Donohue
**Investor Contact:** J. Peschier (312-930-8491)
**Board Members:** T. S. Bitsberger, C. P. Carey, M. Cermak, D. H. Chookaszian, J. M. Clegg, R. F. Corvino, J. A. Donaldson, C. S. Donohue, T. A. Duffy, M. J. Gepsman, L. G. Gerdes, D. R. Glickman, E. Harrington, J. D. Hastert, B. F. Johnson, G. M. Katler, P. B. Lynch, L. Melamed, W. Miller, II, J. Newsome, J. Niciforo, C. C. Odom, II, J. E. Oliff, J. L. Pietrzak, A. J. Pollock, D. Puth, L. Rosenberg, W. G. Salatich, Jr., J. F. Sandner, T. L. Savage, M. S. Scholes, W. R. Shepard, H. J. Siegel, R. H. Steele, C. Stewart, D. Suskind, D. J. Wescott

**Founded:** 1898
**Domicile:** Delaware
**Employees:** 1,970

The McGraw-Hill Companies

# CMS Energy Corp

STANDARD &POOR'S

| S&P Recommendation | HOLD ★★★☆☆ | Price $10.76 (as of Nov 14, 2008) | 12-Mo. Target Price $11.00 | Investment Style Large-Cap Value |
| --- | --- | --- | --- | --- |

**GICS Sector** Utilities
**Sub-Industry** Multi-Utilities

**Summary** This energy holding company's principal subsidiary is Consumers Energy, the largest utility in Michigan and the sixth largest gas and 13th largest electric utility in the U.S.

## Key Stock Statistics (Source S&P, Vickers, company reports)

| | | | | | | | |
| --- | --- | --- | --- | --- | --- | --- | --- |
| 52-Wk Range | $18.07– 8.33 | S&P Oper. EPS 2008E | 1.21 | Market Capitalization(B) | $2.434 | Beta | 1.02 |
| Trailing 12-Month EPS | $0.43 | S&P Oper. EPS 2009E | 1.23 | Yield (%) | 3.35 | S&P 3-Yr. Proj. EPS CAGR(%) | 16 |
| Trailing 12-Month P/E | 25.0 | P/E on S&P Oper. EPS 2008E | 8.9 | Dividend Rate/Share | $0.36 | S&P Credit Rating | BBB- |
| $10K Invested 5 Yrs Ago | $14,472 | Common Shares Outstg. (M) | 226.2 | Institutional Ownership (%) | NM | | |

## Price Performance

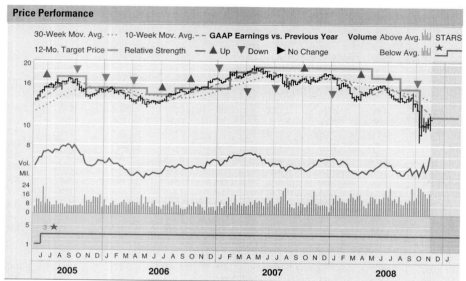

30-Week Mov. Avg. · · · · 10-Week Mov. Avg. – – GAAP Earnings vs. Previous Year Volume Above Avg. STARS
12-Mo. Target Price — Relative Strength — ▲ Up ▼ Down ► No Change Below Avg. ★

Options: ASE, CBOE, P, Ph

Analysis prepared by **Justin McCann** on November 10, 2008, when the stock traded at **$ 10.01**.

## Highlights

➤ We expect operating EPS in 2008 to advance about 44% from 2007 operating EPS of $0.84, which was down 22% from 2006's $1.08. The decline in 2007 reflected the absence of earnings from CMS's divested international businesses and non-utility gas assets in Michigan. The sharp rebound we project for 2008 reflects our expectation that the use of proceeds from asset sales for debt reduction and new investments will result in lower interest expenses and increased earnings. In the first nine months of 2008, operating EPS was $0.95, up 48% from $0.64 in the year-earlier period.

➤ For 2009, we expect operating EPS to increase less than 2% from anticipated results in 2008, reflecting rate base investments and increased operating efficiencies. However, while the auto sector accounted for only 5% of CMS's 2007 electric revenues and 3% of its operating income, we remain concerned about the continuing weakness in the Michigan economy.

➤ In October 2008, the governor of Michigan signed an energy reform package that would modify the state's electric choice program and establish a 12-month deadline for the regulatory resolution of utility rate cases.

## Investment Rationale/Risk

➤ The shares have dropped more than 40% year to date, reflecting, in our view, the crisis in the credit markets and its expected impact on the already weak Michigan economy. With CMS expected to contribute about $160 million to its underfunded pension plan in 2009, it has decided to defer about $180 million in its planned capital expenditures. While we see CMS's financial strength as having greatly improved, and its investment-grade rating restored, we believe that given the worsening outlook for the Michigan economy, there will only be a gradual recovery in the shares.

➤ Risks to our recommendation and target price include a slower-than-expected recovery in both the financial markets and the Michigan economy, as well as a further decrease in the average P/E of the group as a whole.

➤ The decline in share price, combined with the 80% increase in the dividend with the February 29 payment, has effectively raised the recent yield from 1.4% to about 3.5%. However, we do not believe that the still well below-peers yield will benefit the stock. Our 12-month target price is $11, a discount-to-peers P/E of about 8.9X our 2009 EPS estimate of $1.23.

## Qualitative Risk Assessment

| LOW | MEDIUM | HIGH |
| --- | --- | --- |

Our risk assessment reflects the steady cash flow from the regulated electric and gas utility businesses, which operate within a generally supportive regulatory environment, and a substantially improved financial risk profile. The company had used proceeds from recent asset sales to reduce its debt by about $650 million, and its credit rating has been restored to an investment-grade level with a stable outlook.

## Quantitative Evaluations

**S&P Quality Ranking** C

| D | C | B- | B | B+ | A- | A | A+ |
| --- | --- | --- | --- | --- | --- | --- | --- |

**Relative Strength Rank** STRONG

81

LOWEST = 1　　　　HIGHEST = 99

## Revenue/Earnings Data

**Revenue (Million $)**

| | 1Q | 2Q | 3Q | 4Q | Year |
| --- | --- | --- | --- | --- | --- |
| 2008 | 2,184 | 1,365 | 1,428 | -- | -- |
| 2007 | 2,237 | 1,319 | 1,282 | 1,674 | 6,464 |
| 2006 | 2,032 | 1,396 | 1,462 | 1,920 | 6,810 |
| 2005 | 1,845 | 1,230 | 1,307 | 1,906 | 6,288 |
| 2004 | 1,754 | 1,093 | 1,063 | 1,562 | 5,472 |
| 2003 | 1,968 | 1,126 | 1,047 | 1,372 | 5,513 |

**Earnings Per Share ($)**

| | 1Q | 2Q | 3Q | 4Q | Year |
| --- | --- | --- | --- | --- | --- |
| 2008 | 0.44 | 0.20 | 0.33 | E0.25 | E1.21 |
| 2007 | -0.16 | -0.26 | 0.34 | -0.56 | -0.62 |
| 2006 | -0.13 | 0.30 | -0.47 | -0.16 | -0.44 |
| 2005 | 0.74 | 0.12 | -1.21 | -0.09 | -0.51 |
| 2004 | -0.06 | 0.10 | 0.29 | 0.29 | 0.67 |
| 2003 | 0.47 | -0.08 | -0.47 | -0.22 | -0.30 |

Fiscal year ended Dec. 31. Next earnings report expected: Late February. EPS Estimates based on S&P Operating Earnings; historical GAAP earnings are as reported.

## Dividend Data (Dates: mm/dd Payment Date: mm/dd/yy)

| Amount ($) | Date Decl. | Ex-Div. Date | Stk. of Record | Payment Date |
| --- | --- | --- | --- | --- |
| 0.090 | 01/25 | 02/06 | 02/08 | 02/29/08 |
| 0.090 | 04/25 | 05/07 | 05/09 | 05/30/08 |
| 0.090 | 07/25 | 08/06 | 08/08 | 08/29/08 |
| 0.090 | 10/24 | 11/05 | 11/07 | 11/28/08 |

Dividends have been paid since 2007. Source: Company reports.

The McGraw-Hill Companies

# CMS Energy Corp

**STANDARD &POOR'S**

## Business Summary November 10, 2008

CORPORATE OVERVIEW. CMS Energy (CMS) is the energy holding company for Consumers Energy (formerly Consumers Power Co.), a regulated electric and gas utility serving Michigan's Lower Peninsula, and CMS Enterprises, which is engaged in U.S. and international energy-related businesses. CMS operates in three business segments: electric utility, gas utility, and enterprises. CMS's electric utility operations include generation, purchase, distribution and sale of electricity. CMS's gas utility purchases, transports, stores, distributes and sells natural gas. The Enterprises segment, through its various subsidiaries and equity investments, is engaged in diversified energy businesses, including independent power production, electric distribution, and natural gas transmission, storage and processing.

MARKET PROFILE. CMS's electric utility provides electricity to approximately 1.8 million customers in 61 of the 68 counties in the lower peninsula of Michi-

gan. In 2007, the electric utility had total electric deliveries of 39 billion kWh. Consumers' electric utility customer base includes a mix of residential, commercial and diversified industrial customers, the largest segment of which is the automotive industry, which accounted for about 5% of total electric revenues in 2007. CMS's gas utility serves some 1.7 million customers in 46 of the 68 counties in Michigan's lower peninsula. The gas utility also owned 1,671 miles of transmission lines at the end of 2007, and 15 gas storage fields in Michigan, with a storage capacity of 308 bcf. The electric utility segment accounted for 53.3% of consolidated revenues in 2007 (53.9% in 2006); the gas utility segment 40.5% (38.7%); Enterprises 5.9% (7.1%), and other 0.3% (0.2%).

## Company Financials Fiscal Year Ended Dec. 31

| Per Share Data ($) | 2007 | 2006 | 2005 | 2004 | 2003 | 2002 | 2001 | 2000 | 1999 | 1998 |
|---|---|---|---|---|---|---|---|---|---|---|
| Tangible Book Value | 9.46 | 9.90 | 10.53 | 10.51 | 9.69 | 7.47 | 8.11 | 12.15 | 13.23 | 20.30 |
| Earnings | -0.62 | -0.44 | -0.51 | 0.67 | -0.30 | -2.99 | -2.53 | 0.36 | 2.17 | 2.22 |
| S&P Core Earnings | -0.65 | -0.16 | -0.44 | 0.36 | 0.25 | -3.75 | -3.29 | NA | NA | NA |
| Dividends | 0.20 | Nil | Nil | Nil | Nil | 1.09 | 1.46 | 1.46 | 1.39 | 1.26 |
| Payout Ratio | NM | Nil | Nil | Nil | Nil | NM | NM | NM | 64% | 57% |
| Prices:High | 19.55 | 17.00 | 16.80 | 10.65 | 10.74 | 24.80 | 31.80 | 32.25 | 48.44 | 50.13 |
| Prices:Low | 14.98 | 12.09 | 9.70 | 7.81 | 3.41 | 5.45 | 19.49 | 16.06 | 30.31 | 38.75 |
| P/E Ratio:High | NM | NM | NM | 16 | NM | NM | NM | NM | 22 | 23 |
| P/E Ratio:Low | NM | NM | NM | 12 | NM | NM | NM | NM | 14 | 17 |

| Income Statement Analysis (Million $) | | | | | | | | | | |
|---|---|---|---|---|---|---|---|---|---|---|
| Revenue | 6,464 | 6,810 | 6,288 | 5,472 | 5,513 | 8,687 | 9,597 | 8,998 | 6,103 | 5,141 |
| Depreciation | 540 | 576 | 525 | 431 | 428 | 403 | 530 | 637 | 595 | 484 |
| Maintenance | 201 | 326 | 249 | 256 | 226 | 211 | 263 | 298 | 216 | 176 |
| Fixed Charges Coverage | 3.38 | 1.18 | -0.56 | 1.01 | 1.23 | 0.12 | 1.26 | 1.63 | 1.73 | 1.75 |
| Construction Credits | NA | NA | NA | NA | NA | NA | NA | NA | Nil | Nil |
| Effective Tax Rate | 63.3% | NM | NM | NM | NM | NM | NM | 57.7% | 18.8% | 29.2% |
| Net Income | -126 | -85.0 | -98.0 | 127 | -43.0 | -416 | -331 | 41.0 | 277 | 242 |
| S&P Core Earnings | -145 | -31.0 | -93.1 | 63.4 | 40.6 | -522 | -431 | NA | NA | NA |

| Balance Sheet & Other Financial Data (Million $) | | | | | | | | | | |
|---|---|---|---|---|---|---|---|---|---|---|
| Gross Property | 12,894 | 13,293 | 12,448 | 14,751 | 11,790 | 11,344 | 15,195 | 14,087 | 14,278 | 11,253 |
| Capital Expenditures | 1,263 | 670 | 593 | 525 | 535 | 747 | 1,262 | 1,032 | 1,124 | 1,295 |
| Net Property | 8,728 | 7,976 | 7,325 | 8,636 | 6,944 | 5,234 | 8,362 | 7,835 | 8,121 | 6,040 |
| Capitalization:Long Term Debt | 5,832 | 6,466 | 7,286 | 7,307 | 8,652 | 6,399 | 6,983 | 7,913 | 7,075 | 5,486 |
| Capitalization:% Long Term Debt | 71.0 | 72.2 | 73.8 | 75.8 | 84.5 | 85.0 | 78.7 | 77.0 | 74.2 | 71.2 |
| Capitalization:Preferred | 250 | 261 | 261 | 261 | Nil | Nil | Nil | Nil | Nil | Nil |
| Capitalization:% Preferred | 3.00 | 2.91 | 2.64 | 2.71 | Nil | Nil | Nil | Nil | Nil | Nil |
| Capitalization:Common | 2,130 | 2,234 | 2,322 | 2,072 | 1,585 | 1,133 | 1,890 | 2,361 | 2,456 | 2,216 |
| Capitalization:% Common | 25.9 | 24.9 | 23.5 | 21.5 | 15.5 | 15.0 | 21.3 | 23.0 | 25.8 | 28.8 |
| Total Capital | 8,265 | 9,234 | 10,566 | 11,123 | 11,010 | 8,058 | 9,834 | 11,221 | 10,359 | 8,486 |
| % Operating Ratio | 100.4 | 92.8 | 84.8 | 88.2 | 91.5 | 92.1 | 89.6 | 88.9 | 84.7 | 86.9 |
| % Earned on Net Property | 1.8 | NM | NM | 7.6 | 8.1 | 1.8 | 3.7 | 9.1 | 12.9 | 13.5 |
| % Return on Revenue | NM | NM | NM | 2.3 | NM | NM | NM | 0.5 | 4.5 | 4.7 |
| % Return on Invested Capital | 4.4 | 8.1 | 11.0 | 9.5 | 6.7 | 7.9 | 9.4 | 9.5 | 10.0 | 12.0 |
| % Return on Common Equity | NM | NM | NM | 6.3 | NM | NM | NM | 1.7 | 11.9 | 11.5 |

Data as orig reptd.; bef. results of disc opers/spec. items. Per share data adj. for stk. divs.; EPS diluted. E-Estimated. NA-Not Available. NM-Not Meaningful. NR-Not Ranked. UR-Under Review.

**Office:** One Energy Plaza Dr, Jackson, MI 49201-2357.
**Telephone:** 517-788-0550.
**Email:** invest@cmsenergy.com
**Website:** http://www.cmsenergy.com

**Chrmn:** K. Whipple, Jr.
**Pres & CEO:** D.W. Joos
**EVP & CFO:** T.J. Webb
**SVP & Chief Admin Officer:** J.M. Butler

**SVP & General Counsel:** J.E. Brunner
**Investor Contact:** L.L. Mountcastle (517-788-2590)
**Board Members:** M. S. Ayres, J. E. Barfield, R. M. Gabrys, D. W. Joos, P. R. Lochner, Jr., M. T. Monahan, J. F. Paquette, Jr., P. A. Pierre, K. L. Way, K. Whipple, Jr., J. B. Yasinsky

**Founded:** 1987
**Domicile:** Michigan
**Employees:** 7,898

*The McGraw-Hill Companies*

# Coach Inc.

STANDARD &POOR'S

| S&P Recommendation | STRONG BUY ★★★★★ | Price $16.20 (as of Nov 14, 2008) | 12-Mo. Target Price $35.00 | Investment Style Large-Cap Growth |
|---|---|---|---|---|

**GICS Sector** Consumer Discretionary
**Sub-Industry** Apparel, Accessories & Luxury Goods

**Summary** COH designs, makes and markets fine accessories for women and men, including handbags, weekend and travel accessories, outerwear, footwear and business cases.

## Key Stock Statistics (Source S&P, Vickers, company reports)

| | | | | | | | |
|---|---|---|---|---|---|---|---|
| 52-Wk Range | $38.17– 14.52 | S&P Oper. EPS 2009E | 2.25 | Market Capitalization(B) | $5.296 | Beta | 1.69 |
| Trailing 12-Month EPS | $2.22 | S&P Oper. EPS 2010E | 2.70 | Yield (%) | Nil | S&P 3-Yr. Proj. EPS CAGR(%) | 18 |
| Trailing 12-Month P/E | 7.3 | P/E on S&P Oper. EPS 2009E | 7.2 | Dividend Rate/Share | Nil | S&P Credit Rating | NA |
| $10K Invested 5 Yrs Ago | $8,594 | Common Shares Outstg. (M) | 326.9 | Institutional Ownership (%) | 94 | | |

## Price Performance

30-Week Mov. Avg. · · · ·   10-Week Mov. Avg. – – –   **GAAP Earnings vs. Previous Year**   Volume Above Avg. |||| STARS
12-Mo. Target Price —   Relative Strength —   ▲ Up  ▼ Down  ▶ No Change   Below Avg. |||| ★

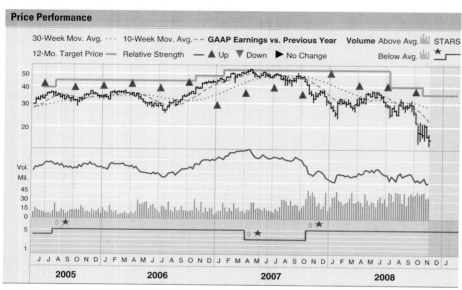

Options: ASE, CBOE, P, Ph

Analysis prepared by **Marie Driscoll, CFA** on October 27, 2008, when the stock traded at **$ 16.66**.

## Highlights

➤ We see ample opportunities for COH to further penetrate the U.S. premium handbag and accessories market, via new store openings, product evolution, and its unique positioning as 'accessible luxury'. We see COH's Japanese market share at 15%+ by 2010, up from 13%, and developing markets, specifically China, providing significant growth prospects as COH opens 50 stores over the coming five years.

➤ We project 10% sales growth for FY 09 (Jun.), down from the 22% increase in FY 08, reflecting muted consumer spending trends expected for the coming 12-18 month period. We see a 20% boost in selling square footage as COH opens approximately 40 North American stores and 10 Japanese stores annually. We project same-store sales to be flat to up 2% at U.S. retail locations, driven by strength in the outlet channel and about a 10% gain in the indirect channel.

➤ We look for a 170 basis point gross margin contraction, to 74% of sales, in FY 09, along with a 150 bps SG&A expense de-leverage reflecting international investment spending. We estimate an EBIT (earnings before interest and taxes) margin of 34%.

## Investment Rationale/Risk

➤ We see favorable long-term sales and earnings prospects for COH and expect prevailing retail weakness to be mitigated by a steady flow of innovative new product at sharp price points this fall and holiday season. September quarter comps rose 1%, as outlet locations post traffic and productivity gains offset by declines at full-price locations due to reduced traffic. Productivity and profitability metrics are more than double those of COH's specialty apparel peers, at an estimated $2,200 trailing 12-months sales per square foot and a 35% EBIT margin. We see the steady flow of new products, elevated service levels and successful brand extensions supporting a three-year EPS CAGR of 18%.

➤ Risks to our recommendation and target price include changes in consumer spending patterns, and risks associated with sourcing, fashion and inventory.

➤ COH recently traded at 7.6X our FY 09 EPS estimate of $2.25, about a 20% discount to specialty apparel retail peers. Our 12-month target price of $35 represents about 16X our FY 09 EPS forecast, a 20% discount to COH's historical five-year average forward P/E of 20X.

## Qualitative Risk Assessment

| LOW | MEDIUM | HIGH |
|---|---|---|

Our risk assessment reflects our view of COH's strong brand equity and growing cash flow, offset by a highly competitive market amid retail consolidation.

## Quantitative Evaluations

**S&P Quality Ranking**                              NR

| D | C | B- | B | B+ | A- | A | A+ |
|---|---|---|---|---|---|---|---|

**Relative Strength Rank**                       MODERATE

40

LOWEST = 1                                      HIGHEST = 99

## Revenue/Earnings Data

**Revenue (Million $)**

| | 1Q | 2Q | 3Q | 4Q | Year |
|---|---|---|---|---|---|
| 2009 | 752.5 | -- | | | |
| 2008 | 676.7 | 978.0 | 744.5 | 781.5 | 3,181 |
| 2007 | 529.4 | 805.6 | 625.3 | 652.1 | 2,612 |
| 2006 | 449.0 | 650.3 | 497.9 | 514.4 | 2,112 |
| 2005 | 344.1 | 531.8 | 415.9 | 418.7 | 1,710 |
| 2004 | 258.4 | 411.5 | 313.1 | 338.2 | 1,321 |

**Earnings Per Share ($)**

| | 1Q | 2Q | 3Q | 4Q | Year |
|---|---|---|---|---|---|
| 2009 | 0.44 | E0.77 | E0.50 | E0.54 | E2.25 |
| 2008 | 0.41 | 0.69 | 0.46 | 0.62 | 2.17 |
| 2007 | 0.31 | 0.57 | 0.39 | 0.42 | 1.69 |
| 2006 | 0.24 | 0.45 | 0.28 | 0.31 | 1.27 |
| 2005 | 0.17 | 0.34 | 0.23 | 0.25 | 1.00 |
| 2004 | 0.11 | 0.25 | 0.15 | 0.17 | 0.68 |

Fiscal year ended Jun. 30. Next earnings report expected: Late January. EPS Estimates based on S&P Operating Earnings; historical GAAP earnings are as reported.

## Dividend Data

No cash dividends have been paid.

# Coach Inc.

**STANDARD &POOR'S**

## Business Summary October 27, 2008

CORPORATE OVERVIEW. Coach is a leading U.S. designer and marketer of high-quality accessories. Founded in 1941, COH has over the past several years transformed the Coach brand, building on its popular core categories by introducing new products in a broader array of materials, styles and categories. The company has also implemented a flexible sourcing and manufacturing model, which it believes enables it to bring a broader range of products to market more rapidly and efficiently.

MARKET PROFILE. Coach is the number one luxury accessories brand in the U.S., with an estimated 20% share of this estimated $8.7 billion market ($100+ handbags). This sub-segment of the handbag/accessories market grew at an estimated 20% pace in 2007 and 2006, 17% in 2005, 30% in 2004, and 23% in 2003. While growth has slowed in 2008 to a 5% -10% pace, it remains one of the best performing categories at retail. Moreover, COH has been able to out-

pace industry growth and add an estimated six market share points in the 2002-2007 period, as it executed its multi-channel growth strategy and continued to do so in 2008, as sales grew 18%. The Japanese consumer makes up about 40% of the global luxury handbag market. COH estimates that it currently has 13% of the domestic Japanese market, and aims to increase its share to 15% over the next five years by expansion and opening new stores. Developing markets represent the next leg of growth, supporting a global market projected at $25 billion in 2010. With a total of 27 locations in Greater China, COH currently holds an estimated 4% share of the market.

## Company Financials Fiscal Year Ended Jun. 30

| Per Share Data ($) | 2008 | 2007 | 2006 | 2005 | 2004 | 2003 | 2002 | 2001 | 2000 | 1999 |
|---|---|---|---|---|---|---|---|---|---|---|
| Tangible Book Value | 3.73 | 4.52 | 2.57 | 2.07 | 2.00 | 1.11 | 0.67 | 0.43 | 0.15 | NA |
| Cash Flow | NA | 1.90 | 1.44 | 1.14 | 0.79 | 0.48 | 0.31 | 0.24 | 0.17 | NA |
| Earnings | 2.17 | 1.69 | 1.27 | 1.00 | 0.68 | 0.40 | 0.24 | 0.19 | 0.10 | NA |
| S&P Core Earnings | 2.17 | 1.69 | 1.26 | 0.91 | 0.61 | 0.35 | 0.21 | 0.17 | NA | NA |
| Dividends | Nil | Nil | Nil | Nil | Nil | Nil | Nil | Nil | NA | NA |
| Payout Ratio | Nil | Nil | Nil | Nil | Nil | Nil | Nil | Nil | NA | NA |
| Prices:High | 37.64 | 54.00 | 44.99 | 36.84 | 28.85 | 20.42 | 8.93 | 5.34 | 3.67 | NA |
| Prices:Low | 14.52 | 29.22 | 25.18 | 24.51 | 16.88 | 7.26 | 4.30 | 2.50 | 2.00 | NA |
| P/E Ratio:High | 17 | 32 | 35 | 37 | 42 | 52 | 38 | 28 | NM | NA |
| P/E Ratio:Low | 7 | 17 | 20 | 25 | 25 | 18 | 18 | 13 | NM | NA |

| Income Statement Analysis (Million $) | 2008 | 2007 | 2006 | 2005 | 2004 | 2003 | 2002 | 2001 | 2000 | 1999 |
|---|---|---|---|---|---|---|---|---|---|---|
| Revenue | 3,181 | 2,612 | 2,112 | 1,710 | 1,321 | 953 | 719 | 616 | 549 | 508 |
| Operating Income | NA | 1,074 | 830 | 679 | 487 | 274 | 163 | 130 | 78.5 | NA |
| Depreciation | 101 | 80.9 | 65.1 | 57.0 | 42.9 | 30.2 | 25.5 | 24.1 | 22.6 | 22.3 |
| Interest Expense | NA | Nil | Nil | 1.22 | 0.81 | 0.70 | 1.12 | 2.26 | 6.60 | NA |
| Pretax Income | 1,195 | 1,035 | 797 | 638 | 448 | 245 | 133 | 99.4 | 51.1 | 19.1 |
| Effective Tax Rate | 34.5% | 38.5% | 38.0% | 36.9% | 37.5% | 37.0% | 35.5% | 35.6% | 30.6% | 12.3% |
| Net Income | 783 | 637 | 494 | 389 | 262 | 147 | 85.8 | 64.0 | 35.4 | 16.7 |
| S&P Core Earnings | 783 | 637 | 492 | 356 | 236 | 129 | 74.9 | 58.3 | NA | NA |

| Balance Sheet & Other Financial Data (Million $) | 2008 | 2007 | 2006 | 2005 | 2004 | 2003 | 2002 | 2001 | 2000 | 1999 |
|---|---|---|---|---|---|---|---|---|---|---|
| Cash | 699 | 557 | 143 | 155 | 263 | 229 | 94.0 | 3.69 | NA | 0.15 |
| Current Assets | NA | 1,740 | 974 | 709 | 706 | 449 | 288 | 152 | 134 | NA |
| Total Assets | 2,274 | 2,450 | 1,627 | 1,347 | 1,029 | 618 | 441 | 259 | 233 | 282 |
| Current Liabilities | NA | 408 | 342 | 266 | 182 | 161 | 159 | 104 | 79.6 | NA |
| Long Term Debt | NA | 2.87 | 3.10 | 3.27 | 3.42 | 3.54 | 3.62 | 3.69 | 87.8 | NA |
| Common Equity | 1,516 | 1,910 | 1,189 | 1,033 | 782 | 427 | 260 | 148 | 65.0 | 203 |
| Total Capital | NA | 1,950 | 1,223 | 1,041 | 842 | 453 | 279 | 152 | 153 | NA |
| Capital Expenditures | 175 | 141 | 134 | 94.6 | 67.7 | 57.1 | 42.8 | 31.9 | 26.1 | 13.5 |
| Cash Flow | NA | 717 | 559 | 446 | 305 | 177 | 111 | 88.2 | 58.0 | NA |
| Current Ratio | 3.1 | 4.3 | 2.9 | 2.7 | 3.9 | 2.8 | 1.8 | 1.5 | 1.7 | 1.7 |
| % Long Term Debt of Capitalization | 0.2 | 0.1 | 0.3 | 0.3 | 0.4 | 0.8 | 1.3 | 2.4 | 57.4 | 1.8 |
| % Net Income of Revenue | 24.6 | 24.4 | 23.4 | 22.7 | 19.8 | 15.4 | 11.9 | 10.4 | 6.4 | 3.3 |
| % Return on Assets | 33.2 | 31.2 | 33.0 | 32.5 | 31.8 | 27.7 | 24.5 | 23.1 | 13.3 | 6.2 |
| % Return on Equity | 45.7 | 41.1 | 44.0 | 42.8 | 43.3 | 42.7 | 42.0 | 35.5 | 18.6 | 8.6 |

Data as orig reptd.; bef. results of disc opers/spec. items. Per share data adj. for stk. divs.; EPS diluted. E-Estimated. NA-Not Available. NM-Not Meaningful. NR-Not Ranked. UR-Under Review.

**Office:** 516 W 34th St, New York, NY 10001-1394.
**Telephone:** 212-594-1850.
**Email:** info@coach.com
**Website:** http://www.coach.com

**Chrmn & CEO:** L. Frankfort
**COO & Co-Pres:** J. Stritzke
**EVP, CFO & Chief Acctg Officer:** M.F. Devine, III
**SVP, Secy & General Counsel:** T. Kahn

**Treas:** N. Walsh
**Investor Contact:** M. Devine (212-594-1850)
**Board Members:** L. Frankfort, S. J. Kropf, G. W. Loveman, I. M. Menezes, I. R. Miller, K. Monda, M. Murphy, J. J. Zeitlin

**Founded:** 1941
**Domicile:** Maryland
**Employees:** 12,000

**The McGraw-Hill Companies**

# Coca-Cola Co (The)

**STANDARD &POOR'S**

| S&P Recommendation | STRONG BUY ★ ★ ★ ★ ★ | Price<br>$45.02 (as of Nov 14, 2008) | 12-Mo. Target Price<br>$55.00 | Investment Style<br>Large-Cap Growth |
|---|---|---|---|---|

**GICS Sector** Consumer Staples
**Sub-Industry** Soft Drinks

**Summary** The world's largest soft drink company, KO also has a sizable fruit juice business. Its bottling interests include a 36% stake in NYSE-listed Coca-Cola Enterprises (CCE).

## Key Stock Statistics (Source S&P, Vickers, company reports)

| | | | | | | | |
|---|---|---|---|---|---|---|---|
| 52-Wk Range | $65.59– 40.29 | S&P Oper. EPS 2008**E** | 3.17 | Market Capitalization(B) | $104.156 | Beta | 0.62 |
| Trailing 12-Month EPS | $2.57 | S&P Oper. EPS 2009**E** | 3.45 | Yield (%) | 3.38 | S&P 3-Yr. Proj. EPS CAGR(%) | 11 |
| Trailing 12-Month P/E | 17.5 | P/E on S&P Oper. EPS 2008**E** | 14.2 | Dividend Rate/Share | $1.52 | S&P Credit Rating | A+ |
| $10K Invested 5 Yrs Ago | $10,937 | Common Shares Outstg. (M) | 2,313.6 | Institutional Ownership (%) | 65 | | |

## Price Performance

30-Week Mov. Avg. · · · 10-Week Mov. Avg. - - **GAAP Earnings vs. Previous Year** Volume Above Avg. STARS

12-Mo. Target Price — Relative Strength — ▲ Up ▼ Down ► No Change Below Avg. ★

Options: ASE, CBOE, P, Ph

Analysis prepared by **Esther Y. Kwon, CFA** on October 15, 2008, when the stock traded at **$ 45.45**.

## Highlights

➤ In 2007, KO acquired Energy Brands (known as glaceau), maker of vitaminwater, for $4.1 billion. We expect the deal to accelerate the growth of KO's non-carb beverage business, an area in which it has lagged chief competitor PepsiCo (PEP: buy, $64). KO's long-term financial objectives include 3% to 4% annual volume growth, 6% to 8% operating income growth, and EPS growth in the high single digits.

➤ For 2008, we see sales growth of 13% on higher prices, positive foreign currency and as distribution for Energy Brands' products is expanded, both domestically and internationally. We look for mid-single digit growth in volumes, with sparkling beverage volumes increasing at a low single digit rate and still beverages up over 10%. We expect operating profits to rise about 17%, as a more favorable product mix, lean initiatives and improved leverage are partially offset by higher commodity costs and healthy marketing spend.

➤ Based on higher interest expense from increased debt to fund 2007 acquisitions, we expect EPS of $3.17 in 2008, up 17% from operating EPS of $2.70 in 2007. In 2009, we see EPS of $3.45.

## Investment Rationale/Risk

➤ We look for volumes in KO's non-carb portfolio to continue to be healthy, as the company widens distribution for its Energy Brands unit in 2008, and for its premium pricing to hold. We view KO's long-term growth targets as reasonable, particularly in light of its high exposure to international markets, which should offset low single digit volume declines at the Coke brand in the U.S. On increasing trial and awareness, we see Coca-Cola Zero driving trademark Coca-Cola volumes worldwide.

➤ Risks to our recommendation and target price include an inability to meet growth targets, adverse foreign currency movements, and unfavorable weather conditions in the company's markets. With regard to corporate governance, we would favor the separation of the chairman and CEO roles.

➤ Our 12-month target price of $55 is based on an analysis of historical and comparative peer P/E multiples. KO's forward P/E has ranged between 16X and 28X over the past few years, while PepsiCo's has been slightly lower. Given a more challenging economic environment, we think a multiple in the lower end of that range and a premium to PepsiCo is appropriate.

## Qualitative Risk Assessment

| LOW | MEDIUM | HIGH |
|---|---|---|

Our risk assessment for the Coca-Cola Company reflects the relatively stable nature of the company's end markets, its dominant market share positions around the world, and our view of its strong balance sheet and cash flow.

## Quantitative Evaluations

**S&P Quality Ranking** A

| D | C | B- | B | B+ | A- | A | A+ |
|---|---|---|---|---|---|---|---|

**Relative Strength Rank** STRONG

79

LOWEST = 1 HIGHEST = 99

## Revenue/Earnings Data

**Revenue (Million $)**

| | 1Q | 2Q | 3Q | 4Q | Year |
|---|---|---|---|---|---|
| 2008 | 7,379 | 9,046 | 8,393 | -- | -- |
| 2007 | 6,103 | 7,733 | 7,690 | 7,331 | 28,857 |
| 2006 | 5,226 | 6,476 | 6,454 | 5,932 | 24,088 |
| 2005 | 5,206 | 6,310 | 6,037 | 5,551 | 23,104 |
| 2004 | 5,078 | 5,965 | 5,662 | 5,257 | 21,962 |
| 2003 | 4,502 | 5,695 | 5,671 | 5,176 | 21,044 |

**Earnings Per Share ($)**

| | | | | | |
|---|---|---|---|---|---|
| 2008 | 0.64 | 0.61 | 0.81 | E0.66 | E3.17 |
| 2007 | 0.54 | 0.80 | 0.71 | 0.52 | 2.57 |
| 2006 | 0.47 | 0.78 | 0.62 | 0.29 | 2.16 |
| 2005 | 0.42 | 0.72 | 0.54 | 0.36 | 2.04 |
| 2004 | 0.46 | 0.65 | 0.39 | 0.50 | 2.00 |
| 2003 | 0.34 | 0.55 | 0.50 | 0.38 | 1.77 |

Fiscal year ended Dec. 31. Next earnings report expected: Mid February. EPS Estimates based on S&P Operating Earnings; historical GAAP earnings are as reported.

## Dividend Data (Dates: mm/dd Payment Date: mm/dd/yy)

| Amount ($) | Date Decl. | Ex-Div. Date | Stk. of Record | Payment Date |
|---|---|---|---|---|
| 0.380 | 02/21 | 03/12 | 03/15 | 04/01/08 |
| 0.380 | 04/17 | 06/11 | 06/15 | 07/01/08 |
| 0.380 | 07/17 | 09/11 | 09/15 | 10/01/08 |
| 0.380 | 10/16 | 11/26 | 12/01 | 12/15/08 |

Dividends have been paid since 1893. Source: Company reports.

---

**Please read the Required Disclosures and Analyst Certification on the last page of this report.**

# Coca-Cola Co (The)

**STANDARD &POOR'S**

## Business Summary October 15, 2008

CORPORATE OVERVIEW. The Coca-Cola Company is the world's largest producer of soft drink concentrates and syrups, as well as the world's biggest producer of juice and juice-related products. Finished soft drink products bearing the company's trademarks have been sold in the U.S. since 1886, and are now sold in more than 200 countries. Sales by operating segment in 2007 were derived as follows: North America (26.9% of revenues); Bottling Investments (26.2%); European Union (14.4%); Pacific (13.9%); Latin America (10.6%); Africa (4.4%); Eurasia (3.4%); and Corporate (0.2%)

The company's business encompasses the production and sale of soft drink and non-carbonated beverage concentrates and syrups. These products are sold to the company's authorized independent and company-owned bottling/canning operations, and fountain wholesalers. These customers then either combine the syrup with carbonated water, or combine the concentrate with sweetener, water and carbonated water to produce finished soft drinks. The finished soft drinks are packaged in containers bearing the company's well-known trademarks, which include Coca-Cola Classic (the best-selling soft drink in the world), caffeine free Coca-Cola, diet Coke (sold as Coke light in many markets outside the U.S.), Cherry Coke, Vanilla Coke, Coke Zero, Fanta, Full Throttle, Sprite, diet Sprite/Sprite Zero, Barq's, Surge, Mr. PiBB, Mello Yello, TAB, Fresca, Hi-C, Fruitopia, and other products developed for specific markets. The company also markets the Schweppes and Canada Dry mixer

(such as tonic water, club soda and ginger ale), Crush and Dr. Pepper brands in more than 160 countries outside the U.S. In 2007, concentrates and syrups for beverages bearing the trademark "Coca-Cola" or including the trademark "Coke" accounted for approximately 53% of the company's total concentrate sales.

In 2007, concentrate sales in the U.S. represented approximately 24% of KO's worldwide sales. About 56% of concentrate sales were beverage concentrates and syrups to 76 authorized bottlers in 393 licensed territories, 33% were fountain syrups sold to fountain retailers, and 491 fountain wholesalers, and the remaining 11% were sales by the company of finished products.

KO has equity positions in approximately 46 unconsolidated bottling, canning and distribution operations for its products worldwide, including bottlers that accounted for approximately 56% of the company's worldwide unit case volume in 2007. Coca-Cola Enterprises (CCE) accounted for approximately 48% of the company's U.S. concentrate sales. KO holds a 35% equity interest in CCE.

## Company Financials Fiscal Year Ended Dec. 31

| Per Share Data ($) | 2007 | 2006 | 2005 | 2004 | 2003 | 2002 | 2001 | 2000 | 1999 | 1998 |
|---|---|---|---|---|---|---|---|---|---|---|
| Tangible Book Value | 8.53 | 5.08 | 5.29 | 5.02 | 4.14 | 3.34 | 3.53 | 2.98 | 3.06 | 3.19 |
| Cash Flow | 3.00 | 2.56 | 2.43 | 2.36 | 2.11 | 1.93 | 1.92 | 1.19 | 1.30 | 1.67 |
| Earnings | 2.57 | 2.16 | 2.04 | 2.00 | 1.77 | 1.60 | 1.60 | 0.88 | 0.98 | 1.42 |
| S&P Core Earnings | 2.51 | 2.04 | 2.03 | 2.08 | 1.77 | 1.62 | 1.46 | NA | NA | NA |
| Dividends | 1.36 | 1.24 | 1.12 | 1.00 | 0.88 | 0.80 | 0.72 | 0.68 | 0.64 | 0.60 |
| Payout Ratio | 53% | 57% | 55% | 50% | 50% | 50% | 45% | 77% | 65% | 42% |
| Prices:High | 64.32 | 49.35 | 45.26 | 53.50 | 50.90 | 57.91 | 62.19 | 66.88 | 70.88 | 88.94 |
| Prices:Low | 45.56 | 39.36 | 40.31 | 38.30 | 37.01 | 42.90 | 42.37 | 42.88 | 47.31 | 53.63 |
| P/E Ratio:High | 25 | 23 | 22 | 27 | 29 | 36 | 39 | 76 | 72 | 63 |
| P/E Ratio:Low | 18 | 18 | 20 | 19 | 21 | 27 | 26 | 49 | 48 | 38 |

| Income Statement Analysis (Million $) | | | | | | | | | | |
|---|---|---|---|---|---|---|---|---|---|---|
| Revenue | 28,857 | 24,088 | 23,104 | 21,962 | 21,044 | 19,564 | 20,092 | 20,458 | 19,805 | 18,813 |
| Operating Income | 8,532 | 7,246 | 7,017 | 6,591 | 6,071 | 6,264 | 6,155 | 4,464 | 4,774 | 5,612 |
| Depreciation | 1,012 | 938 | 932 | 893 | 850 | 806 | 803 | 773 | 792 | 645 |
| Interest Expense | 456 | 220 | 240 | 196 | 178 | 199 | 289 | 447 | 337 | 277 |
| Pretax Income | 7,873 | 6,578 | 6,690 | 6,222 | 5,495 | 5,499 | 5,670 | 3,399 | 3,819 | 5,198 |
| Effective Tax Rate | 24.0% | 22.8% | 27.2% | 22.1% | 20.9% | 27.7% | 29.8% | 36.0% | 36.3% | 32.0% |
| Net Income | 5,981 | 5,080 | 4,872 | 4,847 | 4,347 | 3,976 | 3,979 | 2,177 | 2,431 | 3,533 |
| S&P Core Earnings | 5,827 | 4,797 | 4,854 | 5,063 | 4,350 | 4,021 | 3,654 | NA | NA | NA |

| Balance Sheet & Other Financial Data (Million $) | | | | | | | | | | |
|---|---|---|---|---|---|---|---|---|---|---|
| Cash | 4,308 | 2,590 | 4,767 | 6,768 | 3,482 | 2,345 | 1,934 | 1,892 | 1,812 | 1,807 |
| Current Assets | 12,105 | 8,441 | 10,250 | 12,094 | 8,396 | 7,352 | 7,171 | 6,620 | 6,480 | 6,380 |
| Total Assets | 43,269 | 29,963 | 29,427 | 31,327 | 27,342 | 24,501 | 22,417 | 20,834 | 21,623 | 19,145 |
| Current Liabilities | 13,225 | 8,890 | 9,836 | 10,971 | 7,886 | 7,341 | 8,429 | 9,321 | 9,856 | 8,640 |
| Long Term Debt | 9,329 | 1,314 | 1,154 | 1,157 | 2,517 | 2,701 | 1,219 | 835 | 854 | 687 |
| Common Equity | 21,744 | 16,920 | 16,355 | 15,935 | 14,090 | 11,800 | 11,366 | 9,316 | 9,513 | 8,403 |
| Total Capital | 27,269 | 18,842 | 17,861 | 17,542 | 16,944 | 14,900 | 13,027 | 10,509 | 10,865 | 9,514 |
| Capital Expenditures | 1,648 | 1,407 | 899 | 755 | 812 | 851 | 769 | 733 | 1,069 | 863 |
| Cash Flow | 6,993 | 6,018 | 5,804 | 5,740 | 5,197 | 4,782 | 4,782 | 2,950 | 3,223 | 4,178 |
| Current Ratio | 0.9 | 0.9 | 1.0 | 1.1 | 1.1 | 1.0 | 0.9 | 0.7 | 0.7 | 0.7 |
| % Long Term Debt of Capitalization | 12.9 | 7.0 | 6.5 | 6.6 | 14.9 | 18.1 | 9.4 | 7.9 | 7.9 | 7.2 |
| % Net Income of Revenue | 20.7 | 21.1 | 21.1 | 22.1 | 20.7 | 20.3 | 19.8 | 10.6 | 12.3 | 18.8 |
| % Return on Assets | 16.3 | 17.1 | 16.0 | 16.5 | 16.8 | 16.9 | 18.4 | 10.3 | 11.9 | 19.6 |
| % Return on Equity | 30.9 | 30.5 | 30.2 | 32.3 | 33.6 | 34.3 | 38.5 | 23.1 | 27.1 | 45.0 |

Data as orig reptd.; bef. results of disc opers/spec. items. Per share data adj. for stk. divs.; EPS diluted. E-Estimated. NA-Not Available. NM-Not Meaningful. NR-Not Ranked. UR-Under Review.

**Office:** 1 Coca Cola Plz NW, Atlanta, GA 30313-2499.
**Telephone:** 404-676-2121.
**Website:** http://www.coca-cola.com
**Chrmn:** E.N. Isdell

**Chrmn:** Z.W. Khouri
**Pres, CEO & COO:** M. Kent
**Investor Contact:** G.P. Fayard
**EVP & CFO:** G.P. Fayard

**Board Members:** H. Allen, R. W. Allen, C. P. Black, B. Diller, A. Herman, E. N. Isdell, M. Kent, D. R. Keough, Z. W. Khouri, M. E. Lagomasino, D. McHenry, S. A. Nunn, J. D. Robinson, III, P. V. Ueberroth, J. Wallenberg, J. B. Williams

**Founded:** 1886
**Domicile:** Delaware
**Employees:** 90,500

# Coca-Cola Enterprises Inc.

**STANDARD &POOR'S**

| S&P Recommendation | HOLD ★★★☆☆ | Price | 12-Mo. Target Price | Investment Style |
|---|---|---|---|---|
| | | $9.17 (as of Nov 14, 2008) | $10.00 | Large-Cap Blend |

**GICS Sector** Consumer Staples
**Sub-Industry** Soft Drinks

**Summary** This company is the world's largest bottler of Coca-Cola beverage products, distributing to about 78% of the North American market. Coca-Cola Co. holds 36% of CCE's common stock.

## Key Stock Statistics (Source S&P, Vickers, company reports)

| | | | | | | | |
|---|---|---|---|---|---|---|---|
| 52-Wk Range | $27.09– 8.25 | S&P Oper. EPS 2008E | 1.27 | Market Capitalization(B) | $0.449 | Beta | 0.85 |
| Trailing 12-Month EPS | $-5.75 | S&P Oper. EPS 2009E | 1.35 | Yield (%) | 3.05 | S&P 3-Yr. Proj. EPS CAGR(%) | 6 |
| Trailing 12-Month P/E | NM | P/E on S&P Oper. EPS 2008E | 7.2 | Dividend Rate/Share | $0.28 | S&P Credit Rating | A |
| $10K Invested 5 Yrs Ago | $4,772 | Common Shares Outstg. (M) | 48.9 | Institutional Ownership (%) | NM | | |

## Price Performance

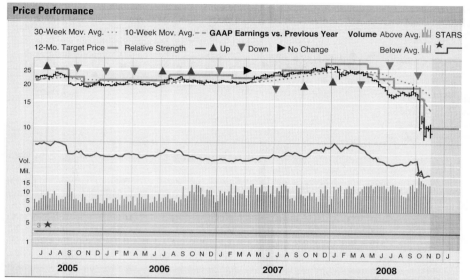

30-Week Mov. Avg. · · · 10-Week Mov. Avg. — — **GAAP Earnings vs. Previous Year** Volume Above Avg. STARS
12-Mo. Target Price — Relative Strength — ▲ Up ▼ Down ▶ No Change Below Avg. ★

Options: ASE, CBOE, P, Ph

Analysis prepared by **Esther Y. Kwon, CFA** on October 23, 2008, when the stock traded at **$ 8.80**.

## Qualitative Risk Assessment

| LOW | MEDIUM | HIGH |
|---|---|---|

Our risk assessment for Coca-Cola Enterprises reflects our view of the relatively stable nature of the company's end markets, its strong cash flow, and its relationship with corporate partner Coca-Cola Company.

## Quantitative Evaluations

**S&P Quality Ranking**     B

| D | C | B- | B | B+ | A- | A | A+ |
|---|---|---|---|---|---|---|---|

**Relative Strength Rank**     MODERATE

34

LOWEST = 1     HIGHEST = 99

## Revenue/Earnings Data

**Revenue (Million $)**

| | 1Q | 2Q | 3Q | 4Q | Year |
|---|---|---|---|---|---|
| 2008 | 4,892 | 5,935 | 5,743 | -- | -- |
| 2007 | 4,567 | 5,665 | 5,405 | 5,299 | 20,936 |
| 2006 | 4,333 | 5,467 | 5,218 | 4,786 | 19,804 |
| 2005 | 4,196 | 5,128 | 4,895 | 4,487 | 18,706 |
| 2004 | 4,240 | 4,844 | 4,670 | 4,404 | 18,158 |
| 2003 | 3,667 | 4,617 | 4,734 | 4,312 | 17,330 |

**Earnings Per Share ($)**

| | | | | | |
|---|---|---|---|---|---|
| 2008 | 0.02 | -6.53 | 0.44 | E0.16 | E1.27 |
| 2007 | 0.03 | 0.56 | 0.55 | 0.32 | 1.46 |
| 2006 | 0.03 | 0.71 | 0.44 | -3.59 | -2.41 |
| 2005 | 0.10 | 0.70 | 0.40 | -0.12 | 1.08 |
| 2004 | 0.22 | 0.43 | 0.44 | 0.17 | 1.26 |
| 2003 | 0.06 | 0.56 | 0.56 | 0.28 | 1.48 |

Fiscal year ended Dec. 31. Next earnings report expected: Mid February. EPS Estimates based on S&P Operating Earnings; historical GAAP earnings are as reported.

## Dividend Data (Dates: mm/dd Payment Date: mm/dd/yy)

| Amount ($) | Date Decl. | Ex-Div. Date | Stk. of Record | Payment Date |
|---|---|---|---|---|
| 0.070 | 02/12 | 03/12 | 03/14 | 03/27/08 |
| 0.070 | 04/22 | 06/11 | 06/13 | 06/26/08 |
| 0.070 | 07/22 | 09/10 | 09/12 | 09/25/08 |
| 0.070 | 10/22 | 11/25 | 11/28 | 12/11/08 |

Dividends have been paid since 1986. Source: Company reports.

## Highlights

➤ In 2008, we expect net revenues to advance at a low single digit rate, reflecting an increase of 4% to 6% in net revenues per case on higher pricing and mix benefits from glaceau, FUZE and Campbell products and a modest positive impact from foreign currency translations. We project that North American volumes will decline due to higher pricing, continued weakness in carbonated soft drinks (CSDs), and softness in the economically sensitive single-serve category.

➤ We see gross margins coming under pressure, as higher pricing is offset by rising sweetener, energy and packaging costs and a mix shift away from higher margin single-serve sales toward lower margin glaceau products. We estimate SG&A expenses will remain flat as a percentage of sales as CCE implements restructuring measures and cost cuts offset some sales deleverage and less funding from Coca-Cola.

➤ On a lower tax rate, we estimate 2008 operating EPS of $1.27, down over 8% from 2007. A difficult operating environment in the U.S. has resulted in deferral of CCE's stock repurchase plan. In 2009, we see EPS rising to $1.35.

## Investment Rationale/Risk

➤ Our hold recommendation reflects our expectation of a challenging operating environment for the company. We see results benefiting from pricing gains, but expect commodity cost inflation, high energy prices and sluggish CSD and bottled water trends to be offsets. We are also concerned that a post-Labor Day price increase in CSDs may further accelerate volume declines in the U.S., and we believe there could be a deterioration in European volumes later in the year.

➤ Risks to our recommendation and target price include more rapid commodity cost inflation than expected, potential consumer reluctance to accept new product introductions, and CCE's ability to achieve sales and earnings growth forecasts. In terms of corporate governance, the board is controlled by a majority of insiders and affiliated outsiders, which we view unfavorably.

➤ Our 12-month target price of $10 is based on the low end of peer multiples and below historical P/E and enterprise value-to-EBITDA multiples, on our view of lower relative international exposure and a rising cost environment.

**STANDARD &POOR'S**

# Coca-Cola Enterprises Inc.

## Business Summary October 23, 2008

CORPORATE OVERVIEW. Coca-Cola Enterprises is the world's largest bottler of Coca-Cola beverage products, distributing about 79% of all bottle/can volumes of carbonated soft-drink products of The Coca-Cola Company (KO) in North America. KO owns about 35% of the company's common stock. CCE's product line also includes other nonalcoholic beverages, such as still and sparkling waters, juices, isotonics and teas. In 2007, the company sold approximately 42 billion bottles and cans throughout its territories, representing about 18% of The Coca-Cola Company's worldwide volume. About 93% of this volume consisted of beverages produced and sold under licenses from The Coca-Cola Company. CCE also distributes Dr Pepper and several other beverage brands.

Based on net operating revenues in 2007, North America accounted for 70%, compared to 72% in 2006, and Europe for 30%, compared to 28%. CCE operates in parts of 46 states in the U.S., the District of Columbia, the U.S. Virgin Islands, all 10 Canadian provinces, and portions of Europe that include Belgium, France, the U.K., Luxembourg, Monaco and The Netherlands. At December 31, 2007, CCE's bottling territories encompassed an aggregate population of 414 million people. The company's five leading brands in North America in 2007 were Coca-Cola Classic, Diet Coke, Sprite, Dasani, and POWERade, while the

five leading brands in Europe were Coca-Cola, Diet Coke/Coke light, Fanta, Coca-Cola Zero and Capri-Sun.

During 2007, the company's package mix (based on wholesale physical case volume) in North America was as follows: 59% cans, 14% 20-ounce bottles, 10.5% 2-liter bottles, and 16.5% other packages. In Europe, the package mix was as follows: 38% cans, 32% multiserve PET (1-liter and greater), 14% single serve PET, and 16% other packages.

In addition to concentrates, sweeteners, juices, and finished product, CCE purchases carbon dioxide, PET preforms, glass and plastic bottles, cans, closures, packaging such as plastic bags in cardboard boxes, and other packaging materials. The beverage agreements with The Coca-Cola Company provide that all authorized containers, closures, cases, cartons and other packages, and labels for the products of The Coca-Cola Company must be purchased from manufacturers approved by The Coca-Cola Company.

## Company Financials Fiscal Year Ended Dec. 31

| Per Share Data ($) | 2007 | 2006 | 2005 | 2004 | 2003 | 2002 | 2001 | 2000 | 1999 | 1998 |
|---|---|---|---|---|---|---|---|---|---|---|
| Tangible Book Value | NM | NM | NM | NM | NM | NM | 6.25 | 6.67 | 6.83 | 6.08 |
| Cash Flow | 3.64 | -0.28 | 3.27 | 3.52 | 3.88 | 3.35 | 3.08 | 3.48 | 3.22 | 3.11 |
| Earnings | 1.46 | -2.41 | 1.08 | 1.26 | 1.48 | 1.07 | -0.05 | 0.54 | 0.13 | 0.35 |
| S&P Core Earnings | 1.45 | -2.34 | 1.01 | 1.19 | 1.22 | 0.78 | -0.34 | NA | NA | NA |
| Dividends | 0.24 | 0.24 | 0.16 | 0.16 | 0.16 | 0.16 | 0.12 | 0.16 | 0.16 | 0.15 |
| Payout Ratio | 16% | NM | 15% | 13% | 11% | 15% | NM | 30% | 123% | 41% |
| Prices:High | 27.09 | 22.49 | 23.92 | 29.34 | 23.30 | 24.50 | 23.90 | 30.25 | 37.50 | 41.56 |
| Prices:Low | 19.78 | 18.83 | 18.52 | 18.45 | 16.85 | 15.94 | 13.46 | 14.00 | 16.81 | 22.88 |
| P/E Ratio:High | 19 | NM | 22 | 23 | 16 | 23 | NM | 56 | NM | NM |
| P/E Ratio:Low | 14 | NM | 17 | 15 | 11 | 15 | NM | 26 | NM | NM |

| Income Statement Analysis (Million $) | | | | | | | | | | |
|---|---|---|---|---|---|---|---|---|---|---|
| Revenue | 20,936 | 19,804 | 18,706 | 18,158 | 17,330 | 16,889 | 15,700 | 14,750 | 14,406 | 13,414 |
| Operating Income | 2,537 | 2,439 | 2,475 | 2,504 | 2,674 | 2,409 | 1,954 | 2,387 | 2,187 | 1,989 |
| Depreciation | 1,067 | 1,012 | 1,044 | 1,068 | 1,097 | 1,045 | 1,353 | 1,261 | 1,348 | 1,120 |
| Interest Expense | 629 | 633 | 633 | 619 | 607 | 662 | 753 | 791 | 751 | 703 |
| Pretax Income | 841 | -2,118 | 790 | 818 | 972 | 705 | -150 | 333 | 88.0 | 169 |
| Effective Tax Rate | 15.4% | NM | 34.9% | 27.1% | 30.5% | 29.9% | NM | 29.1% | 33.0% | 16.0% |
| Net Income | 711 | -1,143 | 514 | 596 | 676 | 494 | -19.0 | 236 | 59.0 | 142 |
| S&P Core Earnings | 708 | -1,110 | 478 | 563 | 563 | 356 | -147 | NA | NA | NA |

| Balance Sheet & Other Financial Data (Million $) | | | | | | | | | | |
|---|---|---|---|---|---|---|---|---|---|---|
| Cash | 170 | 184 | 107 | 155 | 80.0 | 68.0 | 284 | 294 | 141 | 68.0 |
| Current Assets | 4,092 | 3,691 | 3,395 | 3,264 | 3,000 | 2,844 | 2,876 | 2,631 | 2,581 | 2,285 |
| Total Assets | 24,046 | 23,225 | 25,357 | 26,354 | 25,700 | 24,375 | 23,719 | 22,162 | 22,730 | 21,132 |
| Current Liabilities | 5,343 | 3,818 | 3,846 | 3,431 | 3,941 | 3,455 | 4,522 | 3,094 | 3,614 | 3,397 |
| Long Term Debt | 7,391 | 9,218 | 9,165 | 10,523 | 10,552 | 11,236 | 10,365 | 10,348 | 10,153 | 9,605 |
| Common Equity | 5,689 | 4,526 | 5,643 | 5,378 | 4,365 | 3,310 | 2,783 | 2,790 | 2,877 | 2,389 |
| Total Capital | 19,048 | 17,801 | 19,914 | 21,139 | 19,882 | 19,122 | 17,521 | 17,956 | 18,028 | 16,758 |
| Capital Expenditures | 938 | 882 | 914 | 946 | 1,099 | 1,029 | 972 | 1,181 | 1,480 | 1,551 |
| Cash Flow | 1,178 | -131 | 1,558 | 1,664 | 1,771 | 1,536 | 1,331 | 1,494 | 1,404 | 1,262 |
| Current Ratio | 0.8 | 1.0 | 1.0 | 0.9 | 1.0 | 0.8 | 0.8 | 0.6 | 0.9 | 0.7 | 0.7 |
| % Long Term Debt of Capitalization | 38.8 | 51.8 | 46.0 | 49.8 | 53.1 | 58.8 | 59.2 | 57.6 | 56.3 | 57.3 |
| % Net Income of Revenue | 3.3 | NM | 2.7 | 3.3 | 3.9 | 2.9 | NM | 1.6 | 0.4 | 1.1 |
| % Return on Assets | 3.0 | NM | 2.0 | 2.3 | 2.7 | 2.1 | NM | 1.1 | 0.3 | 0.7 |
| % Return on Equity | 13.9 | NM | 9.3 | 12.2 | 17.6 | 16.1 | NM | 8.2 | 2.1 | 6.8 |

Data as orig reptd.; bef. results of disc opers/spec. items. Per share data adj. for stk. divs.; EPS diluted. E-Estimated. NA-Not Available. NM-Not Meaningful. NR-Not Ranked. UR-Under Review.

**Office:** 2500 Windy Ridge Pkwy SE, Atlanta, GA 30339.
**Telephone:** 770-989-3000.
**Website:** http://www.cokecce.com
**Chrmn, Pres & CEO:** J.F. Brock, III

**EVP & Chief Admin Officer:** V.R. Palmer
**SVP & CFO:** W.W. Douglas, III
**SVP & General Counsel:** J.R. Parker, Jr.
**SVP & CIO:** E. Sezer

**Investor Contact:** C. Lischer (770-989-3246)
**Board Members:** F. Aguirre, J. F. Brock, III, C. Darden, I. Finan, M. J. Herb, L. P. Humann, J. Hunter, O. H. Ingram II, D. A. James, T. H. Johnson, S. B. Labarge, C. R. Welling
**Founded:** 1944
**Domicile:** Delaware
**Employees:** 73,000

**The McGraw-Hill Companies**

# Cognizant Technology Solutions Corp

**STANDARD &POOR'S**

| S&P Recommendation | HOLD ★★★☆☆ | Price | 12-Mo. Target Price | Investment Style |
|---|---|---|---|---|
| | | $16.87 (as of Nov 14, 2008) | $23.00 | Large-Cap Growth |

**GICS Sector** Information Technology
**Sub-Industry** IT Consulting & Other Services

**Summary** This company offers full life-cycle solutions to complex software development and maintenance problems.

## Key Stock Statistics (Source S&P, Vickers, company reports)

| | | | | | | | |
|---|---|---|---|---|---|---|---|
| 52-Wk Range | $37.10– 15.47 | S&P Oper. EPS 2008E | 1.45 | Market Capitalization(B) | $4.912 | Beta | 1.98 |
| Trailing 12-Month EPS | $1.38 | S&P Oper. EPS 2009E | 1.67 | Yield (%) | Nil | S&P 3-Yr. Proj. EPS CAGR(%) | 18 |
| Trailing 12-Month P/E | 12.2 | P/E on S&P Oper. EPS 2008E | 11.6 | Dividend Rate/Share | Nil | S&P Credit Rating | NA |
| $10K Invested 5 Yrs Ago | $14,737 | Common Shares Outstg. (M) | 291.2 | Institutional Ownership (%) | 95 | | |

## Price Performance

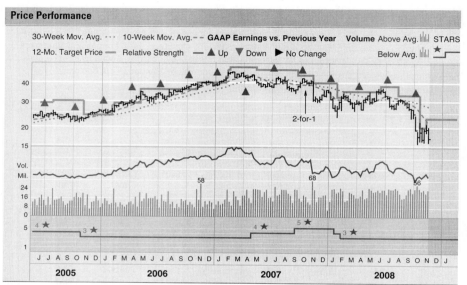

30-Week Mov. Avg. · · · 10-Week Mov. Avg. – – GAAP Earnings vs. Previous Year  Volume Above Avg. STARS
12-Mo. Target Price — Relative Strength — ▲ Up ▼ Down ► No Change  Below Avg.

2-for-1

Options: ASE, CBOE, P, Ph

Analysis prepared by **Dylan Cathers** on November 10, 2008, when the stock traded at **$ 19.13**.

## Highlights

➤ We look for revenue growth of 32% in 2008, slowing to 19% in 2009. CTSH is seeing good growth in its financial services segment, although we believe that could change quickly, given the ongoing reshaping that is occurring in the industry. In general, we believe that IT spending on outsourcing is not falling precipitously, but the services in demand are shifting towards reengineering, projects that are more cost-savings oriented, and that potentially have a rapid return on investment. The other concern we have is delays on IT projects, as companies approach new spending more cautiously. Nonetheless, we think the pipeline is robust and anticipate that CTSH's push into Europe will help offset weakness in the U.S.

➤ We expect operating margins to be down modestly in 2008 and 2009, including projected stock option expense. We think CTSH's investments in the business and rising wages for workers in India will offset falling levels of employee attrition, cost controls, revenue growth, an improved mix of offshore/onsite workers, and a more favorable rupee/U.S. dollar relationship.

➤ We estimate EPS of $1.45 in 2008, rising to $1.67 in 2009.

## Investment Rationale/Risk

➤ Our hold opinion is based on valuation. While we see reduced visibility due to the uncertainty surrounding the U.S. economy, especially in the financial vertical, we think that CTSH's revenue growth will be faster than its peers. Further, we believe the company has done a good job moving into high-growth verticals, such as media, new technology, and telecommunications, and maintaining its margins despite strong headwinds.

➤ Risks to our recommendation and target price include increasing competition in offshore outsourcing, with consequent margin pressures; rising wages of Indian employees; the continuing appreciation of the rupee; and immigration restrictions that could affect personnel. Our corporate governance concerns center around a classified board of directors and a "poison pill" in place.

➤ We use a peer-discount P/E-to-growth (PEG) ratio of 0.77X our 2009 EPS estimate, assuming an expected three-year growth rate of 18%, to arrive at our 12-month target price of $23. At that level, the stock's P/E would be 13.8X our 2009 EPS projection.

## Qualitative Risk Assessment

| LOW | MEDIUM | HIGH |
|---|---|---|

Our risk assessment reflects what we see as CTSH's strong balance sheet, steady cash inflows, and rapid revenue growth, offset by intense competition in the IT services peer group from both companies domiciled in India as well as multinationals.

## Quantitative Evaluations

**S&P Quality Ranking**  B+

| D | C | B- | B | B+ | A- | A | A+ |
|---|---|---|---|---|---|---|---|

**Relative Strength Rank**  MODERATE

46

LOWEST = 1      HIGHEST = 99

## Revenue/Earnings Data

**Revenue (Million $)**

| | 1Q | 2Q | 3Q | 4Q | Year |
|---|---|---|---|---|---|
| 2008 | 643.1 | 685.4 | 734.7 | -- | -- |
| 2007 | 460.3 | 516.5 | 558.8 | 600.0 | 2,136 |
| 2006 | 285.5 | 336.8 | 377.5 | 424.4 | 1,424 |
| 2005 | 181.7 | 211.7 | 235.5 | 256.9 | 885.8 |
| 2004 | 119.7 | 138.7 | 155.4 | 172.8 | 586.7 |
| 2003 | 74.52 | 87.45 | 98.11 | 108.2 | 368.2 |

**Earnings Per Share ($)**

| | | | | | |
|---|---|---|---|---|---|
| 2008 | 0.34 | 0.35 | 0.38 | E0.38 | E1.45 |
| 2007 | 0.25 | 0.27 | 0.32 | 0.32 | 1.15 |
| 2006 | 0.16 | 0.19 | 0.20 | 0.23 | 0.78 |
| 2005 | 0.11 | 0.13 | 0.14 | 0.20 | 0.57 |
| 2004 | 0.07 | 0.09 | 0.09 | 0.11 | 0.35 |
| 2003 | 0.04 | 0.05 | 0.06 | 0.06 | 0.21 |

Fiscal year ended Dec. 31. Next earnings report expected: Early February. EPS Estimates based on S&P Operating Earnings; historical GAAP earnings are as reported.

## Dividend Data

No cash dividends have been paid.

---

**Please read the Required Disclosures and Analyst Certification on the last page of this report.**

The McGraw-Hill Companies

# Cognizant Technology Solutions Corp

**STANDARD &POOR'S**

## Business Summary November 10, 2008

CORPORATE OVERVIEW. Cognizant Technology Solutions began operations in 1994 as an in-house technology development center for Dun & Bradstreet Corp. and its operating units. In its June 1998 IPO, 2,917,000 common shares were sold at $10 each.

The company's objective is to be a leading provider of full life-cycle e-business and application development projects, take full responsibility for ongoing management of a client's software systems, and help clients move legacy transformation projects through to completion. The company's solutions include application development and integration, application management, and re-engineering services.

Applications development services are provided using a full life-cycle application development approach in which the company assumes total start to finish responsibility and accountability for analysis, design, implementation, testing and integration of systems, or through cooperative development, in which CTSH employees work with the customer's in-house IT personnel. In either case, the company's on-site team members work closely with end users

of the application to develop specifications and define requirements.

CTSH applications management services seeks to ensure that a customer's core operational systems are free of defects and responsive to end-users' changing needs. The company is often able to introduce product and process enhancements and improve service levels.

Through its re-engineering services, the company works with customers to migrate systems based on legacy computing environments to newer, open systems-based platforms and client/server architectures, often in response to the more stringent demands of e-business. CTSH's re-engineering tools automate many processes required to implement advanced client/server technologies.

## Company Financials Fiscal Year Ended Dec. 31

| Per Share Data ($) | 2007 | 2006 | 2005 | 2004 | 2003 | 2002 | 2001 | 2000 | 1999 | 1998 |
|---|---|---|---|---|---|---|---|---|---|---|
| Tangible Book Value | 4.42 | 3.60 | 2.44 | 1.61 | 0.98 | 0.62 | 0.42 | 0.29 | 0.20 | 0.14 |
| Cash Flow | 1.33 | 0.89 | 0.64 | 0.41 | 0.26 | 0.17 | 0.12 | 0.07 | 0.12 | 0.04 |
| Earnings | 1.15 | 0.78 | 0.57 | 0.35 | 0.21 | 0.14 | 0.09 | 0.07 | 0.05 | 0.03 |
| S&P Core Earnings | 1.15 | 0.78 | 0.51 | 0.30 | 0.16 | 0.09 | 0.07 | NA | NA | NA |
| Dividends | Nil | Nil | Nil | Nil | Nil | Nil | Nil | Nil | Nil | Nil |
| Payout Ratio | Nil | Nil | Nil | Nil | Nil | Nil | Nil | Nil | Nil | Nil |
| Prices:High | 47.78 | 41.25 | 26.24 | 21.47 | 12.40 | 6.38 | 4.48 | 6.01 | 5.04 | 1.40 |
| Prices:Low | 29.44 | 24.26 | 17.79 | 9.80 | 4.28 | 2.70 | 1.48 | 2.02 | 0.80 | 0.29 |
| P/E Ratio:High | 42 | 53 | 46 | 61 | 59 | 47 | 49 | 83 | NM | 46 |
| P/E Ratio:Low | 26 | 31 | 31 | 28 | 20 | 20 | 16 | 28 | NM | 10 |

| Income Statement Analysis (Million $) | 2007 | 2006 | 2005 | 2004 | 2003 | 2002 | 2001 | 2000 | 1999 | 1998 |
|---|---|---|---|---|---|---|---|---|---|---|
| Revenue | 2,136 | 1,424 | 886 | 587 | 368 | 229 | 178 | 137 | 88.9 | 58.6 |
| Operating Income | 435 | 293 | 199 | 134 | 84.2 | 106 | 42.0 | 30.6 | 19.7 | 11.1 |
| Depreciation | 53.9 | 34.2 | 21.4 | 16.4 | 11.9 | 7.84 | 6.37 | 4.51 | 3.04 | 2.22 |
| Interest Expense | Nil | Nil | Nil | Nil | Nil | Nil | Nil | Nil | Nil | Nil |
| Pretax Income | 414 | 278 | 185 | 122 | 72.2 | 45.1 | 35.4 | 28.2 | 17.9 | 9.64 |
| Effective Tax Rate | 15.5% | 16.2% | 10.3% | 17.9% | 20.6% | 23.4% | 37.4% | 37.4% | 37.4% | 37.4% |
| Net Income | 350 | 233 | 166 | 100 | 57.4 | 34.6 | 22.2 | 17.7 | 11.2 | 6.03 |
| S&P Core Earnings | 350 | 233 | 148 | 85.1 | 42.4 | 23.0 | 16.3 | NA | NA | NA |

| Balance Sheet & Other Financial Data (Million $) | 2007 | 2006 | 2005 | 2004 | 2003 | 2002 | 2001 | 2000 | 1999 | 1998 |
|---|---|---|---|---|---|---|---|---|---|---|
| Cash | 670 | 266 | 197 | 293 | 194 | 126 | 85.0 | 62.0 | 42.6 | 28.4 |
| Current Assets | 1,242 | 1,040 | 663 | 454 | 278 | 176 | 117 | 88.2 | 56.7 | 42.4 |
| Total Assets | 1,838 | 1,326 | 870 | 573 | 361 | 231 | 145 | 110 | 69.0 | 51.7 |
| Current Liabilities | 341 | 250 | 156 | 115 | 62.6 | 41.5 | 21.7 | 26.7 | 13.2 | 13.0 |
| Long Term Debt | Nil | Nil | Nil | Nil | Nil | Nil | Nil | Nil | Nil | Nil |
| Common Equity | 1,468 | 1,073 | 714 | 454 | 274 | 165 | 98.8 | 66.1 | 45.5 | 32.6 |
| Total Capital | 1,483 | 1,073 | 714 | 458 | 298 | 190 | 123 | 82.8 | 55.8 | 38.7 |
| Capital Expenditures | 182 | 105 | 71.8 | 46.6 | 30.0 | 22.3 | 15.0 | 10.7 | 5.92 | 3.74 |
| Cash Flow | 404 | 267 | 188 | 117 | 69.3 | 42.4 | 28.5 | 17.7 | 14.3 | 8.26 |
| Current Ratio | 3.7 | 4.2 | 4.3 | 3.9 | 4.4 | 4.2 | 5.4 | 3.3 | 4.3 | 3.3 |
| % Long Term Debt of Capitalization | Nil | Nil | Nil | Nil | Nil | Nil | Nil | Nil | Nil | Nil |
| % Net Income of Revenue | 16.4 | 16.3 | 18.8 | 17.1 | 15.6 | 15.1 | 12.5 | 12.9 | 12.6 | 10.3 |
| % Return on Assets | 22.1 | 21.2 | 23.1 | 21.4 | 19.4 | 18.4 | 17.4 | 19.8 | 18.6 | 17.2 |
| % Return on Equity | 27.6 | 26.0 | 28.5 | 27.6 | 26.1 | 26.2 | 26.9 | 31.7 | 28.8 | 33.1 |

Data as orig reptd.; bef. results of disc opers/spec. items. Per share data adj. for stk. divs.; EPS diluted. E-Estimated. NA-Not Available. NM-Not Meaningful. NR-Not Ranked. UR-Under Review.

**Office:** 500 Glenpointe Ctr W Ste, Teaneck, NJ 07666-6821.
**Telephone:** 201-801-0233.
**Website:** http://www.cognizant.com
**Chrmn:** J.E. Klein

**Pres & CEO:** F. D'Souza
**Vice Chrmn:** L. Narayanan
**COO, CFO, Chief Acctg Officer & Treas:** G.J. Coburn
**SVP, Secy & General Counsel:** S.E. Schwartz

**Investor Contact:** G. Coburn (201-678-2712)
**Board Members:** F. D'Souza, J. N. Fox, Jr., R. W. Howe, J. E. Klein, L. Narayanan, R. E. Weissman, T. M. Wendel

**Founded:** 1988
**Domicile:** Delaware
**Employees:** 55,400

*The McGraw-Hill Companies*

**STANDARD &POOR'S**

# Colgate-Palmolive Co

| S&P Recommendation | **STRONG BUY** ★★★★★ | Price | 12-Mo. Target Price | Investment Style |
|---|---|---|---|---|
| | | $62.06 (as of Nov 14, 2008) | $84.00 | Large-Cap Growth |

**GICS Sector** Consumer Staples
**Sub-Industry** Household Products

**Summary** This major consumer products company markets oral, personal and household care, and pet nutrition products in more than 200 countries and territories.

## Key Stock Statistics (Source S&P, Vickers, company reports)

| | | | | | | | |
|---|---|---|---|---|---|---|---|
| 52-Wk Range | $81.98– 54.36 | S&P Oper. EPS 2008**E** | 3.85 | Market Capitalization(B) | $31.323 | Beta | 0.27 |
| Trailing 12-Month EPS | $3.49 | S&P Oper. EPS 2009**E** | 4.27 | Yield (%) | 2.58 | S&P 3-Yr. Proj. EPS CAGR(%) | 11 |
| Trailing 12-Month P/E | 17.8 | P/E on S&P Oper. EPS 2008**E** | 16.1 | Dividend Rate/Share | $1.60 | S&P Credit Rating | AA- |
| $10K Invested 5 Yrs Ago | $13,220 | Common Shares Outstg. (M) | 504.7 | Institutional Ownership (%) | 72 | | |

## Price Performance

30-Week Mov. Avg. · · · · 10-Week Mov. Avg. — **GAAP Earnings vs. Previous Year** Volume Above Avg. ⅢⅢ STARS
12-Mo. Target Price — Relative Strength ▲ Up ▼ Down ▶ No Change Below Avg. ⅢⅢ ★

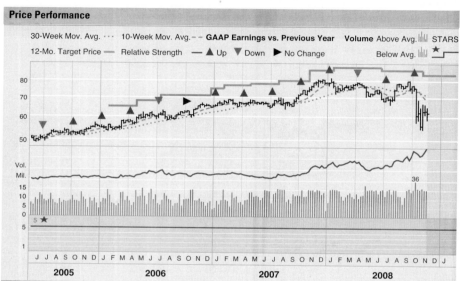

Options: ASE, CBOE, P

Analysis prepared by **Loran Braverman, CFA** on October 31, 2008, when the stock traded at **$ 64.11**.

### Highlights

➤ In December 2004, CL embarked on a four-year restructuring program that involves a 12% work force reduction, the closing of a third of its factories, an increased focus on faster-growing markets, new product innovation, and more efficient spending on marketing.

➤ For 2008, we project a 13% sales gain (assuming about 4% foreign exchange effect) and a slightly lower operating margin, excluding one-time and restructuring charges. We see the benefits of price increases and savings from various restructuring and other programs being more than offset by commodity price pressures and marketing expense increases. We had started 2008 expecting CL to have another year of gross margin improvement, as the company has had for many years, but commodity cost pressures so far have been above our forecasts. For 2009, we see 6.7% revenue growth, including negative foreign exchange, and a modestly higher operating margin.

➤ With our assumption of lower interest expense, a 33% effective tax rate and a 1.5% lower share count, we expect operating EPS to increase to $3.85 in 2008, from 2007's $3.38. Our 2009 EPS estimate is $4.27.

### Investment Rationale/Risk

➤ Our strong buy opinion reflects our view that CL's restructuring plans are likely to drive EPS growth in the low double digits from 2006 onward for at least several years. We expect the company to continue to invest in R&D and marketing, with more resources to be allocated to faster-growing markets. In addition, we have seen a smooth CEO transition, from Reuben Mark, CEO since 1984, to Ian Cook, formerly COO and himself a long-time CL employee, who became CEO on July 1, 2007.

➤ Risks to our recommendation and target price include intensified competition in the global oral care market, unfavorable currency translations, and low consumer acceptance of new products.

➤ Our 12-month target price of $84 is a blend of our three valuation models. Our DCF model assumes a WACC of 8.2% and a terminal growth rate of 3% to arrive at a value of $89. We believe the shares should trade at a premium to peers, which suggests a 16.2X P/E applied to our 2009 EPS estimate, or $69. Our historical analysis uses a P/E of 22.0X, a discount to the 10-year average, to value the stock at $94.

## Qualitative Risk Assessment

| **LOW** | MEDIUM | HIGH |
|---|---|---|

Our risk assessment reflects that demand for household and personal care products is generally static, and not affected by changes in the economy or geopolitical factors. This is partially offset by the mature and competitive nature of these industries.

## Quantitative Evaluations

### S&P Quality Ranking                 A+

| D | C | B- | B | B+ | A- | A | **A+** |
|---|---|---|---|---|---|---|---|

### Relative Strength Rank          STRONG

76

LOWEST = 1                                    HIGHEST = 99

## Revenue/Earnings Data

**Revenue (Million $)**

| | 1Q | 2Q | 3Q | 4Q | Year |
|---|---|---|---|---|---|
| 2008 | 3,713 | 3,965 | 3,988 | -- | -- |
| 2007 | 3,214 | 3,405 | 3,528 | 3,642 | 13,790 |
| 2006 | 2,871 | 3,014 | 3,144 | 3,209 | 12,238 |
| 2005 | 2,743 | 2,838 | 2,912 | 2,905 | 11,397 |
| 2004 | 2,514 | 2,572 | 2,696 | 2,803 | 10,584 |
| 2003 | 2,348 | 2,459 | 2,524 | 2,573 | 9,903 |

**Earnings Per Share ($)**

| | | | | | |
|---|---|---|---|---|---|
| 2008 | 0.87 | 0.92 | 0.94 | E0.98 | E3.85 |
| 2007 | 0.89 | 0.76 | 0.77 | 0.77 | 3.20 |
| 2006 | 0.59 | 0.51 | 0.63 | 0.73 | 2.46 |
| 2005 | 0.53 | 0.62 | 0.63 | 0.65 | 2.43 |
| 2004 | 0.59 | 0.66 | 0.58 | 0.50 | 2.33 |
| 2003 | 0.56 | 0.62 | 0.63 | 0.65 | 2.46 |

Fiscal year ended Dec. 31. Next earnings report expected: Early February. EPS Estimates based on S&P Operating Earnings; historical GAAP earnings are as reported.

## Dividend Data (Dates: mm/dd Payment Date: mm/dd/yy)

| Amount ($) | Date Decl. | Ex-Div. Date | Stk. of Record | Payment Date |
|---|---|---|---|---|
| 0.360 | 01/10 | 01/23 | 01/25 | 02/15/08 |
| 0.400 | 02/27 | 04/22 | 04/24 | 05/15/08 |
| 0.400 | 07/10 | 07/22 | 07/24 | 08/15/08 |
| 0.400 | 10/02 | 10/22 | 10/24 | 11/14/08 |

Dividends have been paid since 1895. Source: Company reports.

---

**Please read the Required Disclosures and Analyst Certification on the last page of this report.**

*The McGraw-Hill Companies*

# Colgate-Palmolive Co

## Business Summary October 31, 2008

CORPORATE OVERVIEW. Colgate-Palmolive Co. is a leading global consumer products company that operates in the oral, personal, and household care, and pet food markets. Its products are marketed in more than 200 countries and territories worldwide. Sales of oral, personal, and home care products accounted for 87% of total worldwide sales in 2007. The balance of revenues was derived from the sale of pet foods. The company's oral care products include toothbrushes, toothpaste and pharmaceutical products for oral health professionals. CL's personal care products include bar and liquid soaps, shampoos, conditioners, deodorants antiperspirants, and shave products. The home care division produces major brands such as Palmolive and Ajax soaps. Oral, personal and home care sales outside of North America accounted for 67% of total sales in 2007. Sales in Latin America, Europe/South Pacific and Greater Asia/Africa accounted for 29%, 28% and 20% of total oral, personal and home care sales segment sales, respectively.

MARKET PROFILE. CL is a dominant player in its categories. According to the company, in 2006, CL expanded upon its number one position in the U.S. tooth-

paste market to a record 37.3%. Furthermore, the company says, over the past decade, CL's global toothpaste market share has increased almost eight percentage points, and CL is now the market leader in 53 of the 71 largest toothpaste markets worldwide. While volume growth for CL's categories in developed countries has been modest, in our view, growth in the developing and emerging markets is projected to rise at a rate two to three times that of developed markets in the near term. Colgate has the advantage of having operated in these markets for an extended period of time (several decades) and this is evident in the leading market shares that the company enjoys. With plans to increase consumer awareness and product innovation, coupled with growing economies, we believe Colgate is well situated to benefit from this market growth.

## Company Financials Fiscal Year Ended Dec. 31

| Per Share Data ($) | 2007 | 2006 | 2005 | 2004 | 2003 | 2002 | 2001 | 2000 | 1999 | 1998 |
|---|---|---|---|---|---|---|---|---|---|---|
| Tangible Book Value | NM | NM | NM | NM | NM | NM | NM | NM | NM | NM |
| Cash Flow | 3.76 | 3.06 | 2.97 | 2.86 | 3.15 | 2.65 | 2.40 | 2.32 | 1.96 | 1.69 |
| Earnings | 3.20 | 2.46 | 2.43 | 2.33 | 2.46 | 2.19 | 1.89 | 1.70 | 1.47 | 1.31 |
| S&P Core Earnings | 3.22 | 2.42 | 2.21 | 2.26 | 2.31 | 2.00 | 1.71 | NA | NA | NA |
| Dividends | 1.40 | 1.25 | 1.11 | 0.96 | 0.90 | 0.72 | 0.68 | 0.63 | 0.59 | 0.55 |
| Payout Ratio | 44% | 51% | 46% | 41% | 37% | 33% | 36% | 37% | 40% | 42% |
| Prices:High | 81.27 | 67.08 | 57.15 | 59.04 | 60.99 | 58.86 | 64.75 | 66.75 | 65.00 | 49.44 |
| Prices:Low | 63.75 | 53.41 | 48.25 | 42.89 | 48.56 | 44.05 | 48.50 | 40.50 | 36.56 | 32.53 |
| P/E Ratio:High | 25 | 27 | 24 | 25 | 25 | 27 | 34 | 39 | 44 | 38 |
| P/E Ratio:Low | 20 | 22 | 20 | 18 | 20 | 20 | 26 | 24 | 25 | 25 |

| Income Statement Analysis (Million $) | | | | | | | | | | |
|---|---|---|---|---|---|---|---|---|---|---|
| Revenue | 13,790 | 12,238 | 11,397 | 10,584 | 9,903 | 9,294 | 9,428 | 9,358 | 9,118 | 8,972 |
| Operating Income | 3,108 | 2,674 | 2,613 | 2,540 | 2,467 | 2,333 | 2,198 | 2,132 | 1,904 | 1,733 |
| Depreciation | 334 | 329 | 329 | 328 | 316 | 297 | 336 | 410 | 340 | 330 |
| Interest Expense | 173 | 159 | 143 | 124 | 124 | 151 | 192 | 200 | 212 | 205 |
| Pretax Income | 2,564 | 2,002 | 2,134 | 2,050 | 2,042 | 1,870 | 1,709 | 1,600 | 1,425 | 1,278 |
| Effective Tax Rate | 29.6% | 32.4% | 34.1% | 32.9% | 30.4% | 31.1% | 30.6% | 31.4% | 32.1% | 31.4% |
| Net Income | 1,737 | 1,353 | 1,351 | 1,327 | 1,421 | 1,288 | 1,147 | 1,064 | 937 | 849 |
| S&P Core Earnings | 1,718 | 1,306 | 1,207 | 1,262 | 1,309 | 1,152 | 1,011 | NA | NA | NA |

| Balance Sheet & Other Financial Data (Million $) | | | | | | | | | | |
|---|---|---|---|---|---|---|---|---|---|---|
| Cash | 451 | 490 | 341 | 320 | 265 | 168 | 173 | 213 | 235 | 182 |
| Current Assets | 3,619 | 3,301 | 2,757 | 2,740 | 2,497 | 2,228 | 2,203 | 2,347 | 2,355 | 2,245 |
| Total Assets | 10,112 | 9,138 | 8,507 | 8,673 | 7,479 | 7,087 | 6,985 | 7,252 | 7,423 | 7,685 |
| Current Liabilities | 3,163 | 3,469 | 2,743 | 2,731 | 2,445 | 2,149 | 2,124 | 2,244 | 2,274 | 2,114 |
| Long Term Debt | 3,508 | 2,720 | 2,918 | 3,090 | 2,685 | 3,211 | 2,812 | 2,537 | 2,243 | 2,301 |
| Common Equity | 2,308 | 1,188 | 1,380 | 971 | 594 | 27.3 | 505 | 1,115 | 1,467 | 1,709 |
| Total Capital | 5,882 | 4,441 | 5,106 | 4,845 | 4,028 | 4,050 | 4,139 | 4,453 | 4,701 | 4,834 |
| Capital Expenditures | 583 | 476 | 389 | 348 | 302 | 344 | 340 | 367 | 373 | 390 |
| Cash Flow | 2,043 | 1,682 | 1,653 | 1,629 | 1,736 | 1,563 | 1,461 | 1,453 | 1,255 | 1,158 |
| Current Ratio | 1.1 | 1.0 | 1.0 | 1.0 | 1.0 | 1.0 | 1.0 | 1.0 | 1.0 | 1.1 |
| % Long Term Debt of Capitalization | 57.4 | 61.3 | 57.1 | 63.8 | 66.7 | 79.3 | 67.9 | 57.0 | 47.7 | 47.6 |
| % Net Income of Revenue | 12.6 | 11.1 | 11.9 | 12.5 | 14.4 | 13.9 | 12.2 | 11.4 | 10.3 | 9.5 |
| % Return on Assets | 17.8 | 15.3 | 15.7 | 16.4 | 19.5 | 18.3 | 16.1 | 14.5 | 12.4 | 11.2 |
| % Return on Equity | 91.2 | 118.5 | 99.5 | 166.2 | 457.2 | 475.7 | 139.0 | 80.8 | 57.6 | 47.3 |

Data as orig reptd.; bef. results of disc opers/spec. items. Per share data adj. for stk. divs.; EPS diluted. E-Estimated. NA-Not Available. NM-Not Meaningful. NR-Not Ranked. UR-Under Review.

**Office:** 300 Park Avenue, New York, NY 10022.
**Telephone:** 212-310-2000.
**Email:** investor_relations@colpal.com
**Website:** http://www.colgate.com

**Chrmn:** R. Mark
**Pres, CEO & COO:** I.M. Cook
**SVP, Secy & General Counsel:** A.D. Hendry
**CFO:** S.C. Patrick

**CTO:** F.J. Moison
**Board Members:** J. T. Cahill, J. K. Conway, I. M. Cook, E. M. Hancock, D. W. Johnson, R. J. Kogan, D. E. Lewis, R. Mark, J. P. Reinhard, S. I. Sadove

**Founded:** 1806
**Domicile:** Delaware
**Employees:** 36,000

# Comcast Corp

| S&P Recommendation **STRONG SELL** ★ ☆ ☆ ☆ ☆ | Price $15.53 (as of Nov 14, 2008) | 12-Mo. Target Price $12.00 | Investment Style Large-Cap Blend |
|---|---|---|---|

**GICS Sector** Consumer Discretionary
**Sub-Industry** Cable & Satellite

**Summary** With about 24.4 million subscribers, this company is the largest U.S. cable multiple system operator (MSO), as well as a provider of cable programming content.

## Key Stock Statistics (Source S&P, Vickers, company reports)

| | | | | | | | |
|---|---|---|---|---|---|---|---|
| 52-Wk Range | $22.86– 9.20 | S&P Oper. EPS 2008**E** | 0.87 | Market Capitalization(B) | $44.576 | Beta | 0.86 |
| Trailing 12-Month EPS | $0.91 | S&P Oper. EPS 2009**E** | 1.07 | Yield (%) | 1.61 | S&P 3-Yr. Proj. EPS CAGR(%) | 10 |
| Trailing 12-Month P/E | 17.1 | P/E on S&P Oper. EPS 2008**E** | 17.9 | Dividend Rate/Share | $0.25 | S&P Credit Rating | BBB |
| $10K Invested 5 Yrs Ago | $7,418 | Common Shares Outstg. (M) | 2,879.8 | Institutional Ownership (%) | 55 | | |

## Price Performance

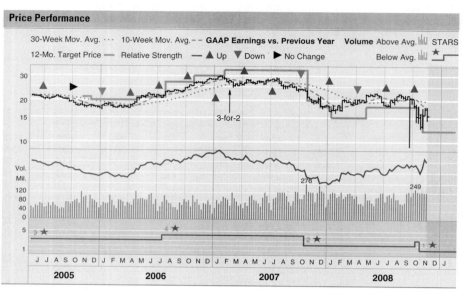

30-Week Mov. Avg. · · · ·    10-Week Mov. Avg. – – –    **GAAP Earnings vs. Previous Year**    Volume Above Avg. � STARS
12-Mo. Target Price —    Relative Strength —    ▲ Up  ▼ Down  ► No Change    Below Avg. ▮▮ ★

Analysis prepared by **Tuna N. Amobi, CFA, CPA** on October 29, 2008, when the stock traded at **$ 16.14.**

Options: ASE, CBOE, P, Ph

## Highlights

➤ We forecast that consolidated revenues will rise 11% in 2008, to about $34.3 billion, consistent with trends in the first nine months. In 2009, we project 8% total revenue growth, to nearly $37.1 billion, reflecting a deceleration of overall revenue-generating unit (RGU) growth and increased promotional pricing for residential high-speed data and phone services at the core cable division, and stagnant advertising growth. This should be partly offset by continued penetration of advanced video services, rate increases, a growing base of commercial data and phone customers, and low double-digit growth in the programming segment.

➤ We see limited opportunities for margin expansion, with declines in phone operating expenses mostly offset by higher marketing and customer service spending, continuing investments in content, technology and wireless initiatives, and higher programming costs.

➤ We project consolidated EBITDA growth of 11% and 7% in 2008 and 2009, respectively. After higher D&A charges, we estimate operating EPS of $0.87 and $1.07 in the respective years, assuming a slower pace of share buybacks under a current $7 billion plan.

## Investment Rationale/Risk

➤ After somewhat encouraging 2008 third quarter results, we see relatively minimal downside risk to management's conservative financial guidance for the full year. However, we expect more headwinds in 2009, on decelerating unit growth and limited margin expansion, amid a slowing economy and increased competition. Still, with seemingly ample liquidity, CMCSA may not need to access volatile capital markets in the foreseeable future. However, we note a retraction in late October of an earlier plan to complete the current buyback authorization in 2009, which seems somewhat ominous given about $5 billion of debt maturities due over the next three years. Also, we note near-term regulatory risk factors.

➤ Risks to our recommendation and target price include a less severe than expected economic contraction, and potential upside from the small and mid-size enterprise market.

➤ Based on 2009 estimates, our 12-month target price of $12 implies cable-only enterprise value near $2,300 per subscriber, or 4.4X total enterprise value to EBITDA, in line with peers. The stock recently had a 1.6% dividend yield.

## Qualitative Risk Assessment

| LOW | MEDIUM | HIGH |
|---|---|---|

Our risk assessment reflects a slowing economy, intensifying competition from satellite operators and telcos, and a potential dividend suspension, offset by economies of scale and what we view as a relatively sound financial condition.

## Quantitative Evaluations

**S&P Quality Ranking** B-

| D | C | B- | B | B+ | A- | A | A+ |
|---|---|---|---|---|---|---|---|

**Relative Strength Rank** MODERATE

69

LOWEST = 1    HIGHEST = 99

## Revenue/Earnings Data

**Revenue (Million $)**

| | 1Q | 2Q | 3Q | 4Q | Year |
|---|---|---|---|---|---|
| 2008 | 8,389 | 8,553 | 8,549 | -- | -- |
| 2007 | 7,388 | 7,712 | 7,781 | 8,014 | 30,895 |
| 2006 | 5,595 | 5,908 | 6,432 | 7,031 | 24,966 |
| 2005 | 5,363 | 5,598 | 5,578 | 5,716 | 22,255 |
| 2004 | 4,908 | 5,066 | 5,098 | 5,235 | 20,307 |
| 2003 | 4,466 | 4,594 | 4,546 | 4,742 | 18,348 |

**Earnings Per Share ($)**

| | | | | | |
|---|---|---|---|---|---|
| 2008 | 0.24 | 0.21 | 0.26 | E0.23 | E0.87 |
| 2007 | 0.26 | 0.19 | 0.18 | 0.20 | 0.83 |
| 2006 | 0.15 | 0.13 | 0.31 | 0.14 | 0.70 |
| 2005 | 0.04 | 0.13 | 0.07 | 0.04 | 0.28 |
| 2004 | 0.02 | 0.08 | 0.07 | 0.13 | 0.29 |
| 2003 | -0.11 | Nil | -0.05 | 0.11 | -0.07 |

Fiscal year ended Dec. 31. Next earnings report expected: Mid February. EPS Estimates based on S&P Operating Earnings; historical GAAP earnings are as reported.

## Dividend Data (Dates: mm/dd Payment Date: mm/dd/yy)

| Amount ($) | Date Decl. | Ex-Div. Date | Stk. of Record | Payment Date |
|---|---|---|---|---|
| 0.063 | 02/14 | 03/31 | 04/02 | 04/30/08 |
| 0.063 | 05/14 | 07/07 | 07/09 | 07/30/08 |
| 0.063 | 08/15 | 10/06 | 10/08 | 10/29/08 |

Dividends have been paid since 2008. Source: Company reports.

# Comcast Corp

STANDARD
&POOR'S

## Business Summary October 29, 2008

CORPORATE OVERVIEW. Comcast Corp. became the largest U.S. cable multiple system operator (MSO) after its acquisition of the former AT&T Broadband (ATTB) in November 2002. As of September 30, 2008, the company counted 24.4 million subscribers to its basic service, about 16.8 million for digital video, more than 14.7 million for high-speed Internet service, and more than 6.1 million for digital phone. The company's content assets include cable networks E! Entertainment Television, The Golf Channel, Outdoor Life Network and G4, among other programming investments.

COMPETITIVE LANDSCAPE. In a typical market, Comcast faces competition from direct broadcast satellite (DBS) providers DirecTV Group and EchoStar Communications, and from incumbent phone companies such as Verizon Communications and AT&T (formerly SBC Communications). In addition, the company competes in several markets that are served by overbuilders that also provide video, voice and data services to residential, and in some cases, enterprise customers.

We expect this competition to intensify in the years ahead, as both DBS companies launch new satellites to drive advanced video offerings, while the telcos accelerate their own deployment of fiber-based video and broadband offerings. A possible national franchising bill could also help the new entrants attain a much quicker time-to-market in head-to-head competition with cable operators. With DSL discounts already aggressive in several markets, we believe the pending AT&T acquisition of BellSouth could create a stronger competitor that could further drive increased promotional activity.

However, we think Comcast has thus far successfully resisted price competition, focusing instead on product differentiation through newer offerings such as VOD, and enhanced features such as higher data speeds and a broadband portal. We expect cable operators to increasingly experiment with package discounts, as the rapidly changing competitive landscape continues to evolve.

## Company Financials Fiscal Year Ended Dec. 31

| Per Share Data ($) | 2007 | 2006 | 2005 | 2004 | 2003 | 2002 | 2001 | 2000 | 1999 | 1998 |
|---|---|---|---|---|---|---|---|---|---|---|
| Tangible Book Value | NM | NM | NM | NM | NM | NM | NM | NM | NM | NM |
| Cash Flow | 2.46 | 2.22 | 1.79 | 1.69 | 0.24 | 1.05 | 0.99 | 3.27 | 1.60 | 1.59 |
| Earnings | 0.83 | 0.70 | 0.28 | 0.29 | -0.07 | -0.17 | -0.89 | 1.44 | 0.63 | 0.83 |
| S&P Core Earnings | 0.74 | 0.48 | 0.33 | 0.14 | -0.30 | 0.47 | -1.03 | NA | NA | NA |
| Dividends | Nil | Nil | Nil | Nil | Nil | Nil | Nil | Nil | 0.01 | 0.03 |
| Payout Ratio | Nil | Nil | Nil | Nil | Nil | Nil | Nil | Nil | 1% | 4% |
| Prices:High | 30.18 | 28.94 | 23.00 | 24.33 | 23.23 | 25.03 | 30.54 | 34.91 | 36.42 | 19.67 |
| Prices:Low | 17.37 | 16.90 | 17.20 | 17.50 | 15.61 | 11.37 | 21.23 | 18.62 | 18.71 | 9.83 |
| P/E Ratio:High | 36 | 41 | 82 | 85 | NM | NM | NM | 24 | 57 | 24 |
| P/E Ratio:Low | 21 | 24 | 61 | 61 | NM | NM | NM | 13 | 30 | 12 |

| Income Statement Analysis (Million $) | | | | | | | | | | |
|---|---|---|---|---|---|---|---|---|---|---|
| Revenue | 30,895 | 24,966 | 22,255 | 20,307 | 18,348 | 12,460 | 19,697 | 8,219 | 6,209 | 5,145 |
| Operating Income | 10,725 | 9,442 | 8,493 | 7,531 | 6,392 | 3,691 | 1,576 | 2,470 | 1,880 | 1,497 |
| Depreciation | 5,107 | 4,823 | 4,803 | 4,623 | 4,438 | 2,032 | 6,345 | 2,631 | 1,216 | 940 |
| Interest Expense | 2,289 | 2,064 | 1,796 | 1,876 | 2,018 | 884 | 2,341 | 691 | 538 | 467 |
| Pretax Income | 4,349 | 3,594 | 1,880 | 1,810 | -137 | 70.0 | -5,927 | 3,602 | 1,500 | 1,557 |
| Effective Tax Rate | 41.4% | 37.5% | 49.6% | 45.6% | NM | NM | NM | 40.0% | 48.2% | 38.1% |
| Net Income | 2,587 | 2,235 | 928 | 970 | -218 | -276 | -3,021 | 2,045 | 781 | 1,008 |
| S&P Core Earnings | 2,313 | 1,541 | 1,090 | 465 | -979 | 792 | -1,482 | NA | NA | NA |

| Balance Sheet & Other Financial Data (Million $) | | | | | | | | | | |
|---|---|---|---|---|---|---|---|---|---|---|
| Cash | 1,061 | 1,239 | 693 | 452 | 1,550 | 781 | 558 | 652 | 922 | 871 |
| Current Assets | 3,667 | 5,202 | 2,594 | 3,535 | 5,403 | 7,076 | 4,944 | 5,144 | 9,759 | 5,624 |
| Total Assets | 113,417 | 110,405 | 103,146 | 104,694 | 109,159 | 113,105 | 109,319 | 35,745 | 28,686 | 14,817 |
| Current Liabilities | 7,952 | 7,440 | 6,269 | 8,635 | 9,654 | 15,383 | 12,489 | 4,042 | 5,527 | 3,093 |
| Long Term Debt | 29,828 | 27,992 | 21,682 | 20,093 | 23,835 | 27,957 | 27,528 | 10,517 | 8,707 | 5,464 |
| Common Equity | 41,340 | 41,167 | 40,219 | 41,422 | 41,662 | 38,329 | 38,451 | 28,113 | 9,772 | 3,243 |
| Total Capital | 98,298 | 96,489 | 89,928 | 88,798 | 91,689 | 92,070 | 94,758 | 45,734 | 23,159 | 10,780 |
| Capital Expenditures | 6,158 | 4,395 | 3,621 | 3,660 | 4,161 | 1,975 | NA | 1,637 | 894 | 899 |
| Cash Flow | 7,694 | 7,058 | 5,731 | 5,593 | 4,220 | 1,756 | 3,324 | 4,653 | 1,967 | 1,918 |
| Current Ratio | 0.5 | 0.7 | 0.4 | 0.4 | 0.6 | 0.5 | 0.4 | 1.3 | 1.8 | 1.8 |
| % Long Term Debt of Capitalization | 30.3 | 29.0 | 24.1 | 22.6 | 26.0 | 30.4 | 29.1 | 23.0 | 37.6 | 50.7 |
| % Net Income of Revenue | 8.4 | 9.0 | 4.2 | 4.8 | NM | NM | NM | 24.9 | 12.6 | 19.6 |
| % Return on Assets | 2.3 | 2.1 | 0.9 | 0.9 | NM | NM | NM | 6.3 | 3.6 | 7.3 |
| % Return on Equity | 6.3 | 5.5 | 2.3 | 2.3 | NM | NM | NM | 8.4 | 11.5 | 45.1 |

Data as orig reptd.; bef. results of disc opers/spec. items. Per share data adj. for stk. divs.; EPS diluted. E-Estimated. NA-Not Available. NM-Not Meaningful. NR-Not Ranked. UR-Under Review.

**Office:** 1500 Market St, Philadelphia, PA 19102-2196.
**Telephone:** 215-665-1700.
**Website:** http://www.comcast.com
**Chrmn, Pres & CEO:** B.L. Roberts

**Vice Chrmn:** J.A. Brodsky
**COO & EVP:** S.B. Burke
**SVP, Chief Acctg Officer & Cntlr:** L.J. Salva
**SVP, Secy & General Counsel:** A. Block

**Investor Contact:** M. Dooner (866-281-2100)
**Board Members:** S. D. Anstrom, K. J. Bacon, S. M. Bonovitz, E. D. Breen, J. A. Brodsky, J. J. Collins, J. M. Cook, G. L. Hassell, J. A. Honickman, B. L. Roberts, R. J. Roberts, J. H. Rodin, F. G. Rohatyn, M. I. Sovern, B. C. Watson, I. A. Wechsler

**Founded:** 1969
**Domicile:** Pennsylvania
**Employees:** 100,000

# Comerica Inc

**STANDARD &POOR'S**

| S&P Recommendation | BUY ★★★★☆ | Price | 12-Mo. Target Price | Investment Style |
|---|---|---|---|---|
| | | $21.95 (as of Nov 14, 2008) | $30.00 | Large-Cap Value |

**GICS Sector** Financials
**Sub-Industry** Diversified Banks

**Summary** This bank holding company operates banking affiliates mainly in Michigan, Texas, California, Arizona and Florida.

## Key Stock Statistics (Source S&P, Vickers, company reports)

| | | | | | | | |
|---|---|---|---|---|---|---|---|
| 52-Wk Range | $54.00– 19.31 | S&P Oper. EPS 2008**E** | 1.73 | Market Capitalization(B) | $3.303 | Beta | 0.67 |
| Trailing 12-Month EPS | $2.06 | S&P Oper. EPS 2009**E** | 2.27 | Yield (%) | 6.01 | S&P 3-Yr. Proj. EPS CAGR(%) | -7 |
| Trailing 12-Month P/E | 10.7 | P/E on S&P Oper. EPS 2008**E** | 12.7 | Dividend Rate/Share | $1.32 | S&P Credit Rating | A |
| $10K Invested 5 Yrs Ago | $5,292 | Common Shares Outstg. (M) | 150.5 | Institutional Ownership (%) | 84 | | |

## Price Performance

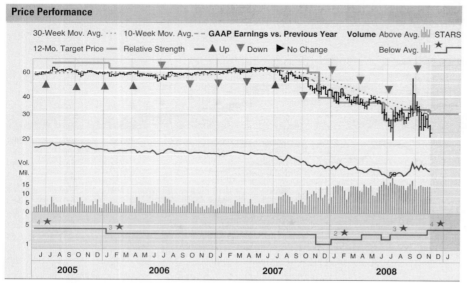

30-Week Mov. Avg. · · · 10-Week Mov. Avg. - - **GAAP Earnings vs. Previous Year** Volume Above Avg. STARS
12-Mo. Target Price — Relative Strength — ▲ Up ▼ Down ► No Change Below Avg. ★

Options: ASE, CBOE, P, Ph

Analysis prepared by **Erik Oja** on November 14, 2008, when the stock traded at **$ 23.52.**

## Qualitative Risk Assessment

| LOW | MEDIUM | HIGH |
|---|---|---|

Our risk assessment reflects CMA's long history of profitability and dividend growth, tempered by its exposure to the California residential real estate market.

## Quantitative Evaluations

**S&P Quality Ranking** A-

| D | C | B- | B | B+ | A- | A | A+ |
|---|---|---|---|---|---|---|---|

**Relative Strength Rank** MODERATE

47

LOWEST = 1 HIGHEST = 99

## Revenue/Earnings Data

**Revenue (Million $)**

| | 1Q | 2Q | 3Q | 4Q | Year |
|---|---|---|---|---|---|
| 2008 | 1,100 | 979.0 | 975.0 | -- | -- |
| 2007 | 1,104 | 1,158 | 1,182 | 1,174 | 4,618 |
| 2006 | 967.0 | 1,048 | 1,088 | 1,174 | 4,277 |
| 2005 | 817.0 | 874.0 | 951.0 | 1,026 | 3,668 |
| 2004 | 763.0 | 773.0 | 764.0 | 794.0 | 3,094 |
| 2003 | 866.0 | 853.0 | 800.0 | 780.0 | 3,299 |

**Earnings Per Share ($)**

| | | | | | |
|---|---|---|---|---|---|
| 2008 | 0.73 | 0.37 | 0.18 | E0.46 | E1.73 |
| 2007 | 1.19 | 1.25 | 1.17 | 0.77 | 4.40 |
| 2006 | 1.26 | 1.19 | 1.20 | 1.16 | 4.81 |
| 2005 | 1.16 | 1.28 | 1.41 | 1.25 | 5.11 |
| 2004 | 0.92 | 1.10 | 1.13 | 1.21 | 4.36 |
| 2003 | 1.00 | 0.97 | 0.89 | 0.89 | 3.75 |

Fiscal year ended Dec. 31. Next earnings report expected: Mid January. EPS Estimates based on S&P Operating Earnings; historical GAAP earnings are as reported.

## Highlights

➤ We expect fee income, ex-gains and losses, to be $220 million in the last quarter of 2008, and to be $230 million per quarter in 2009, for a total of $920 million. Due to the latest Fed rate cut, we expect the net interest margin to be 3.01 % in the last quarter, down from 3.11% in the third quarter. For 2009, we expect a net interest margin of 2.97%, on our expectation that loan yields may fall slightly, while deposit costs, which are already relatively low, remain firm.

➤ CMA's credit quality fell in the third quarter, as $863 million of loans were rated nonperforming, up 18.1% from $731 million at June 30. We see this growth rate as slightly below peers, but are concerned that the level of non-performing loans is now 1.67% of total loans, in-line with peers. We are projecting loan loss provisions of about $650 million in 2008 and about $490 million in 2009. We are basing our estimates on the following assumptions: annualized net chargeoffs of 0.90% of total loans in the fourth quarter of 2008, in-line with the 0.90% figure in the third quarter, plus reserve building of $50 million. For 2009, we expect net chargeoffs of 0.82% of loans, plus reserve building of $70 million.

➤ We forecast 2009 EPS of $2.27.

## Investment Rationale/Risk

➤ CMA has applied to receive $2.25 billion from the US Treasury TARP program. As a result, CMA expects its Tier-1 capital ratio to increase to 10.35%, well above pre-TARP peer median of about 9.00%, from 7.35%, which was low relative to peers. In addition, CMA is taking steps to limit lending exposure to automobile dealers and residential construction. We also view favorably CMA's $8.1 securities portfolio, which consists primarily of AAA mortgage-backed Freddie Mac and Fannie Mae securities. Currently, CMA trades at 10.3X our $2.27 EPS estimate for 2009, a multiple below peers.

➤ Risks to our recommendation and target price include the spread of CMA's credit quality deterioration from California residential construction to CMA's other service territories and other types of loans.

➤ We think CMA should trade above the current industry median of 13.0X 2009 EPS estimates. However, due to the current credit environment, we believe CMA should trade below the high end of the historical range of 10.0X to 15.0X forward EPS estimates we have seen for US regional banks. Our target price of $30 is equal to a P/E of 13.2X our 2009 EPS forecast of $2.27.

## Dividend Data (Dates: mm/dd Payment Date: mm/dd/yy)

| Amount ($) | Date Decl. | Ex-Div. Date | Stk. of Record | Payment Date |
|---|---|---|---|---|
| 0.660 | 01/22 | 03/12 | 03/15 | 04/01/08 |
| 0.660 | 05/20 | 06/11 | 06/15 | 07/01/08 |
| 0.660 | 07/22 | 09/11 | 09/15 | 10/01/08 |
| 0.330 | 09/18 | 12/11 | 12/15 | 01/01/09 |

Dividends have been paid since 1936. Source: Company reports.

---

**Please read the Required Disclosures and Analyst Certification on the last page of this report.**

*The McGraw-Hill Companies*

# Comerica Inc

**STANDARD &POOR'S**

## Business Summary November 14, 2008

CORPORATE OVERVIEW. The owner of one of Michigan's oldest banks, Comerica is a Detroit-based bank holding company that operates banking units mainly in Michigan, California, Texas, Arizona and Florida. It also has banking subsidiaries in Canada and Mexico.

Operations are divided into three major lines of business: the Business Bank, the Retail Bank (formerly known as Small Business and Personal Financial Services), and Wealth & Institutional Management. The Business Bank is primarily comprised of middle market, commercial real estate, national dealer services, global finance, large corporate, leasing, financial services, and technology and life sciences. This business segment offers various products and services, including commercial loans and lines of credit, deposits, cash management, capital market products, international trade finance, letters of credit, foreign exchange management services and loan syndication services.

The Retail Bank includes small business banking (entities with annual sales under $10 million) and personal financial services, consisting of consumer

lending, consumer deposit gathering and mortgage loan origination. In addition to a full range of financial services provided to small businesses and their owners, this business segment offers a variety of consumer products, including deposit accounts, installment loans, credit and debit cards, student loans, home equity loans and lines of credit, and residential mortgage loans.

Wealth & Institutional Management offers products and services consisting of personal trust, which is designed to meet the personal financial needs of the affluent, private banking, institutional trust, retirement services, investment management and advisory services, investment banking, and discount securities brokerage services. This business segment also offers the sale of mutual funds and annuity products, as well as life, disability and long-term care insurance products.

## Company Financials  Fiscal Year Ended Dec. 31

| Per Share Data ($) | 2007 | 2006 | 2005 | 2004 | 2003 | 2002 | 2001 | 2000 | 1999 | 1998 |
|---|---|---|---|---|---|---|---|---|---|---|
| Tangible Book Value | 40.94 | 32.82 | 33.01 | 29.85 | 29.20 | 28.31 | 27.15 | 23.94 | 20.60 | 17.94 |
| Earnings | 4.40 | 4.81 | 5.11 | 4.36 | 3.75 | 3.40 | 3.88 | 4.63 | 4.14 | 3.72 |
| S&P Core Earnings | 4.48 | 4.71 | 4.90 | 4.27 | 3.72 | 3.30 | 3.27 | NA | NA | NA |
| Dividends | 2.56 | 2.36 | 2.20 | 2.08 | 2.00 | 1.92 | 1.76 | 1.60 | 1.40 | 1.25 |
| Payout Ratio | 58% | 49% | 43% | 48% | 53% | 56% | 45% | 35% | 34% | 34% |
| Prices:High | 63.89 | 60.10 | 63.38 | 63.80 | 56.34 | 66.09 | 65.15 | 61.13 | 70.00 | 73.00 |
| Prices:Low | 39.62 | 50.12 | 53.17 | 50.45 | 37.10 | 35.20 | 44.02 | 32.94 | 44.00 | 46.50 |
| P/E Ratio:High | 15 | 12 | 12 | 15 | 15 | 19 | 17 | 13 | 17 | 20 |
| P/E Ratio:Low | 9 | 10 | 10 | 12 | 10 | 10 | 11 | 7 | 11 | 12 |

| Income Statement Analysis (Million $) | 2007 | 2006 | 2005 | 2004 | 2003 | 2002 | 2001 | 2000 | 1999 | 1998 |
|---|---|---|---|---|---|---|---|---|---|---|
| Net Interest Income | 2,003 | 1,983 | 1,956 | 1,810 | 1,926 | 2,132 | 2,102 | 1,659 | 1,547 | 1,461 |
| Tax Equivalent Adjustment | 3.00 | NA | 4.00 | 3.00 | 3.00 | 4.00 | 4.00 | 4.00 | 5.00 | 7.00 |
| Non Interest Income | 881 | 855 | 942 | 857 | 837 | 819 | 784 | 827 | 711 | 597 |
| Loan Loss Provision | 212 | 37.0 | -47.0 | 64.0 | 377 | 635 | 236 | 145 | 114 | 113 |
| % Expense/Operating Revenue | 58.6% | 59.0% | 57.4% | 55.9% | 53.6% | 51.3% | 53.9% | 53.6% | 49.3% | 49.4% |
| Pretax Income | 988 | 1,127 | 1,279 | 1,110 | 953 | 882 | 1,111 | 1,151 | 1,033 | 931 |
| Effective Tax Rate | 31.0% | 30.6% | 32.7% | 31.8% | 30.6% | 31.9% | 36.1% | 34.9% | 34.9% | 34.8% |
| Net Income | 682 | 782 | 861 | 757 | 661 | 601 | 710 | 749 | 673 | 607 |
| % Net Interest Margin | 3.66 | 3.79 | 4.06 | 3.86 | 3.95 | 4.55 | 4.61 | 4.54 | 4.55 | 4.57 |
| S&P Core Earnings | 694 | 766 | 826 | 744 | 657 | 584 | 587 | NA | NA | NA |

| Balance Sheet & Other Financial Data (Million $) | 2007 | 2006 | 2005 | 2004 | 2003 | 2002 | 2001 | 2000 | 1999 | 1998 |
|---|---|---|---|---|---|---|---|---|---|---|
| Money Market Assets | 36.0 | 2,632 | 1,159 | 3,230 | 4,013 | 2,446 | 1,079 | 165 | 613 | 110 |
| Investment Securities | 6,296 | 3,989 | 5,399 | 7,173 | 8,502 | 5,499 | 5,370 | 2,843 | 2,739 | 2,822 |
| Commercial Loans | 38,271 | 35,924 | 33,707 | 31,540 | 32,153 | 33,732 | 32,660 | 28,001 | 25,429 | 23,266 |
| Other Loans | 12,472 | 11,507 | 9,540 | 9,303 | 7,274 | 8,549 | 8,536 | 8,060 | 7,265 | 7,339 |
| Total Assets | 62,331 | 58,001 | 53,013 | 51,766 | 52,592 | 53,301 | 50,732 | 41,985 | 38,653 | 36,601 |
| Demand Deposits | 27,181 | 29,151 | 15,666 | 15,164 | 14,104 | 16,335 | 12,596 | 6,815 | 6,136 | 6,999 |
| Time Deposits | 17,097 | 15,776 | 26,765 | 25,772 | 27,359 | 25,440 | 24,974 | 20,353 | 17,155 | 17,314 |
| Long Term Debt | 8,821 | 5,949 | 3,961 | 4,286 | 4,801 | 5,216 | 5,503 | 8,089 | 8,580 | 5,282 |
| Common Equity | 5,126 | 5,153 | 5,068 | 5,105 | 5,110 | 4,947 | 4,807 | 3,757 | 3,225 | 2,797 |
| % Return on Assets | 1.1 | 1.4 | 1.6 | 1.5 | 1.2 | 1.2 | 1.4 | 1.9 | 1.8 | 1.7 |
| % Return on Equity | 13.3 | 15.3 | 16.9 | 14.8 | 13.1 | 12.3 | 15.4 | 21.0 | 21.8 | 22.2 |
| % Loan Loss Reserve | 1.1 | 1.0 | 1.2 | -1.6 | 2.0 | 1.9 | -1.6 | 1.5 | 1.5 | 1.5 |
| % Loans/Deposits | 110.1 | 105.6 | 101.9 | 99.8 | 99.3 | 101.2 | 109.7 | 132.7 | 140.4 | 125.9 |
| % Equity to Assets | 8.5 | 9.2 | 9.7 | 9.8 | 9.5 | 9.4 | 9.0 | 8.7 | 8.0 | 7.3 |

Data as orig reptd.; bef. results of disc opers/spec. items. Per share data adj. for stk. divs.; EPS diluted. E-Estimated. NA-Not Available. NM-Not Meaningful. NR-Not Ranked. UR-Under Review.

**Office:** 1717 Main St, Dallas, TX 75201-4612.
**Telephone:** 214-969-6476.
**Website:** http://www.comerica.com
**Chrmn, Pres & CEO:** J.W. Babb, Jr.

**Vice Chrmn:** J.J. Buttigieg, III
**EVP & CFO:** B. Acton
**EVP, Secy & General Counsel:** J.W. Bilstrom
**EVP & CIO:** J.R. Beran

**Investor Contact:** D.P. Persons (313-222-2840)
**Board Members:** J. W. Babb, Jr., L. Bauder, J. J. Buttigieg, III, J. F. Cordes, R. A. Cregg, T. K. Denicola, A. F. Earley, Jr., J. P. Kane, R. G. Lindner, A. A. Piergallini, R. S. Taubman, R. M. Turner, Jr., N. G. Vaca, W. P. Vititoe, K. L. Way

**Founded:** 1849
**Domicile:** Delaware
**Employees:** 10,782

The **McGraw·Hill** Companies

# Computer Sciences Corp

**STANDARD &POOR'S**

| S&P Recommendation | BUY ★★★★☆ | Price | 12-Mo. Target Price | Investment Style |
|---|---|---|---|---|
| | | $28.53 (as of Nov 14, 2008) | $34.00 | Large-Cap Blend |

**GICS Sector** Information Technology
**Sub-Industry** Data Processing & Outsourced Services

**Summary** This leading computer services company provides consulting, systems integration and outsourcing services.

## Key Stock Statistics (Source S&P, Vickers, company reports)

| | | | | | | | |
|---|---|---|---|---|---|---|---|
| 52-Wk Range | $55.25– 25.95 | S&P Oper. EPS 2009E | 4.11 | Market Capitalization(B) | $4.318 | Beta | 1.12 |
| Trailing 12-Month EPS | $3.40 | S&P Oper. EPS 2010E | 4.56 | Yield (%) | Nil | S&P 3-Yr. Proj. EPS CAGR(%) | 8 |
| Trailing 12-Month P/E | 8.4 | P/E on S&P Oper. EPS 2009E | 6.9 | Dividend Rate/Share | Nil | S&P Credit Rating | A- |
| $10K Invested 5 Yrs Ago | $6,455 | Common Shares Outstg. (M) | 151.3 | Institutional Ownership (%) | 89 | | |

## Price Performance

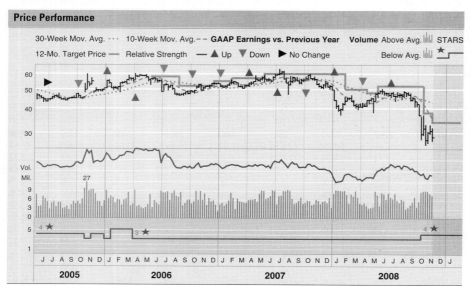

30-Week Mov. Avg. · · · ·  10-Week Mov. Avg. – –  **GAAP Earnings vs. Previous Year**  Volume Above Avg. STARS
12-Mo. Target Price —  Relative Strength —  ▲ Up  ▼ Down  ► No Change  Below Avg.  ★

Options: ASE, CBOE, P, Ph

## Qualitative Risk Assessment

| LOW | MEDIUM | HIGH |
|---|---|---|

Our risk assessment reflects the highly competitive nature of the IT consulting and outsourcing market, offset by our view of CSC's strong balance sheet and the stability afforded the company by the numerous long-term contracts that it has signed with customers.

## Quantitative Evaluations

**S&P Quality Ranking**  B+

| D | C | B- | B | B+ | A- | A | A+ |
|---|---|---|---|---|---|---|---|

**Relative Strength Rank**  MODERATE

52

LOWEST = 1   HIGHEST = 99

## Revenue/Earnings Data

**Revenue (Million $)**

| | 1Q | 2Q | 3Q | 4Q | Year |
|---|---|---|---|---|---|
| 2009 | 4,437 | -- | -- | -- | -- |
| 2008 | 3,838 | 4,017 | 4,160 | 4,484 | 16,500 |
| 2007 | 3,561 | 3,609 | 3,641 | 4,046 | 14,857 |
| 2006 | 3,583 | 3,573 | 3,577 | 3,884 | 14,616 |
| 2005 | 3,736 | 3,935 | 3,517 | 3,879 | 14,059 |
| 2004 | 3,555 | 3,591 | 3,621 | 4,000 | 14,768 |

**Earnings Per Share ($)**

| | 1Q | 2Q | 3Q | 4Q | Year |
|---|---|---|---|---|---|
| 2009 | 0.79 | E0.73 | E1.03 | E1.57 | E4.11 |
| 2008 | 0.61 | 0.43 | 1.05 | 1.15 | 3.20 |
| 2007 | -0.31 | 0.51 | 0.62 | 1.42 | 2.16 |
| 2006 | 0.58 | 0.53 | 0.88 | 1.08 | 3.07 |
| 2005 | 0.58 | 0.68 | 0.69 | 0.86 | 2.59 |
| 2004 | 0.49 | 0.57 | 0.68 | 1.01 | 2.75 |

Fiscal year ended Mar. 31. Next earnings report expected: Late December. EPS Estimates based on S&P Operating Earnings; historical GAAP earnings are as reported.

## Dividend Data

No cash dividends have been paid since 1998.

## Highlights

➤ The 12-month target price for CSC has recently been changed to $34.00 from $38.00. The Highlights section of this Stock Report will be updated accordingly.

## Investment Rationale/Risk

➤ The Investment Rationale/Risk section of this Stock Report will be updated shortly. For the latest News story on CSC from MarketScope, see below.

➤ 11/13/08 12:08 pm ET ... S&P REITERATES BUY OPINION ON SHARES OF CSC CORP. (CSC 28.24****): Sep-Q operating EPS of $0.72 vs. $0.43 is a penny below our estimate. We are lowering our FY 09 (Mar.) revenue growth estimate to 4% from 6%, chiefly to account for adverse currency fluctuations. We see operating margins improving in the second half of the year on a more favorable onshore/offshore mix, improved contract performance, and cost reductions. Still, given the forex headwinds and the possibility of delays in contract signings, we are lowering our FY 09 operating EPS estimate by $0.08, to $4.11, and our 12-month target price by $4, to $34. /D.Cathers

The **McGraw-Hill** Companies

# Computer Sciences Corp

STANDARD
&POOR'S

## Business Summary October 16, 2008

CORPORATE OVERVIEW. Computer Sciences offers what it believes is a broad array of services to clients in the global commercial and government markets. The company specializes in the application of complex information technology (IT) to achieve the strategic objectives of its customers. Offerings include IT and business process outsourcing, and IT and professional services.

Outsourcing involves operating all or a portion of a customer's technology infrastructure, including systems analysis, applications development, network operations, desktop computing, and data center management. CSC also provides business process outsourcing, which involves managing key functions for clients such as claims processing, credit checking, logistics, and customer call centers.

IT and professional services includes systems integration, consulting, and professional services. Systems integration encompasses designing, developing, implementing, and integrating complete information systems. Consulting

and professional services includes advising clients on the strategic acquisition and utilization of IT, and on business strategy, security, modeling, engineering, and business process re-engineering. CSC also licenses sophisticated software systems for healthcare and financial services markets, and provides a broad array of end-to-end e-business solutions to meet the needs of large commercial and government clients.

The company provides services to clients in global commercial industries and to the U.S. federal government. In the global commercial segment, offerings are marketed to clients in a wide variety of industries. In the U.S. federal government market, CSC provides traditional systems integration and outsourcing for complex project management and technical services.

## Company Financials Fiscal Year Ended Mar. 31

| Per Share Data ($) | 2008 | 2007 | 2006 | 2005 | 2004 | 2003 | 2002 | 2001 | 2000 | 1999 |
|---|---|---|---|---|---|---|---|---|---|---|
| Tangible Book Value | 6.35 | 19.51 | 23.85 | 21.71 | 15.44 | 11.78 | 11.58 | 9.26 | 12.78 | 10.98 |
| Cash Flow | NA | 8.95 | 9.42 | 8.56 | 8.29 | 6.95 | 7.02 | 5.17 | 5.59 | 4.85 |
| Earnings | 3.20 | 2.16 | 3.07 | 2.59 | 2.75 | 2.54 | 2.01 | 1.37 | 2.37 | 2.11 |
| S&P Core Earnings | 2.95 | 2.14 | 3.00 | 2.59 | 2.68 | 1.84 | 1.48 | 0.80 | NA | NA |
| Dividends | Nil | NA | Nil | Nil | Nil | Nil | Nil | Nil | Nil | Nil |
| Payout Ratio | Nil | NA | Nil | Nil | Nil | Nil | Nil | Nil | Nil | Nil |
| Calendar Year | 2007 | 2006 | 2005 | 2004 | 2003 | 2002 | 2001 | 2000 | 1999 | 1998 |
| Prices:High | 63.76 | NA | 59.90 | 58.00 | 44.99 | 53.47 | 66.71 | 99.88 | 94.63 | 74.88 |
| Prices:Low | 46.95 | NA | 42.31 | 38.07 | 26.52 | 24.30 | 28.99 | 58.25 | 52.38 | 39.97 |
| P/E Ratio:High | 20 | NA | 20 | 22 | 16 | 21 | 33 | 73 | 40 | 35 |
| P/E Ratio:Low | 15 | NA | 14 | 15 | 10 | 10 | 14 | 43 | 22 | 19 |

### Income Statement Analysis (Million $)

| | 2008 | 2007 | 2006 | 2005 | 2004 | 2003 | 2002 | 2001 | 2000 | 1999 |
|---|---|---|---|---|---|---|---|---|---|---|
| Revenue | 16,500 | 14,857 | 14,616 | 14,059 | 14,768 | 11,347 | 11,426 | 10,524 | 9,371 | 7,660 |
| Operating Income | NA | 2,211 | 2,149 | 1,845 | 1,968 | 1,609 | 1,497 | 1,302 | 1,239 | 990 |
| Depreciation | 1,286 | 1,162 | 1,188 | 1,146 | 1,038 | 858 | 858 | 649 | 546 | 445 |
| Interest Expense | NA | 175 | 104 | 157 | 170 | 143 | 155 | 106 | 58.1 | 48.5 |
| Pretax Income | 918 | 607 | 821 | 715 | 747 | 612 | 497 | 330 | 611 | 511 |
| Effective Tax Rate | 40.7% | 35.9% | 29.7% | 30.6% | 30.5% | 28.0% | 30.7% | 29.4% | 34.1% | 33.3% |
| Net Income | 545 | 389 | 577 | 496 | 519 | 440 | 344 | 233 | 403 | 341 |
| S&P Core Earnings | 502 | 385 | 565 | 495 | 507 | 319 | 254 | 137 | NA | NA |

### Balance Sheet & Other Financial Data (Million $)

| | 2008 | 2007 | 2006 | 2005 | 2004 | 2003 | 2002 | 2001 | 2000 | 1999 |
|---|---|---|---|---|---|---|---|---|---|---|
| Cash | 699 | 1,050 | 1,291 | 1,010 | 610 | 300 | 149 | 185 | 260 | 603 |
| Current Assets | NA | 6,706 | 6,306 | 5,690 | 4,867 | 4,088 | 3,304 | 3,204 | 2,766 | 2,669 |
| Total Assets | 15,775 | 13,731 | 12,943 | 12,634 | 11,804 | 10,433 | 8,611 | 8,175 | 5,874 | 5,008 |
| Current Liabilities | NA | 5,260 | 4,141 | 3,878 | 3,253 | 2,987 | 2,708 | 3,589 | 1,984 | 2,081 |
| Long Term Debt | NA | 1,412 | 1,377 | 1,303 | 2,306 | 2,205 | 1,873 | 1,029 | 652 | 398 |
| Common Equity | 5,462 | 5,886 | 6,772 | 6,495 | 5,504 | 4,606 | 3,624 | 3,215 | 3,044 | 2,400 |
| Total Capital | NA | 7,298 | 8,149 | 7,798 | 7,810 | 6,811 | 5,497 | 4,245 | 3,780 | 2,798 |
| Capital Expenditures | 877 | 686 | 827 | 855 | 725 | 638 | 672 | 897 | 586 | 426 |
| Cash Flow | NA | 1,551 | 1,765 | 1,642 | 1,558 | 1,298 | 1,202 | 882 | 949 | 786 |
| Current Ratio | 1.2 | 1.3 | 1.5 | 1.5 | 1.5 | 1.4 | 1.2 | 0.9 | 1.4 | 1.3 |
| % Long Term Debt of Capitalization | 29.6 | 19.4 | 16.9 | 16.7 | 29.5 | 32.4 | 34.1 | 24.3 | 17.3 | 14.2 |
| % Net Income of Revenue | 3.3 | 2.6 | 3.9 | 3.5 | 3.5 | 3.9 | 3.0 | 2.2 | 4.3 | 4.5 |
| % Return on Assets | 3.7 | 2.9 | 4.5 | 4.1 | 4.7 | 4.6 | 4.1 | 3.3 | 7.2 | 7.5 |
| % Return on Equity | 9.6 | 6.3 | 8.7 | 8.3 | 10.3 | 10.7 | 10.1 | 7.5 | 14.3 | 15.5 |

Data as orig reptd.; bef. results of disc opers/spec. items. Per share data adj. for stk. divs.; EPS diluted. E-Estimated. NA-Not Available. NM-Not Meaningful. NR-Not Ranked. UR-Under Review.

**Office:** 3170 Fairview Park Dr, Falls Church, VA 22042-4516.
**Telephone:** 703-876-1000.
**Email:** investorrelations@csc.com
**Website:** http://www.csc.com

**Chrmn, Pres & CEO:** M.W. Laphen
**CFO, Chief Acctg Officer & Cntlr:** D.G. DeBuck
**Treas:** T.R. Irvin
**Secy & General Counsel:** W.L. Deckelman, Jr.

**Investor Contact:** B. Lackey (310-615-1700)
**Board Members:** I. W. Bailey, II, D. J. Barram, S. L. Baum, R. F. Chase, J. R. Haberkorn, M. W. Laphen, F. W. McFarlan, C. S. Park, T. H. Patrick

**Founded:** 1959
**Domicile:** Nevada
**Employees:** 89,000

# Compuware Corp

**STANDARD &POOR'S**

| | | | | |
|---|---|---|---|---|
| **S&P Recommendation** SELL ★ ★ ☆ ☆ ☆ | | **Price** $5.98 (as of Nov 14, 2008) | **12-Mo. Target Price** $5.50 | **Investment Style** Large-Cap Blend |

**GICS Sector** Information Technology
**Sub-Industry** Application Software

**Summary** This company provides software products and professional services designed to increase the productivity of information systems departments.

## Key Stock Statistics (Source S&P, Vickers, company reports)

| | | | | | | | | |
|---|---|---|---|---|---|---|---|---|
| 52-Wk Range | $11.91– 5.47 | S&P Oper. EPS 2009**E** | 0.46 | Market Capitalization(B) | $1.474 | Beta | | 1.76 |
| Trailing 12-Month EPS | $0.57 | S&P Oper. EPS 2010**E** | 0.45 | Yield (%) | Nil | S&P 3-Yr. Proj. EPS CAGR(%) | | 6 |
| Trailing 12-Month P/E | 10.5 | P/E on S&P Oper. EPS 2009**E** | 13.0 | Dividend Rate/Share | Nil | S&P Credit Rating | | NR |
| $10K Invested 5 Yrs Ago | $10,736 | Common Shares Outstg. (M) | 246.5 | Institutional Ownership (%) | 80 | | | |

## Price Performance

30-Week Mov. Avg. · · · 10-Week Mov. Avg. - - **GAAP Earnings vs. Previous Year** Volume Above Avg. ▮▮▮ STARS
12-Mo. Target Price — Relative Strength — ▲ Up ▼ Down ▶ No Change Below Avg. ▮▮▮ ★

Options: CBOE, P

Analysis prepared by **Jim Yin** on October 28, 2008, when the stock traded at **$ 5.61**.

## Highlights

➤ We estimate that revenue in FY 10 (Mar.) will decrease 1.4%, following our projected 6.3% decline in FY 09. Our outlook reflects our view of a worsening global economy with a recovery in the second half of 2009. We expect software license revenue to fall 1.7% due to customers delaying purchases. We forecast professional service revenue to decrease 4.0%, as CPWR alters its business model, and low-single digit growth for maintenance revenues, reflecting a high maintenance renewal rate.

➤ We forecast that gross margins will increase to 59% in FY 10 from 58% in FY 09. We anticipate that operating margins will remain steady at 15%, due to lower software license revenues offset by a cost savings initiative aimed at a $90 million to $100 million reduction in operating expenses, including a decline in headcount.

➤ Our FY 10 EPS estimate is $0.45, down from $0.46 in FY 09. The expected nominal change in our EPS estimates can be attributed to our projections for flat revenues and operating margins. We expect shares outstanding to remain fairly constant as CPWR recently suspended its share repurchase program.

## Investment Rationale/Risk

➤ Our hold recommendation is based on our concern of further weakness in the global economy. We view CPWR's core business as mature and think the company will be more adversely impacted than other software companies due to its reliance on the auto industry, which accounts for a significant portion of CPWR's revenues. We believe the company will be hurt by unfavorable foreign exchange due to the recent strength in the U.S. dollar. In addition, the company has stopped repurchasing its shares amid the financial crisis.

➤ Risks to our opinion and target price include a recovery in the global economy, being acquired by another company, and higher-than-expected cost savings from restructuring.

➤ Our 12-month target price of $5.50 is based on a blend of our discounted cash flow (DCF) and P/E analyses. Our DCF model assumes a weighted average cost of capital (WACC) of 11.5% and a terminal growth rate of 3%, yielding an intrinsic value of $6.50. For our P/E analysis, we derive a value of $4.50, based on an industry P/E-to-growth ratio of 1.7X, or 10.0X our FY 10 EPS estimate of $0.45.

## Qualitative Risk Assessment

| LOW | MEDIUM | HIGH |
|---|---|---|

Our risk assessment reflects our concern over CPWR's ability to generate future revenue growth, as newer initiatives have been slow to bear fruit, in our opinion. Absent a meaningful pickup in revenue growth, we expect ongoing cost reductions and interest income to drive future earnings growth.

## Quantitative Evaluations

**S&P Quality Ranking** NR

| D | C | B- | B | B+ | A- | A | A+ |
|---|---|---|---|---|---|---|---|

**Relative Strength Rank** MODERATE

| 42 |
|---|

LOWEST = 1      HIGHEST = 99

## Revenue/Earnings Data

**Revenue (Million $)**

| | 1Q | 2Q | 3Q | 4Q | Year |
|---|---|---|---|---|---|
| 2009 | 298.6 | 269.9 | -- | -- | -- |
| 2008 | 279.4 | 302.0 | 309.3 | 338.9 | 1,230 |
| 2007 | 296.3 | 288.5 | 315.2 | 313.0 | 1,213 |
| 2006 | 297.3 | 292.7 | 305.9 | 309.5 | 1,205 |
| 2005 | 287.1 | 295.5 | 330.5 | 318.8 | 1,232 |
| 2004 | 306.0 | 302.8 | 318.2 | 337.7 | 1,265 |

**Earnings Per Share ($)**

| | | | | | |
|---|---|---|---|---|---|
| 2009 | 0.13 | 0.08 | E0.11 | E0.13 | E0.46 |
| 2008 | Nil | 0.13 | 0.13 | 0.23 | 0.47 |
| 2007 | 0.08 | 0.07 | 0.11 | 0.21 | 0.45 |
| 2006 | 0.06 | 0.06 | 0.10 | 0.15 | 0.37 |
| 2005 | Nil | 0.02 | 0.11 | 0.07 | 0.20 |
| 2004 | 0.01 | -0.02 | 0.06 | 0.09 | 0.13 |

Fiscal year ended Mar. 31. Next earnings report expected: Mid January. EPS Estimates based on S&P Operating Earnings; historical GAAP earnings are as reported.

## Dividend Data

No cash dividends have been paid.

*The McGraw-Hill Companies*

# Compuware Corp

STANDARD
&POOR'S

## Business Summary October 28, 2008

CORPORATE OVERVIEW. Originally founded as a professional services company, Compuware provides software, maintenance and professional services intended to increase the productivity of the information technology (IT) departments of businesses. CPWR offers mainframe software for testing, debugging and system maintenance of IBM and IBM-compatible mainframes. The company's distributed products support requirements management (Changepoint), application development (Uniface, Optimal, and DevPartner), testing (QA Center and File-AID/CS), and application performance analysis (Vantage).

LEGAL/REGULATORY ISSUES. On March 21, 2005, Compuware settled all pending litigation with IBM (originally filed in March 2002). Pursuant to the terms of the settlement agreement, IBM also entered into a four-year license and maintenance arrangement with Compuware, worth $140 million, and offered to purchase $260 million of the company's services over a four-year period extending from March 2005 through March 2009. In late 2005, this settlement agreement was amended to extend the period over which IBM could purchase $140 million of Compuware's software and maintenance to five

years (ending March 31, 2010). In addition, according to this amendment, IBM will offer Compuware the opportunity to bid on a minimum of $260 million of IBM-sourced services over a four-and-a-half year period. We do not see the resolution of CPWR's lawsuit against IBM having a meaningful impact on the competitive environment.

FINANCIAL TRENDS. Like those of many of its enterprise software peers, and, in particular, those with sizable mainframe-related revenues, CPWR's revenues peaked in FY 00 (Mar.), driven by Y2K-related spending. Revenues declined annually from FY 00 to FY 06, despite a number of acquisitions, but rose slightly in FY 07. Operating income has followed a similar pattern, although it seems to us to have bottomed in FY 04 due to ongoing expense reductions.

## Company Financials Fiscal Year Ended Mar. 31

| Per Share Data ($) | 2008 | 2007 | 2006 | 2005 | 2004 | 2003 | 2002 | 2001 | 2000 | 1999 |
|---|---|---|---|---|---|---|---|---|---|---|
| Tangible Book Value | 1.95 | 2.57 | 3.33 | 3.15 | 3.11 | 2.93 | 2.60 | 2.02 | 1.51 | 2.70 |
| Cash Flow | NA | 0.70 | 0.51 | 0.34 | 0.27 | 0.41 | -0.40 | 0.60 | 1.10 | 0.97 |
| Earnings | 0.47 | 0.45 | 0.37 | 0.20 | 0.13 | 0.27 | -0.66 | 0.32 | 0.91 | 0.87 |
| S&P Core Earnings | 0.43 | 0.41 | 0.33 | 0.12 | 0.03 | 0.14 | -0.15 | 0.17 | NA | NA |
| Dividends | Nil | Nil | Nil | Nil | Nil | Nil | Nil | Nil | Nil | Nil |
| Payout Ratio | Nil | Nil | Nil | Nil | Nil | Nil | Nil | Nil | Nil | Nil |
| Calendar Year | 2007 | 2006 | 2005 | 2004 | 2003 | 2002 | 2001 | 2000 | 1999 | 1998 |
| Prices:High | 12.56 | 9.55 | 9.99 | 8.95 | 6.52 | 14.00 | 14.50 | 37.81 | 40.00 | 39.91 |
| Prices:Low | 7.32 | 6.02 | 5.51 | 4.35 | 3.22 | 2.35 | 6.25 | 5.63 | 16.38 | 15.56 |
| P/E Ratio:High | 27 | NM | 27 | 45 | 50 | 52 | NM | NM | 44 | 46 |
| P/E Ratio:Low | 16 | NM | 15 | 22 | 25 | 9 | NM | NM | 18 | 18 |

### Income Statement Analysis (Million $)

| | 2008 | 2007 | 2006 | 2005 | 2004 | 2003 | 2002 | 2001 | 2000 | 1999 |
|---|---|---|---|---|---|---|---|---|---|---|
| Revenue | 1,230 | 1,213 | 1,205 | 1,232 | 1,265 | 1,375 | 1,729 | 2,010 | 2,231 | 1,638 |
| Operating Income | NA | 188 | 198 | 143 | 90.5 | 188 | 264 | 296 | 641 | 547 |
| Depreciation | 55.2 | 55.0 | 50.2 | 56.4 | 55.2 | 53.8 | 98.2 | 104 | 71.5 | 41.5 |
| Interest Expense | NA | Nil | Nil | Nil | Nil | 6.10 | 7.43 | 31.3 | 24.5 | Nil |
| Pretax Income | 180 | 193 | 191 | 106 | 56.0 | 156 | -245 | 192 | 562 | 530 |
| Effective Tax Rate | 25.5% | 18.1% | 25.3% | 28.0% | 11.0% | 34.0% | NM | 38.0% | 37.3% | 34.0% |
| Net Income | 134 | 158 | 143 | 76.5 | 49.8 | 103 | -245 | 119 | 352 | 350 |
| S&P Core Earnings | 124 | 143 | 126 | 46.1 | 9.72 | 51.2 | -55.3 | 62.2 | NA | NA |

### Balance Sheet & Other Financial Data (Million $)

| | 2008 | 2007 | 2006 | 2005 | 2004 | 2003 | 2002 | 2001 | 2000 | 1999 |
|---|---|---|---|---|---|---|---|---|---|---|
| Cash | 286 | 261 | 612 | 498 | 455 | 319 | 233 | 53.3 | 30.5 | 193 |
| Current Assets | NA | 921 | 1,445 | 1,358 | 1,143 | 1,050 | 1,063 | 1,004 | 988 | 1,072 |
| Total Assets | 2,019 | 2,029 | 2,511 | 2,478 | 2,234 | 2,123 | 1,994 | 2,279 | 2,416 | 1,677 |
| Current Liabilities | NA | 529 | 545 | 578 | 493 | 469 | 556 | 569 | 596 | 522 |
| Long Term Debt | NA | Nil | Nil | Nil | Nil | Nil | Nil | 140 | 450 | Nil |
| Common Equity | 927 | 1,132 | 1,579 | 1,516 | 1,414 | 1,332 | 1,170 | 1,377 | 1,204 | 1,080 |
| Total Capital | NA | 1,167 | 1,605 | 1,516 | 1,418 | 1,332 | 1,170 | 1,538 | 1,667 | 1,080 |
| Capital Expenditures | 10.5 | 18.6 | 14.5 | 134 | 74.6 | 225 | 90.4 | 39.8 | 34.9 | 26.4 |
| Cash Flow | NA | 213 | 193 | 133 | 105 | 157 | -147 | 223 | 423 | 391 |
| Current Ratio | 1.4 | 1.7 | 2.6 | 2.3 | 2.3 | 2.2 | 1.9 | 1.8 | 1.7 | 2.1 |
| % Long Term Debt of Capitalization | Nil | Nil | Nil | Nil | Nil | Nil | Nil | 9.1 | 27.0 | Nil |
| % Net Income of Revenue | 10.9 | 13.0 | 11.9 | 6.2 | 3.9 | 7.5 | NM | 5.9 | 15.8 | 21.4 |
| % Return on Assets | 6.6 | 7.0 | 5.7 | 3.2 | 2.3 | 5.0 | NM | 5.1 | 17.2 | 25.5 |
| % Return on Equity | 13.1 | 11.7 | 9.2 | 5.2 | 3.6 | 8.2 | NM | 9.2 | 30.8 | 39.1 |

Data as orig reptd.; bef. results of disc opers/spec. items. Per share data adj. for stk. divs.; EPS diluted. E-Estimated. NA-Not Available. NM-Not Meaningful. NR-Not Ranked. UR-Under Review.

**Office:** 1 Campus Martius, Detroit, MI 48226-5099.
**Telephone:** 313-227-7300.
**Email:** investor.relations@compuware.com
**Website:** http://www.compuware.com

**Chrmn & CEO:** P. Karmanos, Jr.
**Pres & COO:** R.C. Paul
**EVP, CFO, Chief Acctg Officer & Treas:** L.L. Fournier
**EVP & Chief Admin Officer:** D.A. Knobblock

**EVP & CTO:** C.J. Bockhausen
**Investor Contact:** L. Elkin (248-737-7345)
**Board Members:** D. W. Archer, G. S. Bedi, W. O. Grabe, W. R. Halling, P. Karmanos, Jr., F. A. Nelson, G. Price, W. J. Prowse, G. S. Romney, T. Thewes

**Founded:** 1973
**Domicile:** Michigan
**Employees:** 6,344

# ConAgra Foods Inc.

STANDARD &POOR'S

| S&P Recommendation BUY ★★★★☆ | Price $15.18 (as of Nov 14, 2008) | 12-Mo. Target Price $25.00 | Investment Style Large-Cap Value |
|---|---|---|---|

**GICS Sector** Consumer Staples
**Sub-Industry** Packaged Foods & Meats

**Summary** This company is one of the largest U.S. packaged food processors.

## Key Stock Statistics (Source S&P, Vickers, company reports)

| | | | | | | | |
|---|---|---|---|---|---|---|---|
| 52-Wk Range | $26.22– 15.00 | S&P Oper. EPS 2009**E** | 1.50 | Market Capitalization(B) | $6.787 | Beta | 0.80 |
| Trailing 12-Month EPS | $2.47 | S&P Oper. EPS 2010**E** | NA | Yield (%) | 5.01 | S&P 3-Yr. Proj. EPS CAGR(%) | 8 |
| Trailing 12-Month P/E | 6.2 | P/E on S&P Oper. EPS 2009**E** | 10.1 | Dividend Rate/Share | $0.76 | S&P Credit Rating | BBB+ |
| $10K Invested 5 Yrs Ago | $7,527 | Common Shares Outstg. (M) | 447.1 | Institutional Ownership (%) | 79 | | |

## Price Performance

30-Week Mov. Avg. ··· 10-Week Mov. Avg. ─ GAAP Earnings vs. Previous Year Volume Above Avg. STARS
12-Mo. Target Price ─ Relative Strength ─ ▲ Up ▼ Down ▶ No Change Below Avg.

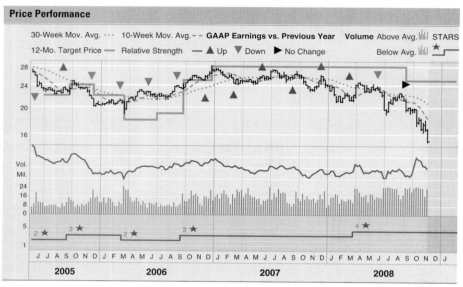

Options: ASE, CBOE, P

Analysis prepared by **Tom Graves, CFA** on September 25, 2008, when the stock traded at **$ 19.61**.

## Highlights

► In June 2008, the company sold its relatively volatile commodity trading and merchandising operations to an investor group for about $2.3 billion of cash and $550 million face value of payment-in-kind debt, subject to adjustments. This was more than what was originally estimated, due to increases in book value.

► In FY 09 (May), we look for the absence of earnings from CAG's commodity trading and merchandising business to be at least partly offset by the impact of stock repurchases, debt repayment and interest income related to proceeds from the sale of that business. After disappointing first quarter results, we expect improved results from CAG's important consumer foods segment, especially in FY 09's second half, helped by higher prices, new products, less pressure from higher input costs, and cost savings from other areas. Before special items, we estimate EPS for FY 09, which has 53 weeks, at $1.50.

► In FY 09's first quarter, CAG utilized about $900 million in an accelerated stock repurchase program, and reduced commercial paper balances by about $1.1 billion.

## Investment Rationale/Risk

► Our buy recommendation reflects our view of CAG being a company in transition. Asset sales since 2003 have generated total pretax proceeds of more than $4 billion. CAG's reported earnings have included a variety of special items, including asset sale gains, restructuring charges, and impairment charges.

► Risks to our recommendation and target price include competitive pressures in CAG's businesses, the potential for increased commodity cost inflation, and the company's ability to generate interest income and to achieve cost savings and efficiency targets.

► With the divestiture of the commodity trading and merchandising business, we anticipate increased profit stability and visibility from a re-shaped ConAgra, and expect the stock to be accorded a higher P/E valuation than it would have otherwise. Our 12-month target price of $25 reflects our view that the stock should receive a P/E discount to what we have targeted, on average, for other food stocks. CAG shares recently had an indicated dividend yield of 3.9%.

## Qualitative Risk Assessment

| LOW | MEDIUM | HIGH |
|---|---|---|

Our risk assessment reflects the relatively stable nature of the company's end markets, and what we view as relatively strong expected cash flows.

## Quantitative Evaluations

**S&P Quality Ranking**     A-

| D | C | B- | B | B+ | A- | A | A+ |
|---|---|---|---|---|---|---|---|

**Relative Strength Rank**     MODERATE

56

LOWEST = 1          HIGHEST = 99

## Revenue/Earnings Data

**Revenue (Million $)**

| | 1Q | 2Q | 3Q | 4Q | Year |
|---|---|---|---|---|---|
| 2009 | 3,066 | -- | -- | -- | -- |
| 2008 | 2,956 | 3,511 | 3,528 | 3,078 | 11,606 |
| 2007 | 2,689 | 3,089 | 2,918 | 3,333 | 12,028 |
| 2006 | 2,700 | 3,026 | 2,879 | 2,975 | 11,579 |
| 2005 | 3,496 | 4,116 | 3,570 | 3,706 | 14,567 |
| 2004 | 4,394 | 3,873 | 3,598 | 3,962 | 14,522 |

**Earnings Per Share ($)**

| | 1Q | 2Q | 3Q | 4Q | Year |
|---|---|---|---|---|---|
| 2009 | 0.23 | E0.41 | E0.42 | E0.42 | E1.50 |
| 2008 | 0.23 | 0.50 | 0.63 | -0.43 | 1.06 |
| 2007 | 0.21 | 0.39 | 0.37 | 0.38 | 1.35 |
| 2006 | 0.63 | 0.24 | 0.18 | 0.10 | 1.15 |
| 2005 | 0.26 | 0.47 | 0.32 | 0.20 | 1.27 |
| 2004 | 0.38 | 0.45 | 0.36 | 0.37 | 1.50 |

Fiscal year ended May 31. Next earnings report expected: Late December. EPS Estimates based on S&P Operating Earnings; historical GAAP earnings are as reported.

## Dividend Data (Dates: mm/dd Payment Date: mm/dd/yy)

| Amount ($) | Date Decl. | Ex-Div. Date | Stk. of Record | Payment Date |
|---|---|---|---|---|
| 0.190 | 11/29 | 01/24 | 01/28 | 02/28/08 |
| 0.190 | 04/03 | 04/29 | 05/01 | 06/02/08 |
| 0.190 | 07/17 | 07/30 | 08/01 | 09/04/08 |
| 0.190 | 09/25 | 10/29 | 10/31 | 12/01/08 |

Dividends have been paid since 1976. Source: Company reports.

---

**Please read the Required Disclosures and Analyst Certification on the last page of this report.**

# ConAgra Foods Inc.

**STANDARD
&POOR'S**

## Business Summary September 25, 2008

CORPORATE OVERVIEW. ConAgra Foods is one of the largest food companies in North America. The company's continuing operations businesses were recently presented in three reporting segments: consumer foods, which provided 59% of total sales in FY 08 (May); food and ingredients (26%); and international foods (6%). CAG's form of segment reporting could be modified in the future. Also, CAG's trading and merchandising segment (12% of FY 07 sales), which was treated as a discontinued operation for full-year FY 08, was sold in June 2008.

The consumer foods segment included branded, private label and customized food products. Major brands include Hunt's, Healthy Choice, Chef Boyardee, Wesson, Orville Redenbacher, Slim Jim, ACT II, Swiss Miss, La Choy, Banquet, Marie Callender's, Kid Cuisine, Hebrew National, Parkay, Blue Bonnet, Egg Beaters, and Reddi-wip.

CAG's foods and ingredients segment included foods and ingredients that are

sold principally to foodservice, food manufacturing and industrial customers. Primary products include specialty potato products, milled grain ingredients, dehydrated vegetables and seasonings, blends, and flavors. CAG's international foods segment included branded food products which are sold principally in retail channels.

In FY 08, CAG's largest customer, Wal-Mart Stores, Inc., and its affiliates, accounted for about 15% of consolidated net sales.

CORPORATE STRATEGY. In recent years, CAG has been pursuing an acquisition and divestiture strategy to shift its focus toward its core branded and value-added food products, while exiting commodity-related businesses.

## Company Financials  Fiscal Year Ended May 31

| Per Share Data ($) | 2008 | 2007 | 2006 | 2005 | 2004 | 2003 | 2002 | 2001 | 2000 | 1999 |
|---|---|---|---|---|---|---|---|---|---|---|
| Tangible Book Value | 2.14 | 0.73 | 0.79 | 0.47 | 0.41 | NM | NM | NM | 1.22 | 1.02 |
| Cash Flow | NA | 2.10 | 1.74 | 1.95 | 2.16 | 2.30 | 2.39 | 2.30 | 1.98 | 1.80 |
| Earnings | 1.06 | 1.35 | 1.15 | 1.27 | 1.50 | 1.58 | 1.47 | 1.33 | 0.86 | 0.75 |
| S&P Core Earnings | 1.05 | 1.29 | 0.91 | 1.14 | 1.39 | 1.42 | 1.27 | 1.20 | NA | NA |
| Dividends | 0.72 | 0.72 | 1.08 | 1.03 | 0.98 | NA | 0.88 | 0.79 | 0.74 | 0.65 |
| Payout Ratio | 68% | 53% | 94% | 81% | 65% | NA | 60% | 59% | 86% | 86% |
| Calendar Year | 2007 | 2006 | 2005 | 2004 | 2003 | 2002 | 2001 | 2000 | 1999 | 1998 |
| Prices:High | 27.73 | 28.35 | 30.24 | 29.65 | 26.41 | 27.65 | 26.00 | 26.19 | 34.38 | 33.63 |
| Prices:Low | 22.81 | 18.85 | 19.99 | 25.38 | 17.75 | 20.90 | 17.50 | 15.06 | 20.63 | 22.56 |
| P/E Ratio:High | 26 | 21 | 26 | 23 | 18 | 18 | 18 | 20 | 40 | 45 |
| P/E Ratio:Low | 22 | 14 | 17 | 20 | 12 | 14 | 12 | 11 | 24 | 30 |

### Income Statement Analysis (Million $)

| | 2008 | 2007 | 2006 | 2005 | 2004 | 2003 | 2002 | 2001 | 2000 | 1999 |
|---|---|---|---|---|---|---|---|---|---|---|
| Revenue | 11,606 | 12,028 | 11,579 | 14,567 | 14,522 | 19,839 | 27,630 | 27,194 | 25,386 | 24,594 |
| Operating Income | NA | 1,577 | 1,184 | 1,618 | 1,735 | 1,123 | 2,144 | 2,026 | 1,828 | 1,940 |
| Depreciation | 297 | 346 | 311 | 351 | 352 | 392 | 474 | 499 | 537 | 500 |
| Interest Expense | NA | 226 | 307 | 341 | 275 | 276 | 402 | 423 | 303 | 354 |
| Pretax Income | 746 | 1,050 | 906 | 1,133 | 1,151 | 1,276 | 1,268 | 1,104 | 666 | 682 |
| Effective Tax Rate | 30.5% | 34.8% | 34.2% | 41.5% | 30.9% | 34.2% | 38.1% | 38.2% | 38.0% | 47.5% |
| Net Income | 519 | 684 | 596 | 663 | 796 | 840 | 785 | 682 | 413 | 358 |
| S&P Core Earnings | 512 | 657 | 470 | 589 | 740 | 750 | 668 | 612 | NA | NA |

### Balance Sheet & Other Financial Data (Million $)

| | 2008 | 2007 | 2006 | 2005 | 2004 | 2003 | 2002 | 2001 | 2000 | 1999 |
|---|---|---|---|---|---|---|---|---|---|---|
| Cash | 141 | 735 | 332 | 208 | 589 | 629 | 158 | 198 | 158 | 62.8 |
| Current Assets | NA | 5,006 | 4,790 | 4,524 | 5,145 | 6,060 | 6,434 | 7,363 | 5,967 | 5,656 |
| Total Assets | 13,683 | 11,836 | 11,970 | 12,792 | 14,230 | 15,071 | 15,496 | 16,481 | 12,296 | 12,146 |
| Current Liabilities | NA | 2,681 | 2,965 | 2,389 | 3,002 | 3,803 | 4,313 | 6,936 | 5,489 | 5,386 |
| Long Term Debt | NA | 3,420 | 3,155 | 4,349 | 5,281 | 5,570 | 5,919 | 4,635 | 3,092 | 3,068 |
| Common Equity | 5,337 | 4,583 | 4,650 | 4,859 | 4,840 | 4,622 | 4,308 | 3,983 | 2,964 | 2,909 |
| Total Capital | NA | 8,003 | 7,805 | 9,209 | 10,120 | 10,192 | 10,227 | 8,618 | 6,056 | 5,977 |
| Capital Expenditures | 490 | 425 | 263 | 453 | 352 | 390 | 531 | 560 | 539 | 662 |
| Cash Flow | NA | 1,030 | 907 | 1,014 | 1,148 | 1,232 | 1,259 | 1,181 | 950 | 858 |
| Current Ratio | 1.7 | 1.9 | 1.6 | 1.9 | 1.7 | 1.6 | 1.5 | 1.1 | 1.1 | 1.1 |
| % Long Term Debt of Capitalization | 38.8 | 42.7 | 40.4 | 47.2 | 52.2 | 54.7 | 57.9 | 53.8 | 51.1 | 51.3 |
| % Net Income of Revenue | 4.5 | 5.7 | 5.1 | 4.6 | 5.5 | 4.2 | 2.8 | 2.5 | 1.6 | 1.5 |
| % Return on Assets | 4.1 | 5.7 | 4.8 | 4.9 | 5.4 | 5.5 | 4.9 | 4.8 | 3.4 | 3.0 |
| % Return on Equity | 10.5 | 14.8 | 12.5 | 13.7 | 16.8 | 18.8 | 18.9 | 19.9 | 14.1 | 12.5 |

Data as orig reptd.; bef. results of disc opers/spec. items. Per share data adj. for stk. divs.; EPS diluted. E-Estimated. NA-Not Available. NM-Not Meaningful. NR-Not Ranked. UR-Under Review.

**Office:** One Conagra Dr, Omaha, NE 68102-5001.
**Telephone:** 402-595-4000.
**Website:** http://www.conagra.com
**Chrmn:** S.F. Goldstone

**Pres & CEO:** G.M. Rodkin
**EVP & CFO:** A.J. Hawaux
**SVP & Treas:** S.E. Messel
**SVP, Secy & General Counsel:** C.R. Batcheler

**Investor Contact:** C.W. Klinefelter (402-595-4154)
**Board Members:** M. C. Bay, K. A. Bousquette, S. G. Butler, S. F. Goldstone, W. G. Jurgensen, R. A. Marshall, S. Martin, G. M. Rodkin, A. J. Schindler, K. Stinson

**Founded:** 1919
**Domicile:** Delaware
**Employees:** 25,000

# ConocoPhillips

STANDARD &POOR'S

| S&P Recommendation | STRONG BUY ★★★★★ | Price $47.39 (as of Nov 14, 2008) | 12-Mo. Target Price $90.00 | Investment Style Large-Cap Blend |
|---|---|---|---|---|

**GICS Sector** Energy
**Sub-Industry** Integrated Oil & Gas

**Summary** This integrated oil and gas company (formerly Phillips Petroleum), the fourth largest integrated oil company in the world, acquired Tosco Corp. in 2001, and merged with Conoco Inc. in 2002.

## Key Stock Statistics (Source S&P, Vickers, company reports)

| | | | | | | | | |
|---|---|---|---|---|---|---|---|---|
| 52-Wk Range | $95.96– 42.15 | S&P Oper. EPS 2008E | 12.52 | Market Capitalization(B) | $70.650 | Beta | | 0.96 |
| Trailing 12-Month EPS | $12.20 | S&P Oper. EPS 2009E | 12.40 | Yield (%) | 3.97 | S&P 3-Yr. Proj. EPS CAGR(%) | | 9 |
| Trailing 12-Month P/E | 3.9 | P/E on S&P Oper. EPS 2008E | 3.8 | Dividend Rate/Share | $1.88 | S&P Credit Rating | | A |
| $10K Invested 5 Yrs Ago | $18,563 | Common Shares Outstg. (M) | 1,490.8 | Institutional Ownership (%) | 76 | | | |

## Price Performance

30-Week Mov. Avg. · · · · 10-Week Mov. Avg. - - **GAAP Earnings vs. Previous Year** Volume Above Avg. STARS
12-Mo. Target Price — Relative Strength — ▲ Up ▼ Down ► No Change Below Avg. ★

Options: ASE, CBOE, P, Ph

Analysis prepared by **Tina J. Vital** on October 22, 2008, when the stock traded at **$ 47.43**.

## Highlights

➤ On September 7, COP agreed to pay up to US$8 billion for a 50% stake in Origin Energy Ltd.'s LNG venture, which plans to develop coal seam reserves in eastern Australia and market LNG to Asian markets. We like the deal, which is expected to close in the fourth quarter, as it enhances COP's LNG position with the creation of an additional hub serving the Asia Pacific markets, and the company gains access to Australia's leading coal bed methane (CBM) resource. However, we view the venture as pricey, at US$32.80 per proved boe, compared to other recent CBM transactions.

➤ Third quarter oil and gas production declined 1% from a year earlier, below our expectations, reflecting maintenance, hurricane impacts and field declines. We project that volumes will drop more than 6% in 2008, but we continue to expect compound annual production growth of about 2% through 2012.

➤ After-tax operating earnings declined 5.6% in 2007, but we expect an increase of 25% in 2008 followed by a slight decline in 2009.

## Investment Rationale/Risk

➤ COP has been reshaping its upstream portfolio to focus on higher-growth assets; Burlington Resources was purchased in 2006, which weakened the company's balance sheet. Since then, strong oil and gas prices and improved production have enabled COP to reduce its balance sheet debt (total debt/capital of 19% as of September 30, 2008). We expect near-term production increases from projects in Canadian heavy oil, Russia, and Asia-Pacific natural gas.

➤ Risks to our recommendation and target price include changes in economic, industrial and operating conditions, including COP's ability to replace its reserves; geopolitical risk; and operational risk.

➤ Blending our DCF ($103 per share, assuming a WACC of 8.6% and a terminal growth rate of 3%), our NAV of $130 (based on a long-term WTI oil price of $90 per barrel), and narrowed relative valuations leads to our 12-month target of $90 per share. This represents an expected enterprise value of about 4.5X our 2009 EBITDA forecast, a discount to U.S. supermajor peers.

## Qualitative Risk Assessment

| LOW | MEDIUM | HIGH |
|---|---|---|

Our risk assessment reflects the company's diversified and strong business profile in volatile, cyclical and capital-intensive segments of the energy industry. While COP has a history of aggressive acquisition activity, we believe its earnings stability is good and its corporate governance practices are sound.

## Quantitative Evaluations

**S&P Quality Ranking** B+

| D | C | B- | B | B+ | A- | A | A+ |
|---|---|---|---|---|---|---|---|

**Relative Strength Rank** MODERATE

45

LOWEST = 1       HIGHEST = 99

## Revenue/Earnings Data

**Revenue (Million $)**

| | 1Q | 2Q | 3Q | 4Q | Year |
|---|---|---|---|---|---|
| 2008 | 54,883 | 71,411 | 71,373 | -- | -- |
| 2007 | 41,320 | 47,370 | 46,062 | 52,685 | 187,437 |
| 2006 | 46,906 | 47,149 | 48,076 | 41,519 | 183,650 |
| 2005 | 37,631 | 41,808 | 48,745 | 51,258 | 179,442 |
| 2004 | 29,813 | 31,528 | 34,350 | 39,385 | 135,076 |
| 2003 | 26,940 | 25,321 | 26,105 | 25,830 | 104,196 |

**Earnings Per Share ($)**

| | | | | | |
|---|---|---|---|---|---|
| 2008 | 2.62 | 3.50 | 3.39 | E3.03 | E12.52 |
| 2007 | 2.12 | 0.18 | 2.23 | 2.71 | 7.22 |
| 2006 | 2.34 | 3.09 | 2.31 | 1.91 | 9.66 |
| 2005 | 2.06 | 2.21 | 2.68 | 2.69 | 9.63 |
| 2004 | 1.16 | 1.44 | 1.44 | 1.76 | 5.79 |
| 2003 | 0.93 | 0.79 | 0.91 | 0.74 | 3.53 |

Fiscal year ended Dec. 31. Next earnings report expected: Late January. EPS Estimates based on S&P Operating Earnings; historical GAAP earnings are as reported.

## Dividend Data (Dates: mm/dd Payment Date: mm/dd/yy)

| Amount ($) | Date Decl. | Ex-Div. Date | Stk. of Record | Payment Date |
|---|---|---|---|---|
| 0.470 | 10/04 | 02/21 | 02/25 | 03/03/08 |
| 0.470 | 05/14 | 07/29 | 07/31 | 09/02/08 |
| 0.470 | 10/01 | 10/29 | 10/31 | 12/01/08 |

Dividends have been paid since 1934. Source: Company reports.

# ConocoPhillips

**STANDARD &POOR'S**

## Business Summary October 22, 2008

CORPORATE OVERVIEW. On August 30, 2002, Phillips Petroleum and Conoco merged, creating ConocoPhillips (COP), the second largest integrated oil company in the U.S. COP operates in six segments: exploration and production (E&P; 26% of 2007 sales, 39% of net income); refining and marketing (R&M; 72%, 50%); midstream (2%, 4%); Lukoil investment; chemicals; and emerging businesses. At year-end 2007, COP owned about a 20% stake in the Russian oil company Lukoil.

Including the Lukoil investment segment, Canadian Syncrude, and COP's share from equity affiliates, oil and gas production declined 1% in 2007, to 2,358,000 boe/d, reflecting the expropriation of the company's Venezuelan oil interests, its exit from Dubai, and the effect of asset dispositions. Net oil and gas production from COP's investment in Lukoil rose 11%, to 443,670 boe/d. Syncrude production increased 9.5%, to 23,000 b/d. Proved reserves (including equity affiliates) declined 7.7%, to 9.57 billion barrels (58% liquids, 73% developed).

Using data from John S. Herold, we estimate COP's three-year (2004-06) finding and development costs at $18.94 per boe, above the peer average; three-year proved acquisition costs at $8.13 per boe, above the peer average; three-year reserve replacement costs at $10.61 per boe, above the peer average; and its three-year reserve replacement at 255%, above the peer average.

As of December 31, 2007, COP owned or had interests in 12 U.S. refineries, five European refineries, and one refinery in Malaysia, with a capacity of 2.71 million b/d. In April 2005, COP unveiled a five-year $3 billion program to expand its ability to refine heavy sour crude oils. At year-end 2007, gasoline and distillates were sold through approximately 10,500 branded outlets in the U.S. (under Phillips 66, Conoco and 76 brands) and Europe (under the JET brand).

## Company Financials Fiscal Year Ended Dec. 31

| Per Share Data ($) | 2007 | 2006 | 2005 | 2004 | 2003 | 2002 | 2001 | 2000 | 1999 | 1998 |
|---|---|---|---|---|---|---|---|---|---|---|
| Tangible Book Value | 41.25 | 29.69 | 25.49 | 18.53 | 12.85 | 9.91 | 14.07 | 10.77 | 8.06 | 7.51 |
| Cash Flow | 12.54 | 14.19 | 12.63 | 8.49 | 5.90 | 5.31 | 5.14 | 5.94 | 2.97 | 2.96 |
| Earnings | 7.22 | 9.66 | 9.63 | 5.79 | 3.53 | 0.74 | 2.79 | 3.63 | 1.20 | 0.46 |
| S&P Core Earnings | 7.49 | 9.59 | 9.72 | 5.88 | 3.43 | 0.64 | 2.60 | NA | NA | NA |
| Dividends | 1.64 | 1.44 | 1.18 | 0.90 | 0.82 | 0.74 | 0.70 | 0.68 | 0.68 | 0.68 |
| Payout Ratio | 23% | 15% | 12% | 15% | 23% | 101% | 25% | 19% | 57% | 149% |
| Prices:High | 90.84 | 74.89 | 71.48 | 45.61 | 33.02 | 32.05 | 34.00 | 35.00 | 28.63 | 26.63 |
| Prices:Low | 61.59 | 54.90 | 41.40 | 32.15 | 26.80 | 22.02 | 25.00 | 17.97 | 18.84 | 20.09 |
| P/E Ratio:High | 13 | 8 | 7 | 8 | 9 | 44 | 12 | 10 | 24 | 59 |
| P/E Ratio:Low | 9 | 6 | 4 | 6 | 8 | 30 | 9 | 5 | 16 | 44 |

| Income Statement Analysis (Million $) | | | | | | | | | | |
|---|---|---|---|---|---|---|---|---|---|---|
| Revenue | 187,437 | 183,650 | 179,442 | 135,076 | 104,196 | 56,748 | 26,868 | 21,113 | 13,751 | 11,545 |
| Operating Income | 31,164 | 37,433 | 24,691 | 17,033 | 11,866 | 4,571 | 8,393 | 5,528 | 2,452 | 1,630 |
| Depreciation, Depletion and Amortization | 8,740 | 7,284 | 4,253 | 3,798 | 3,485 | 4,446 | 1,391 | 1,179 | 902 | 1,302 |
| Interest Expense | 1,801 | 1,087 | 497 | 546 | 864 | 614 | 391 | 422 | 332 | 253 |
| Pretax Income | 23,359 | 28,409 | 23,580 | 14,401 | 8,337 | 2,164 | 3,302 | 3,769 | 1,185 | 421 |
| Effective Tax Rate | 48.7% | 45.0% | 42.0% | 43.5% | 44.9% | 67.0% | 50.2% | 50.6% | 48.6% | 43.7% |
| Net Income | 11,891 | 15,550 | 13,640 | 8,107 | 4,593 | 714 | 1,643 | 1,862 | 609 | 237 |
| S&P Core Earnings | 12,317 | 15,442 | 13,753 | 8,241 | 4,697 | 618 | 1,533 | NA | NA | NA |

| Balance Sheet & Other Financial Data (Million $) | | | | | | | | | | |
|---|---|---|---|---|---|---|---|---|---|---|
| Cash | 1,456 | 817 | 2,214 | 1,387 | 490 | 307 | 142 | 149 | 138 | 97.0 |
| Current Assets | 24,735 | 25,066 | 19,612 | 15,021 | 11,192 | 10,903 | 4,363 | 2,606 | 2,773 | 2,349 |
| Total Assets | 177,757 | 164,781 | 106,999 | 92,861 | 82,455 | 76,836 | 35,217 | 20,509 | 15,201 | 14,216 |
| Current Liabilities | 26,882 | 26,431 | 21,359 | 15,586 | 14,011 | 12,816 | 4,542 | 3,492 | 2,520 | 2,132 |
| Long Term Debt | 26,583 | 23,091 | 10,758 | 14,370 | 16,340 | 19,267 | 9,295 | 7,272 | 4,921 | 4,756 |
| Common Equity | 88,983 | 82,646 | 52,731 | 42,723 | 34,366 | 29,517 | 14,340 | 6,093 | 4,549 | 4,219 |
| Total Capital | 137,757 | 106,939 | 76,137 | 68,583 | 60,113 | 57,796 | 27,650 | 15,259 | 10,950 | 10,292 |
| Capital Expenditures | 11,791 | 15,596 | 11,620 | 9,496 | 6,169 | 4,388 | 3,085 | 2,022 | 1,690 | 2,052 |
| Cash Flow | 20,631 | 22,834 | 17,893 | 11,905 | 8,078 | 5,160 | 3,034 | 3,041 | 1,511 | 1,539 |
| Current Ratio | 0.9 | 0.9 | 0.9 | 1.0 | 0.8 | 0.9 | 1.0 | 0.7 | 1.1 | 1.1 |
| % Long Term Debt of Capitalization | 19.3 | 21.6 | 14.1 | 21.0 | 27.2 | 33.3 | 33.6 | 47.7 | 44.9 | 46.2 |
| % Return on Assets | 6.9 | 11.4 | 13.6 | 9.2 | 5.8 | 1.3 | 5.9 | 10.4 | 4.1 | 1.7 |
| % Return on Equity | 13.9 | 23.0 | 28.6 | 21.0 | 14.4 | 3.3 | 16.1 | 35.0 | 13.9 | 5.2 |

Data as orig reptd.; bef. results of disc opers/spec. items. Per share data adj. for stk. divs.; EPS diluted. E-Estimated. NA-Not Available. NM-Not Meaningful. NR-Not Ranked. UR-Under Review.

**Office:** 600 N Dairy Ashford St, Houston, TX 77079-1175.
**Telephone:** 281-293-1000.
**Website:** http://www.conocophillips.com
**Chrmn & CEO:** J.J. Mulva

**Pres & COO:** J.A. Carrig
**SVP & CFO:** S.L. Cornelius
**SVP, Secy & General Counsel:** J.L. Kelly
**SVP & CIO:** G.L. Batchelder

**Investor Contact:** G. Russell (212-207-1996)
**Board Members:** R. L. Armitage, R. H. Auchinleck, J. Copeland, Jr., K. M. Duberstein, R. R. Harkin, H. McGraw, III, J. J. Mulva, H. J. Norvik, W. K. Reilly, B. Shackouls, V. J. Tschinkel, K. C. Turner, W. E. Wade, Jr.

**Founded:** 1917
**Domicile:** Delaware
**Employees:** 32,600

**The McGraw-Hill Companies**

# Consolidated Edison Inc.

**STANDARD &POOR'S**

| S&P Recommendation **HOLD** ★★★☆☆ | Price $39.19 (as of Nov 14, 2008) | 12-Mo. Target Price $40.00 | Investment Style Large-Cap Value |
|---|---|---|---|

**GICS Sector** Utilities
**Sub-Industry** Multi-Utilities

**Summary** This electric and gas utility holding company serves parts of New York, New Jersey and Pennsylvania.

## Key Stock Statistics (Source S&P, Vickers, company reports)

| | | | | | | |
|---|---|---|---|---|---|---|
| 52-Wk Range | $50.55– 34.11 | S&P Oper. EPS 2008E | 2.95 | Market Capitalization(B) | $10.724 | Beta | 0.25 |
| Trailing 12-Month EPS | $4.55 | S&P Oper. EPS 2009E | 3.00 | Yield (%) | 5.97 | S&P 3-Yr. Proj. EPS CAGR(%) | -2 |
| Trailing 12-Month P/E | 8.6 | P/E on S&P Oper. EPS 2008E | 13.3 | Dividend Rate/Share | $2.34 | S&P Credit Rating | A- |
| $10K Invested 5 Yrs Ago | $12,844 | Common Shares Outstg. (M) | 273.6 | Institutional Ownership (%) | 46 | | |

## Price Performance

30-Week Mov. Avg. · · · 10-Week Mov. Avg. – – GAAP Earnings vs. Previous Year   Volume Above Avg. |ılıl| STARS
12-Mo. Target Price — Relative Strength — ▲ Up ▼ Down ▶ No Change     Below Avg. |ılıl| ★

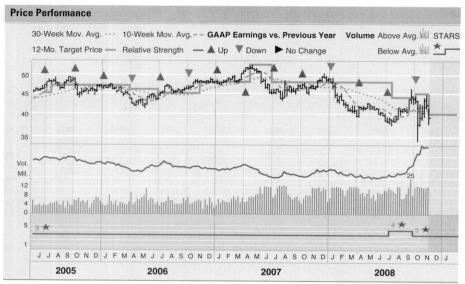

Options: ASE, CBOE, P, Ph

Analysis prepared by **Justin McCann** on November 12, 2008, when the stock traded at **$ 38.77**.

## Highlights

➤ We expect operating EPS in 2008 to decline about 15% from 2007's $3.49. In the first nine months of 2008, operating EPS was down $0.52, to $2.27, on milder weather, higher property taxes, depreciation, and operating expenses, and new stock issuances. Operating EPS for the first nine months excludes net one-time gains of $1.62 and net mark-to-market loss of $0.09.

➤ For 2009 operating EPS, we project only a low single-digit increase from expected results in 2008. We believe the benefit of new rate increases will be nearly offset by higher interest and operating expenses, and an anticipated slowdown in the New York City economy as a result of the turmoil in the financial markets.

➤ On May 9, 2008, Con Edison of New York filed two three-year electric rate increase proposals with the New York PSC. The first requested a $654 million increase (5.8%) that would take effect on April 1, 2009, a second-year increase of 4.2%, and a third-year increase of 3.7%. The second proposed an alternate plan that would raise annual revenues by $557 million (4.9%) in each of the next three years.

## Investment Rationale/Risk

➤ Although the shares are down approximately 20% year to date, they have recovered about 13% from their 2008 low. In addition to the impact of the credit crisis, the expectation of an economic slowdown, and the sharp drop in the stock market, we believe the decline reflects the dilutive impact of new equity issuances, the less than expected increase in electric rates, the lower than anticipated third quarter results, and the negative political and regulatory environment that resulted from an extended power outage in the summer of 2006.

➤ Risks to our recommendation and target price include a significant weakening of the economy in the utility's service territory, unfavorable regulatory rulings, and a sharp decline in the average P/E multiple of the peer group as a whole.

➤ We believe the shares will be supported by a dividend yield (recently 6.0%) that is well above the industry average (around 5.3%). We expect the dividend to continue to increase at an annual rate of around 1%. Our 12-month target price is $40, a premium-to-peers P/E multiple of 13.3X our EPS estimate for 2009.

## Qualitative Risk Assessment

| LOW | MEDIUM | HIGH |
|---|---|---|

Our risk assessment reflects our view of the company's strong and steady cash flows from regulated electric and gas utility operations, its solid balance sheet and A- credit rating, a healthy economy in its service territory, and a supportive regulatory environment historically.

## Quantitative Evaluations

**S&P Quality Ranking** B+

| D | C | B- | B | B+ | A- | A | A+ |
|---|---|---|---|---|---|---|---|

**Relative Strength Rank** STRONG

82

LOWEST = 1     HIGHEST = 99

## Revenue/Earnings Data

**Revenue (Million $)**

| | 1Q | 2Q | 3Q | 4Q | Year |
|---|---|---|---|---|---|
| 2008 | 3,577 | 3,149 | 3,858 | -- | -- |
| 2007 | 3,357 | 2,956 | 3,579 | 3,228 | 13,120 |
| 2006 | 3,317 | 2,555 | 3,441 | 2,824 | 12,137 |
| 2005 | 2,801 | 2,406 | 3,375 | 3,108 | 11,690 |
| 2004 | 2,679 | 2,164 | 2,734 | 2,182 | 9,758 |
| 2003 | 2,570 | 2,175 | 2,801 | 2,279 | 9,827 |

**Earnings Per Share ($)**

| | 1Q | 2Q | 3Q | 4Q | Year |
|---|---|---|---|---|---|
| 2008 | 1.10 | 1.10 | 0.67 | E0.68 | E2.95 |
| 2007 | 0.99 | 0.58 | 1.15 | 0.76 | 3.46 |
| 2006 | 0.74 | 0.51 | 0.92 | 0.78 | 2.95 |
| 2005 | 0.75 | 0.48 | 1.17 | 0.59 | 2.99 |
| 2004 | 0.69 | 0.38 | 1.03 | 0.22 | 2.32 |
| 2003 | 0.72 | 0.29 | 1.16 | 0.19 | 2.36 |

Fiscal year ended Dec. 31. Next earnings report expected: Late January. EPS Estimates based on S&P Operating Earnings; historical GAAP earnings are as reported.

## Dividend Data (Dates: mm/dd Payment Date: mm/dd/yy)

| Amount ($) | Date Decl. | Ex-Div. Date | Stk. of Record | Payment Date |
|---|---|---|---|---|
| 0.585 | 01/24 | 02/11 | 02/13 | 03/15/08 |
| 0.585 | 04/17 | 05/12 | 05/14 | 06/15/08 |
| 0.585 | 07/17 | 08/11 | 08/13 | 09/15/08 |
| 0.585 | 10/16 | 11/07 | 11/12 | 12/15/08 |

Dividends have been paid since 1885. Source: Company reports.

# Consolidated Edison Inc.

**STANDARD &POOR'S**

## Business Summary November 12, 2008

CORPORATE OVERVIEW. Consolidated Edison is a holding company with electric and gas utilities serving a territory that includes New York City (except part of Queens), most of Westchester County, southeastern New York state, northern New Jersey, and northeastern Pennsylvania. Although the company also has some competitive subsidiaries that participate in energy-related businesses, we expect the two regulated utilities to provide substantially all of ED's earnings over the next few years.

MARKET PROFILE. The company's principal business operations are Con Edison of New York's regulated electric, gas and steam utility operations, and Orange and Rockland Utilities' (O&R) regulated electric and gas utility operations. In 2007, electric revenues accounted for 61.8% of consolidated sales (62.9% in 2006); gas revenues 15.4% (15.2%); non-utility revenues 17.5% (16.7%); and steam revenues 5.2% (5.1%). At December 31, 2007, the distribution system of Consolidated Edison Company of New York had about 36,448 miles of overhead distribution lines and around 94,055 miles of underground distribution lines. The distribution system of O&R had about 3,643 miles of overhead distribution lines, and 1,569 miles of underground distribution lines.

The company's Con Edison of New York (CENY) unit provides electric service (75.3% of CENY's operating revenues in 2007) to about 3.2 million customers and gas service (17.8%) to around 1.1 million customers in New York City and Westchester County. It also provides steam service (6.9%) in parts of Manhattan to around 2,000 customers (mostly large office buildings, apartment houses and hospitals). Most of the electricity sold by CENY in 2007 was purchased under firm power contracts (primarily with non-utility generators) or through the wholesale electricity market administered by the New York Independent System Operator (NYISO). We expect this to continue for the foreseeable future.

The company's O&R unit provides electric and gas service in southeastern New York and adjacent areas of eastern Pennsylvania, and electric service in areas of New Jersey adjacent to its New York service territory. In 2007, electric sales accounted for 71.7% of its operating revenues and gas sales, 28.3%.

## Company Financials Fiscal Year Ended Dec. 31

| Per Share Data ($) | 2007 | 2006 | 2005 | 2004 | 2003 | 2002 | 2001 | 2000 | 1999 | 1998 |
|---|---|---|---|---|---|---|---|---|---|---|
| Tangible Book Value | 34.83 | 32.13 | 30.69 | 29.86 | 29.09 | 25.40 | 24.23 | 23.50 | 22.41 | 25.19 |
| Earnings | 3.46 | 2.95 | 2.99 | 2.32 | 2.36 | 3.13 | 3.21 | 2.74 | 3.13 | 3.04 |
| S&P Core Earnings | 2.99 | 2.54 | 2.54 | 1.78 | 1.66 | 0.50 | 0.66 | NA | NA | NA |
| Dividends | 2.32 | 2.30 | 2.28 | 2.26 | 2.24 | 2.22 | 2.20 | 2.18 | 2.14 | 2.12 |
| Payout Ratio | 67% | 78% | 76% | 97% | 95% | 71% | 69% | 80% | 68% | 70% |
| Prices:High | 52.90 | 49.28 | 49.29 | 45.59 | 46.02 | 45.40 | 43.37 | 39.50 | 53.44 | 56.13 |
| Prices:Low | 43.10 | 41.17 | 41.10 | 37.23 | 36.55 | 32.65 | 31.44 | 26.19 | 33.56 | 39.06 |
| P/E Ratio:High | 15 | 17 | 16 | 20 | 20 | 15 | 14 | 14 | 17 | 18 |
| P/E Ratio:Low | 12 | 14 | 14 | 16 | 15 | 10 | 10 | 10 | 11 | 13 |

| Income Statement Analysis (Million $) | 2007 | 2006 | 2005 | 2004 | 2003 | 2002 | 2001 | 2000 | 1999 | 1998 |
|---|---|---|---|---|---|---|---|---|---|---|
| Revenue | 13,120 | 12,137 | 11,690 | 9,758 | 9,827 | 8,482 | 9,634 | 9,431 | 7,491 | 7,093 |
| Depreciation | 645 | 621 | 584 | 551 | 529 | 495 | 526 | 586 | 526 | 519 |
| Maintenance | NA | NA | NA | NA | 353 | 387 | 430 | 458 | 438 | 477 |
| Fixed Charges Coverage | 3.49 | 2.97 | 3.19 | 2.64 | 3.13 | 3.25 | 3.46 | 3.06 | 4.03 | 4.24 |
| Construction Credits | 18.0 | 12.0 | 16.0 | 43.0 | 27.0 | 14.0 | 9.00 | 8.00 | 6.00 | 4.00 |
| Effective Tax Rate | 31.8% | 34.6% | 34.6% | 33.1% | 37.5% | 35.6% | 38.9% | 34.0% | 34.3% | 35.7% |
| Net Income | 925 | 738 | 732 | 549 | 525 | 680 | 696 | 596 | 715 | 730 |
| S&P Core Earnings | 800 | 635 | 621 | 421 | 370 | 106 | 141 | NA | NA | NA |

| Balance Sheet & Other Financial Data (Million $) | 2007 | 2006 | 2005 | 2004 | 2003 | 2002 | 2001 | 2000 | 1999 | 1998 |
|---|---|---|---|---|---|---|---|---|---|---|
| Gross Property | 24,698 | 23,028 | 21,467 | 20,394 | 19,294 | 18,000 | 16,630 | 17,021 | 16,088 | 16,132 |
| Capital Expenditures | 1,928 | 1,847 | 1,617 | 1,359 | 1,292 | 1,216 | 1,104 | 986 | 695 | 626 |
| Net Property | 19,914 | 18,445 | 17,112 | 16,106 | 15,225 | 13,330 | 12,136 | 11,786 | 11,354 | 11,406 |
| Capitalization:Long Term Debt | 7,824 | 8,511 | 7,641 | 6,807 | 6,769 | 6,206 | 5,542 | 5,447 | 4,560 | 4,087 |
| Capitalization:% Long Term Debt | 46.3 | 51.1 | 50.5 | 48.5 | 51.3 | 50.3 | 48.3 | 48.8 | 44.5 | 39.4 |
| Capitalization:Preferred | Nil | Nil | Nil | Nil | Nil | Nil | 250 | 250 | 250 | 250 |
| Capitalization:% Preferred | Nil | Nil | Nil | Nil | Nil | Nil | 2.18 | 2.24 | 2.44 | 2.41 |
| Capitalization:Common | 9,076 | 8,159 | 7,477 | 7,234 | 6,423 | 5,921 | 5,690 | 5,471 | 5,448 | 6,026 |
| Capitalization:% Common | 53.7 | 48.9 | 49.5 | 51.5 | 48.7 | 48.0 | 49.6 | 49.0 | 53.1 | 58.1 |
| Total Capital | 21,408 | 20,806 | 18,804 | 17,806 | 16,406 | 15,037 | 13,835 | 13,602 | 12,666 | 12,911 |
| % Operating Ratio | 89.4 | 89.5 | 90.3 | 90.3 | 88.8 | 74.1 | 88.1 | 117.8 | 86.0 | 85.1 |
| % Earned on Net Property | 9.6 | 7.1 | 7.0 | 5.9 | 6.4 | 8.3 | 9.4 | 8.8 | 9.0 | 9.3 |
| % Return on Revenue | 7.1 | 6.1 | 6.3 | 5.6 | 5.3 | 8.0 | 7.2 | 6.3 | 9.5 | 10.3 |
| % Return on Invested Capital | 6.8 | 6.7 | 6.7 | 5.9 | 7.3 | 7.8 | 8.3 | 7.7 | 8.2 | 11.1 |
| % Return on Common Equity | 11.0 | 9.4 | 10.0 | 7.9 | 8.5 | 11.5 | 12.2 | 10.7 | 12.2 | 11.9 |

Data as orig reptd.; bef. results of disc opers/spec. items. Per share data adj. for stk. divs.; EPS diluted. E-Estimated. NA-Not Available. NM-Not Meaningful. NR-Not Ranked. UR-Under Review.

**Office:** 4 Irving Place, New York, NY 10003-3502.
**Telephone:** 212-460-4600.
**Email:** corpcom@coned.com
**Website:** http://www.coned.com

**Chrmn, Pres & CEO:** K. Burke
**SVP & CFO:** R.N. Hoglund
**Chief Acctg Officer & Cntlr:** E.J. Rasmussen
**Treas:** J.P. O'Brien

**General Counsel:** C.E. McTiernan, Jr.
**Board Members:** K. Burke, V. A. Calarco, G. Campbell, Jr., G. J. Davis, M. J. Del Giudice, E. Futter, S. Hernandez-Pinero, J. F. Killian, P. W. Likins, E. R. McGrath, M. W. Ranger, L. F. Sutherland

**Founded:** 1884
**Domicile:** New York
**Employees:** 15,214

# CONSOL Energy Inc.

STANDARD
&POOR'S

| S&P Recommendation | HOLD ★★★☆☆ | Price $25.52 (as of Nov 14, 2008) | 12-Mo. Target Price $30.00 | Investment Style Large-Cap Blend |
|---|---|---|---|---|

**GICS Sector** Energy
**Sub-Industry** Coal & Consumable Fuels

**Summary** This company is a major producer of high-bituminous coal and coalbed methane gas. We estimate that CNX is the second largest U.S. coal producer by annual production and its coal reserves of 4.5 billion tons.

## Key Stock Statistics (Source S&P, Vickers, company reports)

| | | | | | | | |
|---|---|---|---|---|---|---|---|
| 52-Wk Range | $119.10– 20.28 | S&P Oper. EPS 2008**E** | 1.94 | Market Capitalization(B) | $4.624 | Beta | 1.79 |
| Trailing 12-Month EPS | $1.48 | S&P Oper. EPS 2009**E** | 4.34 | Yield (%) | 1.57 | S&P 3-Yr. Proj. EPS CAGR(%) | 29 |
| Trailing 12-Month P/E | 17.2 | P/E on S&P Oper. EPS 2008**E** | 13.2 | Dividend Rate/Share | $0.40 | S&P Credit Rating | BB+ |
| $10K Invested 5 Yrs Ago | $24,839 | Common Shares Outstg. (M) | 181.2 | Institutional Ownership (%) | 96 | | |

## Price Performance

30-Week Mov. Avg. · · ·   10-Week Mov. Avg. - -   **GAAP Earnings vs. Previous Year**   Volume Above Avg. ||||| STARS
12-Mo. Target Price —   Relative Strength —   ▲ Up  ▼ Down  ► No Change     Below Avg. ||||| ★

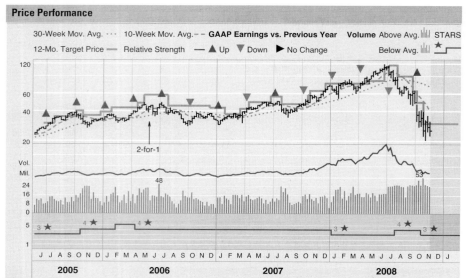

Options: ASE, CBOE, P, Ph

Analysis prepared by **Mathew Christy, CFA** on November 07, 2008, when the stock traded at **$ 25.12**.

## Highlights

➤ We expect revenues to rise 25% in 2008 and more than 30% in 2009, as we forecast a slight increase in produced tons in 2008 and greater average realized prices. We believe that the acquisition of AMVEST, which closed on August 1, 2007, will enable CNX to add over 4 million tons of annual production to its volume for 2008. We calculate that per-ton prices will rise approximately 19% in 2008, as contracts lock in higher prices than 2007 levels and an estimated 4% of total tonnage sold is priced at current spot rates over $100 per ton.

➤ We think EBIT (earnings before interest and taxes) margins will rise in 2008 and continue to increase in 2009 due to higher productivity, cost reduction efforts, and operating leverage from better volume and higher pricing. We forecast that average cash cost per ton will increase 4% in 2008, but rise more than 28% in 2009 on increasing fuel and compensation expenses.

➤ Assuming steady interest expense, tax rates and diluted shares outstanding, we project operating EPS of $1.94 in 2008 and $4.34 in 2009.

## Investment Rationale/Risk

➤ We believe CNX will benefit from increasing volume and improving pricing for coal from Appalachia through its long-term supply contracts that are beginning to display premiums. We view positively CNX's balance sheet due to its 33% average debt-to-capital and 0.8X debt-to-EBITDA ratio for the 12 months ended September 2008. However, we believe recent cost increases, arising from regulatory and labor issues, along with the slowing economy increases operational risks.

➤ Risks to our recommendation and target price include lower-than-expected prices for steam and metallurgical grade coal, reduced productivity, increased supply costs, and slower-than-forecast U.S. economic activity.

➤ Our 12-month target price of $30 is based on a relative valuation analysis. We apply an EV/EBITDA multiple of 3.5X to our 2009 EBITDA estimate, suggesting a $30 value. This multiple is ahead of peers due to CNX's size, but is below the prior historical low multiple of about 4X EBITDA.

## Qualitative Risk Assessment

| LOW | MEDIUM | HIGH |
|---|---|---|

Our risk assessment reflects the cyclical nature of the coal market, our view of unfavorable corporate governance practices concerning takeover defenses, and the heavily regulated nature of the industry and its utilities end market, notwithstanding expected benefits from the pricing cycle and a rising market share.

## Quantitative Evaluations

### S&P Quality Ranking                NR

| D | C | B- | B | B+ | A- | A | A+ |
|---|---|---|---|---|---|---|---|

### Relative Strength Rank            WEAK

| 21 |
|---|

LOWEST = 1                              HIGHEST = 99

## Revenue/Earnings Data

### Revenue (Million $)

| | 1Q | 2Q | 3Q | 4Q | Year |
|---|---|---|---|---|---|
| 2008 | 1,026 | 1,211 | 1,173 | -- | -- |
| 2007 | 915.2 | 1,060 | 868.4 | 918.6 | 3,565 |
| 2006 | 985.9 | 932.3 | 843.4 | 953.7 | 3,715 |
| 2005 | 817.0 | 817.2 | 879.9 | 969.1 | 3,483 |
| 2004 | 650.9 | 674.6 | 659.9 | 791.4 | 2,777 |
| 2003 | 559.8 | 556.5 | 552.2 | 554.0 | 2,222 |

### Earnings Per Share ($)

| | 1Q | 2Q | 3Q | 4Q | Year |
|---|---|---|---|---|---|
| 2008 | 0.41 | 0.54 | 0.49 | E0.50 | E1.94 |
| 2007 | 0.61 | 0.83 | -0.03 | 0.04 | 1.45 |
| 2006 | 0.67 | 0.57 | 0.27 | 0.69 | 2.20 |
| 2005 | 0.41 | 0.22 | 2.02 | 0.47 | 3.13 |
| 2004 | 0.18 | 0.15 | -0.07 | 0.37 | 0.64 |
| 2003 | 0.02 | 0.07 | -0.04 | -0.14 | -0.05 |

Fiscal year ended Dec. 31. Next earnings report expected: Late January. EPS Estimates based on S&P Operating Earnings; historical GAAP earnings are as reported.

## Dividend Data (Dates: mm/dd Payment Date: mm/dd/yy)

| Amount ($) | Date Decl. | Ex-Div. Date | Stk. of Record | Payment Date |
|---|---|---|---|---|
| 0.100 | 01/30 | 02/05 | 02/07 | 02/22/08 |
| 0.100 | 04/25 | 05/02 | 05/06 | 05/27/08 |
| 0.100 | 08/01 | 08/05 | 08/07 | 08/25/08 |
| 0.100 | 10/24 | 11/03 | 11/05 | 11/21/08 |

Dividends have been paid since 1999. Source: Company reports.

---

**Please read the Required Disclosures and Analyst Certification on the last page of this report.**

# CONSOL Energy Inc.

**STANDARD &POOR'S**

## Business Summary November 07, 2008

CORPORATE OVERVIEW. Through expansion and acquisitions, CONSOL Energy has grown from a single fuel mining company formed in 1860 into a multi-energy producer of coal and gas. CNX produces high Btu coal and gas, two fuels that collectively generate two-thirds of all U.S. electric power, from reserves located mainly east of the Mississippi River.

The coal segment (CNX Coal) has 17 mining complexes in the U.S., and sells steam coal to power generators and metallurgical coal to metal and coke producers. The company had an estimated 4.5 billion tons of proven and probable coal reserves at the end of 2007, nearly all of which was located in underground mines. About 63% of CNX's reserves are found in northern Appalachia, with 18% in the Midwest, 13% in central Appalachia, 4% in the western U.S., and 2% in western Canada. The company is a major fuel supplier to the electric power industry in the northeast quadrant of the U.S. Coal produced at CNX's mines is transported to customers via railroad cars, barges, trucks and conveyor belts, or by a combination of such methods. In 2007, the company sold 65.5 million produced tons of coal, down from 68.9 million tons in 2006. Approximately 90% of coal produced in 2007 was sold under contracts with

terms of one year or more. The average sales price per produced ton sold in 2007 was $40.60, versus $38.99 in 2006. In 2007, one customer, Allegheny Energy, accounted for 10% of total company revenue.

CONSOL Energy owns 81.7% of CNX Gas Corporation, which is one of the largest U.S. producers of coalbed methane (CBM), with daily gas production of 155 MMcf. CBM produces pipeline quality gas that is found in coal seams, usually in formations at depths of less than 2,500 feet versus conventional natural gas fields with depths of up to 15,000 feet. At the end of 2007, CNX Gas had 1.3 Tcf of proved CBM reserves, of which approximately 48% was developed, and nearly 3,000 active wells connected to over 1,300 miles of gathering lines. In 2007, the company sold 58.3 Bcf of gas at an average price of $7.20, versus 56.1 Bcf at $7.04 in 2006.

## Company Financials Fiscal Year Ended Dec. 31

| Per Share Data ($) | 2007 | 2006 | 2005 | 2004 | 2003 | 2002 | 2001 | 2000 | 1999 | 1998 |
|---|---|---|---|---|---|---|---|---|---|---|
| Tangible Book Value | 6.77 | 5.84 | 5.54 | 2.59 | NM | 1.03 | 2.23 | 1.62 | 1.59 | NA |
| Cash Flow | 3.24 | 3.80 | 4.54 | 2.17 | 1.40 | 1.74 | 2.71 | 2.24 | 1.24 | NA |
| Earnings | 1.45 | 2.20 | 3.13 | 0.64 | -0.05 | 0.08 | 1.17 | 0.68 | 0.31 | 1.09 |
| S&P Core Earnings | 1.02 | 1.88 | 2.05 | 0.69 | 0.04 | 0.03 | 0.98 | NA | NA | NA |
| Dividends | 0.31 | 0.28 | 0.28 | 0.28 | 0.28 | 0.42 | 0.56 | 0.56 | Nil | NA |
| Payout Ratio | 21% | 13% | 9% | 44% | NM | NM | 48% | 83% | Nil | NA |
| Prices:High | 74.18 | 49.09 | 39.91 | 21.95 | 13.40 | 14.16 | 21.24 | 14.00 | 8.00 | NA |
| Prices:Low | 29.15 | 28.07 | 18.58 | 10.12 | 7.28 | 4.90 | 9.15 | 4.97 | 4.81 | NA |
| P/E Ratio:High | 51 | 22 | 13 | 35 | NM | NM | 18 | 21 | NM | NA |
| P/E Ratio:Low | 20 | 13 | 6 | 16 | NM | NM | 8 | 7 | NM | NA |

| Income Statement Analysis (Million $) | 2007 | 2006 | 2005 | 2004 | 2003 | 2002 | 2001 | 2000 | 1999 | 1998 |
|---|---|---|---|---|---|---|---|---|---|---|
| Revenue | 3,762 | 3,715 | 3,483 | 2,777 | 2,222 | 2,184 | 2,368 | 2,159 | 1,110 | 2,295 |
| Operating Income | 829 | 701 | 617 | 308 | 246 | 268 | 418 | 599 | 409 | NA |
| Depreciation | 329 | 296 | 262 | 280 | 242 | 263 | 243 | 250 | 121 | 256 |
| Interest Expense | 45.4 | 25.1 | 27.3 | 31.4 | 34.5 | 46.2 | 57.6 | 55.0 | 30.5 | 48.1 |
| Pretax Income | 429 | 551 | 655 | 82.6 | -33.5 | -40.4 | 240 | 107 | 40.2 | 212 |
| Effective Tax Rate | 31.7% | 20.4% | 9.83% | NM | NM | NM | 23.6% | NM | 0.30% | 17.8% |
| Net Income | 268 | 409 | 581 | 115 | -12.6 | 11.7 | 184 | 107 | 40.0 | 175 |
| S&P Core Earnings | 190 | 349 | 381 | 125 | 6.95 | 3.70 | 154 | NA | NA | NA |

| Balance Sheet & Other Financial Data (Million $) | 2007 | 2006 | 2005 | 2004 | 2003 | 2002 | 2001 | 2000 | 1999 | 1998 |
|---|---|---|---|---|---|---|---|---|---|---|
| Cash | 41.7 | 224 | 341 | 6.42 | 6.51 | 11.5 | 16.6 | 8.20 | 23.6 | 31.3 |
| Current Assets | 683 | 914 | 998 | 470 | 471 | 623 | 566 | 578 | 623 | NA |
| Total Assets | 6,208 | 5,663 | 5,088 | 4,196 | 4,319 | 4,293 | 3,895 | 3,866 | 3,875 | 3,863 |
| Current Liabilities | 1,016 | 740 | 804 | 705 | 825 | 814 | 934 | 953 | 884 | NA |
| Long Term Debt | 489 | 493 | 438 | 426 | 442 | 488 | 231 | 301 | 313 | NA |
| Common Equity | 1,214 | 984 | 1,025 | 469 | 291 | 162 | 352 | 254 | 255 | -103 |
| Total Capital | 1,866 | 1,612 | 1,557 | 895 | 733 | 650 | 583 | 555 | 567 | NA |
| Capital Expenditures | 743 | 659 | 523 | 411 | 291 | 295 | 214 | 143 | 105 | 260 |
| Cash Flow | 597 | 705 | 843 | 396 | 230 | 275 | 427 | 357 | 161 | NA |
| Current Ratio | 0.7 | 1.2 | 1.2 | 0.7 | 0.6 | 0.8 | 0.6 | 0.6 | 0.7 | 0.5 |
| % Long Term Debt of Capitalization | 26.2 | 30.6 | 28.2 | 47.6 | 60.3 | 75.1 | 39.6 | 54.1 | 55.1 | NM |
| % Net Income of Revenue | 7.1 | 11.5 | 17.2 | 4.1 | NM | NM | 7.8 | 4.9 | 3.6 | 7.6 |
| % Return on Assets | 4.5 | 7.6 | 12.5 | 2.7 | NM | NM | 4.7 | 2.7 | NM | NA |
| % Return on Equity | 23.5 | 40.7 | 77.7 | 30.3 | NM | NM | 60.6 | 42.0 | NM | NM |

Data as orig reptd.; bef. results of disc opers/spec. items. Per share data adj. for stk. divs.; EPS diluted. E-Estimated. NA-Not Available. NM-Not Meaningful. NR-Not Ranked. UR-Under Review.

**Office:** 1800 Washington Road, Pittsburgh, PA 15241.
**Telephone:** 412-831-4000.
**Website:** http://www.consolenergy.com
**Chrmn:** J.L. Whitmire, III

**Pres & CEO:** J.B. Harvey
**Investor Contact:** W.J. Lyons (412-831-4000)
**EVP, CFO & Chief Acctg Officer:** W.J. Lyons
**SVP, Secy & General Counsel:** P.J. Richey

**Board Members:** J. E. Altmeyer, W. E. Davis, R. K. Gupta, P. A. Hammick, D. C. Hardesty, Jr., J. B. Harvey, J. T. Mills, W. P. Powell, J. L. Whitmire, III, J. T. Williams

**Founded:** 1991
**Domicile:** Delaware
**Employees:** 7,728

*The McGraw·Hill Companies*

# Constellation Brands Inc.

**STANDARD &POOR'S**

| S&P Recommendation | **BUY** ★★★★☆ | Price $11.49 (as of Nov 14, 2008) | 12-Mo. Target Price $24.00 | Investment Style Large-Cap Growth |
|---|---|---|---|---|

**GICS Sector** Consumer Staples
**Sub-Industry** Distillers & Vintners

**Summary** This leading international producer and marketer of alcoholic beverages has a broad portfolio of wine, imported beer, and distilled spirits brands.

## Key Stock Statistics (Source S&P, Vickers, company reports)

| | | | | | | | |
|---|---|---|---|---|---|---|---|
| 52-Wk Range | $24.97– 10.66 | S&P Oper. EPS 2009**E** | 1.70 | Market Capitalization(B) | $2.240 | Beta | 0.67 |
| Trailing 12-Month EPS | $-3.28 | S&P Oper. EPS 2010**E** | 1.87 | Yield (%) | Nil | S&P 3-Yr. Proj. EPS CAGR(%) | 11 |
| Trailing 12-Month P/E | NM | P/E on S&P Oper. EPS 2009**E** | 6.8 | Dividend Rate/Share | Nil | S&P Credit Rating | BB- |
| $10K Invested 5 Yrs Ago | $7,389 | Common Shares Outstg. (M) | 218.7 | Institutional Ownership (%) | 92 | | |

## Price Performance

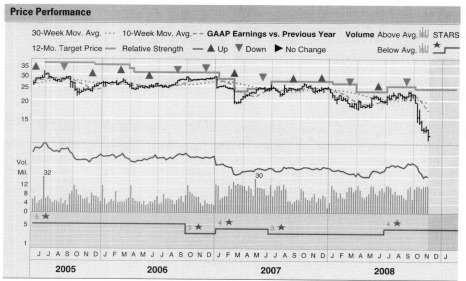

- 30-Week Mov. Avg. · · · 10-Week Mov. Avg. – – **GAAP Earnings vs. Previous Year** Volume Above Avg.▐▌ STARS
- 12-Mo. Target Price — Relative Strength — ▲ Up ▼ Down ► No Change Below Avg.▐▌ ★

Options: ASE, CBOE, P, Ph

Analysis prepared by **Esther Y. Kwon, CFA** on October 02, 2008, when the stock traded at **$ 20.19**.

## Highlights

➤ In 2007, STZ entered into a 50/50 joint venture with Grupo Modelo SA to import and distribute beers, primarily top import brand Corona. As a result, STZ's beer sales have been deconsolidated, with the entity accounted for on an equity basis. The company also sold half of its Matthew Clark wholesale business to a joint venture with Punch Taverns plc.

➤ Following a 25% sales decline in FY 08 (Feb.) on deconsolidation of beer sales, we see FY 09 net revenues rising about 5% on benefits from a stronger portfolio following the purchase of SVEDKA vodka and Fortune Brands' wine business. We project over 200 basis points of operating margin expansion on the restructuring of Australian operations, the consolidation of certain U.S. spirits production processes, and further integration of recent acquisitions in the wines and spirits segments. Longer term, we expect the mix shift toward higher-growth premium-priced wines to benefit margins.

➤ With little change seen in interest expense, and an effective tax rate of 37%, we estimate an increase in FY 09 operating EPS to $1.70, excluding restructuring charges and integration costs. For FY 10, we forecast EPS of $1.87.

## Investment Rationale/Risk

➤ We view favorably STZ's moves into higher-growth segments, divestitures of value-priced, popular brands, and debt reduction. In December 2007, STZ completed the purchase of Fortune Brands' U.S. wine business, which should give STZ a stronger presence in the faster-growing superpremium and above segment. We see healthy global demand for premium wines continuing, and U.S. wine exports benefiting from a relatively weak U.S. dollar. We think recent tax hikes in the U.K. could weigh on results in the near term, but with the write-down and review of wine assets at a competitor in Australia and improving grape supply/demand, we look for competitive conditions to ease in the Australia and U.K. markets.

➤ Risks to our recommendation and target price include continued pricing pressures in the U.K. wine market, resistance to further price increases, and integration risk.

➤ Our 12-month target price of $24 is based on a P/E multiple of 13X our FY 10 EPS estimate of $1.87. We think a discount to the recent historical average of 16X is appropriate amid a backdrop of slowing economic conditions and higher debt levels.

## Qualitative Risk Assessment

| LOW | **MEDIUM** | HIGH |
|---|---|---|

STZ operates in an industry that we believe has demonstrated stable revenue streams. This is offset by our corporate governance concerns relating to STZ's dual class stock structure with unequal voting rights.

## Quantitative Evaluations

**S&P Quality Ranking** **B**

| D | C | B- | **B** | B+ | A- | A | A+ |
|---|---|---|---|---|---|---|---|

**Relative Strength Rank** **MODERATE**

34

LOWEST = 1        HIGHEST = 99

## Revenue/Earnings Data

### Revenue (Million $)

| | 1Q | 2Q | 3Q | 4Q | Year |
|---|---|---|---|---|---|
| 2009 | 931.8 | 956.5 | -- | -- | -- |
| 2008 | 901.2 | 1,168 | 1,406 | 884.4 | 3,773 |
| 2007 | 1,156 | 1,418 | 1,501 | 1,142 | 5,216 |
| 2006 | 1,097 | 1,192 | 1,267 | 1,048 | 4,603 |
| 2005 | 927.3 | 1,037 | 1,086 | 1,038 | 4,088 |
| 2004 | 772.8 | 911.1 | 987.3 | 881.3 | 3,552 |

### Earnings Per Share ($)

| | | | | | |
|---|---|---|---|---|---|
| 2009 | 0.20 | -0.10 | E0.62 | E0.30 | E1.70 |
| 2008 | 0.13 | 0.34 | 0.55 | -3.92 | -2.83 |
| 2007 | 0.36 | 0.28 | 0.45 | 0.29 | 1.38 |
| 2006 | 0.32 | 0.34 | 0.46 | 0.24 | 1.36 |
| 2005 | 0.23 | 0.35 | 0.42 | 0.20 | 1.19 |
| 2004 | 0.21 | 0.17 | 0.37 | 0.28 | 1.03 |

Fiscal year ended Feb. 29. Next earnings report expected: NA. EPS Estimates based on S&P Operating Earnings; historical GAAP earnings are as reported.

## Dividend Data

No cash dividends have been paid.

---

# Constellation Brands Inc.

**STANDARD &POOR'S**

## Business Summary October 02, 2008

CORPORATE OVERVIEW. Through an aggressive acquisition program over the past few years, Constellation Brands (formerly Canandaigua Brands) has become a leading international producer and marketer of alcoholic beverages in North America, Europe and Australia. STZ recently restructured into three divisions -- Constellation Wines, Constellation Spirits, and Crown Imports.

Constellation Wines produces and markets table wines, dessert wines and sparkling wines. It is a leading producer and marketer of wine in the U.S., Canada, Australia, and New Zealand and the largest marketer of wine in the U.K. The company sells wines in the popular, premium, super-premium and ultra-premium categories. The higher category wines are supported by vineyard holdings in California, Canada, Australia, New Zealand and Chile. At the end of FY 08 (Feb.), the company operated 26 wineries in the U.S., 11 in Australia, 10 in Canada, four in New Zealand, and one in South Africa.

STZ has developed a premium wine portfolio through acquisitions, selling 21 of the top 100 U.S. table wines in 2008 compared to 24 in 2007. Leading wine brands include Arbor Mist, Vendange, Woodbridge, Robert Mondavi, Inniskillin, Kim Crawford, Hardys, Nobilo, Alice White, Ruffino, Blackstone, Ravenswood, Estancia, Franciscan Oakville Estate, Simi, Clos du Bois, and Toasted Head.

The former Constellation Beers has been contributed to the Crown Imports joint venture. It imports and markets a diversified line of beer. The company is the largest marketer of imported beer in 25 mostly western states. It distributes six of the top 20 imported beer brands in the U.S.: Corona Extra, the best selling imported beer, Modelo Especial, Corona Light, Pacifico, St. Pauli Girl, and Negra Modelo. It also imports the top-selling Chinese beer, Tsingtao.

Constellation Spirits operates seven facilities where it produces and bottles, imports and markets a diversified line of distilled spirits. Distilled spirits brands are marketed primarily in the value and mid-premium priced category. Principal brands include Black Velvet, Barton, Skol, Fleischmann's Canadian LTD, Montezuma, Ten High, Chi-Chi's, Mr. Boston, Inver House, and Monte Alban. STZ also sells bulk spirits and other related products and services. The company moved to improve its mix of premium brands with the 2007 acquisition of SVEDKA vodka.

## Company Financials Fiscal Year Ended Feb. 29

| Per Share Data ($) | 2008 | 2007 | 2006 | 2005 | 2004 | 2003 | 2002 | 2001 | 2000 | 1999 |
|---|---|---|---|---|---|---|---|---|---|---|
| Tangible Book Value | NM | NM | NM | NM | NM | 0.39 | NM | NM | NM | NM |
| Cash Flow | -2.07 | 1.95 | 1.86 | 1.59 | 1.39 | 1.42 | 1.08 | 0.95 | 0.80 | 0.67 |
| Earnings | -2.83 | -1.38 | 1.36 | 1.19 | 1.03 | 1.10 | 0.79 | 0.65 | 0.52 | 0.41 |
| S&P Core Earnings | 1.13 | 1.41 | 1.24 | 1.02 | 0.96 | 0.97 | 0.66 | 0.54 | NA | NA |
| Dividends | Nil | Nil | Nil | Nil | Nil | Nil | Nil | Nil | Nil | Nil |
| Payout Ratio | Nil | Nil | Nil | Nil | Nil | Nil | Nil | Nil | Nil | Nil |
| Calendar Year | 2007 | 2006 | 2005 | 2004 | 2003 | 2002 | 2001 | 2000 | 1999 | 1998 |
| Prices:High | 29.17 | 29.14 | 31.60 | 23.91 | 17.33 | 16.00 | 11.63 | 7.38 | 7.69 | 7.47 |
| Prices:Low | 18.83 | 23.32 | 21.15 | 14.65 | 10.95 | 10.53 | 6.63 | 5.05 | 5.36 | 4.41 |
| P/E Ratio:High | NM | 22 | 23 | 20 | 17 | 15 | 15 | 11 | 15 | 18 |
| P/E Ratio:Low | NM | 18 | 16 | 12 | 11 | 10 | 8 | 8 | 10 | 11 |

### Income Statement Analysis (Million $)

| | 2008 | 2007 | 2006 | 2005 | 2004 | 2003 | 2002 | 2001 | 2000 | 1999 |
|---|---|---|---|---|---|---|---|---|---|---|
| Revenue | 3,773 | 5,216 | 4,603 | 4,088 | 3,552 | 2,732 | 2,821 | 2,397 | 2,340 | 1,497 |
| Operating Income | 704 | 895 | 840 | 689 | 601 | 470 | 394 | 315 | 281 | 187 |
| Depreciation | 160 | 140 | 128 | 104 | 82.0 | 60.1 | 51.9 | 44.6 | 40.9 | 38.6 |
| Interest Expense | 342 | 269 | 190 | 138 | 145 | 105 | 114 | 109 | 106 | 41.5 |
| Pretax Income | -441 | 535 | 477 | 432 | 344 | 335 | 230 | 162 | 129 | 104 |
| Effective Tax Rate | NM | 38.0% | 31.8% | 36.0% | 36.0% | 39.3% | 40.0% | 40.0% | 40.0% | 59.3% |
| Net Income | -613 | 332 | 325 | 276 | 220 | 203 | 138 | 97.3 | 77.4 | 61.9 |
| S&P Core Earnings | 243 | 334 | 288 | 230 | 199 | 181 | 115 | 80.7 | NA | NA |

### Balance Sheet & Other Financial Data (Million $)

| | 2008 | 2007 | 2006 | 2005 | 2004 | 2003 | 2002 | 2001 | 2000 | 1999 |
|---|---|---|---|---|---|---|---|---|---|---|
| Cash | 20.5 | 33.5 | 10.9 | 17.6 | 37.1 | 13.8 | 8.96 | 146 | 34.3 | 27.6 |
| Current Assets | 3,199 | 3,023 | 2,701 | 2,734 | 2,071 | 1,330 | 1,231 | 1,191 | 996 | 856 |
| Total Assets | 10,053 | 9,438 | 7,401 | 7,804 | 5,559 | 3,196 | 3,069 | 2,512 | 2,349 | 1,794 |
| Current Liabilities | 1,718 | 1,591 | 1,298 | 1,138 | 1,030 | 585 | 595 | 427 | 438 | 832 |
| Long Term Debt | 4,649 | 3,715 | 2,516 | 3,205 | 1,779 | 1,192 | 1,293 | 1,307 | 1,237 | 415 |
| Common Equity | 2,766 | 3,418 | 2,975 | 2,780 | 2,378 | 1,207 | 956 | 616 | 521 | 435 |
| Total Capital | 7,950 | 7,607 | 5,862 | 6,375 | 4,344 | 2,544 | 2,412 | 2,056 | 1,874 | 1,355 |
| Capital Expenditures | 144 | 192 | 132 | 120 | 105 | 71.6 | 71.1 | 68.2 | 57.7 | 49.9 |
| Cash Flow | -454 | 467 | 444 | 370 | 297 | 263 | 190 | 142 | 118 | 101 |
| Current Ratio | 1.9 | 1.9 | 2.1 | 2.4 | 2.0 | 2.3 | 2.1 | 2.8 | 2.3 | 1.0 |
| % Long Term Debt of Capitalization | 58.5 | 48.8 | 42.9 | 50.3 | 41.0 | 46.8 | 53.6 | 63.6 | 66.0 | 30.6 |
| % Net Income of Revenue | NM | 6.4 | 7.1 | 6.8 | 6.2 | 7.4 | 4.9 | 4.1 | 3.3 | 4.1 |
| % Return on Assets | NM | 3.9 | 4.3 | 4.1 | 5.0 | 6.5 | 4.9 | 4.0 | 3.7 | 4.3 |
| % Return on Equity | NM | 10.2 | 11.0 | 10.3 | 12.1 | 18.5 | 17.5 | 17.1 | 16.2 | 14.6 |

Data as orig reptd.; bef. results of disc opers/spec. items. Per share data adj. for stk. divs.; EPS diluted. E-Estimated. NA-Not Available. NM-Not Meaningful. NR-Not Ranked. UR-Under Review.

**Office:** 370 Woodcliff Dr., Suite 300, Fairport, NY 14450-4238.
**Telephone:** 585-218-3600.
**Website:** http://www.cbrands.com
**Chrmn:** R. Sands

**Pres & CEO:** R. Sands
**EVP, CFO & Chief Acctg Officer:** R.P. Ryder
**EVP & Chief Admin Officer:** W.K. Wilson
**EVP & General Counsel:** T.J. Mullin

**Investor Contact:** P. Yahn-Urlaub (585-218-3838)
**Board Members:** B. A. Fromberg, J. K. Hauswald, J. A. Locke, III, T. C. McDermott, P. M. Perez, R. Sands, R. Sands, P. L. Smith, P. H. Soderberg, M. Zupan
**Founded:** 1972
**Domicile:** Delaware
**Employees:** 8,200

**The McGraw-Hill Companies**

# Constellation Energy Group Inc.

**STANDARD &POOR'S**

| S&P Recommendation | HOLD ★★★☆☆ | Price $24.53 (as of Nov 14, 2008) | 12-Mo. Target Price $26.00 | Investment Style Large-Cap Blend |
|---|---|---|---|---|

**GICS Sector** Utilities
**Sub-Industry** Independent Power Producers & Energy Traders

**Summary** This company, the largest wholesale power supplier in the U.S. and the parent of Baltimore Gas and Electric, has agreed to be acquired by MidAmerican Energy Holdings.

## Key Stock Statistics (Source S&P, Vickers, company reports)

| | | | | | | | |
|---|---|---|---|---|---|---|---|
| 52-Wk Range | $107.97– 13.00 | S&P Oper. EPS 2009E | 4.50 | Market Capitalization(B) | $4.374 | Beta | 1.53 |
| Trailing 12-Month EPS | $1.94 | S&P Oper. EPS 2010E | 5.20 | Yield (%) | 7.79 | S&P 3-Yr. Proj. EPS CAGR(%) | 4 |
| Trailing 12-Month P/E | 12.6 | P/E on S&P Oper. EPS 2009E | 5.5 | Dividend Rate/Share | $1.91 | S&P Credit Rating | BBB |
| $10K Invested 5 Yrs Ago | $7,540 | Common Shares Outstg. (M) | 178.3 | Institutional Ownership (%) | 66 | | |

## Price Performance

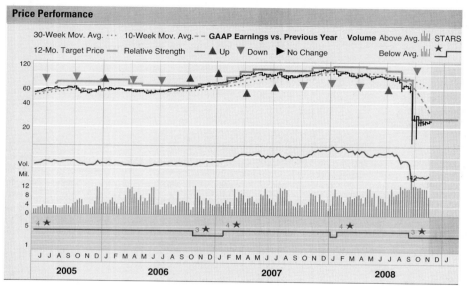

30-Week Mov. Avg. ··· 10-Week Mov. Avg. -- **GAAP Earnings vs. Previous Year** Volume Above Avg. STARS
12-Mo. Target Price — Relative Strength — ▲ Up ▼ Down ▶ No Change Below Avg. ★

Options: ASE, CBOE, P, Ph

Analysis prepared by **Justin McCann** on September 22, 2008, when the stock traded at **$ 27.20**.

## Highlights

➤ We expect the agreed-to acquisition of CEG by MidAmerican Energy Holdings to be completed in the second quarter of 2009, pending shareholder and regulatory approvals. The agreed-to acquisition was sought by CEG to help it overcome a severe liquidity crisis stemming from the adverse effects sharply higher commodity prices had on its derivative assets and liabilities, collateral requirements and counterparty credit exposures. While we expect some shareholder opposition to the $26.50 share price agreed to, we believe that the solid reputation of MidAmerican will facilitate the regulatory approval process.

➤ We expect 2008's operating EPS to grow about 16% from 2007's $4.60. We expect the merchant business to earn around $4.60 a share (up from $3.77 in 2007), and BG&E about $0.72 (down from $0.74). We see other non-regulated units adding around $0.03 (down from $0.09).

➤ On a stand-alone basis, we expect operating EPS in 2009 to grow about 11% from anticipated results in 2008. We expect the growth to again be driven by the merchant energy operations, as below market contracts are replaced by higher-margin, market-based contracts.

## Investment Rationale/Risk

➤ The agreed-to acquisition followed an extraordinarily volatile three-day period in which CEG's shares plummeted 57%. The dramatic decline reflected investor concerns that CEG would be unable to access the liquidity needed for its commodity trading business, and was on the verge of having its credit rating dropped to below investment grade. This would have increased its collateral obligations by an additional $3.2 billion. We believe the agreed-to acquisition will help the company restore its financial strength, as well as its reputation and business with trading counterparties.

➤ Risks to our recommendation and target price include the possibility that the agreed-to acquisition by MidAmerican is not completed. Should it be terminated, we would expect a sharp decline in the shares.

➤ With the sharp drop in the shares, the recent yield from the dividend, assuming four quarterly payments, jumped to about 6.9% (about 5.2% for three quarterly payments). We expect the dividend to be maintained until the close of the deal, with the final payment made on a pro-rata basis. Our target price of $26 approximates the value of the MidAmerican offer.

## Qualitative Risk Assessment

| LOW | MEDIUM | HIGH |
|---|---|---|

Our risk assessment reflects a balance between stable and steady earnings provided by CEG's regulated electric and gas utility operations and cyclical and volatile earnings from the unregulated merchant energy business, including power generation, energy and energy-related marketing and trading.

## Quantitative Evaluations

**S&P Quality Ranking** B+

| D | C | B- | B | B+ | A- | A | A+ |
|---|---|---|---|---|---|---|---|

**Relative Strength Rank** MODERATE

31

LOWEST = 1   HIGHEST = 99

## Revenue/Earnings Data

**Revenue (Million $)**

| | 1Q | 2Q | 3Q | 4Q | Year |
|---|---|---|---|---|---|
| 2008 | 4,827 | 5,077 | 5,324 | -- | -- |
| 2007 | 5,111 | 4,876 | 5,856 | 5,349 | 21,193 |
| 2006 | 4,859 | 4,379 | 5,393 | 4,644 | 19,285 |
| 2005 | 3,630 | 3,549 | 4,922 | 5,159 | 17,132 |
| 2004 | 3,037 | 2,793 | 3,435 | 3,286 | 12,550 |
| 2003 | 2,330 | 2,271 | 2,604 | 2,498 | 9,703 |

**Earnings Per Share ($)**

| | 1Q | 2Q | 3Q | 4Q | Year |
|---|---|---|---|---|---|
| 2008 | 0.81 | 0.95 | -1.26 | E1.17 | E4.70 |
| 2007 | 1.08 | 0.64 | 1.37 | 1.42 | 4.51 |
| 2006 | 0.56 | 0.41 | 1.69 | 1.46 | 4.12 |
| 2005 | 0.67 | 0.66 | 1.02 | 1.04 | 3.38 |
| 2004 | 0.66 | 0.77 | 1.19 | 0.76 | 3.40 |
| 2003 | 0.40 | 0.58 | 1.15 | 0.71 | 2.85 |

Fiscal year ended Dec. 31. Next earnings report expected: Late January. EPS Estimates based on S&P Operating Earnings; historical GAAP earnings are as reported.

## Dividend Data (Dates: mm/dd Payment Date: mm/dd/yy)

| Amount ($) | Date Decl. | Ex-Div. Date | Stk. of Record | Payment Date |
|---|---|---|---|---|
| 0.478 | 01/30 | 03/06 | 03/10 | 04/01/08 |
| 0.478 | 05/16 | 06/06 | 06/10 | 07/01/08 |
| 0.478 | 07/18 | 09/08 | 09/10 | 10/01/08 |
| 0.478 | 10/17 | 12/08 | 12/10 | 01/02/09 |

Dividends have been paid since 1910. Source: Company reports.

# Constellation Energy Group Inc.

**STANDARD &POOR'S**

## Business Summary September 22, 2008

CORPORATE OVERVIEW. Constellation Energy is the largest U.S. wholesale power seller and biggest competitive supplier of electricity to large commercial and industrial customers. It is also the holding company for Baltimore Gas & Electric Company, a regulated utility.

IMPACT OF MAJOR DEVELOPMENTS. On September 19, 2008, the company reached a definitive agreement (tentatively announced on September 18) with MidAmerican Energy Holdings, in which MidAmerican would purchase all of the outstanding shares of CEG for $4.7 billion in cash, or $26.50 a share. Upon the signing of the agreement, CEG issued $1 billion of preferred equity yielding 8.0% to MidAmerican, which is a privately held subsidiary of Berkshire Hathaway. The announcement of the agreement followed several days of unprecedented volatility in the shares, which reflected, we believe, investor fears that the company would risk bankruptcy if it were unable to access the liquidity it needed for its commodities-trading business. The agreement expires nine months after its execution, but may be extended by either company for up to three months. Subject to required shareholder and regulatory approvals, the transaction is expected to be completed by mid-2009.

MARKET PROFILE. We believe CEG is one of the premier players in the merchant energy business. The company's Merchant Energy operations (which accounted for 83% of income from continuing operations in 2007) include wholesale power generation, energy marketing and risk management services for wholesale customers, competitive retail supply services for commercial and industrial customers, and consulting services. Merchant Energy also houses energy marketing and risk management operations, which are conducted by NewEnergy, serving the commercial and industrial (C&I) market, and Constellation Commodities Group, serving the wholesale market. The company's regulated electric (12%) and gas (3%) utility operations are performed by Baltimore Gas and Electric (BGE), which serves around 1.2 million electric customers and approximately 620,000 gas customers in a service territory that covers the city of Baltimore and all or part of 10 counties in central Maryland. CEG's other non-regulated operations accounted for 2% of 2007's income from continuing operations.

## Company Financials Fiscal Year Ended Dec. 31

| Per Share Data ($) | 2008 | 2007 | 2006 | 2005 | 2004 | 2003 | 2002 | 2001 | 2000 | 1999 |
|---|---|---|---|---|---|---|---|---|---|---|
| Tangible Book Value | NA | 28.46 | 24.66 | 26.76 | 25.99 | 23.81 | 22.71 | 23.44 | 20.88 | 19.95 |
| Earnings | 5.35 | 4.51 | 4.12 | 3.38 | 3.40 | 2.85 | 3.20 | 0.52 | 2.30 | 2.18 |
| S&P Core Earnings | NA | 4.26 | 3.93 | 3.31 | 3.33 | 2.66 | 1.75 | 0.34 | NA | NA |
| Dividends | 1.43 | 1.74 | 1.51 | 1.34 | 1.14 | 1.04 | 0.96 | 0.48 | 1.68 | 1.68 |
| Payout Ratio | 27% | 39% | 37% | 40% | 34% | 36% | 30% | 92% | 73% | 77% |
| Prices:High | 107.97 | 104.29 | 70.20 | 62.60 | 44.90 | 39.61 | 32.38 | 50.14 | 52.06 | 31.50 |
| Prices:Low | 13.00 | 68.78 | 50.55 | 43.01 | 35.89 | 25.17 | 19.30 | 20.90 | 27.06 | 24.69 |
| P/E Ratio:High | 20 | 23 | 17 | 19 | 13 | 14 | 10 | 96 | 23 | 14 |
| P/E Ratio:Low | 2 | 15 | 12 | 13 | 11 | 9 | 6 | 40 | 12 | 11 |

| Income Statement Analysis (Million $) | 2008 | 2007 | 2006 | 2005 | 2004 | 2003 | 2002 | 2001 | 2000 | 1999 |
|---|---|---|---|---|---|---|---|---|---|---|
| Revenue | NA | 21,193 | 19,285 | 17,132 | 12,550 | 9,703 | 4,703 | 3,928 | 3,879 | 3,787 |
| Depreciation | NA | 558 | 524 | 542 | 526 | 479 | 481 | 419 | 470 | 450 |
| Maintenance | NA | NA | NA | NA | NA | NA | NA | NA | NA | 186 |
| Fixed Charges Coverage | NA | 5.09 | 4.01 | 3.50 | 3.40 | 3.12 | 2.90 | 3.01 | 3.12 | 2.98 |
| Construction Credits | NA | NA | NA | NA | NA | NA | NA | NA | NA | NA |
| Effective Tax Rate | NA | 33.9% | 31.9% | 25.2% | 22.6% | 36.2% | 37.1% | 31.5% | 40.0% | 36.3% |
| Net Income | NA | 822 | 749 | 607 | 589 | 476 | 526 | 82.4 | 345 | 326 |
| S&P Core Earnings | NA | 777 | 714 | 594 | 578 | 444 | 290 | 54.9 | NA | NA |

| Balance Sheet & Other Financial Data (Million $) | 2008 | 2007 | 2006 | 2005 | 2004 | 2003 | 2002 | 2001 | 2000 | 1999 |
|---|---|---|---|---|---|---|---|---|---|---|
| Gross Property | NA | 14,513 | 13,680 | 14,403 | 14,315 | 13,580 | 12,354 | 11,862 | 10,442 | 8,989 |
| Capital Expenditures | NA | 1,296 | 963 | 760 | 704 | 658 | 850 | 1,318 | 1,079 | 436 |
| Net Property | NA | 9,767 | 9,222 | 10,067 | 10,087 | 9,602 | 7,957 | 7,700 | 6,644 | 5,523 |
| Capitalization:Long Term Debt | NA | 4,851 | 4,222 | 4,559 | 5,003 | 5,229 | 4,804 | 2,903 | 3,349 | 2,765 |
| Capitalization:% Long Term Debt | NA | 47.6 | 47.8 | 48.1 | 51.4 | 55.8 | 55.4 | 43.0 | 51.5 | 48.0 |
| Capitalization:Preferred | NA | Nil | Nil | Nil | Nil | Nil | Nil | Nil | Nil | Nil |
| Capitalization:% Preferred | NA | Nil | Nil | Nil | Nil | Nil | Nil | Nil | Nil | Nil |
| Capitalization:Common | NA | 5,340 | 4,609 | 4,916 | 4,727 | 4,141 | 3,862 | 3,844 | 3,153 | 2,993 |
| Capitalization:% Common | NA | 52.4 | 52.2 | 51.9 | 48.6 | 44.2 | 44.6 | 57.0 | 48.5 | 52.0 |
| Total Capital | NA | 11,798 | 10,419 | 10,720 | 11,105 | 10,833 | 10,083 | 8,271 | 7,943 | 7,157 |
| % Operating Ratio | NA | 95.3 | 94.7 | 94.5 | 92.2 | 91.6 | 87.2 | 78.3 | 84.3 | 84.8 |
| % Earned on Net Property | NA | 15.0 | 13.1 | 10.5 | 17.0 | 17.1 | 17.8 | 5.0 | 13.3 | 13.6 |
| % Return on Revenue | NA | 3.9 | 3.9 | 3.5 | 4.7 | 4.9 | 11.2 | 2.1 | 8.9 | 8.6 |
| % Return on Invested Capital | NA | 10.1 | 11.4 | 9.2 | 9.0 | 8.2 | 9.8 | 10.5 | 8.2 | 7.8 |
| % Return on Common Equity | NA | 16.5 | 15.7 | 12.6 | 13.3 | 11.9 | 13.6 | 2.3 | 11.2 | 10.9 |

Data as orig reptd.; bef. results of disc opers/spec. items. Per share data adj. for stk. divs.; EPS diluted. E-Estimated. NA-Not Available. NM-Not Meaningful. NR-Not Ranked. UR-Under Review.

**Office:** 100 Constellation Way, Baltimore, MD 21202-3142.
**Telephone:** 410-783-2800.
**Website:** http://www.constellation.com
**Chrmn, Pres & CEO:** M.A. Shattuck, III

**COO:** K.W. Hyle
**SVP, Chief Admin Officer & CIO:** B.S. Perlman
**CFO & Treas:** J.W. Thayer
**Chief Acctg Officer & Cntlr:** R.K. Feuerman

**Investor Contact:** K. Hadlock (410-864-6440)
**Board Members:** D. L. Becker, A. C. Berzin, J. T. Brady, J. R. Curtiss, F. A. Hrabowski, III, N. Lampton, R. J. Lawless, L. Martin, M. A. Shattuck, III, J. L. Skolds, M. D. Sullivan, Y. C. de Balmann

**Founded:** 1906
**Domicile:** Maryland
**Employees:** 10,200

**The McGraw-Hill Companies**

# Convergys Corp

**STANDARD & POOR'S**

| S&P Recommendation | BUY ★★★★☆ | Price $5.43 (as of Nov 14, 2008) | 12-Mo. Target Price $12.00 | Investment Style Large-Cap Growth |
|---|---|---|---|---|

**GICS Sector** Information Technology
**Sub-Industry** Data Processing & Outsourced Services

**Summary** This company is a provider of outsourced billing and customer management solutions for communications companies and state governments.

## Key Stock Statistics (Source S&P, Vickers, company reports)

| | | | | | | | |
|---|---|---|---|---|---|---|---|
| 52-Wk Range | $17.94–5.20 | S&P Oper. EPS 2008E | 1.18 | Market Capitalization(B) | $0.663 | Beta | 1.15 |
| Trailing 12-Month EPS | $-0.15 | S&P Oper. EPS 2009E | 1.23 | Yield (%) | Nil | S&P 3-Yr. Proj. EPS CAGR(%) | 7 |
| Trailing 12-Month P/E | NM | P/E on S&P Oper. EPS 2008E | 4.6 | Dividend Rate/Share | Nil | S&P Credit Rating | BB+ |
| $10K Invested 5 Yrs Ago | $3,481 | Common Shares Outstg. (M) | 122.1 | Institutional Ownership (%) | 92 | | |

## Price Performance

30-Week Mov. Avg. ···· 10-Week Mov. Avg. --- GAAP Earnings vs. Previous Year   Volume Above Avg. STARS
12-Mo. Target Price — Relative Strength — ▲ Up ▼ Down ▶ No Change   Below Avg. ★

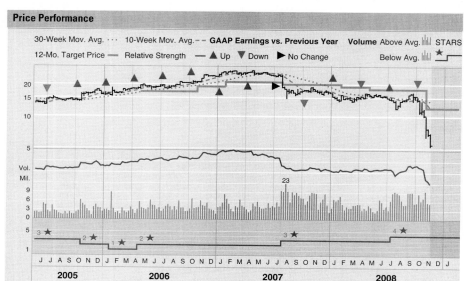

Analysis prepared by **James Moorman, CFA** on October 31, 2008, when the stock traded at **$7.47**.

Options: CBOE, P, Ph

## Highlights

➤ Revenues rose 2.0% in 2007, and we expect a decline of 1% in 2008 and then an increase of 4% in 2009, as we think gains at the larger customer management group (CMG) will be slightly offset by declines in the information management group (IMG). Growth at CMG started to pick up in the third quarter and exceeded our estimates, and we believe it will continue to accelerate into 2009. We think the company has a healthy pipeline and could move forward in the fourth quarter of 2008.

➤ We see operating margins narrowing to 6.5% in 2008, from 8.7% in 2007, before expanding to 7.9% in 2009. We believe that while many of the growth and cost-cutting initiatives of 2007 have started to have an effect, increased spending elsewhere will outweigh the benefits. Notably, we believe increased labor costs at CMG are having a negative impact on margins, although they could dissipate as revenue growth kicks in.

➤ Following EPS of $1.23 in 2007, we estimate $1.18 for 2008 and $1.23 for 2009. The company purchased 3.5 million shares in the second quarter of 2008 and purchased 7.7 million shares so far in 2008.

## Investment Rationale/Risk

➤ We believe recent restructuring efforts and the buildout of the small HR management segment are intended to offset the sizable challenges we see related to customer migration and competition. We are beginning to see business progress in CMG which we believe will continue throughout 2008 and into 2009. We also expect to see growth contribution in 2009 from the Intervoice acquisition. We believe the shares are undervalued.

➤ Risks to our recommendation and target price include reduced business with large customers, below-average growth in demand from non-communications companies, ongoing operating losses in employee care, and currency losses from international operations.

➤ We believe CVG deserves its P/E-to-growth discount to peers given our view of sizable customer migration risk, narrow margins, and sluggish top-line growth. Our 12-month target price is $12, based on a P/E-to-growth ratio of 1.4X, or a P/E of 10X applied to our 2009 EPS estimate. We believe CVG's cash balance provides some support for the shares.

## Qualitative Risk Assessment

| LOW | MEDIUM | HIGH |
|---|---|---|

Our risk assessment for Convergys reflects the competitiveness of serving the communications industry, and concentration of its customer base with approximately 30% of its revenues coming from three companies. This is offset by the company's use of long-term contracts.

## Quantitative Evaluations

**S&P Quality Ranking** B

| D | C | B- | B | B+ | A- | A | A+ |
|---|---|---|---|---|---|---|---|

**Relative Strength Rank** WEAK

12

LOWEST = 1    HIGHEST = 99

## Revenue/Earnings Data

### Revenue (Million $)

| | 1Q | 2Q | 3Q | 4Q | Year |
|---|---|---|---|---|---|
| 2008 | 716.4 | 689.5 | 676.2 | -- | -- |
| 2007 | 719.9 | 707.0 | 703.7 | 713.8 | 2,844 |
| 2006 | 675.3 | 691.8 | 702.7 | 720.0 | 2,790 |
| 2005 | 637.3 | 630.4 | 644.8 | 669.6 | 2,582 |
| 2004 | 573.9 | 601.7 | 639.9 | 672.2 | 2,488 |
| 2003 | 560.4 | 563.2 | 570.7 | 594.5 | 2,289 |

### Earnings Per Share ($)

| | 1Q | 2Q | 3Q | 4Q | Year |
|---|---|---|---|---|---|
| 2008 | 0.28 | 0.32 | -1.15 | E0.25 | E1.18 |
| 2007 | 0.31 | 0.28 | 0.30 | 0.34 | 1.23 |
| 2006 | 0.26 | 0.28 | 0.32 | 0.32 | 1.17 |
| 2005 | 0.22 | 0.18 | 0.30 | 0.16 | 0.86 |
| 2004 | 0.22 | 0.20 | 0.21 | 0.14 | 0.77 |
| 2003 | 0.22 | 0.29 | 0.31 | 0.33 | 1.15 |

Fiscal year ended Dec. 31. Next earnings report expected: Late January. EPS Estimates based on S&P Operating Earnings; historical GAAP earnings are as reported.

## Dividend Data

No cash dividends have been paid.

# Convergys Corp

STANDARD &POOR'S

## Business Summary October 31, 2008

CORPORATE OVERVIEW. Convergys Corp. is a provider of outsourced, integrated billing, and employee and customer care software and services. The information management group, known as IMG (20% of revenues and 13% operating margin in the third quarter of 2008), serves clients principally by providing and managing complex billing and information software that addresses all segments of the communications industry.

The customer management group, known as CMG (71% and 5%), provides outsourced customer management services for clients, utilizing its advanced information systems capabilities and industry experience through call centers and Web-based assistance programs. Communications customers contributed 58% of CMG revenues in 2007. Non-communications clients include technology companies and a number of financial institutions.

The HR management segment (9% and operating losses) helps clients with administration of benefits, and human resources, recruiting and payroll services using a single point of contact system.

The company also has a 45% limited partnership interest in the Cellular Partnership, which operates a cellular telecommunications business in central and southwestern Ohio and northern Kentucky.

COMPETITIVE LANDSCAPE. Convergys's chief competitor for communications business is Amdocs (DOX: buy, $22), which serves the customer care and billing needs of telecom providers such as Sprint Nextel and wireline and wireless operations at AT&T Inc., as well as a number of cable providers. We expect DOX to compete aggressively to capture additional customers given the rollout of triple-play packages of voice, video and data services by telecom and cable providers. In January 2006, Sprint Nextel announced an eight-year agreement with Amdocs to provide a single billing and customer care platform, allowing the wireless phone company to migrate off of Convergys's system. This led to an accelerated decline in billing revenue from Sprint in the second half of 2007. The customer loss followed the migration of Cingular customers off of CVG's billing system, which was largely completed in the first quarter of 2007. The HR management and non-communications customer care businesses compete with companies such as Accenture, Automatic Data Processing and Hewitt Associates.

## Company Financials Fiscal Year Ended Dec. 31

| Per Share Data ($) | 2007 | 2006 | 2005 | 2004 | 2003 | 2002 | 2001 | 2000 | 1999 | 1998 |
|---|---|---|---|---|---|---|---|---|---|---|
| Tangible Book Value | 7.79 | 3.85 | 3.13 | 2.62 | 2.60 | 2.54 | 3.08 | 2.41 | 1.13 | 0.29 |
| Cash Flow | 2.13 | 2.18 | 1.89 | 1.74 | 1.99 | 1.70 | 1.81 | 2.25 | 1.73 | 1.28 |
| Earnings | 1.23 | 1.17 | 0.86 | 0.77 | 1.15 | 0.88 | 0.80 | 1.23 | 0.89 | 0.57 |
| S&P Core Earnings | 1.23 | 1.12 | 0.81 | 0.60 | 0.91 | 0.54 | 0.51 | NA | NA | NA |
| Dividends | Nil | Nil | Nil | Nil | Nil | Nil | Nil | Nil | Nil | Nil |
| Payout Ratio | Nil | Nil | Nil | Nil | Nil | Nil | Nil | Nil | Nil | Nil |
| Prices:High | 27.26 | 24.93 | 17.90 | 19.96 | 20.80 | 37.98 | 50.25 | 55.44 | 31.75 | 23.75 |
| Prices:Low | 14.67 | 15.43 | 12.57 | 12.30 | 11.30 | 12.50 | 24.46 | 26.63 | 14.50 | 9.63 |
| P/E Ratio:High | 22 | 21 | 21 | 26 | 18 | 43 | 63 | 45 | 36 | 42 |
| P/E Ratio:Low | 12 | 13 | 15 | 16 | 10 | 14 | 31 | 22 | 16 | 17 |

| Income Statement Analysis (Million $) | | | | | | | | | | |
|---|---|---|---|---|---|---|---|---|---|---|
| Revenue | 2,844 | 2,790 | 2,582 | 2,488 | 2,289 | 2,286 | 2,321 | 2,163 | 1,763 | 1,447 |
| Operating Income | 378 | 408 | 392 | 327 | 415 | 498 | 543 | 489 | 388 | 313 |
| Depreciation | 124 | 143 | 147 | 141 | 124 | 137 | 176 | 161 | 130 | 101 |
| Interest Expense | 17.5 | 22.8 | 21.2 | 10.3 | 6.90 | 11.0 | 20.0 | 32.9 | 32.5 | 33.9 |
| Pretax Income | 246 | 245 | 213 | 173 | 272 | 244 | 255 | 317 | 223 | 131 |
| Effective Tax Rate | 31.0% | 32.1% | 42.5% | 35.7% | 36.8% | 40.3% | 45.5% | 38.6% | 38.4% | 38.0% |
| Net Income | 170 | 166 | 123 | 112 | 172 | 146 | 139 | 195 | 137 | 81.0 |
| S&P Core Earnings | 169 | 160 | 117 | 87.6 | 133 | 88.9 | 91.3 | NA | NA | NA |

| Balance Sheet & Other Financial Data (Million $) | | | | | | | | | | |
|---|---|---|---|---|---|---|---|---|---|---|
| Cash | 120 | 236 | 196 | 58.4 | 37.2 | 12.2 | 41.1 | 28.2 | 30.8 | 3.80 |
| Current Assets | 862 | 930 | 849 | 593 | 420 | 418 | 523 | 481 | 298 | 361 |
| Total Assets | 2,564 | 2,540 | 2,411 | 2,208 | 1,810 | 1,620 | 1,743 | 1,780 | 1,580 | 1,451 |
| Current Liabilities | 427 | 596 | 618 | 577 | 543 | 462 | 492 | 359 | 387 | 698 |
| Long Term Debt | 259 | 260 | 298 | 302 | 58.8 | 4.60 | 3.60 | 291 | 250 | Nil |
| Common Equity | 1,522 | 1,455 | 1,355 | 1,285 | 1,144 | 1,126 | 1,227 | 1,113 | 927 | 732 |
| Total Capital | 1,862 | 1,759 | 1,697 | 1,588 | 1,202 | 1,131 | 1,230 | 1,403 | 1,178 | 732 |
| Capital Expenditures | 102 | 105 | 131 | 156 | 174 | 90.8 | 114 | 175 | 155 | 93.5 |
| Cash Flow | 294 | 309 | 270 | 253 | 296 | 283 | 315 | 356 | 267 | 182 |
| Current Ratio | 2.0 | 1.6 | 1.4 | 1.0 | 0.8 | 0.9 | 1.1 | 1.3 | 0.8 | 0.5 |
| % Long Term Debt of Capitalization | 14.6 | 14.8 | 17.5 | 19.0 | 4.9 | 0.4 | 0.3 | 20.7 | 21.3 | Nil |
| % Net Income of Revenue | 6.0 | 6.0 | 4.7 | 4.5 | 7.5 | 6.4 | 6.0 | 9.0 | 7.8 | 5.6 |
| % Return on Assets | 6.6 | 6.7 | 5.3 | 5.5 | 10.0 | 8.7 | 7.8 | 11.6 | 9.0 | 7.7 |
| % Return on Equity | 11.4 | 11.8 | 9.3 | 9.2 | 15.1 | 12.4 | 11.8 | 19.1 | 16.5 | 13.9 |

Data as orig reptd.; bef. results of disc opers/spec. items. Per share data adj. for stk. divs.; EPS diluted. E-Estimated. NA-Not Available. NM-Not Meaningful. NR-Not Ranked. UR-Under Review.

**Office:** 201 E 4th St, Cincinnati, OH 45202-4206.
**Telephone:** 513-723-7000.
**Email:** investor@convergys.com
**Website:** http://www.convergys.com

**Chrmn:** P. Odeen
**Pres & CEO:** D.F. Dougherty
**SVP, Chief Acctg Officer, Treas & Cntlr:** T.M. Wesolowski
**SVP, Secy & General Counsel:** K.R. Bowman

**CFO:** E.C. Shanks
**Board Members:** Z. Baird, J. F. Barrett, W. W. Brittain, Jr., D. B. Dillon, D. F. Dougherty, J. E. Gibbs, T. L. Monahan, III, R. L. Nelson, P. Odeen, R. Wallman, D. R. Whitwam

**Founded:** 1998
**Domicile:** Ohio
**Employees:** 75,000

The McGraw-Hill Companies

# Cooper Industries Ltd.

**S&P Recommendation** BUY ★★★★☆

| Price | 12-Mo. Target Price | Investment Style |
|---|---|---|
| $26.92 (as of Nov 14, 2008) | $38.00 | Large-Cap Growth |

**GICS Sector** Industrials
**Sub-Industry** Electrical Components & Equipment

**Summary** This company is a diversified worldwide manufacturer of electrical products, tools and hardware.

## Key Stock Statistics (Source S&P, Vickers, company reports)

| | | | | | | | |
|---|---|---|---|---|---|---|---|
| 52-Wk Range | $55.76– 22.91 | S&P Oper. EPS 2008E | 3.66 | Market Capitalization(B) | $4.666 | Beta | 1.46 |
| Trailing 12-Month EPS | $3.92 | S&P Oper. EPS 2009E | 3.85 | Yield (%) | 3.71 | S&P 3-Yr. Proj. EPS CAGR(%) | 14 |
| Trailing 12-Month P/E | 6.9 | P/E on S&P Oper. EPS 2008E | 7.4 | Dividend Rate/Share | $1.00 | S&P Credit Rating | NA |
| $10K Invested 5 Yrs Ago | $11,117 | Common Shares Outstg. (M) | 173.3 | Institutional Ownership (%) | 86 | | |

## Price Performance

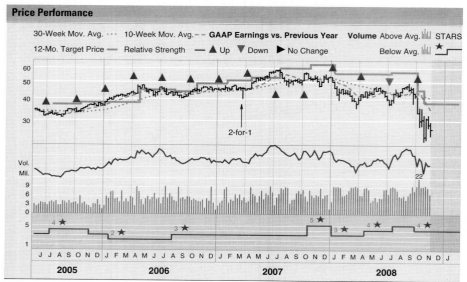

30-Week Mov. Avg. ···· 10-Week Mov. Avg. – – **GAAP Earnings vs. Previous Year** Volume Above Avg. STARS
12-Mo. Target Price — Relative Strength — ▲ Up ▼ Down ► No Change Below Avg. ★

2-for-1

2005  2006  2007  2008

Options: ASE, CBOE, P, Ph

## Qualitative Risk Assessment

| LOW | MEDIUM | HIGH |
|---|---|---|

Our risk assessment reflects our view of favorable growth prospects in markets CBE serves, and what we consider good corporate governance and a healthy balance sheet, offset by vulnerability to slowing real GDP growth in the U.S. or abroad.

## Quantitative Evaluations

**S&P Quality Ranking**  NR

| D | C | B- | B | B+ | A- | A | A+ |
|---|---|---|---|---|---|---|---|

**Relative Strength Rank**  MODERATE

49

LOWEST = 1  HIGHEST = 99

## Revenue/Earnings Data

**Revenue (Million $)**

| | 1Q | 2Q | 3Q | 4Q | Year |
|---|---|---|---|---|---|
| 2008 | 1,546 | 1,724 | 1,728 | -- | -- |
| 2007 | 1,394 | 1,464 | 1,501 | 1,544 | 5,903 |
| 2006 | 1,241 | 1,288 | 1,315 | 1,341 | 5,185 |
| 2005 | 1,145 | 1,189 | 1,210 | 1,186 | 4,730 |
| 2004 | 1,065 | 1,109 | 1,140 | 1,149 | 4,463 |
| 2003 | 957.8 | 1,011 | 1,049 | 1,044 | 4,061 |

**Earnings Per Share ($)**

| | | | | | |
|---|---|---|---|---|---|
| 2008 | 0.86 | 0.92 | 1.08 | E0.87 | E3.66 |
| 2007 | 0.71 | 1.12 | 0.93 | 0.98 | 3.73 |
| 2006 | 0.57 | 0.64 | 0.69 | 0.69 | 2.58 |
| 2005 | 0.46 | 0.51 | 0.54 | 0.55 | 2.06 |
| 2004 | 0.41 | 0.45 | 0.48 | 0.47 | 1.79 |
| 2003 | 0.31 | 0.39 | 0.38 | 0.39 | 1.46 |

Fiscal year ended Dec. 31. Next earnings report expected: Late January. EPS Estimates based on S&P Operating Earnings; historical GAAP earnings are as reported.

## Highlights

► The 12-month target price for CBE has recently been changed to $38.00 from $45.00. The Highlights section of this Stock Report will be updated accordingly.

## Investment Rationale/Risk

► The Investment Rationale/Risk section of this Stock Report will be updated shortly. For the latest News story on CBE from MarketScope, see below.

► 10/23/08 03:07 pm ET ... S&P REITERATES BUY OPINION ON SHARES OF COOPER INDUSTRIES (CBE 25.54****): CBE posts adjusted Q3 EPS of $0.97 vs. $0.83, $0.02 above our estimate. With that outperformance we are maintaining our $3.66 full year '08 EPS projection despite a decrease in our Q4 outlook. However, we are trimming our '09 EPS forecast by $0.06 to $3.85 to reflect slowing global economic activity. We are also cutting our 12-month target price by $7 to $38 on a blend of revised DCF, and historical and peer P/E analysis. We see CBE's cash flows and balance sheet as strong. /ELevy-CFA

## Dividend Data (Dates: mm/dd Payment Date: mm/dd/yy)

| Amount ($) | Date Decl. | Ex-Div. Date | Stk. of Record | Payment Date |
|---|---|---|---|---|
| 0.210 | 11/06 | 11/28 | 11/30 | 01/02/08 |
| 0.250 | 02/12 | 02/27 | 02/29 | 04/01/08 |
| 0.250 | 04/29 | 05/28 | 05/30 | 07/01/08 |
| 0.250 | 08/05 | 11/25 | 11/28 | 01/02/09 |

Dividends have been paid since 1947. Source: Company reports.

The McGraw-Hill Companies

# Cooper Industries Ltd.

**STANDARD &POOR'S**

## Business Summary October 07, 2008

CORPORATE OVERVIEW. Cooper Industries, a diversified, worldwide manufacturer of electrical products, tools and hardware, focuses on leveraging its strong brand name recognition by broadening its product line; strengthening its manufacturing and distribution systems to lower costs and improve customer service; expanding globally via acquisitions and joint ventures to participate in growing economies; and improving working capital efficiency and increasing cash flow to fuel future growth.

Electrical products contributed 87% of revenues in 2007, and tools and hardware provided 13%.

About 29% of sales in 2007 were outside the U.S.

The countries that generate the most international revenues for CBE are Canada, Germany, Mexico and the U.K. The company has several small joint ventures with operations in China.

Cash flow from operations in 2007 was $795 million, up from 2006's 601 million and 2005's $574 million.

CORPORATE STRATEGY. In the four years through 2000, CBE completed 33 ac-

quisitions: 23 in the electrical products group and 10 in the tools and hardware segment. Six acquisitions in 2000 cost about $578 million. The company did not make any acquisitions in 2001 through 2003, but concluded two acquisitions at an aggregate cost of nearly $49 million in 2004. CBE did not complete any acquisitions in 2005. The company's acquisition program resumed in 2006, with four acquisitions for approximately $280 million. It spent $336 million on acquisitions in 2007.

Reflecting slowing demand, the company reduced 2001 capital spending to $115 million, from 2000's $175 million. A further reduction was seen in 2002, to $74 million. Capital spending in 2003 totaled $80 million, but such expenditures increased to $103 million in 2004, as CBE invested in new products, new business systems, and cost reduction programs. However, capital expenditures declined again in both 2005 and 2006, to $97 million and $85 million, respectively. Capital spending totaled more than $115 million in 2007, a level that we believe CBE should exceed again in 2008.

## Company Financials Fiscal Year Ended Dec. 31

| Per Share Data ($) | 2007 | 2006 | 2005 | 2004 | 2003 | 2002 | 2001 | 2000 | 1999 | 1998 |
|---|---|---|---|---|---|---|---|---|---|---|
| Tangible Book Value | 1.98 | 0.76 | 0.66 | 0.77 | 0.33 | 0.04 | 0.63 | NM | 0.02 | 0.46 |
| Cash Flow | 4.37 | 3.27 | 2.74 | 2.40 | 2.11 | 1.79 | 2.36 | 2.84 | 2.53 | 2.10 |
| Earnings | 3.73 | 2.58 | 2.06 | 1.79 | 1.46 | 1.14 | 1.38 | 1.90 | 1.75 | 1.47 |
| Dividends | 0.52 | 0.74 | 0.74 | 0.70 | 0.70 | 0.70 | 0.70 | 0.70 | 0.66 | 0.66 |
| Payout Ratio | 14% | 29% | 36% | 39% | 48% | 61% | 51% | 37% | 38% | 45% |
| Prices:High | 59.05 | 48.06 | 37.88 | 34.22 | 29.43 | 23.51 | 30.23 | 23.50 | 28.38 | 35.19 |
| Prices:Low | 40.00 | 36.02 | 31.04 | 25.67 | 16.93 | 13.57 | 15.81 | 14.69 | 19.81 | 18.44 |
| P/E Ratio:High | 16 | 19 | 18 | 19 | 20 | 21 | 22 | 12 | 16 | 24 |
| P/E Ratio:Low | 11 | 14 | 15 | 14 | 12 | 12 | 11 | 8 | 11 | 13 |

| Income Statement Analysis (Million $) | | | | | | | | | | |
|---|---|---|---|---|---|---|---|---|---|---|
| Revenue | 5,903 | 5,185 | 4,730 | 4,463 | 4,061 | 3,961 | 4,210 | 4,460 | 3,869 | 3,651 |
| Operating Income | 971 | 811 | 671 | 614 | 516 | 516 | 662 | 825 | 725 | 683 |
| Depreciation | 118 | 112 | 111 | 118 | 121 | 122 | 186 | 174 | 148 | 138 |
| Interest Expense | 51.0 | 51.5 | 64.8 | 68.1 | 74.1 | 74.5 | 84.7 | 100 | 55.2 | 102 |
| Pretax Income | 826 | 648 | 495 | 429 | 347 | 280 | 316 | 550 | 519 | 524 |
| Effective Tax Rate | 16.2% | 25.2% | 21.0% | 20.7% | 20.8% | 23.7% | 17.4% | 35.0% | 36.0% | 35.9% |
| Net Income | 692 | 484 | 391 | 340 | 274 | 214 | 261 | 357 | 332 | 336 |

| Balance Sheet & Other Financial Data (Million $) | | | | | | | | | | |
|---|---|---|---|---|---|---|---|---|---|---|
| Cash | 327 | 424 | 453 | 653 | 464 | 302 | 11.5 | 26.4 | 26.9 | 21.0 |
| Current Assets | 2,303 | 2,194 | 2,131 | 2,219 | 1,961 | 1,689 | 1,651 | 1,735 | 1,467 | 1,417 |
| Total Assets | 6,134 | 5,375 | 5,215 | 5,341 | 4,965 | 4,688 | 4,611 | 4,789 | 4,143 | 3,779 |
| Current Liabilities | 1,635 | 1,499 | 1,161 | 1,828 | 1,022 | 960 | 1,106 | 1,174 | 1,086 | 971 |
| Long Term Debt | 910 | 703 | 1,003 | 699 | 1,337 | 1,281 | 1,107 | 1,301 | 894 | 775 |
| Common Equity | 2,842 | 2,475 | 2,205 | 2,287 | 2,118 | 2,002 | 2,023 | 1,904 | 1,743 | 1,563 |
| Total Capital | 3,752 | 3,178 | 3,208 | 2,985 | 3,455 | 3,283 | 3,130 | 3,205 | 2,638 | 2,338 |
| Capital Expenditures | 116 | 85.3 | 96.7 | 103 | 79.9 | 73.8 | 115 | 175 | 166 | 142 |
| Cash Flow | 810 | 596 | 502 | 457 | 396 | 335 | 448 | 532 | 480 | 474 |
| Current Ratio | 1.4 | 1.5 | 1.8 | 1.2 | 1.9 | 1.8 | 1.5 | 1.5 | 1.4 | 1.5 |
| % Long Term Debt of Capitalization | 24.3 | 22.1 | 31.3 | 23.4 | 38.7 | 39.0 | 35.4 | 40.6 | 33.9 | 33.1 |
| % Net Income of Revenue | 11.7 | 9.3 | 8.3 | 7.6 | 6.8 | 5.4 | 6.2 | 8.0 | 8.6 | 9.2 |
| % Return on Assets | 12.0 | 9.1 | 7.4 | 6.6 | 5.7 | 4.6 | 5.6 | 8.0 | 8.4 | 6.8 |
| % Return on Equity | 26.0 | 20.7 | 17.4 | 15.4 | 13.3 | 10.6 | 13.3 | 19.6 | 20.1 | 16.2 |

Data as orig reptd.; bef. results of disc opers/spec. items. Per share data adj. for stk. divs.; EPS diluted. E-Estimated. NA-Not Available. NM-Not Meaningful. NR-Not Ranked. UR-Under Review.

**Office:** 600 Travis St Ste 5600, Houston, TX 77002-1001.
**Telephone:** 713-209-8400.
**Email:** info@cooperindustries.com
**Website:** http://www.cooperindustries.com

**Chrmn, Pres & CEO:** K.S. Hachigian
**Vice Chrmn:** J.R. Wilson
**COO:** L. Ulz
**Investor Contact:** T.A. Klebe (713-209-8400)

**SVP & CFO:** T.A. Klebe
**Board Members:** S. G. Butler, R. M. Devlin, I. J. Evans, K. S. Hachigian, L. A. Hill, L. D. Kingsley, J. J. Postl, D. F. Smith, G. B. Smith, M. S. Thompson, J. R. Wilson

**Founded:** 1833
**Domicile:** Bermuda
**Employees:** 31,504

**The McGraw-Hill Companies**

# Corning Inc

STANDARD
&POOR'S

| S&P Recommendation | HOLD ★★★☆☆ | | Price | 12-Mo. Target Price | Investment Style |
|---|---|---|---|---|---|
| | | | $8.91 (as of Nov 14, 2008) | $12.00 | Large-Cap Blend |

**GICS Sector** Information Technology
**Sub-Industry** Communications Equipment

**Summary** GLW, once an old-line housewares company, is now a leading maker of glass substrates used by the electronics industry and fiber optic equipment used by the telecommunications industry.

## Key Stock Statistics (Source S&P, Vickers, company reports)

| | | | | | | | |
|---|---|---|---|---|---|---|---|
| 52-Wk Range | $28.07– 8.03 | S&P Oper. EPS 2008E | 1.67 | Market Capitalization(B) | $13.849 | Beta | 1.66 |
| Trailing 12-Month EPS | $3.59 | S&P Oper. EPS 2009E | 1.30 | Yield (%) | 2.24 | S&P 3-Yr. Proj. EPS CAGR(%) | 5 |
| Trailing 12-Month P/E | 2.5 | P/E on S&P Oper. EPS 2008E | 5.3 | Dividend Rate/Share | $0.20 | S&P Credit Rating | BBB+ |
| $10K Invested 5 Yrs Ago | $7,810 | Common Shares Outstg. (M) | 1,554.3 | Institutional Ownership (%) | 76 | | |

## Price Performance

- 30-Week Mov. Avg. · · ·   10-Week Mov. Avg. - - -   **GAAP Earnings vs. Previous Year**   Volume Above Avg. STARS
- 12-Mo. Target Price —   Relative Strength —   ▲ Up   ▼ Down   ► No Change   Below Avg. ★

Options: ASE, CBOE, P, Ph

Analysis prepared by **Todd Rosenbluth** on October 30, 2008, when the stock traded at **$ 10.09**.

## Highlights

- ➤ With a projected sharp decline in fourth quarter 2008 sales, due primarily to weakness at the display business, we see sales growth of 4% for all of 2008 and a similar gain in 2009. We believe a weakened macroeconomy and a tight supply chain will pressure the company's liquid glass substrate segment. While we see growth in the telecom unit, with the U.S. automotive industry struggling, we see pressure on the diesel business of the environmental segment.

- ➤ We expect gross margins to narrow to 34% in the fourth quarter of 2008, from 47% in the third quarter, before partially recovering to an average 37% for 2009. We see the typically high-margin display segment being pressured as top customers demand smaller glass sizes and GLW aims to reduce capacity. We also believe that growth in low-margin telecom will be a drag. We see operating margins of 11% in 2009, relative to a projected 22% in 2008.

- ➤ We estimate a 14% tax rate for 2008, and 24% in 2009. We project operating EPS of $1.67 in 2008 and $1.30 in 2009.

## Investment Rationale/Risk

- ➤ We are concerned that an inventory buildup of LCD glass by its Taiwanese customers and diminished consumer demand for end product TVs and computers will limit GLW's traditionally high margin display segment until mid-2009. In addition, we see the slowing U.S. economy hurting its diesel operations. With pressure on revenues and what we view as a relatively high cost structure, we see margin contraction persisting into 2009. However, we believe GLW has strong customer relationships and a cash cushion to provide some support.

- ➤ Risks to our recommendation and target price include softer than expected demand for flat panel displays, unstable pricing on display technologies products, and weaker demand with narrower margins in the telecom unit.

- ➤ Our 12-month target price of $12 is based on a P/E of 9X our 2009 EPS estimate, in line with the peer average. Although we see GLW having a strong balance sheet to weather the weakness in the macroeconomy, we would not add to holdings until visibility improves.

## Qualitative Risk Assessment

| LOW | MEDIUM | HIGH |
|---|---|---|

Our risk assessment reflects Corning's exposure to intense competition in its major businesses, offset by its market leadership and positive cash flow, and our view of its strong balance sheet.

## Quantitative Evaluations

**S&P Quality Ranking**                                    B-

| D | C | B- | B | B+ | A- | A | A+ |
|---|---|---|---|---|---|---|---|

**Relative Strength Rank**                               WEAK

26

LOWEST = 1                                          HIGHEST = 99

## Revenue/Earnings Data

**Revenue (Million $)**

| | 1Q | 2Q | 3Q | 4Q | Year |
|---|---|---|---|---|---|
| 2008 | 1,617 | 1,692 | 1,555 | -- | -- |
| 2007 | 1,307 | 1,418 | 1,553 | 1,582 | 5,860 |
| 2006 | 1,262 | 1,261 | 1,282 | 1,369 | 5,174 |
| 2005 | 1,050 | 1,141 | 1,188 | 1,200 | 4,579 |
| 2004 | 844.0 | 971.0 | 1,006 | 1,033 | 3,854 |
| 2003 | 746.0 | 752.0 | 772.0 | 820.0 | 3,090 |

**Earnings Per Share ($)**

| | | | | | |
|---|---|---|---|---|---|
| 2008 | 0.64 | 2.01 | 0.49 | E0.28 | E1.67 |
| 2007 | 0.20 | 0.30 | 0.38 | 0.45 | 1.34 |
| 2006 | 0.16 | 0.32 | 0.27 | 0.41 | 1.16 |
| 2005 | 0.17 | 0.11 | 0.13 | -0.02 | 0.38 |
| 2004 | 0.04 | 0.07 | -1.79 | 0.11 | -1.57 |
| 2003 | -0.17 | -0.02 | 0.02 | -0.02 | -0.18 |

Fiscal year ended Dec. 31. Next earnings report expected: Late January. EPS Estimates based on S&P Operating Earnings; historical GAAP earnings are as reported.

## Dividend Data (Dates: mm/dd Payment Date: mm/dd/yy)

| Amount ($) | Date Decl. | Ex-Div. Date | Stk. of Record | Payment Date |
|---|---|---|---|---|
| 0.050 | 02/06 | 02/28 | 03/03 | 03/31/08 |
| 0.050 | 04/24 | 05/29 | 06/02 | 06/30/08 |
| 0.050 | 07/16 | 08/27 | 08/29 | 09/30/08 |
| 0.050 | 10/01 | 11/13 | 11/17 | 12/16/08 |

Dividends have been paid since 2007. Source: Company reports.

Please read the **Required Disclosures and Analyst Certification** on the last page of this report.

# Corning Inc

## Business Summary October 30, 2008

CORPORATE OVERVIEW. Corning (GLW) is a maker of high technology fiber optics for the global telecom industry and high performance glass components for the personal computer and television manufacturing industries. Results are reported in the following primary business segments: display technologies (48% of sales in the first nine months of 2008; 55% net profit margin excluding equity income), telecommunications (29%; 4%), environmental technologies (12%; 9%), life sciences (5%; 15%), and specialty materials and other (6%). In 2007, 54% of total sales were in Asia.

PRIMARY BUSINESS DYNAMICS. The display technologies segment manufactures glass substrates for active matrix liquid crystal displays (LCDs), which are used primarily in notebook computers, flat panel desktop monitors, and LCD televisions. In October 2008, GLW said that, due to an increase in inventory build at set assembly customers and worsening economic conditions, the company expected lower segment sales and increased costs from capacity reductions in the fourth quarter of 2008.

In the first half of 2008, GLW believed that growth in the market for Generation 5.5 to Generation 8.0 glass substrates (60% of fourth quarter 2007 production) would accelerate in 2008. In 2008, Corning had been investing in Generation 10

to support a customer initiative. However, due to weaker retail demand for end products, Corning reduced its expectations for glass volume in both the fourth quarter of 2008 (seen as down from third quarter levels) and for all of 2009 (growth of 5% -15%).

The telecom segment produces optical fiber and cable, and hardware and equipment products including cable assemblies, fiber optic hardware, and components. We believe fiber-to-the-premise (FTTP) products, which had sales growth in the third quarter of 2008, will further benefit from increased demand and more stable pricing from large carriers in their fiber deployment spending. In July 2007, GLW said it added a new European FTTP customer and in early 2008, Corning announced that existing customer Verizon will order its new product Clear Curve. This above-average margin product allows equipment to bend around corners with almost no signal loss, and, in our view, could help expand the FTTP market to mutli-dwelling units (40% of global households).

## Company Financials Fiscal Year Ended Dec. 31

| Per Share Data ($) | 2007 | 2006 | 2005 | 2004 | 2003 | 2002 | 2001 | 2000 | 1999 | 1998 |
|---|---|---|---|---|---|---|---|---|---|---|
| Tangible Book Value | 5.97 | 4.43 | 3.43 | 2.38 | 2.65 | 2.14 | 3.39 | 3.56 | 2.60 | 1.72 |
| Cash Flow | 1.72 | 1.56 | 0.71 | -1.20 | 0.23 | -1.04 | -4.74 | 1.34 | 1.15 | 0.85 |
| Earnings | 1.34 | 1.16 | 0.38 | -1.57 | -0.18 | -1.85 | -5.89 | 0.46 | 0.65 | 0.46 |
| S&P Core Earnings | 1.45 | 1.17 | 0.48 | -1.01 | -0.16 | -1.89 | -3.11 | NA | NA | NA |
| Dividends | 0.10 | Nil | Nil | Nil | Nil | Nil | 0.12 | 0.24 | 0.24 | 0.24 |
| Payout Ratio | 7% | Nil | Nil | Nil | Nil | Nil | NM | 52% | 37% | 52% |
| Prices:High | 27.25 | 29.61 | 21.95 | 13.89 | 12.34 | 11.15 | 72.19 | 113.29 | 43.02 | 15.23 |
| Prices:Low | 18.12 | 17.50 | 10.61 | 9.29 | 3.34 | 1.10 | 6.92 | 34.33 | 14.92 | 7.63 |
| P/E Ratio:High | 20 | 26 | 58 | NM | NM | NM | NM | NM | 66 | 33 |
| P/E Ratio:Low | 14 | 15 | 28 | NM | NM | NM | NM | NM | 23 | 16 |

### Income Statement Analysis (Million $)

| | 2007 | 2006 | 2005 | 2004 | 2003 | 2002 | 2001 | 2000 | 1999 | 1998 |
|---|---|---|---|---|---|---|---|---|---|---|
| Revenue | 5,860 | 5,174 | 4,579 | 3,854 | 3,090 | 3,164 | 6,272 | 7,127 | 4,297 | 3,484 |
| Operating Income | 1,869 | 1,489 | 1,284 | 892 | 386 | 21.0 | 805 | 1,929 | 1,053 | 847 |
| Depreciation | 607 | 591 | 512 | 523 | 517 | 661 | 1,080 | 765 | 381 | 298 |
| Interest Expense | 101 | 76.0 | 116 | 141 | 154 | 179 | 153 | 107 | 79.9 | 56.7 |
| Pretax Income | 2,233 | 2,421 | 1,170 | -1,137 | -550 | -2,604 | -5,963 | 840 | 735 | 535 |
| Effective Tax Rate | 3.58% | 22.9% | 49.4% | NM | NM | NM | NM | 48.4% | 25.7% | 24.8% |
| Net Income | 2,150 | 1,855 | 585 | -2,185 | -223 | -1,780 | -5,498 | 410 | 477 | 328 |
| S&P Core Earnings | 2,319 | 1,863 | 738 | -1,420 | -200 | -1,947 | -2,908 | NA | NA | NA |

### Balance Sheet & Other Financial Data (Million $)

| | 2007 | 2006 | 2005 | 2004 | 2003 | 2002 | 2001 | 2000 | 1999 | 1998 |
|---|---|---|---|---|---|---|---|---|---|---|
| Cash | 3,516 | 1,157 | 1,342 | 1,009 | 833 | 1,471 | 1,037 | 138 | 116 | 12.2 |
| Current Assets | 5,294 | 4,798 | 3,860 | 3,281 | 2,694 | 3,825 | 4,107 | 4,634 | 1,783 | 1,310 |
| Total Assets | 15,215 | 13,065 | 11,175 | 9,710 | 10,752 | 11,548 | 12,793 | 17,526 | 6,012 | 4,982 |
| Current Liabilities | 2,512 | 2,319 | 2,216 | 2,336 | 1,553 | 1,680 | 1,994 | 1,949 | 1,488 | 1,075 |
| Long Term Debt | 1,514 | 1,696 | 1,789 | 2,214 | 2,668 | 3,963 | 4,461 | 3,966 | 1,289 | 1,364 |
| Common Equity | 9,496 | 7,246 | 5,609 | 3,752 | 5,379 | 4,536 | 5,414 | 10,633 | 2,227 | 1,506 |
| Total Capital | 11,077 | 8,987 | 7,441 | 6,059 | 8,168 | 8,713 | 10,001 | 14,808 | 3,814 | 3,233 |
| Capital Expenditures | 1,262 | 1,182 | 1,553 | 857 | 366 | 357 | 1,800 | 1,525 | 733 | 714 |
| Cash Flow | 2,757 | 2,446 | 1,097 | -1,662 | 294 | -1,247 | -4,418 | 1,175 | 858 | 626 |
| Current Ratio | 2.1 | 2.1 | 1.7 | 1.4 | 1.7 | 2.3 | 2.1 | 2.4 | 1.2 | 1.2 |
| % Long Term Debt of Capitalization | 13.7 | 18.9 | 24.0 | 36.5 | 32.7 | 45.5 | 44.6 | 26.8 | 33.8 | 42.2 |
| % Net Income of Revenue | 36.7 | 35.9 | 12.8 | NM | NM | NM | NM | NM | 5.7 | 9.4 |
| % Return on Assets | 15.2 | 15.3 | 5.6 | NM | NM | NM | NM | NM | 3.4 | 8.7 | 6.7 |
| % Return on Equity | 25.7 | 29.1 | 12.5 | NM | NM | NM | NM | 6.2 | 25.5 | 23.7 |

Data as orig reptd.; bef. results of disc opers/spec. items. Per share data adj. for stk. divs.; EPS diluted. E-Estimated. NA-Not Available. NM-Not Meaningful. NR-Not Ranked. UR-Under Review.

**Office:** One Riverfront Plaza, Corning, NY 14831-0001.
**Telephone:** 607-974-9000.
**Email:** info@corning.com
**Website:** http://www.corning.com

**Chrmn & CEO:** W.P. Weeks
**Pres & COO:** P.F. Volanakis
**Vice Chrmn & CFO:** J.B. Flaws
**EVP & Chief Admin Officer:** K.P. Gregg

**EVP & CTO:** J.A. Miller, Jr.
**Board Members:** J. S. Brown, R. F. Cummings, Jr., J. B. Flaws, G. Gund, J. R. Houghton, K. M. Landgraf, J. J. O'Connor, D. D. Rieman, H. O. Ruding, W. D. Smithburg, H. E. Tookes, II, P. F. Volanakis, W. P. Weeks

**Founded:** 1851
**Domicile:** New York
**Employees:** 24,800

**STANDARD &POOR'S**

# Costco Wholesale Corp

| S&P Recommendation | **HOLD** ★ ★ ★ ☆ ☆ | Price<br>$48.06 (as of Nov 14, 2008) | 12-Mo. Target Price<br>$66.00 | Investment Style<br>Large-Cap Blend |
|---|---|---|---|---|

**GICS Sector** Consumer Staples
**Sub-Industry** Hypermarkets & Super Centers

**Summary** This company operates over 530 membership warehouses in the U.S., Puerto Rico, Canada, the U.K., Taiwan, Japan, Korea, and Mexico.

## Key Stock Statistics (Source S&P, Vickers, company reports)

| | | | | | | | |
|---|---|---|---|---|---|---|---|
| 52-Wk Range | $75.23–30.70 | S&P Oper. EPS 2009E | 3.15 | Market Capitalization(B) | $20.746 | Beta | 0.71 |
| Trailing 12-Month EPS | $2.89 | S&P Oper. EPS 2010E | NA | Yield (%) | 1.33 | S&P 3-Yr. Proj. EPS CAGR(%) | 11 |
| Trailing 12-Month P/E | 16.6 | P/E on S&P Oper. EPS 2009E | 15.3 | Dividend Rate/Share | $0.64 | S&P Credit Rating | A |
| $10K Invested 5 Yrs Ago | $14,735 | Common Shares Outstg. (M) | 431.7 | Institutional Ownership (%) | 85 | | |

## Price Performance

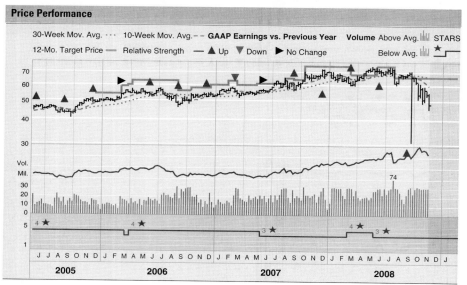

30-Week Mov. Avg. ···· 10-Week Mov. Avg. – – **GAAP Earnings vs. Previous Year**  Volume Above Avg. ▮▮▮ STARS
12-Mo. Target Price — Relative Strength — ▲ Up ▼ Down ► No Change  Below Avg. ▮▮▮ ★

Options: ASE, CBOE, P, Ph

Analysis prepared by **Joseph Agnese** on October 10, 2008, when the stock traded at **$ 52.83**.

## Highlights

➤ We see net sales advancing to about $79 billion in FY 09 (Aug.), from $71 billion in FY 08, reflecting a same-store sales increase of 4%, excluding gasoline and foreign currency effects, and about 5% square footage growth. We look for membership fees to equal 2.1% of sales, benefiting from rising membership and stable retention rates and growing conversions to executive memberships.

➤ We project that margins will narrow, reflecting aggressive pricing as product cost inflation accelerates, partially offset by the benefits from increased sales leverage; a shift in mix toward expanded margin categories such as food and sundries, soft and hard lines, and fresh foods; the impact of a 2% reward on executive memberships; and improved leverage of employee compensation. We see increased pre-opening expenses, reflecting new club openings, and lower interest income due to lower interest rates.

➤ After an expected modest reduction in the share count due to an active share repurchase program, we estimate that FY 09 operating EPS will increase 8.2%, to $3.15, from operating earnings of $2.91 in FY 08.

## Investment Rationale/Risk

➤ We expect COST to increase its market share, as we see the company pricing aggressively as it maintains a strong value proposition and a relatively upscale product mix that appeals to a more affluent customer base. We see category strength in fresh foods and expansion of ancillary businesses offsetting weaker demand for discretionary goods. We think the company is well positioned to generate future earnings growth due to improved labor cost controls and strong new store expansion.

➤ Risks to our recommendation and target price include a slowdown in sales due to weakness in the economy, more difficult foreign currency comparisons, and increased cannibalization from new store expansion.

➤ We believe the stock's valuation will be supported as demand remains strong due to its competitive priced offerings and its less economically sensitive upper income customer base. We apply a P/E of 21X to our FY 09 EPS estimate of $3.15, a 45% premium to the S&P 500 and in line with its five-year average of 21X, to arrive at our 12-month target price of $66.

## Qualitative Risk Assessment

| **LOW** | MEDIUM | HIGH |
|---|---|---|

Our risk assessment for Costco Wholesale incorporates our view of a strong balance sheet, its market leadership position, and our expectation that consistent earnings and dividend growth will continue.

## Quantitative Evaluations

### S&P Quality Ranking A-

| D | C | B- | B | B+ | **A-** | A | A+ |
|---|---|---|---|---|---|---|---|

### Relative Strength Rank MODERATE

**55**

LOWEST = 1  HIGHEST = 99

## Revenue/Earnings Data

### Revenue (Million $)

| | 1Q | 2Q | 3Q | 4Q | Year |
|---|---|---|---|---|---|
| 2008 | 15,810 | 16,960 | 16,614 | 23,100 | 72,483 |
| 2007 | 14,152 | 15,112 | 14,659 | 20,477 | 64,909 |
| 2006 | 12,933 | 14,059 | 13,284 | 19,875 | 60,151 |
| 2005 | 11,578 | 12,658 | 11,997 | 16,702 | 52,935 |
| 2004 | 10,521 | 11,549 | 10,897 | 15,139 | 48,107 |
| 2003 | 9,199 | 10,114 | 9,543 | 13,690 | 42,546 |

### Earnings Per Share ($)

| | | | | | |
|---|---|---|---|---|---|
| 2008 | 0.59 | 0.74 | 0.67 | 0.90 | 2.89 |
| 2007 | 0.51 | 0.54 | 0.49 | 0.83 | 2.37 |
| 2006 | 0.45 | 0.62 | 0.49 | 0.75 | 2.30 |
| 2005 | 0.40 | 0.62 | 0.43 | 0.73 | 2.18 |
| 2004 | 0.34 | 0.48 | 0.42 | 0.62 | 1.85 |
| 2003 | 0.31 | 0.39 | 0.33 | 0.51 | 1.53 |

Fiscal year ended Aug. 31. Next earnings report expected: Mid December. EPS Estimates based on S&P Operating Earnings; historical GAAP earnings are as reported.

## Dividend Data (Dates: mm/dd Payment Date: mm/dd/yy)

| Amount ($) | Date Decl. | Ex-Div. Date | Stk. of Record | Payment Date |
|---|---|---|---|---|
| 0.145 | 01/30 | 02/13 | 02/15 | 02/29/08 |
| 0.160 | 04/29 | 05/14 | 05/16 | 05/30/08 |
| 0.160 | 07/23 | 08/06 | 08/08 | 08/22/08 |
| 0.160 | 10/30 | 11/12 | 11/14 | 11/28/08 |

Dividends have been paid since 2004. Source: Company reports.

# Costco Wholesale Corp

**STANDARD &POOR'S**

## Business Summary October 10, 2008

Costco Wholesale (formerly Costco Companies, Inc., and prior to that, Price/Costco, Inc.) began the pioneering "I can get it for you wholesale" membership warehouse concept in 1976, in San Diego, CA. The company operated 534 warehouses worldwide as of March 2008, mainly in the U.S. and Canada (including 31 stores operated through a joint venture in Mexico). COST also operates an e-commerce Web site, costco.com.

The company believes that low prices on a limited selection of national brand merchandise and selected private-label products in a wide range of merchandise categories produce high sales volume and rapid inventory turnover. According to COST, high levels of turnover, combined with operating efficiencies achieved by volume purchasing in a no-frills, self-service warehouse facility enable the company to operate profitably at significantly narrower gross margins than traditional retailers and even discounters and supermarkets. COST buys virtually all of its merchandise directly from manufacturers, for shipment either directly to warehouse clubs or to a consolidation point (depot), at which

shipments are combined in order to minimize freight and handling costs. The company generally receives cash from the sale of a substantial portion of its inventory at mature warehouse operations before it is required to pay vendors, even though COST often pays early to obtain payment discounts.

COST has two primary types of memberships: Gold Star (individual) and Business members. Individual memberships are available to employees of federal, state and local governments; financial institutions; corporations; utility and transportation companies; public and private educational institutions; and other organizations. Gold Star membership is $50 annually. There were 18.6 million Gold Star memberships as of September 2007, up from 17.3 million as of September 2006.

## Company Financials Fiscal Year Ended Aug. 31

| Per Share Data ($) | 2008 | 2007 | 2006 | 2005 | 2004 | 2003 | 2002 | 2001 | 2000 | 1999 |
|---|---|---|---|---|---|---|---|---|---|---|
| Tangible Book Value | 21.08 | 19.73 | 19.78 | 18.80 | 16.48 | 14.33 | 12.51 | 10.71 | 9.37 | 7.98 |
| Cash Flow | NA | 3.60 | 3.37 | 3.13 | 2.74 | 2.32 | 2.17 | 1.90 | 1.86 | 1.57 |
| Earnings | 2.89 | 2.37 | 2.30 | 2.18 | 1.85 | 1.53 | 1.48 | 1.29 | 1.35 | 1.12 |
| S&P Core Earnings | 2.88 | 2.37 | 2.30 | 2.12 | 1.76 | 1.40 | 1.32 | 1.12 | NA | NA |
| Dividends | NA | 0.55 | 0.49 | 0.43 | 0.20 | Nil | Nil | Nil | Nil | Nil |
| Payout Ratio | NA | 23% | 21% | 20% | 11% | Nil | Nil | Nil | Nil | Nil |
| Prices:High | NA | 72.68 | 57.94 | 51.21 | 50.46 | 39.02 | 46.90 | 46.38 | 60.50 | 49.38 |
| Prices:Low | NA | 51.52 | 46.00 | 39.48 | 35.05 | 27.00 | 27.09 | 29.83 | 25.94 | 32.69 |
| P/E Ratio:High | NA | 31 | 25 | 23 | 27 | 26 | 32 | 36 | 45 | 44 |
| P/E Ratio:Low | NA | 22 | 20 | 18 | 19 | 18 | 18 | 23 | 19 | 29 |

| Income Statement Analysis (Million $) | | | | | | | | | | |
|---|---|---|---|---|---|---|---|---|---|---|
| Revenue | 72,483 | 64,400 | 60,151 | 52,935 | 48,107 | 42,546 | 38,763 | 34,797 | 32,164 | 27,456 |
| Operating Income | NA | 2,189 | 2,146 | 1,969 | 1,827 | 1,567 | 1,494 | 1,312 | 1,299 | 1,141 |
| Depreciation | 653 | 566 | 515 | 478 | 441 | 391 | 342 | 301 | 254 | 225 |
| Interest Expense | NA | 64.1 | 12.6 | 34.4 | 36.7 | 36.9 | 29.1 | 32.0 | 39.3 | 45.5 |
| Pretax Income | 1,999 | 1,710 | 1,751 | 1,549 | 1,401 | 1,158 | 1,138 | 1,003 | 1,052 | 859 |
| Effective Tax Rate | 35.8% | 36.7% | 37.0% | 31.4% | 37.0% | 37.8% | 38.5% | 40.0% | 40.0% | 40.0% |
| Net Income | 1,283 | 1,083 | 1,103 | 1,063 | 882 | 721 | 700 | 602 | 631 | 515 |
| S&P Core Earnings | 1,280 | 1,082 | 1,104 | 1,044 | 837 | 660 | 624 | 525 | NA | NA |

| Balance Sheet & Other Financial Data (Million $) | | | | | | | | | | |
|---|---|---|---|---|---|---|---|---|---|---|
| Cash | 3,275 | 2,780 | 1,511 | 2,063 | 2,823 | 1,545 | 806 | 603 | 525 | 441 |
| Current Assets | NA | 9,324 | 8,232 | 8,086 | 7,269 | 5,712 | 4,631 | 3,882 | 3,470 | 3,316 |
| Total Assets | 20,682 | 19,607 | 17,495 | 16,514 | 15,093 | 13,192 | 11,620 | 10,090 | 8,634 | 7,505 |
| Current Liabilities | NA | 8,582 | 7,819 | 6,609 | 6,171 | 5,011 | 4,450 | 4,112 | 3,404 | 2,866 |
| Long Term Debt | NA | 2,108 | 215 | 711 | 994 | 1,290 | 1,211 | 859 | 790 | 919 |
| Common Equity | 9,192 | 8,623 | 9,143 | 8,881 | 7,625 | 6,555 | 5,694 | 4,883 | 4,240 | 3,532 |
| Total Capital | NA | 10,801 | 9,422 | 9,650 | 8,922 | 8,181 | 7,025 | 5,858 | 5,139 | 4,572 |
| Capital Expenditures | 1,599 | 1,386 | 1,213 | 995 | 706 | 811 | 1,039 | 1,448 | 1,228 | 788 |
| Cash Flow | NA | 1,649 | 1,619 | 1,541 | 1,323 | 1,112 | 1,042 | 903 | 886 | 740 |
| Current Ratio | 1.1 | 1.1 | 1.1 | 1.2 | 1.2 | 1.1 | 1.0 | 0.9 | 1.0 | 1.2 |
| % Long Term Debt of Capitalization | Nil | 19.5 | 2.3 | 7.4 | 11.1 | 15.8 | 17.2 | 14.7 | 15.4 | 20.1 |
| % Net Income of Revenue | 1.8 | 1.7 | 1.8 | 2.0 | 1.8 | 1.7 | 1.8 | 1.7 | 2.0 | 1.9 |
| % Return on Assets | NA | 5.8 | 6.5 | 6.7 | 6.2 | 5.8 | 6.4 | 6.4 | 7.8 | 7.5 |
| % Return on Equity | NA | 12.2 | 12.2 | 12.9 | 12.4 | 11.8 | 13.2 | 13.2 | 16.2 | 15.9 |

Data as orig reptd.; bef. results of disc opers/spec. items. Per share data adj. for stk. divs.; EPS diluted. E-Estimated. NA-Not Available. NM-Not Meaningful. NR-Not Ranked. UR-Under Review.

**Office:** 999 Lake Dr Ste, Issaquah, WA 98027.
**Telephone:** 425-313-8100.
**Email:** investor@costco.com
**Website:** http://www.costco.com

**Chrmn:** J.H. Brotman
**Pres & CEO:** J.D. Sinegal
**COO & EVP:** R.D. DiCerchio
**EVP & CFO:** R. Galanti

**SVP, Chief Acctg Officer & Cntlr:** D.S. Petterson
**Investor Contact:** R.A. Galanti (425-313-8203)
**Board Members:** J. H. Brotman, B. S. Carson, S. Decker, R. D. DiCerchio, D. J. Evans, R. Galanti, W. H. Gates, J. Heisenbach, H. E. James, R. M. Libenson, J. W. Meisenbach, C. Munger, J. S. Ruckelshaus, J. D. Sinegal

**Founded:** 1976
**Domicile:** Washington
**Employees:** 146,000

**The McGraw·Hill Companies**

# Coventry Health Care Inc.

STANDARD &POOR'S

| S&P Recommendation **HOLD** ★★★☆☆ | Price $12.59 (as of Nov 14, 2008) | 12-Mo. Target Price $20.00 | Investment Style Large-Cap Growth |
|---|---|---|---|

**GICS Sector** Health Care
**Sub-Industry** Managed Health Care

**Summary** This national managed health care company operates health plans, insurance companies, network rental/managed care services companies, and workers' compensation services companies.

## Key Stock Statistics (Source S&P, Vickers, company reports)

| | | | | | | | | |
|---|---|---|---|---|---|---|---|---|
| 52-Wk Range | $63.89– 11.40 | S&P Oper. EPS 2008E | 2.70 | Market Capitalization(B) | $1.876 | Beta | 1.26 |
| Trailing 12-Month EPS | $3.14 | S&P Oper. EPS 2009E | 2.70 | Yield (%) | Nil | S&P 3-Yr. Proj. EPS CAGR(%) | NA |
| Trailing 12-Month P/E | 4.0 | P/E on S&P Oper. EPS 2008E | 4.7 | Dividend Rate/Share | Nil | S&P Credit Rating | BBB- |
| $10K Invested 5 Yrs Ago | $4,886 | Common Shares Outstg. (M) | 149.0 | Institutional Ownership (%) | 95 | | |

## Price Performance

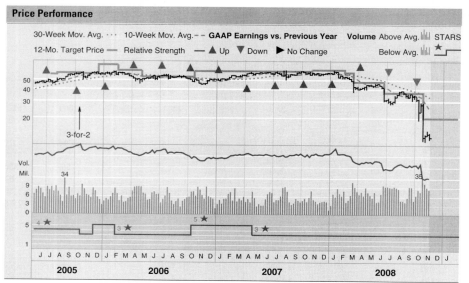

30-Week Mov. Avg. ···· 10-Week Mov. Avg. ─ ─ **GAAP Earnings vs. Previous Year** Volume Above Avg. STARS
12-Mo. Target Price ── Relative Strength ─ ▲ Up ▼ Down ► No Change Below Avg. ★

3-for-2

Options: ASE, CBOE, P, Ph

Analysis prepared by **Phillip M. Seligman** on October 27, 2008, when the stock traded at **$ 12.21**.

### Highlights

➤ We expect revenues to rise by about 8.5% in 2009, to about $13 billion, from the $12.0 billion we look for in 2008. The 21%-plus growth rate we see for 2008 has mostly been driven by three acquisitions in 2007. Given its price hikes to compensate for higher medical cost trends, and the soft economy, we estimate that commercial enrollment will fall by at least 100,000 members. We also forecast 35,000 additional Medicare Advantage (MA) members, 20,000 additional Medicare drug program members and 10,000 more Medicaid members.

➤ Despite our view of no negative prior-year reserve development as CVH experienced in 2008, we still expect the consolidated medical loss ratio (MLR) to rise about 40 basis points (bps) in 2009. Negative impacts on the 2009 MLR we see include an increasing percentage of Medicare and Medicaid revenues in the mix, underpricing in two commercial plans, and adverse member selection in the federal employee HMO business. We forecast a modestly higher SG&A cost ratio, due to MA network buildouts.

➤ We estimate operating EPS of $2.70 in 2008, versus 2007's $4.02, and forecast $2.70 in 2009.

### Investment Rationale/Risk

➤ We are encouraged that CVH has instituted fixes for the underwriting and operational problems that have hurt 2008 EPS. On the commercial front, it is addressing the problem of higher medical cost trends via higher pricing. We expect it to realize some benefit in 2009, but it will not fully benefit until 2010, as most accounts renew in late 2009. CVH also made changes in the 2009 pricing and benefit design of the MA Private Fee-for-Service plan that experienced high provider utilization, causing the MA MLR to spike in 2008. However, we think CVH may not have fully accounted for the cost trends when it submitted its bids to Medicare in June. On a more positive note, the third quarter 2008 investment impairment was modest, in our view, and CVH's financial position looks healthy to us.

➤ Risks to our recommendation and target price include intensified competition, sharply higher medical costs, and a weak economy.

➤ Our 12-month target price of $20 is based on a below-peer forward P/E of 7.5X, reflecting our view of CVH's underperformance and group-wide valuation compression, applied to our 2009 EPS estimate.

## Qualitative Risk Assessment

| LOW | MEDIUM | HIGH |
|---|---|---|

Our risk assessment reflects CVH's increasingly diversified operations and its January 2005 acquisition of First Health, which we think provided good growth prospects. Even so, we think competition amid the soft economy and our view of rising unemployment will take a toll on commercial enrollment, although we see gains in Medicare and Medicaid enrollment.

## Quantitative Evaluations

**S&P Quality Ranking** B+

| D | C | B- | B | B+ | A- | A | A+ |
|---|---|---|---|---|---|---|---|

**Relative Strength Rank** WEAK

15

LOWEST = 1    HIGHEST = 99

## Revenue/Earnings Data

**Revenue (Million $)**

| | 1Q | 2Q | 3Q | 4Q | Year |
|---|---|---|---|---|---|
| 2008 | 2,941 | 2,978 | 2,975 | -- | -- |
| 2007 | 2,237 | 2,332 | 2,523 | 2,788 | 9,880 |
| 2006 | 1,939 | 1,945 | 1,909 | 1,941 | 7,734 |
| 2005 | 1,565 | 1,653 | 1,674 | 1,719 | 6,611 |
| 2004 | 1,288 | 1,310 | 1,330 | 1,384 | 5,312 |
| 2003 | 1,065 | 1,096 | 1,150 | 1,223 | 4,535 |

**Earnings Per Share ($)**

| | | | | | |
|---|---|---|---|---|---|
| 2008 | 0.81 | 0.55 | 0.58 | E0.61 | E2.70 |
| 2007 | 0.76 | 0.96 | 1.08 | 1.18 | 3.98 |
| 2006 | 0.74 | 0.84 | 0.92 | 0.97 | 3.47 |
| 2005 | 0.73 | 0.79 | 0.81 | 0.77 | 3.10 |
| 2004 | 0.55 | 0.62 | 0.64 | 0.67 | 2.48 |
| 2003 | 0.37 | 0.47 | 0.49 | 0.51 | 1.83 |

Fiscal year ended Dec. 31. Next earnings report expected: Mid February. EPS Estimates based on S&P Operating Earnings; historical GAAP earnings are as reported.

## Dividend Data

No cash dividends have been paid.

STANDARD
&POOR'S

# Coventry Health Care Inc.

## Business Summary October 27, 2008

CORPORATE OVERVIEW. Coventry Health Care is a diversified national managed care company. It traditionally offered individual and employer groups a full range of commercial risk products, including health maintenance organization (HMO), preferred provider organization (PPO) and point-of service (POS) products. Through its January 2005 acquisition of First Health Group (FH), it gained a nationwide provider network and high-margin, fee-based service businesses, such as network rental, clinical programs, workers' compensation administration, Medicaid health care management services, and pharmacy benefit management. CVH also gained additional PPO members, including the Federal Employee Health Benefit program, the largest employer-sponsored group health program in the U.S., and an administrative services only (ASO, or non-risk) product for large employers with locations in several states that self-insure. Starting in 2007, CVH combined the enrollment of its existing business with that of FH.

As of September 30, 2008, the company had a total of 3,738,000 members (versus 3,969,000 at December 31, 2007), excluding standalone Medicare prescription drug program members, divided into two operating segments -- the Commercial division and the Individual/Government division.

The Commercial division is comprised of Commercial Group Risk members

(1,497,000, versus 1,580,000), Health Plan ASO (720,000, versus 750,000), and Other ASO (641,000, versus 783,000). Commercial Group Risk membership includes the health plan commercial group business and a small group PPO insurance block that was previously embedded within FH. It excludes the Individual business (under 65 years of age). In the ASO businesses, CVH offers management services and access to its provider networks to employers that self-insure their employee health benefits. The Other ASO membership includes active National Accounts and Federal Employees Health Benefits Plan (FEHBP) administrative services business.

The Individual/Government division consists of Medicare Advantage (377,000, versus 283,000), Medicaid Risk (386,000, versus 480,000) and Individual Risk (117,000, versus 93,000) plans. Medicare Advantage includes Medicare Advantage HMO, Medicare Advantage PPO, and Medicare Advantage PFFS (Private Fee-For-Service). Medicare Part D (Prescription Drug Program) had 910,000 members (versus 704,000).

## Company Financials Fiscal Year Ended Dec. 31

| Per Share Data ($) | 2007 | 2006 | 2005 | 2004 | 2003 | 2002 | 2001 | 2000 | 1999 | 1998 |
|---|---|---|---|---|---|---|---|---|---|---|
| Tangible Book Value | 1.15 | 5.92 | 3.21 | 6.60 | 4.57 | 2.85 | 2.89 | 2.31 | 1.60 | 1.06 |
| Cash Flow | 4.89 | 4.17 | 3.63 | 2.61 | 1.97 | 1.24 | 0.72 | 0.60 | 0.50 | 0.12 |
| Earnings | 3.98 | 3.47 | 3.10 | 2.48 | 1.83 | 1.06 | 0.55 | 0.41 | 0.31 | -0.10 |
| S&P Core Earnings | 3.98 | 3.47 | 3.01 | 2.41 | 1.80 | 1.03 | 0.52 | NA | NA | NA |
| Dividends | Nil | Nil | Nil | Nil | Nil | Nil | Nil | Nil | Nil | Nil |
| Payout Ratio | Nil | Nil | Nil | Nil | Nil | Nil | Nil | Nil | Nil | Nil |
| Prices:High | 64.00 | 61.88 | 60.31 | 36.20 | 29.46 | 16.89 | 12.22 | 13.31 | 6.81 | 8.56 |
| Prices:Low | 48.78 | 44.33 | 34.21 | 24.66 | 10.80 | 8.67 | 5.78 | 3.06 | 2.22 | 1.72 |
| P/E Ratio:High | 16 | 18 | 19 | 15 | 16 | 16 | 22 | 32 | 22 | NM |
| P/E Ratio:Low | 12 | 13 | 11 | 10 | 6 | 8 | 11 | 7 | 7 | NM |

| Income Statement Analysis (Million $) | 2007 | 2006 | 2005 | 2004 | 2003 | 2002 | 2001 | 2000 | 1999 | 1998 |
|---|---|---|---|---|---|---|---|---|---|---|
| Revenue | 9,880 | 7,734 | 6,611 | 5,312 | 4,535 | 3,577 | 3,147 | 2,605 | 2,162 | 2,110 |
| Operating Income | 1,075 | 954 | 878 | 514 | 384 | 220 | 117 | 81.1 | 71.8 | 51.1 |
| Depreciation | 143 | 113 | 86.2 | 17.6 | 18.2 | 18.9 | 25.9 | 27.0 | 28.2 | 25.8 |
| Interest Expense | 73.1 | 52.4 | 58.4 | 14.3 | 15.1 | 13.4 | Nil | Nil | Nil | 8.57 |
| Pretax Income | 995 | 896 | 799 | 527 | 393 | 226 | 135 | 102 | 76.0 | -17.5 |
| Effective Tax Rate | 37.1% | 37.5% | 37.3% | 36.0% | 36.4% | 35.5% | 38.0% | 39.9% | 42.8% | NM |
| Net Income | 626 | 560 | 502 | 337 | 250 | 146 | 83.5 | 61.3 | 43.4 | -11.7 |
| S&P Core Earnings | 627 | 560 | 485 | 328 | 245 | 143 | 78.5 | NA | NA | NA |

| Balance Sheet & Other Financial Data (Million $) | 2007 | 2006 | 2005 | 2004 | 2003 | 2002 | 2001 | 2000 | 1999 | 1998 |
|---|---|---|---|---|---|---|---|---|---|---|
| Cash | 1,101 | 1,371 | 392 | 418 | 253 | 187 | 312 | 256 | 240 | 409 |
| Current Assets | 1,847 | 2,134 | 1,326 | 973 | 534 | 424 | 579 | 507 | 483 | 591 |
| Total Assets | 7,159 | 5,665 | 4,895 | 2,341 | 1,982 | 1,643 | 1,451 | 1,239 | 1,082 | 1,091 |
| Current Liabilities | 1,750 | 1,652 | 1,270 | 932 | 855 | 801 | 752 | 632 | 523 | 566 |
| Long Term Debt | 1,662 | 750 | 760 | 171 | 171 | 175 | Nil | Nil | Nil | 46.4 |
| Common Equity | 3,301 | 2,953 | 2,555 | 1,212 | 929 | 646 | 689 | 662 | 480 | 437 |
| Total Capital | 5,193 | 3,704 | 3,315 | 1,383 | 1,099 | 821 | 689 | 662 | 527 | 483 |
| Capital Expenditures | 61.3 | 72.6 | 71.4 | 15.0 | 13.4 | 13.0 | 11.9 | 16.0 | 14.7 | 3.24 |
| Cash Flow | 769 | 673 | 588 | 355 | 268 | 164 | 109 | 88.4 | 71.6 | 14.1 |
| Current Ratio | 1.1 | 1.3 | 1.0 | 1.0 | 0.6 | 0.5 | 0.8 | 0.8 | 0.9 | 1.0 |
| % Long Term Debt of Capitalization | 33.5 | 20.3 | 22.9 | 12.3 | 15.5 | 21.3 | Nil | Nil | Nil | 9.6 |
| % Net Income of Revenue | 6.3 | 7.2 | 7.6 | 6.3 | 5.5 | 4.1 | 2.7 | 2.4 | 2.0 | NM |
| % Return on Assets | 9.8 | 10.6 | 13.9 | 15.6 | 13.8 | 9.4 | 6.2 | 5.3 | 4.0 | NM |
| % Return on Equity | 20.0 | 20.3 | 26.6 | 31.5 | 31.8 | 21.8 | 13.0 | 10.7 | 9.5 | NM |

Data as orig reptd.; bef. results of disc opers/spec. items. Per share data adj. for stk. divs.; EPS diluted. E-Estimated. NA-Not Available. NM-Not Meaningful. NR-Not Ranked. UR-Under Review.

**Office:** 6705 Rockledge Drive, Bethesda, MD 20817.
**Telephone:** 301-581-0600.
**Email:** investor-relations@cvty.com
**Website:** http://www.coventryhealth.com

**Chrmn:** A.F. Wise
**Pres & CEO:** D.B. Wolf
**CEO:** R.L. Dawson
**EVP, CFO & Treas:** S.M. Guertin

**EVP & General Counsel:** T.C. Zielinski
**Board Members:** J. Ackerman, J. H. Austin, L. D. Crandall, L. N. Kugelman, D. N. Mendelson, R. W. Moorhead, III, E. E. Tallett, T. T. Weglicki, A. F. Wise, D. B. Wolf

**Founded:** 1986
**Domicile:** Delaware
**Employees:** 15,000

# Covidien Ltd

**STANDARD &POOR'S**

| S&P Recommendation **BUY** ★★★★☆ | Price $38.10 (as of Nov 14, 2008) | 12-Mo. Target Price $63.00 | Investment Style Large-Cap Growth |
|---|---|---|---|

**GICS Sector** Health Care
**Sub-Industry** Health Care Equipment

**Summary** Formerly a wholly owned division of Tyco International, Covidien develops, manufactures and distributes medical devices and supplies, diagnostic imaging agents, pharmaceuticals and other health care products used in both clinical and home settings.

## Key Stock Statistics (Source S&P, Vickers, company reports)

| | | | | | | | |
|---|---|---|---|---|---|---|---|
| 52-Wk Range | $57.00–35.33 | S&P Oper. EPS 2008E | 2.60 | Market Capitalization(B) | $19.119 | Beta | NA |
| Trailing 12-Month EPS | $1.96 | S&P Oper. EPS 2009E | 3.10 | Yield (%) | 1.68 | S&P 3-Yr. Proj. EPS CAGR(%) | 10 |
| Trailing 12-Month P/E | 19.4 | P/E on S&P Oper. EPS 2008E | 14.7 | Dividend Rate/Share | $0.64 | S&P Credit Rating | NA |
| $10K Invested 5 Yrs Ago | NA | Common Shares Outstg. (M) | 501.8 | Institutional Ownership (%) | 89 | | |

## Price Performance

30-Week Mov. Avg. · · · 10-Week Mov. Avg. – – **GAAP Earnings vs. Previous Year**  Volume Above Avg. STARS
12-Mo. Target Price —  Relative Strength —  ▲ Up ▼ Down ▶ No Change  Below Avg.  ★

Options: ASE, CBOE, P

Analysis prepared by **Robert M. Gold** on September 15, 2008, when the stock traded at **$ 56.40**.

## Highlights

▶ Excluding the retail products, specialty chemicals and European incontinence businesses that the company intends to divest and has now reclassified as discontinued, we are looking for FY 08 (Sep.) revenues of approximately $10.0 billion, up from a comparable $8.9 billion in FY 07. In our opinion, the company's ongoing product lines can support a sustained currency-neutral revenue growth rate of 7% to 8%. We see FY 09 revenues reaching $11.0 billion.

▶ We see the company reporting substantially higher gross profit margins due to the exclusion of products now classified as discontinued, which should offset higher raw material costs and the adverse impact of foreign currency. However, we anticipate that as a standalone entity, COV will increase spending on both R&D and sales, and we think interest costs will continue to rise following the spinoff from Tyco.

▶ We project FY 08 operating EPS of $2.60, reflecting the dilutive impact of asset sales, and a lower effective tax rate than we originally envisioned. Our FY 09 EPS estimate is $3.10.

## Investment Rationale/Risk

▶ We believe COV will generate sales and earnings growth modestly below comparable large cap medical equipment and supply peers in FY 08, due to its relatively mature product lines, competitive pressures and higher operating costs as it reinvests in its operations following its spinoff from Tyco. However, we think recent decisions to restructure the product portfolio to focus on medical devices and imaging solutions will spur a higher long term revenue growth rate and wider operating margins.

▶ Risks to our recommendation and target price include slower-than-expected sales in the device and imaging categories, more intense competitive pressures, higher raw material cost inflation and a material increase in the value of the U.S. dollar.

▶ Our 12-month target price of $63 is based on an FY 09 P/E of about 20X and an FY 09 price/sales multiple of 2.7X, both in line with the company's medical device and supply peers in our coverage universe. In our opinion, this valuation is justified by the company's recent strategic decisions and potential operating margin growth.

## Qualitative Risk Assessment

| LOW | MEDIUM | HIGH |
|---|---|---|

COV operates in a highly competitive industry subject to pricing pressures, a loss of sales due to patent expirations and the introduction of new and potentially disruptive technologies or products that can adversely impact sales. However, we believe COV is a global leader in many areas of the health care products and supplies markets and has competitive advantages afforded larger players in the industry.

## Quantitative Evaluations

### S&P Quality Ranking   NR

| D | C | B- | B | B+ | A- | A | A+ |
|---|---|---|---|---|---|---|---|

### Relative Strength Rank   MODERATE

56

LOWEST = 1          HIGHEST = 99

## Revenue/Earnings Data

### Revenue (Million $)

| | 1Q | 2Q | 3Q | 4Q | Year |
|---|---|---|---|---|---|
| 2008 | 2,316 | 2,426 | 2,595 | -- | -- |
| 2007 | -- | -- | 2,579 | 2,601 | 10,170 |
| 2006 | -- | -- | -- | -- | 9,647 |
| 2005 | -- | -- | -- | -- | -- |
| 2004 | -- | -- | -- | -- | -- |
| 2003 | -- | -- | -- | -- | -- |

### Earnings Per Share ($)

| | 1Q | 2Q | 3Q | 4Q | Year |
|---|---|---|---|---|---|
| 2008 | 0.89 | 0.50 | 0.66 | E0.63 | E2.60 |
| 2007 | -- | -- | -2.23 | 0.07 | -0.68 |
| 2006 | -- | -- | -- | -- | 2.57 |
| 2005 | -- | -- | -- | -- | -- |
| 2004 | -- | -- | -- | -- | -- |
| 2003 | -- | -- | -- | -- | -- |

Fiscal year ended Sep. 30. Next earnings report expected: NA. EPS Estimates based on S&P Operating Earnings; historical GAAP earnings are as reported.

## Dividend Data (Dates: mm/dd Payment Date: mm/dd/yy)

| Amount ($) | Date Decl. | Ex-Div. Date | Stk. of Record | Payment Date |
|---|---|---|---|---|
| 0.160 | 01/15 | 01/23 | 01/25 | 02/11/08 |
| 0.160 | 03/18 | 03/27 | 03/31 | 05/05/08 |
| 0.160 | 07/16 | 07/24 | 07/28 | 08/11/08 |
| 0.160 | 09/29 | 10/07 | 10/09 | 11/06/08 |

Dividends have been paid since 2007. Source: Company reports.

---

**Please read the Required Disclosures and Analyst Certification on the last page of this report.**

The McGraw·Hill Companies

# Covidien Ltd

**STANDARD &POOR'S**

## Business Summary September 15, 2008

CORPORATE OVERVIEW. Covidien (COV) is a global leader in the development, manufacture and sale of medical products and supplies, diagnostic imaging agents, pharmaceuticals and other health care products used in both clinical and home settings. During FY 07 (Sep.), about 40% of sales were generated in non-U.S. markets. The company was separated from parent Tyco International on July 2, 2007, and NYSE trading commenced under the ticker COV.

The medical devices division (61% of FY 07 sales) develops, makes and sells surgical instruments and devices, respiratory and monitoring products and other products. COV offers a complete line of surgical stapling and laparoscopic instrumentation, and expanded its offerings of surgical mesh for hernia repair through the purchase of a controlling interest in Floreane Medical Implants S.A. during FY 06. Through its Valleylab franchise, COV offers electrosurgery products such as tissue fusing, vessel sealing systems and a radiofrequency ablation system.

The medical device division is also developing and marketing a broad line of innovative biosurgery solutions, including internal sealants, topical adhesives and anti-adhesion products that have potential applications in many types of surgical procedures. It also sells an extensive line of products used to moni-

tor, diagnose and treat respiratory disease and sleep disorders, vascular compression devices, needles and syringes, sharps collection systems, enteral feeding pumps and accessories, tympanic and electronic thermometers, advanced wound care products, urology products and dialysis catheters.

The imaging solutions segment (9%) develops, manufactures and markets contrast agents, contrast delivery systems and radiopharmaceuticals. Its imaging products are used to enhance the quality of images obtained through CT, X-ray, MRI and nuclear medicine procedures. Some of the key products include Optiray non-ionic X-ray contrast agent, OptiMark magnetic resonance imaging agent, OptiVantage contrast delivery system and OctreoScan nuclear medicine imaging agent for cancer. COV also operates its own network of 37 radiopharmacies. In November 2007, the company signed an agreement to supply X-ray contrast imaging agents to customers of MedAssets Supply Chain Systems, a St. Louis-based group purchasing organization.

## Company Financials Fiscal Year Ended Sep. 30

| Per Share Data ($) | 2007 | 2006 | 2005 | 2004 | 2003 | 2002 | 2001 | 2000 | 1999 | 1998 |
|---|---|---|---|---|---|---|---|---|---|---|
| Tangible Book Value | NM | NM | NA | NA | NA | NA | NA | NA | NA | NA |
| Cash Flow | 0.14 | 3.23 | NA | NA | NA | NA | NA | NA | NA | NA |
| Earnings | -0.68 | 2.57 | NA | NA | NA | NA | NA | NA | NA | NA |
| Dividends | Nil | NA | NA | NA | NA | NA | NA | NA | NA | NA |
| Payout Ratio | Nil | NA | NA | NA | NA | NA | NA | NA | NA | NA |
| Prices:High | 49.70 | NA | NA | NA | NA | NA | NA | NA | NA | NA |
| Prices:Low | 36.90 | NA | NA | NA | NA | NA | NA | NA | NA | NA |
| P/E Ratio:High | NM | NA | NA | NA | NA | NA | NA | NA | NA | NA |
| P/E Ratio:Low | NM | NA | NA | NA | NA | NA | NA | NA | NA | NA |

| Income Statement Analysis (Million $) | 2007 | 2006 | 2005 | 2004 | 2003 | 2002 | 2001 | 2000 | 1999 | 1998 |
|---|---|---|---|---|---|---|---|---|---|---|
| Revenue | 10,170 | 9,647 | 9,543 | 9,110 | NA | NA | NA | NA | NA | NA |
| Operating Income | 2,397 | 2,476 | NA | NA | NA | NA | NA | NA | NA | NA |
| Depreciation | 409 | 333 | 320 | 318 | NA | NA | NA | NA | NA | NA |
| Interest Expense | 188 | NA | NA | NA | NA | NA | NA | NA | NA | NA |
| Pretax Income | 151 | 1,858 | 1,751 | 1,990 | NA | NA | NA | NA | NA | NA |
| Effective Tax Rate | NM | 29.8% | 29.6% | 29.2% | NA | NA | NA | NA | NA | NA |
| Net Income | -337 | 1,304 | 1,232 | 1,409 | NA | NA | NA | NA | NA | NA |

| Balance Sheet & Other Financial Data (Million $) | 2007 | 2006 | 2005 | 2004 | 2003 | 2002 | 2001 | 2000 | 1999 | 1998 |
|---|---|---|---|---|---|---|---|---|---|---|
| Cash | 872 | 800 | 141 | NA | NA | NA | NA | NA | NA | NA |
| Current Assets | 7,556 | 7,308 | NA | NA | NA | NA | NA | NA | NA | NA |
| Total Assets | 18,328 | 17,895 | 14,784 | NA | NA | NA | NA | NA | NA | NA |
| Current Liabilities | 5,367 | 8,740 | NA | NA | NA | NA | NA | NA | NA | NA |
| Long Term Debt | 3,565 | 148 | NA | NA | NA | NA | NA | NA | NA | NA |
| Common Equity | 6,742 | 6,803 | 8,116 | NA | NA | NA | NA | NA | NA | NA |
| Total Capital | 10,879 | 6,951 | NA | NA | NA | NA | NA | NA | NA | NA |
| Capital Expenditures | 388 | NA | 331 | 251 | NA | NA | NA | NA | NA | NA |
| Cash Flow | 72.0 | 1,637 | NA | NA | NA | NA | NA | NA | NA | NA |
| Current Ratio | 1.4 | 0.8 | 1.9 | NA | NA | NA | NA | NA | NA | NA |
| % Long Term Debt of Capitalization | 32.7 | 2.1 | 22.9 | Nil | NA | NA | NA | NA | NA | NA |
| % Net Income of Revenue | NM | 13.5 | 12.9 | 15.5 | NA | NA | NA | NA | NA | NA |
| % Return on Assets | NM | NA | NA | NA | NA | NA | NA | NA | NA | NA |
| % Return on Equity | NM | NA | NA | NA | NA | NA | NA | NA | NA | NA |

Data as orig reptd.; bef. results of disc opers/spec. items. Per share data adj. for stk. divs.; EPS diluted. Pro forma data in 2006, bal. sheet & book val. as of March 30, 2007. E-Estimated. NA-Not Available. NM-Not Meaningful. NR-Not Ranked. UR-Under Review.

**Office:** 131 Front St, Hamilton, Bermuda HM12.
**Telephone:** 441-298-2480.
**Website:** http://www.covidien.com
**Chrmn, Pres & CEO:** R.J. Meelia

**COO:** B.D. King
**EVP & CFO:** C.J. Dockendorff
**SVP & General Counsel:** J.H. Masterson
**Chief Acctg Officer & Cntlr:** R.G. Brown, Jr.

**Investor Contact:** C.N. Lannum (508-452-4343)
**Board Members:** C. Arnold, R. H. Brust, J. M. Connors, Jr., C. J. Coughlin, T. M. Donahue, K. J. Herbert, R. J. Hogan, III, R. J. Meelia, D. H. Reilley, T. Yamada, J. A. Zaccagnino

**Founded:** 2000
**Domicile:** Bermuda
**Employees:** 43,800

# CSX Corp

**STANDARD &POOR'S**

| | |
|---|---|
| **S&P Recommendation** BUY ★★★★☆ | |

| Price | 12-Mo. Target Price | Investment Style |
|---|---|---|
| $38.82 (as of Nov 14, 2008) | $60.00 | Large-Cap Value |

**GICS Sector** Industrials
**Sub-Industry** Railroads

**Summary** This company operates a major U.S. rail network, transporting bulk commodities, industrial products and intermodal containers over its network of approximately 21,000 route miles.

## Key Stock Statistics (Source S&P, Vickers, company reports)

| | | | | | | | | |
|---|---|---|---|---|---|---|---|---|
| 52-Wk Range | $70.70– 38.51 | S&P Oper. EPS 2008E | 3.67 | Market Capitalization(B) | $15.313 | Beta | 1.03 |
| Trailing 12-Month EPS | $3.57 | S&P Oper. EPS 2009E | 4.19 | Yield (%) | 2.27 | S&P 3-Yr. Proj. EPS CAGR(%) | 20 |
| Trailing 12-Month P/E | 10.9 | P/E on S&P Oper. EPS 2008E | 10.6 | Dividend Rate/Share | $0.88 | S&P Credit Rating | BBB- |
| $10K Invested 5 Yrs Ago | $24,117 | Common Shares Outstg. (M) | 394.5 | Institutional Ownership (%) | 81 | | |

## Price Performance

30-Week Mov. Avg. · · · 10-Week Mov. Avg. – – **GAAP Earnings vs. Previous Year** Volume Above Avg. STARS
12-Mo. Target Price — Relative Strength — ▲ Up ▼ Down ► No Change Below Avg. ★

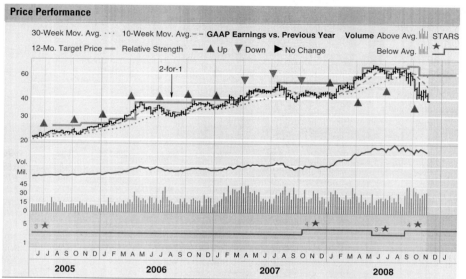

Options: ASE, CBOE, P, Ph

Analysis prepared by **Kevin Kirkeby** on October 17, 2008, when the stock traded at **$ 44.22**.

## Highlights

➤ We see 2008 revenues rising 14%, almost entirely on freight rates, with over half coming from the pass-through of fuel surcharges. Challenges in the building materials and automotive markets, in our view, will mute volumes into 2009. However, we see further rises in carloadings of coal for export due to currency-related pricing differentials. For 2009, we think CSX will again be able to achieve a 6% gain in core pricing, contributing to an 8% overall revenue gain.

➤ We expect margins to widen during the remainder of 2008 on declining diesel fuel prices, as well as contract repricings. We see a modest widening in margins during 2009 as productivity measures take hold. Likewise, lease expenses have been declining recently, and should contribute to the improved profitability we forecast for 2009. We look for fuel prices to have a lessening impact on margins next year.

➤ Reflecting stock buybacks and rising capital investments, we see moderately higher interest expenses in 2009. Including a 3% reduction in average share count, we forecast an EPS increase of about 14%, to $4.19 in 2009, from $3.67 seen in 2008.

## Investment Rationale/Risk

➤ We believe that recent improvements in operating efficiency, despite the near-term impact of volume weakness, are sustainable over the medium term. Further, we see additional gains in coming quarters as CSX strives to narrow the gap between its performance and that of peers on metrics like velocity and dwell time. We believe a valuation near its historical average is warranted as we balance the aggressive earnings targets against above peer-average leverage.

➤ Risks to our opinion and target price include a softening in shipments of export coal, increased regulatory oversight, unusually severe weather, a rapid rise in diesel prices, and increased difficulties reconciling competing agendas within the board of directors.

➤ Our DCF model derives an intrinsic value of $61, assuming a weighted average cost of capital of 9.1% and a 4.0% terminal growth rate. Applying an enterprise value to EBITDA multiple of 7.8X, which is the historical average, to our 12-month forward EBITDA per share estimate, we derive a value of $59. Blending these models, we arrive at our 12-month target price of $60.

## Qualitative Risk Assessment

| LOW | MEDIUM | HIGH |
|---|---|---|

Our risk assessment reflects what we believe is CSX's exposure to economic cycles, freight demand and pricing and fuel prices, offset by its consistently positive cash flow generation and diverse customer base.

## Quantitative Evaluations

**S&P Quality Ranking** B+

| D | C | B- | B | B+ | A- | A | A+ |
|---|---|---|---|---|---|---|---|

**Relative Strength Rank** MODERATE

48

LOWEST = 1        HIGHEST = 99

## Revenue/Earnings Data

### Revenue (Million $)

| | 1Q | 2Q | 3Q | 4Q | Year |
|---|---|---|---|---|---|
| 2008 | 2,713 | 2,907 | 2,961 | -- | -- |
| 2007 | 2,422 | 2,530 | 2,501 | 2,577 | 10,030 |
| 2006 | 2,331 | 2,421 | 2,418 | 2,396 | 9,566 |
| 2005 | 2,108 | 2,166 | 2,125 | 2,219 | 8,618 |
| 2004 | 1,915 | 1,995 | 1,938 | 2,172 | 8,020 |
| 2003 | 2,016 | 1,942 | 1,882 | 1,953 | 7,793 |

### Earnings Per Share ($)

| | | | | | |
|---|---|---|---|---|---|
| 2008 | 0.85 | 0.93 | 0.94 | E0.97 | E3.67 |
| 2007 | 0.52 | 0.71 | 0.67 | 0.86 | 2.74 |
| 2006 | 0.53 | 0.83 | 0.71 | 0.75 | 2.82 |
| 2005 | 0.34 | 0.37 | 0.36 | 0.52 | 1.59 |
| 2004 | 0.06 | 0.26 | 0.26 | 0.36 | 0.94 |
| 2003 | 0.10 | 0.29 | -0.24 | 0.29 | 0.44 |

Fiscal year ended Dec. 31. Next earnings report expected: Late January. EPS Estimates based on S&P Operating Earnings; historical GAAP earnings are as reported.

## Dividend Data (Dates: mm/dd Payment Date: mm/dd/yy)

| Amount ($) | Date Decl. | Ex-Div. Date | Stk. of Record | Payment Date |
|---|---|---|---|---|
| 0.150 | 02/13 | 02/27 | 02/29 | 03/14/08 |
| 0.180 | 03/17 | 05/28 | 05/30 | 06/13/08 |
| 0.220 | 06/25 | 08/27 | 09/01 | 09/15/08 |
| 0.220 | 10/23 | 11/26 | 12/01 | 12/15/08 |

Dividends have been paid since 1922. Source: Company reports.

**Please read the Required Disclosures and Analyst Certification on the last page of this report.**

# CSX Corp

## Business Summary October 17, 2008

CORPORATE OVERVIEW. CSX operates the largest rail network in the eastern U.S., with a 21,000-mile rail network linking commercial markets in 23 states and two Canadian provinces, and owns companies providing intermodal and rail-to-truck transload services. In 1997, the company purchased a 42% stake in Conrail, bringing CSX's system into New York City, Boston, Philadelphia and Buffalo; in 2004, CSX gained direct ownership and control of Conrail's New York Central Lines. With these routes, the company was able to offer shippers broader geographic coverage, access more ports, and expand its share of north-south traffic.

MARKET PROFILE. We consider railroads to be a mature industry, and expect 2.3% annualized U.S. rail tonnage growth between 2006 and 2020. We believe CSX's growth opportunities are at the industry average, as we see above average future growth in intermodal traffic being offset by expected slow coal traffic growth. Even as the U.S. economy recovered over the past five years from a sharp economic slowdown, CSX's intermodal volumes have been relatively flat, near 1.2 million carloadings. Likewise, overall volumes have been flat, versus average annual growth of 1.7% for the overall industry.

We believe growth in CSX's intermodal business, representing 14% of 2007

revenue, will be driven by rising international trade and its cost savings over trucks for long-distance container movements, although we see CSX's service quality as lagging its primary competitor. Coal accounted for 26% of 2007 revenues. Most of this traffic originates from the Appalachian coal fields and is primarily delivered to power utilities. We expect CSX's domestic coal tonnage to experience average growth as its customers balance the high sulfur content of coal against using more costly fuel alternatives. However, export coal is expected to show above average growth due to rising demand from Europe. CSX's merchandise freight provided 50% of freight revenues in 2007, and includes chemical, forest products, metals, and agricultural products. We believe this business is sensitive to U.S. GDP trends, and faces average long-term volume growth prospects. We believe automotive freight, at 8% of revenues in 2007, has a weak volume growth outlook, due to slowing domestic manufacturing and consumer credit trends.

## Company Financials Fiscal Year Ended Dec. 31

| Per Share Data ($) | 2007 | 2006 | 2005 | 2004 | 2003 | 2002 | 2001 | 2000 | 1999 | 1998 |
|---|---|---|---|---|---|---|---|---|---|---|
| Tangible Book Value | 21.14 | 20.42 | 18.25 | 15.77 | 15.01 | 14.52 | 14.32 | 14.13 | 13.20 | 13.55 |
| Cash Flow | 4.71 | 4.67 | 3.41 | 2.55 | 1.94 | 2.62 | 2.16 | 2.76 | 1.46 | 2.73 |
| Earnings | 2.74 | 2.82 | 1.59 | 0.94 | 0.44 | 1.10 | 0.69 | 0.44 | 0.12 | 1.26 |
| S&P Core Earnings | 2.74 | 2.57 | 1.60 | 0.90 | 0.66 | 0.85 | 0.59 | NA | NA | NA |
| Dividends | 0.54 | 0.63 | 0.22 | 0.20 | 0.20 | 0.20 | 0.40 | 0.60 | 0.60 | 0.60 |
| Payout Ratio | 20% | 22% | 14% | 21% | 45% | 18% | 58% | 136% | NM | 48% |
| Prices:High | 51.88 | 38.30 | 25.80 | 20.23 | 18.15 | 20.70 | 20.65 | 16.72 | 26.97 | 30.38 |
| Prices:Low | 33.50 | 24.29 | 18.45 | 14.40 | 12.75 | 12.55 | 12.41 | 9.75 | 14.41 | 18.25 |
| P/E Ratio:High | 19 | 14 | 16 | 22 | 41 | 19 | 30 | 38 | NM | 24 |
| P/E Ratio:Low | 12 | 9 | 12 | 15 | 29 | 11 | 18 | 22 | NM | 15 |

| Income Statement Analysis (Million $) | 2007 | 2006 | 2005 | 2004 | 2003 | 2002 | 2001 | 2000 | 1999 | 1998 |
|---|---|---|---|---|---|---|---|---|---|---|
| Revenue | 10,030 | 9,566 | 8,618 | 8,020 | 7,793 | 8,152 | 8,110 | 8,191 | 10,811 | 9,898 |
| Operating Income | 3,112 | 2,837 | 2,345 | 1,730 | 1,269 | 1,776 | 1,579 | 1,405 | 1,685 | 1,790 |
| Depreciation | 883 | 867 | 833 | 730 | 643 | 649 | 622 | 600 | 621 | 630 |
| Interest Expense | 417 | 392 | 423 | 435 | 418 | 445 | 518 | 543 | 521 | 506 |
| Pretax Income | 1,932 | 1,841 | 1,036 | 637 | 637 | 265 | 723 | 448 | 656 | 130 | 808 |
| Effective Tax Rate | 36.5% | 28.8% | 30.5% | 34.4% | 28.7% | 35.4% | 34.6% | 13.9% | 67.7% | 29.2% |
| Net Income | 1,226 | 1,310 | 720 | 418 | 189 | 467 | 293 | 565 | 51.0 | 537 |
| S&P Core Earnings | 1,228 | 1,194 | 729 | 405 | 280 | 363 | 249 | NA | NA | NA |

| Balance Sheet & Other Financial Data (Million $) | 2007 | 2006 | 2005 | 2004 | 2003 | 2002 | 2001 | 2000 | 1999 | 1998 |
|---|---|---|---|---|---|---|---|---|---|---|
| Cash | 714 | 461 | 309 | 859 | 368 | 264 | 618 | 684 | 974 | 533 |
| Current Assets | 2,491 | 2,672 | 2,372 | 2,987 | 1,903 | 1,789 | 2,074 | 2,046 | 2,563 | 1,984 |
| Total Assets | 25,534 | 25,129 | 24,232 | 24,581 | 21,760 | 20,951 | 20,801 | 20,491 | 20,720 | 20,427 |
| Current Liabilities | 2,671 | 2,522 | 2,979 | 3,317 | 2,210 | 2,454 | 3,303 | 3,280 | 3,473 | 2,600 |
| Long Term Debt | 6,470 | 5,362 | 5,093 | 6,234 | 6,886 | 6,519 | 5,839 | 5,810 | 6,196 | 6,432 |
| Common Equity | 8,685 | 9,863 | 8,918 | 7,858 | 7,569 | 7,091 | 7,060 | 6,017 | 5,756 | 5,880 |
| Total Capital | 21,272 | 21,335 | 20,093 | 20,071 | 18,207 | 17,177 | 16,520 | 15,211 | 15,179 | 15,485 |
| Capital Expenditures | 1,773 | 1,639 | 1,136 | 1,030 | 1,059 | 1,080 | 930 | 913 | 1,517 | 1,479 |
| Cash Flow | 2,109 | 2,177 | 1,553 | 1,148 | 832 | 1,116 | 915 | 1,165 | 623 | 1,167 |
| Current Ratio | 0.9 | 1.1 | 0.8 | 0.9 | 0.9 | 0.7 | 0.6 | 0.6 | 0.7 | 0.8 |
| % Long Term Debt of Capitalization | 30.4 | 25.1 | 25.3 | 31.1 | 37.8 | 38.0 | 35.3 | 38.2 | 40.8 | 41.5 |
| % Net Income of Revenue | 12.2 | 13.7 | 8.4 | 5.2 | 2.4 | 5.7 | 3.6 | 6.9 | 0.5 | 5.4 |
| % Return on Assets | 4.8 | 5.3 | 2.9 | 1.8 | 0.9 | 2.2 | 1.4 | 2.7 | 0.2 | 2.7 |
| % Return on Equity | 13.9 | 14.0 | 8.6 | 5.4 | 2.6 | 6.6 | 4.2 | 9.6 | 0.9 | 9.2 |

Data as orig reptd.; bef. results of disc opers/spec. items. Per share data adj. for stk. divs.; EPS diluted. E-Estimated. NA-Not Available. NM-Not Meaningful. NR-Not Ranked. UR-Under Review.

**Office:** 500 Water Street , Jacksonville , FL 32202.
**Telephone:** 904-359-3200.
**Website:** http://www.csx.com
**Chrmn, Pres & CEO:** M.J. Ward

**EVP & CFO:** O. Munoz
**SVP, Secy & General Counsel:** E.M. Fitzsimmons
**Chief Acctg Officer & Cntlr:** C.T. Sizemore
**Treas:** D.A. Boor

**Investor Contact:** D. Baggs (904-359-4812)
**Board Members:** D. M. Alvarado, A. Behring, J. B. Breaux, A. B. Fogarty, S. T. Halverson, C. Hohn, E. J. Kelly, III, G. H. Lamphere, J. D. McPherson, T. O'Toole, D. M. Ratcliffe, D. J. Shepard, M. J. Ward

**Founded:** 1978
**Domicile:** Virginia
**Employees:** 35,443

# Cummins Inc.

**STANDARD &POOR'S**

| S&P Recommendation | **BUY** ★★★★☆ | Price | 12-Mo. Target Price | Investment Style |
|---|---|---|---|---|
| | | $21.59 (as of Nov 14, 2008) | $35.00 | Large-Cap Value |

**GICS Sector** Industrials
**Sub-Industry** Construction & Farm Machinery & Heavy Trucks

**Summary** This leading manufacturer of truck engines also makes stand-by power equipment and industrial filters.

## Key Stock Statistics (Source S&P, Vickers, company reports)

| | | | | | | | |
|---|---|---|---|---|---|---|---|
| 52-Wk Range | $75.98– 19.55 | S&P Oper. EPS 2008**E** | 4.95 | Market Capitalization(B) | $4.348 | Beta | 1.72 |
| Trailing 12-Month EPS | $4.63 | S&P Oper. EPS 2009**E** | 5.50 | Yield (%) | 3.24 | S&P 3-Yr. Proj. EPS CAGR(%) | 6 |
| Trailing 12-Month P/E | 4.7 | P/E on S&P Oper. EPS 2008**E** | 4.4 | Dividend Rate/Share | $0.70 | S&P Credit Rating | BBB |
| $10K Invested 5 Yrs Ago | $20,372 | Common Shares Outstg. (M) | 201.4 | Institutional Ownership (%) | 91 | | |

## Price Performance

30-Week Mov. Avg. · · · · 10-Week Mov. Avg. – – **GAAP Earnings vs. Previous Year** Volume Above Avg. STARS
12-Mo. Target Price — Relative Strength ▲ Up ▼ Down ▶ No Change Below Avg. ★

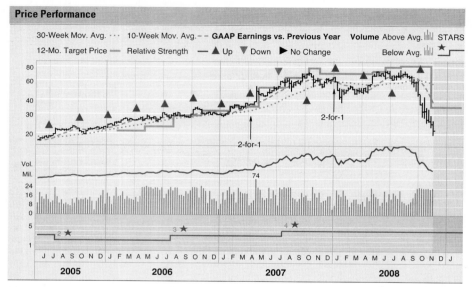

Options: ASE, CBOE, P, Ph

Analysis prepared by **Adrian Compton** on November 13, 2008, when the stock traded at **$ 19.81**.

## Highlights

➤ We expect revenues to increase about 16% in 2008 and then slow to about 3% in 2009. In 2009, we see flat to modest growth across all business segments, as revenues are should be hurt by the slowing global economy. Separately, we see sales benefiting from expected strength in power generation end markets, notably, the proposed economic stimulus pending by international governments geared toward improving power generation infrastructure.

➤ We anticipate that operating margins will rise to about 10% for both 2008 and 2009 from 9.4% in 2007, helped by projected benefits from cost reduction actions implemented over the past few years, the recent pull back in raw materials costs, and price increases are sticking.

➤ We estimate that EPS will rise to $4.95 in 2008 and increase to $5.50 in 2009. We see EPS benefiting from international sales opportunities, notably emerging markets, operating margin expansion, and a modest pre-buy of trucks ahead of the 2010 emission standards expected to be introduced in the U.S., and a reduced share count from the share buy-back program.

## Investment Rationale/Risk

➤ With over 50% of sales outside the U.S., we see CMI benefiting from its leading edge technology in truck engines and power generation equipment. We believe CMI will continue to use technological expertise to increase market share amid a slowing global economy. We also note that strong free cash flow generation enabled CMI to reduce long-term debt by 50% over the past two years, and we think the company will be able to fully fund its pension plan in the near term.

➤ Risks to our recommendation and target price include weaker-than-projected demand in the truck manufacturing and/or power generation markets; slower-than-anticipated economic growth and/or industrial production; and, lower-than-estimated savings from expense reduction initiatives.

➤ Our DCF model, which assumes an 8.8% WACC and a 2.5% terminal growth rate indicates that the stock's intrinsic value is $35. Based on relative metrics, including historical average P/E's and forward P/E of peers, we obtain a value of $35, using 6.4X our EPS FY 09 estimate.

## Qualitative Risk Assessment

| LOW | MEDIUM | HIGH |
|---|---|---|

Our risk assessment reflects the highly cyclical nature of the North America medium (class 5-7) and heavy-duty (class 8) truck markets and significant pension and post-retirement benefit obligations, offset by a geographically diverse mix of business.

## Quantitative Evaluations

**S&P Quality Ranking**      B

| D | C | B- | B | B+ | A- | A | A+ |
|---|---|---|---|---|---|---|---|

**Relative Strength Rank**     WEAK

16

LOWEST = 1         HIGHEST = 99

## Revenue/Earnings Data

**Revenue (Million $)**

| | 1Q | 2Q | 3Q | 4Q | Year |
|---|---|---|---|---|---|
| 2008 | 3,474 | 3,887 | 3,693 | -- | -- |
| 2007 | 2,817 | 3,343 | 3,372 | 3,516 | 13,048 |
| 2006 | 2,678 | 2,842 | 2,809 | 3,033 | 11,362 |
| 2005 | 2,208 | 2,490 | 2,467 | 2,753 | 9,918 |
| 2004 | 1,771 | 2,124 | 2,194 | 2,349 | 8,438 |
| 2003 | 1,387 | 1,539 | 1,634 | 1,736 | 6,296 |

**Earnings Per Share ($)**

| | | | | | |
|---|---|---|---|---|---|
| 2008 | 0.97 | 1.49 | 1.17 | E1.31 | E4.95 |
| 2007 | 0.71 | 1.06 | 0.92 | 1.00 | 3.70 |
| 2006 | 0.68 | 1.10 | 0.84 | 0.94 | 3.55 |
| 2005 | 0.49 | 0.71 | 0.73 | 0.83 | 2.75 |
| 2004 | 0.19 | 0.44 | 0.60 | 0.60 | 1.85 |
| 2003 | -0.20 | 0.09 | 0.15 | 0.27 | 0.34 |

Fiscal year ended Dec. 31. Next earnings report expected: Early February. EPS Estimates based on S&P Operating Earnings; historical GAAP earnings are as reported.

## Dividend Data (Dates: mm/dd Payment Date: mm/dd/yy)

| Amount ($) | Date Decl. | Ex-Div. Date | Stk. of Record | Payment Date |
|---|---|---|---|---|
| 0.125 | 02/12 | 02/20 | 02/22 | 03/03/08 |
| 0.125 | 05/13 | 05/21 | 05/23 | 06/02/08 |
| 0.175 | 07/08 | 08/20 | 08/22 | 09/02/08 |
| 0.175 | 10/14 | 11/19 | 11/21 | 12/01/08 |

Dividends have been paid since 1948. Source: Company reports.

---

**Please read the Required Disclosures and Analyst Certification on the last page of this report.**

The McGraw-Hill Companies

# Cummins Inc.

**STANDARD &POOR'S**

## Business Summary November 13, 2008

This estimated $15 billion in 2008 sales global equipment company makes and services diesel and natural gas engines, electric power generation systems and engine-related component products.

Cummins (CMI), founded in 1919, has long-standing relationships with many of the customers it serves, including Chrysler LLC, Daimler AG, Volvo AB, PAC-CAR Inc., International Truck and Engine Corp. (a unit of Navistar), CNH Global N.V., Komatsu, Scania AB, Ford Motor Corp., and Volkswagen. CMI has over 500 company-owned and independent distributor locations and about 5,200 dealer locations in over 190 countries and territories. CMI's key markets are the on-highway, construction, and general industrial markets.

CMI believes that its competitive strengths include a group of leading brand names, alliances it has established with customers and partners, its global presence (international sales accounted for 54% of total sales in 2007), and its leading technology. In particular, Cummins' technology addresses the reduction of diesel engine emissions. CMI's engines met the EPA's heavy-duty on-highway emission standards that went into effect in January 2007. In addition, its Dodge Ram 6.7-liter Turbo Diesel engine met the EPA's 2010 emission standards ahead of the required date.

The company follows five key business principles in executing its business

strategy: being a low-cost producer in as many of its markets as possible (six sigma, global sourcing, technical productivity); expanding into related markets (for example, CMI's expansion into the light-duty engine market); creating greater shareholder value (measured using return on equity); leveraging complementary businesses (shared technology, common channels and distribution, shared customers and partners, corporate brand image); and creating the right environment for success.

The engine segment (52% of sales in 2007) manufactures and markets a broad range of diesel and natural-gas powered engines under the Cummins brand name for the heavy- and medium-duty truck, bus, recreational vehicle (RV), light-duty automotive, agricultural, construction, mining, marine, oil and gas, rail and governmental equipment markets. CMI manufactures engines with displacements from 1.4 to 91 liters and horsepower ranging from 31 to 3,500. In addition it provides new parts and service, as well as remanufactured parts and engines, through its extensive distribution network.

## Company Financials Fiscal Year Ended Dec. 31

| Per Share Data ($) | 2007 | 2006 | 2005 | 2004 | 2003 | 2002 | 2001 | 2000 | 1999 | 1998 |
|---|---|---|---|---|---|---|---|---|---|---|
| Tangible Book Value | 14.20 | 11.12 | 7.56 | 5.18 | 2.79 | 2.42 | 4.06 | 5.05 | 6.42 | 3.32 |
| Cash Flow | 5.15 | 4.96 | 4.54 | 3.38 | 1.75 | 1.79 | 0.85 | 1.62 | 2.52 | 1.14 |
| Earnings | 3.70 | 3.55 | 2.75 | 1.85 | 0.34 | 0.52 | -0.67 | -0.05 | 1.03 | -0.14 |
| S&P Core Earnings | 3.73 | 3.62 | 2.85 | 2.00 | 0.40 | -0.39 | -1.44 | NA | NA | NA |
| Dividends | 0.43 | 0.33 | 0.30 | 0.30 | 0.30 | 0.30 | 0.30 | 0.30 | 0.28 | 0.28 |
| Payout Ratio | 12% | 9% | 11% | 16% | 88% | 58% | NM | NM | 27% | NM |
| Prices:High | 71.73 | 34.80 | 23.47 | 21.17 | 13.08 | 12.57 | 11.38 | 12.50 | 16.42 | 15.69 |
| Prices:Low | 28.16 | 22.17 | 15.90 | 12.03 | 5.43 | 4.90 | 7.00 | 6.77 | 8.64 | 7.08 |
| P/E Ratio:High | 19 | 10 | 9 | 11 | 38 | 24 | NM | NM | 16 | NM |
| P/E Ratio:Low | 8 | 6 | 6 | 7 | 16 | 10 | NM | NM | 8 | NM |

| Income Statement Analysis (Million $) | | | | | | | | | | |
|---|---|---|---|---|---|---|---|---|---|---|
| Revenue | 13,048 | 11,362 | 9,918 | 8,438 | 6,296 | 5,853 | 5,681 | 6,597 | 6,639 | 6,266 |
| Operating Income | 1,221 | 1,287 | 1,058 | 696 | 316 | 327 | 304 | 479 | 625 | 498 |
| Depreciation | 290 | 296 | 295 | 272 | 223 | 219 | 231 | 240 | 233 | 199 |
| Interest Expense | 59.0 | 96.0 | 109 | 113 | 101 | 82.0 | 87.0 | 86.0 | 75.0 | 71.0 |
| Pretax Income | 1,169 | 1,083 | 798 | 432 | 80.0 | 57.0 | -129 | 3.00 | 221 | -6.00 |
| Effective Tax Rate | 32.6% | 29.9% | 27.1% | 13.0% | 15.0% | NM | NM | NM | 24.9% | NM |
| Net Income | 739 | 715 | 550 | 350 | 54.0 | 79.0 | -102 | 8.00 | 160 | -21.0 |
| S&P Core Earnings | 744 | 729 | 570 | 380 | 62.8 | -61.4 | -221 | NA | NA | NA |

| Balance Sheet & Other Financial Data (Million $) | | | | | | | | | | |
|---|---|---|---|---|---|---|---|---|---|---|
| Cash | 697 | 935 | 840 | 690 | 195 | 298 | 92.0 | 62.0 | 74.0 | 38.0 |
| Current Assets | 4,815 | 4,488 | 3,916 | 3,273 | 2,130 | 1,982 | 1,635 | 1,830 | 2,180 | 1,876 |
| Total Assets | 8,195 | 7,465 | 6,885 | 6,527 | 5,126 | 4,837 | 4,335 | 4,500 | 4,697 | 4,542 |
| Current Liabilities | 2,711 | 2,399 | 2,218 | 2,197 | 1,391 | 1,329 | 970 | 1,223 | 1,314 | 1,071 |
| Long Term Debt | 555 | 647 | 1,213 | 1,299 | 1,380 | 1,290 | 1,206 | 1,032 | 1,092 | 1,137 |
| Common Equity | 3,409 | 2,802 | 1,864 | 2,802 | 949 | 841 | 1,025 | 1,336 | 1,429 | 1,272 |
| Total Capital | 4,257 | 3,703 | 3,302 | 4,309 | 2,452 | 2,223 | 2,314 | 2,440 | 2,595 | 2,471 |
| Capital Expenditures | 353 | 249 | 186 | 151 | 111 | 90.0 | 206 | 228 | 215 | 271 |
| Cash Flow | 1,029 | 1,011 | 845 | 622 | 277 | 298 | 129 | 248 | 393 | 178 |
| Current Ratio | 1.8 | 1.9 | 1.8 | 1.5 | 1.5 | 1.5 | 1.7 | 1.5 | 1.7 | 1.8 |
| % Long Term Debt of Capitalization | 13.0 | 17.5 | 36.7 | 30.1 | 56.3 | 58.0 | 52.1 | 42.3 | 42.1 | 46.0 |
| % Net Income of Revenue | 5.7 | 6.3 | 5.5 | 4.1 | 0.9 | 1.3 | NM | 0.1 | 2.4 | NM |
| % Return on Assets | 9.4 | 10.0 | 8.2 | 6.0 | 1.1 | 1.7 | NM | 0.2 | 3.5 | NM |
| % Return on Equity | 23.8 | 30.6 | 33.7 | 14.9 | 6.0 | 8.7 | NM | 0.6 | 11.8 | NM |

Data as orig reptd.; bef. results of disc opers/spec. items. Per share data adj. for stk. divs.; EPS diluted. E-Estimated. NA-Not Available. NM-Not Meaningful. NR-Not Ranked. UR-Under Review.

**Office:** 500 Jackson Street, Columbus, IN 47202-3005.
**Telephone:** 812-377-3121.
**Email:** investor_relations@cummins.com
**Website:** http://www.cummins.com

**Chrmn & CEO:** T.M. Solso
**Pres, COO & EVP:** N.T. Linebarger
**Vice Chrmn:** F.J. Loughrey
**CFO:** P. Ward

**CTO:** J. Wall
**Investor Contact:** D.A. Cantrell (812-377-3121)
**Board Members:** R. J. Bernhard, R. J. Darnall, R. K. Herdman, A. Herman, F. J. Loughrey, W. I. Miller, G. R. Nelson, T. M. Solso, C. Ware, J. Wilson

**Founded:** 1919
**Domicile:** Indiana
**Employees:** 37,800

# CVS Caremark Corp

STANDARD
&POOR'S

| S&P Recommendation | **STRONG BUY** ★ ★ ★ ★ ★ | Price<br>$29.31 (as of Nov 14, 2008) | 12-Mo. Target Price<br>$36.00 | Investment Style<br>Large-Cap Blend |
|---|---|---|---|---|

**GICS Sector** Consumer Staples
**Sub-Industry** Drug Retail

**Summary** This company is a leading operator of both retail drug stores and pharmacy benefit management services in the U.S.

## Key Stock Statistics (Source S&P, Vickers, company reports)

| | | | | | | | |
|---|---|---|---|---|---|---|---|
| 52-Wk Range | $44.29– 24.25 | S&P Oper. EPS 2008E | 2.44 | Market Capitalization(B) | $42.096 | Beta | 0.79 |
| Trailing 12-Month EPS | $2.09 | S&P Oper. EPS 2009E | 2.74 | Yield (%) | 0.94 | S&P 3-Yr. Proj. EPS CAGR(%) | 13 |
| Trailing 12-Month P/E | 14.0 | P/E on S&P Oper. EPS 2008E | 12.0 | Dividend Rate/Share | $0.28 | S&P Credit Rating | BBB+ |
| $10K Invested 5 Yrs Ago | $17,074 | Common Shares Outstg. (M) | 1,436.2 | Institutional Ownership (%) | 86 | | |

## Price Performance

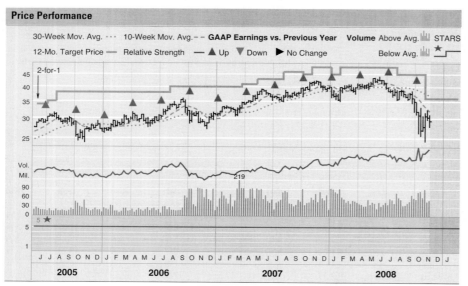

- 30-Week Mov. Avg. · · · 10-Week Mov. Avg. - - **GAAP Earnings vs. Previous Year** Volume Above Avg. STARS
- 12-Mo. Target Price — Relative Strength — ▲ Up ▼ Down ▶ No Change Below Avg. ★

Options: ASE, CBOE, P, Ph

Analysis prepared by **Joseph Agnese** on November 04, 2008, when the stock traded at **$ 31.91**.

## Highlights

➤ We expect total sales in 2009 to increase about 8.0%, to $94.2 billion, from our estimate of $87.2 billion for 2008, reflecting the acquisition of Longs Drug Stores in October 2008, new pharmacy benefit management wins and the continued turnaround of acquired drug stores. Our estimates also assume same-store sales growth of approximately 3.5% and 3.0% in 2008 and 2009, respectively.

➤ We see margins widening in 2009, due to synergies from acquisitions that include increased sales leverage and improved purchasing power, an increased proportion of pharmacy sales coming from wider-margin generic drugs, and improved cost management, due to inventory and pharmacy efficiency programs. Partially offsetting margin benefits, we see a rise in the mix of lower-margin pharmacy sales, higher employee benefit costs and costs associated with expanding services in health care clinics.

➤ We estimate 2009 operating EPS of $2.74, up 12% from our estimate of $2.44 for 2008. Our estimates include dilution from the acquisition of Longs Drug Stores of $0.02 in 2008 and $0.07 in 2009. We expect the acquisition to be accretive to earnings beginning in 2010.

## Investment Rationale/Risk

➤ In October 2008, the company acquired Longs Drug Stores for about $2.9 billion, including the assumption of debt. The acquisition provides access to important growth markets for the company in Northern California and Hawaii, in our view. CVS is an experienced consolidator, and we have confidence in its ability to realize significant long-term synergies.

➤ Risks to our recommendation and target price include potential problems that may arise in implementing and managing the acquisition of Longs Drug Stores, as well as risk from other acquisitions, and exposure to weaker consumer spending in an adverse economic environment.

➤ Due to benefits we see stemming from the acquisitions of Longs Drug Stores and Caremark RX, we believe the shares should trade at a P/E to growth ratio comparable to the S&P 500. Assuming that the shares trade at 1.0X our 2009 estimated EPS growth rate of 13%, compared to 0.8X for the S&P 500, and applying that to our 2009 EPS estimate of $2.74, we arrive at our 12-month target price of $36.

## Qualitative Risk Assessment

| LOW | MEDIUM | HIGH |
|---|---|---|

Our risk assessment reflects our view of the company's leadership position, and strong market share position, in a relatively stable U.S. retail drug industry, offset by the potential for acquisition integration risk and growth of non-traditional competitors.

## Quantitative Evaluations

**S&P Quality Ranking**                                     A

| D | C | B- | B | B+ | A- | A | A+ |
|---|---|---|---|---|---|---|---|

**Relative Strength Rank**                          STRONG

75

LOWEST = 1                                      HIGHEST = 99

## Revenue/Earnings Data

**Revenue (Million $)**

| | 1Q | 2Q | 3Q | 4Q | Year |
|---|---|---|---|---|---|
| 2008 | 21,326 | 21,140 | 20,863 | -- | -- |
| 2007 | 13,189 | 20,703 | 20,495 | 21,942 | 76,330 |
| 2006 | 9,979 | 10,561 | 11,207 | 12,066 | 43,814 |
| 2005 | 9,182 | 9,122 | 8,970 | 9,732 | 37,006 |
| 2004 | 6,819 | 6,943 | 7,909 | 8,923 | 30,594 |
| 2003 | 6,313 | 6,445 | 6,378 | 7,452 | 26,588 |

**Earnings Per Share ($)**

| | | | | | |
|---|---|---|---|---|---|
| 2008 | 0.51 | 0.56 | 0.56 | E0.69 | E2.44 |
| 2007 | 0.43 | 0.47 | 0.45 | 0.55 | 1.92 |
| 2006 | 0.39 | 0.40 | 0.33 | 0.49 | 1.60 |
| 2005 | 0.35 | 0.33 | 0.30 | 0.48 | 1.45 |
| 2004 | 0.29 | 0.28 | 0.22 | 0.31 | 1.10 |
| 2003 | 0.24 | 0.25 | 0.23 | 0.32 | 1.03 |

Fiscal year ended Dec. 31. Next earnings report expected: Early February. EPS Estimates based on S&P Operating Earnings; historical GAAP earnings are as reported.

## Dividend Data (Dates: mm/dd Payment Date: mm/dd/yy)

| Amount<br>($) | Date<br>Decl. | Ex-Div.<br>Date | Stk. of<br>Record | Payment<br>Date |
|---|---|---|---|---|
| 0.060 | 01/09 | 01/17 | 01/22 | 02/01/08 |
| 0.060 | 03/05 | 04/17 | 04/21 | 05/02/08 |
| 0.069 | 07/09 | 07/17 | 07/21 | 08/01/08 |
| 0.069 | 09/24 | 10/17 | 10/21 | 11/03/08 |

Dividends have been paid since 1916. Source: Company reports.

**Please read the Required Disclosures and Analyst Certification on the last page of this report.**

The McGraw-Hill Companies

# CVS Caremark Corp

**STANDARD &POOR'S**

## Business Summary November 04, 2008

CORPORATE OVERVIEW. CVS Corp. operates one of the largest drug store chains in the U.S., based on revenues, net income and store count. The company offers prescription drugs and a wide assortment of general merchandise, including OTC drugs, beauty products and cosmetics, film and photo finishing services, seasonal merchandise, greeting cards and convenience foods. As of December 2007, net selling space in retail and specialty drugstores was 56.5 million sq. ft., with about two-thirds of its store base opened or significantly remodeled within the past five years. Most new stores being built range in size between 10,000 sq. ft. and 13,000 sq. ft. and typically include a drive-thru pharmacy.

MARKET PROFILE. CVS is the largest U.S. drug store chain, based on store count, with about 6,200 stores as of December 2007, in 44 states and the District of Columbia. As of December 2007, the company has stores in 77 of the top 100 U.S. drug store markets, holding the number one or number two market share in 58 of these markets, and 75% of all markets in which it operates. It filled more than 528 million prescriptions in 2007, accounting for about 17% of the U.S. retail pharmacy market. Pharmacy operations are critical to CVS's success, in our view, accounting for 68% of retail store sales in 2007. Pay-

ments by third-party managed care providers under prescription drug plans accounted for 95% of pharmacy sales in 2007. CVS's pharmacy benefit management (PBM) business generated $34.9 billion in sales in 2007.

CORPORATE STRATEGY. CVS's long-term strategy focuses on expanding its retail drug store business in high-growth markets and increasing the size and product offerings of its PBM business. The company expects its pharmacy operations to be a key focus, reflecting its ability to succeed in the rapidly growing managed care arena, and its ongoing purchase of prescription files from independent pharmacies. Historically, the company has grown, in large part, through acquisitions. In June 2006, the company acquired 700 stand-alone drugstores from Albertson's for $2.93 billion in cash. In July 2004, CVS bought 1,268 Eckerd drug stores, as well as Eckerd's mail order, specialty pharmacy and PBM businesses, from J.C. Penney for $2.15 billion.

## Company Financials Fiscal Year Ended Dec. 31

| Per Share Data ($) | 2007 | 2006 | 2005 | 2004 | 2003 | 2002 | 2001 | 2000 | 1999 | 1998 |
|---|---|---|---|---|---|---|---|---|---|---|
| Tangible Book Value | NM | 6.29 | 6.77 | 4.98 | 5.98 | 5.05 | 4.45 | 4.11 | 3.44 | 2.70 |
| Cash Flow | 2.71 | 2.45 | 2.14 | 1.69 | 1.46 | 1.25 | 0.88 | 1.26 | 1.10 | 0.78 |
| Earnings | 1.92 | 1.60 | 1.45 | 1.10 | 1.03 | 0.88 | 0.50 | 0.92 | 0.78 | 0.49 |
| S&P Core Earnings | 1.92 | 1.61 | 1.41 | 1.06 | 0.98 | 0.80 | 0.41 | NA | NA | NA |
| Dividends | 0.23 | 0.16 | 0.15 | 0.13 | 0.12 | 0.12 | 0.12 | 0.12 | 0.12 | 0.14 |
| Payout Ratio | 12% | 10% | 10% | 12% | 11% | 13% | 23% | 13% | 15% | 29% |
| Prices:High | 42.60 | 36.14 | 31.60 | 23.67 | 18.78 | 17.85 | 31.88 | 30.22 | 29.19 | 28.00 |
| Prices:Low | 30.45 | 26.06 | 22.02 | 16.87 | 10.92 | 11.52 | 11.45 | 13.88 | 15.00 | 15.22 |
| P/E Ratio:High | 22 | 23 | 22 | 22 | 18 | 20 | 64 | 33 | 38 | 57 |
| P/E Ratio:Low | 16 | 16 | 15 | 15 | 11 | 13 | 23 | 15 | 19 | 31 |

| Income Statement Analysis (Million $) | | | | | | | | | | |
|---|---|---|---|---|---|---|---|---|---|---|
| Revenue | 76,330 | 43,814 | 37,006 | 30,594 | 26,588 | 24,182 | 22,241 | 20,088 | 18,098 | 15,274 |
| Operating Income | 5,970 | 3,175 | 2,609 | 1,952 | 1,765 | 1,517 | 1,091 | 1,619 | 1,413 | 1,181 |
| Depreciation | 1,095 | 733 | 589 | 497 | 342 | 310 | 321 | 297 | 278 | 250 |
| Interest Expense | 492 | 216 | 111 | 58.3 | 48.0 | 50.4 | 61.0 | 79.3 | 59.1 | 61.0 |
| Pretax Income | 4,359 | 2,226 | 1,909 | 1,396 | 1,376 | 1,156 | 710 | 1,243 | 1,076 | 711 |
| Effective Tax Rate | 39.5% | 38.5% | 35.8% | 34.2% | 38.4% | 38.0% | 41.8% | 40.0% | 41.0% | 44.3% |
| Net Income | 2,637 | 1,369 | 1,225 | 919 | 847 | 717 | 413 | 746 | 635 | 396 |
| S&P Core Earnings | 2,623 | 1,365 | 1,171 | 869 | 785 | 635 | 323 | NA | NA | NA |

| Balance Sheet & Other Financial Data (Million $) | | | | | | | | | | |
|---|---|---|---|---|---|---|---|---|---|---|
| Cash | 1,084 | 531 | 513 | 392 | 843 | 700 | 236 | 337 | 230 | 181 |
| Current Assets | 14,149 | 10,392 | 8,393 | 7,920 | 6,497 | 5,982 | 5,454 | 4,937 | 4,608 | 4,349 |
| Total Assets | 54,722 | 20,570 | 15,283 | 14,547 | 10,543 | 9,645 | 8,628 | 7,950 | 7,275 | 6,736 |
| Current Liabilities | 10,766 | 7,001 | 4,584 | 4,859 | 3,489 | 3,106 | 3,066 | 2,964 | 2,890 | 3,183 |
| Long Term Debt | 8,350 | 2,870 | 1,594 | 1,926 | 753 | 1,076 | 810 | 537 | 558 | 276 |
| Common Equity | 31,163 | 9,704 | 8,109 | 6,759 | 6,022 | 4,991 | 4,306 | 4,037 | 3,404 | 2,830 |
| Total Capital | 43,048 | 12,788 | 9,925 | 8,913 | 6,817 | 6,318 | 12,706 | 4,869 | 4,265 | 3,386 |
| Capital Expenditures | 1,805 | 1,769 | 1,495 | 1,348 | 1,122 | 1,109 | 714 | 695 | 494 | 502 |
| Cash Flow | 3,717 | 2,088 | 1,800 | 1,401 | 1,189 | 1,012 | 719 | 1,028 | 898 | 632 |
| Current Ratio | 1.3 | 1.5 | 1.8 | 1.6 | 1.9 | 1.9 | 1.8 | 1.7 | 1.6 | 1.4 |
| % Long Term Debt of Capitalization | 19.4 | 22.4 | 16.1 | 21.6 | 11.0 | 17.0 | 63.8 | 11.0 | 13.1 | 8.2 |
| % Net Income of Revenue | 3.5 | 3.1 | 3.3 | 3.0 | 3.2 | 3.0 | 1.9 | 3.7 | 3.5 | 2.6 |
| % Return on Assets | 7.0 | 7.6 | 8.2 | 7.3 | 8.4 | 7.8 | 5.0 | 9.8 | 9.1 | 6.4 |
| % Return on Equity | 12.8 | 15.2 | 16.3 | 14.4 | 15.4 | 15.1 | 9.6 | 19.7 | 19.9 | 15.6 |

Data as orig reptd.; bef. results of disc opers/spec. items. Per share data adj. for stk. divs.; EPS diluted. E-Estimated. NA-Not Available. NM-Not Meaningful. NR-Not Ranked. UR-Under Review.

**Office:** One CVS Drive, Woonsocket, RI 02895-6184.
**Telephone:** 401-765-1500.
**Email:** investorinfo@cvs.com
**Website:** http://www.cvs.com

**Chrmn, Pres & CEO:** T.M. Ryan
**EVP, CFO & Chief Admin Officer:** D.B. Rickard
**EVP & General Counsel:** D.A. Sgarro
**SVP, Chief Acctg Officer & Cntlr:** D.M. Denton

**Treas:** C. DeNale
**Investor Contact:** N.R. Christal (914-722-4704)
**Board Members:** E. M. Banks, C. D. Brown, II, D. W. Dorman, M. L. Heard, W. Joyce, J. Millon, T. Murray, C. L. Piccolo, S. Z. Rosenberg, T. M. Ryan, R. J. Swift, K. E. Williams

**Founded:** 1892
**Domicile:** Delaware
**Employees:** 200,000

*The McGraw-Hill Companies*

# Danaher Corp

**STANDARD &POOR'S**

| S&P Recommendation | HOLD ★★★☆☆ | Price $53.92 (as of Nov 14, 2008) | 12-Mo. Target Price $66.00 | Investment Style Large-Cap Growth |
|---|---|---|---|---|

**GICS Sector** Industrials
**Sub-Industry** Industrial Machinery

**Summary** This company is a leading maker of tools, including Sears Craftsman hand tools, and process/environmental controls and telecommunications equipment.

## Key Stock Statistics (Source S&P, Vickers, company reports)

| | | | | | | | |
|---|---|---|---|---|---|---|---|
| 52-Wk Range | $89.22– 49.06 | S&P Oper. EPS 2008E | 4.30 | Market Capitalization(B) | $17.233 | Beta | 1.10 |
| Trailing 12-Month EPS | $4.00 | S&P Oper. EPS 2009E | 4.67 | Yield (%) | 0.22 | S&P 3-Yr. Proj. EPS CAGR(%) | 17 |
| Trailing 12-Month P/E | 13.5 | P/E on S&P Oper. EPS 2008E | 12.5 | Dividend Rate/Share | $0.12 | S&P Credit Rating | A+ |
| $10K Invested 5 Yrs Ago | $13,225 | Common Shares Outstg. (M) | 319.6 | Institutional Ownership (%) | 76 | | |

## Price Performance

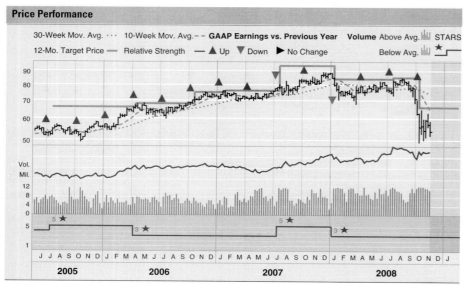

30-Week Mov. Avg. · · · · 10-Week Mov. Avg. - - GAAP Earnings vs. Previous Year Volume Above Avg. STARS
12-Mo. Target Price — Relative Strength — ▲ Up ▼ Down ► No Change Below Avg. ★

Options: ASE, CBOE, P, Ph

Analysis prepared by **Efraim Levy, CFA** on October 07, 2008, when the stock traded at **$ 61.24**.

### Highlights

➤ We expect revenue growth of 12% in 2009, driven by a combination of U.S. and foreign economic growth. We project organic sales growth in all four operating segments, although the pace may be slowed by economic weakness in the U.S and Europe.

➤ We see streamlining activities aiding margins, partly offset by narrower margins at some acquired businesses, and weakening global economies. In July, DHR raised its expectation of EPS for 2008 to between $4.34 and $4.42, excluding non-cash charges related to the Tektronix acquisition. We recently lowered our EPS estimate to $4.30 amid slowing global economic growth and unfavorable currency swings.

➤ For the long term, we look for sales increases to be driven by internal growth, supplemented by acquisitions. We anticipate that a steady flow of new and enhanced products, as well as greater sales of traditional tool lines, will aid comparisons. We expect margins to widen over time, as DHR consolidates acquisitions and likely benefits from higher capacity utilization, productivity gains and cost-cutting efforts. DHR has authorized a 10 million share buyback program that we view positively.

### Investment Rationale/Risk

➤ Our hold opinion is based on our forecast of weakening U.S. and European economic growth. Still, we view the company's balance sheet as strong. Based on several valuation measures, the stock is at a premium to some peers, which we believe reflects DHR's wider net margins and faster growth. Its earnings quality appears high to us, as we expect free cash flow in 2009 to exceed net income.

➤ Risks to our recommendation and target price include slowing demand for DHR's products, and unfavorable changes in foreign exchange rates. Also, we are concerned about some of Danaher's corporate governance practices, particularly its classified board of directors with its staggered terms, which may allow certain policies to be entrenched longer despite shareholders' possible desire to change them.

➤ Given what we see as a sound balance sheet and strong cash flow growth, we think the company could raise its $0.12 annual cash dividend in 2008. Our 12-month target price of $66 is derived by applying a P/E of about 14.2X to our 2009 EPS estimate of $4.67, reflecting relative peer and historical P/E multiples and our concerns our weakening global GDP.

## Qualitative Risk Assessment

| LOW | MEDIUM | HIGH |
|---|---|---|

Our risk assessment reflects our view of favorable growth prospects in most of the company's markets, good corporate leadership, and a solid balance sheet, offset by corporate governance issues.

## Quantitative Evaluations

**S&P Quality Ranking** A+

| D | C | B- | B | B+ | A- | A | A+ |
|---|---|---|---|---|---|---|---|

**Relative Strength Rank** MODERATE

60

LOWEST = 1 HIGHEST = 99

## Revenue/Earnings Data

**Revenue (Million $)**

| | 1Q | 2Q | 3Q | 4Q | Year |
|---|---|---|---|---|---|
| 2008 | 3,029 | 3,284 | 3,208 | -- | -- |
| 2007 | 2,556 | 2,671 | 2,731 | 3,141 | 11,026 |
| 2006 | 2,144 | 2,350 | 2,443 | 2,660 | 9,596 |
| 2005 | 1,826 | 1,929 | 1,966 | 2,264 | 7,985 |
| 2004 | 1,543 | 1,621 | 1,745 | 1,980 | 6,889 |
| 2003 | 1,196 | 1,299 | 1,309 | 1,489 | 5,294 |

**Earnings Per Share ($)**

| | | | | | |
|---|---|---|---|---|---|
| 2008 | 0.83 | 1.09 | 1.11 | E1.24 | E4.30 |
| 2007 | 0.78 | 0.96 | 1.03 | 0.97 | 3.72 |
| 2006 | 0.67 | 0.98 | 0.83 | 1.00 | 3.48 |
| 2005 | 0.58 | 0.70 | 0.70 | 0.78 | 2.76 |
| 2004 | 0.45 | 0.56 | 0.62 | 0.67 | 2.30 |
| 2003 | 0.33 | 0.40 | 0.44 | 0.53 | 1.69 |

Fiscal year ended Dec. 31. Next earnings report expected: Late January. EPS Estimates based on S&P Operating Earnings; historical GAAP earnings are as reported.

## Dividend Data (Dates: mm/dd Payment Date: mm/dd/yy)

| Amount ($) | Date Decl. | Ex-Div. Date | Stk. of Record | Payment Date |
|---|---|---|---|---|
| 0.030 | 12/05 | 12/27 | 12/31 | 01/25/08 |
| 0.030 | 02/21 | 03/26 | 03/28 | 04/25/08 |
| 0.030 | 05/07 | 06/25 | 06/27 | 07/25/08 |
| 0.030 | 09/12 | 09/24 | 09/26 | 10/31/08 |

Dividends have been paid since 1993. Source: Company reports.

# Danaher Corp

## Business Summary October 07, 2008

CORPORATE OVERVIEW. Danaher Corp. is a leading maker of hand tools and process and environmental controls. The company has four reporting segments: professional instrumentation (32% of 2007 sales), industrial technologies (29%), tools and components (12%), and medical technologies, formerly included in professional instrumentation (27%).

The professional instrumentation segment offers professional and technical customers various products and services that are used in connection with the performance of their work.

The industrial technologies segment manufactures products and sub-systems that are typically incorporated by original equipment manufacturers (OEMs) into various end-products and systems, as well as by customers and systems integrators into production and packaging lines.

The tools and components segment encompasses one strategic line of business--mechanics' hand tools--and four focused niche businesses--Delta Consolidated Industries, Hennessy Industries, Jacobs Chuck Manufacturing Company, and Jacobs Vehicle Systems.

Sales in 2007 by geographic destination were: U.S. 49%, Europe 31%, Asia 13%, and other regions 7%.

CORPORATE STRATEGY. The company's strategy is to expand revenues through a combination of internal growth and acquisitions. We expect the company to continue its tradition of successful acquisition integrations. During 2007 the company bought 12 businesses for an aggregate purchase price of about $3.6 billion. This compares to 11 business in 2006 for approximately $2.7 billion and 13 businesses in 2005 for purchase prices totaling about $885 million.

In November 2007, as part of its acquisition strategy, the company purchased Tektronix Inc. for $38 per share, or about $2.8 billion including debt. Tektronix is a supplier of test, measurement and monitoring products, with about $1.1 billion in annual sales.

In May 2006, the company purchased Sybron Dental Specialties Inc. for $47 per share. The total transaction, including the assumption of debt, was valued at about $2 billion. Sybron manufactures a broad range of equipment for the dental industry and had about $650 million in revenues in its fiscal year ended September 30, 2005.

## Company Financials Fiscal Year Ended Dec. 31

| Per Share Data ($) | 2007 | 2006 | 2005 | 2004 | 2003 | 2002 | 2001 | 2000 | 1999 | 1998 |
|---|---|---|---|---|---|---|---|---|---|---|
| Tangible Book Value | NM | NM | NM | NM | 0.99 | 0.01 | NM | 0.28 | 1.46 | 0.25 |
| Cash Flow | 4.50 | 4.12 | 3.28 | 2.75 | 2.07 | 1.87 | 1.57 | 1.63 | 1.33 | 1.05 |
| Earnings | 3.72 | 3.48 | 2.76 | 2.30 | 1.69 | 1.49 | 1.01 | 1.12 | 0.90 | 0.66 |
| S&P Core Earnings | 3.72 | 3.47 | 2.70 | 2.20 | 1.55 | 1.20 | 0.85 | NA | NA | NA |
| Dividends | 0.11 | 0.08 | 0.06 | 0.06 | 0.06 | 0.05 | 0.04 | 0.04 | 0.03 | 0.03 |
| Payout Ratio | 3% | 2% | 2% | 2% | 4% | 3% | 4% | 3% | 3% | 4% |
| Prices:High | 89.22 | 75.28 | 58.40 | 58.90 | 46.18 | 37.73 | 34.34 | 34.91 | 34.50 | 27.63 |
| Prices:Low | 69.11 | 54.04 | 48.32 | 43.83 | 29.78 | 26.30 | 21.95 | 18.22 | 21.38 | 14.00 |
| P/E Ratio:High | 24 | 22 | 21 | 26 | 27 | 25 | 34 | 31 | 39 | 42 |
| P/E Ratio:Low | 19 | 16 | 18 | 19 | 18 | 18 | 22 | 16 | 24 | 21 |

| Income Statement Analysis (Million $) | | | | | | | | | | |
|---|---|---|---|---|---|---|---|---|---|---|
| Revenue | 11,026 | 9,596 | 7,985 | 6,889 | 5,294 | 4,577 | 3,782 | 3,778 | 3,197 | 2,910 |
| Operating Income | 2,055 | 1,719 | 1,446 | 1,253 | 957 | 824 | 750 | 702 | 584 | 475 |
| Depreciation | 268 | 217 | 177 | 156 | 133 | 130 | 178 | 150 | 126 | 109 |
| Interest Expense | 110 | 79.8 | 44.9 | 55.0 | 59.0 | 43.7 | 25.7 | 29.2 | 16.7 | 24.9 |
| Pretax Income | 1,637 | 1,446 | 1,234 | 1,058 | 797 | 657 | 476 | 523 | 430 | 301 |
| Effective Tax Rate | 25.9% | 22.4% | 27.3% | 29.5% | 32.6% | 29.4% | 37.5% | 38.0% | 39.1% | 39.2% |
| Net Income | 1,214 | 1,122 | 898 | 746 | 537 | 464 | 298 | 324 | 262 | 183 |
| S&P Core Earnings | 1,215 | 1,121 | 876 | 715 | 491 | 373 | 249 | NA | NA | NA |

| Balance Sheet & Other Financial Data (Million $) | | | | | | | | | | |
|---|---|---|---|---|---|---|---|---|---|---|
| Cash | 239 | 318 | 316 | 609 | 1,230 | 810 | 707 | 177 | 260 | 41.9 |
| Current Assets | 4,050 | 3,395 | 2,945 | 2,919 | 2,942 | 2,387 | 1,875 | 1,474 | 1,202 | 887 |
| Total Assets | 17,472 | 12,864 | 9,163 | 8,494 | 6,890 | 6,029 | 4,820 | 4,032 | 3,047 | 2,739 |
| Current Liabilities | 2,900 | 2,460 | 2,269 | 2,202 | 1,380 | 1,265 | 1,017 | 1,019 | 709 | 689 |
| Long Term Debt | 3,396 | 2,423 | 858 | 926 | 1,284 | 1,197 | 1,119 | 714 | 341 | 413 |
| Common Equity | 9,086 | 6,645 | 5,080 | 4,620 | 3,647 | 3,010 | 2,229 | 1,942 | 1,709 | 1,352 |
| Total Capital | 12,481 | 9,068 | 5,938 | 5,545 | 4,931 | 4,207 | 3,348 | 2,656 | 2,050 | 1,765 |
| Capital Expenditures | 162 | 138 | 121 | 116 | 80.3 | 65.4 | 80.6 | 88.5 | 88.9 | 90.3 |
| Cash Flow | 1,482 | 1,339 | 1,075 | 902 | 670 | 594 | 476 | 474 | 388 | 292 |
| Current Ratio | 1.4 | 1.4 | 1.3 | 1.3 | 2.1 | 1.9 | 1.8 | 1.4 | 1.7 | 1.3 |
| % Long Term Debt of Capitalization | 27.2 | 26.7 | 14.4 | 16.7 | 26.0 | 28.5 | 33.4 | 26.9 | 16.6 | 23.4 |
| % Net Income of Revenue | 11.0 | 11.7 | 11.2 | 10.8 | 10.1 | 10.1 | 7.9 | 8.6 | 8.2 | 6.3 |
| % Return on Assets | 8.0 | 10.2 | 10.2 | 9.7 | 8.3 | 8.6 | 6.7 | 9.2 | 8.9 | 7.4 |
| % Return on Equity | 15.4 | 19.1 | 18.5 | 18.0 | 16.1 | 17.7 | 14.3 | 17.8 | 16.8 | 14.7 |

Data as orig reptd.; bef. results of disc opers/spec. items. Per share data adj. for stk. divs.; EPS diluted. E-Estimated. NA-Not Available. NM-Not Meaningful. NR-Not Ranked. UR-Under Review.

**Office:** 2099 Pennsylvania Ave NW Fl 12, Washington, DC 20006-6807.
**Telephone:** 202-828-0850.
**Email:** ir@danaher.com
**Website:** http://www.danaher.com

**Chrmn:** S.M. Rales
**Pres & CEO:** H.L. Culp, Jr.
**EVP & CFO:** D.L. Comas
**SVP & General Counsel:** J.P. Graham

**Chief Acctg Officer:** R.S. Lutz
**Board Members:** M. M. Caplin, H. L. Culp, Jr., D. J. Ehrlich, L. L. Hefner, W. G. Lohr, Jr., M. P. Rales, S. M. Rales, J. T. Schwieters, A. G. Spoon

**Founded:** 1969
**Domicile:** Delaware
**Employees:** 50,000

# Darden Restaurants Inc.

**STANDARD &POOR'S**

| S&P Recommendation | BUY ★★★★☆ | Price $17.36 (as of Nov 14, 2008) | 12-Mo. Target Price $34.00 | Investment Style Large-Cap Growth |
|---|---|---|---|---|

**GICS Sector** Consumer Discretionary
**Sub-Industry** Restaurants

**Summary** This restaurant company operates the Red Lobster, Olive Garden, Bahama Breeze and Seasons 52 chains, as well as the LongHorn Steakhouse and Capital Grille chains, which it acquired in 2007.

## Key Stock Statistics (Source S&P, Vickers, company reports)

| | | | | | | | |
|---|---|---|---|---|---|---|---|
| 52-Wk Range | $41.25–16.35 | S&P Oper. EPS 2009E | 2.75 | Market Capitalization(B) | $2.408 | Beta | 0.90 |
| Trailing 12-Month EPS | $2.45 | S&P Oper. EPS 2010E | 3.00 | Yield (%) | 4.61 | S&P 3-Yr. Proj. EPS CAGR(%) | 9 |
| Trailing 12-Month P/E | 7.1 | P/E on S&P Oper. EPS 2009E | 6.3 | Dividend Rate/Share | $0.80 | S&P Credit Rating | BBB |
| $10K Invested 5 Yrs Ago | $9,011 | Common Shares Outstg. (M) | 138.7 | Institutional Ownership (%) | 88 | | |

## Price Performance

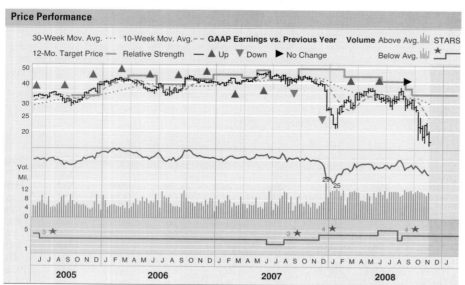

- 30-Week Mov. Avg. ···· 10-Week Mov. Avg. -- **GAAP Earnings vs. Previous Year** Volume Above Avg. STARS
- 12-Mo. Target Price — Relative Strength — ▲ Up ▼ Down ► No Change Below Avg. ★

Options: ASE, CBOE, P, Ph

Analysis prepared by **Mark S. Basham** on September 24, 2008, when the stock traded at **$ 28.21**.

## Qualitative Risk Assessment

| LOW | MEDIUM | HIGH |
|---|---|---|

DRI competes in the stable casual dining industry, and we believe that its Red Lobster and Olive Garden concepts have among the strongest brand name recognition in the industry. However, the casual dining segment over-expanded in recent years, in our opinion, and has begun a consolidation, a part of which includes DRI's disposal of its Smokey Bones Barbeque & Grill chain.

## Quantitative Evaluations

**S&P Quality Ranking** A

| D | C | B- | B | B+ | A- | A | A+ |
|---|---|---|---|---|---|---|---|

**Relative Strength Rank** MODERATE

36

LOWEST = 1    HIGHEST = 99

## Highlights

➤ On October 1, 2007, DRI acquired RARE Hospitality International, Inc. for $1.4 billion in cash. Including RARE from October 1, revenues in FY 08 (May) rose 19%, of which 13% is attributable to RARE.

➤ On August 26, DRI lowered its earnings expectations for FY 09 along with its comparable-store sales forecast to an increase of less than 1% (previously 2%). Reflecting our view that comparable sales will be flat in FY 09, and including a 53rd week in FY 09, we project that total sales will rise 13% on incremental sales of the acquired RARE operations for four months and the opening of about 80 new restaurants.

➤ We expect operating margins in FY 09 to be as much as 75 basis points lower than in FY 08 as costs rise faster than sales. Excluding company estimated integration costs of $0.19 and $0.06 per share in FY 08 and FY 09, we expect EPS to essentially be unchanged in FY 09 at $2.75, compared with $2.74 in FY 08. Our FY 09 estimate includes about $0.05 attributable to the extra week, and reflects about a 2% reduction in shares outstanding, due to likely ongoing repurchases.

## Investment Rationale/Risk

➤ We recommend the purchase of DRI shares. The stock fell about 13% on the disappointing news announced on August 26, and the subsequent price drop has, in our view, resulted in the shares becoming undervalued. We think the company will restore investor confidence that was hurt in the short term when the company lowered its FY 09 forecast in August by delivering its reduced expectations amid tough industry conditions.

➤ Risks to our recommendation and target price include an unexpected further acceleration in food cost inflation. Also, consumers may be more price-sensitive than we expect, suggesting weaker traffic in response to recent price increases and ongoing economic uncertainty.

➤ Our 12-month target price of $34 is based on our discounted cash flow model, which assumes 5% to 6% average annual free cash flow growth, excluding acquisitions and divestitures, through FY 19; a weighted average cost of capital of 9.8%; and a terminal growth rate of 3%. At $34, the shares would trade at 12X our calendar 2009 EPS estimate of $2.85, a multiple that is at the low end of the range for DRI's peer group.

## Revenue/Earnings Data

### Revenue (Million $)

| | 1Q | 2Q | 3Q | 4Q | Year |
|---|---|---|---|---|---|
| 2009 | 1,774 | -- | -- | -- | -- |
| 2008 | 1,468 | 1,522 | 1,811 | 1,826 | 6,627 |
| 2007 | 1,360 | 1,298 | 1,450 | 1,460 | 5,567 |
| 2006 | 1,409 | 1,325 | 1,474 | 1,414 | 5,721 |
| 2005 | 1,279 | 1,229 | 1,376 | 1,394 | 5,278 |
| 2004 | 1,260 | 1,143 | 1,242 | 1,359 | 5,003 |

### Earnings Per Share ($)

| | 1Q | 2Q | 3Q | 4Q | Year |
|---|---|---|---|---|---|
| 2009 | 0.58 | E0.41 | E0.85 | E0.88 | E2.75 |
| 2008 | 0.58 | 0.30 | 0.80 | 0.72 | 2.55 |
| 2007 | 0.62 | 0.45 | 0.79 | 0.67 | 2.53 |
| 2006 | 0.53 | 0.35 | 0.67 | 0.62 | 2.16 |
| 2005 | 0.44 | 0.26 | 0.56 | 0.52 | 1.78 |
| 2004 | 0.40 | 0.18 | 0.46 | 0.32 | 1.36 |

Fiscal year ended May 31. Next earnings report expected: Mid December. EPS Estimates based on S&P Operating Earnings; historical GAAP earnings are as reported.

## Dividend Data (Dates: mm/dd Payment Date: mm/dd/yy)

| Amount ($) | Date Decl. | Ex-Div. Date | Stk. of Record | Payment Date |
|---|---|---|---|---|
| 0.180 | 12/18 | 01/08 | 01/10 | 02/01/08 |
| 0.180 | 03/18 | 04/08 | 04/10 | 05/01/08 |
| 0.200 | 06/24 | 07/08 | 07/10 | 08/01/08 |
| 0.200 | 09/16 | 10/08 | 10/10 | 11/03/08 |

Dividends have been paid since 1995. Source: Company reports.

---

**Please read the Required Disclosures and Analyst Certification on the last page of this report.**

The McGraw·Hill Companies

# Darden Restaurants Inc.

**STANDARD &POOR'S**

## Business Summary September 24, 2008

CORPORATE OVERVIEW. With systemwide sales from continuing operations of more than $6.6 billion in FY 08 (May), Darden Restaurants is the world's largest publicly held casual dining restaurant company. As of May 25, 2008, it operated approximately 1,700 restaurants in the U.S. and Canada, including 680 Red Lobster units, 653 Olive Garden units, 305 LongHorn Steakhouse locations, 32 restaurants in The Capital Grille chain, 23 Bahama Breeze restaurants, seven Seasons 52 locations, and two other restaurants.

Olive Garden is the U.S. market share leader among casual dining Italian food restaurants. FY 08 systemwide sales grew 10%, to $3.1 billion. Same-restaurant sales increased 4.9%, compared to 2.7% in FY 07. Average restaurant sales were $4.9 million. The average check per person was $15 to $16 in FY 07 (latest available).

Red Lobster, founded by William Darden in 1968, is the largest U.S. casual dining seafood-specialty restaurant operator. Systemwide sales totaled $2.6 billion in FY 07, up 1% from FY 07. Average restaurant sales were $3.9 million in FY 08, up from $3.8 million in FY 07. Same-store sales rose 1.1% in FY 08, following a 0.2% increase in FY 07. The average check per person was $18 to $19.

On October 1, 2007, DRI acquired RARE Hospitality International, Inc. in a cash tender offer for all RARE common shares at $38.15 per share, or total consideration of $1.41 billion in cash. Financing was obtained under a $1.2 billion senior interim credit facility and a $700 million senior revolver. Most members of RARE management agreed to join DRI in roles generally similar to those they had at RARE.

RARE operations included the LongHorn Steakhouse chain. Total sales at the chain since being acquired were $575 million. Annual sales per restaurant in FY 08 averaged $2.9 million. Same-store sales decreased 1.1%.

Darden's other concepts, Bahama Breeze, Seasons 52 and Capital Grille (also acquired as part of RARE), are relatively new and have not yet gained enough scale to contribute meaningfully to profits.

## Company Financials Fiscal Year Ended May 31

| Per Share Data ($) | 2008 | 2007 | 2006 | 2005 | 2004 | 2003 | 2002 | 2001 | 2000 | 1999 |
|---|---|---|---|---|---|---|---|---|---|---|
| Tangible Book Value | 2.45 | 7.57 | 8.20 | 8.25 | 7.86 | 7.03 | 6.56 | 5.66 | 5.09 | 4.81 |
| Cash Flow | NA | 3.88 | 3.57 | 3.08 | 2.60 | 2.43 | 2.20 | 1.85 | 1.55 | 1.34 |
| Earnings | 2.55 | 2.53 | 2.16 | 1.78 | 1.36 | 1.31 | 1.30 | 1.06 | 0.89 | 0.66 |
| S&P Core Earnings | 2.54 | 2.53 | 2.10 | 1.68 | 1.27 | 1.18 | 1.16 | 0.97 | NA | NA |
| Dividends | 0.46 | 0.40 | 0.08 | 0.08 | 0.08 | 0.05 | 0.05 | 0.05 | 0.05 | 0.05 |
| Payout Ratio | 18% | 16% | 4% | 4% | 6% | 4% | 4% | 5% | 6% | 8% |
| Calendar Year | 2007 | 2006 | 2005 | 2004 | 2003 | 2002 | 2001 | 2000 | 1999 | 1998 |
| Prices:High | 47.60 | 44.43 | 39.53 | 28.54 | 23.01 | 29.76 | 24.98 | 18.00 | 15.58 | 12.62 |
| Prices:Low | 26.90 | 32.91 | 25.78 | 18.48 | 16.50 | 18.00 | 12.67 | 8.29 | 10.42 | 7.83 |
| P/E Ratio:High | 19 | 18 | 18 | 16 | 17 | 23 | 19 | 17 | 17 | 19 |
| P/E Ratio:Low | 11 | 13 | 12 | 10 | 12 | 14 | 10 | 8 | 12 | 12 |
| **Income Statement Analysis** (Million $) | | | | | | | | | | |
| Revenue | 6,627 | 5,567 | 5,721 | 5,278 | 5,003 | 4,655 | 4,369 | 4,021 | 3,701 | 3,458 |
| Operating Income | NA | 774 | 757 | 685 | 636 | 588 | 563 | 479 | 421 | 352 |
| Depreciation | 246 | 200 | 221 | 213 | 210 | 198 | 166 | 147 | 130 | 125 |
| Interest Expense | NA | 40.7 | 43.1 | 43.1 | 43.7 | 44.1 | 37.8 | 31.5 | 23.1 | 40.6 |
| Pretax Income | 515 | 531 | 483 | 424 | 340 | 348 | 363 | 301 | 274 | 216 |
| Effective Tax Rate | 28.2% | 29.0% | 29.9% | 31.4% | 31.9% | 33.2% | 34.5% | 34.6% | 35.5% | 34.9% |
| Net Income | 370 | 377 | 338 | 291 | 231 | 232 | 238 | 197 | 177 | 141 |
| S&P Core Earnings | 367 | 378 | 330 | 274 | 214 | 208 | 212 | 181 | NA | NA |
| **Balance Sheet & Other Financial Data** (Million $) | | | | | | | | | | |
| Cash | 43.2 | 30.2 | 42.3 | 42.8 | 36.7 | 48.6 | 153 | 61.8 | 26.1 | 41.0 |
| Current Assets | NA | 545 | 378 | 407 | 346 | 326 | 450 | 328 | 290 | 328 |
| Total Assets | 4,731 | 2,881 | 3,010 | 2,938 | 2,780 | 2,665 | 2,530 | 2,218 | 1,971 | 1,906 |
| Current Liabilities | NA | 1,074 | 1,026 | 1,045 | 683 | 640 | 601 | 554 | 607 | 534 |
| Long Term Debt | NA | 492 | 495 | 350 | 653 | 658 | 663 | 518 | 304 | 314 |
| Common Equity | 1,409 | 1,115 | 1,230 | 1,273 | 1,246 | 1,196 | 1,129 | 1,035 | 960 | 964 |
| Total Capital | NA | 1,633 | 1,815 | 1,738 | 2,075 | 2,005 | 1,909 | 1,644 | 1,344 | 1,350 |
| Capital Expenditures | 429 | 345 | 338 | 329 | 354 | 423 | 318 | 355 | 269 | 124 |
| Cash Flow | NA | 578 | 560 | 504 | 441 | 430 | 404 | 344 | 307 | 266 |
| Current Ratio | 0.4 | 0.5 | 0.4 | 0.4 | 0.5 | 0.5 | 0.7 | 0.6 | 0.5 | 0.6 |
| % Long Term Debt of Capitalization | 53.7 | 30.1 | 27.3 | 20.2 | 31.5 | 32.8 | 34.7 | 31.5 | 22.6 | 23.3 |
| % Net Income of Revenue | 5.6 | 6.8 | 5.9 | 5.5 | 4.6 | 5.0 | 5.4 | 4.9 | 4.8 | 4.1 |
| % Return on Assets | 9.7 | 12.8 | 11.4 | 10.2 | 8.5 | 8.9 | 10.0 | 9.4 | 9.2 | 7.2 |
| % Return on Equity | 29.5 | 31.6 | 27.0 | 23.7 | 19.0 | 20.0 | 22.0 | 19.7 | 18.4 | 14.2 |

Data as orig reptd.; bef. results of disc opers/spec. items. Per share data adj. for stk. divs.; EPS diluted. E-Estimated. NA-Not Available. NM-Not Meaningful. NR-Not Ranked. UR-Under Review.

**Office:** 5900 Lake Ellenor Drive, Orlando, FL 32809-4634.
**Telephone:** 407-245-4000.
**Email:** irinfo@darden.com
**Website:** http://www.darden.com

**Chrmn & CEO:** C. Otis, Jr.
**Pres & COO:** A.H. Madsen
**Investor Contact:** C.B. Richmond (407-245-4000)
**SVP, CFO & Chief Acctg Officer:** C.B. Richmond

**SVP, Secy & General Counsel:** P.J. Shives
**Board Members:** L. L. Berry, J. P. Birkelund, O. C. Donald, C. J. Fraleigh, D. H. Hughes, C. A. Ledsinger, Jr., W. M. Lewis, Jr., A. H. Madsen, C. Mcgillicudy, III, C. Otis, Jr., M. D. Rose, M. A. Sastre, J. A. Smith

**Founded:** 1968
**Domicile:** Florida
**Employees:** 178,200

# DaVita Inc

STANDARD &POOR'S

| S&P Recommendation | HOLD ★★★☆☆ | Price $51.36 (as of Nov 14, 2008) | 12-Mo. Target Price $62.00 | Investment Style Large-Cap Growth |
|---|---|---|---|---|

**GICS Sector** Health Care
**Sub-Industry** Health Care Services

**Summary** This company is one of the largest worldwide providers of integrated dialysis services for patients suffering from chronic kidney failure.

## Key Stock Statistics (Source S&P, Vickers, company reports)

| | | | | | | | | |
|---|---|---|---|---|---|---|---|---|
| 52-Wk Range | $62.86– 41.86 | S&P Oper. EPS 2008E | 3.44 | Market Capitalization(B) | $5.331 | Beta | 0.85 |
| Trailing 12-Month EPS | $3.38 | S&P Oper. EPS 2009E | 3.76 | Yield (%) | Nil | S&P 3-Yr. Proj. EPS CAGR(%) | 12 |
| Trailing 12-Month P/E | 15.2 | P/E on S&P Oper. EPS 2008E | 14.9 | Dividend Rate/Share | Nil | S&P Credit Rating | BB- |
| $10K Invested 5 Yrs Ago | $19,744 | Common Shares Outstg. (M) | 103.8 | Institutional Ownership (%) | 95 | | |

## Price Performance

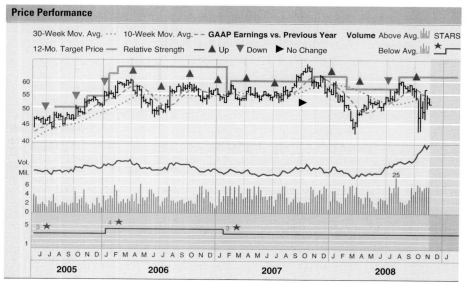

30-Week Mov. Avg. · · · 10-Week Mov. Avg. - - GAAP Earnings vs. Previous Year   Volume Above Avg. STARS
12-Mo. Target Price — Relative Strength — ▲ Up ▼ Down ► No Change   Below Avg.

Options: CBOE, P, Ph

Analysis prepared by **Jeffrey Englander, CFA** on November 06, 2008, when the stock traded at **$ 50.78**.

## Highlights

➤ We see revenues increasing approximately 8% in both 2008 and 2009. Drivers we see include the 1.6% Medicare rate increase that took effect in April 2007, acquisitions in 2007, new dialysis centers, and same-market treatment growth. Partly offsetting these factors should be lower revenue per treatment, reflecting managed care (private payor) reimbursement cuts and lower Medicare reimbursement due to a decline in erythropoietin (EPO) utilization following the FDA's label change on this anemia drug.

➤ We expect gross margins to narrow slightly in 2008 and 2009, on higher dialysis center operating costs, including a rise in Heparin costs, and lower revenue per treatment. We forecast a modest decline in G&A expenses in both years, as a percentage of sales, as higher payroll costs and spending on growth initiatives are offset by Gambro integration synergies. We look for essentially flat bad debt expense as a percentage of net operating revenues.

➤ We forecast operating EPS of $3.44 in 2008, versus 2007's $3.20, and $3.76 in 2009.

## Investment Rationale/Risk

➤ We view dialysis provider fundamentals, including the rising senior population in the U.S., a higher incidence of diabetes, and recurring demand, as favorable, and expect DVA's non-acquired treatment volumes to continue to grow 3.5% to 5% annually. Meanwhile, we see DVA increasingly dependent on commercial pricing, which is sharply above Medicare rates, for its profits. Even so, it continues to experience pricing pressure from private payors, and its performance over the next couple of years looks cloudy to us, as it will depend on how well it fares in contract negotiations with them. While we see early signs EPO utilization has begun to stabilize, favorably impacting results going forward, we see increased Heparin pricing as a challenge.

➤ Risks to our recommendation and target price include headline risk over EPO utilization, unfavorable Medicare rule changes, heightened competition, and reduced reimbursement.

➤ Our 12-month target price of $62 is based on DVA trading at approximately 9X EV/EBITDA based on our 2009 EBITDA estimate, a slight discount to the historical average and approximately 17X our 2009 EPS estimate.

## Qualitative Risk Assessment

| LOW | MEDIUM | HIGH |
|---|---|---|

Our risk assessment reflects our view of stable demand for dialysis services, driven by a rising senior population in the U.S., offset by DVA's dependence on third-party payments, including Medicare and Medicaid.

## Quantitative Evaluations

**S&P Quality Ranking**     B

| D | C | B- | B | B+ | A- | A | A+ |
|---|---|---|---|---|---|---|---|

**Relative Strength Rank**     STRONG

86

LOWEST = 1      HIGHEST = 99

## Revenue/Earnings Data

**Revenue (Million $)**

| | 1Q | 2Q | 3Q | 4Q | Year |
|---|---|---|---|---|---|
| 2008 | 1,345 | 1,407 | 1,447 | -- | -- |
| 2007 | 1,278 | 1,313 | 1,318 | 1,355 | 5,264 |
| 2006 | 1,163 | 1,208 | 1,237 | 1,273 | 4,881 |
| 2005 | 578.6 | 617.1 | 644.9 | 1,133 | 2,974 |
| 2004 | 535.4 | 551.6 | 595.5 | 616.0 | 2,299 |
| 2003 | 459.8 | 489.9 | 513.3 | 553.5 | 2,016 |

**Earnings Per Share ($)**

| | 1Q | 2Q | 3Q | 4Q | Year |
|---|---|---|---|---|---|
| 2008 | 0.80 | 0.90 | 0.89 | E0.86 | E3.44 |
| 2007 | 0.72 | 1.17 | 0.88 | 0.79 | 3.55 |
| 2006 | 0.55 | 0.61 | 0.88 | 0.70 | 2.73 |
| 2005 | 0.50 | 0.49 | 0.49 | 0.54 | 1.99 |
| 2004 | 0.51 | 0.50 | 0.59 | 0.56 | 2.16 |
| 2003 | 0.35 | 0.37 | 0.36 | 0.61 | 1.66 |

Fiscal year ended Dec. 31. Next earnings report expected: Mid February. EPS Estimates based on S&P Operating Earnings; historical GAAP earnings are as reported.

## Dividend Data

No cash dividends have been paid.

---

# DaVita Inc

**STANDARD &POOR'S**

## Business Summary November 06, 2008

CORPORATE OVERVIEW. DaVita is a leading U.S. provider of dialysis and related services for patients suffering from chronic kidney failure, also known as end stage renal disease (ESRD). As of December 31, 2007, DVA provided dialysis and ancillary services to about 107,000 patients through a network of 1,359 outpatient dialysis facilities in 41 states. In addition, the company provided acute inpatient dialysis services at over 800 hospitals.

As a result of DVA's growth through acquisitions, it became highly leveraged, in our opinion. Since a management overhaul in 1999, the company has implemented a new strategy focusing on improving operations and restructuring the balance sheet. In 2005, DVA acquired 492 centers through the Gambro acquisition, as well as 12 independent centers. The company also opened 13 new centers.

In 2007, the company acquired 16 centers, opened 64 new centers, and closed six. As of year end, it owned 1,336 centers outright, held minority interests in 10 centers, and provided administrative services to 13 third-party owned centers. Total treatments in the fourth quarter of 2007 were 3,983,542, up from 3,723,198 in the prior-year period; average dialysis revenue per treatment was $338.11, versus $334.45. In 2007, total treatments were 15,318,995, representing non-acquired treatment growth of 4.6% from 2006. Average revenue per treatment in 2007 was $334.26, up 1.2% from 2006 levels.

Hemodialysis uses an artificial kidney, called a dialyzer, to remove certain toxins, fluids and salt from the patient's blood, together with a machine to control external blood flow and to monitor certain vital signs of the patient. Peritoneal dialysis uses the patient's peritoneal (abdominal) cavity to eliminate fluid and toxins. In 2007, outpatient hemodialysis, peritoneal dialysis and hospital inpatient dialysis accounted for 82%, 9% and 6% of total treatments, respectively.

## Company Financials Fiscal Year Ended Dec. 31

| Per Share Data ($) | 2007 | 2006 | 2005 | 2004 | 2003 | 2002 | 2001 | 2000 | 1999 | 1998 |
|---|---|---|---|---|---|---|---|---|---|---|
| Tangible Book Value | NM | NM | NM | NM | NM | NM | NM | NM | NM | NM |
| Cash Flow | 5.36 | 4.37 | 3.14 | 3.00 | 2.20 | 1.85 | 1.56 | 1.03 | -0.29 | 0.87 |
| Earnings | 3.55 | 2.73 | 1.99 | 2.16 | 1.66 | 1.52 | 1.01 | 0.13 | -1.21 | 0.13 |
| S&P Core Earnings | 3.48 | 2.73 | 1.89 | 2.07 | 1.59 | 1.41 | 0.89 | NA | NA | NA |
| Dividends | Nil | Nil | Nil | Nil | Nil | Nil | Nil | Nil | Nil | Nil |
| Payout Ratio | Nil | Nil | Nil | Nil | Nil | Nil | Nil | Nil | Nil | Nil |
| Prices:High | 67.44 | 60.70 | 53.90 | 41.10 | 26.94 | 17.63 | 16.33 | 11.88 | 19.75 | 24.08 |
| Prices:Low | 50.75 | 46.70 | 38.87 | 25.23 | 12.77 | 12.67 | 9.33 | 1.38 | 3.79 | 12.58 |
| P/E Ratio:High | 19 | 22 | 27 | 19 | 16 | 12 | 16 | 85 | NM | NM |
| P/E Ratio:Low | 14 | 17 | 20 | 12 | 8 | 8 | 9 | 10 | NM | NM |

| Income Statement Analysis (Million $) | 2007 | 2006 | 2005 | 2004 | 2003 | 2002 | 2001 | 2000 | 1999 | 1998 |
|---|---|---|---|---|---|---|---|---|---|---|
| Revenue | 5,264 | 4,881 | 2,974 | 2,299 | 2,016 | 1,855 | 1,651 | 1,486 | 1,445 | 1,205 |
| Operating Income | 1,046 | 911 | 607 | 510 | 461 | 456 | 423 | 291 | 188 | 312 |
| Depreciation | 193 | 173 | 120 | 86.7 | 74.7 | 64.7 | 105 | 112 | 112 | 92.0 |
| Interest Expense | 257 | 277 | 140 | 52.4 | 66.8 | 71.6 | 71.7 | 117 | 111 | 82.6 |
| Pretax Income | 628 | 512 | 353 | 376 | 296 | 325 | 250 | 45.0 | -182 | 64.1 |
| Effective Tax Rate | 39.2% | 36.4% | 35.0% | 37.2% | 38.1% | 39.8% | 41.8% | 62.2% | NM | 64.9% |
| Net Income | 382 | 289 | 207 | 222 | 176 | 187 | 136 | 16.9 | -147 | 15.3 |
| S&P Core Earnings | 374 | 289 | 197 | 213 | 167 | 175 | 118 | NA | NA | NA |

| Balance Sheet & Other Financial Data (Million $) | 2007 | 2006 | 2005 | 2004 | 2003 | 2002 | 2001 | 2000 | 1999 | 1998 |
|---|---|---|---|---|---|---|---|---|---|---|
| Cash | 487 | 310 | 432 | 252 | 61.7 | 96.5 | 36.7 | 31.2 | 108 | 41.5 |
| Current Assets | 1,976 | 1,709 | 1,654 | 869 | 605 | 545 | 475 | 398 | 655 | 560 |
| Total Assets | 6,944 | 6,492 | 6,280 | 2,512 | 1,946 | 1,776 | 1,663 | 1,597 | 2,057 | 1,916 |
| Current Liabilities | 1,087 | 1,112 | 990 | 442 | 363 | 293 | 299 | 250 | 1,699 | 174 |
| Long Term Debt | 3,684 | 3,730 | 4,085 | 1,322 | 1,117 | 1,311 | 811 | 974 | 6.00 | 1,226 |
| Common Equity | 1,732 | 1,246 | 851 | 523 | 307 | 70.3 | 504 | 349 | 326 | 482 |
| Total Capital | 5,733 | 5,224 | 5,100 | 2,048 | 1,563 | 1,474 | 1,359 | 1,342 | 355 | 1,739 |
| Capital Expenditures | 272 | 263 | 161 | 128 | 100 | 103 | 51.2 | 41.1 | 107 | 83.0 |
| Cash Flow | 575 | 463 | 327 | 309 | 250 | 251 | 242 | 129 | -35.0 | 107 |
| Current Ratio | 1.8 | 1.5 | 1.7 | 2.0 | 1.7 | 1.9 | 1.6 | 1.6 | 0.4 | 3.2 |
| % Long Term Debt of Capitalization | 66.2 | 71.4 | 80.1 | 64.6 | 71.4 | 89.0 | 59.7 | 72.5 | 1.7 | 70.5 |
| % Net Income of Revenue | 7.3 | 5.9 | 7.0 | 9.7 | 8.7 | 10.1 | 8.3 | 1.1 | NM | 1.3 |
| % Return on Assets | 5.7 | 4.5 | 4.7 | 10.0 | 9.4 | 10.9 | 8.4 | 0.1 | NM | 1.0 |
| % Return on Equity | 25.6 | 27.6 | 30.2 | 53.6 | 93.2 | 65.1 | 32.0 | 5.0 | NM | 3.4 |

Data as orig reptd.; bef. results of disc opers/spec. items. Per share data adj. for stk. divs.; EPS diluted. E-Estimated. NA-Not Available. NM-Not Meaningful. NR-Not Ranked. UR-Under Review.

**Office:** 601 Hawaii St, El Segundo, CA 90245-4814.
**Telephone:** 310-536-2400.
**Email:** ir@davita.com
**Website:** http://www.davita.com

**Chrmn & CEO:** K.J. Thiry
**COO:** J.C. Mello
**CFO:** R.K. Whitney
**Secy & General Counsel:** J. Schohl

**Investor Contact:** L. Zumwalt (800-310-4872)
**Board Members:** C. G. Berg, W. W. Brittain, Jr., P. J. Diaz, P. T. Grauer, J. M. Nehra, W. Roper, K. J. Thiry, R. J. Valine, R. C. Vaughan

**Founded:** 1994
**Domicile:** Delaware
**Employees:** 31,000

# Dean Foods Co

**STANDARD &POOR'S**

| **S&P Recommendation** HOLD ★★★☆☆ | **Price** $14.55 (as of Nov 14, 2008) | **12-Mo. Target Price** $20.00 | **Investment Style** Large-Cap Blend |
|---|---|---|---|

**GICS Sector** Consumer Staples
**Sub-Industry** Packaged Foods & Meats

**Summary** This leading U.S. dairy processor and distributor was formed in December 2001 when Suiza Foods, the largest U.S. dairy, acquired Dean Foods. Suiza changed its name to Dean Foods.

## Key Stock Statistics (Source S&P, Vickers, company reports)

| | | | | | | | |
|---|---|---|---|---|---|---|---|
| 52-Wk Range | $29.23– 13.45 | S&P Oper. EPS 2008**E** | 1.21 | Market Capitalization(B) | $2.240 | Beta | 0.74 |
| Trailing 12-Month EPS | $1.01 | S&P Oper. EPS 2009**E** | 1.40 | Yield (%) | Nil | S&P 3-Yr. Proj. EPS CAGR(%) | 10 |
| Trailing 12-Month P/E | 14.4 | P/E on S&P Oper. EPS 2008**E** | 12.0 | Dividend Rate/Share | Nil | S&P Credit Rating | BB- |
| $10K Invested 5 Yrs Ago | NA | Common Shares Outstg. (M) | 153.9 | Institutional Ownership (%) | 89 | | |

## Price Performance

30-Week Mov. Avg. · · · 10-Week Mov. Avg. - - - **GAAP Earnings vs. Previous Year** Volume Above Avg. STARS
12-Mo. Target Price — Relative Strength — ▲ Up ▼ Down ► No Change Below Avg. ★

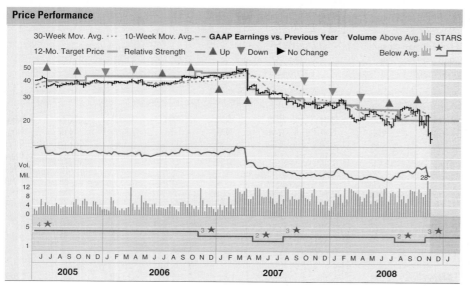

Options: CBOE, P, Ph

## Qualitative Risk Assessment

| LOW | MEDIUM | HIGH |
|---|---|---|

Our risk assessment reflects our view of its leading position in the U.S. milk market, and our expectation of future free cash flow. However, milk prices can be volatile and some products are likely to have stronger demand and growth than others. Also, DF was recently planning a sizeable stock offering, and proceeds were expected to at least partly be used for debt reduction.

## Quantitative Evaluations

**S&P Quality Ranking** B

| D | C | B- | B | B+ | A- | A | A+ |
|---|---|---|---|---|---|---|---|

**Relative Strength Rank** MODERATE

| 37 |
|---|

LOWEST = 1     HIGHEST = 99

## Revenue/Earnings Data

**Revenue (Million $)**

| | 1Q | 2Q | 3Q | 4Q | Year |
|---|---|---|---|---|---|
| 2008 | 3,077 | 3,103 | 3,195 | -- | -- |
| 2007 | 2,630 | 2,844 | 3,117 | 3,232 | 11,822 |
| 2006 | 2,509 | 2,478 | 2,518 | 2,594 | 10,099 |
| 2005 | 2,562 | 2,603 | 2,647 | 2,695 | 10,506 |
| 2004 | 2,452 | 2,807 | 2,773 | 2,791 | 10,822 |
| 2003 | 2,145 | 2,223 | 2,307 | 2,510 | 9,185 |

**Earnings Per Share ($)**

| | 1Q | 2Q | 3Q | 4Q | Year |
|---|---|---|---|---|---|
| 2008 | 0.22 | 0.31 | 0.24 | E0.37 | E1.21 |
| 2007 | 0.47 | 0.21 | 0.05 | 0.24 | 0.95 |
| 2006 | 0.37 | 0.53 | 0.54 | 0.56 | 2.01 |
| 2005 | 0.43 | 0.52 | 0.43 | 0.49 | 1.78 |
| 2004 | 0.43 | 0.47 | 0.21 | 0.64 | 1.78 |
| 2003 | 0.43 | 0.54 | 0.76 | 0.54 | 2.27 |

Fiscal year ended Dec. 31. Next earnings report expected: NA. EPS Estimates based on S&P Operating Earnings; historical GAAP earnings are as reported.

## Dividend Data

A special cash dividend was declared in March 2007.

## Highlights

➤ The STARS recommendation for DF has recently been changed to 3 (hold) from 2 (sell). The Highlights section of this Stock Report will be updated accordingly.

## Investment Rationale/Risk

➤ The Investment Rationale/Risk section of this Stock Report will be updated shortly. For the latest News story on DF from MarketScope, see below.

➤ 11/04/08 12:27 pm ET ... S&P RAISES OPINION ON SHARES OF DEAN FOODS TO HOLD FROM SELL (DF 17.18***): Before special items, Q3 EPS of $0.28 vs. $0.14 is $0.01 above our estimate, helped by a relatively low tax rate. We are reducing our full-year '08 EPS estimate to $1.21 from $1.23. Also, including an estimated $0.06 of dilution related to investing in a new joint venture and $0.03 of estimated incremental pension expense, we are lowering our '09 EPS projection to $1.40 from $1.45. Although we are wary of prospective competitive and cost pressures, we think a weaker outlook is adequately priced into the stock. We are keeping our 12-month target price at $20. /TGraves-CFA

---

**Please read the Required Disclosures and Analyst Certification on the last page of this report.**

# Dean Foods Co

## STANDARD &POOR'S

## Business Summary August 22, 2008

CORPORATE OVERVIEW. Dean Foods Co. is a leading U.S. processor and distributor of milk and other dairy products. In December 2001, Suiza Foods Corp., the largest U.S. dairy, acquired Dean Foods Co. Suiza subsequently changed its name to Dean Foods Co. The company has grown partly through an acquisition strategy and by realizing regional economies of scale and operating efficiencies by consolidating manufacturing and distribution operations. Some of DF's products are sold under licensed brand names.

The company's Dairy Group had $10.4 billion of net sales in 2007, or 88% of DF's total net sales. Segment operating profit, before special items, totaled $624.5 million, down 8.8% from that of the prior year. Fresh milk accounted for 62% of the Dairy Group's 2007 net sales, and ice-cream-related products accounted for 6%. Within the Dairy Group, 60% of sales carried company brands and 40% were private label. In 2007, Wal-Mart, including subsidiaries such as Sam's Club, was the Dairy Group's largest customer, accounting for about 18.5% of the Dairy Group's sales. As of early 2008, the Dairy Group operated 100 manufacturing facilities in 35 states.

The company's WhiteWave Foods business, which had about $1.37 billion of sales in 2007, develops, manufactures and sells a variety of nationally branded soy, dairy, and dairy-related products, such as Silk soy milk and cultured soy products, Horizon Organic dairy products, International Delight coffee creamers, LAND O'LAKES creamers and fluid dairy products, and Rachel's Organic Dairy products. In 2007, combined sales of Horizon organic (including The Organic Cow dairy products) and Silk products represented about 54% of WhiteWave's total. Wal-Mart accounted for about 14.1% of WhiteWave's sales in 2007. Before special items, WhiteWave's segment operating profit in 2007 totaled $118.4 million, down 11% from the year-ago level.

## Company Financials Fiscal Year Ended Dec. 31

| Per Share Data ($) | 2007 | 2006 | 2005 | 2004 | 2003 | 2002 | 2001 | 2000 | 1999 | 1998 |
|---|---|---|---|---|---|---|---|---|---|---|
| Tangible Book Value | NM | NM | NM | NM | NM | NM | NM | NM | NM | NM |
| Cash Flow | 2.64 | 3.63 | 3.22 | 1.58 | 3.41 | 2.71 | 2.44 | 2.35 | 2.05 | 1.55 |
| Earnings | 0.95 | 2.01 | 1.78 | 1.78 | 2.27 | 1.77 | 1.23 | 1.27 | 1.04 | 0.97 |
| S&P Core Earnings | 0.92 | 2.00 | 1.66 | 1.58 | 1.85 | 1.57 | 0.91 | NA | NA | NA |
| Dividends | Nil | Nil | Nil | Nil | Nil | Nil | Nil | Nil | Nil | Nil |
| Payout Ratio | Nil | Nil | Nil | Nil | Nil | Nil | Nil | Nil | Nil | Nil |
| Prices:High | 50.50 | 43.55 | 42.10 | 38.00 | 33.75 | 27.03 | 24.16 | 17.48 | 16.75 | 22.33 |
| Prices:Low | 24.11 | 34.66 | 31.60 | 28.25 | 24.60 | 18.05 | 14.00 | 12.00 | 9.88 | 8.56 |
| P/E Ratio:High | 53 | 22 | 24 | 21 | 15 | 15 | 20 | 14 | 16 | 23 |
| P/E Ratio:Low | 25 | 17 | 18 | 16 | 11 | 10 | 11 | 9 | 10 | 9 |

| Income Statement Analysis (Million $) | 2007 | 2006 | 2005 | 2004 | 2003 | 2002 | 2001 | 2000 | 1999 | 1998 |
|---|---|---|---|---|---|---|---|---|---|---|
| Revenue | 11,822 | 10,099 | 10,506 | 10,822 | 9,185 | 8,991 | 6,230 | 5,756 | 4,482 | 3,321 |
| Operating Income | 810 | 903 | 867 | 919 | 889 | 856 | 542 | 524 | 406 | 334 |
| Depreciation | 232 | 228 | 221 | 224 | 192 | 174 | 155 | 145 | 155 | 91.8 |
| Interest Expense | 322 | 195 | 169 | 205 | 195 | 231 | 135 | 147 | 87.8 | 82.3 |
| Pretax Income | 214 | 456 | 439 | 462 | 574 | 421 | 231 | 234 | 193 | 164 |
| Effective Tax Rate | 39.2% | 38.5% | 37.9% | 38.3% | 38.0% | 36.4% | 36.3% | 38.4% | 39.1% | 36.4% |
| Net Income | 130 | 280 | 272 | 285 | 356 | 268 | 116 | 114 | 109 | 103 |
| S&P Core Earnings | 126 | 278 | 254 | 253 | 288 | 236 | 79.2 | NA | NA | NA |

| Balance Sheet & Other Financial Data (Million $) | 2007 | 2006 | 2005 | 2004 | 2003 | 2002 | 2001 | 2000 | 1999 | 1998 |
|---|---|---|---|---|---|---|---|---|---|---|
| Cash | 32.6 | 31.1 | 25.1 | 27.6 | 47.1 | 45.9 | 78.3 | 31.0 | 25.2 | 54.9 |
| Current Assets | 1,532 | 1,379 | 1,477 | 1,596 | 1,401 | 1,311 | 1,482 | 818 | 639 | 814 |
| Total Assets | 7,033 | 6,770 | 7,051 | 7,756 | 6,993 | 6,582 | 6,732 | 3,780 | 2,659 | 3,014 |
| Current Liabilities | 933 | 1,337 | 1,137 | 1,106 | 1,170 | 1,268 | 1,175 | 700 | 479 | 559 |
| Long Term Debt | 5,271 | 2,872 | 3,329 | 3,116 | 2,611 | 3,140 | 3,556 | 1,809 | 1,373 | 1,576 |
| Common Equity | 51.3 | 1,809 | 1,872 | 2,661 | 2,543 | 1,643 | 1,476 | 599 | 584 | 656 |
| Total Capital | 5,781 | 5,186 | 5,688 | 6,308 | 5,542 | 5,077 | 5,313 | 3,047 | 2,145 | 2,390 |
| Capital Expenditures | 241 | 237 | 307 | 356 | 292 | 242 | 137 | 137 | 188 | 177 |
| Cash Flow | 362 | 508 | 494 | 509 | 548 | 442 | 270 | 259 | 264 | 195 |
| Current Ratio | 1.6 | 1.0 | 1.3 | 1.4 | 1.2 | 1.0 | 1.3 | 1.2 | 1.3 | 1.5 |
| % Long Term Debt of Capitalization | 99.0 | 55.4 | 58.5 | 49.4 | 47.1 | 61.8 | 66.9 | 59.3 | 64.0 | 65.9 |
| % Net Income of Revenue | 1.1 | 2.8 | 2.6 | 2.6 | 3.9 | 3.0 | 1.9 | 1.9 | 2.4 | 3.1 |
| % Return on Assets | 1.9 | 4.1 | 3.7 | 3.9 | 5.2 | 4.0 | 2.2 | 3.5 | 3.8 | 4.7 |
| % Return on Equity | 14.0 | 15.1 | 12.0 | 11.0 | 17.0 | 17.2 | 11.1 | 19.2 | 17.6 | 20.3 |

Data as orig reptd.; bef. results of disc opers/spec. items. Per share data adj. for stk. divs.; EPS diluted. E-Estimated. NA-Not Available. NM-Not Meaningful. NR-Not Ranked. UR-Under Review.

**Office:** 2515 McKinney Avenue, Dallas, TX 75201.
**Telephone:** 214-303-3400.
**Website:** http://www.deanfoods.com
**Chrmn & CEO:** G.L. Engles

**Vice Chrmn:** P. Schenkel
**EVP & CFO:** J.F. Callahan, Jr.
**EVP, Secy & General Counsel:** S.J. Kemps
**SVP & Chief Acctg Officer:** R.L. McCrummen

**Investor Contact:** B. Sievert (214-303-3437)
**Board Members:** L. M. Collens, T. C. Davis, G. L. Engles, S. L. Green, J. S. Hardin, Jr., J. Hill, R. Kirk, J. R. Muse, H. M. Nevares-La Costa, P. Schenkel, J. L. Turner

**Founded:** 1925
**Domicile:** Delaware
**Employees:** 25,585

The McGraw-Hill Companies

# Deere & Co

**STANDARD &POOR'S**

| S&P Recommendation | HOLD ★★★☆☆ | Price $33.79 (as of Nov 14, 2008) | 12-Mo. Target Price $38.00 | Investment Style Large-Cap Blend |
| --- | --- | --- | --- | --- |

**GICS Sector** Industrials
**Sub-Industry** Construction & Farm Machinery & Heavy Trucks

**Summary** The world's largest producer of farm equipment, Deere is also a large maker of construction machinery and lawn and garden equipment.

## Key Stock Statistics (Source S&P, Vickers, company reports)

| | | | | | | |
| --- | --- | --- | --- | --- | --- | --- |
| 52-Wk Range | $94.89– 28.50 | S&P Oper. EPS 2008E | 4.86 | Market Capitalization(B) | $14.429 | Beta | 1.58 |
| Trailing 12-Month EPS | $4.82 | S&P Oper. EPS 2009E | 4.85 | Yield (%) | 3.31 | S&P 3-Yr. Proj. EPS CAGR(%) | 12 |
| Trailing 12-Month P/E | 7.0 | P/E on S&P Oper. EPS 2008E | 7.0 | Dividend Rate/Share | $1.12 | S&P Credit Rating | B |
| $10K Invested 5 Yrs Ago | $11,860 | Common Shares Outstg. (M) | 427.0 | Institutional Ownership (%) | 76 | | |

## Price Performance

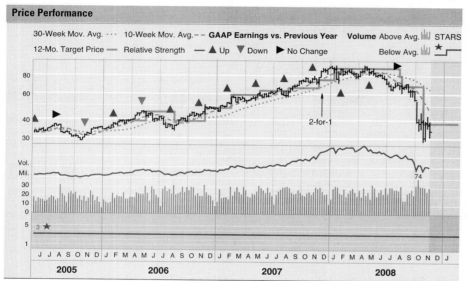

- 30-Week Mov. Avg. ···· 10-Week Mov. Avg. – – GAAP Earnings vs. Previous Year   Volume Above Avg. STARS
- 12-Mo. Target Price — Relative Strength ▲ Up ▼ Down ▶ No Change   Below Avg. ★

Options: ASE, CBOE, Ph

## Qualitative Risk Assessment

| LOW | MEDIUM | HIGH |
| --- | --- | --- |

Our risk assessment for Deere reflects its leading position in many of the markets it serves, and a balance sheet that typically carries large cash balances. On the other hand, the company's businesses are highly cyclical.

## Quantitative Evaluations

**S&P Quality Ranking**      A-

| D | C | B- | B | B+ | A- | A | A+ |
| --- | --- | --- | --- | --- | --- | --- | --- |

**Relative Strength Rank**      MODERATE

37

LOWEST = 1      HIGHEST = 99

## Revenue/Earnings Data

**Revenue (Million $)**

| | 1Q | 2Q | 3Q | 4Q | Year |
| --- | --- | --- | --- | --- | --- |
| 2008 | 5,201 | 809.7 | 7,739 | -- | -- |
| 2007 | 4,425 | 6,883 | 6,634 | 6,141 | 24,082 |
| 2006 | 4,202 | 6,562 | 6,267 | 5,118 | 22,148 |
| 2005 | 4,127 | 6,621 | 6,005 | 5,177 | 21,931 |
| 2004 | 2,912 | 5,877 | 5,418 | 5,207 | 19,986 |
| 2003 | 2,794 | 4,400 | 4,402 | 3,939 | 15,535 |

**Earnings Per Share ($)**

| | | | | | |
| --- | --- | --- | --- | --- | --- |
| 2008 | 0.83 | 1.74 | 1.32 | E0.97 | E4.86 |
| 2007 | 0.52 | 1.36 | 1.32 | 0.94 | 4.00 |
| 2006 | 0.47 | 1.09 | 0.93 | 0.60 | 3.08 |
| 2005 | 0.45 | 1.22 | 0.79 | 0.48 | 2.94 |
| 2004 | 0.34 | 0.94 | 0.79 | 0.71 | 2.78 |
| 2003 | 0.14 | 0.54 | 0.51 | 0.14 | 1.32 |

Fiscal year ended Oct. 31. Next earnings report expected: Late November. EPS Estimates based on S&P Operating Earnings; historical GAAP earnings are as reported.

## Highlights

- The 12-month target price for DE has recently been changed to $38.00 from $68.00. The Highlights section of this Stock Report will be updated accordingly.

## Investment Rationale/Risk

- The Investment Rationale/Risk section of this Stock Report will be updated shortly. For the latest News story on DE from MarketScope, see below.

- 10/22/08 10:40 am ET ... S&P REITERATES HOLD RECOMMENDATION ON SHARES OF DEERE & CO (DE 34.46***): Ahead of Q3 report, we see earnings impacted by the recent sharp decline in agriculture commodity prices, continued high farm input costs, and continued slowdown in construction markets impacting sales of agricultural and construction equipment. Additionally, we see a slowdown in recently strong end-markets such as China, Brazil, Russia, and Australia, and we expect recent strength of the U.S. dollar to hurt forex translation. We are reducing our FY 08 (Oct.) EPS estimate by $0.04 to $4.86, FY 09's by $0.20 to $4.85 and our 12-month target price by $30 to $38. /A.Compton

## Dividend Data (Dates: mm/dd Payment Date: mm/dd/yy)

| Amount ($) | Date Decl. | Ex-Div. Date | Stk. of Record | Payment Date |
| --- | --- | --- | --- | --- |
| 0.250 | 11/29 | 12/27 | 12/31 | 02/01/08 |
| 0.250 | 02/27 | 03/27 | 03/31 | 05/01/08 |
| 0.280 | 05/28 | 06/26 | 06/30 | 08/01/08 |
| 0.280 | 08/27 | 09/26 | 09/30 | 11/03/08 |

Dividends have been paid since 1937. Source: Company reports.

# Deere & Co

**STANDARD &POOR'S**

## Business Summary August 21, 2008

CORPORATE OVERVIEW. Deere & Co. is the world's largest maker of farm tractors and combines, and a leading producer of construction equipment. Its largest competitors include construction equipment behemoth Caterpillar Inc.; Netherlands-based CNH Global N.V., a worldwide maker of both farm and construction equipment; and AGCO Corp., the world's third largest global farm equipment maker.

The agricultural equipment segment (50% of FY 07 (Oct.) revenues; 11.9% operating margin) primarily makes tractors; combine, cotton and sugar cane harvesters; tillage, seeding and soil preparation machinery; hay and forage equipment; material handling equipment; and integrated agricultural management systems technology for the global farming industry. Over the past five years, segment margins averaged about 8.0%.

The commercial and consumer equipment segment (C&CE; 18%; 7.0%) manufactures and distributes equipment and service parts for commercial and residential uses. Products include small tractors for lawn, garden, commercial and utility purposes; riding and walk-behind mowers; golf course equipment; utility vehicles; landscape and irrigation equipment; and other outdoor products. In addition, this division also includes John Deere Landscapes, Inc., a distributor of irrigation equipment, nursery products and landscape products. The company expanded its C&CE division in May 2007, through its $150 million acquisition of LESCO, which supplies consumable lawn care, landscape, golf course and pest control products. Over the past five years, C&CE segment margins averaged 5.5%.

The construction and forestry segment (21%; 11.3%) manufactures and distributes a broad range of machines and service parts used in construction, earth-moving, material handling and timber harvesting. Products include backhoe loaders; crawler dozers and loaders; four-wheel-drive loaders; excavators; motor graders; articulated dump trucks; landscape loaders; skid-steer loaders; and log skidders, feller bunchers, harvesters and related attachments. Over the past five years, margins for this segment averaged 8.6%.

The credit segment (11%; 21.3%; both include other revenues) finances sales and leases by John Deere dealers of new and used agricultural, commercial and consumer, and construction and forestry equipment. In addition, this division provides wholesale financing to dealers, provides operating loans, and finances retail revolving charge accounts. Credit operations had receivables under management of $15.2 billion at April 30, 2008.

## Company Financials Fiscal Year Ended Oct. 31

| Per Share Data ($) | 2007 | 2006 | 2005 | 2004 | 2003 | 2002 | 2001 | 2000 | 1999 | 1998 |
|---|---|---|---|---|---|---|---|---|---|---|
| Tangible Book Value | 13.17 | 13.92 | 12.13 | 10.93 | 5.91 | 4.75 | 6.57 | 7.78 | 8.12 | 8.33 |
| Cash Flow | 5.64 | 4.55 | 4.23 | 4.00 | 2.62 | 2.17 | 1.39 | 2.40 | 1.61 | 2.92 |
| Earnings | 4.00 | 3.08 | 2.94 | 2.78 | 1.32 | 0.67 | -0.14 | 1.03 | 0.51 | 2.08 |
| S&P Core Earnings | 4.22 | 3.25 | 3.02 | 2.84 | 1.54 | -0.19 | -0.82 | NA | NA | NA |
| Dividends | 0.91 | 0.78 | 0.61 | 0.53 | 0.44 | 0.44 | 0.44 | 0.44 | 0.44 | 0.44 |
| Payout Ratio | 23% | 22% | 21% | 19% | 33% | 66% | NM | 43% | 86% | 21% |
| Prices:High | 93.74 | 50.70 | 37.21 | 37.47 | 33.71 | 25.80 | 23.06 | 24.81 | 22.97 | 32.06 |
| Prices:Low | 45.12 | 33.45 | 28.50 | 28.36 | 18.78 | 18.75 | 16.75 | 15.16 | 15.78 | 14.19 |
| P/E Ratio:High | 23 | 14 | 13 | 13 | 26 | 39 | NM | 24 | 45 | 15 |
| P/E Ratio:Low | 11 | 9 | 10 | 10 | 14 | 28 | NM | 15 | 31 | 7 |

| Income Statement Analysis (Million $) | 2007 | 2006 | 2005 | 2004 | 2003 | 2002 | 2001 | 2000 | 1999 | 1998 |
|---|---|---|---|---|---|---|---|---|---|---|
| Revenue | 24,082 | 22,148 | 21,931 | 19,986 | 15,535 | 13,947 | 13,293 | 13,137 | 11,751 | 13,749 |
| Operating Income | 4,571 | 3,883 | 3,553 | 2,976 | 2,231 | 1,696 | 1,274 | 2,102 | 1,435 | 2,497 |
| Depreciation | 744 | 691 | 636 | 621 | 631 | 725 | 718 | 648 | 513 | 418 |
| Interest Expense | 1,151 | 1,018 | 761 | 592 | 1,257 | 637 | 766 | 676 | 557 | 519 |
| Pretax Income | 2,676 | 2,195 | 2,162 | 2,115 | 980 | 578 | -46.3 | 779 | 374 | 1,575 |
| Effective Tax Rate | 33.0% | 33.8% | 33.1% | 33.5% | 34.4% | 44.7% | NM | 37.7% | 36.1% | 35.2% |
| Net Income | 1,822 | 1,453 | 1,447 | 1,406 | 643 | 319 | -64.0 | 486 | 239 | 1,021 |
| S&P Core Earnings | 1,917 | 1,534 | 1,483 | 1,430 | 743 | -94.8 | -385 | NA | NA | NA |

| Balance Sheet & Other Financial Data (Million $) | 2007 | 2006 | 2005 | 2004 | 2003 | 2002 | 2001 | 2000 | 1999 | 1998 |
|---|---|---|---|---|---|---|---|---|---|---|
| Cash | 3,902 | 3,504 | 4,708 | 3,428 | 4,616 | 3,004 | 1,206 | 419 | 612 | 1,177 |
| Current Assets | NA | NA | NA | NA | NA | NA | NA | NA | NA | NA |
| Total Assets | 38,576 | 34,720 | 33,637 | 28,754 | 26,258 | 23,768 | 22,663 | 20,469 | 17,578 | 18,002 |
| Current Liabilities | NA | NA | NA | NA | NA | NA | NA | NA | NA | NA |
| Long Term Debt | 11,798 | 11,584 | 11,739 | 11,090 | 10,404 | 8,950 | 6,561 | 4,764 | 3,806 | 2,792 |
| Common Equity | 7,156 | 7,565 | 6,825 | 6,350 | 2,834 | 1,797 | 3,992 | 4,302 | 4,094 | 4,080 |
| Total Capital | 19,137 | 19,214 | 18,564 | 17,441 | 13,238 | 10,772 | 10,566 | 9,141 | 7,963 | 6,892 |
| Capital Expenditures | 1,023 | 766 | 513 | 364 | 310 | 359 | 491 | 427 | 316 | 435 |
| Cash Flow | 2,566 | 2,145 | 2,083 | 2,027 | 1,275 | 1,045 | 654 | 1,133 | 752 | 1,439 |
| Current Ratio | NA | 2.2 | 2.4 | 3.0 | 2.5 | 2.2 | 1.7 | 1.7 | 1.8 | 1.7 |
| % Long Term Debt of Capitalization | 61.6 | 60.3 | 63.2 | 63.6 | 78.6 | 83.1 | 62.1 | 52.1 | 47.8 | 40.5 |
| % Net Income of Revenue | 7.5 | 6.6 | 6.6 | 7.0 | 4.2 | 2.4 | NM | 3.8 | 2.0 | 7.4 |
| % Return on Assets | 4.9 | 4.3 | 4.6 | 5.1 | 2.6 | 1.4 | NM | 2.6 | 1.3 | 5.9 |
| % Return on Equity | 24.7 | 20.2 | 22.0 | 30.6 | 27.8 | 11.8 | NM | 11.6 | 5.8 | 24.8 |

Data as orig reptd.; bef. results of disc opers/spec. items. Per share data adj. for stk. divs.; EPS diluted. E-Estimated. NA-Not Available. NM-Not Meaningful. NR-Not Ranked. UR-Under Review.

**Office:** One John Deere Place, Moline, IL 61265.
**Telephone:** 309-765-8000.
**Email:** stockholder@deere.com
**Website:** http://www.deere.com

**Chrmn, Pres & CEO:** R.W. Lane
**SVP, CFO & Chief Acctg Officer:** M. Mack, Jr.
**SVP & General Counsel:** J.R. Jenkins
**Treas:** J.A. Davlin

**Secy:** M.K. Jones
**Investor Contact:** M. Ziegler (309-765-4491)
**Board Members:** C. C. Bowles, V. D. Coffman, T. K. Dunnigan, C. O. Holliday, Jr., D. C. Jain, C. M. Jones, A. L. Kelly, R. W. Lane, B. A. Madero, J. Milberg, R. B. Myers, T. H. Patrick, A. L. Peters

**Founded:** 1837
**Domicile:** Delaware
**Employees:** 52,022

# Dell Inc

**STANDARD &POOR'S**

| S&P Recommendation **HOLD** ★★★☆☆ | Price $10.89 (as of Nov 14, 2008) | 12-Mo. Target Price $15.00 | Investment Style Large-Cap Growth |
|---|---|---|---|

**GICS Sector** Information Technology
**Sub-Industry** Computer Hardware

**Summary** This company is the leading direct marketer and one of the world's 10 leading manufacturers of PCs compatible with industry standards established by IBM.

## Key Stock Statistics (Source S&P, Vickers, company reports)

| | | | | | |
|---|---|---|---|---|---|
| 52-Wk Range | $28.40– 8.85 | S&P Oper. EPS 2009**E** | 1.40 | Market Capitalization(B) | $21.326 |
| Trailing 12-Month EPS | $1.34 | S&P Oper. EPS 2010**E** | 1.60 | Yield (%) | Nil |
| Trailing 12-Month P/E | 8.1 | P/E on S&P Oper. EPS 2009**E** | 7.8 | Dividend Rate/Share | Nil |
| $10K Invested 5 Yrs Ago | $3,090 | Common Shares Outstg. (M) | 1,958.4 | Institutional Ownership (%) | 70 |

| | |
|---|---|
| Beta | 1.38 |
| S&P 3-Yr. Proj. EPS CAGR(%) | 11 |
| S&P Credit Rating | A- |

## Price Performance

30-Week Mov. Avg. · · · 10-Week Mov. Avg. - - **GAAP Earnings vs. Previous Year** Volume Above Avg. STARS
12-Mo. Target Price — Relative Strength — ▲ Up ▼ Down ► No Change Below Avg. ★

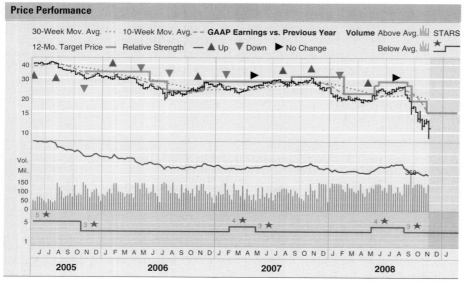

Options: ASE, CBOE, P, Ph

Analysis prepared by **Thomas W. Smith, CFA** on November 06, 2008, when the stock traded at **$ 12.08**.

## Highlights

➤ We project that revenues will rise about 7% in FY 09 (Jan.) and 4% in FY 10, following a September 16 company observation of "softening in global end-user demand." Despite a moderating technology spending climate that we foresee, we believe results will be aided by new corporate strategies, including new products for consumers and small businesses, and the broadening of distribution through retail channels.

➤ We see gross margins dipping below 18% in FY 09 and improving to about 18.2% in FY 10, reflecting pricing pressure and initial costs to reorganize for greater productivity, and the subsequent potential savings we project from improved supply chain management and product mix. We expect SG&A expenses to recede as a percentage of sales in FY 09 and FY 10, as new investments related to customer service are likely to be completed.

➤ We project FY 09 EPS of $1.40 and FY 10 EPS of $1.60. We expect share repurchases, partly paid for with debt, to lend support to EPS.

## Investment Rationale/Risk

➤ We see potential for moderate revenue growth based on new territories and more variety in products and services, as the company executes a new strategy for global expansion. We are less certain about the pace and size of margin improvements, given competitive pricing pressures and the risk that the benefits from higher production volumes or from production in lower-cost regions may be offset by start-up costs. However, we believe the arrival of a new CFO on June 13 added expertise in managing global operations.

➤ Risks to our recommendation and target price include the potential for market share losses, slowdowns in technology spending, and higher facilities reorganization costs than we project. The company's increasing reliance on an international distribution system involving partners, and a need to maintain higher inventory, raises the potential for management errors, in our view.

➤ Applying a target P/E multiple of 10.5X, toward the low end of the historical range and near peers, to our 12-month forward EPS estimate of $1.44, we arrive at our 12-month target price of $15.

## Qualitative Risk Assessment

| LOW | **MEDIUM** | HIGH |
|---|---|---|

Our risk assessment reflects our view of Dell's solid balance sheet and strong execution in asset management, offset by what we see as competitive pressures on product design and pricing, as well as a shift to greater reliance on retail partners around the world.

## Quantitative Evaluations

**S&P Quality Ranking**      B+

| D | C | B- | B | **B+** | A- | A | A+ |
|---|---|---|---|---|---|---|---|

**Relative Strength Rank**      **MODERATE**

35

LOWEST = 1          HIGHEST = 99

## Revenue/Earnings Data

**Revenue (Million $)**

| | 1Q | 2Q | 3Q | 4Q | Year |
|---|---|---|---|---|---|
| 2009 | 16,077 | 16,434 | -- | -- | -- |
| 2008 | 14,722 | 14,776 | 15,646 | 15,989 | 61,133 |
| 2007 | 14,320 | 14,211 | 14,419 | 14,470 | 57,420 |
| 2006 | 13,386 | 13,428 | 13,911 | 15,183 | 55,908 |
| 2005 | 11,540 | 11,706 | 12,502 | 13,457 | 49,205 |
| 2004 | 9,532 | 9,778 | 10,622 | 11,512 | 41,444 |

**Earnings Per Share ($)**

| | | | | | |
|---|---|---|---|---|---|
| 2009 | 0.38 | 0.31 | E0.35 | E0.36 | E1.40 |
| 2008 | 0.34 | 0.31 | 0.34 | 0.31 | 1.31 |
| 2007 | 0.34 | 0.21 | 0.27 | 0.32 | 1.14 |
| 2006 | 0.37 | 0.41 | 0.25 | 0.43 | 1.46 |
| 2005 | 0.28 | 0.31 | 0.33 | 0.26 | 1.18 |
| 2004 | 0.23 | 0.34 | 0.26 | 0.29 | 1.01 |

Fiscal year ended Jan. 31. Next earnings report expected: NA. EPS Estimates based on S&P Operating Earnings; historical GAAP earnings are as reported.

## Dividend Data

No cash dividends have been paid.

# Dell Inc

## Business Summary November 06, 2008

CORPORATE OVERVIEW. We view Dell Inc. (DELL) as a key player in the global market for information technology (IT). According to data from IDC, a market research firm, IT spending growth is slowing to a five-year compound annual rate (CAGR) of about 6%, from double-digit rates last decade, partly on the law of large numbers, but also reflecting intense pricing pressure in many key categories, especially computer hardware. While leading computer hardware manufacturers have been grappling with plunging PC prices over the past decade, DELL has been leading this charge, in our opinion, and we think it has emerged as a key force with which all computer hardware vendors have had to reckon.

DELL is number two in global PC unit shipments, with a 14.9% market share in calendar 2007 according to IDC, well up from 10.5% earlier in the decade, but below 2005's 18.2%. The majority of DELL's sales are from PCs (60% of FY 08 (Jan.) total revenue, the sum of Desktop PCs (32%) and Mobility (28%)), with other categories including Software and Peripherals (16%), Servers and Networking (11%), Services (9%), and Storage (4%). Within the PC category, sales of Mobility (mainly notebook PCs) are rising faster than sales of Desktop PCs. Revenue from notebooks pulled approximately even with desktop revenue for the first time in the FY 08 third quarter, and we expect notebooks to lead in the future.

The customer base is broad, with no single customer accounting for 10% of sales in FY 08 or the prior two fiscal years. The company is expanding in rapid-growth emerging markets including China, India and Brazil. Revenues derived from outside the U.S. rose to 47% of total revenue in FY 08, from 44% in FY 07. Sales in FY 08 were derived 61% from the Americas (including 51% business and 10% U.S. consumer), 25% from EMEA (Europe, Middle-East, Africa), and 14% from APJ (Asia, Pacific, Japan).

## Company Financials Fiscal Year Ended Jan. 31

| Per Share Data ($) | 2008 | 2007 | 2006 | 2005 | 2004 | 2003 | 2002 | 2001 | 2000 | 1999 |
|---|---|---|---|---|---|---|---|---|---|---|
| Tangible Book Value | 1.03 | 1.60 | 1.77 | 2.61 | 2.46 | 1.89 | 1.80 | 2.16 | 2.06 | 0.91 |
| Cash Flow | 1.58 | 1.34 | 1.62 | 1.32 | 1.11 | 0.88 | 0.54 | 0.90 | 0.67 | 0.56 |
| Earnings | 1.31 | 1.14 | 1.46 | 1.18 | 1.01 | 0.80 | 0.46 | 0.81 | 0.61 | 0.53 |
| S&P Core Earnings | 1.28 | 1.13 | 1.03 | 0.88 | 0.68 | 0.49 | 0.28 | 0.58 | NA | NA |
| Dividends | Nil | Nil | Nil | Nil | Nil | Nil | Nil | Nil | Nil | Nil |
| Payout Ratio | Nil | Nil | Nil | Nil | Nil | Nil | Nil | Nil | Nil | Nil |
| Calendar Year | 2007 | 2006 | 2005 | 2004 | 2003 | 2002 | 2001 | 2000 | 1999 | 1998 |
| Prices:High | 30.77 | 30.77 | 42.30 | 42.57 | 37.18 | 31.06 | 31.32 | 59.69 | 55.00 | 37.91 |
| Prices:Low | 21.61 | 21.61 | 28.62 | 31.14 | 22.59 | 21.90 | 16.01 | 16.25 | 31.37 | 9.92 |
| P/E Ratio:High | 23 | 27 | 29 | 36 | 37 | 39 | 68 | 74 | 90 | 73 |
| P/E Ratio:Low | 16 | 19 | 20 | 26 | 22 | 27 | 35 | 20 | 51 | 19 |

### Income Statement Analysis (Million $)

| | 2008 | 2007 | 2006 | 2005 | 2004 | 2003 | 2002 | 2001 | 2000 | 1999 |
|---|---|---|---|---|---|---|---|---|---|---|
| Revenue | 61,133 | 57,420 | 55,908 | 49,205 | 41,444 | 35,404 | 31,168 | 31,888 | 25,265 | 18,243 |
| Operating Income | 4,344 | 3,541 | 4,740 | 4,588 | 3,807 | 3,055 | 2,510 | 3,008 | 2,613 | 2,149 |
| Depreciation | 599 | 471 | 393 | 334 | 263 | 211 | 239 | 240 | 156 | 103 |
| Interest Expense | 45.0 | 45.0 | 28.0 | 16.0 | 14.0 | 17.0 | 29.0 | 47.0 | 34.0 | Nil |
| Pretax Income | 3,856 | 3,345 | 4,574 | 4,445 | 3,724 | 3,027 | 1,731 | 3,194 | 2,451 | 2,084 |
| Effective Tax Rate | 22.8% | 22.8% | 21.9% | 31.5% | 29.0% | 29.9% | 28.0% | 30.0% | 32.0% | 29.9% |
| Net Income | 2,947 | 2,583 | 3,572 | 3,043 | 2,645 | 2,122 | 1,246 | 2,236 | 1,666 | 1,460 |
| S&P Core Earnings | 2,871 | 2,563 | 2,494 | 2,227 | 1,806 | 1,356 | 781 | 1,602 | NA | NA |

### Balance Sheet & Other Financial Data (Million $)

| | 2008 | 2007 | 2006 | 2005 | 2004 | 2003 | 2002 | 2001 | 2000 | 1999 |
|---|---|---|---|---|---|---|---|---|---|---|
| Cash | 7,972 | 9,546 | 7,042 | 4,747 | 4,317 | 4,232 | 3,641 | 4,910 | 3,809 | 3,181 |
| Current Assets | 19,880 | 19,939 | 17,706 | 16,897 | 10,633 | 8,924 | 7,877 | 9,491 | 7,681 | 6,339 |
| Total Assets | 27,561 | 25,635 | 23,109 | 23,215 | 19,311 | 15,470 | 13,535 | 13,435 | 11,471 | 6,877 |
| Current Liabilities | 18,526 | 17,791 | 15,927 | 14,136 | 10,896 | 8,933 | 7,519 | 6,543 | 5,192 | 3,695 |
| Long Term Debt | 362 | 569 | 504 | 505 | 505 | 506 | 520 | 509 | 508 | 512 |
| Common Equity | 3,735 | 4,328 | 4,129 | 6,485 | 6,280 | 4,873 | 4,694 | 5,622 | 5,308 | 2,321 |
| Total Capital | 4,191 | 5,008 | 4,633 | 6,990 | 6,785 | 5,379 | 5,214 | 6,131 | 5,816 | 2,833 |
| Capital Expenditures | 831 | 896 | 728 | 525 | 329 | 305 | 303 | 482 | 397 | 296 |
| Cash Flow | 3,546 | 3,054 | 3,965 | 3,377 | 2,908 | 2,333 | 1,485 | 2,476 | 1,822 | 1,563 |
| Current Ratio | 1.1 | 1.1 | 1.1 | 1.2 | 1.0 | 1.0 | 1.0 | 1.5 | 1.5 | 1.7 |
| % Long Term Debt of Capitalization | 8.6 | 11.4 | 10.9 | 7.2 | 7.4 | 9.4 | 10.0 | 8.3 | 8.7 | 18.1 |
| % Net Income of Revenue | 4.8 | 4.5 | 6.4 | 6.2 | 6.4 | 6.0 | 4.0 | 7.0 | 6.6 | 8.0 |
| % Return on Assets | 11.1 | 10.6 | 15.4 | 14.3 | 15.2 | 14.6 | 9.2 | 18.0 | 18.2 | 26.2 |
| % Return on Equity | 73.1 | 61.1 | 67.3 | 47.7 | 47.4 | 44.4 | 24.2 | 40.9 | 43.7 | 80.8 |

Data as orig reptd.; bef. results of disc opers/spec. items. Per share data adj. for stk. divs.; EPS diluted. E-Estimated. NA-Not Available. NM-Not Meaningful. NR-Not Ranked. UR-Under Review.

**Office:** One Dell Way, Round Rock, TX 78682.
**Telephone:** 512-338-4400.
**Email:** investor_relations_fulfillment@dell.com
**Website:** http://www.dell.com

**Chrmn & CEO:** M.S. Dell
**COO:** M.R. Cannon
**SVP & CFO:** B. Gladden
**SVP, Secy & General Counsel:** L.P. Tu

**SVP & CIO:** S.F. Schuckenbrock
**Investor Contact:** L.A. Tyson (512-723-1130)
**Board Members:** D. J. Carty, M. S. Dell, W. H. Gray, III, S. L. Krawcheck, A. Lafley, J. C. Lewent, T. W. Luce, III, K. S. Luft, A. J. Mandl, M. A. Miles, S. A. Nunn

**Founded:** 1984
**Domicile:** Delaware
**Employees:** 88,200

# DENTSPLY International Inc

**STANDARD &POOR'S**

| S&P Recommendation | SELL ★★☆☆☆ | Price $29.44 (as of Nov 14, 2008) | 12-Mo. Target Price $24.00 | Investment Style Large-Cap Growth |
|---|---|---|---|---|

**GICS Sector** Health Care
**Sub-Industry** Health Care Supplies

**Summary** This company is a designer, developer, manufacturer and marketer of a broad range of products for the dental market.

## Key Stock Statistics (Source S&P, Vickers, company reports)

| | | | | | | | |
|---|---|---|---|---|---|---|---|
| 52-Wk Range | $47.84– 24.78 | S&P Oper. EPS 2008E | 1.89 | Market Capitalization(B) | $4.385 | Beta | 0.55 |
| Trailing 12-Month EPS | $1.85 | S&P Oper. EPS 2009E | 2.00 | Yield (%) | 0.68 | S&P 3-Yr. Proj. EPS CAGR(%) | 12 |
| Trailing 12-Month P/E | 15.9 | P/E on S&P Oper. EPS 2008E | 15.6 | Dividend Rate/Share | $0.20 | S&P Credit Rating | NA |
| $10K Invested 5 Yrs Ago | $13,835 | Common Shares Outstg. (M) | 149.0 | Institutional Ownership (%) | 84 | | |

## Price Performance

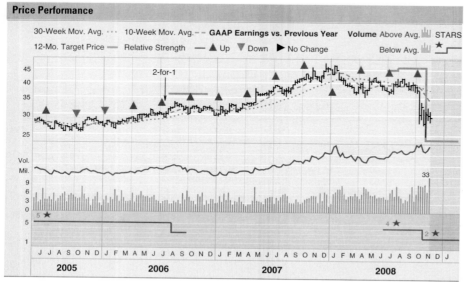

30-Week Mov. Avg. · · · · 10-Week Mov. Avg. - - - **GAAP Earnings vs. Previous Year** Volume Above Avg. STARS
12-Mo. Target Price — Relative Strength — ▲ Up ▼ Down ▶ No Change Below Avg. ★

Options: CBOE, P, Ph

Analysis prepared by **Phillip M. Seligman** on November 11, 2008, when the stock traded at **$ 29.10**.

### Qualitative Risk Assessment

| LOW | MEDIUM | HIGH |
|---|---|---|

Our risk assessment reflects XRAY's long-term trend of relative stability and its broad product and geographic diversification that we believe limits the impact of competition. We also believe XRAY's relatively low long-term debt to capitalization ratio provides some degree of protection from financial difficulties.

### Quantitative Evaluations

**S&P Quality Ranking** A-

| D | C | B- | B | B+ | A- | A | A+ |
|---|---|---|---|---|---|---|---|

**Relative Strength Rank** MODERATE

68

LOWEST = 1    HIGHEST = 99

## Highlights

➤ We forecast net sales, excluding precious metals, in 2009 to be flat to slightly up from the $2.0 billion we project in 2008. Such growth is below the 11% we see for 2008, which has been benefiting from salesforce expansion in 2007, acquisitions and internal sales growth--which excludes precious metals prices, foreign exchange, and recent acquisitions--of 5.0%-5.5%. Drivers we see for 2009 include recent price increases in its consumable lines, strong global growth of the implant business, and new products, offset by continued U.S. economic softness, signs of some dental markets slowing in Europe, and assuming no change from the U.S. dollar's current relative strength.

➤ We foresee the operating margin expanding in line with XRAY's stated goal of improving operating margins by 30 to 50 basis points (bps) per year. We believe the margin expansion will come from an improving product mix and cost control. We also see lower net interest expense, given the low interest rate environment. Lastly, we expect the tax rate to be flat with 2008's.

➤ We estimate operating EPS of $1.89 in 2008, versus 2007's $1.66, and project $2.00 in 2009.

## Investment Rationale/Risk

➤ Long-term fundamentals of the dental products business look good to us. These include an aging population in developed countries and rising standards of living in developing countries. We also like XRAY's broad product and geographic diversification. But given our view of rising unemployment and studies citing a higher percentage of Americans reporting problems paying medical bills, we believe consumers are delaying high-cost, discretionary dental procedures, such as orthodontics, and indications are they are also delaying endodontic care. We would not be surprised if dentists are slowing their order rates. Indeed, XRAY reduced its forecast of internal growth in 2008 to 5.0%-5.5%, from 5.5%-6.5%.

➤ Risks to our recommendation and target price include reduced competition and a sharp increase in discretionary dental care in the U.S. and Europe.

➤ By applying a P/E-to-growth (PEG) ratio of 1.1X, assuming about 12% three-year EPS growth, and our 2008 EPS estimate, we derive a 12-month target price of $24. The PEG ratio is below the medical-device group's on our view of greater sensitivity to the soft U.S. economy.

## Revenue/Earnings Data

**Revenue (Million $)**

| | 1Q | 2Q | 3Q | 4Q | Year |
|---|---|---|---|---|---|
| 2008 | 560.8 | 594.9 | 530.0 | -- | -- |
| 2007 | 472.9 | 507.4 | 488.1 | 541.5 | 2,010 |
| 2006 | 431.0 | 472.4 | 435.7 | 471.3 | 1,811 |
| 2005 | 407.0 | 444.8 | 416.0 | 447.4 | 1,715 |
| 2004 | 414.4 | 424.4 | 390.0 | 465.5 | 1,694 |
| 2003 | 396.2 | 418.0 | 400.4 | 429.7 | 1,571 |

**Earnings Per Share ($)**

| | 1Q | 2Q | 3Q | 4Q | Year |
|---|---|---|---|---|---|
| 2008 | 0.45 | 0.52 | 0.44 | E0.46 | E1.89 |
| 2007 | 0.38 | 0.42 | 0.42 | 0.45 | 1.68 |
| 2006 | 0.31 | 0.37 | 0.31 | 0.42 | 1.41 |
| 2005 | 0.30 | 0.36 | -0.39 | Nil | 0.28 |
| 2004 | 0.28 | 0.30 | 0.29 | 0.42 | 1.28 |
| 2003 | 0.24 | 0.28 | 0.26 | 0.30 | 1.05 |

Fiscal year ended Dec. 31. Next earnings report expected: Early February. EPS Estimates based on S&P Operating Earnings; historical GAAP earnings are as reported.

## Dividend Data (Dates: mm/dd Payment Date: mm/dd/yy)

| Amount ($) | Date Decl. | Ex-Div. Date | Stk. of Record | Payment Date |
|---|---|---|---|---|
| 0.045 | 02/13 | 03/25 | 03/27 | 04/07/08 |
| 0.045 | 05/13 | 06/25 | 06/27 | 07/08/08 |
| 0.045 | 07/28 | 09/24 | 09/26 | 10/07/08 |
| 0.050 | 09/30 | 12/24 | 12/29 | 01/09/09 |

Dividends have been paid since 1994. Source: Company reports.

# DENTSPLY International Inc

## Business Summary November 11, 2008

CORPORATE OVERVIEW. Dentsply International, Inc. (XRAY) was created by a merger of a predecessor Dentsply International Inc. and Gendex Corp. in 1993. The predecessor Dentsply, founded in 1899, manufactured and distributed artificial teeth, dental equipment and dental consumable products. Gendex, founded in 1983, manufactured dental x-ray equipment and handpieces. In early 2004, the company divested the dental x-ray equipment business. Dentsply believes it is the world's largest developer and manufacturer of a broad range of products for the dental market.

Dental consumables (35% of sales in 2007 and 40% in 2006, excluding precious metal content) include dental sundries, such as dental anesthetics, prophylaxis paste, dental sealants, impression materials, restorative materials, bone grafting materials, tooth whiteners, and topical fluoride; and small equipment products, such as high and low speed handpieces, intraoral curing light systems, dental diagnostic systems, and ultrasonic scalers and polishers.

Dental laboratory products (19%;19%) are used in dental laboratories in the preparation of dental appliances. Products include dental prosthetics, including artificial teeth, precious metal dental alloys, dental ceramics, crown and bridge materials, computer aided machining (CAM) ceramics systems, and porcelain furnaces.

Dental specialty products (43%; 38%) include specialized treatment products, such as endodontic (root canal) instruments and materials, implants and related products, bone grafting materials, and orthodontic appliances and accessories.

In addition to the U.S., Dentsply conducts its business in over 120 foreign countries, principally through its foreign subsidiaries. For 2007, 2006 and 2005, net sales, excluding precious metal content, to customers outside the U.S., including export sales, accounted for approximately 59%, 58% and 56%, respectively, of consolidated net sales.

During 2007 and 2006, one customer, Henry Schein Incorporated, a dental distributor, accounted for 11.6% and 10.9%, respectively, of the company's consolidated net sales.

## Company Financials Fiscal Year Ended Dec. 31

| Per Share Data ($) | 2007 | 2006 | 2005 | 2004 | 2003 | 2002 | 2001 | 2000 | 1999 | 1998 |
|---|---|---|---|---|---|---|---|---|---|---|
| Tangible Book Value | 2.07 | 1.39 | 1.52 | 1.17 | NM | NM | NM | 1.13 | 0.75 | 0.43 |
| Cash Flow | 2.00 | 1.71 | 0.59 | 1.58 | 1.34 | 1.20 | 1.11 | 0.91 | 0.82 | 0.45 |
| Earnings | 1.67 | 1.41 | 0.28 | 1.28 | 1.05 | 0.93 | 0.77 | 0.64 | 0.57 | 0.22 |
| S&P Core Earnings | 1.72 | 1.41 | 0.20 | 1.21 | 0.95 | 0.84 | 0.60 | NA | NA | NA |
| Dividends | 0.17 | 0.15 | 0.13 | 0.11 | 0.11 | 0.10 | 0.09 | 0.09 | 0.08 | 0.07 |
| Payout Ratio | 10% | 10% | 45% | 8% | 9% | 10% | 12% | 13% | 13% | 32% |
| Prices:High | 47.84 | 33.76 | 29.22 | 28.42 | 23.70 | 21.75 | 17.34 | 14.46 | 9.77 | 11.71 |
| Prices:Low | 29.44 | 26.07 | 25.37 | 20.88 | 16.05 | 15.63 | 10.83 | 7.71 | 6.83 | 6.67 |
| P/E Ratio:High | 29 | 24 | NM | 22 | 22 | 24 | 23 | 22 | 17 | 54 |
| P/E Ratio:Low | 18 | 18 | NM | 16 | 15 | 17 | 14 | 12 | 12 | 31 |

| Income Statement Analysis (Million $) | 2007 | 2006 | 2005 | 2004 | 2003 | 2002 | 2001 | 2000 | 1999 | 1998 |
|---|---|---|---|---|---|---|---|---|---|---|
| Revenue | 2,010 | 1,810 | 1,715 | 1,694 | 1,571 | 1,514 | 1,129 | 890 | 831 | 795 |
| Operating Income | 416 | 370 | 356 | 352 | 317 | 298 | 238 | 205 | 189 | 179 |
| Depreciation | 50.3 | 47.4 | 50.6 | 49.3 | 45.7 | 43.9 | 54.3 | 41.4 | 39.6 | 37.5 |
| Interest Expense | 23.8 | 10.8 | 17.8 | 25.1 | 26.1 | 29.2 | 21.7 | 10.2 | 15.8 | 15.4 |
| Pretax Income | 358 | 315 | 71.0 | 274 | 251 | 221 | 185 | 152 | 138 | 55.1 |
| Effective Tax Rate | 27.5% | 28.9% | 36.1% | 23.3% | 32.4% | 33.0% | 34.4% | 33.5% | 34.9% | 36.8% |
| Net Income | 260 | 224 | 45.4 | 210 | 170 | 148 | 121 | 101 | 89.9 | 34.8 |
| S&P Core Earnings | 265 | 223 | 32.0 | 198 | 153 | 134 | 94.6 | NA | NA | NA |

| Balance Sheet & Other Financial Data (Million $) | 2007 | 2006 | 2005 | 2004 | 2003 | 2002 | 2001 | 2000 | 1999 | 1998 |
|---|---|---|---|---|---|---|---|---|---|---|
| Cash | 169 | 65.1 | 435 | 506 | 164 | 25.7 | 33.7 | 15.4 | 7.28 | 8.69 |
| Current Assets | 982 | 718 | 1,030 | 1,056 | 727 | 541 | 484 | 325 | 315 | 322 |
| Total Assets | 2,676 | 2,181 | 2,407 | 2,798 | 2,446 | 2,087 | 1,798 | 867 | 860 | 895 |
| Current Liabilities | 312 | 311 | 741 | 405 | 338 | 366 | 359 | 168 | 176 | 194 |
| Long Term Debt | 482 | 367 | 270 | 780 | 790 | 770 | 724 | 110 | 145 | 217 |
| Common Equity | 1,516 | 1,274 | 1,242 | 1,444 | 1,122 | 836 | 610 | 520 | 469 | 414 |
| Total Capital | 2,060 | 1,694 | 1,555 | 2,283 | 1,964 | 1,634 | 1,366 | 651 | 637 | 653 |
| Capital Expenditures | 64.2 | 50.6 | 45.3 | 56.3 | 76.6 | 3.31 | 49.3 | 28.4 | 33.4 | 31.4 |
| Cash Flow | 310 | 271 | 96.0 | 260 | 216 | 192 | 176 | 142 | 129 | 72.3 |
| Current Ratio | 3.1 | 2.3 | 1.4 | 2.6 | 2.2 | 1.5 | 1.4 | 1.9 | 1.8 | 1.7 |
| % Long Term Debt of Capitalization | 23.4 | 21.7 | 17.4 | 34.2 | 40.2 | 47.1 | 53.0 | 16.8 | 22.8 | 33.3 |
| % Net Income of Revenue | 12.9 | 12.4 | 2.6 | 12.4 | 10.8 | 9.8 | 10.8 | 11.4 | 10.8 | 4.4 |
| % Return on Assets | 10.7 | 9.7 | 1.7 | 8.0 | 7.5 | 7.6 | 9.1 | 11.7 | 10.2 | 4.2 |
| % Return on Equity | 18.6 | 17.8 | 3.4 | 16.4 | 17.3 | 20.5 | 21.5 | 20.4 | 20.4 | 8.3 |

Data as orig reptd.; bef. results of disc opers/spec. items. Per share data adj. for stk. divs.; EPS diluted. E-Estimated. NA-Not Available. NM-Not Meaningful. NR-Not Ranked. UR-Under Review.

**Office:** 221 W Philadelphia St, York, PA, USA 17405-0872.
**Telephone:** 717-845-7511.
**Email:** investor@dentsply.com
**Website:** http://www.dentsply.com

**Chrmn, Pres & CEO:** B.W. Wise
**COO & EVP:** C.T. Clark
**Investor Contact:** W.R. Jellison (717-849-4243)
**SVP, CFO & Chief Acctg Officer:** W.R. Jellison

**CTO:** S.R. Jeffries
**Board Members:** M. C. Alfano, E. K. Brandt, P. H. Cholmondeley, M. Coleman, W. L. Dixon, W. F. Hecht, L. A. Jones, F. Lunger, J. C. Miles, II, W. K. Smith, B. W. Wise

**Founded:** 1983
**Domicile:** Delaware
**Employees:** 8,900

# Developers Diversified Realty Corp

STANDARD
&POOR'S

| S&P Recommendation | HOLD ★★★☆☆ | Price $5.22 (as of Nov 14, 2008) | 12-Mo. Target Price $13.00 | Investment Style Large-Cap Blend |
|---|---|---|---|---|

**GICS Sector** Financials
**Sub-Industry** Retail REITS

**Summary** This self-administered and self-managed real estate investment trust acquires, develops, leases, and manages shopping centers across the U.S.

## Key Stock Statistics (Source S&P, Vickers, company reports)

| | | | | | | | |
|---|---|---|---|---|---|---|---|
| 52-Wk Range | $47.68– 4.01 | S&P FFO/Sh. 2008E | 3.22 | Market Capitalization(B) | $0.628 | Beta | 1.05 |
| Trailing 12-Month FFO/Share | NA | S&P FFO/Sh. 2009E | 3.00 | Yield (%) | 28.74 | S&P 3-Yr. FFO/Sh. Proj. CAGR(%) | -7 |
| Trailing 12-Month P/FFO | NA | P/FFO on S&P FFO/Sh. 2008E | 1.6 | Dividend Rate/Share | $1.50 | S&P Credit Rating | BBB- |
| $10K Invested 5 Yrs Ago | $2,191 | Common Shares Outstg. (M) | 120.3 | Institutional Ownership (%) | 94 | | |

## Price Performance

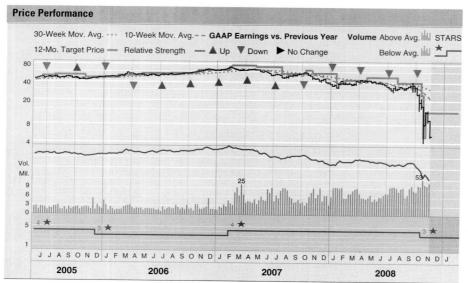

- 30-Week Mov. Avg.
- 10-Week Mov. Avg.
- **GAAP Earnings vs. Previous Year**
- Volume Above Avg. | STARS
- 12-Mo. Target Price — Relative Strength — ▲ Up ▼ Down ► No Change
- Below Avg.

Options: CBOE, P

Analysis prepared by **Robert McMillan** on October 27, 2008, when the stock traded at **$ 8.78**.

## Highlights

➤ We expect DDR to continue to benefit from its strategy of operating shopping centers. We look for total revenues, after increasing 22% in 2007, to drop fractionally in 2008, and we see a 1.4% decrease in 2009 on property dispositions designed to deleverage DDR's balance sheet and enhance liquidity.

➤ Despite our expectations for continued economic softness, we believe that continuing retailer demand for new and existing space will help insulate DDR's portfolio from a weak economy. We see occupancy rates remaining at healthy levels. The core portfolio was 94.5% leased at the end of the third quarter, down from 95.9% a year earlier. We expect moderate demand for space to enable the trust to continue to achieve moderate rent increases on new leases and renewals of expiring leases. During the third quarter, rental rates on new leases and renewal leases were up 8.9%. More stringent commercial real estate financing conditions may also present an opportunity for DDR to make higher-yielding acquisitions that would also help the portfolio.

➤ Our per-share FFO projections are $3.22 for 2008 and $3.00 for 2009.

## Investment Rationale/Risk

➤ Over the long term, we think investors in DDR will benefit from the trust's position as one of the largest owners and managers of shopping centers in the U.S. and established relationships with numerous retailers, which should allow it to continue to generate robust growth.

➤ Risks to our recommendation and target price include slower-than-expected growth in retailer expansion, a large increase in shopping center supply, and sharply higher interest rates.

➤ The shares recently traded at about 2.7X DDR's trailing 12-month FFO per share. Our target price of $13 is equal to 4.5X our forward 12-month FFO estimate of $2.87. Recently, the shares have dropped sharply we think on concerns about DDE's debt maturity amid weakness in the equity and credit markets. We think that management's plan to sell assets, reduce dividends, and curtail development activities will enhance DDR's liquidity and allow the multiple to expand. We think the trust's retailer-dependent business, which is anchored by long-term leases, is somewhat insulated from near-term economic changes and that the valuation multiple will expand as DDR continues to grow.

## Qualitative Risk Assessment

| LOW | MEDIUM | HIGH |
|---|---|---|

Our risk assessment for DDR reflects its position as one of the largest owners of shopping centers in the U.S, its broad customer and geographic base, and our view of its strong financial condition.

## Quantitative Evaluations

**S&P Quality Ranking** B+

| D | C | B- | B | B+ | A- | A | A+ |
|---|---|---|---|---|---|---|---|

**Relative Strength Rank** WEAK

3

LOWEST = 1 — HIGHEST = 99

## Revenue/FFO Data

**Revenue (Million $)**

| | 1Q | 2Q | 3Q | 4Q | Year |
|---|---|---|---|---|---|
| 2008 | 241.9 | 243.9 | 233.9 | -- | -- |
| 2007 | 230.4 | 279.5 | 234.1 | 239.2 | 945.0 |
| 2006 | 200.6 | 198.3 | 204.8 | 214.4 | 818.1 |
| 2005 | 171.9 | 176.3 | 180.5 | 198.5 | 727.2 |
| 2004 | 123.2 | 146.9 | 164.0 | 164.8 | 598.9 |
| 2003 | 102.6 | 123.2 | 123.9 | 126.4 | 476.1 |

**FFO Per Share ($)**

| | 1Q | 2Q | 3Q | 4Q | Year |
|---|---|---|---|---|---|
| 2008 | 0.83 | 0.82 | E0.83 | E0.73 | E3.22 |
| 2007 | 0.91 | 0.89 | 0.80 | 0.82 | 3.79 |
| 2006 | 0.78 | 0.99 | 0.83 | 0.82 | 1.81 |
| 2005 | 0.90 | 0.84 | 0.74 | 0.74 | 2.08 |
| 2004 | 0.71 | 0.84 | 0.72 | 0.69 | 2.95 |
| 2003 | 0.61 | 0.64 | 0.59 | 0.68 | 2.51 |

Fiscal year ended Dec. 31. Next earnings report expected: Mid February. FFO Estimates based on S&P Funds From Operations Est..

## Dividend Data (Dates: mm/dd Payment Date: mm/dd/yy)

| Amount ($) | Date Decl. | Ex-Div. Date | Stk. of Record | Payment Date |
|---|---|---|---|---|
| 0.690 | 01/09 | 03/18 | 03/21 | 04/08/08 |
| 0.690 | 05/15 | 06/18 | 06/20 | 07/08/08 |
| 0.690 | 08/19 | 09/24 | 09/26 | 10/07/08 |

Dividends have been paid since 1993. Source: Company reports.

# Developers Diversified Realty Corp

**STANDARD
&POOR'S**

## Business Summary October 27, 2008

CORPORATE OVERVIEW. Developers Diversified Realty Corp., a self-administered and self-managed REIT, acquires, develops, redevelops, owns, leases and manages shopping centers and business centers. At December 31, 2007, the trust's portfolio consisted of 710 shopping centers (including 317 centers owned through unconsolidated joint ventures and 40 that are otherwise consolidated by the trust) and seven business centers The shopping centers consist of 677 community shopping centers, 26 enclosed malls and seven lifestyle centers. The properties also include more than 1,600 undeveloped acres, primarily shopping centers, development sites and parcels, located adjacent to certain of the shopping centers. The shopping centers aggregate approximately 116.2 million square feet of DDR-owned gross leasable area (GLA) (approximately 148.3 million square feet of total GLA) and are located in 45 states, plus Puerto Rico and Brazil. These centers are principally in the Southeast and Midwest, with significant concentrations in Florida, Georgia and New York. The trust also has assets under development in Canada and Russia. The business centers aggregate 0.8 million square feet of DDR-owned GLA and are located in five states, primarily in Maryland.

The trust's shopping centers are designed to attract local area customers, and are typically anchored by one or more discount department stores. They often include a supermarket, drug store, junior department store and/or other major discount retailer as additional anchors. The shopping centers are typically anchored by two or more strong national tenant anchors such as Wal-Mart, Kohl's, Target, Home Depot or Lowe's Home Improvement and two or more medium-sized national big-box tenants such as Best Buy, Bed Bath & Beyond, TJ Maxx or Michaels.

CORPORATE STRATEGY. For DDR, location and the financial health and growth of its retail tenants are among the most important factors affecting the success of its portfolio, in our view. Further, we believe this industry enjoys relatively high barriers to entry, since developing new shopping centers requires large amounts of capital as well as time-consuming regulatory approval, which has been difficult to obtain in the recent past amid concerns about traffic and pollution. We expect DDR to continue to derive numerous growth opportunities from being large and having a well-located and varied array of shopping center formats and relationships with a broad array of retailers, which should allow DDR to cross-promote its properties and generate growth from the introduction of new retail concepts.

## Company Financials Fiscal Year Ended Dec. 31

| Per Share Data ($) | 2007 | 2006 | 2005 | 2004 | 2003 | 2002 | 2001 | 2000 | 1999 | 1998 |
|---|---|---|---|---|---|---|---|---|---|---|
| Tangible Book Value | 21.26 | 16.44 | 17.12 | 23.42 | 12.35 | 9.63 | 8.92 | 8.64 | 9.15 | 9.69 |
| Earnings | 1.68 | 1.69 | 1.91 | 2.17 | 2.28 | 1.14 | 1.17 | 1.31 | 0.95 | 1.00 |
| S&P Core Earnings | 1.65 | 1.69 | 1.92 | 2.17 | 2.27 | 1.09 | 1.15 | NA | NA | NA |
| Dividends | 2.64 | 2.36 | 2.16 | 1.94 | 1.69 | 1.52 | 1.48 | 1.44 | 1.38 | 0.98 |
| Payout Ratio | 143% | 140% | 113% | 89% | 74% | 133% | 126% | 110% | 145% | 98% |
| Prices:High | 72.33 | 66.36 | 49.49 | 45.85 | 33.90 | 23.65 | 19.38 | 16.25 | 18.50 | 21.47 |
| Prices:Low | 37.42 | 46.96 | 38.74 | 30.80 | 21.22 | 17.25 | 12.88 | 11.00 | 12.31 | 15.88 |
| P/E Ratio:High | 39 | 39 | 26 | 21 | 15 | 21 | 17 | 12 | 19 | 21 |
| P/E Ratio:Low | 20 | 28 | 20 | 14 | 9 | 15 | 11 | 8 | 13 | 16 |

| Income Statement Analysis (Million $) | | | | | | | | | | |
|---|---|---|---|---|---|---|---|---|---|---|
| Rental Income | 861 | 753 | 523 | 439 | 348 | 330 | 291 | 261 | 242 | 214 |
| Mortgage Income | Nil | Nil | Nil | Nil | Nil | Nil | Nil | Nil | Nil | Nil |
| Total Income | 945 | 818 | 727 | 599 | 476 | 357 | 322 | 286 | 264 | 228 |
| General Expenses | 242 | 174 | 153 | 119 | 105 | 73.1 | 59.3 | 47.5 | 69.7 | 33.0 |
| Interest Expense | 261 | 222 | 182 | 130 | 89.7 | 76.8 | 81.8 | 77.0 | 68.0 | 57.2 |
| Provision for Losses | Nil | Nil | Nil | Nil | Nil | Nil | Nil | Nil | Nil | Nil |
| Depreciation | 219 | 192 | 165 | 132 | 94.4 | 77.7 | 64.5 | 54.2 | 52.0 | 43.2 |
| Net Income | 256 | 168 | 176 | 262 | 167 | 101 | 92.4 | 101 | 87.0 | 78.8 |
| S&P Core Earnings | 201 | 184 | 210 | 212 | 189 | 71.2 | 64.4 | NA | NA | NA |

| Balance Sheet & Other Financial Data (Million $) | | | | | | | | | | |
|---|---|---|---|---|---|---|---|---|---|---|
| Cash | 109 | 28.4 | 30.7 | 49.9 | 11.7 | 16.4 | 19.1 | 4.24 | 6.00 | 2.30 |
| Total Assets | 9,090 | 7,180 | 6,863 | 5,584 | 3,941 | 2,777 | 2,497 | 2,332 | 2,321 | 2,127 |
| Real Estate Investment | 8,984 | 7,442 | 7,029 | 5,603 | 3,885 | 2,804 | 2,494 | 2,162 | 2,068 | 1,897 |
| Loss Reserve | Nil | Nil | Nil | Nil | Nil | Nil | Nil | Nil | Nil | Nil |
| Net Investment | 7,961 | 6,581 | 6,337 | 5,035 | 3,427 | 2,395 | 2,142 | 1,865 | 1,818 | 2,041 |
| Short Term Debt | 709 | 429 | Nil | Nil | Nil | 207 | 158 | 261 | 183 | 81.1 |
| Capitalization:Debt | 4,882 | 3,820 | 3,832 | 2,478 | 2,083 | 1,292 | 1,151 | 967 | 969 | 919 |
| Capitalization:Equity | 2,444 | 1,791 | 1,865 | 1,849 | 1,079 | 642 | 530 | 480 | 852 | 599 |
| Capitalization:Total | 7,993 | 6,438 | 6,533 | 5,088 | 3,745 | 2,452 | 2,235 | 1,986 | 2,037 | 1,963 |
| % Earnings & Depreciation/Assets | 5.8 | 5.1 | 5.4 | 8.3 | 7.8 | 6.8 | 6.5 | 6.7 | 6.3 | 5.7 |
| Price Times Book Value:High | 3.4 | 4.0 | 2.9 | 1.9 | 2.7 | 2.5 | 2.2 | 1.9 | 2.0 | 2.2 |
| Price Times Book Value:Low | 1.8 | 2.9 | 2.3 | 1.3 | 1.7 | 1.8 | 1.4 | 1.3 | 1.4 | 1.6 |

Data as orig reptd.; bef. results of disc opers/spec. items. Per share data adj. for stk. divs.; EPS diluted. E-Estimated. NA-Not Available. NM-Not Meaningful. NR-Not Ranked. UR-Under Review.

**Office:** 3300 Enterprise Parkway, Beachwood, OH 44122.
**Telephone:** 216-755-5500.
**Email:** ir@ddrc.com
**Website:** http://www.ddr.com

**Chrmn & CEO:** S.A. Wolstein
**Pres & COO:** D.B. Hurwitz
**EVP & CFO:** W.H. Schafer
**EVP & Secy:** J.U. Allgood

**SVP & Chief Acctg Officer:** C.A. Vesy
**Investor Contact:** S. Schroeder
**Board Members:** D. S. Adler, T. R. Ahern, R. H. Gidel, V. B. MacFarlane, C. Macnab, S. D. Roulston, B. A. Sholem, W. B. Summers, Jr., S. A. Wolstein

**Founded:** 1965
**Domicile:** Ohio
**Employees:** 773

# Devon Energy Corp

**STANDARD &POOR'S**

| S&P Recommendation **BUY** ★★★★☆ | Price $70.14 (as of Nov 14, 2008) | 12-Mo. Target Price $114.00 | Investment Style Large-Cap Blend |
|---|---|---|---|

**GICS Sector** Energy
**Sub-Industry** Oil & Gas Exploration & Production

**Summary** As one of the largest independent oil and gas exploration and production companies in the U.S., the firm has grown through acquisitions of Ocean Energy, Mitchell Energy, Anderson Exploration and Chief Holdings.

## Key Stock Statistics (Source S&P, Vickers, company reports)

| | | | | | | | |
|---|---|---|---|---|---|---|---|
| 52-Wk Range | $127.43– 54.40 | S&P Oper. EPS 2008**E** | 11.70 | Market Capitalization(B) | $30.967 | Beta | 0.92 |
| Trailing 12-Month EPS | $13.32 | S&P Oper. EPS 2009**E** | 10.27 | Yield (%) | 0.91 | S&P 3-Yr. Proj. EPS CAGR(%) | 27 |
| Trailing 12-Month P/E | 5.3 | P/E on S&P Oper. EPS 2008**E** | 6.0 | Dividend Rate/Share | $0.64 | S&P Credit Rating | BBB+ |
| $10K Invested 5 Yrs Ago | $28,821 | Common Shares Outstg. (M) | 441.5 | Institutional Ownership (%) | 81 | | |

## Price Performance

30-Week Mov. Avg. ···   10-Week Mov. Avg. ‐‐   **GAAP Earnings vs. Previous Year**   Volume Above Avg. STARS
12-Mo. Target Price —   Relative Strength —   ▲ Up   ▼ Down   ► No Change   Below Avg. ★

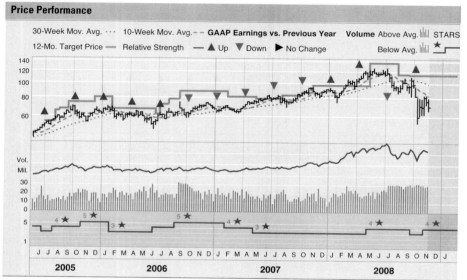

Options: ASE, CBOE, P

Analysis prepared by **Michael Kay** on November 07, 2008, when the stock traded at **$ 73.59.**

### Highlights

➤ Production is up 6% so far in 2008, below expectations on impact of high oil prices on production sharing contracts, hurricane shut-ins, and downtime at the ACG field offshore Azerbaijan. We see strong development results in the U.S., Canada, and Brazil boosting second-half volumes by 5%. Our full-year 2008 production growth outlook is 6%, below original expectations, but we see 14% growth in 2009.

➤ DVN is selling international assets with lower growth to focus on higher-growth assets such as the Barnett, Haynesville and Horn River shale plays. It has completed the majority of its announced divestiture in Africa for proceeds of more than $3 billion. In June, DVN closed on the sale of its assets in Equatorial Guinea for $2.2 billion. DVN has $250 million in transactions remaining to close by the end of 2008.

➤ After-tax operating earnings increased about 8% in 2007, and we expect strong price realizations and production gains will lead to a 82% rise in 2008, before declining 15% in 2009 on weaker prices. We see 2008 EPS of $11.70 (including a $0.13 derivative gain in first nine months) and $10.27 in 2009.

### Investment Rationale/Risk

➤ We believe recent discoveries have shifted DVN's focus to organic growth, from restructuring acquisitions. We estimate that successful results in the Gulf of Mexico's Lower Tertiary Trend, and a strong portfolio of deepwater prospects, have raised production growth prospects through 2015, while also increasing its presence and production outlook in unconventional resources. We see DVN expanding its lease position in the Barnett and Haynesville shales and the Horn River play and to grow oil sands production from its Jackfish project.

➤ Risks to our recommendation and target price include changes in economic, industry and operating conditions, such as rising costs and difficulty in organically replacing reserves.

➤ A drop in oil and gas prices, due to weakening economy and ongoing credit crisis, has caused a similar decline in E&P shares. However, we believe DVN is trading at a discount to our proven reserve NAV of $113 and with low debt levels, we find shares attractive. Our 12-month target of $114 blends our DCF ($102; WACC of 9.5%, terminal growth 3%), relative metrics, and NAV estimate.

## Qualitative Risk Assessment

| LOW | MEDIUM | HIGH |
|---|---|---|

Our risk assessment for DVN reflects our view of its position as a large independent exploration and production company focused on stable, lower-risk assets located in North America, offset by exposure to economic, commodity price and operational risk.

## Quantitative Evaluations

**S&P Quality Ranking**   A-

| D | C | B- | B | B+ | A- | A | A+ |
|---|---|---|---|---|---|---|---|

**Relative Strength Rank**   MODERATE

62

LOWEST = 1                                                    HIGHEST = 99

## Revenue/Earnings Data

**Revenue (Million $)**

| | 1Q | 2Q | 3Q | 4Q | Year |
|---|---|---|---|---|---|
| 2008 | 3,763 | 4,763 | 4,386 | -- | -- |
| 2007 | 2,473 | 2,929 | 2,763 | 3,197 | 11,362 |
| 2006 | 2,684 | 2,589 | 2,696 | 2,609 | 10,578 |
| 2005 | 2,351 | 2,468 | 2,704 | 3,218 | 10,741 |
| 2004 | 2,238 | 2,219 | 2,267 | 2,465 | 9,189 |
| 2003 | 1,671 | 1,813 | 1,948 | 1,921 | 7,352 |

**Earnings Per Share ($)**

| | 1Q | 2Q | 3Q | 4Q | Year |
|---|---|---|---|---|---|
| 2008 | 1.45 | 1.31 | 5.63 | E2.34 | E11.70 |
| 2007 | 1.27 | 1.82 | 1.43 | 2.45 | 6.97 |
| 2006 | 1.56 | 1.92 | 1.57 | 1.26 | 6.29 |
| 2005 | 1.14 | 1.38 | 1.63 | 2.14 | 6.26 |
| 2004 | 1.00 | 1.01 | 1.04 | 1.35 | 4.38 |
| 2003 | 1.29 | 0.81 | 0.86 | 1.13 | 4.00 |

Fiscal year ended Dec. 31. Next earnings report expected: Early February. EPS Estimates based on S&P Operating Earnings; historical GAAP earnings are as reported.

## Dividend Data (Dates: mm/dd Payment Date: mm/dd/yy)

| Amount ($) | Date Decl. | Ex-Div. Date | Stk. of Record | Payment Date |
|---|---|---|---|---|
| 0.140 | 12/03 | 12/12 | 12/14 | 12/28/07 |
| 0.160 | 03/03 | 03/13 | 03/17 | 03/31/08 |
| 0.160 | 06/02 | 06/12 | 06/16 | 06/30/08 |
| 0.160 | 09/02 | 09/12 | 09/16 | 09/30/08 |

Dividends have been paid since 1993. Source: Company reports.

**STANDARD & POOR'S**

# Devon Energy Corp

## Business Summary November 07, 2008

CORPORATE OVERVIEW. Devon Energy Corp. (DVN) is an independent exploration and production company primarily engaged in the exploration, development and production of oil and natural gas; the acquisition of producing properties; the transportation of oil, natural gas and natural gas liquids (NGLs); and the processing of natural gas. The company began operations as a private company in 1971, and its common stock began trading publicly in 1988.

DVN's operations are focused in the U.S. (66% of 2007 revenues; 49% of 2007 earnings), Canada (22%; 20%), and internationally (12%; 31%). U.S. activities are concentrated in four regions: the Mid-Continent (mainly north and east Texas and Oklahoma), the Permian Basin (within Texas and New Mexico), the Rocky Mountains (from the Canadian border into northern New Mexico), offshore areas of the Gulf of Mexico, and onshore areas of the Gulf Coast (mainly in south Texas and south Louisiana). Canadian operations are located in the provinces of Alberta, British Columbia and Saskatchewan. Operations outside North America include Azerbaijan, Brazil and China. In January 2007, DVN announced plans to divest its assets and operations in West Africa.

DVN also has marketing and midstream operations that perform various activities to support its oil and gas operations.

Oil and gas production rose 12% to 224 million barrel oil equivalent (boe; 36% liquids) in 2007. Proved oil and gas reserves rose 9.2%, to 2.496 billion boe (75% developed, 40% liquids) in 2007. We estimate its 2007 organic reserve replacement at 194%. Using data from John S. Herold, an industry research firm, we estimate DVN's three-year (2004-06) finding and development costs at $12.78 per boe, in line with peers; its three-year proved acquisition costs at $10.63 per boe, below the peer average; its three-year reserve replacement costs at $12.57 per boe, in line with peers; and its three-year average reserve replacement at 170%, strong but below the peer average.

## Company Financials Fiscal Year Ended Dec. 31

| Per Share Data ($) | 2007 | 2006 | 2005 | 2004 | 2003 | 2002 | 2001 | 2000 | 1999 | 1998 |
|---|---|---|---|---|---|---|---|---|---|---|
| Tangible Book Value | 35.31 | 26.09 | 20.31 | 16.30 | 11.50 | 3.20 | 4.32 | 11.03 | 16.03 | 5.40 |
| Cash Flow | 13.32 | 11.73 | 10.87 | 8.95 | 8.10 | 4.04 | 3.54 | 5.37 | 2.65 | 0.66 |
| Earnings | 6.97 | 6.29 | 6.26 | 4.38 | 4.00 | 0.16 | 0.17 | 2.75 | 0.73 | -0.63 |
| S&P Core Earnings | 6.99 | 6.29 | 6.01 | 4.30 | 3.99 | 0.47 | 0.09 | NA | NA | NA |
| Dividends | 0.56 | 0.45 | 0.30 | 0.20 | 0.10 | 0.10 | 0.10 | 0.10 | 0.10 | 0.10 |
| Payout Ratio | 8% | 7% | 5% | 5% | 3% | 63% | 59% | 4% | 14% | NM |
| Prices:High | 94.75 | 74.75 | 70.35 | 41.64 | 29.40 | 26.55 | 33.38 | 32.37 | 22.47 | 20.56 |
| Prices:Low | 62.80 | 48.94 | 36.48 | 25.90 | 21.23 | 16.94 | 15.28 | 15.69 | 10.06 | 13.06 |
| P/E Ratio:High | 14 | 12 | 11 | 10 | 7 | NM | NM | 12 | 31 | NM |
| P/E Ratio:Low | 9 | 8 | 6 | 6 | 5 | NM | NM | 6 | 14 | NM |

| Income Statement Analysis (Million $) | | | | | | | | | | |
|---|---|---|---|---|---|---|---|---|---|---|
| Revenue | 11,362 | 10,578 | 10,741 | 9,189 | 7,352 | 4,316 | 3,075 | 2,784 | 734 | 388 |
| Operating Income | 7,380 | 6,938 | 7,290 | 6,038 | 4,589 | 2,403 | 2,350 | 2,094 | 491 | 237 |
| Depreciation, Depletion and Amortization | 2,858 | 2,442 | 2,191 | 2,290 | 1,793 | 1,211 | 876 | 693 | 254 | 124 |
| Interest Expense | 532 | 421 | 533 | 475 | 504 | 533 | 220 | 154 | 66.9 | 22.6 |
| Pretax Income | 4,224 | 4,012 | 4,552 | 3,293 | 2,245 | -134 | 84.0 | 1,142 | 160 | -75.8 |
| Effective Tax Rate | 25.5% | 29.6% | 35.6% | 33.6% | 22.9% | NM | 35.7% | 36.0% | 40.8% | NM |
| Net Income | 3,146 | 2,823 | 2,930 | 2,186 | 1,731 | 59.0 | 54.0 | 730 | 94.6 | -60.3 |
| S&P Core Earnings | 3,144 | 2,815 | 2,801 | 2,136 | 1,715 | 147 | 22.9 | NA | NA | NA |

| Balance Sheet & Other Financial Data (Million $) | | | | | | | | | | |
|---|---|---|---|---|---|---|---|---|---|---|
| Cash | 1,736 | 739 | 1,606 | 2,119 | 1,273 | 292 | 193 | 228 | 167 | 19.2 |
| Current Assets | 3,914 | 3,212 | 4,206 | 3,583 | 2,364 | 1,064 | 1,081 | 934 | 417 | 111 |
| Total Assets | 41,456 | 35,063 | 30,273 | 29,736 | 27,162 | 16,225 | 13,184 | 6,860 | 4,623 | 1,226 |
| Current Liabilities | 3,657 | 4,645 | 2,934 | 3,100 | 2,071 | 1,042 | 919 | 629 | 227 | 80.7 |
| Long Term Debt | 7,928 | 5,568 | 5,957 | 7,031 | 8,635 | 7,562 | 6,589 | 2,049 | 1,787 | 555 |
| Common Equity | 22,005 | 17,441 | 14,999 | 13,673 | 11,055 | 4,652 | 3,258 | 3,276 | 2,024 | 523 |
| Total Capital | 34,972 | 28,660 | 26,362 | 25,505 | 24,061 | 14,842 | 11,990 | 5,953 | 4,204 | 1,111 |
| Capital Expenditures | 6,158 | 7,551 | 4,090 | 3,103 | 2,587 | 3,426 | 5,326 | 1,280 | 315 | 376 |
| Cash Flow | 5,994 | 5,255 | 5,111 | 4,466 | 3,514 | 1,260 | 920 | 1,414 | 345 | 63.6 |
| Current Ratio | 1.1 | 0.7 | 1.4 | 1.2 | 1.1 | 1.0 | 1.2 | 1.5 | 1.8 | 1.4 |
| % Long Term Debt of Capitalization | 23.9 | 19.4 | 22.6 | 27.6 | 35.9 | 51.0 | 55.0 | 34.4 | 42.5 | 49.9 |
| % Return on Assets | 8.2 | 8.6 | 9.7 | 7.7 | 8.0 | NM | 0.5 | 11.3 | 3.2 | NM |
| % Return on Equity | 15.9 | 17.4 | 20.3 | 17.6 | 21.9 | NM | 1.3 | 24.9 | 7.1 | NM |

Data as orig reptd.; bef. results of disc opers/spec. items. Per share data adj. for stk. divs.; EPS diluted. E-Estimated. NA-Not Available. NM-Not Meaningful. NR-Not Ranked. UR-Under Review.

**Office:** 20 N Broadway, Oklahoma City, OK 73102-8260.
**Telephone:** 405-235-3611.
**Website:** http://www.devonenergy.com
**Chrmn & CEO:** J.L. Nichols

**Pres:** J. Richels
**EVP & General Counsel:** L.C. Taylor
**SVP, CFO & Chief Acctg Officer:** D.J. Heatly
**Chief Admin Officer:** R.A. Marcum

**Investor Contact:** V. White (405-552-4526)
**Board Members:** T. F. Ferguson, D. A. Hager, J. A. Hill, R. L. Howard, M. M. Kanovsky, J. T. Mitchell, J. L. Nichols, M. P. Ricciardello, J. Richels

**Founded:** 1988
**Domicile:** Delaware
**Employees:** 5,000

The McGraw-Hill Companies

# DIRECTV Group Inc (The)

**STANDARD &POOR'S**

| S&P Recommendation | BUY ★★★★☆ | Price<br>$20.64 (as of Nov 14, 2008) | 12-Mo. Target Price<br>$32.00 | Investment Style<br>Large-Cap Blend |
|---|---|---|---|---|

**GICS Sector** Consumer Discretionary
**Sub-Industry** Cable & Satellite

**Summary** This company is the larger of the two major U.S. providers of direct broadcast satellite (DBS) television service, with more than 17 million subscribers across the U.S., and nearly 3.5 million in Latin America.

## Key Stock Statistics (Source S&P, Vickers, company reports)

| | | | | | | | |
|---|---|---|---|---|---|---|---|
| 52-Wk Range | $29.10– 11.25 | S&P Oper. EPS 2008E | 1.43 | Market Capitalization(B) | $21.678 | Beta | 0.61 |
| Trailing 12-Month EPS | $1.35 | S&P Oper. EPS 2009E | 1.91 | Yield (%) | Nil | S&P 3-Yr. Proj. EPS CAGR(%) | 15 |
| Trailing 12-Month P/E | 15.3 | P/E on S&P Oper. EPS 2008E | 14.4 | Dividend Rate/Share | Nil | S&P Credit Rating | BBB |
| $10K Invested 5 Yrs Ago | $15,622 | Common Shares Outstg. (M) | 1,050.3 | Institutional Ownership (%) | 56 | | |

## Price Performance

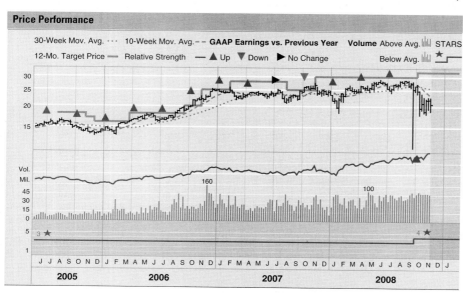

30-Week Mov. Avg. · · · · 10-Week Mov. Avg. – – GAAP Earnings vs. Previous Year Volume Above Avg. ▮▮▮ STARS
12-Mo. Target Price — Relative Strength — ▲ Up ▼ Down ▶ No Change Below Avg. ▮▮▮ ★

Options: ASE, CBOE, P, Ph

Analysis prepared by **Tuna N. Amobi, CFA, CPA** on October 02, 2008, when the stock traded at **$ 25.02.**

## Highlights

➤ We project 2008 gross adds at DTV U.S. near 3.8 million, and near 4.0 million in 2009, mainly driven by the direct sales channel. With a notable reduction in churn after a credit tightening, we expect more than 18.5 million U.S. subscribers by the end of 2009, on net adds of about 900,000 each year. With advanced services driving a projected 6%-7% annual growth in average revenue per U.S. subscriber, combined with continued solid double-digit growth from DTV Latin America and modest advertising revenues, we forecast 15% and 11% total revenue growth for 2008 and 2009, respectively.

➤ We see higher programming costs on the NFL Sunday Ticket, as well as further increases in subscriber acquisition costs (SAC) and retention/upgrade expenses, with an increased penetration of HD DVR services.

➤ Noting a 2007 accounting change under a lease program, we project total 2008 and 2009 EBITDA up nearly 23% and 18%, to more than $5.1 billion and $6.0 billion, respectively. After higher satellite D&A, we forecast EPS of $1.43 and $1.91 in the respective years, with continued share buybacks under a new $3 billion plan.

## Investment Rationale/Risk

➤ We recently upgraded our opinion on the shares to buy from a hold, after a co-branding deal with AT&T (T: strong buy; $28), effective after January 31, 2009. We note DTV now has exclusive pacts with all major telcos which, in recent years, have proven an important channel that offers a vastly incremental marketing base. Separately, we think DTV's encouraging results for the 2008 first half further demonstrate the benefits of a greater mix of higher quality subscribers and a continued aggressive HD deployment. We also note continued strong operating strides at DTV Latin America, and note DTV's ample financial flexibility for buybacks and select acquisitions.

➤ Risks to our recommendation and target price include increased competition from cable operators; high SAC and upgrade/retention expenses; and a sharp economic slowdown.

➤ Our 12-month target price of $32 implies a forward enterprise value per subscriber of about $2,100, deemed ample relative to DISH Network (DISH: hold, $20). DTV recently had about $2.3 billion of foreign net operating carryforward losses, mainly from its Brazilian operations.

## Qualitative Risk Assessment

| LOW | MEDIUM | HIGH |
|---|---|---|

Our risk assessment reflects what we view as ample financial flexibility, and a projected acceleration of free cash flow, offset by increased competition from cable operators' bundled offerings, and uncertainty surrounding a planned change in control.

## Quantitative Evaluations

**S&P Quality Ranking** B-

| D | C | B- | B | B+ | A- | A | A+ |
|---|---|---|---|---|---|---|---|

**Relative Strength Rank** STRONG

71

LOWEST = 1     HIGHEST = 99

## Revenue/Earnings Data

**Revenue (Million $)**

| | 1Q | 2Q | 3Q | 4Q | Year |
|---|---|---|---|---|---|
| 2008 | 4,591 | 4,807 | 4,981 | -- | -- |
| 2007 | 3,908 | 4,135 | 4,327 | 4,876 | 17,246 |
| 2006 | 3,386 | 3,520 | 3,667 | 4,183 | 14,756 |
| 2005 | 3,148 | 3,188 | 3,233 | 3,596 | 13,165 |
| 2004 | 2,493 | 2,643 | 2,862 | 3,362 | 11,360 |
| 2003 | 2,227 | 2,371 | 2,570 | 2,953 | 9,372 |

**Earnings Per Share ($)**

| | | | | | |
|---|---|---|---|---|---|
| 2008 | 0.32 | 0.40 | 0.33 | E0.39 | E1.43 |
| 2007 | 0.27 | 0.36 | 0.27 | 0.30 | 1.19 |
| 2006 | 0.17 | 0.36 | 0.30 | 0.29 | 1.12 |
| 2005 | -0.03 | 0.10 | 0.07 | 0.09 | 0.22 |
| 2004 | 0.13 | -0.01 | -0.67 | -0.20 | -0.77 |
| 2003 | -0.04 | 0.02 | 0.04 | -0.22 | -0.27 |

Fiscal year ended Dec. 31. Next earnings report expected: Mid February. EPS Estimates based on S&P Operating Earnings; historical GAAP earnings are as reported.

## Dividend Data

No cash dividends have been paid since 1997.

---

**Please read the Required Disclosures and Analyst Certification on the last page of this report.**

The McGraw-Hill Companies

# DIRECTV Group Inc (The)

**STANDARD**
**&POOR'S**

## Business Summary October 02, 2008

CORPORATE OVERVIEW. The DIRECTV Group (formerly Hughes Electronics) is a leading provider of direct broadcast satellite (DBS) television service, providing hundreds of digital video and audio channels to more than 17 million monthly subscribers in the U.S., and a selection of local and international programming to nearly 3.5 million subscribers in Latin America (mostly in Brazil, Argentina, Venezuela and Puerto Rico). DTV distributes its services mainly through direct sales and retail channels, and through co-branding partnerships with three of the four RBOCs. In February 2008, as part of a $12 billion swap with News Corp. (NWS: buy, $11; NWS.A: buy, $11), Liberty Media (LINTA: $12) (LCAPA: $12) acquired a 38.4% stake in DTV, subsequently raised to a 49.7% current stake, with Liberty agreeing to limit its stake to 49.7% pursuant to a stand-still pact.

CORPORATE STRATEGY. We see several key strategic initiatives to launch enhanced features and services such as advanced high-definition (HD) and DVR offerings, amid a transition from MPEG-2 to MPEG-4 platform. After a launch of DIRECTV 11 in 2008, we see ample capacity to offer a wide breadth of HD programming. DTV is on track to offer 130 national HD channels by mid-August 2008, and local HD in 121 markets by the end of the year. Other initia-

tives include a new video-on-demand (VOD) offering, broadband video, games, enhanced program guides, home networked DVRs, and portable devices. With NFL Sunday Ticket at the centerpiece of its sports programming offerings, DTV's contract with the pro football league extends through the 2010 season.

In July 2008, DTV acquired 180 Connect Inc., a major installation service provider, which it estimates fulfils 15%-20% of its work orders. In June 2007, DTV and DBS peer DISH Network (DISH: sell; $21) simultaneously unveiled distribution pacts to offer Imax-based wireless high-speed broadband service from Clearwire (CLWR: $10, NR), which in turn will offer their DBS video services, with both DBS companies offering data, video and voice services in CLWR's current and future markets starting in 2007. Earlier, in 2004, the company divested assets such as Hughes Networks Systems and PanAmSat, and separately DTV Latin America emerged from a bankruptcy reorganization.

## Company Financials Fiscal Year Ended Dec. 31

| Per Share Data ($) | 2007 | 2006 | 2005 | 2004 | 2003 | 2002 | 2001 | 2000 | 1999 | 1998 |
|---|---|---|---|---|---|---|---|---|---|---|
| Tangible Book Value | 0.92 | 1.10 | 2.17 | 1.61 | 4.36 | 2.76 | NM | 4.20 | 6.78 | 15.16 |
| Cash Flow | 2.59 | 1.93 | 0.83 | -0.16 | 0.27 | 0.88 | 0.50 | 0.73 | 0.55 | 0.61 |
| Earnings | 1.19 | 1.12 | 0.22 | -0.77 | -0.27 | -0.21 | -0.55 | -0.34 | -0.35 | 0.23 |
| S&P Core Earnings | 1.18 | 1.05 | 0.20 | -0.96 | -0.32 | -0.78 | -0.86 | NA | NA | NA |
| Dividends | Nil | Nil | Nil | Nil | Nil | Nil | Nil | Nil | Nil | Nil |
| Payout Ratio | Nil | Nil | Nil | Nil | Nil | Nil | Nil | Nil | Nil | Nil |
| Prices:High | 27.73 | 25.57 | 17.01 | 18.81 | 16.91 | 17.55 | 28.00 | 46.67 | 32.54 | 19.29 |
| Prices:Low | 20.73 | 13.28 | 13.17 | 14.70 | 9.40 | 8.00 | 11.50 | 21.33 | 12.83 | 10.13 |
| P/E Ratio:High | 23 | 23 | 77 | NM | NM | NM | NM | NM | NM | 85 |
| P/E Ratio:Low | 17 | 12 | 60 | NM | NM | NM | NM | NM | NM | 45 |

| Income Statement Analysis (Million $) | | | | | | | | | | |
|---|---|---|---|---|---|---|---|---|---|---|
| Revenue | 17,246 | 14,756 | 13,165 | 11,360 | 9,372 | 8,935 | 8,262 | 7,288 | 5,560 | 5,964 |
| Operating Income | 4,145 | 3,274 | 1,441 | -1,281 | 617 | 668 | 390 | 594 | 219 | 683 |
| Depreciation | 1,684 | 1,034 | 853 | 838 | 755 | 1,067 | 1,148 | 948 | 647 | 434 |
| Interest Expense | 286 | 246 | 238 | 132 | 156 | 336 | 196 | 218 | 123 | 112 |
| Pretax Income | 2,388 | 542 | 480 | -1,734 | -478 | -140 | -990 | -816 | -660 | 191 |
| Effective Tax Rate | 39.5% | NM | 36.1% | NM | NM | NM | NM | NM | NM | 23.4% |
| Net Income | 1,434 | 1,420 | 305 | -1,056 | -375 | -213 | -614 | -355 | -391 | 260 |
| S&P Core Earnings | 1,410 | 1,336 | 279 | -1,312 | -439 | -862 | -923 | NA | NA | NA |

| Balance Sheet & Other Financial Data (Million $) | | | | | | | | | | |
|---|---|---|---|---|---|---|---|---|---|---|
| Cash | 1,098 | 2,499 | 3,701 | 2,830 | 1,720 | 1,129 | 700 | 1,508 | 238 | 1,342 |
| Current Assets | 3,146 | 4,556 | 6,096 | 4,771 | 10,356 | 3,656 | 3,341 | 4,154 | 3,858 | 3,846 |
| Total Assets | 15,063 | 15,141 | 15,630 | 14,324 | 18,978 | 17,885 | 19,210 | 19,279 | 18,597 | 13,435 |
| Current Liabilities | 3,434 | 3,323 | 2,828 | 2,695 | 5,840 | 3,203 | 4,407 | 2,691 | 2,642 | 2,010 |
| Long Term Debt | 3,347 | 3,395 | 3,405 | 2,410 | 2,435 | 2,390 | 989 | 1,292 | 1,586 | 779 |
| Common Equity | 6,302 | 6,681 | 7,940 | 7,507 | 9,631 | 9,063 | 9,574 | 10,830 | 10,194 | 8,382 |
| Total Capital | 10,227 | 10,138 | 11,395 | 9,965 | 12,305 | 12,590 | 13,339 | 14,941 | 14,501 | 10,286 |
| Capital Expenditures | 2,692 | 1,754 | 889 | 1,023 | 444 | 566 | 799 | 939 | 472 | 344 |
| Cash Flow | 3,118 | 2,455 | 1,158 | -218 | 380 | 808 | 438 | 496 | 205 | 694 |
| Current Ratio | 0.9 | 1.4 | 2.2 | 1.8 | 1.8 | 1.1 | 0.8 | 1.5 | 1.5 | 1.9 |
| % Long Term Debt of Capitalization | 32.7 | 33.5 | 29.9 | 24.2 | 19.8 | 19.0 | 7.4 | 8.6 | 10.9 | 7.6 |
| % Net Income of Revenue | 8.3 | 9.6 | 2.3 | NM | NM | NM | NM | NM | NM | 4.4 |
| % Return on Assets | 9.5 | 9.2 | 2.0 | NM | NM | NM | NM | NM | NM | 2.0 |
| % Return on Equity | 22.1 | 19.4 | 3.9 | NM | NM | NM | NM | NM | NM | 3.1 |

Data as orig reptd.; bef. results of disc opers/spec. items. Per share data adj. for stk. divs.; EPS diluted. E-Estimated. NA-Not Available. NM-Not Meaningful. NR-Not Ranked. UR-Under Review.

**Office:** 2230 E Imperial Hwy, El Segundo, CA 90245-3531.
**Telephone:** 310-964-5000.
**Website:** http://www.directv.com
**Chrmn:** J.C. Malone

**Pres & CEO:** C. Carey
**COO:** M.W. Palkovic
**EVP & CTO:** R. Pontual
**EVP, Secy & General Counsel:** L.D. Hunter

**Investor Contact:** J. Rubin (212-462-5200)
**Board Members:** N. R. Austrian, R. F. Boyd, Jr., C. Carey, M. D. Carleton, J. M. Cornelius, C. R. Lee, P. A. Lund, G. B. Maffei, J. C. Malone, N. S. Newcomb, H. Saban, J. F. Smith, Jr.

**Founded:** 1977
**Domicile:** Delaware
**Employees:** 12,300

*The McGraw-Hill Companies*

# Discover Financial Services Inc

**STANDARD &POOR'S**

| S&P Recommendation HOLD ★★★☆☆ | Price | 12-Mo. Target Price | Investment Style |
|---|---|---|---|
| | $9.47 (as of Nov 14, 2008) | $14.00 | Large-Cap Growth |

**GICS Sector** Financials
**Sub-Industry** Consumer Finance

**Summary** Discover Financial Services is the fourth-largest network and sixth-largest card issuer in the U.S. The company offers credit and prepaid cards and provides payment processing services to merchants and financial institutions.

## Key Stock Statistics (Source S&P, Vickers, company reports)

| | | | | | | | |
|---|---|---|---|---|---|---|---|
| 52-Wk Range | $19.87– 7.52 | S&P Oper. EPS 2008**E** | 1.45 | Market Capitalization(B) | $4.545 | Beta | NA |
| Trailing 12-Month EPS | $0.91 | S&P Oper. EPS 2009**E** | 1.33 | Yield (%) | 2.53 | S&P 3-Yr. Proj. EPS CAGR(%) | -4 |
| Trailing 12-Month P/E | 10.4 | P/E on S&P Oper. EPS 2008**E** | 6.5 | Dividend Rate/Share | $0.24 | S&P Credit Rating | NA |
| $10K Invested 5 Yrs Ago | NA | Common Shares Outstg. (M) | 479.9 | Institutional Ownership (%) | 83 | | |

## Price Performance

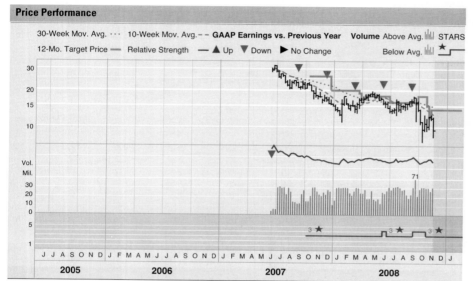

30-Week Mov. Avg. · · · 10-Week Mov. Avg. – – GAAP Earnings vs. Previous Year  Volume Above Avg. STARS
12-Mo. Target Price — Relative Strength — ▲ Up ▼ Down ► No Change   Below Avg.

Options: ASE, CBOE, P

Analysis prepared by **Stuart Plesser** on November 06, 2008, when the stock traded at **$ 11.73**.

## Highlights

▶ We expect average managed credit card loans to increase around 7.0% in FY 09 (Nov.), as DFS should benefit from its cash back programs. Net interest income should grow roughly 10% due to an increase in receivables and a stabilization of the net interest margin. Specifically, we look for a net interest margin of 8.8% in FY 09, versus a projected 8.6% in FY 08. We expect managed revenue to be up 8% in FY 09, to about $6.8 billion.

▶ Although managed chargeoffs were under control in FY 07, in our view, at 4.08%, we expect chargeoffs to rise throughout FY 08 and FY 09 due to the increasing strain on consumers. We forecast chargeoffs will top 6% by the second half of FY 09, and see provisions increasing in the double digits in FY 09 as a result. We expect cost reduction efforts and modifications to DFS's rewards program to gain further traction in FY 09. Thus, we look for expenses to amount to 37% of revenue for FY 09, versus a projected 38% in FY 08.

▶ Based on modest share accretion, we estimate operating EPS of $1.45 in FY 08, versus $1.75 the previous year. For FY 09, we see EPS of $1.33.

## Investment Rationale/Risk

▶ In our view, managed receivables should be able to grow at a solid pace, reflecting DFS's cash back programs. However, higher funding costs, due to relatively high LIBOR rates, will likely weigh on earnings. Although chargeoffs will likely pick up due to higher unemployment levels, we believe they will be manageable due to DFS's more conservative customer base. DFS recently settled a lawsuit against Visa and MasterCard for anticompetitive policies for $2.75 billion. Funds from the settlement should help offset high funding costs associated with a downturn in the securitization market. However, some of these funds may have to be paid out to Morgan Stanley, DFS's former parent, in the form of a special dividend.

▶ Risks to our recommendation and target price include further deterioration in U.S. consumer credit due to rising unemployment.

▶ Our 12-month target price of $14 values the stock at 10.5X our FY 09 EPS estimate. This multiple represents a discount to peers and is at the low end of DFS's historical range.

## Qualitative Risk Assessment

| LOW | MEDIUM | HIGH |
|---|---|---|

Our risk assessment reflects what we see as solid business fundamentals and a growing merchant base, tempered by DFS's exposure to consumer spending habits and the U.S. economy.

## Quantitative Evaluations

**S&P Quality Ranking**   NR

| D | C | B- | B | B+ | A- | A | A+ |
|---|---|---|---|---|---|---|---|

**Relative Strength Rank**   MODERATE

44

LOWEST = 1                    HIGHEST = 99

## Revenue/Earnings Data

**Revenue (Million $)**

| | 1Q | 2Q | 3Q | 4Q | Year |
|---|---|---|---|---|---|
| 2008 | 1,638 | 1,457 | 1,557 | -- | -- |
| 2007 | 1,506 | 1,575 | 1,601 | 1,752 | 6,434 |
| 2006 | -- | -- | -- | -- | 6,211 |
| 2005 | -- | -- | -- | -- | -- |
| 2004 | -- | -- | -- | -- | -- |
| 2003 | -- | -- | -- | -- | -- |

**Earnings Per Share ($)**

| | | | | | |
|---|---|---|---|---|---|
| 2008 | 0.50 | 0.42 | 0.37 | E0.17 | E1.45 |
| 2007 | 0.55 | 0.44 | 0.42 | -0.18 | 1.23 |
| 2006 | -- | 0.72 | 0.51 | 0.39 | 1.89 |
| 2005 | -- | -- | -- | -- | -- |
| 2004 | -- | -- | -- | -- | -- |
| 2003 | -- | -- | -- | -- | -- |

Fiscal year ended Nov. 30. Next earnings report expected: Late December. EPS Estimates based on S&P Operating Earnings; historical GAAP earnings are as reported.

## Dividend Data (Dates: mm/dd Payment Date: mm/dd/yy)

| Amount ($) | Date Decl. | Ex-Div. Date | Stk. of Record | Payment Date |
|---|---|---|---|---|
| 0.060 | 12/20 | 12/31 | 01/03 | 01/22/08 |
| 0.060 | 03/19 | 04/01 | 04/03 | 04/22/08 |
| 0.060 | 06/26 | 06/27 | 07/01 | 07/22/08 |
| 0.060 | 09/16 | 09/29 | 10/01 | 10/22/08 |

Dividends have been paid since 2007. Source: Company reports.

**Please read the Required Disclosures and Analyst Certification on the last page of this report.**

The **McGraw·Hill** Companies

# Discover Financial Services Inc

**STANDARD &POOR'S**

## Business Summary November 06, 2008

CORPORATE OVERVIEW. Discover Financial Services (DFS), formerly a business segment of Morgan Stanley, is a credit card issuer and electronic payment services company. DFS offers credit and prepaid cards and other financial products and services to qualified customers in the United States, and provides payment processing and related services to merchants and financial institutions in the United States. DFS manages its operations through three business segments: U.S. Card, International Card (sold in 2008), and Third-Party Payments. The U.S. Card segment is the major contributor to the company, in terms of income before income taxes. The International Card segment lost money in FY 07 (Nov.), while the Third-Party Payments segment was marginally profitable and continues to comprise a larger portion of DFS's income stream.

The U.S. Card segment offers Discover Card-branded credit cards issued to more than 50 million individuals and small businesses over the Discover Network, which is the company's proprietary credit card network in the United States. The segment also includes DFS's other consumer products and services businesses, including prepaid and other consumer lending and deposit products offered primarily through the company's Discover Bank subsidiary.

The company entered the debit card business in 2006, allowing banks to offer Discover-branded debit cards.

The International Card segment (sold in March 2008) offered consumer finance products and services in the United Kingdom. Its products included Morgan Stanley-branded, Goldfish-branded and various affinity-branded credit cards issued on the MasterCard and Visa networks. The company also has reciprocity alliances with card issuers in Japan (JCB) and China (China Union Pay).

The Third-Party Payments segment includes PULSE and the company's third-party payments business. PULSE, an automated teller machine (ATM), debit and electronic funds transfer network, serves more than 4,400 financial institutions and includes nearly 260,000 ATMs, as well as point-of-sale terminals nationwide.

## Company Financials Fiscal Year Ended Nov. 30

| Per Share Data ($) | 2007 | 2006 | 2005 | 2004 | 2003 | 2002 | 2001 | 2000 | 1999 | 1998 |
|---|---|---|---|---|---|---|---|---|---|---|
| Tangible Book Value | 10.98 | NA | NA | NA | NA | NA | NA | NA | NA | NA |
| Earnings | 1.23 | 1.89 | NA | NA | NA | NA | NA | NA | NA | NA |
| S&P Core Earnings | 1.23 | 2.26 | 1.21 | NA | NA | NA | NA | NA | NA | NA |
| Dividends | 0.06 | Nil | NA | NA | NA | NA | NA | NA | NA | NA |
| Payout Ratio | 5% | NA | NA | NA | NA | NA | NA | NA | NA | NA |
| Prices:High | 32.17 | NA | NA | NA | NA | NA | NA | NA | NA | NA |
| Prices:Low | 14.81 | NA | NA | NA | NA | NA | NA | NA | NA | NA |
| P/E Ratio:High | 26 | NA | NA | NA | NA | NA | NA | NA | NA | NA |
| P/E Ratio:Low | 12 | NA | NA | NA | NA | NA | NA | NA | NA | NA |

| Income Statement Analysis (Million $) | 2007 | 2006 | 2005 | 2004 | 2003 | 2002 | 2001 | 2000 | 1999 | 1998 |
|---|---|---|---|---|---|---|---|---|---|---|
| Net Interest Income | 1,506 | 1,459 | NA | NA | NA | NA | NA | NA | NA | NA |
| Tax Equivalent Adjustment | NA | NA | NA | NA | NA | NA | NA | NA | NA | NA |
| Non Interest Income | 3,546 | 3,539 | NA | NA | NA | NA | NA | NA | NA | NA |
| Loan Loss Provision | 950 | 756 | NA | NA | NA | NA | NA | NA | NA | NA |
| % Expense/Operating Revenue | 49.0% | 55.5% | NA | NA | NA | NA | NA | NA | NA | NA |
| Pretax Income | 945 | 1,467 | 924 | 1,219 | NA | NA | NA | NA | NA | NA |
| Effective Tax Rate | 37.7% | 31.8% | 37.5% | 36.3% | NA | NA | NA | NA | NA | NA |
| Net Income | 589 | 1,001 | 578 | 776 | NA | NA | NA | NA | NA | NA |
| % Net Interest Margin | NA | NA | NA | NA | NA | NA | NA | NA | NA | NA |
| S&P Core Earnings | 587 | 1,078 | 578 | NA | NA | NA | NA | NA | NA | NA |

| Balance Sheet & Other Financial Data (Million $) | 2007 | 2006 | 2005 | 2004 | 2003 | 2002 | 2001 | 2000 | 1999 | 1998 |
|---|---|---|---|---|---|---|---|---|---|---|
| Money Market Assets | 6,270 | Nil | NA | NA | NA | NA | NA | NA | NA | NA |
| Investment Securities | 526 | 86.0 | NA | NA | NA | NA | NA | NA | NA | NA |
| Commercial Loans | 234 | 111 | NA | NA | NA | NA | NA | NA | NA | NA |
| Other Loans | 23,720 | 21,707 | NA | NA | NA | NA | NA | NA | NA | NA |
| Total Assets | 37,376 | 32,403 | 26,944 | NA | NA | NA | NA | NA | NA | NA |
| Demand Deposits | 82.0 | 86.0 | NA | NA | NA | NA | NA | NA | NA | NA |
| Time Deposits | 24,644 | 21,042 | NA | NA | NA | NA | NA | NA | NA | NA |
| Long Term Debt | 2,134 | 1,706 | NA | NA | NA | NA | NA | NA | NA | NA |
| Common Equity | 5,599 | 5,425 | NA | NA | NA | NA | NA | NA | NA | NA |
| % Return on Assets | 1.8 | NM | NA | NA | NA | NA | NA | NA | NA | NA |
| % Return on Equity | 10.4 | NM | NA | NA | NA | NA | NA | NA | NA | NA |
| % Loan Loss Reserve | 3.8 | 3.5 | NA | NA | NA | NA | NA | NA | NA | NA |
| % Loans/Deposits | 96.8 | NM | NA | NA | NA | NA | NA | NA | NA | NA |
| % Equity to Assets | 17.1 | NM | NA | NA | NA | NA | NA | NA | NA | NA |

Data as orig reptd.; bef. results of disc opers/spec. items. Per share data adj. for stk. divs.; EPS diluted. 2006 data pro forma; bal. sheet as of Feb. 28 '07. E-Estimated. NA-Not Available. NM-Not Meaningful. NR-Not Ranked. UR-Under Review.

**Office:** 2500 Lake Cook Road, Riverwoods, IL 60015.
**Telephone:** 224-405-0900.
**Website:** http://www.discover.com
**Chrmn:** D.D. Dammerman

**Pres & COO:** R.C. Hochschild
**CEO:** D.W. Nelms
**EVP & CFO:** R.A. Guthrie
**EVP & CTO:** D.E. Offereins

**Board Members:** J. S. Aronin, M. K. Bush, G. C. Case, D. D. Dammerman, R. M. Devlin, T. G. Maheras, M. H. Moskow, D. W. Nelms, M. L. Rankowitz, E. F. Smith, L. A. Weinbach

**Founded:** 1960
**Domicile:** Delaware
**Employees:** 12,800

**The McGraw-Hill Companies**

# Walt Disney Co (The)

STANDARD &POOR'S

| S&P Recommendation | HOLD ★★★☆☆ | Price | 12-Mo. Target Price | Investment Style |
|---|---|---|---|---|
| | | $21.08 (as of Nov 14, 2008) | $25.00 | Large-Cap Growth |

**GICS Sector** Consumer Discretionary
**Sub-Industry** Movies & Entertainment

**Summary** This media and entertainment conglomerate has diversified global operations in theme parks, motion pictures, and television broadcasting and merchandise licensing.

## Key Stock Statistics (Source S&P, Vickers, company reports)

| | | | | | | | |
|---|---|---|---|---|---|---|---|
| 52-Wk Range | $35.02– 19.58 | S&P Oper. EPS 2009**E** | 2.49 | Market Capitalization(B) | $39.555 | Beta | 0.89 |
| Trailing 12-Month EPS | $2.28 | S&P Oper. EPS 2010**E** | NA | Yield (%) | 1.66 | S&P 3-Yr. Proj. EPS CAGR(%) | 12 |
| Trailing 12-Month P/E | 9.3 | P/E on S&P Oper. EPS 2009**E** | 8.5 | Dividend Rate/Share | $0.35 | S&P Credit Rating | A |
| $10K Invested 5 Yrs Ago | NA | Common Shares Outstg. (M) | 1,876.4 | Institutional Ownership (%) | 66 | | |

## Price Performance

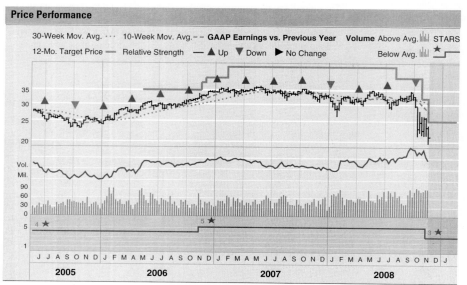

30-Week Mov. Avg. ···  10-Week Mov. Avg. - -  **GAAP Earnings vs. Previous Year**  Volume Above Avg. STARS
12-Mo. Target Price —  Relative Strength —  ▲ Up ▼ Down ▶ No Change  Below Avg.

Options: ASE, CBOE, P, Ph

### Qualitative Risk Assessment

| LOW | MEDIUM | HIGH |
|---|---|---|

Our risk assessment reflects the strength of the company's content-oriented media and entertainment brands, counterbalanced by a relatively high exposure to cyclical advertising-related and theme park businesses.

### Quantitative Evaluations

**S&P Quality Ranking**      A

| D | C | B- | B | B+ | A- | A | A+ |
|---|---|---|---|---|---|---|---|

**Relative Strength Rank**     MODERATE

49

LOWEST = 1       HIGHEST = 99

### Revenue/Earnings Data

**Revenue (Million $)**

| | 1Q | 2Q | 3Q | 4Q | Year |
|---|---|---|---|---|---|
| 2008 | 10,452 | 8,710 | 9,236 | 9,445 | 37,843 |
| 2007 | 9,581 | 7,954 | 9,045 | 8,930 | 35,510 |
| 2006 | 8,854 | 8,027 | 8,620 | 8,784 | 34,285 |
| 2005 | 8,666 | 7,829 | 7,715 | 7,734 | 31,944 |
| 2004 | 8,549 | 7,189 | 7,471 | 7,543 | 30,752 |
| 2003 | 7,170 | 6,500 | 6,377 | 7,014 | 27,061 |

**Earnings Per Share ($)**

| | 1Q | 2Q | 3Q | 4Q | Year |
|---|---|---|---|---|---|
| 2008 | 0.63 | 0.58 | 0.66 | 0.40 | 2.28 |
| 2007 | 0.79 | 0.43 | 0.58 | 0.44 | 2.24 |
| 2006 | 0.37 | 0.37 | 0.53 | 0.36 | 1.64 |
| 2005 | 0.33 | 0.31 | 0.39 | 0.20 | 1.24 |
| 2004 | 0.33 | 0.26 | 0.29 | 0.25 | 1.12 |
| 2003 | 0.06 | 0.15 | 0.24 | 0.20 | 0.65 |

Fiscal year ended Sep. 30. Next earnings report expected: Early February. EPS Estimates based on S&P Operating Earnings; historical GAAP earnings are as reported.

### Dividend Data (Dates: mm/dd Payment Date: mm/dd/yy)

| Amount ($) | Date Decl. | Ex-Div. Date | Stk. of Record | Payment Date |
|---|---|---|---|---|
| 0.350 | 11/28 | 12/05 | 12/07 | 01/11/08 |

Dividends have been paid since 1957. Source: Company reports.

## Highlights

➤ The STARS recommendation for DIS has recently been changed to 3 (hold) from 5 (strong buy) and the 12-month target price has recently been changed to $25.00 from $32.00. The Highlights section of this Stock Report will be updated accordingly.

## Investment Rationale/Risk

➤ The Investment Rationale/Risk section of this Stock Report will be updated shortly. For the latest News story on DIS from MarketScope, see below.

➤ 11/07/08 10:04 am ET ... S&P REDUCES OPINION ON SHARES OF WALT DISNEY CO. TO HOLD FROM STRONG BUY (DIS 21.8***): After $0.03 bad debt charge, Sep-Q EPS of $0.40 on 6% less shares, vs. $0.44, misses S&P and Street estimates by $0.09. Slowdown is starting to weigh on U.S. parks, TV ads (ESPN, ABC), with tough film comps, vs. bright spots in cable (ESPN, Disney Channel), Euro Disney, licensing. In sobering near-term outlook, DIS sees further sharp deterioration in park bookings and ABC/ESPN ads, while halting share buybacks. With likely added N-T challenges for film and North America retail stores, we cut our target price by $7 to $25, on sum-of-the-parts valuation. Dividend yields 1.6%. /T. Amobi - CPA, CFA

---

The McGraw-Hill Companies

# Walt Disney Co (The)

## Business Summary October 21, 2008

CORPORATE OVERVIEW. The Walt Disney Co. is a leading media conglomerate with key operations in theme parks, television, filmed entertainment and merchandise licensing. Theme Parks and Resorts (30% of FY 07 (Sep.) revenues) includes the company's best known assets: Disney World and Disneyland parks in Orlando, FL, and Anaheim, CA, respectively; the Disney Cruise Line; Euro Disney, Paris (39%-owned); and Hong Kong Disneyland (43%-owned).

Media Networks (42% of revenues) includes the ABC broadcast network; 10 television stations; and cable networks ESPN (80%-owned), The Disney Channel, ABC Family and Lifetime (50%). In November 2006, DIS sold its 39.5% stake in the E! cable network to Comcast for $1.23 billion. Studio entertainment (21% of revenues) includes the film, television and home video businesses under the Walt Disney, Touchstone and Miramax brands. Consumer products (6% of revenues) includes merchandise licensing, children's book publishing, video game development, as well as nearly 335 retail stores in North America, and about 104 other stores mainly in Europe.

CORPORATE STRATEGY. As a content-oriented company, DIS's top strategic priorities include creativity and innovation, international expansion, and lever-aging new technology applications. Under CEO Robert Iger, we see senior management aggressively exploring new avenues to offer its branded content, characters and entertainment franchises across emerging digital platforms such as broadband and wireless, while making further investments in other areas such as video games. Recent initiatives include: a deal to provide content from its ABC networks and the film studios on Apple's video iPod, the launch of Disney Mobile cellular phone service, and an ad-supported streaming of ABC's shows.

In April 2008, DIS unveiled a slate of 10 new animated films (from Disney and Pixar) to be released through 2012, and earlier in July 2006, restructured its studio and sharply reduced its annual film (to 10 live-action/animation films plus two to three Touchstone titles), with a focus on Disney-branded films. It has aggressively expanded its Disney Channel in the past few years, and in September 2005, opened Hong Kong Disneyland.

## Company Financials Fiscal Year Ended Sep. 30

| Per Share Data ($) | 2008 | 2007 | 2006 | 2005 | 2004 | 2003 | 2002 | 2001 | 2000 | 1999 |
|---|---|---|---|---|---|---|---|---|---|---|
| Tangible Book Value | NA | 3.15 | 3.10 | 3.24 | 3.15 | 2.01 | 1.78 | 3.99 | 2.24 | 2.59 |
| Cash Flow | NA | 3.08 | 2.40 | 1.93 | 1.69 | 1.17 | 1.11 | 0.89 | 1.48 | 2.22 |
| Earnings | 2.28 | 2.24 | 1.64 | 1.24 | 1.12 | 0.65 | 0.60 | 0.11 | 0.57 | 0.62 |
| S&P Core Earnings | NA | 1.96 | 1.69 | 1.27 | 1.04 | 0.49 | 0.29 | 0.21 | NA | NA |
| Dividends | NA | 0.31 | 0.27 | 0.24 | 0.21 | 0.21 | 0.21 | 0.21 | 0.21 | 0.21 |
| Payout Ratio | NA | 14% | 16% | 19% | 19% | 32% | 35% | 191% | 37% | 34% |
| Prices:High | NA | 36.79 | 34.89 | 29.99 | 28.41 | 23.80 | 25.17 | 34.80 | 43.88 | 38.69 |
| Prices:Low | NA | 30.68 | 23.77 | 22.89 | 20.88 | 14.84 | 13.48 | 15.50 | 26.00 | 23.38 |
| P/E Ratio:High | NA | 16 | 21 | 24 | 25 | 37 | 42 | NM | 77 | 62 |
| P/E Ratio:Low | NA | 14 | 14 | 18 | 19 | 23 | 22 | NM | 46 | 38 |

| Income Statement Analysis (Million $) | | | | | | | | | | |
|---|---|---|---|---|---|---|---|---|---|---|
| Revenue | 37,843 | 35,510 | 34,285 | 31,944 | 30,752 | 27,061 | 25,329 | 25,269 | 25,402 | 23,402 |
| Operating Income | NA | 8,272 | 6,914 | 5,446 | 5,258 | 3,790 | 3,426 | 4,586 | 5,043 | 7,010 |
| Depreciation | 1,582 | 1,491 | 1,436 | 1,339 | 1,210 | 1,077 | 1,042 | 1,754 | 2,195 | 3,323 |
| Interest Expense | NA | 593 | 592 | 605 | 629 | 666 | 453 | 417 | 558 | 717 |
| Pretax Income | 7,402 | 7,725 | 5,447 | 3,987 | 3,739 | 2,254 | 2,190 | 1,283 | 2,633 | 2,314 |
| Effective Tax Rate | 36.1% | 37.2% | 34.7% | 31.1% | 32.0% | 35.0% | 38.9% | 82.5% | 61.0% | 43.8% |
| Net Income | 4,427 | 4,674 | 3,374 | 2,569 | 2,345 | 1,338 | 1,236 | 120 | 920 | 1,300 |
| S&P Core Earnings | NA | 4,074 | 3,479 | 2,635 | 2,201 | 1,006 | 606 | 458 | NA | NA |

| Balance Sheet & Other Financial Data (Million $) | | | | | | | | | | |
|---|---|---|---|---|---|---|---|---|---|---|
| Cash | 3,001 | 3,670 | 2,411 | 1,723 | 2,042 | 1,583 | 1,239 | 618 | 842 | 414 |
| Current Assets | NA | 11,314 | 9,562 | 8,845 | 9,369 | 8,314 | 7,849 | 7,029 | 10,007 | 10,200 |
| Total Assets | 62,497 | 60,928 | 59,998 | 53,158 | 53,902 | 49,988 | 50,045 | 43,699 | 45,027 | 43,679 |
| Current Liabilities | NA | 11,391 | 10,210 | 9,168 | 11,059 | 8,669 | 7,819 | 6,219 | 8,402 | 7,707 |
| Long Term Debt | NA | 11,892 | 10,843 | 10,157 | 9,395 | 10,643 | 12,467 | 8,940 | 6,959 | 9,278 |
| Common Equity | 32,323 | 30,753 | 31,820 | 26,210 | 26,081 | 23,791 | 23,445 | 22,672 | 24,100 | 20,975 |
| Total Capital | NA | 45,218 | 46,657 | 40,045 | 39,224 | 37,574 | 38,943 | 34,724 | 34,248 | 32,913 |
| Capital Expenditures | 1,586 | 1,566 | 1,299 | 1,823 | 1,427 | 1,049 | 1,086 | 1,795 | 2,013 | 2,134 |
| Cash Flow | NA | 6,165 | 4,810 | 3,908 | 3,555 | 2,415 | 2,278 | 1,874 | 3,115 | 4,623 |
| Current Ratio | 1.0 | 1.0 | 0.9 | 1.0 | 0.8 | 1.0 | 1.0 | 1.1 | 1.2 | 1.3 |
| % Long Term Debt of Capitalization | 23.0 | 26.2 | 23.2 | 25.4 | 24.0 | 28.3 | 32.0 | 25.7 | 20.3 | 28.2 |
| % Net Income of Revenue | 11.7 | 13.1 | 9.8 | 8.0 | 7.6 | 4.9 | 4.9 | 0.5 | 3.6 | 5.6 |
| % Return on Assets | 7.2 | 7.7 | 6.0 | 4.8 | 4.5 | 2.7 | 2.6 | 0.3 | 2.1 | 3.1 |
| % Return on Equity | 14.0 | 14.9 | 11.6 | 9.8 | 9.4 | 5.7 | 5.4 | 0.5 | 4.1 | 6.4 |

Data as orig reptd.; bef. results of disc opers/spec. items. Per share data adj. for stk. divs.; EPS diluted. E-Estimated. NA-Not Available. NM-Not Meaningful. NR-Not Ranked. UR-Under Review.

**Office:** 500 South Buena Vista Street, Burbank, CA 91521.
**Telephone:** 818-560-1000.
**Website:** http://www.disney.com
**Chrmn:** J.E. Pepper, Jr.

**Pres & CEO:** R. Iger
**EVP, CFO & Chief Acctg Officer:** T. Staggs
**EVP & Treas:** C.M. McCarthy
**EVP, Secy & General Counsel:** A.N. Braverman

**Investor Contact:** L. Singer
**Board Members:** S. E. Arnold, J. E. Bryson, J. S. Chen, J. L. Estrin, R. Iger, S. P. Jobs, F. H. Langhammer, A. B. Lewis, M. Lozano, R. W. Matschullat, J. E. Pepper, Jr., O. Smith

**Founded:** 1936
**Domicile:** Delaware
**Employees:** 137,000

# Dominion Resources Inc.

**STANDARD &POOR'S**

**S&P Recommendation** BUY ★★★★☆

| | |
|---|---|
| **Price** | **12-Mo. Target Price** | **Investment Style** |
| $36.39 (as of Nov 14, 2008) | $49.00 | Large-Cap Blend |

**GICS Sector** Utilities
**Sub-Industry** Multi-Utilities

**Summary** This energy holding company's principal subsidiaries are Virginia Electric & Power Co. and Consolidated Natural Gas.

## Key Stock Statistics (Source S&P, Vickers, company reports)

| | | | | | | | |
|---|---|---|---|---|---|---|---|
| 52-Wk Range | $49.38– 31.26 | S&P Oper. EPS 2008**E** | 3.15 | Market Capitalization(B) | $21.155 | Beta | 0.32 |
| Trailing 12-Month EPS | $3.08 | S&P Oper. EPS 2009**E** | 3.43 | Yield (%) | 4.34 | S&P 3-Yr. Proj. EPS CAGR(%) | 10 |
| Trailing 12-Month P/E | 11.8 | P/E on S&P Oper. EPS 2008**E** | 11.6 | Dividend Rate/Share | $1.58 | S&P Credit Rating | A- |
| $10K Invested 5 Yrs Ago | $14,338 | Common Shares Outstg. (M) | 581.3 | Institutional Ownership (%) | 60 | | |

## Price Performance

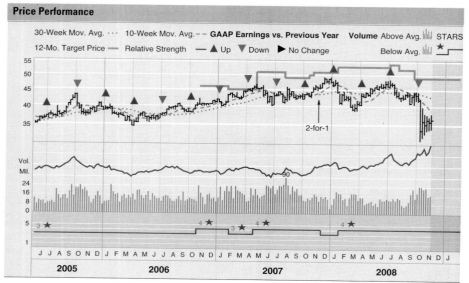

- 30-Week Mov. Avg. ···· 10-Week Mov. Avg. — GAAP Earnings vs. Previous Year  Volume Above Avg. STARS
- 12-Mo. Target Price — Relative Strength — ▲ Up ▼ Down ▶ No Change  Below Avg. ★

2-for-1

Options: ASE, CBOE, P, Ph

Analysis prepared by **Christopher B. Muir** on September 19, 2008, when the stock traded at **$ 43.90.**

### Highlights

► In 2007, D completed transformational transactions by selling a vast majority of its exploration and production (E&P) assets for $14 billion, which will allow the company to focus on its core business of delivering electricity and natural gas. The asset sales have already funded substantial share repurchases, debt reductions and an announced increase in the dividend. We believe that continued share repurchases are likely over the coming year.

► We think revenues will decrease 2.0% in 2008, due to the absence of exploration and production revenues. We expect operating margins to widen in 2008 on lower per-revenue depreciation expense. We see 2009 revenues rising 4.3%, with a continued increase in operating margins. We look for interest costs to decline dramatically in 2008 and 2009 as D reduces debt with cash from the asset sales, but we see lower non-operating income.

► Assuming an effective tax rate of 36.9%, our 2008 operating EPS estimate is $3.15, up 22% from 2007's $2.58. Our 2009 operating EPS forecast is $3.43, an increase of 8.9%.

### Investment Rationale/Risk

► We view the company's recently completed sale of its E&P assets as positive, allowing it to focus on its core businesses. We also view the recently agreed-to sale, pending approvals, of its Pennsylvania and West Virginia utility businesses positively. The reset of rates in Virginia in 2007 should help offset the impact of higher fuel costs. We think D's announced target of a 55% payout ratio by 2010 will support double-digit dividend increases over the next two years. We view positively the company's commitment to sell its international energy-related operations.

► Risks to our recommendation and target price include potential delays or cost overruns related to development projects; a sharp decline in natural gas prices; sharply higher interest rates; and a weaker economy.

► The stock recently traded at about 12.6X our 2009 EPS estimate, a 4% premium to its multi-utility peers. Our 12-month target price of $49 is 14.3X our 2009 EPS estimate, close to even with our peer target, which we think is justified by slightly above peer-average dividend and EPS growth.

## Qualitative Risk Assessment

| LOW | MEDIUM | HIGH |
|---|---|---|

Our risk assessment reflects our view of Dominion's relatively large capitalization and balanced sources of earnings, which include low-risk regulated electric and gas distribution and pipeline operations, offset by higher-risk exploration and production and energy marketing businesses.

## Quantitative Evaluations

**S&P Quality Ranking**  B+

| D | C | B- | B | B+ | A- | A | A+ |
|---|---|---|---|---|---|---|---|

**Relative Strength Rank**  **STRONG**

80

LOWEST = 1   HIGHEST = 99

## Revenue/Earnings Data

**Revenue (Million $)**

| | 1Q | 2Q | 3Q | 4Q | Year |
|---|---|---|---|---|---|
| 2008 | 4,389 | 3,452 | 4,231 | -- | -- |
| 2007 | 4,661 | 3,730 | 3,589 | 3,694 | 15,674 |
| 2006 | 4,951 | 3,548 | 4,016 | 3,967 | 16,482 |
| 2005 | 4,736 | 3,646 | 4,564 | 5,095 | 18,041 |
| 2004 | 3,879 | 3,040 | 3,292 | 3,761 | 13,972 |
| 2003 | 3,579 | 2,630 | 2,853 | 3,016 | 12,078 |

**Earnings Per Share ($)**

| | | | | | |
|---|---|---|---|---|---|
| 2008 | 1.18 | 0.52 | 0.87 | E0.64 | E3.15 |
| 2007 | 0.68 | -0.56 | 3.63 | 0.52 | 4.13 |
| 2006 | 0.78 | 0.24 | 0.93 | 0.28 | 2.23 |
| 2005 | 0.63 | 0.49 | 0.02 | 0.38 | 1.50 |
| 2004 | 0.68 | 0.40 | 0.51 | 0.34 | 1.91 |
| 2003 | 0.66 | 0.39 | 0.51 | -0.05 | 1.49 |

Fiscal year ended Dec. 31. Next earnings report expected: Late January. EPS Estimates based on S&P Operating Earnings; historical GAAP earnings are as reported.

## Dividend Data (Dates: mm/dd Payment Date: mm/dd/yy)

| Amount ($) | Date Decl. | Ex-Div. Date | Stk. of Record | Payment Date |
|---|---|---|---|---|
| 0.395 | 01/25 | 02/27 | 02/29 | 03/20/08 |
| 0.395 | 05/09 | 05/28 | 05/30 | 06/20/08 |
| 0.395 | 08/07 | 08/27 | 08/29 | 09/20/08 |
| 0.395 | 10/24 | 11/26 | 12/01 | 12/20/08 |

Dividends have been paid since 1925. Source: Company reports.

*The McGraw-Hill Companies*

# Dominion Resources Inc.

## Business Summary September 19, 2008

CORPORATE OVERVIEW. D is a fully integrated gas and electric holding company. The company operates in three primary segments: Virginia Power, Energy, and Generation. The Virginia Power segment (22.3% of 2007 operating segment revenue) operates regulated electric transmission and distribution business in Virginia and northeastern North Carolina. The Energy segment (16.0%) operates a regulated natural gas distribution company in Ohio, regulated gas transmission pipeline and storage operations, regulated LNG operations, and the natural gas E&P business, which supports the company's gas distribution business. The Energy segment also includes a producer services business, which aggregates gas supply, provides gas transportation and storage market-based services and engages in associated gas trading and marketing. The Generation segment (61.7%) is involved in generation for the electric utility and merchant power along with energy marketing and risk management activities.

CORPORATE STRATEGY. D focuses its efforts mainly on the Northeast, Mid-Atlantic and Midwest regions of the U.S. As part of a strategy to concentrate on expanding its core businesses in the above-mentioned markets, D is committed to divesting all of its energy-related operations outside the U.S. D believes that focusing on its core businesses will reduce earnings volatility and help to grow EPS 4% to 5% per year. It has a proactive risk management strategy, and has entered into commodity derivative agreements to hedge against commodity price risks.

MARKET PROFILE. As of December 31, 2007, D had total power generation capacity of 26,555 MW, with 15,723 MW of utility generation, 2,076 MY of utility power purchase agreements, and 8,756 MW of merchant generation. The former Delivery segment served a total of 2.36 million electric customers. The Energy segment serves 1.70 million gas utility customers in Ohio and has about 14,000 miles of interstate natural gas transmission, gathering storage pipelines, 975 bcf of storage capacity, and 1.1 trillion cubic feet equivalent of proved gas and oil reserves. This division also operates a liquefied natural gas (LNG) terminal at Cove Point, MD.

## Company Financials Fiscal Year Ended Dec. 31

| Per Share Data ($) | 2007 | 2006 | 2005 | 2004 | 2003 | 2002 | 2001 | 2000 | 1999 | 1998 |
|---|---|---|---|---|---|---|---|---|---|---|
| Tangible Book Value | 9.21 | 11.45 | 8.79 | 16.37 | 9.60 | 9.09 | 7.85 | 7.10 | 12.40 | 13.28 |
| Earnings | 4.13 | 2.22 | 1.50 | 1.91 | 1.49 | 2.41 | 1.08 | 0.88 | 1.41 | 1.38 |
| S&P Core Earnings | 0.46 | 2.21 | 1.47 | 1.90 | 1.58 | 1.92 | 0.66 | NA | NA | NA |
| Dividends | 2.25 | 0.35 | 1.34 | 1.30 | 1.29 | 1.29 | 1.29 | 1.29 | 1.29 | 1.29 |
| Payout Ratio | 54% | 16% | 89% | 68% | 87% | 54% | 120% | 147% | 92% | 94% |
| Prices:High | 49.38 | 42.22 | 43.49 | 34.43 | 32.97 | 33.53 | 35.00 | 33.97 | 24.69 | 24.47 |
| Prices:Low | 39.84 | 34.36 | 33.26 | 30.39 | 25.87 | 17.70 | 27.57 | 17.41 | 18.28 | 18.91 |
| P/E Ratio:High | 12 | 19 | 29 | 18 | 22 | 14 | 33 | 39 | 18 | 18 |
| P/E Ratio:Low | 10 | 15 | 22 | 16 | 17 | 7 | 26 | 20 | 13 | 14 |

| Income Statement Analysis (Million $) | | | | | | | | | | |
|---|---|---|---|---|---|---|---|---|---|---|
| Revenue | 15,674 | 16,482 | 18,041 | 13,972 | 12,078 | 10,218 | 10,558 | 9,260 | 5,520 | 6,086 |
| Depreciation | 1,368 | 1,606 | 1,412 | 1,305 | 1,216 | 1,258 | 1,245 | 1,176 | 716 | 734 |
| Maintenance | NA | NA | NA | NA | NA | NA | NA | NA | NA | NA |
| Fixed Charges Coverage | 4.82 | 3.42 | 2.63 | 3.09 | 2.63 | 3.15 | 2.02 | 1.99 | 2.44 | 1.83 |
| Construction Credits | Nil | Nil | Nil | Nil | Nil | Nil | Nil | Nil | Nil | Nil |
| Effective Tax Rate | 39.5% | 37.0% | 36.0% | 35.6% | 38.6% | 33.3% | 40.5% | 30.5% | 31.3% | 35.2% |
| Net Income | 2,705 | 1,563 | 1,034 | 1,264 | 949 | 1,362 | 544 | 415 | 551 | 536 |
| S&P Core Earnings | 295 | 1,555 | 1,010 | 1,254 | 1,004 | 1,088 | 331 | NA | NA | NA |

| Balance Sheet & Other Financial Data (Million $) | | | | | | | | | | |
|---|---|---|---|---|---|---|---|---|---|---|
| Gross Property | 33,331 | 43,575 | 42,063 | 38,663 | 37,107 | 32,631 | 33,105 | 31,011 | 18,646 | 18,106 |
| Capital Expenditures | 3,972 | 4,052 | 1,683 | 1,451 | 2,138 | 2,828 | 1,224 | 1,385 | 737 | 755 |
| Net Property | 21,352 | 29,382 | 28,940 | 26,716 | 25,850 | 20,257 | 18,681 | 14,849 | 10,764 | 10,637 |
| Capitalization:Long Term Debt | 13,492 | 15,048 | 14,910 | 15,764 | 16,033 | 13,714 | 12,119 | 10,486 | 7,321 | 5,071 |
| Capitalization:% Long Term Debt | 58.9 | 53.8 | 58.9 | 58.0 | 60.3 | 57.3 | 58.1 | 58.3 | 58.2 | 44.2 |
| Capitalization:Preferred | Nil | Nil | Nil | Nil | Nil | Nil | Nil | 509 | 509 | 1,074 |
| Capitalization:% Preferred | Nil | Nil | Nil | Nil | Nil | Nil | Nil | 2.83 | 4.05 | 9.40 |
| Capitalization:Common | 9,406 | 12,913 | 10,397 | 11,426 | 10,538 | 10,213 | 8,368 | 6,992 | 4,752 | 5,315 |
| Capitalization:% Common | 41.1 | 46.2 | 41.1 | 42.0 | 39.7 | 42.7 | 40.1 | 38.9 | 37.8 | 46.4 |
| Total Capital | 27,179 | 33,842 | 30,291 | 32,689 | 31,134 | 28,136 | 24,811 | 20,955 | 14,427 | 13,475 |
| % Operating Ratio | 75.9 | 85.3 | 89.7 | 85.6 | 83.7 | 78.5 | 85.6 | 80.5 | 80.9 | 64.4 |
| % Earned on Net Property | 21.9 | 11.5 | 8.8 | 10.3 | 10.6 | 21.4 | 10.6 | 11.9 | 9.7 | 9.4 |
| % Return on Revenue | 17.3 | 9.5 | 5.7 | 9.0 | 7.9 | 13.3 | 5.2 | 4.5 | 10.0 | 8.8 |
| % Return on Invested Capital | 12.7 | 8.1 | 6.4 | 6.5 | 6.5 | 8.5 | 7.2 | 10.7 | 7.9 | 8.4 |
| % Return on Common Equity | 24.2 | 13.4 | 9.5 | 11.5 | 9.1 | 14.7 | 7.1 | 7.1 | 10.9 | 10.4 |

Data as orig reptd.; bef. results of disc opers/spec. items. Per share data adj. for stk. divs.; EPS diluted. E-Estimated. NA-Not Available. NM-Not Meaningful. NR-Not Ranked. UR-Under Review.

**Office:** 120 Tredegar Street, Richmond, VA 23219.
**Telephone:** 804-819-2000.
**Email:** investor_relations@domres.com
**Website:** http://www.dom.com

**Chrmn, Pres & CEO:** T.F. Farrell, II
**EVP & CFO:** T.N. Chewning
**SVP & Chief Acctg Officer:** T.P. Wohlfarth
**SVP & Treas:** G.S. Hetzer

**SVP & General Counsel:** J.F. Stutts
**Investor Contact:** J. O'Hare (804-819-2156)
**Board Members:** P. W. Brown, G. A. Davidson, Jr., T. F. Farrell, II, J. Harris, R. S. Jepson, Jr., M. J. Kington, B. J. Lambert, III, M. A. McKenna, F. S. Royal, D. A. Wollard

**Founded:** 1909
**Domicile:** Virginia
**Employees:** 17,000

# R.R. Donnelley & Sons Co

**STANDARD &POOR'S**

| S&P Recommendation HOLD ★★★☆☆ | Price $12.47 (as of Nov 14, 2008) | 12-Mo. Target Price $21.00 | Investment Style Large-Cap Value |
|---|---|---|---|

**GICS Sector** Industrials
**Sub-Industry** Commercial Printing

**Summary** R.R. Donnelley, the largest U.S. commercial printer, specializes in the production of catalogs, inserts, magazines, books, directories, and financial and computer documentation.

## Key Stock Statistics (Source S&P, Vickers, company reports)

| | | | | | | | |
|---|---|---|---|---|---|---|---|
| 52-Wk Range | $39.02–11.81 | S&P Oper. EPS 2008**E** | 3.00 | Market Capitalization(B) | $2.556 | Beta | 1.50 |
| Trailing 12-Month EPS | $0.96 | S&P Oper. EPS 2009**E** | 2.90 | Yield (%) | 8.34 | S&P 3-Yr. Proj. EPS CAGR(%) | NM |
| Trailing 12-Month P/E | 13.0 | P/E on S&P Oper. EPS 2008**E** | 4.2 | Dividend Rate/Share | $1.04 | S&P Credit Rating | BBB+ |
| $10K Invested 5 Yrs Ago | $5,207 | Common Shares Outstg. (M) | 205.0 | Institutional Ownership (%) | 89 | | |

## Price Performance

30-Week Mov. Avg. · · · 10-Week Mov. Avg. – – **GAAP Earnings vs. Previous Year** Volume Above Avg. ▫▫▫ STARS
12-Mo. Target Price — Relative Strength — ▲ Up ▼ Down ▶ No Change Below Avg. ▫▫▫ ★

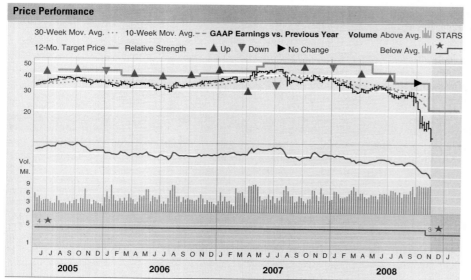

Options: CBOE, P, Ph

Analysis prepared by **Adrian Compton** on November 12, 2008, when the stock traded at **$13.07.**

### Highlights

➤ For 2008, we forecast revenue growth of about 6%, with contributions from the recent acquisitions of Cardinal Brands, Pro Line Printing, Banta, Perry-Judd's, and Von Hoffman. We forecast a revenue decline of about 5% in 2009, reflecting the recessionary economies of the U.S. (77% of 2007 revenues) and Europe (14% of 2007 revenues), RRD's main end-markets. We also foresee more unfavorable foreign exchange comparisons affecting EPS through 2009.

➤ Before restructuring, impairment and acquisition charges, we expect operating margins to widen in 2009, benefiting from operating leverage generated through revenue growth, reduced energy costs, as well as continued productivity advances and cost synergies, as RRD integrates its 2007 acquisitions. We expect these factors to be somewhat offset by pricing pressure and increased paper costs.

➤ After expected higher interest payments and a likely decrease in the effective tax rate, we see 2008 operating EPS of $3.00, versus $2.94 for 2007, before one-time items. We project EPS of $2.90 in 2009 on declining revenues.

### Investment Rationale/Risk

➤ We expect RRD to continue to gain market share by leveraging its geographic and product breadth, and we expect the company to benefit from its low cost operating structure. We believe the company will be able to post ongoing moderate EPS gains in 2008 before a decline in 2009. We think the company will continue to pursue selective acquisitions, as it aims to expand its global reach and further increase its operating leverage.

➤ Risks to our recommendation and target price include acquisition integration problems, substantially higher input costs, a prolonged economic downturn in the company's end-markets, and a greater than expected increase in the amount of information disseminated electronically.

➤ Using our DCF valuation, assuming a 6% increase in revenue in 2008, then declining about 5% in 2009, perpetuity cash flow growth of 2.5%, and a WACC of 9.1%, we calculate intrinsic value of about $21, about 7.2X our 2009 EPS estimate.

## Qualitative Risk Assessment

| LOW | MEDIUM | HIGH |
|---|---|---|

Our risk assessment reflects economies of scale that the company realizes as the largest U.S. commercial printer in a fragmented print industry, offset by industry pricing pressure and the increasingly electronic nature of communication.

## Quantitative Evaluations

**S&P Quality Ranking**      B-

| D | C | B- | B | B+ | A- | A | A+ |
|---|---|---|---|---|---|---|---|

**Relative Strength Rank**      WEAK

24

LOWEST = 1      HIGHEST = 99

## Revenue/Earnings Data

**Revenue (Million $)**

| | 1Q | 2Q | 3Q | 4Q | Year |
|---|---|---|---|---|---|
| 2008 | 2,997 | 2,924 | 2,865 | -- | -- |
| 2007 | 2,793 | 2,796 | 2,910 | 3,088 | 11,587 |
| 2006 | 2,267 | 2,274 | 2,309 | 2,467 | 9,317 |
| 2005 | 1,927 | 1,932 | 2,184 | 2,388 | 8,430 |
| 2004 | 1,289 | 1,843 | 1,913 | 2,112 | 7,156 |
| 2003 | 1,074 | 1,142 | 1,194 | 1,377 | 4,787 |

**Earnings Per Share ($)**

| | 1Q | 2Q | 3Q | 4Q | Year |
|---|---|---|---|---|---|
| 2008 | 0.85 | 0.68 | 0.80 | E0.70 | E3.00 |
| 2007 | 0.63 | -0.32 | 0.80 | -1.37 | -0.22 |
| 2006 | 0.52 | 0.57 | 0.75 | -0.01 | 1.84 |
| 2005 | 0.50 | 0.44 | 0.59 | -1.09 | 0.44 |
| 2004 | -0.35 | -0.06 | 0.52 | 0.61 | 0.88 |
| 2003 | 0.05 | 0.17 | 0.47 | 0.85 | 1.54 |

Fiscal year ended Dec. 31. Next earnings report expected: Late February. EPS Estimates based on S&P Operating Earnings; historical GAAP earnings are as reported.

## Dividend Data (Dates: mm/dd Payment Date: mm/dd/yy)

| Amount ($) | Date Decl. | Ex-Div. Date | Stk. of Record | Payment Date |
|---|---|---|---|---|
| 0.260 | 01/10 | 01/23 | 01/25 | 03/03/08 |
| 0.260 | 04/02 | 04/15 | 04/17 | 06/02/08 |
| 0.260 | 07/23 | 08/05 | 08/07 | 09/02/08 |
| 0.260 | 10/29 | 11/10 | 11/13 | 12/01/08 |

Dividends have been paid since 1911. Source: Company reports.

# R.R. Donnelley & Sons Co

STANDARD
&POOR'S

## Business Summary November 12, 2008

CORPORATE OVERVIEW. RRD is the largest printing company in North America, serving customers in the publishing, health care, advertising, retail, telecommunications, technology, financial services and other industries. The company provides solutions in long- and short-run commercial printing, direct mail, financial printing, print fulfillment, forms and labels, logistics, digital printing, call centers, transactional print-and-mail, print management, online services, digital photography, color services, and content and database management. Geographically, the company derives the majority of its revenues from the U.S. (74% of 2007 revenues), with international accounting for about 26%.

The company has two reportable segments: U.S. Print and Related Services, and International. R.R. Donnelly management changed its reportable segments in the third quarter of 2007 to reflect changes in management reporting structure and the manner in which management assesses information for decision-making purposes.

The U.S. Print and Related Services segment (74% of revenues in 2007) consists of the following U.S. businesses: magazine, catalog and retail, which includes print services to consumer magazine and catalog publishers as well as retailers; book, which serves the consumer, religious, educational and specialty book and telecommunications sectors; directories, which serves the printing needs of yellow and white pages directory publishers; logistics, which delivers company and third-party printed products and distributes time-sensitive and secure material, and performs warehousing and fulfillment services; direct mail, which offers content creation, database management, printing, personalization finishing and distribution services to direct marketing companies; financial print; direct mail; and short-run commercial print, which provides print and print related services to a diversified customer base.

## Company Financials Fiscal Year Ended Dec. 31

| Per Share Data ($) | 2007 | 2006 | 2005 | 2004 | 2003 | 2002 | 2001 | 2000 | 1999 | 1998 |
|---|---|---|---|---|---|---|---|---|---|---|
| Tangible Book Value | NM | 0.54 | NM | 3.81 | 5.14 | 4.51 | 3.92 | 5.89 | 6.01 | 6.85 |
| Cash Flow | 2.52 | 3.96 | 2.40 | 5.07 | 4.43 | 4.32 | 3.41 | 5.34 | 5.29 | 4.66 |
| Earnings | -0.22 | 1.84 | 0.44 | 0.88 | 1.54 | 1.24 | 0.21 | 2.17 | 2.40 | 2.08 |
| S&P Core Earnings | 1.48 | 1.97 | 1.27 | 1.20 | 1.18 | 0.18 | -0.65 | NA | NA | NA |
| Dividends | 1.04 | 1.04 | 1.04 | 1.04 | 1.02 | 0.98 | 0.94 | 0.90 | 0.86 | 0.82 |
| Payout Ratio | NM | 57% | NM | 118% | 66% | 79% | NM | 41% | 36% | 39% |
| Prices:High | 45.25 | 36.00 | 38.27 | 35.37 | 30.15 | 32.10 | 31.90 | 27.50 | 44.75 | 48.00 |
| Prices:Low | 32.59 | 28.50 | 29.54 | 27.62 | 16.94 | 18.50 | 24.30 | 19.00 | 21.50 | 33.75 |
| P/E Ratio:High | NM | 20 | 87 | 40 | 20 | 26 | NM | 13 | 19 | 23 |
| P/E Ratio:Low | NM | 15 | 67 | 31 | 11 | 15 | NM | 9 | 9 | 16 |

| Income Statement Analysis (Million $) | 2007 | 2006 | 2005 | 2004 | 2003 | 2002 | 2001 | 2000 | 1999 | 1998 |
|---|---|---|---|---|---|---|---|---|---|---|
| Revenue | 11,587 | 9,317 | 8,430 | 7,156 | 4,787 | 4,755 | 5,298 | 5,764 | 5,183 | 5,018 |
| Operating Income | 1,752 | 1,420 | 1,295 | 952 | 617 | 686 | 722 | 891 | 905 | 856 |
| Depreciation | 598 | 463 | 425 | 771 | 329 | 352 | 379 | 390 | 374 | 367 |
| Interest Expense | 231 | 139 | 111 | 85.9 | 50.4 | 62.8 | 71.2 | 89.6 | 88.2 | 78.0 |
| Pretax Income | 91.4 | 601 | 332 | 357 | 208 | 176 | 74.9 | 434 | 507 | 510 |
| Effective Tax Rate | NM | 32.6% | 71.5% | 26.0% | 15.3% | 19.1% | 66.6% | 38.5% | 38.5% | 42.2% |
| Net Income | -48.4 | 403 | 95.6 | 265 | 177 | 142 | 25.0 | 267 | 312 | 295 |
| S&P Core Earnings | 322 | 430 | 275 | 243 | 136 | 21.3 | -78.3 | NA | NA | NA |

| Balance Sheet & Other Financial Data (Million $) | 2007 | 2006 | 2005 | 2004 | 2003 | 2002 | 2001 | 2000 | 1999 | 1998 |
|---|---|---|---|---|---|---|---|---|---|---|
| Cash | 443 | 211 | 367 | 642 | 60.8 | 60.5 | 48.6 | 60.9 | 41.9 | 66.0 |
| Current Assets | 3,521 | 2,517 | 2,622 | 2,601 | 1,000 | 866 | 940 | 1,206 | 1,230 | 1,145 |
| Total Assets | 12,087 | 9,636 | 9,374 | 8,554 | 3,189 | 3,152 | 3,400 | 3,914 | 3,853 | 3,788 |
| Current Liabilities | 2,765 | 1,612 | 1,814 | 1,487 | 884 | 955 | 984 | 1,191 | 1,203 | 898 |
| Long Term Debt | 3,602 | 2,359 | 2,365 | 1,581 | 752 | 753 | 881 | 739 | 748 | 999 |
| Common Equity | 3,907 | 4,125 | 3,724 | 3,987 | 983 | 882 | 915 | 1,233 | 1,138 | 1,301 |
| Total Capital | 8,382 | 7,087 | 6,686 | 6,144 | 1,970 | 1,882 | 1,982 | 2,205 | 2,140 | 2,585 |
| Capital Expenditures | 482 | 374 | 471 | 265 | 203 | 242 | 273 | 237 | 276 | 225 |
| Cash Flow | 550 | 866 | 521 | 1,036 | 506 | 495 | 404 | 657 | 686 | 662 |
| Current Ratio | 1.3 | 1.6 | 1.4 | 1.7 | 1.1 | 0.9 | 1.0 | 1.0 | 1.0 | 1.3 |
| % Long Term Debt of Capitalization | 43.0 | 33.3 | 35.4 | 25.7 | 38.2 | 40.0 | 44.5 | 33.5 | 35.0 | 38.6 |
| % Net Income of Revenue | NM | 4.3 | 1.1 | 3.7 | 3.7 | 3.0 | 0.5 | 4.6 | 6.0 | 5.9 |
| % Return on Assets | NM | 4.2 | 1.1 | 4.5 | 5.5 | 4.4 | 0.7 | 6.9 | 8.1 | 7.4 |
| % Return on Equity | NM | 10.3 | 2.5 | 10.7 | 18.6 | 15.8 | 2.4 | 22.5 | 25.5 | 20.4 |

Data as orig reptd.; bef. results of disc opers/spec. items. Per share data adj. for stk. divs.; EPS diluted. E-Estimated. NA-Not Available. NM-Not Meaningful. NR-Not Ranked. UR-Under Review.

**Office:** 111 S Wacker Dr, Chicago, IL 60606-4302.
**Telephone:** 312-326-8000.
**Email:** investor.info@rrd.com
**Website:** http://www.rrdonnelley.com

**Chrmn:** S.M. Wolf
**Pres & CEO:** T.J. Quinlan, III
**COO:** J. Paloian
**EVP, Secy & General Counsel:** S.S. Bettman

**SVP, Chief Acctg Officer & Cntlr:** A.B. Coxhead
**Investor Contact:** M. McHugh (866-425-8272)
**Board Members:** L. A. Chaden, E. V. Goings, J. Hamilton, T. S. Johnson, J. C. Pope, T. J. Quinlan, III, M. T. Riordan, O. R. Sockwell, Jr., S. M. Wolf

**Founded:** 1864
**Domicile:** Delaware
**Employees:** 65,000

The McGraw·Hill Companies

# Dover Corp

**STANDARD &POOR'S**

**S&P Recommendation** HOLD ★★★☆☆

| | | |
|---|---|---|
| **Price** | **12-Mo. Target Price** | **Investment Style** |
| $29.21 (as of Nov 14, 2008) | $35.00 | Large-Cap Growth |

**GICS Sector** Industrials
**Sub-Industry** Industrial Machinery

**Summary** This company manufactures a broad range of specialized industrial products and sophisticated manufacturing equipment.

## Key Stock Statistics (Source S&P, Vickers, company reports)

| | | | | | | | |
|---|---|---|---|---|---|---|---|
| 52-Wk Range | $54.57– 25.21 | S&P Oper. EPS 2008**E** | 3.69 | Market Capitalization(B) | $5.432 | Beta | 1.35 |
| Trailing 12-Month EPS | $3.41 | S&P Oper. EPS 2009**E** | 3.61 | Yield (%) | 3.42 | S&P 3-Yr. Proj. EPS CAGR(%) | 11 |
| Trailing 12-Month P/E | 8.6 | P/E on S&P Oper. EPS 2008**E** | 7.9 | Dividend Rate/Share | $1.00 | S&P Credit Rating | A |
| $10K Invested 5 Yrs Ago | $8,215 | Common Shares Outstg. (M) | 186.0 | Institutional Ownership (%) | 87 | | |

## Price Performance

- 30-Week Mov. Avg. ···· 10-Week Mov. Avg. ─ **GAAP Earnings vs. Previous Year** Volume Above Avg. ▮▮ STARS
- 12-Mo. Target Price ─ Relative Strength ─ ▲ Up ▼ Down ▶ No Change  Below Avg. ▮▮ ★

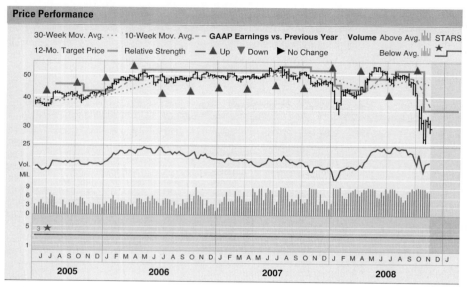

Options: CBOE, P, Ph

Analysis prepared by **Mathew Christy, CFA** on October 28, 2008, when the stock traded at **$ 29.78**.

## Highlights

➤ We believe revenues will increase about 6% in 2008 and 1% in 2009. We see 2% organic growth in 2008, with the balance from recent acquisition contributions, price increases and currency translation. We expect most of the revenue gains to come from strength in the Fluid Management segment, which is heavily involved in the oil and gas industries, and we project revenue growth of 17% in 2008 and 8.5% in 2009 for this unit. We believe the remainder of Dover's businesses, which are weighted towards construction, transportation, electronics, and general industrial, will experience declining organic sales growth offset somewhat by acquisitions.

➤ In our opinion, greater operating leverage, capacity utilization, price increases, and business mix should help expand gross margins this year. However, this is based on stronger results during the first nine months of 2008, as we expect the effects of a slowing economy to negatively effect pricing and product mix later in the year.

➤ On a modestly lower effective tax rate, we project operating EPS of $3.69 in 2008 and $3.61 in 2009.

## Investment Rationale/Risk

➤ We believe DOV continues to improve its ability to generate strong free cash flow as it improves the quality of business within its portfolio. As a result of discontinuing 20 low-margin, capital-intensive businesses over the past two years, and replacing them with 17 new steady-growth, high-margin units, we expect that DOV will drive both top- and bottom-line growth, translating into steady free cash flow and dividend payments. Nevertheless, given increased macroeconomic risk, we believe the shares are appropriately valued at recent levels.

➤ Risks to our recommendation and target price include weaker-than-expected global economic growth, softer industrial, energy and electronics markets, potential value-diminishing acquisitions, and a protracted search for a new CEO.

➤ Our 12-month target price of $35 represents a blend of valuation metrics. Our discounted cash flow model, which assumes a 3% perpetual growth rate and a 10.4% discount rate, indicates intrinsic value of $39. For our relative valuation, we apply an EV/EBITDA multiple of 5.4X, in line with peers, to our 2009 EBITDA projection, implying a value of $30.

## Qualitative Risk Assessment

| LOW | MEDIUM | **HIGH** |
|---|---|---|

Our risk assessment reflects the company's acquisition strategy, its model of operating numerous different businesses as stand-alone entities, and its exposure to several cyclical end markets.

## Quantitative Evaluations

**S&P Quality Ranking**  A-

| D | C | B- | B | B+ | **A-** | A | A+ |
|---|---|---|---|---|---|---|---|

**Relative Strength Rank**  **MODERATE**

52

LOWEST = 1    HIGHEST = 99

## Revenue/Earnings Data

**Revenue (Million $)**

| | 1Q | 2Q | 3Q | 4Q | Year |
|---|---|---|---|---|---|
| 2008 | 1,855 | 2,011 | 1,966 | -- | -- |
| 2007 | 1,780 | 1,859 | 1,844 | 1,860 | 7,226 |
| 2006 | 1,500 | 1,650 | 1,647 | 1,715 | 6,512 |
| 2005 | 1,383 | 1,525 | 1,556 | 1,614 | 6,078 |
| 2004 | 1,242 | 1,380 | 1,444 | 1,421 | 5,488 |
| 2003 | 1,028 | 1,124 | 1,154 | 1,198 | 4,413 |

**Earnings Per Share ($)**

| | | | | | |
|---|---|---|---|---|---|
| 2008 | 0.76 | 0.98 | 1.01 | E0.94 | E3.69 |
| 2007 | 0.67 | 0.85 | 0.88 | 0.86 | 3.22 |
| 2006 | 0.64 | 0.77 | 0.77 | 0.76 | 2.94 |
| 2005 | 0.47 | 0.59 | 0.65 | 0.61 | 2.32 |
| 2004 | 0.41 | 0.53 | 0.58 | 0.48 | 2.00 |
| 2003 | 0.29 | 0.36 | 0.37 | 0.39 | 1.40 |

Fiscal year ended Dec. 31. Next earnings report expected: Late January. EPS Estimates based on S&P Operating Earnings; historical GAAP earnings are as reported.

## Dividend Data (Dates: mm/dd Payment Date: mm/dd/yy)

| Amount ($) | Date Decl. | Ex-Div. Date | Stk. of Record | Payment Date |
|---|---|---|---|---|
| 0.200 | 02/14 | 02/27 | 02/29 | 03/14/08 |
| 0.200 | 05/01 | 05/28 | 05/31 | 06/15/08 |
| 0.250 | 08/07 | 08/27 | 08/31 | 09/15/08 |
| 0.250 | 11/06 | 11/25 | 11/30 | 12/15/08 |

Dividends have been paid since 1947. Source: Company reports.

# Dover Corp

## Business Summary October 28, 2008

CORPORATE OVERVIEW. Dover Corporation is a diversified manufacturer of a broad range of specialized industrial products and manufacturing equipment. The company has evolved largely through acquisitions, with 75 acquisitions costing approximately $4 billion completed between January 2000 and December 2006. There are four operating segments: Industrial Products, Engineered Systems, Fluid Management and Electronic Technologies.

Industrial Products (31% of 2007 sales, with 13% operating margin) manufactures a diverse mix of equipment and components for use in the waste handling, bulk transport and automotive service industries. Its two sub-units are Material Handling and Mobile Equipment. Major units include Paladin, PDQ Manufacturing, Heil Environmental, Rotary Lift, Heil Trailer International, Chief Automotive, and Marathon Equipment.

Engineered Systems (30%, 13%) manufactures food equipment (refrigeration systems, display cases, walk-in coolers, etc.) and packaging machinery. It is composed of two primary sub-groups -- Product Identification and Engineered Products. The food equipment businesses (Hill Phoenix and Unified Brands)

sell to the institutional and commercial foodservice markets. The packaging machinery businesses sell to the beverage and food processing industries.

Fluid Management (21%, 21%) manufactures products primarily for the oil and gas, automotive fueling, fluid handling, engineered components, material handling and chemical equipment industries. This segment consists of two primary sub-units -- Energy and Fluid Solutions.

Electronic Technologies (19%, 13%) manufactures an array of specialized electronic, electromechanical and plastic components for OEMs in multiple end markets, including hearing aids, telecom, defense and aerospace electronics, and life sciences. It also supplies ATM hardware and software for retail applications and financial institutions, and chemical proportioning and dispensing systems for janitorial/sanitation applications.

## Company Financials Fiscal Year Ended Dec. 31

| Per Share Data ($) | 2007 | 2006 | 2005 | 2004 | 2003 | 2002 | 2001 | 2000 | 1999 | 1998 |
|---|---|---|---|---|---|---|---|---|---|---|
| Tangible Book Value | NM | NM | NM | 2.16 | 2.71 | 2.66 | 1.97 | 1.79 | 1.08 | 2.11 |
| Cash Flow | 4.43 | 3.92 | 3.18 | 2.78 | 2.14 | 1.83 | 1.89 | 3.60 | 2.79 | 2.20 |
| Earnings | 3.22 | 2.94 | 2.32 | 2.00 | 1.40 | 1.04 | 0.82 | 2.61 | 1.92 | 1.45 |
| S&P Core Earnings | 3.28 | 2.98 | 2.25 | 1.92 | 1.31 | 0.90 | 0.68 | NA | NA | NA |
| Dividends | 0.77 | 0.71 | 0.66 | 0.62 | 0.57 | 0.54 | 0.52 | 0.48 | 0.44 | 0.40 |
| Payout Ratio | 24% | 24% | 28% | 31% | 41% | 52% | 63% | 18% | 23% | 28% |
| Prices:High | 54.59 | 51.92 | 42.11 | 44.13 | 40.45 | 43.55 | 43.55 | 54.38 | 47.94 | 39.94 |
| Prices:Low | 44.34 | 40.30 | 34.11 | 35.12 | 22.85 | 23.54 | 26.40 | 34.13 | 29.31 | 25.50 |
| P/E Ratio:High | 17 | 18 | 18 | 22 | 29 | 42 | 53 | 21 | 25 | 28 |
| P/E Ratio:Low | 14 | 14 | 15 | 18 | 16 | 23 | 32 | 13 | 15 | 18 |

| Income Statement Analysis (Million $) | | | | | | | | | | |
|---|---|---|---|---|---|---|---|---|---|---|
| Revenue | 7,226 | 6,512 | 6,078 | 5,488 | 4,413 | 4,184 | 4,460 | 5,401 | 4,446 | 3,978 |
| Operating Income | 1,220 | 1,113 | 876 | 773 | 595 | 503 | 518 | 1,047 | 819 | 700 |
| Depreciation | 245 | 202 | 176 | 161 | 151 | 161 | 219 | 203 | 183 | 168 |
| Interest Expense | 89.0 | 77.0 | 72.2 | 61.3 | 62.2 | 70.0 | 91.2 | 97.5 | 53.4 | 60.7 |
| Pretax Income | 888 | 823 | 644 | 552 | 372 | 270 | 238 | 772 | 615 | 489 |
| Effective Tax Rate | 26.4% | 26.7% | 26.3% | 25.9% | 23.3% | 21.7% | 30.0% | 31.0% | 34.1% | 33.2% |
| Net Income | 653 | 603 | 474 | 409 | 285 | 211 | 167 | 533 | 405 | 326 |
| S&P Core Earnings | 667 | 613 | 460 | 392 | 267 | 182 | 138 | NA | NA | NA |

| Balance Sheet & Other Financial Data (Million $) | | | | | | | | | | |
|---|---|---|---|---|---|---|---|---|---|---|
| Cash | 602 | 374 | 191 | 358 | 370 | 295 | 177 | 187 | 138 | 96.8 |
| Current Assets | 2,544 | 2,272 | 1,976 | 2,150 | 1,850 | 1,658 | 1,655 | 1,975 | 1,612 | 1,305 |
| Total Assets | 8,070 | 7,627 | 6,573 | 5,792 | 5,134 | 4,437 | 4,602 | 4,892 | 4,132 | 3,627 |
| Current Liabilities | 1,681 | 1,434 | 1,207 | 1,356 | 911 | 697 | 819 | 1,605 | 1,345 | 990 |
| Long Term Debt | 1,452 | 1,480 | 1,344 | 753 | 1,004 | 1,030 | 1,033 | 632 | 608 | 610 |
| Common Equity | 3,946 | 3,811 | 3,330 | 3,119 | 2,743 | 2,395 | 2,520 | 2,442 | 2,039 | 1,911 |
| Total Capital | 5,714 | 5,656 | 5,046 | 4,168 | 3,980 | 3,561 | 3,656 | 3,141 | 2,689 | 2,571 |
| Capital Expenditures | 174 | 195 | 152 | 107 | 96.4 | 102 | 167 | 198 | 130 | 126 |
| Cash Flow | 898 | 805 | 650 | 570 | 437 | 372 | 386 | 737 | 588 | 494 |
| Current Ratio | 1.5 | 1.6 | 1.6 | 1.6 | 2.0 | 2.4 | 2.0 | 1.2 | 1.2 | 1.3 |
| % Long Term Debt of Capitalization | 25.4 | 26.2 | 26.6 | 18.1 | 25.2 | 28.9 | 28.3 | 20.1 | 22.6 | 23.7 |
| % Net Income of Revenue | 9.0 | 9.3 | 7.8 | 7.5 | 6.5 | 5.0 | 3.7 | 9.9 | 9.1 | 8.2 |
| % Return on Assets | 8.3 | 8.5 | 7.7 | 7.5 | 6.0 | 4.7 | 3.5 | 11.8 | 10.4 | 9.5 |
| % Return on Equity | 16.8 | 16.9 | 14.7 | 14.0 | 11.1 | 8.6 | 6.7 | 23.8 | 20.5 | 17.7 |

Data as orig reptd.; bef. results of disc opers/spec. items. Per share data adj. for stk. divs.; EPS diluted. E-Estimated. NA-Not Available. NM-Not Meaningful. NR-Not Ranked. UR-Under Review.

**Office:** 280 Park Ave Rm, New York, NY 10017-1215.
**Telephone:** 212-922-1640.
**Website:** http://www.dovercorporation.com
**Chrmn:** J.L. Koley

**Pres & COO:** R.A. Livingston
**CEO:** R.L. Hoffman
**CFO:** R.G. Kuhbach
**Chief Acctg Officer & Cntlr:** R.T. McKay, Jr.

**Investor Contact:** P.E. Goldberg (212-922-1640)
**Board Members:** D. H. Benson, R. W. Cremin, T. J. Derosa, J. M. Ergas, P. T. Francis, K. C. Graham, R. L. Hoffman, J. L. Koley, R. K. Lochridge, B. G. Rethore, M. B. Stubbs, M. A. Winston

**Founded:** 1947
**Domicile:** Delaware
**Employees:** 33,400

# Dow Chemical Co (The)

**STANDARD &POOR'S**

**S&P Recommendation** BUY ★ ★ ★ ★ ☆

| Price | 12-Mo. Target Price | Investment Style |
|---|---|---|
| $21.15 (as of Nov 14, 2008) | $30.00 | Large-Cap Blend |

**GICS Sector** Materials
**Sub-Industry** Diversified Chemicals

**Summary** Dow, the largest U.S. chemical company, provides chemical, plastic and agricultural products and services to many consumer markets.

## Key Stock Statistics (Source S&P, Vickers, company reports)

| | | | | | | | |
|---|---|---|---|---|---|---|---|
| 52-Wk Range | $45.50– 19.35 | S&P Oper. EPS 2008E | 2.85 | Market Capitalization(B) | $19.538 | Beta | 1.15 |
| Trailing 12-Month EPS | $2.75 | S&P Oper. EPS 2009E | 2.85 | Yield (%) | 7.94 | S&P 3-Yr. Proj. EPS CAGR(%) | 8 |
| Trailing 12-Month P/E | 7.7 | P/E on S&P Oper. EPS 2008E | 7.4 | Dividend Rate/Share | $1.68 | S&P Credit Rating | A- |
| $10K Invested 5 Yrs Ago | $6,776 | Common Shares Outstg. (M) | 923.8 | Institutional Ownership (%) | 69 | | |

## Price Performance

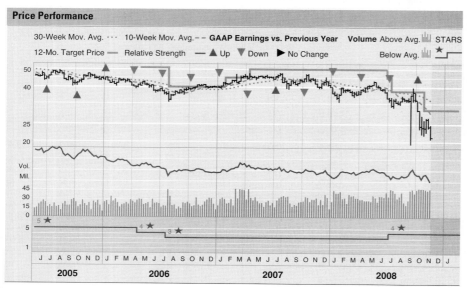

30-Week Mov. Avg. · · · · 10-Week Mov. Avg. – – – **GAAP Earnings vs. Previous Year** Volume Above Avg. STARS
12-Mo. Target Price —— Relative Strength — ▲ Up ▼ Down ▶ No Change Below Avg.

2005 2006 2007 2008

Options: ASE, CBOE, P, Ph

Analysis prepared by **Richard O'Reilly, CFA** on November 12, 2008, when the stock traded at **$ 22.80**.

## Highlights

► We look for sales at Dow as presently constituted to rise 20% in 2008, driven by selling price increases in response to the rapid rise in raw material costs earlier in 2008. Sales for 2009 will likely reflect two major pending transactions-- the formation of a 50%-owned joint venture (annual sales of $14 billion) to consists of all of Dow's global polyethylene and polypropylene businesses and the purchase of Rohm and Haas Co. (ROH: hold, $74), subject to approvals. We expect volume growth to be minimal at best into early 2009 amid softening conditions in the U.S. and Europe.

► Volatile feedstock costs should be lower after averaging about 40% higher in 2008. Prices for many basic plastics and chemicals should remain volatile; industry resin prices have eased since July in response to falling feedstock costs, while caustic soda prices have continued to move up.

► We expect the company to post operating EPS of $2.85 in 2008 and 2009, down from 2007's $3.74 (excluding special charges totaling $0.77, primarily a one-time charge in the fourth quarter for plant shutdowns). We see the purchase of ROH as modestly dilutive in 2009.

## Investment Rationale/Risk

► Our buy opinion is based on valuation. Dow has announced two major pending transactions since late 2007-- the formation of a 50%-owned joint venture with a unit of Kuwait Petroleum Corp. to consist of all of Dow's wholly owned global polyethylene and polypropylene businesses; and the purchase of Rohm and Haas Co. (ROH: hold, $74) for a total of $18.8 billion, subject to approvals. If the transactions are completed, expected by early 2009, specialty chemicals and materials would account for nearly 70% of Dow annual sales and profits.

► Risks to our recommendation and target price include a worse-than-expected softening of the U.S. economy, sharply higher energy costs, and unplanned production outages. We remain somewhat concerned about possible additional asbestos liabilities for Dow, largely related to its Union Carbide unit.

► Our 12-month target price of $30 is based on a historical mid-cycle P/E of about 10.5X applied to an annualized earnings rate of $2.85 that we believe Dow, as currently constituted, should achieve in 2009.

## Qualitative Risk Assessment

| LOW | MEDIUM | HIGH |
|---|---|---|

Our risk assessment reflects Dow's diverse business and geographic sales mix and manufacturing integration, offset by the cyclical nature of the commodity chemical industry and the volatility of raw material costs.

## Quantitative Evaluations

**S&P Quality Ranking** B

| D | C | B- | B | B+ | A- | A | A+ |
|---|---|---|---|---|---|---|---|

**Relative Strength Rank** MODERATE

41

LOWEST = 1          HIGHEST = 99

## Revenue/Earnings Data

**Revenue (Million $)**

| | 1Q | 2Q | 3Q | 4Q | Year |
|---|---|---|---|---|---|
| 2008 | 14,824 | 16,380 | 15,411 | -- | -- |
| 2007 | 12,432 | 13,265 | 13,589 | 14,227 | 53,513 |
| 2006 | 12,020 | 12,509 | 12,359 | 12,236 | 49,124 |
| 2005 | 11,679 | 11,450 | 11,261 | 11,917 | 46,307 |
| 2004 | 9,309 | 9,844 | 10,072 | 10,936 | 40,161 |
| 2003 | 8,081 | 8,242 | 7,977 | 8,332 | 32,632 |

**Earnings Per Share ($)**

| | | | | | |
|---|---|---|---|---|---|
| 2008 | 0.99 | 0.81 | 0.46 | E0.59 | E2.85 |
| 2007 | 1.00 | 1.07 | 0.24 | 0.49 | 2.99 |
| 2006 | 1.24 | 1.05 | 0.53 | 1.00 | 3.82 |
| 2005 | 1.39 | 1.30 | 0.82 | 1.14 | 4.64 |
| 2004 | 0.50 | 0.72 | 0.65 | 1.06 | 2.93 |
| 2003 | 0.09 | 0.43 | 0.36 | 0.94 | 1.88 |

Fiscal year ended Dec. 31. Next earnings report expected: Late January. EPS Estimates based on S&P Operating Earnings; historical GAAP earnings are as reported.

## Dividend Data (Dates: mm/dd Payment Date: mm/dd/yy)

| Amount ($) | Date Decl. | Ex-Div. Date | Stk. of Record | Payment Date |
|---|---|---|---|---|
| 0.420 | 12/10 | 12/27 | 12/31 | 01/30/08 |
| 0.420 | 02/14 | 03/27 | 03/31 | 04/30/08 |
| 0.420 | 05/15 | 06/26 | 06/30 | 07/30/08 |
| 0.420 | 09/11 | 09/26 | 09/30 | 10/30/08 |

Dividends have been paid since 1911. Source: Company reports.

---

**Please read the Required Disclosures and Analyst Certification on the last page of this report.**

*The McGraw-Hill Companies*

# Dow Chemical Co (The)

## Business Summary November 12, 2008

CORPORATE OVERVIEW. The 2001 purchase of Union Carbide Corp., a leading producer of polyethylene, ethylene glycol, solvents and specialty chemicals, made Dow the largest U.S. chemical company. Foreign operations accounted for 66% of 2007 sales.

Chemicals (11% of sales and 15% of profits in 2007) include inorganics (chlorine, caustic soda, chlorinated solvents, calcium chlorides, ethylene dichloride and vinyl chloride), ethylene oxide/glycol, and vinyl acetate monomer, used primarily as raw materials in the manufacture of customer products. Performance chemicals (16%, 17%) consist of latex (including styrene-butadiene) coatings and binders, acrylics, water-based emulsions (acrylic latexes), water soluble polymers, cellulose ethers and resins, ion exchange resins, membranes, biocides, custom manufacturing, fine chemicals, glycine, glycols, amines, surfactants, heat transfer and deicing fluids, coolants, and lubricants and solvents. The segment also includes results of the Dow Corning joint venture.

Dow AgroSciences (7%, 8%) is a leading global maker of herbicides (Clincher, Starane), insecticides (Lorsban, Sentricon termite colony elimination system, Tracer) and fungicides for crop protection and industrial/commercial pest control. It is also building a plant genetics and biotechnology business in crop

seeds (Mycogen, Nexera), traits (Herculex) and value-added grains.

The company, a major producer of plastics (24%, 36%), is the world's largest producer of polyethylene and polystyrene resins, which are used in a broad variety of applications. It also makes polypropylene and has a joint venture for PET polyester plastics. Performance plastics (29%, 25%) consist of engineering plastics (polycarbonates, ABS), elastomers, synthetic rubbers, adhesives and sealants, polyolefins for wire and cable insulation, SARAN resins and films, specialty films, polyurethanes (systems, sealants and adhesives, polyols, isocyanates, propylene oxide/glycol), epoxy resins and intermediates (phenol and acetone), fabricated building products (foams and films, STYROFOAM insulation products, weather barrier products), and technology licensing (UNIPOL for polyethylene and polypropylene, Meteor for ethylene oxide/glycol). The hydrocarbons and energy business (13%, -1%) procures fuels and raw materials and produces ethylene, propylene, aromatics, styrene, and power and steam.

## Company Financials Fiscal Year Ended Dec. 31

| Per Share Data ($) | 2007 | 2006 | 2005 | 2004 | 2003 | 2002 | 2001 | 2000 | 1999 | 1998 |
|---|---|---|---|---|---|---|---|---|---|---|
| Tangible Book Value | 17.00 | 14.50 | 12.14 | 9.01 | 5.79 | 4.19 | 7.59 | 10.78 | 9.59 | 8.77 |
| Cash Flow | 5.09 | 5.83 | 6.83 | 5.12 | 3.93 | 4.57 | 1.55 | 4.14 | 3.91 | 3.83 |
| Earnings | 2.99 | 3.82 | 4.64 | 2.93 | 1.88 | -0.44 | -0.46 | 2.22 | 1.98 | 1.91 |
| S&P Core Earnings | 2.82 | 3.73 | 4.04 | 2.34 | 1.58 | -1.41 | -1.43 | NA | NA | NA |
| Dividends | 1.64 | 1.50 | 1.34 | 1.34 | 1.34 | 1.34 | 1.30 | 1.16 | 1.16 | 1.16 |
| Payout Ratio | 55% | 39% | 29% | 46% | 71% | NM | NM | 52% | 59% | 61% |
| Prices:High | 47.96 | 45.15 | 56.75 | 51.34 | 42.00 | 37.00 | 39.67 | 47.17 | 46.00 | 33.81 |
| Prices:Low | 38.89 | 33.00 | 40.18 | 36.35 | 24.83 | 23.66 | 25.06 | 23.00 | 28.50 | 24.90 |
| P/E Ratio:High | 16 | 12 | 12 | 18 | 22 | NM | NM | 21 | 23 | 18 |
| P/E Ratio:Low | 13 | 9 | 9 | 12 | 13 | NM | NM | 10 | 14 | 13 |

| Income Statement Analysis (Million $) | | | | | | | | | | |
|---|---|---|---|---|---|---|---|---|---|---|
| Revenue | 53,513 | 49,124 | 46,307 | 40,161 | 32,632 | 27,609 | 27,805 | 23,008 | 18,929 | 18,441 |
| Operating Income | 5,903 | 6,675 | 7,437 | 5,466 | 3,922 | 2,925 | 2,953 | 3,462 | 3,407 | 3,498 |
| Depreciation | 2,031 | 1,954 | 2,134 | 2,088 | 1,903 | 1,825 | 1,815 | 1,315 | 1,301 | 1,305 |
| Interest Expense | 669 | 689 | 702 | 747 | 828 | 774 | 733 | 460 | 431 | 493 |
| Pretax Income | 4,229 | 4,972 | 6,399 | 3,796 | 1,751 | -622 | -613 | 2,401 | 2,166 | 2,012 |
| Effective Tax Rate | 29.4% | 23.2% | 27.8% | 23.1% | NM | NM | NM | 34.3% | 35.4% | 34.0% |
| Net Income | 2,887 | 3,724 | 4,535 | 2,797 | 1,739 | -405 | -417 | 1,513 | 1,331 | 1,310 |
| S&P Core Earnings | 2,734 | 3,638 | 3,956 | 2,236 | 1,462 | -1,295 | -1,303 | NA | NA | NA |

| Balance Sheet & Other Financial Data (Million $) | | | | | | | | | | |
|---|---|---|---|---|---|---|---|---|---|---|
| Cash | 1,737 | 2,910 | 3,838 | 3,192 | 2,434 | 1,573 | 264 | 304 | 1,212 | 390 |
| Current Assets | 18,654 | 17,209 | 17,404 | 15,890 | 13,002 | 11,681 | 10,308 | 9,260 | 8,847 | 8,040 |
| Total Assets | 48,801 | 45,581 | 45,934 | 45,885 | 41,891 | 39,562 | 35,515 | 27,645 | 25,499 | 23,830 |
| Current Liabilities | 12,445 | 10,601 | 10,663 | 10,506 | 9,534 | 8,856 | 8,125 | 7,873 | 6,295 | 6,842 |
| Long Term Debt | 7,581 | 8,036 | 10,186 | 12,629 | 12,763 | 12,659 | 10,266 | 5,365 | 5,022 | 4,051 |
| Common Equity | 19,389 | 17,065 | 15,324 | 12,270 | 9,175 | 7,626 | 9,993 | 9,186 | 8,323 | 7,429 |
| Total Capital | 29,238 | 27,465 | 27,241 | 26,649 | 23,438 | 21,645 | 21,376 | 15,848 | 14,642 | 12,802 |
| Capital Expenditures | 2,075 | 1,775 | 1,597 | 1,333 | 1,100 | 1,623 | 1,587 | 1,349 | 1,412 | 1,546 |
| Cash Flow | 4,918 | 5,678 | 6,669 | 4,885 | 3,642 | 1,420 | 1,398 | 2,828 | 2,627 | 2,609 |
| Current Ratio | 1.5 | 1.6 | 1.6 | 1.5 | 1.4 | 1.3 | 1.3 | 1.2 | 1.4 | 1.2 |
| % Long Term Debt of Capitalization | 25.9 | 30.4 | 37.4 | 47.4 | 54.5 | 58.5 | 48.0 | 33.9 | 34.3 | 31.6 |
| % Net Income of Revenue | 5.4 | 7.6 | 9.8 | 7.0 | 5.3 | NM | NM | 6.6 | 7.0 | 7.1 |
| % Return on Assets | 6.1 | 8.1 | 9.9 | 6.4 | 4.3 | NM | NM | 5.7 | 5.4 | 5.5 |
| % Return on Equity | 15.8 | 23.0 | 32.9 | 26.1 | 20.7 | NM | NM | 17.3 | 16.8 | 17.3 |

Data as orig reptd.; bef. results of disc opers/spec. items. Per share data adj. for stk. divs.; EPS diluted. E-Estimated. NA-Not Available. NM-Not Meaningful. NR-Not Ranked. UR-Under Review.

**Office:** 2030 Dow Center, Midland, MI 48674-0001.
**Telephone:** 989-636-1000.
**Website:** http://www.dow.com
**Chrmn, Pres & CEO:** A. Liveris

**EVP & CFO:** G.E. Merszei
**EVP & CTO:** W.F. Banholzer
**EVP, Secy & General Counsel:** C.J. Kalil
**EVP & CIO:** D.E. Kepler, II

**Investor Contact:** T. McNeill (989-636-0626)
**Board Members:** A. A. Allemang, J. K. Barton, J. A. Bell, J. M. Fettig, B. H. Franklin, J. B. Hess, A. Liveris, G. E. Merszei, D. H. Reilley, J. M. Ringler, R. G. Shaw, P. G. Stern

**Founded:** 1897
**Domicile:** Delaware
**Employees:** 45,856

# D.R. Horton Inc.

**STANDARD &POOR'S**

**S&P Recommendation** | BUY ★★★★☆ | | **Price** $5.79 (as of Nov 14, 2008) | **12-Mo. Target Price** $10.00 | **Investment Style** Large-Cap Blend

**GICS Sector** Consumer Discretionary
**Sub-Industry** Homebuilding

**Summary** This company is the largest homebuilder in the U.S., based on number of homes sold.

## Key Stock Statistics (Source S&P, Vickers, company reports)

| | | | | | | | |
|---|---|---|---|---|---|---|---|
| 52-Wk Range | $17.95– 4.33 | S&P Oper. EPS 2008**E** | -6.55 | Market Capitalization(B) | $1.833 | Beta | 1.05 |
| Trailing 12-Month EPS | $-5.97 | S&P Oper. EPS 2009**E** | Nil | Yield (%) | 5.18 | S&P 3-Yr. Proj. EPS CAGR(%) | 5 |
| Trailing 12-Month P/E | NM | P/E on S&P Oper. EPS 2008**E** | NM | Dividend Rate/Share | $0.30 | S&P Credit Rating | BB |
| $10K Invested 5 Yrs Ago | $3,091 | Common Shares Outstg. (M) | 316.6 | Institutional Ownership (%) | 92 | | |

## Price Performance

30-Week Mov. Avg. · · · 10-Week Mov. Avg. — **GAAP Earnings vs. Previous Year** Volume Above Avg. STARS
12-Mo. Target Price — Relative Strength — ▲ Up ▼ Down ▶ No Change Below Avg. 

Options: ASE, CBOE, P, Ph

Analysis prepared by **Kenneth M. Leon, CPA** on October 20, 2008, when the stock traded at **$ 7.19**.

## Highlights

► After an estimated 46% sales decline in FY 08 (Sep.), we forecast a 29% sales decrease in FY 09 and then a rebound to low single digit growth in FY 10, as a multi-year slowdown in the housing industry plays out. At June 30, 2008, the company's backlog value was $1.9 billion, a 56% year-to-year decline. We believe an increase in backlog is not likely until some time in the first half of 2009, when we think the housing market should begin to stabilize.

► We estimate that DHI's homebuilding gross margin will remain at 13% to 15% in FY 08 and FY 09, compared with 20% in FY 07. DHI realized a peak gross margin of 24% in FY 06. Asset impairment charges, which were $1.3 billion in FY 07, should continue, but at a slower pace, in our view; DHI booked $330 million of such charges in the third quarter of FY 08, compared to $834 million in the second quarter.

► To stimulate sales activity in the first half of FY 09, we believe the company will maintain SG&A costs as a percentage of total revenues at the 12% to 13% level, in line with our estimate in FY 08. With other cost control initiatives, we estimate breakeven results in FY 09.

## Investment Rationale/Risk

► As DHI is the largest U.S. homebuilder, we see reduced interest rates raising affordability in its target markets. Despite the company booking over $3.5 billion of asset impairments since the beginning of 2006, we still view DHI as one of the better managed large homebuilders, with strong operating controls. We believe a rebound in the housing market will benefit DHI with a return to more stable home prices and an improved sales pace to complete its communities.

► Risks to our recommendation and target price include the possibility of a prolonged housing recession and deteriorating jobs employment data. We see the potential for further writedowns of inventory and joint venture investments above our target, which would be detrimental to our EPS estimates and book value.

► Our 12-month target price of $10 reflects a target price-to-book multiple just under 0.9X applied to our estimated forward book value just below $11.60, near the middle of the historical range for DHI but still a premium to peers, reflecting its strong balance sheet, operating scale advantages and cost-control efforts.

## Qualitative Risk Assessment

| LOW | MEDIUM | HIGH |
|---|---|---|

Our risk assessment reflects DHI's exposure to an extended downturn in the housing market, offset by its focus on reducing debt with free cash flow from operations. As the largest U.S. homebuilder, DHI has scale advantages to reduce labor costs and material costs, but severe weakness in the housing market may delay profitability.

## Quantitative Evaluations

**S&P Quality Ranking** A

| D | C | B- | B | B+ | A- | A | A+ |
|---|---|---|---|---|---|---|---|

**Relative Strength Rank** WEAK

27

LOWEST = 1          HIGHEST = 99

## Revenue/Earnings Data

**Revenue (Million $)**

| | 1Q | 2Q | 3Q | 4Q | Year |
|---|---|---|---|---|---|
| 2008 | 1,708 | 1,624 | 1,464 | -- | -- |
| 2007 | 3,172 | 2,598 | 2,658 | 2,868 | 11,297 |
| 2006 | 2,903 | 3,598 | 3,668 | 4,883 | 15,051 |
| 2005 | 2,520 | 2,877 | 3,370 | 5,097 | 13,864 |
| 2004 | 2,205 | 2,335 | 2,790 | 3,511 | 10,841 |
| 2003 | 1,745 | 1,909 | 2,212 | 2,862 | 8,728 |

**Earnings Per Share ($)**

| | 1Q | 2Q | 3Q | 4Q | Year |
|---|---|---|---|---|---|
| 2008 | -0.41 | -4.14 | -1.26 | E-0.73 | E-6.55 |
| 2007 | 0.35 | 0.16 | -2.62 | -0.16 | -2.27 |
| 2006 | 0.98 | 1.11 | 0.93 | 0.88 | 3.90 |
| 2005 | 0.76 | 0.92 | 1.17 | 1.77 | 4.62 |
| 2004 | 0.58 | 0.60 | 0.80 | 1.10 | 3.08 |
| 2003 | 0.38 | 0.43 | 0.50 | 0.73 | 2.05 |

Fiscal year ended Sep. 30. Next earnings report expected: Late November. EPS Estimates based on S&P Operating Earnings; historical GAAP earnings are as reported.

## Dividend Data (Dates: mm/dd Payment Date: mm/dd/yy)

| Amount ($) | Date Decl. | Ex-Div. Date | Stk. of Record | Payment Date |
|---|---|---|---|---|
| 0.150 | 10/24 | 11/01 | 11/05 | 11/16/07 |
| 0.150 | 02/01 | 02/08 | 02/12 | 02/20/08 |
| 0.075 | 05/06 | 05/15 | 05/19 | 05/29/08 |
| 0.075 | 08/05 | 08/14 | 08/18 | 08/28/08 |

Dividends have been paid since 1997. Source: Company reports.

---

**Please read the Required Disclosures and Analyst Certification on the last page of this report.**

The **McGraw·Hill** Companies

# D.R. Horton Inc.

STANDARD
&POOR'S

## Business Summary October 20, 2008

CORPORATE OVERVIEW. D.R. Horton was founded in 1978 by Donald Horton, now chairman. In 1992, it went public to gain broader access to capital markets, which has helped fuel its subsequent growth beyond its base in the Dallas/Fort Worth area. With operating divisions in 27 states and 83 markets, D.R. Horton is the largest domestic homebuilder by number of homes closed in FY 07 (Sep.) and the most geographically diversified.

The company was the first U.S. builder to sell 50,000 homes in a single year (FY 05), and it aims to be the first to eclipse the 100,000 unit mark (by FY 10). By emphasizing entry level and first-time move-up buyers, it targets the broadest segments of the population. With an average selling price of $253,000 in FY 07 and $273,900 in FY 06, DHI's homes are among the most affordable of all public builders. Detached homes accounted for 81% of home sales revenue in FY 07.

CORPORATE STRATEGY. Most of D.R. Horton's growth in the past 15 to 20 years has been the result of organic initiatives, in our opinion. Generally, the company has established satellite operations in new markets located in relatively close proximity to existing markets. We think the company has been successful at quickly ramping up volumes in these satellite operations -- often at the expense of smaller competitors -- aided by materials purchasing agreements struck at the regional level and relatively favorable access to capital markets.

Complementing this organic growth has been an aggressive takeover program, with close to 20 acquisitions since DHI went public. Most of these deals have occurred in new markets in an effort to either create a platform for future growth in a locale or to expand an existing satellite operation there. The majority of these acquisitions have been focused on a single market and have been asset-based transactions, rather than purchases of companies. However, in 2002, DHI bought Schuler Homes for about $1.8 billion, in a deal that increased its revenue base about 25%.

## Company Financials Fiscal Year Ended Sep. 30

| Per Share Data ($) | 2007 | 2006 | 2005 | 2004 | 2003 | 2002 | 2001 | 2000 | 1999 | 1998 |
|---|---|---|---|---|---|---|---|---|---|---|
| Tangible Book Value | 17.64 | 18.75 | 15.28 | 10.87 | 7.93 | 5.77 | 4.83 | 3.81 | 3.01 | 2.43 |
| Cash Flow | -2.06 | 4.10 | 4.87 | 3.24 | 2.16 | 1.54 | 1.24 | 0.94 | 0.78 | 0.46 |
| Earnings | -2.27 | 3.90 | 4.62 | 3.08 | 2.05 | 1.44 | 1.10 | 0.84 | 0.69 | 0.43 |
| S&P Core Earnings | -1.29 | 3.90 | 4.61 | 3.07 | 2.04 | 1.44 | 1.16 | NA | NA | NA |
| Dividends | 0.60 | 0.44 | 0.31 | 0.22 | 0.14 | 0.10 | 0.06 | 0.05 | 0.03 | 0.02 |
| Payout Ratio | NM | 11% | 7% | 7% | 7% | 7% | 5% | 5% | 5% | 6% |
| Prices:High | 31.13 | 41.66 | 42.82 | 31.41 | 22.69 | 14.58 | 11.17 | 7.81 | 6.34 | 6.87 |
| Prices:Low | 10.15 | 19.52 | 26.83 | 18.47 | 8.48 | 8.02 | 5.83 | 3.00 | 2.76 | 2.93 |
| P/E Ratio:High | NM | 11 | 9 | 10 | 11 | 10 | 10 | 9 | 9 | 16 |
| P/E Ratio:Low | NM | 5 | 6 | 6 | 4 | 6 | 5 | 4 | 4 | 7 |

| Income Statement Analysis (Million $) | 2007 | 2006 | 2005 | 2004 | 2003 | 2002 | 2001 | 2000 | 1999 | 1998 |
|---|---|---|---|---|---|---|---|---|---|---|
| Revenue | 11,297 | 15,051 | 13,864 | 10,841 | 8,728 | 6,739 | 4,456 | 3,654 | 3,156 | 2,177 |
| Operating Income | -420 | 2,036 | 2,402 | 1,430 | 1,049 | 693 | 480 | 339 | 273 | 189 |
| Depreciation | 64.4 | 61.7 | 52.8 | 49.6 | 41.8 | 32.8 | 31.2 | 22.0 | 20.8 | 9.83 |
| Interest Expense | 328 | 55.0 | 21.2 | 9.30 | 12.6 | 11.5 | 14.1 | 15.8 | 16.5 | 16.2 |
| Pretax Income | -951 | 1,987 | 2,379 | 1,583 | 1,008 | 648 | 408 | 309 | 264 | 159 |
| Effective Tax Rate | 25.1% | 37.9% | 38.2% | 38.4% | 37.9% | 37.5% | 37.5% | 38.0% | 39.4% | 41.3% |
| Net Income | -712 | 1,233 | 1,471 | 975 | 626 | 405 | 255 | 192 | 160 | 93.4 |
| S&P Core Earnings | -404 | 1,233 | 1,463 | 969 | 622 | 406 | 267 | NA | NA | NA |

| Balance Sheet & Other Financial Data (Million $) | 2007 | 2006 | 2005 | 2004 | 2003 | 2002 | 2001 | 2000 | 1999 | 1998 |
|---|---|---|---|---|---|---|---|---|---|---|
| Cash | 275 | 588 | 1,150 | 518 | 583 | 104 | 239 | 72.5 | 129 | 76.8 |
| Current Assets | NA | NA | NA | NA | NA | NA | NA | NA | NA | NA |
| Total Assets | 11,556 | 14,821 | 12,515 | 8,985 | 7,279 | 6,018 | 3,652 | 2,695 | 2,362 | 1,668 |
| Current Liabilities | NA | NA | NA | NA | NA | NA | NA | NA | NA | NA |
| Long Term Debt | 3,746 | 4,861 | 3,660 | 3,032 | 2,665 | 2,636 | 1,884 | 1,344 | 1,191 | 855 |
| Common Equity | 5,587 | 6,453 | 5,360 | 3,961 | 3,031 | 2,270 | 1,250 | 970 | 798 | 549 |
| Total Capital | NA | 11,419 | 9,224 | 7,159 | 5,832 | 4,927 | 3,143 | 2,319 | 1,993 | 1,407 |
| Capital Expenditures | 39.8 | 83.3 | 68.2 | 55.2 | 48.7 | 39.8 | 33.4 | 19.6 | 17.3 | 11.6 |
| Cash Flow | -648 | 1,295 | 1,523 | 1,025 | 668 | 437 | 286 | 214 | 181 | 103 |
| Current Ratio | 4.8 | 3.7 | 3.3 | 4.7 | 4.7 | 4.5 | 4.7 | 5.0 | 4.5 | 5.2 |
| % Long Term Debt of Capitalization | 39.1 | 42.6 | 39.7 | 42.4 | 45.7 | 53.5 | 59.9 | 58.0 | 59.7 | 60.8 |
| % Net Income of Revenue | NM | 8.2 | 10.6 | 8.9 | 7.2 | 6.0 | 5.7 | 5.2 | 5.1 | 4.3 |
| % Return on Assets | NM | 9.0 | 13.7 | 12.0 | 9.4 | 8.4 | 8.0 | 7.6 | 7.9 | 7.8 |
| % Return on Equity | NM | 20.9 | 31.5 | 27.9 | 23.6 | 23.0 | 23.0 | 21.7 | 23.7 | 23.0 |

Data as orig reptd.; bef. results of disc opers/spec. items. Per share data adj. for stk. divs.; EPS diluted. E-Estimated. NA-Not Available. NM-Not Meaningful. NR-Not Ranked. UR-Under Review.

**Office:** 301 Commerce St Ste 500, Fort Worth, TX 76102-4178.
**Telephone:** 817-390-8200.
**Website:** http://www.drhorton.com
**Chrmn:** D.R. Horton

**Pres, Vice Chrmn & CEO:** D.J. Tomnitz
**EVP, CFO & Chief Acctg Officer:** B.W. Wheat
**Investor Contact:** S.H. Dwyer (817-390-8200)
**EVP & Treas:** S.H. Dwyer

**Board Members:** B. S. Anderson, M. R. Buchanan, R. I. Galland, M. W. Hewatt, D. R. Horton, B. G. Scott, D. J. Tomnitz, B. W. Wheat
**Founded:** 1991
**Domicile:** Delaware
**Employees:** 6,231

# Dr Pepper Snapple Group Inc

**S&P Recommendation** BUY ★ ★ ★ ★ ☆

| Price | 12-Mo. Target Price | Investment Style |
|---|---|---|
| $17.56 (as of Nov 14, 2008) | $22.00 | Large-Cap Growth |

**GICS Sector** Consumer Staples
**Sub-Industry** Soft Drinks

**Summary** Spun off from Cadbury Schweppes in May 2008, DPS is the third largest marketer, bottler and distributor of non-alcoholic beverages in North America. Key brands include Dr Pepper, Snapple, 7UP, Mott's, Canada Dry and Schweppes.

## Key Stock Statistics (Source S&P, Vickers, company reports)

| | | | | | | | |
|---|---|---|---|---|---|---|---|
| 52-Wk Range | $30.00– 17.52 | S&P Oper. EPS 2008E | 1.84 | Market Capitalization(B) | $4.455 | Beta | NA |
| Trailing 12-Month EPS | $1.95 | S&P Oper. EPS 2009E | 1.92 | Yield (%) | Nil | S&P 3-Yr. Proj. EPS CAGR(%) | 6 |
| Trailing 12-Month P/E | 9.0 | P/E on S&P Oper. EPS 2008E | 9.5 | Dividend Rate/Share | Nil | S&P Credit Rating | NA |
| $10K Invested 5 Yrs Ago | NA | Common Shares Outstg. (M) | 253.7 | Institutional Ownership (%) | 85 | | |

## Price Performance

30-Week Mov. Avg. · · · 10-Week Mov. Avg. – – **GAAP Earnings vs. Previous Year** Volume Above Avg. STARS

12-Mo. Target Price — Relative Strength — ▲ Up ▼ Down ► No Change Below Avg. ★

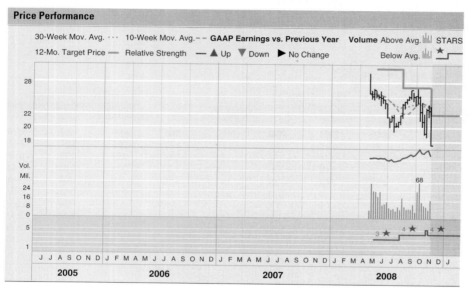

Options: CBOE, P, Ph

Analysis prepared by **Esther Y. Kwon, CFA** on November 13, 2008, when the stock traded at **$ 18.19**.

## Highlights

➤ In 2008, we estimate revenue of approximately $5.8 billion, up from 2007's $5.7 billion, on price increases, as we project volume to be flat to down on declines in the carbonated soft drink category. We expect DPS volume to outperform the carbonated drink category, which we estimate will decline at a single digit rate. In 2009, we look for 3% revenue growth, to $5.9 billion.

➤ On higher prices for ingredients and packaging and increased energy costs, we estimate gross margin contraction of about 40 basis points in 2008. We look for operating margins to decline as higher energy costs are only partially offset by efficiencies related to DPS's October 2007 restructuring, which included a reduction of approximately 470 employees and the closure of manufacturing facilities in Denver, CO, and Waterloo, NY, and which we think could generate $68 million in annual cost savings. In 2009, we look for margin expansion to 17.9%.

➤ On a 37% effective tax rate, we estimate 2008 EPS of $1.84. In 2009, we project EPS of $1.92. We do not anticipate dividends over the short term as DPS repays part of its more than $3.0 billion of debt.

## Investment Rationale/Risk

➤ We think the separation from Cadbury Schweppes will allow management to focus efforts on its own priorities and create a currency for acquisitions. While we are concerned by DPS's high concentration in the declining North America carbonated beverage market, we think DPS is underpenetrated in the high-margin cold drink channel, and we see the launch of a new advertising campaign and several new products in the second half of 2008 driving growth in a sluggish beverage market.

➤ Risks to our recommendation and target price include more rapid commodity cost inflation than expected, potential consumer reluctance to accept new products, and unfavorable weather conditions in the company's markets.

➤ Our 12-month target price of $22 is derived from our peer multiple analysis. Given DPS's limited history as an independent company and limited exposure to the faster-growth non-carbonated beverage category, we apply an 11.5X multiple to our 2009 EPS estimate of $1.92, in line with the multiple we use for bottling peers, but a discount to concentrate companies.

## Qualitative Risk Assessment

| LOW | MEDIUM | HIGH |
|---|---|---|

Our risk assessment for Dr Pepper Snapple Group reflects our view of the relatively stable nature of the company's end markets and its strong cash flow generation ability.

## Quantitative Evaluations

**S&P Quality Ranking** NR

| D | C | B- | B | B+ | A- | A | A+ |
|---|---|---|---|---|---|---|---|

**Relative Strength Rank** MODERATE

47

LOWEST = 1 HIGHEST = 99

## Revenue/Earnings Data

**Revenue (Million $)**

| | 1Q | 2Q | 3Q | 4Q | Year |
|---|---|---|---|---|---|
| 2008 | 1,307 | 1,557 | -- | -- | -- |
| 2007 | -- | -- | -- | -- | 5,748 |
| 2006 | -- | -- | -- | -- | -- |
| 2005 | -- | -- | -- | -- | -- |
| 2004 | -- | -- | -- | -- | -- |
| 2003 | -- | -- | -- | -- | -- |

**Earnings Per Share ($)**

| | | | | | |
|---|---|---|---|---|---|
| 2008 | 0.37 | 0.43 | E0.53 | E0.43 | E1.84 |
| 2007 | -- | -- | -- | -- | 1.79 |
| 2006 | -- | -- | -- | -- | -- |
| 2005 | -- | -- | -- | -- | -- |
| 2004 | -- | -- | -- | -- | -- |
| 2003 | -- | -- | -- | -- | -- |

Fiscal year ended Dec. 31. Next earnings report expected: NA. EPS Estimates based on S&P Operating Earnings; historical GAAP earnings are as reported.

## Dividend Data

No cash dividends have been paid.

---

# Dr Pepper Snapple Group Inc

**STANDARD &POOR'S**

## Business Summary November 13, 2008

CORPORATE OVERVIEW. Dr Pepper Snapple Group is the third largest marketer, bottler and distributor of non-alcoholic beverages in North America and the leading flavored carbonated soft drink (CSD) company in the United States. Its CSD brands include Dr Pepper, 7UP, Sunkist, A&W, Canada Dry, Schweppes, and Squirt. Its non-CSD brands include Snapple, Mott's, Hawaiian Punch and Clamato. The company also distributes Monster energy drink, FIJI mineral water and Big Red soda. Approximately one-third of the company's volume is generated by the Dr Pepper brand.

The company has three main operating segments: beverage concentrates (21% of 2007 sales, with an operating profit margin of 54.5%), finished goods (24% of sales, with a 10.7% operating margin), and bottling (49% of sales with a 4.1% margin). The Mexican and Caribbean segment accounted for the remaining sales, and had a 14.2% margin.

In 2007, DPS generated 89% of its sales in the United States, 4% in Canada, and the remainder in Mexico and the Caribbean.

CORPORATE STRATEGY. DPS's growth strategies include leveraging key brands through line extensions, such as launching Snapple super premium teas and antioxidant waters with functional benefits through its Snapple line. DPS is also targeting opportunities in high growth and high margin categories,

including ready to drink teas, energy drinks and other functional beverages, and plans to increase its presence in higher margin channels and packages. These channels include convenience stores, vending machines and small independent retail outlets, most often offering higher margin single-serve packages. With a slowing economy, however, Standard & Poor's remains cautious on this segment, which is particularly sensitive to changes in discretionary income. The company may also selectively enter into distribution agreements for high growth, third-party brands that can use DPS's bottling and distribution network.

In addition, DPS plans to continue to acquire regional bottling companies to broaden geographic coverage. Management believes the integrated model of brand ownership with bottling capabilities best aligns the economic interests of all parties involved. Finally, the company is targeting improvements in operating efficiencies as it integrates recent bottling acquisitions and reduces distribution costs.

## Company Financials Fiscal Year Ended Dec. 31

| Per Share Data ($) | 2007 | 2006 | 2005 | 2004 | 2003 | 2002 | 2001 | 2000 | 1999 | 1998 |
|---|---|---|---|---|---|---|---|---|---|---|
| Tangible Book Value | NM | NA | NA | NA | NA | NA | NA | NA | NA | NA |
| Cash Flow | 2.19 | NA | NA | NA | NA | NA | NA | NA | NA | NA |
| Earnings | 1.79 | NA | NA | NA | NA | NA | NA | NA | NA | NA |
| S&P Core Earnings | 1.76 | 1.92 | NA | NA | NA | NA | NA | NA | NA | NA |
| Dividends | NA | NA | NA | NA | NA | NA | NA | NA | NA | NA |
| Payout Ratio | NA | NA | NA | NA | NA | NA | NA | NA | NA | NA |
| Prices:High | NA | NA | NA | NA | NA | NA | NA | NA | NA | NA |
| Prices:Low | NA | NA | NA | NA | NA | NA | NA | NA | NA | NA |
| P/E Ratio:High | NA | NA | NA | NA | NA | NA | NA | NA | NA | NA |
| P/E Ratio:Low | NA | NA | NA | NA | NA | NA | NA | NA | NA | NA |

**Income Statement Analysis** (Million $)

| | 2007 | 2006 | 2005 | 2004 | 2003 | 2002 | 2001 | 2000 | 1999 | 1998 |
|---|---|---|---|---|---|---|---|---|---|---|
| Revenue | 5,748 | 4,735 | 3,205 | 3,065 | NA | NA | NA | NA | NA | NA |
| Operating Income | 1,113 | NA | NA | NA | NA | NA | NA | NA | NA | NA |
| Depreciation | 100 | 139 | 79.0 | 84.0 | NA | NA | NA | NA | NA | NA |
| Interest Expense | 250 | NA | NA | NA | NA | NA | NA | NA | NA | NA |
| Pretax Income | 774 | 808 | 808 | 716 | NA | NA | NA | NA | NA | NA |
| Effective Tax Rate | 41.2% | 36.9% | 39.7% | 37.7% | NA | NA | NA | NA | NA | NA |
| Net Income | 455 | 510 | 487 | 446 | NA | NA | NA | NA | NA | NA |
| S&P Core Earnings | 446 | 487 | NA | NA | NA | NA | NA | NA | NA | NA |

**Balance Sheet & Other Financial Data** (Million $)

| | 2007 | 2006 | 2005 | 2004 | 2003 | 2002 | 2001 | 2000 | 1999 | 1998 |
|---|---|---|---|---|---|---|---|---|---|---|
| Cash | 100 | 35.0 | 28.0 | NA | NA | NA | NA | NA | NA | NA |
| Current Assets | 1,179 | NA | NA | NA | NA | NA | NA | NA | NA | NA |
| Total Assets | 9,598 | 9,346 | 7,433 | NA | NA | NA | NA | NA | NA | NA |
| Current Liabilities | 2,764 | NA | NA | NA | NA | NA | NA | NA | NA | NA |
| Long Term Debt | 1,999 | NA | NA | NA | NA | NA | NA | NA | NA | NA |
| Common Equity | 2,922 | 3,250 | 2,426 | NA | NA | NA | NA | NA | NA | NA |
| Total Capital | 6,245 | NA | NA | NA | NA | NA | NA | NA | NA | NA |
| Capital Expenditures | 230 | 158 | 44.0 | 71.0 | NA | NA | NA | NA | NA | NA |
| Cash Flow | 555 | NA | NA | NA | NA | NA | NA | NA | NA | NA |
| Current Ratio | 0.4 | 1.0 | 1.2 | NA | NA | NA | NA | NA | NA | NA |
| % Long Term Debt of Capitalization | 32.0 | 43.8 | 50.3 | Nil | NA | NA | NA | NA | NA | NA |
| % Net Income of Revenue | 7.9 | 10.8 | 15.2 | 14.6 | NA | NA | NA | NA | NA | NA |
| % Return on Assets | NA | 6.1 | NA | NA | NA | NA | NA | NA | NA | NA |
| % Return on Equity | NA | 18.0 | NA | NA | NA | NA | NA | NA | NA | NA |

Data as orig reptd.; bef. results of disc opers/spec. items. Per share data adj. for stk. divs.; EPS diluted. Pro forma data in 2007. E-Estimated. NA-Not Available. NM-Not Meaningful. NR-Not Ranked. UR-Under Review.

**Office:** 5301 Legacy Drive, Plano, TX 75024.
**Telephone:** 972-673-7000.
**Website:** http://www.drpeppersnapple.com
**Chrmn:** W. Sanders

**Pres & CEO:** L.D. Young
**EVP & CFO:** J.O. Stewart
**EVP & General Counsel:** J.L. Baldwin, Jr.
**CSO & CTO:** D.J. Thomas

**Investor Contact:** A. Noormohamed (972-673-6050)
**Board Members:** T. Martin, P. H. Patsley, R. G. Rogers, W. Sanders, J. Stahl, J. O. Stewart, A. Szostak, L. D. Young

**Founded:** 2007
**Domicile:** Delaware
**Employees:** 20,000

# DTE Energy Co

**STANDARD &POOR'S**

## S&P Recommendation  HOLD ★★★☆☆

| Price | 12-Mo. Target Price |
|---|---|
| $36.77 (as of Nov 14, 2008) | $37.00 |

**GICS Sector** Utilities
**Sub-Industry** Multi-Utilities

**Summary** This Detroit-based diversified energy company is involved in the development and management of energy-related businesses and services nationwide.

## Key Stock Statistics (Source S&P, Vickers, company reports)

| | | | | | | | |
|---|---|---|---|---|---|---|---|
| 52-Wk Range | $51.15– 27.82 | S&P Oper. EPS 2008E | 2.95 | Market Capitalization(B) | $5.994 | Beta | 0.65 |
| Trailing 12-Month EPS | $4.14 | S&P Oper. EPS 2009E | 3.17 | Yield (%) | 5.77 | S&P 3-Yr. Proj. EPS CAGR(%) | 7 |
| Trailing 12-Month P/E | 8.9 | P/E on S&P Oper. EPS 2008E | 12.5 | Dividend Rate/Share | $2.12 | S&P Credit Rating | BBB |
| $10K Invested 5 Yrs Ago | $12,843 | Common Shares Outstg. (M) | 163.0 | Institutional Ownership (%) | 56 | | |

## Price Performance

- 30-Week Mov. Avg. ····
- 10-Week Mov. Avg. ─ ─
- **GAAP Earnings vs. Previous Year**
- Volume Above Avg. ▮▮▮ STARS
- 12-Mo. Target Price ──
- Relative Strength ─
- ▲ Up ▼ Down ▶ No Change
- Below Avg. ▮▮▮

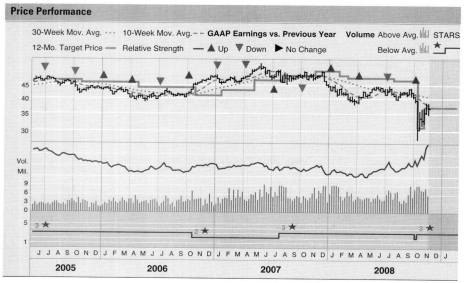

Options: ASE, Ph

Analysis prepared by **Justin McCann** on November 04, 2008, when the stock traded at **$ 38.11**.

## Highlights

▶ We expect operating EPS in 2008 to increase more than 4% from 2007 EPS from continuing operations of $2.82, benefiting from DTE's use of over $1 billion from after-tax proceeds of its asset sales for debt reduction and share buy-backs, as well as lower operation and mainte-nance costs. We believe this will be partially offset by a weakening economy and higher un-collectible reserves at the utilities, as well as higher storm costs.

▶ For 2009, we expect operating EPS to grow about 7% from anticipated results in 2008, with an expected electric rate increase being par-tially offset by the potential impact of a still weak economy. In its updated general rate case filing in February 2008, Detroit Edison re-quested that the test year be changed from the 2008 average rate base of $8.8 billion to a 2009 projected average rate base of $9.2 billion. The Michigan Public Service Commission (MPSC) is expected to make a ruling at the end of 2008.

▶ On October 6, 2008, the governor of Michigan signed into law an energy reform package that would modify the state's electric choice pro-gram and establish a 12-month deadline for the resolution of utility rate cases.

## Investment Rationale/Risk

▶ The shares are down approximately 14% year to date, hurt, in our view, by the decline in both the economy and the stock market. While we see long-term benefits from the energy legisla-tion modifying Michigan's electric choice pro-gram, we believe that given the worsening out-look for the state's economy, which has been exacerbated by the crisis in the financial mar-kets, there will be only a gradual recovery in the shares. While DTE's synfuel tax credits ex-pired at the end of 2007, it expects about $200 million in cash benefits produced from synfuel-related hedges in both 2008 and 2009.

▶ Risks to our recommendation and target price include a slower-than-expected recovery in both the financial markets and the Michigan economy, as well as a sharp decrease in the average P/E of the peer group as a whole.

▶ The shares recently yielded about 5.6% on what we consider a secure dividend, well above the recent peer average of 4.9%. However, given the current market, we do not expect this to benefit the stock. Our 12-month target price is $37, a discount-to-peers P/E of about 11.7X our EPS estimate for 2009.

## Qualitative Risk Assessment

| LOW | MEDIUM | HIGH |
|---|---|---|

Our risk assessment reflects a balance between the steady cash flow that we expect from the regulated utilities, which operate within a generally supportive regulatory environment, and most of the unregulated operations, which continue to contribute a significant portion of DTE's consolidated cash flow. While we expect DTE to benefit from the modification of Michigan's Electric Choice program, we remain concerned about the weak outlook for the state's economy .

## Quantitative Evaluations

### S&P Quality Ranking     B

| D | C | B- | B | B+ | A- | A | A+ |
|---|---|---|---|---|---|---|---|

### Relative Strength Rank     STRONG

86

LOWEST = 1    HIGHEST = 99

## Revenue/Earnings Data

### Revenue (Million $)

| | 1Q | 2Q | 3Q | 4Q | Year |
|---|---|---|---|---|---|
| 2008 | 2,570 | 2,251 | 2,338 | -- | -- |
| 2007 | 2,463 | 1,692 | 2,140 | 2,211 | 8,506 |
| 2006 | 2,635 | 1,895 | 2,196 | 2,296 | 9,022 |
| 2005 | 2,309 | 1,941 | 2,060 | 2,712 | 9,022 |
| 2004 | 2,093 | 1,501 | 1,594 | 1,926 | 7,114 |
| 2003 | 2,095 | 1,600 | 1,654 | 1,692 | 7,041 |

### Earnings Per Share ($)

| | | | | | |
|---|---|---|---|---|---|
| 2008 | 1.23 | 0.17 | 1.03 | E0.95 | E2.95 |
| 2007 | 0.54 | 1.99 | 0.92 | 1.17 | 4.62 |
| 2006 | 0.76 | -0.18 | 1.07 | 0.81 | 2.45 |
| 2005 | 0.72 | 0.19 | 0.17 | 2.18 | 3.27 |
| 2004 | 1.15 | 0.20 | 0.54 | 0.68 | 2.55 |
| 2003 | 0.64 | -0.22 | 1.06 | 1.36 | 2.85 |

Fiscal year ended Dec. 31. Next earnings report expected: Late February. EPS Estimates based on S&P Operating Earnings; historical GAAP earnings are as reported.

## Dividend Data (Dates: mm/dd Payment Date: mm/dd/yy)

| Amount ($) | Date Decl. | Ex-Div. Date | Stk. of Record | Payment Date |
|---|---|---|---|---|
| 0.530 | 12/07 | 12/13 | 12/17 | 01/15/08 |
| 0.530 | 03/07 | 03/17 | 03/19 | 04/15/08 |
| 0.530 | 06/06 | 06/12 | 06/16 | 07/15/08 |
| 0.530 | 09/05 | 09/11 | 09/15 | 10/15/08 |

Dividends have been paid since 1909. Source: Company reports.

---

**Please read the Required Disclosures and Analyst Certification on the last page of this report.**

The McGraw-Hill Companies

# DTE Energy Co

**STANDARD &POOR'S**

## Business Summary November 04, 2008

CORPORATE OVERVIEW. DTE Energy, formed on January 1, 1996, is the holding company for The Detroit Edison Company and Michigan Consolidated Gas (MichCon), regulated electric and gas utilities serving customers within the state of Michigan, and three non-utility operations engaged in a variety of energy-related businesses in various portions of the United States. The regulated utility operations accounted for 79.6% of consolidated revenues in 2007, and the non-utility operations 20.4%.

MARKET PROFILE. Detroit Edison is a regulated electric utility serving approximately 2.2 million customers in southeastern Michigan. In 2007, residential customers accounted for 37.0% of the utility's revenues; commercial customers 36.7%; industrial customers 18.2%; other 5.5%; and wholesale 2.6%. With its high percentage of commercial and industrial customers, the utility has been hurt by the state's Customer Choice program, losing about 4% of retail sales in 2007, 6% in 2006, 12% in 2005, and 18% in 2004. However, the loss of customers also had the effect of reducing the need for purchased power, and allowed it to sell excess power into the wholesale market when conditions were favorable. The utility's generating capability is heavily dependent on the availability of coal, which accounts for approximately 70% of its fuel re-

quirements. The majority of the utility's coal needs are obtained through long-term contracts, with the remainder purchased through short-term agreements or purchases in the spot market.

MichCon is a regulated natural gas utility serving about 1.3 million residential, commercial and industrial customers in the state of Michigan. It also has subsidiaries involved in the gathering and transmission of natural gas in northern Michigan, and operates one of the largest natural gas distribution and transmission systems in the U.S., with connections to interstate pipelines providing access to most of the major natural gas producing regions in the Gulf Coast, Mid-Continent and Canadian regions. The company purchases its natural gas supplies on the open market through a diversified portfolio of supply contracts, and given its storage capacity, should be able to meet its supply requirements.

## Company Financials Fiscal Year Ended Dec. 31

| Per Share Data ($) | 2007 | 2006 | 2005 | 2004 | 2003 | 2002 | 2001 | 2000 | 1999 | 1998 |
|---|---|---|---|---|---|---|---|---|---|---|
| Tangible Book Value | 23.23 | 21.02 | 20.88 | 20.01 | 19.05 | 14.61 | 16.06 | 28.15 | 26.96 | 25.49 |
| Earnings | 4.62 | 2.45 | 3.27 | 2.55 | 2.85 | 3.83 | 2.14 | 3.27 | 3.33 | 3.05 |
| S&P Core Earnings | 1.55 | 2.88 | 2.13 | 1.97 | 3.22 | 2.80 | 2.09 | NA | NA | NA |
| Dividends | 2.12 | 2.08 | 2.06 | 2.06 | 2.06 | 2.06 | 2.06 | 2.06 | 2.06 | 2.06 |
| Payout Ratio | 46% | 85% | 63% | 81% | 72% | 54% | 96% | 63% | 62% | 68% |
| Prices:High | 54.74 | 49.24 | 48.31 | 45.49 | 49.50 | 47.70 | 47.13 | 41.31 | 44.69 | 49.25 |
| Prices:Low | 43.96 | 38.77 | 41.39 | 37.88 | 34.00 | 33.05 | 33.13 | 28.44 | 31.06 | 33.44 |
| P/E Ratio:High | 12 | 20 | 15 | 18 | 17 | 12 | 22 | 13 | 13 | 16 |
| P/E Ratio:Low | 10 | 16 | 13 | 15 | 12 | 9 | 15 | 9 | 9 | 11 |

| Income Statement Analysis (Million $) | 2007 | 2006 | 2005 | 2004 | 2003 | 2002 | 2001 | 2000 | 1999 | 1998 |
|---|---|---|---|---|---|---|---|---|---|---|
| Revenue | 8,506 | 9,022 | 9,022 | 7,114 | 7,041 | 6,749 | 7,849 | 5,597 | 4,728 | 4,221 |
| Depreciation | 932 | 1,014 | 869 | 744 | 687 | 759 | 795 | 758 | 735 | 661 |
| Maintenance | NA | NA | NA | NA | NA | NA | NA | NA | NA | NA |
| Fixed Charges Coverage | 1.55 | 1.82 | 1.21 | 1.35 | 1.49 | 2.00 | 2.04 | 2.42 | 2.60 | 2.84 |
| Construction Credits | NA | NA | NA | NA | NA | NA | NA | NA | NA | Nil |
| Effective Tax Rate | 31.5% | NM | NM | NM | 24.0% | NM | NM | 1.89% | 11.0% | 25.8% |
| Net Income | 787 | 437 | 576 | 443 | 480 | 632 | 329 | 468 | 483 | 443 |
| S&P Core Earnings | 266 | 512 | 374 | 344 | 542 | 463 | 322 | NA | NA | NA |

| Balance Sheet & Other Financial Data (Million $) | 2007 | 2006 | 2005 | 2004 | 2003 | 2002 | 2001 | 2000 | 1999 | 1998 |
|---|---|---|---|---|---|---|---|---|---|---|
| Gross Property | 18,809 | 19,224 | 18,660 | 18,011 | 17,679 | 17,862 | 17,067 | 13,162 | 12,746 | 12,178 |
| Capital Expenditures | 1,299 | 1,403 | 1,065 | 904 | 751 | 984 | 1,096 | 749 | 739 | 555 |
| Net Property | 11,408 | 11,451 | 10,830 | 10,491 | 10,324 | 9,813 | 9,543 | 7,387 | 7,148 | 6,943 |
| Capitalization:Long Term Debt | 6,971 | 7,474 | 7,080 | 7,606 | 7,669 | 7,785 | 7,928 | 4,062 | 4,052 | 4,323 |
| Capitalization:% Long Term Debt | 54.4 | 56.1 | 55.1 | 57.8 | 59.2 | 63.0 | 63.0 | 50.3 | 50.9 | 53.9 |
| Capitalization:Preferred | Nil | Nil | Nil | Nil | Nil | Nil | Nil | Nil | Nil | Nil |
| Capitalization:% Preferred | Nil | Nil | Nil | Nil | Nil | Nil | Nil | Nil | Nil | Nil |
| Capitalization:Common | 5,853 | 5,849 | 5,769 | 5,548 | 5,287 | 4,565 | 4,657 | 4,015 | 3,909 | 3,698 |
| Capitalization:% Common | 45.6 | 43.9 | 44.9 | 42.2 | 40.8 | 37.0 | 37.0 | 49.7 | 49.1 | 46.1 |
| Total Capital | 14,696 | 14,950 | 14,468 | 13,429 | 14,256 | 13,434 | 14,063 | 9,878 | 9,886 | 9,909 |
| % Operating Ratio | 95.2 | 91.2 | 96.1 | 93.4 | 91.1 | 82.8 | 86.3 | 85.3 | 82.2 | 81.4 |
| % Earned on Net Property | 6.8 | 7.4 | 8.9 | 8.1 | 7.2 | 11.4 | 8.2 | 11.4 | 12.8 | 11.8 |
| % Return on Revenue | 9.3 | 4.8 | 6.4 | 6.2 | 6.8 | 9.4 | 4.2 | 8.4 | 10.2 | 10.5 |
| % Return on Invested Capital | 3.1 | 5.4 | 6.0 | 6.1 | 7.5 | 9.1 | 8.9 | 8.1 | 8.3 | 6.2 |
| % Return on Common Equity | 13.5 | 7.5 | 10.2 | 8.2 | 9.7 | 13.8 | 7.6 | 11.8 | 12.7 | 12.2 |

Data as orig reptd.; bef. results of disc opers/spec. items. Per share data adj. for stk. divs.; EPS diluted. E-Estimated. NA-Not Available. NM-Not Meaningful. NR-Not Ranked. UR-Under Review.

**Office:** 2000 2nd Ave, Detroit, MI 48226-1279.
**Telephone:** 313-235-4000.
**Email:** shareholdersvcs@dteenergy.com
**Website:** http://www.dteenergy.com

**Chrmn & CEO:** A.F. Earley, Jr.
**Pres & COO:** G.M. Anderson
**EVP & CFO:** D. Meador
**SVP & General Counsel:** B.D. Peterson

**SVP & CIO:** L. Ellyn
**Investor Contact:** D. McClung (313-235-8030)
**Board Members:** L. Bauder, A. F. Earley, Jr., W. F. Fountain, A. D. Gilmour, A. R. Glancy, III, F. Hennessey, J. E. Lobbia, G. J. McGovern, E. A. Miller, C. W. Pryor, Jr., J. Robles, Jr., R. G. Shaw, J. H. Vandenberghe

**Founded:** 1995
**Domicile:** Michigan
**Employees:** 10,262

# Duke Energy Corp

STANDARD &POOR'S

| S&P Recommendation | HOLD ★★★☆☆ | Price<br>$15.64 (as of Nov 14, 2008) | 12-Mo. Target Price<br>$17.00 | Investment Style<br>Large-Cap Value |
|---|---|---|---|---|

**GICS Sector** Utilities
**Sub-Industry** Electric Utilities

**Summary** DUK provides service to about 3.9 million electric customers in North Carolina, South Carolina, Indiana, Ohio and Kentucky, and 500,000 gas customers in Kentucky and Ohio.

## Key Stock Statistics (Source S&P, Vickers, company reports)

| | | | | | | | |
|---|---|---|---|---|---|---|---|
| 52-Wk Range | $20.78– 13.50 | S&P Oper. EPS 2008**E** | 1.12 | Market Capitalization(B) | $19.789 | Beta | 0.40 |
| Trailing 12-Month EPS | $1.01 | S&P Oper. EPS 2009**E** | 1.33 | Yield (%) | 5.88 | S&P 3-Yr. Proj. EPS CAGR(%) | 5 |
| Trailing 12-Month P/E | 15.5 | P/E on S&P Oper. EPS 2008**E** | 14.0 | Dividend Rate/Share | $0.92 | S&P Credit Rating | A- |
| $10K Invested 5 Yrs Ago | NA | Common Shares Outstg. (M) | 1,265.3 | Institutional Ownership (%) | 57 | | |

## Price Performance

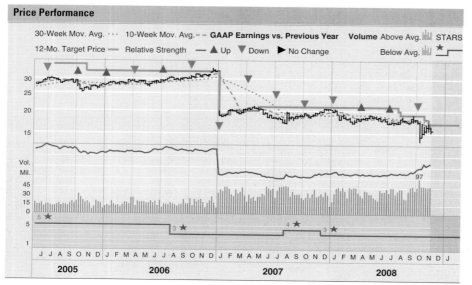

30-Week Mov. Avg. · · · 10-Week Mov. Avg. - - - **GAAP Earnings vs. Previous Year** Volume Above Avg. ▐▌▌▌ STARS
12-Mo. Target Price — Relative Strength — ▲ Up ▼ Down ► No Change Below Avg. ▐▌▌ ★

Options: ASE, CBOE, P, Ph

## Qualitative Risk Assessment

| LOW | MEDIUM | HIGH |
|---|---|---|

Our risk assessment reflects DUK's large market capitalization and a balanced portfolio of businesses that include lower-risk regulated electric and gas utility services, partly offset by higher-risk unregulated businesses, though they make up less than 25% of the company's earnings.

## Quantitative Evaluations

**S&P Quality Ranking**      B

| D | C | B- | B | B+ | A- | A | A+ |
|---|---|---|---|---|---|---|---|

**Relative Strength Rank**      **STRONG**

80

LOWEST = 1      HIGHEST = 99

## Revenue/Earnings Data

**Revenue (Million $)**

| | 1Q | 2Q | 3Q | 4Q | Year |
|---|---|---|---|---|---|
| 2008 | 3,337 | 3,229 | 3,508 | -- | -- |
| 2007 | 3,035 | 2,966 | 3,688 | 3,031 | 12,443 |
| 2006 | 3,106 | 3,865 | 4,143 | 4,070 | 15,184 |
| 2005 | 5,328 | 5,274 | 3,028 | 3,116 | 16,746 |
| 2004 | 5,635 | 5,318 | 5,504 | 6,046 | 22,503 |
| 2003 | 6,228 | 5,235 | 5,609 | 5,457 | 22,529 |

**Earnings Per Share ($)**

| | 1Q | 2Q | 3Q | 4Q | Year |
|---|---|---|---|---|---|
| 2008 | 0.37 | 0.27 | 0.17 | **E**0.18 | **E**1.12 |
| 2007 | 0.27 | 0.24 | 0.48 | 0.21 | 1.20 |
| 2006 | 0.50 | 0.34 | 0.60 | 0.31 | 1.70 |
| 2005 | 0.88 | 0.32 | 0.96 | 0.43 | 2.61 |
| 2004 | 0.07 | 0.43 | 0.42 | 0.36 | 1.27 |
| 2003 | 0.43 | 0.46 | 0.05 | -1.99 | -1.13 |

Fiscal year ended Dec. 31. Next earnings report expected: Early February. EPS Estimates based on S&P Operating Earnings; historical GAAP earnings are as reported.

## Highlights

▸ The 12-month target price for DUK has recently been changed to $17.00 from $18.00. The Highlights section of this Stock Report will be updated accordingly.

## Investment Rationale/Risk

▸ The Investment Rationale/Risk section of this Stock Report will be updated shortly. For the latest News story on DUK from MarketScope, see below.

▸ 11/05/08 09:53 am ET ... S&P MAINTAINS HOLD RECOMMENDATION ON SHARES OF DUKE ENERGY (DUK 16.01***): Q3 recurring EPS of $0.27 vs. $0.45 misses our estimate by $0.18. Mark-to-market losses hurt results by $0.06 and storm costs and mild weather another $0.08. DUK does not provide enough data to compare operations with our expectations until its 10-Q filing, but we note unfavorable EBIT comparisons for all segments. We like DUK's higher-growth Carolina service territories and the prospect for increasing rate base through 2012. However, we are cutting our '08 EPS estimate by $0.22 to $1.12 on the lower Q3, and '09's by $0.03 to $1.33. We also lower our target price by $1 to $17. /CMuir

## Dividend Data (Dates: mm/dd Payment Date: mm/dd/yy)

| Amount ($) | Date Decl. | Ex-Div. Date | Stk. of Record | Payment Date |
|---|---|---|---|---|
| 0.220 | 01/04 | 02/13 | 02/15 | 03/17/08 |
| 0.220 | 05/08 | 05/15 | 05/19 | 06/16/08 |
| 0.230 | 06/24 | 08/13 | 08/15 | 09/16/08 |
| 0.230 | 10/28 | 11/12 | 11/14 | 12/16/08 |

Dividends have been paid since 1926. Source: Company reports.

The McGraw-Hill Companies

# Duke Energy Corp

**STANDARD &POOR'S**

## Business Summary October 20, 2008

CORPORATE OVERVIEW. Duke provides electric and gas utility services, sells wholesale power, has investments in various South American generation plants, and owns 50% of a real estate joint venture. Operating segments include Franchised Electric and Gas, Commercial Power, Duke Energy International (DEI), and Crescent Resources.

MARKET PROFILE. Franchised Electric and Gas serves about 3.9 million electric customers over 47,000 square miles in North Carolina, South Carolina, Indiana, Ohio and Kentucky and about 500,000 gas customers in Kentucky and Ohio, and owns generating assets totaling 27,856 MW (49% coal; 21% natural gas, oil or other; 18% nuclear; and 12% hydro) as of December 2007. Electric sales in 2007 were 29% residential, 32% commercial, 29% industrial and 10% other. We believe the combination with Cinergy effectively reduces the impact that the slowing textile industry in the Carolinas will have on the company's overall sales going forward.

The Commercial Power segment consists of 8,019 MW, mostly supporting regulated operations in Ohio. There are 5,813 MW located in Ohio, 640 MW in Illinois, 620 MW in Pennsylvania, 480 MW in Indiana, and 466 MW in Tennessee. DEI primarily consists of power generation (3,968 MW) in Central and South America. Crescent Resources develops and manages commercial, residential and multi-family real estate projects in the Southeast and Southwest, and manages legacy land holdings in North and South Carolina.

CORPORATE STRATEGY. We believe DUK has become an electric company focused on regulated operations and electric sales to regulated businesses. In September 2005, Duke began disposing a portion of its former wholesale power generation and marketing unit assets (9,860 net MW of generation capacity at 2004 year end) and contracts outside the Midwest. In March 2006, DUK purchased a Cincinnati-based electric distribution company; in September 2006, DUK sold 51% of Crescent Resources to Morgan Stanley; and in January 2007, the company spun off its natural gas businesses to shareholders.

## Company Financials Fiscal Year Ended Dec. 31

| Per Share Data ($) | 2007 | 2006 | 2005 | 2004 | 2003 | 2002 | 2001 | 2000 | 1999 | 1998 |
|---|---|---|---|---|---|---|---|---|---|---|
| Tangible Book Value | 12.55 | 13.54 | 13.65 | 12.54 | 10.74 | 12.51 | 14.11 | 11.21 | 10.69 | 10.09 |
| Earnings | 1.20 | 1.70 | 2.61 | 1.27 | -1.13 | 1.22 | 2.56 | 2.38 | 1.13 | 1.71 |
| S&P Core Earnings | 1.22 | 1.80 | 1.29 | 1.24 | -1.10 | 1.01 | 2.29 | NA | NA | NA |
| Dividends | 0.86 | 0.95 | 1.17 | 1.10 | 1.10 | 1.10 | 1.10 | 1.10 | 1.10 | 1.10 |
| Payout Ratio | 70% | 56% | 45% | 87% | NM | 90% | 43% | 46% | 98% | 64% |
| Prices:High | 21.30 | 34.50 | 30.55 | 26.16 | 21.57 | 40.00 | 47.74 | 45.22 | 32.66 | 35.50 |
| Prices:Low | 16.91 | 26.94 | 24.37 | 18.85 | 12.21 | 16.42 | 32.22 | 22.88 | 23.38 | 26.56 |
| P/E Ratio:High | 17 | 20 | 12 | 21 | NM | 33 | 19 | 19 | 29 | 21 |
| P/E Ratio:Low | 14 | 16 | 9 | 15 | NM | 13 | 13 | 10 | 21 | 16 |

| Income Statement Analysis (Million $) | | | | | | | | | | |
|---|---|---|---|---|---|---|---|---|---|---|
| Revenue | 12,720 | 15,184 | 16,746 | 22,503 | 22,529 | 15,663 | 59,503 | 49,318 | 21,742 | 17,610 |
| Depreciation | 1,746 | 2,049 | 1,728 | 1,851 | 1,803 | 1,571 | 1,336 | 1,167 | 968 | 909 |
| Maintenance | NA | NA | NA | NA | NA | NA | NA | NA | NA | NA |
| Fixed Charges Coverage | 4.03 | 2.77 | 2.91 | 2.40 | 1.96 | 2.46 | 5.33 | 4.25 | 3.16 | 4.78 |
| Construction Credits | NA | NA | NA | NA | NA | NA | 53.0 | 63.0 | 82.0 | 88.0 |
| Effective Tax Rate | 31.8% | 28.8% | 29.5% | 27.5% | NM | 35.1% | 33.1% | 32.9% | 31.4% | 36.4% |
| Net Income | 1,522 | 2,019 | 2,533 | 1,232 | -1,005 | 1,034 | 1,994 | 1,776 | 847 | 1,260 |
| S&P Core Earnings | 1,551 | 2,131 | 1,249 | 1,199 | -994 | 908 | 1,777 | NA | NA | NA |

| Balance Sheet & Other Financial Data (Million $) | | | | | | | | | | |
|---|---|---|---|---|---|---|---|---|---|---|
| Gross Property | 46,056 | 58,330 | 40,574 | 46,806 | 47,157 | 48,677 | 39,464 | 34,615 | 30,436 | 27,128 |
| Capital Expenditures | 3,125 | 3,381 | 2,309 | 2,055 | 2,470 | 4,924 | 5,930 | 5,634 | 5,936 | 2,159 |
| Net Property | 31,110 | 41,447 | 29,200 | 33,506 | 34,986 | 36,219 | 28,415 | 24,469 | 20,995 | 16,875 |
| Capitalization:Long Term Debt | 9,498 | 18,118 | 14,547 | 16,932 | 20,622 | 21,629 | 13,728 | 12,425 | 10,087 | 7,191 |
| Capitalization:% Long Term Debt | 30.9 | 41.0 | 46.9 | 50.5 | 59.8 | 58.9 | 51.5 | 54.7 | 52.0 | 45.9 |
| Capitalization:Preferred | Nil | Nil | Nil | 134 | 134 | 157 | 234 | 247 | 313 | 313 |
| Capitalization:% Preferred | Nil | Nil | Nil | 0.40 | 0.39 | 0.43 | 0.88 | 1.09 | 1.61 | 2.00 |
| Capitalization:Common | 21,199 | 26,102 | 16,439 | 16,441 | 13,748 | 14,944 | 12,689 | 10,056 | 8,998 | 8,150 |
| Capitalization:% Common | 69.1 | 59.0 | 53.1 | 49.1 | 39.8 | 40.7 | 47.6 | 44.2 | 46.4 | 52.1 |
| Total Capital | 35,629 | 52,203 | 36,988 | 40,375 | 40,490 | 43,644 | 33,393 | 29,225 | 24,225 | 19,882 |
| % Operating Ratio | 86.0 | 87.6 | 89.6 | 88.6 | 85.4 | 87.1 | 95.0 | 94.3 | 93.8 | 90.6 |
| % Earned on Net Property | 6.9 | 9.0 | 11.5 | 8.9 | NM | 7.6 | 15.5 | 16.8 | 9.5 | 14.9 |
| % Return on Revenue | 12.0 | 13.3 | 15.1 | 5.5 | NM | 6.6 | 3.4 | 3.6 | 3.9 | 7.2 |
| % Return on Invested Capital | 4.7 | 7.5 | 11.1 | 7.0 | 8.7 | 6.3 | 10.5 | 11.2 | 7.6 | 13.2 |
| % Return on Common Equity | 6.4 | 9.5 | 15.3 | 8.1 | NM | 7.4 | 17.4 | 18.4 | 9.6 | 15.5 |

Data as orig reptd.; bef. results of disc opers/spec. items. Per share data adj. for stk. divs.; EPS diluted. E-Estimated. NA-Not Available. NM-Not Meaningful. NR-Not Ranked. UR-Under Review.

**Office:** 526 South Church Street, Charlotte, NC 28202-1904.
**Telephone:** 704-594-6200.
**Website:** http://www.duke-energy.com
**Chrmn, Pres & CEO:** J.E. Rogers

**EVP & CIO:** A.R. Mullinax
**SVP, Chief Acctg Officer & Cntlr:** S.K. Young
**SVP & Secy:** J.S. Janson
**CFO:** D.L. Hauser

**Investor Contact:** S.G. De May ()
**Board Members:** W. Barnet, III, G. A. Bernhardt, M. G. Browning, D. R. DiMicco, A. M. Gray, J. H. Hance, Jr., J. T. Rhodes, J. E. Rogers, M. L. Schapiro, P. R. Sharp, D. S. Taft

**Founded:** 1916
**Domicile:** North Carolina
**Employees:** 17,800

# E. I. du Pont de Nemours and Co

STANDARD
&POOR'S

**S&P Recommendation** HOLD ★★★☆☆

| | | |
|---|---|---|
| **Price** | **12-Mo. Target Price** | **Investment Style** |
| $27.43 (as of Nov 14, 2008) | $33.00 | Large-Cap Value |

**GICS Sector** Materials
**Sub-Industry** Diversified Chemicals

**Summary** This broadly diversified company is the second largest U.S. chemicals manufacturer.

## Key Stock Statistics (Source S&P, Vickers, company reports)

| | | | | | | | |
|---|---|---|---|---|---|---|---|
| 52-Wk Range | $52.49– 26.08 | S&P Oper. EPS 2008**E** | 3.10 | Market Capitalization(B) | $24.752 | Beta | 1.06 |
| Trailing 12-Month EPS | $3.49 | S&P Oper. EPS 2009**E** | 3.25 | Yield (%) | 5.98 | S&P 3-Yr. Proj. EPS CAGR(%) | 8 |
| Trailing 12-Month P/E | 7.9 | P/E on S&P Oper. EPS 2008**E** | 8.8 | Dividend Rate/Share | $1.64 | S&P Credit Rating | A |
| $10K Invested 5 Yrs Ago | $8,101 | Common Shares Outstg. (M) | 902.4 | Institutional Ownership (%) | 67 | | |

## Price Performance

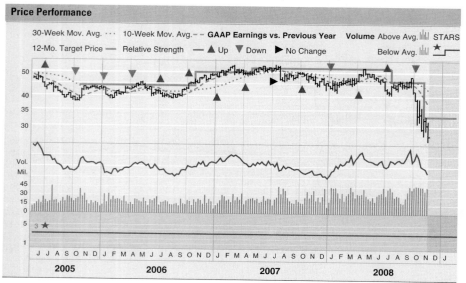

30-Week Mov. Avg. · · · 10-Week Mov. Avg. - - GAAP Earnings vs. Previous Year Volume Above Avg. STARS
12-Mo. Target Price — Relative Strength — ▲ Up ▼ Down ► No Change Below Avg. ★

Options: ASE, CBOE, P, Ph

Analysis prepared by **Richard O'Reilly, CFA** on October 29, 2008, when the stock traded at **$ 31.52**.

## Highlights

➤ We expect sales to grow modestly in 2009. We believe that selling prices, aided by growth of newer products, will continue to advance. We see continuing negative trends in DD's chemicals businesses in 2009, reflecting downturns in key U.S. markets, offset by global economic growth, and unfavorable currency exchange rates. We expect raw material and energy costs to ease after a rapid rise in 2008.

➤ We think the agriculture segment's sales and profits will continue to advance after projected 20% profit growth in 2008 on strong global farm fundamentals. DD believes that its U.S. corn seed market share was equal to 2007's level. Pharmaceuticals profits may begin to see the impact of pending patent expirations in 2010 of Cozaar/Hyzaar.

➤ Our EPS estimate for 2008 includes a $0.24 benefit from a weaker U.S. dollar, and second-half EPS are expected to include about $0.28 in total costs from hurricane-related damage and lost sales. We look for the base tax rate for 2009 to be similar to 22% for 2008.

## Investment Rationale/Risk

➤ While we expect the company to achieve increased profits in 2009 on global volume gains and better agricultural markets, we look for DD to continue to face headwinds from downturns in the U.S. housing and auto markets. Historically, high raw material costs have pressured chemicals margins. The company stabilized its market share in 2008 in the important domestic corn seed market.

➤ Risks to our opinion and target price include weaker-than-expected global industrial activity, higher raw material costs than we assume, adverse weather conditions reducing demand for agricultural products, and an inability to successfully develop and launch new products.

➤ The stock recently traded at a P/E ratio below the S&P 500, at about 9X our 2009 EPS estimate of $3.25. DD also trades below our intrinsic value calculation of $35, which assumes average annual free cash flow growth of 10% over 10 years, terminal growth of 3% a year, and a discount rate of 9.0%. Using a blend of our relative P/E and discounted cash flow metrics, our 12-month target price is $33. DD's recent dividend yield was nearly twice that of the S&P 500.

## Quantitative Evaluations

**S&P Quality Ranking** B

| D | C | B- | **B** | B+ | A- | A | A+ |
|---|---|---|---|---|---|---|---|

**Relative Strength Rank** MODERATE

43

LOWEST = 1 HIGHEST = 99

## Revenue/Earnings Data

**Revenue (Million $)**

| | 1Q | 2Q | 3Q | 4Q | Year |
|---|---|---|---|---|---|
| 2008 | 8,925 | 9,308 | 7,717 | -- | -- |
| 2007 | 7,845 | 7,875 | 6,675 | 6,983 | 29,378 |
| 2006 | 7,394 | 7,442 | 6,309 | 6,276 | 27,421 |
| 2005 | 7,431 | 7,511 | 5,870 | 5,827 | 26,639 |
| 2004 | 8,073 | 7,527 | 5,740 | 6,000 | 27,340 |
| 2003 | 7,008 | 7,369 | 6,142 | 6,477 | 26,996 |

**Earnings Per Share ($)**

| | 1Q | 2Q | 3Q | 4Q | Year |
|---|---|---|---|---|---|
| 2008 | 1.31 | 1.18 | 0.40 | E0.21 | E3.10 |
| 2007 | 1.01 | 1.04 | 0.56 | 0.60 | 3.22 |
| 2006 | 0.88 | 1.04 | 0.52 | 0.94 | 3.38 |
| 2005 | 0.96 | 1.01 | -0.09 | 0.16 | 2.07 |
| 2004 | 0.66 | 0.50 | 0.33 | 0.28 | 1.77 |
| 2003 | 0.56 | 0.50 | -0.88 | 0.63 | 0.99 |

Fiscal year ended Dec. 31. Next earnings report expected: Late January. EPS Estimates based on S&P Operating Earnings; historical GAAP earnings are as reported.

## Dividend Data (Dates: mm/dd Payment Date: mm/dd/yy)

| Amount ($) | Date Decl. | Ex-Div. Date | Stk. of Record | Payment Date |
|---|---|---|---|---|
| 0.410 | 01/30 | 02/13 | 02/15 | 03/14/08 |
| 0.410 | 04/30 | 05/13 | 05/15 | 06/12/08 |
| 0.410 | 07/30 | 08/13 | 08/15 | 09/12/08 |
| 0.410 | 10/29 | 11/12 | 11/14 | 12/12/08 |

Dividends have been paid since 1904. Source: Company reports.

# E. I. du Pont de Nemours and Co

**STANDARD &POOR'S**

## Business Summary October 29, 2008

E.I. du Pont de Nemours and Company, the second largest domestic chemicals producer, has made several major changes in recent years, including expanding its life sciences businesses (now crop pesticides and nutrition). In April 2004, it sold the Textile and Interiors unit (consisting of nylon, polyester and Lycra fibers, with total annual sales of $6.3 billion) for $4.2 billion; proceeds were largely used to repay debt. The sale of the fiber businesses reduced DD's then exposure to raw material cost changes by about 55%.

Foreign sales accounted for 62% of the total in 2007.

The Agricultural and Nutrition segment (23% of sales in 2007, and 18% of pretax operating income) consists of Pioneer Hi-Bred (46% of segment sales in 2006), the world's largest seed company, including corn (70% of sales) and soybeans; DuPont is also a major global supplier of crop protection chemicals (35%). Pioneer estimates that its U.S. corn market share again declined slightly in 2007 to 30%, partly due to a limited supply of certain biotech traits. The segment also includes nutrition and health (including the Solae soy business and food packaging products) and microbial diagnostic testing products. Segment sales rose 14% in 2007 and profits climbed nearly 50% partly due to a restructuring charge in 2006.

The Coatings and Color Technologies unit (22%, 17%) is one of the largest global auto paint suppliers (including OEM and refinish markets) and the largest maker of titanium dioxide pigments (35% of segment sales). The segment also includes industrial and powder coatings, and inks for digital printing. Segment volume grew 1% in 2007 as increases in titanium pigments, particularly in Europe and Asia Pacific, were partially offset by declines in automotive OEM sales, primarily in North America and Europe.

The Electronic and Communication Technologies segment (13%, 12%) includes electronic and advanced display materials and products (photoresins, slurries, films, laminants), and flexographic printing and proofing systems. DD is the world's largest maker of fluorochemicals (refrigerants, blowing agents, aerosols) and fluoropolymers (Teflon resins and coatings).

Performance Materials (22%, 13%) includes engineering polymers for auto, electrical, consumer and industrial uses; packaging and industrial polymers; polyester films; and elastomers.

## Company Financials Fiscal Year Ended Dec. 31

| Per Share Data ($) | 2007 | 2006 | 2005 | 2004 | 2003 | 2002 | 2001 | 2000 | 1999 | 1998 |
|---|---|---|---|---|---|---|---|---|---|---|
| Tangible Book Value | 6.64 | 4.56 | 4.24 | 6.25 | 4.63 | 4.54 | 7.30 | 4.50 | 3.72 | 9.78 |
| Cash Flow | 4.70 | 4.49 | 3.45 | 3.11 | 2.58 | 3.35 | 5.83 | 3.96 | 1.73 | 2.70 |
| Earnings | 3.22 | 3.38 | 2.07 | 1.77 | 0.99 | 1.84 | 4.15 | 2.19 | 0.19 | 1.43 |
| S&P Core Earnings | 2.93 | 2.98 | 1.98 | 2.00 | 1.14 | 0.40 | -1.04 | NA | NA | NA |
| Dividends | 1.52 | 1.48 | 1.46 | 1.40 | 1.40 | 1.40 | 1.40 | 1.40 | 1.40 | 1.37 |
| Payout Ratio | 47% | 44% | 71% | 79% | 141% | 76% | 34% | 64% | NM | 96% |
| Prices:High | 53.90 | 49.68 | 54.90 | 49.39 | 46.00 | 49.80 | 49.88 | 74.00 | 75.19 | 84.44 |
| Prices:Low | 42.25 | 38.52 | 37.60 | 39.88 | 38.60 | 35.02 | 32.64 | 38.19 | 50.06 | 51.69 |
| P/E Ratio:High | 17 | 15 | 27 | 28 | 46 | 27 | 12 | 34 | NM | 59 |
| P/E Ratio:Low | 13 | 11 | 18 | 23 | 39 | 19 | 8 | 17 | NM | 36 |

| Income Statement Analysis (Million $) | 2007 | 2006 | 2005 | 2004 | 2003 | 2002 | 2001 | 2000 | 1999 | 1998 |
|---|---|---|---|---|---|---|---|---|---|---|
| Revenue | 29,378 | 27,421 | 26,639 | 27,340 | 26,996 | 24,006 | 24,726 | 28,268 | 26,918 | 24,767 |
| Operating Income | 4,269 | 3,612 | 3,507 | 3,574 | 3,176 | 4,263 | 4,130 | 5,244 | 5,469 | 5,680 |
| Depreciation | 1,371 | 1,384 | 1,358 | 1,347 | 1,584 | 1,515 | 1,754 | 1,860 | 1,690 | 1,452 |
| Interest Expense | 430 | 460 | 518 | 362 | 347 | 359 | 590 | 810 | 535 | 640 |
| Pretax Income | 3,743 | 3,329 | 3,558 | 1,442 | 143 | 2,124 | 6,844 | 3,447 | 1,690 | 2,613 |
| Effective Tax Rate | 20.0% | 5.89% | 41.3% | NM | NM | 8.71% | 36.0% | 31.1% | 83.4% | 36.0% |
| Net Income | 2,988 | 3,148 | 2,053 | 1,780 | 1,002 | 1,841 | 4,328 | 2,314 | 219 | 1,648 |
| S&P Core Earnings | 2,713 | 2,768 | 1,965 | 2,008 | 1,132 | 398 | -1,087 | NA | NA | NA |

| Balance Sheet & Other Financial Data (Million $) | 2007 | 2006 | 2005 | 2004 | 2003 | 2002 | 2001 | 2000 | 1999 | 1998 |
|---|---|---|---|---|---|---|---|---|---|---|
| Cash | 1,436 | 1,893 | 1,851 | 3,536 | 3,298 | 4,143 | 5,848 | 1,617 | 1,582 | 1,069 |
| Current Assets | 13,160 | 12,870 | 12,422 | 15,211 | 18,462 | 13,459 | 14,801 | 11,656 | 12,653 | 9,236 |
| Total Assets | 34,131 | 31,777 | 33,250 | 35,632 | 37,039 | 34,621 | 40,319 | 39,426 | 40,777 | 38,536 |
| Current Liabilities | 8,541 | 7,940 | 7,463 | 7,939 | 13,043 | 7,096 | 8,067 | 9,255 | 11,228 | 11,610 |
| Long Term Debt | 5,955 | 6,013 | 6,783 | 5,548 | 4,301 | 5,647 | 5,350 | 6,658 | 6,625 | 4,495 |
| Common Equity | 10,899 | 9,185 | 8,670 | 11,140 | 9,544 | 8,826 | 14,215 | 13,062 | 12,638 | 13,717 |
| Total Capital | 18,335 | 16,145 | 17,346 | 19,001 | 15,087 | 18,755 | 24,916 | 22,442 | 21,677 | 19,286 |
| Capital Expenditures | 1,585 | 1,532 | 1,340 | 1,232 | 1,713 | 1,280 | 1,494 | 1,925 | 2,055 | 2,240 |
| Cash Flow | 4,349 | 4,532 | 3,411 | 3,117 | 2,576 | 3,346 | 6,072 | 4,164 | 1,899 | 3,090 |
| Current Ratio | 1.5 | 1.6 | 1.7 | 1.9 | 1.4 | 1.9 | 1.8 | 1.3 | 1.1 | 0.8 |
| % Long Term Debt of Capitalization | 32.5 | 37.2 | 39.1 | 29.2 | 28.5 | 30.1 | 21.5 | 29.7 | 30.6 | 23.3 |
| % Net Income of Revenue | 10.2 | 11.5 | 7.7 | 6.5 | 3.7 | 7.7 | 17.5 | 8.2 | 0.8 | 6.7 |
| % Return on Assets | 9.1 | 9.7 | 6.0 | 4.9 | 2.8 | 4.9 | 10.9 | 5.8 | 0.6 | 4.4 |
| % Return on Equity | 29.7 | 35.2 | 20.6 | 17.1 | 10.8 | 15.9 | 31.7 | 17.9 | 1.6 | 13.3 |

Data as orig reptd.; bef. results of disc opers/spec. items. Per share data adj. for stk. divs.; EPS diluted. E-Estimated. NA-Not Available. NM-Not Meaningful. NR-Not Ranked. UR-Under Review.

**Office:** 1007 Market Street, Wilmington, DE 19898.
**Telephone:** 302-774-1000.
**Email:** info@dupont.com
**Website:** http://www.dupont.com

**Chrmn & CEO:** C.O. Holliday, Jr.
**COO & EVP:** R. Goodmanson
**EVP, CFO & Chief Acctg Officer:** J.L. Keefer
**SVP, CSO & CTO:** U. Chowdhry

**SVP & General Counsel:** T.L. Sager
**Investor Contact:** C.J. Lukach (800-441-7515)
**Board Members:** R. H. Brown, R. A. Brown, B. P. Collomb, C. J. Crawford, A. M. Cutler, J. T. Dillon, M. A. Hewson, C. O. Holliday, Jr., L. D. Juliber, T. D. Pont, II, W. K. Reilly, E. I. du Pont, II

**Founded:** 1802
**Domicile:** Delaware
**Employees:** 60,000

# Dynegy Inc.

**STANDARD &POOR'S**

| S&P Recommendation BUY ★★★★☆ | Price $2.38 (as of Nov 14, 2008) | 12-Mo. Target Price $4.00 | Investment Style Large-Cap Value |
| --- | --- | --- | --- |

**GICS Sector** Utilities
**Sub-Industry** Independent Power Producers & Energy Traders

**Summary** This company generates and sells wholesale power from plants located primarily in the U.S. Midwest, Northeast and South.

## Key Stock Statistics (Source S&P, Vickers, company reports)

| | | | | | | | |
| --- | --- | --- | --- | --- | --- | --- | --- |
| 52-Wk Range | $9.92–2.02 | S&P Oper. EPS 2008E | 0.19 | Market Capitalization(B) | $1.197 | Beta | 2.03 |
| Trailing 12-Month EPS | $0.16 | S&P Oper. EPS 2009E | 0.17 | Yield (%) | Nil | S&P 3-Yr. Proj. EPS CAGR(%) | -10 |
| Trailing 12-Month P/E | 14.9 | P/E on S&P Oper. EPS 2008E | 12.5 | Dividend Rate/Share | Nil | S&P Credit Rating | NA |
| $10K Invested 5 Yrs Ago | $5,920 | Common Shares Outstg. (M) | 842.9 | Institutional Ownership (%) | 84 | | |

## Price Performance

30-Week Mov. Avg. · · · · 10-Week Mov. Avg. - - GAAP Earnings vs. Previous Year   Volume Above Avg. STARS
12-Mo. Target Price — Relative Strength — ▲ Up ▼ Down ▶ No Change   Below Avg.

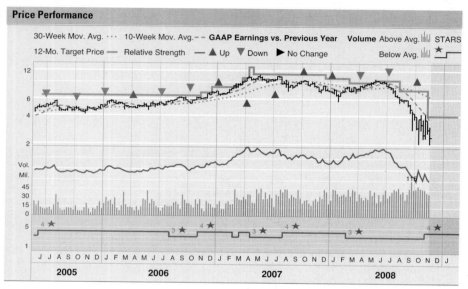

Options: ASE, CBOE, P, Ph

Analysis prepared by **Christopher B. Muir** on November 06, 2008, when the stock traded at **$ 3.00**.

## Highlights

➤ We expect revenues to increase about 23% in 2008 and 7.4% in 2009, reflecting the second-quarter 2007 purchase of LS Power's generation assets as well as expected higher gas prices, which tend to set power prices during times of peak usage. We also expect DYN revenues to see a long-term benefit from capacity auctions in various regions.

➤ We forecast 2008 and 2009 gross margins slightly lower than 2007's, due to the full-year effect of the LS Power acquisition, more than offset by higher per-revenue fuel costs. In addition, we look for operating margins of 18.5% in 2008 and 18.3% in 2009, down from 21.2% in 2007, as we expect lower per-revenue operations and maintenance costs to only partly offset the narrower gross margins. We forecast that interest expense will increase modestly on a full year's worth of acquisition-related interest.

➤ Assuming an effective tax rate of 35.3% and a greater number of shares outstanding stemming from the acquisition, we project 2008 recurring losses per share of $0.32 due to mark-to-market losses, compared to EPS of $0.37 in 2007. Our 2009 EPS estimate is $0.18.

## Investment Rationale/Risk

➤ In April 2007, DYN purchased LS Power's generation portfolio, which we view as accretive to cash flow and earnings. However, partly due to the acquisition, we see the company's debt reduction efforts as stalled, reducing EPS growth potential in the near future. Due to the large amount of hedges that do not qualify for hedge accounting, we see a very volatile earnings stream.

➤ Risks to our recommendation and target price include higher coal transportation costs and lower electricity demand. The variability of sales volumes, fuel and commodity prices and operational activities leads to less earnings visibility, in our opinion.

➤ The shares recently traded at about 17X our 2009 EPS estimate, a large premium to peers. Our 12-month target price of $4.00 is 22X our 2009 EPS forecast, also a very large premium to our peer target. We believe this valuation is warranted by strong power markets, which we think will lead to swift EPS growth in the next several years, and by our perception that the LS Power assets enhance DYN's current power plant portfolio and will add to its earnings.

## Qualitative Risk Assessment

| LOW | MEDIUM | HIGH |
| --- | --- | --- |

Our risk assessment is based on Dynegy's significant exposure to cyclical power markets and volatile commodity markets for fuels that it uses to generate power.

## Quantitative Evaluations

### S&P Quality Ranking    C

| D | C | B- | B | B+ | A- | A | A+ |
| --- | --- | --- | --- | --- | --- | --- | --- |

### Relative Strength Rank    WEAK

23

LOWEST = 1    HIGHEST = 99

## Revenue/Earnings Data

### Revenue (Million $)

| | 1Q | 2Q | 3Q | 4Q | Year |
| --- | --- | --- | --- | --- | --- |
| 2008 | 774.0 | 323.0 | 1,886 | -- | -- |
| 2007 | 505.0 | 828.0 | 1,046 | 724.0 | 3,103 |
| 2006 | 600.0 | 439.0 | 581.0 | 397.0 | 2,017 |
| 2005 | 462.0 | 459.0 | 770.0 | 622.0 | 2,313 |
| 2004 | 1,657 | 1,440 | 1,650 | 1,406 | 6,153 |
| 2003 | 1,879 | 1,067 | 1,385 | 1,456 | 5,787 |

### Earnings Per Share ($)

| | 1Q | 2Q | 3Q | 4Q | Year |
| --- | --- | --- | --- | --- | --- |
| 2008 | -0.18 | -0.32 | 0.72 | E0.04 | E0.19 |
| 2007 | 0.03 | Nil | 0.11 | -0.07 | 0.15 |
| 2006 | -0.01 | -0.48 | -0.14 | -0.12 | -0.80 |
| 2005 | -0.71 | -0.30 | -0.05 | -0.98 | -2.13 |
| 2004 | 0.14 | Nil | 0.16 | -0.47 | -0.09 |
| 2003 | -0.03 | -0.99 | 2.65 | -0.54 | 1.30 |

Fiscal year ended Dec. 31. Next earnings report expected: Late February. EPS Estimates based on S&P Operating Earnings; historical GAAP earnings are as reported.

## Dividend Data

No cash dividends have been paid since 2002.

# Dynegy Inc.

**STANDARD &POOR'S**

## Business Summary November 06, 2008

CORPORATE OVERVIEW. At the end of 2007, DYN owned or leased 19,165 net megawatts (MW) of generating capacity. The company provides energy, capacity and ancillary services primarily through bilateral negotiated contracts with third parties and into regional central markets. The power generation business consists of three segments -- the Midwest (9,230 MW), the West (6,126 MW), and the Northeast (3,809 MW). About 80% of DYN's generation capacity is gas-fired, 18% is coal-fired, and 2% is oil-fired. About 13% of its capacity can be switched to alternate fuels, including gas or oil. In terms of dispatch type, about 19% is base load generation, 32% is intermediate, and 50% is peaking.

By 2006, DYN had completed the fuel conversion of all its Midwest coal generation facilities to exclusively burn Powder River Basin (PRB) coal. PRB coal is a cleaner-burning coal with lower sulfur content, making it more economic to burn while emitting lower amounts of sulfur dioxide. DYN believes the conversion to PRB coal and attendant upgrades to new equipment and technologies will allow its units to improve operating margins and reliability.

CORPORATE STRATEGY. Dynegy has sought to strengthen its balance sheet in the wake of credit, accounting, regulatory and operating difficulties that nega-

tively affected the energy merchant industry in 2002 and 2003. The company raised $389 million in cash from the sale or exchange of businesses and investments in 2006, versus $2.4 billion in 2005, $246 million in 2004, $72 million in 2003, and $1.58 billion in 2002. In recent years, however, we believe the company has gained the financial flexibility to make acquisitions, including Sithe Energies in 2005 and the mostly stock acquisition of LS Power's generation portfolio. Operationally, DYN aims to focus on operational excellence.

IMPACT OF MAJOR DEVELOPMENTS. In January 2005, DYN completed the acquisition of Sithe Energies for $135 million in cash and the assumption of $919 million of project debt. The acquisition included the 1,021 MW Independence power generation facility located near Scriba, NY, four natural gas-fired merchant facilities in New York, and four hydroelectric generation facilities in Pennsylvania. In addition, Dynegy acquired a 750 MW firm capacity sales agreement with Con Edison, which runs through 2014, and provides annual cash receipts of $100 million.

## Company Financials Fiscal Year Ended Dec. 31

| Per Share Data ($) | 2007 | 2006 | 2005 | 2004 | 2003 | 2002 | 2001 | 2000 | 1999 | 1998 |
|---|---|---|---|---|---|---|---|---|---|---|
| Tangible Book Value | 4.26 | 3.86 | 5.58 | 4.87 | 5.04 | 4.57 | 8.85 | 6.49 | 4.03 | 3.15 |
| Cash Flow | 0.59 | -0.20 | -1.06 | 0.64 | -0.05 | -4.00 | 3.23 | 2.71 | 1.22 | 0.93 |
| Earnings | 0.15 | -0.80 | -2.13 | -0.09 | 1.30 | -6.24 | 1.89 | 1.48 | 0.65 | 0.48 |
| S&P Core Earnings | 0.13 | -0.68 | -0.71 | 0.06 | 1.76 | -1.96 | 0.73 | NA | NA | NA |
| Dividends | Nil | Nil | Nil | Nil | Nil | 0.15 | 0.30 | 0.32 | 0.04 | 0.04 |
| Payout Ratio | Nil | Nil | Nil | Nil | Nil | NM | 16% | 22% | 5% | 8% |
| Prices:High | 10.95 | 7.32 | 5.70 | 6.09 | 5.43 | 32.19 | 59.00 | 59.88 | 17.93 | 12.68 |
| Prices:Low | 6.47 | 4.50 | 3.21 | 3.40 | 1.13 | 0.49 | 20.00 | 17.12 | 7.34 | 6.79 |
| P/E Ratio:High | 73 | NM | NM | NM | 4 | NM | 31 | 40 | 27 | 27 |
| P/E Ratio:Low | 43 | NM | NM | NM | 1 | NM | 11 | 12 | 11 | 14 |

| Income Statement Analysis (Million $) | | | | | | | | | | |
|---|---|---|---|---|---|---|---|---|---|---|
| Revenue | 3,103 | 2,017 | 2,313 | 6,153 | 5,787 | 5,553 | 42,242 | 29,445 | 15,430 | 14,258 |
| Operating Income | 917 | 469 | 507 | 620 | 367 | 327 | 1,424 | 1,130 | 343 | 225 |
| Depreciation | 325 | 265 | 284 | 356 | 454 | 613 | 454 | 389 | 129 | 103 |
| Interest Expense | 399 | 382 | 389 | 480 | 509 | 374 | 259 | 251 | 78.2 | 75.0 |
| Pretax Income | 274 | -526 | -1,199 | -74.0 | -675 | -2,546 | 977 | 791 | 243 | 175 |
| Effective Tax Rate | 55.1% | NM | NM | NM | NM | NM | 27.5% | 33.0% | 30.7% | 28.7% |
| Net Income | 116 | -358 | -804 | -10.0 | -474 | -1,955 | 646 | 501 | 152 | 108 |
| S&P Core Earnings | 106 | -310 | -274 | 27.6 | 734 | -711 | 246 | NA | NA | NA |

| Balance Sheet & Other Financial Data (Million $) | | | | | | | | | | |
|---|---|---|---|---|---|---|---|---|---|---|
| Cash | 432 | 371 | 1,549 | 628 | 496 | 774 | 218 | 86.0 | 45.2 | 28.4 |
| Current Assets | 1,663 | 2,082 | 3,706 | 2,752 | 3,030 | 7,586 | 9,507 | 10,150 | 2,805 | 2,117 |
| Total Assets | 13,221 | 7,630 | 10,126 | 9,852 | 13,293 | 20,030 | 24,874 | 21,406 | 6,525 | 5,264 |
| Current Liabilities | 999 | 1,259 | 2,116 | 1,802 | 2,576 | 6,748 | 8,555 | 9,405 | 2,539 | 2,026 |
| Long Term Debt | 5,939 | 3,190 | 4,228 | 4,332 | 5,893 | 5,666 | 3,854 | 3,174 | 1,499 | 1,247 |
| Common Equity | 4,506 | 2,267 | 2,153 | 1,867 | 2,045 | 2,087 | 4,719 | 3,613 | 1,234 | 1,053 |
| Total Capital | 11,718 | 5,926 | 7,326 | 7,302 | 9,221 | 10,062 | 12,694 | 8,214 | 3,144 | 2,692 |
| Capital Expenditures | 379 | 155 | 195 | 311 | 333 | 947 | 1,845 | 769 | 365 | 299 |
| Cash Flow | 441 | -102 | -542 | 324 | -20.0 | -1,672 | 1,097 | 855 | 281 | 211 |
| Current Ratio | 1.7 | 1.7 | 1.8 | 1.5 | 1.2 | 1.1 | 1.1 | 1.1 | 1.1 | 1.0 |
| % Long Term Debt of Capitalization | 56.7 | 53.8 | 57.7 | 59.3 | 63.9 | 56.3 | 30.4 | 38.6 | 47.7 | 46.3 |
| % Net Income of Revenue | 3.7 | NM | NM | NM | NM | NM | 1.5 | 1.7 | 1.0 | 0.8 |
| % Return on Assets | 1.1 | NM | NM | NM | NM | NM | 2.8 | 3.6 | 2.6 | 2.2 |
| % Return on Equity | 3.4 | NM | NM | NM | NM | NM | 15.5 | 19.2 | 13.2 | 10.8 |

Data as orig reptd.; bef. results of disc opers/spec. items. Per share data adj. for stk. divs.; EPS diluted. E-Estimated. NA-Not Available. NM-Not Meaningful. NR-Not Ranked. UR-Under Review.

**Office:** 1000 Louisiana Street, Houston, TX 77002-5050.
**Telephone:** 713-507-6400.
**Email:** ir@dynegy.com
**Website:** http://www.dynegy.com

**Chrmn, Pres & CEO:** B.A. Williamson
**COO:** R.W. Eimer, Jr.
**EVP & CFO:** H.C. Nichols
**SVP, Chief Acctg Officer & Cntlr:** C.J. Stone

**SVP & Treas:** C.C. Cook
**Investor Contact:** N. Grossman (713-507-6466)
**Auditor:** Ernst & Young
**Board Members:** J. Bartlett, D. W. Biegler, T. D. Clark, Jr., V. E. Grijalva, P. A. Hammick, F. E. Hardenbergh, L. A. Lednicky, G. L. Mazanec, H. C. Nichols, M. Segal, H. B. Sheppard, W. L. Trubeck, B. A. Williamson

**Founded:** 1985
**Domicile:** Illinois
**Employees:** 1,800

# Eastman Chemical Co

**STANDARD &POOR'S**

| S&P Recommendation **BUY** ★★★★☆ | Price $35.09 (as of Nov 14, 2008) | 12-Mo. Target Price $50.00 | Investment Style Large-Cap Value |

**GICS Sector** Materials
**Sub-Industry** Diversified Chemicals

**Summary** This global company manufactures and markets more than 1,200 chemicals, fibers and polyester plastics products.

## Key Stock Statistics (Source S&P, Vickers, company reports)

| | | | | | | | |
|---|---|---|---|---|---|---|---|
| 52-Wk Range | $78.29– 30.51 | S&P Oper. EPS 2008**E** | 5.30 | Market Capitalization(B) | $2.546 | Beta | 0.94 |
| Trailing 12-Month EPS | $5.69 | S&P Oper. EPS 2009**E** | 5.75 | Yield (%) | 5.02 | S&P 3-Yr. Proj. EPS CAGR(%) | 10 |
| Trailing 12-Month P/E | 6.2 | P/E on S&P Oper. EPS 2008**E** | 6.6 | Dividend Rate/Share | $1.76 | S&P Credit Rating | BBB |
| $10K Invested 5 Yrs Ago | $11,796 | Common Shares Outstg. (M) | 72.5 | Institutional Ownership (%) | 90 | | |

## Price Performance

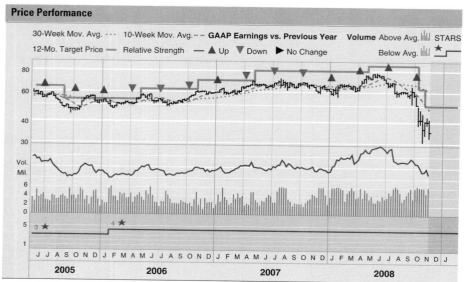

30-Week Mov. Avg. · · · ·   10-Week Mov. Avg. – – –   **GAAP Earnings vs. Previous Year**   Volume Above Avg. ▪▪▪ STARS
12-Mo. Target Price —   Relative Strength — ▲ Up ▼ Down ► No Change   Below Avg. ▪▪▪ ★

Options: ASE, CBOE, P, Ph

Analysis prepared by **Richard O'Reilly, CFA** on October 29, 2008, when the stock traded at **$ 36.69**.

## Highlights

➤ We expect sales to be modestly higher in 2009 on price increases implemented during 2008. The coatings and intermediate chemicals segments should continue to expand, with volumes boosted by overall growing non-U.S. economies and an improving product mix. We forecast overall raw material and energy costs possibly easing in 2009 after a sizable increase during 2008.

➤ We expect the domestic polyester resin business to turn solidly profitable for 2009 as EMN reduced operating costs in 2008, including through the shutdown of high-cost capacity. The fourth quarter of 2008 will include costs for a planned 50% expansion of the new U.S. resin plant that uses new technology. We believe fibers profits in 2009 will be again be modestly higher, helped by a recent capacity expansion.

➤ EMN will likely incur greater development costs related to a coal gasification project. We expect interest expense in 2009 to increase modestly, and the tax rate to remain about 30%, including an investment tax credit.

## Investment Rationale/Risk

➤ Based on our 2009 EPS estimate, the shares were recently trading at what we view as an excessive P/E discount to other major diversified chemical company equities. We expect the coatings, specialty plastics and fibers segments (over 80% of annual profits) to grow through 2009 and we think the challenging domestic polyester resins business will turn profitable as a result of reduced costs and expansion of the new plant technology.

➤ Risks to our recommendation and target price include the cyclical character of polyester resins, unplanned production outages and interruptions, possible greater-than-estimated asbestos liabilities, and higher-than-expected raw material costs.

➤ Applying a P/E of 8.7X, closer to the P/Es of diversified chemicals peers in our coverage universe, to our 2009 EPS estimate of $5.75 results in our 12-month target price of $50. We believe the dividend, which recently provided an above-average yield of almost 5.0%, is secure.

## Qualitative Risk Assessment

| LOW | MEDIUM | HIGH |

Our risk assessment reflects the diverse business and geographic sales mix of the company, offset by the cyclical nature of the chemicals industry and the volatility of raw material costs.

## Quantitative Evaluations

**S&P Quality Ranking** B-

| D | C | B- | B | B+ | A- | A | A+ |

**Relative Strength Rank** MODERATE

39

LOWEST = 1     HIGHEST = 99

## Revenue/Earnings Data

**Revenue (Million $)**

| | 1Q | 2Q | 3Q | 4Q | Year |
|---|---|---|---|---|---|
| 2008 | 1,727 | 1,834 | 1,819 | -- | -- |
| 2007 | 1,795 | 1,895 | 1,813 | 1,737 | 6,830 |
| 2006 | 1,803 | 1,929 | 1,966 | 1,752 | 7,450 |
| 2005 | 1,762 | 1,752 | 1,816 | 1,729 | 7,059 |
| 2004 | 1,597 | 1,676 | 1,649 | 1,658 | 6,580 |
| 2003 | 1,441 | 1,481 | 1,444 | 1,434 | 5,800 |

**Earnings Per Share ($)**

| | 1Q | 2Q | 3Q | 4Q | Year |
|---|---|---|---|---|---|
| 2008 | 1.45 | 1.49 | 1.33 | E0.92 | E5.30 |
| 2007 | 0.91 | 1.22 | 0.24 | 1.25 | 3.83 |
| 2006 | 1.27 | 1.37 | 1.15 | 1.12 | 4.91 |
| 2005 | 2.00 | 2.51 | 1.50 | 0.81 | 6.81 |
| 2004 | -0.07 | 1.07 | 0.49 | 0.68 | 2.18 |
| 2003 | 0.23 | 0.46 | -4.35 | 0.13 | -3.54 |

Fiscal year ended Dec. 31. Next earnings report expected: Late January. EPS Estimates based on S&P Operating Earnings; historical GAAP earnings are as reported.

## Dividend Data (Dates: mm/dd Payment Date: mm/dd/yy)

| Amount ($) | Date Decl. | Ex-Div. Date | Stk. of Record | Payment Date |
|---|---|---|---|---|
| 0.440 | 12/06 | 12/13 | 12/17 | 01/02/08 |
| 0.440 | 02/21 | 03/13 | 03/17 | 04/01/08 |
| 0.440 | 05/01 | 06/12 | 06/16 | 07/01/08 |
| 0.440 | 08/07 | 09/11 | 09/15 | 10/01/08 |

Dividends have been paid since 1994. Source: Company reports.

**Please read the Required Disclosures and Analyst Certification on the last page of this report.**

The McGraw-Hill Companies

STANDARD
&POOR'S

# Eastman Chemical Co

## Business Summary October 29, 2008

CORPORATE OVERVIEW. Eastman Chemical Co. is a large global maker of a broad range of chemicals, plastics and fibers. International operations accounted for 42% of sales in 2007.

The Chemicals and Fibers group consists of three segments. The coatings, adhesive, specialty polymers and inks segment (21% of 2007 sales, operating profits of $235 million) is a leading supplier of alcohols and solvents used in coatings (60% of segment sales) and resins, dispersions and specialty polymers used in adhesives (40%). Performance chemicals and intermediates (31%, $220 million) includes oxo chemicals, acetyls, plasticizers and glycols used for polymers, photographic and home care products, agricultural chemicals and pharmaceutical intermediates; and additives for food and beverage ingredients. The segment also included contract ethylene sales of $314 million under a supply agreement related to a former polyethylene business. About 75% of annual segment sales is generated in North America. In the fibers business (14%, $238 million), EMN is one of the world's two largest suppliers of acetate cigarette filter tow and the leader in acetate yarn. The company projects global growth in demand for filter tow of 3% annually through 2010, with Asia and Eastern Europe having the fastest growth rates. The business also includes acetyl chemicals (acetate flake, acetic anhydride).

The Polyester group consists of polymers (21%, loss of $207 million) and spe-

cialty plastics (13%, profit of $65 million). EMN in 2006 was the world's largest producer of polyester plastics, consisting of polyethylene terephthalate (PET), used for packaging applications and beverage containers such as soft-drink bottles, with annual PET capacity of 3.3 billion lbs. at year-end 2006. EMN in 2007 decided to close or sell its unprofitable polyester production sites outside the U.S.; in December, it sold its two facilities in Latin America (sales of $413 million in 2007 and a loss of $127 million, including a restructuring charge of $115 million). EMN in late March 2008 sold its remaining two European plants (sales of $542 million in 2007, including from a plant in Spain sold in April 2007; reported as discontinued operations beginning in late 2007). Eastman's domestic operations had sales of $1.0 billion in 2007 and a loss of $80 million. In early 2007, EMN completed the start-up of a new U.S. plant with annual capacity of 770 million lbs. using new IntegRex technology. EMN has closed 880 million lbs. of higher-cost domestic capacity and plans to expand the new plant by 50% by year-end 2008. IntegRex would then account for about 65% of EMN's U.S. PET capacity.

## Company Financials Fiscal Year Ended Dec. 31

| Per Share Data ($) | 2007 | 2006 | 2005 | 2004 | 2003 | 2002 | 2001 | 2000 | 1999 | 1998 |
|---|---|---|---|---|---|---|---|---|---|---|
| Tangible Book Value | 26.63 | 20.42 | 15.85 | 10.70 | 9.00 | 9.06 | 9.92 | 15.64 | 16.81 | 24.45 |
| Cash Flow | 6.97 | 8.64 | 10.50 | 6.23 | 1.22 | 6.18 | 3.33 | 9.36 | 5.46 | 7.59 |
| Earnings | 3.83 | 4.91 | 6.81 | 2.18 | -3.54 | 1.02 | -2.33 | 3.94 | 0.61 | 3.13 |
| S&P Core Earnings | 3.79 | 4.42 | 5.63 | 2.23 | -3.45 | 0.26 | -3.06 | NA | NA | NA |
| Dividends | 1.76 | 1.76 | 1.76 | 1.76 | 1.76 | 1.76 | 1.76 | 1.76 | 1.76 | 1.76 |
| Payout Ratio | 46% | 36% | 26% | 81% | NM | 173% | NM | 45% | NM | 56% |
| Prices:High | 72.44 | 61.29 | 61.80 | 58.17 | 39.57 | 49.55 | 55.65 | 54.75 | 60.31 | 72.94 |
| Prices:Low | 57.54 | 47.30 | 44.10 | 38.00 | 27.56 | 34.53 | 29.03 | 33.63 | 36.00 | 43.50 |
| P/E Ratio:High | 19 | 12 | 9 | 27 | NM | 49 | NM | 14 | 99 | 23 |
| P/E Ratio:Low | 15 | 10 | 6 | 17 | NM | 34 | NM | 9 | 59 | 14 |

| Income Statement Analysis (Million $) | | | | | | | | | | |
|---|---|---|---|---|---|---|---|---|---|---|
| Revenue | 6,830 | 7,450 | 7,059 | 6,580 | 5,800 | 5,320 | 5,384 | 5,292 | 4,590 | 4,481 |
| Operating Income | 929 | 981 | 1,092 | 696 | 590 | 610 | 755 | 989 | 663 | 785 |
| Depreciation | 264 | 308 | 304 | 322 | 367 | 397 | 435 | 418 | 383 | 351 |
| Interest Expense | 113 | 80.0 | 100 | 115 | 124 | 128 | 140 | 135 | 126 | 96.0 |
| Pretax Income | 470 | 576 | 783 | 64.0 | -381 | 84.0 | -297 | 452 | 72.0 | 360 |
| Effective Tax Rate | 31.7% | 29.0% | 28.9% | NM | NM | 5.95% | NM | 33.0% | 33.3% | 30.8% |
| Net Income | 321 | 409 | 557 | 170 | -273 | 79.0 | -179 | 303 | 48.0 | 249 |
| S&P Core Earnings | 316 | 368 | 459 | 173 | -266 | 20.4 | -236 | NA | NA | NA |

| Balance Sheet & Other Financial Data (Million $) | | | | | | | | | | |
|---|---|---|---|---|---|---|---|---|---|---|
| Cash | 888 | 939 | 524 | 325 | 558 | 77.0 | 66.0 | 101 | 186 | 29.0 |
| Current Assets | 2,293 | 2,422 | 1,924 | 1,768 | 2,010 | 1,529 | 1,458 | 1,523 | 1,489 | 1,415 |
| Total Assets | 6,009 | 6,173 | 5,773 | 5,872 | 6,230 | 6,273 | 6,086 | 6,550 | 6,303 | 5,876 |
| Current Liabilities | 1,122 | 1,059 | 1,051 | 1,099 | 1,477 | 1,224 | 958 | 1,258 | 1,608 | 985 |
| Long Term Debt | 1,613 | 1,589 | 1,621 | 2,061 | 2,089 | 2,054 | 2,143 | 1,914 | 1,506 | 1,649 |
| Common Equity | 2,082 | 2,029 | 1,612 | 1,184 | 1,913 | 1,271 | 1,378 | 1,812 | 2,521 | 1,934 |
| Total Capital | 3,917 | 3,618 | 3,550 | 3,455 | 4,318 | 3,809 | 3,973 | 4,333 | 4,512 | 3,998 |
| Capital Expenditures | 518 | 389 | 343 | 248 | 230 | 427 | 234 | 226 | 292 | 500 |
| Cash Flow | 585 | 717 | 861 | 492 | 94.0 | 476 | 256 | 721 | 431 | 600 |
| Current Ratio | 2.0 | 2.3 | 1.8 | 1.6 | 1.4 | 1.2 | 1.5 | 1.2 | 0.9 | 1.4 |
| % Long Term Debt of Capitalization | 42.4 | 43.9 | 45.7 | 59.7 | 48.4 | 53.9 | 53.9 | 44.2 | 33.4 | 41.2 |
| % Net Income of Revenue | 4.7 | 5.5 | 7.9 | 2.6 | NM | 1.5 | NM | 5.7 | 1.0 | 5.6 |
| % Return on Assets | 5.3 | 6.8 | 9.6 | 2.8 | NM | 1.3 | NM | 4.7 | 0.8 | 4.3 |
| % Return on Equity | 15.6 | 22.5 | 39.8 | 15.3 | NM | 6.0 | NM | 17.0 | 1.9 | 13.5 |

Data as orig reptd.; bef. results of disc opers/spec. items. Per share data adj. for stk. divs.; EPS diluted. E-Estimated. NA-Not Available. NM-Not Meaningful. NR-Not Ranked. UR-Under Review.

**Office:** 200 S Wilcox Dr, Kingsport, TN, USA 37660-5147.
**Telephone:** 423-229-2000.
**Website:** http://www.eastman.com
**Chrmn & CEO:** J.B. Ferguson

**Pres:** J.P. Rogers
**SVP & CFO:** C.E. Espeland
**SVP & Chief Admin Officer:** N.P. Sneed
**SVP & CTO:** G.W. Nelson

**Investor Contact:** G. Riddle (423-229-8692)
**Board Members:** G. E. Anderson, M. P. Connors, S. R. Demeritt, J. B. Ferguson, R. M. Hernandez, R. Hornbaker, L. M. Kling, H. L. Lance, T. H. McLain, D. W. Raisbeck, P. M. Wood

**Founded:** 1993
**Domicile:** Delaware
**Employees:** 10,800

The McGraw-Hill Companies

# Eastman Kodak Co

| S&P Recommendation | SELL ★ ★ ☆ ☆ ☆ | Price | 12-Mo. Target Price | Investment Style |
|---|---|---|---|---|
| | | $7.89 (as of Nov 14, 2008) | $9.50 | Large-Cap Value |

**GICS Sector** Consumer Discretionary
**Sub-Industry** Photographic Products

**Summary** This multinational company has a large presence in consumer, professional and health imaging.

## Key Stock Statistics (Source S&P, Vickers, company reports)

| | | | | | | | |
|---|---|---|---|---|---|---|---|
| 52-Wk Range | $24.46– 7.24 | S&P Oper. EPS 2008E | 0.08 | Market Capitalization(B) | $2.118 | Beta | 1.51 |
| Trailing 12-Month EPS | $2.41 | S&P Oper. EPS 2009E | 0.27 | Yield (%) | 6.34 | S&P 3-Yr. Proj. EPS CAGR(%) | NM |
| Trailing 12-Month P/E | 3.3 | P/E on S&P Oper. EPS 2008E | 98.6 | Dividend Rate/Share | $0.50 | S&P Credit Rating | B+ |
| $10K Invested 5 Yrs Ago | $3,605 | Common Shares Outstg. (M) | 268.5 | Institutional Ownership (%) | 96 | | |

## Price Performance

30-Week Mov. Avg. · · ·    10-Week Mov. Avg. – –    **GAAP Earnings vs. Previous Year**    Volume Above Avg. STARS
12-Mo. Target Price —    Relative Strength —    ▲ Up    ▼ Down    ► No Change    Below Avg.

Options: ASE, CBOE, P, Ph

Analysis prepared by **Erik Kolb** on November 03, 2008, when the stock traded at **$ 9.49**.

## Highlights

➤ In 2008, we estimate revenue of $10.2 billion, down about 1% from 2007, as we project a sizable decrease in EK's traditional film market being partially offset by double-digit growth in digital businesses as recent restructuring efforts take hold. We believe revenues for the recently launched inkjet printer product line should ramp up, but at this point, we are skeptical of management's near-term goals for the unit. We see a high single digit increase in graphic communications, as EK's digital plates and NEXPRESS commercial printing presses gain market share.

➤ We see further challenges in EK's consumer digital imaging business this year, although we look for overall profitability to benefit from restructuring efforts. Sizable labor reductions over the past few years should help to improve margins this year, and although management says restructuring efforts are complete, we would not be surprised to see further reductions later in 2008 or 2009.

➤ We estimate EPS of $0.08 in 2008, compared to a loss of $0.71 per share in 2007. For 2009, we forecast EPS of $0.27.

## Investment Rationale/Risk

➤ Although we believe EK has made modest progress in its shift toward a more digitally focused product line after completing a four-year restructuring program, which incurred roughly $3.4 billion in charges, we think the ultimate outcome of the transition remains in question. We think a shifting product mix is creating both opportunities for, and significant risk to, profits. Looking ahead, we expect EK to have a narrower focus, including a greater profit dependence on consumer digital imaging and graphic communications, including new product lines such as ink-jet printers, all areas we see with limited margin growth potential.

➤ Risks to our recommendation and target price include a slower than anticipated decline in demand for traditional film product offerings, lower than forecast pricing pressure for digital products, success of new product launches, and increases in market share.

➤ Our 12-month target price of $9.50 reflects a blend of our DCF and relative valuations. Our DCF model assumes a WACC of 10.4% and long-term growth of 1.8%. Our relative model uses an EBITDA multiple below EK's historical average, reflecting the heightened risk we see.

## Qualitative Risk Assessment

| LOW | MEDIUM | HIGH |
|---|---|---|

Our risk assessment is based on the company's ongoing shift toward digital photography. While we think EK has made progress in this endeavor, we are concerned about competitive threats and margin declines in this space.

## Quantitative Evaluations

**S&P Quality Ranking**    B-

| D | C | B- | B | B+ | A- | A | A+ |
|---|---|---|---|---|---|---|---|

**Relative Strength Rank**    WEAK

27

LOWEST = 1    HIGHEST = 99

## Revenue/Earnings Data

**Revenue (Million $)**

| | 1Q | 2Q | 3Q | 4Q | Year |
|---|---|---|---|---|---|
| 2008 | 2,093 | 2,485 | 2,405 | -- | -- |
| 2007 | 2,080 | 2,468 | 2,533 | 3,220 | 10,301 |
| 2006 | 2,889 | 3,360 | 3,204 | 3,821 | 13,274 |
| 2005 | 2,832 | 3,686 | 3,553 | 4,197 | 14,268 |
| 2004 | 2,919 | 3,469 | 3,364 | 3,765 | 13,517 |
| 2003 | 2,740 | 3,352 | 3,447 | 3,778 | 13,317 |

**Earnings Per Share ($)**

| | 1Q | 2Q | 3Q | 4Q | Year |
|---|---|---|---|---|---|
| 2008 | -0.40 | -0.67 | 0.35 | E0.25 | E0.08 |
| 2007 | -0.61 | -0.53 | 0.11 | 0.28 | -0.71 |
| 2006 | -1.04 | -0.98 | -0.13 | 0.06 | -2.09 |
| 2005 | -0.49 | -0.49 | -3.62 | -0.47 | -5.05 |
| 2004 | 0.06 | 0.50 | 0.16 | -0.06 | 0.28 |
| 2003 | -0.01 | 0.39 | 0.42 | 0.03 | 0.83 |

Fiscal year ended Dec. 31. Next earnings report expected: Late January. EPS Estimates based on S&P Operating Earnings; historical GAAP earnings are as reported.

## Dividend Data (Dates: mm/dd Payment Date: mm/dd/yy)

| Amount ($) | Date Decl. | Ex-Div. Date | Stk. of Record | Payment Date |
|---|---|---|---|---|
| 0.250 | 10/16 | 10/30 | 11/01 | 12/14/07 |
| 0.250 | 05/14 | 05/28 | 06/01 | 07/16/08 |
| 0.250 | 10/15 | 10/30 | 11/03 | 12/12/08 |

Dividends have been paid since 1902. Source: Company reports.

# Eastman Kodak Co

**STANDARD &POOR'S**

## Business Summary November 03, 2008

CORPORATE OVERVIEW. Eastman Kodak provides imaging technology products and services to the photographic and graphic communications markets. In 2007, the film products group accounted for 19.1% of net sales from continuing operations, compared to 21.9% in 2006, while consumer digital imaging represented 45.0% (44.6%), graphic communications 34.9% (32.9%), and other activities 1% (0.6%).

The consumer digital imaging group is a global provider of digital photography products and services for consumer markets. Offerings include digital products such as digital cameras and digital picture frames, retail printing, online imaging services, imaging sensors, and all-in-one printers. Kodak holds top three market shares in categories such as digital still cameras, retail printing, and digital picture frames. EK's strategy in this segment is to extend picture taking, picture search/organizing, creativity, sharing and printing to bring innovative new experiences to consumers.

The film products group is composed of traditional photographic products and services used to create motion pictures, and for consumer, professional and industrial imaging applications. The company manufactures and markets films

and one-time-use and re-loadable film cameras.

The graphic communications group serves a variety of customers in the creative, in-plant, data center, commercial printing, packaging, newspaper, and digital service bureau market segments with a range of software, media, and hardware products that provide customers with a variety of solutions for prepress equipment, workflow software, digital and traditional printing, document scanning, and multi-vendor IT services.

Through the years, EK has engaged in extensive and productive efforts in research and development and expenses totaled $535 million (5.2% of sales) in 2007, compared to $578 million (5.5%) in 2006 and $739 million (6.5%) in 2005. The company also holds a portfolio of patents in several areas important to its business.

## Company Financials Fiscal Year Ended Dec. 31

| Per Share Data ($) | 2007 | 2006 | 2005 | 2004 | 2003 | 2002 | 2001 | 2000 | 1999 | 1998 |
|---|---|---|---|---|---|---|---|---|---|---|
| Tangible Book Value | 4.77 | NM | NM | 6.57 | 5.53 | 6.27 | 6.71 | 8.56 | 9.45 | 8.54 |
| Cash Flow | 2.02 | 2.55 | -0.18 | 3.88 | 3.72 | 5.52 | 3.42 | 7.48 | 7.19 | 6.84 |
| Earnings | -0.71 | -2.09 | -5.05 | 0.28 | 0.83 | 2.72 | 0.26 | 4.59 | 4.33 | 4.24 |
| S&P Core Earnings | -1.58 | -2.65 | -4.93 | -0.42 | 0.53 | 0.44 | -1.86 | NA | NA | NA |
| Dividends | 0.50 | 0.50 | 0.50 | 0.50 | 1.15 | 1.80 | 1.77 | 1.76 | 1.76 | 1.76 |
| Payout Ratio | NM | NM | NM | 179% | 139% | 68% | NM | 38% | 41% | 42% |
| Prices:High | 30.20 | 30.91 | 35.19 | 34.74 | 41.08 | 38.48 | 49.95 | 67.50 | 80.38 | 88.94 |
| Prices:Low | 21.42 | 18.93 | 20.77 | 24.25 | 20.39 | 25.58 | 24.40 | 35.31 | 56.63 | 57.94 |
| P/E Ratio:High | NM | NM | NM | NM | 49 | 15 | 19 | 15 | 19 | 21 |
| P/E Ratio:Low | NM | NM | NM | NM | 25 | 10 | 9 | 8 | 13 | 14 |

| Income Statement Analysis (Million $) | 2007 | 2006 | 2005 | 2004 | 2003 | 2002 | 2001 | 2000 | 1999 | 1998 |
|---|---|---|---|---|---|---|---|---|---|---|
| Revenue | 10,301 | 13,274 | 14,268 | 13,517 | 13,317 | 12,835 | 13,234 | 13,994 | 14,089 | 13,406 |
| Operating Income | 1,002 | 1,600 | 1,493 | 1,638 | 1,685 | 2,898 | 1,923 | 3,103 | 2,908 | 2,783 |
| Depreciation | 785 | 1,331 | 1,402 | 1,030 | 830 | 818 | 919 | 889 | 918 | 853 |
| Interest Expense | 113 | 262 | 211 | 168 | 148 | 173 | 219 | 178 | 142 | 110 |
| Pretax Income | -256 | -346 | -762 | -92.0 | 196 | 946 | 97.0 | 2,132 | 2,109 | 2,106 |
| Effective Tax Rate | NM | NM | NM | NM | NM | 16.1% | 33.0% | 34.0% | 34.0% | 34.0% |
| Net Income | -205 | -600 | -1,455 | 81.0 | 238 | 793 | 76.0 | 1,407 | 1,392 | 1,390 |
| S&P Core Earnings | -453 | -757 | -1,419 | -119 | 149 | 127 | -541 | NA | NA | NA |

| Balance Sheet & Other Financial Data (Million $) | 2007 | 2006 | 2005 | 2004 | 2003 | 2002 | 2001 | 2000 | 1999 | 1998 |
|---|---|---|---|---|---|---|---|---|---|---|
| Cash | 2,976 | 1,469 | 1,665 | 1,255 | 1,250 | 569 | 448 | 251 | 393 | 500 |
| Current Assets | 6,053 | 5,557 | 5,781 | 5,648 | 5,455 | 4,534 | 4,683 | 5,491 | 5,444 | 5,599 |
| Total Assets | 13,659 | 14,320 | 14,921 | 14,737 | 14,818 | 13,369 | 13,362 | 14,212 | 14,370 | 14,733 |
| Current Liabilities | 4,446 | 4,971 | 5,489 | 4,990 | 5,307 | 5,377 | 5,354 | 6,215 | 5,769 | 6,178 |
| Long Term Debt | 1,289 | 2,714 | 2,764 | 1,852 | 2,302 | 1,164 | 1,666 | 1,166 | Nil | 504 |
| Common Equity | 3,029 | 1,388 | 1,967 | 3,811 | 3,264 | 2,777 | 2,894 | 3,428 | 3,912 | 3,988 |
| Total Capital | 4,318 | 4,102 | 4,731 | 5,663 | 5,566 | 3,941 | 4,560 | 4,655 | 3,971 | 1,108 |
| Capital Expenditures | 259 | 379 | 472 | 460 | 506 | 577 | 743 | 945 | 1,127 | 4,561 |
| Cash Flow | 580 | 731 | -53.0 | 1,111 | 1,068 | 1,611 | 995 | 2,296 | 2,310 | 2,243 |
| Current Ratio | 1.4 | 1.1 | 1.1 | 1.1 | 1.0 | 0.8 | 0.9 | 0.9 | 0.9 | 0.9 |
| % Long Term Debt of Capitalization | 29.9 | 66.2 | 58.4 | 32.7 | 41.4 | 29.5 | 36.5 | 25.0 | Nil | 11.1 |
| % Net Income of Revenue | NM | NM | NM | NM | 1.8 | 6.2 | 0.6 | 10.1 | 9.9 | 10.4 |
| % Return on Assets | NM | NM | NM | NM | 1.7 | 5.9 | 0.6 | 9.8 | 9.6 | 10.0 |
| % Return on Equity | NM | NM | NM | NM | 7.9 | 27.9 | 2.4 | 38.3 | 35.2 | 38.9 |

Data as orig reptd.; bef. results of disc opers/spec. items. Per share data adj. for stk. divs.; EPS diluted. E-Estimated. NA-Not Available. NM-Not Meaningful. NR-Not Ranked. UR-Under Review.

**Office:** 343 State Street, Rochester, NY 14650.
**Telephone:** 585-724-4000.
**Website:** http://www.kodak.com
**Chrmn & CEO:** A.M. Perez

**Pres & COO:** P.J. Faraci
**EVP & CFO:** F.S. Sklarsky
**SVP & CTO:** B. Lloyd
**SVP & General Counsel:** J.P. Haag

**Investor Contact:** A.P. McCorvey
**Board Members:** R. Braddock, T. M. Donahue, M. Hawley, W. H. Hernandez, D. R. Lebda, D. L. Lee, D. E. Lewis, W. G. Parrett, A. M. Perez, H. D. Ruiz, D. F. Strigl, L. D. Tyson

**Founded:** 1880
**Domicile:** New Jersey
**Employees:** 26,900

*The McGraw-Hill Companies*

# Eaton Corp

STANDARD
&POOR'S

| S&P Recommendation | HOLD ★★★☆☆ | Price | 12-Mo. Target Price | Investment Style |
|---|---|---|---|---|
| | | $41.15 (as of Nov 14, 2008) | $51.00 | Large-Cap Blend |

**GICS Sector** Industrials
**Sub-Industry** Industrial Machinery

**Summary** This diversified industrial manufacturer's products include electrical systems and components for power management, truck transmissions, and fluid power systems and services for industrial, mobile and aircraft equipment.

## Key Stock Statistics (Source S&P, Vickers, company reports)

| | | | | | | | |
|---|---|---|---|---|---|---|---|
| 52-Wk Range | $99.66– 37.69 | S&P Oper. EPS 2008**E** | 7.48 | Market Capitalization(B) | $6.786 | Beta | 1.70 |
| Trailing 12-Month EPS | $7.27 | S&P Oper. EPS 2009**E** | 7.10 | Yield (%) | 4.86 | S&P 3-Yr. Proj. EPS CAGR(%) | 9 |
| Trailing 12-Month P/E | 5.7 | P/E on S&P Oper. EPS 2008**E** | 5.5 | Dividend Rate/Share | $2.00 | S&P Credit Rating | A |
| $10K Invested 5 Yrs Ago | $9,028 | Common Shares Outstg. (M) | 164.9 | Institutional Ownership (%) | 80 | | |

## Price Performance

Options: ASE, CBOE, P, Ph

Analysis prepared by **Mathew Christy, CFA** on October 22, 2008, when the stock traded at **$ 38.83**.

## Highlights

➤ We expect 2008 revenue to increase slightly less than 22%, but increase only 4.8% in 2009, led by contributions from recent acquisitions and organic revenue growth. We project modest growth in the truck component business in 2008, but expect higher growth in 2009 from tougher emissions standards that take effect in 2010. Our forecast for 2009 calls for NAFTA Class 8 truck volume to decline about 10% from 2007 levels, to approximately 202,000 units.

➤ We look for operating margins to expand modestly in 2008, driven primarily by results in the first nine-months of the year and increased profitability in the electrical and hydraulics segments. In 2009, we forecast relatively flat operating margins, as we expect benefits from ongoing expense reduction efforts and a flat pension expense to offset lower operating leverage.

➤ We project operating EPS of $7.48 in 2008 and $7.10 in 2009, representing expected EPS percent change of 10% growth and a 5% decline in the respective years, also on higher interest expenses and higher effective tax rates.

## Investment Rationale/Risk

➤ We think ETN's end market growth will slow over the next 12 months from declining worldwide economic growth and our expectation for reduced commercial construction activity in 2009. However, we are positive about ETN's efforts to obtain a better balanced businesses portfolio that is less cyclical and capital intensive and generates strong returns and cash flows. In addition, we think ETN's recent share price decline adequately discounts our expected decline in earnings.

➤ Risks to our recommendation and target price include weaker-than-expected global economic growth, a greater-than-forecast downturn in heavy-duty truck markets, and an inability to integrate recent acquisitions.

➤ Our 12-month target price of $51 blends two valuation metrics. Our discounted cash flow model, which assumes 3% perpetuity growth and a 11.5% discount rate, indicates a $55 value. Regarding relative peer valuation, we apply a multiple of 5.5X, ahead of peers and equal to historic trough multiples, to our forward 12-month EBITDA estimate, implying a $47 valuation.

## Qualitative Risk Assessment

| LOW | MEDIUM | HIGH |
|---|---|---|

Our risk assessment reflects our view that ETN has good geographic and product diversification, offset by the highly cyclical nature of the company's various end markets, and significant pension and other post-retirement benefit obligations.

## Quantitative Evaluations

**S&P Quality Ranking**      B+

| D | C | B- | B | B+ | A- | A | A+ |
|---|---|---|---|---|---|---|---|

**Relative Strength Rank**     MODERATE

44

LOWEST = 1       HIGHEST = 99

## Revenue/Earnings Data

**Revenue (Million $)**

| | 1Q | 2Q | 3Q | 4Q | Year |
|---|---|---|---|---|---|
| 2008 | 3,496 | 4,279 | 4,114 | -- | -- |
| 2007 | 3,153 | 3,248 | 3,298 | 3,374 | 13,033 |
| 2006 | 2,991 | 3,162 | 3,115 | 3,102 | 12,370 |
| 2005 | 2,654 | 2,834 | 2,789 | 2,838 | 11,115 |
| 2004 | 2,238 | 2,403 | 2,543 | 2,633 | 9,817 |
| 2003 | 1,925 | 2,027 | 2,026 | 2,083 | 8,061 |

**Earnings Per Share ($)**

| | | | | | |
|---|---|---|---|---|---|
| 2008 | 1.62 | 2.04 | 1.87 | E1.75 | E7.48 |
| 2007 | 1.53 | 1.60 | 1.59 | 1.67 | 6.38 |
| 2006 | 1.35 | 1.63 | 1.39 | 1.59 | 5.97 |
| 2005 | 1.19 | 1.37 | 1.30 | 1.38 | 5.23 |
| 2004 | 0.85 | 1.03 | 1.09 | 1.16 | 4.13 |
| 2003 | 0.50 | 0.64 | 0.70 | 0.72 | 2.56 |

Fiscal year ended Dec. 31. Next earnings report expected: Late January. EPS Estimates based on S&P Operating Earnings; historical GAAP earnings are as reported.

## Dividend Data (Dates: mm/dd Payment Date: mm/dd/yy)

| Amount ($) | Date Decl. | Ex-Div. Date | Stk. of Record | Payment Date |
|---|---|---|---|---|
| 0.500 | 01/22 | 01/31 | 02/04 | 02/22/08 |
| 0.500 | 04/23 | 05/01 | 05/05 | 05/23/08 |
| 0.500 | 07/23 | 07/31 | 08/04 | 08/22/08 |
| 0.500 | 10/22 | 10/30 | 11/03 | 11/21/08 |

Dividends have been paid since 1923. Source: Company reports.

---

**Please read the Required Disclosures and Analyst Certification on the last page of this report.**

# Eaton Corp

**STANDARD &POOR'S**

## Business Summary October 22, 2008

CORPORATE OVERVIEW. Eaton Corp., a diversified industrial equipment and parts manufacturer with $13 billion in revenues in 2007, conducts business through four business segments.

ETN's Electrical segment (37% of 2007 revenues with 12.4% operating margins excluding one-time items) makes a wide range of power distribution and control equipment, such as switchboards, circuit boards, circuit breakers, starters, AC and DC Uninterruptible Power Systems (UPS) and power management software. The segment also produces electronic sensors that control industrial machinery, as well as electricity quality-monitoring systems. The unit's primary competitors include GE, Germany-based Siemens and Schneider Electric. Demand for ETN's electrical equipment and components mainly reflects the health of the non-residential (35% of segment sales), power quality (30%), industrial (18%), residential construction (12%) and telecom (5%) industries.

The Fluid Power segment (34%; 12.7%) makes hydraulic pumps, motors, valves cylinders and power steering for everything from jet planes to farm tractors. The segment also sells hydraulic and electromechanical equipment such as actuators, pumps, steering systems cockpit controls and pneumatic systems. It sells primarily to three market channels: mobile (primarily earthmovers and farm tractors; about 40% of sales); stationary (primarily machine tools; 23%);

and aerospace (mainly commercial and military aircraft; 37%).

Parker-Hannifin, the world's largest hydraulics equipment maker, Eaton (the second largest), Germany-based Sauer Danfoss (the third), and Germany-based Mannesmann (fourth) account for about 40% of the $50 billion in revenue global hydraulics equipment industry. The 60% balance is comprised of hundreds of smaller hydraulics equipment makers.

With about 85% of the global truck transmission market (such as drive trains, clutches, gearboxes and shafts), ETN's Truck Component unit (16%; 16.6%) is the world's largest maker of medium and heavy duty truck transmissions. The segment's primary competitor is Germany-based ZedF. ETN is also a major manufacturer of brake clutches. The segment's primary competitor in this segment is Wabco. Other truck transmission and clutch makers include European truck manufacturers, which primarily make transmissions and clutches for their own trucks. Demand for ETN's truck components is mainly driven by the health of the medium and heavy duty truck market.

## Company Financials Fiscal Year Ended Dec. 31

| Per Share Data ($) | 2007 | 2006 | 2005 | 2004 | 2003 | 2002 | 2001 | 2000 | 1999 | 1998 |
|---|---|---|---|---|---|---|---|---|---|---|
| Tangible Book Value | NM | 2.30 | 0.09 | 3.46 | 3.14 | NM | 0.29 | NM | 0.64 | 7.17 |
| Cash Flow | 9.50 | 8.80 | 8.08 | 6.67 | 5.18 | 4.49 | 3.78 | 5.05 | 7.25 | 4.66 |
| Earnings | 6.38 | 5.97 | 5.23 | 4.13 | 2.56 | 1.96 | 1.20 | 2.50 | 4.18 | 2.40 |
| S&P Core Earnings | 6.86 | 6.45 | 5.40 | 4.15 | 2.43 | 0.99 | -0.18 | NA | NA | NA |
| Dividends | 1.72 | 1.48 | 1.24 | 1.08 | 0.92 | 0.88 | 0.88 | 0.88 | 0.88 | 0.88 |
| Payout Ratio | 27% | 24% | 24% | 26% | 36% | 45% | 74% | 35% | 21% | 37% |
| Prices:High | 104.12 | 79.98 | 72.69 | 72.64 | 54.70 | 44.34 | 40.72 | 43.28 | 51.75 | 49.81 |
| Prices:Low | 71.91 | 62.37 | 56.65 | 52.74 | 33.01 | 29.55 | 27.56 | 28.75 | 31.00 | 28.75 |
| P/E Ratio:High | 16 | 13 | 14 | 18 | 21 | 23 | 34 | 17 | 12 | 21 |
| P/E Ratio:Low | 11 | 10 | 11 | 13 | 13 | 15 | 23 | 11 | 7 | 12 |

| Income Statement Analysis (Million $) | | | | | | | | | | |
|---|---|---|---|---|---|---|---|---|---|---|
| Revenue | 13,033 | 12,370 | 11,115 | 9,817 | 8,061 | 7,209 | 7,299 | 8,309 | 8,402 | 6,625 |
| Operating Income | 1,646 | 1,487 | 1,468 | 1,287 | 984 | 870 | 703 | 1,013 | 1,170 | 813 |
| Depreciation | 469 | 434 | 409 | 400 | 394 | 353 | 355 | 364 | 441 | 331 |
| Interest Expense | 147 | 104 | 90.0 | 78.0 | 87.0 | 104 | 142 | 177 | 152 | 88.0 |
| Pretax Income | 1,041 | 989 | 996 | 781 | 508 | 399 | 278 | 552 | 963 | 485 |
| Effective Tax Rate | 7.88% | 7.79% | 19.2% | 17.0% | 24.0% | 29.6% | 39.2% | 34.2% | 35.9% | 28.0% |
| Net Income | 959 | 912 | 805 | 648 | 386 | 281 | 169 | 363 | 617 | 349 |
| S&P Core Earnings | 1,031 | 985 | 832 | 651 | 367 | 141 | -25.0 | NA | NA | NA |

| Balance Sheet & Other Financial Data (Million $) | | | | | | | | | | |
|---|---|---|---|---|---|---|---|---|---|---|
| Cash | 646 | 114 | 110 | 85.0 | 61.0 | 75.0 | 112 | 82.0 | 81.0 | 80.0 |
| Current Assets | 4,767 | 4,408 | 3,578 | 3,182 | 3,093 | 2,457 | 2,387 | 2,571 | 2,782 | 1,982 |
| Total Assets | 13,430 | 11,417 | 10,218 | 9,075 | 8,223 | 7,138 | 7,646 | 8,180 | 8,437 | 5,665 |
| Current Liabilities | 3,659 | 3,407 | 2,968 | 2,262 | 2,126 | 1,734 | 1,669 | 2,107 | 2,649 | 1,516 |
| Long Term Debt | 3,417 | 1,774 | 1,830 | Nil | 1,651 | 1,887 | 2,252 | 2,447 | 1,915 | 1,191 |
| Common Equity | 5,172 | 4,106 | 3,778 | 3,606 | 3,117 | 2,302 | 2,475 | 2,410 | 2,624 | 2,057 |
| Total Capital | 7,604 | 5,880 | 5,608 | 3,606 | 4,768 | 4,752 | 5,307 | 4,857 | 4,539 | 3,248 |
| Capital Expenditures | 354 | 360 | 363 | 330 | 2,733 | 228 | 295 | 386 | 496 | 483 |
| Cash Flow | 1,428 | 1,346 | 1,214 | 1,048 | 780 | 634 | 524 | 727 | 1,058 | 680 |
| Current Ratio | 1.3 | 1.3 | 1.2 | 1.4 | 1.5 | 1.4 | 1.4 | 1.2 | 1.1 | 1.3 |
| % Long Term Debt of Capitalization | 32.0 | 30.2 | 32.6 | Nil | 34.6 | 39.7 | 42.4 | 50.4 | 42.2 | 36.7 |
| % Net Income of Revenue | 7.4 | 7.4 | 7.2 | 6.6 | 4.8 | 3.9 | 2.3 | 4.4 | 7.3 | 5.3 |
| % Return on Assets | 7.7 | 8.4 | 8.3 | 7.5 | 5.0 | 3.8 | 2.1 | 4.4 | 8.8 | 6.3 |
| % Return on Equity | 20.7 | 23.1 | 21.8 | 19.3 | 14.2 | 11.8 | 6.9 | 14.4 | 26.4 | 16.9 |

Data as orig reptd.; bef. results of disc opers/spec. items. Per share data adj. for stk. divs.; EPS diluted. E-Estimated. NA-Not Available. NM-Not Meaningful. NR-Not Ranked. UR-Under Review.

**Office:** Eaton Center, Cleveland, OH 44114-2584.
**Telephone:** 216-523-5000.
**Website:** http://www.eaton.com
**Chrmn, Pres & CEO:** A.M. Cutler

**EVP & CFO:** R.H. Fearon
**EVP & General Counsel:** M.M. McGuire
**SVP & Secy:** T.E. Moran
**CTO:** Y.P. Tsavalas

**Investor Contact:** B. Hartman (216-523-4501)
**Board Members:** C. M. Connor, M. J. Critelli, A. M. Cutler, C. E. Golden, E. Green, N. C. Lautenbach, D. L. McCoy, J. R. Miller, G. Page, V. A. Pelson, G. L. Tooker

**Founded:** 1916
**Domicile:** Ohio
**Employees:** 79,000

**STANDARD &POOR'S**

# eBay Inc

| S&P Recommendation | **BUY** ★★★★☆ | Price<br>$12.36 (as of Nov 14, 2008) | 12-Mo. Target Price<br>$23.00 | Investment Style<br>Large-Cap Growth |
| --- | --- | --- | --- | --- |

**GICS Sector** Information Technology
**Sub-Industry** Internet Software & Services

**Summary** EBAY owns one of the world's most popular e-commerce destinations, which bears its name, as well as PayPal, an online payments company, and Skype, an Internet telephony business.

## Key Stock Statistics (Source S&P, Vickers, company reports)

| | | | | | | | | |
| --- | --- | --- | --- | --- | --- | --- | --- | --- |
| 52-Wk Range | $35.12– 11.39 | S&P Oper. EPS 2008E | 1.51 | Market Capitalization(B) | $15.783 | Beta | | 2.00 |
| Trailing 12-Month EPS | $1.44 | S&P Oper. EPS 2009E | 1.63 | Yield (%) | Nil | S&P 3-Yr. Proj. EPS CAGR(%) | | 11 |
| Trailing 12-Month P/E | 8.6 | P/E on S&P Oper. EPS 2008E | 8.2 | Dividend Rate/Share | Nil | S&P Credit Rating | | NA |
| $10K Invested 5 Yrs Ago | $4,546 | Common Shares Outstg. (M) | 1,276.9 | Institutional Ownership (%) | 70 | | | |

## Price Performance

30-Week Mov. Avg. ···· 10-Week Mov. Avg. --- **GAAP Earnings vs. Previous Year**   Volume Above Avg. ▏▎▍ STARS
12-Mo. Target Price — Relative Strength — ▲ Up ▼ Down ▶ No Change   Below Avg. ▏▎▍ ★

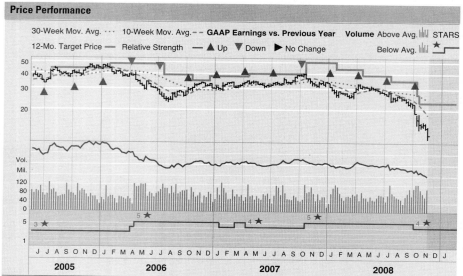

Options: ASE, CBOE, P, Ph

Analysis prepared by **Scott H. Kessler** on October 20, 2008, when the stock traded at **$ 15.26.**

## Highlights

▶ We project that net revenues will increase 13% in 2008 and 8% in 2009. For 2008, we foresee 6% growth in marketplaces (including eBay.com), 27% in payments (PayPal), and 45% in communications (Skype). We believe EBAY will generate marketplaces growth in 2009 largely consistent with that of 2008, given a challenging economic backdrop and following material investment and changes.

▶ We expect EBAY's annual non-GAAP operating margin to fall in 2008 and 2009, reflecting economic difficulties, expected notable retooling of and investment in the core marketplaces businesses around the world, and a less favorable revenue mix.

▶ In October 2008, EBAY announced the proposed purchase of online consumer finance company Bill Me Later for some $945 million in cash and options. In October 2005, EBAY acquired Skype Technologies, a provider of Internet communications offerings, for some $2.5 billion in cash and stock. EBAY announced an additional $2.0 billion share buyback in January 2008, following a plan announced one year before.

## Investment Rationale/Risk

▶ We see EBAY as the clear leader in online auctions, a mainstream Internet retail destination, a major facilitator of large transactions involving cars and real estate, a growing international presence, and the owner of the world's leading purely online payment platform. We are relatively optimistic about its international and payment segments, and believe the new management team can eventually re-ignite growth at the marketplaces unit.

▶ Risks to our recommendation and target price include a sharp weakening of consumer sentiment/spending, significant and increasing international competition, and potential issues related to a recent adverse French court decision related to the sale of counterfeit items on EBAY's platforms.

▶ Our discounted cash flow model, with assumptions that include a weighted average cost of capital of 12.5%, projected average annual free cash flow growth of 11% over the next five years, and a terminal growth rate of 3%, yields an intrinsic value calculation of $23, which is our 12-month target price.

## Qualitative Risk Assessment

| LOW | MEDIUM | **HIGH** |
| --- | --- | --- |

Our risk assessment reflects our view that EBAY is a well-established leader in the Internet segment, operates a business model that we see as attractive, and has a strong balance sheet. However, the company operates in fast-changing areas and faces notable competition. Over the past couple of years, we have viewed EBAY's quarterly results, financial outlook, strategic decisions and management changes as disappointing at times. We believe this has contributed to stock volatility that is greater than that of the S&P 500.

## Quantitative Evaluations

**S&P Quality Ranking**                                    **B**

| D | C | B- | **B** | B+ | A- | A | A+ |
| --- | --- | --- | --- | --- | --- | --- | --- |

**Relative Strength Rank**                        **MODERATE**

| 30 |
| --- |

LOWEST = 1                                               HIGHEST = 99

## Revenue/Earnings Data

**Revenue (Million $)**

| | 1Q | 2Q | 3Q | 4Q | Year |
| --- | --- | --- | --- | --- | --- |
| 2008 | 2,192 | 2,196 | 2,118 | -- | -- |
| 2007 | 1,768 | 1,418 | 1,889 | 2,181 | 7,672 |
| 2006 | 1,390 | 1,411 | 1,449 | 1,720 | 5,970 |
| 2005 | 1,032 | 1,086 | 1,106 | 1,329 | 4,552 |
| 2004 | 756.2 | 773.4 | 805.9 | 935.8 | 3,271 |
| 2003 | 476.5 | 509.3 | 530.9 | 648.4 | 2,165 |

**Earnings Per Share ($)**

| | | | | | |
| --- | --- | --- | --- | --- | --- |
| 2008 | 0.34 | 0.35 | 0.38 | E0.33 | E1.51 |
| 2007 | 0.27 | 0.27 | -0.69 | 0.39 | 0.25 |
| 2006 | 0.17 | 0.17 | 0.20 | 0.25 | 0.79 |
| 2005 | 0.19 | 0.21 | 0.18 | 0.20 | 0.78 |
| 2004 | 0.15 | 0.14 | 0.13 | 0.15 | 0.57 |
| 2003 | 0.08 | 0.07 | 0.08 | 0.11 | 0.34 |

Fiscal year ended Dec. 31. Next earnings report expected: Late January. EPS Estimates based on S&P Operating Earnings; historical GAAP earnings are as reported.

## Dividend Data

No cash dividends have been paid.

*The McGraw-Hill Companies*

# eBay Inc

STANDARD
&POOR'S

## Business Summary October 20, 2008

CORPORATE OVERVIEW. eBay operates the world's largest online trading community. As of September 2008, the marketplaces segment had 85.7 million active users (compared with 83.0 million a year earlier) that accounted for 700.2 million new listings (555.6 million) and operated some 534,000 stores (520,000). Following acquisitions in recent years, the company also owns Half.com (fixed price retail sales), PayPal (online payments), Rent.com (apartment and home rentals), Shopping.com (comparison shopping), Skype (Internet calling), and StubHub (online ticket sales). As of September 2008, PayPal had 65.3 million active registered accounts (54.8 million) and Skype had 370.2 million registered users (245.7 million).

The company and its affiliates have websites directed toward the following geographies: Argentina, Australia, Austria, Belgium, Brazil, Canada, China, France, Germany, Hong Kong, India, Ireland, Italy, Malaysia, Mexico, the Netherlands, New Zealand, the Philippines, Poland, Singapore, South Korea, Spain, Sweden, Switzerland, Taiwan, Turkey, the U.K. and Vietnam. eBay discontinued its website in Japan in early 2002. In December 2006, EBAY announced it would contribute its China operations to a joint venture with Internet portal and wireless services company TOM Online. EBAY owns a 49% stake in the venture, which was created in February 2007.

CORPORATE STRATEGY. The company's stated goal is to become the world's most efficient and abundant marketplace by expanding its community of users, delivering value to buyers and sellers, creating a global marketplace, and providing a faster, easier and safer trading experience. EBAY has increasingly employed acquisitions to fulfill the aforementioned goal, with a focus on international expansion and offering more choices and services to its buyers and sellers. In our view, PayPal was an extremely successful acquisition because it dramatically enhanced the user experience. Moreover, the combination accelerated the benefits the companies already derived from the Network Effect (whereby a product/service becomes more valuable to its users as its number of users increases), in our opinion. Although we are skeptical as to whether the October 2005 purchase of Skype will yield comparable results, and this opinion is underscored by the company taking a related impairment charge of $1.4 billion in 2007, we have grown modestly more optimistic about Skype's longer-term potential as a stand-alone business, and we also see synergies with PayPal.

## Company Financials Fiscal Year Ended Dec. 31

| Per Share Data ($) | 2007 | 2006 | 2005 | 2004 | 2003 | 2002 | 2001 | 2000 | 1999 | 1998 |
|---|---|---|---|---|---|---|---|---|---|---|
| Tangible Book Value | 3.90 | 2.69 | 2.21 | 2.73 | 2.23 | 1.46 | 1.11 | 0.93 | 0.81 | 0.09 |
| Cash Flow | 0.69 | 1.17 | 1.05 | 0.75 | 0.46 | 0.28 | 0.16 | 0.08 | 0.03 | 0.01 |
| Earnings | 0.25 | 0.79 | 0.78 | 0.57 | 0.34 | 0.21 | 0.08 | 0.04 | 0.01 | Nil |
| S&P Core Earnings | 1.26 | 0.79 | 0.61 | 0.43 | 0.21 | 0.04 | -0.00 | NA | NA | NA |
| Dividends | Nil | Nil | Nil | Nil | Nil | Nil | Nil | Nil | Nil | Nil |
| Payout Ratio | Nil | Nil | Nil | Nil | Nil | Nil | Nil | NM | Nil | Nil |
| Prices:High | 40.73 | 47.86 | 58.89 | 59.21 | 32.40 | 17.71 | 18.19 | 31.88 | 29.25 | 12.97 |
| Prices:Low | 28.60 | 22.83 | 30.78 | 31.30 | 16.88 | 12.21 | 7.11 | 6.69 | 6.92 | 0.75 |
| P/E Ratio:High | NM | 61 | 75 | NM | 95 | 83 | NM | NM | NM | NM |
| P/E Ratio:Low | NM | 29 | 39 | NM | 50 | 57 | NM | NM | NM | NM |

| Income Statement Analysis (Million $) | | | | | | | | | | |
|---|---|---|---|---|---|---|---|---|---|---|
| Revenue | 7,672 | 5,970 | 4,552 | 3,271 | 2,165 | 1,214 | 749 | 431 | 225 | 47.4 |
| Operating Income | 2,606 | 1,968 | 1,820 | 1,313 | 828 | 431 | 227 | 74.6 | 23.8 | 8.88 |
| Depreciation | 602 | 545 | 378 | 254 | 159 | 76.6 | 86.6 | 38.1 | 20.7 | 2.79 |
| Interest Expense | 16.6 | 5.92 | 3.48 | 8.88 | 4.31 | 1.49 | 2.85 | 3.37 | 1.94 | 0.04 |
| Pretax Income | 751 | 1,547 | 1,549 | 1,128 | 662 | 398 | 163 | 78.0 | 20.5 | 7.03 |
| Effective Tax Rate | 53.6% | 27.2% | 30.2% | 30.5% | 31.3% | 36.7% | 49.1% | 42.0% | 45.8% | 65.9% |
| Net Income | 348 | 1,126 | 1,082 | 778 | 447 | 250 | 90.4 | 48.3 | 10.8 | 2.40 |
| S&P Core Earnings | 1,739 | 1,126 | 853 | 589 | 270 | 52.2 | -4.04 | NA | NA | NA |

| Balance Sheet & Other Financial Data (Million $) | | | | | | | | | | |
|---|---|---|---|---|---|---|---|---|---|---|
| Cash | 5,984 | 2,663 | 1,314 | 1,330 | 1,382 | 1,109 | 524 | 202 | 220 | 31.8 |
| Current Assets | 7,123 | 4,971 | 3,183 | 2,911 | 2,146 | 1,468 | 884 | 675 | 460 | 83.4 |
| Total Assets | 15,366 | 13,494 | 11,789 | 7,991 | 5,820 | 4,124 | 1,679 | 1,182 | 964 | 92.5 |
| Current Liabilities | 3,100 | 2,518 | 1,485 | 1,085 | 647 | 386 | 180 | 137 | 88.8 | 8.04 |
| Long Term Debt | Nil | Nil | Nil | 0.08 | 124 | 13.8 | 12.0 | 11.4 | 15.0 | Nil |
| Common Equity | 11,705 | 10,905 | 10,048 | 6,728 | 4,896 | 3,556 | 1,429 | 1,014 | 852 | 84.4 |
| Total Capital | 11,705 | 10,905 | 10,264 | 6,868 | 5,139 | 3,715 | 1,479 | 1,038 | 867 | 84.4 |
| Capital Expenditures | 454 | 515 | 338 | 293 | 365 | 139 | 57.4 | 49.8 | 141 | 8.86 |
| Cash Flow | 950 | 1,670 | 1,460 | 1,032 | 606 | 326 | 177 | 86.3 | 31.5 | 5.19 |
| Current Ratio | 2.3 | 2.0 | 2.1 | 2.7 | 3.3 | 3.8 | 4.9 | 4.9 | 5.2 | 10.4 |
| % Long Term Debt of Capitalization | Nil | Nil | Nil | NM | 2.4 | 0.4 | 0.8 | 1.1 | 1.7 | Nil |
| % Net Income of Revenue | 4.5 | 18.9 | 23.8 | 23.8 | 20.7 | 20.6 | 12.1 | 11.2 | 4.8 | 5.1 |
| % Return on Assets | 2.4 | 8.9 | 10.9 | 11.3 | 9.1 | 8.6 | 6.3 | 4.5 | 1.9 | 4.9 |
| % Return on Equity | 3.1 | 10.7 | 12.9 | 13.4 | 10.6 | 10.0 | 7.4 | 5.2 | 2.3 | 5.6 |

Data as orig reptd.; bef. results of disc opers/spec. items. Per share data adj. for stk. divs.; EPS diluted. E-Estimated. NA-Not Available. NM-Not Meaningful. NR-Not Ranked. UR-Under Review.

**Office:** 2145 Hamilton Ave, San Jose, CA 95125-5905.
**Telephone:** 408-376-7400.
**Email:** investor_relations@ebay.com
**Website:** http://www.ebay.com

**Chrmn:** P.M. Omidyar
**Pres & CEO:** J. Donahoe
**SVP & CFO:** R.H. Swan
**SVP, Secy & General Counsel:** M.R. Jacobson

**Chief Acctg Officer:** P. DePaul
**Investor Contact:** T. Ford (408-376-7205)
**Board Members:** F. D. Anderson, M. L. Andreessen, E. W. Barnholt, P. Bourguignon, S. D. Cook, J. Donahoe, W. C. Ford, Jr., D. G. Lepore, D. M. Moffett, P. M. Omidyar, R. T. Schlosberg, III, H. D. Schultz, T. J. Tierney

**Founded:** 1995
**Domicile:** Delaware
**Employees:** 15,500

# Ecolab Inc.

**STANDARD & POOR'S**

| S&P Recommendation | BUY ★★★★☆ | Price $32.77 (as of Nov 14, 2008) | 12-Mo. Target Price $48.00 | Investment Style Large-Cap Growth |

**GICS Sector** Materials
**Sub-Industry** Specialty Chemicals

**Summary** This company is the leading worldwide marketer of cleaning, sanitizing and maintenance products and services for the hospitality, institutional and industrial markets.

## Key Stock Statistics (Source S&P, Vickers, company reports)

| | | | | | | | |
|---|---|---|---|---|---|---|---|
| 52-Wk Range | $52.78 – 29.56 | S&P Oper. EPS 2008E | 1.87 | Market Capitalization(B) | $8.122 | Beta | 0.35 |
| Trailing 12-Month EPS | $1.91 | S&P Oper. EPS 2009E | 2.05 | Yield (%) | 1.59 | S&P 3-Yr. Proj. EPS CAGR(%) | 12 |
| Trailing 12-Month P/E | 17.2 | P/E on S&P Oper. EPS 2008E | 17.5 | Dividend Rate/Share | $0.52 | S&P Credit Rating | A |
| $10K Invested 5 Yrs Ago | $13,224 | Common Shares Outstg. (M) | 247.8 | Institutional Ownership (%) | 56 | | |

## Price Performance

30-Week Mov. Avg. ···· 10-Week Mov. Avg. -- GAAP Earnings vs. Previous Year    Volume Above Avg. ▐▐▌ STARS
12-Mo. Target Price ─ Relative Strength ─ ▲ Up ▼ Down ► No Change    Below Avg. ▐▐▌ ★

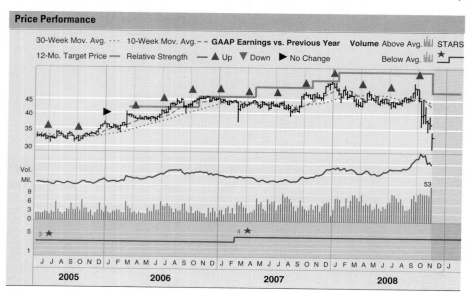

Options: CBOE, P, Ph

Analysis prepared by **Richard O'Reilly, CFA** on November 10, 2008, when the stock traded at **$ 33.65.**

## Highlights

➤ We expect sales growth to be minimal in 2009, hurt by unfavorable currency exchange rates and more challenging end markets. Projected sales growth in 2008 of about 15% includes favorable currency rates. We see organic sales growth from existing businesses rising about 5%, aided by benefits from new products and customers, a forecasted price increase of 3%, and a 4% expansion of the sales force in 2008.

➤ We look for the domestic institutional, Kay, food & beverage, health care and pest elimination units to continue to expand. We believe international sales will increase in most parts of the world, including stronger comparisons in Europe. We project that operating margins in 2009 will remain stable on our estimated sales gain, despite higher raw material costs. We expect the loss from the GCS kitchen repair unit to narrow in 2009.

➤ Interest expense in 2009 should exceed the $61 million expected for 2008, reflecting the planned repurchase of a small portion of the stake held by Henkel AG, which should be accretive to EPS. Recent acquisitions are expected to be less dilutive to EPS in 2009. We assume an effective tax rate of 31%, down slightly from 2008.

## Investment Rationale/Risk

➤ We expect ECL to post ongoing solid sales and EPS gains in coming periods, based on our belief that conditions will remain healthy in the global industries it serves. We believe that the repurchase of a portion of the 29% stake owned by Henkel KGaA will be accretive to EPS.

➤ Risks to our recommendation and target price include unexpected slowdowns in the hospitality, travel, and foodservice industries, an inability to continue to successfully introduce new products and services, and higher-than-projected raw material costs (equal to 20% of sales).

➤ The shares recently traded at about 18X our 2008 EPS forecast, a 40% premium to the S&P 500, but at the low point of ECL's annual P/E for the past decade. We believe that a steady grower such as ECL will be sought by investors as economic growth remains slow, and we think the shares offer solid upside potential. Our 12-month target price of $48 is about 24X our 2009 EPS forecast of $2.05, and reflects a P/E-to-growth (PEG) multiple of 2.0X, coupled with the 12% EPS gains that we see for the next few years. The dividend has been raised for 16 consecutive years.

## Qualitative Risk Assessment

| LOW | MEDIUM | HIGH |

Our risk assessment reflects the company's leading share positions in its core businesses, the stable nature of its end markets and customers, and our view of its strong balance sheet and cash generation. The stock's S&P Quality Ranking is A, the second highest possible, indicating a solid 10-year historical record of earnings and dividend growth.

## Quantitative Evaluations

**S&P Quality Ranking**                    A

| D | C | B- | B | B+ | A- | A | A+ |

**Relative Strength Rank**              MODERATE

53

LOWEST = 1                              HIGHEST = 99

## Revenue/Earnings Data

**Revenue (Million $)**

| | 1Q | 2Q | 3Q | 4Q | Year |
|---|---|---|---|---|---|
| 2008 | 1,458 | 1,570 | 1,626 | -- | -- |
| 2007 | 1,254 | 1,362 | 1,413 | 1,440 | 5,470 |
| 2006 | 1,120 | 1,226 | 1,279 | 1,271 | 4,896 |
| 2005 | 1,070 | 1,159 | 1,165 | 1,142 | 4,535 |
| 2004 | 979.4 | 1,043 | 1,090 | 1,073 | 4,185 |
| 2003 | 875.9 | 946.7 | 982.8 | 956.5 | 3,762 |

**Earnings Per Share ($)**

| | | | | | |
|---|---|---|---|---|---|
| 2008 | 0.41 | 0.55 | 0.50 | E0.46 | E1.87 |
| 2007 | 0.35 | 0.44 | 0.46 | 0.45 | 1.70 |
| 2006 | 0.30 | 0.36 | 0.43 | 0.34 | 1.43 |
| 2005 | 0.27 | 0.31 | 0.38 | 0.27 | 1.23 |
| 2004 | 0.25 | 0.30 | 0.36 | 0.27 | 1.19 |
| 2003 | 0.21 | 0.25 | 0.33 | 0.26 | 1.06 |

Fiscal year ended Dec. 31. Next earnings report expected: Mid February. EPS Estimates based on S&P Operating Earnings; historical GAAP earnings are as reported.

## Dividend Data (Dates: mm/dd Payment Date: mm/dd/yy)

| Amount ($) | Date Decl. | Ex-Div. Date | Stk. of Record | Payment Date |
|---|---|---|---|---|
| 0.130 | 12/06 | 12/14 | 12/18 | 01/15/08 |
| 0.130 | 02/22 | 03/07 | 03/11 | 04/15/08 |
| 0.130 | 05/02 | 06/13 | 06/17 | 07/15/08 |
| 0.130 | 08/01 | 09/12 | 09/16 | 10/15/08 |

Dividends have been paid since 1936. Source: Company reports.

---

**Please read the Required Disclosures and Analyst Certification on the last page of this report.**

The McGraw-Hill Companies

# Ecolab Inc.

**STANDARD &POOR'S**

## Business Summary November 10, 2008

CORPORATE OVERVIEW. Ecolab is a global supplier of cleaning, sanitizing, and maintenance products and services for hospitality, institutional, and industrial markets. In the U.S. cleaning and sanitizing business (44% of 2007 sales, 57% of profits), the institutional division (27% of 2007 total sales) is the leading provider of cleaners and sanitizers for warewashing, on-premise laundry, kitchen cleaning and general housekeeping, product dispensing equipment and dishwashing racks and related kitchen sundries to the food-service, lodging and health care industries. It also provides pool and spa treatment products. In addition, the division includes professional janitorial products (detergents, floor care, disinfectants, odor control) sold under the Airkem brand name.

The Kay division (5%) is the largest supplier of cleaning and sanitizing products (surface cleaners, degreasers, sanitizers and hand care products) for the quick-service restaurant, convenience store and food retail markets. The Food and Beverage division (8%) offers cleaning and sanitizing products and services to farms, dairy plants, food and beverage processors, and pharmaceutical plants.

ECL also sells health care products (skin care, disinfectants and sterilants; 1%) under the Huntington and Microtek names; textile care products (1%) for large institutional and commercial laundries; vehicle care products (soaps, polishes, wheel treatments) for rental, fleet and retail car washes (1%); and water treatment products (1%) to institutional, laundry and food and beverage, and processing markets for boilers, cooling and waste treatment systems.

Other U.S. services (9%, 6%) include institutional and commercial pest elimination and prevention services (6%) and GCS Services, a provider of commercial kitchen equipment repair and maintenance services (3%). ECL bought GCS Service in 1998, and has added to this business through small acquisitions; this business had operating losses for the five years through 2007.

The International business (47%, 37%) provides services similar to those offered in the U.S. to Canada (3%) and about 70 countries in Europe (32%), Latin America (4%), the Asia/Pacific region (7%), and other (1%). The institutional and food & beverage businesses constitute a larger portion of the international business compared to the U.S.

## Company Financials Fiscal Year Ended Dec. 31

| Per Share Data ($) | 2007 | 2006 | 2005 | 2004 | 2003 | 2002 | 2001 | 2000 | 1999 | 1998 |
|---|---|---|---|---|---|---|---|---|---|---|
| Tangible Book Value | 1.33 | 1.67 | 2.00 | 1.33 | 1.14 | 0.83 | 0.41 | 1.77 | 1.98 | 1.76 |
| Cash Flow | 2.85 | 2.48 | 2.22 | 2.13 | 1.93 | 1.67 | 1.35 | 1.35 | 1.15 | 1.03 |
| Earnings | 1.70 | 1.43 | 1.23 | 1.19 | 1.06 | 0.81 | 0.73 | 0.79 | 0.66 | 0.58 |
| S&P Core Earnings | 1.69 | 1.46 | 1.24 | 1.10 | 0.98 | 0.64 | 0.61 | NA | NA | NA |
| Dividends | 0.48 | 0.42 | 0.36 | 0.33 | 0.30 | 0.28 | 0.26 | 0.25 | 0.21 | 0.19 |
| Payout Ratio | 28% | 29% | 29% | 28% | 28% | 34% | 36% | 31% | 32% | 33% |
| Prices:High | 52.78 | 46.40 | 37.15 | 35.59 | 27.92 | 25.20 | 22.09 | 22.84 | 22.22 | 19.00 |
| Prices:Low | 37.01 | 33.64 | 30.68 | 26.12 | 23.08 | 18.27 | 14.25 | 14.00 | 15.84 | 13.06 |
| P/E Ratio:High | 31 | 32 | 30 | 30 | 26 | 31 | 30 | 29 | 34 | 33 |
| P/E Ratio:Low | 22 | 24 | 25 | 22 | 22 | 23 | 20 | 18 | 24 | 23 |

| Income Statement Analysis (Million $) | 2007 | 2006 | 2005 | 2004 | 2003 | 2002 | 2001 | 2000 | 1999 | 1998 |
|---|---|---|---|---|---|---|---|---|---|---|
| Revenue | 5,470 | 4,896 | 4,535 | 4,185 | 3,762 | 3,404 | 2,355 | 2,264 | 2,080 | 1,888 |
| Operating Income | 978 | 880 | 799 | 786 | 713 | 656 | 482 | 471 | 714 | 384 |
| Depreciation | 291 | 269 | 257 | 247 | 230 | 223 | 163 | 148 | 135 | 122 |
| Interest Expense | 58.9 | 51.3 | 49.8 | 45.3 | 45.3 | 43.9 | 28.4 | 24.6 | 22.7 | 25.0 |
| Pretax Income | 616 | 567 | 498 | 489 | 448 | 354 | 306 | 338 | 286 | 256 |
| Effective Tax Rate | 30.7% | 35.0% | 35.9% | 36.5% | 38.1% | 39.6% | 38.4% | 38.3% | 38.4% | 39.7% |
| Net Income | 427 | 369 | 319 | 310 | 277 | 214 | 188 | 209 | 176 | 155 |
| S&P Core Earnings | 424 | 376 | 322 | 283 | 260 | 167 | 157 | NA | NA | NA |

| Balance Sheet & Other Financial Data (Million $) | 2007 | 2006 | 2005 | 2004 | 2003 | 2002 | 2001 | 2000 | 1999 | 1998 |
|---|---|---|---|---|---|---|---|---|---|---|
| Cash | 137 | 484 | 104 | 71.2 | 85.6 | 49.2 | 41.8 | 44.0 | 47.7 | 28.4 |
| Current Assets | 1,717 | 1,854 | 1,422 | 1,279 | 1,150 | 1,016 | 930 | 601 | 577 | 504 |
| Total Assets | 4,723 | 4,419 | 3,797 | 3,716 | 3,229 | 2,878 | 2,525 | 1,714 | 1,586 | 1,471 |
| Current Liabilities | 1,518 | 1,503 | 1,119 | 940 | 851 | 866 | 828 | 532 | 471 | 400 |
| Long Term Debt | 600 | 557 | 519 | Nil | 604 | 540 | 512 | 234 | 169 | 227 |
| Common Equity | 1,936 | 1,680 | 1,649 | 1,563 | 1,295 | 1,100 | 880 | 757 | 929 | 691 |
| Total Capital | 2,536 | 2,237 | 2,169 | 1,563 | 1,900 | 1,639 | 1,393 | 991 | 1,098 | 918 |
| Capital Expenditures | 362 | 288 | 269 | 276 | 212 | 213 | 158 | 150 | 146 | 148 |
| Cash Flow | 718 | 637 | 576 | 558 | 507 | 437 | 351 | 357 | 310 | 276 |
| Current Ratio | 1.1 | 1.2 | 1.3 | 1.4 | 1.4 | 1.2 | 1.1 | 1.1 | 1.2 | 1.3 |
| % Long Term Debt of Capitalization | 23.7 | 24.9 | 23.9 | Nil | 31.8 | 32.9 | 36.8 | 23.6 | 15.4 | 24.7 |
| % Net Income of Revenue | 7.8 | 7.5 | 7.0 | 7.4 | 7.4 | 6.3 | 8.0 | 9.2 | 8.5 | 8.2 |
| % Return on Assets | 9.3 | 9.0 | 8.5 | 8.9 | 9.1 | 7.9 | 8.9 | 12.6 | 11.5 | 10.7 |
| % Return on Equity | 23.6 | 22.1 | 19.7 | 21.7 | 23.2 | 21.6 | 23.0 | 27.5 | 18.9 | 24.9 |

Data as orig reptd.; bef. results of disc opers/spec. items. Per share data adj. for stk. divs.; EPS diluted. E-Estimated. NA-Not Available. NM-Not Meaningful. NR-Not Ranked. UR-Under Review.

**Office:** 370 North Wabasha Street, Saint Paul, MN 55102-1390.
**Telephone:** 800-232-6522.
**Email:** investor.info@ecolab.com
**Website:** http://www.ecolab.com

**Chrmn, Pres & CEO:** D.M. Baker, Jr.
**Pres:** J. Trotter
**SVP & CTO:** S.K. Nestegard
**SVP & CTO:** L.L. Berger

**SVP, Secy & General Counsel:** L.T. Bell
**Investor Contact:** S.L. Fritze (800-232-6522)
**Board Members:** D. M. Baker, Jr., B. Beck, L. S. Biller, R. U. De Schutter, J. A. Grundhofer, J. W. Johnson, J. W. Levin, R. L. Lumpkins, B. M. Pritchard, J. J. Zillmer

**Founded:** 1924
**Domicile:** Delaware
**Employees:** 26,052

# Edison International

**STANDARD &POOR'S**

| S&P Recommendation **BUY** ★★★★☆ | Price $33.47 (as of Nov 14, 2008) | 12-Mo. Target Price $41.00 | Investment Style Large-Cap Blend |
|---|---|---|---|

**GICS Sector** Utilities
**Sub-Industry** Electric Utilities

**Summary** EIX is the holding company for Southern California Edison. Other businesses include electric power generation, financial investments, and real estate development.

## Key Stock Statistics (Source S&P, Vickers, company reports)

| | | | | | | | | |
|---|---|---|---|---|---|---|---|---|
| 52-Wk Range | **$58.00– 26.73** | S&P Oper. EPS 2008**E** | **3.80** | Market Capitalization(B) | **$10.905** | Beta | **0.84** |
| Trailing 12-Month EPS | **$3.66** | S&P Oper. EPS 2009**E** | **4.34** | Yield (%) | **3.65** | S&P 3-Yr. Proj. EPS CAGR(%) | **11** |
| Trailing 12-Month P/E | **9.1** | P/E on S&P Oper. EPS 2008**E** | **8.8** | Dividend Rate/Share | **$1.22** | S&P Credit Rating | **BBB-** |
| $10K Invested 5 Yrs Ago | **$18,991** | Common Shares Outstg. (M) | **325.8** | Institutional Ownership (%) | **77** | | |

## Price Performance

30-Week Mov. Avg. ···· 10-Week Mov. Avg. - - GAAP Earnings vs. Previous Year   Volume Above Avg. |||| STARS
12-Mo. Target Price — Relative Strength   ▲ Up ▼ Down ▶ No Change   Below Avg. |||| ★

Options: ASE, CBOE, P

Analysis prepared by **Justin McCann** on November 11, 2008, when the stock traded at **$ 32.77**.

### Highlights

➤ We expect 2008 operating EPS to rise 3% from 2007's $3.69, on an enhanced rate base at Southern California Edison (SCE). Higher margins at Edison Mission Group (EMG) should be offset by an $0.05 a share charge tied to hedge contracts with Lehman Brothers. We see SCE EPS at about $2.23 a share in 2008 (up from $2.07 in 2007), EMG at $1.71 ($1.72), and a loss of $0.14 (a loss of $0.10) at the parent. In the first nine months of 2008, EIX operating EPS grew to $3.18, from $3.04 in the year-earlier period.

➤ For 2009, we project operating EPS to rise 14% from expected 2008 results. Over the next few years, we see EPS growth driven by SCE's five-year, $19 billion infrastructure development plan, resulting in a steadily growing rate base. The California Public Utility Commission (CPUC) approved an 8.5% increase for 2008, to $12.7 billion. SCE is seeking additional rate base hikes of 22.0%, to $15.5 billion in 2009, 18.1%, to $18.3 billion in 2010, 16.4%, to $21.3 billion in 2011, and 10.8%, to $23.6 billion in 2012.

➤ On September 19, 2008, the CPUC approved $1.63 billion in funding for SCE's 2009-2012 installation of 5.3 million smart meters for its residential and small business customers.

### Investment Rationale/Risk

➤ After a 17.3% advance in 2007, EIX shares are down more than 35% year to date. We believe the shares have been hurt by the impact of the credit crisis, the dramatic downturn in the broader market, and an investor shift away from power generators, and think they are undervalued at a recent discount-to-peers P/E of about 7.6X our EPS estimate for 2009. Given our EPS outlook for the next few years, we recommend the shares for above-average total return. We expect earnings to be aided by the rate increases at SCE and higher wholesale power margins for Edison Mission Energy.

➤ Risks to our recommendation and target price include the potential for unfavorable regulatory or legislative acts, a sharp decline in the gas/coal price spread, and a significant drop in the P/E of the electric utility group as a whole.

➤ After a recent decrease in peer valuations, we believe the stock, despite its below-peers dividend yield (recently about 3.5%), has above-peers total return potential over the next 12 months. Our 12-month target price is $41, derived from a discount-to-peers P/E of about 9.4X our 2009 EPS estimate.

## Qualitative Risk Assessment

| LOW | MEDIUM | HIGH |
|---|---|---|

Our risk assessment reflects our view of the strong and steady earnings and cash flow that we expect from the regulated Southern California Edison utility, with its large and rapidly growing service territory and a generally supportive regulatory environment.

## Quantitative Evaluations

**S&P Quality Ranking**          **B**

| D | C | B- | B | B+ | A- | A | A+ |
|---|---|---|---|---|---|---|---|

**Relative Strength Rank**          **MODERATE**

69

LOWEST = 1          HIGHEST = 99

## Revenue/Earnings Data

**Revenue (Million $)**

| | 1Q | 2Q | 3Q | 4Q | Year |
|---|---|---|---|---|---|
| 2008 | 3,083 | 3,382 | 4,111 | -- | -- |
| 2007 | 2,912 | 3,047 | 3,942 | 3,211 | 13,113 |
| 2006 | 2,751 | 3,001 | 3,802 | 3,067 | 12,622 |
| 2005 | 2,446 | 2,649 | 3,783 | 2,975 | 11,852 |
| 2004 | 2,116 | 2,565 | 3,188 | 2,327 | 10,199 |
| 2003 | 2,523 | 3,125 | 3,833 | 2,654 | 12,135 |

**Earnings Per Share ($)**

| | 1Q | 2Q | 3Q | 4Q | Year |
|---|---|---|---|---|---|
| 2008 | 0.92 | 0.79 | 1.31 | E0.62 | E3.80 |
| 2007 | 1.00 | 0.28 | 1.40 | 0.65 | 3.32 |
| 2006 | 0.56 | 0.53 | 1.39 | 0.80 | 3.28 |
| 2005 | 0.59 | 0.55 | 1.31 | 0.90 | 3.34 |
| 2004 | 0.16 | -1.21 | 0.95 | 0.78 | 0.68 |
| 2003 | 0.19 | 0.07 | 1.52 | 0.59 | 2.37 |

Fiscal year ended Dec. 31. Next earnings report expected: Late February. EPS Estimates based on S&P Operating Earnings; historical GAAP earnings are as reported.

## Dividend Data (Dates: mm/dd Payment Date: mm/dd/yy)

| Amount ($) | Date Decl. | Ex-Div. Date | Stk. of Record | Payment Date |
|---|---|---|---|---|
| 0.305 | 12/13 | 12/27 | 12/31 | 01/31/08 |
| 0.305 | 02/28 | 03/27 | 03/31 | 04/30/08 |
| 0.305 | 04/24 | 06/26 | 06/30 | 07/31/08 |
| 0.305 | 09/04 | 09/26 | 09/30 | 10/31/08 |

Dividends have been paid since 2004. Source: Company reports.

# Edison International

**STANDARD &POOR'S**

## Business Summary November 11, 2008

CORPORATE OVERVIEW. Edison International (EIX) is the holding company of the regulated Southern California Edison (SCE) utility and several non-regulated subsidiaries. The principal non-utility companies are Edison Mission Energy (EME), an independent power producer that also conducts price risk management and energy trading activities, and Edison Capital, which holds equity investments in energy and infrastructure projects. In 2007, SCE accounted for 80.4% of EIX's consolidated revenues, the non-utility power generation business 19.4%, and financial servicers and other operations 0.2%. The utility's retail operations are regulated by the purview of the California Public Utilities Commission (CPUC), while its wholesale operations fall under the oversight of the Federal Energy Regulatory Commission (FERC).

CORPORATE STRATEGY. The company seeks to establish a balanced approach for growth, dividends, and balance sheet strength. It is working to re-duce administration expenses in the non-utility companies and to establish a multi-year productivity effort at the utility. EIX has taken steps to rebalance its capital structure and to further reduce its debt. It has also worked to enhance its liquidity through strong cash flow generation. SCE is working on new projects that should expand its transmission and distribution systems, and intends to implement a comprehensive software system to support the majority of its critical business processes. We also expect to see EIX further strengthen the independent power business, expand investment in renewable energy, and evaluate prospects for growth in the non-utility sector.

## Company Financials Fiscal Year Ended Dec. 31

| Per Share Data ($) | 2007 | 2006 | 2005 | 2004 | 2003 | 2002 | 2001 | 2000 | 1999 | 1998 |
|---|---|---|---|---|---|---|---|---|---|---|
| Tangible Book Value | 25.92 | 23.65 | 20.30 | 18.56 | 13.86 | 11.59 | 8.10 | 7.43 | 14.03 | 13.55 |
| Earnings | 3.32 | 3.28 | 3.34 | 0.68 | 2.37 | 3.46 | 7.36 | -5.84 | 1.79 | 1.84 |
| S&P Core Earnings | 3.26 | 3.28 | 3.35 | 0.60 | 2.45 | 2.81 | 6.78 | NA | NA | NA |
| Dividends | 1.17 | 1.10 | 1.02 | 1.05 | Nil | Nil | Nil | 1.11 | 1.07 | 1.04 |
| Payout Ratio | 35% | 34% | 31% | 154% | Nil | Nil | Nil | NM | 60% | 56% |
| Prices:High | 60.26 | 47.15 | 49.16 | 32.52 | 22.07 | 19.60 | 16.12 | 30.00 | 29.63 | 31.00 |
| Prices:Low | 42.76 | 37.90 | 30.43 | 21.24 | 10.57 | 7.80 | 6.25 | 14.13 | 21.63 | 25.13 |
| P/E Ratio:High | 18 | 14 | 15 | 48 | 9 | 6 | 2 | NM | 17 | 17 |
| P/E Ratio:Low | 13 | 12 | 9 | 31 | 4 | 2 | 1 | NM | 12 | 14 |

| Income Statement Analysis (Million $) | | | | | | | | | | |
|---|---|---|---|---|---|---|---|---|---|---|
| Revenue | 13,113 | 12,622 | 11,852 | 10,199 | 12,135 | 11,488 | 11,436 | 11,717 | 9,670 | 10,208 |
| Depreciation | 1,264 | 1,181 | 1,061 | 1,022 | 1,184 | 1,030 | 973 | 1,933 | 1,794 | 1,662 |
| Maintenance | NA | NA | NA | NA | NA | NA | NA | NA | NA | 411 |
| Fixed Charges Coverage | 3.38 | 3.18 | 3.28 | 2.20 | 1.73 | 1.91 | 3.38 | -0.98 | 1.96 | 1.71 |
| Construction Credits | NA | NA | NA | NA | NA | NA | NA | NA | Nil | 12.0 |
| Effective Tax Rate | 27.4% | 32.3% | 26.4% | NM | 21.5% | 25.6% | 40.7% | NM | 32.0% | 40.4% |
| Net Income | 1,100 | 1,083 | 1,108 | 226 | 779 | 1,135 | 2,402 | -1,943 | 623 | 668 |
| S&P Core Earnings | 1,077 | 1,082 | 1,111 | 199 | 808 | 921 | 2,211 | NA | NA | NA |

| Balance Sheet & Other Financial Data (Million $) | | | | | | | | | | |
|---|---|---|---|---|---|---|---|---|---|---|
| Gross Property | 29,248 | 25,090 | 24,775 | 23,214 | 24,674 | 23,264 | 22,396 | 25,737 | 27,203 | 17,223 |
| Capital Expenditures | 2,826 | 2,536 | 1,868 | 1,733 | 1,288 | 1,590 | 933 | 1,488 | 1,231 | 963 |
| Net Property | 22,309 | 20,269 | 18,588 | 17,397 | 20,288 | 15,170 | 14,427 | 17,903 | 19,683 | 10,326 |
| Capitalization:Long Term Debt | 9,931 | 10,016 | 9,552 | 9,807 | 12,221 | 12,915 | 14,007 | 13,660 | 15,050 | 8,543 |
| Capitalization:% Long Term Debt | 54.0 | 56.5 | 59.1 | 61.3 | 69.4 | 74.4 | 81.1 | 85.0 | 74.3 | 62.6 |
| Capitalization:Preferred | Nil | Nil | Nil | Nil | 9.00 | Nil | Nil | Nil | Nil | Nil |
| Capitalization:% Preferred | Nil | Nil | Nil | Nil | 0.05 | Nil | Nil | Nil | Nil | Nil |
| Capitalization:Common | 8,444 | 7,709 | 6,615 | 6,049 | 5,383 | 4,437 | 3,272 | 2,420 | 5,211 | 5,099 |
| Capitalization:% Common | 46.0 | 43.5 | 40.9 | 37.8 | 30.6 | 25.6 | 18.9 | 15.0 | 25.7 | 37.4 |
| Total Capital | 23,866 | 23,415 | 21,854 | 21,688 | 24,246 | 23,786 | 24,163 | 21,609 | 26,252 | 18,520 |
| % Operating Ratio | 84.6 | 84.7 | 80.7 | 80.6 | 75.2 | 82.8 | 93.2 | 86.4 | 92.9 | 96.9 |
| % Earned on Net Property | 13.1 | 12.8 | 6.9 | 6.6 | 9.1 | 16.0 | 36.9 | NM | 11.6 | 6.4 |
| % Return on Revenue | 8.8 | 8.6 | 9.3 | 2.2 | 6.4 | 9.9 | 21.0 | NM | 6.4 | 6.5 |
| % Return on Invested Capital | 9.4 | 10.2 | 12.2 | 10.4 | 14.9 | 10.9 | 4.8 | 7.8 | 3.6 | 7.9 |
| % Return on Common Equity | 13.6 | 15.1 | 17.1 | 3.8 | 15.9 | 29.4 | 84.4 | NM | 12.1 | 12.6 |

Data as orig reptd.; bef. results of disc opers/spec. items. Per share data adj. for stk. divs.; EPS diluted. E-Estimated. NA-Not Available. NM-Not Meaningful. NR-Not Ranked. UR-Under Review.

**Office:** 2244 Walnut Grove Avenue, Rosemead, CA 91770-3714.
**Telephone:** 877-379-9515.
**Website:** http://www.edison.com
**Chrmn, Pres & CEO:** T.F. Craver, Jr.

**EVP, CFO & Treas:** W.J. Scilacci, Jr.
**EVP & General Counsel:** R.L. Adler
**SVP & CIO:** M. Yazdi
**Chief Acctg Officer & Cntlr:** L.G. Sullivan

**Investor Contact:** S. Cunningham (877-379-9515)
**Board Members:** V. C. Chang, F. A. Cordova, T. F. Craver, Jr., C. B. Curtis, B. M. Freeman, L. G. Nogales, R. L. Olson, J. M. Rosser, R. T. Schlosberg, III, R. H. Smith, T. C. Sutton, B. White

**Founded:** 1886
**Domicile:** California
**Employees:** 17,275

*The McGraw-Hill Companies*

# Electronic Arts Inc

**STANDARD &POOR'S**

| S&P Recommendation **SELL** ★★☆☆☆ | Price $20.44 (as of Nov 14, 2008) | 12-Mo. Target Price $20.00 | Investment Style Large-Cap Growth |
|---|---|---|---|

**GICS Sector** Information Technology
**Sub-Industry** Home Entertainment Software

**Summary** This company produces entertainment software for PCs, home video game consoles and mobile gaming devices.

## Key Stock Statistics (Source S&P, Vickers, company reports)

| | | | | | | | | |
|---|---|---|---|---|---|---|---|---|
| 52-Wk Range | $60.35– 19.28 | S&P Oper. EPS 2009E | -0.75 | Market Capitalization(B) | $6.559 | Beta | 1.67 |
| Trailing 12-Month EPS | $-1.67 | S&P Oper. EPS 2010E | 0.50 | Yield (%) | Nil | S&P 3-Yr. Proj. EPS CAGR(%) | 20 |
| Trailing 12-Month P/E | NM | P/E on S&P Oper. EPS 2009E | NM | Dividend Rate/Share | Nil | S&P Credit Rating | NA |
| $10K Invested 5 Yrs Ago | $4,085 | Common Shares Outstg. (M) | 320.9 | Institutional Ownership (%) | 96 | | |

## Price Performance

30-Week Mov. Avg. ··· 10-Week Mov. Avg. — GAAP Earnings vs. Previous Year    Volume Above Avg. STARS
12-Mo. Target Price — Relative Strength — ▲ Up ▼ Down ► No Change    Below Avg.

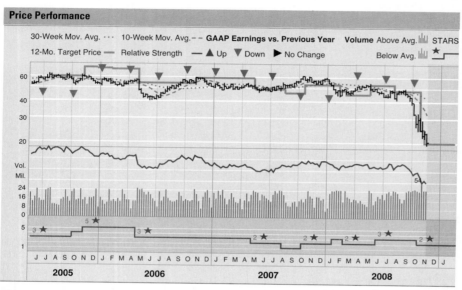

Options: ASE, CBOE, P, Ph

Analysis prepared by **Jim Yin** on November 03, 2008, when the stock traded at **$ 23.16**.

## Highlights

➤ We see revenue, excluding about $50 million of deferred revenue, rising 9.4% in FY 10 (Mar.), following 26% growth we project for FY 09, driven by continued strong sales of FIFA, Spore, The Sims, and new titles from the acquisitions of BioWare and Pandemic Studios. However, we expect sales growth to slow down with difficult global economic conditions and faster growth in non-traditional video game player segments, in which ERTS has smaller market shares. We believe sales of Rock Band have been disappointing and think sales of Madden NFL will decline due to lack of new features.

➤ We see gross margins remaining at 53% in FY 10, the same percentage expected in FY 09, as cost saving measures are offset by higher revenues from distribution, which have lower gross margins. We project that operating margins will improve to 2.7%, from -5.8% seen in FY 09, reflecting headcount reduction and effective control of development costs.

➤ Our EPS estimate for FY 10 is $0.50, versus a loss of $0.75 seen in FY 09. The projected increase reflects higher revenues and expanding margins, partially offset by more shares outstanding.

## Investment Rationale/Risk

➤ Our sell recommendation reflects our view that the global economic slowdown will hurt sales of video games, which have been viewed as a safe haven amid weak consumer spending. We forecast a weak Christmas shopping season and believe key franchises including Madden NFL and NCAA Football have been losing their appeal. After Take-Two Interactive (TTWO: hold, $12) rejected ERTS's $25.74 a share takeover bid, we are concerned that ERTS does not have any new major game titles to offset this decline.

➤ Risks to our recommendation and target price include a recovery in the global economy, stronger sales of next-generation game consoles, and better-than-expected cost savings from recent acquisitions.

➤ Our 12-month target price of $20 is based on a blend of our discounted cash flow (DCF) and P/E analyses. Our DCF model assumes a 12.5% weighted average cost of capital and 4% terminal growth, yielding an intrinsic value of $22. From our P/E analysis, we derive a value of $17, based on an industry P/E-to-growth ratio of 1.7X, or a multiple of 34X our FY 10 EPS estimate of $0.50.

## Qualitative Risk Assessment

| LOW | MEDIUM | HIGH |
|---|---|---|

Our risk assessment takes into account the volatile nature of the home entertainment software industry and the company's focus on the consumer market. These factors are offset, in our view, by ERTS's leading market share position and advantageous financial structure.

## Quantitative Evaluations

### S&P Quality Ranking
B+

| D | C | B- | B | B+ | A- | A | A+ |
|---|---|---|---|---|---|---|---|

### Relative Strength Rank
WEAK

| 25 |
|---|

LOWEST = 1    HIGHEST = 99

## Revenue/Earnings Data

### Revenue (Million $)

| | 1Q | 2Q | 3Q | 4Q | Year |
|---|---|---|---|---|---|
| 2009 | 804.0 | 894.0 | -- | -- | -- |
| 2008 | 395.0 | 640.0 | 1,503 | 1,127 | 3,665 |
| 2007 | 413.0 | 784.0 | 1,281 | 613.0 | 3,091 |
| 2006 | 365.0 | 675.0 | 1,270 | 641.0 | 2,951 |
| 2005 | 431.6 | 715.7 | 1,428 | 553.0 | 3,129 |
| 2004 | 353.4 | 530.0 | 1,475 | 598.4 | 2,957 |

### Earnings Per Share ($)

| | 1Q | 2Q | 3Q | 4Q | Year |
|---|---|---|---|---|---|
| 2009 | -0.52 | -0.97 | E0.65 | E-0.13 | E-0.75 |
| 2008 | -0.42 | -0.62 | -0.10 | -0.29 | -1.45 |
| 2007 | -0.26 | 0.07 | 0.50 | -0.08 | 0.24 |
| 2006 | -0.19 | 0.16 | 0.83 | -0.05 | 0.75 |
| 2005 | 0.08 | 0.31 | 1.18 | 0.02 | 1.59 |
| 2004 | 0.06 | 0.25 | 1.26 | 0.29 | 1.87 |

Fiscal year ended Mar. 31. Next earnings report expected: Early February. EPS Estimates based on S&P Operating Earnings; historical GAAP earnings are as reported.

## Dividend Data

No cash dividends have been paid.

# Electronic Arts Inc

STANDARD &POOR'S

## Business Summary November 03, 2008

CORPORATE OVERVIEW. ERTS is one of the largest third-party developers of video games, which can be played on a variety of platforms including Sony PlayStation, Microsoft Xbox 360, Nintendo Wii, personal computers, and mobile devices. ERTS owns many of today's most popular video game franchises, including Madden NFL, The Sims, and Need for Speed. The company organizes its business into four labels: EA SPORTS, EA Games, EA Casual Entertainment and The Sims. Each label operates with dedicated studio and marketing teams.

ERTS publish titles across all major platforms, including consoles (49% of FY 08 revenues), PCs (12%), and handheld gaming devices (16%). The remaining 23% of revenues come from distribution of third-party developed games, subscription services, licensing, and advertising. Within the console segment, ERTS's revenues are spread among the PlayStation 2 (16%), Xbox 360 (16%), Wii (8%), PlayStation 3 (8%) and Xbox (1%). The company also has a diversified video game portfolio with only one title, Rock Band, accounting for more than 10% of its total revenue in FY 08.

ERTS publishes and distributes games in over 35 countries throughout the world. International revenue accounted for $1.723 billion, or 47% of total revenue, in FY 08.

CORPORATE STRATEGY. One of the company's strategic goals is to increase resources toward developing new titles for the next-generation of game consoles, which includes Microsoft Xbox 360, Nintendo Wii and Sony PlayStation 3. The installed base of these game consoles is expected to increase significantly in 2008 as consumers upgrade their video game systems. ERTS plans to release limited number of titles for prior-generation consoles as product sales for these systems are anticipated to decline.

ERTS has completed several acquisitions to broaden its product portfolio, in particular internally developed video games, which provide higher operating margins than licensed intellectual properties. The most recent were the acquisitions of BioWare Corp. and Pandemic Studios, two privately owned video game studios, for about $860 million in cash and stock in January 2008. The two game studios are known for creating role-playing action/adventure games and have 10 franchises under development. ERTS expects the deal to be mildly dilutive to FY 08 earnings.

## Company Financials Fiscal Year Ended Mar. 31

| Per Share Data ($) | 2008 | 2007 | 2006 | 2005 | 2004 | 2003 | 2002 | 2001 | 2000 | 1999 |
|---|---|---|---|---|---|---|---|---|---|---|
| Tangible Book Value | 9.19 | 9.93 | 8.29 | 10.66 | 8.52 | 11.62 | 3.92 | 3.33 | 2.86 | 2.38 |
| Cash Flow | NA | 0.70 | 1.05 | 1.82 | 2.12 | 2.79 | 0.74 | 0.22 | 0.62 | 0.47 |
| Earnings | -1.45 | 0.24 | 0.75 | 1.59 | 1.87 | 1.09 | 0.36 | -0.04 | 0.44 | 0.29 |
| S&P Core Earnings | -1.22 | 0.24 | 0.49 | 1.35 | 1.59 | 0.82 | 0.10 | -0.25 | NA | NA |
| Dividends | Nil | Nil | Nil | Nil | Nil | Nil | Nil | Nil | Nil | Nil |
| Payout Ratio | Nil | Nil | Nil | Nil | Nil | Nil | Nil | Nil | Nil | Nil |
| Calendar Year | 2007 | 2006 | 2005 | 2004 | 2003 | 2002 | 2001 | 2000 | 1999 | 1998 |
| Prices:High | 61.62 | 59.85 | 71.16 | 63.71 | 52.89 | 36.22 | 33.46 | 28.97 | 31.11 | 14.28 |
| Prices:Low | 46.27 | 39.99 | 47.45 | 43.38 | 23.76 | 24.74 | 17.25 | 12.25 | 9.50 | 8.31 |
| P/E Ratio:High | NM | NM | 95 | 40 | 28 | 33 | 94 | NM | 71 | 50 |
| P/E Ratio:Low | NM | NM | 63 | 27 | 13 | 23 | 49 | NM | 22 | 29 |

| Income Statement Analysis (Million $) | | | | | | | | | | |
|---|---|---|---|---|---|---|---|---|---|---|
| Revenue | 3,665 | 3,091 | 2,951 | 3,129 | 2,957 | 2,482 | 1,725 | 1,322 | 1,420 | 1,222 |
| Operating Income | NA | 204 | 454 | 759 | 863 | 629 | 267 | 42.1 | 207 | 190 |
| Depreciation | 164 | 147 | 95.0 | 75.0 | 77.5 | 91.6 | 111 | 69.7 | 46.7 | 40.4 |
| Interest Expense | NA | Nil | Nil | Nil | Nil | Nil | Nil | Nil | Nil | Nil |
| Pretax Income | -507 | 138 | 389 | 725 | 797 | 461 | 148 | -13.4 | 170 | 118 |
| Effective Tax Rate | 10.5% | 47.8% | 37.8% | 30.5% | 27.5% | 30.9% | 31.0% | NM | 30.9% | 38.3% |
| Net Income | -454 | 76.0 | 236 | 504 | 577 | 317 | 102 | -11.1 | 117 | 72.9 |
| S&P Core Earnings | -382 | 76.0 | 153 | 425 | 482 | 239 | 28.0 | -68.2 | NA | NA |

| Balance Sheet & Other Financial Data (Million $) | | | | | | | | | | |
|---|---|---|---|---|---|---|---|---|---|---|
| Cash | 3,016 | 1,712 | 1,402 | 1,410 | 2,151 | 951 | 804 | 477 | 340 | 318 |
| Current Assets | NA | 3,597 | 3,012 | 3,706 | 2,911 | 1,911 | 1,153 | 819 | 705 | 569 |
| Total Assets | 6,059 | 5,146 | 4,386 | 4,370 | 3,401 | 2,360 | 1,699 | 1,379 | 1,192 | 902 |
| Current Liabilities | NA | 1,026 | 869 | 828 | 722 | 571 | 453 | 340 | 265 | 236 |
| Long Term Debt | NA | Nil | Nil | Nil | Nil | Nil | Nil | Nil | Nil | Nil |
| Common Equity | 4,339 | 4,032 | 3,408 | 3,498 | 2,678 | 1,785 | 1,243 | 1,034 | 923 | 663 |
| Total Capital | NA | 4,040 | 3,449 | 3,509 | 2,678 | 1,789 | 1,246 | 1,039 | 927 | 666 |
| Capital Expenditures | 84.0 | 178 | 123 | 126 | 89.6 | 59.1 | 51.5 | 120 | 135 | 116 |
| Cash Flow | NA | 223 | 331 | 579 | 655 | 409 | 212 | 58.6 | 163 | 119 |
| Current Ratio | 3.0 | 3.5 | 3.5 | 4.5 | 4.0 | 3.3 | 2.5 | 2.4 | 2.7 | 2.4 |
| % Long Term Debt of Capitalization | Nil | Nil | Nil | Nil | Nil | Nil | Nil | Nil | Nil | Nil |
| % Net Income of Revenue | NM | 2.5 | 8.0 | 16.1 | 19.5 | 12.8 | 5.9 | NM | 8.2 | 6.0 |
| % Return on Assets | NM | 1.6 | 5.4 | 12.9 | 20.0 | 15.6 | 6.6 | NM | 11.2 | 8.8 |
| % Return on Equity | NM | 2.0 | 6.8 | 16.3 | 25.9 | 20.9 | 8.9 | NM | 14.7 | 11.9 |

Data as orig reptd.; bef. results of disc opers/spec. items. Per share data adj. for stk. divs.; EPS diluted. E-Estimated. NA-Not Available. NM-Not Meaningful. NR-Not Ranked. UR-Under Review.

Office: 209 Redwood Shores Parkway, Redwood City, CA 94065-1175.
Telephone: 650-628-1500.
Email: investorrelations@ea.com
Website: http://www.ea.com

Chrmn: L.F. Probst, III
CEO: J. Riccitiello
COO: J. Pleasants
EVP & CFO: E.F. Brown

SVP & CTO: G. Entis
Investor Contact: J. Brown (650-628-7922)
Board Members: R. Asher, L. S. Coleman, Jr., G. M. Kusin, G. B. Laybourne, G. B. Maffei, V. Paul, L. F. Probst, III, J. Riccitiello, R. A. Simonson, L. J. Srere

Founded: 1982
Domicile: Delaware
Employees: 9,000

**STANDARD &POOR'S**

# El Paso Corp

| S&P Recommendation HOLD ★★★☆☆ | Price $7.28 (as of Nov 14, 2008) | 12-Mo. Target Price $10.00 | Investment Style Large-Cap Value |
| --- | --- | --- | --- |

**GICS Sector** Energy
**Sub-Industry** Oil & Gas Storage & Transportation

**Summary** This provider of natural gas and related energy products owns North America's largest natural gas pipeline system and is one of its biggest independent natural gas producers.

## Key Stock Statistics (Source S&P, Vickers, company reports)

| | | | | | | | |
| --- | --- | --- | --- | --- | --- | --- | --- |
| 52-Wk Range | $22.47– 6.58 | S&P Oper. EPS 2008E | 1.51 | Market Capitalization(B) | $5.086 | Beta | 1.00 |
| Trailing 12-Month EPS | $1.34 | S&P Oper. EPS 2009E | 1.27 | Yield (%) | 2.75 | S&P 3-Yr. Proj. EPS CAGR(%) | 12 |
| Trailing 12-Month P/E | 5.4 | P/E on S&P Oper. EPS 2008E | 4.8 | Dividend Rate/Share | $0.20 | S&P Credit Rating | BB |
| $10K Invested 5 Yrs Ago | $11,254 | Common Shares Outstg. (M) | 698.6 | Institutional Ownership (%) | 84 | | |

## Price Performance

30-Week Mov. Avg. · · · 10-Week Mov. Avg. – – **GAAP Earnings vs. Previous Year** **Volume** Above Avg. ⅡⅢ STARS
12-Mo. Target Price — Relative Strength ▲ Up ▼ Down ► No Change Below Avg. ⅡⅢ ★

Options: ASE, CBOE, P

Analysis prepared by **Michael Kay** on November 06, 2008, when the stock traded at **$ 8.02**.

## Highlights

► We see 2008 production growth of 5% and flat in 2009. Third quarter volumes declined 6%, reflecting 41 Mmcfe/d of shut-in volumes from hurricanes. Shut-ins currently stand at about 80 Mmcfe/d. EP plans to accelerate the development of Brazilian assets and now sees first production in early 2009; we think this will be crucial to future segment growth. We believe EP has a substantial position in several emerging plays, including the Haynesville Shale.

► Pipelines are benefiting from higher rates and the startup of several new projects, including the completion of the Elba Island LNG terminal, the expansion of the Piceance pipeline and the Cheyenne Plains pipeline, and the start-up of the Cypress Pipeline. In February, EP closed on an agreement to acquire a 50% interest in the Gulf LNG Clean Energy Project, expected to be in service by late 2011, for $1.1 billion. With the addition of three new pipeline projects, EP currently has a project backlog of $8 billion.

► Based on a 2008 capital budget of $3.5 billion, we forecast 12% EBITDA growth and EPS of $1.51, up 49%. In 2009, we see EPS of $1.27 on a capital budget of $3 billion and lower prices.

## Investment Rationale/Risk

► Over the past year, EP has closed the acquisition of Peoples Energy for $879 million, and sold its ANR Pipeline, Michigan storage assets, and its 50% interest in Great Lakes Transmission for $4.14 billion. With these transactions, we believe EP's risk profile will rise, but growth prospects should expand with a higher concentration on E&P. EP expects to sell properties in the Gulf of Mexico, and we expect investor focus to turn to emerging resource plays. We recently downgraded EP to hold, from buy, based on high debt levels and weakening forecasts.

► Risks to our recommendation and target price include a major decline in natural gas prices, difficulty integrating acquisitions, and weaker-than-expected economic conditions.

► While we remain attracted to EP's premier gas pipeline franchise, we see a weakening E&P environment. Also, we would prefer to see emphasis on reserve additions through the drillbit rather than via acquisitions in E&P. Our 12-month target price of $10 is based on a blend of our relative valuations, including an EV to estimated 2009 EBITDA ratio of 4.5X and a projected P/E of 10X our 2009 EPS estimate.

## Qualitative Risk Assessment

| LOW | MEDIUM | HIGH |
| --- | --- | --- |

Our risk assessment is based on our view of the struggling exploration and production (E&P) segment, which has proven to be very volatile. EP's balance sheet is highly leveraged, in our opinion, making it difficult to turn around the E&P segment. Partly offsetting these risks is EP's involvement in several different business lines, including regulated pipelines.

## Quantitative Evaluations

**S&P Quality Ranking** B-

| D | C | B- | B | B+ | A- | A | A+ |
| --- | --- | --- | --- | --- | --- | --- | --- |

**Relative Strength Rank** WEAK

28

LOWEST = 1     HIGHEST = 99

## Revenue/Earnings Data

**Revenue (Million $)**

| | 1Q | 2Q | 3Q | 4Q | Year |
| --- | --- | --- | --- | --- | --- |
| 2008 | 1,269 | 1,153 | 1,598 | -- | -- |
| 2007 | 1,022 | 1,198 | 1,166 | 1,262 | 4,648 |
| 2006 | 1,337 | 1,089 | 942.0 | 913.0 | 4,281 |
| 2005 | 1,108 | 1,184 | 768.0 | 957.0 | 4,017 |
| 2004 | 1,557 | 1,524 | 1,429 | 1,364 | 5,874 |
| 2003 | 1,844 | 1,574 | 1,724 | 1,569 | 6,711 |

**Earnings Per Share ($)**

| | 1Q | 2Q | 3Q | 4Q | Year |
| --- | --- | --- | --- | --- | --- |
| 2008 | 0.33 | 0.25 | 0.58 | E0.26 | E1.51 |
| 2007 | -0.08 | 0.22 | 0.20 | 0.20 | 0.57 |
| 2006 | 0.42 | 0.19 | 0.15 | -0.30 | 0.72 |
| 2005 | 0.18 | -0.34 | -0.51 | -0.45 | -1.13 |
| 2004 | -0.15 | 0.07 | -0.31 | -0.86 | -1.25 |
| 2003 | -0.33 | -0.53 | 0.12 | -0.28 | -1.03 |

Fiscal year ended Dec. 31. Next earnings report expected: Late February. EPS Estimates based on S&P Operating Earnings; historical GAAP earnings are as reported.

## Dividend Data (Dates: mm/dd Payment Date: mm/dd/yy)

| Amount ($) | Date Decl. | Ex-Div. Date | Stk. of Record | Payment Date |
| --- | --- | --- | --- | --- |
| 0.040 | 02/07 | 03/05 | 03/07 | 04/01/08 |
| 0.040 | 03/31 | 06/04 | 06/06 | 07/01/08 |
| 0.050 | 07/25 | 09/03 | 09/05 | 10/01/08 |
| 0.050 | 10/23 | 12/03 | 12/05 | 01/02/09 |

Dividends have been paid since 1992. Source: Company reports.

The McGraw-Hill Companies

# El Paso Corp

**STANDARD &POOR'S**

## Business Summary November 06, 2008

CORPORATE OVERVIEW. Founded in 1928, El Paso originally served as a regional natural gas pipeline company that ultimately expanded geographically and into complimentary business lines. By 2001, its total assets exceeded $44 billion and included natural gas production, power generation, trading operations and its traditional natural gas pipeline businesses. In late 2001 through 2003, various industry and company-specific events led to a substantial decline in EP's fundamentals. In late 2003, EP announced a long-term business strategy principally focused on core pipeline and production businesses. During the past several years, EP has sold off non-core assets to reduce debt and improve liquidity.

Operations are conducted through three primary segments: Pipelines, Exploration and Production and Marketing. EP also has a Power segment that holds its remaining interests in international power plants in Brazil, Asia and Central America.

PRIMARY BUSINESS DYNAMICS. The Pipeline segment is the largest U.S. owner of interstate natural gas pipelines and owns or has interests in 42,000 miles of pipeline. The division also has 230 billion cubic feet (Bcf) of natural gas storage capacity, and a liquefied natural gas terminal at Elba Island, GA with 806 million cubic feet (Mmcf) of daily base load sendout capacity. Each

pipeline system and storage facility operates under Federal Energy Regulatory Commission (FERC) approved tariffs that establish rates, cost recovery mechanisms, and service terms and conditions. The established rates are a function of EP's costs of providing services, including a "reasonable" return on invested capital.

In February 2007, EP sold ANR Pipeline Company (ANR), its Michigan storage assets, and its 50% interest in Great Lakes Gas Transmission, which comprised approximately 12,600 miles of pipeline and 236 Bcf of storage capacity.

EP's strategy to create value in this segment is to: 1) Expand systems into new markets while leveraging existing assets; 2) recontract or contract available or expiring capacity and resolve open rate cases; 3) leverage its coast-to-coast scale economies; and 4) invest in maintenance and pipeline integrity projects to maintain the value and ensure the safety of its pipeline systems and assets.

## Company Financials Fiscal Year Ended Dec. 31

| Per Share Data ($) | 2007 | 2006 | 2005 | 2004 | 2003 | 2002 | 2001 | 2000 | 1999 | 1998 |
|---|---|---|---|---|---|---|---|---|---|---|
| Tangible Book Value | 6.47 | 6.00 | 3.38 | 4.68 | 5.36 | 11.70 | 17.65 | 15.25 | 10.47 | 13.06 |
| Cash Flow | 2.25 | 2.09 | 0.61 | 0.45 | 0.99 | 0.21 | 2.76 | 4.82 | 1.61 | 3.92 |
| Earnings | 0.57 | 0.72 | -1.13 | -1.25 | -1.03 | -2.30 | 0.13 | 2.44 | -1.06 | 1.85 |
| S&P Core Earnings | 0.54 | 0.69 | -1.07 | -0.84 | -0.68 | -1.95 | -0.37 | NA | NA | NA |
| Dividends | 0.16 | 0.16 | 0.16 | 0.16 | 0.16 | 0.87 | 0.85 | 0.82 | 0.79 | 0.76 |
| Payout Ratio | 28% | 22% | NM | NM | NM | NM | NM | 34% | NM | 41% |
| Prices:High | 18.56 | 16.39 | 14.16 | 11.85 | 10.30 | 46.89 | 75.30 | 74.25 | 43.44 | 38.94 |
| Prices:Low | 13.71 | 11.80 | 9.30 | 6.57 | 3.33 | 4.39 | 36.00 | 30.31 | 30.69 | 24.69 |
| P/E Ratio:High | 33 | 23 | NM | NM | NM | NM | NM | 30 | NM | 21 |
| P/E Ratio:Low | 24 | 16 | NM | NM | NM | NM | NM | 12 | NM | 13 |

| Income Statement Analysis (Million $) | | | | | | | | | | |
|---|---|---|---|---|---|---|---|---|---|---|
| Revenue | 4,648 | 4,281 | 4,017 | 5,874 | 6,711 | 12,194 | 57,475 | 21,950 | 10,581 | 5,782 |
| Operating Income | 2,904 | 1,427 | 934 | 2,386 | 2,907 | 2,872 | 4,391 | 2,155 | 1,482 | 775 |
| Depreciation | 1,176 | 1,047 | 1,121 | 1,088 | 1,207 | 1,405 | 1,359 | 589 | 609 | 269 |
| Interest Expense | 1,044 | 1,228 | 1,389 | 1,632 | 1,839 | 1,400 | 1,155 | 538 | 453 | 267 |
| Pretax Income | 664 | 523 | -991 | -777 | -1,200 | -1,567 | 466 | 1,012 | -287 | 377 |
| Effective Tax Rate | 33.4% | NM | NM | NM | NM | NM | 39.1% | 28.3% | NM | 33.7% |
| Net Income | 436 | 531 | -702 | -802 | -616 | -1,289 | 67.0 | 582 | -242 | 225 |
| S&P Core Earnings | 375 | 471 | -696 | -531 | -401 | -1,096 | -194 | NA | NA | NA |

| Balance Sheet & Other Financial Data (Million $) | | | | | | | | | | |
|---|---|---|---|---|---|---|---|---|---|---|
| Cash | 285 | 537 | 2,132 | 2,117 | 1,429 | 1,591 | 1,139 | 688 | 545 | 90.0 |
| Current Assets | 1,712 | 7,167 | 6,185 | 5,632 | 8,922 | 11,924 | 12,659 | 10,076 | 2,911 | 1,209 |
| Total Assets | 24,579 | 27,261 | 31,838 | 31,383 | 37,084 | 46,224 | 48,171 | 27,445 | 16,657 | 10,069 |
| Current Liabilities | 2,413 | 6,151 | 5,712 | 4,572 | 7,074 | 10,350 | 13,565 | 10,467 | 3,702 | 2,162 |
| Long Term Debt | 12,483 | 13,260 | 17,054 | 18,608 | 20,722 | 19,727 | 14,109 | 6,574 | 5,548 | 3,177 |
| Common Equity | 4,530 | 3,436 | 2,639 | 3,439 | 4,474 | 8,377 | 9,356 | 3,569 | 2,947 | 2,108 |
| Total Capital | 19,485 | 18,396 | 21,850 | 23,358 | 25,196 | 31,680 | 31,012 | 14,623 | 11,601 | 6,914 |
| Capital Expenditures | 2,495 | 2,164 | 1,718 | 1,782 | 2,452 | 3,716 | 4,079 | 1,336 | 1,086 | 406 |
| Cash Flow | 1,575 | 1,541 | 392 | 286 | 591 | 116 | 1,426 | 1,171 | 367 | 494 |
| Current Ratio | 0.7 | 1.2 | 1.1 | 1.2 | 1.3 | 1.2 | 0.9 | 1.0 | 0.8 | 0.6 |
| % Long Term Debt of Capitalization | 64.1 | 72.1 | 78.1 | 79.7 | 82.2 | 62.3 | 45.5 | 45.0 | 47.8 | 46.0 |
| % Net Income of Revenue | 9.4 | 12.4 | NM | NM | NM | NM | 0.1 | 2.7 | NM | 3.9 |
| % Return on Assets | 1.7 | 1.8 | NM | NM | NM | NM | 0.1 | 2.6 | NM | 2.3 |
| % Return on Equity | 10.0 | 16.3 | NM | NM | NM | NM | 0.8 | 17.9 | NM | 11.1 |

Data as orig reptd.; bef. results of disc opers/spec. items. Per share data adj. for stk. divs.; EPS diluted. E-Estimated. NA-Not Available. NM-Not Meaningful. NR-Not Ranked. UR-Under Review.

**Office:** El Paso Energy Building, Houston, TX 77002-5089.
**Telephone:** 713-420-2600.
**Email:** investorrelations@epenergy.com
**Website:** http://www.elpaso.com

**Chrmn:** R.L. Kuehn, Jr.
**Pres & CEO:** D.L. Foshee
**CEO:** P.W. Hobby
**EVP & CFO:** D.M. Leland

**EVP & General Counsel:** R.W. Baker
**Investor Contact:** B. Conneny (713-420-5855)
**Board Members:** J. C. Braniff, J. L. Dunlap, D. L. Foshee, R. W. Goldman, A. W. Hall, Jr., T. R. Hix, W. Joyce, R. L. Kuehn, Jr., F. P. McClean, S. J. Shapiro, J. M. Talbert, R. F. Vagt, J. L. Whitmire, III, J. B. Wyatt

**Founded:** 1928
**Domicile:** Delaware
**Employees:** 4,992

The McGraw-Hill Companies

# Embarq Corp

**STANDARD & POOR'S**

| S&P Recommendation | BUY ★★★★☆ | Price | 12-Mo. Target Price | Investment Style |
|---|---|---|---|---|
| | | $30.16 (as of Nov 14, 2008) | $49.00 | Large-Cap Value |

**GICS Sector** Telecommunication Services
**Sub-Industry** Integrated Telecommunication Services

**Summary** Embarq, which provides wireline services to nearly 6 million access lines, is the fourth-largest wireline provider in the U.S. The company was spun off from Sprint Nextel in May 2006 and has agreed to be acquired in a stock deal by CenturyTel, pending necessary approvals.

## Key Stock Statistics (Source S&P, Vickers, company reports)

| | | | | | | | |
|---|---|---|---|---|---|---|---|
| 52-Wk Range | $52.25– 27.05 | S&P Oper. EPS 2008**E** | NA | Market Capitalization(B) | $4.287 | Beta | 0.96 |
| Trailing 12-Month EPS | $5.10 | S&P Oper. EPS 2009**E** | NA | Yield (%) | 9.12 | S&P 3-Yr. Proj. EPS CAGR(%) | 4 |
| Trailing 12-Month P/E | 5.9 | P/E on S&P Oper. EPS 2008**E** | null | Dividend Rate/Share | $2.75 | S&P Credit Rating | BBB- |
| $10K Invested 5 Yrs Ago | NA | Common Shares Outstg. (M) | 142.1 | Institutional Ownership (%) | 95 | | |

## Price Performance

30-Week Mov. Avg. · · · · 10-Week Mov. Avg. - - - GAAP Earnings vs. Previous Year    Volume Above Avg. ▮▮▮▮ STARS
12-Mo. Target Price —    Relative Strength — ▲ Up ▼ Down ► No Change    Below Avg. ▮▮▮▮ ★

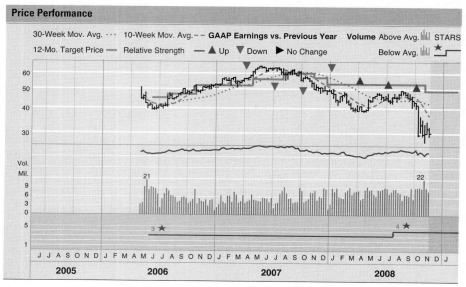

Options: ASE, CBOE, P, Ph

Analysis prepared by **Todd Rosenbluth** on October 28, 2008, when the stock traded at **$ 31.45**.

## Highlights

▸ We see revenues declining to $6.18 billion in 2008 and to $5.9 billion in 2009, from $6.36 billion in 2007, as EQ faces increased competition from cable and wireless carriers in its urban markets and is hurt by slower housing demand. We believe EQ will offset some of the customer losses with the expansion of its DSL and video services through its own service bundle.

▸ Even with revenue weakness in high-margin services and some support of its wireless business, we look for EBITDA margins to widen to 43% in 2008 and hold steady in 2009 from 41% in 2007, as we see benefits from work force reductions in its call center, and additional savings from restructuring.

▸ We expect EPS to be helped by a 6% reduction in the diluted share count in the first nine months of 2008, but see zero added repurchases due to the pending acquisition. Our EPS estimates are $5.46 for 2008 and $5.00 for 2009. We believe that fourth-quarter 2007 EPS was aided by $0.18 per share of tax benefits. Third quarter 2008 results include a $0.29 one-time charge for a workforce reduction.

## Investment Rationale/Risk

▸ We view the pending merger with CenturyTel (CTL: buy $26) as positive. While we see EQ undervalued on its own, we contend it faces customer loyalty challenges and has a thin management team. Combined with CTL, we believe the company will have ample support for its dividend and has opportunities for cost synergies. On a stand alone basis, despite risks from competition and the slowing housing market, we believe EQ's free cash flow will be strong.

▸ Risks to our recommendation and target price include the company's new management team, greater-than-expected cable competition, higher capital spending, and failure to be acquired.

▸ EQ trades at an enterprise value/EBITDA multiple of nearly 4X and a P/E of 7X based on our 2009 estimates, below telecom peers. We believe a discount is warranted given our view of the company's less stable customer base. Our 12-month target price of $49 is based on deal terms and our 12-month target price for CTL of $36. At this level, EQ is valued at an enterprise value/EBITDA multiple of 4.8X and a P/E of about 10X.

## Qualitative Risk Assessment

| LOW | MEDIUM | HIGH |
|---|---|---|

Our risk assessment reflects the competitive nature of the telecom industry and the company's short operating history, offset by our view of the steady operating cash flow that supports its dividend.

## Quantitative Evaluations

**S&P Quality Ranking** NR

| D | C | B- | B | B+ | A- | A | A+ |
|---|---|---|---|---|---|---|---|

**Relative Strength Rank** MODERATE

57

LOWEST = 1    HIGHEST = 99

## Revenue/Earnings Data

**Revenue (Million $)**

| | 1Q | 2Q | 3Q | 4Q | Year |
|---|---|---|---|---|---|
| 2008 | 1,571 | 1,549 | 1,525 | -- | -- |
| 2007 | 1,589 | 1,605 | 1,594 | 1,577 | 6,365 |
| 2006 | 1,561 | 1,579 | 1,606 | 1,617 | 6,363 |
| 2005 | -- | -- | -- | -- | 6,701 |
| 2004 | -- | -- | -- | -- | -- |
| 2003 | -- | -- | -- | -- | -- |

**Earnings Per Share ($)**

| | 1Q | 2Q | 3Q | 4Q | Year |
|---|---|---|---|---|---|
| 2008 | 1.38 | 1.38 | 1.11 | E1.30 | E5.46 |
| 2007 | 1.05 | 1.15 | 1.01 | 1.23 | 4.44 |
| 2006 | 1.42 | 1.44 | 1.06 | 1.28 | 5.21 |
| 2005 | -- | -- | -- | -- | 4.96 |
| 2004 | -- | -- | -- | -- | -- |
| 2003 | -- | -- | -- | -- | -- |

Fiscal year ended Dec. 31. Next earnings report expected: Early February. EPS Estimates based on S&P Operating Earnings; historical GAAP earnings are as reported.

## Dividend Data (Dates: mm/dd Payment Date: mm/dd/yy)

| Amount ($) | Date Decl. | Ex-Div. Date | Stk. of Record | Payment Date |
|---|---|---|---|---|
| 0.688 | 01/09 | 03/06 | 03/10 | 03/31/08 |
| 0.688 | 05/01 | 06/05 | 06/09 | 06/30/08 |
| 0.688 | 07/31 | 09/05 | 09/09 | 09/30/08 |
| 0.688 | 10/14 | 12/08 | 12/10 | 12/31/08 |

Dividends have been paid since 2006. Source: Company reports.

---

**Please read the Required Disclosures and Analyst Certification on the last page of this report.**

The McGraw-Hill Companies

# Embarq Corp

## Business Summary October 28, 2008

CORPORATE OVERVIEW. In mid-May 2006, Sprint Nextel (S) spun off its local telephone business as a separate entity now known as Embarq Corp. (EQ). The corporate action was a tax-free distribution to Sprint's shareholders, who received one share of EQ for every 20 shares of S. As of September 2008, EQ provided local service to 5.85 million access lines in 18 states, down 8.5% from a year earlier and a faster decline than six months earlier. The majority of EQ's access lines are located in Florida, North Carolina, Nevada and Ohio, where home foreclosure rates have recently been high. EQ's offerings include high-speed DSL Internet services for 1.4 million residential customers and whole-sale video services to 284,000 customers.

In early October 2008, The Wall Street Journal reported that EQ had previously hired an adviser to help sell the company, but that due to tight credit markets no deal was possible. However, in late October, EQ agreed to be acquired by rural telecom carrier CenturyTel (CTL) in a stock based transaction originally valued at $40 a share, pending necessary approvals expected in mid-2009. EQ shareholders would receive 1.37 CTL shares per EQ share. As of September 2008, CTL had 2.04 million access lines (down 6% from a year earlier) and 628,000 DSL customers.

CORPORATE STRATEGY. EQ's strategy is to bundle services to sell the com-moditized wireline services with high-growth services such as broadband. To offset what we viewed as slower DSL growth in the first half of 2008, we ex-

pected EQ to increase marketing of broadband and improve connection speeds in the second half of 2008. Meanwhile, in late 2006, EQ began to focus on offering wireless service and signed up 112,000 subscribers by the end of 2007, through a wholesale relationship with Sprint Nextel. In February 2008, EQ said it planned to improve the profitability of the wireless segment, and we believe marketing efforts have been curtailed in 2008.

COMPETITIVE LANDSCAPE. We believe that to date, wireless substitution has been the greatest threat to EQ's access lines. Wireless coverage has im-proved over the past couple of years, and we believe that many of these cus-tomers have dropped their landlines while staying in or moving into EQ's terri-tory. However, with approximately 70% of EQ's access lines being covered by cable competition at the end of 2007 and our expectation that this figure will grow to 80% by the end of 2008, the company should face higher competition on telephony and broadband from cable companies. The largest of the com-petitors in EQ's territory include Time Warner, Comcast, Charter and Cox. EQ has tried to offset the competition by bundling DSL, wireless, and satellite TV for households. At the end of June 2008, monthly revenue per household was $55.92, up 5% from a year earlier.

## Company Financials Fiscal Year Ended Dec. 31

| Per Share Data ($) | 2009 | 2008 | 2007 | 2006 | 2005 | 2004 | 2003 | 2002 | 2001 | 2000 |
|---|---|---|---|---|---|---|---|---|---|---|
| Tangible Book Value | NA | NA | 0.84 | NM | NM | NA | NA | NA | NA | NA |
| Cash Flow | NA | NA | 11.31 | 12.10 | 12.09 | NA | NA | NA | NA | NA |
| Earnings | 5.00 | 5.46 | 4.44 | 5.21 | 4.96 | NA | NA | NA | NA | NA |
| S&P Core Earnings | NA | NA | 4.20 | 4.94 | 5.91 | 6.04 | NA | NA | NA | NA |
| Dividends | NA | 2.75 | 2.38 | 1.00 | Nil | NA | NA | NA | NA | NA |
| Payout Ratio | NA | 50% | 53% | 19% | Nil | NA | NA | NA | NA | NA |
| Prices:High | NA | 50.05 | 65.50 | 53.32 | NA | NA | NA | NA | NA | NA |
| Prices:Low | NA | 29.00 | 46.94 | 38.81 | NA | NA | NA | NA | NA | NA |
| P/E Ratio:High | NA | 9 | 15 | 10 | NA | NA | NA | NA | NA | NA |
| P/E Ratio:Low | NA | 5 | 11 | 7 | NA | NA | NA | NA | NA | NA |

| Income Statement Analysis (Million $) | | | | | | | | | | |
|---|---|---|---|---|---|---|---|---|---|---|
| Revenue | NA | NA | 6,365 | 6,363 | 6,701 | 6,139 | 6,159 | NA | NA | NA |
| Operating Income | NA | NA | 2,587 | 2,571 | 2,911 | NA | NA | NA | NA | NA |
| Depreciation | NA | NA | 1,057 | 1,027 | 1,070 | 1,086 | 1,089 | NA | NA | NA |
| Interest Expense | NA | NA | 432 | 324 | 520 | 102 | 116 | NA | NA | NA |
| Pretax Income | NA | NA | 1,075 | 1,234 | 1,245 | 1,486 | 1,489 | NA | NA | NA |
| Effective Tax Rate | NA | NA | 36.5% | 36.5% | 40.2% | 38.3% | 38.2% | NA | NA | NA |
| Net Income | NA | NA | 683 | 784 | 744 | 917 | 920 | NA | NA | NA |
| S&P Core Earnings | NA | NA | 647 | 745 | 887 | 907 | NA | NA | NA | NA |

| Balance Sheet & Other Financial Data (Million $) | | | | | | | | | | |
|---|---|---|---|---|---|---|---|---|---|---|
| Cash | NA | NA | 69.0 | 53.0 | 200 | 113 | NA | NA | NA | NA |
| Current Assets | NA | NA | 986 | 1,023 | 1,194 | NA | NA | NA | NA | NA |
| Total Assets | NA | NA | 8,901 | 9,091 | 9,473 | 9,329 | NA | NA | NA | NA |
| Current Liabilities | NA | NA | 1,198 | 1,264 | 1,157 | NA | NA | NA | NA | NA |
| Long Term Debt | NA | NA | 5,878 | 6,421 | 7,248 | NA | NA | NA | NA | NA |
| Common Equity | NA | NA | 264 | -468 | -1,071 | 4,960 | NA | NA | NA | NA |
| Total Capital | NA | NA | 7,173 | 6,992 | 7,268 | NA | NA | NA | NA | NA |
| Capital Expenditures | NA | NA | 819 | 923 | NA | 975 | 1,118 | NA | NA | NA |
| Cash Flow | NA | NA | 1,740 | 1,811 | 1,814 | NA | NA | NA | NA | NA |
| Current Ratio | NA | NA | 0.8 | 0.8 | 1.0 | 1.0 | NA | NA | NA | NA |
| % Long Term Debt of Capitalization | NA | NA | 95.6 | 91.8 | 99.7 | 18.2 | Nil | NA | NA | NA |
| % Net Income of Revenue | NA | NA | 10.7 | 12.3 | 11.1 | 14.9 | 14.9 | NA | NA | NA |
| % Return on Assets | NA | NA | 7.6 | 8.4 | NA | NA | NA | NA | NA | NA |
| % Return on Equity | NA | NA | NM | NM | NA | NA | NA | NA | NA | NA |

Data as orig reptd.; bef. results of disc opers/spec. items. Per share data adj. for stk. divs.; EPS diluted. E-Estimated. NA-Not Available. NM-Not Meaningful. NR-Not Ranked. UR-Under Review.

**Office:** 5454 W. 110th Street, Overland Park, KS 66211.
**Telephone:** 913-323-4637.
**Website:** http://www.embarq.com
**Chrmn:** W.A. Owens

**Pres & CEO:** T. Gerke
**CFO:** G.M. Betts
**CTO:** D.G. Huber
**Chief Acctg Officer & Cntlr:** R.B. Green

**Board Members:** P. C. Brown, S. Davis, R. A. Gephardt, T. Gerke, J. P. Mullen, W. A. Owens, D. C. Paliwal, S. M. Shern, L. A. Siegel

**Founded:** 2005
**Domicile:** Delaware
**Employees:** 18,000

# EMC Corp

**STANDARD &POOR'S**

| S&P Recommendation | **STRONG BUY** ★★★★★ | Price | 12-Mo. Target Price | Investment Style |
|---|---|---|---|---|
| | | $9.98 (as of Nov 14, 2008) | $14.00 | Large-Cap Blend |

**GICS Sector** Information Technology
**Sub-Industry** Computer Storage & Peripherals

**Summary** This company is one of the world's largest suppliers of enterprise storage systems, software and services.

## Key Stock Statistics (Source S&P, Vickers, company reports)

| | | | | | | | |
|---|---|---|---|---|---|---|---|
| 52-Wk Range | $20.19– 8.35 | S&P Oper. EPS 2008E | 0.75 | Market Capitalization(B) | $20.367 | Beta | 1.85 |
| Trailing 12-Month EPS | $0.74 | S&P Oper. EPS 2009E | 0.85 | Yield (%) | Nil | S&P 3-Yr. Proj. EPS CAGR(%) | 8 |
| Trailing 12-Month P/E | 13.5 | P/E on S&P Oper. EPS 2008E | 13.3 | Dividend Rate/Share | Nil | S&P Credit Rating | A- |
| $10K Invested 5 Yrs Ago | $7,263 | Common Shares Outstg. (M) | 2,040.8 | Institutional Ownership (%) | 76 | | |

## Price Performance

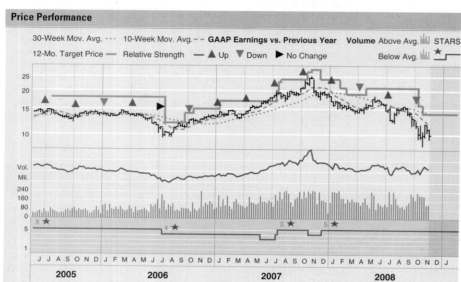

30-Week Mov. Avg. · · · 10-Week Mov. Avg. — **GAAP Earnings vs. Previous Year** Volume Above Avg. STARS
12-Mo. Target Price — Relative Strength — ▲ Up ▼ Down ▶ No Change Below Avg. ★

Options: ASE, CBOE, P, Ph

Analysis prepared by **Rafay Khalid** on October 23, 2008, when the stock traded at **$ 9.98.**

## Highlights

➤ We project that revenues will increase 13% in 2008 and 6% in 2009, based on our expectation for solid international growth and market share gains partially offset by our outlook for weakness in the U.S. financial services end-market. We also foresee sales increases for the information infrastructure business. Although we expect revenue expansion for majority-owned VMware (VMW: not ranked, $20) well above EMC's average in 2008, we believe this rate will decelerate substantially from 2007.

➤ We expect the gross margin to be flat at 55% in 2008 and remain at a similar level in 2009. We forecast slightly higher expenses in 2008 as EMC adds more sales personnel in high-growth markets. However, we think the company's restructuring initiatives will help lower expenses in 2009. We project that adjusted operating margins will remain at 13% in 2008, but increase to 14% in 2009.

➤ Our operating EPS estimates are $0.75 for 2008 and $0.85 for 2009, excluding one-time items. Our estimates assume a tax rate of 21% and that share repurchases will continue based on the company's buyback history.

## Investment Rationale/Risk

➤ We expect global IT spending growth to decline compared to 2007, but remain modestly positive for the rest of 2008 and for 2009. We believe EMC is financially well positioned to weather the economic slowdown, based on our projection that it will end 2008 with $8.6 billion in cash and investments ($4.15 per share) and generate $1.2 billion in free cash flow. We see EMC as undervalued, accounting for its majority stake in VMware.

➤ Risks to our recommendation and target price include substantial purchase delays or cancellations, and developments that negatively affect the business or stock of VMW.

➤ Our intrinsic and peer analyses account for EMC's 85% stake in VMW. Our DCF model assumes a 12.9% weighted average cost of capital and 3% terminal growth, yielding an intrinsic value of $13. Comparing EMC's P/E and P/E-to-growth ratios to those of the S&P 500 Technology sector results in a price of $10. Averaging these calculations and assigning a value of $2.50 for VMW, which we discount due to a variety of risk factors, we arrive at a valuation of $14, our 12-month target price.

## Qualitative Risk Assessment

| LOW | **MEDIUM** | HIGH |
|---|---|---|

Our risk assessment reflects our view that EMC is a market leader, generates consistent free cash flow, and has a strong balance sheet. However, we see the storage segment as somewhat cyclical, highly competitive, and often typified by pricing pressure.

## Quantitative Evaluations

### S&P Quality Ranking                                      B

| D | C | B- | **B** | B+ | A- | A | A+ |
|---|---|---|---|---|---|---|---|

### Relative Strength Rank                           MODERATE

62

LOWEST = 1                                          HIGHEST = 99

## Revenue/Earnings Data

### Revenue (Million $)

| | 1Q | 2Q | 3Q | 4Q | Year |
|---|---|---|---|---|---|
| 2008 | 3,470 | 3,674 | 3,716 | -- | -- |
| 2007 | 2,975 | 3,125 | 3,300 | 3,831 | 13,230 |
| 2006 | 2,551 | 2,575 | 2,815 | 3,215 | 11,155 |
| 2005 | 2,243 | 2,345 | 2,366 | 2,710 | 9,664 |
| 2004 | 1,872 | 1,971 | 2,029 | 2,358 | 8,229 |
| 2003 | 1,384 | 1,479 | 1,511 | 1,863 | 6,237 |

### Earnings Per Share ($)

| | 1Q | 2Q | 3Q | 4Q | Year |
|---|---|---|---|---|---|
| 2008 | 0.13 | 0.18 | 0.20 | E0.23 | E0.75 |
| 2007 | 0.15 | 0.16 | 0.23 | 0.24 | 0.77 |
| 2006 | 0.12 | 0.12 | 0.13 | 0.18 | 0.54 |
| 2005 | 0.11 | 0.12 | 0.17 | 0.06 | 0.47 |
| 2004 | 0.06 | 0.08 | 0.09 | 0.13 | 0.36 |
| 2003 | 0.02 | 0.04 | 0.07 | 0.09 | 0.22 |

Fiscal year ended Dec. 31. Next earnings report expected: Late January. EPS Estimates based on S&P Operating Earnings; historical GAAP earnings are as reported.

## Dividend Data

No cash dividends have been paid.

# EMC Corp

## Business Summary October 23, 2008

CORPORATE OVERVIEW. EMC offers a wide range of storage systems, software and services designed to fulfill customers' needs in terms of performance, functionality, scalability, data availability, and cost. EMC's clients are located around the world and represent a cross-section of economic sectors and government entities. The company's products and services are used in conjunction with a variety of computing platforms that support key business processes, including transaction processing, data warehousing, electronic commerce, and content management.

The company reports revenues in four business segments -- Information Storage, Document Management and Archiving, RSA Information Security, and VMware Infrastructure. Information Storage accounted for 80% of sales in 2007, down from 86% in 2006. Information Storage sales rose 10% in 2007, after increasing 9% in 2006.

Revenues outside the U.S. accounted for 55% of EMC's total in 2007, up from 54% in 2006. Moreover, all of EMC's markets except Asia expanded at a double-digit rate during the year, with Latin America growing the fastest at 22%.

CORPORATE STRATEGY. EMC's strategy focuses on the concept of information lifecycle management (ILM). This idea centers on the management of information across its entire "life," from creation, to usage, to archiving, to disposal. Via its utilization, ILM simultaneously lowers the cost and the risk of managing data, in our view, regardless of its format (documents, images, e-mail, etc.). ILM also provides for cost-effective business continuity and more efficient compliance with regulations.

As part of this plan, EMC has engaged in a number of acquisitions over the past two years. One of its more successful deals, in our opinion, was the purchase of VMware, Inc. (VMW: not ranked, $20), a virtual infrastructure software company, which is operated as an independent subsidiary. VMW's software is designed to enable customers to achieve much higher utilization of the server, storage and network resources deployed within their operations, while dramatically simplifying how the workloads running on those systems are operated and managed. In 2007, VMW's revenues rose 86%, compared to an 83% increase in 2006. In September 2006, EMC acquired RSA Security for $2.1 billion. This transaction marked EMC's entry into the security software segment, and helps serve the needs of customers interested in combined storage and security solutions.

## Company Financials Fiscal Year Ended Dec. 31

| Per Share Data ($) | 2007 | 2006 | 2005 | 2004 | 2003 | 2002 | 2001 | 2000 | 1999 | 1998 |
|---|---|---|---|---|---|---|---|---|---|---|
| Tangible Book Value | 2.42 | 4.39 | 3.20 | 3.22 | 3.19 | 3.05 | 3.31 | 3.72 | 2.38 | 1.60 |
| Cash Flow | 1.02 | 0.87 | 0.73 | 0.61 | 0.45 | 0.24 | 0.07 | 1.02 | 0.66 | 0.46 |
| Earnings | 0.77 | 0.54 | 0.47 | 0.36 | 0.22 | -0.05 | -0.23 | 0.79 | 0.46 | 0.37 |
| S&P Core Earnings | 0.73 | 0.55 | 0.35 | 0.21 | 0.04 | -0.23 | -0.33 | NA | NA | NA |
| Dividends | Nil | Nil | Nil | Nil | Nil | Nil | Nil | Nil | Nil | Nil |
| Payout Ratio | Nil | Nil | Nil | Nil | Nil | Nil | Nil | Nil | Nil | Nil |
| Prices:High | 25.47 | 14.75 | 15.09 | 15.80 | 14.66 | 17.97 | 82.00 | 104.94 | 55.50 | 21.66 |
| Prices:Low | 12.74 | 9.44 | 11.10 | 9.24 | 5.98 | 3.67 | 10.01 | 47.50 | 21.00 | 6.00 |
| P/E Ratio:High | 33 | 27 | 32 | 44 | 67 | NM | NM | NM | NM | 58 |
| P/E Ratio:Low | 17 | 17 | 24 | 26 | 27 | NM | NM | NM | NM | 16 |

| Income Statement Analysis (Million $) | 2007 | 2006 | 2005 | 2004 | 2003 | 2002 | 2001 | 2000 | 1999 | 1998 |
|---|---|---|---|---|---|---|---|---|---|---|
| Revenue | 13,230 | 11,155 | 9,664 | 8,229 | 6,237 | 5,438 | 7,091 | 8,873 | 6,716 | 3,974 |
| Operating Income | 2,302 | 2,170 | 2,222 | 1,716 | 988 | 310 | 355 | 2,774 | 1,897 | 1,185 |
| Depreciation | 530 | 764 | 640 | 616 | 521 | 654 | 655 | 517 | 447 | 203 |
| Interest Expense | 72.9 | 34.1 | 7.99 | 7.52 | 3.03 | 11.4 | 11.3 | 14.6 | 33.5 | 20.2 |
| Pretax Income | 2,060 | 1,390 | 1,652 | 1,185 | 571 | -296 | -577 | 2,441 | 1,357 | 1,058 |
| Effective Tax Rate | 18.4% | 11.7% | 31.4% | 26.5% | 13.1% | NM | NM | 27.0% | 25.5% | 25.0% |
| Net Income | 1,666 | 1,227 | 1,133 | 871 | 496 | -119 | -508 | 1,782 | 1,011 | 793 |
| S&P Core Earnings | 1,569 | 1,241 | 839 | 504 | 84.2 | -477 | -720 | NA | NA | NA |

| Balance Sheet & Other Financial Data (Million $) | 2007 | 2006 | 2005 | 2004 | 2003 | 2002 | 2001 | 2000 | 1999 | 1998 |
|---|---|---|---|---|---|---|---|---|---|---|
| Cash | 6,127 | 1,828 | 2,322 | 1,477 | 1,869 | 1,687 | 2,129 | 1,983 | 1,109 | 705 |
| Current Assets | 10,053 | 6,521 | 6,574 | 4,831 | 4,687 | 4,217 | 4,923 | 6,100 | 4,320 | 3,105 |
| Total Assets | 22,285 | 18,566 | 16,790 | 15,423 | 14,093 | 9,590 | 9,890 | 10,628 | 7,173 | 4,569 |
| Current Liabilities | 4,408 | 3,881 | 3,674 | 2,949 | 2,547 | 2,042 | 2,179 | 2,114 | 1,398 | 653 |
| Long Term Debt | 3,450 | 3,450 | 127 | 128 | 130 | Nil | Nil | 14.5 | 687 | 539 |
| Common Equity | 12,521 | 10,326 | 12,065 | 11,523 | 10,885 | 7,226 | 7,601 | 8,177 | 4,952 | 3,324 |
| Total Capital | 16,448 | 13,776 | 12,368 | 11,793 | 11,015 | 7,226 | 7,601 | 8,494 | 5,764 | 3,914 |
| Capital Expenditures | 699 | 718 | 601 | 371 | 369 | 391 | 889 | 858 | 524 | 373 |
| Cash Flow | 2,196 | 1,992 | 1,773 | 1,488 | 1,017 | 535 | 147 | 2,299 | 1,458 | 997 |
| Current Ratio | 2.3 | 1.7 | 1.8 | 1.6 | 1.8 | 2.1 | 2.3 | 2.9 | 3.1 | 4.8 |
| % Long Term Debt of Capitalization | 21.4 | 25.0 | 1.0 | 1.1 | 1.2 | Nil | Nil | 0.2 | 11.9 | 13.8 |
| % Net Income of Revenue | 12.6 | 11.0 | 11.7 | 10.6 | 8.0 | NM | NM | 20.1 | 15.0 | 20.0 |
| % Return on Assets | 8.2 | 6.9 | 7.0 | 5.9 | 4.2 | NM | NM | 20.0 | 15.8 | 19.7 |
| % Return on Equity | 14.6 | 11.0 | 9.6 | 7.8 | 5.5 | NM | NM | 27.1 | 34.4 | 27.8 |

Data as orig reptd.; bef. results of disc opers/spec. items. Per share data adj. for stk. divs.; EPS diluted. E-Estimated. NA-Not Available. NM-Not Meaningful. NR-Not Ranked. UR-Under Review.

**Office:** 176 South Street, Hopkinton, MA 01748-2230.
**Telephone:** 508-435-1000.
**Email:** emc_ir@emc.com
**Website:** http://www.emc.com

**Chrmn, Pres & CEO:** J.M. Tucci
**EVP & CFO:** D.I. Goulden
**EVP & General Counsel:** P.T. Dacier
**SVP & CTO:** J.M. Nick

**SVP & Chief Acctg Officer:** M.A. Link
**Board Members:** M. W. Brown, M. J. Cronin, G. Deegan, J. R. Egan, W. P. Fitzgerald, O. Kallasvuo, E. F. Kelly, W. B. Priem, P. L. Sagan, D. N. Strohm, J. M. Tucci

**Founded:** 1979
**Domicile:** Massachusetts
**Employees:** 37,700

# Emerson Electric Co.

STANDARD &POOR'S

| S&P Recommendation | BUY ★★★★☆ | Price $33.40 (as of Nov 14, 2008) | 12-Mo. Target Price $39.00 | Investment Style Large-Cap Blend |
|---|---|---|---|---|

**GICS Sector** Industrials
**Sub-Industry** Electrical Components & Equipment

**Summary** This company primarily makes backup power equipment for telecom and Internet providers and users, climate control components, and electric motors.

## Key Stock Statistics (Source S&P, Vickers, company reports)

| | | | | | | | |
|---|---|---|---|---|---|---|---|
| 52-Wk Range | $59.05–29.44 | S&P Oper. EPS 2009E | 2.96 | Market Capitalization(B) | $25.916 | Beta | 1.21 |
| Trailing 12-Month EPS | $3.06 | S&P Oper. EPS 2010E | 3.59 | Yield (%) | 3.95 | S&P 3-Yr. Proj. EPS CAGR(%) | 9 |
| Trailing 12-Month P/E | 10.9 | P/E on S&P Oper. EPS 2009E | 11.3 | Dividend Rate/Share | $1.32 | S&P Credit Rating | A |
| $10K Invested 5 Yrs Ago | $12,530 | Common Shares Outstg. (M) | 775.9 | Institutional Ownership (%) | 74 | | |

## Price Performance

30-Week Mov. Avg. · · ·    10-Week Mov. Avg. - -    **GAAP Earnings vs. Previous Year**    Volume Above Avg. |||| STARS
12-Mo. Target Price —    Relative Strength —    ▲ Up  ▼ Down  ► No Change    Below Avg. |||| ★

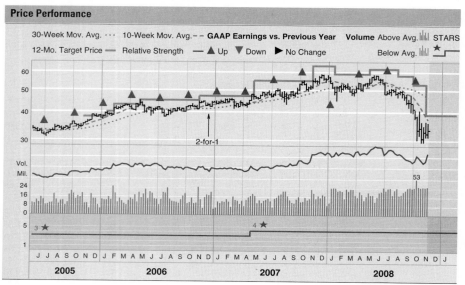

2-for-1

Options: ASE, CBOE, P, Ph

Analysis prepared by **Mathew Christy, CFA** on November 12, 2008, when the stock traded at **$ 31.47**.

## Highlights

➤ We expect that revenues will increase almost 3% in FY 09 (Sep.) and 6.5% in FY 10, led by growth in the process management and network power segments. Our FY 09 forecast reflects slow organic revenue growth, due mainly to continued power demand in international markets, and benefits of acquisitions, offset somewhat by the negative effects of currency translation. Our FY 10 forecast is based on a return to more normalized economic conditions and continued demand for power products.

➤ We think operating margins will decline in FY 09. We see benefits from continued cost rationalization efforts, an improved global supply chain, and increased efficiencies being offset by dilution from acquisition-related costs, raw material cost inflation and ramp-up costs from product transitions and plant realignments, lower gross margins due to product mix and pricing, and lower operating leverage.

➤ We project operating EPS of $2.96 in FY 09 and $3.59 in FY 10, representing a decline of 5% and growth of about 20% in the respective years.

## Investment Rationale/Risk

➤ We believe EMR's business prospects over the next two years remain strong, as the company gains continued organic revenue growth from international sales, globally valued brand platforms, and new product introductions in key business segments, as well as opportunistic bolt-on acquisitions and favorable currency translation. We forecast that EMR's business efficiency and operating metrics will improve, enabling the company to further strengthen its free cash flow growth, providing more cash for acquisitions and share repurchases.

➤ Risks to our recommendation and target price include weaker than expected global economic growth; softer industrial, energy and electronics markets; and potential value-diminishing acquisitions.

➤ Our 12-month target price of $39 represents a blend of two valuation metrics. Our discounted cash flow model, which assumes a 3% perpetual growth rate and a 10.2% discount rate, indicates an intrinsic value of $43. Our relative valuation applies an 11X P/E multiple, a premium to peers but below the historical low multiple of 13X earnings, to our FY 09 EPS estimate, indicating a $33 value.

## Qualitative Risk Assessment

| LOW | MEDIUM | HIGH |
|---|---|---|

Our risk assessment reflects the cyclical nature of several of the company's major end markets, its acquisition strategy, and corporate governance practices that we view as unfavorable versus peers. This is offset by our view of its strong competitive position in major product categories.

## Quantitative Evaluations

**S&P Quality Ranking**   A

| D | C | B- | B | B+ | A- | A | A+ |
|---|---|---|---|---|---|---|---|

**Relative Strength Rank**   MODERATE

68

LOWEST = 1    HIGHEST = 99

## Revenue/Earnings Data

**Revenue (Million $)**

| | 1Q | 2Q | 3Q | 4Q | Year |
|---|---|---|---|---|---|
| 2008 | 5,637 | 6,023 | 6,568 | 6,696 | 24,807 |
| 2007 | 5,051 | 5,513 | 5,874 | 6,134 | 22,572 |
| 2006 | 4,548 | 4,852 | 5,217 | 5,516 | 20,133 |
| 2005 | 3,970 | 4,227 | 4,465 | 4,643 | 17,305 |
| 2004 | 3,600 | 3,859 | 4,036 | 4,120 | 15,615 |
| 2003 | 3,226 | 3,465 | 3,573 | 3,694 | 13,958 |

**Earnings Per Share ($)**

| | | | | | |
|---|---|---|---|---|---|
| 2008 | 0.66 | 0.76 | 0.82 | 0.88 | 3.11 |
| 2007 | 0.55 | 0.61 | 0.72 | 0.78 | 2.66 |
| 2006 | 0.48 | 0.52 | 0.59 | 0.65 | 2.24 |
| 2005 | 0.35 | 0.42 | 0.43 | 0.51 | 1.70 |
| 2004 | 0.29 | 0.38 | 0.41 | 0.42 | 1.49 |
| 2003 | 0.26 | 0.28 | 0.33 | 0.33 | 1.21 |

Fiscal year ended Sep. 30. Next earnings report expected: Early February. EPS Estimates based on S&P Operating Earnings; historical GAAP earnings are as reported.

## Dividend Data (Dates: mm/dd Payment Date: mm/dd/yy)

| Amount ($) | Date Decl. | Ex-Div. Date | Stk. of Record | Payment Date |
|---|---|---|---|---|
| 0.300 | 02/05 | 02/13 | 02/15 | 03/10/08 |
| 0.300 | 05/06 | 05/14 | 05/16 | 06/10/08 |
| 0.300 | 08/05 | 08/13 | 08/15 | 09/10/08 |
| 0.330 | 11/04 | 11/12 | 11/14 | 12/10/08 |

Dividends have been paid since 1947. Source: Company reports.

# Emerson Electric Co.

**STANDARD
&POOR'S**

## Business Summary November 12, 2008

CORPORATE OVERVIEW. Emerson is an industrial conglomerate operating more than 60 diverse businesses in five primary business segments: Process Management, Industrial Automation, Network Power, Climate Technologies, and Appliance and Tools.

The company's Process Management segment, which accounted for 25% of FY 07 (Sep.) total revenues and 31% of operating profits, and had 19% operating margins, produces process management software and systems, analytical instrumentation, valves, control systems for measurement and control of fluid flow, and integrated solutions for process and industrial applications.

The Industrial Automation segment (19%, 19%, 16%) primarily makes industrial motors and drives, transmissions, alternators, controls and equipment for automated equipment.

The Network Power segment (23%, 19%, 13%) mainly makes power systems and precision cooling products used in computer, telecommunications and In-

ternet infrastructure.

The Climate Technologies segment (16%, 15%, 15%) mostly makes home and building thermostats and compressors. Compressors are cooling components used in air conditioning units and refrigerators.

The Appliance and Tools segment (20%, 17%, 13%) mainly makes various household appliances, electric motors and controls for appliances, hand-held tools, and storage solutions.

In terms of geography, total sales in FY 07 broke down as follows: United States 48%, Europe 23%, Asia 16%, Latin America 5%, and other regions 8%.

## Company Financials Fiscal Year Ended Sep. 30

| Per Share Data ($) | 2008 | 2007 | 2006 | 2005 | 2004 | 2003 | 2002 | 2001 | 2000 | 1999 |
|---|---|---|---|---|---|---|---|---|---|---|
| Tangible Book Value | NA | 2.99 | 2.67 | 2.34 | 2.36 | 1.81 | 0.99 | 1.11 | 1.27 | 2.21 |
| Cash Flow | NA | 3.47 | 3.04 | 2.41 | 4.37 | 1.84 | 1.90 | 2.07 | 2.44 | 2.23 |
| Earnings | 3.11 | 2.66 | 2.24 | 1.70 | 1.49 | 1.21 | 1.26 | 1.20 | 1.65 | 1.50 |
| S&P Core Earnings | NA | 2.67 | 2.24 | 1.70 | 1.49 | 1.13 | 0.94 | 0.88 | NA | NA |
| Dividends | NA | 1.05 | 0.89 | 0.83 | 0.80 | 0.79 | 0.78 | 0.77 | 0.72 | 0.65 |
| Payout Ratio | NA | 39% | 40% | 49% | 54% | 65% | 62% | 64% | 44% | 43% |
| Prices:High | NA | 59.05 | 45.21 | 38.92 | 35.44 | 32.50 | 33.04 | 39.63 | 39.88 | 35.72 |
| Prices:Low | NA | 41.26 | 36.78 | 30.35 | 28.11 | 21.89 | 20.87 | 22.02 | 20.25 | 25.72 |
| P/E Ratio:High | NA | 22 | 20 | 23 | 24 | 27 | 26 | 33 | 24 | 24 |
| P/E Ratio:Low | NA | 16 | 16 | 18 | 19 | 18 | 17 | 18 | 12 | 17 |

| Income Statement Analysis (Million $) | | | | | | | | | | |
|---|---|---|---|---|---|---|---|---|---|---|
| Revenue | 24,807 | 22,572 | 20,133 | 17,305 | 15,615 | 13,958 | 13,824 | 15,480 | 15,545 | 14,270 |
| Operating Income | NA | 4,174 | 3,676 | 3,150 | 2,842 | 2,497 | 2,443 | 2,988 | 3,219 | 2,943 |
| Depreciation | 707 | 656 | 607 | 562 | 557 | 534 | 541 | 708 | 678 | 638 |
| Interest Expense | NA | 261 | 225 | 243 | 234 | 246 | 250 | 304 | 288 | 190 |
| Pretax Income | 3,591 | 3,107 | 2,684 | 2,149 | 3,704 | 1,414 | 1,565 | 1,589 | 2,178 | 2,021 |
| Effective Tax Rate | 31.7% | 31.3% | 31.3% | 33.8% | 16.1% | 28.4% | 32.3% | 35.0% | 34.7% | 35.0% |
| Net Income | 2,454 | 2,136 | 1,845 | 1,422 | 3,109 | 1,013 | 1,060 | 1,032 | 1,422 | 1,314 |
| S&P Core Earnings | NA | 2,145 | 1,846 | 1,424 | 1,250 | 951 | 784 | 753 | NA | NA |

| Balance Sheet & Other Financial Data (Million $) | | | | | | | | | | |
|---|---|---|---|---|---|---|---|---|---|---|
| Cash | 1,777 | 1,008 | 810 | 1,233 | 1,346 | 696 | 381 | 356 | 281 | 266 |
| Current Assets | NA | 8,065 | 7,330 | 6,837 | 6,416 | 5,500 | 4,961 | 5,320 | 5,483 | 5,124 |
| Total Assets | 21,040 | 19,680 | 18,672 | 17,227 | 16,361 | 15,194 | 14,545 | 15,046 | 15,164 | 13,624 |
| Current Liabilities | NA | 5,546 | 5,374 | 4,931 | 4,339 | 3,417 | 4,400 | 5,379 | 5,219 | 4,590 |
| Long Term Debt | NA | 3,372 | 3,128 | 3,128 | 3,136 | 3,733 | 2,990 | 2,256 | 2,248 | 1,317 |
| Common Equity | 9,113 | 8,772 | 7,848 | 7,400 | 12,266 | 6,460 | 5,741 | 6,114 | 10,248 | 6,181 |
| Total Capital | NA | 12,144 | 10,976 | 10,528 | 15,402 | 10,193 | 8,731 | 8,370 | 12,496 | 7,498 |
| Capital Expenditures | 714 | 681 | 601 | 518 | 400 | 337 | 384 | 554 | 692 | 592 |
| Cash Flow | NA | 2,792 | 2,452 | 1,984 | 3,666 | 1,547 | 1,601 | 1,740 | 2,101 | 1,951 |
| Current Ratio | 1.4 | 1.5 | 1.4 | 1.4 | 1.5 | 1.6 | 1.1 | 1.0 | 1.1 | 1.1 |
| % Long Term Debt of Capitalization | 26.6 | 27.8 | 28.5 | 29.7 | 20.4 | 36.6 | 34.2 | 26.9 | 18.0 | 17.6 |
| % Net Income of Revenue | 9.9 | 9.5 | 9.2 | 8.2 | 19.9 | 7.3 | 7.7 | 6.7 | 9.2 | 9.2 |
| % Return on Assets | 12.1 | 11.1 | 10.3 | 8.5 | 19.7 | 6.8 | 7.2 | 6.8 | 9.9 | 10.0 |
| % Return on Equity | 27.4 | 25.7 | 24.1 | 19.4 | 26.1 | 16.6 | 17.9 | 16.5 | 14.5 | 21.9 |

Data as orig reptd.; bef. results of disc opers/spec. items. Per share data adj. for stk. divs.; EPS diluted. E-Estimated. NA-Not Available. NM-Not Meaningful. NR-Not Ranked. UR-Under Review.

**Office:** 8000 W Florissant Ave, Saint Louis, MO 63136.
**Telephone:** 314-553-2000.
**Website:** http://www.gotoemerson.com
**Chrmn, Pres & CEO:** D.N. Farr

**COO:** E.L. Monser
**EVP & CFO:** W.J. Galvin
**SVP, Secy & General Counsel:** F.L. Steeves
**Chief Acctg Officer:** R.J. Schlueter

**Investor Contact:** C. Tucker (314-553-2197)
**Board Members:** A. A. Busch, III, D. N. Farr, D. C. Farrell, C. G. Fernandez, W. J. Galvin, A. F. Golden, H. Green, R. Horton, W. R. Johnson, V. R. Loucks, Jr., J. B. Menzer, C. A. Peters, J. W. Prueher, R. L. Ridgway, R. L. Stephenson

**Founded:** 1890
**Domicile:** Missouri
**Employees:** 137,700

# ENSCO International Inc.

**STANDARD
&POOR'S**

| S&P Recommendation | **BUY** ★★★★☆ | Price<br>$32.37 (as of Nov 14, 2008) | 12-Mo. Target Price<br>$47.00 | Investment Style<br>Large-Cap Growth |
|---|---|---|---|---|

**GICS Sector** Energy
**Sub-Industry** Oil & Gas Drilling

**Summary** This company provides offshore contract drilling services to the oil and gas industry worldwide.

## Key Stock Statistics (Source S&P, Vickers, company reports)

| | | | | | | | |
|---|---|---|---|---|---|---|---|
| 52-Wk Range | $83.24– 29.63 | S&P Oper. EPS 2008E | 8.36 | Market Capitalization(B) | $4.591 | Beta | 0.80 |
| Trailing 12-Month EPS | $7.62 | S&P Oper. EPS 2009E | 9.28 | Yield (%) | 0.31 | S&P 3-Yr. Proj. EPS CAGR(%) | 23 |
| Trailing 12-Month P/E | 4.3 | P/E on S&P Oper. EPS 2008E | 3.9 | Dividend Rate/Share | $0.10 | S&P Credit Rating | NR |
| $10K Invested 5 Yrs Ago | $12,157 | Common Shares Outstg. (M) | 141.8 | Institutional Ownership (%) | 97 | | |

## Price Performance

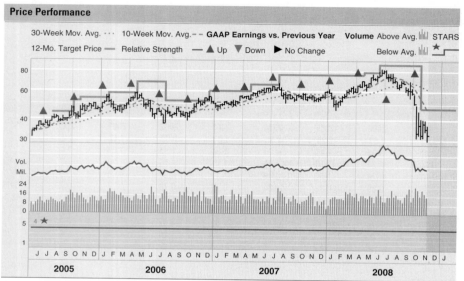

30-Week Mov. Avg. · · · 10-Week Mov. Avg. - - GAAP Earnings vs. Previous Year Volume Above Avg. STARS
12-Mo. Target Price — Relative Strength ▲ Up ▼ Down ► No Change Below Avg. ★

Options: ASE, CBOE, P

Analysis prepared by **Stewart Glickman, CFA** on October 29, 2008, when the stock traded at **$ 37.77**.

## Qualitative Risk Assessment

| LOW | MEDIUM | HIGH |
|---|---|---|

Our risk assessment reflects ESV's exposure to volatile crude oil and natural gas prices, capital spending decisions made by its oil and gas producing customers, and political risk associated with operating in frontier regions. Offsetting these risks is the company's relatively large fleet of premium jackup equipment.

## Quantitative Evaluations

**S&P Quality Ranking**        **B+**

| D | C | B- | B | B+ | A- | A | A+ |
|---|---|---|---|---|---|---|---|

**Relative Strength Rank**      **MODERATE**

32

LOWEST = 1          HIGHEST = 99

## Highlights

➤ Although jackup capacity during the second half of 2008 and in 2009 is expected to rise by virtue of new rig deliveries (a total of 85 new jackups are being built through 2012 industry-wide), we believe there is sufficient growth in demand to enable such rigs to be absorbed without dayrate degradation, at least outside of the Pacific Rim, where we see potential for a modest reduction. In the Middle East alone, where ESV maintains eight jackups, we see potential for significant new demand.

➤ In October, ESV said that its fourth quarter revenues would likely be down about 3% versus the third quarter, as the semisubmersible Ensco 7500 mobilizes to Australia, and the jackup rig Ensco 53 will be in the shipyard for life extension work. However, contract drilling operating expenses are expected to rise about 4% sequentially, due in part to completion of repair and maintenance work that was deferred from the September quarter.

➤ We estimate total revenue growth of 14% in 2008 and 5% in 2009. We expect EPS of $8.36 in 2008, rising to $9.28 in 2009.

## Investment Rationale/Risk

➤ We believe ESV's premium jackup fleet is well positioned in the India and Middle East markets, which we think will face ongoing supply deficits into 2009. Although we think the credit crisis could result in a slowdown in the shallow U.S. Gulf, we note that the decline in the number of rigs in the Gulf has led to some long-term deals for jackups; we also note that only 15% of ESV's projected 2009 revenues come from the U.S. Gulf of Mexico jackup market. In addition, 85% of ESV's customer base for 2009 onwards is comprised of investment-grade companies or nationalized oil companies, which we think are best positioned to manage the impact of the credit crisis.

➤ Risks to our recommendation and target price include reduced dayrates and utilization; lower crude oil and natural gas prices; and delays in newbuild deliveries.

➤ We see ROIC about in line with peers for ESV in 2009, and think this merits a peer valuation. Assuming a 3.5X multiple applied to our 2009 EBITDA estimate and a 5X multiple applied to our 2009 earnings forecast (premiums to peers), and blending with our NAV model, our 12-month target price is $47.

## Revenue/Earnings Data

**Revenue (Million $)**

| | 1Q | 2Q | 3Q | 4Q | Year |
|---|---|---|---|---|---|
| 2008 | 580.3 | 637.1 | 635.8 | -- | -- |
| 2007 | 514.1 | 548.6 | 551.9 | 529.2 | 2,144 |
| 2006 | 381.6 | 475.2 | 486.1 | 470.6 | 1,814 |
| 2005 | 210.6 | 246.3 | 275.1 | 314.9 | 1,047 |
| 2004 | 186.5 | 181.4 | 190.9 | 209.2 | 768.0 |
| 2003 | 195.1 | 196.9 | 199.6 | 199.2 | 790.8 |

**Earnings Per Share ($)**

| | 1Q | 2Q | 3Q | 4Q | Year |
|---|---|---|---|---|---|
| 2008 | 1.90 | 2.07 | 2.13 | E2.20 | E8.36 |
| 2007 | 1.54 | 1.72 | 1.82 | 1.66 | 6.74 |
| 2006 | 0.94 | 1.26 | 1.40 | 1.36 | 4.96 |
| 2005 | 0.27 | 0.39 | 0.52 | 0.67 | 1.86 |
| 2004 | 0.14 | 0.12 | 0.17 | 0.26 | 0.69 |
| 2003 | 0.17 | 0.18 | 0.18 | 0.18 | 0.71 |

Fiscal year ended Dec. 31. Next earnings report expected: Late February. EPS Estimates based on S&P Operating Earnings; historical GAAP earnings are as reported.

## Dividend Data (Dates: mm/dd Payment Date: mm/dd/yy)

| Amount ($) | Date Decl. | Ex-Div. Date | Stk. of Record | Payment Date |
|---|---|---|---|---|
| 0.025 | 02/28 | 03/06 | 03/10 | 03/21/08 |
| 0.025 | 05/22 | 06/05 | 06/09 | 06/20/08 |
| 0.025 | 08/28 | 09/04 | 09/08 | 09/19/08 |
| 0.025 | 11/04 | 12/04 | 12/08 | 12/19/08 |

Dividends have been paid since 1997. Source: Company reports.

# ENSCO International Inc.

STANDARD &POOR'S

## Business Summary October 29, 2008

CORPORATE OVERVIEW. ENSCO International is an international offshore oil and gas contract drilling company. As of February 2008, ESV's offshore drilling fleet was comprised of 44 jackup rigs; one active semisubmersible rig (and four more under construction); and one barge rig. The company is one of the leading international providers of offshore contract drilling services, operating in North and South America, Europe/Africa, and the Asia/Pacific Rim region. As of February 2008, the total backlog of contract drilling work was approximately $3.9 billion, of which approximately 37% was from semisubmersibles, with the remaining 63% largely from jackups.

As of February 2008, ESV had 19 of its 44 jackups in Asia and the Pacific Rim, 15 jackups in North and South America, and 10 jackups in Europe/Africa. Of the four ultra-deepwater semisubmersibles then under construction, the first (the Ensco 8500) is slated for delivery in the third quarter of 2008; the Ensco 8501 is due in the first quarter of 2009; the Ensco 8502, announced in Septem-

ber at a projected capital cost of $385 million, is due in the fourth quarter of 2009; and the Ensco 8503 is due in the third quarter of 2010. In April 2008, ESV announced that it would construct a fifth newbuild semisubmersible, the Ensco 8504, at an expected capital cost of $515 million and with a delivery date in the second half of 2011.

The company's 2007 jackup rig utilization rate was 91%, down from 95% in 2006; dayrates increased to $140,042, from $114,587. Barge rig utilization was 95%, down from 98%; and dayrates rose to $66,699, from $57,168. Semisubmersible rig utilization was 97%, versus 87%, and the average dayrate was $199,432, versus $191,163.

## Company Financials Fiscal Year Ended Dec. 31

| Per Share Data ($) | 2007 | 2006 | 2005 | 2004 | 2003 | 2002 | 2001 | 2000 | 1999 | 1998 |
|---|---|---|---|---|---|---|---|---|---|---|
| Tangible Book Value | 23.74 | 18.97 | 14.32 | 12.14 | 11.55 | 10.85 | 10.70 | 9.59 | 9.05 | 8.25 |
| Cash Flow | 7.99 | 6.11 | 2.92 | 1.69 | 1.61 | 1.29 | 2.41 | 1.32 | 0.76 | 2.40 |
| Earnings | 6.74 | 4.96 | 1.86 | 0.69 | 0.71 | 0.42 | 1.50 | 0.61 | -0.05 | 1.81 |
| S&P Core Earnings | 6.72 | 4.96 | 1.79 | 0.64 | 0.64 | 0.30 | 1.34 | NA | NA | NA |
| Dividends | 0.10 | 0.10 | 0.10 | 0.10 | 0.10 | 0.10 | 0.10 | 0.10 | 0.10 | 0.10 |
| Payout Ratio | 1% | 2% | 5% | 14% | 14% | 24% | 7% | 16% | NM | 6% |
| Prices:High | 67.61 | 58.75 | 50.34 | 34.15 | 31.10 | 35.50 | 44.49 | 43.13 | 25.00 | 33.56 |
| Prices:Low | 45.00 | 37.36 | 29.25 | 24.95 | 23.58 | 20.87 | 12.81 | 20.25 | 8.75 | 8.69 |
| P/E Ratio:High | 10 | 12 | 27 | 49 | 44 | 85 | 30 | 71 | NM | 19 |
| P/E Ratio:Low | 7 | 8 | 16 | 36 | 33 | 50 | 9 | 33 | NM | 5 |

| Income Statement Analysis (Million $) | | | | | | | | | | |
|---|---|---|---|---|---|---|---|---|---|---|
| Revenue | 2,144 | 1,814 | 1,047 | 768 | 791 | 698 | 817 | 534 | 364 | 813 |
| Operating Income | 1,400 | 1,192 | 573 | 323 | 316 | 290 | 442 | 230 | 102 | 469 |
| Depreciation, Depletion and Amortization | 184 | 175 | 161 | 150 | 135 | 124 | 124 | 98.7 | 98.2 | 83.5 |
| Interest Expense | 32.3 | 16.5 | 28.8 | 36.6 | 36.7 | 31.1 | 32.8 | 13.4 | 19.3 | 26.2 |
| Pretax Income | 1,254 | 1,011 | 391 | 140 | 149 | 87.1 | 292 | 125 | 5.20 | 383 |
| Effective Tax Rate | 20.9% | 25.0% | 27.4% | 25.8% | 28.2% | 31.9% | 29.0% | 31.8% | NM | 32.4% |
| Net Income | 992 | 759 | 284 | 104 | 107 | 59.3 | 207 | 85.4 | 6.70 | 254 |
| S&P Core Earnings | 990 | 759 | 273 | 94.8 | 96.1 | 42.5 | 182 | NA | NA | NA |

| Balance Sheet & Other Financial Data (Million $) | | | | | | | | | | |
|---|---|---|---|---|---|---|---|---|---|---|
| Cash | 630 | 566 | 269 | 267 | 354 | 147 | 279 | 107 | 165 | 330 |
| Current Assets | 1,129 | 987 | 578 | 494 | 543 | 388 | 461 | 289 | 273 | 476 |
| Total Assets | 4,969 | 4,334 | 3,618 | 3,322 | 3,183 | 3,062 | 2,324 | 2,108 | 1,978 | 1,993 |
| Current Liabilities | 504 | 385 | 231 | 216 | 187 | 198 | 149 | 117 | 135 | 159 |
| Long Term Debt | 291 | 309 | 475 | 527 | 550 | 548 | 462 | 422 | 371 | 376 |
| Common Equity | 3,752 | 3,216 | 2,533 | 2,182 | 2,081 | 1,967 | 1,440 | 1,329 | 1,241 | 1,245 |
| Total Capital | 4,395 | 3,881 | 3,354 | 3,084 | 2,977 | 2,847 | 2,162 | 1,981 | 1,829 | 1,817 |
| Capital Expenditures | 520 | 529 | 478 | 305 | 187 | 227 | 145 | 256 | 248 | 331 |
| Cash Flow | 1,176 | 934 | 445 | 254 | 242 | 183 | 332 | 184 | 105 | 337 |
| Current Ratio | 2.2 | 2.6 | 2.5 | 2.3 | 2.9 | 2.0 | 3.1 | 2.5 | 2.0 | 3.0 |
| % Long Term Debt of Capitalization | 6.6 | 7.9 | 14.2 | 17.1 | 18.5 | 19.2 | 21.4 | 21.3 | 20.3 | 20.7 |
| % Return on Assets | 21.3 | 19.1 | 8.2 | 3.2 | 3.4 | 2.2 | 9.4 | 4.2 | 0.3 | 13.5 |
| % Return on Equity | 28.5 | 26.4 | 12.0 | 4.9 | 5.3 | 3.5 | 15.0 | 6.7 | 0.5 | 21.9 |

Data as orig reptd.; bef. results of disc opers/spec. items. Per share data adj. for stk. divs.; EPS diluted. E-Estimated. NA-Not Available. NM-Not Meaningful. NR-Not Ranked. UR-Under Review.

**Office:** 500 North Akard Street, Dallas, TX, USA 75201-3331.
**Telephone:** 214-397-3000.
**Email:** hrstaff@enscous.com
**Website:** http://www.enscous.com

**Chrmn, Pres & CEO:** D.W. Rabun
**COO & EVP:** W.S. Chadwick, Jr.
**SVP & CFO:** J.W. Swent, III
**Treas:** R. Yi

**Secy & General Counsel:** C.A. Moomjian, Jr.
**Investor Contact:** R.A. LeBlanc (214-397-3011)
**Board Members:** D. M. Carmichael, J. R. Clark, C. C. Gaut, G. W. Haddock, T. L. Kelly, II, D. W. Rabun, K. O. Rattie, R. M. Rodriguez, P. E. Rowsey, III

**Founded:** 1978
**Domicile:** Delaware
**Employees:** 4,100

# Entergy Corp.

STANDARD &POOR'S

| S&P Recommendation | BUY ★★★★☆ | Price $79.99 (as of Nov 14, 2008) | 12-Mo. Target Price $97.00 | Investment Style Large-Cap Blend |
|---|---|---|---|---|

**GICS Sector** Utilities
**Sub-Industry** Electric Utilities

**Summary** This electric utility holding company serves 2.6 million customers in Arkansas, Louisiana, Mississippi and Texas.

## Key Stock Statistics (Source S&P, Vickers, company reports)

| | | | | | | |
|---|---|---|---|---|---|---|
| 52-Wk Range | $127.48– 61.93 | S&P Oper. EPS 2008**E** | 6.70 | Market Capitalization(B) | $15.324 | Beta | 0.84 |
| Trailing 12-Month EPS | $6.19 | S&P Oper. EPS 2009**E** | 7.65 | Yield (%) | 3.75 | S&P 3-Yr. Proj. EPS CAGR(%) | 12 |
| Trailing 12-Month P/E | 12.9 | P/E on S&P Oper. EPS 2008**E** | 11.9 | Dividend Rate/Share | $3.00 | S&P Credit Rating | BBB |
| $10K Invested 5 Yrs Ago | $17,477 | Common Shares Outstg. (M) | 191.6 | Institutional Ownership (%) | 83 | | |

## Price Performance

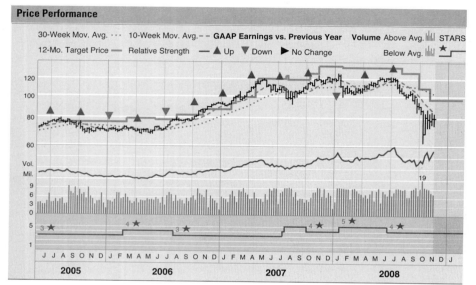

30-Week Mov. Avg. · · ·   10-Week Mov. Avg. - -   **GAAP Earnings vs. Previous Year**   **Volume** Above Avg. STARS
12-Mo. Target Price —   Relative Strength —   ▲ Up   ▼ Down   ▶ No Change   Below Avg. ★

Options: ASE, CBOE, P, Ph

Analysis prepared by **Justin McCann** on November 03, 2008, when the stock traded at **$ 78.05**.

### Highlights

► Due to the turmoil in the financial markets, it is uncertain as to when Entergy's planned tax-free spinoff of its non-utility nuclear assets (into a company to be named Enexus Energy), as well as the equally owned joint venture (EquaGen) to be formed with Enexus, can be implemented. ETR hopes the regulatory approvals will be received by year-end, and it expects to be ready to launch the required financing once market conditions become favorable.

► We expect operating EPS in 2008 to grow about 16% from 2007 operating EPS of $5.76. In the first nine months of 2008, operating EPS grew to $5.51, from $4.63 in the year-earlier period, on higher power prices and a sharp decline in nuclear refueling outage days. Although net revenues for the utilities declined in the third quarter due to the impact of Hurricanes Gustav and Ike, this was more than offset by lower income taxes and operating expenses.

► In addition to expanding nuclear margins, we expect combined 2009 operating EPS to be driven by fewer shares, reflecting ETR's two-year, $1.5 billion share repurchase program. We see these factors resulting in strong EPS growth through the remainder of the decade.

### Investment Rationale/Risk

► We believe the sharp year-to-date drop in the shares reflects the crisis in the credit markets and the dramatic plunge in the stock market. However, we expect them to recover and to realize above-average total return. ETR's plan to spin off its non-utility nuclear operations should enable the new company (Enexus) to realize higher growth and P/E multiples than ETR would as a single combined entity. We would also expect the retained regulated utilities to achieve shareholder value with a targeted 70% to 75% dividend payout, the capacity for a new $2.5 billion share buyback program following the spinoff, and annual EPS growth of 6% to 8%.

► Risks to our recommendation and target price include a sharp drop in the margins of ETR's non-regulated operations, unanticipated problems with its nuclear facilities, and a decline in the average P/E of the group as a whole.

► We believe the stock should benefit from ETR's planned spinoff of its non-utility nuclear assets. With the recent drop in the shares, the yield from the dividend has risen to 3.8%. We expect the shares to trade at a discount-to-peers P/E of 12.7X our combined 2009 EPS estimate, which leads to our 12-month target price of $97.

### Qualitative Risk Assessment

| LOW | MEDIUM | HIGH |
|---|---|---|

Our risk assessment reflects the steady cash flow we expect from most of the regulated utilities and the nuclear operations, offset by uncertainties related to the recovery of the utility operations in New Orleans.

### Quantitative Evaluations

**S&P Quality Ranking**   A-

| D | C | B- | B | B+ | A- | A | A+ |
|---|---|---|---|---|---|---|---|

**Relative Strength Rank**   STRONG

77

LOWEST = 1     HIGHEST = 99

### Revenue/Earnings Data

**Revenue (Million $)**

| | 1Q | 2Q | 3Q | 4Q | Year |
|---|---|---|---|---|---|
| 2008 | 2,865 | 3,264 | -- | -- | -- |
| 2007 | 2,600 | 2,769 | 3,289 | 2,825 | 11,484 |
| 2006 | 2,568 | 2,629 | 3,255 | 2,481 | 10,932 |
| 2005 | 2,323 | 2,710 | 3,130 | 2,652 | 10,106 |
| 2004 | 2,252 | 2,485 | 2,964 | 2,424 | 10,124 |
| 2003 | 2,038 | 2,354 | 2,700 | 2,103 | 9,195 |

**Earnings Per Share ($)**

| | 1Q | 2Q | 3Q | 4Q | Year |
|---|---|---|---|---|---|
| 2008 | 1.56 | 1.37 | E2.32 | E1.18 | E6.70 |
| 2007 | 1.03 | 1.32 | 2.30 | 0.96 | 5.60 |
| 2006 | 0.93 | 1.27 | 1.83 | 1.32 | 5.36 |
| 2005 | 0.79 | 1.33 | 1.65 | 0.59 | 4.40 |
| 2004 | 0.88 | 1.14 | 1.22 | 0.68 | 3.93 |
| 2003 | 1.10 | 0.89 | 1.57 | -0.14 | 3.42 |

Fiscal year ended Dec. 31. Next earnings report expected: NA. EPS Estimates based on S&P Operating Earnings; historical GAAP earnings are as reported.

### Dividend Data (Dates: mm/dd Payment Date: mm/dd/yy)

| Amount ($) | Date Decl. | Ex-Div. Date | Stk. of Record | Payment Date |
|---|---|---|---|---|
| 0.750 | 01/25 | 02/06 | 02/08 | 03/03/08 |
| 0.750 | 04/08 | 05/07 | 05/09 | 06/02/08 |
| 0.750 | 07/25 | 08/06 | 08/08 | 09/02/08 |
| 0.750 | 10/31 | 11/07 | 11/12 | 12/01/08 |

Dividends have been paid since 1988. Source: Company reports.

---

**Please read the Required Disclosures and Analyst Certification on the last page of this report.**

The McGraw-Hill Companies

# Entergy Corp.

STANDARD
&POOR'S

## Business Summary November 03, 2008

CORPORATE OVERVIEW. Entergy is an integrated energy company primarily engaged in electric power production and retail electric distribution operations. It owns and operates power plants with about 30,000 megawatts (MW) of electric generating capacity, and is the second largest nuclear power generator in the U.S. As the holding company for Entergy Arkansas, Entergy Gulf States Louisiana, Entergy Louisiana, Entergy Mississippi, Entergy New Orleans, and Entergy Texas. Entergy Corp. provides electricity to 2.7 million U.S. retail customers. ETR also owns System Energy Resources, which has a 90% interest in the Grand Gulf 1 nuclear plant. The non-utility nuclear business owns and operates five nuclear plants in the northeastern U.S., selling mainly to wholesale customers.

IMPACT OF MAJOR DEVELOPMENTS. On November 5, 2007, Entergy announced that it planned to spin off to shareholders the company's non-utility nuclear business. On April 25, 2008, ETR announced that the name of spun-off company would be Enexus Energy Corp. Entergy also announced that it and Enexus intend to form an equally owned joint venture, to be named EquaGen L.L.C., that will be involved in the operation of the new company's nuclear assets and which will offer ancillary nuclear services to third parties. The company has targeted, pending required approvals, the third quarter of 2008 for the spin-off and joint venture transactions to be completed. The transaction is expected to be tax-free for both the company and the shareholders.

Hurricanes Katrina and Rita in 2005 caused catastrophic damage to large portions of ETR's service territories in Louisiana, Mississippi and Texas, including the effect of extensive flooding in and around greater New Orleans. As of December 31, 2007, Entergy had received $134.5 million on its Katrina and Rita insurance claims. The company estimates that its remaining net insurance recoveries will be approximately $270 million, and that it expects to receive payment for the majority of its estimated recovery through 2009.

On December 31, 2007, Entergy's Gulf States utility completed a jurisdictional separation into two vertically integrated utilities, Entergy Gulf States Louisiana and Entergy Texas. Entergy Gulf States Louisiana was allocated 58.1% of the former entity's assets, and Energy Texas, 41.9%.

On May 8, 2007, Entergy New Orleans emerged from Chapter 11 bankruptcy. This followed the approval of the company's plan of reorganization by the U.S. Bankruptcy Court for the Eastern District of Louisiana. The utility had filed for Chapter 11 reorganization in September 2005, soon after the devastation caused by Hurricane Katrina. Under the reorganization plan, all creditors would be fully compensated.

## Company Financials Fiscal Year Ended Dec. 31

| Per Share Data ($) | 2007 | 2006 | 2005 | 2004 | 2003 | 2002 | 2001 | 2000 | 1999 | 1998 |
|---|---|---|---|---|---|---|---|---|---|---|
| Tangible Book Value | 38.76 | 38.59 | 35.49 | 36.43 | 36.38 | 33.61 | 33.74 | 31.83 | 29.71 | 28.82 |
| Earnings | 5.60 | 5.36 | 4.40 | 3.93 | 3.42 | 2.64 | 3.13 | 2.97 | 2.25 | 3.00 |
| S&P Core Earnings | 5.74 | 5.54 | 4.49 | 3.99 | 3.70 | 2.14 | 2.21 | NA | NA | NA |
| Dividends | 2.58 | 2.16 | 2.16 | 1.89 | 1.60 | 1.34 | 1.28 | 1.22 | 1.20 | 1.50 |
| Payout Ratio | 46% | 40% | 49% | 48% | 47% | 51% | 41% | 41% | 53% | 50% |
| Prices:High | 125.00 | 94.03 | 79.22 | 68.67 | 57.24 | 46.85 | 44.67 | 43.88 | 33.50 | 32.44 |
| Prices:Low | 89.60 | 66.78 | 64.48 | 50.64 | 42.26 | 32.12 | 32.56 | 15.94 | 23.69 | 23.25 |
| P/E Ratio:High | 22 | 18 | 18 | 17 | 17 | 18 | 14 | 15 | 15 | 11 |
| P/E Ratio:Low | 16 | 12 | 15 | 13 | 12 | 12 | 10 | 5 | 11 | 8 |

| Income Statement Analysis (Million $) | | | | | | | | | | |
|---|---|---|---|---|---|---|---|---|---|---|
| Revenue | 11,484 | 10,932 | 10,106 | 10,124 | 9,195 | 8,305 | 9,621 | 10,016 | 8,773 | 11,495 |
| Depreciation | 1,132 | 888 | 856 | 896 | 851 | 839 | 721 | 785 | 745 | 985 |
| Maintenance | NA | NA | NA | NA | NA | NA | NA | NA | NA | NA |
| Fixed Charges Coverage | 3.57 | 3.36 | 3.69 | 3.54 | 2.66 | 2.23 | 2.25 | 2.83 | 2.34 | 1.91 |
| Construction Credits | 67.8 | 63.8 | 75.1 | 65.3 | 75.9 | 57.0 | 48.0 | 56.0 | 52.0 | 23.0 |
| Effective Tax Rate | 30.7% | 28.1% | 36.6% | 28.2% | 37.6% | 32.1% | 38.5% | 40.3% | 37.5% | 24.4% |
| Net Income | 1,135 | 1,133 | 969 | 933 | 813 | 623 | 727 | 711 | 595 | 786 |
| S&P Core Earnings | 1,162 | 1,171 | 961 | 922 | 856 | 487 | 495 | NA | NA | NA |

| Balance Sheet & Other Financial Data (Million $) | | | | | | | | | | |
|---|---|---|---|---|---|---|---|---|---|---|
| Gross Property | 36,302 | 33,366 | 32,437 | 32,055 | 31,181 | 32,964 | 32,403 | 29,865 | 28,178 | 26,892 |
| Capital Expenditures | 1,578 | 1,586 | 1,458 | 1,411 | 1,569 | 1,580 | 1,380 | 1,494 | 1,196 | 1,144 |
| Net Property | 21,194 | 19,651 | 19,426 | 18,915 | 18,561 | 20,657 | 20,597 | 18,501 | 17,279 | 16,816 |
| Capitalization:Long Term Debt | 9,728 | 8,809 | 8,838 | 7,034 | 7,498 | 7,458 | 7,536 | 8,014 | 7,253 | 7,349 |
| Capitalization:% Long Term Debt | 54.3 | 50.8 | 53.2 | 44.5 | 45.2 | 47.6 | 49.1 | 52.2 | 49.3 | 49.7 |
| Capitalization:Preferred | 311 | 345 | Nil | 365 | 334 | 359 | 361 | 335 | 338 | 338 |
| Capitalization:% Preferred | 1.70 | 1.99 | Nil | 2.31 | 2.01 | 2.29 | 2.35 | 2.18 | 2.30 | 2.28 |
| Capitalization:Common | 7,863 | 8,198 | 7,761 | 8,400 | 8,773 | 7,839 | 7,456 | 7,003 | 7,118 | 7,107 |
| Capitalization:% Common | 44.0 | 47.2 | 46.8 | 53.2 | 52.8 | 50.1 | 48.6 | 45.6 | 48.4 | 48.0 |
| Total Capital | 24,625 | 23,531 | 22,399 | 21,266 | 21,805 | 20,355 | 19,399 | 19,095 | 18,539 | 18,942 |
| % Operating Ratio | 87.1 | 88.7 | 63.3 | 87.6 | 89.4 | 85.8 | 88.6 | 89.0 | 88.3 | 86.8 |
| % Earned on Net Property | 10.3 | 9.2 | 9.3 | 8.8 | 8.1 | 5.8 | 8.1 | 8.6 | 7.3 | 8.3 |
| % Return on Revenue | 9.9 | 10.4 | 9.6 | 9.2 | 8.8 | 7.5 | 7.6 | 7.1 | 6.8 | 6.8 |
| % Return on Invested Capital | 7.7 | 7.0 | 6.6 | 6.5 | 2.4 | 7.7 | 7.6 | 7.1 | 7.0 | 14.8 |
| % Return on Common Equity | 14.1 | 14.2 | 11.7 | 10.6 | 9.5 | 7.8 | 9.7 | 9.6 | 7.8 | 10.7 |

Data as orig reptd.; bef. results of disc opers/spec. items. Per share data adj. for stk. divs.; EPS diluted. E-Estimated. NA-Not Available. NM-Not Meaningful. NR-Not Ranked. UR-Under Review.

**Office:** 639 Loyola Ave, New Orleans, LA 70113-3125.
**Telephone:** 504-576-4000.
**Website:** http://www.entergy.com
**Chrmn & CEO:** J.W. Leonard

**Pres & COO:** R.J. Smith
**EVP & CFO:** L.P. Denault
**EVP, Secy & General Counsel:** R.D. Sloan
**SVP & Chief Acctg Officer:** T.H. Bunting, Jr.

**Investor Contact:** N. Morovich (504-576-5506)
**Board Members:** M. S. Bateman, W. Blount, S. D. Debree, G. W. Edwards, A. Herman, D. C. Hintz, J. W. Leonard, S. L. Levenick, J. R. Nichols, W. A. Percy, II, W. J. Tauzin, S. V. Wilkinson

**Founded:** 1989
**Domicile:** Delaware
**Employees:** 14,300

# EOG Resources Inc.

**STANDARD &POOR'S**

| S&P Recommendation **BUY** ★★★★☆ | Price $80.63 (as of Nov 14, 2008) | 12-Mo. Target Price $95.00 | Investment Style Large-Cap Growth |
|---|---|---|---|

**GICS Sector** Energy
**Sub-Industry** Oil & Gas Exploration & Production

**Summary** As one of the largest independent exploration and production companies in the world, this U.S. firm is focused on onshore natural gas production in North America.

## Key Stock Statistics (Source S&P, Vickers, company reports)

| | | | | | | | |
|---|---|---|---|---|---|---|---|
| 52-Wk Range | $144.99– 54.42 | S&P Oper. EPS 2008**E** | 9.56 | Market Capitalization(B) | $20.124 | Beta | 0.77 |
| Trailing 12-Month EPS | $9.32 | S&P Oper. EPS 2009**E** | 7.11 | Yield (%) | 0.67 | S&P 3-Yr. Proj. EPS CAGR(%) | 30 |
| Trailing 12-Month P/E | 8.7 | P/E on S&P Oper. EPS 2008**E** | 8.4 | Dividend Rate/Share | $0.54 | S&P Credit Rating | A- |
| $10K Invested 5 Yrs Ago | $38,260 | Common Shares Outstg. (M) | 249.6 | Institutional Ownership (%) | 94 | | |

## Price Performance

30-Week Mov. Avg. · · · · 10-Week Mov. Avg. - - GAAP Earnings vs. Previous Year   Volume Above Avg. ▮▮▮ STARS
12-Mo. Target Price — Relative Strength — ▲ Up ▼ Down ▶ No Change   Below Avg. ▮▮▮ ★

Options: ASE, CBOE, P, Ph

Analysis prepared by **Michael Kay** on October 28, 2008, when the stock traded at **$ 67.53.**

## Highlights

➤ Production rose 13% in the first half of 2008, slightly above forecast, driven by natural gas increases in the Barnett Shale, Gulf Coast region, the North Dakota Bakken and Mid-Continent areas. In the Bakken, EOG is running an 8 rig program with new wells placed online in June. EOG recently commenced production from two wells in the Horn River Shale Basin of British Columbia. We expect annual production growth of over 15% in 2008 and 13% in 2009.

➤ While industry costs have been rising, we believe EOG has kept increases low versus peers due to its relatively efficient operations in North America and low cost operations in Trinidad. As a result, EOG estimates its North Dakota Bakken, Barnett Shale and Uinta Basin plays offer very high returns relative to other North American developments.

➤ After-tax operating earnings fell 10% in 2007 on increased costs and reduced U.S. natural gas pricing, but we expect a more than 36% gain in 2008 and more than a 25% rise in 2009, reflecting production gains. We see 2008 EPS of $5.88 (with a non-cash derivative loss of $3.08 and a $0.34 asset sale gain). EOG's 2008 capital budget is $4.75 billion versus $3.9 billion in 2007.

## Investment Rationale/Risk

➤ EOG has increased spending to organically raise its production growth, focused on plays such as the Fort Worth Barnett Shale. We believe EOG's expertise in horizontal drilling and technology will aid onshore organic production growth. In February 2008, EOG announced several new onshore plays in the U.S. and expanded the Barnett Shale natural gas play into a promising new oil play. In May 2008, EOG identified a natural gas play in the Mid-Continent region. Separately, EOG has scaled back operations in Trinidad. We expect the ongoing credit crisis and worsening economy to result in drilling capex cutbacks for 2009.

➤ Risks to our recommendation and target price include changes to economic, industrial and operating conditions, such as increased costs and difficulty in replacing reserves.

➤ A drop in oil and gas prices has led to a similar decline in E&P shares. On weaker economic forecasts, we see markets discounting probable reserve potential and now value EOG on proven reserve NAV estimates. We blend our NAV estimate of $100 with DCF ($118; WACC of 9%, terminal growth of 3%) and relative metrics to arrive at a 12-month target price of $95.

## Qualitative Risk Assessment

| LOW | MEDIUM | HIGH |
|---|---|---|

Our risk assessment for EOG is based on our view of its solid business and financial risk profile, reflecting its significant net acreage position, active drilling program and history of relatively low operating costs, offset by its participation in a very competitive, capital intensive and cyclical industry.

## Quantitative Evaluations

**S&P Quality Ranking**  B+

| D | C | B- | B | B+ | A- | A | A+ |
|---|---|---|---|---|---|---|---|

**Relative Strength Rank**  STRONG

84

LOWEST = 1          HIGHEST = 99

## Revenue/Earnings Data

**Revenue (Million $)**

| | 1Q | 2Q | 3Q | 4Q | Year |
|---|---|---|---|---|---|
| 2008 | 1,101 | 1,875 | 3,220 | -- | -- |
| 2007 | 875.2 | 1,055 | 990.5 | 1,251 | 4,098 |
| 2006 | 1,085 | 919.1 | 968.3 | 932.5 | 3,904 |
| 2005 | 688.2 | 783.9 | 934.5 | 1,214 | 3,620 |
| 2004 | 464.3 | 519.0 | 594.2 | 693.7 | 2,271 |
| 2003 | 464.7 | 424.8 | 458.7 | 396.5 | 1,745 |

**Earnings Per Share ($)**

| | | | | | |
|---|---|---|---|---|---|
| 2008 | 0.96 | 0.71 | 6.20 | E1.69 | E9.56 |
| 2007 | 0.88 | 1.24 | 0.82 | 1.44 | 4.37 |
| 2006 | 1.73 | 1.34 | 1.21 | 0.96 | 5.24 |
| 2005 | 0.83 | 1.02 | 1.40 | 1.88 | 5.13 |
| 2004 | 0.42 | 0.60 | 0.71 | 0.85 | 2.58 |
| 2003 | 0.58 | 0.46 | 0.50 | 0.31 | 1.83 |

Fiscal year ended Dec. 31. Next earnings report expected: Early February. EPS Estimates based on S&P Operating Earnings; historical GAAP earnings are as reported.

## Dividend Data (Dates: mm/dd Payment Date: mm/dd/yy)

| Amount ($) | Date Decl. | Ex-Div. Date | Stk. of Record | Payment Date |
|---|---|---|---|---|
| 0.090 | 12/11 | 01/15 | 01/17 | 01/31/08 |
| 0.120 | 02/07 | 04/14 | 04/16 | 04/30/08 |
| 0.120 | 05/09 | 07/15 | 07/17 | 07/31/08 |
| 0.135 | 07/29 | 10/15 | 10/17 | 10/31/08 |

Dividends have been paid since 1990. Source: Company reports.

---

**Please read the Required Disclosures and Analyst Certification on the last page of this report.**

**The McGraw-Hill** Companies

# EOG Resources Inc.

## Business Summary October 28, 2008

CORPORATE OVERVIEW. EOG Resources, Inc. (EOG), a Delaware corporation organized in 1985, together with its subsidiaries, explores for, develops, produces and markets natural gas and crude oil primarily in major producing basins in the U.S., Canada, offshore Trinidad, the U.K. North Sea, and other select regions.

As EOG begins to operate in regions with limited infrastructure, the company is placing more emphasis on gathering and processing operations to support its production activities. This has resulted in the subsidiary formation of Pecan Pipeline Co. and Pecan Pipeline (North Dakota), Inc.

Proved oil and gas reserves rose 14% to 7.745 trillion cubic feet equivalent (Tcfe; 86% natural gas, 77% developed) in 2007. About 67% of EOG's 2007 proved reserves were in the U.S., 16% in Canada, 16% Trinidad, and less than 1% in the U.K. North Sea. Oil and gas production rose 11% to 1.729 billion cubic feet equivalent (Bcfe) per day (85% natural gas) in 2007. We estimate its 2007 organic reserve replacement at 215%. Using data from John S. Herold, we estimate EOG's three-year (2004-06) proved acquisition cost at $6.13 per barrel oil equivalent (boe), below the peer average; its three-year finding & development costs at $12.35 per boe, slightly below the peer average; its three-year reserve replacement costs at $12.10 per boe, slightly below the peer average; and its three-year reserve replacement at 203%, slightly below the peer average.

MARKET PROFILE. As one of the largest independent exploration and production companies in the world, EOG has focused on onshore natural gas operations, primarily in the U.S. and Canada. Substantial portions of its reserves are in long-lived fields with well-established production characteristics.

In the U.S., EOG has interests in the Barnett Shale play of the Fort Worth Basin including the Johnson, Montague, Clay and Archer Counties; Upper Gulf Coast area covering East Texas, Louisiana, and Mississippi; Permian Basin, Rocky Mountain area including the Uinta Basin, Williston Basin and Bakken play in North Dakota; Mid-Continent area including the Hugoton-Deep play in the Southwest Kansas/Oklahoma Panhandle and the Cleveland Horizontal play in the Texas Panhandle; South Texas and the Gulf of Mexico; and Marcellus Shale in Pennsylvania.

In Canada, EOG operates through its subsidiary, EOG Resources Canada, Inc. (EOGRC), with operations focused in the Southeast Alberta/Southwest Saskatchewan shallow natural gas trends; the Pembina/Highvale area of Central Alberta; the Grand Prairie/Wapiti area of Northwest Alberta; the Waskada area in Southwest Manitoba; and the Horn River Basin in northeastern British Columbia.

## Company Financials Fiscal Year Ended Dec. 31

| Per Share Data ($) | 2007 | 2006 | 2005 | 2004 | 2003 | 2002 | 2001 | 2000 | 1999 | 1998 |
|---|---|---|---|---|---|---|---|---|---|---|
| Tangible Book Value | 28.68 | 22.76 | 17.21 | 11.97 | 8.95 | 6.64 | 6.47 | 5.27 | 4.11 | 4.17 |
| Cash Flow | 9.27 | 8.56 | 7.81 | 4.69 | 3.73 | 2.02 | 3.32 | 3.17 | 3.61 | 1.20 |
| Earnings | 4.37 | 5.24 | 5.13 | 2.58 | 1.83 | 0.33 | 1.65 | 1.12 | 2.00 | 0.18 |
| S&P Core Earnings | 4.37 | 5.21 | 5.08 | 2.54 | 1.77 | 0.26 | 1.60 | NA | NA | NA |
| Dividends | 0.33 | 0.22 | 0.15 | 0.12 | 0.09 | 0.08 | 0.08 | 0.07 | 0.06 | 0.06 |
| Payout Ratio | 8% | 4% | 3% | 5% | 5% | 25% | 5% | 6% | 3% | 33% |
| Prices:High | 91.63 | 86.91 | 82.00 | 38.25 | 23.76 | 22.08 | 27.75 | 28.34 | 12.69 | 12.25 |
| Prices:Low | 59.21 | 56.31 | 32.05 | 21.23 | 17.85 | 15.01 | 12.90 | 6.84 | 7.19 | 5.88 |
| P/E Ratio:High | 21 | 17 | 16 | 15 | 13 | 68 | 17 | 25 | 6 | 68 |
| P/E Ratio:Low | 14 | 11 | 6 | 8 | 10 | 46 | 8 | 6 | 4 | 33 |

| Income Statement Analysis (Million $) | | | | | | | | | | |
|---|---|---|---|---|---|---|---|---|---|---|
| Revenue | 4,132 | 3,904 | 3,620 | 2,271 | 1,745 | 1,095 | 1,655 | 1,490 | 801 | 769 |
| Operating Income | 2,802 | 1,895 | 1,992 | 979 | 697 | 648 | 1,181 | 697 | 18.2 | 114 |
| Depreciation, Depletion and Amortization | 1,213 | 817 | 654 | 504 | 442 | 398 | 392 | 370 | 460 | 315 |
| Interest Expense | 76.1 | 43.2 | 62.5 | 63.1 | 58.7 | 59.7 | 45.1 | 61.0 | 61.8 | 48.6 |
| Pretax Income | 1,631 | 1,913 | 1,965 | 926 | 654 | 120 | 631 | 634 | 568 | 60.3 |
| Effective Tax Rate | 33.2% | 32.0% | 35.9% | 32.5% | 33.1% | 27.2% | 36.9% | 37.3% | NM | 6.82% |
| Net Income | 1,090 | 1,300 | 1,260 | 625 | 437 | 87.2 | 399 | 397 | 569 | 56.2 |
| S&P Core Earnings | 1,083 | 1,281 | 1,238 | 605 | 412 | 62.4 | 376 | NA | NA | NA |

| Balance Sheet & Other Financial Data (Million $) | | | | | | | | | | |
|---|---|---|---|---|---|---|---|---|---|---|
| Cash | 54.2 | 218 | 644 | 21.0 | 4.44 | 9.85 | 2.51 | 20.2 | 24.8 | 6.30 |
| Current Assets | 1,292 | 1,350 | 1,563 | 587 | 396 | 395 | 272 | 394 | 201 | 246 |
| Total Assets | 12,089 | 9,402 | 7,753 | 5,799 | 4,749 | 3,814 | 3,414 | 3,001 | 2,611 | 3,018 |
| Current Liabilities | 1,474 | 1,255 | 1,172 | 632 | 477 | 276 | 311 | 370 | 219 | 263 |
| Long Term Debt | 1,185 | 733 | 859 | 1,078 | 1,109 | 1,145 | 856 | 859 | 990 | 1,143 |
| Common Equity | 6,985 | 5,547 | 4,217 | 2,847 | 2,098 | 1,524 | 1,495 | 1,234 | 982 | 1,280 |
| Total Capital | 10,246 | 7,846 | 6,298 | 4,925 | 4,125 | 3,478 | 3,050 | 2,580 | 2,346 | 2,683 |
| Capital Expenditures | 3,679 | 2,819 | 1,725 | 1,417 | 1,204 | 714 | 974 | 603 | 403 | 690 |
| Cash Flow | 2,296 | 2,106 | 1,906 | 1,118 | 868 | 474 | 780 | 756 | 1,028 | 371 |
| Current Ratio | 0.9 | 1.1 | 1.3 | 0.9 | 0.8 | 1.4 | 0.9 | 1.1 | 0.9 | 0.9 |
| % Long Term Debt of Capitalization | 14.5 | 9.3 | 13.6 | 21.9 | 26.9 | 32.9 | 28.1 | 33.3 | 42.2 | 42.6 |
| % Return on Assets | 10.1 | 15.2 | 18.6 | 11.8 | 10.2 | 2.4 | 12.4 | 14.1 | 20.2 | 2.0 |
| % Return on Equity | 17.3 | 26.4 | 35.5 | 24.9 | 23.4 | 5.0 | 28.4 | 34.8 | 50.3 | 4.4 |

Data as orig reptd.; bef. results of disc opers/spec. items. Per share data adj. for stk. divs.; EPS diluted. E-Estimated. NA-Not Available. NM-Not Meaningful. NR-Not Ranked. UR-Under Review.

**Office:** 1111 Bagby St Lbby 2, Houston, TX 77002-2551.
**Telephone:** 877-363-3647.
**Email:** ir@eogresources.com
**Website:** http://www.eogresources.com

**Chrmn & CEO:** M.G. Papa
**COO:** G.L. Thomas
**SVP & General Counsel:** F.J. Plaeger, II
**CFO & Chief Acctg Officer:** T.K. Driggers

**Chief Admin Officer & Secy:** P.L. Edwards
**Investor Contact:** M.A. Baldwin (713-651-6364)
**Board Members:** G. A. Alcorn, C. R. Crisp, J. C. Day, M. G. Papa, H. L. Steward, D. F. Textor, F. G. Wisner

**Founded:** 1985
**Domicile:** Delaware
**Employees:** 1,800

# E TRADE Financial Corporation

STANDARD &POOR'S

| S&P Recommendation | HOLD ★★★☆☆ | Price $1.35 (as of Nov 14, 2008) | 12-Mo. Target Price $2.50 | Investment Style Large-Cap Growth |
|---|---|---|---|---|

**GICS Sector** Financials
**Sub-Industry** Investment Banking & Brokerage

**Summary** This company provides online discount brokerage, mortgage, and banking services, primarily to retail customers.

## Key Stock Statistics (Source S&P, Vickers, company reports)

| | | | | | | | |
|---|---|---|---|---|---|---|---|
| 52-Wk Range | $6.04– 1.27 | S&P Oper. EPS 2008E | -1.31 | Market Capitalization(B) | $0.726 | Beta | 1.75 |
| Trailing 12-Month EPS | $-4.06 | S&P Oper. EPS 2009E | -0.16 | Yield (%) | Nil | S&P 3-Yr. Proj. EPS CAGR(%) | NM |
| Trailing 12-Month P/E | NM | P/E on S&P Oper. EPS 2008E | NM | Dividend Rate/Share | Nil | S&P Credit Rating | B |
| $10K Invested 5 Yrs Ago | $1,303 | Common Shares Outstg. (M) | 537.8 | Institutional Ownership (%) | 52 | | |

## Price Performance

30-Week Mov. Avg. ···· 10-Week Mov. Avg. - - - **GAAP Earnings vs. Previous Year** Volume Above Avg. STARS
12-Mo. Target Price — Relative Strength — ▲ Up ▼ Down ▶ No Change Below Avg. ★

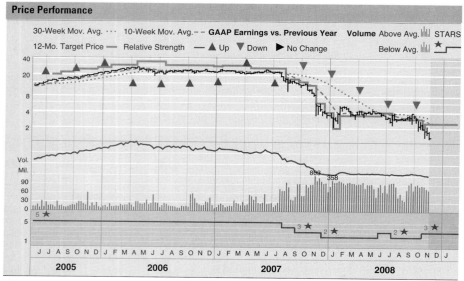

Options: ASE, CBOE, P, Ph

Analysis prepared by **Rikin Pandya** on November 13, 2008, when the stock traded at **$ 1.49**.

## Highlights

➤ ETFC is in the midst of restructuring its operations and balance sheet to focus on its retail clients and reduce exposure to consumer lending and securities investments. While we view the decision to refocus on its core competencies as prudent, we believe significant damage to its balance sheet and future earnings power has already taken place, which puts ETFC in a weaker position relative to peers. Nevertheless, problems at ETFC's bank have not driven away retail clients, as total accounts in Q3 08 were up 4% to 4.44 million, and daily average revenue trades were up 6.6% sequentially.

➤ We expect loan loss provisions will continue to pressure results, as we see the current credit cycle worsening and ETFC reevaluating its home equity loan portfolio. Management is optimistic about receiving assistance from the government's TARP program, and we believe such assistance would add a low-cost capital cushion to ETFC's balance sheet, leaving them in a far more liquid position.

➤ We project losses per share of $1.31 in 2008 and $0.16 in 2009, as loan provisions and other losses will likely continue to mount.

## Investment Rationale/Risk

➤ While we view the move to realign operations to focus on core retail customers as prudent, we see the overhang from its remaining mortgage assets outweighing the near-term positives that we have seen in its retail metrics. We anticipate further write-downs in the home equity loan portfolio through 2009 and continued loan loss provisions for first lien holdings. However, although still uncertain, we believe ETFC may be getting closer to turning the corner with regard to projecting the ultimate damage from the loan portfolio, at which point we think investors will be able move beyond liquidity concerns and concentrate on ETFC's strong retail trading platform. In support of this, ETFC noted that their 2006 vintage loan portfolio, of which suffered much of the losses, is down to just 49% of their original outstanding balance.

➤ Risks to our opinion and target price include greater than expected declines in retail trading volume and client assets, and larger write-downs in the remaining mortgage portfolio.

➤ We arrive at our 12-month target price of $2.50 by applying a 0.5X multiple to projected 12-month book value per share, a discount to peers.

## Qualitative Risk Assessment

| LOW | MEDIUM | HIGH |
|---|---|---|

Our risk assessment reflects our concerns about significant industry volatility and ETFC's exposure to residential mortgage and home equity loans, partially offset by our view of its strong client relationships.

## Quantitative Evaluations

**S&P Quality Ranking**     **C**

| D | C | B- | B | B+ | A- | A | A+ |
|---|---|---|---|---|---|---|---|

**Relative Strength Rank**     **WEAK**

17

LOWEST = 1           HIGHEST = 99

## Revenue/Earnings Data

**Revenue (Million $)**

| | 1Q | 2Q | 3Q | 4Q | Year |
|---|---|---|---|---|---|
| 2008 | 928.1 | 373.6 | 377.7 | -- | -- |
| 2007 | 1,105 | 1,185 | 1,042 | 555.5 | 2,133 |
| 2006 | 598.4 | 611.4 | 581.8 | 628.9 | 2,420 |
| 2005 | 417.4 | 387.7 | 419.8 | 478.9 | 1,704 |
| 2004 | 400.5 | 380.9 | 337.1 | 409.5 | 1,947 |
| 2003 | 322.2 | 381.1 | 397.7 | 382.8 | 1,719 |

**Earnings Per Share ($)**

| | | | | | |
|---|---|---|---|---|---|
| 2008 | -0.20 | -0.24 | -0.60 | E-0.13 | E-1.31 |
| 2007 | 0.39 | 0.37 | -0.14 | -3.98 | -3.40 |
| 2006 | 0.33 | 0.36 | 0.34 | 0.40 | 1.44 |
| 2005 | 0.27 | 0.29 | 0.29 | 0.31 | 1.16 |
| 2004 | 0.23 | 0.24 | 0.21 | 0.24 | 0.92 |
| 2003 | 0.06 | 0.03 | 0.17 | 0.27 | 0.55 |

Fiscal year ended Dec. 31. Next earnings report expected: Late January. EPS Estimates based on S&P Operating Earnings; historical GAAP earnings are as reported.

## Dividend Data

No cash dividends have been paid.

---

# E TRADE Financial Corporation

## Business Summary November 13, 2008

CORPORATE OVERVIEW. E Trade Financial Corporation is one of the industry's leading online financial services concerns. The company provides online discount brokerage and banking services, primarily to retail customers. Although most of the company's business is done over the Internet, ETFC also serves customers through branches, automated and live telephone service, and Internet-enabled wireless devices. Retail customers can move money electronically between brokerage, banking and lending accounts. As of December 31, 2007, ETFC had about 3.6 million brokerage accounts and around 1.1 million banking accounts.

Through its Brokerage segment, ETFC's customers can buy and sell stocks, bonds, options, futures, and over 6,000 non-proprietary mutual funds. Customers can also obtain streaming quotes and charts, access real-time market commentary and research reports, and perform personalized portfolio tracking. Brokerage customers can obtain margin loans collateralized by their securities. The company uses sophisticated proprietary transaction-enabling technology to automate traditionally labor-intensive transactions. The brokerage business continues to be the primary point of introduction for the majority of ETFC's customers, which are typically self-directed investors.

Through its Banking segment, the company has historically offered residential mortgage products, home equity loans and home equity lines of credit (HELOC). The segment also offers credit card, automobile, recreational vehicle (RV), marine, and other consumer loans. In late 2003, the Banking segment began sweeping Brokerage customer money market balances into an FDIC-insured Sweep Deposit Account (SDA) product, which lowered its cost of funds. At the end of 2007, ETFC had $10.1 billion in the SDA product, up from $4.3 billion at the end of 2003. We estimate that nearly half of the bank's customers are also brokerage customers. ETFC's loan portfolio consists of first mortgages, the majority of which are adjustable-rate, home equity lines of credit (HELOC), second mortgage loan products, and consumer loans for RVs, marine, automobile, and credit card loans. Going forward, we expect the asset composition of this segment to change significantly as ETFC completes its restructuring plan announced in September 2007 and realigns its focus on its core retail business.

## Company Financials Fiscal Year Ended Dec. 31

| Per Share Data ($) | 2007 | 2006 | 2005 | 2004 | 2003 | 2002 | 2001 | 2000 | 1999 | 1998 |
|---|---|---|---|---|---|---|---|---|---|---|
| Tangible Book Value | 1.01 | 3.87 | 2.07 | 4.58 | 3.73 | 2.68 | 2.54 | 4.43 | 3.81 | 3.14 |
| Cash Flow | -3.10 | 1.61 | 1.36 | 1.07 | 0.55 | 1.20 | -0.28 | 0.37 | -0.09 | 0.07 |
| Earnings | -3.40 | 1.44 | 1.16 | 0.92 | 0.55 | 0.30 | -0.81 | -0.06 | -0.23 | -0.01 |
| S&P Core Earnings | -3.26 | 1.33 | 0.88 | 0.66 | 0.27 | 0.27 | -0.86 | NA | NA | NA |
| Dividends | Nil | Nil | Nil | Nil | Nil | Nil | Nil | Nil | Nil | Nil |
| Payout Ratio | Nil | Nil | Nil | Nil | Nil | Nil | Nil | Nil | Nil | Nil |
| Prices:High | 26.08 | 27.76 | 21.71 | 15.40 | 12.91 | 12.64 | 15.38 | 34.25 | 72.25 | 16.25 |
| Prices:Low | 3.15 | 18.81 | 10.53 | 9.51 | 3.65 | 2.81 | 4.07 | 6.66 | 12.74 | 2.50 |
| P/E Ratio:High | NM | 19 | 19 | 17 | 23 | 42 | NM | NM | NM | NM |
| P/E Ratio:Low | NM | 13 | 9 | 10 | 7 | 9 | NM | NM | NM | NM |

| Income Statement Analysis (Million $) | 2007 | 2006 | 2005 | 2004 | 2003 | 2002 | 2001 | 2000 | 1999 | 1998 |
|---|---|---|---|---|---|---|---|---|---|---|
| Commissions | 694 | 625 | 459 | 350 | 337 | 302 | 407 | 739 | 356 | 162 |
| Interest Income | 3,570 | 2,775 | 1,650 | 1,146 | 893 | 946 | 1,160 | 960 | 196 | 95.7 |
| Total Revenue | 4,673 | 3,840 | 2,537 | 2,077 | 2,009 | 1,903 | 2,062 | 1,973 | 695 | 285 |
| Interest Expense | 2,133 | 1,527 | 853 | 558 | 532 | 609 | 832 | 630 | 73.4 | 39.7 |
| Pretax Income | -2,178 | 929 | 676 | 514 | 310 | 194 | -310 | 104 | -91.5 | -1.67 |
| Effective Tax Rate | 33.8% | 32.5% | 34.0% | 31.6% | 36.2% | 43.9% | NM | 81.8% | NM | NM |
| Net Income | -1,442 | 627 | 446 | 351 | 203 | 107 | -271 | 19.2 | -54.4 | -0.71 |
| S&P Core Earnings | -1,378 | 580 | 339 | 247 | 101 | 96.1 | -291 | NA | NA | NA |

| Balance Sheet & Other Financial Data (Million $) | 2007 | 2006 | 2005 | 2004 | 2003 | 2002 | 2001 | 2000 | 1999 | 1998 |
|---|---|---|---|---|---|---|---|---|---|---|
| Total Assets | 56,846 | 53,739 | 44,568 | 31,033 | 26,049 | 21,534 | 18,172 | 17,317 | 3,927 | 1,969 |
| Cash Items | 1,778 | 1,212 | 844 | 940 | 921 | 2,223 | 1,601 | 301 | 189 | 26.8 |
| Receivables | 7,179 | 7,636 | 7,174 | 3,035 | 2,298 | 1,500 | 2,139 | 6,543 | 2,913 | 1,310 |
| Securities Owned | 11,385 | 13,922 | 12,565 | 12,589 | 9,876 | 8,702 | 4,726 | 985 | 189 | 503 |
| Securities Borrowed | Nil | Nil | Nil | Nil | Nil | Nil | Nil | NA | NA | NA |
| Due Brokers & Customers | 5,515 | 7,825 | 7,316 | 3,619 | 3,696 | 2,792 | 2,700 | 6,056 | 2,824 | 1,185 |
| Other Liabilities | 38,033 | NA | NA | NA | NA | NA | NA | NA | NA | NA |
| Capitalization:Debt | 10,469 | 7,166 | 6,189 | 586 | 695 | 907 | 605 | 3,336 | Nil | Nil |
| Capitalization:Equity | 2,829 | 4,196 | 3,400 | 2,228 | 1,918 | 1,506 | 1,571 | 1,857 | 914 | 710 |
| Capitalization:Total | 13,298 | 11,363 | 9,589 | 2,814 | 2,614 | 2,412 | 2,175 | 5,192 | 914 | 710 |
| % Return on Revenue | NM | 20.7 | 68.4 | 18.0 | 11.8 | 5.4 | NM | 1.6 | NM | NM |
| % Return on Assets | NM | 1.3 | 1.2 | 1.2 | 0.9 | 0.5 | NM | 0.2 | NM | NM |
| % Return on Equity | NM | 16.5 | 15.9 | 16.9 | 11.9 | 7.0 | NM | 1.2 | NM | NM |

Data as orig reptd.; bef. results of disc opers/spec. items. Per share data adj. for stk. divs.; EPS diluted. E-Estimated. NA-Not Available. NM-Not Meaningful. NR-Not Ranked. UR-Under Review.

**Office:** 135 E 57th St, New York, NY 10022-2050.
**Telephone:** 646-521-4300.
**Email:** ir@etrade.com
**Website:** http://www.etrade.com

**Chrmn & CEO:** D.H. Layton
**Vice Chrmn:** S.H. Willard
**EVP & Cntlr:** M.J. Audette
**CFO:** B.P. Nolop

**Secy & General Counsel:** R.S. Elmer
**Board Members:** R. Druskin, R. D. Fisher, G. A. Hayter, F. W. Kanner, D. H. Layton, M. K. Parks, C. C. Raffaeli, L. E. Randall, J. L. Sclafani, D. L. Weaver, S. H. Willard

**Founded:** 1982
**Domicile:** Delaware
**Employees:** 3,757

# Equifax Inc.

STANDARD &POOR'S

| S&P Recommendation | HOLD ★★★☆☆ | Price $23.53 (as of Nov 14, 2008) | 12-Mo. Target Price $28.00 | Investment Style Large-Cap Growth |
| --- | --- | --- | --- | --- |

**GICS Sector** Industrials
**Sub-Industry** Research & Consulting Services

**Summary** This company is a leading worldwide source of consumer and commercial credit information.

## Key Stock Statistics (Source S&P, Vickers, company reports)

| | | | | | | | |
| --- | --- | --- | --- | --- | --- | --- | --- |
| 52-Wk Range | $39.95–22.05 | S&P Oper. EPS 2008E | 2.49 | Market Capitalization(B) | $2.972 | Beta | 1.04 |
| Trailing 12-Month EPS | $2.08 | S&P Oper. EPS 2009E | 2.55 | Yield (%) | 0.68 | S&P 3-Yr. Proj. EPS CAGR(%) | 11 |
| Trailing 12-Month P/E | 11.3 | P/E on S&P Oper. EPS 2008E | 9.4 | Dividend Rate/Share | $0.16 | S&P Credit Rating | BBB+ |
| $10K Invested 5 Yrs Ago | $9,958 | Common Shares Outstg. (M) | 126.3 | Institutional Ownership (%) | 85 | | |

## Price Performance

30-Week Mov. Avg. · · · 10-Week Mov. Avg. — **GAAP Earnings vs. Previous Year**   Volume Above Avg. ▐▐▌ STARS
12-Mo. Target Price — Relative Strength   ▲ Up   ▼ Down   ▶ No Change   Below Avg. ▐▐▌   ★

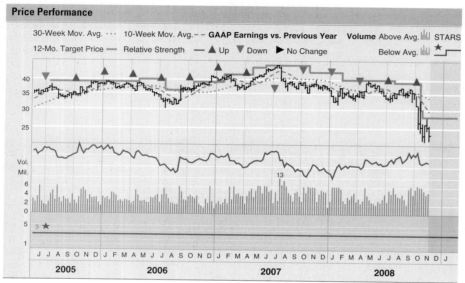

Options: ASE, P, Ph

Analysis prepared by **Zaineb Bokhari** on October 27, 2008, when the stock traded at **$ 22.97**.

### Highlights

➤ We expect revenues to rise 6% in 2008, to $1.95 billion, driven by organic growth and geographic expansion. We expect EFX to pursue acquisitions that broaden its geographic reach and expand existing markets. We think a weak U.S. economy will pressure spending on direct and credit marketing by financial firms, hurting growth for U.S. Consumer Information Solutions. We are also concerned by the recent deterioration in the global economy, particularly Europe. We see revenue growth of about 3% in 2009.

➤ EFX recently realigned and flattened its organizational structure, and we expect this to yield cost savings. However, we expect narrower operating margins for U.S. Consumer Information Solutions, the company's most profitable segment, which includes direct and credit marketing and mortgage reporting solutions. As a result, we see operating margins narrowing modestly in 2008 and remaining flat in 2009.

➤ After higher interest expense following issuance/assumption of debt from the acquisition of TALX, we estimate operating EPS of $2.49 in 2008 (before items), up from $2.32 in 2007. We project EPS of $2.55 in 2009.

### Investment Rationale/Risk

➤ International markets have offered attractive avenues for growth, in our view, particularly in Latin America. We see this being impacted, especially in Europe, by the recent deterioration in the global economy. EFX's U.S. Consumer Information Solutions remains the largest contributor to total revenues (46% in the September 2008 quarter) and retains the highest operating margins, but the business has been in a decline in 2008 year-to-date. We look for a rising revenue contribution in 2008 from TALX, but expect this to limit near-term operating margin expansion. We are more optimistic about settlement and analytical tools and services, which we consider to be counter-cyclical.

➤ Risks to our recommendation and target price include increasing competition from the other major credit bureaus and data providers. In view of the U.S. economic backdrop, we are also concerned about a further slowdown in the company's North American mortgage reporting and direct and credit marketing segments.

➤ Our 12-month target price of $28 is derived by applying an 11X P/E, comparable to the recent average for peers, to our forward 12-month EPS estimate of $2.55.

## Qualitative Risk Assessment

| LOW | MEDIUM | HIGH |
| --- | --- | --- |

Our risk assessment reflects our view that a majority of the company's domestic operations are relatively mature, and have exposure to the financial services sector. We are also concerned about the slowing global economy, particularly in Europe, offset by our positive outlook for the company's Latin American operations, which we see expanding faster than its domestic operations.

## Quantitative Evaluations

**S&P Quality Ranking**                                            B+

| D | C | B- | B | B+ | A- | A | A+ |
| --- | --- | --- | --- | --- | --- | --- | --- |

**Relative Strength Rank**                              MODERATE

54

LOWEST = 1                                              HIGHEST = 99

## Revenue/Earnings Data

**Revenue (Million $)**

| | 1Q | 2Q | 3Q | 4Q | Year |
| --- | --- | --- | --- | --- | --- |
| 2008 | 503.1 | 501.9 | 484.1 | -- | -- |
| 2007 | 405.1 | 454.5 | 492.5 | 490.9 | 1,843 |
| 2006 | 374.0 | 387.7 | 394.6 | 390.0 | 1,546 |
| 2005 | 343.4 | 363.4 | 375.3 | 361.3 | 1,443 |
| 2004 | 309.9 | 315.4 | 319.9 | 327.6 | 1,273 |
| 2003 | 301.6 | 317.0 | 309.8 | 297.0 | 1,225 |

**Earnings Per Share ($)**

| | | | | | |
| --- | --- | --- | --- | --- | --- |
| 2008 | 0.50 | 0.54 | 0.56 | E0.61 | E2.49 |
| 2007 | 0.54 | 0.51 | 0.48 | 0.49 | 2.02 |
| 2006 | 0.48 | 0.53 | 0.61 | 0.50 | 2.12 |
| 2005 | 0.44 | 0.47 | 0.47 | 0.48 | 1.86 |
| 2004 | 0.38 | 0.58 | 0.40 | 0.42 | 1.78 |
| 2003 | 0.33 | 0.36 | 0.39 | 0.23 | 1.31 |

Fiscal year ended Dec. 31. Next earnings report expected: Early February. EPS Estimates based on S&P Operating Earnings; historical GAAP earnings are as reported.

## Dividend Data (Dates: mm/dd Payment Date: mm/dd/yy)

| Amount ($) | Date Decl. | Ex-Div. Date | Stk. of Record | Payment Date |
| --- | --- | --- | --- | --- |
| 0.040 | 02/11 | 02/20 | 02/22 | 03/14/08 |
| 0.040 | 05/09 | 05/21 | 05/23 | 06/13/08 |
| 0.040 | 08/11 | 08/21 | 08/25 | 09/15/08 |
| 0.040 | 11/05 | 11/20 | 11/24 | 12/15/08 |

Dividends have been paid since 1914. Source: Company reports.

# Equifax Inc.

## Business Summary October 27, 2008

CORPORATE OVERVIEW. Equifax is one of three global providers of consumer and commercial credit information. Equifax collects, organizes and manages credit, financial, demographic and marketing information regarding individuals and businesses, which the company collects from various sources. These sources include financial or credit granting institutions (which provide accounts receivable information), government organizations and consumers. The company maintains information in proprietary databases regarding consumers and businesses worldwide. EFX amasses and processes this data using proprietary systems, and makes the data available to customers in various formats.

Products and services include consumer credit information, information database management, marketing information, business credit information, decisioning and analytical tools, and identity verification services that enable businesses to make informed decisions about extending credit or providing services, managing portfolio risk, and developing marketing strategies. According to the company, EFX allows consumers to manage and protect their financial affairs through products that the company sells directly to individuals using the Internet. The company had approximately 7,000 employees in 14 countries in 2007.

Equifax derived 80% of operating revenue from North America in 2007, unchanged from 2006. The U.S. accounted for 73% of operating revenues in 2007 (72%), while Canada accounted for 7% (8%). The company's largest segment, U.S. Consumer Information Solutions (53% of revenues in 2007, down from 63% in 2006), includes Online Consumer Information Solutions (credit information regarding individuals; 35% of 2007 revenues, down from 40% in 2006), Mortgage Reporting Solutions (credit loan origination information; 4%, 5%), Credit Marketing Services (8%, 11%) and Direct Marketing Services (6%, 7%). Other North American operating segments include Personal Solutions (credit information sales to consumers; 8%, 8%) and Commercial Solutions (credit information concerning businesses; 3%, 3%). TALX, acquired in May 2007 (employment, income verification and human resources outsourcing services) accounted for just under 10% of revenues in 2007. EFX's Canadian Consumer business accounted for 6% of total revenues in 2007 and 2006.

## Company Financials Fiscal Year Ended Dec. 31

| Per Share Data ($) | 2007 | 2006 | 2005 | 2004 | 2003 | 2002 | 2001 | 2000 | 1999 | 1998 |
|---|---|---|---|---|---|---|---|---|---|---|
| Tangible Book Value | NM | NM | NM | NM | NM | NM | NM | NM | NM | NM |
| Cash Flow | 2.48 | 2.76 | 2.49 | 2.39 | 2.00 | 1.96 | 1.61 | 2.77 | 2.44 | 2.06 |
| Earnings | 2.02 | 2.12 | 1.86 | 1.78 | 1.31 | 1.39 | 0.84 | 1.68 | 1.55 | 1.34 |
| S&P Core Earnings | 2.02 | 2.07 | 1.88 | 1.59 | 1.18 | 1.04 | 0.52 | NA | NA | NA |
| Dividends | 0.16 | 0.16 | 0.15 | 0.11 | 0.08 | 0.08 | 0.25 | 0.37 | 0.36 | 0.35 |
| Payout Ratio | 8% | 8% | 8% | 6% | 6% | 6% | 29% | 22% | 23% | 26% |
| Prices:High | 46.30 | 41.64 | 39.00 | 28.46 | 27.59 | 31.30 | 38.76 | 36.50 | 39.88 | 45.00 |
| Prices:Low | 35.22 | 30.15 | 26.97 | 22.60 | 17.84 | 18.95 | 18.60 | 19.88 | 20.13 | 29.75 |
| P/E Ratio:High | 23 | 20 | 21 | 16 | 21 | 23 | 46 | 22 | 26 | 34 |
| P/E Ratio:Low | 17 | 14 | 14 | 13 | 14 | 14 | 22 | 12 | 13 | 22 |

| Income Statement Analysis (Million $) | 2007 | 2006 | 2005 | 2004 | 2003 | 2002 | 2001 | 2000 | 1999 | 1998 |
|---|---|---|---|---|---|---|---|---|---|---|
| Revenue | 1,843 | 1,546 | 1,443 | 1,273 | 1,225 | 1,109 | 1,139 | 1,966 | 1,773 | 1,621 |
| Operating Income | 548 | 519 | 504 | 459 | 438 | 432 | 420 | 604 | 540 | 469 |
| Depreciation | 62.0 | 82.8 | 82.2 | 81.1 | 95.3 | 80.5 | 106 | 149 | 125 | 104 |
| Interest Expense | 58.5 | 31.9 | 35.6 | 34.9 | 39.6 | 41.2 | 47.8 | 76.0 | 61.0 | 42.7 |
| Pretax Income | 431 | 420 | 396 | 388 | 286 | 317 | 205 | 385 | 366 | 327 |
| Effective Tax Rate | 35.3% | 33.6% | 36.5% | 38.1% | 36.5% | 39.0% | 41.7% | 40.8% | 41.0% | 40.9% |
| Net Income | 273 | 275 | 247 | 237 | 179 | 191 | 117 | 228 | 216 | 193 |
| S&P Core Earnings | 273 | 268 | 248 | 211 | 162 | 146 | 73.6 | NA | NA | NA |

| Balance Sheet & Other Financial Data (Million $) | 2007 | 2006 | 2005 | 2004 | 2003 | 2002 | 2001 | 2000 | 1999 | 1998 |
|---|---|---|---|---|---|---|---|---|---|---|
| Cash | 81.6 | 67.8 | 37.5 | 52.1 | 39.3 | 30.5 | 33.2 | 89.4 | 137 | 90.6 |
| Current Assets | 425 | 345 | 280 | 300 | 286 | 286 | 358 | 605 | 609 | 520 |
| Total Assets | 3,524 | 1,791 | 1,832 | 1,557 | 1,553 | 1,507 | 1,423 | 2,070 | 1,840 | 1,829 |
| Current Liabilities | 547 | 582 | 295 | 457 | 355 | 428 | 276 | 426 | 505 | 419 |
| Long Term Debt | 1,165 | 174 | 464 | 399 | 663 | 691 | 694 | 994 | 934 | 869 |
| Common Equity | 1,399 | 838 | 820 | 524 | 372 | 221 | 244 | 384 | 393 | 366 |
| Total Capital | 2,842 | 1,083 | 1,410 | 961 | 1,079 | 938 | 1,026 | 1,467 | 1,400 | 1,286 |
| Capital Expenditures | 119 | 52.0 | 17.2 | 16.5 | 14.6 | 12.8 | 13.0 | 37.1 | 39.0 | 44.9 |
| Cash Flow | 335 | 357 | 329 | 318 | 274 | 272 | 224 | 377 | 341 | 297 |
| Current Ratio | 0.8 | 0.6 | 1.0 | 0.7 | 0.8 | 0.7 | 1.3 | 1.4 | 1.2 | 1.2 |
| % Long Term Debt of Capitalization | 41.0 | 16.1 | 32.9 | 41.5 | 61.5 | 73.7 | 67.6 | 67.7 | 66.7 | 67.6 |
| % Net Income of Revenue | 14.8 | 17.8 | 17.1 | 18.6 | 14.6 | 17.2 | 10.3 | 11.6 | 12.2 | 11.9 |
| % Return on Assets | 10.3 | 15.2 | 14.5 | 15.3 | 11.7 | 13.1 | 7.1 | 11.7 | 11.8 | 12.9 |
| % Return on Equity | 24.4 | 33.1 | 36.7 | 53.0 | 60.3 | 82.4 | 37.4 | 76.1 | 49.7 | 54.0 |

Data as orig reptd.; bef. results of disc opers/spec. items. Per share data adj. for stk. divs.; EPS diluted. E-Estimated. NA-Not Available. NM-Not Meaningful. NR-Not Ranked. UR-Under Review.

Office: 1550 Peachtree St NW, Atlanta, GA 30309.
Telephone: 404-885-8000.
Email: investor@equifax.com
Website: http://www.equifax.com

Chrmn & CEO: R.F. Smith
COO: A.S. Bodea
SVP, Chief Acctg Officer & Cntlr: N.M. King
CFO: L. Adrean

Secy: D.C. Arvidson
Board Members: W. W. Canfield, J. Copeland, Jr., R. D. Daleo, W. W. Driver, Jr., M. L. Feidler, L. P. Humann, S. S. Marshall, J. A. McKinley, Jr., R. F. Smith, M. B. Templeton

Founded: 1913
Domicile: Georgia
Employees: 7,000

# Equity Residential

| S&P Recommendation | **SELL** ★★☆☆☆ | Price $27.66 (as of Nov 14, 2008) | 12-Mo. Target Price $29.00 | Investment Style Large-Cap Value |
|---|---|---|---|---|

**GICS Sector** Financials
**Sub-Industry** Residential REITS

**Summary** This equity real estate investment trust (formerly Equity Residential Properties Trust) owns and operates a nationally diversified portfolio of apartment properties.

## Key Stock Statistics (Source S&P, Vickers, company reports)

| | | | | | | | |
|---|---|---|---|---|---|---|---|
| 52-Wk Range | $49.00– 27.22 | S&P FFO/Sh. 2008**E** | 2.48 | Market Capitalization(B) | $7.524 | Beta | 0.70 |
| Trailing 12-Month FFO/Share | NA | S&P FFO/Sh. 2009**E** | 2.50 | Yield (%) | 6.98 | S&P 3-Yr. FFO/Sh. Proj. CAGR(%) | 3 |
| Trailing 12-Month P/FFO | NA | P/FFO on S&P FFO/Sh. 2008**E** | 11.2 | Dividend Rate/Share | $1.93 | S&P Credit Rating | BBB+ |
| $10K Invested 5 Yrs Ago | $11,997 | Common Shares Outstg. (M) | 272.0 | Institutional Ownership (%) | 100 | | |

## Price Performance

- 30-Week Mov. Avg.
- 10-Week Mov. Avg.
- **GAAP Earnings vs. Previous Year**
- Volume Above Avg. STARS
- 12-Mo. Target Price
- Relative Strength
- ▲ Up ▼ Down ▶ No Change
- Below Avg. ★

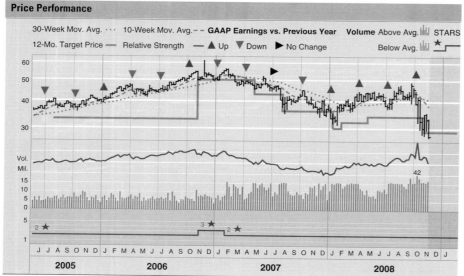

Options: ASE, CBOE, Ph

Analysis prepared by **Royal F. Shepard, CFA** on November 04, 2008, when the stock traded at **$ 33.48**.

## Highlights

- ► We think average rental rate increases will slow for EQR's apartment portfolio to about 2% in 2009, down from an estimated 3.5% in 2008. While occupancy remains solid, at close to 95%, we expect a challenging economic environment will make new tenants increasingly price-sensitive. We are particularly concerned with markets that hold excess housing inventories, including Florida, S. California, and Phoenix.

- ► We think very few attractive acquisition opportunities are presenting themselves in 2008, in light of tight credit market conditions. EQR was a net seller of assets during the first nine months, including 8,795 apartment units for an aggregate price of $807 million. For the full year, we think dispositions will come close to EQR's $1.0 billion target, compared to acquisitions of only about $400 million.

- ► Our 2009 recurring FFO projection, up just $0.02, reflects our outlook for modest rent growth, ongoing increases in operating expenses, and some dilution from dispositions. We expect the cash dividend to be adequately covered, though, and maintains at the annual rate of $1.93 a share.

## Investment Rationale/Risk

- ► Over the last several years, EQR has made significant progress in rebalancing its portfolio toward higher-growth markets. However, we still expect pressure on rental rates in 2009 from legacy assets in overstocked housing markets such as S. Florida, N. Virginia, and Phoenix. As the economy slows, we think it will take several quarters for excess supply to move in balance with demand. We also expect the trust to scale back acquisition activity until credit market conditions improve. Recently at about 13.2X our 2009 FFO per share outlook, EQR traded at a premium to peers, which we view as unwarranted.

- ► Risks to our recommendation and target price include faster-than-anticipated job growth, an improved housing market resulting in less rental competition from single-family homes, and an increase in property values due to investor demand.

- ► Our 12-month target price of $29 is based partly on a multiple of 11.5X our 2009 FFO per share estimate of $2.50, close to peers. We also blend in our dividend discount model, assuming a 10.1% discount rate and a 3% terminal growth rate, which results in intrinsic value of $30.

## Qualitative Risk Assessment

| LOW | MEDIUM | HIGH |
|---|---|---|

Our risk assessment reflects our view that EQR is one of the largest, most diversified residential REITs and has below average financial leverage and moderate stock price volatility.

## Quantitative Evaluations

**S&P Quality Ranking**     A-

| D | C | B- | B | B+ | A- | A | A+ |
|---|---|---|---|---|---|---|---|

**Relative Strength Rank**     MODERATE

44

LOWEST = 1      HIGHEST = 99

## Revenue/FFO Data

**Revenue (Million $)**

| | 1Q | 2Q | 3Q | 4Q | Year |
|---|---|---|---|---|---|---|
| 2008 | 522.8 | 535.5 | 538.3 | -- | -- |
| 2007 | 483.2 | 507.2 | 522.6 | 528.1 | 2,038 |
| 2006 | 470.5 | 490.6 | 511.5 | 517.9 | 1,990 |
| 2005 | 461.6 | 478.9 | 495.5 | 518.9 | 1,955 |
| 2004 | 443.9 | 474.7 | 483.5 | 487.4 | 1,890 |
| 2003 | 448.5 | 455.9 | 459.4 | 459.5 | 1,823 |

**FFO Per Share ($)**

| | | | | | |
|---|---|---|---|---|---|
| 2008 | 0.59 | 0.64 | E0.65 | E0.60 | E2.48 |
| 2007 | 0.55 | 0.60 | 0.58 | 0.67 | 2.39 |
| 2006 | 0.56 | 0.61 | 0.62 | 0.49 | 2.27 |
| 2005 | 0.74 | 0.56 | 0.56 | 0.66 | 2.52 |
| 2004 | 0.52 | 0.56 | 0.50 | 0.56 | 2.14 |
| 2003 | 0.57 | 0.57 | 0.56 | 0.45 | 2.15 |

Fiscal year ended Dec. 31. Next earnings report expected: Early February. FFO Estimates based on S&P Funds From Operations Est..

## Dividend Data (Dates: mm/dd Payment Date: mm/dd/yy)

| Amount ($) | Date Decl. | Ex-Div. Date | Stk. of Record | Payment Date |
|---|---|---|---|---|
| 0.483 | 12/13 | 12/20 | 12/24 | 01/11/08 |
| 0.483 | 02/19 | 03/13 | 03/17 | 04/11/08 |
| 0.483 | 05/19 | 06/12 | 06/16 | 07/11/08 |
| 0.483 | 08/18 | 09/11 | 09/15 | 10/10/08 |

Dividends have been paid since 1993. Source: Company reports.

# Equity Residential

## Business Summary November 04, 2008

CORPORATE OVERVIEW. Equity Residential is one of the largest publicly held owners of multi-family properties. Structured as a real estate investment trust (REIT), it owns, manages and operates properties through its 93.4% interest in its operating limited partnership. At December 31, 2007, EQR owned or had interests in 579 multi-family properties with 152,821 units in 24 states. The trust adopted its current name in May 2002.

During 2006, EQR sold a majority of its ranch style properties, leaving a focus on garden and mid-rise/high-rise assets. Garden-style properties have two or three floors, while mid-rise/high-rise properties have more than three floors. At the end of December 2007, the trust's largest geographic markets as measured by net operating income were the New York Metro Area (10.1%), Los Angeles (8.3%), South Florida (7.8%), Washington DC/N. Virginia (7.7%), and Seattle/Tacoma (7.3%). Average occupancy during the fourth quarter of 2007 was 94.6%, just ahead of 94.5% for the same period in 2006.

MARKET PROFILE. The U.S. housing market is highly fragmented and is broadly characterized by two types of housing units, multifamily and single-family. At the end of 2007, the U.S. Census Bureau estimated that there were 128.65 million housing units in the country, an increase of 1.6% from 2006. Partially due to the high fragmentation, and the fact that residents have the option of

either being owners or tenants (renters), the housing market can be highly competitive. Main demand drivers for apartments are household formation and employment growth. We estimate 1.1 million new households were formed in 2007. Supply is created by new housing unit construction, which could consist of single-family homes, or multifamily apartment buildings or condominiums. We forecast 0.93 million housing unit starts in 2008, down about 31% from 2007.

With apartment tenants on relatively short leases compared to those of commercial and industrial properties, we believe apartment REITs are generally more sensitive to changes in market conditions than REITs in other property categories. Results could be hurt by new construction that adds new space in excess of actual demand. Trends in home price affordability also affect both rent levels and the level of new construction, since the relative price attractiveness of owning versus renting is an important factor in consumer decision making.

## Company Financials Fiscal Year Ended Dec. 31

| Per Share Data ($) | 2007 | 2006 | 2005 | 2004 | 2003 | 2002 | 2001 | 2000 | 1999 | 1998 |
|---|---|---|---|---|---|---|---|---|---|---|
| Tangible Book Value | 17.79 | 18.58 | 16.65 | 15.28 | 15.43 | 15.57 | 16.20 | 20.82 | 16.33 | 16.46 |
| Earnings | 0.23 | 0.20 | 0.51 | 0.37 | 0.43 | 0.78 | 1.36 | 1.67 | 1.15 | 0.82 |
| S&P Core Earnings | 0.21 | 0.20 | 0.51 | 0.34 | 0.41 | 0.72 | 1.38 | NA | NA | NA |
| Dividends | 1.87 | 1.79 | 1.74 | 1.73 | 1.73 | 1.73 | 1.68 | 1.58 | 1.47 | 1.36 |
| Payout Ratio | NM | NM | NM | NM | NM | 222% | 124% | 94% | 128% | 167% |
| Prices:High | 56.46 | 61.50 | 42.17 | 36.75 | 30.30 | 30.96 | 30.45 | 28.63 | 24.19 | 26.28 |
| Prices:Low | 33.79 | 38.84 | 30.70 | 26.65 | 23.12 | 21.55 | 24.80 | 19.34 | 19.06 | 17.34 |
| P/E Ratio:High | NM | NM | 83 | 99 | 70 | 40 | 22 | 17 | 21 | 32 |
| P/E Ratio:Low | NM | NM | 60 | 72 | 54 | 28 | 18 | 12 | 17 | 21 |

| Income Statement Analysis (Million $) | 2007 | 2006 | 2005 | 2004 | 2003 | 2002 | 2001 | 2000 | 1999 | 1998 |
|---|---|---|---|---|---|---|---|---|---|---|
| Rental Income | 2,029 | 1,981 | 1,944 | 1,878 | 1,809 | 1,970 | 2,075 | 1,960 | 1,712 | 1,296 |
| Mortgage Income | Nil | Nil | Nil | Nil | Nil | Nil | 8.79 | 11.2 | 12.6 | 18.6 |
| Total Income | 2,038 | 1,990 | 1,955 | 1,890 | 1,823 | 1,994 | 2,171 | 2,030 | 1,753 | 1,337 |
| General Expenses | 883 | 881 | 925 | 870 | 802 | 841 | 924 | 812 | 673 | 833 |
| Interest Expense | 495 | 436 | 391 | 349 | 333 | 343 | 361 | 388 | 341 | 249 |
| Provision for Losses | Nil | Nil | Nil | Nil | Nil | Nil | Nil | Nil | Nil | Nil |
| Depreciation | 588 | 563 | 508 | 484 | 444 | 462 | 457 | 450 | 409 | 302 |
| Net Income | 93.0 | 101 | 152 | 135 | 212 | 302 | 474 | 555 | 394 | 258 |
| S&P Core Earnings | 58.3 | 59.5 | 98.5 | 74.5 | 86.4 | 194 | 374 | NA | NA | NA |

| Balance Sheet & Other Financial Data (Million $) | 2007 | 2006 | 2005 | 2004 | 2003 | 2002 | 2001 | 2000 | 1999 | 1998 |
|---|---|---|---|---|---|---|---|---|---|---|
| Cash | 71.0 | 260 | 88.8 | 83.5 | 49.6 | 540 | 449 | 417 | 114 | 4.00 |
| Total Assets | 15,690 | 15,062 | 14,099 | 12,645 | 11,467 | 11,811 | 12,236 | 12,264 | 11,716 | 10,700 |
| Real Estate Investment | 18,333 | 17,235 | 16,597 | 14,864 | 12,874 | 13,046 | 13,016 | 12,591 | 12,239 | 10,942 |
| Loss Reserve | Nil | Nil | Nil | Nil | Nil | Nil | Nil | Nil | Nil | Nil |
| Net Investment | 15,163 | 14,217 | 13,709 | 12,264 | 10,578 | 10,934 | 11,297 | 11,239 | 11,168 | 10,224 |
| Short Term Debt | 680 | 921 | NA | NA | NA | 334 | 699 | Nil | 250 | 151 |
| Capitalization:Debt | 8,829 | 7,136 | 7,032 | 5,642 | 4,836 | 5,050 | 5,044 | 5,706 | 5,224 | 4,530 |
| Capitalization:Equity | 4,853 | 5,498 | 4,891 | 4,436 | 4,345 | 4,251 | 4,447 | 4,436 | 4,195 | 5,330 |
| Capitalization:Total | 14,929 | 13,432 | 12,850 | 10,714 | 10,452 | 10,858 | 11,094 | 11,938 | 11,186 | 9,860 |
| % Earnings & Depreciation/Assets | 4.4 | 4.5 | 4.9 | 5.1 | 5.6 | 6.4 | 7.6 | 8.3 | 7.2 | 6.3 |
| Price Times Book Value:High | 3.2 | 3.3 | 2.5 | 2.4 | 2.0 | 2.0 | 1.9 | 1.4 | 1.5 | 1.6 |
| Price Times Book Value:Low | 1.9 | 2.1 | 1.8 | 1.7 | 1.5 | 1.4 | 1.5 | 0.9 | 1.2 | 1.1 |

Data as orig reptd.; bef. results of disc opers/spec. items. Per share data adj. for stk. divs.; EPS diluted. E-Estimated. NA-Not Available. NM-Not Meaningful. NR-Not Ranked. UR-Under Review.

**Office:** Two North Riverside Plaza, Chicago, IL 60606.
**Telephone:** 312-474-1300.
**Email:** investorrelations@eqrworld.com
**Website:** http://www.equityresidential.com

**Chrmn:** S. Zell
**Pres & CEO:** D.J. Neithercut
**Vice Chrmn:** G.A. Spector
**COO:** D.S. Santee

**EVP & CFO:** M.J. Parrell
**Investor Contact:** M. McKenna
**Trustees:** J. W. Alexander, C. L. Atwood, S. O. Evans, B. A. Knox, J. Lynford, J. E. Neal, D. J. Neithercut, D. G. Rogers, S. Z. Rosenberg, G. A. Spector, B. J. White, S. Zell

**Founded:** 1993
**Domicile:** Maryland
**Employees:** 4,800

# Exelon Corp

**STANDARD
&POOR'S**

| S&P Recommendation | BUY ★★★★☆ | Price | 12-Mo. Target Price | Investment Style |
|---|---|---|---|---|
| | | $50.57 (as of Nov 14, 2008) | $61.00 | Large-Cap Blend |

**GICS Sector** Utilities
**Sub-Industry** Electric Utilities

**Summary** Exelon is the holding company for Philadelphia-based PECO Energy and Chicago-based ComEd.

## Key Stock Statistics (Source S&P, Vickers, company reports)

| | | | | | | | |
|---|---|---|---|---|---|---|---|
| 52-Wk Range | $92.13– 41.23 | S&P Oper. EPS 2008E | 4.18 | Market Capitalization(B) | $33.271 | Beta | 0.80 |
| Trailing 12-Month EPS | $3.91 | S&P Oper. EPS 2009E | 4.25 | Yield (%) | 4.15 | S&P 3-Yr. Proj. EPS CAGR(%) | 2 |
| Trailing 12-Month P/E | 12.9 | P/E on S&P Oper. EPS 2008E | 12.1 | Dividend Rate/Share | $2.10 | S&P Credit Rating | BBB |
| $10K Invested 5 Yrs Ago | $18,787 | Common Shares Outstg. (M) | 657.9 | Institutional Ownership (%) | 65 | | |

## Price Performance

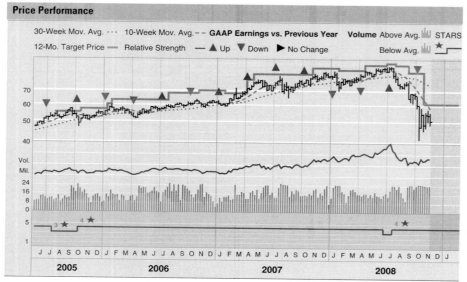

30-Week Mov. Avg. · · · · 10-Week Mov. Avg. - - GAAP Earnings vs. Previous Year Volume Above Avg. STARS
12-Mo. Target Price — Relative Strength — ▲ Up ▼ Down ► No Change Below Avg. ★

Options: ASE, CBOE, P, Ph

Analysis prepared by **Justin McCann** on October 22, 2008, when the stock traded at **$ 50.31**.

### Highlights

▶ If, pending required approvals, EXC completes its unsolicited offer to acquire NRG Energy (NRG: buy, $22), we would expect it to be modestly accretive in the first year, and to result in an expanded presence in the national power market. After expected divestitures of about 3,000 megawatts, the generating capacity of the combined company would be about 47,000 megawatts.

▶ We expect 2008 operating EPS to decline nearly 2% from 2007 operating EPS of $4.32, due to rising operating costs and planned power plant outages. We see the generation segment contributing about $3.32 to operating EPS in 2008, PECO Energy $0.63, and ComEd about $0.40. This should be partially offset by a projected loss of about $0.10 from the holding company.

▶ For 2009, we expect operating EPS to increase about 2% from anticipated results in 2008. Despite the benefit of the reduced shares outstanding, we again expect EPS to be hurt by higher operating costs and planned power plant outages. We project only modest EPS growth in 2010, but expect significant EPS growth in 2011, due to the shift to market-based power contracts with Peco Energy.

### Investment Rationale/Risk

▶ The shares are down more than 30% year to date, reflecting, in our view, the crisis in the credit markets and the extreme volatility in the stock market. If NRG Energy is acquired, EXC would assume more than $8 billion in NRG debt. The company would expect its credit rating to be lowered, but is committed to staying investment grade and believes its rating can be recovered within three years. Since reducing the debt would be a prime priority, EXC has deferred indefinitely its recently announced $1.5 billion share repurchase program.

▶ Risks to our recommendation and target price include an economic recession, sharply reduced wholesale power margins, and a drop in the average P/E of the group as a whole.

▶ With the drop in the shares and the 14% increase in the March dividend payment, the shares recently yielded 4.0%. We believe this is in line with utility holding companies with prospects for above-peers earnings growth. Our 12-month target price is $61, a premium-to-peers P/E of about 14X our EPS estimate for 2009. We believe the premium is warranted by EXC's long-term earnings growth potential.

## Qualitative Risk Assessment

| LOW | MEDIUM | HIGH |
|---|---|---|

Our risk assessment reflects our view of Exelon's strong and steady cash flow from the regulated PECO Energy and ComEd utilities, as well as the healthy earnings and cash flow from very profitable but higher-risk power generating and energy marketing operations.

## Quantitative Evaluations

**S&P Quality Ranking** B+

| D | C | B- | B | B+ | A- | A | A+ |
|---|---|---|---|---|---|---|---|

**Relative Strength Rank** MODERATE

61

LOWEST = 1     HIGHEST = 99

## Revenue/Earnings Data

**Revenue (Million $)**

| | 1Q | 2Q | 3Q | 4Q | Year |
|---|---|---|---|---|---|
| 2008 | 4,517 | 4,622 | 5,228 | -- | -- |
| 2007 | 4,829 | 4,501 | 5,032 | 4,554 | 18,916 |
| 2006 | 3,861 | 3,697 | 4,401 | 3,696 | 15,655 |
| 2005 | 3,561 | 3,484 | 4,473 | 3,838 | 15,357 |
| 2004 | 3,722 | 3,550 | 3,865 | 3,378 | 14,515 |
| 2003 | 4,074 | 3,721 | 4,441 | 3,577 | 15,812 |

**Earnings Per Share ($)**

| | | | | | |
|---|---|---|---|---|---|
| 2008 | 0.88 | 1.13 | 1.06 | E1.05 | E4.18 |
| 2007 | 1.01 | 1.03 | 1.15 | 0.84 | 4.03 |
| 2006 | 0.59 | 0.95 | -0.07 | 0.87 | 2.35 |
| 2005 | 0.77 | 0.76 | 1.07 | -1.19 | 1.40 |
| 2004 | 0.57 | 0.78 | 0.86 | 0.54 | 2.75 |
| 2003 | 0.39 | 0.57 | -0.16 | 0.42 | 1.20 |

Fiscal year ended Dec. 31. Next earnings report expected: Late January. EPS Estimates based on S&P Operating Earnings; historical GAAP earnings are as reported.

## Dividend Data (Dates: mm/dd Payment Date: mm/dd/yy)

| Amount ($) | Date Decl. | Ex-Div. Date | Stk. of Record | Payment Date |
|---|---|---|---|---|
| 0.500 | 12/19 | 02/13 | 02/15 | 03/10/08 |
| 0.500 | 04/30 | 05/13 | 05/15 | 06/10/08 |
| 0.500 | 07/29 | 08/13 | 08/15 | 09/10/08 |
| 0.525 | 10/24 | 11/12 | 11/14 | 12/10/08 |

Dividends have been paid since 1902. Source: Company reports.

---

**Please read the Required Disclosures and Analyst Certification on the last page of this report.**

The McGraw-Hill Companies

# Exelon Corp

STANDARD
&POOR'S

## Business Summary October 22, 2008

CORPORATE OVERVIEW. Exelon Corp. was formed in October 2000 through the acquisition by Philadelphia-based PECO Energy of Chicago-based Unicom Corp. The company, along with its subsidiaries, is engaged in the energy delivery, generation and other businesses. Exelon operates in three business segments: Generation, PECO, and ComEd (Commonwealth Edison). Segment contributions to consolidated net income in 2007 were: Generation, 2,025 million ($1,403 million in 2006); PECO, $507 million ($441 million); ComEd, $165 million (compared to a loss of $112 million, on a goodwill impairment charge of $776 million); and other, $29 million (a loss of $142 million).

IMPACT OF MAJOR DEVELOPMENTS. On October 19, 2008, Exelon announced that it had proposed an unsolicited offer to acquire all of the outstanding common shares of NRG Energy (NRG: buy, $22), one of the leading competitive wholesale power generators in the United States with net generating capacity

of 24,115 megawatts as of December 31, 2007. Under the proposal, which would be subject to the negotiation of a definitive merger agreement and required shareholder and regulatory approvals, NRG shareholders would be offered a fixed exchange ratio of 0.485 EXC shares for each NRG share. Should the acquisition be completed, the combined company would be the largest power company in the U.S. in terms of assets, market capitalization, enterprise value and generating capacity. The announcement comes two years after the September 14, 2006 termination of the merger agreement (that was announced on December 20, 2004) between Exelon and Public Service Enterprise Group (PEG).

## Company Financials Fiscal Year Ended Dec. 31

| Per Share Data ($) | 2007 | 2006 | 2005 | 2004 | 2003 | 2002 | 2001 | 2000 | 1999 | 1998 |
|---|---|---|---|---|---|---|---|---|---|---|
| Tangible Book Value | 11.86 | 11.08 | 8.48 | 7.10 | 5.77 | 4.26 | 4.51 | 3.18 | 4.57 | 6.81 |
| Earnings | 4.03 | 2.35 | 1.40 | 2.75 | 1.20 | 2.58 | 2.20 | 1.44 | 1.58 | 1.16 |
| S&P Core Earnings | 3.92 | 3.49 | 3.01 | 2.79 | 1.74 | 1.64 | 1.49 | NA | NA | NA |
| Dividends | 1.76 | 2.00 | 1.60 | 1.53 | 0.96 | 0.88 | 0.91 | 0.46 | 0.50 | 0.50 |
| Payout Ratio | 44% | 85% | 114% | 56% | 80% | 34% | 41% | 32% | 32% | 43% |
| Prices:High | 86.83 | 63.62 | 57.46 | 44.90 | 33.31 | 28.50 | 35.13 | 35.50 | 25.25 | 21.09 |
| Prices:Low | 58.74 | 51.13 | 41.77 | 30.92 | 23.04 | 18.92 | 19.38 | 16.50 | 15.38 | 9.44 |
| P/E Ratio:High | 22 | 27 | 41 | 16 | 28 | 11 | 16 | 25 | 16 | 18 |
| P/E Ratio:Low | 15 | 22 | 30 | 11 | 19 | 7 | 9 | 11 | 10 | 8 |

| Income Statement Analysis (Million $) | | | | | | | | | | |
|---|---|---|---|---|---|---|---|---|---|---|
| Revenue | 18,916 | 15,655 | 15,357 | 14,515 | 15,812 | 14,955 | 15,140 | 7,499 | 5,437 | 5,210 |
| Depreciation | 1,520 | 1,487 | 1,334 | 1,305 | 1,126 | 1,340 | 1,449 | 458 | 237 | 643 |
| Maintenance | NA | NA | NA | NA | NA | NA | NA | NA | NA | NA |
| Fixed Charges Coverage | 6.03 | 5.19 | 4.88 | 3.94 | 2.19 | 3.56 | 2.98 | 2.94 | 3.24 | 3.52 |
| Construction Credits | NA | NA | NA | NA | NA | NA | NA | Nil | 4.00 | 3.52 |
| Effective Tax Rate | 34.7% | 43.1% | 49.8% | 27.5% | 29.4% | 37.4% | 39.7% | 27.3% | 36.6% | 37.5% |
| Net Income | 2,726 | 1,590 | 951 | 1,841 | 793 | 1,670 | 1,416 | 907 | 619 | 532 |
| S&P Core Earnings | 2,656 | 2,358 | 2,035 | 1,865 | 1,142 | 1,062 | 962 | NA | NA | NA |

| Balance Sheet & Other Financial Data (Million $) | | | | | | | | | | |
|---|---|---|---|---|---|---|---|---|---|---|
| Gross Property | 31,964 | 30,025 | 29,853 | 28,711 | 27,578 | 25,904 | 21,526 | 19,886 | 9,412 | 7,228 |
| Capital Expenditures | 2,674 | 2,418 | 2,165 | 1,921 | 1,954 | 2,150 | 2,041 | 752 | 491 | 415 |
| Net Property | 24,153 | 22,775 | 21,981 | 21,482 | 20,630 | 17,134 | 13,742 | 12,936 | 5,045 | 4,337 |
| Capitalization:Long Term Debt | 12,052 | 11,998 | 11,760 | 12,235 | 13,576 | 14,580 | 13,492 | 14,398 | 6,098 | 3,269 |
| Capitalization:% Long Term Debt | 54.3 | 54.6 | 56.3 | 56.5 | 61.5 | 65.3 | 62.1 | 66.6 | 75.6 | 49.9 |
| Capitalization:Preferred | Nil | Nil | Nil | Nil | Nil | Nil | Nil | Nil | 193 | 230 |
| Capitalization:% Preferred | Nil | Nil | Nil | Nil | Nil | Nil | Nil | Nil | 2.39 | 3.51 |
| Capitalization:Common | 10,137 | 9,973 | 9,125 | 9,423 | 8,503 | 7,742 | 8,230 | 7,215 | 1,773 | 3,057 |
| Capitalization:% Common | 45.7 | 45.4 | 43.7 | 43.5 | 38.5 | 34.7 | 37.9 | 33.4 | 22.0 | 46.6 |
| Total Capital | 27,270 | 27,395 | 25,964 | 26,463 | 26,724 | 26,325 | 26,341 | 26,352 | 10,760 | 9,233 |
| % Operating Ratio | 83.0 | 80.3 | 80.5 | 81.1 | 82.2 | 73.1 | 83.9 | 80.5 | 80.7 | 81.5 |
| % Earned on Net Property | 19.9 | 15.7 | 12.5 | 16.3 | 11.4 | 21.3 | 25.2 | 17.0 | 28.6 | 31.2 |
| % Return on Revenue | 14.4 | 10.2 | 6.2 | 12.7 | 5.0 | 11.2 | 9.4 | 12.1 | 11.4 | 10.2 |
| % Return on Invested Capital | 13.5 | 12.1 | 11.4 | 10.3 | 10.2 | 10.2 | 9.8 | 9.8 | 10.3 | 14.3 |
| % Return on Common Equity | 27.1 | 16.7 | 10.2 | 20.5 | 9.8 | 21.1 | 18.3 | 20.2 | 25.1 | 16.9 |

Data as orig reptd.; bef. results of disc opers/spec. items. Per share data adj. for stk. divs.; EPS diluted. E-Estimated. NA-Not Available. NM-Not Meaningful. NR-Not Ranked. UR-Under Review.

**Office:** 10 S Dearborn St, Chicago, IL 60603-2300.
**Telephone:** 312-394-7398.
**Website:** http://www.exeloncorp.com
**Chrmn & CEO:** J.W. Rowe

**Pres & COO:** C.M. Crane
**SVP, CFO, Chief Acctg Officer & Cntlr:** M.F. Hilzinger
**SVP & Secy:** K.K. Combs
**Investor Contact:** J.F. Young (866-530-8108)

**Investor Contact:** C. Patterson
**Board Members:** J. A. Canning, Jr., M. W. D'Alessio, N. DeBenedictis, B. DeMars, N. Diaz, S. L. Gin, R. B. Greco, P. L. Joskow, J. M. Palms, W. C. Richardson, T. J. Ridge, J. W. Rogers, Jr., J. W. Rowe, S. D. Steinour, D. Thompson

**Founded:** 1887
**Domicile:** Pennsylvania
**Employees:** 17,800

# Expedia Inc

**STANDARD & POOR'S**

| S&P Recommendation | HOLD ★★★☆☆ | Price<br>$7.80 (as of Nov 14, 2008) | 12-Mo. Target Price<br>$14.00 | Investment Style<br>Large-Cap Blend |
|---|---|---|---|---|

**GICS Sector** Consumer Discretionary
**Sub-Industry** Internet Retail

**Summary** Expedia is one of the world's largest online travel-services companies. Businesses include Expedia, Hotels.com, Hotwire and TripAdvisor.

## Key Stock Statistics (Source S&P, Vickers, company reports)

| | | | | | | | |
|---|---|---|---|---|---|---|---|
| 52-Wk Range | $34.66– 7.07 | S&P Oper. EPS 2008**E** | 1.20 | Market Capitalization(B) | $2.038 | Beta | 2.42 |
| Trailing 12-Month EPS | $1.04 | S&P Oper. EPS 2009**E** | 1.35 | Yield (%) | Nil | S&P 3-Yr. Proj. EPS CAGR(%) | 13 |
| Trailing 12-Month P/E | 7.5 | P/E on S&P Oper. EPS 2008**E** | 6.5 | Dividend Rate/Share | Nil | S&P Credit Rating | BB |
| $10K Invested 5 Yrs Ago | NA | Common Shares Outstg. (M) | 286.9 | Institutional Ownership (%) | 85 | | |

## Price Performance

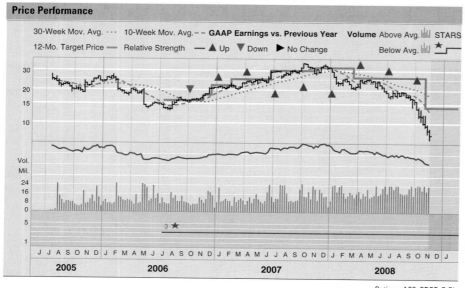

30-Week Mov. Avg. · · ·    10-Week Mov. Avg. - -    **GAAP Earnings vs. Previous Year**    Volume Above Avg. ▐▍▌ STARS
12-Mo. Target Price —    Relative Strength —    ▲ Up    ▼ Down    ▶ No Change    Below Avg. ▐▍▌ ★

Options: ASE, CBOE, P, Ph

Analysis prepared by **Scott H. Kessler** on November 04, 2008, when the stock traded at **$ 9.44**.

## Highlights

➤ We believe EXPE is among the worldwide leaders in the Internet travel segment and will benefit from the continuing migration of associated purchases online. However, we believe the global economic crisis and substantial exposure to Europe, where economic and currency uncertainties are notable, are worrisome. Nonetheless, we forecast revenue growth of 12% in 2008 and 5% in 2009, owing largely to secular growth trends and projected market share gains.

➤ We estimate that annual operating income before amortization (OIBA) and net margins bottomed in 2006, partly due to considerable sales and marketing expenses and technology investments, which have yielded benefits into 2008.

➤ In June 2007, EXPE announced a tender offer to repurchase up to 117 million of its shares at $27.50 to $30 a share. However, credit market uncertainties caused it to reduce this repurchase to 25 million shares (8% of the shares outstanding as of June 2007) at $29 apiece. EXPE had $749 million in cash and investments as of September 2008, and $894 million in long-term debt and a $250 million credit facility.

## Investment Rationale/Risk

➤ We believe EXPE has some of the Internet's best known travel franchises, strong international operations, and a healthy domestic business. We also think it has done a good job over the past few quarters at seizing upon opportunities and executing. However, we believe the company faces many challenges, including significant economic uncertainty and related weak consumer sentiment, a maturing online travel market in the U.S., and significant competition worldwide.

➤ Risks to our recommendation and target price include a notable weakening of global or domestic consumer sentiment or spending, and increasing competitive or pricing pressures.

➤ EXPE's P/E-to-growth multiple was recently higher than that of the other publicly traded online travel company we cover, and the comparison leads to a value of $9. Our DCF assumptions include a WACC of 12.1%, annual free cash flow growth averaging 6% over the next five years, and a perpetuity growth rate of 3%, yielding an intrinsic value of $29. Weighting these methodologies results in our 12-month target price of $14.

## Qualitative Risk Assessment

| LOW | MEDIUM | HIGH |
|---|---|---|

Our risk assessment reflects what we believe is a maturing online travel market in the U.S., an intensely competitive landscape, and relatively low barriers to entry.

## Quantitative Evaluations

**S&P Quality Ranking**      NR

| D | C | B- | B | B+ | A- | A | A+ |
|---|---|---|---|---|---|---|---|

**Relative Strength Rank**      WEAK

22

LOWEST = 1      HIGHEST = 99

## Revenue/Earnings Data

**Revenue (Million $)**

| | 1Q | 2Q | 3Q | 4Q | Year |
|---|---|---|---|---|---|
| 2008 | 687.8 | 795.1 | 833.3 | -- | -- |
| 2007 | 550.5 | 689.9 | 759.6 | 665.3 | 2,677 |
| 2006 | 493.9 | 598.5 | 613.9 | 531.3 | 2,238 |
| 2005 | 485.1 | 555.0 | 584.1 | 494.8 | 2,119 |
| 2004 | 413.3 | 487.0 | 503.8 | 439.0 | 1,843 |
| 2003 | -- | -- | -- | -- | -- |

**Earnings Per Share ($)**

| | 1Q | 2Q | 3Q | 4Q | Year |
|---|---|---|---|---|---|
| 2008 | 0.17 | 0.33 | 0.33 | E0.15 | E1.20 |
| 2007 | 0.11 | 0.30 | 0.32 | 0.22 | 0.94 |
| 2006 | 0.06 | 0.27 | 0.17 | 0.20 | 0.70 |
| 2005 | -- | -- | 0.23 | 0.07 | 0.65 |
| 2004 | -- | -- | -- | -- | 0.37 |
| 2003 | -- | -- | -- | -- | -- |

Fiscal year ended Dec. 31. Next earnings report expected: Early February. EPS Estimates based on S&P Operating Earnings; historical GAAP earnings are as reported.

## Dividend Data

No cash dividends have been paid.

# Expedia Inc

## Business Summary November 04, 2008

CORPORATE OVERVIEW. Expedia, Inc. leverages its portfolio of brands to target a broad range of travelers interested in different travel options. EXPE provides a wide selection of travel products and services, from simple discounted travel to more complex luxury trips. The company's offerings primarily include airline tickets, hotel reservations, car rentals, cruise arrangements, and destination services.

The company's localized Expedia-branded websites (focused on the U.S., as well as Australia, Austria, Canada, Denmark, France, Germany, Ireland, Italy, Japan, the Netherlands, New Zealand, Norway, Spain, Sweden, and the U.K.) offer a large variety of travel products and services. Expedia websites also serve as the travel channel on MSN.com. Expedia Corporate Travel is a full-service travel management firm available to corporate travelers in the U.S., Canada, China, and Europe. Hotels.com provides a multitude of lodging options to travelers, from traditional hotels, to vacation rentals. Part of Hotels.com's strategy is to position itself as a hotel expert offering premium content about lodging properties. These businesses are planning to provide other travel products and services. Hotwire.com is a discount travel website that offers deals to travelers willing to make purchases without knowing certain

itinerary details such as brand, time of departure, and hotel address. eLong (LONG: $7) is a majority-owned online travel services company based in and focused on China (see below for more details).

TripAdvisor is an online travel content destination, with search and directory features, guidebook reviews, and user opinions. We believe TripAdvisor is an extremely valuable asset, not only because we believe it constitutes the Internet's largest and most active travel-related social networking property, but also because it diversifies EXPE operations away from transactions and into media and advertising.

In December 2004, IAC/InterActiveCorp (IACI: buy, $17) announced a plan to spin off what became EXPE. In August 2005, EXPE was spun off as a separate publicly traded company.

## Company Financials Fiscal Year Ended Dec. 31

| Per Share Data ($) | 2007 | 2006 | 2005 | 2004 | 2003 | 2002 | 2001 | 2000 | 1999 | 1998 |
|---|---|---|---|---|---|---|---|---|---|---|
| Tangible Book Value | NM | NM | NM | NA | NA | NA | NA | NA | NA | NA |
| Cash Flow | 1.38 | 1.40 | 1.82 | NA | NA | NA | NA | NA | NA | NA |
| Earnings | 0.94 | 0.70 | 0.65 | 0.37 | NA | NA | NA | NA | NA | NA |
| S&P Core Earnings | 0.94 | 0.79 | 0.69 | 0.48 | 0.27 | 0.26 | -1.04 | NA | NA | NA |
| Dividends | Nil | Nil | Nil | NA | NA | NA | NA | NA | NA | NA |
| Payout Ratio | Nil | Nil | Nil | NA | NA | NA | NA | NA | NA | NA |
| Prices:High | 35.28 | 27.55 | 27.50 | NA | NA | NA | NA | NA | NA | NA |
| Prices:Low | 19.97 | 12.87 | 18.49 | NA | NA | NA | NA | NA | NA | NA |
| P/E Ratio:High | 38 | 39 | 42 | NA | NA | NA | NA | NA | NA | NA |
| P/E Ratio:Low | 21 | 18 | 28 | NA | NA | NA | NA | NA | NA | NA |

| Income Statement Analysis (Million $) | 2007 | 2006 | 2005 | 2004 | 2003 | 2002 | 2001 | 2000 | 1999 | 1998 |
|---|---|---|---|---|---|---|---|---|---|---|
| Revenue | 2,665 | 2,238 | 2,119 | 1,843 | 2,340 | 1,499 | NA | NA | NA | NA |
| Operating Income | 666 | 648 | 678 | NA | NA | NA | NA | NA | NA | NA |
| Depreciation | 137 | 249 | 407 | 157 | 104 | 61.4 | NA | NA | NA | NA |
| Interest Expense | 52.9 | 17.3 | Nil | 7.45 | NA | NA | NA | NA | NA | NA |
| Pretax Income | 497 | 385 | 414 | 219 | 256 | 209 | NA | NA | NA | NA |
| Effective Tax Rate | 40.9% | 36.2% | 44.9% | 40.0% | 38.0% | 39.4% | NA | NA | NA | NA |
| Net Income | 296 | 245 | 229 | 131 | 111 | 76.7 | NA | NA | NA | NA |
| S&P Core Earnings | 296 | 275 | 244 | 163 | 92.3 | 34.2 | -98.1 | NA | NA | NA |

| Balance Sheet & Other Financial Data (Million $) | 2007 | 2006 | 2005 | 2004 | 2003 | 2002 | 2001 | 2000 | 1999 | 1998 |
|---|---|---|---|---|---|---|---|---|---|---|
| Cash | 634 | 853 | 297 | 232 | 882 | NA | NA | NA | NA | NA |
| Current Assets | 1,046 | 1,183 | 590 | 569 | NA | NA | NA | NA | NA | NA |
| Total Assets | 8,295 | 8,269 | 7,757 | 7,803 | 8,755 | NA | NA | NA | NA | NA |
| Current Liabilities | 1,774 | 1,400 | 1,438 | 1,515 | NA | NA | NA | NA | NA | NA |
| Long Term Debt | 1,085 | 500 | Nil | NA | NA | NA | NA | NA | NA | NA |
| Common Equity | 4,818 | 5,904 | 5,734 | 5,820 | 7,554 | NA | NA | NA | NA | NA |
| Total Capital | 6,316 | 6,835 | 6,174 | NA | NA | NA | NA | NA | NA | NA |
| Capital Expenditures | 86.7 | 92.6 | 52.3 | 53.4 | 46.2 | 46.5 | NA | NA | NA | NA |
| Cash Flow | 433 | 494 | 636 | NA | NA | NA | NA | NA | NA | NA |
| Current Ratio | 0.6 | 0.8 | 0.4 | 0.4 | 2.0 | NA | NA | NA | NA | NA |
| % Long Term Debt of Capitalization | 17.2 | 7.3 | Nil | Nil | Nil | Nil | NA | NA | NA | NA |
| % Net Income of Revenue | 11.1 | 10.9 | 10.8 | 7.1 | 4.8 | 5.1 | NA | NA | NA | NA |
| % Return on Assets | 3.6 | 3.1 | 2.6 | 1.8 | NA | NA | NA | NA | NA | NA |
| % Return on Equity | 5.5 | 4.2 | 3.3 | 2.1 | NA | NA | NA | NA | NA | NA |

Data as orig reptd.; bef. results of disc opers/spec. items. Per share data adj. for stk. divs.; EPS diluted. E-Estimated. NA-Not Available. NM-Not Meaningful. NR-Not Ranked. UR-Under Review.

**Office:** 3150 139th Avenue SE, Bellevue, WA 98005-4046.
**Telephone:** 425-679-7200.
**Website:** http://www.expedia.com
**Chrmn:** B. Diller

**Pres & CEO:** D. Khosrowshahi
**Vice Chrmn:** V.A. Kaufman
**CEO:** E. Blachford
**EVP & CFO:** M.B. Adler

**Investor Contact:** S. Haas (425-679-7852)
**Board Members:** A. G. Battle, S. J. Breakwell, B. Diller, J. L. Dolgen, W. R. Fitzgerald, C. A. Jacobson, V. A. Kaufman, P. Kern, D. Khosrowshahi, J. C. Malone

**Founded:** 1996
**Domicile:** Delaware
**Employees:** 7,150

# Expeditors International of Washington Inc

STANDARD &POOR'S

| S&P Recommendation | BUY ★★★★☆ | Price | 12-Mo. Target Price | Investment Style |
|---|---|---|---|---|
| | | $30.68 (as of Nov 14, 2008) | $43.00 | Large-Cap Growth |

**GICS Sector** Industrials
**Sub-Industry** Air Freight & Logistics

**Summary** This company is a global air and ocean freight forwarder and customs broker.

## Key Stock Statistics (Source S&P, Vickers, company reports)

| | | | | | | | | |
|---|---|---|---|---|---|---|---|---|
| 52-Wk Range | $49.92–24.05 | S&P Oper. EPS 2008E | 1.34 | Market Capitalization(B) | $6.506 | Beta | 0.73 |
| Trailing 12-Month EPS | $1.33 | S&P Oper. EPS 2009E | 1.55 | Yield (%) | 1.04 | S&P 3-Yr. Proj. EPS CAGR(%) | 17 |
| Trailing 12-Month P/E | 23.1 | P/E on S&P Oper. EPS 2008E | 22.9 | Dividend Rate/Share | $0.32 | S&P Credit Rating | NA |
| $10K Invested 5 Yrs Ago | $16,275 | Common Shares Outstg. (M) | 212.1 | Institutional Ownership (%) | 97 | | |

## Price Performance

- 30-Week Mov. Avg. · · · ·
- 10-Week Mov. Avg. - - -
- **GAAP Earnings vs. Previous Year**
- Volume Above Avg. ▦▦ STARS
- 12-Mo. Target Price —
- Relative Strength —
- ▲ Up  ▼ Down  ▶ No Change
- Below Avg. ▦▦  ★

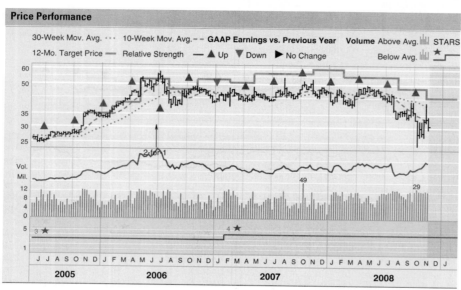

Options: ASE, CBOE, P, Ph

Analysis prepared by **Jim Corridore** on November 03, 2008, when the stock traded at **$ 32.90.**

## Highlights

➤ We expect 2008 net revenues to advance about 10%, following 13% growth in 2007. Revenue growth should be led by higher volumes in air and ocean freight. We expect EXPD to continue to experience strong demand in Europe and Asia, reflecting strengthening economies in these regions, and modest shipping activity in the U.S. We project that airfreight and ocean freight customs net revenues will rise about 11% in 2008, and we see customs brokerage net revenues increasing about 15%.

➤ We expect margins to benefit from the leveraging of SG&A expenses over a higher revenue base. We think that new ocean freight capacity, which has come on line in the past year, could drive ocean freight transportation costs lower, which we believe could allow for additional margin expansion opportunities. Partly offsetting this is likely to be legal costs related to a Department of Justice Investigation related to potential anticompetitive practices.

➤ We forecast 2008 operating EPS of $1.34, which would represent about 11% growth over 2007 EPS of $1.21. For 2009, we see EPS rising 16%, to $1.55.

## Investment Rationale/Risk

➤ With EXPD trading well below our 12-month target price, our recommendation is buy. We think the shares will benefit from stronger than industry average net revenue growth that we expect. While the logistics sector would likely suffer if the U.S. economy slows from current expectations, we believe EXPD's strong international revenue base will allow it to outperform peers. A debt-free balance sheet and what we view as strong projected long-term earnings and cash flow growth are additional positives.

➤ Risks to our recommendation and target price include the potential impact of a sharp economic slowdown. We also see management's communication style, in which it mainly answers questions through 8-K filings, as a risk, in that it may not allow investors to react quickly enough to potentially important news. The company could be hit with a large judgment related to the current Department of Justice Investigation on anticompetitive practices.

➤ Our 12-month target price of $43 values the stock at about 28X our 2009 EPS estimate of $1.55, toward the low end of EXPD's five-year historical P/E range of 24.1X-55.0X EPS.

## Qualitative Risk Assessment

| LOW | MEDIUM | HIGH |
|---|---|---|

Our risk assessment reflects that EXPD operates in a highly cyclical industry and is exposed to currency and global economic risk. We see its communication style as an additional risk. However, we think EXPD has a diversified stream of air, ocean, and customs businesses, and we also believe the balance sheet is strong, with no debt and a relatively large amount of cash.

## Quantitative Evaluations

**S&P Quality Ranking** A+

| D | C | B- | B | B+ | A- | A | A+ |
|---|---|---|---|---|---|---|---|

**Relative Strength Rank** STRONG

75

LOWEST = 1   HIGHEST = 99

## Revenue/Earnings Data

**Revenue (Million $)**

| | 1Q | 2Q | 3Q | 4Q | Year |
|---|---|---|---|---|---|
| 2008 | 1,307 | 1,454 | 1,565 | -- | -- |
| 2007 | 1,119 | 1,259 | 1,411 | 1,447 | 5,235 |
| 2006 | 1,025 | 1,129 | 1,230 | 1,242 | 4,626 |
| 2005 | 825.2 | 928.0 | 1,046 | 1,102 | 3,902 |
| 2004 | 686.9 | 798.7 | 897.2 | 934.8 | 3,318 |
| 2003 | 556.4 | 625.7 | 711.5 | 731.4 | 2,625 |

**Earnings Per Share ($)**

| | | | | | |
|---|---|---|---|---|---|
| 2008 | 0.30 | 0.32 | 0.39 | E0.34 | E1.34 |
| 2007 | 0.27 | 0.30 | 0.34 | 0.32 | 1.21 |
| 2006 | 0.24 | 0.25 | 0.29 | 0.28 | 1.06 |
| 2005 | 0.17 | 0.20 | 0.25 | 0.36 | 0.98 |
| 2004 | 0.15 | 0.17 | 0.20 | 0.20 | 0.71 |
| 2003 | 0.12 | 0.13 | 0.15 | 0.17 | 0.56 |

Fiscal year ended Dec. 31. Next earnings report expected: Mid February. EPS Estimates based on S&P Operating Earnings; historical GAAP earnings are as reported.

## Dividend Data (Dates: mm/dd Payment Date: mm/dd/yy)

| Amount ($) | Date Decl. | Ex-Div. Date | Stk. of Record | Payment Date |
|---|---|---|---|---|
| 0.140 | 11/13 | 11/29 | 12/03 | 12/17/07 |
| 0.160 | 05/08 | 05/29 | 06/02 | 06/16/08 |
| 0.160 | 11/05 | 11/26 | 12/01 | 12/15/08 |

Dividends have been paid since 1993. Source: Company reports.

# Expeditors International of Washington Inc

STANDARD
&POOR'S

## Business Summary November 03, 2008

With an international network supporting the movement and strategic positioning of goods, Expeditors International of Washington is engaged in the business of providing global logistics services to customers diversified in terms of industry specialization and geographic location. In each of its U.S. offices, and in many international offices, the company acts as a customs broker, and also provides additional services, including distribution management, vendor consolidation, cargo insurance, purchase order management, and customized logistics information. EXPD does not compete for domestic freight, overnight courier, or small parcel business, and does not own aircraft or steamships. The company has historically pursued a strategy emphasizing organic growth supplemented by strategic acquisitions. As of May 2008, EXPD had a network of 179 full-service offices, 69 satellite locations and four international service centers located on six continents.

Shipments of computer components, other electronic equipment, housewares, sporting goods, machine parts and toys comprise a significant percentage of the company's business. Import customers include computer retailers and distributors of consumer electronics, department store chains, clothing and shoe wholesalers. Historically, no single customer has accounted for over 5% of revenues.

Air freight services accounted for 46% of net revenues in 2007, and 48% in 2006. EXPD typically acts either as a freight consolidator (purchasing cargo space on airlines and reselling it to customers at lower rates than the airline would charge customers directly), or as an agent for the airlines (receiving shipments from suppliers, and consolidating and forwarding them to the airlines). Shipments are usually characterized by a high value-to-weight ratio, a need for rapid delivery, or both. The company estimates that its average air freight consolidation weighs 3,500 lbs. to 4,500 lbs.

## Company Financials Fiscal Year Ended Dec. 31

| Per Share Data ($) | 2007 | 2006 | 2005 | 2004 | 2003 | 2002 | 2001 | 2000 | 1999 | 1998 |
|---|---|---|---|---|---|---|---|---|---|---|
| Tangible Book Value | 5.69 | 4.95 | 4.21 | 3.70 | 2.98 | 2.49 | 2.01 | 1.76 | 1.40 | 1.10 |
| Cash Flow | 1.39 | 1.27 | 1.12 | 0.82 | 0.67 | 0.62 | 0.55 | 0.48 | 0.37 | 0.30 |
| Earnings | 1.21 | 1.06 | 0.98 | 0.71 | 0.56 | 0.52 | 0.45 | 0.38 | 0.28 | 0.22 |
| S&P Core Earnings | 1.21 | 1.06 | 0.85 | 0.59 | 0.46 | 0.44 | 0.39 | NA | NA | NA |
| Dividends | 0.28 | 0.22 | 0.15 | 0.11 | 0.08 | 0.06 | 0.04 | 0.04 | 0.03 | 0.02 |
| Payout Ratio | 23% | 21% | 15% | 16% | 14% | 12% | 10% | 9% | 9% | 8% |
| Prices:High | 54.46 | 58.32 | 36.37 | 29.20 | 20.42 | 17.22 | 16.48 | 15.03 | 11.59 | 6.03 |
| Prices:Low | 38.31 | 32.83 | 23.59 | 17.85 | 14.81 | 12.47 | 10.49 | 8.16 | 5.08 | 3.11 |
| P/E Ratio:High | 45 | 55 | 37 | 41 | 36 | 33 | 37 | 40 | 42 | 27 |
| P/E Ratio:Low | 32 | 31 | 24 | 25 | 26 | 24 | 24 | 21 | 18 | 14 |

| Income Statement Analysis (Million $) | 2007 | 2006 | 2005 | 2004 | 2003 | 2002 | 2001 | 2000 | 1999 | 1998 |
|---|---|---|---|---|---|---|---|---|---|---|
| Revenue | 5,235 | 4,626 | 3,902 | 3,318 | 2,625 | 2,297 | 1,653 | 1,695 | 1,445 | 1,064 |
| Operating Income | 463 | 411 | 337 | 268 | 211 | 194 | 170 | 150 | 114 | 88.9 |
| Depreciation | 40.0 | 35.4 | 32.3 | 26.7 | 24.4 | 22.7 | 23.5 | 22.5 | 20.8 | 15.5 |
| Interest Expense | Nil | 0.20 | 0.31 | 0.04 | 0.19 | 0.18 | 0.52 | 0.43 | 1.07 | 0.49 |
| Pretax Income | 450 | 396 | 320 | 250 | 196 | 178 | 154 | 133 | 94.6 | 75.6 |
| Effective Tax Rate | 40.0% | 40.6% | 29.6% | 35.4% | 36.4% | 36.8% | 37.0% | 37.7% | 37.5% | 37.4% |
| Net Income | 269 | 235 | 219 | 156 | 122 | 113 | 97.2 | 83.0 | 59.2 | 47.3 |
| S&P Core Earnings | 269 | 235 | 187 | 130 | 98.4 | 92.7 | 83.8 | NA | NA | NA |

| Balance Sheet & Other Financial Data (Million $) | 2007 | 2006 | 2005 | 2004 | 2003 | 2002 | 2001 | 2000 | 1999 | 1998 |
|---|---|---|---|---|---|---|---|---|---|---|
| Cash | 575 | 511 | 464 | 409 | 296 | 212 | 219 | 169 | 71.2 | 49.4 |
| Current Assets | 1,535 | 1,342 | 1,202 | 1,046 | 762 | 605 | 511 | 523 | 382 | 284 |
| Total Assets | 2,069 | 1,822 | 1,566 | 1,364 | 1,041 | 880 | 688 | 662 | 512 | 407 |
| Current Liabilities | 770 | 709 | 613 | 524 | 392 | 356 | 274 | 230 | 229 | 189 |
| Long Term Debt | Nil | Nil | Nil | Nil | Nil | Nil | Nil | Nil | Nil | Nil |
| Common Equity | 1,227 | 1,070 | 914 | 807 | 646 | 524 | 415 | 362 | 282 | 217 |
| Total Capital | 1,299 | 1,113 | 954 | 840 | 649 | 524 | 415 | 362 | 282 | 217 |
| Capital Expenditures | 82.8 | 141 | 90.8 | 66.2 | 20.7 | 81.4 | 37.4 | 25.6 | 26.6 | 52.5 |
| Cash Flow | 309 | 271 | 251 | 183 | 146 | 135 | 121 | 106 | 80.0 | 62.8 |
| Current Ratio | 2.0 | 1.9 | 2.0 | 2.0 | 1.9 | 1.7 | 1.9 | 2.3 | 1.7 | 1.5 |
| % Long Term Debt of Capitalization | Nil | Nil | Nil | Nil | Nil | Nil | Nil | Nil | Nil | Nil |
| % Net Income of Revenue | 5.1 | 5.1 | 5.6 | 4.7 | 4.6 | 4.9 | 5.9 | 4.9 | 4.1 | 4.4 |
| % Return on Assets | 13.8 | 13.9 | 14.9 | 13.0 | 12.7 | 14.3 | 14.4 | 13.9 | 12.9 | 12.6 |
| % Return on Equity | 23.4 | 23.6 | 25.4 | 21.5 | 20.9 | 24.0 | 25.0 | 25.8 | 23.7 | 24.4 |

Data as orig reptd.; bef. results of disc opers/spec. items. Per share data adj. for stk. divs.; EPS diluted. E-Estimated. NA-Not Available. NM-Not Meaningful. NR-Not Ranked. UR-Under Review.

**Office:** 1015 Third Avenue, Seattle, WA 98104-1190.
**Telephone:** 206-674-3400.
**Website:** http://www.expeditors.com
**Chrmn & CEO:** P.J. Rose

**Pres, COO, Chief Acctg Officer & Treas:** R.J. Gates
**SVP & Cntlr:** C.J. Lynch
**SVP & CIO:** J.S. Musser
**CFO:** B.S. Powell

**Investor Contact:** R.J. Gates (206-674-3400)
**Board Members:** J. J. Casey, M. A. Emmert, R. J. Gates, A. L. Howes, D. P. Kourkoumelis, M. J. Malone, J. W. Meisenbach, P. J. Rose, L. Wang, R. R. Wright

**Founded:** 1979
**Domicile:** Washington
**Employees:** 12,310

The McGraw-Hill Companies

# Express Scripts Inc

**STANDARD &POOR'S**

| S&P Recommendation | BUY ★★★★☆ | Price | 12-Mo. Target Price | Investment Style |
|---|---|---|---|---|
| | | $58.49 (as of Nov 14, 2008) | $71.00 | Large-Cap Growth |

**GICS Sector** Health Care
**Sub-Industry** Health Care Services

**Summary** This company offers prescription benefits and disease state management services.

## Key Stock Statistics (Source S&P, Vickers, company reports)

| | | | | | | | |
|---|---|---|---|---|---|---|---|
| 52-Wk Range | $79.10–48.37 | S&P Oper. EPS 2008E | 3.10 | Market Capitalization(B) | $14.474 | Beta | 0.69 |
| Trailing 12-Month EPS | $2.79 | S&P Oper. EPS 2009E | 3.68 | Yield (%) | Nil | S&P 3-Yr. Proj. EPS CAGR(%) | 19 |
| Trailing 12-Month P/E | 21.0 | P/E on S&P Oper. EPS 2008E | 18.9 | Dividend Rate/Share | Nil | S&P Credit Rating | BBB |
| $10K Invested 5 Yrs Ago | $37,160 | Common Shares Outstg. (M) | 247.5 | Institutional Ownership (%) | 95 | | |

## Price Performance

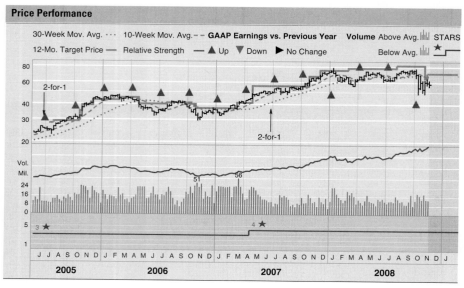

30-Week Mov. Avg. ···  10-Week Mov. Avg. —  **GAAP Earnings vs. Previous Year**  Volume Above Avg. |||| STARS
12-Mo. Target Price —  Relative Strength —  ▲ Up  ▼ Down  ► No Change  Below Avg. |||| ★

Options: ASE, CBOE, P

Analysis prepared by **Phillip M. Seligman** on November 11, 2008, when the stock traded at **$ 60.17**.

## Highlights

▶ We project revenues, which now includes retail co-payments, to be consistent with industry practice, and we see an increase of 1.3% in 2009, to about $22.4 billion, from the $22.15 billion we forecast for 2008. We see growth in 2008 at about 1.5% from the $21.82 billion that ESRX achieved in 2007. Drivers for 2009 include an retention rate in excess of 95% and 226 new accounts covering over 1.4 million lives. However, ESRX expects low utilization, due to tough economic times, and the recent loss of a mail-only client to lead to a 2%-3% reduction in total adjusted claims in 2009 (one mail claim counted as three retail claims). Meanwhile, it expects adjusted scripts to be flat in 2008.

▶ We look for EBITDA per adjusted claim to continue to rise in 2009 on generic drug penetration, mail penetration, and lower drug purchasing costs. Regarding the first factor, the third-quarter 2008 generic drug penetration rate rose 400 basis points from a year earlier, to a record 66.2%.

▶ Our 2008 and 2009 operating EPS estimates are $3.10 and $3.68, respectively, versus 2007's $2.35, bolstered by share buybacks.

## Investment Rationale/Risk

▶ We are encouraged that ESRX has been experiencing strong favorable underlying trends, including lower drug purchasing costs and increasing generic drug penetration, albeit at a slower rate than in 2007. While our estimates for 2008 and 2009 EBITDA per adjusted claim growth are below 2006 and 2007 levels, we think its advance reflects ESRX's ability to help its clients reduce their drug cost trends, which should strengthen the company competitively. We also believe its strong cash flow provides financial flexibility and, in this regard, we are encouraged by the July 2008 acquisition of the workers' comp PBM business of Medical Services Company. Given the high account retention rates among PBMs, we believe ESRX will continue to seek takeover prospects.

▶ Risks to our recommendation and target price include increased government oversight and a potential loss of key clients. We also await the outcome of several legal proceedings.

▶ We derive a 12-month target price of $71 by applying a peer-level P/E-to-growth ratio of 1.2X, assuming three-year EPS growth of 19%, to our 2008 EPS estimate.

## Qualitative Risk Assessment

| LOW | MEDIUM | HIGH |
|---|---|---|

Our risk assessment reflects our view of rising drug demand, and the company's improving financial performance and healthy operating cash flow. However, we believe intense competition and increased government regulation of pharmacy benefit managers (PBMs), which we view as likely, could result in changes in industry conditions.

## Quantitative Evaluations

**S&P Quality Ranking**   B+

| D | C | B- | B | B+ | A- | A | A+ |
|---|---|---|---|---|---|---|---|

**Relative Strength Rank**   STRONG

77

LOWEST = 1     HIGHEST = 99

## Revenue/Earnings Data

**Revenue (Million $)**

| | 1Q | 2Q | 3Q | 4Q | Year |
|---|---|---|---|---|---|
| 2008 | 4,604 | 4,707 | 5,451 | -- | -- |
| 2007 | 4,540 | 4,600 | 4,519 | 4,694 | 18,274 |
| 2006 | 4,380 | 4,421 | 4,330 | 4,529 | 17,660 |
| 2005 | 3,839 | 3,944 | 3,848 | 4,635 | 16,266 |
| 2004 | 3,628 | 3,780 | 3,768 | 3,940 | 15,115 |
| 2003 | 3,224 | 3,334 | 3,249 | 3,488 | 13,295 |

**Earnings Per Share ($)**

| | 1Q | 2Q | 3Q | 4Q | Year |
|---|---|---|---|---|---|
| 2008 | 0.70 | 0.76 | 0.81 | E0.83 | E3.10 |
| 2007 | 0.49 | 0.57 | 0.56 | 0.65 | 2.28 |
| 2006 | 0.35 | 0.38 | 0.42 | 0.54 | 1.67 |
| 2005 | 0.29 | 0.34 | 0.34 | 0.38 | 1.34 |
| 2004 | 0.22 | 0.21 | 0.20 | 0.27 | 0.90 |
| 2003 | 0.19 | 0.19 | 0.20 | 0.22 | 0.80 |

Fiscal year ended Dec. 31. Next earnings report expected: Late February. EPS Estimates based on S&P Operating Earnings; historical GAAP earnings are as reported.

## Dividend Data

No cash dividends have been paid.

# Express Scripts Inc

STANDARD
&POOR'S

## Business Summary November 11, 2008

CORPORATE OVERVIEW. Express Scripts is one of the largest U.S. pharmacy benefits managers (PBMs). Its PBM services (80.2% of 2007 revenue, versus 80.0% in 2006) include retail network pharmacy management, mail pharmacy services, benefit design consultation, drug utilization review, formulary management, disease management, and compliance and therapy management for thousands of client groups that include health insurers, third-party administrators, employers, union-sponsored benefit plans and government health programs.

The SAAS segment (19.8%, versus 19.5%) comprises specialty operations of CuraScript, and its SDS and PMG service lines. The segment's services include delivery of injectable drugs to patient homes, physician offices, and clinics, third party logistics services, and bio-pharma services including reimbursement and customized logistics solutions. The segment also includes distribution of specialty pharmaceuticals requiring special handling or packaging; distribution of pharmaceuticals to low-income patients through manufacturer-sponsored branded and company-sponsored generic patient assistance programs; and distribution of sample units to physicians and verification of practitioner licensure. The infusion business was reclassified as discontinued

operations in 2007's fourth quarter.

Revenues are generated primarily from the delivery of prescription drugs through 60,000 contracted retail pharmacies, three home delivery fulfillment pharmacies, and 25 specialty drug pharmacies, as of December 31, 2007. Revenues from the delivery of prescription drugs to members represented 98.4% of revenues in 2007, versus 98.3% in 2006. Revenues from services, such as the administration of some clients' retail pharmacy networks, and certain services provided by SAAS comprised the remainder.

The five largest clients accounted for 17.4% of revenues in 2007, compared to 17.8% in 2006 and 23.6% in 2005. In 2007, the company processed 380 million network pharmacy claims and 41 million home delivery pharmacy claims, compared to 390 million and 41 million, respectively, in 2006.

## Company Financials Fiscal Year Ended Dec. 31

| Per Share Data ($) | 2007 | 2006 | 2005 | 2004 | 2003 | 2002 | 2001 | 2000 | 1999 | 1998 |
|---|---|---|---|---|---|---|---|---|---|---|
| Tangible Book Value | NM | NM | NM | NM | NM | NM | NM | NM | NM | NM |
| Cash Flow | 2.64 | 2.03 | 1.62 | 1.12 | 0.97 | 0.90 | 0.64 | 0.23 | 0.78 | 0.26 |
| Earnings | 2.28 | 1.67 | 1.34 | 0.90 | 0.79 | 0.64 | 0.39 | -0.03 | 0.53 | 0.16 |
| S&P Core Earnings | 2.24 | 1.67 | 1.30 | 0.87 | 0.75 | 0.60 | 0.36 | NA | NA | NA |
| Dividends | Nil | Nil | Nil | Nil | Nil | Nil | Nil | Nil | Nil | Nil |
| Payout Ratio | Nil | Nil | Nil | Nil | Nil | Nil | Nil | Nil | Nil | Nil |
| Prices:High | 74.40 | 47.50 | 45.40 | 20.30 | 18.86 | 16.48 | 15.36 | 13.38 | 13.19 | 8.63 |
| Prices:Low | 32.32 | 29.40 | 18.27 | 14.58 | 11.58 | 9.66 | 8.71 | 3.56 | 5.55 | 3.38 |
| P/E Ratio:High | 33 | 28 | 34 | 23 | 24 | 26 | 39 | NM | 25 | 54 |
| P/E Ratio:Low | 14 | 18 | 14 | 16 | 15 | 15 | 22 | NM | 10 | 21 |

| Income Statement Analysis (Million $) | | | | | | | | | | |
|---|---|---|---|---|---|---|---|---|---|---|
| Revenue | 18,274 | 17,660 | 16,266 | 15,115 | 13,295 | 12,261 | 9,329 | 6,787 | 4,288 | 2,825 |
| Operating Income | 1,177 | 925 | 727 | 563 | 503 | 454 | 317 | 279 | 241 | 116 |
| Depreciation | 97.5 | 101 | 84.0 | 70.0 | 54.0 | 82.0 | 80.1 | 78.6 | 74.0 | 27.0 |
| Interest Expense | 108 | 95.7 | 37.0 | 41.7 | 41.4 | 42.2 | 34.2 | 47.9 | 60.0 | 20.2 |
| Pretax Income | 945 | 740 | 615 | 451 | 405 | 330 | 208 | -4.47 | 265 | 76.2 |
| Effective Tax Rate | 36.5% | 35.9% | 35.0% | 38.3% | 38.2% | 38.2% | 39.9% | NM | 40.7% | 44.0% |
| Net Income | 600 | 474 | 400 | 278 | 251 | 204 | 125 | -8.02 | 157 | 42.7 |
| S&P Core Earnings | 592 | 474 | 389 | 270 | 239 | 192 | 115 | NA | NA | NA |

| Balance Sheet & Other Financial Data (Million $) | | | | | | | | | | |
|---|---|---|---|---|---|---|---|---|---|---|
| Cash | 437 | 131 | 478 | 166 | 396 | 191 | 178 | 53.2 | 283 | 123 |
| Current Assets | 1,968 | 1,772 | 2,257 | 1,443 | 1,560 | 1,394 | 1,213 | 998 | 1,066 | 657 |
| Total Assets | 5,256 | 5,108 | 5,493 | 3,600 | 3,409 | 3,207 | 2,500 | 2,277 | 2,487 | 1,095 |
| Current Liabilities | 2,475 | 2,429 | 2,394 | 1,813 | 1,626 | 1,544 | 1,246 | 1,116 | 1,100 | 539 |
| Long Term Debt | 1,760 | 1,270 | 1,401 | 412 | 455 | 563 | 346 | 396 | 636 | 306 |
| Common Equity | 696 | 1,125 | 1,465 | 1,196 | 1,194 | 1,003 | 832 | 705 | 699 | 250 |
| Total Capital | 2,735 | 2,395 | 2,866 | 1,608 | 1,649 | 1,565 | 1,178 | 1,102 | 1,335 | 556 |
| Capital Expenditures | 75.0 | 66.8 | 60.0 | 51.5 | 53.1 | 61.3 | 57.3 | 80.2 | 37.0 | 23.9 |
| Cash Flow | 698 | 575 | 484 | 348 | 305 | 286 | 205 | 70.6 | 231 | 69.7 |
| Current Ratio | 0.8 | 0.7 | 0.9 | 0.8 | 1.0 | 0.9 | 1.0 | 0.9 | 1.0 | 1.2 |
| % Long Term Debt of Capitalization | 64.4 | 53.0 | 48.9 | 25.6 | 27.6 | 35.9 | 29.4 | 36.0 | 47.6 | 55.1 |
| % Net Income of Revenue | 3.3 | 2.7 | 2.5 | 1.8 | 1.9 | 1.7 | 1.3 | NM | 3.7 | 1.5 |
| % Return on Assets | 11.6 | 8.9 | 8.8 | 7.9 | 7.6 | 7.1 | 5.2 | NM | 8.8 | 5.7 |
| % Return on Equity | 65.9 | 36.6 | 30.1 | 23.3 | 22.8 | 22.2 | 16.3 | NM | 33.2 | 18.8 |

Data as orig reptd.; bef. results of disc opers/spec. items. Per share data adj. for stk. divs.; EPS diluted. E-Estimated. NA-Not Available. NM-Not Meaningful. NR-Not Ranked. UR-Under Review.

**Office:** 1 Express Way, Saint Louis, MO 63121-1824.
**Telephone:** 314-996-0900.
**Email:** investor.relations@express-scripts.com
**Website:** http://www.express-scripts.com

**Chrmn, Pres & CEO:** G. Paz
**COO, EVP & CIO:** P. McNamee
**EVP & CFO:** J.L. Hall
**EVP & Chief Admin Officer:** M. Holmes

**EVP, Secy & General Counsel:** T.M. Boudreau
**Investor Contact:** D. Myers (314-702-7173)
**Board Members:** G. G. Benanav, F. J. Borelli, M. Breen, N. J. LaHowchic, T. P. MacMahon, W. Myers, Jr., J. O. Parker, Jr., G. Paz, S. K. Skinner, S. Sternberg, B. Toan

**Founded:** 1986
**Domicile:** Delaware
**Employees:** 11,820

# Exxon Mobil Corp

**STANDARD &POOR'S**

| S&P Recommendation | **STRONG BUY** ★★★★★ | Price | 12-Mo. Target Price | Investment Style |
|---|---|---|---|---|
| | | $73.68 (as of Nov 14, 2008) | $105.00 | Large-Cap Blend |

**GICS Sector** Energy
**Sub-Industry** Integrated Oil & Gas

**Summary** XOM, formed through the merger of Exxon and Mobil in late 1999, is the world's largest publicly owned integrated oil company.

## Key Stock Statistics (Source S&P, Vickers, company reports)

| | | | | | | | |
|---|---|---|---|---|---|---|---|
| 52-Wk Range | $96.12–56.51 | S&P Oper. EPS 2008E | 9.03 | Market Capitalization(B) | $374.784 | Beta | 0.71 |
| Trailing 12-Month EPS | $9.24 | S&P Oper. EPS 2009E | 9.45 | Yield (%) | 2.17 | S&P 3-Yr. Proj. EPS CAGR(%) | 10 |
| Trailing 12-Month P/E | 8.0 | P/E on S&P Oper. EPS 2008E | 8.2 | Dividend Rate/Share | $1.60 | S&P Credit Rating | AAA |
| $10K Invested 5 Yrs Ago | $22,594 | Common Shares Outstg. (M) | 5,086.6 | Institutional Ownership (%) | 51 | | |

## Price Performance

30-Week Mov. Avg. · · · 10-Week Mov. Avg. - - **GAAP Earnings vs. Previous Year** Volume Above Avg. STARS
12-Mo. Target Price — Relative Strength — ▲ Up ▼ Down ▶ No Change Below Avg. ★

Options: ASE, CBOE, P, Ph

Analysis prepared by **Tina J. Vital** on November 04, 2008, when the stock traded at **$ 77.18**.

### Highlights

► Third quarter oil and gas production declined 8.2%, below our expectations, reflecting the impact of higher oil prices on production-sharing contracts and Gulf of Mexico hurricane shut-ins. We expect over a 5% decline for 2008. However, with seven major project start-ups in 2007, 12 slated for this year, seven in 2009-2010, and 40 thereafter, we expect XOM to achieve over 2% per annum production growth in 2008-2012.

► In the aftermath of Gulf of Mexico hurricanes, the majority of XOM's Gulf operations are back on line or are completing the final stages of start-up. Third quarter upstream volumes were down by 24,000 boe/d and costs were higher by $50 million (before tax) due to the hurricanes. Damage repairs and lower volumes across all business lines associated with the hurricanes are expected to reduce fourth quarter earnings by about $500 million.

► After-tax operating earnings rose 1.6% in 2007, and we project an increase of 18% in 2008 and about 3% in 2009.

### Investment Rationale/Risk

► We believe XOM will benefit from "big-pocket" upstream growth opportunities in the deepwater, liquefied natural gas (LNG), and ventures with state-owned oil companies. We expect its upstream operations to benefit from strong crude oil prices, and its complex refineries from significant cost discounts due to its ability to refine lower-quality crude feedstocks. We estimate XOM's three-year average upstream costs are below the peer average, and we estimate its three-year average reserve replacement rate is above the peer average.

► Risks to our recommendation and target price include changes in economic, industry and operating conditions, such as difficulty replacing reserves and increased production costs.

► A blend of our discounted cash flow ($110 per share; assuming a WACC of 9.6% and terminal growth of 3%), net asset valuation ($101; assuming a long term WTI oil price of $90 per barrel ), and relative valuations leads to our 12-month target of $105 per share, which reflects an expected enterprise value of 6.3X our 2009 EBITDA estimate, at premium to U.S. supermajor oil peers.

## Qualitative Risk Assessment

| **LOW** | MEDIUM | HIGH |
|---|---|---|

Our risk assessment reflects our view of the company's diversified and strong business profile in volatile, cyclical and capital-intensive segments of the energy industry. We view ExxonMobil's earnings stability and corporate governance practices as above average.

## Quantitative Evaluations

**S&P Quality Ranking** A+

| D | C | B- | B | B+ | A- | A | **A+** |
|---|---|---|---|---|---|---|---|

**Relative Strength Rank** STRONG

88

LOWEST = 1 HIGHEST = 99

## Revenue/Earnings Data

### Revenue (Million $)

| | 1Q | 2Q | 3Q | 4Q | Year |
|---|---|---|---|---|---|
| 2008 | 116,854 | 138,072 | 137,737 | -- | -- |
| 2007 | 87,223 | 98,350 | 102,337 | 116,642 | 404,552 |
| 2006 | 86,317 | 96,024 | 96,268 | 86,858 | 377,635 |
| 2005 | 82,051 | 88,568 | 100,717 | 99,662 | 370,680 |
| 2004 | 67,602 | 70,693 | 76,375 | 83,357 | 298,035 |
| 2003 | 63,780 | 57,165 | 59,841 | 65,952 | 246,738 |

### Earnings Per Share ($)

| | 1Q | 2Q | 3Q | 4Q | Year |
|---|---|---|---|---|---|
| 2008 | 2.03 | 2.22 | 2.86 | E2.13 | E9.03 |
| 2007 | 1.62 | 1.83 | 1.70 | 2.14 | 7.28 |
| 2006 | 1.37 | 1.72 | 1.77 | 1.76 | 6.62 |
| 2005 | 1.22 | 1.20 | 1.58 | 1.71 | 5.71 |
| 2004 | 0.83 | 0.88 | 0.88 | 1.30 | 3.89 |
| 2003 | 0.97 | 0.62 | 0.55 | 1.01 | 3.15 |

Fiscal year ended Dec. 31. Next earnings report expected: Early February. EPS Estimates based on S&P Operating Earnings; historical GAAP earnings are as reported.

## Dividend Data (Dates: mm/dd Payment Date: mm/dd/yy)

| Amount ($) | Date Decl. | Ex-Div. Date | Stk. of Record | Payment Date |
|---|---|---|---|---|
| 0.350 | 01/30 | 02/07 | 02/11 | 03/10/08 |
| 0.400 | 04/30 | 05/09 | 05/13 | 06/10/08 |
| 0.400 | 07/30 | 08/11 | 08/13 | 09/10/08 |
| 0.400 | 10/29 | 11/07 | 11/12 | 12/10/08 |

Dividends have been paid since 1882. Source: Company reports.

# Exxon Mobil Corp

**STANDARD
&POOR'S**

## Business Summary November 04, 2008

CORPORATE OVERVIEW. In late 1999, the FTC allowed Exxon and Mobil to re-unite, creating Exxon Mobil Corp. (XOM). ExxonMobil's businesses include oil and natural gas exploration and production (7% of 2007 sales; 65% of 2007 segment earnings); refining and marketing (83%; 24%); chemicals (9%; 11%); and other operations, such as electric power generation, coal and minerals.

Proved oil and gas reserves declined 3.1% to 13.2 billion barrel oil equivalent (boe; 41% natural gas, 59% liquids), as of year-end 2007. In addition, proved Canadian oil sands reserves declined 3.3% to 694 million barrels as of year-end 2007. Liquids production declined 2.4%, to 2.616 million b/d in 2007, and natural gas production available for sale rose 0.5%, to 9.384 billion cubic feet per day (Bcf)/d in 2007. We estimate XOM's 2007 organic reserve replacement at 105%. Using data from John S. Herold, we estimate XOM's three-year (2004-2006) reserve replacement at 130%, above the peer average; its three-year finding and development cost at $7.00 per boe, below the peer average; its proved acquisition costs at $0.56 per boe, below the peer average; and its reserve replacement costs at $6.07 per boe, below the peer average.

In September 2007, XOM filed a request for arbitration with the International Center for Settlement of Investment Disputes following the June expropriation of assets in Venezuela. XOM's book exposure to Venezuela is about $750 million, related to its Cerro Negro project.

As of year-end 2007, the company had an ownership interest in 38 refineries worldwide, with 6.3 million b/d of atmospheric distillation capacity (U.S. 31%, Europe 28%, Asia Pacific 16%, Japan 12%, Canada 8%, and Latin America/other 5%). In April 2007, ExxonMobil sold its Ingolstadt refinery in Germany (rated capacity of 110,000 b/d) to Petroplus Holdings AG for about $627.5 million (including inventory).

MANAGEMENT. We believe XOM is one of the best managed companies in the energy sector. In January 2006, Lee R. Raymond retired and Rex W. Tillerson became chairman and CEO. We expect Mr. Tillerson to benefit from plans made by Mr. Raymond over the past 12 years, and we see Mr. Tillerson's diplomatic skills as playing an important role in enhancing those plans.

## Company Financials Fiscal Year Ended Dec. 31

| Per Share Data ($) | 2007 | 2006 | 2005 | 2004 | 2003 | 2002 | 2001 | 2000 | 1999 | 1998 |
|---|---|---|---|---|---|---|---|---|---|---|
| Tangible Book Value | 22.62 | 19.87 | 18.13 | 15.90 | 13.69 | 11.13 | 10.74 | 10.21 | 9.13 | 8.83 |
| Cash Flow | 9.48 | 8.89 | 7.34 | 5.38 | 4.50 | 2.84 | 3.32 | 3.43 | 2.30 | 2.38 |
| Earnings | 7.28 | 6.62 | 5.71 | 3.89 | 3.15 | 1.61 | 2.18 | 2.27 | 1.13 | 1.31 |
| S&P Core Earnings | 7.40 | 6.75 | 5.72 | 4.01 | 3.03 | 1.52 | 2.03 | NA | NA | NA |
| Dividends | 1.37 | 1.28 | 1.14 | 1.06 | 0.98 | 0.92 | 0.91 | 0.88 | 0.84 | 0.82 |
| Payout Ratio | 19% | 19% | 20% | 27% | 31% | 57% | 42% | 39% | 74% | 63% |
| Prices:High | 95.27 | 79.00 | 65.96 | 52.05 | 41.13 | 44.58 | 45.84 | 47.72 | 43.63 | 38.66 |
| Prices:Low | 69.02 | 56.42 | 49.25 | 39.91 | 31.58 | 29.75 | 35.01 | 34.94 | 32.16 | 28.31 |
| P/E Ratio:High | 13 | 12 | 12 | 13 | 13 | 28 | 21 | 21 | 39 | 30 |
| P/E Ratio:Low | 9 | 9 | 9 | 10 | 10 | 18 | 16 | 15 | 29 | 22 |

| Income Statement Analysis (Million $) | 2007 | 2006 | 2005 | 2004 | 2003 | 2002 | 2001 | 2000 | 1999 | 1998 |
|---|---|---|---|---|---|---|---|---|---|---|
| Revenue | 404,552 | 377,635 | 370,680 | 298,035 | 246,738 | 204,506 | 213,488 | 232,748 | 185,527 | 117,772 |
| Operating Income | 156,810 | 150,107 | 59,255 | 45,639 | 32,230 | 23,280 | 29,602 | 33,309 | 17,921 | 12,326 |
| Depreciation, Depletion and Amortization | 12,250 | 11,416 | 10,253 | 9,767 | 9,047 | 8,310 | 7,944 | 8,130 | 8,304 | 5,340 |
| Interest Expense | 957 | 654 | 496 | 638 | 207 | 398 | 293 | 589 | 695 | 100 |
| Pretax Income | 71,479 | 68,453 | 60,231 | 42,017 | 32,660 | 17,719 | 24,688 | 27,493 | 11,295 | 9,241 |
| Effective Tax Rate | 41.8% | 40.8% | 38.7% | 37.9% | 33.7% | 36.7% | 36.5% | 40.3% | 28.7% | 28.3% |
| Net Income | 40,610 | 39,500 | 36,130 | 25,330 | 20,960 | 11,011 | 15,105 | 15,990 | 7,910 | 6,440 |
| S&P Core Earnings | 41,250 | 40,263 | 36,164 | 26,089 | 20,214 | 10,418 | 14,042 | NA | NA | NA |

| Balance Sheet & Other Financial Data (Million $) | 2007 | 2006 | 2005 | 2004 | 2003 | 2002 | 2001 | 2000 | 1999 | 1998 |
|---|---|---|---|---|---|---|---|---|---|---|
| Cash | 34,500 | 32,848 | 28,671 | 18,531 | 10,626 | 7,229 | 6,547 | 7,081 | 1,761 | 1,461 |
| Current Assets | 85,963 | 75,777 | 73,342 | 60,377 | 45,960 | 38,291 | 35,681 | 40,399 | 31,141 | 17,593 |
| Total Assets | 242,082 | 219,015 | 208,335 | 195,256 | 174,278 | 152,644 | 143,174 | 149,000 | 144,521 | 92,630 |
| Current Liabilities | 58,312 | 48,817 | 46,307 | 42,981 | 38,386 | 33,175 | 30,114 | 38,191 | 38,733 | 19,412 |
| Long Term Debt | 7,183 | 6,645 | 6,220 | 5,013 | 4,756 | 6,655 | 7,099 | 7,280 | 8,402 | 4,530 |
| Common Equity | 121,762 | 113,844 | 111,186 | 101,756 | 89,915 | 74,597 | 73,161 | 70,757 | 63,466 | 43,645 |
| Total Capital | 156,126 | 141,340 | 138,284 | 131,813 | 118,171 | 100,504 | 99,444 | 97,709 | 91,807 | 63,229 |
| Capital Expenditures | 15,387 | 15,462 | 13,839 | 11,986 | 12,859 | 11,437 | 9,989 | 8,446 | 10,849 | 8,359 |
| Cash Flow | 52,860 | 50,916 | 46,383 | 35,097 | 30,007 | 19,321 | 23,049 | 24,120 | 16,178 | 11,770 |
| Current Ratio | 1.5 | 1.6 | 1.6 | 1.4 | 1.2 | 1.2 | 1.2 | 1.1 | 0.8 | 0.9 |
| % Long Term Debt of Capitalization | 4.6 | 4.7 | 4.4 | 3.8 | 4.0 | 6.6 | 7.1 | 7.5 | 9.2 | 7.2 |
| % Return on Assets | 17.6 | 18.5 | 17.9 | 13.7 | 12.8 | 7.4 | 10.3 | 10.9 | 5.6 | 6.8 |
| % Return on Equity | 34.5 | 35.1 | 33.9 | 26.4 | 25.5 | 14.9 | 21.0 | 23.8 | 12.6 | 14.8 |

Data as orig reptd.; bef. results of disc opers/spec. items. Per share data adj. for stk. divs.; EPS diluted. E-Estimated. NA-Not Available. NM-Not Meaningful. NR-Not Ranked. UR-Under Review.

Office: 5959 Las Colinas Blvd, Irving, TX 75039-2298.
Telephone: 972-444-1000.
Website: http://www.exxonmobil.com
Chrmn, Pres & CEO: R.W. Tillerson

SVP, CFO & Treas: D.D. Humphreys
Chief Acctg Officer & Cntlr: P.T. Mulva
Secy: D.S. Rosenthal
General Counsel: C.W. Matthews

Board Members: M. J. Boskin, L. R. Faulkner, W. W. George, J. R. Houghton, W. R. Howell, R. C. King, P. E. Lippincott, M. C. Nelson, S. J. Palmisano, S. S. Reinemund, W. V. Shipley, R. W. Tillerson, E. E. Whitacre, Jr.

Founded: 1870
Domicile: New Jersey
Employees: 80,800

# Family Dollar Stores Inc.

**STANDARD &POOR'S**

| S&P Recommendation | STRONG BUY ★★★★★ | Price $26.67 (as of Nov 14, 2008) | 12-Mo. Target Price $31.00 | Investment Style Large-Cap Blend |
|---|---|---|---|---|

**GICS Sector** Consumer Discretionary
**Sub-Industry** General Merchandise Stores

**Summary** This company operates a chain of more than 6,500 retail discount stores in 44 states across the U.S.

## Key Stock Statistics (Source S&P, Vickers, company reports)

| | | | | | | | |
|---|---|---|---|---|---|---|---|
| 52-Wk Range | $32.50– 14.62 | S&P Oper. EPS 2009**E** | 1.78 | Market Capitalization(B) | $3.726 | Beta | 0.78 |
| Trailing 12-Month EPS | $1.66 | S&P Oper. EPS 2010**E** | 2.00 | Yield (%) | 1.87 | S&P 3-Yr. Proj. EPS CAGR(%) | 12 |
| Trailing 12-Month P/E | 16.1 | P/E on S&P Oper. EPS 2009**E** | 15.0 | Dividend Rate/Share | $0.50 | S&P Credit Rating | NA |
| $10K Invested 5 Yrs Ago | $7,313 | Common Shares Outstg. (M) | 139.7 | Institutional Ownership (%) | NM | | |

## Price Performance

30-Week Mov. Avg. · · · 10-Week Mov. Avg. - - GAAP Earnings vs. Previous Year    Volume Above Avg. STARS
12-Mo. Target Price — Relative Strength — ▲ Up ▼ Down ▶ No Change    Below Avg. ★

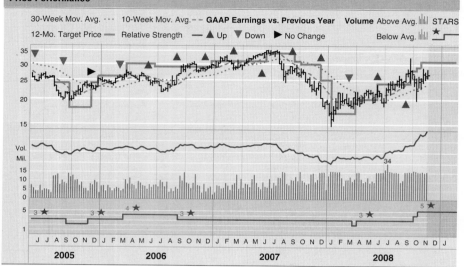

Options: ASE, CBOE, P, Ph

Analysis prepared by **Jason N. Asaeda** on October 22, 2008, when the stock traded at **$ 24.58**.

## Highlights

➤ We project net sales to rise 4% in FY 09 (Aug.) to $7.28 billion. FDO plans to open 125 net new stores, which we estimate will increase total selling square footage by approximately 2%. In an effort to drive sales, we look for the company to maintain a merchandising focus on food and other consumables, to improve its treasure-hunt assortments, and to increase the number of stores that take credit card payments. Balancing these positive factors against a challenging macro-economic environment, we look for same-store sales to rise about 2% in FY 09.

➤ We anticipate gross margin pressure from an increased sales penetration of lower-margin consumables, partially offset by FDO's ongoing efforts to reduce inventory shrinkage, to expand its private label merchandise offerings, and to improve initial mark-ups through global sourcing. We expect the company to achieve modest operating margin expansion on tighter cost controls and expense leverage off of projected same-store sales growth.

➤ Assuming no activity under FDO's $133 million share repurchase authorization, we see FY 09 operating EPS of $1.78.

## Investment Rationale/Risk

➤ Our strong buy recommendation is based on valuation. We look for FDO to weather tough retail conditions over the next year through a merchandising focus on everyday necessities and effective inventory management of more discretionary categories, which we believe will limit the company's markdown exposure. We also believe that FDO will likely gain incremental business from consumers trading down from higher-priced supermarkets, drug stores, and convenience stores. In addition, we note easier same-store sales comparisons for the company in FY 09 and expect to see a lift average customer transaction amounts, a same-store sales driver, from its plan to accept credit card payments in roughly half its chain this holiday season.

➤ Risks to our recommendation and target price include sales shortfalls due to changes in consumer confidence, spending habits, and buying preferences; merchandise availability; and increased promotional activity by competitors.

➤ We derive our 12-month target price of $31 by applying FDO's five-year historical median forward P/E multiple of 17.0X to our calendar 2009 operating EPS estimate of $1.80.

## Qualitative Risk Assessment

| LOW | MEDIUM | HIGH |
|---|---|---|

Our risk assessment reflects our view of FDO's earnings erosion in recent years, partly a result of difficult economic conditions for core lower-income customers. This is offset by what we consider promising new merchandising and productivity initiatives that should, in our opinion, boost sales and profit margins going forward.

## Quantitative Evaluations

**S&P Quality Ranking** A+

| D | C | B- | B | B+ | A- | A | A+ |
|---|---|---|---|---|---|---|---|

**Relative Strength Rank** STRONG

96

LOWEST = 1    HIGHEST = 99

## Revenue/Earnings Data

**Revenue (Million $)**

| | 1Q | 2Q | 3Q | 4Q | Year |
|---|---|---|---|---|---|
| 2008 | 1,683 | 1,833 | 1,702 | 1,766 | 6,984 |
| 2007 | 1,600 | 1,947 | 1,655 | 1,632 | 6,834 |
| 2006 | 1,511 | 1,736 | 1,570 | 1,578 | 6,395 |
| 2005 | 1,380 | 1,587 | 1,428 | 1,430 | 5,825 |
| 2004 | 1,245 | 1,403 | 1,310 | 1,324 | 5,282 |
| 2003 | 1,109 | 1,256 | 1,177 | 1,208 | 4,750 |

**Earnings Per Share ($)**

| | | | | | |
|---|---|---|---|---|---|
| 2008 | 0.37 | 0.45 | 0.46 | 0.38 | 1.66 |
| 2007 | 0.36 | 0.60 | 0.40 | 0.26 | 1.62 |
| 2006 | 0.32 | 0.35 | 0.37 | 0.21 | 1.26 |
| 2005 | 0.32 | 0.48 | 0.32 | 0.18 | 1.30 |
| 2004 | 0.37 | 0.47 | 0.43 | 0.26 | 1.53 |
| 2003 | 0.33 | 0.42 | 0.40 | 0.28 | 1.43 |

Fiscal year ended Aug. 31. Next earnings report expected: NA. EPS Estimates based on S&P Operating Earnings; historical GAAP earnings are as reported.

## Dividend Data (Dates: mm/dd Payment Date: mm/dd/yy)

| Amount ($) | Date Decl. | Ex-Div. Date | Stk. of Record | Payment Date |
|---|---|---|---|---|
| 0.115 | 11/05 | 12/12 | 12/14 | 01/15/08 |
| 0.125 | 01/17 | 03/12 | 03/14 | 04/15/08 |
| 0.125 | 04/25 | 06/11 | 06/13 | 07/15/08 |
| 0.125 | 08/21 | 09/11 | 09/15 | 10/15/08 |

Dividends have been paid since 1976. Source: Company reports.

---

**Please read the Required Disclosures and Analyst Certification on the last page of this report.**

The McGraw-Hill Companies

# Family Dollar Stores Inc.

**STANDARD &POOR'S**

## Business Summary October 22, 2008

CORPORATE OVERVIEW. FDO operates a chain of over 6,500 retail discount stores in 44 states. The company describes its typical customer as a woman in her mid-40s who is the head of her household and has an annual income of under $30,000. Family Dollar stores carry an assortment of hardlines and softlines priced from under $1 to $10 and are operated on a self-service basis, with limited advertising support and promotional activity. The once cash-only stores now accept PIN-based debit card payments in most locations. Food stamp and credit card acceptance is also being rolled out. In our view, broader tender options offer the company an opportunity to improve its share of customer wallet as shopping is more convenient and available cash does not limit basket size.

PRIMARY BUSINESS DYNAMICS. FDO's primary growth drivers are same-store sales (sales results for stores open more than 13 months) and new store openings. In our opinion, the company is driving higher average customer transaction amounts through expanded offerings of frequently purchased hardline consumables such as food, household chemicals and paper products, as well as the addition of opportunistically purchased treasure-hunt items, which added interest to the merchandise mix over the past two years. However, FDO believes macro-economic concerns have prompted its cus-

tomers to consolidate shopping trips in recent years. As a result, annual same-store sales growth weakened from an average 2.6% from FY 04 (Aug.) through FY 06, to 0.9% in FY 07. Same-store sales strengthened in FY 09, rising 1.2%, partially supported by customer spending of fiscal stimulus checks, we think.

FDO continues to be one of the fastest growing retail chains in the U.S. The company's stores are located in rural, small town, suburban, and, increasingly, urban markets. A relatively small store size enables FDO to open new stores in locations that provide neighborhood convenience to its customers in each of these markets. Existing stores are either freestanding or located in shopping centers. From FY 00 through FY 05, the company increased its store count from 3,689 to 5,898 -- a compound annual growth rate (CAGR) of nearly 10%. Since FY 06, FDO has slowed its pace of expansion in an effort to improve the timing of store openings over the course of the year.

## Company Financials Fiscal Year Ended Aug. 31

| Per Share Data ($) | 2008 | 2007 | 2006 | 2005 | 2004 | 2003 | 2002 | 2001 | 2000 | 1999 |
|---|---|---|---|---|---|---|---|---|---|---|
| Tangible Book Value | 8.98 | 8.19 | 8.04 | 8.64 | 8.13 | 7.61 | 6.66 | 5.57 | 4.66 | 4.00 |
| Cash Flow | NA | 2.59 | 2.13 | 1.99 | 2.10 | 1.94 | 1.69 | 1.49 | 1.31 | 1.06 |
| Earnings | 1.66 | 1.62 | 1.26 | 1.30 | 1.53 | 1.43 | 1.25 | 1.10 | 1.00 | 0.81 |
| S&P Core Earnings | 1.66 | 1.71 | 1.44 | 1.21 | 1.45 | 1.39 | 1.22 | 1.08 | NA | NA |
| Dividends | NA | 0.44 | 0.40 | 0.36 | 0.32 | 0.28 | 0.25 | 0.23 | 0.22 | 0.20 |
| Payout Ratio | NA | 27% | 31% | 28% | 21% | 20% | 20% | 21% | 21% | 24% |
| Prices:High | NA | 35.42 | 30.91 | 35.25 | 39.66 | 44.13 | 37.25 | 31.35 | 24.50 | 26.75 |
| Prices:Low | NA | 17.95 | 21.57 | 19.40 | 25.09 | 25.46 | 23.75 | 18.38 | 14.25 | 14.00 |
| P/E Ratio:High | NA | 22 | 24 | 27 | 26 | 31 | 30 | 29 | 25 | 33 |
| P/E Ratio:Low | NA | 11 | 17 | 15 | 16 | 18 | 19 | 17 | 14 | 17 |

| Income Statement Analysis (Million $) | 2008 | 2007 | 2006 | 2005 | 2004 | 2003 | 2002 | 2001 | 2000 | 1999 |
|---|---|---|---|---|---|---|---|---|---|---|
| Revenue | 6,984 | 6,834 | 6,395 | 5,825 | 5,282 | 4,750 | 4,163 | 3,665 | 3,133 | 2,751 |
| Operating Income | NA | 532 | 452 | 458 | 512 | 478 | 419 | 366 | 325 | 266 |
| Depreciation | 150 | 144 | 135 | 115 | 97.9 | 88.3 | 77.0 | 67.7 | 54.5 | 43.8 |
| Interest Expense | NA | 17.0 | 13.1 | Nil | Nil | Nil | Nil | Nil | Nil | Nil |
| Pretax Income | 362 | 382 | 311 | 343 | 414 | 390 | 342 | 298 | 271 | 223 |
| Effective Tax Rate | 35.6% | 36.4% | 37.3% | 36.5% | 36.6% | 36.5% | 36.5% | 36.5% | 36.5% | 37.1% |
| Net Income | 233 | 243 | 195 | 218 | 263 | 247 | 217 | 190 | 172 | 140 |
| S&P Core Earnings | 233 | 257 | 223 | 202 | 250 | 241 | 213 | 186 | NA | NA |

| Balance Sheet & Other Financial Data (Million $) | 2008 | 2007 | 2006 | 2005 | 2004 | 2003 | 2002 | 2001 | 2000 | 1999 |
|---|---|---|---|---|---|---|---|---|---|---|
| Cash | 159 | 87.0 | 79.7 | 105 | 150 | 207 | 220 | 21.8 | 43.6 | 95.3 |
| Current Assets | NA | 1,537 | 1,419 | 1,355 | 1,225 | 1,156 | 1,056 | 807 | 751 | 720 |
| Total Assets | 2,662 | 2,624 | 2,523 | 2,410 | 2,167 | 1,986 | 1,755 | 1,400 | 1,244 | 1,095 |
| Current Liabilities | NA | 1,130 | 986 | 895 | 714 | 595 | 531 | 390 | 412 | 379 |
| Long Term Debt | NA | 250 | 250 | Nil | Nil | Nil | Nil | Nil | Nil | Nil |
| Common Equity | 1,254 | 1,175 | 1,208 | 2,187 | 1,360 | 1,533 | 1,245 | 959 | 798 | 691 |
| Total Capital | NA | 1,494 | 1,537 | 2,274 | 1,454 | 1,612 | 1,314 | 1,009 | 832 | 717 |
| Capital Expenditures | 168 | 132 | 192 | 229 | 218 | 220 | 187 | 163 | 172 | 125 |
| Cash Flow | NA | 387 | 330 | 332 | 361 | 336 | 294 | 257 | 227 | 184 |
| Current Ratio | 1.3 | 1.4 | 1.4 | 1.5 | 1.7 | 1.9 | 2.0 | 2.1 | 1.8 | 1.9 |
| % Long Term Debt of Capitalization | 16.6 | 16.7 | 16.2 | Nil | Nil | Nil | Nil | Nil | Nil | Nil |
| % Net Income of Revenue | 3.3 | 3.5 | 3.1 | 3.7 | 5.0 | 5.2 | 5.2 | 5.2 | 5.5 | 5.1 |
| % Return on Assets | 8.8 | 9.4 | 7.9 | 9.4 | 12.7 | 13.2 | 13.8 | 14.3 | 14.7 | 13.7 |
| % Return on Equity | 19.2 | 20.3 | 8.9 | 10.6 | 19.7 | 17.8 | 18.9 | 21.6 | 23.1 | 22.1 |

Data as orig reptd.; bef. results of disc opers/spec. items. Per share data adj. for stk. divs.; EPS diluted. E-Estimated. NA-Not Available. NM-Not Meaningful. NR-Not Ranked. UR-Under Review.

**Office:** 10401 Monroe Rd, Matthews, NC 28201.
**Telephone:** 704-847-6961.
**Website:** http://www.familydollar.com
**Chrmn & CEO:** H.R. Levine

**Pres & COO:** R.J. Kelly
**SVP & CFO:** K.T. Smith
**SVP & Chief Acctg Officer:** C.M. Sowers
**SVP, Secy & General Counsel:** J.G. Kelley

**Investor Contact:** K.F. Rawlins (704-849-7496)
**Board Members:** M. R. Bernstein, S. A. Decker, E. C. Dolby, G. A. Eisenberg, H. R. Levine, G. R. Mahoney, Jr., J. G. Martin, H. Morgan, D. Pond

**Founded:** 1959
**Domicile:** Delaware
**Employees:** 44,000

The **McGraw·Hill** Companies

# Fastenal Company

**STANDARD &POOR'S**

| S&P Recommendation | STRONG BUY ★★★★★ | Price<br>$33.32 (as of Nov 14, 2008) | 12-Mo. Target Price<br>$61.00 | Investment Style<br>Large-Cap Growth |
|---|---|---|---|---|

**GICS Sector** Industrials
**Sub-Industry** Trading Companies & Distributors

**Summary** This company distributes fasteners and other industrial and construction supplies through 2,300 stores throughout the U.S., and in a few foreign countries.

## Key Stock Statistics (Source S&P, Vickers, company reports)

| | | | | | | | |
|---|---|---|---|---|---|---|---|
| 52-Wk Range | $56.48– 31.52 | S&P Oper. EPS 2008**E** | 1.95 | Market Capitalization(B) | $4.949 | Beta | 0.93 |
| Trailing 12-Month EPS | $1.83 | S&P Oper. EPS 2009**E** | 2.35 | Yield (%) | 1.62 | S&P 3-Yr. Proj. EPS CAGR(%) | 22 |
| Trailing 12-Month P/E | 18.2 | P/E on S&P Oper. EPS 2008**E** | 17.1 | Dividend Rate/Share | $0.54 | S&P Credit Rating | NA |
| $10K Invested 5 Yrs Ago | $14,990 | Common Shares Outstg. (M) | 148.5 | Institutional Ownership (%) | 77 | | |

## Price Performance

30-Week Mov. Avg. · · · 10-Week Mov. Avg. - - **GAAP Earnings vs. Previous Year** Volume Above Avg. STARS
12-Mo. Target Price — Relative Strength — ▲ Up ▼ Down ► No Change Below Avg. ★

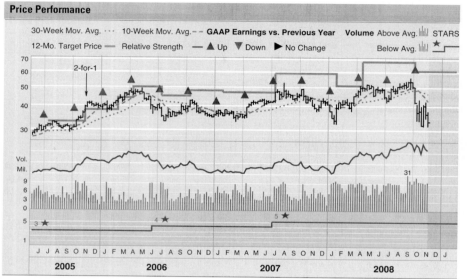

Options: ASE, CBOE, P

Analysis prepared by **Michael W. Jaffe** on October 21, 2008, when the stock traded at **$ 40.03**.

## Highlights

► We expect sales to rise 16% in 2009, despite challenges being seen in the U.S. economy. We see this increase being driven by store openings, the maturation of sites, market share gains, expanded product offerings, and the conversion of sites to a more customer-friendly format. However, we anticipate FAST's sources of sales growth shifting in coming periods, as it announced a new strategy in July 2007 where it is slowing its rate of store growth while increasing the size of the sales staff at its stores.

► We look for slightly wider net margins in 2009, on the improved sales that we forecast, a better product mix, and an ongoing focus on cost controls. We also see margins being aided by cost savings related to the completion of FAST's shift in store models to a more customer-friendly format, and lower occupancy costs driven by its new plan to reduce the level of new stores.

► Our $1.95 a share forecast for 2008 excludes a $0.03 a share third-quarter charge for a preliminary settlement of a class action suit, which was mostly related to overtime provisions for assistant general managers in certain states. In announcing the agreement, FAST said it continued to deny the allegations.

## Investment Rationale/Risk

► We see FAST posting revenue and EPS gains through at least 2009, despite major challenges in the U.S. economy and the industrial markets served by the company. We see these forecasted gains driven in part by Fastenal's recent change in strategy, under which it is now striving to attain sales and margin growth through larger sales staffs and a lower rate of new store openings. We also think its new model will enable FAST to grow its sales and earnings further into the future, as it will be able to expand its store base for a longer period. Based on these factors and our valuation considerations, we find the shares undervalued.

► Risks to our recommendation and target price include a weaker-than-expected U.S. economy, and an unsuccessful change in business model.

► The shares recently traded at 17X our 2009 EPS estimate, a large premium to the S&P 500, but near the bottom of FAST's range for the past decade. Given Fastenal's typically strong profit growth, our very positive view of its recent strategy change, and our forecast of solid EPS gains in coming periods, we think a higher P/E multiple is merited. Our 12-month target price is $61, or 26X our 2009 EPS forecast.

## Qualitative Risk Assessment

| LOW | MEDIUM | HIGH |
|---|---|---|

Our risk assessment for FAST reflects our view of its consistent generation of solid levels of free cash flow, a healthy balance sheet with no long-term debt, and a very well-run business model, with a strong focus on growth and cost controls. This is offset by the cyclical nature of FAST's business, its premium valuation and uncertainties in its recently announced change in business model, to one with less store unit growth and larger sales staffs.

## Quantitative Evaluations

**S&P Quality Ranking**  A

| D | C | B- | B | B+ | A- | A | A+ |
|---|---|---|---|---|---|---|---|

**Relative Strength Rank**  MODERATE

51

LOWEST = 1      HIGHEST = 99

## Revenue/Earnings Data

**Revenue (Million $)**

| | 1Q | 2Q | 3Q | 4Q | Year |
|---|---|---|---|---|---|
| 2008 | 566.2 | 604.2 | 625.0 | -- | -- |
| 2007 | 489.2 | 519.7 | 533.8 | 519.2 | 2,062 |
| 2006 | 431.7 | 458.8 | 470.1 | 448.7 | 1,809 |
| 2005 | 353.8 | 383.3 | 402.2 | 384.0 | 1,523 |
| 2004 | 284.2 | 310.1 | 325.7 | 318.5 | 1,238 |
| 2003 | 235.8 | 249.1 | 258.3 | 251.6 | 994.9 |

**Earnings Per Share ($)**

| | | | | | |
|---|---|---|---|---|---|
| 2008 | 0.46 | 0.51 | 0.49 | E0.46 | E1.95 |
| 2007 | 0.36 | 0.40 | 0.41 | 0.38 | 1.55 |
| 2006 | 0.32 | 0.34 | 0.36 | 0.30 | 1.32 |
| 2005 | 0.25 | 0.29 | 0.31 | 0.26 | 1.10 |
| 2004 | 0.19 | 0.23 | 0.23 | 0.22 | 0.86 |
| 2003 | 0.13 | 0.15 | 0.16 | 0.13 | 0.56 |

Fiscal year ended Dec. 31. Next earnings report expected: Late January. EPS Estimates based on S&P Operating Earnings; historical GAAP earnings are as reported.

## Dividend Data (Dates: mm/dd Payment Date: mm/dd/yy)

| Amount<br>($) | Date<br>Decl. | Ex-Div.<br>Date | Stk. of<br>Record | Payment<br>Date |
|---|---|---|---|---|
| 0.250 | 01/21 | 02/21 | 02/25 | 02/29/08 |
| 0.270 | 07/10 | 08/14 | 08/18 | 08/29/08 |

Dividends have been paid since 1991. Source: Company reports.

---

**Please read the Required Disclosures and Analyst Certification on the last page of this report.**

The McGraw·Hill Companies

# Fastenal Company

STANDARD
&POOR'S

## Business Summary October 21, 2008

CORPORATE OVERVIEW. Fastenal, which sells industrial and construction supplies, began operations in 1967, with a plan to supply threaded fasteners in small- to medium-size cities. It later changed its business plan to include some sites in large cities. At the end of 2007, FAST had 2,160 stores in all 50 states, Puerto Rico, Canada, Mexico, Singapore, China and the Netherlands (1,969 in the U.S.), up 8.0% from 2,000 sites a year earlier. The company's store count had grown to 2,300 at September 30, 2008. Over 70% of the company's stores were opened in the past decade. The closing of a store site during 2007's second quarter marked only the 11th site closed in FAST's history, and three of these were later reopened. FAST distributes products to its store sites from 13 distribution centers, with 11 located throughout the U.S., one in Canada and one in Mexico. Threaded fasteners accounted for 46% of 2007 sales (46% in 2006).

The company offered 10 product lines at the end of 2007, and plans to add more lines in the future. Its original product line now consists of about 349,000 different types of threaded fasteners and supplies. Other product lines offered include 119,000 different types of tools and equipment; 204,000 different cutting tool blades and abrasives; 49,000 types of fluid transfer components and accessories for hydraulic and pneumatic power, plumbing, and heating, ventilating and air-conditioning; 12,000 types of material handling, storage and packaging products; 13,000 kinds of janitorial supplies, chemicals and paint; 19,000 types of electrical supplies; 28,000 welding supply items; 23,000 different safety supplies; and 9,000 types of metals, alloys and materials. FAST sells mostly to customers in the construction industry, and in the manufacturing market for both OEMs and maintenance and repair operations. Its construction customers serve general construction, electrical, plumbing, sheet metal, and road contractor markets.

Most products sold are made by other companies. No supplier accounted for over 5% of FAST's 2007 purchases. No customer accounts for a significant portion of total sales.

COMPETITIVE LANDSCAPE. Fastenal's business is highly competitive. Competition includes both large distributors located primarily in large cities and smaller distributors located in many of the cities in which the company has stores. FAST believes that the principal competitive factors affecting the markets for its products are customer service and convenience.

## Company Financials Fiscal Year Ended Dec. 31

| Per Share Data ($) | 2007 | 2006 | 2005 | 2004 | 2003 | 2002 | 2001 | 2000 | 1999 | 1998 |
|---|---|---|---|---|---|---|---|---|---|---|
| Tangible Book Value | 6.76 | 6.10 | 5.19 | 4.51 | 3.80 | 3.30 | 2.80 | 2.37 | 1.86 | 1.44 |
| Cash Flow | 1.79 | 1.54 | 1.29 | 1.02 | 0.69 | 0.60 | 0.56 | 0.61 | 0.51 | 0.42 |
| Earnings | 1.55 | 1.32 | 1.10 | 0.86 | 0.56 | 0.50 | 0.46 | 0.53 | 0.43 | 0.35 |
| S&P Core Earnings | 1.55 | 1.32 | 1.10 | 0.86 | 0.55 | 0.45 | 0.47 | NA | NA | NA |
| Dividends | 0.44 | 0.40 | 0.31 | 0.20 | 0.11 | 0.03 | 0.02 | 0.02 | 0.01 | 0.01 |
| Payout Ratio | 28% | 30% | 28% | 23% | 19% | 5% | 5% | 4% | 2% | 1% |
| Prices:High | 52.94 | 49.32 | 41.96 | 32.25 | 25.50 | 21.68 | 18.25 | 18.33 | 15.14 | 14.22 |
| Prices:Low | 33.05 | 33.18 | 25.54 | 21.94 | 13.76 | 13.31 | 11.73 | 8.92 | 8.41 | 5.13 |
| P/E Ratio:High | 34 | 37 | 38 | 37 | 46 | 44 | 40 | 34 | 35 | 41 |
| P/E Ratio:Low | 21 | 25 | 23 | 26 | 25 | 27 | 26 | 17 | 19 | 15 |

| Income Statement Analysis (Million $) | | | | | | | | | | |
|---|---|---|---|---|---|---|---|---|---|---|
| Revenue | 2,062 | 1,809 | 1,523 | 1,238 | 995 | 905 | 818 | 746 | 609 | 503 |
| Operating Income | 414 | 354 | 297 | 231 | 156 | 131 | 127 | 141 | 117 | 98.1 |
| Depreciation | 37.4 | 33.5 | 29.0 | 23.6 | 20.4 | 16.9 | 15.0 | 11.8 | 11.8 | 11.0 |
| Interest Expense | Nil | Nil | Nil | Nil | Nil | Nil | Nil | Nil | 0.06 | 1.05 |
| Pretax Income | 378 | 321 | 269 | 208 | 136 | 121 | 114 | 131 | 106 | 86.1 |
| Effective Tax Rate | 38.4% | 38.0% | 38.0% | 37.1% | 38.3% | 38.3% | 38.3% | 38.6% | 38.5% | 38.5% |
| Net Income | 233 | 199 | 167 | 131 | 84.1 | 74.8 | 70.7 | 80.7 | 65.5 | 53.0 |
| S&P Core Earnings | 233 | 199 | 167 | 131 | 82.6 | 68.5 | 70.3 | NA | NA | NA |

| Balance Sheet & Other Financial Data (Million $) | | | | | | | | | | |
|---|---|---|---|---|---|---|---|---|---|---|
| Cash | 57.4 | 33.9 | 70.1 | 74.5 | 95.6 | 51.4 | 68.5 | 32.7 | 28.1 | 2.35 |
| Current Assets | 881 | 768 | 649 | 538 | 454 | 396 | 341 | 293 | 227 | 173 |
| Total Assets | 1,163 | 1,039 | 890 | 1,308 | 652 | 559 | 475 | 402 | 319 | 251 |
| Current Liabilities | 138 | 104 | 91.5 | 71.2 | 60.9 | 47.1 | 40.6 | 36.6 | 33.7 | 30.8 |
| Long Term Debt | Nil | Nil | Nil | Nil | Nil | Nil | Nil | Nil | Nil | Nil |
| Common Equity | 1,010 | 922 | 784 | 684 | 577 | 504 | 425 | 359 | 282 | 218 |
| Total Capital | 1,025 | 935 | 798 | 699 | 591 | 516 | 435 | 366 | 285 | 220 |
| Capital Expenditures | 55.8 | 77.6 | 65.9 | 52.7 | 50.2 | 42.7 | 45.3 | 36.7 | 39.2 | 37.2 |
| Cash Flow | 270 | 233 | 196 | 155 | 105 | 91.8 | 85.1 | 92.5 | 77.2 | 64.0 |
| Current Ratio | 6.4 | 7.4 | 7.1 | 7.6 | 7.5 | 8.4 | 8.4 | 8.0 | 6.8 | 5.6 |
| % Long Term Debt of Capitalization | Nil | Nil | Nil | Nil | Nil | Nil | Nil | Nil | Nil | Nil |
| % Net Income of Revenue | 11.3 | 11.0 | 11.0 | 10.6 | 8.5 | 8.3 | 8.6 | 10.8 | 10.7 | 10.5 |
| % Return on Assets | 21.1 | 20.6 | 20.0 | 10.9 | 13.9 | 14.5 | 16.0 | 22.4 | 23.0 | 23.2 |
| % Return on Equity | 24.1 | 23.3 | 22.7 | 20.8 | 15.6 | 16.1 | 17.9 | 25.2 | 26.2 | 27.6 |

Data as orig reptd.; bef. results of disc opers/spec. items. Per share data adj. for stk. divs.; EPS diluted. E-Estimated. NA-Not Available. NM-Not Meaningful. NR-Not Ranked. UR-Under Review.

**Office:** 2001 Theurer Boulevard, Winona, MN 55987-0978.
**Telephone:** 507-454-5374.
**Email:** info@fastenal.com
**Website:** http://www.fastenal.com

**Chrmn:** R.A. Kierlin
**Pres & CEO:** W.D. Oberton
**EVP, CFO, Chief Acctg Officer & Treas:** D.L. Florness

**Board Members:** M. J. Dolan, M. M. Gostomski, R. A. Hansen, R. A. Kierlin, H. K. McConnon, H. L. Miller, W. D. Oberton, S. M. Slaggie, R. K. Wisecup

**Founded:** 1968
**Domicile:** Minnesota
**Employees:** 12,013

The McGraw-Hill Companies

# Federated Investors Inc.

**STANDARD &POOR'S**

| S&P Recommendation HOLD ★★★★★ | Price $20.96 (as of Nov 14, 2008) | 12-Mo. Target Price $25.00 | Investment Style Large-Cap Growth |
|---|---|---|---|

**GICS Sector** Financials
**Sub-Industry** Asset Management & Custody Banks

**Summary** This leading U.S. investment management company has a strong market share in money market products.

## Key Stock Statistics (Source S&P, Vickers, company reports)

| | | | | | | | |
|---|---|---|---|---|---|---|---|
| 52-Wk Range | $45.01– 17.17 | S&P Oper. EPS 2008E | 2.22 | Market Capitalization(B) | $2.134 | Beta | 0.93 |
| Trailing 12-Month EPS | $2.20 | S&P Oper. EPS 2009E | 2.27 | Yield (%) | 4.58 | S&P 3-Yr. Proj. EPS CAGR(%) | 6 |
| Trailing 12-Month P/E | 9.5 | P/E on S&P Oper. EPS 2008E | 9.4 | Dividend Rate/Share | $0.96 | S&P Credit Rating | NA |
| $10K Invested 5 Yrs Ago | $9,116 | Common Shares Outstg. (M) | 101.8 | Institutional Ownership (%) | 71 | | |

## Price Performance

30-Week Mov. Avg. · · · 10-Week Mov. Avg. — **GAAP Earnings vs. Previous Year** Volume Above Avg. STARS
12-Mo. Target Price — Relative Strength — ▲ Up ▼ Down ► No Change Below Avg. ★

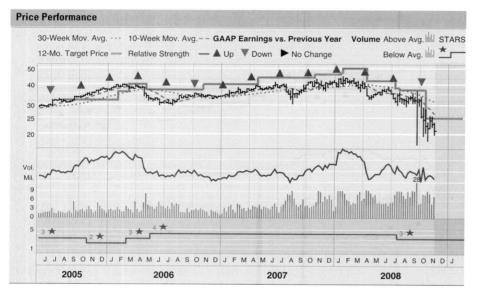

Options: ASE, CBOE

Analysis prepared by **Matthew Albrecht** on October 29, 2008, when the stock traded at **$ 24.97**.

## Highlights

➤ Federated has benefited from recent volatility in the markets, in our view, and money market and ultra-short term bond products have seen strong flows from investors. We think the company may be challenged to retain money market assets when investors again look to invest in equity and debt products, but near-term sentiment suggests to us that we are not at that point yet. We also believe recent government guarantees of money market mutual funds have restored confidence for those products. We expect continued pressure on management fee rates due to an unfavorable asset mix in 2008. We look for growth in assets under management of more than 15% in 2008, but we expect a decline in 2009.

➤ We forecast a decline in the pretax margin in 2008, as continued inflows should result in an increase in marketing and distribution costs, but margins could improve in 2009 as sales slow and underwriting costs come down .We believe compensation costs will remain at about 20% of revenues on a percentage basis for the foreseeable future.

➤ We forecast earnings of $2.22 in 2008 and $2.27 in 2009, aided by modest share repurchases.

## Investment Rationale/Risk

➤ We view a slightly discounted valuation on the shares relative to peers as appropriate, given the firm's focus on lower-margined money market funds. We view favorably the company's direct sales force and strong relationships with wholesalers and intermediaries in our valuation. We also applaud the recent moves to increase FII's exposure to equities, which should help margins. We have a positive view of the company's common share repurchase program, which we estimate could exceed 4 million shares per year.

➤ Risks to our recommendation and target price include potentially increased competition, lower short-term interest rates, and weaker equity fund performance. From a corporate governance perspective, we would like to see a greater percentage of independent directors on the board.

➤ The shares have benefited from market volatility, which has investors seeking safe havens for their cash, and have outperformed the peer group year to date. They recently traded at about 11.3X our 2008 EPS estimate. Our 12-month target price of $25 is equal to 11.0X our 2009 EPS estimate, in line with peers.

## Qualitative Risk Assessment

| LOW | MEDIUM | HIGH |
|---|---|---|

Our risk assessment reflects the company's relatively narrow product offering and significant competition from larger, more diversified fund management companies.

## Quantitative Evaluations

**S&P Quality Ranking** A

| D | C | B- | B | B+ | A- | A | A+ |
|---|---|---|---|---|---|---|---|

**Relative Strength Rank** MODERATE

50

LOWEST = 1          HIGHEST = 99

## Revenue/Earnings Data

**Revenue (Million $)**

| | 1Q | 2Q | 3Q | 4Q | Year |
|---|---|---|---|---|---|
| 2008 | 305.7 | 310.3 | 305.9 | -- | -- |
| 2007 | 264.4 | 276.5 | 286.0 | 300.3 | 1,128 |
| 2006 | 238.8 | 236.4 | 243.9 | 259.7 | 978.9 |
| 2005 | 205.4 | 220.7 | 241.4 | 241.8 | 909.2 |
| 2004 | 220.7 | 213.1 | 205.2 | 208.1 | 847.0 |
| 2003 | 194.1 | 202.5 | 210.0 | 216.8 | 823.3 |

**Earnings Per Share ($)**

| | | | | | |
|---|---|---|---|---|---|
| 2008 | 0.55 | 0.55 | 0.56 | E0.56 | E2.22 |
| 2007 | 0.50 | 0.54 | 0.57 | 0.52 | 2.12 |
| 2006 | 0.43 | 0.44 | 0.43 | 0.51 | 1.80 |
| 2005 | 0.07 | 0.35 | 0.61 | 0.48 | 1.51 |
| 2004 | 0.46 | 0.44 | 0.43 | 0.29 | 1.62 |
| 2003 | 0.43 | 0.44 | 0.46 | 0.38 | 1.71 |

Fiscal year ended Dec. 31. Next earnings report expected: Late January. EPS Estimates based on S&P Operating Earnings; historical GAAP earnings are as reported.

## Dividend Data (Dates: mm/dd Payment Date: mm/dd/yy)

| Amount ($) | Date Decl. | Ex-Div. Date | Stk. of Record | Payment Date |
|---|---|---|---|---|
| 0.240 | 04/24 | 05/06 | 05/08 | 05/15/08 |
| 0.240 | 07/24 | 08/06 | 08/08 | 08/15/08 |
| 2.76 Spl. | 08/19 | 09/05 | 09/09 | 09/15/08 |
| 0.240 | 10/23 | 11/05 | 11/07 | 11/14/08 |

Dividends have been paid since 1998. Source: Company reports.

---

**Please read the Required Disclosures and Analyst Certification on the last page of this report.**

The McGraw-Hill Companies

# Federated Investors Inc.

**STANDARD &POOR'S**

## Business Summary October 29, 2008

CORPORATE OVERVIEW. A leading provider of investment management products and related financial services, Federated Investors (FII) has been in the mutual fund business for more than 40 years. The company is one of the largest mutual fund managers in the United States, based on assets under management. Assets under management at the end of 2007 totaled $302 billion, up from $237 billion at the end of 2006.

Federated manages assets across a wide range of asset categories, including increasing participation in fast-growing areas such as equity and international investments. It is among the industry leaders in money market funds, based on assets under management, and offers one of the industry's most comprehensive product lines. Assets under management by class at the end of 2007 included money market (78% of total), equity (14%), and fixed income (8%). By product type, mutual funds represented about 87% of total assets under management, with the balance held in separately managed accounts.

CORPORATE STRATEGY. Over the past several years, Federated has added

several investment professionals and strengthened its equity and fixed-income product portfolio, in our opinion. The company has more than 170 investment professionals, which includes portfolio managers, analysts and traders. The company ended 2007 with 148 mutual funds and various separately managed accounts. FII has managed institutional separate accounts since 1973, and is focused on growing its managed account business for high-net-worth individuals with investable equity assets of $100,000 or more.

Federated believes that it benefits from a developing industry trend toward intermediary assisted sales (sales of mutual fund products through a financial intermediary), driven by the wide array of options now available to investors, and by a need for financial planning advice that has resulted from a recent increase in the average household's financial assets.

## Company Financials Fiscal Year Ended Dec. 31

| Per Share Data ($) | 2007 | 2006 | 2005 | 2004 | 2003 | 2002 | 2001 | 2000 | 1999 | 1998 |
|---|---|---|---|---|---|---|---|---|---|---|
| Tangible Book Value | 0.53 | 0.39 | 1.59 | 1.36 | 2.05 | 1.46 | 0.79 | 0.86 | 0.62 | 0.28 |
| Cash Flow | 2.37 | 2.07 | 1.75 | 1.79 | 1.95 | 1.90 | 1.65 | 1.40 | 1.10 | 0.88 |
| Earnings | 2.12 | 1.80 | 1.51 | 1.62 | 1.71 | 1.74 | 1.44 | 1.27 | 0.96 | 0.71 |
| S&P Core Earnings | 2.16 | 1.80 | 1.67 | 1.70 | 1.67 | 1.69 | 1.46 | NA | NA | NA |
| Dividends | 0.81 | 0.69 | 0.58 | 0.41 | 0.30 | 0.22 | 0.22 | 0.14 | 0.11 | 0.05 |
| Payout Ratio | 38% | 38% | 38% | 26% | 17% | 12% | 15% | 11% | 11% | 7% |
| Prices:High | 43.35 | 40.17 | 38.11 | 33.79 | 31.90 | 36.18 | 32.80 | 31.69 | 14.12 | 13.46 |
| Prices:Low | 30.31 | 29.56 | 26.99 | 26.72 | 23.85 | 23.43 | 23.31 | 12.46 | 10.04 | 7.33 |
| P/E Ratio:High | 20 | 22 | 25 | 21 | 19 | 21 | 23 | 25 | 15 | 19 |
| P/E Ratio:Low | 14 | 16 | 18 | 16 | 14 | 13 | 16 | 10 | 10 | 10 |

| Income Statement Analysis (Million $) | | | | | | | | | | |
|---|---|---|---|---|---|---|---|---|---|---|
| Income Interest | 5.60 | 2.51 | 8.73 | 3.39 | 2.15 | 2.40 | 9.74 | 19.0 | 13.9 | 8.88 |
| Income Other | 1.20 | 7.02 | 0.05 | -0.11 | 0.00 | 2.27 | 706 | 662 | 587 | 513 |
| Total Income | 1,128 | 979 | 909 | 847 | 823 | 711 | 716 | 681 | 601 | 522 |
| General Expenses | 770 | 694 | 634 | 530 | 531 | 399 | 388 | 394 | 364 | 340 |
| Interest Expense | 5.40 | 8.19 | 17.9 | 21.0 | 4.71 | 4.79 | 29.7 | 34.2 | 31.8 | 27.6 |
| Depreciation | 25.6 | 24.1 | 24.0 | 19.0 | 20.6 | 19.2 | 26.0 | 15.8 | 18.1 | 22.9 |
| Net Income | 217 | 191 | 163 | 179 | 191 | 204 | 173 | 155 | 124 | 92.4 |
| S&P Core Earnings | 222 | 191 | 181 | 188 | 187 | 199 | 175 | NA | NA | NA |

| Balance Sheet & Other Financial Data (Million $) | | | | | | | | | | |
|---|---|---|---|---|---|---|---|---|---|---|
| Cash | 146 | 119 | 246 | 258 | 234 | 151 | 73.5 | 150 | 171 | 186 |
| Receivables | 37.3 | 23.3 | 45.8 | 33.8 | 38.3 | 31.2 | 32.6 | 36.9 | 35.2 | 31.0 |
| Cost of Investments | 25.9 | 16.2 | 38.4 | 2.10 | 1.53 | 1.00 | 4.60 | 85.3 | 66.4 | 13.4 |
| Total Assets | 841 | 810 | 897 | 955 | 879 | 530 | 432 | 705 | 673 | 580 |
| Loss Reserve | Nil | Nil | Nil | Nil | Nil | Nil | 0.32 | 0.09 | 0.18 | 1.27 |
| Short Term Debt | Nil | Nil | Nil | Nil | Nil | Nil | Nil | 14.3 | 14.3 | 0.24 |
| Capitalization:Debt | 63.0 | 113 | 160 | 285 | 328 | 59.2 | 55.0 | 394 | 394 | 372 |
| Capitalization:Equity | 574 | 529 | 540 | 458 | 396 | 341 | 237 | 148 | 119 | 88.7 |
| Capitalization:Total | 667 | 671 | 723 | 767 | 744 | 416 | 299 | 583 | 551 | 491 |
| Price Times Book Value:High | 81.8 | 103 | 24.0 | 24.8 | 15.6 | 24.8 | 41.5 | 36.7 | 22.0 | 49.0 |
| Price Times Book Value:Low | 57.2 | 76.0 | 17.0 | 19.6 | 11.6 | 16.0 | 29.5 | 14.5 | 16.0 | 27.0 |
| Cash Flow | 243 | 215 | 187 | 198 | 212 | 223 | 199 | 171 | 142 | 115 |
| % Expense/Operating Revenue | 68.3 | 71.7 | 71.7 | 65.1 | 65.1 | 56.7 | 58.4 | 62.9 | 65.9 | 70.4 |
| % Earnings & Depreciation/Assets | 29.4 | 25.2 | 20.2 | 19.5 | 25.3 | 46.4 | 35.0 | 24.8 | 22.7 | NA |

Data as orig reptd.; bef. results of disc opers/spec. items. Per share data adj. for stk. divs.; EPS diluted. E-Estimated. NA-Not Available. NM-Not Meaningful. NR-Not Ranked. UR-Under Review.

**Office:** Federated Investors Tower, Pittsburgh, PA 15222-3779.
**Telephone:** 412-288-1900.
**Email:** investors@federatedinv.com
**Website:** http://www.FederatedInvestors.com

**Chrmn:** J.F. Donahue
**Pres & CEO:** J.C. Donahue
**Vice Chrmn:** R.B. Fisher
**Vice Chrmn, EVP, Secy & General Counsel:** J.W. McGonigle

**CFO & Treas:** T.R. Donahue
**Investor Contact:** R. Hanley (412-288-1920)
**Board Members:** L. E. Auriana, J. F. Donahue, J. C. Donahue, M. J. Farrell, R. B. Fisher, D. M. Kelly, J. W. McGonigle, J. L. Murdy, E. G. O'Connor

**Founded:** 1955
**Domicile:** Pennsylvania
**Employees:** 1,270

# FedEx Corp.

STANDARD &POOR'S

| S&P Recommendation | BUY ★★★★☆ | Price $64.37 (as of Nov 14, 2008) | 12-Mo. Target Price $105.00 | Investment Style Large-Cap Growth |
| --- | --- | --- | --- | --- |

**GICS Sector** Industrials
**Sub-Industry** Air Freight & Logistics

**Summary** This company provides guaranteed domestic and international air express, residential and business ground package delivery, heavy freight and logistics services.

## Key Stock Statistics (Source S&P, Vickers, company reports)

| | | | | | | | |
| --- | --- | --- | --- | --- | --- | --- | --- |
| 52-Wk Range | $101.53– 53.90 | S&P Oper. EPS 2009**E** | 5.50 | Market Capitalization(B) | $20.035 | Beta | 0.78 |
| Trailing 12-Month EPS | $3.25 | S&P Oper. EPS 2010**E** | 6.10 | Yield (%) | 0.68 | S&P 3-Yr. Proj. EPS CAGR(%) | 8 |
| Trailing 12-Month P/E | 19.8 | P/E on S&P Oper. EPS 2009**E** | 11.7 | Dividend Rate/Share | $0.44 | S&P Credit Rating | BBB |
| $10K Invested 5 Yrs Ago | $8,524 | Common Shares Outstg. (M) | 311.2 | Institutional Ownership (%) | 79 | | |

## Price Performance

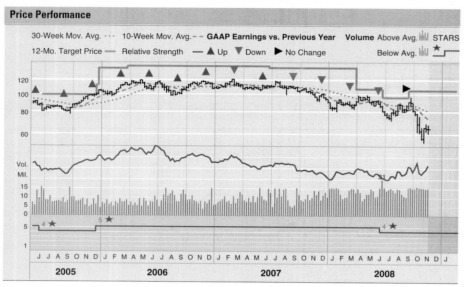

30-Week Mov. Avg. ···· 10-Week Mov. Avg. -- **GAAP Earnings vs. Previous Year** Volume Above Avg. STARS
12-Mo. Target Price — Relative Strength — ▲ Up ▼ Down ► No Change Below Avg. ★

Options: ASE, CBOE, P, PH

Analysis prepared by **Jim Corridore** on September 15, 2008, when the stock traded at **$ 91.72**.

## Highlights

➤ We expect FY 09 (May) revenues to rise 6%, aided by increased surcharges on the rising cost of fuel. We see the U.S. economy slowing, with the largest impact felt at FedEx Express. We project about 6% volume growth at FedEx Ground, with revenues up about 8%. We look for volumes to fall about 2% at Express, with 6% revenue growth, led by international. We see domestic Express volumes down about 4%. We estimate that international revenues will continue to rise in the double digits.

➤ We think operating margins will be hurt by higher fuel costs. However, a recent drop in the price of oil could lessen this impact. We see a mix shift toward more deferred products due to a weakening U.S. economy, and rising personnel costs at Ground due to changes related to disputes over the independent contractor model. The company is attempting to push lower margin shipments into ground and freight channels, which could also aid margins over the long term, freeing up Express capacity for higher-yielding international shipments.

➤ We forecast FY 09 operating EPS of $5.50, representing a 5.7% decline from FY 08's $5.83 (excl. $2.23 in one-time charges at Kinko's).

## Investment Rationale/Risk

➤ While we think FDX's results are likely to be hurt by the slowing U.S. economy, we believe the shares should benefit from increased interest in logistics stocks on any signs of economic improvement. However, we think risks that the economy could take longer to start to show improvement have risen. Our buy recommendation reflects our view that the shares are attractively valued relative to peers and the S&P 500 and have overcorrected on recent EPS misses and reduced guidance. FDX was recently trading at a P/E well below that of the S&P 500, while we expect that over the next three to five years the company's EPS is likely to increase faster than the overall market.

➤ Risks to our recommendation and target price include a possible price war or a recession. In addition, we are concerned about some of FDX's corporate governance practices, such as the presence of affiliated outsiders on the board of directors and the audit committee.

➤ Our 12-month target price of $105 values the shares at 19X our FY 09 EPS estimate of $5.50, near the lower end of the company's five-year historical P/E range of 13.7X-36.6X.

## Qualitative Risk Assessment

| LOW | MEDIUM | HIGH |
| --- | --- | --- |

Our risk assessment reflects our view of the company's strong and stable balance sheet, healthy cash flow generation, and strong earnings growth potential amid the inherent cyclicality of its business segment. This is only partly offset by the potential that FDX could suffer from a material economic slowdown.

## Quantitative Evaluations

**S&P Quality Ranking**     B+

| D | C | B- | B | B+ | A- | A | A+ |
| --- | --- | --- | --- | --- | --- | --- | --- |

**Relative Strength Rank**     STRONG

71

LOWEST = 1     HIGHEST = 99

## Revenue/Earnings Data

**Revenue (Million $)**

| | 1Q | 2Q | 3Q | 4Q | Year |
| --- | --- | --- | --- | --- | --- |
| 2009 | 9,970 | -- | -- | -- | -- |
| 2008 | 9,199 | 9,451 | 9,437 | 9,866 | 37,953 |
| 2007 | 8,545 | 8,926 | 8,592 | 9,151 | 35,214 |
| 2006 | 7,707 | 8,090 | 8,003 | 8,494 | 32,294 |
| 2005 | 6,975 | 7,334 | 7,339 | 7,715 | 29,363 |
| 2004 | 5,687 | 5,920 | 6,062 | 7,041 | 24,710 |

**Earnings Per Share ($)**

| | 1Q | 2Q | 3Q | 4Q | Year |
| --- | --- | --- | --- | --- | --- |
| 2009 | 1.23 | E1.44 | E1.35 | E1.48 | E5.50 |
| 2008 | 1.23 | 1.54 | 1.26 | -0.78 | 3.61 |
| 2007 | 1.53 | 1.64 | 1.35 | 1.96 | 6.48 |
| 2006 | 1.10 | 1.53 | 1.38 | 1.82 | 5.83 |
| 2005 | 1.08 | 1.15 | 1.03 | 1.46 | 4.72 |
| 2004 | 0.42 | 0.30 | 0.68 | 1.36 | 2.76 |

Fiscal year ended May 31. Next earnings report expected: Late December. EPS Estimates based on S&P Operating Earnings; historical GAAP earnings are as reported.

## Dividend Data (Dates: mm/dd Payment Date: mm/dd/yy)

| Amount ($) | Date Decl. | Ex-Div. Date | Stk. of Record | Payment Date |
| --- | --- | --- | --- | --- |
| 0.100 | 11/16 | 12/10 | 12/12 | 01/02/08 |
| 0.100 | 02/22 | 03/07 | 03/11 | 04/01/08 |
| 0.110 | 06/02 | 06/11 | 06/13 | 07/01/08 |
| 0.110 | 08/15 | 09/08 | 09/10 | 10/01/08 |

Dividends have been paid since 2002. Source: Company reports.

**Please read the Required Disclosures and Analyst Certification on the last page of this report.**

**STANDARD & POOR'S**

# FedEx Corp.

## Business Summary September 15, 2008

CORPORATE OVERVIEW. FedEx Corp. provides global time-definite air express services for packages, documents and freight in more than 220 countries, and ground-based delivery of small packages in North America. In addition, the company offers expedited critical shipment delivery, customs brokerage solutions, less-than-truckload (LTL) freight transportation, and customized logistics. In February 2004, FDX paid $2.4 billion in cash for Kinko's, which operates about 1,200 copy centers that also provide business services. Kinko's has annual revenues of about $2 billion. Kinko's joined three other FedEx companies: Express, Ground, and Freight.

CORPORATE STRATEGY. The company intends to leverage and extend the FedEx brand and to provide customers with seamless access to its entire portfolio of integrated transportation services. Sales and marketing activities are coordinated among operating companies. Advanced information technology makes it convenient for customers to use the full range of FedEx services and provides a single point of contact for customers to access shipment tracking, customer service and invoicing information. The company intends to continue to operate independent express, ground and freight networks, but has increased its emphasis on having the individual business units work together to compete more effectively.

## Company Financials Fiscal Year Ended May 31

| Per Share Data ($) | 2008 | 2007 | 2006 | 2005 | 2004 | 2003 | 2002 | 2001 | 2000 | 1999 |
|---|---|---|---|---|---|---|---|---|---|---|
| Tangible Book Value | 35.92 | 29.73 | 28.39 | 22.36 | 17.45 | 21.03 | 18.38 | 16.20 | 14.33 | 14.50 |
| Cash Flow | NA | 12.20 | 10.83 | 9.48 | 7.28 | 7.20 | 6.89 | 6.35 | 6.23 | 5.55 |
| Earnings | 3.61 | 6.48 | 5.83 | 4.72 | 2.76 | 2.74 | 2.39 | 1.99 | 2.32 | 2.10 |
| S&P Core Earnings | 2.77 | 6.32 | 5.60 | 4.48 | 2.61 | 1.38 | 0.95 | 0.44 | NA | NA |
| Dividends | NA | 0.36 | 0.32 | 0.28 | 0.22 | 0.20 | Nil | Nil | Nil | Nil |
| Payout Ratio | NA | 6% | 5% | 6% | 8% | 7% | Nil | Nil | Nil | Nil |
| Calendar Year | 2007 | 2006 | 2005 | 2004 | 2003 | 2002 | 2001 | 2000 | 1999 | 1998 |
| Prices:High | NA | 120.01 | 105.82 | 100.92 | 78.05 | 61.35 | 53.48 | 49.85 | 61.88 | 46.56 |
| Prices:Low | NA | 96.50 | 76.81 | 64.84 | 47.70 | 42.75 | 33.15 | 30.56 | 34.88 | 21.81 |
| P/E Ratio:High | NA | 19 | 18 | 21 | 28 | 22 | 22 | 25 | 27 | 22 |
| P/E Ratio:Low | NA | 15 | 13 | 14 | 17 | 16 | 14 | 15 | 15 | 10 |

| Income Statement Analysis (Million $) | | | | | | | | | | |
|---|---|---|---|---|---|---|---|---|---|---|
| Revenue | 37,953 | 35,214 | 32,294 | 29,363 | 24,710 | 22,487 | 20,607 | 19,629 | 18,257 | 16,773 |
| Operating Income | NA | 5,018 | 4,564 | 3,933 | 3,250 | 2,822 | 2,804 | 2,347 | 2,376 | 2,198 |
| Depreciation | 1,946 | 1,742 | 1,550 | 1,462 | 1,375 | 1,351 | 1,364 | 1,276 | 1,155 | 1,035 |
| Interest Expense | NA | 136 | 142 | 160 | 136 | 118 | 139 | 144 | 106 | 98.0 |
| Pretax Income | 2,016 | 3,215 | 2,899 | 2,313 | 1,319 | 1,338 | 1,160 | 928 | 1,138 | 1,061 |
| Effective Tax Rate | 44.2% | 37.3% | 37.7% | 37.4% | 36.5% | 38.0% | 37.5% | 37.0% | 39.5% | 40.5% |
| Net Income | 1,125 | 2,016 | 1,806 | 1,449 | 838 | 830 | 725 | 584 | 688 | 631 |
| S&P Core Earnings | 868 | 1,966 | 1,733 | 1,376 | 790 | 415 | 286 | 130 | NA | NA |

| Balance Sheet & Other Financial Data (Million $) | | | | | | | | | | |
|---|---|---|---|---|---|---|---|---|---|---|
| Cash | 1,539 | 1,569 | 1,937 | 1,039 | 1,046 | 538 | 331 | 121 | 68.0 | 325 |
| Current Assets | NA | 6,629 | 6,464 | 5,269 | 4,970 | 3,941 | 3,665 | 3,449 | 3,285 | 3,141 |
| Total Assets | 25,633 | 24,000 | 22,690 | 20,404 | 19,134 | 15,385 | 13,812 | 13,340 | 11,527 | 10,648 |
| Current Liabilities | NA | 5,428 | 5,473 | 4,734 | 4,732 | 3,335 | 2,942 | 3,250 | 2,891 | 2,785 |
| Long Term Debt | NA | 2,662 | 1,592 | 2,427 | 2,837 | 1,709 | 1,800 | 1,900 | 1,776 | 1,360 |
| Common Equity | 14,526 | 12,656 | 11,511 | 9,588 | 8,036 | 7,288 | 6,545 | 5,900 | 4,785 | 4,664 |
| Total Capital | NA | 16,215 | 14,470 | 13,221 | 12,054 | 9,879 | 8,944 | 8,256 | 6,906 | 6,317 |
| Capital Expenditures | 2,947 | 2,882 | 2,518 | 2,236 | 1,271 | 1,511 | 1,615 | 1,893 | 1,627 | 1,550 |
| Cash Flow | NA | 3,758 | 3,356 | 2,911 | 2,213 | 2,181 | 2,089 | 1,860 | 1,843 | 1,665 |
| Current Ratio | 1.4 | 1.2 | 1.2 | 1.1 | 1.1 | 1.2 | 1.2 | 1.1 | 1.1 | 1.1 |
| % Long Term Debt of Capitalization | 9.1 | 16.4 | 11.0 | 18.3 | 23.5 | 17.2 | 20.1 | 23.0 | 25.7 | 21.5 |
| % Net Income of Revenue | 3.0 | 5.7 | 5.6 | 4.9 | 3.4 | 3.7 | 3.5 | 3.0 | 3.8 | 3.8 |
| % Return on Assets | 4.5 | 8.6 | 8.4 | 7.3 | 4.9 | 5.7 | 5.3 | 4.7 | 6.2 | 6.2 |
| % Return on Equity | 8.3 | 16.7 | 17.1 | 16.4 | 10.9 | 11.8 | 11.7 | 10.9 | 14.6 | 14.6 |

Data as orig reptd.; bef. results of disc opers/spec. items. Per share data adj. for stk. divs.; EPS diluted. E-Estimated. NA-Not Available. NM-Not Meaningful. NR-Not Ranked. UR-Under Review.

**Office:** 942 South Shady Grove Road, Memphis, TN 38120-4117.
**Telephone:** 901-818-7500.
**Website:** http://www.fedex.com
**Chrmn, Pres & CEO:** F.W. Smith

**Investor Contact:** A.B. Graf, Jr. (901-818-7388)
**EVP & CFO:** A.B. Graf, Jr.
**EVP, Secy & General Counsel:** C.P. Richards
**EVP & CIO:** R.B. Carter

**Board Members:** J. L. Barksdale, A. A. Busch, IV, J. A. Edwardson, J. L. Estrin, J. R. Hyde, III, S. A. Jackson, S. R. Loranger, G. W. Loveman, F. W. Smith, J. I. Smith, P. S. Walsh, P. S. Willmott
**Founded:** 1971
**Domicile:** Delaware
**Employees:** 145,000

**The McGraw-Hill Companies**

# Fidelity National Information Services Inc

**STANDARD &POOR'S**

| S&P Recommendation | BUY ★★★★☆ | Price | 12-Mo. Target Price | Investment Style |
|---|---|---|---|---|
| | | $15.85 (as of Nov 14, 2008) | $18.00 | Large-Cap Growth |

**GICS Sector** Information Technology
**Sub-Industry** Data Processing & Outsourced Services

**Summary** This Florida-based company is a leading provider of core processing services and products to financial institutions.

## Key Stock Statistics (Source S&P, Vickers, company reports)

| | | | | | | | |
|---|---|---|---|---|---|---|---|
| 52-Wk Range | $45.57– 12.35 | S&P Oper. EPS 2008E | 1.50 | Market Capitalization(B) | $3.011 | Beta | 1.11 |
| Trailing 12-Month EPS | $1.51 | S&P Oper. EPS 2009E | 1.65 | Yield (%) | 1.26 | S&P 3-Yr. Proj. EPS CAGR(%) | 12 |
| Trailing 12-Month P/E | 10.5 | P/E on S&P Oper. EPS 2008E | 10.6 | Dividend Rate/Share | $0.20 | S&P Credit Rating | NA |
| $10K Invested 5 Yrs Ago | NA | Common Shares Outstg. (M) | 190.0 | Institutional Ownership (%) | 82 | | |

## Price Performance

30-Week Mov. Avg. ···  10-Week Mov. Avg. --  GAAP Earnings vs. Previous Year  Volume Above Avg. STARS
12-Mo. Target Price —  Relative Strength  ▲ Up  ▼ Down  ▶ No Change  Below Avg. ★

Options: ASE, CBOE, P, Ph

Analysis prepared by **Zaineb Bokhari** on October 30, 2008, when the stock traded at **$ 14.82**.

## Highlights

➤ We expect pro forma revenues to rise nearly 19% in 2008, to $3.5 billion, as FIS continues to sell additional services to its existing customers and broadens its penetration of the mid-sized banks. Our outlook incorporates a contribution from eFunds (acquired September 2007) as well as underlying growth in the mid- to high single digits for FIS's organic business on strong gains from international transaction processing. We see the completion of the Bradesco card portfolio conversions supporting our growth outlook. We forecast 6% revenue growth in 2009.

➤ We expect modestly wider operating margins in 2008, reflecting scale benefits from rising transaction volumes and the anticipated achievement of targeted cost savings from the integration of eFunds. We expect a further widening in 2009.

➤ Our 2008 EPS estimate is $1.50, up from a pro forma $1.23 in 2007. Our estimate excludes projected M&A and acquisition integration costs and charges and purchase price amortization, and is adjusted to reflect the spin-off of Lender Processing Services and the sale of Certegy Australia. We estimate EPS of $1.65 in 2009.

## Investment Rationale/Risk

➤ We recently raised our recommendation on FIS shares to buy, from hold. We expect FIS, now focused on core transaction processing, credit and debit card processing, e-banking, electronic bill payment and item processing, to continue its cost-cutting efforts as it integrates eFunds; we think targeted cost savings of $35 million are achievable. While existing long-term and multi-year contracts will allow FIS to generate recurring revenues, we see organic growth, trending at a mid-to high single digit rate, remaining vulnerable to the slowing macro economy. Nevertheless, we think the company is well managed, and we have a favorable view of its above-peer organic growth rate and attractive valuation.

➤ Risks to our recommendation and target price include ongoing consolidation among financial services customers, which could lead to business loss or disruption. We are also concerned about FIS's exposure to community banks, which could be more vulnerable to the slowing U.S. economy.

➤ We derive our 12-month target price of $18 by applying an 11X P/E to our 2009 EPS estimate, modestly below the 11.5X recent peer average.

## Qualitative Risk Assessment

| LOW | MEDIUM | HIGH |
|---|---|---|

Our risk assessment reflects uncertainty regarding the company's exposure to the financial services industry and ongoing acquisition integration risks. We note that the company's remaining transaction processing business offers a considerable base of recurring revenues, but recent M&A and spinoff transactions have made an objective analysis of long-term historical financials somewhat challenging.

## Quantitative Evaluations

**S&P Quality Ranking**   NR

| D | C | B- | B | B+ | A- | A | A+ |
|---|---|---|---|---|---|---|---|

**Relative Strength Rank**   MODERATE

67

LOWEST = 1                                    HIGHEST = 99

## Revenue/Earnings Data

**Revenue (Million $)**

| | 1Q | 2Q | 3Q | 4Q | Year |
|---|---|---|---|---|---|
| 2008 | 1,291 | 1,339 | 893.8 | -- | -- |
| 2007 | 1,124 | 1,176 | 1,168 | 1,330 | 4,758 |
| 2006 | 900.9 | 1,022 | 1,081 | 1,129 | 4,133 |
| 2005 | 262.5 | 276.0 | 282.8 | 295.9 | 1,117 |
| 2004 | -- | -- | -- | -- | 1,040 |
| 2003 | -- | -- | -- | -- | -- |

**Earnings Per Share ($)**

| | | | | | |
|---|---|---|---|---|---|
| 2008 | 0.35 | 0.38 | 0.24 | E0.44 | E1.50 |
| 2007 | 0.30 | 0.75 | 1.02 | 0.55 | 2.60 |
| 2006 | 0.23 | 0.34 | 0.41 | 0.39 | 1.37 |
| 2005 | 0.34 | 0.40 | 0.36 | 0.57 | 1.66 |
| 2004 | -- | -- | -- | -- | 0.92 |
| 2003 | -- | -- | -- | -- | -- |

Fiscal year ended Dec. 31. Next earnings report expected: Mid February. EPS Estimates based on S&P Operating Earnings; historical GAAP earnings are as reported.

## Dividend Data (Dates: mm/dd Payment Date: mm/dd/yy)

| Amount ($) | Date Decl. | Ex-Div. Date | Stk. of Record | Payment Date |
|---|---|---|---|---|
| 0.050 | 04/17 | 06/11 | 06/13 | 06/27/08 |
| Stk. | 06/16 | 07/03 | 06/24 | 07/01/08 |
| 0.050 | 07/23 | 09/11 | 09/15 | 09/29/08 |
| 0.050 | 10/21 | 12/11 | 12/15 | 12/29/08 |

Dividends have been paid since 2006. Source: Company reports.

---

**Please read the Required Disclosures and Analyst Certification on the last page of this report.**

The McGraw-Hill Companies

# Fidelity National Information Services Inc

STANDARD
&POOR'S

## Business Summary October 30, 2008

CORPORATE OVERVIEW. Fidelity National Information Services, Inc. (FIS) was formed via the combination, on February 1, 2006, of the information processing subsidiary of Fidelity National Financial (FNF), a leading provider of title and specialty insurance, and Certegy, a provider of card and check processing services. As a result of the combination, the company is a leading provider of technology solutions, processing services, and information-based services to the financial industry. The company's primary services include core processing services, check services, card issuer and transaction processing services, risk management services, mortgage loan processing, mortgage-related information products, and outsourcing services.

Until recently, FIS operated in two main business segments: Transaction Processing Services (TPS) and Lender Processing Services (LPS).

The Transaction Processing Services segment is comprised of Certegy's Card and Check Services businesses and the pre-merger financial institution processing businesses of FIS. The segment accounted for 63% of revenue in 2007 and is further segmented into integrated financial solutions (independent community banks, credit unions, and savings banks), enterprise solutions

(large North America-based financial institutions, commercial lenders, etc.), international, and other. At December 31, 2007, FIS had processing and technology relationships with 35 of the top 50 global banks, including nine of the top 10. Through its Lender Processing Services segment (37%), FIS offers a broad range of mortgage-related products and services to support origination, data gathering, risk management, servicing, default management among others. According to the company's 10-K filing for 2007, over 50% of all U.S. residential mortgages (by dollar volume) were processed using its loan servicing platform. On July 2, 2008, FIS completed the spinoff of Lender Processing Services to shareholders.

After the recent spinoff, FIS serves 13,000 financial institution customers in more than 80 countries. In 2007, the company derived 44% of revenues from community banks, 24% from mid- and top-tier U.S. institutions, 11% from the retail, point-of sale channel, and 21% from international customers.

## Company Financials Fiscal Year Ended Dec. 31

| Per Share Data ($) | 2007 | 2006 | 2005 | 2004 | 2003 | 2002 | 2001 | 2000 | 1999 | 1998 |
|---|---|---|---|---|---|---|---|---|---|---|
| Tangible Book Value | NM | NM | 3.53 | 0.55 | NA | NA | NA | NA | NA | NA |
| Cash Flow | 4.04 | 3.66 | 2.48 | 2.40 | NA | NA | NA | NA | NA | NA |
| Earnings | 2.60 | 1.37 | 1.66 | 0.92 | NA | NA | NA | NA | NA | NA |
| S&P Core Earnings | 1.72 | 1.37 | 0.98 | 0.94 | 1.00 | NA | NA | NA | NA | NA |
| Dividends | 0.20 | 0.20 | Nil | Nil | NA | NA | NA | NA | NA | NA |
| Payout Ratio | 8% | 15% | Nil | Nil | NA | NA | NA | NA | NA | NA |
| Prices:High | 57.80 | 42.62 | NA | NA | NA | NA | NA | NA | NA | NA |
| Prices:Low | 39.99 | 33.50 | NA | NA | NA | NA | NA | NA | NA | NA |
| P/E Ratio:High | 22 | 31 | NA | NA | NA | NA | NA | NA | NA | NA |
| P/E Ratio:Low | 15 | 24 | NA | NA | NA | NA | NA | NA | NA | NA |

| Income Statement Analysis (Million $) | 2007 | 2006 | 2005 | 2004 | 2003 | 2002 | 2001 | 2000 | 1999 | 1998 |
|---|---|---|---|---|---|---|---|---|---|---|
| Revenue | 4,758 | 4,133 | 1,117 | 1,040 | 1,945 | 654 | 418 | NA | NA | NA |
| Operating Income | 1,030 | 1,025 | 248 | 227 | NA | NA | NA | NA | NA | NA |
| Depreciation | 284 | 434 | 51.9 | 47.4 | 144 | 18.6 | 9.45 | NA | NA | NA |
| Interest Expense | 201 | 193 | 12.8 | 12.9 | NA | NA | NA | NA | NA | NA |
| Pretax Income | 813 | 409 | 174 | 168 | 362 | 106 | 53.8 | NA | NA | NA |
| Effective Tax Rate | 37.0% | 36.7% | 39.5% | 37.0% | 38.8% | 37.3% | 40.9% | NA | NA | NA |
| Net Income | 510 | 259 | 106 | 106 | 207 | 58.2 | 31.0 | NA | NA | NA |
| S&P Core Earnings | 338 | 259 | 196 | 189 | 200 | NA | NA | NA | NA | NA |

| Balance Sheet & Other Financial Data (Million $) | 2007 | 2006 | 2005 | 2004 | 2003 | 2002 | 2001 | 2000 | 1999 | 1998 |
|---|---|---|---|---|---|---|---|---|---|---|
| Cash | 355 | 212 | 138 | 86.7 | 100 | 56.5 | NA | NA | NA | NA |
| Current Assets | 1,830 | 1,301 | 445 | 409 | NA | NA | NA | NA | NA | NA |
| Total Assets | 9,795 | 7,631 | 972 | 922 | 2,371 | 556 | NA | NA | NA | NA |
| Current Liabilities | 1,254 | 881 | 234 | 290 | NA | NA | NA | NA | NA | NA |
| Long Term Debt | 4,275 | 2,948 | 228 | 274 | NA | NA | NA | NA | NA | NA |
| Common Equity | 3,781 | 3,548 | 459 | 300 | 1,904 | 295 | NA | NA | NA | NA |
| Total Capital | 8,194 | 6,892 | 716 | 614 | NA | NA | NA | NA | NA | NA |
| Capital Expenditures | 114 | 122 | 63.6 | 40.9 | 57.3 | 3.35 | 0.50 | NA | NA | NA |
| Cash Flow | 795 | 693 | 157 | 153 | NA | NA | NA | NA | NA | NA |
| Current Ratio | 1.5 | 1.5 | 1.9 | 1.4 | 1.4 | 1.6 | NA | NA | NA | NA |
| % Long Term Debt of Capitalization | 51.3 | 42.8 | 31.8 | 44.6 | 0.5 | 4.8 | Nil | NA | NA | NA |
| % Net Income of Revenue | 10.7 | 6.3 | 9.4 | 10.2 | 10.6 | 8.9 | 7.4 | NA | NA | NA |
| % Return on Assets | 5.9 | 4.4 | 11.1 | 12.4 | 14.1 | NA | NA | NA | NA | NA |
| % Return on Equity | 14.8 | 12.2 | 27.5 | 37.7 | 18.8 | NA | NA | NA | NA | NA |

Data as orig reptd.; bef. results of disc opers/spec. items. Per share data adj. for stk. divs.; EPS diluted. E-Estimated. NA-Not Available. NM-Not Meaningful. NR-Not Ranked. UR-Under Review.

**Office:** 601 Riverside Ave, Jacksonville, FL 32204-2901.
**Telephone:** 904-854-8100.
**Website:** http://www.fidelityinfoservices.com
**Chrmn:** W.P. Foley, II

**Pres & CEO:** L.A. Kennedy
**Pres & CEO:** J.A. McKinley, Jr.
**COO:** G. Norcross
**EVP & CFO:** G.P. Scanlon

**Board Members:** R. M. Clements, W. P. Foley, II, T. M. Hagerty, K. W. Hughes, D. K. Hunt, L. A. Kennedy, R. N. Massey

**Founded:** 2001
**Domicile:** Georgia
**Employees:** 31,000

# Fifth Third Bancorp

STANDARD
&POOR'S

| S&P Recommendation | HOLD ★★★☆☆ | Price<br>$9.54 (as of Nov 14, 2008) | 12-Mo. Target Price<br>$12.00 | Investment Style<br>Large-Cap Blend |
|---|---|---|---|---|

**GICS Sector** Financials
**Sub-Industry** Regional Banks

**Summary** This regional bank holding company operates banking centers in Ohio and several other states, mostly in the Midwest.

## Key Stock Statistics (Source S&P, Vickers, company reports)

| | | | | | | | |
|---|---|---|---|---|---|---|---|
| 52-Wk Range | $31.21– 7.80 | S&P Oper. EPS 2008E | -0.06 | Market Capitalization(B) | $5.509 | Beta | 1.50 |
| Trailing 12-Month EPS | $0.04 | S&P Oper. EPS 2009E | 0.93 | Yield (%) | 6.29 | S&P 3-Yr. Proj. EPS CAGR(%) | 9 |
| Trailing 12-Month P/E | NM | P/E on S&P Oper. EPS 2008E | NM | Dividend Rate/Share | $0.60 | S&P Credit Rating | A+ |
| $10K Invested 5 Yrs Ago | $2,012 | Common Shares Outstg. (M) | 577.5 | Institutional Ownership (%) | 78 | | |

## Price Performance

30-Week Mov. Avg. · · · · 10-Week Mov. Avg. - - - **GAAP Earnings vs. Previous Year**    Volume Above Avg. |ılıl| STARS
12-Mo. Target Price —— Relative Strength —— ▲ Up  ▼ Down  ► No Change        Below Avg. |ılıl| ★

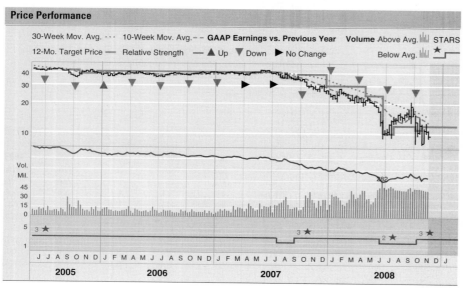

Options: ASE, CBOE, P, Ph

Analysis prepared by **Erik Oja** on November 11, 2008, when the stock traded at **$ 9.90.**

### Highlights

► Excluding purchase accounting adjustments, FITB's third quarter net interest margin was 3.39%, above our 3.30% estimate of the median of peers, a positive in the current environment. Based on FITB's ability to attract large amounts of relatively inexpensive deposits, we expect FITB to maintain a net interest margin of 3.35% in the fourth quarter, and 3.30% in 2009.

► Nonperforming loans of $2.6 billion comprised 3.04% of total loans in the third quarter, worse than most peers, and up 31% from the preceding quarter, a higher sequential growth rate than at most peers. FITB is addressing these serious credit quality issues with three main initiatives: mortgage modifications for homeowners who may be in danger of falling behind; trying to sell problem credits; and halting higher risk lending. We expect loan loss provisions of $2.95 billion in 2008 and $1.785 billion in 2009, based on our expectations for fourth quarter annualized net chargeoffs of 2.00%, and $300 million of reserve building. We expect these figures to fall to 1.25% and $100 million, respectively, by 2009 year end.

► For 2008, we expect a loss per share of $0.06, and for 2009, we expect EPS of $0.93.

### Investment Rationale/Risk

► We see FITB surviving the current banking crisis on the strength of its core net interest income and fee income growth, as well as good capitalization levels. FITB has applied for $3.4 billion from the U.S. Treasury's TARP plan, in exchange for issuing 5.0% preferred stock and warrants to the Treasury. In addition, FITB has shelved plans to sell or spin off its large electronic payment processing division (2008 expected revenues of $920 million, or about 14% of revenues), and was recently selected by the FDIC to assume the assets of a failed bank in Florida. All of these are positives, in our view. However, we think loan loss provisioning expenses will be high in 2009, and possibly in 2010 as well, which may depress profitability for the next five or six quarters.

► Risks to our recommendation and target price include a faster than expected decline in economic conditions in the Midwest, and higher than forecast deposit costs.

► Our 12-month target price of $12 is equal to a below-peers 0.72X multiple of FITB's September 30 tangible book value per share of $16.75, reflecting continued mortgage pressures.

## Qualitative Risk Assessment

| LOW | MEDIUM | HIGH |
|---|---|---|

Our risk assessment reflects what we see as the company's solid business fundamentals and strong customer base. We view FITB as well diversified, but with a concentration in the struggling Midwest.

## Quantitative Evaluations

**S&P Quality Ranking**    A-

| D | C | B- | B | B+ | A- | A | A+ |
|---|---|---|---|---|---|---|---|

**Relative Strength Rank**    MODERATE

46

LOWEST = 1                                    HIGHEST = 99

## Revenue/Earnings Data

**Revenue (Million $)**

| | 1Q | 2Q | 3Q | 4Q | Year |
|---|---|---|---|---|---|
| 2008 | 2,319 | 1,929 | 2,189 | -- | -- |
| 2007 | 2,108 | 2,202 | 2,251 | 2,126 | 8,479 |
| 2006 | 2,015 | 2,132 | 2,196 | 1,765 | 8,108 |
| 2005 | 1,752 | 1,850 | 1,905 | 1,988 | 7,495 |
| 2004 | 1,617 | 1,749 | 1,654 | 1,560 | 6,579 |
| 2003 | 1,588 | 1,641 | 1,666 | 1,587 | 6,474 |

**Earnings Per Share ($)**

| | 1Q | 2Q | 3Q | 4Q | Year |
|---|---|---|---|---|---|
| 2008 | 0.54 | -0.37 | -0.14 | E-0.09 | E-0.06 |
| 2007 | 0.65 | 0.69 | 0.61 | 0.07 | 1.99 |
| 2006 | 0.65 | 0.69 | 0.68 | 0.12 | 2.12 |
| 2005 | 0.72 | 0.75 | 0.71 | 0.60 | 2.77 |
| 2004 | 0.75 | 0.79 | 0.83 | 0.31 | 2.68 |
| 2003 | 0.72 | 0.75 | 0.78 | 0.73 | 2.97 |

Fiscal year ended Dec. 31. Next earnings report expected: Late January. EPS Estimates based on S&P Operating Earnings; historical GAAP earnings are as reported.

## Dividend Data (Dates: mm/dd Payment Date: mm/dd/yy)

| Amount ($) | Date Decl. | Ex-Div. Date | Stk. of Record | Payment Date |
|---|---|---|---|---|
| 0.440 | 03/18 | 03/27 | 03/31 | 04/22/08 |
| 0.150 | 06/18 | 06/26 | 06/30 | 07/22/08 |
| 0.150 | 06/18 | 06/26 | 06/30 | 07/22/08 |
| 0.150 | 09/16 | 09/26 | 09/30 | 10/21/08 |

Dividends have been paid since 1952. Source: Company reports.

# Fifth Third Bancorp

## Business Summary November 11, 2008

CORPORATE OVERVIEW. FITB is divided into five segments: commercial banking, branch banking, consumer lending, investment advisors, and processing solutions. Commercial banking provides a comprehensive range of financial services and products to large and middle-market businesses, governments and professional customers. In addition to traditional lending and depository offerings, commercial banking products and services include cash management, foreign exchange and international trade finance, derivatives and capital markets services, asset-based lending, real estate finance, public finance, commercial leasing, and syndicated finance.

Branch banking provides deposit and loan and lease products to individuals and small businesses through over 1,100 banking centers. Branch banking offers depository and loan products, such as checking and savings accounts, home equity lines of credit, credit cards, and loans for automobiles and other personal financing needs, plus products designed to meet the specific needs of small businesses, including cash management services.

Consumer lending includes mortgage and home equity lending activities and other indirect lending activities. Mortgage and home equity lending activities include the origination, retention and servicing of mortgage and home equity

loans or lines of credit, sales and securitizations of those loans or pools of loans or lines of credit and all associated hedging activities. Other indirect lending activities include loans to consumers through dealers and federal and private student education loans.

Investment advisors provides a full range of investment alternatives for individuals, companies and not-for-profit organizations. Primary services include trust, asset management, retirement plans and custody. Fifth Third Securities, Inc., an indirect wholly owned subsidiary, offers full-service retail brokerage services to individual clients and broker dealer services to the institutional marketplace. Fifth Third Asset Management, Inc., an indirect wholly-owned subsidiary, provides asset management services and also advises a proprietary family of mutual funds, Fifth Third Funds. Fifth Third Processing Solutions provides electronic funds transfer, debit, credit and merchant transaction processing, operates the Jeanie ATM network, and provides other data processing services to affiliated and unaffiliated customers.

## Company Financials Fiscal Year Ended Dec. 31

| Per Share Data ($) | 2007 | 2006 | 2005 | 2004 | 2003 | 2002 | 2001 | 2000 | 1999 | 1998 |
|---|---|---|---|---|---|---|---|---|---|---|
| Tangible Book Value | 12.30 | 13.78 | 12.72 | 13.33 | 13.46 | 13.12 | 13.09 | 10.50 | 8.79 | 7.04 |
| Earnings | 1.99 | 2.12 | 2.77 | 2.68 | 2.97 | 2.76 | 1.86 | 1.83 | 1.43 | 1.17 |
| S&P Core Earnings | 2.19 | 2.14 | 2.78 | 2.69 | 2.84 | 2.56 | 1.63 | NA | NA | NA |
| Dividends | 1.70 | 1.58 | 1.46 | 1.31 | 1.13 | 0.98 | 0.83 | 0.70 | 0.56 | 0.44 |
| Payout Ratio | 85% | 75% | 53% | 49% | 38% | 36% | 45% | 38% | 39% | 37% |
| Prices:High | 43.32 | 41.57 | 48.12 | 60.00 | 62.15 | 69.70 | 64.77 | 60.88 | 50.29 | 49.42 |
| Prices:Low | 24.82 | 35.86 | 35.04 | 45.32 | 47.05 | 55.26 | 45.69 | 29.33 | 38.58 | 31.67 |
| P/E Ratio:High | 22 | 20 | 17 | 22 | 21 | 25 | 35 | 33 | 35 | 42 |
| P/E Ratio:Low | 12 | 17 | 13 | 17 | 16 | 20 | 25 | 16 | 27 | 27 |

| Income Statement Analysis (Million $) | | | | | | | | | | |
|---|---|---|---|---|---|---|---|---|---|---|
| Net Interest Income | 3,009 | 2,873 | 2,965 | 3,012 | 2,905 | 2,700 | 2,433 | 1,470 | 1,405 | 1,003 |
| Tax Equivalent Adjustment | 24.0 | 26.0 | 31.0 | 36.0 | 39.0 | 39.5 | 45.5 | 93.0 | 73.0 | 49.2 |
| Non Interest Income | 2,494 | 1,657 | 2,461 | 2,502 | 2,399 | 2,047 | 1,626 | 1,013 | 876 | 626 |
| Loan Loss Provision | 628 | 343 | 330 | 268 | 399 | 247 | 236 | 89.0 | 134 | 109 |
| % Expense/Operating Revenue | 60.2% | 67.1% | 53.6% | 53.5% | 46.0% | 51.9% | 57.7% | 45.1% | 47.7% | 47.9% |
| Pretax Income | 1,537 | 1,627 | 2,208 | 2,237 | 2,547 | 2,432 | 1,653 | 1,275 | 1,026 | 726 |
| Effective Tax Rate | 30.0% | 27.2% | 29.8% | 31.8% | 31.6% | 31.2% | 33.3% | 32.3% | 34.9% | 34.4% |
| Net Income | 1,076 | 1,184 | 1,549 | 1,525 | 1,722 | 1,635 | 1,101 | 863 | 668 | 476 |
| % Net Interest Margin | 3.36 | 3.06 | 3.23 | 3.48 | 3.62 | 3.96 | 3.82 | 3.77 | 3.99 | 3.94 |
| S&P Core Earnings | 1,183 | 1,191 | 1,555 | 1,529 | 1,650 | 1,513 | 965 | NA | NA | NA |

| Balance Sheet & Other Financial Data (Million $) | | | | | | | | | | |
|---|---|---|---|---|---|---|---|---|---|---|
| Money Market Assets | 171 | 187 | 117 | 77.0 | 55.0 | 312 | 225 | 198 | 355 | 119 |
| Investment Securities | 11,032 | 12,218 | 22,471 | 25,474 | 29,402 | 25,828 | 20,748 | 15,827 | 12,817 | 8,539 |
| Commercial Loans | 40,412 | 36,114 | 33,214 | 30,601 | 28,242 | 22,614 | 10,839 | 12,382 | 11,141 | 9,093 |
| Other Loans | 39,841 | 39,485 | 38,024 | 29,207 | 25,493 | 23,314 | 30,709 | 13,570 | 14,746 | 9,375 |
| Total Assets | 110,962 | 100,669 | 105,225 | 94,456 | 91,143 | 80,894 | 71,026 | 45,857 | 41,589 | 28,922 |
| Demand Deposits | 36,179 | 36,908 | 39,020 | 37,288 | 31,899 | 11,139 | 10,595 | 5,604 | 8,011 | 6,355 |
| Time Deposits | 39,266 | 32,472 | 13,656 | 20,938 | 25,196 | 41,069 | 35,259 | 25,344 | 18,072 | 12,425 |
| Long Term Debt | 12,857 | 12,558 | 15,227 | 13,983 | 9,063 | 8,179 | 7,030 | 4,034 | 1,977 | 2,288 |
| Common Equity | 9,152 | 10,013 | 9,437 | 8,915 | 8,516 | 8,466 | 7,630 | 4,891 | 4,306 | 3,179 |
| % Return on Assets | 1.0 | 1.2 | 1.6 | 1.6 | 2.0 | 2.2 | 1.6 | 2.0 | 1.7 | 1.9 |
| % Return on Equity | 11.2 | 12.2 | 16.9 | 17.3 | 20.3 | 20.3 | 15.4 | 19.2 | 16.6 | 17.5 |
| % Loan Loss Reserve | 1.1 | 1.0 | 1.0 | 1.2 | 1.4 | 1.4 | 1.4 | 1.4 | 4.9 | 1.5 |
| % Loans/Deposits | 106.8 | 108.8 | 105.6 | 103.7 | 94.9 | 94.4 | 95.4 | 85.6 | 100.4 | 94.7 |
| % Equity to Assets | 9.1 | 9.4 | 9.4 | 9.5 | 9.9 | 10.6 | 10.2 | 10.3 | 10.3 | 10.8 |

Data as orig reptd.; bef. results of disc opers/spec. items. Per share data adj. for stk. divs.; EPS diluted. E-Estimated. NA-Not Available. NM-Not Meaningful. NR-Not Ranked. UR-Under Review.

**Office:** 38 Fountain Square Plaza, Cincinnati, OH 45263.
**Telephone:** 513-534-5300.
**Website:** http://www.53.com
**Chrmn, Pres & CEO:** K.T. Kabat

**COO & EVP:** G.D. Carmichael
**EVP, Chief Acctg Officer & Cntlr:** D.T. Poston
**EVP, Secy & General Counsel:** P.L. Reynolds
**SVP & Treas:** M. Sankaran

**Investor Contact:** C.G. Marshall (800-972-3030)
**Board Members:** D. F. Allen, J. F. Barrett, U. L. Bridgeman, Jr., J. P. Hackett, G. R. Heminger, A. M. Hill, K. T. Kabat, R. L. Koch, II, M. D. Livingston, H. G. Meijer, J. E. Rogers, J. J. Schiff, Jr., D. S. Taft, T. W. Traylor

**Founded:** 1862
**Domicile:** Ohio
**Employees:** 21,683

# FirstEnergy Corp.

STANDARD
&POOR'S

| S&P Recommendation | HOLD ★★★☆☆ | Price<br>$52.75 (as of Nov 14, 2008) | 12-Mo. Target Price<br>$62.00 | Investment Style<br>Large-Cap Blend |
|---|---|---|---|---|

**GICS Sector** Utilities
**Sub-Industry** Electric Utilities

**Summary** This electric utility holding company serves about 4.5 million customers in portions of Ohio, Pennsylvania and New Jersey.

## Key Stock Statistics (Source S&P, Vickers, company reports)

| | | | | | | | |
|---|---|---|---|---|---|---|---|
| 52-Wk Range | $84.00–41.20 | S&P Oper. EPS 2008**E** | 4.35 | Market Capitalization(B) | $16.080 | Beta | 0.76 |
| Trailing 12-Month EPS | $4.16 | S&P Oper. EPS 2009**E** | 5.15 | Yield (%) | 4.17 | S&P 3-Yr. Proj. EPS CAGR(%) | 10 |
| Trailing 12-Month P/E | 12.7 | P/E on S&P Oper. EPS 2008**E** | 12.1 | Dividend Rate/Share | $2.20 | S&P Credit Rating | BBB |
| $10K Invested 5 Yrs Ago | $18,053 | Common Shares Outstg. (M) | 304.8 | Institutional Ownership (%) | 73 | | |

## Price Performance

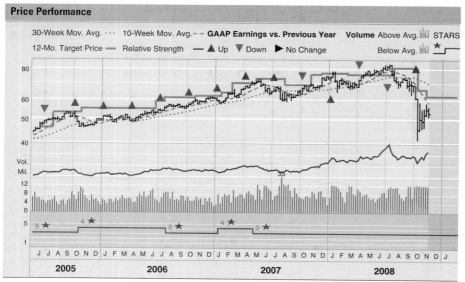

30-Week Mov. Avg. · · · · 10-Week Mov. Avg. - - **GAAP Earnings vs. Previous Year** Volume Above Avg. STARS
12-Mo. Target Price — Relative Strength — ▲ Up ▼ Down ► No Change Below Avg. ★

Options: ASE, CBOE, P, Ph

Analysis prepared by **Justin McCann** on November 10, 2008, when the stock traded at **$55.00**.

## Highlights

➤ We expect operating EPS in 2008 to increase nearly 3% from 2007 operating EPS of $4.23, which rose more than 10% from 2006's $3.82. We believe growth in delivery sales and higher generation margins will be nearly offset by higher amortization, fuel and purchased power costs, and greater expenses related to FE's infrastructure investments. Operating EPS in the first nine months of 2008 was down nearly 2% to $3.29, reflecting planned power plant outages and higher purchased power costs.

➤ For 2009, we expect operating EPS to grow by approximately 18% from anticipated results in 2008. We believe this will be driven by increased power production reflecting the absence of the power plant outages in 2008, as well as by the transition to market-based rates.

➤ Under the coal supply agreement between FE's generation subsidiary and CONSOL Energy (CNX: hold, $30), which was reached in June 2006, CNX would supply a total of more than 128 million tons of high-BTU coal for the 20-year period 2009 through 2028. The agreement replaced an existing agreement that ran through 2020, and should result in the shipment of an additional two million tons per year.

## Investment Rationale/Risk

➤ After a 20% gain in 2007, the shares are down nearly 25% year to date. We believe the decline reflects the crisis in the credit markets and its potential impact on both the overall economy and FE's cost of capital. Over the next 12 months, we expect the stock to recover a substantial portion of its decline. We believe this will largely reflect the sharp increase we project for 2009 earnings.

➤ Risks to our recommendation and target price include the possibility of higher-than-anticipated or inadequately hedged replacement power costs, as well as a reduction in the average P/E of FE's electric utility peers.

➤ FE increased its dividend by 10% with the March 2008 payment. This accelerated the company's new dividend policy, which has targeted future annual increases of 4% to 5% and a dividend payout ratio of 50% to 60%. The targeted growth rate is above both the expected dividend growth rate of the industry and FE's own expected long-term EPS growth rate of 3% to 4%. Our 12-month target price of $62 represents a modest discount-to-peers P/E of 12X our EPS estimate for 2009.

## Qualitative Risk Assessment

| LOW | MEDIUM | HIGH |
|---|---|---|

Our risk assessment reflects the strong and steady cash flow we expect from the company's regulated electric utility subsidiaries; its low-cost baseload power generation in Ohio and Pennsylvania; its low-risk transmission distribution operations in New Jersey and Pennsylvania; and its rate certainty in Ohio. This is partially offset by the company's below-average production performance from nuclear operations and our view of its high level of debt and environmental spending.

## Quantitative Evaluations

**S&P Quality Ranking**                     A-

| D | C | B- | B | B+ | A- | A | A+ |
|---|---|---|---|---|---|---|---|

**Relative Strength Rank**                  MODERATE

70

LOWEST = 1                            HIGHEST = 99

## Revenue/Earnings Data

**Revenue (Million $)**

| | 1Q | 2Q | 3Q | 4Q | Year |
|---|---|---|---|---|---|
| 2008 | 3,277 | 3,245 | 3,904 | -- | -- |
| 2007 | 2,973 | 3,109 | 3,641 | 3,079 | 12,802 |
| 2006 | 2,705 | 2,751 | 3,365 | 2,680 | 11,501 |
| 2005 | 2,813 | 2,900 | 3,588 | 2,892 | 11,989 |
| 2004 | 3,183 | 3,150 | 3,536 | 2,950 | 12,453 |
| 2003 | 3,221 | 2,853 | 3,434 | 2,799 | 12,307 |

**Earnings Per Share ($)**

| | | | | | |
|---|---|---|---|---|---|
| 2008 | 0.90 | 0.86 | 1.53 | E1.07 | E4.35 |
| 2007 | 0.92 | 1.10 | 1.34 | 0.87 | 4.22 |
| 2006 | 0.67 | 0.93 | 1.40 | 0.84 | 3.82 |
| 2005 | 0.42 | 0.54 | 1.01 | 0.67 | 2.65 |
| 2004 | 0.53 | 0.62 | 0.91 | 0.61 | 2.66 |
| 2003 | 0.39 | 0.03 | 0.51 | 0.44 | 1.39 |

Fiscal year ended Dec. 31. Next earnings report expected: Late February. EPS Estimates based on S&P Operating Earnings; historical GAAP earnings are as reported.

## Dividend Data (Dates: mm/dd Payment Date: mm/dd/yy)

| Amount ($) | Date Decl. | Ex-Div. Date | Stk. of Record | Payment Date |
|---|---|---|---|---|
| 0.550 | 12/18 | 02/05 | 02/07 | 03/01/08 |
| 0.550 | 03/18 | 05/05 | 05/07 | 06/01/08 |
| 0.550 | 07/15 | 08/05 | 08/07 | 09/01/08 |
| 0.550 | 09/16 | 11/05 | 11/07 | 12/01/08 |

Dividends have been paid since 1930. Source: Company reports.

---

**Please read the Required Disclosures and Analyst Certification on the last page of this report.**

The McGraw-Hill Companies

# FirstEnergy Corp.

STANDARD
&POOR'S

## Business Summary November 10, 2008

**CORPORATE OVERVIEW.** FirstEnergy (FE) is a diversified energy company involved in the generation, transmission and distribution of electricity as well as energy management and related services. The company operates primarily through two core business segments: Regulated Services, which is comprised of seven electric utility operating companies and provides transmission and distribution services, and Power Supply Management Services, which owns and operates the generation assets and wholesale purchase of electricity, energy management and other energy-related services. The electric utilities accounted for 88.3% of revenues in 2007, with the remaining 11.7% contributed by the unregulated businesses.

**CORPORATE STRATEGY.** FE intends to be a leading regional supplier of energy services in the northeast quadrant of the U.S. On the generation front, the company is working to optimize its generation portfolio and to effectively manage its commodity supplies and risks. FE is committed to reinvesting in the operations of its utilities for a continuous improvement in their customer service quality and reliability. To this end, FE is upgrading its transmission and distribution system, implementing new technologies and incorporating industry best practices. The company has made safety and environmental compliance one of its top priorities, both within the nuclear fleet and across the organization.

**MARKET PROFILE.** FirstEnergy's utility subsidiaries serve around 4.5 million customers within an area of 36,100 square miles in Ohio, Pennsylvania and New Jersey. As of December 31, 2007, FE's power generating facilities produce more than 14,100 megawatts (MW) of electricity, with coal plants accounting for approximately 54.0% of the total; nuclear, nearly 28.5%; oil and natural gas peaking units, 10.9%; hydro, 3.3%; and other, also 3.3%. While we expect FE to benefit from its low-cost fuel sources, with industrial customers accounting for a significant portion of its customer base, it has a greater-than-peers vulnerability to a significant downturn in the regional economy, in our view. In October 2005, four of FE's utility subsidiaries completed an intra-system transfer of 8,132 megawatts of fossil and hydroelectric generation assets to FirstEnergy Generation Corp. for $1.6 billion. The transfer was part of the transitional plans approved by both the Ohio and Pennsylvania public utility commissions requiring the separation of the generation assets from the distribution businesses.

## Company Financials Fiscal Year Ended Dec. 31

| Per Share Data ($) | 2007 | 2006 | 2005 | 2004 | 2003 | 2002 | 2001 | 2000 | 1999 | 1998 |
|---|---|---|---|---|---|---|---|---|---|---|
| Tangible Book Value | 11.06 | 9.83 | 9.63 | 7.70 | 6.55 | 4.11 | 6.04 | 11.42 | 10.47 | 9.62 |
| Earnings | 4.22 | 3.82 | 2.65 | 2.66 | 1.39 | 2.33 | 2.84 | 2.69 | 2.50 | 1.95 |
| S&P Core Earnings | 3.80 | 3.71 | 2.56 | 2.77 | 1.61 | 1.69 | 2.36 | NA | NA | NA |
| Dividends | 2.00 | 1.80 | 1.67 | 1.50 | 1.50 | 1.50 | 1.13 | 1.50 | 1.50 | 1.50 |
| Payout Ratio | 47% | 47% | 63% | 56% | 108% | 64% | 40% | 56% | 60% | 77% |
| Prices:High | 74.98 | 61.70 | 53.36 | 43.41 | 38.90 | 39.12 | 36.98 | 32.13 | 33.19 | 34.06 |
| Prices:Low | 57.77 | 47.75 | 37.70 | 35.24 | 25.82 | 24.85 | 25.10 | 18.00 | 22.13 | 27.06 |
| P/E Ratio:High | 18 | 16 | 20 | 16 | 28 | 17 | 13 | 12 | 13 | 17 |
| P/E Ratio:Low | 14 | 13 | 14 | 13 | 19 | 11 | 9 | 7 | 9 | 14 |

| Income Statement Analysis (Million $) | | | | | | | | | | |
|---|---|---|---|---|---|---|---|---|---|---|
| Revenue | 12,802 | 11,501 | 11,989 | 12,453 | 12,307 | 12,152 | 7,999 | 7,029 | 6,320 | 5,861 |
| Depreciation | 1,657 | 1,457 | 1,870 | 1,756 | 1,282 | 1,106 | 890 | 934 | 938 | 741 |
| Maintenance | NA | NA | NA | NA | NA | NA | NA | NA | NA | NA |
| Fixed Charges Coverage | 3.95 | 3.78 | 3.39 | 3.25 | 1.88 | 2.25 | 2.85 | 2.71 | 2.62 | 2.21 |
| Construction Credits | NA | NA | NA | NA | NA | 24.5 | 35.5 | 27.1 | 13.4 | 7.64 |
| Effective Tax Rate | 40.3% | 38.7% | 46.3% | 43.4% | 49.0% | 44.5% | 42.0% | 38.6% | 41.0% | 42.2% |
| Net Income | 1,309 | 1,258 | 873 | 874 | 422 | 686 | 655 | 599 | 568 | 441 |
| S&P Core Earnings | 1,177 | 1,211 | 841 | 911 | 492 | 496 | 546 | NA | NA | NA |

| Balance Sheet & Other Financial Data (Million $) | | | | | | | | | | |
|---|---|---|---|---|---|---|---|---|---|---|
| Gross Property | 25,731 | 24,722 | 23,790 | 22,892 | 22,374 | 21,231 | 20,589 | 12,839 | 15,013 | 15,255 |
| Capital Expenditures | 1,633 | 1,315 | 1,208 | 846 | 856 | 998 | 852 | 588 | 625 | 653 |
| Net Property | 15,383 | 14,667 | 13,998 | 13,478 | 13,269 | 12,680 | 12,428 | 7,575 | 9,093 | 9,243 |
| Capitalization:Long Term Debt | 8,869 | 8,535 | 8,339 | 10,348 | 9,789 | 11,636 | 12,508 | 6,552 | 6,906 | 7,307 |
| Capitalization:% Long Term Debt | 49.7 | 48.6 | 47.1 | 53.7 | 53.1 | 62.0 | 62.8 | 58.5 | 60.2 | 62.2 |
| Capitalization:Preferred | Nil | Nil | 184 | 335 | 352 | Nil | Nil | Nil | Nil | Nil |
| Capitalization:% Preferred | Nil | Nil | 1.04 | 1.74 | 1.91 | Nil | Nil | Nil | Nil | Nil |
| Capitalization:Common | 8,977 | 9,035 | 9,188 | 8,589 | 8,289 | 7,120 | 7,399 | 4,653 | 4,564 | 4,449 |
| Capitalization:% Common | 50.3 | 51.4 | 51.9 | 44.6 | 45.0 | 38.0 | 37.2 | 41.5 | 39.8 | 37.8 |
| Total Capital | 20,517 | 20,310 | 20,437 | 21,597 | 20,608 | 21,360 | 22,852 | 13,540 | 13,970 | 14,325 |
| % Operating Ratio | 84.9 | 84.3 | 89.0 | 87.3 | 90.4 | 86.6 | 50.8 | 37.8 | 82.0 | 82.2 |
| % Earned on Net Property | 18.7 | 18.2 | 15.0 | 16.5 | 11.2 | 17.4 | 16.8 | 18.1 | 16.7 | NA |
| % Return on Revenue | 10.2 | 10.9 | 7.3 | 7.0 | 3.4 | 5.6 | 8.2 | 8.5 | 9.0 | 7.5 |
| % Return on Invested Capital | 10.1 | 9.6 | 7.3 | 7.4 | 6.5 | 7.4 | 21.8 | 32.0 | 7.8 | NA |
| % Return on Common Equity | 14.5 | 13.8 | 9.8 | 10.4 | 5.5 | 9.5 | 10.9 | 13.0 | 12.6 | 10.3 |

Data as orig reptd.; bef. results of disc opers/spec. items. Per share data adj. for stk. divs.; EPS diluted. E-Estimated. NA-Not Available. NM-Not Meaningful. NR-Not Ranked. UR-Under Review.

**Office:** 76 South Main Street, Akron, OH 44308-1890.
**Telephone:** 800-736-3402.
**Website:** http://www.firstenergycorp.com
**Chrmn:** G.M. Smart

**Pres & CEO:** A.J. Alexander
**EVP & General Counsel:** L.L. Vespoli
**SVP & CFO:** R.H. Marsh
**Chief Acctg Officer & Cntlr:** H.L. Wagner

**Investor Contact:** R.E. Seeholzer (800-736-3402)
**Board Members:** P. T. Addison, A. J. Alexander, M. Anderson, C. Cartwright, W. T. Cottle, R. B. Heisler, Jr., E. J. Novak, Jr., C. A. Rein, G. M. Smart, W. M. Taylor, J. T. Williams

**Founded:** 1996
**Domicile:** Ohio
**Employees:** 14,534

# First Horizon National Corp

**STANDARD & POOR'S**

| S&P Recommendation | SELL ★☆☆☆☆ | Price | 12-Mo. Target Price | Investment Style |
|---|---|---|---|---|
| | | $9.78 (as of Nov 14, 2008) | $8.00 | Large-Cap Blend |

**GICS Sector** Financials
**Sub-Industry** Regional Banks

**Summary** FHN (formerly First Tennessee National) owns First Tennessee Bank and First Horizon Home Loan Corporation.

## Key Stock Statistics (Source S&P, Vickers, company reports)

| | | | | | | | | |
|---|---|---|---|---|---|---|---|---|
| 52-Wk Range | $23.11– 4.39 | S&P Oper. EPS 2008E | -0.88 | Market Capitalization(B) | $1.972 | Beta | 0.71 |
| Trailing 12-Month EPS | $-2.41 | S&P Oper. EPS 2009E | 0.16 | Yield (%) | Nil | S&P 3-Yr. Proj. EPS CAGR(%) | NM |
| Trailing 12-Month P/E | NM | P/E on S&P Oper. EPS 2008E | NM | Dividend Rate/Share | Nil | S&P Credit Rating | BBB |
| $10K Invested 5 Yrs Ago | $2,822 | Common Shares Outstg. (M) | 201.6 | Institutional Ownership (%) | 80 | | |

## Price Performance

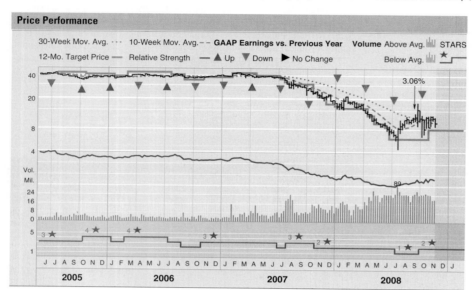

30-Week Mov. Avg. ···  10-Week Mov. Avg. – –  **GAAP Earnings vs. Previous Year**  Volume Above Avg. STARS
12-Mo. Target Price —  Relative Strength —  ▲ Up ▼ Down ▶ No Change  Below Avg.  ★

3.06%

Options: P, Ph

Analysis prepared by **Kevin Cole, CFA** on October 23, 2008, when the stock traded at **$ 10.85.**

## Highlights

➤ In 2008, we expect revenues to be up around 32%, reflecting gains in the mortgage banking business, which suffered from large write-downs in 2007. We look for average earning assets to decrease 8.3%, and the net interest margin to expand to 2.96%, from 2.82% last year. We see non-interest income rising 70%, largely due to significant gains in mortgage banking fees and higher capital markets revenues. However, we believe net interest income will decline 3.5%, as higher margins are offset by significant writedowns on FHN's loan portfolio.

➤ We look for cost-cutting initiatives and asset divestitures to gain traction in late 2008, with expenses down roughly 9%, to about $1.7 billion. We think provisions for losses will nearly quadruple to roughly $1.0 billion, assuming net chargeoffs total roughly 2.5% of average loans. With the allowance for losses at about 84% of nonperforming loans, we believe the company is slightly under-reserved.

➤ Continuing operations recorded a loss of $1.39 a share in 2007, versus EPS of $2.08 in 2006. We project a loss per share of $0.88 in 2008 and EPS of $0.16 in 2009.

## Investment Rationale/Risk

➤ FHN has been one of the more aggressive banks in addressing capital concerns and asset quality issues. In June 2008, FHN agreed to sell mortgage servicing rights and mortgage offices outside its footprint to MetLife. In May 2008, FHN sold $660 million of common shares and announced it would replace its cash dividend with shares. Even considering actions already taken, we still believe FHN will need to raise additional capital if weakness spreads to its commercial loans. Roughly 36% of FHN's portfolio is exposed to commercial and industrial loans. This will likely result in the company taking significant provisions in the quarters ahead, offsetting cost savings associated with the planned mortgage business sale.

➤ Risks to our recommendation and target price include a stabilization of housing prices, a steepening of the yield curve, and better credit conditions than we expect.

➤ Our 12-month target price of $8 is derived by applying a price-to-book value multiple of 0.69X current tangible book value of $11.60, a discount to peers that we think is warranted by what we see as FHN's riskier loan book.

## Qualitative Risk Assessment

| LOW | MEDIUM | HIGH |
|---|---|---|

Our risk assessment takes into account FHN's exposure to a weak residential real estate market, with significant holdings of riskier construction and home equity loans, and what we see as its deteriorating capital base.

## Quantitative Evaluations

**S&P Quality Ranking**      A

| D | C | B- | B | B+ | A- | A | A+ |
|---|---|---|---|---|---|---|---|

**Relative Strength Rank**      STRONG

77

LOWEST = 1        HIGHEST = 99

## Revenue/Earnings Data

**Revenue (Million $)**

| | 1Q | 2Q | 3Q | 4Q | Year |
|---|---|---|---|---|---|
| 2008 | 677.2 | 814.5 | 688.4 | -- | -- |
| 2007 | 866.4 | 875.2 | 786.1 | 638.5 | 3,166 |
| 2006 | 731.0 | 913.6 | 930.4 | 921.0 | 3,496 |
| 2005 | 728.3 | 781.8 | 867.0 | 862.9 | 3,240 |
| 2004 | 624.1 | 630.1 | 627.8 | 647.9 | 2,530 |
| 2003 | 685.6 | 698.3 | 669.7 | 639.8 | 2,693 |

**Earnings Per Share ($)**

| | | | | | |
|---|---|---|---|---|---|
| 2008 | -0.06 | -0.11 | -0.59 | E-0.24 | E-0.88 |
| 2007 | 0.53 | 0.17 | -0.11 | -1.94 | -1.35 |
| 2006 | 0.03 | 0.80 | 0.51 | 0.58 | 3.50 |
| 2005 | 0.82 | 0.78 | 0.87 | 0.84 | 3.32 |
| 2004 | 0.89 | 0.89 | 0.86 | 0.79 | 3.43 |
| 2003 | 0.88 | 0.87 | 0.88 | 0.87 | 3.51 |

Fiscal year ended Dec. 31. Next earnings report expected: Mid January. EPS Estimates based on S&P Operating Earnings; historical GAAP earnings are as reported.

## Dividend Data (Dates: mm/dd Payment Date: mm/dd/yy)

| Amount ($) | Date Decl. | Ex-Div. Date | Stk. of Record | Payment Date |
|---|---|---|---|---|
| 0.200 | 01/17 | 03/12 | 03/14 | 04/01/08 |
| 0.200 | 04/17 | 06/11 | 06/13 | 07/01/08 |
| 3.0615% Stk | 07/17 | 09/10 | 09/12 | 10/01/08 |
| 1.837 Stk. | 10/22 | 12/10 | 12/12 | 01/01/09 |

Dividends have been paid since 1895. Source: Company reports.

# First Horizon National Corp

STANDARD
&POOR'S

## Business Summary October 23, 2008

CORPORATE OVERVIEW. First Horizon National (formerly First Tennessee National) is a Memphis, TN-based regional bank. FHN is one of the 30 largest bank holding companies in the U.S. in terms of asset size, with $37.0 billion in assets at December 31, 2007. Through its three major brands -- First Horizon Home Loan, First Tennessee National and FTN Financial -- the bank provides retail commercial banking services, mortgage banking, and capital markets operations. During 2007, 52% of revenues came from fee income, versus 54% in 2006. This contrasts with the average regional bank, which derives about 32% of its revenues from fee income sources.

Retail/commercial banking contributed 71% of revenues in 2007 (versus 63% in 2006), mortgage banking 9% (22%), capital markets 18% (18%), and corporate 2% (negative 3%).

Income from capital markets operations was the largest contributor to fee income. As of December 2007, First Horizon Home Loan had 500 offices in 42 U.S. states and Hong Kong, and was in the top 20 nationally in mortgage loan originations and the top 15 mortgage loan servicing, at December 31, 2007, as reported by Inside Mortgage Finance.

CORPORATE STRATEGY. Unlike many of its competitors, the company has generally not grown through an aggressive acquisition strategy, but has focused on expanding its nationally ranked specialty lines of business. FHN's strategy is to invest capital and other resources in current markets to expand and gain market share; and to continue to expand the capital markets business into a broader range of products, services, and customers. In 2008, FHN plans to coordinate growth with a focus on stronger and more stable returns on capital.

IMPACT OF MAJOR DEVELOPMENTS. In January 2005, FTN Financial, FHN's capital markets division, acquired the fixed income business of Spear, Leeds & Kellogg, a division of Goldman Sachs, Inc. Following the acquisition, FTN Financial had about 1,000 employees in 15 states, with over 5,000 customers. In March 2006, FHN sold its merchant processing business -- First Horizon Merchant Services -- to NOVA Information Systems, a subsidiary of U.S. Bancorp, for an after-tax gain of $209 million. Partial proceeds from the sale were used to fund a 4 million common share accelerated repurchase program with the goal of minimizing the potentially dilutive effect of the merchant divestiture on future earnings per share.

## Company Financials Fiscal Year Ended Dec. 31

| Per Share Data ($) | 2007 | 2006 | 2005 | 2004 | 2003 | 2002 | 2001 | 2000 | 1999 | 1998 |
|---|---|---|---|---|---|---|---|---|---|---|
| Tangible Book Value | 14.49 | 16.50 | 14.74 | 14.29 | 13.03 | 11.57 | 9.97 | 9.52 | 8.28 | 2.27 |
| Earnings | -1.35 | 3.50 | 3.32 | 3.43 | 3.51 | 2.80 | 2.44 | 1.72 | 1.85 | 1.67 |
| S&P Core Earnings | -0.99 | 1.98 | 3.16 | 3.31 | 3.22 | 2.51 | 1.82 | NA | NA | NA |
| Dividends | 1.75 | 1.75 | 1.69 | 1.58 | 1.26 | 1.02 | 0.88 | 0.85 | 0.74 | 0.64 |
| Payout Ratio | NM | 50% | 51% | 46% | 36% | 36% | 36% | 50% | 40% | 38% |
| Prices:High | 44.09 | 41.79 | 43.47 | 47.21 | 47.06 | 39.78 | 36.38 | 28.44 | 44.03 | 37.24 |
| Prices:Low | 17.13 | 36.00 | 33.75 | 39.58 | 34.52 | 28.88 | 26.32 | 15.46 | 26.56 | 22.68 |
| P/E Ratio:High | NM | 12 | 13 | 14 | 13 | 14 | 15 | 17 | 24 | 22 |
| P/E Ratio:Low | NM | 10 | 10 | 12 | 10 | 10 | 11 | 9 | 14 | 14 |

| Income Statement Analysis (Million $) | | | | | | | | | | |
|---|---|---|---|---|---|---|---|---|---|---|
| Net Interest Income | 941 | 997 | 984 | 856 | 806 | 753 | 686 | 598 | 590 | 541 |
| Tax Equivalent Adjustment | 0.69 | NA | 1.17 | 1.10 | 1.26 | 1.50 | 2.10 | 2.60 | 3.00 | NA |
| Non Interest Income | 861 | 1,233 | 1,400 | 1,342 | 1,638 | 1,550 | 1,321 | 1,068 | 1,121 | 982 |
| Loan Loss Provision | 273 | 83.1 | 67.7 | 48.3 | 86.7 | 92.2 | 93.5 | 67.4 | 57.9 | 51.4 |
| % Expense/Operating Revenue | 102.3% | 78.2% | 70.1% | 68.4% | 67.1% | 71.3% | 67.7% | 75.5% | 74.4% | 73.7% |
| Pretax Income | -316 | 338 | 645 | 667 | 719 | 558 | 494 | 337 | 379 | 353 |
| Effective Tax Rate | 44.6% | 25.8% | 31.6% | 31.9% | 34.2% | 32.5% | 33.2% | 31.0% | 34.8% | 36.0% |
| Net Income | NM | 251 | 441 | 454 | 473 | 376 | 330 | 233 | 248 | 226 |
| % Net Interest Margin | 2.82 | 2.93 | 3.08 | 3.62 | 3.78 | 4.33 | 4.27 | 3.73 | 3.80 | 3.80 |
| S&P Core Earnings | -128 | 261 | 423 | 438 | 434 | 337 | 248 | NA | NA | NA |

| Balance Sheet & Other Financial Data (Million $) | | | | | | | | | | |
|---|---|---|---|---|---|---|---|---|---|---|
| Money Market Assets | 1,129 | 1,221 | 3,629 | 1,676 | 1,182 | 1,157 | 877 | 380 | 430 | 484 |
| Investment Securities | 3,033 | 3,890 | 2,912 | 2,681 | 2,470 | 2,700 | 2,526 | 2,839 | 3,101 | 2,426 |
| Commercial Loans | 8,435 | 8,338 | 9,899 | 7,730 | 6,904 | 5,723 | 5,598 | 5,327 | 4,431 | 4,117 |
| Other Loans | 13,669 | 13,767 | 10,702 | 8,698 | 7,087 | 5,622 | 4,685 | 4,912 | 4,933 | 4,440 |
| Total Assets | 37,015 | 37,918 | 36,579 | 29,772 | 24,507 | 23,823 | 20,617 | 18,555 | 18,373 | 18,734 |
| Demand Deposits | 5,055 | 5,448 | 10,027 | 4,995 | 4,540 | 5,149 | 4,010 | 2,847 | 2,798 | 3,058 |
| Time Deposits | 11,977 | 14,766 | 13,411 | 14,788 | 11,140 | 10,564 | 9,596 | 9,342 | 8,560 | 8,665 |
| Long Term Debt | 6,825 | 6,132 | 3,733 | 2,617 | 1,117 | 1,074 | 3,066 | 3,119 | 459 | 514 |
| Common Equity | 2,136 | 2,462 | 2,312 | 2,041 | 1,850 | 1,691 | 1,478 | 1,384 | 1,241 | 1,100 |
| % Return on Assets | NM | 0.7 | 1.3 | 1.7 | 2.0 | 1.7 | 1.7 | 1.3 | 1.3 | 1.4 |
| % Return on Equity | NM | 10.4 | 20.3 | 23.1 | 26.7 | 23.8 | 23.0 | 17.7 | 21.1 | 23.0 |
| % Loan Loss Reserve | 1.5 | 0.9 | 0.8 | 0.7 | 0.9 | 0.9 | 1.1 | 1.2 | 1.2 | 1.6 |
| % Loans/Deposits | 118.7 | 123.6 | 106.8 | 109.2 | 108.2 | 102.7 | 100.6 | 98.2 | 100.5 | 78.3 |
| % Equity to Assets | 6.1 | 6.5 | 6.6 | 7.2 | 7.3 | 7.1 | 7.3 | 7.1 | 6.3 | 6.2 |

Data as orig reptd.; bef. results of disc opers/spec. items. Per share data adj. for stk. divs.; EPS diluted. E-Estimated. NA-Not Available. NM-Not Meaningful. NR-Not Ranked. UR-Under Review.

**Office:** 165 Madison Avenue, Memphis, TN 38103.
**Telephone:** 901-523-4444.
**Website:** http://www.fhnc.com
**Chrmn:** M.D. Rose

**Pres & CEO:** D.B. Jordan
**Vice Chrmn:** G.L. Baker
**EVP, CFO & Treas:** T.C. Adams, Jr.
**EVP & CTO:** M. McDougall

**Board Members:** G. L. Baker, R. Blattberg, R. B. Carter, S. F. Cooper, J. A. Haslam, III, D. B. Jordan, R. B. Martin, V. R. Palmer, C. V. Reed, M. D. Rose, M. F. Sammons, W. B. Sansom, L. Yancy, III

**Founded:** 1968
**Domicile:** Tennessee
**Employees:** 12,398

The McGraw-Hill Companies

**STANDARD &POOR'S**

# Fiserv Inc

| S&P Recommendation | BUY ★★★★☆ | Price | 12-Mo. Target Price | Investment Style |
|---|---|---|---|---|
| | | $32.75 (as of Nov 14, 2008) | $39.00 | Large-Cap Growth |

**GICS Sector** Information Technology
**Sub-Industry** Data Processing & Outsourced Services

**Summary** This company provides account processing and integrated information management systems for financial institutions. In December 2007, FISV acquired CheckFree Corp. for $4.4 billion.

## Key Stock Statistics (Source S&P, Vickers, company reports)

| | | | | | | | |
|---|---|---|---|---|---|---|---|
| 52-Wk Range | $56.80– 28.57 | S&P Oper. EPS 2008**E** | 3.30 | Market Capitalization(B) | $5.245 | Beta | 1.19 |
| Trailing 12-Month EPS | $3.65 | S&P Oper. EPS 2009**E** | 3.70 | Yield (%) | Nil | S&P 3-Yr. Proj. EPS CAGR(%) | 13 |
| Trailing 12-Month P/E | 9.0 | P/E on S&P Oper. EPS 2008**E** | 9.9 | Dividend Rate/Share | Nil | S&P Credit Rating | BBB |
| $10K Invested 5 Yrs Ago | $8,883 | Common Shares Outstg. (M) | 160.2 | Institutional Ownership (%) | 85 | | |

## Price Performance

30-Week Mov. Avg. · · · 10-Week Mov. Avg. – – **GAAP Earnings vs. Previous Year** Volume Above Avg. ▐▌▐▌ STARS
12-Mo. Target Price — Relative Strength — ▲ Up ▼ Down ► No Change Below Avg. ▐▌▐▌

Options: ASE, CBOE, Ph

Analysis prepared by **Scott H. Kessler** on October 30, 2008, when the stock traded at **$ 32.13**.

## Highlights

➤ We foresee normalized revenue growth of 10% for 2008 and some deceleration in 2009, driven by financial offerings and an unfavorable demand/spending backdrop. We see notable uncertainties related to what we expect will be continuing challenges and consolidation in the financial services segment.

➤ Historically, FISV has used its free cash flow to make acquisitions intended to broaden its offerings and customer base. Acquired companies and businesses once accounted for about 50% of FISV's annual revenue growth. However, in recent years the company de-emphasized acquisitions and has focused more on efforts related to cross-selling and margin improvement.

➤ In December 2007, FISV acquired CheckFree Corp. for $4.4 billion. We believe CheckFree notably broadens and deepens FISV's offerings, technology, and customer base, and will contribute to material market-share gains. In January 2008, FISV sold Fiserv Health for $721 million. In July 2008, FISV sold 51% of its insurance unit for $510 million in after-tax proceeds and announced a related 10 million share buyback.

## Investment Rationale/Risk

➤ Notwithstanding FISV's substantial exposure to financial services customers and activity, which has increased on a percentage basis in recent years, we believe its large size and footprint, diversified customer base, and considerable recurring revenues are appealing. We also believe the recent financial crisis could eventually provide beneficial for new business opportunities.

➤ Risks to our recommendation and target price include weaker demand than we expect for financial services technology offerings, substantial deceleration in internal growth, and a slower and less successful integration of CheckFree than we foresee.

➤ Comparisons to the P/E multiple and P/E-to-growth rate of data processing companies in the S&P 1500 yield a price of $30. Our DCF model (including assumptions of a discount rate of 8.7%, average growth of 9% over the next five years, and a terminal growth rate of 3%) leads to an intrinsic value calculation of $47. Averaging these considerations results in our 12-month target price of $39.

## Qualitative Risk Assessment

| LOW | MEDIUM | HIGH |
|---|---|---|

Our risk assessment reflects our view of FISV's notable size, market position and flexible balance sheet, offset by what we consider its relatively modest internal growth rate and active acquisition strategy.

## Quantitative Evaluations

**S&P Quality Ranking** B+

| D | C | B- | B | B+ | A- | A | A+ |
|---|---|---|---|---|---|---|---|

**Relative Strength Rank** MODERATE

56

LOWEST = 1   HIGHEST = 99

## Revenue/Earnings Data

**Revenue (Million $)**

| | 1Q | 2Q | 3Q | 4Q | Year |
|---|---|---|---|---|---|
| 2008 | 1,310 | 1,295 | 1,080 | -- | -- |
| 2007 | 1,219 | 1,180 | 1,174 | 1,110 | 3,922 |
| 2006 | 1,097 | 1,093 | 1,157 | 1,198 | 4,544 |
| 2005 | 973.1 | 996.4 | 1,012 | 1,078 | 4,059 |
| 2004 | 937.5 | 946.0 | 958.1 | 966.4 | 3,730 |
| 2003 | 707.5 | 738.6 | 796.1 | 837.3 | 3,034 |

**Earnings Per Share ($)**

| | | | | | |
|---|---|---|---|---|---|
| 2008 | 0.59 | 0.60 | 0.45 | E0.93 | E3.30 |
| 2007 | 0.66 | 0.62 | 0.72 | 0.54 | 2.42 |
| 2006 | 0.64 | 0.63 | 0.63 | 0.61 | 2.49 |
| 2005 | 0.71 | 0.59 | 0.58 | 0.80 | 2.68 |
| 2004 | 0.49 | 0.49 | 0.53 | 0.50 | 2.00 |
| 2003 | 0.38 | 0.40 | 0.41 | 0.42 | 1.61 |

Fiscal year ended Dec. 31. Next earnings report expected: Early February. EPS Estimates based on S&P Operating Earnings; historical GAAP earnings are as reported.

## Dividend Data

No cash dividends have been paid.

---

The **McGraw·Hill** Companies

# Fiserv Inc

**STANDARD &POOR'S**

## Business Summary October 30, 2008

CORPORATE OVERVIEW. At the end of 2006, Fiserv made some adjustments to its operating segments. Most notably, it created a new insurance services unit, which included the old health plan management services segment, and insurance operations that were previously classified in the financial institutions segment. In January 2008, FISV sold Fiserv Health, and most of its health-related businesses.

The financial segment (accounting for 77% of total revenues in 2007 and 80% in 2006) provides solutions to more than 9,000 financial institutions, including banks, credit unions, leasing and finance companies, and savings institutions. Many offerings are sold as an integrated suite to clients, and could include core processing (allowing for account servicing and management information functionality for banks, thrifts and credit unions), lending and item processing (providing for the clearing of paper and imaged checks), payments processing (enabling FISV clients to provide their customers with services such as home-banking and bill payment offerings), and a variety of industry-specific products and services.

The insurance segment (21%, 20%) provided solutions to more than 2,500 insurance companies and more than 5,000 agencies and brokerages. These offerings are focused on workers' compensation (involving transaction process-

ing and administration services to that segment), property and casualty insurance associated with flood claims (providing technology to address a broad range of issues from application and claims processing to regulatory compliance), life and annuity products (allowing for everything from educating and licensing agents to reporting on results), and healthcare banking and payments (related to healthcare savings accounts and accounting for associated claims). In mid-2008, FISV sold a majority stake in its insurance segment to Stone Point Capital for after-tax proceeds of $510 million.

In December 2007, FISV acquired CheckFree Corp. for $4.4 billion (and this business accounted for 2% of FISV's total revenues in 2007). We believe this acquisition has bolstered FISV's base of offerings, technology and customers, and see notable cross-selling potential. CheckFree's financial e-commerce products enable consumers to review bank accounts and receive and pay bills electronically. In 2007, CheckFree processed more than 1.4 billion transactions and delivered more than 250 million electronic bills.

## Company Financials Fiscal Year Ended Dec. 31

| Per Share Data ($) | 2007 | 2006 | 2005 | 2004 | 2003 | 2002 | 2001 | 2000 | 1999 | 1998 |
|---|---|---|---|---|---|---|---|---|---|---|
| Tangible Book Value | NM | NM | NM | 0.96 | NM | 2.60 | 2.60 | 2.18 | 1.57 | 1.57 |
| Cash Flow | 2.88 | 3.62 | 3.62 | 2.94 | 2.48 | 2.09 | 1.86 | 1.33 | 1.18 | 1.00 |
| Earnings | 2.42 | 2.49 | 2.68 | 2.00 | 1.61 | 1.37 | 1.09 | 0.93 | 0.73 | 0.60 |
| S&P Core Earnings | 2.42 | 2.50 | 2.28 | 1.91 | 1.47 | 1.26 | 1.00 | NA | NA | NA |
| Dividends | Nil | Nil | Nil | Nil | Nil | Nil | Nil | Nil | Nil | Nil |
| Payout Ratio | Nil | Nil | Nil | Nil | Nil | Nil | Nil | Nil | Nil | Nil |
| Prices:High | 59.85 | 53.60 | 46.89 | 41.01 | 40.77 | 47.24 | 44.61 | 42.75 | 27.17 | 23.83 |
| Prices:Low | 44.16 | 40.29 | 36.33 | 32.20 | 27.23 | 22.50 | 29.08 | 16.21 | 16.08 | 13.33 |
| P/E Ratio:High | 25 | 21 | 17 | 21 | 25 | 34 | 41 | 46 | 37 | 40 |
| P/E Ratio:Low | 18 | 16 | 14 | 16 | 17 | 16 | 27 | 17 | 22 | 22 |

| Income Statement Analysis (Million $) | | | | | | | | | | |
|---|---|---|---|---|---|---|---|---|---|---|
| Revenue | 3,922 | 4,544 | 4,059 | 3,730 | 3,034 | 2,569 | 1,890 | 1,654 | 1,408 | 1,234 |
| Operating Income | 836 | 943 | 925 | 845 | 704 | 734 | 501 | 429 | 347 | 282 |
| Depreciation | 78.0 | 199 | 179 | 185 | 172 | 141 | 148 | 70.1 | 86.3 | 76.5 |
| Interest Expense | 76.0 | 41.0 | 27.8 | 24.9 | 22.9 | 17.8 | 12.1 | 22.1 | 19.4 | 16.0 |
| Pretax Income | 661 | 710 | 818 | 641 | 516 | 436 | 347 | 300 | 234 | 194 |
| Effective Tax Rate | 38.3% | 37.6% | 37.5% | 38.4% | 39.0% | 39.0% | 40.0% | 41.0% | 41.0% | 41.0% |
| Net Income | 408 | 443 | 511 | 395 | 315 | 266 | 208 | 177 | 138 | 114 |
| S&P Core Earnings | 408 | 443 | 435 | 377 | 288 | 246 | 191 | NA | NA | NA |

| Balance Sheet & Other Financial Data (Million $) | | | | | | | | | | |
|---|---|---|---|---|---|---|---|---|---|---|
| Cash | 309 | 185 | 184 | 516 | 203 | 227 | 136 | 98.9 | 80.6 | 71.6 |
| Current Assets | 4,204 | NA | NA | NA | NA | NA | NA | NA | NA | NA |
| Total Assets | 11,846 | 6,208 | 6,040 | 8,383 | 7,214 | 6,439 | 5,322 | 5,586 | 5,308 | 3,958 |
| Current Liabilities | 3,754 | NA | NA | NA | NA | NA | NA | NA | NA | NA |
| Long Term Debt | 5,405 | 747 | 595 | 505 | 699 | 483 | 343 | 335 | 326 | 390 |
| Common Equity | 2,467 | 2,426 | 2,466 | 2,564 | 2,200 | 1,828 | 1,605 | 1,252 | 1,091 | 886 |
| Total Capital | 7,933 | 3,173 | 3,227 | 3,204 | 2,990 | 2,357 | 1,948 | 1,622 | 1,477 | 1,276 |
| Capital Expenditures | 160 | 187 | 165 | 161 | 143 | 142 | 68.0 | 73.0 | 69.7 | 77.5 |
| Cash Flow | 486 | 642 | 691 | 580 | 487 | 407 | 356 | 247 | 224 | 191 |
| Current Ratio | 1.1 | 1.6 | 1.4 | 5.0 | 0.9 | 1.0 | 1.1 | 1.1 | 1.1 | 1.1 |
| % Long Term Debt of Capitalization | 66.5 | 23.6 | 18.4 | 15.8 | 23.4 | 20.5 | 17.6 | 20.7 | 22.1 | 30.6 |
| % Net Income of Revenue | 10.4 | 9.8 | 12.6 | 10.6 | 10.4 | 10.4 | 11.0 | 10.7 | 9.8 | 9.3 |
| % Return on Assets | 4.5 | 7.2 | 7.1 | 5.1 | 4.6 | 4.5 | 3.8 | 3.2 | 3.0 | 3.0 |
| % Return on Equity | 16.7 | 18.1 | 20.3 | 16.6 | 15.6 | 15.5 | 14.6 | 15.1 | 13.9 | 13.8 |

Data as orig reptd.; bef. results of disc opers/spec. items. Per share data adj. for stk. divs.; EPS diluted. E-Estimated. NA-Not Available. NM-Not Meaningful. NR-Not Ranked. UR-Under Review.

Office: 255 Fiserv Drive, Brookfield, WI 53045.
Telephone: 262-879-5000.
Email: general_info@fiserv.com
Website: http://www.fiserv.com

Chrmn: D.F. Dillon
Pres & CEO: J.W. Yabuki
Vice Chrmn: P. Kight
EVP, CFO, Chief Acctg Officer & Treas: T.J. Hirsch

EVP, Chief Admin Officer, Secy & General Counsel: C.W. Sprague
Investor Contact: D. Banks (262-879-5055)
Board Members: D. F. Dillon, D. P. Kearney, P. Kight, G. J. Levy, D. J. O'Leary, G. M. Renwick, K. M. Robak, D. R. Simons, T. Wertheimer, J. W. Yabuki

Founded: 1984
Domicile: Wisconsin
Employees: 25,000

The McGraw-Hill Companies

# Fluor Corp.

**STANDARD & POOR'S**

| S&P Recommendation | BUY ★★★★☆ | Price $39.71 (as of Nov 10, 2008) | 12-Mo. Target Price $50.00 | Investment Style Large-Cap Blend |
| --- | --- | --- | --- | --- |

**GICS Sector** Industrials
**Sub-Industry** Construction & Engineering

**Summary** Fluor is one of the world's largest engineering, procurement and construction companies.

## Key Stock Statistics (Source S&P, Vickers, company reports)

| | | | | | | | |
| --- | --- | --- | --- | --- | --- | --- | --- |
| 52-Wk Range | $101.37– 28.92 | S&P Oper. EPS 2008E | 3.50 | Market Capitalization(B) | $7.108 | Beta | 1.78 |
| Trailing 12-Month EPS | $3.81 | S&P Oper. EPS 2009E | 4.05 | Yield (%) | 1.26 | S&P 3-Yr. Proj. EPS CAGR(%) | 17 |
| Trailing 12-Month P/E | 10.4 | P/E on S&P Oper. EPS 2008E | 11.3 | Dividend Rate/Share | $0.50 | S&P Credit Rating | A |
| $10K Invested 5 Yrs Ago | $23,326 | Common Shares Outstg. (M) | 179.0 | Institutional Ownership (%) | 95 | | |

## Price Performance

- 30-Week Mov. Avg.  ···· 10-Week Mov. Avg. --- **GAAP Earnings vs. Previous Year** Volume Above Avg. STARS
- 12-Mo. Target Price — Relative Strength ▲ Up ▼ Down ▶ No Change Below Avg. ★

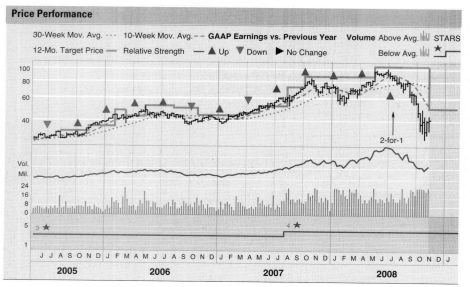

Options: ASE, CBOE, P, Ph

Analysis prepared by **Stewart Scharf** on November 10, 2008, when the stock traded at **$ 39.66.**

## Highlights

➤ We project revenue growth of at least 35% for 2008, but see some moderation in 2009 due to softer demand in certain markets, especially in oil sands. However, we expect the backlog to remain strong for oil and gas, transportation and global services projects, while government work is steady based on DOE projects and nuclear cleanup in the U.K. Demand should slow for power projects as companies are unable to secure permits for coal-fired plants, and oil & gas ventures, which we see FLR targeting more outside the U.S.

➤ In our view, quarterly operating margins may be uneven due to a mix shift, as several large oil and gas projects gradually transition to the construction phase. However, we see higher-margin new awards for industrial and global services projects, and look for margins to expand further in 2009, from our near 6% projection for 2008, aided in part by stabilizing commodities costs. However, we still expect FLR to prioritize profit growth and return on assets (ROA), ahead of margins.

➤ We forecast an effective tax rate of 38% for 2008, and EPS of $3.50 (before a $0.26 gain), advancing 16%, to $4.05, in 2009.

## Investment Rationale/Risk

➤ We maintain our buy recommendation on the stock, based on our valuation models and our view of favorable global growth prospects for most segments. We do not expect the recent drop in oil prices to deter most major oil & gas customers from investing in refinery upgrades and other projects.

➤ Risks to our recommendation and target price include project delays, labor shortages, credit market issues, sharply lower oil prices, and timing issues for new awards. We also are concerned about corporate governance practices, as three or more related-party transactions involved directors or officers other than the CEO.

➤ We believe the shares warrant an above-peers forward P/E multiple, mainly based on the company's strong prospect list and backlog, and diversified business model. Applying a P/E multiple of about 11X to our 2009 EPS estimate results in a value of $45. Our discounted cash flow (DCF) model, which assumes a 3.5% terminal growth rate and an 8.3% weighted average cost of capital suggests the stock's intrinsic value is $55. Using a blend of our DCF and relative P/E metrics, we arrive at our 12-month target price of $50.

## Qualitative Risk Assessment

| LOW | MEDIUM | HIGH |
| --- | --- | --- |

Our risk assessment reflects the cyclical nature of the company's markets, and geopolitical issues, as more projects are in unstable regions of the world. In addition, we see a tight engineering labor market and volatility in new bookings. This is offset by our view of FLR's strong balance sheet, as debt levels are well controlled, and favorable trends continue in the power and oil & gas markets.

## Quantitative Evaluations

**S&P Quality Ranking**     B+

| D | C | B- | B | B+ | A- | A | A+ |
| --- | --- | --- | --- | --- | --- | --- | --- |

**Relative Strength Rank**     MODERATE

37

LOWEST = 1       HIGHEST = 99

## Revenue/Earnings Data

**Revenue (Million $)**

| | 1Q | 2Q | 3Q | 4Q | Year |
| --- | --- | --- | --- | --- | --- |
| 2008 | 4,807 | 5,774 | -- | -- | -- |
| 2007 | 3,642 | 4,222 | 4,155 | 4,712 | 16,691 |
| 2006 | 3,625 | 3,456 | 3,364 | 3,633 | 14,079 |
| 2005 | 2,860 | 2,920 | 3,419 | 3,963 | 13,161 |
| 2004 | 2,063 | 2,214 | 2,363 | 2,740 | 9,380 |
| 2003 | 2,077 | 2,243 | 2,121 | 2,365 | 8,806 |

**Earnings Per Share ($)**

| | | | | | |
| --- | --- | --- | --- | --- | --- |
| 2008 | 0.75 | 1.13 | E0.97 | E0.88 | E3.50 |
| 2007 | 0.47 | 0.52 | 0.51 | 1.42 | 2.93 |
| 2006 | 0.50 | 0.37 | 0.16 | 0.45 | 1.48 |
| 2005 | 0.28 | -0.10 | 0.76 | 0.37 | 1.31 |
| 2004 | 0.29 | 0.27 | 0.29 | 0.29 | 1.13 |
| 2003 | 0.26 | 0.27 | 0.28 | 0.32 | 1.12 |

Fiscal year ended Dec. 31. Next earnings report expected: NA. EPS Estimates based on S&P Operating Earnings; historical GAAP earnings are as reported.

## Dividend Data (Dates: mm/dd Payment Date: mm/dd/yy)

| Amount ($) | Date Decl. | Ex-Div. Date | Stk. of Record | Payment Date |
| --- | --- | --- | --- | --- |
| 0.250 | 05/07 | 06/04 | 06/06 | 07/02/08 |
| 2-for-1 | 05/07 | 07/17 | 06/16 | 07/16/08 |
| 0.125 | 08/01 | 09/03 | 09/05 | 10/02/08 |
| 0.125 | 10/31 | 12/03 | 12/05 | 01/05/09 |

Dividends have been paid since 1974. Source: Company reports.

# Fluor Corp.

**STANDARD &POOR'S**

## Business Summary November 10, 2008

CORPORATE OVERVIEW. Fluor Corp. is one of the world's largest engineering, procurement, construction and maintenance companies. It has five principal operating segments. The Oil and Gas segment provides services to oil, gas, refining, chemical, polymer and petrochemical customers. Industrial and Infrastructure provides EPC services to businesses, including industrial, commercial, telecommunications, mining and technology. Global Services provides operations and maintenance support, and equipment and outsourcing, through TRS Staffing Solutions. Government Services provides support services to the federal government and other government parties.

Contributions to revenues and operating profits in 2007 were as follows: Oil and Gas, 50% of revenues and operating profits of $433 million; Industrial and Infrastructure, 20% and $101 million; Power, 7% and $38 million; Global Services, 15% and $201 million; and Government Services, 7.8% and $29 million.

Total backlog of over $30 billion at year-end 2007, up 38% from a year earlier, was divided by segment as follows: Oil and Gas $18.5 billion, up 54%; Industrial and Infrastructure $6.1 billion, up 11%; Power $2.4 billion, up 86%; Global Services $2.5 billion, up 6%; and Government Services $740 million, down 12%. Backlog by geographic region at the end of 2007 was: U.S. 44%; the Americas 6%; Europe, Africa and the Middle East 43%; and Asia Pacific (including Australia) 7%. Backlog at September 30, 2008, was $36.5 billion, up 31% from a

year earlier and 11% sequentially, and includes a long cycle of larger projects which tend to take three to five years to complete, versus earlier smaller projects which had an 18-to-36 month cycle. As of September 30, 2008, FLR's percentage of fixed price work in backlog had decreased to 25%, from about 30% at the end of 2006, with most of the fixed-price projects in infrastructure and power, while oil & gas is primarily cost reimbursable. About 53% of the backlog was outside the U.S., including 40% in Europe, Africa and the Middle East.

FLR received new awards of $8.8 billion in the third quarter of 2008, up 47% from a year ago. New awards included $3.4 billion for the BP Whiting Modernization Project in the U.S. and a large gas processing project in Russia. New awards by segment in the third quarter of 2008 were: Oil and Gas, 58% of total awards; Industrial and Infrastructure, 24%; Government, 10%; Global Services, 5%; and Power, 3%. The company expects bookings in 2009 to at least the 2008 level.

In the 2007 fourth quarter, FLR recorded a $0.68 tax settlement gain.

## Company Financials Fiscal Year Ended Dec. 31

| Per Share Data ($) | 2007 | 2006 | 2005 | 2004 | 2003 | 2002 | 2001 | 2000 | 1999 | 1998 |
|---|---|---|---|---|---|---|---|---|---|---|
| Tangible Book Value | 12.39 | 9.39 | 8.92 | 7.45 | 6.26 | 5.38 | 4.79 | 9.98 | 9.64 | 9.18 |
| Cash Flow | 3.74 | 2.18 | 1.91 | 1.68 | 1.61 | 1.55 | 1.26 | 2.69 | 2.78 | 3.32 |
| Earnings | 2.93 | 1.48 | 1.31 | 1.13 | 1.12 | 1.07 | 0.81 | 0.66 | 0.69 | 1.49 |
| S&P Core Earnings | 2.93 | 1.50 | 1.31 | 1.04 | 1.17 | 0.90 | 0.57 | NA | NA | NA |
| Dividends | 0.20 | 0.10 | 0.32 | 0.32 | 0.32 | 0.32 | 0.32 | 0.50 | 0.40 | 0.40 |
| Payout Ratio | 7% | 7% | 24% | 28% | 29% | 30% | 40% | 76% | 58% | 27% |
| Prices:High | 86.08 | 51.93 | 39.55 | 27.60 | 20.41 | 22.48 | 31.60 | 24.25 | 23.25 | 26.25 |
| Prices:Low | 37.61 | 36.76 | 25.06 | 18.05 | 13.33 | 10.03 | 15.60 | 11.97 | 13.09 | 17.06 |
| P/E Ratio:High | 29 | 35 | 30 | 25 | 18 | 21 | 39 | 37 | 34 | 18 |
| P/E Ratio:Low | 13 | 25 | 19 | 16 | 12 | 9 | 19 | 18 | 19 | 11 |

| Income Statement Analysis (Million $) | 2007 | 2006 | 2005 | 2004 | 2003 | 2002 | 2001 | 2000 | 1999 | 1998 |
|---|---|---|---|---|---|---|---|---|---|---|
| Revenue | 16,691 | 14,079 | 13,161 | 9,380 | 8,806 | 9,959 | 8,972 | 9,970 | 12,417 | 13,505 |
| Operating Income | 755 | 504 | 396 | 370 | 344 | 332 | 258 | 451 | 654 | 676 |
| Depreciation | 147 | 126 | 104 | 91.9 | 79.7 | 78.0 | 71.9 | 312 | 318 | 289 |
| Interest Expense | 24.0 | 23.0 | 16.3 | 15.4 | 10.1 | 8.93 | 25.0 | 26.3 | 50.9 | 45.0 |
| Pretax Income | 649 | 382 | 300 | 281 | 268 | 261 | 185 | 142 | 186 | 362 |
| Effective Tax Rate | 17.8% | 31.0% | 24.1% | 33.6% | 33.0% | 34.8% | 31.1% | 29.8% | 44.0% | 35.1% |
| Net Income | 533 | 263 | 227 | 187 | 180 | 170 | 128 | 99.8 | 104 | 235 |
| S&P Core Earnings | 533 | 267 | 226 | 171 | 188 | 143 | 90.2 | NA | NA | NA |

| Balance Sheet & Other Financial Data (Million $) | 2007 | 2006 | 2005 | 2004 | 2003 | 2002 | 2001 | 2000 | 1999 | 1998 |
|---|---|---|---|---|---|---|---|---|---|---|
| Cash | 1,714 | 976 | 789 | 605 | 497 | 753 | 573 | 69.4 | 210 | 341 |
| Current Assets | 4,060 | 3,324 | 3,108 | 2,723 | 2,214 | 1,941 | 1,851 | 1,448 | 1,910 | 2,277 |
| Total Assets | 5,796 | 4,875 | 4,574 | 3,970 | 3,449 | 3,142 | 3,091 | 3,653 | 4,886 | 5,019 |
| Current Liabilities | 2,860 | 2,406 | 2,339 | 1,764 | 1,829 | 1,756 | 1,811 | 1,620 | 2,204 | 2,496 |
| Long Term Debt | 325 | 187 | 92.0 | 348 | 44.7 | 17.6 | 17.6 | 17.6 | 318 | 300 |
| Common Equity | 2,274 | 1,730 | 1,631 | 1,336 | 1,082 | 884 | 789 | 1,609 | 1,581 | 1,526 |
| Total Capital | 2,292 | 1,918 | 1,723 | 1,683 | 1,126 | 901 | 807 | 1,627 | 2,061 | 1,932 |
| Capital Expenditures | 284 | 274 | 213 | 104 | 79.2 | 63.0 | 148 | 284 | 504 | 601 |
| Cash Flow | 680 | 390 | 331 | 279 | 259 | 248 | 200 | 412 | 422 | 524 |
| Current Ratio | 1.4 | 1.4 | 1.3 | 1.5 | 1.2 | 1.1 | 1.0 | 0.9 | 0.9 | 0.9 |
| % Long Term Debt of Capitalization | 0.8 | 9.8 | 5.3 | 20.7 | 4.0 | 2.0 | 2.2 | 1.1 | 15.4 | 15.5 |
| % Net Income of Revenue | 3.2 | 1.9 | 1.7 | 2.0 | 2.0 | 1.7 | 1.4 | 1.0 | 0.8 | 1.7 |
| % Return on Assets | 10.0 | 5.6 | 5.3 | 5.0 | 5.4 | 5.4 | 4.4 | 2.3 | 2.1 | 4.8 |
| % Return on Equity | 26.6 | 15.7 | 15.3 | 15.4 | 18.3 | 20.3 | 18.0 | 6.3 | 6.7 | 14.4 |

Data as orig reptd.; bef. results of disc opers/spec. items. Per share data adj. for stk. divs.; EPS diluted. E-Estimated. NA-Not Available. NM-Not Meaningful. NR-Not Ranked. UR-Under Review.

**Office:** 6700 Las Colinas Blvd, Irving, TX 75039-2902.
**Telephone:** 469-398-7000.
**Email:** investor@fluor.com
**Website:** http://www.fluor.com

**Chrmn & CEO:** A. Boeckmann
**COO:** G. Coxon
**EVP & CIO:** R.F. Barnard
**SVP & CFO:** D.M. Steuert

**Treas:** J. Oliva
**Investor Contact:** K. Lockwood (469-398-7220)
**Board Members:** I. Adesida, P. K. Barker, A. Boeckmann, P. J. Fluor, J. T. Hackett, K. Kresa, V. S. Martinez, D. R. O'Hare, J. W. Prueher, P. S. Watson, S. Woolsey

**Founded:** 1924
**Domicile:** Delaware
**Employees:** 41,260

The McGraw-Hill Companies

# Fluor Corp.

**STANDARD &POOR'S**

| S&P Recommendation **BUY** ★★★★☆ | Price<br>$35.73 (as of Nov 14, 2008) | 12-Mo. Target Price<br>$50.00 | Investment Style<br>Large-Cap Blend |
|---|---|---|---|

**GICS Sector** Industrials
**Sub-Industry** Construction & Engineering

**Summary** Fluor is one of the world's largest engineering, procurement and construction companies.

## Key Stock Statistics (Source S&P, Vickers, company reports)

| | | | | | | | |
|---|---|---|---|---|---|---|---|
| 52-Wk Range | $101.37– 28.92 | S&P Oper. EPS 2008**E** | 3.50 | Market Capitalization(B) | $6.485 | Beta | 1.78 |
| Trailing 12-Month EPS | $4.30 | S&P Oper. EPS 2009**E** | 4.05 | Yield (%) | 1.40 | S&P 3-Yr. Proj. EPS CAGR(%) | 17 |
| Trailing 12-Month P/E | 8.3 | P/E on S&P Oper. EPS 2008**E** | 10.2 | Dividend Rate/Share | $0.50 | S&P Credit Rating | A |
| $10K Invested 5 Yrs Ago | $21,011 | Common Shares Outstg. (M) | 181.5 | Institutional Ownership (%) | 95 | | |

## Price Performance

30-Week Mov. Avg. · · · ·   10-Week Mov. Avg. – –   **GAAP Earnings vs. Previous Year**   Volume Above Avg. STARS
12-Mo. Target Price —   Relative Strength —   ▲ Up   ▼ Down   ▶ No Change   Below Avg.   ★

2-for-1

J J A S O N D | J F M A M J J A S O N D | J F M A M J J A S O N D | J F M A M J J A S O N D | J F M A M J J A S O N D J
2005 | 2006 | 2007 | 2008

Options: ASE, CBOE, P, Ph

Analysis prepared by **Stewart Scharf** on November 10, 2008, when the stock traded at **$ 39.66**.

## Highlights

➤ We project revenue growth of at least 35% for 2008, but see some moderation in 2009 due to softer demand in certain markets, especially in oil sands. However, we expect the backlog to remain strong for oil and gas, transportation and global services projects, while government work is steady based on DOE projects and nuclear cleanup in the U.K. Demand should slow for power projects as companies are unable to secure permits for coal-fired plants, and oil & gas ventures, which we see FLR targeting more outside the U.S.

➤ In our view, quarterly operating margins may be uneven due to a mix shift, as several large oil and gas projects gradually transition to the construction phase. However, we see higher-margin new awards for industrial and global services projects, and look for margins to expand further in 2009, from our near 6% projection for 2008, aided in part by stabilizing commodities costs. However, we still expect FLR to prioritize profit growth and return on assets (ROA), ahead of margins.

➤ We forecast an effective tax rate of 38% for 2008, and EPS of $3.50 (before a $0.26 gain), advancing 16%, to $4.05, in 2009.

## Investment Rationale/Risk

➤ We maintain our buy recommendation on the stock, based on our valuation models and our view of favorable global growth prospects for most segments. We do not expect the recent drop in oil prices to deter most major oil & gas customers from investing in refinery upgrades and other projects.

➤ Risks to our recommendation and target price include project delays, labor shortages, credit market issues, sharply lower oil prices, and timing issues for new awards. We also are concerned about corporate governance practices, as three or more related-party transactions involved directors or officers other than the CEO.

➤ We believe the shares warrant an above-peers forward P/E multiple, mainly based on the company's strong prospect list and backlog, and diversified business model. Applying a P/E multiple of about 11X to our 2009 EPS estimate results in a value of $45. Our discounted cash flow (DCF) model, which assumes a 3.5% terminal growth rate and an 8.3% weighted average cost of capital suggests the stock's intrinsic value is $55. Using a blend of our DCF and relative P/E metrics, we arrive at our 12-month target price of $50.

## Qualitative Risk Assessment

| LOW | MEDIUM | HIGH |
|---|---|---|

Our risk assessment reflects the cyclical nature of the company's markets, and geopolitical issues, as more projects are in unstable regions of the world. In addition, we see a tight engineering labor market and volatility in new bookings. This is offset by our view of FLR's strong balance sheet, as debt levels are well controlled, and favorable trends continue in the power and oil & gas markets.

## Quantitative Evaluations

**S&P Quality Ranking**   B+

| D | C | B- | B | B+ | A- | A | A+ |
|---|---|---|---|---|---|---|---|

**Relative Strength Rank**   MODERATE

36

LOWEST = 1                HIGHEST = 99

## Revenue/Earnings Data

**Revenue (Million $)**

| | 1Q | 2Q | 3Q | 4Q | Year |
|---|---|---|---|---|---|
| 2008 | 4,807 | 5,774 | 5,674 | -- | -- |
| 2007 | 3,642 | 4,222 | 4,155 | 4,712 | 16,691 |
| 2006 | 3,625 | 3,456 | 3,364 | 3,633 | 14,079 |
| 2005 | 2,860 | 2,920 | 3,419 | 3,963 | 13,161 |
| 2004 | 2,063 | 2,214 | 2,363 | 2,740 | 9,380 |
| 2003 | 2,077 | 2,243 | 2,121 | 2,365 | 8,806 |

**Earnings Per Share ($)**

| | | | | | |
|---|---|---|---|---|---|
| 2008 | 0.75 | 1.13 | 1.01 | E0.88 | E3.50 |
| 2007 | 0.47 | 0.52 | 0.51 | 1.42 | 2.93 |
| 2006 | 0.50 | 0.37 | 0.16 | 0.45 | 1.48 |
| 2005 | 0.28 | -0.10 | 0.76 | 0.37 | 1.31 |
| 2004 | 0.29 | 0.27 | 0.29 | 0.29 | 1.13 |
| 2003 | 0.26 | 0.27 | 0.28 | 0.32 | 1.12 |

Fiscal year ended Dec. 31. Next earnings report expected: Late February. EPS Estimates based on S&P Operating Earnings; historical GAAP earnings are as reported.

## Dividend Data (Dates: mm/dd Payment Date: mm/dd/yy)

| Amount ($) | Date Decl. | Ex-Div. Date | Stk. of Record | Payment Date |
|---|---|---|---|---|
| 0.250 | 05/07 | 06/04 | 06/06 | 07/02/08 |
| 2-for-1 | 05/07 | 07/17 | 06/16 | 07/16/08 |
| 0.125 | 08/01 | 09/03 | 09/05 | 10/02/08 |
| 0.125 | 10/31 | 12/03 | 12/05 | 01/05/09 |

Dividends have been paid since 1974. Source: Company reports.

STANDARD
&POOR'S

# Fluor Corp.

## Business Summary November 10, 2008

CORPORATE OVERVIEW. Fluor Corp. is one of the world's largest engineering, procurement, construction and maintenance companies. It has five principal operating segments. The Oil and Gas segment provides services to oil, gas, refining, chemical, polymer and petrochemical customers. Industrial and Infrastructure provides EPC services to businesses, including industrial, commercial, telecommunications, mining and technology. Global Services provides operations and maintenance support, and equipment and outsourcing, through TRS Staffing Solutions. Government Services provides support services to the federal government and other government parties.

Contributions to revenues and operating profits in 2007 were as follows: Oil and Gas, 50% of revenues and operating profits of $433 million; Industrial and Infrastructure, 20% and $101 million; Power, 7% and $38 million; Global Services, 15% and $201 million; and Government Services, 7.8% and $29 million.

Total backlog of over $30 billion at year-end 2007, up 38% from a year earlier, was divided by segment as follows: Oil and Gas $18.5 billion, up 54%; Industrial and Infrastructure $6.1 billion, up 11%; Power $2.4 billion, up 86%; Global Services $2.5 billion, up 6%; and Government Services $740 million, down 12%. Backlog by geographic region at the end of 2007 was: U.S. 44%; the Americas 6%; Europe, Africa and the Middle East 43%; and Asia Pacific (including Australia) 7%. Backlog at September 30, 2008, was $36.5 billion, up 31% from a

year earlier and 11% sequentially, and includes a long cycle of larger projects which tend to take three to five years to complete, versus earlier smaller projects which had an 18-to-36 month cycle. As of September 30, 2008, FLR's percentage of fixed price work in backlog had decreased to 25%, from about 30% at the end of 2006, with most of the fixed-price projects in infrastructure and power, while oil & gas is primarily cost reimbursable. About 53% of the backlog was outside the U.S., including 40% in Europe, Africa and the Middle East.

FLR received new awards of $8.8 billion in the third quarter of 2008, up 47% from a year ago. New awards included $3.4 billion for the BP Whiting Modernization Project in the U.S. and a large gas processing project in Russia. New awards by segment in the third quarter of 2008 were: Oil and Gas, 58% of total awards; Industrial and Infrastructure, 24%; Government, 10%; Global Services, 5%; and Power, 3%. The company expects bookings in 2009 to at least the 2008 level.

In the 2007 fourth quarter, FLR recorded a $0.68 tax settlement gain.

## Company Financials Fiscal Year Ended Dec. 31

| Per Share Data ($) | 2007 | 2006 | 2005 | 2004 | 2003 | 2002 | 2001 | 2000 | 1999 | 1998 |
|---|---|---|---|---|---|---|---|---|---|---|
| Tangible Book Value | 12.39 | 9.39 | 8.92 | 7.45 | 6.26 | 5.38 | 4.79 | 9.98 | 9.64 | 9.18 |
| Cash Flow | 3.74 | 2.18 | 1.91 | 1.68 | 1.61 | 1.55 | 1.26 | 2.69 | 2.78 | 3.32 |
| Earnings | 2.93 | 1.48 | 1.31 | 1.13 | 1.12 | 1.07 | 0.81 | 0.66 | 0.69 | 1.49 |
| S&P Core Earnings | 2.93 | 1.50 | 1.31 | 1.31 | 1.04 | 1.17 | 0.90 | 0.57 | NA | NA | NA |
| Dividends | 0.20 | 0.10 | 0.32 | 0.32 | 0.32 | 0.32 | 0.32 | 0.50 | 0.40 | 0.40 |
| Payout Ratio | 7% | 7% | 24% | 28% | 29% | 30% | 40% | 76% | 58% | 27% |
| Prices:High | 86.08 | 51.93 | 39.55 | 27.60 | 20.41 | 22.48 | 31.60 | 24.25 | 23.25 | 26.25 |
| Prices:Low | 37.61 | 36.76 | 25.06 | 18.05 | 13.33 | 10.03 | 15.60 | 11.97 | 13.09 | 17.06 |
| P/E Ratio:High | 29 | 35 | 30 | 25 | 18 | 21 | 39 | 37 | 34 | 18 |
| P/E Ratio:Low | 13 | 25 | 19 | 16 | 12 | 9 | 19 | 18 | 19 | 11 |

| Income Statement Analysis (Million $) | | | | | | | | | | |
|---|---|---|---|---|---|---|---|---|---|---|
| Revenue | 16,691 | 14,079 | 13,161 | 9,380 | 8,806 | 9,959 | 8,972 | 9,970 | 12,417 | 13,505 |
| Operating Income | 755 | 504 | 396 | 370 | 344 | 332 | 258 | 451 | 654 | 676 |
| Depreciation | 147 | 126 | 104 | 91.9 | 79.7 | 78.0 | 71.9 | 312 | 318 | 289 |
| Interest Expense | 24.0 | 23.0 | 16.3 | 15.4 | 10.1 | 8.93 | 25.0 | 26.3 | 50.9 | 45.0 |
| Pretax Income | 649 | 382 | 300 | 281 | 268 | 261 | 185 | 142 | 186 | 362 |
| Effective Tax Rate | 17.8% | 31.0% | 24.1% | 33.6% | 33.0% | 34.8% | 31.1% | 29.8% | 44.0% | 35.1% |
| Net Income | 533 | 263 | 227 | 187 | 180 | 170 | 128 | 99.8 | 104 | 235 |
| S&P Core Earnings | 533 | 267 | 226 | 171 | 188 | 143 | 90.2 | NA | NA | NA |

| Balance Sheet & Other Financial Data (Million $) | | | | | | | | | | |
|---|---|---|---|---|---|---|---|---|---|---|
| Cash | 1,714 | 976 | 789 | 605 | 497 | 753 | 573 | 69.4 | 210 | 341 |
| Current Assets | 4,060 | 3,324 | 3,108 | 2,723 | 2,214 | 1,941 | 1,851 | 1,448 | 1,910 | 2,277 |
| Total Assets | 5,796 | 4,875 | 4,574 | 3,970 | 3,449 | 3,142 | 3,091 | 3,653 | 4,886 | 5,019 |
| Current Liabilities | 2,860 | 2,406 | 2,339 | 1,764 | 1,829 | 1,756 | 1,811 | 1,620 | 2,204 | 2,496 |
| Long Term Debt | 325 | 187 | 92.0 | 348 | 44.7 | 17.6 | 17.6 | 17.6 | 318 | 300 |
| Common Equity | 2,274 | 1,730 | 1,631 | 1,336 | 1,082 | 884 | 789 | 1,609 | 1,581 | 1,526 |
| Total Capital | 2,292 | 1,918 | 1,723 | 1,683 | 1,126 | 901 | 807 | 1,627 | 2,061 | 1,932 |
| Capital Expenditures | 284 | 274 | 213 | 104 | 79.2 | 63.0 | 148 | 284 | 504 | 601 |
| Cash Flow | 680 | 390 | 331 | 279 | 259 | 248 | 200 | 412 | 422 | 524 |
| Current Ratio | 1.4 | 1.4 | 1.3 | 1.5 | 1.2 | 1.1 | 1.0 | 0.9 | 0.9 | 0.9 |
| % Long Term Debt of Capitalization | 0.8 | 9.8 | 5.3 | 20.7 | 4.0 | 2.0 | 2.2 | 1.1 | 15.4 | 15.5 |
| % Net Income of Revenue | 3.2 | 1.9 | 1.7 | 2.0 | 2.0 | 1.7 | 1.4 | 1.0 | 0.8 | 1.7 |
| % Return on Assets | 10.0 | 5.6 | 5.3 | 5.0 | 5.4 | 5.4 | 4.4 | 2.3 | 2.1 | 4.8 |
| % Return on Equity | 26.6 | 15.7 | 15.3 | 15.4 | 18.3 | 20.3 | 18.0 | 6.3 | 6.7 | 14.4 |

Data as orig reptd.; bef. results of disc opers/spec. items. Per share data adj. for stk. divs.; EPS diluted. E-Estimated. NA-Not Available. NM-Not Meaningful. NR-Not Ranked. UR-Under Review.

**Office:** 6700 Las Colinas Blvd, Irving, TX 75039-2902.
**Telephone:** 469-398-7000.
**Email:** investor@fluor.com
**Website:** http://www.fluor.com

**Chrmn & CEO:** A. Boeckmann
**COO:** G. Coxon
**EVP & CIO:** R.F. Barnard
**SVP & CFO:** D.M. Steuert

**Treas:** J. Oliva
**Investor Contact:** K. Lockwood (469-398-7220)
**Board Members:** I. Adesida, P. K. Barker, A. Boeckmann, P. J. Fluor, J. T. Hackett, K. Kresa, V. S. Martinez, D. R. O'Hare, J. W. Prueher, P. S. Watson, S. Woolsey

**Founded:** 1924
**Domicile:** Delaware
**Employees:** 41,260

The McGraw·Hill Companies

# Ford Motor Co

**STANDARD &POOR'S**

## S&P Recommendation HOLD ★★★☆☆

| Price | 12-Mo. Target Price | Investment Style |
|---|---|---|
| $1.80 (as of Nov 14, 2008) | $4.50 | Large-Cap Value |

**GICS Sector** Consumer Discretionary
**Sub-Industry** Automobile Manufacturers

**Summary** Ford, the world's second largest producer of cars and trucks, also has automotive financing and insurance operations.

## Key Stock Statistics (Source S&P, Vickers, company reports)

| | | | | | | | |
|---|---|---|---|---|---|---|---|
| 52-Wk Range | $8.79– 1.72 | S&P Oper. EPS 2008E | -2.26 | Market Capitalization(B) | $4.172 | Beta | 1.63 |
| Trailing 12-Month EPS | $-5.21 | S&P Oper. EPS 2009E | -1.97 | Yield (%) | Nil | S&P 3-Yr. Proj. EPS CAGR(%) | NM |
| Trailing 12-Month P/E | NM | P/E on S&P Oper. EPS 2008E | NM | Dividend Rate/Share | Nil | S&P Credit Rating | B- |
| $10K Invested 5 Yrs Ago | $1,535 | Common Shares Outstg. (M) | 2,388.9 | Institutional Ownership (%) | 77 | | |

## Price Performance

30-Week Mov. Avg. · · · · 10-Week Mov. Avg. - - **GAAP Earnings vs. Previous Year** Volume Above Avg. STARS
12-Mo. Target Price — Relative Strength — ▲ Up ▼ Down ► No Change Below Avg. ★

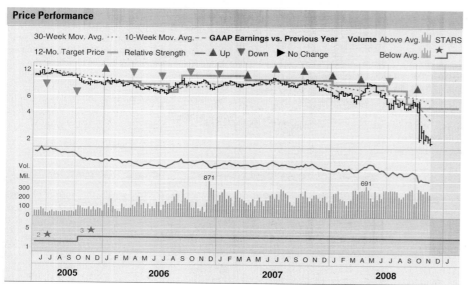

Options: ASE, CBOE, P, Ph

Analysis prepared by **Efraim Levy, CFA** on October 07, 2008, when the stock traded at **$ 3.07**.

### Highlights

➤ We see F's total revenues falling 4% to 5% in 2009. We believe F faces challenges from weakening demand in the U.S. and Europe, intense competition, lower market share, excess capacity, relatively high gasoline prices, and a sharp shift in demand for its important pickup trucks. The financial services segment has historically been an important contributor to sales and earnings, but we think it will report a loss for 2008 given reduced truck residual values.

➤ We see F's contract with the UAW enhancing F's profitability by about $2 billion a year starting in 2010. The agreement includes unprecedented union givebacks in terms of benefits and work rules, personalized to F's needs. In addition, the establishment of a health care trust to be managed by the union should free the company from onerous and uncertain obligations. Still, what is really needed, in our view, is increased demand for Ford's products on styling, quality and value improvements.

➤ In 2008, we expect sizable cash outlays as Ford proceeds with its restructuring plan and faces declining North American sales. We expect the company to post losses through 2009 and to see further operating cash outflows.

### Investment Rationale/Risk

➤ We think Ford's president and CEO, an automotive industry outsider with experience in turning around an international manufacturer, has enhanced Ford's improvement efforts. However, we are less confident in his or Ford's ability to consistently bring to market successful vehicles -- one of the company's most important challenges, in our view. In 2008, we expect the company to lose market share again. While we believe that Ford needs to stabilize volumes, we would hold the shares, as we believe that net income will benefit from restructuring activities.

➤ Risks to our opinion and target price include increased competitive challenges, a decline in expected demand and production, weaker than projected financial services income, and a greater drop in cash balances than we expect. We are also concerned about Ford's corporate governance, with Ford family members having greater voting rights than other shareholders.

➤ As of June 30, 2008, total stockholders' equity was negative. The stock recently traded at a price to sales (P/S) multiple above that of GM. Based on peer comparative P/S multiples, our 12-month target price is $4.50, equal to about 0.07X projected 2009 sales per share.

### Qualitative Risk Assessment

| LOW | MEDIUM | HIGH |
|---|---|---|

Our risk assessment reflects the highly cyclical nature of Ford's markets as well as our view of the current and long-term challenges it faces, including intensifying competition, high fixed and legacy costs, and a weak balance sheet.

### Quantitative Evaluations

**S&P Quality Ranking** C

| D | C | B- | B | B+ | A- | A | A+ |
|---|---|---|---|---|---|---|---|

**Relative Strength Rank** WEAK

17

LOWEST = 1     HIGHEST = 99

### Revenue/Earnings Data

**Revenue (Million $)**

| | 1Q | 2Q | 3Q | 4Q | Year |
|---|---|---|---|---|---|
| 2008 | 43,513 | 38,600 | 32,100 | -- | -- |
| 2007 | 43,019 | 44,200 | 41,100 | 44,100 | 172,455 |
| 2006 | 41,055 | 41,965 | 37,110 | 40,318 | 160,123 |
| 2005 | 45,136 | 44,548 | 40,856 | 46,549 | 177,089 |
| 2004 | 44,691 | 42,802 | 38,996 | 44,930 | 171,652 |
| 2003 | 40,815 | 40,582 | 36,791 | 46,008 | 164,196 |

**Earnings Per Share ($)**

| | | | | | |
|---|---|---|---|---|---|
| 2008 | 0.05 | -3.88 | -0.06 | E-0.80 | E-2.26 |
| 2007 | -0.15 | 0.30 | -0.19 | -1.33 | -1.40 |
| 2006 | -0.64 | -0.14 | -2.79 | -2.98 | -6.72 |
| 2005 | 0.58 | 0.47 | -0.16 | 0.21 | 1.14 |
| 2004 | 0.95 | 0.57 | 0.25 | 0.03 | 1.80 |
| 2003 | 0.45 | 0.22 | 0.13 | -0.35 | 0.50 |

Fiscal year ended Dec. 31. Next earnings report expected: Late January. EPS Estimates based on S&P Operating Earnings; historical GAAP earnings are as reported.

### Dividend Data

No cash dividends have been paid since 2006.

# Ford Motor Co

## Business Summary October 07, 2008

CORPORATE OVERVIEW. Ford is the world's second largest motor vehicle manufacturer. It produces cars and trucks, and many of the vehicles' plastic, glass and electronic components, and replacement parts. It also owns a 33% stake in Mazda Motor Corp. Financial services include Ford Motor Credit (automotive financing and insurance) and American Road Insurance Co.

Despite historically high new light vehicle industry volume, Ford's margins have been pressured by an increase in competition -- primarily from Asian companies -- and a shift away from the more profitable large pickup truck and SUV segments to smaller, less profitable crossover utility vehicles (CUVs). We think this is likely to hurt Ford's market share, at least until the company can introduce more of its own CUVs.

In recent years, the company's business and product portfolio has changed several times as Ford sought to optimize its financial health and performance. In December 2005, Ford sold its Hertz Corp. unit for about $15 billion, including around $5.6 billion in cash proceeds. We believe the sale diluted EPS in 2006, as Hertz had contributed $0.16 per share to EPS in 2004 and $0.19 in the first nine months of 2005, according to company estimates. In 1999, the company acquired the car operations of AB Volvo for $6.45 billion. In 2000, Ford acquired Land Rover from BMW Group for $1.9 billion. In June 2008, the company sold Jaguar and Land Rover to Tata Motors for $2.3 billion, but used about $600 million of the proceeds to fund the Jaguar and Land Rover pension plans.

CORPORATE STRATEGY. Challenged by a shrinking U.S. market share, the company has announced restructuring plans in recent years in an attempt to lower its costs. However, even as Ford works to reduce its costs, the company now faces expenses stemming from assistance F is giving its former in-house parts manufacturing unit, Visteon Corp. In October 2005, Ford acquired 23 money-losing plants and facilities from Visteon. It also provided financial assistance to Visteon. In exchange, it received warrants to purchase Visteon common shares.

In March 2005, the company agreed to relieve Visteon of a portion (about $25 million per month) of its obligation to reimburse Ford for the costs of Ford's employees assigned to Visteon; to reduce by about one-fourth the number of days within which Ford will make payment to Visteon for materials and components it purchases from Visteon; and to acquire up to about $150 million of new machinery and equipment for use by Visteon necessary for its production of components for Ford. In exchange, Visteon agreed to continue to supply Ford with certain components without cost surcharges.

In January 2007, the company reported nearly $10 billion in restructuring-related charges, after taxes. The costs included expenses related to the buyout of approximately 38,000 hourly U.S. as well additional employees outside the U.S and fixed asset impairment charges in North America and at Jaguar and Land Rover.

## Company Financials Fiscal Year Ended Dec. 31

| Per Share Data ($) | 2007 | 2006 | 2005 | 2004 | 2003 | 2002 | 2001 | 2000 | 1999 | 1998 |
|---|---|---|---|---|---|---|---|---|---|---|
| Tangible Book Value | 0.70 | NM | 3.68 | 4.60 | 2.30 | NM | NM | 6.10 | 16.60 | 16.80 |
| Cash Flow | 5.26 | -6.71 | 7.62 | 9.12 | 8.31 | 8.45 | 5.78 | 13.46 | 13.36 | 24.70 |
| Earnings | -1.40 | -6.72 | 1.14 | 1.80 | 0.50 | 0.15 | -3.02 | 3.59 | 5.86 | 17.76 |
| S&P Core Earnings | -0.94 | -5.58 | 0.64 | 1.80 | 1.03 | -1.16 | -4.56 | NA | NA | NA |
| Dividends | Nil | 0.35 | 0.40 | 0.40 | 0.40 | 0.40 | 1.05 | 2.30 | 1.88 | 2.18 |
| Payout Ratio | Nil | NM | 35% | 22% | 80% | NM | NM | 64% | 32% | 12% |
| Prices:High | 9.70 | 9.48 | 14.75 | 17.34 | 17.33 | 18.23 | 31.42 | 57.25 | 67.88 | 65.94 |
| Prices:Low | 6.65 | 1.06 | 7.57 | 12.61 | 6.58 | 6.90 | 14.70 | 21.69 | 46.25 | 37.50 |
| P/E Ratio:High | NM | NM | 13 | 10 | 35 | NM | NM | 16 | 12 | 4 |
| P/E Ratio:Low | NM | NM | 7 | 7 | 13 | NM | NM | 6 | 8 | 2 |

| Income Statement Analysis (Million $) | | | | | | | | | | |
|---|---|---|---|---|---|---|---|---|---|---|
| Revenue | 172,455 | 160,123 | 177,089 | 171,652 | 164,196 | 163,420 | 162,412 | 170,064 | 162,558 | 144,416 |
| Operating Income | 21,189 | 8,286 | 21,052 | 24,945 | 24,770 | 25,034 | 22,941 | 34,530 | 29,311 | 27,400 |
| Depreciation | 13,158 | 16,453 | 14,042 | 13,052 | 14,297 | 15,177 | 15,922 | 14,849 | 9,254 | 8,589 |
| Interest Expense | 10,927 | 8,783 | 7,643 | 7,071 | 7,690 | 8,824 | 10,848 | 10,902 | 9,076 | 8,865 |
| Pretax Income | -3,746 | -15,051 | 1,996 | 4,853 | 1,370 | 953 | -7,584 | 8,234 | 11,026 | 25,396 |
| Effective Tax Rate | NM | NM | NM | 19.3% | 9.85% | 31.7% | NM | 32.9% | 33.3% | 12.5% |
| Net Income | -2,764 | -12,615 | 2,228 | 3,634 | 921 | 284 | -5,453 | 5,410 | 7,237 | 22,071 |
| S&P Core Earnings | -1,866 | -10,472 | 1,146 | 3,637 | 1,905 | -2,202 | -8,266 | NA | NA | NA |

| Balance Sheet & Other Financial Data (Million $) | | | | | | | | | | |
|---|---|---|---|---|---|---|---|---|---|---|
| Cash | 50,031 | 50,366 | 39,082 | 33,018 | 33,642 | 30,521 | 15,028 | 16,490 | 23,585 | 23,805 |
| Total Assets | 279,264 | 278,554 | 269,476 | 292,654 | 304,594 | 289,357 | 276,543 | 284,421 | 276,229 | 237,545 |
| Long Term Debt | 107,478 | 144,373 | 94,428 | 106,540 | 119,751 | 125,806 | 121,430 | 99,560 | 78,734 | 64,898 |
| Total Debt | 168,530 | 172,049 | 154,332 | 172,973 | 179,804 | 167,892 | 168,009 | 166,229 | 152,738 | 132,835 |
| Common Equity | 5,628 | -3,465 | 12,957 | 16,045 | 11,651 | 5,590 | 7,786 | 18,610 | 27,537 | 23,409 |
| Capital Expenditures | 6,022 | 6,848 | 7,517 | 6,745 | 7,749 | 7,278 | 7,008 | 8,348 | 8,535 | 8,617 |
| Cash Flow | 10,394 | -12,615 | 16,270 | 16,686 | 15,218 | 15,446 | 10,454 | 20,244 | 16,476 | 30,553 |
| % Return on Assets | NM | NM | 0.8 | 1.2 | 0.3 | 0.1 | NM | 2.0 | 2.8 | 8.5 |
| % Return on Equity | NM | NM | 15.4 | 26.2 | 10.7 | 4.0 | NM | 23.3 | 28.4 | 81.1 |
| % Long Term Debt of Capitalization | 93.9 | 83.7 | 82.9 | 82.2 | 87.5 | 87.8 | 87.2 | 78.3 | 68.6 | 73.5 |

Data as orig reptd.; bef. results of disc opers/spec. items. Per share data adj. for stk. divs.; EPS diluted. E-Estimated. NA-Not Available. NM-Not Meaningful. NR-Not Ranked. UR-Under Review.

**Office:** 1 American Rd, Dearborn, MI 48126-2798.
**Telephone:** 313-322-3000.
**Website:** http://www.ford.com
**Chrmn & COO:** W.C. Ford, Jr.

**Pres & CEO:** A.R. Mulally
**EVP & CFO:** L.W. Booth
**SVP, Chief Acctg Officer & Cntlr:** P.J. Daniel
**CTO:** G. Schmidt

**Investor Contact:** D.R. Leclair (800-555-5259)
**Board Members:** S. G. Butler, K. A. Casiano, E. B. Ford, II, W. C. Ford, Jr., I. O. Hockaday, Jr., R. A. Manoogian, E. R. Marram, A. R. Mulally, H. A. Neal, G. L. Shaheen, J. L. Thornton

**Founded:** 1903
**Domicile:** Delaware
**Employees:** 246,000

# Forest Laboratories Inc.

**STANDARD &POOR'S**

| S&P Recommendation | HOLD ★★★☆☆ | Price $22.97 (as of Nov 14, 2008) | 12-Mo. Target Price $28.00 | Investment Style Large-Cap Growth |
|---|---|---|---|---|

**GICS Sector** Health Care
**Sub-Industry** Pharmaceuticals

**Summary** This company develops and makes branded and generic ethical drug products, sold primarily in the U.S., Puerto Rico, and Western and Eastern Europe.

## Key Stock Statistics (Source S&P, Vickers, company reports)

| | | | | | | | |
|---|---|---|---|---|---|---|---|
| 52-Wk Range | $42.76–20.00 | S&P Oper. EPS 2009**E** | 3.35 | Market Capitalization(B) | $6.923 | Beta | 0.93 |
| Trailing 12-Month EPS | $3.10 | S&P Oper. EPS 2010**E** | 3.55 | Yield (%) | Nil | S&P 3-Yr. Proj. EPS CAGR(%) | 9 |
| Trailing 12-Month P/E | 7.4 | P/E on S&P Oper. EPS 2009**E** | 6.9 | Dividend Rate/Share | Nil | S&P Credit Rating | NA |
| $10K Invested 5 Yrs Ago | $4,291 | Common Shares Outstg. (M) | 301.4 | Institutional Ownership (%) | 95 | | |

## Price Performance

30-Week Mov. Avg. · · · 10-Week Mov. Avg. - - **GAAP Earnings vs. Previous Year** Volume Above Avg. STARS
12-Mo. Target Price — Relative Strength ▲ Up ▼ Down ► No Change Below Avg. ★

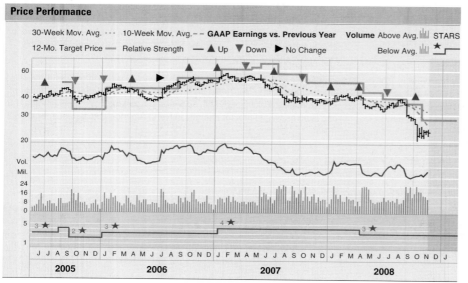

Options: ASE, CBOE, P, Ph

Analysis prepared by **Herman B. Saftlas** on October 24, 2008, when the stock traded at **$ 22.07**.

## Highlights

➤ We expect revenues in FY 09 (Mar.) to rise about 4%. Despite heightened competitive pressures, we see modest growth for Lexapro, reflecting our view of that drug's efficacy and side effect advantages, and higher prices. FDA clearance to market Lexapro for adolescent depression would also boost volume, in our opinion. We look for sales of Namenda Alzheimer's drug to increase in the low double digits, lifted by projected greater acceptance in the medical community. We expect sales of Bystolic beta blocker antihypertensive, launched in January 2008, to reach $55 million in FY 09.

➤ We forecast gross margins to expand somewhat on productivity enhancements. However, R&D spending is expected to be sharply higher, largely reflecting an estimated $100 million in milestone payments on in-licensed drugs during the second half of FY 09. SG&A costs should also rise to support new product launches. Joint venture income is expected to be lower.

➤ We estimate EPS in FY 09 at $3.35 (before an $0.08 special charge), up from $3.06 in FY 08. We see EPS of $3.55 for FY 10.

## Investment Rationale/Risk

➤ This leading specialty drugmaker faces a challenging future, in our view, with patent protection on its two principal products -- Lexapro antidepressant and Namenda Alzheimer's treatment (combined sales accounting for 81% of FY 08 revenues) -- expiring in 2012-2013. While we believe FRX has an impressive pipeline of new products, as well as other in-licensing opportunities, we are uncertain if they will be sufficient to replace Lexapro and Namenda. Key R&D programs include milnacipran for fibromyalgia; linaclotide for constipation and irritable bowel syndrome; dutogliptin for type 2 diabetes; and new uses for Lexapro and Bystolic.

➤ Risks to our recommendation and target price include greater-than-expected competition in principal markets, as well as possible setbacks in the R&D pipeline.

➤ Our 12-month target price of $28 applies a discount-to-peers P/E of 8.4X our FY 09 EPS estimate. This valuation is also supported by our DCF model, which assumes decelerating cash flow growth over the next 10 years, a WACC of 8%, and terminal growth of 1%, and leads to an intrinsic value of $28.

## Qualitative Risk Assessment

| LOW | MEDIUM | HIGH |
|---|---|---|

Our risk assessment reflects that we view positively the company's recent legal victory against generic challengers to its important Lexapro patent. We also think its R&D pipeline shows promise. However, Forest's relatively small size among big pharma competitors and our view of its somewhat limited product line represent negative risk factors.

## Quantitative Evaluations

**S&P Quality Ranking**     B+

| D | C | B- | B | B+ | A- | A | A+ |
|---|---|---|---|---|---|---|---|

**Relative Strength Rank**     MODERATE

66

LOWEST = 1         HIGHEST = 99

## Revenue/Earnings Data

**Revenue (Million $)**

| | 1Q | 2Q | 3Q | 4Q | Year |
|---|---|---|---|---|---|
| 2009 | 947.9 | 972.8 | -- | -- | -- |
| 2008 | 928.3 | 919.0 | 998.2 | 990.9 | 3,718 |
| 2007 | 816.3 | 847.0 | 893.0 | 885.4 | 3,442 |
| 2006 | 711.8 | 736.5 | 757.8 | 756.3 | 2,962 |
| 2005 | -- | -- | -- | 640.6 | 3,114 |
| 2004 | 605.8 | 619.2 | 700.5 | 725.1 | 2,650 |

**Earnings Per Share ($)**

| | | | | | |
|---|---|---|---|---|---|
| 2009 | 0.79 | 0.80 | E0.88 | E0.80 | E3.35 |
| 2008 | 0.83 | 0.71 | 0.96 | 0.55 | 3.06 |
| 2007 | 0.62 | 0.75 | 0.78 | -0.75 | 1.41 |
| 2006 | 0.62 | 0.59 | 0.57 | 0.28 | 2.08 |
| 2005 | 0.60 | 0.79 | 0.70 | 0.15 | 2.25 |
| 2004 | 0.48 | 0.49 | 0.60 | 0.38 | 1.95 |

Fiscal year ended Mar. 31. Next earnings report expected: Mid January. EPS Estimates based on S&P Operating Earnings; historical GAAP earnings are as reported.

## Dividend Data

No cash dividends have been paid.

# Forest Laboratories Inc.

## Business Summary October 24, 2008

CORPORATE OVERVIEW. Forest Laboratories is a leading producer of niche-oriented branded and generic prescription pharmaceuticals. Most of Forest's products were developed in collaboration with licensing partners. FRX's most important products are antidepressants, which accounted for about 65% of net sales in FY 08 (Mar.).

Lexapro antidepressant is the company's single most important product. A single enanitomer version of Celexa (an older, off-patent FRX antidepressant), Lexapro is an advanced selective serotonin reuptake inhibitor (SSRI) indicated for the treatment of both depression and generalized anxiety disorder. Lexapro had sales of $2.3 billion in FY 08, up from $2.1 billion in FY 07. FRX licensed both Celexa and Lexapro from H. Lundbeck A/S, a Danish pharmaceutical company.

FRX's second most important product is Namenda (licensed from Merz Pharmaceuticals of Germany), a treatment for moderate to severe Alzheimer's disease. Sales of Namenda were $830 million in FY 08, up from $660 million in FY 07.

The company's third largest drug is Benicar, a antihypertensive co-promoted with Sankyo. FRX booked income of $212 million from Benicar in FY 08, up from

$175 million in FY 07. In January 2008, FRX launched Bystolic, a novel beta blocker antihypertensive that was in-licensed from Mylan Laboratories. Other products include Tiazac, an antihypertensive; Aerobid, an asthma drug; Campral for alcohol addiction; Combunox for the short-term management of severe pain; Aero-chamber, a device used to improve the delivery of aerosol products; and Cervidil, used to aid in cervical dilation.

COMPETITIVE LANDSCAPE. The U.S. antidepressant drug market totaled about $11.7 billion in the 12 months through March 2008, based on data from IMS Health. We expect this market to shrink in terms of dollar sales over the coming years, reflecting the impact of inexpensive generic versions of many patent-expired branded antidepressants. Pfizer's popular Zoloft antidepressant lost patent protection in 2006, and Wyeth's patent on Effexor antidepressant expires in 2008. Generics now largely comprise previously branded Prozac and Paxil antidepressant markets.

## Company Financials Fiscal Year Ended Mar. 31

| Per Share Data ($) | 2008 | 2007 | 2006 | 2005 | 2004 | 2003 | 2002 | 2001 | 2000 | 1999 |
|---|---|---|---|---|---|---|---|---|---|---|
| Tangible Book Value | 10.19 | 8.93 | 7.69 | 8.21 | 8.03 | 5.66 | 3.75 | 2.60 | 1.79 | 1.60 |
| Cash Flow | NA | 1.55 | 2.20 | 2.32 | 2.01 | 1.80 | 1.06 | 0.71 | 0.44 | 0.29 |
| Earnings | 3.06 | 1.41 | 2.08 | 2.25 | 1.95 | 1.66 | 0.91 | 0.59 | 0.32 | 0.23 |
| S&P Core Earnings | 3.01 | 1.41 | 1.97 | 2.15 | 1.85 | 1.58 | 0.74 | 0.47 | NA | NA |
| Dividends | Nil | Nil | Nil | Nil | Nil | Nil | Nil | Nil | Nil | Nil |
| Payout Ratio | Nil | Nil | Nil | Nil | Nil | Nil | Nil | Nil | Nil | Nil |
| Calendar Year | 2007 | 2006 | 2005 | 2004 | 2003 | 2002 | 2001 | 2000 | 1999 | 1998 |
| Prices:High | 57.97 | 54.70 | 45.21 | 78.81 | 63.23 | 54.99 | 41.60 | 35.33 | 15.44 | 13.31 |
| Prices:Low | 34.89 | 36.18 | 32.46 | 36.10 | 41.85 | 32.12 | 23.25 | 14.34 | 10.31 | 6.08 |
| P/E Ratio:High | 19 | 39 | 22 | 35 | 32 | 33 | 46 | 60 | 48 | 59 |
| P/E Ratio:Low | 11 | 26 | 16 | 16 | 21 | 19 | 26 | 24 | 32 | 27 |

### Income Statement Analysis (Million $)

| | 2008 | 2007 | 2006 | 2005 | 2004 | 2003 | 2002 | 2001 | 2000 | 1999 |
|---|---|---|---|---|---|---|---|---|---|---|
| Revenue | 3,718 | 3,442 | 2,962 | 3,114 | 2,650 | 2,207 | 1,567 | 1,181 | 882 | 546 |
| Operating Income | NA | 754 | 701 | 1,164 | 929 | 833 | 490 | 318 | 181 | 54.3 |
| Depreciation | 86.7 | 45.4 | 40.7 | 25.4 | 22.2 | 51.6 | 54.6 | 43.3 | 40.6 | 21.3 |
| Interest Expense | NA | Nil | Nil | Nil | Nil | Nil | Nil | Nil | Nil | Nil |
| Pretax Income | 1,210 | 709 | 870 | 1,185 | 937 | 821 | 470 | 299 | 157 | 111 |
| Effective Tax Rate | 20.0% | 35.9% | 18.5% | 29.2% | 21.5% | 24.2% | 28.1% | 28.0% | 28.4% | 30.4% |
| Net Income | 968 | 454 | 709 | 839 | 736 | 622 | 338 | 215 | 113 | 77.2 |
| S&P Core Earnings | 953 | 454 | 673 | 800 | 697 | 589 | 272 | 170 | NA | NA |

### Balance Sheet & Other Financial Data (Million $)

| | 2008 | 2007 | 2006 | 2005 | 2004 | 2003 | 2002 | 2001 | 2000 | 1999 |
|---|---|---|---|---|---|---|---|---|---|---|
| Cash | 1,777 | 1,353 | 1,323 | 1,619 | 2,131 | 1,556 | 893 | 506 | 355 | 279 |
| Current Assets | NA | 2,423 | 2,207 | 2,708 | 2,916 | 2,255 | 1,195 | 884 | 645 | 502 |
| Total Assets | 4,525 | 3,653 | 3,120 | 3,705 | 3,863 | 2,918 | 1,952 | 1,447 | 1,098 | 875 |
| Current Liabilities | NA | 628 | 421 | 564 | 605 | 564 | 325 | 224 | 211 | 130 |
| Long Term Debt | NA | Nil | Nil | Nil | Nil | Nil | Nil | Nil | Nil | Nil |
| Common Equity | 3,715 | 3,025 | 2,698 | 3,132 | 3,256 | 2,352 | 1,625 | 1,222 | 885 | 744 |
| Total Capital | NA | 3,026 | 2,699 | 3,141 | 3,258 | 2,354 | 1,627 | 1,223 | 887 | 745 |
| Capital Expenditures | 34.9 | 30.0 | 55.0 | 89.0 | 102 | 79.6 | 36.4 | 30.9 | 35.3 | 17.2 |
| Cash Flow | NA | 500 | 749 | 864 | 758 | 674 | 393 | 258 | 153 | 98.4 |
| Current Ratio | 4.8 | 3.9 | 5.2 | 4.8 | 4.8 | 4.0 | 3.7 | 4.0 | 3.1 | 3.9 |
| % Long Term Debt of Capitalization | Nil | Nil | Nil | Nil | Nil | Nil | Nil | Nil | Nil | Nil |
| % Net Income of Revenue | 26.0 | 13.5 | 24.3 | 26.9 | 27.8 | 28.2 | 21.6 | 18.2 | 12.8 | 14.1 |
| % Return on Assets | 23.7 | 13.4 | 20.8 | 22.2 | 21.7 | 25.5 | 19.9 | 16.7 | 11.4 | 9.5 |
| % Return on Equity | 28.7 | 15.9 | 24.3 | 26.3 | 26.2 | 31.3 | 23.7 | 20.4 | 13.8 | 11.4 |

Data as orig reptd.; bef. results of disc opers/spec. items. Per share data adj. for stk. divs.; EPS diluted. E-Estimated. NA-Not Available. NM-Not Meaningful. NR-Not Ranked. UR-Under Review.

**Office:** 909 3rd Ave, New York, NY 10022-4748.
**Telephone:** 212-421-7850.
**Email:** investor.relations@frx.com
**Website:** http://www.frx.com

**Chrmn & CEO:** H. Solomon
**Pres & COO:** L.S. Olanoff
**Investor Contact:** F.I. Perier, Jr. (212-421-7850)
**SVP, CFO & Chief Acctg Officer:** F.I. Perier, Jr.

**Secy:** W.J. Candee, III
**Board Members:** N. Basgoz, W. J. Candee, III, G. S. Cohan, D. L. Goldwasser, K. E. Goodman, L. S. Olanoff, L. B. Salans, H. Solomon

**Founded:** 1956
**Domicile:** Delaware
**Employees:** 5,211

# Fortune Brands Inc.

**STANDARD & POOR'S**

| S&P Recommendation | HOLD ★★★☆☆ | Price | 12-Mo. Target Price | Investment Style |
|---|---|---|---|---|
| | | $36.07 (as of Nov 14, 2008) | $42.00 | Large-Cap Blend |

**GICS Sector** Consumer Discretionary
**Sub-Industry** Housewares & Specialties

**Summary** This diversified holding company has interests in consumer businesses that include home improvement, spirits, and golf-related products.

## Key Stock Statistics (Source S&P, Vickers, company reports)

| | | | | | | | |
|---|---|---|---|---|---|---|---|
| 52-Wk Range | $79.83–32.00 | S&P Oper. EPS 2008E | 3.93 | Market Capitalization(B) | $5.408 | Beta | 1.14 |
| Trailing 12-Month EPS | $5.12 | S&P Oper. EPS 2009E | 3.95 | Yield (%) | 4.88 | S&P 3-Yr. Proj. EPS CAGR(%) | 8 |
| Trailing 12-Month P/E | 7.0 | P/E on S&P Oper. EPS 2008E | 9.2 | Dividend Rate/Share | $1.76 | S&P Credit Rating | BBB |
| $10K Invested 5 Yrs Ago | NA | Common Shares Outstg. (M) | 149.9 | Institutional Ownership (%) | 78 | | |

## Price Performance

30-Week Mov. Avg. · · · 10-Week Mov. Avg. – – **GAAP Earnings vs. Previous Year** Volume Above Avg. STARS
12-Mo. Target Price — Relative Strength ▲ Up ▼ Down ► No Change Below Avg. ★

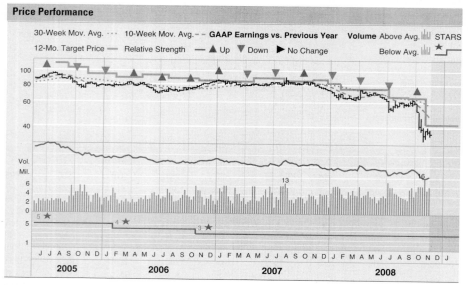

Options: ASE, CBOE, P, Ph

Analysis prepared by **Loran Braverman, CFA** on October 24, 2008, when the stock traded at **$35.73**.

## Highlights

► For 2008, we project a total company sales decline of 10%, with all segments - Spirits, Home & Hardware and Golf - showing down revenues. The Distilled Spirits Council of the U.S.'s forecast is for U.S. revenue for spirits makers to increase by a lesser amount in 2008 than in 2007, on concerns of a weaker economy affecting away-from-home consumption. We expect sales in Spirits to fall 2.5%, the more cyclical Home & Hardware segment to decrease 12% and Golf 2%. For 2009, we look for total sales to be modestly lower.

► We think the operating margin, before restructuring charges, will narrow to 14.2% in 2008 from 16.7%, primarily from the negative operating leverage of lower sales. Also, FO has been experiencing commodity cost pressures from petroleum-based materials, glass, steel, particle board and grains. We expect interest expense to be down 17%. For 2009, we look for the operating margin to widen to 15.0%.

► We expect operating EPS to decrease to $3.93 in 2008 and be close to flat at $3.95 in 2009.

## Investment Rationale/Risk

► Our hold opinion reflects our view that the stock price appropriately reflects FO's growth prospects. Although much of FO's sales in its Home & Hardware segment come from the repair and remodeling of existing homes rather than new home construction, we are now more cautious on both of these components for 2008 and 2009. In August 2008, FO's Absolut Vodka distribution agreement was terminated early in exchange for $230 million payment from Pernod Ricard. As a result, FO will no longer report noncash recognition of about $27 million in annual deferred gains.

► Risks to our recommendation and target price include a slowdown in the economy, a sharp increase in interest rates, and low consumer acceptance of new products.

► Our 12-month target price of $42 is based on a blend of our historical and peer analyses. Our historical analysis applies a P/E close to the low of the 10-year historical range to our 2009 estimate, implying a value of $42. Our sum-of-the-parts peer analysis, weighted by our relative segmental 2009 projected operating income percentages, uses a P/E of 10.6X our 2009 EPS estimate, implying a value of $42, as well.

## Qualitative Risk Assessment

| LOW | MEDIUM | HIGH |
|---|---|---|

Our risk assessment reflects our view that FO has a long track record of consistent sales and earnings growth. While the company has exposure to the homebuilding market, more of its products are geared for remodeling. Its spirits and golf businesses are generally stable, in our opinion.

## Quantitative Evaluations

**S&P Quality Ranking**     **B**

| D | C | B- | **B** | B+ | A- | A | A+ |
|---|---|---|---|---|---|---|---|

**Relative Strength Rank**     **MODERATE**

**47**

LOWEST = 1       HIGHEST = 99

## Revenue/Earnings Data

**Revenue (Million $)**

| | 1Q | 2Q | 3Q | 4Q | Year |
|---|---|---|---|---|---|
| 2008 | 1,711 | 1,967 | 1,799 | -- | -- |
| 2007 | 1,909 | 2,293 | 2,145 | 2,215 | 8,052 |
| 2006 | 2,017 | 2,257 | 2,219 | 2,277 | 8,769 |
| 2005 | 1,518 | 1,783 | 1,802 | 1,959 | 7,061 |
| 2004 | 1,708 | 1,890 | 1,812 | 1,912 | 7,321 |
| 2003 | 1,392 | 1,582 | 1,584 | 1,657 | 6,215 |

**Earnings Per Share ($)**

| | | | | | |
|---|---|---|---|---|---|
| 2008 | 0.69 | 0.17 | 2.01 | E0.82 | E3.93 |
| 2007 | 0.78 | 1.47 | 1.33 | 1.22 | 4.79 |
| 2006 | 1.15 | 1.63 | 0.98 | 1.65 | 5.42 |
| 2005 | 0.95 | 1.22 | 0.52 | 1.17 | 3.87 |
| 2004 | 0.92 | 1.11 | 1.52 | 1.68 | 5.23 |
| 2003 | 0.66 | 1.18 | 0.98 | 1.04 | 3.86 |

Fiscal year ended Dec. 31. Next earnings report expected: Late January. EPS Estimates based on S&P Operating Earnings; historical GAAP earnings are as reported.

## Dividend Data (Dates: mm/dd Payment Date: mm/dd/yy)

| Amount ($) | Date Decl. | Ex-Div. Date | Stk. of Record | Payment Date |
|---|---|---|---|---|
| 0.420 | 01/22 | 02/04 | 02/06 | 03/03/08 |
| 0.420 | 04/29 | 05/12 | 05/14 | 06/02/08 |
| 0.440 | 07/25 | 08/11 | 08/13 | 09/02/08 |
| 0.440 | 09/30 | 11/07 | 11/12 | 12/01/08 |

Dividends have been paid since 1905. Source: Company reports.

# Fortune Brands Inc.

**STANDARD
&POOR'S**

## Business Summary October 24, 2008

CORPORATE OVERVIEW. Fortune Brands is a holding company with subsidiaries that produce home and hardware products, spirits, and golf products.

Major units of FO's Home & Hardware products segment include Master-Brand Cabinets, Moen, Master Lock, Waterloo and Therma-Tru. In 2007, hardware and home improvement products accounted for 53% of total sales and 35% of operating company contributions (before corporate expenses).

Golf products (16%, 12%) operations are conducted through Acushnet, a leading producer of golf balls (Titleist, Pinnacle), golf shoes (FootJoy), golf clubs (Cobra, Titleist), and golf gloves. Other products include bags, carts, dress and athletic shoes, socks and accessories.

Spirits (formerly Spirits & Wine) (31%, 53%) are sold through the Beam Global Spirits & Wine subsidiary. Leading brands include Jim Beam bourbon whiskey, DeKuyper cordials, Gilbey's gin, Kamchatka vodka, and Maker's Mark bourbon. Principal markets are the U.S., the U.K., and Australia. About 49% of the division's sales come from international markets. In July 2005, the company acquired various spirits and wine brands from Pernod Ricard, which

in turn were acquired by Pernod from Allied Domecq PLC. This transaction more than doubled the sales of FO's Spirits & Wine segment. In 2007, the U.S. wine businesses were sold; we believe they had annualized sales of about $225 million.

In 2007, net sales by geographic region for FO, based on country of destination, were the United States, with 73% of net sales, Canada 6%, the United Kingdom 6%, Australia 3%, Spain 2% and all other 10%.

CORPORATE STRATEGY. FO seeks to grow its sales and earnings through continued brand investment and to gain market share by developing and expanding customer relationships. Its first priority is internal growth, followed by expansion through acquisitions and joint ventures. Also, the company continuously looks to improve productivity, as well as the cost and asset structures, of its businesses.

## Company Financials Fiscal Year Ended Dec. 31

| Per Share Data ($) | 2007 | 2006 | 2005 | 2004 | 2003 | 2002 | 2001 | 2000 | 1999 | 1998 |
|---|---|---|---|---|---|---|---|---|---|---|
| Tangible Book Value | NM | NM | NM | NM | NM | NM | 2.06 | 0.89 | 0.83 | 1.91 |
| Cash Flow | 6.58 | 7.37 | 5.35 | 6.70 | 5.14 | 4.57 | 3.89 | 0.63 | -3.96 | 3.09 |
| Earnings | 4.79 | 5.42 | 3.87 | 5.23 | 3.86 | 3.41 | 2.49 | -0.88 | -5.35 | 1.67 |
| S&P Core Earnings | 4.62 | 5.47 | 3.73 | 4.58 | 3.79 | 3.14 | 2.38 | NA | NA | NA |
| Dividends | 1.62 | 1.50 | 1.38 | 1.26 | 1.14 | 1.02 | 0.97 | 0.93 | 0.89 | 0.85 |
| Payout Ratio | 34% | 28% | 36% | 24% | 30% | 30% | 39% | NM | NM | 51% |
| Prices:High | 90.80 | 85.96 | 96.18 | 80.50 | 71.80 | 57.86 | 40.54 | 33.25 | 45.88 | 42.25 |
| Prices:Low | 72.13 | 68.45 | 73.50 | 66.10 | 40.60 | 36.85 | 28.38 | 19.19 | 29.38 | 25.25 |
| P/E Ratio:High | 19 | 16 | 25 | 15 | 19 | 17 | 16 | NM | NM | 25 |
| P/E Ratio:Low | 15 | 13 | 19 | 13 | 11 | 11 | 11 | NM | NM | 15 |

| Income Statement Analysis (Million $) | 2007 | 2006 | 2005 | 2004 | 2003 | 2002 | 2001 | 2000 | 1999 | 1998 |
|---|---|---|---|---|---|---|---|---|---|---|
| Revenue | 8,563 | 8,769 | 7,061 | 7,321 | 6,215 | 5,678 | 5,679 | 5,845 | 5,525 | 5,241 |
| Operating Income | 1,712 | 1,777 | 1,715 | 1,374 | 1,142 | 1,011 | 870 | 938 | 853 | 871 |
| Depreciation | 280 | 298 | 224 | 221 | 193 | 179 | 219 | 237 | 231 | 251 |
| Interest Expense | 294 | 332 | 159 | 87.9 | 73.8 | 74.1 | 96.8 | 134 | 107 | 103 |
| Pretax Income | 1,120 | 1,209 | 926 | 1,086 | 884 | 756 | 492 | 38.9 | -721 | 512 |
| Effective Tax Rate | 30.9% | 25.7% | 35.0% | 26.1% | 32.7% | 28.3% | 19.2% | NM | NM | 42.6% |
| Net Income | 750 | 830 | 582 | 784 | 579 | 526 | 386 | -138 | -891 | 294 |
| S&P Core Earnings | 722 | 837 | 559 | 684 | 567 | 484 | 367 | NA | NA | NA |

| Balance Sheet & Other Financial Data (Million $) | 2007 | 2006 | 2005 | 2004 | 2003 | 2002 | 2001 | 2000 | 1999 | 1998 |
|---|---|---|---|---|---|---|---|---|---|---|
| Cash | 204 | 183 | 93.6 | 165 | 105 | 15.4 | 48.7 | 20.9 | 72.0 | 40.0 |
| Current Assets | 3,781 | 3,930 | 3,193 | 2,642 | 2,282 | 1,903 | 1,970 | 2,265 | 2,313 | 2,265 |
| Total Assets | 13,957 | 14,668 | 13,202 | 7,884 | 7,445 | 5,822 | 5,301 | 5,764 | 6,417 | 7,360 |
| Current Liabilities | 2,094 | 2,515 | 2,818 | 2,036 | 2,134 | 1,515 | 1,258 | 2,040 | 2,003 | 1,845 |
| Long Term Debt | 4,374 | 5,035 | 4,890 | 1,240 | 1,243 | 200 | 950 | 1,152 | 1,205 | 982 |
| Common Equity | 5,680 | 4,722 | 3,639 | 3,203 | 2,712 | 2,305 | 2,094 | 2,127 | 2,728 | 4,087 |
| Total Capital | 11,138 | 11,458 | 9,788 | 5,207 | 4,664 | 2,983 | 3,444 | 3,343 | 3,991 | 5,080 |
| Capital Expenditures | 267 | 266 | 222 | 242 | 194 | 194 | 207 | 227 | 241 | 252 |
| Cash Flow | 1,029 | 1,128 | 805 | 1,005 | 772 | 704 | 605 | 99.0 | -661 | 544 |
| Current Ratio | 1.8 | 1.6 | 1.1 | 1.3 | 1.1 | 1.3 | 1.6 | 1.1 | 1.2 | 1.2 |
| % Long Term Debt of Capitalization | 38.7 | 43.9 | 50.0 | 23.8 | 26.6 | 6.7 | 27.6 | 34.5 | 30.2 | 19.3 |
| % Net Income of Revenue | 8.7 | 9.5 | 8.2 | 10.7 | 9.3 | 9.3 | 6.8 | NM | NM | 5.6 |
| % Return on Assets | 5.2 | 6.0 | 5.5 | 10.2 | 8.7 | 9.5 | 7.0 | NM | NM | 4.1 |
| % Return on Equity | 14.4 | 19.9 | 17.2 | 26.5 | 23.1 | 23.9 | 18.3 | NM | NM | 7.2 |

Data as orig reptd.; bef. results of disc opers/spec. items. Per share data adj. for stk. divs.; EPS diluted. E-Estimated. NA-Not Available. NM-Not Meaningful. NR-Not Ranked. UR-Under Review.

**Office:** 520 Lake Cook Rd, Deerfield, IL 60015-5611.
**Telephone:** 847-484-4400.
**Email:** investorrelations@fortunebrands.com
**Website:** http://www.fortunebrands.com

**Chrmn, Pres & CEO:** B.A. Carbonari
**SVP & CFO:** C.P. Omtvedt
**SVP & Treas:** M. Hausberg
**SVP, Secy & General Counsel:** M.A. Roche

**Cntlr:** E.A. Wiertel
**Board Members:** B. A. Carbonari, R. A. Goldstein, A. F. Hackett, C. C. Hine, P. E. Leroy, A. D. MacKay, A. M. Tatlock, D. M. Thomas, R. V. Waters, III, N. H. Wesley, P. Wilson

**Founded:** 1904
**Domicile:** Delaware
**Employees:** 31,027

# FPL Group Inc.

**STANDARD & POOR'S**

## S&P Recommendation  BUY ★★★★☆

| Price | 12-Mo. Target Price | Investment Style |
|---|---|---|
| $47.30 (as of Nov 14, 2008) | $48.00 | Large-Cap Blend |

**GICS Sector** Utilities
**Sub-Industry** Electric Utilities

**Summary** FPL Group is the holding company for Florida Power & Light and FPL Energy.

### Key Stock Statistics (Source S&P, Vickers, company reports)

| | | | | | | | |
|---|---|---|---|---|---|---|---|
| 52-Wk Range | $73.75–33.81 | S&P Oper. EPS 2010**E** | 4.52 | Market Capitalization(B) | $19.333 | Beta | 0.77 |
| Trailing 12-Month EPS | $3.62 | S&P Oper. EPS 2011**E** | NA | Yield (%) | 3.76 | S&P 3-Yr. Proj. EPS CAGR(%) | 9 |
| Trailing 12-Month P/E | 13.1 | P/E on S&P Oper. EPS 2010**E** | 10.5 | Dividend Rate/Share | $1.78 | S&P Credit Rating | A |
| $10K Invested 5 Yrs Ago | $17,105 | Common Shares Outstg. (M) | 408.7 | Institutional Ownership (%) | 64 | | |

### Price Performance

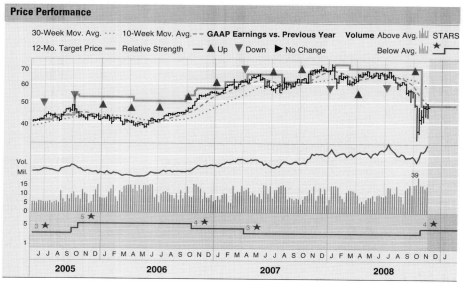

- 30-Week Mov. Avg. · · · 10-Week Mov. Avg. — **GAAP Earnings vs. Previous Year**  Volume Above Avg. STARS
- 12-Mo. Target Price — Relative Strength — ▲ Up ▼ Down ▶ No Change  Below Avg.

Options: ASE, CBOE, P, Ph

Analysis prepared by **Justin McCann** on October 28, 2008, when the stock traded at **$ 43.85**.

### Qualitative Risk Assessment

| LOW | MEDIUM | HIGH |
|---|---|---|

Our risk assessment reflects our view of FPL's strong and steady cash flows from its Florida Power & Light utility, which enjoys well above average customer growth, and a generally supportive regulatory environment. We believe this largely offsets the fast growing but higher-risk cash flows from its independent power subsidiary.

### Quantitative Evaluations

**S&P Quality Ranking**    A-

| D | C | B- | B | B+ | A- | A | A+ |
|---|---|---|---|---|---|---|---|

**Relative Strength Rank**    **STRONG**

83

LOWEST = 1    HIGHEST = 99

### Revenue/Earnings Data

**Revenue (Million $)**

| | 1Q | 2Q | 3Q | 4Q | Year |
|---|---|---|---|---|---|
| 2008 | 3,434 | 3,585 | 5,387 | -- | -- |
| 2007 | 3,075 | 3,929 | 4,575 | 3,683 | 15,263 |
| 2006 | 3,584 | 3,809 | 4,694 | 3,623 | 15,710 |
| 2005 | 2,437 | 2,741 | 3,504 | 3,164 | 11,846 |
| 2004 | 2,331 | 2,619 | 2,983 | 2,589 | 10,522 |
| 2003 | 2,082 | 2,339 | 2,775 | 2,435 | 9,630 |

**Earnings Per Share ($)**

| | 1Q | 2Q | 3Q | 4Q | Year |
|---|---|---|---|---|---|
| 2008 | 0.62 | 0.52 | 1.92 | E0.90 | E3.84 |
| 2007 | 0.38 | 1.01 | 1.33 | 0.56 | 3.28 |
| 2006 | 0.64 | 0.60 | 1.32 | 0.67 | 3.23 |
| 2005 | 0.36 | 0.52 | 0.87 | 0.53 | 2.29 |
| 2004 | 0.39 | 0.72 | 0.88 | 0.47 | 2.46 |
| 2003 | 0.50 | 0.67 | 0.94 | 0.41 | 2.51 |

Fiscal year ended Dec. 31. Next earnings report expected: Late January. EPS Estimates based on S&P Operating Earnings; historical GAAP earnings are as reported.

### Highlights

- We expect operating EPS in 2008 to increase about 10% from 2007 operating EPS of $3.48. We believe earnings from the Florida Power & Light utility will continue to be restricted by a slowdown in customer growth, reflecting the weakness in the Florida economy and housing market. This should be more than offset, however, by continued earnings growth at FPL Energy. We forecast operating EPS of about $2.12 from Florida Power & Light; approximately $1.92 from FPL Energy; and a loss per share of around $0.20 from corporate and other operations.

- On October 27, 2008, FPL announced that due to the current economic environment it would temporarily defer its 2009 capital spending plans by about $1.7 billion, to $5.3 billion. It said the plan was flexible and could be increased or decreased as market conditions warranted.

- For 2009, we expect EPS to grow about 8% from anticipated results in 2008. We believe this will reflect continuing strength at FPL Energy, driven by renewed higher-margin power contracts. While FPL Energy will continue the expansion of its wind power operations, it plans to reduce the expansion planned for 2009 by about 400 megawatts (MW), to 1,100 MW.

### Investment Rationale/Risk

- We recently raised our recommendation on the shares to buy, from hold. The stock was down nearly 40% year to date, reflecting, in our view, the crisis in the credit markets and its impact on the Florida economy and housing market. This decline follows strong gains of 25% in 2007 and 31% in 2006, in which the stock strongly outperformed FPL's electric utility peers. We believe the market will gradually stabilize, and think the stock will realize above-average total return over the next 12 months, driven by the growth prospects projected for FPL Energy.

- Risks to our recommendation and target price include lower than expected results from the unregulated FPL Energy business, and a reduction in the average P/E of the group as a whole.

- With the sharp decline in the shares and the 8.5% increase in the dividend that became effective with the March payment, the recent yield from the dividend was 4.4%. We expect the company to sustain an average annual dividend growth of approximately 8% over the next few years. Our 12-month target price is $48, a discount-to-peers P/E of about 11.6X our 2009 EPS estimate, which reflects, in our view, the weakness in the Florida economy.

### Dividend Data (Dates: mm/dd Payment Date: mm/dd/yy)

| Amount ($) | Date Decl. | Ex-Div. Date | Stk. of Record | Payment Date |
|---|---|---|---|---|
| 0.445 | 02/15 | 02/27 | 02/29 | 03/17/08 |
| 0.445 | 05/23 | 06/04 | 06/06 | 06/16/08 |
| 0.445 | 07/25 | 08/27 | 08/29 | 09/15/08 |
| 0.445 | 10/17 | 11/25 | 11/28 | 12/15/08 |

Dividends have been paid since 1944. Source: Company reports.

# FPL Group Inc.

STANDARD
&POOR'S

## Business Summary October 28, 2008

CORPORATE OVERVIEW. FPL Group, one of the largest providers of electricity-related services in the U.S., is the holding company for Florida Power & Light Co. (FP&L), a regulated and vertically integrated utility, and FPL Energy, a wholesale generator of electricity with operations in 25 states.

MARKET PROFILE. Florida Power & Light provides electricity to about 4.5 million customers in an area covering nearly all of Florida's eastern seaboard, as well as the southern part of the state. As is true of most states in the Southeast, Florida has shown little interest in restructuring its electric utility industry. Although there have been efforts to introduce a competitive wholesale generation market within the state, there has not been any legislation that would allow it to take place, and we do not expect to see any within the next several years.

Electric revenues by customer class in 2007 were: residential 54%; commercial 39%; industrial 3%; and other 4%. Given its unusually low level of exposure to industrial customers, we consider the company to be much less vulnerable to economic downturns. This, along with an above average customer growth rate (2.0% in 2007 ) and a recent regulatory ruling that has provided

rate certainty through 2009 and set up a storm cost recovery mechanism, helps to establish, we think, a more favorable foundation for the utility's long-term annual EPS growth, which we project at 3% to 4%.

IMPACT OF MAJOR DEVELOPMENTS. On October 25, 2006, FPL and Baltimore-based Constellation Energy Group (CEG) announced the termination of the merger agreement that had been announced on December 19, 2005. Since CEG is not only the holding company for Baltimore Gas & Electric Company, but the nation's largest wholesale power seller and its leading competitive supplier of electricity to large commercial and industrial customers, the merger would have made the combined entity one of the biggest electric companies in the U.S. Although we were disappointed that the merger was terminated, we believe the regulatory and judicial uncertainties surrounding the approval process in Maryland justified the decision.

## Company Financials Fiscal Year Ended Dec. 31

| Per Share Data ($) | 2009 | 2008 | 2007 | 2006 | 2005 | 2004 | 2003 | 2002 | 2001 | 2000 |
|---|---|---|---|---|---|---|---|---|---|---|
| Tangible Book Value | NA | NA | 26.35 | 24.52 | 21.52 | 20.24 | 18.93 | 17.46 | 17.09 | 15.89 |
| Earnings | 4.15 | 3.84 | 3.27 | 3.23 | 2.29 | 2.46 | 2.51 | 2.01 | 2.31 | 2.07 |
| S&P Core Earnings | NA | NA | 3.04 | 3.00 | 2.06 | 2.17 | 2.21 | 1.52 | 1.83 | NA |
| Dividends | NA | 1.78 | 1.64 | 1.50 | 1.42 | 1.30 | 1.20 | 1.16 | 1.12 | 1.08 |
| Payout Ratio | NA | 46% | 50% | 46% | 62% | 53% | 48% | 58% | 48% | 52% |
| Prices:High | NA | 73.75 | 72.77 | 55.57 | 48.11 | 38.05 | 34.04 | 32.66 | 35.81 | 36.50 |
| Prices:Low | NA | 33.81 | 53.72 | 37.81 | 35.90 | 30.10 | 26.78 | 22.50 | 25.61 | 18.19 |
| P/E Ratio:High | NA | 19 | 22 | 17 | 21 | 15 | 14 | 16 | 16 | 18 |
| P/E Ratio:Low | NA | 9 | 16 | 12 | 16 | 12 | 11 | 11 | 11 | 9 |

| Income Statement Analysis (Million $) | | | | | | | | | | |
|---|---|---|---|---|---|---|---|---|---|---|
| Revenue | NA | NA | 15,263 | 15,710 | 11,846 | 10,522 | 9,630 | 8,311 | 8,475 | 7,082 |
| Depreciation | NA | NA | 1,261 | 1,185 | 1,285 | 1,198 | 1,105 | 952 | 983 | 1,032 |
| Maintenance | NA | NA | NA | NA | NA | NA | NA | NA | NA | NA |
| Fixed Charges Coverage | NA | NA | 3.18 | 3.30 | 2.87 | 3.26 | 3.95 | 4.52 | 4.51 | 4.55 |
| Construction Credits | NA | NA | 23.0 | 21.0 | 28.0 | 37.0 | NA | NA | NA | Nil |
| Effective Tax Rate | NA | NA | 21.9% | 23.7% | 23.5% | 23.1% | 29.2% | 26.0% | 32.7% | 32.3% |
| Net Income | NA | NA | 1,312 | 1,281 | 885 | 887 | 893 | 695 | 781 | 704 |
| S&P Core Earnings | NA | NA | 1,218 | 1,187 | 797 | 782 | 786 | 527 | 616 | NA |

| Balance Sheet & Other Financial Data (Million $) | | | | | | | | | | |
|---|---|---|---|---|---|---|---|---|---|---|
| Gross Property | NA | NA | 41,040 | 36,152 | 33,351 | 31,720 | 30,272 | 26,505 | 23,388 | 21,022 |
| Capital Expenditures | NA | NA | 1,826 | 1,763 | 1,616 | 1,394 | 1,383 | 1,277 | 1,544 | 1,299 |
| Net Property | NA | NA | 28,652 | 24,499 | 22,463 | 21,226 | 20,297 | 14,304 | 11,662 | 9,934 |
| Capitalization:Long Term Debt | NA | NA | 11,280 | 9,591 | 8,039 | 8,027 | 8,728 | 6,016 | 5,084 | 4,202 |
| Capitalization:% Long Term Debt | NA | NA | 51.2 | 49.1 | 48.6 | 51.6 | 55.6 | 47.4 | 45.8 | 42.9 |
| Capitalization:Preferred | NA | NA | Nil | Nil | Nil | Nil | Nil | Nil | Nil | Nil |
| Capitalization:% Preferred | NA | NA | Nil | Nil | Nil | Nil | Nil | Nil | Nil | Nil |
| Capitalization:Common | NA | NA | 10,735 | 9,930 | 8,499 | 7,537 | 6,967 | 6,688 | 6,015 | 5,593 |
| Capitalization:% Common | NA | NA | 48.8 | 50.9 | 51.4 | 48.4 | 44.4 | 52.6 | 54.2 | 57.1 |
| Total Capital | NA | NA | 25,836 | 22,953 | 19,615 | 15,645 | 17,850 | 14,444 | 12,629 | 11,442 |
| % Operating Ratio | NA | NA | 87.5 | 87.1 | 88.6 | 87.8 | 87.9 | 85.7 | 87.6 | 86.3 |
| % Earned on Net Property | NA | NA | 8.6 | 8.9 | 6.7 | 7.1 | 8.1 | 9.5 | 10.3 | 12.9 |
| % Return on Revenue | NA | NA | 8.6 | 8.2 | 7.5 | 8.4 | 9.3 | 8.4 | 9.2 | 9.9 |
| % Return on Invested Capital | NA | NA | 8.2 | 10.9 | 8.6 | 9.2 | 8.1 | 9.0 | 9.6 | 9.7 |
| % Return on Common Equity | NA | NA | 12.7 | 13.9 | 11.0 | 12.0 | 13.4 | 10.7 | 13.5 | 12.8 |

Data as orig reptd.; bef. results of disc opers/spec. items. Per share data adj. for stk. divs.; EPS diluted. E-Estimated. NA-Not Available. NM-Not Meaningful. NR-Not Ranked. UR-Under Review.

**Office:** 700 Universe Boulevard, Juno Beach, FL 33408-0420.
**Telephone:** 561-694-4000.
**Website:** http://www.fplgroup.com
**Chrmn & CEO:** L. Hay, III

**Pres & COO:** J.L. Robo
**SVP & General Counsel:** E.F. Tancer
**CFO:** A. Pimentel, Jr.
**Chief Acctg Officer & Cntlr:** K.M. Davis

**Investor Contact:** P. Cutler (800-222-4511)
**Board Members:** S. S. Barrat, R. Beall, II, J. H. Brown, J. L. Camaren, J. B. Ferguson, L. Hay, III, T. Jennings, O. D. Kingsley, Jr., R. E. Schupp, M. H. Thaman, H. E. Tookes, II, P. R. Tregurtha

**Founded:** 1984
**Domicile:** Florida
**Employees:** 10,500

The McGraw-Hill Companies

# Franklin Resources Inc.

**STANDARD &POOR'S**

| S&P Recommendation **HOLD** ★★★☆☆ | Price $54.43 (as of Nov 14, 2008) | 12-Mo. Target Price $70.00 | Investment Style Large-Cap Growth |
|---|---|---|---|

**GICS Sector** Financials
**Sub-Industry** Asset Management & Custody Banks

**Summary** This company is one of the world's largest asset managers, serving retail, institutional and high-net-worth clients.

## Key Stock Statistics (Source S&P, Vickers, company reports)

| | | | | | | | |
|---|---|---|---|---|---|---|---|
| 52-Wk Range | $129.08–49.30 | S&P Oper. EPS 2008**E** | 6.67 | Market Capitalization(B) | $12.751 | Beta | 1.32 |
| Trailing 12-Month EPS | $7.14 | S&P Oper. EPS 2009**E** | 6.18 | Yield (%) | 1.47 | S&P 3-Yr. Proj. EPS CAGR(%) | -2 |
| Trailing 12-Month P/E | 7.6 | P/E on S&P Oper. EPS 2008**E** | 8.2 | Dividend Rate/Share | $0.80 | S&P Credit Rating | AA- |
| $10K Invested 5 Yrs Ago | $12,487 | Common Shares Outstg. (M) | 234.3 | Institutional Ownership (%) | 48 | | |

## Price Performance

30-Week Mov. Avg.  · · · 10-Week Mov. Avg. - - **GAAP Earnings vs. Previous Year**  Volume Above Avg. ▥▥ STARS
12-Mo. Target Price — Relative Strength — ▲ Up ▼ Down ► No Change  Below Avg. ▥▥ ★

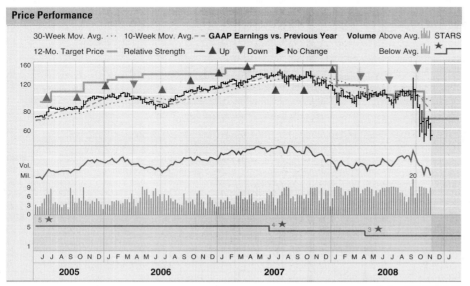

Options: ASE, CBOE, P, Ph

Analysis prepared by **Matthew Albrecht** on October 29, 2008, when the stock traded at **$ 64.21**.

## Highlights

➤ Assets under management at Franklin Resources continue to fall, fueled by equity market declines, as 52% of its assets are in equity funds. We see near-term underperformance in its funds relative to peers also causing a headwind to flows. Modest inflows to fixed income and money market products have provided a modest boost to overall balances, but the unfavorable asset shift has put pressure on the management fee rate. We expect management fees to increase on a percentage basis in FY 09 (Sep.) following the decline we saw in FY 08. We also think reduced performance fees, investment losses and lower earnings on invested cash balances have hurt the top line. After assets under management fell more than 20% in FY 08, we see a modest rebound in FY 09.

➤ We look for compensation costs to moderate in FY 09 after increasing on a relative basis in FY 08 due to revenue declines. We anticipate a slimmer underwriting and distribution margin in the current year following compression in FY 08, and higher advertising costs and international expansion efforts will likely combine to pressure the pretax margin.

➤ We see EPS of $6.18 in FY 09.

## Investment Rationale/Risk

➤ We believe the shares trade at a discount to peers due to the relative underperformance of BEN's funds over the past few years. Until the most recent quarter, fund flows had remained relatively strong and the company's strong international presence has provided a catalyst. We view favorably BEN's strong operating free cash flow, but we would prefer that it raise its dividend or repurchase additional shares, given increasing cash balances.

➤ Risks to our recommendation and target price include potential depreciation in global equity, bond and currency markets that can materially affect assets under management and net investor flows. In addition, we think the shift by investors toward discount brokerage firms could hurt net inflows, given that BEN's funds typically have front-end sales charges.

➤ The shares recently traded at 10.1X our FY 09 EPS estimate, in line with the recent multiples of comparable peers. Our 12-month target price of $70 is equal to 11.3X our FY 09 EPS estimate, in line with falling peer multiples and a discount to BEN's own historical multiple due to recent market declines.

## Qualitative Risk Assessment

| LOW | MEDIUM | HIGH |
|---|---|---|

Our risk assessment reflects our view of the company's strong relative investment performance, consistent net client inflows, and low ratio of debt to total capitalization.

## Quantitative Evaluations

**S&P Quality Ranking**  A-

| D | C | B- | B | B+ | A- | A | A+ |
|---|---|---|---|---|---|---|---|

**Relative Strength Rank**  MODERATE

36

LOWEST = 1      HIGHEST = 99

## Revenue/Earnings Data

**Revenue (Million $)**

| | 1Q | 2Q | 3Q | 4Q | Year |
|---|---|---|---|---|---|
| 2008 | 1,686 | 1,504 | 1,522 | 1,321 | -- |
| 2007 | 1,428 | 1,509 | 1,640 | 1,629 | 6,206 |
| 2006 | 1,181 | 1,255 | 1,317 | 1,297 | 5,051 |
| 2005 | 986.0 | 1,051 | 1,110 | 1,163 | 4,310 |
| 2004 | 809.7 | 879.0 | 867.8 | 881.7 | 3,438 |
| 2003 | 605.5 | 613.1 | 683.9 | 722.0 | 2,624 |

**Earnings Per Share ($)**

| | | | | | |
|---|---|---|---|---|---|
| 2008 | 2.12 | 1.54 | 1.71 | 1.30 | E6.67 |
| 2007 | 1.67 | 1.73 | 1.86 | 1.76 | 7.03 |
| 2006 | 1.21 | 0.74 | 1.41 | 1.49 | 4.86 |
| 2005 | 0.92 | 0.85 | 1.00 | 1.28 | 4.06 |
| 2004 | 0.67 | 0.68 | 0.69 | 0.74 | 2.78 |
| 2003 | 0.43 | 0.43 | 0.52 | 0.61 | 1.97 |

Fiscal year ended Sep. 30. Next earnings report expected: NA. EPS Estimates based on S&P Operating Earnings; historical GAAP earnings are as reported.

## Dividend Data (Dates: mm/dd Payment Date: mm/dd/yy)

| Amount ($) | Date Decl. | Ex-Div. Date | Stk. of Record | Payment Date |
|---|---|---|---|---|
| 0.200 | 12/14 | 12/26 | 12/28 | 01/11/08 |
| 0.200 | 03/04 | 03/26 | 03/28 | 04/11/08 |
| 0.200 | 06/17 | 06/26 | 06/30 | 07/11/08 |
| 0.200 | 09/18 | 10/02 | 10/06 | 10/15/08 |

Dividends have been paid since 1981. Source: Company reports.

---

**Please read the Required Disclosures and Analyst Certification on the last page of this report.**

The McGraw-Hill Companies

**STANDARD &POOR'S**

# Franklin Resources Inc.

## Business Summary October 29, 2008

CORPORATE OVERVIEW. Franklin Resources is one of the largest U.S. money managers, with $507.3 billion in assets under management at the end of FY 08 (Sep.), down from $645.9 billion at the end of FY 07. At the end of FY 08, equity-based investments accounted for 52% of assets under management, fixed-income investments 28%, hybrid funds 19%, and money funds 1%. Global equity and fixed income accounted for 51% of assets under management. We think that a potential decline in the dollar relative to other major currencies would aid BEN, due to the high percentage of assets invested globally. At the end of FY 07, about 40% of assets under management were held by investors domiciled outside the U.S.

The company's sponsored investment products are distributed under five distinct names: Franklin, Templeton, Mutual Series, Bisset and Fiduciary. We are impressed with BEN's broad range of investment products, but we think the company lacks a compelling roster of growth equity products. BEN has targeted key market segments, including retail (58% of assets at the end of FY 08) and institutional and international (42%).

CORPORATE STRATEGY. Despite its acquisitive history, we think BEN's man-

agement favors organic growth. We believe that the interests of BEN's management are closely aligned with those of shareholders given that directors, director nominees and executive officers as a group owned about 35% of the common shares outstanding as of December 4, 2007. We expect BEN to be selective in any acquisition pursuits.

Through several acquisitions, BEN has shifted its asset mix from predominantly fixed-income securities toward equity-based investments. In April 2001, BEN acquired Fiduciary Trust Co. International, an investment management company catering to high-net-worth and institutional clients, for about $776 million. In 1996, BEN acquired certain assets and liabilities of Heine Securities Corp., which managed the value-oriented Mutual Series funds. The Templeton funds were acquired in 1992, with the purchase of Templeton, Galbraith & Hansberger.

## Company Financials Fiscal Year Ended Sep. 30

| Per Share Data ($) | 2007 | 2006 | 2005 | 2004 | 2003 | 2002 | 2001 | 2000 | 1999 | 1998 |
|---|---|---|---|---|---|---|---|---|---|---|
| Tangible Book Value | 21.49 | 18.57 | 14.39 | 12.23 | 9.31 | 8.69 | 7.23 | 7.37 | 5.79 | 4.08 |
| Cash Flow | 7.82 | 5.86 | 5.02 | 3.51 | 2.67 | 2.35 | 2.79 | 3.13 | 2.48 | 2.74 |
| Earnings | 7.03 | 4.86 | 4.06 | 2.78 | 1.97 | 1.65 | 1.91 | 2.28 | 1.69 | 1.98 |
| S&P Core Earnings | 6.64 | 4.72 | 3.97 | 2.47 | 1.70 | 1.56 | 1.61 | NA | NA | NA |
| Dividends | 0.57 | 0.36 | 0.40 | 0.33 | 0.29 | 0.28 | 0.26 | 0.24 | 0.22 | 0.20 |
| Payout Ratio | 8% | 7% | 10% | 12% | 15% | 17% | 14% | 11% | 13% | 10% |
| Prices:High | 145.59 | 114.98 | 98.86 | 71.45 | 52.25 | 44.48 | 48.30 | 45.63 | 45.00 | 57.88 |
| Prices:Low | 108.46 | 80.16 | 63.56 | 46.85 | 29.99 | 27.90 | 30.85 | 24.63 | 27.00 | 25.75 |
| P/E Ratio:High | 21 | 24 | 24 | 26 | 27 | 27 | 25 | 20 | 27 | 29 |
| P/E Ratio:Low | 15 | 16 | 16 | 17 | 15 | 17 | 16 | 11 | 16 | 13 |

| Income Statement Analysis (Million $) | 2007 | 2006 | 2005 | 2004 | 2003 | 2002 | 2001 | 2000 | 1999 | 1998 |
|---|---|---|---|---|---|---|---|---|---|---|
| Income Interest | NA | NA | NA | NA | NA | NA | NA | NA | NA | NA |
| Income Other | NA | NA | NA | NA | NA | NA | NA | NA | NA | NA |
| Total Income | 6,206 | 5,051 | 4,310 | 3,438 | 2,624 | 2,519 | 2,355 | 2,340 | 2,262 | 2,577 |
| General Expenses | 4,138 | 3,417 | 3,004 | NA | NA | NA | NA | NA | NA | NA |
| Interest Expense | 23.2 | 29.2 | 34.0 | 30.7 | 19.9 | 12.3 | 10.6 | 14.0 | 21.0 | 22.5 |
| Depreciation | 199 | 215 | 17.5 | NA | NA | NA | NA | 200 | 200 | 191 |
| Net Income | 1,773 | 1,268 | 1,058 | 702 | 503 | 433 | 485 | 562 | 427 | 500 |
| S&P Core Earnings | 1,674 | 1,229 | 1,033 | 622 | 432 | 410 | 407 | | | |

| Balance Sheet & Other Financial Data (Million $) | 2007 | 2006 | 2005 | 2004 | 2003 | 2002 | 2001 | 2000 | 1999 | 1998 |
|---|---|---|---|---|---|---|---|---|---|---|
| Cash | 3,584 | 3,613 | 3,152 | 2,917 | 1,054 | 981 | 569 | 746 | 819 | 537 |
| Receivables | 1,106 | 711 | 549 | 444 | 441 | 393 | 603 | 693 | 552 | 318 |
| Cost of Investments | NA | NA | 1,566 | NA | NA | NA | NA | NA | NA | NA |
| Total Assets | 9,943 | 9,500 | 8,894 | 8,228 | 6,971 | 6,423 | 6,266 | 4,042 | 3,667 | 3,480 |
| Loss Reserve | NA | NA | Nil | NA | NA | NA | NA | NA | NA | NA |
| Short Term Debt | 420 | 168 | 169 | NA | 0.29 | 7.80 | NA | NA | NA | NA |
| Capitalization:Debt | 162 | 628 | 1,208 | 1,196 | 1,109 | 595 | 566 | 294 | 294 | 612 |
| Capitalization:Equity | 7,332 | 6,685 | 5,684 | 5,107 | 4,310 | 4,267 | 3,978 | 2,965 | 2,657 | 2,281 |
| Capitalization:Total | 8,170 | 7,620 | 7,204 | 6,615 | 5,622 | 5,037 | 4,544 | 3,260 | 2,951 | 2,775 |
| Price Times Book Value:High | 6.8 | 6.2 | 6.9 | NA | 5.5 | 5.1 | NA | NA | NA | NA |
| Price Times Book Value:Low | 5.2 | 4.3 | 4.4 | NA | 3.2 | 3.2 | NA | NA | NA | NA |
| Cash Flow | 1,972 | 1,483 | 1,075 | NA | NA | NA | NA | 762 | 627 | 691 |
| % Expense/Operating Revenue | 66.7 | 67.7 | 70.1 | NA | NA | NA | NA | NA | NA | NA |
| % Earnings & Depreciation/Assets | 20.3 | 16.1 | 12.6 | NA | NA | NA | NA | NA | NA | NA |

Data as orig reptd.; bef. results of disc opers/spec. items. Per share data adj. for stk. divs.; EPS diluted. E-Estimated. NA-Not Available. NM-Not Meaningful. NR-Not Ranked. UR-Under Review.

**Office:** One Franklin Parkway, San Mateo, CA 94403.
**Telephone:** 650-312-2000.
**Website:** http://www.franklintempleton.com
**Chrmn:** C.B. Johnson

**Pres & CEO:** G.E. Johnson
**Vice Chrmn:** R.H. Johnson, Jr.
**COO & CTO:** J.J. Bolt
**EVP, CFO, Chief Acctg Officer & Treas:** K.A. Lewis

**Board Members:** S. H. Armacost, C. Crocker, J. R. Hardiman, F. W. Hellman, R. D. Joffe, C. B. Johnson, G. E. Johnson, R. H. Johnson, Jr., T. H. Kean, S. C. Ratnathicam, P. M. Sacerdote, L. Stein, A. M. Tatlock, L. E. Woodworth

**Founded:** 1947
**Domicile:** Delaware
**Employees:** 8,699

*The McGraw-Hill Companies*

# Freeport-McMoran Copper & Gold Inc.

STANDARD &POOR'S

| S&P Recommendation | BUY ★★★★☆ | Price | 12-Mo. Target Price |
|---|---|---|---|
| | | $24.34 (as of Nov 14, 2008) | $46.00 |

**GICS Sector** Materials
**Sub-Industry** Diversified Metals & Mining

**Summary** Following its acquisition of Phelps Dodge on March 19, 2007, FCX is the world's second largest copper producer.

## Key Stock Statistics (Source S&P, Vickers, company reports)

| | | | | | | | |
|---|---|---|---|---|---|---|---|
| 52-Wk Range | $127.24– 21.50 | S&P Oper. EPS 2008E | 8.02 | Market Capitalization(B) | $9.346 | Beta | 2.26 |
| Trailing 12-Month EPS | $7.27 | S&P Oper. EPS 2009E | 6.93 | Yield (%) | 7.44 | S&P 3-Yr. Proj. EPS CAGR(%) | 2 |
| Trailing 12-Month P/E | 3.4 | P/E on S&P Oper. EPS 2008E | 3.0 | Dividend Rate/Share | $1.81 | S&P Credit Rating | BBB- |
| $10K Invested 5 Yrs Ago | $7,671 | Common Shares Outstg. (M) | 384.0 | Institutional Ownership (%) | 96 | | |

## Price Performance

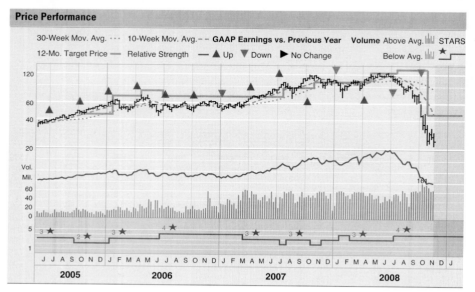

30-Week Mov. Avg. · · · · · 10-Week Mov. Avg. - - - **GAAP Earnings vs. Previous Year**  Volume Above Avg. STARS
12-Mo. Target Price —  Relative Strength —  ▲ Up ▼ Down ► No Change  Below Avg.  ★

Options: ASE, CBOE, P, Ph

Analysis prepared by **Leo J. Larkin** on October 20, 2008, when the stock traded at **$ 35.60.**

## Highlights

► Following an projected sales increase of 40% in 2008, we look for a 15% decline in sales in 2009, on a projected decline in the price of copper. Our copper price outlook is based on our expectation that global copper demand in 2009 will decline 3% to 4%, versus flat demand for 2008. Our estimate for lower copper demand is based on the S&P forecast for global GDP growth of 2.1% in 2009, versus estimated global GDP growth of 2.8% in 2008. In our view, demand from the U.S. (the world's second largest consumer) will decrease again in 2009 on an expected drop in non-residential construction and continued weakness in demand from the homebuilding market. Also, we think that demand growth in China (the world's largest consumer) will be up just 2% in 2009 versus an estimated gain of 4% in 2008.

► Penalized by lower revenue per pound and continued high interest expense, we project EPS of $6.93 in 2009, versus our EPS estimate of $8.29 in 2008.

► Longer term, we expect EPS and reserves to increase on rising copper demand and consolidation of the base metals mining industry.

## Investment Rationale/Risk

► For the long term, we think increased demand for durable goods in China and India, along with less rapid increases in the supply of copper, will support generally higher prices, sales, and profits. Thus, we remain positive on the prospects for FCX. Near term, we believe the PD merger will be mildly dilutive, due to PD's cost of production being higher than that of FCX. Down the road, though, the merger should be positive, given that it achieves geographic diversification for FCX. In our opinion, the concentration of FCX's mining assets in Indonesia prior to the merger was a drag on its valuation. Recently trading at about 4.8X our 2009 estimate and yielding just about 5.5%, we think shares are attractively valued. On that basis, our recommendation is buy.

► Risks to our opinion and target price include a decline in the price of copper in 2009 in excess of what we project.

► Our 12-month target price of $46 assumes that FCX will sell at 6.6X our 2009 EPS estimate, which is about in line with the P/E we project for its base metal peers. Our target P/E is toward the low end of FCX's historical range of the past 10 years.

## Qualitative Risk Assessment

| LOW | MEDIUM | HIGH |
|---|---|---|

Our risk assessment reflects the company's exposure to cyclical demand for copper and gold, along with sizable debt incurred in the merger with Phelps Dodge. Offsetting this is FCX's sizable free cash flow generation and its large share of the global copper market.

## Quantitative Evaluations

**S&P Quality Ranking** — B+

| D | C | B- | B | B+ | A- | A | A+ |
|---|---|---|---|---|---|---|---|

**Relative Strength Rank** — WEAK

12

LOWEST = 1    HIGHEST = 99

## Revenue/Earnings Data

**Revenue (Million $)**

| | 1Q | 2Q | 3Q | 4Q | Year |
|---|---|---|---|---|---|
| 2008 | 5,672 | 5,441 | 4,616 | -- | -- |
| 2007 | 2,303 | 5,807 | 5,066 | 4,184 | 16,939 |
| 2006 | 1,086 | 1,426 | 1,636 | 1,642 | 5,791 |
| 2005 | 803.1 | 902.9 | 983.3 | 1,490 | 4,179 |
| 2004 | 360.2 | 486.3 | 600.6 | 924.8 | 2,372 |
| 2003 | 524.6 | 609.5 | 632.0 | 446.1 | 2,212 |

**Earnings Per Share ($)**

| | | | | | |
|---|---|---|---|---|---|
| 2008 | 2.64 | 2.24 | 1.31 | E1.94 | E8.02 |
| 2007 | 2.02 | 2.62 | 1.85 | 1.07 | 7.41 |
| 2006 | 1.23 | 1.74 | 1.67 | 1.99 | 6.63 |
| 2005 | 0.70 | 0.91 | 0.86 | 2.19 | 4.67 |
| 2004 | -0.10 | -0.30 | 0.10 | 1.08 | 0.85 |
| 2003 | 0.28 | 0.37 | 0.41 | Nil | 1.07 |

Fiscal year ended Dec. 31. Next earnings report expected: Late January. EPS Estimates based on S&P Operating Earnings; historical GAAP earnings are as reported.

## Dividend Data (Dates: mm/dd Payment Date: mm/dd/yy)

| Amount ($) | Date Decl. | Ex-Div. Date | Stk. of Record | Payment Date |
|---|---|---|---|---|
| 0.438 | 03/27 | 04/11 | 04/15 | 05/01/08 |
| 0.438 | 06/26 | 07/11 | 07/15 | 08/01/08 |
| 0.500 | 09/25 | 10/10 | 10/15 | 11/01/08 |
| 0.500 | 09/25 | 10/10 | 10/15 | 11/01/08 |

Dividends have been paid since 2003. Source: Company reports.

---

**Please read the Required Disclosures and Analyst Certification on the last page of this report.**

# Freeport-McMoran Copper & Gold Inc.

STANDARD &POOR'S

## Business Summary October 20, 2008

CORPORATE OVERVIEW. Freeport-McMoRan Copper & Gold is the world's second largest copper producer and is a major producer of gold and molybdenum. FCX has twelve producing mines located in Indonesia, North America, and South America along with exploration projects in Africa.

Copper production totaled 3.9 billion pounds in 2007, versus 1.2 billion pounds in 2006, reflecting the acquisition of Phelps Dodge in March 2007; gold production totaled 2.3 million oz., versus 1.7 million oz. in 2006. Molybdenum production was 70 million pounds in 2007, reflecting the acquisition of Phelps Dodge. In 2007, North America accounted for 34% of copper production, South America 36%, and Indonesia 30%.

At 2007 year end, consolidated proven and probable reserves totaled 93.2 billion pounds of copper, 41.0 million ounces of gold, 2.0 billion pounds of molyb-

denum, 230.9 million ounces of silver and 0.6 billion pounds of cobalt. Some 40% of FCX's copper reserves were in Indonesia, about 28% percent were in South America, 27% were in North America and some 5% were in Africa. Some 96% of FCX's gold reserves were in Indonesia, with the balance located in South America. Some 90% of molybdenum reserves are primarily in North America, with the remaining in South America. At the end of 2006, FCX's proven and probable reserves consisted of 38.7 billion lbs. of copper and 41.1 million oz. of gold.

## Company Financials Fiscal Year Ended Dec. 31

| Per Share Data ($) | 2007 | 2006 | 2005 | 2004 | 2003 | 2002 | 2001 | 2000 | 1999 | 1998 |
|---|---|---|---|---|---|---|---|---|---|---|
| Tangible Book Value | 28.56 | 6.83 | 3.98 | 0.36 | 4.23 | NM | NM | NM | NM | NM |
| Cash Flow | 10.03 | 7.33 | 5.38 | 1.96 | 2.52 | 2.67 | 2.49 | 2.09 | 2.39 | 2.25 |
| Earnings | 7.41 | 6.63 | 4.67 | 0.85 | 1.07 | 0.89 | 0.53 | 0.26 | 0.61 | 0.67 |
| S&P Core Earnings | 7.26 | 6.56 | 4.63 | 0.48 | 1.03 | 0.84 | 0.49 | NA | NA | NA |
| Dividends | 1.25 | 1.25 | 1.25 | 0.85 | 0.27 | Nil | Nil | Nil | Nil | 0.20 |
| Payout Ratio | 17% | 19% | 27% | 100% | 25% | Nil | Nil | Nil | Nil | 30% |
| Prices:High | 120.20 | 72.20 | 56.35 | 44.90 | 46.74 | 20.83 | 17.15 | 21.44 | 21.38 | 21.44 |
| Prices:Low | 48.85 | 43.10 | 31.52 | 27.76 | 16.01 | 9.95 | 8.31 | 6.75 | 9.13 | 9.81 |
| P/E Ratio:High | 16 | 11 | 12 | 53 | 44 | 23 | 32 | 82 | 35 | 32 |
| P/E Ratio:Low | 7 | 7 | 7 | 33 | 15 | 11 | 16 | 26 | 15 | 15 |

| Income Statement Analysis (Million $) | | | | | | | | | | |
|---|---|---|---|---|---|---|---|---|---|---|
| Revenue | 16,939 | 5,791 | 4,179 | 2,372 | 2,212 | 1,910 | 1,839 | 1,869 | 1,887 | 1,757 |
| Operating Income | 7,801 | 3,096 | 2,429 | 823 | 1,054 | 901 | 827 | 778 | 876 | 852 |
| Depreciation | 1,246 | 228 | 252 | 206 | 231 | 260 | 284 | 284 | 293 | 277 |
| Interest Expense | 660 | 75.6 | 132 | 148 | 197 | 171 | 174 | 205 | 194 | 225 |
| Pretax Income | 6,133 | 2,826 | 2,037 | 574 | 584 | 450 | 359 | 273 | 381 | 361 |
| Effective Tax Rate | 39.1% | 42.5% | 44.9% | 57.6% | 57.9% | 54.6% | 56.6% | 58.4% | 51.4% | 47.2% |
| Net Income | 2,942 | 1,457 | 995 | 202 | 197 | 168 | 113 | 77.0 | 136 | 154 |
| S&P Core Earnings | 2,672 | 1,381 | 919 | 77.7 | 167 | 123 | 70.8 | NA | NA | NA |

| Balance Sheet & Other Financial Data (Million $) | | | | | | | | | | |
|---|---|---|---|---|---|---|---|---|---|---|
| Cash | 1,626 | 907 | 764 | 551 | 464 | 7.84 | 7.59 | 7.97 | 6.70 | 5.90 |
| Current Assets | 5,903 | 2,151 | 2,022 | 1,460 | 1,100 | 638 | 548 | 569 | 564 | 46.0 |
| Total Assets | 40,661 | 5,390 | 5,550 | 5,087 | 4,718 | 4,192 | 4,212 | 3,951 | 4,083 | 4,193 |
| Current Liabilities | 3,869 | 972 | 1,369 | 698 | 632 | 538 | 628 | 634 | 515 | 518 |
| Long Term Debt | 7,180 | 661 | 1,003 | 1,874 | 2,076 | 1,961 | 2,133 | 1,988 | 2,033 | 2,329 |
| Common Equity | 14,259 | 1,345 | 743 | 63.6 | 776 | -83.2 | -246 | -312 | -153 | -247 |
| Total Capital | 33,953 | 4,119 | 3,971 | 4,189 | 3,925 | 3,514 | 3,464 | 3,204 | 3,453 | 3,599 |
| Capital Expenditures | 1,755 | 251 | 143 | 141 | 139 | 188 | 167 | 292 | 161 | 292 |
| Cash Flow | 3,980 | 1,624 | 1,186 | 363 | 401 | 391 | 360 | 323 | 394 | 395 |
| Current Ratio | 1.5 | 2.2 | 1.5 | 2.1 | 1.7 | 1.2 | 0.9 | 0.9 | 1.1 | 1.1 |
| % Long Term Debt of Capitalization | 26.9 | 16.0 | 25.2 | 44.7 | 52.9 | 55.8 | 61.6 | 62.0 | 58.9 | 64.7 |
| % Net Income of Revenue | 17.4 | 25.2 | 23.8 | 8.5 | 8.9 | 8.8 | 6.1 | 4.1 | 7.2 | 8.8 |
| % Return on Assets | 11.9 | 26.6 | 18.7 | 4.1 | 4.4 | 4.0 | 2.8 | 1.9 | 3.3 | 3.7 |
| % Return on Equity | 35.0 | 133.7 | 231.7 | 37.3 | 49.0 | NM | NM | NM | NM | NM |

Data as orig reptd.; bef. results of disc opers/spec. items. Per share data adj. for stk. divs.; EPS diluted. E-Estimated. NA-Not Available. NM-Not Meaningful. NR-Not Ranked. UR-Under Review.

Office: 1 N Central Ave, Phoenix, AZ 85004-4414.
Telephone: 602-366-8100.
Email: ir@fmi.com
Website: http://www.fcx.com

Chrmn: J.R. Moffett
Pres & CEO: R.C. Adkerson
Vice Chrmn: B.M. Rankin, Jr.
Investor Contact: K.L. Quirk

EVP, CFO & Treas: K.L. Quirk
Board Members: R. C. Adkerson, R. J. Allison, Jr., R. A. Day, G. J. Ford, H. D. Graham, Jr., J. B. Johnston, C. C. Krulak, B. L. Lackey, J. C. Madonna, D. E. McCoy, G. K. McDonald, J. R. Moffett, B. M. Rankin, Jr., J. S. Roy, S. H. Siegele, J. T. Wharton

Founded: 1987
Domicile: Delaware
Employees: 25,541

# Frontier Communications Corp

**STANDARD &POOR'S**

| S&P Recommendation | **STRONG BUY** ★★★★★ | Price | 12-Mo. Target Price | Investment Style |
|---|---|---|---|---|
| | | $8.49 (as of Nov 14, 2008) | $11.00 | Large-Cap Value |

**GICS Sector** Telecommunication Services
**Sub-Industry** Integrated Telecommunication Services

**Summary** This company, previously known as Citizens Communications, provides wireline communications services in rural areas and small and medium-sized cities. In March 2007, it acquired Commonwealth Telephone Enterprises, a rural telecom carrier.

## Key Stock Statistics (Source S&P, Vickers, company reports)

| | | | | | | | |
|---|---|---|---|---|---|---|---|
| 52-Wk Range | $13.20 – 6.89 | S&P Oper. EPS 2008E | 0.60 | Market Capitalization(B) | $2.643 | Beta | 0.80 |
| Trailing 12-Month EPS | $0.64 | S&P Oper. EPS 2009E | 0.61 | Yield (%) | 11.78 | S&P 3-Yr. Proj. EPS CAGR(%) | 4 |
| Trailing 12-Month P/E | 13.3 | P/E on S&P Oper. EPS 2008E | 14.1 | Dividend Rate/Share | $1.00 | S&P Credit Rating | BB |
| $10K Invested 5 Yrs Ago | $7,935 | Common Shares Outstg. (M) | 311.3 | Institutional Ownership (%) | 59 | | |

## Price Performance

30-Week Mov. Avg. · · · · 10-Week Mov. Avg. - - - **GAAP Earnings vs. Previous Year** Volume Above Avg. STARS
12-Mo. Target Price — Relative Strength — ▲ Up ▼ Down ► No Change Below Avg. ★

Analysis prepared by **Todd Rosenbluth** on November 12, 2008, when the stock traded at **$ 8.25.**

Options: CBOE, P, Ph

### Highlights

▶ We expect revenues of $2.25 billion in 2008, including benefits from acquisitions, and we forecast $2.23 billion in 2009. On an organic basis, we project that revenues will be down, as additional long-distance and DSL penetration is offset by a one-time revenue settlement in 2007 and lower access charges due to a decline in universal service support and access line weakness. Despite a focus on service bundles for retention, we believe access line losses will continue due to macroeconomic pressure.

▶ We think EBITDA margins will narrow slightly to 54% in 2008 and then to 53% in 2009, but will remain among the industry's best. We see benefits from work force cuts, and a billing and call center conversion, but see this being offset by increased promotional activities and weakness in higher-margin voice services.

▶ With rising depreciation and interest charges offset by benefits from past share repurchases, we see operating EPS of $0.60 in 2008 and $0.61 in 2009. First-quarter 2007 results were helped by a one-time gain of $0.07, while there was a $0.02 one-time charge in the third quarter.

### Investment Rationale/Risk

▶ We believe the share price decline in October reflects the potentially negative impact from pending FCC changes to reduced universal service funding (USF) and intercarrier compensation. We expect any changes to be phased in and see less than 10% of FTR's revenues at risk over time. Meanwhile, we believe FTR will continue to expand its customer base for DSL and video offerings and. given cost synergies from acquisitions, we see FTR's cash flow remaining strong and being able to support its dividend. We see FTR using additional cash to reduce its debt leverage.

▶ Risks to our recommendation and target price include a balance sheet that appears more leveraged than peers; not retaining residential and corporate customers; and adverse changes to the universal service fund, from which FTR receives revenues.

▶ Our 12-month target price of $11 is based on an EV/EBITDA multiple of 6X, in line with rural telecom peers and down from historic levels to reflect macroeconomic and regulatory risks. At our target price, FTR's dividend yield would be an above-average 9%.

## Qualitative Risk Assessment

| LOW | **MEDIUM** | HIGH |
|---|---|---|

Our risk assessment for Frontier Communications reflects the rural, less competitive nature of its operations, what we see as the strong and stable cash flow that supports its dividend policy, but sensitivity to the U.S. economy.

## Quantitative Evaluations

**S&P Quality Ranking** B-

| D | C | **B-** | B | B+ | A- | A | A+ |
|---|---|---|---|---|---|---|---|

**Relative Strength Rank** **MODERATE**

66

LOWEST = 1      HIGHEST = 99

## Revenue/Earnings Data

### Revenue (Million $)

| | 1Q | 2Q | 3Q | 4Q | Year |
|---|---|---|---|---|---|
| 2008 | 569.2 | 562.6 | 557.9 | -- | -- |
| 2007 | 556.2 | 578.8 | 575.8 | 577.2 | 2,288 |
| 2006 | 506.9 | 506.9 | 507.2 | 504.4 | 2,025 |
| 2005 | 537.2 | 531.8 | 537.4 | 556.1 | 2,162 |
| 2004 | 558.5 | 544.1 | 545.4 | 545.0 | 2,193 |
| 2003 | 651.9 | 644.0 | 595.0 | 554.1 | 2,445 |

### Earnings Per Share ($)

| | | | | | |
|---|---|---|---|---|---|
| 2008 | 0.14 | 0.15 | 0.15 | E0.15 | E0.60 |
| 2007 | 0.21 | 0.12 | 0.14 | 0.18 | 0.65 |
| 2006 | 0.13 | 0.29 | 0.16 | 0.20 | 0.78 |
| 2005 | 0.11 | 0.13 | 0.11 | 0.23 | 0.59 |
| 2004 | 0.15 | 0.08 | -0.04 | 0.05 | 0.23 |
| 2003 | 0.22 | 0.12 | 0.04 | 0.05 | 0.42 |

Fiscal year ended Dec. 31. Next earnings report expected: Late February. EPS Estimates based on S&P Operating Earnings; historical GAAP earnings are as reported.

## Dividend Data (Dates: mm/dd Payment Date: mm/dd/yy)

| Amount ($) | Date Decl. | Ex-Div. Date | Stk. of Record | Payment Date |
|---|---|---|---|---|
| 0.250 | 02/21 | 03/06 | 03/10 | 03/31/08 |
| 0.250 | 05/14 | 06/05 | 06/09 | 06/30/08 |
| 0.250 | 07/03 | 09/05 | 09/09 | 09/30/08 |
| 0.250 | 11/06 | 12/05 | 12/09 | 12/31/08 |

Dividends have been paid since 2004. Source: Company reports.

---

**Please read the Required Disclosures and Analyst Certification on the last page of this report.**

The McGraw-Hill Companies

# Frontier Communications Corp

**STANDARD &POOR'S**

## Business Summary November 12, 2008

CORPORATE OVERVIEW. Frontier Communications (formerly Citizens Communications) provides wireline services to rural areas and small and medium-sized towns and cities in 24 states, including Arizona, California, New York and Pennsylvania, as an incumbent local exchange carrier (ILEC) for 2.3 million access lines as of September 2008 (with 65% used by residential customers), including lines acquired from Commonwealth Telephone (CTCO) in a largely cash deal in March 2007 and a smaller acquisition in late 2007. The company also had 572,000 DSL subscribers, up 15% from a year earlier. FTR has increased its revenues via greater penetration of its bundle of services, including enhanced features such as caller ID, voicemail and DSL. Electric Lightwave, which the company operated to provide competitive local access services to business customers, was sold in mid-2006, for $247 million.

CORPORATE STRATEGY. In 2007 and in the first half of 2008, FTR focused on expanding by providing rural local residential phone customers with enhanced services as well as long-distance (64% of total lines) and DSL. At the end of September 2008, FTR had DSL penetration of 37% of its residential access lines (25% of total lines). During 2007, the company reduced operating expenses through the consolidation of call centers and by enabling some employees to work from home. For the second half of 2008, the company has identified additional savings from call center and billing consolidation. In certain markets during the fourth quarter of 2007, FTR offered a free computer or

TV to those who sign up for a two-year service bundle that includes broadband or video, in an effort to increase penetration and customer loyalty. During the first half of 2008, the company ran limited marketing programs but was offering gift cards in the fourth quarter of 2008 in exchange for its service bundle.

COMPETITIVE LANDSCAPE. We believe FTR faces challenges from cable telephony and wireless that led to its 6.7% access line erosion in the 12 months ended September 2008, as the lines lost were not fully offset by the organic DSL additions in the period that resulted in second lines being dropped. The company competes with cable providers such as Time Warner in its most competitive Rochester, NY, market, and Comcast in California, which began to offer telephony services in 2006, along with other cable providers in its smallest markets. As of September 2008, approximately 65% of FTR's operating territory faced cable telephony competition, and we think this rate will increase to 70% in 2009. FTR has a partnership with EchoStar Communications to provide digital video services to FTR's wireline customers (112,350 at the end of September 2008).

## Company Financials Fiscal Year Ended Dec. 31

| Per Share Data ($) | 2007 | 2006 | 2005 | 2004 | 2003 | 2002 | 2001 | 2000 | 1999 | 1998 |
|---|---|---|---|---|---|---|---|---|---|---|
| Tangible Book Value | NM | NM | NM | NM | NM | NM | NM | 4.09 | 7.36 | 7.27 |
| Cash Flow | 2.30 | 2.25 | 2.26 | 2.09 | 2.37 | -0.24 | 2.08 | 1.30 | 1.45 | 1.22 |
| Earnings | 0.65 | 0.78 | 0.59 | 0.23 | 0.42 | -2.93 | -0.28 | -0.15 | 0.45 | 0.23 |
| S&P Core Earnings | 0.52 | 0.64 | 0.59 | 0.19 | 0.68 | -2.89 | -0.58 | NA | NA | NA |
| Dividends | 1.00 | 1.00 | 1.00 | 0.50 | Nil | Nil | Nil | Nil | Nil | Nil |
| Payout Ratio | 154% | 128% | 169% | NM | Nil | Nil | Nil | Nil | Nil | Nil |
| Prices:High | 16.05 | 14.95 | 14.05 | 14.80 | 13.40 | 11.52 | 15.88 | 19.00 | 14.31 | 11.18 |
| Prices:Low | 12.03 | 11.97 | 12.08 | 11.37 | 8.81 | 2.51 | 8.20 | 12.50 | 7.25 | 6.89 |
| P/E Ratio:High | 25 | 19 | 24 | 62 | 32 | NM | NM | NM | 32 | 51 |
| P/E Ratio:Low | 19 | 15 | 20 | 47 | 21 | NM | NM | NM | 16 | 31 |

| Income Statement Analysis (Million $) | 2007 | 2006 | 2005 | 2004 | 2003 | 2002 | 2001 | 2000 | 1999 | 1998 |
|---|---|---|---|---|---|---|---|---|---|---|
| Revenue | 2,288 | 2,025 | 2,162 | 2,193 | 2,445 | 2,669 | 2,457 | 1,802 | 1,087 | 1,542 |
| Operating Income | 1,251 | 1,121 | 1,149 | 1,148 | 1,173 | 1,179 | 927 | 549 | 8.07 | 178 |
| Depreciation | 546 | 476 | 542 | 573 | 595 | 756 | 632 | 388 | 262 | 258 |
| Interest Expense | 384 | 336 | 339 | 379 | 423 | 478 | 386 | 194 | 93.2 | 112 |
| Pretax Income | 343 | 390 | 285 | 85.5 | 189 | -1,238 | -78.7 | -44.0 | 158 | 73.9 |
| Effective Tax Rate | 37.4% | 35.0% | 29.6% | 15.6% | 35.5% | NM | NM | NM | 40.8% | 25.4% |
| Net Income | 215 | 254 | 200 | 72.2 | 122 | -823 | -63.9 | -40.1 | 117 | 59.6 |
| S&P Core Earnings | 171 | 206 | 201 | 57.7 | 198 | -811 | -164 | NA | NA | NA |

| Balance Sheet & Other Financial Data (Million $) | 2007 | 2006 | 2005 | 2004 | 2003 | 2002 | 2001 | 2000 | 1999 | 1998 |
|---|---|---|---|---|---|---|---|---|---|---|
| Cash | 226 | 1,041 | 266 | 167 | 584 | 393 | 57.7 | 31.2 | 37.1 | 31.9 |
| Current Assets | 524 | 1,273 | 542 | 450 | 896 | 1,201 | 2,533 | 2,263 | 309 | 414 |
| Total Assets | 7,256 | 6,791 | 6,412 | 6,668 | 7,689 | 8,147 | 10,554 | 6,955 | 5,772 | 5,293 |
| Current Liabilities | 446 | 426 | 617 | 418 | 536 | 771 | 1,567 | 992 | 467 | 508 |
| Long Term Debt | 4,739 | 4,461 | 3,999 | 4,267 | 4,397 | 5,159 | 5,736 | 3,264 | 2,309 | 1,900 |
| Common Equity | 998 | 1,058 | 1,042 | 1,362 | 1,415 | 1,172 | 1,946 | 1,720 | 1,920 | 1,793 |
| Total Capital | 6,446 | 6,033 | 5,366 | 5,629 | 6,259 | 6,468 | 8,112 | 5,474 | 4,700 | 4,669 |
| Capital Expenditures | 316 | 269 | 268 | 276 | 278 | 469 | 531 | 537 | 485 | 483 |
| Cash Flow | 761 | 730 | 742 | 645 | 717 | -67.5 | 568 | 348 | 380 | 318 |
| Current Ratio | 1.2 | 3.0 | 0.9 | 1.1 | 1.7 | 1.6 | 1.6 | 2.3 | 0.7 | 0.8 |
| % Long Term Debt of Capitalization | 82.6 | 73.9 | 74.5 | 75.8 | 70.2 | 79.8 | 70.7 | 59.6 | 49.1 | 52.0 |
| % Net Income of Revenue | 9.4 | 12.5 | 9.3 | 3.3 | 5.0 | NM | NM | NM | 10.8 | 3.9 |
| % Return on Assets | 3.1 | 3.8 | 3.1 | 1.0 | 1.5 | NM | NM | NM | 2.1 | 1.2 |
| % Return on Equity | 20.9 | 24.2 | 16.7 | 5.2 | 9.4 | NM | NM | NM | 6.5 | 3.4 |

Data as orig reptd.; bef. results of disc opers/spec. items. Per share data adj. for stk. divs.; EPS diluted. E-Estimated. NA-Not Available. NM-Not Meaningful. NR-Not Ranked. UR-Under Review.

**Office:** 3 High Ridge Park, Stamford, CT 06905-1337.
**Telephone:** 203-614-5600.
**Email:** citizens@cnz.com
**Website:** http://www.czn.net

**Chrmn, Pres & CEO:** M. Wilderotter
**COO & EVP:** D.J. McCarthy
**EVP & CFO:** D.R. Shassian
**SVP & Chief Acctg Officer:** R.J. Larson

**SVP, Secy & General Counsel:** H.E. Glassman
**Board Members:** K. Q. Abernathy, L. T. Barnes, Jr., P. C. Bynoe, M. T. Dugan, J. Finard, L. W. Fitt, W. M. Kraus, H. L. Schrott, L. Segil, D. H. Ward, M. A. Wick, III, M. Wilderotter

**Founded:** 1927
**Domicile:** Delaware
**Employees:** 5,939

# GameStop Corp.

| S&P Recommendation | STRONG BUY ★★★★★ | Price $23.28 (as of Nov 14, 2008) | 12-Mo. Target Price $40.00 | Investment Style Large-Cap Growth |
|---|---|---|---|---|

**GICS Sector** Consumer Discretionary
**Sub-Industry** Computer & Electronics Retail

**Summary** This company is the largest U.S. video game and PC entertainment software specialty retailer, and operates about 5,000 stores worldwide.

## Key Stock Statistics (Source S&P, Vickers, company reports)

| | | | | | | | |
|---|---|---|---|---|---|---|---|
| 52-Wk Range | $63.77– 21.16 | S&P Oper. EPS 2009**E** | 2.42 | Market Capitalization(B) | $3.811 | Beta | 1.76 |
| Trailing 12-Month EPS | $2.16 | S&P Oper. EPS 2010**E** | 2.79 | Yield (%) | Nil | S&P 3-Yr. Proj. EPS CAGR(%) | 15 |
| Trailing 12-Month P/E | 10.8 | P/E on S&P Oper. EPS 2009**E** | 9.6 | Dividend Rate/Share | Nil | S&P Credit Rating | NA |
| $10K Invested 5 Yrs Ago | $28,794 | Common Shares Outstg. (M) | 163.7 | Institutional Ownership (%) | 97 | | |

## Price Performance

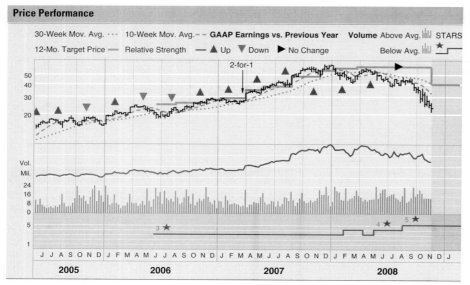

30-Week Mov. Avg. · · · · 10-Week Mov. Avg. - - **GAAP Earnings vs. Previous Year** Volume Above Avg. STARS
12-Mo. Target Price — Relative Strength — ▲ Up ▼ Down ▶ No Change Below Avg. ★

Options: ASE, CBOE, Ph

Analysis prepared by **Michael Souers** on November 07, 2008, when the stock traded at **$ 24.94**.

## Highlights

➤ We see FY 09 (Jan.) revenues rising 23%, following a 33% advance in FY 08. We expect this growth to be driven by the opening of about 600 new stores and by low-teen comp-store sales growth. We expect a relatively new hardware cycle, including Microsoft's Xbox 360, Sony's PlayStation3 and Nintendo Wii, to drive demand for consoles and related software.

➤ We see gross margins widening slightly in FY 09 due to an expected shift in mix to software from hardware following a significant ramp-up in the installed base. We also project that the high-margin used game segment will continue to show strength. Driven by our projections of strong same-store sales results, and the expense leverage generated as a result, we see operating margins widening approximately 60 basis points.

➤ After modestly lower net interest expense driven by GME's continued focus on debt retirement, and taxes at 36.5% versus 34.6%, we see FY 09 operating EPS of $2.42, a 34% increase from the $1.80 the company earned in FY 08, excluding one-time items. We see FY 10 EPS of $2.79.

## Investment Rationale/Risk

➤ We think the video game industry is only partially through a powerful growth cycle unprecedented in strength, and we expect greater than 15% earnings growth from GME over the next two years. Moreover, the industry appears to be somewhat insulated from an overall decline in consumer spending. Longer term, we believe the electronic game industry will benefit from hardware platform technology evolution, a growing used video game market, and broadening demographic appeal. Following a recent decline, we find the shares extremely attractive at a P/E-to-growth rate of under 0.6X, a significant discount to the S&P 500.

➤ Risks to our opinion and target price include a slowdown in consumer spending, inventory shortages, an inability to successfully manage new store openings or merger integration, and corporate governance issues including the existence of a non shareholder-approved poison pill.

➤ Our 12-month target price of $40, or about 14X our FY 10 EPS estimate, is based on our DCF analysis, which assumes a weighted average cost of capital of 11.2% and terminal growth of 4.0%.

## Qualitative Risk Assessment

| LOW | MEDIUM | HIGH |
|---|---|---|

Our risk assessment reflects the company's leading market share position, offset by industry cyclicality, as growth is partly dependent on the timing of new hardware and software releases.

## Quantitative Evaluations

**S&P Quality Ranking** NR

| D | C | B- | B | B+ | A- | A | A+ |
|---|---|---|---|---|---|---|---|

**Relative Strength Rank** MODERATE

36

LOWEST = 1     HIGHEST = 99

## Revenue/Earnings Data

**Revenue (Million $)**

| | 1Q | 2Q | 3Q | 4Q | Year |
|---|---|---|---|---|---|
| 2009 | 1,814 | 1,804 | -- | -- | -- |
| 2008 | 1,279 | 1,338 | 1,611 | 2,866 | 7,094 |
| 2007 | 1,040 | 963.4 | 1,012 | 2,304 | 5,319 |
| 2006 | 474.7 | 415.9 | 534.2 | 1,667 | 3,092 |
| 2005 | 371.7 | 345.6 | 416.7 | 708.7 | 1,843 |
| 2004 | 321.7 | 305.7 | 326.0 | 625.4 | 1,579 |

**Earnings Per Share ($)**

| | 1Q | 2Q | 3Q | 4Q | Year |
|---|---|---|---|---|---|
| 2009 | 0.37 | 0.34 | E0.36 | E1.34 | E2.42 |
| 2008 | 0.15 | 0.34 | 0.31 | 1.14 | 1.75 |
| 2007 | 0.08 | 0.02 | 0.09 | 0.81 | 1.00 |
| 2006 | 0.10 | 0.07 | -0.02 | 0.55 | 0.81 |
| 2005 | 0.06 | 0.07 | 0.11 | 0.32 | 0.53 |
| 2004 | 0.06 | 0.06 | 0.09 | 0.34 | 0.53 |

Fiscal year ended Jan. 31. Next earnings report expected: Late November. EPS Estimates based on S&P Operating Earnings; historical GAAP earnings are as reported.

## Dividend Data

No cash dividends have been paid.

# GameStop Corp.

STANDARD
&POOR'S

## Business Summary November 07, 2008

CORPORATE OVERVIEW. GameStop is the world's largest retailer of video game products and PC entertainment software. The company sells new and used video game hardware, video game software and accessories, as well as PC entertainment software, related accessories and other merchandise. As of February 2, 2008, GameStop operated 5,264 stores in the U.S., Australia, Canada and Europe, primarily under the names GameStop and EB Games. Of the total store count, 4,061 stores are located in the U.S., with the remaining 1,203 located internationally.

In October 2005, GameStop acquired close peer Electronics Boutique Holding Corp., which essentially doubled the company's market share in video game retailing. We estimate GME currently has a global market share of nearly 20%.

MARKET PROFILE. According to NPD Group, Inc., a market research firm, the U.S. electronic games industry generated approximately $18.6 billion in 2007, and, according to the International Development Group, retail sales of video game hardware and software and PC entertainment software totaled $15.6 billion in Europe. The Entertainment Software Association (ESA) estimates that 67% of all American head of households play video or computer games, and that the average game player is 33 years old. We believe that trends such as

hardware platform technology evolution and a broadening demographic appeal will continue to propel growth in this industry.

In addition, as the installed base of video game hardware platforms has increased, and new hardware platforms are introduced, a rising used video game market has evolved in the U.S. We believe that GameStop is the leading retailer of used video games in the world, with the broadest selection of used video game products for both current and previous generation platforms. We think that the company's focus on the used game market enables GameStop to differentiate itself from mass merchants, toy stores and consumer electronics retailers that sell video game products. We note that the used game business, which represented 22% of FY 08 (Jan.) sales, generates significantly higher gross margins than the company average. For example, used game products generated a gross margin of approximately 49% in FY 08, compared to 7% for hardware and 26% for the total company.

## Company Financials Fiscal Year Ended Jan. 31

| Per Share Data ($) | 2008 | 2007 | 2006 | 2005 | 2004 | 2003 | 2002 | 2001 | 2000 | 1999 |
|---|---|---|---|---|---|---|---|---|---|---|
| Tangible Book Value | 2.80 | NM | NM | 2.19 | 2.41 | 2.02 | NM | NM | NA | NA |
| Cash Flow | 2.54 | 1.69 | 1.34 | 0.85 | 0.77 | 0.62 | 0.47 | 0.14 | NA | NA |
| Earnings | 1.75 | 1.00 | 0.81 | 0.53 | 0.53 | 0.44 | 0.09 | -0.17 | -0.43 | NA |
| S&P Core Earnings | 1.75 | 1.00 | 0.76 | 0.92 | 0.47 | 0.37 | 0.09 | NA | NA | NA |
| Dividends | Nil | Nil | Nil | Nil | Nil | Nil | Nil | Nil | NA | NA |
| Payout Ratio | Nil | Nil | Nil | Nil | Nil | Nil | Nil | Nil | NA | NA |
| Calendar Year | 2007 | 2006 | 2005 | 2004 | 2003 | 2002 | 2001 | 2000 | 1999 | 1998 |
| Prices:High | 63.77 | 29.21 | 19.21 | 11.76 | 9.52 | 12.15 | NA | NA | NA | NA |
| Prices:Low | 24.95 | 15.57 | 9.27 | 7.19 | 3.75 | 4.46 | NA | NA | NA | NA |
| P/E Ratio:High | 36 | 29 | 24 | 22 | 18 | 28 | NA | NA | NA | NA |
| P/E Ratio:Low | 14 | 16 | 12 | 14 | 7 | 10 | NA | NA | NA | NA |

**Income Statement Analysis** (Million $)

| | 2008 | 2007 | 2006 | 2005 | 2004 | 2003 | 2002 | 2001 | 2000 | 1999 |
|---|---|---|---|---|---|---|---|---|---|---|
| Revenue | 7,094 | 5,319 | 3,092 | 1,843 | 1,579 | 1,353 | 1,121 | 757 | 553 | 465 |
| Operating Income | 632 | 450 | 273 | 163 | 133 | 110 | 64.4 | 27.8 | NA | NA |
| Depreciation | 130 | 110 | 66.7 | 37.0 | 28.9 | 22.6 | 30.3 | 22.0 | 8.09 | 4.80 |
| Interest Expense | 61.6 | 84.7 | 37.9 | 2.16 | 0.66 | 1.37 | 19.6 | 23.0 | NA | NA |
| Pretax Income | 441 | 254 | 160 | 98.9 | 105 | 87.7 | 14.6 | -17.8 | -5.51 | 21.7 |
| Effective Tax Rate | 34.6% | 37.8% | 37.0% | 38.4% | 39.7% | 40.2% | 52.4% | NM | 38.0% | 40.3% |
| Net Income | 288 | 158 | 101 | 60.9 | 63.5 | 52.4 | 6.96 | -12.0 | -3.42 | 13.0 |
| S&P Core Earnings | 288 | 158 | 94.1 | 53.2 | 55.6 | 44.1 | 6.76 | NA | NA | NA |

**Balance Sheet & Other Financial Data** (Million $)

| | 2008 | 2007 | 2006 | 2005 | 2004 | 2003 | 2002 | 2001 | 2000 | 1999 |
|---|---|---|---|---|---|---|---|---|---|---|
| Cash | 857 | 652 | 402 | 171 | 205 | 232 | 80.8 | 8.70 | 6.61 | NA |
| Current Assets | 1,795 | 1,440 | 1,121 | 424 | 473 | 416 | 237 | 138 | NA | NA |
| Total Assets | 3,776 | 3,350 | 3,015 | 915 | 899 | 804 | 607 | 510 | 308 | NA |
| Current Liabilities | 1,261 | 1,087 | 888 | 314 | 284 | 247 | 206 | 140 | NA | NA |
| Long Term Debt | 574 | 844 | 963 | 24.3 | Nil | Nil | 400 | 385 | NA | NA |
| Common Equity | 1,862 | 1,376 | 1,115 | 543 | 594 | 549 | -3.99 | -20.6 | -8.57 | NA |
| Total Capital | 2,437 | 2,220 | 2,091 | 588 | 612 | 554 | 399 | 367 | NA | NA |
| Capital Expenditures | 176 | 134 | 111 | 98.3 | 63.0 | 39.5 | 20.5 | 25.1 | 16.4 | 6.79 |
| Cash Flow | 419 | 268 | 167 | 97.9 | 92.4 | 75.0 | 37.3 | 10.0 | NA | NA |
| Current Ratio | 1.4 | 1.3 | 1.3 | 1.4 | 1.7 | 1.7 | 1.2 | 1.0 | 0.7 | NA |
| % Long Term Debt of Capitalization | 23.6 | 38.0 | 46.1 | 4.1 | Nil | Nil | 100.2 | 105.0 | 104.4 | Nil |
| % Net Income of Revenue | 4.1 | 3.0 | 3.3 | 3.3 | 4.0 | 3.9 | 0.6 | NM | NM | 2.8 |
| % Return on Assets | 8.1 | 5.0 | 5.1 | 6.7 | 7.5 | 7.4 | 1.2 | NM | NA | NA |
| % Return on Equity | 17.8 | 12.7 | 12.2 | 10.7 | 11.1 | 19.2 | NM | NM | NA | NA |

Data as orig reptd.; bef. results of disc opers/spec. items. Per share data adj. for stk. divs.; EPS diluted. E-Estimated. NA-Not Available. NM-Not Meaningful. NR-Not Ranked. UR-Under Review.

**Office:** 625 Westport Pkwy, Grapevine, TX 76051-6740.
**Telephone:** 817-424-2000.
**Email:** investorrelations@gamestop.com
**Website:** http://www.gamestop.com

**Chrmn:** R.R. Fontaine
**Vice Chrmn & CEO:** D.A. Dematteo
**COO:** J.P. Raines
**EVP & CFO:** D.W. Carlson

**SVP & Chief Acctg Officer:** R.A. Lloyd
**Investor Contact:** M. Hodges (817-424-2000)
**Board Members:** J. L. Davis, D. A. Dematteo, R. R. Fontaine, S. Koonin, L. Riggio, M. N. Rosen, S. M. Shern, S. Steinberg, G. R. Szczepanski, E. A. Volkwein, L. S. Zilavy

**Founded:** 1994
**Domicile:** Delaware
**Employees:** 43,000

# Gannett Co Inc.

**STANDARD &POOR'S**

| **S&P Recommendation** HOLD ★★★☆☆ | **Price** $8.15 (as of Nov 14, 2008) | **12-Mo. Target Price** $13.00 | **Investment Style** Large-Cap Blend |
|---|---|---|---|

**GICS Sector** Consumer Discretionary
**Sub-Industry** Publishing

**Summary** Gannett publishes 90 daily U.S. newspapers, nearly 1,000 non-daily publications in the U.S., and close to 300 U.K. titles, and operates 23 TV stations in the U.S.

## Key Stock Statistics (Source S&P, Vickers, company reports)

| | | | | | | | |
|---|---|---|---|---|---|---|---|
| 52-Wk Range | $39.50– 7.86 | S&P Oper. EPS 2009E | 2.90 | Market Capitalization(B) | $1.859 | Beta | 1.04 |
| Trailing 12-Month EPS | $-7.40 | S&P Oper. EPS 2010E | NA | Yield (%) | 19.63 | S&P 3-Yr. Proj. EPS CAGR(%) | -11 |
| Trailing 12-Month P/E | NM | P/E on S&P Oper. EPS 2009E | 2.8 | Dividend Rate/Share | $1.60 | S&P Credit Rating | BBB- |
| $10K Invested 5 Yrs Ago | $1,084 | Common Shares Outstg. (M) | 228.1 | Institutional Ownership (%) | NM | | |

## Price Performance

30-Week Mov. Avg. · · · 10-Week Mov. Avg. - - **GAAP Earnings vs. Previous Year**   Volume Above Avg. STARS
12-Mo. Target Price — Relative Strength   — ▲ Up ▼ Down ▶ No Change   Below Avg.

Options: ASE, CBOE, P, Ph

Analysis prepared by **Marie Driscoll, CFA** on November 04, 2008, when the stock traded at **$ 11.56**.

## Highlights

➤ We foresee print publishing revenues remaining soft due for the remainder of 2008 and into 2009 due to weak economic environments in the U.S. and U.K., and as we expect classified advertising overall to continue migrating online. We look for strong broadcast revenue growth in 2008, mostly due to an anticipated boost from Olympic and election year advertising. Overall, we expect a revenue drop of about 8% in both 2008 and 2009.

➤ We forecast an operating margin of 18.5% in 2009, down from our estimate for 19.2% in 2008. We see the benefits of recent staff reduction initiatives being more than offset by declines in profitable print classified advertising, higher paper pricing and negative operating leverage from lower revenues.

➤ We forecast 2009 EPS of $2.90, down from our EPS estimate of $3.45 in 2008. Our estimates include severance expense, which we view as recurring due to ongoing restructuring activity at GCI. Our 2008 estimate excludes $0.22 of gains from one-time items and $11.08 in charges related to asset impairment.

## Investment Rationale/Risk

➤ We remain concerned by what we see as a secular decline in newspaper advertising, especially as the company garners only about 6% of its revenues from online operations. We are also concerned by negative trends in the U.S. and U.K. economies that we expect to hurt classified advertising. On a positive note, with a free cash flow/equity yield of about 20%, we think there is long-term value in what we see as GCI's strong free cash flow generating capabilities. We also note GCI's above average dividend yield.

➤ Risks to our recommendation and target price include a worse than expected slowdown in U.S. GDP, declines in audience ratings at network-affiliated TV stations, and a weakening of the British pound versus the U.S. dollar.

➤ Our 12-month target price of $13 is derived by applying an enterprise value/EBITDA ratio of 4.6X to our 2009 EBITDA estimate of $1.46 billion. This multiple is at the low end of the company's historical range and about a 15% discount to peers, which we think is appropriate given significant cyclical, secular and operating challenges we see facing GCI.

## Qualitative Risk Assessment

| LOW | **MEDIUM** | HIGH |
|---|---|---|

Our risk assessment reflects a highly competitive advertising environment, offset by our view of the company's consistently strong free cash flow and profitability, and its relatively low weighted average cost of capital.

## Quantitative Evaluations

**S&P Quality Ranking**   A

| D | C | B- | B | B+ | A- | **A** | A+ |
|---|---|---|---|---|---|---|---|

**Relative Strength Rank**   WEAK

20

LOWEST = 1                    HIGHEST = 99

## Revenue/Earnings Data

**Revenue (Million $)**

| | 1Q | 2Q | 3Q | 4Q | Year |
|---|---|---|---|---|---|
| 2008 | 1,677 | 1,718 | 1,637 | -- | -- |
| 2007 | 1,871 | 1,928 | 1,756 | 1,897 | 7,439 |
| 2006 | 1,883 | 2,028 | 1,915 | 2,208 | 8,033 |
| 2005 | 1,768 | 1,911 | 1,865 | 2,055 | 7,599 |
| 2004 | 1,730 | 1,873 | 1,816 | 1,962 | 7,381 |
| 2003 | 1,552 | 1,705 | 1,631 | 1,822 | 6,711 |

**Earnings Per Share ($)**

| | 1Q | 2Q | 3Q | 4Q | Year |
|---|---|---|---|---|---|
| 2008 | 0.84 | -10.03 | 0.69 | E1.00 | E3.45 |
| 2007 | 0.90 | 1.24 | 1.01 | 1.06 | 4.17 |
| 2006 | 0.99 | 1.31 | 1.11 | 1.51 | 4.90 |
| 2005 | 1.03 | 1.34 | 1.13 | 1.44 | 4.92 |
| 2004 | 1.00 | 1.30 | 1.18 | 1.47 | 4.92 |
| 2003 | 0.93 | 1.20 | 1.03 | 1.31 | 4.46 |

Fiscal year ended Dec. 31. Next earnings report expected: Early February. EPS Estimates based on S&P Operating Earnings; historical GAAP earnings are as reported.

## Dividend Data (Dates: mm/dd Payment Date: mm/dd/yy)

| Amount ($) | Date Decl. | Ex-Div. Date | Stk. of Record | Payment Date |
|---|---|---|---|---|
| 0.400 | 02/27 | 03/05 | 03/07 | 04/01/08 |
| 0.400 | 04/30 | 06/04 | 06/06 | 07/01/08 |
| 0.400 | 07/31 | 09/10 | 09/12 | 10/01/08 |
| 0.400 | 10/30 | 12/10 | 12/12 | 01/02/09 |

Dividends have been paid since 1929. Source: Company reports.

# Gannett Co Inc.

**STANDARD &POOR'S**

## Business Summary November 04, 2008

CORPORATE OVERVIEW. Gannett is the largest newspaper publisher in the U.S. The company publishes newspapers, operates broadcasting stations, runs Web sites in connection with its newspaper and broadcast operations, and is engaged in marketing, commercial printing, a newswire service, data services, and news programming.

The newspaper publishing segment (89% of 2007 revenues) consists of the operations of 85 daily newspapers and about 900 non-daily publications in the U.S., and 17 daily and nearly 300 non-daily titles in the U.K. The segment includes the publication of USA TODAY, the nation's largest selling daily newspaper. The company's strategy for non-daily publications is to target these products at communities of interest, defined by geography, demographics or lifestyle. In the U.K., the company is the second largest regional publisher via its wholly owned subsidiary, Newsquest plc. The segment also includes PointRoll, an Internet ad services business, Planet Discover, a provider of local, integrated online search and advertising technology, commercial printing, newswire, marketing and data services operations.

Newspaper publishing revenues are derived principally from the sale of advertising (74% of 2007 revenues), including Internet advertising, and circulation revenues (19%). Within the advertising category, revenues were derived from local (44%), national (16%) and classified (40%) advertising. The remaining segment revenues (7%) came from commercial printing operations, earnings from a 40.6% stake in the Texas-New Mexico Newspaper Partnership, and a 19.49% equity interest in California Newspapers Partnership. Newsquest operations generated approximately 19% and 12% of segment advertising and circulation revenues, respectively.

The broadcast segment (11% of 2007 revenues) consists of 23 network-affiliated TV stations, including 12 NBC, six CBS, three ABC affiliates and two MyNetworkTV affiliates, and Captivate Network, a national news and entertainment network that delivers programming and full-motion video advertising through video screens located in office tower elevators across North America. The principal sources of GCI's television revenues are: local advertising focusing on the immediate geographic area of the stations; national advertising, compensation paid by the networks for carrying commercial network programs; advertising on the stations' Web sites; and payments by advertisers to television stations for other services, such as the production of advertising material. Captivate derives its revenue principally from national advertising.

## Company Financials Fiscal Year Ended Dec. 31

| Per Share Data ($) | 2008 | 2007 | 2006 | 2005 | 2004 | 2003 | 2002 | 2001 | 2000 | 1999 |
|---|---|---|---|---|---|---|---|---|---|---|
| Tangible Book Value | NA | NM | NM | NM | NM | NM | NM | NM | NM | NM |
| Cash Flow | NA | 5.38 | 6.07 | 6.24 | 6.14 | 5.30 | 5.13 | 4.78 | 4.99 | 3.87 |
| Earnings | 3.51 | 4.17 | 4.90 | 4.92 | 4.92 | 4.46 | 4.31 | 3.12 | 3.63 | 3.26 |
| S&P Core Earnings | NA | 4.01 | 4.86 | 4.43 | 4.45 | 4.23 | 3.70 | 2.39 | NA | NA |
| Dividends | 1.20 | 1.42 | 1.20 | 1.12 | 1.04 | 0.98 | 0.94 | 0.90 | 0.86 | 0.81 |
| Payout Ratio | 34% | 34% | 24% | 23% | 21% | 22% | 22% | 29% | 24% | 25% |
| Prices:High | 39.00 | 63.50 | 64.97 | 82.41 | 91.38 | 89.63 | 79.90 | 71.14 | 81.56 | 83.63 |
| Prices:Low | 14.62 | 34.34 | 51.65 | 58.37 | 78.84 | 66.70 | 62.76 | 53.00 | 48.38 | 60.63 |
| P/E Ratio:High | 11 | 15 | 13 | 17 | 19 | 20 | 19 | 23 | 22 | 26 |
| P/E Ratio:Low | 4 | 8 | 11 | 12 | 16 | 15 | 15 | 17 | 13 | 19 |

| Income Statement Analysis (Million $) | | | | | | | | | | |
|---|---|---|---|---|---|---|---|---|---|---|
| Revenue | NA | 7,439 | 8,033 | 7,599 | 7,381 | 6,711 | 6,422 | 6,344 | 6,222 | 5,260 |
| Operating Income | NA | 2,005 | 2,275 | 2,322 | 2,392 | 2,213 | 2,149 | 2,034 | 2,190 | 1,843 |
| Depreciation | NA | 282 | 277 | 274 | 244 | 232 | 215 | 444 | 376 | 169 |
| Interest Expense | NA | 260 | 288 | 211 | 141 | 139 | 146 | 222 | 219 | 94.6 |
| Pretax Income | NA | 1,449 | 1,719 | 1,818 | 1,995 | 1,840 | 1,765 | 1,371 | 1,609 | 1,527 |
| Effective Tax Rate | NA | 32.7% | 32.5% | 33.4% | 34.0% | 34.2% | 34.3% | 39.4% | 39.6% | 39.8% |
| Net Income | NA | 976 | 1,161 | 1,211 | 1,317 | 1,211 | 1,160 | 831 | 972 | 919 |
| S&P Core Earnings | NA | 939 | 1,151 | 1,092 | 1,191 | 1,150 | 998 | 638 | NA | NA |

| Balance Sheet & Other Financial Data (Million $) | | | | | | | | | | |
|---|---|---|---|---|---|---|---|---|---|---|
| Cash | NA | 77.3 | 94.3 | 163 | 136 | 67.2 | 90.4 | 141 | 193 | 46.2 |
| Current Assets | NA | 1,343 | 1,532 | 1,462 | 1,371 | 1,223 | 1,133 | 1,178 | 1,302 | 1,075 |
| Total Assets | NA | 15,888 | 16,224 | 15,743 | 15,399 | 14,706 | 13,733 | 13,096 | 12,980 | 9,006 |
| Current Liabilities | NA | 962 | 1,117 | 1,096 | 1,005 | 962 | 959 | 1,128 | 1,174 | 884 |
| Long Term Debt | NA | 4,098 | 5,210 | 5,438 | 4,608 | 3,835 | 4,547 | 5,080 | 5,748 | 2,463 |
| Common Equity | NA | 9,017 | 8,382 | 7,571 | 8,164 | 8,423 | 6,912 | 5,736 | 5,103 | 4,630 |
| Total Capital | NA | 13,832 | 14,319 | 13,897 | 13,685 | 13,094 | 12,138 | 11,319 | 11,126 | 7,572 |
| Capital Expenditures | NA | 171 | 201 | 263 | 280 | 281 | 275 | 325 | 351 | 258 |
| Cash Flow | NA | 1,258 | 1,438 | 1,486 | 1,561 | 1,443 | 1,375 | 1,275 | 1,348 | 1,089 |
| Current Ratio | NA | 1.4 | 1.4 | 1.3 | 1.4 | 1.3 | 1.2 | 1.0 | 1.1 | 1.2 |
| % Long Term Debt of Capitalization | NA | 29.6 | 36.4 | 39.1 | 33.7 | 29.3 | 37.5 | 44.9 | 51.7 | 32.5 |
| % Net Income of Revenue | NA | 13.1 | 14.4 | 15.9 | 17.8 | 18.0 | 18.1 | 13.1 | 15.6 | 17.5 |
| % Return on Assets | NA | 6.1 | 7.3 | 7.8 | 8.8 | 8.5 | 8.6 | 6.4 | 8.8 | 11.5 |
| % Return on Equity | NA | 11.2 | 14.6 | 15.4 | 15.9 | 15.8 | 18.3 | 15.3 | 20.0 | 21.4 |

Data as orig reptd.; bef. results of disc opers/spec. items. Per share data adj. for stk. divs.; EPS diluted. E-Estimated. NA-Not Available. NM-Not Meaningful. NR-Not Ranked. UR-Under Review.

**Office:** 7950 Jones Branch Dr, McLean, VA 22107-0910.
**Telephone:** 703-854-6000.
**Email:** gcishare@gannett.com
**Website:** http://www.gannett.com

**Chrmn, Pres & CEO:** C.A. Dubow
**EVP & CFO:** G.C. Martore
**SVP & General Counsel:** K. Wimmer
**Treas:** M.A. Hart

**Secy:** T.A. Mayman
**Investor Contact:** J. Heinz (703-854-6917)
**Board Members:** C. A. Dubow, H. D. Elias, H. D. Elias, A. H. Harper, J. J. Louis, M. Magner, S. K. McCune, D. M. McFarland, D. E. Shalala, N. Shapiro, K. H. Williams

**Founded:** 1906
**Domicile:** Delaware
**Employees:** 46,100

*The McGraw-Hill Companies*

# Gap Inc. (The)

**STANDARD &POOR'S**

| S&P Recommendation **HOLD** ★★★☆☆ | Price<br>$11.55 (as of Nov 14, 2008) | 12-Mo. Target Price<br>$14.00 | Investment Style<br>Large-Cap Blend |
|---|---|---|---|

**GICS Sector** Consumer Discretionary
**Sub-Industry** Apparel Retail

**Summary** This specialty apparel retailer operates Gap, Banana Republic and Old Navy stores, offering casual clothing to moderate, upscale and value-oriented market segments.

## Key Stock Statistics (Source S&P, Vickers, company reports)

| | | | | | | | |
|---|---|---|---|---|---|---|---|
| 52-Wk Range | $22.02– 10.54 | S&P Oper. EPS 2009**E** | 1.32 | Market Capitalization(B) | $8.217 | Beta | 0.78 |
| Trailing 12-Month EPS | $1.31 | S&P Oper. EPS 2010**E** | 1.40 | Yield (%) | 2.94 | S&P 3-Yr. Proj. EPS CAGR(%) | 8 |
| Trailing 12-Month P/E | 8.8 | P/E on S&P Oper. EPS 2009**E** | 8.8 | Dividend Rate/Share | $0.34 | S&P Credit Rating | BB+ |
| $10K Invested 5 Yrs Ago | $5,717 | Common Shares Outstg. (M) | 711.4 | Institutional Ownership (%) | 70 | | |

## Price Performance

30-Week Mov. Avg. ···  10-Week Mov. Avg. —  **GAAP Earnings vs. Previous Year**  Volume Above Avg. ▮▮ STARS
12-Mo. Target Price —  Relative Strength —  ▲ Up  ▼ Down  ▶ No Change  Below Avg. ▮▮ ★

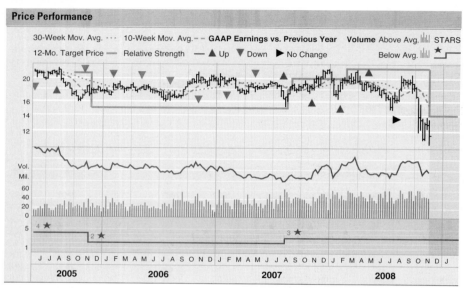

Analysis prepared by **Marie Driscoll, CFA** on November 13, 2008, when the stock traded at **$ 10.96**.

Options: ASE, CBOE, P, Ph

## Highlights

➤ We believe mature, overdistributed brands lacking clear positioning have driven weak operating and financial results since FY 05 (Jan.). FY 08 sales declined 5% to $15.8 billion; down 5% on a comp-store basis after a 7% comp-store decline in FY 07. By division, FY 08 comps were -7% at Old Navy; -5% at Gap NA, -1% at Gap International, and up 1% at Banana Republic. Sales per square foot dropped 5% to $376.

➤ We project a 6% sales decline in FY 09 driven by continued weakness at Old Navy as GPS repositions the brand to a new target, a young woman on a budget who's purchasing for herself and her family. We see a modest decline in Gap NA sales, flat sales at Banana Republic and gains internationally and online (e-commerce). We forecast a 1.5% sales decline in FY 10.

➤ We expect an improvement in gross and operating margins as FY 09 progresses in tandem with the increased impact of new leadership at Gap on merchandise design and inventory flow. We see FY 09 operating margins expanding 200 basis points, to 10.1%, and another increment of 50 bps in FY 10 on improved sourcing and inventory management.

## Investment Rationale/Risk

➤ Quarterly same-store sales comparisons have been negative for the past 17 quarters. October-quarter comps disappointed us at -12%, reflecting negative trends at all brands, with Old Navy -20%. We are disappointed by traffic trends across all brands, but are encouraged by improved merchandise margins and inventory management. We expect further Gap store closures in tandem with improved brand positioning.

➤ Risks to our recommendation and target price include adverse same-store sales trends and a slow learning curve for GPS's new CEO, in addition to typical risks associated with specialty retailers such as employment, consumer income and spending trends, an increase in promotional activity in the mall, and continued access to sourcing.

➤ Our 12-month target price of $14 assumes that GPS will trade at about 10X our FY 10 EPS estimate, about a 25% premium to peers reflecting our view of the company's strong balance sheet and cash flows. This compares with GPS's historical five-year average forward multiple of 18.5X.

## Qualitative Risk Assessment

| LOW | **MEDIUM** | HIGH |
|---|---|---|

Our risk assessment reflects our view of GPS's strong cash flow and balance sheet, offset by weakness in its two largest brands and increased competition.

## Quantitative Evaluations

**S&P Quality Ranking**  A-

| D | C | B- | B | B+ | **A-** | A | A+ |
|---|---|---|---|---|---|---|---|

**Relative Strength Rank**  **MODERATE**

47

LOWEST = 1                HIGHEST = 99

## Revenue/Earnings Data

**Revenue (Million $)**

| | 1Q | 2Q | 3Q | 4Q | Year |
|---|---|---|---|---|---|
| 2009 | 3,384 | 3,499 | -- | -- | -- |
| 2008 | 3,549 | 3,685 | 3,854 | 4,675 | 15,763 |
| 2007 | 3,441 | 3,716 | 3,856 | 4,930 | 15,943 |
| 2006 | 3,626 | 3,716 | 3,860 | 4,821 | 16,023 |
| 2005 | 3,668 | 3,721 | 3,980 | 4,898 | 16,267 |
| 2004 | 3,353 | 3,685 | 3,929 | 4,886 | 15,854 |

**Earnings Per Share ($)**

| | 1Q | 2Q | 3Q | 4Q | Year |
|---|---|---|---|---|---|
| 2009 | 0.34 | 0.32 | E0.33 | E0.35 | E1.32 |
| 2008 | 0.25 | 0.32 | 0.30 | 0.35 | 1.09 |
| 2007 | 0.28 | 0.15 | 0.23 | 0.27 | 0.93 |
| 2006 | 0.31 | 0.30 | 0.24 | 0.39 | 1.24 |
| 2005 | 0.33 | 0.21 | 0.28 | 0.40 | 1.21 |
| 2004 | 0.22 | 0.22 | 0.28 | 0.37 | 1.09 |

Fiscal year ended Jan. 31. Next earnings report expected: Late November. EPS Estimates based on S&P Operating Earnings; historical GAAP earnings are as reported.

## Dividend Data (Dates: mm/dd Payment Date: mm/dd/yy)

| Amount ($) | Date Decl. | Ex-Div. Date | Stk. of Record | Payment Date |
|---|---|---|---|---|
| 0.080 | 11/27 | 01/07 | 01/09 | 01/30/08 |
| 0.085 | 03/26 | 04/04 | 04/08 | 04/29/08 |
| 0.085 | 06/03 | 07/03 | 07/08 | 07/29/08 |
| 0.085 | 10/01 | 10/09 | 10/14 | 10/28/08 |

Dividends have been paid since 1976. Source: Company reports.

---

**Please read the Required Disclosures and Analyst Certification on the last page of this report.**

*The McGraw-Hill Companies*

# Gap Inc. (The)

## Business Summary November 13, 2008

CORPORATE OVERVIEW. Gap, Inc. is a specialty retailer that operates stores selling casual apparel, accessories, and personal care products for men, women and children. As of February 2, 2008, it operated 3,167 stores: 1,249 Gap North America; 555 Banana Republic North America; 1,059 Old Navy North America; and 304 international locations, with 39.6 million sq. ft. of total retail space. In FY 08 (Jan.), international retail locations accounted for an estimated 10% of sales.

MARKET PROFILE. GPS participates in the men's, women's and children's apparel market, which generated approximately $196 billion at U.S. retail in 2007 (up 2.9%), according to NPD Fashionworld consumer estimated data. The apparel market is fragmented, with national brands marketed by 20 companies accounting for about 30% of total apparel sales, and the remaining 70% comprised of smaller and/or private label "store" brands. The market is mature, in our view, with demand largely mirroring population growth, and fashion trends accounting for a modicum of incremental volume. Deflationary pricing

pressure is a function of channel competition and production steadily moving offshore to low-cost producers in India, Asia and China. S&P forecasts flat 2008 apparel sales.

COMPETITIVE LANDSCAPE. By channel, specialty stores account for the largest share of apparel sales, at 31% in 2007, according to NPD. Mass merchants (e.g., Wal-Mart and Target) came in second, at 20%, and department stores came in third, at 16%, down from 19% in 2003. National chains (e.g., Sears and J C Penney) captured 15% of 2007 apparel sales, and off-price retailers (e.g., TJX and Ross Stores) were at 7%. The remaining 11% was divided among factory outlets and direct and e-mail pure plays. GPS is the largest U.S. specialty retailer, with an estimated 22% of the channel's volume.

## Company Financials Fiscal Year Ended Jan. 31

| Per Share Data ($) | 2008 | 2007 | 2006 | 2005 | 2004 | 2003 | 2002 | 2001 | 2000 | 1999 |
|---|---|---|---|---|---|---|---|---|---|---|
| Tangible Book Value | 11.50 | 9.58 | 6.33 | 5.73 | 5.33 | 4.12 | 3.48 | 3.43 | 2.63 | 1.83 |
| Cash Flow | 1.89 | 1.57 | 1.93 | 1.79 | 1.71 | 1.43 | 0.93 | 1.67 | 1.75 | 1.25 |
| Earnings | 1.09 | 0.93 | 1.24 | 1.21 | 1.09 | 0.54 | -0.01 | 1.00 | 1.26 | 0.91 |
| S&P Core Earnings | 1.09 | 0.93 | 1.15 | 1.13 | 1.03 | 0.50 | -0.10 | 0.86 | NA | NA |
| Dividends | 0.32 | 0.20 | 0.09 | 0.09 | 0.09 | 0.09 | 0.09 | 0.09 | 0.09 | 0.09 |
| Payout Ratio | 29% | 22% | 7% | 7% | 8% | 17% | NM | 9% | 7% | 9% |
| Calendar Year | 2007 | 2006 | 2005 | 2004 | 2003 | 2002 | 2001 | 2000 | 1999 | 1998 |
| Prices:High | 22.02 | 21.39 | 22.70 | 25.72 | 23.47 | 17.14 | 34.98 | 53.75 | 52.69 | 40.92 |
| Prices:Low | 15.20 | 15.91 | 15.90 | 18.12 | 12.01 | 8.35 | 11.12 | 18.50 | 30.81 | 15.31 |
| P/E Ratio:High | 20 | 23 | 18 | 21 | 22 | 32 | NM | 54 | 42 | 45 |
| P/E Ratio:Low | 14 | 17 | 13 | 15 | 11 | 15 | NM | 18 | 24 | 17 |

| Income Statement Analysis (Million $) | | | | | | | | | | |
|---|---|---|---|---|---|---|---|---|---|---|
| Revenue | 15,763 | 15,943 | 16,023 | 16,267 | 15,854 | 14,455 | 13,848 | 13,674 | 11,635 | 9,054 |
| Operating Income | 1,984 | 1,701 | 2,370 | 2,705 | 2,543 | 1,794 | 1,148 | 2,035 | 2,253 | 1,659 |
| Depreciation | 635 | 530 | 625 | 620 | 664 | 781 | 810 | 590 | 436 | 326 |
| Interest Expense | 36.0 | 49.0 | 45.0 | 167 | 234 | 249 | 109 | 74.9 | 31.8 | 13.6 |
| Pretax Income | 1,406 | 1,264 | 1,793 | 1,872 | 1,683 | 801 | 242 | 1,382 | 1,785 | 1,319 |
| Effective Tax Rate | 38.3% | 38.5% | 37.9% | 38.6% | 38.8% | 40.4% | NM | 36.5% | 36.9% | 37.5% |
| Net Income | 867 | 778 | 1,113 | 1,150 | 1,030 | 477 | -7.76 | 877 | 1,127 | 825 |
| S&P Core Earnings | 867 | 776 | 1,033 | 1,073 | 978 | 439 | -89.1 | 760 | NA | NA |

| Balance Sheet & Other Financial Data (Million $) | | | | | | | | | | |
|---|---|---|---|---|---|---|---|---|---|---|
| Cash | 1,939 | 2,644 | 2,987 | 7,139 | 2,261 | 3,389 | 1,036 | 409 | 450 | 565 |
| Current Assets | 4,086 | 5,029 | 5,239 | 6,304 | 6,689 | 5,740 | 3,045 | 2,648 | 2,198 | 1,872 |
| Total Assets | 7,838 | 8,544 | 8,821 | 10,048 | 10,343 | 9,902 | 7,591 | 7,013 | 5,189 | 3,964 |
| Current Liabilities | 2,433 | 2,272 | 1,942 | 2,242 | 2,492 | 2,727 | 2,056 | 2,799 | 1,753 | 1,553 |
| Long Term Debt | 50.0 | 188 | 513 | 1,886 | 2,487 | 2,896 | 1,961 | 780 | 785 | 496 |
| Common Equity | 4,274 | 5,174 | 5,425 | 4,936 | 4,783 | 3,658 | 3,010 | 2,928 | 2,233 | 1,574 |
| Total Capital | 4,324 | 5,362 | 5,938 | 6,822 | 7,270 | 6,554 | 4,971 | 3,708 | 3,018 | 2,070 |
| Capital Expenditures | 682 | 572 | 600 | 442 | 272 | 303 | 940 | 1,859 | 1,239 | 798 |
| Cash Flow | 1,502 | 1,308 | 1,738 | 1,770 | 1,694 | 1,258 | 803 | 1,468 | 1,563 | 1,151 |
| Current Ratio | 1.7 | 2.2 | 2.7 | 2.8 | 2.7 | 2.1 | 1.5 | 0.9 | 1.3 | 1.2 |
| % Long Term Debt of Capitalization | 1.2 | 3.5 | 8.6 | 27.6 | 34.2 | 44.2 | 39.5 | 21.0 | 26.0 | 24.0 |
| % Net Income of Revenue | 5.5 | 4.9 | 6.9 | 7.1 | 6.5 | 3.3 | NM | 6.4 | 9.7 | 9.1 |
| % Return on Assets | 10.6 | 9.0 | 11.8 | 11.1 | 10.2 | 5.4 | NM | 14.4 | 24.6 | 22.6 |
| % Return on Equity | 18.4 | 14.7 | 21.5 | 24.0 | 24.4 | 14.3 | NM | 34.0 | 59.2 | 52.2 |

Data as orig reptd.; bef. results of disc opers/spec. items. Per share data adj. for stk. divs.; EPS diluted. E-Estimated. NA-Not Available. NM-Not Meaningful. NR-Not Ranked. UR-Under Review.

**Office:** 2 Folsom St, San Francisco, CA 94105-1205.
**Telephone:** 650-952-4400 .
**Email:** investor_relations@gap.com
**Website:** http://www.gapinc.com

**Chrmn & CEO:** G.K. Murphy
**COO:** A. Peck
**EVP, CFO & Chief Acctg Officer:** S.L. Simmons
**EVP & CIO:** M.B. Tasooji

**SVP & Secy:** M. Banks
**Investor Contact:** E. Price (415-427-2360)
**Board Members:** H. Behar, A. D. Bellamy, D. De Sole, D. G. Fisher, D. F. Fisher, R. J. Fisher, P. Hughes, B. L. Martin, J. P. Montoya, G. K. Murphy, J. M. Schneider, M. A. Shattuck, III, K. C. Youngblood

**Founded:** 1969
**Domicile:** Delaware
**Employees:** 150,000

# General Dynamics Corp

STANDARD &POOR'S

| S&P Recommendation | BUY ★★★★☆ | Price $55.51 (as of Nov 14, 2008) | 12-Mo. Target Price $74.00 | Investment Style Large-Cap Growth |
|---|---|---|---|---|

**GICS Sector** Industrials
**Sub-Industry** Aerospace & Defense

**Summary** General Dynamics is the world's sixth largest military contractor and also one of the world's biggest makers of corporate jets.

## Key Stock Statistics (Source S&P, Vickers, company reports)

| | | | | | | | |
|---|---|---|---|---|---|---|---|
| 52-Wk Range | $95.13– 51.90 | S&P Oper. EPS 2008**E** | 6.18 | Market Capitalization(B) | $21.640 | Beta | 1.15 |
| Trailing 12-Month EPS | $6.02 | S&P Oper. EPS 2009**E** | 6.75 | Yield (%) | 2.52 | S&P 3-Yr. Proj. EPS CAGR(%) | 11 |
| Trailing 12-Month P/E | 9.2 | P/E on S&P Oper. EPS 2008**E** | 9.0 | Dividend Rate/Share | $1.40 | S&P Credit Rating | A |
| $10K Invested 5 Yrs Ago | $14,577 | Common Shares Outstg. (M) | 389.8 | Institutional Ownership (%) | 81 | | |

## Price Performance

30-Week Mov. Avg. ···  10-Week Mov. Avg. - -  **GAAP Earnings vs. Previous Year**  Volume Above Avg. |||| STARS
12-Mo. Target Price —  Relative Strength —  ▲ Up  ▼ Down  ► No Change  Below Avg. |||| ★

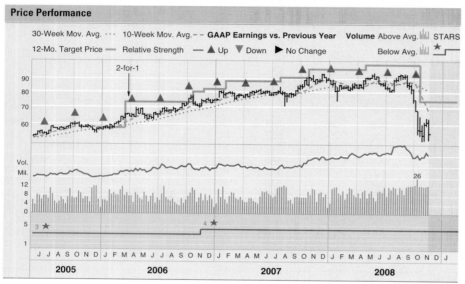

2005 2006 2007 2008

Options: ASE, CBOE, Ph

Analysis prepared by **Richard Tortoriello** on November 07, 2008, when the stock traded at **$ 61.60**.

### Highlights

➤ We look for sales to increase about 8% in 2008 and 2009, with strong growth in combat systems and aerospace, and moderate growth in IS&T and marine. We see increased global spending on armored vehicles and a strong business jet order backlog as multi-year drivers for revenue growth at GD. In addition, we expect growth in the marine segment to increase in 2009 and beyond, as the Navy plans significant fleet additions. The September 2008 funded backlog of $50 billion is 1.6X our 2009 revenue projection.

➤ We expect a 2008 operating margin of about 12.5%, up from 11.4% in 2007, with expected continued improvement in aerospace, combat systems and marine, due to productivity increases and pricing. For 2009, we project further slight improvement. We project EPS of $6.18 in 2008, with growth to $6.75 in 2009.

➤ GD has generated free cash flow (cash flow from operations less capital expenditures) per share in excess of EPS in each of the past five years. We expect FCF per share above EPS again in 2008, with cash to be used for share repurchases, acquisitions, and dividend increases.

### Investment Rationale/Risk

➤ Longer term, we see GD continuing to increase sales and EPS via acquisitions, growth in business jet deliveries, and strength in land vehicles and munitions needed for current operations in Iraq and the replacement of lost and damaged equipment afterward. We see strong supplemental spending by Congress for the on-going wars funding increased defense spending at GD. Also, we expect continued moderate growth (about 6%) in the IS&T segment, and we see significantly increased potential for the marine segment in 2009 and beyond.

➤ Risks to our recommendation and target price include the potential for delays and/or cuts in military budgets and failure of GD to perform well on existing contracts or to win new contracts.

➤ Our 12-month target price of $74 is based on an enterprise value to estimated 2009 EBITDA multiple of 7.5X, below the 10-year average for GD of 11X and the 20-year average of 8X. Given our view of strong near-term growth, offset by risks associated with a slowing global economy and a potential troop drawdown in Iraq, we see a slightly below average multiple as appropriate for the shares.

### Qualitative Risk Assessment

| LOW | MEDIUM | HIGH |
|---|---|---|

Our risk assessment for GD is based on the company's long-term record of consistent earnings and dividend growth, as reflected in its S&P Quality Ranking of A+. In addition, we note the company's conservative capitalization, with a debt-to-total capital ratio of 15% as of September 2008.

### Quantitative Evaluations

**S&P Quality Ranking**                                    **A+**

| D | C | B- | B | B+ | A- | A | A+ |
|---|---|---|---|---|---|---|---|

**Relative Strength Rank**                          **MODERATE**

54

LOWEST = 1                                              HIGHEST = 99

### Revenue/Earnings Data

**Revenue (Million $)**

| | 1Q | 2Q | 3Q | 4Q | Year |
|---|---|---|---|---|---|
| 2008 | 7,005 | 7,303 | 7,140 | -- | -- |
| 2007 | 6,300 | 6,591 | 6,834 | 7,515 | 27,240 |
| 2006 | 5,546 | 5,934 | 6,069 | 6,514 | 24,063 |
| 2005 | 4,819 | 5,214 | 5,380 | 5,831 | 21,244 |
| 2004 | 4,661 | 4,666 | 4,661 | 5,190 | 19,178 |
| 2003 | 3,421 | 3,935 | 4,427 | 4,834 | 16,617 |

**Earnings Per Share ($)**

| | | | | | |
|---|---|---|---|---|---|
| 2008 | 1.42 | 1.60 | 1.59 | E1.58 | E6.18 |
| 2007 | 1.07 | 1.27 | 1.34 | 1.42 | 5.10 |
| 2006 | 0.95 | 1.03 | 1.08 | 1.13 | 4.20 |
| 2005 | 0.85 | 0.85 | 0.92 | 1.00 | 3.63 |
| 2004 | 0.66 | 0.73 | 0.79 | 0.82 | 2.99 |
| 2003 | 0.56 | 0.61 | 0.64 | 0.70 | 2.50 |

Fiscal year ended Dec. 31. Next earnings report expected: Late January. EPS Estimates based on S&P Operating Earnings; historical GAAP earnings are as reported.

### Dividend Data (Dates: mm/dd Payment Date: mm/dd/yy)

| Amount ($) | Date Decl. | Ex-Div. Date | Stk. of Record | Payment Date |
|---|---|---|---|---|
| 0.290 | 12/05 | 01/16 | 01/18 | 02/08/08 |
| 0.350 | 03/05 | 04/09 | 04/11 | 05/09/08 |
| 0.350 | 06/04 | 07/01 | 07/03 | 08/08/08 |
| 0.350 | 08/06 | 10/08 | 10/10 | 11/14/08 |

Dividends have been paid since 1979. Source: Company reports.

---

**Please read the Required Disclosures and Analyst Certification on the last page of this report.**

# General Dynamics Corp

**STANDARD & POOR'S**

## Business Summary November 07, 2008

CORPORATE OVERVIEW. General Dynamics is the world's sixth largest defense contractor and the second largest maker of corporate jets by revenues. The company conducts business through four segments.

Information Systems & Technology (IS&T; 35% of sales and 32% of operating profits in 2007) primarily makes sophisticated electronics for land-, sea- and air-based weapons systems. Customers also include federal civilian agencies and commercial customers. Since it was created in 1997, the group has grown into a business that provides systems integration expertise; hardware and software products; and engineering, management and support services. The group's three principal markets are tactical and strategic mission systems (primarily secure communications systems), information technology and mission services, and intelligence mission systems, which provides specialized intelligence, surveillance, and reconnaissance equipment and services. We believe the $70 billion U.S. government IT market is fragmented; IS&T's main competitors are the IT divisions of Northrop Grumman, Lockheed Martin and Boeing.

Combat Systems (29% and 29%) makes, repairs and supports wheeled and tracked armored vehicles and munitions. The segment also makes armor, threat detection systems, and electronic countermeasures for combat vehi-

cles. GD is also the only U.S. tank maker. Reflecting the U.S. Army's desire to transform itself into a highly agile fighting force, demand is expected to slow for tanks, but to accelerate for its various wheeled combat vehicles. Major current programs include the M1 Abrams tank (upgrade programs), the Stryker wheeled combat vehicle, and the Expeditionary Fighting Vehicle. CS's main competitor is BAE Systems' Land & Armaments division.

Aerospace (18% and 26%) makes the well known Gulfstream business jet. Based on revenues, Gulfstream is the world's second-largest corporate jet maker, behind Canada-based Bombardier. Textron's Cessna division, France's Dassault and Hawker Beechcraft Corp. (formerly Raytheon's aircraft-making unit) are also significant competitors. According to statistics from Bombardier, the total business aircraft market was over $16 billion in 2007, with the top five manufacturers accounting for the majority of sales. Gulfstream sells business jets primarily to the high end of the market. In March 2008, Gulfstream introduced the ultra-large, ultra-long range G650, which it expects to deliver beginning in 2012.

## Company Financials Fiscal Year Ended Dec. 31

| Per Share Data ($) | 2007 | 2006 | 2005 | 2004 | 2003 | 2002 | 2001 | 2000 | 1999 | 1998 |
|---|---|---|---|---|---|---|---|---|---|---|
| Tangible Book Value | 0.46 | 0.25 | 1.40 | NM | NM | 2.81 | 1.92 | 3.22 | 1.64 | 2.74 |
| Cash Flow | 5.78 | 5.16 | 4.48 | 3.57 | 3.20 | 3.14 | 2.99 | 2.80 | 2.66 | 1.93 |
| Earnings | 5.10 | 4.20 | 3.63 | 2.99 | 2.50 | 2.59 | 2.33 | 2.24 | 2.18 | 1.43 |
| S&P Core Earnings | 4.90 | 4.08 | 3.34 | 2.81 | 2.34 | 1.62 | 1.57 | NA | NA | NA |
| Dividends | 1.10 | 0.66 | 0.78 | 0.70 | 0.63 | 0.59 | 0.55 | 0.51 | 0.47 | 0.43 |
| Payout Ratio | 22% | 16% | 22% | 23% | 25% | 23% | 24% | 23% | 22% | 30% |
| Prices:High | 94.55 | 77.98 | 61.14 | 54.99 | 45.40 | 55.59 | 48.00 | 39.50 | 37.72 | 31.00 |
| Prices:Low | 70.61 | 56.68 | 48.80 | 42.48 | 25.00 | 36.63 | 30.25 | 18.13 | 23.09 | 20.13 |
| P/E Ratio:High | 19 | 19 | 17 | 18 | 18 | 21 | 21 | 18 | 17 | 22 |
| P/E Ratio:Low | 14 | 13 | 13 | 14 | 10 | 14 | 13 | 8 | 11 | 14 |

| Income Statement Analysis (Million $) | 2007 | 2006 | 2005 | 2004 | 2003 | 2002 | 2001 | 2000 | 1999 | 1998 |
|---|---|---|---|---|---|---|---|---|---|---|
| Revenue | 27,240 | 24,063 | 21,244 | 19,178 | 16,617 | 13,829 | 12,163 | 10,356 | 8,959 | 4,970 |
| Operating Income | 3,391 | 3,009 | 2,539 | 2,173 | 1,744 | 1,795 | 1,756 | 1,555 | 1,396 | 668 |
| Depreciation | 278 | 384 | 342 | 232 | 277 | 213 | 271 | 226 | 193 | 126 |
| Interest Expense | 131 | 101 | 154 | 157 | 98.0 | 45.0 | 56.0 | 60.0 | 34.0 | 12.0 |
| Pretax Income | 3,047 | 2,527 | 2,100 | 1,785 | 1,372 | 1,584 | 1,424 | 1,262 | 1,126 | 549 |
| Effective Tax Rate | 31.7% | 32.3% | 30.1% | 32.6% | 27.3% | 33.6% | 33.8% | 28.6% | 21.8% | 33.7% |
| Net Income | 2,080 | 1,710 | 1,468 | 1,203 | 997 | 1,051 | 943 | 901 | 880 | 364 |
| S&P Core Earnings | 1,999 | 1,663 | 1,354 | 1,130 | 931 | 658 | 636 | NA | NA | NA |

| Balance Sheet & Other Financial Data (Million $) | 2007 | 2006 | 2005 | 2004 | 2003 | 2002 | 2001 | 2000 | 1999 | 1998 |
|---|---|---|---|---|---|---|---|---|---|---|
| Cash | 3,155 | 1,604 | 2,331 | 976 | 860 | 328 | 442 | 177 | 270 | 220 |
| Current Assets | 12,298 | 9,880 | 9,173 | 7,287 | 6,394 | 5,098 | 4,893 | 3,551 | 3,491 | 1,873 |
| Total Assets | 25,733 | 22,376 | 19,591 | 17,544 | 16,183 | 11,731 | 11,069 | 7,987 | 7,774 | 4,572 |
| Current Liabilities | 9,164 | 7,824 | 6,907 | 5,374 | 5,616 | 4,582 | 4,579 | 2,901 | 3,453 | 1,461 |
| Long Term Debt | 2,118 | 2,774 | 2,781 | 3,291 | 3,296 | 718 | 724 | 162 | 169 | 249 |
| Common Equity | 11,768 | 9,827 | 8,145 | 7,189 | 5,921 | 5,199 | 4,528 | 3,820 | 3,171 | 2,219 |
| Total Capital | 13,886 | 12,601 | 10,926 | 10,480 | 9,217 | 5,917 | 5,252 | 3,982 | 3,340 | 2,468 |
| Capital Expenditures | 474 | 334 | 279 | 266 | 224 | 264 | 356 | 288 | 197 | 158 |
| Cash Flow | 2,358 | 2,094 | 1,810 | 1,435 | 1,274 | 1,264 | 1,214 | 1,127 | 1,073 | 490 |
| Current Ratio | 1.3 | 1.3 | 1.3 | 1.4 | 1.1 | 1.1 | 1.1 | 1.2 | 1.0 | 1.3 |
| % Long Term Debt of Capitalization | 15.3 | 22.0 | 25.5 | 31.4 | 35.8 | 12.1 | 13.8 | 4.1 | 5.1 | 10.1 |
| % Net Income of Revenue | 7.6 | 7.1 | 6.9 | 6.3 | 6.0 | 7.6 | 7.8 | 8.7 | 9.8 | 7.3 |
| % Return on Assets | 8.6 | 8.1 | 7.9 | 7.1 | 7.1 | 9.2 | 9.9 | 11.4 | 12.6 | 8.4 |
| % Return on Equity | 19.3 | 19.0 | 19.1 | 18.4 | 17.9 | 21.6 | 22.6 | 25.8 | 31.5 | 17.6 |

Data as orig reptd.; bef. results of disc opers/spec. items. Per share data adj. for stk. divs.; EPS diluted. E-Estimated. NA-Not Available. NM-Not Meaningful. NR-Not Ranked. UR-Under Review.

**Office:** 2941 Fairview Park Dr Ste 100, Falls Church, VA 22042-4513.
**Telephone:** 703-876-3000.
**Website:** http://www.generaldynamics.com
**Chrmn & CEO:** N.D. Chabraja

**Vice Chrmn:** J.L. Johnson
**SVP & CFO:** L.H. Redd
**SVP, Secy & General Counsel:** D.A. Savner
**Chief Admin Officer:** W.M. Oliver

**Investor Contact:** A. Gilliland (703-876-3748)
**Board Members:** N. D. Chabraja, J. S. Crown, W. P. Fricks, C. H. Goodman, J. L. Johnson, G. A. Joulwan, P. G. Kaminski, J. M. Keane, D. J. Lucas, L. L. Lyles, C. E. Mundy, J. C. Reyes, R. Walmsley

**Founded:** 1899
**Domicile:** Delaware
**Employees:** 83,500

The **McGraw-Hill** Companies

# General Electric Co

STANDARD
&POOR'S

| S&P Recommendation | HOLD ★★★☆☆ | Price $16.02 (as of Nov 14, 2008) | 12-Mo. Target Price $25.00 | Investment Style Large-Cap Blend |
|---|---|---|---|---|

**GICS Sector** Industrials
**Sub-Industry** Industrial Conglomerates

**Summary** This industrial conglomerate sells products ranging from jet engines and gas turbines to consumer appliances, railroad locomotives, and medical equipment. It also owns NBC Universal, and is one of the world's largest providers of consumer and commercial financing.

## Key Stock Statistics (Source S&P, Vickers, company reports)

| | | | | | | | |
|---|---|---|---|---|---|---|---|
| 52-Wk Range | $38.67– 14.58 | S&P Oper. EPS 2008E | 1.96 | Market Capitalization(B) | $159.486 | Beta | 0.69 |
| Trailing 12-Month EPS | $2.04 | S&P Oper. EPS 2009E | 1.97 | Yield (%) | 7.74 | S&P 3-Yr. Proj. EPS CAGR(%) | 7 |
| Trailing 12-Month P/E | 7.9 | P/E on S&P Oper. EPS 2008E | 8.2 | Dividend Rate/Share | $1.24 | S&P Credit Rating | AAA |
| $10K Invested 5 Yrs Ago | $6,670 | Common Shares Outstg. (M) | 9,955.5 | Institutional Ownership (%) | 57 | | |

## Price Performance

30-Week Mov. Avg. · · · 10-Week Mov. Avg. — GAAP Earnings vs. Previous Year    Volume Above Avg. ▐▐▐ STARS
12-Mo. Target Price — Relative Strength — ▲ Up ▼ Down ► No Change    Below Avg. ▐▐▐ ★

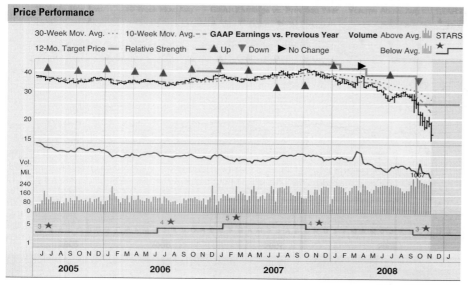

Options: ASE, CBOE, P, Ph

Analysis prepared by **Richard Tortoriello** on October 28, 2008, when the stock traded at **$ 18.80**.

## Highlights

► We estimate revenue growth of about 6% in 2008 and 3% in 2009. We see growth determined by two contrasting dynamics: continued moderate growth in GE's industrial businesses (excluding its household appliance business) offset by declining growth in GE's financial businesses due to lower underwriting volumes and increasing credit losses. On October 2, 2008, GE commenced a secondary share offering of 547 million common shares, priced at $22.25 per share, with an overallotment of up to 82 million shares. GE also announced that Berkshire Hathaway will purchase $3 billion of 10% preferred shares, with a warrant to purchase about 135 million common shares.

► We see operating margins narrowing sharply to 14.0% in 2008 and 2009, from 15.8% in 2007, due primarily to increased loss provisions in GE's financial services businesses, as well as a weaker pricing environment at NBC Universal, and weak performance in the consumer appliance business.

► We estimate earnings per share of $1.96 in 2008 and $1.97 in 2009.

## Investment Rationale/Risk

► GE's valuations are at multi-year lows, due to a financial crisis that has called into question the balance sheets of even the most creditworthy institutions. With a recent capital infusion, as well as a government loan program, we believe that GE Capital's funding position is strong, and we continue to expect good cash flows from GE's industrial businesses, enabling GE to maintain its current dividend through the end of 2009. We also see GE using what we view as its relatively strong balance sheet to purchase attractive financial assets at bargain prices.

► Risks to our recommendation and target price include the possibility of a deep or sustained global recession, which would affect GE's industrial businesses, as well as greater than expected losses in GE's financial businesses.

► Our 12-month target price of $25 is based on a P/E multiple of about 12.7X our 2009 EPS estimate. This compares to a 10-year average forward P/E of 18X, with lows near 10X and highs (during 2000) near 40X. Given current financial market and economic conditions, we believe a P/E closer to historical lows is appropriate.

## Qualitative Risk Assessment

| LOW | MEDIUM | HIGH |
|---|---|---|

Our risk assessment reflects our view of GE's long-term record of steady growth in earnings, cash flow and dividends, which we attribute to good management of a diversified portfolio of growing and profitable businesses, offset by recent financial market turmoil, which has caused GE to access the capital markets.

## Quantitative Evaluations

**S&P Quality Ranking**                                            A+

| D | C | B- | B | B+ | A- | A | A+ |
|---|---|---|---|---|---|---|---|

**Relative Strength Rank**                          MODERATE

| 37 |
|---|

LOWEST = 1                                          HIGHEST = 99

## Revenue/Earnings Data

**Revenue (Million $)**

| | 1Q | 2Q | 3Q | 4Q | Year |
|---|---|---|---|---|---|
| 2008 | 42,243 | 46,891 | 47,234 | -- | -- |
| 2007 | 39,200 | 42,384 | 42,534 | 48,588 | 172,592 |
| 2006 | -- | -- | -- | 44,621 | 163,391 |
| 2005 | -- | -- | -- | 40,705 | 149,702 |
| 2004 | 33,350 | 37,035 | 38,272 | 43,706 | 152,363 |
| 2003 | 30,456 | 33,373 | 33,394 | 36,964 | 134,187 |

**Earnings Per Share ($)**

| | 1Q | 2Q | 3Q | 4Q | Year |
|---|---|---|---|---|---|
| 2008 | 0.44 | 0.54 | 0.45 | E0.54 | E1.96 |
| 2007 | 0.44 | 0.52 | 0.50 | 0.68 | 2.20 |
| 2006 | 0.40 | 0.48 | 0.48 | 0.64 | 1.99 |
| 2005 | 0.33 | 0.41 | 0.43 | 0.55 | 1.72 |
| 2004 | 0.32 | 0.38 | 0.38 | 0.51 | 1.59 |
| 2003 | 0.32 | 0.38 | 0.40 | 0.45 | 1.55 |

Fiscal year ended Dec. 31. Next earnings report expected: Late January. EPS Estimates based on S&P Operating Earnings; historical GAAP earnings are as reported.

## Dividend Data (Dates: mm/dd Payment Date: mm/dd/yy)

| Amount ($) | Date Decl. | Ex-Div. Date | Stk. of Record | Payment Date |
|---|---|---|---|---|
| 0.310 | 12/11 | 12/20 | 12/24 | 01/25/08 |
| 0.310 | 02/08 | 02/21 | 02/25 | 04/25/08 |
| 0.310 | 06/06 | 06/19 | 06/23 | 07/25/08 |
| 0.310 | 08/22 | 09/18 | 09/22 | 10/27/08 |

Dividends have been paid since 1899. Source: Company reports.

**Please read the Required Disclosures and Analyst Certification on the last page of this report.**

# General Electric Co

**STANDARD
&POOR'S**

## Business Summary October 28, 2008

CORPORATE OVERVIEW. This multi-industry, heavy-equipment, media and financing giant does business through six segments: Infrastructure, Industrial, Healthcare, NBC Universal, Commercial Finance, and GE Money (formerly Consumer Finance). Revenue by geographic region in 2007 was: U.S. 50%, Europe 23%, Pacific Basin 13%, Americas 7%, ME and Africa 5%, and Other 2%.

The Infrastructure segment (35% of 2007 revenues, 37% of operating profits) produces, sells, finances and services equipment for the air transportation and energy generation industries (products include jet engines and maintenance services, gas turbines for power generation, windmills, and nuclear reactors). It also produces, sells and services equipment for the rail transportation (locomotives); oil & gas production, transportation, and refining; and water treatment industries. The Aviation and Energy sub-segments, excluding financial services, together made up 68% of 2007 segment revenues and 66% of operating profits.

The Industrial segment (11%, 6%) produces and sells consumer appliances, industrial equipment, and related services. GE makes, sells and services major home appliances, under the Monogram, GE Profile, GE, and Hotpoint brands; it also produces a variety of electrical equipment and motors. The Enterprise Solutions sub-segment offers protection and productivity solutions, including facility safety, plant automation, power control, and sensing applica-

tions. Consumer and industrial products accounted for 75% of 2007 segment revenues and 60% of operating profits; Enterprise Solutions accounted for the remainder. In August 2007, GE sold its low-margin plastics business.

The Healthcare segment (10%, 10%) manufactures, sells and services a wide range of medical equipment, including equipment for magnetic resonance (MR), computed tomography (CT), positron emission tomography (PET) imaging, x-ray, patient monitoring, diagnostic cardiology, nuclear imaging, ultrasound, bone densitometry, anesthesiology and oxygen therapy, neonatal and critical care, and therapy.

NBC Universal (9%, 11%) is principally engaged in the broadcast of network television services to affiliated television stations within the U.S.; the production of live and recorded TV programs; the production and distribution of motion pictures; the operation of TV broadcasting stations; the ownership of several cable/satellite networks around the world; the operation of theme parks; and investment and programming activities in multimedia and the Internet.

## Company Financials Fiscal Year Ended Dec. 31

| Per Share Data ($) | 2007 | 2006 | 2005 | 2004 | 2003 | 2002 | 2001 | 2000 | 1999 | 1998 |
|---|---|---|---|---|---|---|---|---|---|---|
| Tangible Book Value | 2.38 | 2.52 | 2.64 | 2.55 | 2.40 | 1.76 | 2.34 | 2.32 | 1.68 | 1.55 |
| Cash Flow | 3.21 | 2.90 | 2.53 | 2.39 | 2.24 | 2.11 | 2.11 | 2.04 | 1.74 | 1.52 |
| Earnings | 2.20 | 1.99 | 1.72 | 1.59 | 1.55 | 1.51 | 1.41 | 1.27 | 1.07 | 0.93 |
| S&P Core Earnings | 2.07 | 1.90 | 1.66 | 1.54 | 1.41 | 1.10 | 0.98 | NA | NA | NA |
| Dividends | 1.15 | 1.03 | 0.91 | 0.82 | 0.77 | 0.73 | 0.66 | 0.57 | 0.49 | 0.42 |
| Payout Ratio | 52% | 52% | 53% | 52% | 50% | 48% | 47% | 45% | 46% | 45% |
| Prices:High | 42.15 | 38.49 | 37.34 | 37.75 | 32.42 | 41.84 | 53.55 | 60.50 | 53.17 | 34.65 |
| Prices:Low | 33.90 | 32.06 | 32.67 | 28.88 | 21.30 | 21.40 | 28.50 | 41.65 | 31.35 | 23.00 |
| P/E Ratio:High | 19 | 19 | 22 | 24 | 21 | 28 | 38 | 48 | 50 | 37 |
| P/E Ratio:Low | 15 | 16 | 19 | 18 | 14 | 14 | 20 | 33 | 29 | 25 |

| Income Statement Analysis (Million $) | | | | | | | | | | |
|---|---|---|---|---|---|---|---|---|---|---|
| Revenue | 172,738 | 163,391 | 149,702 | 152,363 | 134,187 | 131,698 | 125,913 | 129,853 | 111,630 | 100,469 |
| Operating Income | 69,594 | 53,972 | 46,840 | 40,262 | 36,792 | 35,431 | 38,200 | 38,329 | 32,646 | 29,355 |
| Depreciation | 10,278 | 9,158 | 8,538 | 8,385 | 6,956 | 5,998 | 7,089 | 7,736 | 6,691 | 5,860 |
| Interest Expense | 23,787 | 19,286 | 15,187 | 11,907 | 10,432 | 10,216 | 11,062 | 11,720 | 10,013 | 9,753 |
| Pretax Income | 27,514 | 25,528 | 23,115 | 21,034 | 20,194 | 19,217 | 20,049 | 18,873 | 15,577 | 13,742 |
| Effective Tax Rate | 15.0% | 15.5% | 16.7% | 16.7% | 21.4% | 19.6% | 27.8% | 30.3% | 31.1% | 30.4% |
| Net Income | 22,468 | 20,666 | 18,275 | 16,593 | 15,589 | 15,133 | 14,128 | 12,735 | 10,717 | 9,296 |
| S&P Core Earnings | 21,155 | 19,701 | 17,548 | 16,138 | 14,195 | 11,038 | 9,889 | NA | NA | NA |

| Balance Sheet & Other Financial Data (Million $) | | | | | | | | | | |
|---|---|---|---|---|---|---|---|---|---|---|
| Cash | 17,578 | 14,275 | 9,011 | 150,864 | 133,388 | 125,772 | 110,099 | 99,534 | 90,312 | 83,034 |
| Current Assets | NA | NA | NA | NA | NA | NA | NA | NA | NA | NA |
| Total Assets | 795,337 | 697,239 | 673,342 | 750,330 | 647,483 | 575,244 | 495,023 | 437,006 | 405,200 | 355,935 |
| Current Liabilities | NA | NA | NA | NA | NA | NA | NA | NA | NA | NA |
| Long Term Debt | 319,015 | 260,804 | 212,281 | 213,161 | 170,004 | 140,632 | 79,806 | 82,132 | 71,427 | 59,663 |
| Common Equity | 115,559 | 112,314 | 109,354 | 110,284 | 79,180 | 63,706 | 54,824 | 50,492 | 42,557 | 38,880 |
| Total Capital | 454,722 | 394,867 | 346,019 | 354,242 | 267,611 | 222,328 | 148,975 | 146,250 | 128,436 | 112,158 |
| Capital Expenditures | 17,870 | 16,650 | 14,441 | 13,118 | 9,767 | 13,351 | 15,520 | 13,967 | 15,502 | 8,982 |
| Cash Flow | 32,746 | 29,824 | 26,813 | 24,978 | 22,545 | 21,131 | 21,217 | 20,471 | 17,408 | 15,156 |
| Current Ratio | 1.9 | 1.8 | 1.9 | 1.7 | 1.7 | 1.5 | 1.2 | 1.3 | 1.2 | 1.2 |
| % Long Term Debt of Capitalization | 70.2 | 66.0 | 61.3 | 60.2 | 63.5 | 63.3 | 53.6 | 56.2 | 55.6 | 53.2 |
| % Net Income of Revenue | 13.2 | 12.8 | 12.2 | 10.8 | 11.6 | 11.5 | 11.2 | 9.8 | 9.6 | 9.3 |
| % Return on Assets | 3.0 | 3.0 | 2.6 | 2.4 | 2.5 | 2.8 | 3.0 | 3.0 | 2.8 | 2.8 |
| % Return on Equity | 19.7 | 18.6 | 16.6 | 17.5 | 21.8 | 25.5 | 26.8 | 27.4 | 26.3 | 25.4 |

Data as orig reptd.; bef. results of disc opers/spec. items. Per share data adj. for stk. divs.; EPS diluted. E-Estimated. NA-Not Available. NM-Not Meaningful. NR-Not Ranked. UR-Under Review.

**Office:** 3135 Easton Tpke, Fairfield, CT 06828-0001.
**Telephone:** 203-373-2211.
**Website:** http://www.ge.com
**Chrmn & CEO:** J.R. Immelt

**Pres:** J. Gaspin
**Pres:** P. Ehrenheim
**COO:** W. Hewett
**SVP & CFO:** K.S. Sherin

**Investor Contact:** D. Janki
**Board Members:** J. I. Cash, Jr., W. Castell, A. M. Fudge, S. Hockfield, J. R. Immelt, A. Jung, A. Lafley, R. W. Lane, C. X. Laporte, R. S. Larsen, R. B. Lazarus, J. J. Mulva, S. A. Nunn, R. S. Penske, R. J. Swieringa, D. A. Warner, III

**Founded:** 1892
**Domicile:** New York
**Employees:** 327,000

**The McGraw-Hill Companies**

# General Mills Inc.

**STANDARD &POOR'S**

| S&P Recommendation | STRONG BUY ★★★★★ | Price<br>$66.23 (as of Nov 14, 2008) | 12-Mo. Target Price<br>$78.00 | Investment Style<br>Large-Cap Blend |
|---|---|---|---|---|

**GICS Sector** Consumer Staples
**Sub-Industry** Packaged Foods & Meats

**Summary** This company is a major producer of packaged consumer food products, including Big G cereals and Betty Crocker desserts/baking mixes.

## Key Stock Statistics (Source S&P, Vickers, company reports)

| | | | | | | | |
|---|---|---|---|---|---|---|---|
| 52-Wk Range | $72.01–51.00 | S&P Oper. EPS 2009E | 3.90 | Market Capitalization(B) | $22.130 | Beta | 0.18 |
| Trailing 12-Month EPS | $3.69 | S&P Oper. EPS 2010E | 4.20 | Yield (%) | 2.60 | S&P 3-Yr. Proj. EPS CAGR(%) | 9 |
| Trailing 12-Month P/E | 18.0 | P/E on S&P Oper. EPS 2009E | 17.0 | Dividend Rate/Share | $1.72 | S&P Credit Rating | BBB+ |
| $10K Invested 5 Yrs Ago | $16,880 | Common Shares Outstg. (M) | 334.1 | Institutional Ownership (%) | 83 | | |

## Price Performance

30-Week Mov. Avg. · · · 10-Week Mov. Avg. – – **GAAP Earnings vs. Previous Year** Volume Above Avg. ▐▌▐ STARS
12-Mo. Target Price — Relative Strength — ▲ Up ▼ Down ► No Change Below Avg. ▐▌▐ ★

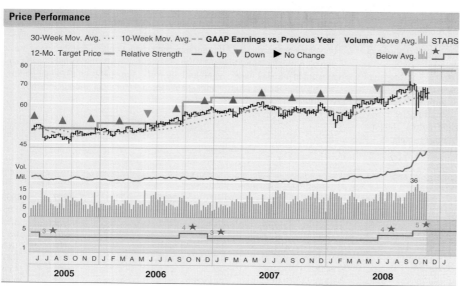

Options: ASE, CBOE, P, Ph

Analysis prepared by **Tom Graves, CFA** on October 07, 2008, when the stock traded at **$ 67.83**.

## Highlights

➤ In FY 09 (May), we look for net sales to advance about 11% from the $13.7 billion reported for FY 08, with higher pricing, and bolstered by investments in consumer marketing and product innovation. We also expect sales to receive a boost from a 53rd week in the fiscal year.

➤ We expect margin pressure from ingredient costs, but we think operating margins will receive support from a combination of productivity gains and higher prices. Excluding some special items, we look for FY 09 EPS of $3.87, up from $3.52 for FY 08. In FY 08, special items included a $0.10 a share net benefit related to mark-to-market valuation of certain commodity positions, and a $0.09 a share benefit from reduction of a tax reserve. Included in our EPS estimate for FY 09 are expenses related to restructuring, impairment and other exit costs. In FY 10, we estimate EPS of $4.20.

➤ FY 09's first quarter included a negative impact of $0.17 a share from mark-to-market valuation of certain commodity positions. This is excluded from our FY 09 EPS estimate. Also in the first quarter, GIS repurchased 8.2 million shares of common stock for a total purchase price of $519.2 million.

## Investment Rationale/Risk

➤ Given concerns about economic weakness ahead, we expect this stock to benefit from investors seeking defensive or lower-risk shares. Also, we look for GIS's important U.S. Retail segment to benefit from consumers eating more at home. We believe the company has opportunities to bolster longer-term profit margins through a focus on such areas as manufacturing and spending efficiency, global sourcing and sales mix. We look for GIS to generate future free cash flow, with at least a portion being used for dividends and stock repurchases.

➤ Risks to our recommendation and target price include competitive pressures, disappointing consumer acceptance of new products, higher-than-expected commodity cost inflation, and an inability to achieve sales and earnings growth forecasts.

➤ Our 12-month target price of $78 reflects a moderate P/E premium to what we project, on average, for other food stocks. Also, GIS shares recently had an indicated dividend yield of 2.5%. The quarterly dividend has been raised twice in 2008.

## Qualitative Risk Assessment

| LOW | MEDIUM | HIGH |
|---|---|---|

Our risk assessment reflects the relatively stable nature of the company's end markets, strong cash flows, and an S&P Quality Ranking of A- that reflects GIS's historical stability of earnings and dividends.

## Quantitative Evaluations

**S&P Quality Ranking** A-

| D | C | B- | B | B+ | A- | A | A+ |
|---|---|---|---|---|---|---|---|

**Relative Strength Rank** STRONG

92

LOWEST = 1      HIGHEST = 99

## Revenue/Earnings Data

**Revenue (Million $)**

| | 1Q | 2Q | 3Q | 4Q | Year |
|---|---|---|---|---|---|
| 2009 | 3,497 | -- | -- | -- | -- |
| 2008 | 3,072 | 3,703 | 3,406 | 3,471 | 13,652 |
| 2007 | 2,860 | 3,467 | 3,054 | 3,061 | 12,442 |
| 2006 | 2,662 | 3,273 | 2,860 | 2,845 | 11,640 |
| 2005 | 2,585 | 3,168 | 2,772 | 2,719 | 11,244 |
| 2004 | 2,518 | 3,060 | 2,703 | 2,789 | 11,070 |

**Earnings Per Share ($)**

| | | | | | |
|---|---|---|---|---|---|
| 2009 | 0.79 | E1.23 | E0.90 | E0.81 | E3.90 |
| 2008 | 0.80 | 1.14 | 1.23 | 0.53 | 3.71 |
| 2007 | 0.74 | 1.08 | 0.74 | 0.62 | 3.18 |
| 2006 | 0.64 | 0.97 | 0.68 | 0.61 | 2.90 |
| 2005 | 0.45 | 0.92 | 0.58 | 1.14 | 3.08 |
| 2004 | 0.59 | 0.81 | 0.63 | 0.72 | 2.75 |

Fiscal year ended May 31. Next earnings report expected: Mid December. EPS Estimates based on S&P Operating Earnings; historical GAAP earnings are as reported.

## Dividend Data (Dates: mm/dd Payment Date: mm/dd/yy)

| Amount ($) | Date Decl. | Ex-Div. Date | Stk. of Record | Payment Date |
|---|---|---|---|---|
| 0.390 | 12/10 | 01/08 | 01/10 | 02/01/08 |
| 0.400 | 03/10 | 04/08 | 04/10 | 05/01/08 |
| 0.430 | 06/23 | 07/08 | 07/10 | 08/01/08 |
| 0.430 | 09/22 | 10/08 | 10/10 | 11/03/08 |

Dividends have been paid since 1898. Source: Company reports.

---

**Please read the Required Disclosures and Analyst Certification on the last page of this report.**

# General Mills Inc.

**STANDARD &POOR'S**

## Business Summary October 07, 2008

CORPORATE OVERVIEW. General Mills (GIS) is the second largest U.S. producer of ready-to-eat breakfast cereals, and a leading producer of other well-known packaged consumer foods. The U.S. Retail segment, which accounted for 66% of net sales in FY 08 (May), consists of cereals, meals, refrigerated and frozen dough products, baking products, snacks, yogurt and organic foods. The Bakeries and Foodservice segment (15%) consists of products marketed to retail and wholesale bakeries and offered to commercial and noncommercial foodservice sectors throughout the U.S. and Canada, such as restaurants and businesses and school cafeterias. The International segment (19%)includes retail business outside the U.S. and foodservice business outside of the U.S. and Canada.

Major cereal brands include Cheerios, Wheaties, Lucky Charms, Total and Chex cereals. Other consumer packaged food products include baking mixes (e.g., Betty Crocker, Bisquick); dry dinners; Progresso soups, Green Giant canned and frozen vegetables; snacks; Pillsbury refrigerated and frozen dough products, frozen pizza; Yoplait and Colombo yogurt; Haagen-Dazs ice cream; and Cascadian Farm and Muir Glen organic products. Some products

may be marketed under licensing arrangements with other parties. GIS also has a grain merchandising operation that holds inventories carried at fair market value, and uses derivatives to hedge its net inventory position and minimize its market exposures.

During FY 08, Wal-Mart Stores, Inc. (or affiliates) accounted for 19% of GIS's consolidated net sales.

GIS joint ventures include a 50% equity interest in Cereal Partners Worldwide (CPW), a joint venture with Nestle S.A. that manufactures and markets cereal products outside the U.S. and Canada; and 50% equity interests in some Asian-related joint ventures for the manufacture, distribution and marketing of Haagen-Dazs frozen ice cream products and novelties.

## Company Financials Fiscal Year Ended May 31

| Per Share Data ($) | 2008 | 2007 | 2006 | 2005 | 2004 | 2003 | 2002 | 2001 | 2000 | 1999 |
|---|---|---|---|---|---|---|---|---|---|---|
| Tangible Book Value | NM | NM | NM | NM | NM | NM | NM | NM | NM | NM |
| Cash Flow | 5.06 | 4.59 | 3.99 | 4.11 | 3.79 | 3.39 | 2.21 | 3.04 | 2.68 | 4.63 |
| Earnings | 3.71 | 3.18 | 2.90 | 3.08 | 2.75 | 2.43 | 1.35 | 2.28 | 2.00 | 1.70 |
| S&P Core Earnings | 3.29 | 3.03 | 2.72 | 2.17 | 2.43 | 1.74 | 0.55 | 1.79 | NA | NA |
| Dividends | 1.44 | 1.44 | 1.34 | 1.24 | 1.10 | 1.10 | 1.10 | 1.10 | 1.10 | 1.08 |
| Payout Ratio | 39% | 42% | 46% | 40% | 40% | 45% | 81% | 48% | 55% | 64% |
| Calendar Year | 2007 | 2006 | 2005 | 2004 | 2003 | 2002 | 2001 | 2000 | 1999 | 1998 |
| Prices:High | 61.52 | 59.23 | 53.89 | 49.96 | 49.66 | 51.73 | 52.86 | 45.31 | 43.94 | 39.84 |
| Prices:Low | 54.17 | 47.05 | 44.67 | 43.01 | 41.43 | 37.38 | 37.26 | 29.38 | 32.50 | 29.59 |
| P/E Ratio:High | 17 | 19 | 19 | 16 | 18 | 21 | 39 | 20 | 22 | 23 |
| P/E Ratio:Low | 15 | 15 | 15 | 14 | 15 | 15 | 28 | 13 | 16 | 17 |

### Income Statement Analysis (Million $)

| | 2008 | 2007 | 2006 | 2005 | 2004 | 2003 | 2002 | 2001 | 2000 | 1999 |
|---|---|---|---|---|---|---|---|---|---|---|
| Revenue | 13,652 | 12,442 | 11,640 | 11,244 | 11,070 | 10,506 | 7,949 | 7,078 | 6,700 | 6,246 |
| Operating Income | 2,687 | 2,515 | 2,420 | 2,435 | 2,442 | 2,290 | 1,569 | 1,392 | 1,308 | 1,212 |
| Depreciation | 459 | 418 | 424 | 443 | 399 | 365 | 296 | 223 | 209 | 194 |
| Interest Expense | 422 | 427 | 427 | 488 | 537 | 589 | 445 | 223 | 168 | 134 |
| Pretax Income | 1,917 | 1,704 | 1,631 | 1,904 | 1,583 | 1,377 | 700 | 1,015 | 950 | 838 |
| Effective Tax Rate | 32.5% | 32.9% | 33.2% | 34.9% | 33.4% | 33.4% | 34.1% | 34.5% | 35.3% | 36.3% |
| Net Income | 1,295 | 1,144 | 1,090 | 1,240 | 1,055 | 917 | 461 | 665 | 614 | 535 |
| S&P Core Earnings | 1,142 | 1,089 | 1,024 | 863 | 931 | 652 | 189 | 512 | NA | NA |

### Balance Sheet & Other Financial Data (Million $)

| | 2008 | 2007 | 2006 | 2005 | 2004 | 2003 | 2002 | 2001 | 2000 | 1999 |
|---|---|---|---|---|---|---|---|---|---|---|
| Cash | 674 | 417 | 647 | 573 | 751 | 703 | 975 | 64.1 | 25.6 | 3.90 |
| Current Assets | 3,620 | 3,054 | 3,176 | 3,055 | 3,215 | 3,179 | 3,437 | 1,408 | 1,190 | 1,103 |
| Total Assets | 19,042 | 18,184 | 18,207 | 18,066 | 18,448 | 18,227 | 16,540 | 5,091 | 4,574 | 4,141 |
| Current Liabilities | 4,856 | 5,845 | 6,138 | 4,184 | 2,757 | 3,444 | 5,747 | 2,209 | 2,529 | 1,700 |
| Long Term Debt | 4,349 | 3,218 | 2,415 | 4,255 | 7,410 | 7,516 | 5,591 | 2,221 | 1,760 | 1,702 |
| Common Equity | 6,216 | 5,319 | 5,772 | 5,676 | 5,248 | 4,175 | 3,576 | 52.2 | -289 | 164 |
| Total Capital | 12,261 | 11,109 | 11,145 | 12,915 | 14,730 | 13,652 | 9,727 | 2,696 | 1,859 | 2,156 |
| Capital Expenditures | 522 | 460 | 360 | 414 | 628 | 711 | 506 | 308 | 268 | 281 |
| Cash Flow | 1,754 | 1,562 | 1,514 | 1,683 | 1,454 | 1,282 | 757 | 888 | 823 | 729 |
| Current Ratio | 0.8 | 0.5 | 0.5 | 0.7 | 1.2 | 0.9 | 0.6 | 0.6 | 0.5 | 0.6 |
| % Long Term Debt of Capitalization | 38.7 | 28.9 | 21.7 | 32.9 | 50.3 | 55.1 | 57.5 | 82.4 | 94.7 | 79.0 |
| % Net Income of Revenue | 9.5 | 9.2 | 9.4 | 11.0 | 9.5 | 8.7 | 5.8 | 9.4 | 9.2 | 8.6 |
| % Return on Assets | 7.0 | 6.3 | 6.0 | 6.8 | 5.8 | 5.3 | 4.3 | 13.8 | 14.1 | 13.4 |
| % Return on Equity | 22.5 | 20.6 | 18.7 | 22.7 | 22.4 | 23.7 | 25.4 | NM | NM | 301.6 |

Data as orig reptd.; bef. results of disc opers/spec. items. Per share data adj. for stk. divs.; EPS diluted. E-Estimated. NA-Not Available. NM-Not Meaningful. NR-Not Ranked. UR-Under Review.

**Office:** 1 General Mills Blvd, Minneapolis, MN 55426-1348.
**Telephone:** 763-764-7600.
**Website:** http://www.generalmills.com
**Chrmn, Pres & CEO:** K.J. Powell

**EVP & CFO:** D.L. Mulligan
**EVP, Secy & General Counsel:** R.A. Palmore
**CTO:** P.C. Erickson
**Chief Acctg Officer & Cntlr:** R.O. Lund

**Investor Contact:** K. Wenker (800-245-5703)
**Board Members:** B. H. Anderson, P. Danos, W. T. Esrey, R. V. Gilmartin, J. R. Hope, H. G. Miller, H. O. Ochoa-Brillembourg, S. Odland, K. J. Powell, L. E. Quam, M. D. Rose, R. L. Ryan, A. Spence, D. A. Terrell

**Founded:** 1928
**Domicile:** Delaware
**Employees:** 29,500

The McGraw-Hill Companies

# General Motors Corp.

**STANDARD &POOR'S**

**S&P Recommendation** SELL ★ ★ ☆ ☆ ☆

| Price | 12-Mo. Target Price | Investment Style |
|---|---|---|
| $3.01 (as of Nov 14, 2008) | $3.00 | Large-Cap Value |

**GICS Sector** Consumer Discretionary
**Sub-Industry** Automobile Manufacturers

**Summary** GM, the world's largest producer of cars and trucks, also has significant finance, aerospace, defense and electronics operations.

## Key Stock Statistics (Source S&P, Vickers, company reports)

| | | | | | | | |
|---|---|---|---|---|---|---|---|
| 52-Wk Range | $29.95– 2.75 | S&P Oper. EPS 2009**E** | -10.12 | Market Capitalization(B) | $1.837 | Beta | 1.74 |
| Trailing 12-Month EPS | $-38.74 | S&P Oper. EPS 2010**E** | 1.31 | Yield (%) | Nil | S&P 3-Yr. Proj. EPS CAGR(%) | -5 |
| Trailing 12-Month P/E | NM | P/E on S&P Oper. EPS 2009**E** | NM | Dividend Rate/Share | Nil | S&P Credit Rating | CCC+ |
| $10K Invested 5 Yrs Ago | $867 | Common Shares Outstg. (M) | 610.5 | Institutional Ownership (%) | NM | | |

## Price Performance

- 30-Week Mov. Avg. ···· 10-Week Mov. Avg. — **GAAP Earnings vs. Previous Year** Volume Above Avg. STARS
- 12-Mo. Target Price — Relative Strength — ▲ Up ▽ Down ► No Change Below Avg. ★

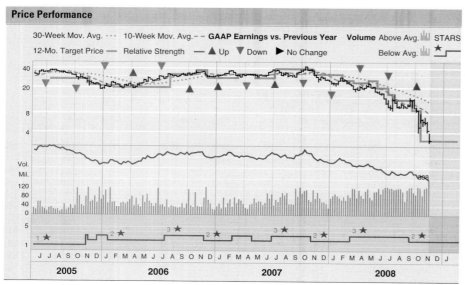

Options: ASE, CBOE, P, Ph

Analysis prepared by **Efraim Levy, CFA** on October 13, 2008, when the stock traded at **$ 5.95**.

## Highlights

➤ We see about a 15% decrease in revenues in 2008, as lower U.S. automotive sales and financial revenues should outweigh higher non-U.S. sales. We forecast that U.S. light vehicle truck sales volume will dip 15%, to 13.7 million units, in 2008, with a decrease to 13.4 million units in 2009, and a partial recovery in 2010. Global vehicle production could rise modestly in 2009.

➤ We look for automotive profits, before special items, to shrink in 2008, due to a less favorable product cycle and a dramatically unfavorable mix shift in North America, partly offset by the absence of a net non-cash charge. We do not expect to see savings from the establishment of a health care trust before 2010. In addition, we see challenges to sustained profitability in North American automotive operations.

➤ Our loss projection for 2008 reflects the negative impact of a supplier strike, as well as weaker results at 49%-owned GMAC and lower U.S. volume and mix, partly offset by relative strength in international markets. Liquidity should benefit from cash flow initiatives, including dividend suspension and other expense-saving actions, but we also see sizable claims on cash.

## Investment Rationale/Risk

➤ Despite near-term challenges, we think GM has sufficient near-term liquidity for its operating needs into 2009, although it may need additional cash later in the year. While the company announced a plan to enhance 2009 cash flows by $10 billion to $15 billion, with our view of unfavorable automotive and capital markets, we are skeptical that asset sales and capital-raising efforts will allow it to achieve the upper end of the range; greater cost-cutting may be needed.

➤ Risks to our recommendation and target price include stronger than expected demand for the company's vehicles, faster and greater cost and restructuring savings, and sharp decreases in gasoline and commodity prices. GMAC, GM's 49%-owned financial services division, could post stronger than projected net income, and savings and efficiencies from UAW negotiations may be greater than we expect.

➤ We consider visibility to be unusually limited, and we see losses through at least 2009. Based on historical multiples, we apply a total enterprise value to EBITDA multiple of about 3.2X to our 2010 EBITDA forecast of $8.055 billion to arrive at our 12-month target price of $3.

## Qualitative Risk Assessment

| LOW | MEDIUM | HIGH |
|---|---|---|

Our risk assessment reflects the highly cyclical nature of GM's markets as well as our view of the current and long-term challenges it faces, its highly leveraged balance sheet, intensifying competition, and high fixed and legacy costs. We also note the detrimental impact that high gasoline prices are expected to have on light vehicle sales.

## Quantitative Evaluations

### S&P Quality Ranking C

| D | C | B- | B | B+ | A- | A | A+ |
|---|---|---|---|---|---|---|---|

### Relative Strength Rank WEAK

7

LOWEST = 1　　　　　　　　　　HIGHEST = 99

## Revenue/Earnings Data

### Revenue (Million $)

| | 1Q | 2Q | 3Q | 4Q | Year |
|---|---|---|---|---|---|
| 2008 | 42,670 | 38,156 | 37,941 | -- | -- |
| 2007 | 43,387 | 46,844 | 43,806 | 47,085 | 181,122 |
| 2006 | 52,376 | 54,464 | 49,300 | 51,209 | 207,349 |
| 2005 | 45,773 | 48,469 | 47,182 | 51,180 | 192,604 |
| 2004 | 47,862 | 49,293 | 44,934 | 51,428 | 193,517 |
| 2003 | 47,146 | 45,944 | 43,351 | 49,084 | 185,524 |

### Earnings Per Share ($)

| | | | | | |
|---|---|---|---|---|---|
| 2008 | -5.74 | -27.33 | -4.45 | E-5.37 | E-23.18 |
| 2007 | -0.07 | 1.37 | -75.12 | -2.70 | -76.52 |
| 2006 | 1.06 | -5.98 | -0.26 | 1.68 | -3.50 |
| 2005 | -2.22 | -1.75 | -2.94 | -11.59 | -18.50 |
| 2004 | 2.12 | 2.42 | 0.56 | -0.17 | 4.95 |
| 2003 | 2.74 | 1.57 | 0.80 | Nil | 5.03 |

Fiscal year ended Dec. 31. Next earnings report expected: Mid February. EPS Estimates based on S&P Operating Earnings; historical GAAP earnings are as reported.

## Dividend Data (Dates: mm/dd Payment Date: mm/dd/yy)

| Amount ($) | Date Decl. | Ex-Div. Date | Stk. of Record | Payment Date |
|---|---|---|---|---|
| 0.250 | 11/06 | 11/14 | 11/16 | 12/10/07 |
| 0.250 | 02/05 | 02/13 | 02/15 | 03/10/08 |
| 0.250 | 05/06 | 05/14 | 05/16 | 06/10/08 |

Dividends have been paid since 1915. Source: Company reports.

---

**Please read the Required Disclosures and Analyst Certification on the last page of this report.**

The McGraw-Hill Companies

# General Motors Corp.

**STANDARD
&POOR'S**

## Business Summary October 13, 2008

CORPORATE OVERVIEW. Due to an adjustment in accounting methods, GM restated filed financial statements and financial information from 2002 through the third quarter of 2006 and delayed filing its full-year 2006 results. While we prefer to not see restatements of past filings, there was no material impact on cash flows during the affected periods. However, we are concerned about GM's admission of a lack of effective internal accounting controls. GM is the world's largest manufacturer of cars and trucks. The majority of its business is derived from the automotive industry, but it also has financing and insurance and financial services operations through 49%-owned GMAC, and it produces products and provides services in other industries. Competition has been increasing for this once dominant market leader. With Toyota Motor (TM: hold, $60), already the world's most profitable automaker, steadily and rapidly expanding its global vehicle sales and production, we believe the Japanese company will overtake GM as the undisputed world volume leader in vehicle sales in 2008.

IMPACT OF MAJOR DEVELOPMENTS. GM's agreement with UAW should improve the company's profits and competitiveness with foreign rivals. However, we do not expect GM to see the benefits from the establishment of a health care trust prior to 2010. The trust will be managed by the UAW, but initially funded by GM. What is really needed, in our view, is sustained improved demand for GM products based on styling, quality and value improvements.

On July 15, 2008, the company announced several initiatives to save or generate between $10 billion and $15 billion in cash through 2009. These included a reduction in salaried employment levels and health care coverage for salaried retirees; deferring $1.7 billion of payments to the new UAW health care VEBA;

truck production capacity reductions; reduced capital spending plans; working capital improvements; and the suspension of cash dividends. It also included the company's plans to raise an additional $4 billion to $5 billion in cash via asset sales and capital market activities. However, we do not consider current automotive and economic conditions conducive to asset sales, such as of the Hummer brand, at attractive prices. Nor do we find the expected cost of capital market fundraising attractive.

In November 2006, GM sold 51% of GMAC to an investor group. At the time, GM believed this would enhance GMAC's credit rating and thereby reduce the unit's borrowing costs, in addition to the funds it raises for the automaker. Instead, it benefited GM by reducing its exposure to recent GMAC losses.

In October 2005, Delphi Corp. (formerly Delphi Automotive Systems) filed for Chapter 11 bankruptcy protection. Delphi is GM's largest parts supplier.

Reported 2007 results include a net non-cash charge of $38.6 billion due to a valuation allowance against deferred tax assets related to operations in the U.S., Canada and Germany.

The company estimates that the 2008 strike at American Axle (AXL: hold, $3) cost it $800 million in profit in the first quarter and $1.8 billion in the second quarter. In addition, GM offered up to $215 million toward settling the strike, which ended in May.

## Company Financials  Fiscal Year Ended Dec. 31

| Per Share Data ($) | 2008 | 2007 | 2006 | 2005 | 2004 | 2003 | 2002 | 2001 | 2000 | 1999 |
|---|---|---|---|---|---|---|---|---|---|---|
| Tangible Book Value | NA | NM | NM | 18.12 | 40.35 | 36.49 | NM | 1.93 | 13.60 | 16.03 |
| Cash Flow | NA | -59.69 | 15.85 | 9.38 | 29.91 | 29.60 | 26.03 | 24.12 | 30.04 | 27.20 |
| Earnings | -22.96 | -76.52 | -3.50 | -18.50 | 4.95 | 5.03 | 3.35 | 1.77 | 6.68 | 8.53 |
| S&P Core Earnings | NA | -75.99 | 3.48 | -11.92 | 7.11 | 7.91 | -1.49 | -5.77 | NA | NA |
| Dividends | 0.50 | 1.00 | 1.00 | 2.00 | 2.00 | 2.00 | 2.00 | 2.00 | 2.00 | 2.00 |
| Payout Ratio | NM | NM | NM | NM | 40% | 40% | 60% | 113% | 30% | 23% |
| Prices:High | 29.28 | 43.20 | 36.56 | 40.80 | 55.55 | 54.39 | 68.17 | 67.80 | 94.63 | 94.88 |
| Prices:Low | 8.81 | 24.50 | 18.47 | 18.33 | 36.90 | 29.75 | 30.80 | 39.17 | 48.44 | 59.75 |
| P/E Ratio:High | NM | NM | NM | NM | 11 | 11 | 20 | 38 | 14 | 11 |
| P/E Ratio:Low | NM | NM | NM | NM | 7 | 6 | 9 | 22 | 7 | 7 |

| Income Statement Analysis (Million $) | | | | | | | | | | |
|---|---|---|---|---|---|---|---|---|---|---|
| Revenue | NA | 181,122 | 207,349 | 192,604 | 193,517 | 185,524 | 186,763 | 177,260 | 184,632 | 176,558 |
| Operating Income | NA | 9,169 | 20,227 | 14,606 | 27,324 | 26,423 | 22,733 | 23,016 | 30,127 | 29,115 |
| Depreciation | NA | 9,513 | 10,950 | 15,769 | 14,152 | 13,978 | 12,938 | 12,908 | 13,411 | 12,318 |
| Interest Expense | NA | 3,307 | 16,945 | 15,768 | 11,980 | 9,464 | 7,715 | 8,590 | 9,552 | 7,750 |
| Pretax Income | NA | -5,729 | -4,763 | -16,336 | 1,894 | 3,593 | 2,080 | 1,518 | 7,164 | 8,722 |
| Effective Tax Rate | NA | NM | NM | NM | NM | 20.3% | 25.6% | 50.6% | 33.4% | 35.7% |
| Net Income | NA | -43,297 | -1,978 | -10,458 | 2,805 | 2,862 | 1,736 | 601 | 4,452 | 5,576 |
| S&P Core Earnings | NA | -42,996 | 1,972 | -6,741 | 4,040 | 4,510 | -838 | -3,209 | NA | NA |

| Balance Sheet & Other Financial Data (Million $) | | | | | | | | | | |
|---|---|---|---|---|---|---|---|---|---|---|
| Cash | NA | 26,956 | 24,261 | 50,452 | 57,730 | 54,769 | 38,274 | 30,014 | 21,040 | 21,250 |
| Total Assets | NA | 148,883 | 186,192 | 476,078 | 479,603 | 448,507 | 370,782 | 323,969 | 303,100 | 274,730 |
| Long Term Debt | NA | 38,292 | 42,505 | 202,177 | 207,174 | 191,133 | 134,272 | 104,638 | 65,843 | 62,963 |
| Total Debt | NA | 44,339 | 48,171 | 285,750 | 300,279 | 271,756 | 201,940 | 166,314 | 144,655 | 131,906 |
| Common Equity | NA | -37,094 | -5,441 | 14,597 | 27,726 | 25,268 | 6,814 | 19,707 | 30,175 | 20,644 |
| Capital Expenditures | NA | 7,542 | 7,933 | 8,179 | 7,753 | 7,330 | 7,443 | 8,631 | 9,722 | 7,384 |
| Cash Flow | NA | -33,784 | 8,972 | 5,311 | 16,957 | 16,840 | 14,627 | 13,410 | 17,753 | 17,814 |
| % Return on Assets | NA | NM | NM | NM | 0.6 | 0.7 | 0.5 | 0.2 | 1.5 | 2.1 |
| % Return on Equity | NA | NM | NM | NM | 10.6 | 17.8 | 12.7 | 2.0 | 17.1 | 30.8 |
| % Long Term Debt of Capitalization | NA | 1361.7 | 114.8 | 91.0 | 85.5 | 85.2 | 89.0 | 79.4 | 63.8 | 69.3 |

Data as orig reptd.; bef. results of disc opers/spec. items. Per share data adj. for stk. divs.; EPS diluted. E-Estimated. NA-Not Available. NM-Not Meaningful. NR-Not Ranked. UR-Under Review.

**Office:** 300 Renaissance Center, Detroit, MI 48265-3000.
**Telephone:** 313-556-5000.
**Website:** http://www.gm.com
**Chrmn & CEO:** G.R. Wagoner, Jr.

**Pres & COO:** F.A. Henderson
**EVP & CFO:** R.G. Young
**Chief Acctg Officer & Cntlr:** N.S. Cyprus
**Treas:** W.G. Borst

**Board Members:** P. Barnevik, E. B. Bowles, J. H. Bryan, Jr., A. M. Codina, E. B. Davis, Jr., G. M. Fisher, E. N. Isdell, K. L. Katen, K. Kresa, E. J. Kullman, P. A. Laskawy, K. V. Marinello, E. Pfeiffer, M. Shannon, G. R. Wagoner, Jr.

**Founded:** 1908
**Domicile:** Delaware
**Employees:** 266,000

*The McGraw-Hill Companies*

# Genuine Parts Co

**STANDARD &POOR'S**

| S&P Recommendation | BUY ★★★★☆ | Price<br>$35.95 (as of Nov 14, 2008) | 12-Mo. Target Price<br>$47.00 | Investment Style<br>Large-Cap Blend |
|---|---|---|---|---|

**GICS Sector** Consumer Discretionary
**Sub-Industry** Distributors

**Summary** This company is a leading wholesale distributor of automotive replacement parts, industrial parts and supplies, and office products.

## Key Stock Statistics (Source S&P, Vickers, company reports)

| | | | | | | | |
|---|---|---|---|---|---|---|---|
| 52-Wk Range | $49.51– 29.92 | S&P Oper. EPS 2008E | 3.16 | Market Capitalization(B) | $5.732 | Beta | 0.83 |
| Trailing 12-Month EPS | $3.11 | S&P Oper. EPS 2009E | 3.34 | Yield (%) | 4.34 | S&P 3-Yr. Proj. EPS CAGR(%) | 6 |
| Trailing 12-Month P/E | 11.6 | P/E on S&P Oper. EPS 2008E | 11.4 | Dividend Rate/Share | $1.56 | S&P Credit Rating | NA |
| $10K Invested 5 Yrs Ago | $13,443 | Common Shares Outstg. (M) | 159.4 | Institutional Ownership (%) | 76 | | |

## Price Performance

30-Week Mov. Avg. · · · ·   10-Week Mov. Avg. – – –   **GAAP Earnings vs. Previous Year**   Volume Above Avg. ▐▌▐▌   STARS

12-Mo. Target Price —   Relative Strength —   ▲ Up   ▼ Down   ▶ No Change   Below Avg. ▐▌▐▌   ★

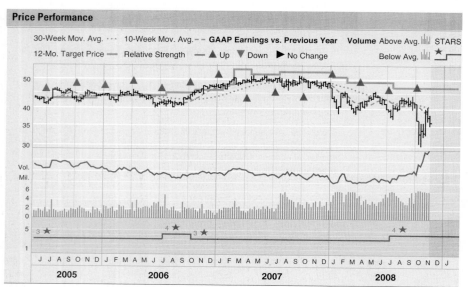

Options: ASE, P, Ph

Analysis prepared by **Efraim Levy, CFA** on September 26, 2008, when the stock traded at **$ 41.47**.

## Highlights

➤ Despite our belief that a recession is likely, we expect revenues to rise 4%-5% in each of 2008 and 2009. We think pricing will remain competitive, and foresee operating margins rising modestly as GPC divests some low-margin businesses and cuts costs. The projected gross margin improvement will be partially offset, in our view, by other lower-margin businesses growing faster than higher-margin segments.

➤ We expect longer-term prospects for GPC's auto parts segment to be enhanced by the rising number and increasing complexity of vehicles. The average vehicle in the U.S. is currently more than eight years old. We believe GPC will benefit from an expanding market share, as long-term industry consolidation continues to drive out smaller participants. We also think GPC is likely to use its distribution strength to leverage sales of acquired parts companies.

➤ What we view as GPC's solid balance sheet, low debt, and strong cash flow are resources that could be used to accelerate earnings growth in the longer term. We see GPC using cash flow to repurchase shares, invest in growing the business, make modest-sized acquisitions, and increase its dividend.

## Investment Rationale/Risk

➤ Based on our 2008 EPS estimate, the stock's recent P/E of about 12.4X is above the average for peers and appropriate, in our view, given the company's greater earnings stability. Earnings quality appears high to us, and an above-average dividend yield adds to GPC's total return potential.

➤ Risks to our recommendation and target price include weaker-than-expected demand for the company's products and a slower-than-anticipated improvement in operating margins.

➤ Our 12-month target price of $47 is based on a blend of our relative and discounted cash flow (DCF) metrics. On a relative basis, we assume a P/E of about 12.9X applied to our 2009 EPS estimate of $3.34, reflecting historical and peer P/E comparisons, leading to a value of about $43. Our DCF model, which assumes a weighted average cost of capital of 9.7%, a compound annual growth rate of 3.5% over the next 15 years, and a terminal growth rate of 3%, calculates an intrinsic value near $51.

## Qualitative Risk Assessment

| LOW | MEDIUM | HIGH |
|---|---|---|

Our risk assessment reflects GPC's long-term record of rising sales and earnings and what we view as strong corporate leadership and a healthy balance sheet.

## Quantitative Evaluations

**S&P Quality Ranking**   A

| D | C | B- | B | B+ | A- | A | A+ |
|---|---|---|---|---|---|---|---|

**Relative Strength Rank**   STRONG

81

LOWEST = 1                 HIGHEST = 99

## Revenue/Earnings Data

**Revenue (Million $)**

| | 1Q | 2Q | 3Q | 4Q | Year |
|---|---|---|---|---|---|
| 2008 | 2,739 | 2,873 | 2,882 | -- | -- |
| 2007 | 2,649 | 2,770 | 2,798 | 2,627 | 10,843 |
| 2006 | 2,554 | 2,662 | 2,700 | 2,543 | 10,458 |
| 2005 | 2,342 | 2,476 | 2,556 | 2,410 | 9,783 |
| 2004 | 2,197 | 2,298 | 2,349 | 2,253 | 9,097 |
| 2003 | 2,022 | 2,153 | 2,189 | 2,085 | 8,449 |

**Earnings Per Share ($)**

| | 1Q | 2Q | 3Q | 4Q | Year |
|---|---|---|---|---|---|
| 2008 | 0.75 | 0.81 | 0.81 | E0.81 | E3.16 |
| 2007 | 0.71 | 0.76 | 0.76 | 0.75 | 2.98 |
| 2006 | 0.66 | 0.70 | 0.71 | 0.70 | 2.76 |
| 2005 | 0.61 | 0.63 | 0.63 | 0.63 | 2.50 |
| 2004 | 0.57 | 0.58 | 0.56 | 0.55 | 2.25 |
| 2003 | 0.51 | 0.52 | 0.51 | 0.50 | 2.03 |

Fiscal year ended Dec. 31. Next earnings report expected: Mid February. EPS Estimates based on S&P Operating Earnings; historical GAAP earnings are as reported.

## Dividend Data (Dates: mm/dd Payment Date: mm/dd/yy)

| Amount ($) | Date Decl. | Ex-Div. Date | Stk. of Record | Payment Date |
|---|---|---|---|---|
| 0.365 | 11/19 | 12/05 | 12/07 | 01/02/08 |
| 0.390 | 02/19 | 03/05 | 03/07 | 04/01/08 |
| 0.390 | 04/21 | 06/04 | 06/06 | 07/01/08 |
| 0.390 | 08/18 | 09/03 | 09/05 | 10/01/08 |

Dividends have been paid since 1948. Source: Company reports.

---

**Please read the Required Disclosures and Analyst Certification on the last page of this report.**

*The McGraw·Hill Companies*

# Genuine Parts Co

## Business Summary September 26, 2008

CORPORATE OVERVIEW. Genuine Parts is the leading independent U.S. distributor of automotive replacement parts. It operates 58 NAPA warehouse distribution centers in the U.S., about 1,100 company-owned jobbing stores, four Rayloc auto parts rebuilding plants, four Balkamp distribution centers, two Altrom import parts distribution centers, eight heavy vehicle parts distribution centers and facilities and one JI Chicago distribution center. The company has been expanding via a combination of internal growth and acquisitions.

The automotive parts segment (49% of 2007 revenues, 47% of profits) serves about 5,800 NAPA Auto Parts stores, including about 1,100 company-owned stores, selling to garages, service stations, car and truck dealers, fleet operators, leasing companies, bus and truck lines, etc.

The industrial parts segment (31%, 32%) distributes around three million industrial replacement parts and related supply items, including bearings, power transmission equipment replacement parts, including hydraulic and pneumatic products, material handling components, agricultural and irrigation equipment, and related items from locations in the U.S. and Canada.

Through S. P. Richards Co., the office products group (16%, 18%) distributes more than 40,000 office product items, including information processing supplies and office furniture, machines and supplies to office suppliers, from facilities in the U.S. and Canada.

The EIS electrical/electronics materials group (4%, 3%) was formed via the 1998 acquisition of EIS, Inc., for $200 million. EIS is a wholesale distributor of material and supplies to the electrical and electronic industries.

The U.S. accounted for almost 89% of sales in 2007. Canada contributed 11% and Mexico represented less than 1%.

## Company Financials Fiscal Year Ended Dec. 31

| Per Share Data ($) | 2007 | 2006 | 2005 | 2004 | 2003 | 2002 | 2001 | 2000 | 1999 | 1998 |
|---|---|---|---|---|---|---|---|---|---|---|
| Tangible Book Value | 15.86 | 4.82 | 15.21 | 14.21 | 12.95 | 11.88 | 10.97 | 10.50 | 9.80 | 9.52 |
| Cash Flow | 3.49 | 3.18 | 2.87 | 2.61 | 2.42 | 2.50 | 2.21 | 2.72 | 2.61 | 2.36 |
| Earnings | 2.98 | 2.76 | 2.50 | 2.25 | 2.03 | 2.10 | 1.71 | 2.20 | 2.11 | 1.98 |
| S&P Core Earnings | 2.98 | 2.76 | 2.40 | 2.22 | 1.95 | 1.80 | 1.53 | NA | NA | NA |
| Dividends | 1.46 | 1.35 | 1.25 | 1.20 | 1.18 | 1.16 | 1.14 | 1.10 | 1.03 | 0.99 |
| Payout Ratio | 49% | 49% | 50% | 53% | 58% | 55% | 67% | 50% | 49% | 50% |
| Prices:High | 51.68 | 48.34 | 46.64 | 44.32 | 33.75 | 38.80 | 37.94 | 26.69 | 35.75 | 38.25 |
| Prices:Low | 46.00 | 40.00 | 40.75 | 32.03 | 27.20 | 27.10 | 23.91 | 18.25 | 22.25 | 28.25 |
| P/E Ratio:High | 17 | 18 | 19 | 20 | 17 | 18 | 22 | 12 | 17 | 19 |
| P/E Ratio:Low | 15 | 14 | 16 | 14 | 13 | 13 | 14 | 8 | 11 | 14 |

| Income Statement Analysis (Million $) | 2007 | 2006 | 2005 | 2004 | 2003 | 2002 | 2001 | 2000 | 1999 | 1998 |
|---|---|---|---|---|---|---|---|---|---|---|
| Revenue | 10,843 | 10,458 | 9,783 | 9,097 | 8,449 | 8,259 | 8,221 | 8,370 | 7,982 | 6,614 |
| Operating Income | 926 | 870 | 804 | 698 | 641 | 676 | 656 | 739 | 718 | 658 |
| Depreciation | 87.7 | 73.4 | 65.5 | 62.2 | 69.0 | 70.2 | 85.8 | 92.3 | 90.0 | 69.3 |
| Interest Expense | 31.3 | 31.6 | 29.6 | Nil | Nil | Nil | Nil | Nil | Nil | Nil |
| Pretax Income | 822 | 771 | 709 | 636 | 572 | 606 | 496 | 647 | 628 | 589 |
| Effective Tax Rate | 37.8% | 38.3% | 38.3% | 37.8% | 38.1% | 39.3% | 40.1% | 40.4% | 39.9% | 39.6% |
| Net Income | 506 | 475 | 437 | 396 | 354 | 368 | 297 | 385 | 378 | 356 |
| S&P Core Earnings | 506 | 475 | 420 | 388 | 339 | 316 | 265 | NA | NA | NA |

| Balance Sheet & Other Financial Data (Million $) | 2007 | 2006 | 2005 | 2004 | 2003 | 2002 | 2001 | 2000 | 1999 | 1998 |
|---|---|---|---|---|---|---|---|---|---|---|
| Cash | 232 | 136 | 189 | 135 | 15.4 | 20.0 | 85.8 | 27.7 | 45.7 | 85.0 |
| Current Assets | 4,053 | 3,835 | 3,807 | 3,633 | 3,418 | 3,336 | 3,146 | 3,019 | 2,895 | 2,683 |
| Total Assets | 4,774 | 4,497 | 4,772 | 4,455 | 4,116 | 4,020 | 4,207 | 4,142 | 3,930 | 3,600 |
| Current Liabilities | 1,548 | 1,199 | 1,249 | 1,133 | 1,017 | 1,070 | 919 | 988 | 916 | 818 |
| Long Term Debt | 250 | 500 | 500 | 500 | 625 | 675 | 836 | 771 | 702 | 589 |
| Common Equity | 2,717 | 2,550 | 2,694 | 2,544 | 2,312 | 2,130 | 2,345 | 2,261 | 2,178 | 2,053 |
| Total Capital | 3,033 | 3,111 | 3,408 | 3,212 | 3,100 | 2,950 | 3,287 | 3,154 | 3,014 | 2,782 |
| Capital Expenditures | 116 | 126 | 85.7 | 72.1 | 73.9 | 64.8 | 41.9 | 71.1 | 88.3 | 88.2 |
| Cash Flow | 594 | 549 | 503 | 458 | 423 | 438 | 383 | 478 | 468 | 425 |
| Current Ratio | 2.6 | 3.2 | 3.0 | 3.2 | 3.4 | 3.1 | 3.4 | 3.1 | 3.2 | 3.3 |
| % Long Term Debt of Capitalization | 8.2 | 16.1 | 14.7 | 15.6 | 20.2 | 22.9 | 25.4 | 24.4 | 23.3 | 21.1 |
| % Net Income of Revenue | 4.7 | 4.5 | 4.5 | 4.3 | 4.2 | 4.4 | 3.6 | 4.6 | 4.7 | 5.4 |
| % Return on Assets | 10.9 | 10.3 | 9.5 | 9.2 | 8.6 | 8.9 | 7.1 | 9.5 | 10.0 | 11.2 |
| % Return on Equity | 19.2 | 18.1 | 16.7 | 16.3 | 15.9 | 16.4 | 12.9 | 17.4 | 17.9 | 18.2 |

Data as orig reptd.; bef. results of disc opers/spec. items. Per share data adj. for stk. divs.; EPS diluted. E-Estimated. NA-Not Available. NM-Not Meaningful. NR-Not Ranked. UR-Under Review.

**Office:** 2999 Cir 75 Pkwy, Atlanta, GA 30339.
**Telephone:** 770-953-1700.
**Website:** http://www.genpt.com
**Chrmn, Pres & CEO:** T. Gallagher

**Vice Chrmn, EVP, CFO & Chief Acctg Officer:** J.W. Nix
**SVP & Treas:** F.M. Howard
**SVP & Secy:** C.B. Yancey
**SVP & General Counsel:** S.C. Smith

**Board Members:** M. B. Bullock, R. W. Courts, II, J. E. Douville, T. Gallagher, G. C. Guynn, J. D. Johns, M. M. Johns, J. H. Lanier, W. B. Needham, J. W. Nix, L. L. Prince, G. W. Rollins, L. G. Steiner

**Founded:** 1928
**Domicile:** Georgia
**Employees:** 32,000

# Genworth Financial Inc

STANDARD
&POOR'S

**S&P Recommendation** **HOLD** ★ ★ ★ ☆ ☆

| | | |
|---|---|---|
| **Price** $1.47 (as of Nov 14, 2008) | **12-Mo. Target Price** $4.00 | **Investment Style** Large-Cap Blend |

**GICS Sector** Financials
**Sub-Industry** Multi-line Insurance

**Summary** This insurance holding company serves lifestyle protection, retirement income, investment and mortgage insurance needs around the world.

## Key Stock Statistics (Source S&P, Vickers, company reports)

| | | | | | | | | |
|---|---|---|---|---|---|---|---|---|
| 52-Wk Range | $28.21– 0.90 | S&P Oper. EPS 2008**E** | 1.95 | Market Capitalization(B) | $0.637 | Beta | 2.12 |
| Trailing 12-Month EPS | $-0.17 | S&P Oper. EPS 2009**E** | 2.27 | Yield (%) | Nil | S&P 3-Yr. Proj. EPS CAGR(%) | -5 |
| Trailing 12-Month P/E | NM | P/E on S&P Oper. EPS 2008**E** | 0.8 | Dividend Rate/Share | Nil | S&P Credit Rating | A- |
| $10K Invested 5 Yrs Ago | NA | Common Shares Outstg. (M) | 433.1 | Institutional Ownership (%) | 100 | | |

## Price Performance

- 30-Week Mov. Avg. ···· 10-Week Mov. Avg. - - **GAAP Earnings vs. Previous Year** **Volume** Above Avg. ▮▮▮ **STARS**
- 12-Mo. Target Price — Relative Strength — ▲ Up ▼ Down ▶ No Change Below Avg. ▮▮▮ ★

Options: ASE, CBOE, P, Ph

Analysis prepared by **Bret Howlett** on November 12, 2008, when the stock traded at **$ 1.00**.

## Highlights

➤ We believe revenues will experience high single-digit growth in 2008, driven by strength in GNW's retirement and protection and international businesses. However, we expect operating earnings to decline given losses in the U.S. mortgage insurance business, and impact from weak equity markets. We expect operating earnings in the retirement and protection business to decline, and be negatively impacted from DAC charges, guaranteed death and withdrawal benefit costs, and lower investment income, but be partially offset by solid growth in fixed annuity sales. We think variable life sales will be weak in 2008, as consumers move away from equity-linked products.

➤ We expect earnings for the international business to benefit from the strong growth we see in the international mortgage unit, based on GNW's aggressive expansion into Europe, and growth in the payment protection business. Due to significant realized losses in its investment portfolio mostly related to real estate exposure, we believe it will be challenging for GNW to reach its goal of a 12% ROE by year-end 2008.

➤ We forecast operating EPS of $1.95 in 2008, and a rise to $2.27 for 2009.

## Investment Rationale/Risk

➤ Despite the share price decline, our hold opinion reflects our view that limited financial flexibility, continued losses in its U.S. mortgage insurance business, and elevated impairments in its investment portfolio will likely weigh on the shares. We believe GNW's capital and liquidity positions are weak relative to peers, and the company remains more vulnerable to turmoil in the financial markets. The company has sub-prime and Alt-A exposure in its mortgage insurance business and investment portfolio. We expect that market concerns regarding the credit environment will result in share price volatility. But with GNW trading at a steep discount to peers, we think the capital, housing, and credit market problems are already reflected in its valuation and that downside should be limited.

➤ Risks to our recommendation and target price include a continued low interest rate environment; increased investment portfolio risks; high concentrations of product line sales associated with certain third parties; and a prolonged slowdown in the housing market.

➤ Our 12-month target price of $4 about 0.2X our 2008 book value per share estimate, below the company's historical average multiple.

## Qualitative Risk Assessment

| LOW | MEDIUM | **HIGH** |
|---|---|---|

Our risk assessment reflects significant exposure to the U.S. housing market from the mortgage insurance business, which may result in volatility. In addition, GNW is vulnerable to investment losses and has a weaker capital position relative to peers, in our view. Our recommendation also reflects the unfavorable operating environment for the life insurance group.

## Quantitative Evaluations

**S&P Quality Ranking** NR

| D | C | B- | B | B+ | A- | A | A+ |
|---|---|---|---|---|---|---|---|

**Relative Strength Rank** WEAK

1

LOWEST = 1     HIGHEST = 99

## Revenue/Earnings Data

**Revenue (Million $)**

| | 1Q | 2Q | 3Q | 4Q | Year |
|---|---|---|---|---|---|
| 2008 | 2,753 | 2,398 | 2,168 | -- | -- |
| 2007 | 2,710 | 2,765 | 2,875 | 2,775 | 11,125 |
| 2006 | 2,625 | 2,754 | 2,804 | 2,846 | 11,029 |
| 2005 | 2,611 | 2,610 | 2,628 | 2,655 | 10,504 |
| 2004 | 3,024 | 2,921 | 2,470 | 2,642 | 11,057 |
| 2003 | -- | -- | -- | -- | 9,775 |

**Earnings Per Share ($)**

| | 1Q | 2Q | 3Q | 4Q | Year |
|---|---|---|---|---|---|
| 2008 | 0.27 | -0.25 | -0.60 | E0.45 | E1.95 |
| 2007 | 0.69 | 0.70 | 0.76 | 0.41 | 2.58 |
| 2006 | 0.69 | 0.68 | 0.65 | 0.81 | 2.83 |
| 2005 | 0.65 | 0.60 | 0.64 | 0.64 | 2.52 |
| 2004 | 0.53 | 0.55 | 0.55 | 0.70 | 2.34 |
| 2003 | -- | -- | -- | -- | 1.82 |

Fiscal year ended Dec. 31. Next earnings report expected: Early February. EPS Estimates based on S&P Operating Earnings; historical GAAP earnings are as reported.

## Dividend Data (Dates: mm/dd Payment Date: mm/dd/yy)

| Amount ($) | Date Decl. | Ex-Div. Date | Stk. of Record | Payment Date |
|---|---|---|---|---|
| 0.100 | 03/19 | 04/09 | 04/11 | 04/28/08 |
| 0.100 | 05/13 | 07/09 | 07/11 | 07/28/08 |
| 0.100 | 09/08 | 10/08 | 10/10 | 10/27/08 |

Dividends have been paid since 2004. Source: Company reports.

The **McGraw-Hill** Companies

# Genworth Financial Inc

**STANDARD &POOR'S**

## Business Summary November 12, 2008

CORPORATE OVERVIEW. Genworth Financial, Inc., carved out from General Electric (GE) in May 2004, is a U.S. insurance company with an expanding international presence. As of February 2007, GNW had operations in 25 countries, and believed it was one of the largest providers of private mortgage insurance outside the U.S. based on new insurance written. According to reports by VARDS, LIMRA International, and Inside Mortgage Finance magazine, in 2005, GNW was the largest U.S. provider of variable income annuities and the second-largest provider of fixed immediate annuities, based on total premiums and deposits, and the fifth-largest provider of mortgage insurance, based on new insurance written.

The company conducts its business through three major segments. The first segment is retirement and protection (68% of 2007 total revenues, 72% of 2006 total revenues). This segment is comprised of managed money (3.0%, 1.9%); retirement income (17%, 21%); spread-based institutional (4.6%, 5.6%); life insurance (18%, 18%); and long-term care (26%, 26%). The second segment is international (24%, 21%). This segment consists of the company's mortgage

insurance business in Canada, Australia, and Europe, in addition to proposals for other target countries for mortgage insurance. The segment also includes payment protection insurance, which helps consumers meet their payment obligations in the event of illness, involuntary unemployment, disability or death. The third segment is U.S. mortgage insurance (7.2%, 6.4%). The mortgage insurance business facilitates home ownership by enabling borrowers to buy homes with low down payment mortgages. These products also help financial institutions manage their capital efficiently by reducing the capital required for low down payment mortgages. The company also has a corporate and other segment (0.6%, 1.1%), which includes unallocated corporate income and expenses, results of a small, non-core business, and most interest and other financing expenses.

## Company Financials Fiscal Year Ended Dec. 31

| Per Share Data ($) | 2007 | 2006 | 2005 | 2004 | 2003 | 2002 | 2001 | 2000 | 1999 | 1998 |
|---|---|---|---|---|---|---|---|---|---|---|
| Tangible Book Value | 31.64 | 24.20 | 24.51 | 21.69 | 20.18 | NA | NA | NA | NA | NA |
| Operating Earnings | NA | NA | NA | NA | NA | NA | NA | NA | NA | NA |
| Earnings | 2.58 | 2.83 | 2.52 | 2.34 | 1.82 | NA | NA | NA | NA | NA |
| S&P Core Earnings | 3.04 | 2.92 | 2.52 | 2.29 | 1.96 | NA | NA | NA | NA | NA |
| Dividends | 0.37 | 0.32 | 0.27 | 0.07 | NA | NA | NA | NA | NA | NA |
| Relative Payout | 14% | 11% | 11% | 3% | NA | NA | NA | NA | NA | NA |
| Prices:High | 37.16 | 36.47 | 35.25 | 27.84 | NA | NA | NA | NA | NA | NA |
| Prices:Low | 23.26 | 31.00 | 25.72 | 18.75 | NA | NA | NA | NA | NA | NA |
| P/E Ratio:High | 14 | 13 | 14 | 12 | NA | NA | NA | NA | NA | NA |
| P/E Ratio:Low | 9 | 11 | 10 | 8 | NA | NA | NA | NA | NA | NA |

| Income Statement Analysis (Million $) | | | | | | | | | | |
|---|---|---|---|---|---|---|---|---|---|---|
| Life Insurance in Force | NA | NA | NA | NA | NA | NA | NA | NA | NA | NA |
| Premium Income:Life A & H | NA | NA | NA | NA | 6,252 | NA | NA | NA | NA | NA |
| Premium Income:Casualty/Property. | NA | NA | NA | NA | Nil | NA | NA | NA | NA | NA |
| Net Investment Income | NA | 3,837 | 3,536 | 3,648 | 2,928 | NA | NA | NA | NA | NA |
| Total Revenue | 11,125 | 11,029 | 10,504 | 11,057 | 9,775 | NA | NA | NA | NA | NA |
| Pretax Income | 1,606 | 1,918 | 1,798 | 1,638 | 1,263 | NA | NA | NA | NA | NA |
| Net Operating Income | NA | NA | NA | NA | NA | NA | NA | NA | NA | NA |
| Net Income | 1,154 | 1,324 | 1,221 | 1,145 | 892 | NA | NA | NA | NA | NA |
| S&P Core Earnings | 1,359 | 1,369 | 1,221 | 1,126 | 956 | NA | NA | NA | NA | NA |

| Balance Sheet & Other Financial Data (Million $) | | | | | | | | | | |
|---|---|---|---|---|---|---|---|---|---|---|
| Cash & Equivalent | 5,369 | 3,222 | 2,608 | 2,125 | 1,630 | NA | NA | NA | NA | NA |
| Premiums Due | NA | NA | NA | NA | NA | NA | NA | NA | NA | NA |
| Investment Assets:Bonds | NA | 55,448 | 53,791 | 52,424 | 50,081 | NA | NA | NA | NA | NA |
| Investment Assets:Stocks | NA | NA | 367 | 374 | 387 | NA | NA | NA | NA | NA |
| Investment Assets:Loans | NA | 9,985 | 8,908 | 7,275 | 6,794 | NA | NA | NA | NA | NA |
| Investment Assets:Total | NA | 73,519 | 66,573 | 65,747 | 61,749 | NA | NA | NA | NA | NA |
| Deferred Policy Costs | NA | NA | 5,586 | 5,020 | 4,421 | NA | NA | NA | NA | NA |
| Total Assets | 114,315 | 110,871 | 105,292 | 103,878 | 100,216 | NA | NA | NA | NA | NA |
| Debt | 7,558 | 3,921 | 3,336 | 3,042 | 3,016 | NA | NA | NA | NA | NA |
| Common Equity | 13,478 | 13,330 | 13,310 | 12,866 | 12,258 | NA | NA | NA | NA | NA |
| Combined Loss-Expense Ratio | NA | NA | NA | NA | NA | NA | NA | NA | NA | NA |
| % Return on Revenue | NA | 12.0 | 11.6 | 10.4 | 9.1 | NA | NA | NA | NA | NA |
| % Return on Equity | 8.6 | 2.2 | 9.3 | 8.0 | NA | NA | NA | NA | NA | NA |
| % Investment Yield | NA | NA | NA | NA | NA | NA | NA | NA | NA | NA |

Data as orig reptd.; bef. results of disc opers/spec. items. Per share data adj. for stk. divs.; EPS diluted. E-Estimated. NA-Not Available. NM-Not Meaningful. NR-Not Ranked. UR-Under Review.

**Office:** 6620 West Broad Street, Richmond, VA 23230.
**Telephone:** 804-281-6000.
**Email:** investorinfo@genworth.com
**Website:** http://www.genworth.com

**Chrmn, Pres & CEO:** M.D. Fraizer
**SVP & CFO:** P.B. Kelleher
**SVP, Secy & General Counsel:** L.E. Roday
**SVP & CIO:** S.J. McKay

**Chief Acctg Officer & Cntlr:** A.R. Corbin
**Investor Contact:** C. English (804-662-2614)
**Board Members:** F. J. Borelli, M. D. Fraizer, N. J. Karch, J. Kerrey, R. J. Lavizzo-Mourey, S. T. Naqvi, J. A. Parke, J. S. Riepe, B. Toan, T. B. Wheeler

**Founded:** 2003
**Domicile:** Delaware
**Employees:** 7,000

# Genzyme Corp

STANDARD &POOR'S

| S&P Recommendation | STRONG BUY ★★★★★ | Price $69.14 (as of Nov 14, 2008) | 12-Mo. Target Price $92.00 | Investment Style Large-Cap Growth |
|---|---|---|---|---|

**GICS Sector** Health Care
**Sub-Industry** Biotechnology

**Summary** This biopharmaceutical concern makes and markets human therapeutic and diagnostic products. Its leading product is Cerezyme, a drug to treat Gaucher disease.

## Key Stock Statistics (Source S&P, Vickers, company reports)

| | | | | | | | |
|---|---|---|---|---|---|---|---|
| 52-Wk Range | $83.97–60.28 | S&P Oper. EPS 2008**E** | 3.52 | Market Capitalization(B) | $18.704 | Beta | 0.26 |
| Trailing 12-Month EPS | $1.48 | S&P Oper. EPS 2009**E** | 4.20 | Yield (%) | Nil | S&P 3-Yr. Proj. EPS CAGR(%) | 20 |
| Trailing 12-Month P/E | 46.7 | P/E on S&P Oper. EPS 2008**E** | 19.6 | Dividend Rate/Share | Nil | S&P Credit Rating | BBB+ |
| $10K Invested 5 Yrs Ago | $15,760 | Common Shares Outstg. (M) | 270.5 | Institutional Ownership (%) | 90 | | |

## Price Performance

30-Week Mov. Avg. · · · ·   10-Week Mov. Avg. — —   **GAAP Earnings vs. Previous Year**   Volume Above Avg. ▮▮ STARS
12-Mo. Target Price —   Relative Strength —   ▲ Up  ▼ Down  ► No Change   Below Avg. ▮▮ ★

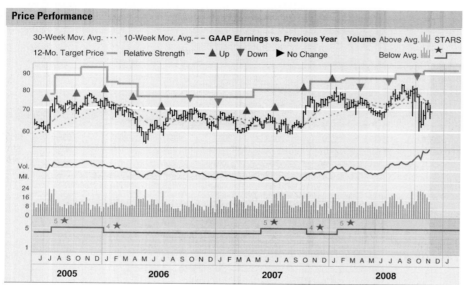

Options: ASE, CBOE, P, Ph

Analysis prepared by **Steven Silver** on October 23, 2008, when the stock traded at **$ 65.15**.

## Highlights

➤ We expect a 22% increase in revenues in 2008, to $4.6 billion, on continued growth across GENZ's diverse product platform. Further, we forecast 14% revenue growth in 2009, to $5.3 billion. We continue to be encouraged by GENZ's revenue diversification, as 2007 Cerezyme sales accounted for 30% of sales, down from 35% in 2006. With approval of Renvela in the U.S. and Synvisc-One in Europe, and clinical progress of GENZ-112638 for Gaucher Disease, we see GENZ successfully advancing next-generation versions of key drugs.

➤ We continue to view GENZ's expense controls favorably, and project expanding operating margins via the selling of new products within an established global infrastructure. We expect 2008 and 2009 operating expenses to total 44% and 43% of respective year product sales, down from 2007's 45%. We see strong operational cash flows funding share repurchase programs, new drug licensing/acquisition deals, and capital investments.

➤ Our 2008 and 2009 EPS estimates are $3.52 and $4.20, respectively. We view GENZ as well positioned to achieve its goal of 20% compound annual EPS growth through 2011.

## Investment Rationale/Risk

➤ We consider GENZ among core biotech holdings, with solid product growth, a robust late-stage pipeline, and a strong financial position ($481 million of third quarter 2008 operating cash flow, and $1.5 billion in cash) after several sizable recent deals. We believe GENZ is well positioned to expand its diverse portfolio, with Myozyme (likely approval of large-scale production facility by end of 2008) and Mozobil (launch expected in 2009) as key drivers. Also, we see catalysts for growth beyond 2011 in oncology with now wholly owned Clolar and Campath (advancing in study for multiple sclerosis) and in the renal unit with in-licensed cholesterol-lowering drug mipomersen and Renvela, successor to Renagel.

➤ Risks to our recommendation and target price include clinical or regulatory setbacks to the new product portfolio, any slowdown in sales growth for key marketed products, and manufacturing issues limiting product supply.

➤ Our 12-month target price of $92 is 22X our 2009 EPS estimate of $4.20, which represents of PEG multiple of 1.1X our 20% long-term growth rate, in line with the large cap biotech peer average in our coverage universe.

## Qualitative Risk Assessment

| LOW | MEDIUM | HIGH |
|---|---|---|

Our risk assessment reflects our belief that Genzyme's portfolio of therapeutic products -- as well as its diagnostic business -- is diverse. With regard to the company's individual drugs of importance, we think Renagel/Renvela faces the most immediate competition, and we see an increasingly competitive landscape for the foreseeable future, which may offset the benefits of product diversity.

## Quantitative Evaluations

**S&P Quality Ranking**                     B-

| D | C | B- | B | B+ | A- | A | A+ |
|---|---|---|---|---|---|---|---|

**Relative Strength Rank**              STRONG

82

LOWEST = 1                          HIGHEST = 99

## Revenue/Earnings Data

**Revenue (Million $)**

| | 1Q | 2Q | 3Q | 4Q | Year |
|---|---|---|---|---|---|
| 2008 | 1,100 | 1,171 | 1,160 | -- | -- |
| 2007 | 883.2 | 933.4 | 960.2 | 1,037 | 3,814 |
| 2006 | 730.8 | 793.4 | 808.6 | 854.2 | 3,187 |
| 2005 | 630.0 | 668.1 | 708.1 | 728.7 | 2,735 |
| 2004 | 491.3 | 549.6 | 569.2 | 591.1 | 2,201 |
| 2003 | 381.9 | 418.9 | 437.0 | 476.1 | 1,714 |

**Earnings Per Share ($)**

| | 1Q | 2Q | 3Q | 4Q | Year |
|---|---|---|---|---|---|
| 2008 | 0.52 | 0.25 | 0.42 | E0.91 | E3.52 |
| 2007 | 0.57 | 0.51 | 0.58 | 0.29 | 1.74 |
| 2006 | 0.37 | 0.49 | 0.06 | -1.02 | -0.06 |
| 2005 | 0.36 | 0.46 | 0.43 | 0.39 | 1.65 |
| 2004 | 0.29 | 0.33 | 0.41 | -0.68 | 0.37 |
| 2003 | 0.28 | 0.32 | -0.43 | 0.25 | 0.42 |

Fiscal year ended Dec. 31. Next earnings report expected: Mid February. EPS Estimates based on S&P Operating Earnings; historical GAAP earnings are as reported.

## Dividend Data

No cash dividends have been paid.

# Genzyme Corp

STANDARD &POOR'S

## Business Summary October 23, 2008

CORPORATE OVERVIEW. Genzyme develops, manufactures and markets therapeutic and diagnostic products. GENZ's leading product is Cerezyme, an enzyme replacement therapy (ERT) for Gaucher disease, a debilitating genetic disorder causing fatigue, anemia and bone erosion. In 2007, Cerezyme sales totaled $1.1 billion (up from $1.0 billion in 2006), accounting for 30% of sales, down from 35% in 2006, and 42% in 2005. GENZ is studying orally administered GENZ-112638 to succeed intravenously infused Cerezyme. The drug is in Phase II study and GENZ plans to start Phase III trials in 2009.

Renagel, which reduces elevated serum phosphorus levels in kidney dialysis patients, generated $603 million in 2007 sales (up 17% from $515 million). In October 2007, the FDA approved Renvela, a buffered form of Renagel, which launched in March 2008. In the same month, an FDA renal committee recommended approval for Renagel/Renvela in earlier pre-dialysis stages of kidney disease, and GENZ expects approval for this indication in 2009.

Fabrazyme is approved in Europe and the U.S. for treating Fabry disease, a

rare genetic disorder. Fabrazyme sales were $424 million in 2007, up from $359 million in 2006. Aldurazyme, an ERT for MPS-I, was approved by the FDA in April 2003 and is partnered with BioMarin through a 50%-owned joint venture. GENZ has developed Myozyme, for treating Pompe disease, a rare and often fatal disorder that afflicts an estimated 10,000 patients worldwide. Myozyme was launched in the U.S. and Europe in mid-2006 and saw 2007 sales of $201 million. GENZ expects approval of a large-scale production facility, on FDA's action date of November 29, 2008. In the biosurgery unit, sales are led by Synvisc, an injectable biomaterial to treat knee osteoarthritis by improving joint lubrication. Synvisc sales were $242 million in 2007, 3% higher than in 2006. A single-injection version, Synvisc-One, is under FDA review with an action date of December 23, 2008. The drug was approved in Europe in December 2007.

## Company Financials Fiscal Year Ended Dec. 31

| Per Share Data ($) | 2007 | 2006 | 2005 | 2004 | 2003 | 2002 | 2001 | 2000 | 1999 | 1998 |
|---|---|---|---|---|---|---|---|---|---|---|
| Tangible Book Value | 13.73 | 10.91 | 7.99 | 8.11 | 6.31 | NM | 6.10 | 4.05 | 5.54 | 5.56 |
| Cash Flow | 2.92 | 2.00 | 2.67 | 1.24 | 0.41 | 1.16 | 0.75 | 0.91 | 1.27 | 1.02 |
| Earnings | 1.74 | -0.06 | 1.65 | 0.37 | 0.42 | 0.81 | 0.19 | 0.68 | 1.00 | 0.74 |
| S&P Core Earnings | 1.94 | 0.32 | 1.23 | -0.03 | -0.26 | 0.59 | 0.02 | NA | NA | NA |
| Dividends | Nil | Nil | Nil | Nil | Nil | Nil | Nil | Nil | Nil | 0.01 |
| Payout Ratio | Nil | Nil | Nil | Nil | Nil | Nil | Nil | Nil | Nil | 1% |
| Prices:High | 76.90 | 75.34 | 77.82 | 59.14 | 52.45 | 58.55 | 64.00 | 51.88 | 31.56 | 25.00 |
| Prices:Low | 58.71 | 54.64 | 55.15 | 40.67 | 28.45 | 15.64 | 34.34 | 19.84 | 15.38 | 11.75 |
| P/E Ratio:High | 44 | NM | 47 | NM | NM | 72 | NM | 77 | 32 | 34 |
| P/E Ratio:Low | 34 | NM | 33 | NM | NM | 19 | NM | 29 | 15 | 16 |

| Income Statement Analysis (Million $) | | | | | | | | | | |
|---|---|---|---|---|---|---|---|---|---|---|
| Revenue | 3,814 | 3,187 | 2,735 | 2,201 | 1,714 | 1,080 | 982 | 752 | 635 | 673 |
| Operating Income | 1,183 | 913 | 915 | 717 | 463 | 318 | 380 | -185 | 280 | 185 |
| Depreciation | 338 | 541 | 285 | 205 | 160 | 96.0 | 118 | 41.2 | 50.2 | 45.8 |
| Interest Expense | 26.7 | 15.5 | 19.6 | 38.2 | 26.6 | 17.8 | 23.2 | 14.2 | 19.9 | 17.1 |
| Pretax Income | 732 | -63.1 | 641 | 222 | 2.82 | 207 | 56.5 | -179 | 226 | 164 |
| Effective Tax Rate | 34.9% | NM | 29.2% | 63.7% | NM | 27.3% | 93.1% | 51.9% | 37.3% | 38.2% |
| Net Income | 480 | -16.8 | 441 | 86.5 | -67.6 | 151 | 3.88 | 85.9 | 142 | 101 |
| S&P Core Earnings | 535 | 90.4 | 326 | -6.61 | -61.0 | 125 | 5.25 | NA | NA | NA |

| Balance Sheet & Other Financial Data (Million $) | | | | | | | | | | |
|---|---|---|---|---|---|---|---|---|---|---|
| Cash | 947 | 492 | 292 | 481 | 293 | 373 | 167 | 136 | 94.5 | 100 |
| Current Assets | 2,609 | 1,990 | 1,665 | 1,634 | 1,323 | 1,100 | 721 | 605 | 605 | 610 |
| Total Assets | 8,302 | 7,191 | 6,879 | 6,069 | 5,005 | 3,556 | 3,225 | 2,499 | 1,400 | 1,646 |
| Current Liabilities | 1,502 | 651 | 550 | 624 | 392 | 275 | 243 | 167 | 117 | 197 |
| Long Term Debt | 717 | 810 | 816 | 811 | 1,415 | 600 | 600 | 454 | 273 | 275 |
| Common Equity | 6,613 | 5,661 | 5,150 | 4,380 | 2,936 | 2,586 | 2,280 | 1,750 | 1,008 | 1,167 |
| Total Capital | 6,727 | 6,481 | 6,301 | 5,417 | 4,558 | 3,268 | 2,961 | 2,329 | 1,280 | 1,442 |
| Capital Expenditures | 413 | 334 | 19.2 | 187 | 260 | 220 | 171 | 72.6 | 52.9 | 55.3 |
| Cash Flow | 818 | 524 | 726 | 292 | 92.9 | 247 | 122 | 127 | 192 | 147 |
| Current Ratio | 1.7 | 3.1 | 3.0 | 2.6 | 3.4 | 4.0 | 3.0 | 3.6 | 5.2 | 3.1 |
| % Long Term Debt of Capitalization | 1.7 | 12.5 | 12.9 | 15.0 | 30.1 | 18.4 | 20.3 | 31.1 | 21.3 | 19.1 |
| % Net Income of Revenue | 12.6 | NM | 16.1 | 3.9 | NM | 14.0 | 0.4 | 11.4 | 22.4 | 15.0 |
| % Return on Assets | 6.2 | NM | 6.8 | 1.6 | NM | 4.4 | 0.2 | 4.0 | 10.1 | 7.1 |
| % Return on Equity | 7.8 | NM | 9.3 | 2.4 | NM | 6.2 | 0.1 | 5.5 | 14.6 | 9.4 |

Data as orig reptd.; bef. results of disc opers/spec. items. Per share data adj. for stk. divs.; EPS diluted. E-Estimated. NA-Not Available. NM-Not Meaningful. NR-Not Ranked. UR-Under Review.

**Office:** 500 Kendall St, Cambridge, MA 02142-1108.
**Telephone:** 617-252-7570.
**Email:** information@genzyme.com
**Website:** http://www.genzyme.com

**Chrmn, Pres & CEO:** H.A. Termeer
**COO:** M.R. Bamforth
**EVP, CFO & Chief Acctg Officer:** M.S. Wyzga
**EVP, Secy & General Counsel:** P. Wirth

**SVP & CSO:** A.E. Smith
**Investor Contact:** K. Galfetti (617-768-6563)
**Board Members:** D. A. Berthiaume, G. K. Boudreaux, R. J. Carpenter, C. Cooney, V. J. Dzau, C. Mack, III, C. Mcgillicudy, III, R. F. Syron, H. A. Termeer

**Founded:** 1991
**Domicile:** Massachusetts
**Employees:** 10,000

# Gilead Sciences Inc

**STANDARD &POOR'S**

| S&P Recommendation | BUY ★★★★☆ | Price $46.92 (as of Nov 14, 2008) | 12-Mo. Target Price $56.00 | Investment Style Large-Cap Growth |
|---|---|---|---|---|

**GICS Sector** Health Care
**Sub-Industry** Biotechnology

**Summary** This biopharmaceutical company is engaged in the discovery, development and commercialization of treatments to fight viral, bacterial and fungal infections.

## Key Stock Statistics (Source S&P, Vickers, company reports)

| | | | | | | | | |
|---|---|---|---|---|---|---|---|---|
| 52-Wk Range | $57.63– 35.60 | S&P Oper. EPS 2009**E** | 2.33 | Market Capitalization(B) | $42.721 | Beta | 0.63 |
| Trailing 12-Month EPS | $1.91 | S&P Oper. EPS 2010**E** | NA | Yield (%) | Nil | S&P 3-Yr. Proj. EPS CAGR(%) | 20 |
| Trailing 12-Month P/E | 24.6 | P/E on S&P Oper. EPS 2009**E** | 20.1 | Dividend Rate/Share | Nil | S&P Credit Rating | NA |
| $10K Invested 5 Yrs Ago | $34,589 | Common Shares Outstg. (M) | 910.5 | Institutional Ownership (%) | 92 | | |

## Price Performance

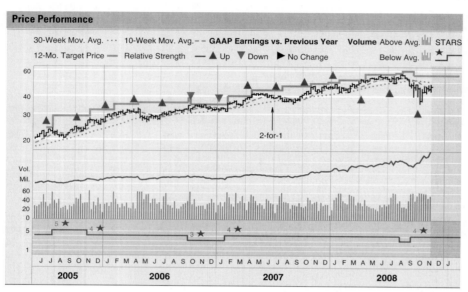

30-Week Mov. Avg. · · · ·   10-Week Mov. Avg. – –   **GAAP Earnings vs. Previous Year**   Volume Above Avg. ▮▮▮ STARS
12-Mo. Target Price —   Relative Strength —   ▲ Up  ▼ Down  ▶ No Change   Below Avg. ▮▮▮ ★

2-for-1

Options: ASE, CBOE, P, Ph

Analysis prepared by **Steven Silver** on October 21, 2008, when the stock traded at **$ 46.30**.

## Highlights

► We see 2008 product sales of $5.1 billion, up 36%, and project a further 17% rise in 2009, to $5.94 billion. We are encouraged by GILD's expanding U.S. HIV drug market share, with 63% of HIV patients on a tenofovir (Viread)-based treatment and 80% of all treatment-naive HIV patients. We think further share expansion is likely, given emerging cardiovascular concerns with chief rival GlaxoSmithKline's abacavir. Further, we see Atripla sales ramping in coming years, following European approval in late 2007, and a country-by-country launch.

► We forecast operating margins of 49% to 50% in 2008 and 2009, reduced from earlier 52% to 53% forecasts. GILD raised expense guidance, expanding investment in its pipeline, which we estimate has been consistently below peer spending levels as a percentage of sales. We believe GILD is well disciplined in managing expenses, as it has supported launch of key new products such as Letairis, which requires a comprehensive risk management program.

► Our 2008 and 2009 EPS estimates are $2.01 and $2.33, respectively. We see GILD opportunistically using its $3 billion share buyback program to support EPS and limit share dilution.

## Investment Rationale/Risk

► We view GILD as a core biotech holding with strong fundamentals. The company generated $555 million in cash from operations in the third quarter of 2008, and had $3.3 billion in cash at September 30, despite repurchasing over $1 billion of shares. In our view, GILD is well positioned to invest in its pipeline and to acquire new clinical assets despite challenges in the global economy. While HIV drugs still account for most of GILD's product sales, we see diversification from Letairis, launched in mid-2007, and recently approved Viread for Hepatitis-B. Despite a recent complete response letter, we ultimately expect approval for Aztreonam lysine for cystic fibrosis.

► Risks to our recommendation and target price include any slowdown in GILD's HIV product sales from competition or a patent challenge, failure of pipeline candidates to gain FDA approval, and increased competition in the heart failure market.

► Our 12-month target price of $56 applies a 24X multiple (1.2X our 20% long-term growth rate) to our 2009 EPS estimate, a premium to its large-cap biotech peers, on our view of GILD's dominant market position and strong cash flows.

## Qualitative Risk Assessment

| LOW | MEDIUM | HIGH |
|---|---|---|

Our risk assessment reflects Gilead's dependence on the growth of its anti-HIV drug portfolio. Also, the company operates in a highly competitive market, and failure to successfully commercialize its pipeline candidates could diminish growth expectations in the future.

## Quantitative Evaluations

**S&P Quality Ranking** B-

| D | C | B- | B | B+ | A- | A | A+ |
|---|---|---|---|---|---|---|---|

**Relative Strength Rank** STRONG

93

LOWEST = 1     HIGHEST = 99

## Revenue/Earnings Data

**Revenue (Million $)**

| | 1Q | 2Q | 3Q | 4Q | Year |
|---|---|---|---|---|---|
| 2008 | 1,258 | 1,278 | 1,371 | -- | -- |
| 2007 | 1,028 | 1,048 | 1,059 | 1,095 | 4,230 |
| 2006 | 692.9 | 685.3 | 748.7 | 899.2 | 3,026 |
| 2005 | 430.4 | 495.3 | 493.5 | 609.3 | 2,028 |
| 2004 | 309.1 | 319.7 | 326.2 | 369.6 | 1,325 |
| 2003 | 165.1 | 238.9 | 200.4 | 263.5 | 867.9 |

**Earnings Per Share ($)**

| | 1Q | 2Q | 3Q | 4Q | Year |
|---|---|---|---|---|---|
| 2008 | 0.51 | 0.46 | 0.53 | E0.52 | E2.01 |
| 2007 | 0.43 | 0.42 | 0.42 | 0.41 | 1.68 |
| 2006 | 0.28 | 0.28 | -0.06 | -1.81 | -1.30 |
| 2005 | 0.17 | 0.21 | 0.19 | 0.29 | 0.86 |
| 2004 | 0.13 | 0.12 | 0.13 | 0.12 | 0.50 |
| 2003 | -0.55 | 0.12 | 0.08 | 0.21 | -0.09 |

Fiscal year ended Dec. 31. Next earnings report expected: Late January. EPS Estimates based on S&P Operating Earnings; historical GAAP earnings are as reported.

## Dividend Data

No cash dividends have been paid.

# Gilead Sciences Inc

STANDARD &POOR'S

## Business Summary October 21, 2008

CORPORATE OVERVIEW. GILD focuses on the research, development and marketing of anti-infective medications, with a primary focus on treatments for HIV.

Truvada continues to be GILD's sales leader, with sales of $1.59 billion in 2007, 33% above 2006's $1.19 billion. Truvada, approved in 2004, is a once-daily combination tablet formulated with previous-generation drugs Viread and Emtriva. Emtriva was the lead product of Triangle Pharmaceuticals, acquired in 2003. Viread was approved in 2001 to treat HIV patients who had become resistant to other reverse transcriptase inhibitors, as well as naive patients in front-line treatment settings. Viread sales were $613 million in 2007, down 11% from $689 million in 2006.

In late 2004, GILD and Bristol-Myers Squibb (BMY) formed a joint venture for a combination tablet with Truvada and BMY's Sustiva. The formulation, marketed as Atripla, was approved and launched in July 2006. GILD books Atripla sales and then pays BMY its 37% share for the Sustiva portion of the drug, which GILD counts as cost of goods on its financial statements. Atripla generated 2007 sales of $903 million. Atripla received EU approval in December 2007 and is being launched throughout 2008. As of June 2008, Atripla was available in four of the five largest European markets, with only France yet to launch.

Hepsera was approved for treatment of Hepatitis B in the U.S. and EU in September 2002 and March 2003, respectively. GILD recorded $303 million of Hepsera sales in 2007, up 31% from $231 million in 2006. GILD out-licensed Asian and Latin American rights to Hepsera to GlaxoSmithKline (GSK) in exchange for milestones and royalties. In June 2007, GILD announced Phase III results for its HIV drug Viread, in treating chronic Hepatitis-B, meeting its primary endpoint of non-inferiority to Hepsera. GILD received FDA approval for this indication in August 2008.

AmBisome is a liposomal formulation of amphotericin B, an antifungal agent that attacks a broad variety of life-threatening fungal infections. AmBisome is co-marketed in the U.S. with Fujisawa Healthcare, and is also approved by the FDA to treat cryptococcal meningitis in AIDS patients. Sales were $263 million in 2007, up 18% from $223 million in 2006.

## Company Financials Fiscal Year Ended Dec. 31

| Per Share Data ($) | 2008 | 2007 | 2006 | 2005 | 2004 | 2003 | 2002 | 2001 | 2000 | 1999 |
|---|---|---|---|---|---|---|---|---|---|---|
| Tangible Book Value | NA | 3.71 | 1.97 | 3.30 | 2.09 | 1.17 | 0.72 | 0.58 | 0.47 | 0.42 |
| Cash Flow | NA | 1.71 | -1.24 | 0.90 | 0.51 | -0.06 | 0.10 | 0.08 | -0.04 | -0.08 |
| Earnings | 1.98 | 1.68 | -1.30 | 0.86 | 0.50 | -0.09 | 0.09 | 0.06 | -0.06 | -0.10 |
| S&P Core Earnings | NA | 1.67 | -1.29 | 0.78 | 0.39 | -0.17 | 0.01 | -0.14 | NA | NA |
| Dividends | Nil | Nil | Nil | Nil | Nil | Nil | Nil | Nil | Nil | Nil |
| Payout Ratio | Nil | Nil | Nil | Nil | Nil | Nil | Nil | Nil | Nil | Nil |
| Prices:High | 57.63 | 47.90 | 35.00 | 28.26 | 19.55 | 17.65 | 10.00 | 9.21 | 7.38 | 5.97 |
| Prices:Low | 42.16 | 30.96 | 26.24 | 15.20 | 12.88 | 7.81 | 6.52 | 3.11 | 2.70 | 2.20 |
| P/E Ratio:High | 29 | 29 | NM | 33 | 39 | NM | NM | NM | NM | NM |
| P/E Ratio:Low | 21 | 18 | NM | 18 | 26 | NM | NM | NM | NM | NM |

| Income Statement Analysis (Million $) | 2008 | 2007 | 2006 | 2005 | 2004 | 2003 | 2002 | 2001 | 2000 | 1999 |
|---|---|---|---|---|---|---|---|---|---|---|
| Revenue | NA | 4,230 | 3,026 | 2,028 | 1,325 | 868 | 467 | 234 | 196 | 169 |
| Operating Income | NA | 2,201 | 1,683 | 1,148 | 656 | 361 | 95.4 | -106 | -40.3 | -39.2 |
| Depreciation | NA | 36.9 | 47.3 | 36.8 | 24.4 | 20.9 | 14.4 | 14.7 | 12.0 | 12.6 |
| Interest Expense | NA | 13.5 | 20.4 | 0.44 | 7.35 | 21.9 | 13.9 | 14.0 | Nil | 6.52 |
| Pretax Income | NA | 2,261 | -644 | 1,158 | 656 | -168 | 73.4 | 55.3 | -41.9 | -65.6 |
| Effective Tax Rate | NA | 29.0% | NM | 30.0% | 31.5% | NM | 1.77% | 7.48% | NM | NM |
| Net Income | NA | 1,615 | -1,190 | 814 | 449 | -72.0 | 72.1 | 51.2 | -43.1 | -66.5 |
| S&P Core Earnings | NA | 1,610 | -1,188 | 737 | 354 | -133 | 8.55 | -108 | NA | NA |

| Balance Sheet & Other Financial Data (Million $) | 2008 | 2007 | 2006 | 2005 | 2004 | 2003 | 2002 | 2001 | 2000 | 1999 |
|---|---|---|---|---|---|---|---|---|---|---|
| Cash | NA | 1,172 | 937 | 2,324 | 1,254 | 707 | 942 | 583 | 513 | 294 |
| Current Assets | NA | 3,028 | 2,429 | 3,092 | 1,850 | 1,266 | 1,184 | 708 | 594 | 372 |
| Total Assets | NA | 5,835 | 4,086 | 3,765 | 2,156 | 1,555 | 1,288 | 795 | 678 | 437 |
| Current Liabilities | NA | 736 | 764 | 455 | 253 | 186 | 105 | 80.1 | 58.2 | 47.9 |
| Long Term Debt | NA | 1,301 | 1,300 | 241 | 0.23 | 345 | 595 | 250 | 252 | 84.8 |
| Common Equity | NA | 3,460 | 1,816 | 3,028 | 1,871 | 1,003 | 571 | 452 | 351 | 297 |
| Total Capital | NA | 4,772 | 3,169 | 3,277 | 1,871 | 1,348 | 1,166 | 703 | 603 | 382 |
| Capital Expenditures | NA | 78.7 | 105 | 2,226 | 51.4 | 38.6 | 17.6 | 26.3 | 15.6 | 12.5 |
| Cash Flow | NA | 1,652 | -1,143 | 851 | 474 | -51.1 | 86.5 | 65.9 | -31.1 | -53.9 |
| Current Ratio | NA | 4.1 | 3.2 | 6.8 | 7.3 | 6.8 | 11.3 | 8.8 | 10.2 | 7.8 |
| % Long Term Debt of Capitalization | NA | 27.2 | 41.0 | 7.3 | NM | 25.6 | 51.0 | 35.6 | 41.8 | 22.2 |
| % Net Income of Revenue | NA | 38.2 | NM | 40.1 | 33.9 | NM | 15.4 | 21.9 | NM | NM |
| % Return on Assets | NA | 32.6 | NM | 27.5 | 24.2 | NM | 6.9 | 6.9 | NM | NM |
| % Return on Equity | NA | 61.2 | NM | 33.2 | 31.3 | NM | 14.1 | 12.7 | NM | NM |

Data as orig reptd.; bef. results of disc opers/spec. items. Per share data adj. for stk. divs.; EPS diluted. E-Estimated. NA-Not Available. NM-Not Meaningful. NR-Not Ranked. UR-Under Review.

**Office:** 333 Lakeside Drive, Foster City, CA 94404.
**Telephone:** 650-574-3000.
**Email:** investor_relations@gilead.com
**Website:** http://www.gilead.com

**Chrmn & CEO:** J.C. Martin
**Pres & COO:** J.F. Milligan
**EVP & CSO:** N.W. Bischofberger
**SVP & CFO:** R.L. Washington

**SVP, Secy & General Counsel:** G.H. Alton
**Investor Contact:** S. Hubbard (650 522-5715)
**Board Members:** P. Berg, J. F. Cogan, E. Davignon, J. M. Denny, C. Hills, J. W. Madigan, J. C. Martin, G. E. Moore, N. G. Moore, R. Whitley, G. E. Wilson

**Founded:** 1987
**Domicile:** Delaware
**Employees:** 2,979

The McGraw-Hill Companies

# Goldman Sachs Group Inc. (The)

STANDARD
&POOR'S

| **S&P Recommendation** HOLD ★★★☆☆ | **Price** $66.73 (as of Nov 14, 2008) | **12-Mo. Target Price** $95.00 | **Investment Style** Large-Cap Growth |
|---|---|---|---|

**GICS Sector** Financials
**Sub-Industry** Investment Banking & Brokerage

**Summary** Goldman Sachs is one of the world's leading investment banking and securities companies.

## Key Stock Statistics (Source S&P, Vickers, company reports)

| | | | | | | | |
|---|---|---|---|---|---|---|---|
| 52-Wk Range | $234.22–61.02 | S&P Oper. EPS 2008**E** | 9.91 | Market Capitalization(B) | $26.388 | Beta | 1.66 |
| Trailing 12-Month EPS | $16.64 | S&P Oper. EPS 2009**E** | 10.49 | Yield (%) | 2.10 | S&P 3-Yr. Proj. EPS CAGR(%) | -19 |
| Trailing 12-Month P/E | 4.0 | P/E on S&P Oper. EPS 2008**E** | 6.7 | Dividend Rate/Share | $1.40 | S&P Credit Rating | AA- |
| $10K Invested 5 Yrs Ago | $7,431 | Common Shares Outstg. (M) | 395.4 | Institutional Ownership (%) | 70 | | |

## Price Performance

30-Week Mov. Avg. · · · · 10-Week Mov. Avg. – – **GAAP Earnings vs. Previous Year** Volume Above Avg. ||||| STARS
12-Mo. Target Price — Relative Strength — ▲ Up ▼ Down ► No Change Below Avg. ||||| 

Options: ASE, CBOE, P, Ph

Analysis prepared by **Matthew Albrecht** on November 12, 2008, when the stock traded at **$ 70.00**.

## Highlights

➤ We believe worsening market conditions will challenge the firm in the year ahead, with credit market struggles causing a decline in M&A activities and reduced underwriting volume. Asset management and prime brokerage operations have been solid performers, but writedowns of leveraged loans and commercial mortgage exposure will likely continue to pressure results. GS's transition to a commercial bank holding company is underway, with the company having raised capital. We expect additional deleveraging as part of the process, and restraints placed on risk at trading desks, as part of a two year transition. We see net revenues declining sharply in FY 08 (Nov.), and declines may persist in FY 09, but the rate of descent should slow.

➤ We look for compensation to consistently approximate 47% of net revenues, but we believe non-compensation expense growth will outpace net revenue growth in the current year, reducing the pretax margin, followed by expansion in FY 09.

➤ We look for earnings per share of $9.91 in FY 08 and $10.49 in FY 09.

## Investment Rationale/Risk

➤ We believe the company's original partnership structure has contributed to an ownership culture within the company, resulting in a competitive advantage for GS. The shares have traditionally traded at a premium valuation to peers, which we believe is based on the company's global reach, significant operating leverage, client relationships, peer-best return on equity and solid balance sheet. We expect that premium to narrow relative to peers as the company transitions to a bank holding company, and its future earnings power remains in question.

➤ Risks to our recommendation and target price include stock and bond market depreciation, sharply higher interest rates, widening credit spreads, and greater regulatory scrutiny. We think GS's global business model also adds risk due to its exposure to geopolitical issues.

➤ The shares recently traded at about 7.1X our FY 08 EPS estimate and 0.8X current tangible book value per share, discounts to historical multiples and the S&P 500. Our 12-month target price of $95 is based on a price-to-tangible book multiple of about 1.0X applied to our 12-month tangible book value projection, in line with peers.

## Qualitative Risk Assessment

| LOW | MEDIUM | HIGH |
|---|---|---|

Our risk assessment reflects our view of the company's global footprint and strong client relationships, offset by industry cyclicality and its high leverage ratio.

## Quantitative Evaluations

**S&P Quality Ranking** A-

| D | C | B- | B | B+ | A- | A | A+ |
|---|---|---|---|---|---|---|---|

**Relative Strength Rank** WEAK

19

LOWEST = 1          HIGHEST = 99

## Revenue/Earnings Data

**Revenue (Million $)**

| | 1Q | 2Q | 3Q | 4Q | Year |
|---|---|---|---|---|---|
| 2008 | 18,629 | 17,643 | 13,625 | -- | -- |
| 2007 | 22,280 | 20,351 | 23,803 | 21,534 | 87,968 |
| 2006 | 17,246 | 18,002 | 15,979 | 18,126 | 69,353 |
| 2005 | 9,964 | 8,949 | 12,333 | 12,145 | 43,391 |
| 2004 | 7,905 | 7,676 | 6,803 | 7,455 | 29,839 |
| 2003 | 6,094 | 5,985 | 5,715 | 5,829 | 23,623 |

**Earnings Per Share ($)**

| | | | | | |
|---|---|---|---|---|---|
| 2008 | 3.24 | 4.58 | 1.81 | E0.28 | E9.91 |
| 2007 | 6.67 | 4.93 | 1.81 | 7.01 | 24.73 |
| 2006 | 5.08 | 4.78 | 3.26 | 6.59 | 19.69 |
| 2005 | 2.94 | 1.71 | 3.25 | 3.35 | 11.21 |
| 2004 | 2.50 | 2.31 | 1.74 | 2.36 | 8.92 |
| 2003 | 1.29 | 1.36 | 1.32 | 1.89 | 5.87 |

Fiscal year ended Nov. 30. Next earnings report expected: NA. EPS Estimates based on S&P Operating Earnings; historical GAAP earnings are as reported.

## Dividend Data (Dates: mm/dd Payment Date: mm/dd/yy)

| Amount ($) | Date Decl. | Ex-Div. Date | Stk. of Record | Payment Date |
|---|---|---|---|---|
| 0.350 | 12/18 | 01/25 | 01/29 | 02/28/08 |
| 0.350 | 03/18 | 04/25 | 04/29 | 05/29/08 |
| 0.350 | 06/17 | 07/25 | 07/29 | 08/28/08 |
| 0.350 | 09/16 | 10/23 | 10/27 | 11/24/08 |

Dividends have been paid since 1999. Source: Company reports.

---

**Please read the Required Disclosures and Analyst Certification on the last page of this report.**

The McGraw-Hill Companies

# Goldman Sachs Group Inc. (The)

**STANDARD &POOR'S**

## Business Summary November 12, 2008

CORPORATE OVERVIEW. Goldman Sachs (GS) is a global investment banking, securities and investment management firm that provides a wide range of services to corporations, financial institutions, governments and high-net-worth individuals. GS operates through three core businesses: Trading and Principal Investments, Investment Banking, and Asset Management and Securities Services.

The Trading and Principal Investments business (68% of FY 07-Nov. net revenues) facilitates customer transactions with a diverse group of corporations, financial institutions, governments and individuals, and takes proprietary positions through market making in, and trading of, fixed income and equity products, currencies, commodities and derivatives. The activities of the Trading and Principal Investments business can be grouped under three segments: Fixed Income, Currency and Commodities (FICC); Equities; and Principal Investments. The FICC business makes markets in and trades interest rate and credit products, mortgage-backed securities, loans and other asset-backed securities, currencies and commodities. The Equities business makes markets in, trades, and acts as a specialist for equities and equity-related products. It

generates commissions from executing and clearing client transactions on major stock, options, and futures exchanges worldwide through its Equities customer franchise and clearing activities.

The Principal Investments business primarily represents net revenues from corporate and real estate merchant banking investments. These net revenues are from four primary sources -- returns on corporate and real estate investments, its investment in the convertible preferred stock of Sumitomo Mitsui Financial Group, Inc. (SMFG), its investment in the ordinary shares of Industrial and Commercial Bank of China Limited (ICBC), and overrides. Overrides represent net revenues from the increased share of the income and gains derived from GS's merchant banking funds when the return on a fund's investments exceeds certain threshold returns.

## Company Financials Fiscal Year Ended Nov. 30

| Per Share Data ($) | 2007 | 2006 | 2005 | 2004 | 2003 | 2002 | 2001 | 2000 | 1999 | 1998 |
|---|---|---|---|---|---|---|---|---|---|---|
| Tangible Book Value | 101.62 | 119.66 | 52.15 | 52.14 | 45.73 | 40.18 | 38.30 | 34.15 | 22.65 | NA |
| Cash Flow | 27.68 | 20.78 | 12.22 | 9.90 | 6.97 | 5.20 | 5.39 | 6.94 | 6.27 | NA |
| Earnings | 24.73 | 19.69 | 11.21 | 8.92 | 5.87 | 4.03 | 4.26 | 6.00 | 5.27 | 2.62 |
| S&P Core Earnings | 24.76 | 19.72 | 11.12 | 8.63 | 5.26 | 3.30 | 3.60 | NA | NA | NA |
| Dividends | 1.40 | 1.30 | 1.00 | 1.00 | 0.74 | 0.48 | 0.48 | 0.48 | 0.24 | NA |
| Payout Ratio | 6% | 7% | 9% | 11% | 13% | 12% | 11% | 8% | 4% | NA |
| Prices:High | 250.70 | 206.70 | 134.99 | 110.88 | 100.78 | 97.25 | 120.00 | 133.63 | 94.81 | NA |
| Prices:Low | 157.38 | 124.23 | 94.75 | 83.29 | 61.02 | 58.57 | 63.27 | 65.50 | 53.00 | NA |
| P/E Ratio:High | 10 | 10 | 12 | 12 | 17 | 24 | 28 | 22 | 17 | NA |
| P/E Ratio:Low | 6 | 6 | 8 | 9 | 10 | 15 | 15 | 11 | 10 | NA |

| Income Statement Analysis (Million $) | | | | | | | | | | |
|---|---|---|---|---|---|---|---|---|---|---|
| Commissions | 12,286 | 10,140 | 6,689 | 5,941 | 4,317 | 3,273 | 3,020 | 2,307 | Nil | 3,368 |
| Interest Income | 45,968 | 35,186 | 21,250 | 11,914 | 10,751 | 11,269 | 16,620 | 17,396 | 12,722 | NA |
| Total Revenue | 87,968 | 69,353 | 43,391 | 29,839 | 23,623 | 22,854 | 31,138 | 33,000 | 25,363 | 22,478 |
| Interest Expense | 41,981 | 31,688 | 18,153 | 8,888 | 7,600 | 8,868 | 15,327 | 16,410 | 12,018 | 13,986 |
| Pretax Income | 17,604 | 14,560 | 8,273 | 6,676 | 4,445 | 3,253 | 3,696 | 5,020 | 1,992 | 2,129 |
| Effective Tax Rate | 34.1% | 34.5% | 32.0% | 31.8% | 32.4% | 35.0% | 37.5% | 38.9% | NM | 41.0% |
| Net Income | 11,599 | 9,537 | 5,626 | 4,553 | 3,005 | 2,114 | 2,310 | 3,067 | 2,708 | 1,256 |
| S&P Core Earnings | 11,419 | 9,416 | 5,560 | 4,406 | 2,693 | 1,737 | 1,949 | NA | NA | NA |

| Balance Sheet & Other Financial Data (Million $) | | | | | | | | | | |
|---|---|---|---|---|---|---|---|---|---|---|
| Total Assets | 1,119,796 | 838,201 | 706,804 | 531,379 | 403,799 | 355,574 | 312,218 | 289,760 | 250,491 | 231,796 |
| Cash Items | 131,821 | 87,283 | 61,666 | 52,544 | 36,802 | 25,211 | 29,043 | 21,002 | 12,190 | 2,702 |
| Receivables | 425,596 | 312,355 | 75,381 | 52,545 | 36,377 | 28,938 | 33,463 | 159,019 | 150,154 | NA |
| Securities Owned | 452,595 | 416,687 | 238,043 | 183,880 | 160,719 | 129,775 | 108,885 | 95,260 | 81,809 | NA |
| Securities Borrowed | 28,624 | 22,208 | 23,331 | 19,394 | 17,528 | 12,238 | 81,579 | 40,211 | 49,352 | NA |
| Due Brokers & Customers | 318,453 | 223,874 | 188,318 | 161,221 | 109,028 | 95,590 | 97,297 | 82,148 | 59,534 | NA |
| Other Liabilities | 38,907 | 31,866 | 13,830 | 10,360 | 8,144 | 6,002 | 7,129 | 11,116 | 110,508 | NA |
| Capitalization:Debt | 164,174 | 122,842 | 100,007 | 80,696 | 57,482 | 38,711 | 31,016 | 31,395 | 20,952 | 20,776 |
| Capitalization:Equity | 39,700 | 32,686 | 26,252 | 25,079 | 21,632 | 19,003 | 18,231 | 16,530 | 10,145 | 7,627 |
| Capitalization:Total | 206,974 | 189,521 | 128,009 | 105,775 | 79,114 | 57,714 | 49,247 | 47,925 | 31,097 | 28,403 |
| % Return on Revenue | 13.1 | 13.8 | 13.0 | 15.3 | 12.7 | 9.3 | 7.4 | 9.3 | 10.7 | 5.6 |
| % Return on Assets | 1.1 | 1.2 | 0.9 | 1.0 | 0.8 | 0.6 | 0.8 | 1.1 | 1.2 | 1.2 |
| % Return on Equity | 32.0 | 31.9 | 21.9 | 19.5 | 14.8 | 11.4 | 13.3 | 23.0 | 30.4 | 37.6 |

Data as orig reptd.; bef. results of disc opers/spec. items. Per share data adj. for stk. divs.; EPS diluted. E-Estimated. NA-Not Available. NM-Not Meaningful. NR-Not Ranked. UR-Under Review.

**Office:** 85 Broad Street, New York, NY 10004.
**Telephone:** 212-902-1000.
**Email:** gs-investor-relations@gs.com
**Website:** http://www.gs.com

**Chrmn & CEO:** L.C. Blankfein
**COO & Co-Pres:** G.D. Cohn
**COO & Co-Pres:** J. Winkelried
**EVP & CFO:** D.A. Viniar

**EVP, Secy & General Counsel:** E.E. Stecher
**Investor Contact:** J. Andrews (212-357-2674)
**Auditor:** PricewaterhouseCoopers
**Board Members:** L. C. Blankfein, J. H. Bryan, Jr., G. D. Cohn, C. Dahlback, S. Friedman, W. W. George, R. K. Gupta, J. A. Johnson, L. D. Juliber, L. N. Mittal, R. J. Simmons, S. Wang, J. Winkelried

**Founded:** 1869
**Domicile:** Delaware
**Employees:** 30,522

*The McGraw-Hill Companies*

# Goodrich Corp

**STANDARD &POOR'S**

| S&P Recommendation HOLD ★★★☆☆ | Price $32.08 (as of Nov 14, 2008) | 12-Mo. Target Price $40.00 | Investment Style Large-Cap Value |
|---|---|---|---|

**GICS Sector** Industrials
**Sub-Industry** Aerospace & Defense

**Summary** This company is one of the world's largest providers of equipment, parts and services to the large commercial, regional, business and military jet markets.

## Key Stock Statistics (Source S&P, Vickers, company reports)

| | | | | | | | |
|---|---|---|---|---|---|---|---|
| 52-Wk Range | $75.74– 28.22 | S&P Oper. EPS 2008E | 4.95 | Market Capitalization(B) | $3.949 | Beta | 1.74 |
| Trailing 12-Month EPS | $5.06 | S&P Oper. EPS 2009E | 5.10 | Yield (%) | 3.12 | S&P 3-Yr. Proj. EPS CAGR(%) | 8 |
| Trailing 12-Month P/E | 6.3 | P/E on S&P Oper. EPS 2008E | 6.5 | Dividend Rate/Share | $1.00 | S&P Credit Rating | BBB+ |
| $10K Invested 5 Yrs Ago | $13,207 | Common Shares Outstg. (M) | 123.1 | Institutional Ownership (%) | 86 | | |

## Price Performance

30-Week Mov. Avg. ⋯ 10-Week Mov. Avg. – – **GAAP Earnings vs. Previous Year** Volume Above Avg. STARS
12-Mo. Target Price — Relative Strength — ▲ Up ▼ Down ▶ No Change Below Avg. ★

Options: ASE, CBOE, P, Ph

Analysis prepared by **Richard Tortoriello** on October 29, 2008, when the stock traded at **$ 35.87**.

## Highlights

> We project 2008 revenues of $7.1 billion, up about 11% from 2007. We see a number of industry trends currently favoring GR's business lines, including a strong large-commercial jet demand cycle, increased global fleet sizes, and aging aircraft in the U.S. However, we also see the likelihood of slowing aftermarket parts and service and business jet demand due to high jet fuel prices and a weakening global economy. We forecast revenue growth will slow to 8% in 2009.

> We expect operating margins of 16.8% in 2008, up from 16.1% in 2007, on increased volume and productivity, offset by a change in mix away from aftermarket services and toward lower-margin original equipment manufacturer (OEM) parts. For 2009, we project an operating margin decrease to 16.3%.

> We estimate 2008 EPS of $4.95, up from EPS of $3.89 in 2007, with growth to $5.10 seen in 2009. We expect free cash flow (cash generated from operations less capital expenditures) of over $3.50 per share, up from $2.64 in 2007.

## Investment Rationale/Risk

> We see strong commercial aviation jet deliveries in 2008 and 2009, but expect results at GR to be constrained by slowing demand for aftermarket parts and services due to slowing growth in global air traffic. Total aftermarket sales rose 16% in 2007, but the company projects growth slowing to 9% to 11% in 2008 and 4% to 7% in 2009. In the aftermarket, GR is benefiting from its strong positions on newer aircraft. Boeing (10% of GR revenues) and Airbus (15%) had backlogs spanning several years of production as of September 2008.

> Risks to our recommendation and target price include the potential for a severe global economic slowdown, the possibility of slowing defense industry orders, and operational and other missteps at GR.

> Our 12-month target price of $40 is based on an enterprise value to estimated 2008 EBITDA multiple of 5.0X. Over the past 10 years, GR's average EV to EBITDA multiple has been 7.8X, with bear market lows near 5.0X. Although we see valuation multiples in the current market dipping below historical benchmarks, we view a 5.0X multiple as appropriate for the shares.

## Qualitative Risk Assessment

| LOW | MEDIUM | HIGH |
|---|---|---|

Our risk assessment reflects GR's history of cyclical earnings growth and its long record of dividend payments, offset by a lack of growth in dividends, as reflected by an S&P Quality Ranking of B (below average). We also take into account GR's recent long-term debt to capital ratio of 36%, which is slightly above average for peers in the aerospace & defense sub-industry.

## Quantitative Evaluations

**S&P Quality Ranking**     **B**

| D | C | B- | **B** | B+ | A- | A | A+ |
|---|---|---|---|---|---|---|---|

**Relative Strength Rank**     **MODERATE**

54

LOWEST = 1        HIGHEST = 99

## Revenue/Earnings Data

**Revenue (Million $)**

| | 1Q | 2Q | 3Q | 4Q | Year |
|---|---|---|---|---|---|
| 2008 | 1,745 | 1,849 | 1,772 | -- | -- |
| 2007 | 1,589 | 1,622 | 1,602 | 1,668 | 6,392 |
| 2006 | 1,424 | 1,483 | 1,436 | 1,535 | 5,878 |
| 2005 | 1,276 | 1,353 | 1,371 | 1,398 | 5,397 |
| 2004 | 1,162 | 1,134 | 1,167 | 1,262 | 4,725 |
| 2003 | 1,094 | 1,095 | 1,064 | 1,130 | 4,383 |

**Earnings Per Share ($)**

| | 1Q | 2Q | 3Q | 4Q | Year |
|---|---|---|---|---|---|
| 2008 | 1.21 | 1.44 | 1.33 | E0.97 | E4.95 |
| 2007 | 0.78 | 0.98 | 1.10 | 1.05 | 3.89 |
| 2006 | 1.59 | 0.64 | 0.80 | 0.78 | 3.80 |
| 2005 | 0.46 | 0.51 | 0.49 | 0.51 | 1.97 |
| 2004 | 0.26 | 0.32 | 0.41 | 0.30 | 1.30 |
| 2003 | -0.28 | 0.12 | 0.29 | 0.19 | 0.33 |

Fiscal year ended Dec. 31. Next earnings report expected: Early February. EPS Estimates based on S&P Operating Earnings; historical GAAP earnings are as reported.

## Dividend Data (Dates: mm/dd Payment Date: mm/dd/yy)

| Amount ($) | Date Decl. | Ex-Div. Date | Stk. of Record | Payment Date |
|---|---|---|---|---|
| 0.225 | 02/19 | 02/28 | 03/03 | 04/01/08 |
| 0.225 | 04/22 | 05/29 | 06/02 | 07/01/08 |
| 0.225 | 07/23 | 08/28 | 09/02 | 10/01/08 |
| 0.250 | 10/21 | 11/26 | 12/01 | 01/02/09 |

Dividends have been paid since 1939. Source: Company reports.

**Please read the Required Disclosures and Analyst Certification on the last page of this report.**

The McGraw-Hill Companies

# Goodrich Corp

**STANDARD &POOR'S**

## Business Summary October 29, 2008

CORPORATE OVERVIEW. Goodrich Corp., a global aircraft components maker and services provider, is also a leading supplier of systems and products to the global defense and aerospace markets. Operations are divided into three segments.

Nacelles and Interior Systems (34% of revenues and 52% of operating profits in 2007) manufactures products and provides maintenance, repair and overhaul associated with aircraft engines, including thrust reversers, cowlings, nozzles and their components (a nacelle is the structure that surrounds an aircraft engine and includes all of the foregoing items), and aircraft interior products, including slides, seats, and cargo and lighting systems. N&IS's largest customers include Airbus, Boeing, Rolls-Royce and global airlines. Primary competitors in this market include Aircelle (a subsidiary of SAFRAN), GE, and Spirit Aerosystems.

Actuation and Landing Systems (38% and 24%) provides systems, components and related services pertaining to aircraft taxi, takeoff, flight control, landing and stopping, as well as engine components, including fuel delivery systems and rotating assemblies. Key products include actuation systems, which use linear, rotary or fly-by-wire actuation to control movement; landing gear; aircraft wheels and brakes. A&LS and Messier-Dowty (a division of France-based SNECMA) each control about 50% of the global landing gear market.

Competitors in other markets include Honeywell (wheels and brakes), Parker Hannifin (actuation), and United Technologies (actuation).

The unit is also a major global provider of aircraft maintenance, repair and overhaul (MRO) services. A&LS's MRO customers mostly comprise the world's major airlines and aircraft leasing companies. Primary aircraft maintenance competitors include TIMCO Aviation Services, SIA Engineering Co., Singapore Technologies and Lufthansa Technik.

Electronic Systems (28% and 24%) produces a wide array of systems and components that provide flight performance measurements, flight management, fuel controls, electrical systems, and control and safety data, as well as reconnaissance and surveillance systems. Key products include sensor systems: aircraft and engine sensors that provide critical measurements for flight control, cockpit information, and engine control systems; and power systems: aircraft electrical power for large commercial airplanes, business jets, and helicopters. Competitors include Honeywell, Thales, United Technologies, and BAE Systems.

## Company Financials Fiscal Year Ended Dec. 31

| Per Share Data ($) | 2007 | 2006 | 2005 | 2004 | 2003 | 2002 | 2001 | 2000 | 1999 | 1998 |
|---|---|---|---|---|---|---|---|---|---|---|
| Tangible Book Value | 7.15 | 1.31 | NM | NM | NM | NM | 4.66 | 3.48 | 1.41 | 9.63 |
| Cash Flow | 5.48 | 5.78 | 3.79 | 3.18 | 2.18 | 3.31 | 3.28 | 4.39 | 3.62 | 5.25 |
| Earnings | 3.89 | 3.80 | 1.97 | 1.30 | 0.33 | 1.57 | 1.65 | 2.68 | 1.53 | 3.04 |
| S&P Core Earnings | 3.77 | 3.94 | 2.10 | 1.57 | 0.42 | 0.42 | 0.41 | NA | NA | NA |
| Dividends | 0.83 | 1.00 | 0.80 | 0.80 | 0.80 | 0.88 | 1.10 | 1.10 | 1.10 | 1.10 |
| Payout Ratio | 21% | 26% | 41% | 62% | 242% | 56% | 67% | 41% | 72% | 36% |
| Prices:High | 75.74 | 47.45 | 45.82 | 33.90 | 30.30 | 34.45 | 44.50 | 43.13 | 45.69 | 56.00 |
| Prices:Low | 44.97 | 37.15 | 30.11 | 26.60 | 12.20 | 14.17 | 15.91 | 21.56 | 21.00 | 26.50 |
| P/E Ratio:High | 19 | 12 | 23 | 26 | 92 | 22 | 27 | 16 | 30 | 18 |
| P/E Ratio:Low | 12 | 10 | 15 | 20 | 37 | 9 | 10 | 8 | 14 | 9 |

| Income Statement Analysis (Million $) | 2007 | 2006 | 2005 | 2004 | 2003 | 2002 | 2001 | 2000 | 1999 | 1998 |
|---|---|---|---|---|---|---|---|---|---|---|
| Revenue | 6,392 | 5,878 | 5,397 | 4,725 | 4,383 | 3,910 | 4,185 | 4,364 | 5,538 | 3,951 |
| Operating Income | 1,086 | 886 | 759 | 636 | 515 | 586 | 666 | 830 | 973 | 653 |
| Depreciation | 205 | 240 | 226 | 223 | 219 | 184 | 174 | 193 | 231 | 165 |
| Interest Expense | 130 | 126 | 131 | 143 | 163 | 117 | 118 | 129 | 138 | 79.0 |
| Pretax Income | 717 | 462 | 375 | 199 | 61.3 | 259 | 271 | 443 | 316 | 374 |
| Effective Tax Rate | 30.8% | NM | 31.8% | 21.7% | 37.2% | 36.0% | 34.8% | 35.4% | 46.3% | 39.1% |
| Net Income | 496 | 481 | 244 | 156 | 38.5 | 166 | 177 | 286 | 170 | 228 |
| S&P Core Earnings | 482 | 499 | 260 | 189 | 48.6 | 44.9 | 44.7 | NA | NA | NA |

| Balance Sheet & Other Financial Data (Million $) | 2007 | 2006 | 2005 | 2004 | 2003 | 2002 | 2001 | 2000 | 1999 | 1998 |
|---|---|---|---|---|---|---|---|---|---|---|
| Cash | 406 | 201 | 251 | 298 | 378 | 150 | 85.8 | 77.5 | 66.4 | 31.7 |
| Current Assets | 3,549 | 3,008 | 2,425 | 2,357 | 2,087 | 2,008 | 1,921 | 3,080 | 2,101 | 1,615 |
| Total Assets | 7,534 | 6,901 | 6,454 | 6,218 | 5,890 | 5,990 | 4,638 | 5,718 | 5,456 | 4,193 |
| Current Liabilities | 1,743 | 1,633 | 1,615 | 1,565 | 1,401 | 1,554 | 1,159 | 2,147 | 1,511 | 991 |
| Long Term Debt | 1,563 | 1,722 | 1,742 | 1,899 | 2,137 | 2,254 | 1,432 | 1,590 | 1,788 | 995 |
| Common Equity | 2,579 | 1,977 | 1,473 | 1,343 | 1,194 | 933 | 1,361 | 1,227 | 1,293 | 1,600 |
| Total Capital | 4,313 | 3,756 | 3,215 | 3,276 | 3,330 | 3,187 | 2,808 | 2,819 | 3,208 | 2,718 |
| Capital Expenditures | 283 | 257 | 216 | 152 | 125 | 107 | 191 | 148 | 246 | 209 |
| Cash Flow | 701 | 721 | 470 | 379 | 258 | 349 | 351 | 479 | 400 | 394 |
| Current Ratio | 2.0 | 1.8 | 1.5 | 1.5 | 1.5 | 1.5 | 1.3 | 1.7 | 1.4 | 1.4 | 1.6 |
| % Long Term Debt of Capitalization | 36.2 | 45.8 | 54.2 | 58.0 | 64.2 | 70.7 | 51.0 | 56.4 | 55.7 | 36.6 |
| % Net Income of Revenue | 7.8 | 8.2 | 4.5 | 3.3 | 0.9 | 4.2 | 4.2 | 6.6 | 3.1 | 5.8 |
| % Return on Assets | 6.9 | 7.2 | 3.8 | 2.6 | 0.6 | 3.0 | 3.6 | 5.3 | 3.2 | 5.9 |
| % Return on Equity | 21.8 | 27.9 | 17.3 | 12.3 | 3.6 | 14.5 | 13.7 | 22.7 | 13.4 | 15.1 |

Data as orig reptd.; bef. results of disc opers/spec. items. Per share data adj. for stk. divs.; EPS diluted. E-Estimated. NA-Not Available. NM-Not Meaningful. NR-Not Ranked. UR-Under Review.

**Office:** Four Coliseum Centre, Charlotte, NC 28217-4578.
**Telephone:** 704-423-7000.
**Website:** http://www.goodrich.com
**Chrmn, Pres & CEO:** M.O. Larsen

**COO & CTO:** J. Witowski
**EVP & CFO:** S.E. Kuechle
**Chief Admin Officer & General Counsel:** T.G. Linnert
**Chief Acctg Officer & Cntlr:** S. Cottrill

**Investor Contact:** P. Gifford (704-423-5517)
**Board Members:** D. C. Creel, G. A. Davidson, Jr., H. E. Deloach, Jr., J. W. Griffith, W. R. Holland, J. P. Jumper, M. O. Larsen, L. W. Newton, D. E. Olesen, A. M. Rankin, Jr., A. T. Young

**Founded:** 1912
**Domicile:** New York
**Employees:** 23,400

The McGraw·Hill Companies

# Goodyear Tire & Rubber Co

STANDARD &POOR'S

| S&P Recommendation | BUY ★★★★☆ | Price | 12-Mo. Target Price | Investment Style |
|---|---|---|---|---|
| | | $5.42 (as of Nov 14, 2008) | $14.00 | Large-Cap Blend |

**GICS Sector** Consumer Discretionary
**Sub-Industry** Tires & Rubber

**Summary** GT is the largest U.S. manufacturer of tires, and one of the biggest worldwide. Operations also include rubber and plastic products and chemicals.

## Key Stock Statistics (Source S&P, Vickers, company reports)

| | | | | | | | |
|---|---|---|---|---|---|---|---|
| 52-Wk Range | $30.10– 5.05 | S&P Oper. EPS 2008**E** | 1.77 | Market Capitalization(B) | $1.308 | Beta | 2.23 |
| Trailing 12-Month EPS | $1.26 | S&P Oper. EPS 2009**E** | 1.95 | Yield (%) | Nil | S&P 3-Yr. Proj. EPS CAGR(%) | 25 |
| Trailing 12-Month P/E | 4.3 | P/E on S&P Oper. EPS 2008**E** | 3.1 | Dividend Rate/Share | Nil | S&P Credit Rating | BB- |
| $10K Invested 5 Yrs Ago | $8,053 | Common Shares Outstg. (M) | 241.3 | Institutional Ownership (%) | 87 | | |

## Price Performance

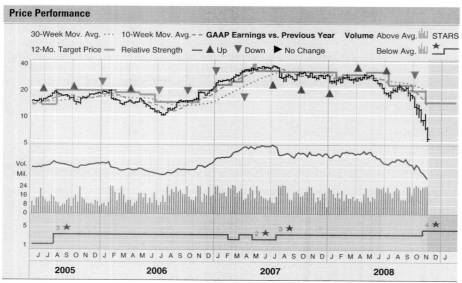

30-Week Mov. Avg. ···· 10-Week Mov. Avg. --- **GAAP Earnings vs. Previous Year** Volume Above Avg. STARS
12-Mo. Target Price — Relative Strength — ▲ Up ▼ Down ► No Change Below Avg.

Options: ASE, CBOE, P, Ph

## Qualitative Risk Assessment

| LOW | MEDIUM | HIGH |
|---|---|---|

Our risk assessment reflects the highly cyclical nature of the company's markets as well as the current and long-term challenges that we believe GT faces due to its highly leveraged balance sheet, intensifying competition, high fixed costs, and legacy costs.

## Quantitative Evaluations

**S&P Quality Ranking**     B-

| D | C | B- | B | B+ | A- | A | A+ |
|---|---|---|---|---|---|---|---|

**Relative Strength Rank**     WEAK

8

LOWEST = 1     HIGHEST = 99

## Revenue/Earnings Data

### Revenue (Million $)

| | 1Q | 2Q | 3Q | 4Q | Year |
|---|---|---|---|---|---|
| 2008 | 4,942 | 5,239 | 5,172 | -- | -- |
| 2007 | 4,499 | 4,921 | 5,064 | 5,160 | 19,644 |
| 2006 | 4,856 | 5,142 | 5,284 | 4,976 | 20,258 |
| 2005 | 4,767 | 4,992 | 5,030 | 4,934 | 19,723 |
| 2004 | 4,302 | 4,519 | 4,714 | 4,835 | 18,370 |
| 2003 | 3,546 | 3,753 | 3,906 | 3,914 | 15,119 |

### Earnings Per Share ($)

| | | | | | |
|---|---|---|---|---|---|
| 2008 | 0.60 | 0.31 | 0.13 | E0.09 | E1.77 |
| 2007 | -0.61 | 0.14 | 0.67 | 0.26 | 0.66 |
| 2006 | 0.37 | 0.01 | -0.27 | -2.02 | -1.86 |
| 2005 | 0.35 | 0.34 | 0.70 | -0.23 | 1.21 |
| 2004 | -0.44 | 0.17 | 0.20 | 0.62 | 0.63 |
| 2003 | -1.12 | -0.30 | -0.67 | -2.49 | -4.58 |

Fiscal year ended Dec. 31. Next earnings report expected: Mid February. EPS Estimates based on S&P Operating Earnings; historical GAAP earnings are as reported.

## Dividend Data

Dividends were last paid in 2002.

## Highlights

➤ The STARS recommendation for GT has recently been changed to 4 (buy) from 3 (hold) and the 12-month target price has recently been changed to $14.00 from $19.00. The Highlights section of this Stock Report will be updated accordingly.

## Investment Rationale/Risk

➤ The Investment Rationale/Risk section of this Stock Report will be updated shortly. For the latest News story on GT from MarketScope, see below.

➤ 11/03/08 12:33 pm ET ... S&P UPGRADES OPINION ON SHARES OF GOODYEAR TIRE & RUBBER TO BUY FROM HOLD (GT 9.78****): Before special items, GT posts Q3 EPS from continuing operations $0.38 vs. $0.68, below our $0.44 estimate. Despite the approval of the transfer responsibility for union healthcare benefits to the union, which we expect will save GT $100M in '09, and other costs savings efforts, we are cutting our '09 EPS estimate by $0.68 to $1.95, given weakening tire demand in the U.S. and abroad for new and replacement tires, with expected higher commodity costs into '09. We are also lowering our 12-month target price by $5 to $14, 7.2X our '09 EPS estimate, based on P/E analysis. /E.Levy-CFA

---

**Please read the Required Disclosures and Analyst Certification on the last page of this report.**

# Goodyear Tire & Rubber Co

**STANDARD &POOR'S**

## Business Summary September 25, 2008

CORPORATE OVERVIEW. Goodyear Tire & Rubber is the largest U.S. manufacturer of tires, and one of the largest worldwide. Operations also include rubber and plastic products and chemicals. Despite efforts to rationalize operations, divest non-core operations, and explore international growth opportunities, the company posted annual losses during 2001 through 2003. However, Goodyear made operational progress and returned to profitability in 2004. Goodyear posted further income gains in 2005, but results in 2006 were dragged down by a fourth-quarter strike against the company. After improvement in 2007, we project additional gains for 2008. GT holds the leading market share in North America, Latin America, China and India.

With the sale of substantially all of its engineered products business in July 2007, the results of that segment have been classified as discontinued operations.

In February 2008, Goodyear formed a new strategic business unit, Europe, Middle East and Africa (EMEA). These regions collectively had about $7.2 billion in revenues in 2007, making the unit the second largest, after North America, in terms of sales. The company began reporting the new segment results in the 2008 first quarter.

CORPORATE STRATEGY. The company plans to achieve more than $2.0 billion

in aggregate cost savings from 2006 through 2009 through a four-point plan. Sources of savings are expected to include continuous improvement in processes, increased low-cost country sourcing, high cost capacity reductions and reduced SG&A expenses, including about $300 million of ongoing savings by 2008 from the master labor agreement with the United Steel Workers.

The company sometimes uses joint ventures to facilitate the growth of its business. In 1999, GT and Sumitomo Rubber Industries (SRI) completed a global alliance that again made GT the world's leading tire manufacturer. GT created a European joint venture with SRI. GT and SRI owned 75% and 25%, respectively, of both the North American and European joint ventures. In Japan, the ownership ratio is reversed.

GT and Pacific Dunlop Ltd. participate in equally owned joint ventures in South Pacific Tyres, an Australian partnership, and South Pacific Tyres N.Z. Ltd., a New Zealand company.

## Company Financials Fiscal Year Ended Dec. 31

| Per Share Data ($) | 2007 | 2006 | 2005 | 2004 | 2003 | 2002 | 2001 | 2000 | 1999 | 1998 |
|---|---|---|---|---|---|---|---|---|---|---|
| Tangible Book Value | 8.58 | NM | NM | NM | NM | NM | 14.06 | 18.49 | 19.87 | 24.01 |
| Cash Flow | 3.25 | 1.95 | 4.16 | 3.87 | -0.62 | -3.01 | 2.71 | 4.22 | 5.18 | 7.63 |
| Earnings | 0.66 | -1.86 | 1.21 | 0.63 | -4.58 | -6.62 | -1.27 | 0.26 | 1.52 | 4.53 |
| S&P Core Earnings | NA | -0.88 | 2.61 | 0.84 | -3.32 | -8.16 | -3.09 | NA | NA | NA |
| Dividends | Nil | Nil | Nil | Nil | Nil | 0.48 | 1.02 | 1.20 | 1.20 | 1.20 |
| Payout Ratio | Nil | Nil | Nil | Nil | Nil | Nil | NM | NM | 79% | 26% |
| Prices:High | 36.90 | 21.35 | 18.59 | 15.01 | 8.19 | 28.85 | 32.10 | 31.63 | 66.75 | 76.75 |
| Prices:Low | 21.40 | 9.75 | 11.24 | 7.06 | 3.35 | 6.50 | 17.37 | 15.60 | 25.50 | 45.88 |
| P/E Ratio:High | 56 | NM | 15 | 24 | NM | NM | NM | NM | 44 | 17 |
| P/E Ratio:Low | 32 | NM | 9 | 11 | NM | NM | NM | NM | 17 | 10 |

| Income Statement Analysis (Million $) | 2007 | 2006 | 2005 | 2004 | 2003 | 2002 | 2001 | 2000 | 1999 | 1998 |
|---|---|---|---|---|---|---|---|---|---|---|
| Revenue | 19,644 | 20,258 | 19,723 | 18,370 | 15,119 | 13,850 | 14,147 | 14,417 | 12,881 | 12,626 |
| Operating Income | 1,677 | 1,256 | 1,706 | 1,457 | -549 | 915 | 916 | 1,173 | 1,094 | 1,560 |
| Depreciation | 614 | 675 | 630 | 629 | 693 | 603 | 637 | 630 | 582 | 488 |
| Interest Expense | 566 | 451 | 411 | 369 | 296 | 241 | 292 | 283 | 179 | 147 |
| Pretax Income | 464 | -113 | 584 | 381 | -655 | 37.9 | -273 | 92.3 | 337 | 1,035 |
| Effective Tax Rate | 55.0% | NM | 42.8% | 54.6% | NM | NM | NM | 20.0% | 16.5% | 27.6% |
| Net Income | 139 | -330 | 239 | 115 | -802 | -1,106 | -204 | 40.3 | 241 | 717 |
| S&P Core Earnings | NA | -157 | 522 | 142 | -584 | -1,362 | -495 | NA | NA | NA |

| Balance Sheet & Other Financial Data (Million $) | 2007 | 2006 | 2005 | 2004 | 2003 | 2002 | 2001 | 2000 | 1999 | 1998 |
|---|---|---|---|---|---|---|---|---|---|---|
| Cash | 3,654 | 3,899 | 2,178 | 1,968 | 1,565 | 947 | 959 | 253 | 241 | 239 |
| Current Assets | 10,172 | 10,179 | 8,680 | 8,632 | 6,988 | 5,227 | 5,255 | 5,467 | 5,261 | 4,529 |
| Total Assets | 17,191 | 17,029 | 15,627 | 16,533 | 15,006 | 13,147 | 13,513 | 13,568 | 13,103 | 10,589 |
| Current Liabilities | 4,664 | 4,666 | 4,811 | 5,113 | 3,686 | 4,071 | 3,327 | 4,226 | 3,960 | 3,277 |
| Long Term Debt | 4,329 | 6,563 | 4,742 | 449 | 4,826 | 2,989 | 3,204 | 2,350 | 2,348 | 1,187 |
| Common Equity | 2,850 | -758 | 73.0 | 72.8 | -13.1 | 651 | 2,864 | 3,503 | 3,617 | 3,746 |
| Total Capital | 8,456 | 7,015 | 5,910 | 1,774 | 5,639 | 4,380 | 6,855 | 6,698 | 6,856 | 5,192 |
| Capital Expenditures | 739 | 671 | 634 | 519 | 375 | 458 | 435 | 614 | 805 | 838 |
| Cash Flow | 753 | 345 | 869 | 744 | -109 | -503 | 433 | 671 | 823 | 1,205 |
| Current Ratio | 2.2 | 2.2 | 1.8 | 1.7 | 1.9 | 1.3 | 1.6 | 1.3 | 1.3 | 1.4 |
| % Long Term Debt of Capitalization | 51.2 | 93.6 | 80.2 | 25.3 | 85.6 | 68.2 | 46.7 | 35.1 | 34.2 | 22.9 |
| % Net Income of Revenue | 0.7 | NM | 1.2 | 0.6 | NM | NM | NM | 0.3 | 1.9 | 5.7 |
| % Return on Assets | 0.8 | NM | 1.5 | 0.7 | NM | NM | NM | 0.3 | 2.0 | 7.0 |
| % Return on Equity | 13.3 | NM | 325.2 | 565.5 | NM | NM | NM | 1.1 | 6.5 | 20.1 |

Data as orig reptd.; bef. results of disc opers/spec. items. Per share data adj. for stk. divs.; EPS diluted. E-Estimated. NA-Not Available. NM-Not Meaningful. NR-Not Ranked. UR-Under Review.

**Office:** 1144 East Market Street, Akron, OH, USA 44316-0001.
**Telephone:** 330-796-2121.
**Email:** goodyear.investor.relations@goodyear.com
**Website:** http://www.goodyear.com

**Chrmn, Pres & CEO:** R.J. Keegan
**EVP & CFO:** D.R. Wells
**SVP & CTO:** J. Kihn
**SVP, Secy & General Counsel:** C.T. Harvie

**Chief Acctg Officer & CIO:** T.A. Connell
**Investor Contact:** G. Dooley (330-796-6704)
**Board Members:** J. C. Boland, J. Firestone, R. J. Keegan, W. A. McCollough, S. A. Minter, D. Morrison, R. O'Neal, S. D. Peterson, S. A. Streeter, G. C. Sullivan, T. H. Weidemeyer, M. R. Wessel

**Founded:** 1898
**Domicile:** Ohio
**Employees:** 72,000

# Google Inc

**STANDARD &POOR'S**

| S&P Recommendation | **STRONG BUY** ★ ★ ★ ★ ★ | Price<br>$310.02 (as of Nov 14, 2008) | 12-Mo. Target Price<br>$500.00 | Investment Style<br>Large-Cap Growth |
|---|---|---|---|---|

**GICS Sector** Information Technology
**Sub-Industry** Internet Software & Services

**Summary** GOOG, which completed its initial public offering in August 2004, is the world's largest Internet company. It specializes in online search and advertising.

## Key Stock Statistics (Source S&P, Vickers, company reports)

| | | | | | | | |
|---|---|---|---|---|---|---|---|
| 52-Wk Range | $724.80– 280.00 | S&P Oper. EPS 2008**E** | 16.19 | Market Capitalization(B) | $97.580 | Beta | 2.02 |
| Trailing 12-Month EPS | $16.56 | S&P Oper. EPS 2009**E** | 17.62 | Yield (%) | Nil | S&P 3-Yr. Proj. EPS CAGR(%) | 17 |
| Trailing 12-Month P/E | 18.7 | P/E on S&P Oper. EPS 2008**E** | 19.1 | Dividend Rate/Share | Nil | S&P Credit Rating | NA |
| $10K Invested 5 Yrs Ago | NA | Common Shares Outstg. (M) | 314.8 | Institutional Ownership (%) | 60 | | |

## Price Performance

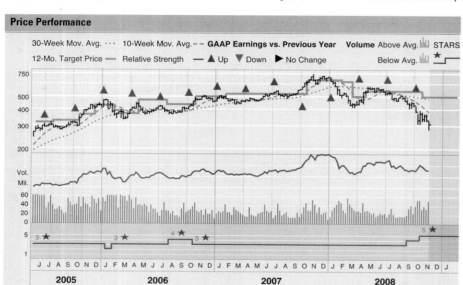

30-Week Mov. Avg. · · · 10-Week Mov. Avg. – – **GAAP Earnings vs. Previous Year** Volume Above Avg. STARS
12-Mo. Target Price — Relative Strength — ▲ Up ▼ Down ► No Change Below Avg.

Options: ASE, CBOE, P, Ph

Analysis prepared by **Scott H. Kessler** on October 20, 2008, when the stock traded at **$ 371.07**.

## Highlights

➤ We believe that gross revenues will increase 38% in 2008 and 23% in 2009, with revenues benefiting from higher spending on Internet advertising, the appeal of keyword search advertising, market share gains in some segments, and international expansion. Revenue increases should continue to be paced, in our view, by revenues derived from GOOG's websites. We believe GOOG continues to face revenue and earnings challenges in many of its businesses not centered on its more traditional Internet search offerings.

➤ We project that annual gross margins will narrow in 2008 and 2009, owing to a less favorable revenue mix that is becoming increasingly tied to large content partners. We expect operating margins to decline in 2008, reflecting continuing aggressive investments for business expansion. We also project interest income to be adversely affected by the DoubleClick purchase and lower interest rates.

➤ Our EPS estimates include notable expenses related to stock-based compensation. We foresee only moderate growth in diluted outstanding shares through 2009.

## Investment Rationale/Risk

➤ We believe global economic uncertainty, competitive pressures, and concerns about GOOG's size and power could detract from revenue growth. Nonetheless, its business model has demonstrated notable resiliency. We are constructive on efforts to broaden its offerings, especially with Web applications (Apps) and mobile services, but believe it has in some cases paid excessive prices to do so. In November 2006, GOOG acquired YouTube for $1.8 billion in stock, and in March 2008 it purchased DoubleClick for $3.2 billion.

➤ Risks to our opinion and target price include possible market share losses, new product or service introductions or partnerships that do not succeed as some expect, and challenges related to legal/regulatory issues.

➤ Our DCF model includes assumptions of a WACC of 10.5%, five-year average annual growth of 23%, and a perpetuity growth rate of 3%, and yields an intrinsic value of roughly $500, which is our 12-month target price. GOOG generates billions of dollars in annual free cash flow and recently had $14.4 billion in cash and marketable securities and no debt.

## Qualitative Risk Assessment

| LOW | MEDIUM | HIGH |
|---|---|---|

Our risk assessment reflects what we see as the Internet segment's emerging nature and relatively low barriers to entry, significant and mounting competition, substantial and increasing investment and related new offerings, our view of somewhat lacking corporate governance practices, and notable share-price volatility.

## Quantitative Evaluations

**S&P Quality Ranking** NR

| D | C | B- | B | B+ | A- | A | A+ |
|---|---|---|---|---|---|---|---|

**Relative Strength Rank** MODERATE

52

LOWEST = 1 HIGHEST = 99

## Revenue/Earnings Data

**Revenue (Million $)**

| | 1Q | 2Q | 3Q | 4Q | Year |
|---|---|---|---|---|---|
| 2008 | 5,186 | 5,367 | 5,541 | -- | -- |
| 2007 | 3,664 | 3,872 | 4,231 | 4,827 | 16,594 |
| 2006 | 2,254 | 2,456 | 2,690 | 3,206 | 10,605 |
| 2005 | 1,257 | 1,385 | 1,578 | 1,919 | 6,139 |
| 2004 | 651.6 | 700.2 | 805.9 | 1,032 | 3,189 |
| 2003 | 248.6 | 311.2 | 393.9 | 512.2 | 1,466 |

**Earnings Per Share ($)**

| | | | | | |
|---|---|---|---|---|---|
| 2008 | 4.12 | 3.91 | 4.24 | E3.92 | E16.19 |
| 2007 | 3.18 | 2.93 | 3.38 | 3.79 | 13.29 |
| 2006 | 1.95 | 2.33 | 2.36 | 3.29 | 9.94 |
| 2005 | 1.29 | 1.19 | 1.32 | 1.22 | 5.02 |
| 2004 | 0.24 | 0.30 | 0.19 | 0.71 | 1.46 |
| 2003 | -- | -- | -- | -- | 0.51 |

Fiscal year ended Dec. 31. Next earnings report expected: Early February. EPS Estimates based on S&P Operating Earnings; historical GAAP earnings are as reported.

## Dividend Data

No cash dividends have been paid.

# Google Inc

**STANDARD &POOR'S**

## Business Summary October 20, 2008

CORPORATE OVERVIEW. Google is a global technology company whose stated mission is to organize the world's information and make it universally accessible and useful. GOOG has amassed and maintains what we believe is the Internet's largest index of information (consisting of billions of items, including Web pages, images and videos), and makes most of it freely accessible and usable to anyone with online access. GOOG's websites are a leading Internet destination, and its brand is one of the most recognized in the world. International sources contributed 51% of revenues in the 2008 third quarter, versus 48% in the prior-year period.

GOOG's advertising program, called AdWords, enables advertisers to present online ads when users are searching for related information. Advertisers employ GOOG's tools to create text-based ads, bid on keywords that trigger display of their ads, and set daily spending budgets. Ads are ranked for presenta-

tion based on the maximum cost per click set by the advertiser, click-through rates, and other factors used to determine ad relevance. This process is designed to favor the most relevant ads. GOOG's AdSense technology enables Google Network websites to provide targeted ads from AdWords advertisers.

Advertising accounted for 97% of revenues in the third quarter of 2008 and 99% in the third quarter of 2007. Google websites accounted for 67% of 2008 third-quarter revenues and 65% of the prior year period's revenues. Google Network websites contributed 30% of 2008 third-quarter revenues and 34% in the 2008 quarter.

## Company Financials Fiscal Year Ended Dec. 31

| Per Share Data ($) | 2007 | 2006 | 2005 | 2004 | 2003 | 2002 | 2001 | 2000 | 1999 | 1998 |
|---|---|---|---|---|---|---|---|---|---|---|
| Tangible Book Value | 63.67 | 49.02 | 31.20 | 10.25 | 7.66 | NA | NA | NA | NA | NA |
| Cash Flow | 16.36 | 11.79 | 5.90 | 1.93 | 0.75 | NA | NA | NA | NA | NA |
| Earnings | 13.29 | 9.94 | 5.02 | 1.46 | 0.51 | 0.45 | 0.04 | -0.22 | -0.14 | NA |
| S&P Core Earnings | 13.18 | 9.92 | 4.68 | 1.85 | 0.40 | 0.44 | NA | NA | NA | NA |
| Dividends | Nil | Nil | Nil | Nil | NA | NA | NA | NA | NA | NA |
| Payout Ratio | Nil | Nil | Nil | Nil | NA | NA | NA | NA | NA | NA |
| Prices:High | 747.24 | 513.00 | 446.21 | 201.60 | NA | NA | NA | NA | NA | NA |
| Prices:Low | 437.00 | 331.55 | 172.57 | 85.00 | NA | NA | NA | NA | NA | NA |
| P/E Ratio:High | 56 | 52 | 89 | NM | NA | NA | NA | NA | NA | NA |
| P/E Ratio:Low | 33 | 33 | 34 | NM | NA | NA | NA | NA | NA | NA |

| Income Statement Analysis (Million $) | 2007 | 2006 | 2005 | 2004 | 2003 | 2002 | 2001 | 2000 | 1999 | 1998 |
|---|---|---|---|---|---|---|---|---|---|---|
| Revenue | 16,594 | 10,605 | 6,139 | 3,189 | 1,466 | 440 | 86.4 | 19.1 | 0.22 | NA |
| Operating Income | 6,052 | 3,550 | 2,274 | 970 | 393 | 204 | 21.0 | NA | NA | NA |
| Depreciation | 968 | 572 | 257 | 129 | 50.2 | 18.0 | 10.0 | NA | NA | NA |
| Interest Expense | 1.30 | 0.26 | 0.78 | 0.86 | 1.93 | 2.57 | 1.76 | NA | NA | NA |
| Pretax Income | 5,674 | 4,011 | 2,142 | 650 | 347 | 185 | 10.1 | -14.7 | -6.08 | NA |
| Effective Tax Rate | 26.0% | 23.3% | 31.6% | 38.6% | 69.5% | 46.1% | 30.6% | Nil | Nil | NA |
| Net Income | 4,204 | 3,077 | 1,465 | 399 | 106 | 99.7 | 6.99 | -14.7 | -6.08 | NA |
| S&P Core Earnings | 4,170 | 3,071 | 1,366 | 503 | 103 | 97.4 | NA | NA | NA | NA |

| Balance Sheet & Other Financial Data (Million $) | 2007 | 2006 | 2005 | 2004 | 2003 | 2002 | 2001 | 2000 | 1999 | 1998 |
|---|---|---|---|---|---|---|---|---|---|---|
| Cash | 14,219 | 11,244 | 8,034 | 2,132 | 1,712 | 146 | 33.6 | 19.1 | 20.0 | NA |
| Current Assets | 17,289 | 13,040 | 9,001 | 2,693 | NA | 232 | NA | NA | NA | NA |
| Total Assets | 25,336 | 18,473 | 10,272 | 3,313 | 2,492 | 286 | 84.5 | 46.9 | 25.8 | NA |
| Current Liabilities | 2,036 | 1,305 | 745 | 340 | NA | 89.5 | NA | NA | NA | NA |
| Long Term Debt | Nil | Nil | Nil | Nil | NA | 6.50 | NA | NA | NA | NA |
| Common Equity | 22,690 | 17,040 | 9,419 | 2,929 | 2,181 | 130 | NA | NA | NA | NA |
| Total Capital | 22,690 | 17,080 | 9,454 | 2,929 | NA | 178 | 50.2 | 27.2 | 20.0 | NA |
| Capital Expenditures | 2,403 | 1,903 | 838 | 319 | 177 | 37.2 | 13.1 | NA | NA | NA |
| Cash Flow | 5,172 | 3,649 | 1,722 | 528 | 156 | 118 | 17.0 | NA | NA | NA |
| Current Ratio | 8.5 | 10.0 | 12.1 | 7.9 | 2.4 | 2.6 | NA | NA | NA | NA |
| % Long Term Debt of Capitalization | Nil | Nil | Nil | Nil | Nil | 3.7 | Nil | NA | NA | NA |
| % Net Income of Revenue | 25.3 | 29.0 | 23.9 | 12.5 | 7.2 | 22.7 | 8.1 | NM | NM | NA |
| % Return on Assets | 19.1 | 21.4 | 21.6 | 19.1 | 18.2 | NA | NA | NA | NA | NA |
| % Return on Equity | 21.1 | 23.3 | 23.7 | 23.0 | 31.4 | NA | NA | NA | NA | NA |

Data as orig reptd.; bef. results of disc opers/spec. items. Per share data adj. for stk. divs.; EPS diluted. E-Estimated. NA-Not Available. NM-Not Meaningful. NR-Not Ranked. UR-Under Review.

**Office:** 1600 Amphitheatre Parkway, Mountain View, CA 94043.
**Telephone:** 650-253-0000.
**Email:** info@google.com
**Website:** http://www.google.com

**Chrmn & CEO:** E.E. Schmidt
**COO:** U. Holzle
**SVP & CFO:** P. Pichette
**SVP, Secy & General Counsel:** D.C. Drummond

**CTO:** S. Brin
**Investor Contact:** M. Shim (650-253-7663)
**Board Members:** S. Brin, J. Doerr, J. L. Hennessy, A. D. Levinson, A. Mather, P. S. Otellini, L. Page, E. E. Schmidt, R. R. Shriram, S. M. Tilghman

**Employees:** 16,805

# Grainger (W W) Inc.

**STANDARD &POOR'S**

| S&P Recommendation | HOLD ★★★☆☆ | Price $65.06 (as of Nov 14, 2008) | 12-Mo. Target Price $74.00 | Investment Style Large-Cap Blend |
|---|---|---|---|---|

**GICS Sector** Industrials
**Sub-Industry** Trading Companies & Distributors

**Summary** Grainger is the largest global distributor of industrial and commercial supplies, such as hand tools, electric motors, light bulbs, and janitorial items.

## Key Stock Statistics (Source S&P, Vickers, company reports)

| | | | | | | | |
|---|---|---|---|---|---|---|---|
| 52-Wk Range | $93.99–61.11 | S&P Oper. EPS 2008E | 6.10 | Market Capitalization(B) | $4.949 | Beta | 0.96 |
| Trailing 12-Month EPS | $5.92 | S&P Oper. EPS 2009E | 5.50 | Yield (%) | 2.46 | S&P 3-Yr. Proj. EPS CAGR(%) | 5 |
| Trailing 12-Month P/E | 11.0 | P/E on S&P Oper. EPS 2008E | 10.7 | Dividend Rate/Share | $1.60 | S&P Credit Rating | AA+ |
| $10K Invested 5 Yrs Ago | $15,607 | Common Shares Outstg. (M) | 76.1 | Institutional Ownership (%) | 74 | | |

## Price Performance

30-Week Mov. Avg. · · · · 10-Week Mov. Avg. - - - **GAAP Earnings vs. Previous Year**   Volume Above Avg. ▯▯▯ STARS
12-Mo. Target Price — Relative Strength — ▲ Up ▼ Down ▶ No Change   Below Avg. ▯▯▯ ★

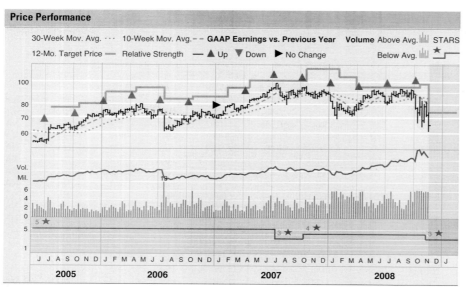

Options: ASE, CBOE, P, Ph

Analysis prepared by **Stewart Scharf** on November 12, 2008, when the stock traded at **$ 65.52.**

## Qualitative Risk Assessment

| LOW | MEDIUM | HIGH |
|---|---|---|

Our risk assessment reflects uncertain economic conditions, pricing pressures, and possible facilities disruptions or shutdowns. This is offset by GWW's S&P Quality Ranking of A, which indicates above average dividend and earnings growth.

## Quantitative Evaluations

**S&P Quality Ranking**   **A**

| D | C | B- | B | B+ | A- | A | A+ |
|---|---|---|---|---|---|---|---|

**Relative Strength Rank**   **MODERATE**

57

LOWEST = 1    HIGHEST = 99

## Highlights

➤ We expect sales to advance about 8% in 2008, with low single digit growth likely in 2009, as weak economic conditions and negative foreign currency effects in Canada and Mexico, due to a stronger U.S. dollar, affect results. In our view, contributions from market and product line expansions in the U.S. branch-based business will continue, but sales to the government, reseller and commercial markets will soften, while further weakness is expected in the retail, contractor, light manufacturing and, especially, heavy manufacturing markets, as well as the lab safety unit.

➤ We see narrower gross margins for 2009 (projected 40.7% for 2008), reflecting the lower volume and a less favorable product mix, despite GWW dissolving low-margin integrated supply and auto contracts. We believe EBITDA margins will also narrow, from near 13% projected for 2008, as competitive pricing pressures and mix issues offset supply chain cost savings and other cost controls.

➤ For 2008, we see a slightly higher effective tax rate of 39%, and operating EPS of $6.10 (before a $0.05 charge), on about 8% fewer shares, declining 10% in 2009, to $5.50.

## Investment Rationale/Risk

➤ We recently downgraded our recommendation to hold, from buy, based on our view of softening market trends, and valuation. However, we expect strategic initiatives to enhance the branch-based distribution network. In our view, strong free cash flow will be targeted mainly for internal investments, while ROIC should continue to expand.

➤ Risks to our recommendation and target price include a significant downturn in industrial production; a negative impact from entering new markets; the need to maintain a large customer base; a sustained strengthening of the U.S. dollar; and an adverse ruling from the Department of Justice related to compliance issues on a U.S. government contract.

➤ Our 12-month target price of $74 is based on a blend of our relative and DCF analyses. Based on historical P/Es and price-to-EBITDA ratios, and forward P/E-to-EPS growth, we believe GWW deserves a below historical P/E multiple of 12.5X our 2009 EPS estimate, which leads to a value of $69. Our DCF-based model, assuming a 3.5% terminal growth rate and an 8.3% weighted average cost of capital, indicates intrinsic value of $79.

## Revenue/Earnings Data

**Revenue (Million $)**

| | 1Q | 2Q | 3Q | 4Q | Year |
|---|---|---|---|---|---|
| 2008 | 1,661 | 1,757 | 1,839 | -- | -- |
| 2007 | 1,547 | 1,601 | 1,659 | 1,612 | 6,418 |
| 2006 | 1,419 | 1,483 | 1,520 | 1,462 | 5,884 |
| 2005 | 1,335 | 1,373 | 1,428 | 1,391 | 5,527 |
| 2004 | 1,228 | 1,256 | 1,301 | 1,265 | 5,050 |
| 2003 | 1,139 | 1,173 | 1,201 | 1,154 | 4,667 |

**Earnings Per Share ($)**

| | | | | | |
|---|---|---|---|---|---|
| 2008 | 1.43 | 1.43 | 1.79 | E1.40 | E6.10 |
| 2007 | 1.17 | 1.21 | 1.29 | 1.28 | 4.94 |
| 2006 | 0.93 | 1.02 | 1.16 | 1.13 | 4.24 |
| 2005 | 0.79 | 0.89 | 0.97 | 1.13 | 3.78 |
| 2004 | 0.69 | 0.72 | 0.74 | 0.98 | 3.13 |
| 2003 | 0.57 | 0.60 | 0.62 | 0.67 | 2.46 |

Fiscal year ended Dec. 31. Next earnings report expected: Late January. EPS Estimates based on S&P Operating Earnings; historical GAAP earnings are as reported.

## Dividend Data (Dates: mm/dd Payment Date: mm/dd/yy)

| Amount ($) | Date Decl. | Ex-Div. Date | Stk. of Record | Payment Date |
|---|---|---|---|---|
| 0.350 | 01/30 | 02/07 | 02/11 | 03/01/08 |
| 0.400 | 04/30 | 05/08 | 05/12 | 06/01/08 |
| 0.400 | 07/30 | 08/07 | 08/11 | 09/01/08 |
| 0.400 | 10/29 | 11/06 | 11/10 | 12/01/08 |

Dividends have been paid since 1965. Source: Company reports.

**Please read the Required Disclosures and Analyst Certification on the last page of this report.**

The McGraw-Hill Companies

# Grainger (W W) Inc.

STANDARD
&POOR'S

## Business Summary November 12, 2008

CORPORATE OVERVIEW. W.W. Grainger distributes facilities maintenance and other industrial and commercial supplies, including pumps, tools, motors, and electrical and safety products. It has more than 600 branches, 18 distribution centers and multiple websites. Starting in 2006, the company began reporting its Canadian branch-based business as a separate segment: Acklands-Grainger. The branch-based business segment mainly consists of 418 U.S. brick and mortar branch stores (two in Puerto Rico) and 20 Will Call Express branches, as well as 20 stores in Mexico, and one branch each in China and Panama (opened in third quarter of 2008). Six Will Call Express locations in China were closed in the third quarter of 2008. These branches sell company-made -- as well as third-party -- industrial supplies, via in-store catalogs and Internet services. GWW estimates China's market for facilities maintenance supplies at $38 billion, and projects that it will exceed $70 billion by 2014.

In 2007, the branch-based unit accounted for 83% of sales and had a pretax return on invested capital (ROIC) of 36.7%. The Acklands unit (154 branches as of early 2008) accounted for 10% of sales, with ROIC of 12.9%. Lab Safety, a direct marketer of safety and other industrial products, was responsible for 6.8% of sales, with ROIC of 29.5%. Approximately 23% of GWW's sales consist of private label items. In 2007, approximately 20% of sales were derived from

heavy manufacturing, close to 20% each from commercial and government, more than 10% each from contractor and light manufacturing, less than 10% each from retailer and reseller, and less than 5% other.

The company's 2008 catalog features about 183,000 products, a 32% increase from 139,000 products in 2007. The 44,000 new products (net) added in 2008 are mainly for power transmission and fleet vehicle maintenance.

In the first nine months of 2008, the company repurchased 4.35 million of its shares for $344 million. Approximately 8.8 million shares remain under GWW's repurchase plan. However, in October 2008, GWW noted that based on current market conditions it would build its cash position. The company also raised its 2008 EPS guidance range to $6.00 to $6.20, from $5.80 to $6.10, including a $0.05 legal reserve charge. In the fourth quarter of 2007, GWW recorded a $4.5 million ($0.03 a share, after tax) severance charge related to staff cuts in information technology.

## Company Financials Fiscal Year Ended Dec. 31

| Per Share Data ($) | 2007 | 2006 | 2005 | 2004 | 2003 | 2002 | 2001 | 2000 | 1999 | 1998 |
|---|---|---|---|---|---|---|---|---|---|---|
| Tangible Book Value | 23.47 | 23.40 | 23.47 | 20.89 | 18.43 | 16.92 | 15.51 | 14.67 | 14.00 | 11.74 |
| Cash Flow | 6.25 | 5.35 | 4.85 | 4.06 | 3.28 | 3.30 | 2.73 | 3.01 | 2.85 | 3.20 |
| Earnings | 4.94 | 4.24 | 3.78 | 3.13 | 2.46 | 2.50 | 1.84 | 2.05 | 1.92 | 2.44 |
| S&P Core Earnings | 4.94 | 4.26 | 3.65 | 2.96 | 2.36 | 2.29 | 1.87 | NA | NA | NA |
| Dividends | 1.34 | 1.11 | 0.92 | 0.79 | 0.74 | 0.72 | 0.70 | 0.67 | 0.63 | 0.58 |
| Payout Ratio | 27% | 26% | 24% | 25% | 30% | 29% | 38% | 33% | 33% | 24% |
| Prices:High | 98.60 | 79.95 | 72.45 | 66.99 | 53.30 | 59.40 | 48.99 | 56.88 | 58.13 | 54.72 |
| Prices:Low | 68.77 | 60.60 | 51.65 | 45.00 | 41.40 | 39.20 | 29.51 | 24.31 | 36.88 | 36.44 |
| P/E Ratio:High | 20 | 19 | 19 | 21 | 22 | 24 | 27 | 28 | 30 | 22 |
| P/E Ratio:Low | 14 | 14 | 14 | 14 | 17 | 16 | 16 | 12 | 19 | 15 |
| **Income Statement Analysis (Million $)** | | | | | | | | | | |
| Revenue | 6,418 | 5,884 | 5,527 | 5,050 | 4,667 | 4,644 | 4,754 | 4,977 | 4,534 | 4,341 |
| Operating Income | 782 | 679 | 617 | 525 | 463 | 467 | 461 | 426 | 406 | 482 |
| Depreciation | 111 | 101 | 98.1 | 85.6 | 76.1 | 75.9 | 83.7 | 90.6 | 88.4 | 74.2 |
| Interest Expense | 4.37 | 1.93 | 1.86 | 4.39 | 6.02 | 6.16 | 10.7 | 24.4 | 15.6 | 6.65 |
| Pretax Income | 682 | 603 | 533 | 445 | 381 | 398 | 297 | 332 | 304 | 401 |
| Effective Tax Rate | 38.4% | 36.4% | 35.0% | 35.5% | 40.4% | 40.8% | 41.3% | 41.8% | 40.5% | 40.5% |
| Net Income | 420 | 383 | 346 | 287 | 227 | 235 | 175 | 193 | 181 | 239 |
| S&P Core Earnings | 420 | 385 | 336 | 272 | 217 | 213 | 177 | NA | NA | NA |
| **Balance Sheet & Other Financial Data (Million $)** | | | | | | | | | | |
| Cash | 134 | 361 | 545 | 429 | 403 | 209 | 169 | 63.4 | 62.7 | 43.1 |
| Current Assets | 1,801 | 1,862 | 1,998 | 1,755 | 1,633 | 1,485 | 1,393 | 1,483 | 1,471 | 1,206 |
| Total Assets | 3,094 | 3,046 | 3,108 | 2,810 | 2,625 | 2,437 | 2,331 | 2,460 | 2,565 | 2,104 |
| Current Liabilities | 826 | 706 | 727 | 662 | 707 | 586 | 554 | 747 | 871 | 664 |
| Long Term Debt | 4.90 | 4.90 | 4.90 | Nil | 4.90 | 120 | 118 | 125 | 125 | 123 |
| Common Equity | 2,098 | 2,178 | 2,289 | 2,068 | 1,845 | 1,668 | 1,603 | 1,537 | 1,481 | 1,279 |
| Total Capital | 27,720 | 2,189 | 2,301 | 2,072 | 1,850 | 1,787 | 1,723 | 1,663 | 1,654 | 1,402 |
| Capital Expenditures | 189 | 128 | 112 | 128 | 74.1 | 134 | 100 | 65.5 | 114 | 130 |
| Cash Flow | 531 | 484 | 444 | 372 | 303 | 311 | 258 | 284 | 269 | 313 |
| Current Ratio | 2.2 | 2.6 | 2.7 | 2.6 | 2.3 | 2.5 | 2.5 | 2.0 | 1.7 | 1.8 |
| % Long Term Debt of Capitalization | NM | 0.2 | 0.2 | Nil | 0.3 | 6.7 | 6.9 | 7.5 | 7.6 | 8.8 |
| % Net Income of Revenue | 6.6 | 6.5 | 6.3 | 5.7 | 4.9 | 5.1 | 3.7 | 3.9 | 4.0 | 5.5 |
| % Return on Assets | 13.7 | 12.5 | 11.7 | 10.6 | 9.0 | 9.9 | 7.3 | 7.7 | 7.7 | 11.6 |
| % Return on Equity | 19.7 | 17.2 | 15.9 | 14.7 | 12.9 | 14.4 | 11.1 | 12.8 | 13.1 | 18.5 |

Data as orig reptd.; bef. results of disc opers/spec. items. Per share data adj. for stk. divs.; EPS diluted. E-Estimated. NA-Not Available. NM-Not Meaningful. NR-Not Ranked. UR-Under Review.

**Office:** 100 Grainger Pkwy, Lake Forest, IL 60045.
**Telephone:** 847-535-1000.
**Website:** http://www.grainger.com
**Chrmn:** R.L. Keyser

**Pres & CEO:** J.T. Ryan
**Vice Chrmn:** P.O. Loux
**SVP & CFO:** R.L. Jadin
**SVP & General Counsel:** J.L. Howard

**Investor Contact:** W.D. Chapman (847-535-0881)
**Board Members:** B. P. Anderson, W. H. Gantz, V. A. Hailey, W. Hall, R. L. Keyser, S. L. Levenick, P. O. Loux, J. W. McCarter, Jr., N. Novich, M. J. Roberts, G. L. Rogers, J. T. Ryan, J. D. Slavik, H. B. Smith

**Founded:** 1927
**Domicile:** Illinois
**Employees:** 18,036

**STANDARD &POOR'S**

# Halliburton Co

| S&P Recommendation | HOLD ★★★☆☆ | Price | 12-Mo. Target Price | Investment Style |
|---|---|---|---|---|
| | | $18.11 (as of Nov 14, 2008) | $26.00 | Large-Cap Growth |

**GICS Sector** Energy
**Sub-Industry** Oil & Gas Equipment & Services

**Summary** This leading oilfield services company provides products and services to the global energy industry.

## Key Stock Statistics (Source S&P, Vickers, company reports)

| | | | | | | | |
|---|---|---|---|---|---|---|---|
| 52-Wk Range | $55.38– 15.52 | S&P Oper. EPS 2008**E** | 2.86 | Market Capitalization(B) | $16.186 | Beta | 1.32 |
| Trailing 12-Month EPS | $1.93 | S&P Oper. EPS 2009**E** | 3.19 | Yield (%) | 1.99 | S&P 3-Yr. Proj. EPS CAGR(%) | 16 |
| Trailing 12-Month P/E | 9.4 | P/E on S&P Oper. EPS 2008**E** | 6.3 | Dividend Rate/Share | $0.36 | S&P Credit Rating | A |
| $10K Invested 5 Yrs Ago | $15,818 | Common Shares Outstg. (M) | 893.8 | Institutional Ownership (%) | 86 | | |

## Price Performance

30-Week Mov. Avg. · · · 10-Week Mov. Avg. – – GAAP Earnings vs. Previous Year   Volume Above Avg. |||| STARS
12-Mo. Target Price — Relative Strength  — ▲ Up  ▼ Down  ► No Change   Below Avg. ||||

Options: ASE, CBOE, P, Ph

Analysis prepared by **Stewart Glickman, CFA** on October 21, 2008, when the stock traded at **$ 20.56**.

## Highlights

➤ In October, HAL said that although some E&P customers have started to scale back their capital spending plans (which we would attribute in part to the credit crisis as well as recently weakened natural gas prices), it anticipated that the cuts would likely affect development of conventional and shallow drilling activity, as opposed to plans for unconventional natural gas plays. HAL also said that reduced access to the capital markets could result in a tightening of supply, and potential market share gains.

➤ During the third quarter, HAL incurred a one-time charge of $693 million for the redemption of convertible debt, but the transaction reduced diluted shares outstanding by 15 million, or about 1.6%. At the end of September, HAL had a debt to capital ratio of 27%, and had access to an undrawn credit facility of $1.2 billion through July 2012. Also during the third quarter, HAL repurchased 3.5 million shares of common stock at an average price of $34.86 per share.

➤ For 2008, we see revenue growth of 18%, with a further 13% gain in 2009. We expect 2008 EPS from continuing operations of $2.86, rising to $3.19 in 2009.

## Investment Rationale/Risk

➤ In the wake of the credit market crisis and recession concerns, we are less sanguine on prospects for 2009 upstream capital spending, although we do see a recovery in 2010. In the near term, we think that HAL (and its major competitors), will see a deceleration in demand growth for oilfield services in North America, which could weigh on margins. Longer term, we think HAL is well positioned to benefit from a trend towards services with higher technology content, as well as interest in North American unconventional resource plays, which typically yield higher service intensity.

➤ Risks to our recommendation and target price include reduced oil and gas drilling activity, especially in North America; lower-than-expected oil and natural gas prices; and political risk.

➤ Our DCF model, assuming a WACC of 11.3% and terminal growth of 3%, shows intrinsic value of $24. We think a peer valuation is merited, with a relatively stronger 2009 ROIC projection offset by higher North American exposure. Using peer-average multiples of 6X estimated 2009 EBITDA and 7.5X projected 2009 cash flow and blending with our DCF model, our 12-month target price is $26.

## Qualitative Risk Assessment

| LOW | MEDIUM | HIGH |
|---|---|---|

Our risk assessment reflects HAL's exposure to volatile crude oil and natural gas prices, leverage to the North American oilfield services market, and political risk associated with operating in frontier regions such as West Africa and the Middle East. A partial offset is HAL's strong number two position in oilfield services.

## Quantitative Evaluations

**S&P Quality Ranking**                     **B**

| D | C | B- | B | B+ | A- | A | A+ |
|---|---|---|---|---|---|---|---|

**Relative Strength Rank**          **MODERATE**

30

LOWEST = 1                                    HIGHEST = 99

## Revenue/Earnings Data

**Revenue (Million $)**

| | 1Q | 2Q | 3Q | 4Q | Year |
|---|---|---|---|---|---|
| 2008 | 4,029 | 4,487 | 4,853 | -- | -- |
| 2007 | 3,422 | 3,735 | 3,928 | 4,179 | 15,264 |
| 2006 | 5,184 | 5,545 | 5,831 | 6,016 | 22,576 |
| 2005 | 4,938 | 5,163 | 5,095 | 5,798 | 20,994 |
| 2004 | 5,519 | 4,956 | 4,790 | 5,201 | 20,466 |
| 2003 | 3,060 | 3,599 | 4,148 | 5,464 | 16,271 |

**Earnings Per Share ($)**

| | | | | | |
|---|---|---|---|---|---|
| 2008 | 0.64 | 0.68 | -0.02 | E0.77 | E2.86 |
| 2007 | 0.52 | 0.63 | 0.79 | 0.74 | 2.66 |
| 2006 | 0.45 | 0.48 | 0.58 | 0.65 | 2.16 |
| 2005 | 0.36 | 0.38 | 0.48 | 1.04 | 2.27 |
| 2004 | 0.09 | -0.07 | 0.21 | 0.20 | 0.44 |
| 2003 | 0.07 | 0.05 | 0.11 | 0.17 | 0.39 |

Fiscal year ended Dec. 31. Next earnings report expected: Late January. EPS Estimates based on S&P Operating Earnings; historical GAAP earnings are as reported.

## Dividend Data (Dates: mm/dd Payment Date: mm/dd/yy)

| Amount ($) | Date Decl. | Ex-Div. Date | Stk. of Record | Payment Date |
|---|---|---|---|---|
| 0.090 | 10/15 | 11/29 | 12/03 | 12/20/07 |
| 0.090 | 02/14 | 02/28 | 03/03 | 03/20/08 |
| 0.090 | 05/21 | 05/29 | 06/02 | 06/20/08 |
| 0.090 | 07/17 | 08/28 | 09/02 | 09/23/08 |

Dividends have been paid since 1947. Source: Company reports.

*The McGraw-Hill Companies*

# Halliburton Co

## Business Summary October 21, 2008

CORPORATE OVERVIEW. Halliburton is a leading global provider of oilfield services to the energy industry, and until April 2007, provided engineering and construction expertise to energy, industrial and governmental customers. In 2006, HAL was comprised of two main business units: the Energy Services Group (ESG), and the KBR unit. In April 2007, HAL effected the complete separation of KBR via a split-off of its 135.6 million share stake in KBR (81% of KBR's outstanding shares) in exchange for HAL shares. Under the transaction, HAL exchanged its stake in KBR for about 85.3 million shares of HAL (about 8% of HAL shares outstanding), which were retired as treasury stock in early April. Following the separation, HAL was transformed into a pure-play oilfield services company. In the second half of 2007, the company reorganized its four ESG operating segments into two new segments: Completion & Production (55% of 2007 revenues excluding KBR, and 60% of 2007 operating income excluding KBR), and Drilling & Evaluation (45%, 40%). Results from the former KBR segment have been reclassified under discontinued operations. Geographically, HAL generated 47% of its total 2007 revenues (excluding KBR) from North America, followed by Europe/CIS/West Africa (24%), Middle East/Asia (17%) and Latin America (12%). Approximately 65% of HAL's North American revenues in 2007 were derived from C&P activity. In contrast, only about 40% of HAL's Latin American revenue stream is derived from C&P.

CORPORATE STRATEGY. Subsequent to the split-off, with HAL's financial

obligations to KBR for the Barracuda-Caratinga project and the Foreign Corrupt Practices Act investigations limited by terms of the Master Separation Agreement with KBR, we view HAL's exposure to such issues as reduced. While we expect HAL to defend its strong market position in North America, we believe that future capital expenditures will increasingly flow to the Eastern Hemisphere, which we see as growing faster in the long term. In 2007, HAL moved its corporate headquarters to Dubai, from Houston, which we view as symbolic of the growing importance of the Eastern Hemisphere to company operations.

UPCOMING CATALYSTS. Geographically, North America remains the dominant source of revenue for HAL, with 47% of total revenues in 2007 (excluding KBR), and is the primary driver for the Completion & Production segment, generating over 65% of both segment revenues and operating income. However, results in the Drilling & Evaluation segment are likely to be increasingly drawn from overseas, in our view, given expectations that offshore rig demand will show the strongest growth outside of North America.

## Company Financials Fiscal Year Ended Dec. 31

| Per Share Data ($) | 2007 | 2006 | 2005 | 2004 | 2003 | 2002 | 2001 | 2000 | 1999 | 1998 |
|---|---|---|---|---|---|---|---|---|---|---|
| Tangible Book Value | 8.72 | 6.61 | 5.46 | 3.55 | 2.14 | 3.25 | 4.65 | 3.90 | 3.98 | 3.74 |
| Cash Flow | 3.27 | 2.66 | 2.76 | 1.01 | 0.98 | 0.18 | 1.26 | 0.77 | 1.53 | 0.65 |
| Earnings | 2.66 | 2.16 | 2.27 | 0.44 | 0.39 | -0.40 | 0.64 | 0.21 | 0.34 | -0.02 |
| S&P Core Earnings | 2.64 | 2.12 | 2.11 | 0.37 | 0.34 | -0.52 | 0.33 | NA | NA | NA |
| Dividends | 0.35 | 0.30 | 0.25 | 0.25 | 0.25 | 0.25 | 0.25 | 0.25 | 0.25 | 0.25 |
| Payout Ratio | 13% | 14% | 11% | 57% | 64% | NM | 39% | 119% | 75% | NM |
| Prices:High | 41.95 | 41.99 | 34.89 | 20.85 | 13.60 | 10.83 | 24.63 | 27.59 | 25.88 | 28.63 |
| Prices:Low | 27.65 | 26.33 | 18.59 | 12.90 | 8.60 | 4.30 | 5.47 | 16.13 | 14.06 | 12.50 |
| P/E Ratio:High | 16 | 19 | 15 | 48 | 35 | NM | 38 | NM | 77 | NM |
| P/E Ratio:Low | 10 | 12 | 8 | 30 | 22 | NM | 9 | NM | 42 | NM |

| Income Statement Analysis (Million $) | | | | | | | | | | |
|---|---|---|---|---|---|---|---|---|---|---|
| Revenue | 15,264 | 22,576 | 20,994 | 20,466 | 16,271 | 12,572 | 13,046 | 11,856 | 14,765 | 17,159 |
| Operating Income | 4,029 | 3,875 | 2,972 | 1,291 | 1,191 | 363 | 1,615 | 789 | 1,069 | 1,769 |
| Depreciation, Depletion and Amortization | 583 | 527 | 504 | 509 | 518 | 505 | 531 | 503 | 599 | 587 |
| Interest Expense | 154 | 175 | 207 | 229 | 139 | 113 | 147 | 146 | 144 | 137 |
| Pretax Income | 3,460 | 3,449 | 2,492 | 651 | 612 | -228 | 954 | 335 | 1,012 | 278 |
| Effective Tax Rate | 26.2% | 33.2% | 3.17% | 37.0% | 38.2% | NM | 40.3% | 38.5% | 21.1% | NM |
| Net Income | 2,524 | 2,272 | 2,357 | 385 | 339 | -346 | 551 | 188 | 755 | -15.0 |
| S&P Core Earnings | 2,505 | 2,220 | 2,181 | 320 | 299 | -445 | 287 | NA | NA | NA |

| Balance Sheet & Other Financial Data (Million $) | | | | | | | | | | |
|---|---|---|---|---|---|---|---|---|---|---|
| Cash | 2,235 | 4,379 | 2,391 | 2,808 | 1,815 | 1,107 | 290 | 231 | 466 | 203 |
| Current Assets | 7,573 | 11,183 | 9,327 | 9,962 | 7,919 | 5,560 | 5,573 | 5,568 | 6,022 | 6,083 |
| Total Assets | 13,135 | 16,820 | 15,010 | 15,796 | 15,463 | 12,844 | 10,966 | 10,103 | 10,728 | 11,112 |
| Current Liabilities | 2,411 | 4,727 | 4,437 | 7,064 | 6,542 | 3,272 | 2,908 | 3,826 | 3,693 | 4,004 |
| Long Term Debt | 2,627 | 2,786 | 2,813 | 3,593 | 3,415 | 1,181 | 1,403 | 1,049 | 1,056 | 1,370 |
| Common Equity | 6,866 | 7,376 | 6,372 | 3,932 | 2,547 | 3,558 | 4,752 | 5,618 | 4,287 | 4,061 |
| Total Capital | 9,587 | 10,609 | 9,330 | 7,633 | 6,062 | 4,810 | 6,196 | 6,705 | 5,496 | 5,601 |
| Capital Expenditures | 1,583 | 891 | 651 | 575 | 515 | 764 | 797 | 578 | 593 | 914 |
| Cash Flow | 3,107 | 2,799 | 2,861 | 894 | 857 | 159 | 1,082 | 691 | 1,354 | 572 |
| Current Ratio | 3.1 | 2.4 | 2.1 | 1.4 | 1.2 | 1.7 | 1.9 | 1.5 | 1.6 | 1.5 |
| % Long Term Debt of Capitalization | 27.4 | 26.3 | 30.2 | 47.1 | 56.3 | 24.6 | 22.6 | 15.6 | 19.2 | 24.5 |
| % Return on Assets | 16.9 | 14.3 | 15.3 | 2.5 | 2.4 | NM | 5.2 | 1.9 | 6.9 | NM |
| % Return on Equity | 35.4 | 33.1 | 45.7 | 14.4 | 11.1 | NM | 12.7 | 3.7 | 18.1 | NM |

Data as orig reptd.; bef. results of disc opers/spec. items. Per share data adj. for stk. divs.; EPS diluted. E-Estimated. NA-Not Available. NM-Not Meaningful. NR-Not Ranked. UR-Under Review.

Office: 1401 McKinney St Ste 2400, Houston, TX 77010-4040.
Telephone: 713-759-2600.
Email: investors@haliburton.com
Website: http://www.halliburton.com

Chrmn, Pres & CEO: D.J. Lesar
EVP & CFO: M.A. McCollum
EVP & General Counsel: A.O. Cornelison, Jr.
SVP & Treas: C.W. Nunez

Chief Admin Officer: L. Pope
Investor Contact: C. Garcia (713-759-2688)
Board Members: A. Bennett, J. R. Boyd, M. Carroll, K. T. Derr, S. M. Gillis, J. T. Hackett, D. J. Lesar, J. L. Martin, J. A. Precourt, D. L. Reed

Founded: 1919
Domicile: Delaware
Employees: 51,000

# Harley-Davidson Inc.

**STANDARD &POOR'S**

| S&P Recommendation | HOLD ★★★☆☆ | Price<br>$15.35 (as of Nov 14, 2008) | 12-Mo. Target Price<br>$38.00 | Investment Style<br>Large-Cap Growth |
|---|---|---|---|---|

**GICS Sector** Consumer Discretionary
**Sub-Industry** Motorcycle Manufacturers

**Summary** This leading maker of heavyweight motorcycles also produces a line of motorcycle parts and accessories.

## Key Stock Statistics (Source S&P, Vickers, company reports)

| | | | | | | | |
|---|---|---|---|---|---|---|---|
| 52-Wk Range | $50.04– 15.05 | S&P Oper. EPS 2008**E** | 3.05 | Market Capitalization(B) | $3.574 | Beta | 1.08 |
| Trailing 12-Month EPS | $3.23 | S&P Oper. EPS 2009**E** | 3.17 | Yield (%) | 8.60 | S&P 3-Yr. Proj. EPS CAGR(%) | NM |
| Trailing 12-Month P/E | 4.8 | P/E on S&P Oper. EPS 2008**E** | 5.0 | Dividend Rate/Share | $1.32 | S&P Credit Rating | A |
| $10K Invested 5 Yrs Ago | $3,568 | Common Shares Outstg. (M) | 232.8 | Institutional Ownership (%) | 84 | | |

## Price Performance

30-Week Mov. Avg. · · ·   10-Week Mov. Avg. - -   GAAP Earnings vs. Previous Year   Volume Above Avg. STARS
12-Mo. Target Price —   Relative Strength —   ▲ Up   ▼ Down   ► No Change   Below Avg.

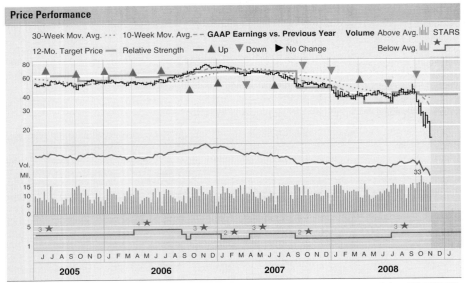

Options: ASE, CBOE, P, Ph

Analysis prepared by **Erik Kolb** on October 14, 2008, when the stock traded at **$ 29.33**.

### Highlights

➤ In July 2008, HOG said it expects third quarter 2008 wholesale shipments of Harley-Davidson brand motorcycles to total between 74,000 and 78,000 units. HOG shipped 86,535 units in the third quarter of 2007.

➤ We look for revenues in 2008 to decrease 1.7% from the $5.7 billion reported for 2007, as HOG attempts to reduce currently bloated inventory levels. We see the company achieving shipment reduction through temporary plant shutdowns and adjustments to production rates. Furthermore, we believe consumers are likely to reduce their discretionary spending because of high gasoline prices and as weakness in the U.S. economy continues. We estimate EPS of $3.14 in 2008 and $3.28 in 2009.

➤ As of June 30, 2008, HOG had cash equivalents and marketable securities totaling about $804 million, down from $1.046 billion two years earlier. In 2007, the company repurchased 20.4 million shares of its common stock at a cost of $1.15 billion, implying an average price of $56.37, well below its current price, and there are 19.3 million shares remaining under the current authorizations.

### Investment Rationale/Risk

➤ We continue to view positively HOG's strong brand and market leadership, but we expect motorcycle sales, especially in the U.S., to be weak in 2008. The company's recent efforts to clear dealer inventory seem to be making some progress of late, although we expect the economic slowdown to continue pressuring domestic sales, partly offset by international sales.

➤ Risks to our recommendation and target price include the possibility that consumers will significantly decrease their discretionary spending and that demand for HOG bikes will be substantially weaker than we expect, especially in the international market segment.

➤ Our 12-month target price of $38 is based on our discounted cash flow model, which assumes a weighted average cost of capital (WACC) of 9.6% and an annual perpetuity cash flow growth rate of 2.1%, and our relative analysis, which applies a P/E slightly below recreationally driven peers given HOG's high U.S. exposure. HOG increased its quarterly dividend payment by 43% over the past year, continuing a series of payout hikes in recent years.

## Qualitative Risk Assessment

| LOW | MEDIUM | HIGH |
|---|---|---|

Our risk assessment reflects our view that this company's market leadership position and strong brand should help offset the prospect that an aging U.S. population will limit future domestic demand for motorcycles. Also, we expect the company to generate free cash flow, with some of it likely to be used for dividend increases and to repurchase stock.

## Quantitative Evaluations

### S&P Quality Ranking                                      A+

| D | C | B- | B | B+ | A- | A | A+ |
|---|---|---|---|---|---|---|---|

### Relative Strength Rank                                   WEAK

15

LOWEST = 1                                          HIGHEST = 99

## Revenue/Earnings Data

### Revenue (Million $)

| | 1Q | 2Q | 3Q | 4Q | Year |
|---|---|---|---|---|---|
| 2008 | 1,306 | 1,573 | 1,535 | -- | -- |
| 2007 | 1,179 | 1,620 | 1,541 | 1,386 | 6,143 |
| 2006 | 1,285 | 1,377 | 1,636 | 1,503 | 5,801 |
| 2005 | 1,235 | 1,333 | 1,431 | 1,342 | 5,342 |
| 2004 | 1,166 | 1,328 | 1,301 | 1,221 | 5,015 |
| 2003 | 1,114 | 1,219 | 1,134 | 1,158 | 4,624 |

### Earnings Per Share ($)

| | | | | | |
|---|---|---|---|---|---|
| 2008 | 0.79 | 0.95 | 0.71 | E0.60 | E3.05 |
| 2007 | 0.74 | 1.14 | 1.07 | 0.78 | 3.74 |
| 2006 | 0.86 | 0.91 | 1.20 | 0.97 | 3.93 |
| 2005 | 0.77 | 0.84 | 0.96 | 0.84 | 3.41 |
| 2004 | 0.68 | 0.83 | 0.77 | 0.71 | 3.00 |
| 2003 | 0.61 | 0.66 | 0.62 | 0.60 | 2.50 |

Fiscal year ended Dec. 31. Next earnings report expected: Late January. EPS Estimates based on S&P Operating Earnings; historical GAAP earnings are as reported.

## Dividend Data (Dates: mm/dd Payment Date: mm/dd/yy)

| Amount ($) | Date Decl. | Ex-Div. Date | Stk. of Record | Payment Date |
|---|---|---|---|---|
| 0.300 | 12/11 | 12/19 | 12/21 | 12/28/07 |
| 0.300 | 02/13 | 03/03 | 03/05 | 03/18/08 |
| 0.330 | 04/26 | 06/03 | 06/05 | 06/20/08 |
| 0.330 | 09/17 | 09/29 | 10/01 | 10/10/08 |

Dividends have been paid since 1993. Source: Company reports.

**Please read the Required Disclosures and Analyst Certification on the last page of this report.**

The McGraw-Hill Companies

# Harley-Davidson Inc.

**STANDARD &POOR'S**

## Business Summary October 14, 2008

CORPORATE OVERVIEW. Harley-Davidson is a leading supplier of heavy-weight motorcycles (engine displacement exceeding about 651 cubic centimeters). The company also sells motorcycle parts, accessories, clothing and collectibles, and has a sizable financial services business.

HOG manufactures five families of Harley-Davidson brand motorcycles: Sportster, Dyna, Softail, Touring and VRSC. As of early 2008, the engines in these product lines ranged in size from 883 cc to 1800 cc. The company's 2008 model year line-up includes 31 models of Harley-Davidson heavyweight motorcycles, with domestic manufacturer's suggested retail prices ranging from $6,595 to $20,195. Also, as of early 2008, HOG was offering some limited-edition custom motorcycles having suggested retail prices ranging from $24,995 to $33,495.

In 2007, HOG shipped 330,619 Harley-Davidson brand motorcycles, down from 348,196 in 2006. Also, HOG shipped 11,513 Buell motorcycles in 2007, down from 12,460 in 2006.

CORPORATE STRATEGY. We expect the company to focus on both current owners of HOG motorcycles and on potential new customers. We believe that many purchasers of a new Harley-Davidson motorcycle previously owned a HOG bike.

We expect HOG's marketing focus to include international markets, where we project that HOG's opportunities for growth are stronger than they are in the U.S. In 2007, HOG's international sales totaled about $1.52 billion (25% of total sales), up from $1.18 million (20%) in 2006.

In addition to selling motorcycle-related products, we see HOG making a sizable profit related to financial services that it provides to independent dealers and to retail customers of those dealers. During 2007, Harley-Davidson Financial Services financed 55% of the new Harley-Davidson motorcycles retailed by independent dealers in the United States, as compared to 48% in 2006.

In July 2008, HOG announced it agreed to acquire 100% of MV Agusta Group, an Italian motorcycle manufacturer, for total consideration of $109 million. In 2007, MVAG shipped 5,819 motorcycles.

## Company Financials Fiscal Year Ended Dec. 31

| Per Share Data ($) | 2007 | 2006 | 2005 | 2004 | 2003 | 2002 | 2001 | 2000 | 1999 | 1998 |
|---|---|---|---|---|---|---|---|---|---|---|
| Tangible Book Value | 16.32 | 10.46 | 11.05 | 10.73 | 9.63 | 7.21 | 5.64 | 4.47 | 3.65 | 3.20 |
| Cash Flow | 4.55 | 4.87 | 4.25 | 3.72 | 3.18 | 2.48 | 1.93 | 1.56 | 1.23 | 0.97 |
| Earnings | 3.74 | 3.93 | 3.41 | 3.00 | 2.50 | 1.90 | 1.43 | 1.13 | 0.87 | 0.69 |
| S&P Core Earnings | 3.76 | 3.95 | 3.44 | 2.98 | 2.51 | 1.85 | 1.34 | NA | NA | NA |
| Dividends | 1.06 | 0.81 | 0.63 | 0.41 | 0.20 | 0.14 | 0.12 | 0.10 | 0.09 | 0.08 |
| Payout Ratio | 28% | 21% | 18% | 13% | 8% | 7% | 8% | 9% | 10% | 11% |
| Prices:High | 74.03 | 75.87 | 62.49 | 63.75 | 52.51 | 57.25 | 55.99 | 50.63 | 32.03 | 23.75 |
| Prices:Low | 44.37 | 47.86 | 44.40 | 45.20 | 35.01 | 42.60 | 32.00 | 29.53 | 21.38 | 12.47 |
| P/E Ratio:High | 20 | 19 | 18 | 21 | 21 | 30 | 39 | 45 | 37 | 34 |
| P/E Ratio:Low | 12 | 12 | 13 | 15 | 14 | 22 | 22 | 26 | 25 | 18 |

| Income Statement Analysis (Million $) | 2007 | 2006 | 2005 | 2004 | 2003 | 2002 | 2001 | 2000 | 1999 | 1998 |
|---|---|---|---|---|---|---|---|---|---|---|
| Revenue | 6,153 | 5,801 | 5,342 | 5,015 | 4,624 | 4,091 | 3,363 | 2,906 | 2,453 | 2,064 |
| Operating Income | 1,721 | 1,431 | 1,676 | 1,576 | 1,346 | 1,059 | 816 | 648 | 530 | 421 |
| Depreciation | 204 | 214 | 206 | 214 | 197 | 176 | 153 | 133 | 114 | 87.4 |
| Interest Expense | 81.5 | Nil | Nil | Nil | Nil | Nil | Nil | Nil | Nil | Nil |
| Pretax Income | 1,448 | 1,624 | 1,488 | 1,379 | 1,166 | 886 | 673 | 549 | 421 | 336 |
| Effective Tax Rate | 35.5% | 35.8% | 35.5% | 35.5% | 34.7% | 34.5% | 35.0% | 36.6% | 36.5% | 36.5% |
| Net Income | 934 | 1,043 | 960 | 890 | 761 | 580 | 438 | 348 | 267 | 214 |
| S&P Core Earnings | 940 | 1,048 | 969 | 881 | 763 | 564 | 411 | NA | NA | NA |

| Balance Sheet & Other Financial Data (Million $) | 2007 | 2006 | 2005 | 2004 | 2003 | 2002 | 2001 | 2000 | 1999 | 1998 |
|---|---|---|---|---|---|---|---|---|---|---|
| Cash | 405 | 897 | 1,046 | 1,612 | 1,323 | 796 | 635 | 420 | 183 | 165 |
| Total Assets | 5,657 | 5,532 | 5,255 | 5,483 | 4,923 | 3,861 | 3,118 | 2,436 | 2,112 | 1,920 |
| Long Term Debt | 980 | 87.0 | 1,000 | 800 | 670 | 380 | 380 | 355 | 280 | 280 |
| Total Debt | 2,100 | 87.0 | 1,205 | 1,295 | 794 | 763 | 597 | 445 | 461 | 427 |
| Common Equity | 2,375 | 2,757 | 3,084 | 3,218 | 2,958 | 2,233 | 1,756 | 1,406 | 1,161 | 1,080 |
| Capital Expenditures | 242 | 220 | 198 | 214 | 227 | 324 | 204 | 204 | 166 | 183 |
| Cash Flow | 1,138 | 1,257 | 1,165 | 1,104 | 958 | 756 | 591 | 481 | 381 | 301 |
| % Return on Assets | 16.7 | 19.3 | 17.9 | 17.1 | 17.3 | 16.6 | 15.8 | 15.3 | 13.3 | 12.2 |
| % Return on Equity | 36.4 | 35.7 | 30.5 | 28.8 | 29.3 | 29.1 | 27.7 | 27.1 | 24.4 | 23.0 |
| % Long Term Debt of Capitalization | 29.2 | 3.1 | 23.6 | 19.7 | 17.8 | 14.4 | 17.6 | 20.2 | 19.4 | 21.4 |

Data as orig reptd.; bef. results of disc opers/spec. items. Per share data adj. for stk. divs.; EPS diluted. E-Estimated. NA-Not Available. NM-Not Meaningful. NR-Not Ranked. UR-Under Review.

**Office:** 3700 W Juneau Ave, Milwaukee, WI 53208.
**Telephone:** 414-342-4680.
**Email:** investor_relations@harley-davidson.com
**Website:** http://www.harley-davidson.com

**Chrmn:** J.L. Bleustein
**Pres & CEO:** J.L. Ziemer
**Investor Contact:** T.E. Bergmann (414-342-4680)
**EVP, CFO & Chief Acctg Officer:** T.E. Bergmann

**EVP, Secy & General Counsel:** G.A. Lione
**Board Members:** B. K. Allen, R. I. Beattie, J. L. Bleustein, G. H. Conrades, J. C. Green, D. A. James, S. Levinson, N. T. Linebarger, G. L. Miles, Jr., J. A. Norling, J. Zeitz, J. L. Ziemer

**Founded:** 1903
**Domicile:** Wisconsin
**Employees:** 9,755

The *McGraw-Hill* Companies

# Harman International Industries Inc.

**STANDARD &POOR'S**

| S&P Recommendation | HOLD ★★★☆☆ | Price $14.88 (as of Nov 14, 2008) | 12-Mo. Target Price $25.00 | Investment Style Large-Cap Growth |
|---|---|---|---|---|

**GICS Sector** Consumer Discretionary
**Sub-Industry** Consumer Electronics

**Summary** This company manufactures and markets high-fidelity audio products and electronic systems targeted at OEM, consumer and professional markets.

## Key Stock Statistics (Source S&P, Vickers, company reports)

| | | | | | | | | |
|---|---|---|---|---|---|---|---|---|
| 52-Wk Range | $75.41– 13.53 | S&P Oper. EPS 2009E | 1.64 | Market Capitalization(B) | $0.871 | Beta | 1.82 |
| Trailing 12-Month EPS | $1.57 | S&P Oper. EPS 2010E | 1.60 | Yield (%) | 0.34 | S&P 3-Yr. Proj. EPS CAGR(%) | 10 |
| Trailing 12-Month P/E | 9.5 | P/E on S&P Oper. EPS 2009E | 9.1 | Dividend Rate/Share | $0.05 | S&P Credit Rating | BB+ |
| $10K Invested 5 Yrs Ago | $2,405 | Common Shares Outstg. (M) | 58.5 | Institutional Ownership (%) | 97 | | |

## Price Performance

30-Week Mov. Avg. ··· 10-Week Mov. Avg. -- **GAAP Earnings vs. Previous Year** Volume Above Avg. STARS
12-Mo. Target Price — Relative Strength — ▲ Up ▼ Down ► No Change Below Avg. ★

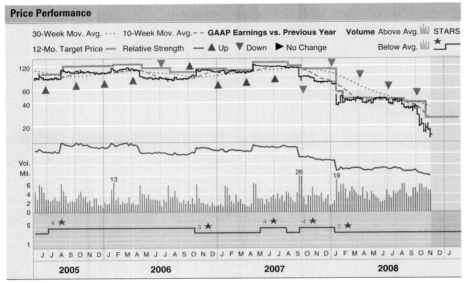

Options: ASE, CBOE, P, Ph

Analysis prepared by **Michael Souers** on November 06, 2008, when the stock traded at **$ 17.54**.

## Highlights

➤ For FY 09 (Jun.), we project overall revenues to decline 9.4%, following a rise of 16% in FY 08. We see this decline being driven by a decrease in demand caused by the deteriorating global economy and dismal environment for automotive sales. In addition, we project a reduction in volume from Mercedes -- which is now dual-sourced. We also see foreign currency translation being a rather significant headwind to revenues for the remainder of FY 09, due to the recent strength in the dollar. However, we note HAR's original equipment manufacturing pipeline for the auto segment is nearly booked through FY 10, which should help provide a sales buffer.

➤ HAR has identified $350 million in cost savings across engineering, sourcing and manufacturing, and we expect these efforts to be ongoing. However, in FY 09, given the significant decline in revenues that we project, we expect the deleveraging of fixed costs leading to a modest narrowing of operating margins.

➤ Excluding anticipated restructuring costs, we project EPS of $1.64 in FY 09, a 24% decline from the $2.17 earned in FY 08. We project EPS of $1.60 in FY 10.

## Investment Rationale/Risk

➤ Given the dramatic downturn in global automotive sales, we think HAR's recently announced plans to sharply reduce costs will not help improve operating margins until FY 10. We think investors are likely to remain skeptical about the company's progress until then, given recent expense guidance misses. We note HAR has announced several unfavorable revisions to its expense outlook over the past year, which we believe has reduced investor confidence in the company. We see no near-term catalyst for the stock, and we would not add to positions.

➤ Risks to our recommendation and target price include higher-than-anticipated research and development costs, further weakness in automotive sales, and a loss of customers.

➤ We derive our 12-month target price of $25, approximately 15X our FY 09 EPS estimate, by applying a 5.0X multiple to our FY 09 EBITDA estimate of $287 million. This multiple is at the bottom of HAR's 10 year historical trading range, reflecting the heightened near-term uncertainty we see in HAR's expense requirements and lack of revenue visibility.

## Qualitative Risk Assessment

| LOW | MEDIUM | HIGH |
|---|---|---|

Our risk assessment reflects our view of HAR's strong balance sheet, offset by its large customer concentration in the automotive segment and sensitivity to the cyclical automobile industry.

## Quantitative Evaluations

**S&P Quality Ranking** A-

| D | C | B- | B | B+ | A- | A | A+ |
|---|---|---|---|---|---|---|---|

**Relative Strength Rank** WEAK

20

LOWEST = 1    HIGHEST = 99

## Revenue/Earnings Data

**Revenue (Million $)**

| | 1Q | 2Q | 3Q | 4Q | Year |
|---|---|---|---|---|---|
| 2009 | 869.2 | -- | -- | -- | -- |
| 2008 | 947.0 | 1,066 | 1,033 | 1,067 | 4,113 |
| 2007 | 825.5 | 931.7 | 882.8 | 911.1 | 3,551 |
| 2006 | 754.7 | 832.7 | 801.5 | 859.1 | 3,248 |
| 2005 | 691.7 | 788.6 | 742.6 | 808.0 | 3,031 |
| 2004 | 597.3 | 691.6 | 690.4 | 732.0 | 2,711 |

**Earnings Per Share ($)**

| | | | | | |
|---|---|---|---|---|---|
| 2009 | 0.40 | E0.47 | E0.21 | E0.46 | E1.64 |
| 2008 | 0.55 | 0.68 | -0.06 | 0.54 | 1.73 |
| 2007 | 0.85 | 1.22 | 1.07 | 1.58 | 4.73 |
| 2006 | 0.79 | 1.07 | 0.94 | 0.95 | 3.75 |
| 2005 | 0.48 | 0.92 | 0.90 | 1.01 | 3.31 |
| 2004 | 0.29 | 0.46 | 0.63 | 0.76 | 2.27 |

Fiscal year ended Jun. 30. Next earnings report expected: Early February. EPS Estimates based on S&P Operating Earnings; historical GAAP earnings are as reported.

## Dividend Data (Dates: mm/dd Payment Date: mm/dd/yy)

| Amount ($) | Date Decl. | Ex-Div. Date | Stk. of Record | Payment Date |
|---|---|---|---|---|
| 0.013 | 01/23 | 02/04 | 02/06 | 02/20/08 |
| 0.013 | 04/24 | 05/05 | 05/07 | 05/21/08 |
| 0.013 | 07/28 | 08/04 | 08/06 | 08/20/08 |
| 0.013 | 10/21 | 11/03 | 11/05 | 11/19/08 |

Dividends have been paid since 1994. Source: Company reports.

# Harman International Industries Inc.

**STANDARD &POOR'S**

## Business Summary November 06, 2008

CORPORATE OVERVIEW. HAR has three operating segments: Automotive (72% of FY 08 (Jun.) sales), Professional (15%), and Consumer (13%). Within Automotive, HAR designs, manufactures and markets audio, electronic and infotainment systems to be installed as original equipment by automotive manufacturers. Infotainment systems are a combination of information and entertainment components that may include or control GPS navigation, traffic information, voice-activated telephone and climate control, rear seat entertainment, wireless Internet access, hard disk recording, MP3 playback, and high-end branded audio systems. Brand names include JBL, Infinity, Mark Levinson, Harman/Kardon, Logic 7, Lexicon and Becker. Customers include DaimlerChrysler, Mercedes Benz, the BMW Group, Toyota/Lexus, Audi/VW, Porsche, Land Rover, Hyundai and PSA Peugeot Citroen. HAR also produces an infotainment system for Harley-Davidson motorcycles, and produces personal navigation devices that are primarily sold in Europe.

In the Consumer segment, HAR makes audio, video and electronic systems for home, mobile and multimedia applications. Mobile products include an array of aftermarket systems to deliver audio entertainment and navigation in vehicles. Products for multimedia applications are primarily focused on enhancing sound for Apple's iPods and iPhones, computers, headphones and MP3 players. Brands include JBL, Infinity, Harman/Kardon, Lexicon, Mark Levinson and Revel. The Professional segment produces loudspeakers and electronics used by audio professionals in concert halls, stadiums, and other buildings for recording, broadcast, cinema and music reproduction applications. In August 2008, the company installed sound systems at venues in China for the Olympics. Brands include JBL Professional, Soundcraft, AKG, Lexicon, BSS and Studer.

DaimlerChrysler accounted for 18% of the company's net sales in FY 08, primarily from the Mercedes-Benz division, while Audi/VW accounted for an additional 11% of revenues. Also, approximately 72% of sales where to automobile manufacturers. Thus, we believe HAR has a significant level of customer concentration risk, though we see no near-term threat to the business.

## Company Financials Fiscal Year Ended Jun. 30

| Per Share Data ($) | 2008 | 2007 | 2006 | 2005 | 2004 | 2003 | 2002 | 2001 | 2000 | 1999 |
|---|---|---|---|---|---|---|---|---|---|---|
| Tangible Book Value | 15.44 | 16.71 | 12.82 | 10.74 | 9.43 | 6.66 | 5.04 | 4.33 | 4.69 | 4.61 |
| Cash Flow | NA | 6.64 | 5.66 | 4.99 | 3.80 | 2.85 | 2.00 | 1.48 | 1.95 | 1.09 |
| Earnings | 1.73 | 4.72 | 3.75 | 3.31 | 2.27 | 1.55 | 0.85 | 0.48 | 1.03 | 0.16 |
| S&P Core Earnings | 1.79 | 4.75 | 3.75 | 3.28 | 2.27 | 1.51 | 0.76 | 0.41 | NA | NA |
| Dividends | 0.05 | 0.05 | 0.05 | 0.05 | 0.05 | 0.05 | 0.05 | 0.05 | 0.04 | 0.05 |
| Payout Ratio | 3% | 1% | 1% | 2% | 2% | 3% | 6% | 10% | 4% | 31% |
| Prices:High | 73.75 | 125.13 | 115.85 | 130.45 | 131.74 | 75.35 | 32.65 | 23.31 | 25.18 | 14.03 |
| Prices:Low | 13.53 | 69.48 | 74.65 | 68.54 | 66.12 | 26.15 | 19.09 | 11.64 | 13.75 | 8.56 |
| P/E Ratio:High | 43 | 27 | 31 | 39 | 58 | 49 | 38 | 49 | 24 | 86 |
| P/E Ratio:Low | 8 | 15 | 20 | 21 | 29 | 17 | 22 | 24 | 13 | 53 |

| Income Statement Analysis (Million $) | | | | | | | | | | |
|---|---|---|---|---|---|---|---|---|---|---|
| Revenue | 4,113 | 3,551 | 3,248 | 3,031 | 2,711 | 2,229 | 1,826 | 1,717 | 1,678 | 1,500 |
| Operating Income | NA | 514 | 527 | 470 | 360 | 255 | 181 | 138 | 186 | 143 |
| Depreciation | 152 | 127 | 130 | 119 | 106 | 88.5 | 78.1 | 67.2 | 64.6 | 66.8 |
| Interest Expense | NA | 1.50 | 13.0 | 10.5 | 17.2 | 22.6 | 22.4 | 25.0 | 18.5 | 23.6 |
| Pretax Income | 124 | 382 | 376 | 335 | 228 | 142 | 80.2 | 45.1 | 103 | 14.4 |
| Effective Tax Rate | 13.8% | 18.4% | 32.4% | 30.6% | 30.6% | 26.0% | 28.2% | 28.2% | 29.1% | 18.7% |
| Net Income | 108 | 314 | 255 | 233 | 158 | 105 | 57.5 | 32.4 | 72.8 | 11.7 |
| S&P Core Earnings | 111 | 316 | 256 | 231 | 158 | 102 | 51.5 | 27.3 | NA | NA |

| Balance Sheet & Other Financial Data (Million $) | | | | | | | | | | |
|---|---|---|---|---|---|---|---|---|---|---|
| Cash | 223 | 106 | 292 | 291 | 378 | 148 | 116 | 2.75 | 4.36 | 2.96 |
| Current Assets | NA | 1,233 | 1,249 | 1,183 | 1,204 | 968 | 877 | 709 | 671 | 647 |
| Total Assets | 2,827 | 2,509 | 2,355 | 2,187 | 1,989 | 1,704 | 1,480 | 1,162 | 1,138 | 1,066 |
| Current Liabilities | NA | 816 | 869 | 729 | 662 | 487 | 433 | 350 | 361 | 287 |
| Long Term Debt | NA | 57.7 | 179 | 331 | 388 | 498 | 470 | Nil | 255 | 280 |
| Common Equity | 1,340 | 1,510 | 1,228 | 1,061 | 875 | 656 | 527 | 423 | 486 | 468 |
| Total Capital | NA | 1,568 | 1,410 | 1,392 | 1,263 | 1,154 | 999 | 424 | 742 | 749 |
| Capital Expenditures | 139 | 175 | 131 | 176 | 135 | 116 | 114 | 88.1 | 80.4 | 67.8 |
| Cash Flow | NA | 441 | 385 | 352 | 264 | 194 | 136 | 99.6 | 137 | 78.5 |
| Current Ratio | 1.6 | 1.5 | 1.4 | 1.6 | 1.8 | 2.0 | 2.0 | 2.0 | 1.9 | 2.3 |
| % Long Term Debt of Capitalization | 24.2 | 3.7 | 12.7 | 23.8 | 30.7 | 43.2 | 47.1 | Nil | 34.3 | 37.4 |
| % Net Income of Revenue | 2.6 | 8.8 | 7.9 | 7.7 | 5.8 | 4.7 | 3.1 | 1.9 | 4.3 | 0.8 |
| % Return on Assets | 4.0 | 12.9 | 11.2 | 11.2 | 8.6 | 6.6 | 4.4 | 2.8 | 6.6 | 1.1 |
| % Return on Equity | 7.6 | 22.8 | 22.3 | 24.1 | 20.6 | 17.8 | 12.1 | 7.1 | 15.3 | 2.4 |

Data as orig reptd.; bef. results of disc opers/spec. items. Per share data adj. for stk. divs.; EPS diluted. E-Estimated. NA-Not Available. NM-Not Meaningful. NR-Not Ranked. UR-Under Review.

**Office:** 1101 Pennsylvania Avenue, N.W., Washington, DC 20004.
**Telephone:** 202-393-1101.
**Website:** http://www.harman.com
**Chrmn & CEO:** D.C. Paliwal

**EVP & CFO:** H.K. Parker
**EVP & CTO:** H. Schinagel
**Chief Acctg Officer:** J. Peter
**Treas:** R.C. Ryan

**Investor Contact:** S.B. Robinson (202-393-1101)
**Board Members:** B. F. Carroll, H. Einsmann, S. M. Hufstedler, A. M. Korologos, E. H. Meyer, D. C. Paliwal, K. Reiss, H. S. Runtagh, G. G. Steel

**Founded:** 1980
**Domicile:** Delaware
**Employees:** 11,694

The **McGraw-Hill** Companies

# Harris Corp

**STANDARD & POOR'S**

| S&P Recommendation **STRONG BUY** ★★★★★ | Price<br>$33.04 (as of Nov 14, 2008) | 12-Mo. Target Price<br>$49.00 | Investment Style<br>Large-Cap Growth |
|---|---|---|---|

**GICS Sector** Information Technology
**Sub-Industry** Communications Equipment

**Summary** This company focuses on communications equipment for voice, data and video applications for commercial and governmental customers.

## Key Stock Statistics (Source S&P, Vickers, company reports)

| | | | | | | | | |
|---|---|---|---|---|---|---|---|---|
| 52-Wk Range | $66.71 – 29.93 | S&P Oper. EPS 2009**E** | 4.09 | Market Capitalization(B) | $4.447 | Beta | 1.53 |
| Trailing 12-Month EPS | $3.41 | S&P Oper. EPS 2010**E** | 4.40 | Yield (%) | 2.42 | S&P 3-Yr. Proj. EPS CAGR(%) | 11 |
| Trailing 12-Month P/E | 9.7 | P/E on S&P Oper. EPS 2009**E** | 8.1 | Dividend Rate/Share | $0.80 | S&P Credit Rating | BBB+ |
| $10K Invested 5 Yrs Ago | $18,771 | Common Shares Outstg. (M) | 134.6 | Institutional Ownership (%) | 83 | | |

## Price Performance

30-Week Mov. Avg. · · · · 10-Week Mov. Avg. - - - GAAP Earnings vs. Previous Year   Volume Above Avg. STARS
12-Mo. Target Price —  Relative Strength — ▲ Up ▼ Down ▶ No Change   Below Avg. ★

Options: ASE, CBOE, P, Ph

Analysis prepared by **Todd Rosenbluth** on November 12, 2008, when the stock traded at **$ 33.74**.

## Highlights

➤ Following a sales advance of 25% in FY 08 (Jun.), with more than half the growth from the acquisition of Multimax, we see an 8.5% sales increase in FY 09. This projected growth reflects our view of strong government-related (38% of total sales in FY 08) product demand from increased spending to support government agencies, as well as improved demand for tactical radios in the U.S. and internationally within the defense communications unit (37%). We also see a modest recovery in the broadcast segment.

➤ Gross margins narrowed slightly to 31% in FY 08, due in part to some cost overruns, but we expect them to widen to 32% in FY 09, with additional cost savings in the second half of the year. We expect operating margins of 15% in FY 09, up from 14% in FY 08, with well contained SG&A expenses.

➤ Despite the absence of non-operating income, we estimate operating EPS of $4.09 in FY 09 and $4.40 in FY 10. Fourth quarter FY 07 results included an $0.08 non-recurring charge, and third quarter FY 08 results included a $0.22 negative impact from cost overruns.

## Investment Rationale/Risk

➤ We think HRS's dependence on U.S. and non-U.S. government spending gives the company better visibility to achieve its earnings guidance due to less sensitivity to the macro economy than its peers. We see growth being driven by new contracts to support tactical radios and IT services. We expect continued demand for HRS offerings as military operations are focused on improving communications even as troop deployments will likely fluctuate amid pending changes in the U.S. government. In mid-2008, HRS entertained offers to sell its business, but no transaction took place and we think tight credit limits a near-term deal.

➤ Risks to our recommendation and target price include reduced funding for U.S. governmental contracts, lower capital spending by service operators, and delays or missed contract orders.

➤ Based on projected 11% EPS growth over the next three years and a slight premium to peers P/E of about 12X our FY 09 EPS estimate, we arrive at our 12-month target price of $49. We believe HRS's strong balance sheet and dividend yield lends support.

## Qualitative Risk Assessment

| LOW | MEDIUM | HIGH |
|---|---|---|

With more than half of total sales coming from governments and government agencies, we believe HRS is exposed to uneven sales patterns and fixed-price contract risks, which may affect profitability. However, we view HRS's balance sheet and competitive position as strong.

## Quantitative Evaluations

**S&P Quality Ranking**    B+

| D | C | B- | B | B+ | A- | A | A+ |
|---|---|---|---|---|---|---|---|

**Relative Strength Rank**    MODERATE

55

LOWEST = 1    HIGHEST = 99

## Revenue/Earnings Data

**Revenue (Million $)**

| | 1Q | 2Q | 3Q | 4Q | Year |
|---|---|---|---|---|---|
| 2009 | 1,368 | -- | -- | -- | -- |
| 2008 | 1,231 | 1,318 | 1,330 | 1,433 | 5,311 |
| 2007 | 946.8 | 1,016 | 1,072 | 1,208 | 4,243 |
| 2006 | 759.7 | 841.6 | 881.1 | 992.4 | 3,475 |
| 2005 | 669.4 | 737.2 | 772.1 | 821.9 | 3,001 |
| 2004 | 547.9 | 593.9 | 654.0 | 722.8 | 2,519 |

**Earnings Per Share ($)**

| | 1Q | 2Q | 3Q | 4Q | Year |
|---|---|---|---|---|---|
| 2009 | 0.88 | E1.02 | E1.07 | E1.12 | E4.09 |
| 2008 | 0.73 | 0.83 | 0.78 | 0.91 | 3.26 |
| 2007 | 0.60 | 0.67 | 1.52 | 0.63 | 3.43 |
| 2006 | 0.36 | 0.22 | 0.52 | 0.61 | 1.71 |
| 2005 | 0.29 | 0.33 | 0.40 | 0.44 | 1.46 |
| 2004 | 0.19 | 0.24 | 0.26 | 0.25 | 0.94 |

Fiscal year ended Jun. 30. Next earnings report expected: Late January. EPS Estimates based on S&P Operating Earnings; historical GAAP earnings are as reported.

## Dividend Data (Dates: mm/dd Payment Date: mm/dd/yy)

| Amount ($) | Date Decl. | Ex-Div. Date | Stk. of Record | Payment Date |
|---|---|---|---|---|
| 0.150 | 02/22 | 02/29 | 03/04 | 03/14/08 |
| 0.150 | 04/25 | 05/28 | 05/30 | 06/13/08 |
| 0.200 | 08/25 | 09/02 | 09/04 | 09/17/08 |
| 0.200 | 10/24 | 11/19 | 11/21 | 12/05/08 |

Dividends have been paid since 1941. Source: Company reports.

# Harris Corp

STANDARD &POOR'S

## Business Summary November 12, 2008

CORPORATE OVERVIEW. Harris Corp. is an international communications equipment company that focuses on providing product, system and service solutions for commercial and governmental customers including communications networks, antennas, aviation electronics, and handheld radios. The company operates under three main business segments: government communications systems, defense communications (which includes the radio frequency communications segment), and broadcast communications. In FY 08 (Jun.), 24% of revenues were from non-U.S. markets.

PRIMARY BUSINESS DYNAMICS. The government communications systems (GCS) segment conducts advanced research, develops prototypes and designs, and develops and produces state-of-the-art airborne, space-borne and terrestrial communications, information processing systems for the Federal Aviation Administration (FAA), the U.S. Census Bureau and other governmental agencies. The government segment has a diverse portfolio of more than 300 programs. In July 2007, HRS was awarded a five-year U.S. government contract to provide IT solutions that support national security systems. In January 2008, Harris won business with the U.S. Air Force in a six-year contract that could be worth more than $400 million. In the first quarter of FY 09, HRS won additional IT business with a U.S. agency. The acquired Multimax business is part of this segment.

The defense communications segment supplies secure wireless voice and data communications products, systems and networks to the U.S. Department of Defense and other federal and state agencies, and foreign government defense agencies. The segment offers a line of secure tactical radio products and systems for person-transportable, mobile, strategic fixed-site and shipboard applications used by military personnel. In June 2007, HRS was awarded a multi-billion dollar contract with the Department of Defense to supply next-generation multi-band handheld radios. In October 2008, in conjunction with $168 million in revenues from tactical radios, HRS said demand for its Falcon radios remained robust, driven by a broad range of customers within the U.S. Department of Defense as well as throughout international markets. Orders in FY 08 were higher than the year before.

The broadcast communications segment serves the digital and analog television and radio infrastructure markets, providing transmission, automation, studio and network management systems. Demand for U.S. digital TV transmission and automation systems was weak in FY 08.

## Company Financials Fiscal Year Ended Jun. 30

| Per Share Data ($) | 2008 | 2007 | 2006 | 2005 | 2004 | 2003 | 2002 | 2001 | 2000 | 1999 |
|---|---|---|---|---|---|---|---|---|---|---|
| Tangible Book Value | 2.69 | NM | 3.90 | 5.79 | 7.96 | 7.21 | 7.05 | 6.82 | 8.75 | 9.52 |
| Cash Flow | NA | 4.75 | 2.53 | 1.94 | 1.36 | 0.87 | 1.04 | 0.75 | 0.68 | 0.71 |
| Earnings | 3.26 | 3.43 | 1.71 | 1.46 | 0.94 | 0.45 | 0.63 | 0.16 | 0.17 | 0.32 |
| S&P Core Earnings | 3.19 | 2.74 | 1.74 | 1.43 | 0.90 | 0.31 | 0.28 | -0.45 | NA | NA |
| Dividends | 0.60 | 0.44 | 0.32 | 0.24 | 0.20 | 0.16 | 0.10 | 0.10 | 0.05 | 0.24 |
| Payout Ratio | 18% | 13% | 19% | 16% | 21% | 36% | 16% | 63% | 29% | 76% |
| Prices:High | 66.71 | 66.94 | 49.78 | 45.78 | 34.58 | 19.74 | 19.35 | 18.50 | 19.69 | 20.31 |
| Prices:Low | 29.93 | 45.85 | 37.69 | 26.94 | 18.92 | 12.68 | 12.05 | 10.40 | 10.38 | 7.75 |
| P/E Ratio:High | 20 | 20 | 29 | 31 | 37 | 44 | 31 | NM | NM | 64 |
| P/E Ratio:Low | 9 | 13 | 22 | 18 | 20 | 28 | 19 | 65 | 61 | 25 |

| Income Statement Analysis (Million $) | 2008 | 2007 | 2006 | 2005 | 2004 | 2003 | 2002 | 2001 | 2000 | 1999 |
|---|---|---|---|---|---|---|---|---|---|---|
| Revenue | 5,311 | 4,243 | 3,475 | 3,001 | 2,519 | 2,093 | 1,876 | 1,955 | 1,807 | 1,744 |
| Operating Income | NA | 676 | 505 | 393 | 264 | 142 | 153 | 167 | 108 | 80.9 |
| Depreciation | 172 | 135 | 98.4 | 71.4 | 55.1 | 56.4 | 55.1 | 79.7 | 68.6 | 63.5 |
| Interest Expense | NA | 41.1 | 36.5 | 24.0 | 24.5 | 24.9 | 26.7 | 34.8 | 25.2 | 9.80 |
| Pretax Income | 638 | 661 | 381 | 298 | 180 | 90.1 | 125 | 72.4 | 38.5 | 78.0 |
| Effective Tax Rate | 31.6% | 28.9% | 37.5% | 32.2% | 30.2% | 34.0% | 34.0% | 70.4% | 35.1% | 36.0% |
| Net Income | 444 | 480 | 238 | 202 | 126 | 59.5 | 82.6 | 21.4 | 25.0 | 49.9 |
| S&P Core Earnings | 435 | 382 | 243 | 199 | 120 | 40.8 | 36.5 | -60.5 | NA | NA |

| Balance Sheet & Other Financial Data (Million $) | 2008 | 2007 | 2006 | 2005 | 2004 | 2003 | 2002 | 2001 | 2000 | 1999 |
|---|---|---|---|---|---|---|---|---|---|---|
| Cash | 392 | 409 | 181 | 378 | 644 | 466 | 278 | 250 | 811 | 101 |
| Current Assets | NA | 1,829 | 1,428 | 1,318 | 1,554 | 1,358 | 1,154 | 1,222 | 1,629 | 1,031 |
| Total Assets | 4,559 | 4,406 | 3,142 | 2,457 | 2,226 | 2,080 | 1,859 | 1,960 | 2,327 | 2,959 |
| Current Liabilities | NA | 1,638 | 752 | 590 | 543 | 496 | 426 | 460 | 556 | 807 |
| Long Term Debt | NA | 409 | 700 | 401 | 401 | 402 | 283 | 384 | 383 | 515 |
| Common Equity | 2,274 | 1,904 | 1,662 | 1,439 | 1,279 | 1,188 | 1,150 | 1,115 | 1,374 | 1,590 |
| Total Capital | NA | 2,701 | 2,390 | 1,867 | 1,683 | 1,590 | 1,433 | 1,500 | 1,757 | 2,151 |
| Capital Expenditures | 113 | 88.8 | 102 | 75.0 | 66.4 | 73.0 | 45.9 | 55.2 | 81.3 | 60.4 |
| Cash Flow | NA | 616 | 336 | 274 | 181 | 116 | 138 | 101 | 93.6 | 113 |
| Current Ratio | 2.1 | 1.1 | 1.9 | 2.2 | 2.9 | 2.7 | 2.7 | 2.7 | 2.9 | 1.3 |
| % Long Term Debt of Capitalization | 24.2 | 15.1 | 29.3 | 21.5 | 23.9 | 25.3 | 19.8 | 25.6 | 21.8 | 23.9 |
| % Net Income of Revenue | 8.4 | 11.3 | 6.8 | 6.7 | 5.0 | 2.8 | 4.4 | 1.1 | 1.4 | 2.9 |
| % Return on Assets | 9.9 | 12.7 | 8.5 | 8.6 | 5.8 | 3.0 | 4.3 | 1.0 | 0.9 | 1.6 |
| % Return on Equity | 21.3 | 26.9 | 15.3 | 14.9 | 10.2 | 5.1 | 7.3 | 1.7 | 1.7 | 3.1 |

Data as orig reptd.; bef. results of disc opers/spec. items. Per share data adj. for stk. divs.; EPS diluted. E-Estimated. NA-Not Available. NM-Not Meaningful. NR-Not Ranked. UR-Under Review.

**Office:** 1025 W. NASA Boulevard, Melbourne, FL 32919.
**Telephone:** 321-727-9100.
**Website:** http://www.harris.com
**Chrmn, Pres & CEO:** H.L. Lance

**COO & EVP:** R.K. Henry
**CFO:** G.L. McArthur
**CTO:** R.K. Buchanan
**Chief Acctg Officer:** L.A. Schwartz

**Investor Contact:** P. Padgett (321-727-9383)
**Board Members:** T. A. Dattilo, T. D. Growcock, L. Hay, III, K. L. Katen, S. Kaufman, L. F. Kenne, H. L. Lance, D. B. Rickard, J. C. Stoffel, G. T. Swienton, H. E. Tookes, II

**Founded:** 1916
**Domicile:** Delaware
**Employees:** 16,500

# Hartford Financial Services Group Inc. (The)

**STANDARD &POOR'S**

| S&P Recommendation | HOLD ★★★☆☆ | Price | 12-Mo. Target Price | Investment Style |
|---|---|---|---|---|
| | | $12.65 (as of Nov 14, 2008) | $14.00 | Large-Cap Blend |

**GICS Sector** Financials
**Sub-Industry** Multi-line Insurance

**Summary** HIG is one of the largest U.S. multi-line insurance holding companies, and is a leading writer of individual variable annuities in the U.S. and Japan.

## Key Stock Statistics (Source S&P, Vickers, company reports)

| | | | | | | | |
|---|---|---|---|---|---|---|---|
| 52-Wk Range | $98.70– 8.23 | S&P Oper. EPS 2008**E** | 4.40 | Market Capitalization(B) | $3.802 | Beta | 1.65 |
| Trailing 12-Month EPS | $-4.35 | S&P Oper. EPS 2009**E** | 6.87 | Yield (%) | 10.12 | S&P 3-Yr. Proj. EPS CAGR(%) | -6 |
| Trailing 12-Month P/E | NM | P/E on S&P Oper. EPS 2008**E** | 2.9 | Dividend Rate/Share | $1.28 | S&P Credit Rating | A |
| $10K Invested 5 Yrs Ago | $2,549 | Common Shares Outstg. (M) | 300.6 | Institutional Ownership (%) | 91 | | |

## Price Performance

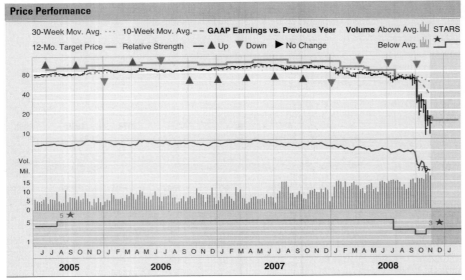

30-Week Mov. Avg. · · · 10-Week Mov. Avg. - - **GAAP Earnings vs. Previous Year** Volume Above Avg. STARS
12-Mo. Target Price — Relative Strength — ▲ Up ▼ Down ▶ No Change  Below Avg.

Options: ASE, CBOE, P, Ph

## Qualitative Risk Assessment

| LOW | MEDIUM | **HIGH** |
|---|---|---|

Our risk assessment reflects our view of HIG's vulnerability to further credit write downs, DAC charge-offs, and potential dilution of shares stemming from the recent capital infusion from Allianz. Also, we think HIG could face the need for an additional capital increases if the market environments worsen.

## Quantitative Evaluations

**S&P Quality Ranking**    B+

| D | C | B- | B | **B+** | A- | A | A+ |
|---|---|---|---|---|---|---|---|

**Relative Strength Rank**    WEAK

6

LOWEST = 1      HIGHEST = 99

## Revenue/Earnings Data

**Revenue (Million $)**

| | 1Q | 2Q | 3Q | 4Q | Year |
|---|---|---|---|---|---|
| 2008 | 1,544 | 7,503 | -393.0 | -- | -- |
| 2007 | 6,759 | 7,660 | 5,823 | 5,674 | 25,916 |
| 2006 | 6,543 | 4,971 | 7,407 | 7,579 | 26,500 |
| 2005 | 6,002 | 6,064 | 7,307 | 7,710 | 27,083 |
| 2004 | 5,732 | 5,444 | 5,416 | 6,101 | 22,693 |
| 2003 | 4,331 | 4,682 | 4,947 | 4,773 | 18,733 |

**Earnings Per Share ($)**

| | 1Q | 2Q | 3Q | 4Q | Year |
|---|---|---|---|---|---|
| 2008 | 0.46 | 1.73 | -8.74 | E1.10 | E4.40 |
| 2007 | 2.71 | 1.96 | 2.68 | 1.88 | 9.24 |
| 2006 | 2.34 | 1.52 | 2.39 | 2.42 | 8.69 |
| 2005 | 2.21 | 1.98 | 1.76 | 1.51 | 7.44 |
| 2004 | 2.01 | 1.46 | 1.66 | 2.08 | 7.20 |
| 2003 | -5.33 | 1.88 | 1.20 | 1.59 | -0.33 |

Fiscal year ended Dec. 31. Next earnings report expected: Late January. EPS Estimates based on S&P Operating Earnings; historical GAAP earnings are as reported.

## Highlights

➤ The 12-month target price for HIG has recently been changed to $14.00 from $16.00. The Highlights section of this Stock Report will be updated accordingly.

## Investment Rationale/Risk

➤ The Investment Rationale/Risk section of this Stock Report will be updated shortly. For the latest News story on HIG from MarketScope, see below.

➤ 11/14/08 04:59 pm ET ... S&P KEEPS HOLD OPINION ON SHARES OF HARTFORD FINANCIAL (HIG 12.65***): HIG agrees to acquire Federal Trust Corp (FDTR 0.23, NR), parent of Federal Trust Bank, for about $10M. In conjunction with this, HIG applied to become an S&L holding company and participate in Treasury's capital purchase program. All applications are subject to approval, and we think HIG's is uncertain, given a disproportionate amount of capital it would be eligible to receive under the program, which HIG estimates at $1.1B-$3.4B, and the acquisition price. We are lowering our target price $2 to $14, a below-peers 0.5X book value, on our concerns about HIG's capital situation. / B.Howlett,K.Cole-CFA

## Dividend Data (Dates: mm/dd Payment Date: mm/dd/yy)

| Amount ($) | Date Decl. | Ex-Div. Date | Stk. of Record | Payment Date |
|---|---|---|---|---|
| 0.530 | 02/21 | 02/28 | 03/03 | 04/01/08 |
| 0.530 | 05/21 | 05/29 | 06/02 | 07/01/08 |
| 0.530 | 07/17 | 08/28 | 09/02 | 10/01/08 |
| 0.320 | 10/15 | 11/26 | 12/01 | 01/02/09 |

Dividends have been paid since 1996. Source: Company reports.

The McGraw·Hill Companies

# Hartford Financial Services Group Inc. (The)

**STANDARD
&POOR'S**

## Business Summary November 06, 2008

CORPORATE OVERVIEW. As a multi-line insurer, HIG underwrites life as well as property-casualty insurance. Segment revenues totaled $25.9 billion in 2007, of which life accounted for 52% and property-casualty for the remaining 48%.

HIG's property-casualty operation provides a wide range of commercial, personal, specialty and reinsurance coverages. It constitutes one of the largest U.S. property-casualty insurance organizations, and is the endorsed provider of automobile and homeowners coverages to members of AARP. Earned premiums of $10.5 billion in 2007 were derived from personal lines (37%), small commercial lines (26%), middle market commercial lines (22%) and specialty commercial (15%).

HIG's life insurance operations are conducted by Hartford Life, Inc. The Retail Investment Products Group (which accounted for 50% of the life division's nearly $2.0 billion of segment operating profits in 2007) provides an array of investment and savings products to individual investors, including annuities,

mutual funds, 401(k) plans and 529 college savings plans. Group Benefits (17% of segment profits in 2007) offers short- and long-term disability insurance, group life and accident insurance, and other specialty products to employers, associations and affinity groups. The Individual Life segment (10%) offers an array of life insurance, including variable universal life, universal life, whole life and term life insurance. The Institutional Solutions Group (7%) provides customized wealth creation and financial protection solutions for institutions, corporations and high-net-worth individuals. The Retirement Plans Group (4% of 2007 segment operating profits) provides retirement plans for corporate clients and non-profit organizations. The International unit (13%) offers fixed and variable annuities in Japan, Brazil and the U.K.

## Company Financials Fiscal Year Ended Dec. 31

| Per Share Data ($) | 2007 | 2006 | 2005 | 2004 | 2003 | 2002 | 2001 | 2000 | 1999 | 1998 |
|---|---|---|---|---|---|---|---|---|---|---|
| Tangible Book Value | 55.69 | 53.12 | 45.05 | 42.58 | 34.80 | 35.31 | 29.87 | 32.88 | 25.07 | 28.17 |
| Operating Earnings | NA | NA | NA | NA | -0.93 | 4.96 | 3.00 | 4.29 | 3.68 | 3.45 |
| Earnings | 9.24 | 8.69 | 7.44 | 7.20 | -0.33 | 3.97 | 2.27 | 4.36 | 3.79 | 4.30 |
| S&P Core Earnings | 11.27 | 8.98 | 7.62 | 6.52 | -1.15 | 4.27 | 2.22 | NA | NA | NA |
| Dividends | 2.03 | 1.70 | 1.17 | 1.13 | 1.09 | 1.05 | 1.01 | 0.97 | 0.90 | 0.85 |
| Relative Payout | 22% | 20% | 16% | 16% | NM | 26% | 44% | 22% | 24% | 20% |
| Prices:High | 106.23 | 94.03 | 89.49 | 69.57 | 59.27 | 70.24 | 71.15 | 80.00 | 66.44 | 60.00 |
| Prices:Low | 83.00 | 79.24 | 65.35 | 52.73 | 31.64 | 37.25 | 45.50 | 29.38 | 36.50 | 37.63 |
| P/E Ratio:High | 11 | 11 | 12 | 10 | NM | 18 | 31 | 18 | 18 | 14 |
| P/E Ratio:Low | 9 | 9 | 9 | 7 | NM | 9 | 20 | 7 | 10 | 9 |

| Income Statement Analysis (Million $) | | | | | | | | | | |
|---|---|---|---|---|---|---|---|---|---|---|
| Life Insurance in Force | 179,483 | 164,227 | 764,293 | 139,889 | 704,369 | 629,028 | 534,489 | 585,582 | 527,285 | 528,608 |
| Premium Income:Life A & H | 15,619 | 15,023 | 14,359 | 13,566 | 11,891 | 4,884 | 4,903 | 4,565 | 4,069 | 4,371 |
| Premium Income:Casualty/Property. | NA | NA | NA | NA | 8,805 | 8,114 | 7,266 | 6,975 | 6,488 | 7,245 |
| Net Investment Income | 5,359 | 6,515 | 8,231 | 5,162 | 3,233 | 2,953 | 2,850 | 2,674 | 2,627 | 3,102 |
| Total Revenue | 25,916 | 26,500 | 27,083 | 22,693 | 18,733 | 15,907 | 15,147 | 14,703 | 13,528 | 15,022 |
| Pretax Income | 4,005 | 3,602 | 2,985 | 2,523 | -550 | 1,068 | 354 | 1,418 | 1,235 | 1,475 |
| Net Operating Income | NA | NA | NA | NA | -253 | 1,250 | 724 | 962 | 837 | 816 |
| Net Income | 2,949 | 2,745 | 2,274 | 2,138 | -91.0 | 1,000 | 549 | 974 | 862 | 1,015 |
| S&P Core Earnings | 3,598 | 2,839 | 2,335 | 1,936 | -315 | 1,078 | 538 | NA | NA | NA |

| Balance Sheet & Other Financial Data (Million $) | | | | | | | | | | |
|---|---|---|---|---|---|---|---|---|---|---|
| Cash & Equivalent | 2,011 | 1,424 | 1,273 | 1,148 | 462 | 377 | 353 | 227 | 182 | 123 |
| Premiums Due | 3,681 | 3,675 | 6,360 | 6,178 | 9,043 | 7,706 | 2,432 | 6,874 | 2,071 | 1,833 |
| Investment Assets:Bonds | 81,657 | 80,755 | 76,440 | 75,100 | 61,263 | 48,889 | 40,046 | 34,492 | 32,875 | 35,331 |
| Investment Assets:Stocks | 38,777 | 31,132 | 25,495 | 14,466 | 565 | 917 | 1,349 | 1,056 | 1,286 | 1,066 |
| Investment Assets:Loans | 7,471 | 5,369 | 3,747 | 2,662 | 2,512 | 2,934 | 3,317 | 3,610 | 4,222 | 6,687 |
| Investment Assets:Total | 131,086 | 119,173 | 106,935 | 94,408 | 65,847 | 54,530 | 46,689 | 40,669 | 39,141 | 43,696 |
| Deferred Policy Costs | 11,742 | 10,268 | 9,702 | 8,509 | 7,599 | 6,689 | 6,420 | 5,305 | 5,038 | 4,579 |
| Total Assets | 360,361 | 326,710 | 285,557 | 259,735 | 225,853 | 182,043 | 181,238 | 171,532 | 167,051 | 150,632 |
| Debt | 3,951 | 3,762 | 4,048 | 4,308 | 4,613 | 4,064 | 3,377 | 3,105 | 2,798 | 2,798 |
| Common Equity | 19,204 | 18,876 | 15,325 | 14,238 | 11,639 | 10,734 | 9,013 | 7,464 | 5,466 | 6,423 |
| Combined Loss-Expense Ratio | 90.8 | 89.3 | 93.2 | 95.3 | 98.0 | 99.2 | 112.4 | 102.4 | 103.3 | 102.9 |
| % Return on Revenue | 11.4 | 10.4 | 8.4 | 9.4 | NM | 6.3 | 3.6 | 6.6 | 6.4 | 6.8 |
| % Return on Equity | 15.5 | 16.1 | 15.4 | 16.5 | NM | 10.1 | 6.7 | 15.1 | 14.5 | 16.2 |
| % Investment Yield | 4.3 | 5.8 | 8.2 | 6.4 | 5.4 | 5.8 | 6.5 | 6.7 | 6.3 | 7.7 |

Data as orig reptd.; bef. results of disc opers/spec. items. Per share data adj. for stk. divs.; EPS diluted. E-Estimated. NA-Not Available. NM-Not Meaningful. NR-Not Ranked. UR-Under Review.

**Office:** 1 Hartford Plz, Hartford, CT 06155-0001.
**Telephone:** 860-547-5000.
**Website:** http://www.thehartford.com
**Chrmn & CEO:** R. Ayer

**Pres & COO:** T.M. Marra
**EVP & CFO:** L.H. Zlatkus
**EVP & General Counsel:** A.J. Kreczko
**SVP, Chief Acctg Officer & Cntlr:** B.A. Bombara

**Investor Contact:** D.M. Johnson (860-547-2537)
**Board Members:** R. B. Allardice, III, R. Ayer, T. Fetter, E. J. Kelly, III, P. G. Kirk, Jr., T. M. Marra, G. J. McGovern, M. G. Morris, C. B. Strauss, H. P. Swygert, R. de Oliveira

**Founded:** 1810
**Domicile:** Delaware
**Employees:** 31,000

The **McGraw·Hill** Companies

# Hasbro Inc.

STANDARD &POOR'S

**S&P Recommendation** HOLD ★★★☆☆

**Price**
$26.94 (as of Nov 14, 2008)

**12-Mo. Target Price**
$34.00

**GICS Sector** Consumer Discretionary
**Sub-Industry** Leisure Products

**Summary** This large toy company has brands that include Monopoly, Playskool and Tonka, as well as various items related to categories such as Star Wars and Pokemon.

## Key Stock Statistics (Source S&P, Vickers, company reports)

| | | | | | | | | |
|---|---|---|---|---|---|---|---|---|
| 52-Wk Range | $41.68– 21.57 | S&P Oper. EPS 2008E | 2.27 | Market Capitalization(B) | $3.750 | Beta | 1.30 |
| Trailing 12-Month EPS | $2.23 | S&P Oper. EPS 2009E | 2.42 | Yield (%) | 2.97 | S&P 3-Yr. Proj. EPS CAGR(%) | 7 |
| Trailing 12-Month P/E | 12.1 | P/E on S&P Oper. EPS 2008E | 11.9 | Dividend Rate/Share | $0.80 | S&P Credit Rating | BBB |
| $10K Invested 5 Yrs Ago | $13,335 | Common Shares Outstg. (M) | 139.2 | Institutional Ownership (%) | 99 | | |

## Price Performance

30-Week Mov. Avg. · · · · 10-Week Mov. Avg. - - - GAAP Earnings vs. Previous Year   Volume Above Avg. ▌▌▌▌ STARS
12-Mo. Target Price —   Relative Strength —   ▲ Up ▼ Down ▶ No Change   Below Avg. ▌▌▌ ★

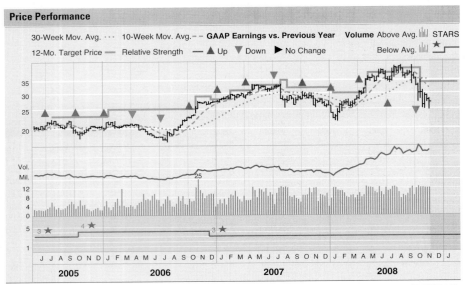

Options: ASE, CBOE, P, Ph

Analysis prepared by **Erik Kolb** on October 17, 2008, when the stock traded at **$ 30.09**.

## Highlights

➤ We see net revenues increasing 4.7% for 2008, to $4.02 billion, as comparisons to 2007 remain tough, since revenues rose 32% last year. However, we see a variety of new products gaining traction this year, especially in the boys category. Indeed, new animated Star Wars theatrical and TV releases, Marvel movie releases, and continued strength of Nerf all augur well for HAS, in our view. Elsewhere, royalties generated from the Electronic Arts agreement will likely be modest in 2008, but we see a ramp-up in 2009 and beyond. For 2009, we expect 4.5% higher net revenues on core growth and the positive impact from the Transformers 2 and GI Joe movie releases.

➤ We expect 2008 operating margins to increase about 50 basis points, to 14.0%, as an improved product mix, greater international sales, and the initial EA licensing contribution are partially offset by rising production costs at Chinese facilities and higher advertising expenses. We expect a modest 20 basis point improvement, to 14.2%, in 2009.

➤ We estimate operating EPS of $2.18 and $2.35 for 2008 and 2009, respectively.

## Investment Rationale/Risk

➤ We have a hold recommendation on HAS, which recently traded at about 14X our 2008 EPS estimate. We think the company is well positioned to grow its market share in the toy category, particularly as it increases the use of technology in its offerings to make toys more interactive, but given the weakened economy, near-term consumer spending habits are less certain. We believe HAS has strong cash flow and an improved balance sheet, which should enable the company to enhance shareholder value through its ongoing share repurchase program.

➤ Risks to our recommendation and target price include more store closings and tight inventory management at toy retailers, weak consumer spending and/or negative consumer sentiment, a lack of market demand for HAS products, and increased competition in the consumer electronic toy category from larger consumer electronics manufacturers.

➤ Our 12-month target price of $34 applies a P/E of about 15X to a blend of our 2008 and 2009 EPS estimates, roughly in line with historical and toy industry peer averages.

## Qualitative Risk Assessment

| LOW | MEDIUM | HIGH |
|---|---|---|

Our risk assessment takes into account our view of HAS's strong market share position and healthy balance sheet, offset by intense industry rivalry and the concentrated buying power of U.S. toy retailers.

## Quantitative Evaluations

**S&P Quality Ranking**     B+

| D | C | B- | B | B+ | A- | A | A+ |
|---|---|---|---|---|---|---|---|

**Relative Strength Rank**     MODERATE

64

LOWEST = 1     HIGHEST = 99

## Revenue/Earnings Data

**Revenue (Million $)**

| | 1Q | 2Q | 3Q | 4Q | Year |
|---|---|---|---|---|---|
| 2008 | 704.2 | 784.3 | 1,302 | -- | -- |
| 2007 | 625.3 | 691.4 | 1,223 | 1,298 | 3,838 |
| 2006 | 468.2 | 527.8 | 1,039 | 1,116 | 3,151 |
| 2005 | 454.9 | 572.4 | 988.1 | 1,072 | 3,088 |
| 2004 | 474.3 | 516.4 | 947.3 | 1,060 | 2,998 |
| 2003 | 461.8 | 581.5 | 581.5 | 1,124 | 3,139 |

**Earnings Per Share ($)**

| | | | | | |
|---|---|---|---|---|---|
| 2008 | 0.25 | 0.25 | 0.89 | E0.88 | E2.27 |
| 2007 | 0.19 | 0.03 | 0.95 | 0.84 | 1.97 |
| 2006 | -0.03 | 0.07 | 0.58 | 0.62 | 1.29 |
| 2005 | -0.02 | 0.13 | 0.47 | 0.48 | 1.09 |
| 2004 | 0.03 | 0.06 | 0.43 | 0.44 | 0.96 |
| 2003 | 0.01 | 0.06 | 0.06 | 0.43 | 0.98 |

Fiscal year ended Dec. 31. Next earnings report expected: Mid February. EPS Estimates based on S&P Operating Earnings; historical GAAP earnings are as reported.

## Dividend Data (Dates: mm/dd Payment Date: mm/dd/yy)

| Amount ($) | Date Decl. | Ex-Div. Date | Stk. of Record | Payment Date |
|---|---|---|---|---|
| 0.160 | 12/06 | 01/30 | 02/01 | 02/15/08 |
| 0.200 | 02/07 | 04/29 | 05/01 | 05/15/08 |
| 0.200 | 05/22 | 07/30 | 08/01 | 08/15/08 |
| 0.200 | 10/03 | 10/30 | 11/03 | 11/17/08 |

Dividends have been paid since 1981. Source: Company reports.

**Please read the Required Disclosures and Analyst Certification on the last page of this report.**

# Hasbro Inc.

## Business Summary October 17, 2008

CORPORATE OVERVIEW. Hasbro is a worldwide leader in children's and family leisure time and entertainment products and services, including the design, manufacture and marketing of games and toys ranging from traditional to high-tech. Some of the company's widely recognized core brands, both internationally and in the U.S., are Playskool, Tonka, Super Soaker, Milton Bradley, Parker Brothers, Tiger And Wizards of the Coast. Offerings in the games segment include traditional board games, hand-held electronic, trading card, plug and play and DVD games, as well as electronic learning aids and puzzles. Toy offerings include boys' action figures, vehicles and playsets, girls' toys, electronic toys, plush products, preschool toys and infant products, children's consumer electronics, electronic interactive products and toy related specialty products.

Part of HAS's growth strategy includes licensing, which has been successful in the past for HAS. In 2005, revenues generated from the sale of Star Wars products produced under its license with Lucas Licensing and Lucasfilm represented approximately 16% of total company revenues. In January 2006, HAS completed a licensing agreement with Marvel Entertainment, Inc. to produce action figures and other toys and games based on their library of intellectual property, including Spiderman and the Fantastic 4. Products related to this license began shipping late in 2006, with full ramp-up realized in 2007.

MARKET PROFILE. According to the NPD Group, a leading consumer and retail information provider, retail sales in the U.S. toy industry decreased approximately 2.2%, to $22.1 billion, in 2007, versus $22.6 billion generated in 2006. This compares to a 15% rise in HAS North American sales for 2007. Although total industry sales declined, certain subcategories that HAS participates in performed well, contributing to the company's market share gains. In particular, Boys' toys rose approximately 79% to $1.02 billion, and Girls' toys increased 29% to $697 million. Excluding HAS's international sales, we estimate that the company had approximately an 11% market share in the U.S. toy industry in 2007.

## Company Financials Fiscal Year Ended Dec. 31

| Per Share Data ($) | 2007 | 2006 | 2005 | 2004 | 2003 | 2002 | 2001 | 2000 | 1999 | 1998 |
|---|---|---|---|---|---|---|---|---|---|---|
| Tangible Book Value | 2.95 | 3.34 | 3.61 | 3.01 | 1.32 | 0.08 | NM | NM | 0.64 | 2.05 |
| Cash Flow | 2.86 | 2.35 | 2.20 | 1.75 | 2.37 | 0.95 | 1.66 | 0.69 | 2.31 | 1.48 |
| Earnings | 1.97 | 1.29 | 1.09 | 0.96 | 0.98 | 0.43 | 0.35 | -0.82 | 0.93 | 1.01 |
| S&P Core Earnings | 1.96 | 1.29 | 1.02 | 0.90 | 0.93 | 0.44 | 0.19 | NA | NA | NA |
| Dividends | 0.60 | 0.45 | 0.33 | 0.21 | 0.12 | 0.12 | 0.12 | 0.24 | 0.23 | 0.21 |
| Payout Ratio | 30% | 35% | 30% | 22% | 12% | 28% | 34% | NM | 25% | 21% |
| Prices:High | 33.49 | 27.69 | 22.35 | 23.33 | 22.63 | 17.30 | 18.44 | 18.94 | 37.00 | 27.29 |
| Prices:Low | 25.25 | 17.00 | 17.75 | 16.90 | 11.23 | 9.87 | 10.31 | 8.38 | 16.88 | 18.67 |
| P/E Ratio:High | 17 | 21 | 21 | 24 | 23 | 40 | 53 | NM | 40 | 27 |
| P/E Ratio:Low | 13 | 13 | 16 | 18 | 11 | 23 | 29 | NM | 18 | 18 |

| Income Statement Analysis (Million $) | 2007 | 2006 | 2005 | 2004 | 2003 | 2002 | 2001 | 2000 | 1999 | 1998 |
|---|---|---|---|---|---|---|---|---|---|---|
| Revenue | 3,838 | 3,151 | 3,088 | 2,998 | 3,139 | 2,816 | 2,856 | 3,787 | 4,232 | 3,304 |
| Operating Income | 686 | 523 | 491 | 439 | 509 | 309 | 435 | 268 | 669 | 442 |
| Depreciation | 157 | 147 | 180 | 146 | 240 | 89.3 | 226 | 264 | 277 | 97.0 |
| Interest Expense | 34.6 | 27.5 | 30.5 | 31.7 | 52.5 | 77.5 | 104 | 114 | 69.3 | 36.1 |
| Pretax Income | 462 | 341 | 311 | 260 | 244 | 104 | 96.2 | -226 | 274 | 303 |
| Effective Tax Rate | 28.0% | 32.6% | 31.8% | 24.6% | 28.3% | 27.9% | 36.8% | NM | 31.0% | 32.0% |
| Net Income | 333 | 230 | 212 | 196 | 175 | 75.1 | 60.8 | -145 | 189 | 206 |
| S&P Core Earnings | 332 | 230 | 199 | 184 | 166 | 79.1 | 33.8 | NA | NA | NA |

| Balance Sheet & Other Financial Data (Million $) | 2007 | 2006 | 2005 | 2004 | 2003 | 2002 | 2001 | 2000 | 1999 | 1998 |
|---|---|---|---|---|---|---|---|---|---|---|
| Cash | 774 | 715 | 942 | 725 | 521 | 495 | 233 | 127 | 280 | 178 |
| Current Assets | 1,888 | 1,718 | 1,830 | 1,718 | 1,509 | 1,432 | 1,369 | 1,580 | 2,132 | 1,790 |
| Total Assets | 3,237 | 3,097 | 3,301 | 3,241 | 3,163 | 3,143 | 3,369 | 3,828 | 4,463 | 3,794 |
| Current Liabilities | 888 | 906 | 911 | 1,149 | 930 | 967 | 759 | 1,240 | 2,071 | 1,366 |
| Long Term Debt | 710 | 495 | 496 | 303 | 687 | 857 | 1,166 | 1,168 | 421 | 407 |
| Common Equity | 1,385 | 1,538 | 1,723 | 1,640 | 1,405 | 1,191 | 1,353 | 1,327 | 1,879 | 1,945 |
| Total Capital | 2,095 | 2,033 | 2,219 | 1,942 | 2,092 | 2,049 | 2,519 | 2,495 | 2,300 | 2,352 |
| Capital Expenditures | 91.5 | 82.1 | 70.6 | 79.2 | 63.1 | 58.7 | 50.0 | 125 | 107 | 142 |
| Cash Flow | 490 | 377 | 392 | 342 | 415 | 164 | 287 | 120 | 466 | 303 |
| Current Ratio | 2.1 | 1.9 | 2.0 | 1.5 | 1.6 | 1.5 | 1.8 | 1.3 | 1.0 | 1.3 |
| % Long Term Debt of Capitalization | 33.8 | 24.3 | 22.3 | 15.6 | 32.8 | 41.8 | 46.3 | 46.8 | 18.3 | 17.3 |
| % Net Income of Revenue | 8.7 | 7.3 | 6.9 | 6.5 | 5.6 | 2.7 | 2.1 | NM | 4.5 | 6.2 |
| % Return on Assets | 10.5 | 7.2 | 6.5 | 6.1 | 5.6 | 2.3 | 1.7 | NM | 4.6 | 6.2 |
| % Return on Equity | 22.8 | 14.1 | 12.6 | 12.9 | 13.5 | 5.9 | 4.5 | NM | 9.9 | 10.9 |

Data as orig reptd.; bef. results of disc opers/spec. items. Per share data adj. for stk. divs.; EPS diluted. E-Estimated. NA-Not Available. NM-Not Meaningful. NR-Not Ranked. UR-Under Review.

**Office:** 1027 Newport Ave, Pawtucket, RI, USA 02861-2500.
**Telephone:** 401-431-8697.
**Website:** http://www.hasbro.com
**Chrmn:** A.J. Verrecchia

**Pres & CEO:** B. Goldner
**Vice Chrmn:** A.R. Batkin
**COO, EVP, CFO & Chief Acctg Officer:** D.D. Hargreaves
**SVP & Treas:** M.R. Trueb

**Investor Contact:** D. Thomas Slater (401-431-8697)
**Board Members:** B. L. Anderson, A. R. Batkin, F. J. Biondi, Jr., K. A. Bronfin, J. M. Connors, Jr., M. W. Garrett, E. G. Gee, B. Goldner, J. M. Greenberg, A. G. Hassenfeld, T. A. Leinbach, E. M. Philip, P. Stern, A. J. Verrecchia

**Founded:** 1926
**Domicile:** Rhode Island
**Employees:** 5,900

**STANDARD &POOR'S**

# HCP Inc

| S&P Recommendation | HOLD ★★★☆☆ | Price<br>$21.58 (as of Nov 14, 2008) | 12-Mo. Target Price<br>$30.00 | Investment Style<br>Large-Cap Value |
|---|---|---|---|---|

**GICS Sector** Financials
**Sub-Industry** Specialized REITS

**Summary** This equity-oriented real estate investment trust, based in California, has direct or joint venture investments in health care-related facilities across the U.S.

## Key Stock Statistics (Source S&P, Vickers, company reports)

| | | | | | | | |
|---|---|---|---|---|---|---|---|
| 52-Wk Range | $42.16– 20.65 | S&P FFO/Sh. 2008E | 2.35 | Market Capitalization(B) | $5.452 | Beta | 1.05 |
| Trailing 12-Month FFO/Share | NA | S&P FFO/Sh. 2009E | 2.40 | Yield (%) | 8.43 | S&P 3-Yr. FFO/Sh. Proj. CAGR(%) | 7 |
| Trailing 12-Month P/FFO | NA | P/FFO on S&P FFO/Sh. 2008E | 9.2 | Dividend Rate/Share | $1.82 | S&P Credit Rating | BBB |
| $10K Invested 5 Yrs Ago | $9,869 | Common Shares Outstg. (M) | 252.7 | Institutional Ownership (%) | 79 | | |

## Price Performance

- 30-Week Mov. Avg.
- 10-Week Mov. Avg.
- 12-Mo. Target Price
- Relative Strength
- GAAP Earnings vs. Previous Year
- ▲ Up  ▼ Down  ► No Change
- Volume Above Avg.  Below Avg.
- STARS

Options: CBOE

Analysis prepared by **Rikin Pandya** on October 23, 2008, when the stock traded at **$ 28.51.**

## Highlights

- During the first six months of 2008, HCP sold non-core assets for gross proceeds of $526 million. Dispositions have focused on the acute care hospital sector, which we expect to reduce the trust's risk from pressure on Medicare and Medicaid reimbursement rates. Due to tight credit market conditions, however, we think HCP may still come up short on its full-year target of $700 million to $800 million in total 2008 asset dispositions.

- We expect HCP's same-property portfolio to deliver low single digit growth in net operating income in 2008. We think its direct debt investments and life sciences facilities will show the strongest performance, with hospitals and senior housing delivering more limited growth. Debt paydown and select acquisitions are likely to aid growth and about offset dilution from HCP's $3.2 billion acquisition of Slough Estates USA in 2007.

- We forecast 2008 per share funds from operations (FFO), including merger costs, of $2.35, up 9.8% from 2007. Our outlook includes about $0.16 a share in expected one-time lease termination fees related to three California facilities leased to a large hospital operator.

## Investment Rationale/Risk

- HCP has reduced its financial leverage through a combination of asset sales and equity offerings. However, we consider still-elevated debt levels as a negative given uncertain credit markets. As of June 30, 2008, total debt was 57.8% of total capitalization. In addition, we remain concerned with the trust's large exposure to the senior housing sector, where we believe fundamentals are weakening. However, HCP has limited exposure to continuing care retirement communities (CCRC), which involve large down payments, usually requiring the sale of primary residences, and are most effected by economic downturns.

- Risks to our recommendation and target price include slower than expected revenue growth or demand for senior housing facilities, inability to refinance maturing debt on favorable terms, and a reduction in government medical reimbursement rates.

- Our 12-month target price of $30 is based on a multiple of 12.5X our 2009 FFO per share estimate, in line with peers.

## Qualitative Risk Assessment

| LOW | MEDIUM | HIGH |
|---|---|---|

Our risk assessment reflects HCP's position as a major and diversified owner of health care-related properties, offset by our view of its leveraged financial position.

## Quantitative Evaluations

**S&P Quality Ranking**     **B+**

| D | C | B- | B | B+ | A- | A | A+ |
|---|---|---|---|---|---|---|---|

**Relative Strength Rank**     **MODERATE**

34

LOWEST = 1       HIGHEST = 99

## Revenue/FFO Data

### Revenue (Million $)

| | 1Q | 2Q | 3Q | 4Q | Year |
|---|---|---|---|---|---|
| 2008 | 252.2 | 251.4 | 269.9 | -- | -- |
| 2007 | 223.8 | 223.2 | 262.5 | 273.1 | 1,001 |
| 2006 | 126.5 | 127.5 | 130.2 | 234.9 | 619.1 |
| 2005 | 108.4 | 118.5 | 124.4 | 127.7 | 477.3 |
| 2004 | 96.56 | 106.1 | 110.7 | 115.5 | 428.7 |
| 2003 | 90.29 | 97.41 | 102.3 | 110.2 | 400.2 |

### FFO Per Share ($)

| | | | | | |
|---|---|---|---|---|---|
| 2008 | 0.55 | 0.51 | E0.66 | E0.58 | E2.35 |
| 2007 | 0.50 | 0.58 | 0.52 | 0.54 | 2.14 |
| 2006 | 0.53 | 0.47 | 0.50 | 0.35 | 1.82 |
| 2005 | 0.44 | 0.47 | 0.50 | 0.48 | 1.89 |
| 2004 | 0.41 | 0.44 | 0.37 | 0.45 | 1.66 |
| 2003 | 0.32 | 0.45 | 0.42 | 0.47 | 1.64 |

Fiscal year ended Dec. 31. Next earnings report expected: Mid February. FFO Estimates based on S&P Funds From Operations Est..

## Dividend Data (Dates: mm/dd Payment Date: mm/dd/yy)

| Amount ($) | Date Decl. | Ex-Div. Date | Stk. of Record | Payment Date |
|---|---|---|---|---|
| 0.455 | 01/28 | 02/05 | 02/07 | 02/21/08 |
| 0.455 | 04/24 | 05/01 | 05/05 | 05/19/08 |
| 0.455 | 07/31 | 08/07 | 08/11 | 08/21/08 |
| 0.455 | 10/30 | 11/06 | 11/10 | 11/21/08 |

Dividends have been paid since 1985. Source: Company reports.

# HCP Inc

STANDARD
&POOR'S

## Business Summary October 23, 2008

CORPORATE OVERVIEW. Organized in 1985 to qualify as a real estate invest-ment trust (REIT), HCP Inc is a self-administered REIT that invests exclusively in health care real estate throughout the U.S. It leases its single-tenant build-ings to health care operators on a long-term basis, and its multi-tenant build-ings to health care providers under various market terms. HCP invests in prop-erties directly, through joint ventures, and provides secured financing to facil-ity operators, depending on the dynamics of the investment opportunity.

At December 31, 2007, HCP's real estate investments consisted of 648 facili-ties, including 37 hospitals, 63 skilled nursing facilities, 246 senior housing fa-cilities, 205 medical office buildings, and 97 life science facilities. HCP saw this portfolio shrink in 2007 as asset dispositions and the transfer of properties in joint ventures offset individual property acquisitions and the Slough Estates life sciences transaction. At year end, mezzanine loans and other debt invest-ments aggregated $1.3 billion.

CORPORATE STRATEGY. HCP's investment strategy is based on three princi-ples: opportunistic investing, portfolio diversification, and a balance sheet that we view as conservative. The company completes real estate transactions when they are expected to drive profitable growth and create long-term stockholder value.

A key to HCP's strategy is maintaining a diversified portfolio of health care-related real estate. The trust believes that diversification within the health care industry reduces the likelihood that a single event will materially harm its business. This allows HCP to take advantage of opportunities in different mar-kets, based on individual market dynamics. We view HCP as one of the most diversified health care REITs in terms of geography, property type and tenant base. The company's largest tenants are Brookdale Senior Living, Sunrise Se-nior Living, Tenet Healthcare, HCA, Inc., and Amgen Inc. During 2007, HCP had one tenant accounting for more than 10% revenues -- Sunrise Senior Living.

HCP routinely acquires and disposes of properties in order to enhance the overall value of its portfolio. During 2007, HCP made investments totaling $4.7 billion, with an average yield of 7.7%. Over 60% of these investments were re-lated to its acquisition of Slough Estates' life sciences property portfolio. We expect HCP to continue to be acquisitive across the various areas of its port-folio in 2008.

## Company Financials Fiscal Year Ended Dec. 31

| Per Share Data ($) | 2007 | 2006 | 2005 | 2004 | 2003 | 2002 | 2001 | 2000 | 1999 | 1998 |
|---|---|---|---|---|---|---|---|---|---|---|
| Tangible Book Value | 14.45 | 12.47 | 7.82 | 8.41 | 8.82 | 8.46 | 8.62 | 8.55 | 9.00 | 6.58 |
| Earnings | 0.67 | 0.57 | 1.02 | 1.03 | 0.94 | 0.97 | 0.89 | 1.07 | 1.13 | 1.27 |
| S&P Core Earnings | 0.67 | 0.57 | 1.02 | 1.02 | 0.94 | 0.96 | 0.88 | NA | NA | NA |
| Dividends | 1.78 | 1.70 | 1.68 | 1.67 | 1.66 | 1.63 | 1.55 | 1.10 | 1.39 | 1.31 |
| Payout Ratio | NM | NM | 165% | 162% | 177% | 169% | 174% | 103% | 124% | 103% |
| Prices:High | 42.11 | 37.84 | 28.92 | 29.67 | 25.85 | 22.54 | 19.52 | 15.22 | 16.56 | 20.00 |
| Prices:Low | 25.11 | 25.12 | 23.13 | 20.00 | 16.53 | 17.90 | 14.63 | 11.53 | 10.84 | 14.13 |
| P/E Ratio:High | 63 | 66 | 28 | 29 | 27 | 23 | 22 | 14 | 15 | 16 |
| P/E Ratio:Low | 37 | 44 | 23 | 19 | 18 | 19 | 16 | 11 | 10 | 11 |

| Income Statement Analysis (Million $) | 2007 | 2006 | 2005 | 2004 | 2003 | 2002 | 2001 | 2000 | 1999 | 1998 |
|---|---|---|---|---|---|---|---|---|---|---|
| Rental Income | 836 | 557 | 452 | 389 | 349 | 332 | 311 | 307 | 190 | 138 |
| Mortgage Income | Nil | Nil | Nil | Nil | Nil | Nil | Nil | 23.0 | 25.2 | 23.1 |
| Total Income | 983 | 619 | 477 | 429 | 400 | 360 | 332 | 330 | 225 | 162 |
| General Expenses | 257 | 137 | 91.1 | 79.3 | 63.4 | 51.1 | 43.3 | 41.0 | 27.8 | 5.05 |
| Interest Expense | 357 | 213 | 107 | 89.1 | 90.7 | 78.0 | 78.5 | 86.7 | 57.7 | 36.8 |
| Provision for Losses | Nil | Nil | Nil | Nil | Nil | Nil | Nil | Nil | Nil | Nil |
| Depreciation | 274 | 144 | 107 | 87.0 | 79.1 | 75.7 | 84.1 | 72.6 | 47.9 | 32.5 |
| Net Income | 161 | 107 | 159 | 158 | 155 | 137 | 121 | 113 | 96.2 | 87.2 |
| S&P Core Earnings | 140 | 85.5 | 138 | 136 | 118 | 112 | 94.5 | NA | NA | NA |

| Balance Sheet & Other Financial Data (Million $) | 2007 | 2006 | 2005 | 2004 | 2003 | 2002 | 2001 | 2000 | 1999 | 1998 |
|---|---|---|---|---|---|---|---|---|---|---|
| Cash | 133 | 764 | 69.9 | 81.1 | 228 | 41.2 | 30.2 | 81.2 | 55.3 | 59.0 |
| Total Assets | 12,522 | 10,013 | 3,597 | 3,103 | 3,036 | 2,748 | 2,431 | 2,399 | 2,469 | 1,357 |
| Real Estate Investment | 9,979 | 7,463 | 3,856 | 3,351 | 2,992 | 2,796 | 2,535 | 2,389 | 2,423 | 1,143 |
| Loss Reserve | Nil | Nil | Nil | Nil | Nil | Nil | Nil | Nil | Nil | Nil |
| Net Investment | 9,250 | 6,867 | 3,242 | 2,816 | 2,506 | 2,371 | 2,195 | 2,101 | 2,193 | 1,131 |
| Short Term Debt | 500 | NA | NA | NA | NA | NA | NA | 4.30 | 3.79 | 10.0 |
| Capitalization:Debt | 7,027 | 4,318 | 1,837 | 1,242 | 1,407 | 1,334 | 358 | 1,155 | 960 | 702 |
| Capitalization:Equity | 3,819 | 3,009 | 1,115 | 1,134 | 1,155 | 1,006 | 972 | 870 | 925 | 408 |
| Capitalization:Total | 11,454 | 7,774 | 3,386 | 2,783 | 2,965 | 2,686 | 1,674 | 2,339 | 2,201 | 1,321 |
| % Earnings & Depreciation/Assets | 3.9 | 3.6 | 7.9 | 8.0 | 8.1 | 8.2 | 8.5 | 7.6 | 7.5 | 10.4 |
| Price Times Book Value:High | 2.9 | 3.0 | 3.7 | 3.5 | 2.9 | 2.7 | 2.3 | 1.8 | 1.8 | 3.0 |
| Price Times Book Value:Low | 1.7 | 2.0 | 3.0 | 2.4 | 1.9 | 2.1 | 1.7 | 1.3 | 1.2 | 2.2 |

Data as orig reptd.; bef. results of disc opers/spec. items. Per share data adj. for stk. divs.; EPS diluted. E-Estimated. NA-Not Available. NM-Not Meaningful. NR-Not Ranked. UR-Under Review.

**Office:** 3760 Kilroy Airport Way Ste 300, Long Beach, CA 90806-6862.
**Telephone:** 562-733-5100.
**Email:** investorrelations@hcpi.com
**Website:** http://www.hcpi.com

**Chrmn, Pres, CEO & COO:** J.F. Flaherty, III
**Investor Contact:** M.A. Wallace
**EVP, CFO & Treas:** M.A. Wallace
**EVP, Chief Admin Officer, Secy & General Counsel:** E.J.Messmer, Jr., P. L. Rhein, K. B. Roath, R. M. Henning

**SVP & Chief Acctg Officer:** G.P. Doyle
**Board Members:** R. Fanning, Jr., J. F. Flaherty, III, C. N. Garvey, D. B. Henry, L. E. Martin, M. D. Mckee, H. M. Rosenberg, J. P. Sullivan

**Founded:** 1985
**Domicile:** Maryland
**Employees:** 153

# Heinz (H J) Co

**STANDARD & POOR'S**

**S&P Recommendation** HOLD ★★★☆☆

**Price** $41.02 (as of Nov 14, 2008)

**12-Mo. Target Price** $53.00

**Investment Style** Large-Cap Blend

**GICS Sector** Consumer Staples
**Sub-Industry** Packaged Foods & Meats

**Summary** This company produces a wide variety of food products worldwide, with a major presence in the U.S. in condiments, frozen potatoes, and convenience meals.

## Key Stock Statistics (Source S&P, Vickers, company reports)

| | | | | | | | |
|---|---|---|---|---|---|---|---|
| 52-Wk Range | $53.00–38.43 | S&P Oper. EPS 2009E | 2.91 | Market Capitalization(B) | $12.811 | Beta | 0.46 |
| Trailing 12-Month EPS | $2.72 | S&P Oper. EPS 2010E | NA | Yield (%) | 4.05 | S&P 3-Yr. Proj. EPS CAGR(%) | NA |
| Trailing 12-Month P/E | 15.1 | P/E on S&P Oper. EPS 2009E | 14.1 | Dividend Rate/Share | $1.66 | S&P Credit Rating | BBB |
| $10K Invested 5 Yrs Ago | $13,420 | Common Shares Outstg. (M) | 312.3 | Institutional Ownership (%) | 72 | | |

## Price Performance

30-Week Mov. Avg. ····  10-Week Mov. Avg. - -  GAAP Earnings vs. Previous Year  Volume Above Avg. STARS
12-Mo. Target Price —  Relative Strength —  ▲ Up  ▼ Down  ► No Change  Below Avg.

Options: ASE, CBOE, P

Analysis prepared by **Tom Graves, CFA** on August 22, 2008, when the stock traded at **$51.83**.

## Highlights

➤ We look for FY 09 (Apr.) net sales from continuing operations to rise about 10% from the $10.1 billion reported for FY 08, reflecting higher volume and prices. We expect sales growth in emerging international markets to exceed that of the overall company.

➤ In FY 09, we expect that HNZ will again face margin pressure from higher commodity costs. However, we look for price increases, productivity gains, and economies of scale to offset at least a portion of higher input costs (e.g., ingredients or packaging). Our FY 09 EPS estimate is $2.91, up about 11% from the $2.63 reported for FY 08.

➤ In May 2008, HNZ outlined a two-year plan that included core annual revenue growth of more than 6%, which we expect will be driven by increased marketing and research and development investments. The launch of new products, accelerated growth in the area of health and wellness, and strong sales growth in emerging markets. HNZ also plans to leverage its global supply chain to identify more cost-saving opportunities and further optimize its manufacturing and distribution infrastructure.

## Investment Rationale/Risk

➤ Our hold recommendation on the shares reflects our view that the stock will receive support from prospects for further sales and profit increases. In FY 09, we do not expect fluctuations in currency exchange rates to be as much of a contributor to reported sales growth as in FY 08, when currency movements contributed nearly half of the 12% rise in sales. We also expect the company to look for acquisition opportunities. We don't expect year-ahead stock repurchases by HNZ to significantly exceed the amount of proceeds received from the exercise of stock options.

➤ Risks to our recommendation and target price include competitive product and pricing pressures in HNZ's markets, raw material cost inflation, and consumer acceptance of new product introductions.

➤ Our 12-month target price of $53 reflects our view that the shares should trade at about 18.7X estimated calendar 2008 EPS, or close to the target P/E that we expect, on average, for a group of other food stocks. HNZ shares have an indicated dividend yield of about 3.2%. The dividend was raised 9.2%, to $0.415 quarterly, with the July 2008 payment.

## Qualitative Risk Assessment

| LOW | MEDIUM | HIGH |
|---|---|---|

Our risk assessment for H. J. Heinz reflects the relatively stable nature of the company's end markets, our view of its strong cash flow, and corporate governance practices that we believe are favorable relative to peers.

## Quantitative Evaluations

**S&P Quality Ranking** B+

| D | C | B- | B | B+ | A- | A | A+ |
|---|---|---|---|---|---|---|---|

**Relative Strength Rank** STRONG

71

LOWEST = 1     HIGHEST = 99

## Revenue/Earnings Data

**Revenue (Million $)**

| | 1Q | 2Q | 3Q | 4Q | Year |
|---|---|---|---|---|---|
| 2009 | 2,583 | -- | -- | -- | -- |
| 2008 | 2,248 | 2,523 | 2,611 | 2,688 | 10,071 |
| 2007 | 2,060 | 2,232 | 2,295 | 2,414 | 9,002 |
| 2006 | 2,110 | 2,339 | 2,187 | 2,400 | 8,643 |
| 2005 | 2,003 | 2,200 | 2,261 | 2,448 | 8,912 |
| 2004 | 1,896 | 2,090 | 2,097 | 2,331 | 8,415 |

**Earnings Per Share ($)**

| | | | | | |
|---|---|---|---|---|---|
| 2009 | 0.72 | E0.76 | E0.75 | E0.68 | E2.91 |
| 2008 | 0.72 | 0.71 | 0.68 | 0.61 | 2.63 |
| 2007 | 0.58 | 0.59 | 0.66 | 0.55 | 2.38 |
| 2006 | 0.45 | 0.50 | 0.40 | Nil | 1.29 |
| 2005 | 0.55 | 0.56 | 0.50 | 0.58 | 2.08 |
| 2004 | 0.60 | 0.54 | 0.57 | 0.56 | 2.20 |

Fiscal year ended Apr. 30. Next earnings report expected: Late November. EPS Estimates based on S&P Operating Earnings; historical GAAP earnings are as reported.

## Dividend Data (Dates: mm/dd Payment Date: mm/dd/yy)

| Amount ($) | Date Decl. | Ex-Div. Date | Stk. of Record | Payment Date |
|---|---|---|---|---|
| 0.380 | 03/12 | 03/19 | 03/24 | 04/10/08 |
| 0.415 | 05/29 | 06/20 | 06/24 | 07/10/08 |
| 0.415 | 08/13 | 09/18 | 09/22 | 10/10/08 |
| 0.415 | 11/12 | 12/18 | 12/22 | 01/10/09 |

Dividends have been paid since 1911. Source: Company reports.

# Heinz (H J) Co

## Business Summary August 22, 2008

CORPORATE OVERVIEW. Although largely known for its familiar ketchup, H.J. Heinz boasts many other branded food products, ranging from Ore-Ida frozen potatoes to Weight Watchers frozen dinners. In FY 08 (Apr.), the North American Consumer Products segment represented 30% of sales, while Europe accounted for 35%, Asia/Pacific for 16%, U.S. Foodservice for 15%, and Rest of World for 4%.

The company's revenues are generated via the manufacture and sale of products in the following categories: ketchup and sauces (40.5% of FY 08 sales); meals and snacks (44.9%); infant/nutrition (10.8%); and other products (3.8%). Brands or trademarks utilized by HNZ include Heinz, Classico, Weight Watchers (licensed), Smart Ones, Boston Market (licensed), and Ore-Ida.

CORPORATE STRATEGY. In May 2008, HNZ presented a two-year performance plan that included core annual growth of more than 6%, driven by increased marketing and research and development investments. HNZ said that over the course of the plan, it expects to launch more than 400 new products supported by an incremental marketing investment of $60 million to $100 million. HNZ said it was targeting 15% of its annual revenue from products launched in the prior 36 months. Also, HNZ said it expects accelerated growth in health and wellness products.

HNZ anticipates annual sales growth in the high teens from its fast-growing emerging markets, accelerating to about 20% of the company's overall sales within five years. The company also plans to leverage its global supply chain to identify more cost-saving opportunities and further optimize its manufacturing and distribution infrastructure. We look for HNZ to exit an additional five to six factories over the next two years. HNZ expects $400 million in supply chain productivity over the next two years and an increase in return on invested capital.

Heinz has focused on exiting non-strategic business operations. In the fourth quarter of FY 06, the company completed the sale of its European seafood business and its Tegel poultry business in New Zealand. All told, portfolio realignment has resulted in the divesture of approximately 20 non-core product lines and businesses and has generated proceeds of about $1 billion. The company believes that by improving the focus of its product portfolio, it will be better positioned to achieve consistent and sustainable growth.

## Company Financials Fiscal Year Ended Apr. 30

| Per Share Data ($) | 2008 | 2007 | 2006 | 2005 | 2004 | 2003 | 2002 | 2001 | 2000 | 1999 |
|---|---|---|---|---|---|---|---|---|---|---|
| Tangible Book Value | NM | NM | NM | NM | NM | NM | NM | NM | NM | NM |
| Cash Flow | NA | 3.88 | 2.07 | 2.82 | 2.86 | 2.17 | 3.22 | 2.26 | 3.32 | 2.11 |
| Earnings | 2.63 | 2.38 | 1.29 | 2.08 | 2.20 | 1.57 | 2.36 | 1.41 | 2.47 | 1.29 |
| S&P Core Earnings | 2.26 | 2.36 | 1.72 | 2.29 | 2.11 | 1.43 | 1.99 | 1.31 | NA | NA |
| Dividends | NA | 1.20 | 1.14 | 1.10 | 1.08 | 1.61 | 1.55 | 1.45 | 1.40 | 1.34 |
| Payout Ratio | NA | 50% | 88% | 53% | 49% | 88% | 65% | 102% | 56% | 104% |
| Calendar Year | 2007 | 2006 | 2005 | 2004 | 2003 | 2002 | 2001 | 2000 | 1999 | 1998 |
| Prices:High | NA | 46.75 | 39.13 | 40.61 | 36.82 | 43.48 | 47.94 | 48.00 | 58.81 | 61.75 |
| Prices:Low | NA | 33.42 | 33.64 | 34.53 | 28.90 | 29.60 | 36.90 | 30.81 | 39.50 | 48.50 |
| P/E Ratio:High | NA | 20 | 30 | 20 | 17 | 24 | 20 | 34 | 24 | 48 |
| P/E Ratio:Low | NA | 14 | 26 | 17 | 13 | 16 | 16 | 22 | 16 | 38 |

### Income Statement Analysis (Million $)

| | 2008 | 2007 | 2006 | 2005 | 2004 | 2003 | 2002 | 2001 | 2000 | 1999 |
|---|---|---|---|---|---|---|---|---|---|---|
| Revenue | 10,071 | 9,002 | 8,643 | 8,912 | 8,415 | 8,237 | 9,431 | 9,430 | 9,408 | 9,300 |
| Operating Income | NA | 1,946 | 1,377 | 1,607 | 1,613 | 1,389 | 1,892 | 1,282 | 1,575 | 1,412 |
| Depreciation | 289 | 500 | 264 | 252 | 234 | 215 | 302 | 299 | 306 | 302 |
| Interest Expense | NA | 333 | 316 | 232 | 212 | 224 | 294 | 333 | 270 | 259 |
| Pretax Income | 1,218 | 1,124 | 693 | 1,059 | 1,169 | 869 | 1,279 | 673 | 1,464 | 835 |
| Effective Tax Rate | 30.6% | 29.6% | 36.2% | 30.5% | 33.3% | 36.1% | 34.8% | 26.5% | 39.2% | 43.2% |
| Net Income | 845 | 792 | 443 | 736 | 779 | 555 | 834 | 495 | 891 | 474 |
| S&P Core Earnings | 725 | 784 | 587 | 809 | 747 | 500 | 702 | 458 | NA | NA |

### Balance Sheet & Other Financial Data (Million $)

| | 2008 | 2007 | 2006 | 2005 | 2004 | 2003 | 2002 | 2001 | 2000 | 1999 |
|---|---|---|---|---|---|---|---|---|---|---|
| Cash | 618 | 653 | 445 | 1,084 | 1,180 | 802 | 207 | 139 | 138 | 116 |
| Current Assets | NA | 3,019 | 2,704 | 3,646 | 3,611 | 3,284 | 3,374 | 3,117 | 3,170 | 2,887 |
| Total Assets | 10,565 | 10,033 | 9,738 | 10,578 | 9,877 | 9,225 | 10,278 | 9,035 | 8,851 | 8,054 |
| Current Liabilities | NA | 2,505 | 2,018 | 2,587 | 2,469 | 1,926 | 2,509 | 3,655 | 2,126 | 2,786 |
| Long Term Debt | NA | 4,414 | 4,357 | 4,122 | 4,538 | 4,776 | 4,643 | 3,015 | 3,936 | 2,472 |
| Common Equity | 1,888 | 2,280 | 2,049 | 2,614 | 8,841 | 2,876 | 1,719 | 1,374 | 1,596 | 1,804 |
| Total Capital | NA | 7,256 | 7,045 | 7,359 | 13,797 | 8,252 | 7,197 | 4,642 | 5,804 | 4,587 |
| Capital Expenditures | 302 | 245 | 231 | 241 | 232 | 154 | 213 | 411 | 452 | 317 |
| Cash Flow | NA | 1,291 | 707 | 988 | 1,013 | 770 | 1,136 | 794 | 1,197 | 776 |
| Current Ratio | 1.3 | 1.2 | 1.3 | 1.4 | 1.5 | 1.7 | 1.3 | 0.9 | 1.5 | 1.0 |
| % Long Term Debt of Capitalization | 62.8 | 60.8 | 61.8 | 56.0 | 32.9 | 57.9 | 64.5 | 64.9 | 67.8 | 53.9 |
| % Net Income of Revenue | 8.4 | 8.8 | 5.1 | 8.3 | 9.3 | 6.7 | 8.8 | 5.2 | 9.5 | 5.1 |
| % Return on Assets | 8.2 | 8.0 | 4.4 | 7.2 | 8.2 | 5.7 | 8.6 | 5.5 | 10.5 | 5.9 |
| % Return on Equity | 45.3 | 34.0 | 19.0 | 26.3 | 8.9 | 17.9 | 53.9 | 33.3 | 52.4 | 23.6 |

Data as orig reptd.; bef. results of disc opers/spec. items. Per share data adj. for stk. divs.; EPS diluted. E-Estimated. NA-Not Available. NM-Not Meaningful. NR-Not Ranked. UR-Under Review.

**Office:** One PPG Place, Pittsburgh, PA 15222.
**Telephone:** 412-456-5700.
**Website:** http://www.heinz.com
**Chrmn, Pres & CEO:** W.R. Johnson

**EVP & CFO:** A.B. Winkleblack
**EVP & General Counsel:** T.N. Bobby
**SVP & Chief Admin Officer:** D.E. Smyth
**SVP, Chief Acctg Officer & Cntlr:** E.J. McMenamin

**Investor Contact:** M.R. Nollen
**Board Members:** C. E. Bunch, L. S. Coleman, Jr., J. G. Drosdick, E. E. Holiday, W. R. Johnson, C. Kendle, D. R. O'Hare, N. Peltz, D. H. Reilley, L. C. Swann, T. J. Usher, M. F. Weinstein

**Founded:** 1869
**Domicile:** Pennsylvania
**Employees:** 32,500

# Hershey Co (The)

STANDARD
&POOR'S

| S&P Recommendation | **SELL** ★★☆☆☆ | Price<br>$35.96 (as of Nov 14, 2008) | 12-Mo. Target Price<br>$33.00 | Investment Style<br>Large-Cap Growth |
|---|---|---|---|---|

**GICS Sector** Consumer Staples
**Sub-Industry** Packaged Foods & Meats

**Summary** Hershey is a major producer of chocolate or confectionery products.

## Key Stock Statistics (Source S&P, Vickers, company reports)

| | | | | | | | | |
|---|---|---|---|---|---|---|---|---|
| 52-Wk Range | $44.32– 32.31 | S&P Oper. EPS 2008**E** | 1.86 | Market Capitalization(B) | $5.984 | Beta | | 0.24 |
| Trailing 12-Month EPS | $1.24 | S&P Oper. EPS 2009**E** | 1.92 | Yield (%) | 3.31 | S&P 3-Yr. Proj. EPS CAGR(%) | | 5 |
| Trailing 12-Month P/E | 29.0 | P/E on S&P Oper. EPS 2008**E** | 19.3 | Dividend Rate/Share | $1.19 | S&P Credit Rating | | A |
| $10K Invested 5 Yrs Ago | $10,360 | Common Shares Outstg. (M) | 227.1 | Institutional Ownership (%) | 77 | | | |

## Price Performance

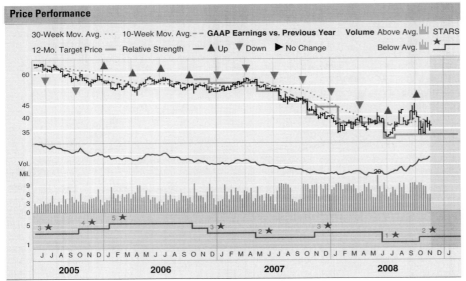

30-Week Mov. Avg. ··· 10-Week Mov. Avg. – – 12-Mo. Target Price — Relative Strength — ▲ Up ▼ Down ► No Change — GAAP Earnings vs. Previous Year — Volume Above Avg. — Below Avg. — STARS

Options: ASE, CBOE, P, Ph

Analysis prepared by **Tom Graves, CFA** on October 27, 2008, when the stock traded at **$ 33.06**.

## Highlights

➤ We look for HSY's sales to grow at least modestly in 2008, from the $4.95 billion reported for 2007. We believe that a 6.4% rise in sales in 2008's third quarter included a boost from customer buy-in related to August price increases. However, we also expect that HSY's U.S. market share has benefited recently from increased marketing support. In 2009, we expect that sales volumes will be limited by higher prices.

➤ We estimate that EPS, before special items, will total $1.86 in 2008 and $1.92 in 2009, down from $2.08 in 2007. This excludes business impairment and realignment charges. In 2007, there was about $1.15 of special charges. We expect that over the next couple of years, HSY will increasingly look to fund investments with savings from a supply chain transformation program.

➤ We see HSY undergoing considerable change. In November 2007, HSY said that six independent directors had resigned at the request of controlling shareholder The Hershey Trust. Also, in late 2007, David J. West became president and CEO of HSY. He was previously HSY's chief operating officer.

## Investment Rationale/Risk

➤ We see HSY's plan for an improved supply chain bolstering longer-term profit growth prospects. We expect a portion of anticipated manufacturing savings to be spent on areas such as brand support, new products and overseas expansion. In terms of corporate governance, the company has a dual class capital structure with unequal voting rights, which we view unfavorably.

➤ Risks to our recommendation and target price include the possibility that sales will be stronger than we anticipate; that profit margins will be more favorable; and that new products or cost-saving efforts will be viewed as better than expected.

➤ We see diminished expectations of HSY being sold to another company. Our 12-month target price of $33 is based on a P/E of 17.7X our 2008 EPS estimate of $1.86, which is a moderate P/E discount to what we expect, on average, from a group of packaged food stocks. Also, HSY shares recently had an indicated dividend yield of about 3.5%.

## Qualitative Risk Assessment

| LOW | MEDIUM | HIGH |
|---|---|---|

Our risk assessment reflects what we see as the relatively stable nature of Hershey's primary end markets, the strength of its U.S. business, and the strength of the company's balance sheet and cash flow.

## Quantitative Evaluations

**S&P Quality Ranking**  B+

| D | C | B- | B | B+ | A- | A | A+ |
|---|---|---|---|---|---|---|---|

**Relative Strength Rank**  STRONG

87

LOWEST = 1    HIGHEST = 99

## Revenue/Earnings Data

**Revenue (Million $)**

| | 1Q | 2Q | 3Q | 4Q | Year |
|---|---|---|---|---|---|
| 2008 | 1,160 | 1,105 | 1,490 | -- | -- |
| 2007 | 1,153 | 1,052 | 1,399 | 1,342 | 4,947 |
| 2006 | 1,140 | 1,052 | 1,416 | 1,337 | 4,944 |
| 2005 | 1,126 | 988.5 | 1,368 | 1,353 | 4,836 |
| 2004 | 1,013 | 893.7 | 1,255 | 1,268 | 4,429 |
| 2003 | 953.2 | 849.1 | 1,191 | 1,179 | 4,173 |

**Earnings Per Share ($)**

| | | | | | |
|---|---|---|---|---|---|
| 2008 | 0.28 | 0.18 | 0.54 | E0.56 | E1.86 |
| 2007 | 0.40 | 0.01 | 0.27 | 0.24 | 0.93 |
| 2006 | 0.50 | 0.41 | 0.78 | 0.65 | 2.34 |
| 2005 | 0.47 | 0.39 | 0.48 | 0.70 | 1.99 |
| 2004 | 0.41 | 0.56 | 0.66 | 0.68 | 2.30 |
| 2003 | 0.37 | 0.27 | 0.58 | 0.55 | 1.76 |

Fiscal year ended Dec. 31. Next earnings report expected: Late January. EPS Estimates based on S&P Operating Earnings; historical GAAP earnings are as reported.

## Dividend Data (Dates: mm/dd Payment Date: mm/dd/yy)

| Amount ($) | Date Decl. | Ex-Div. Date | Stk. of Record | Payment Date |
|---|---|---|---|---|
| 0.298 | 02/13 | 02/21 | 02/25 | 03/14/08 |
| 0.298 | 04/21 | 05/21 | 05/23 | 06/13/08 |
| 0.298 | 08/05 | 08/21 | 08/25 | 09/15/08 |
| 0.298 | 09/30 | 11/21 | 11/25 | 12/15/08 |

Dividends have been paid since 1930. Source: Company reports.

# Hershey Co (The)

**STANDARD &POOR'S**

## Business Summary October 27, 2008

CORPORATE OVERVIEW. This company produces and distributes a variety of chocolate, confectionery and grocery products. The company's brands include Hershey's Kisses and Reese's.

CORPORATE STRATEGY. In February 2007, HSY announced a supply chain transformation program that is expected to be completed by December 2009. HSY has estimated that this program will incur pretax charges and non-recurring project implementation costs (likely including asset write-offs) of $550 million to $575 million, which we expect over the three-year period from 2007 to 2009. In October 2008, HSY said that the amount of non-cash charges could increase by up to $75 million due to pension settlement items. Also, we expect the transformation program to result in increased capital expenditures in those years. Under the program, HSY is expected to significantly increase manufacturing capacity utilization by reducing the number of its production lines; outsource the production of low value-added items; and construct a production facility in Mexico. As a result of the transformation program, HSY has targeted ongoing annual savings of $170 million to $190 million to be generated by 2010. HSY planned to invest a portion of these savings in strategic growth initiatives.

We expect that HSY's strategy will include focus on, and advertising support for, core brands that provide about 60% of U.S. sales.

In 2007, if special items are excluded, HSY had EPS of $2.08, compared with $2.37 in 2006. In 2007, there were special charges of $1.10 a share related to the supply chain transformation program, and $0.05 a share of business re-alignment and impairment charges related to HSY's business in Brazil. In October 2008, HSY estimated business impairment and realignment charges of $0.39 to $0.42 a share for this year.

In 2007, 13.8% of HSY's net sales were from businesses outside the U.S., up from 10.9% in 2006. Longer term, we expect international expansion to include a focus on emerging markets in Asia, particularly India and China, Mexico, and selected markets in South America.

## Company Financials Fiscal Year Ended Dec. 31

| Per Share Data ($) | 2007 | 2006 | 2005 | 2004 | 2003 | 2002 | 2001 | 2000 | 1999 | 1998 |
|---|---|---|---|---|---|---|---|---|---|---|
| Tangible Book Value | NM | 0.18 | 1.63 | 2.03 | 3.29 | 3.55 | 2.65 | 2.57 | 2.34 | 1.79 |
| Cash Flow | 2.27 | 3.17 | 2.96 | 3.17 | 2.44 | 2.17 | 1.44 | 1.84 | 2.21 | 1.71 |
| Earnings | 0.93 | 2.34 | 1.99 | 2.30 | 1.76 | 1.46 | 0.75 | 1.21 | 1.63 | 1.17 |
| S&P Core Earnings | 1.14 | 2.26 | 1.94 | 2.23 | 1.73 | 1.37 | 0.94 | NA | NA | NA |
| Dividends | 1.14 | 1.03 | 0.93 | 0.84 | 0.72 | 0.63 | 0.58 | 0.54 | 0.50 | 0.46 |
| Payout Ratio | 122% | 44% | 47% | 36% | 41% | 43% | 78% | 45% | 31% | 39% |
| Prices:High | 56.75 | 57.65 | 67.37 | 56.75 | 39.33 | 39.75 | 35.08 | 33.22 | 32.44 | 38.19 |
| Prices:Low | 38.21 | 48.20 | 52.49 | 37.28 | 30.35 | 28.23 | 27.56 | 18.88 | 22.88 | 29.84 |
| P/E Ratio:High | 61 | 25 | 34 | 25 | 22 | 27 | 47 | 27 | 20 | 33 |
| P/E Ratio:Low | 41 | 21 | 26 | 16 | 17 | 19 | 37 | 16 | 14 | 26 |

| Income Statement Analysis (Million $) | 2007 | 2006 | 2005 | 2004 | 2003 | 2002 | 2001 | 2000 | 1999 | 1998 |
|---|---|---|---|---|---|---|---|---|---|---|
| Revenue | 4,947 | 4,944 | 4,836 | 4,429 | 4,173 | 4,120 | 4,557 | 4,221 | 3,971 | 4,436 |
| Operating Income | 1,047 | 1,207 | 1,175 | 1,092 | 992 | 904 | 812 | 799 | 722 | 801 |
| Depreciation | 311 | 200 | 218 | 190 | 181 | 178 | 190 | 176 | 163 | 158 |
| Interest Expense | 119 | 116 | 89.5 | 66.5 | 63.5 | 60.7 | 71.5 | 81.0 | 77.3 | 88.6 |
| Pretax Income | 340 | 877 | 773 | 836 | 733 | 638 | 344 | 547 | 728 | 557 |
| Effective Tax Rate | 37.1% | 36.2% | 36.2% | 29.3% | 36.6% | 36.7% | 39.7% | 38.8% | 36.8% | 38.8% |
| Net Income | 214 | 559 | 493 | 591 | 465 | 404 | 207 | 335 | 460 | 341 |
| S&P Core Earnings | 264 | 540 | 482 | 573 | 455 | 377 | 258 | NA | NA | NA |

| Balance Sheet & Other Financial Data (Million $) | 2007 | 2006 | 2005 | 2004 | 2003 | 2002 | 2001 | 2000 | 1999 | 1998 |
|---|---|---|---|---|---|---|---|---|---|---|
| Cash | 129 | 97.1 | 67.2 | 54.8 | 115 | 298 | 134 | 32.0 | 118 | 39.0 |
| Current Assets | 1,427 | 1,418 | 1,409 | 1,182 | 1,132 | 1,264 | 1,168 | 1,295 | 1,280 | 1,134 |
| Total Assets | 4,247 | 4,158 | 4,295 | 3,798 | 3,583 | 3,481 | 3,247 | 3,448 | 3,347 | 3,404 |
| Current Liabilities | 1,619 | 1,454 | 1,518 | 1,285 | 586 | 547 | 606 | 767 | 713 | 815 |
| Long Term Debt | 1,280 | 1,248 | 943 | 691 | 968 | 852 | 877 | 878 | 878 | 879 |
| Common Equity | 593 | 683 | 1,021 | 1,089 | 1,280 | 1,372 | 1,147 | 1,175 | 1,099 | 1,042 |
| Total Capital | 2,084 | 2,218 | 2,364 | 2,109 | 2,626 | 2,572 | 2,280 | 2,353 | 2,303 | 2,243 |
| Capital Expenditures | 190 | 183 | 181 | 182 | 219 | 133 | 160 | 138 | 115 | 161 |
| Cash Flow | 525 | 759 | 711 | 781 | 646 | 581 | 398 | 511 | 624 | 499 |
| Current Ratio | 0.9 | 1.0 | 0.9 | 0.9 | 1.9 | 2.3 | 1.9 | 1.7 | 1.8 | 1.4 |
| % Long Term Debt of Capitalization | 61.4 | 56.3 | 39.9 | 32.7 | 36.9 | 33.1 | 38.5 | 37.3 | 38.1 | 39.2 |
| % Net Income of Revenue | 4.3 | 11.3 | 10.2 | 13.3 | 11.1 | 9.8 | 4.5 | 7.9 | 11.6 | 7.7 |
| % Return on Assets | 5.1 | 13.3 | 12.2 | 16.0 | 13.2 | 12.0 | 6.2 | 9.8 | 13.6 | 10.2 |
| % Return on Equity | 33.6 | 65.8 | 45.7 | 46.4 | 35.1 | 32.0 | 17.8 | 29.4 | 43.0 | 36.0 |

Data as orig reptd.; bef. results of disc opers/spec. items. Per share data adj. for stk. divs.; EPS diluted. E-Estimated. NA-Not Available. NM-Not Meaningful. NR-Not Ranked. UR-Under Review.

**Office:** 100 Crystal A Dr, Hershey, PA 17033-9790.
**Telephone:** 717-534-4200.
**Website:** http://www.hersheys.com
**Chrmn:** K.L. Wolfe

**Pres & CEO:** D.J. West
**COO:** G.J. Kaiser
**SVP & CFO:** H. Alfonso
**SVP, Secy & General Counsel:** B.H. Snyder

**Investor Contact:** M.K. Pogharian (800-539-0261)
**Board Members:** R. H. Campbell, R. F. Cavanaugh, C. A. Davis, A. G. Langbo, J. E. Nevels, T. J. Ridge, D. L. Shedlarz, C. B. Strauss, D. J. West, K. L. Wolfe, L. S. Zimmerman

**Founded:** 1893
**Domicile:** Delaware
**Employees:** 12,800

**STANDARD &POOR'S**

# Hess Corp

**S&P Recommendation** HOLD ★★★☆☆

| | | |
|---|---|---|
| **Price** $55.53 (as of Nov 14, 2008) | **12-Mo. Target Price** $74.00 | **Investment Style** Large-Cap Blend |

**GICS Sector** Energy
**Sub-Industry** Integrated Oil & Gas

**Summary** This integrated oil and natural gas company has exploration and production activities worldwide, and markets refined petroleum products on the U.S. East Coast.

## Key Stock Statistics (Source S&P, Vickers, company reports)

| | | | | | | | |
|---|---|---|---|---|---|---|---|
| 52-Wk Range | $137.00– 41.61 | S&P Oper. EPS 2008E | 9.38 | Market Capitalization(B) | $18.107 | Beta | 1.04 |
| Trailing 12-Month EPS | $9.07 | S&P Oper. EPS 2009E | 7.05 | Yield (%) | 0.72 | S&P 3-Yr. Proj. EPS CAGR(%) | 2 |
| Trailing 12-Month P/E | 6.1 | P/E on S&P Oper. EPS 2008E | 5.9 | Dividend Rate/Share | $0.40 | S&P Credit Rating | BBB- |
| $10K Invested 5 Yrs Ago | $33,873 | Common Shares Outstg. (M) | 326.1 | Institutional Ownership (%) | 81 | | |

## Price Performance

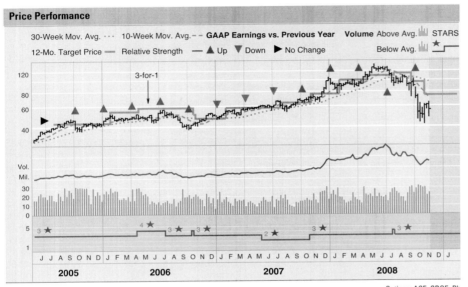

30-Week Mov. Avg. ···· 10-Week Mov. Avg. ─ ─ **GAAP Earnings vs. Previous Year** Volume Above Avg. STARS
12-Mo. Target Price ── Relative Strength ─ ▲ Up ▼ Down ► No Change Below Avg.

3-for-1

Options: ASE, CBOE, Ph

Analysis prepared by **Tina J. Vital** on October 29, 2008, when the stock traded at **$ 53.13**.

## Highlights

➤ Third-quarter oil and gas production rose about 1%, a little less than we expected, reflecting downtime from Gulf hurricanes. As of late October, HES had restored 4,000 boe/d of Gulf production, and the remaining 30,000 boe/d was expected to be back on stream by January 2009. The company reported good progress on developments slated to start up in 2009 (e.g., JDA Phase 2 in the Gulf of Thailand, Shenzi in the deepwater Gulf of Mexico, and Ujung Pangkak in Indonesia). We expect 2008 production to be about flat, slightly below management's guidance of 380,000 boe/d.

➤ While the recent drop in oil prices has boosted U.S. refining margins, the company's fuel margins narrowed 7%, and year-over-year convenience store sales were flat in the third quarter, reflecting weak economic conditions. As of late October, we see U.S. industrywide refining margins narrowing about 18% in 2008 and 2009.

➤ We expect strong pricing to boost after-tax operating earnings about 62% in 2008, but see a decline of about 25% in 2009, reflecting slowed economic growth.

## Investment Rationale/Risk

➤ While we estimate HES's upstream costs as slightly above peers, increased spending has improved its exploration success. HES announced natural gas discoveries on Australia's Northwest Shelf in 2008, and at its Glencoe-1 well. During 2007, major development projects included the Ujung Pangkah field in Indonesia, the Okume Complex in Equatorial Guinea, and the Phu Horn field in Thailand. During 2008, HES expects significant progress at its Shenzi field in the deepwater Gulf of Mexico, and it continues appraisals of the Pony and Tubular Bells discoveries in the deepwater Gulf of Mexico.

➤ Risks to our recommendation and target price include deterioration in economic, industrial and operating conditions, and the company's potential inability to replace oil and gas reserves.

➤ A blend of our DCF ($73 per share; assuming a WACC of 9.7% and terminal growth of 3%), net asset value ($78; assuming a long-term WTI oil price of $90 per barrel) and narrowed relative valuations leads to our 12-month target of $74 per share, representing an expected enterprise value of 3.9X our 2009 EBITDA estimate, in line with peers.

## Qualitative Risk Assessment

| LOW | MEDIUM | HIGH |
|---|---|---|

Our risk assessment reflects HES's diversified business profile in volatile, cyclical and capital-intensive segments of the energy industry. However, we see increased risk from its investments in politically troubled locales, and a relatively high cost structure in exploration and production.

## Quantitative Evaluations

**S&P Quality Ranking** B

| D | C | B- | B | B+ | A- | A | A+ |
|---|---|---|---|---|---|---|---|

**Relative Strength Rank** MODERATE

48

LOWEST = 1     HIGHEST = 99

## Revenue/Earnings Data

### Revenue (Million $)

| | 1Q | 2Q | 3Q | 4Q | Year |
|---|---|---|---|---|---|
| 2008 | 10,667 | 11,717 | 11,398 | -- | -- |
| 2007 | 7,319 | 7,421 | 7,451 | 9,456 | 31,647 |
| 2006 | 7,159 | 6,718 | 7,035 | 7,155 | 28,067 |
| 2005 | 4,956 | 4,963 | 5,769 | 7,059 | 22,747 |
| 2004 | 4,488 | 3,803 | 3,830 | 4,612 | 16,733 |
| 2003 | 4,254 | 3,199 | 3,230 | 3,628 | 14,480 |

### Earnings Per Share ($)

| | | | | | |
|---|---|---|---|---|---|
| 2008 | 2.34 | 2.76 | 2.37 | E1.91 | E9.38 |
| 2007 | 1.17 | 1.75 | 1.23 | 1.59 | 5.74 |
| 2006 | 2.21 | 1.79 | 0.94 | 1.13 | 6.07 |
| 2005 | 0.71 | 0.92 | 0.87 | 1.44 | 3.98 |
| 2004 | 0.92 | 0.92 | 0.58 | 0.74 | 3.17 |
| 2003 | 0.81 | 0.24 | 0.55 | 0.24 | 1.72 |

Fiscal year ended Dec. 31. Next earnings report expected: Late January. EPS Estimates based on S&P Operating Earnings; historical GAAP earnings are as reported.

## Dividend Data (Dates: mm/dd Payment Date: mm/dd/yy)

| Amount ($) | Date Decl. | Ex-Div. Date | Stk. of Record | Payment Date |
|---|---|---|---|---|
| 0.100 | 12/05 | 12/17 | 12/19 | 01/02/08 |
| 0.100 | 03/05 | 03/13 | 03/17 | 03/31/08 |
| 0.100 | 06/04 | 06/12 | 06/16 | 06/30/08 |
| 0.100 | 09/03 | 09/12 | 09/16 | 09/30/08 |

Dividends have been paid since 1922. Source: Company reports.

# Hess Corp

STANDARD &POOR'S

## Business Summary October 29, 2008

CORPORATE OVERVIEW. Hess Corp. (HES; formerly Amerada Hess Corp.) has two operating segments: Exploration and Production (25% of 2007 revenues; 86% of net income), and Marketing and Refining (75%; 14%). Business is conducted in the U.S., Europe, Africa, Asia and elsewhere. As of May 2007, the Hess family and related interests owned about 14% of the common shares.

Oil and gas production rose 5%, to 377,000 boe per day (73% liquids), in 2007. Net proved oil and gas reserves rose 7%, to 1.33 billion barrels of oil equivalent (boe; 56% developed, 67% liquids) in 2007. Using data from John S. Herold, an oil industry consultant, we estimate HES's three-year (2005-06) average proved acquisition costs at $2.44 per boe, in line with peers; its three-year finding & development costs at $18.66 per boe, above the peer average; its three-year reserve replacement costs at $13.07 per boe, slightly above the peer average; and its three-year reserve replacement at 163%, slightly above the peer average.

As of March 31, 2008, the company's outstanding hedge positions included 24,000 b/d of Brent crude oil for each year of 2008-2012. As of March 31, 2008, there were no hedges of WTI crude oil or natural gas production.

HES's refining earnings are mainly derived from its 50% ownership in the refining joint venture HOVENSA, formed in October 1998 with a subsidiary of Petroleos de Venezuela S.A. (PdVSA) in the U.S. Virgin Islands. In addition, HES owns and operates a 65,000 b/d fluid catalytic cracking facility in Port Reading, NJ, to produce gasoline and heating oil.

HOVENSA has a long-term supply contract with PdVSA to purchase 115,000 b/d of Venezuelan Merey heavy crude oil. PdVSA also supplies 155,000 b/d of Venezuelan Masa medium gravity crude oil to HOVENSA under a long-term supply contract. The remaining crude oil requirements are purchased mainly under contracts of one year or less from third parties, and through spot purchases on the open market. After sales of refined products by HOVENSA to third parties, the company purchases 50% of HOVENSA's remaining production at market prices.

## Company Financials Fiscal Year Ended Dec. 31

| Per Share Data ($) | 2007 | 2006 | 2005 | 2004 | 2003 | 2002 | 2001 | 2000 | 1999 | 1998 |
|---|---|---|---|---|---|---|---|---|---|---|
| Tangible Book Value | 26.67 | 21.77 | 16.61 | 14.34 | 13.62 | 12.17 | 14.70 | 14.59 | 11.17 | 9.99 |
| Cash Flow | 10.99 | 9.80 | 7.11 | 6.18 | 5.61 | 4.17 | 7.04 | 6.43 | 4.02 | 0.73 |
| Earnings | 5.74 | 6.07 | 3.98 | 3.17 | 1.72 | -0.83 | 3.42 | 3.79 | 1.62 | -1.71 |
| S&P Core Earnings | 5.83 | 5.38 | 3.78 | 3.06 | 1.75 | -1.28 | 3.25 | NA | NA | NA |
| Dividends | 0.40 | 0.40 | 0.40 | 0.40 | 0.40 | 0.40 | 0.40 | 0.20 | 0.20 | 0.20 |
| Payout Ratio | 7% | 7% | 10% | 13% | 23% | NM | 12% | 5% | 12% | NM |
| Prices:High | 105.85 | 56.45 | 47.50 | 31.30 | 19.07 | 28.23 | 30.13 | 25.42 | 22.10 | 20.35 |
| Prices:Low | 45.96 | 37.62 | 25.94 | 17.75 | 13.71 | 16.47 | 17.92 | 15.94 | 14.58 | 15.33 |
| P/E Ratio:High | 18 | 9 | 12 | 10 | 11 | NM | 9 | 7 | 14 | NM |
| P/E Ratio:Low | 8 | 6 | 7 | 6 | 8 | NM | 5 | 4 | 9 | NM |

| Income Statement Analysis (Million $) | 2007 | 2006 | 2005 | 2004 | 2003 | 2002 | 2001 | 2000 | 1999 | 1998 |
|---|---|---|---|---|---|---|---|---|---|---|
| Revenue | 31,647 | 28,067 | 22,747 | 16,733 | 14,480 | 12,093 | 13,413 | 11,993 | 7,039 | 6,590 |
| Operating Income | 5,259 | 4,812 | 2,967 | 2,769 | 2,127 | 2,382 | 2,399 | 2,264 | 1,214 | 475 |
| Depreciation, Depletion and Amortization | 1,678 | 1,224 | 1,025 | 970 | 1,053 | 1,320 | 967 | 714 | 648 | 657 |
| Interest Expense | 306 | 201 | 224 | 241 | 293 | 269 | 194 | 162 | 158 | 153 |
| Pretax Income | 3,704 | 4,040 | 2,226 | 1,558 | 781 | -51.0 | 1,438 | 1,672 | 702 | -514 |
| Effective Tax Rate | 50.5% | 52.6% | 44.2% | 37.7% | 40.2% | NM | 36.4% | 38.8% | 37.6% | NM |
| Net Income | 1,832 | 1,916 | 1,242 | 970 | 467 | -218 | 914 | 1,023 | 438 | -459 |
| S&P Core Earnings | 1,865 | 1,657 | 1,131 | 888 | 468 | -339 | 870 | NA | NA | NA |

| Balance Sheet & Other Financial Data (Million $) | 2007 | 2006 | 2005 | 2004 | 2003 | 2002 | 2001 | 2000 | 1999 | 1998 |
|---|---|---|---|---|---|---|---|---|---|---|
| Cash | 607 | 383 | 315 | 877 | 518 | 197 | 37.0 | 312 | 41.0 | 74.0 |
| Current Assets | 6,926 | 5,848 | 5,290 | 4,335 | 3,186 | 2,756 | 3,946 | 4,115 | 1,828 | 1,887 |
| Total Assets | 26,131 | 22,404 | 19,115 | 16,312 | 13,983 | 13,262 | 15,369 | 10,274 | 7,728 | 7,883 |
| Current Liabilities | 8,024 | 6,739 | 6,447 | 4,697 | 2,669 | 2,553 | 3,718 | 3,538 | 1,579 | 1,797 |
| Long Term Debt | 3,918 | 3,745 | 3,759 | 3,785 | 3,868 | 4,976 | 5,283 | 1,985 | 2,287 | 2,476 |
| Common Equity | 9,774 | 8,111 | 6,272 | 5,583 | 5,326 | 8,498 | 4,907 | 3,883 | 3,038 | 2,643 |
| Total Capital | 16,054 | 13,955 | 11,446 | 10,566 | 10,352 | 14,518 | 11,301 | 6,378 | 5,767 | 5,603 |
| Capital Expenditures | 3,578 | 3,844 | 2,341 | 1,521 | 1,358 | 1,404 | 2,501 | 938 | 797 | 1,439 |
| Cash Flow | 3,510 | 3,096 | 2,219 | 1,892 | 1,515 | 1,102 | 1,881 | 1,737 | 1,086 | 198 |
| Current Ratio | 0.9 | 0.9 | 0.8 | 0.9 | 1.2 | 1.1 | 1.1 | 1.2 | 1.2 | 1.1 |
| % Long Term Debt of Capitalization | 24.4 | 26.8 | 32.8 | 35.8 | 37.4 | 34.3 | 46.7 | 31.1 | 39.7 | 44.2 |
| % Return on Assets | 7.5 | 9.2 | 7.0 | 6.4 | 3.4 | NM | 7.1 | 11.4 | 5.6 | NM |
| % Return on Equity | 20.5 | 26.0 | 20.1 | 16.9 | 9.7 | NM | 20.8 | 29.6 | 15.4 | NM |

Data as orig reptd.; bef. results of disc opers/spec. items. Per share data adj. for stk. divs.; EPS diluted. E-Estimated. NA-Not Available. NM-Not Meaningful. NR-Not Ranked. UR-Under Review.

**Office:** 1185 Avenue Of The Americas, New York, NY 10036.
**Telephone:** 212-997-8500.
**Email:** investorrelations@hess.com
**Website:** http://www.hess.com

**Chrmn & CEO:** J.B. Hess
**EVP & General Counsel:** J.B. Collins, II
**SVP, CFO & Chief Acctg Officer:** J.P. Rielly
**CTO:** S. Heck

**Treas:** S. Mehra
**Investor Contact:** J.R. Wilson (212-536-8940)
**Board Members:** N. F. Brady, J. B. Collins, II, J. B. Hess, E. E. Holiday, T. H. Kean, R. J. Lavizzo-Mourey, C. G. Matthews, J. H. Mullin, III, J. O'Connor, F. A. Olson, F. B. Walker, R. N. Wilson, E. H. von Metzsch

**Founded:** 1920
**Domicile:** Delaware
**Employees:** 13,300

# Hewlett-Packard Co

STANDARD &POOR'S

| S&P Recommendation | STRONG BUY ★★★★★ | Price $30.46 (as of Nov 14, 2008) | 12-Mo. Target Price $61.00 | Investment Style Large-Cap Blend |
|---|---|---|---|---|

**GICS Sector** Information Technology
**Sub-Industry** Computer Hardware

**Summary** This leading maker of computer products, including printers, servers and PCs, has a large service and support network.

## Key Stock Statistics (Source S&P, Vickers, company reports)

| | | | | | | | | |
|---|---|---|---|---|---|---|---|---|
| 52-Wk Range | $52.90– 28.23 | S&P Oper. EPS 2009E | 4.30 | Market Capitalization(B) | $74.600 | Beta | | 1.09 |
| Trailing 12-Month EPS | $3.23 | S&P Oper. EPS 2010E | 4.95 | Yield (%) | 1.05 | S&P 3-Yr. Proj. EPS CAGR(%) | | 17 |
| Trailing 12-Month P/E | 9.4 | P/E on S&P Oper. EPS 2009E | 7.1 | Dividend Rate/Share | $0.32 | S&P Credit Rating | | A |
| $10K Invested 5 Yrs Ago | $14,544 | Common Shares Outstg. (M) | 2,449.1 | Institutional Ownership (%) | 76 | | | |

## Price Performance

30-Week Mov. Avg. · · · 10-Week Mov. Avg. — **GAAP Earnings vs. Previous Year** Volume Above Avg. ▌▌▌ STARS
12-Mo. Target Price — Relative Strength — ▲ Up ▼ Down ▶ No Change Below Avg. ▌▌▌ ★

Options: ASE, CBOE, P, Ph

Analysis prepared by **Thomas W. Smith, CFA** on October 03, 2008, when the stock traded at **$ 43.00**.

### Highlights

➤ We project revenue will grow 14% in FY 08 (Oct.) and 23% in FY 09, including acquired Electronic Data Services (EDS) operations. Demand for wireless portability is driving strong notebook PC sales. On October 1, HPQ agreed to acquire a storage virtualization provider, LeftHand Networks, for $360 million in cash, subject to customary closing conditions.

➤ On August 26, HPQ acquired information technology services provider Electronic Data Services in a deal worth about $13.9 billion. HPQ paid for EDS with cash and new debt, which we view as a substantial, but manageable, levering of the company's financial position. We expect margins, excluding acquisition-related charges, to narrow for a few quarters as the company begins to integrate EDS operations, and then widen based on cost savings. Staff cuts of 24,600 were announced September 16.

➤ Before acquisition-related charges that we expect near $1.7 billion in the FY 08 fourth quarter, including a $0.3 billion restructuring charge and a $1.4 billion increase in goodwill, we estimate operating EPS of $3.62 in FY 08, followed by $4.30 in FY 09.

### Investment Rationale/Risk

➤ We believe that HPQ has the potential to gain market share in PCs, servers, printers, and IT services. The company has made substantial progress in cost reduction, by our analysis. We think that the major acquisition of EDS will strongly re-test management's cost-cutting skills, but also offer an opportunity to dramatically broaden the services segment, and thus enable HPQ to offer better one-stop shopping for global enterprises' information technology needs. On September 22, the board authorized $8 billion more for share repurchases.

➤ Risks to our recommendation and target price include HPQ's ability to integrate EDS operations effectively. A trend we foresee for moderation in U.S. economic growth and spending on technology equipment could prove more pronounced than we have forecast.

➤ We apply a target P/E near 15X, in the bottom half of a four-year historical range for HPQ and below a recent average for S&P 500 Information Technology sector companies to reflect integration risk, to our 12-month forward operating EPS estimate of $4.11, to arrive at our 12-month target price of $61.

## Qualitative Risk Assessment

| LOW | MEDIUM | HIGH |
|---|---|---|

Our risk assessment reflects the intensely price competitive environment in the computer hardware industry and potential integration risk from planned and completed acquisitions, balanced by our view of the company's broad worldwide customer base and its successful efforts in reducing its cost structure.

## Quantitative Evaluations

**S&P Quality Ranking** B+

| D | C | B- | B | B+ | A- | A | A+ |
|---|---|---|---|---|---|---|---|

**Relative Strength Rank** MODERATE

45

LOWEST = 1    HIGHEST = 99

## Revenue/Earnings Data

**Revenue (Million $)**

| | 1Q | 2Q | 3Q | 4Q | Year |
|---|---|---|---|---|---|
| 2008 | 28,467 | 28,262 | 28,032 | -- | -- |
| 2007 | 25,082 | 25,534 | 25,377 | 28,293 | 104,286 |
| 2006 | 22,659 | 22,554 | 21,890 | 24,555 | 91,658 |
| 2005 | 21,454 | 21,570 | 20,759 | 22,913 | 86,696 |
| 2004 | 19,514 | 20,113 | 18,889 | 21,389 | 79,905 |
| 2003 | 17,877 | 17,983 | 17,348 | 19,853 | 73,061 |

**Earnings Per Share ($)**

| | | | | | |
|---|---|---|---|---|---|
| 2008 | 0.80 | 0.81 | 0.80 | E1.02 | E3.62 |
| 2007 | 0.55 | 0.65 | 0.80 | 0.81 | 2.68 |
| 2006 | 0.42 | 0.66 | 0.48 | 0.60 | 2.18 |
| 2005 | 0.32 | 0.33 | 0.03 | 0.14 | 0.82 |
| 2004 | 0.30 | 0.29 | 0.19 | 0.37 | 1.15 |
| 2003 | 0.24 | 0.22 | 0.10 | 0.28 | 0.83 |

Fiscal year ended Oct. 31. Next earnings report expected: NA. EPS Estimates based on S&P Operating Earnings; historical GAAP earnings are as reported.

## Dividend Data (Dates: mm/dd Payment Date: mm/dd/yy)

| Amount ($) | Date Decl. | Ex-Div. Date | Stk. of Record | Payment Date |
|---|---|---|---|---|
| 0.080 | 11/19 | 12/10 | 12/12 | 01/02/08 |
| 0.080 | 01/18 | 03/10 | 03/12 | 04/02/08 |
| 0.080 | 06/03 | 06/09 | 06/11 | 07/02/08 |
| 0.080 | 07/25 | 09/08 | 09/10 | 10/01/08 |

Dividends have been paid since 1965. Source: Company reports.

# Hewlett-Packard Co

**STANDARD &POOR'S**

## Business Summary October 03, 2008

CORPORATE OVERVIEW. Hewlett-Packard provides computers and printers, and a wide range of related products and services to individual and enterprise customers worldwide. The ongoing elimination of about 15,000 positions through retirement programs and work force restructurings has enabled HPQ to develop a global delivery structure that has improved margins by taking advantage of low-cost technical expertise. In February 2005, chairman and CEO Carly Fiorina stepped down after the company's board was unable to agree on how to execute HPQ's strategy. Effective April 1, 2005, former NCR Corp. CEO Mark Hurd was named CEO and president. In addition, Mr. Hurd took over the chairman's role in late September 2006.

In November 2006, the company revealed that the SEC had begun a formal investigation of HPQ relating to procedures it used in trying to uncover the source of its boardroom leaks. In addition, the Federal Communications Commission and a Congressional committee requested information relating to this matter. While these revelations do not affect HPQ's fundamental business, in our opinion, we are concerned about potential administrative costs and internal distractions associated with these probes. For instance, the company en-

tered an agreement with the California Attorney General to resolve related civil claims, and has paid $14.5 million and taken actions to ensure that HPQ's corporate investigations will be in accordance with state law.

The breadth of the company's customer base is illustrated by the almost 67% of FY 07 revenues that came from outside the U.S. Further, no single customer accounted for more than 10% of sales in FY 07.

PRIMARY BUSINESS DYNAMICS. Large corporations and small offices/home offices are the primary drivers of spending on information technology products and services. Industrywide trends, exchange rates and distribution channels influence HPQ's financial performance. Most players sell broad product lines and have a global sourcing and distribution system.

## Company Financials Fiscal Year Ended Oct. 31

| Per Share Data ($) | 2008 | 2007 | 2006 | 2005 | 2004 | 2003 | 2002 | 2001 | 2000 | 1999 |
|---|---|---|---|---|---|---|---|---|---|---|
| Tangible Book Value | NA | 4.91 | 6.57 | 6.04 | 6.06 | 6.08 | 5.35 | 7.20 | 7.30 | 9.10 |
| Cash Flow | NA | 3.67 | 3.00 | 1.63 | 1.93 | 1.65 | 0.48 | 1.01 | 2.37 | 2.10 |
| Earnings | 3.62 | 2.68 | 2.18 | 0.82 | 1.15 | 0.83 | -0.37 | 0.32 | 1.73 | 1.49 |
| S&P Core Earnings | NA | 2.56 | 2.10 | 0.74 | 0.94 | 0.65 | -0.65 | 0.16 | NA | NA |
| Dividends | 0.32 | 0.32 | 0.32 | 0.32 | 0.32 | 0.32 | 0.32 | 0.32 | 0.32 | 0.32 |
| Payout Ratio | 9% | 12% | 15% | 39% | 28% | 39% | NM | 100% | 18% | 22% |
| Prices:High | 50.98 | 53.48 | 41.70 | 30.25 | 26.28 | 23.90 | 24.12 | 37.95 | 77.75 | 59.22 |
| Prices:Low | 28.23 | 38.15 | 28.37 | 18.89 | 16.08 | 14.18 | 10.75 | 12.50 | 29.13 | 31.69 |
| P/E Ratio:High | 14 | 20 | 19 | 37 | 23 | 29 | NM | NM | 45 | 40 |
| P/E Ratio:Low | 8 | 14 | 13 | 23 | 14 | 17 | NM | NM | 17 | 21 |

| Income Statement Analysis (Million $) | | | | | | | | | | |
|---|---|---|---|---|---|---|---|---|---|---|
| Revenue | NA | 104,286 | 91,658 | 86,696 | 79,905 | 73,061 | 56,588 | 45,226 | 48,782 | 42,370 |
| Operating Income | NA | 11,773 | 9,372 | 7,520 | 7,017 | 6,713 | 4,570 | 3,192 | 5,257 | 5,004 |
| Depreciation | NA | 2,705 | 2,353 | 2,344 | 2,395 | 2,527 | 2,119 | 1,369 | 1,368 | 1,316 |
| Interest Expense | NA | 289 | 249 | 334 | 247 | 277 | 212 | 234 | 233 | 202 |
| Pretax Income | NA | 9,177 | 7,191 | 3,543 | 4,196 | 2,888 | -1,052 | 702 | 4,625 | 4,194 |
| Effective Tax Rate | NA | 20.9% | 13.8% | 32.3% | 16.7% | 12.1% | NM | 11.1% | 23.0% | 26.0% |
| Net Income | NA | 7,264 | 6,198 | 2,398 | 3,497 | 2,539 | -923 | 624 | 3,561 | 3,104 |
| S&P Core Earnings | NA | 6,913 | 5,992 | 2,150 | 2,886 | 1,983 | -1,635 | 285 | NA | NA |

| Balance Sheet & Other Financial Data (Million $) | | | | | | | | | | |
|---|---|---|---|---|---|---|---|---|---|---|
| Cash | NA | 11,293 | 16,400 | 13,911 | 12,663 | 14,188 | 11,192 | 4,197 | 3,415 | 5,411 |
| Current Assets | NA | 47,402 | 48,264 | 43,334 | 42,901 | 40,996 | 36,075 | 21,305 | 23,244 | 21,642 |
| Total Assets | NA | 88,699 | 81,981 | 77,317 | 76,138 | 74,708 | 70,710 | 32,584 | 34,009 | 35,297 |
| Current Liabilities | NA | 39,260 | 2,490 | 31,460 | 28,588 | 26,630 | 24,310 | 13,964 | 15,197 | 14,321 |
| Long Term Debt | NA | 4,997 | 2,490 | 3,392 | 4,623 | 6,494 | 6,035 | 3,729 | 3,402 | 1,764 |
| Common Equity | NA | 38,526 | 38,144 | 37,176 | 37,564 | 37,746 | 36,262 | 13,953 | 14,209 | 18,295 |
| Total Capital | NA | 43,523 | 40,634 | 40,568 | 42,187 | 44,240 | 42,297 | 17,682 | 17,611 | 20,059 |
| Capital Expenditures | NA | 3,040 | 2,536 | 1,995 | 2,126 | 1,995 | 1,710 | 1,527 | 1,737 | 1,134 |
| Cash Flow | NA | 9,969 | 8,551 | 4,742 | 5,892 | 5,066 | 1,196 | 1,993 | 4,929 | 4,420 |
| Current Ratio | NA | 1.2 | 1.3 | 1.4 | 1.5 | 1.5 | 1.5 | 1.5 | 1.5 | 1.5 |
| % Long Term Debt of Capitalization | NA | 11.5 | 6.1 | 8.4 | 11.0 | 14.7 | 14.3 | 21.1 | 19.3 | 8.8 |
| % Net Income of Revenue | NA | 7.0 | 6.8 | 2.8 | 4.4 | 3.5 | NM | 1.4 | 7.3 | 7.3 |
| % Return on Assets | NA | 8.5 | 7.8 | 3.1 | 4.6 | 3.5 | NM | 1.9 | 10.3 | 9.3 |
| % Return on Equity | NA | 19.0 | 16.5 | 6.4 | 9.3 | 6.9 | NM | 4.4 | 21.9 | 17.6 |

Data as orig reptd.; bef. results of disc opers/spec. items. Per share data adj. for stk. divs.; EPS diluted. E-Estimated. NA-Not Available. NM-Not Meaningful. NR-Not Ranked. UR-Under Review.

**Office:** 3000 Hanover Street, Palo Alto, CA 94304-1112.
**Telephone:** 650-857-1501.
**Website:** http://www.hp.com
**Chrmn, Pres & CEO:** M. Hurd

**COO:** G. Bouchard
**EVP & CFO:** C.A. Lesjak
**EVP & Chief Admin Officer:** J.E. Flaxman
**EVP & CTO:** S.V. Robison

**Investor Contact:** B. Humphries (650-857-3342)
**Board Members:** L. T. Babbio, Jr., S. Baldauf, R. A. Hackborn, J. Hammergren, M. Hurd, J. Hyatt, J. R. Joyce, R. L. Ryan, L. S. Salhany, G. K. Thompson

**Founded:** 1939
**Domicile:** Delaware
**Employees:** 172,000

**The McGraw·Hill Companies**

# Home Depot Inc. (The)

**STANDARD &POOR'S**

| **S&P Recommendation** HOLD ★★★☆☆ | **Price** $20.54 (as of Nov 14, 2008) | **12-Mo. Target Price** $24.00 | **Investment Style** Large-Cap Blend |

**GICS Sector** Consumer Discretionary
**Sub-Industry** Home Improvement Retail

**Summary** HD operates a chain of over 2,200 retail warehouse-type stores, selling a wide variety of home improvement products for the do-it-yourself and home remodeling markets.

## Key Stock Statistics (Source S&P, Vickers, company reports)

| | | | | | | | |
|---|---|---|---|---|---|---|---|
| 52-Wk Range | $31.08– 17.05 | S&P Oper. EPS 2009**E** | 1.63 | Market Capitalization(B) | $34.886 | Beta | 0.84 |
| Trailing 12-Month EPS | $1.94 | S&P Oper. EPS 2010**E** | 1.31 | Yield (%) | 4.38 | S&P 3-Yr. Proj. EPS CAGR(%) | 9 |
| Trailing 12-Month P/E | 10.6 | P/E on S&P Oper. EPS 2009**E** | 12.6 | Dividend Rate/Share | $0.90 | S&P Credit Rating | BBB+ |
| $10K Invested 5 Yrs Ago | $6,207 | Common Shares Outstg. (M) | 1,698.5 | Institutional Ownership (%) | 70 | | |

## Price Performance

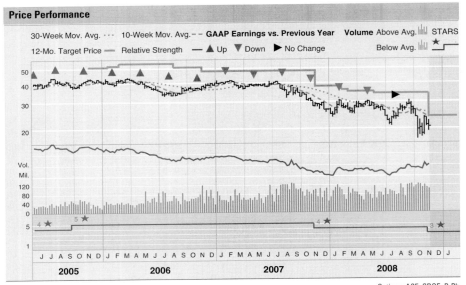

30-Week Mov. Avg. ···· 10-Week Mov. Avg. ──── **GAAP Earnings vs. Previous Year**   Volume Above Avg. STARS
12-Mo. Target Price ── Relative Strength ── ▲ Up ▼ Down ▶ No Change   Below Avg.

Options: ASE, CBOE, P, Ph

Analysis prepared by **Michael Souers** on November 12, 2008, when the stock traded at **$ 19.99**.

## Highlights

➤ We expect retail sales to decline 7.2% in FY 09 (Jan.), following a 2.1% decrease in FY 08, excluding sales from HD Supply -- which is being treated as a discontinued operation. We see revenues reflecting about 40 net new retail store additions, including approximately 20 international store openings, and a same-store sales decline of 8%-9%, as we project continued deterioration in the housing market.

➤ We foresee FY 09 operating margins narrowing 270 basis points, as expenses deleverage due to a projected severe drop in comp-store sales. Furthermore, investment in rapid deployment centers, an action created to improve the supply chain over the longer term, should accelerate the margin decline. Additionally, HD remains committed to reinvesting in its stores in order to improve customer service and retention.

➤ After a diluted share count that is about 9% lower, based on HD's aggressive repurchase plan, we project FY 09 operating EPS of $1.63, a 28% decrease from the $2.27 the company earned in FY 08, excluding HD Supply. We see FY 10 EPS of $1.31.

## Investment Rationale/Risk

➤ We recently lowered our opinion on the shares to hold, from buy. At about 12X our FY 09 EPS estimate, HD recently traded at a slight discount to key peer Lowe's (LOW: hold, $18) and the S&P 500. We expect the housing market to bottom within the next year, and believe HD will reap the rewards from an accelerated focus on customer service once the market recovers. Favorable demographic trends such as the aging of houses and low interest rates should help support home remodeling efforts over the longer term. Although we are concerned the bleak housing market and outlook for consumer spending will limit share price upside over the near term, we favor what we see as HD's strong balance sheet, financial flexibility, and abundant free cash flow generation.

➤ Risks to our recommendation and target price include a sharp slowdown in the economy; a large rise in interest rates; and unfavorable currency movements.

➤ Our 12-month target price of $24, which is equal to about 18X our FY 10 EPS estimate, is derived from our DCF model, which assumes a weighted average cost of capital of 9.6% and a terminal growth rate of 3.0%.

## Qualitative Risk Assessment

| LOW | MEDIUM | HIGH |

Our risk assessment for Home Depot reflects the cyclical nature of the home improvement retail industry, which is reliant on economic growth, more than offset by our view of ample opportunities for growth in the professional market domestically and the retail business overseas, and an S&P Quality Ranking of A+.

## Quantitative Evaluations

**S&P Quality Ranking**  **A+**

| D | C | B- | B | B+ | A- | A | A+ |

**Relative Strength Rank**  **STRONG**

71

LOWEST = 1    HIGHEST = 99

## Revenue/Earnings Data

**Revenue (Million $)**

| | 1Q | 2Q | 3Q | 4Q | Year |
|---|---|---|---|---|---|
| 2009 | 17,907 | 20,990 | -- | -- | -- |
| 2008 | 21,585 | 22,184 | 18,961 | 17,659 | 77,349 |
| 2007 | 21,461 | 26,026 | 23,085 | 20,265 | 90,837 |
| 2006 | 18,973 | 22,305 | 20,744 | 19,489 | 81,511 |
| 2005 | 17,550 | 19,960 | 18,772 | 16,812 | 73,094 |
| 2004 | 15,104 | 17,989 | 16,598 | 15,125 | 64,816 |

**Earnings Per Share ($)**

| | 1Q | 2Q | 3Q | 4Q | Year |
|---|---|---|---|---|---|
| 2009 | 0.21 | 0.71 | E0.35 | E0.16 | E1.63 |
| 2008 | 0.53 | 0.71 | 0.59 | 0.40 | 2.27 |
| 2007 | 0.70 | 0.90 | 0.73 | 0.46 | 2.79 |
| 2006 | 0.57 | 0.82 | 0.72 | 0.60 | 2.72 |
| 2005 | 0.49 | 0.70 | 0.60 | 0.47 | 2.26 |
| 2004 | 0.39 | 0.56 | 0.50 | 0.42 | 1.88 |

Fiscal year ended Jan. 31. Next earnings report expected: Mid November. EPS Estimates based on S&P Operating Earnings; historical GAAP earnings are as reported.

## Dividend Data (Dates: mm/dd Payment Date: mm/dd/yy)

| Amount ($) | Date Decl. | Ex-Div. Date | Stk. of Record | Payment Date |
|---|---|---|---|---|
| 0.225 | 11/15 | 11/27 | 11/29 | 12/13/07 |
| 0.225 | 02/28 | 03/11 | 03/13 | 03/27/08 |
| 0.225 | 05/22 | 06/03 | 06/05 | 06/19/08 |
| 0.225 | 08/21 | 09/02 | 09/04 | 09/18/08 |

Dividends have been paid since 1987. Source: Company reports.

---

**Please read the Required Disclosures and Analyst Certification on the last page of this report.**

The McGraw-Hill Companies

# Home Depot Inc. (The)

**STANDARD &POOR'S**

## Business Summary November 12, 2008

**CORPORATE OVERVIEW.** Home Depot is the world's largest home improvement retailer, with revenues in excess of $75 billion. At February 3, 2008, HD operated 2,234 total stores, including 2,193 Home Depot Stores (165 in Canada, 66 in Mexico and 12 in China), 34 EXPO Design Centers, five Yardbirds stores in California and two THD Design Centers.

Home Depot stores average approximately 105,000 sq. ft., plus 23,000 sq. ft. of garden center and storage space. It stocks 35,000 to 45,000 items, including brand name and proprietary items. Home Depot stores serve three primary customer groups: Do-It-Yourself (DIY) customers, typically homeowners who complete their own projects and installations; Do-It-For-Me (DIFM) customers, usually homeowners who purchase materials and hire third parties to complete the project and/or installation; and Professional Customers, consisting of professional remodelers, general contractors, repairpeople and tradespeople. By product group, plumbing, electrical and kitchen (31% of FY 08 revenues) represented HD's largest source of revenue, followed by hardware and seasonal (28%), building materials, lumber and millwork (22%) and paint, flooring and wall covering (19%).

**CORPORATE STRATEGY.** We believe HD is in a period of transition after years of expanding rapidly as a big-box retailer. We expect Home Depot to confront a rapidly saturating domestic market by accelerating its expansion efforts abroad. Domestically, HD is increasing its focus on service and customer retention as a means to gain market share.

At the end of 2006, Home Depot acquired The Home Way, a Chinese home improvement retailer, including 12 stores in six cities. We anticipate that HD will focus on learning from the Chinese market in FY 08 and FY 09 before embarking on an aggressive expansion of stores over several years starting in FY 10.

In August 2007, Home Depot closed the sale of HD Supply for $8.3 billion, recognizing a $4 million loss, net of tax. In connection with the sale, it purchased a 12.5% equity interest in the newly formed HD Supply for $325 million, and guaranteed a $1.0 billion senior secured loan of HD Supply.

## Company Financials Fiscal Year Ended Jan. 31

| Per Share Data ($) | 2008 | 2007 | 2006 | 2005 | 2004 | 2003 | 2002 | 2001 | 2000 | 1999 |
|---|---|---|---|---|---|---|---|---|---|---|
| Tangible Book Value | 9.75 | 11.81 | 11.12 | 9.54 | 9.56 | 8.39 | 7.53 | 6.32 | 5.22 | 3.83 |
| Cash Flow | 3.19 | 3.65 | 3.45 | 2.85 | 2.35 | 1.95 | 1.62 | 1.35 | 1.19 | 0.86 |
| Earnings | 2.27 | 2.79 | 2.72 | 2.26 | 1.88 | 1.56 | 1.29 | 1.10 | 1.00 | 0.71 |
| S&P Core Earnings | 2.27 | 2.79 | 2.68 | 2.19 | 1.78 | 1.46 | 1.18 | 1.01 | NA | NA |
| Dividends | 0.68 | 0.68 | 0.40 | 0.33 | 0.26 | 0.21 | 0.17 | 0.16 | 0.11 | 0.08 |
| Payout Ratio | 30% | 24% | 15% | 15% | 14% | 13% | 13% | 15% | 11% | 11% |
| Calendar Year | 2007 | 2006 | 2005 | 2004 | 2003 | 2002 | 2001 | 2000 | 1999 | 1998 |
| Prices:High | 42.01 | 43.95 | 43.98 | 44.30 | 37.89 | 52.60 | 53.73 | 70.00 | 69.75 | 41.33 |
| Prices:Low | 25.57 | 32.85 | 34.56 | 32.34 | 20.10 | 23.01 | 30.30 | 34.69 | 34.58 | 18.44 |
| P/E Ratio:High | 19 | 16 | 16 | 20 | 20 | 41 | 43 | 64 | 70 | 58 |
| P/E Ratio:Low | 11 | 12 | 13 | 14 | 11 | 18 | 24 | 32 | 35 | 26 |

| Income Statement Analysis (Million $) | | | | | | | | | | |
|---|---|---|---|---|---|---|---|---|---|---|
| Revenue | 77,349 | 90,837 | 81,511 | 73,094 | 64,816 | 58,247 | 53,553 | 45,738 | 38,434 | 30,219 |
| Operating Income | 9,032 | 11,435 | 10,942 | 9,245 | 7,922 | 6,733 | 5,696 | 4,792 | 4,258 | 3,034 |
| Depreciation | 1,702 | 1,762 | 1,579 | 1,319 | 1,076 | 903 | 764 | 601 | 463 | 373 |
| Interest Expense | 742 | 427 | 143 | 70.0 | 62.0 | 37.0 | 28.0 | 21.0 | 28.0 | 37.0 |
| Pretax Income | 6,620 | 9,308 | 9,282 | 7,912 | 6,843 | 5,872 | 4,957 | 4,217 | 3,804 | 2,654 |
| Effective Tax Rate | 36.4% | 38.1% | 37.1% | 36.8% | 37.1% | 37.6% | 38.6% | 38.8% | 39.0% | 39.2% |
| Net Income | 4,210 | 5,761 | 5,838 | 5,001 | 4,304 | 3,664 | 3,044 | 2,581 | 2,320 | 1,614 |
| S&P Core Earnings | 4,210 | 5,761 | 5,751 | 4,843 | 4,067 | 3,414 | 2,780 | 2,364 | NA | NA |

| Balance Sheet & Other Financial Data (Million $) | | | | | | | | | | |
|---|---|---|---|---|---|---|---|---|---|---|
| Cash | 457 | 614 | 793 | 506 | 2,826 | 2,188 | 2,477 | 167 | 168 | 62.0 |
| Current Assets | 14,674 | 18,000 | 15,346 | 14,190 | 13,328 | 11,917 | 10,361 | 7,777 | 6,390 | 4,933 |
| Total Assets | 44,324 | 52,263 | 44,482 | 38,907 | 34,437 | 30,011 | 26,394 | 21,385 | 17,081 | 13,465 |
| Current Liabilities | 12,706 | 12,931 | 12,901 | 10,529 | 9,554 | 8,035 | 6,501 | 4,385 | 3,656 | 2,857 |
| Long Term Debt | 11,383 | 11,643 | 2,672 | 2,148 | 856 | 1,321 | 1,250 | 1,545 | 750 | 1,566 |
| Common Equity | 17,714 | 25,030 | 26,909 | 24,158 | 22,407 | 19,802 | 18,082 | 15,004 | 12,341 | 8,740 |
| Total Capital | 29,785 | 38,089 | 30,604 | 27,615 | 24,230 | 21,485 | 19,521 | 16,755 | 13,188 | 10,400 |
| Capital Expenditures | 3,558 | 3,542 | 3,881 | 3,948 | 3,508 | 2,749 | 3,393 | 3,558 | 2,581 | 2,059 |
| Cash Flow | 5,912 | 7,523 | 7,417 | 6,320 | 5,380 | 4,567 | 3,808 | 3,182 | 2,783 | 1,987 |
| Current Ratio | 1.2 | 1.4 | 1.2 | 1.3 | 1.4 | 1.5 | 1.6 | 1.8 | 1.7 | 1.7 |
| % Long Term Debt of Capitalization | 38.2 | 31.8 | 8.7 | 7.8 | 3.5 | 6.1 | 6.4 | 9.2 | 5.7 | 15.1 |
| % Net Income of Revenue | 5.4 | 6.3 | 7.2 | 6.8 | 6.6 | 6.3 | 5.7 | 5.6 | 6.0 | 5.3 |
| % Return on Assets | 8.7 | 11.9 | 14.0 | 13.6 | 13.4 | 13.0 | 12.7 | 13.4 | 15.2 | 13.1 |
| % Return on Equity | 19.7 | 22.2 | 22.9 | 21.5 | 20.4 | 19.3 | 18.4 | 18.9 | 22.0 | 20.4 |

Data as orig reptd.; bef. results of disc opers/spec. items. Per share data adj. for stk. divs.; EPS diluted. E-Estimated. NA-Not Available. NM-Not Meaningful. NR-Not Ranked. UR-Under Review.

**Office:** 2455 Paces Ferry Rd, N.W., Atlanta, GA 30339-1834.
**Telephone:** 770-433-8211.
**Website:** http://www.homedepot.com
**Chrmn & CEO:** F.S. Blake

**EVP, CFO & Chief Acctg Officer:** C.B. Tome
**EVP, Secy & General Counsel:** J.A. VanWoerkom
**EVP & CIO:** M. Carey
**Investor Contact:** D. Dayhoff (770-384-2666)

**Board Members:** F. D. Ackerman, D. H. Batchelder, F. S. Blake, A. Bousbib, G. D. Brenneman, A. P. Carey, J. L. Clendenin, A. M. Codina, B. C. Cornell, M. Hart, III, B. Hill, L. P. Jackson, Jr., K. L. Katen, C. X. Laporte
**Founded:** 1978
**Domicile:** Delaware
**Employees:** 331,000

*The McGraw-Hill Companies*

**STANDARD &POOR'S**

# Honeywell International Inc.

| S&P Recommendation **BUY** ★★★★☆ | Price $27.35 (as of Nov 14, 2008) | 12-Mo. Target Price $33.00 | Investment Style Large-Cap Value |
| --- | --- | --- | --- |

**GICS Sector** Industrials
**Sub-Industry** Aerospace & Defense

**Summary** The world's largest maker of cockpit controls, small jet engines and climate control equipment, HON also makes industrial materials and automotive products.

## Key Stock Statistics (Source S&P, Vickers, company reports)

| | | | | | | |
| --- | --- | --- | --- | --- | --- | --- |
| 52-Wk Range | $62.99– 25.46 | S&P Oper. EPS 2008**E** | 3.78 | Market Capitalization(B) | $19.864 | Beta 1.49 |
| Trailing 12-Month EPS | $3.70 | S&P Oper. EPS 2009**E** | 3.70 | Yield (%) | 4.02 | S&P 3-Yr. Proj. EPS CAGR(%) 7 |
| Trailing 12-Month P/E | 7.4 | P/E on S&P Oper. EPS 2008**E** | 7.2 | Dividend Rate/Share | $1.10 | S&P Credit Rating A |
| $10K Invested 5 Yrs Ago | $10,213 | Common Shares Outstg. (M) | 726.3 | Institutional Ownership (%) | 81 | |

## Price Performance

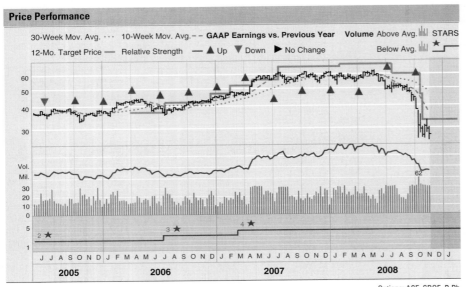

30-Week Mov. Avg. ··· 10-Week Mov. Avg. – – GAAP Earnings vs. Previous Year   Volume Above Avg. ▮▮▮ STARS
12-Mo. Target Price — Relative Strength — ▲ Up ▼ Down ▶ No Change   Below Avg. ▮▮▮

2005   2006   2007   2008

Options: ASE, CBOE, P, Ph

Analysis prepared by **Richard Tortoriello** on October 23, 2008, when the stock traded at **$ 28.88**.

## Highlights

➤ After 8% growth we see in 2008, we project no growth for 2009, reflecting slow growth in Aerospace and Automation & Control Solutions (ACS), and flat sales in Specialty Materials, due to our view of a global economic slowdown. As of the third quarter of 2008, orders in the ACS business remained strong, and we expect the aerospace OEM business to strengthen in 2009, as we anticipate an end to a strike at Boeing. However, we see a steep decline in Transportation Systems sales, due to sharp cutbacks and model introduction delays at automakers.

➤ We estimate operating margins of 13.3% in 2008, down from 13.5% in 2007, primarily driven by volume declines in the Transportation segment, as well as some slowing in Aerospace. We see a slight decline in operating margins in 2009, as productivity and cost cutting programs are offset by slowing volumes and a stronger U.S. dollar.

➤ We estimate EPS of $3.78 in 2008, but project a decline to $3.70 in 2009, on much slower sales growth and a slight decline in operating margins.

## Investment Rationale/Risk

➤ Although we see the likelihood of significantly slower growth in the global economy this year and next, we believe that HON is well positioned to weather adverse conditions. Specifically, we see very high backlogs at large commercial plane and business jet makers supporting aerospace sales in 2009 and into 2010. In addition, we continue to expect some growth in ACS. At the same time, we see HON valuations at or near historical lows on a variety of measures, and view the downturn as an opportunity to buy shares in a world-class company at an attractive price.

➤ Risks to our recommendation and target price include a stronger than expected downturn in the global economy or in any of HON's core markets, the potential for competitive pressures in its core markets, as well as the possibility of manufacturing or other operational difficulties.

➤ Our 12-month target price of $33 is based on an enterprise value to estimated 2008 EBITDA multiple of 5.3X. EV to EBITDA multiples this low for HON have not been seen since just after the 1990 bear market.

## Qualitative Risk Assessment

| LOW | **MEDIUM** | HIGH |
| --- | --- | --- |

Our risk assessment reflects what we believe is above-average exposure to market movements, sensitivity to economic cycles, currency fluctuations, and raw material costs. This is offset by what we view as HON's strong balance sheet and its ability to generate significant amounts of cash.

## Quantitative Evaluations

**S&P Quality Ranking**   B

| D | C | B- | **B** | B+ | A- | A | A+ |
| --- | --- | --- | --- | --- | --- | --- | --- |

**Relative Strength Rank**   MODERATE
41
LOWEST = 1                    HIGHEST = 99

## Revenue/Earnings Data

**Revenue (Million $)**

| | 1Q | 2Q | 3Q | 4Q | Year |
| --- | --- | --- | --- | --- | --- |
| 2008 | 8,895 | 9,674 | 9,275 | -- | -- |
| 2007 | 8,041 | 8,538 | 8,735 | 9,275 | 34,589 |
| 2006 | 7,241 | 7,898 | 7,952 | 8,276 | 31,367 |
| 2005 | 6,453 | 7,026 | 6,899 | 7,275 | 27,653 |
| 2004 | 6,178 | 6,388 | 6,395 | 6,640 | 25,601 |
| 2003 | 5,399 | 5,749 | 5,768 | 6,187 | 23,103 |

**Earnings Per Share ($)**

| | 1Q | 2Q | 3Q | 4Q | Year |
| --- | --- | --- | --- | --- | --- |
| 2008 | 0.85 | 0.96 | 0.97 | E0.99 | E3.78 |
| 2007 | 0.66 | 0.78 | 0.81 | 0.91 | 3.16 |
| 2006 | 0.51 | 0.63 | 0.66 | 0.72 | 2.51 |
| 2005 | 0.42 | 0.33 | 0.51 | 0.61 | 1.86 |
| 2004 | 0.34 | 0.42 | 0.43 | 0.30 | 1.49 |
| 2003 | 0.32 | 0.37 | 0.40 | 0.47 | 1.56 |

Fiscal year ended Dec. 31. Next earnings report expected: Late January. EPS Estimates based on S&P Operating Earnings; historical GAAP earnings are as reported.

## Dividend Data (Dates: mm/dd Payment Date: mm/dd/yy)

| Amount ($) | Date Decl. | Ex-Div. Date | Stk. of Record | Payment Date |
| --- | --- | --- | --- | --- |
| 0.275 | 02/14 | 02/25 | 02/27 | 03/10/08 |
| 0.275 | 04/28 | 05/16 | 05/20 | 06/10/08 |
| 0.275 | 07/25 | 08/18 | 08/20 | 09/10/08 |
| 0.275 | 10/31 | 11/18 | 11/20 | 12/10/08 |

Dividends have been paid since 1887. Source: Company reports.

**The McGraw·Hill Companies**

# Honeywell International Inc.

STANDARD
&POOR'S

## Business Summary October 23, 2008

CORPORATE OVERVIEW. Honeywell International Inc., an aerospace and in-dustrial conglomerate with $35 billion in revenues, conducts business through four operating segments. HON generated about 49% of sales from products sold outside of the U.S. in 2007, primarily in Europe, Canada, Asia, and Latin America.

The Aerospace segment (35% of 2007 revenues and 45% of operating profits) makes a variety of products for commercial and military aircraft including cockpit controls and other avionics, flight safety systems, auxiliary power units, environmental control systems, engine systems, light-ing, and wheels and brakes. It is also a leading maker of jet engines for re-gional and business jet manufacturers, and makes space products and sub-systems. The Aerospace segment is also a major player in the $45 billion glob-al aircraft maintenance, repair and overhaul (MRO) industry, and distributes aircraft hardware.

HON's Automation and Control Solutions segment (36% of revenues and 29% of operating profits) is best known as a global producer of home and office cli-mate controls equipment. It also makes security & life safety products; pro-vides process automation products and solutions to industry; and provides

building solutions and services, including energy management, security and asset management, and HVAC and building control.

The Specialty Materials segment (14% and 14%) makes specialty chemicals and fibers. Products include fluorine products, specialty films and additives, advanced fibers and composites, intermediates, specialty chemicals, elec-tronic materials and chemicals, and catalysts, absorbents, and equipment and technologies for the petrochemical and refining industries. HON sells its in-dustrial materials primarily to the food, pharmaceutical, and electronic pack-aging industries.

The Transportation Systems segment (15% and 12%) consists of a portfolio of brand name car care products, such as FRAM filters, Prestone antifreeze, Au-tolite spark plugs, and Simoniz car waxes. The unit is also a leading manufac-turer of turbochargers for passenger cars and commercial vehicles and brak-ing products.

## Company Financials Fiscal Year Ended Dec. 31

| Per Share Data ($) | 2007 | 2006 | 2005 | 2004 | 2003 | 2002 | 2001 | 2000 | 1999 | 1998 |
|---|---|---|---|---|---|---|---|---|---|---|
| Tangible Book Value | NM | 0.09 | 1.95 | 4.70 | 4.46 | 2.52 | 3.45 | 4.71 | 4.95 | 4.12 |
| Cash Flow | 4.24 | 3.59 | 2.74 | 2.24 | 2.25 | 0.53 | 1.02 | 3.28 | 2.99 | 3.38 |
| Earnings | 3.16 | 2.51 | 1.86 | 1.49 | 1.56 | -0.27 | -0.12 | 2.05 | 1.90 | 2.32 |
| S&P Core Earnings | 3.15 | 2.62 | 1.83 | 1.42 | 1.57 | 0.15 | -0.26 | NA | NA | NA |
| Dividends | 1.00 | 0.91 | 1.03 | 0.75 | 0.75 | 0.75 | 0.75 | 0.75 | 0.68 | 0.60 |
| Payout Ratio | 32% | 36% | 55% | 50% | 48% | NM | NM | 37% | 36% | 26% |
| Prices:High | 62.29 | 45.77 | 39.50 | 38.46 | 33.50 | 40.95 | 53.90 | 60.50 | 68.63 | 47.56 |
| Prices:Low | 43.14 | 35.24 | 32.68 | 31.23 | 20.20 | 18.77 | 22.15 | 32.13 | 37.81 | 32.63 |
| P/E Ratio:High | 20 | 18 | 21 | 26 | 21 | NM | NM | 30 | 36 | 21 |
| P/E Ratio:Low | 14 | 14 | 18 | 21 | 13 | NM | NM | 16 | 20 | 14 |

| Income Statement Analysis (Million $) | 2007 | 2006 | 2005 | 2004 | 2003 | 2002 | 2001 | 2000 | 1999 | 1998 |
|---|---|---|---|---|---|---|---|---|---|---|
| Revenue | 34,589 | 31,367 | 27,653 | 25,601 | 23,103 | 22,274 | 23,652 | 25,023 | 23,735 | 15,128 |
| Operating Income | 4,561 | 3,855 | 3,178 | 2,350 | 2,513 | 2,573 | 1,085 | 3,794 | 2,905 | 2,571 |
| Depreciation | 837 | 794 | 697 | 650 | 595 | 671 | 926 | 995 | 881 | 609 |
| Interest Expense | 456 | 374 | 356 | 331 | 335 | 344 | 405 | 481 | 265 | 162 |
| Pretax Income | 3,321 | 2,798 | 2,323 | 1,680 | 1,647 | -945 | -422 | 2,398 | 2,248 | 1,980 |
| Effective Tax Rate | 26.4% | 25.7% | 31.9% | 23.8% | 18.0% | NM | NM | 30.8% | 31.5% | 30.9% |
| Net Income | 2,444 | 2,078 | 1,581 | 1,281 | 1,344 | -220 | NA | 1,659 | 1,541 | 1,331 |
| S&P Core Earnings | 2,445 | 2,168 | 1,554 | 1,225 | 1,363 | 119 | -207 | NA | NA | NA |

| Balance Sheet & Other Financial Data (Million $) | 2007 | 2006 | 2005 | 2004 | 2003 | 2002 | 2001 | 2000 | 1999 | 1998 |
|---|---|---|---|---|---|---|---|---|---|---|
| Cash | 1,829 | 1,224 | 1,234 | 3,586 | 2,950 | 2,021 | 1,393 | 1,196 | 1,991 | 712 |
| Current Assets | 13,685 | 12,304 | 11,962 | 12,820 | 11,523 | 10,195 | 9,894 | 10,661 | 10,422 | 5,593 |
| Total Assets | 33,805 | 30,941 | 32,294 | 31,062 | 29,344 | 27,559 | 24,226 | 25,175 | 23,527 | 15,560 |
| Current Liabilities | 11,941 | 10,135 | 10,430 | 8,739 | 6,783 | 6,574 | 6,220 | 7,214 | 8,272 | 5,185 |
| Long Term Debt | 5,419 | 3,909 | 3,082 | 4,069 | 4,961 | 4,719 | 4,731 | 3,941 | 2,457 | 1,476 |
| Common Equity | 9,222 | 9,720 | 11,254 | 11,252 | 7,243 | 8,925 | 9,170 | 9,707 | 8,599 | 5,297 |
| Total Capital | 15,375 | 13,981 | 14,839 | 15,718 | 12,520 | 14,063 | 14,776 | 14,821 | 11,920 | 7,568 |
| Capital Expenditures | 767 | 733 | 684 | 629 | 655 | 671 | 876 | 853 | 986 | 684 |
| Cash Flow | 3,281 | 2,872 | 2,278 | 1,931 | 1,939 | 451 | 827 | 2,654 | 2,422 | 1,940 |
| Current Ratio | 1.2 | 1.2 | 1.1 | 1.5 | 1.7 | 1.6 | 1.6 | 1.5 | 1.3 | 1.1 |
| % Long Term Debt of Capitalization | 35.2 | 28.0 | 20.8 | 25.9 | 39.6 | 33.6 | 32.0 | 26.6 | 20.6 | 19.5 |
| % Net Income of Revenue | 7.0 | 6.6 | 5.7 | 5.0 | 5.8 | NM | NM | 6.6 | 6.5 | 8.8 |
| % Return on Assets | 7.5 | 6.5 | 5.0 | 4.2 | 4.7 | NM | NM | 6.8 | 6.7 | 9.1 |
| % Return on Equity | 25.8 | 20.3 | 14.0 | 11.7 | 21.1 | NM | NM | 18.1 | 18.5 | 28.0 |

Data as orig reptd.; bef. results of disc opers/spec. items. Per share data adj. for stk. divs.; EPS diluted. E-Estimated. NA-Not Available. NM-Not Meaningful. NR-Not Ranked. UR-Under Review.

Office: 101 Columbia Rd, Morristown, NJ 07960-4640.
Telephone: 973-455-2000.
Website: http://www.honeywell.com
Chrmn & CEO: D.M. Cote

COO & CTO: L.E. Kittelberger
SVP & CFO: D.J. Anderson
SVP & General Counsel: P.M. Kreindler
Chief Acctg Officer & Cntlr: T.M. Griep

Investor Contact: M. Grainger (973-455-2222)
Board Members: G. Bethune, D. M. Cote, D. S. Davis, L.
F. Deily, C. R. Hollick, J. C. Pardo, B. T. Sheares, E. K.
Shinseki, J. R. Stafford, T. P. Stafford, M. W. Wright

Founded: 1920
Domicile: Delaware
Employees: 122,000

# Hospira Inc

**STANDARD &POOR'S**

| S&P Recommendation **BUY** ★★★★☆ | Price $30.02 (as of Nov 14, 2008) | 12-Mo. Target Price $43.00 | Investment Style Large-Cap Growth |

**GICS Sector** Health Care
**Sub-Industry** Health Care Equipment

**Summary** Spun off from Abbott Laboratories in May 2004, this company provides a variety of hospital products, including injectable generic drugs, pumps, and syringes.

## Key Stock Statistics (Source S&P, Vickers, company reports)

| | | | | | | | |
|---|---|---|---|---|---|---|---|
| 52-Wk Range | $44.64– 23.00 | S&P Oper. EPS 2008**E** | 2.51 | Market Capitalization(B) | $4.791 | Beta | 0.33 |
| Trailing 12-Month EPS | $1.81 | S&P Oper. EPS 2009**E** | 2.86 | Yield (%) | Nil | S&P 3-Yr. Proj. EPS CAGR(%) | 14 |
| Trailing 12-Month P/E | 16.6 | P/E on S&P Oper. EPS 2008**E** | 12.0 | Dividend Rate/Share | Nil | S&P Credit Rating | BBB |
| $10K Invested 5 Yrs Ago | NA | Common Shares Outstg. (M) | 159.6 | Institutional Ownership (%) | 85 | | |

## Price Performance

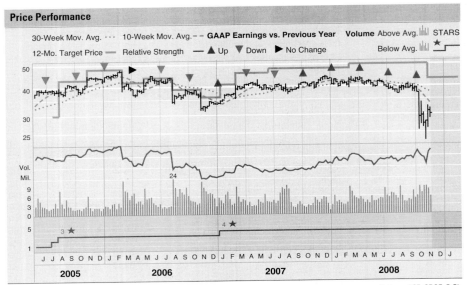

30-Week Mov. Avg. · · · · 10-Week Mov. Avg. – – – GAAP Earnings vs. Previous Year  Volume Above Avg. ▏▍▎ STARS
12-Mo. Target Price —— Relative Strength —— ▲ Up ▼ Down ▶ No Change  Below Avg. ▏▍▎

Options: ASE, CBOE, P, Ph

Analysis prepared by **Jeffrey Englander, CFA** on November 11, 2008, when the stock traded at **$ 30.17**.

## Highlights

➤ We expect revenues to rise about 8% in 2008, reflecting a full year's contribution from the Mayne Pharma acquisition, and about 6% in 2009. We see growth being driven by an improved pipeline and increased international penetration from the Mayne acquisition, and improved growth in medication management systems, offset in part by the need for gradual replacement of lost business in the contract manufacturing area.

➤ We look for gross margins to widen in 2008 as HSP realizes cost synergies from the Mayne acquisition and benefits from manufacturing optimization programs. We look for HSP to transition to higher-margin products, particularly in its medication management systems business. We see operating expenses declining as a percentage of sales in 2008 as decreases in SG&A expenses offset an absolute dollar increase in R&D expenses in support of the new product pipeline. For 2009, we see gross margins narrowing modestly and look for operating expenses to decline slightly as a percentage of sales.

➤ We forecast operating EPS of $2.51 in 2008 and $2.86 in 2009, compared to operating EPS of $2.20 in 2007.

## Investment Rationale/Risk

➤ We expect revenue to be driven by contributions from the Mayne acquisition, a strong pipeline of new products and anticipated launches in 2008, and growth in oncologic products and international sales. Hospira, with its partner Stada, launched its first biogeneric (a generic EPO with trade name Retacrit) in Europe in the first quarter of 2008, and we expect the launch of a second biogeneric by 2010. In addition, we believe HSP is on track to reach its integration savings goals for the Mayne acquisition, and will be able to offset the impact of the $50 million of lost Abbott business in the contract manufacturing segment.

➤ Risks to our recommendation and target price include failure to gain approval or slower than anticipated approval for injectable drugs and biogenerics, lower than anticipated drug pricing, and a decrease in demand for medication delivery products.

➤ Our 12-month target price of $43 assumes that HSP will trade at approximately 15X our 2009 EPS estimate of $2.86, a discount to the historical P/E ratio afforded peers, given HSP's brief history as a public company and uneven, albeit improving, operating performance.

## Qualitative Risk Assessment

| LOW | MEDIUM | HIGH |

Our risk assessment reflects HSP's broad product portfolio, which reduces dependence on any one product category. We see stable demand for hospital products, given our belief that demand for hospital services will remain strong. However, we see minimal growth overall for this industry.

## Quantitative Evaluations

**S&P Quality Ranking**   NR

| D | C | B- | B | B+ | A- | A | A+ |

**Relative Strength Rank**   STRONG

73

LOWEST = 1                    HIGHEST = 99

## Revenue/Earnings Data

**Revenue (Million $)**

| | 1Q | 2Q | 3Q | 4Q | Year |
|---|---|---|---|---|---|
| 2008 | 888.7 | 901.6 | 925.5 | -- | -- |
| 2007 | 782.8 | 869.4 | 838.0 | 946.1 | 3,436 |
| 2006 | 664.3 | 629.9 | 646.6 | 706.5 | 2,689 |
| 2005 | 662.1 | 618.5 | 656.6 | 646.2 | 2,627 |
| 2004 | 609.0 | 667.4 | 656.1 | 700.3 | 2,645 |
| 2003 | -- | -- | -- | -- | 2,545 |

**Earnings Per Share ($)**

| | | | | | |
|---|---|---|---|---|---|
| 2008 | 0.41 | 0.43 | 0.51 | E0.73 | E2.51 |
| 2007 | -0.19 | 0.20 | 0.37 | 0.47 | 0.85 |
| 2006 | 0.49 | 0.34 | 0.35 | 0.30 | 1.48 |
| 2005 | 0.49 | 0.44 | 0.37 | 0.16 | 1.46 |
| 2004 | 0.43 | 0.80 | 0.39 | 0.31 | 1.92 |
| 2003 | -- | -- | -- | -- | 1.65 |

Fiscal year ended Dec. 31. Next earnings report expected: Late February. EPS Estimates based on S&P Operating Earnings; historical GAAP earnings are as reported.

## Dividend Data

No cash dividends have been paid.

# Hospira Inc

STANDARD &POOR'S

## Business Summary November 11, 2008

CORPORATE OVERVIEW. Hospira (HSP) was created on May 3, 2004, as a spinoff from Abbott Laboratories. Abbott shareholders received one share of Hospira for every 10 shares of Abbott. HSP provides medication delivery systems and specialty pharmaceuticals to hospitals, clinics and physicians. The legal separation to become a standalone company was completed in the second quarter of 2006.

Hospira has operations in the Americas (77% of 2007 revenues); Europe, the Middle East and Africa (16%); and Asia-Pacific (6.6%). The company operates 16 manufacturing facilities domestically and internationally.

Operating segments include specialty injectable pharmaceuticals -- including specialty injectables and biogenerics (2007 sales of $1,665.2 million, 49% of sales); medication management systems -- principally infusion pumps as well

as related software and services ($725.6 million, 21%); and other pharmaceuticals -- encompassing large volume I.V. solutions, nutritionals and contract manufacturing services ($725.6 million, 21%), with the balance of sales from other devices. Major competitors include APP Pharmaceuticals, Baxter International, Becton Dickinson, Edwards Lifesciences, Fresenius AG and Patheon.

The specialty injectable pharmaceuticals division provides over 190 generic injectable drugs available in a wide array of dosages and formulations. Therapeutic areas of focus include cardiovascular, anesthesia, anti-infectives, analgesics, and other.

## Company Financials Fiscal Year Ended Dec. 31

| Per Share Data ($) | 2007 | 2006 | 2005 | 2004 | 2003 | 2002 | 2001 | 2000 | 1999 | 1998 |
|---|---|---|---|---|---|---|---|---|---|---|
| Tangible Book Value | NM | 8.03 | 7.57 | 5.74 | NM | NA | NA | NA | NA | NA |
| Cash Flow | 2.32 | 2.45 | 2.42 | 2.84 | NA | NA | NA | NA | NA | NA |
| Earnings | 0.85 | 1.48 | 1.46 | 1.92 | 1.65 | NA | NA | NA | NA | NA |
| S&P Core Earnings | 0.79 | 1.45 | 1.35 | 1.31 | 1.46 | NA | NA | NA | NA | NA |
| Dividends | Nil | Nil | Nil | Nil | NA | NA | NA | NA | NA | NA |
| Payout Ratio | Nil | Nil | Nil | Nil | NA | NA | NA | NA | NA | NA |
| Prices:High | 44.64 | 47.99 | 45.10 | 34.86 | NA | NA | NA | NA | NA | NA |
| Prices:Low | 33.60 | 31.15 | 28.35 | 24.02 | NA | NA | NA | NA | NA | NA |
| P/E Ratio:High | 53 | 32 | 31 | 18 | NA | NA | NA | NA | NA | NA |
| P/E Ratio:Low | 40 | 21 | 19 | 13 | NA | NA | NA | NA | NA | NA |

| Income Statement Analysis (Million $) | 2007 | 2006 | 2005 | 2004 | 2003 | 2002 | 2001 | 2000 | 1999 | 1998 |
|---|---|---|---|---|---|---|---|---|---|---|
| Revenue | 3,436 | 2,689 | 2,627 | 2,645 | 2,624 | 2,603 | 2,514 | 2,348 | NA | NA |
| Operating Income | 763 | 506 | 493 | 509 | 506 | NA | NA | NA | NA | NA |
| Depreciation | 235 | 157 | 156 | 146 | 146 | 134 | 123 | 133 | NA | NA |
| Interest Expense | 145 | 31.0 | 28.3 | 18.8 | Nil | NA | NA | NA | NA | NA |
| Pretax Income | 188 | 324 | 322 | 412 | 359 | 352 | 390 | 421 | NA | NA |
| Effective Tax Rate | 27.2% | 26.9% | 26.8% | 26.7% | 27.5% | 30.0% | 30.0% | 29.5% | NA | NA |
| Net Income | 137 | 237 | 236 | 302 | 260 | 247 | 273 | 297 | NA | NA |
| S&P Core Earnings | 128 | 233 | 217 | 206 | 231 | 187 | NA | NA | NA | NA |

| Balance Sheet & Other Financial Data (Million $) | 2007 | 2006 | 2005 | 2004 | 2003 | 2002 | 2001 | 2000 | 1999 | 1998 |
|---|---|---|---|---|---|---|---|---|---|---|
| Cash | 241 | 322 | 521 | 200 | Nil | NA | NA | NA | NA | NA |
| Current Assets | 1,841 | 1,523 | 1,561 | 1,198 | 1,075 | NA | NA | NA | NA | NA |
| Total Assets | 5,085 | 2,848 | 2,789 | 2,343 | 2,250 | 2,154 | 2,133 | NA | NA | NA |
| Current Liabilities | 794 | 606 | 596 | 536 | 360 | NA | NA | NA | NA | NA |
| Long Term Debt | 2,243 | 702 | 695 | 699 | Nil | NA | NA | NA | NA | NA |
| Common Equity | 1,745 | 1,361 | 1,328 | 984 | 1,453 | 1,334 | 1,461 | NA | NA | NA |
| Total Capital | 3,980 | 2,066 | 2,027 | 1,687 | 1,453 | NA | NA | NA | NA | NA |
| Capital Expenditures | 211 | 235 | 256 | 229 | 197 | 191 | 200 | 199 | NA | NA |
| Cash Flow | 372 | 393 | 392 | 447 | 406 | NA | NA | NA | NA | NA |
| Current Ratio | 2.3 | 2.5 | 2.6 | 2.2 | 3.0 | 2.4 | 2.8 | NA | NA | NA |
| % Long Term Debt of Capitalization | 55.6 | 34.0 | 34.3 | 41.4 | Nil | Nil | Nil | Nil | NA | NA |
| % Net Income of Revenue | 4.0 | 8.8 | 9.0 | 11.4 | 9.9 | 9.5 | 10.9 | 12.7 | NA | NA |
| % Return on Assets | 3.5 | 8.4 | 9.2 | 13.1 | 11.8 | 11.5 | NA | NA | NA | NA |
| % Return on Equity | 8.8 | 17.6 | 20.4 | 24.7 | 18.7 | 17.7 | NA | NA | NA | NA |

Data as orig reptd.; bef. results of disc opers/spec. items. Per share data adj. for stk. divs.; EPS diluted. E-Estimated. NA-Not Available. NM-Not Meaningful. NR-Not Ranked. UR-Under Review.

**Office:** 275 North Field Drive, Lake Forest, IL 60045.
**Telephone:** 847-937-6100.
**Chrmn & CEO:** C.B. Begley
**COO:** T.C. Kearney

**SVP & CFO:** T.E. Werner
**SVP & CSO:** S. Ramachandra
**SVP, Secy & General Counsel:** B.J. Smith
**Investor Contact:** L. McHugh (224-212-2363)

**Board Members:** I. W. Bailey, II, C. B. Begley, B. L. Bowles, C. Curran, R. W. Hale, R. A. Matricaria, J. J. Sokolov, J. C. Staley, M. F. Wheeler

**Founded:** 2003
**Domicile:** Delaware
**Employees:** 14,000

# STANDARD &POOR'S

# Host Hotels & Resorts Inc

| S&P Recommendation | HOLD ★★★☆☆ | Price $7.15 (as of Nov 14, 2008) | 12-Mo. Target Price $10.00 | Investment Style Large-Cap Value |
|---|---|---|---|---|

**GICS Sector** Financials
**Sub-Industry** Specialized REITS

**Summary** This real estate investment trust owns a portfolio of luxury and upper-upscale full-service hotels.

## Key Stock Statistics (Source S&P, Vickers, company reports)

| | | | | | | | |
|---|---|---|---|---|---|---|---|
| 52-Wk Range | $20.06– 6.82 | S&P FFO/Sh. 2008E | 1.75 | Market Capitalization(B) | $3.736 | Beta | 1.26 |
| Trailing 12-Month FFO/Share | NA | S&P FFO/Sh. 2009E | 1.47 | Yield (%) | 11.19 | S&P 3-Yr. FFO/Sh. Proj. CAGR(%) | NM |
| Trailing 12-Month P/FFO | NA | P/FFO on S&P FFO/Sh. 2008E | 4.1 | Dividend Rate/Share | $0.80 | S&P Credit Rating | BB |
| $10K Invested 5 Yrs Ago | $7,711 | Common Shares Outstg. (M) | 522.5 | Institutional Ownership (%) | NM | | |

## Price Performance

30-Week Mov. Avg. · · · 10-Week Mov. Avg. - - GAAP Earnings vs. Previous Year   Volume Above Avg. STARS
12-Mo. Target Price — Relative Strength — ▲ Up ▼ Down ▶ No Change   Below Avg.

Options: ASE, CBOE, P, Ph

Analysis prepared by **Rikin Pandya** on October 20, 2008, when the stock traded at **$ 9.21**.

## Highlights

➤ We think harsh economic conditions will cause increased challenges for hotel owners for the rest of 2008 and into 2009. However, we think HST's concentration in the luxury and upper-upscale segments may provide some protection against industry price competition. On economic pressure, we believe both leisure and business travelers have begun to reduce the number and length of hotel stays.

➤ In the second quarter for HST, comparable revenue per available room (RevPAR) fell 2.1%, driven by a 180 basis point decrease in occupancy rates, and a significant fall off in demand for Hawaiian leisure properties. In 2009, we expect a 400 basis point decline in occupancy rates, a 3.4% drop in average daily rates, and REVPAR to sharply decrease by 7.8%. However, in our view, a tight grip on expenses, including a hiring freeze and cost cutting in food & beverage and hotel departmental expenses, will partially an offset to revenue declines, and we forecast only a 200 basis point reduction in operating margins.

➤ We expect funds from operations of $1.75 in 2008 and $1.47 in 2009.

## Investment Rationale/Risk

➤ We expect overall industry growth rates to decline in 2009, and we believe HST will see further declines in the rate of growth of its key fundamentals. The hotel REIT operating model is one where operating metrics such as daily rates and occupancy can deteriorate substantially faster than metrics for other REITS, where long-term leases drive operating results. Despite current market turmoil, we believe HST will be well positioned to eventually increase profits given recent room renovations and property upgrades. Also, the recent drop in energy prices , and overall economic weakness may ease airfare to HST's markets.

➤ Risks to our recommendation and target price include a greater than expected slowdown in demand for business and leisure travel, and large increases in the cost of energy, insurance, and labor.

➤ Our 12-month target price of $10 is based on a multiple of 6.8X our 2009 FFO per share estimate, a significant premium to lodging REIT peers based on our view strong brand names, and geographic diversification of HST's hotel portfolio.

## Qualitative Risk Assessment

| LOW | MEDIUM | HIGH |
|---|---|---|

Our risk assessment reflects the highly cyclical nature of the lodging industry and the volatility that this may create in earnings and dividends. However, we think HST's large and well-diversified portfolio provides an offset.

## Quantitative Evaluations

**S&P Quality Ranking**   B-

| D | C | B- | B | B+ | A- | A | A+ |
|---|---|---|---|---|---|---|---|

**Relative Strength Rank**   WEAK

29

LOWEST = 1                                        HIGHEST = 99

## Revenue/FFO Data

### Revenue (Million $)

| | 1Q | 2Q | 3Q | 4Q | Year |
|---|---|---|---|---|---|
| 2008 | 1,058 | 1,417 | 1,168 | -- | -- |
| 2007 | 1,031 | 1,385 | 1,201 | 1,809 | 5,437 |
| 2006 | 840.0 | 1,195 | 1,119 | 1,734 | 4,888 |
| 2005 | 802.0 | 976.0 | 831.0 | 1,272 | 3,881 |
| 2004 | 777.0 | 898.0 | 784.0 | 1,181 | 3,640 |
| 2003 | 779.0 | 840.0 | 737.0 | 1,092 | 3,448 |

### FFO Per Share ($)

| | | | | | |
|---|---|---|---|---|---|
| 2008 | 0.33 | 0.56 | E0.30 | E0.56 | E1.75 |
| 2007 | 0.30 | 0.48 | 0.38 | 0.75 | 1.91 |
| 2006 | 0.27 | 0.39 | 0.28 | 0.44 | 1.53 |
| 2005 | 0.19 | 0.22 | 0.19 | 0.35 | 1.15 |
| 2004 | 0.13 | 0.02 | 0.06 | 0.35 | 0.77 |
| 2003 | 0.16 | 0.22 | 0.03 | 0.53 | 0.99 |

Fiscal year ended Dec. 31. Next earnings report expected: Late February. FFO Estimates based on S&P Funds From Operations Est..

## Dividend Data (Dates: mm/dd Payment Date: mm/dd/yy)

| Amount ($) | Date Decl. | Ex-Div. Date | Stk. of Record | Payment Date |
|---|---|---|---|---|
| .2 Spl. | 12/17 | 12/27 | 12/31 | 01/15/08 |
| 0.200 | 03/17 | 03/27 | 03/31 | 04/15/08 |
| 0.200 | 06/16 | 06/26 | 06/30 | 07/15/08 |
| 0.200 | 09/18 | 09/26 | 09/30 | 10/15/08 |

Dividends have been paid since 2004. Source: Company reports.

The McGraw-Hill Companies

# Host Hotels & Resorts Inc

**STANDARD &POOR'S**

## Business Summary October 20, 2008

CORPORATE OVERVIEW. Host Hotels & Resorts operates as a self-managed and self-administered real estate investment trust (REIT). At December 31, 2007, HST owned a portfolio consisting of 119 luxury and upper-upscale hotels containing approximately 64,000 rooms. HST's hotels operate under a number of well-known brands, including Marriott, Ritz-Carlton, Hyatt, Swissotel, Four Seasons, Hilton, Fairmont and Westin. Seventy-five of the company's properties were operated under the Marriott brand name. HST also holds a minority interest in a joint venture that owns 10 hotels in Europe with approximately 3,000 rooms. HST is geographically diversified, with hotels in most of the major metropolitan areas. The company's locations primarily include central business districts of major cities, airport areas, and resort/conference destinations.

HST's hotel revenue has traditionally experienced moderate seasonality, with a greater percentage of revenue falling in the second and fourth quarters. In addition, the fourth quarter reflects 16 or 17 weeks of results, versus 12 weeks in each of the first three fiscal quarters.

MARKET PROFILE. The lodging industry staged a strong recovery following a downturn after September 11, 2001. In the early part of 2004, the industry began to see positive trends in the three key metrics for lodging companies: oc-cupancy, average daily rate (ADR), and revenue per available room (RevPAR). Along with strong demand for both business and leisure travel, lodging companies have benefited from a limited new supply of rooms. A number of factors have kept the supply pipeline slow, including, in our view, the depressed demand environment in 2002 and 2003, increasing construction costs, difficulty obtaining construction financing, and the demand for alternative real estate such as condo conversions.

According to industry data provider Smith Travel Research, the U.S. lodging industry experienced 5.7% RevPAR growth in 2007, compared to 7.5% in 2006, 8.4% in 2005, 7.8% in 2004, and 0.4% in 2003. Driving the recent growth has been, in our view, additional room demand, a significant improvement in the ADR, and minimal new supply. The ADR in the U.S. reached $103.64 in 2007, and occupancy held steady at 63.2%, near the highest level since 2000. In 2007, the industry sold 1.2% more room nights than in 2006, while available rooms increased 1.4%, still below the 2.1% annual average since 1989.

## Company Financials Fiscal Year Ended Dec. 31

| Per Share Data ($) | 2007 | 2006 | 2005 | 2004 | 2003 | 2002 | 2001 | 2000 | 1999 | 1998 |
|---|---|---|---|---|---|---|---|---|---|---|
| Tangible Book Value | 10.22 | 9.83 | NM | 5.64 | 5.57 | 4.87 | 4.77 | 5.50 | 5.82 | 5.81 |
| Earnings | 1.01 | 0.60 | 0.30 | -0.31 | -0.92 | -0.24 | 0.09 | 0.64 | 0.87 | 0.84 |
| S&P Core Earnings | 0.92 | 0.57 | 0.27 | -0.31 | -0.95 | -0.25 | 0.09 | NA | NA | NA |
| Dividends | 0.80 | 0.71 | 0.41 | 0.10 | Nil | Nil | 0.78 | 0.86 | 0.63 | Nil |
| Payout Ratio | 79% | 118% | 137% | NM | Nil | Nil | NM | 106% | 72% | Nil |
| Prices:High | 28.98 | 25.79 | 19.24 | 17.40 | 12.33 | 12.25 | 13.95 | 12.93 | 14.81 | 22.13 |
| Prices:Low | 16.55 | 18.77 | 15.46 | 11.16 | 6.07 | 7.50 | 6.22 | 8.00 | 7.38 | 9.88 |
| P/E Ratio:High | 29 | 43 | 64 | NM | NM | NM | NM | 20 | 17 | 26 |
| P/E Ratio:Low | 16 | 31 | 52 | NM | NM | NM | NM | 13 | 8 | 12 |

| Income Statement Analysis (Million $) | | | | | | | | | | |
|---|---|---|---|---|---|---|---|---|---|---|
| Rental Income | 120 | 119 | 111 | 106 | 100 | 101 | 126 | 1,390 | 1,295 | NA |
| Mortgage Income | Nil | Nil | Nil | Nil | Nil | Nil | Nil | Nil | Nil | NA |
| Total Income | 5,426 | 4,888 | 3,881 | 3,640 | 3,448 | 3,680 | 3,754 | 1,473 | 1,295 | 3,456 |
| General Expenses | 4,007 | 3,665 | 2,936 | 2,812 | 2,765 | 2,823 | 2,821 | 337 | 318 | 2,659 |
| Interest Expense | 422 | 450 | 443 | 483 | 523 | 498 | 492 | 465 | 467 | 335 |
| Provision for Losses | Nil | Nil | Nil | Nil | Nil | Nil | Nil | Nil | Nil | Nil |
| Depreciation | 517 | 459 | 368 | 354 | 367 | 372 | 378 | 331 | 289 | 243 |
| Net Income | 550 | 309 | 138 | -64.0 | -225 | -29.0 | 53.0 | 159 | 196 | 194 |
| S&P Core Earnings | 490 | 276 | 98.0 | -106 | -267 | -65.0 | 20.0 | NA | NA | NA |

| Balance Sheet & Other Financial Data (Million $) | | | | | | | | | | |
|---|---|---|---|---|---|---|---|---|---|---|
| Cash | 553 | 524 | 225 | 416 | 838 | 627 | 608 | 566 | 326 | 469 |
| Total Assets | 11,812 | 11,808 | 8,245 | 8,421 | 8,592 | 8,316 | 8,338 | 8,396 | 8,202 | 8,268 |
| Real Estate Investment | 14,288 | 13,897 | 10,382 | 9,924 | 9,511 | 9,193 | 8,828 | 8,599 | 8,329 | 8,171 |
| Loss Reserve | Nil | Nil | Nil | Nil | Nil | Nil | Nil | Nil | Nil | Nil |
| Net Investment | 10,588 | 10,584 | 7,434 | 7,274 | 7,085 | 7,031 | 6,999 | 7,110 | 49.0 | 72.0 |
| Short Term Debt | 261 | 268 | NA | NA | NA | NA | 148 | 54.0 | 180 | 405 |
| Capitalization:Debt | 5,364 | 5,610 | 5,370 | 5,523 | 3,976 | 5,638 | 5,929 | 5,743 | 5,386 | 5,276 |
| Capitalization:Equity | 5,344 | 5,125 | 2,176 | 2,058 | 1,797 | 1,271 | 1,270 | 1,225 | 1,309 | 1,311 |
| Capitalization:Total | 11,021 | 11,045 | 7,932 | 8,126 | 6,112 | 7,471 | 7,748 | 7,649 | 7,448 | 7,199 |
| % Earnings & Depreciation/Assets | 9.0 | 7.6 | 6.0 | 3.4 | 1.7 | 4.1 | 5.2 | 5.9 | 5.9 | 6.1 |
| Price Times Book Value:High | 2.8 | 2.6 | NM | 3.1 | 2.2 | 2.5 | 2.9 | 2.4 | 2.5 | 3.8 |
| Price Times Book Value:Low | 1.6 | 1.9 | NM | 2.0 | 1.1 | 1.5 | 1.3 | 1.5 | 1.3 | 1.7 |

Data as orig reptd.; bef. results of disc opers/spec. items. Per share data adj. for stk. divs.; EPS diluted. E-Estimated. NA-Not Available. NM-Not Meaningful. NR-Not Ranked. UR-Under Review.

**Office:** 6903 Rockledge Drive, Bethesda, MD 20817.
**Telephone:** 240-744-5121.
**Website:** http://www.hosthotels.com
**Chrmn:** R.E. Marriott

**Pres & CEO:** W.E. Walter
**EVP, CFO & Treas:** L.K. Harvey
**EVP, Secy & General Counsel:** E.A. Abdoo
**Investor Contact:** G.J. Larson (240-744-5120)

**Board Members:** R. M. Baylis, T. C. Golden, A. M. Korologos, R. E. Marriott, J. A. McHale, J. B. Morse, Jr., W. E. Walter

**Founded:** 1927
**Domicile:** Maryland
**Employees:** 243

The McGraw-Hill Companies

**STANDARD &POOR'S**

# Block (H&R) Inc.

**S&P Recommendation** HOLD ★★★☆☆

| Price | 12-Mo. Target Price | Investment Style |
|---|---|---|
| $17.68 (as of Nov 14, 2008) | $24.00 | Large-Cap Blend |

**GICS Sector** Consumer Discretionary
**Sub-Industry** Specialized Consumer Services

**Summary** This diversified company provides a wide range of financial products and services, including income tax preparation, banking, brokerage and investment planning services.

## Key Stock Statistics (Source S&P, Vickers, company reports)

| | | | | | | | | |
|---|---|---|---|---|---|---|---|---|
| 52-Wk Range | $27.97– 15.00 | S&P Oper. EPS 2009**E** | 1.65 | Market Capitalization(B) | $5.801 | Beta | | 0.94 |
| Trailing 12-Month EPS | $-0.43 | S&P Oper. EPS 2010**E** | 1.79 | Yield (%) | 3.39 | S&P 3-Yr. Proj. EPS CAGR(%) | | 12 |
| Trailing 12-Month P/E | NM | P/E on S&P Oper. EPS 2009**E** | 10.7 | Dividend Rate/Share | $0.60 | S&P Credit Rating | | BBB |
| $10K Invested 5 Yrs Ago | $8,153 | Common Shares Outstg. (M) | 328.1 | Institutional Ownership (%) | 92 | | | |

## Price Performance

30-Week Mov. Avg. · · · 10-Week Mov. Avg. - - - **GAAP Earnings vs. Previous Year** Volume Above Avg. STARS
12-Mo. Target Price — Relative Strength — ▲ Up ▼ Down ▶ No Change Below Avg.

Options: ASE, CBOE, P, Ph

Analysis prepared by **Pearl Wang** on September 22, 2008, when the stock traded at **$ 24.07**.

### Highlights

➤ In May 2008, HRB sold its Option One mortgage servicing business to an affiliate of WL Ross & Co. LLC. for about $1.3 billion. We view this sale favorably, as we think it increases HRB's focus on its core tax preparation business, reduces HRB's risk and exposure to mortgage loan servicing, and improves HRB's liquidity. We project about a 4.0% revenue increase in FY 09 (Apr.), helped by expected strength in the tax services segment. This follows FY 08's 9.5% increase.

➤ We expect operating margins to improve to 19% in FY 09, from FY 08's 17%. We forecast that HRB's margin improvement in FY 09 will come from improved pricing, client growth, and continued decreases in expenses.

➤ We project earnings from continuing operations of $1.65 in FY 09, following FY 08's $1.39. In June 2008, HRB increased its annual dividend rate to $0.60 per share. HRB also authorized $2 billion of share repurchases through FY 12, but HRB does not expect purchases to begin until the fourth quarter of FY 09.

### Investment Rationale/Risk

➤ We think HRB is increasing its focus on its core tax preparer business, which we view positively given its strong market share position in that business. We believe management made progress toward narrowing its organizational focus through the May 2008 sale of Option One. We think this will help reduce investor uncertainty about the stock by providing funding for debt paydown and the remaining mortgage operations. We also like HRB's purchase in September of its franchise units in Texas, Arkansas and Oklahoma, as it should allow HRB to convert the region to a higher royalty rate prior to future franchise expansions.

➤ Risks to our opinion and target price include increased competition, ongoing litigation, and additional accounting-related issues following HRB's restatement of its FY 04 and FY 05 results in 2006.

➤ We derive our 12-month target price of $24 by applying a five-year historical average 14.5X EPS multiple to our FY 09 EPS estimate of $1.65.

### Qualitative Risk Assessment

| LOW | MEDIUM | HIGH |
|---|---|---|

Despite HRB's leading tax preparer position in its market, our risk assessment reflects uncertainty surrounding a pending IRS ruling regarding refund anticipation loan products. We are also concerned about internal accounting control issues, which in 2006 caused HRB to restate almost three years of results.

### Quantitative Evaluations

**S&P Quality Ranking**     B+

| D | C | B- | B | B+ | A- | A | A+ |
|---|---|---|---|---|---|---|---|

**Relative Strength Rank**     MODERATE

66

LOWEST = 1      HIGHEST = 99

### Revenue/Earnings Data

**Revenue (Million $)**

| | 1Q | 2Q | 3Q | 4Q | Year |
|---|---|---|---|---|---|---|
| 2009 | 339.6 | -- | -- | -- | -- |
| 2008 | 381.2 | 434.8 | 972.6 | 2,615 | 4,404 |
| 2007 | 342.8 | 396.1 | 931.2 | 2,351 | 4,021 |
| 2006 | 615.0 | 605.0 | 1,157 | 2,496 | 4,873 |
| 2005 | 482.7 | 539.3 | 1,032 | 2,357 | 4,420 |
| 2004 | 494.8 | 579.9 | 977.2 | 2,192 | 4,206 |

**Earnings Per Share ($)**

| | 1Q | 2Q | 3Q | 4Q | Year |
|---|---|---|---|---|---|---|
| 2009 | -0.40 | E-0.37 | E0.17 | E2.18 | E1.65 |
| 2008 | -0.39 | -0.42 | 0.03 | 2.11 | 1.39 |
| 2007 | -0.36 | -0.38 | 0.07 | 1.81 | 1.15 |
| 2006 | -0.08 | -0.25 | 0.04 | 1.77 | 1.47 |
| 2005 | -0.13 | -0.16 | 0.28 | 1.83 | 1.88 |
| 2004 | 0.03 | 0.03 | 0.29 | 1.62 | 1.95 |

Fiscal year ended Apr. 30. Next earnings report expected: Mid December. EPS Estimates based on S&P Operating Earnings; historical GAAP earnings are as reported.

### Dividend Data (Dates: mm/dd Payment Date: mm/dd/yy)

| Amount ($) | Date Decl. | Ex-Div. Date | Stk. of Record | Payment Date |
|---|---|---|---|---|
| 0.143 | 11/28 | 12/10 | 12/12 | 01/02/08 |
| 0.143 | 02/26 | 03/07 | 03/11 | 04/01/08 |
| 0.143 | 05/06 | 06/06 | 06/10 | 07/01/08 |
| 0.150 | 08/27 | 09/08 | 09/10 | 10/01/08 |

Dividends have been paid since 1962. Source: Company reports.

Please read the **Required Disclosures and Analyst Certification** on the last page of this report.

_The McGraw-Hill Companies_

# Block (H&R) Inc.

**STANDARD &POOR'S**

## Business Summary September 22, 2008

CORPORATE OVERVIEW. HRB provides various financial products and services, which the company believes are complementary. In FY 08 (Apr.), Tax Services accounted for 67.9% of revenues and 106% of profits, Business Services 21% and 1.4%, and Consumer Financial Services 10% and 1.4%; the corporate division accounted for (19)% of profits.

The Tax Services division served about 23.5 million clients in FY 08 vs. 22.9 million clients in FY 07 and 21.9 million in FY 06, including 16.5 million retail clients (up 3.8% in FY 08 vs. FY 07) and 4.2 million clients (down 5%). Tax Services also offers refund anticipation loans (RALs), which contributed 4.3% of revenues and $87 million to the Tax Services division's pretax results in FY 08. There were 13,038 company-owned and franchised U.S. H&R Block offices at April 30, 2008. In addition, HRB offers tax preparation services at hundreds of H&R Block Premium offices for more complex returns. International operations are located primarily in Australia, Canada, and the U.K., with combined company owned and franchise offices numbering 1,509 at April 30, 2008. Tax Services also offers online tax preparation, tax preparation software, and guarantee programs.

HRB also provides brokerage services, investment planning, accounting, tax and consulting services, and tax, estate planning, and financial planning services.

MARKET PROFILE. HRB's largest segment, Tax Services, competes with other tax service chains, professional CPA/accounting firms, "mom and pop" local tax service providers and do-it-yourselfers DIYers). In addition, HRB and some other online tax service product providers participate in the Free Filing Alliance, which offers free online federal return preparation with no income limitations. We believe HRB competes successfully by offering many services at what customers believe is an acceptable price-to-value relationship. These services include: the convenience of the largest retail tax office network in the U.S.; a "Peace of Mind" Guarantee" (POM) whereby HRB commits to representing its clients if they are audited by the IRS, and assuming the cost of additional taxes resulting from errors attributable to an HRB tax professional; "Refund Anticipation Loans" and "Refund Anticipation Checks" and a service whereby DIYers using HRB's online service can have an HRB tax professional check their returns and receive the POM guarantee. By offering increased value, HRB has been able to raise its rates 5%-7% annually since 2002.

## Company Financials Fiscal Year Ended Apr. 30

| Per Share Data ($) | 2008 | 2007 | 2006 | 2005 | 2004 | 2003 | 2002 | 2001 | 2000 | 1999 |
|---|---|---|---|---|---|---|---|---|---|---|
| Tangible Book Value | NM | 0.74 | 1.90 | 1.64 | 1.41 | 1.69 | 0.73 | 0.67 | 0.32 | 1.68 |
| Cash Flow | NA | 1.62 | 2.05 | 2.43 | 2.42 | 2.02 | 1.57 | 2.61 | 1.01 | 0.77 |
| Earnings | 1.39 | 1.15 | 1.47 | 1.88 | 1.95 | 1.58 | 1.16 | 0.76 | 0.64 | 0.59 |
| S&P Core Earnings | 1.40 | 1.15 | 1.53 | 1.76 | 1.85 | 1.44 | 1.07 | 0.73 | NA | NA |
| Dividends | 0.53 | 0.49 | 0.54 | 0.39 | 0.39 | 0.35 | 0.29 | 0.27 | 0.26 | 0.21 |
| Payout Ratio | 38% | 42% | 37% | 21% | 20% | 22% | 25% | 35% | 40% | 36% |
| Calendar Year | 2007 | 2006 | 2005 | 2004 | 2003 | 2002 | 2001 | 2000 | 1999 | 1998 |
| Prices:High | 24.95 | 25.75 | 30.00 | 30.50 | 27.89 | 26.75 | 23.19 | 12.38 | 14.88 | 12.27 |
| Prices:Low | 17.57 | 19.80 | 22.99 | 22.08 | 17.64 | 14.50 | 9.16 | 6.73 | 9.50 | 8.83 |
| P/E Ratio:High | 18 | 22 | 20 | 16 | 14 | 17 | 20 | 16 | 23 | 21 |
| P/E Ratio:Low | 13 | 17 | 16 | 12 | 9 | 9 | 8 | 9 | 15 | 15 |

| Income Statement Analysis (Million $) | 2008 | 2007 | 2006 | 2005 | 2004 | 2003 | 2002 | 2001 | 2000 | 1999 |
|---|---|---|---|---|---|---|---|---|---|---|
| Revenue | 4,404 | 4,021 | 4,873 | 4,420 | 4,206 | 3,780 | 3,318 | 3,002 | 2,452 | 1,645 |
| Operating Income | NA | 810 | 128 | 215 | 1,411 | 240 | 987 | 913 | 704 | 499 |
| Depreciation | 146 | 150 | 192 | 184 | 172 | 162 | 155 | 206 | 147 | 74.6 |
| Interest Expense | NA | 46.9 | 49.1 | 62.4 | 84.6 | 92.6 | 116 | 243 | 154 | 69.3 |
| Pretax Income | 745 | 636 | 827 | 1,018 | 1,164 | 987 | 717 | 473 | 412 | 384 |
| Effective Tax Rate | 39.0% | 41.1% | 40.7% | 37.5% | 39.5% | 41.2% | 39.4% | 41.5% | 38.9% | 38.0% |
| Net Income | 454 | 374 | 490 | 636 | 704 | 580 | 434 | 277 | 252 | 238 |
| S&P Core Earnings | 458 | 374 | 509 | 593 | 665 | 527 | 400 | 268 | NA | NA |

| Balance Sheet & Other Financial Data (Million $) | 2008 | 2007 | 2006 | 2005 | 2004 | 2003 | 2002 | 2001 | 2000 | 1999 |
|---|---|---|---|---|---|---|---|---|---|---|
| Cash | 729 | 1,254 | 1,088 | 1,617 | 1,617 | 1,337 | 617 | 326 | 442 | 250 |
| Current Assets | NA | 3,454 | 2,824 | 3,071 | 2,961 | 2,747 | 2,245 | 2,271 | 3,864 | 1,087 |
| Total Assets | 5,623 | 7,499 | 5,989 | 5,539 | 5,380 | 4,604 | 4,231 | 4,122 | 5,699 | 1,910 |
| Current Liabilities | NA | 5,176 | 2,893 | 2,209 | 2,472 | 1,897 | 1,880 | 1,988 | 3,520 | 554 |
| Long Term Debt | NA | 520 | 418 | 923 | 546 | 822 | 868 | 871 | 872 | 250 |
| Common Equity | 988 | 1,414 | 2,148 | 1,976 | 1,897 | 1,664 | 1,369 | 1,174 | 1,219 | 1,062 |
| Total Capital | NA | 1,934 | 2,565 | 2,899 | 2,443 | 2,486 | 2,238 | 2,045 | 2,091 | 1,312 |
| Capital Expenditures | 106 | 161 | 251 | 209 | 128 | 151 | 112 | 90.0 | 113 | 78.8 |
| Cash Flow | NA | 525 | 682 | 820 | 876 | 742 | 590 | 482 | 399 | 312 |
| Current Ratio | 0.8 | 0.7 | 1.0 | 1.4 | 1.2 | 1.4 | 1.2 | 1.1 | 1.1 | 2.0 |
| % Long Term Debt of Capitalization | 48.4 | 26.9 | 16.3 | 31.8 | 22.3 | 33.1 | 38.8 | 42.6 | 41.7 | 19.0 |
| % Net Income of Revenue | 10.3 | 9.3 | 12.4 | 14.3 | 16.7 | 21.4 | 13.1 | 9.2 | 10.3 | 14.5 |
| % Return on Assets | 6.9 | 5.6 | 8.5 | 11.8 | 13.9 | 13.1 | 10.4 | 5.6 | 6.6 | 9.9 |
| % Return on Equity | 37.8 | 21.0 | 23.9 | 33.5 | 39.6 | 38.2 | 34.2 | 23.1 | 22.1 | 19.8 |

Data as orig reptd.; bef. results of disc opers/spec. items. Per share data adj. for stk. divs.; EPS diluted. E-Estimated. NA-Not Available. NM-Not Meaningful. NR-Not Ranked. UR-Under Review.

**Office:** 1 H&R Block Way, Kansas City, MO 64105.
**Telephone:** 816-854-3000.
**Email:** investorrelations@hrblock.com
**Website:** http://www.hrblock.com

**Chrmn:** R.C. Breeden
**Pres & CEO:** R.P. Smyth
**EVP & General Counsel:** C. Graebner
**SVP, CFO & Treas:** B.S. Shulman

**SVP & CIO:** R. Agar
**Investor Contact:** S. Dudley (816-854-4505)
**Board Members:** A. Bennett, T. M. Bloch, R. C. Breeden, R. A. Gerard, L. J. Lauer, D. B. Lewis, T. D. Seip, L. E. Shaw, Jr., R. P. Smyth, C. Wood

**Founded:** 1946
**Domicile:** Missouri
**Employees:** 137,200

**STANDARD & POOR'S**

# Hudson City Bancorp Inc

| S&P Recommendation | BUY ★★★★☆ | Price $17.51 (as of Nov 14, 2008) | 12-Mo. Target Price $19.00 | Investment Style Large-Cap Blend |
| --- | --- | --- | --- | --- |

**GICS Sector** Financials
**Sub-Industry** Thrifts & Mortgage Finance

**Summary** Hudson City Bancorp, through Hudson City Savings Bank, operates over 100 branches in the New York metropolitan area. It caters to high median household income counties and focuses on jumbo mortgage loan funding, largely through time deposits.

## Key Stock Statistics (Source S&P, Vickers, company reports)

| | | | | | | | | |
| --- | --- | --- | --- | --- | --- | --- | --- | --- |
| 52-Wk Range | $25.05– 13.28 | S&P Oper. EPS 2008**E** | 0.91 | Market Capitalization(B) | $9.127 | Beta | | 0.27 |
| Trailing 12-Month EPS | $0.81 | S&P Oper. EPS 2009**E** | 1.16 | Yield (%) | 2.97 | S&P 3-Yr. Proj. EPS CAGR(%) | | 13 |
| Trailing 12-Month P/E | 21.6 | P/E on S&P Oper. EPS 2008**E** | 19.2 | Dividend Rate/Share | $0.52 | S&P Credit Rating | | NA |
| $10K Invested 5 Yrs Ago | $18,289 | Common Shares Outstg. (M) | 521.2 | Institutional Ownership (%) | 79 | | | |

## Price Performance

| 30-Week Mov. Avg. · · · | 10-Week Mov. Avg. – – | GAAP Earnings vs. Previous Year | Volume Above Avg. | STARS |
| --- | --- | --- | --- | --- |
| 12-Mo. Target Price — | Relative Strength — | ▲ Up  ▼ Down  ► No Change | Below Avg. | |

3.206-for-

141    120    97

2005    2006    2007    2008

Options: ASE, CBOE, Ph

Analysis prepared by **Kevin Cole, CFA** on November 12, 2008, when the stock traded at **$ 17.30**.

## Highlights

➤ We anticipate that loan growth and higher fee income will result in revenues increasing 39% in 2008, versus 5.6% in 2007. Our 2008 estimate assumes a net interest margin of 1.90% (up from 1.65% in 2007), average earning asset growth of 24%, and non-interest income growth of 20%. We look for loan growth to be strong in 2008 as HCBK will likely take advantage of attractive spreads and add to its securities portfolio.

➤ HCBK has a strong record of expense control. We look for HCBK's efficiency ratio to be 22.7% in 2008, due largely to a higher revenue base. Given the company's concentration on fixed rate mortgages for higher median income families with higher loan-to-value ratios, we see relatively modest net chargeoffs this year. Non-performing assets to total assets is running toward the low end of the industry at 0.29%, reflecting HCBK's higher loan standards. Even so, we look for provisions to more than triple in 2008, to $15.0 million.

➤ Assuming an effective tax rate of 38.6%, we see 2008 operating EPS of $0.91, and $1.16 in 2009, up from 2007's $0.58.

## Investment Rationale/Risk

➤ We are not sure how the Treasury's new mandate to inject capital into financial institutions will affect HCBK. As competitors receive capital, we believe competition in the jumbo, home-loan market will increase. But, we think it is more likely that funds will be used predominately for acquisitions, leaving HCBK's loan spreads at historically high levels. We think HCBK's avoidance of subprime, Alt-A, and high-LTV loans will enable it to weather the current housing price decline better than most. However, we do see HCBK's chargeoffs and provisions increasing to levels not seen over the past few years on general economic weakness.

➤ Risks to our opinion and target price include larger-than-expected job losses in the tri-state area, and a severe deterioration in the prime loan segment.

➤ Our 12-month target price of $19 equates to roughly 2.0X HCBK's tangible book value of $9.52 a share. This multiple is above peers, but warranted, we believe, by what we see as HCBK's strong credit quality.

## Qualitative Risk Assessment

| LOW | MEDIUM | HIGH |
| --- | --- | --- |

Our risk assessment reflects our view of the solid credit quality of HCBK's loan portfolio and its history of profitability. While the company operates in a highly competitive and fragmented industry, companies in the industry tend to produce relatively stable financial results.

## Quantitative Evaluations

**S&P Quality Ranking**   **A**

| D | C | B- | B | B+ | A- | A | A+ |
| --- | --- | --- | --- | --- | --- | --- | --- |

**Relative Strength Rank**   **STRONG**

89

LOWEST = 1                    HIGHEST = 99

## Revenue/Earnings Data

**Revenue (Million $)**

| | 1Q | 2Q | 3Q | 4Q | Year |
| --- | --- | --- | --- | --- | --- |
| 2008 | 615.5 | 648.8 | 683.5 | -- | -- |
| 2007 | 481.2 | 513.3 | 550.3 | 590.0 | 2,135 |
| 2006 | 361.0 | 385.6 | 423.7 | 449.0 | 1,621 |
| 2005 | 257.5 | 280.5 | 315.2 | 333.8 | 1,187 |
| 2004 | 216.7 | 224.7 | 239.2 | 251.1 | 931.6 |
| 2003 | 204.0 | 202.6 | 196.1 | 204.3 | 807.0 |

**Earnings Per Share ($)**

| | | | | | |
| --- | --- | --- | --- | --- | --- |
| 2008 | 0.18 | 0.22 | 0.25 | E0.26 | E0.91 |
| 2007 | 0.13 | 0.14 | 0.15 | 0.16 | 0.58 |
| 2006 | 0.13 | 0.13 | 0.13 | 0.13 | 0.53 |
| 2005 | 0.11 | 0.11 | 0.13 | 0.13 | 0.48 |
| 2004 | 0.09 | 0.10 | 0.11 | 0.11 | 0.40 |
| 2003 | 0.09 | 0.09 | 0.08 | 0.09 | 0.35 |

Fiscal year ended Dec. 31. Next earnings report expected: Late January. EPS Estimates based on S&P Operating Earnings; historical GAAP earnings are as reported.

## Dividend Data (Dates: mm/dd Payment Date: mm/dd/yy)

| Amount ($) | Date Decl. | Ex-Div. Date | Stk. of Record | Payment Date |
| --- | --- | --- | --- | --- |
| 0.090 | 01/23 | 02/07 | 02/11 | 03/01/08 |
| 0.110 | 04/22 | 05/07 | 05/09 | 05/31/08 |
| 0.120 | 07/23 | 08/07 | 08/11 | 08/29/08 |
| 0.130 | 10/15 | 11/06 | 11/10 | 11/29/08 |

Dividends have been paid since 1999. Source: Company reports.

The McGraw-Hill Companies

# Hudson City Bancorp Inc

**STANDARD &POOR'S**

## Business Summary November 12, 2008

CORPORATE OVERVIEW. Hudson City Bancorp, Inc. (HCBK), a community- and consumer-oriented retail savings bank holding company, offers traditional deposit products, residential real estate mortgage loans and consumer loans. In addition, HCBK purchases mortgages, mortgage-backed securities, securities issued by the U.S. government and government-sponsored agencies and other investments permitted by applicable laws and regulations. HCBK is the holding company of its only subsidiary, Hudson City Savings Bank (Hudson City). The company's revenues are derived principally from interest on mortgage loans & mortgage-backed securities and interest & dividends on investment securities. The bank's primary sources of funds are customer deposits, borrowings, scheduled amortization and prepayments of mortgage loans and mortgage-backed securities, maturities and calls of investment securities and funds provided by operations.

PRIMARY BUSINESS DYNAMICS. As of December 31, 2007, HCBK had total loans of $24.19 billion. Hudson's loan portfolio primarily consists of one-to-four family residential first mortgage loans. HCBK's first mortgage loans totaled $23.79 billion as of December 31, 2007, representing 98.3% of the total loan portfolio. Of the first mortgage loans outstanding at that date, fixed-rate mortgage loans represented 80.5%, while adjustable-rate mortgage loans accounted for the remaining 19.5%. HCBK's loan portfolio also includes multi-family and commercial mortgage loans, construction loans and consumer and other loans, which primarily consist of fixed-rate second mortgage loans and home equity credit lines. The company does not originate or purchase sub-prime loans, negative amortization loans or option ARM loans.

CORPORATE STRATEGY. HCBK seeks to continue its growth by focusing on the origination and purchase of mortgage loans, while purchasing mortgage-backed securities and investment securities as a supplement. It intends to fund its growth with customer deposits and borrowed funds. The company aims to increase customer deposits by continuing to offer desirable products at competitive rates and by opening new branch offices. HCBK continues to focus on high median household income counties, in line with its jumbo mortgage loan and consumer deposit business model.

## Company Financials Fiscal Year Ended Dec. 31

| Per Share Data ($) | 2007 | 2006 | 2005 | 2004 | 2003 | 2002 | 2001 | 2000 | 1999 | 1998 |
|---|---|---|---|---|---|---|---|---|---|---|
| Tangible Book Value | 15.08 | 8.54 | 8.83 | 2.35 | 2.18 | 2.14 | 2.03 | 2.04 | NA | NA |
| Earnings | 0.58 | 0.53 | 0.48 | 0.40 | 0.35 | 0.32 | 0.21 | 0.16 | NA | NA |
| S&P Core Earnings | 0.58 | 0.53 | 0.47 | 0.39 | 0.34 | 0.31 | 0.20 | NA | NA | NA |
| Dividends | 0.33 | 0.30 | 0.27 | 0.22 | 0.16 | 0.11 | 0.07 | 0.03 | NA | NA |
| Payout Ratio | 57% | 57% | 56% | 54% | 47% | 34% | 35% | 21% | NA | NA |
| Prices:High | 16.08 | 14.09 | 12.61 | 12.79 | 12.00 | 6.71 | 4.14 | 3.16 | NA | NA |
| Prices:Low | 11.45 | 11.90 | 10.09 | 9.79 | 5.79 | 4.04 | 2.72 | 1.97 | NA | NA |
| P/E Ratio:High | 28 | 27 | 26 | 32 | 35 | 21 | 20 | 19 | NA | NA |
| P/E Ratio:Low | 20 | 22 | 21 | 24 | 17 | 13 | 13 | 12 | NA | NA |

| Income Statement Analysis (Million $) | | | | | | | | | | |
|---|---|---|---|---|---|---|---|---|---|---|
| Net Interest Income | 647 | 613 | 562 | 485 | 401 | 388 | 287 | 254 | NA | NA |
| Loan Loss Provision | 4.80 | Nil | 0.07 | 0.79 | 0.90 | 1.50 | 1.88 | 2.13 | NA | NA |
| Non Interest Income | 7.27 | 6.29 | 5.27 | 16.6 | 5.34 | 5.95 | 4.69 | 4.54 | NA | NA |
| Non Interest Expenses | 168 | 159 | 128 | 118 | 103 | 93.5 | 81.8 | 79.0 | NA | NA |
| Pretax Income | 482 | 461 | 442 | 382 | 327 | 301 | 208 | 177 | NA | NA |
| Effective Tax Rate | 38.6% | 37.3% | 37.6% | 37.4% | 36.6% | 36.3% | 35.3% | 35.3% | NA | NA |
| Net Income | 296 | 289 | 276 | 239 | 207 | 192 | 135 | 115 | NA | NA |
| % Net Interest Margin | 1.64 | 1.96 | 2.35 | 3.66 | 2.65 | 3.10 | 2.87 | 2.90 | NA | NA |
| S&P Core Earnings | 294 | 287 | 272 | 235 | 204 | 186 | 128 | NA | NA | NA |

| Balance Sheet & Other Financial Data (Million $) | | | | | | | | | | |
|---|---|---|---|---|---|---|---|---|---|---|
| Total Assets | 44,424 | 35,507 | 28,075 | 20,146 | 17,033 | 14,145 | 11,427 | 9,380 | NA | NA |
| Loans | 24,198 | 19,069 | 15,037 | 11,328 | 8,766 | 6,932 | 5,932 | 4,841 | NA | NA |
| Deposits | 15,153 | 13,416 | 11,383 | 11,477 | 10,454 | 9,139 | 7,913 | 6,604 | NA | NA |
| Capitalization:Debt | 24,141 | 16,966 | 11,350 | 7,150 | 5,150 | 3,600 | 2,150 | 650 | NA | NA |
| Capitalization:Equity | 4,611 | 4,930 | 5,201 | 1,403 | 1,329 | 1,316 | 1,289 | 1,465 | NA | NA |
| Capitalization:Total | 28,752 | 21,896 | 16,551 | 8,553 | 6,479 | 4,916 | 3,439 | 2,115 | NA | NA |
| % Return on Assets | 0.7 | 0.9 | 1.1 | 1.3 | 1.3 | 1.5 | 1.3 | 1.3 | NA | NA |
| % Return on Equity | 6.2 | 5.7 | 8.4 | 17.5 | 15.7 | 14.7 | 9.8 | 7.8 | NA | NA |
| % Loan Loss Reserve | 0.1 | 0.2 | 0.2 | 0.2 | 0.2 | 0.4 | 0.4 | NA | NA | NA |
| % Risk Based Capital | 24.8 | 31.0 | 41.3 | 17.5 | 7.5 | 26.8 | 32.0 | 43.0 | NA | NA |
| Price Times Book Value:High | 1.1 | 1.6 | 1.4 | 5.4 | 5.5 | 3.1 | 2.0 | 1.5 | NA | NA |
| Price Times Book Value:Low | 0.8 | 1.4 | 1.1 | 4.2 | 2.7 | 1.9 | 1.3 | 0.9 | NA | NA |

Data as orig reptd.; bef. results of disc opers/spec. items. Per share data adj. for stk. divs.; EPS diluted. E-Estimated. NA-Not Available. NM-Not Meaningful. NR-Not Ranked. UR-Under Review.

**Office:** 80 W Century Rd, Paramus, NJ, USA 07652-1405.
**Telephone:** 201-967-1900.
**Website:** http://www.hcbk.com
**Chrmn, Pres & CEO:** R.E. Hermance, Jr.

**COO & EVP:** D.J. Salamone
**EVP & CFO:** J.C. Kranz
**SVP, Treas & Secy:** V.A. Olszewski
**Investor Contact:** S. Munhall (201-967-8290)

**Board Members:** M. W. Azzara, W. G. Bardel, S. A. Belair, V. H. Bruni, W. J. Cosgrove, R. E. Hermance, Jr., D. O. Quest, D. J. Salamone, J. G. Sponholz

**Founded:** 1868
**Domicile:** Delaware
**Employees:** 1,362

*The McGraw-Hill Companies*

**STANDARD &POOR'S**

# Humana Inc.

| S&P Recommendation **BUY** ★★★★☆ | Price $30.63 (as of Nov 14, 2008) | 12-Mo. Target Price $46.00 | Investment Style Large-Cap Growth |
| --- | --- | --- | --- |

**GICS Sector** Health Care
**Sub-Industry** Managed Health Care

**Summary** This company provides a broad range of managed health care services to more than 11.5 million individuals.

## Key Stock Statistics (Source S&P, Vickers, company reports)

| | | | | | |
| --- | --- | --- | --- | --- | --- |
| 52-Wk Range | $88.10– 25.01 | S&P Oper. EPS 2008**E** | 4.30 | Market Capitalization(B) | $5.168 |
| Trailing 12-Month EPS | $4.22 | S&P Oper. EPS 2009**E** | 5.70 | Yield (%) | Nil |
| Trailing 12-Month P/E | 7.3 | P/E on S&P Oper. EPS 2008**E** | 7.1 | Dividend Rate/Share | Nil |
| $10K Invested 5 Yrs Ago | $14,819 | Common Shares Outstg. (M) | 168.7 | Institutional Ownership (%) | 89 |

| | |
| --- | --- |
| Beta | 1.06 |
| S&P 3-Yr. Proj. EPS CAGR(%) | 15 |
| S&P Credit Rating | BBB |

## Price Performance

30-Week Mov. Avg. · · · · 10-Week Mov. Avg. – · – **GAAP Earnings vs. Previous Year**   **Volume** Above Avg. ⅢⅢ   STARS
12-Mo. Target Price —   Relative Strength —   ▲ Up ▼ Down ▶ No Change   Below Avg. ⅢⅢ

Options: ASE, CBOE, Ph

Analysis prepared by **Phillip M. Seligman** on November 05, 2008, when the stock traded at **$ 36.01**.

### Highlights

➤ We forecast that premium and ASO fee revenues will rise 6.7% in 2009, to about $30.4 billion, from the $28.5 billion we see in 2008. Drivers for 2009 include organic growth of 50,000 Medicare Advantage (MA), but 700,000 fewer members in the Medicare standalone PDP program (of which 308,000 are low-income, subsidized seniors), 93,000 fewer Medicaid members, flat to modestly lower commercial enrollment, and no change in TRICARE enrollment. Revenue growth is below the 14.8% we project for 2008, which benefited from acquisitions and aggressive MA member recruitment. On the commercial side, we see premium yields (rates minus buydowns) in 2009 on a same-store basis in line with expected 6%-7% medical cost trends, similar to 2008 levels.

➤ We believe the consolidated medical cost ratio (MCR) will be 90 basis points (bps) below 2008 levels, mainly on PDP repricing and higher cost-sharing in its MA PFFS plans. We see the SG&A cost ratio modestly below the 13.7% we look for in 2008, partly on revenue leverage.

➤ We estimate operating EPS of $4.30 in 2008 and $5.70 in 2009, also assuming lower investment income than the level HUM is guiding.

### Investment Rationale/Risk

➤ We think HUM has made a strategic decision to focus more on profitability in 2009 than on gaining MA market share, as it has done until this year. We believe its higher PDP pricing and greater Private Fee-for-Service (PFFS) cost-sharing will lead many healthy PDP and PFFS members to switch to rivals. But we expect it will also cause unhealthy members to leave, and encourage other PFFS members to switch to its PPO offerings ahead of the mandated conversion in 2011 of PFFS plans into network-based ones. Meanwhile, its consistent favorable prior-period reserve development suggests to us a conservative medical cost reserving policy. Elsewhere, HUM recently terminated interest rate swaps, receiving $108 million in cash, which matched its third-quarter predominantly non-cash investment losses. We view HUM as well-capitalized and its operating cash flow as healthy, providing financial flexibility.

➤ Risks to our recommendation and target price include intensified competition, a medical cost spike, and MA rate cuts.

➤ Our 12-month target price of $46 assumes a peer-level forward P/E multiple of 8X applied to our 2009 EPS estimate.

### Qualitative Risk Assessment

| LOW | MEDIUM | **HIGH** |
| --- | --- | --- |

Our risk assessment reflects HUM's strong reliance on Medicare Advantage (MA) for growth. We also believe that intense competition will continue to limit commercial enrollment growth.

### Quantitative Evaluations

**S&P Quality Ranking**   B+

| D | C | B- | B | **B+** | A- | A | A+ |
| --- | --- | --- | --- | --- | --- | --- | --- |

**Relative Strength Rank**   MODERATE

| 54 |
| --- |

LOWEST = 1   HIGHEST = 99

### Revenue/Earnings Data

**Revenue (Million $)**

| | 1Q | 2Q | 3Q | 4Q | Year |
| --- | --- | --- | --- | --- | --- |
| 2008 | 6,960 | 7,351 | 7,148 | -- | -- |
| 2007 | 6,205 | 6,427 | 6,320 | 6,339 | 25,290 |
| 2006 | 4,704 | 5,407 | 5,650 | 5,655 | 21,417 |
| 2005 | 3,887 | 3,546 | 3,821 | 3,663 | 14,418 |
| 2004 | 3,287 | 3,431 | 3,176 | 3,210 | 13,104 |
| 2003 | 2,932 | 3,030 | 3,112 | 3,153 | 12,226 |

**Earnings Per Share ($)**

| | | | | | |
| --- | --- | --- | --- | --- | --- |
| 2008 | 0.47 | 1.24 | 1.09 | E1.10 | E4.30 |
| 2007 | 0.42 | 1.28 | 1.78 | 1.43 | 4.91 |
| 2006 | 0.50 | 0.53 | 0.95 | 0.92 | 2.90 |
| 2005 | 0.54 | 0.51 | 0.30 | 0.39 | 1.87 |
| 2004 | 0.41 | 0.50 | 0.52 | 0.29 | 1.72 |
| 2003 | 0.19 | 0.43 | 0.38 | 0.41 | 1.41 |

Fiscal year ended Dec. 31. Next earnings report expected: Early February. EPS Estimates based on S&P Operating Earnings; historical GAAP earnings are as reported.

### Dividend Data

No cash dividends have been paid since 1993.

# Humana Inc.

STANDARD
&POOR'S

## Business Summary November 05, 2008

CORPORATE OVERVIEW. Humana is one of the largest managed care organizations, with medical membership of 11,527,300 (8,438,300 excluding Medicare Prescription Drug Program (PDP) enrollment) as of September 30, 2008, versus 11,467,100 (8,025,500) at December 31, 2007.

The Commercial segment consists of members enrolled in products marketed to employer groups and individuals, including fully insured medical (1,931,200 versus 1,808,600), administrative services only (ASO; 1,622,800 versus 1,643,000), and specialty (6,727,400 versus 6,783,800). Health maintenance organizations (HMOs; 8.1% of total premium and fee revenues in 2007) require members to use only doctors in their networks and generally reimburse providers on a capitated basis. Preferred provider organizations (PPOs; 14.7%) allow members the option to go to doctors outside of the network, with the members paying a portion of the provider's fees. ASO products (1.2%), which include HMOs, PPOs and consumer-directed health plans, are offered to employers that self-insure their employee health plans. Specialty products (2.2%) include dental, group and individual life, and short-term disability.

The Government segment consists of Medicare Advantage (MA; HMO: 502,300 versus 453,100; PPO: 171,000 versus 74,100; private fee-for-service, or

PFFS: 694,700 versus 615,800); Medicare PDP (Standard: 1,495,700 versus 2,131,900, Enhanced: 1,433,800 versus 1,091,500, Complete: 159,500 versus 218,600); Medicaid (insured: 385,100 versus 384,400; ASO: 177,300 versus 180,600), and the Dept. of Defense health program, TRICARE (fully insured: 1,734,400 versus 1,719,100; ASO: 1,219,500 versus 1,146,800).

In 2007, MA revenues were $11.2 billion (45.0%) and Medicare PDP revenues were $3.7 billion (14.8%). As of April, 2008, MA plans included 13 local HMOs, 41 local PPOs, a regional PPO in 25 states, and private fee-for-service (PFFS) programs in 50 states, and HUM offered the Medicare Prescription Drug Program in 50 states.

The Medicaid unit (2.3%) has contracts in Puerto Rico and Florida.

HUM's current TRICARE South Region contract (fully insured: 11.4%; administrative services fees: 0.3%) covers beneficiaries in 10 states.

## Company Financials Fiscal Year Ended Dec. 31

| Per Share Data ($) | 2007 | 2006 | 2005 | 2004 | 2003 | 2002 | 2001 | 2000 | 1999 | 1998 |
|---|---|---|---|---|---|---|---|---|---|---|
| Tangible Book Value | 13.91 | 10.46 | 7.41 | 7.52 | 6.54 | 5.09 | 4.33 | 3.43 | 2.75 | 2.98 |
| Cash Flow | 6.00 | 3.79 | 2.68 | 2.45 | 2.20 | 1.57 | 1.67 | 1.42 | -1.53 | 1.53 |
| Earnings | 4.91 | 2.90 | 1.87 | 1.72 | 1.41 | 0.85 | 0.70 | 0.54 | -2.28 | 0.77 |
| S&P Core Earnings | 4.87 | 2.64 | 1.99 | 1.55 | 1.23 | 0.87 | 0.63 | NA | NA | NA |
| Dividends | Nil | Nil | Nil | Nil | Nil | Nil | Nil | Nil | Nil | Nil |
| Payout Ratio | Nil | Nil | Nil | Nil | Nil | Nil | Nil | Nil | Nil | Nil |
| Prices:High | 81.50 | 68.24 | 55.70 | 31.02 | 23.39 | 17.45 | 15.63 | 15.81 | 20.75 | 32.13 |
| Prices:Low | 51.00 | 41.08 | 28.92 | 15.20 | 8.68 | 9.78 | 8.38 | 4.75 | 5.88 | 12.25 |
| P/E Ratio:High | 17 | 24 | 30 | 18 | 17 | 21 | 22 | 29 | NM | 42 |
| P/E Ratio:Low | 10 | 14 | 15 | 9 | 6 | 12 | 12 | 9 | NM | 16 |
| **Income Statement Analysis** (Million $) | | | | | | | | | | |
| Revenue | 25,290 | 21,417 | 14,418 | 13,104 | 12,226 | 11,261 | 10,195 | 10,395 | 9,959 | 9,597 |
| Operating Income | 1,543 | 974 | 590 | 415 | 489 | 384 | 114 | 171 | 59.0 | 228 |
| Depreciation | 185 | 149 | 129 | 118 | 127 | 121 | 162 | 147 | 124 | 128 |
| Interest Expense | 68.9 | 63.1 | 39.3 | 23.2 | 17.4 | 17.0 | 25.0 | 29.0 | 33.0 | 47.0 |
| Pretax Income | 1,289 | 762 | 422 | 416 | 345 | 210 | 183 | 114 | -404 | 203 |
| Effective Tax Rate | 35.3% | 36.0% | 26.9% | 32.7% | 33.6% | 32.0% | 36.1% | 21.1% | NM | 36.5% |
| Net Income | 834 | 487 | 308 | 280 | 229 | 143 | 117 | 90.0 | -382 | 129 |
| S&P Core Earnings | 826 | 443 | 330 | 252 | 200 | 145 | 104 | NA | NA | NA |
| **Balance Sheet & Other Financial Data** (Million $) | | | | | | | | | | |
| Cash | 5,676 | 1,740 | 732 | 580 | 931 | 721 | 651 | 2,067 | 2,485 | 2,812 |
| Current Assets | 8,733 | 7,333 | 4,206 | 3,596 | 3,321 | 2,795 | 2,623 | 2,499 | 3,064 | 3,119 |
| Total Assets | 12,879 | 10,127 | 6,870 | 5,658 | 5,293 | 4,600 | 4,404 | 4,167 | 4,900 | 5,496 |
| Current Liabilities | 5,792 | 5,192 | 3,220 | 2,327 | 2,265 | 2,390 | 2,307 | 2,665 | 3,164 | 2,643 |
| Long Term Debt | 1,688 | 1,269 | 514 | 637 | 643 | 340 | 315 | Nil | 324 | 1,011 |
| Common Equity | 4,029 | 3,054 | 2,474 | 2,090 | 1,836 | 1,606 | 1,508 | 1,374 | 1,268 | 1,688 |
| Total Capital | 5,717 | 4,323 | 2,988 | 2,727 | 2,479 | 1,946 | 1,823 | 1,374 | 1,592 | 2,699 |
| Capital Expenditures | 239 | 193 | 166 | 114 | 101 | 112 | 115 | 135 | 89.0 | 104 |
| Cash Flow | 1,018 | 636 | 437 | 398 | 356 | 264 | 279 | 237 | -258 | 257 |
| Current Ratio | 1.5 | 1.4 | 1.3 | 1.5 | 1.5 | 1.2 | 1.1 | 0.9 | 1.0 | 1.2 |
| % Long Term Debt of Capitalization | 29.5 | 29.4 | 17.2 | 23.3 | 25.9 | 17.5 | 17.3 | Nil | 20.4 | 37.5 |
| % Net Income of Revenue | 3.3 | 2.3 | 2.1 | 102.6 | 1.9 | 1.3 | 1.2 | 0.9 | NM | 1.3 |
| % Return on Assets | 7.3 | 5.7 | 4.9 | 5.1 | 4.5 | 3.2 | 2.7 | 2.0 | NM | 2.4 |
| % Return on Equity | 23.5 | 17.5 | 13.5 | 14.3 | 13.3 | 9.2 | 8.2 | 6.8 | NM | 8.1 |

Data as orig reptd.; bef. results of disc opers/spec. items. Per share data adj. for stk. divs.; EPS diluted. E-Estimated. NA-Not Available. NM-Not Meaningful. NR-Not Ranked. UR-Under Review.

**Office:** 500 W Main St, Louisville, KY 40202-4268.
**Telephone:** 502-580-1000.
**Website:** http://www.humana.com
**Chrmn:** D.A. Jones, Jr.

**Pres & CEO:** M.B. McCallister
**COO & SVP:** J.E. Murray
**SVP, CFO & Treas:** J.H. Bloem
**SVP & General Counsel:** C.M. Todoroff

**Investor Contact:** R.C. Nethery (502-580-3644)
**Board Members:** F. D'Amelio, W. R. Dunbar, K. J. Hilzinger, D. A. Jones, Jr., M. B. McCallister, W. J. McDonald, J. J. O'Brien, M. T. Peterson, W. A. Reynolds

**Founded:** 1964
**Domicile:** Delaware
**Employees:** 25,000

The McGraw·Hill Companies

STANDARD &POOR'S

# Huntington Bancshares Inc

**S&P Recommendation** BUY ★★★★☆

| | |
|---|---|
| **Price** | $7.79 (as of Nov 14, 2008) |
| **12-Mo. Target Price** | $11.00 |
| **Investment Style** | Large-Cap Blend |

**GICS Sector** Financials
**Sub-Industry** Regional Banks

**Summary** This $55 billion regional bank holding company has a network of branches throughout the Midwest.

## Key Stock Statistics (Source S&P, Vickers, company reports)

| | | | | | | |
|---|---|---|---|---|---|---|
| 52-Wk Range | $16.86– 4.37 | S&P Oper. EPS 2008**E** | 0.94 | Market Capitalization(B) | $2.852 | Beta | 0.86 |
| Trailing 12-Month EPS | $0.27 | S&P Oper. EPS 2009**E** | 1.07 | Yield (%) | 6.80 | S&P 3-Yr. Proj. EPS CAGR(%) | 75 |
| Trailing 12-Month P/E | 28.9 | P/E on S&P Oper. EPS 2008**E** | 8.3 | Dividend Rate/Share | $0.53 | S&P Credit Rating | BBB+ |
| $10K Invested 5 Yrs Ago | $4,518 | Common Shares Outstg. (M) | 366.2 | Institutional Ownership (%) | 64 | | |

## Price Performance

Options: CBOE, Ph

## Qualitative Risk Assessment

LOW **MEDIUM** HIGH

Our risk assessment reflects HBAN's exposure to the Midwestern economy and housing-related issues.

## Quantitative Evaluations

**S&P Quality Ranking** B+

D | C | B- | B | **B+** | A- | A | A+

**Relative Strength Rank** MODERATE 69

LOWEST = 1     HIGHEST = 99

## Revenue/Earnings Data

**Revenue (Million $)**

| | 1Q | 2Q | 3Q | 4Q | Year |
|---|---|---|---|---|---|
| 2008 | 989.2 | 933.1 | 912.2 | -- | -- |
| 2007 | 689.1 | 698.7 | 1,056 | 985.0 | 3,420 |
| 2006 | 624.3 | 684.9 | 636.9 | 685.5 | 2,632 |
| 2005 | 544.2 | 558.5 | 581.6 | 589.8 | 2,274 |
| 2004 | 553.6 | 542.3 | 527.9 | 542.2 | 2,166 |
| 2003 | 599.6 | 604.7 | 606.1 | 564.6 | 2,375 |

**Earnings Per Share ($)**

| | | | | | |
|---|---|---|---|---|---|
| 2008 | 0.35 | 0.25 | 0.28 | E0.15 | E0.94 |
| 2007 | 0.40 | 0.34 | 0.38 | -0.65 | 0.25 |
| 2006 | 0.45 | 0.46 | 0.65 | 0.37 | 1.92 |
| 2005 | 0.41 | 0.45 | 0.47 | 0.44 | 1.77 |
| 2004 | 0.45 | 0.47 | 0.40 | 0.39 | 1.71 |
| 2003 | 0.39 | 0.42 | 0.45 | 0.40 | 1.67 |

Fiscal year ended Dec. 31. Next earnings report expected: Mid January. EPS Estimates based on S&P Operating Earnings; historical GAAP earnings are as reported.

## Highlights

► The STARS recommendation for HBAN has recently been changed to 4 (buy) from 3 (hold) and the 12-month target price has recently been changed to $11.00 from $12.00. The Highlights section of this Stock Report will be updated accordingly.

## Investment Rationale/Risk

► The Investment Rationale/Risk section of this Stock Report will be updated shortly. For the latest News story on HBAN from MarketScope, see below.

► 11/10/08 02:18 pm ET ... S&P RAISES OPINION ON SHARES OF HUNTINGTON BANCSHARES TO BUY FROM HOLD (HBAN 8.96****): Our upgrade is based on valuation, as HBAN shares have fallen almost 17% from a recent peak. The S&P Regional Bank index declined 12%, we think due to general economic fears and the implication for credit costs at HBAN and its peers. However, we think HBAN has relatively high reserve levels, acceptable credit quality and a sustainable $0.13 dividend. We keep our '09 EPS estimate at $1.07; we also keep our $11 target price, based on a discount-to-peers 10.2X multiple on our '09 EPS forecast, a discount 0.70X book value, reflecting our view of HBAN's credit-related challenges. /E. Oja

## Dividend Data (Dates: mm/dd Payment Date: mm/dd/yy)

| Amount ($) | Date Decl. | Ex-Div. Date | Stk. of Record | Payment Date |
|---|---|---|---|---|
| 0.265 | 01/16 | 03/12 | 03/14 | 04/01/08 |
| 0.133 | 04/15 | 06/11 | 06/13 | 07/01/08 |
| 0.133 | 07/16 | 09/10 | 09/12 | 10/01/08 |
| 0.133 | 10/15 | 12/10 | 12/13 | 01/02/09 |

Dividends have been paid since 1912. Source: Company reports.

# Huntington Bancshares Inc

## Business Summary September 04, 2008

CORPORATE OVERVIEW. Huntington Bancshares Inc. (HBAN) is a multi-state diversified financial holding company focused on the Midwest region of the United States. It provides full-service commercial and consumer banking services, mortgage banking services, automobile financing, equipment leasing, investment management, trust services, and brokerage services. The company also offers insurance services.

The regional banking line of business provides traditional banking products and services to consumer, small business, and commercial customers located in its eight operating regions within the six states of Ohio, Pennsylvania, Michigan, West Virginia, Indiana, and Kentucky. It provides these services through a banking network of 600 branches, over 1,400 ATMs, along with Internet and telephone banking channels. It also provides certain services outside of these five states, including mortgage banking and equipment leasing. Each region is further divided into retail and commercial banking units.

On July 1, 2007, HBAN completed the acquisition of Sky Financial Group for

approximately $3.5 billion, in a 90% stock, 10% cash deal. Under the terms of the deal HBAN paid 1.098 shares of HBAN for each share of Sky Financial, and issued approximately 131.3 million shares of its own stock to acquire Sky Financial's 119.6 million outstanding shares. These 131.3 million extra shares represented a 55% increase in HBAN's share count. The merger added nearly $13 billion in loans to HBAN's June 30, 2007 level of $26.8 billion, and added $13.1 billion in total deposits to HBAN's June 30, 2007 level of $$24.6 billion. The original intent of this merger was to help HBAN to cut costs through consolidation and to increase customer convenience. St the time of this merger, however, we questioned HBAN's strategy of expanding its concentration in the highly competitive Midwestern markets.

## Company Financials Fiscal Year Ended Dec. 31

| Per Share Data ($) | 2007 | 2006 | 2005 | 2004 | 2003 | 2002 | 2001 | 2000 | 1999 | 1998 |
|---|---|---|---|---|---|---|---|---|---|---|
| Tangible Book Value | 7.14 | 10.12 | 11.41 | 10.02 | 8.99 | 8.95 | 6.77 | 9.43 | 8.66 | 8.43 |
| Earnings | 0.25 | 1.92 | 1.77 | 1.71 | 1.67 | 1.49 | 0.71 | 1.32 | 1.65 | 1.17 |
| S&P Core Earnings | 0.32 | 1.95 | 1.73 | 1.66 | 1.56 | 0.67 | 0.60 | NA | NA | NA |
| Dividends | 1.06 | 1.00 | 0.85 | 0.75 | 0.67 | 0.64 | 0.72 | 0.74 | 0.68 | 0.62 |
| Payout Ratio | NM | 52% | 48% | 44% | 40% | 43% | 101% | 56% | 41% | 53% |
| Prices:High | 24.14 | 24.97 | 25.41 | 25.38 | 22.55 | 21.77 | 19.28 | 21.82 | 30.89 | 28.55 |
| Prices:Low | 13.50 | 22.56 | 20.97 | 20.89 | 17.78 | 16.00 | 12.63 | 12.52 | 19.49 | 18.18 |
| P/E Ratio:High | 97 | 13 | 14 | 15 | 14 | 15 | 27 | 17 | 19 | 25 |
| P/E Ratio:Low | 54 | 12 | 12 | 12 | 11 | 11 | 18 | 9 | 12 | 16 |

| Income Statement Analysis (Million $) | | | | | | | | | | |
|---|---|---|---|---|---|---|---|---|---|---|
| Net Interest Income | 1,302 | 1,019 | 962 | 911 | 849 | 984 | 996 | 942 | 1,042 | 1,021 |
| Tax Equivalent Adjustment | 19.3 | 16.0 | 13.4 | NA | 9.68 | 5.21 | 6.35 | 8.31 | 9.42 | 10.3 |
| Non Interest Income | 706 | 634 | 640 | 803 | 1,064 | 680 | 509 | 494 | 561 | 408 |
| Loan Loss Provision | 644 | 65.2 | 81.3 | 55.1 | 164 | 227 | 309 | 90.5 | 88.4 | 105 |
| % Expense/Operating Revenue | 65.3% | 60.0% | 60.5% | 65.5% | 64.3% | 50.6% | 67.4% | 61.7% | 56.6% | 63.9% |
| Pretax Income | 22.6 | 514 | 544 | 553 | 524 | 589 | 173 | 460 | 615 | 440 |
| Effective Tax Rate | NM | 10.3% | 24.2% | 27.8% | 26.4% | 38.4% | NM | 28.6% | 31.3% | 31.4% |
| Net Income | 75.2 | 461 | 412 | 399 | 386 | 363 | 179 | 328 | 422 | 302 |
| % Net Interest Margin | 3.36 | 3.29 | 3.33 | 3.33 | 3.49 | 4.19 | 4.02 | 3.73 | 4.11 | 4.28 |
| S&P Core Earnings | 96.8 | 467 | 405 | 388 | 360 | 165 | 152 | NA | NA | NA |

| Balance Sheet & Other Financial Data (Million $) | | | | | | | | | | |
|---|---|---|---|---|---|---|---|---|---|---|
| Money Market Assets | 1,965 | 551 | 105 | 960 | 138 | 86.6 | 118 | 143 | 28.9 | 243 |
| Investment Securities | 4,500 | 4,363 | 4,527 | 4,239 | 4,929 | 3,411 | 2,862 | 4,107 | 4,889 | 4,806 |
| Commercial Loans | 22,308 | 12,354 | 10,845 | 10,303 | 9,486 | 9,336 | 10,415 | 8,887 | 8,452 | 6,027 |
| Other Loans | 17,746 | 13,799 | 13,627 | 13,257 | 11,590 | 11,619 | 11,187 | 11,723 | 12,216 | 13,428 |
| Total Assets | 54,697 | 35,329 | 32,765 | 32,565 | 30,484 | 27,579 | 28,500 | 28,599 | 29,037 | 28,296 |
| Demand Deposits | 5,372 | 3,616 | 3,390 | 3,392 | 2,987 | 3,074 | 3,741 | 3,505 | 7,594 | 7,771 |
| Time Deposits | 32,371 | 21,432 | 19,020 | 17,376 | 15,500 | 14,425 | 16,446 | 16,272 | 11,613 | 11,951 |
| Long Term Debt | 6,955 | 4,513 | 4,597 | 6,227 | 6,808 | 3,304 | 3,039 | 3,338 | 4,269 | 3,247 |
| Common Equity | 5,949 | 3,014 | 2,594 | 2,538 | 2,275 | 2,304 | 2,416 | 2,366 | 2,182 | 2,149 |
| % Return on Assets | 0.2 | 1.4 | 1.3 | 1.3 | 1.3 | 1.3 | 0.6 | 1.1 | 1.5 | 1.1 |
| % Return on Equity | 1.7 | 16.6 | 16.0 | 16.6 | 17.3 | 15.4 | 7.5 | 14.4 | 19.5 | 14.5 |
| % Loan Loss Reserve | 1.4 | 1.0 | -0.7 | 1.1 | 1.6 | 1.7 | 1.8 | 1.4 | -1.4 | 1.5 |
| % Loans/Deposits | 105.4 | 105.5 | 171.3 | 114.5 | 115.2 | 122.8 | 110.1 | 105.0 | 106.5 | 98.6 |
| % Equity to Assets | 10.0 | 8.2 | 7.8 | 7.6 | 7.7 | 8.4 | 8.4 | 7.9 | 7.6 | 7.6 |

Data as orig reptd.; bef. results of disc opers/spec. items. Per share data adj. for stk. divs.; EPS diluted. E-Estimated. NA-Not Available. NM-Not Meaningful. NR-Not Ranked. UR-Under Review.

**Office:** 41 S High St, Columbus, OH 43287.
**Telephone:** 614-480-8300.
**Website:** http://www.huntington.com
**Chrmn, Pres & CEO:** T.E. Hoaglin

**COO & CTO:** W. Dolloff
**EVP & CFO:** D.R. Kimble
**EVP & Treas:** M. Sankaran
**EVP, Secy & General Counsel:** R.A. Cheap

**Investor Contact:** D.R. Kimble (614-480-5676)
**Board Members:** R. J. Biggs, D. M. Casto, III, M. J. Endres, M. Fennell, J. B. Gerlach, Jr., D. J. Hilliker, T. E. Hoaglin, D. P. Lauer, J. A. Levy, W. J. Lhota, G. E. Little, G. P. Mastroianni, D. L. Porteous, K. H. Ransier

**Founded:** 1966
**Domicile:** Maryland
**Employees:** 11,925

# STANDARD &POOR'S

# Illinois Tool Works Inc.

| **S&P Recommendation** HOLD ★★★☆☆ | **Price** $31.84 (as of Nov 14, 2008) | **12-Mo. Target Price** $40.00 | **Investment Style** Large-Cap Growth |
|---|---|---|---|

**GICS Sector** Industrials
**Sub-Industry** Industrial Machinery

**Summary** This diversified manufacturer operates a portfolio of about 750 industrial and consumer businesses located throughout the world.

## Key Stock Statistics (Source S&P, Vickers, company reports)

| | | | | | | | |
|---|---|---|---|---|---|---|---|
| 52-Wk Range | $58.97– 28.50 | S&P Oper. EPS 2008**E** | 3.29 | Market Capitalization(B) | $16.275 | Beta | 1.03 |
| Trailing 12-Month EPS | $3.31 | S&P Oper. EPS 2009**E** | 3.61 | Yield (%) | 3.89 | S&P 3-Yr. Proj. EPS CAGR(%) | 10 |
| Trailing 12-Month P/E | 9.6 | P/E on S&P Oper. EPS 2008**E** | 9.7 | Dividend Rate/Share | $1.24 | S&P Credit Rating | AA- |
| $10K Invested 5 Yrs Ago | $9,107 | Common Shares Outstg. (M) | 511.2 | Institutional Ownership (%) | 84 | | |

## Price Performance

- 30-Week Mov. Avg. ···· 10-Week Mov. Avg. -- GAAP Earnings vs. Previous Year   Volume Above Avg. STARS
- 12-Mo. Target Price — Relative Strength — ▲ Up ▼ Down ► No Change   Below Avg. ★

Options: ASE, CBOE, Ph

Analysis prepared by **Mathew Christy, CFA** on October 21, 2008, when the stock traded at **$ 35.40**.

## Highlights

➤ Excluding discontinued operations, we see revenues increasing nearly 11% in 2008 and 6% in 2009, driven mainly by the positive effects of acquisitions and currency fluctuations, offset by flat to slightly negative organic growth in ITW's end markets. We foresee end-market conditions weakening due to lower North American auto production and commercial construction activity along with slowing international economic growth. We expect ITW's domestic auto revenues to be hampered by soft demand and high inventories.

➤ We expect the operating margin in 2008 to contract due to acquisition and restructuring costs, increased input costs, and lower pricing. In 2009, we forecast a slight decline in operating margins, as lower pricing and higher costs in the first half of the year hurt profitability, slightly offset by improving results in the second half of 2009.

➤ With steady interest expense and a stable tax rate, we forecast EPS of $3.29 and $3.61 in 2008 and 2009, respectively.

## Investment Rationale/Risk

➤ While we expect improving results, we think a large part of the gains will be via non-organic growth, including acquisitions, currency effects and share repurchases, as favorable international conditions in many of ITW's end markets are offset by the exposure to other markets, including the automotive and construction sectors. We believe the shares are appropriately valued at recent levels.

➤ Risks to our recommendation and target price include an unexpected downturn in industrial activity and/or capital spending; execution risk associated with acquisitions; continued escalation of raw material costs; and a greater-than-anticipated slowing of the residential housing and/or automotive markets.

➤ Our 12-month target price of $40 represents a weighted blend of two valuation metrics. Our discounted cash flow model, which assumes 3% growth in perpetuity and a 10.3% weighted average cost of capital, indicates intrinsic value of about $50. In terms of relative valuation, we apply a target P/E multiple of about 9.5X, ahead of peers and near historical trough multiples, to our forward 12-month EPS estimate of $3.48, which suggests a value of about $34 a share.

## Qualitative Risk Assessment

| LOW | MEDIUM | HIGH |
|---|---|---|

Our risk assessment reflects an S&P Quality Ranking of A+ for ITW, a balance sheet we see as strong with a relatively low amount of debt, and free cash flow that has averaged about 97% of net income over the past 10 years.

## Quantitative Evaluations

**S&P Quality Ranking**    A+

| D | C | B- | B | B+ | A- | A | A+ |
|---|---|---|---|---|---|---|---|

**Relative Strength Rank**    MODERATE

58

LOWEST = 1    HIGHEST = 99

## Revenue/Earnings Data

**Revenue (Million $)**

| | 1Q | 2Q | 3Q | 4Q | Year |
|---|---|---|---|---|---|
| 2008 | 4,139 | 4,570 | 4,148 | -- | -- |
| 2007 | 3,759 | 4,160 | 4,094 | 4,244 | 16,171 |
| 2006 | 3,297 | 3,579 | 3,538 | 3,641 | 14,055 |
| 2005 | 3,074 | 3,296 | 3,258 | 3,294 | 12,922 |
| 2004 | 2,710 | 3,002 | 2,967 | 3,052 | 11,731 |
| 2003 | 2,314 | 2,564 | 2,532 | 2,626 | 10,036 |

**Earnings Per Share ($)**

| | | | | |
|---|---|---|---|---|
| 2008 | 0.57 | 1.01 | 0.85 | E0.86 | E3.29 |
| 2007 | 0.71 | 0.90 | 0.89 | 0.87 | 3.28 |
| 2006 | 0.65 | 0.81 | 0.78 | 0.77 | 3.01 |
| 2005 | 0.53 | 0.65 | 0.72 | 0.71 | 2.60 |
| 2004 | 0.47 | 0.58 | 0.55 | 0.61 | 2.20 |
| 2003 | 0.33 | 0.46 | 0.44 | 0.47 | 1.69 |

Fiscal year ended Dec. 31. Next earnings report expected: Mid December. EPS Estimates based on S&P Operating Earnings; historical GAAP earnings are as reported.

## Dividend Data (Dates: mm/dd Payment Date: mm/dd/yy)

| Amount ($) | Date Decl. | Ex-Div. Date | Stk. of Record | Payment Date |
|---|---|---|---|---|
| 0.280 | 02/08 | 03/27 | 03/31 | 04/14/08 |
| 0.280 | 05/02 | 06/26 | 06/30 | 07/14/08 |
| 0.310 | 08/08 | 09/26 | 09/30 | 10/14/08 |
| 0.310 | 10/30 | 12/29 | 12/31 | 01/13/09 |

Dividends have been paid since 1933. Source: Company reports.

---

The *McGraw-Hill* Companies

# Illinois Tool Works Inc.

STANDARD
&POOR'S

## Business Summary October 21, 2008

CORPORATE OVERVIEW. Illinois Tool Works (ITW) operates about 750 small industrial businesses in a highly decentralized structure that places responsibility on managers at the lowest level possible, in order to focus each business unit on the needs of its particular customers. Each business unit manager is responsible, and is held strictly accountable, for the results of his or her individual business.

ITW is diversified not only by customer and industry, but also by geographic region, with about 49% of revenues derived overseas. At the end of 2007, ITW diversified its business segmentation beyond its former four reporting segments and now reports on the basis of eight reportable segments, including Industrial Packaging, Power Systems and Electronics, Transportation, Construction Products, Food Equipment, Decorative Surfaces, Polymers & Fluids and All Others.

The Industrial Packaging segment (15% of revenues and 12% of operating income in 2007; with 13% operating profit margin) produces steel, plastic and paper products used for bundling, shipping and protecting transported goods. In 2007, this segment mainly served the primary metals (25%) general industrial (21%) construction (14%) and food and beverage (13%) markets.

The Power Systems & Electronics segment (14% and 17%; 20%) produces equipment and consumables associated with specialty power conversion, metallurgy and electronics. In 2007, this segment primarily served the general industrial (36%), electronics (20%) and construction (10%) markets.

The Transportation segment (14% and 14%; 17%) produces components, fasteners, fluids and polymers for transportation-related applications. In 2007 this segment primarily served the automotive original equipment manufacturers (72%) and auto aftermarket (21%)

The Construction segment (13% and 11%; 14%) produces fasteners and related fastening tools for wood applications; anchors, fasteners and related tools for concrete and wood applications; metal plate truss components and related equipment and software; and packaged hardware fasteners, anchors and other products for retail.

## Company Financials Fiscal Year Ended Dec. 31

| Per Share Data ($) | 2007 | 2006 | 2005 | 2004 | 2003 | 2002 | 2001 | 2000 | 1999 | 1998 |
|---|---|---|---|---|---|---|---|---|---|---|
| Tangible Book Value | 7.37 | 6.94 | 6.89 | 7.59 | 8.22 | 6.90 | 5.42 | 4.82 | 4.64 | 4.30 |
| Cash Flow | 4.22 | 3.79 | 3.26 | 2.78 | 2.18 | 2.01 | 1.94 | 2.25 | 1.94 | 1.75 |
| Earnings | 3.28 | 3.01 | 2.60 | 2.20 | 1.69 | 1.51 | 1.31 | 1.58 | 1.38 | 1.34 |
| S&P Core Earnings | 3.27 | 3.03 | 2.60 | 2.13 | 1.63 | 1.38 | 1.13 | NA | NA | NA |
| Dividends | 0.98 | 0.92 | 0.61 | 0.52 | 0.47 | 0.45 | 0.42 | 0.38 | 0.34 | 0.26 |
| Payout Ratio | 30% | 30% | 23% | 24% | 28% | 30% | 32% | 24% | 25% | 19% |
| Prices:High | 60.00 | 53.54 | 47.32 | 48.35 | 42.35 | 38.90 | 36.00 | 34.50 | 41.00 | 36.59 |
| Prices:Low | 45.60 | 41.54 | 39.25 | 36.46 | 27.28 | 27.52 | 24.58 | 24.75 | 29.06 | 22.59 |
| P/E Ratio:High | 18 | 18 | 18 | 22 | 25 | 26 | 27 | 22 | 30 | 27 |
| P/E Ratio:Low | 14 | 14 | 15 | 17 | 16 | 18 | 19 | 16 | 21 | 17 |

| Income Statement Analysis (Million $) | 2007 | 2006 | 2005 | 2004 | 2003 | 2002 | 2001 | 2000 | 1999 | 1998 |
|---|---|---|---|---|---|---|---|---|---|---|
| Revenue | 16,171 | 14,055 | 12,922 | 11,731 | 10,036 | 9,468 | 9,293 | 9,984 | 9,333 | 5,648 |
| Operating Income | 3,147 | 2,865 | 2,558 | 2,410 | 1,940 | 1,812 | 1,692 | 1,977 | 1,830 | 1,291 |
| Depreciation | 523 | 444 | 383 | 353 | 307 | 306 | 386 | 413 | 343 | 212 |
| Interest Expense | 102 | 85.6 | 87.0 | 69.2 | 70.7 | 68.5 | 68.1 | 72.4 | 67.5 | 14.2 |
| Pretax Income | 2,581 | 2,445 | 2,182 | 1,999 | 1,576 | 1,434 | 1,231 | 1,478 | 1,353 | 1,060 |
| Effective Tax Rate | 29.3% | 29.8% | 31.5% | 33.0% | 34.0% | 35.0% | 34.8% | 35.2% | 37.8% | 36.5% |
| Net Income | 1,826 | 1,718 | 1,495 | 1,340 | 1,040 | 932 | 802 | 958 | 841 | 673 |
| S&P Core Earnings | 1,818 | 1,729 | 1,493 | 1,299 | 1,009 | 851 | 691 | NA | NA | NA |

| Balance Sheet & Other Financial Data (Million $) | 2007 | 2006 | 2005 | 2004 | 2003 | 2002 | 2001 | 2000 | 1999 | 1998 |
|---|---|---|---|---|---|---|---|---|---|---|
| Cash | 828 | 590 | 370 | 667 | 1,684 | 1,058 | 282 | 151 | 233 | 93.5 |
| Current Assets | 6,166 | 5,206 | 4,112 | 4,322 | 4,783 | 3,879 | 3,163 | 3,329 | 3,273 | 1,834 |
| Total Assets | 15,526 | 13,880 | 11,446 | 11,352 | 11,193 | 10,623 | 9,822 | 9,603 | 9,060 | 6,118 |
| Current Liabilities | 2,960 | 2,637 | 2,001 | 1,851 | 1,489 | 1,567 | 1,518 | 1,818 | 2,045 | 1,222 |
| Long Term Debt | 2,299 | 956 | 958 | 921 | 920 | 1,460 | 1,267 | 1,549 | 1,361 | 947 |
| Common Equity | 9,351 | 9,018 | 7,547 | 7,628 | 7,874 | 6,649 | 6,041 | 5,401 | 4,815 | 3,338 |
| Total Capital | 11,501 | 9,973 | 8,505 | 8,549 | 8,795 | 8,109 | 7,308 | 6,950 | 6,176 | 4,285 |
| Capital Expenditures | 353 | 301 | 293 | 283 | 258 | 271 | 257 | 314 | 336 | 208 |
| Cash Flow | 2,349 | 2,162 | 1,878 | 1,693 | 1,347 | 1,238 | 1,189 | 1,371 | 1,184 | 885 |
| Current Ratio | 2.1 | 2.0 | 2.1 | 2.3 | 3.2 | 2.5 | 2.1 | 1.8 | 1.6 | 1.5 |
| % Long Term Debt of Capitalization | 16.8 | 9.6 | 11.3 | 10.8 | 10.5 | 18.0 | 17.3 | 22.3 | 22.0 | 22.1 |
| % Net Income of Revenue | 11.3 | 12.2 | 11.6 | 11.4 | 10.4 | 9.8 | 8.6 | 9.6 | 9.0 | 11.9 |
| % Return on Assets | 12.4 | 13.6 | 13.1 | 11.9 | 9.5 | 9.1 | 8.3 | 10.3 | 9.7 | 11.7 |
| % Return on Equity | 19.9 | 20.7 | 19.7 | 17.3 | 14.3 | 14.7 | 14.0 | 18.8 | 18.6 | 21.9 |

Data as orig reptd.; bef. results of disc opers/spec. items. Per share data adj. for stk. divs.; EPS diluted. E-Estimated. NA-Not Available. NM-Not Meaningful. NR-Not Ranked. UR-Under Review.

**Office:** 3600 W. Lake Avenue, Glenview, IL 60026-5811.
**Telephone:** 847-724-7500.
**Website:** http://www.itw.com
**Chrmn & CEO:** D.B. Speer

**SVP, CFO, Chief Acctg Officer & Cntlr:** R.D. Kropp
**SVP, Secy & General Counsel:** J.H. Wooten, Jr.
**CTO:** M.W. Croll
**Investor Contact:** J. Brooklier (847-657-4104)

**Board Members:** W. F. Aldinger, III, M. D. Brailsford, S. M. Crown, D. H. Davis, Jr., R. C. McCormack, R. S. Morrison, J. A. Skinner, H. B. Smith, D. B. Speer, P. B. Strobel

**Founded:** 1912
**Domicile:** Delaware
**Employees:** 60,000

The McGraw-Hill Companies

**STANDARD &POOR'S**

# IMS Health Inc

| S&P Recommendation | BUY ★★★★☆ | Price<br>$12.47 (as of Nov 14, 2008) | 12-Mo. Target Price<br>$19.00 | Investment Style<br>Large-Cap Growth |
|---|---|---|---|---|

**GICS Sector** Health Care
**Sub-Industry** Health Care Technology

**Summary** IMS provides information solutions to the health care sector.

## Key Stock Statistics (Source S&P, Vickers, company reports)

| | | | | | | | |
|---|---|---|---|---|---|---|---|
| 52-Wk Range | $25.50– 10.99 | S&P Oper. EPS 2008**E** | 1.68 | Market Capitalization(B) | $2.268 | Beta | 1.09 |
| Trailing 12-Month EPS | $1.24 | S&P Oper. EPS 2009**E** | 1.85 | Yield (%) | 0.96 | S&P 3-Yr. Proj. EPS CAGR(%) | 11 |
| Trailing 12-Month P/E | 10.1 | P/E on S&P Oper. EPS 2008**E** | 7.4 | Dividend Rate/Share | $0.12 | S&P Credit Rating | NA |
| $10K Invested 5 Yrs Ago | $5,465 | Common Shares Outstg. (M) | 181.9 | Institutional Ownership (%) | 92 | | |

## Price Performance

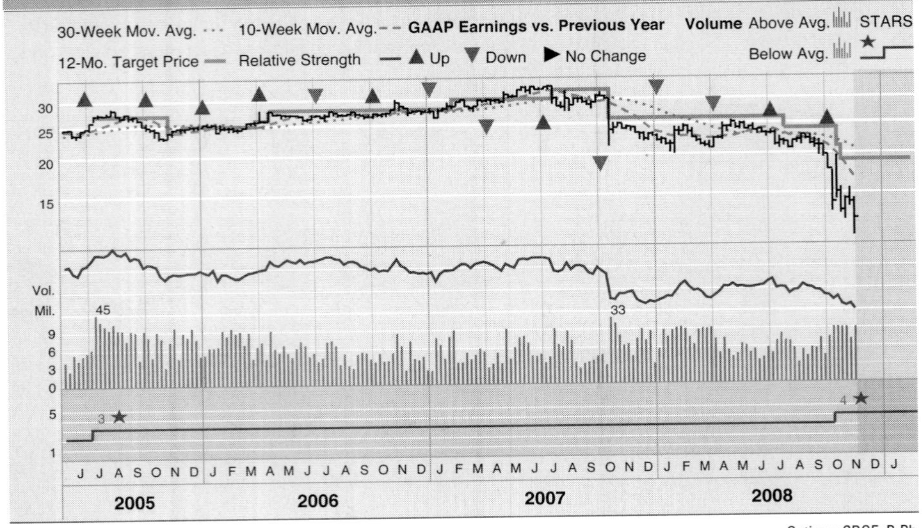

30-Week Mov. Avg. ···· 10-Week Mov. Avg. — **GAAP Earnings vs. Previous Year**  Volume Above Avg. � STARS
12-Mo. Target Price — Relative Strength — ▲ Up ▼ Down ► No Change  Below Avg. ıIII ★

Options: CBOE, P, Ph

Analysis prepared by **Michael W. Jaffe** on November 04, 2008, when the stock traded at **$ 15.10**.

## Highlights

➤ We expect revenues to increase 5% in 2009. Our forecast reflects our outlook for modest growth in demand and RX's new offerings. We see the strongest growth in the U.S. and emerging markets, and think RX's consulting offerings will be the most favorable business area. At the same time, we believe the level of RX's growth will be limited somewhat by the likelihood that the global pharmaceutical market will grow at the below historical pace that it has been experiencing in recent years. We also expect the recent strengthening of the U.S. dollar to result in less favorable currency translation.

➤ We see operating margins turning slightly wider in 2009, on incremental cost savings likely to be generated via the company's recently implemented restructuring program. We see that factor partly offset by the impact of our outlook for ongoing challenging trends in IMS Health's client markets.

➤ Our 2008 and 2009 EPS forecasts compare with EPS of $1.51 before one-time items in 2007.

## Investment Rationale/Risk

➤ We believe IMS Health has been facing challenging business trends in its client base, as sales growth has slowed at many pharmaceutical companies in recent years. However, we have a favorable view of RX's efforts to improve operating efficiencies and cut costs through a recent restructuring program, and are also positive about its ongoing new product introductions. Based on these factors and valuation considerations, we believe the shares are undervalued.

➤ Risks to our recommendation and target price include weaker than anticipated conditions in the health care and pharmaceutical markets served by RX, and limited success of its current restructuring program.

➤ The shares recently traded at about 8X our 2009 EPS forecast, falling below all valuations of the past decade. Based on our belief that RX will face challenging industry conditions for some time, but still manage to record modest EPS growth, we think a low end multiple is merited, but believe the shares are discounting worse conditions than we anticipate. Our 12-month target price is $19 or about 10X our 2009 forecast.

## Qualitative Risk Assessment

| LOW | MEDIUM | HIGH |
|---|---|---|

Our risk assessment reflects our view of RX's usually solid levels of free cash flow, offset by the company's relatively high level of debt leverage. Also, its income statements typically have numerous one-time items, which raises questions about earnings quality.

## Quantitative Evaluations

**S&P Quality Ranking**                                             B+

| D | C | B- | B | B+ | A- | A | A+ |
|---|---|---|---|---|---|---|---|

**Relative Strength Rank**                              MODERATE

40

LOWEST = 1                                              HIGHEST = 99

## Revenue/Earnings Data

**Revenue (Million $)**

| | 1Q | 2Q | 3Q | 4Q | Year |
|---|---|---|---|---|---|
| 2008 | 574.2 | 600.7 | 573.7 | -- | -- |
| 2007 | 510.4 | 537.5 | 538.8 | 605.9 | 2,193 |
| 2006 | 446.2 | 486.2 | 482.7 | 543.5 | 1,959 |
| 2005 | 411.0 | 433.3 | 432.8 | 477.7 | 1,755 |
| 2004 | 361.6 | 379.6 | 384.2 | 443.7 | 1,569 |
| 2003 | 313.9 | 337.8 | 346.0 | 384.1 | 1,382 |

**Earnings Per Share ($)**

| | | | | | |
|---|---|---|---|---|---|
| 2008 | 0.32 | 0.42 | 0.41 | E0.48 | E1.68 |
| 2007 | 0.43 | 0.36 | 0.29 | 0.09 | 1.18 |
| 2006 | 0.56 | 0.30 | 0.34 | 0.32 | 1.53 |
| 2005 | 0.13 | 0.41 | 0.30 | 0.38 | 1.22 |
| 2004 | 0.34 | 0.27 | 0.28 | 0.32 | 1.20 |
| 2003 | -0.20 | 0.23 | 0.29 | 0.28 | 0.56 |

Fiscal year ended Dec. 31. Next earnings report expected: Early February. EPS Estimates based on S&P Operating Earnings; historical GAAP earnings are as reported.

## Dividend Data (Dates: mm/dd Payment Date: mm/dd/yy)

| Amount<br>($) | Date<br>Decl. | Ex-Div.<br>Date | Stk. of<br>Record | Payment<br>Date |
|---|---|---|---|---|
| 0.030 | 02/12 | 02/27 | 03/01 | 03/28/08 |
| 0.030 | 04/15 | 04/29 | 05/01 | 06/06/08 |
| 0.030 | 07/14 | 07/30 | 08/01 | 09/05/08 |
| 0.030 | 10/21 | 10/24 | 10/28 | 12/05/08 |

Dividends have been paid since 1997. Source: Company reports.

# IMS Health Inc

## Business Summary November 04, 2008

IMS Health is a global provider of market intelligence to the pharmaceutical and health care industries, with operations covering more than 100 countries (63% of revenues from foreign operations in 2007). In November 2005, the company's planned agreement to be acquired by VNU N.V., a global information and media company, was mutually terminated. The cash and stock deal, valued at $7.0 billion at the time it was announced, was called off because of opposition from a group of major VNU shareholders.

IMS provides critical business intelligence, including information, analytics and consulting services, to the pharmaceutical and health care industries worldwide. This includes offerings in the areas of sales force effectiveness (46% of revenues in 2007), portfolio optimization (29%), and launch, brand management and other (25%). Sales to the pharmaceutical industry account for about 80% of RX's revenues.

The company's sales force effectiveness services are used principally by pharmaceutical manufacturers to measure, forecast and optimize the effectiveness and efficiency of sales representatives, and to focus on sales and marketing efforts. They include sales territory and prescription tracking re-

ports.

RX's portfolio optimization services provide customers with the intelligence and tools to identify and optimize pharmaceutical product portfolios, including currently marketed products and the new product pipeline. Integrating prescriptions, sales, disease/treatment and industry intelligence, RX's portfolio optimization services provide a comprehensive picture of the worldwide market. The company's offerings include syndicated pharmaceutical, medical, hospital and prescription audits.

In the area of launch, brand management and other services, RX's offerings combine information and analytical tools to address client needs relevant to each stage in the life of a pharmaceutical product. The areas covered include brand planning, pricing and market access, promotion management, and performance management.

## Company Financials Fiscal Year Ended Dec. 31

| Per Share Data ($) | 2007 | 2006 | 2005 | 2004 | 2003 | 2002 | 2001 | 2000 | 1999 | 1998 |
|---|---|---|---|---|---|---|---|---|---|---|
| Tangible Book Value | NM | NM | NM | NM | NM | 0.13 | 0.24 | NM | 0.51 | 1.45 |
| Cash Flow | 1.57 | 1.88 | 1.67 | 1.65 | 0.87 | 1.14 | 0.69 | 0.69 | 1.10 | 0.82 |
| Earnings | 1.18 | 1.53 | 1.22 | 1.20 | 0.56 | 0.93 | 0.46 | 0.39 | 0.78 | 0.53 |
| S&P Core Earnings | 1.14 | 1.36 | 1.09 | 0.95 | 0.47 | 0.82 | 0.52 | NA | NA | NA |
| Dividends | 0.12 | 0.12 | 0.08 | 0.08 | 0.08 | 0.08 | 0.08 | 0.08 | 0.08 | 0.06 |
| Payout Ratio | 10% | 8% | 7% | 7% | 14% | 9% | 17% | 21% | 10% | 11% |
| Prices:High | 33.12 | 30.13 | 28.60 | 26.80 | 25.07 | 22.59 | 30.50 | 28.69 | 39.19 | 38.46 |
| Prices:Low | 21.20 | 23.94 | 22.01 | 20.16 | 13.68 | 12.90 | 17.30 | 14.25 | 21.50 | 21.34 |
| P/E Ratio:High | 28 | 20 | 23 | 22 | 45 | 24 | 66 | 74 | 50 | 73 |
| P/E Ratio:Low | 18 | 16 | 18 | 17 | 24 | 14 | 38 | 37 | 28 | 40 |

| Income Statement Analysis (Million $) | | | | | | | | | | |
|---|---|---|---|---|---|---|---|---|---|---|
| Revenue | 2,193 | 1,959 | 1,755 | 1,569 | 1,382 | 1,428 | 1,333 | 1,424 | 1,398 | 1,187 |
| Operating Income | 557 | 524 | 543 | 517 | 437 | 510 | 494 | 459 | 439 | 310 |
| Depreciation | 77.7 | 73.8 | 105 | 93.5 | 75.1 | 61.8 | 69.2 | 92.0 | 100 | 96.4 |
| Interest Expense | 37.9 | 40.4 | 22.7 | 19.5 | 15.4 | 14.4 | 18.1 | 17.6 | 7.59 | 1.17 |
| Pretax Income | 357 | 449 | 454 | 415 | 305 | 397 | 177 | 257 | 152 | 271 |
| Effective Tax Rate | 32.3% | 29.7% | 37.5% | 31.2% | 54.4% | 32.9% | 21.7% | 54.7% | NM | 34.1% |
| Net Income | 234 | 316 | 284 | 285 | 139 | 266 | 138 | 116 | 250 | 178 |
| S&P Core Earnings | 226 | 282 | 252 | 226 | 116 | 236 | 155 | NA | NA | NA |

| Balance Sheet & Other Financial Data (Million $) | | | | | | | | | | |
|---|---|---|---|---|---|---|---|---|---|---|
| Cash | 218 | 157 | 363 | 460 | 385 | 415 | 268 | 119 | 116 | 206 |
| Current Assets | 840 | 693 | 821 | 937 | 779 | 827 | 657 | 569 | 607 | 634 |
| Total Assets | 2,244 | 1,907 | 1,973 | 1,891 | 1,644 | 1,619 | 1,368 | 1,243 | 1,451 | 1,732 |
| Current Liabilities | 635 | 543 | 549 | 554 | 837 | 679 | 635 | 827 | 723 | 550 |
| Long Term Debt | 1,203 | 975 | 611 | 627 | 152 | 325 | 150 | Nil | Nil | Nil |
| Common Equity | -40.3 | 33.9 | 415 | 256 | 190 | 222 | 218 | 147 | 494 | 825 |
| Total Capital | 1,264 | 1,110 | 1,126 | 984 | 443 | 727 | 513 | 282 | 619 | 972 |
| Capital Expenditures | 61.2 | 27.5 | 52.0 | 22.5 | 23.7 | 44.4 | 34.3 | 33.4 | 33.0 | 30.9 |
| Cash Flow | 312 | 389 | 389 | 379 | 214 | 328 | 208 | 208 | 351 | 275 |
| Current Ratio | 1.3 | 1.3 | 1.5 | 1.7 | 0.9 | 1.2 | 1.0 | 0.7 | 0.8 | 1.2 |
| % Long Term Debt of Capitalization | 95.2 | 87.9 | 54.3 | 63.7 | 34.3 | 44.7 | 29.2 | Nil | Nil | Nil |
| % Net Income of Revenue | 10.7 | 16.1 | 16.2 | 18.2 | 10.1 | 18.6 | 10.4 | 8.2 | 17.9 | 15.0 |
| % Return on Assets | 11.3 | 16.3 | 14.7 | 16.1 | 8.5 | 17.8 | 10.3 | 8.7 | 15.8 | 11.0 |
| % Return on Equity | NM | 140.6 | 84.7 | 128.2 | 67.6 | 120.8 | 86.0 | 34.7 | 38.0 | 21.9 |

Data as orig reptd.; bef. results of disc opers/spec. items. Per share data adj. for stk. divs.; EPS diluted. E-Estimated. NA-Not Available. NM-Not Meaningful. NR-Not Ranked. UR-Under Review.

**Office:** 901 Main Ave, Norwalk, CT 06851-1170.
**Telephone:** 203-845-5200.
**Website:** http://www.imshealth.com
**Chrmn, Pres & CEO:** D.R. Carlucci

**COO & EVP:** G.V. Pajot
**SVP & CFO:** L.G. Katz
**SVP, Secy & General Counsel:** R.H. Steinfeld
**Chief Acctg Officer & Cntlr:** H. Bhangdia

**Investor Contact:** D. Peck (203-845-5237)
**Board Members:** D. R. Carlucci, C. L. Clemente, J. D. Edwards, K. E. Giusti, J. P. Imlay, Jr., H. E. Lockhart, M. B. Puckett, W. C. Vanfaasen, B. W. Wise

**Founded:** 1998
**Domicile:** Delaware
**Employees:** 7,950

**STANDARD &POOR'S**

# Ingersoll-Rand Co Ltd

| S&P Recommendation | HOLD ★★★☆☆ | Price $15.11 (as of Nov 14, 2008) | 12-Mo. Target Price $19.00 | Investment Style Large-Cap Blend |
|---|---|---|---|---|

**GICS Sector** Industrials
**Sub-Industry** Industrial Machinery

**Summary** This company manufactures a wide range of industrial and commercial products, including climate control, industrial technology and security products.

## Key Stock Statistics (Source S&P, Vickers, company reports)

| | | | | | |
|---|---|---|---|---|---|
| 52-Wk Range | $52.20– 14.18 | S&P Oper. EPS 2008**E** | 3.34 | Market Capitalization(B) | $4.817 |
| Trailing 12-Month EPS | $10.87 | S&P Oper. EPS 2009**E** | 2.68 | Yield (%) | 4.77 |
| Trailing 12-Month P/E | 1.4 | P/E on S&P Oper. EPS 2008**E** | 4.5 | Dividend Rate/Share | $0.72 |
| $10K Invested 5 Yrs Ago | $5,529 | Common Shares Outstg. (M) | 318.8 | Institutional Ownership (%) | 79 |

| | |
|---|---|
| Beta | 1.73 |
| S&P 3-Yr. Proj. EPS CAGR(%) | 11 |
| S&P Credit Rating | NA |

## Price Performance

- 30-Week Mov. Avg.  ···· 10-Week Mov. Avg. --- GAAP Earnings vs. Previous Year  Volume Above Avg. STARS
- 12-Mo. Target Price — Relative Strength — ▲ Up ▼ Down ► No Change  Below Avg. ★

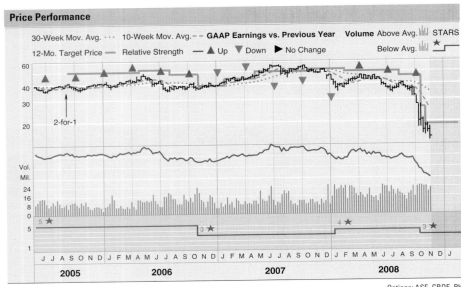

Options: ASE, CBOE, Ph

Analysis prepared by **Mathew Christy, CFA** on November 07, 2008, when the stock traded at **$ 16.20**.

## Highlights

► We expect revenue of $13.6 billion in 2008, with growth mainly due to the recent Trane acquisition, and an estimated 3% expansion in legacy businesses including the Industrial Solutions and Climate Control segments. We forecast organic revenue to decline in 2009, on much weaker first-half results and nearly flat organic results later in the year. However, we expect total 2009 revenue to expand to $16.2 billion, or nearly 19%, due to acquisitions.

► We see operating margins declining to about 9.6% in 2008, on higher commodity costs and overhead expenses, and forecast 2009 operating margins falling to about 8.5%. We expect IR's operating margins to steadily decline through the first half of 2009 and trough at about 8%. Our 2009 operating margin forecast is based on gross margins narrowing to about 25%, from an estimated 26.6% in 2008, and SG&A expenses averaging 16.5% of sales.

► Reflecting our forecast of higher effective tax rates in 2008, we project EPS from continuing operations of $3.34 in 2008 and $2.68 in 2009.

## Investment Rationale/Risk

► In our view, IR's portfolio rebalancing, including the sale of the Road Development and Bobcat businesses, has reduced its capital intensity and cyclicality, but it remains exposed to end markets that are cyclical, including general industrial and construction. We expect slowing end markets and higher costs to lead to reduced margins in both 2008 and 2009 and lower EPS results in 2009. However, we believe IR's share price fairly discounts a decline in earnings, as the stock recently traded around 6.5X our 2009 EPS estimate, a discount to peers and somewhat below historical trough multiples.

► Risks to our recommendation and target price include sharply weaker-than-expected global economic growth, softer industrial, energy and electronics markets, and integration risks of the Trane acquisition.

► Our 12-month target price of $19 is based on a relative valuation analysis, applying a P/E multiple of 7X to our 2009 EPS estimate. This valuation multiple represents about a 22% discount to peers and is equal to historical low multiples, which we believe is warranted given the uncertain economic environment.

## Qualitative Risk Assessment

| LOW | MEDIUM | HIGH |
|---|---|---|

Our risk assessment reflects the cyclical nature of several of IR's major end markets, and its active acquisition strategy, offset by an expanding recurring revenue base, a strong history of cash flow generation, and leading returns.

## Quantitative Evaluations

**S&P Quality Ranking**  NR

| D | C | B- | B | B+ | A- | A | A+ |
|---|---|---|---|---|---|---|---|

**Relative Strength Rank**  WEAK

22

LOWEST = 1    HIGHEST = 99

## Revenue/Earnings Data

**Revenue (Million $)**

| | 1Q | 2Q | 3Q | 4Q | Year |
|---|---|---|---|---|---|
| 2008 | 2,163 | 3,081 | 4,313 | -- | -- |
| 2007 | 2,668 | 2,225 | 2,239 | 2,323 | 8,763 |
| 2006 | 2,711 | 3,042 | 2,766 | 2,891 | 11,409 |
| 2005 | 2,459 | 2,760 | 2,615 | 2,713 | 10,547 |
| 2004 | 2,292 | 2,714 | 2,368 | 2,459 | 9,394 |
| 2003 | 2,182 | 2,509 | 2,520 | 2,666 | 9,876 |

**Earnings Per Share ($)**

| | | | | | |
|---|---|---|---|---|---|
| 2008 | 0.77 | 0.90 | 0.72 | E0.56 | E3.34 |
| 2007 | 0.70 | 0.68 | 0.68 | 0.62 | 2.48 |
| 2006 | 0.79 | 0.97 | 0.79 | 0.74 | 3.31 |
| 2005 | 0.67 | 0.86 | 0.75 | 0.81 | 3.09 |
| 2004 | 0.47 | 0.72 | 0.59 | 0.64 | 2.37 |
| 2003 | 0.28 | 0.45 | 0.44 | 0.56 | 1.72 |

Fiscal year ended Dec. 31. Next earnings report expected: Mid February. EPS Estimates based on S&P Operating Earnings; historical GAAP earnings are as reported.

## Dividend Data (Dates: mm/dd Payment Date: mm/dd/yy)

| Amount ($) | Date Decl. | Ex-Div. Date | Stk. of Record | Payment Date |
|---|---|---|---|---|
| 0.180 | 04/05 | 11/12 | 11/14 | 12/01/08 |

Dividends have been paid since 1910. Source: Company reports.

---

# Ingersoll-Rand Co Ltd

**STANDARD &POOR'S**

## Business Summary November 07, 2008

CORPORATE OVERVIEW. Ingersoll-Rand is a global provider of climate control equipment, construction equipment, industrial solutions, and security and safety products.

The Climate Control segment (39% of 2007 revenue from continuing operations; 24% of operating profits; 11% margin) makes transport temperature control units, HVAC systems, refrigerated display merchandisers, beverage coolers, and walk-in storage coolers and freezers. Its brand names include Hussmann and Thermo-King. Thermo-King is the world's largest maker of commercial refrigeration equipment used in truck trailers, seagoing containers and railcars. Hussmann is one of the world's largest makers of refrigerated supermarket displays.

The Industrial Solutions segment (33%; 34%; 14%) provides solutions to enhance customer industrial efficiency in the areas of air solutions, productivity solutions and energy systems, and makes air compressors, fluid products, energy generation systems and industrial tools.

The Security segment (29%; 37%; 17%) makes doors and locks for the commercial and do-it-yourself markets, electronic security products, and security and scheduling software. The segment makes products that include Schlage locks, door control hardware, and steel and power-operated doors.

PRIMARY BUSINESS DYNAMICS. We believe that IR has substantially completed the transformation of its business portfolio to become a less cyclical company with stronger long-term growth prospects. It did so by divesting deeply cyclical, capital-intensive, low-growth businesses, to instead concentrate on what we view as its high-potential businesses. We think that organic growth derived by IR in coming years will be powered by strength in its end markets, new product introductions, a rising recurring revenue stream, and an expansion in international markets. We anticipate that approximately one-half of revenue growth will occur in international markets. In 2007, the U.S. accounted for 54% of total revenues. We expect the company to continue generating strong free cash flow going forward, which management is likely to use for bolt-on acquisitions, share repurchases and dividend increases. In 2007, IR spent nearly $2 billion on stock repurchases and over $26 million on bolt-on acquisitions (not including the $10 billion Trane deal that is expected to close in May 2008).

## Company Financials Fiscal Year Ended Dec. 31

| Per Share Data ($) | 2007 | 2006 | 2005 | 2004 | 2003 | 2002 | 2001 | 2000 | 1999 | 1998 |
|---|---|---|---|---|---|---|---|---|---|---|
| Tangible Book Value | 11.70 | 0.21 | 1.60 | 2.54 | NM | NM | NM | NM | NM | NM |
| Cash Flow | 2.95 | 4.10 | 3.66 | 2.81 | 2.28 | 1.68 | 1.83 | 2.60 | 2.46 | 2.39 |
| Earnings | 2.48 | 3.31 | 3.09 | 2.37 | 1.72 | 1.08 | 0.74 | 1.68 | 1.65 | 1.54 |
| Dividends | 0.18 | 0.68 | 0.57 | 0.44 | 0.36 | 0.34 | 0.34 | 0.34 | 0.32 | 0.30 |
| Payout Ratio | 7% | 21% | 18% | 19% | 21% | 31% | 46% | 20% | 19% | 19% |
| Prices:High | 56.66 | 49.00 | 43.96 | 41.45 | 34.10 | 27.20 | 25.14 | 28.88 | 36.91 | 27.00 |
| Prices:Low | 38.25 | 34.95 | 35.13 | 29.52 | 17.26 | 14.85 | 15.20 | 14.75 | 22.31 | 17.00 |
| P/E Ratio:High | 23 | 15 | 14 | 18 | 20 | 25 | 34 | 17 | 22 | 18 |
| P/E Ratio:Low | 15 | 11 | 11 | 12 | 10 | 14 | 21 | 9 | 14 | 11 |

| Income Statement Analysis (Million $) | 2007 | 2006 | 2005 | 2004 | 2003 | 2002 | 2001 | 2000 | 1999 | 1998 |
|---|---|---|---|---|---|---|---|---|---|---|
| Revenue | 8,763 | 11,409 | 10,547 | 9,394 | 9,876 | 8,951 | 9,682 | 8,798 | 7,667 | 8,292 |
| Operating Income | 1,224 | 1,632 | 1,558 | 1,295 | 1,061 | 891 | 979 | 1,488 | 1,372 | 1,327 |
| Depreciation | 138 | 191 | 196 | 174 | 194 | 206 | 363 | 297 | 272 | 283 |
| Interest Expense | 136 | 132 | 144 | 153 | 177 | 230 | 253 | 254 | 203 | 226 |
| Pretax Income | 952 | 1,315 | 1,270 | 984 | 703 | 402 | 263 | 869 | 874 | 843 |
| Effective Tax Rate | 21.5% | 17.6% | 16.1% | 14.1% | 13.4% | 5.05% | NM | 32.6% | 34.3% | 33.2% |
| Net Income | 733 | 1,068 | 1,053 | 830 | 594 | 367 | 246 | 546 | 545 | 509 |

| Balance Sheet & Other Financial Data (Million $) | 2007 | 2006 | 2005 | 2004 | 2003 | 2002 | 2001 | 2000 | 1999 | 1998 |
|---|---|---|---|---|---|---|---|---|---|---|
| Cash | 4,735 | 363 | 1,037 | 1,704 | 460 | 342 | 121 | 200 | 223 | 77.6 |
| Current Assets | 7,701 | 4,096 | 4,248 | 4,610 | 3,539 | 4,112 | 3,188 | 3,323 | 2,868 | 2,428 |
| Total Assets | 14,376 | 12,146 | 11,756 | 11,415 | 10,665 | 10,810 | 11,064 | 10,529 | 8,400 | 8,310 |
| Current Liabilities | 3,236 | 3,614 | 3,200 | 2,877 | 3,053 | 3,798 | 2,851 | 3,967 | 1,739 | 1,849 |
| Long Term Debt | 713 | 905 | 1,184 | 1,268 | 1,519 | 2,092 | 2,901 | 1,943 | 2,516 | 2,569 |
| Common Equity | 7,908 | 5,405 | 5,762 | 5,734 | 4,493 | 3,478 | 3,917 | 3,495 | 3,083 | 2,708 |
| Total Capital | 8,718 | 6,310 | 6,946 | 7,001 | 6,133 | 5,685 | 7,098 | 5,548 | 5,695 | 5,410 |
| Capital Expenditures | 120 | 212 | 112 | 109 | 108 | 123 | 201 | 187 | 191 | 14.5 |
| Cash Flow | 871 | 1,259 | 1,249 | 1,004 | 788 | 573 | 609 | 843 | 817 | 792 |
| Current Ratio | 2.4 | 1.1 | 1.3 | 1.6 | 1.2 | 1.1 | 1.1 | 0.8 | 1.6 | 1.3 |
| % Long Term Debt of Capitalization | 8.2 | 14.3 | 17.0 | 18.1 | 24.8 | 36.8 | 40.9 | 35.0 | 44.2 | 47.5 |
| % Net Income of Revenue | 8.4 | 9.4 | 10.0 | 8.8 | 6.0 | 4.1 | 2.5 | 6.2 | 7.1 | 6.1 |
| % Return on Assets | 5.5 | 8.9 | 9.1 | 7.5 | 5.5 | 3.3 | 2.2 | 5.8 | 6.7 | 6.1 |
| % Return on Equity | 11.0 | 19.1 | 18.3 | 16.2 | 14.9 | 9.9 | 6.7 | 16.6 | 18.7 | 20.2 |

Data as orig reptd.; bef. results of disc opers/spec. items. Per share data adj. for stk. divs.; EPS diluted. E-Estimated. NA-Not Available. NM-Not Meaningful. NR-Not Ranked. UR-Under Review.

**Office:** Clarendon House 2 Church Street, Hamilton, Bermuda HM 11.
**Telephone:** 441-295-2838.
**Email:** seekinfo@irco.com
**Website:** http://www.ingersollrand.com

**Chrmn, Pres & CEO:** H.L. Henkel
**SVP & CFO:** S.R. Shawley
**SVP & General Counsel:** P. Nachtigal
**Chief Acctg Officer & Cntlr:** R.J. Weller

**Treas:** D. Kuhl
**Investor Contact:** B.L. Brasier
**Board Members:** A. C. Berzin, J. L. Cohon, G. D. Forsee, P. C. Godsoe, E. E. Hagenlocker, H. L. Henkel, C. J. Horner, H. W. Lichtenberger, T. E. Martin, P. Nachtigal, O. R. Smith, R. J. Swift, T. L. White

**Founded:** 1905
**Domicile:** Bermuda
**Employees:** 35,560

**STANDARD &POOR'S**

# Integrys Energy Group Inc

| S&P Recommendation HOLD ★★★☆☆ | Price $43.38 (as of Nov 14, 2008) | 12-Mo. Target Price $49.00 | Investment Style Large-Cap Blend |
|---|---|---|---|

**GICS Sector** Utilities
**Sub-Industry** Multi-Utilities

**Summary** This utility holding company serves about 485,000 regulated electric and 1,674,000 regulated gas customers. The company also operates an unregulated energy supply and services business.

## Key Stock Statistics (Source S&P, Vickers, company reports)

| | | | | | | | |
|---|---|---|---|---|---|---|---|
| 52-Wk Range | $53.92–36.91 | S&P Oper. EPS 2008**E** | 3.57 | Market Capitalization(B) | $3.315 | Beta | 0.61 |
| Trailing 12-Month EPS | $2.42 | S&P Oper. EPS 2009**E** | 3.94 | Yield (%) | 6.18 | S&P 3-Yr. Proj. EPS CAGR(%) | 5 |
| Trailing 12-Month P/E | 17.9 | P/E on S&P Oper. EPS 2008**E** | 12.2 | Dividend Rate/Share | $2.68 | S&P Credit Rating | A- |
| $10K Invested 5 Yrs Ago | $12,372 | Common Shares Outstg. (M) | 76.4 | Institutional Ownership (%) | 52 | | |

## Price Performance

- 30-Week Mov. Avg. · · · 10-Week Mov. Avg. – – GAAP Earnings vs. Previous Year   Volume Above Avg. | STARS
- 12-Mo. Target Price — Relative Strength ▲ Up ▼ Down ▶ No Change   Below Avg. |

Options: P, Ph

## Highlights

- ► The 12-month target price for TEG has recently been changed to $49.00 from $52.00. The Highlights section of this Stock Report will be updated accordingly.

## Investment Rationale/Risk

- ► The Investment Rationale/Risk section of this Stock Report will be updated shortly. For the latest News story on TEG from MarketScope, see below.

- ► 11/06/08 05:31 pm ET ... S&P MAINTAINS HOLD OPINION ON SHARES OF INTEGRYS ENERGY GROUP (TEG 43.62***): Q3 recurring EPS of $0.20 vs. $0.17 misses our estimate by a penny. Revenues were higher than expected and per-revenue non-fuel operating expenses were lower, though per-revenue cost of fuel and purchased power was higher. We continue to like TEG's growth in its unregulated energy business and its relatively high dividend yield of 6.1%. We also expect to see cost savings from the recent merger with Peoples Gas. We are keeping our '08 EPS estimate at $3.57 and '09's at $3.94. We lower our target price by $3 to $49 to reflect lower peer valuations. /C.Muir

## Qualitative Risk Assessment

| LOW | MEDIUM | HIGH |
|---|---|---|

Our risk assessment reflects what we see as a balanced portfolio of operations, which includes lower risk gas and electric utility businesses as well as higher risk unregulated wholesale and retail energy marketing services.

## Quantitative Evaluations

**S&P Quality Ranking**                     A-

| D | C | B- | B | B+ | A- | A | A+ |
|---|---|---|---|---|---|---|---|

**Relative Strength Rank**          STRONG

75

LOWEST = 1                    HIGHEST = 99

## Revenue/Earnings Data

**Revenue (Million $)**

| | 1Q | 2Q | 3Q | 4Q | Year |
|---|---|---|---|---|---|
| 2008 | 3,989 | 3,417 | 3,223 | -- | -- |
| 2007 | 2,747 | 2,362 | 2,123 | 3,062 | 10,292 |
| 2006 | 1,996 | 1,475 | 1,555 | 1,865 | 6,891 |
| 2005 | 1,462 | 1,328 | 1,757 | 2,391 | 6,826 |
| 2004 | 1,373 | 1,046 | 1,073 | 1,399 | 4,891 |
| 2003 | 1,283 | 981.8 | 1,012 | 1,121 | 4,321 |

**Earnings Per Share ($)**

| | 1Q | 2Q | 3Q | 4Q | Year |
|---|---|---|---|---|---|
| 2008 | 1.77 | -0.31 | -0.77 | E1.18 | E3.57 |
| 2007 | 2.01 | -0.53 | 0.14 | 1.19 | 2.48 |
| 2006 | 1.44 | 0.97 | 0.63 | 0.50 | 3.50 |
| 2005 | 1.62 | 0.62 | 1.25 | 0.53 | 4.11 |
| 2004 | 1.22 | 0.26 | 0.99 | 1.60 | 4.07 |
| 2003 | 0.92 | 0.08 | 1.04 | 0.91 | 3.24 |

Fiscal year ended Dec. 31. Next earnings report expected: Late February. EPS Estimates based on S&P Operating Earnings; historical GAAP earnings are as reported.

## Dividend Data (Dates: mm/dd Payment Date: mm/dd/yy)

| Amount ($) | Date Decl. | Ex-Div. Date | Stk. of Record | Payment Date |
|---|---|---|---|---|
| 0.670 | 02/18 | 02/27 | 02/29 | 03/20/08 |
| 0.670 | 04/15 | 05/28 | 05/30 | 06/20/08 |
| 0.670 | 07/10 | 08/27 | 08/29 | 09/20/08 |
| 0.670 | 10/14 | 11/24 | 11/26 | 12/20/08 |

Dividends have been paid since 1940. Source: Company reports.

# Integrys Energy Group Inc

**STANDARD &POOR'S**

## Business Summary September 22, 2008

CORPORATE OVERVIEW. Integrys Energy Group (TEG) is a holding company with regulated and unregulated business units. As of December 31, 2007, the company's subsidiaries were organized in three operating segments: electric utility, gas utility, and Integrys Energy Services. A holding company and other segment includes operations that don't fit into the other segments, including nonutility operations of the regulated utilities. In 2007, ESI was the largest contributor to TEG's revenues, at 68%. The electric utility segment contributed 12%, while the gas utility segment contributed 20%.

The electric utility segment includes the electric operations of Wisconsin Public Service Corporation (WPSC) and Upper Peninsula Power Company (UPPCO). The gas utility segment includes the gas operations of WPSC, Michigan Gas Utilities Corporation (MGUC), Minnesota Energy Resources Corporation (MERC), The Peoples Gas Light and Coke Company (PGL); and North Shore Gas Company (NSG). Integrys Energy Services, Inc. (ESI) is an unregulated subsidiary that operates electric generation facilities and energy marketing operations and provides energy generation and management services.

IMPACT OF MAJOR DEVELOPMENTS. On July 10, 2006, TEG announced a merger agreement with Chicago-based Peoples Energy Corporation (PGL), which distributes natural gas to approximately 970,000 customers in Chicago and northeastern Illinois. The companies completed the merger on February 21, 2007. Under the agreement, PGL shareholders received 0.825 of a share of TEG common stock for each PGL share. Following the completion of the merger, former PGL shareholders became owners of about 42% of the company. We believe the combined entity will be able to realize cost savings through the elimination of overlapping functions. The combination adds nearly 970,000 natural gas customers to the 360,000 from the recently completed acquisitions from Aquila, and increases TEG's total natural gas customer base to more than 1,630,000, more than four times the level at the end of 2005.

On July 3, 2006, TEG completed the acquisition (announced in September 2005) of Aquila's natural gas distribution operations in Minnesota for $333 million in cash. Earlier, on April 3, 2006, it completed the acquisition of Aquila's Michigan operations for nearly $270 million plus an adjustment for working capital. The Minnesota and Michigan operations provide gas services to 200,000 and 161,000 customers, respectively. We believe the acquisitions have greatly expanded TEG's utility operations in a growing region and are helping to realize the company's strategy to become a strong regional energy company.

## Company Financials Fiscal Year Ended Dec. 31

| Per Share Data ($) | 2007 | 2006 | 2005 | 2004 | 2003 | 2002 | 2001 | 2000 | 1999 | 1998 |
|---|---|---|---|---|---|---|---|---|---|---|
| Tangible Book Value | 29.97 | 28.36 | 31.69 | 29.12 | 27.25 | 24.48 | 22.91 | 20.42 | 19.97 | 19.45 |
| Earnings | 2.48 | 3.50 | 4.11 | 4.07 | 3.24 | 3.42 | 2.74 | 2.53 | 2.24 | 1.76 |
| S&P Core Earnings | 2.49 | 3.58 | 2.86 | 3.82 | 3.12 | 1.48 | 0.99 | NA | NA | NA |
| Dividends | 2.50 | 2.28 | 2.24 | 2.20 | 2.16 | 2.12 | 2.08 | 2.04 | 2.00 | 1.96 |
| Payout Ratio | 101% | 62% | 55% | 54% | 67% | 62% | 76% | 81% | 89% | 111% |
| Prices:High | 60.63 | 57.75 | 60.00 | 50.53 | 46.80 | 42.68 | 36.80 | 39.00 | 35.75 | 37.50 |
| Prices:Low | 48.10 | 47.39 | 47.67 | 43.50 | 36.80 | 30.47 | 31.00 | 22.63 | 24.44 | 29.94 |
| P/E Ratio:High | 24 | 16 | 15 | 12 | 14 | 12 | 13 | 15 | 16 | 21 |
| P/E Ratio:Low | 19 | 13 | 12 | 11 | 11 | 9 | 11 | 9 | 11 | 17 |
| **Income Statement Analysis (Million $)** | | | | | | | | | | |
| Revenue | 10,292 | 6,891 | 6,826 | 4,891 | 4,321 | 2,675 | 2,676 | 1,952 | 516 | 1,064 |
| Depreciation | 195 | 106 | 142 | 107 | 138 | 98.0 | 86.6 | 99.8 | 83.7 | 86.3 |
| Maintenance | NA | NA | NA | NA | NA | NA | NA | 73.0 | 60.6 | 52.8 |
| Fixed Charges Coverage | 2.57 | 2.85 | 3.80 | 4.31 | 3.55 | 3.97 | 2.32 | 2.14 | 3.03 | 3.56 |
| Construction Credits | NA | NA | NA | NA | NA | NA | NA | 4.46 | 3.62 | 0.35 |
| Effective Tax Rate | 32.2% | 23.3% | 20.7% | 16.1% | 22.0% | 18.5% | 5.83% | 8.23% | 33.3% | 33.8% |
| Net Income | 181 | 152 | 148 | 153 | 114 | 109 | 77.6 | 67.0 | 59.6 | 46.6 |
| S&P Core Earnings | 179 | 152 | 111 | 144 | 103 | 47.1 | 28.2 | NA | NA | NA |
| **Balance Sheet & Other Financial Data (Million $)** | | | | | | | | | | |
| Gross Property | 7,066 | 3,961 | 3,099 | 3,308 | 3,065 | 3,186 | 2,979 | 2,716 | 2,444 | 2,045 |
| Capital Expenditures | 393 | 342 | 414 | 290 | 176 | 229 | 249 | 191 | 273 | 111 |
| Net Property | 4,464 | 2,535 | 2,044 | 2,003 | 1,829 | 1,610 | 1,464 | 1,351 | 1,319 | 839 |
| Capitalization:Long Term Debt | 2,316 | 1,338 | 918 | 866 | 923 | 926 | 829 | 761 | 686 | 394 |
| Capitalization:% Long Term Debt | 41.7 | 46.6 | 41.3 | 42.0 | 47.9 | 53.7 | 53.7 | 58.4 | 56.1 | 40.9 |
| Capitalization:Preferred | Nil | Nil | Nil | Nil | Nil | Nil | Nil | Nil | Nil | 51.2 |
| Capitalization:% Preferred | Nil | Nil | Nil | Nil | Nil | Nil | Nil | Nil | Nil | 5.30 |
| Capitalization:Common | 3,236 | 1,534 | 1,304 | 1,114 | 1,003 | 798 | 716 | 543 | 536 | 517 |
| Capitalization:% Common | 58.3 | 53.4 | 58.7 | 58.0 | 52.1 | 46.3 | 46.3 | 41.6 | 43.9 | 53.8 |
| Total Capital | 6,046 | 2,970 | 2,317 | 2,062 | 2,024 | 1,816 | 1,635 | 1,428 | 1,359 | 1,061 |
| % Operating Ratio | 97.3 | 97.0 | 98.2 | 96.7 | 97.8 | 95.3 | 96.2 | 94.5 | 195.4 | 92.8 |
| % Earned on Net Property | 10.5 | 10.9 | 9.2 | 9.9 | 7.4 | 9.8 | 7.6 | 8.6 | 59.2 | 12.6 |
| % Return on Revenue | 1.8 | 2.2 | 2.2 | 3.1 | 2.6 | 4.1 | 2.9 | 3.4 | 11.5 | 4.4 |
| % Return on Invested Capital | 7.7 | 9.4 | 25.0 | 18.6 | 9.3 | 10.1 | 9.1 | 9.1 | 8.2 | 10.3 |
| % Return on Common Equity | 7.5 | 10.5 | 13.3 | 14.5 | 12.8 | 14.5 | 12.3 | 12.4 | 11.3 | 9.4 |

Data as orig reptd.; bef. results of disc opers/spec. items. Per share data adj. for stk. divs.; EPS diluted. E-Estimated. NA-Not Available. NM-Not Meaningful. NR-Not Ranked. UR-Under Review.

**Office:** 130 E Randolph St, Chicago, IL 60601-6207.
**Telephone:** 800-699-1269.
**Email:** investor@integrysgroup.com
**Website:** http://www.integrysgroup.com

**Pres & CEO:** L.L. Weyers
**SVP & CFO:** J.P. O'Leary
**Chief Acctg Officer & Cntlr:** D.L. Ford
**Treas:** B.A. Johnson

**Secy:** P. Kauffman
**Investor Contact:** S.P. Eschbach (312-228-5408)
**Board Members:** K. E. Bailey, R. Bemis, W. J. Brodsky, A. J. Budney, Jr., P. S. Cafferty, E. Carnahan, R. C. Gallagher, K. M. Hasselblad-Pascale, J. W. Higgins, J. L. Kemerling, M. E. Lavin, J. C. Meng, W. F. Protz, Jr., L. L. Weyers

**Founded:** 1883
**Domicile:** Wisconsin
**Employees:** 5,231

*The McGraw-Hill Companies*

STANDARD
&POOR'S

# Intel Corp

| S&P Recommendation | BUY ★★★★☆ | Price $13.32 (as of Nov 14, 2008) | 12-Mo. Target Price $16.00 | Investment Style Large-Cap Growth |
| --- | --- | --- | --- | --- |

**GICS Sector** Information Technology
**Sub-Industry** Semiconductors

**Summary** This company is the world's largest manufacturer of microprocessors, the central processing units of PCs, and also produces other semiconductor products.

## Key Stock Statistics (Source S&P, Vickers, company reports)

| | | | | | | | |
| --- | --- | --- | --- | --- | --- | --- | --- |
| 52-Wk Range | $27.99– 12.87 | S&P Oper. EPS 2008**E** | 1.15 | Market Capitalization(B) | $74.086 | Beta | 1.22 |
| Trailing 12-Month EPS | $1.26 | S&P Oper. EPS 2009**E** | 1.00 | Yield (%) | 4.20 | S&P 3-Yr. Proj. EPS CAGR(%) | 3 |
| Trailing 12-Month P/E | 10.6 | P/E on S&P Oper. EPS 2008**E** | 11.6 | Dividend Rate/Share | $0.56 | S&P Credit Rating | A+ |
| $10K Invested 5 Yrs Ago | $4,430 | Common Shares Outstg. (M) | 5,562.0 | Institutional Ownership (%) | 65 | | |

## Price Performance

30-Week Mov. Avg. ···  10-Week Mov. Avg. - - -  GAAP Earnings vs. Previous Year   Volume Above Avg. ▐▌▊  STARS
12-Mo. Target Price —  Relative Strength —  ▲ Up  ▼ Down  ▶ No Change   Below Avg. ▐▌▊  ★

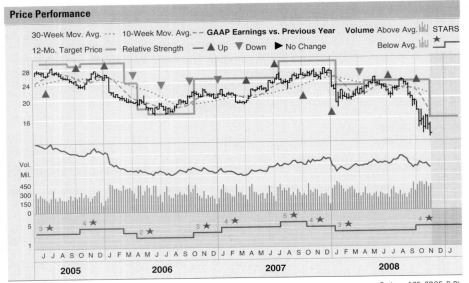

Options: ASE, CBOE, P, Ph

Analysis prepared by **Clyde Montevirgen** on November 14, 2008, when the stock traded at **$ 13.33**.

## Qualitative Risk Assessment

| LOW | MEDIUM | HIGH |
| --- | --- | --- |

Our view is that Intel's results reflect the sales cycles of the semiconductor industry and demand trends for personal computers. In addition, its above-average beta reflects high share price volatility. This is offset, in our opinion, by its large size, long corporate history, and its low debt levels compared to peers.

## Quantitative Evaluations

**S&P Quality Ranking** — B+

| D | C | B- | B | B+ | A- | A | A+ |
| --- | --- | --- | --- | --- | --- | --- | --- |

**Relative Strength Rank** — MODERATE

46

LOWEST = 1                                HIGHEST = 99

## Revenue/Earnings Data

### Revenue (Million $)

| | 1Q | 2Q | 3Q | 4Q | Year |
| --- | --- | --- | --- | --- | --- |
| 2008 | 9,673 | 9,470 | 10,217 | -- | -- |
| 2007 | 8,852 | 8,680 | 10,090 | 10,712 | 38,334 |
| 2006 | 8,940 | 8,009 | 8,739 | 9,694 | 35,382 |
| 2005 | 9,434 | 9,231 | 9,960 | 10,201 | 38,826 |
| 2004 | 8,091 | 8,049 | 8,471 | 9,598 | 34,209 |
| 2003 | 6,751 | 6,816 | 7,833 | 8,741 | 30,141 |

### Earnings Per Share ($)

| | | | | | |
| --- | --- | --- | --- | --- | --- |
| 2008 | 0.25 | 0.28 | 0.35 | E0.28 | E1.15 |
| 2007 | 0.28 | 0.22 | 0.30 | 0.38 | 1.18 |
| 2006 | 0.23 | 0.15 | 0.22 | 0.26 | 0.86 |
| 2005 | 0.35 | 0.33 | 0.32 | 0.40 | 1.40 |
| 2004 | 0.26 | 0.27 | 0.30 | 0.33 | 1.16 |
| 2003 | 0.14 | 0.14 | 0.25 | 0.33 | 0.85 |

Fiscal year ended Dec. 31. Next earnings report expected: NA. EPS Estimates based on S&P Operating Earnings; historical GAAP earnings are as reported.

## Highlights

▶ We think sales will fall 10% in 2009, following projected flat sales for 2008, reflecting an anticipated slowdown in PC sales. Macroeconomic pressure will likely lead to slower orders as the supply chain tightens inventory, in our view. However, we believe that Intel's new and soon to be released microprocessors will outperform competitors' offerings, which should lead to market share gains and increasing sales to higher-end segments, supporting longer-term growth. We also see INTC's Atom processor and upcoming product releases providing growth opportunities in addition to those from its traditional microprocessor base.

▶ We forecast gross margins narrowing to around the 54% area for 2009, versus an anticipated 56% in 2008. We see negative impact from its 32-nm process implementation in early 2009 and from slower orders, but believe gross margins will widen in the second half on higher utilization and sales of higher-end chips. Similarly, we project operating margins to narrow to 22% for 2009 from an estimated 26% in 2008, as sales decline.

▶ We estimate GAAP EPS of $1.00 for 2009, compared to a projected $1.15 for 2008.

## Investment Rationale/Risk

▶ Although we expect slowing orders as the industry faces macroeconomic weakness, we think INTC will have notable longer-term earnings growth potential after it ramps new production lines, which should provide leading-technology chips and cost benefits. The Atom processor and future release of its graphics chip should provide new growth opportunities, while its latest laptop and server microprocessors should lead to market share gains and lead to a more favorable sales mix, in our opinion. We also think Intel's ASPs will benefit from weaker competition as Advanced Micro Devices (AMD: hold, $3) tries to improve its financial position and product offerings. In our view, INTC has a strong balance sheet, healthy free cash flows, and offers lower business risk than that of other chipmakers.

▶ Risks to our recommendation and target price include worse-than-expected demand for PCs, accelerated ASP erosion, and less traction for its latest chips.

▶ Our 12-month target price of $16 reflects our P/E analysis, in which we apply a multiple of about 16X, modestly above the industry average, to our 2009 EPS estimate.

## Dividend Data (Dates: mm/dd  Payment Date: mm/dd/yy)

| Amount ($) | Date Decl. | Ex-Div. Date | Stk. of Record | Payment Date |
| --- | --- | --- | --- | --- |
| 0.128 | 01/17 | 02/05 | 02/07 | 03/01/08 |
| 0.140 | 03/20 | 05/05 | 05/07 | 06/01/08 |
| 0.140 | 07/17 | 08/05 | 08/07 | 09/01/08 |
| 0.140 | 09/10 | 11/05 | 11/07 | 12/01/08 |

Dividends have been paid since 1992. Source: Company reports.

---

**Please read the Required Disclosures and Analyst Certification on the last page of this report.**

The *McGraw-Hill* Companies

# Intel Corp

STANDARD
&POOR'S

## Business Summary November 14, 2008

CORPORATE OVERVIEW. Intel is the world's largest semiconductor chip maker based on revenue and unit shipments, and is well known for its dominant market share in microprocessors for personal computers (PCs). In the first quarter of 2005, the company reorganized its operating segments to reflect a more customer-focused strategy.

The Digital Enterprise Group, or DEG (53% of 2007 total sales), designs and delivers computing and communications platforms for business and service providers. Revenues from microprocessors within DEG represented 41% of total sales in 2006. DEG serves the desktop computing market, including consumer and enterprise desktops, as well as the networking and storage markets.

The Mobility Group (38%) makes microprocessors and related chipsets and motherboards primarily for the notebook computing market. Intel's Centrino mobile platform, consisting of a processor, chipset, and wireless network connection, represented most of the revenue for the Mobility Group in 2006.

The Flash Memory Group makes NOR and NAND flash memory products for a variety of digital devices including: cellular phones, set-top boxes, networking equipment, DVD players, modems, digital audio devices, among others. The company did not formally state the percentage of revenues for this group in 2007 because it was in the process of completing a divestment of its NOR

Flash assets to Numonyx (which closed in March 2008).

Intel also has three other operating segments, the Digital Home Group, Digital Health Group, and Channel Platform Group, which have made limited contributions to total revenues.

CORPORATE STRATEGY. Intel's stated mission is to be the preeminent supplier of silicon chips and platform solutions to the worldwide digital economy. Owning 77% of total microprocessors shipped in late 2007, the company is a clear share leader in the worldwide microprocessor market. Although INTC has a sizable lead over competitors, runner-up Advanced Micro Devices (AMD), with about 23% of market share, has effectively increased its presence over the past couple of years. In 2005, when Intel was focusing on creating faster microprocessors, AMD went in a different direction and focused on creating chips that were not only fast but also power efficient, a quality that became increasingly attractive to enterprises with large energy bills because of computing activities, and to laptop customers who faced short battery lives, among others.

## Company Financials Fiscal Year Ended Dec. 31

| Per Share Data ($) | 2007 | 2006 | 2005 | 2004 | 2003 | 2002 | 2001 | 2000 | 1999 | 1998 |
|---|---|---|---|---|---|---|---|---|---|---|
| Tangible Book Value | 6.51 | 5.70 | 5.46 | 5.57 | 5.26 | 4.74 | 4.59 | 4.67 | 4.14 | 3.53 |
| Cash Flow | 1.98 | 1.65 | 2.15 | 1.91 | 1.62 | 1.25 | 1.13 | 2.20 | 1.57 | 0.63 |
| Earnings | 1.18 | 0.86 | 1.40 | 1.16 | 0.85 | 0.46 | 0.19 | 1.51 | 1.05 | 0.87 |
| S&P Core Earnings | 1.18 | 0.77 | 1.22 | 0.99 | 0.83 | 0.35 | 0.11 | NA | NA | NA |
| Dividends | 0.45 | 0.40 | 0.32 | 0.16 | 0.08 | 0.08 | 0.08 | 0.07 | 0.07 | 0.03 |
| Payout Ratio | 38% | 47% | 23% | 14% | 9% | 17% | 42% | 4% | 7% | 4% |
| Prices:High | 27.99 | 26.63 | 28.84 | 34.60 | 34.51 | 36.78 | 38.59 | 75.81 | 44.75 | 31.55 |
| Prices:Low | 18.75 | 16.75 | 21.94 | 19.64 | 14.88 | 12.95 | 18.96 | 29.81 | 25.06 | 16.41 |
| P/E Ratio:High | 24 | 31 | 21 | 30 | 41 | 80 | NM | 50 | 42 | 37 |
| P/E Ratio:Low | 16 | 19 | 16 | 17 | 18 | 28 | NM | 20 | 24 | 19 |

| Income Statement Analysis (Million $) | | | | | | | | | | |
|---|---|---|---|---|---|---|---|---|---|---|
| Revenue | 38,334 | 35,382 | 38,826 | 34,209 | 30,141 | 26,764 | 26,539 | 33,726 | 29,389 | 26,273 |
| Operating Income | 13,643 | 10,861 | 16,685 | 15,019 | 13,225 | 9,746 | 8,923 | 15,339 | 13,756 | 11,351 |
| Depreciation | 4,798 | 4,654 | 4,595 | 4,889 | 5,070 | 5,344 | 6,469 | 4,835 | 3,597 | 2,807 |
| Interest Expense | 15.0 | 1,202 | 19.0 | 50.0 | 62.0 | 84.0 | 56.0 | 35.0 | 36.0 | 34.0 |
| Pretax Income | 9,166 | 7,068 | 12,610 | 10,417 | 7,442 | 4,204 | 2,183 | 15,141 | 11,228 | 9,137 |
| Effective Tax Rate | 23.9% | 28.6% | 31.3% | 27.8% | 24.2% | 25.9% | 40.9% | 30.4% | 34.9% | 33.6% |
| Net Income | 6,976 | 5,044 | 8,664 | 7,516 | 5,641 | 3,117 | 1,291 | 10,535 | 7,314 | 6,068 |
| S&P Core Earnings | 6,978 | 4,518 | 7,555 | 6,374 | 5,467 | 2,332 | 740 | NA | NA | NA |

| Balance Sheet & Other Financial Data (Million $) | | | | | | | | | | |
|---|---|---|---|---|---|---|---|---|---|---|
| Cash | 15,363 | 6,598 | 7,324 | 8,407 | 7,971 | 7,404 | 7,970 | 2,976 | 3,695 | 2,038 |
| Current Assets | 23,885 | 18,280 | 21,194 | 24,058 | 22,882 | 18,925 | 17,633 | 21,150 | 17,819 | 13,475 |
| Total Assets | 55,651 | 48,368 | 48,314 | 48,143 | 47,143 | 44,224 | 44,395 | 47,945 | 43,849 | 31,471 |
| Current Liabilities | 8,571 | 8,514 | 9,234 | 8,006 | 6,879 | 6,595 | 6,570 | 8,650 | 7,099 | 5,804 |
| Long Term Debt | 1,980 | 1,848 | 2,106 | 703 | 936 | 929 | 1,050 | 707 | 955 | 702 |
| Common Equity | 42,762 | 36,752 | 36,182 | 38,579 | 37,846 | 35,468 | 35,830 | 37,322 | 32,535 | 23,377 |
| Total Capital | 45,153 | 38,865 | 38,991 | 40,137 | 40,264 | 37,629 | 37,825 | 39,295 | 36,750 | 25,667 |
| Capital Expenditures | 5,000 | 5,779 | 5,818 | 3,843 | 3,656 | 4,703 | 7,309 | 6,674 | 3,403 | 3,557 |
| Cash Flow | 11,774 | 9,698 | 13,259 | 12,405 | 10,711 | 8,461 | 7,760 | 15,370 | 10,911 | 8,875 |
| Current Ratio | 2.8 | 2.1 | 2.3 | 3.0 | 3.3 | 2.9 | 2.7 | 2.4 | 2.5 | 2.3 |
| % Long Term Debt of Capitalization | 4.4 | 4.8 | 5.4 | 1.8 | 2.3 | 2.5 | 2.8 | 1.8 | 2.6 | 2.7 |
| % Net Income of Revenue | 18.2 | 14.3 | 22.3 | 22.0 | 18.7 | 11.6 | 4.9 | 31.2 | 24.9 | 23.1 |
| % Return on Assets | 13.4 | 10.4 | 18.0 | 15.8 | 12.3 | 7.0 | 2.8 | 23.0 | 19.4 | 20.1 |
| % Return on Equity | 17.6 | 13.8 | 23.2 | 19.7 | 15.4 | 8.7 | 3.5 | 30.1 | 26.0 | 27.0 |

Data as orig reptd.; bef. results of disc opers/spec. items. Per share data adj. for stk. divs.; EPS diluted. E-Estimated. NA-Not Available. NM-Not Meaningful. NR-Not Ranked. UR-Under Review.

**Office:** 2200 Mission College Boulevard, Santa Clara, CA 95054-1549.
**Telephone:** 408-765-8080.
**Website:** http://www.intc.com
**Chrmn:** C.R. Barrett

**Pres & CEO:** P.S. Otellini
**EVP & Chief Admin Officer:** A. Bryant
**SVP & General Counsel:** D.B. Sewell
**CFO & Chief Acctg Officer:** S.J. Smith

**Investor Contact:** N. Knupffer (408-653-5324)
**Board Members:** C. R. Barrett, C. Barshefsky, C. A. Bartz, S. Decker, D. J. Guzy, R. E. Hundt, P. S. Otellini, J. Plummer, D. S. Pottruck, J. E. Shaw, J. L. Thornton, D. B. Yoffie

**Founded:** 1968
**Domicile:** Delaware
**Employees:** 86,300

**STANDARD &POOR'S**

# IntercontinentalExchange Inc

| S&P Recommendation | BUY ★★★★☆ | Price | 12-Mo. Target Price | Investment Style |
|---|---|---|---|---|
| | | $70.86 (as of Nov 14, 2008) | $120.00 | Large-Cap Growth |

**GICS Sector** Financials
**Sub-Industry** Specialized Finance

**Summary** ICE is a fully electronic marketplace that offers exchange-based and over-the-counter trading of a variety of energy and soft commodity products.

## Key Stock Statistics (Source S&P, Vickers, company reports)

| | | | | | | | | |
|---|---|---|---|---|---|---|---|---|
| 52-Wk Range | $194.92–53.02 | S&P Oper. EPS 2008E | 4.58 | Market Capitalization(B) | $5.119 | Beta | | 2.57 |
| Trailing 12-Month EPS | $4.42 | S&P Oper. EPS 2009E | 5.04 | Yield (%) | Nil | S&P 3-Yr. Proj. EPS CAGR(%) | | 28 |
| Trailing 12-Month P/E | 16.0 | P/E on S&P Oper. EPS 2008E | 15.5 | Dividend Rate/Share | Nil | S&P Credit Rating | | NA |
| $10K Invested 5 Yrs Ago | NA | Common Shares Outstg. (M) | 72.2 | Institutional Ownership (%) | 85 | | | |

## Price Performance

30-Week Mov. Avg. ···· 10-Week Mov. Avg. --- GAAP Earnings vs. Previous Year  Volume Above Avg. STARS
12-Mo. Target Price — Relative Strength  ▲ Up  ▼ Down  ▶ No Change  Below Avg.

Options: ASE, CBOE, P, Ph

Analysis prepared by **Rikin Pandya** on November 11, 2008, when the stock traded at **$ 73.02**.

## Highlights

➤ By embracing electronic trading and being an innovator with its centrally cleared over-the-counter (OTC) offerings, ICE has established itself as a leading marketplace for trading energy products. With its exchange and OTC product offerings, fully electronic platform, and leading position in energy and soft commodity products, we believe ICE's marketplaces are attractive to a growing pool of traders looking at alternative investments. The CTFC has increased oversight and regulation in order to curb speculation in the commodities market in hopes of easing crude prices. Nevertheless, we believe industry-wide trends remain favorable.

➤ In the third quarter, ICE continued to benefit from historically high trading volumes. ICE Futures Europe volume grew 5% to 27.5 million contracts, ICE Futures U.S. and Canada rose 36% to 18.7 million contracts, and over the counter (OTC) transaction fees increased 55% to $89.6 million. Although expenses grew over 18% in Q3 08, we believe ICE has the resources to manage expenses in a depressed market.

➤ Assuming an effective tax rate of 35%, we see EPS of $4.58 in 2008 and $5.04 in 2009.

## Investment Rationale/Risk

➤ While near-term earnings visibility remains somewhat cloudy stemming from what we believe will be reduced trading volumes amidst de-leveraging on a macro level, we are very positive about ICE's long-term prospects. The recent announcement of an agreement with nine major banks regarding their support of a central credit-default swap (CDS) clearinghouse leaves ICE in a favorable situation, in our view. Further, due to the complexities that are sure to arise, we see ICE's acquisition of The Clearing Corp as an important step in developing a clearing house, which has the sole focus of clearing CDS. We believe ICE remains well positioned to grow as a standalone entity or provide strong technology capabilities and product diversification for a potential partner, as we expect further consolidation among exchanges.

➤ Risks to our recommendation and target price include slower trading volumes, enhanced regulatory scrutiny of OTC markets, increasing competition, and migration to in-house clearing.

➤ Our 12-month target price of $120 is based on a P/E of 24X our 2009 EPS estimate, which is a premium to the current peer average.

## Qualitative Risk Assessment

| LOW | MEDIUM | HIGH |
|---|---|---|

Our risk assessment reflects the potential volatility in results due to changes in energy product trading volumes, recent acquisition activity in the sector, and a changing regulatory environment.

## Quantitative Evaluations

**S&P Quality Ranking** NR

| D | C | B- | B | B+ | A- | A | A+ |
|---|---|---|---|---|---|---|---|

**Relative Strength Rank** MODERATE

66

LOWEST = 1    HIGHEST = 99

## Revenue/Earnings Data

**Revenue (Million $)**

| | 1Q | 2Q | 3Q | 4Q | Year |
|---|---|---|---|---|---|
| 2008 | 207.2 | 197.2 | 201.4 | -- | -- |
| 2007 | 126.6 | 136.7 | 151.7 | 159.3 | 574.3 |
| 2006 | 73.59 | 73.59 | 94.66 | 95.26 | 313.8 |
| 2005 | -- | -- | -- | -- | 155.9 |
| 2004 | -- | -- | -- | -- | 108.4 |
| 2003 | -- | -- | -- | -- | 93.70 |

**Earnings Per Share ($)**

| | | | | | |
|---|---|---|---|---|---|
| 2008 | 1.29 | 1.19 | 1.04 | E1.06 | E4.58 |
| 2007 | 0.80 | 0.75 | 0.93 | 0.90 | 3.39 |
| 2006 | 0.33 | 0.52 | 0.73 | 0.81 | 2.40 |
| 2005 | -- | -- | -- | -- | 0.39 |
| 2004 | -- | -- | -- | -- | 0.41 |
| 2003 | -- | -- | -- | -- | 0.37 |

Fiscal year ended Dec. 31. Next earnings report expected: Early February. EPS Estimates based on S&P Operating Earnings; historical GAAP earnings are as reported.

## Dividend Data

No cash dividends have been paid.

# IntercontinentalExchange Inc

## Business Summary November 11, 2008

CORPORATE OVERVIEW. IntercontinentalExchange, Inc. operates a fully electronic marketplace offering exchange-based and over-the-counter (OTC) trading of a variety of energy products, and is the leading global exchange for soft commodities. The company's primary products include futures contracts for Brent crude oil and West Texas Intermediary crude oil, OTC trading of Henry Hub natural gas contracts, and various soft commodity futures. ICE provides trading for financial settlement and contracts for physical delivery of the underlying commodity.

ICE was formed in May 2000, to provide a platform for OTC energy trading. In June 2001, the company acquired the International Petroleum Exchange (IPE), which was mainly a floor-based futures exchange. In early 2002, the company introduced the industry's first cleared OTC contract through its partnership with LCH.Clearnet. In April 2005, ICE closed the IPE trading floor and moved to an entirely electronic marketplace. In January 2007, ICE acquired the New York Board of Trade (NYBOT) for approximately $1.1 billion. NYBOT, which has been renamed ICE Futures U.S., is a leading soft commodity exchange for products such as sugar, coffee, cocoa, orange juice, pulp, and cotton, as well as several financial products. In 2007, ICE derived approximately 85% of its

revenue from commission fees associated with trading its products on its exchange and OTC platforms. ICE generates a majority of its trading commissions from a relatively small amount of crude, gas oil, and North American power futures and OTC contracts.

We view ICE's move to offer cleared OTC contracts as one of the key growth drivers for the OTC business. Transaction fees for cleared OTC contracts grew from $6.0 million in 2003 to over $150 million in 2007, and now represent almost 80% of OTC revenue, up from 14% in 2003. By offering cleared contracts for the traditionally bilaterally settled OTC market, we believe ICE has helped to simplify and reduce the credit risk for OTC transactions, facilitating greater trading activity. Through its current OTC clearing arrangement with LCH.Clearnet, ICE does not receive any of the clearing fees associated with the centrally cleared products on its OTC platform. ICE does receive its standard commissions on these transactions.

## Company Financials Fiscal Year Ended Dec. 31

| Per Share Data ($) | 2007 | 2006 | 2005 | 2004 | 2003 | 2002 | 2001 | 2000 | 1999 | 1998 |
|---|---|---|---|---|---|---|---|---|---|---|
| Tangible Book Value | NM | 6.42 | 2.82 | 2.56 | NA | NA | NA | NA | NA | NA |
| Cash Flow | 3.85 | 2.63 | 1.04 | 0.73 | 0.72 | 0.89 | NA | NA | NA | NA |
| Earnings | 3.39 | 2.40 | 0.39 | 0.41 | 0.37 | 0.37 | NA | NA | NA | NA |
| S&P Core Earnings | 3.30 | 2.39 | 0.82 | 0.32 | 0.18 | NA | NA | NA | NA | NA |
| Dividends | Nil | Nil | Nil | NA | NA | NA | NA | NA | NA | NA |
| Payout Ratio | Nil | Nil | Nil | NA | NA | NA | NA | NA | NA | NA |
| Prices:High | 194.92 | 113.85 | 44.21 | NA | NA | NA | NA | NA | NA | NA |
| Prices:Low | 108.15 | 36.00 | 26.00 | NA | NA | NA | NA | NA | NA | NA |
| P/E Ratio:High | 57 | 47 | NM | NA | NA | NA | NA | NA | NA | NA |
| P/E Ratio:Low | 32 | 15 | NM | NA | NA | NA | NA | NA | NA | NA |

| Income Statement Analysis (Million $) | | | | | | | | | | |
|---|---|---|---|---|---|---|---|---|---|---|
| Revenue | 574 | 314 | 156 | 108 | 93.7 | 125 | NA | NA | NA | NA |
| Operating Income | 397 | 218 | 91.1 | 49.4 | 38.3 | 65.3 | NA | NA | NA | NA |
| Depreciation | 32.7 | 13.7 | 15.1 | 17.0 | 19.3 | 14.4 | NA | NA | NA | NA |
| Interest Expense | 18.6 | 0.23 | 0.61 | 0.14 | 0.08 | 0.40 | NA | NA | NA | NA |
| Pretax Income | 358 | 213 | 60.0 | 33.7 | 19.9 | 25.4 | NA | NA | NA | NA |
| Effective Tax Rate | 32.9% | 32.6% | 32.6% | 34.7% | 32.7% | 33.8% | NA | NA | NA | NA |
| Net Income | 241 | 143 | 40.4 | 21.9 | 13.4 | 34.7 | NA | NA | NA | NA |
| S&P Core Earnings | 234 | 143 | 43.8 | 17.0 | 9.81 | NA | NA | NA | NA | NA |

| Balance Sheet & Other Financial Data (Million $) | | | | | | | | | | |
|---|---|---|---|---|---|---|---|---|---|---|
| Cash | 280 | 204 | 32.6 | 89.2 | 56.9 | NA | NA | NA | NA | NA |
| Current Assets | 1,142 | 341 | 164 | NA | NA | NA | NA | NA | NA | NA |
| Total Assets | 2,796 | 493 | 266 | 208 | 215 | NA | NA | NA | NA | NA |
| Current Liabilities | 911 | 37.9 | 26.4 | NA | NA | NA | NA | NA | NA | NA |
| Long Term Debt | 184 | Nil | Nil | Nil | NA | NA | NA | NA | NA | NA |
| Common Equity | 1,477 | 454 | 233 | 221 | 186 | NA | NA | NA | NA | NA |
| Total Capital | 1,770 | 454 | 238 | 221 | NA | NA | NA | NA | NA | NA |
| Capital Expenditures | 43.3 | 12.4 | 8.61 | 1.70 | 1.61 | 14.8 | NA | NA | NA | NA |
| Cash Flow | 273 | 157 | 55.5 | 38.9 | 39.3 | 49.1 | NA | NA | NA | NA |
| Current Ratio | 1.3 | 9.0 | 6.2 | 2.9 | 5.9 | NA | NA | NA | NA | NA |
| % Long Term Debt of Capitalization | 10.4 | Nil | Nil | Nil | Nil | Nil | NA | NA | NA | NA |
| % Net Income of Revenue | 41.9 | 45.5 | 25.9 | 20.3 | 14.3 | 27.8 | NA | NA | NA | NA |
| % Return on Assets | 14.6 | 37.7 | NM | 10.4 | NA | NA | NA | NA | NA | NA |
| % Return on Equity | 24.9 | 41.6 | NM | 13.1 | NA | NA | NA | NA | NA | NA |

Data as orig reptd.; bef. results of disc opers/spec. items. Per share data adj. for stk. divs.; EPS diluted. E-Estimated. NA-Not Available. NM-Not Meaningful. NR-Not Ranked. UR-Under Review.

Office: 2100 RiverEdge Parkway, Atlanta, GA 30328.
Telephone: 770-857-4700.
Email: ir@theice.com
Website: http://www.theice.com

Chrmn & CEO: J.C. Sprecher
Pres & COO: C.A. Vice
SVP, CFO & Chief Acctg Officer: S.A. Hill
SVP & CTO: E.D. Marcial

SVP, Secy & General Counsel: J.H. Short
Board Members: C. R. Crisp, J. Forneri, F. W. Hatfield, T. F. Martell, R. Reid, F. V. Salerno, F. W. Schneider, F. W. Schoenhut, J. C. Sprecher, J. A. Sprieser, V. Tese

Founded: 2000
Domicile: Delaware
Employees: 506

**STANDARD &POOR'S**

# International Business Machines Corp

| S&P Recommendation | STRONG BUY ★ ★ ★ ★ ★ | Price $80.33 (as of Nov 14, 2008) | 12-Mo. Target Price $130.00 | Investment Style Large-Cap Growth |
|---|---|---|---|---|

**GICS Sector** Information Technology
**Sub-Industry** Computer Hardware

**Summary** IBM, the world's largest technology company, offers a diversified line of computer hardware equipment, application and system software, and related services.

## Key Stock Statistics (Source S&P, Vickers, company reports)

| | | | | | | | |
|---|---|---|---|---|---|---|---|
| 52-Wk Range | $130.93– 75.40 | S&P Oper. EPS 2008E | 8.83 | Market Capitalization(B) | $107.920 | Beta | 1.05 |
| Trailing 12-Month EPS | $8.48 | S&P Oper. EPS 2009E | 9.80 | Yield (%) | 2.49 | S&P 3-Yr. Proj. EPS CAGR(%) | 14 |
| Trailing 12-Month P/E | 9.5 | P/E on S&P Oper. EPS 2008E | 9.1 | Dividend Rate/Share | $2.00 | S&P Credit Rating | A+ |
| $10K Invested 5 Yrs Ago | $9,470 | Common Shares Outstg. (M) | 1,343.5 | Institutional Ownership (%) | 61 | | |

## Price Performance

30-Week Mov. Avg. · · · · 10-Week Mov. Avg. – – **GAAP Earnings vs. Previous Year** Volume Above Avg. STARS
12-Mo. Target Price — Relative Strength — ▲ Up ▼ Down ► No Change Below Avg. ★

Options: ASE, CBOE, P, Ph

Analysis prepared by **Thomas W. Smith, CFA** on October 17, 2008, when the stock traded at **$ 91.52**.

## Qualitative Risk Assessment

| LOW | MEDIUM | HIGH |
|---|---|---|

Our risk assessment reflects what we view as IBM's competitively positioned solutions offerings, global market presence, and significant economies of scale, offset by what we see as an intensely competitive pricing environment.

## Quantitative Evaluations

**S&P Quality Ranking** A

| D | C | B- | B | B+ | A- | A | A+ |
|---|---|---|---|---|---|---|---|

**Relative Strength Rank** MODERATE

53

LOWEST = 1 HIGHEST = 99

## Revenue/Earnings Data

### Revenue (Million $)

| | 1Q | 2Q | 3Q | 4Q | Year |
|---|---|---|---|---|---|
| 2008 | 24,502 | 26,820 | 25,302 | -- | -- |
| 2007 | 22,029 | 23,772 | 24,119 | 28,866 | 98,785 |
| 2006 | 20,659 | 21,890 | 22,617 | 26,257 | 91,424 |
| 2005 | 22,908 | 22,270 | 21,529 | 24,427 | 91,134 |
| 2004 | 22,175 | 23,098 | 23,349 | 27,671 | 96,293 |
| 2003 | 20,065 | 21,631 | 21,522 | 25,913 | 89,131 |

### Earnings Per Share ($)

| | | | | | |
|---|---|---|---|---|---|
| 2008 | 1.65 | 1.98 | 2.05 | E3.15 | E8.83 |
| 2007 | 1.21 | 1.55 | 1.68 | 2.80 | 7.18 |
| 2006 | 1.08 | 1.30 | 1.45 | 2.30 | 6.06 |
| 2005 | 0.85 | 1.14 | 0.94 | 2.01 | 4.91 |
| 2004 | 0.93 | 1.16 | 1.06 | 1.81 | 4.94 |
| 2003 | 0.79 | 0.98 | 1.02 | 1.56 | 4.34 |

Fiscal year ended Dec. 31. Next earnings report expected: Mid January. EPS Estimates based on S&P Operating Earnings; historical GAAP earnings are as reported.

## Highlights

➤ We expect revenues to rise about 8% in 2008 amid a slower growing U.S. economy and weakness at some financial industry customers, and then we see an increase of 4% for 2009. We believe the services segment will continue to gain traction. We project robust growth in IBM's Software division, reflecting recent acquisitions, including Cognos and Platform Solutions, and the strength of some of the company's key middleware platforms (including WebSphere and Tivoli). We look for some softness in Systems & Technology sales despite good customer acceptance of new hardware products.

➤ We look for gross margins to widen to 43.7% in 2008 and 44% in 2009, from 42.3% in 2007, on ongoing cost reduction efforts and an improved sales mix. We think pretax margins will expand as well. Effective tax rates should benefit from more international business.

➤ We estimate EPS of $8.83 in 2008 and $9.80 in 2009. We expect a $15 billion share buyback plan, announced February 26, to bolster EPS. The company has a long-term goal of achieving EPS of $10.00 to $11.00 in 2010.

## Investment Rationale/Risk

➤ IBM's results should benefit, in our view, from strong revenue growth in emerging markets and a widening of margins reflecting cost cutting and improved profitability in more mature markets. We project modest, but relatively consistent, near-term revenue growth.

➤ Risks to our recommendation and target price include execution risks with regard to the global services operations, which might further elongate the sales cycle. Pricing pressure and managing a transition to new hardware products are also risks. Regarding corporate governance practices, we are somewhat concerned that the roles of chairman and CEO are combined.

➤ Our 12-month target price of $130 reflects a target P/E near 14X, which is toward the low end of the recent five-year historical range for IBM, applied to our 12-month forward EPS estimate of $9.39. Our target P/E is a bit above a recent P/E near 13X for Information Technology Sector companies in the S&P 500 Index, which we view as a reasonable premium for IBM shares given its economies of scale and relatively steady earnings performance.

## Dividend Data (Dates: mm/dd Payment Date: mm/dd/yy)

| Amount ($) | Date Decl. | Ex-Div. Date | Stk. of Record | Payment Date |
|---|---|---|---|---|
| 0.400 | 01/29 | 02/06 | 02/08 | 03/10/08 |
| 0.500 | 04/29 | 05/07 | 05/09 | 06/10/08 |
| 0.500 | 07/29 | 08/06 | 08/08 | 09/10/08 |
| 0.500 | 10/28 | 11/06 | 11/10 | 12/10/08 |

Dividends have been paid since 1916. Source: Company reports.

---

# International Business Machines Corp

STANDARD
&POOR'S

## Business Summary October 17, 2008

CORPORATE OVERVIEW. With a corporate history dating back to 1911, International Business Machines has grown to be a major contributor to each major category that comprises the total information technology market: hardware, software, and services. The company is a leading server vendor, among the largest software vendors (behind Microsoft Corp. and Oracle Corp.), and has the largest global services organization.

The company strives for innovation as a means of product differentiation and, with a research and development budget of $6.1 billion in 2007, it claims to have been awarded more patents in 2007 than any other company.

The global scope of operations is reflected in the mix of revenue sources in 2007, with the Americas representing about 42%, EMEA 35%, Asia Pacific 20%, and an OEM category 3%. Regional growth was decisively stronger outside the Americas in 2007. Revenue from EMEA grew at a 14.5% pace in 2007, and 11.8% in Asia Pacific, compared to only 5.2% for the Americas and an 8.9% rate for all IBM. The company's revenue from the so-called BRIC countries (Brazil, Russia, India and China) grew 26% in 2007 (18% adjusted for currency fluctuations).

CORPORATE STRATEGY. IBM has evolved from being a computer hardware vendor to a systems, services and software company. While computer hardware (included in the Systems & Technology Group) accounted for about 22% of sales in 2007, IBM has emphasized -- through acquisitions and investments -- services and software. These areas serving adjacent markets to hardware have gained momentum as IBM leverages its ability to offer total solutions to customers. IBM's focus on higher value added segments such as services (55% of 2007 sales) and software (20%) resulted in these areas together representing almost 76% of revenue and 77% of pretax profits in 2007. Global financing represented almost 3% of 2007 revenues, and is primarily used to leverage IBM's financial structuring and portfolio management, and to expand the customer base.

## Company Financials Fiscal Year Ended Dec. 31

| Per Share Data ($) | 2007 | 2006 | 2005 | 2004 | 2003 | 2002 | 2001 | 2000 | 1999 | 1998 |
|---|---|---|---|---|---|---|---|---|---|---|
| Tangible Book Value | 8.72 | 8.93 | 13.97 | 11.86 | 12.36 | 10.84 | 12.96 | 11.08 | 10.65 | 9.84 |
| Cash Flow | 10.22 | 9.39 | 8.10 | 7.82 | 7.01 | 5.61 | 7.08 | 6.95 | 7.40 | 5.64 |
| Earnings | 7.18 | 6.06 | 4.91 | 4.94 | 4.34 | 3.07 | 4.35 | 4.44 | 4.12 | 3.28 |
| S&P Core Earnings | 6.94 | 5.88 | 3.93 | 4.06 | 3.00 | 0.08 | 1.33 | NA | NA | NA |
| Dividends | 1.50 | 1.10 | 0.78 | 0.70 | 0.63 | 0.59 | 0.55 | 0.51 | 0.47 | 0.44 |
| Payout Ratio | 21% | 18% | 16% | 14% | 15% | 19% | 13% | 11% | 11% | 13% |
| Prices:High | 121.46 | 97.88 | 99.10 | 100.43 | 94.54 | 126.39 | 124.70 | 134.94 | 139.19 | 94.97 |
| Prices:Low | 88.77 | 72.73 | 71.85 | 90.82 | 73.17 | 54.01 | 83.75 | 80.06 | 80.88 | 47.81 |
| P/E Ratio:High | 17 | 16 | 20 | 20 | 22 | 41 | 29 | 30 | 34 | 29 |
| P/E Ratio:Low | 12 | 12 | 15 | 18 | 17 | 18 | 19 | 18 | 20 | 15 |

| Income Statement Analysis (Million $) | | | | | | | | | | |
|---|---|---|---|---|---|---|---|---|---|---|
| Revenue | 98,786 | 91,424 | 91,134 | 96,293 | 89,131 | 81,186 | 85,866 | 88,396 | 87,548 | 81,667 |
| Operating Income | 18,765 | 16,912 | 14,564 | 15,890 | 14,790 | 11,175 | 14,115 | 16,147 | 18,086 | 13,639 |
| Depreciation | 4,405 | 4,983 | 5,188 | 4,915 | 4,701 | 4,379 | 4,820 | 4,513 | 6,159 | 4,475 |
| Interest Expense | 1,431 | 278 | 220 | 139 | 145 | 145 | 238 | 717 | 727 | 713 |
| Pretax Income | 14,489 | 13,317 | 12,226 | 12,028 | 10,874 | 7,524 | 10,953 | 11,534 | 11,757 | 9,040 |
| Effective Tax Rate | 28.1% | 29.3% | 34.6% | 29.8% | 30.0% | 29.1% | 29.5% | 29.8% | 34.4% | 30.0% |
| Net Income | 10,418 | 9,416 | 7,994 | 8,448 | 7,613 | 5,334 | 7,723 | 8,093 | 7,712 | 6,328 |
| S&P Core Earnings | 10,073 | 9,116 | 6,395 | 6,923 | 5,270 | 111 | 2,302 | NA | NA | NA |

| Balance Sheet & Other Financial Data (Million $) | | | | | | | | | | |
|---|---|---|---|---|---|---|---|---|---|---|
| Cash | 16,146 | 10,656 | 13,686 | 10,570 | 7,647 | 5,975 | 6,393 | 3,722 | 5,831 | 5,768 |
| Current Assets | 53,177 | 44,660 | 45,661 | 46,970 | 44,998 | 41,652 | 42,461 | 43,880 | 43,155 | 42,360 |
| Total Assets | 120,431 | 103,234 | 105,748 | 109,183 | 104,457 | 96,484 | 88,313 | 88,349 | 87,495 | 86,100 |
| Current Liabilities | 44,310 | 40,091 | 35,152 | 39,798 | 37,900 | 34,550 | 35,119 | 36,406 | 39,578 | 36,827 |
| Long Term Debt | 23,039 | 13,780 | 15,425 | 14,828 | 16,986 | 19,986 | 15,963 | 18,371 | 14,124 | 15,508 |
| Common Equity | 28,470 | 28,506 | 33,098 | 29,747 | 27,864 | 22,782 | 23,614 | 20,624 | 20,264 | 19,186 |
| Total Capital | 51,509 | 42,286 | 48,523 | 44,575 | 44,850 | 42,768 | 39,577 | 38,995 | 36,236 | 36,455 |
| Capital Expenditures | 4,630 | 4,362 | 3,842 | 4,368 | 4,393 | 4,753 | 5,660 | 5,616 | 5,959 | 6,520 |
| Cash Flow | 14,823 | 14,399 | 13,182 | 13,363 | 12,314 | 9,713 | 12,533 | 12,586 | 13,851 | 10,783 |
| Current Ratio | 1.2 | 1.1 | 1.3 | 1.2 | 1.2 | 1.2 | 1.2 | 1.2 | 1.1 | 1.2 |
| % Long Term Debt of Capitalization | 44.7 | 32.6 | 31.7 | 33.3 | 37.9 | 46.7 | 40.3 | 47.1 | 39.2 | 42.5 |
| % Net Income of Revenue | 10.6 | 10.3 | 8.8 | 8.8 | 8.5 | 6.6 | 9.0 | 9.2 | 8.8 | 7.7 |
| % Return on Assets | 9.3 | 9.0 | 7.4 | 7.9 | 7.6 | 5.7 | 8.7 | 9.2 | 8.9 | 7.6 |
| % Return on Equity | 36.6 | 30.6 | 24.7 | 29.3 | 30.1 | 23.1 | 35.1 | 39.7 | 39.0 | 32.7 |

Data as orig reptd.; bef. results of disc opers/spec. items. Per share data adj. for stk. divs.; EPS diluted. E-Estimated. NA-Not Available. NM-Not Meaningful. NR-Not Ranked. UR-Under Review.

**Office:** New Orchard Road, Armonk, NY 10504.
**Telephone:** 914-499-1900.
**Website:** http://www.ibm.com
**Chrmn, Pres & CEO:** S.J. Palmisano

**SVP & CFO:** M. Loughridge
**SVP & General Counsel:** R.C. Weber
**Treas:** M. Schroeter
**Secy:** A. Bonzani

**Investor Contact:** T.S. Shaughnessy (914-499-1900)
**Board Members:** A. J. Belda, C. P. Black, W. R. Brody, K. I. Chenault, M. L. Eskew, S. A. Jackson, T. Nishimuro, L. A. Noto, J. W. Owens, S. J. Palmisano, J. Spero, S. Taurel, L. Zambrano

**Founded:** 1910
**Domicile:** New York
**Employees:** 386,558

The McGraw-Hill Companies

**STANDARD &POOR'S**

# International Flavors & Fragrances Inc.

| **S&P Recommendation** HOLD ★★★☆☆ | **Price** $27.86 (as of Nov 14, 2008) | **12-Mo. Target Price** $39.00 | **Investment Style** Large-Cap Growth |
|---|---|---|---|

**GICS Sector** Materials
**Sub-Industry** Specialty Chemicals

**Summary** This leading producer of flavors and fragrances used in a wide variety of consumer goods derives over two-thirds of its sales and earnings from operations outside the U.S.

## Key Stock Statistics (Source S&P, Vickers, company reports)

| | | | | | |
|---|---|---|---|---|---|
| 52-Wk Range | $50.34– 27.00 | S&P Oper. EPS 2008E | 2.85 | Market Capitalization(B) | $2.191 |
| Trailing 12-Month EPS | $2.83 | S&P Oper. EPS 2009E | 3.00 | Yield (%) | 3.59 |
| Trailing 12-Month P/E | 9.8 | P/E on S&P Oper. EPS 2008E | 9.8 | Dividend Rate/Share | $1.00 |
| $10K Invested 5 Yrs Ago | $9,676 | Common Shares Outstg. (M) | 78.6 | Institutional Ownership (%) | 83 |

| | | | |
|---|---|---|---|
| Beta | 0.80 | | |
| S&P 3-Yr. Proj. EPS CAGR(%) | 10 | | |
| S&P Credit Rating | BBB | | |

## Price Performance

30-Week Mov. Avg. · · · 10-Week Mov. Avg. – – **GAAP Earnings vs. Previous Year**   **Volume** Above Avg. ▐▊▌ STARS
12-Mo. Target Price — Relative Strength — ▲ Up ▼ Down ▶ No Change   Below Avg. ▐▪▌ ★ ⌐_

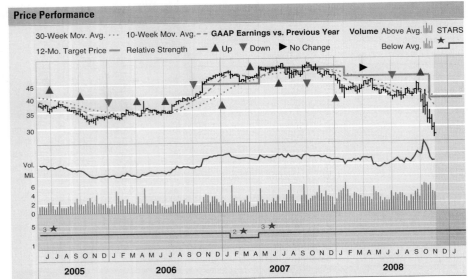

Options: CBOE

Analysis prepared by **Richard O'Reilly, CFA** on November 04, 2008, when the stock traded at **$ 32.50**.

## Highlights

➤ We expect sales in 2009 to be similar to those forecasted for 2008, helped by introductions of new customer products and modestly higher selling prices, offset by expected unfavorable currency exchange rates and slowdowns in domestic and European consumer markets. Sales growth of 7% in the first nine months of 2008 was helped by 5% from favorable currency rates. We believe that IFF in 2008 continued to gain share with major customers for flavors, but we expect the retail environment for fine fragrances to be challenging into 2009.

➤ We forecast a gross margin of 42.0% for 2009, up from an expected 41.5% in 2008, which was hurt by escalating costs for raw materials and freight. Profits for the first nine months of 2008 included special charges totaling $0.09 a share. We see 2008 interest expense of about $73 million, as a result of increased debt incurred in an accelerated stock buyback plan.

➤ We project that the effective tax rate for 2009 will remain at about 28%. EPS comparisons in 2008 should be helped by 10% fewer average shares outstanding as a result of the company's stock repurchase program.

## Investment Rationale/Risk

➤ We expect the company in 2009 to continue to achieve sales growth, driven by an improved win rate of new business, especially in flavors, although currency exchange rates could be a negative factor. We believe IFF's has strong cash flows and ample liquidity, including revolving credit facilities.

➤ Risks to our recommendation and target price include increased economic and political uncertainties in global markets, greater currency fluctuations, an inability to maintain close relationships with customers, lack of customers' success in new product launches, and unexpected increases in raw material costs.

➤ The shares recently yielded 3.1% and traded at a P/E of about 11X our 2008 EPS estimate, in line with the corresponding multiples accorded to the shares of other major specialty chemical concerns, based on our forecasts. We think the stock will perform in line with the S&P 500 over the next 12 months, reflecting what we see as a favorable EPS outlook for 2009. Assuming a P/E multiple close to peers, our 12-month target price is $39.

## Qualitative Risk Assessment

| LOW | **MEDIUM** | HIGH |
|---|---|---|

Our risk assessment reflects our view of the stable nature of the company's businesses and end markets, and its leadership positions, offset by a somewhat concentrated customer base.

## Quantitative Evaluations

**S&P Quality Ranking**      B+

| D | C | B- | B | **B+** | A- | A | A+ |
|---|---|---|---|---|---|---|---|

**Relative Strength Rank**      MODERATE

47

LOWEST = 1          HIGHEST = 99

## Revenue/Earnings Data

### Revenue (Million $)

| | 1Q | 2Q | 3Q | 4Q | Year |
|---|---|---|---|---|---|
| 2008 | 596.6 | 636.1 | 617.5 | -- | -- |
| 2007 | 566.1 | 573.7 | 583.3 | 553.5 | 2,277 |
| 2006 | 511.4 | 530.5 | 539.1 | 514.3 | 2,095 |
| 2005 | 523.1 | 515.6 | 493.1 | 461.7 | 1,993 |
| 2004 | 535.0 | 524.2 | 506.2 | 468.2 | 2,034 |
| 2003 | 466.2 | 482.6 | 480.9 | 471.8 | 1,902 |

### Earnings Per Share ($)

| | | | | | |
|---|---|---|---|---|---|
| 2008 | 0.69 | 0.83 | 0.73 | E0.54 | E2.85 |
| 2007 | 0.69 | 0.87 | 0.67 | 0.58 | 2.82 |
| 2006 | 0.58 | 0.67 | 0.70 | 0.53 | 2.48 |
| 2005 | 0.55 | 0.60 | 0.72 | 0.16 | 2.04 |
| 2004 | 0.59 | 0.59 | 0.44 | 0.43 | 2.05 |
| 2003 | 0.34 | 0.54 | 0.54 | 0.40 | 1.83 |

Fiscal year ended Dec. 31. Next earnings report expected: Late January. EPS Estimates based on S&P Operating Earnings; historical GAAP earnings are as reported.

## Dividend Data (Dates: mm/dd Payment Date: mm/dd/yy)

| Amount ($) | Date Decl. | Ex-Div. Date | Stk. of Record | Payment Date |
|---|---|---|---|---|
| 0.230 | 12/11 | 12/19 | 12/21 | 01/07/08 |
| 0.230 | 03/04 | 03/18 | 03/20 | 04/03/08 |
| 0.230 | 05/06 | 06/17 | 06/19 | 07/03/08 |
| 0.250 | 07/22 | 09/16 | 09/18 | 10/02/08 |

Dividends have been paid since 1956. Source: Company reports.

---

**Please read the Required Disclosures and Analyst Certification on the last page of this report.**

*The McGraw·Hill Companies*

# International Flavors & Fragrances Inc.

## Business Summary November 04, 2008

CORPORATE OVERVIEW. International Flavors & Fragrances, founded in 1909, is a leading global maker of products used by other manufacturers to enhance the aromas and tastes of consumer products. The November 2000 purchase of Bush Boake Allen Inc. (BOA) for $970 million boosted annual sales to nearly $2 billion.

IFF receives more than 70% of its sales outside the U.S. In 2007, North America contributed 28% of sales; Europe 37%; Latin America 13%; and Asia-Pacific 22%.

Fragrance products accounted for 56% of sales and 53% of operating profits in 2007. Fragrances are used in the manufacture of soaps, detergents, cosmetic creams, lotions and powders, lipsticks, after shave lotions, deodorants, hair preparations, air fresheners, perfumes and colognes and other consumer products. Most major U.S. companies in these industries are IFF customers. Cosmetics (including perfumes and toiletries) and household products (soaps and detergents) are the two largest customer groups.

Flavor products account for IFF's remaining sales and profits. Flavors are sold principally to the food, beverage and other industries for use in consumer products such as soft drinks, candies, cake mixes, desserts, prepared foods, dietary foods, dairy products, drink powders, pharmaceuticals, oral care products, alcoholic beverages and tobacco. Two of the largest customers for flavor products are major U.S. producers of prepared foods and beverages.

By category, 44% of sales in 2007 were from flavor compounds, 24% functional fragrances, 20% fine fragrances and toiletries, and 12% ingredients.

The company uses both synthetic and natural ingredients in its compounds. IFF manufactures most of the synthetic ingredients, of which a substantial portion (45% in 2007) is sold to others. It has had a consistent commitment to R&D spending, and anticipates that R&D expense will approximate 9% of annual sales over the next several years. R&D is conducted in 31 laboratories in 23 countries.

## Company Financials Fiscal Year Ended Dec. 31

| Per Share Data ($) | 2007 | 2006 | 2005 | 2004 | 2003 | 2002 | 2001 | 2000 | 1999 | 1998 |
|---|---|---|---|---|---|---|---|---|---|---|
| Tangible Book Value | NM | 1.78 | 1.54 | 1.28 | NM | NM | NM | NM | 8.19 | 8.91 |
| Cash Flow | 3.77 | 3.46 | 3.07 | 3.01 | 2.77 | 2.72 | 2.47 | 1.90 | 2.06 | 2.35 |
| Earnings | 2.82 | 2.48 | 2.04 | 2.05 | 1.83 | 1.84 | 1.20 | 1.22 | 1.53 | 1.90 |
| S&P Core Earnings | 2.75 | 2.35 | 2.04 | 1.82 | 1.70 | 1.37 | 0.70 | NA | NA | NA |
| Dividends | 0.88 | 0.77 | 0.73 | 0.69 | 0.63 | 0.60 | 0.60 | 1.52 | 1.52 | 1.48 |
| Payout Ratio | 31% | 31% | 36% | 33% | 34% | 33% | 50% | 125% | 99% | 78% |
| Prices:High | 54.75 | 49.88 | 42.90 | 43.20 | 36.61 | 37.45 | 31.69 | 37.94 | 48.50 | 51.88 |
| Prices:Low | 45.71 | 32.53 | 31.19 | 32.77 | 29.18 | 26.05 | 19.75 | 14.69 | 33.63 | 32.06 |
| P/E Ratio:High | 19 | 20 | 21 | 21 | 20 | 20 | 26 | 31 | 32 | 27 |
| P/E Ratio:Low | 16 | 13 | 15 | 16 | 16 | 14 | 16 | 12 | 22 | 17 |

| Income Statement Analysis (Million $) | | | | | | | | | | |
|---|---|---|---|---|---|---|---|---|---|---|
| Revenue | 2,277 | 2,095 | 1,993 | 2,034 | 1,902 | 1,809 | 1,844 | 1,463 | 1,439 | 1,407 |
| Operating Income | 452 | 421 | 382 | 433 | 415 | 396 | 409 | 322 | 338 | 356 |
| Depreciation | 82.8 | 89.7 | 91.9 | 91.0 | 86.7 | 84.5 | 123 | 69.3 | 56.4 | 49.0 |
| Interest Expense | 41.5 | 25.5 | 24.0 | 24.0 | 28.5 | 37.0 | 70.4 | 25.1 | 5.15 | 2.04 |
| Pretax Income | 329 | 313 | 246 | 281 | 252 | 266 | 188 | 184 | 243 | 311 |
| Effective Tax Rate | 24.8% | 27.7% | 21.6% | 30.2% | 31.5% | 34.0% | 38.2% | 33.2% | 33.5% | 34.5% |
| Net Income | 247 | 227 | 193 | 196 | 173 | 176 | 116 | 123 | 162 | 204 |
| S&P Core Earnings | 241 | 214 | 193 | 174 | 161 | 131 | 68.5 | NA | NA | NA |

| Balance Sheet & Other Financial Data (Million $) | | | | | | | | | | |
|---|---|---|---|---|---|---|---|---|---|---|
| Cash | 152 | 115 | 273 | 32.6 | 12.1 | 14.9 | 48.5 | 129 | 62.1 | 116 |
| Current Assets | 1,190 | 1,080 | 1,191 | 961 | 903 | 867 | 896 | 1,019 | 835 | 848 |
| Total Assets | 2,727 | 2,479 | 2,638 | 2,363 | 2,307 | 2,233 | 2,268 | 2,489 | 1,401 | 1,388 |
| Current Liabilities | 539 | 447 | 1,203 | 400 | 526 | 359 | 560 | 1,179 | 370 | 273 |
| Long Term Debt | 1,060 | 791 | 131 | 669 | 690 | 1,007 | 939 | 417 | 3.83 | 4.34 |
| Common Equity | 617 | 873 | 915 | 910 | 743 | 575 | 524 | 631 | 858 | 945 |
| Total Capital | 1,677 | 1,665 | 1,047 | 1,579 | 1,433 | 1,582 | 1,508 | 1,152 | 895 | 1,084 |
| Capital Expenditures | 65.6 | 58.3 | 93.4 | 70.6 | 6.40 | 81.8 | 52.0 | 60.7 | 102 | 89.7 |
| Cash Flow | 330 | 316 | 285 | 287 | 259 | 260 | 239 | 192 | 218 | 253 |
| Current Ratio | 2.2 | 2.4 | 1.0 | 2.4 | 1.7 | 2.4 | 1.6 | 0.9 | 2.3 | 3.1 |
| % Long Term Debt of Capitalization | 63.2 | 47.5 | 12.5 | 42.4 | 48.2 | 63.7 | 62.3 | 36.2 | 0.4 | 0.4 |
| % Net Income of Revenue | 10.9 | 10.8 | 9.7 | 9.6 | 9.1 | 9.7 | 6.3 | 8.4 | 11.3 | 14.5 |
| % Return on Assets | 9.1 | 8.9 | 7.7 | 8.4 | 7.6 | 7.8 | 4.9 | 6.3 | 11.6 | 14.5 |
| % Return on Equity | 33.2 | 26.0 | 21.1 | 23.7 | 26.2 | 32.0 | 20.1 | 16.5 | 18.0 | 20.9 |

Data as orig reptd.; bef. results of disc opers/spec. items. Per share data adj. for stk. divs.; EPS diluted. E-Estimated. NA-Not Available. NM-Not Meaningful. NR-Not Ranked. UR-Under Review.

**Office:** 521 W 57th St, New York, NY 10019-2960.
**Telephone:** 212-765-5500.
**Email:** investor.relations@iff.com
**Website:** http://www.iff.com

**Chrmn & CEO:** R.M. Amen
**Pres:** B.M. Tansky
**SVP, Secy & General Counsel:** D.M. Meany
**CFO:** R.A. O'Leary

**Treas:** C.D. Weller
**Investor Contact:** Y. Rudich (212-708-7164)
**Board Members:** M. H. Adame, R. M. Amen, G. Blobel, M. Bottoli, L. B. Buck, J. M. Cook, P. A. Georgescu, A. A. Herzan, H. W. Howell, Jr., K. M. Hudson, A. C. Martinez, B. M. Tansky, D. D. Tough

**Founded:** 1909
**Domicile:** New York
**Employees:** 5,300

**STANDARD &POOR'S**

# International Game Technology

**S&P Recommendation** HOLD ★★★☆☆

| Price | 12-Mo. Target Price | Investment Style |
|---|---|---|
| $10.74 (as of Nov 14, 2008) | $14.00 | Large-Cap Growth |

**GICS Sector** Consumer Discretionary
**Sub-Industry** Casinos & Gaming

**Summary** This company is a leading maker of gaming machines and proprietary software systems for gaming machine networks.

## Key Stock Statistics (Source S&P, Vickers, company reports)

| | | | | | |
|---|---|---|---|---|---|
| 52-Wk Range | $49.41– 9.76 | S&P Oper. EPS 2009**E** | 1.27 | Market Capitalization(B) | $3.189 |
| Trailing 12-Month EPS | $1.10 | S&P Oper. EPS 2010**E** | NA | Yield (%) | 5.40 |
| Trailing 12-Month P/E | 9.8 | P/E on S&P Oper. EPS 2009**E** | 8.5 | Dividend Rate/Share | $0.58 |
| $10K Invested 5 Yrs Ago | $3,488 | Common Shares Outstg. (M) | 296.9 | Institutional Ownership (%) | 81 |

| | |
|---|---|
| Beta | 1.66 |
| S&P 3-Yr. Proj. EPS CAGR(%) | 7 |
| S&P Credit Rating | BBB |

## Price Performance

30-Week Mov. Avg. · · · · 10-Week Mov. Avg. - - - **GAAP Earnings vs. Previous Year** Volume Above Avg. ▮▮▮ STARS
12-Mo. Target Price — Relative Strength — ▲ Up ▼ Down ▶ No Change  Below Avg. ▮▮▮ ★

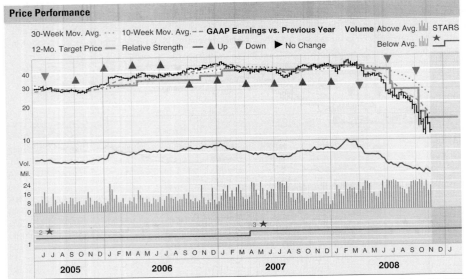

Options: ASE, CBOE

## Qualitative Risk Assessment

| LOW | MEDIUM | HIGH |
|---|---|---|

Our risk assessment reflects the company's industry-leading position as a supplier of gaming machines. We expect the company to generate free cash flow, with at least some of it used for stock repurchases. This is offset by our projection that IGT will continue to spend heavily on research and development and our view that growth prospects depend on regulatory factors and technology changes, including the legalization of gaming markets.

## Quantitative Evaluations

**S&P Quality Ranking**          B+

| D | C | B- | B | B+ | A- | A | A+ |
|---|---|---|---|---|---|---|---|

**Relative Strength Rank**          MODERATE

30

LOWEST = 1          HIGHEST = 99

## Highlights

▶ The 12-month target price for IGT has recently been changed to $14.00 from $16.00. The Highlights section of this Stock Report will be updated accordingly.

## Investment Rationale/Risk

▶ The Investment Rationale/Risk section of this Stock Report will be updated shortly. For the latest News story on IGT from MarketScope, see below.

▶ 10/30/08 02:24 pm ET ... S&P MAINTAINS HOLD RECOMMENDATION ON SHARES OF INTERNATIONAL GAME TECHOLOGY (IGT 12.3***): Adjusted Sep-Q EPS of $0.28 vs. $0.38 misses our estimate by $0.02 as gaming operations revenue and margins fell short of our projections. Against normal seasonality, play levels declined across all jurisdictions as consumers, particularly in Vegas, continued to pull back. Expenses rose, helping drive operating margins down 640 bps. While IGT has embarked on cost cuts and is revamping its product team, we think measures will take time, especially as its customers focus on preserving capital. We cut our FY 09 (Sep.) EPS estimate by $0.06 to $1.27 and target price by $2 to $14. /E.Kwon-CFA

## Revenue/Earnings Data

**Revenue (Million $)**

| | 1Q | 2Q | 3Q | 4Q | Year |
|---|---|---|---|---|---|
| 2008 | 645.8 | 573.2 | 677.4 | 632.2 | 2,529 |
| 2007 | 642.3 | 609.7 | 706.5 | 662.9 | 2,621 |
| 2006 | 616.2 | 644.4 | 612.4 | 638.7 | 2,512 |
| 2005 | 641.2 | 551.0 | 579.6 | 607.6 | 2,379 |
| 2004 | 608.1 | 636.1 | 618.9 | 621.7 | 2,485 |
| 2003 | 489.6 | 529.1 | 561.9 | 547.5 | 2,128 |

**Earnings Per Share ($)**

| | | | | | |
|---|---|---|---|---|---|
| 2008 | 0.36 | 0.22 | 0.35 | 0.18 | 1.10 |
| 2007 | 0.35 | 0.38 | 0.41 | 0.38 | 1.51 |
| 2006 | 0.34 | 0.35 | 0.33 | 0.33 | 1.34 |
| 2005 | 0.33 | 0.26 | 0.32 | 0.30 | 1.20 |
| 2004 | 0.33 | 0.32 | 0.38 | 0.15 | 1.18 |
| 2003 | 0.25 | 0.27 | 0.30 | 0.29 | 1.07 |

Fiscal year ended Sep. 30. Next earnings report expected: Mid January. EPS Estimates based on S&P Operating Earnings; historical GAAP earnings are as reported.

## Dividend Data (Dates: mm/dd Payment Date: mm/dd/yy)

| Amount ($) | Date Decl. | Ex-Div. Date | Stk. of Record | Payment Date |
|---|---|---|---|---|
| 0.140 | 12/10 | 12/20 | 12/24 | 01/07/08 |
| 0.140 | 02/26 | 03/17 | 03/19 | 04/02/08 |
| 0.140 | 05/19 | 06/09 | 06/11 | 07/01/08 |
| 0.145 | 08/19 | 09/09 | 09/11 | 10/02/08 |

Dividends have been paid since 2003. Source: Company reports.

# International Game Technology

**STANDARD &POOR'S**

## Business Summary October 08, 2008

CORPORATE OVERVIEW. International Game Technology (IGT) is a leading maker of gaming machines. In addition to selling machines, IGT's business includes the placement of machines from which it receives recurring revenues.

In FY 07 (Sep.), 48% of IGT revenues came from product sales compared to 50% in FY 06, and the remainder from gaming operations, including progressive systems.

Product sales in FY 07 included the sale of 105,900 machines, down from 112,000 machines in FY 06, and down from 141,900 in FY 05. FY 07 sales included 43,000 for North America vs. 51,100 and 50,500 in FY 06 and FY 05, respectively. Shipments to international markets totaled 62,900, up from 60,900 machines in FY 06 but down from 91,400 in FY 05. International sales may include some lower-priced machines with relatively low-value prizes. In addition to machines for casinos, IGT has made video gaming terminals (VGTs) for government-sponsored programs, including lotteries.

IGT's gaming operations segment includes the placement of games in both casinos and government-sponsored gaming markets, under a variety of recurring revenue pricing arrangements, including wide-area progressive systems, standalone participation and flat fee, equipment leasing and rental, as well as hybrid pricing or premium products that include a product sale and a recurring fee.

CORPORATE STRATEGY. In FY 07, IGT's research and development spending totaled $202.2 million (about 7.7% of revenues), up from $188.5 million (7.5%) in FY 06, and up from $138.4 million (5.8%) in FY 05. We expect that the company's ability to develop successful machines and games, with features that appeal to gamblers and casinos, will be a significant factor in the amount of product sales it has.

PRIMARY BUSINESS DYNAMICS. We see opportunities for IGT gaming machines including: racetracks in Indiana; a new opening in the Las Vegas locals market, East Side Cannery; the expansion of Native American casinos in California, Connecticut and Oklahoma; and, the continued build out in Pennsylvania. Longer term, resort openings in Las Vegas and Atlantic City, as well as Singapore, should also drive demand for slots.

Overall, during the next few years, we expect a shift toward sales or licensing of server-based games to become more evident, creating opportunities for increased IGT revenues from sales or licensing of replacement machines or games for use in such locations as U.S. casinos.

## Company Financials Fiscal Year Ended Sep. 30

| Per Share Data ($) | 2008 | 2007 | 2006 | 2005 | 2004 | 2003 | 2002 | 2001 | 2000 | 1999 |
|---|---|---|---|---|---|---|---|---|---|---|
| Tangible Book Value | NA | 0.29 | 2.06 | 1.56 | 1.98 | 1.42 | 0.55 | 0.40 | NM | 0.26 |
| Cash Flow | NA | 2.30 | 1.99 | 1.78 | 1.56 | 1.45 | 1.23 | 0.91 | 0.67 | 0.29 |
| Earnings | 1.10 | 1.51 | 1.34 | 1.20 | 1.18 | 1.07 | 0.80 | 0.70 | 0.50 | 0.16 |
| S&P Core Earnings | NA | 1.47 | 1.33 | 1.15 | 1.11 | 1.02 | 0.79 | 0.67 | NA | NA |
| Dividends | NA | 0.52 | 0.50 | 0.48 | 0.30 | 0.18 | Nil | Nil | Nil | 0.03 |
| Payout Ratio | NA | 34% | 37% | 40% | 25% | 16% | Nil | Nil | Nil | 18% |
| Prices:High | NA | 48.79 | 46.76 | 34.63 | 47.12 | 37.00 | 20.03 | 17.99 | 12.34 | 6.03 |
| Prices:Low | NA | 33.57 | 30.12 | 24.20 | 28.22 | 18.05 | 11.94 | 8.93 | 4.36 | 3.53 |
| P/E Ratio:High | NA | 32 | 35 | 29 | 40 | 35 | 25 | 26 | 25 | 37 |
| P/E Ratio:Low | NA | 22 | 22 | 20 | 24 | 17 | 15 | 13 | 9 | 22 |

### Income Statement Analysis (Million $)

| | 2008 | 2007 | 2006 | 2005 | 2004 | 2003 | 2002 | 2001 | 2000 | 1999 |
|---|---|---|---|---|---|---|---|---|---|---|
| Revenue | 2,529 | 2,621 | 2,512 | 2,379 | 2,485 | 2,128 | 1,848 | 1,199 | 1,004 | 930 |
| Operating Income | NA | 1,066 | 960 | 886 | 964 | 800 | 646 | 315 | 343 | 267 |
| Depreciation | 276 | 266 | 235 | 222 | 150 | 134 | 146 | 63.3 | 54.4 | 52.3 |
| Interest Expense | NA | 77.6 | 50.8 | 58.1 | 90.5 | 117 | 117 | 102 | 102 | 72.8 |
| Pretax Income | 591 | 805 | 747 | 681 | 653 | 599 | 110 | 339 | 245 | 101 |
| Effective Tax Rate | 42.0% | 36.9% | 36.6% | 35.9% | 34.2% | 37.3% | NM | 37.0% | 36.0% | 35.6% |
| Net Income | 343 | 508 | 474 | 437 | 430 | 375 | 277 | 214 | 157 | 65.3 |
| S&P Core Earnings | NA | 493 | 470 | 415 | 405 | 357 | 273 | 204 | NA | NA |

### Balance Sheet & Other Financial Data (Million $)

| | 2008 | 2007 | 2006 | 2005 | 2004 | 2003 | 2002 | 2001 | 2000 | 1999 |
|---|---|---|---|---|---|---|---|---|---|---|
| Cash | 266 | 261 | 295 | 289 | 765 | 1,316 | 424 | 364 | 245 | 426 |
| Current Assets | NA | 1,287 | 1,376 | 1,437 | 1,510 | 2,078 | 1,195 | 968 | 814 | 975 |
| Total Assets | 4,557 | 4,168 | 3,903 | 3,864 | 3,873 | 4,185 | 3,316 | 1,923 | 1,624 | 1,765 |
| Current Liabilities | NA | 692 | 1,247 | 1,218 | 560 | 945 | 511 | 371 | 259 | 213 |
| Long Term Debt | NA | 1,503 | 200 | 200 | 792 | 1,146 | 971 | 985 | 992 | 990 |
| Common Equity | 909 | 1,453 | 2,042 | 1,906 | 1,977 | 1,687 | 1,433 | 296 | 96.6 | 242 |
| Total Capital | NA | 2,956 | 2,242 | 2,106 | 2,768 | 2,833 | 2,413 | 1,281 | 1,088 | 1,233 |
| Capital Expenditures | 298 | 344 | 311 | 239 | 211 | 30.8 | 33.8 | 34.7 | 18.5 | 17.8 |
| Cash Flow | NA | 774 | 709 | 659 | 580 | 509 | 423 | 277 | 211 | 118 |
| Current Ratio | 2.0 | 1.9 | 1.1 | 1.2 | 2.7 | 2.2 | 2.3 | 2.6 | 3.1 | 4.6 |
| % Long Term Debt of Capitalization | 70.8 | 50.9 | 8.9 | 9.5 | 28.6 | 40.4 | 40.3 | 76.9 | 91.1 | 80.3 |
| % Net Income of Revenue | 13.6 | 19.4 | 18.9 | 18.3 | 17.3 | 17.6 | 15.0 | 17.8 | 15.6 | 7.0 |
| % Return on Assets | 7.9 | 12.6 | 12.2 | 11.3 | 10.7 | 10.0 | 10.6 | 12.1 | 9.3 | 3.9 |
| % Return on Equity | 29.0 | 29.1 | 24.0 | 22.5 | 23.5 | 24.1 | 32.0 | 109.0 | 92.6 | 16.7 |

Data as orig reptd.; bef. results of disc opers/spec. items. Per share data adj. for stk. divs.; EPS diluted. E-Estimated. NA-Not Available. NM-Not Meaningful. NR-Not Ranked. UR-Under Review.

**Office:** 9295 Prototype Drive, Reno, NV 89521.
**Telephone:** 775-448-7777.
**Website:** http://www.igt.com
**Chrmn, Pres & CEO:** T.J. Matthews

**EVP, Secy & General Counsel:** D.D. Johnson
**CFO, Chief Acctg Officer & Treas:** D.R. Siciliano
**Treas:** L. Rosenthal
**Investor Contact:** P. Cavanaugh (866-296-4232)

**Board Members:** R. A. Bittman, R. R. Burt, P. S. Hart, R. A. Mathewson, T. J. Matthews, R. J. Miller, F. B. Rentschler
**Founded:** 1980
**Domicile:** Nevada
**Employees:** 5,400

**STANDARD &POOR'S**

# International Paper Co

**S&P Recommendation** BUY ★★★★☆

| Price | 12-Mo. Target Price | Investment Style |
|---|---|---|
| $12.52 (as of Nov 14, 2008) | $22.00 | Large-Cap Value |

**GICS Sector** Materials
**Sub-Industry** Paper Products

**Summary** This company is a leading worldwide producer and distributor of printing papers and packaging products.

## Key Stock Statistics (Source S&P, Vickers, company reports)

| | | | | | | |
|---|---|---|---|---|---|---|
| 52-Wk Range | $34.75–11.24 | S&P Oper. EPS 2008**E** | 2.15 | Market Capitalization(B) | $5.353 | Beta | 1.28 |
| Trailing 12-Month EPS | $1.97 | S&P Oper. EPS 2009**E** | 1.80 | Yield (%) | 7.99 | S&P 3-Yr. Proj. EPS CAGR(%) | 2 |
| Trailing 12-Month P/E | 6.4 | P/E on S&P Oper. EPS 2008**E** | 5.8 | Dividend Rate/Share | $1.00 | S&P Credit Rating | BBB |
| $10K Invested 5 Yrs Ago | $3,942 | Common Shares Outstg. (M) | 427.5 | Institutional Ownership (%) | 92 | | |

## Price Performance

30-Week Mov. Avg. · · · 10-Week Mov. Avg. – – GAAP Earnings vs. Previous Year  Volume Above Avg. STARS
12-Mo. Target Price — Relative Strength — ▲ Up ▼ Down ► No Change  Below Avg.

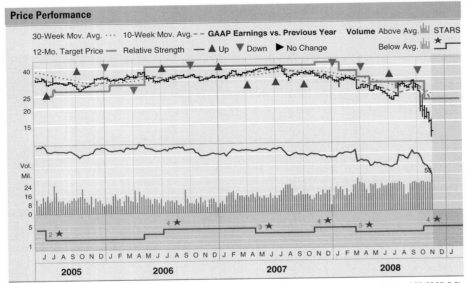

Options: ASE, CBOE, P, Ph

Analysis prepared by **Stuart J. Benway, CFA** on November 04, 2008, when the stock traded at **$ 17.06**.

## Highlights

➤ We expect sales in 2008 to rise 15%-20%, primarily due to the acquisition of a major corrugated packaging business. However, we also forecast higher prices for paper and packaging and expanded volume in the distribution business. Further gains should come from an increasing contribution from overseas units. In 2009, the addition of the packaging business should add about 10%-12% to revenue growth, but we are concerned about economic weakness hurting demand.

➤ We expect operating margins from continuing operations to decline moderately in 2008. This projected narrowing should result from sharply higher input costs including energy, wood fiber, and chemicals. Partially offsetting this, in our view, will be continuing cost-reductions from a program that targeted $400 million of savings in 2007. We think that price increases will also help margins, but interest expense is expected to rise significantly. We see further margin erosion in 2009.

➤ We see operating EPS of $2.15 for 2008, a slight decrease from $2.22 in 2007, and for 2009 we see a moderate decline to $1.80.

## Investment Rationale/Risk

➤ We believe that IP's restructuring moves have allowed it to strengthen its balance sheet, invest in faster-growing regions, and repurchase shares. The company has investments and joint ventures in Brazil, China, and Russia that will begin to contribute meaningfully to earnings growth in 2008, in our opinion. Although, we are concerned about rapidly rising input costs and a weakening domestic economy, we think the shares are undervalued at recent levels.

➤ Risks to our recommendation and target price include sharply reduced economic strength, worse-than-projected demand and pricing trends for uncoated paper and packaging, and the failure of new ventures to achieve targeted returns.

➤ Our discounted cash flow model, which assumes a 7.3% weighted average cost of capital, strong free cash flow generation in 2010, and a 2.5% terminal growth rate, calculates intrinsic value of $28. Applying a peer forward P/E of 7.6X to our 2009 EPS estimate, we derive a value of $14. Our 12-month target price of $22 is a weighted blend of these two measures.

## Qualitative Risk Assessment

| LOW | MEDIUM | HIGH |
|---|---|---|

IP operates in a cyclical and capital-intensive industry and is affected by changes in industrial production, interest rates, and economic growth. However, this is offset as it is one of the largest companies in the sector, and has greater economies of scale than many of its competitors.

## Quantitative Evaluations

**S&P Quality Ranking** B+

| D | C | B- | B | B+ | A- | A | A+ |
|---|---|---|---|---|---|---|---|

**Relative Strength Rank** WEAK

22

LOWEST = 1    HIGHEST = 99

## Revenue/Earnings Data

**Revenue (Million $)**

| | 1Q | 2Q | 3Q | 4Q | Year |
|---|---|---|---|---|---|
| 2008 | 5,668 | 5,807 | 6,808 | -- | -- |
| 2007 | 5,217 | 5,291 | 5,541 | 5,841 | 21,890 |
| 2006 | 5,668 | 6,270 | 5,867 | 5,324 | 21,995 |
| 2005 | 6,011 | 5,916 | 6,036 | 6,134 | 24,097 |
| 2004 | 6,138 | 6,229 | 6,578 | 6,603 | 25,548 |
| 2003 | 6,075 | 6,264 | 6,373 | 6,500 | 25,179 |

**Earnings Per Share ($)**

| | | | | | |
|---|---|---|---|---|---|
| 2008 | 0.35 | 0.54 | 0.35 | E0.34 | E2.15 |
| 2007 | 1.02 | 0.46 | 0.52 | 0.80 | 2.81 |
| 2006 | 0.14 | 0.24 | 0.23 | 4.53 | 2.65 |
| 2005 | 0.22 | 0.19 | 1.48 | -0.17 | 1.74 |
| 2004 | 0.10 | 0.13 | 0.42 | 0.32 | 0.98 |
| 2003 | 0.11 | 0.19 | 0.25 | 0.11 | 0.66 |

Fiscal year ended Dec. 31. Next earnings report expected: Mid February. EPS Estimates based on S&P Operating Earnings; historical GAAP earnings are as reported.

## Dividend Data (Dates: mm/dd Payment Date: mm/dd/yy)

| Amount ($) | Date Decl. | Ex-Div. Date | Stk. of Record | Payment Date |
|---|---|---|---|---|
| 0.250 | 01/08 | 02/13 | 02/15 | 03/14/08 |
| 0.250 | 05/12 | 05/21 | 05/23 | 06/16/08 |
| 0.250 | 07/08 | 08/14 | 08/18 | 09/15/08 |
| 0.250 | 10/14 | 11/13 | 11/17 | 12/15/08 |

Dividends have been paid since 1946. Source: Company reports.

---

**Please read the Required Disclosures and Analyst Certification on the last page of this report.**

The **McGraw-Hill** Companies

# International Paper Co

STANDARD
&POOR'S

## Business Summary November 04, 2008

CORPORATE OVERVIEW. International Paper is the world's largest paper and forest products company. According to Pulp & Paper magazine, its market share is about 25% in uncoated free sheet (UFS), used in copiers and for envelopes and forms, giving it the number-two position in that major category. It is the third-largest linerboard producer, used to make corrugated boxes, with nearly 14% of the market. It also manufactures bleached paperboard used to package cosmetics, food, beverages, and pharmaceuticals, and is the second-largest boxboard producer in the U.S., with a share of 11%.

IMPACT OF MAJOR DEVELOPMENTS. On March 17, 2008, International Paper agreed to acquire the corrugated packaging business of Weyerhaeuser for $6 billion in cash and closed the deal on August 4, 2008. Because the transaction is a purchase of assets rather than stock, IP said that it would realize a tax benefit with a net present value of approximately $1.4 billion. This business had sales in 2007 of $5.2 billion and EBITDA of $670 million. IP expects to generate $400 million of synergies on an annual basis after three years with $175 million coming in the first year. This savings are expected to come from reduced overhead, improved logistics, greater efficiency, and better customer mix. The deal gives IP just under a 30% share of the North American corrugated packaging market. We think the move is a good strategic fit for IP, but we are concerned about the near-term earnings dilution and potential economic weakness that appears to be spreading in the domestic economy.

MARKET PROFILE. IP operates in a highly cyclical and capital-intensive industry. Demand for the company's products are dependent on a number of factors, including industrial non-durable goods production, consumer spending, commercial printing and advertising activity, white collar employment levels, and movements in currency exchange rates. Historical prices for paper and wood products have been volatile, and, despite its size, IP has had only a limited direct influence over the timing and extent of price changes for its products. Pricing is significantly affected by the relationship between supply and demand, and supply is mainly influenced by fluctuations in available manufacturing capacity. Technology seems to be having an impact on paper demand, especially in UFS, IP's largest category, where demand has grown more slowly than the economy in recent years. We doubt the trend is likely to improve, as industry forecaster Resource Information Systems Inc. (RISI) projects that demand for UFS will grow at less than a 0.5% compound annual growth rate (CAGR) through 2009.

## Company Financials Fiscal Year Ended Dec. 31

| Per Share Data ($) | 2007 | 2006 | 2005 | 2004 | 2003 | 2002 | 2001 | 2000 | 1999 | 1998 |
|---|---|---|---|---|---|---|---|---|---|---|
| Tangible Book Value | 14.08 | 11.10 | 6.75 | 6.69 | 6.01 | 4.31 | 7.78 | 11.89 | 18.65 | 20.45 |
| Cash Flow | 5.31 | 4.99 | 4.38 | 4.19 | 4.07 | 3.90 | 1.51 | 4.28 | 4.16 | 4.65 |
| Earnings | 2.81 | 2.65 | 1.74 | 0.98 | 0.66 | 0.61 | -2.37 | 0.82 | 0.48 | 0.77 |
| S&P Core Earnings | 2.45 | 1.13 | 1.67 | 0.84 | 0.51 | 0.92 | -2.25 | NA | NA | NA |
| Dividends | 1.00 | 1.00 | 1.00 | 1.00 | 1.00 | 1.00 | 1.00 | 1.00 | 1.00 | 1.00 |
| Payout Ratio | 36% | 38% | 57% | 102% | 152% | 164% | NM | 122% | NM | 130% |
| Prices:High | 41.57 | 37.98 | 42.59 | 45.01 | 43.32 | 46.20 | 43.31 | 60.00 | 59.50 | 55.25 |
| Prices:Low | 31.05 | 30.69 | 26.97 | 37.12 | 33.09 | 31.35 | 30.70 | 26.31 | 39.50 | 35.50 |
| P/E Ratio:High | 15 | 14 | 24 | 46 | 66 | 76 | NM | 73 | NM | 72 |
| P/E Ratio:Low | 11 | 12 | 15 | 38 | 50 | 51 | NM | 32 | NM | 46 |

| Income Statement Analysis (Million $) | 2007 | 2006 | 2005 | 2004 | 2003 | 2002 | 2001 | 2000 | 1999 | 1998 |
|---|---|---|---|---|---|---|---|---|---|---|
| Revenue | 21,890 | 21,995 | 24,097 | 25,548 | 25,179 | 24,976 | 26,363 | 28,180 | 24,573 | 19,541 |
| Operating Income | 2,796 | 2,609 | 3,228 | 3,251 | 3,293 | 3,576 | 3,305 | 5,432 | 3,061 | 2,202 |
| Depreciation | 1,086 | 1,158 | 1,376 | 1,565 | 1,644 | 1,587 | 1,870 | 1,916 | 1,520 | 1,186 |
| Interest Expense | 483 | 651 | 593 | 743 | 766 | 783 | 929 | 791 | 541 | 496 |
| Pretax Income | 1,654 | 3,188 | 586 | 746 | 346 | 371 | -1,265 | 497 | 448 | 392 |
| Effective Tax Rate | 25.1% | 59.3% | NM | 27.6% | NM | NM | NM | 23.5% | 19.2% | 20.4% |
| Net Income | 1,215 | 1,282 | 859 | 478 | 315 | 295 | -1,142 | 142 | 199 | 236 |
| S&P Core Earnings | 1,058 | 539 | 819 | 402 | 242 | 444 | -1,091 | NA | NA | NA |

| Balance Sheet & Other Financial Data (Million $) | 2007 | 2006 | 2005 | 2004 | 2003 | 2002 | 2001 | 2000 | 1999 | 1998 |
|---|---|---|---|---|---|---|---|---|---|---|
| Cash | 905 | 1,624 | 1,641 | 2,596 | 2,363 | 1,074 | 1,224 | 1,198 | 453 | 477 |
| Current Assets | 6,735 | 8,637 | 7,409 | 9,319 | 9,337 | 7,738 | 8,312 | 10,455 | 7,241 | 6,010 |
| Total Assets | 24,159 | 24,034 | 28,771 | 34,217 | 35,525 | 33,792 | 37,158 | 42,109 | 30,268 | 26,356 |
| Current Liabilities | 3,842 | 4,641 | 4,844 | 4,872 | 6,803 | 4,579 | 5,374 | 7,413 | 4,382 | 3,636 |
| Long Term Debt | 6,620 | 6,531 | 11,023 | 14,132 | 13,450 | 13,042 | 14,262 | 14,453 | 9,325 | 8,212 |
| Common Equity | 8,672 | 10,839 | 8,351 | 8,254 | 8,237 | 7,374 | 10,291 | 12,034 | 10,304 | 8,902 |
| Total Capital | 18,172 | 19,816 | 20,311 | 25,631 | 25,085 | 25,435 | 29,804 | 32,541 | 24,554 | 21,582 |
| Capital Expenditures | 1,288 | 1,009 | 1,155 | 1,262 | 1,166 | 1,009 | 1,049 | 1,352 | 1,139 | 1,049 |
| Cash Flow | 2,301 | 2,440 | 2,235 | 2,043 | 1,959 | 1,882 | 728 | 2,058 | 1,719 | 1,422 |
| Current Ratio | 1.8 | 1.9 | 1.5 | 1.9 | 1.4 | 1.7 | 1.5 | 1.4 | 1.7 | 1.7 |
| % Long Term Debt of Capitalization | 41.7 | 33.0 | 54.3 | 55.1 | 53.6 | 51.3 | 47.9 | 44.4 | 38.0 | 38.1 |
| % Net Income of Revenue | 5.6 | 5.8 | 3.6 | 1.9 | 1.3 | 1.2 | NM | 0.5 | 0.8 | 1.2 |
| % Return on Assets | 5.0 | 4.9 | 2.7 | 1.4 | 0.9 | 0.8 | NM | 0.4 | 0.6 | 0.9 |
| % Return on Equity | 14.6 | 13.4 | 10.3 | 5.8 | 4.0 | 3.3 | NM | 1.3 | 1.9 | 2.7 |

Data as orig reptd.; bef. results of disc opers/spec. items. Per share data adj. for stk. divs.; EPS diluted. E-Estimated. NA-Not Available. NM-Not Meaningful. NR-Not Ranked. UR-Under Review.

**Office:** 6400 Poplar Ave, Memphis, TN 38197-0198.
**Telephone:** 901-419-7000.
**Email:** comm@ipaper.com
**Website:** http://www.internationalpaper.com

**Chrmn & CEO:** J.V. Faraci
**EVP & CTO:** N.A. Lesko
**SVP & CFO:** T.S. Nicholls
**SVP, Secy & General Counsel:** M.A. Smith

**SVP & CIO:** J.N. Balboni
**Investor Contact:** T.A. Cleves (901-419-7566)
**Board Members:** D. J. Bronczek, M. F. Brooks, L. L. Elsenhans, J. V. Faraci, S. G. Gibara, D. McHenry, S. J. Mobley, J. L. Townsend, III, J. F. Turner, W. G. Walter, A. Weisser, J. S. Whisler

**Founded:** 1898
**Domicile:** New York
**Employees:** 51,500

STANDARD
&POOR'S

# Interpublic Group of Companies Inc. (The)

| S&P Recommendation BUY ★★★★☆ | Price $3.90 (as of Nov 14, 2008) | 12-Mo. Target Price $8.00 | Investment Style Large-Cap Blend |
|---|---|---|---|

**GICS Sector** Consumer Discretionary
**Sub-Industry** Advertising

**Summary** Interpublic is one of the world's largest organizations of advertising agencies and marketing communications companies.

## Key Stock Statistics (Source S&P, Vickers, company reports)

| | | | | | | |
|---|---|---|---|---|---|---|
| 52-Wk Range | $10.47 – 3.48 | S&P Oper. EPS 2008**E** | 0.43 | Market Capitalization(B) | $1.859 | Beta | 1.17 |
| Trailing 12-Month EPS | $0.42 | S&P Oper. EPS 2009**E** | 0.50 | Yield (%) | Nil | S&P 3-Yr. Proj. EPS CAGR(%) | 26 |
| Trailing 12-Month P/E | 9.3 | P/E on S&P Oper. EPS 2008**E** | 9.1 | Dividend Rate/Share | Nil | S&P Credit Rating | B+ |
| $10K Invested 5 Yrs Ago | $2,591 | Common Shares Outstg. (M) | 476.5 | Institutional Ownership (%) | NM | | |

## Price Performance

30-Week Mov. Avg. · · · · 10-Week Mov. Avg. - - - GAAP Earnings vs. Previous Year   Volume Above Avg. ▮▮▮ STARS
12-Mo. Target Price —  Relative Strength — ▲ Up ▼ Down ► No Change   Below Avg. ▮▮▮ ★

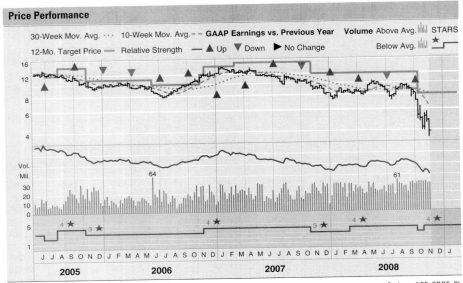

Options: ASE, CBOE, Ph

Analysis prepared by **Mark S. Basham** on November 07, 2008, when the stock traded at **$ 4.86**.

### Qualitative Risk Assessment

| LOW | MEDIUM | HIGH |
|---|---|---|

Our risk assessment reflects our view of a highly competitive advertising industry, and economic cyclicality associated with advertising spending, offset by what we see as a conservative balance sheet structure and an improving profitability outlook for IPG.

### Quantitative Evaluations

**S&P Quality Ranking**   C

| D | C | B- | B | B+ | A- | A | A+ |
|---|---|---|---|---|---|---|---|

**Relative Strength Rank**   WEAK

23

LOWEST = 1   HIGHEST = 99

### Revenue/Earnings Data

**Revenue (Million $)**

| | 1Q | 2Q | 3Q | 4Q | Year |
|---|---|---|---|---|---|
| 2008 | 1,485 | 1,836 | 1,740 | -- | -- |
| 2007 | 1,359 | 1,653 | 1,560 | 1,983 | 6,554 |
| 2006 | 1,327 | 1,533 | 1,454 | 1,877 | 6,191 |
| 2005 | 1,328 | 1,611 | 1,440 | 1,896 | 6,274 |
| 2004 | 1,389 | 1,513 | 1,519 | 1,966 | 6,387 |
| 2003 | 1,316 | 1,499 | 1,419 | 1,629 | 5,863 |

**Earnings Per Share ($)**

| | | | | | |
|---|---|---|---|---|---|
| 2008 | -0.15 | 0.17 | 0.08 | E0.32 | E0.43 |
| 2007 | -0.29 | 0.24 | -0.06 | 0.31 | 0.26 |
| 2006 | -0.43 | 0.09 | -0.03 | 0.11 | -0.20 |
| 2005 | -0.36 | 0.01 | -0.25 | -0.10 | -0.70 |
| 2004 | -0.21 | -0.23 | -1.22 | 0.22 | -1.36 |
| 2003 | -0.03 | -0.06 | -1.08 | -0.26 | -1.43 |

Fiscal year ended Dec. 31. Next earnings report expected: Early March. EPS Estimates based on S&P Operating Earnings; historical GAAP earnings are as reported.

### Dividend Data

No cash dividends have been paid since 2002.

## Highlights

➤ We see revenues rising 7.7% in 2008, with a further projected advance of about 3.9% in 2009. We think organic revenue growth will slow as 2009 progresses, given our outlook for recessionary conditions in the U.S. We no longer expect IPG to benefit from a weak U.S. dollar in 2009, compared to an estimated positive effect of 2.4% on revenues in 2008. We believe IPG may selectively pursue acquisitions in 2009, although tight credit conditions and market uncertainty could deter M&A.

➤ We anticipate IPG's operating margin will rise to 8.9% in 2008 from 5.7% in 2007. We see higher revenues leading to fixed cost leverage, with cost reductions enacted by IPG at recent acquisitions benefiting margins, as well. However, in 2009, we expect margins will dip to a still relatively healthy 8.2%, as costs grow faster than revenues. We also expect margins to benefit from a decline in Sarbanes-Oxley compliance related professional fees in 2008 and 2009.

➤ We forecast EPS of $0.43 in 2008, rising to $0.50 in 2009 on a reduction in the effective tax rate from 45% to 40%.

## Investment Rationale/Risk

➤ Following expected strong revenue growth in 2008, we think revenue growth momentum will moderate in 2009 on recessionary conditions in the U.S. This reflects IPG's comments in late October that the global financial situation had begun to weigh on marketers' spending plans. Likely mitigating the effects of the economic slowdown, in our view, is that IPG has gained market share in 2008 on the strength of several recent new business wins. In international markets, we expect continued revenue and market share gains in 2009, though at a more moderate pace given the deteriorating economic environment in Europe and slowing elsewhere.

➤ Risks to our recommendation and target price include significant business losses, adverse accounting-related developments, a significant U.S. recession, and higher-than-expected severance expenses or professional fees.

➤ Our 12-month target price of $8 is derived by applying a discount-to-peer-average enterprise value/EBITDA multiple of 7.5X to our 2009 EBITDA estimate of approximately $800 million. We believe a discount is warranted to reflect IPG's historical lower-than-peer level of profitability.

# Interpublic Group of Companies Inc. (The)

STANDARD &POOR'S

## Business Summary November 07, 2008

CORPORATE OVERVIEW. The Interpublic Group of Companies, along with its subsidiaries, is one of the world's largest advertising and marketing services companies, made up of communication agencies around the world that deliver custom marketing solutions to clients. These agencies cover the spectrum of marketing disciplines and specialties, from traditional services such as consumer advertising and direct marketing, to emerging services such as mobile and search engine marketing.

The company generates revenue from planning, creating and placing advertising in various media and from planning and executing other communications or marketing programs. IPG also receives commissions from clients for planning and supervising work done by outside contractors in the physical preparation of finished print advertisements and the production of TV and radio commercials and other forms of advertising. In addition, IPG derives revenue in a number of other ways, including the planning and placement in media of advertising produced by unrelated advertising agencies, the creation and publication of brochures, billboards, point of sale materials and direct marketing pieces for clients, the planning and carrying out of specialized marketing research, public relations campaigns, and creating and managing special events at which client products are featured.

IPG has two reportable segments: the Integrated Agency Network (IAN), comprised of Draftfcb, Lowe, McCann, media agencies and other standalone agencies, and the Constituent Management Group (CMG), which is made up of the bulk of IPG's specialist marketing service offerings. Draftfcb was formed from the merger of two IPG companies in 2006, and is focused on consumer advertising and behavioral, data-driven direct marketing. Lowe is a creative advertising agency operating in the world's largest advertising markets. McCann is a marketing communications company that consists of McCann Erickson Advertising, MRM Worldwide for relationship marketing and digital expertise, Momentum Worldwide for experiential marketing, and McCann Healthcare for health care communications, as well as various other brands. Interpublic also has two leading media specialists, Initiative (which was aligned with Draftfcb in 2006) and Universal McCann (aligned with McCann Erickson). The company maintains separate brands in competing disciplines in order to serve a broad range of clients.

## Company Financials Fiscal Year Ended Dec. 31

| Per Share Data ($) | 2007 | 2006 | 2005 | 2004 | 2003 | 2002 | 2001 | 2000 | 1999 | 1998 |
|---|---|---|---|---|---|---|---|---|---|---|
| Tangible Book Value | NM | NM | NM | NM | NM | NM | NM | NM | NM | NM |
| Cash Flow | 0.63 | 0.21 | -0.30 | -0.91 | -0.90 | 0.83 | -0.36 | 1.99 | 1.77 | 1.67 |
| Earnings | 0.26 | -0.20 | -0.70 | -1.36 | -1.43 | 0.26 | -1.37 | 1.15 | 1.11 | 1.11 |
| S&P Core Earnings | 0.29 | -0.18 | -0.62 | -0.82 | -0.84 | 0.36 | -0.60 | NA | NA | NA |
| Dividends | Nil | Nil | Nil | Nil | Nil | 0.38 | 0.38 | 0.37 | 0.33 | 0.29 |
| Payout Ratio | Nil | Nil | Nil | Nil | Nil | 146% | NM | 32% | 30% | 26% |
| Prices:High | 13.94 | 12.83 | 13.80 | 17.31 | 16.50 | 34.98 | 47.44 | 57.69 | 58.38 | 40.31 |
| Prices:Low | 7.91 | 7.79 | 9.08 | 10.47 | 7.20 | 9.85 | 18.25 | 32.69 | 34.41 | 22.56 |
| P/E Ratio:High | 54 | NM | NM | NM | NM | NM | NM | 50 | 53 | 36 |
| P/E Ratio:Low | 30 | NM | NM | NM | NM | NM | NM | 28 | 31 | 20 |

### Income Statement Analysis (Million $)

| | 2007 | 2006 | 2005 | 2004 | 2003 | 2002 | 2001 | 2000 | 1999 | 1998 |
|---|---|---|---|---|---|---|---|---|---|---|
| Revenue | 6,554 | 6,191 | 6,274 | 6,387 | 5,863 | 6,204 | 6,727 | 5,626 | 4,427 | 3,844 |
| Operating Income | 547 | 341 | 156 | 589 | 719 | 762 | 1,113 | 1,096 | 791 | 656 |
| Depreciation | 177 | 174 | 169 | 185 | 204 | 218 | 372 | 263 | 190 | 159 |
| Interest Expense | 237 | 219 | 182 | 172 | 173 | 146 | 165 | 109 | 66.4 | 58.7 |
| Pretax Income | 243 | 2.00 | -173 | -261 | -330 | 271 | -519 | 672 | 592 | 570 |
| Effective Tax Rate | 24.2% | NM | NM | NM | NM | 51.8% | NM | 40.7% | 39.9% | 40.7% |
| Net Income | 168 | -36.7 | -272 | -545 | -553 | 99.5 | -505 | 359 | 322 | 310 |
| S&P Core Earnings | 150 | -75.8 | -265 | -363 | -325 | 136 | -217 | NA | NA | NA |

### Balance Sheet & Other Financial Data (Million $)

| | 2007 | 2006 | 2005 | 2004 | 2003 | 2002 | 2001 | 2000 | 1999 | 1998 |
|---|---|---|---|---|---|---|---|---|---|---|
| Cash | 2,083 | 1,957 | 2,192 | 1,970 | 2,006 | 933 | 935 | 748 | 1,018 | 841 |
| Current Assets | 7,686 | 7,209 | 7,497 | 7,637 | 7,350 | 6,322 | 6,467 | 6,026 | 5,768 | 4,777 |
| Total Assets | 12,458 | 11,864 | 11,945 | 12,272 | 12,235 | 11,794 | 11,515 | 10,238 | 8,727 | 6,943 |
| Current Liabilities | 7,121 | 6,663 | 6,857 | 7,563 | 6,625 | 7,090 | 6,434 | 6,106 | 5,637 | 4,658 |
| Long Term Debt | 2,044 | 2,249 | 2,183 | Nil | 2,192 | 1,818 | 2,481 | 1,505 | 867 | 507 |
| Common Equity | 1,807 | 1,416 | 1,047 | 1,345 | 2,721 | 2,100 | 2,384 | 2,046 | 2,407 | 1,265 |
| Total Capital | 4,376 | 4,236 | 4,178 | 1,773 | 5,356 | 3,988 | 4,953 | 3,637 | 3,394 | 1,828 |
| Capital Expenditures | 148 | 128 | 141 | 194 | 160 | 183 | 268 | 202 | 150 | 137 |
| Cash Flow | 317 | 89.3 | -129 | -380 | -349 | 317 | -133 | 622 | 512 | 469 |
| Current Ratio | 1.1 | 1.1 | 1.1 | 1.0 | 1.1 | 0.9 | 1.0 | 1.0 | 1.0 | 1.0 |
| % Long Term Debt of Capitalization | 46.7 | 53.1 | 52.3 | Nil | 40.9 | 45.6 | 50.1 | 41.4 | 25.5 | 27.7 |
| % Net Income of Revenue | 2.6 | NM | NM | NM | NM | 1.6 | NM | 6.4 | 7.3 | 8.1 |
| % Return on Assets | 1.4 | NM | NM | NM | NM | 0.9 | NM | 3.7 | 4.1 | 4.9 |
| % Return on Equity | 10.4 | NM | NM | NM | NM | 5.1 | NM | 18.8 | 14.7 | 23.7 |

Data as orig reptd.; bef. results of disc opers/spec. items. Per share data adj. for stk. divs.; EPS diluted. E-Estimated. NA-Not Available. NM-Not Meaningful. NR-Not Ranked. UR-Under Review.

**Office:** 1114 Avenue Of The Americas, New York, NY 10035.
**Telephone:** 212-704-1200.
**Website:** http://www.interpublic.com
**Chrmn, Pres & CEO:** M.I. Roth

**EVP & CFO:** F. Mergenthaler
**SVP, Chief Acctg Officer & Cntlr:** C.F. Carroll
**SVP & Treas:** E.T. Johnson
**SVP, Secy & General Counsel:** N.J. Camera

**Investor Contact:** J. Leshne (212-704-1439)
**Board Members:** F. J. Borelli, R. K. Brack, Jr., J. Carter-Miller, J. M. Considine, R. A. Goldstein, H. J. Greeniaus, M. J. Guilfoile, W. T. Kerr, M. I. Roth, D. M. Thomas

**Founded:** 1902
**Domicile:** Delaware
**Employees:** 43,000

**STANDARD &POOR'S**

# Intuitive Surgical Inc

| | | |
|---|---|---|
| **S&P Recommendation** HOLD ★★★☆☆ | **Price** $148.41 (as of Nov 14, 2008) | **12-Mo. Target Price** $234.00 |

**Investment Style**
Large-Cap Blend

**GICS Sector** Health Care
**Sub-Industry** Health Care Equipment

**Summary** This company has developed the da Vinci Surgical System, which uses advanced robotics and computerized visualization technology for minimally invasive surgeries.

## Key Stock Statistics (Source S&P, Vickers, company reports)

| | | | | | | | |
|---|---|---|---|---|---|---|---|
| 52-Wk Range | $359.59–144.31 | S&P Oper. EPS 2008**E** | 5.30 | Market Capitalization(B) | $5.805 | Beta | 1.25 |
| Trailing 12-Month EPS | $5.08 | S&P Oper. EPS 2009**E** | 6.40 | Yield (%) | Nil | S&P 3-Yr. Proj. EPS CAGR(%) | 25 |
| Trailing 12-Month P/E | 29.2 | P/E on S&P Oper. EPS 2008**E** | 28.0 | Dividend Rate/Share | Nil | S&P Credit Rating | NA |
| $10K Invested 5 Yrs Ago | $103,278 | Common Shares Outstg. (M) | 39.1 | Institutional Ownership (%) | 85 | | |

## Price Performance

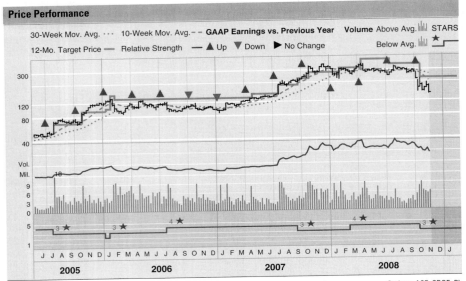

30-Week Mov. Avg. · · · 10-Week Mov. Avg. – – GAAP Earnings vs. Previous Year  Volume Above Avg. ▥ STARS
12-Mo. Target Price — Relative Strength  ▲ Up ▼ Down ► No Change   Below Avg. ▥  ★

Options: ASE, CBOE, Ph

Analysis prepared by **Robert M. Gold** on October 17, 2008, when the stock traded at **$ 193.09**.

## Highlights

➤ Our 2008 sales forecast is $901 million, including instrument/accessory revenues of $298 million, systems sales of $472 million and service/training revenues of $131 million. We think total procedures will approximate 133,500 in 2008, representing 57% growth versus 2007. We believe 2009 revenue growth will approximate 22%, a deceleration from recent years, which we believe will reflect a reduced hospital capital spending environment and lower procedure rates.

➤ We believe gross margins in 2008 will approach 71%, aided by higher service margins and reduced instrument costs, but negatively impacted by lower selling prices and costs incurred on manufacturing expansion. We anticipate that R&D costs will absorb a marginally lower portion of sales this year, but expect significant SG&A spending as management continues to invest in salesforce expansion. We have some concern regarding gross margins in 2009 amid tighter credit market conditions and an anticipated economic slowdown.

➤ Our 2008 EPS estimate is $5.30, and we see an approximate 21% advance in 2009, to $6.40.

## Investment Rationale/Risk

➤ We think ISRG's technology represents the leading edge in minimally invasive surgery and will continue to gain validity through use in a broadening number of surgical procedures. The company has one of the highest projected growth rates in our health care coverage universe. We believe ISRG has the ability to generate a compound annual growth rate (CAGR) of 25% in sales and operating EPS during the three-year period from 2008 through 2011.

➤ Risks to our recommendation and target price include pricing pressure on equipment, lower-than-expected sales of the da Vinci System, and tighter credit markets, which could impact purchasing decisions among the company's customer base. Longer term, competitive advances in surgical tools could become more of a threat to the da Vinci System.

➤ Based on our projected three-year EPS growth forecast of 25%, and assuming a forward PEG of 1.46X, a steep premium to midcap medical device peers that we believe is justified by the company's superior growth rate, applied to our 2009 EPS forecast of $6.40, our 12-month target price is $234.

## Qualitative Risk Assessment

| LOW | MEDIUM | HIGH |
|---|---|---|

Our risk assessment reflects risks that we would characterize as specific to a maker of medical devices such as ISRG, including those associated with protecting its intellectual property rights, failing to comply with regulations of U.S. and foreign health agencies, and legal liability for injury that may result from use of the company's products, such as inappropriate or "off-label" use. ISRG's common stock also bears the risk of being valued as a high-growth investment, and a failure to meet investor growth expectations could hurt the share price.

## Quantitative Evaluations

**S&P Quality Ranking**  NR

| D | C | B- | B | B+ | A- | A | A+ |
|---|---|---|---|---|---|---|---|

**Relative Strength Rank**  MODERATE

32

LOWEST = 1              HIGHEST = 99

## Revenue/Earnings Data

**Revenue (Million $)**

| | 1Q | 2Q | 3Q | 4Q | Year |
|---|---|---|---|---|---|
| 2008 | 118.2 | 219.2 | 236.0 | -- | -- |
| 2007 | 114.2 | 140.3 | 156.9 | 189.5 | 600.8 |
| 2006 | 77.26 | 87.03 | 95.83 | 112.6 | 372.7 |
| 2005 | 41.61 | 52.76 | 60.87 | 72.10 | 227.3 |
| 2004 | 27.06 | 31.06 | 35.49 | 45.19 | 138.8 |
| 2003 | 19.24 | 21.45 | 23.39 | 27.59 | 91.68 |

**Earnings Per Share ($)**

| | | | | | |
|---|---|---|---|---|---|
| 2008 | 1.12 | 1.28 | 1.44 | E1.46 | E5.30 |
| 2007 | 0.62 | 0.79 | 1.04 | 1.24 | 3.70 |
| 2006 | 0.38 | 0.44 | 0.45 | 0.62 | 1.89 |
| 2005 | 0.25 | 0.40 | 0.55 | 1.31 | 2.51 |
| 2004 | 0.02 | 0.14 | 0.17 | 0.32 | 0.67 |
| 2003 | -0.12 | 0.05 | -0.12 | -0.16 | -0.41 |

Fiscal year ended Dec. 31. Next earnings report expected: Early February. EPS Estimates based on S&P Operating Earnings; historical GAAP earnings are as reported.

## Dividend Data

No cash dividends have been paid.

*The McGraw-Hill Companies*

# Intuitive Surgical Inc

STANDARD
&POOR'S

## Business Summary October 17, 2008

Intuitive Surgical (ISRG) has designed the da Vinci Surgical System, a product that incorporates advanced robotics and computerized visualization technologies to improve the ability of surgeons to perform complex, minimally invasive procedures. As of 2007 year-end, the company had sold over 800 da Vinci Surgical Systems, and surgeons using the company's technology had successfully completed more than 150,000 surgical procedures of various types, including urologic, gynecologic, cardiothoracic and general surgery.

The da Vinci Surgical System consists of a surgeon's console, a patient-side cart, a high performance vision system, and proprietary wristed instruments. By placing computer-enhanced technology between the surgeon and patient, ISRG believes da Vinci lets surgeons perform better surgery in a manner never before experienced. The system translates a surgeon's natural hand movements on instrument controls on a console into corresponding micro-movements of instruments positioned inside the patient through small puncture incisions (ports). It gives a surgeon the intuitive control, range of motion, fine tissue manipulation capability, and 3-D visualization characteristics of open surgery, while simultaneously allowing use of the small ports of minimally invasive surgery. During 2007, surgeons using ISRG products performed

over 55,000 prostatectomy procedures and over 13,000 hysterectomy procedures worldwide.

Intuitive's strategy is targeted at establishing Intuitive surgery as the standard for complex surgical procedures and many other procedures. Over time, the company hopes to broaden the number of procedures performed using the da Vinci Surgical System and to educate surgeons and hospitals about the benefits of Intuitive surgery.

The da Vinci System is covered by over 255 U.S. patents and 46 foreign patents that are licensed or owned by the company. The manufacture, marketing, and use of Class II medical devices such as the da Vinci System is governed by extensive regulations administered by the FDA, which we think act as significant barriers to entry by competitors.

## Company Financials Fiscal Year Ended Dec. 31

| Per Share Data ($) | 2007 | 2006 | 2005 | 2004 | 2003 | 2002 | 2001 | 2000 | 1999 | 1998 |
|---|---|---|---|---|---|---|---|---|---|---|
| Tangible Book Value | 19.61 | 12.55 | 8.64 | 4.83 | 3.87 | 3.46 | 4.14 | 4.86 | 5.42 | NA |
| Cash Flow | 4.04 | 2.15 | 2.64 | 0.82 | -0.23 | -0.80 | -0.76 | -1.42 | -1.46 | NA |
| Earnings | 3.70 | 1.89 | 2.51 | 0.67 | -0.41 | -1.02 | -0.94 | -1.56 | -1.58 | -16.27 |
| S&P Core Earnings | 3.70 | 1.89 | 2.14 | 0.39 | -0.57 | -1.10 | -1.14 | NA | NA | NA |
| Dividends | Nil | Nil | Nil | Nil | Nil | Nil | Nil | Nil | NA | NA |
| Payout Ratio | Nil | Nil | Nil | Nil | Nil | Nil | Nil | Nil | NA | NA |
| Prices:High | 359.59 | 139.50 | 124.79 | 40.60 | 18.61 | 22.50 | 29.56 | 38.13 | NA | NA |
| Prices:Low | 86.20 | 85.63 | 35.69 | 15.08 | 7.34 | 11.20 | 6.00 | 10.75 | NA | NA |
| P/E Ratio:High | 97 | 74 | 50 | 61 | NM | NM | NM | NM | NA | NA |
| P/E Ratio:Low | 23 | 45 | 14 | 23 | NM | NM | NM | NM | NA | NA |

| Income Statement Analysis (Million $) | 2007 | 2006 | 2005 | 2004 | 2003 | 2002 | 2001 | 2000 | 1999 | 1998 |
|---|---|---|---|---|---|---|---|---|---|---|
| Revenue | 601 | 373 | 227 | 139 | 91.7 | 72.0 | 51.7 | 26.6 | 10.2 | Nil |
| Operating Income | 220 | 117 | 73.6 | 26.3 | -7.73 | -16.3 | -17.3 | -20.7 | -18.1 | -29.5 |
| Depreciation | 13.0 | 10.0 | 4.86 | 5.10 | 4.15 | 3.89 | 3.12 | 1.60 | 1.44 | 1.27 |
| Interest Expense | Nil | Nil | 0.02 | 0.09 | 0.20 | 0.20 | 0.27 | 0.40 | 0.41 | 0.22 |
| Pretax Income | 237 | 120 | 73.8 | 24.2 | -9.62 | -18.4 | -16.7 | -18.5 | -18.4 | -29.4 |
| Effective Tax Rate | 39.1% | 40.0% | NM | 3.00% | NM | NM | NM | NM | NM | NM |
| Net Income | 145 | 72.0 | 94.1 | 23.5 | -9.62 | -18.4 | -16.7 | -18.5 | -18.4 | -29.4 |
| S&P Core Earnings | 145 | 72.0 | 80.1 | 13.6 | -13.6 | -20.0 | -20.3 | NA | NA | NA |

| Balance Sheet & Other Financial Data (Million $) | 2007 | 2006 | 2005 | 2004 | 2003 | 2002 | 2001 | 2000 | 1999 | 1998 |
|---|---|---|---|---|---|---|---|---|---|---|
| Cash | 427 | 34.4 | 5.51 | 5.77 | 11.3 | 17.6 | 10.5 | 22.7 | 95.5 | 23.2 |
| Current Assets | 610 | 374 | 209 | 177 | 152 | 78.6 | 89.2 | 104 | NA | NA |
| Total Assets | 1,040 | 672 | 502 | 354 | 315 | 91.6 | 100 | 112 | 106 | 28.2 |
| Current Liabilities | 132 | 80.7 | 58.0 | 38.4 | 34.2 | 26.1 | 21.3 | 19.8 | NA | NA |
| Long Term Debt | Nil | Nil | Nil | Nil | 0.70 | 1.84 | 0.77 | 1.86 | 2.47 | NA |
| Common Equity | 889 | 590 | 443 | 315 | 279 | 63.7 | 78.3 | 90.7 | 93.2 | 20.6 |
| Total Capital | 889 | 590 | 443 | 315 | 280 | 65.5 | 79.1 | 92.6 | 95.6 | NA |
| Capital Expenditures | 20.3 | 15.9 | 30.1 | 22.4 | 2.53 | 5.79 | 5.53 | 3.56 | 0.93 | 1.68 |
| Cash Flow | 158 | 82.1 | 99.0 | 28.6 | -5.47 | -14.5 | -13.6 | -16.9 | -17.0 | NA |
| Current Ratio | 4.6 | 4.6 | 3.6 | 4.6 | 4.4 | 3.0 | 4.2 | 5.2 | 3.3 | 4.9 |
| % Long Term Debt of Capitalization | Nil | Nil | Nil | Nil | 0.2 | 2.8 | 1.0 | 2.0 | 2.6 | 10.2 |
| % Net Income of Revenue | 24.1 | 19.3 | 41.4 | 16.9 | NM | NM | NM | NM | NM | NA |
| % Return on Assets | 16.9 | 12.3 | 22.0 | 7.0 | NM | NM | NM | NM | NM | NA |
| % Return on Equity | 19.6 | 14.0 | 24.9 | 7.9 | NM | NM | NM | NM | NM | NA |

Data as orig reptd.; bef. results of disc opers/spec. items. Per share data adj. for stk. divs.; EPS diluted. E-Estimated. NA-Not Available. NM-Not Meaningful. NR-Not Ranked. UR-Under Review.

Office: 1266 Kifer Rd, Sunnyvale, CA, USA 94086-5304.
Telephone: 408-523-2100 .
Email: ir@intusurg.com
Website: http://www.intuitivesurgical.com

Chrmn & CEO: L.M. Smith
Pres & COO: G.S. Guthart
SVP, CFO & Chief Acctg Officer: M.L. Mohr
SVP & General Counsel: M.J. Meltzer

Cntlr: J.J. Skoglund
Board Members: R. W. Duggan, D. K. Grossman, E. H. Halvorson, R. J. Kramer, A. J. Levy, F. D. Loop, M. J. Rubash, L. M. Smith, G. Stalk, Jr.

Founded: 1995
Domicile: Delaware
Employees: 764

**STANDARD & POOR'S**

# Intuit Inc

| | |
|---|---|
| **S&P Recommendation** HOLD ★★★☆☆ | **Price** $21.58 (as of Nov 14, 2008) |

| **12-Mo. Target Price** | **Investment Style** |
|---|---|
| $26.00 | Large-Cap Growth |

**GICS Sector** Information Technology
**Sub-Industry** Application Software

**Summary** This company develops and markets small business accounting and management, tax preparation and personal finance software.

## Key Stock Statistics (Source S&P, Vickers, company reports)

| | | | | | | | | |
|---|---|---|---|---|---|---|---|---|
| 52-Wk Range | $32.16–20.50 | S&P Oper. EPS 2009E | 1.64 | Market Capitalization(B) | $6.991 | Beta | 0.80 |
| Trailing 12-Month EPS | $1.41 | S&P Oper. EPS 2010E | NA | Yield (%) | Nil | S&P 3-Yr. Proj. EPS CAGR(%) | 13 |
| Trailing 12-Month P/E | 15.3 | P/E on S&P Oper. EPS 2009E | 13.2 | Dividend Rate/Share | Nil | S&P Credit Rating | BBB |
| $10K Invested 5 Yrs Ago | $8,973 | Common Shares Outstg. (M) | 324.0 | Institutional Ownership (%) | 87 | | |

## Price Performance

30-Week Mov. Avg. · · · ·    10-Week Mov. Avg. – – –    **GAAP Earnings vs. Previous Year**    Volume Above Avg. ▮▮▮▮    STARS
12-Mo. Target Price —    Relative Strength —    ▲ Up    ▼ Down    ▶ No Change    Below Avg. ▮▮▮▮

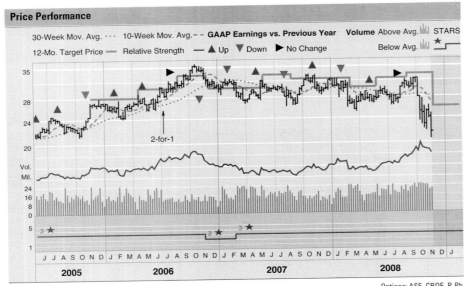

Options: ASE, CBOE, P, Ph

## Qualitative Risk Assessment

| LOW | MEDIUM | **HIGH** |
|---|---|---|

Our risk assessment reflects our view of the company's strong market position within the consumer and professional tax and small business accounting software segments, and its liquid balance sheet. Our optimism is tempered by what we see as challenges that the company faces as it tries to grow beyond its core market segments.

## Quantitative Evaluations

**S&P Quality Ranking**     B+

| D | C | B- | B | **B+** | A- | A | A+ |
|---|---|---|---|---|---|---|---|

**Relative Strength Rank**     MODERATE

57

LOWEST = 1     HIGHEST = 99

## Revenue/Earnings Data

**Revenue (Million $)**

| | 1Q | 2Q | 3Q | 4Q | Year |
|---|---|---|---|---|---|
| 2008 | 444.9 | 834.9 | 1,313 | 478.2 | 3,071 |
| 2007 | 350.5 | 750.6 | 1,139 | 432.7 | 2,673 |
| 2006 | 304.1 | 742.7 | 952.6 | 342.9 | 2,342 |
| 2005 | 266.0 | 662.6 | 849.5 | 301.8 | 2,038 |
| 2004 | 242.5 | 636.3 | 713.0 | 275.9 | 1,868 |
| 2003 | 223.3 | 558.1 | 634.7 | 245.1 | 1,651 |

**Earnings Per Share ($)**

| | | | | | |
|---|---|---|---|---|---|
| 2008 | -0.14 | 0.34 | 1.33 | -0.19 | 1.33 |
| 2007 | -0.17 | 0.40 | 1.04 | -0.19 | 1.25 |
| 2006 | -0.17 | 0.43 | 0.84 | -0.06 | 1.05 |
| 2005 | -0.11 | 0.39 | 0.81 | -0.06 | 1.00 |
| 2004 | -0.14 | 0.37 | 0.67 | -0.11 | 0.79 |
| 2003 | -0.13 | 0.29 | 0.53 | -0.06 | 0.82 |

Fiscal year ended Jul. 31. Next earnings report expected: Mid November. EPS Estimates based on S&P Operating Earnings; historical GAAP earnings are as reported.

## Highlights

➤ The 12-month target price for INTU has recently been changed to $26.00 from $33.00. The Highlights section of this Stock Report will be updated accordingly.

## Investment Rationale/Risk

➤ The Investment Rationale/Risk section of this Stock Report will be updated shortly. For the latest News story on INTU from MarketScope, see below.

➤ 11/14/08 11:04 am ET ... S&P MAINTAINS HOLD RECOMMENDATION ON SHARES OF INTUIT INC. (INTU 21.86***): Ahead of Oct-Q results expected 11/19, we maintain our estimate of a $0.19 loss vs. year-ago $0.15 loss. We trim our Oct-Q sales estimate by $4M to $488M. We remain concerned about the slow economy's impact on INTU's small business customers and the reduction in our sales outlook reflects additional conservatism about the growth outlook for this segment. For FY 09 (July), we trim our revenue forecast to $3.40B from $3.42B and lower our FY 09 EPS estimate by $0.03 to $1.64. We are reducing our target price by $7 to $26, using a blend of relative and intrinsic valuation measures. /Z. Bokhari

## Dividend Data

No cash dividends have been paid.

# Intuit Inc

## Business Summary August 26, 2008

CORPORATE OVERVIEW. Intuit is a leading provider of accounting, financial management, personal finance and tax software for consumers and small businesses. The company's flagship products include QuickBooks, TurboTax, Lacerte, and Quicken, among others. In FY 06, the company had five business segments including: QuickBooks, Payroll and Payments, Consumer tax, Professional tax and Other Businesses.

QuickBooks products and services (which accounted for 22% of total net revenues in FY 07 ended in July) provide bookkeeping capabilities and business management tools. As part of the company's "Right for Me" strategy, INTU offers QuickBooks Simple Start for very small, less complex businesses; QuickBooks Pro, for slightly larger businesses that have additional payroll needs, QuickBooks Pro for Mac; QuickBooks Premier, to support businesses that need advanced accounting capabilities and business planning tools; and QuickBooks Enterprise Solutions, designed for mid-sized companies. INTU also offers an online version of QuickBooks and Premier and Enterprise versions that cater to specific industries, such as Accountant, Manufacturing and Wholesale, Retail, Non-Profit, Contractor, and Professional Services.

Payroll and Payments (19%) consist of miscellaneous business management solutions. Outsourced payroll services include QuickBooks Payroll in different varieties and QuickBooks Online Payroll, for use with QuickBooks Online Edition. Direct deposit and electronic tax payment and filing services are available with some of these offerings for additional fees. This segment also includes Innovative Merchant Solutions (IMS), which offers credit card, debit card, electronic benefits, check guarantee and gift card processing, Web-based transaction processing services for online merchants as well as customer service, charge-back retrieval and support, and fraud and loss prevention screening.

The Consumer Tax segment (30%) is centered on TurboTax. TurboTax software enables individuals and small businesses to prepare and file income tax returns using computers. TurboTax for the Web allows individuals to prepare tax returns online. Versions of TurboTax Premier software are designed to address the special income tax needs of different types of users, including investors, those planning for retirement, and rental property owners. Electronic tax filing services are also provided.

## Company Financials Fiscal Year Ended Jul. 31

| Per Share Data ($) | 2008 | 2007 | 2006 | 2005 | 2004 | 2003 | 2002 | 2001 | 2000 | 1999 |
|---|---|---|---|---|---|---|---|---|---|---|
| Tangible Book Value | 0.32 | 0.66 | 3.41 | 3.61 | 2.75 | 3.44 | 4.02 | 4.15 | 4.00 | 2.75 |
| Cash Flow | NA | 1.51 | 1.34 | 1.31 | 1.03 | 0.81 | 0.30 | -0.09 | 1.23 | 1.36 |
| Earnings | 1.33 | 1.25 | 1.05 | 1.00 | 0.79 | 0.82 | 0.30 | -0.24 | 0.73 | 0.99 |
| S&P Core Earnings | 1.22 | 1.19 | 1.04 | 0.86 | 0.61 | 0.41 | NA | -0.32 | NA | NA |
| Dividends | Nil | Nil | Nil | Nil | Nil | Nil | Nil | Nil | NA | NA |
| Payout Ratio | Nil | Nil | Nil | Nil | Nil | Nil | Nil | Nil | Nil | Nil |
| Prices:High | 32.00 | 33.10 | 35.98 | 27.97 | 26.63 | 26.95 | 27.52 | 23.69 | 45.00 | 32.00 |
| Prices:Low | 20.50 | 26.14 | 23.99 | 18.62 | 17.92 | 16.65 | 17.26 | 11.31 | 12.88 | 11.25 |
| P/E Ratio:High | 24 | 26 | 34 | 28 | 34 | 33 | NM | NM | 62 | 32 |
| P/E Ratio:Low | 15 | 21 | 23 | 19 | 23 | 20 | NM | NM | 18 | 11 |

| Income Statement Analysis (Million $) | | | | | | | | | | |
|---|---|---|---|---|---|---|---|---|---|---|
| Revenue | 3,071 | 2,673 | 2,342 | 2,038 | 1,868 | 1,651 | 1,358 | 1,261 | 1,094 | 848 |
| Operating Income | NA | 773 | 677 | 659 | 561 | 461 | 343 | 265 | 200 | 254 |
| Depreciation | 216 | 135 | 104 | 118 | 97.0 | 76.5 | 59.9 | 59.9 | 213 | 141 |
| Interest Expense | NA | 27.1 | Nil | Nil | Nil | Nil | Nil | Nil | Nil | Nil |
| Pretax Income | 698 | 696 | 610 | 556 | 453 | 393 | 84.9 | -96.5 | 513 | 617 |
| Effective Tax Rate | 35.2% | 36.1% | 38.0% | 32.6% | 30.0% | 33.0% | 17.9% | NM | 40.4% | 39.0% |
| Net Income | 451 | 443 | 377 | 375 | 317 | 263 | 69.8 | -97.1 | 306 | 377 |
| S&P Core Earnings | 415 | 422 | 372 | 323 | 245 | 172 | -0.77 | -129 | NA | NA |

| Balance Sheet & Other Financial Data (Million $) | | | | | | | | | | |
|---|---|---|---|---|---|---|---|---|---|---|
| Cash | 828 | 255 | 180 | 83.8 | 27.2 | 1,207 | 452 | 535 | 643 | 950 |
| Current Assets | NA | 1,952 | 1,817 | 1,614 | 1,517 | 1,669 | 1,995 | 2,148 | 2,129 | 1,586 |
| Total Assets | 4,667 | 4,252 | 2,770 | 2,716 | 2,696 | 2,790 | 2,963 | 2,962 | 2,879 | 2,328 |
| Current Liabilities | NA | 1,160 | 1,016 | 1,003 | 857 | 796 | 733 | 788 | 807 | 781 |
| Long Term Debt | NA | 998 | 15.4 | 17.5 | 5.77 | 29.3 | 14.6 | 12.4 | 0.54 | 36.3 |
| Common Equity | 2,073 | 2,035 | 1,738 | 1,695 | 1,822 | 1,965 | 2,216 | 2,170 | 4,143 | 1,511 |
| Total Capital | NA | 3,034 | 1,754 | 1,713 | 1,828 | 1,994 | 2,230 | 2,182 | 4,143 | 1,547 |
| Capital Expenditures | 306 | 105 | 44.6 | 38.2 | 52.3 | 50.4 | 42.6 | 77.1 | 94.9 | 80.0 |
| Cash Flow | NA | 538 | 482 | 493 | 414 | 340 | 130 | -37.2 | 519 | 518 |
| Current Ratio | 1.2 | 1.7 | 1.8 | 1.6 | 1.8 | 2.1 | 2.7 | 2.7 | 2.6 | 2.0 |
| % Long Term Debt of Capitalization | 32.4 | 32.9 | 0.9 | 1.0 | 0.3 | 1.5 | 0.7 | 0.6 | 0.0 | 2.3 |
| % Net Income of Revenue | 14.7 | 16.6 | 16.1 | 18.4 | 17.0 | 15.9 | 5.1 | NM | 27.9 | 44.4 |
| % Return on Assets | 10.1 | 24.1 | 13.8 | 13.8 | 11.6 | 9.2 | 2.4 | NM | 11.4 | 19.7 |
| % Return on Equity | 22.0 | 23.5 | 22.0 | 21.3 | 16.7 | 12.6 | 3.2 | NM | 8.4 | 29.0 |

Data as orig reptd.; bef. results of disc opers/spec. items. Per share data adj. for stk. divs.; EPS diluted. E-Estimated. NA-Not Available. NM-Not Meaningful. NR-Not Ranked. UR-Under Review.

**Office:** 2700 Coast Ave, Mountain View, CA 94043-1140.
**Telephone:** 650-944-6000.
**Email:** investor_relations@intuit.com
**Website:** http://www.intuit.com

**Chrmn:** W.V. Campbell
**Pres & CEO:** B.D. Smith
**SVP & CFO:** R.N. Williams
**SVP & CTO:** P. Halvorsen

**SVP, Secy & General Counsel:** L.A. Fennell
**Investor Contact:** K. Patel (650-944-3560)
**Board Members:** S. M. Bennett, C. W. Brody, W. V. Campbell, S. D. Cook, D. B. Greene, M. R. Hallman, B. Harris, Jr., S. N. Johnson, E. Kangas, D. D. Powell, S. Sclavos, B. D. Smith

**Founded:** 1984
**Domicile:** Delaware
**Employees:** 8,200

# STANDARD &POOR'S

# Invesco Ltd

**S&P Recommendation** HOLD ★★★☆☆

| | | |
|---|---|---|
| **Price** | **12-Mo. Target Price** | **Investment Style** |
| $11.96 (as of Nov 14, 2008) | $17.00 | Large-Cap Blend |

**GICS Sector** Financials
**Sub-Industry** Asset Management & Custody Banks

**Summary** This diversified investment manager offers an array of investment options to individuals and institutions through offices around the world.

## Key Stock Statistics (Source S&P, Vickers, company reports)

| | | | | | | | |
|---|---|---|---|---|---|---|---|
| 52-Wk Range | $32.25– 10.20 | S&P Oper. EPS 2008**E** | 1.48 | Market Capitalization(B) | $4.604 | Beta | 2.00 |
| Trailing 12-Month EPS | $1.56 | S&P Oper. EPS 2009**E** | 1.59 | Yield (%) | 3.34 | S&P 3-Yr. Proj. EPS CAGR(%) | 4 |
| Trailing 12-Month P/E | 7.7 | P/E on S&P Oper. EPS 2008**E** | 8.1 | Dividend Rate/Share | $0.40 | S&P Credit Rating | BBB+ |
| $10K Invested 5 Yrs Ago | $8,622 | Common Shares Outstg. (M) | 385.0 | Institutional Ownership (%) | 80 | | |

## Price Performance

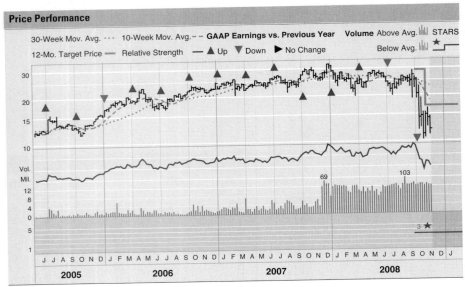

30-Week Mov. Avg. ···· 10-Week Mov. Avg. ─ ─ **GAAP Earnings vs. Previous Year**   Volume  Above Avg. |||| STARS
12-Mo. Target Price ─ Relative Strength  ─ ▲ Up  ▼ Down  ▶ No Change   Below Avg. |||| ★

Analysis prepared by **Matthew Albrecht** on November 06, 2008, when the stock traded at **$ 13.62**.

## Highlights

➤ We expect declines in equity markets and net client outflows to cause assets under management to decline in 2008, but we see a measured recovery in 2009. We expect pressure on revenues this year as well. Specifically, we look for equity market declines and outflows, combined with relative strength in lower-margined fixed income and money market products, to result in an unfavorable asset mix. Client outflows from long-term accounts totaled nearly $18 billion in 2008 through September, but have seen improved trends, and we expect them to turn positive in the first half of 2009. We also look for the private equity and ETF managers to post solid results. We see revenues declining about 10% this year on lower average asset balances, followed by 3% growth in 2009.

➤ Despite IVZ's variable cost structure, we expect margins to be pressured somewhat in the current year as the fixed cost base is spread over a smaller revenue total. We see distribution costs coming down on a percentage basis, but those costs could rebound if we see a recovery in fund flows.

➤ We look for EPS of $1.48 in 2008 and $1.59 in 2009, supported by share repurchases.

## Investment Rationale/Risk

➤ We think that Invesco, with its broad product offerings and global reach, is in position to attract and increase client assets. We note that the firm's client asset base is biased toward equities, but it also has achieved international diversification, and its customer base is composed of both retail and institutional clients. We think its current valuation accurately discounts the firm's future earnings power in this uncertain environment. We have a positive view of Invesco's corporate governance policies, including the independence of the majority of directors and separation of the chairman and chief executive roles.

➤ Risks to our recommendation and target price include market depreciation, poor relative investment performance, and increased government regulation within the industry.

➤ IVZ recently traded at 10.4X our 2008 earnings estimate, a discount to its peer group average multiple. We believe a discount is warranted as asset flows remain negative as productwide performance has lagged, in our view. Our 12-month target price of $17 assumes a 10.7X multiple applied to our 2009 earnings estimate, still a discount to peers.

## Qualitative Risk Assessment

| LOW | MEDIUM | HIGH |
|---|---|---|

Our risk assessment reflects our view of the company's strong market share, broad product base and improving investment performance, offset by economic and industry cyclicality, the firm's bias toward equity products, and recent relative fund underperformance.

## Quantitative Evaluations

**S&P Quality Ranking**                    NR

| D | C | B- | B | B+ | A- | A | A+ |
|---|---|---|---|---|---|---|---|

**Relative Strength Rank**        MODERATE

30

LOWEST = 1                                  HIGHEST = 99

## Revenue/Earnings Data

**Revenue (Million $)**

| | 1Q | 2Q | 3Q | 4Q | Year |
|---|---|---|---|---|---|
| 2008 | 910.4 | 935.6 | 827.2 | -- | -- |
| 2007 | 900.2 | 979.0 | 976.6 | 1,023 | 3,879 |
| 2006 | 584.1 | 588.1 | 587.1 | 655.3 | 2,415 |
| 2005 | 537.8 | 547.8 | 536.2 | 551.4 | 2,173 |
| 2004 | 530.4 | 525.7 | 508.2 | 576.9 | 2,224 |
| 2003 | 427.9 | 467.8 | 505.1 | 536.2 | 2,061 |

**Earnings Per Share ($)**

| | | | | | |
|---|---|---|---|---|---|
| 2008 | 0.39 | 0.41 | 0.33 | E0.35 | E1.48 |
| 2007 | 0.38 | 0.43 | 0.41 | 0.43 | 1.64 |
| 2006 | 0.26 | 0.30 | 0.26 | 0.40 | 1.20 |
| 2005 | 0.18 | 0.18 | 0.18 | -0.02 | 0.52 |
| 2004 | 0.04 | 0.03 | -0.84 | Nil | -0.84 |
| 2003 | -0.03 | -0.13 | 0.07 | 0.02 | -0.08 |

Fiscal year ended Dec. 31. Next earnings report expected: Early February. EPS Estimates based on S&P Operating Earnings; historical GAAP earnings are as reported.

## Dividend Data (Dates: mm/dd Payment Date: mm/dd/yy)

| Amount ($) | Date Decl. | Ex-Div. Date | Stk. of Record | Payment Date |
|---|---|---|---|---|
| 0.220 | -- | 03/18 | 03/19 | 04/07/08 |
| 0.100 | 04/24 | 05/19 | 05/21 | 06/09/08 |
| 0.100 | 07/24 | 08/18 | 08/20 | 09/09/08 |
| 0.100 | 10/27 | 11/24 | 11/26 | 12/17/08 |

Dividends have been paid since 1995. Source: Company reports.

The McGraw-Hill Companies

# Invesco Ltd

STANDARD
&POOR'S

## Business Summary November 06, 2008

CORPORATE OVERVIEW. Invesco is an independent global investment management company that provides an array of investment choices for retail, institutional and high-net-worth clients around the globe. It is incorporated under the laws of Bermuda, and it is headquartered in Atlanta, Georgia. Prior to May 2007, the company was called AMVESCAP PLC, formed through the 1997 merger of Invesco and AIM. Through its subsidiaries, it offers equity, fixed income, and alternative strategies to investors domiciled throughout the world. Assets under management (AUM) totaled $500.1 billion at December 31, 2007. Retail assets accounted for 52% of AUM, institutional assets were 45% of the total, and assets in the private wealth management unit accounted for the remaining 3%. Clients domiciled in the U.S. accounted for 58% of AUM at the end of 2007, U.K. clients owned 18%, and clients in Canada, Europe, and Asia each represented less than 10% of assets.

The company distributes its products utilizing a number of brands through various distribution channels. Its retail products are distributed through Invesco AIM in the U.S., Invesco Trimark in Canada, Invesco Perpetual in the U.K., Invesco in Europe and Asia, and PowerShares for exchange traded funds (ETFs). Retail products are primarily distributed through third parties, including broker-dealers, retirement platforms, financial advisors and insurance companies. Its assets in China are managed through its joint-venture called In-

vesco Great Wall. It offers a full array of investment options, including money market, fixed income, balanced, equity and alternative fund choices.

Its institutional clients are served throughout the world through Invesco and Invesco AIM. It offers a range of products, including equities, fixed income, real estate, financial structures and absolute return strategies. Private equity options are offered through W.L. Ross & Co. A global salesforce distributes products and provides service to clients around the world. Clients include public entities, corporate, union, non-profit, endowments, foundations, and financial institutions.

Invesco's private wealth management services are offered through Atlantic Trust. It provides high-net-worth individuals with personalized service, including financial counseling, estate planning, asset allocation, investment management, private equity, trust, custody and other services. It had offices in 11 cities at December 31, 2007.

## Company Financials Fiscal Year Ended Dec. 31

| Per Share Data ($) | 2007 | 2006 | 2005 | 2004 | 2003 | 2002 | 2001 | 2000 | 1999 | 1998 |
|---|---|---|---|---|---|---|---|---|---|---|
| Tangible Book Value | NM | NM | NM | NM | NM | NM | NM | NM | NM | NM |
| Cash Flow | 1.85 | 1.37 | 0.76 | -0.60 | 0.80 | 0.89 | 1.27 | 1.65 | 1.26 | 0.73 |
| Earnings | 1.64 | 1.20 | 0.52 | -0.84 | -0.08 | 0.06 | 0.54 | 1.22 | 0.88 | 0.50 |
| Dividends | 0.37 | 0.36 | 0.33 | 0.32 | 0.37 | 0.36 | 0.30 | 0.46 | 0.27 | 0.40 |
| Payout Ratio | 23% | 30% | 63% | NM | NM | NM | 56% | 38% | 31% | 80% |
| Prices:High | 32.25 | 25.04 | 15.92 | 17.33 | 18.16 | 31.80 | 48.00 | 61.19 | 23.40 | 24.90 |
| Prices:Low | 26.10 | 15.46 | 11.15 | 9.62 | 7.65 | 7.62 | 16.20 | 20.60 | 14.40 | 8.60 |
| P/E Ratio:High | 20 | 21 | 31 | NM | NM | NM | 89 | 51 | 27 | 50 |
| P/E Ratio:Low | 16 | 13 | 21 | NM | NM | NM | 30 | 17 | 16 | 17 |

| Income Statement Analysis (Million $) | | | | | | | | | | |
|---|---|---|---|---|---|---|---|---|---|---|
| Revenue | 3,879 | 2,415 | 2,173 | 1,158 | 1,158 | 1,345 | 1,620 | 1,629 | 1,072 | 802 |
| Operating Income | 1,058 | 853 | 595 | -63.3 | 362 | 427 | 591 | 591 | 393 | 235 |
| Depreciation | 64.1 | 67.6 | 94.5 | 45.6 | 200 | 210 | 206 | 110 | 77.4 | 47.4 |
| Interest Expense | 71.3 | 81.3 | 85.1 | 44.1 | 48.3 | 52.6 | 55.9 | 51.6 | 44.7 | 38.2 |
| Pretax Income | 1,244 | 755 | 360 | -138 | 36.4 | 102 | 280 | 446 | 283 | 161 |
| Effective Tax Rate | 28.7% | 35.0% | 40.7% | NM | NM | 83.5% | 44.8% | 35.3% | 36.0% | 41.7% |
| Net Income | 674 | 490 | 212 | -173 | -17.3 | 16.9 | 155 | 289 | 181 | 94.1 |

| Balance Sheet & Other Financial Data (Million $) | | | | | | | | | | |
|---|---|---|---|---|---|---|---|---|---|---|
| Cash | 1,130 | 924 | 1,957 | 369 | 393 | 424 | 209 | 466 | 250 | 199 |
| Current Assets | 4,194 | 3,497 | 2,706 | 1,385 | 1,297 | 1,150 | 785 | 1,152 | 926 | 679 |
| Total Assets | 12,925 | 9,292 | 7,578 | 3,907 | 4,110 | 4,138 | 4,432 | 4,296 | 1,827 | 1,611 |
| Current Liabilities | 3,641 | 3,582 | 2,523 | 1,253 | 1,070 | 1,139 | 641 | 764 | 706 | 544 |
| Long Term Debt | 1,276 | 973 | 1,212 | 683 | 730 | 596 | 844 | 960 | 659 | 686 |
| Common Equity | 6,591 | 4,270 | 3,613 | 1,863 | 2,232 | 2,283 | 2,282 | 2,103 | 437 | 331 |
| Total Capital | 8,988 | 5,248 | 4,872 | 2,590 | 2,993 | 2,918 | 3,126 | 3,063 | 1,096 | 1,017 |
| Capital Expenditures | 36.7 | 37.7 | 38.2 | 27.6 | 36.6 | 54.6 | 68.0 | 62.0 | 56.7 | 54.6 |
| Cash Flow | 738 | 558 | 307 | -128 | 183 | 227 | 361 | 399 | 258 | 142 |
| Current Ratio | 1.2 | 1.0 | 1.1 | 1.1 | 1.2 | 1.0 | 1.2 | 1.5 | 1.3 | 1.2 |
| % Long Term Debt of Capitalization | 14.2 | 18.5 | 24.9 | 26.4 | 24.4 | 20.4 | 27.0 | 31.3 | 60.2 | 67.5 |
| % Net Income of Revenue | 17.4 | 20.3 | 9.8 | NM | NM | 1.3 | 9.6 | 17.7 | 16.9 | 11.7 |
| % Return on Assets | 5.3 | 5.8 | 2.8 | NM | NM | 0.4 | 3.6 | 9.4 | 10.5 | 9.3 |
| % Return on Equity | 10.6 | 12.4 | 5.9 | NM | NM | 0.7 | 7.1 | 22.7 | 47.2 | 60.8 |

Data as orig reptd.; bef. results of disc opers/spec. items. Per share data adj. for stk. divs.; EPS diluted. Prior to 2005 balance sheet and income statement in pounds. E-Estimated. NA-Not Available. NM-Not Meaningful. NR-Not Ranked. UR-Under Review.

**Office:** 1360 Peachtree St NE, Atlanta, GA 30309-3233.
**Telephone:** 404-892-0896.
**Email:** AMVESCAPContactUs@amvescap.com
**Website:** http://www.invesco.com

**Chrmn:** R.D. Adams
**Pres & CEO:** M.L. Flanagan
**COO:** J.I. Robertson
**SVP & CFO:** L.M. Starr

**Chief Admin Officer:** C.D. Meadows
**Investor Contact:** M.S. Perman (44-0-20-7065-3942)
**Board Members:** R. D. Adams, J. Banham, J. R. Canion, R. Canion, M. L. Flanagan, J. P. Kenney, D. Kessler, E. P. Lawrence, J. T. Presby, J. I. Robertson

**Founded:** 1935
**Domicile:** Bermuda
**Employees:** 5,475

The McGraw-Hill Companies

STANDARD
&POOR'S

# ITT Corp

**S&P Recommendation** BUY ★★★★☆

| | |
|---|---|
| **Price** $40.99 (as of Nov 14, 2008) | **12-Mo. Target Price** $46.00 |

**Investment Style** Large-Cap Growth

**GICS Sector** Industrials
**Sub-Industry** Industrial Machinery

**Summary** This company is a diversified industrial manufacturer of advanced technology products.

## Key Stock Statistics (Source S&P, Vickers, company reports)

| | | | | | | | |
|---|---|---|---|---|---|---|---|
| 52-Wk Range | $69.73–35.81 | S&P Oper. EPS 2008E | 4.03 | Market Capitalization(B) | $7.443 | Beta | 1.30 |
| Trailing 12-Month EPS | $4.18 | S&P Oper. EPS 2009E | 4.05 | Yield (%) | 1.71 | S&P 3-Yr. Proj. EPS CAGR(%) | 14 |
| Trailing 12-Month P/E | 9.8 | P/E on S&P Oper. EPS 2008E | 10.2 | Dividend Rate/Share | $0.70 | S&P Credit Rating | BBB+ |
| $10K Invested 5 Yrs Ago | $13,011 | Common Shares Outstg. (M) | 181.6 | Institutional Ownership (%) | 82 | | |

## Price Performance

30-Week Mov. Avg. · · · ·  10-Week Mov. Avg. - - -  GAAP Earnings vs. Previous Year  Volume Above Avg. STARS
12-Mo. Target Price —  Relative Strength —  ▲ Up  ▼ Down  ► No Change  Below Avg.

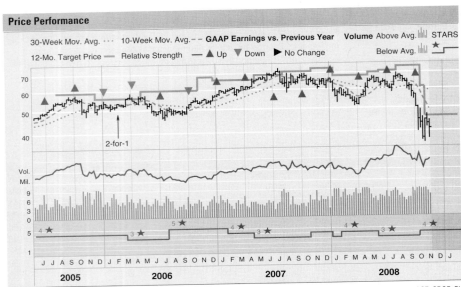

Options: ASE, CBOE, Ph

Analysis prepared by **Efraim Levy, CFA** on October 27, 2008, when the stock traded at **$ 37.51**.

## Highlights

➤ After an expected 28% revenue gain in 2008, we expect growth to slow in 2009 due to the weakening global economy. Still, with more than half of ITT's expected sales in the defense electronics and services segment, with its high visibility backlog, as well as the company's product and geographic diversity, we expect ITT to post mid-single digit sales growth in 2009.

➤ We think the EDO acquisition, including integration costs, will restrain operating margins, despite higher sales, an improved cost structure, and a reduction in restructuring expenses (included in ongoing estimates). In addition to ongoing restructuring efforts, ITT expects to incur about $0.17 per share of costs associated with staffing reductions that should benefit results beginning in the second quarter of 2009. We estimate a 32.0% effective tax rate in 2009.

➤ Although we consider the balance sheet and cash flows as strong, the company said it will focus on liquidity and temporarily cut back on share buybacks and acquisition activity. Looking long term, we expect the company to post 8% to 10% average annual revenue growth reflecting new products, expanded markets, and potential acquisitions.

## Investment Rationale/Risk

➤ We believe strong cash flow will support a modest cash dividend, debt reduction, share buybacks, and strategic acquisitions. We expect the cash dividend payment to be increased on an annual basis. With long-term debt at less than 10% of total capitalization, which is below most peers, we see the company's balance sheet as solid.

➤ Risks to our recommendation and target price include reduced demand at ITT's operating segments, competitive price pressures, and slower-than-expected economic growth.

➤ Applying a P/E multiple of about 10X, reflecting peer and historical P/E comparisons, to our 2009 EPS estimate of $4.05, leads to a value of nearly $41. Our discounted cash flow model, which assumes a weighted average cost of capital of 13.2%, compound annual growth of 7.7% over the next 15 years, and a terminal growth rate of 3.0%, generates intrinsic value of nearly $51. Based on a blend of these metrics, our 12-month target price is $46. We would buy ITT shares for total return potential.

## Qualitative Risk Assessment

| LOW | MEDIUM | HIGH |
|---|---|---|

Our risk assessment reflects our view of ITT's favorable growth prospects in most of the markets it serves and our view of a as strong management team and solid balance sheet. This is offset by our outlook for U.S. defense spending growth, which we think may slow in coming years.

## Quantitative Evaluations

**S&P Quality Ranking** B+

| D | C | B- | B | B+ | A- | A | A+ |
|---|---|---|---|---|---|---|---|

**Relative Strength Rank** MODERATE

58

LOWEST = 1    HIGHEST = 99

## Revenue/Earnings Data

### Revenue (Million $)

| | 1Q | 2Q | 3Q | 4Q | Year |
|---|---|---|---|---|---|
| 2008 | 2,806 | 3,064 | 2,879 | -- | -- |
| 2007 | 2,070 | 2,223 | 2,181 | 2,529 | 9,003 |
| 2006 | 1,792 | 1,964 | 2,001 | 2,051 | 7,808 |
| 2005 | 1,776 | 1,874 | 1,828 | 1,950 | 7,427 |
| 2004 | 1,511 | 1,647 | 1,663 | 1,943 | 6,764 |
| 2003 | 1,296 | 1,438 | 1,375 | 1,517 | 5,627 |

### Earnings Per Share ($)

| | | | | | |
|---|---|---|---|---|---|
| 2008 | 0.93 | 1.22 | 1.20 | E0.80 | E4.03 |
| 2007 | 0.74 | 1.08 | 0.92 | 0.70 | 3.44 |
| 2006 | 0.55 | 0.72 | 0.75 | 0.65 | 2.67 |
| 2005 | 0.65 | 0.70 | 0.79 | -0.48 | 1.67 |
| 2004 | 0.47 | 0.60 | 0.58 | 0.66 | 2.32 |
| 2003 | 0.46 | 0.49 | 0.55 | 0.58 | 2.08 |

Fiscal year ended Dec. 31. Next earnings report expected: Early February. EPS Estimates based on S&P Operating Earnings; historical GAAP earnings are as reported.

## Dividend Data (Dates: mm/dd Payment Date: mm/dd/yy)

| Amount ($) | Date Decl. | Ex-Div. Date | Stk. of Record | Payment Date |
|---|---|---|---|---|
| 0.175 | 02/15 | 03/05 | 03/07 | 04/01/08 |
| 0.175 | 05/13 | 05/21 | 05/23 | 07/01/08 |
| 0.175 | 08/07 | 08/20 | 08/22 | 10/01/08 |
| 0.175 | 10/07 | 11/12 | 11/14 | 01/01/09 |

Dividends have been paid since 1996. Source: Company reports.

# ITT Corp

## Business Summary October 27, 2008

CORPORATE OVERVIEW. ITT Corp. (name changed from ITT Industries in July 2006) is primarily a producer of defense electronics and fluid technology products.

Fluid technology products (39% of 2007 sales) include pumps, valves, heat exchangers, mixers and fluid measuring instruments and controls for residential, agricultural, commercial, municipal and industrial applications. The fluid technology segment became the world's largest pump manufacturer (formerly third largest) following its 1997 acquisition of Goulds Pumps, Inc.

Defense electronics and services (46%) are sold to the military and to government agencies. Products include traffic control systems, jamming devices that guard military planes against radar guided missiles, digital combat radios, night vision devices, radar, satellite instruments and other. About 83% of segment sales in 2006 (latest available) were to the U.S. government.

Motion and flow control (15%) products include switches and valves for in-

dustrial and aerospace applications, products for the marine and leisure markets, and fluid handling materials such as tubing systems and connectors for various automotive and industrial markets for the transportation industry.

CORPORATE STRATEGY. The company's strategy is to expand revenues through a combination of internal growth and acquisitions. We expect the company to continue its tradition of successful acquisition integrations.

At the same time, ITT plans to divest operations that do not fit its strategic goals or provide adequate returns. A recent example is the 2007 divestiture of the switches components operations, which accounted for about half of the electronics segment's 2006 revenues.

## Company Financials Fiscal Year Ended Dec. 31

### Per Share Data ($)

| | 2007 | 2006 | 2005 | 2004 | 2003 | 2002 | 2001 | 2000 | 1999 | 1998 |
|---|---|---|---|---|---|---|---|---|---|---|
| Tangible Book Value | NM | 1.72 | 1.38 | NM | 0.78 | NM | NM | NM | NM | 2.27 |
| Cash Flow | 4.45 | 3.58 | 2.71 | 3.37 | 3.08 | 2.94 | 2.37 | 2.59 | 2.25 | 0.43 |
| Earnings | 3.44 | 2.67 | 1.67 | 2.32 | 2.08 | 2.03 | 1.20 | 1.47 | 1.27 | -0.43 |
| S&P Core Earnings | 3.35 | 2.74 | 2.28 | 2.13 | 1.94 | 0.69 | -0.18 | NA | NA | NA |
| Dividends | 0.56 | 0.55 | 0.36 | 0.34 | 0.32 | 0.30 | 0.30 | 0.30 | 0.30 | 0.30 |
| Payout Ratio | 16% | 21% | 22% | 15% | 15% | 15% | 25% | 20% | 24% | NM |
| Prices:High | 73.44 | 58.73 | 58.05 | 43.36 | 37.70 | 35.43 | 26.00 | 19.81 | 20.75 | 20.44 |
| Prices:Low | 56.30 | 45.34 | 40.24 | 35.52 | 25.06 | 22.90 | 17.78 | 11.19 | 15.25 | 14.06 |
| P/E Ratio:High | 21 | 22 | 35 | 19 | 18 | 17 | 22 | 13 | 16 | NM |
| P/E Ratio:Low | 16 | 17 | 24 | 15 | 12 | 11 | 15 | 8 | 12 | NM |

### Income Statement Analysis (Million $)

| | 2007 | 2006 | 2005 | 2004 | 2003 | 2002 | 2001 | 2000 | 1999 | 1998 |
|---|---|---|---|---|---|---|---|---|---|---|
| Revenue | 9,003 | 7,808 | 7,427 | 6,764 | 5,627 | 4,985 | 4,676 | 4,829 | 4,632 | 4,493 |
| Operating Income | 1,229 | 1,024 | 985 | 871 | 559 | 706 | 707 | 695 | 592 | 525 |
| Depreciation | 185 | 172 | 197 | 199 | 188 | 171 | 213 | 202 | 181 | 196 |
| Interest Expense | 115 | 86.2 | 75.0 | 50.4 | Nil | 68.8 | 85.5 | 93.1 | 84.8 | 126 |
| Pretax Income | 898 | 727 | 448 | 610 | 531 | 509 | 333 | 420 | 370 | -160 |
| Effective Tax Rate | 29.6% | 31.3% | 29.8% | 28.3% | 26.3% | 25.3% | 35.0% | 37.0% | 37.0% | NM |
| Net Income | 633 | 500 | 314 | 438 | 391 | 380 | 217 | 265 | 233 | -98.0 |
| S&P Core Earnings | 616 | 512 | 429 | 400 | 364 | 129 | -31.7 | NA | NA | NA |

### Balance Sheet & Other Financial Data (Million $)

| | 2007 | 2006 | 2005 | 2004 | 2003 | 2002 | 2001 | 2000 | 1999 | 1998 |
|---|---|---|---|---|---|---|---|---|---|---|
| Cash | 1,840 | 937 | 451 | 263 | 414 | 202 | 121 | 88.7 | 182 | 880 |
| Current Assets | 4,930 | 3,348 | 2,772 | 2,329 | 2,106 | 1,701 | 1,459 | 1,506 | 1,628 | 2,382 |
| Total Assets | 11,553 | 7,430 | 7,063 | 7,277 | 5,938 | 5,390 | 4,508 | 4,611 | 4,530 | 5,049 |
| Current Liabilities | 5,456 | 2,759 | 2,560 | 2,446 | 1,687 | 1,730 | 1,897 | 2,233 | 2,110 | 2,151 |
| Long Term Debt | 3,566 | 500 | 516 | 543 | 461 | 492 | 456 | 408 | 479 | 516 |
| Common Equity | 3,945 | 3,362 | 2,723 | 2,343 | 1,848 | 1,137 | 1,376 | 1,211 | 1,099 | 1,299 |
| Total Capital | 4,637 | 3,863 | 3,240 | 2,886 | 2,309 | 1,630 | 1,832 | 1,620 | 1,578 | 1,815 |
| Capital Expenditures | 239 | 177 | 179 | 165 | 154 | 153 | 174 | 181 | 228 | 213 |
| Cash Flow | 818 | 671 | 511 | 636 | 579 | 551 | 430 | 466 | 414 | 98.0 |
| Current Ratio | 0.9 | 1.2 | 1.1 | 1.0 | 1.2 | 1.0 | 0.8 | 0.7 | 0.8 | 1.1 |
| % Long Term Debt of Capitalization | 10.9 | 13.0 | 15.9 | 18.8 | 20.0 | 30.2 | 24.9 | 25.2 | 30.3 | 28.4 |
| % Net Income of Revenue | 7.0 | 6.4 | 4.2 | 6.5 | 6.9 | 7.6 | 4.6 | 5.5 | 5.0 | NM |
| % Return on Assets | 6.7 | 6.9 | 4.4 | 6.6 | 6.9 | 7.7 | 4.8 | 5.8 | 4.9 | NM |
| % Return on Equity | 18.6 | 16.1 | 12.4 | 20.9 | 26.2 | 30.2 | 16.8 | 22.9 | 19.4 | NM |

Data as orig reptd.; bef. results of disc opers/spec. items. Per share data adj. for stk. divs.; EPS diluted. E-Estimated. NA-Not Available. NM-Not Meaningful. NR-Not Ranked. UR-Under Review.

Office: 4 West Red Oak Lane, White Plains, NY 10604-3617.
Telephone: 914-641-2000.
Website: http://www.itt.com
Chrmn, Pres & CEO: S.R. Loranger

COO: H.J. Driesse
SVP & CFO: D.L. Ramos
SVP & CTO: B.L. Reichelderfer
SVP & Treas: D.E. Foley

Investor Contact: P.J. Milligan
Board Members: C. J. Crawford, C. A. Gold, R. F. Hake, J. J. Hamre, P. J. Kern, S. R. Loranger, F. T. MacInnis, S. N. Mohapatra, L. S. Sanford, M. I. Tambakeras

Founded: 1920
Domicile: Indiana
Employees: 39,700

**STANDARD &POOR'S**

# Jabil Circuit Inc

| S&P Recommendation **HOLD** ★★★☆☆ | Price<br>$6.33 (as of Nov 14, 2008) | 12-Mo. Target Price<br>$13.00 | Investment Style<br>Large-Cap Growth |
|---|---|---|---|

**GICS Sector** Information Technology
**Sub-Industry** Electronic Manufacturing Services

**Summary** This company manufactures circuit board assemblies for international OEMs in the PC, peripheral, communications and automotive markets.

## Key Stock Statistics (Source S&P, Vickers, company reports)

| | | | | | | | | |
|---|---|---|---|---|---|---|---|---|
| 52-Wk Range | $18.78– 6.03 | S&P Oper. EPS 2009**E** | 1.16 | Market Capitalization(B) | $1.333 | Beta | 1.16 |
| Trailing 12-Month EPS | $0.65 | S&P Oper. EPS 2010**E** | 1.35 | Yield (%) | 4.42 | S&P 3-Yr. Proj. EPS CAGR(%) | 15 |
| Trailing 12-Month P/E | 9.7 | P/E on S&P Oper. EPS 2009**E** | 5.5 | Dividend Rate/Share | $0.28 | S&P Credit Rating | BB+ |
| $10K Invested 5 Yrs Ago | $2,292 | Common Shares Outstg. (M) | 210.6 | Institutional Ownership (%) | 90 | | |

## Price Performance

30-Week Mov. Avg. · · · 10-Week Mov. Avg. - - **GAAP Earnings vs. Previous Year**   **Volume** Above Avg. ⅠⅠⅡ **STARS**
12-Mo. Target Price — Relative Strength — ▲ Up ▼ Down ▶ No Change   Below Avg. ⅠⅠⅡ ★ ⌐

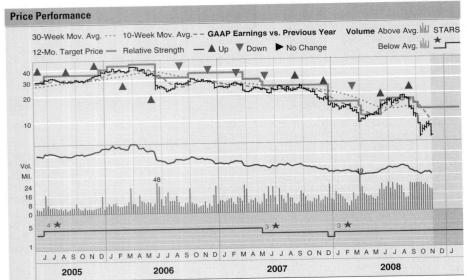

Options: ASE, CBOE, P, Ph

Analysis prepared by **Thomas W. Smith, CFA** on September 30, 2008, when the stock traded at **$ 9.28**.

## Highlights

➤ We forecast revenue to rise about 7% for FY 09 (Aug.), and a further 7% for FY 10. We project that pressure on consumer segment revenues will continue in FY 09, due to a realignment in operations. We see a continued push into low-cost geographies providing some offset to a moderating U.S. economy. While JBL benefits from providing end-to-end solutions to a well-diversified customer base, we believe it lacks some opportunities for scale efficiencies that are enjoyed by the biggest industry players.

➤ We expect gross margins to improve gradually to 7.1% in FY 09 and 7.3% in FY 10, as higher volumes combine with fewer costs associated with the buildout of the electromechanical business, and with more benefits from restructuring activities. We see pressure on operating margins from restructuring in FY 08 fading in FY 09.

➤ We see JBL benefiting from favorable tax jurisdictions in offshore locations. On an operating basis, excluding restructuring-related charges but including stock-based compensation expense, we project EPS of $1.16 for FY 09 and $1.35 for FY 10.

## Investment Rationale/Risk

➤ We believe the longer-term outlook for the electronic manufacturing services industry remains favorable. However, we think that market segments affected by U.S. consumer and enterprise spending are currently experiencing a slowdown. Despite JBL's push to diversify its business mix, the consumer segment accounted for 30% of revenues in the FY 08 fourth quarter, which think creates an overall drag on revenues and margins. Long-term debt has increased since FY 06, which we view as a minor caution sign.

➤ Risks to our recommendation and target price include potential market share losses, slower implementation of new contracts and facilities than we project, and less smooth acquisition integration and restructuring than we foresee.

➤ Our 12-month target price of $13 is derived mainly by applying a target P/E multiple of 11X, which is near the level for electronic manufacturing services (EMS) peers but toward the low end of JBL's historical range to reflect moderating end-market growth, to our 12-month forward EPS estimate of $1.16.

## Qualitative Risk Assessment

| LOW | MEDIUM | **HIGH** |
|---|---|---|

Our risk assessment reflects our view of the historically volatile nature of the electronic manufacturing services industry as well as what we see as the company's relatively high exposure to fluctuations in commodity prices.

## Quantitative Evaluations

**S&P Quality Ranking**   B

| D | C | B- | **B** | B+ | A- | A | A+ |
|---|---|---|---|---|---|---|---|

**Relative Strength Rank**   **WEAK**

26

LOWEST = 1   HIGHEST = 99

## Revenue/Earnings Data

**Revenue (Million $)**

| | 1Q | 2Q | 3Q | 4Q | Year |
|---|---|---|---|---|---|
| 2008 | 3,368 | 3,059 | 3,088 | 3,265 | 12,780 |
| 2007 | 3,224 | 2,935 | 3,002 | 3,130 | 12,291 |
| 2006 | 2,404 | 2,315 | 2,592 | 2,954 | 10,265 |
| 2005 | 1,833 | 1,716 | 1,938 | 2,037 | 7,524 |
| 2004 | 1,509 | 1,492 | 1,626 | 1,626 | 6,253 |
| 2003 | 1,068 | 1,146 | 1,219 | 1,296 | 4,729 |

**Earnings Per Share ($)**

| | | | | | |
|---|---|---|---|---|---|
| 2008 | 0.30 | -0.12 | 0.19 | 0.28 | 0.65 |
| 2007 | 0.20 | 0.07 | 0.03 | 0.06 | 0.35 |
| 2006 | 0.37 | 0.32 | 0.30 | -0.22 | 0.77 |
| 2005 | 0.27 | 0.22 | 0.29 | 0.34 | 1.12 |
| 2004 | 0.20 | 0.19 | 0.19 | 0.22 | 0.81 |
| 2003 | 0.04 | 0.05 | 0.02 | 0.10 | 0.21 |

Fiscal year ended Aug. 31. Next earnings report expected: Late December. EPS Estimates based on S&P Operating Earnings; historical GAAP earnings are as reported.

## Dividend Data (Dates: mm/dd Payment Date: mm/dd/yy)

| Amount ($) | Date Decl. | Ex-Div. Date | Stk. of Record | Payment Date |
|---|---|---|---|---|
| 0.070 | 01/22 | 02/13 | 02/15 | 03/03/08 |
| 0.070 | 04/17 | 05/13 | 05/15 | 06/02/08 |
| 0.070 | 07/17 | 08/13 | 08/15 | 09/02/08 |
| 0.070 | 10/24 | 11/13 | 11/17 | 12/01/08 |

Dividends have been paid since 2006. Source: Company reports.

# Jabil Circuit Inc

**STANDARD &POOR'S**

## Business Summary September 30, 2008

CORPORATE OVERVIEW. This provider of electronic manufacturing services (EMS) works with customers in a variety of industries at facilities around the world. Between FY 05 (Aug.) and FY 07, sales increased over 60%, to more than $12.2 billion, with much of the growth generated internally.

In FY 07, Cisco Systems and Nokia Corp. were the only customers accounting for more than 10% of sales, with Cisco at 15% (under 10% of FY 06 sales) and Nokia Corp. at 13% (21%). In FY 07, 50 customers accounted for 90% of JBL's revenues, which represents a broadening of the customer base from the 40 customers it took to represent 90% of FY 06 sales. Royal Philips Electronics represented 12% of FY 06 sales. We think the FY 07 acquisition of Taiwan Greenpoint enhanced JBL's position with most of its existing customers, and brought higher operating margins to JBL's core business.

MARKET PROFILE. We believe the EMS industry remains well positioned to capture new business from original equipment manufacturers (OEMs). This is due to our view that the cost advantages associated with the outsourcing model are becoming better understood by potential participants. We think the benefits of this strategy are ample, with companies being able to reduce costs and reallocate resources toward their core competencies (e.g., marketing and research and development). We expect the industry to grow near 10% annually over the next several years.

We see a number of key trends emerging in the EMS landscape. For instance, OEMs have begun to limit the number of EMS providers with which they conduct business. We think this move results from customers' desire to streamline their operations. While in the past they may have utilized five or six vendors, many now seek to limit that total to just one or two.

## Company Financials Fiscal Year Ended Aug. 31

### Per Share Data ($)

| | 2008 | 2007 | 2006 | 2005 | 2004 | 2003 | 2002 | 2001 | 2000 | 1999 |
|---|---|---|---|---|---|---|---|---|---|---|
| Tangible Book Value | 6.90 | 5.97 | 8.26 | 8.22 | 7.29 | 6.06 | 6.63 | 6.43 | 6.68 | 3.32 |
| Cash Flow | NA | 1.51 | 1.71 | 2.18 | 1.89 | 1.32 | 1.11 | 1.35 | 1.31 | 0.90 |
| Earnings | 0.65 | 0.35 | 0.77 | 1.12 | 0.81 | 0.21 | 0.17 | 0.59 | 0.78 | 0.56 |
| S&P Core Earnings | 0.64 | 0.35 | 0.77 | 0.64 | 0.59 | 0.04 | NA | 0.46 | NA | NA |
| Dividends | 0.28 | 0.28 | 0.14 | Nil | Nil | Nil | Nil | Nil | Nil | Nil |
| Payout Ratio | 43% | 80% | 18% | Nil | Nil | Nil | Nil | Nil | Nil | Nil |
| Prices:High | 18.78 | 27.86 | 43.70 | 39.00 | 32.40 | 31.66 | 26.79 | 40.99 | 68.00 | 38.97 |
| Prices:Low | 6.03 | 14.27 | 22.01 | 21.80 | 19.18 | 21.20 | 11.13 | 14.00 | 18.63 | 14.25 |
| P/E Ratio:High | 29 | 80 | 57 | 35 | 40 | NM | NM | 69 | 87 | 70 |
| P/E Ratio:Low | 9 | 41 | 29 | 19 | 24 | NM | 65 | 24 | 24 | 25 |

### Income Statement Analysis (Million $)

| | 2008 | 2007 | 2006 | 2005 | 2004 | 2003 | 2002 | 2001 | 2000 | 1999 |
|---|---|---|---|---|---|---|---|---|---|---|
| Revenue | 12,780 | 12,291 | 10,265 | 7,524 | 6,253 | 4,729 | 3,545 | 4,331 | 3,558 | 2,000 |
| Operating Income | NA | 494 | 522 | 507 | 439 | 369 | 296 | 353 | 317 | 197 |
| Depreciation | 276 | 240 | 199 | 220 | 222 | 224 | 188 | 155 | 99.3 | 56.0 |
| Interest Expense | NA | 86.1 | 23.5 | 24.8 | 19.4 | 17.0 | 13.1 | 5.86 | 7.61 | 1.69 |
| Pretax Income | 157 | 94.5 | 225 | 276 | 198 | 37.0 | 44.8 | 166 | 213 | 140 |
| Effective Tax Rate | 16.0% | 22.6% | 26.9% | 16.1% | 15.5% | NM | 22.4% | 28.7% | 31.5% | 34.4% |
| Net Income | 134 | 73.2 | 165 | 232 | 167 | 43.0 | 34.7 | 119 | 146 | 91.5 |
| S&P Core Earnings | 131 | 73.9 | 165 | 134 | 122 | 8.12 | -0.11 | 93.4 | NA | NA |

### Balance Sheet & Other Financial Data (Million $)

| | 2008 | 2007 | 2006 | 2005 | 2004 | 2003 | 2002 | 2001 | 2000 | 1999 |
|---|---|---|---|---|---|---|---|---|---|---|
| Cash | 773 | 664 | 774 | 796 | 621 | 700 | 641 | 431 | 338 | 114 |
| Current Assets | NA | 3,666 | 3,679 | 2,686 | 2,183 | 2,094 | 1,588 | 1,447 | 1,387 | 588 |
| Total Assets | 7,032 | 6,295 | 5,412 | 4,077 | 3,329 | 3,245 | 2,548 | 2,358 | 2,018 | 921 |
| Current Liabilities | NA | 2,991 | 2,701 | 1,568 | 1,159 | 1,263 | 593 | 505 | 692 | 331 |
| Long Term Debt | NA | 760 | 330 | 327 | 305 | 297 | 355 | 362 | 25.0 | 33.3 |
| Common Equity | 2,716 | 2,443 | 2,294 | 2,135 | 1,819 | 1,588 | 1,507 | 1,414 | 1,270 | 546 |
| Total Capital | NA | 3,226 | 2,632 | 2,462 | 2,125 | 1,905 | 1,903 | 1,813 | 1,323 | 588 |
| Capital Expenditures | 338 | 302 | 280 | 257 | 218 | 117 | 85.5 | 309 | 333 | 150 |
| Cash Flow | NA | 313 | 363 | 452 | 389 | 267 | 223 | 274 | 245 | 147 |
| Current Ratio | 1.4 | 1.2 | 1.4 | 1.7 | 1.9 | 1.7 | 2.7 | 2.9 | 2.0 | 1.8 |
| % Long Term Debt of Capitalization | 26.9 | 23.6 | 12.5 | 13.3 | 14.4 | 15.6 | 18.6 | 20.0 | 1.9 | 5.7 |
| % Net Income of Revenue | 1.1 | 0.6 | 1.6 | 3.1 | 2.7 | 0.9 | 1.0 | 2.7 | 4.1 | 4.6 |
| % Return on Assets | 2.0 | 1.3 | 3.5 | 6.3 | 5.1 | 1.5 | 1.4 | 5.4 | 9.5 | 12.7 |
| % Return on Equity | 5.2 | 3.1 | 7.4 | 11.7 | 9.8 | 2.8 | 2.4 | 8.8 | 15.8 | 23.0 |

Data as orig reptd.; bef. results of disc opers/spec. items. Per share data adj. for stk. divs.; EPS diluted. E-Estimated. NA-Not Available. NM-Not Meaningful. NR-Not Ranked. UR-Under Review.

**Office:** 10560 Dr. Martin Luther King Jr. Street North, St. Petersburg, FL 33716.
**Telephone:** 727-577-9749.
**Email:** investor_relations@jabil.com
**Website:** http://www.jabil.com

**Chrmn:** W.D. Morean
**Pres & CEO:** T.L. Main
**Vice Chrmn:** T.A. Sansone
**COO:** M.T. Mondello

**CFO & Chief Acctg Officer:** F.I. Alexander
**Investor Contact:** B. Walters (727-803-3349)
**Board Members:** L. S. Grafstein, M. S. Lavitt, T. L. Main, W. D. Morean, L. J. Murphy, F. Newman, S. A. Raymund, T. A. Sansone, K. A. Walters

**Founded:** 1969
**Domicile:** Delaware
**Employees:** 61,000

The McGraw Hill Companies

STANDARD
&POOR'S

# Jacobs Engineering Group Inc.

| S&P Recommendation | STRONG BUY ★★★★★ | Price $31.01 (as of Nov 14, 2008) | 12-Mo. Target Price $60.00 | Investment Style Large-Cap Growth |
| --- | --- | --- | --- | --- |

**GICS Sector** Industrials
**Sub-Industry** Construction & Engineering

**Summary** This company provides engineering, construction and maintenance services to private industry and federal government agencies on a worldwide basis.

## Key Stock Statistics (Source S&P, Vickers, company reports)

| | | | | | | | |
| --- | --- | --- | --- | --- | --- | --- | --- |
| 52-Wk Range | $103.29– 28.25 | S&P Oper. EPS 2009**E** | 3.95 | Market Capitalization(B) | $3.796 | Beta | 1.79 |
| Trailing 12-Month EPS | $3.38 | S&P Oper. EPS 2010**E** | 4.50 | Yield (%) | Nil | S&P 3-Yr. Proj. EPS CAGR(%) | 18 |
| Trailing 12-Month P/E | 9.2 | P/E on S&P Oper. EPS 2009**E** | 7.9 | Dividend Rate/Share | Nil | S&P Credit Rating | NA |
| $10K Invested 5 Yrs Ago | $14,423 | Common Shares Outstg. (M) | 122.4 | Institutional Ownership (%) | 83 | | |

## Price Performance

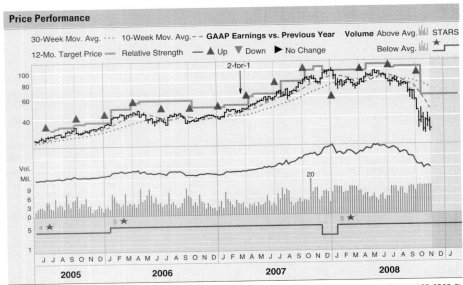

30-Week Mov. Avg. · · · · 10-Week Mov. Avg. - - - GAAP Earnings vs. Previous Year   Volume Above Avg. STARS
12-Mo. Target Price —   Relative Strength —   ▲ Up ▼ Down ► No Change   Below Avg.

2-for-1

Options: ASE, CBOE, Ph

Analysis prepared by **Stewart Scharf** on November 07, 2008, when the stock traded at **$ 34.51**.

## Highlights

➤ We expect total revenue growth of about 20% in FY 09 (Sep.), mainly on further demand in the refining, national government and infrastructure segments. We still see solid growth in the oil & gas business, athough we see some work in the Canadian oil sands being postponed due to uncertain market conditions. We still expect new bookings in the Middle East, while environmental nuclear cleanup in the U.K., U.S. defense and institutional building projects remain strong. We also see JEC seeking an oil & gas or infrastructure acquisition.

➤ We believe gross margins will begin to widen at a slower pace by FY 09 (15.4% through the first nine months of FY 08), as the mix gradually shifts toward the lower-margin construction phase from professional services. Operating margins should improve on increased global engineering work at low-cost centers mainly in India, higher wage rates, some synergies from acquisitions and other cost control efforts; SG&A expenses (mostly salaries) will likely stabilize near 10% of revenues.

➤ We expect the effective tax rate to remain near 36% in FY 09, with EPS of $3.95, advancing 14%, to $4.50, in FY 10.

## Investment Rationale/Risk

➤ We base our strong buy opinion on our valuation metrics following near-term volatility, along with the company's diversified customer and geographic base, and relationship-based business model, which we view as a positive in a challenging environment.

➤ Risks to our recommendation and target price include a downturn in some key markets such as oil & gas due to a recessionary environment; project delays or cancellations based on customer liquidity issues or a further sharp drop in oil prices; an inability to offset a shortage of skilled labor via outsourcing overseas; and a lack of acquisition opportunities.

➤ Our discounted cash flow (DCF) model suggests an intrinsic value of $67, assuming a perpetuity growth rate of 4% and a weighted average cost of capital (WACC) of about 8%. Based on our view of favorable global prospects in most core segments, and JEC's relatively low-risk business model, we think the stock deserves a premium-to-peers P/E of about 13X our FY 09 EPS estimate, resulting in a value of $52. Blending these metrics, we arrive at our 12-month target price of $60.

## Qualitative Risk Assessment

| LOW | MEDIUM | HIGH |
| --- | --- | --- |

Our risk assessment reflects the cyclical nature of the company's various markets, its growth-by-acquisition strategy, changes in global political conditions, timing issues related to new awards, and fluctuations in interest rates and foreign currencies. These factors are offset by what we see as JEC's strong cash position and virtually no debt.

## Quantitative Evaluations

**S&P Quality Ranking** B+

| D | C | B- | B | B+ | A- | A | A+ |
| --- | --- | --- | --- | --- | --- | --- | --- |

**Relative Strength Rank** WEAK

27

LOWEST = 1     HIGHEST = 99

## Revenue/Earnings Data

### Revenue (Million $)

| | 1Q | 2Q | 3Q | 4Q | Year |
| --- | --- | --- | --- | --- | --- |
| 2008 | 2,472 | 2,665 | 2,919 | 3,197 | 11,252 |
| 2007 | 2,019 | 2,092 | 2,084 | 2,280 | 8,474 |
| 2006 | 1,683 | 1,832 | 1,926 | 1,979 | 7,421 |
| 2005 | 1,283 | 1,383 | 1,449 | 1,519 | 5,635 |
| 2004 | 1,135 | 1,124 | 1,120 | 1,216 | 4,594 |
| 2003 | 1,135 | 1,203 | 1,131 | 1,063 | 4,616 |

### Earnings Per Share ($)

| | | | | | |
| --- | --- | --- | --- | --- | --- |
| 2008 | 0.79 | 0.80 | 0.87 | 0.92 | 3.38 |
| 2007 | 0.51 | 0.55 | 0.61 | 0.68 | 2.35 |
| 2006 | 0.36 | 0.37 | 0.42 | 0.49 | 1.64 |
| 2005 | 0.28 | 0.31 | 0.34 | 0.36 | 1.29 |
| 2004 | 0.29 | 0.31 | 0.26 | 0.26 | 1.13 |
| 2003 | 0.29 | 0.28 | 0.29 | 0.29 | 1.14 |

Fiscal year ended Sep. 30. Next earnings report expected: Late January. EPS Estimates based on S&P Operating Earnings; historical GAAP earnings are as reported.

## Dividend Data

No cash dividends have been paid since 1984.

---

The McGraw-Hill Companies

# Jacobs Engineering Group Inc.

STANDARD &POOR'S

## Business Summary November 07, 2008

CORPORATE OVERVIEW. Jacobs Engineering focuses on providing a broad range of technical, professional and construction services to a large number of industrial, commercial and governmental clients worldwide. The company offers project services; consulting services; operations and maintenance services; and construction services via offices primarily in North America, Europe, Asia and Australia. In November 2007, the company was moved into the S&P 500 Index from S&P's MidCap 400 Index.

In FY 08 (Sep.), revenues by sector were: chemicals, 13%; buildings, 6%; national government (environmental, defense and NASA), 18%; pharmaBio (pharmaceutical and biotech), 9%; oil and gas (upstream), 10%; refining (downstream), 33%; infrastructure, 8%; and pulp and paper, high tech, food and consumer products, 3%. The higher-margin technical professional services component accounted for 52% of revenues and 48% of backlog in FY 08, with the balance derived from field services. At the end of FY 08, total backlog was $16.7 billion ($8.1 billion technical professional services), up 23% from $13.6 billion a year earlier, driven by new awards for oil & gas, refining, infrastructure and national government projects. The company expects about 65% of its backlog to be realized as revenues within the next fiscal year. In FY 07 (latest available), about 40% of revenues were generated from operations outside of the U.S., up from 35% in FY 06.

Project services include the engineering and design of process plants and high-technology facilities. Construction services offers traditional field services to private and public sector clients. Process, scientific and systems consulting includes market analyses to determine the feasibility of a project. Operations and maintenance services include all tasks required to keep a process plant in day-to-day operation.

In FY 07, revenues derived from agencies of the U.S. government accounted for 16.6% of the total, up from 16.4% in FY 06. JEC sees total federal contracts (40%) gradually rising to 50% of its business. Cost-reimbursable projects accounted for 88% of the FY 07 total.

At the end of FY 07, the company's pension plans were underfunded by $110 million, down from $184 million a year earlier.

## Company Financials Fiscal Year Ended Sep. 30

| Per Share Data ($) | 2008 | 2007 | 2006 | 2005 | 2004 | 2003 | 2002 | 2001 | 2000 | 1999 |
|---|---|---|---|---|---|---|---|---|---|---|
| Tangible Book Value | NA | 8.42 | 7.36 | 5.10 | 4.04 | 4.00 | 2.73 | 2.55 | 2.15 | 1.95 |
| Cash Flow | NA | 2.85 | 2.04 | 1.70 | 1.44 | 1.45 | 1.31 | 1.16 | 0.86 | 0.92 |
| Earnings | 3.38 | 2.35 | 1.64 | 1.29 | 1.13 | 1.14 | 0.99 | 0.81 | 0.48 | 0.62 |
| S&P Core Earnings | NA | 2.38 | 1.68 | 1.16 | 1.02 | 0.91 | 0.75 | 0.53 | NA | NA |
| Dividends | Nil | Nil | Nil | Nil | Nil | Nil | Nil | Nil | Nil | Nil |
| Payout Ratio | Nil | Nil | Nil | Nil | Nil | Nil | Nil | Nil | Nil | Nil |
| Prices:High | 103.29 | 99.62 | 46.64 | 34.71 | 24.11 | 24.97 | 21.45 | 18.92 | 12.30 | 10.69 |
| Prices:Low | 28.25 | 38.25 | 33.90 | 22.33 | 18.43 | 17.48 | 13.05 | 10.56 | 6.55 | 7.31 |
| P/E Ratio:High | 31 | 42 | 29 | 27 | 21 | 22 | 22 | 24 | 25 | 17 |
| P/E Ratio:Low | 8 | 16 | 21 | 17 | 16 | 15 | 13 | 13 | 14 | 12 |

| Income Statement Analysis (Million $) | | | | | | | | | | |
|---|---|---|---|---|---|---|---|---|---|---|
| Revenue | 11,252 | 8,474 | 7,421 | 5,635 | 4,594 | 4,616 | 4,556 | 3,957 | 3,419 | 2,875 |
| Operating Income | NA | 498 | 350 | 288 | 232 | 232 | 207 | 183 | 165 | 140 |
| Depreciation | NA | 55.7 | 48.3 | 46.4 | 34.2 | 35.4 | 35.1 | 38.9 | 40.1 | 31.6 |
| Interest Expense | NA | 8.00 | 7.50 | 6.47 | 3.57 | 3.25 | 7.50 | 11.7 | 11.4 | 8.77 |
| Pretax Income | 657 | 449 | 305 | 236 | 198 | 197 | 169 | 138 | 81.3 | 105 |
| Effective Tax Rate | 36.0% | 36.0% | 35.5% | 36.0% | 35.0% | 35.0% | 35.0% | 36.5% | 37.3% | 37.4% |
| Net Income | 421 | 287 | 197 | 151 | 129 | 128 | 110 | 87.8 | 51.0 | 65.4 |
| S&P Core Earnings | NA | 290 | 202 | 136 | 118 | 102 | 82.3 | 57.5 | NA | NA |

| Balance Sheet & Other Financial Data (Million $) | | | | | | | | | | |
|---|---|---|---|---|---|---|---|---|---|---|
| Cash | NA | 613 | 434 | 240 | 100 | 126 | 48.5 | 49.3 | 65.8 | 53.5 |
| Current Assets | NA | 2,278 | 1,818 | 1,337 | 1,084 | 970 | 975 | 946 | 851 | 730 |
| Total Assets | NA | 3,389 | 2,854 | 2,354 | 2,071 | 1,671 | 1,674 | 1,557 | 1,384 | 1,220 |
| Current Liabilities | NA | 1,276 | 1,041 | 785 | 686 | 611 | 740 | 701 | 684 | 585 |
| Long Term Debt | NA | 40.0 | 77.7 | 89.6 | 78.8 | 17.8 | 85.7 | 164 | 147 | 135 |
| Common Equity | NA | 1,844 | 1,423 | 1,141 | 1,005 | 842 | 690 | 592 | 496 | 449 |
| Total Capital | NA | 1,884 | 1,508 | 1,237 | 1,089 | 865 | 781 | 761 | 648 | 590 |
| Capital Expenditures | NA | 64.6 | 54.0 | 43.9 | 37.1 | 25.8 | 37.2 | 28.8 | 44.4 | 39.0 |
| Cash Flow | NA | 343 | 245 | 197 | 163 | 163 | 145 | 127 | 91.1 | 97.0 |
| Current Ratio | NA | 1.8 | 1.7 | 1.7 | 1.6 | 1.6 | 1.3 | 1.4 | 1.2 | 1.2 |
| % Long Term Debt of Capitalization | Nil | 2.1 | 5.2 | 7.2 | 7.2 | 2.1 | 11.0 | 21.6 | 22.7 | 22.9 |
| % Net Income of Revenue | 3.7 | 3.3 | 2.7 | 2.7 | 2.8 | 2.8 | 2.4 | 2.2 | 1.5 | 2.3 |
| % Return on Assets | NA | 9.1 | 7.5 | 6.8 | 6.9 | 7.7 | 6.8 | 6.0 | 3.9 | 6.5 |
| % Return on Equity | NA | 17.5 | 15.2 | 14.1 | 14.0 | 16.7 | 17.1 | 16.1 | 10.8 | 16.0 |

Data as orig reptd.; bef. results of disc opers/spec. items. Per share data adj. for stk. divs.; EPS diluted. E-Estimated. NA-Not Available. NM-Not Meaningful. NR-Not Ranked. UR-Under Review.

Office: 1111 South Arroyo Parkway, Pasadena, CA, USA 91105.
Telephone: 626-578-3500.
Website: http://www.jacobs.com
Chrmn: N.G. Watson

Pres & CEO: C.L. Martin
EVP, CFO, Chief Admin Officer & Treas: J. Prosser, Jr.
SVP, Chief Acctg Officer & Cntlr: N.G. Thawerbhoy
SVP, Secy & General Counsel: W.C. Markley, III

Investor Contact: J.W. Prosser, Jr. (626-578-6803)
Board Members: J. R. Bronson, J. F. Coyne, R. C. Davidson, Jr., E. V. Fritzky, R. B. Gwyn, J. P. Jumper, L. F. Levinson, C. L. Martin, B. Montoya, T. M. Niles, N. G. Watson

Founded: 1957
Domicile: Delaware
Employees: 49,200

The McGraw-Hill Companies

STANDARD
&POOR'S

# Janus Capital Group Inc

**S&P Recommendation** HOLD ★★★☆☆

| | | |
|---|---|---|
| **Price** $7.27 (as of Nov 14, 2008) | **12-Mo. Target Price** $13.00 | **Investment Style** Large-Cap Blend |

**GICS Sector** Financials
**Sub-Industry** Asset Management & Custody Banks

**Summary** Janus is a U.S.-based investment management company that focuses on equity growth and quantitative strategies.

## Key Stock Statistics (Source S&P, Vickers, company reports)

| | | | | | | | |
|---|---|---|---|---|---|---|---|
| 52-Wk Range | $36.88– 6.44 | S&P Oper. EPS 2008E | 0.94 | Market Capitalization(B) | $1.148 | Beta | 1.78 |
| Trailing 12-Month EPS | $0.91 | S&P Oper. EPS 2009E | 1.02 | Yield (%) | 0.55 | S&P 3-Yr. Proj. EPS CAGR(%) | 3 |
| Trailing 12-Month P/E | 8.0 | P/E on S&P Oper. EPS 2008E | 7.7 | Dividend Rate/Share | $0.04 | S&P Credit Rating | BBB+ |
| $10K Invested 5 Yrs Ago | $5,440 | Common Shares Outstg. (M) | 157.9 | Institutional Ownership (%) | 97 | | |

## Price Performance

30-Week Mov. Avg. ···· 10-Week Mov. Avg. ─ ─ **GAAP Earnings vs. Previous Year**   Volume Above Avg. ▮▮▮  **STARS**
12-Mo. Target Price ─── Relative Strength — ▲ Up ▼ Down ▶ No Change   Below Avg. ▮▮▮ ★

Options: CBOE, P, Ph

Analysis prepared by **Matthew Albrecht** on November 03, 2008, when the stock traded at **$ 11.74**.

## Highlights

➤ We think good performance from Janus funds continues to attract assets, though in current market conditions, we think net inflows may be difficult to come by. Its INTECH subsidiary continues to see flows, which be believe is due to its strong track record. We see strong relative performance, as well as improving non-U.S. distribution and increased penetration in the institutional market, continuing to attract assets. We expect modest inflows across products and channels to offset some of the steep equity market declines this year, but we still see assets under management falling more than 20% in 2008, but balances could rebound next year. We expect revenues to decline in each of the next two years as average asset balances fall.

➤ We see compensation falling in 2008 on a relative basis, helped by staff reductions and flexible accrual rates, but we see an increase in that expense in 2009. We also expect investment losses and fund support costs to pressure pretax margins. Longer term, we see efficiencies in the cost structure helping pretax margins expand.

➤ We forecast EPS of $0.94 in 2008 and $1.02 in 2009.

## Investment Rationale/Risk

➤ As of September 30, 2008, 52%, 74% and 79% of JNS's equity fund family were in the top half of their categories on a one-, three- and five-year performance basis, respectively, which we believe should help attract additional flows in the quarters to come. Client redemptions in legacy products have only recently been stemmed, however. Investor preference for growth products and JNS's strong fund performance had previously warranted this stock's premium multiple, in our view, but we think its close ties to equity markets are reflected in its recent peer-average multiple as markets slide.

➤ Risks to our recommendation and target price include potential equity and bond market depreciation, and increasing competition. We view Janus's corporate governance practices negatively and would like to see a higher proportion of independent directors.

➤ The shares recently traded at about 11.5X our 2008 EPS estimate, in line with the peer group average that has declined significantly recently, which we believe is due to steep declines in the equity markets. Our 12-month target price of $13 is equal to 12.7X our 2009 EPS estimate, in line with peers.

## Qualitative Risk Assessment

| LOW | MEDIUM | HIGH |
|---|---|---|

Our risk assessment reflects the company's lack of product diversification, previous regulatory issues, and turnover of investment personnel.

## Quantitative Evaluations

**S&P Quality Ranking**   NR

| D | C | B- | B | B+ | A- | A | A+ |
|---|---|---|---|---|---|---|---|

**Relative Strength Rank**   WEAK

10

LOWEST = 1                     HIGHEST = 99

## Revenue/Earnings Data

**Revenue (Million $)**

| | 1Q | 2Q | 3Q | 4Q | Year |
|---|---|---|---|---|---|
| 2008 | 281.2 | 304.2 | 275.4 | -- | -- |
| 2007 | 247.9 | 273.0 | 284.6 | 311.5 | 1,117 |
| 2006 | 256.1 | 254.6 | 250.1 | 265.9 | 1,027 |
| 2005 | 239.0 | 229.3 | 237.5 | 247.3 | 953.1 |
| 2004 | 274.4 | 258.8 | 237.8 | 239.8 | 1,011 |
| 2003 | 231.2 | 245.5 | 256.6 | 261.4 | 994.7 |

**Earnings Per Share ($)**

| | | | | | |
|---|---|---|---|---|---|
| 2008 | 0.24 | 0.40 | 0.16 | E0.20 | E0.94 |
| 2007 | 0.20 | 0.28 | 0.29 | 0.30 | 1.07 |
| 2006 | 0.17 | 0.15 | 0.15 | 0.19 | 0.66 |
| 2005 | 0.09 | 0.12 | 0.15 | 0.05 | 0.40 |
| 2004 | -0.10 | 0.54 | 0.20 | 0.08 | 0.73 |
| 2003 | 0.17 | 0.22 | 0.24 | 3.51 | 4.17 |

Fiscal year ended Dec. 31. Next earnings report expected: Late January. EPS Estimates based on S&P Operating Earnings; historical GAAP earnings are as reported.

## Dividend Data (Dates: mm/dd Payment Date: mm/dd/yy)

| Amount ($) | Date Decl. | Ex-Div. Date | Stk. of Record | Payment Date |
|---|---|---|---|---|
| 0.040 | 05/01 | 05/14 | 05/16 | 05/30/08 |

Dividends have been paid since 2000. Source: Company reports.

---

The **McGraw·Hill** Companies

# Janus Capital Group Inc

STANDARD
&POOR'S

## Business Summary November 03, 2008

CORPORATE OVERVIEW. Janus Capital Group, a single-branded global asset management company, was created through the January 1, 2003 merger of Janus Capital Corp. into its parent company, Stilwell Financial Inc., which had been spun off from Kansas City Southern Industries in July 2000 via a stock offering. The company had total assets under management of nearly $207 billion at the end of 2007, up from $168 billion at the end of 2006. The company distributes its products through one global distribution network directly to investors, and through advisers and financial intermediaries.

Wholly owned Janus Capital Management focuses on growth equities, and uses both fundamental and quantitative investment research. It also offers core, international, specialty fixed-income, and money market products. Its largest funds include Janus Fund (JANSX), Janus Worldwide (JAWWX) and Janus Twenty (JAVLX).

The company owns 86.5% of Enhanced Investment Technologies, LLC (INTECH), which focuses on mathematically driven equity investing strategies. INTECH's assets under management totaled about $70 billion at the end of 2007, up from $7.3 billion at the end of 2002. INTECH, which manages assets for large institutions and endowments, seeks to achieve long-term returns

that outperform a passive index, while controlling risks and trading costs.

JNS owns about 80% of Perkins, Wolf, McDonnell and Co., which focuses on value investing and sub-advises a number of Janus's small- and mid-cap value products. Bay Isle employs a bottom-up analysis, with a focus on what it believes to be quality companies that trade at discounts to their fair market value. Vontobel Asset Management is a sub-adviser for several Janus mutual funds and products, focusing on value equities.

In December 2003, JNS exchanged 32.3 million DST Systems shares for all shares of a DST unit, referred to as JCG Partners, which owns a commercial printing business worth about $115 million, and has $999 million in cash. In December 2003, JNS said it would no longer use the equity method to account for its remaining investment. In 2004, JNS sold its remaining 7.4 million shares of DST stock.

## Company Financials Fiscal Year Ended Dec. 31

### Per Share Data ($)

| | 2007 | 2006 | 2005 | 2004 | 2003 | 2002 | 2001 | 2000 | 1999 | 1998 |
|---|---|---|---|---|---|---|---|---|---|---|
| Tangible Book Value | NM | NM | 0.88 | 1.43 | 1.00 | NM | NM | 3.50 | NA | NA |
| Cash Flow | 1.21 | 0.93 | 0.64 | 0.99 | 4.46 | 0.70 | 1.93 | 3.30 | 1.51 | NA |
| Earnings | 1.07 | 0.66 | 0.40 | 0.73 | 4.17 | 0.38 | 1.31 | 2.90 | 1.31 | 0.67 |
| S&P Core Earnings | 1.05 | 0.61 | 0.42 | 0.32 | 1.60 | 0.42 | 1.18 | NA | NA | NA |
| Dividends | 0.04 | 0.04 | 0.04 | 0.04 | 0.04 | 0.05 | 0.04 | 0.01 | NA | NA |
| Payout Ratio | 4% | 6% | 10% | 5% | 1% | 13% | 3% | NM | NA | NA |
| Prices:High | 37.08 | 24.20 | 20.59 | 17.90 | 19.00 | 29.24 | 46.63 | 54.50 | NA | NA |
| Prices:Low | 19.35 | 15.50 | 12.75 | 12.60 | 9.46 | 8.97 | 18.20 | 30.75 | NA | NA |
| P/E Ratio:High | 35 | 37 | 51 | 25 | 5 | 77 | 36 | 19 | NA | NA |
| P/E Ratio:Low | 18 | 23 | 32 | 17 | 2 | 24 | 14 | 11 | NA | NA |

### Income Statement Analysis (Million $)

| | 2007 | 2006 | 2005 | 2004 | 2003 | 2002 | 2001 | 2000 | 1999 | 1998 |
|---|---|---|---|---|---|---|---|---|---|---|
| Revenue | 1,117 | 1,027 | 953 | 1,011 | 995 | 1,145 | 1,556 | 2,248 | 1,212 | 671 |
| Operating Income | 375 | 267 | 224 | 264 | 396 | 441 | 872 | 1,118 | 554 | 297 |
| Depreciation | 24.9 | 47.1 | 50.1 | 60.4 | 67.6 | 72.3 | 131 | 81.2 | 35.4 | 16.8 |
| Interest Expense | 58.8 | 32.3 | 28.6 | 38.4 | 60.5 | 57.8 | 34.8 | 7.70 | 5.90 | 6.50 |
| Pretax Income | 330 | 237 | 176 | 272 | 895 | 320 | 620 | 1,202 | 587 | 289 |
| Effective Tax Rate | 35.3% | 34.5% | 38.6% | 33.9% | NM | 72.6% | 35.1% | 35.5% | 36.8% | 35.8% |
| Net Income | 192 | 134 | 87.8 | 170 | 956 | 84.7 | 302 | 664 | 313 | 152 |
| S&P Core Earnings | 189 | 124 | 92.5 | 74.1 | 367 | 92.4 | 276 | NA | NA | NA |

### Balance Sheet & Other Financial Data (Million $)

| | 2007 | 2006 | 2005 | 2004 | 2003 | 2002 | 2001 | 2000 | 1999 | 1998 |
|---|---|---|---|---|---|---|---|---|---|---|
| Cash | 691 | 560 | 553 | 527 | 1,223 | 161 | 237 | 364 | 324 | 139 |
| Current Assets | 954 | 925 | 1,004 | 1,065 | 1,466 | 346 | 478 | 641 | 525 | 259 |
| Total Assets | 3,564 | 3,538 | 3,629 | 3,768 | 4,332 | 3,322 | 3,392 | 1,581 | 1,232 | 823 |
| Current Liabilities | 227 | 186 | 268 | 155 | 301 | 185 | 881 | 196 | 163 | 71.1 |
| Long Term Debt | 1,128 | 537 | 262 | 378 | 769 | 856 | 400 | Nil | Nil | 16.6 |
| Common Equity | 1,724 | 2,306 | 2,581 | 2,735 | 2,661 | 1,508 | 1,363 | 1,058 | 815 | 540 |
| Total Capital | 3,272 | 3,261 | 3,283 | 3,553 | 3,997 | 3,097 | 2,466 | 1,342 | 1,024 | 710 |
| Capital Expenditures | 16.7 | 17.0 | 23.6 | 26.5 | 23.9 | 16.3 | 34.3 | 107 | 50.5 | 35.0 |
| Cash Flow | 217 | 181 | 138 | 230 | 1,023 | 157 | 433 | 745 | 348 | 169 |
| Current Ratio | 4.2 | 5.0 | 3.7 | 6.9 | 4.9 | 1.9 | 0.5 | 3.3 | 3.2 | 3.6 |
| % Long Term Debt of Capitalization | 39.3 | 16.5 | 8.0 | 10.6 | 19.2 | 27.6 | 16.2 | Nil | Nil | 2.3 |
| % Net Income of Revenue | 17.2 | 13.0 | 9.2 | 16.8 | 96.1 | 7.4 | 19.4 | 29.5 | 25.8 | 22.7 |
| % Return on Assets | 5.4 | 3.7 | 2.4 | 4.2 | 25.0 | 2.5 | 12.2 | 47.2 | 30.5 | NA |
| % Return on Equity | 9.5 | 5.5 | 3.3 | 6.3 | 45.9 | 5.9 | 25.0 | 70.9 | 46.2 | 34.3 |

Data as orig reptd.; bef. results of disc opers/spec. items. Per share data adj. for stk. divs.; EPS diluted. E-Estimated. NA-Not Available. NM-Not Meaningful. NR-Not Ranked. UR-Under Review.

**Office:** 151 Detroit St, Denver, CO 80206-4928.
**Telephone:** 303-333-3863.
**Website:** http://www.janus.com
**Chrmn:** S.L. Scheid

**CEO:** G.D. Black
**EVP & CFO:** G.A. Frost
**EVP, Secy & General Counsel:** K.D. Howes
**Chief Acctg Officer & Cntlr:** R.W. Blakley

**Board Members:** T. K. Armour, P. F. Balser, G. D. Black, G. A. Cox, J. J. Diermeier, J. Fredericks, D. R. Gatzek, L. E. Kochard, R. T. Parry, J. Patton, L. H. Rowland, G. S. Schafer, S. L. Scheid, R. J. Skidelskiy

**Founded:** 1998
**Domicile:** Delaware
**Employees:** 1,213

**STANDARD &POOR'S**

# JDS Uniphase Corp

| S&P Recommendation | HOLD ★★★☆☆ | Price | 12-Mo. Target Price | Investment Style |
|---|---|---|---|---|
| | | $3.06 (as of Nov 14, 2008) | $4.00 | Large-Cap Blend |

**GICS Sector** Information Technology
**Sub-Industry** Communications Equipment

**Summary** This company manufactures fiber optic products and communications test and measurement solutions.

## Key Stock Statistics (Source S&P, Vickers, company reports)

| | | | | | | | | |
|---|---|---|---|---|---|---|---|---|
| 52-Wk Range | $15.33– 2.95 | S&P Oper. EPS 2009**E** | 0.18 | Market Capitalization(B) | $0.658 | Beta | | 1.68 |
| Trailing 12-Month EPS | $-0.14 | S&P Oper. EPS 2010**E** | 0.38 | Yield (%) | Nil | S&P 3-Yr. Proj. EPS CAGR(%) | | 25 |
| Trailing 12-Month P/E | NM | P/E on S&P Oper. EPS 2009**E** | 17.0 | Dividend Rate/Share | Nil | S&P Credit Rating | | NA |
| $10K Invested 5 Yrs Ago | $1,138 | Common Shares Outstg. (M) | 214.9 | Institutional Ownership (%) | 81 | | | |

## Price Performance

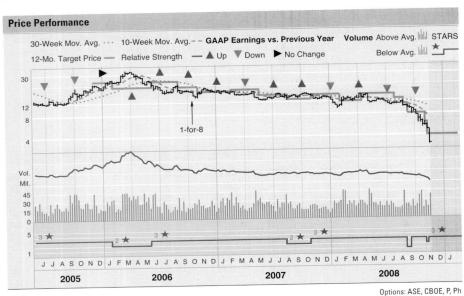

30-Week Mov. Avg. · · · ·    10-Week Mov. Avg. - - -    GAAP Earnings vs. Previous Year    Volume Above Avg. STARS
12-Mo. Target Price —    Relative Strength —    ▲ Up ▼ Down ► No Change    Below Avg. ★

1-for-8

2005    2006    2007    2008

Options: ASE, CBOE, P, Ph

Analysis prepared by **Ari Bensinger** on November 12, 2008, when the stock traded at **$ 3.24**.

## Qualitative Risk Assessment

| LOW | MEDIUM | HIGH |
|---|---|---|

Our risk assessment reflects the highly competitive nature of the industry, the company's dependence on telecom carrier spending, which tends to be uneven due to the uncertain timing of network projects and upgrades, and a high degree of stock price volatility.

## Quantitative Evaluations

**S&P Quality Ranking**                                          C

| D | C | B- | B | B+ | A- | A | A+ |
|---|---|---|---|---|---|---|---|

**Relative Strength Rank**                                  WEAK

9

LOWEST = 1                                          HIGHEST = 99

## Highlights

➤ Following a 10% sales increase in FY 08 (Jun.), we see sales being relatively flat during FY 09, reflecting weakening trends in enterprise spending. Demand for optical communication products, particularly tunable lasers and ROADMs, should remain strong on accelerated buildouts of broadband networks. Results in test and measurement are being hurt by order deferrals by the company's wireline and cable customers.

➤ The company is in the midst of a major restructuring program. As a result of a favorable product mix and continued cost cutting, we believe FY 09 gross margins will widen to 44%, up from the 43% registered in FY 08. We forecast FY 09 operating expenses as a percentage of sales declining from the prior period.

➤ After minimal taxes due to loss carryovers and a material decline in interest income on lower interest rates, we forecast FY 09 operating EPS of $0.18, versus the $0.21 posted in FY 08. Our estimate includes projected stock option expense of $0.20 a share. We see FY 10 EPS of $0.38.

## Investment Rationale/Risk

➤ We expect JDSU to benefit over the long term from increased demand for optical systems and test measurement systems, as service operators expand their network bandwidth capabilities to handle sharply higher data traffic patterns. Over the near term, however, we see customers increasingly scrutinizing spending habits and deferring projects. Based on our valuation analysis, we believe the current stock price adequately reflects the challenging operating environment.

➤ Risks to our recommendation and target price include decreased telecom capital spending, market share losses, and slower-than-expected margin improvement.

➤ Our 12-month target price of $4 is based on 1X the company's cash position and 0.5X our FY 09 sales estimate, below the peer mean, warranted by our view that a more disciplined telecom spending environment will hamper near-term sales and earnings growth. While we see the potential for material operating leverage in the company's business model, we see considerable uncertainty in future earnings power.

## Revenue/Earnings Data

**Revenue (Million $)**

| | 1Q | 2Q | 3Q | 4Q | Year |
|---|---|---|---|---|---|
| 2009 | 380.7 | -- | -- | -- | -- |
| 2008 | 356.7 | 399.2 | 383.9 | 390.3 | 1,530 |
| 2007 | 318.1 | 366.3 | 361.7 | 350.7 | 1,397 |
| 2006 | 258.3 | 312.9 | 314.9 | 318.2 | 1,204 |
| 2005 | 194.5 | 180.5 | 166.3 | 170.9 | 712.2 |
| 2004 | 147.4 | 152.6 | 161.4 | 174.5 | 635.9 |

**Earnings Per Share ($)**

| | | | | | |
|---|---|---|---|---|---|
| 2009 | -0.08 | E0.05 | E0.02 | E0.07 | E0.18 |
| 2008 | -0.03 | 0.09 | -0.03 | -0.13 | -0.10 |
| 2007 | -0.08 | 0.10 | -0.07 | -0.08 | -0.12 |
| 2006 | -0.32 | -0.24 | 0.02 | -0.24 | -0.72 |
| 2005 | -0.16 | -0.24 | -0.24 | -0.80 | -1.44 |
| 2004 | -0.16 | -0.32 | -0.08 | -0.16 | -0.64 |

Fiscal year ended Jun. 30. Next earnings report expected: Early February. EPS Estimates based on S&P Operating Earnings; historical GAAP earnings are as reported.

## Dividend Data

No cash dividends have been paid.

# JDS Uniphase Corp

**STANDARD &POOR'S**

## Business Summary November 12, 2008

CORPORATE OVERVIEW. JDS Uniphase supplies optical components, as well as communications test and measurement solutions for the communications market. The company also leverages its optical science capabilities on non-communications applications, offering products for display, security, medical environmental instrumentation, decorative, aerospace and defense applications.

The company operates in three principal segments: optical communications, (37% of FY 07 (Jun.)revenue); communications test and measurement (44%); and advanced optical technologies (12%). In addition, the commercial lasers business unit accounted for approximately 7% of net revenue in FY 07.

PRIMARY BUSINESS DYNAMICS. JDSU supplies the basic building blocks for fiber optic networks, which enable the rapid transmission of large amounts of data over long distances via light waves. The optical communications product group provides fiber optic components, modules and subsystems. Products include tunable transmitters, receivers, amplifiers, multiplexers and demultiplexers, reconfigurable optical add/drop multiplexers (ROADMs), switches, optical performance monitors, couplers, splitters and circulators. In addition, the company provides optical communications solutions required to build and maintain Agile Optical Networks (AONs). AONs are designed to be dynamically and remotely reconfigurable, so that they can quickly and easily meet changes in network traffic patterns and demand. We believe that a growing

demand for network capacity and bandwidth will result in increased demand on the metro and long-haul infrastructures into which these services feed.

The communications test and measurement segment provides instruments, software, systems and services that help communications equipment manufacturers and service providers accelerate the deployment of broadband networks and services from the core of the network to the home, including deployment over fiber to the curb, node or premise and digital networks.

The advanced optical technologies segment provides document authentication, brand protection and product differentiation solutions for a range of commercial and consumer applications. It also offers thin film coated optics for applications, including computer monitors and flat panel displays, projection systems, photocopiers, facsimile machines, scanners, as well as optically variable micro flakes for security applications and decorative surface treatments. JDSU's technology protects approximately 100 currencies worldwide and has been widely adopted by leading pharmaceutical and biotechnology companies on prescription drug packaging.

## Company Financials Fiscal Year Ended Jun. 30

| Per Share Data ($) | 2008 | 2007 | 2006 | 2005 | 2004 | 2003 | 2002 | 2001 | 2000 | 1999 |
|---|---|---|---|---|---|---|---|---|---|---|
| Tangible Book Value | 2.73 | 2.80 | 2.72 | 5.76 | 7.12 | 7.92 | 11.44 | 22.24 | 20.88 | 2.16 |
| Cash Flow | NA | 0.48 | -0.46 | -1.11 | -0.32 | -4.82 | -52.00 | -370.58 | 0.52 | -3.52 |
| Earnings | -0.10 | -0.12 | -0.72 | -1.44 | -0.64 | -5.28 | -42.21 | -411.20 | -10.08 | -4.30 |
| S&P Core Earnings | -0.12 | -0.21 | -0.88 | -2.24 | -2.56 | -7.84 | -32.88 | -175.60 | NA | NA |
| Dividends | Nil | Nil | Nil | Nil | Nil | Nil | Nil | Nil | Nil | Nil |
| Payout Ratio | Nil | Nil | Nil | Nil | Nil | Nil | Nil | Nil | Nil | Nil |
| Prices:High | 15.33 | 17.99 | 34.40 | 26.08 | 47.08 | 37.68 | 82.72 | 519.50 | 1227 | 710.00 |
| Prices:Low | 2.95 | 12.41 | 13.93 | 10.56 | 22.72 | 19.84 | 12.64 | 40.96 | 296.00 | 59.25 |
| P/E Ratio:High | NM | NM | NM | NM | NM | NM | NM | NM | NM | NM |
| P/E Ratio:Low | NM | NM | NM | NM | NM | NM | NM | NM | NM | NM |

| Income Statement Analysis (Million $) | | | | | | | | | | |
|---|---|---|---|---|---|---|---|---|---|---|
| Revenue | 1,530 | 1,397 | 1,204 | 712 | 636 | 676 | 1,098 | 3,233 | 1,430 | 283 |
| Operating Income | NA | 36.8 | -107 | -83.9 | -58.5 | -306 | -374 | -62.5 | 446 | 94.6 |
| Depreciation | 145 | 128 | 57.4 | 61.3 | 55.9 | 79.2 | 1,645 | 5,542 | 951 | 30.7 |
| Interest Expense | NA | 7.10 | 27.7 | Nil | Nil | Nil | Nil | Nil | 0.50 | 0.02 |
| Pretax Income | -19.3 | -24.3 | -152 | -255 | -128 | -920 | -8,501 | -56,494 | -830 | -151 |
| Effective Tax Rate | NM | NM | NM | NM | NM | NM | NM | NM | NM | NM |
| Net Income | -21.7 | -26.3 | -151 | -261 | -113 | -934 | -8,738 | -56,122 | -905 | -171 |
| S&P Core Earnings | -27.5 | -45.7 | -181 | -394 | -446 | -1,399 | -5,534 | -23,966 | NA | NA |

| Balance Sheet & Other Financial Data (Million $) | | | | | | | | | | |
|---|---|---|---|---|---|---|---|---|---|---|
| Cash | 874 | 363 | 365 | 511 | 328 | 242 | 412 | 763 | 319 | 75.4 |
| Current Assets | NA | 1,661 | 1,805 | 1,588 | 1,866 | 1,515 | 1,857 | 3,036 | 1,973 | 928 |
| Total Assets | 2,906 | 3,025 | 3,065 | 2,080 | 2,422 | 2,138 | 3,005 | 12,245 | 26,389 | 8,192 |
| Current Liabilities | NA | 348 | 422 | 240 | 350 | 423 | 483 | 848 | 647 | 298 |
| Long Term Debt | NA | 808 | 900 | 467 | 465 | Nil | 5.50 | 12.8 | 41.0 | Nil |
| Common Equity | 1,817 | 1,736 | 1,584 | 1,335 | 1,571 | 1,671 | 2,471 | 10,706 | 24,779 | 3,619 |
| Total Capital | NA | 2,544 | 2,484 | 1,802 | 2,063 | 1,699 | 2,519 | 11,392 | 25,722 | 3,937 |
| Capital Expenditures | 51.7 | 75.7 | 67.2 | 35.8 | 66.4 | 47.2 | 133 | 732 | 280 | 46.6 |
| Cash Flow | NA | 102 | -93.8 | -200 | -56.7 | -855 | -7,093 | -50,580 | 46.0 | -140 |
| Current Ratio | 3.2 | 4.8 | 4.3 | 6.6 | 5.3 | 3.6 | 3.8 | 3.6 | 3.0 | 3.1 |
| % Long Term Debt of Capitalization | 18.3 | 31.8 | 36.2 | 25.9 | 22.5 | Nil | 0.2 | 0.1 | 0.2 | Nil |
| % Net Income of Revenue | NM | NM | NM | NM | NM | NM | NM | NM | NM | NM |
| % Return on Assets | NM | NM | NM | NM | NM | NM | NM | NM | NM | NM |
| % Return on Equity | NM | NM | NM | NM | NM | NM | NM | NM | NM | NM |

Data as orig reptd.; bef. results of disc opers/spec. items. Per share data adj. for stk. divs.; EPS diluted. E-Estimated. NA-Not Available. NM-Not Meaningful. NR-Not Ranked. UR-Under Review.

**Office:** 430 N McCarthy Blvd, Milpitas, CA 95035-5116.
**Telephone:** 408-546-5000.
**Email:** investor.relations@jdsu.com
**Website:** http://www.jdsu.com

**Chrmn:** M.A. Kaplan
**Pres & CEO:** K.J. Kennedy
**Investor Contact:** D. Vellequette (408-546-4445)
**EVP, CFO & Chief Acctg Officer:** D. Vellequette

**SVP & CTO:** S. Lumish
**Board Members:** R. E. Belluzzo, H. L. Covert, Jr., B. Day, K. A. DeNuccio, P. A. Herscher, M. A. Jabbar, M. A. Kaplan, K. J. Kennedy, R. T. Liebhaber, C. S. Skrzypczak

**Founded:** 1979
**Domicile:** Delaware
**Employees:** 7,100

*The McGraw-Hill Companies*

**STANDARD &POOR'S**

# Johnson Controls Inc.

| S&P Recommendation **BUY** ★★★★☆ | Price $15.36 (as of Nov 14, 2008) | 12-Mo. Target Price $34.00 | Investment Style Large-Cap Blend |
| --- | --- | --- | --- |

**GICS Sector** Consumer Discretionary
**Sub-Industry** Auto Parts & Equipment

**Summary** This company supplies building controls and energy management systems, automotive seating, and batteries.

## Key Stock Statistics (Source S&P, Vickers, company reports)

| | | | | | | | |
| --- | --- | --- | --- | --- | --- | --- | --- |
| 52-Wk Range | $39.64– 14.58 | S&P Oper. EPS 2009**E** | 2.10 | Market Capitalization(B) | $9.120 | Beta | 1.00 |
| Trailing 12-Month EPS | $1.63 | S&P Oper. EPS 2010**E** | NA | Yield (%) | 3.39 | S&P 3-Yr. Proj. EPS CAGR(%) | 16 |
| Trailing 12-Month P/E | 9.4 | P/E on S&P Oper. EPS 2009**E** | 7.3 | Dividend Rate/Share | $0.52 | S&P Credit Rating | A- |
| $10K Invested 5 Yrs Ago | $9,278 | Common Shares Outstg. (M) | 593.8 | Institutional Ownership (%) | 78 | | |

## Price Performance

30-Week Mov. Avg. · · · 10-Week Mov. Avg. – – GAAP Earnings vs. Previous Year  Volume Above Avg. STARS
12-Mo. Target Price — Relative Strength — ▲ Up ▼ Down ▶ No Change  Below Avg. ★

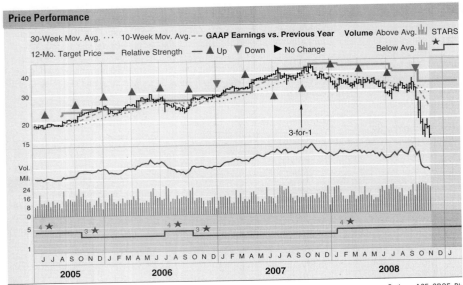

Options: ASE, CBOE, Ph

Analysis prepared by **Efraim Levy, CFA** on October 07, 2008, when the stock traded at **$ 26.14**.

## Highlights

➤ We expect FY 09 (Sep.) sales to advance in the upper single digits, reflecting an expansion of the facilities management business, expected new automotive business, higher global automobile production, pass-through of lead costs and acquisitions. We see facilities management benefiting from new customers as outsourcing trends continue and the backlog of orders for installed systems continues to grow. Automotive revenues will likely benefit from new contracts and expanding business with Asian and European vehicle makers. Restraining growth should be weakening U.S. and global economies and lower vehicle sales for the U.S. and Western European industries.

➤ We see operating margins contracting slightly as JCI suffers from weak domestic demand and incurs higher health care expenses, pricing pressures from customers, higher raw material costs, and lower margins from pass-through lead sales. Partially offsetting should be benefits from rising sales, plus restructuring activities, especially in Europe.

➤ Our FY 08 EPS estimate is $2.33, up from $2.09 in FY 07, which excludes non-recurring tax benefits.

## Investment Rationale/Risk

➤ We expect growth to exceed that of peers, and with greater earnings stability. We project that diversification in geography, products and customers will help JCI withstand weakness in the domestic auto manufacturers. The stock's P/E multiple was recently below that of the S&P 500 based on our calendar 2008 estimates. We view the balance sheet as strong, with long-term debt generally at 20% to 36% of capitalization over the past decade.

➤ Risks to our recommendation and target price include lower-than-expected demand, especially for automotive parts, higher raw material costs, failure to achieve expected acquisition synergies, and pricing pressure from customers.

➤ Applying a P/E multiple of 13X, a premium to peers but in the lower to middle portion of JCI's historical average range, to our FY 09 EPS estimate of $2.46 leads to a value of $32. Our DCF model, which assumes a weighted average cost of capital of 10.7%, a compound annual growth rate of 7.1% over the next 15 years, and a terminal growth rate of 3.5%, leads to an intrinsic value of $36. Our 12-month target price of $34 is a blend of these two methodologies.

## Qualitative Risk Assessment

| LOW | MEDIUM | HIGH |
| --- | --- | --- |

Our risk assessment reflects favorable growth prospects in the building controls markets that JCI serves and what we view as a strong management team and a healthy balance sheet, offset by the challenges faced by the automotive operations.

## Quantitative Evaluations

**S&P Quality Ranking** A+

| D | C | B- | B | B+ | A- | A | A+ |
| --- | --- | --- | --- | --- | --- | --- | --- |

**Relative Strength Rank** WEAK

29

LOWEST = 1    HIGHEST = 99

## Revenue/Earnings Data

**Revenue (Million $)**

| | 1Q | 2Q | 3Q | 4Q | Year |
| --- | --- | --- | --- | --- | --- |
| 2008 | 9,484 | 9,406 | 9,865 | 9,307 | 38,062 |
| 2007 | 8,210 | 8,492 | 8,911 | 9,011 | 34,624 |
| 2006 | 7,528 | 8,167 | 8,390 | 8,150 | 32,235 |
| 2005 | 6,618 | 6,899 | 7,062 | 6,900 | 27,479 |
| 2004 | 6,384 | 6,620 | 6,792 | 6,757 | 26,553 |
| 2003 | 5,183 | 5,503 | 5,960 | 6,000 | 22,646 |

**Earnings Per Share ($)**

| | | | | | |
| --- | --- | --- | --- | --- | --- |
| 2008 | 0.40 | 0.48 | 0.73 | 0.03 | 1.63 |
| 2007 | 0.28 | 0.44 | 0.66 | 0.77 | 2.16 |
| 2006 | 0.29 | 0.28 | 0.57 | 0.62 | 1.75 |
| 2005 | 0.28 | 0.09 | 0.44 | 0.50 | 1.30 |
| 2004 | 0.29 | 0.27 | 0.38 | 0.47 | 1.41 |
| 2003 | 0.25 | 0.23 | 0.33 | 0.39 | 1.20 |

Fiscal year ended Sep. 30. Next earnings report expected: Late January. EPS Estimates based on S&P Operating Earnings; historical GAAP earnings are as reported.

## Dividend Data (Dates: mm/dd Payment Date: mm/dd/yy)

| Amount ($) | Date Decl. | Ex-Div. Date | Stk. of Record | Payment Date |
| --- | --- | --- | --- | --- |
| 0.130 | 11/14 | 12/12 | 12/14 | 01/03/08 |
| 0.130 | 01/23 | 03/12 | 03/14 | 04/02/08 |
| 0.130 | 05/20 | 06/11 | 06/13 | 07/03/08 |
| 0.130 | 07/23 | 09/10 | 09/12 | 10/02/08 |

Dividends have been paid since 1887. Source: Company reports.

The **McGraw-Hill** Companies

# Johnson Controls Inc.

**STANDARD &POOR'S**

## Business Summary October 07, 2008

CORPORATE OVERVIEW. Johnson Controls, founded in 1885, is a leading manufacturer of automotive interior systems, automotive batteries and automated building control systems. It also provides facility management services for commercial buildings. In FY 07 (Sep.), the automotive segment accounted for 63% of sales and 55% of income, with the balance coming from controls and facility management.

The automotive interior segment manufactures complete seats and seating components for North American and European car and light-truck manufacturers. The segment has grown rapidly in recent years, gaining contracts to produce seats formerly manufactured in-house by automakers, and expanding in Europe. Seating accounted for nearly 51% of sales in FY 07.

The power solutions unit, the largest automotive battery operation in North America, makes lead-acid batteries primarily for the automotive replacement market and for OEMs. Batteries accounted for about 12% of FY 07 sales and the unit is expanding operations in Europe.

The building efficiency (formerly called controls) segment manufactures, installs and services controls and control systems, principally for nonresidential buildings, which are used for temperature and energy management, and fire safety and security maintenance. The segment also includes custom engineering, installation and servicing of process control systems and a growing facilities management business. Building efficiency sales accounted for 37% of FY 07 revenues. As of March 2008, JCI had an unearned backlog of building systems and services contracts totaling $4.5 billion.

Government building trends promoting facility management outsourcing and energy efficiency programs are creating, in our view, additional opportunities.

GM, DaimlerChrysler (now Daimler AG and Chrysler LLC) and Ford accounted for an aggregate of 28% of FY 07 sales, although none of the companies individually accounted for more than 10% of sales. We expect the share of revenues from the largest three customers to shrink as the company expands its sales outside the U.S. and with non-domestic customers expanding in the U.S.

## Company Financials Fiscal Year Ended Sep. 30

| Per Share Data ($) | 2008 | 2007 | 2006 | 2005 | 2004 | 2003 | 2002 | 2001 | 2000 | 1999 |
|---|---|---|---|---|---|---|---|---|---|---|
| Tangible Book Value | NA | 3.38 | 1.10 | 3.52 | 1.93 | 1.27 | 0.74 | 1.17 | 0.61 | 0.08 |
| Cash Flow | NA | 3.38 | 2.95 | 2.41 | 2.48 | 2.17 | 1.97 | 1.77 | 1.79 | 1.55 |
| Earnings | 1.63 | 2.16 | 1.75 | 1.30 | 1.41 | 1.20 | 1.06 | 0.85 | 0.85 | 0.75 |
| S&P Core Earnings | NA | 2.16 | 1.74 | 1.31 | 1.42 | 1.16 | 0.89 | 0.70 | NA | NA |
| Dividends | 0.63 | 0.33 | 0.37 | 0.33 | 0.30 | 0.24 | 0.22 | 0.21 | 0.19 | 0.17 |
| Payout Ratio | 39% | 15% | 21% | 26% | 21% | 20% | 21% | 24% | 22% | 22% |
| Prices:High | 36.52 | 44.46 | 30.00 | 25.07 | 21.33 | 19.37 | 15.53 | 13.78 | 10.85 | 12.78 |
| Prices:Low | 14.58 | 28.09 | 22.12 | 17.52 | 16.52 | 11.96 | 11.52 | 8.66 | 7.64 | 8.17 |
| P/E Ratio:High | 22 | 21 | 17 | 19 | 15 | 16 | 15 | 16 | 13 | 17 |
| P/E Ratio:Low | 9 | 13 | 13 | 13 | 12 | 10 | 11 | 10 | 9 | 11 |

### Income Statement Analysis (Million $)

| | 2008 | 2007 | 2006 | 2005 | 2004 | 2003 | 2002 | 2001 | 2000 | 1999 |
|---|---|---|---|---|---|---|---|---|---|---|
| Revenue | 38,062 | 34,624 | 32,235 | 27,479 | 26,553 | 22,646 | 20,103 | 18,427 | 17,155 | 16,139 |
| Operating Income | NA | 2,527 | 2,184 | 1,913 | 1,918 | 1,720 | 1,639 | 1,477 | 1,427 | 1,300 |
| Depreciation | 783 | 732 | 705 | 636 | 617 | 558 | 517 | 516 | 462 | 446 |
| Interest Expense | NA | 277 | 248 | 121 | 111 | 114 | 122 | 129 | 128 | 153 |
| Pretax Income | 1,324 | 1,607 | 1,138 | 1,003 | 1,212 | 1,058 | 1,006 | 867 | 856 | 770 |
| Effective Tax Rate | 24.2% | 18.7% | 5.54% | 20.4% | 26.0% | 31.0% | 34.6% | 38.7% | 39.6% | 40.5% |
| Net Income | 979 | 1,295 | 1,033 | 757 | 818 | 683 | 600 | 478 | 472 | 420 |
| S&P Core Earnings | NA | 1,292 | 1,025 | 764 | 818 | 650 | 497 | 385 | NA | NA |

### Balance Sheet & Other Financial Data (Million $)

| | 2008 | 2007 | 2006 | 2005 | 2004 | 2003 | 2002 | 2001 | 2000 | 1999 |
|---|---|---|---|---|---|---|---|---|---|---|
| Cash | 384 | 674 | 293 | 171 | 170 | 136 | 262 | 375 | 276 | 276 |
| Current Assets | NA | 10,872 | 9,264 | 7,139 | 6,377 | 5,620 | 4,946 | 4,544 | 4,277 | 3,849 |
| Total Assets | 25,318 | 24,105 | 21,921 | 16,144 | 15,091 | 13,127 | 11,165 | 9,912 | 9,428 | 8,614 |
| Current Liabilities | NA | 9,920 | 8,146 | 6,841 | 6,602 | 5,584 | 4,806 | 4,580 | 4,510 | 4,267 |
| Long Term Debt | NA | 3,255 | 4,166 | 1,578 | 1,631 | 1,777 | 1,827 | 1,395 | 1,315 | 1,283 |
| Common Equity | 9,411 | 8,907 | 7,355 | 6,058 | 5,206 | 4,164 | 3,396 | 2,862 | 2,447 | 2,135 |
| Total Capital | NA | 11,290 | 11,650 | 7,831 | 7,106 | 6,260 | 5,515 | 4,588 | 3,891 | 3,553 |
| Capital Expenditures | 807 | 828 | 711 | 664 | 862 | 664 | 496 | 622 | 547 | 514 |
| Cash Flow | NA | 2,027 | 1,738 | 1,394 | 1,434 | 1,234 | 1,110 | 985 | 924 | 856 |
| Current Ratio | 1.1 | 1.1 | 1.1 | 1.0 | 1.0 | 1.0 | 1.0 | 1.0 | 0.9 | 0.9 |
| % Long Term Debt of Capitalization | 24.9 | 28.8 | 35.8 | 20.1 | 22.9 | 28.4 | 33.1 | 30.4 | 33.8 | 36.1 |
| % Net Income of Revenue | 2.6 | 3.7 | 3.2 | 2.8 | 3.1 | 3.0 | 3.0 | 2.6 | 2.8 | 2.6 |
| % Return on Assets | 4.0 | 5.6 | 5.4 | 4.9 | 5.8 | 5.6 | 5.7 | 4.9 | 5.2 | 5.1 |
| % Return on Equity | 10.7 | 15.9 | 15.4 | 13.4 | 17.4 | 17.9 | 18.9 | 17.7 | 20.2 | 20.8 |

Data as orig reptd.; bef. results of disc opers/spec. items. Per share data adj. for stk. divs.; EPS diluted. E-Estimated. NA-Not Available. NM-Not Meaningful. NR-Not Ranked. UR-Under Review.

**Office:** 5757 N. Green Bay Avenue, Milwaukee, WI 53209-4408.
**Telephone:** 414-524-1200.
**Website:** http://www.johnsoncontrols.com
**Chrmn & CEO:** S.A. Roell

**Pres & COO:** K. Wandell
**EVP & CFO:** R.B. McDonald
**Chief Acctg Officer & Cntlr:** S.M. Kreh
**Treas:** F.A. Voltolina

**Investor Contact:** D.M. Zutz (414-524-1200)
**Board Members:** D. W. Archer, R. L. Barnett, J. M. Barth, N. A. Black, R. A. Cornog, R. Goodman, J. A. Joerres, W. H. Lacy, S. J. Morcott, E. C. Reyes-Retana, S. A. Roell, R. F. Teerlink

**Founded:** 1900
**Domicile:** Wisconsin
**Employees:** 140,000

*The McGraw-Hill Companies*

**STANDARD &POOR'S**

# Johnson & Johnson

| S&P Recommendation | **STRONG BUY** ★★★★★ | Price | 12-Mo. Target Price | Investment Style |
|---|---|---|---|---|
| | | $60.05 (as of Nov 14, 2008) | $80.00 | Large-Cap Growth |

**GICS Sector** Health Care
**Sub-Industry** Pharmaceuticals

**Summary** This company is a leader in the pharmaceutical, medical device and consumer products industries. The company has one of the largest market capitalizations within the S&P 500 Index.

## Key Stock Statistics (Source S&P, Vickers, company reports)

| | | | | | | | | |
|---|---|---|---|---|---|---|---|---|
| 52-Wk Range | $72.76–52.06 | S&P Oper. EPS 2008**E** | 4.53 | Market Capitalization(B) | $166.613 | Beta | | 0.36 |
| Trailing 12-Month EPS | $4.42 | S&P Oper. EPS 2009**E** | 4.75 | Yield (%) | 3.06 | S&P 3-Yr. Proj. EPS CAGR(%) | | 8 |
| Trailing 12-Month P/E | 13.6 | P/E on S&P Oper. EPS 2008**E** | 13.3 | Dividend Rate/Share | $1.84 | S&P Credit Rating | | AAA |
| $10K Invested 5 Yrs Ago | $12,888 | Common Shares Outstg. (M) | 2,774.6 | Institutional Ownership (%) | 64 | | | |

## Price Performance

- 30-Week Mov. Avg. ····
- 10-Week Mov. Avg. - - -
- GAAP Earnings vs. Previous Year
- Volume Above Avg. STARS
- 12-Mo. Target Price —
- Relative Strength —
- ▲ Up ▼ Down ► No Change
- Below Avg.

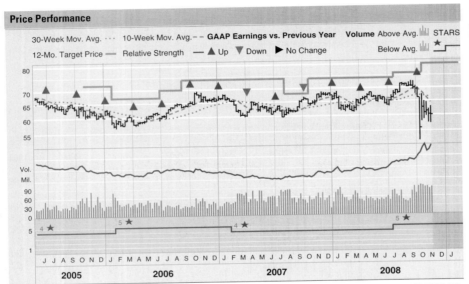

Options: ASE, CBOE, P, Ph

Analysis prepared by **Herman B. Saftlas** on October 17, 2008, when the stock traded at **$ 63.50**.

## Highlights

➤ We expect revenues in 2009 to approximate the $64.5 billion indicated for 2008. Despite expected less favorable foreign exchange comparisons, we forecast top line growth in medical devices and consumer products, supported by new products, higher prices and greater penetration of overseas markets. However, pharmaceutical sales will probably decline in 2009, reflecting generic erosion in large selling drugs such as Risperdal anti-psychotic and Topamax epilepsy treatment. But other drugs such as Remicade, Concerta and Velcade should show further gains.

➤ We expect gross margins will face pressures from a less profitable sales mix, largely reflecting a projected decline in higher-margined pharmaceutical sales. However, we expect net margins to benefit from synergies from recent acquisitions, reduced staffing levels and other operating economies. Pretax savings from restructuring actions taken in 2008 were indicated at $1.6 billion.

➤ After taxes estimated in the 23%-24% range, we see 2009 operating EPS of $4.75, up from an indicated $4.53 in 2008.

## Investment Rationale/Risk

➤ We believe JNJ's diversified sales base across pharmaceuticals, medical devices and consumer products, along with its decentralized business model, has served it well in the past, and should continue to do so in the years ahead. In our opinion, revenue and cost synergies from the purchase of Pfizer's consumer products unit should drive cash EPS accretion, and boost cash flow amid challenging device and drug conditions. We also expect restructuring savings to help expand the pipeline. We think JNJ shares are particularly appealing during the present volatile stock market.

➤ Risks to our recommendation and target price include faster than expected generic erosion in several drug lines, an inability to sustain growth in the device area, possible pipeline disappointments, and adverse foreign exchange.

➤ Our 12-month target price of $80 applies a P/E of 16.8X to our 2009 EPS estimate, a valuation that is roughly in line with peer large capitalization, diversified healthcare stocks. Our DCF analysis also shows intrinsic value of $80, assuming a 7.7% WACC and 2% terminal growth.

## Qualitative Risk Assessment

| LOW | MEDIUM | HIGH |
|---|---|---|

Our risk assessment reflects our belief that JNJ has products that are largely immune from economic cycles, its modest reliance on any single product category or customer for sustained growth, and competitive advantages owing to its large financial resources, business scale and global sales capabilities.

## Quantitative Evaluations

**S&P Quality Ranking** A+

| D | C | B- | B | B+ | A- | A | A+ |
|---|---|---|---|---|---|---|---|

**Relative Strength Rank** STRONG

80

LOWEST = 1          HIGHEST = 99

## Revenue/Earnings Data

**Revenue (Million $)**

| | 1Q | 2Q | 3Q | 4Q | Year |
|---|---|---|---|---|---|
| 2008 | 16,194 | 16,450 | 15,921 | -- | -- |
| 2007 | 15,037 | 15,131 | 14,970 | 15,957 | 61,095 |
| 2006 | 12,992 | 13,363 | 13,287 | 13,682 | 53,324 |
| 2005 | 12,832 | 12,762 | 12,310 | 12,610 | 50,514 |
| 2004 | 11,559 | 11,484 | 11,553 | 12,752 | 47,348 |
| 2003 | 9,821 | 10,332 | 10,455 | 11,254 | 41,862 |

**Earnings Per Share ($)**

| | 1Q | 2Q | 3Q | 4Q | Year |
|---|---|---|---|---|---|
| 2008 | 1.26 | 1.17 | 1.17 | E0.93 | E4.53 |
| 2007 | 0.88 | 1.05 | 0.88 | 0.82 | 3.64 |
| 2006 | 1.10 | 0.95 | 0.94 | 0.74 | 3.73 |
| 2005 | 0.97 | 0.89 | 0.87 | 0.73 | 3.46 |
| 2004 | 0.83 | 0.82 | 0.78 | 0.41 | 2.84 |
| 2003 | 0.69 | 0.40 | 0.69 | 0.62 | 2.40 |

Fiscal year ended Dec. 31. Next earnings report expected: Late January. EPS Estimates based on S&P Operating Earnings; historical GAAP earnings are as reported.

## Dividend Data (Dates: mm/dd Payment Date: mm/dd/yy)

| Amount ($) | Date Decl. | Ex-Div. Date | Stk. of Record | Payment Date |
|---|---|---|---|---|
| 0.415 | 01/02 | 02/22 | 02/26 | 03/11/08 |
| 0.460 | 04/24 | 05/22 | 05/27 | 06/10/08 |
| 0.460 | 07/21 | 08/22 | 08/26 | 09/09/08 |
| 0.460 | 10/16 | 11/21 | 11/25 | 12/09/08 |

Dividends have been paid since 1944. Source: Company reports.

---

**Please read the Required Disclosures and Analyst Certification on the last page of this report.**

**The McGraw-Hill Companies**

# Johnson & Johnson

STANDARD
&POOR'S

## Business Summary October 17, 2008

CORPORATE OVERVIEW. Johnson & Johnson ranks as one of the largest and most diversified health care firms, with products spanning across the pharmaceutical and medical device industries. The company is also a major participant in the global consumer products business, and, in December 2006, purchased the consumer products unit of Pfizer for $16.6 billion. In February 2007, JNJ consummated its acquisition of Conor Medsystems, Inc. for $1.4 billion in cash.

The pharmaceutical segment (41% of 2007 sales) includes products in therapeutic areas including anti-infective, antipsychotic, cardiovascular, contraceptive, dermatology, gastrointestinal, hematology, immunology, neurology, oncology, pain management, urology and virology. In 2007, eight products each generated at least $1 billion of sales: Risperdal/Risperdal Consta ($4.6 billion, down 9% from 2006), Procrit/Eprex ($2.9 billion, down 9%), Remicade ($3.3 billion, up 10%), Topamax ($2.5 billion, up 21%), Floxin/Levaquin ($1.6 billion, up 8%), Duragesic ($1.2 billion, down 10%), Aciphex/Pariet ($1.4 billion, up 10%), and Concerta ($1.0 billion, up 11%). Generic competition against Risperdal commenced in mid-2008.

The medical devices and diagnostics segment (35%) sells a wide range of products, including Ethicon's wound care, surgical sports medicine and women's health care products; Cordis's circulatory disease management products; Lifescan's blood glucose monitoring products; Ortho-Clinical Diagnostic's professional diagnostic products; Depuy's orthopaedic joint reconstruction and spinal products; and Vistakon's disposable contact lenses.

The consumer segment (24%) primarily sells personal care products, including nonprescription drugs, adult skin and hair care products, baby care products, oral care products, first aid products, women's health products, and nutritional products. Major brands include Band-Aid Brand Adhesive Bandages, Imodium A-D antidiarrheal, Johnson's Baby line of products, Neutrogena skin and hair care products, and Tylenol pain reliever.

## Company Financials Fiscal Year Ended Dec. 31

| Per Share Data ($) | 2007 | 2006 | 2005 | 2004 | 2003 | 2002 | 2001 | 2000 | 1999 | 1998 |
|---|---|---|---|---|---|---|---|---|---|---|
| Tangible Book Value | 5.13 | 3.67 | 8.64 | 6.72 | 5.17 | 4.53 | 4.97 | 4.15 | 3.11 | 2.38 |
| Cash Flow | 4.59 | 4.57 | 4.20 | 3.58 | 3.01 | 2.67 | 2.35 | 2.23 | 1.98 | 1.57 |
| Earnings | 3.63 | 3.73 | 3.46 | 2.84 | 2.40 | 2.16 | 1.84 | 1.70 | 1.47 | 1.12 |
| S&P Core Earnings | 3.61 | 3.65 | 3.38 | 2.77 | 2.26 | 1.99 | 1.66 | NA | NA | NA |
| Dividends | 1.62 | 1.46 | 1.28 | 1.10 | 0.93 | 0.80 | 0.70 | 0.62 | 0.55 | 0.49 |
| Payout Ratio | 45% | 39% | 37% | 39% | 39% | 37% | 38% | 36% | 37% | 43% |
| Prices:High | 68.75 | 69.41 | 69.99 | 64.25 | 59.08 | 65.89 | 60.97 | 52.97 | 53.44 | 44.88 |
| Prices:Low | 59.72 | 56.65 | 59.76 | 49.25 | 48.05 | 41.40 | 40.25 | 33.06 | 38.50 | 31.69 |
| P/E Ratio:High | 19 | 19 | 20 | 23 | 25 | 31 | 33 | 31 | 36 | 40 |
| P/E Ratio:Low | 16 | 15 | 17 | 17 | 20 | 19 | 22 | 19 | 26 | 28 |

| Income Statement Analysis (Million $) | | | | | | | | | | |
|---|---|---|---|---|---|---|---|---|---|---|
| Revenue | 61,035 | 53,324 | 50,514 | 47,348 | 41,862 | 36,298 | 33,004 | 29,139 | 27,471 | 23,657 |
| Operating Income | 17,930 | 15,886 | 15,464 | 14,987 | 12,740 | 11,340 | 9,490 | 7,992 | 7,370 | 6,291 |
| Depreciation | 2,777 | 2,177 | 2,093 | 2,124 | 1,869 | 1,662 | 1,605 | 1,515 | 1,444 | 1,246 |
| Interest Expense | 426 | 63.0 | 54.0 | 187 | 207 | 160 | 153 | 146 | 197 | 110 |
| Pretax Income | 13,283 | 14,587 | 13,656 | 12,838 | 10,308 | 9,291 | 7,898 | 6,622 | 5,753 | 4,269 |
| Effective Tax Rate | 20.4% | 24.2% | 23.8% | 33.7% | 30.2% | 29.0% | 28.2% | 27.5% | 27.6% | 28.3% |
| Net Income | 10,576 | 11,053 | 10,411 | 8,509 | 7,197 | 6,597 | 5,668 | 4,800 | 4,167 | 3,059 |
| S&P Core Earnings | 10,534 | 10,814 | 10,161 | 8,263 | 6,785 | 6,052 | 5,090 | NA | NA | NA |

| Balance Sheet & Other Financial Data (Million $) | | | | | | | | | | |
|---|---|---|---|---|---|---|---|---|---|---|
| Cash | 9,315 | 4,084 | 16,138 | 12,884 | 9,523 | 7,596 | 8,941 | 6,013 | 4,320 | 2,994 |
| Current Assets | 29,945 | 22,975 | 31,394 | 27,320 | 22,995 | 19,266 | 18,473 | 15,450 | 13,200 | 11,132 |
| Total Assets | 80,954 | 70,556 | 58,025 | 53,317 | 48,263 | 40,556 | 38,488 | 31,321 | 29,163 | 26,211 |
| Current Liabilities | 19,837 | 19,161 | 12,635 | 13,927 | 13,448 | 11,449 | 8,044 | 7,140 | 7,454 | 8,162 |
| Long Term Debt | 7,074 | 2,014 | 2,017 | 2,565 | 2,955 | 2,022 | 2,217 | 2,037 | 2,450 | 1,269 |
| Common Equity | 43,319 | 61,266 | 37,871 | 31,813 | 26,869 | 22,697 | 24,233 | 18,808 | 16,213 | 13,590 |
| Total Capital | 51,886 | 64,599 | 40,099 | 34,781 | 30,604 | 25,362 | 26,943 | 21,100 | 18,950 | 15,437 |
| Capital Expenditures | 2,942 | 2,666 | 2,632 | 2,175 | 2,262 | 2,099 | 1,731 | 1,646 | 1,728 | 1,460 |
| Cash Flow | 13,353 | 13,230 | 12,504 | 10,633 | 9,066 | 8,259 | 7,273 | 6,315 | 5,611 | 4,305 |
| Current Ratio | 1.5 | 1.2 | 2.5 | 2.0 | 1.7 | 1.7 | 2.3 | 2.2 | 1.8 | 1.4 |
| % Long Term Debt of Capitalization | 13.6 | 3.1 | 5.0 | 7.4 | 9.7 | 8.0 | 8.2 | 9.7 | 12.9 | 8.2 |
| % Net Income of Revenue | 17.3 | 20.7 | 20.6 | 18.0 | 17.2 | 18.2 | 17.2 | 16.5 | 15.2 | 12.9 |
| % Return on Assets | 14.9 | 17.1 | 18.7 | 16.8 | 16.2 | 16.7 | 15.6 | 15.9 | 14.8 | 12.8 |
| % Return on Equity | 20.2 | 19.8 | 29.9 | 29.0 | 29.0 | 28.1 | 25.4 | 27.4 | 27.5 | 23.6 |

Data as orig reptd.; bef. results of disc opers/spec. items. Per share data adj. for stk. divs.; EPS diluted. E-Estimated. NA-Not Available. NM-Not Meaningful. NR-Not Ranked. UR-Under Review.

**Office:** One Johnson & Johnson Plaza, New Brunswick, NJ 08933.
**Telephone:** 732-524-0400.
**Website:** http://www.jnj.com
**Chrmn & CEO:** W.C. Weldon

**Vice Chrmn:** C.A. Poon
**CFO:** D.J. Caruso
**Chief Acctg Officer & Cntlr:** S.J. Cosgrove
**Treas:** J.A. Papa

**Investor Contact:** L. Mehrotra (732-524-6491)
**Board Members:** M. S. Coleman, J. G. Cullen, M. M. Johns, A. G. Langbo, S. Lindquist, L. F. Mullin, W. D. Perez, C. A. Poon, C. Prince, III, D. Satcher, W. C. Weldon

**Founded:** 1887
**Domicile:** New Jersey
**Employees:** 119,500

The McGraw-Hill Companies

# Jones Apparel Group Inc.

**STANDARD &POOR'S**

| S&P Recommendation **HOLD** ★★★☆☆ | Price $6.32 (as of Nov 14, 2008) | 12-Mo. Target Price $10.00 | Investment Style Large-Cap Blend |
| --- | --- | --- | --- |

**GICS Sector** Consumer Discretionary
**Sub-Industry** Apparel, Accessories & Luxury Goods

**Summary** JNY is a leading designer, marketer and wholesaler of women's apparel, footwear and accessories, with brands that include Jones New York, Nine West and Evan-Picone.

## Key Stock Statistics (Source S&P, Vickers, company reports)

| | | | | | | | |
| --- | --- | --- | --- | --- | --- | --- | --- |
| 52-Wk Range | $22.12– 6.24 | S&P Oper. EPS 2008**E** | 0.97 | Market Capitalization(B) | $0.527 | Beta | 1.68 |
| Trailing 12-Month EPS | $-0.38 | S&P Oper. EPS 2009**E** | 1.15 | Yield (%) | 8.86 | S&P 3-Yr. Proj. EPS CAGR(%) | 8 |
| Trailing 12-Month P/E | NM | P/E on S&P Oper. EPS 2008**E** | 6.5 | Dividend Rate/Share | $0.56 | S&P Credit Rating | BB- |
| $10K Invested 5 Yrs Ago | $2,026 | Common Shares Outstg. (M) | 83.4 | Institutional Ownership (%) | NM | | |

## Price Performance

30-Week Mov. Avg. · · ·  10-Week Mov. Avg. – –  **GAAP Earnings vs. Previous Year**  Volume Above Avg. STARS
12-Mo. Target Price —  Relative Strength —  ▲ Up  ▼ Down  ► No Change  Below Avg.

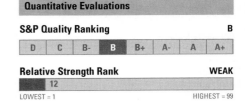

Options: ASE, CBOE, P, Ph

Analysis prepared by **Marie Driscoll, CFA** on November 06, 2008, when the stock traded at **$ 8.96**.

## Highlights

➤ We see 2008 as a transitional year for JNY as it right-sizes its wholesale apparel business amid retailers' retrenchment. JNY plans to focus on a handful of core brands -- Jones New York, Anne Klein, Nine West, Gloria Vanderbilt and l.e.i. -- as growth opportunities, having exited most of its moderate sportswear business (about $1 billion) in 2007.

➤ We expect sales of $3.6 billion in 2008, at the low end of JNY's guidance. The launch of l.e.i. jeans in 3,000 Wal-Mart stores in time for Back-to-School 2008 was a plus this fall, and we are cautiously optimistic regarding this initiative. We see a 4% sales decline in 2009 reflecting weak consumer spending, promotional pressures, and tight inventory levels at retail.

➤ We see margin pressure from inflationary costs along with retail pressure for additional markdown support in the prevailing macro environment. We project an operating margin of 5.2% in 2008 and expect modest margin expansion in 2009 to 5.6%, reflecting improvement at Nine West retail. We see share buybacks benefiting per-share results in 2008, which we estimate at $0.97, versus an adjusted $1.26 in 2007, and we project $1.15 for 2009.

## Investment Rationale/Risk

➤ We consider many of JNY's 20-some apparel and footwear brands as mature and think the decision to exit or sell them is difficult, but correct. As the company rationalizes its portfolio of branded apparel, we believe it will be able to focus better on a few recently acquired businesses that could provide significant growth opportunities along with potential cost synergies. Kasper and Anne Klein provide opportunity in women's better apparel, but we think shoeWoo, a footwear retail concept currently in test, is more promising, as we believe shoppers will increasingly opt for the selections of multi-brand venues. If the l.e.i. launch at Wal-Mart is successful, we see potential for brand repositioning of some of JNY's mature lines.

➤ Risks to our opinion and target price include changes in consumer spending, fashion and inventory risk, and management's ability to integrate recent acquisitions.

➤ Our 12-month target price of $10 is derived by applying a 25% discount to the peer forward P/E multiple of 12X to our 2009 EPS estimate reflecting execution risk at Nine-West.

## Qualitative Risk Assessment

| LOW | **MEDIUM** | HIGH |
| --- | --- | --- |

Our risk assessment is based on the company's exposure to department store channel contraction, offset by a diversified brand portfolio spanning multiple channels.

## Quantitative Evaluations

**S&P Quality Ranking** B

| D | C | B- | **B** | B+ | A- | A | A+ |
| --- | --- | --- | --- | --- | --- | --- | --- |

**Relative Strength Rank** WEAK

12

LOWEST = 1          HIGHEST = 99

## Revenue/Earnings Data

**Revenue (Million $)**

| | 1Q | 2Q | 3Q | 4Q | Year |
| --- | --- | --- | --- | --- | --- |
| 2008 | 975.4 | 829.4 | 964.7 | -- | -- |
| 2007 | 1,079 | 903.9 | 1,028 | 838.5 | 3,849 |
| 2006 | 1,215 | 1,074 | 1,241 | 1,213 | 4,743 |
| 2005 | 1,349 | 1,176 | 1,328 | 1,221 | 5,074 |
| 2004 | 1,218 | 1,053 | 1,296 | 1,083 | 4,650 |
| 2003 | 1,234 | 980.4 | 1,181 | 980.2 | 4,375 |

**Earnings Per Share ($)**

| | | | | | |
| --- | --- | --- | --- | --- | --- |
| 2008 | 0.23 | 0.13 | 0.32 | E0.05 | E0.97 |
| 2007 | 0.41 | -0.48 | 1.37 | -1.01 | 0.45 |
| 2006 | 0.21 | 0.32 | 0.56 | -2.51 | -1.32 |
| 2005 | 0.71 | 0.46 | 0.65 | 0.48 | 2.30 |
| 2004 | 0.73 | 0.61 | 0.77 | 0.28 | 2.39 |
| 2003 | 0.90 | 0.54 | 0.71 | 0.33 | 2.48 |

Fiscal year ended Dec. 31. Next earnings report expected: Mid February. EPS Estimates based on S&P Operating Earnings; historical GAAP earnings are as reported.

## Dividend Data (Dates: mm/dd Payment Date: mm/dd/yy)

| Amount ($) | Date Decl. | Ex-Div. Date | Stk. of Record | Payment Date |
| --- | --- | --- | --- | --- |
| 0.140 | 02/13 | 02/27 | 02/29 | 03/14/08 |
| 0.140 | 04/30 | 05/14 | 05/16 | 05/30/08 |
| 0.140 | 07/30 | 08/13 | 08/15 | 08/29/08 |
| 0.140 | 10/29 | 11/12 | 11/14 | 11/28/08 |

Dividends have been paid since 2003. Source: Company reports.

# Jones Apparel Group Inc.

**STANDARD**
**&POOR'S**

## Business Summary November 06, 2008

CORPORATE OVERVIEW. Jones Apparel Group, Inc. (JNY) is a multi-branded apparel and accessories company operating on both the wholesale and retail level.

MARKET PROFILE. JNY participates in the women's apparel market, which represented 53% of domestic apparel retail purchases, or $103 billion, in 2007, according to NPD Fashionworld consumer estimated data. The apparel market is fragmented, with national brands marketed by 20 companies accounting for about 30% of total apparel sales, and the remaining 70% comprised of smaller and/or private label "store" brands. The market is mature, in our view, with demand largely mirroring population growth and fashion trends accounting for a modicum of incremental volume. Deflationary pricing pressure is a function, we think, of channel competition and production steadily moving offshore to low-cost producers in India, Asia and China. S&P forecasts flat 2008 apparel sales, versus a 3% gain in 2007, 5% in 2006, and a 4% year-to-year advance in the 2003-2005 period.

COMPETITIVE LANDSCAPE. By channel, specialty stores account for the largest share of apparel sales, at 31% in 2007, according to NPD. Mass mer-

chants (Wal-Mart and Target) came in second at 20%, and department stores, JNY's primary channel, came in third at 16%, followed closely by national chains (Sears and JC Penney), which grew at a 5% pace in 2007 and captured 15% of 2007 sales. Off-price retailers (TJX and Ross Stores) accounted for 7% of apparel sales, with the remaining 11% divided among factory outlets and direct and e-mail pure plays. JNY holds meaningful market shares in department stores and national chains, where it competes with Liz Claiborne, Polo Ralph Lauren and VF Corp., as well as private label offerings, which garner about a third of total apparel purchases and are an important differentiator for retailers. JNY also sells directly to consumers through 396 specialty retail and 638 outlet stores in the U.S. and Canada. The company formerly participated in the luxury retail market via the Barneys New York flagship store, three regional stores and eight Barneys New York CO-OP stores, which were sold in September 2007.

## Company Financials Fiscal Year Ended Dec. 31

| Per Share Data ($) | 2007 | 2006 | 2005 | 2004 | 2003 | 2002 | 2001 | 2000 | 1999 | 1998 |
|---|---|---|---|---|---|---|---|---|---|---|
| Tangible Book Value | 23.82 | 1.30 | NM | NM | 0.98 | 0.66 | 0.03 | 0.16 | NM | 2.33 |
| Cash Flow | 1.21 | -0.37 | 3.16 | 3.24 | 3.04 | 3.03 | 1.96 | 3.37 | 2.05 | 1.68 |
| Earnings | 0.45 | -1.32 | 2.30 | 2.39 | 2.48 | 2.46 | 1.82 | 2.48 | 1.60 | 1.47 |
| S&P Core Earnings | 0.88 | 2.92 | 2.32 | 2.34 | 2.40 | 2.35 | 1.63 | NA | NA | NA |
| Dividends | 0.56 | 0.50 | 0.44 | 0.36 | 0.16 | Nil | Nil | Nil | Nil | Nil |
| Payout Ratio | 124% | NM | 19% | 15% | 6% | Nil | Nil | Nil | Nil | Nil |
| Prices:High | 35.54 | 36.10 | 37.48 | 40.00 | 37.44 | 41.68 | 47.43 | 35.00 | 35.88 | 37.75 |
| Prices:Low | 15.98 | 27.30 | 26.47 | 33.00 | 25.61 | 26.18 | 23.75 | 20.13 | 21.50 | 15.88 |
| P/E Ratio:High | 79 | NM | 16 | 17 | 15 | 17 | 26 | 14 | 22 | 26 |
| P/E Ratio:Low | 36 | NM | 12 | 14 | 10 | 11 | 13 | 8 | 13 | 11 |

### Income Statement Analysis (Million $)

| | 2007 | 2006 | 2005 | 2004 | 2003 | 2002 | 2001 | 2000 | 1999 | 1998 |
|---|---|---|---|---|---|---|---|---|---|---|
| Revenue | 3,849 | 4,743 | 5,074 | 4,650 | 4,375 | 4,341 | 4,073 | 4,143 | 3,151 | 1,685 |
| Operating Income | 228 | 475 | 600 | 636 | 664 | 679 | 506 | 714 | 431 | 283 |
| Depreciation | 76.7 | 105 | 103 | 108 | 84.3 | 88.8 | 25.7 | 109 | 53.1 | 21.2 |
| Interest Expense | 52.0 | 58.2 | 76.2 | 51.2 | 58.8 | 62.7 | 84.6 | 104 | 66.9 | 11.8 |
| Pretax Income | -58.5 | -200 | 425 | 483 | 529 | 534 | 400 | 503 | 315 | 252 |
| Effective Tax Rate | NM | NM | 35.5% | 37.5% | 37.5% | 37.7% | 40.9% | 40.0% | 40.1% | 38.5% |
| Net Income | 45.9 | -146 | 274 | 302 | 331 | 332 | 236 | 302 | 188 | 155 |
| S&P Core Earnings | 89.2 | 322 | 275 | 295 | 318 | 318 | 210 | NA | NA | NA |

### Balance Sheet & Other Financial Data (Million $)

| | 2007 | 2006 | 2005 | 2004 | 2003 | 2002 | 2001 | 2000 | 1999 | 1998 |
|---|---|---|---|---|---|---|---|---|---|---|
| Cash | 303 | 71.5 | 34.9 | 45.0 | 350 | 283 | 76.5 | 60.5 | 47.0 | 129 |
| Current Assets | 1,294 | 1,279 | 1,284 | 1,296 | 1,456 | 1,318 | 1,141 | 1,182 | 1,131 | 632 |
| Total Assets | 3,237 | 3,787 | 4,578 | 4,551 | 4,188 | 3,853 | 3,374 | 2,979 | 2,792 | 1,189 |
| Current Liabilities | 396 | 615 | 836 | 684 | 629 | 427 | 378 | 887 | 661 | 174 |
| Long Term Debt | 778 | Nil | 790 | 1,017 | 835 | 978 | 977 | 576 | 834 | 415 |
| Common Equity | 1,997 | 2,212 | 2,666 | 2,654 | 2,538 | 2,304 | 1,905 | 1,477 | 1,241 | 594 |
| Total Capital | 2,775 | 2,254 | 3,632 | 3,806 | 3,503 | 3,380 | 2,963 | 2,053 | 2,075 | 1,009 |
| Capital Expenditures | 111 | 171 | 87.5 | 56.6 | 53.3 | 52.6 | 56.4 | 46.8 | 29.7 | 48.5 |
| Cash Flow | 123 | -40.8 | 377 | 410 | 415 | 421 | 262 | 411 | 242 | 176 |
| Current Ratio | 3.3 | 2.1 | 1.5 | 1.9 | 2.3 | 3.1 | 3.0 | 1.3 | 1.7 | 3.6 |
| % Long Term Debt of Capitalization | 28.0 | Nil | 21.7 | 26.7 | 23.8 | 28.9 | 33.0 | 28.1 | 40.2 | 41.1 |
| % Net Income of Revenue | 1.2 | NM | 5.4 | 6.5 | 7.6 | 7.7 | 5.8 | 7.3 | 6.0 | 9.2 |
| % Return on Assets | 1.3 | NM | 6.0 | 6.9 | 8.2 | 9.2 | 7.4 | 10.5 | 9.5 | 17.5 |
| % Return on Equity | 2.2 | NM | 10.3 | 11.6 | 13.7 | 15.8 | 14.0 | 22.2 | 20.5 | 30.1 |

Data as orig reptd.; bef. results of disc opers/spec. items. Per share data adj. for stk. divs.; EPS diluted. E-Estimated. NA-Not Available. NM-Not Meaningful. NR-Not Ranked. UR-Under Review.

**Office:** 1411 Broadway, New York, NY 10018-3496.
**Telephone:** 212-642-3860.
**Website:** http://www.jny.com
**Chrmn:** S. Kimmel

**Pres & CEO:** W.R. Card
**COO:** C. DiPietrantonio
**EVP & CTO:** P. Lanham
**EVP, Chief Acctg Officer & Cntlr:** C.R. Cade

**Investor Contact:** J.T. McClain (212-642-3860)
**Board Members:** W. R. Card, G. C. Crotty, M. H.
Kamens, J. Kerrey, S. Kimmel, A. N. Reese, L. W.
Robinson, D. F. Zarcone, F. van Paasschen

**Founded:** 1975
**Domicile:** Pennsylvania
**Employees:** 13,830

**STANDARD &POOR'S**

# JPMorgan Chase & Co.

| S&P Recommendation **STRONG BUY** ★★★★★ | Price $34.47 (as of Nov 14, 2008) | 12-Mo. Target Price $50.00 | Investment Style Large-Cap Value |
|---|---|---|---|

**GICS Sector** Financials
**Sub-Industry** Other Diversified Financial Services

**Summary** JPMorgan Chase is a leading global financial services company with assets of $2.3 trillion and operations in more than 50 countries.

## Key Stock Statistics (Source S&P, Vickers, company reports)

| | | | | | | | |
|---|---|---|---|---|---|---|---|
| 52-Wk Range | $50.63– 29.24 | S&P Oper. EPS 2008**E** | 1.87 | Market Capitalization(B) | $128.654 | Beta | 0.48 |
| Trailing 12-Month EPS | $2.17 | S&P Oper. EPS 2009**E** | 3.21 | Yield (%) | 4.41 | S&P 3-Yr. Proj. EPS CAGR(%) | -1 |
| Trailing 12-Month P/E | 15.9 | P/E on S&P Oper. EPS 2008**E** | 18.4 | Dividend Rate/Share | $1.52 | S&P Credit Rating | AA- |
| $10K Invested 5 Yrs Ago | $11,528 | Common Shares Outstg. (M) | 3,732.4 | Institutional Ownership (%) | 71 | | |

## Price Performance

- 30-Week Mov. Avg. · · · 10-Week Mov. Avg. – – GAAP Earnings vs. Previous Year    Volume Above Avg. STARS
- 12-Mo. Target Price — Relative Strength ▲ Up ▼ Down ► No Change    Below Avg.

Options: ASE, CBOE, P, Ph

Analysis prepared by **Stuart Plesser** on October 20, 2008, when the stock traded at **$ 39.96**.

## Highlights

➤ We look for revenue to rise 25% in 2009, largely due to the acquisition of Washington Mutual but also reflecting lower securities write-downs. We see double-digit growth in average earning assets, as JPM should continue to gain market share in most of its business lines due to the exit of weaker players. Net interest income should grow in the double digits, by our analysis, reflecting a more favorable interest rate environment.

➤ We look for provisions to increase roughly 25% in 2009 from elevated 2008 levels as JPM will likely need to continue to add to reserves, as its mortgage and credit card portfolio will likely continue to deteriorate. We look favorably upon JPM's reserve ratios, which totaled 2.57% of loans, near the top of peers. JPM's exposure to leveraged loans and Alt-A securities has been reduced in recent quarters; we look for continued write-downs but at lower levels in the coming quarters. We expect expenses to amount to roughly 55% of revenues in 2009, lower than projected for 2008.

➤ We estimate operating EPS of $1.87 in 2008, versus $4.38 in 2007. In 2009, project EPS of $3.21.

## Investment Rationale/Risk

➤ We think JPM's large customer base and above-peers Tier 1 capital ratio of 8.9% will allow it the flexibility to move toward higher-growth products and markets as well as absorb potential challenges that may be ahead. We are particularly encouraged by the build-up of reserves, especially in light of the credit difficulties we continue to foresee. Although we view market conditions and the consumer credit environment as challenging, we consider JPM's balance sheet as strong relative to peers. Still, we do not think JPM is immune to the weak credit environment. We see the acquisition of Bear Stearns and most of the operations of Washington Mutual (WM) as offering limited downside risk, with the possibility of solid upside potential. Indeed, WM significantly expands JPM's footprint, particularly in California.

➤ Risks to our recommendation and target price include legal and regulatory risk; integration risk; unexpected further turmoil in the credit markets; a severe economic downturn; and an inverted yield curve.

➤ Our 12-month target price of $50 is equal to 15.6X our 2009 EPS estimate of $3.21, a premium to the peer group average.

## Qualitative Risk Assessment

| LOW | MEDIUM | HIGH |
|---|---|---|

Our risk assessment of JPMorgan Chase reflects our view of the company's strong fundamentals, well-reserved balance sheet and high capital ratios. We also believe JPM's diversity in its geographic presence and product offerings provides significant protection from a local or regional downturn.

## Quantitative Evaluations

**S&P Quality Ranking**     **B**

| D | C | B- | B | B+ | A- | A | A+ |
|---|---|---|---|---|---|---|---|

**Relative Strength Rank**     **MODERATE**

68

LOWEST = 1      HIGHEST = 99

## Revenue/Earnings Data

### Revenue (Million $)

| | 1Q | 2Q | 3Q | 4Q | Year |
|---|---|---|---|---|---|
| 2008 | 26,763 | 26,634 | 23,069 | -- | -- |
| 2007 | 29,486 | 30,082 | 16,112 | 28,104 | 116,353 |
| 2006 | 23,477 | 24,175 | 24,957 | 26,693 | 99,302 |
| 2005 | 19,054 | 18,691 | 21,048 | 21,109 | 79,902 |
| 2004 | 11,625 | 11,227 | 16,546 | 17,483 | 56,931 |
| 2003 | 11,454 | 11,842 | 10,396 | 10,671 | 44,363 |

### Earnings Per Share ($)

| | | | | | |
|---|---|---|---|---|---|
| 2008 | 0.68 | 0.54 | -0.06 | E0.54 | E1.87 |
| 2007 | 1.34 | 1.20 | 0.97 | 0.86 | 4.38 |
| 2006 | 0.86 | 0.98 | 0.90 | 1.26 | 3.82 |
| 2005 | 0.63 | 0.28 | 0.71 | 0.76 | 2.38 |
| 2004 | 0.92 | -0.27 | 0.39 | 0.46 | 1.55 |
| 2003 | 0.69 | 0.89 | 0.78 | 0.89 | 3.24 |

Fiscal year ended Dec. 31. Next earnings report expected: NA. EPS Estimates based on S&P Operating Earnings; historical GAAP earnings are as reported.

## Dividend Data (Dates: mm/dd Payment Date: mm/dd/yy)

| Amount ($) | Date Decl. | Ex-Div. Date | Stk. of Record | Payment Date |
|---|---|---|---|---|
| 0.380 | 12/11 | 01/02 | 01/04 | 01/31/08 |
| 0.380 | 03/18 | 04/02 | 04/04 | 04/30/08 |
| 0.380 | 05/20 | 07/01 | 07/03 | 07/31/08 |
| 0.380 | 09/16 | 10/02 | 10/06 | 10/31/08 |

Dividends have been paid since 1827. Source: Company reports.

# JPMorgan Chase & Co.

STANDARD
&POOR'S

## Business Summary October 20, 2008

CORPORATE OVERVIEW. JPMorgan Chase's operations are divided into six major business lines: Investment Banking, Retail Financial Services (RFS), Card Services (CS), Commercial Banking (CB), Treasury & Securities Services (TSS), and Asset Management (AM).

JPM is one of the world's leading investment banks, with clients consisting of corporations, financial institutions, governments, and institutional investors worldwide. Its products and services include advising on corporate strategy and structure, equity and debt capital raising, sophisticated risk management, research, and market making in cash securities and derivative instruments.

RFS includes Home Finance, Consumer & Small Business Banking, Auto & Education Finance and Insurance. At year-end 2007, RFS had over 3,100 bank branches, 9,100 ATMs and 290 mortgage offices. In 2007 JPM added 73 net new branches, versus 438 in 2006.

CS had over 155 million cards in circulation and $157 billion in managed loans as of December 31, 2007. Card Services offers a wide variety of products to satisfy the needs of its card members, including cards issued on behalf of

many well-known partners, such as major airlines, hotels, universities, retailers, and other financial institutions.

CB provides lending, treasury services, investment banking and investment management services to corporations, municipalities, financial institutions and not-for-profit entities.

TSS offers transaction, investment and information services to support the needs of corporations, issuers and institutional investors worldwide. TSS reported assets under custody of $15.9 trillion in 2007, up 15% from 2006.

AM provides investment management to retail and institutional investors, financial intermediaries and high-net-worth families and individuals globally. Assets under management reached $1.2 trillion in AM in 2007.

## Company Financials Fiscal Year Ended Dec. 31

| Per Share Data ($) | 2007 | 2006 | 2005 | 2004 | 2003 | 2002 | 2001 | 2000 | 1999 | 1998 |
|---|---|---|---|---|---|---|---|---|---|---|
| Tangible Book Value | 18.77 | 16.11 | 15.88 | 14.77 | 14.77 | 15.82 | 12.54 | 12.95 | 18.59 | 17.93 |
| Earnings | 4.38 | 3.82 | 2.38 | 1.55 | 3.24 | 0.80 | 0.81 | 2.86 | 4.18 | 2.83 |
| S&P Core Earnings | 4.44 | 3.88 | 2.76 | 2.25 | 3.12 | 0.65 | 0.34 | NA | NA | NA |
| Dividends | 1.44 | 1.36 | 1.36 | 1.36 | 1.36 | 1.36 | 1.34 | 1.23 | 1.06 | 0.93 |
| Payout Ratio | 33% | 34% | 57% | 88% | 42% | 170% | 165% | 43% | 25% | 33% |
| Prices:High | 53.25 | 49.00 | 40.56 | 43.84 | 38.26 | 39.68 | 57.33 | 67.17 | 60.75 | 51.71 |
| Prices:Low | 40.15 | 37.88 | 32.92 | 34.62 | 20.13 | 15.26 | 29.04 | 32.38 | 43.87 | 23.71 |
| P/E Ratio:High | 12 | 12 | 17 | 28 | 12 | 50 | 71 | 23 | 15 | 18 |
| P/E Ratio:Low | 9 | 9 | 14 | 22 | 6 | 19 | 36 | 11 | 10 | 8 |

| Income Statement Analysis (Million $) | | | | | | | | | | |
|---|---|---|---|---|---|---|---|---|---|---|
| Net Interest Income | 26,406 | 21,242 | 19,831 | 16,761 | 12,337 | 11,526 | 10,802 | 9,512 | 8,744 | 8,566 |
| Tax Equivalent Adjustment | 377 | NA | 269 | NA | NA | NA | NA | NA | NA | NA |
| Non Interest Income | 44,802 | 17,959 | 34,702 | 26,336 | 19,473 | 16,525 | 17,382 | 23,193 | 13,372 | 9,692 |
| Loan Loss Provision | 6,864 | 3,270 | 3,483 | NA | NA | 4,331 | 3,185 | 1,377 | 1,621 | 1,343 |
| % Expense/Operating Revenue | 58.6% | 97.7% | 66.5% | 85.6% | 73.0% | 81.2% | 82.7% | 69.8% | 55.3% | 63.5% |
| Pretax Income | 22,805 | 19,886 | 12,215 | 6,194 | 10,028 | 2,519 | 2,566 | 8,733 | 8,375 | 5,930 |
| Effective Tax Rate | 32.6% | 31.4% | 30.6% | 27.9% | 33.0% | 34.0% | 33.0% | 34.4% | 35.0% | 36.2% |
| Net Income | 15,365 | 13,649 | 8,483 | 4,466 | 6,719 | 1,663 | 1,719 | 5,727 | 5,446 | 3,782 |
| % Net Interest Margin | 2.39 | 2.16 | 2.19 | 2.27 | 2.10 | 2.09 | 1.99 | 1.87 | 2.98 | 2.89 |
| S&P Core Earnings | 15,563 | 13,852 | 9,802 | 6,456 | 6,439 | 1,290 | 698 | NA | NA | NA |

| Balance Sheet & Other Financial Data (Million $) | | | | | | | | | | |
|---|---|---|---|---|---|---|---|---|---|---|
| Money Market Assets | 662,306 | 506,262 | 432,358 | 390,168 | 329,739 | 314,110 | 265,875 | 293,429 | 115,168 | 83,391 |
| Investment Securities | 169,634 | 172,022 | 128,578 | 149,675 | 109,328 | 126,834 | 105,537 | 117,494 | 61,513 | 64,490 |
| Commercial Loans | 238,210 | 188,372 | 150,111 | 135,067 | 83,097 | 91,548 | 104,864 | 119,460 | 88,120 | 88,056 |
| Other Loans | 281,164 | 294,755 | 269,037 | 267,047 | 136,421 | 124,816 | 112,580 | 96,590 | 88,039 | 83,756 |
| Total Assets | 1,562,147 | 1,351,520 | 1,198,942 | 1,157,248 | 770,912 | 758,800 | 693,575 | 715,348 | 406,105 | 365,875 |
| Demand Deposits | 135,748 | 140,443 | 143,075 | 136,188 | 79,465 | 82,029 | 76,974 | 62,713 | 55,529 | 51,623 |
| Time Deposits | 604,980 | 498,345 | 411,916 | 385,268 | 247,027 | 222,724 | 216,676 | 216,652 | 186,216 | 160,814 |
| Long Term Debt | 197,878 | 117,358 | 119,886 | 105,718 | 54,782 | 45,190 | 44,172 | 47,788 | 20,690 | 18,375 |
| Common Equity | 123,221 | 115,790 | 107,072 | 105,314 | 45,145 | 41,297 | 40,090 | 40,818 | 22,689 | 22,810 |
| % Return on Assets | 1.1 | 1.1 | 0.7 | 0.5 | 0.9 | 0.2 | 0.2 | 0.8 | 1.4 | 1.0 |
| % Return on Equity | 12.9 | 12.2 | 8.0 | 5.9 | 15.4 | 4.0 | 4.1 | 15.2 | 23.6 | 17.2 |
| % Loan Loss Reserve | 1.8 | 1.5 | 1.7 | 1.8 | 2.1 | 2.5 | 2.1 | 1.7 | 2.0 | 2.1 |
| % Loans/Deposits | 72.6 | 75.6 | 75.5 | 77.1 | 67.2 | 71.0 | 74.0 | 77.3 | 72.9 | 84.0 |
| % Equity to Assets | 8.2 | 8.7 | 9.0 | 7.8 | 5.7 | 5.6 | 5.7 | 5.4 | 5.9 | 5.9 |

Data as orig reptd.; bef. results of disc opers/spec. items. Per share data adj. for stk. divs.; EPS diluted. E-Estimated. NA-Not Available. NM-Not Meaningful. NR-Not Ranked. UR-Under Review.

**Office:** 270 Park Ave, New York, NY 10017-2070.
**Telephone:** 212-270-6000.
**Website:** http://www.jpmorganchase.com
**Chrmn, Pres & CEO:** J. Dimon

**Vice Chrmn:** B.J. Taylor
**Vice Chrmn:** M. Breuer
**EVP & CFO:** M.J. Cavanagh
**EVP & General Counsel:** S.M. Cutler

**Investor Contact:** J. Bates (212-270-7318)
**Board Members:** C. C. Bowles, M. Breuer, S. B. Burke, B. Cormier, D. M. Cote, J. S. Crown, J. Dimon, E. Futter, W. H. Gray, III, L. P. Jackson, Jr., D. C. Novak, L. R. Raymond, W. C. Weldon.

**Founded:** 1823
**Domicile:** Delaware
**Employees:** 180,667

The McGraw-Hill Companies

# Juniper Networks Inc

**STANDARD &POOR'S**

**S&P Recommendation** BUY ★★★★☆

| | | |
|---|---|---|
| **Price** | **12-Mo. Target Price** | **Investment Style** |
| $15.03 (as of Nov 14, 2008) | $24.00 | Large-Cap Blend |

**GICS Sector** Information Technology
**Sub-Industry** Communications Equipment

**Summary** This company provides Internet Protocol networking products and services, with a specific emphasis on telecom routing solutions.

## Key Stock Statistics (Source S&P, Vickers, company reports)

| | | | | | | | | |
|---|---|---|---|---|---|---|---|---|
| 52-Wk Range | $34.95– 14.20 | S&P Oper. EPS 2008**E** | 1.03 | Market Capitalization(B) | $8.169 | Beta | 1.82 |
| Trailing 12-Month EPS | $0.89 | S&P Oper. EPS 2009**E** | 1.25 | Yield (%) | Nil | S&P 3-Yr. Proj. EPS CAGR(%) | 17 |
| Trailing 12-Month P/E | 16.9 | P/E on S&P Oper. EPS 2008**E** | 14.6 | Dividend Rate/Share | Nil | S&P Credit Rating | BB |
| $10K Invested 5 Yrs Ago | $8,468 | Common Shares Outstg. (M) | 543.5 | Institutional Ownership (%) | 95 | | |

## Price Performance

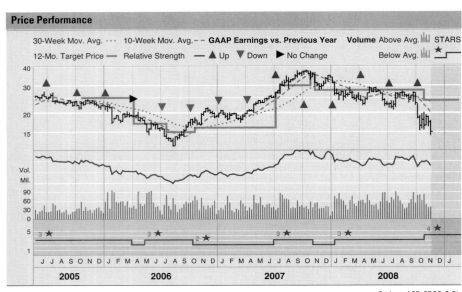

30-Week Mov. Avg. · · · · 10-Week Mov. Avg. — **GAAP Earnings vs. Previous Year** Volume Above Avg. ▮▮▮ STARS
12-Mo. Target Price — Relative Strength — ▲ Up ▼ Down ► No Change Below Avg. ▮▮▮ ★

Options: ASE, CBOE, P, Ph

Analysis prepared by **Ari Bensinger** on October 27, 2008, when the stock traded at **$ 16.50**.

## Highlights

➤ Following an estimated 27% increase in 2008, we forecast sales advancing 18% in 2009, to $4.2 billion, mainly reflecting accelerating demand for network infrastructure products from the service provider market. We are optimistic about recent portfolio enhancements and new product introductions, specifically the launch of a new ethernet switch and core router. Still, we believe JNPR needs to expand its distribution base and product application features to better compete in the enterprise market.

➤ We expect 2009 gross margins to decline moderately from 2008, to the 67% level, owing to an increasing mix of lower-margin enterprise sales and industry pricing pressure. We look for 2009 operating expenses as a percentage of sales to decrease from the prior year on the higher volume that we project.

➤ After a rebound in interest income, which we expect to fall sharply in 2008 due to lower interest rates, and a stable tax rate of 28%, we look for EPS of $1.25 in 2009, up from the $1.03 that we estimate for 2008. Estimates for both years include projected stock option expense of $0.13.

## Investment Rationale/Risk

➤ While we see near-term sales at risk from more disciplined information technology and carrier spending amid a weakening economic climate, we think recent product upgrades in core routing, as well as new opportunities in the carrier ethernet space, bode well for future growth opportunities. We view JNPR as well positioned to benefit from accelerating demand for higher speed routers to handle an increase in network bandwidth needs.

➤ Risks to our recommendation and target price include a decline in carrier spending, material market share losses in the routing market, and weaker than expected sales traction in the enterprise sector.

➤ Our 12-month target price of $24 is largely based on a forward P/E of 19X our 2009 EPS estimate of $1.25, above the industry average. This is warranted, in our view, by JNPR's strong position in IP transport, which is expanding at a rapid rate due to the proliferation of digital video. Using our three-year earnings growth estimate of 17%, our target price represents a forward P/E to growth ratio of 1.1X, in line with peers.

## Qualitative Risk Assessment

| LOW | MEDIUM | **HIGH** |
|---|---|---|

Our risk assessment reflects the highly competitive nature of the industry and execution risks related to the company's planned expansion into the enterprise market.

## Quantitative Evaluations

**S&P Quality Ranking** B

| D | C | B- | **B** | B+ | A- | A | A+ |
|---|---|---|---|---|---|---|---|

**Relative Strength Rank** MODERATE
42
LOWEST = 1 HIGHEST = 99

## Revenue/Earnings Data

**Revenue (Million $)**

| | 1Q | 2Q | 3Q | 4Q | Year |
|---|---|---|---|---|---|
| 2008 | 822.9 | 879.0 | 947.0 | -- | -- |
| 2007 | 626.9 | 664.9 | 735.1 | 809.2 | 2,836 |
| 2006 | 566.7 | 567.5 | 573.6 | 595.8 | 2,304 |
| 2005 | 449.1 | 493.0 | 546.4 | 575.5 | 2,064 |
| 2004 | 224.1 | 306.9 | 375.0 | 430.1 | 1,336 |
| 2003 | 157.2 | 165.1 | 172.1 | 207.0 | 701.4 |

**Earnings Per Share ($)**

| | | | | | |
|---|---|---|---|---|---|
| 2008 | 0.20 | 0.22 | 0.27 | E0.29 | E1.03 |
| 2007 | 0.11 | 0.15 | 0.15 | 0.22 | 0.62 |
| 2006 | 0.13 | -2.13 | 0.10 | 0.12 | -1.76 |
| 2005 | 0.13 | 0.15 | 0.14 | 0.17 | 0.59 |
| 2004 | 0.08 | -0.02 | 0.08 | 0.11 | 0.25 |
| 2003 | 0.01 | 0.03 | 0.02 | 0.04 | 0.10 |

Fiscal year ended Dec. 31. Next earnings report expected: Late January. EPS Estimates based on S&P Operating Earnings; historical GAAP earnings are as reported.

## Dividend Data

No cash dividends have been paid.

# Juniper Networks Inc

STANDARD
&POOR'S

## Business Summary October 27, 2008

CORPORATE OVERVIEW. Juniper Networks, founded in 1996, makes secure Internet Protocol (IP) networking solutions that are designed to address the needs at the core and at the edge of the network, and for wireless access. The company's core product is IP backbone routers for service providers. The acquisition of NetScreen in 2004 added a broad family of network security solutions aimed at enterprises, service providers, and government entities.

JNPR has strategic distribution relationships with Nokia Siemens Networks, Ericsson A.B., and Lucent Technologies, allowing for the resale of its products on a worldwide, non-exclusive basis, providing for discounts based upon the volume of products sold and specifying other general terms of sale. Nokia Siemens Networks accounted for more than 10% of total sales during 2007. Operations are organized into three operating segments: infrastructure, service layer technologies (SLT), and service.

PRIMARY BUSINESS DYNAMICS. The infrastructure segment (62% of total sales in 2007) primarily offers scalable router products that are used to control and direct network traffic from the core, through the edge, aggregation and the customer premise equipment level. The company has experienced an increased demand for infrastructure products due to the adoption and expan-

sion of IP networks as a result of peer to peer interaction, increased broadband usage, video, and IP television.

Infrastructure products include the M-series and T-series routers, geared to service providers, offering carrier class reliability and scalability. The M-series, which can be deployed at the edge of operator networks, in small and medium core networks, includes the M320, M160, M40e, M20, M10i and M7i platforms. The MX-Series addresses the Carrier Ethernet market. The T-series, T1600, T640 and T320, and TX Matrix are primarily designed for core IP infrastructures. Other product platforms include E-series and J-series (wireless routers, developed through JNPR's joint venture with Ericsson). In January 2008, the company introduced the EX-series family of Ethernet switches. Products run on JNPR's JUNOS Internet software, and are differentiated from their competition in that they also feature the company's high-performance, ASIC-based packet forwarding technology.

## Company Financials Fiscal Year Ended Dec. 31

| Per Share Data ($) | 2007 | 2006 | 2005 | 2004 | 2003 | 2002 | 2001 | 2000 | 1999 | 1998 |
|---|---|---|---|---|---|---|---|---|---|---|
| Tangible Book Value | 3.09 | 4.08 | 3.04 | 2.89 | 1.48 | 1.18 | 2.36 | 1.87 | 1.47 | 0.80 |
| Cash Flow | 0.96 | -1.46 | 0.82 | 0.52 | 0.27 | -0.16 | 0.42 | 0.53 | -0.01 | -1.35 |
| Earnings | 0.62 | -1.76 | 0.59 | 0.25 | 0.10 | -0.34 | -0.04 | 0.43 | -0.05 | -0.14 |
| S&P Core Earnings | 0.60 | -0.27 | 0.26 | 0.12 | -0.06 | -0.51 | -0.38 | NA | NA | NA |
| Dividends | Nil | Nil | Nil | Nil | Nil | Nil | Nil | Nil | Nil | NA |
| Payout Ratio | Nil | Nil | Nil | Nil | Nil | Nil | Nil | Nil | Nil | NA |
| Prices:High | 37.95 | 22.63 | 27.65 | 31.25 | 19.38 | 23.01 | 145.00 | 244.50 | 64.06 | NA |
| Prices:Low | 17.21 | 12.09 | 19.65 | 18.75 | 6.88 | 4.15 | 8.90 | 48.83 | 5.67 | NA |
| P/E Ratio:High | 61 | NM | 47 | NM | NM | NM | NM | NM | NM | NA |
| P/E Ratio:Low | 28 | NM | 33 | NM | NM | NM | NM | NM | NM | NA |

| Income Statement Analysis (Million $) | | | | | | | | | | |
|---|---|---|---|---|---|---|---|---|---|---|
| Revenue | 2,836 | 2,304 | 2,064 | 1,336 | 701 | 547 | 887 | 674 | 103 | 3.81 |
| Operating Income | 610 | 496 | 595 | 376 | 141 | 42.2 | 205 | 249 | -9.31 | -30.1 |
| Depreciation | 193 | 173 | 139 | 145 | 70.0 | 63.0 | 148 | 34.8 | 5.31 | 2.17 |
| Interest Expense | 1.70 | 3.59 | 3.93 | 5.38 | 39.1 | 55.6 | 61.4 | 52.7 | Nil | Nil |
| Pretax Income | 511 | -897 | 502 | 219 | 59.0 | -115 | 16.5 | 230 | -6.61 | -31.0 |
| Effective Tax Rate | 29.3% | NM | 29.5% | 38.0% | 33.6% | NM | NM | 35.8% | NM | NM |
| Net Income | 361 | -1,001 | 354 | 136 | 39.2 | -120 | -13.4 | 148 | -9.03 | -31.0 |
| S&P Core Earnings | 353 | -156 | 156 | 65.9 | -25.6 | -180 | -122 | NA | NA | NA |

| Balance Sheet & Other Financial Data (Million $) | | | | | | | | | | |
|---|---|---|---|---|---|---|---|---|---|---|
| Cash | 1,956 | 1,596 | 918 | 713 | 396 | 194 | 607 | 563 | 158 | 20.1 |
| Current Assets | 2,555 | 2,522 | 1,818 | 1,414 | 691 | 681 | 1,126 | 1,349 | 378 | 28.8 |
| Total Assets | 6,885 | 7,368 | 8,027 | 7,000 | 2,411 | 2,615 | 2,390 | 2,103 | 513 | 36.7 |
| Current Liabilities | 1,380 | 763 | 627 | 503 | 291 | 242 | 242 | 216 | 55.7 | 14.4 |
| Long Term Debt | Nil | 400 | 400 | Nil | 558 | 942 | 1,150 | 1,120 | Nil | 5.20 |
| Common Equity | 5,354 | 6,115 | 6,900 | 5,993 | 1,562 | 1,431 | 997 | 730 | 458 | 17.1 |
| Total Capital | 5,354 | 6,515 | 7,300 | 5,993 | 2,120 | 2,373 | 2,147 | 1,850 | 458 | 22.3 |
| Capital Expenditures | 147 | 102 | 98.2 | 63.2 | 19.4 | 36.1 | 241 | 35.0 | 10.0 | 6.53 |
| Cash Flow | 554 | -828 | 493 | 281 | 109 | -56.6 | 134 | 183 | -3.73 | -28.8 |
| Current Ratio | 1.9 | 3.3 | 2.9 | 2.8 | 2.4 | 2.8 | 4.6 | 6.2 | 6.8 | 2.0 |
| % Long Term Debt of Capitalization | Nil | 6.1 | 5.5 | Nil | 26.3 | 39.7 | 53.6 | 60.5 | Nil | 23.4 |
| % Net Income of Revenue | 12.7 | NM | 17.2 | 10.2 | 5.6 | NM | NM | 22.0 | NM | NM |
| % Return on Assets | 5.1 | NM | 4.7 | 2.9 | 1.6 | NM | NM | 11.3 | NM | NM |
| % Return on Equity | 6.3 | NM | 5.5 | 3.6 | 2.6 | NM | NM | 24.9 | NM | NM |

Data as orig reptd.; bef. results of disc opers/spec. items. Per share data adj. for stk. divs.; EPS diluted. E-Estimated. NA-Not Available. NM-Not Meaningful. NR-Not Ranked. UR-Under Review.

**Office:** 1194 North Mathilda Avenue, Sunnyvale, CA 94089.
**Telephone:** 408-745-2000.
**Email:** investor-relations@juniper.net
**Website:** http://www.juniper.net

**Chrmn & Pres:** S.G. Kriens
**Vice Chrmn & CTO:** P. Sindhu
**CEO:** K.R. Johnson
**COO:** M.J. Rose

**EVP, CFO & Chief Acctg Officer:** R.M. Denholm
**Board Members:** R. M. Calderoni, M. B. Cranston, K. R. Johnson, S. G. Kriens, J. M. Lawrie, S. Sclavos, P. Sindhu, W. R. Stensrud

**Founded:** 1996
**Domicile:** Delaware
**Employees:** 5,879

# KB Home

**STANDARD &POOR'S**

| S&P Recommendation | HOLD ★★★☆☆ | Price<br>$12.01 (as of Nov 14, 2008) | 12-Mo. Target Price<br>$18.00 | Investment Style<br>Large-Cap Blend |
|---|---|---|---|---|

**GICS Sector** Consumer Discretionary
**Sub-Industry** Homebuilding

**Summary** This large, diversified homebuilder has operations in most of the largest markets in the U.S.

## Key Stock Statistics (Source S&P, Vickers, company reports)

| | | | | | | | |
|---|---|---|---|---|---|---|---|
| 52-Wk Range | $28.99– 10.77 | S&P Oper. EPS 2008**E** | -10.00 | Market Capitalization(B) | $1.076 | Beta | 1.14 |
| Trailing 12-Month EPS | $-18.62 | S&P Oper. EPS 2009**E** | -3.00 | Yield (%) | 2.08 | S&P 3-Yr. Proj. EPS CAGR(%) | 5 |
| Trailing 12-Month P/E | NM | P/E on S&P Oper. EPS 2008**E** | NM | Dividend Rate/Share | $0.25 | S&P Credit Rating | BB |
| $10K Invested 5 Yrs Ago | $3,960 | Common Shares Outstg. (M) | 89.6 | Institutional Ownership (%) | NM | | |

## Price Performance

30-Week Mov. Avg. ···· 10-Week Mov. Avg. ── GAAP Earnings vs. Previous Year    Volume Above Avg. STARS
12-Mo. Target Price ── Relative Strength    ▲ Up ▼ Down ▶ No Change    Below Avg. ★

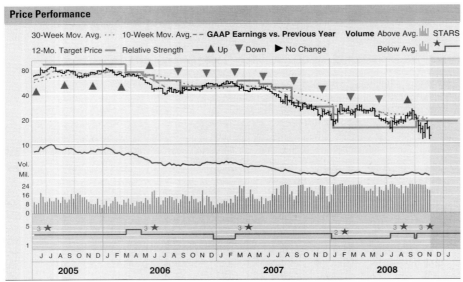

Options: ASE, CBOE, P, Ph

Analysis prepared by **Kenneth M. Leon, CPA** on October 09, 2008, when the stock traded at **$ 15.90**.

## Qualitative Risk Assessment

| LOW | MEDIUM | **HIGH** |
|---|---|---|

Our risk assessment reflects our opinion that market conditions have worsened and that a housing turnaround is not likely until at least late 2008. KBH has taken large write offs to adjust inventory, land and goodwill to its view of market value. Partly offsetting these risks is KBH's cash and borrowing capacity.

## Quantitative Evaluations

**S&P Quality Ranking**    A-

| D | C | B- | B | B+ | **A-** | A | A+ |
|---|---|---|---|---|---|---|---|

**Relative Strength Rank**    MODERATE

37

LOWEST = 1                              HIGHEST = 99

## Revenue/Earnings Data

**Revenue (Million $)**

| | 1Q | 2Q | 3Q | 4Q | Year |
|---|---|---|---|---|---|
| 2008 | 794.2 | 639.1 | 681.6 | -- | -- |
| 2007 | 1,389 | 1,413 | 1,544 | 2,071 | 6,417 |
| 2006 | 2,192 | 2,592 | 2,674 | 3,546 | 11,004 |
| 2005 | 1,636 | 2,130 | 2,525 | 3,150 | 9,442 |
| 2004 | 1,353 | 1,570 | 1,748 | 2,381 | 7,053 |
| 2003 | 1,095 | 1,440 | 1,442 | 1,873 | 5,851 |

**Earnings Per Share ($)**

| | | | | | |
|---|---|---|---|---|---|
| 2008 | -3.47 | -3.30 | -1.87 | E-1.37 | E-10.00 |
| 2007 | 0.14 | -2.26 | -6.19 | -9.99 | -18.33 |
| 2006 | 2.01 | 2.45 | 1.90 | -0.64 | 5.82 |
| 2005 | 1.41 | 2.06 | 2.55 | 3.51 | 9.53 |
| 2004 | 0.88 | 1.20 | 1.42 | 2.21 | 5.70 |
| 2003 | 0.63 | 0.97 | 1.17 | 1.66 | 4.40 |

Fiscal year ended Nov. 30. Next earnings report expected: NA. EPS Estimates based on S&P Operating Earnings; historical GAAP earnings are as reported.

## Highlights

➤ Following a 36% revenue decline in FY 07 (Nov.), we forecast that KB Home revenues will decrease nearly 60% in FY 08, and then decline 11% in FY 09. We believe that KBH, like many homebuilders, is enduring weak orders and declining sales despite offering aggressive pricing. The company responded to the depressed new housing market by booking $2.7 billion of asset writedowns in FY 07 for home inventory, land acquisitions and investments in joint ventures. KBH booked $507 million of asset write offs in the first nine months of FY 08.

➤ Gross proceeds of $800 million from the sale of its French operations in July 2007 enabled KBH to reduce its total debt outstanding to $2.2 billion, or to 45% of total capitalization, in line with peers. With $942 million in cash at August 31, 2008, we believe KBH can survive what we view as its weak position in the West and the Southeast.

➤ We estimate losses per share of $10.00 for FY 08 and $3.00 for FY 09. We believe KBH may be prompted to take additional writedowns, but we think the worst was posted in FY 07.

## Investment Rationale/Risk

➤ With a sales backlog value that declined from $6 billion in early FY 06 to $1.1 billion at August 31, 2008, we believe KBH is exposed to weak sales comparisons, with uncertainties about customer contract cancellations, average selling prices and asset impairments. Nonetheless, we believe KBH has a strong balance sheet with $942 million in cash to meet its debt obligations, and we think KBH will survive the housing downturn.

➤ Risks to our recommendation and target price include the key drivers that would decrease buyers' confidence levels, such as higher mortgage rates, employment losses and weaker home affordability than we project. With KBH focused on entry-level and move-up products, its middle income base of buyers is sensitive to any signs of less favorable credit availability and terms.

➤ We believe the shares are below our view of appropriate value. Our 12-month target price if $18 is based on a target price-to-book multiple of 1.23X -- toward the mid range of the historical range for KBH but still above large builders -- applied to our 12-month forward book value estimate of $14.60.

## Dividend Data (Dates: mm/dd Payment Date: mm/dd/yy)

| Amount<br>($) | Date<br>Decl. | Ex-Div.<br>Date | Stk. of<br>Record | Payment<br>Date |
|---|---|---|---|---|
| 0.250 | 12/06 | 02/05 | 02/07 | 02/21/08 |
| 0.250 | 04/03 | 05/06 | 05/08 | 05/22/08 |
| 0.250 | 05/28 | 07/08 | 07/10 | 07/24/08 |
| 0.063 | 11/04 | 11/12 | 11/14 | 11/25/08 |

Dividends have been paid since 1986. Source: Company reports.

# KB Home

**STANDARD
&POOR'S**

## Business Summary October 09, 2008

CORPORATE OVERVIEW. From its base in California, KB Home has become one of the five largest single-family homebuilders in the country. In doing so, it has helped establish what has become the industry model for rapid growth: using the acquisition of smaller builders as platforms for growth into new markets. Since 1993, KBH has expanded into Nevada, Arizona, Colorado, New Mexico, Texas, Florida, Georgia, North Carolina, South Carolina, Illinois and Indiana.

KBH entered Georgia and North Carolina in March 2003, through the acquisition of Colony Homes; re-entered Illinois through the September 2003 takeover of Zale Homes in Chicago; South Carolina through the January 2004 purchase of Palmetto Traditional Homes; and Indiana through the June 2004 purchase of Dura Builders.

In FY 07 (Nov.), the company delivered a total of 23,743 homes, down from 32,124 in FY 06. The company reports in four geographic segments. In FY 07, the West Coast accounted for 21% of unit deliveries (22% in FY 06), the Southwest 20% (22%), Central 27% (30%), and the Southeast 32% (26%).

Reflecting housing market conditions that show significant slowing, the number of lots under option was reduced to 20,000 at year-end FY 07, from 56,316 a year before. Similarly bracing for a slower market ahead, the company reduced its total lots owned or under option to 65,000 as of year-end FY 07, from 130,548 at year-end FY 06.

At the end of FY 07, KBH's backlog totaled 6,322 units, representing $1.5 billion. These levels were down 40% and 47%, respectively, from a year earlier. In our opinion, a 9% decline in average selling prices in FY 07 reflected a credit crunch that negatively affected mortgage availability and homebuyer demand. At the end of the FY 08 third quarter, the company's backlog totaled 4,774 units, or $1.1 billion, while deliveries in the quarter were only 2,788 units, compared to 5,699 units in the prior year's third quarter.

## Company Financials Fiscal Year Ended Nov. 30

| Per Share Data ($) | 2007 | 2006 | 2005 | 2004 | 2003 | 2002 | 2001 | 2000 | 1999 | 1998 |
|---|---|---|---|---|---|---|---|---|---|---|
| Tangible Book Value | 23.06 | 30.09 | 27.50 | 19.34 | 14.63 | 11.25 | 8.95 | 6.63 | 5.35 | 5.37 |
| Cash Flow | -18.10 | 6.11 | 9.76 | 5.96 | 4.65 | 3.77 | 3.32 | 3.14 | 1.95 | 1.38 |
| Earnings | -18.33 | 5.82 | 9.53 | 5.70 | 4.40 | 3.58 | 2.75 | 2.62 | 1.54 | 1.16 |
| S&P Core Earnings | -17.41 | 5.61 | 9.28 | 11.32 | 8.69 | 7.00 | 5.32 | NA | NA | NA |
| Dividends | 1.00 | 1.00 | 0.56 | 0.15 | 0.15 | 0.15 | 0.15 | 0.15 | 0.15 | 0.15 |
| Payout Ratio | NM | 17% | 6% | 3% | 3% | 4% | 5% | 6% | 10% | 13% |
| Prices:High | 56.08 | 81.99 | 85.45 | 53.76 | 37.48 | 27.20 | 20.72 | 19.16 | 15.13 | 17.50 |
| Prices:Low | 18.44 | 37.89 | 49.25 | 30.14 | 21.28 | 18.57 | 12.34 | 8.41 | 8.38 | 8.56 |
| P/E Ratio:High | NM | 14 | 9 | 9 | 9 | 8 | 8 | 7 | 10 | 15 |
| P/E Ratio:Low | NM | 7 | 5 | 5 | 5 | 5 | 4 | 3 | 5 | 7 |

| Income Statement Analysis (Million $) | | | | | | | | | | |
|---|---|---|---|---|---|---|---|---|---|---|
| Revenue | 6,417 | 11,004 | 9,442 | 7,053 | 5,851 | 5,031 | 4,574 | 3,931 | 3,836 | 2,449 |
| Operating Income | 1,329 | 790 | 1,387 | 796 | 584 | 539 | 448 | 373 | 333 | 203 |
| Depreciation | 19.8 | 24.2 | 20.5 | 21.8 | 21.5 | 17.2 | 43.9 | 41.3 | 40.0 | 18.1 |
| Interest Expense | Nil | 18.8 | 24.0 | 22.7 | 30.2 | 44.2 | 59.5 | 50.9 | 45.0 | 38.4 |
| Pretax Income | -1,461 | 766 | 1,374 | 787 | 580 | 486 | 352 | 329 | 257 | 154 |
| Effective Tax Rate | NM | 28.1% | 33.0% | 30.1% | 31.5% | 31.9% | 31.3% | 26.6% | 30.7% | 33.4% |
| Net Income | -1,415 | 482 | 842 | 481 | 371 | 314 | 214 | 210 | 147 | 95.3 |
| S&P Core Earnings | -1,344 | 465 | 808 | 467 | 357 | 302 | 207 | NA | NA | NA |

| Balance Sheet & Other Financial Data (Million $) | | | | | | | | | | |
|---|---|---|---|---|---|---|---|---|---|---|
| Cash | 1,325 | 655 | 145 | 234 | 138 | 330 | 281 | 33.1 | 28.0 | 63.4 |
| Current Assets | NA | NA | NA | NA | NA | NA | NA | NA | NA | NA |
| Total Assets | 5,706 | 9,014 | 7,747 | 5,836 | 4,236 | 4,026 | 3,693 | 2,829 | 2,664 | 1,860 |
| Current Liabilities | NA | NA | NA | NA | NA | NA | NA | NA | NA | NA |
| Long Term Debt | 2,162 | 3,027 | 2,433 | 2,048 | 1,393 | 1,181 | 1,111 | 1,208 | 1,308 | 800 |
| Common Equity | 1,851 | 2,923 | 2,852 | 2,056 | 1,593 | 1,274 | 1,092 | 655 | 676 | 475 |
| Total Capital | 4,013 | 6,139 | 5,429 | 4,231 | 3,075 | 2,530 | 2,267 | 1,919 | 1,994 | 1,472 |
| Capital Expenditures | 0.69 | 22.1 | 24.0 | 23.2 | 13.1 | 31.1 | 12.2 | 18.5 | 19.0 | Nil |
| Cash Flow | -1,397 | 503 | 863 | 503 | 392 | 332 | 258 | 251 | 187 | 113 |
| Current Ratio | 2.9 | 2.7 | 3.0 | 3.1 | 2.7 | 3.5 | 3.7 | 4.1 | 3.4 | 4.2 |
| % Long Term Debt of Capitalization | 53.8 | 49.3 | 44.8 | 48.4 | 45.3 | 46.7 | 49.0 | 62.9 | 65.6 | 54.3 |
| % Net Income of Revenue | NM | 4.4 | 8.9 | 6.8 | 6.3 | 6.2 | 4.7 | 5.3 | 3.8 | 3.9 |
| % Return on Assets | NM | 5.8 | 12.4 | 9.5 | 9.0 | 8.1 | 6.6 | 7.6 | 6.5 | 5.8 |
| % Return on Equity | NM | 16.9 | 34.3 | 26.4 | 25.9 | 26.6 | 24.5 | 31.6 | 25.6 | 22.2 |

Data as orig reptd.; bef. results of disc opers/spec. items. Per share data adj. for stk. divs.; EPS diluted. E-Estimated. NA-Not Available. NM-Not Meaningful. NR-Not Ranked. UR-Under Review.

**Office:** 10990 Wilshire Blvd, Los Angeles, CA 90024-3913.
**Telephone:** 310-231-4000.
**Website:** http://www.kbhome.com
**Chrmn:** S.F. Bollenbach

**Pres & CEO:** J. Mezger
**EVP, Secy & General Counsel:** W.C. Shiba
**SVP, Chief Acctg Officer & Cntlr:** W.R. Hollinger
**SVP & Treas:** K.K. Masuda

**Investor Contact:** K. Masuda (310-893-7434)
**Board Members:** S. F. Bollenbach, R. W. Burkle, T. W. Finchem, K. M. Jastrow, II, R. L. Johnson, J. Lanni, M. Lora, M. G. McCaffery, J. Mezger, L. Moonves, L. G. Nogales

**Founded:** 1957
**Domicile:** Delaware
**Employees:** 3,100

**The McGraw-Hill Companies**

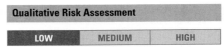

# Kellogg Co

**S&P Recommendation** HOLD ★★★☆☆

| Price | 12-Mo. Target Price | Investment Style |
|---|---|---|
| $46.93 (as of Nov 14, 2008) | $56.00 | Large-Cap Growth |

**GICS Sector** Consumer Staples
**Sub-Industry** Packaged Foods & Meats

**Summary** Kellogg is a leading producer of ready-to-eat cereal, and also sells convenience foods such as cookies, crackers, cereal bars, fruit snacks, and frozen waffles.

## Key Stock Statistics (Source S&P, Vickers, company reports)

| | | | | | | | | |
|---|---|---|---|---|---|---|---|---|
| 52-Wk Range | $58.51– 45.25 | S&P Oper. EPS 2008**E** | 2.99 | Market Capitalization(B) | $17.913 | Beta | | 0.21 |
| Trailing 12-Month EPS | $2.95 | S&P Oper. EPS 2009**E** | 3.20 | Yield (%) | 2.90 | S&P 3-Yr. Proj. EPS CAGR(%) | | 9 |
| Trailing 12-Month P/E | 15.9 | P/E on S&P Oper. EPS 2008**E** | 15.7 | Dividend Rate/Share | $1.36 | S&P Credit Rating | | BBB+ |
| $10K Invested 5 Yrs Ago | $14,938 | Common Shares Outstg. (M) | 381.7 | Institutional Ownership (%) | 82 | | | |

## Price Performance

30-Week Mov. Avg. · · · ·  10-Week Mov. Avg. – –  **GAAP Earnings vs. Previous Year**  Volume Above Avg. ▍▍▍ STARS
12-Mo. Target Price —  Relative Strength —  ▲ Up  ▼ Down  ► No Change  Below Avg. ▍▍▍ ★

[Price performance chart showing years 2005, 2006, 2007, 2008 with price scale 44–56, Vol. Mil. scale, monthly markers J J A S O N D, STARS ratings 4★ and 3★]

Options: CBOE, Ph

Analysis prepared by **Tom Graves, CFA** on September 19, 2008, when the stock traded at **$ 56.01**.

## Highlights

➤ In 2008, which includes a 53rd week, we look for sales to increase about 11% from the $11.8 billion reported for 2007. We expect that there will again be a favorable impact from currency exchange rates. Also, we believe that profit margins again will be pressured by commodity costs. However, we think that Kellogg will receive benefits from cost-reduction projects, and that it will incur expenses related to such initiatives. We anticipate that these costs will total about $0.14 a share in 2008, compared to $0.18 of these costs in 2007, of which about $0.08 was incurred in 2007's second quarter.

➤ We estimate net income in 2008 of $1.14 billion ($2.99 a share), up from the $1.10 billion ($2.76) reported for 2007. In 2009, we look for EPS of $3.27.

➤ In July 2008, Kellogg said that its board of directors had authorized an additional $500 million share repurchase program, to be executed within the next 12 months. Kellogg's initial 2008 authorization of $650 million has been completed. Kellogg said that repurchases related to the additional program were expected to start late in 2008.

## Investment Rationale/Risk

➤ Looking ahead, we expect profit growth to be bolstered by product innovation. In 2008, we expect overall profit improvement to be limited by a higher tax rate and commodity cost pressure. We expect that incremental benefits from a 53rd week will at least partly be spent on integrating acquisitions.

➤ Risks to our recommendation and target price include competitive pressures in K's businesses, consumer acceptance of new product introductions, commodity cost inflation, and the company's ability to achieve sales and earnings growth forecasts.

➤ In our view, the prospect of strong company cash flow (after capital expenditures) should help to give the stock some appeal. In 2007, such cash flow totaled about $1 billion. Our 12-month target price of $56 reflects our view that the stock should receive a P/E valuation (on estimated 2008 EPS) that is similar to the average of what we expect from a group of packaged foods stocks. The stock recently had an indicated dividend yield of 2.4%.

## Qualitative Risk Assessment

| LOW | MEDIUM | HIGH |
|---|---|---|

Our risk assessment for Kellogg Company reflects the relatively stable nature of the company's end markets, what we consider its strong balance sheet and cash flow, and corporate governance practices that we view as favorable versus peers.

## Quantitative Evaluations

**S&P Quality Ranking**  A

| D | C | B- | B | B+ | A- | A | A+ |
|---|---|---|---|---|---|---|---|

**Relative Strength Rank**  STRONG

74

LOWEST = 1    HIGHEST = 99

## Revenue/Earnings Data

**Revenue (Million $)**

| | 1Q | 2Q | 3Q | 4Q | Year |
|---|---|---|---|---|---|
| 2008 | 3,258 | 3,343 | 3,288 | -- | -- |
| 2007 | 2,963 | 3,015 | 3,004 | 2,794 | 11,776 |
| 2006 | 2,727 | 2,774 | 2,822 | 2,584 | 10,907 |
| 2005 | 2,572 | 2,587 | 2,623 | 2,394 | 10,177 |
| 2004 | 2,391 | 2,387 | 2,445 | 2,391 | 9,614 |
| 2003 | 2,148 | 2,247 | 2,282 | 2,135 | 8,812 |

**Earnings Per Share ($)**

| | 1Q | 2Q | 3Q | 4Q | Year |
|---|---|---|---|---|---|
| 2008 | 0.81 | 0.82 | 0.89 | E0.47 | E2.99 |
| 2007 | 0.80 | 0.75 | 0.76 | 0.44 | 2.76 |
| 2006 | 0.68 | 0.67 | 0.70 | 0.45 | 2.51 |
| 2005 | 0.61 | 0.62 | 0.66 | 0.47 | 2.36 |
| 2004 | 0.53 | 0.57 | 0.59 | 0.45 | 2.14 |
| 2003 | 0.40 | 0.50 | 0.56 | 0.46 | 1.92 |

Fiscal year ended Dec. 31. Next earnings report expected: Early February. EPS Estimates based on S&P Operating Earnings; historical GAAP earnings are as reported.

## Dividend Data (Dates: mm/dd Payment Date: mm/dd/yy)

| Amount ($) | Date Decl. | Ex-Div. Date | Stk. of Record | Payment Date |
|---|---|---|---|---|
| 0.310 | 02/22 | 02/29 | 03/04 | 03/18/08 |
| 0.310 | 04/25 | 05/29 | 06/02 | 06/17/08 |
| 0.340 | 07/25 | 08/28 | 09/02 | 09/16/08 |
| 0.340 | 10/24 | 12/01 | 12/03 | 12/16/08 |

Dividends have been paid since 1923. Source: Company reports.

---

**Please read the Required Disclosures and Analyst Certification on the last page of this report.**

The McGraw-Hill Companies

# Kellogg Co

## Business Summary September 19, 2008

CORPORATE OVERVIEW. Kellogg Co., incorporated in 1922, is a leading producer of ready-to-eat cereal. Also, the company has expanded its operations to include convenience food products such as Pop-Tarts toaster pastries, Eggo frozen waffles, Nutri-Grain cereal bars, and Rice Krispies Treats squares.

With the 2001 acquisition of the Keebler Foods Co., the company also markets cookies, crackers and other convenience food products under brand names such as Keebler, Cheez-It, Murray and Famous Amos, and manufactures private label cookies, crackers and other products.

Sales contributions by geographic region in 2007 were: North America 66%, Europe 20%, Latin America 8%, and Asia Pacific 6%. Also, in 2007, cereal sold through North American retail channels represented 24% of total net sales, while international cereal sales represented 28%. Other sales categories in-

cluded North American retail snacks (30%), North American frozen and specialty channels (12%), and international convenience foods (5%).

In 2007, Kellogg's top five customers accounted for about 32% of net sales collectively, and about 40% of U.S. net sales. Kellogg's largest customer, Wal-Mart Stores, Inc., and its affiliates, accounted for about 19% of net sales during 2007.

Kellogg's expenditures for research and development were about $179 million in 2007, and $191 million in 2006.

## Company Financials Fiscal Year Ended Dec. 31

| Per Share Data ($) | 2007 | 2006 | 2005 | 2004 | 2003 | 2002 | 2001 | 2000 | 1999 | 1998 |
|---|---|---|---|---|---|---|---|---|---|---|
| Tangible Book Value | NM | NM | NM | NM | NM | NM | NM | 1.21 | 1.28 | 1.26 |
| Cash Flow | 3.69 | 3.39 | 3.30 | 3.15 | 2.83 | 2.60 | 2.26 | 2.16 | 1.54 | 1.91 |
| Earnings | 2.76 | 2.51 | 2.36 | 2.14 | 1.92 | 1.75 | 1.18 | 1.45 | 0.83 | 1.23 |
| S&P Core Earnings | 2.74 | 2.62 | 2.29 | 2.10 | 1.86 | 1.24 | 0.77 | NA | NA | NA |
| Dividends | 1.49 | 1.14 | 1.06 | 1.01 | 1.01 | 1.01 | 1.01 | 1.00 | 0.96 | 0.92 |
| Payout Ratio | 54% | 45% | 45% | 47% | 53% | 58% | 86% | 69% | 116% | 75% |
| Prices:High | 56.89 | 50.95 | 46.99 | 45.32 | 38.57 | 37.00 | 34.00 | 32.00 | 42.25 | 50.19 |
| Prices:Low | 48.68 | 42.41 | 42.35 | 37.00 | 27.85 | 29.02 | 24.25 | 20.75 | 30.00 | 28.50 |
| P/E Ratio:High | 21 | 20 | 20 | 21 | 20 | 21 | 29 | 22 | 51 | 41 |
| P/E Ratio:Low | 18 | 17 | 18 | 17 | 15 | 17 | 21 | 14 | 36 | 23 |

| Income Statement Analysis (Million $) | | | | | | | | | | |
|---|---|---|---|---|---|---|---|---|---|---|
| Revenue | 11,776 | 10,907 | 10,177 | 9,614 | 8,812 | 8,304 | 8,853 | 6,955 | 6,984 | 6,762 |
| Operating Income | 2,347 | 2,119 | 2,142 | 2,091 | 1,917 | 1,857 | 1,640 | 1,367 | 1,361 | 1,243 |
| Depreciation | 372 | 353 | 392 | 410 | 373 | 348 | 439 | 291 | 288 | 278 |
| Interest Expense | 324 | 307 | 300 | 309 | 371 | 391 | 352 | 138 | 119 | 119 |
| Pretax Income | 1,547 | 1,471 | 1,425 | 1,366 | 1,170 | 1,144 | 804 | 868 | 537 | 783 |
| Effective Tax Rate | 28.7% | 31.7% | 31.2% | 34.8% | 32.7% | 37.0% | 40.1% | 32.3% | 37.0% | 35.8% |
| Net Income | 1,103 | 1,004 | 980 | 891 | 787 | 721 | 482 | 588 | 338 | 503 |
| S&P Core Earnings | 1,093 | 1,047 | 953 | 875 | 763 | 510 | 312 | NA | NA | NA |

| Balance Sheet & Other Financial Data (Million $) | | | | | | | | | | |
|---|---|---|---|---|---|---|---|---|---|---|
| Cash | 524 | 411 | 219 | 417 | 141 | 101 | 2,318 | 204 | 151 | 136 |
| Current Assets | 2,717 | 2,427 | 2,197 | 2,122 | 1,797 | 1,763 | 1,902 | 1,607 | 1,569 | 1,497 |
| Total Assets | 11,397 | 10,714 | 10,575 | 10,790 | 10,231 | 10,219 | 10,369 | 4,896 | 4,809 | 5,052 |
| Current Liabilities | 4,044 | 4,020 | 3,163 | 2,846 | 2,766 | 3,015 | 2,208 | 2,493 | 1,588 | 1,719 |
| Long Term Debt | 3,276 | 3,053 | 3,703 | 3,893 | 4,265 | 4,519 | 5,619 | 709 | 1,613 | 1,614 |
| Common Equity | 2,526 | 2,069 | 2,284 | 2,257 | 1,443 | 895 | 871 | 898 | 813 | 890 |
| Total Capital | 6,443 | 5,122 | 5,986 | 6,150 | 5,709 | 5,415 | 6,491 | 1,607 | 2,426 | 2,504 |
| Capital Expenditures | 472 | 453 | 374 | 279 | 247 | 254 | 277 | 231 | 266 | 344 |
| Cash Flow | 1,475 | 1,357 | 1,372 | 1,301 | 1,160 | 1,069 | 921 | 878 | 626 | 781 |
| Current Ratio | 0.7 | 0.6 | 0.7 | 0.7 | 0.6 | 0.6 | 0.9 | 0.6 | 1.0 | 0.9 |
| % Long Term Debt of Capitalization | 50.9 | 59.6 | 61.9 | 63.3 | 74.7 | 83.5 | 86.6 | 44.1 | 66.5 | 64.5 |
| % Net Income of Revenue | 9.4 | 9.2 | 9.6 | 9.3 | 8.9 | 8.7 | 5.4 | 8.5 | 4.8 | 7.4 |
| % Return on Assets | 10.0 | 9.4 | 9.3 | 8.5 | 7.7 | 7.0 | 6.3 | 12.1 | 6.9 | 10.1 |
| % Return on Equity | 48.0 | 46.1 | 43.2 | 48.1 | 67.3 | 81.6 | 54.5 | 68.7 | 39.7 | 53.3 |

Data as orig reptd.; bef. results of disc opers/spec. items. Per share data adj. for stk. divs.; EPS diluted. E-Estimated. NA-Not Available. NM-Not Meaningful. NR-Not Ranked. UR-Under Review.

**Office:** One Kellogg Sq, Battle Creek, MI, USA 49016-3599.
**Telephone:** 269-961-2000.
**Website:** http://www.kelloggcompany.com
**Chrmn:** J.M. Jenness

**Pres & CEO:** A.D. MacKay
**Investor Contact:** J.A. Bryant (269-961-2800)
**COO & CFO:** J.A. Bryant
**SVP & CIO:** R.E. Bruch

**Board Members:** B. S. Carson, J. T. Dillon, G. Gund, J. M. Jenness, D. A. Johnson, D. R. Knauss, A. M. Korologos, A. D. MacKay, R. M. Rebolledo, S. K. Speirn, R. A. Steele, J. L. Zabriskie

**Founded:** 1906
**Domicile:** Delaware
**Employees:** 26,494

# KeyCorp

**S&P Recommendation** HOLD ★★★★★

**Price**
$9.60 (as of Nov 14, 2008)

**12-Mo. Target Price**
$12.00

**Investment Style**
Large-Cap Value

**GICS Sector** Financials
**Sub-Industry** Regional Banks

**Summary** This multiregional bank holding company operates 985 branch offices in Ohio, New York, Washington State, Oregon, Maine, Indiana, and eight other states.

### Key Stock Statistics (Source S&P, Vickers, company reports)

| | | | | | | | |
|---|---|---|---|---|---|---|---|
| 52-Wk Range | $27.23– 5.75 | S&P Oper. EPS 2008**E** | -2.15 | Market Capitalization(B) | $4.752 | Beta | 1.16 |
| Trailing 12-Month EPS | $-2.19 | S&P Oper. EPS 2009**E** | 0.81 | Yield (%) | 7.81 | S&P 3-Yr. Proj. EPS CAGR(%) | -15 |
| Trailing 12-Month P/E | NM | P/E on S&P Oper. EPS 2008**E** | NM | Dividend Rate/Share | $0.75 | S&P Credit Rating | A- |
| $10K Invested 5 Yrs Ago | $4,309 | Common Shares Outstg. (M) | 495.0 | Institutional Ownership (%) | 75 | | |

### Price Performance

30-Week Mov. Avg. · · · · 10-Week Mov. Avg. —— **GAAP Earnings vs. Previous Year** **Volume** Above Avg. ▯▮▯ **STARS**
12-Mo. Target Price —— Relative Strength —— ▲ Up ▼ Down ▶ No Change Below Avg. ▮▯▮ ★

Options: ASE, CBOE, P, Ph

Analysis prepared by **Stuart Plesser** on October 24, 2008, when the stock traded at **$ 10.37**.

### Highlights

➤ We forecast total loan portfolio growth of 3.0% in 2009, down from a projected 8.5% in 2008, reflecting current softness in the U.S. economy. Our estimate is for a modest increase in fee income in 2009, assuming the likelihood of continued market volatility in KEY's capital markets-driven businesses. We expect total non-interest income (fee income plus gains and losses) to increase modestly in 2009 absent any gains from the Visa public stock offering and derivative losses.

➤ Non-performing loans totaled 1.26% of total loans at the end of the third quarter, up from 1.07% at the end of the second quarter. Annualized chargeffs declined to 1.40% of loans, from 2.74% the previous quarter, which was elevated due to KEY's attempt to aggressively sell non-performing loans. We estimate an annualized chargeoff rate of 1.45% in the fourth quarter. We estimate loan loss provisions of $1.6 billion in 2008, declining to $1.2 billion in 2009, assuming annualized chargeoffs of 1.45%.

➤ We project a loss per share of $2.15 in 2008. For 2009, we expect EPS rebounding to a gain of $0.81.

### Investment Rationale/Risk

➤ We think KEY is making good inroads containing non-performing loans and charging them off, but we believe visibility on future credit trends is still murky. We are concerned about an increase in commercial lending as companies make use of pre-existing revolver loans. We expect KEY's net interest margin to come under pressure in coming quarters, reflecting its asset-sensitive balance sheet. While we maintain our positive view of KEY's non-interest expense controls, low exposure to CDOs (collateralized debt obligations) and SIVs (structured investment vehicles), and relatively high capital levels, we remain cautious on the shares due to KEY's exposure to possible further declines in credit quality in real estate construction and commercial lending.

➤ Risks to our recommendation and target price include a slower than expected economic recovery causing higher-than-expected provisions.

➤ Our 12-month target price of $12 is derived by applying a below historical 0.95X multiple to KEY's tangible book value of $12.66. We think this multiple is warranted given the weak credit quality of KEY's loan book.

### Qualitative Risk Assessment

| LOW | MEDIUM | HIGH |
|---|---|---|

Our risk assessment reflects our view of the company's large-cap valuation, and its history of profitability, partly offset by its exposure to possible declines in the value of its investment securities and the possibility of further declines in lending credit quality.

### Quantitative Evaluations

**S&P Quality Ranking** B

| D | C | B- | B | B+ | A- | A | A+ |
|---|---|---|---|---|---|---|---|

**Relative Strength Rank** MODERATE

58

LOWEST = 1 HIGHEST = 99

### Revenue/Earnings Data

**Revenue (Million $)**

| | 1Q | 2Q | 3Q | 4Q | Year |
|---|---|---|---|---|---|
| 2008 | 1,882 | 1,435 | 1,620 | -- | -- |
| 2007 | 2,022 | 2,044 | 1,872 | 1,935 | 7,621 |
| 2006 | 1,732 | 1,872 | 1,932 | 1,971 | 7,507 |
| 2005 | 1,565 | 1,602 | 1,705 | 1,823 | 6,695 |
| 2004 | 1,370 | 1,358 | 1,388 | 1,448 | 5,564 |
| 2003 | 1,418 | 1,456 | 1,434 | 1,422 | 5,730 |

**Earnings Per Share ($)**

| | | | | | |
|---|---|---|---|---|---|
| 2008 | 0.55 | -2.70 | -0.07 | E0.13 | E-2.15 |
| 2007 | 0.89 | 0.85 | 0.57 | 0.06 | 2.38 |
| 2006 | 0.66 | 0.75 | 0.74 | 0.76 | 2.91 |
| 2005 | 0.64 | 0.70 | 0.67 | 0.72 | 2.73 |
| 2004 | 0.59 | 0.58 | 0.61 | 0.51 | 2.30 |
| 2003 | 0.51 | 0.53 | 0.53 | 0.55 | 2.12 |

Fiscal year ended Dec. 31. Next earnings report expected: Late January. EPS Estimates based on S&P Operating Earnings; historical GAAP earnings are as reported.

### Dividend Data (Dates: mm/dd Payment Date: mm/dd/yy)

| Amount ($) | Date Decl. | Ex-Div. Date | Stk. of Record | Payment Date |
|---|---|---|---|---|
| 0.365 | 11/15 | 11/23 | 11/27 | 12/14/07 |
| 0.375 | 12/20 | 02/29 | 03/04 | 03/14/08 |
| 0.375 | 05/15 | 05/22 | 05/27 | 06/13/08 |
| 0.188 | 07/18 | 08/28 | 09/02 | 09/15/08 |

Dividends have been paid since 1963. Source: Company reports.

---

**Please read the Required Disclosures and Analyst Certification on the last page of this report.**

# KeyCorp

STANDARD
&POOR'S

## Business Summary October 24, 2008

CORPORATE OVERVIEW. KEY owns KeyBank, located in Ohio, New York, Washington, Oregon, Maine, Colorado, Indiana, Utah, Idaho, Vermont, Alaska and Kentucky. The company has two business groups: Community Banking, and National Banking.

The Community Banking segment generates about 52% of total revenues, and houses Regional Banking and Commercial Banking.

National Banking generates about 48% of total revenues, and houses Real Estate Capital, Equipment Finance, Institutional and Capital Markets, Consumer Finance, Indirect Lending, Commercial Floor Plan Lending, and National Home Equity.

MARKET PROFILE. As of June 30, 2007 (latest available FDIC data), KEY had 958 branches and $57.3 billion in deposits, with about 60% of its deposits and 45% of its branches concentrated in Ohio and New York, according to Highline Data. In Ohio, KEY had 227 branches, $18.1 billion in deposits, and a deposit market share of about 8.1%, which ranks third. In New York, KEY had 198 branches, $13.0 billion in deposits, and a deposit market share of about 1.7%, which ranks twelfth. In Washington State, KEY had 152 branches, $8.0 billion in deposits, and a deposit market share of about 6.4%, which ranks fourth. In Oregon, KEY had 64 branches, $3.2 billion in deposits, and a deposit market share of about 5.4%, which ranks sixth. In Maine, KEY had 63 branches, $2.6 billion in deposits, and a deposit market share of about 10.9%, which ranks second. In Indiana, KEY had 64 branches, $2.6 billion in deposits, and a deposit market share of about 2.5%, which ranks sixth. In Colorado, KEY had 48 branches, $2.3 billion in deposits, and a deposit market share of about 2.5%, which ranks seventh. In addition, KEY had a number three ranking in Idaho, and a number five market ranking in Vermont and in Alaska. Finally, KEY had offices in Utah, Michigan and Florida, with a small presence in Kentucky.

## Company Financials Fiscal Year Ended Dec. 31

| Per Share Data ($) | 2007 | 2006 | 2005 | 2004 | 2003 | 2002 | 2001 | 2000 | 1999 | 1998 |
|---|---|---|---|---|---|---|---|---|---|---|
| Tangible Book Value | 16.39 | 15.99 | 15.05 | 13.91 | 13.87 | 13.34 | 11.85 | 12.39 | 11.13 | 10.28 |
| Earnings | 2.38 | 2.91 | 2.73 | 2.30 | 2.12 | 2.27 | 0.37 | 2.30 | 2.45 | 2.23 |
| S&P Core Earnings | 2.12 | 2.93 | 2.72 | 2.41 | 2.12 | 2.10 | 0.43 | NA | NA | NA |
| Dividends | 1.46 | 1.38 | 1.30 | 1.24 | 1.22 | 1.20 | 1.18 | 1.12 | 1.04 | 0.94 |
| Payout Ratio | 61% | 47% | 48% | 54% | 58% | 53% | NM | 49% | 42% | 42% |
| Prices:High | 39.90 | 38.63 | 35.00 | 34.50 | 29.41 | 29.40 | 29.25 | 28.50 | 38.13 | 44.88 |
| Prices:Low | 21.04 | 32.90 | 30.10 | 28.23 | 22.31 | 20.98 | 20.49 | 15.56 | 21.00 | 23.38 |
| P/E Ratio:High | 17 | 13 | 13 | 15 | 14 | 13 | 79 | 12 | 16 | 20 |
| P/E Ratio:Low | 9 | 11 | 11 | 12 | 11 | 9 | 55 | 7 | 9 | 10 |

| Income Statement Analysis (Million $) | | | | | | | | | | |
|---|---|---|---|---|---|---|---|---|---|---|
| Net Interest Income | 2,769 | 2,815 | 2,790 | 2,637 | 2,725 | 2,749 | 2,825 | 2,730 | 2,787 | 2,749 |
| Tax Equivalent Adjustment | 99.0 | 103 | 121 | 94.0 | 71.0 | 120 | 45.0 | 28.0 | 32.0 | 34.0 |
| Non Interest Income | 2,264 | 2,126 | 2,077 | 1,742 | 1,749 | 1,763 | 1,690 | 2,222 | 2,265 | 1,566 |
| Loan Loss Provision | 529 | 150 | 143 | 185 | 501 | 553 | 1,350 | 490 | 348 | 297 |
| % Expense/Operating Revenue | 64.5% | 62.4% | 64.5% | 62.8% | 60.3% | 57.3% | 64.5% | 58.6% | 60.0% | 58.6% |
| Pretax Income | 1,221 | 1,643 | 1,588 | 1,388 | 1,242 | 1,312 | 259 | 1,517 | 1,684 | 1,479 |
| Effective Tax Rate | 22.9% | 27.4% | 28.9% | 31.3% | 27.3% | 25.6% | 39.4% | 33.9% | 34.3% | 32.7% |
| Net Income | 941 | 1,193 | 1,129 | 954 | 903 | 976 | 157 | 1,002 | 1,107 | 996 |
| % Net Interest Margin | 3.46 | 3.67 | 3.69 | 3.64 | 3.80 | 3.97 | 3.81 | 3.69 | 3.93 | 4.18 |
| S&P Core Earnings | 840 | 1,198 | 1,125 | 1,006 | 898 | 896 | 179 | NA | NA | NA |

| Balance Sheet & Other Financial Data (Million $) | | | | | | | | | | |
|---|---|---|---|---|---|---|---|---|---|---|
| Money Market Assets | 1,056 | Nil | Nil | NA | NA | NA | NA | NA | NA | NA |
| Investment Securities | 7,860 | NA | NA | NA | NA | NA | NA | NA | NA | NA |
| Commercial Loans | 52,705 | 48,306 | 39,291 | 43,276 | 36,189 | 36,612 | 38,063 | 39,610 | 36,672 | 22,685 |
| Other Loans | 18,748 | 17,520 | 20,078 | 25,188 | 26,522 | 25,845 | 25,246 | 27,295 | 27,550 | 39,327 |
| Total Assets | 99,983 | 92,337 | 93,126 | 90,739 | 84,487 | 85,202 | 80,938 | 87,270 | 83,395 | 80,020 |
| Demand Deposits | 11,028 | 13,553 | 13,335 | 11,581 | 11,175 | 10,630 | 23,128 | 9,076 | 8,607 | 9,540 |
| Time Deposits | 52,071 | 45,563 | 45,430 | 39,683 | 39,683 | 38,716 | 21,667 | 39,573 | 34,626 | 33,043 |
| Long Term Debt | 11,957 | 14,533 | 13,939 | 14,846 | 15,294 | 16,865 | 15,842 | 15,404 | 17,124 | 13,964 |
| Common Equity | 7,746 | 7,703 | 7,598 | 7,117 | 6,969 | 6,835 | 6,155 | 6,623 | 6,389 | 6,167 |
| % Return on Assets | 1.0 | 1.3 | 1.2 | 1.1 | 1.1 | 1.2 | 0.2 | 1.2 | 1.4 | 1.3 |
| % Return on Equity | 12.2 | 15.6 | 15.3 | 13.5 | 13.1 | 15.0 | 2.5 | 15.4 | 17.6 | 17.5 |
| % Loan Loss Reserve | 1.7 | 1.4 | 1.4 | 1.7 | 2.2 | 2.3 | 2.7 | 1.5 | 1.4 | 1.5 |
| % Loans/Deposits | 111.8 | 117.5 | 118.9 | 118.4 | 123.3 | 126.6 | 138.0 | 137.5 | 148.5 | 145.6 |
| % Equity to Assets | 8.0 | 8.3 | 8.0 | 8.0 | 8.1 | 7.8 | 7.6 | 7.6 | 7.7 | 7.4 |

Data as orig reptd.; bef. results of disc opers/spec. items. Per share data adj. for stk. divs.; EPS diluted. E-Estimated. NA-Not Available. NM-Not Meaningful. NR-Not Ranked. UR-Under Review.

**Office:** 127 Public Square, Cleveland, OH 44114-1306.
**Telephone:** 216-689-6300.
**Website:** http://www.key.com
**Chrmn, Pres & CEO:** H.L. Meyer, III

**Vice Chrmn & Chief Admin Officer:** T.C. Stevens
**EVP & CFO:** J.B. Weeden
**EVP & Treas:** J.M. Vayda
**EVP & General Counsel:** P.N. Harris

**Board Members:** R. Alvarez, W. G. Bares, E. P. Campbell, C. Cartwright, A. M. Cutler, H. J. Dallas, L. E. Martin, E. R. Menasce, H. L. Meyer, III, B. R. Sanford, T. C. Stevens, P. G. Ten Eyck, II

**Founded:** 1849
**Domicile:** Ohio
**Employees:** 18,934

# Kimberly-Clark Corp

STANDARD
&POOR'S

| S&P Recommendation | BUY ★★★★☆ | Price $57.37 (as of Nov 14, 2008) | 12-Mo. Target Price $64.00 | Investment Style Large-Cap Blend |
|---|---|---|---|---|

**GICS Sector** Consumer Staples
**Sub-Industry** Household Products

**Summary** This leading consumer products company's global tissue, personal care and health care brands include Huggies, Pull-Ups, Kotex, Depend, Kleenex, Scott and Kimberly-Clark.

## Key Stock Statistics (Source S&P, Vickers, company reports)

| | | | | | | | | |
|---|---|---|---|---|---|---|---|---|
| 52-Wk Range | $70.35– 50.42 | S&P Oper. EPS 2008E | 4.15 | Market Capitalization(B) | $23.737 | Beta | | 0.48 |
| Trailing 12-Month EPS | $4.10 | S&P Oper. EPS 2009E | 4.45 | Yield (%) | 4.04 | S&P 3-Yr. Proj. EPS CAGR(%) | | 8 |
| Trailing 12-Month P/E | 14.0 | P/E on S&P Oper. EPS 2008E | 13.8 | Dividend Rate/Share | $2.32 | S&P Credit Rating | | A |
| $10K Invested 5 Yrs Ago | NA | Common Shares Outstg. (M) | 413.8 | Institutional Ownership (%) | 77 | | | |

## Price Performance

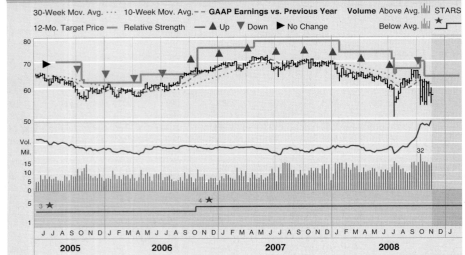

30-Week Mov. Avg. ···· 10-Week Mov. Avg. – – GAAP Earnings vs. Previous Year  Volume Above Avg. ▮▮▮ STARS
12-Mo. Target Price — Relative Strength — ▲ Up ▼ Down ► No Change    Below Avg. ▮▮▮ ★

Options: ASE, CBOE, P

Analysis prepared by **Loran Braverman, CFA** on October 22, 2008, when the stock traded at **$ 57.22**.

## Highlights

➤ In 2008, we expect sales growth of 7.5%, with Personal Care segment revenues up 11%, driven by new products and growth in developing markets. We see Consumer Tissue segment sales rising 5%, K-C Professional & Other 8% and Health Care 1%. Our 2009 sales growth estimate is 2.6%, with the slowdown from 2008's pace largely reflecting currency shifts.

➤ We project an operating margin decline in 2008 of 120 basis points, excluding restructuring costs, despite KMB making good strides in cost reduction and raising prices. We look for continued substantial commodity cost pressures, particularly from oil, natural gas and pulp, and also planned strategic investments in advertising and promotions. For 2009, we see the margin widening as commodity cost pressures moderate. We expect contributions to pension plans to rise in both 2008 and 2009.

➤ Assuming an effective tax rate of 28.5%, versus 24% in 2007, and a 6% decline in average shares outstanding, partly due to an accelerated share repurchase program in July 2007, we project operating EPS in 2008 of $4.15, versus $4.25 in 2007. Our 2009 EPS estimate is $4.45.

## Investment Rationale/Risk

➤ Although we continue to see intense competition in developed countries and in consumer tissue and personal care categories, we believe the company's efforts to expand in non-traditional (for KMB) categories and its focus on certain developing markets will support sales growth. In addition, we expect further benefits to KMB's earnings in 2008 from the strategic cost reduction program begun in late 2005, although this is likely to be masked by higher commodity costs. In 2009, we expect margins to start to widen.

➤ Risks to our recommendation and target price include increased promotional activity in the consumer paper category, higher commodity costs, a lack of product innovation, unfavorable foreign currency shifts, and decreased consumer acceptance of KMB's products.

➤ Our 12-month target price of $64 is based on a blend of our historical and relative analyses. Our historical analysis suggests a value of $74, using a P/E close to the 10-year low applied to our 2009 EPS forecast of $4.45. Our peer analysis applies a discount to the group average, implying a value of $54.

## Qualitative Risk Assessment

| LOW | MEDIUM | HIGH |
|---|---|---|

Our risk assessment reflects the generally static demand for household and personal care products, which is usually not affected by changes in the economy or geopolitical factors.

## Quantitative Evaluations

**S&P Quality Ranking**                    A

| D | C | B- | B | B+ | A- | A | A+ |
|---|---|---|---|---|---|---|---|

**Relative Strength Rank**          STRONG

82

LOWEST = 1                        HIGHEST = 99

## Revenue/Earnings Data

**Revenue (Million $)**

| | 1Q | 2Q | 3Q | 4Q | Year |
|---|---|---|---|---|---|
| 2008 | 4,813 | 5,006 | 4,998 | -- | -- |
| 2007 | 4,385 | 4,502 | 4,621 | 4,758 | 18,266 |
| 2006 | 4,068 | 4,161 | 4,210 | 4,307 | 16,747 |
| 2005 | 3,906 | 3,987 | 4,001 | 4,009 | 15,903 |
| 2004 | 3,712 | 3,687 | 3,783 | 3,901 | 15,083 |
| 2003 | 3,460 | 3,545 | 3,642 | 3,702 | 14,348 |

**Earnings Per Share ($)**

| | | | | | |
|---|---|---|---|---|---|
| 2008 | 1.04 | 1.01 | 0.99 | E1.02 | E4.15 |
| 2007 | 0.98 | 1.00 | 1.04 | 1.07 | 4.09 |
| 2006 | 0.60 | 0.82 | 0.79 | 1.05 | 3.25 |
| 2005 | 0.93 | 0.88 | 0.68 | 0.82 | 3.31 |
| 2004 | 0.88 | 0.88 | 0.87 | 0.92 | 3.55 |
| 2003 | 0.78 | 0.82 | 0.83 | 0.91 | 3.33 |

Fiscal year ended Dec. 31. Next earnings report expected: Late January. EPS Estimates based on S&P Operating Earnings; historical GAAP earnings are as reported.

## Dividend Data (Dates: mm/dd Payment Date: mm/dd/yy)

| Amount ($) | Date Decl. | Ex-Div. Date | Stk. of Record | Payment Date |
|---|---|---|---|---|
| 0.580 | 02/21 | 03/05 | 03/07 | 04/02/08 |
| 0.580 | 04/17 | 06/04 | 06/06 | 07/02/08 |
| 0.580 | 08/01 | 09/03 | 09/05 | 10/02/08 |
| 0.580 | 11/13 | 12/03 | 12/05 | 01/05/09 |

Dividends have been paid since 1935. Source: Company reports.

# Kimberly-Clark Corp

STANDARD
&POOR'S

## Business Summary October 22, 2008

CORPORATE OVERVIEW. Kimberly-Clark, best known for brand names such as Kleenex, Scott, Huggies and Kotex, sells consumer and other products in more than 150 countries. After operating as a broadly diversified enterprise, KMB made a major transition since the early 1990s, transforming itself into a global consumer products company. The company further developed its health care business through the acquisitions of Technol Medical Products, Ballard Medical Products, and Safeskin Corp. Reflecting more than 30 strategic acquisitions and 20 strategic divestitures since 1992, KMB has become a leading global manufacturer of tissue, personal care and health care products, manufactured in 39 countries. In 2004, KMB distributed to its shareholders all of the outstanding shares of Neenah Paper, Inc., which was formed in 2004 to facilitate the spin-off of KMB's U.S. fine paper and technical paper businesses and its Canadian pulp mills.

KMB classifies its business into four reportable global segments: Personal Care; Consumer Tissue; K-C Professional & Other; and Health Care. In 2007, Personal Care contributed 41% of sales and 53% of segment operating profits; Consumer Tissue 35% and 24%; K-C Professional & Other 17% and 16%; and Health Care 7% and 7%.

In 2007, sales in the U.S. and Canada contributed about 54% to sales, Europe 18%, and Asia, Latin America and other 28%. Wal-Mart Stores, Inc. is KMB's single largest customer, accounting for about 13% of net sales in each of 2005, 2006 and 2007.

CORPORATE STRATEGY. In mid-2003, KMB introduced a new strategic plan called the Global Business Plan (GBP), which involves prioritizing growth opportunities and applying greater financial discipline to KMB's global operations. The annual goals established by the GBP are: top-line growth of 3%-5%; EPS growth in the mid- to high-single digits; an operating margin improvement of 40 to 50 basis points; capital spending of 5%-6% of net sales; an ROIC improvement of 40 to 50 basis points; and dividend increases in the high single digits to the low double digits. On average, in the 2004 through 2007 period, we believe KMB met or exceeded all these goals but an operating margin improvement, which was adversely affected by unusually high inflationary cost pressures. Also, under the GBP, capital allocation focused on more targeted expansion activity and an increased emphasis on innovation and cost reduction.

## Company Financials Fiscal Year Ended Dec. 31

| Per Share Data ($) | 2007 | 2006 | 2005 | 2004 | 2003 | 2002 | 2001 | 2000 | 1999 | 1998 |
|---|---|---|---|---|---|---|---|---|---|---|
| Tangible Book Value | 5.92 | 7.10 | 6.22 | 8.13 | 8.21 | 6.65 | 7.10 | 7.04 | 7.12 | 6.12 |
| Cash Flow | 5.90 | 5.34 | 5.08 | 5.32 | 4.80 | 4.60 | 1.39 | 4.55 | 4.17 | 3.11 |
| Earnings | 4.09 | 3.25 | 3.31 | 3.55 | 3.33 | 3.24 | 3.02 | 3.34 | 3.09 | 2.13 |
| S&P Core Earnings | 4.09 | 3.32 | 3.32 | 3.56 | 3.35 | 2.74 | 2.49 | NA | NA | NA |
| Dividends | 2.12 | 1.96 | 1.80 | 1.60 | 1.36 | 1.20 | 1.12 | 1.08 | 1.03 | 0.99 |
| Payout Ratio | 52% | 60% | 54% | 45% | 41% | 37% | 37% | 32% | 33% | 46% |
| Prices:High | 72.79 | 68.58 | 68.29 | 69.00 | 59.30 | 66.79 | 72.19 | 73.25 | 69.56 | 59.44 |
| Prices:Low | 63.79 | 56.59 | 55.60 | 56.19 | 42.92 | 45.30 | 52.06 | 42.00 | 44.81 | 35.88 |
| P/E Ratio:High | 18 | 21 | 21 | 19 | 18 | 21 | 24 | 22 | 23 | 28 |
| P/E Ratio:Low | 16 | 17 | 17 | 16 | 13 | 14 | 17 | 13 | 15 | 17 |

| Income Statement Analysis (Million $) | | | | | | | | | | |
|---|---|---|---|---|---|---|---|---|---|---|
| Revenue | 18,266 | 16,747 | 15,903 | 15,083 | 14,348 | 13,566 | 14,524 | 13,982 | 13,007 | 12,298 |
| Operating Income | 3,553 | 3,034 | 3,155 | 3,358 | 3,158 | 3,170 | 3,162 | 3,203 | 2,815 | 2,320 |
| Depreciation | 806 | 933 | 844 | 800 | 746 | 707 | 740 | 673 | 586 | 542 |
| Interest Expense | 283 | 220 | 190 | 163 | 168 | 182 | 192 | 222 | 213 | 199 |
| Pretax Income | 2,488 | 2,064 | 2,106 | 2,328 | 2,153 | 2,411 | 2,319 | 2,622 | 2,441 | 1,763 |
| Effective Tax Rate | 21.6% | 22.7% | 20.8% | 20.8% | 23.9% | 27.7% | 27.8% | 28.9% | 29.9% | 31.9% |
| Net Income | 1,823 | 1,500 | 1,581 | 1,770 | 1,694 | 1,686 | 1,610 | 1,801 | 1,668 | 1,177 |
| S&P Core Earnings | 1,820 | 1,533 | 1,581 | 1,777 | 1,708 | 1,424 | 1,329 | NA | NA | NA |

| Balance Sheet & Other Financial Data (Million $) | | | | | | | | | | |
|---|---|---|---|---|---|---|---|---|---|---|
| Cash | 762 | 361 | 364 | 594 | 291 | 495 | 405 | 207 | 323 | 144 |
| Current Assets | 6,097 | 5,270 | 4,783 | 4,962 | 4,438 | 4,274 | 3,922 | 3,790 | 3,562 | 3,367 |
| Total Assets | 18,440 | 17,067 | 16,303 | 17,018 | 16,780 | 15,586 | 15,008 | 14,480 | 12,816 | 11,510 |
| Current Liabilities | 4,929 | 5,016 | 4,643 | 4,537 | 3,919 | 4,038 | 4,168 | 4,574 | 3,846 | 3,791 |
| Long Term Debt | 4,394 | 3,069 | 3,352 | 3,021 | 3,301 | 3,398 | 2,962 | Nil | 1,927 | 2,068 |
| Common Equity | 5,224 | 6,097 | 5,558 | 6,630 | 6,766 | 5,650 | 5,647 | 5,767 | 5,093 | 3,887 |
| Total Capital | 11,476 | 9,981 | 9,878 | 10,859 | 10,366 | 10,158 | 9,923 | 7,036 | 8,101 | 6,819 |
| Capital Expenditures | 989 | 972 | 710 | 535 | 878 | 871 | 1,100 | 1,170 | 786 | 670 |
| Cash Flow | 2,629 | 2,432 | 2,425 | 2,571 | 2,440 | 2,393 | 740 | 2,474 | 2,254 | 1,719 |
| Current Ratio | 1.2 | 1.1 | 1.0 | 1.1 | 1.1 | 1.1 | 0.9 | 0.8 | 0.9 | 0.9 |
| % Long Term Debt of Capitalization | 38.3 | 30.8 | 33.9 | 27.8 | 31.8 | 33.4 | 29.9 | Nil | 23.8 | 30.3 |
| % Net Income of Revenue | 10.0 | 9.0 | 9.9 | 11.7 | 11.8 | 12.4 | 11.1 | 12.9 | 12.8 | 9.6 |
| % Return on Assets | 10.3 | 9.0 | 9.5 | 10.5 | 10.5 | 11.0 | 10.9 | 13.2 | 13.6 | 10.3 |
| % Return on Equity | 32.2 | 25.7 | 25.9 | 26.4 | 27.3 | 29.8 | 28.2 | 33.2 | 37.1 | 29.4 |

Data as orig reptd.; bef. results of disc opers/spec. items. Per share data adj. for stk. divs.; EPS diluted. E-Estimated. NA-Not Available. NM-Not Meaningful. NR-Not Ranked. UR-Under Review.

**Office:** P.O. Box 619100, Dallas, TX 75261-9100.
**Telephone:** 972-281-1200.
**Website:** http://www.kimberly-clark.com
**Chrmn, Pres & CEO:** T.J. Falk

**SVP & CFO:** M.A. Buthman
**Chief Acctg Officer & Cntlr:** R.J. Vest
**Secy:** T.C. Everett
**Investor Contact:** M.D. Masseth (972-281-1478)

**Board Members:** J. R. Alm, D. Beresford, J. F. Bergstrom, A. E. Bru, R. W. Decherd, T. J. Falk, M. C. Jemison, J. M. Jenness, I. C. Read, L. J. Rice, M. J. Shapiro, G. C. Sullivan

**Founded:** 1872
**Domicile:** Delaware
**Employees:** 53,000

# Kimco Realty Corp

**STANDARD &POOR'S**

| S&P Recommendation | HOLD ★★★☆☆ | Price<br>$17.25 (as of Nov 14, 2008) | 12-Mo. Target Price<br>$20.00 | Investment Style<br>Large-Cap Blend |
|---|---|---|---|---|

**GICS Sector** Financials
**Sub-Industry** Retail REITS

**Summary** This real estate investment trust is one of the largest U.S. owners and operators of neighborhood and community shopping centers.

## Key Stock Statistics (Source S&P, Vickers, company reports)

| | | | | | | | |
|---|---|---|---|---|---|---|---|
| 52-Wk Range | $47.80– 16.02 | S&P FFO/Sh. 2008E | 2.25 | Market Capitalization(B) | $4.382 | Beta | 0.85 |
| Trailing 12-Month FFO/Share | NA | S&P FFO/Sh. 2009E | 2.30 | Yield (%) | 10.20 | S&P 3-Yr. FFO/Sh. Proj. CAGR(%) | 1 |
| Trailing 12-Month P/FFO | NA | P/FFO on S&P FFO/Sh. 2008E | 7.7 | Dividend Rate/Share | $1.76 | S&P Credit Rating | A- |
| $10K Invested 5 Yrs Ago | $9,762 | Common Shares Outstg. (M) | 254.0 | Institutional Ownership (%) | 83 | | |

## Price Performance

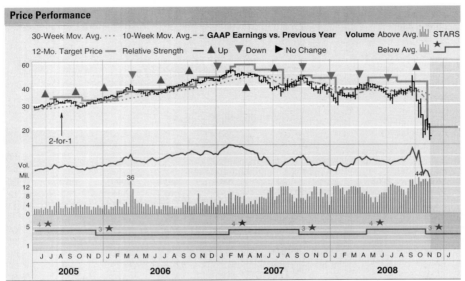

- 30-Week Mov. Avg.  ···· 10-Week Mov. Avg.  — GAAP Earnings vs. Previous Year  Volume Above Avg. STARS
- 12-Mo. Target Price — Relative Strength  ▲ Up  ▼ Down  ► No Change  Below Avg. ★

Options: ASE, CBOE, P, Ph

Analysis prepared by **Robert McMillan** on November 11, 2008, when the stock traded at **$ 18.62**.

## Highlights

➤ We expect the trust to continue to benefit from what we view as a successful strategy of operating neighborhood and community shopping centers in North America and expanding into high-growth international markets via joint ventures.

➤ We look for total revenues, after rising about 16% in 2007, to advance about 11% in 2008 and 9% in 2009 on higher rents at established properties and contributions from acquisitions and development activities. Occupancy of KIM's total portfolio dropped to 95.3% at the end of the third quarter, from 96.4% a year earlier. Despite our expectations of a soft economy and more store closures, we believe ongoing retailer demand for new and existing space, on top of limited new construction, will help results. Rents on new and renewal leases in the U.S. rose a combined 10.6% during the third quarter. Nevertheless, sharp declines in KIM's merchant building business will restrict growth. Management is focused on enhancing liquidity given the current credit freeze. KIM does not have any onerous near-term debt maturities.

➤ We project FFO per share of $2.25 for 2008 and $2.30 for 2009.

## Investment Rationale/Risk

➤ We believe that KIM, as one of the largest owners and operators of neighborhood and community shopping centers in the U.S. with a broad array of established relationships, will generate above-average rent growth, and we think the company it deserves to trade at a premium to peers on a valuation basis.

➤ Risks to our recommendation and target price include slower-than-expected growth in retailer expansion and rental rates, higher-than-normal retailer bankruptcies, and increases in interest rates.

➤ The shares recently traded at about 7.5X trailing 12-month FFO per share. Our 12-month target price of $20 is equal to about 10X our forward 12-month FFO estimate of $1.95. We believe the stock has been volatile over the past year in part due to concerns about the soft economy, a rise in store closures, and declines in transactional volumes. Although we do not expect transaction volume to recover in the foreseeable future, we think the valuation multiple will expand over time as KIM demonstrates that it's core portfolio, which is anchored by long term leases, continues to grow.

## Qualitative Risk Assessment

| LOW | MEDIUM | HIGH |
|---|---|---|

Our risk assessment reflects our view of KIM's strong fundamentals, healthy credit quality, and diversified customer base. We also believe KIM's diversity in its geographic presence helps provide significant protection from a local or regional downturn.

## Quantitative Evaluations

**S&P Quality Ranking**    A+

| D | C | B- | B | B+ | A- | A | A+ |
|---|---|---|---|---|---|---|---|

**Relative Strength Rank**    WEAK

24

LOWEST = 1    HIGHEST = 99

## Revenue/FFO Data

**Revenue (Million $)**

| | 1Q | 2Q | 3Q | 4Q | Year |
|---|---|---|---|---|---|
| 2008 | 190.5 | 199.9 | 208.6 | -- | -- |
| 2007 | 158.3 | 170.8 | 210.3 | 179.7 | 750.6 |
| 2006 | 138.1 | 147.9 | 150.7 | 157.3 | 653.0 |
| 2005 | 129.3 | 126.7 | 129.6 | 137.0 | 580.6 |
| 2004 | 139.9 | 129.7 | 122.7 | 124.7 | 517.0 |
| 2003 | 119.7 | 115.0 | 118.5 | 126.6 | 479.7 |

**FFO Per Share ($)**

| | 1Q | 2Q | 3Q | 4Q | Year |
|---|---|---|---|---|---|
| 2008 | 0.64 | 0.66 | E0.64 | E0.27 | E2.25 |
| 2007 | 0.78 | 0.71 | 0.57 | 0.53 | 2.59 |
| 2006 | 0.53 | 0.54 | 0.56 | 0.58 | 2.21 |
| 2005 | 0.53 | 0.54 | 0.56 | 0.55 | 2.00 |
| 2004 | 0.47 | 0.48 | 0.50 | 0.45 | 1.78 |
| 2003 | 0.39 | 0.40 | 0.41 | 0.43 | 1.62 |

Fiscal year ended Dec. 31. Next earnings report expected: Early February. FFO Estimates based on S&P Funds From Operations Est..

## Dividend Data (Dates: mm/dd Payment Date: mm/dd/yy)

| Amount ($) | Date Decl. | Ex-Div. Date | Stk. of Record | Payment Date |
|---|---|---|---|---|
| 0.400 | 03/17 | 04/02 | 04/04 | 04/15/08 |
| 0.400 | 06/16 | 07/01 | 07/03 | 07/15/08 |
| 0.440 | 07/29 | 10/01 | 10/03 | 10/15/08 |
| 0.440 | 11/05 | 12/30 | 01/02 | 01/15/09 |

Dividends have been paid since 1992. Source: Company reports.

---

**Please read the Required Disclosures and Analyst Certification on the last page of this report.**

# Kimco Realty Corp

**STANDARD &POOR'S**

## Business Summary November 11, 2008

Kimco Realty specializes in the acquisition, development and management of shopping centers that it believes are well-located and have strong growth potential. At the end of 2007, KIM had interests in 1,973 properties, totaling approximately 183 million square feet of gross leasable area ("GLA") located in 45 states, Canada, Mexico, Puerto Rico and Chile. The trust's ownership interests in real estate consist of its consolidated portfolio and in portfolios where it owns an economic interest, such as properties in its investment management programs, where it partners with institutional investors and also retains management.

The trust's investment objective has been to increase cash flow, current income, and, consequently, the value of its existing portfolio of properties, and to seek continued growth through the strategic re-tenanting, renovation and expansion of its existing centers, and through the selective acquisition of established income-producing real estate properties and properties requiring significant re-tenanting and redevelopment. These properties are mainly located in neighborhood and community shopping centers in geographic regions in which KIM presently operates.

For KIM as well as other retail-oriented REITs, we believe that location and the financial health and growth of its retail tenants are among the most important factors affecting the success of its portfolio. KIM's neighborhood and community shopping center properties are designed to attract local area customers and typically are anchored by a discount department store, a supermarket or a drugstore tenant offering day-to-day necessities rather than high-priced luxury items. The trust seeks to reduce operating and leasing risks through diversification achieved by the geographic distribution of its properties and a large tenant base. At December 31, 2007, the single largest neighborhood and community shopping center accounted for 1.7% of annualized base rental revenues and 0.8% of total shopping center GLA. At December 31, 2007, the five largest tenants were The Home Depot, TJX Companies, Sears Holdings, Kohl's, and Wal-Mart.

## Company Financials Fiscal Year Ended Dec. 31

| Per Share Data ($) | 2007 | 2006 | 2005 | 2004 | 2003 | 2002 | 2001 | 2000 | 1999 | 1998 |
|---|---|---|---|---|---|---|---|---|---|---|
| Tangible Book Value | 12.88 | 13.24 | 9.70 | 9.17 | 8.87 | 8.04 | 7.95 | 7.26 | 6.98 | 6.94 |
| Earnings | 1.33 | 1.36 | 1.40 | 1.19 | 1.04 | 1.10 | 1.08 | 0.96 | 0.82 | 0.67 |
| S&P Core Earnings | 1.33 | 1.36 | 1.40 | 1.18 | 1.03 | 1.08 | 1.07 | NA | NA | NA |
| Dividends | 1.52 | 1.38 | 1.27 | 1.16 | 1.10 | 1.05 | 0.98 | 0.91 | 0.79 | 0.66 |
| Payout Ratio | 114% | 101% | 91% | 97% | 105% | 96% | 91% | 95% | 96% | 98% |
| Prices:High | 53.60 | 47.13 | 33.35 | 29.64 | 22.93 | 16.94 | 17.03 | 14.92 | 13.58 | 13.88 |
| Prices:Low | 33.74 | 32.02 | 25.90 | 19.77 | 15.13 | 12.98 | 13.58 | 10.92 | 10.29 | 11.15 |
| P/E Ratio:High | 40 | 35 | 24 | 25 | 22 | 15 | 16 | 16 | 17 | 21 |
| P/E Ratio:Low | 25 | 24 | 18 | 17 | 14 | 12 | 13 | 11 | 13 | 17 |

| Income Statement Analysis (Million $) | | | | | | | | | | |
|---|---|---|---|---|---|---|---|---|---|---|
| Rental Income | 682 | 594 | 523 | 517 | 480 | 451 | 469 | 459 | 434 | 339 |
| Mortgage Income | 14.2 | 18.8 | NA | NA | NA | NA | NA | NA | NA | NA |
| Total Income | 751 | 653 | 581 | 517 | 480 | 451 | 469 | 466 | 434 | 339 |
| General Expenses | 104 | 164 | 128 | 111 | 104 | 9.15 | 89.7 | 138 | 136 | 110 |
| Interest Expense | 214 | 173 | 128 | 108 | 103 | 86.9 | 89.4 | 92.1 | 83.6 | 64.9 |
| Provision for Losses | Nil | Nil | Nil | Nil | Nil | Nil | Nil | Nil | Nil | Nil |
| Depreciation | 190 | 141 | 106 | 102 | 86.2 | 76.7 | 74.2 | 71.1 | 67.4 | 51.3 |
| Net Income | 362 | 343 | 334 | 282 | 247 | 249 | 237 | 205 | 177 | 127 |
| S&P Core Earnings | 342 | 333 | 322 | 268 | 222 | 227 | 209 | NA | NA | NA |

| Balance Sheet & Other Financial Data (Million $) | | | | | | | | | | |
|---|---|---|---|---|---|---|---|---|---|---|
| Cash | 87.5 | 1,616 | 1,018 | 757 | 581 | 36.0 | 93.8 | 19.1 | 28.1 | 43.9 |
| Total Assets | 9,098 | 7,869 | 5,535 | 4,747 | 4,604 | 3,757 | 3,385 | 3,171 | 3,007 | 3,051 |
| Real Estate Investment | 6,181 | 6,002 | 4,560 | 4,877 | 4,137 | 3,399 | 3,201 | 3,112 | 2,951 | 3,024 |
| Loss Reserve | Nil | Nil | Nil | Nil | Nil | Nil | Nil | Nil | Nil | Nil |
| Net Investment | 6,348 | 5,195 | 3,820 | 4,242 | 3,569 | 2,882 | 2,748 | 2,720 | 2,627 | 2,768 |
| Short Term Debt | 281 | 209 | NA | NA | 570 | 147 | 123 | 4.60 | 229 | 129 |
| Capitalization:Debt | 3,936 | 3,378 | 2,397 | 1,860 | 1,585 | 1,430 | 1,205 | 1,321 | 1,021 | 1,169 |
| Capitalization:Equity | 3,894 | 3,366 | 2,387 | 2,236 | 2,135 | 1,906 | 1,889 | 1,703 | 1,604 | 1,584 |
| Capitalization:Total | 8,279 | 7,170 | 4,907 | 4,203 | 3,820 | 3,431 | 3,103 | 3,039 | 2,640 | 2,759 |
| % Earnings & Depreciation/Assets | 6.5 | 7.2 | 8.5 | 8.2 | 8.0 | 9.1 | 9.5 | 8.9 | 8.1 | 8.1 |
| Price Times Book Value:High | 4.2 | 3.6 | 3.4 | 3.2 | 2.6 | 2.1 | 2.1 | 2.1 | 2.0 | 2.0 |
| Price Times Book Value:Low | 2.6 | 2.4 | 2.7 | 2.2 | 1.7 | 1.6 | 1.7 | 1.5 | 1.5 | 1.6 |

Data as orig reptd.; bef. results of disc opers/spec. items. Per share data adj. for stk. divs.; EPS diluted. E-Estimated. NA-Not Available. NM-Not Meaningful. NR-Not Ranked. UR-Under Review.

**Office:** 3333 New Hyde Park Road, New Hyde Park, NY 11042-0020.
**Telephone:** 800-285-4626.
**Email:** ir@kimcorealty.com
**Website:** http://www.kimcorealty.com

**Chrmn & CEO:** M.E. Cooper
**Pres & Vice Chrmn:** D.B. Henry
**Vice Chrmn:** M.J. Flynn
**COO & EVP:** D.R. Lukes

**EVP, CFO & Chief Admin Officer:** M.V. Pappagallo
**Investor Contact:** B. Pooley (516-869-2530)
**Board Members:** M. E. Cooper, P. E. Coviello, R. G. Dooley, M. J. Flynn, J. Grills, D. B. Henry, F. P. Hughes, F. Lourenso, R. B. Saltzman

**Founded:** 1966
**Domicile:** Maryland
**Employees:** 682

**The McGraw·Hill Companies**

# King Pharmaceuticals Inc.

STANDARD
&POOR'S

| S&P Recommendation | HOLD ★★★☆☆ | Price $9.64 (as of Nov 14, 2008) | 12-Mo. Target Price $13.00 | Investment Style Large-Cap Blend |
|---|---|---|---|---|

**GICS Sector** Health Care
**Sub-Industry** Pharmaceuticals

**Summary** This company makes and markets a line of prescription pharmaceuticals. Altace, a treatment for hypertension and congestive heart failure, is its most important product.

## Key Stock Statistics (Source S&P, Vickers, company reports)

| | | | | | | | |
|---|---|---|---|---|---|---|---|
| 52-Wk Range | $12.60–6.98 | S&P Oper. EPS 2008E | 1.20 | Market Capitalization(B) | $2.376 | Beta | 0.67 |
| Trailing 12-Month EPS | $1.05 | S&P Oper. EPS 2009E | 0.90 | Yield (%) | Nil | S&P 3-Yr. Proj. EPS CAGR(%) | -20 |
| Trailing 12-Month P/E | 9.2 | P/E on S&P Oper. EPS 2008E | 8.0 | Dividend Rate/Share | Nil | S&P Credit Rating | BB |
| $10K Invested 5 Yrs Ago | $7,265 | Common Shares Outstg. (M) | 246.5 | Institutional Ownership (%) | 99 | | |

## Price Performance

30-Week Mov. Avg. · · · ·   10-Week Mov. Avg. - -   GAAP Earnings vs. Previous Year   Volume Above Avg. STARS
12-Mo. Target Price —   Relative Strength —   ▲ Up   ▼ Down   ▶ No Change   Below Avg.

Options: ASE, CBOE, P, Ph

Analysis prepared by **Herman B. Saftlas** on September 15, 2008, when the stock traded at **$ 10.74**.

## Qualitative Risk Assessment

| LOW | MEDIUM | HIGH |
|---|---|---|

Our risk assessment reflects King Pharmaceuticals' reliance on in-licensing drugs from other companies and on aggressive marketing for its sales growth. KG recently lost patent protection on its principal Altace heart drug. While we believe generic threats to Skelaxin, KG's second most important drug, have diminished with a recent patent settlement, we still think King's prospects are heavily dependent on the success of its R&D program and future in-licensing opportunities.

## Quantitative Evaluations

**S&P Quality Ranking**     B-

| D | C | B- | B | B+ | A- | A | A+ |
|---|---|---|---|---|---|---|---|

**Relative Strength Rank**     STRONG

94

LOWEST = 1         HIGHEST = 99

## Highlights

➤ Based on King's present operations, we expect 2008 revenues to decline about 30%, largely reflecting generic erosion in the Altace line. However, we think King has a good chance of blocking near-term generic competition to its important Skelaxin muscle relaxant line, partly due to a recent patent settlement with CorePharma LLC that delays generics from that firm until 2012. We see higher sales from Avinza pain treatment, as well as from Meridian injection devices. However, sales in the Thrombin-JMI and Levoxyl lines are likely to decline under increased competitive pressures.

➤ We expect 2008 gross margins to contract to about 75%, from 2007's 78.6%, on reduced volume and a less profitable sales mix. Although R&D expenses will likely increase on stepped-up spending on new products, we see sharp reductions in SG&A costs, Altace co-promotion fees (payable to Wyeth), and other operating expenses.

➤ We project operating EPS of $1.15 for 2008, down from 2007's $1.95. Reflecting the effects of projected worsening generic erosion, we see EPS slipping to $0.95 in 2009.

## Investment Rationale/Risk

➤ In mid-September 2008, King commenced a hostile tender offer to purchase all the outstanding common shares of specialty drugmaker Alpharma (ALO: hold, $37), at $37 a share in cash, raised from a prior bid of $33, representing a total value of $1.6 billion. We view this as a strategically compelling deal for KG, whose existing drugs face significant generic erosion. Key positives we see include strong cash flow from ALO's animal health division, and operating synergies from the combination of both firms' growing pain treatment franchises. KG expects a potential deal to deliver synergies of between $50 million and $70 million.

➤ Risks to our recommendation and target price include failure to complete the takeover of ALO, competitive pressures in key lines, and pipeline uncertainties.

➤ Our 12-month target price of $13 applies a discount-to-peers P/E of about 11.3X to our 2008 EPS estimate. Our DCF model, which assumes decelerating cash flow growth over the next 10 years, a WACC of 8.5%, and terminal growth of 1%, also indicates intrinsic value of about $13.

## Revenue/Earnings Data

### Revenue (Million $)

| | 1Q | 2Q | 3Q | 4Q | Year |
|---|---|---|---|---|---|
| 2008 | 432.0 | 396.9 | 388.5 | -- | -- |
| 2007 | 516.0 | 542.7 | 544.9 | 533.3 | 2,137 |
| 2006 | 484.2 | 499.7 | 491.7 | 512.9 | 1,989 |
| 2005 | 368.6 | 462.9 | 518.0 | 423.3 | 1,773 |
| 2004 | 291.5 | 275.1 | 394.7 | 342.6 | 1,304 |
| 2003 | 343.8 | 370.7 | 424.2 | 382.6 | 1,521 |

### Earnings Per Share ($)

| | 1Q | 2Q | 3Q | 4Q | Year |
|---|---|---|---|---|---|
| 2008 | 0.36 | 0.18 | 0.35 | E0.23 | E1.20 |
| 2007 | 0.48 | 0.26 | -0.17 | 0.18 | 0.75 |
| 2006 | 0.21 | 0.46 | 0.37 | 0.15 | 1.19 |
| 2005 | 0.28 | 0.08 | 0.50 | -0.39 | 0.48 |
| 2004 | -0.01 | -0.27 | -0.01 | 0.06 | -0.21 |
| 2003 | -0.03 | -0.15 | 0.44 | 0.17 | 0.44 |

Fiscal year ended Dec. 31. Next earnings report expected: Late February. EPS Estimates based on S&P Operating Earnings; historical GAAP earnings are as reported.

## Dividend Data

No cash dividends have been paid.

---

# King Pharmaceuticals Inc.

STANDARD &POOR'S

## Business Summary September 15, 2008

CORPORATE OVERVIEW. King Pharmaceuticals is a vertically integrated branded pharmaceutical company. A key part of its business strategy consists of the acquisition of branded prescription drugs being divested by large global pharmaceutical companies. To date, King has successfully acquired and commercialized more than 35 branded products, and has introduced several product line extensions.

Sales of branded pharmaceuticals accounted for 87% of total net revenues in 2007, Meridian Medical Technologies (a maker of auto-injectors acquired in January 2003) 7%, royalties from licensed drugs 4%, and contract manufacturing and other 2%.

The company's most important drug in 2007 was Altace, a heart drug whose sales totaled $646 million, down from $653 million in 2006. Altace is an angiotensin converting enzyme (ACE) inhibitor indicated for the treatment of hypertension and congestive heart failure. However, generics entered the Altace market in late 2007, and we expect Altace sales to drop precipitously in 2008. Other cardiovascular drugs include Corzide and Corgard beta blocker treatments for high blood pressure.

King's key neuroscience product is Skelaxin (sales of $440 million in 2007), a muscle relaxant indicated for the relief of discomforts associated with acute, painful musculoskeletal conditions. Other neuroscience drugs include Avinza ($109 million), a once-daily, extended-release formulation of morphine sulfate for severe pain; and Sonata ($79 million), a nonbenzodiazepine treatment for insomnia. Levoxyl ($100 million) and Cytomel ($48 million) are treatments of thyroid disorders.

King's primary hospital/acute care product is Thrombin-JMI ($267 million), a drug used to control minor bleeding during surgery. Other products include Bicillin ($59 million), an anti-infective; Synercid, an injectable antibiotic; and Intal, an oral multi-dose inhaler of a non-steroidal anti-inflammatory agent to treat asthma. The Meridian Medical Technologies division markets auto-injectors, which are pre-filled, pen-like devices that allow patients or care-givers to automatically inject precise drug dosages.

## Company Financials Fiscal Year Ended Dec. 31

| Per Share Data ($) | 2007 | 2006 | 2005 | 2004 | 2003 | 2002 | 2001 | 2000 | 1999 | 1998 |
|---|---|---|---|---|---|---|---|---|---|---|
| Tangible Book Value | 6.51 | 5.41 | 3.66 | 7.67 | 0.68 | 2.90 | 3.47 | 0.85 | NM | NM |
| Cash Flow | 1.43 | 1.79 | 1.09 | 0.46 | 0.95 | 0.98 | 1.20 | 0.66 | 1.12 | 0.86 |
| Earnings | 0.75 | 1.19 | 0.48 | -0.21 | 0.44 | 0.74 | 0.99 | 0.47 | 0.47 | 0.28 |
| S&P Core Earnings | 0.78 | 1.31 | 0.47 | -0.06 | 0.41 | 0.71 | 0.94 | NA | NA | NA |
| Dividends | Nil | Nil | Nil | Nil | Nil | Nil | Nil | Nil | Nil | Nil |
| Payout Ratio | Nil | Nil | Nil | Nil | Nil | Nil | Nil | Nil | Nil | Nil |
| Prices:High | 22.25 | 20.00 | 17.99 | 20.62 | 18.13 | 42.13 | 46.05 | 41.63 | 34.00 | 9.58 |
| Prices:Low | 9.75 | 15.15 | 7.50 | 10.01 | 9.46 | 15.00 | 24.79 | 14.81 | 6.46 | 3.54 |
| P/E Ratio:High | 30 | 17 | 37 | NM | 41 | 57 | 47 | 88 | 72 | 34 |
| P/E Ratio:Low | 13 | 13 | 16 | NM | 22 | 20 | 25 | 31 | 14 | 13 |

| Income Statement Analysis (Million $) | | | | | | | | | | |
|---|---|---|---|---|---|---|---|---|---|---|
| Revenue | 2,137 | 1,989 | 1,773 | 1,304 | 1,521 | 1,128 | 872 | 620 | 348 | 163 |
| Operating Income | 834 | 700 | 551 | 272 | 403 | 426 | 429 | 326 | 155 | 64.7 |
| Depreciation | 167 | 148 | 147 | 162 | 125 | 59.3 | 48.0 | 41.9 | 26.9 | 9.30 |
| Interest Expense | 8.10 | 9.86 | 11.9 | 12.6 | 13.4 | 12.4 | 12.7 | 37.0 | 55.4 | 14.9 |
| Pretax Income | 251 | 424 | 178 | -58.0 | 177 | 268 | 371 | 192 | 73.0 | 40.7 |
| Effective Tax Rate | 27.0% | 32.0% | 34.5% | NM | 40.2% | 31.8% | 37.2% | 45.4% | 37.5% | 37.8% |
| Net Income | 183 | 289 | 117 | -50.6 | 106 | 183 | 233 | 105 | 45.7 | 25.3 |
| S&P Core Earnings | 191 | 318 | 115 | -13.1 | 98.4 | 175 | 222 | NA | NA | NA |

| Balance Sheet & Other Financial Data (Million $) | | | | | | | | | | |
|---|---|---|---|---|---|---|---|---|---|---|
| Cash | 1,366 | 114 | 48.5 | 359 | 146 | 815 | 924 | 76.4 | 8.50 | 1.16 |
| Current Assets | 1,820 | 1,673 | 1,248 | 1,127 | 946 | 1,262 | 1,238 | 317 | 131 | 75.6 |
| Total Assets | 3,427 | 3,330 | 2,965 | 2,924 | 3,178 | 2,751 | 2,507 | 1,282 | 806 | 668 |
| Current Liabilities | 453 | 618 | 971 | 689 | 669 | 370 | 151 | 105 | 89.8 | 44.5 |
| Long Term Debt | 400 | 400 | Nil | 345 | 345 | 345 | 346 | 99.0 | 553 | 514 |
| Common Equity | 2,511 | 2,289 | 1,973 | 1,849 | 2,042 | 1,931 | 1,908 | 988 | 148 | 101 |
| Total Capital | 2,911 | 2,689 | 1,973 | 2,194 | 2,387 | 2,310 | 2,292 | 1,104 | 716 | 623 |
| Capital Expenditures | 49.6 | 45.8 | 53.3 | 55.1 | 51.2 | 73.6 | 40.2 | 25.1 | 8.80 | 81.1 |
| Cash Flow | 350 | 436 | 264 | 111 | 230 | 242 | 281 | 147 | 22.6 | 34.6 |
| Current Ratio | 4.0 | 2.7 | 1.3 | 1.6 | 1.4 | 3.4 | 8.2 | 3.0 | 1.5 | 1.7 |
| % Long Term Debt of Capitalization | 13.7 | 14.9 | Nil | 15.7 | 14.5 | 14.9 | 15.1 | 9.0 | 77.2 | 82.5 |
| % Net Income of Revenue | 8.6 | 14.5 | 6.6 | NM | 7.0 | 16.2 | 26.7 | 16.9 | 13.1 | 15.5 |
| % Return on Assets | 5.4 | 9.2 | 4.0 | NM | 3.6 | 6.9 | 12.3 | 8.5 | 6.2 | 6.5 |
| % Return on Equity | 7.6 | 13.5 | 6.1 | NM | 5.3 | 9.5 | 16.1 | 14.1 | 36.7 | 38.9 |

Data as orig reptd.; bef. results of disc opers/spec. items. Per share data adj. for stk. divs.; EPS diluted. E-Estimated. NA-Not Available. NM-Not Meaningful. NR-Not Ranked. UR-Under Review.

**Office:** 501 Fifth Street, Bristol, TN 37620-2304.
**Telephone:** 423-989-8000.
**Email:** investorrelations@kingpharm.com
**Website:** http://www.kingpharm.com

**Chrmn, Pres & CEO:** B.A. Markison
**Investor Contact:** J.E. Green (423-989-8125)
**CFO & Chief Acctg Officer:** J. Squicciarino
**CSO:** E.G. Carter

**CTO:** E.J. Bruce
**Board Members:** E. W. Deavenport, Jr., E. M. Greetham, P. A. Incarnati, G. D. Jordan, B. A. Markison, R. Moyer, D. G. Rooker, T. G. Wood

**Founded:** 1993
**Domicile:** Tennessee
**Employees:** 2,052

# KLA Tencor Corp

**STANDARD &POOR'S**

| **S&P Recommendation** | BUY ★★★★☆ | **Price** $18.16 (as of Nov 14, 2008) | **12-Mo. Target Price** $25.00 | **Investment Style** Large-Cap Growth |

**GICS Sector** Information Technology
**Sub-Industry** Semiconductor Equipment

**Summary** This company is the world's leading manufacturer of yield monitoring and process control systems for the semiconductor industry.

## Key Stock Statistics (Source S&P, Vickers, company reports)

| | | | | | | | |
|---|---|---|---|---|---|---|---|
| 52-Wk Range | $51.85– 16.67 | S&P Oper. EPS 2009**E** | 0.49 | Market Capitalization(B) | $3.066 | Beta | 1.81 |
| Trailing 12-Month EPS | $1.62 | S&P Oper. EPS 2010**E** | NA | Yield (%) | 3.30 | S&P 3-Yr. Proj. EPS CAGR(%) | -15 |
| Trailing 12-Month P/E | 11.2 | P/E on S&P Oper. EPS 2009**E** | 37.1 | Dividend Rate/Share | $0.60 | S&P Credit Rating | NA |
| $10K Invested 5 Yrs Ago | $3,308 | Common Shares Outstg. (M) | 168.9 | Institutional Ownership (%) | 94 | | |

## Price Performance

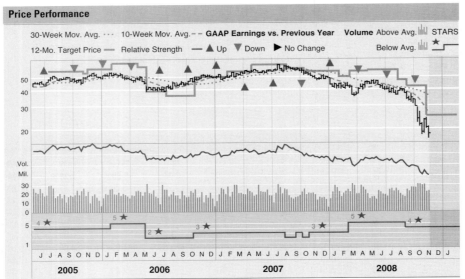

30-Week Mov. Avg. ···· 10-Week Mov. Avg. ─ ─ GAAP Earnings vs. Previous Year  Volume Above Avg. ⅢⅢ STARS
12-Mo. Target Price ── Relative Strength ▲ Up ▼ Down ► No Change  Below Avg. ⅢⅢ

Options: ASE, CBOE, P, Ph

Analysis prepared by **Angelo Zino** on November 03, 2008, when the stock traded at **$ 22.59**.

## Highlights

➤ Following a decline of 8% in FY 08 (Jun.), we see revenues falling 31% in FY 09. We anticipate muted demand for memory and foundry related equipment but expect logic orders to remain strong. Logic represented 77% of total orders during the September quarter. We believe the transition to 32- and 45-nanometer nodes will cause yield and defectivity challenges, which we believe will stimulate KLA-Tencor's customers to increase spending. We think this transition will increase KLAC's total available market by about 30%.

➤ We project an annual gross margin of 50% for FY 09, below the 55% margin posted in FY 08, reflecting lower volume. We view KLAC's yield management and process control systems only moderately susceptible to pricing pressure due to the critical value they add to semiconductor customers. We expect KLAC to reduce operating expenses to about $170 million by the middle of calendar year 2009, which would lower its quarterly breakeven revenue level to $350 million to $400 million.

➤ We think the ICOS acquisition expands KLAC into high-growth adjacent markets including back-end inspection and LED products.

## Investment Rationale/Risk

➤ We view KLAC's competitive position in both inspection and metrology as strong, and see long-term growth in yield management and process control. While we expect KLAC to benefit from challenges relating to new materials being used in the chip manufacturing process, we are concerned about near-term equipment spending. We view positively KLAC's leading market share position in its respective markets, healthy backlog and solid business model. In our opinion, the company is well-positioned to manage current industry conditions and benefit from the next cyclical upturn. We expect the yield monitoring and process control systems products to do better than other types of front-end semiconductor equipment.

➤ Risks to our recommendation and target price include an industry downturn, competition pressuring KLAC's market share position, and a weakening of the global economy.

➤ Our 12-month target price of $25 is based on a peer-premium price-to-sale (P/S) multiple of 2.5X our FY 09 sales per share estimate of $9.96, warranted, in our view, given its leading market position. This is below the company's three- and five-year historical averages.

## Qualitative Risk Assessment

| LOW | MEDIUM | HIGH |

Our risk assessment reflects the company's exposure to the cyclicality of the semiconductor equipment industry and the amount of change in relevant technologies, only partially offset by limited pricing pressure and our view of KLAC's strong market position, size and financial condition.

## Quantitative Evaluations

**S&P Quality Ranking**  B

| D | C | B- | B | B+ | A- | A | A+ |

**Relative Strength Rank**  MODERATE

31

LOWEST = 1                    HIGHEST = 99

## Revenue/Earnings Data

**Revenue (Million $)**

| | 1Q | 2Q | 3Q | 4Q | Year |
|---|---|---|---|---|---|
| 2009 | 532.5 | -- | -- | -- | -- |
| 2008 | 693.0 | 635.8 | 602.2 | 590.7 | 2,522 |
| 2007 | 629.4 | 649.3 | 716.2 | 736.4 | 2,731 |
| 2006 | 484.3 | 487.7 | 519.7 | 579.0 | 2,071 |
| 2005 | 518.8 | 532.9 | 541.6 | 491.9 | 2,085 |
| 2004 | 318.0 | 338.5 | 389.8 | 450.4 | 1,497 |

**Earnings Per Share ($)**

| | | | | | |
|---|---|---|---|---|---|
| 2009 | 0.11 | E0.01 | E0.06 | E0.10 | E0.49 |
| 2008 | 0.46 | 0.45 | 0.61 | 0.43 | 1.95 |
| 2007 | 0.67 | 0.44 | 0.76 | 0.75 | 2.61 |
| 2006 | 0.37 | 0.38 | 0.47 | 0.65 | 1.86 |
| 2005 | 0.58 | 0.61 | 0.61 | 0.52 | 2.32 |
| 2004 | 0.18 | 0.22 | 0.33 | 0.48 | 1.21 |

Fiscal year ended Jun. 30. Next earnings report expected: Late January. EPS Estimates based on S&P Operating Earnings; historical GAAP earnings are as reported.

## Dividend Data (Dates: mm/dd Payment Date: mm/dd/yy)

| Amount ($) | Date Decl. | Ex-Div. Date | Stk. of Record | Payment Date |
|---|---|---|---|---|
| 0.150 | 02/13 | 02/21 | 02/25 | 03/03/08 |
| 0.150 | 05/07 | 05/15 | 05/19 | 06/02/08 |
| 0.150 | 08/06 | 08/14 | 08/18 | 09/02/08 |
| 0.150 | 11/13 | 11/20 | 11/24 | 12/01/08 |

Dividends have been paid since 2005. Source: Company reports.

# KLA Tencor Corp

**STANDARD &POOR'S**

## Business Summary November 03, 2008

CORPORATE OVERVIEW. KLAC is the world's leading manufacturer of yield management and process monitoring systems for the semiconductor industry.

Maximizing yields, or the number of good die (chips) per wafer, is a key goal in manufacturing integrated circuits (ICs). Higher yields increase revenues obtained for each semiconductor wafer processed. As IC line widths decrease, yields become more sensitive to microscopic-sized defects. KLAC's systems are used to improve yields by identifying defects, analyzing them to determine process problems and patterns, and facilitate corrective actions. These systems monitor subsequent results to ensure that problems have been contained. With in-line systems, corrections can be made while the wafer is still in the production line, rather than waiting for end-of-process testing and feedback.

KLAC offers a broad range of inspection and yield management. The company's wafer inspection systems include unpatterned and patterned wafer inspection tools used to find, count and characterize particles and pattern defects on wafers both in engineering applications and in-line at various stages during the semiconductor manufacturing process. KLAC's brightfiled inspection systems are extremely sensitive to small defects and capture a large range of defect types, which is critical as customers move to 45nm and small-er production.

Reticle inspection systems look for defects on the quartz plates used in copying circuit designs onto an IC during the photolithography process. Film measurement products measure a variety of optical and electrical properties of thin films. Scanning electron beam microscopes (SEMs) can measure the critical dimensions (CDs) of tiny semiconductor features. For chip manufacturing below 90nm, e-beam inspection is becoming increasingly important, not only during the research and development phase, where the highest levels of sensitivity are needed to highlight and eradicate potential design problems, but also in production, where dedicated high-speed e-beam inspection systems.

At the end of FY 08 (Jun.), KLAC's revenues by geographic region were divided as follows: United States 21% (24% in FY 07), Europe & Israel 12% (10%), Japan 24% (22%), Taiwan 23% (20%), Korea 9% (11%), and Asia Pacific 11% (13%). No customer accounted for greater than 10% of revenues during FY 08 or FY 07.

## Company Financials Fiscal Year Ended Jun. 30

### Per Share Data ($)

| | 2008 | 2007 | 2006 | 2005 | 2004 | 2003 | 2002 | 2001 | 2000 | 1999 |
|---|---|---|---|---|---|---|---|---|---|---|
| Tangible Book Value | 11.96 | 16.00 | 17.56 | 15.49 | 13.34 | 11.56 | 10.70 | 9.38 | 9.11 | 6.95 |
| Cash Flow | NA | 3.15 | 2.20 | 2.67 | 1.62 | 1.07 | 1.45 | 2.22 | 1.65 | 0.48 |
| Earnings | 1.95 | 2.61 | 1.86 | 2.32 | 1.21 | 0.70 | 1.10 | 1.93 | 1.32 | 0.22 |
| S&P Core Earnings | 2.05 | 2.64 | 1.89 | 1.88 | 0.77 | 0.12 | 0.49 | 1.45 | NA | NA |
| Dividends | NA | 0.48 | 0.48 | 0.12 | Nil | Nil | Nil | 1.45 | NA | NA |
| Payout Ratio | NA | 18% | 26% | 5% | Nil | Nil | Nil | Nil | Nil | Nil |
| Prices:High | NA | 62.67 | 55.03 | 55.00 | 62.82 | 61.25 | 70.58 | 61.00 | 97.75 | 56.56 |
| Prices:Low | NA | 46.59 | 38.38 | 37.39 | 35.02 | 31.20 | 25.16 | 28.61 | 25.50 | 21.19 |
| P/E Ratio:High | NA | 24 | 30 | 24 | 52 | 88 | 64 | 32 | 74 | NM |
| P/E Ratio:Low | NA | 18 | 21 | 16 | 29 | 45 | 23 | 15 | 19 | 99 |

### Income Statement Analysis (Million $)

| | 2008 | 2007 | 2006 | 2005 | 2004 | 2003 | 2002 | 2001 | 2000 | 1999 |
|---|---|---|---|---|---|---|---|---|---|---|
| Revenue | 2,522 | 2,731 | 2,071 | 2,085 | 1,497 | 1,323 | 1,637 | 2,104 | 1,499 | 843 |
| Operating Income | NA | 699 | 379 | 653 | 380 | 201 | 314 | 512 | 370 | 80.6 |
| Depreciation | 126 | 109 | 69.4 | 70.9 | 82.9 | 71.4 | 69.6 | 55.6 | 63.3 | 48.2 |
| Interest Expense | NA | Nil | Nil | Nil | Nil | 0.39 | Nil | Nil | Nil | Nil |
| Pretax Income | 560 | 680 | 378 | 627 | 325 | 181 | 287 | 513 | 353 | 50.3 |
| Effective Tax Rate | 35.9% | 22.1% | NM | 25.0% | 24.9% | 24.0% | 24.8% | 27.2% | 28.1% | 22.1% |
| Net Income | 359 | 528 | 380 | 467 | 244 | 137 | 216 | 373 | 254 | 39.2 |
| S&P Core Earnings | 379 | 535 | 386 | 377 | 156 | 22.4 | 96.5 | 281 | NA | NA |

### Balance Sheet & Other Financial Data (Million $)

| | 2008 | 2007 | 2006 | 2005 | 2004 | 2003 | 2002 | 2001 | 2000 | 1999 |
|---|---|---|---|---|---|---|---|---|---|---|
| Cash | 1,579 | 1,711 | 2,326 | 2,195 | 1,876 | 1,488 | 1,334 | 697 | 844 | 696 |
| Current Assets | NA | 3,253 | 3,543 | 3,203 | 2,192 | 1,806 | 1,619 | 1,897 | 1,552 | 942 |
| Total Assets | 4,848 | 4,623 | 4,576 | 3,986 | 3,539 | 2,867 | 2,718 | 2,745 | 2,204 | 1,585 |
| Current Liabilities | NA | 1,073 | 1,002 | 932 | 912 | 651 | 687 | 984 | 495 | 352 |
| Long Term Debt | NA | Nil | Nil | Nil | Nil | Nil | Nil | Nil | Nil | Nil |
| Common Equity | 2,982 | 3,550 | 3,568 | 3,045 | 2,628 | 2,216 | 2,030 | 1,760 | 1,709 | 1,233 |
| Total Capital | NA | 3,550 | 3,573 | 3,055 | 2,628 | 2,216 | 2,030 | 1,760 | 1,709 | 1,233 |
| Capital Expenditures | 57.3 | 83.8 | 73.8 | 59.7 | 55.5 | 134 | 68.7 | 162 | 78.7 | 56.8 |
| Cash Flow | NA | 637 | 450 | 538 | 327 | 209 | 286 | 429 | 317 | 87.4 |
| Current Ratio | 3.2 | 3.0 | 3.5 | 3.4 | 2.4 | 2.8 | 2.4 | 1.9 | 3.1 | 2.7 |
| % Long Term Debt of Capitalization | 20.0 | Nil | Nil | Nil | Nil | Nil | Nil | Nil | Nil | Nil |
| % Net Income of Revenue | 14.2 | 19.3 | 18.4 | 22.4 | 16.3 | 10.4 | 13.2 | 17.7 | 16.9 | 4.7 |
| % Return on Assets | 7.6 | 11.5 | 8.8 | 12.4 | 7.6 | 4.9 | 7.9 | 15.1 | 13.4 | 2.5 |
| % Return on Equity | 11.0 | 14.8 | 11.4 | 16.5 | 10.1 | 6.5 | 11.4 | 21.5 | 17.3 | 3.2 |

Data as orig reptd.; bef. results of disc opers/spec. items. Per share data adj. for stk. divs.; EPS diluted. E-Estimated. NA-Not Available. NM-Not Meaningful. NR-Not Ranked. UR-Under Review.

**Office:** One Technology Dr, Milpitas, CA 95035.
**Telephone:** 408-875-3000.
**Website:** http://www.tencor.com
**Chrmn:** E.W. Barnholt

**CEO:** R.P. Wallace
**EVP & CFO:** M.P. Dentinger
**EVP & CTO:** B.B. Tsai
**SVP & Chief Admin Officer:** J.L. Titinger

**Investor Contact:** W. Lin (408-875-3000)
**Board Members:** R. P. Akins, E. W. Barnholt, R. T. Bond, R. M. Calderoni, J. T. Dickson, S. Kaufman, K. J. Kennedy, K. M. Patel, R. P. Wallace, D. C. Wang

**Founded:** 1975
**Domicile:** Delaware
**Employees:** 6,000

# Kohl's Corp

## STANDARD &POOR'S

| S&P Recommendation | SELL ★ ★ ☆ ☆ ☆ | Price $29.09 (as of Nov 14, 2008) | 12-Mo. Target Price $26.00 | Investment Style Large-Cap Growth |
| --- | --- | --- | --- | --- |

**GICS Sector** Consumer Discretionary
**Sub-Industry** Department Stores

**Summary** This company operates over 950 specialty department stores in 47 states, featuring moderately priced apparel, shoes, accessories, and products for the home.

## Key Stock Statistics (Source S&P, Vickers, company reports)

| | | | | | | | | |
| --- | --- | --- | --- | --- | --- | --- | --- | --- |
| 52-Wk Range | $56.00– 25.18 | S&P Oper. EPS 2009E | 2.73 | Market Capitalization(B) | $8.860 | Beta | | 0.78 |
| Trailing 12-Month EPS | $3.19 | S&P Oper. EPS 2010E | 2.20 | Yield (%) | Nil | S&P 3-Yr. Proj. EPS CAGR(%) | | -6 |
| Trailing 12-Month P/E | 9.1 | P/E on S&P Oper. EPS 2009E | 10.7 | Dividend Rate/Share | Nil | S&P Credit Rating | | BBB+ |
| $10K Invested 5 Yrs Ago | $5,616 | Common Shares Outstg. (M) | 304.6 | Institutional Ownership (%) | 92 | | | |

## Price Performance

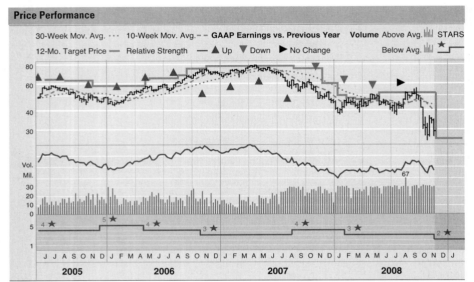

30-Week Mov. Avg. · · · · 10-Week Mov. Avg. – – GAAP Earnings vs. Previous Year Volume Above Avg. STARS
12-Mo. Target Price — Relative Strength — ▲ Up ▼ Down ▶ No Change Below Avg. ★

Options: ASE, CBOE, P, Ph

## Qualitative Risk Assessment

| LOW | MEDIUM | HIGH |
| --- | --- | --- |

Our risk assessment reflects our view of KSS's improving sales, increasing market share in the moderate department store sector, and healthy balance sheet and cash flow, offset by uncertainty over consumer discretionary spending in light of economic conditions and debt levels.

## Quantitative Evaluations

**S&P Quality Ranking**　　　　　　　　B+

| D | C | B- | B | B+ | A- | A | A+ |
| --- | --- | --- | --- | --- | --- | --- | --- |

**Relative Strength Rank**　　　　　　　MODERATE

46

LOWEST = 1　　　　　　　　　　　　　HIGHEST = 99

## Revenue/Earnings Data

**Revenue (Million $)**

| | 1Q | 2Q | 3Q | 4Q | Year |
| --- | --- | --- | --- | --- | --- |
| 2009 | 3,624 | 3,725 | -- | -- | -- |
| 2008 | 3,572 | 3,589 | 3,825 | 5,487 | 16,474 |
| 2007 | 3,185 | 3,291 | 3,637 | 5,431 | 15,544 |
| 2006 | 2,743 | 2,888 | 3,119 | 4,652 | 13,402 |
| 2005 | 2,380 | 2,498 | 2,744 | 4,079 | 11,701 |
| 2004 | 2,118 | 2,208 | 2,394 | 3,562 | 10,282 |

**Earnings Per Share ($)**

| | 1Q | 2Q | 3Q | 4Q | Year |
| --- | --- | --- | --- | --- | --- |
| 2009 | 0.49 | 0.77 | E0.55 | E0.95 | E2.73 |
| 2008 | 0.64 | 0.77 | 0.61 | 1.31 | 3.39 |
| 2007 | 0.48 | 0.69 | 0.68 | 1.48 | 3.31 |
| 2006 | 0.36 | 0.54 | 0.45 | 1.08 | 2.43 |
| 2005 | 0.32 | 0.45 | 0.41 | 0.94 | 2.12 |
| 2004 | 0.32 | 0.33 | 0.35 | 0.72 | 1.72 |

Fiscal year ended Jan. 31. Next earnings report expected: Mid November. EPS Estimates based on S&P Operating Earnings; historical GAAP earnings are as reported.

## Dividend Data

No cash dividends have been paid.

## Highlights

➤ The STARS recommendation for KSS has recently been changed to 2 (sell) from 3 (hold) and the 12-month target price has recently been changed to $26.00 from $52.00. The Highlights section of this Stock Report will be updated accordingly.

## Investment Rationale/Risk

➤ The Investment Rationale/Risk section of this Stock Report will be updated shortly. For the latest News story on KSS from MarketScope, see below.

➤ 11/14/08 12:14 pm ET ... S&P LOWERS OPINION ON SHARES OF KOHL'S CORP. TO SELL FROM HOLD, ON VALUATION (KSS 29.19**): Oct-Q EPS of $0.52 vs. $0.61 misses our $0.55 estimate on weak sales. We look for higher penetration of private and exclusive brands and effective inventory controls to support modest gross margin improvement in the Jan-Q and next year. But we do not expect KSS to be able to leverage expenses on same-store sales, given that we see declines of 7% in FY 09 (Jan.) and 6% in FY 10. As a result, we lower our FY 09 EPS estimate to $2.73 from $3.15, and FY 10's to $2.20 from $3.45. We also reduce our P/E-based 12-month target price to $26 from $52 on significantly lower peer multiples. /J.Asaeda

---

# Kohl's Corp

**STANDARD &POOR'S**

## Business Summary August 21, 2008

CORPORATE OVERVIEW. Kohl's (KSS), with its "Expect Great Things" line, has positioned itself as a preferred shopping destination for busy women. Its traditional customers are married women aged 25 to 54. The company's stores feature easy-to-shop layouts and emphasize moderately priced exclusive and national brand family apparel and shoes, accessories, cosmetics, home furnishings, and housewares. KSS uses a "nine-box grid" merchandising strategy. Product assortments fall into three categories, "good," "better," and "best," differentiated by price and quality, and also reflect three distinct customer styles: the "classic" customer who wants a coordinated look without bending the rules; the "updated" customer who likes classic styles with a twist; and the more fashion-forward "contemporary" customer.

PRIMARY BUSINESS DYNAMICS. KSS is one of the fastest-growing retail chains in the U.S. From FY 01 through FY 06, the company increased its selling square footage at a compound annual growth rate (CAGR) of 19% as it expanded its store count from 320 to 732. From FY 07 through FY 11, KSS expects to open about 500 new stores. Based on this aggressive five-year growth plan, the company's store count should top 1,200 by the end of FY 11. As we see this level of expansion unlikely to be matched by other department stores, we think KSS is in a position to potentially capture market share. The company opened 85 new stores in FY 07 and an additional 112 in FY 08, ending FY 08 with 929 stores.

From a merchandising standpoint, we believe KSS fell behind competitors such as J.C. Penney and Macy's in delivering newness and better quality merchandise sought by its customers in FY 04. Since then, however, we have seen the company prove itself capable of creating a more compelling sales mix by investing in new contemporary brands such as Candie's in juniors and young girls, and by entering the beauty business. KSS also responded successfully, in our view, to dress clothing trends in FY 06 with the launch of Chaps (by Ralph Lauren) in men's career casual sportswear.

In FY 07, the company filled out its contemporary apparel offerings, and expanded its most popular brands into additional product categories (e.g., Chaps into women's and boys), creating true lifestyle brands. We think these rollouts complemented KSS's ongoing efforts to capture more share of wallet among empty nesters aged 45 to 54 and single women aged 25 to 34.

## Company Financials Fiscal Year Ended Jan. 31

| Per Share Data ($) | 2008 | 2007 | 2006 | 2005 | 2004 | 2003 | 2002 | 2001 | 2000 | 1999 |
|---|---|---|---|---|---|---|---|---|---|---|
| Tangible Book Value | 21.77 | 18.32 | 16.62 | 13.78 | 11.60 | 9.85 | 7.78 | 6.21 | 4.70 | 3.55 |
| Cash Flow | 4.80 | 4.47 | 3.42 | 2.95 | 2.43 | 2.41 | 1.93 | 1.48 | 1.05 | 0.81 |
| Earnings | 3.39 | 3.31 | 2.43 | 2.12 | 1.72 | 1.87 | 1.35 | 1.10 | 0.78 | 0.59 |
| S&P Core Earnings | 3.39 | 3.31 | 2.43 | 2.04 | 1.62 | 1.78 | 1.38 | 1.04 | NA | NA |
| Dividends | Nil | Nil | Nil | Nil | Nil | Nil | Nil | Nil | Nil | Nil |
| Payout Ratio | Nil | Nil | Nil | Nil | Nil | Nil | Nil | Nil | Nil | Nil |
| Calendar Year | 2007 | 2006 | 2005 | 2004 | 2003 | 2002 | 2001 | 2000 | 1999 | 1998 |
| Prices:High | 79.55 | 75.54 | 58.90 | 54.10 | 65.44 | 78.83 | 72.24 | 66.50 | 40.63 | 30.75 |
| Prices:Low | 44.16 | 42.78 | 43.63 | 39.59 | 42.40 | 44.00 | 41.95 | 33.50 | 28.63 | 16.20 |
| P/E Ratio:High | 23 | 23 | 24 | 26 | 38 | 42 | 54 | 60 | 52 | 52 |
| P/E Ratio:Low | 13 | 13 | 18 | 19 | 25 | 24 | 31 | 30 | 37 | 27 |

### Income Statement Analysis (Million $)

| | 2008 | 2007 | 2006 | 2005 | 2004 | 2003 | 2002 | 2001 | 2000 | 1999 |
|---|---|---|---|---|---|---|---|---|---|---|
| Revenue | 16,474 | 15,544 | 13,402 | 11,701 | 10,282 | 9,120 | 7,489 | 6,152 | 4,557 | 3,682 |
| Operating Income | 2,257 | 2,202 | 1,755 | 1,525 | 1,260 | 1,282 | 1,002 | 779 | 537 | 408 |
| Depreciation | 452 | 388 | 339 | 288 | 237 | 191 | 152 | 128 | 83.3 | 70.0 |
| Interest Expense | 98.7 | 74.4 | 72.1 | 64.1 | 75.2 | 59.4 | 57.4 | Nil | 29.5 | 22.9 |
| Pretax Income | 1,742 | 1,774 | 1,346 | 1,174 | 950 | 1,034 | 800 | 605 | 421 | 317 |
| Effective Tax Rate | 37.8% | 37.5% | 37.4% | 37.8% | 37.8% | 37.8% | 38.0% | 38.5% | 38.7% | 39.3% |
| Net Income | 1,084 | 1,109 | 842 | 730 | 591 | 643 | 496 | 372 | 258 | 192 |
| S&P Core Earnings | 1,084 | 1,109 | 842 | 703 | 557 | 608 | 471 | 349 | NA | NA |

### Balance Sheet & Other Financial Data (Million $)

| | 2008 | 2007 | 2006 | 2005 | 2004 | 2003 | 2002 | 2001 | 2000 | 1999 |
|---|---|---|---|---|---|---|---|---|---|---|
| Cash | 664 | 620 | 127 | 117 | 113 | 90.1 | 107 | 124 | 12.6 | 29.6 |
| Current Assets | 3,724 | 3,401 | 4,266 | 3,643 | 3,025 | 3,284 | 2,464 | 1,922 | 1,367 | 939 |
| Total Assets | 10,560 | 9,041 | 9,153 | 7,979 | 6,698 | 6,316 | 4,930 | 3,855 | 2,915 | 1,936 |
| Current Liabilities | 1,771 | 1,919 | 1,746 | 1,456 | 1,122 | 1,508 | 880 | 723 | 634 | 380 |
| Long Term Debt | 2,052 | 1,040 | 1,046 | 1,103 | 1,076 | 1,059 | 1,095 | 803 | 495 | 311 |
| Common Equity | 6,102 | 5,603 | 5,957 | 4,967 | 4,191 | 3,512 | 2,791 | 2,203 | 1,686 | 1,163 |
| Total Capital | 8,416 | 6,887 | 7,221 | 6,367 | 5,504 | 4,743 | 4,001 | 3,090 | 2,247 | 1,527 |
| Capital Expenditures | 1,542 | 1,142 | 799 | 890 | 832 | 716 | 662 | 481 | 625 | 249 |
| Cash Flow | 1,536 | 1,496 | 1,181 | 1,019 | 828 | 835 | 648 | 500 | 341 | 262 |
| Current Ratio | 2.1 | 1.8 | 2.4 | 2.5 | 2.7 | 2.2 | 2.8 | 2.7 | 2.2 | 2.5 |
| % Long Term Debt of Capitalization | 24.4 | 15.7 | 14.5 | 17.3 | 19.5 | 22.3 | 27.4 | 26.0 | 22.0 | 20.4 |
| % Net Income of Revenue | 6.6 | 7.1 | 6.3 | 6.2 | 5.7 | 7.1 | 6.6 | 6.0 | 5.7 | 5.2 |
| % Return on Assets | 11.1 | 12.2 | 9.8 | 10.0 | 9.1 | 11.4 | 11.3 | 10.9 | 10.6 | 10.8 |
| % Return on Equity | 18.5 | 19.2 | 15.3 | 16.0 | 15.3 | 20.4 | 19.9 | 19.1 | 18.1 | 18.2 |

Data as orig reptd.; bef. results of disc opers/spec. items. Per share data adj. for stk. divs.; EPS diluted. E-Estimated. NA-Not Available. NM-Not Meaningful. NR-Not Ranked. UR-Under Review.

**Office:** N56W17000 Ridgewood Dr, Menomonee Falls, WI 53051-5660.
**Telephone:** 262-703-7000.
**Website:** http://www.kohls.com
**Chrmn:** L. Montgomery

**Pres & CEO:** K. Mansell
**Investor Contact:** W.S. McDonald (262-703-1893)
**EVP, CFO & Chief Acctg Officer:** W.S. McDonald
**EVP, Secy & General Counsel:** R.D. Schepp

**Board Members:** P. Boneparth, S. Burd, W. Embry, J. F. Herma, D. E. Jones, W. S. Kellogg, K. Mansell, L. Montgomery, F. V. Sica, P. M. Sommerhauser, S. A. Streeter, S. E. Watson

**Founded:** 1986
**Domicile:** Wisconsin
**Employees:** 125,000

*The McGraw-Hill Companies*

# Kraft Foods Inc.

**STANDARD &POOR'S**

| S&P Recommendation | STRONG BUY ★★★★★ | Price $27.44 (as of Nov 14, 2008) | 12-Mo. Target Price $37.00 | Investment Style Large-Cap Blend |
|---|---|---|---|---|

**GICS Sector** Consumer Staples
**Sub-Industry** Packaged Foods & Meats

**Summary** Kraft Foods is the largest U.S. branded food and beverage company, and the second largest in the world.

## Key Stock Statistics (Source S&P, Vickers, company reports)

| | | | | | | | |
|---|---|---|---|---|---|---|---|
| 52-Wk Range | $35.29– 25.56 | S&P Oper. EPS 2008**E** | 1.90 | Market Capitalization(B) | $40.313 | Beta | 0.52 |
| Trailing 12-Month EPS | $2.18 | S&P Oper. EPS 2009**E** | 2.03 | Yield (%) | 4.23 | S&P 3-Yr. Proj. EPS CAGR(%) | 7 |
| Trailing 12-Month P/E | 12.6 | P/E on S&P Oper. EPS 2008**E** | 14.4 | Dividend Rate/Share | $1.16 | S&P Credit Rating | A- |
| $10K Invested 5 Yrs Ago | $10,392 | Common Shares Outstg. (M) | 1,469.1 | Institutional Ownership (%) | 75 | | |

## Price Performance

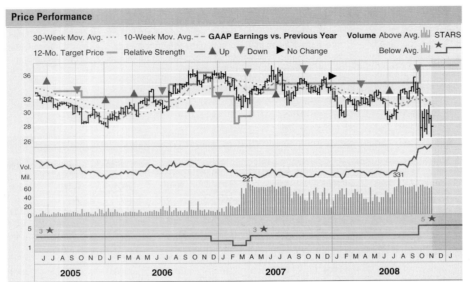

30-Week Mov. Avg. ···· 10-Week Mov. Avg. – – GAAP Earnings vs. Previous Year  Volume Above Avg. STARS
12-Mo. Target Price — Relative Strength ▲ Up ▼ Down ► No Change  Below Avg.

Options: ASE, CBOE, P, Ph

Analysis prepared by **Tom Graves, CFA** on October 07, 2008, when the stock traded at **$ 31.21**.

## Highlights

➤ KFT is in the midst of a multi-year restructuring program that we expect will better position the company for growth. Also, at least near-term, we look for KFT sales to be aided by consumers eating more at home. While a stronger U.S. dollar would likely hurt translation of overseas sales and profits, KFT could benefit from commodity price declines.

➤ In August 2008, KFT completed the divestiture of its Post cereal business. In connection with this transaction, KFT shareholders had an option to exchange KFT common shares for what would become common shares of Ralcorp (RAH: hold, $69), which acquired the Post business. KFT was able to accept a maximum of 46.1 million shares in the exchange offer, and we estimate that KFT shareholders will end up owning about 54% of the newly constituted Ralcorp.

➤ In 2008, we look for revenue growth from continuing operations of more than 10%, with much of this coming from the November 2007 acquisition of the Danone biscuit business. Excluding special items (e.g., restructuring costs), we estimate 2008 EPS from continuing operations of $1.91. In 2009, we look for an increase to $2.06.

## Investment Rationale/Risk

➤ We expect this stock to benefit from investors seeking defensive or lower-risk shares. Also, KFT shares have an above-average dividend yield, and we think the company has the potential for improved long-term EPS growth as it completes its restructuring plan. However, we have concerns about challenging competitive conditions we see in some product categories, plus possible margin pressure from commodity costs, along with the operational and execution risk associated with the company's strategic growth plan and restructuring.

➤ Risks to our recommendation and target price include higher than anticipated commodity costs, possible disappointing consumer acceptance of new product introductions, and the extent to which the company meets sales and earnings expectations.

➤ Our 12-month target price of $37 reflects our view that the stock should trade at about 19.4X our estimate of 2008 EPS, which is modestly above the average P/E that we expect from a group of food company stocks. KFT recently had an indicated dividend yield of 3.7%.

## Qualitative Risk Assessment

| LOW | MEDIUM | HIGH |
|---|---|---|

Our risk assessment reflects the execution risk that we see KFT facing from its internal restructuring, and other factors such as competitive conditions. This is offset by the relatively stable nature of the company's end markets, our view of its strong balance sheet and cash flow, and its leading global market share positions.

## Quantitative Evaluations

**S&P Quality Ranking**  NR

| D | C | B- | B | B+ | A- | A | A+ |
|---|---|---|---|---|---|---|---|

**Relative Strength Rank**  STRONG

76

LOWEST = 1    HIGHEST = 99

## Revenue/Earnings Data

**Revenue (Million $)**

| | 1Q | 2Q | 3Q | 4Q | Year |
|---|---|---|---|---|---|
| 2008 | 10,372 | 11,176 | 10,462 | -- | -- |
| 2007 | 8,586 | 9,205 | 9,054 | 10,396 | 37,241 |
| 2006 | 8,123 | 8,619 | 8,243 | 9,371 | 34,356 |
| 2005 | 8,059 | 8,334 | 8,057 | 9,663 | 34,113 |
| 2004 | 7,575 | 8,091 | 7,718 | 8,784 | 32,168 |
| 2003 | 7,359 | 7,841 | 7,480 | 8,330 | 31,010 |

**Earnings Per Share ($)**

| | 1Q | 2Q | 3Q | 4Q | Year |
|---|---|---|---|---|---|
| 2008 | 0.42 | 0.48 | 0.36 | E0.43 | E1.90 |
| 2007 | 0.43 | 0.44 | 0.38 | 0.38 | 1.63 |
| 2006 | 0.61 | 0.41 | 0.45 | 0.38 | 1.85 |
| 2005 | 0.41 | 0.45 | 0.40 | 0.46 | 1.72 |
| 2004 | 0.32 | 0.40 | 0.45 | 0.40 | 1.55 |
| 2003 | 0.49 | 0.55 | 0.47 | 0.50 | 2.01 |

Fiscal year ended Dec. 31. Next earnings report expected: Late January. EPS Estimates based on S&P Operating Earnings; historical GAAP earnings are as reported.

## Dividend Data (Dates: mm/dd Payment Date: mm/dd/yy)

| Amount ($) | Date Decl. | Ex-Div. Date | Stk. of Record | Payment Date |
|---|---|---|---|---|
| 0.270 | 12/07 | 12/21 | 12/26 | 01/04/08 |
| 0.270 | 02/22 | 03/12 | 03/14 | 04/04/08 |
| 0.270 | 06/16 | 06/25 | 06/27 | 07/16/08 |
| 0.290 | 09/09 | 09/22 | 09/24 | 10/08/08 |

Dividends have been paid since 2001. Source: Company reports.

# Kraft Foods Inc.

STANDARD &POOR'S

## Business Summary October 07, 2008

CORPORATE OVERVIEW. Kraft Foods is one of the world's largest branded food and beverage companies. In 2007, U.S. operations accounted for $21.5 billion, or approximately 58%, of total company net revenues. European operations accounted for $9.4 billion (25%), and other operations provided $6.3 billion (17%).

Business segments include North America Beverages (8.7% of 2007 net revenues), North America Cheese & Foodservice (17.1%), North America Convenient Meals (13.7%), North America Grocery (7.2%), North America Snacks & Cereals (17.5%), European Union (21.4%), and Developing Markets (14.4%). Wal-Mart Stores, Inc. accounted for about 15% of KFT's net revenues in 2007.

We believe that Kraft has at least eight or nine brands with annual revenue of at least about $1 billion each. These include Kraft cheeses, dinners and dressings; Oscar Mayer meats; Philadelphia cream cheese; Maxwell House coffee; Nabisco cookies and crackers and its Oreo brand; Jacobs coffees; Milka chocolates; and LU biscuits.

Divestitures by KFT have included its hot cereal assets and trademarks, which were sold in the first quarter of 2007; and its pet snacks brand and assets, which were sold in the third quarter of 2006.

CORPORATE STRATEGY. We see KFT aiming to achieve long-term EPS growth of 7% to 9% annually, with annual organic revenue growth of 4% and operating profit margin expansion.

In January 2004, the company announced a strategic plan that we view as part of an effort to stem market share losses and improve growth prospects. Elements of the plan included a higher level of investment in brand building, a transformation of the product portfolio, an expanded global scale, and a reduction in the cost structure. In 2006, the restructuring plan was extended through 2008. We expect the entire program to result in about $2.8 billion of pretax charges (cash portion about $1.7 billion), including asset disposals, severance and implementation costs. Annual savings from the program are expected to reach $1.2 billion.

## Company Financials Fiscal Year Ended Dec. 31

| Per Share Data ($) | 2007 | 2006 | 2005 | 2004 | 2003 | 2002 | 2001 | 2000 | 1999 | 1998 |
|---|---|---|---|---|---|---|---|---|---|---|
| Tangible Book Value | NM | NM | NM | NM | NM | NM | NM | NM | NA | NA |
| Cash Flow | 2.18 | 2.39 | 2.27 | 2.07 | 2.48 | 2.37 | 2.19 | 2.02 | NA | NA |
| Earnings | 1.63 | 1.85 | 1.72 | 1.55 | 2.01 | 1.96 | 1.17 | 1.03 | 1.21 | 1.12 |
| S&P Core Earnings | 1.65 | 1.80 | 1.74 | 1.53 | 1.93 | 1.65 | 0.81 | NA | NA | NA |
| Dividends | 1.04 | 0.96 | 0.87 | 0.77 | 0.66 | 0.56 | 0.26 | NA | NA | NA |
| Payout Ratio | 64% | 52% | 51% | 50% | 33% | 29% | 22% | NA | NA | NA |
| Prices:High | 37.20 | 36.67 | 35.65 | 36.06 | 39.40 | 43.95 | 35.57 | NA | NA | NA |
| Prices:Low | 29.95 | 27.44 | 27.88 | 29.45 | 26.35 | 32.50 | 29.50 | NA | NA | NA |
| P/E Ratio:High | 23 | 20 | 21 | 23 | 20 | 22 | 30 | NA | NA | NA |
| P/E Ratio:Low | 18 | 15 | 16 | 19 | 13 | 17 | 25 | NA | NA | NA |

| Income Statement Analysis (Million $) | | | | | | | | | | |
|---|---|---|---|---|---|---|---|---|---|---|
| Revenue | 37,241 | 34,356 | 34,113 | 32,168 | 31,010 | 29,723 | 33,875 | 34,679 | 26,797 | 27,311 |
| Operating Income | 5,794 | 6,065 | 6,002 | 6,108 | 6,786 | 6,892 | 6,526 | 6,284 | NA | NA |
| Depreciation | 886 | 898 | 879 | 879 | 813 | 716 | 1,642 | 1,722 | 1,030 | 1,038 |
| Interest Expense | 701 | 510 | 636 | 666 | 678 | 854 | 1,437 | NA | NA | NA |
| Pretax Income | 3,730 | 4,016 | 4,116 | 3,946 | 5,346 | 5,267 | 3,447 | 3,214 | 3,040 | 2,999 |
| Effective Tax Rate | 30.5% | 23.7% | 29.4% | 32.3% | 34.9% | 35.5% | 45.4% | 44.4% | 42.3% | 45.6% |
| Net Income | 2,590 | 3,060 | 2,904 | 2,669 | 3,476 | 3,394 | 1,882 | 1,787 | 1,753 | 1,632 |
| S&P Core Earnings | 2,640 | 2,963 | 2,930 | 2,632 | 3,337 | 2,861 | 1,308 | NA | NA | NA |

| Balance Sheet & Other Financial Data (Million $) | | | | | | | | | | |
|---|---|---|---|---|---|---|---|---|---|---|
| Cash | 567 | 239 | 316 | 282 | 514 | 215 | 162 | 191 | 95.0 | NA |
| Current Assets | 10,737 | 8,254 | 8,153 | 9,722 | 8,124 | 7,456 | 7,006 | NA | NA | NA |
| Total Assets | 67,993 | 55,574 | 57,628 | 59,928 | 59,285 | 57,100 | 55,798 | 52,071 | 30,336 | NA |
| Current Liabilities | 17,086 | 10,473 | 8,724 | 9,078 | 7,861 | 7,169 | 8,875 | NA | NA | NA |
| Long Term Debt | 12,902 | 7,081 | 8,475 | 9,723 | 11,591 | 10,416 | 13,134 | 15,677 | NA | NA |
| Common Equity | 27,295 | 28,555 | 29,593 | 29,911 | 28,530 | 25,832 | 23,478 | 22,755 | 13,461 | NA |
| Total Capital | 45,073 | 39,566 | 44,135 | 45,484 | 45,977 | 41,676 | 41,643 | 38,432 | NA | NA |
| Capital Expenditures | 1,241 | 1,169 | 1,171 | 1,006 | 1,085 | 1,184 | 1,101 | 1,151 | 860 | 841 |
| Cash Flow | 3,476 | 3,958 | 3,783 | 3,548 | 4,289 | 4,110 | 3,524 | 3,509 | NA | NA |
| Current Ratio | 0.6 | 0.8 | 0.9 | 1.1 | 1.0 | 1.0 | 0.8 | 0.9 | 1.1 | NA |
| % Long Term Debt of Capitalization | 28.6 | 17.9 | 19.2 | 21.4 | 25.2 | 25.0 | 31.5 | 40.8 | 34.2 | Nil |
| % Net Income of Revenue | 7.0 | 8.9 | 8.5 | 8.3 | 11.2 | 11.4 | 5.6 | 5.2 | 6.5 | 6.0 |
| % Return on Assets | 4.2 | 5.4 | 4.9 | 4.5 | 6.0 | 6.0 | 3.5 | 4.9 | NA | NA |
| % Return on Equity | 9.3 | 10.5 | 9.8 | 9.1 | 12.8 | 13.8 | 10.0 | 14.6 | NA | NA |

Data as orig reptd.; bef. results of disc opers/spec. items. Per share data adj. for stk. divs.; EPS diluted. E-Estimated. NA-Not Available. NM-Not Meaningful. NR-Not Ranked. UR-Under Review.

**Office:** Three Lakes Drive, Northfield, IL 60093.
**Telephone:** 847-646-2000.
**Website:** http://www.kraft.com
**Chrmn & CEO:** I.B. Rosenfeld

**COO:** D.A. Brearton
**EVP & CFO:** T.R. McLevish
**EVP & General Counsel:** M.S. Firestone
**SVP & CSO:** J. Ruff

**Board Members:** A. Banga, J. Bennink, M. M. Hart, L. D. Juliber, M. Ketchum, R. A. Lerner, J. C. Pope, F. G. Reynolds, I. B. Rosenfeld, M. L. Schapiro, D. C. Wright, F. G. Zarb

**Founded:** 2000
**Domicile:** Virginia
**Employees:** 103,000

# Kroger Co. (The)

| S&P Recommendation | BUY ★★★★☆ | Price $28.02 (as of Nov 14, 2008) | 12-Mo. Target Price $31.00 | Investment Style Large-Cap Blend |
|---|---|---|---|---|

**GICS Sector** Consumer Staples
**Sub-Industry** Food Retail

**Summary** This supermarket operator, with about 2,500 stores in 31 states, also operates convenience stores, jewelry stores, supermarket fuel centers, and food processing plants.

## Key Stock Statistics (Source S&P, Vickers, company reports)

| | | | | | | | | |
|---|---|---|---|---|---|---|---|---|
| 52-Wk Range | $30.99– 22.30 | S&P Oper. EPS 2009**E** | 1.95 | Market Capitalization(B) | $18.282 | Beta | | 0.48 |
| Trailing 12-Month EPS | $1.84 | S&P Oper. EPS 2010**E** | 2.15 | Yield (%) | 1.28 | S&P 3-Yr. Proj. EPS CAGR(%) | | 11 |
| Trailing 12-Month P/E | 15.2 | P/E on S&P Oper. EPS 2009**E** | 14.4 | Dividend Rate/Share | $0.36 | S&P Credit Rating | | BBB- |
| $10K Invested 5 Yrs Ago | $16,008 | Common Shares Outstg. (M) | 652.5 | Institutional Ownership (%) | 86 | | | |

## Price Performance

| 30-Week Mov. Avg. · · · · | 10-Week Mov. Avg. - - - | **GAAP Earnings vs. Previous Year** | Volume | Above Avg. ⅲⅲ | STARS |
|---|---|---|---|---|---|
| 12-Mo. Target Price — | Relative Strength — | ▲ Up ▼ Down ▶ No Change | | Below Avg. ⅲⅲ | ★ |

Options: ASE, CBOE, P

Analysis prepared by **Joseph Agnese** on September 17, 2008, when the stock traded at **$ 27.72**.

## Highlights

➤ We expect sales to increase 12%, to $78.4 billion, in FY 09 (Jan.), from $70 billion in FY 08, reflecting about 2.5% square footage growth, 5% identical-store sales gains, and store relocations. Total sales should benefit from increased gasoline sales and from food cost inflation in the low to mid single digits.

➤ We believe EBIT margins will narrow slightly, reflecting the company's pursuit of a price reduction strategy and higher sales of lower margin gasoline, partially offset by increased sales leverage, an improved ability to pass on product cost increases, a more stable promotional spending budget, and cost-saving opportunities that we forecast in areas such as administration, labor, shrinkage, warehousing and transportation. We think the company's sales growth strategy will focus on both service and merchandise improvements in addition to price reductions. In our opinion, these strategies will help the company compete against lower-priced mass merchants.

➤ After benefits from significantly fewer shares outstanding due to an active repurchase program, we expect FY 09 operating EPS to increase 15%, to $1.95, from $1.69 in FY 08.

## Investment Rationale/Risk

➤ We have a buy recommendation on the shares, as we believe the company is well positioned to continue growing market share. We think results will benefit from KR's strategy of boosting sales through targeted marketing, price reductions, and improved service levels, which, in our view, should limit downside risk despite intense competition in the food/retail industry.

➤ Risks to our recommendation and target price include potential weakness in the economy that would cause consumers to become more price conscious, increased price competition, and losses of market share to new competitors.

➤ Our 12-month target price of $31 is based on our P/E and EV/EBITDA analyses. Based on our expectations of improving trends, we think the shares should trade at about 14.5X our FY 10 EPS estimate of $2.15, in line with its 10% 5-year historical 12-month P/E multiple discount of 10% to that of S&P 500, leading to a projected value of $31. Applying a 6X multiple, slightly below peers, to our FY 10 EBITDA estimate of $4.4 billion, also results in a share price of $31.

## Qualitative Risk Assessment

| LOW | MEDIUM | HIGH |
|---|---|---|

Our risk assessment reflects our view of the company's diversification through multiple format offerings, strong market share positions, and potential opportunities from industry consolidation.

## Quantitative Evaluations

**S&P Quality Ranking** B

| D | C | B- | **B** | B+ | A- | A | A+ |
|---|---|---|---|---|---|---|---|

**Relative Strength Rank** **STRONG**

95

LOWEST = 1       HIGHEST = 99

## Revenue/Earnings Data

**Revenue (Million $)**

| | 1Q | 2Q | 3Q | 4Q | Year |
|---|---|---|---|---|---|
| 2009 | 23,107 | 18,053 | -- | -- | -- |
| 2008 | 20,726 | 16,139 | 16,135 | 17,235 | 70,235 |
| 2007 | 19,415 | 15,138 | 14,999 | 16,859 | 66,111 |
| 2006 | 17,948 | 13,865 | 14,021 | 14,720 | 60,553 |
| 2005 | 16,905 | 12,980 | 12,854 | 13,695 | 56,434 |
| 2004 | 16,266 | 12,351 | 12,141 | 13,034 | 53,791 |

**Earnings Per Share ($)**

| | | | | | |
|---|---|---|---|---|---|
| 2009 | 0.58 | 0.42 | E0.38 | E0.56 | E1.95 |
| 2008 | 0.47 | 0.42 | 0.37 | 0.48 | 1.69 |
| 2007 | 0.42 | 0.29 | 0.30 | 0.54 | 1.54 |
| 2006 | 0.40 | 0.27 | 0.25 | 0.39 | 1.31 |
| 2005 | 0.35 | 0.19 | 0.19 | -0.89 | -0.14 |
| 2004 | 0.46 | 0.25 | 0.15 | -0.45 | 0.42 |

Fiscal year ended Jan. 31. Next earnings report expected: Mid December. EPS Estimates based on S&P Operating Earnings; historical GAAP earnings are as reported.

## Dividend Data (Dates: mm/dd Payment Date: mm/dd/yy)

| Amount ($) | Date Decl. | Ex-Div. Date | Stk. of Record | Payment Date |
|---|---|---|---|---|
| 0.075 | 01/18 | 02/13 | 02/15 | 03/01/08 |
| 0.090 | 03/13 | 05/13 | 05/15 | 06/01/08 |
| 0.090 | 06/26 | 08/13 | 08/15 | 09/01/08 |
| 0.090 | 09/18 | 11/12 | 11/14 | 12/01/08 |

Dividends have been paid since 2006. Source: Company reports.

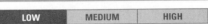

# Kroger Co. (The)

STANDARD
&POOR'S

## Business Summary September 17, 2008

CORPORATE OVERVIEW. Kroger is one of the largest U.S. supermarket chains, with 2,486 supermarkets as of February 2008. The company's principal operating format is combination food and drug stores (combo stores). In addition to combo stores, KR also operates multi-department stores, marketplace stores, price-impact warehouses, convenience stores, fuel centers, jewelry stores, and food processing plants. Total food store square footage exceeded 145 million as of February 2008.

Retail food stores are operated under three formats: combo stores, multi-department stores, and price-impact warehouse stores. Combo stores are considered neighborhood stores, and include many specialty departments, such as whole health sections, pharmacies, general merchandise, pet centers, and perishables, such as fresh seafood and organic produce. Combo banners include Kroger, Ralphs, King Soopers, City Market, Dillons, Smith's, Fry's, QFC, Hilander, Owen's, Jay C, Baker's, Pay Less and Gerbes.

Multi-department stores offer one-stop shopping, are significantly larger in size than combo stores, and sell a wider selection of general merchandise items, including apparel, home fashion and furnishings, electronics, automotive, toys, and fine jewelry. Multi-department formats include Fred Meyer, Fry's Marketplace, Smith's Marketplace and Kroger Marketplace. Many combination and multi-department stores include a fuel center.

Price-impact warehouse stores offer everyday low prices, plus promotions for a wide selection of grocery and health and beauty care items. Price-impact warehouse stores include Food 4 Less and Foods Co.

## Company Financials Fiscal Year Ended Jan. 31

### Per Share Data ($)

| | 2008 | 2007 | 2006 | 2005 | 2004 | 2003 | 2002 | 2001 | 2000 | 1999 |
|---|---|---|---|---|---|---|---|---|---|---|
| Tangible Book Value | 7.07 | 5.61 | 3.04 | 1.85 | 1.18 | 0.36 | NM | NM | NM | NM |
| Cash Flow | 3.64 | 3.30 | 3.04 | 1.57 | 2.02 | 2.93 | 2.44 | 2.11 | 1.86 | 1.66 |
| Earnings | 1.69 | 1.54 | 1.31 | -0.14 | 0.42 | 1.56 | 1.26 | 1.04 | 0.74 | 0.85 |
| S&P Core Earnings | 1.70 | 1.59 | 1.27 | 0.99 | 0.98 | 1.40 | 1.12 | 0.96 | NA | NA |
| Dividends | 0.20 | Nil | Nil | Nil | Nil | Nil | Nil | Nil | Nil | Nil |
| Payout Ratio | 12% | Nil | Nil | Nil | Nil | Nil | Nil | Nil | Nil | Nil |
| Calendar Year | 2007 | 2006 | 2005 | 2004 | 2003 | 2002 | 2001 | 2000 | 1999 | 1998 |
| Prices:High | 31.94 | 24.48 | 20.88 | 19.67 | 19.70 | 23.81 | 27.66 | 27.94 | 34.91 | 18.66 |
| Prices:Low | 22.94 | 18.05 | 15.15 | 14.65 | 12.05 | 11.00 | 19.60 | 14.06 | 14.88 | 11.34 |
| P/E Ratio:High | 19 | 16 | 16 | NM | 47 | 15 | 22 | 27 | 47 | 22 |
| P/E Ratio:Low | 14 | 12 | 12 | NM | 29 | 7 | 16 | 14 | 20 | 13 |

### Income Statement Analysis (Million $)

| | 2008 | 2007 | 2006 | 2005 | 2004 | 2003 | 2002 | 2001 | 2000 | 1999 |
|---|---|---|---|---|---|---|---|---|---|---|
| Revenue | 70,235 | 66,111 | 60,553 | 56,434 | 53,791 | 51,760 | 50,098 | 49,000 | 45,352 | 28,203 |
| Operating Income | 3,657 | 3,508 | 3,300 | 3,003 | 3,147 | 3,676 | 3,567 | 3,397 | 3,125 | 1,410 |
| Depreciation | 1,356 | 1,272 | 1,265 | 1,256 | 1,209 | 1,087 | 973 | 907 | 961 | 430 |
| Interest Expense | 474 | 488 | 510 | 557 | 604 | 600 | 648 | 675 | 652 | 267 |
| Pretax Income | 1,827 | 1,748 | 1,525 | 290 | 770 | 1,973 | 1,711 | 1,508 | 1,129 | 713 |
| Effective Tax Rate | 35.4% | 36.2% | 37.2% | NM | 59.1% | 37.5% | 39.0% | 41.6% | 43.5% | 36.9% |
| Net Income | 1,181 | 1,115 | 958 | -100 | 315 | 1,233 | 1,043 | 880 | 638 | 450 |
| S&P Core Earnings | 1,193 | 1,155 | 928 | 720 | 745 | 1,105 | 914 | 816 | NA | NA |

### Balance Sheet & Other Financial Data (Million $)

| | 2008 | 2007 | 2006 | 2005 | 2004 | 2003 | 2002 | 2001 | 2000 | 1999 |
|---|---|---|---|---|---|---|---|---|---|---|
| Cash | 918 | 803 | 210 | 144 | 159 | 171 | 161 | 161 | 281 | 122 |
| Current Assets | 7,114 | 6,755 | 6,466 | 6,406 | 5,619 | 5,566 | 5,512 | 5,416 | 5,531 | 2,673 |
| Total Assets | 22,299 | 21,215 | 20,482 | 20,491 | 20,184 | 20,102 | 19,087 | 18,190 | 17,966 | 6,700 |
| Current Liabilities | 8,689 | 7,581 | 6,715 | 6,316 | 5,586 | 5,608 | 5,485 | 5,591 | 5,728 | 3,192 |
| Long Term Debt | 6,529 | 6,154 | 6,678 | 7,900 | 8,116 | 8,222 | 8,412 | 8,210 | 8,045 | 3,229 |
| Common Equity | 4,914 | 4,923 | 4,390 | 3,540 | 4,011 | 3,850 | 3,502 | 3,089 | 2,683 | -388 |
| Total Capital | 11,810 | 11,799 | 11,911 | 12,379 | 13,117 | 12,072 | 11,914 | 11,299 | 10,728 | 3,042 |
| Capital Expenditures | 2,126 | 1,683 | 1,306 | 1,634 | 2,000 | 1,891 | 2,139 | 1,623 | 1,701 | 923 |
| Cash Flow | 2,537 | 2,387 | 2,223 | 1,156 | 1,524 | 2,320 | 2,016 | 1,787 | 1,599 | 880 |
| Current Ratio | 0.8 | 0.9 | 1.0 | 1.0 | 1.0 | 1.0 | 1.0 | 1.0 | 1.0 | 0.8 |
| % Long Term Debt of Capitalization | 55.3 | 55.6 | 56.1 | 63.8 | 61.9 | 68.1 | 70.6 | 72.7 | 75.0 | 106.1 |
| % Net Income of Revenue | 1.7 | 1.7 | 1.6 | NM | 0.6 | 2.4 | 2.1 | 1.8 | 1.4 | 1.6 |
| % Return on Assets | 5.4 | 5.4 | 4.7 | NM | 1.6 | 6.3 | 5.6 | 4.9 | 3.7 | 1.6 |
| % Return on Equity | 24.0 | 24.0 | 23.9 | NM | 8.0 | 33.5 | 31.6 | 30.5 | 27.7 | NM |

Data as orig reptd.; bef. results of disc opers/spec. items. Per share data adj. for stk. divs.; EPS diluted. E-Estimated. NA-Not Available. NM-Not Meaningful. NR-Not Ranked. UR-Under Review.

**Office:** 1014 Vine St, Cincinnati, OH 45202.
**Telephone:** 513-762-4000.
**Email:** investors@kroger.com
**Website:** http://www.kroger.com

**Chrmn & CEO:** D.B. Dillon
**Pres & COO:** D.W. McGeorge
**Vice Chrmn:** W.R. McMullen
**EVP, Secy & General Counsel:** P.W. Heldman

**SVP & CFO:** J.M. Schlotman
**Investor Contact:** C. Fike (513-762-4969)
**Board Members:** R. V. Anderson, R. D. Beyer, D. B. Dillon, S. J. Kropf, J. T. Lamacchia, D. B. Lewis, D. W. McGeorge, W. R. McMullen, J. P. Montoya, C. R. Moore, S. M. Phillips, S. R. Rogel, J. A. Runde, R. L. Sargent, B. Shackouls

**Founded:** 1883
**Domicile:** Ohio
**Employees:** 323,000

# Laboratory Corporation of America Holdings

STANDARD &POOR'S

| S&P Recommendation | **BUY** ★★★★☆ | Price $64.62 (as of Nov 14, 2008) | 12-Mo. Target Price $84.00 | Investment Style Large-Cap Growth |
|---|---|---|---|---|

**GICS Sector** Health Care
**Sub-Industry** Health Care Services

**Summary** This clinical laboratory organization offers a broad range of clinical tests through a national network of laboratories.

## Key Stock Statistics (Source S&P, Vickers, company reports)

| | | | | | | | | |
|---|---|---|---|---|---|---|---|---|
| 52-Wk Range | $80.77– 52.93 | S&P Oper. EPS 2008**E** | 4.60 | Market Capitalization(B) | $6.979 | Beta | | 0.67 |
| Trailing 12-Month EPS | $4.04 | S&P Oper. EPS 2009**E** | 5.15 | Yield (%) | Nil | S&P 3-Yr. Proj. EPS CAGR(%) | | 12 |
| Trailing 12-Month P/E | 16.0 | P/E on S&P Oper. EPS 2008**E** | 14.0 | Dividend Rate/Share | Nil | S&P Credit Rating | | BBB |
| $10K Invested 5 Yrs Ago | $18,152 | Common Shares Outstg. (M) | 108.0 | Institutional Ownership (%) | NM | | | |

## Price Performance

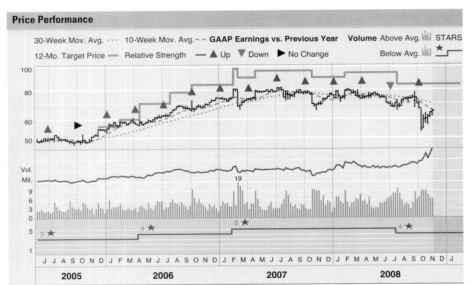

30-Week Mov. Avg. ···· 10-Week Mov. Avg. – – GAAP Earnings vs. Previous Year   Volume Above Avg. STARS
12-Mo. Target Price — Relative Strength ▲ Up ▼ Down ► No Change   Below Avg. ★

Options: ASE, CBOE, P, Ph

Analysis prepared by **Jeffrey Loo, CFA** on November 13, 2008, when the stock traded at **$ 62.48**.

## Highlights

➤ We expect sales to rise 11% in 2008, to $4.5 billion. Our sales forecast includes the consolidation of LH's Canadian joint venture, Gamma-Dynacare (GD). We see volume rising 10% and prices advancing 1%, as we expect GD to increase the routine testing mix versus higher-priced esoteric testing. Under its 10-year deal with UnitedHealthcare (UNH), effective January 1, 2007, LH agreed to reimburse UNH up to $200 million for transitional costs over three years. In the first nine months 2008, UNH billed LH $31.3 million, as we think LH's rapid network buildout helped minimize potential leakage and transition costs. We expect a lower amount in 2009. But we see a higher bad debt level, an increased sales allowance along with GD adversely affecting EBITDA margins by 140 basis points. In 2009, we forecast sales growth of 5%, but we think LH will continue to make acquisitions to supplement organic growth.

➤ LH continues to repurchase shares, with about 4.6 million repurchased in the first nine months 2008. As of September 2008, $95 million remains available under its repurchase program.

➤ We forecast EPS of $4.60 and $5.15 for 2008 and 2009, respectively.

## Investment Rationale/Risk

➤ Amid a challenging economic environment and higher unemployment levels we believe LH's core lab testing business is fundamentally sound and we expect LH to expand faster than the industry's estimated mid-single digit growth rate, aided by the addition of its joint venture and small acquisitions. We also see the potential benefit of more genomic testing, albeit a modest one in 2008, but think the growth in molecular diagnostics should aid volume and pricing beyond 2008. However, in October, LH withdrew its OvaSure ovarian cancer test after the FDA determined the test must receive FDA approval before marketed. We think the shares, recently trading at 12.2X our 2009 EPS forecast, well below historical levels, are undervalued.

➤ Risks to our recommendation and target price include greater-than-expected pricing pressure and an inability to efficiently establish a lab network to absorb the UNH business.

➤ Our 12-month target price of $84 is based on our DCF analysis (assuming a WACC of 9.3% and a terminal growth rate of 3%) and a P/E to growth (PEG) ratio of 1.35X applied to our 2009 EPS estimate, in line with peers.

## Qualitative Risk Assessment

| LOW | MEDIUM | HIGH |
|---|---|---|

Our risk assessment reflects LH's leadership position in a large, mature industry, its broad geographic service area with clients in all 50 states, and our view of its diverse and balanced payer mix.

## Quantitative Evaluations

**S&P Quality Ranking** B+

| D | C | B- | B | B+ | A- | A | A+ |
|---|---|---|---|---|---|---|---|

**Relative Strength Rank** STRONG

90

LOWEST = 1          HIGHEST = 99

## Revenue/Earnings Data

**Revenue (Million $)**

| | 1Q | 2Q | 3Q | 4Q | Year |
|---|---|---|---|---|---|
| 2008 | 1,103 | 1,148 | 1,135 | -- | -- |
| 2007 | 998.7 | 1,043 | 1,021 | 1,006 | 4,068 |
| 2006 | 878.6 | 903.7 | 909.9 | 898.6 | 3,591 |
| 2005 | 799.1 | 853.3 | 852.9 | 822.3 | 3,328 |
| 2004 | 752.5 | 784.3 | 781.5 | 766.5 | 3,085 |
| 2003 | 712.2 | 743.7 | 752.0 | 731.5 | 2,939 |

**Earnings Per Share ($)**

| | 1Q | 2Q | 3Q | 4Q | Year |
|---|---|---|---|---|---|
| 2008 | 1.14 | 0.92 | 1.00 | E1.11 | E4.60 |
| 2007 | 0.98 | 1.05 | 0.92 | 0.98 | 3.93 |
| 2006 | 0.76 | 0.87 | 0.81 | 0.81 | 3.24 |
| 2005 | 0.67 | 0.74 | 0.66 | 0.64 | 2.71 |
| 2004 | 0.58 | 0.66 | 0.66 | 0.58 | 2.45 |
| 2003 | 0.51 | 0.60 | 0.58 | 0.54 | 2.22 |

Fiscal year ended Dec. 31. Next earnings report expected: Early February. EPS Estimates based on S&P Operating Earnings; historical GAAP earnings are as reported.

## Dividend Data

No cash dividends have been paid.

---

# Laboratory Corporation of America Holdings

STANDARD
&POOR'S

## Business Summary November 13, 2008

CORPORATE OVERVIEW. Laboratory Corporation of America Holdings is the second largest independent U.S. clinical laboratory. Clinical laboratory tests are used by medical professionals in routine testing, patient diagnosis, and in the monitoring and treatment of disease. As of December 2007, LH had 37 primary testing facilities and more than 1,600 service sites consisting of branches, patient service centers, and STAT laboratories that have the ability to perform certain routine tests quickly and report results to the physician immediately. The company's laboratory services involve the testing of both bodily fluids and human tissues. LH offers more than 4,400 different tests, consisting of routine tests and specialty and niche testing (esoteric). The most frequently administered routine tests include blood chemistry analyses, urinalysis, blood cell counts, pap tests, HIV tests, microbiology cultures and procedures, and alcohol and other substance abuse tests. The company's esoteric tests include testing for infectious diseases, allergies, diagnostic genetics, identity, and oncology. An average of 420,000 specimens were being processed daily as of December 2007, with routine testing results generally available within 24 hours.

The company provides testing services to a broad range of health care providers, including independent physicians, hospitals, HMOs and other managed care groups, and governmental and other institutions. During 2005, no client accounted for over 4% of net sales. Most testing services are billed to a party other than the physician or other authorized person who ordered the test. Payers other than the direct patient include insurance companies, managed care organizations, Medicare and Medicaid. Client-billed accounted for 27% of revenue in 2007 (27% in 2006), and generated an average of $31.60 ($29.30 in 2006) in revenue per requisition; patients-billed 9% (9% in 2006) and $158.84 ($148.91 in 2006); managed care clients 46% (43% in 2006) and $35.74 ($37.01 in 2006); and Medicare, Medicaid and Insurance 18% (21% in 2006) and $40.66 ($40.11 in 2006). In May 2005, the company acquired Esoterix, Inc., a provider of specialty reference testing. In February 2005, LH bought US Labs, located in Irvine, CA. In March 2004, LH purchased laboratory operations in Poughkeepsie, NY, and Atlanta, GA, from MDS Diagnostic Services. In July 2007, LH acquired DSI Labs, expanding its operations in southwest Florida.

## Company Financials Fiscal Year Ended Dec. 31

| Per Share Data ($) | 2007 | 2006 | 2005 | 2004 | 2003 | 2002 | 2001 | 2000 | 1999 | 1998 |
|---|---|---|---|---|---|---|---|---|---|---|
| Tangible Book Value | NM | NM | NM | 1.04 | 0.27 | 2.67 | 0.83 | 0.09 | NM | NM |
| Cash Flow | 5.26 | 4.80 | 4.24 | 3.33 | 3.18 | 2.47 | 2.03 | 1.74 | 0.19 | 2.17 |
| Earnings | 3.93 | 3.24 | 2.71 | 2.45 | 2.22 | 1.77 | 1.29 | 0.81 | 0.29 | 0.50 |
| S&P Core Earnings | 3.89 | 3.21 | 2.53 | 2.25 | 2.04 | 1.56 | 1.15 | NA | NA | NA |
| Dividends | Nil | Nil | Nil | Nil | Nil | Nil | Nil | Nil | Nil | Nil |
| Payout Ratio | Nil | Nil | Nil | Nil | Nil | Nil | Nil | Nil | Nil | Nil |
| Prices:High | 82.32 | 74.30 | 55.00 | 50.03 | 37.72 | 52.38 | 45.68 | 45.75 | 9.69 | 6.88 |
| Prices:Low | 65.13 | 52.58 | 44.63 | 36.70 | 22.21 | 18.51 | 24.88 | 7.81 | 3.13 | 2.81 |
| P/E Ratio:High | 21 | 23 | 20 | 20 | 17 | 30 | 35 | 57 | 33 | 14 |
| P/E Ratio:Low | 17 | 16 | 16 | 15 | 10 | 10 | 19 | 10 | 11 | 6 |

| Income Statement Analysis (Million $) | 2007 | 2006 | 2005 | 2004 | 2003 | 2002 | 2001 | 2000 | 1999 | 1998 |
|---|---|---|---|---|---|---|---|---|---|---|
| Revenue | 4,068 | 3,591 | 3,328 | 3,085 | 2,939 | 2,508 | 2,200 | 1,919 | 1,699 | 1,613 |
| Operating Income | 989 | 853 | 785 | 736 | 671 | 554 | 472 | 340 | 234 | 212 |
| Depreciation | 161 | 155 | 150 | 139 | 136 | 102 | 104 | 89.6 | 84.5 | 84.2 |
| Interest Expense | 56.6 | 47.8 | 34.4 | 36.1 | 40.9 | 19.2 | 27.0 | 38.5 | 41.6 | 48.7 |
| Pretax Income | 802 | 721 | 641 | 615 | 540 | 432 | 332 | 208 | 106 | 81.5 |
| Effective Tax Rate | 40.6% | 40.1% | 39.7% | 41.0% | 40.6% | 41.1% | 45.0% | 46.0% | 38.0% | 15.6% |
| Net Income | 477 | 432 | 386 | 363 | 321 | 255 | 183 | 112 | 65.4 | 68.8 |
| S&P Core Earnings | 472 | 428 | 368 | 339 | 295 | 226 | 162 | NA | NA | NA |

| Balance Sheet & Other Financial Data (Million $) | 2007 | 2006 | 2005 | 2004 | 2003 | 2002 | 2001 | 2000 | 1999 | 1998 |
|---|---|---|---|---|---|---|---|---|---|---|
| Cash | 166 | 51.5 | 45.4 | 187 | 123 | 56.4 | 149 | 48.8 | 40.3 | 22.7 |
| Current Assets | 938 | 887 | 702 | 740 | 658 | 597 | 624 | 512 | 500 | 519 |
| Total Assets | 4,368 | 4,001 | 3,876 | 3,601 | 3,415 | 2,612 | 1,930 | 1,667 | 1,590 | 1,641 |
| Current Liabilities | 968 | 931 | 888 | 301 | 758 | 229 | 201 | 312 | 246 | 251 |
| Long Term Debt | 1,078 | 603 | 604 | 892 | 361 | 522 | 509 | 354 | 483 | 576 |
| Common Equity | 1,725 | 1,977 | 1,886 | 1,999 | 1,896 | 1,612 | 1,085 | 877 | 176 | 154 |
| Total Capital | 3,310 | 2,989 | 2,899 | 3,213 | 2,530 | 2,133 | 1,594 | 1,231 | 1,217 | 1,257 |
| Capital Expenditures | 143 | 116 | 93.6 | 95.0 | 83.6 | 74.3 | 88.1 | 55.5 | 69.4 | 58.7 |
| Cash Flow | 638 | 587 | 536 | 502 | 457 | 356 | 287 | 167 | 99.5 | 109 |
| Current Ratio | 1.0 | 1.0 | 0.8 | 2.5 | 0.9 | 2.6 | 3.1 | 1.6 | 2.0 | 2.1 |
| % Long Term Debt of Capitalization | 32.6 | 20.2 | 20.9 | 27.8 | 14.3 | 24.4 | 31.9 | 28.7 | 39.7 | 45.8 |
| % Net Income of Revenue | 11.7 | 12.0 | 11.6 | 11.8 | 10.9 | 10.2 | 8.3 | 5.8 | 3.9 | 4.3 |
| % Return on Assets | 11.4 | 11.0 | 10.3 | 10.3 | 10.7 | 11.2 | 10.2 | 6.9 | 4.0 | 4.2 |
| % Return on Equity | 25.8 | 22.3 | 19.9 | 18.6 | 18.3 | 18.9 | 18.6 | 14.8 | 9.1 | 17.2 |

Data as orig reptd.; bef. results of disc opers/spec. items. Per share data adj. for stk. divs.; EPS diluted. E-Estimated. NA-Not Available. NM-Not Meaningful. NR-Not Ranked. UR-Under Review.

**Office:** 358 South Main Street, Burlington, NC 27215.
**Telephone:** 336-229-1127.
**Website:** http://www.labcorp.com
**Chrmn:** T.P. MacMahon

**Pres & CEO:** D.P. King
**Vice Chrmn, EVP, Secy & General Counsel:** B. Smith
**COO & EVP:** D.M. Hardison
**EVP, CFO, Chief Acctg Officer & Treas:** W.B. Hayes

**Investor Contact:** S. Fleming (336-436-4879)
**Board Members:** K. B. Anderson, J. Belingard, D. P. King, W. Lane, T. P. MacMahon, R. E. Mittelstaedt, Jr., A. H. Rubenstein, B. Smith, M. K. Weikel, R. S. Williams

**Founded:** 1971
**Domicile:** Delaware
**Employees:** 26,000

The *McGraw-Hill* Companies

# Estee Lauder Companies Inc. (The)

| S&P Recommendation | HOLD ★★★☆☆ | Price<br>$29.93 (as of Nov 14, 2008) | 12-Mo. Target Price<br>$39.00 | Investment Style<br>Large-Cap Growth |
|---|---|---|---|---|

**GICS Sector** Consumer Staples
**Sub-Industry** Personal Products

**Summary** This company is one of the world's leading manufacturers and marketers of skin care, makeup, and fragrance products.

## Key Stock Statistics (Source S&P, Vickers, company reports)

| | | | | | | | | |
|---|---|---|---|---|---|---|---|---|
| 52-Wk Range | $54.75– 28.80 | S&P Oper. EPS 2009E | 2.30 | Market Capitalization(B) | $3.541 | Beta | | 0.45 |
| Trailing 12-Month EPS | $2.46 | S&P Oper. EPS 2010E | NA | Yield (%) | 1.84 | S&P 3-Yr. Proj. EPS CAGR(%) | | NA |
| Trailing 12-Month P/E | 12.2 | P/E on S&P Oper. EPS 2009E | 13.0 | Dividend Rate/Share | $0.55 | S&P Credit Rating | | A |
| $10K Invested 5 Yrs Ago | $8,386 | Common Shares Outstg. (M) | 196.4 | Institutional Ownership (%) | NM | | | |

## Price Performance

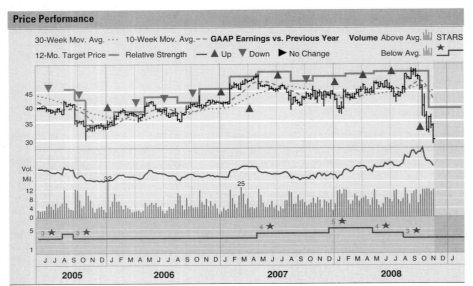

30-Week Mov. Avg. ···· 10-Week Mov. Avg. – – GAAP Earnings vs. Previous Year Volume Above Avg. STARS
12-Mo. Target Price — Relative Strength — ▲ Up ▼ Down ▶ No Change Below Avg.

Options: ASE, CBOE, Ph

Analysis prepared by **Loran Braverman, CFA** on October 29, 2008, when the stock traded at **$34.96**.

### Highlights

➤ In FY 08 (Jun.), sales increased 12.4%, including a positive 4.2% from foreign currency. The Americas segment rose 4%, with weakness in the still important U.S. department store channel offset by strength in other channels in the U.S. and growth in Canada and Latin America. Our FY 09 sales growth outlook is a decline of 2.5%, which assumes a negative 6.5% impact from foreign currency. We are looking for a slowing in local currency sales, particularly in the Europe, the Middle East & Africa segment. EL and a number of other consumer products companies first reported a slowing in sales in some Western European countries late in the June quarter.

➤ The operating margin narrowed by 40 basis points (bps) in FY 08, versus FY 07, due primarily to EL's previously announced acceleration and increase in investments in its business. In FY 09, we think margin pressure from continuing investments and a lower sales base can be largely offset by benefits from previous investments and an accelleration in EL's cost cutting plans. We also project lower interest expense and a 35.1% tax rate.

➤ Our FY 09 EPS estimate is $2.30.

### Investment Rationale/Risk

➤ Our hold recommendation reflects our view that EL's good long-term growth prospects are adequately reflected in the stock price. Also, we are concerned about a prolonged consumer spending slowdown in Western Europe and other important markets at the same time that the U.S. is experiencing a difficult consumer discretionary environment.

➤ Risks to our recommendation and target price include a prolonged decline in the economies in EL's major country markets, low consumer acceptance of new products and unfavorable foreign exchange translation. We are concerned about EL's corporate governance practices given the majority voting power of insiders.

➤ Our 12-month target price of $39 is based on a blend of our DCF model and our historical and relative analyses. Our DCF model assumes terminal values of 10.2% for the weighted average cost of capital and 3% for growth, implying a value of $44. Our historical analysis suggests a value of $40 based on a multiple of 15.1X, at the low end of the 10-year range, applied to our calendar 2009 EPS estimate of $2.62. Our peer analysis uses a P/E of 13.0X, a premium to the peer average, to value the stock at $34.

### Qualitative Risk Assessment

| LOW | MEDIUM | HIGH |
|---|---|---|

Our risk assessment reflects our view of EL's market share advantage, leading brands, scale leverage, and a strong balance sheet. However, the company is exposed to short-term events such as changes in the retail industry, geopolitical events, and consumer spending.

### Quantitative Evaluations

**S&P Quality Ranking**          A-

| D | C | B- | B | B+ | A- | A | A+ |
|---|---|---|---|---|---|---|---|

**Relative Strength Rank**          MODERATE

40

LOWEST = 1          HIGHEST = 99

### Revenue/Earnings Data

**Revenue (Million $)**

| | 1Q | 2Q | 3Q | 4Q | Year |
|---|---|---|---|---|---|
| 2009 | 1,904 | -- | -- | -- | -- |
| 2008 | 1,710 | 2,309 | 1,880 | 2,012 | 7,911 |
| 2007 | 1,594 | 1,991 | 1,691 | 1,762 | 7,038 |
| 2006 | 1,497 | 1,784 | 1,578 | 1,605 | 6,464 |
| 2005 | 1,504 | 1,750 | 1,538 | 1,544 | 6,336 |
| 2004 | 1,352 | 1,619 | 1,422 | 1,403 | 5,790 |

**Earnings Per Share ($)**

| | | | | | |
|---|---|---|---|---|---|
| 2009 | 0.26 | E0.97 | E0.45 | E0.62 | E2.30 |
| 2008 | 0.20 | 1.14 | 0.46 | 0.61 | 2.40 |
| 2007 | 0.27 | 0.99 | 0.45 | 0.45 | 2.16 |
| 2006 | 0.28 | 0.70 | 0.28 | 0.23 | 1.49 |
| 2005 | 0.41 | 0.60 | 0.46 | 0.30 | 1.78 |
| 2004 | 0.34 | 0.54 | 0.43 | 0.31 | 1.62 |

Fiscal year ended Jun. 30. Next earnings report expected: Early February. EPS Estimates based on S&P Operating Earnings; historical GAAP earnings are as reported.

### Dividend Data (Dates: mm/dd Payment Date: mm/dd/yy)

| Amount ($) | Date Decl. | Ex-Div. Date | Stk. of Record | Payment Date |
|---|---|---|---|---|
| 0.550 | 11/09 | 12/05 | 12/07 | 12/27/07 |
| 0.550 | 11/06 | 11/26 | 12/01 | 12/17/08 |

Dividends have been paid since 1996. Source: Company reports.

---

**Please read the Required Disclosures and Analyst Certification on the last page of this report.**

# Estee Lauder Companies Inc. (The)

**STANDARD & POOR'S**

## Business Summary October 29, 2008

CORPORATE OVERVIEW. The Estee Lauder Companies was founded in 1946 by Estee and Joseph Lauder. EL has grown into one of the world's largest manufacturers and marketers of skin care, makeup and fragrance products, sold in more than 140 countries and territories worldwide. EL has historically been a dominant player in the high-end fragrance and cosmetic categories, with brand names such as Estee Lauder, Clinique, Aramis, Prescriptives, Origins, M.A.C, Bobbi Brown, La Mer, Aveda, Stila, Jo Malone, and Bumble and Bumble. EL is also the global licensee for fragrances and cosmetics sold under the Tommy Hilfiger, Donna Karan and Michael Kors brands. Each brand is distinctly positioned within the cosmetics market, according to the company.

EL reports sales and operating income by three regions. The Americas accounted for 47% of sales and 28% of profits in FY 08 (Jun.), Europe, the Middle East and Africa 38% of sales and 53% of profits, and Asia/Pacific 15% and 19%, respectively.

The skin care division (38% of FY 08 net sales) addresses various skin care needs of women and men. Products include moisturizers, creams, lotions, cleansers, sun screens and self-tanning products. The makeup division (38%) manufactures, markets and sells a full array of makeup products, including lipsticks, mascaras, foundations, eyeshadows, nail polishes and powders. The fragrance division (18%) offers a variety of fragrance products, including eau de parfum sprays and colognes, as well as lotions, powders, creams and soaps that are based on a particular fragrance. The products of the hair care division (5%) are offered mainly in salons and in freestanding retail stores and include styling products, shampoos, conditioners and finishing sprays. Other is less than 1%.

As is customary in the cosmetics industry, EL accepts returns of its products from retailers under certain conditions. In recognition of this practice and in according with generally accepted accounting principals, EL reports sales on a net basis, which is computed by deducting the amount of actual returns received and an amount established for anticipated returns from gross sales. As a percentage of gross sales, returns were 4.4% in FY 08, 4.2% in FY 07 and 5.0% in FY 06.

In FY 08, Macy's, Inc. accounted for 11% of EL's accounts receivable and 12% of consolidated net sales.

## Company Financials Fiscal Year Ended Jun. 30

| Per Share Data ($) | 2008 | 2007 | 2006 | 2005 | 2004 | 2003 | 2002 | 2001 | 2000 | 1999 |
|---|---|---|---|---|---|---|---|---|---|---|
| Tangible Book Value | 3.86 | 2.23 | 4.29 | 6.79 | 4.35 | 2.92 | 3.20 | 2.64 | 1.77 | 1.33 |
| Cash Flow | NA | 3.16 | 2.41 | 2.64 | 2.45 | 2.01 | 1.46 | 1.82 | 1.73 | 1.45 |
| Earnings | 2.40 | 2.16 | 1.49 | 1.78 | 1.62 | 1.26 | 0.78 | 1.17 | 1.20 | 1.03 |
| S&P Core Earnings | 2.28 | 2.18 | 1.52 | 1.69 | 1.51 | 1.17 | 0.70 | 1.01 | NA | NA |
| Dividends | 0.55 | 0.50 | 0.40 | 0.40 | 0.30 | 0.20 | 0.20 | 0.20 | 0.15 | 0.18 |
| Payout Ratio | 23% | 23% | 27% | 22% | 19% | 16% | 26% | 17% | 12% | 17% |
| Prices:High | 54.75 | 52.31 | 43.60 | 47.50 | 49.34 | 40.20 | 38.80 | 44.35 | 55.88 | 56.50 |
| Prices:Low | 28.80 | 38.41 | 32.79 | 29.98 | 37.55 | 25.73 | 25.20 | 29.25 | 33.75 | 37.25 |
| P/E Ratio:High | 23 | 24 | 29 | 27 | 30 | 32 | 50 | 38 | 47 | 55 |
| P/E Ratio:Low | 12 | 18 | 22 | 17 | 23 | 20 | 32 | 25 | 28 | 36 |

| Income Statement Analysis (Million $) | 2008 | 2007 | 2006 | 2005 | 2004 | 2003 | 2002 | 2001 | 2000 | 1999 |
|---|---|---|---|---|---|---|---|---|---|---|
| Revenue | 7,911 | 7,038 | 6,464 | 6,336 | 5,790 | 5,118 | 4,744 | 4,608 | 4,367 | 3,962 |
| Operating Income | NA | 958 | 910 | 917 | 836 | 712 | 614 | 706 | 645 | 556 |
| Depreciation | 251 | 207 | 198 | 197 | 192 | 175 | 162 | 156 | 129 | 99.6 |
| Interest Expense | NA | 38.9 | 23.8 | 13.9 | 27.1 | 8.10 | 9.80 | 12.3 | 17.1 | 16.7 |
| Pretax Income | 744 | 711 | 596 | 707 | 617 | 474 | 332 | 483 | 499 | 440 |
| Effective Tax Rate | 34.9% | 35.9% | 43.6% | 41.2% | 37.7% | 33.9% | 34.5% | 36.0% | 37.0% | 38.0% |
| Net Income | 474 | 449 | 325 | 406 | 375 | 320 | 213 | 307 | 314 | 273 |
| S&P Core Earnings | 450 | 453 | 332 | 390 | 351 | 274 | 171 | 245 | NA | NA |

| Balance Sheet & Other Financial Data (Million $) | 2008 | 2007 | 2006 | 2005 | 2004 | 2003 | 2002 | 2001 | 2000 | 1999 |
|---|---|---|---|---|---|---|---|---|---|---|
| Cash | 402 | 254 | 369 | 553 | 612 | 364 | 547 | 347 | 320 | 348 |
| Current Assets | NA | 2,239 | 2,177 | 2,303 | 2,199 | 1,845 | 1,928 | 1,739 | 1,619 | 1,570 |
| Total Assets | 5,011 | 4,126 | 3,784 | 3,886 | 3,708 | 3,350 | 3,417 | 3,219 | 3,043 | 2,747 |
| Current Liabilities | NA | 1,501 | 1,438 | 1,498 | 1,322 | 1,054 | 960 | 857 | 902 | 862 |
| Long Term Debt | NA | 1,028 | 432 | 451 | 462 | 284 | 404 | 411 | 418 | 423 |
| Common Equity | 1,653 | 1,199 | 1,622 | 1,693 | 1,733 | 1,424 | 1,462 | 1,352 | 1,160 | 924 |
| Total Capital | NA | 2,248 | 2,079 | 2,160 | 2,211 | 2,080 | 2,226 | 2,123 | 1,939 | 1,707 |
| Capital Expenditures | 358 | 312 | 261 | 230 | 207 | 163 | 203 | 192 | 181 | 118 |
| Cash Flow | NA | 656 | 523 | 603 | 567 | 471 | 351 | 440 | 420 | 349 |
| Current Ratio | 1.6 | 1.5 | 1.5 | 1.5 | 1.7 | 1.8 | 2.0 | 2.0 | 1.8 | 1.8 |
| % Long Term Debt of Capitalization | 39.5 | 45.7 | 20.8 | 20.9 | 20.9 | 13.6 | 18.1 | 19.4 | 21.6 | 24.8 |
| % Net Income of Revenue | 6.0 | 6.4 | 5.0 | 6.4 | 6.5 | 6.2 | 4.5 | 6.7 | 7.2 | 6.9 |
| % Return on Assets | 10.4 | 11.3 | 8.5 | 10.7 | 10.6 | 9.5 | 6.4 | 9.8 | 10.8 | 10.4 |
| % Return on Equity | 33.2 | 31.8 | 19.6 | 23.7 | 23.8 | 20.5 | 13.4 | 22.6 | 27.9 | 30.8 |

Data as orig reptd.; bef. results of disc opers/spec. items. Per share data adj. for stk. divs.; EPS diluted. E-Estimated. NA-Not Available. NM-Not Meaningful. NR-Not Ranked. UR-Under Review.

**Office:** 767 5th Avenue, New York, NY 10153-0023.
**Telephone:** 212-572-4200.
**Email:** irdept@estee.com
**Website:** http://www.elcompanies.com

**Chrmn:** L.A. Lauder
**Pres & COO:** F. Freda
**Vice Chrmn:** D.J. Brestle
**CEO:** W.P. Lauder

**EVP, CFO & Chief Acctg Officer:** R.W. Kunes
**Investor Contact:** D. D'Andrea (212-572-4384)
**Board Members:** C. Barshefsky, R. M. Bravo, D. J. Brestle, P. J. Fribourg, M. L. Hobson, I. O. Hockaday, Jr., A. Lauder, L. A. Lauder, R. S. Lauder, W. P. Lauder, R. D. Parsons, B. S. Sternlicht, L. F. de Rothschild

**Founded:** 1946
**Domicile:** Delaware
**Employees:** 32,000

*The McGraw-Hill Companies*

# Leggett & Platt Inc

**STANDARD &POOR'S**

| S&P Recommendation HOLD ★★★☆☆ | Price $14.88 (as of Nov 14, 2008) | 12-Mo. Target Price $20.00 | Investment Style Large-Cap Blend |
| --- | --- | --- | --- |

**GICS Sector** Consumer Discretionary
**Sub-Industry** Home Furnishings

**Summary** This company makes a broad line of bedding and furniture components and other home, office and commercial furnishings, as well as diversified products for non-furnishings markets.

## Key Stock Statistics (Source S&P, Vickers, company reports)

| | | | | | | | |
| --- | --- | --- | --- | --- | --- | --- | --- |
| 52-Wk Range | $24.60– 13.89 | S&P Oper. EPS 2008E | 1.05 | Market Capitalization(B) | $2.324 | Beta | 0.70 |
| Trailing 12-Month EPS | $-0.53 | S&P Oper. EPS 2009E | 1.30 | Yield (%) | 6.72 | S&P 3-Yr. Proj. EPS CAGR(%) | 5 |
| Trailing 12-Month P/E | NM | P/E on S&P Oper. EPS 2008E | 14.2 | Dividend Rate/Share | $1.00 | S&P Credit Rating | A |
| $10K Invested 5 Yrs Ago | $8,530 | Common Shares Outstg. (M) | 156.2 | Institutional Ownership (%) | 89 | | |

## Price Performance

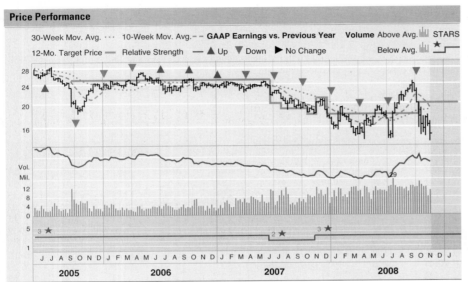

30-Week Mov. Avg. ···· 10-Week Mov. Avg. ─ ─ GAAP Earnings vs. Previous Year   Volume Above Avg. ▮▮▮ STARS
12-Mo. Target Price ── Relative Strength ── ▲ Up ▼ Down ► No Change   Below Avg. ▮▮▮

Options: ASE, Ph

Analysis prepared by **Pearl Wang** on November 10, 2008, when the stock traded at **$ 16.60.**

## Highlights

➤ Including the recent divestment of the Aluminum Products operation and the planned closing of six other business units by the end of 2008, we project that revenues will decrease about 3% in 2008 and about another 1% in 2009, largely reflecting our view of challenging economic conditions in the next 12 months. Economic trends are critical to LEG's residential furnishings and commercial fixtures units.

➤ Facing weak volumes, high and rising raw material costs, and poor capacity utilization, LEG announced in November 2007 that it was seeking opportunities to consolidate, close or divest production or warehouse facilities. In July 2008, LEG closed the sale of its Aluminum Products business for $300 million in cash, a $25 million subordinated note, and preferred stock valued at up to $25 million depending on future performance of the segment. We expect the other business units to be divested this year.

➤ LEG believes the proposed elimination of businesses will cut approximately $1.2 billion from total sales in 2008. We forecast EPS of $1.05 in 2008 and $1.30 in 2009.

## Investment Rationale/Risk

➤ We believe LEG is still challenged by a slump in U.S. housing markets and a weak economy that will likely hurt demand in its Commercial Fixturing & Components and Industrial Materials segments. Narrowing its focus to fewer businesses with the planned restructuring should enable the company to improve operating efficiencies, in our opinion. We see execution risk in planned business divestments and continued restructuring of remaining businesses.

➤ Risks to our recommendation and target price include any further weakness in economic and market conditions, and rising costs of raw materials, fuel and energy.

➤ Applying a price to book multiple of 1.55X to LEG's $12.94 book value at June 30, 2008, our 12-month target price is $20. This is a discount to LEG's five-year historical average -- warranted, in our view, by a lack of visibility for improved sales growth. With the stock's above-average dividend yield (recently 6.1%), we would hold the shares for their total return potential.

## Qualitative Risk Assessment

| LOW | MEDIUM | HIGH |
| --- | --- | --- |

Our risk assessment takes into account our view of LEG's long history of profitability and strong free cash flow, offset by the cyclical industry in which the company operates. We believe LEG faces execution risk in its planned corporate restructuring designed to improve returns on investment.

## Quantitative Evaluations

**S&P Quality Ranking**      B

| D | C | B- | B | B+ | A- | A | A+ |
| --- | --- | --- | --- | --- | --- | --- | --- |

**Relative Strength Rank**      MODERATE

56

LOWEST = 1      HIGHEST = 99

## Revenue/Earnings Data

### Revenue (Million $)

| | 1Q | 2Q | 3Q | 4Q | Year |
| --- | --- | --- | --- | --- | --- |
| 2008 | 998.3 | 1,063 | 1,132 | -- | -- |
| 2007 | 1,064 | 1,316 | 1,325 | 1,054 | 4,306 |
| 2006 | 1,378 | 1,403 | 1,415 | 1,311 | 5,505 |
| 2005 | 1,301 | 1,310 | 1,349 | 1,340 | 5,299 |
| 2004 | 1,187 | 1,278 | 1,338 | 1,282 | 5,086 |
| 2003 | 1,038 | 1,053 | 1,157 | 1,141 | 4,388 |

### Earnings Per Share ($)

| | | | | | |
| --- | --- | --- | --- | --- | --- |
| 2008 | 0.23 | 0.25 | 0.29 | E0.19 | E1.05 |
| 2007 | 0.31 | 0.30 | 0.36 | -0.71 | 0.28 |
| 2006 | 0.33 | 0.45 | 0.45 | 0.38 | 1.61 |
| 2005 | 0.37 | 0.41 | 0.28 | 0.24 | 1.30 |
| 2004 | 0.32 | 0.39 | 0.41 | 0.33 | 1.45 |
| 2003 | 0.25 | 0.24 | 0.26 | 0.30 | 1.05 |

Fiscal year ended Dec. 31. Next earnings report expected: Late January. EPS Estimates based on S&P Operating Earnings; historical GAAP earnings are as reported.

## Dividend Data (Dates: mm/dd Payment Date: mm/dd/yy)

| Amount ($) | Date Decl. | Ex-Div. Date | Stk. of Record | Payment Date |
| --- | --- | --- | --- | --- |
| 0.250 | 02/21 | 03/12 | 03/14 | 04/15/08 |
| 0.250 | 05/08 | 06/11 | 06/13 | 07/15/08 |
| 0.250 | 08/07 | 09/11 | 09/15 | 10/15/08 |
| 0.250 | 11/06 | 12/11 | 12/15 | 01/15/09 |

Dividends have been paid since 1939. Source: Company reports.

# Leggett & Platt Inc

**STANDARD &POOR'S**

## Business Summary November 10, 2008

CORPORATE OVERVIEW. Leggett & Platt, founded in 1883, is a diversified manufacturer that conceives, designs and produces a wide range of engineered components and products that can be found in most homes, offices, retail stores and automobiles.

LEG's business is organized into five business segments. Residential Furnishings, which accounted for 50% of 2007 sales (47% in 2006), consists of the Bedding, Home Furniture & Consumer Products, and Fabric, Foam & Fiber Groups. The Commercial Fixturing & Components segment, 18% of 2007 sales (17%), consists of Fixture & Display and Office Furniture Components. Industrial Materials, 17% of 2007 sales (13%), consists of the Wire and Tubing Groups, while Specialized Products, 15% (13%), consists of the Automotive, Machinery and Commercial Vehicles Groups, and Aluminum Products (divested in mid-2008), less than 1% (10%), makes up the balance.

Although no customer accounted for more than 5% of total company revenues in 2007, LEG has several significant customers within its segments. In Commercial Fixturing & Components, one customer accounted for 14% of 2007 segment sales. In Specialized Products, one customer provided 12% of segment sales.

PRIMARY BUSINESS DYNAMICS. In the past 20 years, about two-thirds of LEG's sales growth has come from acquisitions. Over the past 10 years, the average acquisition target had revenues of $15 million to $20 million, which the company believes serves to minimize the risk of any single acquisition. In 2007, LEG generated $614 million in cash from operations; the company expects it will need about $300 million annually to fund, collectively, capital expenditures and dividends. LEG believes much of the excess cash will be used to repurchase shares.

## Company Financials Fiscal Year Ended Dec. 31

| Per Share Data ($) | 2007 | 2006 | 2005 | 2004 | 2003 | 2002 | 2001 | 2000 | 1999 | 1998 |
|---|---|---|---|---|---|---|---|---|---|---|
| Tangible Book Value | 5.73 | 5.72 | 5.55 | 6.38 | 5.62 | 5.36 | 4.81 | 4.61 | 4.50 | 4.59 |
| Cash Flow | 1.16 | 2.67 | 2.18 | 2.35 | 1.89 | 1.99 | 1.92 | 2.18 | 2.19 | 1.87 |
| Earnings | 0.28 | 1.61 | 1.30 | 1.45 | 1.05 | 1.17 | 0.94 | 1.32 | 1.45 | 1.24 |
| S&P Core Earnings | 0.90 | 1.57 | 1.27 | 1.38 | 1.02 | 1.11 | 0.85 | NA | NA | NA |
| Dividends | 0.78 | 0.84 | 0.63 | 0.58 | 0.54 | 0.50 | 0.48 | 0.42 | 0.35 | 0.31 |
| Payout Ratio | NM | 52% | 48% | 40% | 51% | 43% | 51% | 32% | 24% | 25% |
| Prices:High | 24.73 | 27.04 | 29.61 | 30.68 | 23.69 | 27.40 | 24.45 | 22.56 | 28.31 | 28.75 |
| Prices:Low | 17.14 | 21.93 | 18.19 | 21.19 | 17.16 | 18.60 | 16.85 | 14.19 | 18.63 | 16.88 |
| P/E Ratio:High | 88 | 17 | 23 | 21 | 23 | 23 | 26 | 17 | 20 | 23 |
| P/E Ratio:Low | 61 | 14 | 14 | 15 | 16 | 16 | 18 | 11 | 13 | 14 |

| Income Statement Analysis (Million $) | 2007 | 2006 | 2005 | 2004 | 2003 | 2002 | 2001 | 2000 | 1999 | 1998 |
|---|---|---|---|---|---|---|---|---|---|---|
| Revenue | 4,306 | 5,505 | 5,299 | 5,086 | 4,388 | 4,272 | 4,114 | 4,276 | 3,779 | 3,370 |
| Operating Income | 492 | 666 | 605 | 622 | 520 | 582 | 558 | 660 | 650 | 555 |
| Depreciation | 157 | 175 | 171 | 177 | 167 | 165 | 197 | 173 | 149 | 128 |
| Interest Expense | 58.6 | 56.2 | 46.7 | 45.9 | 46.9 | 42.1 | 58.8 | 66.3 | 43.0 | 38.5 |
| Pretax Income | 128 | 435 | 356 | 423 | 315 | 364 | 297 | 419 | 463 | 396 |
| Effective Tax Rate | 60.3% | 30.9% | 29.4% | 32.5% | 34.7% | 35.9% | 36.9% | 36.9% | 37.2% | 37.3% |
| Net Income | 51.0 | 300 | 251 | 285 | 206 | 233 | 188 | 264 | 291 | 248 |
| S&P Core Earnings | 161 | 291 | 245 | 272 | 202 | 221 | 169 | NA | NA | NA |

| Balance Sheet & Other Financial Data (Million $) | 2007 | 2006 | 2005 | 2004 | 2003 | 2002 | 2001 | 2000 | 1999 | 1998 |
|---|---|---|---|---|---|---|---|---|---|---|
| Cash | 205 | 132 | 64.9 | 491 | 444 | 225 | 187 | 37.3 | 20.6 | 83.5 |
| Current Assets | 1,834 | 1,894 | 1,763 | 2,065 | 1,819 | 1,488 | 1,422 | 1,405 | 1,256 | 1,137 |
| Total Assets | 4,073 | 4,265 | 4,053 | 4,197 | 3,890 | 3,501 | 3,413 | 3,373 | 2,978 | 2,535 |
| Current Liabilities | 800 | 691 | 738 | 960 | 626 | 598 | 457 | 477 | 432 | 401 |
| Long Term Debt | 1,001 | 1,060 | 922 | 779 | 1,012 | 809 | 978 | 988 | 787 | 574 |
| Common Equity | 2,133 | 2,351 | 2,249 | 2,313 | 2,114 | 1,977 | 1,867 | 1,794 | 1,646 | 1,437 |
| Total Capital | 3,176 | 3,478 | 3,230 | 3,178 | 3,221 | 2,865 | 2,909 | 2,854 | 2,502 | 2,086 |
| Capital Expenditures | 149 | 166 | 164 | 157 | 137 | 124 | 128 | 170 | 159 | 148 |
| Cash Flow | 208 | 476 | 422 | 463 | 373 | 398 | 384 | 437 | 440 | 376 |
| Current Ratio | 2.3 | 2.7 | 2.4 | 2.2 | 2.9 | 2.5 | 3.1 | 2.9 | 2.9 | 2.8 |
| % Long Term Debt of Capitalization | 31.5 | 30.5 | 28.5 | 24.5 | 31.4 | 28.2 | 33.6 | 34.6 | 31.5 | 27.5 |
| % Net Income of Revenue | 1.2 | 5.5 | 4.7 | 5.6 | 4.7 | 5.5 | 4.6 | 6.2 | 7.7 | 7.4 |
| % Return on Assets | 1.2 | 7.2 | 6.1 | 7.1 | 5.6 | 6.7 | 5.5 | 8.3 | 10.5 | 10.7 |
| % Return on Equity | 2.3 | 13.1 | 11.0 | 12.9 | 10.1 | 12.1 | 10.3 | 15.4 | 18.8 | 19.0 |

Data as orig reptd.; bef. results of disc opers/spec. items. Per share data adj. for stk. divs.; EPS diluted. E-Estimated. NA-Not Available. NM-Not Meaningful. NR-Not Ranked. UR-Under Review.

**Office:** No. 1 Leggett Road, Carthage, MO 64836-9649.
**Telephone:** 417-358-8131.
**Email:** invest@leggett.com
**Website:** http://www.leggett.com

**Chrmn:** R.T. Fisher
**Pres & CEO:** D.S. Haffner
**COO & EVP:** K.G. Glassman
**SVP & CFO:** M.C. Flanigan

**SVP, Secy & General Counsel:** E.C. Jett
**Investor Contact:** S.R. McCoy (417-358-8131)
**Board Members:** R. F. Bentele, R. W. Clark, R. T. Enloe, III, R. T. Fisher, K. G. Glassman, D. S. Haffner, J. McClanathan, J. C. Odom, M. E. Purnell, Jr., P. A. Wood

**Founded:** 1883
**Domicile:** Missouri
**Employees:** 24,000

# Legg Mason Inc

| S&P Recommendation | HOLD ★★★☆☆ | Price | 12-Mo. Target Price | Investment Style |
|---|---|---|---|---|
| | | $15.65 (as of Nov 14, 2008) | $19.00 | Large-Cap Growth |

**GICS Sector** Financials
**Sub-Industry** Asset Management & Custody Banks

**Summary** This diversified investment manager serves individual and institutional investors through offices around the United States.

## Key Stock Statistics (Source S&P, Vickers, company reports)

| | | | | | | | |
|---|---|---|---|---|---|---|---|
| 52-Wk Range | $79.94 – 11.09 | S&P Oper. EPS 2009E | 0.52 | Market Capitalization(B) | $2.221 | Beta | 1.72 |
| Trailing 12-Month EPS | $-1.67 | S&P Oper. EPS 2010E | 3.31 | Yield (%) | 6.13 | S&P 3-Yr. Proj. EPS CAGR(%) | 29 |
| Trailing 12-Month P/E | NM | P/E on S&P Oper. EPS 2009E | 30.1 | Dividend Rate/Share | $0.96 | S&P Credit Rating | BBB+ |
| $10K Invested 5 Yrs Ago | $3,044 | Common Shares Outstg. (M) | 141.9 | Institutional Ownership (%) | 86 | | |

## Price Performance

30-Week Mov. Avg. ·····   10-Week Mov. Avg. —   **GAAP Earnings vs. Previous Year**   Volume Above Avg. ⅢⅢ STARS
12-Mo. Target Price —   Relative Strength —   ▲ Up   ▼ Down   ▶ No Change   Below Avg. ⅢⅢ ☆

Options: ASE, CBOE, P, Ph

Analysis prepared by **Matthew Albrecht** on November 10, 2008, when the stock traded at **$ 18.17**.

## Highlights

➤ We project assets under management to fall about 20% in FY 09 (Mar.) because significant fund underperformance in recent years, particularly at some flagship funds, has resulted in significant net outflows. Equity market declines have also tilted the asset mix toward fixed income and money market products, reducing the average management fee rate, and performance fees will be hard to come by, in our view. LM is expanding its distribution network around the globe and extending its reach with the wirehouses, but we do not anticipate a return to positive flows until fund performance improves. We expect a decline in operating revenues in FY 09 and FY 10, based on lower average asset balances.

➤ The distribution expense ratio decreased in FY 08, to about 42%, and we anticipate a similar ratio in FY 09 and FY 10. We expect costs to support structured investment vehicle investments to continue into FY 09, and we see further pressure on pretax margins in the current year before costs decline in FY 10, allowing for margin growth.

➤ We forecast operating EPS of $0.52 in FY 09 and $3.31 in FY 10.

## Investment Rationale/Risk

➤ We believe that Legg Mason has completed the integration of Citigroup's asset management division and that expected cost synergies have been realized. LM has overcome fund redemptions triggered by the deal, but is struggling with flows at some of its legacy funds. Equity fund performance has lagged peers, and continued concerns surrounding its exposure to SIVs and related costs result in what we see as its discounted valuation, which we think is accurately reflected in the recent price.

➤ Risks to our recommendation and target price include further market declines and poor relative investment performance.

➤ The shares recently traded at 34.9X our FY 09 EPS estimate but just 5.5X FY 10's estimate. Our 12-month target price of $19 is derived by applying a P/E multiple of 6.2X to our forward 12-month earnings projection, a discount to peer multiples due to recent fund underperformance and continued equity fund outflows.

## Qualitative Risk Assessment

| LOW | MEDIUM | HIGH |
|---|---|---|

Our risk assessment reflects our view of the company's strong market share and impressive relative investment performance, offset by industry cyclicality and integration challenges we foresee from recent acquisitions.

## Quantitative Evaluations

**S&P Quality Ranking**                                      A

| D | C | B- | B | B+ | A- | A | A+ |
|---|---|---|---|---|---|---|---|

**Relative Strength Rank**                              WEAK

| 18 |
|---|

LOWEST = 1                                    HIGHEST = 99

## Revenue/Earnings Data

**Revenue (Million $)**

| | 1Q | 2Q | 3Q | 4Q | Year |
|---|---|---|---|---|---|
| 2009 | 1,054 | 966.1 | -- | -- | -- |
| 2008 | 1,206 | 1,172 | 1,187 | 1,069 | 4,634 |
| 2007 | 1,038 | 1,031 | 1,133 | 1,142 | 4,344 |
| 2006 | 437.7 | 466.4 | 689.0 | 1,052 | 2,645 |
| 2005 | 554.9 | 585.5 | 658.3 | 690.8 | 2,490 |
| 2004 | 440.2 | 585.5 | 521.2 | 576.5 | 2,004 |

**Earnings Per Share ($)**

| | | | | | |
|---|---|---|---|---|---|
| 2009 | -0.22 | -0.74 | E0.74 | E0.74 | E0.52 |
| 2008 | 1.32 | 1.23 | 1.07 | -1.81 | 1.86 |
| 2007 | 1.08 | 1.00 | 1.21 | 1.19 | 4.48 |
| 2006 | 0.93 | 0.75 | 0.77 | 1.04 | 3.30 |
| 2005 | 0.76 | 0.81 | 0.98 | 0.98 | 3.53 |
| 2004 | 0.55 | 0.81 | 0.71 | 0.81 | 2.64 |

Fiscal year ended Mar. 31. Next earnings report expected: Late January. EPS Estimates based on S&P Operating Earnings; historical GAAP earnings are as reported.

## Dividend Data (Dates: mm/dd Payment Date: mm/dd/yy)

| Amount ($) | Date Decl. | Ex-Div. Date | Stk. of Record | Payment Date |
|---|---|---|---|---|
| 0.240 | 01/29 | 03/04 | 03/06 | 04/07/08 |
| 0.240 | 04/29 | 06/06 | 06/10 | 07/07/08 |
| 0.240 | 07/22 | 09/30 | 10/02 | 10/20/08 |
| 0.240 | 10/28 | 12/08 | 12/10 | 01/05/09 |

Dividends have been paid since 1983. Source: Company reports.

---

**Please read the Required Disclosures and Analyst Certification on the last page of this report.**

The McGraw-Hill Companies

# Legg Mason Inc

**STANDARD &POOR'S**

## Business Summary November 10, 2008

CORPORATE OVERVIEW. Legg Mason is a holding company which, through subsidiaries, is principally engaged in providing asset management and other related financial services to individuals, institutions, corporations, governments, and government agencies. We are pleased with the company's recent efforts to focus on its asset management business, which we think makes LM a much larger, broader, and more focused asset management company. At the end of FY 08 (Mar.), total assets under management were about $950 billion, down from about $969 billion a year earlier. Headquartered in Baltimore, MD, LM's offices are mainly in the U.S., as well as in the U.K., Canada and Singapore. At the end of March 2008, fixed income assets represented 53% of total assets under management, equity assets 29%, and liquidity assets 18%. We are pleased with the company's success in diversifying its product offerings, but would like to see more sector and industry-specific mutual funds.

We think LM has a diverse collection of asset management subsidiaries, which include Western Asset, Legg Mason Capital Management, Brandywine,

and Permal. LM's Asset Management business provides asset management services to institutional and individual clients and investment advisory services to company-sponsored investment funds. Investment products include proprietary mutual funds ranging from money market and fixed income funds to equity funds managed in a wide variety of investing styles, non-U.S. funds, and a number of unregistered, alternative investment products. LM's mutual funds group sponsors domestic and international equity, fixed income and money market mutual funds, closed-end funds, and other proprietary funds. Legg Mason Value Trust (LMVTX), managed by Bill Miller, had been the only equity mutual fund to have surpassed the S&P 500 Index for 15 straight years, with the streak ending in 2006. We do not doubt his investment strategy, however, and we still believe the fund will outperform the market frequently.

## Company Financials Fiscal Year Ended Mar. 31

| Per Share Data ($) | 2008 | 2007 | 2006 | 2005 | 2004 | 2003 | 2002 | 2001 | 2000 | 1999 |
|---|---|---|---|---|---|---|---|---|---|---|
| Tangible Book Value | NA | NM | NM | 11.66 | 6.50 | 3.32 | 1.52 | 8.25 | 7.07 | 5.89 |
| Cash Flow | NA | 5.95 | 3.90 | 3.83 | 2.62 | 1.85 | 1.49 | 1.53 | 1.56 | 1.03 |
| Earnings | 1.86 | 4.48 | 3.30 | 3.53 | 2.64 | 1.85 | 1.49 | 1.53 | 1.55 | 1.03 |
| S&P Core Earnings | 1.86 | 4.48 | 3.25 | 3.41 | 2.57 | 1.63 | 1.35 | 1.44 | NA | NA |
| Dividends | 0.81 | 0.69 | 0.40 | 0.37 | 0.29 | 0.29 | 0.23 | 0.20 | 0.18 | 0.15 |
| Payout Ratio | 44% | 15% | 12% | 11% | 11% | 15% | 16% | 13% | 12% | 15% |
| Calendar Year | 2007 | 2006 | 2005 | 2004 | 2003 | 2002 | 2001 | 2000 | 1999 | 1998 |
| Prices:High | 110.17 | 140.00 | 129.00 | 73.70 | 56.77 | 38.10 | 37.99 | 40.17 | 28.58 | 21.52 |
| Prices:Low | 68.35 | 81.01 | 68.10 | 48.95 | 29.47 | 24.74 | 22.83 | 20.46 | 17.62 | 11.54 |
| P/E Ratio:High | 59 | 31 | 39 | 21 | 22 | 21 | 25 | 26 | 18 | 24 |
| P/E Ratio:Low | 37 | 18 | 21 | 14 | 11 | 13 | 15 | 13 | 11 | 13 |

| Income Statement Analysis (Million $) | 2008 | 2007 | 2006 | 2005 | 2004 | 2003 | 2002 | 2001 | 2000 | 1999 |
|---|---|---|---|---|---|---|---|---|---|---|
| Commissions | NA | Nil | Nil | 358 | 344 | 317 | 331 | 359 | 363 | 279 |
| Interest Income | NA | 58.9 | 48.0 | 119 | 84.3 | 109 | 168 | 282 | 223 | 160 |
| Total Revenue | 4,634 | 4,344 | 2,645 | 2,490 | 2,004 | 1,615 | 1,579 | 1,536 | 1,371 | 1,046 |
| Interest Expense | NA | 71.5 | 52.6 | 80.8 | 63.2 | 87.1 | 127 | 175 | 134 | 94.9 |
| Pretax Income | 444 | 1,044 | 703 | 659 | 472 | 308 | 253 | 266 | 239 | 149 |
| Effective Tax Rate | 39.7% | 38.1% | 39.2% | 38.0% | 38.5% | 38.1% | 39.6% | 41.2% | 40.4% | 40.0% |
| Net Income | 268 | 646 | 434 | 408 | 291 | 191 | 153 | 156 | 143 | 89.3 |
| S&P Core Earnings | 268 | 646 | 421 | 394 | 283 | 168 | 138 | 146 | NA | NA |

| Balance Sheet & Other Financial Data (Million $) | 2008 | 2007 | 2006 | 2005 | 2004 | 2003 | 2002 | 2001 | 2000 | 1999 |
|---|---|---|---|---|---|---|---|---|---|---|
| Total Assets | 11,830 | 9,604 | 9,302 | 8,219 | 7,263 | 6,067 | 5,940 | 4,688 | 4,785 | 3,474 |
| Cash Items | 2,557 | 1,184 | 1,023 | 3,554 | 3,744 | 3,274 | 2,970 | 2,498 | 1,628 | 1,582 |
| Receivables | NA | 852 | 850 | 1,564 | 1,458 | 1,155 | 1,230 | 1,333 | 1,652 | 921 |
| Securities Owned | NA | 273 | 142 | 1,298 | 870 | 419 | 458 | 374 | 774 | 144 |
| Securities Borrowed | NA | Nil | Nil | 588 | 488 | 220 | 280 | 253 | 688 | 309 |
| Due Brokers & Customers | NA | Nil | Nil | 3,419 | 3,657 | 75.0 | 35.0 | 2,955 | 15.2 | 2,181 |
| Other Liabilities | NA | 1,079 | 1,633 | 1,108 | 764 | 462 | 410 | 328 | 334 | 541 |
| Capitalization:Debt | NA | 1,108 | 1,166 | 811 | 794 | 787 | 877 | 219 | 339 | 99.7 |
| Capitalization:Equity | 6,621 | 6,678 | 5,850 | 2,293 | 1,560 | 1,248 | 1,075 | 917 | 752 | 554 |
| Capitalization:Total | NA | 8,229 | 7,016 | 3,104 | 2,354 | 2,035 | 1,952 | 1,136 | 1,091 | 654 |
| % Return on Revenue | 5.8 | 14.9 | 16.4 | 19.2 | 17.5 | 14.7 | 12.3 | 13.3 | 14.1 | 12.9 |
| % Return on Assets | 2.5 | 6.8 | 5.0 | 5.3 | 4.4 | 3.2 | 2.9 | 3.3 | 3.5 | 2.8 |
| % Return on Equity | 4.1 | 10.2 | 10.7 | 21.2 | 20.7 | 16.4 | 15.4 | 18.7 | 21.8 | 16.9 |

Data as orig reptd.; bef. results of disc opers/spec. items. Per share data adj. for stk. divs.; EPS diluted. E-Estimated. NA-Not Available. NM-Not Meaningful. NR-Not Ranked. UR-Under Review.

**Office:** 100 Light Street, Baltimore, MD 21202-1099.
**Telephone:** 410-539-0000.
**Website:** http://www.leggmason.com
**Chrmn:** R.A. Mason

**Pres & CEO:** M.R. Fetting
**SVP, CFO, Chief Acctg Officer & Treas:** C.J. Daley, Jr.
**SVP & General Counsel:** T.P. Lemke
**Chief Admin Officer:** J.A. Sullivan

**Investor Contact:** M. Rosati (212-805-6036)
**Board Members:** H. L. Adams, R. E. Angelica, D. Beresford, M. R. Fetting, R. P. Hearn, J. E. Koerner, III, C. G. Krongard, R. A. Mason, S. C. Nuttall, W. A. Reed, M. M. Richardson, R. W. Schipke, K. L. Schmoke, N. J. St. George, R. M. Tarola, J. E. Ukrop

**Founded:** 1899
**Domicile:** Maryland
**Employees:** 4,220

# Lennar Corp

**STANDARD &POOR'S**

| S&P Recommendation **HOLD** ★★★☆☆ | Price $6.30 (as of Nov 14, 2008) | 12-Mo. Target Price $15.00 | Investment Style Large-Cap Blend |
|---|---|---|---|

**GICS Sector** Consumer Discretionary
**Sub-Industry** Homebuilding

**Summary** Lennar, one of the largest, most geographically diversified U.S. home builders, concentrates on moderately priced homes.

## Key Stock Statistics (Source S&P, Vickers, company reports)

| | | | | | | | |
|---|---|---|---|---|---|---|---|
| 52-Wk Range | $22.73– 5.31 | S&P Oper. EPS 2008**E** | -2.20 | Market Capitalization(B) | $0.817 | Beta | 1.68 |
| Trailing 12-Month EPS | $-9.79 | S&P Oper. EPS 2009**E** | -0.75 | Yield (%) | 2.54 | S&P 3-Yr. Proj. EPS CAGR(%) | 8 |
| Trailing 12-Month P/E | NM | P/E on S&P Oper. EPS 2008**E** | NM | Dividend Rate/Share | $0.16 | S&P Credit Rating | BB- |
| $10K Invested 5 Yrs Ago | $1,496 | Common Shares Outstg. (M) | 160.6 | Institutional Ownership (%) | NM | | |

## Price Performance

30-Week Mov. Avg. · · · 10-Week Mov. Avg. — **GAAP Earnings vs. Previous Year** Volume Above Avg. STARS
12-Mo. Target Price — Relative Strength — ▲ Up ▼ Down ► No Change Below Avg.

Options: ASE, CBOE, P, Ph

Analysis prepared by **Kenneth M. Leon, CPA** on September 23, 2008, when the stock traded at **$ 12.71**.

## Highlights

➤ Following a 37% revenue decline in FY 07 (Nov.), we project that revenues will decrease 57% in FY 08, reflecting a deepening of the housing downturn, and then decline a further 5% in FY 09. Home deliveries and average selling prices continued to be weak in the first nine months of FY 08. With low demand and perhaps worsening market conditions, we believe a lower backlog of contracts will lead to reduced future home deliveries in FY 09.

➤ We believe LEN faces weaker housing demand than we previously forecasted in its markets, which may lead to wider operating losses. However, we believe the size of asset writeoffs is beginning to decline significantly from peak levels in the second half of FY 07. Asset impairments were $132 million in the third quarter of FY 08 compared to $857 million, in the prior year's quarter.

➤ We estimate a loss per share of $2.20 for FY 08, including $265 million of inventory writedowns, and a loss of $0.75 a share for FY 09. We believe that additional joint venture investment writedowns are possible over the next six months, although LEN continues to reduce its exposure in this area.

## Investment Rationale/Risk

➤ While the company has posted just under $4 billion of asset impairments since the beginning of 2006, we believe writeoffs will continue but ease in FY 09. We think LEN's joint venture with Morgan Stanley (formed in December 2007), whereby that firm paid $525 million to LEN for an 80% equity stake in acquired land, will support LEN's liquidity to meet its working capital and debt obligations.

➤ Risks to our recommendation and target price include higher levels for 30-year mortgage interest rates and the possibility that LEN's large land position might be exposed to large asset writedowns if industry conditions weaken further than we expect.

➤ With $1.8 billion of asset impairments in the November 2007 quarter, followed by $338 million in the next three quarters, we believe the company's net tangible book value of $21.65 may not decline as rapidly this year as in FY 07. Applying a price-to-book value multiple of slightly below 0.7X, near that of large homebuilders, our 12-month target price is $15.

## Qualitative Risk Assessment

| LOW | MEDIUM | **HIGH** |
|---|---|---|

Our risk assessment reflects that despite LEN being among the least leveraged homebuilders in our coverage universe, the company's off balance sheet operations, including a 50%-owned development joint venture and a relatively significant proportion of land controlled through option contracts, suggest to us relatively limited financial transparency.

## Quantitative Evaluations

**S&P Quality Ranking** B+

| D | C | B- | B | **B+** | A- | A | A+ |
|---|---|---|---|---|---|---|---|

**Relative Strength Rank** WEAK

24

LOWEST = 1 HIGHEST = 99

## Revenue/Earnings Data

**Revenue (Million $)**

| | 1Q | 2Q | 3Q | 4Q | Year |
|---|---|---|---|---|---|
| 2008 | 1,063 | 1,128 | 1,107 | -- | -- |
| 2007 | 2,792 | 2,876 | 2,342 | 2,177 | 10,187 |
| 2006 | 3,241 | 4,578 | 4,182 | 4,266 | 16,267 |
| 2005 | 2,406 | 2,933 | 3,498 | 5,030 | 13,867 |
| 2004 | 1,863 | 2,343 | 2,748 | 3,551 | 10,505 |
| 2003 | 1,600 | 2,103 | 2,268 | 2,936 | 8,908 |

**Earnings Per Share ($)**

| | 1Q | 2Q | 3Q | 4Q | Year |
|---|---|---|---|---|---|
| 2008 | -0.56 | -0.76 | -0.56 | E-0.32 | E-2.20 |
| 2007 | 0.43 | -1.55 | -3.25 | -7.92 | -12.31 |
| 2006 | 1.58 | 2.00 | 1.30 | -1.24 | 3.69 |
| 2005 | 1.17 | 1.55 | 2.06 | 3.54 | 8.17 |
| 2004 | 0.84 | 1.22 | 1.36 | 2.29 | 5.70 |
| 2003 | 0.68 | 1.02 | 1.22 | 1.69 | 4.65 |

Fiscal year ended Nov. 30. Next earnings report expected: Late January. EPS Estimates based on S&P Operating Earnings; historical GAAP earnings are as reported.

## Dividend Data (Dates: mm/dd Payment Date: mm/dd/yy)

| Amount ($) | Date Decl. | Ex-Div. Date | Stk. of Record | Payment Date |
|---|---|---|---|---|
| 0.160 | 01/28 | 02/06 | 02/08 | 02/19/08 |
| 0.160 | 04/08 | 05/01 | 05/05 | 05/15/08 |
| 0.160 | 07/01 | 07/22 | 07/24 | 08/05/08 |
| 0.040 | 10/07 | 10/21 | 10/23 | 11/13/08 |

Dividends have been paid since 1978. Source: Company reports.

# Lennar Corp

STANDARD &POOR'S

## Business Summary September 23, 2008

CORPORATE OVERVIEW. Lennar Corp., one of the largest homebuilders in the U.S. (based on FY 07 (Nov.) U.S. home closings), constructs homes for first-time, move-up and active adult buyers, and also provides various financial services. It takes part in all phases of planning and building, and subcontracts nearly all development and construction work.

The financial services division provides mortgage financing, title insurance, closing services and insurance agency services for LEN homebuyers and others, and sells the loans it originates in the secondary mortgage market.

CORPORATE STRATEGY. Lennar greatly expanded its operations through the May 2000 purchase of U.S. Home Corp. (UH), and maintained an active acquisition program for several years. The company entered the North Carolina and South Carolina markets, and extended its positions in Colorado and Arizona, through the acquisition of various operations of Fortress Group in two separate transactions in late 2001 and mid-2002. It expanded its California business by acquiring Pacific Century Homes and Cambridge Homes (combined annual deliveries of about 2,000 homes) in 2002.

In 2005, the company entered the metropolitan New York City and Boston markets by acquiring rights to develop a portfolio of properties in New Jersey facing mid-town Manhattan and waterfront properties near Boston. It also entered the Reno, NV, market through the acquisition of Barker Coleman. In addition, LEN expanded its presence in Jacksonville through the acquisition of Admiral Homes that same year.

IMPACT OF MAJOR DEVELOPMENTS. In July 2008, President Bush signing into law a sweeping housing bill designed to revive the stagnant housing market and bolster the U.S. economy. LEN is particularly positive about the bill's $7,500 tax credit for first-time home buyers. This provision has the potential to create demand among first-time buyers who have been undecided about buying a new home. And if first-time buyers enter the market, then existing homeowners may trade up, creating an upward spiral of demand.

## Company Financials Fiscal Year Ended Nov. 30

### Per Share Data ($)

| | 2007 | 2006 | 2005 | 2004 | 2003 | 2002 | 2001 | 2000 | 1999 | 1998 |
|---|---|---|---|---|---|---|---|---|---|---|
| Tangible Book Value | 25.67 | 34.42 | 32.09 | 24.05 | 20.68 | 15.71 | 12.14 | 8.92 | 7.08 | 6.16 |
| Cash Flow | -11.95 | 4.03 | 8.60 | 5.98 | 5.11 | 4.32 | 3.45 | 2.23 | 1.69 | 1.44 |
| Earnings | -12.31 | 3.69 | 8.17 | 5.70 | 4.65 | 3.86 | 3.01 | 1.82 | 1.37 | 1.25 |
| S&P Core Earnings | -12.36 | 3.62 | 8.10 | 5.63 | 4.61 | 3.83 | 2.90 | NA | NA | NA |
| Dividends | 0.64 | 0.64 | 0.57 | 0.39 | 0.14 | 0.03 | 0.03 | 0.03 | 0.03 | 0.03 |
| Payout Ratio | NM | 17% | 7% | 7% | 3% | 1% | 1% | 1% | 2% | 2% |
| Prices:High | 56.54 | 66.44 | 68.86 | 57.20 | 50.90 | 31.99 | 24.94 | 19.69 | 13.94 | 18.09 |
| Prices:Low | 14.00 | 38.66 | 50.30 | 40.30 | 24.10 | 21.60 | 15.52 | 7.63 | 6.53 | 7.44 |
| P/E Ratio:High | NM | 18 | 8 | 10 | 11 | 8 | 8 | 11 | 10 | 15 |
| P/E Ratio:Low | NM | 10 | 6 | 7 | 5 | 6 | 5 | 4 | 5 | 6 |

### Income Statement Analysis (Million $)

| | 2007 | 2006 | 2005 | 2004 | 2003 | 2002 | 2001 | 2000 | 1999 | 1998 |
|---|---|---|---|---|---|---|---|---|---|---|
| Revenue | 10,187 | 16,267 | 13,867 | 10,505 | 8,908 | 7,320 | 6,029 | 4,707 | 3,119 | 2,417 |
| Operating Income | -2,626 | 941 | 2,124 | 1,426 | 1,158 | 1,094 | 868 | 533 | 382 | NA |
| Depreciation | 57.0 | 56.5 | 79.6 | 55.6 | 54.5 | 72.4 | 68.7 | 58.5 | 47.7 | 24.4 |
| Interest Expense | Nil | Nil | Nil | Nil | 141 | 146 | 120 | 98.6 | 48.9 | 47.6 |
| Pretax Income | -3,081 | 956 | 2,205 | 1,519 | 1,207 | 876 | 679 | 376 | 285 | 240 |
| Effective Tax Rate | NM | 36.5% | 37.0% | 37.8% | 37.8% | 37.8% | 38.5% | 39.0% | 39.5% | 40.0% |
| Net Income | -1,942 | 594 | 1,344 | 946 | 751 | 545 | 418 | 229 | 173 | 144 |
| S&P Core Earnings | -1,948 | 582 | 1,331 | 934 | 744 | 541 | 404 | NA | NA | NA |

### Balance Sheet & Other Financial Data (Million $)

| | 2007 | 2006 | 2005 | 2004 | 2003 | 2002 | 2001 | 2000 | 1999 | 1998 |
|---|---|---|---|---|---|---|---|---|---|---|
| Cash | 642 | 778 | 910 | 1,322 | 1,201 | 731 | 824 | 288 | 83.3 | 34.7 |
| Current Assets | NA | NA | NA | NA | NA | NA | NA | NA | NA | NA |
| Total Assets | 9,103 | 12,408 | 12,541 | 9,165 | 6,775 | 5,756 | 4,714 | 3,778 | 2,058 | 1,918 |
| Current Liabilities | NA | NA | NA | NA | NA | NA | NA | NA | NA | NA |
| Long Term Debt | 2,295 | 2,614 | 2,565 | 2,918 | 1,552 | 1,521 | 1,488 | 1,240 | 524 | 799 |
| Common Equity | 3,822 | 5,702 | 5,251 | 4,053 | 3,264 | 2,229 | 1,659 | 1,229 | 881 | 716 |
| Total Capital | 6,146 | 8,283 | 7,895 | 6,971 | 4,816 | 3,751 | 3,147 | 2,468 | 1,405 | 1,515 |
| Capital Expenditures | Nil | 26.8 | 21.7 | 27.4 | 29.6 | 4.09 | 13.1 | 16.0 | 15.3 | 13.2 |
| Cash Flow | -1,885 | 650 | 1,424 | 1,001 | 806 | 618 | 487 | 288 | 220 | 168 |
| Current Ratio | 5.5 | 4.3 | 5.9 | 3.0 | 3.3 | 2.9 | 3.6 | 2.5 | 2.8 | NA |
| % Long Term Debt of Capitalization | 37.3 | 31.2 | 32.5 | 41.9 | 32.2 | 40.6 | 47.3 | 50.2 | 37.3 | 52.7 |
| % Net Income of Revenue | NM | 3.7 | 9.7 | 9.0 | 8.4 | 7.4 | 6.9 | 4.9 | 5.5 | 6.0 |
| % Return on Assets | NM | 4.8 | 12.4 | 11.9 | 12.0 | 10.4 | 9.8 | 7.9 | 8.7 | 8.8 |
| % Return on Equity | NM | 10.8 | 28.9 | 25.8 | 27.4 | 28.0 | 28.9 | 21.7 | 21.6 | 25.0 |

Data as orig reptd.; bef. results of disc opers/spec. items. Per share data adj. for stk. divs.; EPS diluted. E-Estimated. NA-Not Available. NM-Not Meaningful. NR-Not Ranked. UR-Under Review.

**Office:** 700 NW 107th Ave, Miami, FL 33172.
**Telephone:** 305-559-4000.
**Website:** http://www.lennar.com
**Pres & CEO:** S. Miller

**COO:** J.M. Jaffe
**CFO:** B.E. Gross
**Chief Acctg Officer & Treas:** D.J. Bessette
**Secy & General Counsel:** M. Sustana

**Investor Contact:** M.H. Ames (800-741-4663)
**Board Members:** I. Bolotin, S. Gerard, S. W. Hudson, R. K. Landon, S. Lapidus, S. Miller, D. E. Shalala, J. Sonnenfeld

**Founded:** 1954
**Domicile:** Delaware
**Employees:** 6,934

# STANDARD &POOR'S

# Leucadia National Corp

| S&P Recommendation | HOLD ★★★☆☆ | Price $19.88 (as of Nov 14, 2008) | 12-Mo. Target Price $26.00 | Investment Style Large-Cap Growth |
|---|---|---|---|---|

**GICS Sector** Financials
**Sub-Industry** Multi-Sector Holdings

**Summary** This diversified holding company has subsidiaries engaged in manufacturing, real estate, medical product development, gaming entertainment, mining, and energy.

## Key Stock Statistics (Source S&P, Vickers, company reports)

| | | | | | | | | |
|---|---|---|---|---|---|---|---|---|
| 52-Wk Range | $56.90– 16.41 | S&P Oper. EPS 2008**E** | -2.00 | Market Capitalization(B) | $4.630 | Beta | | 1.28 |
| Trailing 12-Month EPS | $2.49 | S&P Oper. EPS 2009**E** | 0.50 | Yield (%) | 1.26 | S&P 3-Yr. Proj. EPS CAGR(%) | | 5 |
| Trailing 12-Month P/E | 8.0 | P/E on S&P Oper. EPS 2008**E** | NM | Dividend Rate/Share | $0.25 | S&P Credit Rating | | BB+ |
| $10K Invested 5 Yrs Ago | $14,683 | Common Shares Outstg. (M) | 232.9 | Institutional Ownership (%) | 61 | | | |

## Price Performance

30-Week Mov. Avg. · · · · 10-Week Mov. Avg. - - - GAAP Earnings vs. Previous Year    Volume Above Avg. ▮▮▮ STARS
12-Mo. Target Price —    Relative Strength — ▲ Up ▼ Down ► No Change    Below Avg. ▮▮▮

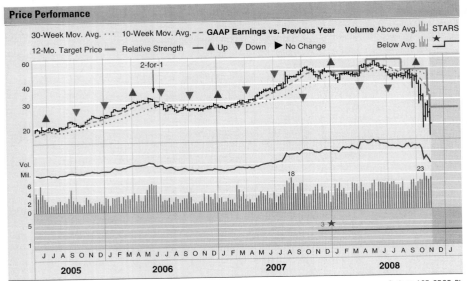

Options: ASE, CBOE, Ph

## Highlights

➤ The 12-month target price for LUK has recently been changed to $26.00 from $32.00. The Highlights section of this Stock Report will be updated accordingly.

## Investment Rationale/Risk

➤ The Investment Rationale/Risk section of this Stock Report will be updated shortly. For the latest News story on LUK from MarketScope, see below.

➤ 11/07/08 11:16 am ET ... S&P KEEPS HOLD OPINION ON SHARES OF LEUCADIA NATIONAL (LUK 22.98***): LUK reports Q3 EPS of $0.37 vs. $0.02, compared with our $0.32 estimate. However, a major part of its profit was related to its investment in Jeffries Group (JEF 14.10**) and other holdings that increased in Q3. Subsequently, the value of these assets has fallen sharply. Therefore, we expect a large loss in Q4 and our '08 estimate is now for a loss of $2.00, cut from EPS of $0.25. We have also lowered our '09 forecast to EPS of $0.50 from $0.75. We are reducing our 12-month target price to $26 from $32 to reflect a decline in estimated book value. /S.Benway-CFA

## Qualitative Risk Assessment

| LOW | MEDIUM | HIGH |
|---|---|---|

Our risk assessment reflects the broad diversity of the company's investments and what we view as a strong management team, offset by its exposure to certain development stage businesses.

## Quantitative Evaluations

**S&P Quality Ranking**    B-

| D | C | B- | B | B+ | A- | A | A+ |
|---|---|---|---|---|---|---|---|

**Relative Strength Rank**    WEAK

21

LOWEST = 1    HIGHEST = 99

## Revenue/Earnings Data

### Revenue (Million $)

| | 1Q | 2Q | 3Q | 4Q | Year |
|---|---|---|---|---|---|
| 2008 | 333.1 | 337.6 | 251.6 | -- | -- |
| 2007 | 197.2 | 344.0 | 331.2 | 282.6 | 1,155 |
| 2006 | 291.6 | 224.4 | 170.2 | 176.4 | 862.7 |
| 2005 | 121.3 | 258.7 | 343.3 | 317.9 | 1,041 |
| 2004 | 509.7 | 569.6 | 633.6 | 549.2 | 2,262 |
| 2003 | 56.90 | 67.30 | 76.09 | 356.1 | 556.4 |

### Earnings Per Share ($)

| | | | | | |
|---|---|---|---|---|---|
| 2008 | -0.43 | -0.76 | 0.36 | E-1.80 | E-2.00 |
| 2007 | 0.04 | 0.12 | 0.01 | 1.87 | 2.09 |
| 2006 | 0.37 | 0.17 | 0.02 | 0.03 | 0.60 |
| 2005 | -0.03 | 5.23 | 0.22 | -0.10 | 5.36 |
| 2004 | -0.06 | 0.17 | 0.34 | 0.24 | 0.70 |
| 2003 | -0.08 | 0.06 | 0.30 | 0.16 | 0.46 |

Fiscal year ended Dec. 31. Next earnings report expected: Early March. EPS Estimates based on S&P Operating Earnings; historical GAAP earnings are as reported.

## Dividend Data (Dates: mm/dd Payment Date: mm/dd/yy)

| Amount ($) | Date Decl. | Ex-Div. Date | Stk. of Record | Payment Date |
|---|---|---|---|---|
| 0.250 | 12/04 | 12/13 | 12/17 | 12/28/07 |

Dividends have been paid since 1999. Source: Company reports.

The McGraw-Hill Companies

# Leucadia National Corp

STANDARD
&POOR'S

## Business Summary November 06, 2008

CORPORATE OVERVIEW. Leucadia National is a diversified holding company that is involved in a wide variety of businesses, including timber and plastics manufacturing, telecommunications, real estate activities, medical product development, and winery operations. The company also owns equity interests in operating businesses and investment partnerships including gaming entertainment, land-based contract oil and gas drilling, real estate activities, and development of a copper mine in Spain and a major iron ore project in Australia. In addition, Leucadia has significant investments in several partnerships that invest in domestic and international debt and equity securities. Revenues by major business segment in 2007 were as follows: Telecommunications 31%; Idaho Timber 25%; Conwed Plastics 9%; property management and services 7%; and gaming 3%.

CORPORATE STRATEGY. Leucadia's approach to its investments is to focus on return on investment and cash flow to build long-term shareholder value. Management continuously evaluates the retention and disposition of its existing operations, and investigates possible acquisition targets. In selecting potential acquisitions, LUK seeks assets and companies that are troubled or out of favor, and that are selling below apparent value as a result. We expect the composition of Leucadia's assets to change continuously as certain businesses are divested and others are acquired.

PRIMARY BUSINESS DYNAMICS. Leucadia's telecommunications business is conducted through STi Prepaid and consists primarily of prepaid international long distance calling cards. Consumers located in the U.S. who make international calls often use calling cards because they provide lower rates than those offered by traditional long distance providers. STi Prepaid's cards are primarily marketed to ethnic communities in urban areas. Through its Idaho Timber business, the company remanufactures dimension lumber that is used in general construction and home improvement. Idaho Timber purchases low quality lumber and upgrades it into higher grade products through cutting, trimming and planing. This unit also makes boards for home centers and decking products. Demand in this business is closely tied to the level of housing starts and home size.

## Company Financials Fiscal Year Ended Dec. 31

### Per Share Data ($)

| | 2007 | 2006 | 2005 | 2004 | 2003 | 2002 | 2001 | 2000 | 1999 | 1998 |
|---|---|---|---|---|---|---|---|---|---|---|
| Tangible Book Value | 24.66 | 17.72 | 16.87 | 17.32 | 10.04 | 8.78 | 7.05 | 7.26 | 6.58 | 9.97 |
| Cash Flow | 2.26 | 0.75 | NA | NA | NA | NA | NA | NA | NA | NA |
| Earnings | 2.09 | 0.60 | 5.36 | 0.70 | 0.46 | 0.91 | 0.39 | 0.69 | 1.09 | 0.24 |
| S&P Core Earnings | 1.79 | NA | 4.69 | 0.05 | 0.42 | 1.05 | 0.27 | NA | NA | NA |
| Dividends | 0.25 | 0.25 | 0.13 | 0.13 | 0.08 | 0.08 | 0.08 | 0.08 | 4.53 | Nil |
| Payout Ratio | 12% | 42% | 2% | 18% | 18% | 9% | 21% | 12% | NM | Nil |
| Prices:High | 52.67 | 32.62 | 24.64 | 23.50 | 15.40 | 13.42 | 11.90 | 12.50 | 11.13 | 13.71 |
| Prices:Low | 26.52 | 23.26 | 16.20 | 15.02 | 10.86 | 9.21 | 8.77 | 6.88 | 6.71 | 8.75 |
| P/E Ratio:High | 25 | 54 | 5 | 34 | 34 | 15 | 31 | 18 | 10 | 56 |
| P/E Ratio:Low | 13 | 39 | 3 | 21 | 24 | 10 | 22 | 10 | 6 | 36 |

### Income Statement Analysis (Million $)

| | 2007 | 2006 | 2005 | 2004 | 2003 | 2002 | 2001 | 2000 | 1999 | 1998 |
|---|---|---|---|---|---|---|---|---|---|---|
| Revenue | 1,155 | 863 | 1,041 | 2,262 | 556 | 242 | 375 | 715 | 710 | 507 |
| Operating Income | 58.1 | 222 | NA | NA | NA | NA | NA | NA | NA | NA |
| Depreciation | 49.8 | 43.6 | 190 | 233 | 65.7 | 18.7 | 17.5 | 21.4 | 15.4 | 10.3 |
| Interest Expense | 112 | 79.4 | 68.4 | 96.8 | 43.6 | 33.5 | 55.2 | 57.7 | 50.7 | 45.1 |
| Pretax Income | -79.0 | 172 | 93.0 | 132 | 42.9 | 13.2 | 53.7 | 193 | 243 | 29.4 |
| Effective Tax Rate | 708.9% | 24.4% | NM | NM | NM | NM | NM | 37.6% | 18.3% | NM |
| Net Income | 481 | 130 | 1,224 | 152 | 84.4 | 153 | 64.8 | 115 | 193 | 46.2 |
| S&P Core Earnings | 411 | -9.43 | 1,071 | 5.47 | 77.7 | 177 | 45.7 | NA | NA | NA |

### Balance Sheet & Other Financial Data (Million $)

| | 2007 | 2006 | 2005 | 2004 | 2003 | 2002 | 2001 | 2000 | 1999 | 1998 |
|---|---|---|---|---|---|---|---|---|---|---|
| Cash | 1,440 | 3,430 | 3,063 | 2,781 | 2,033 | 1,044 | 1,183 | 1,613 | 1,467 | 2,230 |
| Current Assets | 1,720 | 1,366 | NA | NA | NA | NA | NA | NA | NA | NA |
| Total Assets | 8,127 | 5,304 | 5,261 | 4,800 | 4,397 | 2,542 | 2,577 | 3,144 | 3,070 | 3,959 |
| Current Liabilities | 460 | 327 | NA | NA | NA | NA | NA | NA | NA | NA |
| Long Term Debt | 2,004 | 975 | NA | NA | NA | NA | NA | NA | NA | NA |
| Common Equity | 5,570 | 3,893 | 3,662 | 2,259 | 2,134 | 1,487 | 1,195 | 1,204 | 1,122 | 1,853 |
| Total Capital | 7,596 | 4,887 | 4,665 | 3,760 | 3,307 | 1,893 | 1,666 | 1,631 | 1,720 | 2,685 |
| Capital Expenditures | 135 | 111 | 136 | 97.4 | 84.7 | NA | NA | NA | NA | NA |
| Cash Flow | 531 | 173 | NA | NA | NA | NA | NA | NA | NA | NA |
| Current Ratio | 3.7 | 4.2 | 4.7 | 3.1 | 2.1 | 8.4 | 5.6 | 4.5 | 3.5 | 4.6 |
| % Long Term Debt of Capitalization | 26.4 | 19.9 | 20.8 | 38.8 | 34.7 | 17.5 | 25.7 | 24.4 | 28.6 | 26.9 |
| % Net Income of Revenue | 41.6 | 15.7 | 117.6 | 6.8 | 15.2 | 63.1 | 16.2 | 16.8 | 27.3 | 9.1 |
| % Return on Assets | 77.2 | 2.5 | 24.3 | 3.3 | 2.4 | 6.0 | 2.3 | 3.7 | 5.5 | 1.1 |
| % Return on Equity | 10.2 | 3.4 | 41.4 | 6.9 | 4.7 | 11.4 | 5.4 | 9.9 | 13.0 | 2.5 |

Data as orig reptd.; bef. results of disc opers/spec. items. Per share data adj. for stk. divs.; EPS diluted. E-Estimated. NA-Not Available. NM-Not Meaningful. NR-Not Ranked. UR-Under Review.

Office: 315 Park Ave S Fl, New York, NY 10010.
Telephone: 212-460-1900.
Chrmn & CEO: I.M. Cumming
Pres & COO: J.S. Steinberg

CFO: J.A. Orlando
Chief Acctg Officer & Cntlr: B.L. Lowenthal
Treas: R.J. Nittoli
Investor Contact: L.E. Ulbrandt (212-460-1900)

Board Members: I. M. Cumming, P. M. Dougan, L. D. Glaubinger, A. J. Hirschfield, J. E. Jordan, J. C. Keil, J. C. Nichols, III, J. S. Steinberg

Founded: 1854
Domicile: New York
Employees: 4,057

The McGraw-Hill Companies

# Lexmark International Inc.

| S&P Recommendation | HOLD ★★★☆☆ | Price | 12-Mo. Target Price | Investment Style |
|---|---|---|---|---|
| | | $23.97 (as of Nov 14, 2008) | $29.00 | Large-Cap Growth |

**GICS Sector** Information Technology
**Sub-Industry** Computer Storage & Peripherals

**Summary** Lexmark develops, manufactures and supplies laser and inkjet printers and associated consumable supplies for the office and home markets.

## Key Stock Statistics (Source S&P, Vickers, company reports)

| | | | | | | | | |
|---|---|---|---|---|---|---|---|---|
| 52-Wk Range | $37.88– 22.13 | S&P Oper. EPS 2008E | 2.92 | Market Capitalization(B) | $1.879 | Beta | 1.20 |
| Trailing 12-Month EPS | $3.46 | S&P Oper. EPS 2009E | 2.40 | Yield (%) | Nil | S&P 3-Yr. Proj. EPS CAGR(%) | 1 |
| Trailing 12-Month P/E | 6.9 | P/E on S&P Oper. EPS 2008E | 8.2 | Dividend Rate/Share | Nil | S&P Credit Rating | NA |
| $10K Invested 5 Yrs Ago | $3,154 | Common Shares Outstg. (M) | 78.4 | Institutional Ownership (%) | NM | | |

## Price Performance

30-Week Mov. Avg. ··· 10-Week Mov. Avg. — **GAAP Earnings vs. Previous Year** Volume Above Avg. STARS
12-Mo. Target Price — Relative Strength — ▲ Up ▼ Down ► No Change Below Avg.

Options: ASE, CBOE, P, Ph

Analysis prepared by **Thomas W. Smith, CFA** on November 05, 2008, when the stock traded at **$ 27.09**.

## Highlights

➤ We project that revenues will decrease about 8% in 2008, and decline 5% in 2009, continuing a recent trend of lackluster top-line performance. We believe results will benefit from new product introductions, continued growth from laser units and supplies, and further penetration of its enterprise customer base. However, the inkjet printer business has been slowing, and we expect the pricing environment to remain intense, given updated offerings by competitors.

➤ We look for operating margins to widen a bit for 2008, as the company follows through on a restructuring plan announced in October 2007, before narrowing back in 2009 on lower volumes. We view LXK as on track to achieve annual cost savings from the restructuring of $40 million in 2008, and $70 million annually thereafter. However, we think margin results could be volatile, based on changes in LXK's business mix. The company took on new debt in May 2008, and we expect additional share repurchase activity.

➤ We forecast 2008 EPS of $2.92, excluding restructuring charges. We project 2009 EPS of $2.40.

## Investment Rationale/Risk

➤ We think that LXK has been innovative in its product line in the past, owns some important intellectual property, and should be able to expand its branded products and laser printer businesses. We believe that market conditions supporting low-end systems will continue to pressure the company's growth, but also foresee LXK making progress on cost controls. Although we view LXK as a potential takeover candidate, we believe that it has some contractual agreements that may prevent such a deal from occurring.

➤ Risks to our recommendation and target price include the possibility that competition from Hewlett-Packard (HPQ: strong buy, $38) will be greater than we anticipate, that savings from restructuring come in below our estimates, and that penetration of high-growth segments is slower than we project.

➤ Our 12-month target price of $29 reflects our P/E analysis. We apply a target P/E of 14X, which is toward the low end of a five-year historical range for LXK to reflect a slow revenue environment that we foresee, to our 12-month forward EPS estimate of $2.04.

## Qualitative Risk Assessment

| LOW | MEDIUM | HIGH |
|---|---|---|

Our risk assessment reflects what we see as a difficult competitive pricing environment in the printer market, offset by our view of LXK's strides in improving its product portfolio and cost position.

## Quantitative Evaluations

**S&P Quality Ranking** B+

| D | C | B- | B | B+ | A- | A | A+ |
|---|---|---|---|---|---|---|---|

**Relative Strength Rank** MODERATE

56

LOWEST = 1    HIGHEST = 99

## Revenue/Earnings Data

**Revenue (Million $)**

| | 1Q | 2Q | 3Q | 4Q | Year |
|---|---|---|---|---|---|
| 2008 | 1,175 | 1,139 | 1,131 | -- | -- |
| 2007 | 1,261 | 1,208 | 1,195 | 1,310 | 4,974 |
| 2006 | 1,275 | 1,229 | 1,235 | 1,369 | 5,108 |
| 2005 | 1,358 | 1,283 | 1,216 | 1,365 | 5,222 |
| 2004 | 1,256 | 1,248 | 1,266 | 1,544 | 5,314 |
| 2003 | 1,108 | 1,120 | 1,157 | 1,370 | 4,755 |

**Earnings Per Share ($)**

| | | | | | |
|---|---|---|---|---|---|
| 2008 | 1.07 | 0.89 | 0.42 | E0.50 | E2.92 |
| 2007 | 0.95 | 0.67 | 0.48 | 1.04 | 3.14 |
| 2006 | 0.78 | 0.74 | 0.85 | 0.91 | 3.27 |
| 2005 | 0.96 | 0.64 | 0.59 | 0.71 | 2.91 |
| 2004 | 0.91 | 1.02 | 1.17 | 1.18 | 4.28 |
| 2003 | 0.73 | 0.77 | 0.79 | 1.05 | 3.34 |

Fiscal year ended Dec. 31. Next earnings report expected: Late January. EPS Estimates based on S&P Operating Earnings; historical GAAP earnings are as reported.

## Dividend Data

No cash dividends have been paid.

# Lexmark International Inc.

STANDARD &POOR'S

## Business Summary November 05, 2008

CORPORATE OVERVIEW. Lexmark shook up the printer industry with the introduction of the first desktop color printer priced under $100 with its November 1997 launch of the $99 color inkjet printer, aimed at building brand awareness and an installed base. We think LXK's competitive advantage in the past was its low cost structure and its ability to price aggressively. However, in recent quarters, it has been on the defensive, in our view, as peers have undercut its prices and LXK's product mix was not focused on some of the more compelling printer areas. Going forward, LXK management believes that its commitment to R&D should bear fruit and help revive unit growth and subsequently high-margin supplies sales, but we view this as a multi-year process. New products in 2007 included a new family of wireless inkjet printers.

The company operates mainly in two segments. The Business segment represented 60% of sales in 2007 (56% of 2006 sales) and saw revenue rise 5% to nearly $3 billion. Laser printer hardware unit shipments decreased 3% in 2007, despite strength in laser multi-function printers and branded workgroup printers. The Consumer segment represented 40% of 2007 sales (44%), and suffered a 12% revenue decline to nearly $2 billion. Inkjet hardware unit shipments fell 18% in 2007 and average selling prices per unit declined. Part of the slowdown was based on a planned transition to more favorable printer place-

ments in every geographic territory.

Lexmark distributes to Business customers via many channels, including the company's network of authorized distributors. The company distributes to Consumer customers through retail outlets worldwide. The company also sells through alliances and OEM arrangements. One customer, Dell, accounted for 14% of revenues in 2007, down from 15% in 2006.

MARKET PROFILE. The company estimates the total distributed office and home printing revenue market opportunity for hardware, supplies and related services was about $95 billion in 2007. Informed by industry market research, we project this market to grow at a compound annual growth rate (CAGR) of approximately 4% over the next few years. A key trend we see is that printer vendors are cutting prices on printers to expand their installed base and subsequently capitalize on the growth in margin-rich supplies sales.

## Company Financials Fiscal Year Ended Dec. 31

| Per Share Data ($) | 2007 | 2006 | 2005 | 2004 | 2003 | 2002 | 2001 | 2000 | 1999 | 1998 |
|---|---|---|---|---|---|---|---|---|---|---|
| Tangible Book Value | 15.76 | 10.67 | 12.77 | NM | 17.46 | NM | 8.25 | 6.11 | 6.24 | 5.22 |
| Cash Flow | 5.13 | 5.21 | 4.21 | 5.29 | 4.48 | 3.84 | 2.98 | 2.80 | 2.89 | 2.23 |
| Earnings | 3.14 | 3.27 | 2.91 | 4.28 | 3.34 | 2.79 | 2.05 | 2.13 | 2.32 | 1.70 |
| S&P Core Earnings | 3.10 | 3.28 | 2.52 | 3.94 | 3.04 | 2.27 | 1.57 | NA | NA | NA |
| Dividends | Nil | Nil | Nil | Nil | Nil | Nil | Nil | Nil | Nil | Nil |
| Payout Ratio | Nil | Nil | Nil | Nil | Nil | Nil | Nil | Nil | Nil | Nil |
| Prices:High | 73.20 | 74.68 | 86.62 | 97.50 | 79.65 | 69.50 | 70.75 | 135.88 | 104.00 | 51.00 |
| Prices:Low | 32.35 | 44.09 | 39.33 | 76.00 | 56.57 | 41.94 | 40.81 | 28.75 | 42.09 | 17.50 |
| P/E Ratio:High | 23 | 23 | 30 | 23 | 24 | 25 | 35 | 64 | 45 | 30 |
| P/E Ratio:Low | 10 | 13 | 14 | 18 | 17 | 15 | 20 | 13 | 18 | 10 |

| Income Statement Analysis (Million $) | 2007 | 2006 | 2005 | 2004 | 2003 | 2002 | 2001 | 2000 | 1999 | 1998 |
|---|---|---|---|---|---|---|---|---|---|---|
| Revenue | 4,974 | 5,108 | 5,222 | 5,314 | 4,755 | 4,356 | 4,143 | 3,807 | 3,452 | 3,021 |
| Operating Income | 564 | 715 | 692 | 867 | 743 | 643 | 525 | 548 | 557 | 458 |
| Depreciation | 191 | 201 | 159 | 135 | 149 | 138 | 126 | 91.2 | 80.1 | 75.6 |
| Interest Expense | 13.0 | 12.1 | 11.2 | 12.3 | 12.5 | 9.00 | 14.8 | 12.8 | 10.7 | 11.0 |
| Pretax Income | 350 | 459 | 554 | 746 | 594 | 496 | 318 | 396 | 459 | 365 |
| Effective Tax Rate | 13.9% | 26.3% | 35.7% | 23.8% | 26.0% | 26.0% | 13.9% | 28.0% | 30.6% | 33.5% |
| Net Income | 301 | 338 | 356 | 569 | 439 | 367 | 274 | 285 | 319 | 243 |
| S&P Core Earnings | 297 | 340 | 308 | 524 | 399 | 298 | 210 | NA | NA | NA |

| Balance Sheet & Other Financial Data (Million $) | 2007 | 2006 | 2005 | 2004 | 2003 | 2002 | 2001 | 2000 | 1999 | 1998 |
|---|---|---|---|---|---|---|---|---|---|---|
| Cash | 796 | 551 | 889 | 1,567 | 1,196 | 498 | 90.7 | 68.5 | 93.9 | 149 |
| Current Assets | 2,067 | 1,830 | 2,170 | 3,001 | 2,444 | 1,799 | 1,493 | 1,244 | 1,089 | 1,020 |
| Total Assets | 3,121 | 2,849 | 3,330 | 4,124 | 3,450 | 2,808 | 2,450 | 2,073 | 1,703 | 1,483 |
| Current Liabilities | 1,497 | 1,324 | 1,234 | 1,468 | 1,183 | 1,099 | 931 | 979 | 736 | 606 |
| Long Term Debt | Nil | 150 | 150 | 150 | 149 | 149 | 149 | 149 | 149 | 149 |
| Common Equity | 1,278 | 1,035 | 1,429 | 2,083 | 1,643 | 1,082 | 1,076 | 777 | 659 | 578 |
| Total Capital | 1,278 | 1,185 | 1,578 | 2,232 | 1,792 | 1,231 | 1,225 | 926 | 808 | 727 |
| Capital Expenditures | 183 | 200 | 201 | 198 | 93.8 | 112 | 214 | 297 | 220 | 102 |
| Cash Flow | 492 | 539 | 515 | 704 | 588 | 505 | 399 | 377 | 399 | 319 |
| Current Ratio | 1.4 | 1.4 | 1.8 | 2.0 | 2.1 | 1.6 | 1.6 | 1.3 | 1.5 | 1.7 |
| % Long Term Debt of Capitalization | Nil | 12.6 | 9.5 | 6.7 | 8.3 | 12.1 | 12.2 | 16.1 | 18.4 | 20.5 |
| % Net Income of Revenue | 6.1 | 6.6 | 6.8 | 10.7 | 9.2 | 8.4 | 6.6 | 7.5 | 9.2 | 8.0 |
| % Return on Assets | 10.1 | 11.0 | 9.6 | 15.0 | 14.0 | 13.9 | 12.1 | 15.1 | 20.0 | 18.1 |
| % Return on Equity | 26.0 | 27.5 | 20.3 | 30.5 | 32.2 | 34.0 | 29.5 | 39.7 | 51.5 | 45.1 |

Data as orig reptd.; bef. results of disc opers/spec. items. Per share data adj. for stk. divs.; EPS diluted. E-Estimated. NA-Not Available. NM-Not Meaningful. NR-Not Ranked. UR-Under Review.

**Office:** 740 West New Circle Rd, Lexington, KY 40550.
**Telephone:** 859-232-2000.
**Website:** http://www.lexmark.com
**Chrmn & CEO:** P.J. Curlander

**Investor Contact:** J.W. Gamble, Jr. (859-232-2000)
**EVP & CFO:** J.W. Gamble, Jr.
**Chief Acctg Officer & Cntlr:** G.D. Stromquist
**Treas:** R.A. Pelini

**Board Members:** T. Beck, P. J. Curlander, W. R. Fields, R. E. Gomory, S. R. Hardis, J. F. Hardymon, R. Holland, Jr., M. L. Mann, M. J. Maples, J. L. Montupet, K. P. Seifert

**Founded:** 1990
**Domicile:** Delaware
**Employees:** 13,800

# Eli Lilly and Co

**STANDARD
&POOR'S**

**S&P Recommendation** HOLD ★★★☆☆

| Price | 12-Mo. Target Price | Investment Style |
|---|---|---|
| $32.06 (as of Nov 14, 2008) | $40.00 | Large-Cap Blend |

**GICS Sector** Health Care
**Sub-Industry** Pharmaceuticals

**Summary** This leading producer of prescription drugs offers a wide range of treatments for neurological disorders, diabetes, cancer, and other conditions. The company also sells animal health products.

## Key Stock Statistics (Source S&P, Vickers, company reports)

| | | | | | | | | |
|---|---|---|---|---|---|---|---|---|
| 52-Wk Range | $57.52– 29.25 | S&P Oper. EPS 2008**E** | 4.00 | Market Capitalization(B) | $36.451 | Beta | | 0.76 |
| Trailing 12-Month EPS | $2.21 | S&P Oper. EPS 2009**E** | 4.05 | Yield (%) | 5.86 | S&P 3-Yr. Proj. EPS CAGR(%) | | 5 |
| Trailing 12-Month P/E | 14.5 | P/E on S&P Oper. EPS 2008**E** | 8.0 | Dividend Rate/Share | $1.88 | S&P Credit Rating | | AA |
| $10K Invested 5 Yrs Ago | $5,241 | Common Shares Outstg. (M) | 1,137.0 | Institutional Ownership (%) | 78 | | | |

## Price Performance

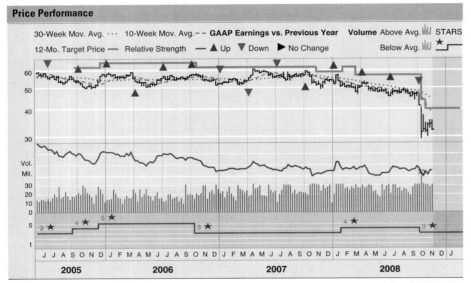

30-Week Mov. Avg. ··· 10-Week Mov. Avg.- - **GAAP Earnings vs. Previous Year** Volume Above Avg. STARS
12-Mo. Target Price — Relative Strength — ▲ Up ▼ Down ▶ No Change Below Avg.

Options: ASE, CBOE, P, Ph

Analysis prepared by **Herman B. Saftlas** on November 07, 2008, when the stock traded at **$ 33.33**.

## Highlights

➤ We forecast mid-single digit revenue growth in 2009. Sales of Cymbalta should show continued robust growth, boosted by expanded direct-to-consumer advertising, new indications, and expansion in foreign markets. We also see gains in other drugs such as Humalog, Cialis and Alimta. However, sales of Zyprexa are likely to show little or no growth, impacted by generic erosion abroad. Augmented by new products, we see animal health sales rising modestly. Volume should also benefit from sales of Erbitux anticancer drug, assuming completion of the planned acquisition of Im-clone Systems.

➤ We expect gross margins in 2009 to show modest expansion from the 78% that we estimate for 2008. However, operating margins are likely to come under pressure from dilution associated with the planned $6.5 billion cash acquisition of Erbitux, which is expected to require some $2.5 billion to $3 billion of outside financing.

➤ We project operating EPS of $4.05 for 2009, up from the $4.00 estimated for 2008, excluding acquisition-related charges and other non-recurring expenses in each year.

## Investment Rationale/Risk

➤ In early October, LLY agreed to acquire ImClone Systems (IMCL: hold, $69) for $6.5 billion in cash. The combination will give LLY access to Erbitux, a blockbuster anticancer drug that we expect to grow rapidly in the years ahead, supported by new indications. The acquisition should also expand LLY's biologics manufacturing capacity, and provide important operating and cost synergies. However, we expect the deal to dilute EPS through 2011, and become accretive on a cash basis in 2012. In addition, we think LLY will face a legal battle with Bristol-Myers Squibb over rights to a next-generation Erbitux that is now under development.

➤ Risks to our recommendation and target price include greater-than-expected competitive pressures, as well as failure to develop and commercialize new drugs.

➤ Our 12-month target price of $40 applies a below-peers P/E of 9.9X to our 2009 EPS estimate. Our DCF model, which assumes decelerating cash flow growth over the next 10 years, a WACC of 7.0%, and perpetuity growth of 1%, also indicates intrinsic value of $40. The dividend recently yielded 5.6%.

## Qualitative Risk Assessment

| LOW | MEDIUM | HIGH |
|---|---|---|

Our risk assessment reflects generic challenges to the company's branded patents, and drug development and regulatory risks. This is offset by our view of LLY's diverse drug portfolio, limited patent expiration exposure, and robust pipeline.

## Quantitative Evaluations

**S&P Quality Ranking** B+

| D | C | B- | B | B+ | A- | A | A+ |
|---|---|---|---|---|---|---|---|

**Relative Strength Rank** MODERATE

59

LOWEST = 1 HIGHEST = 99

## Revenue/Earnings Data

**Revenue (Million $)**

| | 1Q | 2Q | 3Q | 4Q | Year |
|---|---|---|---|---|---|
| 2008 | 4,808 | 5,150 | 5,210 | -- | -- |
| 2007 | 4,226 | 4,631 | 4,587 | 5,190 | 18,634 |
| 2006 | 3,715 | 3,867 | 3,864 | 4,245 | 15,691 |
| 2005 | 3,497 | 3,668 | 3,601 | 3,879 | 14,645 |
| 2004 | 3,377 | 3,556 | 3,280 | 3,644 | 13,858 |
| 2003 | 2,889 | 3,088 | 3,139 | 3,466 | 12,583 |

**Earnings Per Share ($)**

| | 1Q | 2Q | 3Q | 4Q | Year |
|---|---|---|---|---|---|
| 2008 | 0.97 | 0.88 | -0.43 | E1.05 | E4.00 |
| 2007 | 0.47 | 0.61 | 0.85 | 0.78 | 2.71 |
| 2006 | 0.77 | 0.76 | 0.80 | 0.12 | 2.45 |
| 2005 | 0.68 | -0.23 | 0.73 | 0.66 | 1.83 |
| 2004 | 0.37 | 0.60 | 0.69 | Nil | 1.66 |
| 2003 | 0.38 | 0.64 | 0.66 | 0.69 | 2.37 |

Fiscal year ended Dec. 31. Next earnings report expected: Late January. EPS Estimates based on S&P Operating Earnings; historical GAAP earnings are as reported.

## Dividend Data (Dates: mm/dd Payment Date: mm/dd/yy)

| Amount ($) | Date Decl. | Ex-Div. Date | Stk. of Record | Payment Date |
|---|---|---|---|---|
| 0.470 | 12/17 | 02/13 | 02/15 | 03/10/08 |
| 0.470 | 04/21 | 05/13 | 05/15 | 06/10/08 |
| 0.470 | 06/20 | 08/13 | 08/15 | 09/10/08 |
| 0.470 | 10/20 | 11/12 | 11/14 | 12/10/08 |

Dividends have been paid since 1885. Source: Company reports.

---

**Please read the Required Disclosures and Analyst Certification on the last page of this report.**

*The McGraw-Hill Companies*

# Eli Lilly and Co

STANDARD
&POOR'S

## Business Summary November 07, 2008

CORPORATE OVERVIEW. Eli Lilly and Co. is a leading maker of prescription drugs, offering a wide range of treatments for neurological disorders, diabetes, cancer, and other conditions. Animal health products are also sold. In January 2007, the company acquired ICOS Corp. for $2.3 billion in cash. The acquisition gave LLY full ownership of Cialis, a treatment for erectile dysfunction, which had previously been marketed through a 50/50 venture with ICOS. Revenues by geographic region in 2007 broke down as follows: U.S. 54%, Europe 26%, and other areas 20%.

LLY's largest selling drug is Zyprexa, a treatment for schizophrenia and bipolar disorder that offers clinical advantages over older antipsychotic drugs. Sales of Zyprexa totaled $4.8 billion in 2007, up from $4.4 billion in 2006. U.S. sales of Zyprexa rose 6% in 2007 (mostly due to higher prices), while foreign sales climbed 12%, driven by better demand and favorable currency exchange rates. LLY also offers Symbyax, a combination of Zyprexa and Prozac, to treat bipolar depression.

In August 2004, the company launched Cymbalta, a potent antidepressant. Cymbalta works on two body chemicals involved in depression -- serotonin and norepinephrine -- while most conventional antidepressants affect only serotonin. Sales of Cymbalta were $2.1 billion in 2007, up from $1.3 billion in 2006.

Diabetes care products (sales of $3.2 billion in 2007) include Humulin, a human insulin produced through recombinant DNA technology; Humalog, a rapid-acting injectable human insulin analog; Iletin, an animal-source insulin; and Actos, an oral agent for Type 2 diabetes that is manufactured by Takeda Chemical Industries of Japan and co-marketed by Lilly and Takeda. In May 2005, the FDA approved Byetta (generically known as exenatide) for Type 2 diabetes. Lilly shares in the profits from Byetta with Amylin Pharmaceuticals, co-developer of the drug.

Other important drugs are Gemzar, a treatment for lung cancer and pancreatic cancer (sales of $1.6 billion); Cialis, a treatment for erectile dysfunction ($1.2 billion); Evista, a drug used to prevent and treat osteoporosis in postmenopausal women ($1.1 billion); Alimta, a treatment for lung cancer ($854 million); Forteo for severe osteoporosis ($709 million); and Humatrope, a recombinant human growth hormone ($441 million). Animal health products ($996 million) include cattle feed additives, antibiotics and related items.

## Company Financials Fiscal Year Ended Dec. 31

### Per Share Data ($)

| | 2007 | 2006 | 2005 | 2004 | 2003 | 2002 | 2001 | 2000 | 1999 | 1998 |
|---|---|---|---|---|---|---|---|---|---|---|
| Tangible Book Value | 10.64 | 9.70 | 9.55 | 9.51 | 8.69 | 7.37 | 6.32 | 5.37 | 4.49 | 2.66 |
| Cash Flow | 3.49 | 3.06 | 2.41 | 2.21 | 2.87 | 2.85 | 2.91 | 3.18 | 2.70 | 2.31 |
| Earnings | 2.71 | 2.45 | 1.83 | 1.66 | 2.37 | 2.50 | 2.58 | 2.79 | 2.30 | 1.87 |
| S&P Core Earnings | 2.78 | 2.90 | 1.85 | 1.42 | 2.09 | 1.96 | 2.17 | NA | NA | NA |
| Dividends | 1.70 | 1.60 | 1.52 | 1.42 | 1.34 | 1.24 | 1.12 | 1.04 | 0.92 | 0.80 |
| Payout Ratio | 63% | 65% | 83% | 86% | 57% | 50% | 43% | 37% | 40% | 43% |
| Prices:High | 61.00 | 59.24 | 60.98 | 76.95 | 73.89 | 81.09 | 95.00 | 109.00 | 97.75 | 91.31 |
| Prices:Low | 49.09 | 50.19 | 49.47 | 50.34 | 52.77 | 43.75 | 70.01 | 54.00 | 60.56 | 57.69 |
| P/E Ratio:High | 23 | 24 | 33 | 46 | 31 | 32 | 37 | 39 | 42 | 49 |
| P/E Ratio:Low | 18 | 20 | 27 | 30 | 22 | 17 | 27 | 19 | 26 | 31 |

### Income Statement Analysis (Million $)

| | 2007 | 2006 | 2005 | 2004 | 2003 | 2002 | 2001 | 2000 | 1999 | 1998 |
|---|---|---|---|---|---|---|---|---|---|---|
| Revenue | 18,634 | 15,691 | 14,645 | 13,858 | 12,583 | 11,078 | 11,543 | 10,862 | 10,003 | 9,237 |
| Operating Income | 5,658 | 4,927 | 4,375 | 4,256 | 4,050 | 3,821 | 4,185 | 3,996 | 3,803 | 3,315 |
| Depreciation | 855 | 802 | 726 | 598 | 548 | 493 | 455 | 436 | 440 | 490 |
| Interest Expense | 324 | Nil | 105 | 274 | 61.0 | 79.7 | 147 | 182 | 242 | 181 |
| Pretax Income | 3,877 | 3,418 | 2,718 | 2,942 | 3,262 | 3,458 | 3,552 | 3,859 | 3,245 | 2,665 |
| Effective Tax Rate | 23.8% | 22.1% | 26.3% | 38.5% | 21.5% | 21.7% | 20.9% | 20.8% | 21.5% | 21.4% |
| Net Income | 2,953 | 2,663 | 2,002 | 1,810 | 2,561 | 2,708 | 2,809 | 3,058 | 2,547 | 2,096 |
| S&P Core Earnings | 3,028 | 3,153 | 2,016 | 1,558 | 2,261 | 2,128 | 2,359 | NA | NA | NA |

### Balance Sheet & Other Financial Data (Million $)

| | 2007 | 2006 | 2005 | 2004 | 2003 | 2002 | 2001 | 2000 | 1999 | 1998 |
|---|---|---|---|---|---|---|---|---|---|---|
| Cash | 4,831 | 3,109 | 3,007 | 5,365 | 2,756 | 1,946 | 2,702 | 4,115 | 3,700 | 1,496 |
| Current Assets | 12,257 | 9,694 | 10,796 | 12,836 | 8,759 | 7,804 | 6,939 | 7,943 | 7,056 | 5,407 |
| Total Assets | 26,788 | 21,955 | 24,581 | 24,867 | 21,678 | 19,042 | 16,434 | 14,691 | 12,825 | 12,596 |
| Current Liabilities | 5,268 | 5,086 | 5,716 | 7,594 | 5,551 | 5,064 | 5,203 | 4,961 | 3,935 | 4,607 |
| Long Term Debt | 4,594 | 3,494 | 5,764 | 4,492 | 4,688 | 4,358 | 3,132 | 2,634 | 2,812 | 2,186 |
| Common Equity | 13,664 | 11,081 | 11,000 | 10,920 | 9,765 | 8,274 | 7,104 | 8,682 | 5,013 | 4,430 |
| Total Capital | 18,545 | 14,638 | 17,459 | 16,032 | 14,453 | 12,632 | 10,236 | 11,407 | 7,962 | 6,864 |
| Capital Expenditures | 1,082 | 1,078 | 1,298 | 1,898 | 1,707 | 1,131 | 884 | 678 | 528 | 420 |
| Cash Flow | 3,808 | 3,465 | 2,728 | 2,408 | 3,109 | 3,201 | 3,264 | 3,494 | 2,986 | 2,586 |
| Current Ratio | 2.3 | 1.9 | 1.9 | 1.7 | 1.6 | 1.5 | 1.3 | 1.6 | 1.8 | 1.2 |
| % Long Term Debt of Capitalization | 24.8 | 23.9 | 33.0 | 28.0 | 32.4 | 34.5 | 30.6 | 23.1 | 35.3 | 31.8 |
| % Net Income of Revenue | 15.9 | 17.0 | 13.7 | 13.1 | 20.4 | 24.4 | 24.3 | 28.2 | 25.5 | 22.7 |
| % Return on Assets | 12.1 | 11.4 | 8.1 | 7.8 | 12.6 | 15.3 | 18.1 | 22.2 | 20.0 | 16.7 |
| % Return on Equity | 24.0 | 24.2 | 18.1 | 17.5 | 28.4 | 35.2 | 42.7 | 44.7 | 53.9 | 46.2 |

Data as orig reptd.; bef. results of disc opers/spec. items. Per share data adj. for stk. divs.; EPS diluted. E-Estimated. NA-Not Available. NM-Not Meaningful. NR-Not Ranked. UR-Under Review.

**Office:** Lilly Corporate Center, Indianapolis, IN 46285.
**Telephone:** 317-276-2000.
**Website:** http://www.lilly.com
**Chrmn:** S. Taurel

**Pres & CEO:** J.C. Lechleiter
**CEO:** J. Millon
**SVP & CFO:** D.W. Rice
**SVP & General Counsel:** R.A. Armitage

**Investor Contact:** P. Johnson (317-276-2000)
**Board Members:** W. W. Bischoff, J. M. Cook, D. M. Edgar, M. L. Eskew, M. Feldstein, J. E. Fyrwald, A. G. Gilman, K. N. Horn, J. C. Lechleiter, E. R. Marram, F. G. Prendergast, K. P. Seifert, S. Taurel

**Founded:** 1876
**Domicile:** Indiana
**Employees:** 40,600

The McGraw-Hill Companies

# Limited Brands Inc.

**STANDARD &POOR'S**

| S&P Recommendation **HOLD** ★★★☆☆ | Price | 12-Mo. Target Price | Investment Style |
|---|---|---|---|
| | $9.01 (as of Nov 14, 2008) | $12.00 | Large-Cap Blend |

**GICS Sector** Consumer Discretionary
**Sub-Industry** Apparel Retail

**Summary** This specialty retailer of women's apparel, lingerie and personal care and beauty products operates about 3,000 specialty stores.

## Key Stock Statistics (Source S&P, Vickers, company reports)

| | | | | | | |
|---|---|---|---|---|---|---|
| 52-Wk Range | $22.16– 8.11 | S&P Oper. EPS 2009**E** | 1.35 | Market Capitalization(B) | $3.061 | Beta | 1.25 |
| Trailing 12-Month EPS | $1.71 | S&P Oper. EPS 2010**E** | 1.30 | Yield (%) | 6.66 | S&P 3-Yr. Proj. EPS CAGR(%) | 8 |
| Trailing 12-Month P/E | 5.3 | P/E on S&P Oper. EPS 2009**E** | 6.7 | Dividend Rate/Share | $0.60 | S&P Credit Rating | BBB- |
| $10K Invested 5 Yrs Ago | $6,071 | Common Shares Outstg. (M) | 339.7 | Institutional Ownership (%) | 79 | | |

## Price Performance

- 30-Week Mov. Avg. · · · 10-Week Mov. Avg. — **GAAP Earnings vs. Previous Year** Volume Above Avg. STARS
- 12-Mo. Target Price — Relative Strength — ▲ Up ▼ Down ▶ No Change Below Avg. ★

Options: ASE, CBOE, P, Ph

Analysis prepared by **Marie Driscoll, CFA** on November 14, 2008, when the stock traded at **$ 9.01**.

### Highlights

➤ We see FY 09 (Jan.) as a period of infrastructure investment as LTD prepares to grow businesses globally with its intimates and personal care retail brands, Victoria's Secret (VS) and Bath and Body Works (BBW). We see potential line extensions, sub-brands, and additional fragrance and beauty launches for VS in the intermediate term, but we believe heightened category competition and brand repositioning will weaken near-term results.

➤ Same-store sales fell 2% in FY 08 (-2% at VS and -4% at BBW). We project FY 09 sales at $9.22 billion, a 9% decline, reflecting about a 10% same-store sales drop, partially offset by store expansion and a 10% gain in direct sales. We see a 3% lower sales in FY 10. LTD reported a 7% drop in same-store sales for the first nine months of FY 09.

➤ We project about 80 basis points of operating margin improvement in FY 09 to 9.3%, on reduced inventory investment, improved merchandise margins and an improved SG&A expense rate. We see FY 10's operating margin declining to 8.9%, as heightened competition and a difficult retail environment may necessitate additional marketing and sales support.

### Investment Rationale/Risk

➤ We see no near-term catalyst for share outperformance, with the shares recently trading at about 7X our FY 10 EPS estimate. We expect LTD to focus on cost controls and merchandise margin expansion in FY 09 and FY 10, with a growth strategy of developing new concepts. Its FY 08 acquisition of La Senza launched LTD into the international intimate apparel market and should provide a platform for further international expansion, which we believe will be important given the relative maturity of LTD's many domestic retail concepts. The dividend recently provided a yield of about 6.3%.

➤ Risks to our recommendation and target price include fashion and inventory risk, weakening trends in consumer spending, integration risk relative to La Senza, and weak same-store sales trends. With an estimated 65%-plus of LTD's profits earned in the fiscal fourth quarter, earnings risk is heightened.

➤ We derive our 12-month target price of $12 by applying a 9X forward multiple to our FY 10 EPS estimate of $1.30, about a 15% premium to peers on the less discretionary nature of LTD's merchandise, and compared to a 5-year average forward multiple of 15X.

### Qualitative Risk Assessment

| LOW | MEDIUM | HIGH |
|---|---|---|

Our risk assessment reflects LTD's strong cash flow, offset by execution risk in the company's attempt to re-position its Victoria's Secret brand in an increasingly competitive marketplace.

### Quantitative Evaluations

**S&P Quality Ranking** B+

| D | C | B- | B | B+ | A- | A | A+ |
|---|---|---|---|---|---|---|---|

**Relative Strength Rank** WEAK

26

LOWEST = 1    HIGHEST = 99

### Revenue/Earnings Data

**Revenue (Million $)**

| | 1Q | 2Q | 3Q | 4Q | Year |
|---|---|---|---|---|---|
| 2009 | 1,925 | 2,284 | -- | -- | -- |
| 2008 | 2,311 | 2,624 | 1,923 | 3,276 | 10,134 |
| 2007 | 2,077 | 2,454 | 2,115 | 4,025 | 10,671 |
| 2006 | 1,975 | 2,291 | 1,892 | 3,542 | 9,699 |
| 2005 | 1,975 | 2,211 | 1,891 | 3,328 | 9,408 |
| 2004 | 1,842 | 2,014 | 1,847 | 3,231 | 8,934 |

**Earnings Per Share ($)**

| | | | | | |
|---|---|---|---|---|---|
| 2009 | 0.29 | 0.30 | E0.01 | E0.95 | E1.35 |
| 2008 | 0.13 | 0.30 | -0.03 | 1.10 | 1.89 |
| 2007 | 0.25 | 0.28 | 0.06 | 1.08 | 1.68 |
| 2006 | 0.16 | 0.20 | Nil | 1.28 | 1.62 |
| 2005 | 0.06 | 0.31 | 0.16 | 0.87 | 1.47 |
| 2004 | 0.19 | 0.19 | 0.25 | 0.74 | 1.36 |

Fiscal year ended Jan. 31. Next earnings report expected: Late November. EPS Estimates based on S&P Operating Earnings; historical GAAP earnings are as reported.

### Dividend Data (Dates: mm/dd Payment Date: mm/dd/yy)

| Amount ($) | Date Decl. | Ex-Div. Date | Stk. of Record | Payment Date |
|---|---|---|---|---|
| 0.150 | 02/04 | 02/26 | 02/28 | 03/14/08 |
| 0.150 | 05/19 | 05/27 | 05/29 | 06/13/08 |
| 0.150 | 08/08 | 08/26 | 08/28 | 09/12/08 |
| 0.150 | 11/06 | 11/24 | 11/26 | 12/12/08 |

Dividends have been paid since 1970. Source: Company reports.

# Limited Brands Inc.

STANDARD
&POOR'S

## Business Summary November 14, 2008

CORPORATE OVERVIEW. Limited Brands (formerly The Limited) is a specialty retailer that conducts its business in two primary segments: Victoria's Secret, a women's intimate apparel, personal care products and accessories retail brand; and Bath & Body Works, a personal care and home fragrance products retail brand. At February 2, 2008, the store base consisted of 1,020 Victoria's Secret, 312 La Senza and 1,592 Bath & Body Works locations. LTD also operates two Henri Bendel stores and six C.O. Bigelows, an upscale apothecary. The company adopted its current name in May 2002.

In FY 08 (Jan. ), LTD attempted to divest its apparel businesses and sold a 67% interest in Express and a 75% interest in The Limited for a net gain of $250 million. The divested apparel businesses generated $870 million of revenues in the FY 08 first half, accounting for 9% of FY 08 consolidated sales. Victoria's Secret accounted for 55%, and Bath & Body Works for 25%. The remaining 11% was Mast Industries external sales to third parties, including second half sales to the divested apparel businesses.

Victoria's Secret (VS) is the leading specialty retailer of women's intimate ap-

parel and beauty products, with FY 08 sales of $5.6 billion, which includes $1.4 billion at Victoria's Secret Direct, a catalog and e-commerce retailer of women's intimate and other apparel and beauty products. Bath & Body Works (BBW) is a specialty retailer of personal care and home fragrance products. FY 08 sales were $2.5 billion, including White Barn Candle Company.

MARKET PROFILE. The mature and fragmented U.S. women's apparel market generated about $104 billion at retail in 2007, according to NPD Fashionworld consumer estimated data. S&P forecasts that 2008 apparel sales will be flat to up modestly, following 2% growth in 2007 and 4% annual gains in the 2004-2006 period. The domestic personal care market is mature as well, with the demand function reflecting population trends in addition to the development of new categories.

## Company Financials Fiscal Year Ended Jan. 31

### Per Share Data ($)

| | 2008 | 2007 | 2006 | 2005 | 2004 | 2003 | 2002 | 2001 | 2000 | 1999 |
|---|---|---|---|---|---|---|---|---|---|---|
| Tangible Book Value | NM | 2.34 | 1.69 | 1.31 | 6.78 | 5.93 | 6.40 | 5.43 | 5.00 | 4.92 |
| Cash Flow | 2.82 | 2.46 | 2.45 | 2.17 | 1.90 | 1.48 | 1.83 | 1.58 | 1.61 | 4.76 |
| Earnings | 1.89 | 1.68 | 1.62 | 1.47 | 1.36 | 0.95 | 0.94 | 0.96 | 1.00 | 4.16 |
| S&P Core Earnings | 1.47 | 1.68 | 1.57 | 1.27 | 1.03 | 0.94 | 0.80 | 0.91 | NA | NA |
| Dividends | 0.79 | 0.60 | 0.48 | 0.40 | 0.40 | 0.30 | 0.30 | 0.30 | 0.30 | 0.26 |
| Payout Ratio | 42% | 36% | 30% | 27% | 29% | 32% | 32% | 31% | 30% | 6% |

| Calendar Year | 2007 | 2006 | 2005 | 2004 | 2003 | 2002 | 2001 | 2000 | 1999 | 1998 |
|---|---|---|---|---|---|---|---|---|---|---|
| Prices:High | 30.03 | 32.60 | 25.50 | 27.89 | 18.46 | 22.34 | 21.29 | 27.88 | 25.31 | 18.25 |
| Prices:Low | 16.50 | 21.62 | 18.81 | 17.35 | 10.88 | 12.53 | 9.00 | 14.44 | 13.75 | 10.25 |
| P/E Ratio:High | 16 | 19 | 16 | 19 | 14 | 24 | 23 | 29 | 25 | 4 |
| P/E Ratio:Low | 9 | 13 | 12 | 12 | 8 | 13 | 10 | 15 | 14 | 2 |

### Income Statement Analysis (Million $)

| | 2008 | 2007 | 2006 | 2005 | 2004 | 2003 | 2002 | 2001 | 2000 | 1999 |
|---|---|---|---|---|---|---|---|---|---|---|
| Revenue | 10,086 | 10,671 | 9,699 | 9,408 | 8,934 | 8,445 | 9,363 | 10,105 | 9,766 | 9,347 |
| Operating Income | 1,208 | 1,492 | 1,285 | 1,360 | 1,246 | 1,148 | 1,025 | 1,148 | 1,169 | 984 |
| Depreciation | 352 | 316 | 299 | 333 | 28.3 | 276 | 277 | 272 | 272 | 286 |
| Interest Expense | 149 | 102 | 94.0 | 58.0 | 62.0 | 30.0 | 34.0 | 58.0 | 78.0 | 69.0 |
| Pretax Income | 1,107 | 1,097 | 960 | 1,116 | 1,166 | 843 | 968 | 828 | 905 | 2,428 |
| Effective Tax Rate | 37.1% | 38.5% | 30.3% | 36.8% | 38.5% | 40.5% | 39.8% | 40.0% | 41.0% | 12.8% |
| Net Income | 718 | 675 | 669 | 705 | 717 | 496 | 519 | 428 | 461 | 2,054 |
| S&P Core Earnings | 561 | 675 | 638 | 609 | 540 | 492 | 352 | 406 | NA | NA |

### Balance Sheet & Other Financial Data (Million $)

| | 2008 | 2007 | 2006 | 2005 | 2004 | 2003 | 2002 | 2001 | 2000 | 1999 |
|---|---|---|---|---|---|---|---|---|---|---|
| Cash | 1,018 | 500 | 1,208 | 1,161 | 3,129 | 2,262 | 1,375 | 563 | 817 | 1,222 |
| Current Assets | 2,919 | 2,771 | 2,784 | 2,684 | 4,433 | 3,606 | 2,682 | 2,068 | 2,285 | 2,318 |
| Total Assets | 7,437 | 7,093 | 6,346 | 6,089 | 7,873 | 7,246 | 4,719 | 4,088 | 4,126 | 4,550 |
| Current Liabilities | 1,374 | 1,709 | 1,575 | 1,451 | 1,392 | 1,259 | 1,319 | 1,000 | 1,236 | 1,248 |
| Long Term Debt | 2,905 | 1,665 | 1,669 | 1,646 | 648 | 547 | 250 | 400 | 400 | 550 |
| Common Equity | 2,219 | 2,955 | 2,471 | 2,335 | 5,266 | 4,860 | 2,744 | 2,317 | 2,147 | 2,233 |
| Total Capital | 5,354 | 4,864 | 4,319 | 4,191 | 6,048 | 5,532 | 3,171 | 2,860 | 2,666 | 2,894 |
| Capital Expenditures | 749 | 548 | 480 | 431 | 293 | 306 | 337 | 446 | 375 | 347 |
| Cash Flow | 1,070 | 991 | 968 | 1,038 | 1,000 | 772 | 796 | 700 | 733 | 2,340 |
| Current Ratio | 2.1 | 1.6 | 1.8 | 1.8 | 3.2 | 2.9 | 2.0 | 2.1 | 1.8 | 1.9 |
| % Long Term Debt of Capitalization | 54.3 | 35.5 | 38.6 | 39.3 | 10.7 | 9.9 | 7.9 | 14.0 | 15.0 | 19.0 |
| % Net Income of Revenue | 7.1 | 6.3 | 6.9 | 7.5 | 8.0 | 5.9 | 5.5 | 4.2 | 4.7 | 22.0 |
| % Return on Assets | 9.9 | 10.1 | 10.8 | 10.1 | 9.5 | 8.0 | 11.8 | 10.4 | 10.7 | 46.4 |
| % Return on Equity | 27.8 | 24.9 | 27.9 | 18.6 | 14.2 | 13.0 | 20.5 | 19.2 | 21.4 | 96.0 |

Data as orig reptd.; bef. results of disc opers/spec. items. Per share data adj. for stk. divs.; EPS diluted. E-Estimated. NA-Not Available. NM-Not Meaningful. NR-Not Ranked. UR-Under Review.

**Office:** Three Limited Parkway, Columbus, OH 43216.
**Telephone:** 614-415-7000.
**Website:** http://www.limitedbrands.com
**Chrmn & CEO:** L.H. Wexner

**EVP & CFO:** S.B. Burgdoerfer
**EVP & Chief Admin Officer:** M.R. Redgrave
**SVP, Secy & General Counsel:** S.P. Fried
**CTO:** J.J. Ricker

**Investor Contact:** T.J. Faber ()
**Board Members:** D. S. Hersch, J. L. Heskett, D. A. James, D. T. Kollat, W. R. Loomis, Jr., J. H. Miro, J. Swartz, A. R. Tessler, A. S. Wexner, L. H. Wexner, R. Zimmerman

**Founded:** 1967
**Domicile:** Delaware
**Employees:** 97,500

# Lincoln National Corp

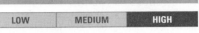

| S&P Recommendation | HOLD ★ ★ ★ ☆ ☆ | Price $14.35 (as of Nov 14, 2008) | 12-Mo. Target Price $25.00 | Investment Style Large-Cap Value |
|---|---|---|---|---|

**GICS Sector** Financials
**Sub-Industry** Life & Health Insurance

**Summary** This company offers annuities, life insurance, mutual funds, asset management, and related advisory services to affluent individuals.

## Key Stock Statistics (Source S&P, Vickers, company reports)

| | | | | | | | |
|---|---|---|---|---|---|---|---|
| 52-Wk Range | $63.26– 12.62 | S&P Oper. EPS 2008**E** | 4.70 | Market Capitalization(B) | $3.685 | Beta | 2.14 |
| Trailing 12-Month EPS | $2.57 | S&P Oper. EPS 2009**E** | 5.35 | Yield (%) | 5.85 | S&P 3-Yr. Proj. EPS CAGR(%) | 3 |
| Trailing 12-Month P/E | 5.6 | P/E on S&P Oper. EPS 2008**E** | 3.1 | Dividend Rate/Share | $0.84 | S&P Credit Rating | A+ |
| $10K Invested 5 Yrs Ago | $4,370 | Common Shares Outstg. (M) | 256.8 | Institutional Ownership (%) | 72 | | |

## Price Performance

30-Week Mov. Avg. ···  10-Week Mov. Avg. ‑ ‑  **GAAP Earnings vs. Previous Year**  Volume Above Avg. ▊▊ STARS
12-Mo. Target Price ▬  Relative Strength ▬  ▲ Up ▼ Down ► No Change  Below Avg. ▊▊ ★

Options: ASE, CBOE, P, Ph

Analysis prepared by **Bret Howlett** on October 30, 2008, when the stock traded at **$ 17.71**.

## Highlights

➤ We see operating earnings of the company's life insurance operations declining in 2008 due to poor flows, unfavorable DAC unlocking, reduced spreads and hedge breakage related to its variable annuity business. We expect sales to be weak for annuities as competition increases from other deposit-oriented products, and the volatile equity markets reduce demand for equity-linked annuities. In addition, we are concerned that LNC might have to raise prices for some products with living benefit riders, and potential disruption in its distribution network as a result of the recent consolidation of various wirehouses.

➤ We anticipate that earnings from the group protection business will advance in the mid-single digits based on higher premium growth, expanded distribution, and favorable persistency. We are concerned, however, about the decline in fee income from reduced average account balances in LNC's variable annuity and defined contribution business, and poor alternative investment returns.

➤ We forecast 2008 income from operations of $4.70 a share. Our EPS estimate for 2009 is $5.35.

## Investment Rationale/Risk

➤ Our hold recommendation is based on our concern that LNC will face further investment losses, and headwinds challenging its revenue growth for 2008. In addition, we believe that unfavorable DAC adjustments and hedge breakage costs related to the volatile capital markets could pressure earnings. However, LNC's business fundamentals are solid despite the unfavorable operating environment, and we believe the diversified earnings mix positions the company well for stable earnings over time. Although we believe LNC's capital position should allow it to absorb current investment losses, we remain concerned about the sharp buildup in unrealized investment losses, which stood at $4.9 billion as of the end of the third quarter.

➤ Risks to our recommendation and target price include worse than expected product spreads, deterioration in life insurance and annuity sales, unfavorable economic conditions and future instability in the credit markets.

➤ Our 12-month target price is $25, or about 0.7X our 2009 book value estimate, below LNC's historical multiples.

## Qualitative Risk Assessment

| LOW | MEDIUM | HIGH |
|---|---|---|

Our risk assessment reflects LNC's significant exposure to the equity markets and potential for further investment losses.

## Quantitative Evaluations

**S&P Quality Ranking** B+

| D | C | B- | B | B+ | A- | A | A+ |
|---|---|---|---|---|---|---|---|

**Relative Strength Rank** WEAK

10

LOWEST = 1          HIGHEST = 99

## Revenue/Earnings Data

**Revenue (Million $)**

| | 1Q | 2Q | 3Q | 4Q | Year |
|---|---|---|---|---|---|
| 2008 | 2,524 | 2,582 | 2,436 | -- | -- |
| 2007 | 2,670 | 2,740 | 2,681 | 2,606 | 10,594 |
| 2006 | 1,417 | 2,496 | 2,487 | 2,658 | 9,063 |
| 2005 | 1,313 | 1,373 | 1,413 | 1,388 | 5,488 |
| 2004 | 1,259 | 1,359 | 1,406 | 1,347 | 5,371 |
| 2003 | 1,099 | 1,213 | 1,269 | 1,327 | 5,284 |

**Earnings Per Share ($)**

| | | | | | |
|---|---|---|---|---|---|
| 2008 | 1.12 | 0.48 | 0.58 | E0.95 | E4.70 |
| 2007 | 1.42 | 1.37 | 1.21 | 0.89 | 4.82 |
| 2006 | 1.24 | 1.23 | 1.29 | 1.36 | 5.13 |
| 2005 | 1.01 | 1.13 | 1.30 | 1.28 | 4.72 |
| 2004 | 0.86 | 1.04 | 1.12 | 1.07 | 4.09 |
| 2003 | 0.23 | 0.80 | 0.74 | 1.08 | 2.85 |

Fiscal year ended Dec. 31. Next earnings report expected: Early February. EPS Estimates based on S&P Operating Earnings; historical GAAP earnings are as reported.

## Dividend Data (Dates: mm/dd Payment Date: mm/dd/yy)

| Amount ($) | Date Decl. | Ex-Div. Date | Stk. of Record | Payment Date |
|---|---|---|---|---|
| 0.415 | 02/08 | 04/07 | 04/09 | 05/01/08 |
| 0.415 | 05/08 | 07/08 | 07/10 | 08/01/08 |
| 0.415 | 08/07 | 10/08 | 10/10 | 11/01/08 |
| 0.210 | 10/10 | 01/07 | 01/09 | 02/01/09 |

Dividends have been paid since 1920. Source: Company reports.

# Lincoln National Corp

**STANDARD &POOR'S**

## Business Summary October 30, 2008

CORPORATE OVERVIEW. Lincoln National is a holding company with subsidiaries that operate multiple insurance and investment management businesses. Primary operating subsidiaries include The Lincoln National Life Insurance Company, First Penn-Pacific Life Insurance Company, Lincoln Life & Annuity Company of New York, Delaware Management Holdings, Inc., Lincoln National (UK) plc, Lincoln Financial Advisors (LFA), a retailing distribution unit, and Lincoln Financial Distributors (LFD), a wholesaling distribution unit.

Following the acquisition of Jefferson-Pilot in April 2006, LNC's segments were restructured, and operations are currently divided into five business segments: Individual Markets (61% of 2007 operating revenue), Employer Markets (28%), Investment Management (5.5%), Lincoln U.K. (3.5%), and Other Operations (2.6%).

The Individual Markets segment encompasses the individual annuities and individual life insurance business lines. According to Variable Annuity Research and Data Services (VARDS), LNC ranked seventh in assets and eighth in individual variable annuity net premiums written in 2006 in the U.S. The life insurance business targets the affluent market, and underwrites and sells universal life, variable universal life, interest-sensitive whole life, corporate-owned life insurance (COLI), term-life insurance, and linked products such as univer-

sal life linked with long-term care benefits. The employer markets segment encompasses the retirement products, executive benefits and benefit partners businesses.

The Investment Management segment offers retail and institutional mutual funds, separate and managed accounts, 529 college savings plans, and retirement plans and services, including 401(k) plans and administration services. Lincoln U.K. is licensed to do business throughout the U.K., and focuses primarily on retaining its existing customers and managing expenses for a closed block of business in the U.K., including accepting new deposits from, and offering new products to, existing policyholders. Offerings consist principally of unit-linked life and pension products, similar to U.S. variable life and annuity products. The Other Operations segment includes the financial data for the operations of Lincoln Financial Advisors (LFA) and Lincoln Financial Distributors (LFD), LNC's retail and wholesale distributors, operations that are not directly related to the business segments.

## Company Financials Fiscal Year Ended Dec. 31

| Per Share Data ($) | 2007 | 2006 | 2005 | 2004 | 2003 | 2002 | 2001 | 2000 | 1999 | 1998 |
|---|---|---|---|---|---|---|---|---|---|---|
| Tangible Book Value | 15.20 | 27.92 | 22.47 | 22.25 | 18.74 | 15.62 | 14.10 | 11.06 | 5.59 | 10.17 |
| Operating Earnings | NA | NA | NA | NA | NA | 2.56 | 3.56 | 3.27 | 2.32 | 2.61 |
| Earnings | 4.82 | 5.13 | 4.72 | 4.09 | 2.85 | 0.49 | 3.13 | 3.19 | 2.30 | 2.51 |
| S&P Core Earnings | 5.00 | 5.05 | 4.71 | 3.78 | 4.36 | 1.16 | 3.10 | NA | NA | NA |
| Dividends | 1.58 | 1.52 | 1.46 | 1.40 | 1.34 | 1.28 | 1.22 | 1.16 | 1.10 | 1.30 |
| Payout Ratio | 31% | 30% | 31% | 34% | 47% | NM | 39% | 36% | 48% | 52% |
| Prices:High | 74.72 | 66.72 | 54.41 | 50.38 | 41.32 | 53.65 | 52.75 | 56.38 | 57.50 | 49.44 |
| Prices:Low | 54.40 | 52.00 | 41.59 | 39.98 | 24.73 | 25.11 | 38.00 | 22.63 | 36.00 | 33.50 |
| P/E Ratio:High | 15 | 13 | 12 | 12 | 14 | NM | 17 | 18 | 25 | 20 |
| P/E Ratio:Low | 11 | 10 | 9 | 10 | 9 | NM | 12 | 7 | 16 | 13 |

### Income Statement Analysis (Million $)

| | 2007 | 2006 | 2005 | 2004 | 2003 | 2002 | 2001 | 2000 | 1999 | 1998 |
|---|---|---|---|---|---|---|---|---|---|---|
| Life Insurance in Force | 748,200 | 702,600 | 339,100 | 325,700 | 307,800 | 873,595 | 651,900 | 637,100 | 516,600 | 400,800 |
| Premium Income:Life | 4,258 | 3,354 | 2,069 | 1,882 | 1,694 | 1,730 | 2,907 | 3,064 | 2,721 | 2,260 |
| Premium Income:A & H | 941 | 656 | 1.30 | 3.52 | 3.98 | 20.3 | 341 | 410 | 698 | 635 |
| Net Investment Income | 4,384 | 3,981 | 2,702 | 2,704 | 2,639 | 2,608 | 2,680 | 2,747 | 2,808 | 2,681 |
| Total Revenue | 10,594 | 9,063 | 5,488 | 5,371 | 5,284 | 4,635 | 6,381 | 6,852 | 6,798 | 6,087 |
| Pretax Income | 1,874 | 1,811 | 1,075 | 1,036 | 1,048 | 1.62 | 764 | 836 | 570 | 697 |
| Net Operating Income | NA | NA | NA | NA | NA | 474 | 689 | 639 | 457 | NA |
| Net Income | 1,321 | 1,316 | 831 | 732 | 767 | 91.6 | 606 | 621 | 460 | 510 |
| S&P Core Earnings | 1,371 | 1,298 | 831 | 675 | 782 | 215 | 600 | NA | NA | NA |

### Balance Sheet & Other Financial Data (Million $)

| | 2007 | 2006 | 2005 | 2004 | 2003 | 2002 | 2001 | 2000 | 1999 | 1998 |
|---|---|---|---|---|---|---|---|---|---|---|
| Cash & Equivalent | 6,667 | 2,487 | 2,838 | 2,187 | 2,234 | 2,227 | 3,659 | 2,474 | 2,429 | 2,433 |
| Premiums Due | 401 | 356 | 343 | 233 | 352 | 213 | 400 | 297 | 260 | 775 |
| Investment Assets:Bonds | 56,276 | 55,853 | 33,443 | 34,701 | 32,769 | 32,767 | 28,346 | 27,450 | 27,689 | 30,233 |
| Investment Assets:Stocks | 518 | 701 | 3,391 | 3,399 | 3,319 | 337 | 471 | 550 | 604 | 543 |
| Investment Assets:Loans | 10,258 | 10,144 | 5,525 | 5,728 | 6,119 | 6,151 | 6,475 | 6,624 | 6,628 | 6,233 |
| Investment Assets:Total | 71,922 | 71,488 | 43,168 | 44,507 | 42,778 | 40,000 | 36,113 | 35,369 | 35,578 | 37,929 |
| Deferred Policy Costs | 9,580 | 8,420 | 4,092 | 3,445 | 3,192 | 2,971 | 2,885 | 3,071 | 2,800 | 1,964 |
| Total Assets | 191,435 | 178,494 | 124,788 | 116,219 | 106,745 | 93,133 | 98,001 | 99,844 | 103,096 | 99,836 |
| Debt | 5,168 | 4,116 | 1,333 | 1,083 | 1,459 | 1,512 | 1,336 | 1,457 | 1,457 | 712 |
| Common Equity | 11,718 | 71,017 | 6,384 | 6,175 | 5,811 | 5,296 | 5,263 | 4,953 | 4,264 | 5,388 |
| % Return on Revenue | 12.5 | 14.5 | 15.1 | 13.6 | 14.5 | 2.0 | 9.5 | 9.1 | 6.8 | 28.6 |
| % Return on Assets | 0.7 | 0.1 | 0.1 | 0.1 | 0.1 | 0.1 | 0.6 | 0.6 | 0.5 | 0.6 |
| % Return on Equity | 11.1 | 2.3 | 13.2 | 12.2 | 13.8 | 1.7 | 11.9 | 13.5 | 0.4 | 9.8 |
| % Investment Yield | 6.1 | 6.8 | 6.1 | 6.8 | 7.1 | 6.9 | 7.5 | 7.7 | 7.6 | 7.9 |

Data as orig reptd.; bef. results of disc opers/spec. items. Per share data adj. for stk. divs.; EPS diluted. E-Estimated. NA-Not Available. NM-Not Meaningful. NR-Not Ranked. UR-Under Review.

**Office:** 150 N Radnor Chester Rd Ste A305, Radnor, PA 19087-5238.
**Telephone:** 484-583-1400.
**Email:** investorrelations@lnc.com
**Website:** http://www.lfg.com

**Chrmn:** J.P. Barrett
**Pres & CEO:** D.R. Glass
**SVP & CFO:** F.J. Crawford
**SVP & General Counsel:** D.L. Schoff

**SVP & CIO:** C.C. Cornelio
**Board Members:** W. J. Avery, J. P. Barrett, W. H. Cunningham, D. R. Glass, G. W. Henderson, III, E. G. Johnson, M. L. Lachman, M. F. Mee, W. B. Payne, P. S. Pittard, D. A. Stonecipher, I. Tidwell

**Founded:** 1905
**Domicile:** Indiana
**Employees:** 10,870

# Linear Technology Corp

STANDARD
&POOR'S

| S&P Recommendation | HOLD ★★★☆☆ | Price | 12-Mo. Target Price | Investment Style |
|---|---|---|---|---|
| | | $21.95 (as of Nov 14, 2008) | $26.00 | Large-Cap Growth |

**GICS Sector** Information Technology
**Sub-Industry** Semiconductors

**Summary** This company manufactures high-performance linear integrated circuits.

## Key Stock Statistics (Source S&P, Vickers, company reports)

| | | | | | | | | |
|---|---|---|---|---|---|---|---|---|
| 52-Wk Range | $37.77– 18.52 | S&P Oper. EPS 2009**E** | 1.49 | Market Capitalization(B) | $4.867 | Beta | | 1.26 |
| Trailing 12-Month EPS | $1.80 | S&P Oper. EPS 2010**E** | NA | Yield (%) | 3.83 | S&P 3-Yr. Proj. EPS CAGR(%) | | 1 |
| Trailing 12-Month P/E | 12.2 | P/E on S&P Oper. EPS 2009**E** | 14.7 | Dividend Rate/Share | $0.84 | S&P Credit Rating | | NA |
| $10K Invested 5 Yrs Ago | $5,649 | Common Shares Outstg. (M) | 221.7 | Institutional Ownership (%) | NM | | | |

## Price Performance

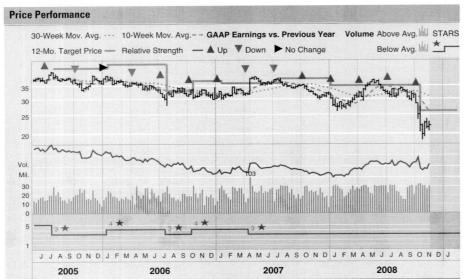

30-Week Mov. Avg. · · · 10-Week Mov. Avg. · · · — **GAAP Earnings vs. Previous Year** Volume Above Avg. ‖‖ STARS
12-Mo. Target Price — Relative Strength — ▲ Up ▼ Down ► No Change Below Avg. ‖‖

Options: ASE, CBOE, P, Ph

Analysis prepared by **Clyde Montevirgen** on October 16, 2008, when the stock traded at **$ 22.04**.

## Highlights

➤ We think that revenues will decrease 8% in FY 09 (Jun.), below the 9% growth pace in FY 08. The credit crisis and slowing global economy have started to hurt orders, and will likely weigh on top-line results as smaller businesses look to preserve cash and keep inventories lean. Given healthy growth last fiscal year, we see unfavorable comparisons ahead. Over the longer-term, we see the usage of analog semiconductors in devices proliferating, which should provide LLTC growth opportunities. We believe that LLTC is effectively executing on its goal to further penetrate the higher-end analog segment, and we see the company taking market share gains in the communications, computing, industrial and automotive markets.

➤ We anticipate gross margins narrowing to the 76% area in FY 09 from around 77% in FY 08. We view favorably LLTC's focus on high-end analog, as pricing should remain relatively stable, helping preserve margins during the slowdown. Similarly, we project non-GAAP operating margins around 44% in FY 09, below 48% in FY 08, reflecting the impact of lower sales levels.

➤ We expect non-GAAP EPS of $1.49 in FY 09, compared to $1.71 in FY 08.

## Investment Rationale/Risk

➤ Our hold recommendation reflects our view of an attractive valuation balanced by declining earnings. We believe that Linear is one of the better run companies in our coverage universe. LLTC's valuation multiples are nearing historical trough levels and the shares are fairly inexpensive, in our view. In the next upcycle, we expect LLTC to expand revenues by further penetrating several faster growing end markets, such as automotive and certain industrial markets. However, the depth and length of the current slowdown is unknown, which adds substantial risk. Given LLTC's operational structure and anticipated lower sales levels, we see weakening profitability ahead.

➤ Risks to our recommendation and target price include increasing competition, higher than anticipated operating expenses, and a longer than expected downturn.

➤ Our 12-month target price of $26 is based on a blend of our DCF and P/E analyses. Our DCF model, which assumes a WACC of 10% and a terminal growth rate of 4%, shows intrinsic value of $28. We apply a P/E of 17X, above peer average, to our FY 09 EPS estimate to derive a value of around $25.

## Qualitative Risk Assessment

| LOW | MEDIUM | HIGH |
|---|---|---|

Our risk assessment reflects the company's exposure to the sales cycles of the semiconductor industry. This is offset by stabilizing factors such as a high level of proprietary circuit design content, a varied customer base, diverse end markets, and wider margins than most competitors.

## Quantitative Evaluations

**S&P Quality Ranking** A

| D | C | B- | B | B+ | A- | A | A+ |
|---|---|---|---|---|---|---|---|

**Relative Strength Rank** MODERATE

63

LOWEST = 1     HIGHEST = 99

## Revenue/Earnings Data

**Revenue (Million $)**

| | 1Q | 2Q | 3Q | 4Q | Year |
|---|---|---|---|---|---|
| 2009 | 310.4 | -- | -- | -- | -- |
| 2008 | 281.5 | 288.7 | 297.9 | 307.1 | 1,175 |
| 2007 | 292.1 | 267.9 | 255.0 | 268.1 | 1,083 |
| 2006 | 256.0 | 265.2 | 278.9 | 292.9 | 1,093 |
| 2005 | 253.0 | 250.1 | 290.7 | 255.8 | 1,050 |
| 2004 | 174.1 | 186.0 | 209.1 | 238.1 | 807.3 |

**Earnings Per Share ($)**

| | | | | | |
|---|---|---|---|---|---|
| 2009 | 0.48 | E0.32 | E0.33 | E0.36 | E1.49 |
| 2008 | 0.40 | 0.41 | 0.44 | 0.46 | 1.71 |
| 2007 | 0.37 | 0.34 | 0.32 | 0.36 | 1.39 |
| 2006 | 0.31 | 0.33 | 0.35 | 0.37 | 1.37 |
| 2005 | 0.33 | 0.33 | 0.39 | 0.34 | 1.38 |
| 2004 | 0.22 | 0.23 | 0.27 | 0.31 | 1.02 |

Fiscal year ended Jun. 30. Next earnings report expected: Mid January. EPS Estimates based on S&P Operating Earnings; historical GAAP earnings are as reported.

## Dividend Data (Dates: mm/dd Payment Date: mm/dd/yy)

| Amount ($) | Date Decl. | Ex-Div. Date | Stk. of Record | Payment Date |
|---|---|---|---|---|
| 0.210 | 01/16 | 02/13 | 02/15 | 02/27/08 |
| 0.210 | 04/15 | 05/14 | 05/16 | 05/28/08 |
| 0.210 | 07/22 | 08/13 | 08/15 | 08/27/08 |
| 0.210 | 10/14 | 11/12 | 11/14 | 11/26/08 |

Dividends have been paid since 1992. Source: Company reports.

# Linear Technology Corp

**STANDARD &POOR'S**

## Business Summary October 16, 2008

CORPORATE OVERVIEW. Linear Technology Corp. (LLTC) designs, makes and markets a broad line of high-performance standard linear integrated circuits (ICs) that address a wide range of real-world signal processing applications. Its principal product lines include operational and high-speed amplifiers, voltage regulators, voltage references, data converters, interface circuits, and other linear circuits, including buffers, battery monitors, comparators, drivers and filters.

LLTC's products are used in a wide variety of applications, including wireless and wireline telecommunications, networking, satellite systems, notebook and desk-top PCs, computer peripherals, video/multimedia, industrial instrumentation, medical devices, and high-end consumer products such as digital cameras and MP3 players.

The company has consistently expanded its customer base throughout its history. LLTC initially served primarily an industrial customer base, with a high percentage of revenues from the military market. Since the late 1980s, new products led to growth in the PC and hand-held device markets, and commu-

nication and networking markets contributed to growth significantly in recent years. The company now sells its products to more than 15,000 original equipment manufacturers directly or through a sales distributor channel. Its largest customer in FY 07 (Jun.) was the distributor Arrow Electronics, which accounted for 14% of total revenue. No other single company comprised over 10% of sales.

Linear has fabrication plants in Camas, WA, and Milpitas, CA. The company currently produces semiconductors on six-inch diameter (150 millimeter) wafers. Processed wafers are then shipped to its assembly plant in Penang, Malaysia, or other independent assembly contractors for "back-end" functions such as separating and packaging. The chips are then sent to its Singapore facility for final testing and inspection. The process from manufacturing to final testing can take up to 16 weeks.

## Company Financials Fiscal Year Ended Jun. 30

### Per Share Data ($)

| | 2008 | 2007 | 2006 | 2005 | 2004 | 2003 | 2002 | 2001 | 2000 | 1999 |
|---|---|---|---|---|---|---|---|---|---|---|
| Tangible Book Value | NM | NM | 6.94 | 6.55 | 5.87 | 5.80 | 5.63 | 5.59 | 4.20 | 2.95 |
| Cash Flow | NA | 1.56 | 1.53 | 1.53 | 1.17 | 0.88 | 0.74 | 1.39 | 0.95 | 0.68 |
| Earnings | 1.71 | 1.39 | 1.37 | 1.38 | 1.02 | 0.74 | 0.60 | 1.29 | 0.88 | 0.61 |
| S&P Core Earnings | 1.71 | 1.39 | 1.37 | 0.99 | 0.79 | 0.50 | 0.40 | 1.10 | NA | NA |
| Dividends | 0.78 | 0.66 | 0.50 | 0.36 | 0.28 | 0.21 | 0.17 | 0.13 | 0.08 | 0.08 |
| Payout Ratio | 46% | 47% | 36% | 26% | 27% | 28% | 28% | 10% | 9% | 12% |
| Prices:High | 37.77 | 38.84 | 39.35 | 41.67 | 45.09 | 44.80 | 47.50 | 65.13 | 74.75 | 41.59 |
| Prices:Low | 18.52 | 29.62 | 27.80 | 32.83 | 34.01 | 24.76 | 18.92 | 29.45 | 35.06 | 20.88 |
| P/E Ratio:High | 22 | 28 | 29 | 30 | 44 | 61 | 79 | 50 | 85 | 68 |
| P/E Ratio:Low | 11 | 21 | 20 | 24 | 33 | 33 | 32 | 23 | 40 | 34 |

### Income Statement Analysis (Million $)

| | 2008 | 2007 | 2006 | 2005 | 2004 | 2003 | 2002 | 2001 | 2000 | 1999 |
|---|---|---|---|---|---|---|---|---|---|---|
| Revenue | 1,175 | 1,083 | 1,093 | 1,050 | 807 | 607 | 512 | 973 | 706 | 507 |
| Operating Income | NA | 575 | 613 | 638 | 485 | 340 | 271 | 582 | 399 | 280 |
| Depreciation | 48.1 | 50.7 | 49.3 | 48.8 | 48.7 | 45.9 | 46.3 | 35.8 | 25.0 | 22.0 |
| Interest Expense | NA | 12.1 | Nil | Nil | Nil | Nil | Nil | Nil | Nil | Nil |
| Pretax Income | 541 | 570 | 617 | 620 | 462 | 333 | 278 | 611 | 417 | 286 |
| Effective Tax Rate | 28.4% | 27.8% | 30.5% | 30.0% | 29.0% | 29.0% | 29.0% | 30.0% | 31.0% | 32.0% |
| Net Income | 388 | 412 | 429 | 434 | 328 | 237 | 198 | 427 | 288 | 194 |
| S&P Core Earnings | 388 | 412 | 429 | 311 | 253 | 161 | 132 | 366 | NA | NA |

### Balance Sheet & Other Financial Data (Million $)

| | 2008 | 2007 | 2006 | 2005 | 2004 | 2003 | 2002 | 2001 | 2000 | 1999 |
|---|---|---|---|---|---|---|---|---|---|---|
| Cash | 967 | 156 | 541 | 323 | 204 | 136 | 212 | 321 | 230 | 787 |
| Current Assets | NA | 861 | 2,077 | 2,007 | 1,832 | 1,776 | 1,728 | 1,728 | 1,310 | 905 |
| Total Assets | 1,584 | 1,219 | 2,391 | 2,286 | 2,088 | 2,057 | 1,988 | 2,017 | 1,507 | 1,047 |
| Current Liabilities | NA | 180 | 237 | 208 | 203 | 162 | 169 | 202 | 169 | 125 |
| Long Term Debt | NA | 1,700 | Nil | Nil | Nil | Nil | Nil | Nil | Nil | Nil |
| Common Equity | -434 | -708 | 2,104 | 2,007 | 1,811 | 1,815 | 1,781 | 1,782 | 1,322 | 907 |
| Total Capital | NA | 1,005 | 2,104 | 2,007 | 1,811 | 1,815 | 1,819 | 1,815 | 1,339 | 922 |
| Capital Expenditures | 35.3 | 62.0 | 69.4 | 62.1 | 20.7 | 6.61 | 17.9 | 128 | 80.3 | 39.1 |
| Cash Flow | NA | 462 | 478 | 483 | 377 | 282 | 244 | 463 | 313 | 216 |
| Current Ratio | 7.1 | 4.8 | 8.8 | 9.7 | 9.0 | 11.0 | 10.2 | 8.5 | 7.8 | 7.2 |
| % Long Term Debt of Capitalization | 134.3 | 169.2 | Nil | Nil | Nil | Nil | Nil | Nil | Nil | Nil |
| % Net Income of Revenue | 33.0 | 38.0 | 39.2 | 41.3 | 40.7 | 39.0 | 38.6 | 43.9 | 40.8 | 38.3 |
| % Return on Assets | 27.7 | 22.8 | 18.3 | 19.8 | 15.8 | 11.7 | 9.9 | 24.3 | 22.5 | 20.0 |
| % Return on Equity | NM | 59.0 | 20.9 | 22.7 | 18.1 | 13.2 | 11.1 | 27.5 | 25.8 | 23.3 |

Data as orig reptd.; bef. results of disc opers/spec. items. Per share data adj. for stk. divs.; EPS diluted. E-Estimated. NA-Not Available. NM-Not Meaningful. NR-Not Ranked. UR-Under Review.

**Office:** 1630 McCarthy Boulevard, Milpitas, CA 95035-7487.
**Telephone:** 408-432-1900.
**Website:** http://www.linear.com
**Chrmn:** R.H. Swanson, Jr.

**CEO:** L. Maier
**COO:** A.R. McCann
**Investor Contact:** P. Coghlan (408-432-1900)
**CFO, Chief Acctg Officer & Secy:** P. Coghlan

**Board Members:** D. S. Lee, L. Maier, R. M. Moley, R. H. Swanson, Jr., T. S. Volpe

**Founded:** 1981
**Domicile:** Delaware
**Employees:** 4,173

The McGraw-Hill Companies

**STANDARD &POOR'S**

# Liz Claiborne Inc.

**S&P Recommendation** `HOLD` ★★★☆☆

| | | |
|---|---|---|
| **Price** $3.69 (as of Nov 14, 2008) | **12-Mo. Target Price** $6.00 | **Investment Style** Large-Cap Blend |

**GICS Sector** Consumer Discretionary
**Sub-Industry** Apparel, Accessories & Luxury Goods

**Summary** This company designs and markets women's and men's apparel made by independent suppliers and sold through department and specialty stores worldwide.

---

### Key Stock Statistics (Source S&P, Vickers, company reports)

| | | | | | | | |
|---|---|---|---|---|---|---|---|
| 52-Wk Range | $25.92– 3.55 | S&P Oper. EPS 2008**E** | 0.95 | Market Capitalization(B) | $0.350 | Beta | 0.81 |
| Trailing 12-Month EPS | $-4.78 | S&P Oper. EPS 2009**E** | 0.85 | Yield (%) | 6.23 | S&P 3-Yr. Proj. EPS CAGR(%) | 0 |
| Trailing 12-Month P/E | NM | P/E on S&P Oper. EPS 2008**E** | 3.9 | Dividend Rate/Share | $0.23 | S&P Credit Rating | BB+ |
| $10K Invested 5 Yrs Ago | $1,085 | Common Shares Outstg. (M) | 94.8 | Institutional Ownership (%) | NM | | |

## Price Performance

30-Week Mov. Avg. ··· 10-Week Mov. Avg. – – **GAAP Earnings vs. Previous Year** Volume Above Avg. ▮▮▮ STARS
12-Mo. Target Price — Relative Strength — ▲ Up ▼ Down ▶ No Change Below Avg. ▮▮▮ ★

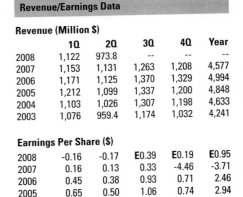

Options: CBOE, P

### Highlights

▶ The STARS recommendation for LIZ has recently been changed to 3 (hold) from 2 (sell). The Highlights section of this Stock Report will be updated accordingly.

### Investment Rationale/Risk

▶ The Investment Rationale/Risk section of this Stock Report will be updated shortly. For the latest News story on LIZ from MarketScope, see below.

▶ 11/13/08 02:47 pm ET ... S&P RAISES OPINION ON SHARES OF LIZ CLAIBORNE TO HOLD FROM SELL, ON VALUATION (LIZ 4.59***): LIZ has fallen below our target price, and while we expect dismal sales and earnings reports over the coming 12 months given our deteriorating outlook on employment, consumer sentiment and discretionary income, we believe this is now adequately reflected in the share price. The next positive data point is the Jan. '09 re-launch of Liz Claiborne brand, designed by Issac Mizrahi. We see the bulk of LIZ's portfolio constituents under pressure through 2009 and we expect more rapid brand maturation in this cycle. We maintain our 12-month target price at $6. /M. Driscoll-CFA

## Qualitative Risk Assessment

| LOW | MEDIUM | **HIGH** |
|---|---|---|

Our risk assessment reflects our view of LIZ's exposure to department store consolidation, partly offset by its broad diversification and strong cash flows.

## Quantitative Evaluations

**S&P Quality Ranking**          A-

| D | C | B- | B | B+ | **A-** | A | A+ |
|---|---|---|---|---|---|---|---|

**Relative Strength Rank**       WEAK

  4

LOWEST = 1                  HIGHEST = 99

## Revenue/Earnings Data

**Revenue (Million $)**

| | 1Q | 2Q | 3Q | 4Q | Year |
|---|---|---|---|---|---|
| 2008 | 1,122 | 973.8 | -- | -- | -- |
| 2007 | 1,153 | 1,131 | 1,263 | 1,208 | 4,577 |
| 2006 | 1,171 | 1,125 | 1,370 | 1,329 | 4,994 |
| 2005 | 1,212 | 1,099 | 1,337 | 1,200 | 4,848 |
| 2004 | 1,103 | 1,026 | 1,307 | 1,198 | 4,633 |
| 2003 | 1,076 | 959.4 | 1,174 | 1,032 | 4,241 |

**Earnings Per Share ($)**

| | 1Q | 2Q | 3Q | 4Q | Year |
|---|---|---|---|---|---|
| 2008 | -0.16 | -0.17 | E0.39 | E0.19 | E0.95 |
| 2007 | 0.16 | 0.13 | 0.33 | -4.46 | -3.71 |
| 2006 | 0.45 | 0.38 | 0.93 | 0.71 | 2.46 |
| 2005 | 0.65 | 0.50 | 1.06 | 0.74 | 2.94 |
| 2004 | 0.62 | 0.46 | 1.03 | 0.75 | 2.85 |
| 2003 | 0.59 | 0.41 | 0.89 | 0.66 | 2.55 |

Fiscal year ended Dec. 31. Next earnings report expected: NA. EPS Estimates based on S&P Operating Earnings; historical GAAP earnings are as reported.

## Dividend Data (Dates: mm/dd Payment Date: mm/dd/yy)

| Amount ($) | Date Decl. | Ex-Div. Date | Stk. of Record | Payment Date |
|---|---|---|---|---|
| 0.056 | 01/23 | 02/20 | 02/22 | 03/17/08 |
| 0.056 | 05/15 | 05/20 | 05/22 | 06/16/08 |
| 0.056 | 07/15 | 08/20 | 08/22 | 09/15/08 |
| 0.056 | 10/15 | 11/19 | 11/21 | 12/15/08 |

Dividends have been paid since 1984. Source: Company reports.

---

# Liz Claiborne Inc.

**STANDARD & POOR'S**

## Business Summary October 24, 2008

CORPORATE OVERVIEW. Liz Claiborne is one of the largest U.S. branded apparel companies, with a portfolio of about 20 apparel and accessory brands.

MARKET PROFILE. The women's apparel market represented 53% of 2007 domestic apparel retail purchases, or $103 billion, according to NPD Fashionworld consumer estimated data. The apparel market is fragmented, with national brands marketed by 20 companies accounting for about 30% of total apparel sales, and the remaining 70% comprised of smaller and/or private label "store" brands. The market is mature, with demand largely mirroring population growth and fashion trends accounting for a modicum of incremental volume. Deflationary pricing pressure is a function of channel competition and production steadily moving offshore to low-cost producers in India, Asia and China. S&P forecasts flat to a modest 1% increase in 2008 apparel sales, generally in line with GDP growth, versus gains of 3% in 2007, 5% in 2006 and 4% in 2004 and 2005.

COMPETITIVE LANDSCAPE. By channel, specialty stores account for the largest share of apparel sales, at 31% in 2007, flat with 2006, according to NPD. Mass merchants (Wal-Mart and Target) came in second at 20%, and department stores came in third at 16%. National chains (Sears and JC Penney) captured 15% of 2007 apparel sales and off-price retailers (TJX and Ross Stores) 7%. The remaining 11% was divided among factory outlets and direct and email pure plays. LIZ holds meaningful market shares in department stores and national chains, where it competes with Jones Apparel Group, Polo Ralph Lauren and VF Corp., as well as private label offerings, which garner about a third of total apparel purchases and are an important differentiator for retailers. LIZ also sells directly to consumers through 433 specialty retail stores and 350 outlet stores throughout the world as well as 680 international concession stores.

## Company Financials Fiscal Year Ended Dec. 31

### Per Share Data ($)

| | 2007 | 2006 | 2005 | 2004 | 2003 | 2002 | 2001 | 2000 | 1999 | 1998 |
|---|---|---|---|---|---|---|---|---|---|---|
| Tangible Book Value | 37.60 | 6.86 | 7.74 | 7.13 | 6.73 | 5.43 | 5.71 | 5.45 | 5.95 | 7.67 |
| Cash Flow | -2.11 | 3.82 | 4.12 | 3.95 | 3.51 | 3.06 | 2.79 | 2.43 | 2.11 | 1.71 |
| Earnings | -3.71 | 2.46 | 2.94 | 2.85 | 2.55 | 2.16 | 1.83 | 1.72 | 1.56 | 1.29 |
| S&P Core Earnings | -0.30 | 2.44 | 2.88 | 2.60 | 2.39 | 2.00 | 1.68 | NA | NA | NA |
| Dividends | 0.23 | 0.23 | 0.23 | 0.23 | 0.23 | 0.23 | 0.23 | 0.23 | 0.23 | 0.23 |
| Payout Ratio | NM | 9% | 8% | 8% | 9% | 10% | 12% | 13% | 14% | 18% |
| Prices:High | 46.84 | 44.50 | 43.82 | 42.47 | 38.90 | 33.25 | 27.48 | 24.16 | 20.34 | 27.44 |
| Prices:Low | 19.91 | 33.40 | 33.70 | 32.09 | 26.23 | 23.55 | 18.00 | 15.47 | 15.44 | 12.50 |
| P/E Ratio:High | NM | 18 | 15 | 15 | 15 | 15 | 15 | 14 | 13 | 21 |
| P/E Ratio:Low | NM | 14 | 11 | 11 | 10 | 11 | 10 | 9 | 10 | 10 |

### Income Statement Analysis (Million $)

| | 2007 | 2006 | 2005 | 2004 | 2003 | 2002 | 2001 | 2000 | 1999 | 1998 |
|---|---|---|---|---|---|---|---|---|---|---|
| Revenue | 4,577 | 4,994 | 4,848 | 4,633 | 4,241 | 3,718 | 3,449 | 3,104 | 2,807 | 2,535 |
| Operating Income | 429 | 576 | 652 | 628 | 575 | 493 | 780 | 402 | 368 | 340 |
| Depreciation | 160 | 140 | 128 | 116 | 105 | 96.4 | 101 | 77.0 | 67.8 | 55.8 |
| Interest Expense | 52.5 | Nil | 31.8 | 32.2 | 30.5 | 25.1 | 28.1 | 21.9 | 1.61 | Nil |
| Pretax Income | -471 | 407 | 491 | 480 | 438 | 362 | 300 | 288 | 302 | 267 |
| Effective Tax Rate | 21.7% | 37.4% | 35.4% | 34.7% | 36.2% | 36.2% | 36.0% | 36.0% | 36.2% | 36.5% |
| Net Income | -370 | 255 | 317 | 314 | 280 | 231 | 192 | 185 | 192 | 169 |
| S&P Core Earnings | -27.2 | 252 | 309 | 284 | 259 | 213 | 176 | NA | NA | NA |

### Balance Sheet & Other Financial Data (Million $)

| | 2007 | 2006 | 2005 | 2004 | 2003 | 2002 | 2001 | 2000 | 1999 | 1998 |
|---|---|---|---|---|---|---|---|---|---|---|
| Cash | 206 | 195 | 343 | 393 | 344 | 276 | 161 | 54.4 | 37.9 | 230 |
| Current Assets | 1,565 | 1,470 | 1,457 | 1,509 | 1,348 | 1,203 | 1,106 | 911 | 859 | 1,075 |
| Total Assets | 3,268 | 3,496 | 3,152 | 3,030 | 2,607 | 2,296 | 1,951 | 1,512 | 1,412 | 1,393 |
| Current Liabilities | 770 | 674 | 608 | 638 | 527 | 591 | 447 | 358 | 352 | 363 |
| Long Term Debt | 837 | 570 | 418 | 485 | 440 | 378 | 387 | 269 | 116 | Nil |
| Common Equity | 1,516 | 2,130 | 2,003 | 1,812 | 1,600 | 1,286 | 1,056 | 834 | 902 | 981 |
| Total Capital | 2,357 | 2,758 | 2,478 | 2,359 | 2,094 | 1,705 | 1,480 | 1,139 | 1,044 | 999 |
| Capital Expenditures | 173 | 169 | 140 | 134 | 96.7 | 80.0 | 82.2 | 66.7 | 75.1 | 88.5 |
| Cash Flow | -210 | 395 | 445 | 429 | 385 | 328 | 294 | 262 | 260 | 225 |
| Current Ratio | 2.0 | 2.2 | 2.4 | 2.4 | 2.6 | 2.0 | 2.5 | 2.5 | 2.4 | 3.0 |
| % Long Term Debt of Capitalization | 35.5 | 20.7 | 16.9 | 20.6 | 21.0 | 22.2 | 26.1 | 23.6 | 11.1 | Nil |
| % Net Income of Revenue | NM | 5.1 | 6.5 | 6.8 | 6.6 | 6.2 | 5.6 | 5.9 | 6.9 | 6.7 |
| % Return on Assets | NM | 7.7 | 10.3 | 11.1 | 11.5 | 10.9 | 11.1 | 12.6 | 13.7 | 12.6 |
| % Return on Equity | NM | 12.3 | 16.5 | 18.4 | 19.3 | 19.7 | 20.3 | 21.3 | 20.4 | 17.8 |

Data as orig reptd.; bef. results of disc opers/spec. items. Per share data adj. for stk. divs.; EPS diluted. E-Estimated. NA-Not Available. NM-Not Meaningful. NR-Not Ranked. UR-Under Review.

**Office:** 1441 Broadway, New York, NY 10018.
**Telephone:** 212-354-4900.
**Email:** investor_relations@liz.com
**Website:** http://www.lizclaiborne.com

**Chrmn:** K. Koplovitz
**CEO:** W.L. McComb
**COO:** M. Scarpa
**CFO:** A.C. Warren

**Chief Acctg Officer & Cntlr:** E.H. Goodell
**Board Members:** B. W. Aronson, D. A. Carp, R. J. Fernandez, K. B. Gilman, N. J. Karch, K. P. Kopelman, K. Koplovitz, A. C. Martinez, W. L. McComb, O. R. Sockwell, Jr.

**Founded:** 1976
**Domicile:** Delaware
**Employees:** 16,500

**STANDARD &POOR'S**

# Lockheed Martin Corp

| S&P Recommendation BUY ★★★★☆ | Price $72.26 (as of Nov 14, 2008) | 12-Mo. Target Price $100.00 | Investment Style Large-Cap Growth |

**GICS Sector** Industrials
**Sub-Industry** Aerospace & Defense

**Summary** This company is the world's largest military weapons manufacturer and is also a significant supplier to NASA and other government agencies.

## Key Stock Statistics (Source S&P, Vickers, company reports)

| | | | | | | | |
|---|---|---|---|---|---|---|---|
| 52-Wk Range | $120.30– 68.82 | S&P Oper. EPS 2008**E** | 7.60 | Market Capitalization(B) | $28.948 | Beta | 0.62 |
| Trailing 12-Month EPS | $7.71 | S&P Oper. EPS 2009**E** | 7.90 | Yield (%) | 3.16 | S&P 3-Yr. Proj. EPS CAGR(%) | 6 |
| Trailing 12-Month P/E | 9.4 | P/E on S&P Oper. EPS 2008**E** | 9.5 | Dividend Rate/Share | $2.28 | S&P Credit Rating | A- |
| $10K Invested 5 Yrs Ago | $17,326 | Common Shares Outstg. (M) | 400.6 | Institutional Ownership (%) | 89 | | |

## Price Performance

30-Week Mov. Avg. ···· 10-Week Mov. Avg. --- **GAAP Earnings vs. Previous Year** Volume Above Avg. STARS
12-Mo. Target Price — Relative Strength — ▲ Up ▼ Down ► No Change Below Avg. ★

Options: ASE, CBOE, P, Ph

Analysis prepared by **Richard Tortoriello** on October 29, 2008, when the stock traded at **$ 80.31**.

## Highlights

➤ We project a 1% rise in sales in 2008, as we see growth in LMT's Information Systems & Global Services (IS&GS) and Electronic Systems (ES) segments being offset by declines in Aeronautics and flat results in Space Systems (SS). We expect Aeronautics to be weak in the short term but to show strong growth in future years, with LMT projecting strong revenues from the F-22, F-35, and C-130J programs beginning in 2009, as the programs transition into production. For 2009, we see sales rising about 6%, with strong gains in Aeronautics and IS&GS, moderate growth in ES and slow growth in SS.

➤ We expect operating margins to widen to 11.7% in 2008, from 10.8% in 2007 and 9.5% in 2006, with the strongest improvement in Space Systems. Margin improvement has been a big part of LMT's growth story in recent years, in our view, allowing for significantly better profitability and free cash flow.

➤ We estimate EPS growth of 7% in 2008 to $7.60, and 4% in 2009 to $7.90. We expect free cash flow (cash from operating activities less capital expenditures) per share in 2008 of over $9, well ahead of EPS.

## Investment Rationale/Risk

➤ We see significant long-term opportunities for Lockheed in Aeronautics, given both the average age of the U.S. Air Force fleet of about 25 years and the need for next-generation fighter planes. We believe the F-35 Lightning II and the F-22 Raptor hold strong long-term promise for LMT. We also have a positive view of LMT's efforts to pursue more non-defense opportunities with the government, see the possibility of strong defense export sales, and view recent overall contract wins as a sign that LMT continues to execute well across its businesses.

➤ Risks to our recommendation and target price include the potential for decreases in defense spending, as recommended by the president or as enacted by Congress; time or cost overruns on major projects; and the failure to win significant new contracts.

➤ Our 12-month target price of $100 is based on a P/E of 12.7X our 2009 EPS estimate. This is below a 10-year average historical forward P/E of 17.7X for LMT, with lows of 9X. Given our view of investor concerns regarding the defense budget, we believe a lower than historical average multiple is warranted.

## Qualitative Risk Assessment

| LOW | MEDIUM | HIGH |

Our risk assessment reflects the company's leading position in military markets and what we view as a healthy balance sheet, with long-term debt representing about 28% of LMT's total capitalization as of September 2008. However, our risk evaluation also factors in the cyclical nature of Lockheed's business, especially its dependence on government defense programs.

## Quantitative Evaluations

**S&P Quality Ranking** B+

| D | C | B- | B | B+ | A- | A | A+ |

**Relative Strength Rank** MODERATE
47
LOWEST = 1    HIGHEST = 99

## Revenue/Earnings Data

**Revenue (Million $)**

| | 1Q | 2Q | 3Q | 4Q | Year |
|---|---|---|---|---|---|---|
| 2008 | 9,983 | 11,039 | 10,577 | -- | -- |
| 2007 | 9,275 | 10,651 | 11,095 | 10,841 | 41,862 |
| 2006 | 9,214 | 9,961 | 9,605 | 10,840 | 39,620 |
| 2005 | 8,488 | 9,295 | 9,201 | 10,229 | 37,213 |
| 2004 | 8,347 | 8,776 | 8,438 | 9,965 | 35,526 |
| 2003 | 7,059 | 7,709 | 8,078 | 8,978 | 31,824 |

**Earnings Per Share ($)**

| | 1Q | 2Q | 3Q | 4Q | Year |
|---|---|---|---|---|---|---|
| 2008 | 1.75 | 2.15 | 1.92 | E1.78 | E7.60 |
| 2007 | 1.60 | 1.82 | 1.80 | 1.89 | 7.10 |
| 2006 | 1.34 | 1.34 | 1.46 | 1.68 | 5.80 |
| 2005 | 0.83 | 1.02 | 0.96 | 1.29 | 4.10 |
| 2004 | 0.65 | 0.66 | 0.69 | 0.83 | 2.83 |
| 2003 | 0.55 | 0.54 | 0.48 | 0.77 | 2.34 |

Fiscal year ended Dec. 31. Next earnings report expected: Late January. EPS Estimates based on S&P Operating Earnings; historical GAAP earnings are as reported.

## Dividend Data (Dates: mm/dd Payment Date: mm/dd/yy)

| Amount ($) | Date Decl. | Ex-Div. Date | Stk. of Record | Payment Date |
|---|---|---|---|---|
| 0.420 | 01/24 | 02/28 | 03/03 | 03/28/08 |
| 0.420 | 04/24 | 05/29 | 06/02 | 06/27/08 |
| 0.420 | 06/26 | 08/28 | 09/02 | 09/26/08 |
| 0.570 | 09/25 | 11/26 | 12/01 | 12/26/08 |

Dividends have been paid since 1995. Source: Company reports.

# Lockheed Martin Corp

**STANDARD &POOR'S**

## Business Summary October 29, 2008

CORPORATE OVERVIEW. Lockheed Martin is the world's largest military weapons maker. During 2007, the company derived 84% of its net sales from the U.S. government, including both Department of Defense and non-Department of Defense agencies. Sales to foreign governments were 13% of net sales, with 3% of net sales to commercial and other customers. Lockheed Martin conducts business through four operating segments:

The Aeronautics segment (29% of revenues and 32% of operating profits in 2007) primarily makes fighter jets and military transport planes. Major development and production programs include the F-35 Lightning II, the F-22 Raptor, the F-16 Fighting Falcon, and the C-130J Super Hercules transport. In addition, LMT's "Skunk Works" research & development laboratory is well known for its advanced R&D efforts. It is currently focused on unmanned military aircraft.

Electronic Systems (27% and 30%) primarily makes land-, sea- and air-based missiles and missile defense systems. Other offerings include various electronic surveillance and reconnaissance systems. About 41% of the segment's 2007 sales came from maritime systems & sensors, with another 37% coming from missiles & fire control products. Major current programs include the Terminal High-Altitude Area Defense System (THAAD), the Patriot Advanced Capability (PAC-3) missile, the VH-71 Presidential Helicopter, the AEGIS weapon system, and the Arrowhead fire control system for the Apache helicopter.

Space Systems (24% and 20%) mostly makes satellites, strategic and defensive missile systems and space transportation systems. Satellites include both government and commercial products. Space transportation systems include NASA's next-generation space flight systems, including the Orion crew exploration vehicle. Satellites accounted for 68% of segment sales in 2007. LMT is the prime contractor for the Space-Based Infrared System (SBIRS) missile detection program and the Advanced Extremely High Frequency (AEHF) communications system. LMT's 50/50 joint venture with Boeing, the United Launch Alliance, provides satellite launch services to the U.S. government.

Information Systems & Global Services (20% and 18%) is engaged in a wide variety of information technology, IT services, and other technology services to federal agencies and other customers. Major product lines include: IT integration and management; enterprise solutions; application development and maintenance; business processing management; consulting on strategic programs for the Department of Defense and other civil government agencies; mission operations and engineering for the military, homeland security, and NASA; mission readiness, peacekeeping, and nation-building programs; and support of nuclear weapons stewardship and naval reactor programs.

## Company Financials Fiscal Year Ended Dec. 31

| Per Share Data ($) | 2007 | 2006 | 2005 | 2004 | 2003 | 2002 | 2001 | 2000 | 1999 | 1998 |
|---|---|---|---|---|---|---|---|---|---|---|
| Tangible Book Value | NM | NM | NM | NM | NM | NM | NM | NM | NM | NM |
| Cash Flow | 9.02 | 7.55 | 5.68 | 4.39 | 3.69 | 2.40 | 2.08 | 1.36 | 3.30 | 5.27 |
| Earnings | 7.10 | 5.80 | 4.10 | 2.83 | 2.34 | 1.18 | 0.18 | -1.05 | 1.92 | 2.63 |
| S&P Core Earnings | 6.65 | 5.70 | 4.11 | 3.23 | 2.20 | -0.78 | -2.29 | NA | NA | NA |
| Dividends | 1.47 | 1.25 | 1.05 | 0.91 | 0.58 | 0.44 | 0.44 | 0.44 | 0.88 | 0.82 |
| Payout Ratio | 21% | 22% | 26% | 32% | 25% | 37% | NM | NM | 46% | 31% |
| Prices:High | 113.74 | 93.24 | 65.46 | 61.77 | 58.95 | 71.52 | 52.98 | 37.58 | 46.00 | 58.94 |
| Prices:Low | 88.86 | 62.52 | 52.54 | 43.10 | 40.64 | 45.85 | 31.00 | 16.50 | 16.38 | 41.00 |
| P/E Ratio:High | 16 | 16 | 16 | 22 | 25 | 61 | NM | NM | 24 | 22 |
| P/E Ratio:Low | 13 | 11 | 13 | 15 | 17 | 39 | NM | NM | 9 | 16 |

| Income Statement Analysis (Million $) | | | | | | | | | | |
|---|---|---|---|---|---|---|---|---|---|---|
| Revenue | 41,862 | 39,620 | 37,213 | 35,526 | 31,824 | 26,578 | 23,990 | 25,329 | 25,530 | 26,266 |
| Operating Income | 5,032 | 4,198 | 3,242 | 2,624 | 2,585 | 2,507 | 2,366 | 2,582 | 2,634 | 3,357 |
| Depreciation | 819 | 764 | 705 | 656 | 609 | 558 | 823 | 968 | 969 | 1,005 |
| Interest Expense | 352 | 361 | 370 | 425 | 487 | 581 | 700 | 919 | 809 | 861 |
| Pretax Income | 4,368 | 3,592 | 2,616 | 1,664 | 1,532 | 577 | 188 | 286 | 1,200 | 1,661 |
| Effective Tax Rate | 30.6% | 29.6% | 30.2% | 23.9% | 31.3% | 7.63% | 58.0% | NM | 38.6% | 39.7% |
| Net Income | 3,033 | 2,529 | 1,825 | 1,266 | 1,053 | 533 | 79.0 | -424 | 737 | 1,001 |
| S&P Core Earnings | 2,844 | 2,486 | 1,830 | 1,448 | 994 | -353 | -989 | NA | NA | NA |

| Balance Sheet & Other Financial Data (Million $) | | | | | | | | | | |
|---|---|---|---|---|---|---|---|---|---|---|
| Cash | 2,981 | 1,912 | 2,244 | 1,060 | 1,010 | 2,738 | 912 | 1,505 | 455 | 285 |
| Current Assets | 10,940 | 10,164 | 10,529 | 8,953 | 9,401 | 10,626 | 10,778 | 11,259 | 10,696 | 10,611 |
| Total Assets | 28,926 | 28,231 | 27,744 | 25,554 | 26,175 | 25,758 | 27,654 | 30,349 | 30,012 | 28,744 |
| Current Liabilities | 9,871 | 9,553 | 9,428 | 8,566 | 8,893 | 9,821 | 9,689 | 10,175 | 8,812 | 10,267 |
| Long Term Debt | 4,303 | 4,405 | 4,784 | 5,104 | 6,072 | 6,217 | 7,422 | 9,065 | 11,427 | 8,957 |
| Common Equity | 9,805 | 6,884 | 7,867 | 7,021 | 6,756 | 5,865 | 6,443 | 7,160 | 6,361 | 6,137 |
| Total Capital | 14,108 | 11,289 | 12,651 | 12,125 | 12,828 | 12,082 | 14,857 | 16,961 | 17,788 | 15,094 |
| Capital Expenditures | 940 | 893 | 865 | 769 | 687 | 662 | 619 | 500 | 669 | 697 |
| Cash Flow | 3,852 | 3,293 | 2,530 | 1,922 | 1,662 | 1,091 | 902 | 544 | 1,266 | 2,006 |
| Current Ratio | 1.1 | 1.1 | 1.1 | 1.0 | 1.1 | 1.1 | 1.1 | 1.1 | 1.2 | 1.0 |
| % Long Term Debt of Capitalization | 30.5 | 39.0 | 37.8 | 42.1 | 47.3 | 51.5 | 50.0 | 53.4 | 64.2 | 59.3 |
| % Net Income of Revenue | 7.3 | 6.4 | 4.9 | 3.6 | 3.3 | 2.0 | 0.3 | NM | 2.9 | 3.8 |
| % Return on Assets | 10.6 | 9.0 | 6.8 | 4.9 | 4.0 | 2.0 | 0.3 | NM | 2.5 | 3.5 |
| % Return on Equity | 36.4 | 34.3 | 24.5 | 18.4 | 16.7 | 8.7 | 1.2 | NM | 11.8 | 17.7 |

Data as orig reptd.; bef. results of disc opers/spec. items. Per share data adj. for stk. divs.; EPS diluted. E-Estimated. NA-Not Available. NM-Not Meaningful. NR-Not Ranked. UR-Under Review.

**Office:** 6801 Rockledge Drive, Bethesda, MD 20817.
**Telephone:** 301-897-6000.
**Website:** http://www.lockheedmartin.com
**Chrmn, Pres & CEO:** R.J. Stevens

**Pres:** M.S. Williams
**COO:** R. Nakamoto
**EVP & CFO:** B.L. Tanner
**SVP & CTO:** R. Johnson

**Board Members:** E. C. Aldridge, Jr., N. D. Archibald, M. C. Barrett, D. B. Burritt, J. O. Ellis, Jr., G. S. King, J. M. Loy, D. H. McCorkindale, J. W. Ralston, F. Savage, J. M. Schneider, A. Stevens, R. J. Stevens, J. R. Ukropina
**Founded:** 1909
**Domicile:** Maryland
**Employees:** 140,000

**The McGraw-Hill Companies**

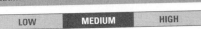

**STANDARD
&POOR'S**

# Loews Corp

**S&P Recommendation** HOLD ★★★☆☆

| | |
|---|---|
| **Price** | $27.94 (as of Nov 14, 2008) |
| **12-Mo. Target Price** | $30.00 |
| **Investment Style** | Large-Cap Value |

**GICS Sector** Financials
**Sub-Industry** Multi-line Insurance

**Summary** This conglomerate includes holdings in property/casualty insurance, offshore drilling, hotels, and natural gas pipelines.

## Key Stock Statistics (Source S&P, Vickers, company reports)

| | | | | | | | | |
|---|---|---|---|---|---|---|---|---|
| 52-Wk Range | $51.51– 23.27 | S&P Oper. EPS 2008**E** | **NA** | Market Capitalization(B) | **$12.184** | Beta | **1.34** |
| Trailing 12-Month EPS | $11.28 | S&P Oper. EPS 2009**E** | **NA** | Yield (%) | **0.89** | S&P 3-Yr. Proj. EPS CAGR(%) | **10** |
| Trailing 12-Month P/E | 2.5 | P/E on S&P Oper. EPS 2008**E** | **null** | Dividend Rate/Share | **$0.25** | S&P Credit Rating | **A** |
| $10K Invested 5 Yrs Ago | $20,043 | Common Shares Outstg. (M) | **436.1** | Institutional Ownership (%) | **63** | | |

## Price Performance

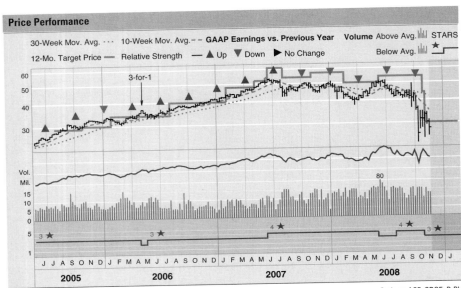

Options: ASE, CBOE, P, Ph

Analysis prepared by **Bret Howlett** on October 30, 2008, when the stock traded at **$ 30.69**.

### Highlights

➤ We expect L's revenues to decline in 2008 mainly on poor performance from its principal subsidiary - 90%-owned CNA Financial (CNA: hold, $17). We believe CNA's revenues will be adversely affected by lower investment income and declining P&C rates. We expect 50%-owned Diamond Offshore (DO: buy, $97) to benefit from rising demand in deepwater floaters and midwater floaters, and a robust backlog should provide strong earnings viability. We forecast solid operating earnings growth for 70%-owned Boardwalk Pipeline Partners (BWP: NR) on our estimate of expanding natural gas storage capacity and improved operating efficiencies. We expect HighMount E&P earnings to benefit from a strong demand for natural gas.

➤ Due to the softening P&C rate environment, we expect operating earnings to decline for CNA in 2008, although our we believe the company will benefit from an improved outlook in 2009. We believe L's recent $1.25 billion purchase of CNA preferred shares will help stabilize capital levels of the subsidiary amid investment losses.

➤ Our operating EPS forecasts are $1.79 for 2008 and $4.60 for 2009.

### Investment Rationale/Risk

➤ Although we see strong fundamentals for L's energy subsidiaries, we believe over the near-term, L will be weighed down by the turbulent operating environment and overall uncertainty at CNA. We expected further investment losses, and a unfavorable operating environment at CNA to be a drag on L's results over the next several quarters. However, we think that demand for rigs will prove to be a boon for Diamond Offshore and that increased demand for natural gas should benefit the Boardwalk Pipeline and HighMount E&P subsidiaries. Also, we expect CNA to benefit if the down-phase in the commercial underwriting pricing cycle stabilizes, or reverses in 2009.

➤ Risks to our recommendation and target price include a decline in the level of oil and gas production for Diamond Offshore; higher-than-projected catastrophe losses; greater-than-expected losses in the investment portfolio; asbestos and environmental losses for CNA; and, a slowdown in consumer spending affecting Loews Hotels.

➤ Our 12-month target price is $30, 6.5X our 2009 operating estimate and below its historical multiples.

## Qualitative Risk Assessment

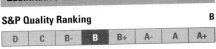

| LOW | MEDIUM | HIGH |
|---|---|---|

Our risk assessment reflects the company's exposure to investment losses from its subsidiary CNA Financial, regulation risks, litigation risk, and catastrophic events. This is offset by this diversified group of holdings and substantial free cash flow.

## Quantitative Evaluations

**S&P Quality Ranking**      **B**

| D | C | B- | B | B+ | A- | A | A+ |
|---|---|---|---|---|---|---|---|

**Relative Strength Rank**      **MODERATE**

53

LOWEST = 1      HIGHEST = 99

## Revenue/Earnings Data

### Revenue (Million $)

| | 1Q | 2Q | 3Q | 4Q | Year |
|---|---|---|---|---|---|---|
| 2008 | 4,543 | 3,922 | 2,970 | -- | -- |
| 2007 | 4,660 | 4,637 | 4,653 | 4,567 | 18,380 |
| 2006 | 4,245 | 4,277 | 4,507 | 4,882 | 17,911 |
| 2005 | 3,741 | 4,031 | 4,138 | 4,108 | 16,018 |
| 2004 | 3,491 | 3,915 | 3,785 | 4,051 | 15,242 |
| 2003 | 3,949 | 4,250 | 3,940 | 4,336 | 16,461 |

### Earnings Per Share ($)

| | 1Q | 2Q | 3Q | 4Q | Year |
|---|---|---|---|---|---|---|
| 2008 | 0.89 | 0.80 | -0.33 | E1.00 | E1.79 |
| 2007 | 1.19 | 0.96 | 0.76 | 0.71 | 3.64 |
| 2006 | 0.86 | 0.85 | 0.93 | 1.15 | 3.80 |
| 2005 | 0.53 | 0.68 | 0.42 | 0.07 | 1.69 |
| 2004 | 0.02 | 0.66 | 0.40 | 0.80 | 1.88 |
| 2003 | 0.29 | 0.34 | -2.53 | 0.60 | -1.30 |

Fiscal year ended Dec. 31. Next earnings report expected: Mid February. EPS Estimates based on S&P Operating Earnings; historical GAAP earnings are as reported.

## Dividend Data (Dates: mm/dd Payment Date: mm/dd/yy)

| Amount ($) | Date Decl. | Ex-Div. Date | Stk. of Record | Payment Date |
|---|---|---|---|---|
| 0.063 | 02/12 | 02/28 | 03/03 | 03/14/08 |
| 0.063 | 05/09 | 05/21 | 05/23 | 06/06/08 |
| 0.063 | 08/12 | 08/28 | 09/02 | 09/15/08 |
| 0.063 | 11/11 | 11/26 | 12/01 | 12/12/08 |

Dividends have been paid since 1967. Source: Company reports.

# Loews Corp

STANDARD &POOR'S

## Business Summary October 30, 2008

CORPORATE OVERVIEW. Loews Corp. is a holding company with interests in property/casualty insurance (CNA Financial Corp., 89% stake), hotels (Loews Hotels Holding Corp.), offshore oil and gas drilling (Diamond Offshore Drilling, Inc., 51% stake), exploration, production and marketing of natural gas and natural gas liquids (HighMount Exploration & Production LLC), and interstate natural gas pipelines (Boardwalk Pipeline Partners, LP, 70% stake).

CNA Financial Corp. (NYSE: CNA; 54% of consolidated total revenues in 2007) is an insurance holding company with subsidiaries that primarily consist of property and casualty insurance companies. The Loews Hotels division (2.1%) owns and/or operates 18 hotels in the U.S. and Canada. Diamond Offshore (NYSE: DO; 14%) operates 44 offshore drilling rigs that are chartered on a con-

tract basis for fixed terms by energy exploration companies. Boardwalk Pipeline (NYSE: BWP; 3.7%) owns and operates two interstate natural gas pipeline systems, Gulf South Pipeline and Texas Gas Transmission. High-Mount Exploration & Production LLC (1.7%) is involved in the exploration, production and marketing of natural gas, NGLs (predominantly ethane and propane) and oil. Other activities accounted for about 2.4% of consolidated total revenue in 2007.

## Company Financials Fiscal Year Ended Dec. 31

| Per Share Data ($) | 2009 | 2008 | 2007 | 2006 | 2005 | 2004 | 2003 | 2002 | 2001 | 2000 |
|---|---|---|---|---|---|---|---|---|---|---|
| Tangible Book Value | NA | NA | 25.44 | NM | NM | 21.35 | NM | 19.88 | 16.23 | 18.28 |
| Operating Earnings | NA | NA | NA | NA | NA | NA | NA | 1.71 | -2.27 | 1.90 |
| Earnings | 4.60 | 1.79 | 3.64 | 3.80 | 1.69 | 1.88 | -1.30 | 1.50 | -0.92 | 3.15 |
| S&P Core Earnings | NA | NA | 3.76 | 3.65 | 1.49 | 2.17 | -2.00 | 2.63 | -2.47 | NA |
| Dividends | NA | 0.19 | 0.25 | 0.18 | 0.20 | 0.20 | 0.20 | 0.20 | 0.19 | 0.17 |
| Relative Payout | NA | 10% | 7% | 5% | 12% | 11% | NM | 13% | NM | 5% |
| Prices:High | NA | 51.51 | 53.46 | 42.18 | 32.90 | 23.67 | 16.49 | 20.77 | 24.17 | 34.98 |
| Prices:Low | NA | 23.27 | 40.21 | 30.42 | 22.35 | 16.36 | 12.75 | 12.50 | 13.68 | 12.75 |
| P/E Ratio:High | NA | 29 | 15 | 11 | 19 | 13 | NM | 14 | NM | 11 |
| P/E Ratio:Low | NA | 13 | 11 | 8 | 13 | 9 | NM | 8 | NM | 4 |

| Income Statement Analysis (Million $) | 2009 | 2008 | 2007 | 2006 | 2005 | 2004 | 2003 | 2002 | 2001 | 2000 |
|---|---|---|---|---|---|---|---|---|---|---|
| Life Insurance in Force | NA | NA | 14,090 | 15,652 | 20,548 | 56,645 | 388,968 | 437,751 | 497,732 | 534,781 |
| Premium Income:Life A & H | NA | NA | 618 | 641 | 704 | 901 | 2,275 | 3,382 | 4,351 | 4,549 |
| Premium Income:Casualty/Property. | NA | NA | 6,866 | 6,962 | 6,865 | 7,304 | 6,935 | 6,828 | 5,010 | 6,923 |
| Net Investment Income | NA | NA | 2,891 | 2,915 | 2,099 | 1,869 | 1,732 | 1,867 | 2,145 | 2,388 |
| Total Revenue | NA | NA | 18,380 | 17,911 | 16,018 | 15,242 | 16,461 | 17,495 | 19,417 | 21,338 |
| Pretax Income | NA | NA | 4,575 | 1,237 | 1,016 | 1,822 | -751 | 1,647 | -813 | 3,206 |
| Net Operating Income | NA | NA | NA | NA | NA | NA | NA | 1,099 | -1,328 | 1,134 |
| Net Income | NA | NA | 2,481 | 760 | 623 | 1,231 | -468 | 983 | -536 | 1,877 |
| S&P Core Earnings | NA | NA | 2,014 | 2,024 | 831 | 1,205 | -1,112 | 1,594 | -1,447 | NA |

| Balance Sheet & Other Financial Data (Million $) | 2009 | 2008 | 2007 | 2006 | 2005 | 2004 | 2003 | 2002 | 2001 | 2000 |
|---|---|---|---|---|---|---|---|---|---|---|
| Cash & Equivalent | NA | NA | 141 | 132 | 151 | 220 | 181 | 185 | 181 | 195 |
| Premiums Due | NA | NA | 11,677 | 12,423 | 15,314 | 18,807 | 20,468 | 16,601 | 19,453 | 15,302 |
| Investment Assets:Bonds | NA | NA | 34,663 | 37,570 | 33,381 | 33,502 | 28,781 | 27,434 | 31,191 | 27,244 |
| Investment Assets:Stocks | NA | NA | 1,347 | 1,309 | 1,107 | 664 | 888 | 1,121 | 1,646 | 2,683 |
| Investment Assets:Loans | NA | NA | Nil | Nil | Nil | Nil | Nil | NA | NA | NA |
| Investment Assets:Total | NA | NA | 47,923 | 52,020 | 43,547 | 44,299 | 42,515 | 40,137 | 41,159 | 40,396 |
| Deferred Policy Costs | NA | NA | 1,161 | 1,190 | 1,197 | 1,268 | 2,533 | 2,551 | 2,424 | 2,418 |
| Total Assets | NA | NA | 76,079 | 75,325 | 69,548 | 73,750 | 77,881 | 70,520 | 75,251 | 70,877 |
| Debt | NA | NA | 6,900 | 1,230 | 1,627 | 5,980 | 2,032 | 5,652 | 5,920 | 6,040 |
| Common Equity | NA | NA | 17,591 | 15,580 | -201 | 45,428 | -729 | 11,235 | 9,649 | 11,191 |
| Combined Loss-Expense Ratio | NA | NA | 110.1 | 109.1 | 120.3 | 105.9 | 146.6 | 110.3 | 158.6 | 113.6 |
| % Return on Revenue | NA | NA | 13.5 | 4.2 | 3.9 | 8.1 | 14.2 | 5.6 | NM | 8.8 |
| % Return on Equity | NA | NA | 15.0 | 14.2 | 2.6 | 2.8 | NM | 8.1 | NM | 4.9 |
| % Investment Yield | NA | NA | 5.8 | 6.1 | 2.6 | 4.3 | 4.2 | 4.6 | 5.2 | 5.9 |

Data as orig reptd.; bef. results of disc opers/spec. items. Per share data adj. for stk. divs.; EPS diluted. E-Estimated. NA-Not Available. NM-Not Meaningful. NR-Not Ranked. UR-Under Review.

**Office:** 667 Madison Ave, New York, NY 10021-8087.
**Telephone:** 212-521-2000.
**Website:** http://www.loews.com
**Co-Chrmn:** J.M. Tisch

**Co-Chrmn:** A. Tisch
**Pres & CEO:** J.S. Tisch
**SVP & CFO:** P.W. Keegan
**SVP, Secy & General Counsel:** G.W. Garson

**Investor Contact:** D. Daugherty (212-521-2788)
**Board Members:** A. E. Berman, J. L. Bower, C. M. Diker, P. J. Fribourg, W. L. Harris, P. A. Laskawy, K. Miller, G. R. Scott, A. Tisch, J. S. Tisch, J. M. Tisch

**Founded:** 1954
**Domicile:** Delaware
**Employees:** 21,700

STANDARD &POOR'S

# Lorillard Inc

| S&P Recommendation | HOLD ★★★☆☆ | Price | 12-Mo. Target Price | Investment Style |
|---|---|---|---|---|
| | | $60.78 (as of Nov 14, 2008) | $65.00 | Large-Cap Blend |

**GICS Sector** Consumer Staples
**Sub-Industry** Tobacco

**Summary** Lorillard is the third largest U.S. tobacco company and the leading manufacturer and marketer of menthol cigarettes.

## Key Stock Statistics (Source S&P, Vickers, company reports)

| | | | | | | | |
|---|---|---|---|---|---|---|---|
| 52-Wk Range | $92.79– 53.30 | S&P Oper. EPS 2008**E** | 5.16 | Market Capitalization(B) | $10.215 | Beta | 0.71 |
| Trailing 12-Month EPS | $4.86 | S&P Oper. EPS 2009**E** | 5.48 | Yield (%) | 6.05 | S&P 3-Yr. Proj. EPS CAGR(%) | 9 |
| Trailing 12-Month P/E | 12.5 | P/E on S&P Oper. EPS 2008**E** | 11.8 | Dividend Rate/Share | $3.68 | S&P Credit Rating | A |
| $10K Invested 5 Yrs Ago | $26,401 | Common Shares Outstg. (M) | 168.1 | Institutional Ownership (%) | 92 | | |

## Price Performance

30-Week Mov. Avg. ···· 10-Week Mov. Avg. --- GAAP Earnings vs. Previous Year  Volume Above Avg. STARS
12-Mo. Target Price — Relative Strength — ▲ Up ▼ Down ▶ No Change  Below Avg.

Analysis prepared by **Esther Y. Kwon, CFA** on October 30, 2008, when the stock traded at **$ 64.67**.

### Highlights

➤ Lorillard, formerly a division of Loews Corp., was spun off in June 2008. Its operating performance had previously been followed as a tracking stock (Loews Corp. - Carolina Group; CG). We see 2008 revenues rising at a mid-single digit rate, as we expect moderate growth in premium volumes and a higher mix of discount brands. Lorillard has significantly increased its marketing efforts behind the Newport brand, and we look for the resulting positive trend to continue in 2008. However, we believe this projected improvement in market share will be somewhat limited by an overall decline in industry volumes.

➤ For 2008, we see discount brand volumes to continue to accelerate, resulting in a slight expected deterioration in gross margins but offset by a recent price increase. Although we believe marketing costs will rise, we see only a modest increase in selling, general and administrative expenses. We expect operating margins to be down slightly but operating profit to increase at a mid-single digit rate.

➤ On a higher tax rate and significantly reduced investment income, we expect 2008 EPS of $5.16. For 2009, we see EPS rising to $5.42.

### Investment Rationale/Risk

➤ We view positively LO's continued market share gains for its leading brand, Newport, in both the menthol and premium categories. We believe efforts to increase its investment in this brand will result in long term volume growth ahead of peers, less promotional activity, and higher average prices, but we are concerned about LO's dependence on the Northeast, especially with exposure to financial services and New York's recent excise tax boost.

➤ Risks to our recommendation and target price include increasing menthol competition from the premium and deep discount segments, a slowdown in industry volume trends, and a worsening of the litigation environment.

➤ Applying a below recent average P/E of 12X to our 2009 estimate, we arrive at our 12-month target price of $65. Our P/E assumption is a discount to the peer average, as we see operating margins eroding on mix shift and higher expenses. While we are concerned about relatively high geographic concentration and see limited margin expansion potential, we think LO may be attractive to strategic acquirers given the separation from Loews, which could be supportive to the shares.

### Qualitative Risk Assessment

| LOW | MEDIUM | HIGH |
|---|---|---|

Our risk assessment reflects the relatively stable revenue and income streams enjoyed by the tobacco industry, offset by significant ongoing litigation.

### Quantitative Evaluations

**S&P Quality Ranking**　　　　NR

| D | C | B- | B | B+ | A- | A | A+ |
|---|---|---|---|---|---|---|---|

**Relative Strength Rank**　　　　STRONG

80

LOWEST = 1　　　　HIGHEST = 99

### Revenue/Earnings Data

**Revenue (Million $)**

| | 1Q | 2Q | 3Q | 4Q | Year |
|---|---|---|---|---|---|
| 2008 | 932.0 | 886.0 | 936.0 | -- | -- |
| 2007 | 947.3 | 1,055 | 1,044 | 957.0 | 3,281 |
| 2006 | 880.8 | 998.6 | 1,016 | 936.7 | 3,866 |
| 2005 | -- | -- | -- | 916.0 | 3,640 |
| 2004 | 776.1 | 868.0 | 887.4 | 832.5 | 3,388 |
| 2003 | 852.8 | 790.0 | 845.7 | 787.7 | 3,288 |

**Earnings Per Share ($)**

| | | | | | |
|---|---|---|---|---|---|
| 2008 | 1.00 | 1.25 | 1.38 | E1.38 | E5.16 |
| 2007 | 1.08 | 1.30 | 1.34 | 1.18 | 5.16 |
| 2006 | 0.86 | 1.09 | 1.17 | 1.26 | 4.46 |
| 2005 | 0.68 | 0.82 | 0.99 | 1.11 | 3.62 |
| 2004 | 0.59 | 0.70 | 0.92 | 0.93 | 3.15 |
| 2003 | 0.72 | 0.63 | 0.67 | 0.74 | 2.76 |

Fiscal year ended Dec. 31. Next earnings report expected: Mid February. EPS Estimates based on S&P Operating Earnings; historical GAAP earnings are as reported.

### Dividend Data (Dates: mm/dd Payment Date: mm/dd/yy)

| Amount ($) | Date Decl. | Ex-Div. Date | Stk. of Record | Payment Date |
|---|---|---|---|---|
| 0.455 | 11/13 | 11/29 | 12/03 | 12/14/07 |
| 0.455 | 02/12 | 02/28 | 03/03 | 03/14/08 |
| 0.455 | 05/09 | 05/21 | 05/23 | 06/06/08 |
| 0.920 | 08/21 | 08/28 | 09/02 | 09/12/08 |

Dividends have been paid since 2002. Source: Company reports.

The McGraw-Hill Companies

# Lorillard Inc

**STANDARD &POOR'S**

## Business Summary October 30, 2008

CORPORATE OVERVIEW. The company produces and markets cigarettes primarily in the U.S. The tobacco used in Lorillard cigarettes includes burley leaf, flue-cured tobacco grown in the U.S. and abroad, and aromatic tobacco grown primarily in Turkey and other Near Eastern countries. Through Alliance One International, Inc., Lorillard directs the purchase of nearly 90% of its U.S. leaf tobacco needs. The company stores the various types and grades of its tobacco in 29 warehouses at its Danville, VA, facility. Its sole manufacturing plant, located in Greensboro, NC, has an annual production capacity of about 43 billion cigarettes.

The company primarily sells its cigarettes to distributors that resell them to chain store organizations and government agencies. As of December 31, 2007, Lorillard had approximately 600 direct buying customers servicing more than 400,000 retail accounts. Lorillard does not sell cigarettes directly to consumers. During 2007, 2006, 2005, 2004 and 2003, sales made by Lorillard to McLane Company, Inc. comprised 24%, 23%, 21%, 20% and 20%, respectively,

of Lorillard's revenues. No other customer accounted for more than 10% of sales.

REGULATORY ENVIRONMENT. Lorillard's business operations are subject to a variety of federal, state and local laws and regulations governing, among other things, the publication of health warnings on cigarette packaging, advertising and sales of tobacco products, restrictions on smoking in public places, and fire safety standards. The U.S. cigarette industry faces a number of issues that have affected and may continue to affect its operations, including substantial litigation that seeks billions of dollars of damages. As of February 15, 2008, Lorillard was a defendant in about 3,775 cases facing the industry.

## Company Financials Fiscal Year Ended Dec. 31

### Per Share Data ($)

| | 2007 | 2006 | 2005 | 2004 | 2003 | 2002 | 2001 | 2000 | 1999 | 1998 |
|---|---|---|---|---|---|---|---|---|---|---|
| Tangible Book Value | 6.34 | NM | NM | NM | NM | NM | NA | NA | NA | NA |
| Cash Flow | 4.91 | NA | NA | NA | 8.08 | NA | NA | NA | NA | NA |
| Earnings | 4.91 | 4.46 | 3.62 | 3.15 | 2.76 | 3.50 | NA | NA | NA | NA |
| S&P Core Earnings | 5.31 | 4.46 | 3.63 | 3.13 | 3.31 | 2.92 | NA | NA | NA | NA |
| Dividends | 1.82 | 1.82 | 1.82 | 1.82 | 1.81 | 1.34 | NA | NA | NA | NA |
| Payout Ratio | 37% | 41% | 50% | 58% | 66% | 38% | NA | NA | NA | NA |
| Prices:High | 92.79 | 64.83 | 46.06 | 30.00 | 28.10 | 34.05 | NA | NA | NA | NA |
| Prices:Low | 64.00 | 43.83 | 28.47 | 22.49 | 17.18 | 16.80 | NA | NA | NA | NA |
| P/E Ratio:High | 19 | 15 | 13 | 10 | 10 | 10 | NA | NA | NA | NA |
| P/E Ratio:Low | 13 | 10 | 8 | 7 | 6 | 5 | NA | NA | NA | NA |

### Income Statement Analysis (Million $)

| | 2007 | 2006 | 2005 | 2004 | 2003 | 2002 | 2001 | 2000 | 1999 | 1998 |
|---|---|---|---|---|---|---|---|---|---|---|
| Revenue | 3,969 | 3,866 | 3,640 | 3,388 | 3,288 | 3,798 | 3,868 | NA | NA | NA |
| Operating Income | 1,392 | 1,352 | 1,156 | 1,041 | 934 | NA | NA | NA | NA | NA |
| Depreciation | 40.0 | 47.0 | 48.0 | 40.0 | NA | NA | NA | NA | NA | NA |
| Interest Expense | 74.0 | 116 | 141 | 158 | 183 | 178 | 0.70 | NA | NA | NA |
| Pretax Income | 1,318 | 1,237 | 1,016 | 884 | 751 | 1,121 | 1,105 | NA | NA | NA |
| Effective Tax Rate | 35.1% | 38.5% | 38.6% | 38.2% | 37.7% | 39.2% | 39.0% | NA | NA | NA |
| Net Income | 855 | 760 | 623 | 546 | 468 | 682 | 673 | NA | NA | NA |
| S&P Core Earnings | 577 | 417 | 252 | 184 | 138 | 117 | 672 | NA | NA | NA |

### Balance Sheet & Other Financial Data (Million $)

| | 2007 | 2006 | 2005 | 2004 | 2003 | 2002 | 2001 | 2000 | 1999 | 1998 |
|---|---|---|---|---|---|---|---|---|---|---|
| Cash | 2.00 | 1.50 | 2.50 | 36.0 | 1.90 | 2.20 | 1.70 | NA | NA | NA |
| Current Assets | NA | NA | NA | NA | NA | NA | NA | NA | NA | NA |
| Total Assets | 2,702 | 2,861 | 2,897 | 2,278 | 2,725 | 2,927 | 2,769 | NA | NA | NA |
| Current Liabilities | NA | NA | NA | NA | NA | NA | NA | NA | NA | NA |
| Long Term Debt | 424 | 1,230 | 1,627 | 1,871 | 2,032 | 2,438 | Nil | NA | NA | NA |
| Common Equity | 685 | 0.16 | -201 | -502 | -729 | -884 | 1,275 | NA | NA | NA |
| Total Capital | 1,109 | 1,230 | 1,426 | 1,369 | 1,303 | 1,555 | 1,275 | NA | NA | NA |
| Capital Expenditures | 51.0 | 29.7 | 31.2 | 50.8 | 56.4 | 51.7 | 41.2 | NA | NA | NA |
| Cash Flow | NA | NA | NA | NA | NA | NA | NA | NA | NA | NA |
| Current Ratio | 1.8 | 1.8 | 1.7 | NA | NA | NA | NA | NA | NA | NA |
| % Long Term Debt of Capitalization | 38.2 | 100.0 | 114.1 | 136.7 | 156.0 | 156.8 | Nil | NA | NA | NA |
| % Net Income of Revenue | 21.5 | 19.7 | 17.1 | 16.1 | 14.2 | 17.9 | 17.4 | NA | NA | NA |
| % Return on Assets | 30.7 | 26.4 | 22.0 | 19.8 | 16.6 | 23.9 | NA | NA | NA | NA |
| % Return on Equity | 203.4 | 5.4 | NM | NM | NM | 348.6 | NA | NA | NA | NA |

Data as orig reptd.; bef. results of disc opers/spec. items. Per share data adj. for stk. divs.; EPS diluted. Prior to June 11, 2008, data and historical prices reflect the former Loews Corp-Carolina Group. E-Estimated. NA-Not Available. NM-Not Meaningful. NR-Not Ranked. UR-Under Review.

**Office:** 667 Madison Avenue, New York, NY 10065-8029.
**Telephone:** 212-521-2000.
**Email:** ir@loews.com
**Website:** http://www.loews.com

**Chrmn, Pres & CEO:** M.L. Orlowsky
**EVP & CFO:** D.H. Taylor
**SVP, Chief Acctg Officer & Treas:** T.R. Staab
**SVP, Secy & General Counsel:** R.S. Milstein

**Treas:** H. Lewis
**Investor Contact:** P.W. Keegan (212-521-2000)
**Board Members:** R. C. Almon, V. W. Colbert, D. E. Dangoor, K. D. Dietz, M. L. Orlowsky, R. W. Roedel, D. H. Taylor, N. Travis

**Founded:** 1969
**Domicile:** Delaware
**Employees:** 2,800

# Lowe's Companies Inc.

**STANDARD &POOR'S**

| S&P Recommendation | HOLD ★★★☆☆ | Price $18.23 (as of Nov 14, 2008) | 12-Mo. Target Price $30.00 | Investment Style Large-Cap Growth |
|---|---|---|---|---|

**GICS Sector** Consumer Discretionary
**Sub-Industry** Home Improvement Retail

**Summary** This company retails building materials and supplies, lumber, hardware and appliances through about 1,600 stores in 49 states and Canada.

## Key Stock Statistics (Source S&P, Vickers, company reports)

| | | | | | |
|---|---|---|---|---|---|
| 52-Wk Range | $28.49– 15.76 | S&P Oper. EPS 2009**E** | 1.54 | Market Capitalization(B) | $26.719 |
| Trailing 12-Month EPS | $1.75 | S&P Oper. EPS 2010**E** | 1.55 | Yield (%) | 1.87 |
| Trailing 12-Month P/E | 10.4 | P/E on S&P Oper. EPS 2009**E** | 11.8 | Dividend Rate/Share | $0.34 |
| $10K Invested 5 Yrs Ago | $6,446 | Common Shares Outstg. (M) | 1,465.7 | Institutional Ownership (%) | 83 |

| | |
|---|---|
| Beta | 0.98 |
| S&P 3-Yr. Proj. EPS CAGR(%) | 12 |
| S&P Credit Rating | A+ |

## Price Performance

- 30-Week Mov. Avg. · · · ·
- 10-Week Mov. Avg. - -
- **GAAP Earnings vs. Previous Year**
- Volume Above Avg. ▏▍▊ STARS
- 12-Mo. Target Price —
- Relative Strength —
- ▲ Up ▼ Down ▶ No Change
- Below Avg. ▏▍▊ ★ —

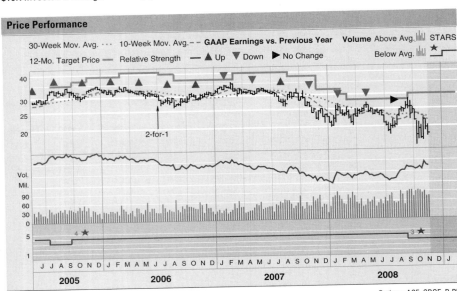

2-for-1

Options: ASE, CBOE, P, Ph

Analysis prepared by **Michael Souers** on September 25, 2008, when the stock traded at **$ 24.05**.

## Highlights

➤ We forecast sales growth of 4.2% in FY 10 (Jan.), following our projection of a 1.3% advance in FY 09. We expect this growth to be driven by an estimated 75-85 net new store openings, reflecting an approximate 5% increase in total square footage. However, we look for same-store sales to decrease approximately 1%, as we project further declines in average ticket and foot traffic due to the challenging macro-environment. We expect the housing market to remain under pressure throughout much of 2009 and see a related slowdown in consumer spending.

➤ We project FY 10 operating margins to decline slightly, as higher occupancy costs, increasing payroll expenses and a deleveraging of expenses due to declining same-store sales results are only partially offset by lower sourcing costs and an improved product mix.

➤ We see flat interest expense, taxes at an effective rate of 38.0%, and about 1% fewer shares outstanding, reflecting LOW's active share repurchase plan. We forecast FY 10 EPS of $1.55, a slight increase from the $1.54 we project the company will earn in FY 09.

## Investment Rationale/Risk

➤ We think the aging of homes and home ownership rates near historical highs are powerful long term demographic drivers that should help mitigate the continued weakness in housing turnover that we see for 2009. In addition, despite concerns about consumer spending, we believe consumers will continue to allocate a fair portion of their discretionary income to home improvement projects, as they view their homes as investments. We also favor international expansion opportunities in Canada and Mexico. However, with LOW trading at over 15X our FY 10 EPS, we think upside will remain limited until the housing market improves.

➤ Risks to our recommendation and target price include a sharp slowdown in the economy; a large rise in long term interest rates; and failure by LOW to execute its metro market expansion strategy.

➤ At about 15X our FY 10 EPS estimate, LOW shares recently traded at a slight premium to key peer Home Depot (HD: buy, $26). Our 12-month target price of $30 is derived from our discounted cash flow (DCF) analysis, which assumes a weighted average cost of capital of 9.4% and a terminal growth rate of 3.0%.

## Qualitative Risk Assessment

| LOW | MEDIUM | HIGH |
|---|---|---|

Our risk assessment reflects the cyclical nature of the home improvement retail industry, which is reliant on economic growth, offset by our view of ample opportunities for retail growth both domestically and abroad, and an S&P Quality Ranking of A+, reflecting LOW's consistent historical earnings and dividend growth.

## Quantitative Evaluations

**S&P Quality Ranking**          A+

| D | C | B- | B | B+ | A- | A | A+ |
|---|---|---|---|---|---|---|---|

**Relative Strength Rank**          MODERATE

67

LOWEST = 1                    HIGHEST = 99

## Revenue/Earnings Data

**Revenue (Million $)**

| | 1Q | 2Q | 3Q | 4Q | Year |
|---|---|---|---|---|---|
| 2009 | 12,009 | 14,509 | -- | -- | -- |
| 2008 | 12,172 | 14,167 | 11,565 | 10,379 | 48,283 |
| 2007 | 11,921 | 13,389 | 11,211 | 10,406 | 46,927 |
| 2006 | 9,913 | 11,929 | 10,592 | 10,808 | 43,243 |
| 2005 | 8,681 | 10,169 | 9,064 | 8,550 | 36,464 |
| 2004 | 7,118 | 8,666 | 7,802 | 7,252 | 30,838 |

**Earnings Per Share ($)**

| | | | | | |
|---|---|---|---|---|---|
| 2009 | 0.41 | 0.64 | E0.30 | E0.19 | E1.54 |
| 2008 | 0.48 | 0.64 | 0.43 | 0.28 | 1.86 |
| 2007 | 0.53 | 0.60 | 0.46 | 0.40 | 1.99 |
| 2006 | 0.37 | 0.52 | 0.41 | 0.44 | 1.73 |
| 2005 | 0.28 | 0.44 | 0.32 | 0.32 | 1.36 |
| 2004 | 0.26 | 0.38 | 0.28 | 0.25 | 1.16 |

Fiscal year ended Jan. 31. Next earnings report expected: Late November. EPS Estimates based on S&P Operating Earnings; historical GAAP earnings are as reported.

## Dividend Data (Dates: mm/dd Payment Date: mm/dd/yy)

| Amount ($) | Date Decl. | Ex-Div. Date | Stk. of Record | Payment Date |
|---|---|---|---|---|
| 0.080 | 11/19 | 01/16 | 01/18 | 02/01/08 |
| 0.080 | 03/24 | 04/16 | 04/18 | 05/02/08 |
| 0.085 | 05/30 | 07/16 | 07/18 | 08/01/08 |
| 0.085 | 08/25 | 10/15 | 10/17 | 10/31/08 |

Dividends have been paid since 1961. Source: Company reports.

# Lowe's Companies Inc.

**STANDARD &POOR'S**

## Business Summary September 25, 2008

CORPORATE OVERVIEW. Lowe's Companies is the world's second largest home improvement retailer. It focuses on retail do-it-yourself (DIY) customers, do-it-for-me (DIFM) customers who utilize LOW's installation services, and commercial business customers. Lowe's offers a complete line of products and services for home decorating, maintenance, repair, remodeling, and the maintenance of commercial buildings.

As of February 1, 2008, LOW operated 1,534 stores in 50 states and Canada, representing 174 million sq. ft. of selling space. The company has two primary prototype stores--a 117,000-square-foot store for larger markets and a 94,000-square-foot store used primarily to serve smaller markets. Both prototypes include a lawn and garden center, averaging an additional 31,000 square feet for larger stores and 26,000 square feet for smaller stores. Of the total stores operating at February 1, 2008, approximately 87% were owned, including stores on leased land, while the remaining 14% were leased from unaffiliated third parties. Typical LOW stores stock more than 40,000 items, with hundreds of thousands of items available through the company's special order system.

CORPORATE STRATEGY. LOW is focusing much of its future expansion on metropolitan markets with populations of 500,000 or more. The company expects that the majority of its FY 09 expansion plans will be comprised of the 117,000 square-foot stores in larger markets, but it also plans to open 103,000 square-foot and 94,000 square-foot stores in smaller to mid-sized markets.

Lowe's opened six stores in the greater Toronto area in the second half of 2007, and will continue its Canadian expansion in FY 09. Additionally, LOW plans on expanding into Mexico, with three to five stores expected to open in Monterrey in 2009.

## Company Financials Fiscal Year Ended Jan. 31

### Per Share Data ($)

| | 2008 | 2007 | 2006 | 2005 | 2004 | 2003 | 2002 | 2001 | 2000 | 1999 |
|---|---|---|---|---|---|---|---|---|---|---|
| Tangible Book Value | 11.04 | 10.31 | 9.15 | 7.45 | 6.55 | 5.31 | 4.30 | 3.59 | 3.07 | 2.22 |
| Cash Flow | 2.77 | 2.73 | 2.44 | 1.92 | 1.68 | 1.32 | 0.98 | 0.79 | 0.66 | 0.53 |
| Earnings | 1.86 | 1.99 | 1.73 | 1.36 | 1.16 | 0.93 | 0.65 | 0.52 | 0.44 | 0.34 |
| S&P Core Earnings | 1.86 | 1.99 | 1.73 | 1.33 | 1.13 | 0.87 | 0.61 | 0.50 | NA | NA |
| Dividends | 0.18 | 0.11 | 0.08 | 0.06 | 0.06 | 0.04 | 0.04 | 0.04 | 0.03 | 0.03 |
| Payout Ratio | 10% | 6% | 4% | 4% | 5% | 5% | 0% | 7% | 7% | 9% |
| Calendar Year | 2007 | 2006 | 2005 | 2004 | 2003 | 2002 | 2001 | 2000 | 1999 | 1998 |
| Prices:High | 35.74 | 34.83 | 34.85 | 30.27 | 30.21 | 25.00 | 24.44 | 16.81 | 16.61 | 13.05 |
| Prices:Low | 21.01 | 26.15 | 25.36 | 22.95 | 16.69 | 16.25 | 10.94 | 8.56 | 10.75 | 5.40 |
| P/E Ratio:High | 19 | 17 | 20 | 22 | 26 | 27 | 38 | 32 | 38 | 38 |
| P/E Ratio:Low | 11 | 13 | 15 | 17 | 14 | 18 | 17 | 16 | 25 | 16 |

### Income Statement Analysis (Million $)

| | 2008 | 2007 | 2006 | 2005 | 2004 | 2003 | 2002 | 2001 | 2000 | 1999 |
|---|---|---|---|---|---|---|---|---|---|---|
| Revenue | 48,283 | 46,927 | 43,243 | 36,464 | 30,838 | 26,491 | 22,111 | 18,779 | 15,906 | 12,245 |
| Operating Income | 6,071 | 6,314 | 5,715 | 4,878 | 3,959 | 3,186 | 2,332 | 1,811 | 1,511 | 1,105 |
| Depreciation | 1,366 | 1,162 | 1,051 | 920 | 781 | 645 | 534 | 409 | 337 | 272 |
| Interest Expense | 304 | 238 | 158 | 176 | 180 | 203 | 199 | 146 | 123 | 95.0 |
| Pretax Income | 4,511 | 4,998 | 4,506 | 3,536 | 2,998 | 2,359 | 1,624 | 1,283 | 1,065 | 758 |
| Effective Tax Rate | 37.7% | 37.9% | 38.5% | 38.5% | 37.9% | 37.6% | 37.0% | 36.9% | 36.8% | 36.4% |
| Net Income | 2,809 | 3,105 | 2,771 | 2,176 | 1,862 | 1,471 | 1,023 | 810 | 673 | 482 |
| S&P Core Earnings | 2,809 | 3,105 | 2,763 | 2,134 | 1,801 | 1,386 | 968 | 773 | NA | NA |

### Balance Sheet & Other Financial Data (Million $)

| | 2008 | 2007 | 2006 | 2005 | 2004 | 2003 | 2002 | 2001 | 2000 | 1999 |
|---|---|---|---|---|---|---|---|---|---|---|
| Cash | 530 | 796 | 423 | 813 | 1,624 | 1,126 | 799 | 456 | 491 | 223 |
| Current Assets | 8,686 | 8,314 | 7,831 | 6,974 | 6,687 | 5,568 | 4,920 | 4,175 | 3,710 | 2,586 |
| Total Assets | 30,869 | 27,767 | 24,682 | 21,209 | 19,042 | 16,109 | 13,736 | 11,376 | 9,012 | 6,345 |
| Current Liabilities | 7,751 | 6,539 | 5,832 | 5,719 | 4,368 | 3,578 | 3,017 | 2,929 | 2,386 | 1,765 |
| Long Term Debt | 5,576 | 4,325 | 3,499 | 3,060 | 3,678 | 3,736 | 3,734 | 2,698 | 1,727 | 1,283 |
| Common Equity | 16,098 | 15,725 | 14,339 | 11,535 | 10,309 | 8,302 | 6,675 | 5,494 | 4,695 | 3,136 |
| Total Capital | 22,344 | 20,785 | 18,573 | 15,331 | 14,644 | 12,516 | 10,713 | 8,443 | 6,622 | 4,579 |
| Capital Expenditures | 4,010 | 3,916 | 3,379 | 2,927 | 2,444 | 2,362 | 2,199 | 2,332 | 1,472 | 928 |
| Cash Flow | 4,175 | 4,267 | 3,822 | 3,096 | 2,643 | 2,116 | 1,557 | 1,219 | 1,010 | 754 |
| Current Ratio | 1.1 | 1.3 | 1.3 | 1.2 | 1.5 | 1.6 | 1.6 | 1.4 | 1.6 | 1.5 |
| % Long Term Debt of Capitalization | 25.0 | 21.6 | 18.8 | 20.0 | 25.1 | 29.8 | 34.9 | 32.0 | 26.1 | 28.0 |
| % Net Income of Revenue | 5.8 | 6.6 | 6.4 | 6.0 | 6.0 | 5.6 | 4.6 | 4.3 | 4.2 | 3.9 |
| % Return on Assets | 9.6 | 11.9 | 12.1 | 10.9 | 10.6 | 9.9 | 8.2 | 7.9 | 8.4 | 8.3 |
| % Return on Equity | 17.7 | 20.7 | 21.4 | 20.0 | 20.0 | 19.6 | 16.8 | 15.9 | 16.2 | 16.8 |

Data as orig reptd.; bef. results of disc opers/spec. items. Per share data adj. for stk. divs.; EPS diluted. E-Estimated. NA-Not Available. NM-Not Meaningful. NR-Not Ranked. UR-Under Review.

**Office:** 1000 Lowes Blvd, Mooresville, NC 28117-8520.
**Telephone:** 704-758-1000.
**Website:** http://www.lowes.com
**Chrmn & CEO:** R.A. Niblock

**Pres & COO:** L.D. Stone
**EVP & CFO:** R.F. Hull, Jr.
**SVP & Chief Acctg Officer:** M.V. Hollifield
**SVP, Secy & General Counsel:** G.M. Keener, Jr.

**Board Members:** D. W. Bernauer, L. L. Berry, P. C. Browning, D. Hudson, R. A. Ingram, R. L. Johnson, M. O. Larsen, R. K. Lochridge, R. A. Niblock, S. F. Page, O. T. Sloan, III

**Founded:** 1952
**Domicile:** North Carolina
**Employees:** 216,000

**The McGraw-Hill Companies**

**STANDARD &POOR'S**

# L-3 Communications Holdings Inc

| | | Price | 12-Mo. Target Price | Investment Style |
|---|---|---|---|---|
| **S&P Recommendation** BUY ★★★★☆ | | $69.33 (as of Nov 14, 2008) | $100.00 | Large-Cap Blend |

**GICS Sector** Industrials
**Sub-Industry** Aerospace & Defense

**Summary** This company is a provider of intelligence, surveillance, and reconnaissance systems; secure communications systems; aircraft modernization, training and government services; among other defense, intelligence, and security products.

## Key Stock Statistics (Source S&P, Vickers, company reports)

| | | | | | | | |
|---|---|---|---|---|---|---|---|
| 52-Wk Range | $115.33– 65.70 | S&P Oper. EPS 2008**E** | 7.48 | Market Capitalization(B) | $8.278 | Beta | 0.90 |
| Trailing 12-Month EPS | $7.14 | S&P Oper. EPS 2009**E** | 7.45 | Yield (%) | 1.73 | S&P 3-Yr. Proj. EPS CAGR(%) | 11 |
| Trailing 12-Month P/E | 9.7 | P/E on S&P Oper. EPS 2008**E** | 9.3 | Dividend Rate/Share | $1.20 | S&P Credit Rating | BBB- |
| $10K Invested 5 Yrs Ago | $15,849 | Common Shares Outstg. (M) | 119.4 | Institutional Ownership (%) | 84 | | |

## Price Performance

30-Week Mov. Avg. · · · 10-Week Mov. Avg. — **GAAP Earnings vs. Previous Year**    Volume Above Avg. STARS
12-Mo. Target Price — Relative Strength — ▲ Up ▼ Down ▶ No Change    Below Avg.

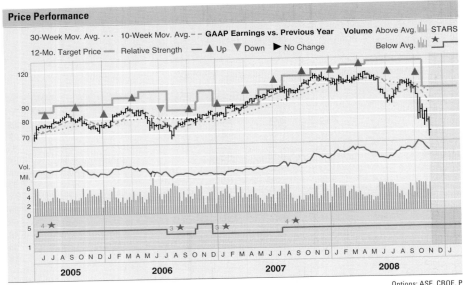

Options: ASE, CBOE, P

Analysis prepared by **Richard Tortoriello** on November 10, 2008, when the stock traded at **$ 75.32**.

### Highlights

▶ We anticipate revenue growth of about 5% in 2008 and 8% in 2009, versus organic growth of 9.6% that was recorded in 2007. We see the decline in growth in 2008 as due in part to the loss of the "Linguist" contract to supply transla- tion services to the military to a competitor. We expect revenue growth in 2008 and 2009 to be driven by strong growth in C3ISR, due to the de- fense department's continued focus on defense electronics, as well as strong growth in the Specialized Products, driven by a variety of mil- itary and commercial applications.

▶ For 2008, we expect a slight increase in operat- ing margins, to 10.5% from 10.4% in 2007, on im- proved contract performance and cost efficien- cies. We are modeling a further modest in- crease in operating margins to 10.8% for 2009.

▶ We project EPS of $7.48 in 2008, which includes $0.71 in special gains, and $7.45 in 2009, or growth of 10% excluding one-time items. We expect the company to generate free cash flow (cash from operations less capital expendi- tures) of over $9.50 per share in 2008.

### Investment Rationale/Risk

▶ Following the June 2006 death of L-3's founder, we see new management focusing on more se- lective acquisitions, improving profit margins, creating more products that span business lines, and maximizing cash flow. We also antici- pate a greater focus on moderate share repur- chases and dividend increases. We see L-3's mix of defense electronics and communications and government services as well matched with current military priorities, and expect investors to benefit from what we view as strong organic sales growth, strong cash flow generation, and an attractive valuation.

▶ Risks to our recommendation and target price include the potential for delays and/or cuts in military budgets and the failure to perform well on existing contracts or to win new contracts.

▶ Our 12-month target price of $100 is based on an enterprise value to estimated 2009 EBITDA multiple of 8X, below an average historical mul- tiple of 12X, but in line with EV to EBITDA multi- ples we are using to value other defense con- tractors. We believe the likelihood of a troop drawdown from Iraq and slower-than-historical growth at LLL warrant this multiple.

## Qualitative Risk Assessment

| LOW | MEDIUM | HIGH |
|---|---|---|

Our risk assessment reflects our view of LLL's strong historical record of earnings growth, offset by the company's current low dividend payout ratio and relatively high financial leverage, and risks inherent in its dependence on government spending.

## Quantitative Evaluations

**S&P Quality Ranking**                                        A-

| D | C | B- | B | B+ | A- | A | A+ |
|---|---|---|---|---|---|---|---|

**Relative Strength Rank**                            MODERATE

51

LOWEST = 1                                         HIGHEST = 99

## Revenue/Earnings Data

**Revenue (Million $)**

| | 1Q | 2Q | 3Q | 4Q | Year |
|---|---|---|---|---|---|
| 2008 | 3,506 | 3,722 | 3,662 | -- | -- |
| 2007 | 3,300 | 3,408 | 3,448 | 3,806 | 13,961 |
| 2006 | 2,904 | 3,083 | 3,105 | 3,385 | 12,477 |
| 2005 | 1,963 | 2,076 | 2,506 | 2,900 | 9,445 |
| 2004 | 1,522 | 1,680 | 1,784 | 1,911 | 6,897 |
| 2003 | 1,089 | 1,227 | 1,265 | 1,481 | 5,062 |

**Earnings Per Share ($)**

| | | | | | |
|---|---|---|---|---|---|
| 2008 | 1.54 | 2.24 | 1.73 | E1.96 | E7.48 |
| 2007 | 1.29 | 1.49 | 1.56 | 1.63 | 5.98 |
| 2006 | 1.13 | 0.40 | 1.31 | 1.37 | 4.22 |
| 2005 | 0.86 | 0.99 | 1.11 | 1.24 | 4.20 |
| 2004 | 0.67 | 0.81 | 0.93 | 1.01 | 3.33 |
| 2003 | 0.50 | 0.53 | 0.74 | 0.94 | 2.71 |

Fiscal year ended Dec. 31. Next earnings report expected: Early February. EPS Estimates based on S&P Operating Earnings; historical GAAP earnings are as reported.

## Dividend Data (Dates: mm/dd Payment Date: mm/dd/yy)

| Amount ($) | Date Decl. | Ex-Div. Date | Stk. of Record | Payment Date |
|---|---|---|---|---|
| 0.300 | 02/05 | 02/14 | 02/19 | 03/17/08 |
| 0.300 | 04/29 | 05/14 | 05/16 | 06/16/08 |
| 0.300 | 07/08 | 08/14 | 08/18 | 09/15/08 |
| 0.300 | 10/07 | 11/13 | 11/17 | 12/15/08 |

Dividends have been paid since 2004. Source: Company reports.

# L-3 Communications Holdings Inc

**STANDARD
&POOR'S**

## Business Summary November 10, 2008

CORPORATE OVERVIEW. L-3 Communications (LLL), an acquisitive $15 billion in revenues maker of military and homeland security electronics, conducts business through four operating segments.

The Command, Control, Communications, Intelligence, Surveillance, and Reconnaissance (C3ISR) business segment (17% of sales and 16% of operating income in 2007), specializes in signals intelligence (SIGINT) and communications intelligence (COMINT) products. These products provide troops the ability to collect and analyze unknown electronic signals from command centers, communications nodes and air defense systems for real-time situation awareness and response. C3ISR also provides C3 systems, networked communications systems, and secure communications products for military and other U.S. government agencies and foreign governments.

The Government Services segment (31% of sales and 28% of operating profits) provides a wide range of engineering, technical, information technology, advisory, training, and support services to the Department of Defense (DoD), Dept. of State, Dept. of Justice, U.S. Government intelligence agencies, and allied foreign governments. Major services include communication software support; high-end engineering and information systems support for command, control, communications and ISR architectures; developing and managing programs in the U.S. and internationally that focus on teaching, training and education, logistics, strategic planning, leadership development, etc.; human intelligence support; aviation and maritime services support; intelligence support; technical and management services; and high-end IT support to the DoD and other federal agencies.

The Aircraft Modernization & Maintenance segment (18% of sales and 17% of operating profits) provides modernization, upgrades and sustainment, maintenance and logistics support services for various government aircraft and other platforms. Services are sold primarily to the U.S. DoD, the Canadian Department of National Defense, and other allied foreign governments. Major products and services include aircraft modernization, including life extension, maintenance, upgrades, and support; and base operations support and aircraft services, including logistics support, maintenance and refurbishment, quick response teams, and contractor operated and managed base supply.

The Specialized Products segment (34% of sales and 39% of operating profits) provides a broad range of products, including components, subsystems, and systems, to military and commercial customers in several diverse niche markets. Product lines include power & control systems, microwave, avionics & displays, training & simulation, electro-optic/infrared (EO/IR), precision engagement, security & detection systems, propulsion systems, undersea warfare, and telemetry and advanced technology.

## Company Financials Fiscal Year Ended Dec. 31

| Per Share Data ($) | 2007 | 2006 | 2005 | 2004 | 2003 | 2002 | 2001 | 2000 | 1999 | 1998 |
|---|---|---|---|---|---|---|---|---|---|---|
| Tangible Book Value | NM | NM | NM | NM | NM | NM | NM | NM | NM | NM |
| Cash Flow | 7.53 | 5.30 | 5.46 | 4.27 | 3.52 | 2.96 | 2.37 | 2.25 | 16.75 | 1.41 |
| Earnings | 5.98 | 4.22 | 4.20 | 3.33 | 2.71 | 2.29 | 1.48 | 1.18 | 0.88 | 0.63 |
| S&P Core Earnings | 5.68 | 4.93 | 4.07 | 3.22 | 2.66 | 1.87 | 1.08 | NA | NA | NA |
| Dividends | 1.00 | 0.75 | 0.50 | 0.40 | Nil | Nil | Nil | Nil | Nil | Nil |
| Payout Ratio | 17% | 18% | 12% | 12% | Nil | Nil | Nil | Nil | Nil | Nil |
| Prices:High | 115.29 | 88.50 | 84.84 | 77.26 | 51.83 | 66.78 | 49.04 | 39.66 | 27.13 | 24.75 |
| Prices:Low | 79.26 | 66.50 | 64.66 | 49.31 | 34.22 | 40.60 | 30.35 | 17.84 | 17.13 | 11.00 |
| P/E Ratio:High | 19 | 21 | 20 | 23 | 19 | 29 | 33 | 33 | 31 | 39 |
| P/E Ratio:Low | 13 | 16 | 15 | 15 | 13 | 18 | 21 | 15 | 20 | 17 |

| Income Statement Analysis (Million $) | | | | | | | | | | |
|---|---|---|---|---|---|---|---|---|---|---|
| Revenue | 13,961 | 12,477 | 9,445 | 6,897 | 5,062 | 4,011 | 2,347 | 1,910 | 1,405 | 1,037 |
| Operating Income | 1,645 | 1,376 | 1,150 | 868 | 676 | 530 | 362 | 297 | 204 | 141 |
| Depreciation | 196 | 136 | 153 | 119 | 95.4 | 75.9 | 87.0 | 74.3 | 53.7 | 40.4 |
| Interest Expense | 296 | 296 | 204 | 145 | 133 | 122 | 86.4 | 93.0 | 60.6 | 49.6 |
| Pretax Income | 1,183 | 835 | 798 | 606 | 437 | 336 | 191 | 134 | 95.4 | 53.5 |
| Effective Tax Rate | 35.3% | 35.7% | 35.1% | 35.5% | 35.7% | 35.0% | 37.1% | 38.3% | 38.5% | 39.1% |
| Net Income | 756 | 526 | 509 | 382 | 278 | 212 | 115 | 82.7 | 58.7 | 32.6 |
| S&P Core Earnings | 719 | 615 | 493 | 370 | 274 | 171 | 82.0 | NA | NA | NA |

| Balance Sheet & Other Financial Data (Million $) | | | | | | | | | | |
|---|---|---|---|---|---|---|---|---|---|---|
| Cash | 780 | 348 | 394 | 653 | 135 | 135 | 361 | 32.7 | 42.8 | 26.1 |
| Current Assets | 4,763 | 3,930 | 3,644 | 2,808 | 1,938 | 1,639 | 1,239 | 830 | 568 | 405 |
| Total Assets | 14,391 | 13,287 | 11,909 | 7,781 | 6,493 | 5,242 | 3,335 | 2,464 | 1,634 | 1,285 |
| Current Liabilities | 2,582 | 2,376 | 1,854 | 1,176 | 924 | 697 | 524 | 469 | 318 | 248 |
| Long Term Debt | 4,547 | 4,535 | 4,634 | 2,190 | 2,457 | 1,848 | 1,315 | 1,095 | 605 | 605 |
| Common Equity | 5,989 | 5,306 | 4,491 | 3,800 | 2,574 | 2,202 | 1,214 | 693 | 583 | 300 |
| Total Capital | 10,857 | 10,069 | 9,325 | 6,067 | 5,108 | 4,123 | 2,599 | 1,788 | 1,188 | 905 |
| Capital Expenditures | 157 | 156 | 120 | 80.5 | 82.9 | 62.1 | 48.1 | 33.6 | 23.5 | 23.4 |
| Cash Flow | 952 | 662 | 661 | 501 | 373 | 288 | 202 | 157 | 112 | 72.9 |
| Current Ratio | 1.9 | 1.7 | 2.0 | 2.4 | 2.1 | 2.4 | 2.4 | 1.8 | 1.8 | 1.6 |
| % Long Term Debt of Capitalization | 41.8 | 45.0 | 49.7 | 36.1 | 48.1 | 44.8 | 50.6 | 61.3 | 50.9 | 66.9 |
| % Net Income of Revenue | 5.4 | 4.2 | 5.4 | 5.5 | 5.5 | 5.3 | 4.9 | 4.3 | 4.2 | 3.1 |
| % Return on Assets | 5.5 | 4.2 | 5.2 | 5.3 | 4.7 | 5.0 | 4.0 | 4.0 | 4.2 | 3.3 |
| % Return on Equity | 13.4 | 10.7 | 12.3 | 12.0 | 11.6 | 12.4 | 12.1 | 13.0 | 13.3 | 15.0 |

Data as orig reptd.; bef. results of disc opers/spec. items. Per share data adj. for stk. divs.; EPS diluted. E-Estimated. NA-Not Available. NM-Not Meaningful. NR-Not Ranked. UR-Under Review.

**Office:** 600 3rd Ave, New York, NY 10016.
**Telephone:** 212-697-1111.
**Website:** http://www.L3com.com
**Chrmn, Pres & CEO:** M.T. Strianese

**COO:** D.T. Butler, III
**SVP, Secy & General Counsel:** S.M. Post
**CFO:** R.G. D'Ambrosio
**Chief Admin Officer:** S.M. Sheridan

**Investor Contact:** E. Boyriven (212-850-5600)
**Board Members:** C. R. Canizares, P. A. Cohen, T. A. Corcoran, R. B. Millard, J. M. Shalikashvili, A. L. Simon, M. T. Strianese, A. H. Washkowitz, J. P. White

**Founded:** 1997
**Domicile:** Delaware
**Employees:** 64,600

**The McGraw-Hill Companies**

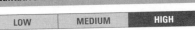
**STANDARD &POOR'S**

# LSI Corp

**S&P Recommendation** **BUY** ★★★★☆

| Price | 12-Mo. Target Price | Investment Style |
|---|---|---|
| $3.12 (as of Nov 14, 2008) | $5.00 | Large-Cap Blend |

**GICS Sector** Information Technology
**Sub-Industry** Semiconductors

**Summary** This leading supplier of complex, high-performance semiconductors and storage systems acquired Agere Systems in April 2007.

## Key Stock Statistics (Source S&P, Vickers, company reports)

| | | | | | | | | |
|---|---|---|---|---|---|---|---|---|
| 52-Wk Range | $7.87– 3.00 | S&P Oper. EPS 2008**E** | 0.38 | Market Capitalization(B) | $2.013 | Beta | | 2.06 |
| Trailing 12-Month EPS | $-3.05 | S&P Oper. EPS 2009**E** | 0.44 | Yield (%) | Nil | S&P 3-Yr. Proj. EPS CAGR(%) | | 14 |
| Trailing 12-Month P/E | NM | P/E on S&P Oper. EPS 2008**E** | 8.2 | Dividend Rate/Share | Nil | S&P Credit Rating | | BB |
| $10K Invested 5 Yrs Ago | $3,184 | Common Shares Outstg. (M) | 645.1 | Institutional Ownership (%) | 89 | | | |

## Price Performance

30-Week Mov. Avg. ···  10-Week Mov. Avg. ─  **GAAP Earnings vs. Previous Year**  Volume Above Avg. ▥▥▥ STARS
12-Mo. Target Price ─  Relative Strength ─  ▲ Up  ▼ Down  ▶ No Change  Below Avg. ▥▥▥ ★

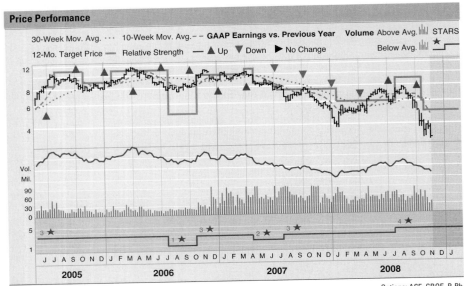

Options: ASE, CBOE, P, Ph

Analysis prepared by **Rafay Khalid** on October 27, 2008, when the stock traded at **$ 3.50**.

### Highlights

➤ We project that revenues will advance 6% in 2008 and 2% in 2009. Our outlook is based on solid sales growth from the company's storage semiconductor and storage system businesses, supported by new product cycles. In addition, we see market share gains in hard disk drive (HDD) semiconductor products due to the completed acquisition of Infineon Technologies' HDD business and new design wins. We believe revenues will remain stable for legacy networking products in 2008, but decline slightly in 2009.

➤ We expect a non-GAAP gross margin of 47% in 2008, wider than the 44% posted last year, reflecting our expectation of better cost absorption from higher sales and improved product mix. The company has been making progress in integrating Agere Systems, in our opinion, and we think that synergies and cost-cutting measures will support a wider operating margin of 10% in 2008 versus 4% in 2007. We project operating margins will expand to 12% in 2009.

➤ Our operating EPS estimate is $0.38 in 2008, excluding one-time acquisition-related charges, compared to $0.19 in 2007. We project operating EPS of $0.44 next year.

### Investment Rationale/Risk

➤ Despite a weak macroeconomic environment, we believe the storage markets will grow this year, supporting LSI's sales. We think the Agere and Infineon HDD acquisitions will help LSI gain market share with large customers. Combined with our view of more efficient operations, we see notable earnings growth this year and a solid increase next year. We view LSI's balance sheet as solid, reflecting our projection of $1.83 per share in cash and investments for the end of 2008, along with our expectation of solid free cash flow generation.

➤ Risks to our recommendation and target price include weaker-than-expected product adoption rates and slower realization of acquisition-related cost savings.

➤ Our 12-month target price of $5 is based on a blend of our P/E and DCF analyses. We apply a peer-premium P/E ratio of 11.3X on our 2009 operating EPS estimate to derive a $5 valuation. We think LSI warrants a peer premium due to what we see as sales and earnings growth above the industry. Our DCF model assumes a 16.2% weighted average cost of capital and 2% terminal growth, and yields an intrinsic value of $5.

### Qualitative Risk Assessment

| LOW | MEDIUM | **HIGH** |
|---|---|---|

LSI is subject to the sales cycles of the semiconductor industry and of consumer electronics and data storage end markets. The company faces competition from makers of programmable logic devices as well as from many custom logic chip makers. We view the balance sheet as weaker than the peer group average.

### Quantitative Evaluations

**S&P Quality Ranking** C

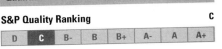

| D | **C** | B- | B | B+ | A- | A | A+ |
|---|---|---|---|---|---|---|---|

**Relative Strength Rank** WEAK

28

LOWEST = 1                                 HIGHEST = 99

### Revenue/Earnings Data

**Revenue (Million $)**

| | 1Q | 2Q | 3Q | 4Q | Year |
|---|---|---|---|---|---|
| 2008 | 660.8 | 692.1 | 714.3 | -- | -- |
| 2007 | 465.4 | 669.9 | 727.4 | 740.9 | 2,604 |
| 2006 | 475.9 | 489.6 | 493.0 | 523.7 | 1,982 |
| 2005 | 450.0 | 481.3 | 481.7 | 506.2 | 1,919 |
| 2004 | 452.4 | 447.9 | 380.2 | 419.7 | 1,700 |
| 2003 | 372.8 | 407.2 | 450.2 | 462.9 | 1,693 |

**Earnings Per Share ($)**

| | | | | | |
|---|---|---|---|---|---|
| 2008 | -0.02 | -0.02 | 0.02 | E0.09 | E0.38 |
| 2007 | 0.07 | -0.50 | -0.20 | -2.88 | -3.87 |
| 2006 | 0.03 | 0.13 | 0.11 | 0.14 | 0.42 |
| 2005 | 0.01 | 0.06 | -0.19 | 0.09 | -0.01 |
| 2004 | 0.02 | 0.02 | -0.73 | -0.51 | -1.21 |
| 2003 | -0.33 | -0.43 | -0.08 | 0.02 | -0.82 |

Fiscal year ended Dec. 31. Next earnings report expected: Late January. EPS Estimates based on S&P Operating Earnings; historical GAAP earnings are as reported.

### Dividend Data

No cash dividends have been paid.

# LSI Corp

STANDARD
&POOR'S

## Business Summary October 27, 2008

CORPORATE OVERVIEW. LSI Corp. (formerly LSI Logic) is best known as a leading supplier of application-specific and standard integrated circuits, and since 1998 has diversified into storage components. In March 2006, the company announced plans to focus on growth opportunities in storage and consumer markets. Following its 2007 merger with Agere Systems, and divestiture of its consumer and mobility business segments, LSI focuses on two main segments: semiconductor and storage systems.

In 2007, the semiconductor segment accounted for 68% of revenues, compared to 62% in 2006; and storage systems represented 32% (38%). Revenues for the semiconductor group were up 45.4% in 2007, while Storage Systems revenues increased 8.7%.

MARKET PROFILE. Customers are generally electronic original equipment manufacturers (OEMs). LSI focuses on larger companies that make products

in high volume.

The company emphasizes complex system-on-a-chip products that employ its CoreWare design methodology. Using sophisticated electronic design automation tools, customers add product features to pre-wired cores of industry-standard architecture protocols and algorithms that are electronically stitched together on a single chip. CoreWare methodology is based on application-specific integrated circuit (ASIC) technology: these semiconductors are designed to satisfy particular customer requirements. LSI is a large player in the global ASIC market, competing with companies such as IBM, Philips Electronics, Texas Instruments and Broadcom.

## Company Financials Fiscal Year Ended Dec. 31

| Per Share Data ($) | 2007 | 2006 | 2005 | 2004 | 2003 | 2002 | 2001 | 2000 | 1999 | 1998 |
|---|---|---|---|---|---|---|---|---|---|---|
| Tangible Book Value | 1.12 | 2.24 | 1.66 | 1.38 | 2.39 | 2.80 | 3.15 | 5.96 | 5.21 | 4.17 |
| Cash Flow | -3.48 | 0.62 | 0.36 | -0.75 | -0.12 | 0.15 | -1.32 | 1.81 | 1.62 | 0.41 |
| Earnings | -3.87 | 0.42 | -0.01 | -1.21 | -0.82 | -0.79 | -2.84 | 0.70 | 0.52 | -0.47 |
| S&P Core Earnings | -1.80 | 0.35 | -0.20 | -1.51 | -1.33 | -1.36 | -3.47 | NA | NA | NA |
| Dividends | Nil | Nil | Nil | Nil | Nil | Nil | Nil | Nil | Nil | Nil |
| Payout Ratio | Nil | Nil | Nil | Nil | Nil | Nil | Nil | Nil | Nil | Nil |
| Prices:High | 10.68 | 11.81 | 10.75 | 11.50 | 12.90 | 18.60 | 26.10 | 90.38 | 35.69 | 14.69 |
| Prices:Low | 5.06 | 7.41 | 4.92 | 4.01 | 3.78 | 3.97 | 9.70 | 16.30 | 8.06 | 5.25 |
| P/E Ratio:High | NM | 28 | NM | NM | NM | NM | NM | NM | 69 | NM |
| P/E Ratio:Low | NM | 18 | NM | NM | NM | NM | NM | NM | 16 | NM |

| Income Statement Analysis (Million $) | | | | | | | | | | |
|---|---|---|---|---|---|---|---|---|---|---|
| Revenue | 2,604 | 1,982 | 1,919 | 1,700 | 1,693 | 1,817 | 1,785 | 2,738 | 2,089 | 1,491 |
| Operating Income | 168 | 236 | 283 | 172 | 171 | 155 | -157 | 815 | 568 | 198 |
| Depreciation | 253 | 82.3 | 146 | 177 | 263 | 349 | 533 | 404 | 367 | 248 |
| Interest Expense | 31.0 | 24.3 | 25.3 | 25.3 | 30.7 | 52.0 | 44.6 | 41.6 | 40.0 | 8.48 |
| Pretax Income | -2,475 | 185 | 20.9 | -439 | -284 | -291 | -1,030 | 380 | 224 | -124 |
| Effective Tax Rate | NM | 8.46% | NM | NM | NM | NM | NM | 37.6% | 29.0% | NM |
| Net Income | -2,487 | 170 | -5.62 | -464 | -309 | -292 | -992 | 237 | 159 | -132 |
| S&P Core Earnings | -1,157 | 140 | -80.0 | -582 | -505 | -507 | -1,214 | NA | NA | NA |

| Balance Sheet & Other Financial Data (Million $) | | | | | | | | | | |
|---|---|---|---|---|---|---|---|---|---|---|
| Cash | 1,398 | 328 | 265 | 219 | 270 | 449 | 757 | 236 | 251 | 200 |
| Current Assets | 2,193 | 1,636 | 1,620 | 1,365 | 1,390 | 1,626 | 1,769 | 2,072 | 1,288 | 820 |
| Total Assets | 4,396 | 2,852 | 2,796 | 2,874 | 3,448 | 4,143 | 4,626 | 4,197 | 3,207 | 2,800 |
| Current Liabilities | 762 | 527 | 743 | 396 | 391 | 398 | 510 | 627 | 475 | 593 |
| Long Term Debt | 718 | 350 | 350 | 782 | 866 | 1,241 | 1,336 | 846 | 672 | 556 |
| Common Equity | 2,485 | 1,896 | 1,628 | 1,618 | 2,042 | 2,300 | 2,480 | 2,498 | 1,856 | 1,510 |
| Total Capital | 3,388 | 2,246 | 1,978 | 2,400 | 2,916 | 3,665 | 3,995 | 3,481 | 2,610 | 2,207 |
| Capital Expenditures | 103 | 58.7 | 48.1 | 52.8 | 78.2 | 39.0 | 224 | 277 | 205 | 329 |
| Cash Flow | -2,234 | 252 | 141 | -287 | -45.8 | 57.0 | -459 | 641 | 526 | 116 |
| Current Ratio | 2.9 | 3.1 | 2.2 | 3.4 | 3.6 | 4.1 | 3.5 | 3.3 | 2.7 | 1.4 |
| % Long Term Debt of Capitalization | 21.2 | 15.6 | 17.7 | 32.6 | 29.7 | 33.8 | 33.4 | 24.3 | 25.7 | 25.2 |
| % Net Income of Revenue | NM | 8.6 | NM | NM | NM | NM | NM | 8.6 | 7.6 | NM |
| % Return on Assets | NM | 6.0 | NM | NM | NM | NM | NM | 6.4 | 5.3 | NM |
| % Return on Equity | NM | 9.6 | NM | NM | NM | NM | NM | 10.9 | 9.4 | NM |

Data as orig reptd.; bef. results of disc opers/spec. items. Per share data adj. for stk. divs.; EPS diluted. E-Estimated. NA-Not Available. NM-Not Meaningful. NR-Not Ranked. UR-Under Review.

**Office:** 1621 Barber Lane, Milpitas, CA 95035.
**Telephone:** 408-433-8000.
**Email:** investorrelations@lsil.com
**Website:** http://www.lsi.com

**Chrmn:** G. Reyes
**Pres & CEO:** A.Y. Talwalkar
**EVP, CFO & Chief Acctg Officer:** B. Look
**EVP & CTO:** C. Simson

**EVP, Secy & General Counsel:** J.F. Rankin
**Investor Contact:** S. Shah (610-712-5471)
**Board Members:** T. Chen, C. A. Haggerty, R. Hill, M. J. Mancuso, J. H. Miner, A. Netravali, M. J. O'Rourke, G. Reyes, A. Y. Talwalkar

**Founded:** 1980
**Domicile:** Delaware
**Employees:** 6,193

The McGraw-Hill Companies

**STANDARD &POOR'S**

# Macy's Inc

| S&P Recommendation | HOLD ★★★☆☆ | Price $7.52 (as of Nov 14, 2008) | 12-Mo. Target Price $10.00 | Investment Style Large-Cap Blend |
|---|---|---|---|---|

**GICS Sector** Consumer Discretionary
**Sub-Industry** Department Stores

**Summary** This company operates more than 800 department stores under the Macy's and Bloomingdale's names.

## Key Stock Statistics (Source S&P, Vickers, company reports)

| | | | | | | | |
|---|---|---|---|---|---|---|---|
| 52-Wk Range | $31.55– 6.92 | S&P Oper. EPS 2009**E** | 1.40 | Market Capitalization(B) | $3.163 | Beta | 1.30 |
| Trailing 12-Month EPS | $1.86 | S&P Oper. EPS 2010**E** | 1.15 | Yield (%) | 7.05 | S&P 3-Yr. Proj. EPS CAGR(%) | -7 |
| Trailing 12-Month P/E | 4.0 | P/E on S&P Oper. EPS 2009**E** | 5.4 | Dividend Rate/Share | $0.53 | S&P Credit Rating | BBB |
| $10K Invested 5 Yrs Ago | $3,173 | Common Shares Outstg. (M) | 420.5 | Institutional Ownership (%) | 96 | | |

## Price Performance

30-Week Mov. Avg. ···· 10-Week Mov. Avg. --- **GAAP Earnings vs. Previous Year**   Volume Above Avg. ▮▮▮ STARS
12-Mo. Target Price —   Relative Strength —   ▲ Up   ▼ Down   ▶ No Change     Below Avg. ▮▮▮

Options: ASE, CBOE, P, Ph

## Qualitative Risk Assessment

| LOW | MEDIUM | HIGH |
|---|---|---|

Our risk assessment reflects our view of M's strong brand and geographical presence in a consolidating industry, outweighed by perceived merchandise localization challenges and an uncertain outlook for consumer discretionary spending.

## Quantitative Evaluations

**S&P Quality Ranking**                         B

| D | C | B- | B | B+ | A- | A | A+ |
|---|---|---|---|---|---|---|---|

**Relative Strength Rank**                    WEAK

| 16 | |
|---|---|
| LOWEST = 1 | HIGHEST = 99 |

## Highlights

➤ The 12-month target price for M has recently been changed to $10.00 from $12.00. The Highlights section of this Stock Report will be updated accordingly.

## Investment Rationale/Risk

➤ The Investment Rationale/Risk section of this Stock Report will be updated shortly. For the latest News story on M from MarketScope, see below.

➤ 11/12/08 11:34 am ET ... S&P MAINTAINS HOLD RECOMMENDATION ON SHARES OF MACY'S (M 8.87***): Oct-Q operating loss per share of $0.08 vs. EPS of $0.10 beats our loss estimate of $0.24 on tight inventory controls and sales growth in private labels. We see M gaining marketshare from competitors on strength of its brands and marketing. But with sales trends deteriorating in the Oct-Q, we see aggressive markdowns and higher marketing spend driving holiday sales. We raise our FY 09 (Jan.) operating EPS estimate by $0.10 to $1.40 but keep FY 10's at $1.15. On lower peer multiples, we reduce our P/E-based 12-month target price by $2 to $10. /J.Asaeda

## Revenue/Earnings Data

**Revenue (Million $)**

| | 1Q | 2Q | 3Q | 4Q | Year |
|---|---|---|---|---|---|
| 2009 | 5,747 | 5,718 | -- | -- | -- |
| 2008 | 5,921 | 5,892 | 5,906 | 8,594 | 26,313 |
| 2007 | 5,930 | 5,995 | 5,886 | 9,159 | 26,970 |
| 2006 | 3,641 | 3,623 | 5,785 | 9,571 | 22,390 |
| 2005 | 3,517 | 3,548 | 3,491 | 5,074 | 15,630 |
| 2004 | 3,291 | 3,434 | 3,486 | 5,053 | 15,264 |

**Earnings Per Share ($)**

| | 1Q | 2Q | 3Q | 4Q | Year |
|---|---|---|---|---|---|
| 2009 | -0.14 | 0.17 | E-0.24 | E1.17 | E1.40 |
| 2008 | 0.11 | 0.17 | 0.08 | 1.73 | 2.01 |
| 2007 | -0.13 | 0.51 | 0.03 | 1.45 | 1.80 |
| 2006 | 0.36 | 0.84 | 0.89 | 1.23 | 3.16 |
| 2005 | 0.26 | 0.22 | 0.21 | 1.28 | 1.93 |
| 2004 | 0.12 | 0.32 | 0.18 | 1.25 | 1.86 |

Fiscal year ended Jan. 31. Next earnings report expected: Mid November. EPS Estimates based on S&P Operating Earnings; historical GAAP earnings are as reported.

## Dividend Data (Dates: mm/dd Payment Date: mm/dd/yy)

| Amount ($) | Date Decl. | Ex-Div. Date | Stk. of Record | Payment Date |
|---|---|---|---|---|
| 0.130 | 02/22 | 03/12 | 03/14 | 04/01/08 |
| 0.133 | 05/16 | 06/11 | 06/13 | 07/01/08 |
| 0.133 | 08/22 | 09/11 | 09/15 | 10/01/08 |
| 0.133 | 10/24 | 12/11 | 12/15 | 01/02/09 |

Dividends have been paid since 2003. Source: Company reports.

*The McGraw-Hill Companies*

# Macy's Inc

**STANDARD &POOR'S**

## Business Summary October 14, 2008

CORPORATE OVERVIEW. In February 2005, M and The May Department Stores Co. announced merger plans. At that time, May was in need of new leadership to revive its business, and M was in the midst of a successful turnaround and on the lookout for acquisitions that would expand its presence in underserved markets. Both companies viewed the merger as a win-win proposition, as M would roll out its profit-driving merchandising, pricing, and service initiatives to May's stores, and May would extend M's presence into 15 new states.

As a result of the $17 billion May merger, which closed in August 2005, M is now the fourth largest U.S. mass merchandiser in annual revenues, with over 800 department stores in 45 states under the Macy's and Bloomingdale's names.

CORPORATE STRATEGY. Since 2005, M has focused on three key priorities to better position its business for long-term growth: growing "better" and "affordable luxury" assortments, with an emphasis on private label merchandise; improving customer perceptions of fair value in less discounted prices; and enriching the overall shopping experience. With its merger with May, the company also expanded its core Macy's brand nationwide.

Going forward, M sees an opportunity to accelerate the sales performance in

about 400 former May locations that were rebranded Macy's on September 9, 2006. As part of its efforts to increase public awareness of Macy's, which contributes about 90% of the company's revenues, M changed its corporate name to Macy's, Inc. from Federated Department Stores, Inc. on June 1, 2007. On that date, the company's shares also began trading under the ticker symbol "M" (replacing "FD") on the New York Stock Exchange.

UPCOMING CATALYSTS. In February 2008, M announced "My Macy's," a new initiative aimed at accelerating same-store sales growth through custom-tailoring of merchandise assortments, size ranges, marketing programs, and shopping experiences to the needs of core customers surrounding each Macy's store. In support of My Macy's, the company plans to roll out new systems and technology during FY 09 designed to help merchants more accurately assort each Macy's store with customer preferred items, brands, garment sizes and colors.

## Company Financials Fiscal Year Ended Jan. 31

| Per Share Data ($) | 2008 | 2007 | 2006 | 2005 | 2004 | 2003 | 2002 | 2001 | 2000 | 1999 |
|---|---|---|---|---|---|---|---|---|---|---|
| Tangible Book Value | NM | 5.56 | 5.34 | 16.55 | NM | 13.47 | 12.16 | 12.47 | 11.26 | 12.15 |
| Cash Flow | 4.90 | 4.11 | 4.29 | 4.09 | 3.92 | 3.31 | 2.94 | 1.32 | 3.49 | 2.91 |
| Earnings | 2.01 | 1.80 | 3.16 | 1.93 | 1.86 | 1.61 | 1.30 | -0.45 | 1.81 | 1.53 |
| S&P Core Earnings | 1.90 | 1.62 | 2.21 | 1.83 | 1.69 | 1.24 | 0.91 | 0.25 | NA | NA |
| Dividends | 0.51 | 0.45 | 0.26 | 0.19 | Nil | Nil | Nil | Nil | NA | NA |
| Payout Ratio | 25% | 25% | 8% | 10% | Nil | Nil | Nil | Nil | Nil | Nil |
| Calendar Year | 2007 | 2006 | 2005 | 2004 | 2003 | 2002 | 2001 | 2000 | 1999 | 1998 |
| Prices:High | 46.70 | 45.01 | 39.03 | 29.08 | 25.30 | 22.13 | 24.95 | 26.94 | 28.53 | 28.09 |
| Prices:Low | 24.70 | 32.38 | 27.10 | 21.40 | 11.76 | 11.80 | 13.03 | 10.50 | 18.22 | 16.41 |
| P/E Ratio:High | 23 | 25 | 12 | 15 | 14 | 14 | 19 | NM | 16 | 18 |
| P/E Ratio:Low | 12 | 18 | 9 | 11 | 6 | 7 | 10 | NM | 10 | 11 |

### Income Statement Analysis (Million $)

| | 2008 | 2007 | 2006 | 2005 | 2004 | 2003 | 2002 | 2001 | 2000 | 1999 |
|---|---|---|---|---|---|---|---|---|---|---|
| Revenue | 26,313 | 26,970 | 22,390 | 15,630 | 15,264 | 15,435 | 15,651 | 18,407 | 17,716 | 15,833 |
| Operating Income | 3,167 | 2,910 | 3,087 | 2,143 | 2,047 | 2,019 | 1,923 | 2,239 | 2,443 | 2,085 |
| Depreciation | 1,304 | 1,265 | 974 | 743 | 706 | 676 | 657 | 727 | 742 | 630 |
| Interest Expense | 590 | 520 | 422 | 299 | 266 | 311 | 331 | 444 | 368 | 304 |
| Pretax Income | 1,320 | 1,446 | 2,044 | 1,116 | 1,084 | 1,048 | 780 | 113 | 1,346 | 1,163 |
| Effective Tax Rate | 31.1% | 31.7% | 32.8% | 38.3% | 36.1% | 39.1% | 33.6% | NM | 40.9% | 41.1% |
| Net Income | 909 | 988 | 1,373 | 689 | 693 | 638 | 518 | -184 | 795 | 685 |
| S&P Core Earnings | 860 | 888 | 967 | 655 | 628 | 490 | 364 | 102 | NA | NA |

### Balance Sheet & Other Financial Data (Million $)

| | 2008 | 2007 | 2006 | 2005 | 2004 | 2003 | 2002 | 2001 | 2000 | 1999 |
|---|---|---|---|---|---|---|---|---|---|---|
| Cash | 583 | 1,211 | 248 | 868 | 925 | 716 | 636 | 322 | 218 | 307 |
| Current Assets | 6,324 | 7,422 | 10,145 | 7,510 | 7,452 | 7,154 | 7,280 | 8,700 | 8,522 | 5,972 |
| Total Assets | 27,789 | 29,550 | 33,168 | 14,885 | 14,550 | 14,441 | 15,044 | 17,012 | 17,692 | 13,464 |
| Current Liabilities | 5,360 | 6,359 | 7,590 | 4,301 | 3,883 | 3,601 | 3,714 | 4,869 | 4,552 | 3,068 |
| Long Term Debt | 9,087 | 7,847 | 8,860 | 2,637 | 3,151 | 3,408 | 3,859 | 4,374 | 4,589 | 3,057 |
| Common Equity | 9,907 | 12,254 | 13,519 | 6,167 | 5,940 | 5,762 | 5,564 | 5,822 | 6,552 | 5,709 |
| Total Capital | 20,440 | 21,829 | 24,083 | 10,003 | 10,089 | 10,168 | 10,768 | 11,589 | 12,585 | 9,826 |
| Capital Expenditures | 994 | 1,317 | 568 | 467 | 508 | 568 | 615 | 742 | 770 | 695 |
| Cash Flow | 2,213 | 2,253 | 2,347 | 1,432 | 1,399 | 1,314 | 1,175 | 543 | 1,537 | 1,315 |
| Current Ratio | 1.2 | 1.2 | 1.3 | 1.7 | 1.9 | 2.0 | 2.0 | 1.8 | 1.9 | 1.9 |
| % Long Term Debt of Capitalization | 44.5 | 39.0 | 36.8 | 26.4 | 31.2 | 33.5 | 35.8 | 37.7 | 36.5 | 31.1 |
| % Net Income of Revenue | 3.5 | 3.7 | 6.1 | 4.4 | 4.5 | 4.1 | 3.3 | NM | 4.5 | 4.3 |
| % Return on Assets | 3.2 | 3.2 | 5.7 | 4.7 | 4.8 | 4.2 | 3.4 | NM | 4.5 | 5.0 |
| % Return on Equity | 8.2 | 7.7 | 13.9 | 11.4 | 11.8 | 11.3 | 9.1 | NM | 13.0 | 12.5 |

Data as orig reptd.; bef. results of disc opers/spec. items. Per share data adj. for stk. divs.; EPS diluted. E-Estimated. NA-Not Available. NM-Not Meaningful. NR-Not Ranked. UR-Under Review.

**Office:** 7 W Seventh St, Cincinnati, OH 45202.
**Telephone:** 513-579-7000.
**Website:** http://www.fds.com
**Chrmn, Pres & CEO:** T.J. Lundgren

**Vice Chrmn:** S.D. Kronick
**Vice Chrmn:** R.J. Borneo
**Investor Contact:** K.M. Hoguet (212-494-1602)
**EVP & CFO:** K.M. Hoguet

**Board Members:** S. F. Bollenbach, D. P. Connelly, M. Feldberg, S. D. Kronick, S. Levinson, T. J. Lundgren, J. Neubauer, J. A. Pichler, J. M. Roche, M. S. Traub, K. M. Von Der Heyden, C. E. Weatherup, M. C. Whittington
**Founded:** 1858
**Domicile:** Delaware
**Employees:** 188,000

# Manitowoc Company Inc. (The)

| S&P Recommendation **SELL** ★ ★ ☆ ☆ ☆ | Price $6.92 (as of Nov 14, 2008) | 12-Mo. Target Price $6.50 | Investment Style Large-Cap Growth |
|---|---|---|---|

**GICS Sector** Industrials
**Sub-Industry** Construction & Farm Machinery & Heavy Trucks

**Summary** This Wisconsin company is a leading provider of cranes and commercial foodservice equipment. It has agreed to sell its shipbuilding and ship repair business.

## Key Stock Statistics (Source S&P, Vickers, company reports)

| | | | | | | | |
|---|---|---|---|---|---|---|---|
| 52-Wk Range | $51.49– 6.84 | S&P Oper. EPS 2008**E** | 2.95 | Market Capitalization(B) | $0.902 | Beta | 2.11 |
| Trailing 12-Month EPS | $2.37 | S&P Oper. EPS 2009**E** | 1.85 | Yield (%) | 1.16 | S&P 3-Yr. Proj. EPS CAGR(%) | 1 |
| Trailing 12-Month P/E | 2.9 | P/E on S&P Oper. EPS 2008**E** | 2.3 | Dividend Rate/Share | $0.08 | S&P Credit Rating | BB |
| $10K Invested 5 Yrs Ago | $11,900 | Common Shares Outstg. (M) | 130.3 | Institutional Ownership (%) | 77 | | |

## Price Performance

30-Week Mov. Avg. ····   10-Week Mov. Avg. – –   GAAP Earnings vs. Previous Year   Volume Above Avg. STARS
12-Mo. Target Price —   Relative Strength — ▲ Up ▼ Down ► No Change   Below Avg. ★

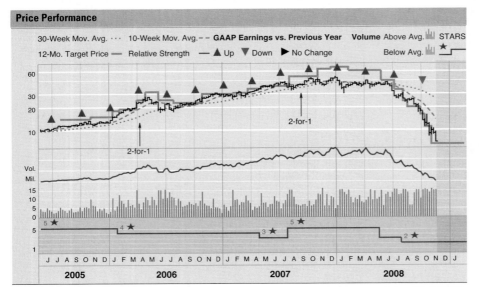

2-for-1
2-for-1

| 2005 | 2006 | 2007 | 2008 |

Options: ASE, CBOE, P, Ph

## Highlights

➤ The 12-month target price for MTW has recently been changed to $6.50 from $11.00. The Highlights section of this Stock Report will be updated accordingly.

## Investment Rationale/Risk

➤ The Investment Rationale/Risk section of this Stock Report will be updated shortly. For the latest News story on MTW from MarketScope, see below.

➤ 10/29/08 01:04 pm ET ... S&P MAINTAINS SELL OPINION ON SHARES OF MANITOWOC (MTW 8.94**): Q3 EPS of $0.80 before charges, vs. $0.56, beats our forecast by $0.01. But the shares are down 14% so far today, as MTW cuts Q4 guidance 16%-29% below our prior forecast, citing slower demand for its cranes in Europe, Russia, Africa and China, mostly from financing challenges. We are cutting our '08 EPS estimate by $0.30 to $2.95 and '09's by $1.40 to $1.85 on our much dimmer view of crane prospects and our negative outlook for the just-finished purchase of foodservice equipment maker Enodis plc. We are also cutting our target price by $4.50 to $6.50, 3.5X our '09 estimate. /M.Jaffe

## Qualitative Risk Assessment

| LOW | MEDIUM | **HIGH** |
|---|---|---|

Our risk assessment reflects the highly cyclical nature of the crane market. We also think MTW's expected addition of over $2 billion of debt to fund its planned acquisition of foodservice equipment supplier Enodis plc would reduce the health of its balance sheet.

## Quantitative Evaluations

**S&P Quality Ranking**     B

| D | C | B- | **B** | B+ | A- | A | A+ |
|---|---|---|---|---|---|---|---|

**Relative Strength Rank**     WEAK

10

LOWEST = 1      HIGHEST = 99

## Revenue/Earnings Data

**Revenue (Million $)**

| | 1Q | 2Q | 3Q | 4Q | Year |
|---|---|---|---|---|---|
| 2008 | 1,077 | 1,305 | 1,107 | -- | -- |
| 2007 | 862.1 | 1,019 | 1,006 | 1,118 | 4,005 |
| 2006 | 633.0 | 746.2 | 779.0 | 775.2 | 2,933 |
| 2005 | 510.3 | 589.6 | 564.9 | 589.3 | 2,254 |
| 2004 | 411.8 | 526.2 | 491.2 | 534.9 | 1,964 |
| 2003 | 365.9 | 419.3 | 412.1 | 395.9 | 1,593 |

**Earnings Per Share ($)**

| | 1Q | 2Q | 3Q | 4Q | Year |
|---|---|---|---|---|---|
| 2008 | 0.78 | 1.01 | -0.29 | E0.60 | E2.95 |
| 2007 | 0.51 | 0.77 | 0.59 | 0.74 | 2.62 |
| 2006 | 0.24 | 0.34 | 0.40 | 0.35 | 1.33 |
| 2005 | 0.05 | 0.20 | 0.17 | 0.07 | 0.48 |
| 2004 | 0.06 | 0.14 | 0.12 | 0.05 | 0.37 |
| 2003 | 0.01 | 0.06 | 0.08 | 0.03 | 0.18 |

Fiscal year ended Dec. 31. Next earnings report expected: Early February. EPS Estimates based on S&P Operating Earnings; historical GAAP earnings are as reported.

## Dividend Data (Dates: mm/dd Payment Date: mm/dd/yy)

| Amount ($) | Date Decl. | Ex-Div. Date | Stk. of Record | Payment Date |
|---|---|---|---|---|
| 0.020 | 02/15 | 03/05 | 03/07 | 03/17/08 |
| 0.020 | 05/05 | 05/29 | 06/02 | 06/12/08 |
| 0.020 | 07/24 | 08/27 | 09/01 | 09/11/08 |
| 0.020 | 10/20 | 11/26 | 12/01 | 12/11/08 |

Dividends have been paid since 1945. Source: Company reports.

# Manitowoc Company Inc. (The)

**STANDARD & POOR'S**

## Business Summary October 13, 2008

CORPORATE OVERVIEW. The Manitowoc Co. manufactures cranes, foodservice equipment and marine vessels. MTW derived 51% of its sales in foreign markets in 2007 (48% in 2006), with Europe accounting for the majority (30% of total sales in 2007 and 28% in 2006).

In June 2008, MTW was the high bidder in an auction for Enodis plc, a global food and beverage equipment maker. Its bid totaled $2.7 billion (based on currency exchange at that time), consisting of 328 pence per share (over $2.4 billion) in cash, plus the assumption of about $249 million of debt. The transaction received antitrust clearance in the U.S. and Europe, after MTW agreed to sell Enodis' ice machine operations. The deal was expected to close in late October, subject to certain approvals by a U.K. court. In August 2008, MTW agreed to sell its marine segment to a unit of Fincantieri-Cantieri Navali Italani SpA, for $120 million in cash. The deal was expected to close at the end of the year, subject to approvals.

The crane division (81% and 84% of 2007 sales and operating profits, respectively; 14.5% operating margin) designs and manufactures a diversified line of lattice-boom crawler cranes with lifting capacities of up to 1,433 U.S. tons, which are used to lift material and equipment in a wide variety of applications and end markets; tower cranes, which offer the ability to lift and distribute material at the point of use more quickly and accurately than other types of lifting machinery; mobile telescopic cranes, which are used to lift and move material at job sites; and boom trucks, of which telescopic boom trucks are used mostly for lifting material at a job site, and articulated boom trucks are used mostly to load and unload truck beds. MTW's crane segment also has a parts and services operation. The division serves applications such as energy, petrochemical and industrial projects; infrastructure development; commercial and high-rise residential construction; and mining and dredging.

The foodservice segment (11% and 11%; 14.0%) is a broad-line producer of "cold-side" commercial foodservice products. It offers commercial ice-cube machines and storage bins; refrigerators and freezers; refrigerated undercounters and food preparation tables; ice/beverage dispensers; cast aluminum cold plates; compressor racks; and modular refrigeration systems. The foodservice segment has sold products primarily in the U.S., but has been increasing its global focus in recent years. The division sells to lodging, restaurant, health care, convenience, and soft-drink bottling markets.

The marine division (8% and 5%; 8.1%) provides new construction services for commercial, government and military vessels. It also provides inspection, maintenance, conversion, and repair of freshwater and saltwater vessels.

## Company Financials Fiscal Year Ended Dec. 31

### Per Share Data ($)

| | 2007 | 2006 | 2005 | 2004 | 2003 | 2002 | 2001 | 2000 | 1999 | 1998 |
|---|---|---|---|---|---|---|---|---|---|---|
| Tangible Book Value | 4.85 | 1.23 | NM | NM | NM | NM | NM | NM | NM | NM |
| Cash Flow | 3.31 | 1.92 | 1.00 | 0.78 | 0.63 | 0.71 | 0.85 | 0.81 | 0.80 | 0.63 |
| Earnings | 2.62 | 1.33 | 0.48 | 0.37 | 0.18 | 0.39 | 0.50 | 0.60 | 0.64 | 0.49 |
| S&P Core Earnings | 2.64 | 1.33 | 0.51 | 0.32 | 0.14 | 0.34 | 0.48 | NA | NA | NA |
| Dividends | 0.08 | 0.07 | 0.07 | 0.07 | 0.07 | 0.07 | 0.08 | 0.08 | 0.08 | 0.08 |
| Payout Ratio | 3% | 5% | 15% | 19% | 39% | 18% | 15% | 12% | 12% | 15% |
| Prices:High | 51.49 | 31.33 | 13.50 | 9.96 | 7.95 | 11.10 | 8.21 | 8.72 | 10.94 | 7.83 |
| Prices:Low | 25.67 | 12.41 | 8.58 | 6.90 | 4.18 | 5.53 | 5.58 | 4.41 | 6.05 | 4.08 |
| P/E Ratio:High | 20 | 24 | 28 | 27 | 44 | 28 | 17 | 15 | 17 | 16 |
| P/E Ratio:Low | 10 | 9 | 18 | 19 | 23 | 14 | 11 | 7 | 9 | 8 |

### Income Statement Analysis (Million $)

| | 2007 | 2006 | 2005 | 2004 | 2003 | 2002 | 2001 | 2000 | 1999 | 1998 |
|---|---|---|---|---|---|---|---|---|---|---|
| Revenue | 4,005 | 2,933 | 2,254 | 1,964 | 1,593 | 1,407 | 1,117 | 873 | 805 | 695 |
| Operating Income | 592 | 375 | 200 | 162 | 132 | 159 | 152 | 131 | 136 | 107 |
| Depreciation | 88.1 | 72.3 | 63.5 | 54.0 | 48.4 | 35.1 | 33.4 | 18.1 | 16.7 | 14.6 |
| Interest Expense | 36.3 | 46.3 | 53.8 | 56.9 | 56.9 | 52.0 | 37.5 | 14.5 | 10.8 | 9.74 |
| Pretax Income | 463 | 245 | 73.9 | 49.1 | 22.6 | 62.8 | 79.7 | 96.1 | 106 | 81.4 |
| Effective Tax Rate | 27.9% | 32.0% | 20.0% | 19.0% | 18.0% | 36.0% | 38.7% | 37.3% | 37.0% | 36.9% |
| Net Income | 334 | 167 | 59.1 | 39.8 | 18.5 | 40.2 | 48.9 | 60.3 | 66.8 | 51.4 |
| S&P Core Earnings | 336 | 167 | 62.2 | 34.7 | 14.6 | 34.6 | 46.9 | NA | NA | NA |

### Balance Sheet & Other Financial Data (Million $)

| | 2007 | 2006 | 2005 | 2004 | 2003 | 2002 | 2001 | 2000 | 1999 | 1998 |
|---|---|---|---|---|---|---|---|---|---|---|
| Cash | 366 | 176 | 232 | 179 | 47.2 | 30.4 | 25.7 | 16.0 | 12.0 | 12.4 |
| Current Assets | 1,576 | 1,143 | 953 | 846 | 646 | 647 | 331 | 224 | 191 | 191 |
| Total Assets | 2,869 | 2,220 | 1,962 | 1,928 | 1,603 | 1,577 | 1,081 | 643 | 530 | 481 |
| Current Liabilities | 1,075 | 935 | 690 | 653 | 545 | 460 | 296 | 239 | 189 | 198 |
| Long Term Debt | 218 | 264 | 474 | 512 | 567 | 624 | 23.1 | 20.3 | 79.2 | 79.8 |
| Common Equity | 1,350 | 774 | 543 | 519 | 298 | 295 | 264 | 234 | 232 | 173 |
| Total Capital | 1,567 | 1,039 | 1,017 | 1,031 | 866 | 919 | 287 | 254 | 311 | 252 |
| Capital Expenditures | 120 | 67.6 | 54.9 | 44.4 | 32.0 | 33.0 | 29.3 | 13.4 | 13.7 | 11.7 |
| Cash Flow | 422 | 239 | 123 | 93.8 | 66.9 | 75.3 | 82.2 | 78.3 | 83.5 | 66.0 |
| Current Ratio | 1.5 | 1.2 | 1.4 | 1.3 | 1.2 | 1.4 | 1.1 | 0.9 | 1.0 | 1.0 |
| % Long Term Debt of Capitalization | 13.9 | 25.4 | 46.6 | 49.7 | 65.5 | 67.9 | 8.0 | 8.0 | 25.4 | 31.6 |
| % Net Income of Revenue | 8.3 | 5.7 | 2.6 | 2.0 | 1.2 | 2.9 | 4.4 | 6.9 | 8.3 | 7.4 |
| % Return on Assets | 13.1 | 8.0 | 3.0 | 2.2 | 1.2 | 3.0 | 5.7 | 10.3 | 13.2 | 11.7 |
| % Return on Equity | 31.4 | 25.3 | 11.1 | 9.1 | 6.2 | 14.4 | 19.6 | 25.9 | 33.0 | 34.1 |

Data as orig reptd.; bef. results of disc opers/spec. items. Per share data adj. for stk. divs.; EPS diluted. E-Estimated. NA-Not Available. NM-Not Meaningful. NR-Not Ranked. UR-Under Review.

**Office:** 2400 South 44th Street, Manitowoc, WI 54220-5846.
**Telephone:** 920-684-4410.
**Website:** http://www.manitowoc.com
**Chrmn:** T.D. Growcock

**Pres & CEO:** G.E. Tellock
**COO:** J. Wheeler
**SVP & CFO:** C.J. Laurino
**SVP, Secy & General Counsel:** M.D. Jones

**Investor Contact:** S.C. Khail (920-684-4410)
**Board Members:** D. H. Anderson, V. W. Colbert, D. W. Duval, C. M. Egnotovich, T. D. Growcock, K. W. Krueger, K. D. Nosbusch, J. L. Packard, R. C. Stift, G. E. Tellock
**Founded:** 1853
**Domicile:** Wisconsin
**Employees:** 10,460

# Marathon Oil Corp

| S&P Recommendation BUY ★★★★☆ | Price $26.69 (as of Nov 14, 2008) | 12-Mo. Target Price $46.00 | Investment Style Large-Cap Blend |
|---|---|---|---|

**GICS Sector** Energy
**Sub-Industry** Integrated Oil & Gas

**Summary** One of the largest integrated oil companies in the U.S., Marathon has international operations in oil and gas exploration and production, and domestic refining, marketing and transportation.

## Key Stock Statistics (Source S&P, Vickers, company reports)

| | | | | | | | |
|---|---|---|---|---|---|---|---|
| 52-Wk Range | $63.22– 21.50 | S&P Oper. EPS 2008**E** | 6.99 | Market Capitalization(B) | $18.923 | Beta | 1.25 |
| Trailing 12-Month EPS | $5.94 | S&P Oper. EPS 2009**E** | 7.23 | Yield (%) | 3.60 | S&P 3-Yr. Proj. EPS CAGR(%) | 14 |
| Trailing 12-Month P/E | 4.5 | P/E on S&P Oper. EPS 2008**E** | 3.8 | Dividend Rate/Share | $0.96 | S&P Credit Rating | BBB+ |
| $10K Invested 5 Yrs Ago | $20,036 | Common Shares Outstg. (M) | 709.0 | Institutional Ownership (%) | 81 | | |

## Price Performance

30-Week Mov. Avg. ···· 10-Week Mov. Avg. -- GAAP Earnings vs. Previous Year   Volume Above Avg. STARS
12-Mo. Target Price — Relative Strength ▲ Up ▼ Down ► No Change   Below Avg. ★

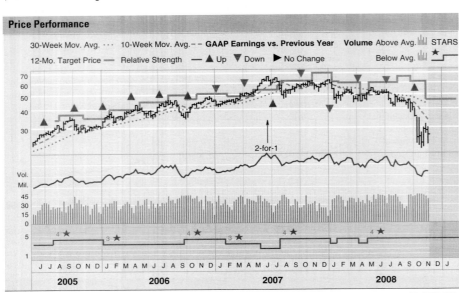

Options: ASE, CBOE, P, Ph

Analysis prepared by **Tina J. Vital** on November 07, 2008, when the stock traded at **$ 27.93**.

### Highlights

➤ MRO has increased its exposure toward more higher-growth but politically challenging regions (Africa, Libya), and has placed emphasis on larger, longer lead time projects (deepwater Gulf of Mexico, western Canada). Start-ups in Norway and the U.S. Gulf of Mexico should lead to about 8% production growth in 2008, at the low end of guidance, and we expect over 8% per annum production growth during 2008-2012, within the range of management guidance.

➤ Third quarter refinery throughputs declined 7.8% from last year, reflecting the temporary shutdown of its Houston and Texas City refineries due to Gulf hurricanes. During the quarter, U.S. gasoline inventories fell and gasoline prices climbed. Combined with lower crude pricing, third quarter refining and wholesale marketing gross margins rose 47%. Industry-wide, we expect U.S. Gulf Coast 321 refining cracks will narrow by about 18% in 2008 and 2009.

➤ After-tax operating earnings declined 19% in 2007, but we expect increases of 32% in 2008, and 3% in 2009.

### Investment Rationale/Risk

➤ In July 2008, MRO was evaluating the potential separation of its exploration and production and refining and marketing units into two independent, publicly traded companies. A decision by MRO's directors is expected in the fourth quarter, subject to necessary approvals, with a potential separation seen in the first quarter of 2009. We believe such a separation would unlock value in its businesses and permit increased upstream investment.

➤ Risks to our recommendation and target price include changes in economic, industry, and operating conditions, such as rising industry costs and difficulty replacing reserves.

➤ A blend of our discounted cash flow ($26 per share, assuming a WACC of 10.0% and terminal growth of 3%), net asset ($67 per share; assuming a long-term WTI oil price of $90 per barrel) and narrowed relative valuations leads to our 12-month target price of $46 per share, at an expected enterprise value of 3.2X our 2009 EBITDA estimate, a slight premium to peers.

### Qualitative Risk Assessment

| LOW | MEDIUM | HIGH |

Our risk assessment reflects our view of the company's diversified and solid business profile in volatile and cyclical segments of the energy industry. We consider MRO's earnings stability to be good, and its corporate governance practices sound.

### Quantitative Evaluations

**S&P Quality Ranking**                    B+

| D | C | B- | B | B+ | A- | A | A+ |

**Relative Strength Rank**          MODERATE

52

LOWEST = 1                    HIGHEST = 99

### Revenue/Earnings Data

**Revenue (Million $)**

| | 1Q | 2Q | 3Q | 4Q | Year |
|---|---|---|---|---|---|
| 2008 | 18,100 | 20,617 | 21,841 | -- | -- |
| 2007 | 12,869 | 16,736 | 16,762 | 18,185 | 64,552 |
| 2006 | 16,418 | 18,179 | 16,492 | 13,807 | 64,896 |
| 2005 | 12,932 | 16,019 | 17,248 | 17,314 | 63,673 |
| 2004 | 10,652 | 12,514 | 12,249 | 14,183 | 49,598 |
| 2003 | 10,033 | 9,643 | 10,253 | 11,034 | 40,963 |

**Earnings Per Share ($)**

| | | | | | |
|---|---|---|---|---|---|
| 2008 | 1.02 | 1.08 | 2.90 | E1.98 | E6.99 |
| 2007 | 1.04 | 2.24 | 1.49 | 0.94 | 5.68 |
| 2006 | 1.07 | 2.04 | 2.26 | 1.53 | 6.87 |
| 2005 | 0.47 | 0.96 | 1.04 | 1.74 | 4.25 |
| 2004 | 0.42 | 0.51 | 0.32 | 0.62 | 1.86 |
| 2003 | 0.49 | 0.40 | 0.45 | 0.32 | 1.63 |

Fiscal year ended Dec. 31. Next earnings report expected: Early February. EPS Estimates based on S&P Operating Earnings; historical GAAP earnings are as reported.

### Dividend Data (Dates: mm/dd Payment Date: mm/dd/yy)

| Amount ($) | Date Decl. | Ex-Div. Date | Stk. of Record | Payment Date |
|---|---|---|---|---|
| 0.240 | 01/28 | 02/15 | 02/20 | 03/10/08 |
| 0.240 | 04/30 | 05/19 | 05/21 | 06/10/08 |
| 0.240 | 07/31 | 08/18 | 08/20 | 09/10/08 |
| 0.240 | 10/29 | 11/17 | 11/19 | 12/10/08 |

Dividends have been paid since 1991. Source: Company reports.

# Marathon Oil Corp

## Business Summary November 07, 2008

CORPORATE OVERVIEW. As one of the largest integrated oil companies and refiners in the U.S., Marathon Oil (MRO; formerly USX-Marathon Group, a part of USX Corp.) is engaged in four operating segments: Exploration and Production (E&P; 14% of 2007 revenues; $1.73 billion of 2007 segment income); Oil Sands Mining (OSM; less than 1%; loss of $63 million), Refining, Marketing and Transportation (RM&T; 85%; $2.1 billion); and Integrated Gas (IG; less than 1%; $132 million).

The E&P segment conducts exploration in the U.S., Angola, Norway and Indonesia, and production activities in the U.S., the U.K., Norway, Ireland, Equatorial Guinea and Libya. Proved oil and gas reserves declined 2.9% to 1.225 billion barrel oil equivalent (boe; 72% developed, 53% liquids) in 2007. Oil and gas production declined 7% to 351,000 boe per day (boe/d; 56% liquids) in 2007. We estimate MRO's 2007 organic reserve replacement at 69% of production. Using data from John S. Herold, we estimate MRO's three-year (2004-06) finding and development costs at $12.46 per boe, below the peer average; its three-year proved acquisition costs at $2.40 per boe, below the peer average;

and its three-year reserve replacement rate at 171%, above the peer average.

Through MRO's October 2007 acquisition of Western Oil Sands Inc. (WTO) for about US$6.9 billion (including assumed debt of US$1.1 billion), MRO gained a 20% interest in the Athabasca Oil Sands Project (AOSP) in Alberta, Canada. The venture produces bitumen (net production of 31,000 b/d of bitumen in 2007, expected to rise to 130,000 b/d by 2020; and net proved mining reserves of 436 million barrels of bitumen) from oil sands deposits and upgrades the bitumen to synthetic crude oil. As a result, MRO's directors approved a $1.9 billion expansion and heavy oil upgrade project at its Detroit refinery to raise its heavy oil processing capacity, by about 80,000 b/d, and its total oil refining capacity from 100,000 b/d to 115,000 b/d. Completion is slated for late 2010.

## Company Financials Fiscal Year Ended Dec. 31

| Per Share Data ($) | 2007 | 2006 | 2005 | 2004 | 2003 | 2002 | 2001 | 2000 | 1999 | 1998 |
|---|---|---|---|---|---|---|---|---|---|---|
| Tangible Book Value | 24.30 | 18.72 | 13.90 | 11.17 | 9.20 | 7.57 | 7.99 | 7.77 | 7.70 | 7.00 |
| Cash Flow | 7.91 | 9.30 | 6.14 | 3.57 | 3.53 | 2.80 | 4.12 | 2.69 | 2.59 | 2.14 |
| Earnings | 5.68 | 6.87 | 4.25 | 1.86 | 1.63 | 0.86 | 2.13 | 0.70 | 1.05 | 0.52 |
| S&P Core Earnings | 5.69 | 6.85 | 4.20 | 1.91 | 1.63 | 0.69 | 2.21 | NA | NA | NA |
| Dividends | 0.92 | 0.77 | 0.61 | 0.52 | 0.48 | 0.46 | 0.46 | 0.44 | 0.42 | 0.42 |
| Payout Ratio | 16% | 11% | 14% | 28% | 29% | 53% | 75% | 63% | 40% | 80% |
| Prices:High | 67.04 | 49.37 | 36.34 | 21.30 | 16.81 | 15.15 | 16.87 | 15.19 | 16.94 | 20.25 |
| Prices:Low | 41.50 | 31.01 | 17.76 | 15.15 | 9.93 | 9.41 | 12.48 | 10.34 | 9.81 | 12.50 |
| P/E Ratio:High | 12 | 7 | 9 | 11 | 10 | 18 | 28 | 22 | 16 | 39 |
| P/E Ratio:Low | 7 | 5 | 4 | 8 | 6 | 11 | 20 | 15 | 9 | 24 |
| **Income Statement Analysis** (Million $) | | | | | | | | | | |
| Revenue | 64,552 | 64,896 | 63,673 | 49,598 | 40,963 | 31,464 | 33,019 | 34,487 | 24,212 | 21,726 |
| Operating Income | 7,598 | 9,932 | 6,660 | 8,379 | 2,988 | 2,253 | 4,215 | 3,521 | 1,997 | 1,530 |
| Depreciation, Depletion and Amortization | 1,613 | 1,518 | 1,358 | 1,217 | 1,175 | 1,201 | 1,236 | 1,245 | 950 | 941 |
| Interest Expense | 290 | 108 | 145 | 161 | 238 | 288 | 196 | 260 | 290 | 311 |
| Pretax Income | 6,846 | 8,969 | 5,157 | 2,509 | 1,898 | 1,098 | 2,781 | 1,412 | 1,425 | 701 |
| Effective Tax Rate | 42.4% | 44.8% | 33.5% | 29.0% | 30.8% | 35.4% | 27.3% | 34.1% | 22.7% | 20.3% |
| Net Income | 3,948 | 4,957 | 3,051 | 1,257 | 1,012 | 536 | 1,318 | 432 | 654 | 310 |
| S&P Core Earnings | 3,953 | 4,949 | 3,013 | 1,290 | 1,014 | 428 | 1,367 | NA | NA | NA |
| **Balance Sheet & Other Financial Data** (Million $) | | | | | | | | | | |
| Cash | 1,199 | 2,585 | 2,617 | 3,369 | 1,396 | 488 | 657 | 340 | 111 | 137 |
| Current Assets | 10,587 | 10,096 | 9,383 | 8,867 | 6,040 | 4,479 | 4,411 | 4,985 | 4,102 | 2,976 |
| Total Assets | 42,746 | 30,831 | 28,498 | 23,423 | 19,482 | 17,812 | 16,129 | 15,232 | 15,705 | 14,544 |
| Current Liabilities | 11,260 | 8,061 | 8,154 | 5,253 | 4,207 | 3,659 | 3,468 | 4,012 | 3,149 | 2,610 |
| Long Term Debt | 6,084 | 3,061 | 3,698 | 4,057 | 4,085 | 4,410 | 3,432 | 4,196 | 3,504 | 3,640 |
| Common Equity | 19,223 | 14,607 | 11,705 | 8,111 | 6,075 | 5,082 | 4,940 | 4,845 | 4,800 | 4,312 |
| Total Capital | 28,696 | 20,083 | 17,868 | 16,411 | 12,171 | 12,908 | 11,632 | 12,235 | 11,552 | 10,992 |
| Capital Expenditures | 4,466 | 3,433 | 2,890 | 2,237 | 1,892 | 1,574 | 1,639 | 1,669 | 1,378 | 1,270 |
| Cash Flow | 5,500 | 6,475 | 4,409 | 2,474 | 2,187 | 1,737 | 2,546 | 1,677 | 1,604 | 1,251 |
| Current Ratio | 0.9 | 1.3 | 1.2 | 1.7 | 1.4 | 1.2 | 1.3 | 1.2 | 1.3 | 1.1 |
| % Long Term Debt of Capitalization | 21.2 | 15.2 | 20.7 | 24.7 | 33.6 | 34.2 | 29.5 | 34.3 | 30.3 | 33.1 |
| % Return on Assets | 10.7 | 16.7 | 11.8 | 5.9 | 5.4 | 3.2 | 7.9 | 2.8 | 4.3 | 2.5 |
| % Return on Equity | 23.3 | 37.7 | 30.8 | 17.7 | 18.1 | 10.7 | 22.4 | 9.0 | 14.4 | 7.8 |

Data as orig reptd.; bef. results of disc opers/spec. items. Per share data adj. for stk. divs.; EPS diluted. E-Estimated. NA-Not Available. NM-Not Meaningful. NR-Not Ranked. UR-Under Review.

**Office:** 5555 San Felipe St Bsmt, Houston, TX 77056-2701.
**Telephone:** 713-629-6600.
**Website:** http://www.marathon.com
**Chrmn:** T.J. Usher

**Pres & CEO:** C.P. Cazalot, Jr.
**EVP & CFO:** J.F. Clark
**CTO:** S.B. Hinchman
**Chief Acctg Officer & Cntlr:** M.K. Stewart

**Investor Contact:** H. Thill (713-296-4140)
**Board Members:** C. F. Bolden, Jr., G. H. Boyce, C. P. Cazalot, Jr., D. A. Daberko, W. J. Davis, S. A. Jackson, P. Lader, C. R. Lee, D. H. Reilley, S. E. Schofield, J. W. Snow, T. J. Usher

**Founded:** 1901
**Domicile:** Delaware
**Employees:** 29,524

# Marriott International Inc.

**STANDARD &POOR'S**

| S&P Recommendation **SELL** ★ ★ ☆ ☆ ☆ | Price $15.66 (as of Nov 14, 2008) | 12-Mo. Target Price $15.00 | Investment Style Large-Cap Growth |
|---|---|---|---|

**GICS Sector** Consumer Discretionary
**Sub-Industry** Hotels, Resorts & Cruise Lines

**Summary** MAR's lodging brands include over 3,100 properties, most of which are managed by the company or are operated by others through franchise relationships.

## Key Stock Statistics (Source S&P, Vickers, company reports)

| | | | | | | | |
|---|---|---|---|---|---|---|---|
| 52-Wk Range | $37.89– 15.32 | S&P Oper. EPS 2008**E** | 1.60 | Market Capitalization(B) | $5.467 | Beta | 0.94 |
| Trailing 12-Month EPS | $1.47 | S&P Oper. EPS 2009**E** | 1.20 | Yield (%) | 2.23 | S&P 3-Yr. Proj. EPS CAGR(%) | -10 |
| Trailing 12-Month P/E | 10.7 | P/E on S&P Oper. EPS 2008**E** | 9.8 | Dividend Rate/Share | $0.35 | S&P Credit Rating | BBB |
| $10K Invested 5 Yrs Ago | $7,023 | Common Shares Outstg. (M) | 349.1 | Institutional Ownership (%) | 56 | | |

## Price Performance

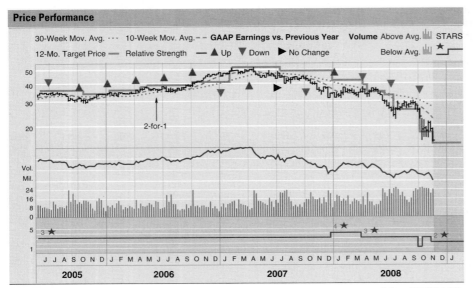

30-Week Mov. Avg. · · · 10-Week Mov. Avg. - - - **GAAP Earnings vs. Previous Year** Volume Above Avg. STARS
12-Mo. Target Price — Relative Strength — ▲ Up ▼ Down ► No Change Below Avg.

2-for-1

Vol. Mil.

2005 2006 2007 2008

Options: ASE, CBOE, P, Ph

## Qualitative Risk Assessment

| LOW | MEDIUM | **HIGH** |
|---|---|---|

Our risk assessment reflects our view that MAR is subject to cyclical economic and industry changes that suggest a period that will be difficult for it to grow earnings may be in the offing. However, we believe MAR's finances are relatively strong, and we expect that internal cash flow will be sufficient to finance future minimum capital needs, although outside capital, particularly to finance timeshare receivables, is likely to be more costly, if available at all.

## Quantitative Evaluations

**S&P Quality Ranking** A

| D | C | B- | B | B+ | A- | **A** | A+ |
|---|---|---|---|---|---|---|---|

**Relative Strength Rank** MODERATE

36

LOWEST = 1 HIGHEST = 99

## Highlights

> The STARS recommendation for MAR has recently been changed to 2 (sell) from 3 (hold) and the 12-month target price has recently been changed to $15.00 from $18.00. The Highlights section of this Stock Report will be updated accordingly.

## Investment Rationale/Risk

> The Investment Rationale/Risk section of this Stock Report will be updated shortly. For the latest News story on MAR from MarketScope, see below.

> 11/13/08 10:07 am ET ... S&P LOWERS OPINION ON SHARES OF MARRIOTT INTERNATIONAL TO SELL FROM HOLD (MAR 16.26**): In conjunction with our reiteration this morning of our negative fundamental outlook for the hotel industry, we reduce our '08 EPS estimate for MAR by $0.05 to $1.60 to reflect the sharp slowdown seen so far in Q4. For 2009, we now see revenues declining 5% from '08 and we cut our EPS estimate by $0.20 to $1.20. Our downgrade reflects our view that MAR no longer warrants the slight valuation premium we have historically awarded its shares. On revised 8.5X enterprise value/EBITDA multiple, we lower our 12-month target price by $3 to $15, below the current share price. /M.Basham

## Revenue/Earnings Data

**Revenue (Million $)**

| | 1Q | 2Q | 3Q | 4Q | Year |
|---|---|---|---|---|---|
| 2008 | 2,947 | 3,185 | 2,963 | -- | -- |
| 2007 | 2,836 | 3,122 | 2,943 | 4,089 | 12,990 |
| 2006 | 2,705 | 2,891 | 2,703 | 3,861 | 12,160 |
| 2005 | 2,534 | 2,661 | 2,714 | 3,641 | 11,550 |
| 2004 | 2,252 | 2,402 | 2,304 | 3,141 | 10,099 |
| 2003 | 2,023 | 2,016 | 2,109 | 2,866 | 9,014 |

**Earnings Per Share ($)**

| | | | | | |
|---|---|---|---|---|---|
| 2008 | 0.33 | 0.41 | 0.26 | E0.43 | E1.60 |
| 2007 | 0.40 | 0.43 | 0.31 | 0.62 | 1.75 |
| 2006 | 0.39 | 0.43 | 0.33 | 0.52 | 1.66 |
| 2005 | 0.31 | 0.29 | 0.33 | 0.54 | 1.45 |
| 2004 | 0.24 | 0.34 | 0.28 | 0.40 | 1.24 |
| 2003 | 0.18 | 0.26 | 0.19 | 0.35 | 0.97 |

Fiscal year ended Dec. 31. Next earnings report expected: Late January. EPS Estimates based on S&P Operating Earnings; historical GAAP earnings are as reported.

## Dividend Data (Dates: mm/dd Payment Date: mm/dd/yy)

| Amount ($) | Date Decl. | Ex-Div. Date | Stk. of Record | Payment Date |
|---|---|---|---|---|
| 0.075 | 02/07 | 04/01 | 04/03 | 05/01/08 |
| 0.088 | 05/02 | 06/24 | 06/26 | 08/01/08 |
| 0.088 | 08/07 | 09/09 | 09/11 | 10/03/08 |
| 0.088 | 11/07 | 11/26 | 12/01 | 01/09/09 |

Dividends have been paid since 1998. Source: Company reports.

---

# Marriott International Inc.

STANDARD
&POOR'S

## Business Summary October 20, 2008

CORPORATE OVERVIEW. As of September 5, 2008, Marriott International's lodging and timeshare businesses included 3,105 properties, with 550,453 rooms or suites. This compares with 2,999 properties with 535,093 rooms or suites as of December 28, 2007. Of the 3,105 properties, about 2,612 were full and limited service hotels located in the U.S.

At year-end 2007, MAR had 1,077 properties (275,796 rooms or suites) that MAR operated under long-term management or lease agreements, and had six owned properties (1,916). With its management agreements, the company typically earns a base fee, and may receive an incentive management fee that is based on hotel profits. MAR also had 1,922 franchised properties, with 259,297 rooms, that were operated by other parties. With franchise properties, the company generally receives an initial application fee and continuing royalty fees.

By brand (including franchises), as of year-end 2007, MAR's business included 520 Marriott Hotels & Resorts, Marriott Conference Centers or JW Marriott Hotels & Resorts properties; 68 Ritz-Carlton hotels; 141 Renaissance hotels; 767 Courtyard hotels; 537 Fairfield Inn properties; 177 SpringHill Suites properties, 546 Residence Inn hotels; 141 TownPlace Suites properties; two Bulgari

Hotel & Resorts properties, 61 timeshare properties; and 39 corporate housing and residential units. Two brands for which the first properties are in planning or development are Nickelodeon Resorts by Marriott, and Edition, a global boutique hotel brand for which the company has partnered with hotelier Ian Schrager.

For 2007, MAR's North American full-service lodging segment, which included Marriott full-service and Renaissance businesses, accounted for 42% of total revenues, while North American limited service accounted for 17%. In addition, international accounted for 12%, luxury 12%, timeshare 16%, and other 1%.

The company's international presence as of year-end 2007 included: 172 properties (41,073 rooms or suites) in Europe or the United Kingdom, 85 properties (29,439) in Asia, 35 (10,772) in the Middle East or Africa, 119 (27,571) in the Americas ex-U.S., and eight (2,354) in Australia.

## Company Financials Fiscal Year Ended Dec. 31

| Per Share Data ($) | 2007 | 2006 | 2005 | 2004 | 2003 | 2002 | 2001 | 2000 | 1999 | 1998 |
|---|---|---|---|---|---|---|---|---|---|---|
| Tangible Book Value | 1.42 | 2.88 | 4.52 | 5.85 | 5.17 | 4.57 | 3.56 | 2.81 | 2.13 | 1.68 |
| Cash Flow | 2.25 | 2.32 | 1.84 | 1.68 | 1.30 | 1.23 | 0.89 | 1.33 | 1.04 | 0.97 |
| Earnings | 1.75 | 1.66 | 1.45 | 1.24 | 0.97 | 0.87 | 0.46 | 0.95 | 0.76 | 0.73 |
| S&P Core Earnings | 1.78 | 1.57 | 1.25 | 1.00 | 0.68 | 0.77 | 0.35 | NA | NA | NA |
| Dividends | 0.29 | 0.24 | 0.20 | 0.17 | 0.15 | 0.14 | 0.13 | 0.12 | 0.11 | 0.07 |
| Payout Ratio | 16% | 14% | 14% | 13% | 15% | 16% | 28% | 12% | 13% | 10% |
| Prices:High | 52.00 | 48.31 | 35.39 | 32.00 | 23.60 | 23.23 | 25.25 | 21.75 | 22.25 | 18.97 |
| Prices:Low | 31.34 | 32.31 | 29.01 | 20.32 | 14.28 | 13.13 | 13.65 | 13.06 | 14.50 | 9.69 |
| P/E Ratio:High | 30 | 29 | 24 | 26 | 24 | 27 | 55 | 23 | 28 | 26 |
| P/E Ratio:Low | 18 | 19 | 20 | 16 | 15 | 15 | 30 | 14 | 18 | 13 |

| Income Statement Analysis (Million $) | | | | | | | | | | |
|---|---|---|---|---|---|---|---|---|---|---|
| Revenue | 12,990 | 12,160 | 11,550 | 10,099 | 9,014 | 8,441 | 10,152 | 10,017 | 8,739 | 7,968 |
| Operating Income | 1,385 | 1,199 | 739 | 643 | 537 | 634 | 779 | 997 | 828 | 766 |
| Depreciation | 197 | 188 | 184 | 166 | 160 | 187 | 222 | 195 | 162 | 140 |
| Interest Expense | 184 | 124 | 106 | 99.0 | 110 | 86.0 | 109 | 100 | 61.0 | 30.0 |
| Pretax Income | 1,137 | 997 | 717 | 654 | 488 | 471 | 370 | 757 | 637 | 632 |
| Effective Tax Rate | 39.0% | 28.7% | 13.1% | 15.3% | NM | 6.79% | 36.2% | 36.7% | 37.2% | 382.0% |
| Net Income | 697 | 717 | 668 | 594 | 476 | 439 | 236 | 479 | 400 | 390 |
| S&P Core Earnings | 711 | 680 | 579 | 484 | 330 | 381 | 180 | NA | NA | NA |

| Balance Sheet & Other Financial Data (Million $) | | | | | | | | | | |
|---|---|---|---|---|---|---|---|---|---|---|
| Cash | 332 | 193 | 203 | 770 | 229 | 198 | 817 | 334 | 489 | 390 |
| Current Assets | 3,572 | 3,314 | 2,010 | 1,946 | 1,235 | 1,744 | 2,130 | 1,415 | 1,600 | 1,333 |
| Total Assets | 8,942 | 8,588 | 8,530 | 8,668 | 8,177 | 8,296 | 9,107 | 8,237 | 7,324 | 6,233 |
| Current Liabilities | 2,876 | 2,522 | 1,992 | 2,356 | 1,770 | 2,207 | 1,802 | 1,917 | 1,743 | 1,412 |
| Long Term Debt | 2,790 | 1,818 | 1,681 | 836 | 1,391 | 1,553 | 2,815 | 2,016 | 1,676 | 1,267 |
| Common Equity | 1,429 | 2,618 | 3,252 | 4,081 | 3,838 | 3,573 | 3,478 | 3,267 | 2,908 | 2,570 |
| Total Capital | 4,219 | 4,436 | 4,944 | 4,929 | 5,398 | 5,232 | 6,293 | 5,283 | 4,584 | 3,837 |
| Capital Expenditures | 671 | 529 | 780 | 181 | 210 | 292 | 560 | 1,095 | 929 | 937 |
| Cash Flow | 894 | 905 | 852 | 760 | 636 | 626 | 458 | 674 | 562 | 530 |
| Current Ratio | 1.2 | 1.3 | 1.0 | 0.8 | 0.7 | 0.8 | 1.2 | 0.7 | 0.9 | 0.9 |
| % Long Term Debt of Capitalization | 66.1 | 41.0 | 34.0 | 16.9 | 25.7 | 29.7 | 44.7 | 38.2 | 36.6 | 33.0 |
| % Net Income of Revenue | 5.3 | 5.9 | 5.8 | 5.9 | 5.3 | 5.2 | 2.3 | 4.8 | 4.6 | 4.9 |
| % Return on Assets | 7.9 | 8.4 | 7.8 | 7.1 | 5.8 | 5.0 | 2.7 | 6.2 | 5.9 | 6.8 |
| % Return on Equity | 34.4 | 24.4 | 18.2 | 15.0 | 12.8 | 12.5 | 7.0 | 15.5 | 14.6 | 15.1 |

Data as orig reptd.; bef. results of disc opers/spec. items. Per share data adj. for stk. divs.; EPS diluted. E-Estimated. NA-Not Available. NM-Not Meaningful. NR-Not Ranked. UR-Under Review.

**Office:** 10400 Fernwood Road, Bethesda, MD 20817-1102.
**Telephone:** 301-380-3000.
**Website:** http://www.marriott.com
**Chrmn & CEO:** J.W. Marriott, Jr.

**Pres & COO:** W.J. Shaw
**Vice Chrmn:** J.W. Marriott, III
**EVP & CFO:** A.M. Sorenson
**EVP & Chief Acctg Officer:** C.T. Berquist

**Investor Contact:** T. Marder (301-380-2553)
**Board Members:** M. K. Bush, L. Kellner, D. L. Lee, J. W. Marriott, III, J. W. Marriott, Jr., G. Munoz, H. J. Pearce, S. S. Reinemund, M. W. Romney, W. J. Shaw, L. M. Small

**Founded:** 1971
**Domicile:** Delaware
**Employees:** 151,000

# Marshall & Ilsley Corp

**STANDARD &POOR'S**

**S&P Recommendation** HOLD ★ ★ ★ ☆ ☆

| Price | 12-Mo. Target Price | Investment Style |
|---|---|---|
| $14.70 (as of Nov 14, 2008) | $19.00 | Large-Cap Blend |

**GICS Sector** Financials
**Sub-Industry** Regional Banks

**Summary** This bank holding company operates mainly in Wisconsin, and is also in Missouri, Arizona, Minnesota, Florida, Kansas, and four other states.

## Key Stock Statistics (Source S&P, Vickers, company reports)

| | | | | | | | |
|---|---|---|---|---|---|---|---|
| 52-Wk Range | $33.04– 10.90 | S&P Oper. EPS 2008**E** | -0.37 | Market Capitalization(B) | $3.814 | Beta | 0.81 |
| Trailing 12-Month EPS | $1.26 | S&P Oper. EPS 2009**E** | 1.39 | Yield (%) | 8.71 | S&P 3-Yr. Proj. EPS CAGR(%) | 3 |
| Trailing 12-Month P/E | 11.7 | P/E on S&P Oper. EPS 2008**E** | NM | Dividend Rate/Share | $1.28 | S&P Credit Rating | A |
| $10K Invested 5 Yrs Ago | $5,863 | Common Shares Outstg. (M) | 259.4 | Institutional Ownership (%) | 62 | | |

## Price Performance

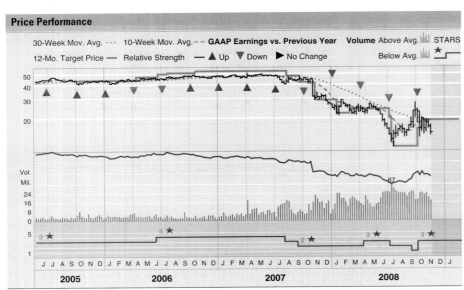

30-Week Mov. Avg. ···· 10-Week Mov. Avg. ─ ─ **GAAP Earnings vs. Previous Year** Volume Above Avg. STARS
12-Mo. Target Price ── Relative Strength ── ▲ Up ▼ Down ► No Change Below Avg. ★

Options: ASE, CBOE, P, Ph

Analysis prepared by **Erik Oja** on November 04, 2008, when the stock traded at **$ 18.80**.

## Highlights

➤ We forecast 1.7% growth in net interest income in 2009, accompanied by a decline in the net interest margin, to 2.95%, down from our forecast of 3.00% for 2008, and below the 3.14% reported for 2007, driven by the recent string of Fed rate cuts. However, we expect MI's fee income, excluding gains and losses, to climb 3.1% in 2009, to $760 million, driven by wealth management revenues.

➤ MI expects core non-interest expenses as a percentage of revenues to improve to 52%, down from 62.5% in 2006, the last full year in which Metavante was a part of MI. We are forecasting a total ratio of 56.5% in 2008, and 59.0% in 2009. Our estimate of loan loss provisions for 2008 is about $1.34 billion (first quarter $146 million, second quarter $886 million, third quarter $155 million, and fourth quarter estimate of $156 million), up from $320 million in 2007. We expect loan loss provisions of $565 million for all of 2009.

➤ We expect a loss per share of $0.37 in 2008, versus EPS of $1.87 in 2007. However, we see EPS of $1.39 for 2009, on our expectation for a reduction in loan loss provisions.

## Investment Rationale/Risk

➤ Second-quarter loan loss provisioning expense of $886 million, or $485 million in excess of net chargeoffs of $401 million (an annualized 3.3% of loans), was primarily due to housing price-related declines in the credit quality of MI's $5.0 billion in residential real estate construction loans, particularly those made in Florida and Arizona. We believe that visibility on these loans is not good, while the risk of additional quarters of high loan loss provisions, in the range of $155 million in the third and fourth quarters, remains high. MI recently traded at 13.5X our 2009 EPS estimate of $1.39, a multiple that is below our estimation of 15.9X for the industry.

➤ Risks to our recommendation and target price include lower than expected credit quality, higher than expected loan loss provisions, deposit costs above our expectations, and loan yields and growth lower than our forecasts.

➤ Our target price of $19 is based on a discount-to-peers 13.7X multiple on our 2009 EPS estimate of $1.39, reflecting MI's current credit challenges.

## Qualitative Risk Assessment

| LOW | MEDIUM | HIGH |
|---|---|---|

Our risk assessment reflects our view of the company's large-cap valuation, and its history of profitability, offset by the risk that credit quality will suffer from continuing downtrends in the Sunbelt and Midwest.

## Quantitative Evaluations

**S&P Quality Ranking** A

| D | C | B- | B | B+ | A- | **A** | A+ |
|---|---|---|---|---|---|---|---|

**Relative Strength Rank** **MODERATE**

60

LOWEST = 1     HIGHEST = 99

## Revenue/Earnings Data

**Revenue (Million $)**

| | 1Q | 2Q | 3Q | 4Q | Year |
|---|---|---|---|---|---|
| 2008 | 3,880 | 3,846 | 3,745 | -- | -- |
| 2007 | 1,386 | 1,438 | 1,474 | 3,873 | 4,398 |
| 2006 | 1,139 | 1,290 | 1,381 | 1,317 | 5,128 |
| 2005 | 895.1 | 975.8 | 1,014 | 1,076 | 3,963 |
| 2004 | 702.5 | 728.0 | 792.2 | 882.5 | 3,112 |
| 2003 | 548.7 | 682.2 | 696.3 | 818.5 | 2,746 |

**Earnings Per Share ($)**

| | | | | | |
|---|---|---|---|---|---|
| 2008 | 0.56 | -1.52 | 0.32 | E0.26 | E-0.37 |
| 2007 | 0.83 | 0.83 | 0.85 | -0.09 | 1.87 |
| 2006 | 0.72 | 0.74 | 0.92 | 0.79 | 3.17 |
| 2005 | 0.73 | 0.81 | 0.78 | 0.78 | 3.10 |
| 2004 | 0.65 | 0.67 | 0.69 | 0.76 | 2.77 |
| 2003 | 0.56 | 0.59 | 0.61 | 0.62 | 2.38 |

Fiscal year ended Dec. 31. Next earnings report expected: Late January. EPS Estimates based on S&P Operating Earnings; historical GAAP earnings are as reported.

## Dividend Data (Dates: mm/dd Payment Date: mm/dd/yy)

| Amount ($) | Date Decl. | Ex-Div. Date | Stk. of Record | Payment Date |
|---|---|---|---|---|
| 0.310 | 02/21 | 02/28 | 03/03 | 03/14/08 |
| 0.320 | 04/22 | 05/28 | 05/30 | 06/13/08 |
| 0.320 | 08/21 | 08/28 | 09/02 | 09/12/08 |
| 0.320 | 10/16 | 11/25 | 11/28 | 12/12/08 |

Dividends have been paid since 1938. Source: Company reports.

# Marshall & Ilsley Corp

STANDARD
&POOR'S

## Business Summary November 04, 2008

CORPORATE OVERVIEW. MI owns banking subsidiaries with operations in Wisconsin and the metropolitan areas of Phoenix and Tucson, AZ, Minneapolis/St. Paul, MN, St. Louis, MO, Las Vegas, NV, and Naples and Bonita Springs, FL. MI also owns nonbanking subsidiaries that are related or incidental to banking. The company also has other business operations that include trust services, residential mortgage banking, capital markets, brokerage and insurance, commercial leasing, commercial mortgage banking, and community development investments.

PRIMARY BUSINESS DYNAMICS. On April 3, 2007, MI announced that it would separate MI and Metavante Corporation into two separate publicly held companies by the end of 2007. Warburg Pincus, a global private equity investor, invested $625 million to acquire an equity stake of 25% in Metavante Corp. MI shareholders own the remaining 75% of Metavante. By the terms of the deal, each share of the "old" MI was entitled to receive one share of "new" Marshall & Ilsley Corp., plus one-third of a share of Metavante Corp. MI received a cash infusion of about $1.665 billion, which may be invested, used to improve MI's capital ratios, buy back shares, or increase the dividend. This deal closed on November 1, 2007.

Starting in the 1990s, the company made several sizable bank acquisitions,

mostly in Wisconsin. Beginning in 2000, it shifted its bank acquisition focus outside Wisconsin. Between 1994 and 1998, the company acquired six Wisconsin banks, with assets totaling $9.3 billion, for $2.0 billion. In 2001 and 2002, MI acquired three banks in Minnesota and one bank in Missouri, with combined assets of $4.3 billion, for a total of $994 million. On April 3, 2006, MI closed its acquisition of Gold Banc Corp. in Kansas, with assets of $4.1 billion, for $715 million. On March 1, 2006, the company completed its acquisition of Trustcorp Financial in Missouri, with assets of $705 million, for $181 million. On December 4, 2006, MI announced the pending acquisition of United Heritage Bank of Orlando, for $217 million; this deal closed on April 2, 2007. On February 12, 2007, MI announced the acquisition of Excel Bank Corp. for $101 million, and this transaction closed July 2, 2007. MI's most recent acquisition was First Indiana Corp, for $538 million cash, and the closing date was January 3, 2008. We estimate that this acquisition accounted for about half of MI's growth of loans, deposits, and fee income, in the first quarter of 2008.

## Company Financials Fiscal Year Ended Dec. 31

### Per Share Data ($)

| | 2007 | 2006 | 2005 | 2004 | 2003 | 2002 | 2001 | 2000 | 1999 | 1998 |
|---|---|---|---|---|---|---|---|---|---|---|
| Tangible Book Value | 19.82 | 11.51 | 9.02 | 7.76 | 9.96 | 8.61 | 9.00 | 9.06 | 8.12 | 8.67 |
| Earnings | 1.87 | 3.17 | 3.10 | 2.77 | 2.38 | 2.16 | 1.54 | 1.45 | 1.57 | 1.31 |
| S&P Core Earnings | 1.87 | 3.17 | 2.99 | 2.66 | 2.28 | 2.07 | 1.49 | NA | NA | NA |
| Dividends | 1.20 | 1.05 | 0.93 | 0.81 | 0.70 | 0.55 | 0.57 | 0.52 | 0.47 | 0.43 |
| Payout Ratio | 64% | 33% | 30% | 29% | 29% | 25% | 37% | 36% | 30% | 33% |
| Prices:High | 51.48 | 49.10 | 47.40 | 44.70 | 38.46 | 32.12 | 32.12 | 31.13 | 36.38 | 31.13 |
| Prices:Low | 26.04 | 40.83 | 40.05 | 35.67 | 24.60 | 23.11 | 23.54 | 19.13 | 27.19 | 19.69 |
| P/E Ratio:High | 28 | 15 | 15 | 16 | 16 | 15 | 21 | 22 | 23 | 24 |
| P/E Ratio:Low | 14 | 13 | 13 | 13 | 10 | 11 | 15 | 13 | 17 | 15 |

### Income Statement Analysis (Million $)

| | 2007 | 2006 | 2005 | 2004 | 2003 | 2002 | 2001 | 2000 | 1999 | 1998 |
|---|---|---|---|---|---|---|---|---|---|---|
| Net Interest Income | 1,616 | 1,490 | 1,233 | 1,132 | 1,057 | 1,006 | 843 | 673 | 705 | 676 |
| Tax Equivalent Adjustment | 28.2 | NA | 33.3 | NA | NA | 32.2 | 31.2 | 31.0 | 28.7 | 26.2 |
| Non Interest Income | 729 | 1,906 | 1,704 | 1,411 | 1,194 | 1,089 | 1,020 | 978 | 850 | 726 |
| Loan Loss Provision | 320 | 50.6 | 44.8 | 38.0 | 63.0 | 74.4 | 54.1 | 30.4 | 25.4 | 27.1 |
| % Expense/Operating Revenue | 56.1% | 63.6% | 62.2% | 62.7% | 64.5% | 61.9% | 68.1% | 65.4% | 64.2% | 67.1% |
| Pretax Income | 711 | 1,196 | 1,090 | 945 | 758 | 719 | 501 | 470 | 528 | 465 |
| Effective Tax Rate | 30.1% | 32.4% | 33.3% | 33.6% | 28.3% | 33.2% | 32.6% | 32.5% | 32.9% | 35.2% |
| Net Income | 497 | 808 | 727 | 627 | 544 | 480 | 338 | 317 | 355 | 301 |
| % Net Interest Margin | 3.14 | 3.27 | 3.31 | 3.52 | 3.65 | 3.96 | 3.67 | 2.81 | 3.58 | 3.69 |
| S&P Core Earnings | 496 | 808 | 705 | 605 | 519 | 453 | 319 | NA | NA | NA |

### Balance Sheet & Other Financial Data (Million $)

| | 2007 | 2006 | 2005 | 2004 | 2003 | 2002 | 2001 | 2000 | 1999 | 1998 |
|---|---|---|---|---|---|---|---|---|---|---|
| Money Market Assets | 587 | 293 | 330 | 191 | 163 | 250 | 947 | 163 | 175 | 146 |
| Investment Securities | 7,818 | 7,473 | 6,320 | 6,085 | 5,607 | 5,209 | 4,464 | 5,848 | 5,575 | 5,192 |
| Commercial Loans | 26,526 | 23,717 | 19,023 | 16,646 | 14,254 | 6,586 | 10,815 | 9,649 | 4,754 | 4,078 |
| Other Loans | 19,770 | 17,917 | 14,866 | 12,810 | 10,896 | 17,011 | 8,480 | 7,938 | 11,580 | 9,918 |
| Total Assets | 59,849 | 56,230 | 46,213 | 40,437 | 34,373 | 32,875 | 27,254 | 26,078 | 24,370 | 21,566 |
| Demand Deposits | 6,174 | 6,112 | 5,525 | 15,005 | 4,715 | 4,462 | 3,559 | 3,130 | 2,831 | 2,929 |
| Time Deposits | 29,017 | 27,972 | 22,149 | 11,450 | 17,555 | 15,932 | 12,934 | 16,119 | 13,604 | 12,991 |
| Long Term Debt | 9,873 | 8,026 | 6,669 | 5,027 | 2,735 | 2,284 | 1,560 | 921 | 665 | 794 |
| Common Equity | 7,033 | 6,151 | 4,769 | 3,970 | 3,329 | 3,037 | 2,536 | 3,200 | 2,117 | 2,282 |
| % Return on Assets | 0.9 | 1.6 | 1.7 | 1.7 | 1.6 | 1.6 | 1.3 | 1.3 | 1.5 | 1.5 |
| % Return on Equity | 7.5 | 14.7 | 16.6 | 17.1 | 17.1 | 17.4 | 13.8 | 10.6 | 13.8 | 14.0 |
| % Loan Loss Reserve | 1.1 | 1.0 | 1.1 | 1.2 | 1.4 | 1.4 | 1.4 | 1.3 | 1.4 | 1.6 |
| % Loans/Deposits | 125.8 | 123.0 | 123.5 | 111.6 | 113.1 | 117.2 | 117.0 | 91.4 | 99.4 | 88.0 |
| % Equity to Assets | 11.4 | 10.7 | 9.9 | 9.8 | 9.5 | 9.2 | 9.0 | 11.9 | 11.0 | 10.2 |

Data as orig reptd.; bef. results of disc opers/spec. items. Per share data adj. for stk. divs.; EPS diluted. E-Estimated. NA-Not Available. NM-Not Meaningful. NR-Not Ranked. UR-Under Review.

**Office:** 770 N Water St, Milwaukee, WI 53202.
**Telephone:** 414-765-7801.
**Website:** http://www.micorp.com
**Chrmn:** D.J. Kuester

**Pres & CEO:** M.F. Furlong
**Vice Chrmn:** P.M. Platten, III
**SVP & CFO:** G.A. Smith
**SVP, Chief Admin Officer & General Counsel:** R.J. Erickson

**Investor Contact:** D.L. Urban
**Board Members:** A. N. Baur, J. F. Chait, J. Daniels, Jr., M. F. Furlong, T. D. Kellner, D. J. Kuester, D. J. Lubar, K. C. Lyall, J. A. Mellowes, R. J. O'Toole, S. W. Orr, Jr., P. M. Platten, III, J. S. Shiely, D. S. Waller, G. E. Wardeberg, J. B. Wigdale

**Founded:** 1959
**Domicile:** Wisconsin
**Employees:** 9,670

# Marsh & McLennan Companies Inc.

STANDARD
&POOR'S

| S&P Recommendation | BUY ★★★★☆ | Price<br>$23.85 (as of Nov 14, 2008) | 12-Mo. Target Price<br>$36.00 | Investment Style<br>Large-Cap Blend |
|---|---|---|---|---|

**GICS Sector** Financials
**Sub-Industry** Insurance Brokers

**Summary** This global professional services concern provides risk and insurance services, investment management, and consulting services through its operating companies.

## Key Stock Statistics (Source S&P, Vickers, company reports)

| | | | | | | | | |
|---|---|---|---|---|---|---|---|---|
| 52-Wk Range | $36.82– 22.20 | S&P Oper. EPS 2008E | 1.48 | Market Capitalization(B) | $12.261 | Beta | | 0.66 |
| Trailing 12-Month EPS | $-0.13 | S&P Oper. EPS 2009E | 1.91 | Yield (%) | 3.35 | S&P 3-Yr. Proj. EPS CAGR(%) | | 5 |
| Trailing 12-Month P/E | NM | P/E on S&P Oper. EPS 2008E | 16.1 | Dividend Rate/Share | $0.80 | S&P Credit Rating | | BBB- |
| $10K Invested 5 Yrs Ago | $6,087 | Common Shares Outstg. (M) | 514.1 | Institutional Ownership (%) | 81 | | | |

## Price Performance

30-Week Mov. Avg. · · · 10-Week Mov. Avg. – – GAAP Earnings vs. Previous Year   Volume Above Avg. STARS
12-Mo. Target Price — Relative Strength — ▲ Up ▼ Down ► No Change   Below Avg.

Options: ASE, CBOE, P, Ph

Analysis prepared by **Bret Howlett** on November 11, 2008, when the stock traded at **$ 23.76**.

## Highlights

➤ We anticipate that total revenues in 2008 will rise in the high single-digits, driven by MMC's diversified portfolio of businesses including its international and consumer segments, partially offset by lower investment income. We see risk and insurance services segment revenue increasing modestly in 2008, reflecting solid growth in EMEA and Asia-Pacific. We estimate that consulting revenues will grow in the mid-single digits this year, however, we are concerned that the weakening U.S. and global economy will limit growth in 2009. We believe profitability in the risk consulting and technology segment will improve due to recent restructuring initiatives at Kroll. Overall, we are encouraged by MMC's improved client retention rates and solid new business production.

➤ We believe MMC's restructuring initiatives are on track, and we anticipate margin improvement this year. We expect expenses to be lowered given the various cost-cutting initiatives set by the company, which we see resulting in $125 million of savings next year.

➤ We forecast 2008 EPS from continuing operations of $1.48. Our 2009 projection of EPS from continuing operations is $1.91.

## Investment Rationale/Risk

➤ So far, 2008 has proven to be a transitional year for MMC, and we believe the company is making progress with its restructuring initiatives, and should benefit from an improved pricing environment in 2009. MMC has been successful in expanding revenues and cutting expenses, and we have been impressed with MMC's solid organic growth and improving customer retention rates despite a soft environment. We believe earnings power has been re-established at MMC and see considerable room for margin expansion given cost-cutting efforts and restructured operations. We remain confident in MMC's new leadership team and believe recent solid results have increased its credibility.

➤ Risks to our recommendation and target price include lower-than-expected revenue on rate increases and/or deteriorating client retention; lower-than-projected cost savings from restructurings and layoffs; lower-than-anticipated cost savings and growth at Kroll; and, unfavorable legal and regulatory developments.

➤ Our 12-month target price is $36, about 18.8X estimated 2009 EPS, in line with MMC's historical multiples.

## Qualitative Risk Assessment

| LOW | MEDIUM | HIGH |
|---|---|---|

Our risk assessment reflects the company's leading market share position, diversified businesses, and global scale, offset by regulatory scrutiny and business model changes as a result of contingent commissions.

## Quantitative Evaluations

**S&P Quality Ranking** B+

| D | C | B- | B | B+ | A- | A | A+ |
|---|---|---|---|---|---|---|---|

**Relative Strength Rank** MODERATE

62

LOWEST = 1    HIGHEST = 99

## Revenue/Earnings Data

### Revenue (Million $)

| | 1Q | 2Q | 3Q | 4Q | Year |
|---|---|---|---|---|---|
| 2008 | 3,047 | 3,048 | 2,838 | -- | -- |
| 2007 | 2,812 | 2,819 | 2,794 | 2,925 | 11,350 |
| 2006 | 3,016 | 2,970 | 2,872 | 3,063 | 11,921 |
| 2005 | 3,070 | 2,977 | 2,779 | 2,826 | 11,652 |
| 2004 | 3,196 | 3,028 | 2,950 | 2,985 | 12,159 |
| 2003 | 2,852 | 2,865 | 2,837 | 3,034 | 11,588 |

### Earnings Per Share ($)

| | | | | | |
|---|---|---|---|---|---|
| 2008 | -0.41 | 0.11 | 0.03 | E0.39 | E1.48 |
| 2007 | 0.41 | 0.25 | 0.15 | 0.17 | 0.98 |
| 2006 | 0.43 | 0.31 | 0.32 | 0.39 | 1.45 |
| 2005 | 0.24 | 0.30 | 0.11 | 0.03 | 0.67 |
| 2004 | 0.83 | 0.73 | 0.04 | -1.29 | 0.33 |
| 2003 | 0.81 | 0.66 | 0.65 | 0.69 | 2.81 |

Fiscal year ended Dec. 31. Next earnings report expected: Mid February. EPS Estimates based on S&P Operating Earnings; historical GAAP earnings are as reported.

## Dividend Data (Dates: mm/dd Payment Date: mm/dd/yy)

| Amount ($) | Date Decl. | Ex-Div. Date | Stk. of Record | Payment Date |
|---|---|---|---|---|
| 0.200 | 01/17 | 01/24 | 01/28 | 02/15/08 |
| 0.200 | 03/19 | 04/04 | 04/08 | 05/15/08 |
| 0.200 | 05/15 | 07/03 | 07/08 | 08/15/08 |
| 0.200 | 09/17 | 10/14 | 10/16 | 11/14/08 |

Dividends have been paid since 1923. Source: Company reports.

The McGraw-Hill Companies

# Marsh & McLennan Companies Inc.

STANDARD
&POOR'S

## Business Summary November 11, 2008

CORPORATE OVERVIEW. Marsh & McLennan is one of the world's largest insurance brokers. The insurance brokerage industry has suffered in recent years from probes into bid rigging and contingent commissions. We believe recent settlements and corporate restructurings have improved the outlook at MMC, but ongoing legal and regulatory proceedings and uncertainty regarding implementing a new business model present weak near-term earnings visibility, in our view.

MMC operates in four main segments: risk and insurance services, risk consulting and technology, investment management, and consulting. Risk and insurance services (49% of operating segment revenues in 2007; 51% in 2006) includes insurance services, reinsurance services and risk capital holdings, risk management and consulting, insurance broking, and insurance program management. Reinsurance broking and catastrophe and financial modeling services are done under the Guy Carpenter name. Risk consulting and technology (8.7% in 2007; 9.2% in 2006) is conducted under the Kroll name. Con-

sulting and human resource outsourcing (43% in 2007; 40% in 2006) is done under the Mercer and Oliver Wyman Group names.

LEGAL/REGULATORY ISSUES. In April 2004, Putnam entered into the final settlements of charges by the SEC and the Massachusetts Secretary of the Commonwealth related to alleged short-term trading of Putnam mutual funds by employees in their personal accounts. Under the settlements, Putnam agreed, without admitting or denying the charges, to pay $110 million in penalties and restitution, and to implement a number of remedial actions. In March 2005, an independent consultant concluded that Putnam should pay fund shareholders $108.5 million, of which $83.5 million was in addition to previous settlement amounts.

## Company Financials Fiscal Year Ended Dec. 31

| Per Share Data ($) | 2007 | 2006 | 2005 | 2004 | 2003 | 2002 | 2001 | 2000 | 1999 | 1998 |
|---|---|---|---|---|---|---|---|---|---|---|
| Tangible Book Value | 0.13 | NM | NM | NM | NM | NM | NM | 9.47 | NM | NM |
| Cash Flow | 1.80 | 2.34 | 1.58 | 1.18 | 3.52 | 3.10 | 2.61 | 2.94 | 2.07 | 1.98 |
| Earnings | 0.98 | 1.45 | 0.67 | 0.33 | 2.81 | 2.45 | 1.70 | 2.05 | 1.31 | 1.49 |
| S&P Core Earnings | 0.70 | 1.30 | 0.38 | 1.11 | 2.29 | 1.60 | 0.91 | NA | NA | NA |
| Dividends | 0.76 | 0.68 | 0.68 | 0.99 | 1.18 | 1.09 | 1.03 | 0.95 | 0.85 | 0.73 |
| Payout Ratio | 71% | 47% | 101% | NM | 42% | 44% | 61% | 46% | 65% | 49% |
| Prices:High | 33.90 | 32.73 | 34.25 | 49.69 | 54.97 | 57.30 | 59.03 | 67.84 | 48.38 | 32.16 |
| Prices:Low | 23.12 | 24.00 | 26.67 | 22.75 | 38.27 | 34.61 | 39.50 | 35.25 | 28.56 | 21.69 |
| P/E Ratio:High | 35 | 23 | 51 | NM | 19 | 23 | 35 | 33 | 37 | 22 |
| P/E Ratio:Low | 24 | 17 | 40 | NM | 14 | 14 | 23 | 17 | 22 | 15 |

| Income Statement Analysis (Million $) | | | | | | | | | | |
|---|---|---|---|---|---|---|---|---|---|---|
| Revenue | 11,350 | 11,921 | 11,652 | 12,159 | 11,588 | 10,440 | 9,943 | 10,157 | 9,157 | 7,190 |
| Operating Income | 1,586 | 1,946 | 1,386 | 2,073 | 2,887 | 2,633 | 2,283 | 2,179 | 1,859 | 1,671 |
| Depreciation | 442 | 488 | 490 | 456 | 391 | 359 | 520 | 488 | 400 | 251 |
| Interest Expense | 267 | 303 | 332 | 219 | 185 | 160 | 196 | 247 | 233 | 140 |
| Pretax Income | 847 | 1,219 | 571 | 450 | 2,335 | 2,133 | 1,590 | 1,955 | 1,247 | 1,305 |
| Effective Tax Rate | 34.8% | 31.8% | 33.6% | 57.6% | 33.0% | 35.0% | 37.7% | 38.5% | 41.8% | 39.0% |
| Net Income | 538 | 818 | 369 | 176 | 1,540 | 1,365 | 974 | 1,181 | 726 | 796 |
| S&P Core Earnings | 375 | 732 | 211 | 590 | 1,254 | 890 | 525 | NA | NA | NA |

| Balance Sheet & Other Financial Data (Million $) | | | | | | | | | | |
|---|---|---|---|---|---|---|---|---|---|---|
| Cash | 2,133 | 2,089 | 2,020 | 1,396 | 665 | 546 | 537 | 240 | 428 | 610 |
| Current Assets | 5,454 | 5,834 | 5,262 | 4,887 | 3,901 | 3,664 | 3,792 | 3,639 | 3,283 | 3,245 |
| Total Assets | 17,359 | 18,137 | 17,892 | 18,337 | 15,053 | 13,855 | 13,293 | 13,769 | 13,021 | 11,871 |
| Current Liabilities | 3,493 | 5,549 | 4,351 | 4,735 | 4,089 | 3,863 | 3,938 | 4,119 | 4,318 | 5,002 |
| Long Term Debt | 3,604 | 3,860 | 5,044 | 4,691 | 2,910 | 2,891 | 2,334 | 2,347 | 2,357 | 1,590 |
| Common Equity | 7,822 | 5,819 | 5,360 | 5,056 | 5,451 | 5,018 | 5,173 | 5,228 | 4,170 | 3,659 |
| Total Capital | 11,426 | 9,679 | 10,404 | 9,747 | 8,361 | 7,909 | 7,507 | 7,575 | 6,527 | 5,249 |
| Capital Expenditures | 378 | 307 | 345 | 376 | 436 | 423 | 433 | 472 | 358 | 297 |
| Cash Flow | 980 | 1,306 | 859 | 632 | 1,931 | 1,724 | 1,494 | 1,669 | 1,126 | 1,047 |
| Current Ratio | 1.6 | 1.1 | 1.2 | 1.0 | 1.0 | 0.9 | 1.0 | 0.9 | 0.8 | 0.6 |
| % Long Term Debt of Capitalization | 31.5 | 39.9 | 48.5 | 48.1 | 34.8 | 36.6 | 31.1 | 31.0 | 36.1 | 30.3 |
| % Net Income of Revenue | 4.7 | 6.9 | 3.2 | 1.4 | 13.3 | 13.1 | 9.8 | 11.6 | 7.9 | 11.1 |
| % Return on Assets | 3.0 | 4.5 | 2.0 | 1.1 | 10.7 | 10.1 | 7.2 | 8.8 | 5.8 | 8.0 |
| % Return on Equity | 7.9 | 14.6 | 7.1 | 3.4 | 29.4 | 26.8 | 18.7 | 25.1 | 18.5 | 23.2 |

Data as orig reptd.; bef. results of disc opers/spec. items. Per share data adj. for stk. divs.; EPS diluted. E-Estimated. NA-Not Available. NM-Not Meaningful. NR-Not Ranked. UR-Under Review.

**Office:** 1166 Avenue Of The Americas Bsmt, New York, NY 10036-2708.
**Telephone:** 212-345-5000.
**Email:** shareowner-svcs@email.bankofny.com
**Website:** http://www.mmc.com

**Chrmn:** S.R. Hardis
**Pres, CEO & CFO:** B. Duperreault
**Vice Chrmn:** M. Neely
**EVP & General Counsel:** P.J. Beshar

**SVP & Chief Admin Officer:** M.A. Petrullo
**Investor Contact:** M.B. Bartley (212-345-5000)
**Board Members:** L. M. Baker, Jr., Z. W. Carter, B. Duperreault, O. Fanjul Martin, S. R. Hardis, G. S. King, I. B. Lang, B. P. Nolop, M. D. Oken, D. A. Olsen, M. Schapiro, A. Simmons

**Founded:** 1923
**Domicile:** Delaware
**Employees:** 56,100

The *McGraw-Hill* Companies

# Masco Corp

**STANDARD &POOR'S**

**S&P Recommendation** HOLD ★ ★ ★ ☆ ☆

| Price | 12-Mo. Target Price | Investment Style |
|---|---|---|
| $7.69 (as of Nov 14, 2008) | $11.00 | Large-Cap Blend |

**GICS Sector** Industrials
**Sub-Industry** Building Products

**Summary** This company is one of the world's leading makers of faucets, cabinets, coatings, and other consumer brand-name home improvement and building products.

## Key Stock Statistics (Source S&P, Vickers, company reports)

| | | | | | | |
|---|---|---|---|---|---|---|
| 52-Wk Range | $25.00 – 7.14 | S&P Oper. EPS 2008**E** | 0.30 | Market Capitalization(B) | $2.768 | Beta | 1.44 |
| Trailing 12-Month EPS | $-0.10 | S&P Oper. EPS 2009**E** | 0.30 | Yield (%) | 12.22 | S&P 3-Yr. Proj. EPS CAGR(%) | -30 |
| Trailing 12-Month P/E | NM | P/E on S&P Oper. EPS 2008**E** | 25.6 | Dividend Rate/Share | $0.94 | S&P Credit Rating | BBB+ |
| $10K Invested 5 Yrs Ago | $3,337 | Common Shares Outstg. (M) | 359.9 | Institutional Ownership (%) | NM | | |

## Price Performance

- 30-Week Mov. Avg. ··· 10-Week Mov. Avg. - - **GAAP Earnings vs. Previous Year** Volume Above Avg. STARS
- 12-Mo. Target Price — Relative Strength — ▲ Up ▼ Down ► No Change Below Avg. ★

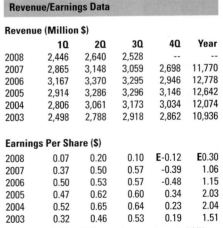

Options: ASE, CBOE, P, Ph

Analysis prepared by **Michael W. Jaffe** on November 07, 2008, when the stock traded at **$ 8.83**.

## Qualitative Risk Assessment

| LOW | MEDIUM | HIGH |
|---|---|---|

Our risk assessment for Masco reflects MAS's relatively consistent generation of strong levels of free cash flow, which in our view, has enabled it to frequently raise its cash dividend. However, it also operates in a very cyclical area, as evidenced by the recent major downturn in its operating performance. We additionally think that Masco's risk profile has been raised by an executive transition, with its chairman and CEO giving up his CEO role in July 2007, and its president retiring at the end of 2007.

## Quantitative Evaluations

**S&P Quality Ranking** B+

| D | C | B- | B | B+ | A- | A | A+ |
|---|---|---|---|---|---|---|---|

**Relative Strength Rank** WEAK

19

LOWEST = 1    HIGHEST = 99

## Highlights

➤ We expect another 8% fall in sales in 2009, after a steep drop so far in 2008. We think demand will remain hurt by a very slow U.S. housing market. We also see fewer refinancings and home equity loans crimping big-ticket consumer spending. Moreover, we see much lower sales in the now faltering European region.

➤ We project narrower operating margins in 2009, on our outlook for ongoing very challenging sales conditions, and the likelihood of less favorable foreign currency exchange, as the U.S. dollar has been strengthening against the euro in recent periods. We see these factors offset slightly by expected benefits from recent cost cuts, particularly major head count reductions. We also see a much lower expected effective tax rate; Masco's rate in 2008 was to be well above its traditional level, as MAS was repatriating foreign earnings to utilize favorable U.S. tax law provisions. However, its effective rate should return to normal in 2009.

➤ Our EPS forecasts for 2008 and 2009 compare with income before one-time items of $1.76 in 2007, with most of the charges related to impairment of goodwill and other intangibles.

## Investment Rationale/Risk

➤ We think very soft U.S. housing markets and slow home improvement spending, combined with the recent major downturn in the European economy, will limit MAS's sales through 2009. However, we favor Masco's strong brand names, and the government is exploring financial options to end the U.S.'s deep housing downturn. Our valuation model finds MAS shares near a fair valuation.

➤ Risks to our recommendation and target price include a longer than expected U.S. housing downturn, and a weaker than expected performance in foreign markets served by MAS.

➤ MAS's business has been in a deep cyclical downturn, but we applaud its major cost cuts of the past two years. In addition, with the government now taking actions to firm up both financing and housing markets, we think investors will treat Masco as if a bottom will be reached over the next year. Using price-to-sales analysis, the shares recently traded at 0.4X projected sales per share, based on our $8.9 billion sales forecast for 2009. We think that valuation, which falls below Masco's traditional trough valuation, is appropriate, and set a 12-month target price of $11, or 0.45X projected sales.

## Revenue/Earnings Data

**Revenue (Million $)**

| | 1Q | 2Q | 3Q | 4Q | Year |
|---|---|---|---|---|---|
| 2008 | 2,446 | 2,640 | 2,528 | -- | -- |
| 2007 | 2,865 | 3,148 | 3,059 | 2,698 | 11,770 |
| 2006 | 3,167 | 3,370 | 3,295 | 2,946 | 12,778 |
| 2005 | 2,914 | 3,286 | 3,296 | 3,146 | 12,642 |
| 2004 | 2,806 | 3,061 | 3,173 | 3,034 | 12,074 |
| 2003 | 2,498 | 2,788 | 2,918 | 2,862 | 10,936 |

**Earnings Per Share ($)**

| | | | | | |
|---|---|---|---|---|---|
| 2008 | 0.07 | 0.20 | 0.10 | E-0.12 | E0.30 |
| 2007 | 0.37 | 0.50 | 0.57 | -0.39 | 1.06 |
| 2006 | 0.50 | 0.53 | 0.57 | -0.48 | 1.15 |
| 2005 | 0.47 | 0.62 | 0.60 | 0.34 | 2.03 |
| 2004 | 0.52 | 0.65 | 0.64 | 0.23 | 2.04 |
| 2003 | 0.32 | 0.46 | 0.53 | 0.19 | 1.51 |

Fiscal year ended Dec. 31. Next earnings report expected: Mid February. EPS Estimates based on S&P Operating Earnings; historical GAAP earnings are as reported.

## Dividend Data (Dates: mm/dd Payment Date: mm/dd/yy)

| Amount ($) | Date Decl. | Ex-Div. Date | Stk. of Record | Payment Date |
|---|---|---|---|---|
| 0.230 | 12/05 | 01/02 | 01/04 | 02/04/08 |
| 0.230 | 03/28 | 04/09 | 04/11 | 05/12/08 |
| 0.230 | 06/20 | 07/01 | 07/03 | 08/04/08 |
| 0.235 | 09/12 | 10/08 | 10/10 | 11/10/08 |

Dividends have been paid since 1944. Source: Company reports.

# Masco Corp

## Business Summary November 07, 2008

Masco is one of the largest U.S. makers of brand name consumer products for home improvement and new construction markets; it derives most of its revenues from the sale of faucets, kitchen and bath cabinets, plumbing supplies and architectural coatings. Operations are focused on North America (79% of 2007 sales) and Europe (most of the rest). Home Depot contributed 20% of 2007 sales.

The plumbing products division (29% of 2007 sales) is a major global faucet maker. Masco revolutionized faucets in 1954 with the Delta line, and also offers the Peerless, Brizo and Newport Brass brands, among others. In addition, the division offers other bath products, including plumbing fittings and valves, bathtubs and shower enclosures, and spa items; brand names include Alsons, Aqua Glass and HotSpring. It makes cabinets and related products (24%), including cabinetry for kitchen, bath, storage, home office and home entertainment applications, featuring the Kraftmaid, Merillat and Mill's Pride brands. According to the company, it is the largest U.S. maker of kitchen and bath cabinetry.

Masco sells decorative architectural items (15%), including paints and stains, and decorative bath and shower accessories. Trade names include Behr in paints and stains and Franklin Brass in bath and shower. It also supplies and installs insulation products and other building products such as fireplaces, cabinetry, gutters, shelving and windows (22%), and sells other specialty products (10%), such as windows and patio doors, electric staple guns, and radiators.

We believe that an aggressive acquisition program enabled Masco to build large positions in the markets it serves. Since 2003, however, the company has pursued a business plan that shifted it away from a focus on takeovers. It now concentrates on internal growth, with an increased emphasis on cash flow and return on invested capital.

In July 2007, Richard Manoogian, Masco's chairman and CEO, gave up his CEO duties and moved into a new post as executive chairman. Based on Mr. Manoogian's recommendation, Timothy Wadhams, Masco's senior vice president and CFO since 2001, was appointed to the CEO role. In addition, Alan Barry, Masco's president, stepped down from his post at the end of 2007, when he reached normal retirement age, with Mr. Wadhams also assuming that title.

## Company Financials Fiscal Year Ended Dec. 31

| Per Share Data ($) | 2007 | 2006 | 2005 | 2004 | 2003 | 2002 | 2001 | 2000 | 1999 | 1998 |
|---|---|---|---|---|---|---|---|---|---|---|
| Tangible Book Value | NM | 0.54 | 0.88 | 1.54 | 1.36 | 1.31 | 1.30 | 2.78 | 3.14 | 4.99 |
| Cash Flow | 1.71 | 1.76 | 2.66 | 2.56 | 2.00 | 1.85 | 1.02 | 1.84 | 1.68 | 1.78 |
| Earnings | 1.06 | 1.15 | 2.03 | 2.04 | 1.51 | 1.33 | 0.42 | 1.31 | 1.28 | 1.39 |
| S&P Core Earnings | 1.56 | 2.17 | 2.17 | 2.25 | 1.67 | 1.52 | 1.12 | NA | NA | NA |
| Dividends | 0.91 | 0.86 | 0.78 | 0.66 | 0.58 | 0.55 | 0.52 | 0.49 | 0.45 | 0.43 |
| Payout Ratio | 86% | 75% | 38% | 32% | 38% | 41% | 125% | 37% | 35% | 31% |
| Prices:High | 34.72 | 33.70 | 38.43 | 37.02 | 28.44 | 29.43 | 26.94 | 27.00 | 33.69 | 33.00 |
| Prices:Low | 20.89 | 25.85 | 27.15 | 25.88 | 16.59 | 17.25 | 17.76 | 14.50 | 22.50 | 20.75 |
| P/E Ratio:High | 33 | 29 | 19 | 18 | 19 | 22 | 64 | 21 | 26 | 24 |
| P/E Ratio:Low | 20 | 22 | 13 | 13 | 11 | 13 | 42 | 11 | 18 | 15 |

**Income Statement Analysis** (Million $)

| | 2007 | 2006 | 2005 | 2004 | 2003 | 2002 | 2001 | 2000 | 1999 | 1998 |
|---|---|---|---|---|---|---|---|---|---|---|
| Revenue | 11,770 | 12,778 | 12,642 | 12,074 | 10,936 | 9,419 | 8,358 | 7,243 | 6,307 | 4,345 |
| Operating Income | 1,419 | 1,700 | 1,881 | 1,944 | 1,738 | 1,683 | 1,309 | 1,295 | 1,093 | 817 |
| Depreciation | 241 | 244 | 241 | 237 | 244 | 220 | 269 | 238 | 182 | 136 |
| Interest Expense | 258 | 240 | 247 | 217 | 262 | 237 | 239 | 191 | 120 | 85.3 |
| Pretax Income | 770 | 900 | 1,412 | 1,518 | 1,216 | 1,031 | 301 | 893 | 904 | 755 |
| Effective Tax Rate | 43.6% | 45.8% | 36.7% | 37.5% | 38.1% | 33.8% | 34.0% | 33.8% | 37.0% | 37.0% |
| Net Income | 397 | 461 | 872 | 930 | 740 | 682 | 199 | 592 | 570 | 476 |
| S&P Core Earnings | 582 | 866 | 936 | 1,027 | 816 | 779 | 528 | NA | NA | NA |

**Balance Sheet & Other Financial Data** (Million $)

| | 2007 | 2006 | 2005 | 2004 | 2003 | 2002 | 2001 | 2000 | 1999 | 1998 |
|---|---|---|---|---|---|---|---|---|---|---|
| Cash | 922 | 1,958 | 1,964 | 1,256 | 795 | 1,067 | 312 | 169 | 231 | 542 |
| Current Assets | 3,808 | 5,115 | 5,123 | 4,402 | 3,804 | 3,950 | 2,627 | 2,308 | 2,110 | 1,863 |
| Total Assets | 10,907 | 12,325 | 12,559 | 12,541 | 12,149 | 12,050 | 9,183 | 7,744 | 6,635 | 5,167 |
| Current Liabilities | 1,908 | 3,389 | 2,894 | 2,147 | 2,099 | 1,932 | 1,237 | 1,078 | 846 | 847 |
| Long Term Debt | 3,966 | 3,533 | 3,915 | 4,187 | 3,848 | 4,316 | 3,628 | 3,018 | 2,431 | 1,391 |
| Common Equity | 4,025 | 4,471 | 4,848 | 5,596 | 5,456 | 5,294 | 4,120 | 3,426 | 3,137 | 2,729 |
| Total Capital | 7,991 | 8,004 | 9,665 | 9,783 | 9,304 | 9,610 | 7,747 | 6,444 | 5,788 | 4,321 |
| Capital Expenditures | 248 | 388 | 282 | 310 | 271 | 285 | 274 | 388 | 351 | 189 |
| Cash Flow | 638 | 705 | 1,113 | 1,167 | 984 | 902 | 468 | 830 | 751 | 612 |
| Current Ratio | 2.0 | 1.5 | 1.8 | 2.1 | 1.8 | 2.0 | 2.1 | 2.1 | 2.5 | 2.2 |
| % Long Term Debt of Capitalization | 49.6 | 44.1 | 40.5 | 42.8 | 41.4 | 44.9 | 46.8 | 46.8 | 42.0 | 32.2 |
| % Net Income of Revenue | 3.4 | 3.6 | 6.9 | 7.7 | 6.8 | 7.2 | 2.4 | 8.2 | 9.0 | 11.0 |
| % Return on Assets | 3.4 | 3.7 | 6.9 | 7.5 | 6.1 | 6.5 | 2.3 | 8.2 | 9.0 | 11.0 |
| % Return on Equity | 9.4 | 9.9 | 17.0 | 16.6 | 13.8 | 14.7 | 5.3 | 18.0 | 19.3 | 19.2 |

Data as orig reptd.; bef. results of disc opers/spec. items. Per share data adj. for stk. divs.; EPS diluted. E-Estimated. NA-Not Available. NM-Not Meaningful. NR-Not Ranked. UR-Under Review.

**Office:** 21001 Van Born Road, Taylor, MI 48180.
**Telephone:** 313-274-7400.
**Website:** http://www.masco.com
**Chrmn:** R.A. Manoogian

**Pres & CEO:** T. Wadhams
**COO & EVP:** D. Demarie, Jr.
**SVP & General Counsel:** J.R. Leekley
**CFO, Chief Acctg Officer & Treas:** J.G. Sznewajs

**Investor Contact:** M.C. Duey (313-274-7400)
**Board Members:** D. W. Archer, T. G. Denomme, A. F. Earley, Jr., V. G. Istock, D. L. Johnston, J. M. Losh, R. A. Manoogian, L. A. Payne, M. A. Van Lokeren, T. Wadhams

**Founded:** 1929
**Domicile:** Delaware
**Employees:** 52,000

# Massey Energy Co

**STANDARD & POOR'S**

## S&P Recommendation  HOLD ★★★☆☆

**Price**
$16.20 (as of Nov 14, 2008)

**12-Mo. Target Price**
$27.00

**GICS Sector** Energy
**Sub-Industry** Coal & Consumable Fuels

**Summary** Massey Energy is the fourth largest U.S. coal producer.

### Key Stock Statistics (Source S&P, Vickers, company reports)

| | | | | | | | |
|---|---|---|---|---|---|---|---|
| 52-Wk Range | $95.70– 15.25 | S&P Oper. EPS 2008**E** | 3.57 | Market Capitalization(B) | $1.379 | Beta | 1.81 |
| Trailing 12-Month EPS | $0.10 | S&P Oper. EPS 2009**E** | 5.24 | Yield (%) | 1.48 | S&P 3-Yr. Proj. EPS CAGR(%) | 20 |
| Trailing 12-Month P/E | NM | P/E on S&P Oper. EPS 2008**E** | 4.5 | Dividend Rate/Share | $0.24 | S&P Credit Rating | NA |
| $10K Invested 5 Yrs Ago | $12,045 | Common Shares Outstg. (M) | 85.1 | Institutional Ownership (%) | 97 | | |

### Price Performance

30-Week Mov. Avg. · · · 10-Week Mov. Avg. - - **GAAP Earnings vs. Previous Year**  Volume Above Avg. STARS
12-Mo. Target Price — Relative Strength — ▲ Up ▼ Down ► No Change  Below Avg.

Options: ASE, CBOE, P, Ph

Analysis prepared by **Mathew Christy, CFA** on November 05, 2008, when the stock traded at **$ 20.24**.

### Highlights

➤ We expect revenues to increase about 27% in 2008, led by 25% projected growth in average realized coal prices and a 3% increase in volume produced, followed by a 26% revenue rise in 2009. We believe average realized prices will increase 25% and volume will rise 2% in 2009, based on higher committed steam coal prices and much higher metallurgical coal pricing, and expansion plans offset somewhat by lower demand due to the slowing economy.

➤ We think operating margins will expand in 2008 as coal pricing and cost reduction efforts benefit results, partly offset by greater regulatory burdens. We see the 2008 operating margin increasing to 14.5%, as operating margin per ton increases to 23% on higher pricing and better volumes, from 16% in 2007. We see further margin expansion in 2009 and expect operating margins greater than 15% and operating margin per ton of more than 25%, mainly due to higher pricing.

➤ Our forecast calls for tax rates to drop in 2008 and remain flat in 2009. We estimate operating EPS of $3.57 in 2008 and $5.24 in 2009.

### Investment Rationale/Risk

➤ We believe Massey will see healthy revenue growth as its below-market price contracts expire, higher-priced contracts become a greater percentage of sales, and volume benefits from global demand. With China becoming a net importer, Europe looking to source more U.S. coal, and domestic coal consumption increasing, we expect volume and prices for steam coal to rise, but we believe that metallurgical coal volumes could decline in 2009 due to production cutbacks at steel producers.

➤ Risks to our recommendation and target price include a negative settlement of the EPA lawsuit, lower-than-expected coal prices and productivity, and transportation constraints leading to lower than projected volumes.

➤ Our 12-month target price of $27 is a weighted blend of two valuation methodologies. In terms of relative valuation, we apply an EV/EBITDA multiple of 3X, in line with the peer average, to our 2009 EBITDA estimate, suggesting a $24 value. Our net asset valuation model, which assumes a discount rate of 15.8% and coal prices declining after 2010, indicates a $32 value.

### Qualitative Risk Assessment

| LOW | MEDIUM | HIGH |
|---|---|---|

Our risk assessment reflects the cyclicality of the coal market, MEE's and the industry's high fixed-cost structure, the concentration of company reserves in the central Appalachian region, the heavy regulation of the industry and its utilities end market, and recent lawsuits pending against the company.

### Quantitative Evaluations

**S&P Quality Ranking**  NR

| D | C | B- | B | B+ | A- | A | A+ |
|---|---|---|---|---|---|---|---|

**Relative Strength Rank**  WEAK

12

LOWEST = 1  HIGHEST = 99

### Revenue/Earnings Data

**Revenue (Million $)**

| | 1Q | 2Q | 3Q | 4Q | Year |
|---|---|---|---|---|---|
| 2008 | 644.6 | 826.8 | 763.3 | -- | -- |
| 2007 | 607.3 | 617.8 | 603.4 | 585.0 | 2,396 |
| 2006 | 559.5 | 556.1 | 555.9 | 548.4 | 2,220 |
| 2005 | 570.0 | 582.5 | 533.7 | 518.0 | 2,204 |
| 2004 | 410.9 | 466.7 | 436.7 | 452.4 | 1,767 |
| 2003 | 374.6 | 393.4 | 390.8 | 394.6 | 1,553 |

**Earnings Per Share ($)**

| | | | | | |
|---|---|---|---|---|---|
| 2008 | 0.52 | -1.16 | 0.64 | E1.04 | E3.57 |
| 2007 | 0.40 | 0.43 | 0.27 | 0.06 | 1.17 |
| 2006 | 0.08 | 0.04 | 0.30 | 0.10 | 0.51 |
| 2005 | 0.59 | 0.44 | 0.28 | -2.37 | -1.33 |
| 2004 | -0.03 | 0.16 | 0.03 | 0.02 | 0.18 |
| 2003 | -0.13 | -0.03 | -0.05 | -0.22 | -0.43 |

Fiscal year ended Dec. 31. Next earnings report expected: Early February. EPS Estimates based on S&P Operating Earnings; historical GAAP earnings are as reported.

### Dividend Data (Dates: mm/dd Payment Date: mm/dd/yy)

| Amount ($) | Date Decl. | Ex-Div. Date | Stk. of Record | Payment Date |
|---|---|---|---|---|
| 0.050 | 02/19 | 03/20 | 03/25 | 04/08/08 |
| 0.050 | 05/13 | 06/20 | 06/24 | 07/08/08 |
| 0.050 | 08/19 | 09/26 | 09/30 | 10/14/08 |
| 0.060 | 11/11 | 12/15 | 12/17 | 12/31/08 |

Dividends have been paid since 2001. Source: Company reports.

# Massey Energy Co

STANDARD
&POOR'S

## Business Summary November 05, 2008

CORPORATE OVERVIEW. Massey Energy (formerly Fluor Corp.) produces low-sulfur coal for electric generation, steel-making, and various industrial applications. In November 2000, the company spun off Fluor Corp., which assumed all of its non-coal businesses. The spin-off was accomplished through the distribution to MEE common stockholders of all Fluor common stock. The company declared a special dividend of one Fluor common share for every MEE share held of record on November 30, 2000. MEE is the fourth largest U.S. coal company by our calculation, and the largest in the central Appalachian region. It produces, processes and sells bituminous, low-sulfur coal of steam and metallurgical grades from 35 underground mines and 12 surface mines in West Virginia, Kentucky and Virginia. Its steam coal is primarily purchased by utilities and industrial clients as fuel for power plants. Its metallurgical coal is used primarily to make coke for use in the manufacture of steel. Coal tons sold rose to 39.9 million tons in 2007, from 39.1 million tons in 2006. Revenue per ton increased to $51.55, from $48.71. Average cash cost per ton was $45.14, up from $43.10. In 2007, approximately 95% of coal sales volumes was sold under long-term contracts.

The breakdown of tonnage sold by end market in 2007 was as follows: electric utility, 69%; metallurgical (steel industry sector), 21%; and general industrial, 10%. In 2007, American Electric Power accounted for 11% of total produced coal revenue. The company produces coal using four distinct mining methods: underground room and pillar, underground longwall, surface, and highwall. Use of continuous miner machines in the room and pillar method of underground mining accounted for 40% of production in 2007, underground longwall mining operations provided 7% of production, surface mining accounted for 46%, and highwall 7%. MEE estimated that it had total recoverable reserves of about 2.3 billion tons as of December 31, 2007. The company projected that 62% of its reserves were comprised of coal containing less than 1% sulfur. Low-sulfur coal is vital to utility customers seeking to reduce emissions and reduce costs of compliance with the Clean Air Act.

## Company Financials Fiscal Year Ended Dec. 31

### Per Share Data ($)

| | 2007 | 2006 | 2005 | 2004 | 2003 | 2002 | 2001 | 2000 | 1999 | 1998 |
|---|---|---|---|---|---|---|---|---|---|---|
| Tangible Book Value | 10.17 | 8.60 | 10.26 | 10.16 | 10.05 | 10.73 | 11.55 | NM | NM | NA |
| Cash Flow | 4.22 | 3.34 | 1.74 | 3.12 | 2.20 | 2.35 | 2.38 | 3.39 | 3.28 | NA |
| Earnings | 1.17 | 0.51 | -1.33 | 0.18 | -0.43 | -0.44 | -0.07 | 1.07 | 1.01 | 1.74 |
| S&P Core Earnings | 1.09 | 0.27 | -1.83 | 0.14 | -0.60 | -0.33 | -0.30 | NA | NA | NA |
| Dividends | 0.17 | 0.16 | 0.16 | 0.16 | 0.16 | 0.16 | 0.12 | Nil | NA | NA |
| Payout Ratio | 15% | 31% | NM | 89% | NM | NM | NM | Nil | NA | NA |
| Prices:High | 37.99 | 44.34 | 57.00 | 36.96 | 21.60 | 22.41 | 28.95 | 13.19 | NA | NA |
| Prices:Low | 16.01 | 18.77 | 31.80 | 17.99 | 7.30 | 4.55 | 11.25 | 9.94 | NA | NA |
| P/E Ratio:High | 32 | 87 | NM | NM | NM | NM | NM | 12 | NA | NA |
| P/E Ratio:Low | 14 | 37 | NM | NM | NM | NM | NM | 9 | NA | NA |

### Income Statement Analysis (Million $)

| | 2007 | 2006 | 2005 | 2004 | 2003 | 2002 | 2001 | 2000 | 1999 | 1998 |
|---|---|---|---|---|---|---|---|---|---|---|
| Revenue | 2,414 | 2,220 | 2,204 | 1,767 | 1,553 | 1,630 | 1,432 | 1,141 | 1,114 | 1,154 |
| Operating Income | 433 | 348 | 426 | 280 | 179 | 181 | 191 | 268 | 307 | NA |
| Depreciation | 246 | 231 | 235 | 225 | 196 | 208 | 181 | 171 | 168 | 150 |
| Interest Expense | 85.8 | 86.1 | 67.1 | 60.7 | 48.3 | 35.3 | 34.2 | 0.35 | 0.80 | 0.51 |
| Pretax Income | 130 | 45.0 | -75.4 | -5.64 | -60.7 | -57.5 | -15.9 | 122 | 153 | 186 |
| Effective Tax Rate | 27.3% | 7.57% | NM | NM | NM | NM | NM | 35.5% | 32.4% | 30.9% |
| Net Income | 94.1 | 41.6 | -102 | 13.9 | -32.3 | -32.6 | -5.42 | 78.8 | 103 | 128 |
| S&P Core Earnings | 87.6 | 22.8 | -140 | 10.6 | -44.8 | -24.0 | -22.1 | NA | NA | NA |

### Balance Sheet & Other Financial Data (Million $)

| | 2007 | 2006 | 2005 | 2004 | 2003 | 2002 | 2001 | 2000 | 1999 | 1998 |
|---|---|---|---|---|---|---|---|---|---|---|
| Cash | 365 | 239 | 319 | 123 | 88.8 | 2.73 | 5.66 | 6.93 | 8.05 | 3.65 |
| Current Assets | 887 | 800 | 1,044 | 791 | 703 | 510 | 458 | 384 | 287 | NA |
| Total Assets | 2,861 | 2,741 | 2,986 | 2,651 | 2,377 | 2,241 | 2,271 | 2,161 | 1,980 | 1,837 |
| Current Liabilities | 368 | 355 | 374 | 332 | 259 | 573 | 542 | 275 | 243 | NA |
| Long Term Debt | 1,103 | 1,102 | 1,103 | 900 | 784 | 286 | 300 | Nil | Nil | NA |
| Common Equity | 784 | 697 | 841 | 777 | 759 | 808 | 861 | 1,375 | 1,277 | 1,181 |
| Total Capital | 2,041 | 1,916 | 2,177 | 1,894 | 1,770 | 1,339 | 1,411 | 1,629 | 1,503 | NA |
| Capital Expenditures | 270 | 298 | 347 | 347 | 164 | 135 | 248 | 205 | 230 | 308 |
| Cash Flow | 340 | 272 | 133 | 238 | 164 | 175 | 176 | 250 | 271 | NA |
| Current Ratio | 2.4 | 2.3 | 2.8 | 2.4 | 2.7 | 0.9 | 0.8 | 1.4 | 1.2 | 1.0 |
| % Long Term Debt of Capitalization | 54.0 | 57.5 | 50.6 | 47.5 | 44.3 | 21.4 | 21.3 | Nil | Nil | Nil |
| % Net Income of Revenue | 3.9 | 1.9 | NM | NM | NM | NM | NM | 6.9 | 9.3 | 11.1 |
| % Return on Assets | 3.4 | 1.5 | NM | NM | NM | NM | NM | 3.8 | 5.4 | NA |
| % Return on Equity | 12.7 | 5.4 | NM | NM | NM | NM | NM | 5.9 | 8.4 | 8.8 |

Data as orig reptd.; bef. results of disc opers/spec. items. Per share data adj. for stk. divs.; EPS diluted. E-Estimated. NA-Not Available. NM-Not Meaningful. NR-Not Ranked. UR-Under Review.

**Office:** 4 North 4th Street, Richmond, VA 23219.
**Telephone:** 804-788-1800.
**Website:** http://www.masseyenergyco.com
**EVP & Chief Admin Officer:** B.F. Phillips, Jr.

**Founded:** 1912

**Board Members:** J. B. Crawford, R. M. Gabrys, E. G. Gee

**Founded:** 1912
**Domicile:** Delaware
**Employees:** 5,407

# MasterCard Inc

| S&P Recommendation HOLD ★★★☆☆ | Price $143.68 (as of Nov 14, 2008) | 12-Mo. Target Price $175.00 | Investment Style Large-Cap Growth |
|---|---|---|---|

**GICS Sector** Information Technology
**Sub-Industry** Data Processing & Outsourced Services

**Summary** MasterCard is a global leader in transaction processing and brand licensing providing services in over 210 countries and territories, with more than 25 million acceptance locations.

## Key Stock Statistics (Source S&P, Vickers, company reports)

| | | | | | | |
|---|---|---|---|---|---|---|
| 52-Wk Range | $320.30– 120.02 | S&P Oper. EPS 2008**E** | 9.01 | Market Capitalization(B) | $14.136 | Beta 2.13 |
| Trailing 12-Month EPS | $-1.44 | S&P Oper. EPS 2009**E** | 11.33 | Yield (%) | 0.42 | S&P 3-Yr. Proj. EPS CAGR(%) 24 |
| Trailing 12-Month P/E | NM | P/E on S&P Oper. EPS 2008**E** | 15.9 | Dividend Rate/Share | $0.60 | S&P Credit Rating NA |
| $10K Invested 5 Yrs Ago | NA | Common Shares Outstg. (M) | 129.2 | Institutional Ownership (%) | 98 | |

## Price Performance

- 30-Week Mov. Avg.
- 10-Week Mov. Avg.
- GAAP Earnings vs. Previous Year
- Volume Above Avg.
- STARS
- 12-Mo. Target Price
- Relative Strength
- ▲ Up ▼ Down ▶ No Change
- Below Avg.

Options: ASE, CBOE, P, Ph

Analysis prepared by **Stuart Plesser** on November 05, 2008, when the stock traded at **$ 159.99**.

## Qualitative Risk Assessment

| LOW | MEDIUM | HIGH |
|---|---|---|

Our risk assessment reflects what we view as an oligopolistic market environment, tempered somewhat by pending litigation risks and an evolving competitive environment.

## Quantitative Evaluations

**S&P Quality Ranking** NR

| D | C | B- | B | B+ | A- | A | A+ |
|---|---|---|---|---|---|---|---|

**Relative Strength Rank** MODERATE

55

LOWEST = 1    HIGHEST = 99

## Revenue/Earnings Data

### Revenue (Million $)

| | 1Q | 2Q | 3Q | 4Q | Year |
|---|---|---|---|---|---|
| 2008 | 1,182 | 1,247 | 1,338 | -- | |
| 2007 | 915.1 | 997.0 | 1,083 | 1,073 | 4,068 |
| 2006 | 738.5 | 846.5 | 902.0 | 839.2 | 3,326 |
| 2005 | -- | -- | -- | -- | 2,938 |
| 2004 | -- | -- | -- | -- | -- |
| 2003 | -- | -- | -- | -- | -- |

### Earnings Per Share ($)

| | 1Q | 2Q | 3Q | 4Q | Year |
|---|---|---|---|---|---|
| 2008 | 3.38 | -5.74 | -1.49 | E1.83 | E9.01 |
| 2007 | 1.57 | 1.85 | 2.31 | 2.26 | 8.00 |
| 2006 | 0.94 | -2.30 | 1.42 | 0.30 | 0.37 |
| 2005 | -- | -- | -- | -- | -- |
| 2004 | -- | -- | -- | -- | -- |
| 2003 | -- | -- | -- | -- | -- |

Fiscal year ended Dec. 31. Next earnings report expected: Early February. EPS Estimates based on S&P Operating Earnings; historical GAAP earnings are as reported.

## Highlights

- We expect revenue to advance 9% in 2009, mainly reflecting our expectations for a slow-down in growth of both gross dollar volume (GDV) and processed transactions. We forecast more emphasis on international growth, as U.S. GDV shows signs of deceleration. While we anticipate that spending growth will slow, especially in the U.S., we expect GDV to continue to exceed transaction growth in 2009.

- We anticipate expenses in 2009 to remain in line with 2008's projected levels, as MA is instituting cost-cutting initiatives in anticipation of a slowdown in revenues. As such, we forecast operating margins to improve significantly in 2009 on lower expenses as a percentage of revenue. Indeed, we are particularly encouraged by the strong operating leverage of the company's business model. Longer term, we see the expansion of revenue growth emanating from MA's PayPass program, prepaid cards, as well as from a bigger push for its debit cards.

- Our EPS estimate for 2008 is $9.01. For 2009, we look for EPS of $11.33.

## Investment Rationale/Risk

- We believe there are plenty of opportunities for MA to generate strong growth, including international expansion, debit card growth, and contactless payment solutions. We expect transaction volumes to remain solid despite a general slowdown in consumer spending, as consumers shift to greater credit usage. That said, cross border fees will likely rise at a less robust rate in 2009 due a slowdown in travel. We also see a slowdown in U.S. spending reflecting weakness in the economy. While we also have concerns about regulatory issues, we believe much of this is reflected in the stock price.

- Risks to our recommendation and target price include deterioration in domestic consumer spending, a slowdown in business spending, a rise in unemployment that would pressure spending, and negative outcomes concerning possible regulatory issues. Customer retention, though, is also a concern.

- Our 12-month target price of $175 is about 15.4X our 2009 EPS forecast, a discount to Visa (V: hold, $54) that we think is justified by MA's lower exposure to debit cards and fewer cards outstanding.

## Dividend Data (Dates: mm/dd Payment Date: mm/dd/yy)

| Amount ($) | Date Decl. | Ex-Div. Date | Stk. of Record | Payment Date |
|---|---|---|---|---|
| 0.150 | 12/06 | 01/09 | 01/11 | 02/11/08 |
| 0.150 | 02/05 | 04/07 | 04/09 | 05/09/08 |
| 0.150 | 06/03 | 07/09 | 07/11 | 08/11/08 |
| 0.150 | 09/09 | 10/08 | 10/10 | 11/10/08 |

Dividends have been paid since 2006. Source: Company reports.

# MasterCard Inc

## Business Summary November 05, 2008

CORPORATE OVERVIEW. MasterCard Incorporated (MA), a leading global payment solutions company, provides a variety of services in support of the credit, debit and related payment programs of about 25,000 financial institutions. MA follows a three-tiered business model as a franchisor, processor and advisor. The company, through its businesses, develops and markets payment solutions, processes payment transactions, and provides consulting services to its customers and merchants. MA manages a family of payment card brands, including MasterCard, MasterCard Electronic, Maestro, and Cirrus, which it licenses to its customers.

MasterCard generates revenues from two sources: operations fees and assessments. The company follows a "four-party" payment system, which typically involves four parties in addition to the company: the cardholder, the merchant, the issuer (the cardholder's bank) and the acquirer (the merchant's bank). Issuers typically pay operations fees and assessments, while acquirers principally pay assessments on gross dollar volume (GDV) or cards and, to a lesser extent, certain operations fees.

MA charges operations fees to its customers for providing transaction processing and other payment-related services. Operations fees include core authorization, clearing and settlement fees, cross-border and currency con-

version fees, switch fees, connectivity fees and other operations fees, such as acceptance development fees, warning bulletins, holograms, fees for compliance programs, and user-pay fees for a variety of transaction enhancement services. The company charges assessments based on customers' GDV of activity on the cards that carry its brands, and rates vary by region. GDV includes the aggregated dollar amount of usage (purchases, cash disbursements, balance transfers and convenience checks) on MasterCard-branded cards.

On an aggregate basis, MA received approximately 74% of its revenues in connection with operations fees and approximately 26% in connection with assessments in 2006. The company processed 18.7 billion transactions (including PIN-based online transactions) during that year, a 16.2% increase over the number of transactions processed in 2005. GDV on cards carrying the MasterCard brand, as reported by MA's customers, increased 18.4% year over year to approximately $2.3 trillion in 2007.

## Company Financials Fiscal Year Ended Dec. 31

| Per Share Data ($) | 2007 | 2006 | 2005 | 2004 | 2003 | 2002 | 2001 | 2000 | 1999 | 1998 |
|---|---|---|---|---|---|---|---|---|---|---|
| Tangible Book Value | 18.79 | 13.90 | 6.99 | NA | NA | NA | NA | NA | NA | NA |
| Cash Flow | 8.37 | NA | NA | NA | NA | NA | NA | NA | NA | NA |
| Earnings | 8.00 | 0.37 | 2.67 | 2.38 | -3.91 | 1.35 | 1.98 | 1.65 | NA | NA |
| S&P Core Earnings | 7.04 | 0.53 | 2.97 | 2.56 | 1.06 | NA | NA | NA | NA | NA |
| Dividends | 0.54 | 0.09 | NA | NA | NA | NA | NA | NA | NA | NA |
| Payout Ratio | 7% | 24% | NA | NA | NA | NA | NA | NA | NA | NA |
| Prices:High | 227.18 | 108.60 | NA | NA | NA | NA | NA | NA | NA | NA |
| Prices:Low | 95.30 | 39.00 | NA | NA | NA | NA | NA | NA | NA | NA |
| P/E Ratio:High | 28 | NM | NA | NA | NA | NA | NA | NA | NA | NA |
| P/E Ratio:Low | 12 | NM | NA | NA | NA | NA | NA | NA | NA | NA |

| Income Statement Analysis (Million $) | | | | | | | | | | |
|---|---|---|---|---|---|---|---|---|---|---|
| Revenue | 4,068 | 3,326 | 2,938 | 2,593 | 2,231 | 1,892 | 1,611 | 1,445 | NA | NA |
| Operating Income | 1,161 | 713 | NA | NA | NA | NA | NA | NA | NA | NA |
| Depreciation | 49.3 | 43.5 | 110 | 123 | 120 | 90.5 | 70.0 | 59.4 | NA | NA |
| Interest Expense | 57.3 | 61.2 | NA | NA | NA | NA | NA | NA | NA | NA |
| Pretax Income | 1,671 | 294 | 407 | 324 | -612 | 158 | 229 | 193 | NA | NA |
| Effective Tax Rate | 35.0% | 82.9% | 34.5% | 26.5% | 36.1% | 26.5% | 39.7% | 42.5% | NA | NA |
| Net Income | 1,086 | 50.2 | 267 | 238 | -391 | 116 | 142 | 118 | NA | NA |
| S&P Core Earnings | 954 | 72.8 | 297 | 257 | 107 | NA | NA | NA | NA | NA |

| Balance Sheet & Other Financial Data (Million $) | | | | | | | | | | |
|---|---|---|---|---|---|---|---|---|---|---|
| Cash | 2,970 | 2,484 | 1,282 | 1,138 | 911 | 872 | 670 | NA | NA | NA |
| Current Assets | 4,592 | 3,577 | NA | NA | NA | NA | NA | NA | NA | NA |
| Total Assets | 6,260 | 5,082 | 3,701 | 3,265 | 2,901 | 2,261 | 1,486 | NA | NA | NA |
| Current Liabilities | 2,363 | 1,812 | NA | NA | NA | NA | NA | NA | NA | NA |
| Long Term Debt | 150 | 230 | 229 | NA | NA | NA | NA | NA | NA | NA |
| Common Equity | 3,027 | 2,364 | 1,169 | 975 | 699 | 1,023 | 607 | NA | NA | NA |
| Total Capital | 3,253 | 2,665 | NA | NA | NA | NA | NA | NA | NA | NA |
| Capital Expenditures | 81.6 | 61.2 | 43.9 | 30.5 | 76.3 | 54.2 | 57.9 | 113 | NA | NA |
| Cash Flow | 1,135 | NA | NA | NA | NA | NA | NA | NA | NA | NA |
| Current Ratio | 1.9 | 2.0 | 1.4 | 1.5 | 1.4 | 1.6 | 1.7 | NA | NA | NA |
| % Long Term Debt of Capitalization | 4.6 | 8.8 | 16.4 | 19.0 | 24.6 | 7.3 | 11.7 | Nil | NA | NA |
| % Net Income of Revenue | 26.7 | 1.5 | 9.1 | 9.2 | NM | 6.2 | 8.8 | 8.2 | NA | NA |
| % Return on Assets | 19.2 | 1.1 | 7.7 | 7.7 | NM | 6.2 | NA | NA | NA | NA |
| % Return on Equity | 40.3 | 2.8 | 24.9 | 28.5 | NM | 14.3 | NA | NA | NA | NA |

Data as orig reptd.; bef. results of disc opers/spec. items. Per share data adj. for stk. divs.; EPS diluted. E-Estimated. NA-Not Available. NM-Not Meaningful. NR-Not Ranked. UR-Under Review.

**Office:** 2000 Purchase Street, Purchase, NY 10577.
**Telephone:** 914-249-2000.
**Website:** http://www.mastercard.com
**Chrmn:** R.N. Haythornthwaite

**Pres & CEO:** R.W. Selander
**Vice Chrmn:** A.J. Heuer
**CFO:** M. Hund-Mejean
**Chief Admin Officer:** M.W. Michl

**Investor Contact:** B. Gasper (914-249-4565)
**Board Members:** S. Barzi, D. R. Carlucci, S. J. Freiberg, B. S. Fung, R. N. Haythornthwaite, A. J. Heuer, N. J. Karch, J. O. Lagunes, M. Olivie, M. Schwartz, R. W. Selander, E. T. Suning, J. Tai

**Founded:** 1966
**Domicile:** Delaware
**Employees:** 5,000

# STANDARD &POOR'S

# Mattel Inc.

| S&P Recommendation | HOLD ★★★☆☆ | Price $13.91 (as of Nov 14, 2008) | 12-Mo. Target Price $17.00 | Investment Style Large-Cap Blend |
|---|---|---|---|---|

**GICS Sector** Consumer Discretionary
**Sub-Industry** Leisure Products

**Summary** This large toy company's brands and products include Barbie dolls, Fisher-Price toys, American Girl dolls and books, and Hot Wheels.

## Key Stock Statistics (Source S&P, Vickers, company reports)

| | | | | | | | | |
|---|---|---|---|---|---|---|---|---|
| 52-Wk Range | $23.63–12.53 | S&P Oper. EPS 2008**E** | 1.36 | Market Capitalization(B) | $4.986 | Beta | 0.86 |
| Trailing 12-Month EPS | $1.46 | S&P Oper. EPS 2009**E** | 1.65 | Yield (%) | 5.39 | S&P 3-Yr. Proj. EPS CAGR(%) | 4 |
| Trailing 12-Month P/E | 9.5 | P/E on S&P Oper. EPS 2008**E** | 10.2 | Dividend Rate/Share | $0.75 | S&P Credit Rating | BBB- |
| $10K Invested 5 Yrs Ago | $8,249 | Common Shares Outstg. (M) | 358.4 | Institutional Ownership (%) | 95 | | |

## Price Performance

30-Week Mov. Avg. · · · · 10-Week Mov. Avg. - - - GAAP Earnings vs. Previous Year   Volume Above Avg. STARS
12-Mo. Target Price — Relative Strength — ▲ Up ▼ Down ▶ No Change   Below Avg.

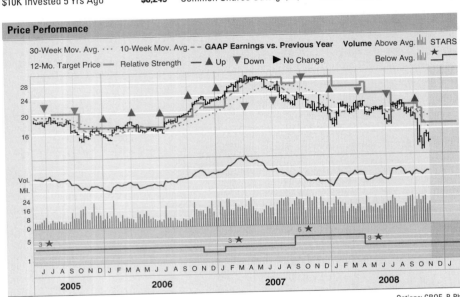

Options: CBOE, P, Ph

Analysis prepared by **Erik Kolb** on October 28, 2008, when the stock traded at **$ 13.75**.

### Highlights

➤ Against the backdrop of a weak economic outlook, leading to reduced consumer spending on toys, we expect revenues to rise 4.4% in 2008 and 2.2% in 2009, compared to 2007 growth of 5.7%. Mattel Boys and Girls brands ought to hold steady, as we believe the Hot Wheels property and girls' brands should be decent contributors. Fisher-Price brands may well prove weak, and we believe this brand also has lower margins. We expect Barbie to remain a key product for MAT, but mostly on international sales growth. In addition to modest projected volume growth, a mid-single-digit price increase will likely boost sales. Geographically, we expect international growth to significantly outpace domestic growth.

➤ We see gross profit margins of 45.8% in 2008, down slightly from 2007, as modest productivity initiatives related to reducing headcount and administrative expenses are offset by continued external cost pressures, such as higher raw material and transportation costs. Prices increases should help modestly. We see margins of 46.1% in 2009.

➤ We see 2008 EPS of $1.36, vs. $1.54 in 2007, and our 2009 estimate is $1.65.

### Investment Rationale/Risk

➤ Although we have confidence in MAT's portfolio of leading consumer brands and its strong cash flow, its first quarter results indicated that products, particularly in the Fisher-Price segment, are seeing some near-term weakness. So while we expect international growth to continue, domestic weakness may mostly offset this. We think strong cash flow should enable the company to raise the dividend and increase share buybacks. In 2007, MAT recalled a substantial number of toys, some of which contained lead paint and were produced in China by third-party manufacturers, but we believe the company will be able to restore consumer confidence in the safety of its products.

➤ Risks to our recommendation and target price include an uncertain toy retailing environment and the possibility of continued toy store closings, an inability to reinvigorate the top line, continued cost pressures, and a material impact resulting from recent toy recalls.

➤ Our 12-month target price of $17 is based on a P/E multiple of 13.0X, roughly in line with peers and trough historical averages, applied to our forward four quarter estimate.

### Qualitative Risk Assessment

| LOW | MEDIUM | HIGH |
|---|---|---|

Our risk assessment reflects our favorable view of MAT's leading market share position and strong balance sheet, offset by our negative view of the intense industry rivalry and concentrated buying power of U.S. toy retailers.

### Quantitative Evaluations

**S&P Quality Ranking**   B

| D | C | B- | B | B+ | A- | A | A+ |
|---|---|---|---|---|---|---|---|

**Relative Strength Rank**   MODERATE

63

LOWEST = 1     HIGHEST = 99

### Revenue/Earnings Data

**Revenue (Million $)**

| | 1Q | 2Q | 3Q | 4Q | Year |
|---|---|---|---|---|---|
| 2008 | 919.3 | 1,112 | 1,946 | -- | -- |
| 2007 | 940.3 | 1,003 | 1,839 | 2,189 | 5,970 |
| 2006 | 793.3 | 957.7 | 1,790 | 2,109 | 5,650 |
| 2005 | 783.1 | 886.8 | 1,666 | 1,843 | 5,179 |
| 2004 | 780.9 | 804.0 | 1,667 | 1,850 | 5,103 |
| 2003 | 745.3 | 769.0 | 1,705 | 1,741 | 4,960 |

**Earnings Per Share ($)**

| | 1Q | 2Q | 3Q | 4Q | Year |
|---|---|---|---|---|---|
| 2008 | -0.13 | 0.03 | 0.66 | E0.80 | E1.36 |
| 2007 | 0.03 | 0.06 | 0.61 | 0.89 | 1.54 |
| 2006 | 0.08 | 0.10 | 0.62 | 0.75 | 1.53 |
| 2005 | 0.02 | -0.23 | 0.55 | 0.69 | 1.01 |
| 2004 | 0.02 | 0.06 | 0.61 | 0.68 | 1.35 |
| 2003 | 0.07 | 0.05 | 0.61 | 0.49 | 1.22 |

Fiscal year ended Dec. 31. Next earnings report expected: Early February. EPS Estimates based on S&P Operating Earnings; historical GAAP earnings are as reported.

### Dividend Data (Dates: mm/dd Payment Date: mm/dd/yy)

| Amount ($) | Date Decl. | Ex-Div. Date | Stk. of Record | Payment Date |
|---|---|---|---|---|
| 0.750 | 11/16 | 11/28 | 11/30 | 12/14/07 |

Dividends have been paid since 1990. Source: Company reports.

---

**Please read the Required Disclosures and Analyst Certification on the last page of this report.**

The McGraw-Hill Companies

# Mattel Inc.

STANDARD &POOR'S

## Business Summary October 28, 2008

CORPORATE OVERVIEW. Mattel markets a wide variety of toy products on a worldwide basis. Brands are grouped in the following categories: Mattel Girls & Boys Brands, Fisher-Price Brands and American Girl Brands. Mattel brands include Barbie, Polly Pocket, Disney Classics, Hot Wheels, Matchbox and Tyco R/C vehicles and playsets, Nickelodeon, Harry Potter, Yu-Gi-Oh!, Batman, Justice League, and Megaman, among others. Fisher-Price brands include Fisher-Price, Power Wheels, Sesame Street, Little People, Winnie the Pooh, Rescue Heroes, Barney, See 'N Say, Dora the Explorer, BabyGear, and View-Master. American Girl brand products are sold directly to consumers, and its children's publications are sold to certain retailers. Brand names include American Girl Today, the American Girls Collection, Just Like You and Bitty Baby.

MAT operates in the U.S. and internationally. Revenues from the international segment provided 49% of consolidated gross sales in 2007. In the international segment, the geographic breakdown was as follows: Europe, 56% of 2007 sales; Latin America, 28%; Asia Pacific, 9%; and Other, 7%.

CORPORATE STRATEGY. We believe that two key elements of MAT's growth strategy are to build its brands and cut costs. With declining sales in its core Barbie brand, MAT has been focused on reinvigorating this product line, while driving growth in other key brands. To further leverage its brands, MAT also pursues licensing arrangements and strategic partnerships, which we think helps to extend its portfolio of brands into areas outside of traditional toys.

## Company Financials Fiscal Year Ended Dec. 31

### Per Share Data ($)

| | 2007 | 2006 | 2005 | 2004 | 2003 | 2002 | 2001 | 2000 | 1999 | 1998 |
|---|---|---|---|---|---|---|---|---|---|---|
| Tangible Book Value | 4.04 | 4.13 | 3.51 | 3.97 | 3.49 | 2.92 | 1.46 | 0.59 | 1.36 | 1.64 |
| Cash Flow | 1.97 | 1.98 | 1.44 | 1.79 | 1.63 | 1.47 | 1.31 | 1.00 | 0.73 | 1.78 |
| Earnings | 1.54 | 1.53 | 1.01 | 1.35 | 1.22 | 1.03 | 0.71 | 0.40 | -0.21 | 1.10 |
| S&P Core Earnings | 1.54 | 1.55 | 0.88 | 1.25 | 1.14 | 1.00 | 0.66 | NA | NA | NA |
| Dividends | 0.75 | 0.65 | 0.50 | 0.45 | 0.40 | 0.05 | 0.05 | 0.27 | 0.34 | 0.30 |
| Payout Ratio | 49% | 42% | 50% | 33% | 33% | 5% | 7% | 67% | NM | 27% |
| Prices:High | 29.71 | 23.98 | 21.64 | 19.79 | 23.20 | 22.36 | 19.92 | 15.13 | 30.31 | 46.56 |
| Prices:Low | 18.83 | 14.75 | 14.52 | 15.94 | 18.57 | 15.05 | 13.52 | 8.94 | 11.69 | 21.25 |
| P/E Ratio:High | 19 | 16 | 21 | 15 | 19 | 22 | 28 | 38 | NM | 42 |
| P/E Ratio:Low | 12 | 10 | 14 | 12 | 15 | 15 | 19 | 22 | NM | 19 |

### Income Statement Analysis (Million $)

| | 2007 | 2006 | 2005 | 2004 | 2003 | 2002 | 2001 | 2000 | 1999 | 1998 |
|---|---|---|---|---|---|---|---|---|---|---|
| Revenue | 5,970 | 5,650 | 5,179 | 5,103 | 4,960 | 4,885 | 4,804 | 4,670 | 5,515 | 4,782 |
| Operating Income | 1,011 | 901 | 840 | 913 | 974 | 934 | 881 | 652 | 671 | 841 |
| Depreciation | 170 | 172 | 175 | 182 | 184 | 192 | 263 | 256 | 390 | 215 |
| Interest Expense | 71.0 | 79.9 | 76.5 | 77.8 | 80.6 | 114 | 155 | 153 | 152 | 111 |
| Pretax Income | 703 | 684 | 652 | 696 | 741 | 621 | 430 | 225 | -111 | 465 |
| Effective Tax Rate | 14.7% | 13.3% | 36.0% | 17.7% | 27.4% | 26.8% | 27.7% | 24.5% | NM | 28.6% |
| Net Income | 600 | 593 | 417 | 573 | 538 | 455 | 311 | 170 | -82.4 | 332 |
| S&P Core Earnings | 601 | 600 | 359 | 531 | 502 | 439 | 288 | NA | NA | NA |

### Balance Sheet & Other Financial Data (Million $)

| | 2007 | 2006 | 2005 | 2004 | 2003 | 2002 | 2001 | 2000 | 1999 | 1998 |
|---|---|---|---|---|---|---|---|---|---|---|
| Cash | 901 | 1,206 | 998 | 1,157 | 1,153 | 1,267 | 617 | 232 | 275 | 212 |
| Current Assets | 2,593 | 2,850 | 2,413 | 2,637 | 2,395 | 2,389 | 2,093 | 1,751 | 2,420 | 2,058 |
| Total Assets | 4,805 | 4,956 | 4,372 | 4,756 | 4,511 | 4,460 | 4,541 | 4,313 | 5,127 | 4,262 |
| Current Liabilities | 1,570 | 1,583 | 1,463 | 1,727 | 1,468 | 1,649 | 1,597 | 1,502 | 1,818 | 1,317 |
| Long Term Debt | 550 | 636 | 525 | 400 | 589 | 640 | 1,021 | 1,242 | 1,184 | 984 |
| Common Equity | 2,307 | 2,433 | 2,102 | 2,386 | 2,216 | 1,979 | 1,738 | 1,403 | 1,963 | 1,819 |
| Total Capital | 2,857 | 3,069 | 2,627 | 2,786 | 2,805 | 2,619 | 2,759 | 2,645 | 3,147 | 2,804 |
| Capital Expenditures | 147 | 64.1 | 137 | 144 | 101 | 167 | 101 | 162 | 212 | 783 |
| Cash Flow | 770 | 765 | 592 | 755 | 721 | 647 | 573 | 427 | 304 | 539 |
| Current Ratio | 1.7 | 1.8 | 1.6 | 1.5 | 1.6 | 1.4 | 1.3 | 1.2 | 1.3 | 1.6 |
| % Long Term Debt of Capitalization | 19.3 | 20.7 | 20.0 | 14.4 | 21.0 | 24.4 | 37.0 | 47.0 | 37.6 | 35.1 |
| % Net Income of Revenue | 10.0 | 10.5 | 8.1 | 11.2 | 10.8 | 9.3 | 6.5 | 3.6 | NM | 6.9 |
| % Return on Assets | 12.3 | 12.7 | 9.1 | 12.4 | 12.0 | 10.1 | 7.0 | 3.8 | NM | 8.2 |
| % Return on Equity | 25.3 | 26.2 | 18.6 | 24.9 | 25.6 | 24.5 | 19.8 | 10.1 | NM | 17.8 |

Data as orig reptd.; bef. results of disc opers/spec. items. Per share data adj. for stk. divs.; EPS diluted. E-Estimated. NA-Not Available. NM-Not Meaningful. NR-Not Ranked. UR-Under Review.

**Office:** 333 Continental Boulevard, El Segundo, CA 90245-5012.
**Telephone:** 310-252-2000.
**Website:** http://www.mattel.com
**Chrmn & CEO:** R.A. Eckert

**COO:** T.A. Debrowski
**SVP, Chief Acctg Officer & Cntlr:** H.S. Topham
**SVP, Secy & General Counsel:** R. Normile
**CFO:** K.M. Farr

**Board Members:** M. J. Dolan, R. A. Eckert, F. D. Fergusson, T. M. Friedman, R. Gelbart, D. Ng, V. M. Prabhu, A. L. Rich, R. L. Sargent, D. A. Scarborough, C. Sinclair, G. C. Sullivan, K. B. White

**Founded:** 1945
**Domicile:** Delaware
**Employees:** 31,000

**STANDARD &POOR'S**

# MBIA Inc.

| S&P Recommendation | HOLD ★★★☆☆ | Price<br>$5.90 (as of Nov 14, 2008) | 12-Mo. Target Price<br>$6.00 | Investment Style<br>Large-Cap Blend |
|---|---|---|---|---|

**GICS Sector** Financials
**Sub-Industry** Property & Casualty Insurance

**Summary** This company provides financial guarantee insurance and related services to public finance clients and financial institutions around the world.

## Key Stock Statistics (Source S&P, Vickers, company reports)

| | | | | | | | |
|---|---|---|---|---|---|---|---|
| 52-Wk Range | $38.19– 3.62 | S&P Oper. EPS 2008**E** | -5.94 | Market Capitalization(B) | $1.612 | Beta | 2.36 |
| Trailing 12-Month EPS | $-19.66 | S&P Oper. EPS 2009**E** | 1.50 | Yield (%) | Nil | S&P 3-Yr. Proj. EPS CAGR(%) | NM |
| Trailing 12-Month P/E | NM | P/E on S&P Oper. EPS 2008**E** | NM | Dividend Rate/Share | Nil | S&P Credit Rating | A- |
| $10K Invested 5 Yrs Ago | $1,110 | Common Shares Outstg. (M) | 273.3 | Institutional Ownership (%) | 85 | | |

## Price Performance

- 30-Week Mov. Avg. ···· 10-Week Mov. Avg. -- - GAAP Earnings vs. Previous Year  Volume Above Avg. STARS
- 12-Mo. Target Price — Relative Strength —  ▲ Up  ▼ Down  ▶ No Change  Below Avg. ★

Options: ASE, CBOE, P, Ph

## Qualitative Risk Assessment

| LOW | MEDIUM | HIGH |
|---|---|---|

Our risk assessment reflects our view that the company faces a number of challenges as it seeks to maintain and rebuild its business. In addition to risks associated with interest rate fluctuations and macro credit trends, we believe MBIA faces a high degree of "reputation risk," driven primarily by concerns the company may face additional challenges after losing its top-tier financial strength rating.

## Quantitative Evaluations

**S&P Quality Ranking**  NR

| D | C | B- | B | B+ | A- | A | A+ |
|---|---|---|---|---|---|---|---|

**Relative Strength Rank**  WEAK

28

LOWEST = 1          HIGHEST = 99

## Revenue/Earnings Data

**Revenue (Million $)**

| | 1Q | 2Q | 3Q | 4Q | Year |
|---|---|---|---|---|---|
| 2008 | -2,956 | 3,289 | 319.8 | -- | -- |
| 2007 | 369.6 | 779.1 | 428.3 | -2,220 | -384.7 |
| 2006 | 351.8 | 689.2 | 707.4 | 693.3 | 2,712 |
| 2005 | 326.0 | 339.3 | 605.2 | 600.0 | 2,301 |
| 2004 | 327.5 | 340.4 | 476.0 | 345.5 | 2,001 |
| 2003 | 280.9 | 310.7 | 313.0 | 325.8 | 1,770 |

**Earnings Per Share ($)**

| | 1Q | 2Q | 3Q | 4Q | Year |
|---|---|---|---|---|---|
| 2008 | -13.03 | -7.14 | -3.48 | E-2.00 | E-5.94 |
| 2007 | 1.46 | 1.61 | -0.29 | -18.55 | -15.17 |
| 2006 | 1.45 | 1.61 | 1.58 | 1.30 | 5.95 |
| 2005 | 1.52 | 1.37 | 1.05 | 1.34 | 5.19 |
| 2004 | 1.42 | 1.47 | 1.29 | 1.36 | 5.61 |
| 2003 | 1.54 | 1.51 | 1.31 | 1.25 | 5.61 |

Fiscal year ended Dec. 31. Next earnings report expected: Early February. EPS Estimates based on S&P Operating Earnings; historical GAAP earnings are as reported.

## Highlights

➤ The 12-month target price for MBI has recently been changed to $6.00 from $10.00. The Highlights section of this Stock Report will be updated accordingly.

## Investment Rationale/Risk

➤ The Investment Rationale/Risk section of this Stock Report will be updated shortly. For the latest News story on MBI from MarketScope, see below.

➤ 11/13/08 02:09 pm ET ... S&P MAINTAINS HOLD RECOMMENDATION ON SHARES OF MBIA INC. (MBI 5.53***): The shares of this bond insurer, which have fallen more than 70% year to date, have weakened again today. We attribute the most recent weakness in the stock to a downgrade of MBI's financial strength, and to a shift in the focus of the U.S. Treasury's rescue efforts away from an intended purchase of troubled mortgage-backed assets. Despite the shares' discounted valuation (currently trading at 45% of MBI's Sept. 30 stated book value), we would not add to positions. Our lowering of our target price by $4 to $6 assumes the shares remain discounted to historical averages. / C.Seifert

## Dividend Data (Dates: mm/dd Payment Date: mm/dd/yy)

| Amount ($) | Date Decl. | Ex-Div. Date | Stk. of Record | Payment Date |
|---|---|---|---|---|
| 0.340 | 12/06 | 12/19 | 12/21 | 01/15/08 |
| Div Omitted | -- | -- | -- | 02/25/08 |

Dividends have been paid since 1987. Source: Company reports.

# MBIA Inc.

**STANDARD &POOR'S**

## Business Summary October 01, 2008

CORPORATE OVERVIEW. MBIA Inc. (MBI), as of year-end 2007, was the leading municipal bond insurer, and had a significant presence in the structured finance market. It is also engaged in asset management operations.

MBI offers insurance for new issues of municipal bonds, and for bonds traded in the secondary market, including bonds held in unit investment trusts and mutual funds. The economic value of municipal bond insurance to the governmental unit or agency offering bonds is a saving in interest costs reflecting the difference in yield on an insured bond from that on the same bond if uninsured.

At December 31, 2007, the net par value of the company's insured debt obligations was $678.7 billion, of which general obligation municipal bonds accounted for 25%, utility bonds 11%, tax-backed bonds 7%, transportation bonds 5%, health care bonds 4%, other U.S. municipal bonds 8%, non-U.S. municipal obligations 5%, U.S. structured finance obligations (asset/mortgage backed)

23%, and international structured finance 12%. Of the $678.7 billion of net outstanding insured debt obligations at December 31, 2007, 17% had been issued outside the U.S., 11% had been issued by California, 6% by New York, 4% by Florida, and about 3% each by Texas, New Jersey and Illinois.

MBI in recent years has expanded its presence in the structured finance (or asset-backed) markets. Adjusted direct premiums (which include upfront and installment premiums) in the global public finance segment advanced 3% in 2007, to $597.1 million, from $578.9 million in 2006. Global structured finance adjusted direct premiums (including upfront and installment premiums) surged 99% in 2007, to $899.8 million, from $451.9 million in 2006.

## Company Financials Fiscal Year Ended Dec. 31

| Per Share Data ($) | 2007 | 2006 | 2005 | 2004 | 2003 | 2002 | 2001 | 2000 | 1999 | 1998 |
|---|---|---|---|---|---|---|---|---|---|---|
| Tangible Book Value | 24.76 | 53.15 | 48.36 | 46.63 | 42.87 | 37.32 | 31.56 | 27.86 | 23.01 | 24.59 |
| Operating Earnings | NA | NA | NA | 5.25 | 4.80 | 4.27 | 3.88 | 3.41 | 3.15 | 3.05 |
| Earnings | -15.17 | 5.95 | 5.19 | 5.61 | 5.61 | 3.98 | 3.91 | 3.55 | 2.13 | 2.88 |
| S&P Core Earnings | -15.48 | 5.88 | 5.75 | 5.33 | 5.25 | 3.91 | 3.81 | NA | NA | NA |
| Dividends | 1.36 | 1.24 | 1.12 | 0.96 | 0.80 | 0.68 | 0.60 | 0.55 | 0.53 | 0.52 |
| Payout Ratio | NM | 21% | 22% | 17% | 14% | 17% | 15% | 15% | 25% | 18% |
| Prices:High | 76.02 | 73.49 | 64.00 | 67.34 | 60.72 | 60.11 | 57.49 | 50.79 | 47.92 | 53.96 |
| Prices:Low | 17.79 | 56.00 | 49.07 | 52.55 | 34.14 | 34.93 | 36.00 | 24.21 | 30.08 | 30.71 |
| P/E Ratio:High | NM | 12 | 12 | 12 | 11 | 15 | 15 | 14 | 23 | 19 |
| P/E Ratio:Low | NM | 9 | 9 | 9 | 6 | 9 | 9 | 7 | 14 | 11 |

| Income Statement Analysis (Million $) | | | | | | | | | | |
|---|---|---|---|---|---|---|---|---|---|---|
| Premium Income | 824 | 836 | 843 | 822 | 733 | 589 | 524 | 446 | 443 | 425 |
| Net Investment Income | 2,184 | 1,863 | 492 | 474 | 447 | 442 | 413 | 394 | 359 | 332 |
| Other Revenue | -3,290 | 13.5 | 1,458 | 704 | 590 | 120 | 197 | 217 | 605 | 156 |
| Total Revenue | -283 | 2,712 | 2,301 | 2,001 | 1,770 | 1,151 | 1,134 | 1,057 | 964 | 912 |
| Pretax Income | -3,066 | 1,133 | 1,016 | 1,130 | 1,149 | 793 | 791 | 715 | 388 | 565 |
| Net Operating Income | NA | NA | NA | NA | NA | NA | NA | NA | NA | NA |
| Net Income | -1,922 | 813 | 712 | 813 | 814 | 587 | 583 | 529 | 321 | 433 |
| S&P Core Earnings | -1,961 | 804 | 789 | 773 | 761 | 577 | 568 | NA | NA | NA |

| Balance Sheet & Other Financial Data (Million $) | | | | | | | | | | |
|---|---|---|---|---|---|---|---|---|---|---|
| Cash & Equivalent | 854 | 796 | 629 | 678 | 452 | 298 | 297 | 246 | 229 | 148 |
| Premiums Due | 326 | 363 | 408 | 505 | 536 | 522 | 507 | NA | NA | NA |
| Investment Assets:Bonds | 29,589 | 27,756 | 23,747 | 19,680 | 17,391 | 16,195 | 14,087 | 11,737 | 10,274 | 9,562 |
| Investment Assets:Stocks | Nil | Nil | Nil | Nil | Nil | Nil | Nil | Nil | Nil | Nil |
| Investment Assets:Loans | Nil | Nil | Nil | Nil | Nil | Nil | Nil | Nil | Nil | Nil |
| Investment Assets:Total | 42,066 | 46,399 | 40,562 | 41,556 | 27,707 | 17,095 | 14,516 | 12,233 | 10,694 | 10,080 |
| Deferred Policy Costs | 473 | 450 | 427 | 360 | 320 | 302 | 278 | 274 | 252 | 230 |
| Total Assets | 47,415 | 39,763 | 34,561 | 33,027 | 30,268 | 18,852 | 16,200 | 13,894 | 12,264 | 11,797 |
| Debt | 15,412 | 13,619 | 10,033 | 8,877 | 8,870 | 1,033 | 805 | 795 | 689 | 689 |
| Common Equity | 3,656 | 7,204 | 6,592 | 6,579 | 6,259 | 5,493 | 4,783 | 4,223 | 3,513 | 3,792 |
| Property & Casualty:Loss Ratio | 105.2 | 9.7 | 10.0 | 10.0 | 9.2 | 9.4 | 9.3 | 6.2 | 12.3 | 8.0 |
| Property & Casualty:Expense Ratio | 23.6 | 26.6 | 24.9 | 22.0 | 12.8 | 16.8 | 13.4 | 22.1 | 23.6 | 16.8 |
| Property & Casualty Combined Ratio | 128.6 | 36.3 | 34.9 | 32.0 | 22.0 | 26.2 | 22.7 | 28.3 | 35.9 | 24.8 |
| % Return on Revenue | NM | 30.0 | 31.0 | 40.6 | 46.0 | 51.0 | 51.4 | 50.0 | 33.2 | 47.5 |
| % Return on Equity | NM | 11.8 | 10.8 | 12.7 | 13.8 | 11.4 | 13.0 | 13.7 | 8.8 | 12.7 |

Data as orig reptd.; bef. results of disc opers/spec. items. Per share data adj. for stk. divs.; EPS diluted. E-Estimated. NA-Not Available. NM-Not Meaningful. NR-Not Ranked. UR-Under Review.

**Office:** 113 King Street, Armonk, NY 10504-1610.
**Telephone:** 914-273-4545.
**Website:** http://www.mbia.com
**Chrmn & CEO:** J.W. Brown, Jr.

**Pres & COO:** W.C. Fallon
**Pres, CFO & Chief Admin Officer:** C.E. Chaplin
**EVP, Secy & General Counsel:** R.D. Wertheim
**Chief Acctg Officer & Cntlr:** D.C. Hamilton

**Investor Contact:** G. Diamond (914-765-3190)
**Board Members:** J. W. Brown, Jr., D. A. Coulter, C. L. Gaudiani, D. P. Kearney, K. Lee, L. H. Meyer, J. A. Rolls, R. C. Vaughan

**Founded:** 1973
**Domicile:** Connecticut
**Employees:** 486

**The McGraw-Hill Companies**

# McCormick & Company Inc

STANDARD
&POOR'S

**S&P Recommendation** HOLD ★★★☆☆

| Price | 12-Mo. Target Price | Investment Style |
|---|---|---|
| $30.79 (as of Nov 14, 2008) | $41.00 | Large-Cap Growth |

**GICS Sector** Consumer Staples
**Sub-Industry** Packaged Foods & Meats

**Summary** This company primarily produces spices, seasonings and flavorings for the retail food, foodservice and industrial markets. Trademarks include McCormick and Schilling.

## Key Stock Statistics (Source S&P, Vickers, company reports)

| | | | | | | | | |
|---|---|---|---|---|---|---|---|---|
| 52-Wk Range | $42.06– 29.64 | S&P Oper. EPS 2008**E** | 2.13 | Market Capitalization(B) | $3.618 | Beta | 0.54 |
| Trailing 12-Month EPS | $1.99 | S&P Oper. EPS 2009**E** | 2.34 | Yield (%) | 2.86 | S&P 3-Yr. Proj. EPS CAGR(%) | 10 |
| Trailing 12-Month P/E | 15.5 | P/E on S&P Oper. EPS 2008**E** | 14.5 | Dividend Rate/Share | $0.88 | S&P Credit Rating | A- |
| $10K Invested 5 Yrs Ago | $11,786 | Common Shares Outstg. (M) | 130.0 | Institutional Ownership (%) | 81 | | |

## Price Performance

30-Week Mov. Avg. · · · · 10-Week Mov. Avg. – – – **GAAP Earnings vs. Previous Year** Volume Above Avg. STARS
12-Mo. Target Price — Relative Strength — ▲ Up ▼ Down ► No Change Below Avg.

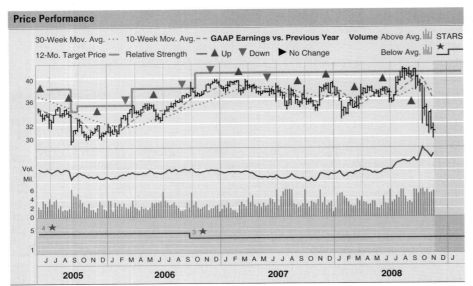

Options: Ph

Analysis prepared by **Tom Graves, CFA** on August 22, 2008, when the stock traded at **$ 40.60**.

## Highlights

➤ In August 2008, MKC said that it had completed the purchase of assets of the Lawry's seasoning and marinade business, for $604 million.

➤ With partial-year inclusion of the Lawry's business, we look for FY 08 (Nov.) net sales to increase about 9%, from the $2.92 billion reported for FY 07. We expect FY 08 profit margins (before restructuring charges) to be bolstered by cost reduction efforts and product mix. Excluding restructuring charges and other special ,items, we project EPS of $2.13, up from $1.92 in FY 07. This includes $0.03 of accretion from the Lawry's acquisition. We look for MKC to have restructuring charges totaling about $0.10 a share in FY 08, compared to about an $0.18 negative impact in FY 07. For FY 09, we estimate EPS of $2.34.

➤ In FY 07, MKC repurchased 4.3 million of its common shares for $157.0 million. As of February 29, 2008, $49 million remained under a $400 million share repurchase authorization. However, in view of the Lawry's acquisition, we expect MKC to be emphasizing debt repayment as a use of cash in the year ahead.

## Investment Rationale/Risk

➤ Regarding the recent Lawry's acquisition, we like the idea of MKC expanding in related businesses. We believe that long-term prospects for the company to generate free cash flow are favorable. With respect to its restructuring program, MKC was projecting up to $55 million (pretax) of annual cost savings, including $10 million realized in FY 06 and another $35 million realized in FY 07.

➤ Risks to our recommendation and target price relate to competitive pressures in MKC's businesses, consumer acceptance of new product introductions, and commodity cost inflation. In terms of corporate governance, the company has a dual class capital structure with unequal voting rights, which we view unfavorably.

➤ Our 12-month target price of $41 is 19.1X our calendar year 2008 EPS estimate of $2.15, which is about a 7% premium to what we expect, on average, from a small group of peers or competitors. The stock recently had an indicated dividend yield of about 2.2%.

## Qualitative Risk Assessment

| LOW | MEDIUM | HIGH |
|---|---|---|

Our risk assessment reflects the relatively stable nature of the company's end markets, our view of its strong balance sheet and cash flow, and an S&P Quality Ranking of A+, which reflects historical stability of earnings and dividends.

## Quantitative Evaluations

**S&P Quality Ranking** A+

| D | C | B- | B | B+ | A- | A | A+ |
|---|---|---|---|---|---|---|---|

**Relative Strength Rank** MODERATE

67

LOWEST = 1 HIGHEST = 99

## Revenue/Earnings Data

**Revenue (Million $)**

| | 1Q | 2Q | 3Q | 4Q | Year |
|---|---|---|---|---|---|
| 2008 | 724.0 | 764.1 | 781.6 | -- | -- |
| 2007 | 652.6 | 687.2 | 716.2 | 860.1 | 2,916 |
| 2006 | 609.7 | 639.9 | 663.1 | 803.7 | 2,716 |
| 2005 | 603.6 | 628.6 | 622.7 | 737.1 | 2,592 |
| 2004 | 572.4 | 596.2 | 613.5 | 744.1 | 2,526 |
| 2003 | 485.4 | 527.9 | 557.6 | 698.7 | 2,270 |

**Earnings Per Share ($)**

| | | | | | |
|---|---|---|---|---|---|
| 2008 | 0.39 | 0.41 | 0.52 | E0.84 | E2.13 |
| 2007 | 0.33 | 0.31 | 0.43 | 0.67 | 1.73 |
| 2006 | 0.11 | 0.46 | 0.32 | 0.62 | 1.50 |
| 2005 | 0.26 | 0.31 | 0.35 | 0.65 | 1.56 |
| 2004 | 0.27 | 0.30 | 0.33 | 0.62 | 1.52 |
| 2003 | 0.23 | 0.27 | 0.28 | 0.61 | 1.40 |

Fiscal year ended Nov. 30. Next earnings report expected: Late January. EPS Estimates based on S&P Operating Earnings; historical GAAP earnings are as reported.

## Dividend Data (Dates: mm/dd Payment Date: mm/dd/yy)

| Amount ($) | Date Decl. | Ex-Div. Date | Stk. of Record | Payment Date |
|---|---|---|---|---|
| 0.220 | 11/27 | 12/26 | 12/28 | 01/18/08 |
| 0.220 | 04/02 | 04/10 | 04/14 | 04/25/08 |
| 0.220 | 06/24 | 07/02 | 07/07 | 07/21/08 |
| 0.220 | 09/23 | 10/01 | 10/03 | 10/17/08 |

Dividends have been paid since 1925. Source: Company reports.

# McCormick & Company Inc

## Business Summary August 22, 2008

CORPORATE PROFILE. Founded by Willoughby M. McCormick in 1889, Mc-Cormick & Co. is the world's largest spice company, with operations in the manufacture, marketing and distribution of spices, seasonings, flavorings and other specialty food products. The company markets its products to retail food, foodservice and industrial markets under the McCormick and Schilling names.

McCormick's consumer segment, which accounted for 57% of sales and 82% of operating profits (before restructuring costs) in FY 07 (Nov.), sells spices, herbs, extracts, seasoning blends, sauces, marinades and specialty foods to the consumer food market. The industrial segment (43%, 19%) sells seasoning blends, natural spices and herbs, wet flavors, coating systems and compound flavors to food manufacturers and the food service industry, both directly and through distributors. Many spices and herbs purchased by the company are imported into the U.S., although significant quantities of some materials, such as paprika, dehydrated vegetables, onion and garlic, and food ingredients other than spices and herbs, originate in the U.S.

MKC says that many of its products are prepared from confidential formulas developed by its research laboratories and product development teams. Expenditures for research and development were $49.3 million in FY 07, compared to $45.0 million in FY 06.

CORPORATE STRATEGY. We see MKC aiming to improve profitability with cost reduction efforts and a focus on higher-margin, higher-value-added products.

A restructuring program announced in 2005 is expected to extend through 2008. Related to this plan, we look for MKC to have a total pretax negative impact (net) of $115 million to $125 million, including a transaction-related gain of $34 million. With its restructuring program, MKC has projected at least $55 million (pretax) of annual cost savings, including $10 million realized in FY 06 and another $35 million realized in FY 07. We expect the restructuring plan to include the consolidation of global manufacturing, the rationalization of distribution facilities, efforts to improve its go-to-market strategy, the elimination of administrative redundancies, and the rationalization of joint venture partnerships. We expect that a portion of the savings may be invested in potential growth drivers such as brand advertising.

## Company Financials Fiscal Year Ended Nov. 30

| Per Share Data ($) | 2007 | 2006 | 2005 | 2004 | 2003 | 2002 | 2001 | 2000 | 1999 | 1998 |
|---|---|---|---|---|---|---|---|---|---|---|
| Tangible Book Value | NM | NM | NM | 0.45 | 0.28 | 0.62 | NM | NM | 1.70 | 1.57 |
| Cash Flow | 2.36 | 2.14 | 2.10 | 2.11 | 1.85 | 1.73 | 1.57 | 1.43 | 1.12 | 1.07 |
| Earnings | 1.73 | 1.50 | 1.56 | 1.52 | 1.40 | 1.26 | 1.05 | 0.99 | 0.72 | 0.71 |
| S&P Core Earnings | 1.81 | 1.40 | 1.51 | 1.43 | 1.28 | 1.12 | 0.90 | NA | NA | NA |
| Dividends | 0.80 | 0.72 | 0.64 | 0.56 | 0.46 | 0.37 | 0.40 | 0.38 | 0.34 | 0.32 |
| Payout Ratio | 46% | 48% | 41% | 37% | 33% | 29% | 38% | 38% | 48% | 45% |
| Prices:High | 39.73 | 39.82 | 39.14 | 38.94 | 30.21 | 27.25 | 23.27 | 18.88 | 17.31 | 18.22 |
| Prices:Low | 33.89 | 30.09 | 28.95 | 28.60 | 21.71 | 20.70 | 17.00 | 11.88 | 13.31 | 13.53 |
| P/E Ratio:High | 23 | 27 | 25 | 26 | 22 | 22 | 22 | 19 | 24 | 26 |
| P/E Ratio:Low | 20 | 20 | 19 | 19 | 16 | 16 | 16 | 12 | 19 | 19 |

| Income Statement Analysis (Million $) | 2007 | 2006 | 2005 | 2004 | 2003 | 2002 | 2001 | 2000 | 1999 | 1998 |
|---|---|---|---|---|---|---|---|---|---|---|
| Revenue | 2,916 | 2,716 | 2,592 | 2,526 | 2,270 | 2,320 | 2,372 | 2,124 | 2,007 | 1,881 |
| Operating Income | 468 | 429 | 429 | 402 | 366 | 353 | 324 | 287 | 252 | 240 |
| Depreciation | 83.0 | 86.8 | 74.6 | 72.0 | 65.3 | 66.8 | 73.0 | 61.3 | 57.4 | 54.8 |
| Interest Expense | 61.0 | 53.7 | 48.2 | 41.0 | 38.6 | 43.6 | 52.9 | 39.7 | 32.4 | 36.9 |
| Pretax Income | 302 | 270 | 316 | 308 | 286 | 257 | 212 | 204 | 163 | 159 |
| Effective Tax Rate | 30.4% | 24.0% | 30.6% | 28.9% | 29.1% | 28.9% | 29.7% | 32.6% | 36.8% | 34.6% |
| Net Income | 230 | 202 | 215 | 215 | 199 | 180 | 147 | 138 | 103 | 104 |
| S&P Core Earnings | 240 | 189 | 208 | 202 | 182 | 158 | 126 | NA | NA | NA |

| Balance Sheet & Other Financial Data (Million $) | 2007 | 2006 | 2005 | 2004 | 2003 | 2002 | 2001 | 2000 | 1999 | 1998 |
|---|---|---|---|---|---|---|---|---|---|---|
| Cash | 46.0 | 49.0 | 30.3 | 70.3 | 25.1 | 47.3 | 31.3 | 23.9 | 12.0 | 17.7 |
| Current Assets | 983 | 899 | 800 | 864 | 762 | 725 | 636 | 620 | 491 | 504 |
| Total Assets | 2,788 | 2,568 | 2,273 | 2,370 | 2,148 | 1,931 | 1,772 | 1,660 | 1,189 | 1,259 |
| Current Liabilities | 861 | 780 | 699 | 773 | 713 | 673 | 714 | 1,027 | 471 | 518 |
| Long Term Debt | 574 | 570 | 464 | 465 | 449 | 454 | 454 | 160 | 241 | 250 |
| Common Equity | 1,085 | 933 | 800 | 890 | 755 | 592 | 463 | 359 | 382 | 468 |
| Total Capital | 1,669 | 1,575 | 1,293 | 1,386 | 1,226 | 1,046 | 943 | 523 | 628 | 643 |
| Capital Expenditures | 79.0 | 84.8 | 73.8 | 69.8 | 91.6 | 111 | 112 | 53.6 | 49.3 | 54.8 |
| Cash Flow | 313 | 289 | 290 | 287 | 265 | 247 | 220 | 199 | 161 | 159 |
| Current Ratio | 1.1 | 1.2 | 1.1 | 1.1 | 1.1 | 1.1 | 0.9 | 0.6 | 1.0 | 1.0 |
| % Long Term Debt of Capitalization | 34.3 | 37.8 | 35.9 | 33.6 | 36.6 | 43.4 | 48.2 | 30.6 | 38.5 | 38.9 |
| % Net Income of Revenue | 7.8 | 7.4 | 8.3 | 8.5 | 8.8 | 7.8 | 6.2 | 6.5 | 5.1 | 5.5 |
| % Return on Assets | 8.5 | 8.4 | 9.3 | 9.5 | 9.8 | 9.7 | 8.5 | 9.7 | 8.4 | 8.3 |
| % Return on Equity | 22.7 | 23.3 | 25.4 | 26.1 | 29.6 | 34.1 | 35.7 | 37.1 | 26.8 | 24.1 |

Data as orig reptd.; bef. results of disc opers/spec. items. Per share data adj. for stk. divs.; EPS diluted. E-Estimated. NA-Not Available. NM-Not Meaningful. NR-Not Ranked. UR-Under Review.

**Office:** 18 Loveton Circle, Sparks, MD 21152-6000.
**Telephone:** 410-771-7301.
**Website:** http://www.mccormick.com
**Chrmn:** R.J. Lawless

**Pres & CEO:** A.D. Wilson
**EVP & CFO:** G.M. Stetz, Jr.
**SVP, Secy & General Counsel:** R.W. Skelton
**Chief Acctg Officer & Cntlr:** K.A. Kelly, Jr.

**Investor Contact:** J. Brooks (410-771-7244)
**Board Members:** J. P. Bilbrey, J. T. Brady, J. M. Fitzpatrick, F. A. Hrabowski, III, R. J. Lawless, M. D. Mangan, J. W. McGrath, M. M. Preston, G. A. Roche, W. E. Stevens, A. D. Wilson

**Founded:** 1889
**Domicile:** Maryland
**Employees:** 7,500

# McDonald's Corp

STANDARD &POOR'S

| S&P Recommendation | STRONG BUY ★★★★★ | Price $56.13 (as of Nov 14, 2008) | 12-Mo. Target Price $66.00 | Investment Style Large-Cap Growth |

**GICS Sector** Consumer Discretionary
**Sub-Industry** Restaurants

**Summary** MCD is the largest fast-food restaurant company in the world, with more than 31,600 restaurants in 118 countries.

## Key Stock Statistics (Source S&P, Vickers, company reports)

| | | | | | | | |
|---|---|---|---|---|---|---|---|
| 52-Wk Range | $67.00– 45.79 | S&P Oper. EPS 2008**E** | 3.70 | Market Capitalization(B) | $62.559 | Beta | 0.94 |
| Trailing 12-Month EPS | $3.96 | S&P Oper. EPS 2009**E** | 3.80 | Yield (%) | 3.56 | S&P 3-Yr. Proj. EPS CAGR(%) | 11 |
| Trailing 12-Month P/E | 14.2 | P/E on S&P Oper. EPS 2008**E** | 15.2 | Dividend Rate/Share | $2.00 | S&P Credit Rating | A |
| $10K Invested 5 Yrs Ago | $24,328 | Common Shares Outstg. (M) | 1,114.5 | Institutional Ownership (%) | 75 | | |

## Price Performance

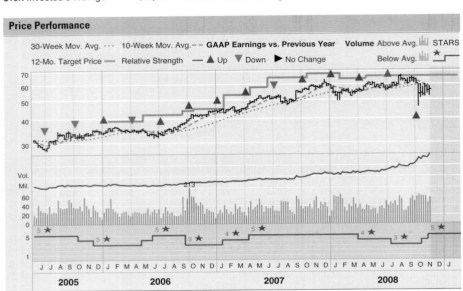

- 30-Week Mov. Avg. · · · 10-Week Mov. Avg. — GAAP Earnings vs. Previous Year   Volume Above Avg. STARS
- 12-Mo. Target Price — Relative Strength — ▲ Up ▼ Down ► No Change   Below Avg.

Options: ASE, CBOE, P, Ph

## Qualitative Risk Assessment

| LOW | MEDIUM | HIGH |

McDonald's competes in the global fast food industry, where it has a very strong brand name presence. However, results can vary widely due to fluctuations in food costs, competitive discounting, and exchange rate volatility. Recent economic softness in the U.S. is likely to weigh on short-term domestic financial results, but may allow the company to gain market share in the long run.

## Quantitative Evaluations

**S&P Quality Ranking** A-

| D | C | B- | B | B+ | A- | A | A+ |

**Relative Strength Rank** STRONG

86

LOWEST = 1          HIGHEST = 99

## Highlights

➤ The STARS recommendation for MCD has recently been changed to 5 (strong buy) from 4 (buy). The Highlights section of this Stock Report will be updated accordingly.

## Investment Rationale/Risk

➤ The Investment Rationale/Risk section of this Stock Report will be updated shortly. For the latest News story on MCD from MarketScope, see below.

➤ 11/11/08 09:49 am ET ... S&P RAISES OPINION ON MCDONALD'S CORP SHARES TO STRONG BUY FROM BUY (MCD 56.56*****): The shares have substantially given back gains early Monday following MCD's announcement that October comparable sales rose 8.2%. With the exception of next February, we think easy sales comparisons in upcoming months will allow MCD to continue to report strong sales gains, which we attribute to food service industry marketshare shifts away from full service options. We have factored in likely unfavorable forex benefit shifts in Q4 and 2009 into our $3.70 and $3.80 EPS estimates for '08 and '09. We keep our DCF-based 12-month target price of $66. /M.Basham

## Revenue/Earnings Data

**Revenue (Million $)**

| | 1Q | 2Q | 3Q | 4Q | Year |
|---|---|---|---|---|---|
| 2008 | 5,615 | 6,075 | 6,267 | -- | -- |
| 2007 | 5,293 | 5,839 | 5,901 | 5,754 | 22,787 |
| 2006 | 4,914 | 5,367 | 5,671 | 5,634 | 21,586 |
| 2005 | 4,803 | 5,096 | 5,327 | 5,235 | 20,460 |
| 2004 | 4,400 | 4,729 | 4,926 | 5,010 | 19,065 |
| 2003 | 3,800 | 4,281 | 4,505 | 4,555 | 17,141 |

**Earnings Per Share ($)**

| | 1Q | 2Q | 3Q | 4Q | Year |
|---|---|---|---|---|---|
| 2008 | 0.81 | 1.04 | 1.05 | E0.90 | E3.70 |
| 2007 | 0.63 | -0.59 | 0.83 | 1.06 | 1.93 |
| 2006 | 0.46 | 0.56 | 0.67 | 0.61 | 2.30 |
| 2005 | 0.56 | 0.42 | 0.58 | 0.48 | 2.04 |
| 2004 | 0.40 | 0.47 | 0.61 | 0.31 | 1.79 |
| 2003 | 0.29 | 0.37 | 0.43 | 0.10 | 1.18 |

Fiscal year ended Dec. 31. Next earnings report expected: Late January. EPS Estimates based on S&P Operating Earnings; historical GAAP earnings are as reported.

## Dividend Data (Dates: mm/dd Payment Date: mm/dd/yy)

| Amount ($) | Date Decl. | Ex-Div. Date | Stk. of Record | Payment Date |
|---|---|---|---|---|
| 0.375 | 01/24 | 02/28 | 03/03 | 03/17/08 |
| 0.375 | 05/22 | 06/05 | 06/09 | 06/23/08 |
| 0.375 | 07/17 | 08/28 | 09/02 | 09/16/08 |
| 0.500 | 09/25 | 11/26 | 12/01 | 12/15/08 |

Dividends have been paid since 1976. Source: Company reports.

---

**Please read the Required Disclosures and Analyst Certification on the last page of this report.**

The McGraw-Hill Companies

# McDonald's Corp

## Business Summary October 27, 2008

CORPORATE OVERVIEW. With one of the world's most widely known brand names, McDonald's operates and franchises more than 31,600 restaurants in 118 countries. Systemwide sales totaled $64.1 billion in 2007, up from $57.5 billion in 2006.

In the U.S., the McDonald's chain dominates the $150 billion quick-service restaurant industry. With U.S. systemwide sales of nearly $29 billion, its domestic business is several times larger than its closest competitors, Burger King and Wendy's Old Fashioned Hamburgers. MCD's international segment has supplied much of its earnings growth over the past two decades, and, in 2007, contributed 55% of operating income (before corporate expenses and one-time charges). All restaurants are operated by MCD, franchisees, or affiliates under joint venture agreements.

In August 2007, the company completed the sale of its existing businesses in Brazil, Argentina, Mexico, Puerto Rico, Venezuela and 13 other countries in Latin America and the Caribbean to a developmental licensee (the Latam transaction). The company recorded impairment charges totaling approximately $1.7 billion, substantially all of which was non-cash. The charges included approximately $892 million for the difference between the net book value of the Latam business and the approximately $680 million in cash proceeds,

and $773 million in foreign currency translation losses previously included in comprehensive income.

CORPORATE STRATEGY. In 2003, the company introduced a new corporate strategy that focuses on product development and investment in existing properties, rather than on expansion and price discounting. MCD's stated operating priorities include fixing operating inadequacies in existing restaurants; taking a more integrated and focused approach to growth, with an emphasis on increasing sales, margins and returns in existing restaurants; and ensuring the correct operating structure and resources, aligned behind focusing priorities that create benefits for its customers and restaurants.

A significant part of the new corporate strategy has been to de-emphasize Partner Brands concepts in order to focus on the McDonald's brand. In 2006 and 2007, MCD disposed of interests in the Chipotle Mexican Grill restaurant concept as well as the Boston Market chain.

## Company Financials Fiscal Year Ended Dec. 31

| Per Share Data ($) | 2007 | 2006 | 2005 | 2004 | 2003 | 2002 | 2001 | 2000 | 1999 | 1998 |
|---|---|---|---|---|---|---|---|---|---|---|
| Tangible Book Value | 11.14 | 11.01 | 10.45 | 9.74 | 8.18 | 6.88 | 6.30 | 5.86 | 6.20 | 6.26 |
| Cash Flow | 2.87 | 3.29 | 3.05 | 2.73 | 2.08 | 1.59 | 2.08 | 2.20 | 2.07 | 1.73 |
| Earnings | 1.93 | 2.30 | 2.04 | 1.79 | 1.18 | 0.77 | 1.25 | 1.46 | 1.39 | 1.10 |
| S&P Core Earnings | 1.88 | 2.28 | 2.00 | 1.66 | 0.96 | 0.51 | 1.01 | 1.46 | 1.39 | 1.10 |
| Dividends | 1.50 | 1.00 | 0.67 | 0.55 | 0.40 | 0.24 | 0.23 | 0.22 | 0.20 | 0.18 |
| Payout Ratio | 78% | 43% | 33% | 31% | 34% | 31% | 18% | 15% | 14% | 16% |
| Prices:High | 63.69 | 44.68 | 35.69 | 32.96 | 27.01 | 30.72 | 35.06 | 43.63 | 49.56 | 39.75 |
| Prices:Low | 42.31 | 31.73 | 27.36 | 24.54 | 12.12 | 15.17 | 24.75 | 26.38 | 35.94 | 22.31 |
| P/E Ratio:High | 33 | 19 | 17 | 18 | 23 | 40 | 28 | 30 | 36 | 36 |
| P/E Ratio:Low | 22 | 14 | 13 | 14 | 10 | 20 | 20 | 18 | 26 | 20 |

| Income Statement Analysis (Million $) | 2007 | 2006 | 2005 | 2004 | 2003 | 2002 | 2001 | 2000 | 1999 | 1998 |
|---|---|---|---|---|---|---|---|---|---|---|
| Revenue | 22,787 | 21,586 | 20,460 | 19,065 | 17,141 | 15,406 | 14,870 | 14,243 | 13,259 | 12,421 |
| Operating Income | 6,683 | 5,829 | 5,243 | 4,742 | 3,980 | 3,164 | 3,983 | 4,144 | 4,171 | 3,903 |
| Depreciation | 1,145 | 1,250 | 1,250 | 1,201 | 1,148 | 1,051 | 1,086 | 1,011 | 956 | 881 |
| Interest Expense | 417 | 402 | 356 | 358 | 388 | 360 | 452 | 430 | 396 | 414 |
| Pretax Income | 3,572 | 4,166 | 3,702 | 3,202 | 2,346 | 1,662 | 2,330 | 2,882 | 2,884 | 2,307 |
| Effective Tax Rate | 34.6% | 31.0% | 29.7% | 28.9% | 35.7% | 40.3% | 29.8% | 31.4% | 32.5% | 32.8% |
| Net Income | 2,335 | 2,873 | 2,602 | 2,279 | 1,508 | 992 | 1,637 | 1,977 | 1,948 | 1,550 |
| S&P Core Earnings | 2,277 | 2,848 | 2,540 | 2,100 | 1,226 | 667 | 1,328 | NA | NA | NA |

| Balance Sheet & Other Financial Data (Million $) | 2007 | 2006 | 2005 | 2004 | 2003 | 2002 | 2001 | 2000 | 1999 | 1998 |
|---|---|---|---|---|---|---|---|---|---|---|
| Cash | 1,981 | 2,136 | 4,260 | 1,380 | 493 | 330 | 418 | 422 | 420 | 299 |
| Current Assets | 3,582 | 3,625 | 5,850 | 2,858 | 1,885 | 1,715 | 1,819 | 1,662 | 1,572 | 1,309 |
| Total Assets | 29,392 | 29,024 | 29,989 | 27,838 | 25,525 | 23,971 | 22,535 | 21,683 | 20,983 | 19,784 |
| Current Liabilities | 4,499 | 3,008 | 4,036 | 3,521 | 2,486 | 2,422 | 2,248 | 2,361 | 3,274 | 2,497 |
| Long Term Debt | 7,310 | 8,417 | 8,937 | 8,357 | 9,343 | 9,704 | 8,556 | 7,844 | 5,632 | 6,189 |
| Common Equity | 15,280 | 15,458 | 15,146 | 14,202 | 11,982 | 10,281 | 9,488 | 9,204 | 9,639 | 9,464 |
| Total Capital | 23,551 | 24,941 | 25,060 | 23,340 | 22,340 | 20,988 | 19,156 | 18,133 | 16,445 | 17,228 |
| Capital Expenditures | 1,947 | 1,742 | 1,607 | 1,419 | 1,307 | 2,004 | 1,906 | 1,945 | 1,868 | 1,879 |
| Cash Flow | 3,480 | 4,123 | 3,852 | 3,480 | 2,656 | 2,043 | 2,723 | 2,988 | 2,904 | 2,431 |
| Current Ratio | 0.8 | 1.2 | 1.4 | 0.8 | 0.8 | 0.7 | 0.8 | 0.7 | 0.5 | 0.5 |
| % Long Term Debt of Capitalization | 31.0 | 33.7 | 35.7 | 35.8 | 41.8 | 46.2 | 44.7 | 43.3 | 34.2 | 35.9 |
| % Net Income of Revenue | 10.3 | 13.3 | 12.7 | 12.0 | 8.8 | 6.4 | 11.0 | 13.9 | 14.7 | 12.5 |
| % Return on Assets | 8.9 | 9.7 | 9.0 | 8.5 | 6.1 | 4.3 | 7.4 | 9.3 | 9.6 | 8.2 |
| % Return on Equity | 15.2 | 18.8 | 17.7 | 17.4 | 13.5 | 10.0 | 17.5 | 21.0 | 20.4 | 16.9 |

Data as orig reptd.; bef. results of disc opers/spec. items. Per share data adj. for stk. divs.; EPS diluted. E-Estimated. NA-Not Available. NM-Not Meaningful. NR-Not Ranked. UR-Under Review.

**Office:** McDonald's Plaza, Oak Brook, IL 60523.
**Telephone:** 630-623-3000.
**Website:** http://www.mcdonalds.com
**Chrmn:** A.J. McKenna

**Pres & COO:** R. Alvarez
**Vice Chrmn & CEO:** J.A. Skinner
**EVP & CFO:** P.J. Bensen
**EVP, Secy & General Counsel:** G. Santona

**Board Members:** R. Alvarez, S. E. Arnold, R. A. Eckert, E. Hernandez, Jr., J. P. Jackson, R. H. Lenny, W. E. Massey, A. J. McKenna, C. D. McMillan, S. A. Penrose, J. W. Rogers, Jr., J. A. Skinner, R. W. Stone

**Founded:** 1948
**Domicile:** Delaware
**Employees:** 390,000

# McGraw-Hill Companies Inc. (The)

**STANDARD &POOR'S**

**S&P Recommendation** `NOT RANKED`

**Price**
$23.36 (as of Nov 14, 2008)

**Investment Style**
Large-Cap Growth

**GICS Sector** Consumer Discretionary
**Sub-Industry** Publishing

**Summary** This leading information services organization serves worldwide markets in education, business, industry, other professions and government.

## Key Stock Statistics (Source S&P, Vickers, company reports)

| | | | | | | | |
|---|---|---|---|---|---|---|---|
| 52-Wk Range | $49.13– 17.15 | S&P Oper. EPS 2008**E** | NA | Market Capitalization(B) | $7.347 | Beta | 1.30 |
| Trailing 12-Month EPS | $2.55 | S&P Oper. EPS 2009**E** | NA | Yield (%) | 3.77 | S&P 3-Yr. Proj. EPS CAGR(%) | |
| Trailing 12-Month P/E | 9.2 | P/E on S&P Oper. EPS 2008**E** | NA | Dividend Rate/Share | $0.88 | S&P Credit Rating | NR |
| $10K Invested 5 Yrs Ago | $7,464 | Common Shares Outstg. (M) | 314.5 | Institutional Ownership (%) | 80 | | |

## Price Performance

30-Week Mov. Avg. ···   10-Week Mov. Avg. ──   GAAP Earnings vs. Previous Year   Volume Above Avg. STARS
12-Mo. Target Price ── Relative Strength ── ▲ Up ▼ Down ► No Change   Below Avg.

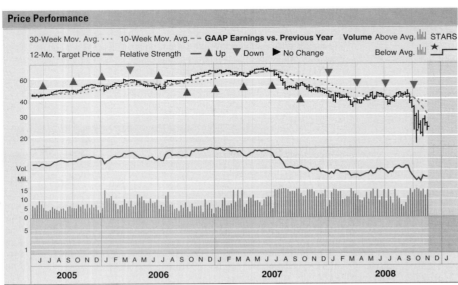

Options: ASE, CBOE, P, Ph

Analysis prepared by **Tom Graves, CFA** on October 31, 2008, when the stock traded at **$ 26.47**.

## Qualitative Risk Assessment

A Qualitative Risk Assessment is not available for this company.

## Quantitative Evaluations

**S&P Quality Ranking**   NR

| D | C | B- | B | B+ | A- | A | A+ |
|---|---|----|---|----|----|---|----|

**Relative Strength Rank**   **MODERATE**

47

LOWEST = 1                                          HIGHEST = 99

## Revenue/Earnings Data

### Revenue (Million $)

| | 1Q | 2Q | 3Q | 4Q | Year |
|---|---|---|---|---|---|
| 2008 | 1,218 | 1,673 | 2,049 | -- | -- |
| 2007 | 1,296 | 1,718 | 2,188 | 1,570 | 6,772 |
| 2006 | 1,141 | 1,528 | 1,993 | 1,594 | 6,255 |
| 2005 | 1,029 | 1,456 | 1,977 | 1,541 | 6,004 |
| 2004 | 919.9 | 1,246 | 1,723 | 1,362 | 5,251 |
| 2003 | 830.8 | 1,172 | 1,603 | 1,222 | 4,828 |

### Earnings Per Share ($)

| | | | | | |
|---|---|---|---|---|---|
| 2008 | 0.25 | 0.66 | 1.23 | -- | -- |
| 2007 | 0.40 | 0.79 | 1.34 | 0.43 | 2.94 |
| 2006 | 0.20 | 0.60 | 1.06 | 0.56 | 2.40 |
| 2005 | 0.21 | 0.51 | 1.00 | 0.50 | 2.21 |
| 2004 | 0.20 | 0.43 | 0.85 | 0.49 | 1.96 |
| 2003 | 0.11 | 0.37 | 0.76 | 0.56 | 1.79 |

Fiscal year ended Dec. 31. Next earnings report expected: Late January. EPS Estimates based on S&P Operating Earnings; historical GAAP earnings are as reported.

## Highlights

► In October 2008, MHP said it expects 2008 revenue from its Financial Services segment to be down 11%-12%, with low visibility in the credit markets. In the first nine months of 2008, transaction revenue from S&P's Credit Market Services business was down 54%. MHP also said it expects Education segment revenue in 2008 to decline 1%-2%, and noted a slowdown in the el-hi market in August and September. In the Information & Media Services segment, MHP expects 2008 revenue to be up 4%-6%.

► MHP expects an operating margin decline in the Financial Services segment of 425 to 475 basis points in 2008, from 44.6% in 2007, and margin contraction in Education of 300 to 350 basis points, from 14.8% in 2007. However, the company anticipates operating margin improvement in Information & Media Services, from 6.2% in 2007.

► In October 2008, MHP forecast 2008 EPS of $2.63-$2.65, excluding restructuring charges, but including associated benefits. In 2008's first nine months, MHP had $47.1 million (pretax) of restructuring charges, which was largely related to the reduction of about 670 positions.

## Investment Rationale/Risk

► For 2008, the company anticipates $270 million of pre-publication investment, down from $299 million in 2007. Purchases of property and equipment are expected to decline to $115 million, from $230 million in 2007, and depreciation and amortization charges are expected to increase to about $452 million, from $401 million in 2007. The company projects overall free cash flow of about $500 million prior to acquisitions or share repurchases. In late October, MHP said that year-to-date purchases of common stock totaled 10.9 million shares for a total cost of $447.2 million.

► MHP noted in its 2007 10-K report filed with the SEC in February 2008 that possible risk factors for the company include the health of capital and equity markets, including future interest rate changes; loss of market share or revenue due to competition or regulation; and the level of educational funding, both domestically and internationally.

► Recent average EPS estimates for MHP by other analysts were $2.63 for 2008 and $2.66 for 2009. Standard & Poor's is a division of MHP, and provides no EPS estimates, target price or recommendation for the company.

## Dividend Data (Dates: mm/dd Payment Date: mm/dd/yy)

| Amount ($) | Date Decl. | Ex-Div. Date | Stk. of Record | Payment Date |
|---|---|---|---|---|
| 0.220 | 01/30 | 02/25 | 02/27 | 03/12/08 |
| 0.220 | 04/30 | 05/23 | 05/28 | 06/11/08 |
| 0.220 | 07/30 | 08/22 | 08/26 | 09/10/08 |
| 0.220 | 10/22 | 11/21 | 11/25 | 12/10/08 |

Dividends have been paid since 1937. Source: Company reports.

# McGraw-Hill Companies Inc. (The)

**STANDARD
&POOR'S**

## Business Summary October 31, 2008

CORPORATE PROFILE. The McGraw-Hill Companies, Inc. is a leading provider of information products and services to business, professional, and education markets worldwide. The company believes that through acquisitions, new product and service development, and a strong commitment to customer service, many of its business units have grown to be leaders in their respective fields. Well known brands include BusinessWeek, Standard & Poor's, Platts, F.W. Dodge, and Sweet's.

The Financial Services segment (45% of revenues and 75% of operating profit) operates under the Standard & Poor's brand and provides credit ratings, evaluation services, and analyses globally on corporations, financial institutions, securitized and project financings, and local, state and sovereign governments. The company believes it is the world's leading provider of credit analysis and information, incorporating the largest global network of credit ratings professionals. In June 2005, MHP acquired majority ownership of Crisil Limited, a leading provider of credit ratings, financial news and risk and policy advisory services in India. In February 2007, the company announced the sale of its mutual fund data business to Morningstar, Inc. In April 2005, the company

acquired Vista Research Inc., a leading provider of primary research. In September 2004, the company acquired privately owned Capital IQ, a leading provider of high-impact information solutions to the global investment and financial services communities.

McGraw-Hill Education (40%, 22%) is comprised of two operating groups -- the School Education Group (SEG) and the Higher Education, Professional and International Group (HPI). SEG provides educational and professional materials in the U.S. to the pre-K to 12th grade market, and is a leading provider of assessment and reporting services. In July 2004, MHP acquired The Grow Network, a privately held company now part of SEG that provides assessment reporting and customized content for states and large school districts across the country.

## Company Financials Fiscal Year Ended Dec. 31

| Per Share Data ($) | 2007 | 2006 | 2005 | 2004 | 2003 | 2002 | 2001 | 2000 | 1999 | 1998 |
|---|---|---|---|---|---|---|---|---|---|---|
| Tangible Book Value | NM | 1.00 | 2.04 | 2.72 | 2.24 | 0.94 | 0.09 | 0.17 | 1.12 | 0.74 |
| Cash Flow | 3.41 | 2.85 | 3.21 | 2.98 | 2.84 | 1.71 | 2.04 | 2.13 | 1.85 | 1.61 |
| Earnings | 2.94 | 2.40 | 2.21 | 1.96 | 1.79 | 1.48 | 0.96 | 1.21 | 1.07 | 0.86 |
| S&P Core Earnings | 2.89 | 2.38 | 2.05 | 1.80 | 1.44 | 1.15 | 0.60 | NA | NA | NA |
| Dividends | 0.82 | 0.73 | 0.66 | 0.60 | 0.54 | 0.51 | 0.49 | 0.47 | 0.43 | 0.39 |
| Payout Ratio | 28% | 30% | 30% | 31% | 30% | 34% | 51% | 39% | 40% | 46% |
| Prices:High | 72.50 | 69.25 | 53.97 | 46.06 | 35.00 | 34.85 | 35.44 | 33.84 | 31.56 | 25.83 |
| Prices:Low | 43.46 | 46.37 | 40.51 | 34.55 | 25.87 | 25.36 | 24.35 | 20.94 | 23.56 | 17.13 |
| P/E Ratio:High | 25 | 29 | 24 | 23 | 20 | 24 | 37 | 28 | 29 | 30 |
| P/E Ratio:Low | 15 | 19 | 18 | 18 | 14 | 17 | 25 | 17 | 22 | 20 |

| Income Statement Analysis (Million $) | | | | | | | | | | |
|---|---|---|---|---|---|---|---|---|---|---|
| Revenue | 6,772 | 6,255 | 6,004 | 5,251 | 4,828 | 4,788 | 4,646 | 4,281 | 3,992 | 3,729 |
| Operating Income | 1,846 | 1,580 | 1,749 | 1,467 | 1,369 | 1,037 | 1,044 | 1,128 | 984 | 851 |
| Depreciation | 161 | 162 | 385 | 393 | 403 | 89.6 | 421 | 362 | 308 | 299 |
| Interest Expense | 40.6 | 13.6 | 5.20 | 5.79 | 7.10 | 22.5 | 55.1 | 52.8 | 42.0 | 48.0 |
| Pretax Income | 1,623 | 1,405 | 1,360 | 1,169 | 1,130 | 905 | 615 | 767 | 698 | 560 |
| Effective Tax Rate | 37.5% | 37.2% | 37.9% | 35.3% | 39.1% | 36.3% | 38.7% | 38.5% | 39.0% | 39.0% |
| Net Income | 1,014 | 882 | 844 | 756 | 688 | 577 | 377 | 472 | 426 | 342 |
| S&P Core Earnings | 995 | 874 | 786 | 694 | 552 | 446 | 233 | NA | NA | NA |

| Balance Sheet & Other Financial Data (Million $) | | | | | | | | | | |
|---|---|---|---|---|---|---|---|---|---|---|
| Cash | 396 | 353 | 749 | 681 | 696 | 58.2 | 53.5 | 3.17 | 6.49 | 10.5 |
| Current Assets | 2,333 | 2,258 | 2,591 | 2,448 | 2,256 | 1,674 | 1,813 | 1,802 | 1,554 | 1,429 |
| Total Assets | 6,357 | 6,043 | 6,396 | 5,863 | 5,394 | 5,032 | 5,161 | 4,931 | 4,089 | 3,788 |
| Current Liabilities | 2,657 | 2,468 | 2,225 | 1,969 | 1,994 | 1,775 | 1,876 | 1,781 | 1,525 | 1,291 |
| Long Term Debt | 1,197 | 0.31 | 0.34 | 0.51 | 0.39 | 459 | 834 | 818 | 355 | 452 |
| Common Equity | 1,607 | 7,785 | 3,113 | 4,952 | 2,557 | 2,202 | 1,884 | 1,761 | 1,691 | 1,565 |
| Total Capital | 2,943 | 7,936 | 3,432 | 5,185 | 2,758 | 2,861 | 2,908 | 2,742 | 2,182 | 2,147 |
| Capital Expenditures | 230 | 127 | 120 | 139 | 115 | 70.0 | 117 | 97.7 | 154 | 179 |
| Cash Flow | 1,175 | 1,044 | 1,230 | 1,149 | 1,091 | 666 | 798 | 834 | 734 | 641 |
| Current Ratio | 0.9 | 0.9 | 1.2 | 1.2 | 1.1 | 0.9 | 1.0 | 1.0 | 1.0 | 1.1 |
| % Long Term Debt of Capitalization | 40.7 | NM | 0.0 | 0.0 | 0.0 | 16.0 | 28.7 | 29.8 | 16.3 | 21.1 |
| % Net Income of Revenue | 15.0 | 14.1 | 14.1 | 14.4 | 14.2 | 12.0 | 8.1 | 11.0 | 10.7 | 9.2 |
| % Return on Assets | 16.3 | 14.2 | 13.8 | 13.5 | 13.2 | 11.3 | 7.5 | 10.4 | 10.8 | 9.1 |
| % Return on Equity | 47.3 | 12.8 | 27.7 | 16.5 | 29.1 | 28.2 | 20.5 | 27.7 | 26.3 | 22.7 |

Data as orig reptd.; bef. results of disc opers/spec. items. Per share data adj. for stk. divs.; EPS diluted. E-Estimated. NA-Not Available. NM-Not Meaningful. NR-Not Ranked. UR-Under Review.

**Office:** 1221 Avenue Of The Americas, New York, NY 10020-1095.
**Telephone:** 212-512-2000.
**Email:** investor_relations@mcgraw-hill.com
**Website:** http://www.mcgraw-hill.com

**Chrmn, Pres & CEO:** H. McGraw, III
**EVP & CFO:** R.J. Bahash
**EVP & General Counsel:** K.M. Vittor
**EVP & CIO:** B.D. Marcus

**SVP & Secy:** S.L. Bennett
**Investor Contact:** D.S. Rubin (212-512-4321)
**Board Members:** P. Aspe Armella, W. W. Bischoff, D. Daft, L. K. Lorimer, R. P. McGraw, H. McGraw, III, H. O. Ochoa-Brillembourg, M. Rake, J. H. Ross, E. B. Rust, Jr., K. L. Schmoke, S. Taurel

**Founded:** 1899
**Domicile:** New York
**Employees:** 21,171

The **McGraw·Hill** Companies

**STANDARD &POOR'S**

# McKesson Corp

| S&P Recommendation | **STRONG BUY** ★★★★★ | Price $35.26 (as of Nov 14, 2008) | 12-Mo. Target Price $62.00 | Investment Style Large-Cap Blend |
|---|---|---|---|---|

**GICS Sector** Health Care
**Sub-Industry** Health Care Distributors

**Summary** This company (formerly McKesson HBOC) provides pharmaceutical supply management and information technologies to a broad range of health care customers.

## Key Stock Statistics (Source S&P, Vickers, company reports)

| | | | | | | | |
|---|---|---|---|---|---|---|---|
| 52-Wk Range | $68.43– 33.11 | S&P Oper. EPS 2009**E** | 4.00 | Market Capitalization(B) | $9.643 | Beta | 0.57 |
| Trailing 12-Month EPS | $3.72 | S&P Oper. EPS 2010**E** | 4.25 | Yield (%) | 1.36 | S&P 3-Yr. Proj. EPS CAGR(%) | 11 |
| Trailing 12-Month P/E | 9.5 | P/E on S&P Oper. EPS 2009**E** | 8.8 | Dividend Rate/Share | $0.48 | S&P Credit Rating | BBB+ |
| $10K Invested 5 Yrs Ago | $12,123 | Common Shares Outstg. (M) | 273.5 | Institutional Ownership (%) | 90 | | |

## Price Performance

30-Week Mov. Avg. ···· 10-Week Mov. Avg. --- GAAP Earnings vs. Previous Year   Volume Above Avg. STARS
12-Mo. Target Price — Relative Strength — ▲ Up ▼ Down ► No Change   Below Avg.

Options: ASE, CBOE, P, Ph

Analysis prepared by **Phillip M. Seligman** on November 11, 2008, when the stock traded at **$ 37.14**.

## Highlights

➤ For FY 09 (Mar.), we look for companywide revenue growth of about 6%. Growth drivers we see include almost 6% higher drug distribution (part of McKesson Distribution Solutions, MDS) revenues on account wins, growing demand from existing accounts, and the October 2007 Oncology Therapeutics Network (OTN) acquisition, partly offset by generic drugs' lower prices than their brand equivalents, and a large account loss. We also forecast 6.5% higher medical-surgical (also part of MDS) sales and 5.5% higher McKesson Technology Solutions (MTS) revenues. The deceleration we see for MTS in FY 09 is due to lapping of the January 2007 Per-Se acquisition, a revenue spike in FY 08's June quarter, and delayed hospital purchase decisions amid the weaker economy.

➤ We expect companywide operating margins to narrow slightly, as generic drug penetration and cost controls are outweighed by internal investments, the impact of several acquisitions, and slower MTS revenue growth. We also see lower interest income due to the lower interest rate environment

➤ We project FY 09 operating EPS of $4.00, versus FY 08's $3.39, and look for $4.25 in FY 10.

## Investment Rationale/Risk

➤ We are encouraged by our view of MCK's resilience in the weaker economy. Its organic direct-store pharmaceutical revenue grew 7% in the September quarter, outpacing the market's 1%-2% as determined by IMS Health for calendar 2008. Looking ahead, we believe margins will benefit from generic sales growth we see impelled by the soft economy. Also, MTS has been benefiting from a recurring stream of maintenance revenues from a large installed base, and from some product sales. Given hospitals' needs to improve efficiency and cut medical errors, we view the slowdown in hospital purchasing decisions as temporary. Meanwhile, we view MCK as financially sound, and like its decision to manage the company and balance sheet more conservatively until financial markets stabilize.

➤ Risks to our recommendation and target price include the loss of major accounts and unfavorable regulatory changes.

➤ Our 12-month target price of $62 is derived by applying an above-peers P/E of 15X to our calendar 2009 EPS estimate of $4.12. The P/E reflects groupwide valuation compression, but is above peers on our view of superior execution.

## Qualitative Risk Assessment

| LOW | MEDIUM | HIGH |
|---|---|---|

Our risk assessment reflects our view of MCK's improving profitability and the growing demand for its highly profitable IT products and services, offset by our belief that the company is more price competitive than peers and that future drugmaker-distributor contract negotiations might be less favorable for distributors.

## Quantitative Evaluations

**S&P Quality Ranking**          B+

| D | C | B- | B | B+ | A- | A | A+ |
|---|---|---|---|---|---|---|---|

**Relative Strength Rank**          MODERATE

47

LOWEST = 1          HIGHEST = 99

## Revenue/Earnings Data

**Revenue (Million $)**

| | 1Q | 2Q | 3Q | 4Q | Year |
|---|---|---|---|---|---|
| 2009 | 26,704 | 26,574 | -- | -- | -- |
| 2008 | 24,528 | 24,450 | 26,494 | 26,231 | 101,703 |
| 2007 | 23,315 | 22,386 | 23,111 | 24,165 | 92,977 |
| 2006 | 20,968 | 21,515 | 22,510 | 23,057 | 88,050 |
| 2005 | 19,187 | 19,934 | 20,782 | 20,612 | 80,515 |
| 2004 | 16,524 | 16,810 | 18,232 | 17,940 | 69,506 |

**Earnings Per Share ($)**

| | 1Q | 2Q | 3Q | 4Q | Year |
|---|---|---|---|---|---|
| 2009 | 0.83 | 1.19 | E0.94 | E1.15 | E4.00 |
| 2008 | 0.77 | 0.83 | 0.68 | 1.05 | 3.32 |
| 2007 | 0.60 | 0.94 | 0.79 | 0.85 | 3.17 |
| 2006 | 0.55 | 0.49 | 0.61 | 0.70 | 2.34 |
| 2005 | 0.55 | 0.29 | -2.26 | 0.85 | -0.53 |
| 2004 | 0.53 | 0.53 | 0.41 | 0.73 | 2.19 |

Fiscal year ended Mar. 31. Next earnings report expected: Early February. EPS Estimates based on S&P Operating Earnings; historical GAAP earnings are as reported.

## Dividend Data (Dates: mm/dd Payment Date: mm/dd/yy)

| Amount ($) | Date Decl. | Ex-Div. Date | Stk. of Record | Payment Date |
|---|---|---|---|---|
| 0.060 | 01/23 | 02/28 | 03/03 | 04/01/08 |
| 0.120 | 05/21 | 06/04 | 06/06 | 07/01/08 |
| 0.120 | 07/23 | 08/28 | 09/02 | 10/01/08 |
| 0.120 | 10/24 | 11/26 | 12/01 | 01/02/09 |

Dividends have been paid since 1995. Source: Company reports.

# McKesson Corp

STANDARD
&POOR'S

## Business Summary November 11, 2008

CORPORATE OVERVIEW. McKesson Corp. is a leading distributor of medical products and supplies and health care information technology products and services. Beginning in FY 08 (Mar.), MCK started reporting its results in two segments:

McKesson Distribution Solutions (MDS; 97.1% of FY 08 revenue on a pro forma basis) includes what was previously reported as Pharmaceutical Solutions and Medical-Surgical Solutions, with the exception of its Payor business. The pharmaceutical distribution unit primarily distributes ethical and proprietary drugs and health and beauty care, and focuses on three customer segments: retail independent pharmacies, retail chains, and institutions, in all 50 states and Canada. The medical-surgical distribution unit provides medical-surgical supplies, equipment, logistics and related services to alternate-site health care providers, including physicians' offices, long-term care and home care. Through its investment in Parata Systems, MDS also markets automated pharmacy systems to hospitals and retail pharmacies.

McKesson Technology Solutions (MTS; 2.9%) consists primarily of the former

Provider Technologies segment and the aforementioned Payor business. MTS delivers enterprise-wide patient care, clinical, financial, supply chain, and strategic management software solutions, pharmacy automation for hospitals, as well as connectivity, outsourcing and other services, to health care organizations throughout North America, the United Kingdom and other European countries. Its customers include hospitals, physicians, home care providers, retail pharmacies and payors.

CORPORATE STRATEGY. Distribution agreements between distributors and most drugmakers have transitioned toward a more fee-based approach, with the distributors appropriately and predictably compensated for distribution and related logistic and administrative services and data, in our opinion. MCK and its peers see over 80% of their drugmaker compensation as fixed and not dependent upon drug price inflation.

## Company Financials Fiscal Year Ended Mar. 31

| Per Share Data ($) | 2008 | 2007 | 2006 | 2005 | 2004 | 2003 | 2002 | 2001 | 2000 | 1999 |
|---|---|---|---|---|---|---|---|---|---|---|
| Tangible Book Value | 10.42 | 9.10 | 13.36 | 12.47 | 12.66 | 10.57 | 9.81 | 8.55 | 8.40 | 5.89 |
| Cash Flow | 4.09 | 4.14 | 3.28 | 0.32 | 2.94 | 2.65 | 2.20 | 0.72 | 1.37 | 0.98 |
| Earnings | 3.32 | 3.17 | 2.34 | -0.53 | 2.19 | 1.90 | 1.43 | -0.15 | 0.66 | 0.31 |
| S&P Core Earnings | 3.33 | 3.16 | 2.07 | 1.93 | 1.29 | 1.24 | 0.87 | -0.39 | NA | NA |
| Dividends | 0.24 | 0.24 | 0.24 | 0.24 | 0.24 | 0.24 | 0.24 | 0.24 | 0.31 | 0.50 |
| Payout Ratio | 7% | 8% | 10% | NM | 11% | 13% | 17% | NM | 46% | 161% |
| Calendar Year | 2007 | 2006 | 2005 | 2004 | 2003 | 2002 | 2001 | 2000 | 1999 | 1998 |
| Prices:High | 68.43 | 55.10 | 52.89 | 35.90 | 37.14 | 42.09 | 41.50 | 37.00 | 89.75 | 96.25 |
| Prices:Low | 50.80 | 44.60 | 30.13 | 22.61 | 22.61 | 24.99 | 23.40 | 16.00 | 18.56 | 47.88 |
| P/E Ratio:High | 21 | 17 | 23 | NM | 17 | 22 | 29 | NM | NM | NM |
| P/E Ratio:Low | 15 | 14 | 13 | NM | 10 | 13 | 16 | NM | NM | NM |

| Income Statement Analysis (Million $) | | | | | | | | | | |
|---|---|---|---|---|---|---|---|---|---|---|
| Revenue | 101,703 | 92,977 | 88,050 | 80,515 | 69,506 | 57,121 | 50,006 | 42,010 | 36,734 | 30,382 |
| Operating Income | 1,736 | 1,553 | 1,425 | 1,260 | 1,216 | 1,134 | 923 | 454 | 359 | 531 |
| Depreciation | 231 | 295 | 266 | 251 | 232 | 204 | 208 | 246 | 201 | 199 |
| Interest Expense | 142 | 99.0 | 94.0 | 118 | 120 | 121 | 119 | 118 | 120 | 124 |
| Pretax Income | 1,457 | 1,297 | 1,158 | -240 | 911 | 855 | 601 | 9.60 | 307 | 202 |
| Effective Tax Rate | 32.1% | 25.4% | 36.4% | NM | 29.1% | 34.3% | 30.4% | NM | 39.7% | 57.9% |
| Net Income | 989 | 968 | 737 | -157 | 646 | 562 | 419 | -42.7 | 185 | 85.0 |
| S&P Core Earnings | 991 | 964 | 650 | 565 | 380 | 364 | 255 | -113 | NA | NA |

| Balance Sheet & Other Financial Data (Million $) | | | | | | | | | | |
|---|---|---|---|---|---|---|---|---|---|---|
| Cash | 1,362 | 1,954 | 2,142 | 1,809 | 718 | 534 | 563 | 446 | 606 | 269 |
| Current Assets | 17,786 | 17,856 | 16,919 | 15,332 | 13,004 | 11,254 | 10,699 | 9,164 | 7,966 | 6,500 |
| Total Assets | 24,603 | 23,943 | 20,975 | 18,775 | 16,240 | 14,353 | 13,324 | 11,530 | 10,373 | 9,082 |
| Current Liabilities | 15,348 | 15,126 | 13,515 | 11,793 | 9,456 | 7,974 | 7,588 | 6,550 | 5,122 | 4,800 |
| Long Term Debt | 1,795 | 1,803 | 965 | 1,202 | 1,210 | 1,487 | 1,485 | 1,232 | 1,440 | 1,142 |
| Common Equity | 6,121 | 6,273 | 5,907 | 5,275 | 5,165 | 4,529 | 3,940 | 3,493 | 4,213 | 2,882 |
| Total Capital | 7,916 | 8,076 | 6,872 | 6,477 | 6,375 | 6,016 | 5,425 | 4,724 | 5,653 | 4,024 |
| Capital Expenditures | 195 | 126 | 167 | 140 | 115 | 116 | 132 | 159 | 145 | 251 |
| Cash Flow | 1,220 | 1,263 | 1,003 | 94.2 | 879 | 766 | 626 | 203 | 386 | 284 |
| Current Ratio | 1.2 | 1.2 | 1.3 | 1.3 | 1.4 | 1.4 | 1.4 | 1.4 | 1.6 | 1.4 |
| % Long Term Debt of Capitalization | 22.7 | 22.3 | 14.0 | 18.6 | 19.0 | 24.7 | 27.4 | 26.1 | 25.5 | 28.4 |
| % Net Income of Revenue | 1.0 | 1.0 | 0.8 | NM | 0.9 | 1.0 | 0.8 | NM | 0.5 | 0.3 |
| % Return on Assets | 4.1 | 4.3 | 3.7 | NM | 4.2 | 4.1 | 3.4 | NM | 1.9 | 1.2 |
| % Return on Equity | 16.0 | 15.9 | 13.2 | NM | 13.3 | 13.3 | 11.3 | NM | 4.8 | 3.9 |

Data as orig reptd.; bef. results of disc opers/spec. items. Per share data adj. for stk. divs.; EPS diluted. E-Estimated. NA-Not Available. NM-Not Meaningful. NR-Not Ranked. UR-Under Review.

**Office:** One Post St McKesson Plaza, San Francisco, CA 94104-5296.
**Telephone:** 415-983-8300.
**Email:** investors@mckesson.com
**Website:** http://www.mckesson.com

**Chrmn, Pres & CEO:** J. Hammergren
**EVP & CFO:** J. Campbell
**EVP, Secy & General Counsel:** L.E. Seeger
**EVP & CIO:** R.N. Spratt

**Chief Acctg Officer & Cntlr:** N.A. Rees
**Investor Contact:** J.C. Campbell (800-826-9360)
**Board Members:** A. Bryant, W. A. Budd, J. Hammergren, A. F. Irby, III, M. C. Jacobs, M. L. Knowles, D. M. Lawrence, E. A. Mueller, J. V. Napier, J. E. Shaw

**Founded:** 1994
**Domicile:** Delaware
**Employees:** 32,900

# MeadWestvaco Corp

STANDARD
&POOR'S

| S&P Recommendation | HOLD ★★★☆☆ | Price $12.23 (as of Nov 14, 2008) | 12-Mo. Target Price $15.00 | Investment Style Large-Cap Value |
|---|---|---|---|---|

**GICS Sector** Materials
**Sub-Industry** Paper Products

**Summary** This company is primarily a major producer of paperboard packaging used in a variety of consumer markets.

## Key Stock Statistics (Source S&P, Vickers, company reports)

| | | | | | | | | |
|---|---|---|---|---|---|---|---|---|
| 52-Wk Range | $34.61–11.19 | S&P Oper. EPS 2008**E** | 0.80 | Market Capitalization(B) | $2.089 | Beta | 1.13 |
| Trailing 12-Month EPS | $1.45 | S&P Oper. EPS 2009**E** | 0.80 | Yield (%) | 7.52 | S&P 3-Yr. Proj. EPS CAGR(%) | 2 |
| Trailing 12-Month P/E | 8.4 | P/E on S&P Oper. EPS 2008**E** | 15.3 | Dividend Rate/Share | $0.92 | S&P Credit Rating | BBB |
| $10K Invested 5 Yrs Ago | $5,551 | Common Shares Outstg. (M) | 170.8 | Institutional Ownership (%) | 88 | | |

## Price Performance

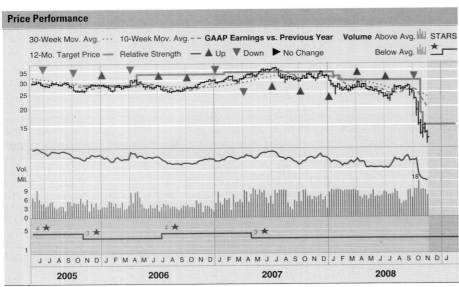

30-Week Mov. Avg. · · · 10-Week Mov. Avg. ─ ─ **GAAP Earnings vs. Previous Year** Volume Above Avg. ⅲⅲ STARS
12-Mo. Target Price ── Relative Strength ── ▲ Up ▼ Down ▶ No Change Below Avg. ⅲⅲ ★

Options: ASE, CBOE, P

Analysis prepared by **Stuart J. Benway, CFA** on November 13, 2008, when the stock traded at **$ 11.63**.

## Highlights

➤ We expect sales to fall 1%-3% in 2008 largely due to the divestiture of a kraft paper mill, partly offset by the addition of a modest acquisition and higher average prices across most of MWV's businesses. We expect growth in the personal care, beverage, and health care categories, especially overseas, but demand in the media and office products sector is likely to continue to be weak. We see a modest revenue decline in 2009.

➤ We anticipate lower margins in 2008. We expect a positive impact from higher prices, improved manufacturing efficiencies from the shutdown of high-cost capacity, and the anticipated benefits of other cost-cutting initiatives. We see these factors being more than offset by higher costs for manufacturing inputs as well as underutilized capacity. Lower energy costs should help margins modestly in 2009.

➤ Our operating EPS forecast for 2008 is $0.80, down 27% from operating EPS of $1.09 in 2007, and for 2009 we also project EPS of $0.80. These estimates include only modest land sales gains, which could be significant in certain quarters.

## Investment Rationale/Risk

➤ We believe that volume trends in the packaging sector will remain subdued in the near term due to reduced compact disc sales, an increased emphasis on packaging reduction, and a sluggish economy. However, we think that MWV is well positioned over the long term due to its high market share in mostly non-commodity markets and its geographic diversification into higher-growth regions.

➤ Risks to our recommendation and target price include a weaker-than-expected global economy, softer-than-projected demand and pricing trends for the company's packaging grades, a renewed rise in energy and raw material costs, and poor execution of MWV's planned cost-cutting initiatives.

➤ MeadWestvaco's peer group trades at 8.5X our 2009 EPS estimates. Applying this valuation to our 2009 EPS estimate, we derive a value of $7 for the shares. Our DCF model values the shares at $20, assuming a weighted average cost of capital of 8.4%, significant land sales, and growth in perpetuity of 2.5%. Our 12-month target price of $15 is a weighted blend of these two measures.

## Qualitative Risk Assessment

| LOW | MEDIUM | HIGH |
|---|---|---|

MWV operates in a moderately cyclical and seasonal sector and is subject to swings in certain commodity prices. However, it has some pricing power due to its high market share, and its debt levels are low relative to many of its peers.

## Quantitative Evaluations

**S&P Quality Ranking** B-

| D | C | B- | B | B+ | A- | A | A+ |
|---|---|---|---|---|---|---|---|

**Relative Strength Rank** WEAK

27

LOWEST = 1    HIGHEST = 99

## Revenue/Earnings Data

**Revenue (Million $)**

| | 1Q | 2Q | 3Q | 4Q | Year |
|---|---|---|---|---|---|
| 2008 | 1,518 | 1,709 | 1,811 | -- | -- |
| 2007 | 1,552 | 1,706 | 1,796 | 1,852 | 6,906 |
| 2006 | 1,434 | 1,570 | 1,751 | 1,775 | 6,530 |
| 2005 | 1,373 | 1,587 | 1,583 | 1,627 | 6,170 |
| 2004 | 1,833 | 2,095 | 2,148 | 2,151 | 8,227 |
| 2003 | 1,694 | 1,915 | 1,999 | 1,945 | 7,553 |

**Earnings Per Share ($)**

| | 1Q | 2Q | 3Q | 4Q | Year |
|---|---|---|---|---|---|
| 2008 | -0.05 | 0.33 | 0.26 | E0.27 | E0.80 |
| 2007 | -0.09 | 0.17 | 0.66 | 0.82 | 1.55 |
| 2006 | 0.02 | -0.04 | 0.31 | 0.23 | 0.52 |
| 2005 | 0.08 | -0.06 | 0.30 | 0.33 | 0.62 |
| 2004 | -0.01 | 0.24 | 0.52 | -2.45 | -1.73 |
| 2003 | -0.36 | -0.04 | 0.14 | 0.25 | -0.01 |

Fiscal year ended Dec. 31. Next earnings report expected: Early February. EPS Estimates based on S&P Operating Earnings; historical GAAP earnings are as reported.

## Dividend Data (Dates: mm/dd Payment Date: mm/dd/yy)

| Amount ($) | Date Decl. | Ex-Div. Date | Stk. of Record | Payment Date |
|---|---|---|---|---|
| 0.230 | 01/23 | 07/30 | 08/01 | 09/02/08 |

Dividends have been paid since 1892. Source: Company reports.

---

# MeadWestvaco Corp

**STANDARD &POOR'S**

## Business Summary November 13, 2008

CORPORATE OVERVIEW. Through a series of mergers and divestitures, Mead-Westvaco has molded itself into one of the largest producers of packaging products in the world, and it is also a major supplier of consumer and office products and specialty chemicals. The Packaging Resources segment (41% of 2007 revenues) produces bleached paperboard, coated paperboard, kraft paperboard, linerboard and saturating kraft, and packaging for consumer products including beverage and dairy, cosmetics, tobacco, pharmaceuticals, and health care products. Some of the company's major customers include Altria, Anheuser-Busch, Coca-Cola and Procter & Gamble. The Consumer Solutions segment (33%) sells a full range of consumer packaging products, including printed plastic packaging and injection-molded products used for packaging DVDs, CDs, cosmetics, and pharmaceuticals, and plastic dispensing and spraying systems for worldwide personal care, health care, fragrance, and lawn and garden markets. The Consumer and Office Products segment (16%) makes, markets and distributes school and office products, time management products, and envelopes. The Specialty Chemicals segment (7%) produces, markets and distributes specialty chemicals derived from sawdust and other by-products of the pulp and papermaking process. These chemicals include activated carbon, printing ink resins, emulsifiers used in asphalt paving, and

dyestuffs. Corporate and other accounted for 3% of sales in 2007. The company also owns about 900,000 acres of forest lands in the U.S.

MARKET PROFILE. MeadWestvaco is the largest producer of paperboard, also known as folding boxboard or cartonboard, in North America, with a share of about 16%, according to Pulp & Paper magazine. The market is somewhat fragmented, with more than 15 companies accounting for at least a 1% share, although the top three producers control 36% of the industry. Unlike containerboard, paperboard has a bendable quality for creasing, scoring and shaping, and usually packages single items meant for consumer purchase. It is used in a variety of consumer applications where print quality, strength and customer appeal are important. Folding carton demand is primarily driven by consumer spending and industrial production. We believe the company's market position, technical expertise and product line diversity give it a moderate level of control over pricing.

## Company Financials Fiscal Year Ended Dec. 31

### Per Share Data ($)

| | 2007 | 2006 | 2005 | 2004 | 2003 | 2002 | 2001 | 2000 | 1999 | 1998 |
|---|---|---|---|---|---|---|---|---|---|---|
| Tangible Book Value | 13.52 | 14.74 | 14.58 | 18.44 | 19.89 | 20.44 | 17.34 | 23.17 | 21.65 | 22.39 |
| Cash Flow | 4.13 | 3.37 | 3.17 | 1.87 | 3.60 | 3.49 | 4.29 | 5.63 | 3.90 | 4.06 |
| Earnings | 1.56 | 0.52 | 0.62 | -1.73 | -0.01 | -0.01 | 0.87 | 2.53 | 1.11 | 1.30 |
| S&P Core Earnings | 0.21 | -0.11 | 0.27 | -2.67 | -0.81 | -1.37 | -1.04 | NA | NA | NA |
| Dividends | Nil | 0.92 | 0.92 | 0.92 | 0.92 | 0.92 | 0.88 | 0.88 | 0.88 | 0.88 |
| Payout Ratio | Nil | 177% | 148% | NM | NM | NM | 101% | 35% | 79% | 68% |
| Prices:High | 36.50 | 30.85 | 34.33 | 34.34 | 29.83 | 36.50 | 32.10 | 34.75 | 33.50 | 34.13 |
| Prices:Low | 28.39 | 24.76 | 25.06 | 25.16 | 21.37 | 15.57 | 22.68 | 24.06 | 20.81 | 21.00 |
| P/E Ratio:High | 23 | 59 | 55 | NM | NM | NM | 37 | 14 | 30 | 26 |
| P/E Ratio:Low | 18 | 48 | 40 | NM | NM | NM | 26 | 10 | 19 | 16 |

### Income Statement Analysis (Million $)

| | 2007 | 2006 | 2005 | 2004 | 2003 | 2002 | 2001 | 2000 | 1999 | 1998 |
|---|---|---|---|---|---|---|---|---|---|---|
| Revenue | 6,906 | 6,530 | 6,170 | 8,227 | 7,553 | 7,242 | 3,935 | 3,663 | 2,802 | 2,886 |
| Operating Income | 893 | 743 | 818 | 1,042 | 855 | 859 | 677 | 869 | 601 | 577 |
| Depreciation | 473 | 517 | 491 | 726 | 724 | 674 | 347 | 314 | 280 | 281 |
| Interest Expense | 219 | 211 | 208 | 278 | 291 | 309 | 208 | 192 | 124 | 110 |
| Pretax Income | 400 | 98.0 | 135 | -454 | -29.0 | -15.0 | 119 | 404 | 148 | 204 |
| Effective Tax Rate | 28.8% | 5.10% | 11.9% | NM | NM | NM | 25.6% | 36.9% | 24.9% | 35.4% |
| Net Income | 285 | 93.0 | 119 | -349 | -2.00 | -3.00 | 88.2 | 255 | 111 | 132 |
| S&P Core Earnings | 36.7 | -22.1 | 50.6 | -539 | -164 | -264 | -104 | NA | NA | NA |

### Balance Sheet & Other Financial Data (Million $)

| | 2007 | 2006 | 2005 | 2004 | 2003 | 2002 | 2001 | 2000 | 1999 | 1998 |
|---|---|---|---|---|---|---|---|---|---|---|
| Cash | 245 | 156 | 297 | 270 | 225 | 372 | 81.2 | 255 | 109 | 105 |
| Current Assets | 2,167 | 2,015 | 2,030 | 2,562 | 2,426 | 2,431 | 1,016 | 1,064 | 738 | 739 |
| Total Assets | 9,837 | 9,285 | 8,908 | 11,681 | 12,487 | 12,921 | 6,787 | 6,570 | 4,897 | 5,009 |
| Current Liabilities | 1,455 | 1,465 | 1,042 | 1,751 | 1,501 | 1,620 | 701 | 567 | 425 | 467 |
| Long Term Debt | 2,375 | 2,372 | 2,417 | 3,427 | 3,969 | 4,233 | 2,660 | 2,687 | 1,502 | 1,526 |
| Common Equity | 3,708 | 3,533 | 3,483 | 4,317 | 4,768 | 4,831 | 2,341 | 2,333 | 2,171 | 2,246 |
| Total Capital | 7,311 | 7,082 | 7,052 | 9,249 | 10,415 | 10,821 | 6,009 | 5,927 | 4,472 | 4,541 |
| Capital Expenditures | 347 | 302 | 305 | 407 | 393 | 377 | 290 | 214 | 229 | 423 |
| Cash Flow | 758 | 610 | 610 | 377 | 722 | 671 | 436 | 569 | 392 | 413 |
| Current Ratio | 1.5 | 1.4 | 1.9 | 1.5 | 1.6 | 1.5 | 1.4 | 1.9 | 1.7 | 1.6 |
| % Long Term Debt of Capitalization | 32.5 | 33.5 | 34.3 | 37.1 | 38.1 | 39.1 | 44.3 | 45.3 | 33.6 | 33.6 |
| % Net Income of Revenue | 4.1 | 1.4 | 1.9 | NM | NM | NM | 2.2 | 7.0 | 4.0 | 4.6 |
| % Return on Assets | 3.0 | 1.0 | 1.2 | NM | NM | NM | 1.3 | 4.4 | 2.2 | 2.7 |
| % Return on Equity | 7.9 | 2.7 | 3.1 | NM | NM | NM | 3.8 | 11.3 | 5.0 | 5.8 |

Data as orig reptd.; bef. results of disc opers/spec. items. Per share data adj. for stk. divs.; EPS diluted. E-Estimated. NA-Not Available. NM-Not Meaningful. NR-Not Ranked. UR-Under Review.

**Office:** 11013 West Broad St, Glen Allen, VA 23060-5937.
**Telephone:** 804-327-5200.
**Website:** http://www.meadwestvaco.com
**Chrmn & CEO:** J.A. Luke, Jr.

**Pres:** J.A. Buzzard
**SVP & CFO:** E.M. Rajkowski
**SVP & CTO:** M.T. Watkins
**SVP, Secy & General Counsel:** W.L. Willkie, II

**Investor Contact:** E.M. Rajkowski (804-327-5200)
**Board Members:** M. E. Campbell, T. W. Cole, Jr., J. G. Kaiser, R. B. Kelson, J. M. Kilts, S. J. Kropf, D. S. Luke, J. A. Luke, Jr., R. C. McCormack, T. H. Powers, E. M. Straw, J. L. Warner

**Founded:** 1846
**Domicile:** Delaware
**Employees:** 24,000

# Medco Health Solutions Inc.

STANDARD &POOR'S

| S&P Recommendation BUY ★★★★☆ | Price $39.93 (as of Nov 14, 2008) | 12-Mo. Target Price $49.00 | Investment Style Large-Cap Blend |
|---|---|---|---|

**GICS Sector** Health Care
**Sub-Industry** Health Care Services

**Summary** Medco, spun off from Merck & Co. in August 2003, is the largest U.S. pharmacy benefit manager (PBM) in terms of revenues and script count.

## Key Stock Statistics (Source S&P, Vickers, company reports)

| | | | | | | | |
|---|---|---|---|---|---|---|---|
| 52-Wk Range | $54.63– 29.80 | S&P Oper. EPS 2008**E** | 2.33 | Market Capitalization(B) | $19.886 | Beta | 0.53 |
| Trailing 12-Month EPS | $1.96 | S&P Oper. EPS 2009**E** | 2.77 | Yield (%) | Nil | S&P 3-Yr. Proj. EPS CAGR(%) | 21 |
| Trailing 12-Month P/E | 20.4 | P/E on S&P Oper. EPS 2008**E** | 17.1 | Dividend Rate/Share | Nil | S&P Credit Rating | BBB |
| $10K Invested 5 Yrs Ago | $22,061 | Common Shares Outstg. (M) | 498.0 | Institutional Ownership (%) | 79 | | |

## Price Performance

30-Week Mov. Avg. · · · · 10-Week Mov. Avg. — GAAP Earnings vs. Previous Year   Volume Above Avg. STARS
12-Mo. Target Price — Relative Strength — ▲ Up ▼ Down ▶ No Change   Below Avg.

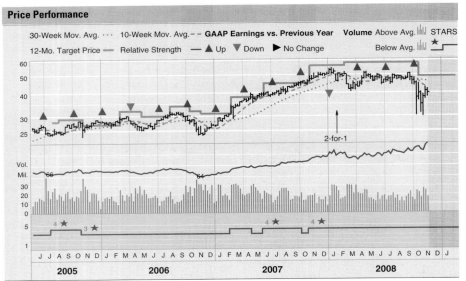

Options: ASE, CBOE, P, Ph

Analysis prepared by **Phillip M. Seligman** on November 12, 2008, when the stock traded at **$ 38.49**.

### Qualitative Risk Assessment

| LOW | MEDIUM | HIGH |
|---|---|---|

Our risk assessment reflects rising drug demand and our view of MHS's improving financial performance and declining debt leverage. However, we believe that intense competition and increased government regulation of pharmacy benefit managers, which we view as likely, could slow long-term progress in profits.

### Quantitative Evaluations

**S&P Quality Ranking** NR

| D | C | B- | B | B+ | A- | A | A+ |
|---|---|---|---|---|---|---|---|

**Relative Strength Rank** STRONG

82

LOWEST = 1   HIGHEST = 99

### Revenue/Earnings Data

**Revenue (Million $)**

| | 1Q | 2Q | 3Q | 4Q | Year |
|---|---|---|---|---|---|
| 2008 | 12,963 | 12,775 | 12,559 | -- | -- |
| 2007 | 11,160 | 11,050 | 10,919 | 11,379 | 44,506 |
| 2006 | 10,564 | 10,589 | 10,461 | 10,930 | 42,544 |
| 2005 | 8,743 | 8,999 | 9,325 | 10,803 | 37,871 |
| 2004 | 8,906 | 8,836 | 8,697 | 8,913 | 35,352 |
| 2003 | 8,334 | 8,405 | 8,524 | 9,002 | 34,265 |

**Earnings Per Share ($)**

| | 1Q | 2Q | 3Q | 4Q | Year |
|---|---|---|---|---|---|
| 2008 | 0.50 | 0.51 | 0.58 | E0.59 | E2.33 |
| 2007 | 0.47 | 0.38 | 0.39 | 0.38 | 1.63 |
| 2006 | 0.08 | 0.28 | 0.31 | 0.39 | 1.05 |
| 2005 | 0.24 | 0.24 | 0.26 | 0.29 | 1.03 |
| 2004 | 0.19 | 0.23 | 0.22 | 0.24 | 0.88 |
| 2003 | 0.19 | 0.20 | 0.19 | 0.22 | 0.79 |

Fiscal year ended Dec. 31. Next earnings report expected: Mid February. EPS Estimates based on S&P Operating Earnings; historical GAAP earnings are as reported.

### Dividend Data (Dates: mm/dd Payment Date: mm/dd/yy)

| Amount ($) | Date Decl. | Ex-Div. Date | Stk. of Record | Payment Date |
|---|---|---|---|---|
| 2-for-1 | 11/29 | 01/25 | 01/10 | 01/24/08 |

Source: Company reports.

## Highlights

➤ We expect revenues to rise 8% in 2009, to $55.3 billion, from the $51.2 billion we see in 2008. Drivers we see include net new business of $4.9 billion so far for 2009 and the full-year benefit of 2008's new business, with growth tempered by the weak economy and the penetration of generic drugs, which carry lower prices but wider margins than branded drugs. Top-line growth should be below the 15% we see in 2008, which benefited from the acquisition of PolyMedica, a provider of diabetes testing supplies and drugs, and the launches of generic Fosamax (for osteoporosis) and Protonix (for acid reflux).

➤ We believe EBITDA per adjusted script, a measure of PBM profitability, will expand more slowly than the 14%-15% growth we see in 2008, since 2009 account wins have lower mail penetration rates and MHS lost accounts with higher mail order volumes. We expect most of the gain to come from SG&A cost control.

➤ We look for operating EPS before amortization charges of $2.33 in 2008, versus 2007's $1.82, and $2.77 in 2009. MHS expects $0.11 from generic drug launches slated for 2009, less than contributions from 2008 launches.

## Investment Rationale/Risk

➤ We continue to view long-term fundamentals in the PBM space as bright, as health plans, governments and employers seek to control drug costs. MHS's third-quarter revenue growth was healthy, in our view. Interestingly, MHS sees PBMs poised to benefit under President-elect Obama, assuming he tries to solve the uninsured problem, and supports e-prescribing and a biogenerics pathway. Also, MHS does not see its business being affected should the federal government negotiate directly with drugmakers on Medicare Part D drug pricing. Meanwhile, we are encouraged that MHS has not seen a deterioration in its accounts receivable as of September 30, despite some clients' financial difficulties. We view MHS's cash flow as healthy, providing financial flexibility.

➤ Risks to our recommendation and target price include intensifying competition and more regulatory oversight.

➤ Our 12-month target price of $49 is derived by applying a P/E-to-growth ratio of 1.0X, assuming three-year EPS growth of 21%, to our 2009 operating EPS estimate. The PEG ratio reflects groupwide valuation compression and the historical discount to peers.

# Medco Health Solutions Inc.

**STANDARD**
**&POOR'S**

## Business Summary November 12, 2008

CORPORATE OVERVIEW. Medco Health Solutions was spun off to Merck & Co. (MRK) shareholders in a tax-free transaction on August 19, 2003. The company is one of the largest U.S. pharmacy benefit managers (PBMs). It provides programs and services to clients and members of PBMs, and to physicians and pharmacies that they use.

In 2007, MHS processed about 560 million prescriptions, compared to 553 million in 2006. Revenues and net income are derived from: rebates and discounts on prescription drugs from pharmaceutical manufacturers; competitive discounts from retail pharmacies; the negotiation of favorable client pricing, including rebate sharing terms; the shift in dispensing volumes from retail to home delivery; and the provision of services in a cost-efficient manner.

We believe that MHS is facing some risks, including pending lawsuits by plaintiffs alleging that MHS breached fiduciary obligations under the Employee Retirement Income Security Act (ERISA).

Gross rebates recorded as received from MRK totaled $301.1 million through the separation date of August 19, 2003, $443.9 million in 2002, and $439.4 million in 2001. According to MHS, effective as of the end of March 2006, the agreement entered into with MRK in July 2002 was terminated. Under that agreement, MRK provided MHS with rebates based, in part, on whether MRK products were included in formularies that MHS offers clients, and on whether MRK products achieve specified market share targets under MHS's plans. If MHS had failed to achieve the targets, it may have had to pay damages. That agreement was replaced with one that is similar to other rebate agreements that MHS has with other major drugmakers.

## Company Financials Fiscal Year Ended Dec. 31

### Per Share Data ($)

| | 2007 | 2006 | 2005 | 2004 | 2003 | 2002 | 2001 | 2000 | 1999 | 1998 |
|---|---|---|---|---|---|---|---|---|---|---|
| Tangible Book Value | NM | NM | NM | 0.49 | NM | NM | 0.85 | 0.66 | NA | NA |
| Cash Flow | 2.33 | 1.69 | 1.63 | 1.56 | 1.31 | 1.07 | 1.08 | 0.94 | NA | NA |
| Earnings | 1.63 | 1.05 | 1.03 | 0.88 | 0.79 | 0.59 | 0.48 | 0.40 | NA | NA |
| S&P Core Earnings | 1.62 | 1.21 | 0.93 | 0.74 | 0.52 | 0.54 | 0.36 | NA | NA | NA |
| Dividends | Nil | Nil | Nil | Nil | Nil | NA | NA | NA | NA | NA |
| Payout Ratio | Nil | Nil | Nil | Nil | Nil | NA | NA | NA | NA | NA |
| Prices:High | 51.67 | 32.06 | 28.98 | 20.95 | 19.00 | NA | NA | NA | NA | NA |
| Prices:Low | 26.26 | 23.54 | 20.28 | 14.70 | 10.10 | NA | NA | NA | NA | NA |
| P/E Ratio:High | 32 | 31 | 28 | 24 | 24 | NA | NA | NA | NA | NA |
| P/E Ratio:Low | 16 | 22 | 20 | 17 | 13 | NA | NA | NA | NA | NA |

### Income Statement Analysis (Million $)

| | 2007 | 2006 | 2005 | 2004 | 2003 | 2002 | 2001 | 2000 | 1999 | 1998 |
|---|---|---|---|---|---|---|---|---|---|---|
| Revenue | 44,506 | 42,544 | 37,871 | 35,352 | 34,265 | 32,959 | 29,071 | 22,266 | NA | NA |
| Operating Income | 2,000 | 1,470 | 1,350 | 1,244 | 1,025 | 886 | 837 | 731 | NA | NA |
| Depreciation | 397 | 392 | 358 | 378 | 283 | 257 | 323 | 289 | NA | NA |
| Interest Expense | 134 | 65.9 | 73.9 | Nil | Nil | 73.5 | Nil | Nil | NA | NA |
| Pretax Income | 1,503 | 1,012 | 953 | 806 | 729 | 547 | 518 | 448 | NA | NA |
| Effective Tax Rate | 39.3% | 37.7% | 36.8% | 40.3% | 41.6% | 41.7% | 50.5% | 51.6% | NA | NA |
| Net Income | 912 | 630 | 602 | 482 | 426 | 319 | 257 | 217 | NA | NA |
| S&P Core Earnings | 908 | 726 | 544 | 404 | 279 | 287 | 188 | NA | NA | NA |

### Balance Sheet & Other Financial Data (Million $)

| | 2007 | 2006 | 2005 | 2004 | 2003 | 2002 | 2001 | 2000 | 1999 | 1998 |
|---|---|---|---|---|---|---|---|---|---|---|
| Cash | 844 | 818 | 888 | 1,146 | 638 | 203 | 16.3 | NA | NA | NA |
| Current Assets | 6,303 | 5,855 | 5,061 | 4,320 | 3,760 | 3,044 | 2,534 | NA | NA | NA |
| Total Assets | 16,218 | 14,388 | 13,703 | 10,542 | 10,263 | 9,714 | 9,252 | 8,915 | NA | NA |
| Current Liabilities | 5,129 | 4,827 | 3,761 | 2,645 | 2,605 | 2,370 | 1,809 | NA | NA | NA |
| Long Term Debt | 2,894 | 866 | 944 | 1,093 | 1,346 | 1,385 | Nil | Nil | NA | NA |
| Common Equity | 6,875 | 7,504 | 7,724 | 5,719 | 5,080 | 4,738 | 6,268 | 6,358 | NA | NA |
| Total Capital | 10,937 | 9,531 | 9,882 | 6,812 | 7,604 | 7,305 | 7,423 | 7,502 | NA | NA |
| Capital Expenditures | 178 | 151 | 132 | 98.1 | 125 | 235 | 322 | 251 | NA | NA |
| Cash Flow | 1,309 | 1,022 | 960 | 859 | 709 | 576 | 580 | 506 | NA | NA |
| Current Ratio | 1.2 | 1.2 | 1.3 | 1.6 | 1.4 | 1.3 | 1.4 | NA | NA | NA |
| % Long Term Debt of Capitalization | 26.5 | 9.1 | 9.6 | 16.0 | 17.7 | 19.0 | Nil | Nil | NA | NA |
| % Net Income of Revenue | 2.1 | 1.5 | 1.6 | 1.4 | 1.2 | 1.0 | 0.9 | 1.0 | NA | NA |
| % Return on Assets | 6.0 | 4.4 | 5.0 | 4.6 | 4.2 | NA | 2.8 | NA | NA | NA |
| % Return on Equity | 12.7 | 8.3 | 9.0 | 8.9 | 7.3 | NA | 4.1 | NA | NA | NA |

Data as orig reptd.; bef. results of disc opers/spec. items. Per share data adj. for stk. divs.; EPS diluted. E-Estimated. NA-Not Available. NM-Not Meaningful. NR-Not Ranked. UR-Under Review.

**Office:** 100 Parsons Pond Drive, Franklin Lakes, NJ 07417-2603.
**Telephone:** 201-269-3400.
**Website:** http://www.medco.com
**Chrmn & CEO:** D.B. Snow, Jr.

**Pres & COO:** K.O. Klepper
**SVP & CFO:** R.J. Rubino
**SVP, Chief Acctg Officer & Cntlr:** G.R. Cappucci
**SVP, Secy & General Counsel:** T.M. Moriarty

**Board Members:** H. W. Barker, Jr., J. L. Cassis, N. M. DeParle, M. Goldstein, C. M. Lillis, M. S. Potter, W. Roper, D. B. Snow, Jr., D. D. Stevens, B. J. Wilson

**Founded:** 1983
**Domicile:** Delaware
**Employees:** 20,800

# Medtronic Inc.

**STANDARD &POOR'S**

**S&P Recommendation** HOLD ★★★☆☆

| | | |
|---|---|---|
| **Price** $37.45 (as of Nov 14, 2008) | **12-Mo. Target Price** $55.00 | **Investment Style** Large-Cap Growth |

**GICS Sector** Health Care
**Sub-Industry** Health Care Equipment

**Summary** This global medical device manufacturer has leadership positions in the pacemaker, defibrillator, orthopedic, diabetes management and other medical markets.

## Key Stock Statistics (Source S&P, Vickers, company reports)

| | | | | | | | |
|---|---|---|---|---|---|---|---|
| 52-Wk Range | $56.97–34.61 | S&P Oper. EPS 2009**E** | 3.00 | Market Capitalization(B) | $42.255 | Beta | 0.16 |
| Trailing 12-Month EPS | $2.03 | S&P Oper. EPS 2010**E** | 3.40 | Yield (%) | 2.00 | S&P 3-Yr. Proj. EPS CAGR(%) | 13 |
| Trailing 12-Month P/E | 18.5 | P/E on S&P Oper. EPS 2009**E** | 12.5 | Dividend Rate/Share | $0.75 | S&P Credit Rating | AA- |
| $10K Invested 5 Yrs Ago | $8,581 | Common Shares Outstg. (M) | 1,128.3 | Institutional Ownership (%) | 77 | | |

## Price Performance

30-Week Mov. Avg. · · · ·  10-Week Mov. Avg. - - -  **GAAP Earnings vs. Previous Year**  **Volume** Above Avg. ▮▮▮  STARS

12-Mo. Target Price —  Relative Strength —  ▲ Up  ▼ Down  ► No Change  Below Avg. ▮▮▮  ★⌐

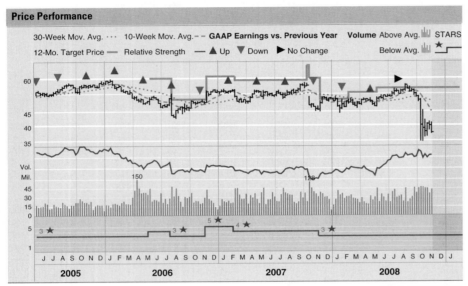

Options: ASE, CBOE, P, Ph

Analysis prepared by **Robert M. Gold** on September 25, 2008, when the stock traded at **$ 52.61**.

## Highlights

➤ We expect FY 09 (Apr.) sales of $15.2 billion, reflecting projected sales of $5.2 billion in the cardiac rhythm management division, $3.6 billion in the spinal category, cardiovascular sales of $2.6 billion, $1.4 billion in neuromodulation, $1.2 billion in diabetes, $900 million in surgical technologies and about $300 million from Physio-Control. In August 2008, MDT reiterated FY 09 revenue guidance of $15.0 billion to $15.5 billion, but we have a slightly less bullish forecast for the global ICD market and are therefore more comfortable at the lower end of that range.

➤ We think FY 09 gross margin expansion will be restricted by general pricing pressures across many product categories, partially offset by manufacturing efficiencies and the inclusion of Kyphon sales. We expect R&D and SG&A costs to consume 10% and 34%, respectively, of sales. We expect FY 09 free cash flow to approximate $3.0 billion, and anticipate that MDT will use this capital to raise the dividend, repurchase stock and/or pursue strategic acquisitions.

➤ We see FY 09 operating EPS of $3.00, up from the comparable $2.58 earned in FY 08. Looking into FY 10, we project EPS of $3.40.

## Investment Rationale/Risk

➤ We believe the global ICD market will rise 4%-6% in 2009, aided by the resolution of product safety issues and steady sales growth overseas. In our view, MDT has significant growth opportunities in the cardiac stent markets, driven by rising demand for its Endeavor drug-coated product in Europe and the U.S. We also look for contributions from the launch of new heart valve products, and think the diabetes franchise will continue to grow in excess of 20%.

➤ Risks to our recommendation and target price include a loss of share in key markets, unfavorable patent litigation, adverse reimbursement rate changes, and further weakness in the U.S. ICD market.

➤ Although we are cautious on the domestic ICD and spine markets, we think the company's diversified product line, new product pipeline, and free cash flow generation warrant a forward P/E-to-growth (PEG) ratio in line with large-cap device peers in our coverage. Our 12-month target price is $55, or about 18.5X our calendarized 2008 EPS estimate of $2.97, resulting in a forward PEG ratio of 1.4X.

## Qualitative Risk Assessment

| LOW | MEDIUM | HIGH |
|---|---|---|

Our risk assessment reflects MDT's exposure to intensely competitive areas of the medical equipment markets, which are typically characterized by relatively short product life cycles, pricing pressures, and the threat of new market entrants. However, we believe this is offset by MDT's many competitive advantages due to the scale of its operations and sales force, product breadth and what we see as its financial strength.

## Quantitative Evaluations

**S&P Quality Ranking**  A-

| D | C | B- | B | B+ | A- | A | A+ |
|---|---|---|---|---|---|---|---|

**Relative Strength Rank**  MODERATE

60

LOWEST = 1     HIGHEST = 99

## Revenue/Earnings Data

**Revenue (Million $)**

| | 1Q | 2Q | 3Q | 4Q | Year |
|---|---|---|---|---|---|
| 2009 | 3,706 | -- | -- | -- | -- |
| 2008 | 3,127 | 3,124 | 3,405 | 3,860 | 13,515 |
| 2007 | 2,897 | 3,075 | 3,048 | 3,280 | 12,299 |
| 2006 | 2,690 | 2,765 | 2,770 | 3,077 | 11,292 |
| 2005 | 2,346 | 2,400 | 2,531 | 2,778 | 10,055 |
| 2004 | 2,064 | 2,164 | 2,194 | 2,665 | 9,087 |

**Earnings Per Share ($)**

| | | | | | |
|---|---|---|---|---|---|
| 2009 | 0.66 | E0.72 | E0.76 | E0.80 | E3.00 |
| 2008 | 0.66 | 0.58 | 0.07 | 0.72 | 1.95 |
| 2007 | 0.51 | 0.59 | 0.61 | 0.70 | 2.41 |
| 2006 | 0.26 | 0.67 | 0.55 | 0.62 | 2.09 |
| 2005 | 0.43 | 0.44 | 0.45 | 0.16 | 1.48 |
| 2004 | 0.37 | 0.39 | 0.38 | 0.47 | 1.60 |

Fiscal year ended Apr. 30. Next earnings report expected: Late November. EPS Estimates based on S&P Operating Earnings; historical GAAP earnings are as reported.

## Dividend Data (Dates: mm/dd Payment Date: mm/dd/yy)

| Amount ($) | Date Decl. | Ex-Div. Date | Stk. of Record | Payment Date |
|---|---|---|---|---|
| 0.125 | 02/21 | 04/02 | 04/04 | 04/25/08 |
| 0.188 | 06/26 | 07/01 | 07/03 | 07/25/08 |
| 0.188 | 08/21 | 10/01 | 10/03 | 10/24/08 |
| 0.188 | 10/16 | 12/30 | 01/02 | 01/23/09 |

Dividends have been paid since 1977. Source: Company reports.

---

**Please read the Required Disclosures and Analyst Certification on the last page of this report.**

The McGraw-Hill Companies

# Medtronic Inc.

STANDARD &POOR'S

## Business Summary September 25, 2008

CORPORATE OVERVIEW. Medtronic has leading positions in medical device categories, including cardiac rhythm management, spinal, vascular, neurology and cardiac surgery.

Cardiac rhythm management products (39% of FY 08 (Apr.) revenues) include implantable pacemakers to treat slow or irregular heartbeats. Bradycardia systems include pacemakers, leads and accessories. Some models are non-invasively programmed by a physician to adjust sensing, electrical pulse intensity, duration, rate and other factors, as well as pacers that can sense in both upper and lower heart chambers and produce appropriate impulses. In May 2005, FDA approval was received for EnRhythm, the company's newest dual-chamber pacemaker, and the first to offer an exclusive pacing mode, called Managed Ventricular Pacing, which enables the device to be programmed to minimize pacing pulses to the right ventricle.

Implantable cardioverter defibrillators (ICDs) treat abnormally fast heart beats by monitoring the heart; when a rapid rhythm is detected, electrical impulses or shocks are delivered. Cardiac resynchronization therapy (CRT) devices

synchronize contractions of multiple heart chambers. The company's InSynch ICD offers CRT for heart failure, as well as advanced defibrillation capabilities for patients also at risk for potentially lethal tachyarrhythmias that may lead to cardiac arrest. The Insynch Marquis system combines the cardiac resynchronization of InSynch devices with defibrillation therapies of the Marquis ICD platform. During FY 05, MDT launched its highest energy CRT-D device, the InSynch Maximo, and the InSynch Sentry CRT-D, which incorporates automatic fluid status monitoring. It also added a ventricle-to-ventricle feature to both InSynch Maximo and InSynch Sentry that allows physicians to separately adjust the timing of electrical therapy delivered to the two ventricles to optimize the beating of the heart and enhance blood flow. MDT also sells external defibrillators through its Physio-Control unit.

## Company Financials Fiscal Year Ended Apr. 30

| Per Share Data ($) | 2008 | 2007 | 2006 | 2005 | 2004 | 2003 | 2002 | 2001 | 2000 | 1999 |
|---|---|---|---|---|---|---|---|---|---|---|
| Tangible Book Value | 1.62 | 4.56 | 2.98 | 4.26 | 3.18 | 2.21 | 1.10 | 3.53 | 2.61 | 1.99 |
| Cash Flow | NA | 2.91 | 2.54 | 1.86 | 1.96 | 1.64 | 1.07 | 1.10 | 1.10 | 0.58 |
| Earnings | 1.95 | 2.41 | 2.09 | 1.48 | 1.60 | 1.30 | 0.80 | 0.85 | 0.90 | 0.40 |
| S&P Core Earnings | 2.12 | 2.44 | 2.00 | 1.65 | 1.46 | 1.10 | 0.76 | 0.91 | NA | NA |
| Dividends | 0.44 | 0.39 | 0.34 | 0.29 | 0.25 | 0.25 | 0.20 | 0.12 | 0.15 | 0.12 |
| Payout Ratio | 23% | 16% | 16% | 20% | 16% | 19% | 25% | 14% | 16% | 30% |
| Calendar Year | 2007 | 2006 | 2005 | 2004 | 2003 | 2002 | 2001 | 2000 | 1999 | 1998 |
| Prices:High | 57.99 | 59.87 | 58.91 | 53.70 | 52.92 | 50.69 | 60.81 | 62.00 | 44.63 | 38.38 |
| Prices:Low | 44.87 | 42.37 | 48.70 | 43.99 | 42.90 | 32.50 | 36.64 | 32.75 | 29.94 | 22.72 |
| P/E Ratio:High | 30 | 25 | 28 | 36 | 33 | 39 | 72 | 61 | 50 | 97 |
| P/E Ratio:Low | 23 | 18 | 23 | 30 | 27 | 25 | 43 | 32 | 33 | 58 |

### Income Statement Analysis (Million $)

| | 2008 | 2007 | 2006 | 2005 | 2004 | 2003 | 2002 | 2001 | 2000 | 1999 |
|---|---|---|---|---|---|---|---|---|---|---|
| Revenue | 13,515 | 12,299 | 11,292 | 10,055 | 9,087 | 7,665 | 6,411 | 5,552 | 5,015 | 4,134 |
| Operating Income | NA | 4,322 | 4,248 | 3,907 | 3,583 | 3,062 | 2,479 | 2,176 | 1,871 | 1,535 |
| Depreciation | 637 | 583 | 544 | 463 | 443 | 408 | 330 | 297 | 243 | 213 |
| Interest Expense | NA | 228 | Nil | 55.1 | 56.5 | 7.20 | Nil | 74.0 | 13.0 | 28.8 |
| Pretax Income | 2,885 | 3,515 | 3,161 | 2,544 | 2,797 | 2,341 | 1,524 | 1,549 | 1,630 | 822 |
| Effective Tax Rate | 22.7% | 20.3% | 19.4% | 29.1% | 29.9% | 31.7% | 35.4% | 32.5% | 32.6% | 43.0% |
| Net Income | 2,231 | 2,802 | 2,547 | 1,804 | 1,959 | 1,600 | 984 | 1,046 | 1,099 | 468 |
| S&P Core Earnings | 2,423 | 2,841 | 2,450 | 2,006 | 1,790 | 1,347 | 936 | 1,121 | NA | NA |

### Balance Sheet & Other Financial Data (Million $)

| | 2008 | 2007 | 2006 | 2005 | 2004 | 2003 | 2002 | 2001 | 2000 | 1999 |
|---|---|---|---|---|---|---|---|---|---|---|
| Cash | 1,613 | 1,256 | 2,994 | 2,232 | 1,594 | 1,470 | 411 | 1,030 | 448 | 376 |
| Current Assets | NA | 7,918 | 10,377 | 7,422 | 5,313 | 4,606 | 3,488 | 3,757 | 3,013 | 2,395 |
| Total Assets | 22,198 | 19,512 | 19,665 | 16,617 | 14,111 | 12,321 | 10,905 | 7,039 | 5,669 | 4,870 |
| Current Liabilities | NA | 2,563 | 4,406 | 3,380 | 4,241 | 1,813 | 3,985 | 1,359 | 992 | 990 |
| Long Term Debt | NA | 5,578 | 5,486 | 1,973 | 1.10 | 1,980 | 9.50 | 13.0 | 14.0 | 17.6 |
| Common Equity | 11,536 | 10,977 | 9,383 | 10,450 | 9,077 | 7,906 | 6,431 | 5,510 | 4,491 | 3,655 |
| Total Capital | NA | 16,555 | 14,891 | 12,901 | 9,486 | 10,191 | 6,674 | 5,523 | 4,520 | 3,703 |
| Capital Expenditures | 513 | 573 | 407 | 452 | 425 | 380 | 386 | 440 | 342 | 226 |
| Cash Flow | NA | 3,385 | 3,090 | 2,267 | 2,402 | 2,008 | 1,314 | 1,343 | 1,342 | 681 |
| Current Ratio | 2.1 | 3.1 | 2.4 | 2.2 | 1.3 | 2.5 | 0.9 | 2.8 | 3.0 | 2.4 |
| % Long Term Debt of Capitalization | 32.9 | 33.7 | 36.8 | 15.3 | 0.0 | 19.4 | 0.1 | 0.2 | 0.3 | 0.5 |
| % Net Income of Revenue | 16.5 | 22.8 | 22.6 | 17.9 | 21.6 | 20.9 | 15.3 | 18.8 | 21.9 | 11.3 |
| % Return on Assets | 10.7 | 14.3 | 14.0 | 11.7 | 14.8 | 13.8 | 11.0 | 16.5 | 20.6 | 11.0 |
| % Return on Equity | 19.8 | 27.5 | 25.7 | 18.5 | 23.1 | 22.3 | 16.5 | 20.9 | 26.6 | 14.8 |

Data as orig reptd.; bef. results of disc opers/spec. items. Per share data adj. for stk. divs.; EPS diluted. E-Estimated. NA-Not Available. NM-Not Meaningful. NR-Not Ranked. UR-Under Review.

**Office:** 710 Medtronic Parkway, Minneapolis, MN 55432-5604.
**Telephone:** 763-514-4000.
**Website:** http://www.medtronic.com
**Chrmn & CEO:** W.A. Hawkins, III

**Pres:** P. Rajadurai
**COO:** H.J. Dallas
**SVP, CFO & Chief Acctg Officer:** G. Ellis
**SVP, Secy & General Counsel:** T.L. Carlson

**Investor Contact:** J. Warren (763-505-2696)
**Board Members:** R. H. Anderson, D. Calhoun, V. J. Dzau, W. A. Hawkins, III, S. A. Jackson, J. T. Lenehan, D. M. O'Leary, K. J. Powell, R. C. Pozen, J. Rosso, J. W. Schuler

**Founded:** 1957
**Domicile:** Minnesota
**Employees:** 40,000

# MEMC Electronic Materials Inc.

| S&P Recommendation **HOLD** ★★★☆☆ | Price $15.34 (as of Nov 14, 2008) | 12-Mo. Target Price $18.00 | Investment Style Large-Cap Growth |
|---|---|---|---|

**GICS Sector** Information Technology
**Sub-Industry** Semiconductor Equipment

**Summary** This company is a worldwide producer of silicon wafers used in semiconductors for microelectronic applications. It also provides silicon materials to the solar industry.

## Key Stock Statistics (Source S&P, Vickers, company reports)

| | | | | | | | |
|---|---|---|---|---|---|---|---|
| 52-Wk Range | $96.08–13.79 | S&P Oper. EPS 2008**E** | 3.61 | Market Capitalization(B) | $3.443 | Beta | 2.30 |
| Trailing 12-Month EPS | $3.01 | S&P Oper. EPS 2009**E** | 3.62 | Yield (%) | Nil | S&P 3-Yr. Proj. EPS CAGR(%) | 15 |
| Trailing 12-Month P/E | 5.1 | P/E on S&P Oper. EPS 2008**E** | 4.2 | Dividend Rate/Share | Nil | S&P Credit Rating | NA |
| $10K Invested 5 Yrs Ago | $15,188 | Common Shares Outstg. (M) | 224.5 | Institutional Ownership (%) | 89 | | |

## Price Performance

30-Week Mov. Avg. ···· 10-Week Mov. Avg. – – GAAP Earnings vs. Previous Year  Volume Above Avg. ▉▉▉ STARS
12-Mo. Target Price —  Relative Strength —  ▲ Up  ▼ Down  ► No Change   Below Avg. ▪▪▪ ★

[Price chart showing WFR stock from 2005 to 2008, with price axis marked at 20, 40, 60, 80; Volume axis marked at 0, 10, 20, 30 Mil.; monthly markers J J A S O N D for years 2005, 2006, 2007, 2008; value "63" noted on chart; STARS line showing 3★, 4★, 3★, 2★, 5★, 4★, 3★]

Options: ASE, CBOE, P, Ph

Analysis prepared by **Angelo Zino** on October 28, 2008, when the stock traded at **$ 17.10.**

## Highlights

➤ We expect revenues to increase 12% in 2008 and 10% in 2009. While we anticipate the production of polysilicon and delivery of solar wafers to remain strong, semiconductor wafer demand is projected to decline sharply, mainly due to customer inventory reduction efforts amid uncertain economic conditions. Management estimates that $1 of polysilicon at long-term prices can convert into $2 of solar revenue or $4 to $7 of revenue for a semiconductor wafer.

➤ We project the annual gross margin to narrow to 48% in 2009 compared with our forecast of 51% in 2008. While we expect lower sales from the higher-margin semiconductor business, we think this will be partially offset by rising sales from the aggressive expansion of its solar business. We remain wary of polysilicon production issues, which have impacted margins at times over the last several quarters. We see operating expenses representing about 7% of sales for 2009.

➤ We expect WFR to have total polysilicon capacity of 8,000 metric tons by the end of 2008, 11,500 metric tons by the end of 2009 and 15,000 metric tons by 2010.

## Investment Rationale/Risk

➤ We project that the solar industry will grow at a 30% compound annual growth rate (CAGR) through 2010, and see elevated demand for polysilicon. We expect WFR's revenues to incrementally shift towards the solar segment from the semiconductor industry and think WFR can drive sales up to $800-$900 million per quarter when its Unit 3 & 4 plants are fully operational. WFR has signed separate agreements with Suntech, Gintech, Conergy and Tainergy to supply a total of $15-$18 billion of solar wafers over a 10-year period.

➤ Risks to our recommendation and target price include faster expansion of industry capacity than we expect, changes in governmental policy related to alternative energy technology, a slowdown in the global economy, and slower-than-expected growth in the solar or semiconductor industries.

➤ Our 12-month target price of $18 is based on a P/E ratio of 5X our 2009 operating EPS forecast of $3.62, a discount to both the S&P 500 and comparable solar manufacturers, reflecting investor concern regarding recent polysilicon production issues.

## Qualitative Risk Assessment

| LOW | MEDIUM | **HIGH** |
|---|---|---|

Our risk assessment reflects WFR's exposure to the historical cyclicality of the semiconductor equipment industry and intense competition, partly offset by what we view as WFR's strong market position and size.

## Quantitative Evaluations

**S&P Quality Ranking** B-

| D | C | **B-** | B | B+ | A- | A | A+ |
|---|---|---|---|---|---|---|---|

**Relative Strength Rank** WEAK

17

LOWEST = 1                                        HIGHEST = 99

## Revenue/Earnings Data

**Revenue (Million $)**

| | 1Q | 2Q | 3Q | 4Q | Year |
|---|---|---|---|---|---|
| 2008 | 501.4 | 531.4 | 546.0 | -- | -- |
| 2007 | 440.4 | 472.7 | 472.8 | 535.9 | 1,922 |
| 2006 | 341.6 | 370.5 | 408.0 | 420.6 | 1,541 |
| 2005 | 250.9 | 272.3 | 280.7 | 303.4 | 1,107 |
| 2004 | 228.8 | 255.5 | 275.3 | 268.4 | 1,028 |
| 2003 | 188.4 | 191.8 | 195.9 | 205.0 | 781.1 |

**Earnings Per Share ($)**

| | | | | | |
|---|---|---|---|---|---|
| 2008 | -0.18 | 0.76 | 0.80 | E0.99 | E3.61 |
| 2007 | 0.58 | 0.70 | 0.65 | 1.62 | 3.56 |
| 2006 | 0.29 | 0.36 | 0.40 | 0.56 | 1.61 |
| 2005 | 0.25 | 0.18 | 0.45 | 0.22 | 1.10 |
| 2004 | 0.16 | 0.27 | 0.27 | 0.31 | 1.02 |
| 2003 | 0.09 | 0.13 | 0.16 | 0.15 | 0.53 |

Fiscal year ended Dec. 31. Next earnings report expected: Late January. EPS Estimates based on S&P Operating Earnings; historical GAAP earnings are as reported.

## Dividend Data

No cash dividends have been paid.

The **McGraw·Hill** Companies

# MEMC Electronic Materials Inc.

STANDARD &POOR'S

## Business Summary October 28, 2008

CORPORATE OVERVIEW. MEMC Electronic Materials, Inc. (WFR) is a global leader in the manufacture of silicon wafers. The company designs, manufactures and provides wafers and intermediate products for use in the semiconductor, solar and related industries. WFR operates manufacturing facilities in every major semiconductor manufacturing region, including Europe, Japan, Malaysia, South Korea, Taiwan, and the U.S. Its customers include virtually all of the world's major semiconductor device manufacturers, such as the major memory, microprocessor, and applications specific integrated circuit (ASIC) manufacturers, as well as the world's largest foundries.

WFR's products include prime polish wafers, epitaxial wafers and test and monitor wafers. The company markets its products primarily through a global direct sales force, with about 61% of 2007 sales in the Asia-Pacific region, 24% in the U.S., and 15% in Europe. WFR has a network of customer service and support centers globally.

In 2007, Samsung and Yingli Green Energy each accounted for greater than 10% of total revenues. At year-end 2007, WFR had 219 U.S. patents and 453 foreign patents. It also had 58 and 275 pending U.S. and foreign patent applications, respectively.

CORPORATE STRATEGY. The company's strategy is to strengthen its leadership position through continuous improvement of the technology, with the goal of increasing both market share and profits. In 2007, the company announced two agreements to supply solar wafers worth approximately $8 billion-$9 billion in incremental revenue over a ten-year period. At the end of 2007, WFR had agreements to supply wafers to solar customers worth approximately $15 billion-$18 billion in revenue over the next ten years, up from the $7 billion-$9 billion at the end of 2006.

Although WFR has some long-term supply agreements, its agreements are generally one year or less, which specify price and usually only indicate expected volumes or market share. While we expect new production of polysilicon to come on line in 2008, we believe demand will continue to exceed supply for the next few years. For that reason, we expect a favorable pricing environment for polysilicon wafers in the foreseeable future. Sales of polysilicon raw material accounted for approximately 22% and 19% of total sales in 2007 and 2006, respectively.

## Company Financials Fiscal Year Ended Dec. 31

| Per Share Data ($) | 2007 | 2006 | 2005 | 2004 | 2003 | 2002 | 2001 | 2000 | 1999 | 1998 |
|---|---|---|---|---|---|---|---|---|---|---|
| Tangible Book Value | 8.98 | 5.23 | 3.21 | 2.13 | 0.94 | NM | NM | 4.61 | 5.55 | 8.66 |
| Cash Flow | 3.90 | 1.91 | 1.35 | 1.22 | 0.68 | 0.09 | -4.65 | 1.86 | 0.12 | -3.95 |
| Earnings | 3.56 | 1.61 | 1.10 | 1.02 | 0.53 | -0.17 | -7.51 | -0.62 | -2.43 | -7.80 |
| S&P Core Earnings | 3.57 | 1.62 | 1.06 | 0.96 | 0.49 | -0.33 | -7.60 | NA | NA | NA |
| Dividends | Nil | Nil | Nil | Nil | Nil | Nil | Nil | Nil | Nil | Nil |
| Payout Ratio | Nil | Nil | Nil | Nil | Nil | Nil | Nil | Nil | Nil | Nil |
| Prices:High | 96.08 | 48.90 | 24.68 | 13.28 | 14.51 | 11.50 | 11.90 | 24.25 | 21.62 | 19.00 |
| Prices:Low | 39.51 | 22.60 | 10.70 | 7.33 | 7.00 | 2.25 | 1.05 | 6.25 | 5.37 | 2.94 |
| P/E Ratio:High | 27 | 30 | 17 | 13 | 27 | NM | NM | NM | NM | NM |
| P/E Ratio:Low | 11 | 14 | 7 | 7 | 13 | NM | NM | NM | NM | NM |

| Income Statement Analysis (Million $) | | | | | | | | | | |
|---|---|---|---|---|---|---|---|---|---|---|
| Revenue | 1,922 | 1,541 | 1,107 | 1,028 | 781 | 687 | 618 | 872 | 694 | 759 |
| Operating Income | 929 | 629 | 314 | 304 | 174 | 114 | -9.69 | 161 | 0.11 | -31.1 |
| Depreciation | 79.3 | 70.3 | 57.2 | 44.1 | 31.0 | 34.2 | 169 | 173 | 159 | 156 |
| Interest Expense | 2.40 | 2.43 | 7.26 | 13.5 | 12.9 | 73.4 | 78.4 | 78.8 | 66.1 | 45.8 |
| Pretax Income | 1,112 | 590 | 252 | 175 | 162 | 20.8 | -259 | -65.6 | -222 | -417 |
| Effective Tax Rate | 25.4% | 36.4% | NM | NM | 22.7% | NM | NM | NM | NM | NM |
| Net Income | 826 | 369 | 249 | 226 | 117 | -5.07 | -489 | -43.4 | -151 | -316 |
| S&P Core Earnings | 827 | 370 | 240 | 212 | 108 | -41.9 | -529 | NA | NA | NA |

| Balance Sheet & Other Financial Data (Million $) | | | | | | | | | | |
|---|---|---|---|---|---|---|---|---|---|---|
| Cash | 1,316 | 528 | 126 | 92.3 | 96.9 | 166 | 107 | 94.8 | 28.6 | 16.2 |
| Current Assets | 1,590 | 900 | 436 | 390 | 365 | 364 | 264 | 410 | 276 | 299 |
| Total Assets | 2,887 | 1,766 | 1,148 | 1,010 | 727 | 632 | 549 | 1,891 | 1,725 | 1,774 |
| Current Liabilities | 444 | 258 | 225 | 216 | 244 | 286 | 222 | 324 | 190 | 259 |
| Long Term Debt | 25.6 | 29.4 | 34.8 | 116 | 59.3 | 161 | 145 | 943 | 870 | 871 |
| Common Equity | 2,035 | 1,167 | 711 | 443 | 194 | -24.7 | -9.74 | 366 | 433 | 399 |
| Total Capital | 2,096 | 1,235 | 791 | 605 | 317 | 194 | 186 | 1,384 | 1,346 | 1,318 |
| Capital Expenditures | 276 | 148 | 163 | 150 | 85.2 | 22.0 | 7.00 | 57.8 | 49.3 | 195 |
| Cash Flow | 906 | 440 | 307 | 270 | 148 | 12.1 | -324 | 130 | 7.60 | -160 |
| Current Ratio | 3.6 | 3.5 | 1.9 | 1.8 | 1.5 | 1.3 | 1.2 | 1.3 | 1.5 | 1.2 |
| % Long Term Debt of Capitalization | 1.2 | 2.4 | 4.4 | 19.2 | 18.7 | 82.9 | 77.8 | 68.1 | 64.6 | 66.1 |
| % Net Income of Revenue | 43.0 | 24.0 | 22.5 | 22.0 | 14.9 | NM | NM | NM | NM | NM |
| % Return on Assets | 35.5 | 25.3 | 22.9 | 26.0 | 17.2 | NM | NM | NM | NM | NM |
| % Return on Equity | 51.6 | 39.3 | 43.2 | 71.1 | 138.1 | NM | NM | NM | NM | NM |

Data as orig reptd.; bef. results of disc opers/spec. items. Per share data adj. for stk. divs.; EPS diluted. E-Estimated. NA-Not Available. NM-Not Meaningful. NR-Not Ranked. UR-Under Review.

**Office:** 501 Pearl Drive, St. Peters, MO 63376.
**Telephone:** 636-474-5000.
**Email:** invest@memc.com
**Website:** http://www.memc.com

**Chrmn:** J.W. Marren
**CEO:** M. Turner, Jr.
**SVP, CFO & Chief Acctg Officer:** K.H. Hannah
**Secy & General Counsel:** B.D. Kohn

**Investor Contact:** B. Michalek (636-474-5443)
**Board Members:** P. Blackmore, R. J. Boehlke, N. K. Gareeb, J. W. Marren, C. D. Marsh, M. M. McNamara, W. E. Stevens, M. Turner, Jr., J. B. Williams

**Founded:** 1984
**Domicile:** Delaware
**Employees:** 5,350

# Merck & Co Inc.

| S&P Recommendation | HOLD ★★★☆☆ | Price $27.33 (as of Nov 14, 2008) | 12-Mo. Target Price $34.00 | Investment Style Large-Cap Blend |
|---|---|---|---|---|

**GICS Sector** Health Care
**Sub-Industry** Pharmaceuticals

**Summary** Merck is one of the world's largest prescription pharmaceuticals concerns.

## Key Stock Statistics (Source S&P, Vickers, company reports)

| | | | | | | | |
|---|---|---|---|---|---|---|---|
| 52-Wk Range | $61.62– 23.64 | S&P Oper. EPS 2008**E** | 3.30 | Market Capitalization(B) | $57.781 | Beta | 1.04 |
| Trailing 12-Month EPS | $2.09 | S&P Oper. EPS 2009**E** | 3.50 | Yield (%) | 5.56 | S&P 3-Yr. Proj. EPS CAGR(%) | 6 |
| Trailing 12-Month P/E | 13.1 | P/E on S&P Oper. EPS 2008**E** | 8.3 | Dividend Rate/Share | $1.52 | S&P Credit Rating | AA- |
| $10K Invested 5 Yrs Ago | $7,135 | Common Shares Outstg. (M) | 2,114.2 | Institutional Ownership (%) | 72 | | |

## Price Performance

30-Week Mov. Avg. · · · 10-Week Mov. Avg. – – GAAP Earnings vs. Previous Year   Volume Above Avg. ıllıl   STARS
12-Mo. Target Price —   Relative Strength   — ▲ Up ▼ Down ▶ No Change   Below Avg. ıllıl   ★

Options: ASE, CBOE, P, Ph

Analysis prepared by **Herman B. Saftlas** on November 14, 2008, when the stock traded at **$ 28.47**.

## Highlights

➤ We expect 2009 revenues to rise modestly from the $24 billion that we estimate for 2008. Key growth drivers, in our opinion, should be Januvia/Janumet diabetes treatments, Singulair respiratory therapy and vaccines. Sales in the latter segment are expected to be augmented by gains in newer products such as Gardasil HPV, and RotaTeq pediatric and Zostavax shingles vaccines. We expect sales of Cozaar/Hyzaar to be relatively flat, and sales of Fosamax, Zocor and other off-patent drugs to decline.

➤ By our analysis, gross margins in 2009 will probably be modestly above the 77.5% indicated for 2008, helped by manufacturing efficiencies. SG&A expenses are expected to decline, and R&D spending will probably be flat. However, we expect joint venture equity income to decline, reflecting lower sales of Vytorin/Zetia cholesterol drugs, which have been hurt by unfavorable clinical trial results, as well as reduced income from AstraZeneca's sales of Nexium.

➤ We project 2009 operating EPS of $3.50, up from an estimated $3.30 in 2008, before restructuring charges and other nonrecurring items.

## Investment Rationale/Risk

➤ Although we believe MRK faces declining equity income from its Vytorin/Zetia cholesterol joint venture with Schering-Plough (from studies showing Vytorin was no more effective than generic Zocor in reducing arterial plaque), we think Merck has other growth drivers, combined with extensive cost restructuring measures, that should facilitate modest EPS growth over the next few years. One of the positive key drivers, in our opinion, is the new Januvia/Janumet Type 2 diabetes franchise, which we believe offers a better side effect profile than older therapies. With respect to cost savings, MRK expects to achieve cumulative restructuring savings of $3.8 billion to $4.2 billion over the 2008-2013 period.

➤ Risks to our recommendation and target price include lower than expected equity income from the Vytorin/Zetia joint venture, negative new studies affecting the latter franchise, and possible R&D pipeline disappointments.

➤ Our 12-month target price of $34 applies a discount to peers P/E of about 9.7X to our EPS estimate for 2009. Merck's $1.52 annual dividend recently provided a yield of over 5%.

## Qualitative Risk Assessment

| LOW | MEDIUM | HIGH |
|---|---|---|

Our risk assessment for MRK reflects risks that the company shares with other major pharmaceutical producers, such as challenges to branded patents, new drug development, and regulatory risks. In addition, we think MRK's joint venture Vytorin/Zetia franchise has been negatively affected by disappointing results from the ENHANCE and SEAS trials. However, we still think MRK has one of the stronger R&D pipelines in the drug sector.

## Quantitative Evaluations

**S&P Quality Ranking**                                  B+

| D | C | B- | B | B+ | A- | A | A+ |
|---|---|---|---|---|---|---|---|

**Relative Strength Rank**                          MODERATE

70

LOWEST = 1                                            HIGHEST = 99

## Revenue/Earnings Data

**Revenue (Million $)**

| | 1Q | 2Q | 3Q | 4Q | Year |
|---|---|---|---|---|---|
| 2008 | 5,822 | 6,052 | 5,944 | -- | -- |
| 2007 | 5,769 | 6,111 | 6,074 | 6,243 | 24,198 |
| 2006 | 5,410 | 5,772 | 5,410 | 6,044 | 22,636 |
| 2005 | 5,362 | 5,468 | 5,416 | 5,766 | 22,012 |
| 2004 | 5,631 | 6,022 | 5,538 | 5,748 | 22,939 |
| 2003 | 5,571 | 5,525 | 5,762 | 5,627 | 22,486 |

**Earnings Per Share ($)**

| | 1Q | 2Q | 3Q | 4Q | Year |
|---|---|---|---|---|---|
| 2008 | 1.52 | 0.82 | 0.51 | E0.75 | E3.30 |
| 2007 | 0.78 | 0.77 | 0.70 | -0.74 | 1.49 |
| 2006 | 0.69 | 0.69 | 0.43 | 0.22 | 2.03 |
| 2005 | 0.62 | 0.33 | 0.65 | 0.51 | 2.10 |
| 2004 | 1.06 | 1.26 | 1.28 | 0.50 | 2.61 |
| 2003 | 0.68 | 0.79 | 0.83 | 0.62 | 2.92 |

Fiscal year ended Dec. 31. Next earnings report expected: Late January. EPS Estimates based on S&P Operating Earnings; historical GAAP earnings are as reported.

## Dividend Data (Dates: mm/dd Payment Date: mm/dd/yy)

| Amount ($) | Date Decl. | Ex-Div. Date | Stk. of Record | Payment Date |
|---|---|---|---|---|
| 0.380 | 11/27 | 12/05 | 12/07 | 01/02/08 |
| 0.380 | 02/26 | 03/05 | 03/07 | 04/01/08 |
| 0.380 | 05/27 | 06/04 | 06/06 | 07/01/08 |
| 0.380 | 07/22 | 09/03 | 09/05 | 10/01/08 |

Dividends have been paid since 1935. Source: Company reports.

---

**Please read the Required Disclosures and Analyst Certification on the last page of this report.**

# Merck & Co Inc.

STANDARD
&POOR'S

## Business Summary November 14, 2008

CORPORATE OVERVIEW. Merck & Co. is a leading global drugmaker, producing a wide range of prescription drugs in many therapeutic classes in the U.S. and abroad. Foreign operations accounted for 39% of total pharmaceutical and vaccine sales in 2007.

MRK's largest-selling products include Singulair (sales of $4.3 billion in 2007), a treatment for asthma and seasonal allergic rhinitis; Cozaar/Hyzaar ($3.4 billion), treatments for high blood pressure and congestive heart failure; and Fosamax ($3.0 billion), a drug for osteoporosis (a bone-thinning disease that affects postmenopausal women). Fosamax's key patent expired in February 2008.

Other drugs include Vasotec/Vaseretic antihypertensives; Primaxin, an intravenous antibiotic; Proscar, a treatment for enlarged prostates; Cosopt/Trusopt, glaucoma treatments; and Januvia, a novel treatment for type 2 diabetes.

Merck is also a leading maker of vaccines, which accounted for 18% of sales in 2007. Key vaccines include Gardasil ($1.5 billion) for human papillomavirus, the main cause of cervical cancer; RotaTeq pediatric vaccine, and Zostavax for shingles.

Through a joint venture with Schering-Plough, Merck also markets Zetia -- a

novel type of cholesterol therapy that works by blocking cholesterol absorption in the intestines -- as well as Vytorin, a combination pill containing both Zocor and Zetia. During 2007, Vytorin had sales of $2.8 billion, and Zetia had sales of $2.4 billion. Merck books only equity income from the Schering-Plough joint venture.

OTC medications such as Pepcid AC are offered through a venture with Johnson & Johnson. Merial, a leading animal health products company, is owned jointly by Merck and Rhone-Poulenc SA. Through a venture with AstraZeneca, Merck books sales of Nexium and other drugs.

MARKET PROFILE. The dollar value of the global pharmaceutical market was indicated at $712 billion in 2007, up 6.4% from 2006, based on data from IMS Health. Although drug sales continue to grow faster than most segments of the world economy, we expect industry growth to decelerate over the balance of the decade, reflecting the loss of patent protection on many large selling drugs, tighter reimbursement from government and private health insurance payors, and relatively sluggish new product flow.

## Company Financials Fiscal Year Ended Dec. 31

| Per Share Data ($) | 2007 | 2006 | 2005 | 2004 | 2003 | 2002 | 2001 | 2000 | 1999 | 1998 |
|---|---|---|---|---|---|---|---|---|---|---|
| Tangible Book Value | 11.76 | 7.00 | 7.48 | 7.03 | 6.13 | 4.88 | 3.77 | 3.23 | 2.43 | 1.91 |
| Cash Flow | 2.19 | 3.06 | 2.88 | 3.29 | 3.51 | 3.79 | 3.77 | 3.44 | 3.02 | 2.67 |
| Earnings | 1.49 | 2.03 | 2.10 | 2.61 | 2.92 | 3.14 | 3.14 | 2.90 | 2.45 | 2.15 |
| S&P Core Earnings | 2.85 | 2.28 | 2.09 | 2.56 | 2.71 | 2.81 | 2.87 | NA | NA | NA |
| Dividends | 1.52 | 1.52 | 1.52 | 1.49 | 1.45 | 1.41 | 1.37 | 1.26 | 1.10 | 0.95 |
| Payout Ratio | 102% | 75% | 72% | 57% | 50% | 45% | 44% | 43% | 45% | 44% |
| Prices:High | 61.62 | 46.37 | 35.36 | 49.33 | 63.50 | 64.50 | 95.25 | 96.69 | 87.38 | 80.88 |
| Prices:Low | 42.35 | 31.81 | 25.50 | 25.60 | 40.57 | 38.50 | 56.80 | 52.00 | 60.94 | 50.69 |
| P/E Ratio:High | 41 | 23 | 17 | 19 | 22 | 21 | 30 | 33 | 36 | 38 |
| P/E Ratio:Low | 28 | 16 | 12 | 10 | 14 | 12 | 18 | 18 | 25 | 24 |

| Income Statement Analysis (Million $) | | | | | | | | | | |
|---|---|---|---|---|---|---|---|---|---|---|
| Revenue | 24,198 | 22,636 | 22,012 | 22,939 | 22,486 | 51,790 | 47,716 | 40,363 | 32,714 | 26,898 |
| Operating Income | 7,779 | 5,955 | 7,567 | 8,074 | 9,912 | 11,361 | 11,192 | 10,686 | 9,056 | 7,655 |
| Depreciation | 1,528 | 2,268 | 1,708 | 1,451 | 1,314 | 1,488 | 1,464 | 1,277 | 1,145 | 1,279 |
| Interest Expense | 384 | 375 | 386 | 294 | 351 | 391 | 465 | 484 | 317 | 206 |
| Pretax Income | 3,492 | 6,342 | 7,486 | 8,129 | 9,220 | 10,428 | 10,693 | 10,133 | 8,842 | 8,295 |
| Effective Tax Rate | 2.73% | 28.2% | 36.5% | 26.6% | 26.7% | 29.3% | 29.2% | 29.6% | 30.9% | 34.8% |
| Net Income | 3,275 | 4,434 | 4,631 | 5,813 | 6,590 | 7,150 | 7,282 | 6,822 | 5,891 | 5,248 |
| S&P Core Earnings | 6,255 | 4,973 | 4,582 | 5,699 | 6,089 | 6,395 | 6,649 | NA | NA | NA |

| Balance Sheet & Other Financial Data (Million $) | | | | | | | | | | |
|---|---|---|---|---|---|---|---|---|---|---|
| Cash | 8,231 | 5,915 | 9,585 | 2,879 | 1,201 | 2,243 | 2,144 | 2,537 | 2,022 | 2,606 |
| Current Assets | 15,045 | 15,230 | 21,049 | 13,475 | 11,527 | 14,834 | 12,962 | 13,353 | 11,259 | 10,229 |
| Total Assets | 48,351 | 44,570 | 44,846 | 42,573 | 40,588 | 47,561 | 44,007 | 39,910 | 35,635 | 31,853 |
| Current Liabilities | 12,258 | 12,723 | 13,304 | 11,744 | 9,570 | 12,375 | 11,544 | 9,710 | 8,759 | 6,069 |
| Long Term Debt | 3,916 | 5,551 | 5,126 | 4,692 | 5,096 | 4,879 | 4,799 | 3,601 | 3,144 | 3,221 |
| Common Equity | 18,185 | 17,560 | 17,917 | 17,288 | 15,576 | 18,200 | 16,050 | 14,832 | 13,242 | 12,802 |
| Total Capital | 24,903 | 25,517 | 25,449 | 24,387 | 24,588 | 28,008 | 25,686 | 23,454 | 19,847 | 19,728 |
| Capital Expenditures | 1,011 | 980 | 1,403 | 1,726 | 1,916 | 2,370 | 2,725 | 2,728 | 2,561 | 1,973 |
| Cash Flow | 4,803 | 6,702 | 6,339 | 7,264 | 7,904 | 8,638 | 8,746 | 8,099 | 7,035 | 6,527 |
| Current Ratio | 1.2 | 1.2 | 1.6 | 1.1 | 1.2 | 1.2 | 1.1 | 1.4 | 1.3 | 1.7 |
| % Long Term Debt of Capitalization | 15.7 | 21.8 | 20.1 | 19.2 | 20.7 | 17.4 | 18.7 | 15.4 | 15.8 | 16.3 |
| % Net Income of Revenue | 13.5 | 19.6 | 21.0 | 25.3 | 29.3 | 13.8 | 15.3 | 16.9 | 18.0 | 19.5 |
| % Return on Assets | 7.1 | 9.9 | 10.6 | 14.0 | 15.0 | 15.6 | 17.3 | 18.1 | 17.4 | 18.2 |
| % Return on Equity | 18.3 | 25.0 | 26.3 | 35.4 | 39.0 | 41.7 | 47.2 | 48.6 | 20.1 | 41.3 |

Data as orig reptd.; bef. results of disc opers/spec. items. Per share data adj. for stk. divs.; EPS diluted. E-Estimated. NA-Not Available. NM-Not Meaningful. NR-Not Ranked. UR-Under Review.

**Office:** One Merck Drive, Whitehouse Station, NJ 08889-0100.
**Telephone:** 908-423-1000.
**Website:** http://www.merck.com
**Chrmn, Pres & CEO:** R.T. Clark

**EVP & CFO:** P.N. Kellogg
**EVP & General Counsel:** B.N. Kuhlik
**EVP & CIO:** J.C. Scalet
**SVP, Chief Acctg Officer & Cntlr:** J. Canan

**Investor Contact:** G. Bell (908-423-5185)
**Board Members:** W. G. Bowen, L. A. Brun, R. T. Clark, J. B. Cole, T. H. Glocer, S. F. Goldstone, W. B. Harrison, Jr., H. R. Jacobson, W. N. Kelley, R. B. Lazarus, T. E. Shenk, A. M. Tatlock, S. O. Thier, W. P. Weeks, P. C. Wendell

**Founded:** 1891
**Domicile:** New Jersey
**Employees:** 59,800

The McGraw-Hill Companies

**STANDARD &POOR'S**

# Meredith Corp

| S&P Recommendation **HOLD** ★★★☆☆ | Price | 12-Mo. Target Price | Investment Style |
|---|---|---|---|
| | $16.11 (as of Nov 14, 2008) | $22.00 | Large-Cap Growth |

**GICS Sector** Consumer Discretionary
**Sub-Industry** Publishing

**Summary** This company derives the bulk of its earnings from publishing magazines (primarily Better Homes and Gardens and Ladies' Home Journal) and the ownership of 13 TV stations.

## Key Stock Statistics (Source S&P, Vickers, company reports)

| | | | | | | | |
|---|---|---|---|---|---|---|---|
| 52-Wk Range | $58.28– 15.09 | S&P Oper. EPS 2009**E** | 2.51 | Market Capitalization(B) | $0.579 | Beta | 1.01 |
| Trailing 12-Month EPS | $2.57 | S&P Oper. EPS 2010**E** | 2.80 | Yield (%) | 5.34 | S&P 3-Yr. Proj. EPS CAGR(%) | -2 |
| Trailing 12-Month P/E | 6.3 | P/E on S&P Oper. EPS 2009**E** | 6.4 | Dividend Rate/Share | $0.86 | S&P Credit Rating | NA |
| $10K Invested 5 Yrs Ago | $3,482 | Common Shares Outstg. (M) | 45.1 | Institutional Ownership (%) | NM | | |

## Price Performance

30-Week Mov. Avg. ··· 10-Week Mov. Avg. – – **GAAP Earnings vs. Previous Year**   Volume Above Avg. ▍▌▏ STARS
12-Mo. Target Price — Relative Strength — ▲ Up ▼ Down ▶ No Change    Below Avg. ▍▌▏ ★

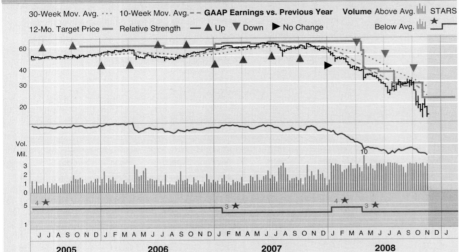

Options: ASE

Analysis prepared by **Jason N. Asaeda** on October 31, 2008, when the stock traded at **$ 18.33**.

## Highlights

➤ We expect total revenues to fall 5% in FY 09 (Jun.), to $1.5 billion. We anticipate strong election year broadcasting advertising. However, as we expect MDP's core advertising categories to be impacted by the current economic downturn, we see an 11% decline in overall advertising revenues, to $850 million. In view of a soft retail sales environment, we also expect a 6% decrease in circulation revenues, to $295 million. Finally, we see other revenues up 11%, supported by the company's new brand licensing deal with Wal-Mart, and growth in MDP's custom publishing and integrated marketing businesses.

➤ We forecast an operating margin contraction to about 13.9% in FY 09 from 16.8% in FY 08. We expect negative operating leverage from lower revenues and higher paper and postage costs to be only partially offset by an increase in highly profitable licensing and integrated marketing revenues and initiatives to reduce labor and vendor costs.

➤ Assuming modest share buybacks, we see EPS falling to $2.51 in FY 09 from $3.14 in FY 08. FY 08 EPS excludes $0.33 of non-recurring costs.

## Investment Rationale/Risk

➤ Our hold recommendation is based on valuation. With what we view as a conservative debt/EBITDA ratio of 1.6X, we expect MDP to continue to supplement organic growth with selective acquisitions. We also believe recent licensing deals demonstrate the company's ability to leverage its strong brands into incremental and profitable revenue streams. In addition, we see incremental revenue growth opportunities for MDP in its non-core advertising categories. However, our optimism is tempered by a difficult economic environment that we see hurting the company's core advertising revenues and reducing earnings in the near-term.

➤ Risks to our recommendation and target price include a longer-than-expected advertising downturn. We also are concerned about MDP's corporate governance, as we do not believe policies such as a dual class voting structure are in the best interests of common shareholders.

➤ Our 12-month target price of $22 is based on a peer-median EV/EBITDA multiple of 5.6X our FY 09 EBITDA estimate of $254 million.

## Qualitative Risk Assessment

| LOW | MEDIUM | HIGH |
|---|---|---|

Our risk assessment reflects a highly competitive environment for advertising among publishers and other media, offset by our view of the company's consistent record of earnings growth, its low weighted average cost of capital, and the stock's low beta.

## Quantitative Evaluations

**S&P Quality Ranking** A-

| D | C | B- | B | B+ | A- | A | A+ |
|---|---|---|---|---|---|---|---|

**Relative Strength Rank** MODERATE

36

LOWEST = 1      HIGHEST = 99

## Revenue/Earnings Data

**Revenue (Million $)**

| | 1Q | 2Q | 3Q | 4Q | Year |
|---|---|---|---|---|---|
| 2009 | 370.4 | -- | -- | -- | -- |
| 2008 | 404.1 | 396.3 | 401.0 | 385.2 | 1,587 |
| 2007 | 386.4 | 399.4 | 401.8 | 428.5 | 1,616 |
| 2006 | 390.3 | 386.0 | 394.9 | 426.4 | 1,598 |
| 2005 | 288.9 | 294.6 | 305.5 | 332.4 | 1,221 |
| 2004 | 272.7 | 280.4 | 299.6 | 309.1 | 1,162 |

**Earnings Per Share ($)**

| | 1Q | 2Q | 3Q | 4Q | Year |
|---|---|---|---|---|---|
| 2009 | 0.41 | E0.50 | E0.78 | E0.82 | E2.51 |
| 2008 | 0.68 | 0.73 | 0.98 | 0.41 | 2.82 |
| 2007 | 0.62 | 0.73 | 1.08 | 1.01 | 3.44 |
| 2006 | 0.52 | 0.58 | 0.97 | 0.97 | 2.86 |
| 2005 | 0.46 | 0.52 | 0.69 | 0.83 | 2.50 |
| 2004 | 0.37 | 0.38 | 0.67 | 0.76 | 2.14 |

Fiscal year ended Jun. 30. Next earnings report expected: Late January. EPS Estimates based on S&P Operating Earnings; historical GAAP earnings are as reported.

## Dividend Data (Dates: mm/dd Payment Date: mm/dd/yy)

| Amount ($) | Date Decl. | Ex-Div. Date | Stk. of Record | Payment Date |
|---|---|---|---|---|
| 0.215 | 02/04 | 02/27 | 02/29 | 03/14/08 |
| 0.215 | 05/15 | 05/28 | 05/30 | 06/13/08 |
| 0.215 | 08/13 | 08/27 | 08/29 | 09/15/08 |
| 0.215 | 11/05 | 11/24 | 11/26 | 12/15/08 |

Dividends have been paid since 1930. Source: Company reports.

---

**Please read the Required Disclosures and Analyst Certification on the last page of this report.**

The **McGraw·Hill** Companies

# Meredith Corp

## Business Summary October 31, 2008

CORPORATE OVERVIEW. Meredith Corp. is a diversified media and marketing company with operations in publishing (78% of FY 07 (Jun.) revenues) and broadcasting (22%). Advertising accounted for about 60% of total revenues, followed by magazine circulation (27%) and other (13%).

The publishing segment focuses on the home and family market. Meredith has more than 25 subscription-based magazines, including Better Homes and Gardens, Family Circle, Ladies' Home Journal and approximately 180 special interest publications. The segment also includes book publishing, integrated marketing, a large consumer database, 25 websites, brand licensing and other related activities. Books are published under the Better Homes and Gardens trademark and under licensed trademarks such as The Home Depot books. Meredith Integrated Marketing offers integrated promotional, database management, relationship and direct marketing capabilities for corporate customers. In April 2006, Meredith acquired O'Grady Meyers (OGM), an interactive marketing services agency that specializes in online customer relationship marketing. Overall FY 07 publishing segment revenues were derived from

advertising (50%), circulation (27%) and other (23%).

The broadcasting segment consists of 13 network-affiliated TV stations and one AM radio station. Broadcasting affiliations include CBS (six stations), FOX (three), MyNetwork TV (two), CW (one) and NBC (one). Local and national advertising contributed approximately 98% of segment revenues in FY 07, and the company states that 30% to 40% of a market's television ad revenues are generated by local news on major network-affiliated stations. The other 2% of revenues comes primarily from broadcast retransmission fees. Given current industry trends, we expect the company to negotiate substantially higher retransmission fees when most of its retransmission agreements expire in FY 09. The segment also includes 18 related websites.

## Company Financials Fiscal Year Ended Jun. 30

| Per Share Data ($) | 2008 | 2007 | 2006 | 2005 | 2004 | 2003 | 2002 | 2001 | 2000 | 1999 |
|---|---|---|---|---|---|---|---|---|---|---|
| Tangible Book Value | NM | NM | NM | NM | NM | NM | NM | NM | NM | NM |
| Cash Flow | NA | 4.94 | 3.76 | 3.19 | 2.82 | 2.40 | 3.64 | 2.39 | 3.01 | 3.20 |
| Earnings | 2.82 | 3.44 | 2.86 | 2.50 | 2.14 | 1.78 | 1.79 | 1.39 | 1.35 | 1.67 |
| S&P Core Earnings | 2.69 | 3.48 | 2.84 | 2.49 | 2.01 | 1.64 | 0.92 | 0.92 | NA | NA |
| Dividends | 0.80 | 0.69 | 0.60 | 0.52 | 0.43 | 0.37 | 0.35 | 0.33 | 0.16 | 0.29 |
| Payout Ratio | 28% | 20% | 20% | 21% | 20% | 22% | 20% | 24% | 12% | 17% |
| Prices:High | 55.08 | 63.41 | 57.29 | 54.33 | 55.94 | 50.32 | 47.75 | 38.97 | 41.06 | 42.00 |
| Prices:Low | 15.09 | 48.15 | 45.04 | 44.51 | 48.24 | 47.09 | 33.42 | 26.50 | 22.38 | 30.63 |
| P/E Ratio:High | 20 | 18 | 20 | 22 | 26 | 28 | 27 | 28 | 30 | 25 |
| P/E Ratio:Low | 5 | 14 | 16 | 18 | 23 | 26 | 19 | 19 | 17 | 18 |

### Income Statement Analysis (Million $)

| | 2008 | 2007 | 2006 | 2005 | 2004 | 2003 | 2002 | 2001 | 2000 | 1999 |
|---|---|---|---|---|---|---|---|---|---|---|
| Revenue | 1,587 | 1,616 | 1,598 | 1,221 | 1,162 | 1,080 | 988 | 1,053 | 1,097 | 1,036 |
| Operating Income | NA | 365 | 312 | 263 | 238 | 209 | 212 | 204 | 249 | 254 |
| Depreciation | 49.2 | 73.8 | 45.7 | 35.3 | 35.2 | 31.4 | 93.8 | 51.6 | 87.6 | 82.6 |
| Interest Expense | NA | 27.2 | 30.2 | Nil | 22.7 | 27.8 | 33.2 | 32.9 | 34.9 | 22.0 |
| Pretax Income | 220 | 263 | 237 | 209 | 181 | 149 | 149 | 116 | 128 | 152 |
| Effective Tax Rate | 39.1% | 35.7% | 39.0% | 38.7% | 38.7% | 38.7% | 38.7% | 38.7% | 44.3% | 41.1% |
| Net Income | 134 | 169 | 145 | 128 | 111 | 91.1 | 91.4 | 71.3 | 71.0 | 89.7 |
| S&P Core Earnings | 128 | 171 | 144 | 127 | 104 | 83.5 | 46.8 | 47.6 | NA | NA |

### Balance Sheet & Other Financial Data (Million $)

| | 2008 | 2007 | 2006 | 2005 | 2004 | 2003 | 2002 | 2001 | 2000 | 1999 |
|---|---|---|---|---|---|---|---|---|---|---|
| Cash | 37.6 | 39.2 | 30.7 | 29.8 | 58.7 | 22.3 | 28.2 | 36.3 | 22.9 | 11.0 |
| Current Assets | NA | 453 | 432 | 304 | 314 | 268 | 272 | 291 | 289 | 256 |
| Total Assets | 2,060 | 2,090 | 2,041 | 1,491 | 1,466 | 1,437 | 1,460 | 1,438 | 1,440 | 1,423 |
| Current Liabilities | NA | 487 | 464 | 439 | 371 | 297 | 307 | 371 | 359 | 344 |
| Long Term Debt | NA | 375 | 515 | 125 | 225 | 375 | 385 | 400 | 455 | 485 |
| Common Equity | 788 | 833 | 698 | 652 | 589 | 501 | 508 | 448 | 423 | 413 |
| Total Capital | NA | 1,375 | 1,338 | 871 | 912 | 948 | 985 | 907 | 926 | 932 |
| Capital Expenditures | 29.6 | 42.6 | 29.2 | 23.8 | 24.5 | 26.6 | 23.4 | 56.0 | 39.4 | 25.7 |
| Cash Flow | NA | 243 | 190 | 163 | 146 | 123 | 185 | 123 | 159 | 172 |
| Current Ratio | 0.9 | 0.9 | 0.9 | 0.7 | 0.8 | 0.9 | 0.9 | 0.8 | 0.8 | 0.7 |
| % Long Term Debt of Capitalization | 32.2 | 27.3 | 38.5 | 14.4 | 24.7 | 39.6 | 39.1 | 44.1 | 49.1 | 52.0 |
| % Net Income of Revenue | 8.5 | 10.4 | 9.1 | 10.5 | 9.5 | 8.4 | 9.3 | 6.8 | 6.5 | 8.7 |
| % Return on Assets | 6.5 | 8.2 | 8.2 | 8.7 | 7.6 | 6.3 | 6.3 | 5.0 | 5.0 | 8.7 |
| % Return on Equity | 16.6 | 22.1 | 21.5 | 20.3 | 20.4 | 18.1 | 19.1 | 16.4 | 17.0 | 22.7 |

Data as orig reptd.; bef. results of disc opers/spec. items. Per share data adj. for stk. divs.; EPS diluted. E-Estimated. NA-Not Available. NM-Not Meaningful. NR-Not Ranked. UR-Under Review.

**Office:** 1716 Locust Street, Des Moines, IA 50309-3023.
**Telephone:** 515-284-3000.
**Website:** http://www.meredith.com
**Chrmn:** W.T. Kerr

**Pres & CEO:** S.M. Lacy
**CFO:** J.H. Ceryanec
**Secy & General Counsel:** J.S. Zieser
**Investor Contact:** S.V. Radia (515-284-3357)

**Board Members:** H. M. Baum, H. M. Bount, M. S. Coleman, J. R. Craigie, A. H. Drewes, D. M. Frazier, F. B. Henry, J. W. Johnson, W. T. Kerr, S. M. Lacy, D. J. Londoner, P. A. Marineau, E. E. Tallett

**Founded:** 1902
**Domicile:** Iowa
**Employees:** 3,570

**STANDARD &POOR'S**

# Merrill Lynch & Co Inc

| S&P Recommendation | HOLD ★★★☆☆ | Price $13.20 (as of Nov 14, 2008) | 12-Mo. Target Price $24.00 | Investment Style Large-Cap Value |
|---|---|---|---|---|

**GICS Sector** Financials
**Sub-Industry** Investment Banking & Brokerage

**Summary** Merrill Lynch is one of the world's largest and most diversified securities brokerage concerns. In mid-September, the company agreed to be acquired by Bank of America in an all stock deal.

## Key Stock Statistics (Source S&P, Vickers, company reports)

| | | | | | | | |
|---|---|---|---|---|---|---|---|
| 52-Wk Range | $63.11–11.65 | S&P Oper. EPS 2008E | -12.81 | Market Capitalization(B) | $21.135 | Beta | 1.69 |
| Trailing 12-Month EPS | $-23.69 | S&P Oper. EPS 2009E | 1.31 | Yield (%) | 10.61 | S&P 3-Yr. Proj. EPS CAGR(%) | NM |
| Trailing 12-Month P/E | NM | P/E on S&P Oper. EPS 2008E | NM | Dividend Rate/Share | $1.40 | S&P Credit Rating | A+ |
| $10K Invested 5 Yrs Ago | $2,597 | Common Shares Outstg. (M) | 1,601.2 | Institutional Ownership (%) | 53 | | |

## Price Performance

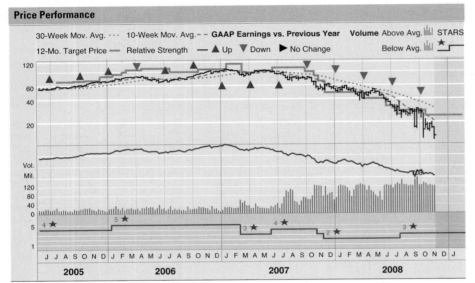

30-Week Mov. Avg. · · · 10-Week Mov. Avg. - - GAAP Earnings vs. Previous Year  Volume Above Avg. ▗▖ STARS
12-Mo. Target Price — Relative Strength — ▲ Up ▼ Down ► No Change  Below Avg. ▗▖ ★

Options: ASE, CBOE, P, Ph

Analysis prepared by **Matthew Albrecht** on October 22, 2008, when the stock traded at **$ 18.47**.

## Highlights

➤ The company has agreed to be acquired by Bank of America (BAC: buy, $24) in an all stock deal, pending shareholder and customary regulatory approvals. MER shareholders are slated to receive 0.8595 shares of BAC stock for each MER common share. The deal comes on the heels of a tumultuous period for the investment banking industry that saw the market question the standalone investment banking business model. We believe the MER business will benefit from the permanent capital base provided by BAC's customer deposits, and its brokerage operations could flourish with exposure to new clients and resulting cross-selling opportunities.

➤ Recent sales and markdowns have significantly reduced MER's exposure to troubled mortgage and leveraged finance markets, and markdowns should decline. Still, we anticipate a slowdown in all major business lines this year, and we expect a sizeable drop in net revenues and earnings for 2008 before a rebound in 2009.

➤ On a standalone basis, we see a loss of $12.81 a share in 2008 and EPS of $1.31 in 2009.

## Investment Rationale/Risk

➤ We believe fixed income and investment banking operations remain a drag on results, while other trading, brokerage, and asset management units perform relatively well. Conditions for the bulge-bracket investment banks have continued to decline, and we are cognizant of the magnitude of exposures to various risky markets. We believe moves to solidify the balance sheet through asset sales and capital raises, although unfavorable for current shareholders, are a positive for the long-term health of the company.

➤ Risks to our opinion and target price include the failure of BAC to consummate the acquisition, further stock and bond market declines and increased competition in major business lines.

➤ The stock recently traded at about 1.2X current tangible book value, below its historical average. Our 12-month target price of $24 assumes a multiple of about 1.5X applied to projected tangible book value in 12 months. We do not anticipate book value and multiple growth until the balance sheet can be cleaned up and profitability can be consistently reached.

## Qualitative Risk Assessment

| LOW | MEDIUM | HIGH |
|---|---|---|

Our risk assessment reflects our view of the company's broad business diversification, strong customer relationships, and significant proportion of asset management and portfolio fees, partially offset by industry cyclicality and mortgage market exposures.

## Quantitative Evaluations

**S&P Quality Ranking**  A-

| D | C | B- | B | B+ | A- | A | A+ |
|---|---|---|---|---|---|---|---|

**Relative Strength Rank**  WEAK

24

LOWEST = 1                    HIGHEST = 99

## Revenue/Earnings Data

**Revenue (Million $)**

| | 1Q | 2Q | 3Q | 4Q | Year |
|---|---|---|---|---|---|
| 2008 | 2,934 | 8,172 | 7,830 | -- | -- |
| 2007 | 21,112 | 23,429 | 13,702 | 4,432 | 62,675 |
| 2006 | 15,561 | 16,689 | 17,379 | 18,959 | 68,622 |
| 2005 | 10,562 | 11,326 | 12,395 | 13,500 | 47,783 |
| 2004 | 7,963 | 7,334 | 7,553 | 9,617 | 32,467 |
| 2003 | 6,923 | 7,292 | 6,857 | 6,673 | 27,745 |

**Earnings Per Share ($)**

| | 1Q | 2Q | 3Q | 4Q | Year |
|---|---|---|---|---|---|
| 2008 | -2.20 | -4.95 | -5.56 | E-0.08 | E-12.81 |
| 2007 | 2.12 | 2.10 | -2.99 | -12.57 | -10.73 |
| 2006 | 0.44 | 1.63 | 3.17 | 2.41 | 7.59 |
| 2005 | 1.21 | 1.14 | 1.40 | 1.41 | 5.16 |
| 2004 | 1.21 | 1.05 | 0.93 | 1.19 | 4.38 |
| 2003 | 0.72 | 1.05 | 1.04 | 1.23 | 4.05 |

Fiscal year ended Dec. 31. Next earnings report expected: Mid January. EPS Estimates based on S&P Operating Earnings; historical GAAP earnings are as reported.

## Dividend Data (Dates: mm/dd Payment Date: mm/dd/yy)

| Amount ($) | Date Decl. | Ex-Div. Date | Stk. of Record | Payment Date |
|---|---|---|---|---|
| 0.350 | 01/28 | 02/12 | 02/14 | 03/05/08 |
| 0.350 | 04/24 | 05/06 | 05/08 | 05/28/08 |
| 0.350 | 07/30 | 08/12 | 08/14 | 09/03/08 |
| 0.350 | 10/27 | 11/10 | 11/13 | 12/03/08 |

Dividends have been paid since 1961. Source: Company reports.

*The McGraw·Hill Companies*

# Merrill Lynch & Co Inc

**STANDARD &POOR'S**

## Business Summary October 22, 2008

CORPORATE OVERVIEW. Merrill Lynch is one of the world's largest financial management and advisory companies, consistently ranking among the largest debt and equity underwriters and mergers and acquisitions advisers on a global basis. MER has two operating segments: Global Markets and Investment Banking (GMI); and the Global Wealth Management group (GWM), including the Private Client Group (GPC) and its nearly 50% stake in BlackRock, which is included in its Global Investment Management unit. In 2006, GMI accounted for 57% of total net revenues, but exposure to mortgage securities resulted in a significant loss for the business in 2007. GWM accounted for 43% of net revenues in 2006, including 37% from GPC and 6% from the divested asset management business, and saw its top line advance 18% in 2007. GMI provides comprehensive investment banking and strategic advisory services, including debt and equity trading, underwriting and origination, and mergers and acquisitions. We remain concerned about rising competition from large commercial banks, which have been gaining market share in investment banking.

We think MER's Global Private Client Group is an undervalued franchise. We believe the company's Private Wealth and Wealth Management Advisors maintain strong relationships with MER's mostly affluent clients and high-net-worth individuals, respectively. MER's Financial Advisory Center serves more than a million clients that have more basic financial needs. At the end of 2007, MER had about 16,740 private client advisers with more than $1.7 trillion

in total client assets in GPC. We think MER is focused on attracting higher net worth clients and emphasizing asset-priced accounts.

In early October 2006, MER combined its asset management business (MLIM) with BlackRock Inc. (BLK: buy, $130). Although MER did not receive a majority stake or voting control, it did obtain approximately a 49% equity stake and a 45% voting stake in a premier asset management company, which we think should see improved growth opportunities. BlackRock is one of the world's largest investment managers, and it holds nearly $1.4 trillion in assets under management as of December 31, 2007. MER reports its share of earnings from the investment, net of expenses and taxes, as revenues on its income statement.

The company has faced pressure to raise capital in the face of substantial write-downs of its mortgage portfolio, and has agreed to sell its 20% stake in financial news and data provider Bloomberg, L.P. and a controlling interest in Financial Data Services, a mutual fund administrator. These moves should raise approximately $8 billion, according to management, and should provide some capital to offset some of its outsized write-downs.

## Company Financials Fiscal Year Ended Dec. 31

| Per Share Data ($) | 2007 | 2006 | 2005 | 2004 | 2003 | 2002 | 2001 | 2000 | 1999 | 1998 |
|---|---|---|---|---|---|---|---|---|---|---|
| Tangible Book Value | 42.64 | 38.67 | 29.37 | 26.48 | 23.69 | 20.76 | 18.38 | 16.67 | 10.67 | 6.09 |
| Cash Flow | -9.94 | 7.59 | 5.16 | 5.77 | 4.05 | 2.63 | 0.57 | 4.11 | 3.09 | 1.50 |
| Earnings | -10.73 | 7.59 | 5.16 | 4.38 | 4.05 | 2.63 | 0.57 | 4.11 | 3.09 | 1.50 |
| S&P Core Earnings | -10.74 | 6.44 | 5.18 | 4.41 | 3.79 | 1.80 | -0.51 | NA | NA | NA |
| Dividends | 1.40 | 1.00 | 0.76 | 0.64 | 0.64 | 0.64 | 0.64 | 0.60 | 0.52 | 0.46 |
| Payout Ratio | NM | 13% | 15% | 15% | 16% | 24% | 112% | 15% | 17% | 31% |
| Prices:High | 98.68 | 93.93 | 69.34 | 64.89 | 60.47 | 59.32 | 80.00 | 74.63 | 51.25 | 54.56 |
| Prices:Low | 50.50 | 64.58 | 52.00 | 47.35 | 30.75 | 28.21 | 33.50 | 36.31 | 31.00 | 17.88 |
| P/E Ratio:High | NM | 12 | 13 | 15 | 15 | 23 | NM | 18 | 17 | 36 |
| P/E Ratio:Low | NM | 9 | 10 | 11 | 8 | 11 | NM | 9 | 10 | 12 |

| Income Statement Analysis (Million $) | | | | | | | | | | |
|---|---|---|---|---|---|---|---|---|---|---|
| Commissions | 7,284 | 5,952 | 5,371 | 4,877 | 4,396 | 4,657 | 5,266 | 6,977 | 6,334 | 5,779 |
| Interest Income | 56,974 | 40,588 | 26,571 | 14,973 | 11,678 | 13,178 | 20,143 | 21,196 | 15,097 | 19,314 |
| Total Revenue | 62,675 | 68,622 | 47,783 | 32,467 | 27,745 | 28,253 | 38,757 | 44,872 | 34,879 | 35,853 |
| Interest Expense | 51,425 | 35,932 | 21,774 | 10,444 | 7,782 | 9,836 | 17,072 | 18,280 | 13,205 | 18,306 |
| Pretax Income | -12,831 | 10,426 | 7,231 | 5,836 | 5,458 | 3,566 | 1,182 | 5,522 | 3,883 | 1,972 |
| Effective Tax Rate | NM | 28.1% | 29.2% | 24.0% | 26.9% | 29.5% | 51.5% | 31.5% | 32.6% | 36.2% |
| Net Income | -8,637 | 7,499 | 5,116 | 4,436 | 3,988 | 2,513 | 573 | 3,784 | 2,618 | 1,259 |
| S&P Core Earnings | -8,923 | 6,191 | 5,066 | 4,418 | 3,689 | 1,694 | -441 | NA | NA | NA |

| Balance Sheet & Other Financial Data (Million $) | | | | | | | | | | |
|---|---|---|---|---|---|---|---|---|---|---|
| Total Assets | 1,020,050 | 841,299 | 681,015 | 648,059 | 494,518 | 447,928 | 419,419 | 407,200 | 328,071 | 299,804 |
| Cash Items | 292,147 | 45,558 | 26,535 | 44,302 | 25,321 | 17,586 | 15,537 | 29,297 | 16,707 | 19,120 |
| Receivables | 479,013 | 459,388 | 134,238 | 124,988 | 105,182 | 100,462 | 86,039 | 103,482 | 77,336 | 135,422 |
| Securities Owned | 234,669 | 203,848 | 148,710 | 181,950 | 134,309 | 100,216 | 92,883 | 91,514 | 106,734 | 107,845 |
| Securities Borrowed | 291,631 | 266,116 | 217,487 | 177,032 | 107,219 | 93,018 | 87,186 | 103,883 | 99,741 | 81,417 |
| Due Brokers & Customers | 88,081 | 73,696 | 55,147 | 60,750 | 47,968 | 45,110 | 40,636 | 34,276 | 34,119 | 28,871 |
| Other Liabilities | 154,830 | 113,977 | 108,053 | 137,028 | 109,720 | 95,804 | 79,654 | 72,765 | 71,880 | 117,432 |
| Capitalization:Debt | 201,087 | 147,033 | 135,501 | 119,576 | 85,969 | 59,070 | 79,267 | 72,937 | 56,190 | 78,869 |
| Capitalization:Equity | 27,549 | 70,129 | 32,927 | 30,740 | 27,226 | 22,450 | 19,583 | 17,879 | 12,377 | 9,707 |
| Capitalization:Total | 233,019 | 220,307 | 171,101 | 150,946 | 113,620 | 81,945 | 99,275 | 91,241 | 68,992 | 85,576 |
| % Return on Revenue | NM | 12.0 | 10.7 | 13.7 | 14.4 | 10.7 | 1.7 | 10.0 | 9.2 | 3.5 |
| % Return on Assets | NM | 1.0 | 0.8 | 1.0 | 0.8 | 0.6 | 0.1 | 1.1 | 0.8 | 0.4 |
| % Return on Equity | NM | 12.3 | 15.9 | 14.8 | 15.9 | 11.8 | 2.9 | 24.6 | 23.4 | 13.9 |

Data as orig reptd.; bef. results of disc opers/spec. items. Per share data adj. for stk. divs.; EPS diluted. E-Estimated. NA-Not Available. NM-Not Meaningful. NR-Not Ranked. UR-Under Review.

**Office:** 4 World Financial Ctr, New York, NY 10080-0002.
**Telephone:** 212-449-1000.
**Website:** http://www.ml.com
**Chrmn & CEO:** J.A. Thain

**Pres & COO:** G.J. Fleming
**Vice Chrmn:** H. Sullivan
**Vice Chrmn:** M.A. Ellman
**Vice Chrmn:** D.J. Barrett

**Investor Contact:** J. Blum (866-607-1234)
**Board Members:** D. J. Barrett, R. T. Berkery, C. T. Christ, A. M. Codina, V. W. Colbert, G. B. Dunn, M. A. Ellman, J. D. Finnegan, D. J. Jonas, A. L. Peters, J. W. Prueher, A. N. Reese, C. O. Rossotti, H. Sullivan, J. A. Thain

**Founded:** 1820
**Domicile:** Delaware
**Employees:** 64,200

**STANDARD &POOR'S**

# Metlife Inc.

| S&P Recommendation | HOLD ★★★☆☆ | Price<br>$28.14 (as of Nov 14, 2008) | 12-Mo. Target Price<br>$40.00 | Investment Style<br>Large-Cap Blend |
|---|---|---|---|---|

**GICS Sector** Financials
**Sub-Industry** Life & Health Insurance

**Summary** This company is a leading publicly traded diversified U.S. life insurance and financial services concern.

## Key Stock Statistics (Source S&P, Vickers, company reports)

| | | | | | | | |
|---|---|---|---|---|---|---|---|
| 52-Wk Range | $67.21– 25.00 | S&P Oper. EPS 2008**E** | 4.36 | Market Capitalization(B) | $22.332 | Beta | 1.46 |
| Trailing 12-Month EPS | $4.37 | S&P Oper. EPS 2009**E** | 5.00 | Yield (%) | 2.63 | S&P 3-Yr. Proj. EPS CAGR(%) | -1 |
| Trailing 12-Month P/E | 6.4 | P/E on S&P Oper. EPS 2008**E** | 6.5 | Dividend Rate/Share | $0.74 | S&P Credit Rating | A |
| $10K Invested 5 Yrs Ago | $9,955 | Common Shares Outstg. (M) | 793.6 | Institutional Ownership (%) | 59 | | |

## Price Performance

Legend: 30-Week Mov. Avg. · · · 10-Week Mov. Avg. — GAAP Earnings vs. Previous Year   Volume Above Avg. | STARS
12-Mo. Target Price — Relative Strength   ▲ Up ▼ Down ► No Change   Below Avg. |

Options: ASE, CBOE, P

Analysis prepared by **Bret Howlett** on October 31, 2008, when the stock traded at **$ 33.45**.

## Highlights

➤ We expect operating earnings from institutional operations to experience high single digit growth in 2008, on improving results from the Travelers acquisition, growth in the non-medical health segment, better results in the retirement and savings segment, and improved mortality trends. We see operating earnings in the individual segment declining significantly due to unfavorable DAC adjustments as a result of the weak equity markets. We expect volatility in the auto and home segment on recent bad weather in the U.S., and we see further losses in 2008.

➤ We see double-digit operating earnings growth in the company's international segment. We look for Korea, Mexico and Japan to contribute to operating profits as MET focuses on increasing sales, expanding its marketing efforts, and upgrading its network. We see variable investment income to continue to be weak in this environment. We believe MET's investment portfolio is vulnerable to a sharp downturn in the economy due to its considerable holdings in below investment grade securities.

➤ We estimate 2008 operating EPS of $4.36 and 2009 operating EPS of $5.00.

## Investment Rationale/Risk

➤ Although we acknowledge MET's strong excess capital position and its overall solid business fundamentals, we think the company's balance sheet will likely come under pressure from further investment losses due to the turmoil in the financial markets and a potential severe downturn in the economy. In particular, we are concerned about MET's above-average exposure to structured securities, commercial real estate, and below investment-grade corporate debt. However, we believe MET maintains a leading position in the life insurance industry and is poised to benefit from its scale, diverse business mix, strong organic growth, global presence. Following MET's recent secondary offering, we think the company could pursue an acquisition.

➤ Risks to our recommendation and target price include credit and interest rate risk; a material decline in the equity markets; the potential need for additional capital; exposure to asbestos-related liability claims.

➤ Our 12-month target price of $40 is roughly 0.8X our estimated 2009 book value per share projection (excluding SFAS 115) , below MET's historical multiples.

## Qualitative Risk Assessment

| LOW | MEDIUM | HIGH |
|---|---|---|

Our risk assessment reflects our view of the company's consistent earnings growth, strong brand identity, diversified product offerings, and geographic footprint, offset by the potential for further investment losses in its investment portfolio.

## Quantitative Evaluations

**S&P Quality Ranking**   NR

| D | C | B- | B | B+ | A- | A | A+ |
|---|---|---|---|---|---|---|---|

**Relative Strength Rank**   MODERATE

34

LOWEST = 1                                   HIGHEST = 99

## Revenue/Earnings Data

**Revenue (Million $)**

| | 1Q | 2Q | 3Q | 4Q | Year |
|---|---|---|---|---|---|
| 2008 | 13,027 | 13,715 | 13,378 | -- | -- |
| 2007 | 12,908 | 13,216 | 13,053 | 13,830 | 53,007 |
| 2006 | 11,565 | 11,387 | 12,551 | 12,893 | 48,396 |
| 2005 | 10,257 | 10,961 | 12,012 | 11,546 | 44,776 |
| 2004 | 9,426 | 9,479 | 10,047 | 10,062 | 39,014 |
| 2003 | 8,364 | 8,862 | 8,816 | 9,747 | 35,790 |

**Earnings Per Share ($)**

| | 1Q | 2Q | 3Q | 4Q | Year |
|---|---|---|---|---|---|
| 2008 | 0.84 | 1.26 | 1.42 | E1.10 | E4.36 |
| 2007 | 1.29 | 1.47 | 1.25 | 1.44 | 5.44 |
| 2006 | 0.92 | 0.74 | 1.19 | 1.00 | 3.85 |
| 2005 | 1.08 | 1.36 | 0.96 | 0.77 | 4.16 |
| 2004 | 0.86 | 1.11 | 0.93 | 0.68 | 3.59 |
| 2003 | 0.38 | 0.78 | 0.74 | 0.68 | 2.57 |

Fiscal year ended Dec. 31. Next earnings report expected: Early February. EPS Estimates based on S&P Operating Earnings; historical GAAP earnings are as reported.

## Dividend Data (Dates: mm/dd Payment Date: mm/dd/yy)

| Amount ($) | Date Decl. | Ex-Div. Date | Stk. of Record | Payment Date |
|---|---|---|---|---|
| 0.740 | 10/23 | 11/02 | 11/06 | 12/14/07 |
| 0.740 | 10/29 | 11/06 | 11/10 | 12/15/08 |

Dividends have been paid since 2000. Source: Company reports.

---

**Please read the Required Disclosures and Analyst Certification on the last page of this report.**

The McGraw-Hill Companies

# Metlife Inc.

STANDARD &POOR'S

## Business Summary October 31, 2008

CORPORATE OVERVIEW. MetLife (MET) is one of the largest insurance and financial services companies in the U.S. The company benefits from a strong brand, a solid financial position, and a large distribution network, in our view. According to the American Council of Life Insurers, MetLife was the largest life insurer in 2005, based on total assets. As of February 2006, MetLife had access to 71% of the world's life insurance markets, up from 36% in 2004. Formerly a mutual insurance company, MetLife demutualized and issued publicly traded stock in April 2000.

MET is organized into five business segments: institutional, individual, auto and home, international, and reinsurance. The institutional segment accounted for 41% of consolidated revenues in 2007 (41% in 2006), the individual segment 29% (30%), the auto and home segment 5.9% (6.2%), the international segment 9.9% (9.0%), and the reinsurance segment 11% (10%). Corporate and

other activities, including MetLife Bank operations, accounted for 2.9% (2.4%) of consolidated revenues in 2007.

CORPORATE STRATEGY. On July 1, 2005, MET acquired Travelers Life & Annuity from Citigroup, Inc. and substantially all of Citigroup's international insurance businesses for $11.8 billion, including approximately $1 billion in MET shares and $10.8 billion in cash. The Travelers acquisition greatly enhances MET's size and scope in its core businesses, in our view. We also see the acquisition leading to strong top-line growth in MET's international operations.

## Company Financials Fiscal Year Ended Dec. 31

### Per Share Data ($)

|  | 2007 | 2006 | 2005 | 2004 | 2003 | 2002 | 2001 | 2000 | 1999 | 1998 |
|---|---|---|---|---|---|---|---|---|---|---|
| Tangible Book Value | 34.79 | 35.64 | 32.06 | 31.16 | 27.94 | 24.83 | 22.43 | 21.53 | NA | NA |
| Operating Earnings | NA | NA | NA | NA | NA | NA | NA | NA | NA | NA |
| Earnings | 5.44 | 3.85 | 4.16 | 3.59 | 2.57 | 1.58 | 0.62 | 1.49 | NA | NA |
| S&P Core Earnings | 5.91 | 5.01 | 4.12 | 3.41 | 2.87 | 2.06 | 0.91 | NA | 1.21 | NA |
| Dividends | 0.74 | 0.59 | 0.52 | 0.46 | 0.23 | 0.21 | 0.20 | 0.20 | NA | NA |
| Payout Ratio | 14% | 15% | 13% | 13% | 9% | 13% | 32% | 13% | NA | NA |
| Prices:High | 71.23 | 60.00 | 52.57 | 41.27 | 34.14 | 34.85 | 36.63 | 36.50 | NA | NA |
| Prices:Low | 58.48 | 48.00 | 37.29 | 32.30 | 23.51 | 20.60 | 24.70 | 14.25 | NA | NA |
| P/E Ratio:High | 13 | 16 | 13 | 11 | 13 | 22 | 59 | 24 | NA | NA |
| P/E Ratio:Low | 11 | 12 | 9 | 9 | 9 | 13 | 40 | 10 | NA | NA |

### Income Statement Analysis (Million $)

|  | 2007 | 2006 | 2005 | 2004 | 2003 | 2002 | 2001 | 2000 | 1999 | 1998 |
|---|---|---|---|---|---|---|---|---|---|---|
| Life Insurance in Force | 6,135,797 | 5,707,215 | 5,125,427 | 4,346,898 | 3,875,110 | 2,679,870 | 2,419,341 | 2,572,261 | NA | NA |
| Premium Income:Life | 19,254 | 18,368 | 17,399 | 15,341 | 14,065 | 13,070 | 11,611 | 11,224 | NA | NA |
| Premium Income:A & H | 5,666 | 4,991 | 4,489 | 4,016 | 3,537 | 3,052 | 2,744 | 2,377 | NA | NA |
| Net Investment Income | 19,006 | 17,192 | 14,910 | 12,418 | 11,636 | 11,329 | 11,923 | 11,768 | 7,639 | NA |
| Total Revenue | 53,007 | 49,746 | 44,869 | 39,014 | 36,147 | 33,147 | 31,928 | 31,947 | 19,244 | NA |
| Pretax Income | 6,279 | 4,221 | 4,399 | 3,779 | 2,630 | 1,671 | 739 | 1,416 | 1,357 | NA |
| Net Operating Income | NA | NA | NA | NA | NA | NA | NA | NA | NA | NA |
| Net Income | 4,280 | 3,105 | 3,139 | 2,708 | 1,943 | 1,155 | 473 | 953 | 918 | NA |
| S&P Core Earnings | 4,495 | 3,867 | 3,123 | 2,574 | 2,144 | 1,512 | 697 | NA | NA | NA |

### Balance Sheet & Other Financial Data (Million $)

|  | 2007 | 2006 | 2005 | 2004 | 2003 | 2002 | 2001 | 2000 | 1999 | 1998 |
|---|---|---|---|---|---|---|---|---|---|---|
| Cash & Equivalent | 13,998 | 10,454 | 7,054 | 6,389 | 5,919 | 4,411 | 9,535 | 5,484 | 4,097 | NA |
| Premiums Due | 14,607 | 14,490 | 12,186 | 6,696 | 7,047 | 7,669 | 6,437 | 8,343 | 6,552 | NA |
| Investment Assets:Bonds | 242,242 | 243,428 | 230,050 | 176,763 | 167,752 | 140,553 | 115,398 | 112,979 | 75,252 | NA |
| Investment Assets:Stocks | 6,829 | 5,890 | 4,163 | 2,188 | 1,598 | 1,348 | 3,063 | 2,193 | 2,006 | NA |
| Investment Assets:Loans | 57,449 | 52,467 | 47,170 | 41,305 | 34,998 | 33,666 | 31,893 | 30,109 | 16,805 | NA |
| Investment Assets:Total | 334,734 | 324,689 | 301,709 | 234,985 | 218,099 | 188,335 | 162,222 | 156,527 | 105,187 | NA |
| Deferred Policy Costs | 21,521 | 20,851 | 19,641 | 14,336 | 12,943 | 11,727 | 11,167 | 10,618 | 4,416 | NA |
| Total Assets | 558,562 | 527,715 | 481,645 | 356,808 | 326,841 | 277,385 | 256,898 | 255,018 | 226,791 | NA |
| Debt | 19,535 | 13,759 | 12,022 | 5,944 | 5,703 | 5,690 | 4,884 | 3,516 | 3,350 | NA |
| Common Equity | 35,178 | 33,797 | 29,100 | 22,824 | 21,149 | 17,385 | 16,062 | 16,389 | 13,873 | NA |
| % Return on Revenue | 8.1 | 6.2 | 7.0 | 6.9 | 5.4 | 3.5 | 1.5 | 3.0 | 4.8 | NA |
| % Return on Assets | 0.8 | 0.6 | 0.7 | 0.8 | 0.6 | 0.4 | 0.2 | 0.4 | NA | NA |
| % Return on Equity | 12.0 | 9.4 | 11.8 | 12.3 | 10.1 | 6.9 | 2.9 | 6.3 | NA | NA |
| % Investment Yield | 5.8 | 5.5 | 5.6 | 6.8 | 5.7 | 6.5 | 7.5 | 8.0 | NA | NA |

Data as orig reptd.; bef. results of disc opers/spec. items. Per share data adj. for stk. divs.; EPS diluted. E-Estimated. NA-Not Available. NM-Not Meaningful. NR-Not Ranked. UR-Under Review.

**Office:** 200 Park Ave, New York, NY 10166-0188.
**Telephone:** 212-578-2211.
**Website:** http://www.metlife.com
**Chrmn & Pres:** C.R. Henrikson

**Pres:** R.A. Liddy
**CEO:** E. Gardner
**COO & CTO:** M.R. Morris
**EVP & CFO:** W.J. Wheeler

**Board Members:** S. M. Burwell, E. Castro-Wright, B. A. Dole, Jr., C. W. Grise, M. Haydel, C. R. Henrikson, R. G. Hubbard, J. M. Keane, J. M. Kilts, H. B. Price, D. Satcher, K. J. Sicchitano, W. C. Steere, Jr., L. C. Wang

**Founded:** 1999
**Domicile:** Delaware
**Employees:** 49,000

**STANDARD &POOR'S**

# Microchip Technology Inc

| S&P Recommendation | BUY ★★★★☆ | Price $19.75 (as of Nov 14, 2008) | 12-Mo. Target Price $27.00 | Investment Style Large-Cap Growth |
|---|---|---|---|---|

**GICS Sector** Information Technology
**Sub-Industry** Semiconductors

**Summary** This company supplies microcontrollers, analog, and other semiconductor products for a wide variety of high-volume embedded control applications.

## Key Stock Statistics (Source S&P, Vickers, company reports)

| | | | | | | | |
|---|---|---|---|---|---|---|---|
| 52-Wk Range | $38.37–19.34 | S&P Oper. EPS 2009**E** | 1.44 | Market Capitalization(B) | $3.592 | Beta | 1.00 |
| Trailing 12-Month EPS | $1.58 | S&P Oper. EPS 2010**E** | 1.34 | Yield (%) | 6.87 | S&P 3-Yr. Proj. EPS CAGR(%) | 2 |
| Trailing 12-Month P/E | 12.5 | P/E on S&P Oper. EPS 2009**E** | 13.7 | Dividend Rate/Share | $1.36 | S&P Credit Rating | NA |
| $10K Invested 5 Yrs Ago | $6,855 | Common Shares Outstg. (M) | 181.9 | Institutional Ownership (%) | NM | | |

## Price Performance

30-Week Mov. Avg. ···   10-Week Mov. Avg. - -   GAAP Earnings vs. Previous Year   Volume Above Avg. ▮▮▮   STARS

12-Mo. Target Price —   Relative Strength —   ▲ Up  ▼ Down  ▶ No Change   Below Avg. ▮▮▮ ★

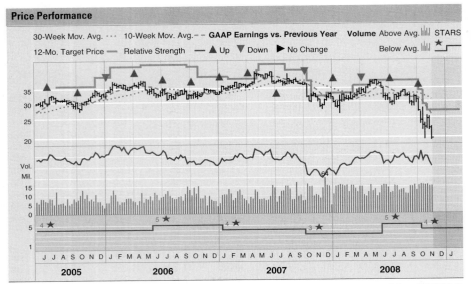

Options: ASE, CBOE, Ph

Analysis prepared by **Clyde Montevirgen** on October 24, 2008, when the stock traded at **$ 22.41**.

### Highlights

➤ We are looking for sales to decline 3% in FY 09 (Mar.), compared to essentially flat sales in FY 08, reflecting softening orders due to macro-economic weakness. However, we believe the sales slide will be similar to peers' and not a result of market share loss. In fact, we see more share gains in the 8-bit and 16-bit microcontroller markets, and also expect MCHP's analog business to grow faster than peers. The company has a high exposure to a wide range of end markets, which should help reduce sales variability.

➤ We expect gross margins to narrow modestly but remain around the 60% range in FY 09, similar to FY 08 results, as a richer product mix and lower depreciation charges balance the negative impact of lower utilization of its manufacturing plants. However, we expect non-GAAP operating margins to narrow to 31% for FY 09, from 32% in FY 08, as we see sales falling faster than expenses.

➤ We anticipate FY 09 operating EPS of $1.44, versus FY 08 EPS of $1.42. MCHP recently repurchased a sizable number of shares as part of a $1.03 billion recapitalization and buyback initiative.

### Investment Rationale/Risk

➤ We view MCHP as having a very profitable business model featuring unusually diverse end markets and a low cost structure. The company is a share leader in the 8-bit microcontroller business, and we believe it will continue to take more share in that market as well as further penetrate the 16-bit microcontroller and analog markets. We think MCHP faces less risk than peers due to its ability to reduce volatility in earnings through effectively managing sales and gross margins. In addition to anticipated share price appreciation, we see the dividend yield of over 6% providing an attractive total return.

➤ Risks to our recommendation and target price include industry cyclicality, maintaining global operations, numerous competitors, and the challenges of entering new markets for 16-bit microcontrollers.

➤ Our 12-month target price of $27 is based on a weighted blend of relative metrics. We apply a P/E multiple of 17X, above the peer average, to our FY 09 EPS estimate to derive a value of $25. We use a price-to-sales multiple of around 6X our forward 12-month sales per share forecast, implying a value of $30.

### Qualitative Risk Assessment

| LOW | MEDIUM | HIGH |
|---|---|---|

Microchip operates in the cyclical semiconductor industry, and the shares have above-average volatility. Offsetting positive factors that we see include a very broad customer base, a breadth of end markets, a low cost structure, no debt, and one of the highest dividend yields among peers.

### Quantitative Evaluations

**S&P Quality Ranking**     **B+**

| D | C | B- | B | B+ | A- | A | A+ |
|---|---|---|---|---|---|---|---|

**Relative Strength Rank**     **MODERATE**

**43**

LOWEST = 1      HIGHEST = 99

### Revenue/Earnings Data

**Revenue (Million $)**

| | 1Q | 2Q | 3Q | 4Q | Year |
|---|---|---|---|---|---|
| 2009 | 268.2 | 269.7 | -- | -- | -- |
| 2008 | 264.1 | 258.7 | 252.6 | 260.4 | 1,036 |
| 2007 | 262.6 | 267.9 | 251.0 | 258.2 | 1,040 |
| 2006 | 218.5 | 227.3 | 234.9 | 247.2 | 927.9 |
| 2005 | 212.8 | 220.7 | 205.4 | 208.1 | 846.9 |
| 2004 | 161.3 | 168.5 | 178.0 | 191.5 | 699.3 |

**Earnings Per Share ($)**

| | 1Q | 2Q | 3Q | 4Q | Year |
|---|---|---|---|---|---|
| 2009 | 0.40 | 0.41 | E0.33 | E0.31 | E1.44 |
| 2008 | 0.36 | 0.27 | 0.38 | 0.40 | 1.40 |
| 2007 | 0.35 | 0.36 | 0.33 | 0.57 | 1.62 |
| 2006 | 0.29 | 0.31 | 0.19 | 0.35 | 1.13 |
| 2005 | 0.21 | 0.29 | 0.25 | 0.27 | 1.01 |
| 2004 | 0.06 | 0.17 | 0.19 | 0.23 | 0.65 |

Fiscal year ended Mar. 31. Next earnings report expected: Late January. EPS Estimates based on S&P Operating Earnings; historical GAAP earnings are as reported.

### Dividend Data (Dates: mm/dd Payment Date: mm/dd/yy)

| Amount ($) | Date Decl. | Ex-Div. Date | Stk. of Record | Payment Date |
|---|---|---|---|---|
| 0.320 | 01/24 | 02/05 | 02/07 | 02/21/08 |
| 0.330 | 04/28 | 05/08 | 05/12 | 05/27/08 |
| 0.338 | 07/24 | 08/05 | 08/07 | 08/21/08 |
| 0.339 | 10/23 | 11/12 | 11/14 | 11/28/08 |

Dividends have been paid since 2002. Source: Company reports.

---

**Please read the Required Disclosures and Analyst Certification on the last page of this report.**

# Microchip Technology Inc

**STANDARD &POOR'S**

## Business Summary October 24, 2008

CORPORATE OVERVIEW. Microchip Technology Inc. (MCHP) develops and manufactures specialized chips used in a wide variety of embedded control applications. MCHP is a leading microcontroller company, serving more than 60,000 end customers worldwide and having shipped over 6 billion PIC microcontrollers since 1990. MCHP also offers a broad range of high-performance linear, mixed-signal, power management, thermal management, battery management, and interface devices, and serial EEPROMs.

Microcontrollers are low-cost components that form the brains of the vast majority of electronic devices, except for PCs. MCHP's signature products include a broad family of proprietary 8- and 16-bit field programmable microcontrollers under the PIC name, designed for applications requiring high performance, fast time-to-market, and user programmability. The company offers a comprehensive set of low cost and easy-to-learn application development tools that let system designers program a PIC microcontroller for specific applications.

By main product lines, microcontrollers provided 80.4% of sales in FY 08 (Mar.) (80.2% in FY 07), memory products 11.6% (11.8%), and analog and interface products 8% (8%). Average selling prices are relatively stable for the microcontrollers and for analog products with significant proprietary content, which is about half the analog segment. Pricing for some of its commodity-type products, such as EEPROMs, tend to fluctuate.

Foreign sales accounted for 75% of FY 08 net sales, up from 74% in FY 07. By major region, FY 08 sales came from Asia (43.8%), Europe (29.8%), and the Americas (26.4%). Approximately 20% of FY 08 sales were sourced from China, including Hong Kong, and Taiwan accounted for about 10% of sales. About 64% of net sales in FY 08 were made through distributors.

## Company Financials Fiscal Year Ended Mar. 31

### Per Share Data ($)

| | 2008 | 2007 | 2006 | 2005 | 2004 | 2003 | 2002 | 2001 | 2000 | 1999 |
|---|---|---|---|---|---|---|---|---|---|---|
| Tangible Book Value | 5.39 | 9.03 | 7.89 | 6.95 | 6.19 | 5.58 | 5.36 | 4.80 | 3.52 | 2.07 |
| Cash Flow | NA | 2.14 | 1.64 | 1.58 | 1.32 | 1.00 | 0.98 | 1.20 | 0.93 | 0.64 |
| Earnings | 1.40 | 1.62 | 1.13 | 1.01 | 0.65 | 0.47 | 0.45 | 0.69 | 0.56 | 0.28 |
| S&P Core Earnings | 1.48 | 1.62 | 1.05 | 0.89 | 0.47 | 0.30 | 0.28 | 0.57 | NA | NA |
| Dividends | 0.97 | 0.57 | 0.21 | 0.11 | 0.04 | 0.04 | Nil | Nil | NA | NA |
| Payout Ratio | 69% | 35% | 18% | 11% | 6% | 9% | Nil | Nil | Nil | Nil |
| Calendar Year | 2007 | 2006 | 2005 | 2004 | 2003 | 2002 | 2001 | 2000 | 1999 | 1998 |
| Prices:High | 42.46 | 38.56 | 34.98 | 34.88 | 36.50 | 33.99 | 28.29 | 34.39 | 22.81 | 12.15 |
| Prices:Low | 27.50 | 30.63 | 24.06 | 25.12 | 17.85 | 15.02 | 14.00 | 12.92 | 7.54 | 5.04 |
| P/E Ratio:High | 30 | 24 | 31 | 35 | 56 | 72 | 62 | 50 | 41 | 44 |
| P/E Ratio:Low | 20 | 19 | 21 | 25 | 27 | 32 | 31 | 19 | 14 | 18 |

### Income Statement Analysis (Million $)

| | 2008 | 2007 | 2006 | 2005 | 2004 | 2003 | 2002 | 2001 | 2000 | 1999 |
|---|---|---|---|---|---|---|---|---|---|---|
| Revenue | 1,036 | 1,040 | 928 | 847 | 699 | 651 | 571 | 716 | 496 | 406 |
| Operating Income | NA | 464 | 567 | 400 | 314 | 286 | 232 | 304 | 204 | 164 |
| Depreciation | 100 | 116 | 111 | 120 | 142 | 111 | 109 | 104 | 68.5 | 65.2 |
| Interest Expense | NA | 5.42 | 1.97 | 0.94 | 0.25 | 0.49 | 0.57 | 0.75 | 1.05 | 2.96 |
| Pretax Income | 351 | 401 | 359 | 277 | 178 | 128 | 127 | 196 | 140 | 68.6 |
| Effective Tax Rate | 15.2% | 11.0% | 32.5% | 22.9% | 22.8% | 22.3% | 25.5% | 27.2% | 27.0% | 27.0% |
| Net Income | 298 | 357 | 242 | 214 | 137 | 99.7 | 94.8 | 143 | 102 | 50.1 |
| S&P Core Earnings | 314 | 357 | 226 | 190 | 100 | 63.5 | 58.2 | 117 | NA | NA |

### Balance Sheet & Other Financial Data (Million $)

| | 2008 | 2007 | 2006 | 2005 | 2004 | 2003 | 2002 | 2001 | 2000 | 1999 |
|---|---|---|---|---|---|---|---|---|---|---|
| Cash | 1,325 | 167 | 565 | 68.7 | 105 | 53.9 | 281 | 130 | 188 | 30.8 |
| Current Assets | NA | 1,085 | 1,119 | 1,075 | 884 | 609 | 549 | 372 | 365 | 203 |
| Total Assets | 2,512 | 2,270 | 2,351 | 1,818 | 1,622 | 1,428 | 1,276 | 1,161 | 812 | 505 |
| Current Liabilities | NA | 256 | 609 | 307 | 270 | 215 | 168 | 195 | 169 | 110 |
| Long Term Debt | NA | Nil | Nil | Nil | Nil | Nil | Nil | Nil | Nil | 25.0 |
| Common Equity | 1,036 | 2,004 | 1,726 | 1,486 | 1,321 | 1,179 | 1,076 | 943 | 624 | 359 |
| Total Capital | NA | 2,013 | 1,741 | 1,510 | 1,351 | 1,212 | 1,107 | 966 | 643 | 396 |
| Capital Expenditures | 69.8 | 60.0 | 76.3 | 63.2 | 63.5 | 80.4 | 44.7 | 441 | 212 | 39.5 |
| Cash Flow | NA | 473 | 353 | 334 | 279 | 211 | 204 | 247 | 171 | 115 |
| Current Ratio | 9.0 | 4.2 | 1.8 | 3.5 | 3.3 | 2.8 | 3.3 | 1.9 | 2.2 | 1.8 |
| % Long Term Debt of Capitalization | 52.6 | Nil | Nil | Nil | Nil | Nil | Nil | Nil | Nil | 6.3 |
| % Net Income of Revenue | 28.8 | 34.3 | 26.1 | 25.2 | 19.6 | 15.3 | 16.6 | 20.0 | 20.6 | 12.3 |
| % Return on Assets | 12.5 | 15.5 | 11.6 | 12.4 | 9.0 | 7.4 | 7.8 | 14.1 | 15.5 | 9.7 |
| % Return on Equity | 19.6 | 19.1 | 15.1 | 15.2 | 11.0 | 8.8 | 9.4 | 17.8 | 20.8 | 13.8 |

Data as orig reptd.; bef. results of disc opers/spec. items. Per share data adj. for stk. divs.; EPS diluted. E-Estimated. NA-Not Available. NM-Not Meaningful. NR-Not Ranked. UR-Under Review.

**Office:** 2355 West Chandler Boulevard, Chandler, AZ 85224-6199.
**Telephone:** 480-792-7200.
**Email:** ir@mail.microchip.com
**Website:** http://www.microchip.com

**Chrmn, Pres & CEO:** S. Sanghi
**CFO & Chief Acctg Officer:** G. Parnell
**Secy:** J.E. Bjornholt
**Investor Contact:** D.L. Wussler (480-792-7373)

**Board Members:** M. W. Chapman, L. Day, IV, A. J. Hugo-Martinez, W. Meyercord, S. Sanghi

**Founded:** 1989
**Domicile:** Delaware
**Employees:** 4,811

**STANDARD &POOR'S**

# Micron Technology Inc.

| **S&P Recommendation** `HOLD` ★★★☆☆ | **Price** $2.75 (as of Nov 14, 2008) | **12-Mo. Target Price** $6.00 | **Investment Style** Large-Cap Value |
|---|---|---|---|

**GICS Sector** Information Technology
**Sub-Industry** Semiconductors

**Summary** MU is a manufacturer of semiconductor memory products, including DRAM and NAND flash memory, as well as image sensors.

## Key Stock Statistics (Source S&P, Vickers, company reports)

| | | | | | | | |
|---|---|---|---|---|---|---|---|
| 52-Wk Range | $9.31–2.63 | S&P Oper. EPS 2009**E** | -0.65 | Market Capitalization(B) | $2.100 | Beta | 1.79 |
| Trailing 12-Month EPS | $-2.10 | S&P Oper. EPS 2010**E** | NA | Yield (%) | Nil | S&P 3-Yr. Proj. EPS CAGR(%) | NM |
| Trailing 12-Month P/E | NM | P/E on S&P Oper. EPS 2009**E** | NM | Dividend Rate/Share | Nil | S&P Credit Rating | B+ |
| $10K Invested 5 Yrs Ago | $2,109 | Common Shares Outstg. (M) | 763.8 | Institutional Ownership (%) | 88 | | |

## Price Performance

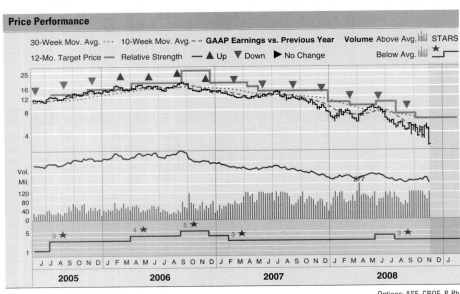

30-Week Mov. Avg. · · · 10-Week Mov. Avg. - - **GAAP Earnings vs. Previous Year** Volume Above Avg. ▏▍▏ STARS
12-Mo. Target Price — Relative Strength — ▲ Up ▼ Down ► No Change   Below Avg. ▏▏ ★

Options: ASE, CBOE, P, Ph

Analysis prepared by **Clyde Montevirgen** on October 03, 2008, when the stock traded at **$ 4.48**.

## Highlights

➤ We think sales will grow 6% in FY 09 (Aug.), faster than the 3% advance in FY 08. With memory chipmakers cutting capital spending to help alleviate an oversupply problem, we anticipate healthy memory bit growth due to continuing strength in demand for PCs and electronic devices and more stable average selling prices (ASPs) ahead. We believe that MU's focus on NAND flash memories and CMOS image sensors will help diversify sales and reduce volatile results.

➤ We estimate gross margins of around 12% in FY 09, up from negative 1% in FY 08, reflecting our view of improving ASPs and per-chip cost reductions. Gross margins are sensitive to industry factors such as the supply of memory chips, and demand for PCs and consumer electronics. Memory supply recently exceeded demand, but we think this imbalance is reversing, which should lead to higher margins ahead. Consequently, we see a negative, yet improving, Non-GAAP operating margin of 7% in FY 09, compared to an adjusted negative 20% in FY 08.

➤ We estimate a non-GAAP loss per share of $0.65 for FY 09, versus a Non-GAAP $1.57 loss in FY 08.

## Investment Rationale/Risk

➤ We believe MU is in a better financial position compared to some competitors, as they try to survive the memory downturn. With our view of healthy PC sales growth over the next year, we believe DRAM prices will improve as excessive supply digests. However, NAND flash prices remain a concern. Although we think that memory chipmakers are taking corrective action in order to prevent an extended oversupply situation, we see pressure on demand as the macroeconomic slowdown could lead to lower sales of the consumer electronic products that use NAND flash memory. Consequently, margins will remain under pressure and losses will continue until demand improves, in our opinion.

➤ Risks to our opinion and target price include sudden downturns in end-market demand for PCs, slower-than-expected sales of consumer electronic products, sharp increases in DRAM production by competitors, and lower than anticipated unit cost reductions.

➤ Our 12-month target price of $6 is derived primarily by applying a multiple of around 0.8X, below the historical average, to our forward 12-month sales per share estimate.

## Qualitative Risk Assessment

| LOW | MEDIUM | **HIGH** |
|---|---|---|

Micron is subject to semiconductor industry cyclicality and to sudden changes in pricing for commodity memory products. It is a relatively large semiconductor company and is the lone American survivor in the global DRAM industry, which has been consolidating in recent years.

## Quantitative Evaluations

**S&P Quality Ranking**  C

| D | **C** | B- | B | B+ | A- | A | A+ |
|---|---|---|---|---|---|---|---|

**Relative Strength Rank**  **WEAK**

`25`

LOWEST = 1                HIGHEST = 99

## Revenue/Earnings Data

**Revenue (Million $)**

| | 1Q | 2Q | 3Q | 4Q | Year |
|---|---|---|---|---|---|
| 2008 | 1,535 | 1,359 | 1,498 | 1,449 | 5,841 |
| 2007 | 1,530 | 1,427 | 1,294 | 1,437 | 5,688 |
| 2006 | 1,362 | 1,225 | 1,312 | 1,373 | 5,272 |
| 2005 | 1,260 | 1,308 | 1,054 | 1,258 | 4,880 |
| 2004 | 1,107 | 991.0 | 1,117 | 1,189 | 4,404 |
| 2003 | 685.1 | 785.0 | 732.7 | 888.5 | 3,091 |

**Earnings Per Share ($)**

| | | | | | |
|---|---|---|---|---|---|
| 2008 | -0.34 | -1.01 | -0.30 | -0.45 | -2.10 |
| 2007 | 0.15 | -0.07 | -0.29 | -0.21 | -0.42 |
| 2006 | 0.09 | 0.27 | 0.12 | 0.08 | 0.57 |
| 2005 | 0.23 | 0.17 | -0.20 | 0.07 | 0.29 |
| 2004 | Nil | -0.04 | 0.13 | 0.14 | 0.24 |
| 2003 | -0.52 | -1.02 | -0.36 | -0.20 | -2.11 |

Fiscal year ended Aug. 31. Next earnings report expected: Late December. EPS Estimates based on S&P Operating Earnings; historical GAAP earnings are as reported.

## Dividend Data

No Dividend Data Available

---

The **McGraw·Hill** Companies

# Micron Technology Inc.

**STANDARD &POOR'S**

## Business Summary October 03, 2008

CORPORATE OVERVIEW. Micron Technology is a global manufacturer and marketer of dynamic random access memory (DRAM), NAND flash memory, and complementary metal-oxide semiconductor (CMOS) image sensors. The company's products are used in an increasingly broad range of electronic devices, including personal computers, workstations, network servers, mobile phones, digital still cameras, MP3 players and other consumer electronics products. About 50% of FY 07 (Aug.) total sales were to the computing market, and Hewlett-Packard accounted for 10% of FY 07 sales.

The company has been in the DRAM business since 1980, and is currently one of the world's largest DRAM suppliers. DRAM products are high-density, low-cost per bit, random access memory devices that provide high-speed data storage and retrieval. Micron offers DRAM products with a variety of performance, pricing, and other characteristics. The company's DRAM products may be classified as core DRAM or specialty memory.

Micron has two segments, memory, which includes both DRAM and NAND

flash memory, and imaging. The memory segment comprised 88% of total revenues in FY 07. By memory type, DRAM sales accounted for 65% of the total in FY 07, down from 76% in FY 06, reflecting an expansion into flash memory and CMOS image sensors over the last couple of years. NAND flash memory sales comprised 23% of sales in FY 07, reflecting growing market demand for memory devices that can retain memory when the power is turned off, for use in handheld electronic devices such as digital still cameras.

The imaging segment made up 12% of total revenues in FY 07. This segment's main product is the CMOS image sensor. Micron offers a broad range of image sensors, including lower-end pixel resolutions from its VGA (video graphics array) products to its higher resolution 8-megapixel products. The company's main image sensor customers are camera module integrators.

## Company Financials Fiscal Year Ended Aug. 31

### Per Share Data ($)

| | 2008 | 2007 | 2006 | 2005 | 2004 | 2003 | 2002 | 2001 | 2000 | 1999 |
|---|---|---|---|---|---|---|---|---|---|---|
| Tangible Book Value | 7.56 | 9.00 | 9.64 | 9.07 | 8.73 | 7.68 | 9.93 | 11.59 | 11.34 | 7.00 |
| Cash Flow | NA | 1.81 | 2.33 | 2.07 | 2.13 | -0.10 | 0.45 | 1.00 | 4.13 | 1.49 |
| Earnings | -2.10 | -0.42 | 0.57 | 0.29 | 0.24 | -2.11 | -1.51 | -0.88 | 2.56 | -0.13 |
| S&P Core Earnings | -1.54 | -0.38 | 0.40 | -0.12 | -0.09 | -2.60 | -2.14 | -1.06 | NA | NA |
| Dividends | NA | Nil | Nil | Nil | Nil | Nil | Nil | Nil | NA | NA |
| Payout Ratio | NA | Nil | Nil | Nil | Nil | Nil | Nil | Nil | Nil | Nil |
| Prices:High | NA | 14.31 | 18.65 | 14.82 | 18.25 | 15.66 | 39.50 | 49.61 | 97.50 | 42.50 |
| Prices:Low | NA | 7.11 | 13.12 | 9.32 | 10.89 | 6.60 | 9.50 | 16.39 | 28.00 | 17.13 |
| P/E Ratio:High | NA | NM | 33 | 51 | 76 | NM | NM | NM | 38 | NM |
| P/E Ratio:Low | NA | NM | 23 | 32 | 45 | NM | NM | NM | 11 | NM |

### Income Statement Analysis (Million $)

| | 2008 | 2007 | 2006 | 2005 | 2004 | 2003 | 2002 | 2001 | 2000 | 1999 |
|---|---|---|---|---|---|---|---|---|---|---|
| Revenue | 5,841 | 5,688 | 5,272 | 4,880 | 4,404 | 3,091 | 2,589 | 3,936 | 7,336 | 3,764 |
| Operating Income | NA | 1,381 | 1,631 | 1,458 | 1,445 | 133 | 152 | 138 | 3,288 | 796 |
| Depreciation | 2,060 | 1,718 | 1,281 | 1,265 | 1,218 | 1,210 | 1,177 | 1,114 | 994 | 843 |
| Interest Expense | NA | 40.0 | 25.0 | 46.9 | 36.0 | 36.5 | 17.1 | 16.7 | 104 | 130 |
| Pretax Income | -1,611 | -168 | 433 | 199 | 232 | -1,200 | -998 | -960 | 2,317 | -91.5 |
| Effective Tax Rate | NM | NM | 4.16% | 5.34% | 32.2% | NM | NM | NM | 34.4% | NM |
| Net Income | -1,619 | -320 | 408 | 188 | 157 | -1,273 | -907 | -521 | 1,504 | -68.9 |
| S&P Core Earnings | -1,190 | -290 | 288 | -75.8 | -62.2 | -1,578 | -1,288 | -626 | NA | NA |

### Balance Sheet & Other Financial Data (Million $)

| | 2008 | 2007 | 2006 | 2005 | 2004 | 2003 | 2002 | 2001 | 2000 | 1999 |
|---|---|---|---|---|---|---|---|---|---|---|
| Cash | 1,362 | 2,192 | 1,431 | 525 | 486 | 570 | 398 | 469 | 702 | 295 |
| Current Assets | NA | 5,234 | 5,101 | 2,926 | 2,639 | 2,037 | 2,119 | 3,138 | 4,904 | 2,830 |
| Total Assets | 13,430 | 14,818 | 12,221 | 8,006 | 7,760 | 7,158 | 7,555 | 8,363 | 9,632 | 6,965 |
| Current Liabilities | NA | 2,026 | 1,661 | 979 | 972 | 993 | 753 | 687 | 1,648 | 922 |
| Long Term Debt | NA | 1,987 | 405 | 1,020 | 1,028 | 997 | 361 | 445 | 934 | 1,528 |
| Common Equity | 6,178 | 7,752 | 8,114 | 5,847 | 5,615 | 5,038 | 6,367 | 7,135 | 6,432 | 3,964 |
| Total Capital | NA | 12,371 | 10,115 | 6,902 | 6,685 | 6,035 | 6,727 | 7,599 | 7,899 | 5,969 |
| Capital Expenditures | 2,529 | 3,603 | 1,365 | 1,065 | 1,081 | 822 | 760 | 1,489 | 1,188 | 804 |
| Cash Flow | NA | 1,398 | 1,689 | 1,453 | 1,375 | -63.3 | 270 | 593 | 2,499 | 774 |
| Current Ratio | 2.4 | 2.6 | 3.1 | 3.0 | 2.7 | 2.1 | 2.8 | 4.6 | 3.0 | 3.1 |
| % Long Term Debt of Capitalization | 20.8 | 16.1 | 4.0 | 14.8 | 15.4 | 16.5 | 5.4 | 5.9 | 11.8 | 25.6 |
| % Net Income of Revenue | NM | NM | 7.7 | 3.9 | 3.6 | NM | NM | NM | 20.5 | NM |
| % Return on Assets | NM | NM | 4.0 | 2.4 | 2.1 | NM | NM | NM | 18.1 | NM |
| % Return on Equity | NM | NM | 5.8 | 3.3 | 3.0 | NM | NM | NM | 28.9 | NM |

Data as orig reptd.; bef. results of disc opers/spec. items. Per share data adj. for stk. divs.; EPS diluted. E-Estimated. NA-Not Available. NM-Not Meaningful. NR-Not Ranked. UR-Under Review.

**Office:** 8000 South Federal Way, Boise, ID 83716-9632.
**Telephone:** 208-368-4000.
**Email:** invrel@micron.com
**Website:** http://www.micron.com

**Chrmn & CEO:** S.R. Appleton
**Pres & COO:** D.M. Durcan
**CFO & Chief Acctg Officer:** R.C. Foster
**Treas:** N.L. Schlachter

**Secy & General Counsel:** R.W. Lewis
**Investor Contact:** K.A. Bedard (208-368-4400)
**Board Members:** T. Aoki, S. R. Appleton, J. W. Bageley, R. L. Bailey, M. Johnson, L. Mondry, R. E. Switz

**Founded:** 1978
**Domicile:** Delaware
**Employees:** 22,800

*The McGraw-Hill Companies*

STANDARD
&POOR'S

# Microsoft Corp

**S&P Recommendation** HOLD ★★★☆☆

| Price | 12-Mo. Target Price | Investment Style |
|---|---|---|
| $20.06 (as of Nov 14, 2008) | $28.00 | Large-Cap Growth |

**GICS Sector** Information Technology
**Sub-Industry** Systems Software

**Summary** Microsoft, the world's largest software company, develops PC software, including the Windows operating system and the Office application suite.

## Key Stock Statistics (Source S&P, Vickers, company reports)

| | | | | | | | | |
|---|---|---|---|---|---|---|---|---|
| 52-Wk Range | $36.72–18.74 | S&P Oper. EPS 2009E | 2.07 | Market Capitalization(B) | $178.445 | Beta | | 0.81 |
| Trailing 12-Month EPS | $1.89 | S&P Oper. EPS 2010E | 2.33 | Yield (%) | 2.59 | S&P 3-Yr. Proj. EPS CAGR(%) | | 7 |
| Trailing 12-Month P/E | 10.6 | P/E on S&P Oper. EPS 2009E | 9.7 | Dividend Rate/Share | $0.52 | S&P Credit Rating | | AAA |
| $10K Invested 5 Yrs Ago | $9,242 | Common Shares Outstg. (M) | 8,895.6 | Institutional Ownership (%) | 61 | | | |

## Price Performance

30-Week Mov. Avg. · · ·   10-Week Mov. Avg. – –   **GAAP Earnings vs. Previous Year**   **Volume** Above Avg. STARS
12-Mo. Target Price —   Relative Strength —   ▲ Up  ▼ Down  ► No Change   Below Avg. ★

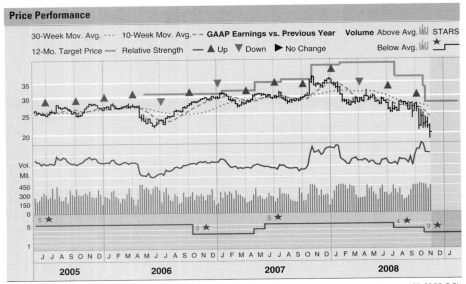

Options: ASE, CBOE, P, Ph

Analysis prepared by **Jim Yin** on November 05, 2008, when the stock traded at **$ 22.71**.

## Highlights

➤ We see total revenues rising 8.3% in FY 09 (Jun.), driven by increased PC sales, particularly in developing countries, and continued growth in online advertising. However, this growth is significantly lower than the 18% achieved in FY 08, reflecting an economic slowdown. We expect client revenue to rise 5.0%. Our growth estimate is based on our forecast for 8%-12% growth in worldwide PC unit shipments, partially offset by lower selling prices in emerging markets. We estimate that server and tools revenue will rise 13%; Microsoft Business division 12%; and Entertainment and Devices division (EDD) 0.9%, down from 34% in FY 08.

➤ We look for gross margins to remain steady at 80.5% in FY 09, down slightly from 80.8% in FY 08, as margin improvement in EDD is offset by higher spending in the online services group. We see operating margins widening to 38.4% in FY 09, from 37.2% in FY 08, reflecting better operating efficiency due to economies of scale.

➤ We estimate EPS of $2.07 for FY 09, compared to $1.87 in FY 08, on 3.8% fewer shares due to the company's repurchase program. MSFT had $20.7 billion in cash and short-term investments as of September 30, 2008.

## Investment Rationale/Risk

➤ We recently lowered our recommendation to hold, from buy, based on our concern over a worsening global economy. MSFT lowered its revenue growth outlook by about 3% and its earnings forecast by 5% as business conditions weakened in September 2008. We think the company faces more difficult year-over-year comparisons following the releases of Vista, Microsoft Office and Windows Server in prior years. We believe losses in its online services business will accelerate as the company boosts investments. All told, we view the shares as fairly valued at recent levels.

➤ Risks to our recommendation and target price include lower than projected PC sales, further deterioration in the global economy, and failure to achieve cost synergies from acquisitions.

➤ Our 12-month target price of $28 is based on a weighted blend of our discounted cash flow (DCF) and P/E analyses. Our DCF model assumes a 10.4% weighted average cost of capital and 3% terminal growth, yielding an intrinsic value of $30. Our P/E analysis derives a value of $25, based on an industry P/E-to-growth multiple of 1.7X, or 12X our FY 09 EPS estimate.

## Qualitative Risk Assessment

| LOW | MEDIUM | HIGH |
|---|---|---|

Our risk assessment reflects MSFT's ongoing antitrust-related issues, the risk that its applications and operating systems may lose market share to open source rivals, and potential difficulties releasing new products in a timely manner, mitigated by the company's current leading market positions and financial strength.

## Quantitative Evaluations

**S&P Quality Ranking**  B+

| D | C | B- | B | B+ | A- | A | A+ |
|---|---|---|---|---|---|---|---|

**Relative Strength Rank**  MODERATE

60

LOWEST = 1   HIGHEST = 99

## Revenue/Earnings Data

**Revenue (Million $)**

| | 1Q | 2Q | 3Q | 4Q | Year |
|---|---|---|---|---|---|
| 2009 | 15,061 | -- | -- | -- | -- |
| 2008 | 13,762 | 16,367 | 14,454 | 15,837 | 60,420 |
| 2007 | 10,811 | 12,542 | 14,398 | 13,371 | 51,122 |
| 2006 | 9,741 | 11,837 | 10,900 | 11,804 | 44,282 |
| 2005 | 9,189 | 10,818 | 9,620 | 10,161 | 39,788 |
| 2004 | 8,215 | 10,153 | 9,175 | 9,292 | 36,835 |

**Earnings Per Share ($)**

| | 1Q | 2Q | 3Q | 4Q | Year |
|---|---|---|---|---|---|
| 2009 | 0.48 | E0.54 | E0.50 | E0.56 | E2.07 |
| 2008 | 0.45 | 0.50 | 0.47 | 0.46 | 1.87 |
| 2007 | 0.35 | 0.26 | 0.50 | 0.31 | 1.42 |
| 2006 | 0.29 | 0.34 | 0.29 | 0.28 | 1.20 |
| 2005 | 0.23 | 0.32 | 0.23 | 0.34 | 1.12 |
| 2004 | 0.24 | 0.14 | 0.12 | 0.25 | 0.75 |

Fiscal year ended Jun. 30. Next earnings report expected: Late January. EPS Estimates based on S&P Operating Earnings; historical GAAP earnings are as reported.

## Dividend Data (Dates: mm/dd Payment Date: mm/dd/yy)

| Amount ($) | Date Decl. | Ex-Div. Date | Stk. of Record | Payment Date |
|---|---|---|---|---|
| 0.110 | 12/19 | 02/19 | 02/21 | 03/13/08 |
| 0.110 | 03/17 | 05/13 | 05/15 | 06/12/08 |
| 0.110 | 06/11 | 08/19 | 08/21 | 09/11/08 |
| 0.130 | 09/22 | 11/18 | 11/20 | 12/11/08 |

Dividends have been paid since 2003. Source: Company reports.

---

**Please read the Required Disclosures and Analyst Certification on the last page of this report.**

The McGraw-Hill Companies

# Microsoft Corp

**STANDARD &POOR'S**

## Business Summary November 05, 2008

CORPORATE OVERVIEW. Microsoft is the world's largest software maker, primarily as a result of its dominant position in operating systems, which run 90% of all PCs currently in use, and business productivity applications, where its Office productivity suite has over 400 million users. The combination of these two strongholds provides MSFT with a strong barrier to entry for competitors, in our opinion. With MSFT generating over $1 billion every month in free cash flow, it had $23.7 billion in cash and investments as of June 2008, despite having paid out more than $116 billion for dividends and share buybacks from FY 04 to FY 08 (Jun.).

MARKET PROFILE. According to IDC, global spending on packaged software totaled $211.3 billion in 2005, with MSFT's share totaling $35.0 billion or 17% of the total market. IDC expects the system infrastructure market, which comprises roughly half of MSFT's software revenues, to expand at a compound annual growth rate (CAGR) of 9.1% from 2005 through 2010. The applications market, which constitutes more than a third of revenues, is expected to increase 7.0%, and the application development and deployment market, more

than 10% of revenues, is forecast to rise 7.1%. We look for MSFT to expand at slightly faster rates for the most part, as the Windows platform continues to gain market share.

CORPORATE STRATEGY. Ray Ozzie, when he was MSFT's chief technical officer (he replaced Bill Gates as chief software architect in June 2006), described the core of the company's business strategy as centered on software as a service rather than as a transactional purchase. This strategy is a further refinement of the .NET strategy described by Gates in 2002, and essentially is driven by three key themes: the power of advertising-supported business models, the effectiveness of online discovery and trial-version downloads as a model for new software adoption, and the demand from users for integrated user experiences that "just work."

## Company Financials Fiscal Year Ended Jun. 30

| Per Share Data ($) | 2008 | 2007 | 2006 | 2005 | 2004 | 2003 | 2002 | 2001 | 2000 | 1999 |
|---|---|---|---|---|---|---|---|---|---|---|
| Tangible Book Value | 2.43 | 2.71 | 3.55 | 4.14 | 6.55 | 5.34 | 2.05 | 4.39 | 3.92 | 2.69 |
| Cash Flow | NA | 1.57 | 1.28 | 1.20 | 0.86 | 1.05 | 0.80 | 0.83 | 0.92 | 0.80 |
| Earnings | 1.87 | 1.42 | 1.20 | 1.12 | 0.75 | 0.92 | 0.71 | 0.66 | 0.85 | 0.71 |
| S&P Core Earnings | 1.99 | 1.38 | 1.27 | 1.20 | 0.83 | 0.75 | 0.65 | 0.58 | NA | NA |
| Dividends | NA | 0.39 | 0.34 | 3.32 | 0.16 | 0.08 | Nil | Nil | Nil | Nil |
| Payout Ratio | NA | 27% | 28% | NM | 21% | 9% | Nil | Nil | Nil | Nil |
| Prices:High | NA | 37.50 | 30.26 | 28.25 | 30.20 | 30.00 | 35.31 | 38.08 | 59.31 | 59.97 |
| Prices:Low | NA | 26.60 | 21.46 | 23.82 | 24.86 | 22.55 | 20.71 | 21.44 | 20.13 | 34.00 |
| P/E Ratio:High | NA | 26 | 25 | 25 | 40 | 33 | 50 | 58 | 70 | 84 |
| P/E Ratio:Low | NA | 19 | 18 | 21 | 33 | 25 | 29 | 32 | 24 | 48 |

| Income Statement Analysis (Million $) | 2008 | 2007 | 2006 | 2005 | 2004 | 2003 | 2002 | 2001 | 2000 | 1999 |
|---|---|---|---|---|---|---|---|---|---|---|
| Revenue | 60,420 | 51,122 | 44,282 | 39,788 | 36,835 | 32,187 | 28,365 | 25,296 | 22,956 | 19,747 |
| Operating Income | NA | 19,964 | 17,375 | 15,416 | 10,220 | 14,656 | 12,994 | 13,256 | 11,685 | 10,938 |
| Depreciation | 2,056 | 1,440 | 903 | 855 | 1,186 | 1,439 | 1,084 | 1,536 | 748 | 1,010 |
| Interest Expense | NA | Nil | Nil | Nil | Nil | Nil | Nil | Nil | Nil | Nil |
| Pretax Income | 23,814 | 20,101 | 18,262 | 16,628 | 12,196 | 14,726 | 11,513 | 11,525 | 14,275 | 11,891 |
| Effective Tax Rate | 25.8% | 30.0% | 31.0% | 26.3% | 33.0% | 32.1% | 32.0% | 33.0% | 34.0% | 34.5% |
| Net Income | 17,681 | 14,065 | 12,599 | 12,254 | 8,168 | 9,993 | 7,829 | 7,721 | 9,421 | 7,785 |
| S&P Core Earnings | 18,873 | 13,643 | 13,329 | 13,107 | 9,042 | 8,155 | 7,051 | 6,518 | NA | NA |

| Balance Sheet & Other Financial Data (Million $) | 2008 | 2007 | 2006 | 2005 | 2004 | 2003 | 2002 | 2001 | 2000 | 1999 |
|---|---|---|---|---|---|---|---|---|---|---|
| Cash | 21,171 | 6,111 | 6,714 | 4,851 | 15,982 | 6,438 | 3,016 | 3,922 | 4,846 | 17,236 |
| Current Assets | NA | 40,168 | 49,010 | 48,737 | 70,566 | 58,973 | 48,576 | 39,637 | 30,308 | 20,233 |
| Total Assets | 72,793 | 63,171 | 69,597 | 70,815 | 92,389 | 79,571 | 67,646 | 59,257 | 52,150 | 37,156 |
| Current Liabilities | NA | 23,754 | 22,442 | 16,877 | 14,969 | 13,974 | 12,744 | 11,132 | 9,755 | 8,718 |
| Long Term Debt | NA | Nil | Nil | Nil | Nil | Nil | Nil | Nil | Nil | Nil |
| Common Equity | 36,286 | 31,097 | 40,104 | 48,115 | 74,825 | 61,020 | 52,180 | 47,289 | 41,368 | 27,458 |
| Total Capital | NA | 31,097 | 40,104 | 48,115 | 74,825 | 62,751 | 52,578 | 48,125 | 42,753 | 28,438 |
| Capital Expenditures | 3,182 | 2,264 | 1,578 | 812 | 1,109 | 891 | 770 | 1,103 | 879 | 583 |
| Cash Flow | NA | 15,505 | 13,502 | 13,109 | 9,354 | 11,432 | 8,913 | 9,257 | 10,156 | 8,767 |
| Current Ratio | 1.5 | 1.7 | 2.2 | 2.9 | 4.7 | 4.2 | 3.8 | 3.6 | 3.1 | 2.3 |
| % Long Term Debt of Capitalization | Nil | Nil | Nil | Nil | Nil | Nil | Nil | Nil | Nil | Nil |
| % Net Income of Revenue | 29.3 | 27.5 | 28.5 | 30.8 | 22.2 | 31.0 | 27.6 | 30.5 | 41.0 | 39.4 |
| % Return on Assets | 26.0 | 21.2 | 17.9 | 14.8 | 9.4 | 13.6 | 12.4 | 13.9 | 20.8 | 26.2 |
| % Return on Equity | 52.5 | 39.5 | 28.6 | 19.9 | 11.7 | 17.7 | 15.7 | 17.4 | 27.3 | 36.0 |

Data as orig reptd.; bef. results of disc opers/spec. items. Per share data adj. for stk. divs.; EPS diluted. E-Estimated. NA-Not Available. NM-Not Meaningful. NR-Not Ranked. UR-Under Review.

Office: 1 Microsoft Way, Redmond, WA 98052-8300.
Telephone: 425-882-8080.
Email: msft@microsoft.com
Website: http://www.microsoft.com

Chrmn: W.H. Gates, III
CEO: S.A. Ballmer
COO: B.K. Turner
SVP & CFO: C.P. Liddell

SVP, Secy & General Counsel: B.L. Smith
Investor Contact: F. Brod (800-285-7772)
Board Members: S. A. Ballmer, J. I. Cash, Jr., D. Dublon, W. H. Gates, III, R. V. Gilmartin, R. Hastings, D. F. Marquardt, C. H. Noski, H. Panke, J. A. Shirley

Founded: 1975
Domicile: Washington
Employees: 91,000

**STANDARD &POOR'S**

# Millipore Corp

| S&P Recommendation | HOLD ★★★★★ | Price $52.26 (as of Nov 14, 2008) | 12-Mo. Target Price $62.00 | Investment Style Large-Cap Growth |
|---|---|---|---|---|

**GICS Sector** Health Care
**Sub-Industry** Life Sciences Tools & Services

**Summary** This company provides technologies, tools and services for the discovery, development and production of new therapeutic drugs.

## Key Stock Statistics (Source S&P, Vickers, company reports)

| | | | | | | | | |
|---|---|---|---|---|---|---|---|---|
| 52-Wk Range | $83.20– 45.95 | S&P Oper. EPS 2008**E** | 3.49 | Market Capitalization(B) | $2.887 | Beta | | 0.71 |
| Trailing 12-Month EPS | $2.83 | S&P Oper. EPS 2009**E** | 3.91 | Yield (%) | Nil | S&P 3-Yr. Proj. EPS CAGR(%) | | 13 |
| Trailing 12-Month P/E | 18.5 | P/E on S&P Oper. EPS 2008**E** | 15.0 | Dividend Rate/Share | Nil | S&P Credit Rating | | BB+ |
| $10K Invested 5 Yrs Ago | $12,502 | Common Shares Outstg. (M) | 55.2 | Institutional Ownership (%) | NM | | | |

## Price Performance

30-Week Mov. Avg. · · · 10-Week Mov. Avg. – – **GAAP Earnings vs. Previous Year** Volume Above Avg. |||| STARS
12-Mo. Target Price — Relative Strength — ▲ Up ▼ Down ▶ No Change  Below Avg. |||| ★

Options: ASE, CBOE, P, Ph

Analysis prepared by **Jeffrey Loo, CFA** on November 05, 2008, when the stock traded at **$ 54.82**.

## Highlights

➤ We see 2008 sales rising 6% to $1.6 billion, reflecting solid 12% growth in Bioscience on strong demand from drug discovery. We expect Bioprocess increases to moderate to 2%, as sluggish demand from large biotech firms in North America has limited growth. But we see improvement in the second half of 2008 and into 2009, partially offset by softening in the European market. The slowdown seen at Bioprocess was the result of several large North American biotech customers lowering inventories and reducing purchases. In 2009, we expect sales gains of 5% to $1.68 billion.

➤ We foresee gross margins improving by 10 basis points on product mix, including higher-margin Serologicals products, but we expect only a 20 bps improvement in operating margins, aided by cost cutting but partially offset by higher R&D costs. We believe MIL's net debt obligation of $1.09 billion as of September 30, 2008, primarily from financing the Serologicals deal, will hurt net margins by 150 basis points, but we see good progress as MIL has been paying down debt.

➤ Our 2008 and 2009 EPS estimates are $3.49 and $3.91, respectively.

## Investment Rationale/Risk

➤ We see ongoing uncertainty within MIL's Bioprocess unit although we expect some stability in late 2008 and into 2009. Despite uncertainty at Bioprocess, we remain encouraged by MIL's product line expansion through internal and external growth efforts. We think these efforts will drive sales growth, and we believe the product portfolio expansion better positions the company for uncertainties in various units. The Serologicals integration is complete, and we believe the combination will provide attractive product line expansion and geographic revenue synergies, as the companies have minimal global sales overlap, particularly in Asia.

➤ Risks to our recommendation and target price include deterioration in the pharmaceutical and biotech R&D spending environment, and a longer-than-expected slowdown in bioprocess sales.

➤ Our 12-month target price of $62 is based on an in-line-with-peers P/E-to-growth (PEG) ratio of about 1.2X, with a three-year EPS growth rate of 13%, applied to our 2009 EPS estimate.

## Qualitative Risk Assessment

| LOW | MEDIUM | HIGH |
|---|---|---|

Our risk assessment reflects MIL's broad product line and geographic reach, offset by a highly competitive marketplace and the company's proactive acquisition strategy, which we believe increases its risk profile.

## Quantitative Evaluations

**S&P Quality Ranking**     **B**

| D | C | B- | B | B+ | A- | A | A+ |
|---|---|---|---|---|---|---|---|

**Relative Strength Rank**     **MODERATE**

65

LOWEST = 1        HIGHEST = 99

## Revenue/Earnings Data

**Revenue (Million $)**

| | 1Q | 2Q | 3Q | 4Q | Year |
|---|---|---|---|---|---|
| 2008 | 396.2 | 414.2 | 395.0 | -- | -- |
| 2007 | 372.0 | 383.2 | 371.2 | 405.2 | 1,532 |
| 2006 | 268.4 | 273.8 | 330.1 | 383.1 | 1,255 |
| 2005 | 250.2 | 245.0 | 293.6 | 256.3 | 991.0 |
| 2004 | 222.5 | 224.7 | 210.7 | 225.4 | 883.3 |
| 2003 | 187.5 | 196.4 | 200.1 | 215.8 | 799.6 |

**Earnings Per Share ($)**

| | | | | | |
|---|---|---|---|---|---|
| 2008 | 0.59 | 0.72 | 0.71 | E0.92 | E3.49 |
| 2007 | 0.49 | 0.52 | 0.66 | 0.82 | 2.48 |
| 2006 | 0.64 | 0.54 | 0.27 | 0.34 | 1.79 |
| 2005 | 0.64 | 0.47 | 0.44 | 0.02 | 1.55 |
| 2004 | 0.55 | 0.57 | 0.50 | 0.49 | 2.10 |
| 2003 | 0.44 | 0.46 | 0.50 | 0.66 | 2.06 |

Fiscal year ended Dec. 31. Next earnings report expected: Early February. EPS Estimates based on S&P Operating Earnings; historical GAAP earnings are as reported.

## Dividend Data

No cash dividends have been paid since January 2002.

---

The McGraw-Hill Companies

# Millipore Corp

## Business Summary November 05, 2008

COMPANY OVERVIEW. Millipore provides tools and services for the development and production of therapeutic drugs. MIL focuses on solutions for drug manufacturing and other production processes, and on research and development tools for the life science industry. MIL's offerings include consumable products, capital equipment, and services sold mainly to pharmaceutical, biotechnology and life science research companies. In 2007, consumables and services accounted for about 86% of sales, with the remaining 14% from hardware. The company sells more than 5,000 products, including process filtration and chromatography products, hardware components and systems used to manufacture and process biopharmaceuticals, process monitoring tools to test for contamination, laboratory sample preparation products, and laboratory water products used to create ultra pure water for laboratory analysis and clinical testing.

The company concentrates its in-house R&D on the development of new products and has augmented its product offerings and research capabilities through acquisitions and alliances, including the $1.5 billion acquisition of Serologicals in July 2006. MIL has said that its operations could be affected by an increasing number of biologic therapeutics being developed and approved over time, since its products are used in research laboratories, drug development programs, and drug manufacturing. According to the company, the drug industry is developing about 2,200 biologic compounds, including about 565 antibodies.

MIL sells its products through a global sales network. In the U.S., it mainly uses a direct sales force and Web site sales. Outside the U.S., MIL has subsidiaries and branches in more than 30 countries, and also employs independent distributors. Revenues by geographic region were as follows: the Americas 42% in 2007 (45% in 2006), Europe 41% (39%), and Asia Pacific (the majority derived from Japan) 17% (16%). Competitors include Amersham Biosciences, Apogent Technologies (now part of Thermo Fisher Scientific), Pall Corp., Qiagen, and United States Filter Corp.

## Company Financials Fiscal Year Ended Dec. 31

### Per Share Data ($)

| | 2007 | 2006 | 2005 | 2004 | 2003 | 2002 | 2001 | 2000 | 1999 | 1998 |
|---|---|---|---|---|---|---|---|---|---|---|
| Tangible Book Value | NM | NM | 12.74 | 12.24 | 8.72 | 5.16 | 7.60 | 5.25 | 2.36 | 1.37 |
| Cash Flow | 4.73 | 3.16 | 2.53 | 2.99 | 2.88 | 2.39 | 1.96 | 3.51 | 2.40 | 1.23 |
| Earnings | 2.48 | 1.79 | 1.55 | 2.10 | 2.06 | 1.67 | 1.32 | 2.53 | 1.42 | 0.22 |
| S&P Core Earnings | 2.48 | 1.81 | 1.43 | 1.27 | 1.67 | 1.41 | 1.08 | NA | NA | NA |
| Dividends | Nil | Nil | Nil | Nil | Nil | Nil | 0.44 | 0.44 | 0.44 | 0.42 |
| Payout Ratio | Nil | Nil | Nil | Nil | Nil | Nil | 33% | 17% | 31% | 191% |
| Prices:High | 83.20 | 76.95 | 67.95 | 57.20 | 49.37 | 60.95 | 66.85 | 77.38 | 42.13 | 38.44 |
| Prices:Low | 65.29 | 59.58 | 42.01 | 42.13 | 29.90 | 27.25 | 42.65 | 36.25 | 23.44 | 17.25 |
| P/E Ratio:High | 34 | 43 | 44 | 27 | 24 | 36 | 51 | 31 | 30 | NM |
| P/E Ratio:Low | 26 | 33 | 27 | 20 | 15 | 16 | 32 | 14 | 17 | NM |

### Income Statement Analysis (Million $)

| | 2007 | 2006 | 2005 | 2004 | 2003 | 2002 | 2001 | 2000 | 1999 | 1998 |
|---|---|---|---|---|---|---|---|---|---|---|
| Revenue | 1,532 | 1,255 | 991 | 883 | 800 | 704 | 657 | 954 | 771 | 699 |
| Operating Income | 376 | 219 | 195 | 182 | 166 | 160 | 150 | 216 | 149 | 89.2 |
| Depreciation | 124 | 74.4 | 50.7 | 44.5 | 40.5 | 35.0 | 30.7 | 46.1 | 44.3 | 44.4 |
| Interest Expense | 69.0 | 45.3 | 6.71 | 9.45 | 16.5 | 19.0 | 25.3 | 26.9 | 30.2 | 29.5 |
| Pretax Income | 152 | 120 | 138 | 130 | 112 | 104 | 78.4 | 154 | 82.4 | 8.54 |
| Effective Tax Rate | 8.15% | 17.8% | 41.7% | 19.1% | 10.1% | 22.0% | 19.0% | 22.4% | 21.9% | NM |
| Net Income | 136 | 97.0 | 80.2 | 106 | 101 | 80.8 | 63.5 | 119 | 64.3 | 9.86 |
| S&P Core Earnings | 136 | 97.9 | 74.6 | 64.0 | 82.0 | 68.5 | 51.8 | NA | NA | NA |

### Balance Sheet & Other Financial Data (Million $)

| | 2007 | 2006 | 2005 | 2004 | 2003 | 2002 | 2001 | 2000 | 1999 | 1998 |
|---|---|---|---|---|---|---|---|---|---|---|
| Cash | 36.2 | 77.5 | 651 | 152 | 147 | 101 | 62.5 | 58.4 | 51.1 | 36.0 |
| Current Assets | 690 | 709 | 1,067 | 541 | 516 | 390 | 312 | 465 | 359 | 305 |
| Total Assets | 2,777 | 2,771 | 1,647 | 1,014 | 951 | 786 | 916 | 875 | 793 | 762 |
| Current Liabilities | 282 | 402 | 243 | 163 | 222 | 134 | 134 | 235 | 270 | 299 |
| Long Term Debt | 1,260 | 1,316 | 552 | 147 | 216 | 334 | 320 | 300 | 313 | 299 |
| Common Equity | 1,137 | 948 | 792 | 639 | 461 | 288 | 394 | 305 | 177 | 137 |
| Total Capital | 2,412 | 2,286 | 1,350 | 793 | 677 | 622 | 759 | 605 | 490 | 436 |
| Capital Expenditures | 102 | 110 | 86.4 | 63.7 | 71.9 | 79.3 | 72.3 | 52.2 | 31.3 | 59.8 |
| Cash Flow | 260 | 171 | 131 | 150 | 141 | 116 | 94.2 | 165 | 109 | 54.3 |
| Current Ratio | 2.5 | 1.8 | 4.4 | 3.3 | 2.3 | 2.9 | 2.3 | 2.0 | 1.3 | 1.0 |
| % Long Term Debt of Capitalization | 52.2 | 57.6 | 40.9 | 18.5 | 31.9 | 53.7 | 42.1 | 49.6 | 63.9 | 68.6 |
| % Net Income of Revenue | 8.9 | 7.7 | 8.1 | 12.0 | 12.6 | 11.5 | 9.7 | 12.5 | 8.3 | 1.4 |
| % Return on Assets | 4.9 | 4.4 | 6.0 | 10.7 | 11.5 | 9.3 | 7.3 | 14.3 | 8.3 | 1.3 |
| % Return on Equity | 13.1 | 11.1 | 11.2 | 19.1 | 26.9 | 23.7 | 18.2 | 49.4 | 41.4 | 6.9 |

Data as orig reptd.; bef. results of disc opers/spec. items. Per share data adj. for stk. divs.; EPS diluted. E-Estimated. NA-Not Available. NM-Not Meaningful. NR-Not Ranked. UR-Under Review.

**Office:** 290 Concord Road, Billerica, MA 01821.
**Telephone:** 978-715-4321 .
**Website:** http://www.millipore.com
**Chrmn, Pres & CEO:** M.D. Madaus

**CFO:** C.F. Wagner, Jr.
**CSO:** D.W. Harris
**Chief Acctg Officer & Cntlr:** A.L. Mattacchione
**Treas:** G. Helliwell

**Investor Contact:** J. Young (978-715-1527)
**Board Members:** D. Bellus, R. C. Bishop, M. D. Booth, R. A. Classon, M. A. Hendricks, M. H. Hoffman, M. D. Madaus, J. F. Reno, E. M. Scolnick, K. E. Welke
**Founded:** 1954
**Domicile:** Massachusetts
**Employees:** 6,000

# Molex Inc

**STANDARD &POOR'S**

| S&P Recommendation | HOLD ★★★☆☆ | Price $13.05 (as of Nov 14, 2008) | 12-Mo. Target Price $16.00 | Investment Style Large-Cap Growth |
|---|---|---|---|---|

**GICS Sector** Information Technology
**Sub-Industry** Electronic Manufacturing Services

**Summary** This company makes electrical and electronic devices primarily for OEMs in the computer, telecommunications, home appliance and home entertainment industries.

## Key Stock Statistics (Source S&P, Vickers, company reports)

| | | | | | | | |
|---|---|---|---|---|---|---|---|
| 52-Wk Range | $30.61–11.63 | S&P Oper. EPS 2009**E** | 1.25 | Market Capitalization(B) | $1.273 | Beta | 1.35 |
| Trailing 12-Month EPS | $1.15 | S&P Oper. EPS 2010**E** | 1.60 | Yield (%) | 4.67 | S&P 3-Yr. Proj. EPS CAGR(%) | 10 |
| Trailing 12-Month P/E | 11.4 | P/E on S&P Oper. EPS 2009**E** | 10.4 | Dividend Rate/Share | $0.61 | S&P Credit Rating | NA |
| $10K Invested 5 Yrs Ago | $4,294 | Common Shares Outstg. (M) | 176.1 | Institutional Ownership (%) | 65 | | |

## Price Performance

30-Week Mov. Avg. · · · · 10-Week Mov. Avg. – – **GAAP Earnings vs. Previous Year** Volume Above Avg. STARS
12-Mo. Target Price — Relative Strength — ▲ Up ▼ Down ► No Change Below Avg. ★

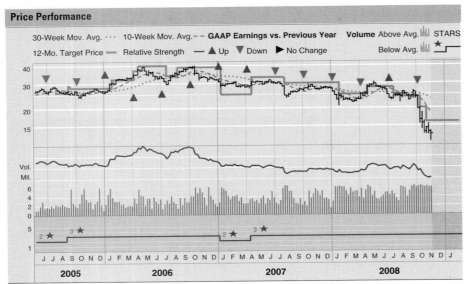

Options: CBOE, P, Ph

Analysis prepared by **Stewart Scharf** on October 29, 2008, when the stock traded at **$ 13.63**.

### Highlights

➤ We project low single digit revenue growth for FY 09 (Jun.), as demand softens for telecom and data infrastructure products, as well as consumer electronics, especially in North America and Europe. We still see some demand for entry level phones with lower connector content in developing global regions. We expect industrial and automotive sales to remain very weak, and we believe the company will pursue some strategic acquisitions.

➤ We believe gross margins will expand sequentially during FY 09, from 30.5% in FY 08, as new products and lower gold, copper and resin costs offset soft volume and a negative effect from a strengthening U.S. dollar. We expect adjusted EBITDA margins to widen from 18% in FY 08, as SG&A expenses fall below 20% of sales, reflecting cost savings from a restructuring program; we project total annual pretax savings of about $110 million, with the plan likely to be completed in early FY 10.

➤ We estimate an effective tax rate of 32% in FY 09, and operating EPS of $1.25 (before at least $0.27 of restructuring charges), advancing 28% in FY 10, to $1.60.

### Investment Rationale/Risk

➤ We base our hold recommendation on our valuation metrics, along with our expectations of a gradual sequential rebound in bookings later in 2009 as the company focuses on expanding its market share. We also project potential cost benefits from a restructuring plan and stabilizing commodities prices.

➤ Risks to our recommendation and target price include a further significant rise in copper, gold and plastics prices; a stronger dollar against the yen and the euro; and a prolonged global economic downturn. Corporate governance practices are also a concern to us as MOLX has two classes of stock, and the board consists mostly of insiders.

➤ Based on our relative and historical valuation metrics, our 12-month target price is $16. We arrive at this calculation by applying a P/E multiple of 13X to our FY 09 EPS estimate, a premium to our projected FY 09 P/E for the S&P 500 and the multiple for S&P's electronic manufacturing services sub-industry, but at a discount to the company's five-year average historical forward P/E.

## Qualitative Risk Assessment

| LOW | MEDIUM | HIGH |
|---|---|---|

Our risk assessment reflects the cyclicality in MOLX's global markets, price and product competition, volatile raw material costs, and weaker foreign currency exchange rates. However, we view the company's balance sheet as strong.

## Quantitative Evaluations

**S&P Quality Ranking** B+

| D | C | B- | B | B+ | A- | A | A+ |
|---|---|---|---|---|---|---|---|

**Relative Strength Rank** MODERATE

37

LOWEST = 1    HIGHEST = 99

## Revenue/Earnings Data

### Revenue (Million $)

| | 1Q | 2Q | 3Q | 4Q | Year |
|---|---|---|---|---|---|
| 2009 | 839.0 | -- | -- | -- | -- |
| 2008 | 792.6 | 841.6 | 822.3 | 871.9 | 3,328 |
| 2007 | 829.6 | 837.5 | 807.0 | 791.9 | 3,266 |
| 2006 | 659.8 | 697.4 | 720.3 | 783.8 | 2,861 |
| 2005 | 640.2 | 651.8 | 612.8 | 643.8 | 2,549 |
| 2004 | 496.8 | 549.0 | 569.2 | 631.8 | 2,247 |

### Earnings Per Share ($)

| | 1Q | 2Q | 3Q | 4Q | Year |
|---|---|---|---|---|---|
| 2009 | 0.25 | E0.24 | E0.32 | E0.35 | E1.25 |
| 2008 | 0.29 | 0.33 | 0.28 | 0.29 | 1.19 |
| 2007 | 0.41 | 0.36 | 0.35 | 0.18 | 1.30 |
| 2006 | 0.25 | 0.31 | 0.33 | 0.38 | 1.26 |
| 2005 | 0.29 | 0.27 | 0.24 | 0.03 | 0.81 |
| 2004 | 0.17 | 0.21 | 0.24 | 0.30 | 0.92 |

Fiscal year ended Jun. 30. Next earnings report expected: Late January. EPS Estimates based on S&P Operating Earnings; historical GAAP earnings are as reported.

## Dividend Data (Dates: mm/dd Payment Date: mm/dd/yy)

| Amount ($) | Date Decl. | Ex-Div. Date | Stk. of Record | Payment Date |
|---|---|---|---|---|
| 0.113 | 12/26 | 12/27 | 12/31 | 01/25/08 |
| 0.113 | 07/26 | 03/27 | 03/31 | 04/25/08 |
| 0.113 | 07/26 | 06/26 | 06/30 | 07/25/08 |
| 0.153 | 08/05 | 09/26 | 09/30 | 10/24/08 |

Dividends have been paid since 1976. Source: Company reports.

# Molex Inc

**STANDARD &POOR'S**

## Business Summary October 29, 2008

CORPORATE OVERVIEW. Molex is the world's second largest connector maker, operating 45 plants in 17 countries, and offering more than 100,000 products.

MOLX's products include electrical and electronic devices such as terminals, cable assemblies, interconnection systems, fiber-optic interconnection systems, and mechanical and electronic switches. In FY 08 (Jun.), these products were sold to the following industries: data products (22%), telecommunications (26%), consumer products (18%), automotive (18%), industrial (13%), and other (3%). Revenues by segment were: Connector, 56%; Transportation, 15%; Custom & Electrical, 28%; and Corporate and other, less than 1%.

MOLX sells primarily to original equipment manufacturers (OEMs), subcontractors and suppliers. Customers include Arrow, Cisco, Dell, Ford, General Motors, Hewlett-Packard, IBM, Matsushita, Motorola and Nokia.

Revenues outside the U.S. accounted for 73% of the FY 08 total. About 52% of net revenues were generated in Asia/Pacific (including 22% in China and 16% in Japan), 20% in Europe and 28% in the Americas. Some 48% of manufacturing capacity is in lower-cost regions such as Eastern Europe, Mexico and China.

At September 30, 2008, order backlog was $386 million, up 9% from a year earlier. New orders in the first fiscal quarter were $796 million, down 1.9% from a

year earlier and 7% sequentially. Orders were as follows: telecom rose 11%, year to year, but fell 5% sequentially. Data declined 6% and 4%; consumer electronics slipped 2% but rose 2% sequentially; medical electronics fell 4% and 12%; industrial dropped 7% and 15%; and automotive orders declined 13% and 17%. The company expects significant long-term growth in medical electronics (3% of revenues in FY 08) as the population ages and demand increases for small home-monitoring equipment. In FY 08, the company generated 23% of sales from new products (introduced within the past 36 months).

In FY 08, MOLX repurchased 6.58 million of its Class A common shares and 1.4 million common shares for nearly $200 million. In the first quarter of FY 09 (Jun.), the company bought back 732,000 Cl. A common shares and 900,000 common shares for $39 million. About $161 million remains under the authorization.

In FY 08, MOLX recorded a pretax restructuring charge of $31 million ($0.12 a share, after tax) and a charge related to a change in the foreign tax credit of $17 million ($0.09).

## Company Financials Fiscal Year Ended Jun. 30

### Per Share Data ($)

| | 2008 | 2007 | 2006 | 2005 | 2004 | 2003 | 2002 | 2001 | 2000 | 1999 |
|---|---|---|---|---|---|---|---|---|---|---|
| Tangible Book Value | 12.66 | 10.64 | 11.60 | 10.78 | 10.05 | 9.10 | 8.64 | 8.25 | 7.83 | 6.94 |
| Cash Flow | NA | 2.58 | 2.41 | 2.02 | 2.10 | 1.62 | 1.53 | 2.13 | 2.11 | 1.77 |
| Earnings | 1.19 | 1.30 | 1.26 | 0.81 | 0.92 | 0.44 | 0.39 | 1.03 | 1.12 | 0.91 |
| S&P Core Earnings | 1.13 | 1.30 | 1.27 | 0.76 | 0.85 | 0.39 | 0.39 | 1.01 | NA | NA |
| Dividends | NA | 0.30 | 0.23 | 0.15 | 0.10 | 0.10 | 0.10 | 0.10 | 0.07 | 0.04 |
| Payout Ratio | NA | 23% | 18% | 19% | 11% | 23% | 26% | 10% | 6% | 4% |
| Prices:High | NA | 32.34 | 40.10 | 30.00 | 36.10 | 35.12 | 39.61 | 48.00 | 63.75 | 45.60 |
| Prices:Low | NA | 23.50 | 25.63 | 23.75 | 27.07 | 19.98 | 19.43 | 25.76 | 34.19 | 20.40 |
| P/E Ratio:High | NA | 25 | 32 | 37 | 39 | 80 | NM | 47 | 57 | 50 |
| P/E Ratio:Low | NA | 18 | 20 | 29 | 29 | 45 | 50 | 25 | 31 | 22 |

### Income Statement Analysis (Million $)

| | 2008 | 2007 | 2006 | 2005 | 2004 | 2003 | 2002 | 2001 | 2000 | 1999 |
|---|---|---|---|---|---|---|---|---|---|---|
| Revenue | 3,328 | 3,266 | 2,861 | 2,549 | 2,247 | 1,843 | 1,712 | 2,366 | 2,217 | 1,712 |
| Operating Income | NA | 596 | 552 | 481 | 450 | -120 | 324 | 498 | 512 | 395 |
| Depreciation | 252 | 238 | 215 | 231 | 228 | 229 | 224 | 218 | 196 | 169 |
| Interest Expense | NA | Nil | Nil | Nil | Nil | Nil | Nil | Nil | Nil | Nil |
| Pretax Income | 339 | 338 | 329 | 217 | 240 | 110 | 93.2 | 291 | 324 | 230 |
| Effective Tax Rate | 36.4% | 28.8% | 28.0% | 28.8% | 26.5% | 22.5% | 17.9% | 30.0% | 31.1% | 22.7% |
| Net Income | 215 | 241 | 237 | 154 | 176 | 84.9 | 76.5 | 204 | 222 | 178 |
| S&P Core Earnings | 205 | 241 | 238 | 143 | 164 | 76.1 | 76.7 | 200 | NA | NA |

### Balance Sheet & Other Financial Data (Million $)

| | 2008 | 2007 | 2006 | 2005 | 2004 | 2003 | 2002 | 2001 | 2000 | 1999 |
|---|---|---|---|---|---|---|---|---|---|---|
| Cash | 510 | 461 | 486 | 498 | 339 | 350 | 313 | 208 | 241 | 183 |
| Current Assets | NA | 1,591 | 1,548 | 1,374 | 1,169 | 962 | 915 | 892 | 1,023 | 881 |
| Total Assets | 3,600 | 3,316 | 2,973 | 2,728 | 2,572 | 2,335 | 2,254 | 2,214 | 2,247 | 1,902 |
| Current Liabilities | NA | 531 | 595 | 470 | 428 | 356 | 360 | 374 | 475 | 342 |
| Long Term Debt | NA | 128 | 8.81 | 9.98 | 14.0 | 16.9 | 17.8 | 25.5 | 21.6 | 20.1 |
| Common Equity | 2,677 | 2,523 | 2,281 | 2,168 | 2,066 | 1,897 | 1,828 | 1,766 | 1,706 | 1,501 |
| Total Capital | NA | 2,651 | 2,290 | 2,180 | 2,081 | 1,914 | 1,846 | 1,793 | 1,734 | 1,526 |
| Capital Expenditures | 235 | 297 | 277 | 231 | 190 | 171 | 172 | 376 | 337 | 229 |
| Cash Flow | NA | 479 | 452 | 385 | 404 | 314 | 300 | 422 | 419 | 347 |
| Current Ratio | 2.8 | 3.0 | 2.6 | 2.9 | 2.7 | 2.7 | 2.5 | 2.4 | 2.2 | 2.6 |
| % Long Term Debt of Capitalization | 5.2 | 4.8 | 0.4 | 0.5 | 0.7 | 0.9 | 1.0 | 1.4 | 1.2 | 1.3 |
| % Net Income of Revenue | 6.5 | 7.4 | 8.3 | 6.1 | 7.8 | 4.6 | 4.5 | 8.6 | 10.0 | 10.4 |
| % Return on Assets | 6.2 | 7.7 | 8.3 | 5.8 | 7.2 | 3.7 | 3.4 | 9.1 | 10.0 | 10.1 |
| % Return on Equity | 8.3 | 10.0 | 10.7 | 7.3 | 8.9 | 4.6 | 4.3 | 11.7 | 13.9 | 12.9 |

Data as orig reptd.; bef. results of disc opers/spec. items. Per share data adj. for stk. divs.; EPS diluted. E-Estimated. NA-Not Available. NM-Not Meaningful. NR-Not Ranked. UR-Under Review.

**Office:** 2222 Wellington Court, Lisle, IL 60532.
**Telephone:** 630-969-4550.
**Website:** http://www.molex.com
**Co-Chrmn:** J.H. Krehbie, Jr.

**Co-Chrmn:** F.A. Krehbiel
**Pres & COO:** L.G. McCarthy
**Vice Chrmn & CEO:** M.P. Slark
**Investor Contact:** D.D. Johnson (630-969-4550)

**Board Members:** M. J. Birck, M. L. Collins, E. D. Jannotta, J. H. Krehbie, Jr., F. L. Krehbiel, F. A. Krehbiel, K. Kusaka, D. L. Landsittel, J. W. Laymon, D. G. Lubin, J. S. Metcalf, R. J. Potter, M. P. Slark

**Founded:** 1938
**Domicile:** Delaware
**Employees:** 32,160

**The McGraw-Hill Companies**

# Molson Coors Brewing Co

**STANDARD &POOR'S**

| S&P Recommendation | BUY ★★★★☆ | Price | 12-Mo. Target Price | Investment Style |
|---|---|---|---|---|
| | | $42.55 (as of Nov 14, 2008) | $46.00 | Large-Cap Blend |

**GICS Sector** Consumer Staples
**Sub-Industry** Brewers

**Summary** TAP, the fifth largest brewer in the world, was formed in early 2005 via the combination of Adolph Coors Co. and Molson, Inc.

## Key Stock Statistics (Source S&P, Vickers, company reports)

| | | | | | | | |
|---|---|---|---|---|---|---|---|
| 52-Wk Range | $59.51–35.00 | S&P Oper. EPS 2008**E** | 2.96 | Market Capitalization(B) | $6.651 | Beta | 0.77 |
| Trailing 12-Month EPS | $2.51 | S&P Oper. EPS 2009**E** | 3.50 | Yield (%) | 1.88 | S&P 3-Yr. Proj. EPS CAGR(%) | 12 |
| Trailing 12-Month P/E | 17.0 | P/E on S&P Oper. EPS 2008**E** | 14.4 | Dividend Rate/Share | $0.80 | S&P Credit Rating | BBB |
| $10K Invested 5 Yrs Ago | $16,197 | Common Shares Outstg. (M) | 183.6 | Institutional Ownership (%) | 88 | | |

## Price Performance

30-Week Mov. Avg. ···· 10-Week Mov. Avg. - - **GAAP Earnings vs. Previous Year** Volume Above Avg. |||| STARS
12-Mo. Target Price — Relative Strength — ▲ Up ▼ Down ▶ No Change    Below Avg. |||| ★

Options: CBOE, P, Ph

Analysis prepared by **Esther Y. Kwon, CFA** on October 30, 2008, when the stock traded at **$ 39.05.**

## Highlights

➤ TAP has combined its U.S. operations into a joint venture with SABMiller. By pooling their breweries, distribution resources and brand marketing, the companies believe they can achieve $500 million of cost synergies annually. The deal gives TAP a 50% voting and 42% economic interest in the joint venture and closed at the end of June.

➤ Excluding the impact of the joint venture, we see sales rising in the mid single digits in 2008, on volume increases and pricing. We expect continued growth for Coors Light in the U.S. and Canada, and strong double digit growth for Blue Moon in the U.S. However, we see continued pressures in the U.K. market hurting overall sales growth, although we expect improvement as the Scottish and Newcastle brewing agreement begins to contribute in the second half. We see incremental cost reductions, estimated at $80 million, offsetting some commodities and packaging cost pressures.

➤ On lower interest expense but a higher effective tax rate, we estimate 2008 operating EPS of $3.05, before special items, versus an adjusted $2.80 in 2007. For 2009, we forecast EPS of $3.55, on a lower tax rate.

## Investment Rationale/Risk

➤ We have been concerned about raw materials inflation, particularly in Canada and the U.K., where TAP has limited ability to hedge adverse impact, but recent declines in key commodities has made us more positive on TAP's outlook. We see TAP benefiting from potential disruption as Anheuser-Busch is integrated into In-Bev, and we project improving results based on new business and easing comparisons in the U.K. in the second half of 2008 and on continuing strength in core brands, Coors Light, Keystone Light and Blue Moon in the U.S. With close of joint venture at the end of June 2008, we think management could take actions to return value to shareholders through share buy-back or dividend increase.

➤ Risks to our opinion and target price include a weakening of Coors Light volumes in the U.S. and Canada. Commodity cost increases could pose additional risks. We see significant execution risk in the joint venture.

➤ Our 12-month target price of $46 is supported by our P/E analyses. Applying a forward P/E multiple of 13X, below of TAP's recent average, to our 2009 EPS estimate, we derive a value of $46.

## Qualitative Risk Assessment

| LOW | MEDIUM | HIGH |
|---|---|---|

Our risk assessment reflects the stable revenue streams of the brewing industry, in which TAP is a major player. We have some corporate governance concerns with respect to TAP's multi-class stock structure and its more than 50% controlling family interest.

## Quantitative Evaluations

**S&P Quality Ranking**                                          A-

| D | C | B- | B | B+ | A- | A | A+ |
|---|---|---|---|---|---|---|---|

**Relative Strength Rank**                            **STRONG**

LOWEST = 1                                          HIGHEST = 99

## Revenue/Earnings Data

**Revenue (Million $)**

| | 1Q | 2Q | 3Q | 4Q | Year |
|---|---|---|---|---|---|
| 2008 | 1,357 | 1,757 | 921.1 | -- | -- |
| 2007 | 1,229 | 1,676 | 1,685 | 1,600 | 6,191 |
| 2006 | 1,154 | 1,583 | 1,577 | 1,531 | 5,845 |
| 2005 | 1,048 | 1,547 | 1,527 | 1,385 | 5,507 |
| 2004 | 923.5 | 1,151 | 1,104 | 1,127 | 4,306 |
| 2003 | 828.1 | 1,100 | 1,049 | 1,023 | 4,000 |

**Earnings Per Share ($)**

| | | | | | |
|---|---|---|---|---|---|
| 2008 | 0.25 | 0.50 | 0.92 | E0.76 | E2.96 |
| 2007 | 0.11 | 1.02 | 0.74 | 0.96 | 2.84 |
| 2006 | -0.11 | 0.91 | 0.71 | 0.65 | 2.16 |
| 2005 | -0.24 | 0.56 | 0.76 | 0.20 | 1.44 |
| 2004 | 0.07 | 0.95 | 0.84 | 0.73 | 2.60 |
| 2003 | 0.01 | 1.04 | 0.84 | 0.49 | 2.39 |

Fiscal year ended Dec. 31. Next earnings report expected: Mid February. EPS Estimates based on S&P Operating Earnings; historical GAAP earnings are as reported.

## Dividend Data (Dates: mm/dd Payment Date: mm/dd/yy)

| Amount ($) | Date Decl. | Ex-Div. Date | Stk. of Record | Payment Date |
|---|---|---|---|---|
| 0.160 | 02/15 | 02/27 | 02/29 | 03/17/08 |
| 0.200 | 05/19 | 05/28 | 05/30 | 06/16/08 |
| 0.200 | 07/29 | 08/27 | 08/29 | 09/15/08 |
| 0.200 | 11/14 | 11/25 | 11/28 | 12/15/08 |

Dividends have been paid since 1970. Source: Company reports.

---

**Please read the Required Disclosures and Analyst Certification on the last page of this report.**

*The McGraw·Hill Companies*

# Molson Coors Brewing Co

**STANDARD &POOR'S**

## Business Summary October 30, 2008

CORPORATE OVERVIEW. Molson Coors Brewing Company was formed in February 2005 by the combination of Adolph Coors Co. and Canadian brewer Molson, Inc. Total combined sales are estimated at about 61 million hectoliters, making it the fifth largest brewer in the world. The transaction resulted in each Molson Class B voting share being converted to shares with 0.126 voting rights and 0.234 non-voting rights of Molson Coors stock, and each Molson Class A converted to shares with a 0.360 non-voting share of Molson Coors.

Molson Inc. was the world's 14th largest brewer in 2004, pre-merger, with operations in Canada, Brazil and the United States. A global brewer with C$3.5 billion in gross annual sales, Molson traces its roots back to 1786, making it North America's oldest beer brand. Adolph Coors Co. was the third largest U.S. brewer, with a 10.3% share of the U.S. beer market in 2004, selling 32.7 million barrels of beer and other malt beverage products, up 3% from the level of 2003. The company was founded in 1873.

TAP's stable of well known U.S. brands includes Coors Light, Original Coors, and Coors Non-Alcoholic premium beers; above-premium brews such as George Killian's Irish Red and Blue Moon Belgian White Ale, and Aspen Edge;

and lower-priced beers, including Extra Gold, Keystone Premium, Keystone Light, and Keystone Ice. Coors produces Zima and Zima Citrus malt-based beverages. Brands sold primarily in Canada include Molson Canadian, Molson Dry, Molson Export, Creemore Springs, Rickard's Red Ale, Carling and Pilsner. Brands sold primarily in the U.K. include Carling, Coors Fine Light Beer, Worthington's Caffrey's, Reef, Screamers, and Stones. Approximately 58% of TAP's 2007 volume was sold in the United States segment, 19% in the Canada segment, and 23% in the Europe segment.

CORPORATE STRATEGY. We look favorably on TAP's strategy to gain market share in each area by cross marketing its products. We are particularly pleased with the gains we see for Coors Light brand in Canada, where it now has a 10% market share, making it the largest selling light-beer, and second largest-selling beer brand overall in Canada.

## Company Financials Fiscal Year Ended Dec. 31

| Per Share Data ($) | 2007 | 2006 | 2005 | 2004 | 2003 | 2002 | 2001 | 2000 | 1999 | 1998 |
|---|---|---|---|---|---|---|---|---|---|---|
| Tangible Book Value | NM | NM | NM | 1.72 | NM | NM | 12.03 | 12.16 | 11.03 | 10.26 |
| Cash Flow | 4.74 | 4.68 | 3.89 | 6.13 | 5.71 | 5.36 | 3.28 | 3.19 | 2.88 | 2.45 |
| Earnings | 2.84 | 2.16 | 1.44 | 2.60 | 2.39 | 2.21 | 1.66 | 1.47 | 1.23 | 0.91 |
| S&P Core Earnings | 2.53 | 1.87 | 1.07 | 2.13 | 2.10 | 0.77 | 0.68 | NA | NA | NA |
| Dividends | 0.64 | 0.64 | 0.64 | 0.41 | 0.41 | 0.41 | 0.40 | 0.36 | 0.32 | 0.30 |
| Payout Ratio | 23% | 31% | 44% | 16% | 17% | 19% | 24% | 25% | 26% | 33% |
| Prices:High | 57.70 | 38.50 | 40.00 | 40.06 | 32.41 | 35.08 | 40.59 | 41.16 | 32.91 | 28.38 |
| Prices:Low | 37.56 | 30.38 | 28.69 | 26.87 | 22.93 | 25.25 | 21.33 | 18.69 | 22.63 | 14.63 |
| P/E Ratio:High | 20 | 18 | 28 | 15 | 14 | 16 | 25 | 28 | 27 | 31 |
| P/E Ratio:Low | 13 | 15 | 20 | 10 | 10 | 11 | 13 | 13 | 18 | 16 |

| Income Statement Analysis (Million $) | | | | | | | | | | |
|---|---|---|---|---|---|---|---|---|---|---|
| Revenue | 6,191 | 5,845 | 5,507 | 4,306 | 4,000 | 3,776 | 2,429 | 2,414 | 2,057 | 1,900 |
| Operating Income | 1,099 | 1,097 | 960 | 609 | 551 | 535 | 296 | 295 | 271 | 239 |
| Depreciation | 346 | 438 | 393 | 268 | 244 | 230 | 121 | 129 | 124 | 116 |
| Interest Expense | 136 | 143 | 131 | 72.4 | 81.2 | 70.9 | 2.01 | 6.41 | 4.36 | 9.80 |
| Pretax Income | 534 | 472 | 295 | 308 | 254 | 257 | 198 | 170 | 151 | 111 |
| Effective Tax Rate | 0.78% | 17.5% | 17.0% | 30.9% | 31.2% | 37.0% | 37.9% | 35.3% | 38.7% | 39.0% |
| Net Income | 515 | 374 | 230 | 197 | 175 | 162 | 123 | 110 | 92.3 | 67.8 |
| S&P Core Earnings | 459 | 324 | 172 | 161 | 154 | 56.1 | 50.7 | NA | NA | NA |

| Balance Sheet & Other Financial Data (Million $) | | | | | | | | | | |
|---|---|---|---|---|---|---|---|---|---|---|
| Cash | 377 | 182 | 39.4 | 123 | 19.4 | 59.2 | 310 | 120 | 164 | 256 |
| Current Assets | 1,777 | 1,458 | 1,468 | 1,268 | 1,079 | 1,054 | 607 | 498 | 613 | 549 |
| Total Assets | 13,452 | 11,603 | 11,799 | 4,658 | 4,486 | 4,297 | 1,740 | 1,629 | 1,546 | 1,461 |
| Current Liabilities | 1,736 | 1,800 | 2,237 | 1,177 | 1,134 | 1,148 | 518 | 379 | 393 | 384 |
| Long Term Debt | 2,261 | 2,130 | 2,137 | 894 | 1,160 | 1,383 | 20.0 | 105 | 105 | 105 |
| Common Equity | 7,149 | 5,817 | 5,325 | 1,601 | 1,267 | 982 | 951 | 932 | 842 | 775 |
| Total Capital | 10,059 | 8,601 | 8,151 | 2,682 | 2,623 | 2,522 | 1,033 | 1,127 | 1,025 | 946 |
| Capital Expenditures | 428 | 446 | 406 | 212 | 240 | 240 | 245 | 154 | 134 | 105 |
| Cash Flow | 861 | 812 | 623 | 465 | 418 | 392 | 244 | 239 | 216 | 184 |
| Current Ratio | 1.0 | 0.8 | 0.7 | 1.1 | 1.0 | 0.9 | 1.2 | 1.3 | 1.6 | 1.4 |
| % Long Term Debt of Capitalization | 22.5 | 24.8 | 26.2 | 33.3 | 44.2 | 54.9 | 1.9 | 9.3 | 10.2 | 11.1 |
| % Net Income of Revenue | 8.3 | 6.4 | 4.2 | 4.6 | 4.4 | 4.3 | 5.1 | 4.5 | 4.5 | 3.6 |
| % Return on Assets | 4.1 | 3.2 | 2.8 | 4.3 | 4.0 | 5.4 | 7.3 | 6.9 | 6.1 | 4.7 |
| % Return on Equity | 7.9 | 6.7 | 6.7 | 13.7 | 15.5 | 16.7 | 13.1 | 12.4 | 11.4 | 9.0 |

Data as orig reptd.; bef. results of disc opers/spec. items. Per share data adj. for stk. divs.; EPS diluted. E-Estimated. NA-Not Available. NM-Not Meaningful. NR-Not Ranked. UR-Under Review.

**Office:** 1225 17th St, Denver, CO 80202-5534.
**Telephone:** 303-279-6565.
**Website:** http://www.molsoncoors.com
**Chrmn:** E.H. Molson

**Pres & CEO:** P. Swinburn
**Vice Chrmn:** P.H. Coors
**SVP, Secy & General Counsel:** S.D. Walker
**CFO:** S. Glendinning

**Investor Contact:** J. Frye (303-279-6565)
**Board Members:** F. Bellini, R. G. Brewer, J. E. Cleghorn, P. H. Coors, C. M. Herington, F. W. Hobbs, A. T. Molson, E. H. Molson, I. Napier, D. P. O'Brien, M. E. Osborn, P. H. Patsley, H. Riley

**Founded:** 1873
**Domicile:** Delaware
**Employees:** 9,700

**STANDARD &POOR'S**

# Monsanto Co

| S&P Recommendation | HOLD ★★★☆☆ | Price $74.10 (as of Nov 14, 2008) | 12-Mo. Target Price $88.00 | Investment Style Large-Cap Blend |
|---|---|---|---|---|

**GICS Sector** Materials
**Sub-Industry** Fertilizers & Agricultural Chemicals

**Summary** This company is a global provider of agricultural products and integrated solutions for farmers.

## Key Stock Statistics (Source S&P, Vickers, company reports)

| | | | | | | | |
|---|---|---|---|---|---|---|---|
| 52-Wk Range | $145.80–68.02 | S&P Oper. EPS 2009**E** | 4.40 | Market Capitalization(B) | $40.603 | Beta | 1.17 |
| Trailing 12-Month EPS | $3.62 | S&P Oper. EPS 2010**E** | 4.85 | Yield (%) | 1.30 | S&P 3-Yr. Proj. EPS CAGR(%) | 15 |
| Trailing 12-Month P/E | 20.5 | P/E on S&P Oper. EPS 2009**E** | 16.8 | Dividend Rate/Share | $0.96 | S&P Credit Rating | A+ |
| $10K Invested 5 Yrs Ago | $60,803 | Common Shares Outstg. (M) | 547.9 | Institutional Ownership (%) | 84 | | |

## Price Performance

30-Week Mov. Avg. · · · · 10-Week Mov. Avg. – – — GAAP Earnings vs. Previous Year    Volume Above Avg. ▂▃▅ STARS
12-Mo. Target Price —— Relative Strength — ▲ Up ▼ Down ► No Change    Below Avg. ▂▃▅ ★

Options: ASE, CBOE, P

Analysis prepared by **Kevin Kirkeby** on October 09, 2008, when the stock traded at **$ 81.44**.

## Highlights

➤ Following a 33% increase in FY 08 (Aug.), we forecast revenue growth to slow to about 14% in FY 09 as planted acreage in the U.S. stabilizes. We still see elevated grain prices encouraging farmers to seek additional yield by using MON's premium seeds. Growth outside the U.S. will likely benefit from the July 2008 acquisition of Cristiani, which added about 900 distributors in Central America, and new product launches in Brazil and Argentina. Fertilizer prices will stabilize in the coming year, in our view, after rising sharply in FY 08.

➤ We look for wider margins in FY 09 on growing sales of higher value-added seeds and traits, including its double and triple stacked varieties. Additionally, we see modestly lower selling and administrative expenses supporting an operating margin, after depreciation, near 27% in FY 09. Our model assumes research and development spending around 9% of FY 09 revenues.

➤ We project a 23% rise in FY 09 operating EPS to $4.40. This assumes no change in the share count, as we believe the buyback authorization merely covers the dilutive effect of stock options.

## Investment Rationale/Risk

➤ MON shares trade at a valuation premium to the S&P 500, reflecting what we see as above-average earnings growth prospects over the coming decade. We expect the primary contributors to be the introduction of next-generation seeds, and the development of its smaller product segments. Also, we anticipate that recent trait approvals will boost crop penetration outside the United States. However, given current market uncertainty, we believe the stock, recently trading at a much smaller premium to the market, is fairly valued.

➤ Risks to our recommendation and target price include unfavorable weather affecting planting, exchange rate fluctuations, the possibility of lower-than-anticipated margins, and a sharp decline in grain prices.

➤ Our three stage DCF model, which assumes a 10.5% cost of equity and annual free cash flow growth of 19% for three years, slowing over the following 10 years to 4% terminal growth, calculates intrinsic value of $96. Our relative valuation model targets a four quarter forward P/E multiple of 18X, and produces a value of $80. Blending these two metrics results in our 12-month target price of $88.

## Qualitative Risk Assessment

| LOW | MEDIUM | HIGH |
|---|---|---|

Our risk assessment for MON reflects its exposure to global agricultural markets and currencies, adverse weather, unfavorable legal and regulatory developments, and risks relating to the enforcement of intellectual property rights. This is offset by relatively low exposure to economic cycles and our view of consistent cash flow generation.

## Quantitative Evaluations

**S&P Quality Ranking**  B+

| D | C | B- | B | B+ | A- | A | A+ |
|---|---|---|---|---|---|---|---|

**Relative Strength Rank**   MODERATE

50

LOWEST = 1                                          HIGHEST = 99

## Revenue/Earnings Data

**Revenue (Million $)**

| | 1Q | 2Q | 3Q | 4Q | Year |
|---|---|---|---|---|---|
| 2008 | 2,049 | 3,727 | 3,538 | 2,051 | 11,365 |
| 2007 | 1,539 | 2,609 | 2,842 | 1,573 | 8,563 |
| 2006 | 1,405 | 2,200 | 2,348 | 1,391 | 7,344 |
| 2005 | 1,072 | 1,908 | 2,040 | 1,274 | 6,294 |
| 2004 | 1,028 | 1,492 | 1,679 | 1,258 | 5,457 |
| 2003 | -- | -- | -- | -- | 3,373 |

**Earnings Per Share ($)**

| | | | | | |
|---|---|---|---|---|---|
| 2008 | 0.45 | 2.00 | 1.46 | -0.32 | 3.59 |
| 2007 | 0.17 | 0.99 | 1.02 | -0.52 | 1.66 |
| 2006 | 0.11 | 0.80 | 0.61 | -0.25 | 1.27 |
| 2005 | -0.24 | 0.68 | 0.08 | -0.24 | 0.29 |
| 2004 | -0.15 | 0.29 | 0.43 | -0.07 | 0.51 |
| 2003 | -- | -- | -- | -- | -0.02 |

Fiscal year ended Aug. 31. Next earnings report expected: Early January. EPS Estimates based on S&P Operating Earnings; historical GAAP earnings are as reported.

## Dividend Data (Dates: mm/dd Payment Date: mm/dd/yy)

| Amount ($) | Date Decl. | Ex-Div. Date | Stk. of Record | Payment Date |
|---|---|---|---|---|
| 0.175 | 12/11 | 01/02 | 01/04 | 01/25/08 |
| 0.175 | 01/16 | 04/02 | 04/04 | 04/25/08 |
| 0.240 | 06/18 | 07/01 | 07/03 | 07/25/08 |
| 0.240 | 08/06 | 10/01 | 10/03 | 10/24/08 |

Dividends have been paid since 2001. Source: Company reports.

---

**Please read the Required Disclosures and Analyst Certification on the last page of this report.**

The McGraw-Hill Companies

# Monsanto Co

STANDARD
&POOR'S

## Business Summary October 09, 2008

CORPORATE OVERVIEW. Monsanto (MON) produces leading seed brands and develops biotechnology traits that assist farmers in controlling insects and weeds, and provides other seed companies with genetic material and biotech traits. MON's Roundup herbicides are used for agricultural, industrial and residential weed control, and are sold in more than 80 countries.

MARKET PROFILE. The company operates in two segments: agricultural productivity, and seeds and genomics. Agricultural productivity (45% of sales and 38% of gross profits in FY 08 (Aug.)) consists of MON's crop protection products (Roundup herbicide and other glyphosate products), its animal agriculture, and the Roundup lawn and garden products. In FY 08, Roundup and other glyphosate-based herbicides accounted for 36% of total sales. Patent protection for the active ingredient in Roundup herbicides expired in the U.S. in 2000. Since then, MON has repositioned itself as one of the lowest cost producers in an effort to mitigate declining herbicide pricing and margins.

Seeds and genomics (55% of sales and 62% of gross profits) consists of the global seeds and related traits businesses, and technology platforms based on plant genomics, which increases the speed and power of genetic research. MON's seeds and genomics segment focuses on corn, soybeans and other oilseeds, cotton and wheat. Given the loss of patent protection for Roundup, we believe MON has focused on capturing value and profitability in its patent-protected seeds and traits business, and expanded its product line through its acquisition of Seminis in 2005. Given this trend, we think that the growth and margin outlook for MON's seeds and genomics segment is superior to that of its agricultural productivity segment.

## Company Financials Fiscal Year Ended Aug. 31

| Per Share Data ($) | 2008 | 2007 | 2006 | 2005 | 2004 | 2003 | 2002 | 2001 | 2000 | 1999 |
|---|---|---|---|---|---|---|---|---|---|---|
| Tangible Book Value | 8.59 | 6.35 | 6.95 | 5.99 | 7.71 | 7.26 | 7.24 | 7.84 | 7.24 | NM |
| Cash Flow | NA | 2.61 | 2.25 | 1.21 | 1.37 | 0.56 | 1.12 | 1.61 | 1.40 | 1.59 |
| Earnings | 3.59 | 1.66 | 1.27 | 0.29 | 0.51 | -0.02 | 0.25 | 0.57 | 0.34 | 0.52 |
| S&P Core Earnings | 3.27 | 1.72 | 1.36 | 0.67 | 0.68 | 0.61 | 0.01 | 0.52 | NA | NA |
| Dividends | 0.77 | 0.48 | 0.39 | 0.33 | 0.27 | 0.25 | 0.24 | 0.23 | Nil | NA |
| Payout Ratio | 21% | 29% | 30% | 113% | 53% | NM | 98% | 40% | Nil | NA |
| Prices:High | 145.80 | 116.25 | 53.49 | 39.93 | 28.22 | 14.45 | 17.00 | 19.40 | 13.69 | NA |
| Prices:Low | 68.02 | 49.10 | 37.91 | 25.00 | 14.04 | 6.78 | 6.60 | 13.44 | 9.88 | NA |
| P/E Ratio:High | 41 | 70 | 42 | NM | 55 | NM | 69 | 34 | 40 | NA |
| P/E Ratio:Low | 19 | 30 | 30 | 86 | 28 | NM | 27 | 24 | 29 | NA |

| Income Statement Analysis (Million $) | | | | | | | | | | |
|---|---|---|---|---|---|---|---|---|---|---|
| Revenue | 11,365 | 8,563 | 7,344 | 6,294 | 5,457 | 3,373 | 4,673 | 5,462 | 5,493 | 5,248 |
| Operating Income | NA | 2,138 | 1,694 | 1,503 | 1,254 | 768 | 882 | 1,335 | 1,216 | 1,179 |
| Depreciation | 573 | 527 | 519 | 488 | 452 | 302 | 460 | 554 | 546 | 547 |
| Interest Expense | NA | 139 | 134 | 115 | 91.0 | 57.0 | 59.0 | 99.0 | 214 | 269 |
| Pretax Income | 2,926 | 1,336 | 1,055 | 261 | 402 | -38.0 | 202 | 463 | 334 | 263 |
| Effective Tax Rate | 30.7% | 30.1% | 32.2% | 39.8% | 32.6% | NM | 36.1% | 35.9% | 47.6% | 43.0% |
| Net Income | 2,007 | 922 | 698 | 157 | 271 | -11.0 | 129 | 297 | 175 | 150 |
| S&P Core Earnings | 1,830 | 951 | 745 | 363 | 362 | 317 | 5.45 | 277 | NA | NA |

| Balance Sheet & Other Financial Data (Million $) | | | | | | | | | | |
|---|---|---|---|---|---|---|---|---|---|---|
| Cash | 1,613 | 866 | 1,460 | 525 | 1,037 | 511 | 428 | 307 | 131 | 26.0 |
| Current Assets | NA | 5,084 | 5,461 | 4,644 | 4,931 | 4,962 | 4,424 | 4,797 | 4,973 | 4,027 |
| Total Assets | 17,993 | 12,983 | 11,728 | 10,579 | 9,164 | 9,461 | 8,890 | 11,429 | 11,726 | 11,101 |
| Current Liabilities | NA | 3,075 | 2,279 | 2,159 | 1,894 | 1,944 | 1,810 | 2,377 | 2,757 | 1,704 |
| Long Term Debt | NA | 1,150 | 1,639 | 1,458 | 1,075 | 1,258 | 851 | 893 | 962 | 4,278 |
| Common Equity | 9,374 | 7,503 | 6,680 | 5,613 | 5,258 | 5,156 | 5,180 | 7,483 | 7,341 | 4,645 |
| Total Capital | NA | 8,653 | 8,319 | 7,071 | 6,333 | 6,414 | 6,031 | 8,376 | 8,303 | 8,923 |
| Capital Expenditures | 918 | 509 | 370 | 281 | 210 | 114 | 224 | 382 | 582 | 632 |
| Cash Flow | NA | 1,449 | 1,217 | 645 | 723 | 291 | 589 | 851 | 721 | 697 |
| Current Ratio | 1.7 | 1.7 | 2.4 | 2.2 | 2.6 | 2.6 | 2.4 | 2.0 | 1.8 | 2.4 |
| % Long Term Debt of Capitalization | 16.1 | 13.3 | 19.7 | 20.6 | 17.0 | 19.6 | 14.1 | 10.7 | 11.6 | 47.9 |
| % Net Income of Revenue | 17.7 | 10.8 | 9.5 | 2.5 | 5.0 | NM | 2.8 | 5.4 | 3.2 | 2.9 |
| % Return on Assets | 13.0 | 7.5 | 6.3 | 1.6 | 2.9 | NM | 1.3 | 2.6 | 1.5 | 1.4 |
| % Return on Equity | 23.8 | 13.0 | 11.2 | 2.9 | 5.2 | NM | 2.0 | 4.0 | 2.9 | 3.4 |

Data as orig reptd.; bef. results of disc opers/spec. items. Per share data adj. for stk. divs.; EPS diluted. E-Estimated. NA-Not Available. NM-Not Meaningful. NR-Not Ranked. UR-Under Review.

**Office:** 800 North Lindbergh Boulevard, St. Louis, MO 63167.
**Telephone:** 314-694-1000.
**Email:** info@monsanto.com
**Website:** http://www.monsanto.com

**Chrmn, Pres & CEO:** H. Grant
**COO:** C.M. Casale
**EVP & CFO:** T.K. Crews
**EVP & CTO:** R.T. Fraley

**SVP, Secy & General Counsel:** D.F. Snively
**Investor Contact:** S.L. Foster (314-694-8148)
**Board Members:** F. V. AtLee, III, J. W. Bachmann, J. Fields, H. Grant, A. H. Harper, G. S. King, C. S. McMillan, W. U. Parfet, G. H. Poste, R. J. Stevens

**Founded:** 2000
**Domicile:** Delaware
**Employees:** 26,400

STANDARD
&POOR'S

# Monster Worldwide Inc

| S&P Recommendation **HOLD** ★★★☆☆ | Price<br>$11.62 (as of Nov 14, 2008) | 12-Mo. Target Price<br>$15.00 | Investment Style<br>Large-Cap Blend |
|---|---|---|---|

**GICS Sector** Industrials
**Sub-Industry** Human Resource & Employment Services

**Summary** Monster Worldwide operates a multinational online career network. It also provides offerings to help consumers develop and direct their careers.

## Key Stock Statistics (Source S&P, Vickers, company reports)

| | | | | | | | |
|---|---|---|---|---|---|---|---|
| 52-Wk Range | $36.47– 9.99 | S&P Oper. EPS 2008**E** | 1.35 | Market Capitalization(B) | $1.376 | Beta | 1.86 |
| Trailing 12-Month EPS | $1.15 | S&P Oper. EPS 2009**E** | 1.10 | Yield (%) | Nil | S&P 3-Yr. Proj. EPS CAGR(%) | -2 |
| Trailing 12-Month P/E | 10.1 | P/E on S&P Oper. EPS 2008**E** | 8.6 | Dividend Rate/Share | Nil | S&P Credit Rating | NA |
| $10K Invested 5 Yrs Ago | $4,862 | Common Shares Outstg. (M) | 123.2 | Institutional Ownership (%) | NM | | |

## Price Performance

30-Week Mov. Avg. · · · 10-Week Mov. Avg. – – GAAP Earnings vs. Previous Year   Volume Above Avg. ▪▪▪ STARS
12-Mo. Target Price — Relative Strength   ▲ Up ▼ Down ► No Change   Below Avg. ▪▪▪ ★

Options: ASE, CBOE, P

Analysis prepared by **Michael W. Jaffe** on November 03, 2008, when the stock traded at **$ 14.03**.

## Highlights

► We expect revenues to be relatively unchanged in 2009. We see ongoing gains in foreign revenues in the coming year, but with the recent moderation in foreign labor trends, we anticipate only modest revenue advances in MNST's international segment. We also forecast the full-year inclusion of several small recent acquisitions to add to the top line. We expect these factors to be offset by a likely ongoing downturn in the North American segment, as we see further weakness in U.S. labor markets.

► We see narrower net margins in 2009, when we expect MNST's overall performance to be limited by ongoing challenges in the U.S. labor market, and by less robust activity in its international business. We also project that the recent strengthening of the U.S. dollar against many foreign currencies will result in a negative currency impact. These conditions should be partly offset by some likely incremental benefits from MNST's restructuring program, announced in mid-2007, which we think has brought considerable cost-cutting discipline.

► Our 2009 EPS forecast compares with operating earnings in 2008 that exclude $0.34 a share of charges in the first nine months of the year.

## Investment Rationale/Risk

► We think demand for MNST's services will moderate on a global basis in coming periods. Although we think these trends will result in an earnings decline in 2009, we are nonetheless impressed by the actions that MNST is taking to support its operating performance. MNST's discovery in 2006 of substantial stock option backdating also makes us question its corporate governance practices, but the executives involved are gone from the company. Based on these mixed factors and our valuation, we would hold the shares.

► Risks to our recommendation and target price include weaker-than-projected global labor markets, and less successful results of MNST's restructuring initiatives than we anticipate.

► The shares recently traded at 13X our 2009 EPS estimate, a premium to MNST's peer group. We recognize several negative characteristics about MNST and its business. Yet, we also think MNST has been taking proper steps to improve its operations, and that its business model typically allows for growth above that of peers. On these views, we think MNST is near an appropriate valuation. Our 12-month target price is $15, or 13.6X our 2009 EPS estimate.

## Qualitative Risk Assessment

| LOW | MEDIUM | **HIGH** |
|---|---|---|

Our risk assessment reflects the cyclicality of the help wanted industry, as it strongly correlates with the economy. It also reflects that despite what we view as a solid level of earnings in both 2006 and 2007, MNST's return on invested capital in those years fell below its weighted average cost of capital. In addition, foreign operations carry operating and exchange rate risks.

## Quantitative Evaluations

**S&P Quality Ranking**     B-

| D | C | **B-** | B | B+ | A- | A | A+ |
|---|---|---|---|---|---|---|---|

**Relative Strength Rank**     MODERATE

49

LOWEST = 1                    HIGHEST = 99

## Revenue/Earnings Data

**Revenue (Million $)**

| | 1Q | 2Q | 3Q | 4Q | Year |
|---|---|---|---|---|---|
| 2008 | 370.4 | 354.3 | 332.2 | -- | -- |
| 2007 | 329.0 | 331.2 | 337.1 | 354.0 | 1,351 |
| 2006 | 257.0 | 275.2 | 285.9 | 298.6 | 1,117 |
| 2005 | 232.1 | 239.0 | 249.3 | 266.6 | 986.9 |
| 2004 | 182.4 | 202.1 | 224.2 | 236.8 | 845.5 |
| 2003 | 168.5 | 166.7 | 173.7 | 170.8 | 679.6 |

**Earnings Per Share ($)**

| | | | | | |
|---|---|---|---|---|---|
| 2008 | 0.18 | 0.15 | 0.36 | E0.31 | E1.35 |
| 2007 | 0.30 | 0.21 | 0.25 | 0.36 | 1.13 |
| 2006 | 0.26 | 0.29 | 0.31 | 0.31 | 1.17 |
| 2005 | 0.19 | 0.21 | 0.25 | 0.28 | 0.92 |
| 2004 | 0.11 | 0.14 | 0.18 | 0.20 | 0.62 |
| 2003 | -1.04 | 0.08 | 0.08 | 0.11 | 0.06 |

Fiscal year ended Dec. 31. Next earnings report expected: Early February. EPS Estimates based on S&P Operating Earnings; historical GAAP earnings are as reported.

## Dividend Data

No cash dividends have been paid.

---

**Please read the Required Disclosures and Analyst Certification on the last page of this report.**

The McGraw-Hill Companies

# Monster Worldwide Inc

STANDARD
&POOR'S

## Business Summary November 03, 2008

CORPORATE OVERVIEW. Monster Worldwide is a leading online recruitment and career management services provider through its Monster.com Web site. MNST's clients range from Fortune 100 companies, to small and medium-sized enterprises and government agencies. During 2007, the company derived 52% of its revenues from its Monster Careers North America division, 36% from Monster Careers International, and 12% from its Advertising & Fees division. No client accounts for more than 5% of MNST's revenues.

Among the most visited brands on the Internet, the Monster network is designed to connect companies with qualified job seekers, offering innovative technology and services that provide greater control over the recruiting process. At year-end 2007, the Monster.com network was available in about 40 countries.

Monster's job search, resume posting services and basic networking are free to the job seeker. It also offers premium career services to job seekers at a

fee, including resume writing, resume priority listing, and premium networking. MNST charges a fee to employers and human resources professionals who want to post jobs, search its resume database, and use its career site hosting and other ancillary services.

The company's Internet Advertising & Fees division provides consumers with content, services and offers, to help them manage the development and direction of their current and future careers. The majority of its services are free to users and are primarily available in North America at present, although MNST plans to expand its offerings across its global network. Revenues for the division are derived mostly from lead generation, display advertising, and products sold to consumers for a fee.

## Company Financials Fiscal Year Ended Dec. 31

| Per Share Data ($) | 2007 | 2006 | 2005 | 2004 | 2003 | 2002 | 2001 | 2000 | 1999 | 1998 |
|---|---|---|---|---|---|---|---|---|---|---|
| Tangible Book Value | 3.97 | 3.65 | 1.47 | 0.27 | 0.18 | 2.02 | 2.61 | 5.16 | 0.18 | NM |
| Cash Flow | 1.49 | 1.47 | 1.22 | 0.92 | 0.31 | -0.46 | 1.28 | 1.11 | 0.35 | 0.43 |
| Earnings | 1.13 | 1.17 | 0.92 | 0.62 | 0.06 | -0.96 | 0.61 | 0.53 | -0.09 | 0.07 |
| S&P Core Earnings | 1.13 | 1.17 | 0.47 | 0.37 | -0.08 | -1.48 | 0.10 | NA | NA | NA |
| Dividends | Nil | Nil | Nil | Nil | Nil | Nil | Nil | Nil | Nil | Nil |
| Payout Ratio | Nil | Nil | Nil | Nil | Nil | Nil | Nil | Nil | Nil | Nil |
| Prices:High | 54.79 | 59.99 | 42.03 | 34.25 | 29.65 | 48.13 | 68.73 | 94.69 | 80.50 | 21.31 |
| Prices:Low | 31.07 | 34.75 | 22.44 | 17.60 | 7.63 | 7.94 | 25.21 | 45.00 | 18.50 | 7.75 |
| P/E Ratio:High | 48 | 51 | 46 | 55 | NM | NM | NM | NM | NM | NM |
| P/E Ratio:Low | 27 | 30 | 24 | 28 | NM | NM | NM | NM | NM | NM |

| Income Statement Analysis (Million $) | | | | | | | | | | |
|---|---|---|---|---|---|---|---|---|---|---|
| Revenue | 1,351 | 1,117 | 987 | 846 | 680 | 1,115 | 1,448 | 1,292 | 766 | 407 |
| Operating Income | 303 | 270 | 214 | 152 | 101 | 112 | 262 | 222 | 109 | 69.4 |
| Depreciation | 47.0 | 39.8 | 38.0 | 37.6 | 28.0 | 55.5 | 76.0 | 62.6 | 35.0 | 22.2 |
| Interest Expense | Nil | Nil | Nil | Nil | Nil | 4.90 | 10.6 | 9.49 | 17.0 | 13.7 |
| Pretax Income | 232 | 241 | 179 | 112 | 23.6 | -130 | 125 | 114 | -1.50 | 12.7 |
| Effective Tax Rate | 36.5% | 36.3% | 35.8% | 34.6% | 69.0% | NM | 46.1% | 50.5% | NM | 66.6% |
| Net Income | 147 | 154 | 115 | 73.1 | 7.32 | -107 | 69.0 | 56.9 | -7.40 | 4.25 |
| S&P Core Earnings | 147 | 154 | 59.2 | 44.0 | -8.08 | -165 | 11.4 | NA | NA | NA |

| Balance Sheet & Other Financial Data (Million $) | | | | | | | | | | |
|---|---|---|---|---|---|---|---|---|---|---|
| Cash | 578 | 58.7 | 320 | 198 | 142 | 192 | 341 | 572 | 57.0 | 28.9 |
| Current Assets | 1,185 | 1,124 | 773 | 704 | 567 | 809 | 1,006 | 1,248 | 557 | 343 |
| Total Assets | 2,078 | 1,970 | 1,679 | 1,544 | 1,122 | 1,631 | 2,206 | 1,992 | 945 | 608 |
| Current Liabilities | 829 | 826 | 697 | 731 | 640 | 799 | 930 | 853 | 565 | 360 |
| Long Term Debt | 0.23 | 0.42 | 15.7 | 34.0 | 2.09 | 3.93 | 9.13 | 28.0 | 71.0 | 118 |
| Common Equity | 1,117 | 1,110 | 920 | 756 | 468 | 813 | 1,229 | 1,058 | 281 | 123 |
| Total Capital | 1,136 | 1,143 | 981 | 789 | 470 | 817 | 1,238 | 1,086 | 352 | 241 |
| Capital Expenditures | 64.1 | 55.6 | 39.8 | 24.3 | 21.6 | 46.7 | 73.6 | 78.9 | 40.4 | 21.7 |
| Cash Flow | 194 | 193 | 153 | 111 | 35.4 | -51.0 | 145 | 119 | 27.6 | 26.4 |
| Current Ratio | 1.4 | 1.4 | 1.1 | 1.0 | 0.9 | 1.0 | 1.1 | 1.5 | 1.0 | 1.0 |
| % Long Term Debt of Capitalization | 0.0 | 0.0 | 1.6 | 4.3 | 0.4 | 0.5 | 0.7 | 2.6 | 19.6 | 48.9 |
| % Net Income of Revenue | 10.9 | 13.8 | 11.7 | 8.6 | 1.1 | NM | 4.8 | 4.4 | NM | 1.0 |
| % Return on Assets | 7.3 | 8.4 | 7.1 | 5.5 | 0.5 | NM | 3.2 | 3.7 | NM | 0.8 |
| % Return on Equity | 13.2 | 15.0 | 13.7 | 11.9 | 1.1 | NM | 6.0 | 8.2 | NM | 3.9 |

Data as orig reptd.; bef. results of disc opers/spec. items. Per share data adj. for stk. divs.; EPS diluted. E-Estimated. NA-Not Available. NM-Not Meaningful. NR-Not Ranked. UR-Under Review.

**Office:** 622 Third Ave, New York, NY 10017-6707.
**Telephone:** 212-351-7000.
**Email:**
corporate.communications@monsterworldwide.com
**Website:** http://www.monsterworldwide.com

**Chrmn, Pres & CEO:** S. Iannuzzi
**EVP & CFO:** T. Yates
**EVP & CIO:** D. Dejanovic
**SVP & Chief Acctg Officer:** J.M. Langrock

**Secy & General Counsel:** E. Kornrich
**Investor Contact:** T.T. Yates
**Board Members:** R. J. Chrenc, J. R. Gaulding, E. P. Giambastiani, Jr., S. Iannuzzi, R. J. Kramer, D. A. Stein, R. Tunioli, T. Yates

**Founded:** 1967
**Domicile:** Delaware
**Employees:** 5,210

# Moody's Corp.

**STANDARD &POOR'S**

| **S&P Recommendation** HOLD ★★★☆☆ | **Price** $19.33 (as of Nov 14, 2008) | **12-Mo. Target Price** $23.00 | **Investment Style** Large-Cap Growth |
|---|---|---|---|

**GICS Sector** Financials
**Sub-Industry** Specialized Finance

**Summary** Moody's is a leading global credit rating, research, and risk analysis concern.

## Key Stock Statistics (Source S&P, Vickers, company reports)

| | | | | | | |
|---|---|---|---|---|---|---|
| 52-Wk Range | $46.36– 17.75 | S&P Oper. EPS 2008E | 1.74 | Market Capitalization(B) | $4.635 | Beta | 1.38 |
| Trailing 12-Month EPS | $1.98 | S&P Oper. EPS 2009E | 2.00 | Yield (%) | 2.07 | S&P 3-Yr. Proj. EPS CAGR(%) | -2 |
| Trailing 12-Month P/E | 9.8 | P/E on S&P Oper. EPS 2008E | 11.1 | Dividend Rate/Share | $0.40 | S&P Credit Rating | NA |
| $10K Invested 5 Yrs Ago | $6,957 | Common Shares Outstg. (M) | 239.8 | Institutional Ownership (%) | NM | | |

## Price Performance

30-Week Mov. Avg. ···· 10-Week Mov. Avg. --- **GAAP Earnings vs. Previous Year** **Volume** Above Avg. STARS
12-Mo. Target Price — Relative Strength ▲ Up ▼ Down ▶ No Change Below Avg. ★

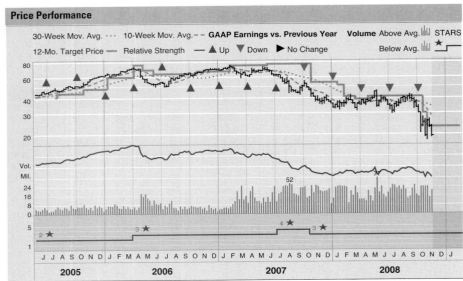

Options: ASE, CBOE, P, Ph

Analysis prepared by **Royal F. Shepard, CFA** on November 06, 2008, when the stock traded at **$ 23.38**.

## Highlights

➤ We expect revenues from MCO's ratings agency business to decline over 34% in 2008, driven by a 56% decline in the structured finance segment. Total revenues, in our estimation, will decline about 23%, due to a positive contribution from global analytical services, which benefits from recurring consulting and research contracts. All told, we see a gradually improving credit environment leading to revenues about even with those to be reported for 2008.

➤ We forecast an operating margin of 50.2% in 2009, up from 43.8% in 2008 but down from 52.2% in 2007. MCO has continued to invest in growth initiatives despite a challenging credit environment, which we believe has hurt the company's profitability in 2008 but will boost its operating margins in 2009 as overall economic conditions gradually improve.

➤ We expect October's purchase of Fermat International to dilute 2008 earnings by $0.05 - $0.07 a share, before having a more neutral impact on 2009 results. On fewer shares outstanding, we see operating EPS of $2.00 in 2009, up from our forecast for EPS of $1.74 in 2008.

## Investment Rationale/Risk

➤ We believe MCO is in a favorable position, with limited competition, high margins, and a risk-averse corporate environment that should lead to above-average long-term growth. We also expect growth to come from the need to rate new products and capital markets development overseas. However, we think deteriorating economic environments in the U.S. and Europe, along with a tight U.S. credit market, will reduce the near-term demand to rate securities.

➤ Risks to our opinion and target price include a greater than anticipated decline in the volume of debt issued in domestic and global capital markets, regulatory changes that increase competition, and persistently high long-term interest rates.

➤ Our 12-month target price of $23 is based primarily on applying an 8.0X EV/EBITDA multiple to our 2009 EBITDA estimate of $890 million. This multiple is at the bottom of MCO's historical range, which we think is appropriate given an uncertain regulatory outlook and tight credit markets. Our DCF model yields an intrinsic value of $25 and assumes a 10.6% WACC and 2.0% terminal growth.

## Qualitative Risk Assessment

| LOW | MEDIUM | HIGH |
|---|---|---|

Our risk assessment reflects Moody's significant market share in the high barrier to entry ratings industry, and what we consider the company's net positive balance sheet cash position, offset by ratings business sensitivity to higher interest rates, and the possibility of regulatory reform designed to increase competition.

## Quantitative Evaluations

**S&P Quality Ranking** B+

| D | C | B- | B | B+ | A- | A | A+ |
|---|---|---|---|---|---|---|---|

**Relative Strength Rank** MODERATE

32

LOWEST = 1 HIGHEST = 99

## Revenue/Earnings Data

**Revenue (Million $)**

| | 1Q | 2Q | 3Q | 4Q | Year |
|---|---|---|---|---|---|
| 2008 | 430.7 | 487.6 | 433.4 | -- | -- |
| 2007 | 583.0 | 646.1 | 525.0 | 504.9 | 2,259 |
| 2006 | 440.2 | 511.4 | 495.5 | 590.0 | 2,037 |
| 2005 | 390.5 | 446.8 | 421.1 | 473.2 | 1,732 |
| 2004 | 331.2 | 357.6 | 357.9 | 391.6 | 1,438 |
| 2003 | 278.2 | 312.7 | 305.0 | 350.7 | 1,247 |

**Earnings Per Share ($)**

| | | | | | |
|---|---|---|---|---|---|
| 2008 | 0.48 | 0.55 | 0.46 | E0.26 | E1.74 |
| 2007 | 0.62 | 0.95 | 0.51 | 0.49 | 2.58 |
| 2006 | 0.49 | 0.59 | 0.55 | 0.97 | 2.58 |
| 2005 | 0.39 | 0.47 | 0.48 | 0.50 | 1.84 |
| 2004 | 0.34 | 0.34 | 0.32 | 0.40 | 1.40 |
| 2003 | 0.31 | 0.33 | 0.28 | 0.28 | 1.20 |

Fiscal year ended Dec. 31. Next earnings report expected: Early February. EPS Estimates based on S&P Operating Earnings; historical GAAP earnings are as reported.

## Dividend Data (Dates: mm/dd Payment Date: mm/dd/yy)

| Amount ($) | Date Decl. | Ex-Div. Date | Stk. of Record | Payment Date |
|---|---|---|---|---|
| 0.100 | 12/18 | 02/15 | 02/20 | 03/10/08 |
| 0.100 | 04/22 | 05/16 | 05/20 | 06/10/08 |
| 0.100 | 07/30 | 08/18 | 08/20 | 09/10/08 |
| 0.100 | 10/29 | 11/18 | 11/20 | 12/10/08 |

Dividends have been paid since 1934. Source: Company reports.

# Moody's Corp.

STANDARD
&POOR'S

## Business Summary November 06, 2008

CORPORATE PROFILE. Moody's Investors Service and the Dun & Bradstreet (D&B) operating company were separated into stand-alone entities on September 30, 2000. Old D&B changed its name to Moody's Corp. (MCO), and new D&B assumed the name Dun & Bradstreet Corp. (DNB).

Moody's is a provider of credit ratings, research and analysis covering debt instruments and securities in the global capital markets, and a provider of quantitative credit assessment services, credit training services and credit process software to banks and other financial institutions. Moody's credit ratings and research help investors analyze the credit risks associated with fixed-income securities. Beyond credit rating services for issuers, Moody's provides research services, data, and analytic tools that are utilized by institutional investors and other credit and capital markets professionals.

Moody's provides ratings and credit research on governmental and commercial entities in more than 100 countries, and its customers include a wide range of corporate and governmental issuers of securities as well as institutional investors, depositors, creditors, investment banks, commercial banks, and other financial intermediaries. In 2007, no single customer accounted for 10% or more of total revenue.

Moody's operates in two reportable segments: Moody's Investors Service, and Moody's KMV. Moody's Investors Service consists of a research group (14% of 2007 revenues, up from 13% in 2006) and four ratings groups: structured finance (39%, 44%), corporate finance (21%, 19%), financial institutions and sovereign risk (13%,13%), and public finance (5%, 4%). The research group primarily generates revenue from the sale of investor-oriented credit research, principally produced by the ratings groups. The ratings groups generate revenue mainly from the assignment of credit ratings on fixed-income instruments in the debt markets.

## Company Financials Fiscal Year Ended Dec. 31

### Per Share Data ($)

| | 2007 | 2006 | 2005 | 2004 | 2003 | 2002 | 2001 | 2000 | 1999 | 1998 |
|---|---|---|---|---|---|---|---|---|---|---|
| Tangible Book Value | NM | NM | 0.30 | 0.39 | NM | NM | NM | NM | NM | NM |
| Cash Flow | 2.73 | 2.72 | 1.95 | 1.51 | 1.30 | 1.00 | 0.72 | 0.54 | 1.21 | 1.13 |
| Earnings | 2.58 | 2.58 | 1.84 | 1.40 | 1.20 | 0.92 | 0.66 | 0.49 | 0.78 | 0.72 |
| S&P Core Earnings | 2.61 | 2.26 | 1.83 | 1.35 | 1.12 | 0.85 | 0.64 | NA | NA | NA |
| Dividends | 0.32 | 0.28 | 0.20 | 0.15 | 0.09 | 0.07 | 0.11 | 0.28 | 0.37 | 0.41 |
| Payout Ratio | 12% | 11% | 11% | 11% | 8% | 7% | 17% | 57% | 47% | 56% |
| Prices:High | 76.09 | 73.29 | 62.50 | 43.86 | 30.43 | 26.20 | 20.55 | 18.09 | 20.00 | 18.34 |
| Prices:Low | 35.05 | 49.76 | 39.55 | 29.85 | 19.75 | 17.90 | 12.78 | 11.31 | 11.69 | 10.88 |
| P/E Ratio:High | 29 | 28 | 34 | 31 | 25 | 29 | 31 | 37 | 26 | 25 |
| P/E Ratio:Low | 14 | 19 | 21 | 21 | 17 | 20 | 19 | 23 | 15 | 15 |

### Income Statement Analysis (Million $)

| | 2007 | 2006 | 2005 | 2004 | 2003 | 2002 | 2001 | 2000 | 1999 | 1998 |
|---|---|---|---|---|---|---|---|---|---|---|
| Revenue | 2,259 | 2,037 | 1,732 | 1,438 | 1,247 | 1,023 | 797 | 602 | 1,972 | 1,935 |
| Operating Income | 1,222 | 1,138 | 975 | 820 | 696 | 563 | 416 | 305 | 621 | 591 |
| Depreciation | 41.2 | 39.5 | 35.2 | 34.1 | 32.6 | 25.0 | 17.0 | 16.6 | 141 | 142 |
| Interest Expense | 62.2 | 15.2 | 21.0 | 16.2 | 21.8 | 21.0 | 16.5 | 3.60 | 5.00 | 12.0 |
| Pretax Income | 1,117 | 1,261 | 935 | 771 | 656 | 517 | 382 | 284 | 457 | 400 |
| Effective Tax Rate | 37.2% | 40.2% | 40.0% | 44.9% | 44.6% | 44.1% | 44.4% | 44.2% | 39.1% | 38.5% |
| Net Income | 702 | 754 | 561 | 425 | 364 | 289 | 212 | 159 | 256 | 246 |
| S&P Core Earnings | 710 | 662 | 558 | 413 | 340 | 269 | 203 | NA | NA | NA |

### Balance Sheet & Other Financial Data (Million $)

| | 2007 | 2006 | 2005 | 2004 | 2003 | 2002 | 2001 | 2000 | 1999 | 1998 |
|---|---|---|---|---|---|---|---|---|---|---|
| Cash | 441 | 408 | 486 | 606 | 269 | 40.0 | 163 | 119 | 113 | 91.0 |
| Current Assets | 989 | 1,002 | 1,052 | 1,023 | 569 | 272 | 371 | 278 | 785 | 764 |
| Total Assets | 1,715 | 1,498 | 1,457 | 1,376 | 941 | 631 | 505 | 398 | 1,786 | 1,789 |
| Current Liabilities | 1,349 | 700 | 579 | 837 | 432 | 462 | 359 | 253 | 1,415 | 1,353 |
| Long Term Debt | 600 | 300 | 300 | Nil | 300 | 300 | 300 | 300 | Nil | Nil |
| Common Equity | -784 | 167 | 309 | 318 | -32.1 | -327 | -304 | -283 | -417 | -371 |
| Total Capital | -184 | 467 | 609 | 318 | 268 | -27.0 | -4.10 | 17.5 | -115 | -70.0 |
| Capital Expenditures | 182 | 31.1 | 31.3 | 21.3 | 17.9 | 18.0 | 14.8 | 12.3 | 44.1 | 55.0 |
| Cash Flow | 743 | 793 | 596 | 459 | 397 | 314 | 229 | 175 | 397 | 388 |
| Current Ratio | 0.7 | 1.4 | 1.8 | 1.2 | 1.3 | 0.6 | 1.0 | 1.1 | 0.6 | 0.6 |
| % Long Term Debt of Capitalization | -326.8 | 64.2 | 49.2 | Nil | 112.0 | NM | NM | NM | Nil | Nil |
| % Net Income of Revenue | 31.1 | 37.0 | 32.4 | 29.6 | 29.2 | 28.2 | 26.6 | 26.3 | 13.0 | 12.7 |
| % Return on Assets | 43.7 | 51.0 | 39.4 | 36.5 | 46.3 | 50.9 | 47.0 | 47.1 | 14.3 | NA |
| % Return on Equity | NM | 316.2 | 178.9 | 297.9 | NM | NM | NM | NM | NM | NM |

Data as orig reptd.; bef. results of disc opers/spec. items. Per share data adj. for stk. divs.; EPS diluted. E-Estimated. NA-Not Available. NM-Not Meaningful. NR-Not Ranked. UR-Under Review.

**Office:** 250 Greenwich St, New York, NY 10007-2140.
**Telephone:** 212-553-0300.
**Website:** http://www.moodys.com
**Chrmn & CEO:** R.W. McDaniel, Jr.

**EVP & CFO:** L.S. Huber
**SVP, Chief Acctg Officer & Cntlr:** J. McCabe
**SVP & General Counsel:** J.J. Goggins
**SVP & CIO:** P. Rotella

**Investor Contact:** L. Westlake (212-553-7179)
**Board Members:** B. L. Anderson, J. D. Duffie, R. R. Glauber, E. Kist, C. Mack, III, R. W. McDaniel, Jr., H. McKinnell, Jr., C. Mcgillicudy, III, N. S. Newcomb, J. K. Wulff

**Founded:** 1998
**Domicile:** Delaware
**Employees:** 3,600

**STANDARD &POOR'S**

# Morgan Stanley

| S&P Recommendation | **BUY** ★★★★☆ | Price $12.03 (as of Nov 14, 2008) | 12-Mo. Target Price $20.00 | Investment Style Large-Cap Blend |
|---|---|---|---|---|

**GICS Sector** Financials
**Sub-Industry** Investment Banking & Brokerage

**Summary** Morgan Stanley is among the largest financial services firms in the U.S., with operations in investment banking, securities, and investment and wealth management.

## Key Stock Statistics (Source S&P, Vickers, company reports)

| | | | | | | | |
|---|---|---|---|---|---|---|---|
| 52-Wk Range | $55.39–6.71 | S&P Oper. EPS 2008**E** | 4.09 | Market Capitalization(B) | $12.776 | Beta | 2.27 |
| Trailing 12-Month EPS | $0.33 | S&P Oper. EPS 2009**E** | 3.19 | Yield (%) | 8.98 | S&P 3-Yr. Proj. EPS CAGR(%) | 24 |
| Trailing 12-Month P/E | 36.5 | P/E on S&P Oper. EPS 2008**E** | 2.9 | Dividend Rate/Share | $1.08 | S&P Credit Rating | A+ |
| $10K Invested 5 Yrs Ago | NA | Common Shares Outstg. (M) | 1,062.0 | Institutional Ownership (%) | 76 | | |

## Price Performance

30-Week Mov. Avg. · · · 10-Week Mov. Avg. - - GAAP Earnings vs. Previous Year   Volume Above Avg. ▥▥▥ STARS
12-Mo. Target Price — Relative Strength   — ▲ Up ▼ Down ▶ No Change   Below Avg. ▥▥▥ ★

Options: ASE, CBOE, P, Ph

Analysis prepared by **Matthew Albrecht** on November 06, 2008, when the stock traded at **$ 15.43**.

## Highlights

➤ We believe the shares have been pressured as the market appears to have lost confidence in the independent investment banking model. We think the transition to a commercial bank holding company, the $9 billion preferred investment in the firm by Mitsubishi UFJ (MTU: hold, $6), and government investment are all positive signs for the long-term health of the firm. While we see these moves diluting current shareholder stakes, we think they will also provide a solid base from which the company can deleverage and transition to a new business model over the next few years.

➤ We see asset write-downs declining, but still expect markdowns of commercial and residential mortgages and leveraged lending commitments. We anticipate a significant decline in M&A and underwriting activity for FY 08 (Nov.), and think the wealth and asset management businesses should also post effects of tough equity and credit markets. We expect compensation and other costs to remain elevated relative to historical levels in FY 08, but we look for pretax margins to expand in each of the next two fiscal years.

➤ We see EPS of $4.09 in FY 08 and $3.19 in FY 09.

## Investment Rationale/Risk

➤ We expect some continued but measured growth in the adviser force through new hires and increased productivity, and this valuable asset should provide some stability as other businesses should struggle in the current environment. We believe the Institutional Securities segment faces a number of challenges, including reduced activity in its investment banking operations and markdowns and trading losses elsewhere, but we think a global footprint should provide some mitigating business opportunities. Looking ahead, we expect the price-to-book valuation gap to narrow versus peers, which is why we have a buy opinion on the shares.

➤ Risks to our recommendation and target price include stock and bond market depreciation and widening credit spreads, as well as additional industry regulation.

➤ MS recently traded at a sizable discount to the overall market and its historical average multiples. Our 12-month target price of $20 is about 0.6X our 12-month forward projected book value per share, which represents a discount to comparable peer multiples.

## Qualitative Risk Assessment

| LOW | **MEDIUM** | HIGH |
|---|---|---|

Our risk assessment reflects our favorable view of the company's diversification by product and by region, offset by our concerns about corporate governance and our view that certain segments lack competitive advantages.

## Quantitative Evaluations

**S&P Quality Ranking**     **B+**

| D | C | B- | B | **B+** | A- | A | A+ |
|---|---|---|---|---|---|---|---|

**Relative Strength Rank**     **WEAK**

14

LOWEST = 1        HIGHEST = 99

## Revenue/Earnings Data

**Revenue (Million $)**

| | 1Q | 2Q | 3Q | 4Q | Year |
|---|---|---|---|---|---|
| 2008 | 21,184 | 16,523 | 16,699 | -- | -- |
| 2007 | 23,192 | 26,195 | 21,230 | 14,711 | 85,328 |
| 2006 | 18,119 | 19,062 | 20,055 | 19,473 | 76,551 |
| 2005 | 11,641 | 11,845 | 13,157 | 15,525 | 52,081 |
| 2004 | 9,992 | 9,802 | 9,854 | 10,420 | 39,549 |
| 2003 | 8,502 | 8,418 | 8,929 | 9,092 | 34,933 |

**Earnings Per Share ($)**

| | 1Q | 2Q | 3Q | 4Q | Year |
|---|---|---|---|---|---|
| 2008 | 1.45 | 0.95 | 1.32 | E0.37 | E4.09 |
| 2007 | 2.17 | 2.24 | 1.32 | -3.61 | 2.37 |
| 2006 | 1.50 | 1.85 | 1.75 | 2.08 | 7.09 |
| 2005 | 1.23 | 0.86 | 1.09 | 1.69 | 4.81 |
| 2004 | 1.11 | 1.10 | 0.78 | 1.09 | 4.08 |
| 2003 | 0.82 | 0.55 | 1.15 | 0.92 | 3.45 |

Fiscal year ended Nov. 30. Next earnings report expected: NA. EPS Estimates based on S&P Operating Earnings; historical GAAP earnings are as reported.

## Dividend Data (Dates: mm/dd Payment Date: mm/dd/yy)

| Amount ($) | Date Decl. | Ex-Div. Date | Stk. of Record | Payment Date |
|---|---|---|---|---|
| 0.270 | 12/24 | 01/09 | 01/11 | 01/31/08 |
| 0.270 | 03/19 | 04/09 | 04/11 | 04/30/08 |
| 0.270 | 06/18 | 07/09 | 07/11 | 07/31/08 |
| 0.270 | 09/16 | 10/15 | 10/17 | 10/31/08 |

Dividends have been paid since 1993. Source: Company reports.

*The McGraw-Hill Companies*

# Morgan Stanley

**STANDARD &POOR'S**

## Business Summary November 06, 2008

CORPORATE OVERVIEW. Morgan Stanley is a global financial services firm that provides a comprehensive suite of products to a diverse group of clients and customers, including corporations, governments, financial institutions and individuals. MS currently has three operating segments: Institutional Securities, Global Wealth Management Group and Asset Management.

The Institutional Securities segment includes capital raising; financial advisory services; corporate lending; sales, trading, financing and market-making activities for equity and fixed-income securities and related products such as foreign exchange and commodities; benchmark indices and risk management analytics; research; and investment activities. The investment banking business is included in this segment, and includes capital raising activities, financial advisory services and corporate lending. This business is one of the largest in the world, ranking second globally in 2006 in completed mergers and acquisitions and initial public offerings, and fifth in global debt issuance. This segment accounted for approximately 57% of net revenues and 24% of pretax profits in FY 07 (Nov.).

The Global Wealth Management Group provides brokerage and investment

advisory services; financial and wealth planning services; annuity and insurance products; credit and other lending products; banking and cash management services; retirement services; and trust and fiduciary services. It provides these services to clients through a network of more than 8,000 global representatives, overseeing $758 billion in client assets at the end of FY 07. The segment accounted for about 24% of net revenues and 34% of pretax profits in FY 07.

The Asset Management segment provides global asset management products and services in equity, fixed income, alternative investments and private equity to institutional and retail clients through proprietary and third-party channels. It had $597 billion of assets under management or supervision at the end of FY 07, and its activities are principally conducted under the Morgan Stanley and Van Kampen brands. The segment accounted for 19% of net revenues and 42% of pretax profits in FY 07.

## Company Financials Fiscal Year Ended Nov. 30

| Per Share Data ($) | 2007 | 2006 | 2005 | 2004 | 2003 | 2002 | 2001 | 2000 | 1999 | 1998 |
|---|---|---|---|---|---|---|---|---|---|---|
| Tangible Book Value | 25.75 | 34.89 | 25.23 | 23.93 | 21.52 | 19.43 | 17.36 | 16.91 | 14.79 | 11.88 |
| Earnings | 2.37 | 7.09 | 4.81 | 4.08 | 3.45 | 2.69 | 3.19 | 4.73 | 4.10 | 2.76 |
| S&P Core Earnings | 2.17 | 7.12 | 5.00 | 4.18 | 3.48 | 2.38 | 2.84 | NA | NA | NA |
| Dividends | 1.08 | 1.08 | 1.08 | 1.00 | 0.92 | 0.92 | 0.92 | 0.80 | 0.48 | 0.40 |
| Payout Ratio | 46% | 15% | 22% | 25% | 27% | 34% | 29% | 17% | 12% | 14% |
| Prices:High | 90.95 | 83.40 | 60.51 | 62.83 | 58.78 | 60.02 | 90.49 | 110.00 | 71.44 | 48.75 |
| Prices:Low | 47.25 | 54.52 | 47.66 | 46.54 | 32.46 | 28.80 | 35.75 | 58.63 | 35.41 | 18.25 |
| P/E Ratio:High | 38 | 12 | 13 | 15 | 17 | 22 | 28 | 23 | 17 | 18 |
| P/E Ratio:Low | 20 | 8 | 10 | 11 | 9 | 11 | 11 | 12 | 9 | 7 |

| Income Statement Analysis (Million $) | 2007 | 2006 | 2005 | 2004 | 2003 | 2002 | 2001 | 2000 | 1999 | 1998 |
|---|---|---|---|---|---|---|---|---|---|---|
| Net Interest Income | 2,781 | 3,279 | 3,750 | 3,731 | 2,935 | 3,896 | 3,348 | 3,058 | 2,365 | 2,922 |
| Non Interest Income | 25,245 | 45,558 | 23,906 | 20,959 | 19,189 | 16,549 | 19,600 | 24,179 | 20,110 | 14,656 |
| Loan Loss Provision | 831 | 756 | 878 | 925 | 1,267 | 1,336 | 1,052 | 810 | 529 | 1,173 |
| Non Interest Expenses | 24,858 | 23,614 | 20,857 | 18,333 | 16,636 | 15,725 | 17,264 | 18,746 | 14,281 | 15,530 |
| % Expense/Operating Revenue | 96.0% | 84.6% | 84.2% | 80.8% | 79.9% | 81.3% | 84.6% | 79.5% | 75.7% | 81.1% |
| Pretax Income | 3,394 | 10,772 | 7,050 | 6,312 | 5,334 | 4,633 | 5,684 | 8,526 | 7,728 | 5,385 |
| Effective Tax Rate | 24.5% | 30.4% | 26.4% | 28.6% | 29.0% | 35.5% | 36.5% | 36.0% | 38.0% | 37.0% |
| Net Income | 2,563 | 7,497 | 5,192 | 4,509 | 3,787 | 2,988 | 3,610 | 5,456 | 4,791 | 3,393 |
| % Net Interest Margin | NA | NA | NA | NA | 5.40 | 5.50 | 5.57 | 6.08 | 8.47 | 9.00 |
| S&P Core Earnings | 2,284 | 7,511 | 5,401 | 4,624 | 3,830 | 2,658 | 3,203 | NA | NA | NA |

| Balance Sheet & Other Financial Data (Million $) | 2007 | 2006 | 2005 | 2004 | 2003 | 2002 | 2001 | 2000 | 1999 | 1998 |
|---|---|---|---|---|---|---|---|---|---|---|
| Money Market Assets | 126,887 | 174,866 | 174,330 | 123,041 | 78,205 | 76,910 | 54,618 | 50,992 | 70,366 | 90,101 |
| Investment Securities | 457,192 | 680,484 | 304,172 | 260,640 | 228,904 | 185,588 | 164,011 | 130,818 | 112,042 | 41,689 |
| Earning Assets:Total Loans | 11,629 | 24,173 | 23,754 | 21,169 | 20,384 | 24,322 | 20,955 | 21,870 | 20,229 | 22,388 |
| Total Assets | 1,045,409 | 1,120,645 | 898,523 | 775,410 | 602,843 | 529,499 | 482,628 | 426,794 | 366,967 | 317,590 |
| Demand Deposits | 27,186 | 14,872 | 2,629 | 1,117 | 1,264 | 1,441 | 1,741 | 1,589 | 1,458 | 1,355 |
| Time Deposits | 3,993 | 13,471 | 16,034 | 12,660 | 11,575 | 12,316 | 10,535 | 10,341 | 8,939 | 6,842 |
| Long Term Debt | 190,624 | 144,978 | 110,465 | 95,286 | 68,410 | 43,985 | 40,851 | 36,830 | 28,604 | 27,435 |
| Common Equity | 30,169 | 34,264 | 29,248 | 28,272 | 24,933 | 21,951 | 20,437 | 18,796 | 16,344 | 13,445 |
| % Return on Assets | 0.2 | 0.7 | 0.6 | 0.7 | 0.7 | 0.6 | 0.8 | 1.4 | 1.4 | NA |
| % Return on Equity | 7.7 | 23.5 | 18.9 | 16.9 | 16.2 | 14.1 | 18.2 | 30.3 | 30.3 | 25.2 |
| % Loan Loss Reserve | Nil | 3.3 | 3.5 | 4.5 | 4.9 | 3.8 | 4.0 | 3.6 | 3.7 | NA |
| % Loans/Deposits | 78.0 | 85.2 | 127.3 | 153.7 | 158.8 | 176.8 | 170.7 | 183.3 | 229.2 | 272.8 |
| % Loans/Assets | 2.1 | 2.3 | 2.7 | 3.0 | 3.9 | 4.5 | 4.7 | 5.4 | 6.2 | 7.5 |
| % Equity to Assets | 3.0 | 3.1 | 3.3 | 3.9 | 4.1 | 4.2 | 4.3 | 4.5 | 4.4 | 4.3 |

Data as orig reptd.; bef. results of disc opers/spec. items. Per share data adj. for stk. divs.; EPS diluted. E-Estimated. NA-Not Available. NM-Not Meaningful. NR-Not Ranked. UR-Under Review.

**Office:** 1585 Broadway, New York, NY 10036.
**Telephone:** 212-761-4000.
**Website:** http://www.morganstanley.com
**Chrmn & CEO:** J. Mack

**EVP & CFO:** T.C. Kelleher
**EVP, Chief Admin Officer & Secy:** T.R. Nides
**EVP & General Counsel:** G.G. Lynch
**CTO:** P. Heller

**Investor Contact:** W. Pike (212-761-0008)
**Board Members:** R. J. Bostock, E. B. Bowles, H. Davies, C. R. Kidder, J. Mack, F. P. McClean, D. Nicolaisen, C. H. Noski, H. S. Olayan, C. E. Phillips, Jr., O. G. Sexton, L. D. Tyson

**Auditor:** Deloitte & Touche
**Founded:** 1981
**Domicile:** Delaware
**Employees:** 48,256

The McGraw-Hill Companies

# Motorola Inc.

**S&P Recommendation** HOLD

| | | |
|---|---|---|
| **Price** | **12-Mo. Target Price** | **Investment Style** |
| $4.08 (as of Nov 14, 2008) | $7.00 | Large-Cap Blend |

**GICS Sector** Information Technology
**Sub-Industry** Communications Equipment

**Summary** Motorola provides wireless and networking equipment for cable, fixed-line and wireless service providers. In early 2008, MOT announced plans to spin off its handset segment as a separate company but has since delayed the possible action beyond 2009.

## Key Stock Statistics (Source S&P, Vickers, company reports)

| | | | | | | | |
|---|---|---|---|---|---|---|---|
| 52-Wk Range | $16.70– 3.90 | S&P Oper. EPS 2008**E** | NA | Market Capitalization(B) | $9.247 | Beta | 2.10 |
| Trailing 12-Month EPS | $-0.21 | S&P Oper. EPS 2009**E** | NA | Yield (%) | 4.90 | S&P 3-Yr. Proj. EPS CAGR(%) | 5 |
| Trailing 12-Month P/E | NM | P/E on S&P Oper. EPS 2008**E** | null | Dividend Rate/Share | $0.20 | S&P Credit Rating | BBB |
| $10K Invested 5 Yrs Ago | NA | Common Shares Outstg. (M) | 2,266.3 | Institutional Ownership (%) | 77 | | |

## Price Performance

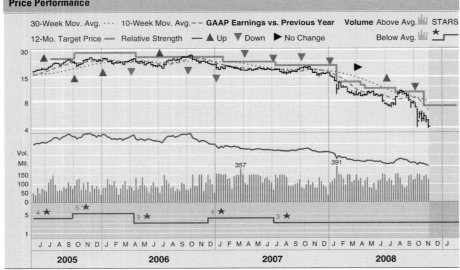

- 30-Week Mov. Avg. · · ·
- 10-Week Mov. Avg. – –
- **GAAP Earnings vs. Previous Year**
- Volume Above Avg.
- STARS
- 12-Mo. Target Price —
- Relative Strength —
- ▲ Up ▼ Down ► No Change
- Below Avg.

2005  2006  2007  2008

Options: ASE, CBOE, P, Ph

Analysis prepared by **Todd Rosenbluth** on November 03, 2008, when the stock traded at **$ 5.06**.

## Highlights

➤ We project a sales decline of 14% in 2008 and a modest 1% improvement in 2009, resulting from weakness in MOT's still large mobile devices unit as an unfavorable product mix and a reduced number of devices should cut demand. We see a double-digit decrease in volumes being partially offset by stability in average selling prices. We expect greater prospects in home and networks mobility in 2009 (5% annual revenue growth) on demand from telecom and cable customers, and in enterprise mobility (4%) from public safety sales.

➤ Despite pressure on sales, we expect 2008 gross margins to widen slightly to 28% before narrowing to 27.5% in 2009, as MOT improves its handset manufacturing process as part of its operational savings focus while benefiting from growth in other segments. We see a reduction in SG&A helping to generate slight operating income.

➤ We see 2008 operating EPS of $0.02 and 2009 EPS of $0.14, including projected stock option expense. We think interest income will remain a contributor in 2008 and 2009.

## Investment Rationale/Risk

➤ We are encouraged by MOT's efforts to lower costs and consolidate its mobile device operations in an effort to return the business to profitability. However, we believe execution will not only take time but will be difficult in light of high competition, a delay in the release of major products, and we note previously failed attempts. We anticipate operating strength in non-handset operations to persist despite some pressure on customer spending. However, our belief that a previously planned spinoff will not occur until 2010 making it harder for us to see the full benefits.

➤ Risks to our recommendation and target price include execution risks involving the handset unit, failure to successfully introduce and ship new handset products, and a slowdown in telecom equipment capital spending.

➤ Based on a below-peers price-to-sales multiple of less than 1X our 2009 estimate, our 12-month target price is $7. The stock is trading at a near 1X its tangible book value, which in our view should provide some support.

## Qualitative Risk Assessment

| LOW | MEDIUM | HIGH |
|---|---|---|

Our risk assessment reflects the company's exposure to the economic health of the telecom and broadband industries and risks related to high-volume manufacturing and distribution to service providers. This is offset by our view of MOT's strong balance sheet.

## Quantitative Evaluations

**S&P Quality Ranking** B

| D | C | B- | B | B+ | A- | A | A+ |
|---|---|---|---|---|---|---|---|

**Relative Strength Rank** WEAK

27

LOWEST = 1     HIGHEST = 99

## Revenue/Earnings Data

**Revenue (Million $)**

| | 1Q | 2Q | 3Q | 4Q | Year |
|---|---|---|---|---|---|
| 2008 | 7,448 | 8,082 | 7,480 | -- | -- |
| 2007 | 9,433 | 8,732 | 8,811 | 9,646 | 36,622 |
| 2006 | 9,608 | 10,876 | 10,603 | 11,792 | 42,879 |
| 2005 | 8,161 | 8,825 | 9,424 | 10,433 | 36,843 |
| 2004 | 7,441 | 7,541 | 7,499 | 8,842 | 31,323 |
| 2003 | 6,043 | 6,163 | 6,829 | 8,023 | 27,058 |

**Earnings Per Share ($)**

| | | | | | |
|---|---|---|---|---|---|
| 2008 | -0.09 | Nil | -0.18 | E0.02 | E0.02 |
| 2007 | -0.09 | -0.02 | 0.02 | 0.05 | -0.05 |
| 2006 | 0.26 | 0.54 | 0.29 | 0.21 | 1.30 |
| 2005 | 0.28 | 0.38 | 0.69 | 0.47 | 1.82 |
| 2004 | 0.19 | 0.25 | 0.18 | 0.28 | 0.90 |
| 2003 | 0.07 | 0.05 | 0.05 | 0.20 | 0.38 |

Fiscal year ended Dec. 31. Next earnings report expected: Late January. EPS Estimates based on S&P Operating Earnings; historical GAAP earnings are as reported.

## Dividend Data (Dates: mm/dd Payment Date: mm/dd/yy)

| Amount ($) | Date Decl. | Ex-Div. Date | Stk. of Record | Payment Date |
|---|---|---|---|---|
| 0.050 | 01/31 | 03/12 | 03/14 | 04/15/08 |
| 0.050 | 05/06 | 06/12 | 06/16 | 07/15/08 |
| 0.050 | 07/29 | 09/11 | 09/15 | 10/15/08 |
| 0.050 | 11/12 | 12/11 | 12/15 | 01/15/09 |

Dividends have been paid since 1942. Source: Company reports.

# Motorola Inc.

**STANDARD &POOR'S**

## Business Summary November 03, 2008

CORPORATE OVERVIEW. Motorola provides wireless and networking equipment for cable and telecom service providers. We believe all these markets are exposed to increased buyer's power due to the industry consolidation of service providers. The Mobile Devices segment (42% of sales in the first nine months of 2008, down from 53% a year earlier) manufactures wireless handsets for GSM and CDMA standards. With the sale of 160 million handsets in 2007 and 70 million in the first nine months of 2008, we estimate that MOT's global handset market share declined to 13% and 8.5%, respectively, from 22% in 2006. The Mobile Devices segment had an operating loss in the first nine months of 2008, even as MOT reduced inventory. Upon reporting third quarter 2008 results, the company has delayed its previous plans to separate its handset business from the rest of Motorola until beyond 2009.

In October 2008, MOT announced efforts to revamp its handset software platforms, which we contend will result in a number of product cancellations, to reduce its cost structure and better align its offerings with customer demand for both smartphones and low-end handsets. We believe this will result in further pressure to handset volumes in the first half of 2009.

The remainder of revenues come from the Home and Networks Mobility (32%)

and Enterprise Mobility (25%) segments. Within Home and Networks, during the third quarter of 2008, MOT shipped 4.1 million digital entertainment devices down from 4.9 million in the second quarter, used primarily by U.S. telecom and cable companies, and 3.1 million broadband gateway devices, up from the prior year. In addition, MOT provided infrastructure for CDMA, GSM and iDEN wireless networks. Within Enterprise Mobility, sales to the government and public safety segments comprised nearly 75% of sales, with the remainder from enterprises such as the U.S. Postal Service.

COMPETITIVE LANDSCAPE. Within the handset market, we see ongoing pressure from diversified manufacturers such as Nokia and Samsung and smartphone specialists such as Apple and Research in Motion that have been gaining market share as consumers look to use their phones for data services. Mobile phone manufacturers shipped a total of 299 million handsets in the third quarter of 2008, up 3.2% from last year but at slower than typical rate due to macroeconomic challenges.

## Company Financials Fiscal Year Ended Dec. 31

### Per Share Data ($)

| | 2009 | 2008 | 2007 | 2006 | 2005 | 2004 | 2003 | 2002 | 2001 | 2000 |
|---|---|---|---|---|---|---|---|---|---|---|
| Tangible Book Value | NA | NA | 4.28 | 7.15 | 6.67 | 5.45 | 5.43 | 4.85 | 6.07 | 8.50 |
| Cash Flow | NA | NA | 0.35 | 1.53 | 2.06 | 1.15 | 1.09 | -0.17 | -0.63 | 1.70 |
| Earnings | 0.17 | NA | -0.05 | 1.30 | 1.82 | 0.90 | 0.38 | -1.09 | -1.78 | 0.58 |
| S&P Core Earnings | NA | NA | 0.07 | 1.24 | 1.18 | 0.78 | 0.08 | -0.93 | -2.23 | NA |
| Dividends | NA | NA | 0.20 | 0.19 | 0.16 | 0.16 | 0.16 | 0.16 | 0.16 | 0.16 |
| Payout Ratio | NA | NA | NM | 15% | 9% | 18% | 42% | NM | NM | 28% |
| Prices:High | NA | NA | 20.91 | 26.30 | 24.99 | 20.89 | 14.40 | 17.12 | 25.13 | 61.54 |
| Prices:Low | NA | NA | 14.87 | 18.66 | 14.48 | 13.83 | 7.59 | 7.30 | 10.50 | 15.81 |
| P/E Ratio:High | NA | NA | NM | 20 | 14 | 23 | 38 | NM | NM | NM |
| P/E Ratio:Low | NA | NA | NM | 14 | 8 | 15 | 20 | NM | NM | NM |

### Income Statement Analysis (Million $)

| | 2009 | 2008 | 2007 | 2006 | 2005 | 2004 | 2003 | 2002 | 2001 | 2000 |
|---|---|---|---|---|---|---|---|---|---|---|
| Revenue | NA | NA | 36,622 | 42,879 | 36,843 | 31,323 | 27,058 | 26,679 | 30,004 | 37,580 |
| Operating Income | NA | NA | 1,349 | 4,675 | 4,851 | 3,887 | 2,694 | 2,059 | -2,595 | 4,544 |
| Depreciation | NA | NA | 906 | 558 | 613 | 659 | 1,667 | 2,108 | 2,552 | 2,522 |
| Interest Expense | NA | NA | 365 | 335 | 325 | 199 | 295 | 668 | 645 | 494 |
| Pretax Income | NA | NA | -390 | 4,610 | 6,520 | 3,252 | 1,293 | -3,446 | -5,511 | 2,231 |
| Effective Tax Rate | NA | NA | 73.1% | 29.3% | 29.5% | 32.6% | 30.9% | NM | NM | 40.9% |
| Net Income | NA | NA | -105 | 3,261 | 4,599 | 2,191 | 893 | -2,485 | -3,937 | 1,318 |
| S&P Core Earnings | NA | NA | 186 | 3,132 | 2,964 | 1,899 | 164 | -2,084 | -4,893 | NA |

### Balance Sheet & Other Financial Data (Million $)

| | 2009 | 2008 | 2007 | 2006 | 2005 | 2004 | 2003 | 2002 | 2001 | 2000 |
|---|---|---|---|---|---|---|---|---|---|---|
| Cash | NA | NA | 8,606 | 15,416 | 14,641 | 10,556 | 7,877 | 6,507 | 6,082 | 3,301 |
| Current Assets | NA | NA | 22,222 | 30,975 | 27,869 | 21,082 | 17,907 | 17,134 | 17,149 | 19,885 |
| Total Assets | NA | NA | 34,812 | 38,593 | 35,649 | 30,889 | 32,098 | 31,152 | 33,398 | 42,343 |
| Current Liabilities | NA | NA | 12,500 | 15,425 | 12,488 | 10,573 | 9,433 | 9,810 | 9,698 | 16,257 |
| Long Term Debt | NA | NA | 3,991 | 2,704 | 3,806 | 4,578 | 7,161 | 7,674 | 8,857 | 4,778 |
| Common Equity | NA | NA | 15,447 | 17,142 | 16,673 | 13,331 | 12,689 | 11,239 | 13,691 | 18,612 |
| Total Capital | NA | NA | 20,371 | 19,846 | 20,479 | 17,909 | 19,850 | 18,913 | 22,548 | 24,894 |
| Capital Expenditures | NA | NA | 527 | 649 | 583 | 494 | 655 | 607 | 1,321 | 4,131 |
| Cash Flow | NA | NA | 801 | 3,819 | 5,212 | 2,850 | 2,560 | -377 | -1,385 | 3,840 |
| Current Ratio | NA | NA | 1.8 | 2.0 | 2.2 | 2.0 | 1.9 | 1.7 | 1.8 | 1.2 |
| % Long Term Debt of Capitalization | NA | NA | 19.6 | 13.6 | 18.6 | 25.6 | 36.1 | 40.6 | 39.3 | 19.2 |
| % Net Income of Revenue | NA | NA | NM | 7.6 | 12.5 | 7.0 | 3.3 | NM | NM | 3.5 |
| % Return on Assets | NA | NA | NM | 8.8 | 13.8 | 7.0 | 2.8 | NM | NM | 3.2 |
| % Return on Equity | NA | NA | NM | 19.3 | 30.7 | 16.8 | 7.5 | NM | NM | 7.1 |

Data as orig reptd.; bef. results of disc opers/spec. items. Per share data adj. for stk. divs.; EPS diluted. E-Estimated. NA-Not Available. NM-Not Meaningful. NR-Not Ranked. UR-Under Review.

**Office:** 1303 East Algonquin Road, Schaumburg, IL 60196.
**Telephone:** 800-262-8509.
**Email:** investors@motorola.com
**Website:** http://www.motorola.com

**Chrmn:** D.W. Dorman
**Pres & Co-CEO:** G.Q. Brown
**Co-CEO:** S.K. Jha
**EVP & CFO:** P.J. Liska

**EVP, Secy & General Counsel:** A.P. Lawson
**Investor Contact:** D. Lindroth (847-576-6899)
**Board Members:** F. J. Biondi, Jr., G. Q. Brown, R. E. Burger, D. W. Dorman, W. R. Hambrecht, S. K. Jha, L. Kimerling, J. C. Lewent, K. A. Meister, T. J. Meredith, N. Negroponte, S. C. Scott, III, R. Sommer, J. R. Stengel, A. J. Vinciquerra, D. A. Warner, III, J. A. White, M. D. White

**Founded:** 1928
**Domicile:** Delaware
**Employees:** 66,000

**The McGraw·Hill Companies**

# M&T Bank Corp

| S&P Recommendation SELL ★ ★ ☆ ☆ ☆ | Price $65.83 (as of Nov 14, 2008) | 12-Mo. Target Price $75.00 | Investment Style Large-Cap Blend |
|---|---|---|---|

**GICS Sector** Financials
**Sub-Industry** Regional Banks

**Summary** This bank holding company for M&T Bank and M&T Bank, N.A. has offices in New York, Pennsylvania, Maryland, Virginia, West Virginia, New Jersey, Delaware, and DC.

## Key Stock Statistics (Source S&P, Vickers, company reports)

| | | | | | | | |
|---|---|---|---|---|---|---|---|
| 52-Wk Range | $108.53– 53.61 | S&P Oper. EPS 2008**E** | 5.39 | Market Capitalization(B) | $7.255 | Beta | 0.17 |
| Trailing 12-Month EPS | $4.69 | S&P Oper. EPS 2009**E** | 5.38 | Yield (%) | 4.25 | S&P 3-Yr. Proj. EPS CAGR(%) | 10 |
| Trailing 12-Month P/E | 14.0 | P/E on S&P Oper. EPS 2008**E** | 12.2 | Dividend Rate/Share | $2.80 | S&P Credit Rating | NA |
| $10K Invested 5 Yrs Ago | $7,799 | Common Shares Outstg. (M) | 110.2 | Institutional Ownership (%) | 79 | | |

## Price Performance

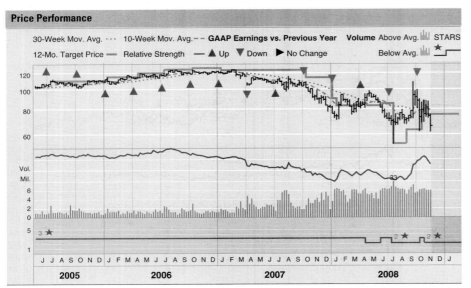

30-Week Mov. Avg. · · · 10-Week Mov. Avg. – – GAAP Earnings vs. Previous Year   Volume Above Avg. STARS
12-Mo. Target Price — Relative Strength   ▲ Up  ▼ Down  ► No Change   Below Avg.

Options: ASE, CBOE, P, Ph

Analysis prepared by **Stuart Plesser** on October 31, 2008, when the stock traded at **$ 79.41**.

## Highlights

➤ We estimate that loan growth will slow to the low single digits in 2009, from projected low-single digit growth in 2008, reflecting business conditions in the Northeast, as well as MTB's cautionary stance on credit quality. The net interest margin may come under pressure due to high funding costs and an asset-sensitive balance sheet. Excluding the writedown of MTB's GSE exposure in 2008, we expect 3% non-interest income growth in 2009, reflecting stable fee revenue and a decline in losses from its Bayview partnership in the second half of 2009.

➤ We expect MTB's non-interest expense to total revenue to remain low relative to other regional banks of similar size. Our 2009 estimate is 59.0%, versus 58.5% projected for 2008, a figure that is distorted somewhat by the writedown of securities. However, we project a 35% increase in loan loss provisions to $520 million in 2009, from $380 million projected for 2008, driven by further writedowns of its loan portfolio.

➤ Given capital restraints, we expect minimal share repurchases in 2009. We project operating EPS of $5.39 in 2008 and $5.38 in 2009.

## Investment Rationale/Risk

➤ We view MTB as one of the more conservative banks in our coverage universe. MTB should benefit from a flight to quality and increase its deposit base. Still, MTB is not immune to overall credit deterioration, which will likely result in chargeoffs of about 1.05% of average loans in 2009, versus 0.70% projected for 2008. As a result, we think provisions will rise next year, largely due to further writedowns of its roughly $2.0 billion home construction portfolio, with general consumer weakness also adding some stress. We are also concerned about deteriorating earnings in BayView Lending, a commercial lender that securitizes loans, in which MTB owns a 20% stake. We think MTB may soon have to take an impairment charge on its investment.

➤ Risks to our recommendation and target price include a net interest margin increase and better-than-expected credit quality.

➤ Our 12-month target price of $75 is 13.9X our 2009 EPS estimate of $5.38, a slight premium to peers.

## Qualitative Risk Assessment

| LOW | MEDIUM | HIGH |
|---|---|---|

Our risk assessment reflects the company's large-cap valuation, our view of the strong credit quality of its loan portfolio, and its history of profitability. While the company operates in a highly competitive and fragmented industry, the industry tends to produce relatively stable financial results.

## Quantitative Evaluations

**S&P Quality Ranking**   A

| D | C | B- | B | B+ | A- | A | A+ |
|---|---|---|---|---|---|---|---|

**Relative Strength Rank**   MODERATE

64

LOWEST = 1   HIGHEST = 99

## Revenue/Earnings Data

**Revenue (Million $)**

| | 1Q | 2Q | 3Q | 4Q | Year |
|---|---|---|---|---|---|
| 2008 | 1,197 | 1,089 | 915.1 | -- | -- |
| 2007 | 1,098 | 1,161 | 1,146 | 1,073 | 4,478 |
| 2006 | 1,030 | 1,076 | 1,127 | 1,127 | 4,360 |
| 2005 | 872.6 | 921.9 | 942.3 | 1,002 | 3,738 |
| 2004 | 774.3 | 792.9 | 828.0 | 846.5 | 3,242 |
| 2003 | 568.4 | 809.3 | 795.7 | 784.2 | 2,958 |

**Earnings Per Share ($)**

| | 1Q | 2Q | 3Q | 4Q | Year |
|---|---|---|---|---|---|
| 2008 | 1.82 | 1.44 | 0.82 | E1.30 | E5.39 |
| 2007 | 1.57 | 1.95 | 1.83 | 0.60 | 5.95 |
| 2006 | 1.77 | 1.87 | 1.85 | 1.88 | 7.37 |
| 2005 | 1.62 | 1.69 | 1.64 | 1.78 | 6.73 |
| 2004 | 1.30 | 1.53 | 1.56 | 1.62 | 6.00 |
| 2003 | 1.23 | 1.10 | 1.28 | 1.35 | 4.95 |

Fiscal year ended Dec. 31. Next earnings report expected: NA. EPS Estimates based on S&P Operating Earnings; historical GAAP earnings are as reported.

## Dividend Data (Dates: mm/dd Payment Date: mm/dd/yy)

| Amount ($) | Date Decl. | Ex-Div. Date | Stk. of Record | Payment Date |
|---|---|---|---|---|
| 0.700 | 11/20 | 12/13 | 12/17 | 12/31/07 |
| 0.700 | 02/20 | 02/27 | 02/29 | 03/31/08 |
| 0.700 | 04/15 | 05/29 | 06/02 | 06/30/08 |
| 0.700 | 07/23 | 08/28 | 09/02 | 09/30/08 |

Dividends have been paid since 1979. Source: Company reports.

# M&T Bank Corp

**STANDARD &POOR'S**

## Business Summary October 31, 2008

CORPORATE OVERVIEW. M&T Bank Corporation is a New York-based bank holding company with $64.9 billion in assets as of December 31, 2007. Its primary subsidiaries are M&T Bank, a New York State chartered bank that focuses its lending on consumers and small- and medium-sized businesses in the Mid-Atlantic region, and National Association (N.A.), a national banking association that offers selected deposit and loan products on a nationwide basis through direct mail and telephone marketing. MTB also operates other subsidiaries that provide insurance, securities, investments, leasing, mortgage, mortgage reinsurance, real estate and other financial products and services.

Following MTB's acquisition of Allfirst Financial Inc., a bank holding company in Baltimore, MD, from Allied Irish Banks, p.l.c. (AIB) on April 1, 2003, AIB gained a 22.5% stake in MTB. As of December 31, 2007, the foreign bank owned 24.3% of MTB's common stock. As long as AIB maintains a significant ownership in MTB, each bank will have representation on the other's board.

MARKET PROFILE. As of June 30, 2007, MTB had 674 branches and $33.1 billion in deposits, with about 55% of its deposits and 41% of its branches concentrated in New York, according to the Federal Deposit Insurance Corporation. In addition, 98.1% of MTB's deposits and 96.7% of branches were concentrated in the three adjoining states of New York, Pennsylvania, and Maryland. In New York, MTB had 275 branches, $18.2 billion in deposits, and a deposit market share of about 2.5%, ranking seventh. In Pennsylvania, MTB had 227 branches, $7.2 billion in deposits, and a deposit market share of about 2.8%, ranking eighth. In Maryland, MTB has 150 branches, $7.1 billion in deposits, and a deposit market share of about 7%, ranking fourth. Finally, MTB has a small presence in the District of Columbia, Virginia, West Virginia and Delaware.

## Company Financials Fiscal Year Ended Dec. 31

| Per Share Data ($) | 2007 | 2006 | 2005 | 2004 | 2003 | 2002 | 2001 | 2000 | 1999 | 1998 |
|---|---|---|---|---|---|---|---|---|---|---|
| Tangible Book Value | 30.62 | 30.05 | 25.56 | 24.52 | 21.43 | 20.23 | 17.84 | 16.10 | 14.88 | 13.72 |
| Earnings | 5.95 | 7.37 | 6.73 | 6.00 | 4.95 | 5.07 | 3.82 | 3.44 | 3.28 | 2.62 |
| S&P Core Earnings | 5.87 | 7.36 | 6.64 | 5.97 | 4.95 | 4.60 | 3.40 | NA | NA | NA |
| Dividends | 2.60 | 2.25 | 1.75 | 1.60 | 1.20 | 1.05 | 1.00 | 0.62 | 0.45 | 0.38 |
| Payout Ratio | 44% | 31% | 26% | 27% | 24% | 21% | 26% | 18% | 14% | 15% |
| Prices:High | 125.13 | 124.98 | 112.50 | 108.75 | 98.98 | 90.05 | 82.11 | 68.42 | 58.25 | 58.20 |
| Prices:Low | 77.39 | 105.72 | 96.71 | 82.90 | 74.71 | 67.70 | 59.80 | 35.70 | 40.60 | 40.00 |
| P/E Ratio:High | 21 | 17 | 17 | 18 | 20 | 18 | 21 | 20 | 18 | 22 |
| P/E Ratio:Low | 13 | 14 | 14 | 14 | 15 | 13 | 16 | 10 | 12 | 15 |

| Income Statement Analysis (Million $) | 2007 | 2006 | 2005 | 2004 | 2003 | 2002 | 2001 | 2000 | 1999 | 1998 |
|---|---|---|---|---|---|---|---|---|---|---|
| Net Interest Income | 1,850 | 1,818 | 1,794 | 1,735 | 1,599 | 1,248 | 1,158 | 854 | 759 | 664 |
| Tax Equivalent Adjustment | 20.8 | NA | 17.3 | NA | 16.3 | 14.0 | 17.5 | 10.5 | 7.71 | 7.19 |
| Non Interest Income | 1,059 | 1,043 | 978 | 940 | 831 | 513 | 476 | 325 | 282 | 269 |
| Loan Loss Provision | 192 | 80.0 | 88.0 | 95.0 | 131 | 122 | 104 | NA | 44.5 | 43.2 |
| % Expense/Operating Revenue | 55.9% | 54.2% | 53.2% | 56.7% | 59.6% | 51.9% | 57.4% | 61.6% | 59.4% | 60.2% |
| Pretax Income | 964 | 1,232 | 1,171 | 1,067 | 851 | 716 | 584 | 446 | 418 | 326 |
| Effective Tax Rate | 32.1% | 31.9% | 33.2% | 32.3% | 32.5% | 32.3% | 35.2% | 35.9% | 36.5% | 36.1% |
| Net Income | 654 | 839 | 782 | 723 | 574 | 485 | 378 | 286 | 266 | 208 |
| % Net Interest Margin | 3.60 | 3.70 | 3.77 | 3.88 | 4.09 | 4.36 | 4.23 | 4.02 | 4.02 | 3.97 |
| S&P Core Earnings | 646 | 838 | 772 | 718 | 574 | 440 | 336 | NA | NA | NA |

| Balance Sheet & Other Financial Data (Million $) | 2007 | 2006 | 2005 | 2004 | 2003 | 2002 | 2001 | 2000 | 1999 | 1998 |
|---|---|---|---|---|---|---|---|---|---|---|
| Money Market Assets | 348 | 143 | 211 | 199 | 250 | 380 | 84.4 | 57.8 | 1,286 | 403 |
| Investment Securities | 8,962 | 7,371 | 8,400 | 8,475 | 7,259 | 3,955 | 3,024 | 3,310 | 1,901 | 2,786 |
| Commercial Loans | 25,715 | 23,165 | 23,940 | 22,886 | 20,869 | 14,522 | 14,071 | 13,399 | 6,141 | 3,657 |
| Other Loans | 22,637 | 20,042 | 16,614 | 15,758 | 15,169 | 11,415 | 11,117 | 9,571 | 11,431 | 12,348 |
| Total Assets | 64,876 | 57,065 | 55,146 | 52,939 | 49,826 | 33,175 | 31,450 | 28,949 | 22,409 | 20,584 |
| Demand Deposits | 9,322 | 8,820 | 9,044 | 9,246 | 10,150 | 5,101 | 4,634 | 4,218 | 2,844 | 2,576 |
| Time Deposits | 31,944 | 25,660 | 28,056 | 26,183 | 20,756 | 16,564 | 16,946 | 16,014 | 12,530 | 12,161 |
| Long Term Debt | 10,318 | 6,891 | 5,586 | 6,349 | 5,535 | 4,497 | 3,462 | 3,415 | 1,744 | 1,568 |
| Common Equity | 6,485 | 6,281 | 5,876 | 5,730 | 5,717 | 3,182 | 2,939 | 38.0 | 44.5 | 1,602 |
| % Return on Assets | 1.1 | 1.5 | 1.4 | 1.4 | 1.4 | 1.5 | 1.3 | 1.1 | 1.2 | 1.2 |
| % Return on Equity | 10.3 | 13.8 | 13.5 | 12.6 | 12.9 | 15.8 | 13.4 | 12.7 | 15.6 | 15.9 |
| % Loan Loss Reserve | 1.6 | 1.5 | 1.6 | 1.6 | 1.7 | 1.7 | 1.7 | 1.6 | -2.0 | 1.9 |
| % Loans/Deposits | 112.1 | 107.6 | 108.7 | 108.4 | 108.0 | 119.7 | 116.7 | 112.4 | 115.4 | 107.2 |
| % Equity to Assets | 10.5 | 10.8 | 10.7 | 11.1 | 10.8 | 9.5 | 9.3 | 8.8 | 7.9 | 7.6 |

Data as orig reptd.; bef. results of disc opers/spec. items. Per share data adj. for stk. divs.; EPS diluted. E-Estimated. NA-Not Available. NM-Not Meaningful. NR-Not Ranked. UR-Under Review.

**Office:** 1 M And T Plz, Buffalo, NY 14203-2399.
**Telephone:** 716-842-5445.
**Email:** ir@mandtbank.com
**Website:** http://www.mandtbank.com

**Chrmn & CEO:** R.G. Wilmers
**Pres:** M.J. Czarnecki
**Vice Chrmn:** J.G. Pereira
**Vice Chrmn:** R.E. Sadler, Jr.

**Vice Chrmn:** M.P. Pinto
**Investor Contact:** D.J. MacLeod (716-842-5462)
**Board Members:** B. D. Baird, R. J. Bennett, C. A. Bontempo, R. T. Brady, M. Buckley, T. J. Cunningham, III, M. J. Czarnecki, C. E. Doherty, R. E. Garman, D. R. Hawbaker, P. W. Hodgson, R. G. King, R. B. Newman, II, J. G. Pereira, M. P. Pinto, R. E. Sadler, Jr., E. Sheehy, S. G. Sheetz, H. L. Washington, R. G. Wilmers

**Founded:** 1969
**Domicile:** New York
**Employees:** 13,869

The McGraw-Hill Companies

# Murphy Oil Corp

**STANDARD &POOR'S**

**S&P Recommendation** HOLD ★★★☆☆

| Price | 12-Mo. Target Price | Investment Style |
|---|---|---|
| $46.86 (as of Nov 14, 2008) | $60.00 | Large-Cap Blend |

**GICS Sector** Energy
**Sub-Industry** Integrated Oil & Gas

**Summary** This international integrated oil company has exploration and production interests worldwide, and refining and marketing operations in the U.S.

## Key Stock Statistics (Source S&P, Vickers, company reports)

| | | | | | | | |
|---|---|---|---|---|---|---|---|
| 52-Wk Range | $101.47–38.01 | S&P Oper. EPS 2008**E** | 9.57 | Market Capitalization(B) | $8.926 | Beta | 0.97 |
| Trailing 12-Month EPS | $9.46 | S&P Oper. EPS 2009**E** | 9.88 | Yield (%) | 2.13 | S&P 3-Yr. Proj. EPS CAGR(%) | 39 |
| Trailing 12-Month P/E | 5.0 | P/E on S&P Oper. EPS 2008**E** | 4.9 | Dividend Rate/Share | $1.00 | S&P Credit Rating | BBB |
| $10K Invested 5 Yrs Ago | $16,357 | Common Shares Outstg. (M) | 190.5 | Institutional Ownership (%) | 80 | | |

## Price Performance

30-Week Mov. Avg. · · · ·   10-Week Mov. Avg. — —   **GAAP Earnings vs. Previous Year**   Volume Above Avg. STARS
12-Mo. Target Price —   Relative Strength —   ▲ Up   ▼ Down   ► No Change   Below Avg.

Options: ASE, CBOE, P, Ph

Analysis prepared by **Tina J. Vital** on November 07, 2008, when the stock traded at **$ 48.87**.

## Highlights

➤ Third quarter oil and gas production climbed 30% from a year earlier, reflecting contributions from the August 2007 start-up of the Kikeh Field, offshore Sabah Malaysia, but were below our expectations due to Gulf hurricane shut-ins. We expect MUR's production will rise by about 26% in 2008, and see about 33% per annum growth during 2007 to 2010 on contributions from Kikeh. Initial natural gas production from Malaysia and the Tupper area in western Canada is slated for 2008, and we see these volumes as helping to offset anticipated field declines in the Gulf of Mexico, onshore southern Louisiana, Hibernia, and Terra Nova.

➤ U.S. industry-wide refining margins have weakened, as refined product prices failed to keep pace with the sharp increase in crude oil prices, and we expect U.S. Gulf Coast 321 refining cracks will narrow about 18% in 2008 and 2009.

➤ We expect after-tax operating earnings will increase 126% in 2008, and remain near these levels in 2009. During the 2008 second quarter, MUR sold its Lloydminster properties in Western Canada for an after-tax gain of $67.9 million (or $0.35 per share).

## Investment Rationale/Risk

➤ While MUR's primary focus is in the U.S. in the deepwater Gulf of Mexico, the company's new international interests have added significant new opportunities. The Kikeh project offshore Malaysia, which commenced in August 2007, has improved the company's upstream prospects, but we see increased risk from its dependence on Kikeh. Also, we view MUR's upstream cost structure as still unfavorable compared to peers. Despite weak exploration results over the past few years, we estimate MUR's 2007 organic reserve replacement at 144%.

➤ Risks to our recommendation and target price include unfavorable changes to economic, industrial and operating conditions, such as difficulty in replacing oil and gas reserves.

➤ A blend of our discounted cash flow ($59 per share; assuming a WACC of 8.7% and terminal growth of 3%), net asset ($84 per share, based on a long term WTI oil price of $90 per barrel), and narrowed relative valuations leads to our 12-month target of $60 per share. This represents an expected enterprise value of 2.7X our 2009 EBITDA estimate, a discount to U.S. peers.

## Qualitative Risk Assessment

| LOW | MEDIUM | **HIGH** |
|---|---|---|

Our risk assessment reflects our view of MUR's moderate financial policies and integrated operations in a volatile, cyclical and capital-intensive segment of the energy industry. We believe its low reserve-to-production ratio limits its operating flexibility, increasing dependence on long-term projects.

## Quantitative Evaluations

**S&P Quality Ranking**                    A-

| D | C | B- | B | B+ | **A-** | A | A+ |
|---|---|---|---|---|---|---|---|

**Relative Strength Rank**        MODERATE

55

LOWEST = 1                    HIGHEST = 99

## Revenue/Earnings Data

**Revenue (Million $)**

| | 1Q | 2Q | 3Q | 4Q | Year |
|---|---|---|---|---|---|
| 2008 | 6,533 | 8,363 | 8,186 | -- | -- |
| 2007 | 3,435 | 4,614 | 4,781 | 5,610 | 18,424 |
| 2006 | 2,991 | 3,799 | 4,153 | 3,364 | 14,307 |
| 2005 | 2,415 | 2,950 | 3,317 | 3,195 | 11,877 |
| 2004 | 1,628 | 2,096 | 2,291 | 2,301 | 8,360 |
| 2003 | 1,322 | 1,278 | 1,297 | 1,449 | 5,345 |

**Earnings Per Share ($)**

| | | | | | |
|---|---|---|---|---|---|
| 2008 | 2.14 | 3.22 | 3.04 | E1.39 | E9.57 |
| 2007 | 0.58 | 1.32 | 1.04 | 1.07 | 4.01 |
| 2006 | 0.60 | 1.13 | 1.18 | 0.46 | 3.37 |
| 2005 | 0.60 | 1.85 | 1.18 | 0.82 | 4.46 |
| 2004 | 0.43 | 0.90 | 0.62 | 0.71 | 2.66 |
| 2003 | 0.51 | 0.43 | 0.37 | 0.32 | 1.63 |

Fiscal year ended Dec. 31. Next earnings report expected: Late January. EPS Estimates based on S&P Operating Earnings; historical GAAP earnings are as reported.

## Dividend Data (Dates: mm/dd Payment Date: mm/dd/yy)

| Amount ($) | Date Decl. | Ex-Div. Date | Stk. of Record | Payment Date |
|---|---|---|---|---|
| 0.188 | 02/06 | 02/14 | 02/19 | 03/03/08 |
| 0.188 | 04/02 | 05/14 | 05/16 | 06/02/08 |
| 0.250 | 08/06 | 08/14 | 08/18 | 09/02/08 |
| 0.250 | 09/30 | 11/12 | 11/14 | 12/01/08 |

Dividends have been paid since 1961. Source: Company reports.

---

# Murphy Oil Corp

**STANDARD &POOR'S**

## Business Summary November 07, 2008

CORPORATE OVERVIEW. Originally incorporated in Louisiana in 1950 as Murphy Corp., the company was reincorporated in Delaware in 1964 under the name Murphy Oil Corp. (MUR). As an international integrated oil and gas company, MUR explores for oil and gas worldwide, but has refining and marketing interests in the U.S. The company operates in two business segments: Exploration and Production (11% of 2007 revenues; 76% of earnings), and Refining and Marketing (89%; 24%).

The Exploration and Production segment produces oil and gas in the U.S., Canada, U.K. North Sea, Malaysia and Ecuador, and conducts exploration activities worldwide. In the U.S., the company has interests in eight oil and gas fields (six in the deepwater Gulf of Mexico, and two onshore Louisiana), four operated by MUR and four by others. MUR's primary focus in the U.S. is in the deepwater Gulf of Mexico, where its primary asset is the Medusa field (MUR 60% stake; contributed 40% of its 2007 oil and gas production) in the Mississippi Canyon Block 538/582.

In Canada, MUR owns an interest in three nonoperated long-lived assets, the Hibernia (6.5%) and Terra Nova (12%) fields offshore Newfoundland and Syncrude Canada Ltd. (5%) in northern Alberta. In addition, the company owns interests in two heavy oil areas and one natural gas area in the Western Canadian Sedimentary Basin (WCSB).

In Malaysia, the company has majority interests in eight separate production sharing contracts (PSCs), and serves as operator. In 2002, MUR made an important discovery at the Kikeh field (80%) in deepwater Block K, offshore Sabah, and added another important discovery at Kakap in 2004. In Ecuador, MUR owns a 20% interest in Block 16, which is operated by Repsol YPF (REP) under a participation contract that expires in 2012. The company also has interests in PSCs covering two offshore blocks in the Republic of Congo.

Proved oil and gas reserves rose 5.7%, to 276.7 million barrels of oil equivalent (boe; 64% liquids, 53% developed), in 2007. Also, MUR's synthetic oil reserves rose 1.9%, to 128.4 million barrels. Oil and gas production increased 1.3%, to 101,702 boe per day (90% liquids). We estimate MUR's 2007 organic reserve replacement at 144%. Using data from John S. Herold, we estimate MUR's three-year (2004-06) proved acquisition costs at $8.73 per boe, above the peer average; its three-year finding & development costs at $23.12 per boe, above peers; its three-year reserve replacement costs at $22.32 per boe, below the peer average; and its three-year reserve replacement at 113%, above peers.

## Company Financials Fiscal Year Ended Dec. 31

| Per Share Data ($) | 2007 | 2006 | 2005 | 2004 | 2003 | 2002 | 2001 | 2000 | 1999 | 1998 |
|---|---|---|---|---|---|---|---|---|---|---|
| Tangible Book Value | 26.47 | 21.37 | 18.38 | 14.16 | 10.27 | 8.41 | 7.99 | 6.72 | 5.87 | 5.44 |
| Cash Flow | 6.75 | 5.40 | 6.57 | 4.38 | 3.39 | 2.16 | 3.07 | 2.87 | 1.80 | 1.05 |
| Earnings | 4.01 | 3.37 | 4.46 | 2.66 | 1.63 | 0.53 | 1.82 | 1.69 | 0.67 | -0.08 |
| S&P Core Earnings | 4.03 | 3.32 | 3.85 | 2.40 | 1.40 | 0.39 | 1.30 | NA | NA | NA |
| Dividends | 0.68 | 0.52 | 0.45 | 0.43 | 0.40 | 0.39 | 0.38 | 0.36 | 0.35 | 0.35 |
| Payout Ratio | 17% | 16% | 10% | 16% | 25% | 73% | 21% | 21% | 53% | NM |
| Prices:High | 85.94 | 60.18 | 57.07 | 43.69 | 34.35 | 24.86 | 21.96 | 17.27 | 15.41 | 13.61 |
| Prices:Low | 45.45 | 44.72 | 37.80 | 28.45 | 19.27 | 15.95 | 13.81 | 12.05 | 8.22 | 8.63 |
| P/E Ratio:High | 21 | 18 | 13 | 16 | 21 | 47 | 12 | 10 | 23 | NM |
| P/E Ratio:Low | 11 | 13 | 8 | 11 | 12 | 30 | 8 | 7 | 12 | NM |

| Income Statement Analysis (Million $) | | | | | | | | | | |
|---|---|---|---|---|---|---|---|---|---|---|
| Revenue | 18,439 | 14,307 | 11,877 | 8,360 | 5,345 | 3,967 | 4,479 | 4,639 | 2,037 | 1,694 |
| Operating Income | 1,845 | 1,514 | 1,854 | 1,110 | 781 | 492 | 768 | 723 | 400 | 288 |
| Depreciation, Depletion and Amortization | 523 | 384 | 397 | 321 | 328 | 300 | 229 | 213 | 204 | 203 |
| Interest Expense | 75.5 | 9.48 | 8.77 | 34.1 | 20.5 | 27.0 | 19.0 | 16.3 | 20.3 | 10.5 |
| Pretax Income | 1,237 | 1,028 | 1,372 | 805 | 419 | 152 | 506 | 465 | 179 | -8.28 |
| Effective Tax Rate | 38.1% | 37.9% | 38.9% | 38.3% | 28.1% | 35.7% | 34.6% | 34.3% | 32.9% | NM |
| Net Income | 767 | 638 | 838 | 496 | 301 | 97.5 | 331 | 306 | 120 | -14.4 |
| S&P Core Earnings | 772 | 630 | 725 | 448 | 259 | 71.4 | 236 | NA | NA | NA |

| Balance Sheet & Other Financial Data (Million $) | | | | | | | | | | |
|---|---|---|---|---|---|---|---|---|---|---|
| Cash | 674 | 543 | 585 | 536 | 252 | 165 | 82.7 | 133 | 34.1 | 28.3 |
| Current Assets | 2,887 | 2,107 | 1,839 | 1,629 | 1,039 | 854 | 599 | 817 | 593 | 437 |
| Total Assets | 10,536 | 7,446 | 6,369 | 5,458 | 4,713 | 3,886 | 3,259 | 3,134 | 2,446 | 2,164 |
| Current Liabilities | 2,109 | 1,311 | 1,287 | 1,205 | 810 | 718 | 560 | 745 | 488 | 381 |
| Long Term Debt | 1,516 | 840 | 610 | 613 | 1,090 | 863 | 521 | 525 | 393 | 333 |
| Common Equity | 5,066 | 4,053 | 3,461 | 2,649 | 1,951 | 1,594 | 1,498 | 1,260 | 1,057 | 978 |
| Total Capital | 7,526 | 5,498 | 4,685 | 3,263 | 3,463 | 2,784 | 2,322 | 2,014 | 1,604 | 1,436 |
| Capital Expenditures | 1,949 | 1,192 | 1,246 | 938 | 938 | 834 | 814 | 512 | 387 | 389 |
| Cash Flow | 1,290 | 1,022 | 1,235 | 818 | 630 | 398 | 560 | 519 | 324 | 188 |
| Current Ratio | 1.4 | 1.6 | 1.4 | 1.4 | 1.3 | 1.2 | 1.1 | 1.1 | 1.2 | 1.1 |
| % Long Term Debt of Capitalization | 20.2 | 15.3 | 13.0 | 18.8 | 31.5 | 31.0 | 22.4 | 26.1 | 24.5 | 23.2 |
| % Return on Assets | 8.5 | 9.2 | 14.2 | 9.8 | 7.0 | 2.7 | 10.4 | 11.0 | 5.2 | NM |
| % Return on Equity | 16.8 | 17.0 | 27.4 | 21.6 | 17.0 | 6.3 | 24.0 | 26.4 | 11.8 | NM |

Data as orig reptd.; bef. results of disc opers/spec. items. Per share data adj. for stk. divs.; EPS diluted. E-Estimated. NA-Not Available. NM-Not Meaningful. NR-Not Ranked. UR-Under Review.

**Office:** 200 Peach Street, El Dorado, AR 71730-7000.
**Telephone:** 870-862-6411.
**Email:** murphyoil@murphyoilcorp.com
**Website:** http://www.murphyoilcorp.com

**Chrmn:** W.C. Nolan, Jr.
**Pres & CEO:** C.P. Deming
**EVP & General Counsel:** S.A. Cosse
**SVP & CFO:** K.G. Fitzgerald

**Chief Acctg Officer & Cntlr:** J.W. Eckart
**Investor Contact:** M. West (870-864-6315)
**Board Members:** F. W. Blue, C. P. Deming, R. A. Hermes, J. V. Kelley, R. M. Murphy, W. C. Nolan, Jr., I. B. Ramberg, N. E. Schmale, D. J. Smith, C. G. Theus

**Founded:** 1950
**Domicile:** Delaware
**Employees:** 7,539

# Mylan Inc

STANDARD
&POOR'S

| S&P Recommendation **HOLD** ★★★☆☆ | Price $9.13 (as of Nov 14, 2008) | 12-Mo. Target Price $12.00 | Investment Style Large-Cap Growth |
|---|---|---|---|

**GICS Sector** Health Care
**Sub-Industry** Pharmaceuticals

**Summary** This leading manufacturer of generic pharmaceuticals produces a broad range of generic drugs in varying strengths. In early October 2007, Mylan acquired the generic drug division of German drugmaker Merck KGaA for some $7.0 billion in cash.

## Key Stock Statistics (Source S&P, Vickers, company reports)

| | | | | | |
|---|---|---|---|---|---|
| 52-Wk Range | $15.49– 5.75 | S&P Oper. EPS 2008**E** | 0.65 | Market Capitalization(B) | $2.782 | Beta | 0.87 |
| Trailing 12-Month EPS | $-5.47 | S&P Oper. EPS 2009**E** | 1.00 | Yield (%) | Nil | S&P 3-Yr. Proj. EPS CAGR(%) | 40 |
| Trailing 12-Month P/E | NM | P/E on S&P Oper. EPS 2008**E** | 14.0 | Dividend Rate/Share | Nil | S&P Credit Rating | BB- |
| $10K Invested 5 Yrs Ago | $4,100 | Common Shares Outstg. (M) | 304.7 | Institutional Ownership (%) | NM | | |

## Price Performance

30-Week Mov. Avg. · · · ·  10-Week Mov. Avg. - -  **GAAP Earnings vs. Previous Year**  Volume Above Avg. ▮▮▮ STARS
12-Mo. Target Price —  Relative Strength —  ▲ Up  ▼ Down  ► No Change  Below Avg. ▮▮▮

Options: ASE, CBOE, P, Ph

Analysis prepared by **Herman B. Saftlas** on November 04, 2008, when the stock traded at **$ 8.77**.

## Qualitative Risk Assessment

| LOW | MEDIUM | HIGH |
|---|---|---|

Our risk assessment reflects risks inherent in the generic pharmaceutical business, which include the ability to successfully develop generic products, obtain regulatory approvals, and legally challenge branded patents. However, we believe these risks are offset at Mylan, given its wide and diverse generic portfolio, and promising branded drug business. We also think the recent acquisition of Merck KGaA's generic business holds long-term promise.

## Quantitative Evaluations

**S&P Quality Ranking**  A-

| D | C | B- | B | B+ | A- | A | A+ |
|---|---|---|---|---|---|---|---|

**Relative Strength Rank**  STRONG

79

LOWEST = 1  HIGHEST = 99

## Highlights

➤ We forecast 2009 revenues of $5.1 billion, up from $4.6 billion that we estimate for 2008, which excludes some $466 million in revenues related to the sale of a divested drug. Revenues in 2008 were boosted by the acquisition of Merck KGaA's generics division in October 2007. Revenues in 2009 should see strong growth in North American generics, driven by a robust lineup of new products. MYL has some 112 AN-DAs presently pending FDA approval. We also see growth in sales of international generics, as well as increased revenues in the Matrix and Dey divisions.

➤ We look for gross margins in 2009 to widen somewhat on the projected better volume and productivity enhancements. We also see tight control of SG&A costs and R&D spending, helped by ongoing merger synergies (estimated at $100 million in 2008). However, the effective tax rate is expected to rise in 2009.

➤ After preferred dividend payments, we project 2009 operating cash EPS of $1.00, before acquisition-related charges and other specified items, up from an estimated $0.65 in 2008.

## Investment Rationale/Risk

➤ We believe Mylan's efforts to expand its base through the acquisitions of Merck KGaA's generic business and India-based Matrix Laboratories hold long-term promise. Besides broadening the company's geographic reach to Europe, Asia and Japan, these acquisitions also provided access to in-house sourcing of active pharmaceutical ingredients and newer areas such as generic biologics. MYL expects accrued merger synergies to reach $300 million by the end of 2010. However, we believe MYL still faces daunting integration issues with these acquisitions. Funding these deals also required Mylan to assume significant long-term debt.

➤ Risks to our recommendation and target price include possible problems integrating the Merck KGaA business, as well as the need to obtain FDA approval for new generics and mount legal challenges to branded patents.

➤ Based on our analysis, MYL shares are valued in line with peers on an EV/EBITDA basis. Our 12 month target price of $12 is supported by our DCF model, which assumes a WACC of 8% and a perpetuity growth rate of 1%.

## Revenue/Earnings Data

**Revenue (Million $)**

| | 1Q | 2Q | 3Q | 4Q | Year |
|---|---|---|---|---|---|
| 2008 | 1,074 | 477.1 | 1,657 | -- | -- |
| 2007 | 356.1 | 366.7 | 401.8 | 487.3 | 1,612 |
| 2006 | 323.4 | 298.0 | 311.3 | 324.6 | 1,257 |
| 2005 | 339.0 | 307.0 | 291.0 | 316.4 | 1,253 |
| 2004 | 331.4 | 360.1 | 349.8 | 333.4 | 1,375 |
| 2003 | 275.5 | 319.5 | 320.5 | 353.7 | 1,269 |

**Earnings Per Share ($)**

| | | | | | |
|---|---|---|---|---|---|
| 2008 | -1.46 | 0.60 | 0.45 | E0.17 | -4.49 |
| 2007 | 0.35 | 0.36 | 0.63 | -0.31 | 0.99 |
| 2006 | 0.16 | 0.16 | 0.22 | 0.27 | 0.79 |
| 2005 | 0.30 | 0.18 | 0.13 | 0.14 | 0.74 |
| 2004 | 0.31 | 0.33 | 0.31 | 0.27 | 1.21 |
| 2003 | 0.22 | 0.24 | 0.25 | 0.27 | 0.97 |

Fiscal year ended Dec. 31. Next earnings report expected: NA. EPS Estimates based on S&P Operating Earnings; historical GAAP earnings are as reported.

## Dividend Data

No Dividend Data Available

# Mylan Inc

**STANDARD &POOR'S**

## Business Summary November 04, 2008

CORPORATE PROFILE. Mylan Laboratories is a leading manufacturer of generic pharmaceutical products in finished tablet, capsule and powder dosage forms. Generic drugs are the chemical equivalents of branded drugs, and are marketed after patents on the primary products expire. Generics are typically sold at prices significantly below those of comparable branded products.

MYL's U.S. generic division markets about 180 generic products, primarily solid oral dose drugs encompassing some 50 therapeutic categories. Some 16 generics are extended-release drugs. The company's UDL Laboratories is the largest U.S. repackager of pharmaceuticals in unit dose formats, which are used primarily in hospitals, nursing homes and similar settings. Mylan Technologies develops and markets products using transdermal drug delivery systems.

IMPACT OF MAJOR DEVELOPMENTS. With the early October 2007 acquisition of a generic drug business from German drugmaker Merck KGaA, Mylan now ranks as the third largest producer of generic pharmaceuticals in the world. The acquired business (referred to as Merck Generics) markets over 400 products, and had sales of $2.3 billion in 2006. The operation has a strong presence in key foreign generic markets, including France, the U.K., Japan,

Canada and Australia. Under terms of the acquisition agreement, MYL has rights to purchase Merck KGaA's generic businesses in 17 additional countries in Latin America, Europe and Asia until October 2009.

As part of the Merck Generics acquisition, MYL also acquired Dey, a producer of branded specialty respiratory and allergy drugs. Key Dey products are EpiPen, an auto-injector treatment for allergic reactions; and DuoNeb, a nebulized treatment for COPD. Mylan expects Merck Generics, which was acquired for about $7.0 billion in cash, to be dilutive to cash EPS in year one, to break even in year two, and to be accretive thereafter.

In January 2007, MYL acquired about 72% of the voting shares of Indian drugmaker Matrix Laboratories for about $776 million in cash. Matrix is the second largest maker of active pharmaceutical ingredients (APIs) in the world. Matrix produces high-quality APIs for Mylan's own generics, as well as for third parties.

## Company Financials Fiscal Year Ended Dec. 31

### Per Share Data ($)

| | 2007 | 2006 | 2005 | 2004 | 2003 | 2002 | 2001 | 2000 | 1999 | 1998 |
|---|---|---|---|---|---|---|---|---|---|---|
| Tangible Book Value | 2.75 | 2.76 | 6.03 | 5.30 | 4.39 | 3.97 | 2.97 | 3.00 | 2.49 | 2.24 |
| Cash Flow | 1.27 | 0.99 | 0.91 | 1.37 | 1.11 | 1.07 | 0.28 | 0.65 | 0.50 | 0.44 |
| Earnings | 0.99 | 0.79 | 0.74 | 1.21 | 0.97 | 0.91 | 0.13 | 0.52 | 0.43 | 0.36 |
| S&P Core Earnings | -4.50 | 0.78 | 0.64 | 1.05 | 0.89 | 0.84 | 0.40 | NA | NA | NA |
| Dividends | 0.24 | 0.12 | 0.10 | 0.08 | 0.08 | 0.07 | 0.07 | 0.07 | 0.07 | 0.07 |
| Payout Ratio | 24% | 15% | 14% | 7% | 18% | 8% | 55% | 14% | 17% | 20% |
| Prices:High | NA | 25.00 | 21.69 | 26.35 | 28.75 | 16.56 | 16.94 | 14.33 | 14.22 | 15.97 |
| Prices:Low | NA | 18.65 | 15.21 | 14.24 | 15.56 | 11.15 | 8.96 | 7.11 | 7.58 | 7.58 |
| P/E Ratio:High | NA | 25 | 27 | 36 | 24 | 17 | 19 | NM | 27 | 37 |
| P/E Ratio:Low | NA | 19 | 19 | 19 | 13 | 12 | 12 | NM | 14 | 18 |

### Income Statement Analysis (Million $)

| | 2007 | 2006 | 2005 | 2004 | 2003 | 2002 | 2001 | 2000 | 1999 | 1998 |
|---|---|---|---|---|---|---|---|---|---|---|
| Revenue | 1,612 | 1,257 | 1,253 | 1,375 | 1,269 | 1,104 | 847 | 790 | 721 | 555 |
| Operating Income | 586 | 347 | 321 | 504 | 452 | 441 | 209 | 259 | 224 | 146 |
| Depreciation | 61.5 | 46.8 | 45.1 | 44.3 | 40.6 | 46.1 | 42.4 | 35.7 | 26.9 | 21.7 |
| Interest Expense | 52.3 | 31.3 | Nil | Nil | Nil | Nil | Nil | Nil | Nil | Nil |
| Pretax Income | 426 | 275 | 312 | 513 | 427 | 408 | 58.0 | 243 | 192 | 148 |
| Effective Tax Rate | 48.9% | 32.8% | 34.8% | 34.7% | 36.1% | 36.3% | 36.0% | 36.5% | 40.0% | 32.1% |
| Net Income | 217 | 185 | 204 | 335 | 272 | 260 | 37.1 | 154 | 115 | 101 |
| S&P Core Earnings | -1,155 | 184 | 175 | 286 | 247 | 241 | 113 | NA | NA | NA |

### Balance Sheet & Other Financial Data (Million $)

| | 2007 | 2006 | 2005 | 2004 | 2003 | 2002 | 2001 | 2000 | 1999 | 1998 |
|---|---|---|---|---|---|---|---|---|---|---|
| Cash | 1,427 | 518 | 808 | 687 | 687 | 617 | 285 | 303 | 260 | 104 |
| Current Assets | 2,412 | 1,192 | 1,528 | 1,318 | 1,228 | 1,062 | 879 | 687 | 583 | 430 |
| Total Assets | 4,254 | 1,871 | 2,136 | 1,875 | 1,745 | 1,617 | 1,466 | 1,341 | 1,207 | 848 |
| Current Liabilities | 701 | 265 | 246 | 174 | 266 | 175 | 291 | 87.8 | 96.4 | 71.3 |
| Long Term Debt | 1,655 | 685 | 19.3 | 19.1 | 19.9 | 21.9 | 23.3 | 30.6 | 26.8 | 26.2 |
| Common Equity | 1,649 | 4,242 | 2,786 | 2,600 | 1,446 | 1,607 | 1,133 | 1,204 | 1,060 | 744 |
| Total Capital | 3,390 | 4,948 | 2,830 | 2,642 | 1,479 | 1,646 | 1,175 | 1,253 | 1,110 | 776 |
| Capital Expenditures | 162 | 104 | 90.7 | 118 | 32.6 | 20.6 | 24.7 | 28.8 | 16.7 | 28.9 |
| Cash Flow | 279 | 231 | 249 | 379 | 313 | 306 | 79.5 | 190 | 142 | 122 |
| Current Ratio | 3.4 | 4.5 | 6.2 | 7.6 | 4.6 | 6.1 | 3.0 | 7.8 | 6.0 | 6.0 |
| % Long Term Debt of Capitalization | 48.8 | 13.8 | 0.7 | 0.7 | 1.3 | 1.3 | 2.0 | 2.4 | 2.4 | 3.4 |
| % Net Income of Revenue | 13.5 | 14.7 | 16.2 | 24.3 | 21.5 | 23.6 | 4.4 | 19.5 | 16.0 | 18.1 |
| % Return on Assets | 7.1 | 9.2 | 10.1 | 18.5 | 16.2 | 16.9 | 2.6 | 12.1 | 11.2 | 12.4 |
| % Return on Equity | 17.8 | 5.3 | 7.6 | 14.1 | 19.1 | 17.7 | 3.2 | 13.6 | 12.8 | 14.4 |

Data as orig reptd.; bef. results of disc opers/spec. items. Per share data adj. for stk. divs.; EPS diluted. E-Estimated. NA-Not Available. NM-Not Meaningful. NR-Not Ranked. UR-Under Review.

**Office:** 1500 Corporate Dr, Canonsburg, PA 15317-8580.
**Telephone:** 724-514-1800.
**Email:** investor_relations@mylan.com
**Website:** http://www.mylan.com

**Chrmn:** M. Puskar
**Vice Chrmn & CEO:** R.J. Coury
**COO & EVP:** H. Bresch
**EVP & CFO:** E.J. Borkowski

**EVP & CTO:** R. Malik
**Investor Contact:** K. King (724-514-1800)
**Board Members:** W. Cameron, R. J. Coury, N. Dimick, D. J. Leech, J. Maroon, N. Nimmagadda, R. L. Piatt, N. Prasad, M. Puskar, C. B. Todd, R. L. Vanderveen

**Founded:** 1970
**Domicile:** Pennsylvania
**Employees:** 12,000

The **McGraw-Hill** Companies

# Nabors Industries Ltd

**STANDARD &POOR'S**

| S&P Recommendation | **HOLD** ★★★☆☆ | Price | 12-Mo. Target Price | Investment Style |
|---|---|---|---|---|
| | | $13.61 (as of Nov 14, 2008) | $18.00 | Large-Cap Growth |

**GICS Sector** Energy
**Sub-Industry** Oil & Gas Drilling

**Summary** This Bermuda company, based in Barbados, is the world's largest oil and gas land drilling contractor.

## Key Stock Statistics (Source S&P, Vickers, company reports)

| | | | | | | | | |
|---|---|---|---|---|---|---|---|---|
| 52-Wk Range | $50.58– 11.21 | S&P Oper. EPS 2008**E** | 3.08 | Market Capitalization(B) | $3.873 | Beta | | 0.98 |
| Trailing 12-Month EPS | $2.99 | S&P Oper. EPS 2009**E** | 2.95 | Yield (%) | Nil | S&P 3-Yr. Proj. EPS CAGR(%) | | -1 |
| Trailing 12-Month P/E | 4.6 | P/E on S&P Oper. EPS 2008**E** | 4.4 | Dividend Rate/Share | Nil | S&P Credit Rating | | A- |
| $10K Invested 5 Yrs Ago | $7,052 | Common Shares Outstg. (M) | 284.6 | Institutional Ownership (%) | 98 | | | |

## Price Performance

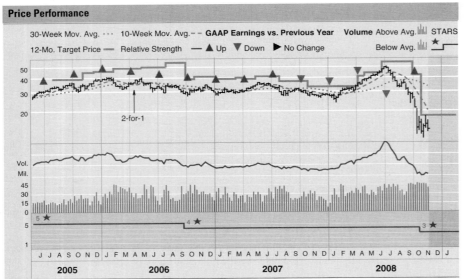

30-Week Mov. Avg. · · · 10-Week Mov. Avg. - - GAAP Earnings vs. Previous Year Volume Above Avg. STARS
12-Mo. Target Price — Relative Strength — ▲ Up ▼ Down ► No Change Below Avg.

Options: ASE, CBOE, P, Ph

Analysis prepared by **Michael Kay** on October 27, 2008, when the stock traded at **$ 13.00**.

## Highlights

► Third quarter cash margins increased by $1,174 per day, to $10,065, on a rise in working rig count of 21. As of October, NBR sees rigs up 10 from 263 in the third quarter. However, NBR has stated that its rig count could fall by 40-50 rigs on cutbacks to drilling plans. NBR believes it can handle the industry downturn better than in prior years, given 81 newly deployed rigs and its long-term contract exposure. Furthermore, over 30 newbuilds are expected to be deployed between mid-2009 and mid-2010. NBR estimates 30% of its fleet is in shale plays, where it sees drilling budget cuts as less likely.

► We have been disappointed by NBR's performance in its international markets and recently lowered our expectations. However, NBR expects to deploy 14 international rigs over the next several months and we see segment income growing by 21% in 2009.

► We see 2008 EPS of $3.08, down from $3.17, on higher interest expense and income taxes, declining to $2.95 in 2009 as dayrates and utilization weaken. We expect NBR to cut discretionary capex in 2009 to $1.5 billion, down $500 million. We believe NBR, with $1.1 billion in cash, can fund $250 million in debt due in 2009.

## Investment Rationale/Risk

► North American onshore drilling faces challenges due to capacity additions and spending cutbacks. While we view NBR as somewhat protected through long-term contracts, its emphasis on larger operators, and segment diversification, we expect volatility in the sector amid continued market turmoil. NBR has strong drilling prospects related to unconventional natural gas plays, given technology advantages and its newbuild program. NBR expects the international segment to benefit from the start-up of some offshore jackup rigs, but is also seeing delays in Mexico.

► Risks to our recommendation and target price include reduced oil and natural gas prices; lower land drilling dayrates; slower-than-expected deliveries of new rigs; and rising cost inflation.

► We now use lower multiples to value land drilling stocks for the following factors: an overall decline in land drilling valuations, a weaker outlook for dayrates and utilization going forward, worsening economic conditions, and the ongoing credit crisis. Blending a target of 4X our 2009 EBITDA estimate, 3.5X our 2009 cash flow projection, and 5X our 2009 EPS estimate, we arrive at our 12-month target price of $18.

## Qualitative Risk Assessment

| LOW | MEDIUM | **HIGH** |
|---|---|---|

Our risk assessment reflects NBR's sensitivity to volatile crude oil and natural gas prices (especially the latter), capital spending decisions made by oil and gas producing customers, and the rising number of newbuild land rigs on order. Partly offsetting these risks is NBR's diversified fleet, including overseas operations, and its leadership position in the industry.

## Quantitative Evaluations

### S&P Quality Ranking — NR

| D | C | B- | B | B+ | A- | A | A+ |
|---|---|---|---|---|---|---|---|

### Relative Strength Rank — WEAK

25

LOWEST = 1     HIGHEST = 99

## Revenue/Earnings Data

### Revenue (Million $)

| | 1Q | 2Q | 3Q | 4Q | Year |
|---|---|---|---|---|---|
| 2008 | 1,322 | 1,282 | 1,455 | -- | -- |
| 2007 | 1,261 | 1,157 | 1,226 | 1,309 | 4,939 |
| 2006 | 1,164 | 1,144 | 1,244 | 1,329 | 4,943 |
| 2005 | 783.7 | 786.1 | 893.3 | 1,016 | 3,551 |
| 2004 | 607.7 | 546.7 | 585.7 | 701.0 | 2,394 |
| 2003 | 455.7 | 433.4 | 476.0 | 524.6 | 1,880 |

### Earnings Per Share ($)

| | | | | | |
|---|---|---|---|---|---|
| 2008 | 0.81 | 0.67 | 0.73 | E0.87 | E3.08 |
| 2007 | 0.92 | 0.79 | 0.68 | 0.78 | 3.13 |
| 2006 | 0.79 | 0.77 | 1.02 | 0.97 | 3.40 |
| 2005 | 0.40 | 0.41 | 0.56 | 0.65 | 2.00 |
| 2004 | 0.23 | 0.15 | 0.24 | 0.34 | 0.96 |
| 2003 | 0.16 | 0.10 | 0.17 | 0.21 | 0.63 |

Fiscal year ended Dec. 31. Next earnings report expected: Early February. EPS Estimates based on S&P Operating Earnings; historical GAAP earnings are as reported.

## Dividend Data

No cash dividends have been paid.

---

The **McGraw·Hill** Companies

# Nabors Industries Ltd

STANDARD
&POOR'S

## Business Summary October 27, 2008

CORPORATE OVERVIEW. The world's largest land drilling contractor, Nabors Industries Ltd. owns a fleet of about 535 land drilling rigs. Formed as a Bermuda-exempt company in December 2001, but operating continuously in the drilling sector since the early 1900s, Nabors conducts oil, gas and geothermal land drilling operations in the lower 48 U.S. states, Alaska and Canada, and internationally, mainly in South and Central America, the Middle East and Africa. NBR actively markets approximately 564 land workover and well servicing rigs in the U.S. Southwest and West, and approximately 173 well servicing and workover rigs in Canada. In addition, it markets 35 platform, 12 jackup and four barge rigs in the Gulf of Mexico and international markets; these rigs provide well servicing, workover and drilling services. NBR also has a 51% ownership interest in a joint venture in Saudi Arabia, which actively markets 9 rigs.

The contract drilling segment (88% of 2007 revenues, and 92% of segment operating income) provides drilling, workover, well servicing and related services in the U.S. (including the lower 48, Alaska and offshore), Canada, and in-

ternationally. During 2007, 59% of contract drilling revenues served customers in the Lower 48, either for land drilling or land well-servicing. Well servicing and workover services are provided for existing wells where some form of artificial lift is required to bring oil to the surface. To supplement its primary business, NBR offers ancillary wellsite services, such as oilfield management, engineering, transportation, construction, maintenance, and well logging. As of December 2007, NBR had a fleet of 29 marine transportation and support vessels, primarily in the Gulf of Mexico, Trinidad, and the Middle East, providing marine transportation of drilling materials, supplies and crews for offshore rig operations and support for other offshore facilities. The supply vessels are used as freight-carrying vessels for bringing drill pipe, tubing, casing, drilling mud, and other equipment to drilling rigs and production platforms.

## Company Financials Fiscal Year Ended Dec. 31

| Per Share Data ($) | 2007 | 2006 | 2005 | 2004 | 2003 | 2002 | 2001 | 2000 | 1999 | 1998 |
|---|---|---|---|---|---|---|---|---|---|---|
| Tangible Book Value | 16.37 | 11.46 | 10.83 | 8.68 | 7.35 | 6.39 | 5.89 | 5.51 | 4.76 | 4.30 |
| Cash Flow | 5.01 | 4.77 | 3.04 | 1.84 | 1.36 | 1.06 | 1.59 | 0.94 | 0.53 | 0.93 |
| Earnings | 3.13 | 3.40 | 2.00 | 0.96 | 0.63 | 0.41 | 1.09 | 0.45 | 0.12 | 0.58 |
| Dividends | Nil | Nil | Nil | Nil | Nil | Nil | Nil | Nil | Nil | Nil |
| Payout Ratio | Nil | Nil | Nil | Nil | Nil | Nil | Nil | Nil | Nil | Nil |
| Prices:High | 36.42 | 41.35 | 39.94 | 27.13 | 22.93 | 24.99 | 31.56 | 30.24 | 15.63 | 15.78 |
| Prices:Low | 26.00 | 27.26 | 23.10 | 20.01 | 16.10 | 13.07 | 9.00 | 14.06 | 5.38 | 5.88 |
| P/E Ratio:High | 12 | 12 | 20 | 28 | 37 | 62 | 29 | 68 | NM | 27 |
| P/E Ratio:Low | 8 | 8 | 12 | 21 | 26 | 32 | 8 | 32 | NM | 10 |

| Income Statement Analysis (Million $) | | | | | | | | | | |
|---|---|---|---|---|---|---|---|---|---|---|
| Revenue | 4,941 | 4,943 | 3,551 | 2,394 | 1,880 | 1,466 | 2,121 | 1,327 | 639 | 968 |
| Operating Income | 1,750 | 1,952 | 1,304 | 626 | 438 | 351 | 0.69 | 377 | 155 | 267 |
| Depreciation, Depletion and Amortization | 540 | 409 | 339 | 300 | 235 | 195 | 190 | 152 | 99.9 | 84.9 |
| Interest Expense | 63.6 | 46.6 | 44.8 | 48.5 | 70.7 | 67.1 | 60.7 | 35.4 | 30.4 | 15.5 |
| Pretax Income | 1,135 | 1,471 | 874 | 336 | 175 | 141 | 542 | 227 | 45.6 | 200 |
| Effective Tax Rate | 21.1% | 30.6% | 25.8% | 9.94% | NM | 13.7% | 35.9% | 40.2% | 39.3% | 37.5% |
| Net Income | 896 | 1,021 | 649 | 302 | 192 | 121 | 348 | 135 | 27.7 | 125 |

| Balance Sheet & Other Financial Data (Million $) | | | | | | | | | | |
|---|---|---|---|---|---|---|---|---|---|---|
| Cash | 767 | 701 | 565 | 1,253 | 1,532 | 1,331 | 919 | 551 | 112 | 47.3 |
| Current Assets | 2,205 | 2,505 | 2,617 | 1,581 | 1,516 | 1,370 | 1,031 | 1,018 | 461 | 266 |
| Total Assets | 10,103 | 9,142 | 7,230 | 5,863 | 5,603 | 5,064 | 4,152 | 3,137 | 2,398 | 1,450 |
| Current Liabilities | 1,494 | 854 | 1,352 | 1,199 | 598 | 751 | 330 | 279 | 265 | 244 |
| Long Term Debt | 3,306 | 4,004 | 1,252 | 1,202 | 1,986 | 1,615 | 1,568 | 855 | 483 | 217 |
| Common Equity | 4,514 | 3,537 | 3,758 | 2,929 | 2,490 | 2,158 | 1,858 | 1,806 | 1,470 | 867 |
| Total Capital | 8,363 | 8,125 | 5,727 | 4,517 | 4,849 | 4,175 | 3,711 | 2,759 | 2,046 | 1,157 |
| Capital Expenditures | 2,014 | 1,927 | 907 | 544 | 353 | 317 | 701 | 301 | 82.1 | 276 |
| Cash Flow | 1,436 | 1,430 | 987 | 603 | 427 | 317 | 538 | 288 | 128 | 210 |
| Current Ratio | 1.5 | 2.9 | 1.9 | 1.3 | 2.5 | 1.8 | 3.1 | 3.6 | 1.7 | 1.1 |
| % Long Term Debt of Capitalization | 39.5 | 49.3 | 21.9 | 26.6 | 41.0 | 38.7 | 42.2 | 31.0 | 23.6 | 18.8 |
| % Return on Assets | 9.3 | 12.5 | 9.9 | 5.3 | 3.6 | 2.6 | 9.5 | 4.9 | 1.4 | 9.3 |
| % Return on Equity | 22.3 | 28.0 | 19.4 | 11.2 | 8.3 | 6.0 | 19.0 | 8.3 | 2.4 | 15.7 |

Data as orig reptd.; bef. results of disc opers/spec. items. Per share data adj. for stk. divs.; EPS diluted. E-Estimated. NA-Not Available. NM-Not Meaningful. NR-Not Ranked. UR-Under Review.

**Office:** 8 Par-La_Ville Road, Hamilton, St. Michael , Barbados HM08.
**Telephone:** 441.292.1510.
**Website:** http://www.nabors.com
**Chrmn & CEO:** E.M. Isenberg

**Pres, Vice Chrmn & COO:** A.G. Petrello
**CFO & Chief Acctg Officer:** B.P. Koch
**Secy:** M.D. Andrews
**Investor Contact:** D.A. Smith (281-775-8038)

**Board Members:** W. T. Comfort, III, E. M. Isenberg, J. L. Payne, A. G. Petrello, H. W. Schmidt, M. M. Sheinfeld, M. J. Whitman

**Founded:** 1968
**Domicile:** Bermuda
**Employees:** 20,921

The McGraw-Hill Companies

**STANDARD &POOR'S**

# Nasdaq OMX Group Inc (The)

| S&P Recommendation HOLD ★★★☆☆ | Price $21.90 (as of Nov 14, 2008) | 12-Mo. Target Price $35.00 | Investment Style Large-Cap Blend |
|---|---|---|---|

**GICS Sector** Financials
**Sub-Industry** Specialized Finance

**Summary** The Nasdaq Stock Market is the largest electronic equity securities market in the U.S., both in terms of listed companies and trading volume.

## Key Stock Statistics (Source S&P, Vickers, company reports)

| | | | | | | | |
|---|---|---|---|---|---|---|---|
| 52-Wk Range | $50.00– 19.97 | S&P Oper. EPS 2008**E** | 1.93 | Market Capitalization(B) | $4.384 | Beta | 2.04 |
| Trailing 12-Month EPS | $1.93 | S&P Oper. EPS 2009**E** | 2.16 | Yield (%) | Nil | S&P 3-Yr. Proj. EPS CAGR(%) | NM |
| Trailing 12-Month P/E | 11.4 | P/E on S&P Oper. EPS 2008**E** | 11.3 | Dividend Rate/Share | Nil | S&P Credit Rating | BBB- |
| $10K Invested 5 Yrs Ago | NA | Common Shares Outstg. (M) | 200.2 | Institutional Ownership (%) | 73 | | |

## Price Performance

30-Week Mov. Avg. ···· 10-Week Mov. Avg. — **GAAP Earnings vs. Previous Year**   **Volume** Above Avg. STARS
12-Mo. Target Price — Relative Strength — ▲ Up ▼ Down ▶ No Change   Below Avg.

Options: ASE, CBOE, P, Ph

Analysis prepared by **Rikin Pandya** on November 11, 2008, when the stock traded at **$ 24.93**.

## Highlights

➤ We believe NDAQ has established itself as a leading equity securities exchange through its strong technology platform and aggressive pricing strategy. We expect the company's trading volumes to continue to benefit from growing demand for fast electronic trade execution and increased market volatility. However, we expect trading volumes to pull back in 2009 from peak levels in the 2008 second half. Also, we are somewhat concerned about short-term benefits from the OMX acquisition not meeting expectations as a result of the severe pullback in the equity markets OMX operates in.

➤ From a margin perspective, we are encouraged that NDAQ is working to establish multiple clearing facilities in the U.S. and Europe to take advantage of their fixed-cost structure, and enabling diminishing marginal costs. Further, NDAQ appears to be ahead of schedule with regard to expense reduction from the recently acquired Philadelphia Stock Exchange. Accordingly, we expect operating margins to improve to 20.1% in 2009 from our projection of 17.4% in 2008.

➤ We see EPS of $1.93 in 2008 and $2.16 in 2009.

## Investment Rationale/Risk

➤ We believe NDAQ has made solid progress in integrating its recent acquisitions and leveraging its advantages in electronic trading to take market share from the NYSE. We expect the U.S. equity markets to become increasingly competitive with the implementation of the Regulation National Market System, but we see NDAQ as well positioned to grow its market presence. We are encouraged by the integration of the OMX acquisition, but in the short term we are concerned that OMX trade revenues are a function of the market value of trades as opposed to a fixed fee. Nevertheless, we believe NDAQ is taking the long-term steps necessary to build the scale needed to maximize profit growth.

➤ Risks to our recommendation and target price include a decrease in trading volumes, changes in the regulatory environment driving increased competition, and integration risk.

➤ Our 12-month target price of $35 is based on a P/E multiple of 16X our 2009 EPS estimate, a discount to historical trading levels. We see this discount as warranted given greater competition in equity markets, and the likelihood of lower trading volumes.

## Qualitative Risk Assessment

| LOW | MEDIUM | HIGH |
|---|---|---|

Our risk assessment reflects the potential volatility in results due to changes in equity trading volumes, the potential impact of future regulatory changes, and the uncertainty surrounding NDAQ's international strategy.

## Quantitative Evaluations

**S&P Quality Ranking** NR

| D | C | B- | B | B+ | A- | A | A+ |
|---|---|---|---|---|---|---|---|

**Relative Strength Rank** MODERATE

40

LOWEST = 1     HIGHEST = 99

## Revenue/Earnings Data

**Revenue (Million $)**

| | 1Q | 2Q | 3Q | 4Q | Year |
|---|---|---|---|---|---|
| 2008 | 813.8 | 821.5 | 990.3 | -- | -- |
| 2007 | 562.0 | 558.2 | 652.0 | 664.5 | 2,437 |
| 2006 | 396.2 | 411.0 | 402.9 | 447.2 | 1,658 |
| 2005 | 180.2 | 219.7 | 220.5 | 259.6 | 879.9 |
| 2004 | 128.4 | 120.0 | 124.0 | 168.1 | 540.4 |
| 2003 | 111.6 | 147.6 | 141.9 | 189.0 | 590.0 |

**Earnings Per Share ($)**

| | | | | | |
|---|---|---|---|---|---|
| 2008 | 0.69 | 0.48 | 0.28 | E0.51 | E1.93 |
| 2007 | 0.14 | 0.39 | 2.41 | 0.57 | 3.46 |
| 2006 | 0.16 | 0.13 | 0.22 | 0.43 | 0.95 |
| 2005 | 0.13 | 0.13 | 0.16 | 0.15 | 0.57 |
| 2004 | 0.02 | 0.02 | -0.08 | -0.10 | -0.14 |
| 2003 | 0.06 | -0.45 | -0.13 | -0.04 | -0.68 |

Fiscal year ended Dec. 31. Next earnings report expected: Early February. EPS Estimates based on S&P Operating Earnings; historical GAAP earnings are as reported.

## Dividend Data

No cash dividends have been paid.

The *McGraw-Hill* Companies

# Nasdaq OMX Group Inc (The)

STANDARD
&POOR'S

## Business Summary November 11, 2008

CORPORATE OVERVIEW. The Nasdaq Stock Market, Inc. operates The Nasdaq Stock Market, the largest electronic equity securities market in the U.S., with 3,135 listed companies as of the end of December 31, 2007. NDAQ's matched volume in all U.S. securities was 442 billion in 2007, up from 331 billion in 2006. The company earns revenue from a number of products and services including trade execution, reselling market data, listing fees, intellectual property licensing, and corporate client services.

NDAQ's business is divided into two segments -- Market Services and Issuer Services. In the three months ended June 30, 2008, Market Services accounted for approximately 84% of the company's revenue. This segment consists of NDAQ's transaction-based business, the Nasdaq Market Center, and its market information services. The largest portion of the Market Services segment is transaction fees NDAQ receives for executing trades on its electronic platforms. A smaller revenue source is the fees the company earns from aggregating and reselling trade and quote information from its systems.

The remainder of NDAQ's revenue is generated through its Issuer Services segment, which includes fees from its securities listings business and other financial products. Revenue in this segment is primarily derived from annual fees from companies whose shares are listed on the Nasdaq Stock Market, fees for listing additional shares, and fees for new listings (initial public offerings). Issuer Services also generates revenue from developing and licensing the NDAQ brand for other financial products such as indexes.

COMPETITIVE LANDSCAPE. We see NDAQ competing with other domestic exchanges, primarily the NYSE Euronext (NYSE) and the American Stock Exchange, for company listings, and competing with these exchanges, regional exchanges and electronic communication networks (ECNs) for trade execution volume. While consolidation, particularly among ECNs, has decreased the number of domestic competitors, we believe technology advancements and regulatory changes have kept the U.S. equity exchange business highly competitive. We believe NDAQ competes on the basis of liquidity, speed and price in its core trade execution services. The company plans to be the low price provider in the market for trade execution, and we expect it to continue offering lower listing fees than the NYSE.

## Company Financials Fiscal Year Ended Dec. 31

| Per Share Data ($) | 2007 | 2006 | 2005 | 2004 | 2003 | 2002 | 2001 | 2000 | 1999 | 1998 |
|---|---|---|---|---|---|---|---|---|---|---|
| Tangible Book Value | 7.54 | 2.44 | NM | NM | 2.04 | NA | NA | NA | NA | NA |
| Cash Flow | 3.65 | 1.20 | 1.08 | 0.99 | 0.57 | NA | NA | NA | NA | NA |
| Earnings | 3.46 | 0.95 | 0.57 | -0.14 | -0.68 | 0.40 | 0.35 | 1.34 | 0.86 | 0.35 |
| S&P Core Earnings | 1.59 | 0.96 | 0.53 | -0.19 | -0.69 | 0.31 | NA | NA | NA | NA |
| Dividends | Nil | Nil | Nil | Nil | Nil | NA | NA | NA | NA | NA |
| Payout Ratio | Nil | Nil | Nil | Nil | Nil | NA | NA | NA | NA | NA |
| Prices:High | 50.47 | 46.75 | 45.23 | NA | NA | NA | NA | NA | NA | NA |
| Prices:Low | 26.57 | 23.91 | 8.15 | NA | NA | NA | NA | NA | NA | NA |
| P/E Ratio:High | 15 | 49 | 79 | NM | NA | NA | NA | NA | NA | NA |
| P/E Ratio:Low | 8 | 25 | 14 | NM | NA | NA | NA | NA | NA | NA |

| Income Statement Analysis (Million $) | 2007 | 2006 | 2005 | 2004 | 2003 | 2002 | 2001 | 2000 | 1999 | 1998 |
|---|---|---|---|---|---|---|---|---|---|---|
| Revenue | 2,437 | 1,658 | 880 | 540 | 590 | 799 | 857 | 868 | 634 | 451 |
| Operating Income | 440 | 288 | 181 | 85.0 | 126 | NA | NA | NA | NA | NA |
| Depreciation | 38.9 | 45.1 | 67.0 | 76.0 | 90.0 | 97.9 | 93.4 | 65.6 | 43.7 | 35.0 |
| Interest Expense | 72.9 | 91.1 | 20.0 | 11.0 | 19.0 | NA | NA | NA | NA | NA |
| Pretax Income | 794 | 212 | 106 | 2.60 | -66.0 | 71.7 | 73.1 | 254 | 145 | 61.0 |
| Effective Tax Rate | 34.7% | 40.2% | 41.8% | 29.3% | NM | 57.3% | 52.4% | 41.3% | 40.4% | 42.7% |
| Net Income | 518 | 128 | 62.0 | 1.80 | -45.0 | 43.1 | 40.5 | 150 | 86.2 | 35.0 |
| S&P Core Earnings | 233 | 129 | 50.5 | -15.2 | -54.1 | 26.4 | NA | NA | NA | NA |

| Balance Sheet & Other Financial Data (Million $) | 2007 | 2006 | 2005 | 2004 | 2003 | 2002 | 2001 | 2000 | 1999 | 1998 |
|---|---|---|---|---|---|---|---|---|---|---|
| Cash | 1,325 | 1,950 | 165 | 58.0 | 149 | 445 | 522 | 516 | 175 | NA |
| Current Assets | 1,682 | 2,313 | 597 | 406 | 530 | NA | NA | NA | NA | NA |
| Total Assets | 2,979 | 3,716 | 2,047 | 815 | 851 | 1,176 | 1,326 | 1,075 | 578 | NA |
| Current Liabilities | 411 | 461 | 325 | 208 | 238 | NA | NA | NA | NA | NA |
| Long Term Debt | 118 | 1,493 | 1,185 | 265 | 265 | NA | NA | NA | NA | NA |
| Common Equity | 2,208 | 1,457 | 253 | 157 | 27.0 | 137 | 518 | 765 | 352 | NA |
| Total Capital | 2,419 | 3,066 | 1,533 | 452 | 467 | NA | NA | NA | NA | NA |
| Capital Expenditures | 18.5 | 21.0 | 25.0 | 26.0 | 32.0 | 85.4 | 123 | 187 | 106 | 29.4 |
| Cash Flow | 557 | 172 | 129 | 77.8 | 45.0 | NA | NA | NA | NA | NA |
| Current Ratio | 4.1 | 5.0 | 1.8 | 2.0 | 2.2 | 2.4 | 2.8 | 3.2 | 2.1 | NA |
| % Long Term Debt of Capitalization | 4.9 | 50.6 | 77.2 | 58.6 | 56.7 | 60.9 | 35.5 | 3.1 | 6.6 | Nil |
| % Net Income of Revenue | 21.3 | 7.7 | 7.0 | 0.0 | NM | 5.4 | 4.7 | 17.3 | 13.6 | 7.8 |
| % Return on Assets | 15.5 | 4.4 | 4.3 | 0.0 | NM | 3.5 | 3.4 | 18.2 | NA | NA |
| % Return on Equity | 28.3 | 15.8 | 30.2 | 6.7 | NM | 13.2 | 6.3 | 26.9 | NA | NA |

Data as orig reptd.; bef. results of disc opers/spec. items. Per share data adj. for stk. divs.; EPS diluted. E-Estimated. NA-Not Available. NM-Not Meaningful. NR-Not Ranked. UR-Under Review.

**Office:** 1 Liberty Plz, New York, NY 10006.
**Telephone:** 212-401-8700.
**Website:** http://www.nasdaq.com
**Chrmn:** H.F. Baldwin

**Pres:** M. Bocker
**Vice Chrmn:** M. Oxley
**CEO:** R. Greifeld
**Investor Contact:** D. Warren (212-401-8742)

**Board Members:** S. Ba'alawi, U. Backstrom, H. F. Baldwin, M. Casey, L. Gorman, R. Greifeld, G. H. Hutchins, B. Kantola, E. Kazim, J. D. Markese, H. M. Nielsen, T. F. O'Neill, M. Oxley, J. S. Riepe, M. R. Splinter, L. Wedenborn, D. L. Wince-Smith

**Founded:** 1979
**Domicile:** Delaware
**Employees:** 891

The McGraw-Hill Companies

# National City Corp

**STANDARD &POOR'S**

**S&P Recommendation** HOLD ★★★☆☆

| Price | 12-Mo. Target Price | Investment Style |
|---|---|---|
| $2.33 (as of Nov 14, 2008) | $2.50 | Large-Cap Blend |

**GICS Sector** Financials
**Sub-Industry** Regional Banks

**Summary** One of the largest US regional banks, Cleveland, Ohio based NCC also has banking offices in Michigan, Kentucky, Indiana, Illinois, Missouri and Pennsylvania.

## Key Stock Statistics (Source S&P, Vickers, company reports)

| | | | | | | | |
|---|---|---|---|---|---|---|---|
| 52-Wk Range | $20.83– 1.25 | S&P Oper. EPS 2008**E** | -3.90 | Market Capitalization(B) | $4.744 | Beta | -0.22 |
| Trailing 12-Month EPS | $-12.22 | S&P Oper. EPS 2009**E** | -0.33 | Yield (%) | 1.72 | S&P 3-Yr. Proj. EPS CAGR(%) | 27 |
| Trailing 12-Month P/E | NM | P/E on S&P Oper. EPS 2008**E** | NM | Dividend Rate/Share | $0.04 | S&P Credit Rating | A- |
| $10K Invested 5 Yrs Ago | $870 | Common Shares Outstg. (M) | 2,036.1 | Institutional Ownership (%) | 36 | | |

## Price Performance

30-Week Mov. Avg. · · · ·   10-Week Mov. Avg. - - -   **GAAP Earnings vs. Previous Year**   Volume Above Avg. ▌▌▌▌   STARS

12-Mo. Target Price —   Relative Strength —   ▲ Up  ▼ Down  ▶ No Change   Below Avg. ▌▌▌▌

Options: CBOE

Analysis prepared by **Erik Oja** on November 12, 2008, when the stock traded at **$ 2.43**.

## Highlights

➤ NCC reported nonperforming loans of $3.537 billion in the third quarter, up only 13.2% from the second quarter, a growth rate far below peers. However, these nonperforming loans totaled 3.08% of NCC's total loans, a level higher than most major regional banks. Reserves of $3.752 billion are adequate to cover the current level of nonperforming loans.

➤ We are forecasting loan loss provisioning expenses of nearly $5.1 billion in 2008, based on the $4.17 billion taken already through the third quarter, which included net chargeoffs of $2.18 billion and reserve building of $1.99 billion. For the fourth quarter, we assume an annualized net chargeoff rate of 2.50%, down from 3.10% in the third quarter, plus reserve building of $250 million. For 2009, we expect annualized net chargeoffs in the 2.00% range, falling to 1.00% by the end of the year, plus reserve building of about $200 million, leading to loan loss provisions of about $2.045 billion.

➤ We see a 2008 operating loss per share of $3.90. We expect loan loss provisions to moderate in 2009, and see a loss per share of $0.33. We expect NCC, on a stand-alone basis, to return to profitability in the 2009 fourth quarter.

## Investment Rationale/Risk

➤ Ohio-based NCC is planning to be acquired by Pittsburgh-based PNC Financial Services, in an all-stock transaction which was announced on October 24. This deal, which was agreed to on friendly terms, requires the approval of regulators and shareholders, and is expected to close at the end of 2008. The deal specifies that each of NCC's nearly 2.036 billion shares outstanding is to be exchanged for .0392 of a share of PNC, equal to about 79.8 million shares of PNC, a deal currently worth about $5.075 billion, or $2.49 per share of NCC. PNC will also assume $384 million payable to NCC warrant holders. Our $2.50 target price approximates the terms of this deal.

➤ Risks to our recommendation and target price include the possibility of a delay in the acquisition by PNC, or a termination of the merger agreement. Additional risks include a slower than expected recovery of the U.S. housing market, a decrease in credit quality, higher net hedging losses than we expect, and a decrease in corporate loan demand.

➤ Our 12-month target price of $2.50 equates to a discount-to-peers 0.41X September 30 tangible book value per share of $6.09.

## Qualitative Risk Assessment

| LOW | MEDIUM | HIGH |
|---|---|---|

Our risk assessment reflects our view of NCC's long history of net interest income and fee income growth, offset by the recent credit deterioration and high loan loss provisioning expenses.

## Quantitative Evaluations

**S&P Quality Ranking** A-

| D | C | B- | B | B+ | A- | A | A+ |
|---|---|---|---|---|---|---|---|

**Relative Strength Rank** MODERATE

33

LOWEST = 1    HIGHEST = 99

## Revenue/Earnings Data

**Revenue (Million $)**

| | 1Q | 2Q | 3Q | 4Q | Year |
|---|---|---|---|---|---|
| 2008 | 3,270 | 2,310 | 2,228 | -- | -- |
| 2007 | 2,831 | 3,012 | 2,977 | 2,978 | 11,791 |
| 2006 | 2,801 | 3,020 | 3,168 | 3,965 | 12,953 |
| 2005 | 2,554 | 2,839 | 2,773 | 2,883 | 11,036 |
| 2004 | 2,462 | 2,261 | 2,639 | 3,198 | 10,560 |
| 2003 | 2,622 | 2,534 | 2,037 | 2,400 | 9,594 |

**Earnings Per Share ($)**

| | | | | | |
|---|---|---|---|---|---|
| 2008 | -0.27 | -2.45 | -5.86 | E-0.43 | E-3.90 |
| 2007 | 0.50 | 0.60 | -0.03 | -0.53 | 0.51 |
| 2006 | 0.74 | 0.77 | 0.86 | 1.36 | 3.72 |
| 2005 | 0.74 | 0.97 | 0.74 | 0.64 | 3.09 |
| 2004 | 1.16 | 0.83 | 0.86 | 1.46 | 4.31 |
| 2003 | 1.05 | 0.94 | 0.56 | 0.88 | 3.43 |

Fiscal year ended Dec. 31. Next earnings report expected: Late January. EPS Estimates based on S&P Operating Earnings; historical GAAP earnings are as reported.

## Dividend Data (Dates: mm/dd Payment Date: mm/dd/yy)

| Amount ($) | Date Decl. | Ex-Div. Date | Stk. of Record | Payment Date |
|---|---|---|---|---|
| 0.210 | 01/02 | 01/10 | 01/14 | 02/01/08 |
| 0.010 | 04/21 | 04/29 | 05/01 | 05/16/08 |
| 0.010 | 07/01 | 07/09 | 07/11 | 08/01/08 |
| 0.010 | 10/02 | 10/08 | 10/13 | 11/03/08 |

Dividends have been paid since 1936. Source: Company reports.

---

**Please read the Required Disclosures and Analyst Certification on the last page of this report.**

The **McGraw·Hill** Companies

# National City Corp

**STANDARD &POOR'S**

## Business Summary November 12, 2008

CORPORATE OVERVIEW. NCC operates five major lines of business: Retail Banking (RB), Commercial Banking - Regional, Commercial Banking - National, Mortgage Banking (NMB), and Asset Management. RB provides banking services to consumers and small businesses within NCC's seven-state footprint. In addition to deposit gathering and direct lending services provided through the retail bank branch network, call centers, and the Internet, RB's activities also include small business banking services, education finance, retail brokerage, and lending-related insurance services. Consumer lending products include home equity, government or privately guaranteed student loans, and credit cards and other unsecured personal and small business lines of credit.

Commercial banking provides credit-related and treasury management services, as well as capital markets and international services, to large- and medium-sized corporations. Major products and services include: lines of credit, term loans, leases, automobile floor plan lending, investment real es-

tate lending, asset-based lending, structured finance, syndicated lending, equity and mezzanine capital, treasury management, and international payment and clearing services.

The mortgage banking line primarily originates conventional residential mortgage and home equity loans both within NCC's banking footprint and nationally. NMB's activities also include servicing mortgage loans for third-party investors. Mortgage loans originated by NMB generally represent loans collateralized by one-to-four-family residential real estate and are made to borrowers in good credit standing. These loans are typically sold to primary mortgage market aggregators and jumbo loan investors.

## Company Financials Fiscal Year Ended Dec. 31

| Per Share Data ($) | 2007 | 2006 | 2005 | 2004 | 2003 | 2002 | 2001 | 2000 | 1999 | 1998 |
|---|---|---|---|---|---|---|---|---|---|---|
| Tangible Book Value | 8.05 | 2.46 | 14.85 | 14.36 | 13.47 | 11.70 | 12.15 | 11.06 | 9.44 | 10.69 |
| Earnings | 0.51 | 4.11 | 3.09 | 4.31 | 3.43 | 2.59 | 2.27 | 2.13 | 2.22 | 1.61 |
| S&P Core Earnings | 0.96 | 2.67 | 2.99 | 3.44 | 3.30 | 2.31 | 1.95 | NA | NA | NA |
| Dividends | 1.60 | Nil | 1.44 | 1.34 | 1.25 | 1.20 | 1.16 | 1.14 | 1.06 | 0.94 |
| Payout Ratio | NM | Nil | 47% | 31% | 36% | 46% | 51% | 54% | 48% | 58% |
| Prices:High | 38.94 | 30.50 | 40.00 | 39.66 | 34.97 | 33.75 | 32.70 | 29.75 | 37.81 | 38.75 |
| Prices:Low | 15.76 | 19.91 | 29.75 | 32.14 | 26.53 | 24.60 | 23.69 | 16.00 | 22.13 | 28.47 |
| P/E Ratio:High | 76 | 7 | 13 | 9 | 10 | 13 | 14 | 14 | 17 | 24 |
| P/E Ratio:Low | 31 | 5 | 10 | 7 | 8 | 9 | 10 | 8 | 10 | 18 |

### Income Statement Analysis (Million $)

| | 2007 | 2006 | 2005 | 2004 | 2003 | 2002 | 2001 | 2000 | 1999 | 1998 |
|---|---|---|---|---|---|---|---|---|---|---|
| Net Interest Income | 4,396 | 4,604 | 4,696 | 4,504 | 4,368 | 4,005 | 3,439 | 2,958 | 3,000 | 2,912 |
| Tax Equivalent Adjustment | 29.0 | NA | 31.3 | NA | 28.0 | 30.4 | 33.3 | 33.7 | 36.9 | 40.3 |
| Non Interest Income | 2,584 | 4,019 | 3,225 | 4,444 | 3,549 | 2,731 | 2,533 | 2,427 | 2,242 | 1,695 |
| Loan Loss Provision | 1,326 | 483 | 287 | 323 | 638 | 682 | 605 | 287 | 250 | 201 |
| % Expense/Operating Revenue | 76.0% | 54.7% | 60.0% | 51.0% | 51.6% | 55.4% | 56.0% | 59.1% | 56.9% | 73.3% |
| Pretax Income | 371 | 3,423 | 2,961 | 4,078 | 3,237 | 2,406 | 2,167 | 1,972 | 2,149 | 1,647 |
| Effective Tax Rate | 15.3% | 32.8% | 33.0% | 31.8% | 34.6% | 33.8% | 35.9% | 34.0% | 34.6% | 35.0% |
| Net Income | 314 | 2,300 | 1,985 | 2,780 | 2,117 | 1,594 | 1,388 | 1,302 | 1,405 | 1,071 |
| % Net Interest Margin | 3.49 | 3.75 | 3.74 | 4.09 | 4.11 | 4.34 | 4.71 | 3.85 | 3.99 | 4.11 |
| S&P Core Earnings | 596 | 1,607 | 1,924 | 2,225 | 2,038 | 1,429 | 1,201 | NA | NA | NA |

### Balance Sheet & Other Financial Data (Million $)

| | 2007 | 2006 | 2005 | 2004 | 2003 | 2002 | 2001 | 2000 | 1999 | 1998 |
|---|---|---|---|---|---|---|---|---|---|---|
| Money Market Assets | 100 | 1,551 | 301 | 303 | 162 | 136 | 171 | 81.0 | 556 | 930 |
| Investment Securities | 8,731 | 15,378 | 10,285 | 10,518 | 7,859 | 10,217 | 10,463 | 10,673 | 15,135 | 15,701 |
| Commercial Loans | 549 | 47,755 | 53,392 | 40,847 | 50,446 | 34,107 | 34,033 | 52,247 | 29,415 | 22,243 |
| Other Loans | 3,741 | 47,737 | 62,646 | 59,290 | 60,115 | 38,028 | 34,007 | 13,357 | 30,789 | 35,768 |
| Total Assets | 150,374 | 140,191 | 142,397 | 139,280 | 113,933 | 118,258 | 105,817 | 88,535 | 87,121 | 88,246 |
| Demand Deposits | 55,232 | 47,873 | 45,733 | 47,916 | 43,435 | 39,179 | 34,324 | 28,763 | 27,744 | 29,523 |
| Time Deposits | 42,323 | 39,361 | 38,253 | 38,039 | 20,495 | 25,940 | 28,806 | 26,494 | 22,322 | 28,724 |
| Long Term Debt | 28,277 | 18,656 | 19,370 | 28,444 | 23,666 | 22,730 | 17,316 | 18,145 | 15,038 | 9,009 |
| Common Equity | 13,408 | 14,581 | 12,613 | 12,804 | 9,329 | 8,308 | 7,381 | 6,740 | 5,698 | 6,977 |
| % Return on Assets | 0.2 | 1.6 | 1.4 | 2.2 | 1.8 | 1.4 | 1.4 | 1.5 | 1.6 | 1.5 |
| % Return on Equity | 2.2 | 16.9 | 15.6 | 25.1 | 24.2 | 20.3 | 19.7 | 20.9 | 22.2 | 18.7 |
| % Loan Loss Reserve | 1.5 | 1.0 | 10.3 | 1.2 | 1.2 | 1.1 | 1.2 | 1.3 | 1.5 | 1.7 |
| % Loans/Deposits | 9.3 | 124.2 | 126.3 | 116.5 | 148.0 | 141.7 | 130.0 | 125.3 | 114.9 | 106.3 |
| % Equity to Assets | 9.6 | 9.6 | 9.0 | 8.7 | 7.5 | 7.0 | 7.3 | 7.1 | 7.2 | 8.2 |

Data as orig reptd.; bef. results of disc opers/spec. items. Per share data adj. for stk. divs.; EPS diluted. E-Estimated. NA-Not Available. NM-Not Meaningful. NR-Not Ranked. UR-Under Review.

**Office:** 1900 E 9th St, Cleveland, OH, USA 44114-3484.
**Telephone:** 216-222-2000.
**Email:** investor.relation@nationalcity.com
**Website:** http://www.nationalcity.com

**Chrmn, Pres & CEO:** P.E. Raskind
**Vice Chrmn:** R.L. Michel
**EVP, Secy & General Counsel:** D.L. Zoeller
**SVP, CFO, Chief Acctg Officer & Treas:** T.A. Richlovsky

**Investor Contact:** J. Hennessey (800-622-4204)
**Board Members:** J. E. Barfield, J. S. Broadhurst, C. M. Connor, B. P. Healy, A. H. Koranda, M. B. McCallister, R. L. Michel, P. Ormond, P. E. Raskind, G. L. Shaheen, R. E. Thornburgh, J. S. Thornton, M. Weiss

**Founded:** 1845
**Domicile:** Delaware
**Employees:** 32,064

*The McGraw·Hill Companies*

# National Oilwell Varco Inc

STANDARD
&POOR'S

| S&P Recommendation BUY ★★★★☆ | Price $25.81 (as of Nov 14, 2008) | 12-Mo. Target Price $39.00 | Investment Style Large-Cap Growth |
|---|---|---|---|

**GICS Sector** Energy
**Sub-Industry** Oil & Gas Equipment & Services

**Summary** This company designs and manufactures drill rig equipment, provides downhole tools and services, and also provides supply chain integration services to the upstream oil and gas industry.

## Key Stock Statistics (Source S&P, Vickers, company reports)

| | | | | | | |
|---|---|---|---|---|---|---|
| 52-Wk Range | $92.70– 20.16 | S&P Oper. EPS 2008**E** | 4.88 | Market Capitalization(B) | $10.771 | Beta 1.57 |
| Trailing 12-Month EPS | $4.54 | S&P Oper. EPS 2009**E** | 5.82 | Yield (%) | Nil | S&P 3-Yr. Proj. EPS CAGR(%) 44 |
| Trailing 12-Month P/E | 5.7 | P/E on S&P Oper. EPS 2008**E** | 5.3 | Dividend Rate/Share | Nil | S&P Credit Rating A- |
| $10K Invested 5 Yrs Ago | $26,431 | Common Shares Outstg. (M) | 417.3 | Institutional Ownership (%) | 88 | |

## Price Performance

30-Week Mov. Avg. · · ·   10-Week Mov. Avg. – – –   **GAAP Earnings vs. Previous Year**   Volume Above Avg. |||| STARS
12-Mo. Target Price —   Relative Strength —   ▲ Up   ▼ Down   ▶ No Change   Below Avg. |||| ★

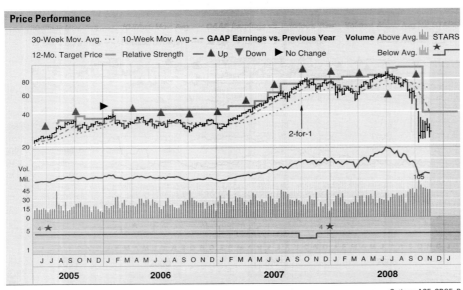

Options: ASE, CBOE, P

Analysis prepared by **Stewart Glickman, CFA** on October 29, 2008, when the stock traded at **$ 25.49**.

### Highlights

➤ New orders for capital equipment totaled $2.4 billion in the third quarter of 2008, up $200 million from the second quarter, and the total backlog at the end of June 2008 was a record $11.8 billion. Although a large number of jackup newbuild announcements have occurred over the past 12 months (with the orderbook standing at about 181 new offshore rigs, roughly half of which are jackups), we think there is the potential for further newbuilds among drillships and semisubmersibles. In the third quarter, NOV said it obtained orders for capital equipment on six newbuild floaters, making it 19 orders year to date.

➤ NOV completed the Grant Prideco acquisition in April 2008, issuing 56.9 million shares of NOV stock and paying $2.93 billion in cash. We estimate the deal to be modestly accretive in 2008, and see potential for revenue synergies, particularly between NOV's downhole motors and the Reed Hycalog drill bit franchise that it acquired in the deal.

➤ Factoring in the impact of the Grant Prideco acquisition, we estimate operating EPS of $4.88 in 2008, rising to $5.82 in 2009.

### Investment Rationale/Risk

➤ We view NOV as an attractive play on the growing need for new rig equipment for the oil and gas industry, particularly for deepwater and unconventional natural gas developments. While the current book of 181 rigs either on order or under construction (85 jackups, 54 semi-submersibles, and 42 drillships) implies about a 30% addition to the existing worldwide fleet, we think that currently unsatisfied demand will absorb most new additions over the next several years, especially for deepwater rigs.

➤ Risks to our opinion and target price include lower-than-expected prices for crude oil and natural gas; a slowdown in drilling activity; and delays in meeting capital equipment orders.

➤ Our discounted cash flow (DCF) model, assuming terminal growth of 3% and a WACC of 13.2%, yields an intrinsic value of about $45. We estimate ROIC of about 17% in 2009, below NOV's capital equipment peers, so we think a modest discount is merited. Based on an assumed 4X multiple of enterprise value to projected 2009 EBITDA, 6X estimated 2009 cash flow (below peers), and our DCF model, our 12-month target price is $39.

### Qualitative Risk Assessment

| LOW | MEDIUM | HIGH |
|---|---|---|

Our risk assessment reflects NOV's exposure to volatile crude oil and natural gas prices, and capital spending decisions made by its contract driller and exploration and production customers. Offsetting these risks is what we view as NOV's leading industry position as a manufacturer of rig capital equipment.

### Quantitative Evaluations

**S&P Quality Ranking** B+

| D | C | B- | B | B+ | A- | A | A+ |
|---|---|---|---|---|---|---|---|

**Relative Strength Rank** WEAK

23

LOWEST = 1          HIGHEST = 99

### Revenue/Earnings Data

**Revenue (Million $)**

| | 1Q | 2Q | 3Q | 4Q | Year |
|---|---|---|---|---|---|
| 2008 | 2,685 | 3,324 | 3,612 | -- | -- |
| 2007 | 2,166 | 2,385 | 2,580 | 2,659 | 9,789 |
| 2006 | 1,512 | 1,657 | 1,778 | 2,079 | 7,026 |
| 2005 | 814.9 | 1,216 | 1,237 | 1,377 | 4,645 |
| 2004 | 496.2 | 533.5 | 618.9 | 669.5 | 2,318 |
| 2003 | 500.6 | 475.4 | 498.6 | 530.4 | 2,005 |

**Earnings Per Share ($)**

| | 1Q | 2Q | 3Q | 4Q | Year |
|---|---|---|---|---|---|
| 2008 | 1.11 | 1.04 | 1.31 | E1.42 | E4.88 |
| 2007 | 0.78 | 0.90 | 1.02 | 1.05 | 3.76 |
| 2006 | 0.34 | 0.42 | 0.50 | 0.68 | 1.94 |
| 2005 | 0.17 | 0.18 | 0.25 | 0.29 | 0.91 |
| 2004 | 0.07 | 0.13 | 0.16 | 0.29 | 0.64 |
| 2003 | 0.12 | 0.12 | 0.14 | 0.09 | 0.45 |

Fiscal year ended Dec. 31. Next earnings report expected: Early February. EPS Estimates based on S&P Operating Earnings; historical GAAP earnings are as reported.

### Dividend Data

No cash dividends have been paid.

The **McGraw-Hill** Companies

# National Oilwell Varco Inc

STANDARD
&POOR'S

## Business Summary October 29, 2008

CORPORATE OVERVIEW. Formerly known as National-Oilwell, this company changed its name to National Oilwell Varco (NOV) on March 14, 2005, following the completion of the merger with Varco International. NOV, a worldwide designer, manufacturer and marketer of comprehensive systems and components used in oil and gas drilling and production, as well as a provider of downhole tools and services, also provides supply chain integration services to the upstream oil and gas industry. The company estimates that more than 90% of the mobile offshore rig fleet and the majority of the world's larger land rigs (2,000 horsepower and greater) manufactured in the past 20 years use drawworks, mud pumps and other drilling components manufactured by NOV.

The combined company generated 2007 revenues of about $9.8 billion, and operating income of $2.0 billion, for an operating margin of approximately 20.9%. The company's Rig Technology segment ($5.75 billion of revenue in 2007, and $1.39 billion of 2007 segment operating income) designs, manufactures and sells drilling systems and components for both land and offshore drilling rigs, as well as complete land drilling and well servicing rigs. The major mechanical components include drawworks, mud pumps, power swivels, SCR houses, solids control equipment, traveling equipment and rotary tables. Many of

these components are designed specifically for applications in offshore, extended reach and deep land drilling. This equipment is installed on new rigs and is often replaced during the upgrade and refurbishment of existing rigs. As of March 31, 2008, total backlog in this segment was about $9.9 billion, up nearly 55% from one year earlier.

The company's Petroleum Services & Supplies segment ($3.06 billion, $732 million) provides a variety of consumable goods and services used in the drilling, completion, workover and remediation of oil and gas wells, service pipelines, flowlines, and other oilfield tubular goods. Products include transfer pumps, solids control systems, drilling motors and other downhole tools, rig instrumentation systems, and mud pump consumables. Following the April 2008 acquisition of Grant Prideco, this segment now offers drill pipe and drill bits.

## Company Financials Fiscal Year Ended Dec. 31

| Per Share Data ($) | 2007 | 2006 | 2005 | 2004 | 2003 | 2002 | 2001 | 2000 | 1999 | 1998 |
|---|---|---|---|---|---|---|---|---|---|---|
| Tangible Book Value | 9.65 | 5.91 | 4.20 | 3.33 | 2.49 | 2.17 | 3.19 | 2.72 | 1.90 | 2.16 |
| Cash Flow | 4.19 | 2.39 | 1.27 | 0.89 | 0.68 | 0.60 | 0.87 | 0.30 | 0.21 | 0.83 |
| Earnings | 3.76 | 1.94 | 0.91 | 0.64 | 0.45 | 0.45 | 0.64 | 0.08 | 0.02 | 0.65 |
| S&P Core Earnings | 3.76 | 1.94 | 0.90 | 0.58 | 0.41 | 0.38 | 0.57 | NA | NA | NA |
| Dividends | Nil | Nil | Nil | Nil | Nil | Nil | Nil | Nil | Nil | Nil |
| Payout Ratio | Nil | Nil | Nil | Nil | Nil | Nil | Nil | Nil | Nil | Nil |
| Prices:High | 82.00 | 38.80 | 34.17 | 18.69 | 12.43 | 14.41 | 20.62 | 19.84 | 9.25 | 20.22 |
| Prices:Low | 26.88 | 25.81 | 16.54 | 10.83 | 8.75 | 7.60 | 6.20 | 7.00 | 4.25 | 3.81 |
| P/E Ratio:High | 22 | 20 | 38 | 29 | 28 | 32 | 32 | 7.00 | NM | 31 |
| P/E Ratio:Low | 7 | 13 | 18 | 17 | 19 | 17 | 10 | NM | NM | 6 |

| Income Statement Analysis (Million $) | 2007 | 2006 | 2005 | 2004 | 2003 | 2002 | 2001 | 2000 | 1999 | 1998 |
|---|---|---|---|---|---|---|---|---|---|---|
| Revenue | 9,789 | 7,026 | 4,645 | 2,318 | 2,005 | 1,522 | 1,747 | 1,150 | 745 | 1,172 |
| Operating Income | 2,198 | 1,280 | 623 | 213 | 198 | 159 | 228 | 97.6 | 45.1 | 157 |
| Depreciation, Depletion and Amortization | 153 | 161 | 115 | 44.0 | 39.2 | 25.0 | 38.9 | 35.0 | 23.2 | 19.2 |
| Interest Expense | 50.3 | 48.7 | 52.9 | 38.4 | 38.9 | 27.3 | 24.9 | Nil | Nil | 12.5 |
| Pretax Income | 2,029 | 1,049 | 430 | 132 | 117 | 112 | 168 | 27.0 | 4.52 | 109 |
| Effective Tax Rate | 33.3% | 33.9% | 32.3% | 14.6% | 28.9% | 35.0% | 38.1% | 51.4% | 66.4% | 36.9% |
| Net Income | 1,337 | 684 | 287 | 110 | 76.8 | 73.1 | 104 | 13.1 | 1.52 | 68.9 |
| S&P Core Earnings | 1,338 | 685 | 283 | 99.2 | 69.3 | 61.6 | 93.6 | NA | NA | NA |

| Balance Sheet & Other Financial Data (Million $) | 2007 | 2006 | 2005 | 2004 | 2003 | 2002 | 2001 | 2000 | 1999 | 1998 |
|---|---|---|---|---|---|---|---|---|---|---|
| Cash | 1,842 | 957 | 209 | 143 | 74.2 | 118 | 43.2 | 42.5 | 12.4 | 11.4 |
| Current Assets | 7,594 | 4,966 | 2,998 | 1,537 | 1,246 | 1,115 | 909 | 743 | 478 | 558 |
| Total Assets | 12,115 | 9,019 | 6,679 | 2,599 | 2,243 | 1,969 | 1,472 | 1,279 | 782 | 818 |
| Current Liabilities | 4,027 | 2,665 | 1,187 | 800 | 452 | 346 | 277 | 263 | 176 | 211 |
| Long Term Debt | 738 | 835 | 836 | 350 | 594 | 595 | 300 | 222 | 196 | 206 |
| Common Equity | 6,661 | 5,024 | 4,194 | 1,296 | 1,090 | 933 | 868 | 767 | 395 | 387 |
| Total Capital | 8,026 | 6,283 | 5,428 | 1,767 | 1,753 | 1,592 | 1,188 | 1,006 | 597 | 597 |
| Capital Expenditures | 252 | 200 | 105 | 39.0 | 32.4 | 24.8 | 27.4 | 24.6 | 15.4 | 27.8 |
| Cash Flow | 1,490 | 845 | 402 | 154 | 116 | 98.1 | 143 | 48.2 | 24.8 | 88.1 |
| Current Ratio | 1.9 | 1.9 | 2.5 | 1.9 | 2.8 | 3.2 | 3.3 | 2.8 | 2.7 | 2.6 |
| % Long Term Debt of Capitalization | 9.2 | 13.3 | 15.4 | 19.8 | 33.9 | 37.3 | 25.3 | 22.1 | 32.8 | 34.5 |
| % Return on Assets | 12.7 | 8.7 | 6.2 | 4.6 | 3.6 | 4.2 | 7.6 | 1.2 | 0.2 | 9.9 |
| % Return on Equity | 22.9 | 14.8 | 10.5 | 9.2 | 7.6 | 8.1 | 12.7 | 1.9 | 0.4 | 20.7 |

Data as orig reptd.; bef. results of disc opers/spec. items. Per share data adj. for stk. divs.; EPS diluted. E-Estimated. NA-Not Available. NM-Not Meaningful. NR-Not Ranked. UR-Under Review.

**Office:** 7909 Parkwood Circle Dr, Houston, TX 77036-6565.
**Telephone:** 713-346-7500.
**Email:** investor.relations@natoil.com
**Website:** http://www.natoil.com

**Chrmn, Pres & CEO:** M.A. Miller, Jr.
**SVP & CFO:** C.C. Williams
**Chief Acctg Officer & Cntlr:** R.W. Blanchard
**Secy & General Counsel:** D.W. Rettig

**Board Members:** G. L. Armstrong, R. E. Beauchamp, B. A. Guill, D. Harrison, R. L. Jarvis, E. Mattson, M. A. Miller, Jr., J. A. Smisek

**Founded:** 1987
**Domicile:** Delaware
**Employees:** 31,198

# National Semiconductor Corp

**STANDARD &POOR'S**

| S&P Recommendation | BUY ★★★★☆ | Price $11.52 (as of Nov 14, 2008) | 12-Mo. Target Price $15.00 | Investment Style Large-Cap Growth |
| --- | --- | --- | --- | --- |

**GICS Sector** Information Technology
**Sub-Industry** Semiconductors

**Summary** This company is a leading manufacturer of a broad line of semiconductors, including analog, digital and mixed-signal integrated circuits.

## Key Stock Statistics (Source S&P, Vickers, company reports)

| | | | | | | | | |
| --- | --- | --- | --- | --- | --- | --- | --- | --- |
| 52-Wk Range | $24.96– 10.23 | S&P Oper. EPS 2009**E** | 1.18 | Market Capitalization(B) | $2.644 | Beta | | 1.81 |
| Trailing 12-Month EPS | $1.29 | S&P Oper. EPS 2010**E** | NA | Yield (%) | 2.78 | S&P 3-Yr. Proj. EPS CAGR(%) | | 6 |
| Trailing 12-Month P/E | 8.9 | P/E on S&P Oper. EPS 2009**E** | 9.8 | Dividend Rate/Share | $0.32 | S&P Credit Rating | | BBB |
| $10K Invested 5 Yrs Ago | $5,746 | Common Shares Outstg. (M) | 229.5 | Institutional Ownership (%) | 91 | | | |

## Price Performance

30-Week Mov. Avg. · · · 10-Week Mov. Avg. - - GAAP Earnings vs. Previous Year Volume Above Avg. STARS
12-Mo. Target Price — Relative Strength — ▲ Up ▼ Down ▶ No Change Below Avg.

Options: ASE, CBOE, P, Ph

Analysis prepared by **Clyde Montevirgen** on November 14, 2008, when the stock traded at **$ 11.66**.

## Qualitative Risk Assessment

| LOW | MEDIUM | HIGH |
| --- | --- | --- |

NSM operates in the semiconductor industry, which tends to be cyclical. Sudden slowdowns can result from downturns in demand for electronics or from chip inventory buildup and industry overcapacity. Share price volatility for the stock is well above average.

## Quantitative Evaluations

**S&P Quality Ranking** B-

| D | C | B- | B | B+ | A- | A | A+ |
| --- | --- | --- | --- | --- | --- | --- | --- |

**Relative Strength Rank** MODERATE

43

LOWEST = 1     HIGHEST = 99

## Highlights

➤ We project sales to fall 7.5% in FY 09 (May), after a decline of 2.3% in FY 08. We believe there are near-term headwinds to growth due to NSM's exposure to the slowing wireless handset market and general macroeconomic weakness. However, NSM has cut lower-margin product lines and transformed its product portfolio, now consisting of higher-margin chips for faster-growing markets. We see healthy sales of power management products, and better penetration in end-markets, where it currently has limited exposure, supporting healthy longer-term revenue advances.

➤ We see gross margins narrowing to the 63% level in FY 09, from above 64% in FY 08, reflecting slower orders and lower plant utilization. However, we think NSM has improved manufacturing efficiency, and believe that margins will expand notably when orders rebound. We expect non-GAAP operating margins to fall to 26% in FY 09, from 28% in FY 08, as sales decline faster than expenses do.

➤ We forecast operating EPS of $1.18 for FY 09, compared to an adjusted $1.27 in FY 08.

## Investment Rationale/Risk

➤ Our buy opinion reflects our view of strong longer-term growth. We believe NSM has effectively transitioned from a commodity chipmaker into a producer of high-performance analog. NSM has a formidable power management product portfolio that we see gaining market share ahead. Gross margins have widened, due in part to a more favorable sales mix, and we anticipate margin expansion when sales rebound. Although we think there are near-term risks related to weak trends in the wireless handset end-market, we believe NSM is attractively valued given our longer-term growth expectations.

➤ Risks to our recommendation and target price include worse-than-anticipated conditions in the wireless handset and consumer end-markets, and above-average share price volatility.

➤ Our 12-month target price of $15 is derived from a blend our price-to-sales and P/E analyses. Applying a P/S multiple of 1.9X, near peer averages, to our forward 12-month sales per share estimate, implies a $13 value. A P/E multiple of about 14X, around the peer average, to our FY 09 EPS estimate, results in a $17 value.

## Revenue/Earnings Data

**Revenue (Million $)**

| | 1Q | 2Q | 3Q | 4Q | Year |
| --- | --- | --- | --- | --- | --- |
| 2009 | 465.6 | -- | -- | -- | -- |
| 2008 | 471.5 | 499.0 | 453.4 | 462.0 | 1,886 |
| 2007 | 541.4 | 501.6 | 431.0 | 455.9 | 1,930 |
| 2006 | 493.8 | 544.0 | 547.7 | 572.6 | 2,158 |
| 2005 | 548.0 | 448.9 | 449.2 | 467.0 | 1,913 |
| 2004 | 424.8 | 473.5 | 513.6 | 571.2 | 1,983 |

**Earnings Per Share ($)**

| | 1Q | 2Q | 3Q | 4Q | Year |
| --- | --- | --- | --- | --- | --- |
| 2009 | 0.33 | E0.27 | E0.25 | E0.31 | E1.18 |
| 2008 | 0.33 | 0.33 | 0.29 | 0.34 | 1.26 |
| 2007 | 0.35 | 0.27 | 0.22 | 0.28 | 1.12 |
| 2006 | 0.24 | 0.32 | 0.37 | 0.34 | 1.26 |
| 2005 | 0.31 | 0.24 | 0.21 | 0.36 | 1.11 |
| 2004 | 0.08 | 0.17 | 0.24 | 0.24 | 0.74 |

Fiscal year ended May 31. Next earnings report expected: Early December. EPS Estimates based on S&P Operating Earnings; historical GAAP earnings are as reported.

## Dividend Data (Dates: mm/dd Payment Date: mm/dd/yy)

| Amount ($) | Date Decl. | Ex-Div. Date | Stk. of Record | Payment Date |
| --- | --- | --- | --- | --- |
| 0.060 | 03/06 | 03/13 | 03/17 | 04/07/08 |
| 0.060 | 06/05 | 06/12 | 06/16 | 07/07/08 |
| 0.060 | 09/05 | 09/16 | 09/18 | 10/06/08 |
| 0.080 | 09/25 | 12/11 | 12/15 | 01/05/09 |

Dividends have been paid since 2005. Source: Company reports.

# National Semiconductor Corp

**STANDARD &POOR'S**

## Business Summary November 14, 2008

CORPORATE OVERVIEW. National Semiconductor designs, develops, manufactures and markets a wide range of semiconductor products. Leading-edge products include power management circuits, display drivers, audio and operational amplifiers, communication interface products and data conversion solutions. The company targets a broad range of markets and applications such as wireless handsets, medical applications, displays, automotive applications, networks, test and measurement applications, industrial markets, and a broad range of portable applications. Most of its products are analog and mixed-signal integrated circuits, comprising about 90% of FY 07 (May) total revenue.

NSM classifies its product lines in two groups, Power Management and Analog Signal Path. The Power Management group makes products that converts and manages power consumption in electronic systems. The Analog Signal Path group makes analog technology that is used during the path that information or data enters the electronic products, is conditioned, converted and processed to the point it is sent out. This technology is used to connect and convert analog signals to digital information.

The company markets its products globally to original equipment manufacturers (OEMs) and original design manufacturers through a direct sales force. In FY 07, 55% of sales came from distributors. Leading distributors include Avnet

(which accounted for 14% of NSM's FY 07 sales) and Arrow (13%). International sales accounted for 78% of total sales in FY 07.

CORPORATE STRATEGY. National Semiconductor's CEO, Brian Halla, who joined the company in 1996, has led an effort to form a "new" NSM. The company's expertise has been primarily in analog intensive, digital and mixed-signal complex integrated circuits. In 1996, NSM spun off its logic, memory and discrete products (considered commodity-type components) as a separate company, Fairchild Semiconductor. The company now focuses on high-end analog chips.

Wafer fabrication is concentrated in two facilities in the U.S. and one in Scotland. Nearly all product assembly and final test operations are performed in several facilities in Asia. The Singapore assembly and test facility is scheduled for closure in 2007; most operations were transferred to the Malaysia and China plants during FY 06.

## Company Financials Fiscal Year Ended May 31

### Per Share Data ($)

| | 2008 | 2007 | 2006 | 2005 | 2004 | 2003 | 2002 | 2001 | 2000 | 1999 |
|---|---|---|---|---|---|---|---|---|---|---|
| Tangible Book Value | 0.59 | 5.43 | 5.57 | 5.65 | 4.21 | 4.18 | 4.46 | 4.70 | 4.63 | 2.67 |
| Cash Flow | NA | 1.56 | 1.72 | 1.63 | 1.27 | 0.54 | 0.31 | 1.30 | 2.33 | -1.81 |
| Earnings | 1.26 | 1.12 | 1.26 | 1.11 | 0.74 | -0.09 | -0.34 | 0.65 | 1.64 | -3.02 |
| S&P Core Earnings | 1.24 | 1.11 | 1.21 | 1.15 | 0.26 | -0.59 | -0.84 | 0.29 | NA | NA |
| Dividends | 0.14 | 0.10 | 0.04 | Nil | Nil | Nil | Nil | Nil | Nil | Nil |
| Payout Ratio | 11% | 9% | 3% | Nil | Nil | Nil | Nil | Nil | Nil | Nil |

| Calendar Year | 2007 | 2006 | 2005 | 2004 | 2003 | 2002 | 2001 | 2000 | 1999 | 1998 |
|---|---|---|---|---|---|---|---|---|---|---|
| Prices:High | 29.69 | 30.93 | 28.75 | 24.35 | 22.63 | 18.65 | 17.55 | 42.97 | 25.94 | 14.13 |
| Prices:Low | 21.54 | 20.56 | 18.36 | 11.85 | 6.27 | 4.98 | 9.85 | 8.56 | 4.44 | 3.72 |
| P/E Ratio:High | 24 | 28 | 23 | 22 | 31 | NM | NM | 66 | 16 | NM |
| P/E Ratio:Low | 17 | 18 | 15 | 11 | 8 | NM | NM | 13 | 3 | NM |

### Income Statement Analysis (Million $)

| | 2008 | 2007 | 2006 | 2005 | 2004 | 2003 | 2002 | 2001 | 2000 | 1999 |
|---|---|---|---|---|---|---|---|---|---|---|
| Revenue | 1,886 | 1,930 | 2,158 | 1,913 | 1,983 | 1,673 | 1,495 | 2,113 | 2,140 | 1,957 |
| Operating Income | NA | 642 | 844 | 626 | 582 | 248 | 81.9 | 517 | 550 | 20.2 |
| Depreciation | 133 | 145 | 166 | 194 | 210 | 229 | 230 | 243 | 264 | 406 |
| Interest Expense | NA | Nil | Nil | Nil | Nil | Nil | 3.90 | 5.00 | 17.9 | Nil |
| Pretax Income | 451 | 531 | 695 | 410 | 334 | -23.3 | -123 | 307 | 642 | -1,085 |
| Effective Tax Rate | 26.4% | 29.3% | 35.4% | NM | 14.7% | NM | NM | 19.4% | 2.32% | NM |
| Net Income | 332 | 375 | 449 | 415 | 285 | -33.3 | -122 | 246 | 628 | -1,010 |
| S&P Core Earnings | 326 | 372 | 433 | 430 | 102 | -215 | -298 | 108 | NA | NA |

### Balance Sheet & Other Financial Data (Million $)

| | 2008 | 2007 | 2006 | 2005 | 2004 | 2003 | 2002 | 2001 | 2000 | 1999 |
|---|---|---|---|---|---|---|---|---|---|---|
| Cash | 737 | 829 | 932 | 867 | 643 | 802 | 681 | 818 | 850 | 419 |
| Current Assets | NA | 1,291 | 1,541 | 1,514 | 1,246 | 1,281 | 1,073 | 1,275 | 1,468 | 989 |
| Total Assets | 2,149 | 2,202 | 2,511 | 2,504 | 2,280 | 2,245 | 2,289 | 2,362 | 2,382 | 2,044 |
| Current Liabilities | NA | 300 | 398 | 285 | 461 | 367 | 404 | 472 | 628 | 665 |
| Long Term Debt | NA | 20.6 | 21.1 | 23.0 | Nil | 19.9 | 20.4 | 26.0 | 48.6 | 416 |
| Common Equity | 197 | 1,749 | 1,926 | 2,062 | 1,681 | 1,706 | 1,781 | 1,768 | 1,643 | 701 |
| Total Capital | NA | 1,769 | 1,947 | 2,085 | 1,681 | 1,726 | 1,802 | 1,794 | 1,692 | 1,317 |
| Capital Expenditures | 111 | 107 | 163 | 96.6 | 215 | 171 | 138 | 228 | 170 | 303 |
| Cash Flow | NA | 520 | 616 | 610 | 495 | 195 | 109 | 489 | 891 | -604 |
| Current Ratio | 3.8 | 4.3 | 3.9 | 5.3 | 2.7 | 3.5 | 2.7 | 2.7 | 2.3 | 1.5 |
| % Long Term Debt of Capitalization | 84.5 | 1.2 | 1.1 | 1.1 | Nil | 1.2 | 1.1 | 1.4 | 2.9 | 31.6 |
| % Net Income of Revenue | 17.6 | 19.4 | 20.8 | 21.7 | 14.4 | NM | NM | 11.6 | 29.3 | NM |
| % Return on Assets | 15.3 | 15.9 | 17.9 | 17.4 | 12.6 | NM | NM | 10.3 | 28.4 | NM |
| % Return on Equity | 34.2 | 20.4 | 22.6 | 22.1 | 16.8 | NM | NM | 14.4 | 49.3 | NM |

Data as orig reptd.; bef. results of disc opers/spec. items. Per share data adj. for stk. divs.; EPS diluted. E-Estimated. NA-Not Available. NM-Not Meaningful. NR-Not Ranked. UR-Under Review.

**Office:** 2900 Semiconductor Dr, Santa Clara, CA 85052-8090.
**Telephone:** 408-721-5000.
**Email:** invest.group@nsc.com
**Website:** http://www.national.com
**Chrmn & CEO:** B.L. Halla
**Pres & COO:** D. Macleod
**SVP & CFO:** L. Chew
**SVP, Secy & General Counsel:** T.M. DuChene
**CTO:** M. Yegnashankaran
**Investor Contact:** R.E. Debarr ()
**Board Members:** S. R. Appleton, G. P. Arnold, R. J. Danzig, J. T. Dickson, R. J. Frankenberg, B. L. Halla, M. A. Maidique, E. McCracken
**Founded:** 1959
**Domicile:** Delaware
**Employees:** 7,300

*The McGraw·Hill Companies*

# NetApp Inc

**STANDARD &POOR'S**

| S&P Recommendation **HOLD** ★★★☆☆ | Price $12.30 (as of Nov 14, 2008) | 12-Mo. Target Price $12.00 | Investment Style Large-Cap Growth |
|---|---|---|---|

**GICS Sector** Information Technology
**Sub-Industry** Computer Storage & Peripherals

**Summary** This company provides storage hardware, software and services to a variety of enterprise customers.

## Key Stock Statistics (Source S&P, Vickers, company reports)

| | | | | | |
|---|---|---|---|---|---|
| 52-Wk Range | $27.49– 10.39 | S&P Oper. EPS 2009**E** | 0.67 | Market Capitalization(B) | $4.027 |
| Trailing 12-Month EPS | $0.89 | S&P Oper. EPS 2010**E** | 0.68 | Yield (%) | Nil |
| Trailing 12-Month P/E | 13.8 | P/E on S&P Oper. EPS 2009**E** | 18.4 | Dividend Rate/Share | Nil |
| $10K Invested 5 Yrs Ago | $4,904 | Common Shares Outstg. (M) | 327.4 | Institutional Ownership (%) | 93 |

| | |
|---|---|
| Beta | 1.96 |
| S&P 3-Yr. Proj. EPS CAGR(%) | -4 |
| S&P Credit Rating | NA |

## Price Performance

- 30-Week Mov. Avg.
- 10-Week Mov. Avg.
- **GAAP Earnings vs. Previous Year**
- Volume Above Avg. STARS
- 12-Mo. Target Price
- Relative Strength
- ▲ Up ▼ Down ▶ No Change
- Below Avg.

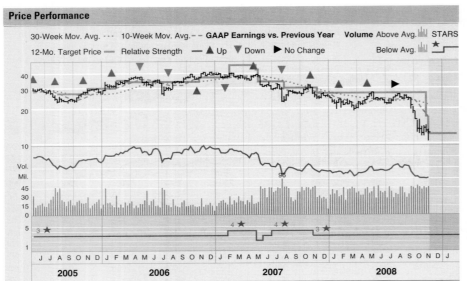

Options: ASE, CBOE, P, Ph

## Highlights

➤ The 12-month target price for NTAP has recently been changed to $12.00 from $17.00. The Highlights section of this Stock Report will be updated accordingly.

## Investment Rationale/Risk

➤ The Investment Rationale/Risk section of this Stock Report will be updated shortly. For the latest News story on NTAP from MarketScope, see below.

➤ 11/13/08 08:56 am ET ... S&P REITERATES HOLD OPINION ON SHARES OF NETAPP INC (NTAP 10.39***): NTAP reports Oct-Q operating EPS of $0.17 vs. $0.20, above our $0.15 estimate. While we believe NTAP's market-share initiatives will help fend off competitors, we expect a weak pricing and order environment amid the economic slowdown. As a result, we are cutting our operating EPS projections by $0.17 to $0.67 for FY 09 (Apr.) and by $0.38 to $0.68 for FY 10. We are also reducing our 12-month target price by $5 to $12 on lower peer valuations. Our target price blends a revised peer-premium P/E of 16.2X our FY 10 forecast with our DCF analysis yielding $13. /RKhalid, CFA

## Qualitative Risk Assessment

| LOW | MEDIUM | HIGH |
|---|---|---|

Our risk assessment accounts for the rapid pace of technological change that typifies the segment, and associated business and stock volatility. However, we believe these factors are offset by NTAP's strong market position and history of earnings growth.

## Quantitative Evaluations

**S&P Quality Ranking**    B

| D | C | B- | B | B+ | A- | A | A+ |
|---|---|---|---|---|---|---|---|

**Relative Strength Rank**    MODERATE

41

LOWEST = 1      HIGHEST = 99

## Revenue/Earnings Data

**Revenue (Million $)**

| | 1Q | 2Q | 3Q | 4Q | Year |
|---|---|---|---|---|---|
| 2009 | 868.8 | -- | -- | -- | -- |
| 2008 | 689.2 | 792.2 | 884.0 | 937.7 | 3,303 |
| 2007 | 621.3 | 652.5 | 729.3 | 801.2 | 2,804 |
| 2006 | 448.4 | 483.1 | 537.0 | 598.0 | 2,066 |
| 2005 | 358.4 | 375.2 | 412.7 | 451.8 | 1,598 |
| 2004 | 260.5 | 275.6 | 297.3 | 337.0 | 1,170 |

**Earnings Per Share ($)**

| | | | | | |
|---|---|---|---|---|---|
| 2009 | 0.11 | E0.15 | E0.21 | E0.20 | E0.67 |
| 2008 | 0.11 | 0.23 | 0.29 | 0.26 | 0.86 |
| 2007 | 0.14 | 0.22 | 0.17 | 0.23 | 0.77 |
| 2006 | 0.16 | 0.18 | 0.20 | 0.15 | 0.69 |
| 2005 | 0.13 | 0.15 | 0.16 | 0.16 | 0.59 |
| 2004 | 0.08 | 0.13 | 0.11 | 0.10 | 0.42 |

Fiscal year ended Apr. 30. Next earnings report expected: Mid November. EPS Estimates based on S&P Operating Earnings; historical GAAP earnings are as reported.

## Dividend Data

No cash dividends have been paid.

# NetApp Inc

STANDARD
&POOR'S

## Business Summary November 07, 2008

CORPORATE OVERVIEW. NetApp Inc. (formerly known as Network Appliance) is a provider of enterprise-level storage hardware and data-management software products and services. NTAP's solutions help global enterprises meet major information technology challenges such as managing the continuing growth in the volume of data, scaling existing infrastructure, complying with regulatory regimes, and security corporate networks and information.

The NTAP family of modular and scalable networked systems provides seamless access to a full range of enterprise data for users working with a variety of platforms, including Fibre Channel (FC), network-attached storage (NAS), storage area network (SAN), and iSCSI environments, as well as online data residing in central locations. NTAP refers to this as fabric-attached storage (FAS). Products include the 200, 900, 3000 and 6000 series.

NTAP's V-Series is a network-based solution that consolidates storage arrays from different suppliers, enabling unified SAN and file access to data stored in heterogeneous FC SAN storage arrays. The V-Series family supports products from Hewlett-Packard, Hitachi and IBM.

CORPORATE STRATEGY. NearStore products focus on optimizing data protection and retention applications. This system offers an alternative to customers by providing faster data access than off-line storage at a significantly lower cost than primary storage. Offerings in this category include the Virtual Tape Library (VTL), a disk-to-disk backup appliance that appears as a tape library to a back-up software application.

The NetCache suite of solutions is designed to manage, control and improve access to Web-based information. Working with a range of software partners, NetCache provides large enterprises with the ability to manage Internet access and security. It essentially enables IT managers to control user access to information, based on profiles, actions, timing, etc.

## Company Financials Fiscal Year Ended Apr. 30

| Per Share Data ($) | 2008 | 2007 | 2006 | 2005 | 2004 | 2003 | 2002 | 2001 | 2000 | 1999 |
|---|---|---|---|---|---|---|---|---|---|---|
| Tangible Book Value | 2.72 | 3.56 | 3.62 | 3.67 | 2.91 | 2.75 | 2.39 | 2.21 | 1.54 | 1.02 |
| Cash Flow | NA | 1.05 | 0.90 | 0.77 | 0.58 | 0.38 | 0.14 | 0.33 | 0.26 | 0.14 |
| Earnings | 0.86 | 0.77 | 0.69 | 0.59 | 0.42 | 0.22 | 0.01 | 0.21 | 0.21 | 0.12 |
| S&P Core Earnings | 0.84 | 0.73 | 0.45 | 0.39 | 0.16 | -0.28 | -0.77 | -0.52 | NA | NA |
| Dividends | Nil | Nil | Nil | Nil | Nil | Nil | Nil | Nil | Nil | Nil |
| Payout Ratio | Nil | Nil | Nil | Nil | Nil | Nil | Nil | Nil | Nil | Nil |
| Calendar Year | 2007 | 2006 | 2005 | 2004 | 2003 | 2002 | 2001 | 2000 | 1999 | 1998 |
| Prices:High | 40.89 | 41.56 | 34.98 | 34.99 | 26.69 | 27.95 | 74.98 | 152.75 | 45.94 | 12.00 |
| Prices:Low | 22.51 | 25.85 | 22.50 | 15.92 | 9.26 | 5.18 | 6.00 | 33.88 | 9.53 | 3.25 |
| P/E Ratio:High | 48 | 54 | 51 | 59 | 64 | NM | NM | NM | NM | NM |
| P/E Ratio:Low | 26 | 34 | 33 | 27 | 22 | NM | NM | NM | NM | NM |

| Income Statement Analysis (Million $) | | | | | | | | | | |
|---|---|---|---|---|---|---|---|---|---|---|
| Revenue | 3,303 | 2,804 | 2,066 | 1,598 | 1,170 | 892 | 798 | 1,006 | 579 | 289 |
| Operating Income | NA | 387 | 395 | 319 | 228 | 146 | 76.5 | 179 | 121 | 63.3 |
| Depreciation | 144 | 111 | 81.8 | 65.6 | 59.5 | 57.4 | 65.3 | 42.3 | 15.7 | 8.15 |
| Interest Expense | NA | 11.6 | 1.28 | Nil | Nil | Nil | Nil | Nil | Nil | 0.78 |
| Pretax Income | 383 | 360 | 350 | 276 | 170 | 97.8 | 2.53 | 133 | 114 | 57.0 |
| Effective Tax Rate | 19.1% | 17.2% | 23.9% | 18.3% | 10.8% | 21.8% | NM | 43.7% | 35.5% | 37.5% |
| Net Income | 310 | 298 | 266 | 226 | 152 | 76.5 | 3.03 | 74.9 | 73.8 | 35.6 |
| S&P Core Earnings | 303 | 282 | 175 | 148 | 59.5 | -98.0 | -256 | -167 | NA | NA |

| Balance Sheet & Other Financial Data (Million $) | | | | | | | | | | |
|---|---|---|---|---|---|---|---|---|---|---|
| Cash | 1,164 | 489 | 461 | 194 | 241 | 284 | 211 | 272 | 279 | 221 |
| Current Assets | NA | 2,241 | 2,033 | 1,576 | 1,089 | 853 | 679 | 636 | 533 | 315 |
| Total Assets | 4,071 | 3,658 | 3,261 | 2,373 | 1,877 | 1,319 | 1,109 | 1,036 | 592 | 346 |
| Current Liabilities | NA | 1,188 | 917 | 520 | 344 | 265 | 216 | 219 | 113 | 50.5 |
| Long Term Debt | NA | Nil | 138 | 4.47 | 4.86 | 3.10 | 3.73 | 0.15 | 0.05 | 0.09 |
| Common Equity | 1,700 | 1,989 | 1,923 | 1,661 | 1,416 | 987 | 858 | 804 | 479 | 296 |
| Total Capital | NA | 1,989 | 2,061 | 1,665 | 1,421 | 990 | 862 | 805 | 479 | 296 |
| Capital Expenditures | 188 | 166 | 133 | 93.6 | 48.6 | 61.3 | 284 | 83.7 | 40.8 | 15.5 |
| Cash Flow | NA | 409 | 348 | 291 | 212 | 134 | 47.4 | 117 | 89.5 | 43.8 |
| Current Ratio | 1.5 | 1.9 | 2.2 | 3.0 | 3.2 | 3.2 | 3.2 | 2.9 | 4.7 | 6.2 |
| % Long Term Debt of Capitalization | 9.2 | Nil | 6.7 | 0.3 | 0.3 | 0.3 | 0.4 | 0.0 | 0.0 | 0.0 |
| % Net Income of Revenue | 9.4 | 10.6 | 12.9 | 14.1 | 13.0 | 8.6 | 0.4 | 7.4 | 12.7 | 12.3 |
| % Return on Assets | 8.0 | 8.6 | 9.5 | 10.6 | 9.5 | 6.3 | 0.3 | 9.2 | 15.7 | 15.4 |
| % Return on Equity | 16.8 | 15.2 | 14.9 | 14.7 | 12.7 | 8.3 | 0.4 | 11.7 | 19.1 | 18.6 |

Data as orig reptd.; bef. results of disc opers/spec. items. Per share data adj. for stk. divs.; EPS diluted. E-Estimated. NA-Not Available. NM-Not Meaningful. NR-Not Ranked. UR-Under Review.

**Office:** 495 East Java Drive, Sunnyvale, CA 94089.
**Telephone:** 408-822-6000.
**Email:** investor_relations@netapp.com
**Website:** http://www.netapp.com

**Chrmn & CEO:** D.J. Warmenhoven
**Pres & COO:** T. Georgens
**Vice Chrmn:** T. Mendoza
**Investor Contact:** S. Gomo ()

**EVP, CFO & Chief Acctg Officer:** S. Gomo
**Board Members:** J. R. Allen, C. A. Bartz, A. L. Earhart, T. Georgens, E. R. Kozel, M. Leslie, T. Mendoza, N. G. Moore, G. T. Shaheen, D. T. Valentine, R. T. Wall, D. J. Warmenhoven

**Founded:** 1992
**Domicile:** Delaware
**Employees:** 7,645

# Newell Rubbermaid Inc.

**STANDARD &POOR'S**

| S&P Recommendation | HOLD ★★★☆☆ | Price | 12-Mo. Target Price | Investment Style |
|---|---|---|---|---|
| | | $12.05 (as of Nov 14, 2008) | $16.00 | Large-Cap Value |

**GICS Sector** Consumer Discretionary
**Sub-Industry** Housewares & Specialties

**Summary** This high volume, brand name consumer products concern has grown through acquisitions. Major product lines include housewares, home furnishings, office products and hardware.

## Key Stock Statistics (Source S&P, Vickers, company reports)

| | | | | | | | |
|---|---|---|---|---|---|---|---|
| 52-Wk Range | $28.84– 11.27 | S&P Oper. EPS 2008**E** | 1.40 | Market Capitalization(B) | $3.339 | Beta | 1.12 |
| Trailing 12-Month EPS | $1.16 | S&P Oper. EPS 2009**E** | 1.55 | Yield (%) | 6.97 | S&P 3-Yr. Proj. EPS CAGR(%) | 9 |
| Trailing 12-Month P/E | 10.4 | P/E on S&P Oper. EPS 2008**E** | 8.6 | Dividend Rate/Share | $0.84 | S&P Credit Rating | BBB+ |
| $10K Invested 5 Yrs Ago | $6,310 | Common Shares Outstg. (M) | 277.1 | Institutional Ownership (%) | 88 | | |

## Price Performance

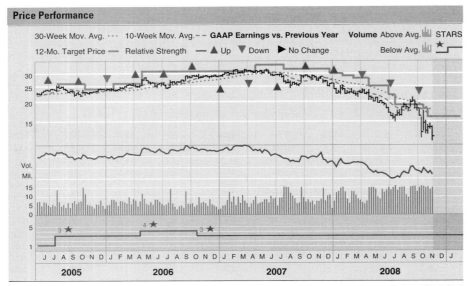

30-Week Mov. Avg. · · · ·  10-Week Mov. Avg. —  **GAAP Earnings vs. Previous Year**  Volume Above Avg. STARS
12-Mo. Target Price —  Relative Strength —  ▲ Up  ▼ Down  ▶ No Change  Below Avg.  ★

Options: ASE, CBOE, P

Analysis prepared by **Loran Braverman, CFA** on November 03, 2008, when the stock traded at **$ 13.76**.

### Highlights

➤ In 2008, we look for 4% sales growth, largely from acquisitions. We estimate a sales increase of close to 4% for the cleaning, organization & decor segment and 18% for home & family segment, both benefiting from acquisitions, while we think the tools & hardware and office products segments will be close to flat. For 2009, our sales growth forecast is 0.9%, with all segments close to flat.

➤ In 2007, the pre-corporate overhead operating margin, excluding restructuring charges, widened by 130 basis points, with higher pricing and productivity gains more than offsetting increases in brand building and other expenses. For 2008, we think commodity cost pressures will contribute to a 270 basis point narrowing in the operating margin, and we expect net interest & other expense to be higher. We look for an effective tax rate in 2008 of 27%, versus 2007's 24%. For 2009, we think moderation in commodity cost pressures could allow the operating margin to widen by 70bps.

➤ We estimate that operating EPS will decrease to $1.40 in 2008, from $1.82 in 2007. Our 2009 EPS estimate is $1.55.

### Investment Rationale/Risk

➤ We think the current stock price adequately reflects NWL's improved long-term growth prospects but current difficult environment. We believe the company, under new leadership, is poised for better innovation and efficiency, and we expect NWL to continue to shed lower-margin, often resin-intensive product lines and invest in more profitable categories. While the categories in which it competes are competitive, we believe NWL will be able to gain market share through better consumer research and greater product innovation.

➤ Risks to our recommendation and target price include poor consumer acceptance of new products, a low level of cost savings associated with the company's reorganization program, negative currency translation and a material increase in prices of key raw materials such as resin and steel.

➤ Our 12-month target price of $16 is a blend of our historical and relative analyses. Our historical model uses a P/E of 11.9X our 2009 EPS estimate, at the low end of the 10-year range, to arrive at an $18 valuation. Our peer analysis uses an in-line multiple of 8.3X, implying a $13 value.

## Qualitative Risk Assessment

| LOW | MEDIUM | HIGH |
|---|---|---|

Our risk assessment reflects that housewares companies' products are generally affordable, low-priced goods that are modestly affected by swings in the economy. However, there is a greater level of import competition for commodity-type goods.

## Quantitative Evaluations

### S&P Quality Ranking                                    B

| D | C | B- | B | B+ | A- | A | A+ |
|---|---|---|---|---|---|---|---|

### Relative Strength Rank                         MODERATE

48

LOWEST = 1                                          HIGHEST = 99

## Revenue/Earnings Data

### Revenue (Million $)

| | 1Q | 2Q | 3Q | 4Q | Year |
|---|---|---|---|---|---|
| 2008 | 1,434 | 1,825 | 1,760 | -- | -- |
| 2007 | 1,384 | 1,693 | 1,687 | 1,643 | 6,407 |
| 2006 | 1,343 | 1,634 | 1,586 | 1,638 | 6,201 |
| 2005 | 1,363 | 1,646 | 1,585 | 1,749 | 6,343 |
| 2004 | 1,541 | 1,736 | 1,672 | 1,809 | 6,748 |
| 2003 | 1,736 | 1,976 | 1,945 | 2,093 | 7,750 |

### Earnings Per Share ($)

| | | | | | |
|---|---|---|---|---|---|
| 2008 | 0.21 | 0.33 | 0.20 | E0.28 | E1.40 |
| 2007 | 0.23 | 0.51 | 0.61 | 0.36 | 1.72 |
| 2006 | 0.47 | 0.49 | 0.41 | 0.33 | 1.71 |
| 2005 | 0.33 | 0.30 | 0.37 | 0.31 | 1.29 |
| 2004 | 0.12 | 0.21 | -0.86 | 0.45 | -0.07 |
| 2003 | 0.06 | 0.27 | 0.27 | -0.77 | -0.17 |

Fiscal year ended Dec. 31. Next earnings report expected: Early February. EPS Estimates based on S&P Operating Earnings; historical GAAP earnings are as reported.

## Dividend Data (Dates: mm/dd Payment Date: mm/dd/yy)

| Amount ($) | Date Decl. | Ex-Div. Date | Stk. of Record | Payment Date |
|---|---|---|---|---|
| 0.210 | 02/14 | 02/27 | 02/29 | 03/14/08 |
| 0.210 | 05/08 | 05/28 | 05/30 | 06/13/08 |
| 0.210 | 08/07 | 08/27 | 08/29 | 09/15/08 |
| 0.210 | 11/13 | 11/25 | 11/28 | 12/15/08 |

Dividends have been paid since 1946. Source: Company reports.

# Newell Rubbermaid Inc.

STANDARD &POOR'S

## Business Summary November 03, 2008

CORPORATE OVERVIEW. Newell Rubbermaid is a global manufacturer and marketer of name brand consumer products and their commercial extensions, serving a wide array of retail channels including department stores, warehouse clubs, home centers, hardware stores, commercial distributors, office superstores, contract stationers, automotive stores and small superstores. Products are sold through four business segments: cleaning, organization & decor (33% of 2007 sales, 30% of segment operating profits), office products (32%, 35%), tools & hardware (20%, 20%), and home & family (15%, 15%). About 28% of 2007 sales were made outside the U.S. Sales to Wal-Mart Stores, Inc. and its subsidiaries amounted to about 13% of sales in 2007.

NWL's cleaning, organization & decor segment is composed of the following global business units (GBUs): Home Products, Foodservice Products, Commercial Products and Decor. These businesses design, manufacture or source, package and distribute semi-durable products primarily for use in the home and commercial settings. These products include indoor and outdoor organization, home storage, food storage, cleaning, refuse, material handling, drapery hardware, custom and stock horizontal and vertical blinds, as well as pleated, cellular and roller shades. Brands include Rubbermaid, Brute, Rough-

neck, TakeAlongs, Levolor and Kirsch.

The office products segment is comprised of the following GBUs: Markers, Highlighters & Art Products, Everyday Writing & Coloring, Technology, Fine Writing & Luxury Accessories and Office Organization. Brands include Sharpie, Paper-Mate, Waterman, Parker, and DYMO.

The tools & hardware business is composed of the following GBUs: Industrial Products & Services, Construction Accessories, Construction Tools and Cabinet, Window & Door. It sells hand tools, power tool accessories, propane torches, manual paint applicator products, cabinet hardware, and window hardware under brand names such as Irwin, Lenox, and BernzOmatic.

The home & family segment is comprised of the following GBUs: Culinary Lifestyle, Baby & Parenting Essentials and Beauty & Style. Brand names include Calphalon, Katana and Goody.

## Company Financials Fiscal Year Ended Dec. 31

| Per Share Data ($) | 2007 | 2006 | 2005 | 2004 | 2003 | 2002 | 2001 | 2000 | 1999 | 1998 |
|---|---|---|---|---|---|---|---|---|---|---|
| Tangible Book Value | NM | NM | NM | NM | NM | NM | 0.44 | 0.97 | 2.38 | 1.57 |
| Cash Flow | 2.18 | 2.41 | 2.07 | 0.84 | 0.84 | 2.21 | 2.22 | 2.57 | 1.30 | 3.14 |
| Earnings | 1.72 | 1.71 | 1.29 | -0.07 | -0.17 | 1.16 | 0.99 | 1.57 | 0.34 | 2.38 |
| S&P Core Earnings | 1.73 | 1.73 | 1.22 | 0.56 | 0.39 | 0.86 | 0.71 | NA | NA | NA |
| Dividends | 0.84 | 0.84 | 0.84 | 0.84 | 0.84 | 0.84 | 0.84 | 0.84 | 0.80 | 0.72 |
| Payout Ratio | 49% | 49% | 65% | NM | NM | 72% | 85% | 54% | 235% | 30% |
| Prices:High | 32.19 | 29.98 | 25.69 | 26.41 | 32.00 | 36.70 | 29.50 | 31.88 | 52.00 | 55.19 |
| Prices:Low | 24.22 | 23.25 | 20.50 | 19.05 | 20.27 | 26.11 | 20.50 | 18.25 | 25.25 | 35.69 |
| P/E Ratio:High | 19 | 18 | 20 | NM | NM | 32 | 30 | 20 | NM | 23 |
| P/E Ratio:Low | 14 | 14 | 16 | NM | NM | 23 | 21 | 12 | NM | 15 |

| Income Statement Analysis (Million $) | | | | | | | | | | |
|---|---|---|---|---|---|---|---|---|---|---|
| Revenue | 6,407 | 6,201 | 6,343 | 6,748 | 7,750 | 7,454 | 6,909 | 6,935 | 6,413 | 3,720 |
| Operating Income | 970 | 916 | 843 | 870 | 992 | 1,033 | 966 | 1,173 | 862 | 736 |
| Depreciation | 143 | 193 | 214 | 249 | 278 | 281 | 329 | 293 | 272 | 148 |
| Interest Expense | 132 | 155 | 142 | 130 | 140 | 111 | 137 | 130 | 100 | 60.4 |
| Pretax Income | 632 | 515 | 418 | 86.3 | 20.1 | 495 | 443 | 685 | 231 | 685 |
| Effective Tax Rate | 23.7% | 8.58% | 14.8% | NM | NM | 31.7% | 34.2% | 38.5% | 58.7% | 42.1% |
| Net Income | 479 | 471 | 356 | -19.1 | -46.6 | 312 | 265 | 422 | 95.4 | 396 |
| S&P Core Earnings | 481 | 476 | 333 | 153 | 108 | 232 | 190 | NA | NA | NA |

| Balance Sheet & Other Financial Data (Million $) | | | | | | | | | | |
|---|---|---|---|---|---|---|---|---|---|---|
| Cash | 329 | 201 | 116 | 506 | 144 | 55.1 | 6.80 | 31.7 | 102 | 57.5 |
| Current Assets | 2,652 | 2,477 | 2,473 | 3,012 | 3,000 | 3,080 | 2,851 | 2,897 | 2,739 | 1,591 |
| Total Assets | 6,683 | 6,311 | 6,446 | 6,666 | 7,481 | 7,389 | 7,266 | 7,262 | 6,724 | 4,328 |
| Current Liabilities | 2,564 | 1,897 | 1,798 | 1,871 | 2,022 | 2,614 | 2,534 | 1,551 | 1,630 | 821 |
| Long Term Debt | 1,197 | 1,972 | 2,430 | 2,424 | 2,869 | 2,357 | 1,865 | 2,815 | 1,956 | 1,366 |
| Common Equity | 2,247 | 1,890 | 1,643 | 1,764 | 2,016 | 2,064 | 2,433 | 2,449 | 2,697 | 1,912 |
| Total Capital | 3,445 | 3,863 | 4,073 | 4,189 | 4,887 | 4,426 | 4,373 | 5,358 | 4,738 | 3,300 |
| Capital Expenditures | 157 | 138 | 92.2 | 122 | 300 | 252 | 250 | 317 | 200 | 148 |
| Cash Flow | 622 | 664 | 570 | 230 | 232 | 592 | 593 | 714 | 367 | 544 |
| Current Ratio | 1.0 | 1.3 | 1.4 | 1.6 | 1.5 | 1.2 | 1.1 | 1.9 | 1.7 | 1.9 |
| % Long Term Debt of Capitalization | 34.8 | 51.1 | 59.7 | 57.9 | 58.7 | 53.2 | 42.7 | 52.5 | 41.3 | 41.3 |
| % Net Income of Revenue | 7.5 | 7.6 | 5.6 | NM | NM | 4.2 | 3.8 | 6.1 | 1.5 | 10.6 |
| % Return on Assets | 7.4 | 7.4 | 5.4 | NM | NM | 4.3 | 3.6 | 6.0 | 1.5 | 9.5 |
| % Return on Equity | 23.2 | 26.6 | 20.9 | NM | NM | 13.9 | 10.8 | 16.4 | 3.4 | 21.7 |

Data as orig reptd.; bef. results of disc opers/spec. items. Per share data adj. for stk. divs.; EPS diluted. E-Estimated. NA-Not Available. NM-Not Meaningful. NR-Not Ranked. UR-Under Review.

**Office:** 10 B Glenlake Pkwy Ste 300, Atlanta, GA 30328-7266.
**Telephone:** 770-407-3800.
**Email:** investor.relations@newellco.com
**Website:** http://www.newellrubbermaid.com

**Chrmn:** W. Marohn
**Pres & CEO:** M. Ketchum
**Investor Contact:** J.P. Robinson (770-407-3994)
**EVP & CFO:** J.P. Robinson

**SVP, Secy & General Counsel:** D.L. Matschullat
**Board Members:** T. E. Clarke, S. S. Cowen, M. T. Cowhig, E. Cuthbert-Millett, D. De Sole, M. Ketchum, W. Marohn, C. A. Montgomery, S. J. Strobel, G. R. Sullivan, M. A. Todman, R. Viault

**Founded:** 1903
**Domicile:** Delaware
**Employees:** 22,000

The McGraw-Hill Companies

# Newmont Mining Corp

**STANDARD &POOR'S**

| S&P Recommendation | STRONG BUY ★ ★ ★ ★ ★ | Price $24.23 (as of Nov 14, 2008) | 12-Mo. Target Price $40.00 | Investment Style Large-Cap Growth |
| --- | --- | --- | --- | --- |

**GICS Sector** Materials
**Sub-Industry** Gold

**Summary** Newmont is the world's second largest gold producer.

## Key Stock Statistics (Source S&P, Vickers, company reports)

| | | | | | | | |
| --- | --- | --- | --- | --- | --- | --- | --- |
| 52-Wk Range | $57.55– 21.40 | S&P Oper. EPS 2008**E** | 2.29 | Market Capitalization(B) | $10.696 | Beta | 0.44 |
| Trailing 12-Month EPS | $1.22 | S&P Oper. EPS 2009**E** | 2.66 | Yield (%) | 1.65 | S&P 3-Yr. Proj. EPS CAGR(%) | 35 |
| Trailing 12-Month P/E | 19.9 | P/E on S&P Oper. EPS 2008**E** | 10.6 | Dividend Rate/Share | $0.40 | S&P Credit Rating | BBB+ |
| $10K Invested 5 Yrs Ago | $5,705 | Common Shares Outstg. (M) | 454.3 | Institutional Ownership (%) | 85 | | |

## Price Performance

30-Week Mov. Avg. · · · 10-Week Mov. Avg. – – **GAAP Earnings vs. Previous Year**  Volume Above Avg. ▏▍▎ STARS
12-Mo. Target Price ── Relative Strength ── ▲ Up ▼ Down ► No Change  Below Avg. ▏▍▎ ★

Options: ASE, CBOE, P, Ph

## Qualitative Risk Assessment

| LOW | MEDIUM | HIGH |
| --- | --- | --- |

Our risk assessment is based on our belief that Newmont's current reserve growth profile is stagnant and could worsen if output from the Yanacocha mine declines more than currently expected. This is offset by our view of Newmont's strong balance sheet and future production from new mines.

## Quantitative Evaluations

**S&P Quality Ranking**  C

| D | C | B- | B | B+ | A- | A | A+ |
| --- | --- | --- | --- | --- | --- | --- | --- |

**Relative Strength Rank**  MODERATE

38

LOWEST = 1   HIGHEST = 99

## Highlights

➤ The 12-month target price for NEM has recently been changed to $40.00 from $64.00. The Highlights section of this Stock Report will be updated accordingly.

## Investment Rationale/Risk

➤ The Investment Rationale/Risk section of this Stock Report will be updated shortly. For the latest News story on NEM from MarketScope, see below.

➤ 10/29/08 12:18 pm ET ... S&P REITERATES STRONG BUY RECOMMENDATION ON SHARES OF NEWMONT MINING (NEM 26.3*****): NEM posts Q3 EPS of $0.39 vs. $0.73 on a 14% sales decline, very shy of our $0.54 estimate on a larger-than-expected drop in copper sales. We cut our '08 estimate to $2.29 from $2.61 to reflect the EPS shortfall, and cut '09's estimate to $2.66 from $3.13 assuming reduced by-product credits stemming from a lower average copper price. On our revised '09 estimate and view the P/E on our '09 estimate will be toward the low end of its historical range in the context of less buoyant commodity prices, we cut our target price to $40 from $64. /L.Larkin

## Revenue/Earnings Data

### Revenue (Million $)

| | 1Q | 2Q | 3Q | 4Q | Year |
| --- | --- | --- | --- | --- | --- |
| 2008 | 1,943 | 1,522 | 1,392 | -- | -- |
| 2007 | 1,256 | 1,302 | 1,646 | 1,410 | 5,526 |
| 2006 | 1,132 | 1,293 | 1,102 | 1,460 | 4,987 |
| 2005 | 945.0 | 998.0 | 1,158 | 1,305 | 4,406 |
| 2004 | 1,122 | 1,009 | 1,163 | 1,230 | 4,524 |
| 2003 | 748.5 | 747.2 | 897.0 | 821.4 | 3,214 |

### Earnings Per Share ($)

| | | | | | |
| --- | --- | --- | --- | --- | --- |
| 2008 | 0.80 | 0.61 | 0.39 | E0.49 | E2.29 |
| 2007 | 0.15 | -0.90 | 0.72 | -2.03 | -2.13 |
| 2006 | 0.46 | 0.34 | 0.59 | 0.47 | 1.86 |
| 2005 | 0.19 | 0.19 | 0.29 | 0.16 | 0.83 |
| 2004 | 0.30 | 0.08 | 0.29 | 0.43 | 1.10 |
| 2003 | 0.38 | 0.22 | 0.28 | 0.36 | 1.23 |

Fiscal year ended Dec. 31. Next earnings report expected: Late February. EPS Estimates based on S&P Operating Earnings; historical GAAP earnings are as reported.

## Dividend Data (Dates: mm/dd Payment Date: mm/dd/yy)

| Amount ($) | Date Decl. | Ex-Div. Date | Stk. of Record | Payment Date |
| --- | --- | --- | --- | --- |
| 0.100 | 02/20 | 03/05 | 03/07 | 03/28/08 |
| 0.100 | 04/23 | 06/04 | 06/06 | 06/27/08 |
| 0.100 | 07/23 | 09/03 | 09/05 | 09/26/08 |
| 0.100 | 10/22 | 12/03 | 12/05 | 12/29/08 |

Dividends have been paid since 1934. Source: Company reports.

# Newmont Mining Corp

STANDARD &POOR'S

## Business Summary September 17, 2008

CORPORATE OVERVIEW. Newmont Mining Corp. is the world's second largest gold company. It has significant assets and operations in the United States, Australia, Peru, Indonesia, Ghana, Canada, Bolivia, New Zealand and Mexico. Newmont has two large development projects in Ghana, West Africa. Newmont is also engaged in the production of copper, principally through its Batu Hijau operation in Indonesia.

Proven and probable gold reserves totaled 86.5 million oz. at the end of 2007 using a gold price assumption of $575 an oz., versus 93.9 million oz. at the end of 2006, using a gold price assumption of $500 an oz.

At year-end 2007, 29.4 million oz. of NEM's gold reserves were located in Nevada, 14.2 million oz. in Peru, 17.4 million oz. in Ghana, 19.4 million oz. in Australia/New Zealand, 4.2 million oz. in Indonesia, and 2.0 million oz. in other operations located in Mexico and Bolivia.

Copper reserves totaled 7.6 billion lbs. at the end of 2007, using a copper price assumption of $1.75 per lb., versus 8.0 billion lbs. at the end of 2006, using a copper price assumption of $1.25 a pound.

In 2007, 29% of Newmont's equity gold sales came from the United States,

20% from Peru, 15% from Australia/New Zealand, 28% from Indonesia, 6% from Ghana, and 2% from other.

As of December 31, 2007, 39% of the company's total long-lived assets were located in the U.S., 11% in Peru, 12% in Australia/New Zealand, 15% in Indonesia, 8% in Ghana and 15% in other.

CORPORATE STRATEGY. NEM's main strategy is to increase its portfolio of low-cost, long-life mines. In 2007's second quarter, NEM incurred a charge to eliminate its remaining gold hedges, as it anticipates higher gold prices over the long term, and seeks to provide shareholders with maximum leverage to the price of gold. NEM plans to spend $1.8 billion in capital development from 2006 to 2010 to offset the decline in the production of mature operations. NEM estimates that its new mines will have project lives of over 16 years and add 2.6 million oz. of annual equity production at costs below the industry average.

## Company Financials Fiscal Year Ended Dec. 31

| Per Share Data ($) | 2007 | 2006 | 2005 | 2004 | 2003 | 2002 | 2001 | 2000 | 1999 | 1998 |
|---|---|---|---|---|---|---|---|---|---|---|
| Tangible Book Value | 16.27 | 14.98 | 12.27 | 11.02 | 8.39 | 2.77 | 7.49 | 8.58 | 8.66 | 8.62 |
| Cash Flow | -0.59 | 3.27 | 2.27 | 2.66 | 2.60 | 1.75 | 1.38 | 1.61 | 1.58 | -0.45 |
| Earnings | -2.13 | 1.86 | 0.83 | 1.10 | 1.23 | 0.39 | -0.16 | -0.06 | 0.15 | -2.27 |
| S&P Core Earnings | 0.42 | 1.45 | 0.79 | 1.22 | 1.05 | 0.25 | -0.26 | NA | NA | NA |
| Dividends | 0.40 | 0.40 | 0.40 | 0.30 | 0.17 | 0.12 | 0.12 | 0.12 | 0.12 | 0.12 |
| Payout Ratio | NM | 22% | 48% | 28% | 14% | 31% | NM | NM | 80% | NM |
| Prices:High | 56.35 | 62.72 | 53.93 | 50.20 | 50.28 | 32.75 | 25.23 | 28.38 | 30.06 | 34.88 |
| Prices:Low | 38.01 | 39.84 | 34.90 | 34.70 | 24.08 | 18.52 | 14.00 | 12.75 | 16.38 | 13.25 |
| P/E Ratio:High | NM | 34 | 65 | 46 | 41 | 84 | NM | NM | NM | NM |
| P/E Ratio:Low | NM | 21 | 42 | 32 | 20 | 47 | NM | NM | NM | NM |

| Income Statement Analysis (Million $) | | | | | | | | | | |
|---|---|---|---|---|---|---|---|---|---|---|
| Revenue | 5,526 | 4,987 | 4,406 | 4,524 | 3,214 | 2,658 | 1,656 | 1,555 | 1,399 | 1,454 |
| Operating Income | 2,041 | 2,059 | 1,621 | 1,878 | 1,219 | 852 | 435 | 502 | 493 | 500 |
| Depreciation | 695 | 636 | 644 | 697 | 564 | 506 | 300 | 293 | 240 | 289 |
| Interest Expense | 155 | 97.0 | 98.0 | 97.6 | 88.6 | 130 | 86.4 | 79.6 | 62.6 | 78.8 |
| Pretax Income | -353 | 1,627 | 1,068 | 1,102 | 890 | 268 | -10.2 | 94.2 | 112 | -471 |
| Effective Tax Rate | NM | 26.1% | 29.4% | 25.0% | 23.2% | 7.43% | NM | 12.1% | 12.9% | NM |
| Net Income | -963 | 840 | 374 | 490 | 510 | 150 | -23.3 | -10.5 | 24.8 | -360 |
| S&P Core Earnings | 192 | 657 | 356 | 540 | 435 | 96.7 | -52.8 | NA | NA | NA |

| Balance Sheet & Other Financial Data (Million $) | | | | | | | | | | |
|---|---|---|---|---|---|---|---|---|---|---|
| Cash | 1,292 | 1,275 | 1,899 | 1,726 | 1,459 | 402 | 149 | 60.3 | 55.3 | 79.1 |
| Current Assets | 2,672 | 2,642 | 3,036 | 2,721 | 2,360 | 1,113 | 709 | 512 | 534 | 513 |
| Total Assets | 15,598 | 15,601 | 13,992 | 12,771 | 11,050 | 10,155 | 4,062 | 3,510 | 3,383 | 3,187 |
| Current Liabilities | 1,500 | 1,739 | 1,350 | 1,101 | 834 | 693 | 486 | 291 | 274 | 212 |
| Long Term Debt | 2,683 | Nil | 1,733 | 1,311 | 887 | 1,701 | 1,090 | 976 | 1,014 | 1,201 |
| Common Equity | 7,548 | 9,865 | 8,376 | 7,938 | 7,385 | 5,419 | 1,469 | 1,466 | 1,452 | 1,440 |
| Total Capital | 12,705 | 10,963 | 11,489 | 10,500 | 9,251 | 8,132 | 2,955 | 2,695 | 2,627 | 2,733 |
| Capital Expenditures | 1,670 | 1,551 | 1,226 | 718 | 501 | 300 | 402 | 378 | 221 | 216 |
| Cash Flow | -268 | 1,476 | 1,018 | 1,187 | 1,075 | 652 | 269 | 283 | 264 | -71.4 |
| Current Ratio | 1.8 | 1.5 | 2.2 | 2.5 | 2.8 | 1.6 | 1.5 | 1.8 | 2.0 | 2.4 |
| % Long Term Debt of Capitalization | 21.1 | Nil | 15.1 | 12.5 | 9.6 | 20.9 | 40.3 | 36.2 | 38.6 | 43.9 |
| % Net Income of Revenue | NM | 16.8 | 8.5 | 10.8 | 15.9 | 5.7 | NM | NM | 1.8 | NM |
| % Return on Assets | NM | 5.7 | 2.8 | 4.2 | 4.8 | 2.1 | NM | NM | 0.7 | NM |
| % Return on Equity | NM | 9.0 | 4.5 | 6.4 | 8.0 | 4.4 | NM | NM | 1.7 | NM |

Data as orig reptd.; bef. results of disc opers/spec. items. Per share data adj. for stk. divs.; EPS diluted. E-Estimated. NA-Not Available. NM-Not Meaningful. NR-Not Ranked. UR-Under Review.

**Office:** 1700 Lincoln Street, Denver, CO 80203-4500.
**Telephone:** 303-863-7414.
**Website:** http://www.newmont.com
**Chrmn:** V.A. Calarco

**Pres & CEO:** R.T. O'Brien
**COO:** B.A. Hill
**EVP & CFO:** R. Ball
**CTO:** D.S. Barr

**Investor Contact:** J. Seaberg (303-837-5743)
**Board Members:** G. A. Barton, V. A. Calarco, J. A. Carrabba, N. Doyle, V. M. Hagen, M. S. Hamson, R. J. Miller, R. T. O'Brien, J. B. Prescott, D. C. Roth, J. V. Taranik, S. R. Thompson

**Founded:** 1916
**Domicile:** Delaware
**Employees:** 15,000

# New York Times Co (The)

**STANDARD &POOR'S**

| S&P Recommendation SELL ★ ★ ☆ ☆ ☆ | Price $7.34 (as of Nov 14, 2008) | 12-Mo. Target Price $10.00 | Investment Style Large-Cap Blend |
|---|---|---|---|

**GICS Sector** Consumer Discretionary
**Sub-Industry** Publishing

**Summary** This diversified communications company publishes newspapers, operates radio and television stations, and has equity holdings in newsprint and paper mills.

## Key Stock Statistics (Source S&P, Vickers, company reports)

| | | | | | | | |
|---|---|---|---|---|---|---|---|
| 52-Wk Range | $21.14– 7.25 | S&P Oper. EPS 2008E | 0.58 | Market Capitalization(B) | $1.049 | Beta | 0.45 |
| Trailing 12-Month EPS | $-0.23 | S&P Oper. EPS 2009E | 0.64 | Yield (%) | 12.53 | S&P 3-Yr. Proj. EPS CAGR(%) | 2 |
| Trailing 12-Month P/E | NM | P/E on S&P Oper. EPS 2008E | 12.7 | Dividend Rate/Share | $0.92 | S&P Credit Rating | BB- |
| $10K Invested 5 Yrs Ago | $1,788 | Common Shares Outstg. (M) | 143.8 | Institutional Ownership (%) | 88 | | |

## Price Performance

| 30-Week Mov. Avg. · · · | 10-Week Mov. Avg. ▬ | **GAAP Earnings vs. Previous Year** | Volume Above Avg. ▐▌ STARS |
|---|---|---|---|
| 12-Mo. Target Price ▬ | Relative Strength ▬ | ▲ Up ▼ Down ► No Change | Below Avg. ▐▌ |

Options: ASE, CBOE, P, Ph

Analysis prepared by **Loran Braverman, CFA** on October 24, 2008, when the stock traded at **$ 9.83**.

## Highlights

➤ We believe NYT's revenues will fare better than other pure-play peers exposed to cyclical and secular challenges in the print publishing industry, partly due to the company's above-average revenues from fast-growing Internet operations. We expect NYT to generate revenue gains from circulation price increases, print outsourcing contracts and from incremental lease revenues. But we see these gains more than offset by weak print advertising, and we forecast an overall revenue decline of 3.7% in 2009, following a drop of 6.1% we anticipate for 2008.

➤ We look for operating margin expansion to 6.3% in 2009, up from our forecast for 6.1% in 2008 but still down from 8.4% in 2007. Including an estimated 3% rate of expense inflation, we see overall costs falling in 2009 as NYT benefits from various expense reduction initiatives. Despite the anticipated gain, we note NYT's margin remains well below peer levels.

➤ We forecast operating 2009 EPS of $0.64, up from our 2008 EPS projection of $0.58. Our EPS estimates include severance expenses, which we view as operational due to ongoing restructuring activity at the company.

## Investment Rationale/Risk

➤ We expect NYT's free cash flow to increase in 2009 as the company reduces its capital expenditures and realizes significant cost savings from recent expense reduction initiatives. We also think the company distinguishes itself by deriving about 11% of overall revenues from its high-growth Internet operations, versus an estimated 8% for peers. However, given a difficult print ad revenue environment we see persisting for the foreseeable future, we see no near-term catalyst for the stock.

➤ Risks to our recommendation and target price include a significant improvement in the health of the New York City and Boston economies, where NYT derives most of its newspaper advertising revenues.

➤ Our 12-month target price of $10 is derived from a blend of our relative valuation and DCF analyses. Our DCF model yields an intrinsic value of $13, and includes assumptions of a 7.5% WACC and 1.0% terminal growth. Applying a slight premium to peer enterprise value/EBITDA multiple of 5.6X to our 2009 EBITDA forecast of $373 million leads to an $8 valuation.

## Qualitative Risk Assessment

| LOW | MEDIUM | HIGH |
|---|---|---|

Our risk assessment reflects our view of a highly competitive advertising environment for publishers and other media, offset by the company's better-than-peer opportunity, in our opinion, to leverage its brand, and NYT's low weighted average cost of capital (WACC).

## Quantitative Evaluations

**S&P Quality Ranking** B+

| D | C | B- | B | B+ | A- | A | A+ |
|---|---|---|---|---|---|---|---|

**Relative Strength Rank** WEAK

24

LOWEST = 1     HIGHEST = 99

## Revenue/Earnings Data

### Revenue (Million $)

| | 1Q | 2Q | 3Q | 4Q | Year |
|---|---|---|---|---|---|
| 2008 | 747.9 | 741.9 | 687.0 | -- | -- |
| 2007 | 786.0 | 788.9 | 754.4 | 865.8 | 3,195 |
| 2006 | 799.2 | 819.6 | 739.6 | 931.5 | 3,290 |
| 2005 | 805.6 | 845.1 | 791.1 | 931.0 | 3,373 |
| 2004 | 801.9 | 823.9 | 773.8 | 903.9 | 3,304 |
| 2003 | 783.7 | 801.9 | 759.3 | 882.3 | 3,227 |

### Earnings Per Share ($)

| | | | | | |
|---|---|---|---|---|---|
| 2008 | Nil | 0.15 | -0.01 | E0.39 | E0.58 |
| 2007 | 0.14 | 0.15 | 0.10 | 0.37 | 0.76 |
| 2006 | 0.21 | 0.37 | 0.06 | -4.59 | -3.93 |
| 2005 | 0.76 | 0.42 | 0.16 | 0.49 | 1.82 |
| 2004 | 0.38 | 0.50 | 0.33 | 0.75 | 1.96 |
| 2003 | 0.45 | 0.47 | 0.33 | 0.73 | 1.98 |

Fiscal year ended Dec. 31. Next earnings report expected: Early February. EPS Estimates based on S&P Operating Earnings; historical GAAP earnings are as reported.

## Dividend Data (Dates: mm/dd Payment Date: mm/dd/yy)

| Amount ($) | Date Decl. | Ex-Div. Date | Stk. of Record | Payment Date |
|---|---|---|---|---|
| 0.230 | 11/15 | 11/29 | 12/03 | 12/12/07 |
| 0.230 | 02/21 | 02/28 | 03/03 | 03/12/08 |
| 0.230 | 04/22 | 05/29 | 06/02 | 06/11/08 |
| 0.230 | 06/19 | 08/28 | 09/02 | 09/15/08 |

Dividends have been paid since 1958. Source: Company reports.

# New York Times Co (The)

STANDARD
&POOR'S

## Business Summary October 24, 2008

CORPORATE OVERVIEW. The New York Times Company is a media company that includes newspapers, Internet businesses, a radio station, investments in paper mills and other investments. In 2007, NYT classified its businesses into two segments, the News Media Group (about 97% of revenues) and About.com (3%).

The News Media Group primarily consists of The New York Times, the International Herald Tribune, The Boston Globe, the Worcester Telegram & Gazette, 14 daily newspapers in Alabama, California, Florida, Louisiana, North Carolina and South Carolina, and related print and digital businesses, such as NYT.com. The majority of the News Media Group's revenue comes from advertising sold in its newspapers and other publications and on its Web sites. In 2007, revenues were derived from national advertising (49%), classified (25%), retail and pre-print (23%), and other (3%). We note that as one of only three national newspapers (along with USA Today and The Wall Street Journal), the New York Times garners a disproportionate amount of its advertising from national advertisers relative to most other newspapers. According to TNS Media Intelligence, the New York Times had a 50.0% market share of national advertising revenue among national newspapers in 2007.

The About group consists of the websites of About.com, ConsumerSearch.com, UCompareHealthCare.com and Calorie-Count.com.

About.com provides users with information and advice on thousands of topics, and the site was one of the top 15 most visited Web sites in 2007. About.com generates revenues through display advertising relevant to adjacent content, cost-per-click advertising, and e-commerce. ConsumerSearch.com is a leading online aggregator and publisher of reviews of consumer products. UCompareHealthCare.com provides Web-based interactive tools to enable users to measure the quality of certain healthcare services. Calorie-Count.com offers weight loss tools and nutritional information.

NYT also owns equity interests in a Canadian newsprint company and a supercalendered paper manufacturing partnership in Maine; approximately 17.5% of New England Sports Ventures, LLC (NESV), which owns the Boston Red Sox, Fenway Park and adjacent real estate, approximately 80% of the New England Sports Network (the regional cable sports network that televises the Red Sox games) and 50% of Roush Fenway Racing, a NASCAR team; and 49% of Metro Boston LLC (Metro Boston), which publishes a free daily newspaper catering to young professionals and students in the Boston metropolitan area.

## Company Financials Fiscal Year Ended Dec. 31

| Per Share Data ($) | 2007 | 2006 | 2005 | 2004 | 2003 | 2002 | 2001 | 2000 | 1999 | 1998 |
|---|---|---|---|---|---|---|---|---|---|---|
| Tangible Book Value | 1.16 | 0.25 | NM | NM | NM | NM | NM | NM | 0.83 | 1.12 |
| Cash Flow | 1.82 | -2.76 | 2.81 | 2.94 | 2.95 | 2.93 | 2.48 | 3.65 | 2.83 | 2.46 |
| Earnings | 0.76 | -3.93 | 1.82 | 1.96 | 1.98 | 1.94 | 1.26 | 2.32 | 1.73 | 1.49 |
| S&P Core Earnings | 0.91 | 1.13 | 1.41 | 1.62 | 1.77 | 1.35 | 0.72 | NA | NA | NA |
| Dividends | 0.87 | 0.69 | 0.65 | 0.61 | 0.57 | 0.53 | 0.49 | 0.45 | 0.41 | 0.37 |
| Payout Ratio | 114% | NM | 36% | 31% | 29% | 27% | 39% | 19% | 24% | 25% |
| Prices:High | 26.90 | 28.98 | 40.90 | 49.23 | 49.06 | 53.00 | 47.98 | 49.88 | 49.94 | 40.69 |
| Prices:Low | 16.02 | 21.54 | 26.09 | 38.47 | 43.29 | 38.60 | 35.48 | 32.63 | 26.50 | 20.50 |
| P/E Ratio:High | 35 | NM | 22 | 25 | 25 | 27 | 38 | 21 | 29 | 27 |
| P/E Ratio:Low | 21 | NM | 14 | 20 | 22 | 20 | 28 | 14 | 15 | 14 |

| Income Statement Analysis (Million $) | | | | | | | | | | |
|---|---|---|---|---|---|---|---|---|---|---|
| Revenue | 3,195 | 3,290 | 3,373 | 3,304 | 3,227 | 3,079 | 3,016 | 3,489 | 3,131 | 2,937 |
| Operating Income | 492 | 464 | 502 | 657 | 687 | 698 | 568 | 864 | 769 | 703 |
| Depreciation | 153 | 170 | 144 | 147 | 148 | 153 | 194 | 228 | 197 | 188 |
| Interest Expense | 59.1 | 50.7 | 49.2 | 44.2 | 44.8 | 48.7 | 51.4 | 64.1 | 52.5 | 46.9 |
| Pretax Income | 185 | -552 | 446 | 477 | 500 | 491 | 340 | 673 | 538 | 506 |
| Effective Tax Rate | 41.2% | NM | 40.4% | 38.5% | 39.6% | 39.0% | 40.5% | 40.9% | 42.4% | 43.3% |
| Net Income | 109 | -568 | 266 | 293 | 303 | 300 | 202 | 398 | 310 | 287 |
| S&P Core Earnings | 129 | 164 | 205 | 242 | 268 | 208 | 116 | NA | NA | NA |

| Balance Sheet & Other Financial Data (Million $) | | | | | | | | | | |
|---|---|---|---|---|---|---|---|---|---|---|
| Cash | 51.5 | 72.4 | 44.9 | 42.4 | 39.4 | 37.0 | 52.0 | 69.0 | 63.9 | 36.0 |
| Current Assets | 664 | 1,185 | 658 | 614 | 603 | 563 | 560 | 611 | 615 | 522 |
| Total Assets | 3,473 | 3,856 | 4,533 | 3,950 | 3,805 | 3,634 | 3,439 | 3,607 | 3,496 | 3,465 |
| Current Liabilities | 976 | 1,298 | 1,067 | 1,120 | 760 | 736 | 861 | 877 | 674 | 628 |
| Long Term Debt | 679 | 795 | 898 | 471 | 726 | 729 | 599 | 637 | 598 | 598 |
| Common Equity | 978 | 820 | 1,516 | 1,401 | 1,392 | 1,362 | 1,150 | 1,281 | 1,449 | 1,531 |
| Total Capital | 1,663 | 1,621 | 2,683 | 2,139 | 2,350 | 2,164 | 1,813 | 2,024 | 2,188 | 2,295 |
| Capital Expenditures | 380 | 332 | 221 | 154 | 121 | 161 | 90.4 | 85.3 | 73.4 | 82.6 |
| Cash Flow | 262 | -398 | 409 | 439 | 450 | 453 | 396 | 626 | 508 | 475 |
| Current Ratio | 0.7 | 0.9 | 0.6 | 0.5 | 0.8 | 0.8 | 0.7 | 0.7 | 0.9 | 0.8 |
| % Long Term Debt of Capitalization | 40.8 | 49.1 | 33.5 | 22.0 | 30.9 | 33.7 | 33.0 | 31.5 | 27.3 | 26.1 |
| % Net Income of Revenue | 3.4 | NM | 7.9 | 8.9 | 9.4 | 9.7 | 6.7 | 11.4 | 9.9 | 9.8 |
| % Return on Assets | 3.0 | NM | 6.3 | 7.5 | 8.1 | 8.5 | 5.7 | 11.2 | 8.9 | 8.1 |
| % Return on Equity | 12.1 | NM | 18.2 | 21.0 | 22.7 | 23.9 | 16.6 | 29.1 | 20.8 | 17.6 |

Data as orig reptd.; bef. results of disc opers/spec. items. Per share data adj. for stk. divs.; EPS diluted. E-Estimated. NA-Not Available. NM-Not Meaningful. NR-Not Ranked. UR-Under Review.

**Office:** 680 8th Ave, New York, NY 10036-7114.
**Telephone:** 212-556-1234.
**Website:** http://www.nytco.com
**Chrmn:** A.O. Sulzberger, Jr.

**Pres & CEO:** J.L. Robinson
**SVP & CFO:** R. Caputo
**SVP, Chief Acctg Officer & Cntlr:** R.A. Benten
**SVP & General Counsel:** K.A. Richieri

**Investor Contact:** C.J. Mathis (212-556-1981)
**Board Members:** R. E. Cesan, D. H. Cohen, R. E. Denham, L. Dolnick, S. Galloway, M. Golden, W. E. Kennard, J. A. Kohlberg, D. G. Lepore, D. E. Liddle, E. R. Marram, T. Middelhoff, J. L. Robinson, A. O. Sulzberger, Jr., D. A. Toben

**Founded:** 1896
**Domicile:** New York
**Employees:** 10,231

# News Corp

**STANDARD &POOR'S**

**S&P Recommendation** SELL ★ ★ ☆ ☆ ☆

| Price | 12-Mo. Target Price | Investment Style |
|---|---|---|
| $7.43 (as of Nov 14, 2008) | $6.50 | Large-Cap Blend |

**GICS Sector** Consumer Discretionary
**Sub-Industry** Movies & Entertainment

**Summary** This leading media conglomerate, with controlling interests in leading content and distribution assets across the globe, including Fox Entertainment, SKY Italia, BSkyB and STAR Asia, acquired Dow Jones in late 2007.

## Key Stock Statistics (Source S&P, Vickers, company reports)

| | | | | | | | | |
|---|---|---|---|---|---|---|---|---|
| 52-Wk Range | $21.57– 6.49 | S&P Oper. EPS 2009**E** | 0.94 | Market Capitalization(B) | $13.486 | Beta | | 1.17 |
| Trailing 12-Month EPS | $1.82 | S&P Oper. EPS 2010**E** | 1.23 | Yield (%) | 1.62 | S&P 3-Yr. Proj. EPS CAGR(%) | | 6 |
| Trailing 12-Month P/E | 4.1 | P/E on S&P Oper. EPS 2009**E** | 7.9 | Dividend Rate/Share | $0.12 | S&P Credit Rating | | BBB+ |
| $10K Invested 5 Yrs Ago | $5,345 | Common Shares Outstg. (M) | 2,613.6 | Institutional Ownership (%) | 88 | | | |

## Price Performance

30-Week Mov. Avg. · · · 10-Week Mov. Avg. – – **GAAP Earnings vs. Previous Year** Volume Above Avg. ▍▍▍ STARS
12-Mo. Target Price — Relative Strength ▲ Up ▼ Down ► No Change Below Avg. ▍▍▍ ★

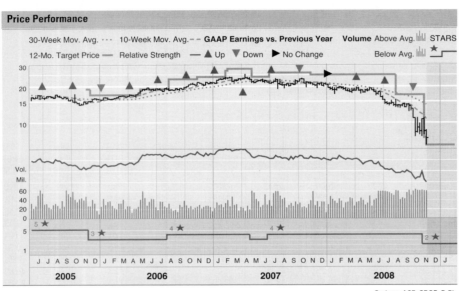

Options: ASE, CBOE, P, Ph

Analysis prepared by **Tuna N. Amobi, CFA, CPA** on November 14, 2008, when the stock traded at **$ 7.63**.

## Highlights

➤ Including Dow Jones (since mid-December 2007), we see total revenues up 2.3% in FY 09 (Jun.) and 7.1% in FY 10, to about $36.2 billion, mainly on the cable networks and SKY Italia. This contrasts with sharp FY 09 declines to modest FY 10 growth at the TV, film and print (magazines, inserts, book publishing, newspapers) units, with the absence of the Super Bowl and recent station divestitures also posing adverse FY 09 comparisons for the TV segment.

➤ We see FY 09 margins narrowing significantly, partly on ad weakness and the economic slowdown, further pressured by TV and online start-up losses, and network programming and film marketing costs. This should improve in FY 10, with upside seen on affiliate renewals at Fox News and FX, international cable channels, SKY Italia, Fox Interactive Media (including MySpace), and WSJ online revenues.

➤ From $5.4 billion in FY 08, we forecast FY 09 total EBIT declining about 13% to $4.7 billion, before rebounding 18% to more than $5.5 billion in FY 10. After interest and taxes, we project operating EPS of $0.94 and $1.23 in the respective years, assuming some share buybacks.

## Investment Rationale/Risk

➤ After a recent decline that began in the 2008 second half, the shares have sold off more sharply in early November after what we saw as mixed September-quarter results, and a disappointing near-term outlook. Citing ad weakness, currency fluctuations, and a deterioration in overall business trends, management reduced its FY 09 EBIT target, to a low- to mid-teens percentage decline (from a 4%-6% growth), which we think bodes ill for the broadcast and print businesses. We see continued ample financial flexibility, but think a number of recent capital allocation moves now seem questionable, amid a severe credit crunch.

➤ Risks to our recommendation and target price include a better-than-expected economic contraction and ad recovery; favorable currency fluctuations (versus U.S. dollar); accretive acquisitions; and positive governance developments on the Murdoch family's control.

➤ Our 12-month target price of $6.50 blends our DCF ($7.50, on 11% WACC, mid- to high single-digit long-term free cash flow growth, 2% perpetuity growth) and sum-of-the-parts ($5.50, including equity affiliates) analyses.

## Qualitative Risk Assessment

| LOW | MEDIUM | HIGH |
|---|---|---|

Our risk assessment reflects the company's portfolio of leading properties with balanced business and geographic diversification, and our view of its strong balance sheet, offset by a high cyclical ad exposure, film volatility, currency risk, and some corporate governance issues.

## Quantitative Evaluations

**S&P Quality Ranking**  A-

| D | C | B- | B | B+ | A- | A | A+ |
|---|---|---|---|---|---|---|---|

**Relative Strength Rank**  MODERATE

32

LOWEST = 1    HIGHEST = 99

## Revenue/Earnings Data

**Revenue (Million $)**

| | 1Q | 2Q | 3Q | 4Q | Year |
|---|---|---|---|---|---|
| 2009 | 7,509 | -- | -- | -- | -- |
| 2008 | 7,067 | 8,590 | 8,750 | 8,589 | 32,996 |
| 2007 | 5,914 | 7,844 | 7,530 | 7,367 | 28,655 |
| 2006 | 5,682 | 6,665 | 6,198 | 6,782 | 25,327 |
| 2005 | 5,191 | 6,562 | 6,043 | 6,108 | 23,859 |
| 2004 | 4,649 | 5,588 | 5,201 | 5,521 | 20,579 |

**Earnings Per Share ($)**

| | | | | | |
|---|---|---|---|---|---|
| 2009 | 0.20 | E0.26 | E0.26 | E0.28 | E0.94 |
| 2008 | 0.23 | 0.27 | 0.91 | 0.43 | 1.81 |
| 2007 | 0.28 | 0.27 | 0.29 | 0.30 | 1.08 |
| 2006 | 0.19 | 0.22 | 0.27 | 0.24 | 0.92 |
| 2005 | 0.16 | 0.56 | 0.14 | 0.23 | 0.73 |
| 2004 | 0.14 | 0.13 | 0.16 | 0.13 | 0.58 |

Fiscal year ended Jun. 30. Next earnings report expected: Early February. EPS Estimates based on S&P Operating Earnings; historical GAAP earnings are as reported.

## Dividend Data (Dates: mm/dd Payment Date: mm/dd/yy)

| Amount ($) | Date Decl. | Ex-Div. Date | Stk. of Record | Payment Date |
|---|---|---|---|---|
| 0.060 | 02/04 | 03/10 | 03/12 | 04/16/08 |
| 0.060 | 09/05 | 09/08 | 09/10 | 10/15/08 |

Dividends have been paid since 1995. Source: Company reports.

---

**Please read the Required Disclosures and Analyst Certification on the last page of this report.**

The **McGraw·Hill** Companies

# News Corp

**STANDARD &POOR'S**

## Business Summary November 14, 2008

CORPORATE OVERVIEW. News Corp., once a small publisher of Australian newspapers, has grown into one of the world's premier media conglomerates. In December 2004, the company moved its domicile to the U.S., followed in March 2005 by a tender offer for the public's 18% minority stake in its Fox Entertainment Group, which we believe helped to simplify its corporate structure. Dow Jones was acquired in December 2007.

Key U.S. assets include Fox film studio and 20th Century Fox TV; Fox broadcast network and TV stations; Fox News, FX and regional sports networks (including FSN Ohio, FSN Florida and 40% of FSN Bay Area); HarperCollins (book publishers); the New York Post newspaper; and an inserts business. International assets include several newspaper businesses in the U.K. and Australia (including The Times, The Sun, News of the World and The Australian); the wholly owned DBS provider SKY Italia; a 39% controlling stake in U.K. DBS provider BSkyB; and several other associated entities in the U.S., Australia and Latin America. About 51% of FY 08 (Jun.) revenues were derived from the U.S. and Canada, 33% from Europe, and 16% from Australasia/other.

CORPORATE STRATEGY. Over the past few years, News Corp. has completed

a number of strategic acquisitions and divestitures. In December 2007, the company acquired Dow Jones in a $5.6 billion transaction. In February 2008, it raised its stake in German pay TV operator Premiere AG to 19.9%, from 14.6%. Also in February, it divested its 38.4% stake in DirecTV, plus three regional sports networks and $550 million of cash, in exchange for Liberty Media's 16.3% voting stake.

In 2005, the company acquired MySpace.com, a leading social networking site, for about $650 million (now the core of its Fox Interactive Media unit, which also includes IGN Entertainment and Scout Media). Revenues at the Fox Interactive Media unit grew to more than $900 million in FY 08 (versus $550 million in FY 07), aided by a multi-year search deal with Google that provides for a minimum revenue guarantee of $900 million over its term. The company's TV shows are also available from Apple's iTunes and mobile content destination Mobizzo.

## Company Financials Fiscal Year Ended Jun. 30

| Per Share Data ($) | 2008 | 2007 | 2006 | 2005 | 2004 | 2003 | 2002 | 2001 | 2000 | 1999 |
|---|---|---|---|---|---|---|---|---|---|---|
| Tangible Book Value | NM | 2.37 | 1.86 | 1.81 | 1.85 | NM | 0.68 | 3.34 | 0.76 | 1.67 |
| Cash Flow | NA | 1.38 | 1.62 | 1.40 | 0.79 | 0.65 | -2.39 | -0.01 | 0.48 | 0.58 |
| Earnings | 1.81 | 1.14 | 0.92 | 0.73 | 0.58 | 0.46 | -2.75 | 0.32 | 0.39 | 0.50 |
| Dividends | 0.12 | 0.12 | 0.13 | 0.11 | 0.10 | 0.08 | 0.07 | 0.07 | 0.07 | 0.08 |
| Payout Ratio | 7% | 11% | 14% | 14% | 17% | 17% | NM | 22% | 18% | 16% |
| Prices:High | 20.55 | 25.40 | 21.94 | 18.88 | 18.77 | 15.54 | 13.60 | 18.70 | 28.59 | 18.44 |
| Prices:Low | 6.49 | 19.00 | 15.17 | 13.94 | 14.57 | 9.33 | 7.54 | 9.80 | 13.44 | 11.47 |
| P/E Ratio:High | 11 | 22 | 24 | 26 | 32 | 34 | NM | 58 | 73 | 37 |
| P/E Ratio:Low | 4 | 17 | 16 | 19 | 25 | 20 | NM | 31 | 34 | 23 |

| Income Statement Analysis (Million $) | | | | | | | | | | |
|---|---|---|---|---|---|---|---|---|---|---|
| Revenue | 32,996 | 28,655 | 25,327 | 23,859 | 29,428 | 29,913 | 29,014 | 25,578 | 22,443 | 21,774 |
| Operating Income | NA | 5,331 | 4,643 | 4,329 | 5,146 | 4,372 | 4,291 | 3,799 | 2,913 | NA |
| Depreciation | 1,287 | 879 | 775 | 765 | 844 | 776 | 749 | 706 | 562 | 510 |
| Interest Expense | NA | 843 | 791 | 736 | 958 | 1,094 | 1,384 | 1,358 | 1,248 | NA |
| Pretax Income | 7,321 | 5,306 | 4,405 | 3,561 | 3,855 | 3,000 | -10,959 | -562 | 1,587 | 1,913 |
| Effective Tax Rate | 24.6% | 34.2% | 34.6% | 34.3% | 32.3% | 25.8% | NM | NM | 20.7% | 15.0% |
| Net Income | 5,387 | 3,426 | 2,812 | 2,128 | 2,312 | 1,808 | -11,962 | -746 | 1,259 | 1,471 |

| Balance Sheet & Other Financial Data (Million $) | | | | | | | | | | |
|---|---|---|---|---|---|---|---|---|---|---|
| Cash | 4,662 | 7,654 | 5,783 | 6,470 | 6,217 | 6,746 | 6,337 | 5,615 | 4,638 | 7,483 |
| Current Assets | NA | 15,906 | 13,123 | 12,779 | 15,012 | 14,861 | 14,647 | 16,173 | 13,127 | 13,555 |
| Total Assets | 62,308 | 62,343 | 56,649 | 54,692 | 73,738 | 67,747 | 71,441 | 84,961 | 65,585 | 53,972 |
| Current Liabilities | NA | 7,494 | 6,373 | 6,649 | 10,437 | 9,303 | 11,005 | 9,776 | 9,008 | 7,447 |
| Long Term Debt | NA | 12,147 | 11,385 | 10,087 | 12,972 | 14,480 | 15,275 | 23,345 | 18,396 | 15,516 |
| Common Equity | 28,623 | 32,922 | 29,874 | 29,377 | 39,387 | 31,834 | 34,101 | 42,050 | 29,389 | 27,109 |
| Total Capital | NA | 51,530 | 46,740 | 44,500 | 59,473 | 53,867 | 54,743 | 70,940 | 51,056 | 42,625 |
| Capital Expenditures | 1,443 | 1,308 | 976 | 901 | 517 | 551 | 505 | 1,113 | 671 | 702 |
| Cash Flow | NA | 4,305 | 3,587 | 2,883 | 3,156 | 2,584 | -11,213 | -40.0 | 1,598 | 1,981 |
| Current Ratio | 1.6 | 2.1 | 2.1 | 1.9 | 1.4 | 1.6 | 1.3 | 1.7 | 1.5 | 1.8 |
| % Long Term Debt of Capitalization | 30.7 | 23.6 | 24.4 | 22.7 | 21.8 | 26.9 | 27.9 | 32.9 | 36.0 | 36.4 |
| % Net Income of Revenue | 16.3 | 12.0 | 11.1 | 8.9 | 7.9 | 6.0 | NM | NM | 5.6 | 6.8 |
| % Return on Assets | 8.6 | 5.8 | 5.1 | 4.1 | 3.3 | 2.6 | NM | NM | 2.1 | 2.7 |
| % Return on Equity | 17.5 | 10.9 | 9.5 | 8.4 | 6.5 | 5.5 | NM | NM | 4.0 | 4.4 |

Data as orig reptd.; bef. results of disc opers/spec. items. Per share data adj. for stk. divs.; EPS diluted. Income and balance sheet data in Australian $ prior to 2005. E-Estimated. NA-Not Available. NM-Not Meaningful. NR-Not Ranked. UR-Under Review.

**Office:** 1211 Avenue Of The Americas, New York, NY 10036-8701.
**Telephone:** 212-852-7000.
**Website:** http://www.newscorp.com
**Chrmn & CEO:** K.R. Murdoch

**Pres & COO:** P. Chernin
**EVP, CFO & Chief Acctg Officer:** D.F. DeVoe
**EVP & General Counsel:** L.A. Jacobs
**Investor Contact:** R. Nolte (212-852-7017)

**Board Members:** J. M. Aznar, N. Bancroft, P. L. Barnes, P. Chernin, K. E. Cowley, D. F. DeVoe, V. D. Dinh, R. Eddington, M. Hurd, A. S. Knight, J. Murdoch, K. R. Murdoch, L. K. Murdoch, T. J. Perkins, A. M. Siskind, J. L. Thornton

**Founded:** 1922
**Domicile:** Delaware
**Employees:** 64,000

# Nicor Inc.

| S&P Recommendation HOLD ★★★☆☆ | Price $39.29 (as of Nov 14, 2008) | 12-Mo. Target Price $48.00 | Investment Style Large-Cap Blend |
|---|---|---|---|

**GICS Sector** Utilities
**Sub-Industry** Gas Utilities

**Summary** This holding company's Nicor Gas subsidiary is one of the largest U.S. distributors of natural gas.

## Key Stock Statistics (Source S&P, Vickers, company reports)

| | | | | | | |
|---|---|---|---|---|---|---|
| 52-Wk Range | $51.99–32.35 | S&P Oper. EPS 2008**E** | 2.33 | Market Capitalization(B) | $1.776 | Beta | 0.30 |
| Trailing 12-Month EPS | $2.80 | S&P Oper. EPS 2009**E** | 2.91 | Yield (%) | 4.73 | S&P 3-Yr. Proj. EPS CAGR(%) | 7 |
| Trailing 12-Month P/E | 14.0 | P/E on S&P Oper. EPS 2008**E** | 16.9 | Dividend Rate/Share | $1.86 | S&P Credit Rating | AA |
| $10K Invested 5 Yrs Ago | $15,001 | Common Shares Outstg. (M) | 45.2 | Institutional Ownership (%) | 72 | | |

## Price Performance

30-Week Mov. Avg. ··· 10-Week Mov. Avg. — GAAP Earnings vs. Previous Year   Volume Above Avg. STARS
12-Mo. Target Price — Relative Strength — ▲ Up ▼ Down ▶ No Change   Below Avg.

Options: P

Analysis prepared by **Christopher B. Muir** on September 25, 2008, when the stock traded at **$ 49.01**.

### Highlights

➤ We see a revenue increase of 17% in 2008 and 5.6% in 2009, based on our projection of higher revenues for both the utility and non-utility segments. We see utility revenues being aided by customer growth and higher gas prices partly offset by lower customer usage. We see Tropical Shipping's revenues growing more modestly due to the economic slowdown. Revenues at Other Energy Ventures should also grow more slowly, in our view.

➤ We project operating margins of 4.6% in 2008 and 5.4% in 2009, down from 6.3% in 2007, reflecting higher per-revenue cost of gas, partly offset by lower per-revenue general tax expense and non-utility operating expenses. We expect other cost categories to grow about as fast as revenues. We project pretax margins of 4.0% in 2008 and 4.7% in 2009, down from 5.3% in 2007, a slower decline than observed with operating margins as we see lower interest expense and higher non-operating income.

➤ Assuming an effective tax rate of 26.6% and a small increase in the number of shares outstanding, we estimate EPS of $2.40 in 2008, a 12% decline from 2007's $2.74. Our 2009 EPS projection is $2.94, a rise of 23%.

### Investment Rationale/Risk

➤ Our 2008 projected payout ratio of 78% is higher than the peer average of around 50%. However, we think the dividend is safe, and the shares recently yielded 3.9%. We think GAS could be granted a substantial rate increase that would become effective in early 2009, adding to profits and pushing the payout ratio substantially lower. Once economic growth in the U.S. recovers, we see strong earnings growth returning to GAS's unregulated businesses.

➤ Risks to our recommendation and target price include a possible unfavorable resolution of the pending rate case and slower-than-projected growth in unregulated operations.

➤ The shares recently traded at about 16.7X our 2009 EPS estimate, a 9% premium to natural gas utility peers. Our 12-month target price of $48 equals a P/E of 16.3X our 2009 EPS estimate, about even with our peer forecast. We think this valuation is warranted by the absence of dividend increases in the near-term, and the uncertainty surrounding the outcome of the pending rate case, partly offset by what we see as an extremely strong balance sheet and above peer average EPS growth assuming a rate increase.

### Qualitative Risk Assessment

| LOW | MEDIUM | HIGH |
|---|---|---|

Our risk assessment reflects the low risk nature of the company's main subsidiary, a regulated natural gas distribution company, slightly offset by the higher risk nature of its much smaller competitive operations. The company benefits from being the lone delivery agent of natural gas to customers within its service territory.

### Quantitative Evaluations

**S&P Quality Ranking**   B

| D | C | B- | B | B+ | A- | A | A+ |
|---|---|---|---|---|---|---|---|

**Relative Strength Rank**   STRONG

74

LOWEST = 1   HIGHEST = 99

### Revenue/Earnings Data

**Revenue (Million $)**

| | 1Q | 2Q | 3Q | 4Q | Year |
|---|---|---|---|---|---|
| 2008 | 1,596 | 699.8 | 440.3 | -- | -- |
| 2007 | 1,335 | 556.9 | 365.2 | 919.5 | 3,176 |
| 2006 | 1,319 | 451.3 | 351.1 | 838.2 | 2,960 |
| 2005 | 1,180 | 484.4 | 336.0 | 1,358 | 3,358 |
| 2004 | 1,116 | 429.5 | 299.9 | 894.6 | 2,740 |
| 2003 | 1,171 | 452.8 | 294.8 | 743.9 | 2,663 |

**Earnings Per Share ($)**

| | 1Q | 2Q | 3Q | 4Q | Year |
|---|---|---|---|---|---|
| 2008 | 0.91 | 0.64 | 0.03 | E0.75 | E2.33 |
| 2007 | 1.04 | 0.40 | 0.32 | 1.23 | 2.99 |
| 2006 | 0.99 | 0.19 | 0.39 | 1.29 | 2.87 |
| 2005 | 0.99 | 0.75 | -0.06 | 1.40 | 3.07 |
| 2004 | 0.44 | 0.36 | -0.26 | 1.08 | 1.70 |
| 2003 | 1.14 | 0.54 | 0.01 | 0.79 | 2.48 |

Fiscal year ended Dec. 31. Next earnings report expected: Late February. EPS Estimates based on S&P Operating Earnings; historical GAAP earnings are as reported.

### Dividend Data (Dates: mm/dd Payment Date: mm/dd/yy)

| Amount ($) | Date Decl. | Ex-Div. Date | Stk. of Record | Payment Date |
|---|---|---|---|---|
| 0.465 | 11/29 | 12/27 | 12/31 | 02/01/08 |
| 0.465 | 03/27 | 04/03 | 04/07 | 05/01/08 |
| 0.465 | 04/24 | 06/26 | 06/30 | 08/01/08 |
| 0.465 | 07/24 | 09/26 | 09/30 | 11/01/08 |

Dividends have been paid since 1954. Source: Company reports.

# Nicor Inc.

STANDARD
&POOR'S

## Business Summary September 25, 2008

CORPORATE OVERVIEW. Nicor Inc. is a holding company, whose principal subsidiaries are Northern Illinois Gas Company (doing business as Nicor Gas Company ), one of the nation's largest distributors of natural gas, and Tropical Shipping, a transporter of containerized freight in the Bahamas and the Caribbean region. Nicor also owns several energy-related ventures, including Nicor Services and Nicor Solutions, which provide energy-related products and services to retail markets, and Nicor Enerchange, a wholesale natural gas marketing company.

PRIMARY BUSINESS DYNAMICS. Nicor seeks earnings growth through investment in unregulated operations, including its Tropical Shipping and Other Energy Ventures divisions. However, the company's main operating segment remains its regulated gas utility operations.

As of the end of 2007, Nicor Gas (62% of 2007 segment operating profits) served 2.2 million customers in a service area that covers most of northern Illinois, excluding Chicago. In 2007, gas deliveries climbed to 468.3 billion cubic feet (Bcf) from 438.7 Bcf in 2006. The company has an extensive storage and transmission system that is directly connected to eight interstate pipelines, and includes eight owned underground gas storage facilities, with

about 150 Bcf of annual storage capacity. In addition, Nicor Gas has about 40 Bcf of purchased storage from an affiliated party under contracts that expire between 2009 and 2012.

Nicor Gas is also engaged in non-traditional natural gas storage and transportation activities through its Chicago Hub, which serves marketers, other distributors, and electric power facilities.

GAS's Tropical Shipping unit (22%) is one of the largest containerized cargo carriers in the Caribbean, with a fleet of 11 owned and eight chartered vessels, with total container capacity of about 5,900 20-foot equivalent units (TEU), serving 26 ports. Total volumes shipped in 2007 were 206,600 TEU, up from 203,100 TEU in 2006, but down from 214,200 TEU in 2005. However, revenues per TEU remained relatively high at $1,955 in 2007 versus $1,961 in 2006 and $1,764 in 2005.

## Company Financials Fiscal Year Ended Dec. 31

| Per Share Data ($) | 2007 | 2006 | 2005 | 2004 | 2003 | 2002 | 2001 | 2000 | 1999 | 1998 |
|---|---|---|---|---|---|---|---|---|---|---|
| Tangible Book Value | 20.51 | 19.43 | 18.36 | 16.99 | 17.15 | 16.55 | 16.39 | 15.56 | 16.76 | 15.97 |
| Cash Flow | 6.64 | 6.44 | 6.55 | 5.05 | 5.73 | 6.00 | 6.46 | 4.12 | 5.58 | 5.25 |
| Earnings | 2.99 | 2.87 | 3.07 | 1.70 | 2.48 | 2.88 | 3.17 | 1.00 | 2.62 | 2.42 |
| S&P Core Earnings | 2.74 | 2.83 | 2.47 | 1.97 | 2.45 | 2.30 | 1.99 | NA | NA | NA |
| Dividends | 1.86 | 1.86 | 1.86 | 1.86 | 1.86 | 1.84 | 1.76 | 1.66 | 1.54 | 1.46 |
| Payout Ratio | 62% | 65% | 61% | 109% | 75% | 64% | 56% | 166% | 59% | 60% |
| Prices:High | 53.66 | 49.92 | 42.97 | 39.65 | 39.30 | 49.00 | 42.38 | 43.88 | 42.94 | 44.44 |
| Prices:Low | 37.80 | 38.72 | 35.50 | 32.04 | 23.70 | 18.09 | 34.00 | 29.38 | 31.19 | 37.13 |
| P/E Ratio:High | 18 | 17 | 14 | 23 | 16 | 17 | 13 | 44 | 16 | 18 |
| P/E Ratio:Low | 13 | 13 | 12 | 19 | 10 | 6 | 11 | 29 | 12 | 15 |

| Income Statement Analysis (Million $) | 2007 | 2006 | 2005 | 2004 | 2003 | 2002 | 2001 | 2000 | 1999 | 1998 |
|---|---|---|---|---|---|---|---|---|---|---|
| Revenue | 3,176 | 2,960 | 3,358 | 2,740 | 2,663 | 1,897 | 2,544 | 2,298 | 1,615 | 1,465 |
| Operating Income | 372 | 366 | 202 | 138 | 189 | 227 | 244 | 507 | 352 | 345 |
| Depreciation | 166 | 160 | 155 | 149 | 144 | 138 | 149 | 144 | 140 | 137 |
| Interest Expense | 38.2 | 49.8 | 48.0 | 41.6 | 37.3 | 38.5 | 44.9 | 48.6 | 45.1 | 46.6 |
| Pretax Income | 184 | 174 | 171 | 105 | 169 | 186 | 217 | 61.1 | 190 | 178 |
| Effective Tax Rate | 26.6% | 26.3% | 20.3% | 28.7% | 35.2% | 31.0% | 33.8% | 23.6% | 34.6% | 34.4% |
| Net Income | 135 | 128 | 136 | 75.1 | 110 | 128 | 144 | 46.7 | 124 | 116 |
| S&P Core Earnings | 124 | 127 | 110 | 87.7 | 108 | 102 | 90.4 | NA | NA | NA |

| Balance Sheet & Other Financial Data (Million $) | 2007 | 2006 | 2005 | 2004 | 2003 | 2002 | 2001 | 2000 | 1999 | 1998 |
|---|---|---|---|---|---|---|---|---|---|---|
| Cash | 91.9 | 41.1 | 119 | 12.9 | 50.3 | 75.2 | 10.7 | 55.8 | 42.5 | 13.0 |
| Current Assets | 1,024 | 911 | 1,346 | 1,021 | 916 | 708 | 518 | 915 | 508 | 465 |
| Total Assets | 4,252 | 4,090 | 4,391 | 3,975 | 3,797 | 2,899 | 2,575 | 2,885 | 2,452 | 2,365 |
| Current Liabilities | 1,276 | 1,142 | 1,623 | 1,174 | 1,069 | 1,099 | 826 | 1,312 | 746 | 579 |
| Long Term Debt | 423 | 498 | 486 | 495 | 497 | 396 | 446 | 347 | 436 | 557 |
| Common Equity | 945 | 873 | 811 | 749 | 755 | 728 | 728 | 708 | 788 | 759 |
| Total Capital | 1,769 | 1,787 | 1,751 | 1,873 | 1,813 | 1,514 | 1,548 | 1,173 | 1,539 | 1,606 |
| Capital Expenditures | 173 | 592 | 202 | 190 | 181 | 193 | 186 | 158 | 154 | 136 |
| Cash Flow | 301 | 288 | 291 | 224 | 253 | 266 | 292 | 191 | 264 | 253 |
| Current Ratio | 0.8 | 0.8 | 0.8 | 0.9 | 0.9 | 0.6 | 0.6 | 0.7 | 0.7 | 0.8 |
| % Long Term Debt of Capitalization | 23.9 | 27.9 | 27.7 | 26.4 | 27.4 | 26.1 | 28.8 | 29.6 | 28.3 | 34.7 |
| % Net Income of Revenue | 4.3 | 4.3 | 4.5 | 2.7 | 4.1 | 6.7 | 5.6 | 2.0 | 7.7 | 7.9 |
| % Return on Assets | 3.2 | 3.0 | 11.4 | 7.8 | 3.3 | 4.7 | 5.3 | 1.8 | 5.1 | 4.9 |
| % Return on Equity | 14.9 | 15.2 | 17.4 | 9.9 | 14.8 | 12.3 | 20.0 | 6.2 | 16.0 | 15.4 |

Data as orig reptd.; bef. results of disc opers/spec. items. Per share data adj. for stk. divs.; EPS diluted. E-Estimated. NA-Not Available. NM-Not Meaningful. NR-Not Ranked. UR-Under Review.

**Office:** 1844 Ferry Road, Naperville, IL 60563-9600.
**Telephone:** 630-305-9500.
**Website:** http://www.nicorinc.com
**Chrmn, Pres & CEO:** R.M. Strobel

**EVP & CFO:** R.L. Hawley
**SVP, Secy & General Counsel:** P.C. Gracey, Jr.
**Chief Acctg Officer & Cntlr:** K.K. Pepping
**Treas:** D.M. Ruschau

**Investor Contact:** M. Knox (630-388-2529)
**Board Members:** R. M. Beavers, Jr., B. P. Bickner, J. H. Birdsall, III, N. R. Bobins, B. J. Gaines, R. A. Jean, D. J. Keller, R. E. Martin, G. R. Nelson, J. E. Rau, J. C. Staley, R. M. Strobel
**Founded:** 1953
**Domicile:** Illinois
**Employees:** 3,900

The McGraw-Hill Companies

# NIKE Inc.

**STANDARD &POOR'S**

| S&P Recommendation **BUY** ★★★★☆ | Price $46.53 (as of Nov 14, 2008) | 12-Mo. Target Price $78.00 | Investment Style Large-Cap Growth |
|---|---|---|---|

**GICS Sector** Consumer Discretionary
**Sub-Industry** Footwear

**Summary** NIKE is the world's leading designer and marketer of high-quality athletic footwear, athletic apparel, and accessories.

## Key Stock Statistics (Source S&P, Vickers, company reports)

| | | | | | | | |
|---|---|---|---|---|---|---|---|
| 52-Wk Range | $70.60– 43.50 | S&P Oper. EPS 2009**E** | 3.95 | Market Capitalization(B) | $18.102 | Beta | 0.54 |
| Trailing 12-Month EPS | $3.64 | S&P Oper. EPS 2010**E** | 4.40 | Yield (%) | 1.98 | S&P 3-Yr. Proj. EPS CAGR(%) | 13 |
| Trailing 12-Month P/E | 12.8 | P/E on S&P Oper. EPS 2009**E** | 11.8 | Dividend Rate/Share | $0.92 | S&P Credit Rating | A+ |
| $10K Invested 5 Yrs Ago | $16,093 | Common Shares Outstg. (M) | 485.2 | Institutional Ownership (%) | 93 | | |

## Price Performance

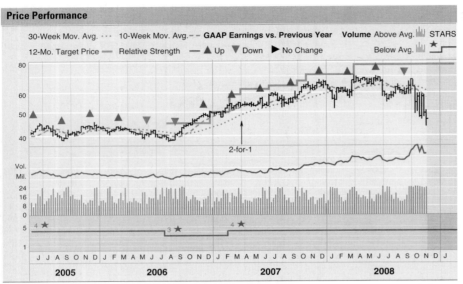

30-Week Mov. Avg. ···· 10-Week Mov. Avg. — — **GAAP Earnings vs. Previous Year** **Volume** Above Avg. STARS
12-Mo. Target Price — Relative Strength — ▲ Up ▼ Down ► No Change Below Avg. ★

2-for-1

Options: ASE, CBOE, P, Ph

Analysis prepared by **Marie Driscoll, CFA** on September 25, 2008, when the stock traded at **$ 65.07**.

## Highlights

➤ The Beijing Summer Olympics benefited NIKE as an official sponsor (it dressed 22 of 28 Chinese Olympic teams); August quarter China revenues were up 50%. China is NKE's second largest market, growing at a 50% clip in FY 08 (May) and surpassing $1 billion in sales. We project revenue growth overall of about 9% in FY 09 as double digit growth in Asia/Pacific offsets low single digit sales gains in the U.S. We see European growth slowing to a 9% pace, from a currency-charged 19% gain in FY 08. NKE's broad geographic exposure (more than 60% of sales are outside the U.S.) positions it well for growth, in our view.

➤ We forecast 10 basis points of operating margin expansion in FY 09, to 13.2%, as gross margin expansion is offset by SG&A expenses increasing faster than sales.

➤ We expect NKE, with about $2.7 billion in cash and short-term investments on its balance sheet and ample free cash flow, to continue to increase its dividend and buy back shares. Incorporating share repurchases and a higher effective tax rate (29% versus 25%), we estimate EPS of $3.95 in FY 09.

## Investment Rationale/Risk

➤ In the past three years, NIKE more than doubled its quarterly dividend and repurchased nearly $3.3 billion of its shares. We see these factors, along with strong fundamentals, including having the dominant global brand with exceptional international growth opportunities, supporting the stock price. Furthermore, NKE has launched key marketing and sales strategies to more closely align it with its key markets. We expect increased global brand awareness related to the Beijing Summer Olympics to benefit FY 09 and beyond. August quarter Chinese future orders were up 50%.

➤ Risks to our recommendation and target price include an economic slowdown domestically and a greater than expected moderation in consumer spending. International risks include economic weakness, supply disruptions, and unfavorable currency fluctuations.

➤ Our 12-month target price of $78 is equal to about 20X our FY 09 EPS estimate of $3.95, in the middle of the 14X-26X range in which the stock has traded over the past five years.

## Qualitative Risk Assessment

| LOW | MEDIUM | HIGH |
|---|---|---|

Our risk assessment reflects what we see as NKE's strong financial and operating metrics, offset by an increasingly competitive global marketplace and prospects for slowing consumer spending in the U.S.

## Quantitative Evaluations

**S&P Quality Ranking**          A+

| D | C | B- | B | B+ | A- | A | A+ |
|---|---|---|---|---|---|---|---|

**Relative Strength Rank**          **MODERATE**

59

LOWEST = 1          HIGHEST = 99

## Revenue/Earnings Data

**Revenue (Million $)**

| | 1Q | 2Q | 3Q | 4Q | Year |
|---|---|---|---|---|---|
| 2009 | 5,432 | -- | -- | -- | -- |
| 2008 | 4,655 | 4,340 | 4,544 | 5,088 | 18,627 |
| 2007 | 4,194 | 3,822 | 3,927 | 4,383 | 16,326 |
| 2006 | 3,862 | 3,475 | 3,613 | 4,005 | 14,955 |
| 2005 | 3,562 | 3,148 | 3,308 | 3,721 | 13,740 |
| 2004 | 3,025 | 2,837 | 2,904 | 3,487 | 12,253 |

**Earnings Per Share ($)**

| | | | | | |
|---|---|---|---|---|---|
| 2009 | 1.03 | E0.85 | E0.91 | E1.13 | E3.95 |
| 2008 | 1.12 | 0.71 | 0.92 | 0.98 | 3.74 |
| 2007 | 0.74 | 0.64 | 0.68 | 0.86 | 2.93 |
| 2006 | 0.81 | 0.57 | 0.62 | 0.64 | 2.64 |
| 2005 | 0.61 | 0.49 | 0.51 | 0.65 | 2.24 |
| 2004 | 0.49 | 0.33 | 0.37 | 0.57 | 1.76 |

Fiscal year ended May 31. Next earnings report expected: Late December. EPS Estimates based on S&P Operating Earnings; historical GAAP earnings are as reported.

## Dividend Data (Dates: mm/dd Payment Date: mm/dd/yy)

| Amount ($) | Date Decl. | Ex-Div. Date | Stk. of Record | Payment Date |
|---|---|---|---|---|
| 0.230 | 11/16 | 12/06 | 12/10 | 01/02/08 |
| 0.230 | 02/14 | 03/06 | 03/10 | 04/01/08 |
| 0.230 | 05/12 | 06/05 | 06/09 | 07/01/08 |
| 0.230 | 08/11 | 09/04 | 09/08 | 10/01/08 |

Dividends have been paid since 1984. Source: Company reports.

# NIKE Inc.

**STANDARD &POOR'S**

## Business Summary September 25, 2008

CORPORATE OVERVIEW. Nike is the world's largest supplier of athletic footwear, with an estimated 50% of this $20 billion market (at wholesale). Sports apparel and equipment are also sold under the Nike banner, and the company's Other segment (13% of sales) houses its affiliated brands including Cole Haan, Converse and Hurley.

MARKET PROFILE. Innovation, marketing and the sports cycle drive the global footwear and athletic apparel markets, in our view. Technologically superior performance products, we think, convey the idea of extraordinary ability to the wearer and are the root of the marketing campaigns aimed at lifestyle consumers (individuals attracted to a brand's attributes of an active lifestyle regardless of sports participation). The global market for athletic apparel is several times as large as the footwear market, and totals over $100 billion, according to industry sources. An estimated 30% of this market consists of active sports apparel (purchased with the intent to be used in an active sport), and the remainder is lifestyle or casual wear. We see apparel representing a significant opportunity for NKE via its brand extensions and market penetra-

tion. According to NPD Fashionworld consumer estimated data, U.S. athletic footwear sales increased 2.6% in 2007, to $19.8 billion, following several years of low single digit gains, with skateboarding enjoying the strongest momentum. Frequent technological innovation enables manufacturers to hold and increase prices while building brand equity. S&P projects a low single digit annual gain for these markets through 2008.

COMPETITIVE LANDSCAPE. Both the athletic footwear and apparel markets are fragmented, providing opportunities for growing market share, in our view. Significant domestic footwear retail channels include athletic footwear specialty shops (18% market share), sporting goods stores (17%), and discounters or mass merchants (11%). Online athletic footwear retailers' sales grew 9% in 2007 (2%).

## Company Financials Fiscal Year Ended May 31

### Per Share Data ($)

| | 2008 | 2007 | 2006 | 2005 | 2004 | 2003 | 2002 | 2001 | 2000 | 1999 |
|---|---|---|---|---|---|---|---|---|---|---|
| Tangible Book Value | 13.51 | 12.93 | 11.23 | 9.77 | 8.14 | 7.22 | 6.39 | 5.77 | 5.05 | 5.14 |
| Cash Flow | NA | 3.51 | 3.17 | 2.72 | 2.22 | 1.83 | 3.51 | 1.44 | 1.37 | 1.13 |
| Earnings | 3.74 | 2.93 | 2.64 | 2.24 | 1.76 | 1.39 | 1.23 | 1.08 | 1.04 | 0.79 |
| S&P Core Earnings | 3.67 | 2.89 | 2.56 | 2.14 | 1.68 | 1.31 | 1.16 | 1.03 | NA | NA |
| Dividends | 0.68 | 0.56 | 0.45 | 0.45 | 0.34 | 0.26 | 0.24 | 0.24 | 0.24 | 0.24 |
| Payout Ratio | 18% | 19% | 17% | 20% | 19% | 19% | 20% | 22% | 23% | 31% |
| Calendar Year | 2007 | 2006 | 2005 | 2004 | 2003 | 2002 | 2001 | 2000 | 1999 | 1998 |
| Prices:High | 67.93 | 50.60 | 45.77 | 46.22 | 34.27 | 32.14 | 30.03 | 28.50 | 33.47 | 26.34 |
| Prices:Low | 47.46 | 37.76 | 37.55 | 32.91 | 21.19 | 19.27 | 17.75 | 12.91 | 19.38 | 15.50 |
| P/E Ratio:High | 18 | 17 | 17 | 21 | 20 | 26 | 24 | 26 | 32 | 34 |
| P/E Ratio:Low | 13 | 13 | 14 | 15 | 12 | 16 | 14 | 12 | 19 | 20 |

### Income Statement Analysis (Million $)

| | 2008 | 2007 | 2006 | 2005 | 2004 | 2003 | 2002 | 2001 | 2000 | 1999 |
|---|---|---|---|---|---|---|---|---|---|---|
| Revenue | 18,627 | 16,326 | 14,955 | 13,740 | 12,253 | 10,697 | 9,893 | 9,489 | 8,995 | 8,777 |
| Operating Income | NA | 2,402 | 23,912 | 2,151 | 1,802 | 1,485 | 1,291 | 1,212 | 1,150 | 1,054 |
| Depreciation | 313 | 270 | 282 | 257 | 252 | 239 | 224 | 197 | 188 | 198 |
| Interest Expense | NA | Nil | Nil | 39.7 | 40.3 | 42.9 | 47.6 | 58.7 | 45.0 | 44.0 |
| Pretax Income | 2,503 | 2,200 | 2,142 | 1,860 | 1,450 | 1,123 | 2,035 | 921 | 919 | 745 |
| Effective Tax Rate | 24.8% | 32.2% | 35.0% | 34.9% | 34.8% | 34.1% | 17.2% | 36.0% | 37.0% | 39.5% |
| Net Income | 1,883 | 1,492 | 1,392 | 1,212 | 946 | 740 | 1,686 | 590 | 579 | 451 |
| S&P Core Earnings | 1,848 | 1,472 | 1,346 | 1,148 | 897 | 698 | 632 | 559 | NA | NA |

### Balance Sheet & Other Financial Data (Million $)

| | 2008 | 2007 | 2006 | 2005 | 2004 | 2003 | 2002 | 2001 | 2000 | 1999 |
|---|---|---|---|---|---|---|---|---|---|---|
| Cash | 2,776 | 1,857 | 954 | 1,388 | 828 | 634 | 576 | 304 | 254 | 198 |
| Current Assets | NA | 8,077 | 7,359 | 6,351 | 5,512 | 4,680 | 4,158 | 3,625 | 3,596 | 3,265 |
| Total Assets | 12,443 | 10,688 | 9,870 | 8,794 | 7,892 | 6,714 | 6,443 | 5,820 | 5,857 | 5,248 |
| Current Liabilities | NA | 2,584 | 2,623 | 1,999 | 2,009 | 2,015 | 1,836 | 1,787 | 2,140 | 1,447 |
| Long Term Debt | NA | Nil | Nil | 687 | 682 | 552 | 626 | 436 | 470 | 386 |
| Common Equity | 7,825 | 7,025 | 6,285 | 5,644 | 4,782 | 3,991 | 3,839 | 3,495 | 3,136 | 3,335 |
| Total Capital | NA | 7,026 | 6,286 | 6,332 | 5,464 | 4,543 | 4,465 | 3,931 | 3,607 | 3,721 |
| Capital Expenditures | 449 | 314 | 334 | 257 | 214 | 186 | 283 | 318 | 420 | 384 |
| Cash Flow | NA | 1,761 | 1,674 | 1,469 | 1,198 | 979 | 1,909 | 787 | 767 | 645 |
| Current Ratio | 2.7 | 3.1 | 2.8 | 3.2 | 2.7 | 2.3 | 2.3 | 2.0 | 1.7 | 2.3 |
| % Long Term Debt of Capitalization | 5.3 | Nil | Nil | 10.9 | 12.5 | 12.1 | 14.0 | 11.1 | 13.0 | 10.4 |
| % Net Income of Revenue | 10.1 | 9.1 | 9.3 | 8.8 | 7.7 | 6.9 | 17.0 | 6.2 | 6.4 | 5.1 |
| % Return on Assets | 16.3 | 14.5 | 14.9 | 14.5 | 12.9 | 11.3 | 27.5 | 10.1 | 10.4 | 8.5 |
| % Return on Equity | 25.4 | 22.4 | 23.3 | 23.2 | 21.6 | 18.9 | 46.0 | 17.8 | 17.9 | 13.7 |

Data as orig reptd.; bef. results of disc opers/spec. items. Per share data adj. for stk. divs.; EPS diluted. E-Estimated. NA-Not Available. NM-Not Meaningful. NR-Not Ranked. UR-Under Review.

**Office:** 1 Bowerman Dr, Beaverton, OR 97005-0979.
**Telephone:** 503-641-6453.
**Website:** http://www.nikebiz.com
**Chrmn:** P.H. Knight

**Pres & CEO:** M.G. Parker
**COO:** G.M. DeStefano
**CFO:** D.W. Blair
**Chief Admin Officer:** R.D. McCray

**Investor Contact:** P.M. Catlett (800-640-8007)
**Board Members:** J. G. Connors, J. K. Conway, T. D. Cook, R. D. DeNunzio, A. B. Graf, Jr., D. G. Houser, J. P. Jackson, P. H. Knight, M. G. Parker, J. A. Rodgers, O. Smith, J. R. Thompson, Jr.

**Founded:** 1964
**Domicile:** Oregon
**Employees:** 32,500

*The McGraw-Hill Companies*

# NiSource Inc.

STANDARD
&POOR'S

| S&P Recommendation HOLD ★★★☆☆ | Price<br>$11.55 (as of Nov 14, 2008) | 12-Mo. Target Price<br>$15.00 | Investment Style<br>Large-Cap Value |
|---|---|---|---|

**GICS Sector** Utilities
**Sub-Industry** Multi-Utilities

**Summary** NI, the third largest U.S. gas distribution utility and the fourth largest gas pipeline company, also provides electric utility services.

## Key Stock Statistics (Source S&P, Vickers, company reports)

| | | | | | | | |
|---|---|---|---|---|---|---|---|
| 52-Wk Range | $19.82– 10.51 | S&P Oper. EPS 2008**E** | 1.35 | Market Capitalization(B) | $3.168 | Beta | 0.56 |
| Trailing 12-Month EPS | $-0.06 | S&P Oper. EPS 2009**E** | 1.35 | Yield (%) | 7.97 | S&P 3-Yr. Proj. EPS CAGR(%) | 2 |
| Trailing 12-Month P/E | NM | P/E on S&P Oper. EPS 2008**E** | 8.6 | Dividend Rate/Share | $0.92 | S&P Credit Rating | NA |
| $10K Invested 5 Yrs Ago | $6,992 | Common Shares Outstg. (M) | 274.2 | Institutional Ownership (%) | 82 | | |

## Price Performance

30-Week Mov. Avg. ··· 10-Week Mov. Avg. – – **GAAP Earnings vs. Previous Year** Volume Above Avg. ▮▮▮ STARS
12-Mo. Target Price — Relative Strength — ▲ Up ▼ Down ▶ No Change Below Avg. ▮▮▮ ★

Options: ASE, CBOE, Ph

## Qualitative Risk Assessment

| LOW | MEDIUM | HIGH |
|---|---|---|

Our risk assessment reflects the company's reliance on fairly stable regulated sources of earnings including gas distribution, gas transmission, and electric utility services.

## Quantitative Evaluations

**S&P Quality Ranking**      B

| D | C | B- | B | B+ | A- | A | A+ |
|---|---|---|---|---|---|---|---|

**Relative Strength Rank**      MODERATE

57

LOWEST = 1      HIGHEST = 99

## Revenue/Earnings Data

**Revenue (Million $)**

| | 1Q | 2Q | 3Q | 4Q | Year |
|---|---|---|---|---|---|
| 2008 | 3,290 | 1,792 | 1,409 | -- | -- |
| 2007 | 2,894 | 1,577 | 1,241 | 2,245 | 7,940 |
| 2006 | 2,972 | 1,312 | 1,156 | 2,050 | 7,490 |
| 2005 | 2,683 | 1,356 | 1,165 | 2,695 | 7,899 |
| 2004 | 2,473 | 1,245 | 979.8 | 1,968 | 6,666 |
| 2003 | 2,525 | 1,141 | 898.3 | 1,683 | 6,247 |

**Earnings Per Share ($)**

| | 1Q | 2Q | 3Q | 4Q | Year |
|---|---|---|---|---|---|
| 2008 | 0.69 | 0.08 | 0.12 | E0.47 | E1.35 |
| 2007 | 0.76 | 0.11 | 0.03 | 0.24 | 1.14 |
| 2006 | 0.63 | 0.08 | 0.10 | 0.33 | 1.14 |
| 2005 | 0.77 | 0.03 | -0.02 | 0.27 | 1.04 |
| 2004 | 0.82 | 0.13 | 0.08 | 0.58 | 1.62 |
| 2003 | 0.87 | 0.15 | 0.09 | 0.53 | 1.63 |

Fiscal year ended Dec. 31. Next earnings report expected: Late January. EPS Estimates based on S&P Operating Earnings; historical GAAP earnings are as reported.

## Highlights

➤ The 12-month target price for NI has recently been changed to $15.00 from $16.00. The Highlights section of this Stock Report will be updated accordingly.

## Investment Rationale/Risk

➤ The Investment Rationale/Risk section of this Stock Report will be updated shortly. For the latest News story on NI from MarketScope, see below.

➤ 11/04/08 09:02 am ET ... S&P MAINTAINS HOLD OPINION ON SHARES OF NISOURCE INC. (NI 13.22***): Q3 recurring EPS of $0.02 vs. $0.08 misses our estimate by $0.10. Revenues nearly matched our estimate, and per-revenue non-fuel operating expenses were lower than expected, but per-revenue cost of sales was much higher. NI continues to move forward with several regulatory initiatives, including an electric-rate case for its Indiana utility; however, we continue to see little EPS growth through '10. We are lowering our '08 EPS estimate by $0.10 to $1.25 and keeping '09's at $1.35. We are lowering our 12-month target price by $1 to $15. The shares are yielding 7.0%. /CMuir

## Dividend Data (Dates: mm/dd Payment Date: mm/dd/yy)

| Amount<br>($) | Date<br>Decl. | Ex-Div.<br>Date | Stk. of<br>Record | Payment<br>Date |
|---|---|---|---|---|
| 0.230 | 01/09 | 01/29 | 01/31 | 02/20/08 |
| 0.230 | 03/26 | 04/28 | 04/30 | 05/20/08 |
| 0.230 | 05/14 | 07/29 | 07/31 | 08/20/08 |
| 0.230 | 08/27 | 10/29 | 10/31 | 11/20/08 |

Dividends have been paid since 1987. Source: Company reports.

---

**Please read the Required Disclosures and Analyst Certification on the last page of this report.**

The McGraw·Hill Companies

# NiSource Inc.

STANDARD
&POOR'S

## Business Summary September 24, 2008

CORPORATE OVERVIEW. NiSource is the third largest U.S. natural gas distributor (measured by customers served), the fourth largest owner of U.S. natural gas interstate pipelines (by route miles), and one of the largest owners of underground natural gas storage. It also provides electric utility services in northern Indiana. The company's operating divisions include Gas Distribution (36% of year end-2007 segment operating income), Gas Transmission and Storage (39%), Electric Operations (28%), Other Operations (0%) and Corporate (-3%).

Gas Distribution operations provide gas utility service to 3.3 million customers in nine states. The division owns and operates 58,362 miles of pipeline, 28,479 acres of underground storage, and 90 storage wells. In 2007, total sales and transportation volumes were 923 MM Dth, up from 827 MM Dth in 2006.

Gas Transmission and Storage operates 15,832 miles of interstate natural gas pipelines and 867,000 acres of underground storage systems with a capacity of about 637 billion cubic feet (Bcf). In 2007, total throughput was 1,423 MM Dth, up 21% from 2006 due to strong market area storage injections, higher

transport usage by natural gas fired electric power generators, enhanced market access through new pipeline interconnects and the addition of new natural gas supply. The division is working to develop the proposed Millennium Pipeline to access additional Canadian gas supply. The Millennium project, a 186-mile section in New York State, is expected to be in service by November 2008. The 12 Bcf Hardy storage project in West Virginia is expected to be fully operational in 2009. NI said it is in the process of a potential separation of Columbia Gas into a master limited partnership structure.

NI's Northern Indiana subsidiary, NIPSCO, generates and distributes electricity for 457,076 electric utility customers. The utility operates four coal-fired plants (2,574 MW), six gas-fired plants (323 MW), and two hydroelectric plants (10 MW). In 2007, the utility generated 78.5% of its electric requirements, and purchased 21.5%. NI said it was considering a possible sale of this business.

## Company Financials Fiscal Year Ended Dec. 31

| Per Share Data ($) | 2007 | 2006 | 2005 | 2004 | 2003 | 2002 | 2001 | 2000 | 1999 | 1998 |
|---|---|---|---|---|---|---|---|---|---|---|
| Tangible Book Value | 3.58 | 3.29 | 2.79 | 2.14 | 0.70 | NM | NM | NM | 9.88 | 9.20 |
| Cash Flow | 3.17 | 3.16 | 3.04 | 3.54 | 3.53 | 4.70 | 4.07 | 3.84 | NA | NA |
| Earnings | 1.14 | 1.14 | 1.04 | 1.62 | 1.63 | 2.00 | 1.01 | 1.08 | 1.27 | 1.59 |
| S&P Core Earnings | 1.09 | 1.13 | 1.20 | 1.62 | 1.67 | 1.43 | 0.32 | NA | NA | NA |
| Dividends | 0.92 | 0.92 | 0.92 | 0.92 | 1.10 | 1.16 | 1.16 | 1.08 | 1.02 | 0.96 |
| Payout Ratio | 78% | 81% | 88% | 57% | 67% | 58% | 115% | 100% | 80% | 60% |
| Prices:High | 25.43 | 24.80 | 25.50 | 22.82 | 21.97 | 24.99 | 32.55 | 31.50 | 30.94 | 33.75 |
| Prices:Low | 17.49 | 19.51 | 20.44 | 19.65 | 16.39 | 14.51 | 18.25 | 12.75 | 16.38 | 24.66 |
| P/E Ratio:High | 22 | 22 | 25 | 14 | 13 | 12 | 32 | 29 | 24 | 21 |
| P/E Ratio:Low | 15 | 17 | 20 | 12 | 10 | 7 | 18 | 12 | 13 | 16 |

| Income Statement Analysis (Million $) | 2007 | 2006 | 2005 | 2004 | 2003 | 2002 | 2001 | 2000 | 1999 | 1998 |
|---|---|---|---|---|---|---|---|---|---|---|
| Revenue | 7,940 | 7,490 | 7,899 | 6,666 | 6,247 | 6,492 | 9,459 | 6,031 | 3,145 | 2,933 |
| Operating Income | 1,493 | 880 | 1,520 | 1,072 | 1,116 | 1,203 | 1,009 | 568 | 773 | 678 |
| Depreciation | 559 | 549 | 545 | 510 | 497 | 574 | 642 | 374 | 311 | 256 |
| Interest Expense | 418 | 7,304 | 425 | 408 | 469 | 533 | 605 | 325 | 184 | 129 |
| Pretax Income | 484 | 484 | 433 | 671 | 662 | 680 | 416 | 298 | 269 | 295 |
| Effective Tax Rate | 35.6% | 35.3% | 34.5% | 35.9% | 35.4% | 34.4% | 44.1% | 43.7% | 33.5% | 34.2% |
| Net Income | 312 | 314 | 284 | 430 | 426 | 426 | 212 | 147 | 160 | 194 |
| S&P Core Earnings | 298 | 310 | 324 | 429 | 437 | 305 | 67.9 | NA | NA | NA |

| Balance Sheet & Other Financial Data (Million $) | 2007 | 2006 | 2005 | 2004 | 2003 | 2002 | 2001 | 2000 | 1999 | 1998 |
|---|---|---|---|---|---|---|---|---|---|---|
| Cash | 95.4 | 33.1 | 69.4 | 30.1 | 27.3 | 56.2 | 128 | 193 | 43.5 | 60.9 |
| Current Assets | 2,455 | 2,783 | 3,061 | 2,286 | 2,063 | 1,869 | 2,567 | 4,918 | NA | NA |
| Total Assets | 18,005 | 18,157 | 17,959 | 16,988 | 16,624 | 16,897 | 17,374 | 19,697 | 6,835 | 4,987 |
| Current Liabilities | 3,393 | 3,821 | 3,843 | 3,602 | 2,609 | 4,177 | 4,729 | 6,893 | NA | NA |
| Long Term Debt | 5,594 | 5,146 | 5,271 | 4,917 | 6,075 | 5,448 | 6,214 | 6,148 | NA | NA |
| Common Equity | 5,077 | 5,014 | 4,933 | 4,787 | 4,416 | 4,175 | 3,469 | 3,415 | 1,354 | 1,150 |
| Total Capital | 12,234 | 11,775 | 11,866 | 11,448 | 10,490 | 11,581 | 11,515 | 11,483 | 4,903 | 3,725 |
| Capital Expenditures | 788 | 637 | 590 | 517 | 575 | 622 | 668 | 366 | 341 | 246 |
| Cash Flow | 871 | 863 | 829 | 940 | 923 | 1,000 | 854 | 521 | NA | NA |
| Current Ratio | 0.7 | 0.7 | 0.8 | 0.6 | 0.8 | 0.4 | 0.5 | 0.7 | 0.5 | 0.7 |
| % Long Term Debt of Capitalization | 45.7 | 43.7 | 44.4 | 42.9 | 57.9 | 47.0 | 54.0 | 53.5 | 60.3 | 59.1 |
| % Net Income of Revenue | 3.9 | 4.2 | 3.6 | 6.5 | 6.8 | 6.6 | 2.2 | 2.4 | 5.1 | 6.6 |
| % Return on Assets | 1.7 | 1.7 | 1.6 | 2.6 | 2.5 | 2.5 | 1.1 | 1.1 | NA | NA |
| % Return on Equity | 6.2 | 6.3 | 5.8 | 9.3 | 9.9 | 11.1 | 6.2 | 6.2 | 12.8 | 16.1 |

Data as orig reptd.; bef. results of disc opers/spec. items. Per share data adj. for stk. divs.; EPS diluted. E-Estimated. NA-Not Available. NM-Not Meaningful. NR-Not Ranked. UR-Under Review.

**Office:** 801 East 86th Avenue, Merrillville, IN, USA 46410-6272.
**Telephone:** 877-647-5990.
**Email:** questions@nisource.com
**Website:** http://www.nisource.com

**Chrmn:** I.M. Rolland
**Pres & CEO:** R.C. Skaggs, Jr.
**EVP & CFO:** S.P. Smith
**EVP & General Counsel:** C.J. Hightman

**Chief Admin Officer:** V.G. Sistovaris
**Investor Contact:** D.J. Vajda (877-647-5990)
**Board Members:** R. A. Abdoo, S. C. Beering, D. S. Coleman, D. E. Foster, M. E. Jesanis, M. R. Kittrell, W. L. Nutter, D. S. Parker, I. M. Rolland, R. C. Skaggs, Jr., R. L. Thompson, C. Y. Woo

**Founded:** 1912
**Domicile:** Delaware
**Employees:** 7,607

The *McGraw-Hill* Companies

**STANDARD &POOR'S**

# Noble Corp

| S&P Recommendation | STRONG BUY ★★★★★ | Price $26.89 (as of Nov 14, 2008) | 12-Mo. Target Price $43.00 | Investment Style Large-Cap Growth |
| --- | --- | --- | --- | --- |

**GICS Sector** Energy
**Sub-Industry** Oil & Gas Drilling

**Summary** This company principally provides contract drilling services for the oil and gas industry worldwide.

## Key Stock Statistics (Source S&P, Vickers, company reports)

| | | | | | |
| --- | --- | --- | --- | --- | --- |
| 52-Wk Range | $68.99–22.25 | S&P Oper. EPS 2008**E** | 5.97 | Market Capitalization(B) | $7.097 |
| Trailing 12-Month EPS | $5.55 | S&P Oper. EPS 2009**E** | 7.20 | Yield (%) | 0.60 |
| Trailing 12-Month P/E | 4.9 | P/E on S&P Oper. EPS 2008**E** | 4.5 | Dividend Rate/Share | $0.16 |
| $10K Invested 5 Yrs Ago | $15,662 | Common Shares Outstg. (M) | 263.9 | Institutional Ownership (%) | 79 |

| | |
| --- | --- |
| Beta | 1.43 |
| S&P 3-Yr. Proj. EPS CAGR(%) | 39 |
| S&P Credit Rating | A- |

## Price Performance

30-Week Mov. Avg. · · · ·   10-Week Mov. Avg. – –   **GAAP Earnings vs. Previous Year**   Volume Above Avg. ▍▏▎ STARS
12-Mo. Target Price —   Relative Strength —   ▲ Up   ▼ Down   ▶ No Change   Below Avg. ▍▏▎   ★

Options: ASE, CBOE, Ph

Analysis prepared by **Stewart Glickman, CFA** on October 30, 2008, when the stock traded at **$ 32.51**.

## Highlights

➤ In the third quarter, daily operating expenses for the company's contract drilling segment were down 1.3% sequentially, better than our expectations and a marked improvement over the second quarter. In October, NE said that it anticipated that contract drilling expenses, for all of 2008, would likely be about $1.1 billion, at the low end of the previously guided range. We note that the sizable third-quarter improvement on cost inflation was obtained not via project deferrals, but rather by improved performance on repairs and maintenance.

➤ In April 2008, NE announced a special dividend of $0.75 per share. While NE did not provide any indications for the timing or magnitude of any more such dividends, we believe that with its strong cash flow generation, the company should have the capacity to do so, should it choose to return cash to shareholders in this fashion. Through September 2008, cash from operations was $1.33 billion, about 55% of total revenues.

➤ We see revenue growth of 20% in 2008, rising a further 25% in 2009. We estimate EPS of $5.97 in 2008, increasing to $7.20 in 2009.

## Investment Rationale/Risk

➤ Although the credit crisis has roiled stock markets, we believe that NE's revenue stream is well-protected by a sizable backlog of contracts, which, outside of Mexico, do not have early termination provisions. Excluding the three low-spec submersible rigs, NE has 77% of total operating days contracted for 2009, and 70% for jackups. While there is some uncertainty in Mexico, we think demand from PEMEX will increase given declines at Mexico's key Cantarell field. For 2009, we expect shallow-water drilling equipment (jackups and submersibles) to contribute about 60% of total revenues, with floaters (semisubmersibles and drillships) accounting for the remaining 40%.

➤ Risks to our recommendation and target price include reduced rig dayrates; higher-than-expected unscheduled shipyard repair days; and decreased oil and natural gas prices.

➤ We think the shares merit a premium valuation, given expected 2009 ROIC of about 28%, above peers. Using multiples of 4.5X 2009 projected EBITDA and 6.5X estimated 2009 earnings (premiums to compressed peer averages), and blending with our NAV model, our 12-month target price is $43.

## Qualitative Risk Assessment

| LOW | MEDIUM | HIGH |
| --- | --- | --- |

Our risk assessment reflects NE's exposure to volatile crude oil and natural gas prices, capital spending decisions made by its oil and gas producing customers, and political risk associated with operating in frontier regions. Offsetting these risks is the company's strong historical financial performance relative to peers.

## Quantitative Evaluations

**S&P Quality Ranking**      **B**

| D | C | B- | B | B+ | A- | A | A+ |
| --- | --- | --- | --- | --- | --- | --- | --- |

**Relative Strength Rank**      **MODERATE**

| 39 |
| --- |

LOWEST = 1        HIGHEST = 99

## Revenue/Earnings Data

### Revenue (Million $)

| | 1Q | 2Q | 3Q | 4Q | Year |
| --- | --- | --- | --- | --- | --- |
| 2008 | 861.4 | 812.9 | 862.0 | -- | -- |
| 2007 | 646.4 | 726.0 | 791.3 | 831.6 | 2,995 |
| 2006 | 461.9 | 517.5 | 562.0 | 558.8 | 2,100 |
| 2005 | 310.3 | 344.0 | 367.2 | 360.6 | 1,382 |
| 2004 | 245.4 | 253.0 | 265.6 | 302.2 | 1,066 |
| 2003 | 245.0 | 247.9 | 254.7 | 239.8 | 987.4 |

### Earnings Per Share ($)

| | | | | | |
| --- | --- | --- | --- | --- | --- |
| 2008 | 1.43 | 1.40 | 1.43 | E1.71 | E5.97 |
| 2007 | 0.93 | 1.08 | 1.18 | 1.29 | 4.48 |
| 2006 | 0.52 | 0.65 | 0.76 | 0.74 | 2.66 |
| 2005 | 0.17 | 0.26 | 0.28 | 0.37 | 1.08 |
| 2004 | 0.11 | 0.13 | 0.12 | 0.20 | 0.55 |
| 2003 | 0.15 | 0.17 | 0.20 | 0.12 | 0.63 |

Fiscal year ended Dec. 31. Next earnings report expected: Late January. EPS Estimates based on S&P Operating Earnings; historical GAAP earnings are as reported.

## Dividend Data (Dates: mm/dd Payment Date: mm/dd/yy)

| Amount ($) | Date Decl. | Ex-Div. Date | Stk. of Record | Payment Date |
| --- | --- | --- | --- | --- |
| .75 Spl. | 04/17 | 04/28 | 04/30 | 05/16/08 |
| 0.040 | 04/30 | 05/12 | 05/14 | 05/30/08 |
| 0.040 | 08/04 | 08/11 | 08/13 | 08/29/08 |
| 0.040 | 10/31 | 11/07 | 11/12 | 12/01/08 |

Dividends have been paid since 2005. Source: Company reports.

---

**Please read the Required Disclosures and Analyst Certification on the last page of this report.**

The McGraw-Hill Companies

# Noble Corp

**STANDARD**
**&POOR'S**

## Business Summary October 30, 2008

CORPORATE OVERVIEW. In April 2002, Noble Drilling Corp. shareholders approved a corporate restructuring that effectively changed the company's place of incorporation from Delaware to the Cayman Islands. The restructuring was completed April 30, 2002, upon the merger of an indirect subsidiary of Noble Corp., a newly formed Cayman Islands company, with Noble Drilling. Noble Corp. (NE) became the parent holding company of Noble Drilling and the other companies in the Noble corporate group.

NE provides contract drilling services in offshore markets worldwide. The company has a fleet of 62 offshore drilling rigs. Company-owned rigs include floating deepwater units, including 13 semisubmersibles and three dynamically positioned drillships, 43 independent leg, cantilever jackup rigs, and three submersibles. As of January 2008, approximately 85% of the fleet was deployed in international markets, mainly in the Middle East, Mexico, the North

Sea, Brazil, West Africa, and India. Contract drilling operations accounted for 91% of total revenues in 2007. As of January 11, 2008, contracted backlog totaled $6.7 billion, and NE had 81% of its available operating days committed for 2008, 40% for 2009, and about 15% for 2010.

Within contract drilling operations, international activity accounted for 76% of revenues in 2007. PEMEX accounted for 15% of total revenues in 2007; no other customer comprised more than 10% of revenues. In 2007, average utilization for NE's international fleet was 95%, down 1% from 2006. NE's average dayrate was $139,948 in 2007, up 43% from $97,837 per day in 2006.

## Company Financials Fiscal Year Ended Dec. 31

| Per Share Data ($) | 2007 | 2006 | 2005 | 2004 | 2003 | 2002 | 2001 | 2000 | 1999 | 1998 |
|---|---|---|---|---|---|---|---|---|---|---|
| Tangible Book Value | 16.06 | 11.96 | 9.97 | 8.87 | 8.16 | 7.45 | 6.72 | 5.90 | 5.30 | 5.00 |
| Cash Flow | 5.28 | 3.66 | 1.97 | 1.32 | 1.18 | 1.25 | 1.43 | 1.02 | 0.69 | 0.89 |
| Earnings | 4.49 | 2.67 | 1.08 | 0.55 | 0.63 | 0.79 | 0.99 | 0.61 | 0.36 | 0.62 |
| Dividends | 0.08 | 0.08 | 0.05 | Nil | Nil | Nil | Nil | Nil | Nil | Nil |
| Payout Ratio | 2% | 3% | 5% | Nil | Nil | Nil | Nil | Nil | Nil | Nil |
| Prices:High | 57.64 | 43.08 | 37.81 | 25.27 | 19.20 | 22.98 | 27.00 | 26.75 | 16.44 | 17.34 |
| Prices:Low | 33.81 | 29.26 | 23.52 | 16.77 | 15.23 | 13.50 | 10.40 | 13.63 | 6.00 | 5.38 |
| P/E Ratio:High | 13 | 16 | 35 | 46 | 31 | 29 | 27 | 44 | 46 | 28 |
| P/E Ratio:Low | 8 | 11 | 22 | 31 | 24 | 17 | 11 | 22 | 17 | 9 |

| Income Statement Analysis (Million $) | | | | | | | | | | |
|---|---|---|---|---|---|---|---|---|---|---|
| Revenue | 2,995 | 2,100 | 1,382 | 1,066 | 987 | 986 | 1,002 | 883 | 706 | 788 |
| Operating Income | 1,751 | 1,170 | 585 | 396 | 366 | 400 | 503 | 379 | 245 | 301 |
| Depreciation, Depletion and Amortization | 217 | 253 | 242 | 209 | 148 | 125 | 119 | 111 | 89.0 | 72.0 |
| Interest Expense | 63.5 | 16.2 | 19.8 | 34.4 | 40.3 | 42.6 | 47.8 | 54.6 | 33.2 | 5.20 |
| Pretax Income | 1,489 | 921 | 364 | 162 | 187 | 243 | 350 | 226 | 124 | 231 |
| Effective Tax Rate | 19.0% | 20.6% | 18.5% | 9.72% | 11.0% | 13.9% | 24.6% | 26.8% | 24.3% | 29.8% |
| Net Income | 1,206 | 732 | 297 | 146 | 166 | 210 | 264 | 166 | 95.3 | 162 |

| Balance Sheet & Other Financial Data (Million $) | | | | | | | | | | |
|---|---|---|---|---|---|---|---|---|---|---|
| Cash | 161 | 61.7 | 166 | 58.8 | 139 | 274 | 288 | 177 | 137 | 217 |
| Current Assets | 860 | 570 | 522 | 425 | 422 | 466 | 494 | 379 | 291 | 438 |
| Total Assets | 5,876 | 4,586 | 4,346 | 3,308 | 3,190 | 3,066 | 2,751 | 2,596 | 2,432 | 2,179 |
| Current Liabilities | 493 | 426 | 259 | 214 | 244 | 281 | 208 | 205 | 233 | 350 |
| Long Term Debt | 774 | 684 | 1,129 | 503 | 542 | 590 | 550 | 650 | 731 | 461 |
| Common Equity | 4,308 | 3,229 | 2,732 | 2,384 | 2,178 | 1,989 | 1,778 | 1,577 | 1,398 | 1,310 |
| Total Capital | 5,318 | 4,126 | 4,097 | 3,086 | 2,927 | 2,779 | 2,526 | 2,372 | 2,197 | 1,828 |
| Capital Expenditures | 1,179 | 1,053 | 434 | 261 | 307 | 268 | 134 | 125 | 422 | 541 |
| Cash Flow | 1,423 | 985 | 538 | 355 | 315 | 335 | 382 | 276 | 184 | 234 |
| Current Ratio | 1.8 | 1.3 | 2.0 | 2.0 | 1.7 | 1.7 | 2.4 | 1.8 | 1.2 | 1.3 |
| % Long Term Debt of Capitalization | 14.6 | 16.6 | 27.6 | 16.3 | 18.5 | 21.2 | 21.8 | 27.4 | 33.3 | 25.2 |
| % Return on Assets | 23.1 | 16.4 | 7.8 | 4.5 | 5.3 | 7.2 | 9.9 | 6.6 | 4.1 | 8.8 |
| % Return on Equity | 32.0 | 24.6 | 11.6 | 6.4 | 8.0 | 11.1 | 15.7 | 11.1 | 7.0 | 13.2 |

Data as orig reptd.; bef. results of disc opers/spec. items. Per share data adj. for stk. divs.; EPS diluted. E-Estimated. NA-Not Available. NM-Not Meaningful. NR-Not Ranked. UR-Under Review.

**Office:** 13135 South Dairy Ashford, Sugar Land, TX, USA 77478.
**Telephone:** 281-276-6100.
**Website:** http://www.noblecorp.com
**Chrmn, Pres & CEO:** D.W. Williams

**EVP & Secy:** J.J. Robertson
**SVP, CFO, Chief Acctg Officer & Treas:** T.L. Mitchell
**Investor Contact:** L.M. Ahlstrom (281-276-6100)

**Auditor:** Pricewaterhousecoopers
**Board Members:** M. A. Cawley, L. J. Chazen, L. R. Corbett, J. H. Edwards, M. E. Leland, J. E. Little, M. P. Ricciardello, D. W. Williams

**Founded:** 1939
**Domicile:** Cayman Islands
**Employees:** 6,600

# Noble Energy Inc

| S&P Recommendation HOLD ★★★☆☆ | Price $50.61 (as of Nov 14, 2008) | 12-Mo. Target Price $55.00 | Investment Style Large-Cap Growth |
|---|---|---|---|

**GICS Sector** Energy
**Sub-Industry** Oil & Gas Exploration & Production

**Summary** This independent exploration and production company (formerly Noble Affiliates) is engaged in the exploration, production and marketing of oil and natural gas worldwide.

## Key Stock Statistics (Source S&P, Vickers, company reports)

| | | | | | | | | |
|---|---|---|---|---|---|---|---|---|
| 52-Wk Range | $105.11– 30.89 | S&P Oper. EPS 2008**E** | 7.59 | Market Capitalization(B) | $8.743 | Beta | | 1.37 |
| Trailing 12-Month EPS | $7.57 | S&P Oper. EPS 2009**E** | 6.72 | Yield (%) | 1.42 | S&P 3-Yr. Proj. EPS CAGR(%) | | 13 |
| Trailing 12-Month P/E | 6.7 | P/E on S&P Oper. EPS 2008**E** | 6.7 | Dividend Rate/Share | $0.72 | S&P Credit Rating | | BBB- |
| $10K Invested 5 Yrs Ago | $26,829 | Common Shares Outstg. (M) | 172.7 | Institutional Ownership (%) | 94 | | | |

## Price Performance

30-Week Mov. Avg. · · · 10-Week Mov. Avg. - - **GAAP Earnings vs. Previous Year** Volume Above Avg. ▮▮▮ STARS
12-Mo. Target Price — Relative Strength — ▲ Up ▼ Down ► No Change Below Avg. ▮▮▮ ★

Options: ASE, CBOE, P, Ph

Analysis prepared by **Michael Kay** on November 04, 2008, when the stock traded at **$ 53.95.**

### Highlights

➤ Driven by developing Rocky Mountain assets, the start-up of Gulf of Mexico (GOM) projects, the start-up of Phase II at Dumbarton in the North Sea, and increased sales in Israel, we see 2008 and 2009 production increases of 11% and 8%, respectively. We expect the completion of an LNG plant and improved volumes in Equatorial Guinea to boost West Africa operations and help offset production declines from the disposal of GOM assets. During the third quarter, NBL made its largest discovery in the GOM at the Gunflint prospect (37.5% interest) and saw testing success at the Diega oil discovery offshore Equatorial Guinea.

➤ We see lease operating expense per unit up 20% in 2008 on a continuing rising service cost environment. We see exploration expense increasing 4% this year, and DD&A up 9%. We expect production increases and higher crude oil prices to boost 2008 EBITDA by 28%, but see lower prices in 2009 leading to a 12% drop.

➤ NBL's 2008 capital budget is $2 billion, up from $1.6 billion (excluding acquisitions) in 2007. We see 2008 EPS of $7.59 (with $0.05 of derivative gains), up from $5.70 in 2007, and $6.72 in 2009 on lower prices.

### Investment Rationale/Risk

➤ In our view, acquisitions have extended NBL's reserve life and made its reserve replacement efforts less dependent on non-operated projects. As a result, we see improvement in NBL's business profile due to increased U.S. onshore operations, operational synergies, and a stronger balance sheet. We view NBL as a low-cost and geographically balanced producer with more financial flexibility than it previously had. NBL increased production by 10% in the first nine months of 2008, in line with our tempered forecasts, reflecting plant maintenance, hurricane shut-ins and natural declines.

➤ Risks to our recommendation and target price include declines in oil and gas prices and production, and an inability to replace reserves.

➤ A drop in oil and gas prices, due to a weakening economy and the ongoing credit crisis, has caused a similar decline in E&P shares. Given instability in financial markets, we expect unproven resource potential to be discounted, and we now value NBL on proven reserve NAV estimates. Our 12-month target price of $55 blends our proved NAV estimate of $60 with our DCF ($59; WACC of 13%; terminal growth of 3%) and peer average relative valuations.

### Qualitative Risk Assessment

| LOW | MEDIUM | HIGH |
|---|---|---|

Our risk assessment reflects our view of NBL's aggressive financial profile, and a satisfactory business profile limited by participation in the cyclical, competitive and capital-intensive exploration and production sector, and by U.S. and international oil and gas operations that carry heightened political and operational risk.

### Quantitative Evaluations

**S&P Quality Ranking** B+

| D | C | B- | B | B+ | A- | A | A+ |
|---|---|---|---|---|---|---|---|

**Relative Strength Rank** STRONG

78

LOWEST = 1 HIGHEST = 99

### Revenue/Earnings Data

**Revenue (Million $)**

| | 1Q | 2Q | 3Q | 4Q | Year |
|---|---|---|---|---|---|
| 2008 | 1,025 | 1,205 | 1,098 | -- | -- |
| 2007 | 742.6 | 794.2 | 813.8 | 921.5 | 3,272 |
| 2006 | 712.0 | 772.6 | 741.3 | 714.2 | 2,940 |
| 2005 | 368.2 | 485.4 | 632.1 | 701.0 | 2,187 |
| 2004 | 317.6 | 335.2 | 320.2 | 378.2 | 1,351 |
| 2003 | 266.7 | 247.2 | 244.3 | 252.8 | 1,011 |

**Earnings Per Share ($)**

| | | | | | |
|---|---|---|---|---|---|
| 2008 | 1.21 | -0.84 | 5.37 | E1.48 | E7.59 |
| 2007 | 1.22 | 1.21 | 1.28 | 1.73 | 5.45 |
| 2006 | 1.26 | -0.17 | 1.75 | 0.94 | 3.79 |
| 2005 | 0.92 | 0.91 | 0.99 | 1.18 | 4.12 |
| 2004 | 0.65 | 0.60 | 0.68 | 0.73 | 2.70 |
| 2003 | 0.28 | 0.23 | 0.28 | Nil | 0.78 |

Fiscal year ended Dec. 31. Next earnings report expected: Late February. EPS Estimates based on S&P Operating Earnings; historical GAAP earnings are as reported.

### Dividend Data (Dates: mm/dd Payment Date: mm/dd/yy)

| Amount ($) | Date Decl. | Ex-Div. Date | Stk. of Record | Payment Date |
|---|---|---|---|---|
| 0.120 | 01/22 | 01/31 | 02/04 | 02/19/08 |
| 0.180 | 04/21 | 05/01 | 05/05 | 05/19/08 |
| 0.180 | 07/22 | 07/31 | 08/04 | 08/18/08 |
| 0.180 | 10/21 | 10/30 | 11/03 | 11/17/08 |

Dividends have been paid since 1975. Source: Company reports.

---

**Please read the Required Disclosures and Analyst Certification on the last page of this report.**

The McGraw-Hill Companies

# Noble Energy Inc

STANDARD
&POOR'S

## Business Summary November 04, 2008

CORPORATE OVERVIEW. Noble Energy (NBL; formerly Noble Affiliates, Inc.) is a large international independent exploration and production concern, engaged in exploration, production and marketing of oil and natural gas. The company has operations in the U.S. (offshore the Gulf of Mexico and California, the Gulf Coast region, the Mid-Continent region, and the Rocky Mountain region) and internationally (in Argentina, China, Ecuador, Equatorial Guinea, the Mediterranean Sea, and the North Sea).

As of December 31, 2007, NBL had estimated proved reserves of 5.28 Bcfe, of which 63% was natural gas and 74% was proved developed. This compares with estimated proved reserves of 5.01 Bcfe, 65% natural gas and 71% proved developed, at the end of 2006, a 5% increase. We forecast NBL's reserve life to be 12.1 years, compared to 12.8 years at the end of 2006.

In February 2008, NBL estimated its 2007 reserve replacement at 166%. NBL organically replaced 165% of its production in 2007. Reserve additions from all sources in North America were 96 million Boe; international reserve additions from all sources totaled 24 million Boe. Companywide at year-end 2007, reserves were 880 million Boe, and reserve additions from all sources were 120 million Boe, at a finding and development cost of $14.71 per Boe. NBL's production grew 6% in 2007. NBL has been reducing its investment in the Gulf of Mexico's conventional shallow shelf and shifting its domestic offshore explo-

ration focus to deepwater Gulf of Mexico areas. NBL is now a larger, more-diversified company with greater opportunities for both domestic and international growth, in our view, through high-impact exploration drilling as well as lower-risk exploitation projects.

IMPACT OF MAJOR DEVELOPMENTS. On July 14, 2006, NBL closed on a $625 million sale of its Gulf of Mexico shelf assets to Coldren Resources LP. After-tax cash proceeds from the sale totaled $504 million, including proceeds received from parties that exercised preferential rights to purchase certain minor properties.

On May 16, 2005, NBL acquired Patina Oil and Gas Corp. As a result of the transaction, Patina shareholders received 0.6014 of a share of NBL common stock, or $39.3398 in cash, for each Patina share. NBL incurred about $1.7 billion of debt in the deal, of which $1.1 billion funded the cash contribution and $611 million repaid Patina's debt. We estimate that the Patina merger extended NBL's reserve life and made its reserve replacement less dependent on international and Gulf of Mexico projects operated by other companies.

## Company Financials Fiscal Year Ended Dec. 31

| Per Share Data ($) | 2007 | 2006 | 2005 | 2004 | 2003 | 2002 | 2001 | 2000 | 1999 | 1998 |
|---|---|---|---|---|---|---|---|---|---|---|
| Tangible Book Value | 23.51 | 19.35 | 12.68 | 12.37 | 9.38 | 8.80 | 8.86 | 7.58 | 5.99 | 5.64 |
| Cash Flow | 9.65 | 7.27 | 6.61 | 5.26 | 3.47 | 2.62 | 3.64 | 3.72 | 2.65 | 1.31 |
| Earnings | 5.45 | 3.79 | 4.12 | 2.70 | 0.78 | 0.16 | 1.17 | 1.69 | 0.43 | -1.44 |
| S&P Core Earnings | 5.42 | 3.05 | 4.08 | 2.58 | 0.70 | 0.08 | 1.08 | NA | NA | NA |
| Dividends | 0.44 | 0.28 | 0.15 | 0.10 | 0.09 | 0.08 | 0.08 | 0.08 | 0.08 | 0.08 |
| Payout Ratio | 8% | 7% | 4% | 4% | 11% | 52% | 7% | 5% | 19% | NM |
| Prices:High | 81.71 | 54.64 | 48.75 | 32.30 | 23.00 | 20.38 | 25.55 | 24.19 | 17.50 | 23.09 |
| Prices:Low | 46.04 | 36.14 | 27.78 | 21.33 | 16.19 | 13.33 | 13.75 | 9.59 | 9.56 | 10.97 |
| P/E Ratio:High | 15 | 14 | 12 | 12 | 29 | NM | 22 | 14 | 41 | NM |
| P/E Ratio:Low | 8 | 9 | 7 | 8 | 21 | NM | 12 | 6 | 22 | NM |
| **Income Statement Analysis** (Million $) | | | | | | | | | | |
| Revenue | 3,272 | 2,940 | 2,187 | 1,351 | 1,011 | 1,444 | 1,572 | 1,381 | 887 | 894 |
| Operating Income | 2,029 | 2,019 | 1,423 | 884 | 539 | 376 | 535 | 550 | 352 | 315 |
| Depreciation, Depletion and Amortization | 728 | 623 | 391 | 309 | 309 | 285 | 284 | 231 | 255 | 313 |
| Interest Expense | 130 | 117 | 87.5 | 48.2 | 47.0 | 47.7 | 26.0 | 31.6 | 43.0 | 43.8 |
| Pretax Income | 1,368 | 1,096 | 969 | 516 | 142 | 42.6 | 225 | 299 | 77.6 | -247 |
| Effective Tax Rate | 31.0% | 38.1% | 33.3% | 39.2% | 36.5% | 58.6% | 40.5% | 36.0% | 36.3% | NM |
| Net Income | 944 | 678 | 646 | 314 | 89.9 | 17.7 | 134 | 192 | 49.5 | -164 |
| S&P Core Earnings | 938 | 548 | 640 | 305 | 81.0 | 8.88 | 123 | NA | NA | NA |
| **Balance Sheet & Other Financial Data** (Million $) | | | | | | | | | | |
| Cash | 660 | 153 | 110 | 180 | 62.4 | 15.4 | 73.2 | 23.2 | 2.93 | 19.1 |
| Current Assets | 1,569 | 1,069 | 1,176 | 734 | 478 | 310 | 352 | 271 | 148 | 188 |
| Total Assets | 10,831 | 9,589 | 8,878 | 3,443 | 2,843 | 2,730 | 2,480 | 1,879 | 1,450 | 1,686 |
| Current Liabilities | 1,636 | 1,184 | 1,240 | 665 | 655 | 472 | 381 | 325 | 184 | 139 |
| Long Term Debt | 1,851 | 1,801 | 2,031 | 880 | 776 | 977 | 837 | 525 | 445 | 745 |
| Common Equity | 4,809 | 4,114 | 3,231 | 1,460 | 1,074 | 1,009 | 1,010 | 850 | 2,134 | 642 |
| Total Capital | 8,644 | 7,673 | 5,262 | 2,524 | 2,013 | 2,188 | 2,024 | 1,492 | 2,662 | 1,494 |
| Capital Expenditures | 1,415 | 1,357 | 786 | 661 | 527 | 596 | 739 | 537 | 123 | 432 |
| Cash Flow | 1,672 | 1,301 | 1,036 | 623 | 399 | 303 | 418 | 422 | 304 | 149 |
| Current Ratio | 1.0 | 0.9 | 0.9 | 1.1 | 0.7 | 0.7 | 0.9 | 0.8 | 0.8 | 1.4 |
| % Long Term Debt of Capitalization | 21.4 | 23.5 | 38.6 | 34.9 | 38.6 | 44.6 | 41.4 | 35.2 | 16.7 | 49.9 |
| % Return on Assets | 9.2 | 7.3 | 10.5 | 10.0 | 3.2 | 0.7 | 6.1 | 11.6 | 3.2 | NM |
| % Return on Equity | 51.7 | 18.8 | 27.5 | 24.8 | 8.6 | 1.7 | 14.4 | 25.0 | 2.2 | NM |

Data as orig reptd.; bef. results of disc opers/spec. items. Per share data adj. for stk. divs.; EPS diluted. E-Estimated. NA-Not Available. NM-Not Meaningful. NR-Not Ranked. UR-Under Review.

Office: 100 Glenborough Drive, Houston, TX 77067.
Telephone: 281-872-3100.
Email: info@nobleenergyinc.com
Website: http://www.nobleenergyinc.com

Chrmn, Pres & CEO: C.D. Davidson
COO & EVP: D.L. Stover
SVP & CFO: C. Tong
Chief Acctg Officer: F. Bruning

Treas: G.M. Stevenson
Investor Contact: D. Larson (281-872-3100)
Auditor: KPMG
Board Members: J. L. Berenson, M. A. Cawley, E. F. Cox, C. D. Davidson, T. J. Edelman, K. L. Hedrick, S. D. Urban, W. T. Van Kleef

Founded: 1969
Domicile: Delaware
Employees: 1,398

The McGraw-Hill Companies

# Nordstrom Inc.

STANDARD
&POOR'S

| **S&P Recommendation** HOLD ★★★☆☆ | **Price**<br>$11.74 (as of Nov 14, 2008) | **12-Mo. Target Price**<br>$13.00 | **Investment Style**<br>Large-Cap Growth |
|---|---|---|---|

**GICS Sector** Consumer Discretionary
**Sub-Industry** Department Stores

**Summary** This Seattle-based specialty retailer of apparel and accessories, widely known for its emphasis on service, operates about 159 stores in 28 states.

## Key Stock Statistics (Source S&P, Vickers, company reports)

| | | | | | | | | |
|---|---|---|---|---|---|---|---|---|
| 52-Wk Range | $40.59–11.10 | S&P Oper. EPS 2009**E** | 1.87 | Market Capitalization(B) | $2.530 | Beta | 1.49 |
| Trailing 12-Month EPS | $2.79 | S&P Oper. EPS 2010**E** | 1.60 | Yield (%) | 5.45 | S&P 3-Yr. Proj. EPS CAGR(%) | 0 |
| Trailing 12-Month P/E | 4.2 | P/E on S&P Oper. EPS 2009**E** | 6.3 | Dividend Rate/Share | $0.64 | S&P Credit Rating | A- |
| $10K Invested 5 Yrs Ago | $8,013 | Common Shares Outstg. (M) | 215.5 | Institutional Ownership (%) | 79 | | |

## Price Performance

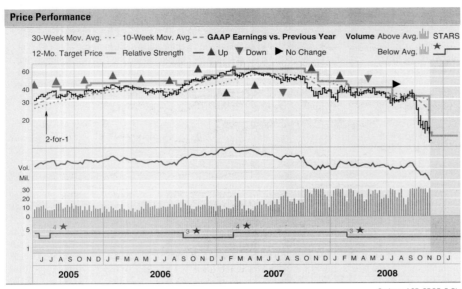

Options: ASE, CBOE, P, Ph

## Qualitative Risk Assessment

| LOW | MEDIUM | HIGH |
|---|---|---|

Our risk assessment reflects our view of JWN's improving sales and profit margins, increasing market share in the better department store sector, and healthy balance sheet and cash flow. This is offset by uncertainty over consumer discretionary spending in light of higher interest rates and debt levels.

## Quantitative Evaluations

**S&P Quality Ranking** A-

| D | C | B- | B | B+ | A- | A | A+ |
|---|---|---|---|---|---|---|---|

**Relative Strength Rank** WEAK

16

LOWEST = 1                    HIGHEST = 99

## Revenue/Earnings Data

**Revenue (Million $)**

| | 1Q | 2Q | 3Q | 4Q | Year |
|---|---|---|---|---|---|
| 2009 | 1,879 | 2,287 | -- | -- | -- |
| 2008 | 1,954 | 2,390 | 1,970 | 2,514 | 8,828 |
| 2007 | 1,787 | 2,270 | 1,872 | 2,631 | 8,561 |
| 2006 | 1,654 | 2,106 | 1,666 | 2,296 | 7,723 |
| 2005 | 1,535 | 1,953 | 1,542 | 2,100 | 7,131 |
| 2004 | 1,344 | 1,795 | 1,421 | 1,933 | 6,492 |

**Earnings Per Share ($)**

| | 1Q | 2Q | 3Q | 4Q | Year |
|---|---|---|---|---|---|
| 2009 | 0.54 | 0.65 | E0.34 | E0.57 | E1.87 |
| 2008 | 0.60 | 0.65 | 0.68 | 0.92 | 2.88 |
| 2007 | 0.48 | 0.67 | 0.52 | 0.89 | 2.55 |
| 2006 | 0.38 | 0.53 | 0.39 | 0.69 | 1.98 |
| 2005 | 0.24 | 0.38 | 0.27 | 0.50 | 1.39 |
| 2004 | 0.10 | 0.24 | 0.17 | 0.37 | 0.88 |

Fiscal year ended Jan. 31. Next earnings report expected: Late November. EPS Estimates based on S&P Operating Earnings; historical GAAP earnings are as reported.

## Highlights

➤ The 12-month target price for JWN has recently been changed to $13.00 from $14.00. The Highlights section of this Stock Report will be updated accordingly.

## Investment Rationale/Risk

➤ The Investment Rationale/Risk section of this Stock Report will be updated shortly. For the latest News story on JWN from MarketScope, see below.

➤ 11/14/08 12:58 pm ET ... S&P MAINTAINS HOLD OPINION ON SHARES OF NORDSTROM INC (JWN 12.05***): Oct-Q EPS of $0.33 vs. $0.59 misses our estimate by a penny. We see some underlying positives in JWN's business, including an improving value proposition on high-quality merchandise, terrific customer service, and now, a lower capex plan for FY 10 (Jan.). But we think it will take a few more quarters of heavy markdowns before inventories are more closely aligned with forecasted sales declines. We cut our FY 09 EPS estimate by $0.23 to $1.87 and FY 10's by $0.40 to $1.60. We also lower our historical P/E-based 12-month target price by $1 to $13. /J.Asaeda

## Dividend Data (Dates: mm/dd Payment Date: mm/dd/yy)

| Amount ($) | Date Decl. | Ex-Div. Date | Stk. of Record | Payment Date |
|---|---|---|---|---|
| 0.135 | 11/19 | 11/28 | 11/30 | 12/14/07 |
| 0.160 | 02/20 | 02/27 | 02/29 | 03/14/08 |
| 0.160 | 05/20 | 05/28 | 05/30 | 06/16/08 |
| 0.160 | 08/19 | 08/27 | 08/29 | 09/15/08 |

Dividends have been paid since 1971. Source: Company reports.

# Nordstrom Inc.

STANDARD
&POOR'S

## Business Summary August 25, 2008

CORPORATE OVERVIEW. In our view, JWN is the clear leader in the U.S. better department store sector, reflecting its focus on high-quality, differentiated merchandise; personalized customer service; and a consistent upscale shopping experience across its entire Nordstrom store base. The company derives its revenues from retail, credit and direct sales channels. JWN formerly owned Faconnable, a wholly owned wholesaler and retailer of high-quality men's, women's and boy's apparel and accessories. In FY 08 (Jan.), merchandise category sales were: women's apparel 35%; shoes 20%; men's apparel 18%; women's accessories 11%; cosmetics 11%; children's apparel 3%; and other 2%.

IMPACT OF MAJOR DEVELOPMENTS. JWN spends about $150 million annually on information technology (IT). In FY 03, the company invested in a perpetual inventory system that has enabled its merchant teams to more accurately forecast sales trends and to better track and plan store-level inventory and expenses, resulting in improved sales performance and profitability, in our

opinion. In FY 05, JWN put into place a new point of sales system that includes Personal Book, a tool that allows salespeople to tailor service to the needs of each customer by organizing and tracking customer preferences, purchases, and contact information. The company has noted that Personal Book has driven incremental sales volume.

In July 2007, JWN agreed to sell Faconnable to M1 Group, a Lebanon-based, family-owned diversified business, for $210 million. As part of the agreement, JWN will continue to buy Faconnable merchandise at historical levels for at least the next three years and will continue to offer Faconnable in Nordstrom stores. The company realized a gain of $33.9 million on the sale ($0.09 per share, after-tax), which closed in the third quarter of FY 08.

## Company Financials Fiscal Year Ended Jan. 31

### Per Share Data ($)

| | 2008 | 2007 | 2006 | 2005 | 2004 | 2003 | 2002 | 2001 | 2000 | 1999 |
|---|---|---|---|---|---|---|---|---|---|---|
| Tangible Book Value | 4.81 | 7.90 | 7.26 | 6.10 | 5.40 | 4.55 | 4.38 | 4.06 | 4.49 | 4.63 |
| Cash Flow | NA | 3.62 | 2.98 | 2.31 | 1.78 | 1.24 | 1.27 | 1.16 | 1.44 | 1.32 |
| Earnings | 2.88 | 2.55 | 1.98 | 1.39 | 0.88 | 0.38 | 0.46 | 0.39 | 0.73 | 0.71 |
| S&P Core Earnings | 2.80 | 2.55 | 1.93 | 2.62 | 1.67 | 0.62 | 0.80 | 0.83 | NA | NA |
| Dividends | 0.42 | 0.32 | 0.24 | 0.21 | 0.21 | 0.19 | 0.18 | 0.16 | 0.18 | 0.15 |
| Payout Ratio | 15% | 13% | 12% | 15% | 23% | 50% | 38% | 41% | 24% | 21% |
| Calendar Year | 2007 | 2006 | 2005 | 2004 | 2003 | 2002 | 2001 | 2000 | 1999 | 1998 |
| Prices:High | 59.70 | 51.40 | 39.00 | 23.68 | 17.75 | 13.44 | 11.49 | 17.25 | 22.41 | 20.19 |
| Prices:Low | 30.46 | 31.77 | 22.71 | 16.55 | 7.50 | 7.80 | 6.90 | 7.06 | 10.84 | 10.71 |
| P/E Ratio:High | 21 | 20 | 20 | 17 | 20 | 35 | 25 | 44 | 31 | 29 |
| P/E Ratio:Low | 11 | 12 | 11 | 12 | 9 | 20 | 15 | 18 | 15 | 15 |

### Income Statement Analysis (Million $)

| | | | | | | | | | | |
|---|---|---|---|---|---|---|---|---|---|---|
| Revenue | 8,828 | 8,561 | 7,723 | 7,131 | 6,492 | 5,975 | 5,634 | 5,529 | 5,124 | 5,028 |
| Operating Income | NA | 1,195 | 1,010 | 817 | 585 | 424 | 363 | 335 | 467 | 458 |
| Depreciation | 269 | 285 | 276 | 265 | 251 | 234 | 218 | 203 | 194 | 180 |
| Interest Expense | NA | 62.4 | 45.3 | 85.4 | 91.0 | 86.2 | 73.5 | 63.0 | 54.0 | 49.0 |
| Pretax Income | 1,173 | 1,106 | 885 | 647 | 398 | 196 | 204 | 167 | 332 | 338 |
| Effective Tax Rate | 39.1% | 38.7% | 37.7% | 39.2% | 39.0% | 47.1% | 39.0% | 38.9% | 38.9% | 38.8% |
| Net Income | 715 | 678 | 551 | 393 | 243 | 104 | 125 | 102 | 203 | 207 |
| S&P Core Earnings | 697 | 677 | 536 | 373 | 229 | 83.9 | 107 | 109 | NA | NA |

### Balance Sheet & Other Financial Data (Million $)

| | | | | | | | | | | |
|---|---|---|---|---|---|---|---|---|---|---|
| Cash | 358 | 403 | 463 | 361 | 476 | 208 | 331 | 25.0 | 27.0 | 241 |
| Current Assets | NA | 2,742 | 2,874 | 2,572 | 2,455 | 2,073 | 2,055 | 1,813 | 1,565 | 1,680 |
| Total Assets | 5,600 | 4,822 | 4,921 | 4,605 | 4,466 | 4,096 | 4,049 | 3,608 | 3,062 | 3,115 |
| Current Liabilities | NA | 1,433 | 1,623 | 1,341 | 1,050 | 870 | 948 | 951 | 867 | 769 |
| Long Term Debt | NA | 624 | 628 | 929 | 1,605 | 1,342 | 1,351 | 1,100 | 747 | 805 |
| Common Equity | 1,115 | 2,169 | 2,093 | 1,789 | 1,634 | 1,372 | 1,314 | 1,229 | 1,185 | 1,317 |
| Total Capital | NA | 2,792 | 2,720 | 2,718 | 3,239 | 2,714 | 2,666 | 2,329 | 1,932 | 2,122 |
| Capital Expenditures | 501 | 264 | 272 | 247 | 258 | 328 | 390 | 321 | 305 | 291 |
| Cash Flow | NA | 963 | 828 | 658 | 494 | 338 | 342 | 305 | 397 | 387 |
| Current Ratio | 2.1 | 1.9 | 1.8 | 1.9 | 2.3 | 2.4 | 2.2 | 1.9 | 1.8 | 2.2 |
| % Long Term Debt of Capitalization | 61.9 | 22.3 | 23.1 | 34.2 | 49.5 | 49.4 | 50.7 | 47.2 | 38.7 | 37.9 |
| % Net Income of Revenue | 8.1 | 7.9 | 7.1 | 5.5 | 3.7 | 1.7 | 2.2 | 1.8 | 4.0 | 4.1 |
| % Return on Assets | 13.7 | 13.9 | 11.6 | 8.6 | 5.7 | 2.5 | 3.3 | 3.1 | 6.6 | 6.9 |
| % Return on Equity | 43.6 | 31.8 | 28.4 | 23.0 | 16.2 | 7.7 | 9.8 | 8.5 | 16.3 | 14.8 |

Data as orig reptd.; bef. results of disc opers/spec. items. Per share data adj. for stk. divs.; EPS diluted. E-Estimated. NA-Not Available. NM-Not Meaningful. NR-Not Ranked. UR-Under Review.

**Office:** 1617 Sixth Ave, Seattle, WA 98101-1707.
**Telephone:** 206-628-2111.
**Email:** invrelations@nordstrom.com
**Website:** http://www.nordstrom.com

**Chrmn:** E. Hernandez, Jr.
**Pres & CEO:** B.W. Nordstrom
**EVP & CFO:** M.G. Koppel
**EVP & Chief Admin Officer:** D.F. Little

**EVP, Secy & General Counsel:** L.G. Iglesias
**Investor Contact:** C. Holloway (206-303-3200)
**Board Members:** P. Campbell, E. Hernandez, Jr., J. P. Jackson, R. G. Miller, B. W. Nordstrom, E. B. Nordstrom, P. E. Nordstrom, P. G. Satre, A. A. Winter

**Founded:** 1901
**Domicile:** Washington
**Employees:** 55,000

The McGraw-Hill Companies

# Norfolk Southern Corp

**STANDARD &POOR'S**

**S&P Recommendation** BUY ★★★★☆

| | | |
|---|---|---|
| **Price** $51.98 (as of Nov 14, 2008) | **12-Mo. Target Price** $75.00 | **Investment Style** Large-Cap Blend |

**GICS Sector** Industrials
**Sub-Industry** Railroads

**Summary** This railroad operates 21,200 route miles serving 22 eastern states, the District of Columbia, and Ontario, Canada.

## Key Stock Statistics (Source S&P, Vickers, company reports)

| | | | | | | | |
|---|---|---|---|---|---|---|---|
| 52-Wk Range | $75.53–41.36 | S&P Oper. EPS 2008**E** | 4.43 | Market Capitalization(B) | $19.247 | Beta | 0.97 |
| Trailing 12-Month EPS | $4.33 | S&P Oper. EPS 2009**E** | 4.87 | Yield (%) | 2.46 | S&P 3-Yr. Proj. EPS CAGR(%) | 12 |
| Trailing 12-Month P/E | 12.0 | P/E on S&P Oper. EPS 2008**E** | 11.7 | Dividend Rate/Share | $1.28 | S&P Credit Rating | BBB+ |
| $10K Invested 5 Yrs Ago | $26,656 | Common Shares Outstg. (M) | 370.3 | Institutional Ownership (%) | 71 | | |

## Price Performance

30-Week Mov. Avg. · · · ·    10-Week Mov. Avg. - - -    **GAAP Earnings vs. Previous Year**    Volume Above Avg. ▎▍▌ STARS
12-Mo. Target Price —    Relative Strength —    ▲ Up    ▼ Down    ▶ No Change    Below Avg. ▎▍▌    ★

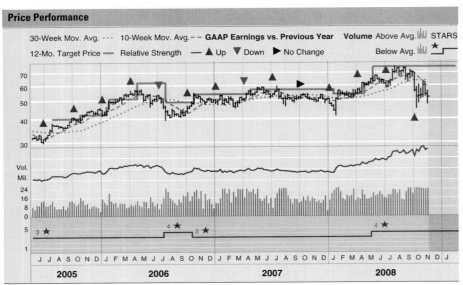

Options: ASE, CBOE, P, Ph

Analysis prepared by **Kevin Kirkeby** on September 29, 2008, when the stock traded at **$ 65.50**.

## Highlights

➤ We consider NSC to be on track for revenue growth of 13% in 2008, with nearly all of the increase coming from pricing and fuel surcharges. Volumes will be modestly negative this year, in our view, due mostly to construction and automotive weakness. Our forecast for 6.5% revenue growth in 2009 reflects a modest rise in volumes and a flattening in the growth of fuel surcharges. Volume gains from the restart of several coal mines and additional exports are expected to continue into 2009. Likewise, we see NSC gaining additional intermodal traffic due to route changes by ocean carriers.

➤ We see operating margins relatively flat for the remainder of 2008 as rising wages are offset by improved asset utilization rates and a stabilizing in diesel prices. Margins should receive a boost during 2009 as fuel prices moderate and fuel cost recovery mechanisms catch up, in our view.

➤ Net interest expenses are likely to increase in 2008 and 2009 as share repurchases reduce its cash position. As of June 2008, NSC had 20 million shares remaining under its buyback authorization.

## Investment Rationale/Risk

➤ Medium-term trends in NSC's primary markets remain favorable and support rising traffic and prices, in our opinion. We see investments in its network improving capacity on heavily trafficked lines like the Heartland Corridor, and leading to higher railcar utilization and greater system fluidity. Looking beyond near-term weakness in NSC's autos and intermodal segments, we believe a valuation near the historical high, and in line with peers is warranted.

➤ Risks to our recommendation and target price include weaker-than-anticipated coal shipments, rising competition in its shorter routes where trucks are able to compete effectively, severe weather, a new round of production cuts by auto manufacturers, and unfavorable changes in regulatory framework.

➤ Blending a forward P/E of about 17.5X our next 12 months EPS estimate, at the five-year high but near the peer average, with our DCF model, which assumes a 8.9% weighted average cost of capital, 14% average EPS growth over the next five years and a 3.5% terminal growth rate (yielding an intrinsic value of $71), we arrive at our 12-month target price of $75.

## Qualitative Risk Assessment

| LOW | **MEDIUM** | HIGH |
|---|---|---|

Our risk assessment reflects what we see as NSC's exposure to economic cycles, regulations, labor and fuel costs, significant capital expenditure requirements, and challenges in maintaining system fluidity, offset by our view of a diverse customer base, historically positive free cash flow, and moderate financial leverage.

## Quantitative Evaluations

**S&P Quality Ranking**    B+

| D | C | B- | B | **B+** | A- | A | A+ |
|---|---|---|---|---|---|---|---|

**Relative Strength Rank**    MODERATE

68

LOWEST = 1    HIGHEST = 99

## Revenue/Earnings Data

**Revenue (Million $)**

| | 1Q | 2Q | 3Q | 4Q | Year |
|---|---|---|---|---|---|
| 2008 | 2,500 | 2,765 | 2,894 | -- | -- |
| 2007 | 2,247 | 2,378 | 2,353 | 2,454 | 9,432 |
| 2006 | 2,303 | 2,392 | 2,393 | 2,319 | 9,407 |
| 2005 | 1,961 | 2,154 | 2,155 | 2,257 | 8,527 |
| 2004 | 1,693 | 1,813 | 1,857 | 1,949 | 7,312 |
| 2003 | 1,561 | 1,633 | 1,598 | 1,676 | 6,468 |

**Earnings Per Share ($)**

| | | | | | |
|---|---|---|---|---|---|
| 2008 | 0.76 | 1.18 | 1.37 | E1.12 | E4.43 |
| 2007 | 0.71 | 0.98 | 1.02 | 1.02 | 3.68 |
| 2006 | 0.72 | 0.89 | 1.02 | 0.95 | 3.57 |
| 2005 | 0.47 | 1.04 | 0.73 | 0.87 | 3.11 |
| 2004 | 0.40 | 0.54 | 0.72 | 0.65 | 2.31 |
| 2003 | 0.54 | 0.35 | 0.35 | 0.13 | 1.05 |

Fiscal year ended Dec. 31. Next earnings report expected: Late January. EPS Estimates based on S&P Operating Earnings; historical GAAP earnings are as reported.

## Dividend Data (Dates: mm/dd Payment Date: mm/dd/yy)

| Amount ($) | Date Decl. | Ex-Div. Date | Stk. of Record | Payment Date |
|---|---|---|---|---|
| 0.290 | 01/22 | 01/30 | 02/01 | 03/10/08 |
| 0.290 | 04/22 | 04/30 | 05/02 | 06/10/08 |
| 0.320 | 07/22 | 07/30 | 08/01 | 09/10/08 |
| 0.320 | 10/21 | 11/05 | 11/07 | 12/10/08 |

Dividends have been paid since 1901. Source: Company reports.

Please read the **Required Disclosures and Analyst Certification** on the last page of this report.

**The McGraw-Hill Companies**

# Norfolk Southern Corp

STANDARD
&POOR'S

## Business Summary September 29, 2008

CORPORATE OVERVIEW. Norfolk Southern provides rail transportation service in the eastern U.S., operating over 21,000 miles of road, with an extensive intermodal and coal service network and a significant general freight business, including an automotive business that is the largest in North America. NSC owns 58% of Conrail's shares, with CSX holding the remainder, and holds 50% voting rights. NSC and CSX operate separate portions of Conrail's rail routes and assets. NSC's non-rail activities includes real estate and natural resources.

MARKET PROFILE. We believe NSC's intermodal business, representing 20% of 2007 freight revenues, will be NSC's fastest-growing segment longer term, driven by rising international trade and its cost savings over trucks for long-distance container movements. We think the superior system fluidity of its extensive intermodal network on the East Coast, supported by ongoing investment in facilities, will provide NSC with a continuing edge in garnering East Coast intermodal traffic. Coal, which we believe is NSC's most profitable segment, accounted for 25% of 2007 freight revenues. Most of this traffic originates from the Appalachian coal fields, and is primarily delivered to power utilities. General merchandise, sensitive to U.S. GDP trends, provided 55% of freight revenues in 2007. We believe chemicals and automotive, representing

12% and 10% of 2007 freight revenues, respectively, are significant general merchandise subsegments that are facing low long-term volume growth prospects. We consider NSC to have considerable exposure to the auto market since it serves 29 assembly plants, the majority of which belong to the domestic manufacturers Ford, Chrysler and General Motors.

COMPETITIVE LANDSCAPE. The U.S. rail industry has an oligopoly-like structure, with over 80% of revenues generated by the four largest railroads: NSC and CSX Corp. operating on the East Coast, and Union Pacific Corp. and Burlington Northern Santa Fe Corp. operating on the West Coast. Railroads simultaneously compete for customers while cooperating by sharing assets, interfacing systems, and completing customer movements. Key suppliers include locomotive and rail equipment manufacturers, fuel suppliers, and labor. NSC's employees, about 85% of whom are unionized, enjoy above national average compensation due to their significant bargaining power.

## Company Financials Fiscal Year Ended Dec. 31

### Per Share Data ($)

| | 2007 | 2006 | 2005 | 2004 | 2003 | 2002 | 2001 | 2000 | 1999 | 1998 |
|---|---|---|---|---|---|---|---|---|---|---|
| Tangible Book Value | 27.12 | 24.19 | 22.66 | 19.98 | 17.83 | 16.71 | 15.78 | 15.17 | 15.53 | 15.61 |
| Cash Flow | 5.63 | 5.50 | 5.02 | 3.83 | 2.40 | 2.50 | 2.27 | 1.80 | 1.91 | 2.83 |
| Earnings | 3.68 | 3.57 | 3.11 | 2.31 | 1.05 | 1.18 | 0.94 | 0.45 | 0.63 | 1.65 |
| S&P Core Earnings | 3.48 | 3.43 | 2.97 | 2.13 | 0.95 | 0.70 | 0.41 | NA | NA | NA |
| Dividends | 0.96 | 0.68 | 0.48 | 0.46 | 0.30 | 0.26 | 0.24 | 0.80 | 0.80 | 0.80 |
| Payout Ratio | 26% | 19% | 15% | 20% | 29% | 22% | 26% | 178% | 127% | 48% |
| Prices:High | 59.77 | 57.71 | 45.81 | 36.69 | 24.62 | 26.98 | 24.11 | 22.75 | 36.44 | 41.75 |
| Prices:Low | 45.38 | 39.10 | 29.60 | 20.38 | 17.35 | 17.20 | 13.41 | 11.94 | 19.63 | 27.44 |
| P/E Ratio:High | 16 | 16 | 15 | 16 | 23 | 23 | 26 | 51 | 58 | 25 |
| P/E Ratio:Low | 12 | 11 | 10 | 9 | 17 | 15 | 14 | 27 | 31 | 17 |

### Income Statement Analysis (Million $)

| | 2007 | 2006 | 2005 | 2004 | 2003 | 2002 | 2001 | 2000 | 1999 | 1998 |
|---|---|---|---|---|---|---|---|---|---|---|
| Revenue | 9,406 | 9,407 | 8,527 | 7,312 | 6,468 | 6,270 | 6,170 | 6,159 | 5,195 | 4,221 |
| Operating Income | 3,334 | 3,307 | 2,904 | 2,311 | 1,592 | 1,158 | 1,521 | 1,150 | 1,207 | 1,502 |
| Depreciation | 775 | 750 | 787 | 609 | 528 | 515 | 514 | 517 | 489 | 450 |
| Interest Expense | 482 | 493 | 500 | 506 | 497 | 518 | 553 | 551 | 561 | 516 |
| Pretax Income | 2,237 | 2,230 | 1,697 | 1,302 | 586 | 706 | 553 | 250 | 351 | 845 |
| Effective Tax Rate | 34.6% | 33.6% | 24.5% | 29.1% | 29.9% | 34.8% | 34.5% | 31.2% | 31.9% | 25.4% |
| Net Income | 1,464 | 1,481 | 1,281 | 923 | 411 | 460 | 362 | 172 | 239 | 630 |
| S&P Core Earnings | 1,377 | 1,417 | 1,224 | 849 | 365 | 270 | 155 | NA | NA | NA |

### Balance Sheet & Other Financial Data (Million $)

| | 2007 | 2006 | 2005 | 2004 | 2003 | 2002 | 2001 | 2000 | 1999 | 1998 |
|---|---|---|---|---|---|---|---|---|---|---|
| Cash | 206 | 527 | 289 | 579 | 284 | 184 | 204 | Nil | 37.0 | 5.00 |
| Current Assets | 1,675 | 2,400 | 2,650 | 1,967 | 1,425 | 1,299 | 1,047 | 849 | 1,371 | 913 |
| Total Assets | 26,144 | 26,028 | 25,861 | 24,750 | 20,596 | 19,956 | 19,418 | 18,976 | 19,250 | 18,180 |
| Current Liabilities | 1,948 | 2,093 | 1,921 | 2,201 | 1,801 | 1,853 | 2,386 | 1,887 | 1,924 | 1,117 |
| Long Term Debt | 6,132 | 6,109 | 6,616 | 6,863 | 6,800 | 7,006 | 7,027 | 7,339 | 7,556 | 7,483 |
| Common Equity | 9,727 | 9,615 | 9,289 | 7,990 | 6,976 | 6,500 | 6,090 | 5,824 | 5,932 | 5,921 |
| Total Capital | 22,290 | 22,168 | 22,525 | 21,403 | 17,008 | 16,561 | 15,943 | 15,958 | 16,225 | 15,998 |
| Capital Expenditures | 1,341 | 1,178 | 1,025 | 1,041 | 720 | 689 | 746 | 731 | 912 | 956 |
| Cash Flow | 2,239 | 2,231 | 2,068 | 1,532 | 939 | 975 | 876 | 689 | 728 | 1,080 |
| Current Ratio | 0.9 | 1.1 | 1.4 | 0.9 | 0.8 | 0.7 | 0.4 | 0.4 | 0.7 | 0.8 |
| % Long Term Debt of Capitalization | 27.5 | 27.6 | 29.4 | 32.1 | 40.0 | 42.3 | 44.1 | 46.0 | 46.6 | 46.8 |
| % Net Income of Revenue | 15.6 | 15.7 | 15.0 | 12.6 | 6.4 | 7.3 | 5.9 | 2.8 | 4.6 | 14.9 |
| % Return on Assets | 5.6 | 5.7 | 5.1 | 4.1 | 2.0 | 2.3 | 1.9 | 0.9 | 1.3 | 3.5 |
| % Return on Equity | 15.1 | 15.7 | 14.8 | 12.3 | 6.1 | 7.3 | 6.1 | 2.9 | 4.0 | 11.1 |

Data as orig reptd.; bef. results of disc opers/spec. items. Per share data adj. for stk. divs.; EPS diluted. E-Estimated. NA-Not Available. NM-Not Meaningful. NR-Not Ranked. UR-Under Review.

**Office:** 3 Commercial Pl, Norfolk, VA 23510-2191.
**Telephone:** 757-629-2680.
**Website:** http://www.nscorp.com
**Chrmn, Pres & CEO:** C.W. Moorman, IV

**COO:** S.C. Tobias
**EVP & CFO:** J.A. Squires
**EVP & CIO:** D.H. Butler
**Chief Admin Officer:** J.P. Rathbone

**Investor Contact:** M. Parkerson (757-533-4939)
**Board Members:** G. L. Baliles, D. A. Carp, G. R. Carter, A. D. Correll, L. Hilliard, K. N. Horn, B. M. Joyce, S. F. Leer, M. D. Lockhart, C. W. Moorman, IV, J. P. Reason

**Founded:** 1980
**Domicile:** Virginia
**Employees:** 30,806

# Northern Trust Corp

STANDARD
&POOR'S

| S&P Recommendation | HOLD ★★★☆☆ | Price $44.92 (as of Nov 14, 2008) | 12-Mo. Target Price $65.00 | Investment Style Large-Cap Growth |
|---|---|---|---|---|

**GICS Sector** Financials
**Sub-Industry** Asset Management & Custody Banks

**Summary** Northern Trust is a leading provider of fiduciary, asset management and private banking services.

## Key Stock Statistics (Source S&P, Vickers, company reports)

| | | | | | | | |
|---|---|---|---|---|---|---|---|
| 52-Wk Range | $88.92– 43.02 | S&P Oper. EPS 2008E | 2.47 | Market Capitalization(B) | $10.019 | Beta | 1.10 |
| Trailing 12-Month EPS | $2.56 | S&P Oper. EPS 2009E | 3.99 | Yield (%) | 2.49 | S&P 3-Yr. Proj. EPS CAGR(%) | 11 |
| Trailing 12-Month P/E | 17.6 | P/E on S&P Oper. EPS 2008E | 18.2 | Dividend Rate/Share | $1.12 | S&P Credit Rating | AA- |
| $10K Invested 5 Yrs Ago | $10,744 | Common Shares Outstg. (M) | 223.0 | Institutional Ownership (%) | 73 | | |

## Price Performance

- 30-Week Mov. Avg. · · ·
- 10-Week Mov. Avg. - -
- **GAAP Earnings vs. Previous Year**
- Volume Above Avg.
- STARS
- 12-Mo. Target Price —
- Relative Strength —
- ▲ Up ▼ Down ► No Change
- Below Avg.

Options: ASE, CBOE, P, Ph

Analysis prepared by **Stuart Plesser** on October 29, 2008, when the stock traded at **$ 56.55**.

### Highlights

➤ In 2009, we look for double-digit average earning asset growth, new business wins, offset by a decline in NTRS' securities lending fees and below historical growth in assets under management. All told, we look for revenue growth of 4% in 2009 down from projected 13.7% in 2008. We expect new business wins to increase in light of disruptions at its competitors. We forecast a 13% decrease in non-interest expense in 2009, assuming the absence of client support charges.

➤ Asset quality has remained solid, with nonperforming assets as a percent of total loans and other real estate owned at 0.21% in the third quarter. New international business growth and foreign exchange trading income should support solid domestic growth, and we expect Northern Trust's private client business to make up an increasing portion of its business. We expect a slightly lower effective tax rate due to NTRS' growing international exposure.

➤ We estimate operating EPS of $2.47 in 2008, versus $3.61 in 2007. For 2009, we look for EPS of $3.99.

### Investment Rationale/Risk

➤ We have a positive view of the company's product and geographic diversity. We believe the company's leading position in the affluent market, should result in above-peers average revenue. We are also encouraged by the defensive positioning of NTRS' securities portfolio. We are cautious, however, about a reduction of funds under management due to recent market declines. We also are wary of the possibility that NTRS will need to continue to support its clients in light of turmoil in the credit markets. Although we look at the government's purchase of $1.5 billion of preferred stock with a 5% coupon as inexpensive capital, it is unclear at present how NTRS will deploy the capital.

➤ Risks to our recommendation and target price include a failure to generate new business from existing and new clients, a significant decline in economic activity, legal and regulatory risks.

➤ Over the past five years, on average, the shares have traded at 20.9X their trailing 12-month EPS. Our 12-month target price of $65 is equal to approximately 16.2X our 2009 EPS estimate of $3.99, a discount to its historical average, we think justified by credit turmoil.

## Qualitative Risk Assessment

| LOW | MEDIUM | HIGH |
|---|---|---|

Our risk assessment reflects what we see as solid business fundamentals and a strong customer base. We view NTRS as well diversified geographically and able to withstand a major economic downturn.

## Quantitative Evaluations

**S&P Quality Ranking** A-

| D | C | B- | B | B+ | A- | A | A+ |
|---|---|---|---|---|---|---|---|

**Relative Strength Rank** MODERATE

38

LOWEST = 1          HIGHEST = 99

## Revenue/Earnings Data

**Revenue (Million $)**

| | 1Q | 2Q | 3Q | 4Q | Year |
|---|---|---|---|---|---|
| 2008 | 1,146 | -- | -- | -- | -- |
| 2007 | 1,250 | 1,338 | 1,385 | 1,699 | 5,395 |
| 2006 | 1,030 | 1,134 | 1,117 | 1,192 | 4,473 |
| 2005 | 792.9 | 902.4 | 912.0 | 947.1 | 3,554 |
| 2004 | 680.9 | 695.9 | 686.7 | 765.6 | 2,829 |
| 2003 | 630.2 | 671.3 | 645.9 | 650.5 | 2,598 |

**Earnings Per Share ($)**

| | | | | | |
|---|---|---|---|---|---|
| 2008 | 1.71 | 0.96 | -0.67 | E1.07 | E2.47 |
| 2007 | 0.84 | 0.92 | 0.93 | 0.55 | 3.24 |
| 2006 | 0.74 | 0.76 | 0.74 | 0.77 | 3.00 |
| 2005 | 0.63 | 0.68 | 0.67 | 0.67 | 2.64 |
| 2004 | 0.57 | 0.59 | 0.52 | 0.59 | 2.26 |
| 2003 | 0.43 | 0.36 | 0.51 | 0.58 | 1.89 |

Fiscal year ended Dec. 31. Next earnings report expected: NA. EPS Estimates based on S&P Operating Earnings; historical GAAP earnings are as reported.

## Dividend Data (Dates: mm/dd Payment Date: mm/dd/yy)

| Amount ($) | Date Decl. | Ex-Div. Date | Stk. of Record | Payment Date |
|---|---|---|---|---|
| 0.280 | 02/19 | 03/06 | 03/10 | 04/01/08 |
| 0.280 | 04/15 | 06/06 | 06/10 | 07/01/08 |
| 0.280 | 07/15 | 09/08 | 09/10 | 10/01/08 |
| 0.280 | 10/21 | 12/08 | 12/10 | 01/02/09 |

Dividends have been paid since 1896. Source: Company reports.

---

# Northern Trust Corp

**STANDARD &POOR'S**

## Business Summary October 29, 2008

CORPORATE OVERVIEW. NTRS organizes its services globally around its two principal business units: Corporate and Institutional Services (C&IS) and Personal Financial Services (PFS). C&IS is a leading worldwide provider of asset servicing, asset management and related services to corporate and public entity retirement funds, foundation and endowment clients, fund managers, insurance companies and government funds. C&IS also offers a full range of commercial banking services through the bank, placing special emphasis on developing and supporting institutional relationships in two target markets: large and mid-sized corporations and financial institutions (both U.S. and non-U.S.). Asset servicing, asset management and related services encompass a full range of capabilities including: global master trust and custody, trade, settlement, and reporting; fund administration,; cash management; and investment risk and performance analytical services.

In 2005, NTRS completed its acquisition of the Financial Services Group Limited (FSG) from Baring Asset Management Holdings Limited. The purchase of FSG brought to C&IS expanded capabilities in institutional fund administration,

custody, trust and related services as well as new capabilities in hedge fund and private equity administration, in our view.

PFS provides personal trust, investment management, custody and philanthropic services; financial consulting; guardianship and estate administration; qualified retirement plans; banking (including private banking); personal lending; and residential real estate mortgage lending. PFS focuses on high net worth individuals, business owners, executives, retirees and established privately-held businesses in its target markets. PFS also includes the Wealth Management Group, which provides customized products and services to meet the complex financial needs of families and individuals in the U.S. and throughout the world, with assets typically exceeding $75 million.

## Company Financials Fiscal Year Ended Dec. 31

| Per Share Data ($) | 2007 | 2006 | 2005 | 2004 | 2003 | 2002 | 2001 | 2000 | 1999 | 1998 |
|---|---|---|---|---|---|---|---|---|---|---|
| Tangible Book Value | 18.50 | 15.53 | 14.72 | 14.14 | 13.88 | 13.04 | 11.97 | 10.54 | 9.25 | 7.54 |
| Earnings | 3.24 | 3.00 | 2.64 | 2.26 | 1.89 | 1.97 | 2.11 | 2.08 | 1.74 | 1.52 |
| S&P Core Earnings | 3.69 | 3.04 | 2.51 | 2.19 | 1.63 | 1.64 | 1.82 | NA | NA | NA |
| Dividends | 1.03 | 0.94 | 0.86 | 0.78 | 0.70 | 0.68 | 0.64 | 0.56 | 0.48 | 0.42 |
| Payout Ratio | 32% | 31% | 33% | 35% | 37% | 35% | 30% | 27% | 28% | 28% |
| Prices:High | 83.17 | 61.40 | 55.00 | 51.35 | 48.75 | 62.67 | 82.25 | 92.13 | 54.63 | 44.94 |
| Prices:Low | 56.52 | 49.12 | 41.60 | 38.40 | 27.64 | 30.41 | 41.40 | 46.75 | 40.16 | 27.88 |
| P/E Ratio:High | 26 | 20 | 21 | 23 | 26 | 32 | 39 | 44 | 31 | 30 |
| P/E Ratio:Low | 17 | 16 | 16 | 17 | 15 | 15 | 20 | 22 | 23 | 18 |

| Income Statement Analysis (Million $) | 2007 | 2006 | 2005 | 2004 | 2003 | 2002 | 2001 | 2000 | 1999 | 1998 |
|---|---|---|---|---|---|---|---|---|---|---|
| Net Interest Income | 832 | 730 | 661 | 561 | 548 | 602 | 595 | 569 | 519 | 477 |
| Tax Equivalent Adjustment | 62.5 | 64.8 | 60.9 | 54.4 | 52.4 | 48.7 | 52.6 | 53.3 | 38.6 | 35.9 |
| Non Interest Income | 2,326 | 2,018 | 1,783 | 1,711 | 1,542 | 1,537 | 1,580 | 1,537 | 1,235 | 1,070 |
| Loan Loss Provision | 18.0 | 15.0 | 2.50 | -15.0 | 2.50 | 37.5 | 66.5 | 24.0 | 12.5 | 9.00 |
| % Expense/Operating Revenue | 77.0% | 69.6% | 69.2% | 65.9% | 68.1% | 67.2% | 61.8% | 62.6% | 62.8% | 63.0% |
| Pretax Income | 1,061 | 1,024 | 888 | 754 | 631 | 669 | 732 | 730 | 616 | 543 |
| Effective Tax Rate | 31.5% | 35.0% | 34.2% | 33.1% | 32.9% | 33.2% | 33.4% | 33.6% | 34.3% | 34.8% |
| Net Income | 727 | 665 | 584 | 505 | 423 | 447 | 488 | 485 | 405 | 354 |
| % Net Interest Margin | 1.67 | 1.73 | 1.79 | 1.66 | 1.73 | 1.93 | 2.02 | 2.02 | 2.05 | 2.08 |
| S&P Core Earnings | 828 | 674 | 561 | 491 | 365 | 369 | 418 | NA | NA | NA |

| Balance Sheet & Other Financial Data (Million $) | 2007 | 2006 | 2005 | 2004 | 2003 | 2002 | 2001 | 2000 | 1999 | 1998 |
|---|---|---|---|---|---|---|---|---|---|---|
| Money Market Assets | 25,051 | 16,790 | 16,036 | 13,168 | 9,565 | 9,332 | 10,546 | 5,865 | 3,439 | 1,174 |
| Investment Securities | 8,888 | 12,365 | 11,109 | 9,042 | 9,471 | 6,594 | 6,331 | 7,270 | 6,244 | 5,848 |
| Commercial Loans | 7,907 | 6,515 | 5,064 | 4,498 | 4,702 | 5,137 | 5,767 | 5,708 | 5,485 | 4,615 |
| Other Loans | 17,433 | 16,094 | 14,905 | 13,445 | 13,111 | 12,927 | 12,213 | 12,437 | 9,890 | 9,032 |
| Total Assets | 67,611 | 60,712 | 53,414 | 45,277 | 41,450 | 39,478 | 39,665 | 36,022 | 28,708 | 27,870 |
| Demand Deposits | 10,118 | 9,315 | 7,427 | 6,377 | 5,767 | 6,602 | 7,110 | 5,375 | 4,945 | 3,928 |
| Time Deposits | 41,095 | 34,505 | 31,093 | 24,681 | 20,503 | 19,460 | 17,909 | 17,453 | 16,426 | 14,275 |
| Long Term Debt | 5,721 | 2,421 | 2,791 | 1,340 | 1,341 | 1,284 | 1,485 | 1,356 | 1,427 | 1,426 |
| Common Equity | 4,509 | 3,944 | 3,601 | 3,296 | 3,055 | 2,880 | 2,653 | 2,342 | 2,055 | 1,820 |
| % Return on Assets | 1.1 | 1.2 | 3.0 | 1.2 | 1.0 | 1.1 | 1.3 | 1.5 | 1.4 | 1.3 |
| % Return on Equity | 17.2 | 17.6 | 42.7 | 15.9 | 14.2 | 16.1 | 19.4 | 21.8 | 20.7 | 20.3 |
| % Loan Loss Reserve | 0.6 | 0.6 | 0.6 | 0.7 | 0.8 | 0.9 | 0.9 | 0.9 | 1.0 | 1.1 |
| % Loans/Deposits | 50.5 | 51.6 | 51.8 | 57.8 | 67.8 | 69.3 | 71.9 | 79.5 | 71.9 | 75.0 |
| % Equity to Assets | 6.6 | 6.6 | 7.0 | 7.3 | 7.3 | 7.0 | 6.6 | 6.8 | 6.8 | 6.5 |

Data as orig reptd.; bef. results of disc opers/spec. items. Per share data adj. for stk. divs.; EPS diluted. E-Estimated. NA-Not Available. NM-Not Meaningful. NR-Not Ranked. UR-Under Review.

**Office:** 50 S La Salle St, Chicago, IL 60603-1003.
**Telephone:** 312-630-6000.
**Website:** http://www.northerntrust.com
**Chrmn:** W.A. Osborn

**Pres & CEO:** F.H. Waddell
**Investor Contact:** S.L. Fradkin
**EVP & CFO:** S.L. Fradkin
**EVP & Chief Admin Officer:** T.P. Moen

**Board Members:** L. W. Bynoe, N. D. Chabraja, S. M. Crown, D. C. Jain, A. L. Kelly, R. C. McCormack, E. J. Mooney, W. A. Osborn, J. W. Rowe, H. B. Smith, W. D. Smithburg, E. J. Sosa, C. A. Tribbett, III, F. H. Waddell

**Founded:** 1889
**Domicile:** Delaware
**Employees:** 10,918

*The McGraw-Hill Companies*

# Northrop Grumman Corp

**STANDARD & POOR'S**

| S&P Recommendation | BUY ★★★★☆ | Price $40.34 (as of Nov 14, 2008) | 12-Mo. Target Price $56.00 | Investment Style Large-Cap Blend |
| --- | --- | --- | --- | --- |

**GICS Sector** Industrials
**Sub-Industry** Aerospace & Defense

**Summary** This company is the world's third largest producer of military arms and equipment, and also has a government IT services business.

## Key Stock Statistics (Source S&P, Vickers, company reports)

| | | | | | |
| --- | --- | --- | --- | --- | --- |
| 52-Wk Range | $83.49– 37.23 | S&P Oper. EPS 2008**E** | 5.09 | Market Capitalization(B) | $13.189 |
| Trailing 12-Month EPS | $5.00 | S&P Oper. EPS 2009**E** | 6.15 | Yield (%) | 3.97 |
| Trailing 12-Month P/E | 8.1 | P/E on S&P Oper. EPS 2008**E** | 7.9 | Dividend Rate/Share | $1.60 |
| $10K Invested 5 Yrs Ago | $9,707 | Common Shares Outstg. (M) | 326.9 | Institutional Ownership (%) | 91 |

| | |
| --- | --- |
| Beta | 0.72 |
| S&P 3-Yr. Proj. EPS CAGR(%) | 9 |
| S&P Credit Rating | BBB+ |

## Price Performance

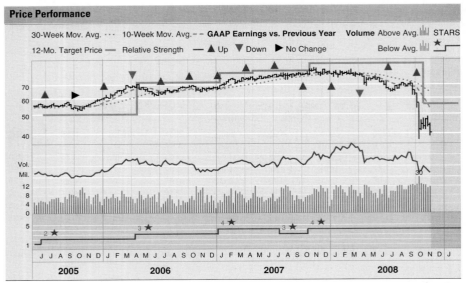

30-Week Mov. Avg. ···· 10-Week Mov. Avg. — **GAAP Earnings vs. Previous Year** Volume Above Avg. STARS
12-Mo. Target Price — Relative Strength — ▲ Up ▼ Down ▶ No Change Below Avg. ★

Options: ASE, CBOE, P

## Highlights

➤ The 12-month target price for NOC has recently been changed to $56.00 from $89.00. The Highlights section of this Stock Report will be updated accordingly.

## Investment Rationale/Risk

➤ The Investment Rationale/Risk section of this Stock Report will be updated shortly. For the latest News story on NOC from MarketScope, see below.

➤ 10/22/08 03:39 pm ET ... S&P REITERATES BUY RECOMMENDATION ON SHARES OF NORTHROP GRUMMAN (NOC 45.73****): Q3 EPS of $1.50 vs. $1.41 on 6% sales growth exceeds our $1.41 estimate. Funded backlog rose 13% to $34B. We are raising our '08 EPS estimate by $0.09 to $5.18, but lower our '09 estimate by $0.50 to $5.65 on projected FAS/CAS pension plan adjustments based on the weak stock market. We are also lowering our 12-month target price by $33 to $56 on our '09 estimate change, as well as compressed valuation multiples. We see aging military equipment and global threat environment favoring NOC's product line of ships, electronics, planes, and services. /R.Tortoriello

## Qualitative Risk Assessment

| LOW | MEDIUM | HIGH |
| --- | --- | --- |

Our risk assessment reflects our view of NOC's typically strong levels of cash flow and a solid balance sheet with a relatively low level of debt. This is offset by the cyclical nature of the company's business, particularly its dependence on government defense programs.

## Quantitative Evaluations

**S&P Quality Ranking**          A-

| D | C | B- | B | B+ | A- | A | A+ |
| --- | --- | --- | --- | --- | --- | --- | --- |

**Relative Strength Rank**          MODERATE

43

LOWEST = 1          HIGHEST = 99

## Revenue/Earnings Data

**Revenue (Million $)**

| | 1Q | 2Q | 3Q | 4Q | Year |
| --- | --- | --- | --- | --- | --- |
| 2008 | 7,724 | 8,628 | 8,381 | -- | -- |
| 2007 | 7,340 | 7,926 | 7,928 | 8,824 | 32,018 |
| 2006 | 7,093 | 7,601 | 7,433 | 8,021 | 30,148 |
| 2005 | 7,453 | 7,962 | 7,446 | 7,860 | 30,721 |
| 2004 | 7,105 | 7,374 | 7,408 | 7,846 | 29,853 |
| 2003 | 5,866 | 6,627 | 6,619 | 7,094 | 26,206 |

**Earnings Per Share ($)**

| | 1Q | 2Q | 3Q | 4Q | Year |
| --- | --- | --- | --- | --- | --- |
| 2008 | 0.76 | 1.40 | 1.50 | E1.53 | E5.09 |
| 2007 | 1.11 | 1.33 | 1.41 | 1.32 | 5.16 |
| 2006 | 1.03 | 1.26 | 0.87 | 1.29 | 4.44 |
| 2005 | 1.08 | 1.00 | 0.80 | 0.92 | 3.81 |
| 2004 | 0.63 | 0.79 | 0.80 | 0.81 | 2.99 |
| 2003 | 0.46 | 0.55 | 0.61 | 0.56 | 2.16 |

Fiscal year ended Dec. 31. Next earnings report expected: Late January. EPS Estimates based on S&P Operating Earnings; historical GAAP earnings are as reported.

## Dividend Data (Dates: mm/dd Payment Date: mm/dd/yy)

| Amount ($) | Date Decl. | Ex-Div. Date | Stk. of Record | Payment Date |
| --- | --- | --- | --- | --- |
| 0.370 | 02/20 | 02/28 | 03/03 | 03/15/08 |
| 0.400 | 04/24 | 05/29 | 06/02 | 06/14/08 |
| 0.400 | 07/25 | 08/21 | 08/25 | 09/06/08 |
| 0.400 | 10/20 | 11/26 | 12/01 | 12/13/08 |

Dividends have been paid since 1951. Source: Company reports.

# Northrop Grumman Corp

**STANDARD &POOR'S**

## Business Summary September 22, 2008

CORPORATE OVERVIEW. This $33 billion in revenues defense electronics, aerospace, and warship-making giant, which operated through seven reportable segments and four primary businesses in 2007, conducts most of its business with the U.S. government, principally the Department of Defense. NOC also transacts with foreign governments and makes commercial sales both domestically and overseas.

The Information & Services business consists of the Mission Systems (18% of 2007 revenue and 18% of operating profit), Information Technology (13% and 10%) and Technical Services (7% and 4%) segments. Mission Systems is a leading global integrator of complex, mission-enabling systems, in the areas of command, control and communications; intelligence, surveillance, and reconnaissance; and missile systems. Information Technology provides IT services and solutions in four business areas: intelligence; defense; civilian agencies; and commercial, state & local. Technical Services provides infrastructure managment and maintenance, training and preparedness, and logistics and life-cycle management to a wide variety of government agencies and commercial and international customers.

The Aerospace business consists of the Integrated Systems (15% of revenue and 18% of operating profit) and Space Technology (10% and 8%) segments. Integrated Systems designs, develops, produces and supports fully missionized integrated systems and subsystems in the areas of battlespace awareness, command and control systems, integrated combat systems, and airborne ground surveillance. Space Technology develops a broad range of systems at the leading edge of space, defense and electronics technology.

The Electronics business (20% of revenue and 25% of operating profit) develops, produces, integrates and supports high-performance sensors, intelligence processing, and navigation systems operating in all environments from undersea to outer space and cyberspace. It also makes and supports power, power control and ship controls for commercial and naval ships. The segment is composed of five areas of business: aerospace systems; defensive systems; government systems; naval & marine systems; and navigation systems.

## Company Financials Fiscal Year Ended Dec. 31

| Per Share Data ($) | 2007 | 2006 | 2005 | 2004 | 2003 | 2002 | 2001 | 2000 | 1999 | 1998 |
|---|---|---|---|---|---|---|---|---|---|---|
| Tangible Book Value | NM | NM | NM | NM | NM | NM | NM | NM | NM | NM |
| Cash Flow | 7.09 | 6.34 | 5.94 | 5.01 | 4.05 | 5.29 | 6.31 | 7.08 | 6.23 | 4.25 |
| Earnings | 5.16 | 4.44 | 3.81 | 2.99 | 2.16 | 2.86 | 2.40 | 4.41 | 3.47 | 1.40 |
| S&P Core Earnings | 4.09 | 3.67 | 2.84 | 2.63 | 2.42 | -0.95 | -2.85 | NA | NA | NA |
| Dividends | 1.48 | 1.16 | 1.01 | 0.89 | 0.80 | 0.80 | 0.80 | 0.80 | 0.80 | 0.80 |
| Payout Ratio | 29% | 26% | 27% | 30% | 37% | 28% | 33% | 18% | 23% | 57% |
| Prices:High | 85.21 | 71.37 | 60.26 | 58.15 | 50.55 | 67.50 | 55.28 | 46.94 | 37.97 | 69.50 |
| Prices:Low | 66.23 | 59.10 | 51.10 | 46.91 | 41.50 | 43.60 | 38.20 | 21.31 | 23.50 | 29.66 |
| P/E Ratio:High | 17 | 16 | 16 | 19 | 23 | 24 | 23 | 11 | 11 | 50 |
| P/E Ratio:Low | 13 | 13 | 13 | 16 | 19 | 15 | 16 | 5 | 7 | 21 |

| Income Statement Analysis (Million $) | | | | | | | | | | |
|---|---|---|---|---|---|---|---|---|---|---|
| Revenue | 32,018 | 30,148 | 30,721 | 29,853 | 26,206 | 17,206 | 13,558 | 7,618 | 8,995 | 8,902 |
| Operating Income | 3,716 | 3,159 | 2,951 | 2,740 | 1,538 | 1,391 | 1,649 | 1,479 | 1,358 | 1,149 |
| Depreciation | 710 | 705 | 773 | 734 | 682 | 525 | 645 | 381 | 389 | 393 |
| Interest Expense | 336 | 347 | 388 | 431 | 497 | 422 | 373 | 175 | 224 | 233 |
| Pretax Income | 2,686 | 2,276 | 2,044 | 1,615 | 1,131 | 1,009 | 699 | 975 | 762 | 312 |
| Effective Tax Rate | 32.9% | 31.2% | 32.3% | 32.3% | 28.6% | 30.9% | 38.9% | 35.9% | 36.6% | 37.8% |
| Net Income | 1,803 | 1,567 | 1,383 | 1,093 | 808 | 697 | 427 | 625 | 483 | 194 |
| S&P Core Earnings | 1,426 | 1,288 | 1,026 | 961 | 892 | -223 | -487 | NA | NA | NA |

| Balance Sheet & Other Financial Data (Million $) | | | | | | | | | | |
|---|---|---|---|---|---|---|---|---|---|---|
| Cash | 963 | 1,015 | 1,605 | 1,230 | 342 | 1,412 | 464 | 319 | 142 | 44.0 |
| Current Assets | 6,772 | 6,719 | 7,549 | 6,907 | 5,745 | 15,835 | 4,589 | 2,526 | 2,793 | 3,033 |
| Total Assets | 33,373 | 32,009 | 34,214 | 33,361 | 33,009 | 42,266 | 20,886 | 9,622 | 9,285 | 9,536 |
| Current Liabilities | 6,432 | 6,753 | 7,974 | 6,223 | 6,361 | 11,373 | 5,132 | 2,688 | 2,464 | 2,367 |
| Long Term Debt | 4,268 | 3,992 | 3,881 | 5,116 | 5,410 | 9,398 | 5,033 | 1,605 | 2,000 | 2,562 |
| Common Equity | 17,687 | 16,615 | 16,825 | 16,970 | 15,785 | 14,322 | 7,391 | 3,919 | 3,257 | 2,850 |
| Total Capital | 22,285 | 20,957 | 21,651 | 22,942 | 22,067 | 24,209 | 13,443 | 5,800 | 5,321 | 5,412 |
| Capital Expenditures | 685 | 737 | 824 | 672 | 635 | 538 | 393 | 274 | 201 | 211 |
| Cash Flow | 2,513 | 2,272 | 2,156 | 1,827 | 1,490 | 1,222 | 1,072 | 1,006 | 872 | 587 |
| Current Ratio | 1.1 | 1.0 | 0.9 | 1.1 | 0.9 | 1.4 | 0.9 | 0.9 | 1.1 | 1.3 |
| % Long Term Debt of Capitalization | 19.2 | 19.0 | 17.9 | 22.3 | 24.5 | 38.8 | 37.4 | 27.7 | 37.6 | 47.3 |
| % Net Income of Revenue | 5.6 | 5.2 | 4.5 | 3.7 | 3.1 | 4.1 | 3.1 | 8.2 | 5.4 | 2.2 |
| % Return on Assets | 5.5 | 4.7 | 4.1 | 3.3 | 2.1 | 2.2 | 2.8 | 6.6 | 5.1 | 2.0 |
| % Return on Equity | 10.5 | 9.4 | 8.2 | 6.6 | 5.4 | 6.4 | 7.6 | 17.4 | 15.8 | 7.1 |

Data as orig reptd.; bef. results of disc opers/spec. items. Per share data adj. for stk. divs.; EPS diluted. E-Estimated. NA-Not Available. NM-Not Meaningful. NR-Not Ranked. UR-Under Review.

**Office:** 1840 Century Park E, Los Angeles, CA 90067-2199.
**Telephone:** 310-553-6262.
**Email:** investor_relations@mail.northgrum.com
**Website:** http://www.northropgrumman.com

**Chrmn & CEO:** R.D. Sugar
**Pres & COO:** W.G. Bush
**CFO:** B. Niland
**Chief Admin Officer:** I.V. Ziskin

**CTO:** D.H. Barakat
**Investor Contact:** G. Kent (310-553-6262)
**Board Members:** L. W. Coleman, T. B. Fargo, V. Fazio, D. E. Felsinger, S. E. Frank, P. Frost, B. S. Gordon, M. Kleiner, K. J. Krapek, C. R. Larson, R. B. Myers, A. L. Peters, K. W. Sharer, R. D. Sugar

**Founded:** 1939
**Domicile:** Delaware
**Employees:** 122,600

The **McGraw-Hill** Companies

# Novell Inc

STANDARD &POOR'S

| S&P Recommendation | HOLD ★★★☆☆ | Price $4.17 (as of Nov 14, 2008) | 12-Mo. Target Price $7.00 | Investment Style Large-Cap Blend |
|---|---|---|---|---|

**GICS Sector** Information Technology
**Sub-Industry** Systems Software

**Summary** This company is a leading vendor of directory-enabled networking software, with its NetWare product line and Linux-based offerings.

## Key Stock Statistics (Source S&P, Vickers, company reports)

| | | | | | | | | |
|---|---|---|---|---|---|---|---|---|
| 52-Wk Range | $7.59– 2.49 | S&P Oper. EPS 2008E | 0.06 | Market Capitalization(B) | $1.440 | Beta | | 1.42 |
| Trailing 12-Month EPS | $-0.03 | S&P Oper. EPS 2009E | 0.20 | Yield (%) | Nil | S&P 3-Yr. Proj. EPS CAGR(%) | | NM |
| Trailing 12-Month P/E | NM | P/E on S&P Oper. EPS 2008E | 69.5 | Dividend Rate/Share | Nil | S&P Credit Rating | | NA |
| $10K Invested 5 Yrs Ago | $4,518 | Common Shares Outstg. (M) | 345.3 | Institutional Ownership (%) | 74 | | | |

## Price Performance

30-Week Mov. Avg. · · · · 10-Week Mov. Avg. - - - **GAAP Earnings vs. Previous Year** Volume Above Avg. STARS
12-Mo. Target Price — Relative Strength — ▲ Up ▼ Down ► No Change Below Avg.

Options: ASE, CBOE, P, Ph

Analysis prepared by **Jim Yin** on September 03, 2008, when the stock traded at **$ 6.23**.

## Highlights

➤ We estimate that total revenue will increase 1.5% in FY 09 (Oct.), compared to 2.1% growth in FY 08. We see a 30% rise in open platform solutions revenue. However, we expect the amount of invoicing to decline, as many corporate customers signed up for multi-year service agreements following the company's announcement of its partnership with Microsoft (MSFT: buy, $27). We believe growth in open platform solutions will be partially offset by declines in systems and resource management, and work group and business consulting.

➤ We expect gross margins in FY 09 to rise to 75%, from 74% in FY 08, on a favorable revenue mix. We expect total operating expenses to decrease as a result of further head count reductions and lower research and development expenses, partially offset by higher stock-based compensation. We see FY 09 operating margins widening to 8.3%, from 2.6% in FY 08.

➤ We estimate EPS of $0.20 in FY 09, compared to the $0.06 we see in FY 08. The expected increase reflects our view of better operating margins, higher revenue, and a lower effective tax rate.

## Investment Rationale/Risk

➤ Our hold recommendation reflects our concern about NOVL's ability to transform itself into a solution provider in a mixed operating system environment through its NetWare business, which has been declining. We believe the company needs to continue developing solutions in areas such as system integration to counter increased competition from Red Hat (RHT: sell, $20) and Oracle (ORCL: strong buy, $21). However, the company has stabilized its NetWare product revenue and improved operating margins in recent quarters. We also believe NOVL's net cash and investments of $943 million, or about $2.68 per share, as of June 30, 2008, will lend some support to the share price.

➤ Risks to our opinion and target price include slower-than-expected growth in Linux products, lower-than-expected cost savings from cost-cutting initiatives, and a slowdown in the global economy.

➤ Our 12-month target price of $7 is based on an enterprise value/sales ratio of 1.5X, which is below the industry average of 2.6X. We believe this discount is appropriate in view of our projections of flat revenue and lower profitability than peers.

## Qualitative Risk Assessment

| LOW | MEDIUM | HIGH |
|---|---|---|

Our risk assessment reflects the volatile market conditions in the Linux and open source software markets, the continuing decline in sales of NOVL's NetWare products, and our belief that NOVL is having difficulty gaining sufficient traction in Linux to offset the decrease in NetWare revenues.

## Quantitative Evaluations

**S&P Quality Ranking** B-

| D | C | B- | B | B+ | A- | A | A+ |
|---|---|---|---|---|---|---|---|

**Relative Strength Rank** MODERATE

62

LOWEST = 1 HIGHEST = 99

## Revenue/Earnings Data

**Revenue (Million $)**

| | 1Q | 2Q | 3Q | 4Q | Year |
|---|---|---|---|---|---|
| 2008 | 230.9 | 235.7 | 245.2 | -- | -- |
| 2007 | 218.4 | 232.4 | 236.8 | 244.9 | 932.5 |
| 2006 | 274.4 | 278.3 | 241.4 | 244.9 | 967.3 |
| 2005 | 290.1 | 297.1 | 290.2 | 320.3 | 1,198 |
| 2004 | 267.1 | 293.6 | 304.6 | 300.7 | 1,166 |
| 2003 | 260.0 | 276.0 | 282.8 | 286.8 | 1,105 |

**Earnings Per Share ($)**

| | | | | | |
|---|---|---|---|---|---|
| 2008 | 0.04 | 0.04 | -0.04 | E0.04 | E0.06 |
| 2007 | -0.04 | Nil | -0.04 | -0.03 | -0.08 |
| 2006 | Nil | 0.01 | 0.03 | 0.06 | 0.02 |
| 2005 | 0.90 | -0.04 | Nil | -0.01 | 0.86 |
| 2004 | 0.03 | -0.04 | 0.06 | 0.03 | 0.08 |
| 2003 | -0.03 | -0.08 | -0.03 | -0.29 | -0.44 |

Fiscal year ended Oct. 31. Next earnings report expected: NA. EPS Estimates based on S&P Operating Earnings; historical GAAP earnings are as reported.

## Dividend Data

No cash dividends have been paid.

# Novell Inc

STANDARD
&POOR'S

## Business Summary September 03, 2008

CORPORATE OVERVIEW. NOVL is a provider of software and services that help customers manage their information technology infrastructure. The company's legacy products are based on its proprietary network operating system, NetWare. Sales of NetWare have been declining, and IDC, an independent market research firm, expects NetWare revenue to decrease at a 32% CAGR (compound annual growth rate) from 2006 through 2011.

In the past few years, NOVL has embraced and promoted Linux and open source computing. The company is the second largest provider of Linux operating systems and subsystems, capturing 26% of the market by revenue in 2006 according to IDC, up from 21% in 2004. As a result of increased use of open source software in enterprise applications, NOVL has repositioned the company as a solution provider in a mixed operating system environment that includes open source and proprietary technologies, thus reducing reliance on its legacy products, such as NetWare.

NOVL reorganized into four product-related business units and a consulting unit. The four business unit segments are open platform solutions, which encompasses SUSE Linux operating system; identity and security management,

which helps to provide secured logon and protect information assets; systems and resource management, which includes software to manage multiple infrastructure resources in a virtual environment; and workgroup, which helps customers to collaborate across the enterprise.

CORPORATE STRATEGY. NOVL relies on a series of alliances and partnerships to drive sales growth; its partners include IBM, HP, Dell, Intel, Oracle, SAP, AMD, CA, EMC and Adobe. NOVL believes it has created an ecosystem around it to combine its strengths with those of its partners; however, these partners are also counted among the strategic partners of many other software firms, and we doubt the partnerships provide a significant competitive advantage. In addition, NOVL's go-to market strategy embraces both a direct and indirect sales channel, with the indirect channel including independent distributors, value-added resellers, systems integrators and hardware OEMs.

## Company Financials Fiscal Year Ended Oct. 31

| Per Share Data ($) | 2007 | 2006 | 2005 | 2004 | 2003 | 2002 | 2001 | 2000 | 1999 | 1998 |
|---|---|---|---|---|---|---|---|---|---|---|
| Tangible Book Value | 2.05 | 1.86 | 2.42 | 1.39 | 1.89 | 2.31 | 2.98 | 3.80 | 4.57 | 4.42 |
| Cash Flow | 0.04 | 0.15 | 0.98 | 0.22 | -0.27 | -0.09 | -0.53 | 0.39 | 0.75 | 0.50 |
| Earnings | -0.08 | 0.02 | 0.86 | 0.08 | -0.44 | -0.28 | -0.79 | 0.15 | 0.55 | 0.29 |
| S&P Core Earnings | -0.09 | -0.02 | -0.11 | -0.07 | -0.45 | -0.47 | -1.27 | NA | NA | NA |
| Dividends | Nil | Nil | Nil | Nil | Nil | Nil | Nil | Nil | Nil | Nil |
| Payout Ratio | Nil | Nil | Nil | Nil | Nil | Nil | Nil | Nil | Nil | Nil |
| Prices:High | 8.26 | 9.83 | 9.27 | 14.24 | 10.77 | 5.64 | 9.13 | 44.56 | 41.19 | 19.00 |
| Prices:Low | 5.76 | 5.70 | 4.94 | 5.62 | 2.14 | 1.57 | 2.96 | 4.88 | 16.06 | 6.81 |
| P/E Ratio:High | NM | NM | 11 | NM | NM | NM | NM | NM | 75 | 66 |
| P/E Ratio:Low | NM | NM | 6 | NM | NM | NM | NM | 33 | 29 | 23 |

| Income Statement Analysis (Million $) | | | | | | | | | | |
|---|---|---|---|---|---|---|---|---|---|---|
| Revenue | 933 | 967 | 1,198 | 1,166 | 1,105 | 1,134 | 1,040 | 1,162 | 1,273 | 1,084 |
| Operating Income | 30.4 | 27.8 | 99.3 | 140 | 52.3 | 103 | 46.1 | 98.2 | 293 | 175 |
| Depreciation | 40.4 | 47.0 | 56.3 | 53.5 | 61.1 | 68.8 | 86.7 | 81.9 | 70.2 | 76.2 |
| Interest Expense | 25.9 | 8.02 | 9.63 | Nil | Nil | Nil | Nil | Nil | Nil | Nil |
| Pretax Income | 8.40 | 30.9 | 466 | 75.0 | -55.0 | -92.2 | -277 | 70.7 | 244 | 142 |
| Effective Tax Rate | NM | 75.3% | 19.2% | 23.7% | NM | NM | NM | 30.0% | 21.8% | 28.0% |
| Net Income | -26.3 | 7.63 | 377 | 57.2 | -162 | -103 | -262 | 49.5 | 191 | 102 |
| S&P Core Earnings | -29.5 | -8.34 | -52.6 | -30.8 | -167 | -172 | -384 | NA | NA | NA |

| Balance Sheet & Other Financial Data (Million $) | | | | | | | | | | |
|---|---|---|---|---|---|---|---|---|---|---|
| Cash | 1,080 | 676 | 811 | 434 | 752 | 636 | 705 | 698 | 895 | 1,007 |
| Current Assets | 2,154 | 1,761 | 2,009 | 1,535 | 1,031 | 920 | 1,027 | 1,007 | 1,336 | 1,436 |
| Total Assets | 2,854 | 2,450 | 2,762 | 2,292 | 1,568 | 1,665 | 1,904 | 1,712 | 1,942 | 1,924 |
| Current Liabilities | 822 | 686 | 753 | 693 | 626 | 592 | 611 | 455 | 440 | 415 |
| Long Term Debt | 600 | 600 | 600 | 600 | Nil | Nil | Nil | Nil | Nil | Nil |
| Common Equity | 1,158 | 1,105 | 1,386 | 963 | 934 | 1,066 | 1,271 | 1,245 | 1,492 | 1,493 |
| Total Capital | 1,758 | 1,718 | 2,004 | 1,599 | 941 | 1,074 | 1,293 | 1,257 | 1,503 | 1,509 |
| Capital Expenditures | 25.2 | 26.7 | 30.8 | 27.0 | 39.5 | 27.6 | 33.3 | 57.8 | 69.2 | 57.4 |
| Cash Flow | 14.1 | 54.6 | 433 | 84.6 | -101 | -34.3 | -175 | 131 | 261 | 178 |
| Current Ratio | 2.6 | 2.6 | 2.7 | 2.2 | 1.6 | 1.6 | 1.7 | 2.2 | 3.0 | 3.5 |
| % Long Term Debt of Capitalization | 34.1 | 34.9 | 29.9 | 37.5 | Nil | Nil | Nil | Nil | Nil | Nil |
| % Net Income of Revenue | NM | 0.8 | 31.5 | 4.9 | NM | NM | NM | 4.3 | 15.0 | 9.4 |
| % Return on Assets | NM | 0.3 | 14.9 | 3.0 | NM | NM | NM | 2.7 | 9.9 | 5.3 |
| % Return on Equity | NM | 0.6 | 32.1 | 3.3 | NM | NM | NM | 3.6 | 12.8 | 6.7 |

Data as orig reptd.; bef. results of disc opers/spec. items. Per share data adj. for stk. divs.; EPS diluted. E-Estimated. NA-Not Available. NM-Not Meaningful. NR-Not Ranked. UR-Under Review.

**Office:** 404 Wyman St Ste 500, Waltham, MA 02451-1212.
**Telephone:** 781-464-8000.
**Website:** http://www.novell.com
**Chrmn:** R.L. Crandall

**Pres & CEO:** R.W. Hovsepian
**EVP & CTO:** J. Jaffe
**SVP, CFO, Chief Acctg Officer & Cntlr:** D.C. Russell
**SVP & General Counsel:** S. Semel

**Investor Contact:** E.M. Hennessy (781-464-8553)
**Board Members:** A. Aiello, Jr., F. Corrado, R. L. Crandall, R. W. Hovsepian, P. S. Jones, C. B. Malone, R. L. Nolan, T. G. Plaskett, J. W. Poduska, J. D. Robinson, III, K. B. White

**Founded:** 1983
**Domicile:** Delaware
**Employees:** 4,100

The *McGraw-Hill* Companies

# Novellus Systems Inc

STANDARD &POOR'S

| S&P Recommendation **HOLD** ★★★☆☆ | Price $12.18 (as of Nov 14, 2008) | 12-Mo. Target Price $16.00 | Investment Style Large-Cap Growth |
|---|---|---|---|

**GICS Sector** Information Technology
**Sub-Industry** Semiconductor Equipment

**Summary** This company manufactures, markets and services automated wafer fabrication systems for the deposition of thin films.

## Key Stock Statistics (Source S&P, Vickers, company reports)

| | | | | | | | | |
|---|---|---|---|---|---|---|---|---|
| 52-Wk Range | $28.11–11.54 | S&P Oper. EPS 2008E | 0.23 | Market Capitalization(B) | $1.190 | Beta | 1.77 |
| Trailing 12-Month EPS | $0.66 | S&P Oper. EPS 2009E | 0.17 | Yield (%) | Nil | S&P 3-Yr. Proj. EPS CAGR(%) | -16 |
| Trailing 12-Month P/E | 18.5 | P/E on S&P Oper. EPS 2008E | 53.0 | Dividend Rate/Share | Nil | S&P Credit Rating | NA |
| $10K Invested 5 Yrs Ago | $2,884 | Common Shares Outstg. (M) | 97.7 | Institutional Ownership (%) | 89 | | |

## Price Performance

30-Week Mov. Avg. · · · 10-Week Mov. Avg. — **GAAP Earnings vs. Previous Year** Volume Above Avg. STARS
12-Mo. Target Price — Relative Strength — ▲ Up ▼ Down ▶ No Change Below Avg.

Options: ASE, CBOE, P, Ph

Analysis prepared by **Angelo Zino** on October 16, 2008, when the stock traded at **$ 14.50**.

## Highlights

➤ We project that sales will decline about 32% in 2008 and 10% in 2009. Depressed memory prices and production cuts by many manufacturers have led us to believe demand will remain muted over the next several quarters. We now project equipment spending to be down an additional 10% next year and see oversupply in memory remaining through the first half of 2009. We expect customer capacity utilization rates to decline near-term, as end-market demand remains uncertain.

➤ We anticipate an annual gross margin of 44% in 2009, flat compared to our 2008 projection. We believe that NVLS has enough flexibility in its manufacturing fixed cost structure to maintain margins during various stages of the business cycle. Long term, we see gross margins widening modestly due to higher sales and lower operating costs. Recent cost cutting efforts have reduced NVLS's operating expenses to under $110 million and the revenue breakeven point to about $245 million to $250 million per quarter.

➤ Following operating EPS of $1.75 in 2007, we forecast operating EPS of $0.23 in 2008 and $0.17 for 2009. We currently project an effective tax rate of 30% for 2009.

## Investment Rationale/Risk

➤ We believe the uncertain economic landscape, lack of profitability from most memory manufacturers, and oversupply of memory chips will cause semiconductor makers to continue being extremely conservative with capital spending plans for 2009. We believe that revenues and margins will be constrained over the next several quarters, as memory customers continue to push-out capacity expansion plans. We expect inventory levels across the supply chain to tighten in 2009, and do not project a significant increase in revenues until chipmaker's become more optimistic of end-market demand. We expect NVLS to modestly repurchase shares.

➤ Risks to our recommendation and target price include a longer than expected semiconductor equipment downturn, weaker than projected global economic growth, and higher than expected R&D expense growth.

➤ We apply a price-to-sales multiple of approximately 1.6X, modestly higher than the peer average, to our 2009 sales per share estimate to arrive at our 12-month target price of $16. We think this multiple is warranted based on NVLS's large market share position.

## Qualitative Risk Assessment

| LOW | MEDIUM | **HIGH** |
|---|---|---|

Our risk assessment reflects the historical cyclicality of the semiconductor equipment industry, the lack of visibility in the medium term, the dynamic nature of semiconductor technology, and intense competition. We believe these risks are partially offset by our view of the company's strong market position, size, and financial condition.

## Quantitative Evaluations

**S&P Quality Ranking**  B-

| D | C | **B-** | B | B+ | A- | A | A+ |
|---|---|---|---|---|---|---|---|

**Relative Strength Rank**  MODERATE

36

LOWEST = 1    HIGHEST = 99

## Revenue/Earnings Data

**Revenue (Million $)**

| | 1Q | 2Q | 3Q | 4Q | Year |
|---|---|---|---|---|---|
| 2008 | 314.7 | 257.7 | 250.1 | -- | -- |
| 2007 | 397.0 | 416.3 | 393.3 | 363.5 | 1,570 |
| 2006 | 365.9 | 410.1 | 444.0 | 438.5 | 1,659 |
| 2005 | 339.7 | 329.6 | 338.9 | 332.3 | 1,340 |
| 2004 | 262.9 | 338.2 | 415.9 | 340.3 | 1,357 |
| 2003 | 238.4 | 239.1 | 221.1 | 226.5 | 925.1 |

**Earnings Per Share ($)**

| | 1Q | 2Q | 3Q | 4Q | Year |
|---|---|---|---|---|---|
| 2008 | 0.15 | -0.02 | 0.01 | ENil | E0.23 |
| 2007 | 0.42 | 0.45 | 0.41 | 0.47 | 1.75 |
| 2006 | 0.18 | 0.42 | 0.57 | 0.34 | 1.49 |
| 2005 | 0.22 | 0.24 | 0.17 | 0.17 | 0.80 |
| 2004 | 0.11 | 0.25 | 0.45 | 0.27 | 1.06 |
| 2003 | 0.08 | 0.05 | -0.23 | 0.07 | -0.03 |

Fiscal year ended Dec. 31. Next earnings report expected: Late January. EPS Estimates based on S&P Operating Earnings; historical GAAP earnings are as reported.

## Dividend Data

No cash dividends have been paid.

# Novellus Systems Inc

STANDARD
&POOR'S

## Business Summary October 16, 2008

CORPORATE OVERVIEW. Novellus is the second largest maker of deposition equipment used to deposit conductive and insulating layers on semiconductor wafers to form integrated circuits (ICs). The company entered the market for wafer surface preparation equipment in 2001. NVLS also entered the chemical mechanical planarization (CMP) equipment market in 2002. These two types of equipment are complementary to deposition equipment.

NVLS's product line of deposition equipment includes chemical vapor deposition (CVD), physical vapor deposition (PVD) and electrochemical deposition (ECD), all of which are used to form the layers of wiring and insulation, known as the interconnect, of ICs. High-density plasma CVD (HDP) and plasma-enhanced CVD (PECVD) systems employ chemical plasma to deposit all of the insulating layers and some of the conductive layers on the surface of a wafer. PVD systems deposit conductive layers through a process known as sputtering, where ions of an inert gas such as argon are electrically accelerated in a high vacuum toward a target of pure metal, such as tantalum or copper. ECD systems are used to build the copper conductive layers on wafers.

Although NVLS's original tool sets established it as a leader in CVD, the company has centered its product strategy on the emergence of the copper inter-connect market. Copper has lower resistance and capacitance values than aluminum, the conductive metal generally used in ICs, offering increased speed and decreased chip size. The company's SABRE tool offers a complete solution for the deposition of copper interconnects and holds the leading market share in copper.

Surface preparation products, including photoresist strip and clean, are becoming more important with the industry's migration to copper interconnects. Surface preparation systems remove photoresist and other potential contaminants from a wafer before proceeding with the next deposition step. CMP systems polish the surface of a wafer after a deposition step to create a flat topography before moving on to subsequent manufacturing steps. Since copper is more difficult to polish and smooth than previous generation aluminum interconnects, and low-k dielectrics are much more porous than predecessors, NVLS's products in this category have become very important, in our view.

## Company Financials Fiscal Year Ended Dec. 31

| Per Share Data ($) | 2007 | 2006 | 2005 | 2004 | 2003 | 2002 | 2001 | 2000 | 1999 | 1998 |
|---|---|---|---|---|---|---|---|---|---|---|
| Tangible Book Value | 11.98 | 12.54 | 11.29 | 11.06 | 12.42 | 12.69 | 13.04 | 11.49 | 6.47 | 3.63 |
| Cash Flow | 2.30 | 2.05 | 1.39 | 1.66 | 0.43 | 0.45 | 1.32 | 2.04 | 0.89 | 0.73 |
| Earnings | 1.75 | 1.49 | 0.80 | 1.06 | -0.03 | 0.15 | 0.97 | 1.75 | 0.64 | 0.50 |
| S&P Core Earnings | 1.71 | 1.47 | 0.43 | 0.74 | -0.42 | -0.33 | 0.52 | NA | NA | NA |
| Dividends | Nil | Nil | Nil | Nil | Nil | Nil | Nil | Nil | Nil | Nil |
| Payout Ratio | Nil | Nil | Nil | Nil | Nil | Nil | Nil | Nil | Nil | Nil |
| Prices:High | 34.97 | 35.00 | 30.77 | 44.52 | 45.50 | 54.48 | 58.70 | 70.25 | 42.79 | 19.77 |
| Prices:Low | 25.40 | 22.28 | 20.83 | 22.89 | 24.93 | 19.40 | 25.37 | 24.94 | 14.96 | 6.96 |
| P/E Ratio:High | 20 | 23 | 38 | 42 | NM | NM | 61 | 40 | 67 | 39 |
| P/E Ratio:Low | 15 | 15 | 26 | 22 | NM | NM | 26 | 14 | 23 | 14 |

| Income Statement Analysis (Million $) | | | | | | | | | | |
|---|---|---|---|---|---|---|---|---|---|---|
| Revenue | 1,570 | 1,659 | 1,340 | 1,357 | 925 | 840 | 1,339 | 1,174 | 593 | 519 |
| Operating Income | 329 | 388 | 228 | 308 | 56.5 | 46.3 | 273 | 328 | 130 | 103 |
| Depreciation | 66.9 | 69.7 | 82.8 | 89.3 | 69.6 | 44.3 | 51.9 | 40.1 | 29.8 | 23.8 |
| Interest Expense | 6.38 | 4.29 | 3.51 | 2.13 | 0.91 | 1.02 | 1.15 | 2.34 | 1.70 | 4.87 |
| Pretax Income | 315 | 339 | 159 | 223 | -15.3 | 22.9 | 209 | 342 | 114 | 80.0 |
| Effective Tax Rate | 32.1% | 44.2% | 30.6% | 29.8% | NM | NM | 31.0% | 31.0% | 33.0% | 34.0% |
| Net Income | 214 | 189 | 110 | 157 | -5.03 | 22.9 | 144 | 236 | 76.6 | 52.8 |
| S&P Core Earnings | 209 | 186 | 59.8 | 108 | -67.2 | -50.7 | 81.6 | NA | NA | NA |

| Balance Sheet & Other Financial Data (Million $) | | | | | | | | | | |
|---|---|---|---|---|---|---|---|---|---|---|
| Cash | 593 | 58.5 | 649 | 106 | 497 | 616 | 551 | 571 | 182 | 81.2 |
| Current Assets | 1,224 | 1,505 | 1,364 | 1,369 | 1,572 | 1,634 | 2,517 | 1,827 | 733 | 399 |
| Total Assets | 2,077 | 2,362 | 2,290 | 2,402 | 2,339 | 2,494 | 3,010 | 2,015 | 910 | 552 |
| Current Liabilities | 329 | 361 | 344 | 324 | 221 | 382 | 1,138 | 505 | 140 | 111 |
| Long Term Debt | 143 | 128 | 125 | 161 | Nil | Nil | Nil | Nil | Nil | 65.0 |
| Common Equity | 1,529 | 1,835 | 1,779 | 1,862 | 2,072 | 2,056 | 1,872 | 1,511 | 770 | 375 |
| Total Capital | 1,700 | 1,963 | 1,904 | 2,023 | 2,072 | 2,075 | 1,872 | 1,511 | 770 | 440 |
| Capital Expenditures | 33.2 | 39.4 | 44.7 | 31.7 | 31.1 | 26.8 | 80.0 | 68.5 | 28.8 | 36.1 |
| Cash Flow | 281 | 259 | 193 | 246 | 64.5 | 67.2 | 196 | 276 | 106 | 76.7 |
| Current Ratio | 3.7 | 4.2 | 4.0 | 4.2 | 7.1 | 4.3 | 2.2 | 3.6 | 5.2 | 3.6 |
| % Long Term Debt of Capitalization | 8.4 | 6.5 | 6.6 | 8.0 | Nil | Nil | Nil | Nil | Nil | 14.7 |
| % Net Income of Revenue | 13.6 | 11.4 | 8.2 | 11.5 | NM | 2.7 | 10.8 | 20.1 | 12.9 | 10.2 |
| % Return on Assets | 9.6 | 8.1 | 4.7 | 6.6 | NM | 0.8 | 5.5 | 16.1 | 10.5 | 10.1 |
| % Return on Equity | 12.7 | 10.5 | 6.0 | 8.0 | NM | 1.2 | 8.2 | 20.7 | 13.4 | 15.6 |

Data as orig reptd.; bef. results of disc opers/spec. items. Per share data adj. for stk. divs.; EPS diluted. E-Estimated. NA-Not Available. NM-Not Meaningful. NR-Not Ranked. UR-Under Review.

**Office:** 4000 North First Street, San Jose, CA 95134-1568.
**Telephone:** 408-943-9700.
**Email:** info@novellus.com
**Website:** http://www.novellus.com

**Chrmn & CEO:** R. Hill
**COO:** G. Addiego
**EVP, CFO & Chief Admin Officer:** J.C. Benzing
**EVP & CTO:** F.E. Chen

**SVP, Secy & General Counsel:** M.J. Collins
**Investor Contact:** R. Yim (408-943-9700)
**Board Members:** N. R. Bonke, Y. A. El-mansy, R. Hill, J. D. Litster, Y. Nishi, G. G. Possley, A. D. Rhoads, W. R. Spivey, J. D. Ulster, D. A. Whitaker

**Founded:** 1984
**Domicile:** California
**Employees:** 3,698

# Nucor Corp

STANDARD &POOR'S

**S&P Recommendation** BUY ★ ★ ★ ★ ☆

| | | |
|---|---|---|
| **Price** $32.73 (as of Nov 14, 2008) | **12-Mo. Target Price** $39.00 | **Investment Style** Large-Cap Blend |

**GICS Sector** Materials
**Sub-Industry** Steel

**Summary** As the largest minimill steelmaker in the U.S., Nucor has one of the most diverse product lines of any steelmaker in the Americas.

## Key Stock Statistics (Source S&P, Vickers, company reports)

| | | | | | | |
|---|---|---|---|---|---|---|
| 52-Wk Range | $83.56– 26.30 | S&P Oper. EPS 2008**E** | 6.78 | Market Capitalization(B) | $10.276 | Beta | 1.11 |
| Trailing 12-Month EPS | $6.98 | S&P Oper. EPS 2009**E** | 5.07 | Yield (%) | 3.91 | S&P 3-Yr. Proj. EPS CAGR(%) | 3 |
| Trailing 12-Month P/E | 4.7 | P/E on S&P Oper. EPS 2008**E** | 4.8 | Dividend Rate/Share | $1.28 | S&P Credit Rating | AA- |
| $10K Invested 5 Yrs Ago | $27,647 | Common Shares Outstg. (M) | 314.0 | Institutional Ownership (%) | 78 | | |

## Price Performance

- 30-Week Mov. Avg. · · ·  10-Week Mov. Avg. – –  **GAAP Earnings vs. Previous Year**  Volume Above Avg. STARS
- 12-Mo. Target Price —  Relative Strength —  ▲ Up  ▼ Down  ► No Change  Below Avg.

2-for-1

Options: ASE, CBOE, P, Ph

Analysis prepared by **Leo J. Larkin** on November 11, 2008, when the stock traded at **$ 34.07**.

## Highlights

➤ We look a 15% sales decline in 2009 on a forecasted decrease in revenue per ton and shipped volume. Our sales forecast rests on several assumptions. First, S&P forecasts negative GDP of 0.1% in 2009 versus GDP growth of 1.6% estimated for 2008. Second, S&P expects a 13.8% decline in non-residential construction spending versus an estimated increase 11% in 2008. We see this depressing sales of both structural steel products for construction markets and sales of fabricated building products. Third, we think distributors will reduce inventories through most of 2009, thereby leading to lower demand for most steel products. Finally, we think reduced domestic steel production will result in lower sales for David J. Joseph's scrap products.

➤ We look for lower operating profit as reduced volume should offset lower costs for energy and scrap. After higher interest expense and more shares outstanding, we project EPS of $5.07 in 2009 versus estimated EPS of $6.78 for 2008.

➤ Longer term, we see EPS rising on industry consolidation, the introduction of new steelmaking technology, a better product mix, acquisitions, and better control of raw material costs.

## Investment Rationale/Risk

➤ We view Nucor as a vehicle for capitalizing on the consolidation of the global steel industry. With the industry becoming more consolidated via mergers, the increased concentration of production among fewer companies should result in greater pricing discipline. Also, we see free cash flow growth accelerating on a combination of rising net income and generally moderate capital spending for the next several years. We believe this will enable NUE to raise its dividend, make acquisitions and invest in new steelmaking technology. We believe the stock, recently trading at about 7X our 2009 estimate and yielding about 3.7%, is attractively valued. Our recommendation is buy on that basis.

➤ Risks to our opinion and target price include the possibility that nonresidential construction declines by more than we currently project in 2009.

➤ The P/E multiple of 7.7X that we apply to our 2009 EPS estimate of $5.07 is toward the low end of the stock's historical range of the past 10 years and at a slight premium to the P/E we project for peers. On that basis, our 12-month target price is $39.

## Qualitative Risk Assessment

| LOW | MEDIUM | HIGH |
|---|---|---|

Our risk assessment reflects that despite Nucor's exposure to cyclical markets such as non-residential construction, the company has a solid share of the markets in which it competes, has a very low ratio of total debt to assets, and generates what we view as substantial free cash flow.

## Quantitative Evaluations

**S&P Quality Ranking**  B

| D | C | B- | B | B+ | A- | A | A+ |
|---|---|---|---|---|---|---|---|

**Relative Strength Rank**  MODERATE

52

LOWEST = 1    HIGHEST = 99

## Revenue/Earnings Data

**Revenue (Million $)**

| | 1Q | 2Q | 3Q | 4Q | Year |
|---|---|---|---|---|---|
| 2008 | 4,974 | 7,091 | 7,448 | -- | -- |
| 2007 | 3,769 | 4,168 | 4,259 | 4,397 | 16,593 |
| 2006 | 3,545 | 3,806 | 3,931 | 3,469 | 14,751 |
| 2005 | 3,323 | 3,145 | 3,026 | 3,207 | 12,701 |
| 2004 | 2,286 | 2,762 | 3,240 | 3,089 | 11,376 |
| 2003 | 1,480 | 1,520 | 1,604 | 1,661 | 6,266 |

**Earnings Per Share ($)**

| | 1Q | 2Q | 3Q | 4Q | Year |
|---|---|---|---|---|---|
| 2008 | 1.41 | 1.94 | 2.31 | E1.12 | E6.78 |
| 2007 | 1.26 | 1.14 | 1.29 | 1.26 | 4.94 |
| 2006 | 1.21 | 1.45 | 1.68 | 1.35 | 5.68 |
| 2005 | 1.10 | 1.02 | 0.93 | 1.09 | 4.13 |
| 2004 | 0.36 | 0.79 | 1.30 | 1.06 | 3.51 |
| 2003 | 0.06 | 0.03 | 0.05 | 0.07 | 0.20 |

Fiscal year ended Dec. 31. Next earnings report expected: Late January. EPS Estimates based on S&P Operating Earnings; historical GAAP earnings are as reported.

## Dividend Data (Dates: mm/dd Payment Date: mm/dd/yy)

| Amount ($) | Date Decl. | Ex-Div. Date | Stk. of Record | Payment Date |
|---|---|---|---|---|
| .20 Ext. | 02/20 | 03/26 | 03/28 | 05/09/08 |
| .2 Ext. | 06/03 | 06/26 | 06/30 | 08/11/08 |
| 0.320 | 06/03 | 06/26 | 06/30 | 08/11/08 |
| .20 Ext. | 09/04 | 09/26 | 09/30 | 11/11/08 |

Dividends have been paid since 1973. Source: Company reports.

# Nucor Corp

## Business Summary November 11, 2008

CORPORATE OVERVIEW. Nucor is the largest U.S. minimill steelmaker. In 2007, production was 22.1 million tons and outside shipments were 20.2 million tons.

CORPORATE STRATEGY. Nucor's growth strategy involves four initiatives. The first is to optimize existing operations. The second is to make strategic acquisitions. The third involves construction of new plants and development of new technologies for markets where the company believes it has a major cost advantage. The fourth initiative is to expand globally through joint ventures that leverage new technologies.

MARKET PROFILE. The primary factors affecting demand for steel products are economic growth in general and growth in demand for durable goods in particular. The two largest end markets for steel products in the U.S. are autos and construction. In 2007, these two markets accounted for 29.5% of shipments in the U.S. market. Other end markets include appliances, containers, machinery, and oil and gas. Distributors, also known as service centers, accounted for 20.4% of industry shipments in the U.S. market in 2007. Distribu-

tors are the largest single market for the steel industry in the U.S. Because distributors sell to a wide variety of OEMs, it is impossible to trace the final destination of much of the industry's shipments. Consequently, demand for steel from the auto, construction and other industries may be higher than the shipment data would suggest. Construction accounts for some 60% of the demand for Nucor's products, oil and gas 15%, autos and appliances 15%, and other markets 10%. In terms of production, the size of the U.S. market was 108.2 million tons in 2007, and Nucor's market share was 20.4%. In the U.S. market, consumption increased at a compound annual growth rate (CAGR) of 1.4% from 1997 through 2006. Global steel production was 1.34 billion metric tons in 2007. Consumption grew at a CAGR of 5.2% from 1997 through 2006 (latest available data).

## Company Financials Fiscal Year Ended Dec. 31

| Per Share Data ($) | 2007 | 2006 | 2005 | 2004 | 2003 | 2002 | 2001 | 2000 | 1999 | 1998 |
|---|---|---|---|---|---|---|---|---|---|---|
| Tangible Book Value | 13.18 | 15.56 | 13.80 | 10.84 | 7.45 | 7.43 | 7.07 | 6.87 | 6.49 | 5.93 |
| Cash Flow | 6.38 | 7.05 | 5.43 | 4.72 | 1.36 | 1.50 | 1.29 | 1.74 | 1.44 | 1.47 |
| Earnings | 4.94 | 5.68 | 4.13 | 3.51 | 0.20 | 0.52 | 0.36 | 0.95 | 0.70 | 0.75 |
| S&P Core Earnings | 4.94 | 5.68 | 4.09 | 3.49 | 0.15 | 0.46 | 0.33 | NA | NA | NA |
| Dividends | 0.63 | 0.40 | 0.30 | 0.24 | 0.20 | 0.19 | 0.17 | 0.15 | 0.13 | 0.12 |
| Payout Ratio | 13% | 7% | 7% | 7% | 100% | 37% | 47% | 16% | 18% | 15% |
| Prices:High | 69.93 | 67.55 | 35.11 | 27.74 | 14.70 | 17.54 | 14.13 | 14.11 | 15.45 | 15.16 |
| Prices:Low | 41.62 | 33.63 | 22.78 | 13.04 | 8.76 | 9.00 | 8.36 | 7.38 | 10.41 | 8.81 |
| P/E Ratio:High | 14 | 12 | 9 | 8 | 73 | 34 | 39 | 15 | 22 | 20 |
| P/E Ratio:Low | 8 | 6 | 6 | 4 | 44 | 17 | 23 | 8 | 15 | 12 |

| Income Statement Analysis (Million $) | | | | | | | | | | |
|---|---|---|---|---|---|---|---|---|---|---|
| Revenue | 16,593 | 14,751 | 12,701 | 11,377 | 6,266 | 4,802 | 4,139 | 4,586 | 4,009 | 4,151 |
| Operating Income | 2,980 | 3,240 | 2,497 | 2,216 | 468 | 601 | 469 | 737 | 631 | 665 |
| Depreciation | 428 | 364 | 375 | 383 | 364 | 307 | 289 | 259 | 257 | 253 |
| Interest Expense | 51.1 | Nil | 4.20 | 22.4 | 24.6 | 22.9 | 22.0 | 24.1 | 20.5 | 10.0 |
| Pretax Income | 2,547 | 2,913 | 2,127 | 1,812 | 90.8 | 310 | 174 | 478 | 379 | 415 |
| Effective Tax Rate | 30.7% | 32.1% | 33.2% | 33.6% | 4.51% | 22.0% | 35.0% | 35.0% | 35.5% | 36.5% |
| Net Income | 1,472 | 1,758 | 1,310 | 1,121 | 62.8 | 162 | 113 | 311 | 245 | 264 |
| S&P Core Earnings | 1,472 | 1,758 | 1,296 | 1,114 | 47.9 | 143 | 101 | NA | NA | NA |

| Balance Sheet & Other Financial Data (Million $) | | | | | | | | | | |
|---|---|---|---|---|---|---|---|---|---|---|
| Cash | 1,576 | 786 | 1,838 | 779 | 350 | 219 | 462 | 491 | 572 | 309 |
| Current Assets | 5,073 | 4,675 | 4,072 | 3,175 | 1,621 | 1,424 | 1,374 | 1,381 | 1,539 | 1,129 |
| Total Assets | 9,826 | 7,885 | 7,139 | 6,133 | 4,492 | 4,381 | 3,759 | 3,722 | 3,730 | 3,227 |
| Current Liabilities | 1,582 | 1,450 | 1,256 | 1,066 | 630 | 592 | 484 | 558 | 531 | 487 |
| Long Term Debt | 2,250 | 922 | 922 | 924 | 904 | 879 | 460 | 460 | 390 | 215 |
| Common Equity | 5,113 | 4,826 | 4,280 | 3,456 | 2,342 | 2,323 | 2,201 | 2,131 | 2,262 | 2,073 |
| Total Capital | 7,651 | 5,987 | 5,396 | 4,553 | 3,423 | 3,419 | 2,946 | 2,904 | 2,934 | 2,570 |
| Capital Expenditures | 520 | 338 | 331 | 286 | 215 | 244 | 261 | 415 | 375 | 503 |
| Cash Flow | 1,900 | 2,122 | 1,685 | 1,505 | 427 | 469 | 402 | 570 | 501 | 517 |
| Current Ratio | 3.2 | 3.2 | 3.2 | 3.0 | 2.6 | 2.4 | 2.8 | 2.5 | 2.9 | 2.3 |
| % Long Term Debt of Capitalization | 29.4 | 15.4 | 17.1 | 20.3 | 26.4 | 25.7 | 15.6 | 15.9 | 13.3 | 8.4 |
| % Net Income of Revenue | 8.9 | 11.9 | 10.3 | 9.9 | 1.0 | 3.4 | 2.7 | 6.8 | 6.1 | 6.4 |
| % Return on Assets | 16.6 | 23.4 | 19.7 | 21.1 | 1.4 | 4.0 | 3.0 | 8.3 | 7.0 | 8.5 |
| % Return on Equity | 29.6 | 38.6 | 33.9 | 38.7 | 2.7 | 5.1 | 5.2 | 14.2 | 11.3 | 13.4 |

Data as orig reptd.; bef. results of disc opers/spec. items. Per share data adj. for stk. divs.; EPS diluted. E-Estimated. NA-Not Available. NM-Not Meaningful. NR-Not Ranked. UR-Under Review.

**Office:** 1915 Rexford Rd, Charlotte, NC 28211-3441.
**Telephone:** 704-366-7000.
**Email:** info@nucor.com
**Website:** http://www.nucor.com

**Chrmn, Pres & CEO:** D.R. DiMicco
**COO:** J.J. Ferriola
**EVP, CFO & Treas:** T.S. Lisenby
**Secy:** A.R. Eagle

**Cntlr:** J.D. Frias
**Board Members:** P. C. Browning, C. C. Daley, Jr., D. R. DiMicco, H. B. Gantt, V. F. Haynes, J. D. Hlavacek, B. L. Kasriel, C. J. Kearney, J. H. Walker

**Founded:** 1940
**Domicile:** Delaware
**Employees:** 18,000

# NVIDIA Corp

**STANDARD &POOR'S**

| S&P Recommendation **HOLD** ★★★☆☆ | Price $7.17 (as of Nov 14, 2008) | 12-Mo. Target Price $14.00 | Investment Style Large-Cap Growth |

**GICS Sector** Information Technology
**Sub-Industry** Semiconductors

**Summary** This company develops and markets 3D graphics processors for personal computers, workstations and digital entertainment platforms.

## Key Stock Statistics (Source S&P, Vickers, company reports)

| | | | | | | | |
|---|---|---|---|---|---|---|---|
| 52-Wk Range | $36.40– 5.97 | S&P Oper. EPS 2009**E** | 0.57 | Market Capitalization(B) | $3.991 | Beta | 2.98 |
| Trailing 12-Month EPS | $0.63 | S&P Oper. EPS 2010**E** | 0.52 | Yield (%) | Nil | S&P 3-Yr. Proj. EPS CAGR(%) | NM |
| Trailing 12-Month P/E | 11.4 | P/E on S&P Oper. EPS 2009**E** | 12.6 | Dividend Rate/Share | Nil | S&P Credit Rating | BB- |
| $10K Invested 5 Yrs Ago | $10,663 | Common Shares Outstg. (M) | 556.6 | Institutional Ownership (%) | 74 | | |

## Price Performance

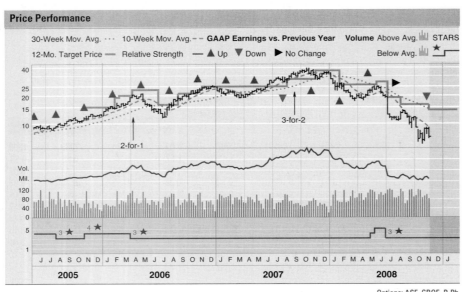

30-Week Mov. Avg. ···  10-Week Mov. Avg. - - **GAAP Earnings vs. Previous Year**  Volume Above Avg. ▐▐▐ STARS
12-Mo. Target Price —  Relative Strength —  ▲ Up ▼ Down ► No Change   Below Avg. ▐▐▐ ★

Options: ASE, CBOE, P, Ph

Analysis prepared by **Clyde Montevirgen** on November 11, 2008, when the stock traded at **$ 8.16**.

### Highlights

➤ We anticipate revenues will decrease 7% for FY 10 (Jan.), following a similar decrease that we see for FY 09. Although we think long-term drivers, such as healthy growth for computers and graphics-intensive applications, remain intact, we see near-term growth limited by a deceleration in computer sales due to macroeconomic headwinds. We are also concerned about slowing sales of desktop computers as laptops gain popularity. However, NVIDIA has strong brand recognition, technologically leading higher-end products, and new products for laptops, which should lead to market share gains, in our opinion.

➤ We believe non-GAAP gross margins will widen to around 44% for FY 10, from an anticipated 42% for FY 09, as NVDA recovers from an exceptionally weak pricing period due to a bad product transition. However, we think adjusted operating margins will decrease to around 9% for FY 10 from an estimated 10% in FY 09, reflecting our view that sales will fall faster than expenses.

➤ We forecast operating EPS of $0.52 in FY 10, versus a projected $0.57 in FY 09.

### Investment Rationale/Risk

➤ Our hold recommendation reflects our view of healthy anticipated long-term growth balanced by near-term hurdles. NVIDIA has benefited from strong computer growth, favorable brand awareness amongst gamers, and increasing graphics intensity in applications. Although we think NVDA's quality products will help it take share in high-end markets that use graphics intensive applications, we are concerned about slowing demand for desktop computers pressuring growth and existing inventory of older, 65 nanometer products, limiting margin expansion.

➤ Risks to our opinion and target price include the possibility that relatively lower economic growth slows PC sales and that AMD gains market share faster than anticipated.

➤ Our 12-month target price of $14 is based on a blend of relative metrics. We apply a target P/E ratio of approximately 24X, which is near the company's historical average, to our FY 10 EPS projection, implying a value of around $13. We also use a price-to-sales multiple of about 2.4X our forward 12-month sales per share estimate, yielding a value of around $15.

### Qualitative Risk Assessment

| LOW | MEDIUM | **HIGH** |

Our risk assessment reflects the cyclicality of the semiconductor industry and of demand trends for electronics goods that benefit from advanced visual displays, and revenue volatility resulting from wins and losses of deals with big accounts.

### Quantitative Evaluations

**S&P Quality Ranking**                              B

| D | C | B- | **B** | B+ | A- | A | A+ |

**Relative Strength Rank**                    MODERATE

41

LOWEST = 1                                      HIGHEST = 99

### Revenue/Earnings Data

**Revenue (Million $)**

| | 1Q | 2Q | 3Q | 4Q | Year |
|---|---|---|---|---|---|
| 2009 | 1,153 | 892.7 | 897.7 | -- | -- |
| 2008 | 844.3 | 935.3 | 1,116 | 1,203 | 4,098 |
| 2007 | 681.8 | 687.5 | 820.6 | 878.9 | 3,069 |
| 2006 | 583.9 | 574.8 | 583.4 | 633.6 | 2,376 |
| 2005 | 471.9 | 456.1 | 515.6 | 566.5 | 2,010 |
| 2004 | 405.0 | 459.8 | 486.1 | 472.1 | 1,823 |

**Earnings Per Share ($)**

| | | | | | |
|---|---|---|---|---|---|
| 2009 | 0.30 | -0.22 | 0.11 | E0.08 | E0.57 |
| 2008 | 0.22 | -0.22 | 0.38 | 0.42 | 1.32 |
| 2007 | 0.15 | 0.15 | 0.18 | 0.27 | 0.77 |
| 2006 | 0.12 | 0.14 | 0.12 | 0.18 | 0.55 |
| 2005 | 0.04 | 0.01 | 0.05 | 0.09 | 0.19 |
| 2004 | 0.04 | 0.05 | 0.01 | 0.05 | 0.15 |

Fiscal year ended Jan. 31. Next earnings report expected: Mid February. EPS Estimates based on S&P Operating Earnings; historical GAAP earnings are as reported.

### Dividend Data

No cash dividends have been paid.

The McGraw-Hill Companies

# NVIDIA Corp

## Business Summary November 11, 2008

CORPORATE OVERVIEW. NVIDIA Corp. designs, develops and markets high-performance graphics processing units (GPUs), media and communications processors (MCPs), handheld GPUs, and related software for PCs and digital entertainment platforms, ranging from professional workstations to video game consoles to handheld electronic devices. The company's products are designed to generate realistic, interactive graphics on consumer and professional computing devices. It aims to be the leading supplier of performance GPUs, MCPs and handheld GPUs.

NVDA has four major product line operating segments: the graphics processing units business, the professional solutions business (PSB), the media and communications processor (MCP) business, and the consumer product business (CPB).

Interactive 3D graphics displays are an integral part of many computing applications for workstations, consumer and commercial desktop and laptop PCs, personal digital assistants, cellular phones, and gaming consoles. NVDA's products are designed into products offered by nearly all leading PC OEMs.

The company supplied graphics chips for Microsoft's Xbox video game console, but lost to rival AMD/ATI Technologies for the GPU for the next-generation Xbox. However, the company presently supplies GPU products for Sony's PlayStation 3 video game console.

CORPORATE STRATEGY. NVDA's goal is to become the leading supplier of performance GPUs, MCPs, and handheld GPUs and application processors. The elements behind the strategy include: building award-winning and architecturally compatible graphics and media products for various platforms; targeting leading OEMs, ODMs, and system builders; sustaining technology and product leadership in graphics and media products; increasing market share; creating synergy by combining expertise in graphics and media; and using its intellectual property and resources to enter into license and development contracts.

## Company Financials Fiscal Year Ended Jan. 31

### Per Share Data ($)

| | 2008 | 2007 | 2006 | 2005 | 2004 | 2003 | 2002 | 2001 | 2000 | 1999 |
|---|---|---|---|---|---|---|---|---|---|---|
| Tangible Book Value | 4.35 | 3.32 | 2.52 | 2.08 | 1.83 | 1.81 | 1.52 | 0.93 | 0.34 | 0.19 |
| Cash Flow | 1.54 | 0.95 | 0.73 | 0.38 | 0.30 | 0.29 | 0.43 | 0.24 | 0.14 | 0.02 |
| Earnings | 1.32 | 0.77 | 0.55 | 0.19 | 0.14 | 0.18 | 0.34 | 0.21 | 0.09 | 0.01 |
| S&P Core Earnings | 1.31 | 0.79 | 0.42 | 0.03 | -0.00 | -0.22 | 0.10 | 0.12 | NA | NA |
| Dividends | Nil | Nil | Nil | Nil | Nil | Nil | Nil | Nil | Nil | Nil |
| Payout Ratio | Nil | Nil | Nil | Nil | Nil | Nil | Nil | Nil | Nil | Nil |
| Calendar Year | 2007 | 2006 | 2005 | 2004 | 2003 | 2002 | 2001 | 2000 | 1999 | 1998 |
| Prices:High | 39.67 | 25.97 | 12.83 | 9.12 | 9.25 | 24.22 | 23.42 | 14.67 | 3.96 | NA |
| Prices:Low | 18.69 | 11.45 | 6.82 | 3.10 | 3.11 | 2.40 | 4.71 | 2.92 | 1.00 | NA |
| P/E Ratio:High | 30 | 34 | 23 | 48 | 65 | NM | 68 | 71 | 42 | NA |
| P/E Ratio:Low | 14 | 15 | 12 | 16 | 22 | NM | 14 | 14 | 11 | NA |

### Income Statement Analysis (Million $)

| | 2008 | 2007 | 2006 | 2005 | 2004 | 2003 | 2002 | 2001 | 2000 | 1999 |
|---|---|---|---|---|---|---|---|---|---|---|
| Revenue | 4,098 | 3,069 | 2,376 | 2,010 | 1,823 | 1,909 | 1,369 | 735 | 375 | 158 |
| Operating Income | 976 | 593 | 452 | 216 | 172 | 202 | 299 | 146 | 63.4 | 8.52 |
| Depreciation | 136 | 108 | 98.0 | 103 | 82.0 | 58.2 | 43.5 | 15.7 | 9.00 | 4.01 |
| Interest Expense | 0.05 | 0.02 | 0.07 | 0.16 | 12.0 | Nil | 16.2 | 4.85 | Nil | Nil |
| Pretax Income | 901 | 494 | 360 | 125 | 86.7 | 151 | 253 | 147 | 56.2 | 4.49 |
| Effective Tax Rate | 11.5% | 9.37% | 16.0% | 20.0% | 14.1% | 39.7% | 30.0% | 31.9% | 32.1% | 7.96% |
| Net Income | 798 | 448 | 303 | 100 | 74.4 | 90.8 | 177 | 100 | 38.1 | 4.13 |
| S&P Core Earnings | 798 | 460 | 230 | 14.6 | -1.44 | -104 | 49.4 | 54.7 | NA | NA |

### Balance Sheet & Other Financial Data (Million $)

| | 2008 | 2007 | 2006 | 2005 | 2004 | 2003 | 2002 | 2001 | 2000 | 1999 |
|---|---|---|---|---|---|---|---|---|---|---|
| Cash | 1,809 | 1,118 | 950 | 670 | 604 | 1,028 | 791 | 674 | 61.6 | 50.3 |
| Current Assets | 2,889 | 2,032 | 1,549 | 1,305 | 1,053 | 1,352 | 1,234 | 930 | 173 | 101 |
| Total Assets | 3,748 | 2,675 | 1,915 | 1,629 | 1,399 | 1,617 | 1,503 | 1,017 | 203 | 113 |
| Current Liabilities | 967 | 639 | 439 | 421 | 334 | 379 | 433 | 110 | 76.2 | 47.1 |
| Long Term Debt | Nil | Nil | Nil | Nil | 0.86 | 305 | 306 | 300 | 1.46 | 2.00 |
| Common Equity | 2,618 | 2,007 | 1,458 | 1,178 | 1,051 | 933 | 764 | 406 | 125 | 64.2 |
| Total Capital | 2,705 | 2,007 | 1,466 | 1,199 | 1,061 | 1,238 | 1,070 | 706 | 126 | 66.2 |
| Capital Expenditures | 188 | 145 | 79.6 | 67.3 | 128 | 63.1 | 97.0 | 36.3 | 11.6 | 7.90 |
| Cash Flow | 933 | 556 | 401 | 203 | 156 | 149 | 220 | 114 | 50.0 | 8.14 |
| Current Ratio | 3.0 | 3.2 | 3.5 | 3.1 | 3.2 | 3.6 | 2.8 | 8.4 | 2.3 | 2.1 |
| % Long Term Debt of Capitalization | Nil | Nil | Nil | Nil | 0.1 | 24.6 | 28.6 | 42.4 | 1.2 | 3.0 |
| % Net Income of Revenue | 19.5 | 14.6 | 12.7 | 5.0 | 4.1 | 4.8 | 12.9 | 13.4 | 10.9 | 2.6 |
| % Return on Assets | 24.8 | 19.4 | 17.1 | 6.6 | 4.9 | 5.8 | 14.0 | 16.1 | 25.9 | 5.8 |
| % Return on Equity | 34.5 | 25.6 | 23.0 | 9.0 | 7.5 | 10.7 | 30.2 | 36.9 | 42.9 | 11.3 |

Data as orig reptd.; bef. results of disc opers/spec. items. Per share data adj. for stk. divs.; EPS diluted. E-Estimated. NA-Not Available. NM-Not Meaningful. NR-Not Ranked. UR-Under Review.

**Office:** 2701 San Tomas Expressway, Santa Clara, CA 95050.
**Telephone:** 408-486-2000.
**Email:** ir@nvidia.com
**Website:** http://www.nvidia.com

**Pres & CEO:** J. Huang
**COO:** D. Shoquist
**SVP, Secy & General Counsel:** D.M. Shannon
**CSO:** D.B. Kirk

**Investor Contact:** M. Hara (408-486-2511)
**Board Members:** S. Chu, T. Coxe, J. C. Gaither, J. Huang, H. C. Jones, Jr., W. J. Miller, M. L. Perry, B. B. Seawell, M. A. Stevens

**Founded:** 1993
**Domicile:** Delaware
**Employees:** 4,985

# NYSE Euronext

| S&P Recommendation **BUY** ★★★★☆ | Price<br>$24.84 (as of Nov 14, 2008) | 12-Mo. Target Price<br>$45.00 | Investment Style<br>Large-Cap Growth |
|---|---|---|---|

**GICS Sector** Financials
**Sub-Industry** Specialized Finance

**Summary** NYX is a holding company created by the merger of NYSE Group and Euronext. NYX operates six cash equities exchanges in five countries and six derivatives exchanges in six countries.

## Key Stock Statistics (Source S&P, Vickers, company reports)

| | | | | | | | |
|---|---|---|---|---|---|---|---|
| 52-Wk Range | **$92.73–21.77** | S&P Oper. EPS 2008**E** | 2.80 | Market Capitalization(B) | **$6.607** | Beta | 1.53 |
| Trailing 12-Month EPS | **$2.84** | S&P Oper. EPS 2009**E** | 3.19 | Yield (%) | 4.83 | S&P 3-Yr. Proj. EPS CAGR(%) | 23 |
| Trailing 12-Month P/E | 8.8 | P/E on S&P Oper. EPS 2008**E** | 8.9 | Dividend Rate/Share | $1.20 | S&P Credit Rating | NA |
| $10K Invested 5 Yrs Ago | NA | Common Shares Outstg. (M) | 266.0 | Institutional Ownership (%) | 59 | | |

## Price Performance

30-Week Mov. Avg. · · · ·   10-Week Mov. Avg. - - -   **GAAP Earnings vs. Previous Year**   Volume Above Avg. STARS
12-Mo. Target Price —   Relative Strength —   ▲ Up   ▼ Down   ► No Change   Below Avg.  ★

Analysis prepared by **Rikin Pandya** on October 22, 2008, when the stock traded at **$ 31.62**.

## Highlights

➤ We view NYX and its New York Stock Exchange, NYSE Arca, and Euronext operations as the leading exchange group in the world. With the completion of its acquisition of Euronext in April 2007, we see NYX taking the lead in the rapidly consolidating global financial exchange landscape. While we believe 2007 was a transitional year for NYX as it integrated Euronext, we see profit growth in 2008 continuing into 2009 as NYX realizes larger expense synergies.

➤ In the second quarter, NYX saw trading volumes, particularly in the U.S., decline from first quarter levels. Although we believe NYX's broad product and geographic exposure position it well for earnings growth, and we expect more significant expense synergies in 2008, lower trading volumes will likely pressure short-term earnings. We see a number of future growth drivers, including U.S. derivatives, bonds, and further geographic expansion.

➤ We forecast EPS of $3.09 in 2008, rising to $3.85 in 2009. Our estimates include results from Euronext, which we expect will be accretive to earnings in both years.

## Investment Rationale/Risk

➤ We believe NYX is in the midst of a significant transformational phase, highlighted by its acquisition of European derivatives and equity exchange Euronext, and the implementation of Regulation National Market System in the U.S. and MiFD in Europe. We believe NYX is taking the right steps to position itself for what we view as a global competitive environment. However, we expect NYX's results to come under pressure from lower trading volume this year, and we are also concerned with market share losses in U.S. equities, and the risk of a large dilutive transaction to expand its U.S. derivatives business.

➤ Risks to our recommendation and target price include an uncertain regulatory environment, Euronext integration problems, migration to a hybrid trading model, and a slowdown in equity and option trading volumes.

➤ Our 12-month target price of $45 is based on a P/E multiple of 11.6X our 2009 EPS estimate, a discount to the current peer average. The shares are trading at a considerable discount to our target price, which we believe represents an attractive buying opportunity.

## Qualitative Risk Assessment

| LOW | MEDIUM | HIGH |
|---|---|---|

Our risk assessment reflects the potential volatility in results due to changes in equity and equity options trading volumes, the impact of current and future regulatory changes, and the integration of a number of recent acquisitions.

## Quantitative Evaluations

### S&P Quality Ranking        NR

| D | C | B- | B | B+ | A- | A | A+ |
|---|---|---|---|---|---|---|---|

### Relative Strength Rank        MODERATE

41

LOWEST = 1                                                    HIGHEST = 99

## Revenue/Earnings Data

### Revenue (Million $)

| | 1Q | 2Q | 3Q | 4Q | Year |
|---|---|---|---|---|---|
| 2008 | 1,191 | 1,112 | 1,159 | -- | -- |
| 2007 | 702.0 | 1,078 | 1,198 | 1,180 | 3,602 |
| 2006 | 478.9 | 659.5 | 602.9 | 658.5 | 2,376 |
| 2005 | -- | -- | -- | -- | 1,667 |
| 2004 | -- | -- | -- | -- | -- |
| 2003 | -- | -- | -- | -- | -- |

### Earnings Per Share ($)

| | | | | | |
|---|---|---|---|---|---|
| 2008 | 0.87 | 0.73 | 0.64 | E0.55 | E2.80 |
| 2007 | 0.43 | 0.62 | 0.97 | 0.59 | 2.70 |
| 2006 | 0.24 | 0.39 | 0.43 | 0.29 | 1.36 |
| 2005 | -- | -- | -- | -- | 0.58 |
| 2004 | -- | -- | -- | -- | -- |
| 2003 | -- | -- | -- | -- | -- |

Fiscal year ended Dec. 31. Next earnings report expected: Early February. EPS Estimates based on S&P Operating Earnings; historical GAAP earnings are as reported.

## Dividend Data (Dates: mm/dd Payment Date: mm/dd/yy)

| Amount ($) | Date Decl. | Ex-Div. Date | Stk. of Record | Payment Date |
|---|---|---|---|---|
| 0.300 | 03/18 | 06/11 | 06/13 | 06/30/08 |
| 0.300 | 06/19 | 09/11 | 09/15 | 09/30/08 |
| 0.300 | 06/19 | 12/11 | 12/15 | 12/31/08 |
| 0.300 | 06/19 | 03/11 | 03/13 | 03/31/09 |

Dividends have been paid since 2007. Source: Company reports.

# NYSE Euronext

**STANDARD &POOR'S**

## Business Summary October 22, 2008

CORPORATE OVERVIEW. NYSE Euronext (NYX) is a holding company created by the combination of NYSE Group and Euronext on April 4, 2007. NYX operates the world's largest and most liquid exchange group and offers a diverse array of financial products and services. The company, which brings together six cash equities exchanges in five countries and six derivatives exchanges in six countries, offers listings, trading in cash equities, equity and interest rate derivatives, bonds and the distribution of market data. As of December 31, 2007, NYX combined listed companies represented over $30.5 trillion in total market capitalization and average daily trading value of approximately $141 billion.

NYX generates revenue primarily from transactions, company listing fees, market data, regulatory fees, and exchange licenses. The company also records activity assessment revenue, which is a pass through netted against section 31 fee expense. We have excluded this revenue line item when examining NYX's revenue from operations. Following the combination of the NYSE with Archipelago (now NYSE Arca), transaction fees have become the largest revenue driver for NYX (47% of total revenue for 2007). Transaction revenue is

generated from fees paid for trading on NYX's exchanges, and benefits from higher trading volumes. Listing fees are NYX's second largest revenue contributor (9.3%) and include initial fees charged for companies listing on one of NYX's exchanges and an ongoing annual listing fee. We view transactional revenue as the key growth driver for NYX moving forward.

CORPORATE STRATEGY. We believe NYX is in the middle of a transformational phase as it fully integrates the NYSE Arca assets with the NYSE, transitions the NYSE from a floor-based trading system to a hybrid floor/electronic model, completes its merger with Euronext, and readies for significant regulatory and structural changes in U.S. and European equity and equity options trading. We expect the number and scope of ongoing projects and regulatory changes to likely make for uneven financial performance and difficult historical and peer comparisons over the coming quarters.

## Company Financials Fiscal Year Ended Dec. 31

| Per Share Data ($) | 2007 | 2006 | 2005 | 2004 | 2003 | 2002 | 2001 | 2000 | 1999 | 1998 |
|---|---|---|---|---|---|---|---|---|---|---|
| Tangible Book Value | NM | 3.51 | NA | NA | NA | NA | NA | NA | NA | NA |
| Cash Flow | 3.76 | 2.27 | 1.50 | NA | NA | NA | NA | NA | NA | NA |
| Earnings | 2.70 | 1.36 | 0.58 | NA | NA | NA | NA | NA | NA | NA |
| S&P Core Earnings | 2.55 | 1.28 | 0.35 | 0.31 | NA | NA | NA | NA | NA | NA |
| Dividends | 0.75 | Nil | NA | NA | NA | NA | NA | NA | NA | NA |
| Payout Ratio | 28% | Nil | NA | NA | NA | NA | NA | NA | NA | NA |
| Prices:High | 109.50 | 112.00 | NA | NA | NA | NA | NA | NA | NA | NA |
| Prices:Low | 64.26 | 48.62 | NA | NA | NA | NA | NA | NA | NA | NA |
| P/E Ratio:High | 41 | 82 | NA | NA | NA | NA | NA | NA | NA | NA |
| P/E Ratio:Low | 24 | 36 | NA | NA | NA | NA | NA | NA | NA | NA |

### Income Statement Analysis (Million $)

| | 2007 | 2006 | 2005 | 2004 | 2003 | 2002 | 2001 | 2000 | 1999 | 1998 |
|---|---|---|---|---|---|---|---|---|---|---|
| Revenue | 4,158 | 2,376 | 1,667 | 1,044 | 1,034 | 1,018 | 1,035 | NA | NA | NA |
| Operating Income | 1,228 | 424 | 3.18 | NA | NA | NA | NA | NA | NA | NA |
| Depreciation | 252 | 136 | 143 | 95.7 | 67.6 | 61.9 | 60.6 | NA | NA | NA |
| Interest Expense | 129 | Nil | Nil | NA | NA | NA | NA | NA | NA | NA |
| Pretax Income | 921 | 328 | 176 | NA | 87.3 | 42.1 | 52.8 | NA | NA | NA |
| Effective Tax Rate | 27.5% | 36.7% | 47.6% | NA | 41.7% | 27.8% | 33.6% | NA | NA | NA |
| Net Income | 643 | 205 | 90.0 | NA | 49.6 | 28.1 | 31.8 | NA | NA | NA |
| S&P Core Earnings | 609 | 193 | 54.1 | 42.3 | NA | NA | NA | NA | NA | NA |

### Balance Sheet & Other Financial Data (Million $)

| | 2007 | 2006 | 2005 | 2004 | 2003 | 2002 | 2001 | 2000 | 1999 | 1998 |
|---|---|---|---|---|---|---|---|---|---|---|
| Cash | 973 | 298 | 328 | 930 | 880 | 963 | 963 | NA | NA | NA |
| Current Assets | 2,278 | 1,443 | 1,204 | NA | NA | NA | NA | NA | NA | NA |
| Total Assets | 16,618 | 3,466 | 3,154 | NA | 1,777 | 1,757 | 1,730 | NA | NA | NA |
| Current Liabilities | 3,462 | 832 | 823 | NA | NA | NA | NA | NA | NA | NA |
| Long Term Debt | 522 | Nil | Nil | NA | NA | NA | NA | NA | NA | NA |
| Common Equity | 9,384 | 1,669 | 1,366 | NA | 952 | 896 | 882 | NA | NA | NA |
| Total Capital | 12,469 | 1,934 | 1,646 | NA | NA | NA | NA | NA | NA | NA |
| Capital Expenditures | 182 | 97.8 | NA | 84.6 | 68.5 | 113 | 89.0 | NA | NA | NA |
| Cash Flow | 895 | 341 | 233 | NA | NA | NA | NA | NA | NA | NA |
| Current Ratio | 0.7 | 1.7 | 1.5 | 2.6 | 2.9 | 3.4 | 3.0 | NA | NA | NA |
| % Long Term Debt of Capitalization | 4.2 | Nil | Nil | Nil | Nil | Nil | Nil | NA | NA | NA |
| % Net Income of Revenue | 15.5 | 8.6 | 5.4 | 2.9 | 4.8 | 2.8 | 3.1 | NA | NA | NA |
| % Return on Assets | 6.4 | 7.2 | NA | 1.6 | 2.8 | 1.6 | NA | NA | NA | NA |
| % Return on Equity | 11.6 | 16.6 | NA | 3.5 | 5.4 | 3.2 | NA | NA | NA | NA |

Data as orig reptd.; bef. results of disc opers/spec. items. Per share data adj. for stk. divs.; EPS diluted. E-Estimated. NA-Not Available. NM-Not Meaningful. NR-Not Ranked. UR-Under Review.

**Office:** 11 Wall Street, New York, NY 10005.
**Telephone:** 212-656-3000.
**Website:** http://www.nyse.com
**Chrmn:** J. Hessels

**Pres & COO:** C.R. Kinney
**Vice Chrmn:** M.N. Carter
**CEO:** D.L. Niederauer
**EVP & CFO:** M.S. Geltzeiler

**Investor Contact:** R. Adamonis (212-656-2140)
**Board Members:** E. L. Brown, M. N. Carter, G. Cox, W. E. Ford, S. Hefes, J. Hessels, D. Hoenn, S. A. Jackson, J. S. McDonald, D. M. McFarland, J. J. McNulty, D. L. Niederauer, B. J. Peterbroeck, A. M. Rivlin, R. E. Salgado, J. Theodore, R. Van Tets, B. Williamson

**Founded:** 2006
**Domicile:** Delaware
**Employees:** 3,083

The **McGraw-Hill** Companies

**STANDARD
&POOR'S**

# Occidental Petroleum Corp

| S&P Recommendation **BUY** ★★★★☆ | Price | 12-Mo. Target Price | Investment Style |
|---|---|---|---|
| | $48.19 (as of Nov 14, 2008) | $70.00 | Large-Cap Blend |

**GICS Sector** Energy
**Sub-Industry** Integrated Oil & Gas

**Summary** As one of the largest oil and gas companies in the U.S., OXY has global operations in exploration and production. Its subsidiary OxyChem is the largest U.S. merchant marketer of chlorine and caustic soda.

## Key Stock Statistics (Source S&P, Vickers, company reports)

| | | | | | | | |
|---|---|---|---|---|---|---|---|
| 52-Wk Range | $100.04– 39.93 | S&P Oper. EPS 2008**E** | 9.50 | Market Capitalization(B) | $39.028 | Beta | 1.03 |
| Trailing 12-Month EPS | $9.52 | S&P Oper. EPS 2009**E** | 8.70 | Yield (%) | 2.66 | S&P 3-Yr. Proj. EPS CAGR(%) | 16 |
| Trailing 12-Month P/E | 5.1 | P/E on S&P Oper. EPS 2008**E** | 5.1 | Dividend Rate/Share | $1.28 | S&P Credit Rating | A |
| $10K Invested 5 Yrs Ago | $28,759 | Common Shares Outstg. (M) | 809.9 | Institutional Ownership (%) | 80 | | |

## Price Performance

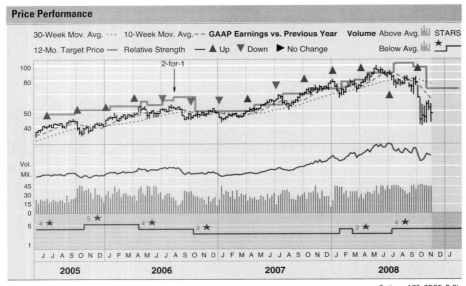

30-Week Mov. Avg. · · · · 10-Week Mov. Avg. - - GAAP Earnings vs. Previous Year   Volume Above Avg. ⅊ STARS
12-Mo. Target Price — Relative Strength — ▲ Up ▼ Down ► No Change   Below Avg. ⅊ ★

Options: ASE, CBOE, P, Ph

Analysis prepared by **Tina J. Vital** on October 28, 2008, when the stock traded at **$ 49.70**.

## Highlights

▶ Third quarter oil and gas production rose 3.2%, reflecting 31,000 boe per day contributions from the Dolphin project, which began production in the 2007 third quarter. However, volumes were below our expectations reflecting impacts from Gulf hurricanes and lower production in Libya as a result of a new contract during the quarter. Based on upwardly revised guidance, we project growth of over 5% in 2008 and over 6% in 2009.

▶ To accelerate prospects in the U.S. (mainly California, Texas and Colorado), as well as in Argentina, Colombia and Libya, OXY raised its 2008 capital expenditure budget to $4.5 to $4.7 billion, from $4.0 billion. So far this year, OXY has spend $3.3 billion on the acquisition of oil and gas assets in North America, and forged exploration deals in the Middle East and Africa.

▶ We expect that after-tax operating earnings will increase 73% in 2008 on production gains and strong pricing, before declining about 9% in 2009 on lower projected price realizations.

## Investment Rationale/Risk

▶ While the majority of OXY's proved reserves and production is in the U.S., we expect its growth to be driven by new projects in the Middle East and North Africa. In June 2008, OXY signed agreements with Libyan National Oil Corp. (NOC) to develop major oil fields in the prolific Sirte Basin. In 2007, OXY joined a 75/25 joint venture with the Austrian firm OMV to develop certain fields in this region. Over the next five years, gross production from these joint venture fields is slated to increase 200%, to 300,000 boe/d. OXY expects to receive 10%-12% of the gross production on an after-tax basis.

▶ Risks to our recommendation and target price include a worsening of economic, industrial and operating conditions, including increased geopolitical risk and difficulty in organically replacing reserves.

▶ A blend of our DCF ($72 per share; assuming a WACC of 11.2% and terminal growth of 3%), net asset ($100 per share; assuming a long term WTI oil price of $90 per barrel) and relative valuations leads to our 12-month target of $70 per share. This represents an enterprise value of 3.5X our 2009 EBITDA estimate, a slight discount to U.S. peers.

## Qualitative Risk Assessment

| LOW | **MEDIUM** | HIGH |
|---|---|---|

Our risk assessment reflects our view of OXY's strong business profile and modest financial risk profile. The company has a large, geographically diverse reserve base, predictable production, and substantial liquidity. However, we believe its strengths are limited by participation in volatile, competitive and capital-intensive businesses, and a penchant for debt-financed acquisitions.

## Quantitative Evaluations

**S&P Quality Ranking**                          **A-**

| D | C | B- | B | B+ | **A-** | A | A+ |
|---|---|---|---|---|---|---|---|

**Relative Strength Rank**          **MODERATE**

| 52 |
|---|

LOWEST = 1                                HIGHEST = 99

## Revenue/Earnings Data

**Revenue (Million $)**

| | 1Q | 2Q | 3Q | 4Q | Year |
|---|---|---|---|---|---|
| 2008 | 6,074 | 7,220 | 7,119 | -- | -- |
| 2007 | 4,015 | 4,411 | 4,841 | 5,517 | 18,784 |
| 2006 | 4,396 | 4,599 | 4,522 | 4,144 | 17,661 |
| 2005 | 3,303 | 3,518 | 4,057 | 4,330 | 15,208 |
| 2004 | 2,557 | 2,724 | 3,005 | 3,082 | 11,368 |
| 2003 | 2,371 | 2,266 | 2,319 | 2,370 | 9,326 |

**Earnings Per Share ($)**

| | | | | | |
|---|---|---|---|---|---|
| 2008 | 2.20 | 2.79 | 2.78 | E1.74 | E9.50 |
| 2007 | 1.38 | 1.36 | 1.57 | 1.74 | 6.05 |
| 2006 | 1.34 | 1.39 | 1.35 | 1.08 | 5.15 |
| 2005 | 1.04 | 1.89 | 2.12 | 1.40 | 6.45 |
| 2004 | 0.62 | 0.73 | 0.94 | 0.96 | 3.25 |
| 2003 | 0.52 | 0.49 | 0.57 | 0.49 | 2.06 |

Fiscal year ended Dec. 31. Next earnings report expected: Late January. EPS Estimates based on S&P Operating Earnings; historical GAAP earnings are as reported.

## Dividend Data (Dates: mm/dd Payment Date: mm/dd/yy)

| Amount ($) | Date Decl. | Ex-Div. Date | Stk. of Record | Payment Date |
|---|---|---|---|---|
| 0.250 | 02/14 | 03/06 | 03/10 | 04/15/08 |
| 0.320 | 05/01 | 06/06 | 06/10 | 07/15/08 |
| 0.320 | 07/17 | 09/08 | 09/10 | 10/15/08 |
| 0.320 | 10/09 | 12/08 | 12/10 | 01/15/09 |

Dividends have been paid since 1975. Source: Company reports.

---

# Occidental Petroleum Corp

STANDARD &POOR'S

## Business Summary October 28, 2008

CORPORATE OVERVIEW. As one of the largest oil and gas companies in the U.S., Occidental Petroleum Corp. (OXY) engages in oil and gas exploration and production in three core regions: the U.S. (75% of 2007 oil and gas reserves), the Middle East/North Africa (16%), and Latin America (9%). OxyChem, a wholly owned subsidiary, manufactures and markets chlor-alkali products and vinyls, and is the largest merchant marketer of chlorine and caustic soda in the U.S.

OXY's businesses operate in three industry segments: Oil and Gas (74% of 2007 net sales; 93% of 2007 earnings), Chemicals (25%; 7%), and Other (1%; nil). In early 2008, OXY reclassified its midstream assets (marketing, gas processing, pipelines, power generation, and CO2 source fields and facilities) out of its Oil and Gas segment into a new segment called Midstream, Marketing and Other.

The Oil and Gas segment explores for, develops, produces and markets crude oil and natural gas. Oil and gas production rose 4.6%, to 570,000 boe per day (79% liquids) in 2007. Proved oil and gas reserves (including other interests) rose 1.4%, to 2.87 billion barrel oil equivalent (boe; 80% developed, 78% liquids) at year-end 2007. We estimate OXY's 2007 organic reserve replacement at 87%. Using data from John S. Herold, an industry research firm, we esti-

mate OXY's three-year (2004-06) proved acquisition costs at $10.93 per boe, below the peer average; three-year finding and development costs at $12.26 per boe, in line with peers; three-year reserve replacement costs at $11.69, below peers; and three-year reserve replacement at 185%, below the peer average.

OxyChem manufactures and markets basic chemicals, vinyls, and performance chemicals, focused on the chlorovinyls chain beginning with chlorine. The company owns and operates chemical plants at 23 domestic sites in the U.S., and at three international sits in Brazil, Canada and Chile.

MARKET PROFILE. OXY's oil and gas operations are focused on large, long-lived "legacy" oil and gas assets, such as those in California (such as the Elk Hills oil and gas field) and the Permian Basin (OXY is the largest producer in the Permian Basin, as of year-end 2007), that tend to have moderate decline rates, enhanced secondary and tertiary recovery opportunities and economies of scale that lead to cost-effective production.

## Company Financials Fiscal Year Ended Dec. 31

### Per Share Data ($)

| | 2007 | 2006 | 2005 | 2004 | 2003 | 2002 | 2001 | 2000 | 1999 | 1998 |
|---|---|---|---|---|---|---|---|---|---|---|
| Tangible Book Value | 27.63 | 22.84 | 18.69 | 13.30 | 10.25 | 8.35 | 7.53 | 6.45 | 4.79 | 4.49 |
| Cash Flow | 8.86 | 7.71 | 8.26 | 4.93 | 3.56 | 2.87 | 2.88 | 3.35 | 1.92 | 1.63 |
| Earnings | 6.05 | 5.15 | 6.45 | 3.25 | 2.06 | 1.54 | 1.59 | 2.13 | 0.79 | 0.44 |
| S&P Core Earnings | 5.19 | 4.97 | 5.78 | 3.26 | 2.03 | 1.28 | 1.70 | NA | NA | NA |
| Dividends | 0.94 | NA | 0.65 | 0.41 | 0.52 | 0.50 | 0.50 | 0.50 | 0.50 | 0.50 |
| Payout Ratio | 16% | NA | 10% | 13% | 25% | 33% | 32% | 23% | 63% | 114% |
| Prices:High | 79.25 | NA | 44.90 | 30.38 | 21.49 | 15.38 | 15.55 | 12.78 | 12.28 | 15.22 |
| Prices:Low | 42.06 | NA | 27.09 | 20.98 | 13.59 | 11.49 | 10.94 | 7.88 | 7.31 | 8.31 |
| P/E Ratio:High | 13 | NA | 7 | 9 | 10 | 10 | 10 | 6 | 16 | 35 |
| P/E Ratio:Low | 7 | NA | 4 | 6 | 7 | 7 | 7 | 4 | 9 | 19 |

### Income Statement Analysis (Million $)

| | 2007 | 2006 | 2005 | 2004 | 2003 | 2002 | 2001 | 2000 | 1999 | 1998 |
|---|---|---|---|---|---|---|---|---|---|---|
| Revenue | 18,784 | 17,661 | 15,208 | 11,368 | 9,326 | 7,338 | 13,985 | 13,574 | 7,610 | 6,596 |
| Operating Income | 10,044 | 9,664 | 7,860 | 5,573 | 4,281 | 3,119 | 3,638 | 3,826 | 1,831 | 1,297 |
| Depreciation, Depletion and Amortization | 2,356 | 2,042 | 1,485 | 1,303 | 1,177 | 1,012 | 971 | 901 | 805 | 835 |
| Interest Expense | 396 | 291 | 293 | 260 | 332 | 295 | 392 | 518 | 498 | 559 |
| Pretax Income | 8,660 | 8,012 | 7,365 | 4,389 | 2,884 | 1,662 | 1,892 | 3,196 | 1,257 | 688 |
| Effective Tax Rate | 40.5% | 43.3% | 27.4% | 38.9% | 42.5% | 25.4% | 29.8% | 45.1% | 50.2% | 52.8% |
| Net Income | 5,078 | 4,435 | 5,272 | 2,606 | 1,595 | 1,163 | 1,186 | 1,569 | 568 | 325 |
| S&P Core Earnings | 4,360 | 4,280 | 4,729 | 2,607 | 1,568 | 963 | 1,273 | NA | NA | NA |

### Balance Sheet & Other Financial Data (Million $)

| | 2007 | 2006 | 2005 | 2004 | 2003 | 2002 | 2001 | 2000 | 1999 | 1998 |
|---|---|---|---|---|---|---|---|---|---|---|
| Cash | 1,964 | 1,339 | 2,189 | 1,449 | 683 | 146 | 199 | 97.0 | 214 | 96.0 |
| Current Assets | 8,595 | 6,006 | 6,574 | 4,431 | 2,474 | 1,873 | 1,483 | 2,067 | 1,688 | 2,795 |
| Total Assets | 36,519 | 32,355 | 26,108 | 21,391 | 18,168 | 16,548 | 17,850 | 19,414 | 14,125 | 15,252 |
| Current Liabilities | 6,266 | 4,724 | 4,280 | 3,423 | 2,526 | 2,235 | 1,890 | 2,740 | 1,967 | 2,931 |
| Long Term Debt | 1,742 | 2,619 | 2,873 | 3,345 | 3,993 | 4,452 | 4,528 | 5,658 | 4,854 | 5,367 |
| Common Equity | 22,823 | 19,184 | 15,032 | 10,550 | 7,929 | 6,318 | 5,634 | 4,774 | 3,523 | 3,120 |
| Total Capital | 26,923 | 24,470 | 19,207 | 15,470 | 13,235 | 12,085 | 13,489 | 13,977 | 9,372 | 9,555 |
| Capital Expenditures | 3,497 | 3,005 | 2,423 | 1,843 | 1,601 | 1,236 | 1,401 | 952 | 601 | 1,074 |
| Cash Flow | 7,434 | 6,477 | 6,757 | 3,909 | 2,772 | 2,175 | 2,157 | 2,470 | 1,366 | 1,143 |
| Current Ratio | 1.4 | 1.3 | 1.5 | 1.3 | 1.0 | 0.8 | 0.8 | 0.8 | 0.9 | 1.0 |
| % Long Term Debt of Capitalization | 6.5 | 10.7 | 15.0 | 21.6 | 30.2 | 36.8 | 33.6 | 40.5 | 51.8 | 56.2 |
| % Return on Assets | 14.7 | 15.2 | 22.2 | 13.2 | 9.2 | 6.8 | 6.4 | 9.4 | 3.9 | 2.1 |
| % Return on Equity | 24.2 | 25.9 | 41.2 | 28.2 | 22.4 | 19.5 | 22.8 | 37.8 | 16.9 | 12.6 |

Data as orig reptd.; bef. results of disc opers/spec. items. Per share data adj. for stk. divs.; EPS diluted. E-Estimated. NA-Not Available. NM-Not Meaningful. NR-Not Ranked. UR-Under Review.

Office: 10889 Wilshire Boulevard, Los Angeles, CA 90024-4201.
Telephone: 310-208-8800.
Email: investorrelations_newyork@oxy.com
Website: http://www.oxy.com

Chrmn & CEO: R.R. Irani
Pres & CFO: S.I. Chazen
EVP, Secy & General Counsel: D.P. de Brier
Treas: J.R. Havert

Investor Contact: C.G. Stavros (212-603-8184)
Board Members: S. Abraham, R. W. Burkle, J. S. Chalsty, E. P. Djerejian, J. E. Feick, R. R. Irani, I. W. Maloney, A. B. Poladian, R. Segovia, A. R. Syriani, R. Tomich, W. L. Weisman

Founded: 1920
Domicile: Delaware
Employees: 9,700

# Office Depot Inc

**STANDARD &POOR'S**

**S&P Recommendation** BUY ★★★★☆

| Price | 12-Mo. Target Price | Investment Style |
|---|---|---|
| $2.03 (as of Nov 14, 2008) | $5.00 | Large-Cap Growth |

**GICS Sector** Consumer Discretionary
**Sub-Industry** Specialty Stores

**Summary** Office Depot is a leading operator of office products superstores and mail order catalogs.

## Key Stock Statistics (Source S&P, Vickers, company reports)

| | | | | | | | |
|---|---|---|---|---|---|---|---|
| 52-Wk Range | $19.23– 1.51 | S&P Oper. EPS 2008**E** | 0.31 | Market Capitalization(B) | $0.558 | Beta | 1.65 |
| Trailing 12-Month EPS | $0.29 | S&P Oper. EPS 2009**E** | 0.09 | Yield (%) | Nil | S&P 3-Yr. Proj. EPS CAGR(%) | 10 |
| Trailing 12-Month P/E | 7.0 | P/E on S&P Oper. EPS 2008**E** | 6.5 | Dividend Rate/Share | Nil | S&P Credit Rating | BB |
| $10K Invested 5 Yrs Ago | $1,354 | Common Shares Outstg. (M) | 274.9 | Institutional Ownership (%) | 87 | | |

## Price Performance

30-Week Mov. Avg. · · · ·  10-Week Mov. Avg. — **GAAP Earnings vs. Previous Year**  Volume Above Avg. STARS
12-Mo. Target Price —  Relative Strength —  ▲ Up  ▼ Down  ► No Change  Below Avg.  ★

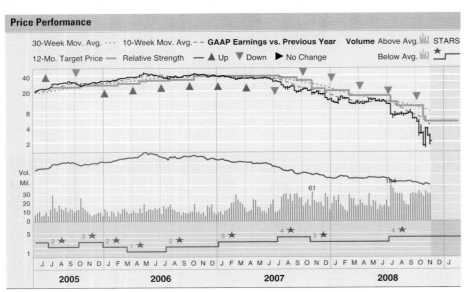

Options: ASE, CBOE, P, Ph

Analysis prepared by **Michael Souers** on November 03, 2008, when the stock traded at **$ 2.88**.

## Highlights

➤ We expect sales to decrease 2.1% in 2009, following our projection of a 4.8% decline in 2008. We expect a slight drop in sales in the U.S. contract business, reflecting weak sales to small and mid-sized businesses, and see a 7% decline in same-store sales. Offsetting these negative drivers somewhat, in our view, will be expansion of ODP's retail and delivery operations in the Northeast, continued international penetration, and the opening of approximately 40 new stores in 2008.

➤ We project flattish gross margins in 2009, reflecting a product mix shift and an increase in occupancy costs, offset by improved sourcing, inventory optimization and a continued push toward selling higher-margin private label brands. We expect ODP's operating margins to narrow slightly on a de-leveraging of fixed expenses caused by the expected same-store sales decline.

➤ We project a slight increase in net interest expense and an effective tax rate of 30%. Our 2009 EPS estimate of $0.09 is a 71% decline from the $0.31 we project the company to earn in 2008, excluding special items.

## Investment Rationale/Risk

➤ We think poor execution and macro-related challenges have created an overhang of uncertainty over the shares, leading to a greater than 80% drop in share price over the past year. Following this decline, we believe the shares are undervalued, trading at a price/sales ratio of under 0.1X and under 5X projected 2009 EBITDA of $367 million. We believe that ODP has the potential to realize intermediate-term operational improvement due to widespread cost-cutting efforts, despite our concern that the retail market for office supply stores may be approaching saturation levels. In addition, we view liquidity concerns as overblown, and think the company has ample liquidity to survive a multi-year economic downturn, if necessary.

➤ Risks to our recommendation and target price include a smaller than expected increase in capital spending by businesses, an inability to post solid same-store sales gains in ODP's North American Retail division, and unfavorable currency fluctuations.

➤ Our 12-month target price of $5 is based on our DCF analysis, which assumes a weighted average cost of capital of 9.7% and a terminal growth rate of 3.0%.

## Qualitative Risk Assessment

| LOW | MEDIUM | HIGH |
|---|---|---|

Our risk assessment reflects the cyclical nature of the office supply retailing industry, which is highly dependent on consumer and business spending, and the company's fairly large exposure to international markets, offset by what we view as a relatively strong balance sheet.

## Quantitative Evaluations

**S&P Quality Ranking**  B

| D | C | B- | B | B+ | A- | A | A+ |
|---|---|---|---|---|---|---|---|

**Relative Strength Rank**  WEAK

10

LOWEST = 1          HIGHEST = 99

## Revenue/Earnings Data

**Revenue (Million $)**

| | 1Q | 2Q | 3Q | 4Q | Year |
|---|---|---|---|---|---|
| 2008 | 3,962 | 3,605 | 3,658 | -- | -- |
| 2007 | 4,094 | 3,632 | 3,935 | 3,867 | 15,528 |
| 2006 | 3,816 | 3,495 | 3,857 | 3,843 | 15,011 |
| 2005 | 3,703 | 3,364 | 3,493 | 3,719 | 14,279 |
| 2004 | 3,605 | 3,162 | 3,328 | 3,469 | 13,565 |
| 2003 | 3,056 | 2,816 | 3,236 | 3,251 | 12,359 |

**Earnings Per Share ($)**

| | 1Q | 2Q | 3Q | 4Q | Year |
|---|---|---|---|---|---|
| 2008 | 0.25 | -0.01 | -0.02 | E-0.09 | E0.31 |
| 2007 | 0.55 | 0.38 | 0.43 | 0.07 | 1.43 |
| 2006 | 0.43 | 0.41 | 0.47 | 0.48 | 1.79 |
| 2005 | 0.37 | 0.31 | -0.15 | 0.34 | 0.87 |
| 2004 | 0.37 | 0.25 | 0.28 | 0.17 | 1.06 |
| 2003 | 0.33 | 0.19 | 0.29 | 0.15 | 0.96 |

Fiscal year ended Dec. 31. Next earnings report expected: Late February. EPS Estimates based on S&P Operating Earnings; historical GAAP earnings are as reported.

## Dividend Data

No cash dividends have been paid.

# Office Depot Inc

## Business Summary November 03, 2008

CORPORATE OVERVIEW. Office Depot is a global supplier of office products and services. It generated net sales of $15.5 billion in 2007 to customers and businesses of all sizes through three business segments: the North American Retail division (44% of revenues), the North American Business Solutions division (29%), and the International division (27%). Sales by product group were as follows: supplies 63%; technology 26%; and furniture and other 11%.

At December 31, 2007, ODP's North American Retail division operated 1,222 office supply stores in 49 states, the District of Columbia and Canada. North American Retail sells a broad assortment of merchandise, including brand name and private brand office supplies, business machines and computers, computer software, office furniture, and other business-related products through its chain of office supply stores. Most stores also contain a copy and print center that offers printing, reproduction mailing, shipping, and other services.

ODP's North American Business Solutions division provides office supply products and services directly to businesses, selling branded and private label products by means of a dedicated sales force, through catalogs and electronically through its Internet sites.

ODP's International division served customers in 43 countries outside the U.S. and Canada through 148 company-owned stores and 157 additional stores operating under licensing and joint venture agreements as of December 31, 2007. It also participates in 92 franchised stores in South Korea and Thailand.

MARKET PROFILE. The U.S. office products industry totaled approximately $332 billion in sales in 2006 (latest available), according to the School, Home and Office Products Association. The market is mature, and S&P forecasts an industry growth rate of 3% a year for the next five years. Growth in the higher-margin commercial segment (36% of the total industry) will likely continue to outpace that of the retail segment (64%) over the next several years due to a solid macro environment for capital spending. While behemoths Staples, Office Depot and OfficeMax are often regarded as the dominant players, the office products industry remains quite fragmented, with the aforementioned trio comprising an approximate 13% share of U.S. sales in 2006, including only about 11% of the retail channel.

## Company Financials Fiscal Year Ended Dec. 31

### Per Share Data ($)

| | 2007 | 2006 | 2005 | 2004 | 2003 | 2002 | 2001 | 2000 | 1999 | 1998 |
|---|---|---|---|---|---|---|---|---|---|---|
| Tangible Book Value | 6.20 | 5.11 | 6.26 | 6.96 | 5.77 | 6.61 | 5.28 | 4.66 | 5.06 | 4.86 |
| Cash Flow | 2.46 | 2.76 | 1.72 | 1.92 | 1.75 | 1.59 | 1.27 | 0.86 | 1.08 | 0.93 |
| Earnings | 1.43 | 1.79 | 0.87 | 1.06 | 0.96 | 0.98 | 0.66 | 0.16 | 0.69 | 0.61 |
| S&P Core Earnings | 1.42 | 1.74 | 0.86 | 1.03 | 0.91 | 0.92 | 0.58 | NA | NA | NA |
| Dividends | Nil | Nil | Nil | Nil | Nil | Nil | Nil | Nil | Nil | Nil |
| Payout Ratio | Nil | Nil | Nil | Nil | Nil | Nil | Nil | Nil | Nil | Nil |
| Prices:High | 39.66 | 46.52 | 31.76 | 19.50 | 18.50 | 21.96 | 18.70 | 14.88 | 26.00 | 24.83 |
| Prices:Low | 13.08 | 30.64 | 16.50 | 13.87 | 10.28 | 10.60 | 7.13 | 5.88 | 9.00 | 10.58 |
| P/E Ratio:High | 28 | 26 | 37 | 18 | 19 | 22 | 28 | 93 | 38 | 41 |
| P/E Ratio:Low | 9 | 17 | 19 | 13 | 11 | 11 | 11 | 37 | 13 | 17 |

### Income Statement Analysis (Million $)

| | 2007 | 2006 | 2005 | 2004 | 2003 | 2002 | 2001 | 2000 | 1999 | 1998 |
|---|---|---|---|---|---|---|---|---|---|---|
| Revenue | 15,528 | 15,011 | 14,279 | 13,565 | 12,359 | 11,357 | 11,154 | 11,570 | 10,263 | 8,998 |
| Operating Income | 797 | 998 | 750 | 799 | 719 | 707 | 562 | 433 | 615 | 659 |
| Depreciation | 282 | 279 | 268 | 269 | 248 | 201 | 199 | 206 | 169 | 141 |
| Interest Expense | 63.1 | 40.8 | 32.4 | 61.1 | 54.8 | 46.2 | 44.3 | 33.9 | 26.1 | 22.4 |
| Pretax Income | 459 | 727 | 362 | 461 | 445 | 479 | 314 | 92.5 | 414 | 389 |
| Effective Tax Rate | 13.7% | 29.0% | 24.3% | 27.3% | 32.1% | 35.0% | 36.0% | 46.6% | 37.8% | 40.0% |
| Net Income | 396 | 516 | 274 | 336 | 302 | 311 | 201 | 49.3 | 258 | 233 |
| S&P Core Earnings | 392 | 500 | 270 | 327 | 286 | 292 | 178 | NA | NA | NA |

### Balance Sheet & Other Financial Data (Million $)

| | 2007 | 2006 | 2005 | 2004 | 2003 | 2002 | 2001 | 2000 | 1999 | 1998 |
|---|---|---|---|---|---|---|---|---|---|---|
| Cash | 223 | 174 | 703 | 794 | 791 | 877 | 563 | 151 | 219 | 705 |
| Current Assets | 3,716 | 3,455 | 3,530 | 3,916 | 3,577 | 3,210 | 2,806 | 2,699 | 2,631 | 2,780 |
| Total Assets | 7,257 | 6,570 | 6,099 | 6,767 | 6,145 | 4,766 | 4,332 | 4,196 | 4,276 | 4,113 |
| Current Liabilities | 2,973 | 2,970 | 2,469 | 2,618 | 2,277 | 1,992 | 2,102 | 1,908 | 1,944 | 1,531 |
| Long Term Debt | 607 | 571 | 569 | 584 | 829 | 412 | 318 | 598 | 321 | 471 |
| Common Equity | 3,084 | 2,610 | 2,739 | 3,223 | 2,794 | 2,297 | 1,848 | 1,601 | 1,908 | 2,029 |
| Total Capital | 3,707 | 3,197 | 3,308 | 3,957 | 3,868 | 2,774 | 2,230 | 2,200 | 2,229 | 2,500 |
| Capital Expenditures | 461 | 343 | 261 | 391 | 212 | 202 | 207 | 268 | 396 | 255 |
| Cash Flow | 678 | 795 | 542 | 605 | 550 | 512 | 400 | 255 | 426 | 374 |
| Current Ratio | 1.3 | 1.2 | 1.4 | 1.5 | 1.6 | 1.6 | 1.3 | 1.4 | 1.4 | 1.8 |
| % Long Term Debt of Capitalization | 16.4 | 17.9 | 17.2 | 14.8 | 21.4 | 14.9 | 14.2 | 27.2 | 14.4 | 18.8 |
| % Net Income of Revenue | 2.6 | 3.4 | 1.9 | 2.5 | 2.4 | 2.7 | 1.8 | 0.4 | 2.5 | 2.6 |
| % Return on Assets | 5.7 | 8.1 | 4.2 | 5.2 | 5.5 | 6.8 | 4.7 | 1.2 | 6.2 | 6.6 |
| % Return on Equity | 13.9 | 19.3 | 9.2 | 11.2 | 11.9 | 15.0 | 11.7 | 2.8 | 13.1 | 13.9 |

Data as orig reptd.; bef. results of disc opers/spec. items. Per share data adj. for stk. divs.; EPS diluted. E-Estimated. NA-Not Available. NM-Not Meaningful. NR-Not Ranked. UR-Under Review.

**Office:** 2200 Old Germantown Road, Delray Beach, FL 33445.
**Telephone:** 561-438-4800.
**Email:** investor.relations@officedepot.com
**Website:** http://www.officedepot.com

**Chrmn & CEO:** S. Odland
**EVP & CFO:** M. Newman
**EVP, Secy & General Counsel:** E.D. Garcia
**SVP, Chief Acctg Officer & Cntlr:** M.E. Hutchens

**SVP & CIO:** T. Toews
**Investor Contact:** R. Tharpe (561-438-4540)
**Board Members:** L. A. Ault, III, N. R. Austrian, D. W. Bernauer, A. E. Bru, M. J. Evans, D. I. Fuente, B. J. Gaines, M. M. Hart, W. Hedrick, K. Mason, M. J. Myers, S. Odland

**Founded:** 1986
**Domicile:** Delaware
**Employees:** 49,000

# Omnicom Group Inc.

**STANDARD &POOR'S**

| S&P Recommendation HOLD ★★★☆☆ | Price $25.40 (as of Nov 14, 2008) | 12-Mo. Target Price $40.00 | Investment Style Large-Cap Growth |
|---|---|---|---|

**GICS Sector** Consumer Discretionary
**Sub-Industry** Advertising

**Summary** This company owns DDB Worldwide, BBDO Worldwide and TBWA Worldwide advertising agency networks; it also owns more than 100 marketing and specialty services firms.

## Key Stock Statistics (Source S&P, Vickers, company reports)

| | | | | | | | |
|---|---|---|---|---|---|---|---|
| 52-Wk Range | $50.51– 22.51 | S&P Oper. EPS 2008E | 3.25 | Market Capitalization(B) | $7.894 | Beta | 0.96 |
| Trailing 12-Month EPS | $3.26 | S&P Oper. EPS 2009E | 3.20 | Yield (%) | 2.36 | S&P 3-Yr. Proj. EPS CAGR(%) | 4 |
| Trailing 12-Month P/E | 7.8 | P/E on S&P Oper. EPS 2008E | 7.8 | Dividend Rate/Share | $0.60 | S&P Credit Rating | A- |
| $10K Invested 5 Yrs Ago | $6,775 | Common Shares Outstg. (M) | 310.8 | Institutional Ownership (%) | 93 | | |

## Price Performance

30-Week Mov. Avg. ··· 10-Week Mov. Avg. -- GAAP Earnings vs. Previous Year  Volume Above Avg. STARS
12-Mo. Target Price — Relative Strength — ▲ Up ▼ Down ► No Change  Below Avg.

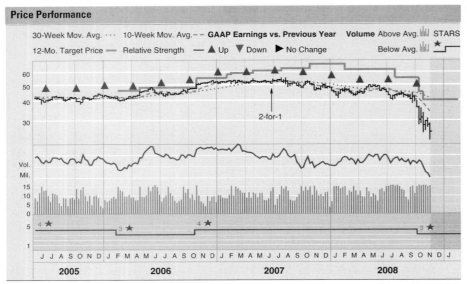

Options: ASE, CBOE, P, Ph

Analysis prepared by **Mark S. Basham** on October 27, 2008, when the stock traded at **$ 27.87**.

## Highlights

➤ We forecast 2008 revenue growth of about 7.8%, reflecting decelerating organic growth as well as foreign currency effects turning negative in the fourth quarter. Looking ahead to 2009, we expect recessionary conditions to push domestic revenues lower, and for foreign exchange effects to be negative as well. The company may seek strategic acquisitions where it makes sense. Following an overseas revenue advance we forecast at 12% for 2008, we expect sharply lower growth in 2009. All told, we project revenue growth of 1.6% in 2009.

➤ We see OMC's operating margin dipping slightly to 12.8% in 2008 from 13.1% in 2007. While we expect OMC to realize operating leverage from higher revenues on its fixed costs, we also see this being more than offset by the company continuing to invest heavily in its infrastructure. In 2009, we see margins dipping to 12.2% as cost increases exceed revenue gains.

➤ We see EPS of $3.20 in 2009, down slightly from our $3.25 projection for 2008. The lower margins that we foresee are expected to more than offset anticipated share repurchases.

## Investment Rationale/Risk

➤ Our hold recommendation reflects our view of a slowing U.S. economy leading to a decelerating pace of domestic organic growth for OMC in 2009. We think a tighter credit environment in the U.S. is likely to reduce acquisition multiples and increase accretive acquisition opportunities. Thus, we see OMC utilizing what we view as a strong balance sheet to pursue market share growth through acquisitions. We note that OMC derives a lower than peer average percentage of its revenues from traditional media advertising (44%), which we view positively, given that economic weakness usually leads to a reduction in overall advertising levels.

➤ Risks to our recommendation and target price include deterioration in global GDP, lost accounts, and possible stock dilution from convertible liquid yield options.

➤ We derive our 12-month target price of $40 by applying an EV/EBITDA multiple of 8.0X to our 2009 EBITDA estimate of $1.94 billion. This multiple is at the low end of OMC's historical range, which we believe is appropriate given the likely deteriorating global economy.

## Qualitative Risk Assessment

| LOW | MEDIUM | HIGH |
|---|---|---|

Our risk assessment primarily reflects a highly competitive advertising industry, offset partly by OMC's diversified geographic and product revenue sources coupled with its position as the world's largest advertising agency by revenue, and our view of its strong track record of EPS and free cash flow growth.

## Quantitative Evaluations

**S&P Quality Ranking**  A+

| D | C | B- | B | B+ | A- | A | A+ |
|---|---|---|---|---|---|---|---|

**Relative Strength Rank**  MODERATE

42

LOWEST = 1    HIGHEST = 99

## Revenue/Earnings Data

**Revenue (Million $)**

| | 1Q | 2Q | 3Q | 4Q | Year |
|---|---|---|---|---|---|
| 2008 | 3,195 | 3,477 | 3,316 | -- | -- |
| 2007 | 2,841 | 3,126 | 3,101 | 3,626 | 12,694 |
| 2006 | 2,563 | 2,823 | 2,774 | 3,216 | 11,377 |
| 2005 | 2,403 | 2,616 | 2,523 | 2,939 | 10,481 |
| 2004 | 2,231 | 2,408 | 2,319 | 2,789 | 9,747 |
| 2003 | 1,937 | 2,150 | 2,029 | 2,506 | 8,621 |

**Earnings Per Share ($)**

| | | | | | |
|---|---|---|---|---|---|
| 2008 | 0.65 | 0.96 | 0.69 | E0.97 | E3.25 |
| 2007 | 0.55 | 0.84 | 0.62 | 0.96 | 2.95 |
| 2006 | 0.47 | 0.71 | 0.52 | 0.81 | 2.50 |
| 2005 | 0.41 | 0.62 | 0.45 | 0.71 | 2.18 |
| 2004 | 0.36 | 0.55 | 0.40 | 0.64 | 1.94 |
| 2003 | 0.35 | 0.51 | 0.36 | 0.58 | 1.80 |

Fiscal year ended Dec. 31. Next earnings report expected: Mid February. EPS Estimates based on S&P Operating Earnings; historical GAAP earnings are as reported.

## Dividend Data (Dates: mm/dd Payment Date: mm/dd/yy)

| Amount ($) | Date Decl. | Ex-Div. Date | Stk. of Record | Payment Date |
|---|---|---|---|---|
| 0.150 | 12/07 | 12/13 | 12/17 | 01/04/08 |
| 0.150 | 02/13 | 03/05 | 03/07 | 04/04/08 |
| 0.150 | 05/16 | 06/04 | 06/06 | 07/03/08 |
| 0.150 | 07/17 | 09/17 | 09/19 | 10/03/08 |

Dividends have been paid since 1986. Source: Company reports.

# Omnicom Group Inc.

STANDARD
&POOR'S

## Business Summary October 27, 2008

CORPORATE OVERVIEW. Omnicom Group, a global advertising and marketing services company, is one of the world's largest corporate communications companies. OMC is comprised of more than 1,500 subsidiary agencies, operating in over 100 countries. It operates as three independent global agency networks: the BBDO Worldwide Network, the DDB Worldwide Network, and the TBWA Worldwide Network. Each agency network has its own clients, and the networks compete with each other in the same markets.

OMC's companies provide an extensive range of services, which it groups into four disciplines: traditional media advertising (43% of 2007 revenues), customer relationship management (37%), public relations (10%), and specialty communications (11%). In 2007, the company's 10 and 100 largest clients accounted for approximately 16.7% and 46.2% of consolidated revenue, respectively. The largest client accounted for about 2.8% of 2007 revenues; no other single client accounted for more than 2.4% of revenues. Operations cover the major regions of North America, the U.K., Europe, the Middle East, Africa, Latin America, the Far East and Australia. In 2007, 53% of revenues were derived from the U.S., 21% from euro-denominated markets, 11% from the U.K., and 15% from other international markets.

The services in these categories include but are not limited to: advertising, brand consultancy, crisis communications, database management, digital and interactive marketing, direct marketing, directory advertising, experiential marketing, field marketing, health care communications, in-store design, investor relations, marketing research, media planning and buying, organizational communications, product placement, promotional marketing, public relations, recruitment communications, reputation consulting, retail marketing, and sports and event marketing.

In our opinion, the breadth, depth and diversity of OMC's business reduces exposure to any single industry, and to an economic reversal in any world region. It also provides the company with significant opportunities to benefit from growth in non-advertising services, such as public relations and event marketing, expenditures for which are growing faster than for traditional advertising.

## Company Financials Fiscal Year Ended Dec. 31

| Per Share Data ($) | 2007 | 2006 | 2005 | 2004 | 2003 | 2002 | 2001 | 2000 | 1999 | 1998 |
|---|---|---|---|---|---|---|---|---|---|---|
| Tangible Book Value | NM | NM | NM | NM | NM | NM | NM | NM | NM | NM |
| Cash Flow | 3.45 | 3.13 | 2.71 | 2.40 | 2.10 | 2.03 | 1.88 | 1.81 | 1.30 | 1.19 |
| Earnings | 2.95 | 2.50 | 2.18 | 1.94 | 1.80 | 1.72 | 1.35 | 1.37 | 1.01 | 0.84 |
| S&P Core Earnings | 2.95 | 2.50 | 2.18 | 1.92 | 1.69 | 1.56 | 1.24 | NA | NA | NA |
| Dividends | 0.50 | 0.50 | 0.46 | 0.45 | 0.40 | 0.40 | 0.39 | 0.35 | 0.30 | 0.25 |
| Payout Ratio | 17% | 20% | 21% | 23% | 22% | 23% | 29% | 26% | 30% | 30% |
| Prices:High | 55.45 | 53.03 | 45.74 | 44.41 | 43.80 | 48.68 | 49.10 | 50.47 | 53.75 | 29.25 |
| Prices:Low | 45.82 | 39.38 | 37.88 | 33.22 | 23.25 | 18.25 | 29.55 | 34.06 | 27.97 | 18.50 |
| P/E Ratio:High | 19 | 21 | 21 | 23 | 24 | 28 | 36 | 37 | 53 | 35 |
| P/E Ratio:Low | 16 | 16 | 17 | 17 | 13 | 11 | 22 | 25 | 28 | 22 |

| Income Statement Analysis (Million $) | | | | | | | | | | |
|---|---|---|---|---|---|---|---|---|---|---|
| Revenue | 12,694 | 11,377 | 10,481 | 9,747 | 8,621 | 7,536 | 6,889 | 6,154 | 5,131 | 4,092 |
| Operating Income | 1,823 | 1,674 | 1,515 | 1,388 | 1,289 | 1,224 | 1,179 | 1,065 | 821 | 693 |
| Depreciation | 164 | 190 | 175 | 172 | 124 | 120 | 211 | 187 | 97.1 | 133 |
| Interest Expense | 107 | 125 | 78.0 | 51.1 | 57.9 | 45.5 | 72.8 | 76.5 | 84.9 | 69.6 |
| Pretax Income | 1,624 | 1,422 | 1,308 | 1,196 | 1,137 | 1,087 | 908 | 923 | 689 | 545 |
| Effective Tax Rate | 33.1% | 32.8% | 33.3% | 33.1% | 33.5% | 34.5% | 38.8% | 40.0% | 39.7% | 39.6% |
| Net Income | 976 | 864 | 791 | 724 | 676 | 643 | 503 | 499 | 363 | 285 |
| S&P Core Earnings | 976 | 866 | 790 | 715 | 631 | 584 | 456 | NA | NA | NA |

| Balance Sheet & Other Financial Data (Million $) | | | | | | | | | | |
|---|---|---|---|---|---|---|---|---|---|---|
| Cash | 1,841 | 1,740 | 836 | 1,166 | 1,529 | 667 | 472 | 517 | 576 | 648 |
| Current Assets | 10,504 | 9,647 | 7,967 | 8,095 | 7,286 | 5,637 | 5,234 | 5,367 | 4,712 | 3,981 |
| Total Assets | 19,272 | 18,164 | 15,920 | 16,002 | 14,499 | 11,820 | 10,617 | 9,891 | 9,018 | 6,910 |
| Current Liabilities | 11,227 | 10,296 | 8,700 | 8,744 | 7,762 | 6,840 | 6,644 | 6,625 | 6,009 | 4,796 |
| Long Term Debt | 3,055 | 3,055 | 2,357 | 2,358 | 2,537 | 1,945 | 1,340 | 1,245 | 712 | 716 |
| Common Equity | 4,092 | 3,871 | 3,948 | 4,079 | 3,466 | 2,569 | 2,178 | 1,548 | 1,553 | 1,086 |
| Total Capital | 7,563 | 7,562 | 6,921 | 6,949 | 6,394 | 4,687 | 3,677 | 2,970 | 2,708 | 1,893 |
| Capital Expenditures | 223 | 178 | 163 | 160 | 141 | 117 | 149 | 150 | 130 | 89.7 |
| Cash Flow | 1,140 | 1,054 | 966 | 896 | 800 | 763 | 714 | 685 | 460 | 418 |
| Current Ratio | 0.9 | 0.9 | 0.9 | 0.9 | 0.9 | 0.8 | 0.8 | 0.8 | 0.8 | 0.8 |
| % Long Term Debt of Capitalization | 40.4 | 40.4 | 34.1 | 33.9 | 39.7 | 41.5 | 36.4 | 41.9 | 26.3 | 37.8 |
| % Net Income of Revenue | 7.7 | 7.6 | 7.5 | 7.4 | 7.8 | 8.5 | 7.3 | 8.1 | 7.1 | 7.0 |
| % Return on Assets | 5.2 | 5.1 | 5.0 | 4.7 | 5.1 | 5.7 | 4.9 | 5.3 | 4.5 | 4.8 |
| % Return on Equity | 24.5 | 22.1 | 19.7 | 18.8 | 22.4 | 27.1 | 27.0 | 32.2 | 27.9 | 27.6 |

Data as orig reptd.; bef. results of disc opers/spec. items. Per share data adj. for stk. divs.; EPS diluted. E-Estimated. NA-Not Available. NM-Not Meaningful. NR-Not Ranked. UR-Under Review.

**Office:** 437 Madison Ave Bsmt, New York, NY 10022-7000.
**Telephone:** 212-415-3600.
**Email:** IR@OmnicomGroup.com
**Website:** http://www.omnicomgroup.com

**Chrmn:** B.A. Crawford
**Pres & CEO:** J. Wren
**Investor Contact:** R.J. Weisenburger (212-415-3393)
**EVP & CFO:** R.J. Weisenburger

**SVP, Chief Acctg Officer & Cntlr:** P.J. Angelastro
**Board Members:** A. R. Batkin, R. C. Clark, L. S. Coleman, Jr., E. M. Cook, B. A. Crawford, S. Denison, M. A. Henning, J. R. Murphy, J. R. Purcell, L. J. Rice, G. L. Roubos, J. Wren

**Founded:** 1944
**Domicile:** New York
**Employees:** 70,000

The **McGraw-Hill** Companies

# Oracle Corp

| S&P Recommendation | STRONG BUY ★★★★★ | Price<br>$16.90 (as of Nov 14, 2008) | 12-Mo. Target Price<br>$23.00 | Investment Style<br>Large-Cap Growth |
|---|---|---|---|---|

**GICS Sector** Information Technology
**Sub-Industry** Systems Software

**Summary** This company is a leading supplier of enterprise database management systems and business applications.

## Key Stock Statistics (Source S&P, Vickers, company reports)

| | | | | | | | |
|---|---|---|---|---|---|---|---|
| 52-Wk Range | $23.62– 15.00 | S&P Oper. EPS 2009**E** | 1.46 | Market Capitalization(B) | $87.110 | Beta | 1.33 |
| Trailing 12-Month EPS | $1.10 | S&P Oper. EPS 2010**E** | 1.65 | Yield (%) | Nil | S&P 3-Yr. Proj. EPS CAGR(%) | 15 |
| Trailing 12-Month P/E | 15.4 | P/E on S&P Oper. EPS 2009**E** | 11.6 | Dividend Rate/Share | Nil | S&P Credit Rating | A |
| $10K Invested 5 Yrs Ago | $13,751 | Common Shares Outstg. (M) | 5,154.5 | Institutional Ownership (%) | 59 | | |

## Price Performance

30-Week Mov. Avg. · · · 10-Week Mov. Avg. — **GAAP Earnings vs. Previous Year** Volume Above Avg. STARS
12-Mo. Target Price — Relative Strength — ▲ Up ▼ Down ▶ No Change Below Avg.

Options: ASE, CBOE, P, Ph

Analysis prepared by **Zaineb Bokhari** on November 11, 2008, when the stock traded at **$ 17.32**.

## Highlights

➤ We forecast healthy organic growth rates but expect acquisitions (BEA Systems in April 2008, among others) to aid growth we project in FY 09 (May). We expect ongoing strength in database sales, fueled by new products and add-on features that we think give ORCL a technology lead over competitors. We look for middleware to remain an area of strength. We are projecting modest growth for applications, due to what we think are tough year-ago comparisons and a weak global economy. We see a rise in non-GAAP revenue of 10% in FY 09 to $25 billion, slowing from 24% in FY 08. We forecast a 9% rise in FY 10.

➤ We expect non-GAAP operating margins to widen modestly to about 44% in FY 09 from 42.7% in FY 08, as management continues to derive cost efficiencies from recent acquisitions. In view of ORCL's success in expanding operating margins while integrating numerous sizable acquisitions, we expect targeted cost synergies and scale benefits to be achieved. We see a further modest widening in FY 10.

➤ With a projected effective tax rate of about 27%, we expect non-GAAP operating EPS of $1.46 in FY 09, rising to $1.65 in FY 10.

## Investment Rationale/Risk

➤ We think ORCL enjoys a formidable market position, enviable operating margins, and generates considerable free cash. While no company is immune to a global economic slowdown, we think ORCL's broad product portfolio, geographic diversity, and sizable maintenance revenue streams, will allow it to grow during a period of global economic softness.

➤ Risks to our recommendation and target price include acquisition integration risks, intense competition, and pricing pressure within enterprise software. We also note that while ORCL is diversified in its customer base, it has exposure to the financial services sector, which could curtail IT spending in view of ongoing problems in credit markets.

➤ Our 12-month target price of $23 is based on a blend of our relative and intrinsic valuation measures. In our valuation of discounted free cash flow, we incorporate assumptions for a 9.8% weighted average cost of capital and 4% terminal growth, yielding an intrinsic value of $28. For our P/E analysis, we apply a 12.4X multiple to our forward 12-month EPS estimate of $1.51, resulting in a price of approximately $19.

## Qualitative Risk Assessment

| LOW | MEDIUM | HIGH |
|---|---|---|

Our risk assessment reflects potential acquisition integration risks faced by the company following a series of large purchases over the past several years. This is offset by our view of ORCL's strong balance sheet, considerable free cash flow, and what we see as a deep management bench.

## Quantitative Evaluations

### S&P Quality Ranking                B

| D | C | B- | **B** | B+ | A- | A | A+ |
|---|---|---|---|---|---|---|---|

### Relative Strength Rank          STRONG

74

LOWEST = 1                                     HIGHEST = 99

## Revenue/Earnings Data

### Revenue (Million $)

| | 1Q | 2Q | 3Q | 4Q | Year |
|---|---|---|---|---|---|
| 2009 | 5,331 | -- | -- | -- | -- |
| 2008 | 4,529 | 5,313 | 5,349 | 7,239 | 22,430 |
| 2007 | 3,591 | 4,163 | 4,414 | 5,828 | 17,996 |
| 2006 | 2,768 | 3,292 | 3,470 | 4,851 | 14,380 |
| 2005 | 2,215 | 2,756 | 2,950 | 3,878 | 11,799 |
| 2004 | 2,072 | 2,498 | 2,509 | 3,076 | 10,156 |

### Earnings Per Share ($)

| | 1Q | 2Q | 3Q | 4Q | Year |
|---|---|---|---|---|---|
| 2009 | 0.21 | E0.32 | E0.33 | E0.53 | E1.46 |
| 2008 | 0.16 | 0.25 | 0.26 | 0.39 | 1.06 |
| 2007 | 0.13 | 0.18 | 0.20 | 0.31 | 0.81 |
| 2006 | 0.10 | 0.15 | 0.14 | 0.24 | 0.64 |
| 2005 | 0.10 | 0.16 | 0.10 | 0.20 | 0.55 |
| 2004 | 0.08 | 0.12 | 0.12 | 0.19 | 0.50 |

Fiscal year ended May 31. Next earnings report expected: Late December. EPS Estimates based on S&P Operating Earnings; historical GAAP earnings are as reported.

## Dividend Data

No cash dividends have been paid.

# Oracle Corp

**STANDARD &POOR'S**

## Business Summary November 11, 2008

CORPORATE OVERVIEW. Oracle Corp. is a leading provider of enterprise software. The company is organized into two businesses: software and services. The company further segments its software business into new software licenses (33% of revenues in FY 08 (May) and 32% in FY 07) and software license updates, and product support (46% and 47% of revenue in FY 08 and FY 07, respectively). The company's services business is divided into consulting (15%, 16%), On Demand (3%, 3%), and education (2%, 2%). Oracle's software products fall into two broad categories: database and middleware, and application software. Database and middleware products accounted for about 65% of total software revenues in FY 08 (66% in FY 06).

MARKET PROFILE. We estimate that corporate spending on enterprise software rose at a mid-to-high single-digit rate in 2007, comparable to 2006. We see growth remaining within this range in 2008, although we think it will slow from 2007, given the slowing global macro picture. In this moderate growth environment, large enterprise software deals are sporadic and tend to be susceptible to delays and disruptions due to long sales cycles and the increasing number of approvals needed to close such deals. As a result, visibility can be limited and quarters can be back-end loaded. To offset this risk and to tap into a market that we still see as underserved, enterprise application vendors are increasingly focusing their attention on small and mid-sized businesses. While this is not a new strategy, it requires the development of a strong partner channel to effectively leverage sales resources.

With some exceptions, we favor large software providers with significant installed bases and diversified technology assets over small- and mid-cap best-of-breed vendors. We see installed bases as key to our forecasts, because we think deeper penetration into existing customers is a less expensive way to grow. We think corporate buyers are evaluating not just the initial cost of the software, but also the long-term cost of support and viability of the vendor. We believe this favors large diversified software vendors.

## Company Financials Fiscal Year Ended May 31

### Per Share Data ($)

| | 2008 | 2007 | 2006 | 2005 | 2004 | 2003 | 2002 | 2001 | 2000 | 1999 |
|---|---|---|---|---|---|---|---|---|---|---|
| Tangible Book Value | NM | NM | 0.13 | 0.09 | 1.55 | 1.21 | 1.13 | 1.12 | 1.15 | 1.29 |
| Cash Flow | NA | 1.03 | 0.79 | 0.63 | 0.55 | 0.49 | 0.45 | 0.50 | 1.10 | 0.43 |
| Earnings | 1.06 | 0.81 | 0.64 | 0.55 | 0.50 | 0.43 | 0.39 | 0.44 | 1.05 | 0.22 |
| S&P Core Earnings | 1.05 | 0.80 | 0.62 | 0.52 | 0.46 | 0.37 | 0.34 | 0.36 | NA | NA |
| Dividends | Nil | Nil | Nil | Nil | Nil | Nil | Nil | Nil | Nil | Nil |
| Payout Ratio | Nil | Nil | Nil | Nil | Nil | Nil | Nil | Nil | Nil | Nil |
| Calendar Year | 2007 | 2006 | 2005 | 2004 | 2003 | 2002 | 2001 | 2000 | 1999 | 1998 |
| Prices:High | 23.31 | 19.75 | 14.51 | 15.51 | 14.03 | 17.50 | 35.00 | 46.47 | 28.34 | 7.48 |
| Prices:Low | 15.97 | 12.06 | 11.25 | 9.78 | 10.64 | 7.25 | 10.16 | 21.50 | 5.25 | 2.96 |
| P/E Ratio:High | 22 | 24 | 23 | 28 | 28 | 41 | 90 | NM | 27 | 34 |
| P/E Ratio:Low | 15 | 15 | 18 | 18 | 21 | 17 | 26 | NM | 5 | 14 |

### Income Statement Analysis (Million $)

| | 2008 | 2007 | 2006 | 2005 | 2004 | 2003 | 2002 | 2001 | 2000 | 1999 |
|---|---|---|---|---|---|---|---|---|---|---|
| Revenue | 22,430 | 17,996 | 14,380 | 11,799 | 10,156 | 9,475 | 9,673 | 10,860 | 10,130 | 8,827 |
| Operating Income | NA | 726 | 5,764 | 4,802 | 4,098 | 3,767 | 3,934 | 4,124 | 3,472 | 2,248 |
| Depreciation | 1,480 | 1,127 | 806 | 425 | 234 | 327 | 363 | 347 | 391 | 375 |
| Interest Expense | NA | 343 | 169 | 135 | 21.0 | 16.0 | 20.0 | 24.0 | 18.9 | 21.4 |
| Pretax Income | 7,834 | 5,986 | 4,810 | 4,051 | 3,945 | 3,425 | 3,408 | 3,971 | 10,123 | 1,982 |
| Effective Tax Rate | 29.5% | 28.6% | 29.7% | 28.8% | 32.0% | 32.6% | 34.7% | 35.5% | 37.8% | 34.9% |
| Net Income | 5,521 | 4,274 | 3,381 | 2,886 | 2,681 | 2,307 | 2,224 | 2,561 | 6,297 | 1,290 |
| S&P Core Earnings | 5,481 | 4,224 | 3,237 | 2,750 | 2,459 | 2,049 | 1,923 | 2,119 | NA | NA |

### Balance Sheet & Other Financial Data (Million $)

| | 2008 | 2007 | 2006 | 2005 | 2004 | 2003 | 2002 | 2001 | 2000 | 1999 |
|---|---|---|---|---|---|---|---|---|---|---|
| Cash | 11,043 | 7,020 | 7,605 | 4,802 | 4,138 | 4,737 | 3,095 | 4,449 | 7,429 | 1,786 |
| Current Assets | NA | 12,883 | 11,974 | 8,479 | 11,336 | 9,227 | 8,728 | 8,963 | 10,883 | 5,447 |
| Total Assets | 47,268 | 34,572 | 29,029 | 20,687 | 12,763 | 11,064 | 10,800 | 11,030 | 13,077 | 7,260 |
| Current Liabilities | NA | 9,387 | 6,930 | 8,063 | 4,272 | 4,158 | 3,960 | 3,917 | 5,862 | 3,046 |
| Long Term Debt | NA | 6,235 | 5,735 | 159 | 163 | 175 | 298 | 301 | 301 | 304 |
| Common Equity | 23,025 | 16,919 | 15,012 | 10,837 | 7,995 | 6,320 | 6,117 | 6,278 | 6,461 | 3,695 |
| Total Capital | NA | 24,275 | 21,311 | 12,006 | 8,217 | 6,681 | 6,619 | 6,906 | 7,028 | 4,135 |
| Capital Expenditures | 243 | 319 | 236 | 188 | 189 | 291 | 278 | 313 | 263 | 347 |
| Cash Flow | NA | 5,401 | 4,187 | 3,311 | 2,915 | 2,634 | 2,587 | 2,908 | 6,611 | 1,290 |
| Current Ratio | 1.8 | 1.4 | 1.7 | 1.1 | 2.7 | 2.2 | 2.2 | 2.3 | 1.9 | 1.8 |
| % Long Term Debt of Capitalization | 29.6 | 25.7 | 26.9 | 1.3 | 2.0 | 2.6 | 4.5 | 4.4 | 4.3 | 7.3 |
| % Net Income of Revenue | 24.6 | 22.7 | 23.5 | 24.4 | 26.4 | 24.3 | 23.0 | 23.6 | 62.2 | 14.6 |
| % Return on Assets | 13.5 | 13.4 | 13.6 | 17.3 | 22.6 | 21.1 | 20.4 | 21.2 | 61.9 | 19.7 |
| % Return on Equity | 27.6 | 26.8 | 26.2 | 30.7 | 37.5 | 37.1 | 35.9 | 40.2 | 124.0 | 19.4 |

Data as orig reptd.; bef. results of disc opers/spec. items. Per share data adj. for stk. divs.; EPS diluted. E-Estimated. NA-Not Available. NM-Not Meaningful. NR-Not Ranked. UR-Under Review.

**Office:** 500 Oracle Parkway, Redwood Shores, CA 94065-1675.
**Telephone:** 650-506-7000.
**Email:** investor_us@oracle.com
**Website:** http://www.oracle.com

**Chrmn:** J.O. Henley
**Pres:** T.C. Chou
**CEO:** L.J. Ellison
**COO:** J.L. Minton

**EVP & CFO:** J. Epstein
**Investor Contact:** K. Bessinger (650-506-4073)
**Board Members:** J. S. Berg, H. R. Bingham, M. J. Boskin, S. A. Catz, B. R. Chizen, G. H. Conrades, L. J. Ellison, H. M. Garcia-Molina, J. O. Henley, J. F. Kemp, D. L. Lucas, C. E. Phillips, Jr., N. Seligman

**Founded:** 1977
**Domicile:** Delaware
**Employees:** 84,233

# PACCAR Inc

**S&P Recommendation** [BUY] ★★★★☆

| Price | 12-Mo. Target Price | Investment Style |
|---|---|---|
| $28.11 (as of Nov 14, 2008) | $43.00 | Large-Cap Blend |

**GICS Sector** Industrials
**Sub-Industry** Construction & Farm Machinery & Heavy Trucks

**Summary** This heavy-duty truck manufacturer produces the well-known Peterbilt and Kenworth brand heavy-duty highway trucks.

## Key Stock Statistics (Source S&P, Vickers, company reports)

| | | | | | | | | |
|---|---|---|---|---|---|---|---|---|
| 52-Wk Range | $58.09– 21.96 | S&P Oper. EPS 2008**E** | 3.27 | Market Capitalization(B) | $10.195 | Beta | 1.52 |
| Trailing 12-Month EPS | $3.17 | S&P Oper. EPS 2009**E** | 3.75 | Yield (%) | 2.56 | S&P 3-Yr. Proj. EPS CAGR(%) | 1 |
| Trailing 12-Month P/E | 8.9 | P/E on S&P Oper. EPS 2008**E** | 8.6 | Dividend Rate/Share | $0.72 | S&P Credit Rating | AA- |
| $10K Invested 5 Yrs Ago | $14,689 | Common Shares Outstg. (M) | 362.7 | Institutional Ownership (%) | 52 | | |

## Price Performance

30-Week Mov. Avg. · · · · 10-Week Mov. Avg. - - **GAAP Earnings vs. Previous Year** Volume Above Avg. STARS
12-Mo. Target Price — Relative Strength — ▲ Up ▼ Down ▶ No Change Below Avg.

Options: ASE, CBOE, P, Ph

Analysis prepared by **Adrian Compton** on October 03, 2008, when the stock traded at **$ 32.85.**

## Highlights

➤ We see net sales growing 4% in 2008, largely on strength overseas. We also expect the domestic market for heavy trucks to start improving in late 2008 to early 2009, driven by fleet owners replacing older vehicles and positioning their fleets ahead of a more stringent set of emission standards scheduled to take effect in 2010. We anticipate that sales will rise another 6% in 2009 on continued pre-buying and an expected improvement in freight market conditions.

➤ We expect margin pressure this year as increased raw material costs are only partly offset by new cost controls. We believe margins will widen in 2009 as a result of recently reduced raw material costs and fixed costs being allocated across a greater number of vehicles. For the longer term, we expect margins (and earnings) to continue to exhibit large swings, due to the highly cyclical nature of the global truck industry and frequent regulatory changes.

➤ We estimate 2008 EPS of $3.27, increasing by 15% in 2009 to $3.75, based on the expected increase in production and utilization rate.

## Investment Rationale/Risk

➤ We see the international truck market being affected in the second half of 2008 and into early 2009 by economic headwinds being experienced in Europe and North America. We expect some of the short-term weakness in truck sales to be offset by PCAR's aftermarket parts and leasing operations in Europe, which should help augment earnings growth. We believe current R&D spending in support of new engine technologies and an updated range of products will position PCAR favorably.

➤ Risks to our recommendation and target price include a greater than expected downturn in the North American and/or European truck markets; potential supply disruptions; and further increases in raw material costs.

➤ In valuing PCAR, we apply an EV/EBITDA multiple of about 10.5X, which is a premium to peers and the S&P 500 reflecting PCAR's market position, to obtain a value of $45. For our DCF analysis, we assume compound annual revenue growth of 4% in 2008, 6% in 2009 and 2.5% in perpetuity, and a WACC of 14.4% to arrive at an intrinsic value of $38. Blending these two valuation metrics results in our 12-month target price of $43.

## Qualitative Risk Assessment

| LOW | MEDIUM | HIGH |
|---|---|---|

Our risk assessment for Paccar reflects the highly cyclical nature of the heavy-duty (Class 8) truck market, offset by our view of a strong balance sheet with a relatively low amount of manufacturing debt and a geographical sales mix that is increasingly diversified.

## Quantitative Evaluations

**S&P Quality Ranking** B+

| D | C | B- | B | B+ | A- | A | A+ |
|---|---|---|---|---|---|---|---|

**Relative Strength Rank** MODERATE

63

LOWEST = 1 HIGHEST = 99

## Revenue/Earnings Data

**Revenue (Million $)**

| | 1Q | 2Q | 3Q | 4Q | Year |
|---|---|---|---|---|---|
| 2008 | 3,938 | 4,113 | 4,005 | -- | -- |
| 2007 | 3,985 | 3,716 | 3,762 | 3,759 | 15,222 |
| 2006 | 3,852 | 3,937 | 3,959 | 3,968 | 16,454 |
| 2005 | 3,422 | 3,555 | 3,541 | 3,426 | 14,057 |
| 2004 | 2,501 | 2,787 | 2,775 | 3,190 | 11,396 |
| 2003 | 1,803 | 1,895 | 1,940 | 2,083 | 8,195 |

**Earnings Per Share ($)**

| | | | | | |
|---|---|---|---|---|---|
| 2008 | 0.79 | 0.86 | 0.82 | E0.80 | E3.27 |
| 2007 | 0.97 | 0.79 | 0.81 | 0.71 | 3.29 |
| 2006 | 0.90 | 0.98 | 1.07 | 1.01 | 3.97 |
| 2005 | 0.69 | 0.62 | 0.79 | 0.81 | 2.92 |
| 2004 | 0.46 | 0.60 | 0.63 | 0.61 | 2.29 |
| 2003 | 0.28 | 0.31 | 0.33 | 0.40 | 1.33 |

Fiscal year ended Dec. 31. Next earnings report expected: Early December. EPS Estimates based on S&P Operating Earnings; historical GAAP earnings are as reported.

## Dividend Data (Dates: mm/dd Payment Date: mm/dd/yy)

| Amount ($) | Date Decl. | Ex-Div. Date | Stk. of Record | Payment Date |
|---|---|---|---|---|
| 0.180 | 12/04 | 02/14 | 02/19 | 03/05/08 |
| 0.180 | 04/22 | 05/15 | 05/19 | 06/05/08 |
| 0.180 | 07/08 | 08/14 | 08/18 | 09/05/08 |
| 0.180 | 09/17 | 11/14 | 11/18 | 12/05/08 |

Dividends have been paid since 1943. Source: Company reports.

---

**Please read the Required Disclosures and Analyst Certification on the last page of this report.**

# PACCAR Inc

STANDARD &POOR'S

## Business Summary October 03, 2008

CORPORATE OVERVIEW. Originally incorporated in 1924 as the Pacific Car and Foundry Company, and tracing its roots back to the Seattle Car Manufacturing Company, PACCAR has grown into a multinational company with principal businesses that include the design, manufacture and distribution of high-quality light, medium and heavy-duty commercial trucks and related aftermarket parts. The company's heavy-duty (Class 8) diesel trucks are marketed under the Peterbilt, Kenworth, DAF and Foden names. In addition, through its Peterbilt and Kenworth divisions, PCAR competes in the North American medium-duty (Class 6/7) markets and the European light/medium (6 to 15 metric ton) commercial vehicle market with DAF cab-over-engine trucks.

In 2007, the company's truck production and related aftermarket parts distribution businesses accounted for 92% of revenues and 83% of operating income. Segment profit margins in 2007, 2006, 2005, and 2004, were 9.7%, 1.9%, 11.5%, and 10.6%, respectively; in the previous cycle, during the boom years of 2000, 1999 and 1998, segment profit margins were 6.9%, 9.0% and 7.4%, re-

spectively.

PCAR also manufactures industrial winches under the Braden, Carco and Gearmatic names. Sales of winches provided less than 1% of net sales in 2006, 2005 and 2004.

Like other big truck makers, the company aims to capitalize on a growing trend toward truck leasing and financing. The Finance Services segment accounted for 7.8% of 2007 revenues, but generated 17% of operating income; it posted 24%, 26%, 26%, and 30% operating margins in 2007, 2006, 2005, and 2004, respectively. In 2007, 2006, 2005, and 2004, provisions for loan losses were $41 million, $34 million, $40 million, and $18 million, respectively.

## Company Financials Fiscal Year Ended Dec. 31

| Per Share Data ($) | 2007 | 2006 | 2005 | 2004 | 2003 | 2002 | 2001 | 2000 | 1999 | 1998 |
|---|---|---|---|---|---|---|---|---|---|---|
| Tangible Book Value | 13.66 | 11.98 | 10.27 | 9.61 | 7.36 | 6.08 | 5.64 | 5.64 | 5.13 | 4.46 |
| Cash Flow | 4.70 | 5.12 | 3.87 | 3.09 | 2.00 | 1.50 | 0.91 | 1.54 | 1.85 | 1.37 |
| Earnings | 3.29 | 3.97 | 2.92 | 2.29 | 1.33 | 0.95 | 0.45 | 1.13 | 1.46 | 1.05 |
| S&P Core Earnings | 3.24 | 3.97 | 2.92 | 2.25 | 1.32 | 0.89 | 0.37 | NA | NA | NA |
| Dividends | 0.83 | 0.64 | 0.39 | 0.33 | 0.46 | 0.29 | 0.24 | 0.24 | 0.47 | 0.41 |
| Payout Ratio | 25% | 16% | 13% | 15% | 35% | 30% | 53% | 21% | 32% | 40% |
| Prices:High | 65.75 | 46.17 | 36.17 | 36.19 | 25.95 | 15.70 | 13.68 | 10.72 | 12.44 | 13.19 |
| Prices:Low | 42.15 | 30.12 | 28.13 | 22.05 | 12.37 | 9.09 | 8.44 | 7.16 | 7.80 | 7.31 |
| P/E Ratio:High | 20 | 12 | 12 | 16 | 20 | 17 | 31 | 9 | 9 | 13 |
| P/E Ratio:Low | 13 | 8 | 10 | 10 | 9 | 10 | 19 | 6 | 5 | 7 |

### Income Statement Analysis (Million $)

| | 2007 | 2006 | 2005 | 2004 | 2003 | 2002 | 2001 | 2000 | 1999 | 1998 |
|---|---|---|---|---|---|---|---|---|---|---|
| Revenue | 15,222 | 16,454 | 14,057 | 11,396 | 8,195 | 7,219 | 6,089 | 7,437 | 9,021 | 7,895 |
| Operating Income | 2,932 | 3,136 | 2,572 | 1,972 | 1,313 | 1,012 | 672 | 1,122 | 1,243 | 931 |
| Depreciation | 526 | 435 | 370 | 315 | 268 | 218 | 180 | 156 | 147 | 124 |
| Interest Expense | 737 | 573 | 445 | 331 | 3.50 | 249 | 275 | 294 | 223 | 192 |
| Pretax Income | 1,764 | 2,175 | 1,774 | 1,368 | 806 | 574 | 255 | 665 | 923 | 653 |
| Effective Tax Rate | 30.4% | 31.2% | 36.1% | 33.7% | 34.6% | 35.2% | 32.0% | 33.6% | 36.8% | 36.1% |
| Net Income | 1,227 | 1,496 | 1,133 | 907 | 527 | 372 | 174 | 442 | 584 | 417 |
| S&P Core Earnings | 1,208 | 1,496 | 1,134 | 889 | 523 | 349 | 145 | NA | NA | NA |

### Balance Sheet & Other Financial Data (Million $)

| | 2007 | 2006 | 2005 | 2004 | 2003 | 2002 | 2001 | 2000 | 1999 | 1998 |
|---|---|---|---|---|---|---|---|---|---|---|
| Cash | 1,948 | 2,628 | 2,290 | 2,220 | 1,724 | 1,308 | 1,062 | 910 | 1,059 | 837 |
| Current Assets | 3,919 | 4,200 | 3,508 | 3,332 | 2,599 | 2,102 | 1,834 | 1,861 | 2,119 | 2,070 |
| Total Assets | 17,228 | 16,107 | 13,715 | 12,228 | 9,940 | 8,703 | 7,914 | 8,271 | 7,933 | 6,795 |
| Current Liabilities | 2,503 | 2,738 | 2,182 | 2,151 | 1,482 | 1,258 | 1,134 | 1,268 | 1,534 | 1,519 |
| Long Term Debt | 3,039 | 498 | 936 | 2,314 | 1,557 | 1,552 | 1,547 | 1,655 | 1,475 | 1,311 |
| Common Equity | 5,013 | 4,456 | 3,901 | 3,762 | 3,246 | 2,601 | 2,253 | 2,249 | 2,111 | 1,764 |
| Total Capital | 8,052 | 4,954 | 4,837 | 6,077 | 4,803 | 4,152 | 3,800 | 3,904 | 3,585 | 3,075 |
| Capital Expenditures | 1,267 | 312 | 300 | 232 | 111 | 78.8 | 83.9 | 143 | 256 | 193 |
| Cash Flow | 1,754 | 1,931 | 1,503 | 1,222 | 794 | 590 | 354 | 598 | 730 | 541 |
| Current Ratio | 1.6 | 1.5 | 1.6 | 1.5 | 1.8 | 1.7 | 1.6 | 1.5 | 1.4 | 1.4 |
| % Long Term Debt of Capitalization | 37.7 | 10.1 | 19.3 | 38.1 | 32.4 | 37.4 | 40.7 | 42.4 | 41.1 | 42.6 |
| % Net Income of Revenue | 8.1 | 9.1 | 8.1 | 8.0 | 6.4 | 5.2 | 2.9 | 5.9 | 6.5 | 5.3 |
| % Return on Assets | 7.4 | 10.0 | 8.7 | 8.2 | 5.6 | 4.5 | 2.1 | 5.5 | 7.9 | 6.7 |
| % Return on Equity | 25.9 | 35.8 | 29.6 | 25.9 | 18.0 | 15.3 | 7.7 | 20.3 | 30.1 | 25.6 |

Data as orig reptd.; bef. results of disc opers/spec. items. Per share data adj. for stk. divs.; EPS diluted. E-Estimated. NA-Not Available. NM-Not Meaningful. NR-Not Ranked. UR-Under Review.

**Office:** 777 106th Avenue NE, Bellevue, WA 98004-5027.
**Telephone:** 425-468-7400.
**Website:** http://www.paccar.com
**Chrmn & CEO:** M.C. Pigott

**Pres:** J.G. Cardillo
**Vice Chrmn:** T.E. Plimpton
**Vice Chrmn & CFO:** M.A. Tembreull
**Chief Acctg Officer & Cntlr:** M.T. Barkley

**Investor Contact:** R. Easton
**Board Members:** A. J. Carnwath, J. Fluke, Jr., S. F. Page, R. T. Parry, J. C. Pigott, M. C. Pigott, T. E. Plimpton, W. G. Reed, Jr., G. M. Spierkel, M. A. Tembreull, C. R. Williamson

**Founded:** 1905
**Domicile:** Delaware
**Employees:** 21,800

**STANDARD &POOR'S**

# Pactiv Corp

| S&P Recommendation | HOLD ★★★☆☆ | Price | 12-Mo. Target Price | Investment Style |
|---|---|---|---|---|
| | | $24.53 (as of Nov 14, 2008) | $28.00 | Large-Cap Growth |

**GICS Sector** Materials
**Sub-Industry** Metal & Glass Containers

**Summary** Spun off by Tenneco in 1999, this company is a leading provider of advanced packaging solutions for consumer, institutional, and industrial markets.

## Key Stock Statistics (Source S&P, Vickers, company reports)

| | | | | | | | |
|---|---|---|---|---|---|---|---|
| 52-Wk Range | $65.20–18.98 | S&P Oper. EPS 2008**E** | 1.70 | Market Capitalization(B) | $3.223 | Beta | 0.79 |
| Trailing 12-Month EPS | $1.56 | S&P Oper. EPS 2009**E** | 2.00 | Yield (%) | Nil | S&P 3-Yr. Proj. EPS CAGR(%) | 5 |
| Trailing 12-Month P/E | 15.7 | P/E on S&P Oper. EPS 2008**E** | 14.4 | Dividend Rate/Share | Nil | S&P Credit Rating | BBB |
| $10K Invested 5 Yrs Ago | $11,025 | Common Shares Outstg. (M) | 131.4 | Institutional Ownership (%) | 94 | | |

## Price Performance

30-Week Mov. Avg. · · · 10-Week Mov. Avg. – – GAAP Earnings vs. Previous Year  Volume Above Avg. STARS
12-Mo. Target Price — Relative Strength — ▲ Up ▼ Down ► No Change  Below Avg. ★

Options: ASE, CBOE, Ph

Analysis prepared by **Stewart Scharf** on October 23, 2008, when the stock traded at **$ 25.41**.

## Qualitative Risk Assessment

| LOW | MEDIUM | HIGH |
|---|---|---|

Our risk assessment reflects increased foreign competition and demand for unbranded products, supplier and customer consolidation, and volatile energy costs. However, we believe the balance sheet is improving as the company generates cash to pay down debt.

## Quantitative Evaluations

**S&P Quality Ranking** — B

| D | C | B- | B | B+ | A- | A | A+ |
|---|---|---|---|---|---|---|---|

**Relative Strength Rank** — STRONG — 89

LOWEST = 1   HIGHEST = 99

## Revenue/Earnings Data

**Revenue (Million $)**

| | 1Q | 2Q | 3Q | 4Q | Year |
|---|---|---|---|---|---|
| 2008 | 808.0 | 951.0 | 925.0 | -- | -- |
| 2007 | 677.0 | 828.0 | 872.0 | 876.0 | 3,253 |
| 2006 | 680.0 | 750.0 | 749.0 | 738.0 | 2,917 |
| 2005 | 613.0 | 707.0 | 695.0 | 741.0 | 2,756 |
| 2004 | 775.0 | 858.0 | 865.0 | 884.0 | 3,382 |
| 2003 | 717.0 | 810.0 | 793.0 | 818.0 | 3,138 |

**Earnings Per Share ($)**

| | | | | | |
|---|---|---|---|---|---|
| 2008 | 0.27 | 0.49 | 0.40 | E0.56 | E1.70 |
| 2007 | 0.43 | 0.52 | 0.45 | 0.45 | 1.84 |
| 2006 | 0.35 | 0.49 | 0.75 | 0.39 | 1.98 |
| 2005 | 0.14 | 0.24 | 0.28 | 0.30 | 0.96 |
| 2004 | Nil | 0.33 | 0.37 | 0.31 | 1.01 |
| 2003 | 0.27 | 0.37 | 0.16 | 0.41 | 1.21 |

Fiscal year ended Dec. 31. Next earnings report expected: Late January. EPS Estimates based on S&P Operating Earnings; historical GAAP earnings are as reported.

## Dividend Data

No cash dividends have been paid.

## Highlights

► We expect about 5% organic sales growth (before 6% from Prairie Packaging) in 2008, driven by pricing initiatives, while unit volume for consumer and food service/food packaging products grows modestly into 2009 due to soft market conditions and, to some extent, customers shifting to less expensive private label products. However, PTV participates in all private label categories except for trash bags.

► Although resin costs should decline as oil prices fall, we project that gross margins (before D&A) in 2008 will narrow to near 25%, from 28.6% in 2007, based on a lag effect for pricing pass throughs. We believe margins will rebound sequentially during 2009, on the lower expected raw material costs and projected cost savings of $10 million resulting from asset rationalizations and headcount reductions.

► We estimate a tax rate of 35% for 2008, and operating EPS of $1.70, before an estimated $0.08 restructuring charge, but after $0.05 cost savings and $0.23 of pension income; we see 18% growth to $2.00 in 2009.

## Investment Rationale/Risk

► Our hold opinion is based on our valuation models and a better outlook for raw material costs. We still project fairly strong cash flow generation targeted for debt paydowns.

► Risks to our recommendation and target price include a significant rise in resin prices that the company is unable to pass through to consumers, further deterioration in the global economy, and a more significant impact from customers seeking lower-priced packaging products. Regarding corporate governance, we are somewhat concerned that the positions of chairman and CEO are held by the same person.

► We blend our DCF valuation with relative metrics to arrive at our 12-month target price of $28. Our DCF model, which assumes a 3% terminal growth rate and a 7.5% weighted average cost of capital (WACC), shows intrinsic value of $30. Based on relative metrics, we apply a P/E of 13X to our 2009 EPS estimate, a premium to peers, to arrive at a value of $26. We think this P/E, which is below PTV's five-year historical average, is warranted based on PTV's leading brand names and focus on controlling costs.

The **McGraw-Hill** Companies

# Pactiv Corp

**STANDARD &POOR'S**

## Business Summary October 23, 2008

CORPORATE OVERVIEW. Pactiv Corp., a global supplier of specialty packaging and consumer products, derives more than 80% of its sales from markets in which it holds the No. 1 or No. 2 market share position. It operates 44 manufacturing plants in North America and one in Germany. It also has a 62.5%-owned joint venture corrugated-converting facility and a 51%-owned folding carton operation in China. In 2007, 95% of sales were generated in North America. Wal-Mart accounted for 20% of total sales.

After discontinuing the protective and flexible packaging division during 2005, PTV operated two units: consumer products (Hefty) and foodservice/food packaging. Consumer products sales accounted for 38% of total sales in 2007 ($227 million of operating income, before restructuring charges), and foodservice/food packaging 62% ($247 million). Foreign sales to external customers accounted for 9.4% of the total. In June 2007, PTV acquired Prairie Packaging Inc., a manufacturer of disposable tableware products with sales of over $500 million, broadening its cups and cutlery business.

The company manufactures consumer products such as plastic storage bags and waste bags; foam and molded fiber disposable tableware; and disposable aluminum cookware. It sells many products under recognized brand names

such as Hefty, Baggies, Hefty One-Zip, Zoo Pals, Kordite, The Gripper, and E-Z Foil. In early 2007, PTV rolled out Hefty One Zip travel bags for liquid carry-on items at airports and OneZip big bags for storing or transporting large items. The company expects new product innovations to generate $100 million in annual retail sales over the next few years.

PTV makes food packaging products for the food processing industry, including molded fiber egg cartons, foam meat trays, aluminum containers, and modified atmosphere packaging. The company also offers tableware products such as plates, bowls, cups, and takeout-service containers.

We believe the company will maintain its leading brand name position in the specialty packaging industry and will continue to develop new products.

The company estimates that a 1% change in resin costs equates to a $0.03 effect on EPS on an annualized basis, assuming no pricing actions.

## Company Financials Fiscal Year Ended Dec. 31

### Per Share Data ($)

| | 2007 | 2006 | 2005 | 2004 | 2003 | 2002 | 2001 | 2000 | 1999 | 1998 |
|---|---|---|---|---|---|---|---|---|---|---|
| Tangible Book Value | NM | 0.68 | 0.23 | 0.98 | 0.77 | 1.79 | 4.91 | 3.79 | 2.19 | NA |
| Cash Flow | 3.08 | 3.02 | 1.94 | 2.10 | 2.24 | 2.35 | 2.14 | 1.84 | 0.43 | 1.43 |
| Earnings | 1.84 | 1.98 | 0.96 | 1.01 | 1.21 | 1.37 | 1.03 | 0.70 | -0.67 | 0.39 |
| S&P Core Earnings | 1.51 | 1.71 | 0.56 | 0.64 | 1.00 | -0.23 | -0.57 | NA | NA | NA |
| Dividends | Nil | Nil | Nil | Nil | Nil | Nil | Nil | Nil | Nil | NA |
| Payout Ratio | Nil | Nil | Nil | Nil | Nil | Nil | Nil | Nil | Nil | NA |
| Prices:High | 36.91 | 36.53 | 25.58 | 25.73 | 24.03 | 24.47 | 18.10 | 13.31 | 14.50 | NA |
| Prices:Low | 22.79 | 21.50 | 16.50 | 19.80 | 17.55 | 15.35 | 11.26 | 7.50 | 9.31 | NA |
| P/E Ratio:High | 20 | 18 | 27 | 25 | 20 | 18 | 18 | 19 | NM | NA |
| P/E Ratio:Low | 12 | 11 | 17 | 20 | 15 | 11 | 11 | 11 | NM | NA |

### Income Statement Analysis (Million $)

| | 2007 | 2006 | 2005 | 2004 | 2003 | 2002 | 2001 | 2000 | 1999 | 1998 |
|---|---|---|---|---|---|---|---|---|---|---|
| Revenue | 3,253 | 2,917 | 2,756 | 3,382 | 3,138 | 2,880 | 2,812 | 3,134 | 2,921 | 2,791 |
| Operating Income | 644 | 568 | 452 | 954 | 630 | 617 | 574 | 570 | 498 | 466 |
| Depreciation | 165 | 145 | 146 | 169 | 163 | 158 | 177 | 185 | 184 | 175 |
| Interest Expense | 98.0 | 73.0 | 82.0 | 101 | 96.0 | 96.0 | 107 | 134 | 146 | 164 |
| Pretax Income | 381 | 391 | 224 | 244 | 314 | 367 | 284 | 207 | -159 | 124 |
| Effective Tax Rate | 35.4% | 29.2% | 36.2% | 36.9% | 37.6% | 39.8% | 41.5% | 44.0% | NM | 46.0% |
| Net Income | 244 | 277 | 143 | 155 | 195 | 220 | 165 | 113 | -112 | 66.0 |
| S&P Core Earnings | 200 | 239 | 82.3 | 96.9 | 160 | -36.1 | -91.1 | NA | NA | NA |

### Balance Sheet & Other Financial Data (Million $)

| | 2007 | 2006 | 2005 | 2004 | 2003 | 2002 | 2001 | 2000 | 1999 | 1998 |
|---|---|---|---|---|---|---|---|---|---|---|
| Cash | 95.0 | 181 | 172 | 222 | 140 | 127 | 41.0 | 26.0 | 12.0 | 18.0 |
| Current Assets | 797 | 838 | 820 | 1,079 | 982 | 904 | 740 | 900 | 866 | 1,031 |
| Total Assets | 3,765 | 2,758 | 2,820 | 3,741 | 3,706 | 3,412 | 4,060 | 4,341 | 4,588 | 4,749 |
| Current Liabilities | 460 | 549 | 456 | 984 | 474 | 501 | 459 | 512 | 920 | 1,703 |
| Long Term Debt | 1,574 | 771 | 869 | 869 | 1,336 | 1,224 | 1,211 | 1,560 | 1,741 | 1,186 |
| Common Equity | 1,226 | 853 | 820 | 1,083 | 1,061 | 897 | 1,689 | 1,539 | 1,350 | 1,286 |
| Total Capital | 3,032 | 1,753 | 1,802 | 2,209 | 2,617 | 2,282 | 3,502 | 3,595 | 3,432 | 2,848 |
| Capital Expenditures | 151 | 78.0 | 121 | 100 | 112 | 126 | 145 | 135 | 1,129 | NA |
| Cash Flow | 409 | 422 | 289 | 324 | 358 | 378 | 342 | 298 | 72.0 | 241 |
| Current Ratio | 1.7 | 1.5 | 1.8 | 1.1 | 2.1 | 1.8 | 1.6 | 1.8 | 0.9 | 0.6 |
| % Long Term Debt of Capitalization | 51.9 | 44.0 | 48.2 | 39.3 | 51.1 | 53.6 | 34.6 | 43.4 | 50.7 | 41.6 |
| % Net Income of Revenue | 7.5 | 9.5 | 5.2 | 4.6 | 6.2 | 7.6 | 5.9 | 3.6 | NM | 2.4 |
| % Return on Assets | 7.5 | 9.9 | 4.4 | 4.2 | 5.5 | 5.9 | 4.0 | 2.5 | NM | NA |
| % Return on Equity | 23.5 | 33.1 | 15.0 | 14.5 | 19.9 | 17.0 | 10.2 | 7.8 | NM | NA |

Data as orig reptd.; bef. results of disc opers/spec. items. Per share data adj. for stk. divs.; EPS diluted. E-Estimated. NA-Not Available. NM-Not Meaningful. NR-Not Ranked. UR-Under Review.

**Office:** 1900 West Field Court, Lake Forest, IL 60045-4828.
**Telephone:** 847-482-2000.
**Email:** investorrelations@pactiv.com
**Website:** http://www.pactiv.com

**Chrmn, Pres & CEO:** R.L. Wambold
**SVP, CFO & Cntlr:** E.T. Walters
**Secy & General Counsel:** J.E. Doyle
**Investor Contact:** C. Hanneman (847-482-2429)

**Board Members:** L. D. Brady, II, K. D. Brooksher, R. J. Darnall, N. Henderson, N. T. Linebarger, R. B. Porter, R. L. Wambold, N. H. Wesley
**Founded:** 1965
**Domicile:** Delaware
**Employees:** 13,000

**The McGraw-Hill Companies**

# Pall Corp

STANDARD
&POOR'S

| S&P Recommendation | HOLD ★★★☆☆ | Price | 12-Mo. Target Price |
|---|---|---|---|
| | | $24.43 (as of Nov 14, 2008) | $38.00 |

**GICS Sector** Industrials
**Sub-Industry** Industrial Machinery

**Summary** This company is a leading producer of filters for the health care, aerospace, microelectronics and other industries.

## Key Stock Statistics (Source S&P, Vickers, company reports)

| | | | | | | | | |
|---|---|---|---|---|---|---|---|---|
| 52-Wk Range | $43.19– 21.79 | S&P Oper. EPS 2009E | 2.20 | Market Capitalization(B) | $2.916 | Beta | 1.33 |
| Trailing 12-Month EPS | $1.76 | S&P Oper. EPS 2010E | 2.50 | Yield (%) | 2.13 | S&P 3-Yr. Proj. EPS CAGR(%) | 13 |
| Trailing 12-Month P/E | 13.9 | P/E on S&P Oper. EPS 2009E | 11.1 | Dividend Rate/Share | $0.52 | S&P Credit Rating | BBB |
| $10K Invested 5 Yrs Ago | $10,555 | Common Shares Outstg. (M) | 119.4 | Institutional Ownership (%) | 91 | | |

## Price Performance

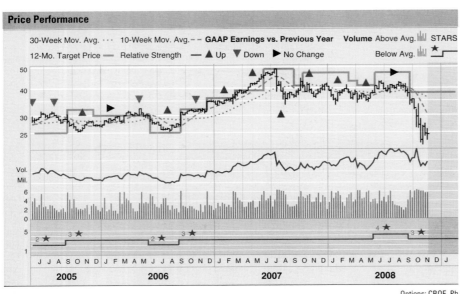

30-Week Mov. Avg. ··· 10-Week Mov. Avg.— **GAAP Earnings vs. Previous Year** Volume Above Avg. ▐█▌ STARS
12-Mo. Target Price — Relative Strength — ▲ Up ▼ Down ▶ No Change Below Avg. ▐█▌ ★

Options: CBOE, Ph

Analysis prepared by **Stewart Scharf** on September 17, 2008, when the stock traded at **$ 35.25**.

### Highlights

➤ We expect FY 09 (Jul.) total sales to advance close to 6% (before about 3% projected negative foreign currency effect), driven by strength in the biopharm and general industrial (renamed Energy, Water and Process Technologies) segments, primarily in Asia. We still see medical sales being affected by lower demand for blood filters, while microelectronics sales should advance 5% assuming that the semiconductor market remains soft, with similar growth seen for aerospace & technologies.

➤ We see gross margins in FY 09 expanding by nearly 150 basis points, to 48.5%, reflecting a more favorable product mix, improved systems engineering and pricing, and product line rationalizations. We expect operating margins (EBITDA) to widen somewhat from 17.5% of sales in FY 08, on improved productivity and cost-cutting initiatives, while SG&A expenses should remain well controlled at about 29% of sales.

➤ We forecast a lower effective tax rate of 32% for FY 09, and project pro forma EPS of $2.20 (before restructuring charges), advancing 14%, to $2.50, in FY 10.

### Investment Rationale/Risk

➤ We recently downgraded our recommendation to a hold, based on valuation metrics as well as our view of foreign currency headwinds and inflationary pressures. We still see favorable trends in most global markets, and expect PLL to continue to focus on rationalizations.

➤ Risks to our recommendation and target price include an extended cyclical downturn in semiconductors, negative foreign currency translations and a significant rise in raw material costs. We have some corporate governance concerns, as PLL found a material weakness in its internal controls related to its financial reporting, although accounting personnel changes have been made and the company recently restated earnings dating back seven years.

➤ Our relative valuation results in a value of $37 using a P/E of 17X our FY 09 EPS estimate, a discount to PLL's five-year historical forward average. Our intrinsic value estimate of $40 is based on our DCF model, which assumes a terminal growth rate of 3.5% and a weighted average cost of capital of 8.5%. Blending these metrics, our 12-month target price is $38.

## Qualitative Risk Assessment

| LOW | MEDIUM | HIGH |
|---|---|---|

Our risk assessment reflects the historically cyclical semiconductor sector, PLL's exposure to foreign markets, and a pending settlement with the IRS and other civil lawsuits related to understating tax payments, even though the SEC inquiry and restatements have been completed. Also, an IRS audit and U.S. Attorney inquiry are still pending. This is offset by our view of PLL's reduced debt levels and strong cash generation.

## Quantitative Evaluations

**S&P Quality Ranking** B+

| D | C | B- | B | B+ | A- | A | A+ |
|---|---|---|---|---|---|---|---|

**Relative Strength Rank** MODERATE

52

LOWEST = 1 HIGHEST = 99

## Revenue/Earnings Data

**Revenue (Million $)**

| | 1Q | 2Q | 3Q | 4Q | Year |
|---|---|---|---|---|---|
| 2008 | 561.0 | 625.8 | 661.7 | 723.2 | 2,572 |
| 2007 | 499.3 | 544.9 | 559.4 | 646.3 | 2,250 |
| 2006 | 431.2 | 478.4 | 510.0 | 597.3 | 2,017 |
| 2005 | 414.7 | 469.5 | 493.5 | 524.5 | 1,902 |
| 2004 | 374.3 | 428.1 | 463.9 | 504.5 | 1,771 |
| 2003 | 332.2 | 388.5 | 421.5 | 471.4 | 1,614 |

**Earnings Per Share ($)**

| | | | | | |
|---|---|---|---|---|---|
| 2008 | 0.29 | 0.39 | 0.51 | 0.57 | 1.76 |
| 2007 | 0.13 | 0.36 | 0.40 | 0.57 | 1.03 |
| 2006 | 0.20 | 0.26 | 0.20 | 0.50 | 1.16 |
| 2005 | 0.17 | 0.26 | 0.35 | 0.34 | 1.12 |
| 2004 | 0.19 | 0.20 | 0.37 | 0.44 | 1.20 |
| 2003 | -0.19 | 0.25 | 0.33 | 0.44 | 0.83 |

Fiscal year ended Jul. 31. Next earnings report expected: NA. EPS Estimates based on S&P Operating Earnings; historical GAAP earnings are as reported.

## Dividend Data (Dates: mm/dd Payment Date: mm/dd/yy)

| Amount ($) | Date Decl. | Ex-Div. Date | Stk. of Record | Payment Date |
|---|---|---|---|---|
| 0.120 | 01/17 | 01/30 | 02/01 | 02/15/08 |
| 0.130 | 03/12 | 04/23 | 04/25 | 05/09/08 |
| 0.130 | 07/15 | 07/31 | 08/04 | 08/19/08 |
| 0.130 | 10/21 | 10/28 | 10/30 | 11/12/08 |

Dividends have been paid since 1974. Source: Company reports.

# Pall Corp

STANDARD &POOR'S

## Business Summary September 17, 2008

CORPORATE OVERVIEW. Pall Corp. is a global producer of filters for health care, aerospace and industrial markets. Pall divides these markets into the following subsegments: Medical and BioPharmaceuticals (Life Sciences), Energy, Water & Process Technologies (formerly General Industrial), Aerospace & Transportation (formed in early FY 07 (Jul.) by integrating the sales and marketing teams of Aerospace and Commercial OEMs), and Microelectronics (the Industrial business). The company's Industrial group includes machinery and equipment, food and beverage, fuels and chemicals, power generation, and municipal water. Systems sales represented 12% of total sales in FY 08, up from 10% in FY 07.

The Industrial segment (62% of revenues in FY 08; $246 million of profits) makes filters and separation products for three markets. Aerospace & Transportation (12% of the segment's sales) includes both commercial and military markets. Energy, Water & Process Technologies (38%) produces filters for the aluminum, paper, automobile, oil, gas, chemical, petrochemical and power industries. Microelectronics (12%) makes products for the semiconductor, data storage and photographic film industries. PLL noted that over $300 million of FY 07 sales (latest available) were derived from water filtration, with municipalities accounting for more than 20%. Consumer electronics accounted for about 40% of division sales in FY 07, up from 25% in 2000. Main competitors in general industrial include 3M's CUNO, GE's GE Infrastructure unit, Siemens's

U.S. Filter, Rohm & Haas, and Parker Hannifin. The segment's five-year sales CAGR was 8.1% between FY 04 and FY 08.

The Life Sciences segment contributed 38% of total revenues ($198 million in operating profits) in FY 08. The BioPharmaceuticals division makes filter products used in the development of drugs, and food and beverage filters that help produce yeast- and bacteria-free water. The rapidly expanding blood division offers hospitals and blood centers blood filters that reduce leukocyte (white cells) and other bloodborne viral contaminants, such as bacteria. Biopharmaceutical sales accounted for nearly 50% of the segment's total sales in FY 08, while medical products (blood and cardiovascular filtration) accounted for the balance. PLL estimates the market potential for medical filters at $4.3 billion. The segment's five-year sales CAGR was 5.2% between FY 04 and FY 08.

In FY 08, the Western Hemisphere accounted for 32% of sales, Europe for 43%, and Asia for 25%. Pro forma EPS was $1.97, before restructuring charges of $0.21.

## Company Financials Fiscal Year Ended Jul. 31

### Per Share Data ($)

| | 2008 | 2007 | 2006 | 2005 | 2004 | 2003 | 2002 | 2001 | 2000 | 1999 |
|---|---|---|---|---|---|---|---|---|---|---|
| Tangible Book Value | 6.94 | 6.14 | 7.21 | 6.73 | 6.21 | 5.16 | NM | 6.29 | 5.41 | 5.09 |
| Cash Flow | NA | 1.78 | 1.92 | 1.85 | 1.90 | 1.51 | 1.19 | 1.53 | 1.68 | 1.01 |
| Earnings | 1.76 | 1.03 | 1.16 | 1.12 | 1.20 | 0.83 | 0.59 | 0.95 | 1.18 | 0.41 |
| S&P Core Earnings | 1.67 | 1.05 | 1.22 | 1.13 | 1.16 | 0.70 | 0.42 | 0.83 | NA | NA |
| Dividends | 0.50 | 0.35 | 0.53 | 0.38 | 0.27 | 0.36 | 0.52 | 0.68 | 0.50 | 0.64 |
| Payout Ratio | 28% | 34% | 46% | 34% | 23% | 43% | 88% | 71% | 42% | 156% |
| Prices:High | 43.19 | 49.00 | 35.57 | 31.52 | 29.80 | 27.00 | 24.48 | 26.25 | 25.00 | 26.19 |
| Prices:Low | 21.79 | 33.23 | 25.26 | 25.21 | 22.00 | 15.01 | 14.68 | 17.50 | 25.00 | 26.19 |
| P/E Ratio:High | 25 | 48 | 31 | 28 | 25 | 33 | 41 | 28 | 21 | 64 |
| P/E Ratio:Low | 12 | 32 | 22 | 23 | 18 | 18 | 25 | 18 | 15 | 38 |

### Income Statement Analysis (Million $)

| | 2008 | 2007 | 2006 | 2005 | 2004 | 2003 | 2002 | 2001 | 2000 | 1999 |
|---|---|---|---|---|---|---|---|---|---|---|
| Revenue | 2,572 | 2,250 | 2,017 | 1,902 | 1,771 | 1,614 | 1,291 | 1,235 | 1,224 | 1,147 |
| Operating Income | NA | NA | 341 | 337 | 320 | 299 | 215 | 256 | 274 | 160 |
| Depreciation | 93.2 | 94.0 | 95.7 | 90.9 | 88.9 | 83.9 | 74.0 | 71.5 | 63.4 | 74.8 |
| Interest Expense | NA | NA | 23.0 | 26.0 | 20.5 | 24.4 | 14.3 | 16.6 | 14.1 | 18.4 |
| Pretax Income | 326 | 261 | 210 | 181 | 198 | 143 | 100.0 | 150 | 188 | 58.9 |
| Effective Tax Rate | 33.3% | 51.1% | 30.8% | 22.2% | 23.4% | 27.9% | 26.7% | 21.5% | 22.2% | 12.6% |
| Net Income | 217 | 128 | 145 | 141 | 152 | 103 | 73.2 | 118 | 147 | 51.5 |
| S&P Core Earnings | 205 | 131 | 153 | 142 | 148 | 87.4 | 52.1 | 102 | NA | NA |

### Balance Sheet & Other Financial Data (Million $)

| | 2008 | 2007 | 2006 | 2005 | 2004 | 2003 | 2002 | 2001 | 2000 | 1999 |
|---|---|---|---|---|---|---|---|---|---|---|
| Cash | 454 | 443 | 318 | 165 | 199 | 127 | 105 | 54.9 | 81.0 | 86.7 |
| Current Assets | NA | NA | 1,377 | 1,160 | 1,070 | 938 | 916 | 779 | 753 | 744 |
| Total Assets | 2,957 | 2,709 | 2,553 | 2,265 | 2,140 | 2,017 | 2,027 | 1,549 | 1,507 | 1,488 |
| Current Liabilities | NA | NA | 531 | 457 | 419 | 421 | 438 | 314 | 438 | 558 |
| Long Term Debt | NA | NA | 640 | 510 | 489 | 490 | 620 | 359 | 224 | 117 |
| Common Equity | 1,139 | 1,061 | 1,179 | 1,140 | 1,054 | 935 | 820 | 770 | 761 | 731 |
| Total Capital | NA | NA | 1,826 | 1,660 | 1,559 | 1,439 | 1,478 | 1,149 | 1,006 | 869 |
| Capital Expenditures | 124 | 97.8 | 96.0 | 86.2 | 61.3 | 62.2 | 69.9 | 77.8 | 66.5 | 71.2 |
| Cash Flow | NA | NA | 241 | 232 | 241 | 187 | 147 | 190 | 210 | 126 |
| Current Ratio | 2.9 | 1.9 | 2.6 | 2.5 | 2.6 | 2.2 | 2.1 | 2.5 | 1.7 | 1.3 |
| % Long Term Debt of Capitalization | 39.6 | 35.8 | 35.0 | 30.7 | 31.3 | 34.0 | 41.9 | 31.2 | 22.3 | 13.4 |
| % Net Income of Revenue | 8.5 | 5.7 | 7.2 | 7.4 | 8.6 | 6.4 | 5.7 | 9.6 | 12.0 | 4.5 |
| % Return on Assets | 7.7 | 4.9 | 6.0 | 6.3 | 7.3 | 5.1 | 4.1 | 7.7 | 9.8 | 3.6 |
| % Return on Equity | 19.8 | 11.4 | 12.5 | 12.8 | 15.2 | 11.8 | 9.2 | 15.4 | 19.7 | 6.9 |

Data as orig reptd.; bef. results of disc opers/spec. items. Per share data adj. for stk. divs.; EPS diluted. E-Estimated. NA-Not Available. NM-Not Meaningful. NR-Not Ranked. UR-Under Review.

**Office:** 2200 Northern Boulevard, East Hills, NY 11548.
**Telephone:** 516-484-5400.
**Email:** invrel@pall.com
**Website:** http://www.pall.com

**Chrmn & CEO:** E. Krasnoff
**Pres & COO:** D.B. Stevens
**SVP, Secy & General Counsel:** S. Marino
**CFO & Treas:** L. McDermott

**Chief Acctg Officer & Cntlr:** F. Moschella
**Investor Contact:** P. Iannucci (516-801-9848)
**Board Members:** D. J. Carroll, Jr., C. W. Grise, J. H. Haskell, Jr., U. S. Haynes, Jr., R. L. Hoffman, E. Krasnoff, D. N. Longstreet, E. W. Martin, Jr., K. L. Plourde, H. Shelley, E. L. Snyder, E. Travaglianti

**Founded:** 1946
**Domicile:** New York
**Employees:** 10,600

# Parker-Hannifin Corp

**STANDARD &POOR'S**

| S&P Recommendation | **BUY** ★★★★☆ | Price<br>$35.95 (as of Nov 14, 2008) | 12-Mo. Target Price<br>$52.00 | Investment Style<br>Large-Cap Blend |
|---|---|---|---|---|

**GICS Sector** Industrials
**Sub-Industry** Industrial Machinery

**Summary** This company is a global maker of industrial pumps, valves and hydraulics. Its products are used in everything from jet engines to trucks and autos and utility turbines.

## Key Stock Statistics (Source S&P, Vickers, company reports)

| | | | | | | | |
|---|---|---|---|---|---|---|---|
| 52-Wk Range | $86.91– 32.88 | S&P Oper. EPS 2009**E** | 5.45 | Market Capitalization(B) | $5.793 | Beta | 1.85 |
| Trailing 12-Month EPS | $5.70 | S&P Oper. EPS 2010**E** | 5.80 | Yield (%) | 2.78 | S&P 3-Yr. Proj. EPS CAGR(%) | 8 |
| Trailing 12-Month P/E | 6.3 | P/E on S&P Oper. EPS 2009**E** | 6.6 | Dividend Rate/Share | $1.00 | S&P Credit Rating | A |
| $10K Invested 5 Yrs Ago | $10,610 | Common Shares Outstg. (M) | 161.2 | Institutional Ownership (%) | 83 | | |

## Price Performance

30-Week Mov. Avg.  ···· 10-Week Mov. Avg. - - **GAAP Earnings vs. Previous Year**  **Volume** Above Avg. ▯▮▯ STARS
12-Mo. Target Price — Relative Strength — ▲ Up ▼ Down ► No Change   Below Avg. ▯▯▯ ★

Options: ASE, CBOE, Ph

Analysis prepared by **Richard Tortoriello** on November 07, 2008, when the stock traded at **$ 36.57**.

## Highlights

➤ We anticipate overall FY 09 (Jun.) revenue growth of 1%. We expect slow growth in the North American Industrial and Aerospace segments, offset by flat growth in International Industrial, and a modest decline in sales in Climate & Industrial Controls, due to the company's exposure to the U.S. residential housing market. We project 3% growth in FY 10.

➤ We expect segment operating margins to decline to 13.5% in FY 09, from 14.1% in FY 08, due to a strengthening U.S. dollar and lower volumes in some product lines. For FY 10, we expect a slight margin increase to 13.7%.

➤ We expect a 1% EPS decline in FY 09, to $5.45, from $5.53 reported for FY 08. For FY 10, we project a 5% increase, to $5.80. We expect FY 09 free cash flow (cash flow from operations less capital expenditures) per share of at least 100% of EPS, as we do not expect PH to need significant working capital additions in FY 09. We see excess cash being used for share repurchases, dividend increases, and business acquisitions.

## Investment Rationale/Risk

➤ Although we see weakness in the automotive, heavy truck and residential housing markets affecting PH's orders, we continue to project slow growth in its North American industrial business. In addition, we view the aerospace cycle as strong, despite projected aftermarket weakness, with large aircraft backlogs at Boeing and Airbus. We view PH as a world-class industrial company recently selling at historical low valuation levels on a variety of measures.

➤ Risks to our recommendation and target price include a strong or prolonged decline in global economic growth, an extended downturn in the aerospace market, and the potential for production and other problems at PH.

➤ Our 12-month target price of $52 is based on an enterprise value to estimated 2008 EBITDA multiple of 6X, modestly above a 20-year low EV to EBITDA multiple of 5X and below a 20-year average of 8X. Given risks associated with slowing global economic growth, we believe a valuation multiple close to historical lows is appropriate for the shares.

## Qualitative Risk Assessment

| LOW | **MEDIUM** | HIGH |
|---|---|---|

Our risk assessment reflects the highly cyclical nature of the company's industrial and aviation markets, volatile energy costs and a competitive environment. This is offset by our view of PH's favorable earnings and dividend track record.

## Quantitative Evaluations

**S&P Quality Ranking** A-

| D | C | B- | B | B+ | **A-** | A | A+ |
|---|---|---|---|---|---|---|---|

**Relative Strength Rank** **MODERATE**

44

LOWEST = 1    HIGHEST = 99

## Revenue/Earnings Data

**Revenue (Million $)**

| | 1Q | 2Q | 3Q | 4Q | Year |
|---|---|---|---|---|---|
| 2009 | 3,065 | -- | -- | -- | -- |
| 2008 | 2,787 | 2,829 | 3,183 | 3,347 | 12,146 |
| 2007 | 2,552 | 2,511 | 2,781 | 2,874 | 10,718 |
| 2006 | 2,114 | 2,158 | 2,498 | 2,617 | 9,386 |
| 2005 | 1,947 | 1,943 | 2,142 | 2,211 | 8,215 |
| 2004 | 1,587 | 1,621 | 1,906 | 1,993 | 7,107 |

**Earnings Per Share ($)**

| | 1Q | 2Q | 3Q | 4Q | Year |
|---|---|---|---|---|---|
| 2009 | 1.50 | E1.35 | E1.18 | E1.43 | E5.45 |
| 2008 | 1.33 | 1.23 | 1.49 | 1.47 | 5.53 |
| 2007 | 1.17 | 1.09 | 1.19 | 1.23 | 4.67 |
| 2006 | 0.79 | 0.71 | 0.97 | 1.03 | 3.52 |
| 2005 | 0.74 | 0.63 | 0.79 | 0.89 | 3.03 |
| 2004 | 0.32 | 0.31 | 0.60 | 0.70 | 1.94 |

Fiscal year ended Jun. 30. Next earnings report expected: Mid January. EPS Estimates based on S&P Operating Earnings; historical GAAP earnings are as reported.

## Dividend Data (Dates: mm/dd Payment Date: mm/dd/yy)

| Amount<br>($) | Date<br>Decl. | Ex-Div.<br>Date | Stk. of<br>Record | Payment<br>Date |
|---|---|---|---|---|
| 0.210 | 01/25 | 02/19 | 02/21 | 03/07/08 |
| 0.210 | 04/17 | 05/13 | 05/15 | 06/06/08 |
| 0.250 | 08/14 | 08/21 | 08/25 | 09/05/08 |
| 0.250 | 10/22 | 11/18 | 11/20 | 12/05/08 |

Dividends have been paid since 1949. Source: Company reports.

*The McGraw-Hill Companies*

# Parker-Hannifin Corp

**STANDARD &POOR'S**

## Business Summary November 07, 2008

CORPORATE OVERVIEW. With $13 billion in estimated annual revenues in FY 09 (Jun.), Parker-Hannifin is one of the world's largest makers of components that control the flow of industrial fluids. It is also a major global maker of components that move and/or control the operation of a variety of machinery and equipment. In addition to motion control products, PH also produces fluid purification, fluid and fuel control, process instrumentation, air conditioning, refrigeration, electromagnetic shielding, and thermal management products and systems. PH's offerings include a wide range of valves, pumps, hydraulics, filters and related products. The company's components are used in everything from jet engines to medical devices, farm tractors and utility turbines.

Although U.S. markets still account for most of the company's revenues, PH is expanding its overseas presence; in FY 08, international sales accounted for 47% of total revenues, up from 40% in FY 07.

PH's Industrial business (76% of FY 08 sales and 82% of segment operating earnings) makes valves, pumps, filters, seals and hydraulic components for a broad range of industries, as well as pneumatic and electromechanical components and systems. The company's industrial components are sold to manufacturers (as part of original equipment) and to end users (as replacement

parts). Replacement part sales are generally more profitable than original equipment sales. PH's industrial components are designed for both standard and custom specifications. Custom-made components are typically more profitable than standard components. The industrial business is reported as two segments: Industrial North America (35% of sales and 36% of operating profits) and Industrial International (41% and 46%). Sales through distributors account for about half of PH's total industrial business.

Aerospace (15% of sales and 15% of segment operating profits) primarily makes hydraulic, pneumatic and fuel equipment used in civilian and military airframes and jet engines. It also makes aircraft wheels and brakes for small planes and military aircraft. PH sells aircraft components to aircraft manufacturers as new equipment, and to end-users (such as airlines) as replacement parts. As with industrial components, aircraft-related replacement parts sales are generally more profitable than are original equipment sales.

## Company Financials Fiscal Year Ended Jun. 30

| Per Share Data ($) | 2008 | 2007 | 2006 | 2005 | 2004 | 2003 | 2002 | 2001 | 2000 | 1999 |
|---|---|---|---|---|---|---|---|---|---|---|
| Tangible Book Value | 8.59 | 10.69 | 9.75 | 9.23 | 9.39 | 7.63 | 8.18 | 8.95 | 9.96 | 8.41 |
| Cash Flow | NA | 6.45 | 5.07 | 4.50 | 3.34 | 2.57 | 2.37 | 3.53 | 3.44 | 3.12 |
| Earnings | 5.53 | 4.67 | 3.52 | 3.03 | 1.94 | 1.12 | 0.75 | 1.99 | 2.21 | 1.89 |
| S&P Core Earnings | 5.10 | 4.77 | 3.83 | 3.08 | 2.00 | 0.61 | 0.37 | 1.19 | NA | NA |
| Dividends | 0.84 | 0.69 | 0.61 | 0.52 | 0.51 | 0.49 | 0.48 | 0.47 | 0.34 | 0.43 |
| Payout Ratio | 15% | 15% | 17% | 17% | 26% | 44% | 64% | 23% | 15% | 23% |
| Prices:High | 86.91 | 86.56 | 58.67 | 50.82 | 52.28 | 39.87 | 36.59 | 33.40 | 36.00 | 34.29 |
| Prices:Low | 32.88 | 50.41 | 43.44 | 37.87 | 34.49 | 23.88 | 23.01 | 20.27 | 20.67 | 19.67 |
| P/E Ratio:High | 16 | 19 | 17 | 17 | 27 | 36 | 49 | 17 | 16 | 18 |
| P/E Ratio:Low | 6 | 11 | 12 | 12 | 18 | 21 | 31 | 10 | 9 | 10 |

| Income Statement Analysis (Million $) | | | | | | | | | | |
|---|---|---|---|---|---|---|---|---|---|---|
| Revenue | 12,146 | 10,718 | 9,386 | 8,215 | 7,107 | 6,411 | 6,149 | 5,980 | 5,355 | 4,959 |
| Operating Income | NA | 1,513 | 1,263 | 1,100 | 817 | 639 | 628 | 836 | 829 | 741 |
| Depreciation | 327 | 295 | 281 | 265 | 253 | 259 | 282 | 265 | 206 | 202 |
| Interest Expense | NA | 83.4 | 75.8 | 67.0 | 73.4 | 81.6 | 82.0 | 90.4 | 59.2 | 63.7 |
| Pretax Income | 1,327 | 1,159 | 900 | 756 | 494 | 297 | 218 | 534 | 562 | 478 |
| Effective Tax Rate | 28.4% | 28.4% | NM | 27.6% | 30.0% | 34.0% | 40.3% | 35.5% | 34.5% | 35.0% |
| Net Income | 949 | 830 | 638 | 548 | 346 | 196 | 130 | 344 | 368 | 311 |
| S&P Core Earnings | 876 | 846 | 694 | 557 | 357 | 107 | 65.0 | 204 | NA | NA |

| Balance Sheet & Other Financial Data (Million $) | | | | | | | | | | |
|---|---|---|---|---|---|---|---|---|---|---|
| Cash | 326 | 173 | 172 | 336 | 184 | 246 | 46.0 | 23.7 | 68.5 | 33.3 |
| Current Assets | NA | 3,386 | 3,139 | 2,786 | 2,537 | 2,397 | 2,236 | 2,196 | 2,153 | 1,775 |
| Total Assets | 10,387 | 8,441 | 8,173 | 6,899 | 6,257 | 5,986 | 5,733 | 5,338 | 4,646 | 3,706 |
| Current Liabilities | NA | 1,925 | 1,681 | 1,336 | 1,260 | 1,424 | 1,360 | 1,413 | 1,186 | 755 |
| Long Term Debt | NA | 1,087 | 1,059 | 938 | 954 | 966 | 1,089 | 857 | 702 | 725 |
| Common Equity | 5,259 | 4,712 | 4,241 | 3,340 | 2,982 | 2,521 | 2,584 | 2,529 | 2,309 | 1,854 |
| Total Capital | NA | 5,913 | 5,419 | 4,314 | 4,015 | 3,508 | 3,750 | 3,518 | 3,089 | 2,610 |
| Capital Expenditures | 280 | 238 | 198 | 157 | 142 | 158 | 207 | 345 | 230 | 230 |
| Cash Flow | NA | 1,125 | 919 | 813 | 599 | 455 | 412 | 609 | 575 | 513 |
| Current Ratio | 1.9 | 1.8 | 1.9 | 2.1 | 2.0 | 1.7 | 1.6 | 1.6 | 1.8 | 2.3 |
| % Long Term Debt of Capitalization | 27.1 | 18.4 | 19.6 | 21.8 | 23.8 | 27.5 | 29.0 | 24.4 | 22.7 | 27.8 |
| % Net Income of Revenue | 7.8 | 7.7 | 6.8 | 6.7 | 4.9 | 3.1 | 2.1 | 5.8 | 6.9 | 6.3 |
| % Return on Assets | 10.1 | 10.0 | 8.5 | 8.3 | 5.6 | 3.3 | 2.3 | 6.9 | 8.8 | 8.6 |
| % Return on Equity | 19.1 | 18.5 | 16.8 | 17.3 | 12.6 | 7.7 | 5.1 | 14.2 | 17.7 | 17.6 |

Data as orig reptd.; bef. results of disc opers/spec. items. Per share data adj. for stk. divs.; EPS diluted. E-Estimated. NA-Not Available. NM-Not Meaningful. NR-Not Ranked. UR-Under Review.

**Office:** 6035 Parkland Boulevard, Cleveland, OH 44124-4141.
**Telephone:** 216-896-3000.
**Website:** http://www.parker.com
**Chrmn, Pres & CEO:** D.E. Washkewicz

**EVP, CFO & Chief Admin Officer:** T.K. Pistell
**CTO:** M.C. Maxwell
**Chief Acctg Officer & Cntlr:** J.P. Marten
**Investor Contact:** P.J. Huggins (216-896-2240)

**Board Members:** L. S. Harty, W. E. Kassling, R. J. Kohlhepp, G. Mazzalupi, K. Muller, C. M. Obourn, J. M. Scaminace, W. R. Schmitt, M. I. Tambakeras, D. E. Washkewicz

**Founded:** 1924
**Domicile:** Ohio
**Employees:** 61,722

The McGraw-Hill Companies

# Patterson Companies Inc

**STANDARD &POOR'S**

**S&P Recommendation** HOLD ★★★☆☆

| Price | 12-Mo. Target Price | Investment Style |
|---|---|---|
| $22.04 (as of Nov 14, 2008) | $37.00 | Large-Cap Growth |

**GICS Sector** Health Care
**Sub-Industry** Health Care Distributors

**Summary** This company is one of the largest distributors of dental supplies in North America and also sells veterinary supplies and rehabilitative equipment.

## Key Stock Statistics (Source S&P, Vickers, company reports)

| | | | | | | | |
|---|---|---|---|---|---|---|---|
| 52-Wk Range | $37.83– 20.64 | S&P Oper. EPS 2009**E** | 1.95 | Market Capitalization(B) | $2.677 | Beta | 0.60 |
| Trailing 12-Month EPS | $1.74 | S&P Oper. EPS 2010**E** | 2.20 | Yield (%) | Nil | S&P 3-Yr. Proj. EPS CAGR(%) | 15 |
| Trailing 12-Month P/E | 12.7 | P/E on S&P Oper. EPS 2009**E** | 11.3 | Dividend Rate/Share | Nil | S&P Credit Rating | NA |
| $10K Invested 5 Yrs Ago | $6,538 | Common Shares Outstg. (M) | 121.4 | Institutional Ownership (%) | 68 | | |

## Price Performance

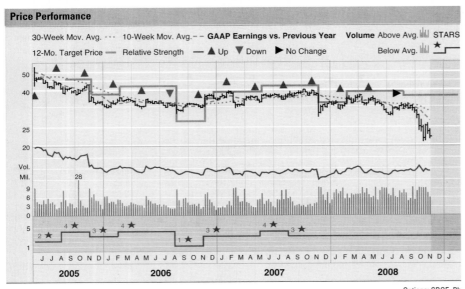

30-Week Mov. Avg. ···  10-Week Mov. Avg. ─ ─  **GAAP Earnings vs. Previous Year**  Volume Above Avg. STARS
12-Mo. Target Price ─  Relative Strength ─  ▲ Up  ▼ Down  ▶ No Change  Below Avg.  ★

Options: CBOE, Ph

Analysis prepared by **Phillip M. Seligman** on August 22, 2008, when the stock traded at **$ 31.98**.

## Highlights

➤ We now project that PDCO's sales will rise about 7% in FY 09 (Apr.), close to FY 08's 7.2% growth. We expect dental equipment and software sales to benefit from easy comps, partly due to tepid October- and April-quarter FY 08 sales. While we expect PDCO to benefit from upgrades to existing CEREC dental restorative systems, we think the company has much to do to revitalize sales of digital x-ray systems.

➤ We forecast healthy medical segment sales growth in FY 09, aided by sales force expansion, while veterinary segment sales should benefit from the veterinary equipment business expansion. We expect the firmwide operating margin to widen slightly, partly on an improved firmwide product mix, higher pricing and freight management in the medical unit, and lapping in the fiscal fourth quarter of a pricing adjustment of the commercial paper used as the source for customer financing contracts. Elsewhere, we see the positive EPS impact from share buybacks outweighing the higher interest costs from recent debt issuance.

➤ We look for EPS of $1.95 in FY 09, versus $1.69 in FY 08, and $2.20 in FY 10.

## Investment Rationale/Risk

➤ We see strong dental supply market fundamentals over the long term, partly driven by an aging population. Meanwhile, we expect some sales to be affected by weaker U.S. economic growth. We view PDCO's tepid April- and July-quarter dental equipment and software sales performance partly as company-specific, given better performance by a rival's dental equipment business over much of the same period. PDCO has rolled out initiatives to reinvigorate digital x-ray system sales, including a revamp of its commission structure, the redesign of the customer loyalty program, and the offer of the EagleSoft Practice Management Software free of charge with the goal of winning new dentists to its digital x-ray solution. Nonetheless, we are taking a wait-and-see attitude.

➤ Risks to our recommendation and target price include a worse than expected performance in PDCO's operating segments, leading to deteriorating profit margins and EPS growth.

➤ Our 12-month target price of $37 is based on a P/E of 19.5X our calendar 2008 EPS estimate of $1.89, below PDCO's 10-year average historical forward P/E of 22X.

## Qualitative Risk Assessment

| LOW | MEDIUM | HIGH |
|---|---|---|

Our risk assessment is based on our view of PDCO's strong long-term record of earnings growth, offset by historically high valuation multiples relative to the overall stock market. Given its high multiples, we view the stock as vulnerable to price declines in the event of an earnings disappointment.

## Quantitative Evaluations

**S&P Quality Ranking**                                        B+

| D | C | B- | B | B+ | A- | A | A+ |
|---|---|---|---|---|---|---|---|

**Relative Strength Rank**                            MODERATE

57

LOWEST = 1                                              HIGHEST = 99

## Revenue/Earnings Data

**Revenue (Million $)**

| | 1Q | 2Q | 3Q | 4Q | Year |
|---|---|---|---|---|---|
| 2009 | 743.9 | -- | -- | -- | -- |
| 2008 | 701.4 | 742.0 | 777.0 | 778.4 | 2,999 |
| 2007 | 655.5 | 694.3 | 709.5 | 739.1 | 2,798 |
| 2006 | 595.9 | 641.7 | 682.4 | 695.2 | 2,615 |
| 2005 | 577.9 | 578.2 | 638.0 | 627.3 | 2,421 |
| 2004 | 433.3 | 477.5 | 521.2 | 537.4 | 1,969 |

**Earnings Per Share ($)**

| | 1Q | 2Q | 3Q | 4Q | Year |
|---|---|---|---|---|---|
| 2009 | 0.39 | E0.46 | E0.53 | E0.57 | E1.95 |
| 2008 | 0.39 | 0.39 | 0.45 | 0.51 | 1.69 |
| 2007 | 0.30 | 0.35 | 0.43 | 0.44 | 1.51 |
| 2006 | 0.31 | 0.32 | 0.39 | 0.41 | 1.43 |
| 2005 | 0.29 | 0.31 | 0.36 | 0.36 | 1.32 |
| 2004 | 0.22 | 0.26 | 0.29 | 0.33 | 1.09 |

Fiscal year ended Apr. 30. Next earnings report expected: Late November. EPS Estimates based on S&P Operating Earnings; historical GAAP earnings are as reported.

## Dividend Data

No cash dividends have been paid.

# Patterson Companies Inc

STANDARD
&POOR'S

## Business Summary August 22, 2008

CORPORATE OVERVIEW. Patterson Companies (formerly Patterson Dental), one of two large distributors of dental products in North America, is a full-service supplier to dentists, dental laboratories, institutions, physicians, and other health care professionals. Through the July 2001 acquisition of J.A. Webster, PDCO became the second largest U.S. distributor of companion-pet veterinary supplies. Also, through the August 2003 acquisition of AbilityOne Products Corp. (now Patterson Medical), PDCO became the largest distributor of non-wheelchair assistive products for patient rehabilitation in the U.S. and the U.K.

PDCO's Patterson Dental subsidiary, 72.7% of FY 08 (Apr.) sales, versus 73.8% in FY 07, provides a broad range of consumables (X-ray film, restorative materials, and sterilization products), advanced technology dental equipment, practice management software, and office forms and stationery.

Consumables and printed products accounted for 55.8% of dental supply sales in FY 08, slightly below FY 07's 55.9%. The company offers its own private label line of anesthetics, instruments, reventative and restorative products, as well as brand name supplies, including X-ray film, protective clothing, toothbrushes, and other dental accessories. Printed products include insurance and billing forms, stationery, appointment books, and other stock office supply products.

PDCO offers a wide range of dental equipment, which accounted for 34.1% of dental supply sales in FY 08, down from 34.6% in FY 07. The product line includes X-ray machines, sterilizers, dental chairs, dental lights and diagnostic equipment. Two of PDCO's fastest growing product lines are the CEREC chairside ceramic dental-restorative system and digital radiography (X-ray) systems. CEREC sales slowed in FY 07 and FY 08's first half, but picked up afterward. Not only do we think that dentists were awaiting the launch of a rival's system, but, in addition, the manufacturer of CEREC had production glitches. However, sales of digital radiography systems slowed sharply in FY 08's final quarter.

Other products, which accounted for 10.1% of dental supply sales in FY 08 and 9.5% in FY 07, include software services, equipment installation and repair, dental office design, and equipment financing.

## Company Financials Fiscal Year Ended Apr. 30

### Per Share Data ($)

| | 2008 | 2007 | 2006 | 2005 | 2004 | 2003 | 2002 | 2001 | 2000 | 1999 |
|---|---|---|---|---|---|---|---|---|---|---|
| Tangible Book Value | 1.01 | 3.70 | 2.73 | 1.95 | 0.76 | 3.66 | 2.85 | 2.64 | 2.08 | 1.62 |
| Cash Flow | NA | 1.70 | 1.60 | 1.52 | 1.27 | 0.94 | 0.80 | 0.65 | 0.55 | 0.43 |
| Earnings | 1.69 | 1.51 | 1.43 | 1.32 | 1.09 | 0.85 | 0.70 | 0.57 | 0.48 | 0.37 |
| S&P Core Earnings | 1.69 | 1.51 | 1.39 | 1.30 | 1.08 | 0.84 | 0.70 | 0.57 | NA | NA |
| Dividends | Nil | Nil | Nil | Nil | Nil | Nil | Nil | Nil | NA | NA |
| Payout Ratio | Nil | Nil | Nil | Nil | Nil | Nil | Nil | Nil | Nil | Nil |
| Calendar Year | 2007 | 2006 | 2005 | 2004 | 2003 | 2002 | 2001 | 2000 | 1999 | 1998 |
| Prices:High | 40.08 | 38.28 | 53.85 | 44.20 | 35.75 | 27.56 | 21.03 | 17.25 | 12.53 | 11.59 |
| Prices:Low | 28.32 | 29.61 | 33.21 | 29.70 | 17.71 | 19.00 | 13.75 | 8.13 | 8.28 | 7.03 |
| P/E Ratio:High | 24 | 25 | 38 | 33 | 33 | 32 | 30 | 31 | 26 | 31 |
| P/E Ratio:Low | 17 | 20 | 23 | 22 | 16 | 22 | 20 | 14 | 17 | 19 |

### Income Statement Analysis (Million $)

| | 2008 | 2007 | 2006 | 2005 | 2004 | 2003 | 2002 | 2001 | 2000 | 1999 |
|---|---|---|---|---|---|---|---|---|---|---|
| Revenue | 2,999 | 2,798 | 2,615 | 2,421 | 1,969 | 1,657 | 1,416 | 1,156 | 1,040 | 879 |
| Operating Income | NA | 361 | 347 | 329 | 262 | 192 | 161 | 391 | 205 | 86.6 |
| Depreciation | 26.3 | 25.5 | 23.7 | 26.9 | 19.4 | 12.8 | 14.3 | 11.1 | 10.2 | 8.20 |
| Interest Expense | NA | 14.2 | 13.4 | 15.1 | 9.60 | 0.07 | 0.11 | 0.12 | 0.13 | 0.52 |
| Pretax Income | 357 | 330 | 317 | 293 | 240 | 186 | 152 | 122 | 103 | 79.7 |
| Effective Tax Rate | 37.1% | 36.8% | 37.4% | 37.4% | 37.6% | 37.6% | 37.4% | 37.4% | 37.4% | 37.4% |
| Net Income | 225 | 208 | 198 | 184 | 150 | 116 | 95.3 | 76.5 | 64.5 | 49.9 |
| S&P Core Earnings | 225 | 208 | 194 | 180 | 147 | 115 | 95.3 | 76.5 | NA | NA |

### Balance Sheet & Other Financial Data (Million $)

| | 2008 | 2007 | 2006 | 2005 | 2004 | 2003 | 2002 | 2001 | 2000 | 1999 |
|---|---|---|---|---|---|---|---|---|---|---|
| Cash | 308 | 242 | 224 | 233 | 287 | 195 | 126 | 160 | 113 | 78.7 |
| Current Assets | NA | 886 | 847 | 800 | 778 | 606 | 529 | 443 | 351 | 287 |
| Total Assets | 2,076 | 1,940 | 1,912 | 1,685 | 1,589 | 824 | 718 | 549 | 452 | 373 |
| Current Liabilities | NA | 377 | 410 | 322 | 264 | 184 | 198 | 133 | 113 | 98.7 |
| Long Term Debt | NA | 130 | 210 | 302 | 480 | 0.13 | Nil | Nil | Nil | 1.68 |
| Common Equity | 1,005 | 1,379 | 1,243 | 1,015 | 802 | 634 | 514 | 409 | 330 | 265 |
| Total Capital | NA | 1,563 | 1,502 | 1,363 | 1,325 | 634 | 514 | 409 | 330 | 269 |
| Capital Expenditures | 36.0 | 19.5 | 49.2 | 31.5 | 19.6 | 11.4 | 11.1 | 10.0 | 15.4 | 7.09 |
| Cash Flow | NA | 234 | 222 | 211 | 169 | 129 | 110 | 87.6 | 74.7 | 58.1 |
| Current Ratio | 2.1 | 2.3 | 2.1 | 2.5 | 2.9 | 3.3 | 2.7 | 3.3 | 3.1 | 2.9 |
| % Long Term Debt of Capitalization | 31.6 | 8.3 | 14.0 | 22.1 | 36.2 | Nil | Nil | Nil | Nil | 0.6 |
| % Net Income of Revenue | 7.5 | 7.4 | 7.6 | 7.6 | 7.6 | 7.0 | 6.7 | 6.6 | 6.2 | 5.7 |
| % Return on Assets | 11.2 | 10.8 | 11.0 | 11.2 | 12.4 | 15.1 | 15.0 | 15.3 | 15.6 | 14.5 |
| % Return on Equity | 18.9 | 15.9 | 17.6 | 20.2 | 20.8 | 20.3 | 20.7 | 20.7 | 21.6 | 21.0 |

Data as orig reptd.; bef. results of disc opers/spec. items. Per share data adj. for stk. divs.; EPS diluted. E-Estimated. NA-Not Available. NM-Not Meaningful. NR-Not Ranked. UR-Under Review.

**Office:** 1031 Mendota Heights Road, St. Paul, MN 55120-1419.
**Telephone:** 612-686-1600.
**Email:** investors@pattersondental.com
**Website:** http://www.pattersondental.com

**Chrmn:** P.L. Frechette
**Pres & CEO:** J.W. Wiltz
**COO:** D.H. Peckskamp
**EVP, CFO, Chief Acctg Officer & Treas:** R.S. Armstrong

**Secy & General Counsel:** M.L. Levitt
**Board Members:** J. D. Buck, R. E. Ezerski, P. L. Frechette, A. B. Lacy, C. Reich, E. A. Rudnick, H. C. Slavkin, J. W. Wiltz

**Founded:** 1877
**Domicile:** Minnesota
**Employees:** 6,850

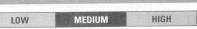

# Paychex Inc

STANDARD
&POOR'S

| S&P Recommendation **BUY** ★★★★☆ | Price $25.70 (as of Nov 14, 2008) | 12-Mo. Target Price $37.00 | Investment Style Large-Cap Growth |
|---|---|---|---|

**GICS Sector** Information Technology
**Sub-Industry** Data Processing & Outsourced Services

**Summary** Paychex provides payroll accounting services to small- and medium-sized concerns throughout the U.S.

## Key Stock Statistics (Source S&P, Vickers, company reports)

| | | | | | | | |
|---|---|---|---|---|---|---|---|
| 52-Wk Range | $40.68– 23.70 | S&P Oper. EPS 2009**E** | 1.64 | Market Capitalization(B) | $9.272 | Beta | 0.79 |
| Trailing 12-Month EPS | $1.58 | S&P Oper. EPS 2010**E** | 1.78 | Yield (%) | 4.82 | S&P 3-Yr. Proj. EPS CAGR(%) | 11 |
| Trailing 12-Month P/E | 16.3 | P/E on S&P Oper. EPS 2009**E** | 15.7 | Dividend Rate/Share | $1.24 | S&P Credit Rating | NA |
| $10K Invested 5 Yrs Ago | $7,404 | Common Shares Outstg. (M) | 360.8 | Institutional Ownership (%) | 70 | | |

## Price Performance

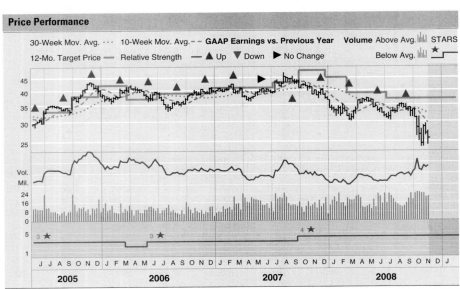

30-Week Mov. Avg. · · · · 10-Week Mov. Avg. - - **GAAP Earnings vs. Previous Year** Volume Above Avg. STARS
12-Mo. Target Price — Relative Strength — ▲ Up ▼ Down ▶ No Change Below Avg. ★

Options: ASE, CBOE, Ph

Analysis prepared by **Dylan Cathers** on September 26, 2008, when the stock traded at **$ 33.36.**

### Highlights

➤ We look for total revenue growth to decelerate to about 6.5% in FY 09 (May) from 9.5% last year. We think the core payroll business will be affected by a number of issues, including an increased number of bankruptcies, fewer hires among its clients, and more clients moving to non-processing status, which could keep growth under 6% this year. We see HR services growth of about 19%, which should help offset some of the slower growth in payroll. We think interest on funds held for clients will be down sharply, due to lower short-term interest rates. We look for 8.5% growth in FY 10.

➤ PAYX is doing a good job holding the line on expenses, in our opinion, and we think operating margins will be roughly flat versus last year. We believe expenses from rising personnel levels and the promotion of new products will be offset by solid cost controls, reduced attrition levels, and high customer retention rates.

➤ In December, PAYX completed a $1 billion share repurchase plan. This, along with an increased dividend, is adversely affecting corporate investment income, but the reduced share count should offset this decrease. We estimate EPS of $1.64 in FY 09 and $1.78 in FY 10.

### Investment Rationale/Risk

➤ Our buy recommendation is based on valuation and our positive long-term view of the company. We see PAYX's earnings benefiting from solid execution, higher retention rates, falling attrition, and strong profitability. However, we think near-term results will be adversely affected by the difficult economic environment in the U.S.

➤ Risks to our recommendation and target price stem from volatility in the small- to medium-sized business environment, and the impact of competition on pricing and margins. Automatic Data Processing (ADP: buy, $44) is the leader in the payroll processing space, and is promoting a payroll processing and tax filing software solution coupled with Microsoft's small business software. We see this product potentially affecting Paychex's growth in the small office market.

➤ Using our calendar 2009 EPS estimate of $1.68, we blend valuations using a peer-based P/E multiple of 22X, a P/E to growth (PEG) ratio of 2.0X, and an estimated three-year growth rate of 11% to arrive at our 12-month target price of $37. This is a slight premium to its payroll processing peers.

## Qualitative Risk Assessment

| LOW | MEDIUM | HIGH |
|---|---|---|

Our risk assessment reflects what we see as the company's strong balance sheet and regular cash inflows, offset by the highly competitive nature of the outsourcing industry as well as the threat of new entrants into the human resources segment.

## Quantitative Evaluations

**S&P Quality Ranking** A+

| D | C | B- | B | B+ | A- | A | A+ |
|---|---|---|---|---|---|---|---|

**Relative Strength Rank** MODERATE

67

LOWEST = 1    HIGHEST = 99

## Revenue/Earnings Data

### Revenue (Million $)

| | 1Q | 2Q | 3Q | 4Q | Year |
|---|---|---|---|---|---|
| 2009 | 534.1 | -- | -- | -- | -- |
| 2008 | 507.1 | 307.8 | 532.2 | 519.2 | 2,066 |
| 2007 | 459.4 | 455.0 | 485.3 | 487.4 | 1,887 |
| 2006 | 403.7 | 399.8 | 430.6 | 440.5 | 1,675 |
| 2005 | 345.0 | 347.3 | 373.9 | 379.0 | 1,445 |
| 2004 | 309.3 | 312.1 | 342.6 | 330.4 | 1,294 |

### Earnings Per Share ($)

| | 1Q | 2Q | 3Q | 4Q | Year |
|---|---|---|---|---|---|
| 2009 | 0.41 | E0.41 | E0.41 | E0.41 | E1.64 |
| 2008 | 0.40 | 0.40 | 0.39 | 0.38 | 1.56 |
| 2007 | 0.35 | 0.35 | 0.33 | 0.32 | 1.39 |
| 2006 | 0.30 | 0.30 | 0.30 | 0.32 | 1.22 |
| 2005 | 0.23 | 0.23 | 0.24 | 0.27 | 0.97 |
| 2004 | 0.21 | 0.21 | 0.21 | 0.16 | 0.80 |

Fiscal year ended May 31. Next earnings report expected: Mid December. EPS Estimates based on S&P Operating Earnings; historical GAAP earnings are as reported.

## Dividend Data (Dates: mm/dd Payment Date: mm/dd/yy)

| Amount ($) | Date Decl. | Ex-Div. Date | Stk. of Record | Payment Date |
|---|---|---|---|---|
| 0.300 | 01/11 | 01/30 | 02/01 | 02/15/08 |
| 0.300 | 04/10 | 04/29 | 05/01 | 05/15/08 |
| 0.310 | 07/09 | 07/30 | 08/01 | 08/15/08 |
| 0.310 | 10/07 | 10/29 | 11/01 | 11/15/08 |

Dividends have been paid since 1988. Source: Company reports.

# Paychex Inc

STANDARD &POOR'S

## Business Summary September 26, 2008

CORPORATE OVERVIEW. Paychex is a leading provider of payroll processing, human resources and benefits services. The company was founded in 1971, and began by serving the payroll accounting services of businesses with fewer than 200 employees. It currently has more than 100 locations and serves over 572,000 clients throughout the U.S.

The company's payroll segment prepares payroll checks, earnings statements, internal accounting records, all federal, state and local payroll tax returns, and provides collection and remittance of payroll obligations. PAYX's tax filing and payment services provide automatic tax filing and payment, preparation and submission of tax returns, plus deposit of funds with tax authorities. Employee Payment Services provides a variety of ways for businesses to pay employees.

In our opinion, PAYX has shown an ability to expand its client base and increase the use of ancillary services, which we believe will lead to consistent growth for its mainstay payroll segment.

The Human Resources/Professional Employer Organization (HRS/PEO) segment provides employee benefits, management and human resources ser-

vices. The Paychex Administrative Services (PAS) product offers businesses a bundled package that includes payroll, employer compliance, and human resource and employee benefit administration. PAYX also offers 401(k) plan services.

MARKET PROFILE. The worldwide market for HR services totaled $98.4 billion in calendar 2007, according to market researcher IDC. Between 2007 and 2012, IDC expects this area to post a compound annual growth rate (CAGR) of 8.0%, with the market in the U.S. increasing at a CAGR of 8.2% from $53.3 billion in 2007. For the more narrow U.S. payroll services market, where we believe Automatic Data Processing is the market leader, IDC sees a CAGR of 6.3% between 2007 and 2012. In contrast, in the U.S. market for business process outsourcing (BPO) services, IDC expects a CAGR of 11.2% over the same time frame.

## Company Financials Fiscal Year Ended May 31

| Per Share Data ($) | 2008 | 2007 | 2006 | 2005 | 2004 | 2003 | 2002 | 2001 | 2000 | 1999 |
|---|---|---|---|---|---|---|---|---|---|---|
| Tangible Book Value | NA | 3.87 | 3.12 | 2.40 | 1.88 | 1.55 | 2.43 | 2.00 | 1.50 | 1.18 |
| Cash Flow | NA | 1.54 | 1.39 | 1.13 | 1.02 | 0.89 | 0.80 | 0.75 | 0.57 | 0.43 |
| Earnings | 1.56 | 1.39 | 1.22 | 0.97 | 0.80 | 0.78 | 0.73 | 0.68 | 0.51 | 0.37 |
| S&P Core Earnings | 1.55 | 1.41 | 1.17 | 0.93 | 0.80 | 0.72 | 0.66 | 0.65 | NA | NA |
| Dividends | 0.79 | 0.61 | 0.51 | 0.47 | 0.44 | 0.33 | 0.33 | 0.22 | 0.18 | 0.12 |
| Payout Ratio | 51% | 44% | 42% | 48% | 55% | 56% | 45% | 32% | 35% | 32% |
| Calendar Year | 2007 | 2006 | 2005 | 2004 | 2003 | 2002 | 2001 | 2000 | 1999 | 1998 |
| Prices:High | 47.14 | 42.37 | 43.37 | 39.12 | 40.54 | 42.15 | 51.00 | 61.25 | 29.92 | 24.47 |
| Prices:Low | 35.96 | 32.98 | 28.60 | 28.83 | 23.76 | 20.39 | 28.27 | 24.17 | 15.71 | 13.37 |
| P/E Ratio:High | 30 | 30 | 36 | 40 | 51 | 54 | 70 | 90 | 59 | 66 |
| P/E Ratio:Low | 23 | 24 | 23 | 30 | 30 | 26 | 39 | 36 | 31 | 36 |

### Income Statement Analysis (Million $)

| | 2008 | 2007 | 2006 | 2005 | 2004 | 2003 | 2002 | 2001 | 2000 | 1999 |
|---|---|---|---|---|---|---|---|---|---|---|
| Revenue | 2,066 | 1,887 | 1,675 | 1,445 | 1,294 | 1,099 | 955 | 870 | 728 | 597 |
| Operating Income | NA | 775 | 716 | 596 | 516 | 444 | 393 | 700 | 283 | 210 |
| Depreciation | 80.6 | 73.4 | 66.5 | 62.0 | 82.8 | 43.4 | 29.5 | 26.4 | 23.9 | 22.1 |
| Interest Expense | NA | Nil | Nil | Nil | Nil | Nil | Nil | Nil | Nil | Nil |
| Pretax Income | 855 | 743 | 675 | 546 | 450 | 432 | 395 | 364 | 275 | 200 |
| Effective Tax Rate | 32.6% | 30.7% | 31.1% | 32.5% | 32.6% | 32.0% | 30.5% | 30.0% | 31.0% | 30.5% |
| Net Income | 576 | 515 | 465 | 369 | 303 | 293 | 275 | 255 | 190 | 139 |
| S&P Core Earnings | 572 | 537 | 445 | 353 | 304 | 272 | 252 | 243 | NA | NA |

### Balance Sheet & Other Financial Data (Million $)

| | 2008 | 2007 | 2006 | 2005 | 2004 | 2003 | 2002 | 2001 | 2000 | 1999 |
|---|---|---|---|---|---|---|---|---|---|---|
| Cash | 393 | 79.4 | 137 | 281 | 219 | 79.9 | 61.9 | 45.8 | 47.1 | 343 |
| Current Assets | NA | 4,861 | 4,444 | 3,689 | 3,280 | 3,033 | 2,815 | 2,791 | 2,363 | 1,793 |
| Total Assets | 5,310 | 6,247 | 5,549 | 4,379 | 3,950 | 3,691 | 2,953 | 2,907 | 2,456 | 1,873 |
| Current Liabilities | NA | 4,237 | 3,838 | 2,942 | 2,722 | 2,588 | 2,023 | 2,144 | 1,887 | 1,432 |
| Long Term Debt | NA | Nil | Nil | Nil | Nil | Nil | Nil | Nil | Nil | Nil |
| Common Equity | 1,197 | 1,985 | 1,670 | 1,411 | 1,235 | 1,077 | 924 | 745 | 563 | 436 |
| Total Capital | NA | 1,994 | 1,686 | 1,429 | 1,249 | 1,084 | 924 | 745 | 563 | 436 |
| Capital Expenditures | 82.3 | 79.0 | 81.1 | 70.7 | 50.6 | 60.2 | 54.4 | 45.3 | 32.9 | 22.1 |
| Cash Flow | NA | 589 | 531 | 431 | 386 | 337 | 304 | 281 | 214 | 161 |
| Current Ratio | 1.1 | 1.1 | 1.2 | 1.3 | 1.2 | 1.2 | 1.4 | 1.3 | 1.3 | 1.3 |
| % Long Term Debt of Capitalization | Nil | Nil | Nil | Nil | Nil | Nil | Nil | Nil | Nil | Nil |
| % Net Income of Revenue | 27.9 | 27.3 | 27.8 | 25.5 | 23.4 | 26.7 | 28.7 | 29.3 | 26.1 | 23.3 |
| % Return on Assets | 10.0 | 8.7 | 9.1 | 8.9 | 7.9 | 8.8 | 9.4 | 9.5 | 8.8 | 8.1 |
| % Return on Equity | 36.6 | 28.2 | 30.2 | 27.9 | 26.2 | 29.3 | 32.6 | 38.7 | 38.0 | 36.3 |

Data as orig reptd.; bef. results of disc opers/spec. items. Per share data adj. for stk. divs.; EPS diluted. E-Estimated. NA-Not Available. NM-Not Meaningful. NR-Not Ranked. UR-Under Review.

**Office:** 911 Panorama Trail South, Rochester, NY 14625-2396.
**Telephone:** 585-385-6666.
**Website:** http://www.paychex.com
**Chrmn:** T. Golisano

**Pres & CEO:** J.J. Judge
**COO:** M. Mucci
**SVP, CFO, Chief Acctg Officer & Secy:** J.M. Morphy
**CTO:** D.A. Canzano

**Investor Contact:** T.J. Allen (585-383-3406)
**Board Members:** D. J. Flaschen, T. Golisano, P. Horsley, G. M. Inman, P. A. Joseph, J. J. Judge, J. M. Tucci, J. M. Velli

**Founded:** 1979
**Domicile:** Delaware
**Employees:** 12,200

# Peabody Energy Corp

STANDARD
&POOR'S

| S&P Recommendation | BUY ★★★★☆ | Price<br>$27.07 (as of Nov 14, 2008) | 12-Mo. Target Price<br>$40.00 | Investment Style<br>Large-Cap Blend |
|---|---|---|---|---|

**GICS Sector** Energy
**Sub-Industry** Coal & Consumable Fuels

**Summary** BTU is the world's largest private sector coal company, with 10.2 billion tons of coal reserves. Its coal fuels about 10% of U.S. electricity generation and 2% of worldwide electricity generation.

## Key Stock Statistics (Source S&P, Vickers, company reports)

| | | | | | | | |
|---|---|---|---|---|---|---|---|
| 52-Wk Range | $88.69– 24.08 | S&P Oper. EPS 2008E | 3.27 | Market Capitalization(B) | $7.218 | Beta | 1.85 |
| Trailing 12-Month EPS | $2.56 | S&P Oper. EPS 2009E | 5.22 | Yield (%) | 0.89 | S&P 3-Yr. Proj. EPS CAGR(%) | 8 |
| Trailing 12-Month P/E | 10.6 | P/E on S&P Oper. EPS 2008E | 8.3 | Dividend Rate/Share | $0.24 | S&P Credit Rating | BB+ |
| $10K Invested 5 Yrs Ago | NA | Common Shares Outstg. (M) | 266.6 | Institutional Ownership (%) | 91 | | |

## Price Performance

30-Week Mov. Avg. · · · 10-Week Mov. Avg. – – GAAP Earnings vs. Previous Year   Volume Above Avg. ▐▌▌ STARS
12-Mo. Target Price — Relative Strength — ▲ Up ▼ Down ▶ No Change   Below Avg. ▐▌▌ ★

Options: ASE, CBOE, P, Ph

Analysis prepared by **Mathew Christy, CFA** on October 20, 2008, when the stock traded at **$ 35.97**.

## Qualitative Risk Assessment

| LOW | MEDIUM | HIGH |
|---|---|---|

Our risk assessment reflects the industry's high cyclicality, extensive industry regulation, the potential for geological difficulties with mines, transportation problems, and volatility in the prices of competing fuels and a narrow customer focus. This is offset by the company's leading market position and geographically well-diversified coal holdings.

## Quantitative Evaluations

**S&P Quality Ranking**  NR

| D | C | B- | B | B+ | A- | A | A+ |
|---|---|---|---|---|---|---|---|

**Relative Strength Rank**  WEAK

| 29 |
|---|

LOWEST = 1                    HIGHEST = 99

## Revenue/Earnings Data

**Revenue (Million $)**

| | 1Q | 2Q | 3Q | 4Q | Year |
|---|---|---|---|---|---|
| 2008 | 1,276 | 1,531 | 1,906 | -- | -- |
| 2007 | 1,365 | 1,322 | 1,494 | 1,212 | 4,575 |
| 2006 | 1,312 | 1,316 | 1,265 | 1,363 | 5,256 |
| 2005 | 1,077 | 1,109 | 1,224 | 1,235 | 4,644 |
| 2004 | 788.6 | 920.1 | 923.1 | 1,024 | 3,632 |
| 2003 | 681.3 | 693.3 | 702.0 | 753.0 | 2,829 |

**Earnings Per Share ($)**

| | | | | | |
|---|---|---|---|---|---|
| 2008 | 0.26 | 0.89 | 1.38 | E0.75 | E3.27 |
| 2007 | 0.33 | 0.40 | 0.12 | 0.71 | 1.56 |
| 2006 | 0.48 | 0.57 | 0.53 | 0.65 | 2.23 |
| 2005 | 0.20 | 0.36 | 0.42 | 0.61 | 1.58 |
| 2004 | 0.10 | 0.16 | 0.17 | 0.27 | 0.70 |
| 2003 | Nil | Nil | 0.10 | 0.10 | 0.19 |

Fiscal year ended Dec. 31. Next earnings report expected: Early February. EPS Estimates based on S&P Operating Earnings; historical GAAP earnings are as reported.

## Dividend Data (Dates: mm/dd Payment Date: mm/dd/yy)

| Amount ($) | Date Decl. | Ex-Div. Date | Stk. of Record | Payment Date |
|---|---|---|---|---|
| 0.060 | 01/29 | 02/08 | 02/12 | 03/04/08 |
| 0.060 | 04/24 | 05/06 | 05/08 | 05/29/08 |
| 0.060 | 07/25 | 08/06 | 08/08 | 08/29/08 |
| 0.060 | 10/23 | 11/04 | 11/06 | 11/28/08 |

Dividends have been paid since 2001. Source: Company reports.

## Highlights

➤ We expect revenues to rise more than 38% in 2008 and about 23% in 2009, led by per-ton price increases of 36% and 27%, respectively. We believe BTU will realize higher pricing as supplies tighten due mainly to industry supply-side issues, including higher production costs, tighter permitting, and curtailed international supplies, along with roll-off of legacy contracts at lower prices. Sales should also increase on growth in produced tons sold of 2.9% in 2008. However, we forecast that tons sold will decline 3% in 2009 from slowing demand, a result of weakening economic growth.

➤ We look for the EBITDA margin to expand to nearly 27% this year on increased volume and higher prices. In addition, we expect the EBITDA margin to expand to nearly 38% in 2009 due mainly to continued pricing gains despite our expectation for lower volumes and a 5% rise in costs per ton. We believe, BTU is successfully reducing high-cost production, which will help lower per-ton costs.

➤ On steadily higher projected taxes, we expect operating EPS of $3.27 for 2008 and $5.22 for 2009.

## Investment Rationale/Risk

➤ We believe BTU will benefit from improved pricing and demand in 2008 and 2009, driven by higher global energy needs, particularly from China and India, partly offset by increased taxes from a release of valuation allowances. BTU's focus on its western and international assets, especially with the Patriot spin-off, should help solidify its profile in rapidly growing and increasingly profitable markets, thereby creating a greater opportunity for margin expansion. We believe the shares are attractively priced at current levels.

➤ Risks to our recommendation and target price include lower-than-expected prices for steam and metallurgical grade coal, lower productivity, increased supply costs, and machinery procurement.

➤ Our 12-month target price of $40 is a weighted blend of two valuation methodologies. In terms of relative valuation, we apply an EV/EBITDA multiple of 5X, equal to historic trough multiples, to our 2009 EBITDA estimate, suggesting a $41 value. Our net asset valuation model, which assumes a discount rate of 15% and a decline in coal prices after 2010, indicates a $39 value.

# Peabody Energy Corp

**STANDARD &POOR'S**

## Business Summary October 20, 2008

CORPORATE OVERVIEW. Peabody Energy Corp. (BTU) was founded in 1883 as Peabody, Daniels and Co., a retail coal supplier. BTU is currently the world's largest private sector coal company. In 2007, it produced over 214 million tons of coal, representing almost a 21% share of U.S. production, by our calculation. BTU sold 237.8 million tons of coal, almost double its nearest U.S. competitor and 50% more than any global peer. It sold coal to more than 400 electricity generating and industrial plants in 20 countries, and fueled the generation of nearly 10% of all electricity in the U.S., and 2% of all electricity in the world. At December 31, 2007, BTU had 9.3 billion tons of proven and probable coal reserves. BTU owns majority interests in 40 coal operations located throughout all major U.S. coal producing regions and in Australia. It also owns a minority interest in one Venezuelan mine through a joint venture agreement. In 2007, 81% of the U.S. mining operation's coal sales were shipped from the U.S. West, and the remaining 19% from the East. Most production in the West is low sulfur coal from the Powder River Basin, which has seen the fastest growth of all U.S. coal regions, according to the Energy Information Administration (EIA). In the West, the company owns and operates mines in Arizona, Colorado, New Mexico and Wyoming. In the East, BTU owns and operates

mines in Illinois, Indiana, Kentucky and West Virginia.

In 2007, 85% of sales were to U.S. electricity generators, 2% to the U.S. industrial sector, and 13% to foreign customers. About 94% of 2007 coal sales were under long-term contracts with an average volume-weighted term of approximately five years, with terms ranging from one to 17 years. As of January 31, 2008, the company had 80 million to 90 million and 140 million to 150 million tons of total unpriced planned production for 2009 and 2010, respectively. In addition to its mining operations, BTU markets and trades coal and emission allowances. Total tons traded amounted to 24.1 million in 2007 (21.4 million tons in 2006). Other energy-related businesses include coalbed methane production, transportation services, and the development of coal-fueled generation plants.

## Company Financials Fiscal Year Ended Dec. 31

### Per Share Data ($)

| | 2007 | 2006 | 2005 | 2004 | 2003 | 2002 | 2001 | 2000 | 1999 | 1998 |
|---|---|---|---|---|---|---|---|---|---|---|
| Tangible Book Value | 9.33 | 7.95 | 8.27 | 3.33 | 5.18 | 5.16 | 4.98 | 5.72 | NA | NA |
| Cash Flow | 2.91 | 3.63 | 2.76 | 0.88 | 1.26 | 1.57 | 0.96 | 3.12 | NA | NA |
| Earnings | 1.56 | 2.23 | 1.58 | 0.70 | 0.19 | 0.49 | 0.10 | 0.74 | 0.10 | NA |
| S&P Core Earnings | 1.42 | 2.00 | 1.43 | 0.63 | 0.11 | 0.27 | -0.03 | NA | NA | NA |
| Dividends | 0.24 | 0.24 | 0.17 | 0.13 | 0.11 | 0.10 | 0.05 | 0.05 | NA | NA |
| Payout Ratio | 15% | 11% | 11% | 19% | 59% | 20% | 53% | 7% | NA | NA |
| Prices:High | 62.55 | 76.29 | 43.48 | 21.70 | 10.75 | 7.69 | 9.51 | NA | NA | NA |
| Prices:Low | 36.20 | 32.94 | 18.37 | 9.10 | 6.13 | 4.38 | 5.55 | NA | NA | NA |
| P/E Ratio:High | 40 | 34 | 28 | 31 | 57 | 16 | NM | NA | NA | NA |
| P/E Ratio:Low | 23 | 15 | 12 | 13 | 32 | 9 | NM | NA | NA | NA |

### Income Statement Analysis (Million $)

| | 2007 | 2006 | 2005 | 2004 | 2003 | 2002 | 2001 | 2000 | 1999 | 1998 |
|---|---|---|---|---|---|---|---|---|---|---|
| Revenue | 4,575 | 5,256 | 4,644 | 3,632 | 2,829 | 2,717 | 2,027 | 2,670 | 2,387 | 2,244 |
| Operating Income | 827 | 884 | 703 | 519 | 385 | 390 | 276 | 405 | NA | NA |
| Depreciation | 362 | 377 | 316 | 270 | 234 | 232 | 175 | 241 | 210 | 203 |
| Interest Expense | 237 | 143 | 103 | 96.8 | 98.5 | 102 | 89.0 | 198 | 180 | 33.6 |
| Pretax Income | 341 | 531 | 426 | 153 | -3.18 | 78.8 | 29.0 | 153 | 26.0 | 251 |
| Effective Tax Rate | NM | NM | 0.23% | NM | NM | NM | 12.9% | 27.9% | 51.6% | 36.0% |
| Net Income | 421 | 601 | 423 | 178 | 41.5 | 106 | 19.0 | 103 | 10.7 | 160 |
| S&P Core Earnings | 383 | 541 | 382 | 160 | 23.9 | 58.5 | -5.74 | NA | NA | NA |

### Balance Sheet & Other Financial Data (Million $)

| | 2007 | 2006 | 2005 | 2004 | 2003 | 2002 | 2001 | 2000 | 1999 | 1998 |
|---|---|---|---|---|---|---|---|---|---|---|
| Cash | 45.3 | 327 | 503 | 390 | 118 | 71.2 | 39.0 | 67.7 | 194 | 96.8 |
| Current Assets | 1,927 | 1,274 | 1,325 | 1,055 | 683 | 550 | 527 | 630 | NA | NA |
| Total Assets | 9,668 | 9,514 | 6,852 | 6,179 | 5,280 | 5,140 | 5,151 | 5,209 | 7,024 | 6,355 |
| Current Liabilities | 2,187 | 1,368 | 1,023 | 774 | 632 | 632 | 684 | 777 | NA | NA |
| Long Term Debt | 3,139 | 3,168 | 1,383 | 1,406 | 1,173 | 982 | 985 | 1,369 | NA | NA |
| Common Equity | 2,520 | 2,339 | 2,178 | 1,725 | 1,132 | 1,081 | 1,040 | 631 | 495 | 1,688 |
| Total Capital | 5,975 | 5,735 | 3,902 | 3,526 | 2,742 | 2,599 | 2,590 | 2,613 | NA | NA |
| Capital Expenditures | 649 | 478 | 384 | 267 | 156 | 209 | 194 | 151 | 196 | 166 |
| Cash Flow | 783 | 978 | 739 | 448 | 276 | 338 | 194 | 344 | NA | NA |
| Current Ratio | 0.9 | 0.9 | 1.3 | 1.4 | 1.1 | 0.9 | 0.8 | 0.8 | 1.4 | 1.3 |
| % Long Term Debt of Capitalization | 52.5 | 55.2 | 35.4 | 39.9 | 42.8 | 37.8 | 38.0 | 52.4 | 81.6 | 24.4 |
| % Net Income of Revenue | 9.2 | 11.4 | 9.1 | 4.9 | NM | 3.9 | 0.1 | 3.8 | 0.5 | 7.1 |
| % Return on Assets | 4.4 | 7.3 | 6.5 | 3.1 | NM | 2.1 | 0.3 | 1.9 | NA | NA |
| % Return on Equity | 17.3 | 26.6 | 21.7 | 12.5 | NM | 10.0 | 2.3 | 18.0 | 1.0 | 9.5 |

Data as orig reptd.; bef. results of disc opers/spec. items. Per share data adj. for stk. divs.; EPS diluted. E-Estimated. NA-Not Available. NM-Not Meaningful. NR-Not Ranked. UR-Under Review.

**Office:** 701 Market St, St. Louis, MO 63101-1826.
**Telephone:** 314-342-3400.
**Email:** publicrelations@peabodyenergy.com
**Website:** http://www.peabodyenergy.com

**Chrmn & CEO:** G.H. Boyce
**Pres:** R.A. Navarre
**COO & EVP:** E. Ford
**EVP & CFO:** M.C. Crews

**EVP & Chief Admin Officer:** S.D. Fiehler
**Investor Contact:** C. Morrow (314-342-7900)
**Board Members:** G. H. Boyce, W. A. Coley, W. E. James, R. B. Karn, III, H. E. Lentz, Jr., W. C. Rusnack, B. M. Touhill, J. F. Turner, S. A. Van Trease, A. H. Washkowitz

**Founded:** 1883
**Domicile:** Delaware
**Employees:** 7,000

The McGraw-Hill Companies

# J. C. Penney Company Inc.

**S&P Recommendation** HOLD ★ ★ ★ ☆ ☆

| Price | 12-Mo. Target Price | Investment Style |
|---|---|---|
| $17.27 (as of Nov 14, 2008) | $20.00 | Large-Cap Blend |

**GICS Sector** Consumer Discretionary
**Sub-Industry** Department Stores

**Summary** JCP is the leading mall-based family department store operator in the U.S., with about 1,083 retail locations and catalog/Internet operations.

## Key Stock Statistics (Source S&P, Vickers, company reports)

| | | | | | | | | |
|---|---|---|---|---|---|---|---|---|
| 52-Wk Range | $51.42– 16.39 | S&P Oper. EPS 2009**E** | 2.61 | Market Capitalization(B) | $3.835 | Beta | 1.36 |
| Trailing 12-Month EPS | $4.16 | S&P Oper. EPS 2010**E** | 1.70 | Yield (%) | 4.63 | S&P 3-Yr. Proj. EPS CAGR(%) | -17 |
| Trailing 12-Month P/E | 4.2 | P/E on S&P Oper. EPS 2009**E** | 6.6 | Dividend Rate/Share | $0.80 | S&P Credit Rating | BBB- |
| $10K Invested 5 Yrs Ago | $7,865 | Common Shares Outstg. (M) | 222.1 | Institutional Ownership (%) | 93 | | |

## Price Performance

- 30-Week Mov. Avg. · · · 10-Week Mov. Avg. - - **GAAP Earnings vs. Previous Year** Volume Above Avg. STARS
- 12-Mo. Target Price — Relative Strength — ▲ Up ▼ Down ▶ No Change Below Avg. ★

Options: ASE, CBOE, P

## Qualitative Risk Assessment

| LOW | MEDIUM | HIGH |
|---|---|---|

Our risk assessment reflects our view of JCP's improving sales and profit margins, increasing market share in the moderate department store sector, and what we see as a healthy balance sheet and cash flow, offset by uncertainty over consumer discretionary spending in light of higher interest rates and debt levels.

## Quantitative Evaluations

**S&P Quality Ranking**      **B**

| D | C | B- | B | B+ | A- | A | A+ |
|---|---|---|---|---|---|---|---|

**Relative Strength Rank**      **WEAK**

25

LOWEST = 1      HIGHEST = 99

## Revenue/Earnings Data

**Revenue (Million $)**

| | 1Q | 2Q | 3Q | 4Q | Year |
|---|---|---|---|---|---|---|
| 2009 | 4,127 | 4,282 | -- | -- | -- |
| 2008 | 4,350 | 4,391 | 4,729 | 6,390 | 19,860 |
| 2007 | 4,220 | 4,238 | 4,781 | 6,664 | 19,903 |
| 2006 | 4,192 | 3,981 | 4,479 | 6,203 | 18,781 |
| 2005 | 4,033 | 3,857 | 4,461 | 6,073 | 18,424 |
| 2004 | 7,493 | 7,313 | 7,985 | 6,098 | 17,786 |

**Earnings Per Share ($)**

| | 1Q | 2Q | 3Q | 4Q | Year |
|---|---|---|---|---|---|---|
| 2009 | 0.54 | 0.52 | E0.55 | E1.00 | E2.61 |
| 2008 | 1.04 | 0.52 | 1.17 | 1.93 | 4.91 |
| 2007 | 0.90 | 0.75 | 1.26 | 2.00 | 4.88 |
| 2006 | 0.63 | 0.46 | 0.94 | 1.92 | 3.83 |
| 2005 | 0.38 | 0.23 | 0.53 | 1.16 | 2.23 |
| 2004 | 0.05 | -0.03 | 0.31 | 0.83 | 1.21 |

Fiscal year ended Jan. 31. Next earnings report expected: Mid November. EPS Estimates based on S&P Operating Earnings; historical GAAP earnings are as reported.

## Highlights

➤ The 12-month target price for JCP has recently been changed to $20.00 from $21.00. The Highlights section of this Stock Report will be updated accordingly.

## Investment Rationale/Risk

➤ The Investment Rationale/Risk section of this Stock Report will be updated shortly. For the latest News story on JCP from MarketScope, see below.

➤ 11/14/08 01:53 pm ET ... S&P MAINTAINS HOLD RECOMMENDATION ON SHARES OF J.C. PENNEY (JCP 17.43***): JCP Oct-Q operating EPS of $0.55 vs. $1.03 matches our estimate. In our view, ongoing investments in new brands and more creative advertising support are strengthening JCP's market positioning. But with consumers growing more cautious about spending, we look for the company to maintain an aggressive promotional strategy to drive sales. Based on this and our expectation for higher pension expense next year, we trim our FY 09 (Jan.) operating EPS estimate by $0.24 to $2.61 and FY 10's by $0.30 to $1.70. We lower our peer-P/E-based 12-month target price by $1 to $20. / J.Asaeda

## Dividend Data (Dates: mm/dd Payment Date: mm/dd/yy)

| Amount ($) | Date Decl. | Ex-Div. Date | Stk. of Record | Payment Date |
|---|---|---|---|---|
| 0.200 | 12/12 | 01/08 | 01/10 | 02/04/08 |
| 0.200 | 03/27 | 04/08 | 04/10 | 05/01/08 |
| 0.200 | 05/16 | 07/08 | 07/10 | 08/01/08 |
| 0.200 | 09/19 | 10/08 | 10/10 | 11/01/08 |

Dividends have been paid since 1922. Source: Company reports.

# J. C. Penney Company Inc.

**STANDARD &POOR'S**

## Business Summary November 12, 2008

CORPORATE OVERVIEW. In our view, JCP is the leading mall-based family department store operator, with 1,083 JCPenney stores in 49 states and Puerto Rico, as of August 2008. The company is also adeptly addressing the needs of time-strapped shoppers with the shopping convenience afforded by its direct business, comprised of JCPenney catalogs and the jcpenney.com web site, as well as its growing off-mall retail presence.

CORPORATE STRATEGY. From FY 01 (Jan.) to FY 06, JCP executed a turnaround plan to improve the profitability of its JCPenney stores. The company focused on delivering competitive, fashionable merchandise assortments; developing a compelling and appealing marketing program; improving store environments; reducing its expense structure; and attracting and retaining an experienced and professional work force. In support of these objectives, JCP moved from decentralized to centralized merchandising, marketing and operating functions, and invested in a new store distribution network and in new merchandise planning, allocation and replenishment systems.

With what we view as the success of its turnaround, JCP has mapped out a new FY 06-FY 10 plan for making JCPenney the preferred shopping choice for "Middle America," which it defines as customers aged 35 to 54 with annual household incomes of $35,000 to $85,000. Key strategies include offering styles that make an emotional connection with the customer; making it easier for the customer to shop seamlessly across store/catalog/Internet channels; creating and sustaining a customer-focused culture; and using the off-mall store format to expand the company's presence in high-potential markets. JCP sees the potential for up to 400 new stores, relocations or expansions on a long-term basis.

## Company Financials Fiscal Year Ended Jan. 31

### Per Share Data ($)

| | 2008 | 2007 | 2006 | 2005 | 2004 | 2003 | 2002 | 2001 | 2000 | 1999 |
|---|---|---|---|---|---|---|---|---|---|---|
| Tangible Book Value | 23.93 | 18.97 | 17.20 | 17.92 | 18.54 | 12.04 | 11.46 | NM | 14.28 | 15.04 |
| Cash Flow | 6.80 | 6.57 | 5.79 | 3.33 | 2.68 | 3.45 | 3.00 | 0.36 | 3.87 | 4.40 |
| Earnings | 4.91 | 4.88 | 3.83 | 2.23 | 1.21 | 1.25 | 0.32 | -2.29 | 1.16 | 2.19 |
| S&P Core Earnings | 4.37 | 4.66 | 3.77 | 2.26 | 1.24 | 0.66 | 0.15 | -2.47 | NA | NA |
| Dividends | 0.72 | 0.50 | 0.50 | 0.50 | 0.50 | 0.50 | 0.50 | 0.50 | 2.19 | 2.18 |
| Payout Ratio | 15% | 10% | 13% | 22% | 41% | 40% | 156% | NM | 188% | 100% |
| Calendar Year | 2007 | 2006 | 2005 | 2004 | 2003 | 2002 | 2001 | 2000 | 1999 | 1998 |
| Prices:High | 87.18 | 82.49 | 57.99 | 41.82 | 26.42 | 27.75 | 29.50 | 22.50 | 54.44 | 78.75 |
| Prices:Low | 39.98 | 54.18 | 40.26 | 25.29 | 15.57 | 14.07 | 10.50 | 8.63 | 17.69 | 42.63 |
| P/E Ratio:High | 18 | 17 | 15 | 19 | 22 | 22 | 92 | NM | 47 | 36 |
| P/E Ratio:Low | 8 | 11 | 11 | 11 | 13 | 11 | 33 | NM | 15 | 19 |

### Income Statement Analysis (Million $)

| | 2008 | 2007 | 2006 | 2005 | 2004 | 2003 | 2002 | 2001 | 2000 | 1999 |
|---|---|---|---|---|---|---|---|---|---|---|
| Revenue | 19,860 | 19,903 | 18,781 | 18,424 | 17,786 | 32,347 | 32,004 | 31,846 | 32,510 | 30,678 |
| Operating Income | 2,268 | 2,277 | 1,949 | 1,680 | 1,184 | 1,681 | 1,473 | 873 | 1,681 | 2,253 |
| Depreciation | 426 | 389 | 372 | 368 | 394 | 667 | 717 | 695 | 710 | 637 |
| Interest Expense | 278 | 270 | 169 | 233 | 261 | 388 | 386 | 427 | 673 | 663 |
| Pretax Income | 1,723 | 1,792 | 1,444 | 1,020 | 546 | 584 | 203 | -886 | 531 | 955 |
| Effective Tax Rate | 35.9% | 36.7% | 32.3% | 34.6% | 33.3% | 36.5% | 43.8% | NM | 36.7% | 37.8% |
| Net Income | 1,105 | 1,134 | 977 | 667 | 345 | 371 | 114 | -568 | 336 | 594 |
| S&P Core Earnings | 986 | 1,081 | 960 | 662 | 345 | 171 | 41.0 | -650 | NA | NA |

### Balance Sheet & Other Financial Data (Million $)

| | 2008 | 2007 | 2006 | 2005 | 2004 | 2003 | 2002 | 2001 | 2000 | 1999 |
|---|---|---|---|---|---|---|---|---|---|---|
| Cash | 2,471 | 2,747 | 3,016 | 4,687 | 2,994 | 2,474 | 2,840 | 944 | 1,233 | 96.0 |
| Current Assets | 6,751 | 6,648 | 6,702 | 8,427 | 6,515 | 8,353 | 8,677 | 7,257 | 8,472 | 11,125 |
| Total Assets | 14,309 | 12,673 | 12,461 | 14,127 | 18,300 | 17,867 | 18,048 | 19,742 | 20,888 | 23,638 |
| Current Liabilities | 3,338 | 3,492 | 2,762 | 3,447 | 3,754 | 4,159 | 4,499 | 4,235 | 4,465 | 5,970 |
| Long Term Debt | 3,505 | 3,010 | 3,444 | 3,464 | 5,114 | 4,940 | 5,179 | 5,448 | 5,844 | 7,143 |
| Common Equity | 5,312 | 4,288 | 4,007 | 4,856 | 5,121 | 6,037 | 5,766 | 5,860 | 6,782 | 6,694 |
| Total Capital | 10,280 | 8,504 | 8,738 | 9,638 | 11,756 | 12,701 | 12,539 | 12,843 | 14,087 | 15,829 |
| Capital Expenditures | 1,243 | 772 | 535 | 412 | 373 | 658 | 631 | 648 | 631 | 744 |
| Cash Flow | 1,531 | 1,523 | 1,349 | 1,023 | 733 | 1,011 | 802 | 94.0 | 1,010 | 1,193 |
| Current Ratio | 2.0 | 1.9 | 2.4 | 2.4 | 1.7 | 2.0 | 1.9 | 1.7 | 1.9 | 1.9 |
| % Long Term Debt of Capitalization | 34.1 | 41.2 | 39.4 | 35.9 | 43.5 | 38.9 | 41.3 | 42.4 | 41.5 | 45.1 |
| % Net Income of Revenue | 5.6 | 5.7 | 5.2 | 3.6 | 2.0 | 1.1 | 0.4 | NM | 1.0 | 1.9 |
| % Return on Assets | 8.2 | 9.0 | 7.3 | 4.1 | 2.0 | 2.1 | 0.1 | NM | 1.5 | 2.5 |
| % Return on Equity | 23.0 | 27.3 | 22.0 | 13.1 | 6.1 | 5.8 | 1.9 | NM | 4.5 | 8.2 |

Data as orig reptd.; bef. results of disc opers/spec. items. Per share data adj. for stk. divs.; EPS diluted. E-Estimated. NA-Not Available. NM-Not Meaningful. NR-Not Ranked. UR-Under Review.

**Office:** 6501 Legacy Drive, Plano, TX 75024-3698.
**Telephone:** 972-431-1000.
**Website:** http://www.jcpenney.net
**Chrmn & CEO:** M.E. Ullman, III

**Pres:** K.C. Hicks
**EVP & CFO:** R.B. Cavanaugh
**EVP & Chief Admin Officer:** M.T. Theilmann
**EVP & CIO:** T.M. Nealon

**Investor Contact:** R. Johnson (972-431-8167)
**Board Members:** C. C. Barrett, M. A. Burns, M. Clark, T. J. Engibous, K. B. Foster, K. C. Hicks, B. Osborne, L. H. Roberts, J. G. Teruel, R. G. Turner, M. E. Ullman, III, M. B. West

**Founded:** 1902
**Domicile:** Delaware
**Employees:** 155,000

# People's United Financial Inc

**STANDARD &POOR'S**

| S&P Recommendation | STRONG BUY ★★★★★ | Price $18.15 (as of Nov 14, 2008) | 12-Mo. Target Price $22.00 | Investment Style Large-Cap Blend |
|---|---|---|---|---|

**GICS Sector** Financials
**Sub-Industry** Thrifts & Mortgage Finance

**Summary** This company provides banking and financial services in four states, with most of its business concentrated in Connecticut.

## Key Stock Statistics (Source S&P, Vickers, company reports)

| | | | | | | |
|---|---|---|---|---|---|---|
| 52-Wk Range | $21.76– 13.92 | S&P Oper. EPS 2008**E** | 0.57 | Market Capitalization(B) | $6.296 | Beta | 0.42 |
| Trailing 12-Month EPS | $0.47 | S&P Oper. EPS 2009**E** | 0.70 | Yield (%) | 3.31 | S&P 3-Yr. Proj. EPS CAGR(%) | 11 |
| Trailing 12-Month P/E | 38.6 | P/E on S&P Oper. EPS 2008**E** | 31.8 | Dividend Rate/Share | $0.60 | S&P Credit Rating | A- |
| $10K Invested 5 Yrs Ago | $30,893 | Common Shares Outstg. (M) | 346.9 | Institutional Ownership (%) | 69 | | |

## Price Performance

30-Week Mov. Avg. · · · · 10-Week Mov. Avg. – – **GAAP Earnings vs. Previous Year** Volume Above Avg. ⁜⁜ STARS
12-Mo. Target Price — Relative Strength — ▲ Up ▼ Down ► No Change Below Avg. ⁜⁜ ★

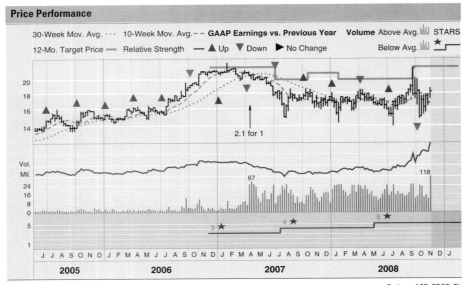

Options: ASE, CBOE, Ph

Analysis prepared by **Stuart Plesser** on October 20, 2008, when the stock traded at **$ 17.68**.

## Highlights

➤ We believe a modest increase in average earning assets, combined with an assumption of a 2.0% yield on securities from the recently completed second-step conversion, will result in a 2.5% increase in revenue for PBCT in 2009. Our 2009 estimates include a net interest margin of 3.60%, basically flat from projected 2008 net interest margin, assuming no further rate cuts.

➤ We see expenses as a percentage of revenue declining in 2009, helped largely by cost-cutting efforts from the Chittenden acquisition. All and all, we look for expenses as a percentage of revenue to total 61.5% in 2009 vs. projected 68% in 2008. Asset quality remains good, in our view, but will likely deteriorate somewhat due to a turn in the credit cycle. We expect 2009 provisions of roughly $29 million, versus projected $24.0 million in 2008, based on an increase in loans outstanding and a 0.20% annualized charge-off/average loan assumption, as credit will likely trend toward historical levels.

➤ Assuming an effective tax rate of 34.0% and a decline in shares outstanding, we see 2008 operating EPS of $0.57, versus 2007's $0.65. Our 2009 EPS assumption is $0.70.

## Investment Rationale/Risk

➤ People's United Financial completed its second-step conversion in April 2007, raising $3.4 billion. It has since purchased Chittenden (CHZ) for $1.9 billion in a cash/stock deal, which closed in early January 2008. We estimate that PBCT has about $2.5 billion of capital remaining to use for share repurchases or to fund another deal. Although we believe the company may have paid a bit too much for CHZ, we believe that PBCT will be able to realize significant cost savings from the acquisition. We underscore PBCT's current liquidity, which, although in the short term may hurt the net interest margin, should ultimately lead to PBCT purchasing a distressed bank at an attractive price, by our analysis. Given our view of PBCT's high credit quality, excess liquidity, and an attractive share price, our recommendation is strong buy.

➤ Risks to our recommendation and target price include detrimental changes in the slope of the yield curve, and possible integration problems related to the recent acquisition.

➤ Our 12-month target price of $22 is based on a roughly 1.40X multiple of current book value of $15.66 per share, a premium to peers.

## Qualitative Risk Assessment

| LOW | MEDIUM | HIGH |
|---|---|---|

Our risk assessment reflects our view of the good credit quality of PBCT's loan portfolio and its history of profitability, offset by execution risk, mostly stemming from the investment of the proceeds from the company's second-step conversion.

## Quantitative Evaluations

**S&P Quality Ranking** B+

| D | C | B- | B | B+ | A- | A | A+ |
|---|---|---|---|---|---|---|---|

**Relative Strength Rank** STRONG
96
LOWEST = 1    HIGHEST = 99

## Revenue/Earnings Data

**Revenue (Million $)**

| | 1Q | 2Q | 3Q | 4Q | Year |
|---|---|---|---|---|---|
| 2008 | 337.2 | 300.9 | 296.6 | -- | -- |
| 2007 | 193.0 | 233.0 | 239.6 | 226.8 | 892.4 |
| 2006 | 179.5 | 183.5 | 161.4 | 195.9 | 729.5 |
| 2005 | 157.2 | 164.3 | 172.7 | 185.5 | 679.7 |
| 2004 | 141.7 | 143.7 | 149.6 | 152.9 | 587.9 |
| 2003 | 202.5 | 193.6 | 182.1 | 187.3 | 765.5 |

**Earnings Per Share ($)**

| | | | | | |
|---|---|---|---|---|---|
| 2008 | 0.05 | 0.13 | 0.14 | E0.15 | E0.57 |
| 2007 | 0.11 | 0.05 | 0.20 | 0.16 | 0.51 |
| 2006 | 0.11 | 0.11 | 0.05 | 0.13 | 0.40 |
| 2005 | 0.10 | 0.10 | 0.11 | 0.11 | 0.42 |
| 2004 | -0.26 | 0.08 | 0.08 | 0.09 | -0.02 |
| 2003 | 0.06 | 0.05 | 0.05 | 0.06 | 0.22 |

Fiscal year ended Dec. 31. Next earnings report expected: Mid January. EPS Estimates based on S&P Operating Earnings; historical GAAP earnings are as reported.

## Dividend Data (Dates: mm/dd Payment Date: mm/dd/yy)

| Amount ($) | Date Decl. | Ex-Div. Date | Stk. of Record | Payment Date |
|---|---|---|---|---|
| 0.133 | 01/17 | 01/30 | 02/01 | 02/15/08 |
| 0.150 | 04/17 | 04/29 | 05/01 | 05/15/08 |
| 0.150 | 07/17 | 07/30 | 08/01 | 08/15/08 |
| 0.150 | 10/17 | 10/29 | 11/01 | 11/15/08 |

Dividends have been paid since 1993. Source: Company reports.

# People's United Financial Inc

**STANDARD &POOR'S**

## Business Summary October 20, 2008

CORPORATE OVERVIEW. People's United Financial (formerly People's Bank of Connecticut), formed in 1842, is a state-chartered stock savings bank head-quartered in Bridgeport, CT. As of March 31, 2008, assets totaled roughly $21.0 billion. The company offers a full range of financial services to individual, corporate and municipal customers. In addition to traditional banking activities, People's provides specialized services tailored to specific markets, including personal, institutional and employee benefits; cash management; and municipal banking and finance. PBCT offers brokerage, financial advisory services and life insurance through its People's Securities subsidiary; equipment financing through People's Capital and Leasing (PCLC); asset management through Olsen Mobeck Investment Advisors, Inc; and insurance services through R.C. Knox and Company, Inc. Services are delivered through a network of eight financial centers, 71 traditional branches, 75 supermarket branches, seven limited-service branches, 23 investment and brokerage offices (22 of which are located in branches), five wealth management and trust offices, nine PCLC offices, and six commercial banking offices.

PBCT has increased its residential mortgage and home equity lending activi-

ties in the contiguous markets of New York and Massachusetts. In addition, PBCT maintains a loan production office in Massachusetts, and PCLC has offices in six states in addition to Connecticut.

PRIMARY BUSINESS DYNAMICS. As of March 31, 2008, total loans of $15.0 billion were 29% residential real estate loans (versus 36% in 2007); 26% commercial loans (29%); 31% commercial real estate (21%); and 14% consumer loans (14%).

As of March 31, 2008, deposits comprised 97.9% of funding costs versus 99.3% at December 31, 2007. At year-end 2007, deposits consisted of non-interest 24% (versus 25% in 2006); low interest 34% (35%); and time deposits 42% (40%).

## Company Financials Fiscal Year Ended Dec. 31

### Per Share Data ($)

| | 2007 | 2006 | 2005 | 2004 | 2003 | 2002 | 2001 | 2000 | 1999 | 1998 |
|---|---|---|---|---|---|---|---|---|---|---|
| Tangible Book Value | 15.77 | 8.68 | 3.98 | 5.53 | 4.55 | 2.83 | 2.82 | 2.61 | 2.25 | 2.38 |
| Earnings | 0.51 | 0.40 | 0.42 | -0.02 | 0.22 | 0.19 | 0.30 | 0.37 | 0.38 | 0.30 |
| S&P Core Earnings | 0.51 | 0.41 | 0.41 | -0.01 | 0.22 | 0.16 | 0.09 | NA | NA | NA |
| Dividends | 0.52 | 0.46 | 0.41 | 0.45 | 0.32 | 0.30 | 0.28 | 0.25 | 0.22 | 0.22 |
| Payout Ratio | 102% | 115% | 96% | NM | 148% | 158% | 96% | 68% | 57% | 73% |
| Prices:High | 22.81 | 21.62 | 16.07 | 14.12 | 7.20 | 5.94 | 6.01 | 5.71 | 6.83 | 8.78 |
| Prices:Low | 14.78 | 14.29 | 11.43 | 6.88 | 5.13 | 4.37 | 4.37 | 3.47 | 4.07 | 3.98 |
| P/E Ratio:High | 45 | 54 | 38 | NM | 33 | 31 | 20 | 15 | 18 | 29 |
| P/E Ratio:Low | 29 | 36 | 27 | NM | 23 | 23 | 15 | 9 | 11 | 13 |

### Income Statement Analysis (Million $)

| | | | | | | | | | | |
|---|---|---|---|---|---|---|---|---|---|---|
| Net Interest Income | 487 | 382 | 370 | 327 | 320 | 351 | 354 | 385 | 338 | 287 |
| Loan Loss Provision | 8.00 | 3.40 | 8.60 | 13.3 | 48.6 | 77.7 | 101 | 59.9 | 54.5 | 45.8 |
| Non Interest Income | 180 | 175 | 172 | 155 | 252 | 251 | 339 | 290 | 282 | 273 |
| Non Interest Expenses | 439 | 347 | 343 | 479 | 436 | 441 | 441 | 453 | 414 | 379 |
| Pretax Income | 225 | 180 | 190 | -14.2 | 86.9 | 80.4 | 133 | 166 | 170 | 173 |
| Effective Tax Rate | 33.6% | 32.2% | 33.7% | NM | 26.6% | 31.1% | 34.8% | 34.5% | 34.3% | 47.1% |
| Net Income | 149 | 122 | 126 | -5.60 | 63.8 | 55.4 | 86.7 | 108 | 112 | 91.7 |
| % Net Interest Margin | 4.12 | 3.87 | 3.68 | 3.33 | 2.95 | 3.40 | 4.33 | 4.47 | 4.26 | 4.34 |
| S&P Core Earnings | 147 | 124 | 124 | -4.16 | 63.9 | 46.6 | 27.2 | NA | NA | NA |

### Balance Sheet & Other Financial Data (Million $)

| | | | | | | | | | | |
|---|---|---|---|---|---|---|---|---|---|---|
| Total Assets | 13,555 | 10,687 | 10,933 | 10,718 | 11,672 | 12,261 | 11,891 | 11,571 | 10,738 | 9,919 |
| Loans | 8,877 | 9,298 | 8,498 | 7,861 | 8,122 | 7,336 | 6,931 | 7,345 | 6,970 | 6,481 |
| Deposits | 8,881 | 9,083 | 9,083 | 8,862 | 8,714 | 8,426 | 7,983 | 7,761 | 7,191 | 6,938 |
| Capitalization:Debt | 65.4 | 65.3 | 109 | 122 | 1,162 | 1,165 | 1,478 | 1,824 | 1,046 | 1,234 |
| Capitalization:Equity | 4,445 | 1,340 | 1,289 | 1,200 | 1,002 | 940 | 935 | 882 | 782 | 852 |
| Capitalization:Total | 4,511 | 1,405 | 1,398 | 1,322 | 2,164 | 2,104 | 2,413 | 2,706 | 1,828 | 2,086 |
| % Return on Assets | 1.2 | 1.1 | 1.2 | NM | 0.5 | 0.5 | 0.7 | 1.0 | 1.1 | 1.0 |
| % Return on Equity | 5.2 | 9.3 | 10.1 | NM | 6.6 | 5.9 | 9.5 | 13.0 | 13.7 | 11.7 |
| % Loan Loss Reserve | 0.8 | 0.8 | 0.9 | 0.9 | 1.4 | 1.5 | 1.6 | 1.4 | 1.5 | 1.6 |
| % Risk Based Capital | 33.4 | 16.1 | 16.4 | 16.7 | 13.1 | 12.5 | 12.3 | 11.6 | 10.9 | 11.7 |
| Price Times Book Value:High | 1.4 | NA | 4.0 | 2.6 | 1.6 | 2.1 | 2.1 | 2.2 | 3.0 | 3.7 |
| Price Times Book Value:Low | 0.9 | NA | 2.9 | 1.2 | 1.1 | 1.5 | 1.6 | 1.3 | 1.8 | 1.7 |

Data as orig reptd.; bef. results of disc opers/spec. items. Per share data adj. for stk. divs.; EPS diluted. E-Estimated. NA-Not Available. NM-Not Meaningful. NR-Not Ranked. UR-Under Review.

**Office:** 850 Main St, Bridgeport, CT 06604-4904.
**Telephone:** 203-338-7171.
**Website:** http://www.peoples.com
**Chrmn:** G.P. Carter

**Pres & CEO:** P.R. Sherringham
**COO:** M.K. Vitelli
**EVP & CFO:** P.D. Burner
**EVP & Chief Admin Officer:** J.P. Barnes

**Investor Contact:** J. Shaw
**Board Members:** C. P. Baron, G. P. Carter, J. K. Dwight, J. Franklin, E. S. Groark, J. M. Hansen, R. M. Hoyt, J. J. Lowney, Jr., M. W. Richards, P. R. Sherringham, J. A. Thomas

**Founded:** 1842
**Domicile:** Connecticut
**Employees:** 2,856

The *McGraw-Hill* Companies

# Pepco Holdings Inc.

| S&P Recommendation  BUY ★★★★☆ | Price<br>$17.74 (as of Nov 14, 2008) | 12-Mo. Target Price<br>$23.00 | Investment Style<br>Large-Cap Blend |
|---|---|---|---|

**GICS Sector** Utilities
**Sub-Industry** Electric Utilities

**Summary** This electric utility holding company was formed through the 2002 merger of Potomac Electric Power Co. (Pepco) and Conectiv.

## Key Stock Statistics (Source S&P, Vickers, company reports)

| | | | | | | |
|---|---|---|---|---|---|---|
| 52-Wk Range | $30.10– 15.27 | S&P Oper. EPS 2008**E** | 1.90 | Market Capitalization(B) | $3.579 | Beta | 0.78 |
| Trailing 12-Month EPS | $1.45 | S&P Oper. EPS 2009**E** | 2.00 | Yield (%) | 6.09 | S&P 3-Yr. Proj. EPS CAGR(%) | 14 |
| Trailing 12-Month P/E | 12.2 | P/E on S&P Oper. EPS 2008**E** | 9.3 | Dividend Rate/Share | $1.08 | S&P Credit Rating | BBB |
| $10K Invested 5 Yrs Ago | $12,103 | Common Shares Outstg. (M) | 201.8 | Institutional Ownership (%) | 60 | | |

## Price Performance

30-Week Mov. Avg. · · ·   10-Week Mov. Avg. - -   **GAAP Earnings vs. Previous Year**   Volume Above Avg. STARS
12-Mo. Target Price —   Relative Strength —   ▲ Up   ▼ Down   ▶ No Change   Below Avg.

[Price performance chart showing 2005, 2006, 2007, 2008 data with price range roughly 16–30, volume in millions, and STARS ranking]

Options: Ph

Analysis prepared by **Justin McCann** on October 17, 2008, when the stock traded at **$ 18.35**.

## Highlights

➤ We expect EPS in 2008 to advance about 30% from 2007 operating EPS of $1.53, driven by rate increases and new transmission rates at the utilities, and continued earnings growth at the unregulated operations. In the first half of 2008, operating EPS grew 81% to $1.03. In addition to the higher rates for the utilities, earnings at Conectiv Energy benefited from fuel price volatility and its fuel hedges.

➤ For 2009, we expect operating EPS to grow more than 4% from anticipated results in 2008. We see Conectiv continuing to benefit from renewal contracts at higher power prices, most of which are already contracted. However, earnings could be restricted by higher operating expenses and a slowdown in the economy.

➤ On January 30, 2008, the District of Columbia Public Service Commission authorized a $28.3 million increase in electric rates for Pepco, effective as of February 20, 2008. On January 2, 2008, Delmarva Power completed the sale of its Virginia electric distribution assets and substantially all of its transmission assets for about $54.2 million. The sale resulted in a $1.8 million after-tax gain, and eliminated Delmarva's obligation to provide default service in Virginia.

## Investment Rationale/Risk

➤ The shares are down more than 30% year-to-date. We believe the stock, after gaining 13% in 2007, has been hurt by the crisis in the credit markets and extreme volatility in the stock market, with a sharp investor shift away from the electric utility sector. However, in our view, the stock has been oversold. We expect it to recover and to outperform the company's electric utility peers over the next 12 months. We recommend the shares for what we consider their above-average total return potential.

➤ Risks to our recommendation and target price include the extent to which POM may be unable to recover incremental purchased power costs; much weaker than expected earnings from the unregulated Conectiv Energy; and the potential for a significant shift in the average P/E of the group as a whole.

➤ Reflecting the 3.8% increase in POM's dividend (effective with the March payment), the recent yield from the dividend was 5.8%, compared to the prior dividend yield of 3.9% and an average peer yield of about 5.4%. Looking forward, we expect the stock to trade at a discount-to-peers P/E of about 11.1X our EPS estimate for 2009. Our 12-month target price is $23.

## Qualitative Risk Assessment

| LOW | MEDIUM | HIGH |
|---|---|---|

Our risk assessment reflects our view of the steady cash flows expected from the regulated electric transmission and distribution businesses, which account for approximately 70% of consolidated cash flows and reflect a healthy economy in the company's service territories. We believe this should largely offset the less predictable earnings and cash flow from the company's unregulated wholesale and retail power marketing businesses.

## Quantitative Evaluations

**S&P Quality Ranking**  B

| D | C | B- | B | B+ | A- | A | A+ |
|---|---|---|---|---|---|---|---|

**Relative Strength Rank**  MODERATE

62

LOWEST = 1        HIGHEST = 99

## Revenue/Earnings Data

**Revenue (Million $)**

| | 1Q | 2Q | 3Q | 4Q | Year |
|---|---|---|---|---|---|
| 2008 | 2,641 | 2,518 | 3,060 | -- | -- |
| 2007 | 2,179 | 2,084 | 2,770 | 2,333 | 9,366 |
| 2006 | 1,952 | 1,917 | 2,590 | 1,905 | 8,363 |
| 2005 | 1,805 | 1,712 | 2,489 | 2,063 | 8,066 |
| 2004 | 1,764 | 1,692 | 2,047 | 1,720 | 7,222 |
| 2003 | 1,929 | 1,698 | 2,131 | 1,514 | 7,271 |

**Earnings Per Share ($)**

| | | | | | |
|---|---|---|---|---|---|
| 2008 | 0.49 | 0.07 | 0.59 | E0.29 | E1.90 |
| 2007 | 0.27 | 0.30 | 0.87 | 0.29 | 1.72 |
| 2006 | 0.29 | 0.27 | 0.54 | 0.19 | 1.30 |
| 2005 | 0.24 | 0.34 | 0.90 | 0.43 | 1.91 |
| 2004 | 0.30 | 0.53 | 0.64 | 0.03 | 1.47 |
| 2003 | -0.15 | 0.22 | 0.92 | -0.36 | 0.63 |

Fiscal year ended Dec. 31. Next earnings report expected: Early March. EPS Estimates based on S&P Operating Earnings; historical GAAP earnings are as reported.

## Dividend Data (Dates: mm/dd Payment Date: mm/dd/yy)

| Amount ($) | Date Decl. | Ex-Div. Date | Stk. of Record | Payment Date |
|---|---|---|---|---|
| 0.260 | 10/25 | 12/06 | 12/10 | 01/02/08 |
| 0.270 | 01/24 | 03/06 | 03/10 | 03/31/08 |
| 0.270 | 05/26 | 12/08 | 12/10 | 12/31/08 |

Dividends have been paid since 1904. Source: Company reports.

---

The McGraw-Hill Companies

# Pepco Holdings Inc.

STANDARD
&POOR'S

## Business Summary October 17, 2008

CORPORATE OVERVIEW. Pepco Holdings (POM) is an energy holding company involved in two principal business operations: power delivery and competitive energy. POM's power delivery business, which provides transmission and distribution of electricity and distribution of natural gas, contributed 53.3% of the company's consolidated operating revenues in 2007. Its operations are conducted through three regulated utility subsidiaries: Potomac Electric Power Company (Pepco), Delmarva Power & Light Company (DPL), and Atlantic City Electric Company (ACE). POM's competitive energy business provides non-regulated generation, marketing and supply of electricity and natural gas, and related energy management services through the Conectiv Energy and Pepco Energy Services subsidiaries. In 2007, the competitive energy business contributed 46.7% of consolidated operating revenues.

CORPORATE STRATEGY. The company's business strategy is to stay focused on the low-risk, stable, power delivery business. Over the next five years, the company plans to invest nearly $5 billion in the utility infrastructure. The utility business has targeted approximately 4% annual average earnings growth by focusing on sales growth, operational excellence, and constructive regulatory outcomes. POM's financial strategy has been to reduce debt, which should result in a stronger balance sheet and enhanced returns for shareholders. The Conectiv Energy division plans to adopt a proactive hedging strategy for risk management and evaluate inorganic growth possibilities.

## Company Financials Fiscal Year Ended Dec. 31

| Per Share Data ($) | 2007 | 2006 | 2005 | 2004 | 2003 | 2002 | 2001 | 2000 | 1999 | 1998 |
|---|---|---|---|---|---|---|---|---|---|---|
| Tangible Book Value | 13.01 | 11.48 | 11.34 | 10.28 | 9.12 | 9.20 | 17.01 | 16.77 | 16.05 | 15.84 |
| Earnings | 1.72 | 1.30 | 1.91 | 1.47 | 0.63 | 1.61 | 1.50 | 2.96 | 1.98 | 1.73 |
| S&P Core Earnings | 1.60 | 1.28 | 1.37 | 1.38 | 0.87 | 1.31 | 1.20 | NA | NA | NA |
| Dividends | 1.04 | 1.04 | 1.00 | 1.00 | 1.00 | 0.92 | 1.17 | 1.66 | 1.66 | 1.66 |
| Payout Ratio | 60% | 80% | 52% | 68% | 159% | 57% | 78% | 56% | 84% | 96% |
| Prices:High | 30.71 | 26.99 | 24.46 | 21.71 | 20.56 | 23.83 | 24.90 | 27.88 | 31.75 | 27.81 |
| Prices:Low | 24.20 | 21.79 | 20.26 | 16.94 | 16.10 | 15.37 | 20.08 | 19.06 | 21.25 | 23.06 |
| P/E Ratio:High | 18 | 21 | 13 | 15 | 33 | 15 | 17 | 9 | 16 | 16 |
| P/E Ratio:Low | 14 | 17 | 11 | 12 | 26 | 10 | 13 | 6 | 11 | 13 |

| Income Statement Analysis (Million $) | | | | | | | | | | |
|---|---|---|---|---|---|---|---|---|---|---|
| Revenue | 9,366 | 8,363 | 8,066 | 7,222 | 7,271 | 4,325 | 2,503 | 2,624 | 2,476 | 2,064 |
| Depreciation | 366 | 413 | 423 | 441 | 422 | 240 | 171 | 248 | 273 | 240 |
| Maintenance | NA | NA | NA | NA | NA | NA | NA | NA | NA | 91.5 |
| Fixed Charges Coverage | 2.41 | 2.25 | 2.37 | 2.06 | 1.43 | 2.47 | 3.06 | 4.32 | 2.71 | 3.08 |
| Construction Credits | NA | NA | NA | NA | NA | NA | NA | NA | NA | 5.50 |
| Effective Tax Rate | 36.0% | 39.4% | 41.3% | 40.1% | 38.0% | 37.1% | 33.1% | 49.2% | 31.7% | 36.0% |
| Net Income | 334 | 248 | 362 | 259 | 108 | 211 | 168 | 352 | 247 | 326 |
| S&P Core Earnings | 311 | 246 | 259 | 241 | 147 | 171 | 130 | NA | NA | NA |

| Balance Sheet & Other Financial Data (Million $) | | | | | | | | | | |
|---|---|---|---|---|---|---|---|---|---|---|
| Gross Property | 12,307 | 11,820 | 11,384 | 11,045 | 10,747 | 10,625 | 4,367 | 4,339 | 6,862 | 6,658 |
| Capital Expenditures | 623 | 475 | 467 | 517 | 564 | 504 | 245 | 226 | 200 | 212 |
| Net Property | 7,877 | 7,577 | 7,312 | 7,088 | 6,965 | 6,798 | 2,758 | 2,776 | 4,602 | 4,521 |
| Capitalization:Long Term Debt | 4,735 | 4,367 | 4,885 | 5,128 | 5,373 | 5,122 | 1,722 | 1,985 | 2,992 | 2,142 |
| Capitalization:% Long Term Debt | 54.1 | 54.7 | 57.7 | 60.4 | 63.7 | 62.2 | 45.9 | 50.4 | 59.8 | 51.4 |
| Capitalization:Preferred | Nil | Nil | Nil | Nil | 63.2 | 111 | 210 | 90.3 | 100 | 150 |
| Capitalization:% Preferred | Nil | Nil | Nil | Nil | 0.75 | 1.35 | 5.59 | 2.29 | 2.00 | 3.60 |
| Capitalization:Common | 4,018 | 3,612 | 3,584 | 3,366 | 3,003 | 2,996 | 1,823 | 1,863 | 1,910 | 1,877 |
| Capitalization:% Common | 45.9 | 45.3 | 42.3 | 39.6 | 35.6 | 36.4 | 48.5 | 47.3 | 38.2 | 45.0 |
| Total Capital | 10,903 | 10,134 | 10,455 | 10,532 | 8,439 | 9,833 | 4,282 | 4,384 | 6,105 | 5,272 |
| % Operating Ratio | 93.7 | 93.2 | 92.4 | 91.6 | 92.6 | 90.3 | 87.1 | 91.9 | 81.4 | 82.3 |
| % Earned on Net Property | 10.0 | 9.3 | 12.6 | 11.0 | 18.6 | 16.4 | 27.5 | 16.0 | 10.0 | 7.9 |
| % Return on Revenue | 3.6 | 3.0 | 4.5 | 3.6 | 1.5 | 4.9 | 6.7 | 13.4 | 10.0 | 10.9 |
| % Return on Invested Capital | 6.0 | 6.2 | 8.0 | 6.7 | 8.3 | 6.4 | 9.6 | 11.8 | 7.6 | 7.1 |
| % Return on Common Equity | 8.8 | 6.9 | 10.5 | 8.1 | 3.4 | 8.7 | 8.9 | 18.4 | 12.6 | 11.5 |

Data as orig reptd.; bef. results of disc opers/spec. items. Per share data adj. for stk. divs.; EPS diluted. E-Estimated. NA-Not Available. NM-Not Meaningful. NR-Not Ranked. UR-Under Review.

**Office:** 701 Ninth Street N.W., Washington, DC 20068.
**Telephone:** 202-872-2000.
**Email:** shareholder@pepco.com
**Website:** http://www.pepcoholdings.com

**Chrmn & CEO:** D.R. Wraase
**Pres & COO:** J.M. Rigby
**Vice Chrmn & General Counsel:** W.T. Torgerson
**SVP & CFO:** P.H. Barry

**Chief Acctg Officer & Cntlr:** R.K. Clark
**Investor Contact:** E.J. Bourscheid (202-872-2797)
**Board Members:** J. B. Dunn, IV, T. C. Golden, F. O. Heintz, B. J. Krumsiek, G. F. MacCormack, R. B. McGlynn, L. C. Nussdorf, F. K. Ross, P. A. Schneider, L. P. Silverman, W. T. Torgerson, D. R. Wraase

**Founded:** 1896
**Domicile:** Delaware
**Employees:** 5,131

**STANDARD &POOR'S**

# PepsiCo Inc

| S&P Recommendation | BUY ★★★★☆ | Price | 12-Mo. Target Price | Investment Style |
|---|---|---|---|---|
| | | $53.52 (as of Nov 14, 2008) | $61.00 | Large-Cap Growth |

**GICS Sector** Consumer Staples
**Sub-Industry** Soft Drinks

**Summary** This company is a major international producer of branded beverage and snack food products.

## Key Stock Statistics (Source S&P, Vickers, company reports)

| | | | | | | | |
|---|---|---|---|---|---|---|---|
| 52-Wk Range | $79.79– 50.41 | S&P Oper. EPS 2008**E** | 3.68 | Market Capitalization(B) | $83.123 | Beta | 0.22 |
| Trailing 12-Month EPS | $3.51 | S&P Oper. EPS 2009**E** | 4.06 | Yield (%) | 3.18 | S&P 3-Yr. Proj. EPS CAGR(%) | 10 |
| Trailing 12-Month P/E | 15.3 | P/E on S&P Oper. EPS 2008**E** | 14.5 | Dividend Rate/Share | $1.70 | S&P Credit Rating | A+ |
| $10K Invested 5 Yrs Ago | $12,435 | Common Shares Outstg. (M) | 1,553.1 | Institutional Ownership (%) | 68 | | |

## Price Performance

30-Week Mov. Avg. · · · 10-Week Mov. Avg. - - - GAAP Earnings vs. Previous Year   Volume Above Avg. |||| STARS
12-Mo. Target Price — Relative Strength — ▲ Up ▼ Down ► No Change   Below Avg. |||| ★

Options: ASE, CBOE, P, Ph

Analysis prepared by **Esther Y. Kwon, CFA** on October 15, 2008, when the stock traded at **$ 54.40**.

## Highlights

➤ We expect net sales to rise over 11% in 2008, aided by new products, acquisitions, penetration of international markets, and foreign currency. We see segment operating income rising less than sales growth on higher cooking oil, grain, energy and PET resin costs, offset slightly by favorable pricing and product mix benefits, operating efficiencies, and productivity gains. We expect commodity price pressure to be especially pronounced for snack products, and we see price increases driving volume growth below historical rates in the near term.

➤ By segment, we see operating profits for PepsiCo Americas Beverages flat to up low-single digits in 2008, and we expect growth at Frito-Lay North America (FLNA) of 3% to 4%. For the PepsiCo International (PI) segment, we believe profits will climb more than 15%, while we think the Quaker Foods (QFNA) business will see a low-single digit gain.

➤ With about 3% fewer shares outstanding, we estimate 2008 operating EPS of $3.68, approximately 9% higher than 2007's $3.38. We expect further growth to $4.06 in 2009. For the next three years, we see annual EPS growth of 10%.

## Investment Rationale/Risk

➤ Our buy recommendation reflects our view of PEP's domestic and international growth opportunities, pricing power and healthy cash flow growth. In addition to the company's leading market positions, we view PEP's product innovation strategy as trend-setting for the industry. Its focus on health and wellness, not only at QFNA, but also at FLNA and PepsiCo Americas Beverages, in addition to its continued penetration of international markets, should continue to drive the top line.

➤ Risks to our recommendation and target price include unfavorable weather conditions in the company's markets and increased competitive activity. As PEP boosts its exposure to foreign markets, political and currency risks also increase.

➤ Our relative valuation model, derived from an analysis of peer P/E and historical P/E multiples, indicates a value of $61, which is our 12-month target price. This reflects a P/E multiple below the low end of the recent historical range on projected 2009 EPS, in a range of 19X to 27X. We believe a lower multiple is appropriate on higher commodity costs and a weak macroeconomic environment.

## Qualitative Risk Assessment

| LOW | MEDIUM | HIGH |
|---|---|---|

Our risk assessment reflects the relatively stable nature of the company's end markets, strong cash flow, leading global market positions, corporate governance practices that we view as favorable versus peers, and an S&P Quality Ranking of A+, reflecting the highest ranking of historical growth and stability of earnings and dividends.

## Quantitative Evaluations

**S&P Quality Ranking**    A+

| D | C | B- | B | B+ | A- | A | A+ |
|---|---|---|---|---|---|---|---|

**Relative Strength Rank**    MODERATE

68

LOWEST = 1    HIGHEST = 99

## Revenue/Earnings Data

### Revenue (Million $)

| | 1Q | 2Q | 3Q | 4Q | Year |
|---|---|---|---|---|---|
| 2008 | 8,333 | 10,945 | 11,244 | -- | -- |
| 2007 | 7,350 | 9,607 | 10,171 | 12,346 | 39,474 |
| 2006 | 7,205 | 8,599 | 8,950 | 10,383 | 35,137 |
| 2005 | 6,585 | 7,697 | 8,184 | 10,096 | 32,562 |
| 2004 | 6,131 | 7,070 | 7,257 | 8,803 | 29,261 |
| 2003 | 5,530 | 6,538 | 6,830 | 8,073 | 26,971 |

### Earnings Per Share ($)

| | | | | | |
|---|---|---|---|---|---|
| 2008 | 0.70 | 1.05 | 0.99 | E0.89 | E3.68 |
| 2007 | 0.65 | 0.94 | 1.06 | 0.77 | 3.41 |
| 2006 | 0.60 | 0.80 | 0.88 | 1.06 | 3.34 |
| 2005 | 0.53 | 0.70 | 0.51 | 0.65 | 2.39 |
| 2004 | 0.46 | 0.61 | 0.79 | 0.55 | 2.41 |
| 2003 | 0.45 | 0.58 | 0.62 | 0.52 | 2.05 |

Fiscal year ended Dec. 31. Next earnings report expected: Early February. EPS Estimates based on S&P Operating Earnings; historical GAAP earnings are as reported.

## Dividend Data (Dates: mm/dd Payment Date: mm/dd/yy)

| Amount ($) | Date Decl. | Ex-Div. Date | Stk. of Record | Payment Date |
|---|---|---|---|---|
| 0.375 | 02/01 | 03/05 | 03/07 | 03/31/08 |
| 0.425 | 05/07 | 06/04 | 06/06 | 06/30/08 |
| 0.425 | 07/18 | 09/03 | 09/05 | 09/30/08 |
| 0.425 | 11/14 | 12/03 | 12/05 | 01/02/09 |

Dividends have been paid since 1952. Source: Company reports.

---

**Please read the Required Disclosures and Analyst Certification on the last page of this report.**

*The McGraw·Hill Companies*

# PepsiCo Inc

**STANDARD & POOR'S**

## Business Summary October 15, 2008

CORPORATE OVERVIEW. Originally incorporated in 1919, PepsiCo is a leader in the global snack and beverage industry. The company manufactures, markets and sells a variety of salty, convenient, sweet and grain-based snacks, carbonated and non-carbonated beverages, and foods. PepsiCo is organized into four business segments: Frito-Lay North America (FLNA), PepsiCo Beverages North America (PBNA), PepsiCo International (PI) and Quaker Foods North America (QFNA). The company's North American divisions operate in the U.S. and Canada. PepsiCo's international divisions operate in more than 200 countries and accounted for 44% and 35% of PEP's net revenue and operating profits, respectively, with Mexico, the United Kingdom and Canada representing 19% of net revenue in 2007.

FLNA (29% of 2007 net revenue, 36% of operating profits before corporate overhead) produces the best-selling line of snack foods in the U.S., including Fritos brand corn chips, Lay's and Ruffles potato chips, Doritos and Tostitos tortilla chips, Cheetos cheese-flavored snacks, Rold Gold pretzels, SunChips multigrain snacks, Grandma's cookies, Quaker Fruit and Oatmeal bars, Quaker Chewy granola bars, Lay's Stax potato crisps, Cracker Jack candy-coated popcorn and Quaker Quakes corn and rice snacks. FLNA branded products

are sold to independent distributors and retailers. Products are transported from Frito-Lay's manufacturing plants to major distribution centers, principally by company-owned trucks.

PBNA (26%, 28%) manufactures or uses contract manufacturers, markets and sells beverage concentrates, fountain syrups and finished goods, under the brands Pepsi, Mountain Dew, Gatorade, Tropicana Pure Premium, Sierra Mist, SoBe Life Water, Tropicana juice drinks, Propel, Naked juice drinks and Izze. PBNA also manufactures, markets and sells ready-to-drink tea and coffee products through joint ventures with Lipton and Starbucks. In addition, it markets the Aquafina water brand and licenses it to its bottlers. Pepsi-Cola bottlers are licensed by PepsiCo to manufacture, sell and distribute, within defined territories, beverages and syrups bearing the Pepsi-Cola beverage trademarks.

## Company Financials Fiscal Year Ended Dec. 31

### Per Share Data ($)

| | 2007 | 2006 | 2005 | 2004 | 2003 | 2002 | 2001 | 2000 | 1999 | 1998 |
|---|---|---|---|---|---|---|---|---|---|---|
| Tangible Book Value | 6.80 | 1.93 | 2.17 | 1.96 | 3.82 | 2.37 | 1.90 | 1.91 | 1.48 | NM |
| Cash Flow | 4.27 | 4.30 | 3.25 | 2.45 | 2.75 | 2.47 | 2.07 | 2.13 | 2.06 | 2.12 |
| Earnings | 3.41 | 3.34 | 2.39 | 2.41 | 2.05 | 1.85 | 1.47 | 1.48 | 1.37 | 1.31 |
| S&P Core Earnings | 3.38 | 3.30 | 2.37 | 2.44 | 2.03 | 1.54 | 1.20 | NA | NA | NA |
| Dividends | 1.43 | 1.16 | 1.01 | 0.85 | 0.63 | 0.60 | 0.58 | 0.56 | 0.53 | 0.51 |
| Payout Ratio | 42% | 35% | 42% | 35% | 31% | 32% | 39% | 38% | 39% | 39% |
| Prices:High | 79.00 | 65.99 | 60.34 | 55.71 | 48.88 | 53.50 | 50.46 | 49.94 | 42.56 | 44.81 |
| Prices:Low | 61.89 | 56.00 | 51.34 | 45.30 | 36.24 | 34.00 | 40.25 | 29.69 | 30.13 | 27.56 |
| P/E Ratio:High | 23 | 20 | 25 | 23 | 24 | 29 | 34 | 34 | 31 | 34 |
| P/E Ratio:Low | 18 | 17 | 21 | 19 | 18 | 18 | 27 | 20 | 22 | 21 |

### Income Statement Analysis (Million $)

| | 2007 | 2006 | 2005 | 2004 | 2003 | 2002 | 2001 | 2000 | 1999 | 1998 |
|---|---|---|---|---|---|---|---|---|---|---|
| Revenue | 39,474 | 35,137 | 32,562 | 29,261 | 26,971 | 25,112 | 26,935 | 20,438 | 20,367 | 22,348 |
| Operating Income | 8,596 | 7,845 | 7,230 | 6,673 | 6,208 | 6,066 | 5,490 | 4,185 | 3,915 | 4,106 |
| Depreciation | 1,426 | 1,406 | 1,308 | 1,264 | 1,221 | 1,112 | 1,082 | 960 | 1,032 | 1,234 |
| Interest Expense | 224 | 239 | 256 | 167 | 163 | 178 | 219 | 221 | 363 | 395 |
| Pretax Income | 7,631 | 6,989 | 6,382 | 5,546 | 4,992 | 4,868 | 4,029 | 3,210 | 3,656 | 2,263 |
| Effective Tax Rate | 25.8% | 19.3% | 36.1% | 24.7% | 28.5% | 31.9% | 33.9% | 32.0% | 43.9% | 11.9% |
| Net Income | 5,658 | 5,642 | 4,078 | 4,174 | 3,568 | 3,313 | 2,662 | 2,183 | 2,050 | 1,993 |
| S&P Core Earnings | 5,602 | 5,565 | 4,028 | 4,191 | 3,543 | 2,749 | 2,164 | NA | NA | NA |

### Balance Sheet & Other Financial Data (Million $)

| | 2007 | 2006 | 2005 | 2004 | 2003 | 2002 | 2001 | 2000 | 1999 | 1998 |
|---|---|---|---|---|---|---|---|---|---|---|
| Cash | 910 | 1,651 | 1,716 | 1,280 | 820 | 1,638 | 683 | 864 | 964 | 311 |
| Current Assets | 10,151 | 9,130 | 10,454 | 8,639 | 6,930 | 6,413 | 5,853 | 4,604 | 4,173 | 4,362 |
| Total Assets | 34,628 | 29,930 | 31,727 | 27,987 | 25,327 | 23,474 | 21,695 | 18,339 | 17,551 | 22,660 |
| Current Liabilities | 7,753 | 6,860 | 9,406 | 6,752 | 6,415 | 6,052 | 4,998 | 3,935 | 3,788 | 7,914 |
| Long Term Debt | 4,203 | 2,550 | 2,313 | 2,397 | 1,702 | 2,187 | 2,651 | 2,346 | 2,812 | 4,028 |
| Common Equity | 17,325 | 15,327 | 14,210 | 13,572 | 11,896 | 9,250 | 8,648 | 7,249 | 6,881 | 6,401 |
| Total Capital | 22,174 | 18,446 | 17,998 | 17,226 | 14,837 | 13,196 | 12,821 | 10,956 | 10,902 | 12,432 |
| Capital Expenditures | 2,430 | 2,068 | 1,736 | 1,387 | 1,345 | 1,437 | 1,324 | 1,067 | 1,118 | 1,405 |
| Cash Flow | 7,084 | 7,047 | 5,384 | 4,109 | 4,786 | 4,421 | 3,744 | 3,143 | 3,082 | 3,227 |
| Current Ratio | 1.3 | 1.3 | 1.1 | 1.3 | 1.1 | 1.1 | 1.2 | 1.2 | 1.1 | 0.6 |
| % Long Term Debt of Capitalization | 18.9 | 13.8 | 12.9 | 13.9 | 11.5 | 16.6 | 20.7 | 21.4 | 25.8 | 32.4 |
| % Net Income of Revenue | 14.3 | 16.1 | 12.5 | 14.3 | 13.2 | 13.2 | 9.9 | 10.7 | 10.1 | 8.9 |
| % Return on Assets | 17.5 | 18.3 | 13.7 | 15.7 | 14.6 | 14.7 | 12.5 | 12.2 | 10.2 | 9.3 |
| % Return on Equity | 34.6 | 38.2 | 29.4 | 22.3 | 33.3 | 37.0 | 32.8 | 30.9 | 30.9 | 29.9 |

Data as orig reptd.; bef. results of disc opers/spec. items. Per share data adj. for stk. divs.; EPS diluted. E-Estimated. NA-Not Available. NM-Not Meaningful. NR-Not Ranked. UR-Under Review.

**Office:** 700 Anderson Hill Road, Purchase, NY 10577.
**Telephone:** 914-253-2000.
**Website:** http://www.pepsico.com
**Chrmn, Pres & CEO:** I.K. Indra

**Vice Chrmn:** M.D. White
**SVP, Chief Acctg Officer & Cntlr:** P.A. Bridgman
**SVP & Treas:** L.L. Nowell, III
**SVP, Secy & General Counsel:** L.D. Thompson

**Board Members:** I. M. Cook, D. Dublon, V. J. Dzau, R. L. Hunt, A. Ibarguen, I. K. Indra, A. C. Martinez, S. P. Rockefeller, J. J. Schiro, L. G. Trotter, D. L. Vasella, M. D. White

**Founded:** 1916
**Domicile:** North Carolina
**Employees:** 185,000

# Pepsi Bottling Group Inc.

STANDARD
&POOR'S

**S&P Recommendation** HOLD ★★★☆☆

| Price | 12-Mo. Target Price | Investment Style |
|---|---|---|
| $20.84 (as of Nov 14, 2008) | $32.00 | Large-Cap Blend |

**GICS Sector** Consumer Staples
**Sub-Industry** Soft Drinks

**Summary** This company is the world's largest manufacturer, seller and distributor of carbonated and non-carbonated Pepsi-Cola beverages.

## Key Stock Statistics (Source S&P, Vickers, company reports)

| | | | | | | | |
|---|---|---|---|---|---|---|---|
| 52-Wk Range | $43.03– 19.92 | S&P Oper. EPS 2008**E** | 2.36 | Market Capitalization(B) | $4.400 | Beta | 0.85 |
| Trailing 12-Month EPS | $2.28 | S&P Oper. EPS 2009**E** | 2.55 | Yield (%) | 3.26 | S&P 3-Yr. Proj. EPS CAGR(%) | 9 |
| Trailing 12-Month P/E | 9.1 | P/E on S&P Oper. EPS 2008**E** | 8.8 | Dividend Rate/Share | $0.68 | S&P Credit Rating | A |
| $10K Invested 5 Yrs Ago | $9,847 | Common Shares Outstg. (M) | 211.2 | Institutional Ownership (%) | 61 | | |

## Price Performance

30-Week Mov. Avg. · · · ·   10-Week Mov. Avg. —   **GAAP Earnings vs. Previous Year**   Volume Above Avg. STARS
12-Mo. Target Price —   Relative Strength —   ▲ Up   ▼ Down   ▶ No Change   Below Avg.

Options: ASE, CBOE, P, Ph

Analysis prepared by **Esther Y. Kwon, CFA** on October 06, 2008, when the stock traded at **$ 26.38**.

## Highlights

➤ In 2008, we expect net revenues to rise about 4%, primarily reflecting flat to lower comparable worldwide volume comparisons and a 4% to 5% increase in net revenue per case. Volume comparisons should benefit from the addition of new beverage products, but we expect overall category growth to be negative on sluggish carbonated soft drink (CSD) trends, weakening non-CSD trends and accelerated declines in unflavored water for PBG as it focuses on profitability rather than volume. By geographic segment, we see flat to lower volume in the U.S. and a low single digit increase in Europe, led by Russia.

➤ We expect margins to be aided by cost saving and efficiency initiatives. However, we think that higher raw material and packaging costs will likely lead to a 6% increase in cost of goods sold per case. In total, we project slight operating margin compression based on gross margin pressure, partially offset by expenses remaining flattish as a percentage of sales.

➤ After an effective tax rate of 33% to 34% and about a 5% reduction in the number of shares outstanding, we forecast EPS of $2.36 in 2008. In 2009, we project EPS of $2.55.

## Investment Rationale/Risk

➤ Our hold recommendation reflects our expectation for strong brand momentum, cost structure improvements, and better EPS visibility in coming quarters, coupled with valuation. We expect to see modest market share gains behind new product introductions and line extensions and better revenue per case growth. We think the pending deal for a majority interest in Russia's top juice producer Lebedyansky will bolster PBG's position in this higher growth market.

➤ Risks to our recommendation and target price include rising competitive pressures for PBG's business in Mexico, increasing commodity cost pressures, an inability to meet volume and revenue growth targets, and unfavorable weather conditions in the company's markets. In terms of corporate governance, the company has a dual class capital structure with unequal voting rights, which we view unfavorably.

➤ Our 12-month target price of $32 is derived from a blended analysis of historical P/E and EV/EBITDA multiples. Given the slowdown in volume trends and an unfavorable raw material cost environment, we believe a multiple at the low end of the historical range is appropriate.

## Qualitative Risk Assessment

| LOW | MEDIUM | HIGH |
|---|---|---|

Our risk assessment reflects the relatively stable nature of the company's end markets, strong cash flows and market share positions, and its relationship with corporate partner PepsiCo.

## Quantitative Evaluations

**S&P Quality Ranking**    A

| D | C | B- | B | B+ | A- | A | A+ |
|---|---|---|---|---|---|---|---|

**Relative Strength Rank**    MODERATE

57

LOWEST = 1                    HIGHEST = 99

## Revenue/Earnings Data

**Revenue (Million $)**

| | 1Q | 2Q | 3Q | 4Q | Year |
|---|---|---|---|---|---|
| 2008 | 2,651 | 3,522 | 3,814 | -- | -- |
| 2007 | 2,466 | 3,360 | 3,729 | 4,036 | 13,591 |
| 2006 | 2,367 | 3,138 | 3,460 | 3,765 | 12,730 |
| 2005 | 2,147 | 2,862 | 3,214 | 3,662 | 11,885 |
| 2004 | 2,067 | 2,675 | 2,934 | 3,230 | 10,906 |
| 2003 | 1,874 | 2,532 | 2,810 | 3,049 | 10,265 |

**Earnings Per Share ($)**

| | | | | | |
|---|---|---|---|---|---|
| 2008 | 0.12 | 0.78 | 1.06 | E0.41 | E2.36 |
| 2007 | 0.12 | 0.70 | 1.12 | 0.35 | 2.28 |
| 2006 | 0.14 | 0.61 | 0.86 | 0.55 | 2.16 |
| 2005 | 0.15 | 0.59 | 0.82 | 0.30 | 1.86 |
| 2004 | 0.19 | 0.53 | 0.73 | 0.29 | 1.73 |
| 2003 | 0.14 | 0.47 | 0.67 | 0.26 | 1.52 |

Fiscal year ended Dec. 31. Next earnings report expected: Late January. EPS Estimates based on S&P Operating Earnings; historical GAAP earnings are as reported.

## Dividend Data (Dates: mm/dd Payment Date: mm/dd/yy)

| Amount ($) | Date Decl. | Ex-Div. Date | Stk. of Record | Payment Date |
|---|---|---|---|---|
| 0.140 | 01/30 | 03/05 | 03/07 | 03/31/08 |
| 0.170 | 03/27 | 06/04 | 06/06 | 06/30/08 |
| 0.170 | 07/16 | 09/03 | 09/05 | 09/30/08 |
| 0.170 | 10/03 | 12/03 | 12/05 | 01/02/09 |

Dividends have been paid since 1999. Source: Company reports.

Stock Report | November 15, 2008 | NYS Symbol: **PBG**

# Pepsi Bottling Group Inc.

STANDARD
&POOR'S

## Business Summary October 06, 2008

CORPORATE OVERVIEW. The Pepsi Bottling Group is the world's largest manufacturer, seller and distributor of carbonated and non-carbonated Pepsi-Cola beverages. The company was separated from PepsiCo (PEP) via a March 1999 IPO. As of January 25, 2008, PepsiCo's ownership represented 41.7% of the voting power of all classes of PBG's voting stock. In addition, PEP owned a 6.7% interest in Bottling Group, LLC, PBG's main operating subsidiary.

The company has exclusive rights to manufacture, sell and distribute Pepsi-Cola beverages in all or a portion of 41 states, the District of Columbia, nine Canadian provinces, Spain, Greece, Turkey, Mexico and Russia. In 2007, approximately 76% of PBG's net revenues were generated in the U.S. and Canada, 14% were derived from Europe, and the remaining 10% came from Mexico.

The company's brands include some of the world's best recognized trademarks, and include Pepsi, Diet Pepsi, Mountain Dew, Lipton's Iced Tea, Sierra Mist, Tropicana juice drinks, Tropicana Twister, Mug Root Beer, SoBe, Dole, Aquafina, Starbucks Frappuccino and Mirinda, which are bottled under licenses from PepsiCo or PepsiCo joint ventures. In some markets, PBG also has the rights to bottle and sell non-PEP beverages such as Dr Pepper and Squirt.

The company has established an extensive production and distribution system to deliver products directly to stores without using wholesalers or middlemen. In Europe, PBG uses a combination of direct store distribution and distribution through wholesalers, depending on local market conditions. At December 31, 2007, it operated 100 soft drink production facilities worldwide, as well as 529 distribution facilities. PBG also owns or leases and operates approximately 38,300 vehicles, and owns more than 2 million coolers and soft drink dispensing and vending machines.

## Company Financials Fiscal Year Ended Dec. 31

### Per Share Data ($)

| | 2007 | 2006 | 2005 | 2004 | 2003 | 2002 | 2001 | 2000 | 1999 | 1998 |
|---|---|---|---|---|---|---|---|---|---|---|
| Tangible Book Value | NM | NM | NM | NM | NM | NM | NM | NM | NM | NM |
| Cash Flow | 5.16 | 4.84 | 4.38 | 3.99 | 3.57 | 3.00 | 2.77 | 2.23 | 2.43 | 2.96 |
| Earnings | 2.29 | 2.16 | 1.86 | 1.73 | 1.52 | 1.46 | 1.03 | 0.77 | 0.46 | -0.39 |
| S&P Core Earnings | 2.40 | 2.27 | 1.71 | 1.64 | 1.42 | 1.18 | 0.78 | NA | NA | NA |
| Dividends | 0.53 | 0.52 | 0.29 | 0.16 | 0.04 | 0.04 | 0.04 | 0.04 | 0.02 | NA |
| Payout Ratio | 23% | 24% | 16% | 9% | 3% | 3% | 4% | 5% | 4% | NA |
| Prices:High | 43.38 | 35.83 | 30.35 | 31.40 | 27.62 | 34.80 | 25.00 | 21.25 | 12.63 | NA |
| Prices:Low | 30.13 | 27.99 | 26.00 | 24.00 | 17.00 | 21.65 | 15.81 | 8.13 | 7.75 | NA |
| P/E Ratio:High | 19 | 17 | 16 | 18 | 18 | 24 | 24 | 28 | 27 | NA |
| P/E Ratio:Low | 13 | 13 | 14 | 14 | 11 | 15 | 15 | 11 | 17 | NA |

### Income Statement Analysis (Million $)

| | 2007 | 2006 | 2005 | 2004 | 2003 | 2002 | 2001 | 2000 | 1999 | 1998 |
|---|---|---|---|---|---|---|---|---|---|---|
| Revenue | 13,591 | 12,730 | 11,885 | 10,906 | 10,265 | 9,216 | 8,443 | 7,982 | 7,505 | 7,041 |
| Operating Income | 1,793 | 1,666 | 1,653 | 1,568 | 1,524 | 1,349 | 1,190 | 1,025 | 901 | 749 |
| Depreciation | 669 | 649 | 630 | 593 | 568 | 451 | 514 | 435 | 505 | 472 |
| Interest Expense | 305 | 266 | 250 | 230 | 239 | 191 | 194 | 192 | 202 | 221 |
| Pretax Income | 803 | 740 | 772 | 745 | 710 | 700 | 482 | 397 | 209 | -192 |
| Effective Tax Rate | 22.0% | 21.5% | 32.0% | 31.1% | 33.5% | 31.6% | 28.2% | 34.0% | 33.5% | NM |
| Net Income | 532 | 522 | 466 | 457 | 422 | 428 | 305 | 229 | 118 | -146 |
| S&P Core Earnings | 559 | 549 | 431 | 435 | 394 | 347 | 229 | NA | NA | NA |

### Balance Sheet & Other Financial Data (Million $)

| | 2007 | 2006 | 2005 | 2004 | 2003 | 2002 | 2001 | 2000 | 1999 | 1998 |
|---|---|---|---|---|---|---|---|---|---|---|
| Cash | 647 | 629 | 502 | 305 | 1,235 | 222 | 277 | 318 | 190 | 36.0 |
| Current Assets | 3,086 | 2,749 | 2,412 | 2,039 | 3,039 | 1,737 | 1,548 | 1,584 | 1,493 | 1,318 |
| Total Assets | 13,115 | 11,927 | 11,524 | 10,793 | 11,544 | 10,027 | 7,857 | 7,736 | 7,619 | 7,322 |
| Current Liabilities | 2,215 | 2,051 | 2,598 | 1,581 | 2,478 | 1,248 | 1,081 | 967 | 947 | 1,025 |
| Long Term Debt | 4,770 | 4,754 | 3,939 | 4,489 | 4,493 | 4,523 | 3,285 | 3,271 | 3,268 | 3,361 |
| Common Equity | 2,615 | 2,084 | 2,043 | 1,949 | 1,881 | 1,824 | 1,601 | 1,646 | 1,563 | -238 |
| Total Capital | 9,714 | 8,671 | 7,899 | 8,298 | 8,191 | 7,960 | 6,226 | 6,295 | 6,287 | 4,325 |
| Capital Expenditures | 854 | 725 | 715 | 717 | 644 | 623 | 593 | 515 | 560 | 507 |
| Cash Flow | 1,201 | 1,171 | 1,096 | 1,050 | 990 | 879 | 819 | 664 | 623 | 326 |
| Current Ratio | 1.4 | 1.3 | 0.9 | 1.3 | 1.2 | 1.4 | 1.4 | 1.6 | 1.6 | 1.3 |
| % Long Term Debt of Capitalization | 49.1 | 54.8 | 49.9 | 54.1 | 54.9 | 56.8 | 52.8 | 52.0 | 51.9 | 77.7 |
| % Net Income of Revenue | 3.9 | 4.1 | 3.9 | 4.2 | 4.1 | 4.6 | 3.6 | 2.9 | 1.6 | NM |
| % Return on Assets | 4.3 | 4.5 | 4.1 | 4.1 | 3.9 | 4.8 | 3.9 | 3.0 | 1.6 | NM |
| % Return on Equity | 22.6 | 25.3 | 23.3 | 23.9 | 22.8 | 25.0 | 18.8 | 14.3 | 17.8 | NM |

Data as orig reptd.; bef. results of disc opers/spec. items. Per share data adj. for stk. divs.; EPS diluted. E-Estimated. NA-Not Available. NM-Not Meaningful. NR-Not Ranked. UR-Under Review.

**Office:** 1 Pepsi Way, Somers, NY 10589-2212.
**Telephone:** 914-767-6000.
**Email:** shareholder.relations@pepsi.com
**Website:** http://www.pbg.com

**Chrmn, Pres & CEO:** E.J. Foss
**Pres:** R. Shabel
**COO:** V.L. Crawford
**SVP & CFO:** A.H. Drewes

**SVP, Secy & General Counsel:** S.M. Rapp
**Investor Contact:** M. Settino (914-767-7216)
**Board Members:** L. G. Alvarado, J. C. Compton, E. J. Foss, I. D. Hall, S. D. Kronick, B. J. McGarvie, J. A. Quelch, J. G. Teruel, C. M. Trudell

**Founded:** 1999
**Domicile:** Delaware
**Employees:** 69,100

The McGraw-Hill Companies

# PerkinElmer Inc.

**STANDARD &POOR'S**

| S&P Recommendation **BUY** ★★★★☆ | Price $16.80 (as of Nov 14, 2008) | 12-Mo. Target Price $24.00 | Investment Style Large-Cap Value |
|---|---|---|---|

**GICS Sector** Health Care
**Sub-Industry** Life Sciences Tools & Services

**Summary** This diversified technology company provides advanced scientific and technical products and services worldwide to pharmaceutical and industrial markets.

## Key Stock Statistics (Source S&P, Vickers, company reports)

| | | | | | | | |
|---|---|---|---|---|---|---|---|
| 52-Wk Range | $29.95– 15.42 | S&P Oper. EPS 2008E | 1.46 | Market Capitalization(B) | $1.984 | Beta | 1.25 |
| Trailing 12-Month EPS | $1.25 | S&P Oper. EPS 2009E | 1.70 | Yield (%) | 1.67 | S&P 3-Yr. Proj. EPS CAGR(%) | 12 |
| Trailing 12-Month P/E | 13.4 | P/E on S&P Oper. EPS 2008E | 11.5 | Dividend Rate/Share | $0.28 | S&P Credit Rating | BBB |
| $10K Invested 5 Yrs Ago | $10,633 | Common Shares Outstg. (M) | 118.1 | Institutional Ownership (%) | 83 | | |

## Price Performance

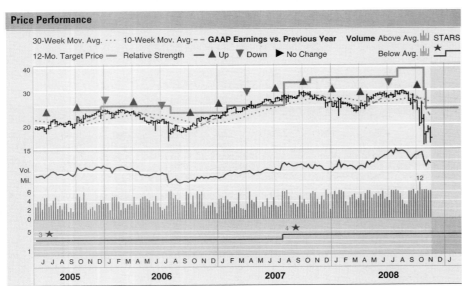

30-Week Mov. Avg. · · · · 10-Week Mov. Avg. – – GAAP Earnings vs. Previous Year  Volume Above Avg. STARS
12-Mo. Target Price — Relative Strength — ▲ Up ▼ Down ► No Change  Below Avg.

Options: ASE, CBOE, Ph

Analysis prepared by **Jeffrey Loo, CFA** on October 30, 2008, when the stock traded at **$ 17.65.**

## Highlights

➤ We see 2008 sales increasing 16%, to $2.07 billion, on contributions from acquisitions, including recently acquired ViaCell, and solid organic growth within Life and Analytical Sciences, driven by new products, and in Optoelectronics, which should benefit from recent capacity expansion. We think recent divestitures narrowed PKI's portfolio and should enable it to focus on higher-margin and faster-growing products. We see continued robust growth in genetic screening as developing countries increasingly adopt prenatal screening, and on strong medical imaging sales, partially offset by slow growth in biopharmaceuticals. We believe the ViaCell deal will expand PKI's neonatal and prenatal product lines, although we expect the deal to be dilutive to earnings in 2008. In 2009, we forecast sales to rise 5% to $2.17 billion.

➤ We see 2008 gross margins improving 140 basis points (bps) as a higher-margin product mix is partially offset by increased investments. However, we expect operating margins to rise only 40 bps on much higher SG&A and R&D costs.

➤ Excluding intangible amortization, we estimate 2008 and 2009 operating EPS at $1.46 and $1.70, respectively.

## Investment Rationale/Risk

➤ We believe PKI is benefiting from its R&D investments, recent acquisitions and portfolio restructuring, which should result in improving sales and margins in 2008. We think its acquisitions, product development efforts and recent divestitures will allow the company to focus on the faster-growing, higher-margin health sciences end market, which should account for about 85% of sales. We believe PKI will remain acquisitive to supplement organic growth, but think integration costs and related issues will adversely affect margins in the short term.

➤ Risks to our recommendation and target price include slower-than-anticipated growth in health sciences end markets, greater-than-expected integration challenges from recent acquisitions, and a slowdown in PKI's fastest-growing markets, including Asia.

➤ Our 12-month target price of $24 is based on a blend of our discounted cash flow analysis, using a weighted average cost of capital of 10.8% and a terminal growth rate of 3%, and our relative valuation analysis, using a P/E-to-growth ratio of 1.2X and our 2009 EPS estimate, in line with peers.

## Qualitative Risk Assessment

| LOW | MEDIUM | HIGH |
|---|---|---|

Our risk assessment reflects PKI's broad product mix and diverse global client base. However, the company has been actively restructuring its business units and product portfolio, which we believe could increase operating risks.

## Quantitative Evaluations

**S&P Quality Ranking**  B

| D | C | B- | B | B+ | A- | A | A+ |
|---|---|---|---|---|---|---|---|

**Relative Strength Rank**  MODERATE

44

LOWEST = 1    HIGHEST = 99

## Revenue/Earnings Data

**Revenue (Million $)**

| | 1Q | 2Q | 3Q | 4Q | Year |
|---|---|---|---|---|---|
| 2008 | 482.3 | 528.6 | 505.1 | -- | -- |
| 2007 | 402.9 | 437.3 | 435.7 | 511.5 | 1,787 |
| 2006 | 355.5 | 377.0 | 386.9 | 427.0 | 1,546 |
| 2005 | 358.2 | 368.0 | 360.0 | 387.7 | 1,474 |
| 2004 | 392.6 | 412.6 | 403.4 | 478.6 | 1,687 |
| 2003 | 358.5 | 377.1 | 367.1 | 432.6 | 1,535 |

**Earnings Per Share ($)**

| | 1Q | 2Q | 3Q | 4Q | Year |
|---|---|---|---|---|---|
| 2008 | 0.20 | 0.27 | 0.37 | E0.47 | E1.46 |
| 2007 | 0.12 | 0.28 | 0.26 | 0.46 | 1.11 |
| 2006 | 0.17 | 0.21 | 0.23 | 0.33 | 0.94 |
| 2005 | 0.12 | 0.23 | 0.20 | -0.05 | 0.51 |
| 2004 | 0.11 | 0.17 | 0.19 | 0.29 | 0.75 |
| 2003 | 0.03 | 0.08 | 0.11 | 0.21 | 0.43 |

Fiscal year ended Dec. 31. Next earnings report expected: Late January. EPS Estimates based on S&P Operating Earnings; historical GAAP earnings are as reported.

## Dividend Data (Dates: mm/dd Payment Date: mm/dd/yy)

| Amount ($) | Date Decl. | Ex-Div. Date | Stk. of Record | Payment Date |
|---|---|---|---|---|
| 0.070 | 01/23 | 04/16 | 04/18 | 05/09/08 |
| 0.070 | 05/28 | 07/16 | 07/18 | 08/08/08 |
| 0.070 | 07/23 | 10/15 | 10/17 | 11/07/08 |
| 0.070 | 10/22 | 01/14 | 01/16 | 02/06/09 |

Dividends have been paid since 1965. Source: Company reports.

# PerkinElmer Inc.

STANDARD &POOR'S

## Business Summary October 30, 2008

CORPORATE OVERVIEW. PerkinElmer is a global technology company with operations in more than 125 countries. It develops, manufactures and provides scientific instruments, consumables and services to the pharmaceutical, biomedical, environmental testing and general industrial markets. Collectively, these markets are commonly referred to as the health sciences and industrial sciences markets. In 2005, PKI operated three business segments within its end markets: Life and Analytical Sciences, Optoelectronics, and Fluid Sciences. However, in 2005 and 2006, PKI divested its Fluid Sciences unit in an effort to focus on the health sciences market, which PKI believes has greater growth and profitability potential. The health sciences markets include all of the businesses in the Life and Analytical Sciences unit and the medical imaging, medical sensors and lighting business in the Optoelectronics unit. The industrial sciences markets include the remaining businesses in Optoelectronics.

Life and Analytical Sciences provides drug discovery, genetic screening, and environmental and chemical analysis tools, including instruments, reagents, consumables and services. Its instruments are used for scientific research and clinical applications. For drug discovery, PKI offers a wide range of in-

strumentation, software and consumables, including reagents, based on its core expertise in fluorescent, chemiluminescent and radioactive labeling, and the detection of nucleic acids and proteins. For genetic screening laboratories, it provides software, reagents and analysis tools to test for various inherited disorders. For chemical analysis, the company offers analytical tools employing technologies such as molecular and atomic spectroscopy, high-pressure liquid chromatography, gas chromatography and thermal analysis.

The Optoelectronics unit makes products that include digital imaging, sensor and specialty lighting components to customers in biomedical, consumer products and other specialty end markets. PKI supplies amorphous silicon digital X-ray detectors, a technology for medical imaging and radiation therapy. The company's specialty lighting technologies include xenon flashtubes, ceramic xenon light sources, and laser pump sources.

## Company Financials Fiscal Year Ended Dec. 31

### Per Share Data ($)

| | 2007 | 2006 | 2005 | 2004 | 2003 | 2002 | 2001 | 2000 | 1999 | 1998 |
|---|---|---|---|---|---|---|---|---|---|---|
| Tangible Book Value | NM | 0.45 | 1.91 | NM | NM | NM | NM | NM | NM | 0.92 |
| Cash Flow | 1.76 | 1.52 | 1.03 | 1.35 | 1.07 | 0.58 | 0.77 | 1.62 | 1.01 | 1.66 |
| Earnings | 1.11 | 0.94 | 0.51 | 0.75 | 0.43 | -0.03 | -0.01 | 1.32 | 0.31 | 1.11 |
| S&P Core Earnings | 1.03 | 0.91 | 0.40 | 0.63 | 0.25 | -0.34 | -0.68 | NA | NA | NA |
| Dividends | 0.28 | 0.28 | 0.28 | 0.28 | 0.28 | 0.28 | 0.28 | 0.28 | 0.28 | 0.28 |
| Payout Ratio | 25% | 30% | 55% | 37% | 65% | NM | NM | 21% | 92% | 25% |
| Prices:High | 30.00 | 24.17 | 24.02 | 23.28 | 18.71 | 36.30 | 52.31 | 60.50 | 22.50 | 16.88 |
| Prices:Low | 21.28 | 16.31 | 17.92 | 15.05 | 7.22 | 4.28 | 21.28 | 19.00 | 12.75 | 9.44 |
| P/E Ratio:High | 27 | 26 | 47 | 31 | 44 | NM | NM | 46 | 74 | 15 |
| P/E Ratio:Low | 19 | 17 | 35 | 20 | 17 | NM | NM | 14 | 42 | 9 |

### Income Statement Analysis (Million $)

| | 2007 | 2006 | 2005 | 2004 | 2003 | 2002 | 2001 | 2000 | 1999 | 1998 |
|---|---|---|---|---|---|---|---|---|---|---|
| Revenue | 1,787 | 1,546 | 1,474 | 1,687 | 1,535 | 1,505 | 1,330 | 1,695 | 1,363 | 1,408 |
| Operating Income | 249 | 221 | 229 | 253 | 211 | 131 | 196 | 263 | 177 | 144 |
| Depreciation | 78.0 | 69.2 | 67.0 | 76.2 | 80.2 | 76.6 | 80.5 | 79.1 | 66.1 | 50.4 |
| Interest Expense | 15.3 | 9.16 | 74.3 | 38.0 | Nil | Nil | Nil | Nil | 28.3 | 11.4 |
| Pretax Income | 151 | 151 | 66.7 | 137 | 80.9 | -8.55 | 34.2 | 144 | 44.9 | 156 |
| Effective Tax Rate | 11.5% | 21.5% | 0.19% | 28.2% | 32.0% | NM | NM | 40.4% | 36.8% | 34.6% |
| Net Income | 134 | 118 | 66.5 | 98.3 | 55.0 | -4.14 | -0.62 | 86.1 | 28.4 | 102 |
| S&P Core Earnings | 124 | 114 | 53.8 | 81.3 | 31.2 | -43.1 | -71.3 | NA | NA | NA |

### Balance Sheet & Other Financial Data (Million $)

| | 2007 | 2006 | 2005 | 2004 | 2003 | 2002 | 2001 | 2000 | 1999 | 1998 |
|---|---|---|---|---|---|---|---|---|---|---|
| Cash | 203 | 199 | 502 | 208 | 202 | 317 | 138 | 126 | 127 | 95.6 |
| Current Assets | 843 | 745 | 999 | 748 | 766 | 991 | 997 | 893 | 815 | 565 |
| Total Assets | 2,949 | 2,510 | 2,693 | 2,576 | 2,608 | 2,836 | 2,919 | 2,260 | 1,715 | 1,185 |
| Current Liabilities | 548 | 477 | 495 | 446 | 452 | 698 | 708 | 718 | 852 | 524 |
| Long Term Debt | 516 | 152 | 243 | 365 | 544 | 614 | 598 | 583 | 115 | 130 |
| Common Equity | 1,575 | 1,578 | 1,651 | 1,460 | 1,349 | 1,252 | 1,364 | 728 | 551 | 400 |
| Total Capital | 2,159 | 1,730 | 1,894 | 1,825 | 1,893 | 1,866 | 1,962 | 1,312 | 666 | 530 |
| Capital Expenditures | 47.0 | 44.5 | 25.1 | 19.0 | 16.6 | 37.8 | 88.7 | 70.6 | 41.1 | 46.5 |
| Cash Flow | 212 | 188 | 134 | 174 | 135 | 72.4 | 79.9 | 165 | 94.5 | 152 |
| Current Ratio | 1.5 | 1.6 | 2.0 | 1.7 | 1.7 | 1.4 | 1.4 | 1.2 | 1.0 | 1.1 |
| % Long Term Debt of Capitalization | 23.9 | 8.8 | 12.8 | 20.0 | 28.7 | 32.9 | 30.5 | 44.5 | 17.3 | 24.5 |
| % Net Income of Revenue | 7.5 | 7.7 | 4.5 | 5.8 | 3.6 | NM | NM | 5.1 | 2.1 | 7.2 |
| % Return on Assets | 4.9 | 4.5 | 2.5 | 3.8 | 2.0 | NM | NM | 4.3 | 2.0 | 10.1 |
| % Return on Equity | 8.5 | 7.3 | 4.3 | 7.0 | 4.2 | NM | NM | 13.5 | 6.0 | 28.0 |

Data as orig reptd.; bef. results of disc opers/spec. items. Per share data adj. for stk. divs.; EPS diluted. E-Estimated. NA-Not Available. NM-Not Meaningful. NR-Not Ranked. UR-Under Review.

Office: 940 Winter St, Wellesley, MA 02481-4008.
Telephone: 781-663-6900.
Website: http://www.perkinelmer.com
Chrmn: G.L. Summe

Pres & CEO: R.F. Friel
SVP & Chief Admin Officer: R.F. Walsh
SVP & CSO: D.R. Marshak
CFO, Chief Acctg Officer & Cntlr: M.L. Battles

Board Members: R. F. Friel, N. A. Lopardo, A. P. Michas, J. C. Mullen, V. L. Sato, G. Schmergel, K. J. Sicchitano, P. J. Sullivan, G. L. Summe, G. R. Tod

Founded: 1947
Domicile: Massachusetts
Employees: 8,700

# Pfizer Inc.

**STANDARD &POOR'S**

## S&P Recommendation HOLD ★★★☆☆

| Price | 12-Mo. Target Price | Investment Style |
|---|---|---|
| $16.28 (as of Nov 14, 2008) | $21.00 | Large-Cap Blend |

**GICS Sector** Health Care
**Sub-Industry** Pharmaceuticals

**Summary** The world's largest pharmaceutical company, Pfizer produces a wide range of drugs across a broad therapeutic spectrum.

## Key Stock Statistics (Source S&P, Vickers, company reports)

| | | | | | |
|---|---|---|---|---|---|
| 52-Wk Range | $24.50–14.31 | S&P Oper. EPS 2008E | 2.37 | Market Capitalization(B) | $109.775 |
| Trailing 12-Month EPS | $1.56 | S&P Oper. EPS 2009E | 2.52 | Yield (%) | 7.86 |
| Trailing 12-Month P/E | 10.4 | P/E on S&P Oper. EPS 2008E | 6.9 | Dividend Rate/Share | $1.28 |
| $10K Invested 5 Yrs Ago | $5,823 | Common Shares Outstg. (M) | 6,742.9 | Institutional Ownership (%) | 68 |

| | |
|---|---|
| Beta | 0.47 |
| S&P 3-Yr. Proj. EPS CAGR(%) | 6 |
| S&P Credit Rating | AAA |

## Price Performance

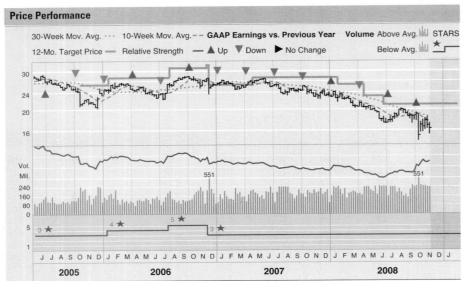

30-Week Mov. Avg. · · ·   10-Week Mov. Avg. – –   **GAAP Earnings vs. Previous Year**   Volume Above Avg. STARS
12-Mo. Target Price —   Relative Strength —   ▲ Up   ▼ Down   ► No Change   Below Avg. ★

Options: ASE, CBOE, P, Ph

Analysis prepared by **Herman B. Saftlas** on October 24, 2008, when the stock traded at **$ 16.55**.

## Qualitative Risk Assessment

| LOW | MEDIUM | HIGH |
|---|---|---|

Our risk assessment reflects PFE's leading position in the global pharmaceutical market, which we believe affords the company significant competitive advantages in terms of marketing and R&D. We also think PFE has unmatched financial flexibility in the pharmaceutical sector. However, we see these pluses offset by the effects of patent expirations and pipeline uncertainties.

## Quantitative Evaluations

### S&P Quality Ranking B+

| D | C | B- | B | B+ | A- | A | A+ |
|---|---|---|---|---|---|---|---|

### Relative Strength Rank STRONG

77

LOWEST = 1   HIGHEST = 99

## Revenue/Earnings Data

### Revenue (Million $)

| | 1Q | 2Q | 3Q | 4Q | Year |
|---|---|---|---|---|---|
| 2008 | 11,848 | 12,129 | 11,973 | -- | -- |
| 2007 | 12,474 | 11,084 | 11,990 | 12,870 | 48,418 |
| 2006 | 11,747 | 11,741 | 12,280 | 12,603 | 48,371 |
| 2005 | 13,091 | 12,425 | 12,189 | 13,592 | 51,298 |
| 2004 | 12,487 | 12,274 | 12,831 | 14,924 | 52,516 |
| 2003 | 8,525 | 9,993 | 12,504 | 14,167 | 45,188 |

### Earnings Per Share ($)

| | | | | | |
|---|---|---|---|---|---|
| 2008 | 0.41 | 0.41 | 0.33 | E0.59 | E2.37 |
| 2007 | 0.48 | 0.19 | 0.12 | 0.40 | 1.18 |
| 2006 | 0.55 | 0.31 | 0.44 | 0.21 | 1.52 |
| 2005 | 0.04 | 0.47 | 0.22 | 0.37 | 1.09 |
| 2004 | 0.30 | 0.38 | 0.43 | 0.39 | 1.49 |
| 2003 | 0.40 | -0.49 | 0.29 | 0.08 | 0.22 |

Fiscal year ended Dec. 31. Next earnings report expected: Late January. EPS Estimates based on S&P Operating Earnings; historical GAAP earnings are as reported.

## Highlights

➤ We expect revenues in 2009 to increase slightly from the $48.5 billion that we estimate for 2008. Despite likely less favorable foreign exchange, we believe the 2009 top line should benefit from reduced overall generic erosion, growth in newer lines such as Lyrica treatment for neuropathic pain and Sutent anticancer therapy. Boosted by a new fibromyalgia indication, we expect Lyrica sales to increase 15% in 2009. We also see modest gains in Lipitor cholesterol-lowering drug and Celebrex arthritis therapy, helped by higher prices. Alliance revenues and animal health sales should also increase. Sales of Norvasc, now off patent, are expected to decline sharply.

➤ We think gross margins will improve modestly, helped by cost efficiencies. SG&A and R&D spending should also show further declines under PFE's aggressive ongoing cost reduction program, which is expected to yield savings of up to $2.0 billion by the end of 2008.

➤ Helped by common share buybacks, we project operating EPS of $2.52 in 2009, up from the $2.37 that we estimate for 2008.

## Investment Rationale/Risk

➤ PFE recently reached an agreement with generic drugmaker Ranbaxy delaying that company's U.S. launch of a generic version of Lipitor until the end of November 2011. We had been expecting generics in the first half of 2010. We believe this deal adds cash flow and eases near-term dividend jitters. However, we think PFE still faces a major patent cliff in 2011-2013, as well as safety concerns on several recent launches and a relatively sparse late-stage pipeline. On the plus side, PFE has a cost restructuring program designed to yield up to $2 billion in savings by the end of 2008. We believe stability of the $1.28 dividend is a high priority, and PFE will continue to adjust costs to maintain it.

➤ Risks to our recommendation and target price include competitive pressures in key drug lines, and possible pipeline setbacks.

➤ Our 12-month target price of $21 applies a below-peers P/E of about 8.9X to our 2008 EPS estimate. Our target price is also close to our calculation of intrinsic value, derived from our DCF model, which assumes a WACC of 7.2% and a terminal growth rate of 1%.

## Dividend Data (Dates: mm/dd Payment Date: mm/dd/yy)

| Amount ($) | Date Decl. | Ex-Div. Date | Stk. of Record | Payment Date |
|---|---|---|---|---|
| 0.320 | 12/17 | 02/06 | 02/08 | 03/04/08 |
| 0.320 | 04/24 | 05/07 | 05/09 | 06/03/08 |
| 0.320 | 06/26 | 08/06 | 08/08 | 09/03/08 |
| 0.320 | 10/23 | 11/05 | 11/07 | 12/02/08 |

Dividends have been paid since 1901. Source: Company reports.

The McGraw-Hill Companies

# Pfizer Inc.

STANDARD
&POOR'S

## Business Summary October 24, 2008

CORPORATE OVERVIEW. Pfizer stands out above its peers in the $670 billion global pharmaceutical sector, in our opinion. Growth over the past 10 years was largely augmented by two major acquisitions -- Warner-Lambert Co. in 2000 and Pharmacia Corp. in 2003 -- as well as by in-licensed products. In December 2006, PFE sold its consumer health care products business (sales of $3.9 billion in 2005) to Johnson & Johnson for $16.6 billion in cash.

MARKET PROFILE. Worldwide pharmaceutical industry revenue growth has slowed in recent years, reflecting the effects of tighter reimbursements from key managed care markets, the loss of patent protection on blockbuster drugs, and relatively sluggish new product flow stemming from reduced R&D productivity. IMS Health projects that the global drug market will grow 5%-6% in 2008, from $712 billion in 2007. For the U.S. and Europe's top five markets, IMS estimates market growth of 4%-5% in 2008.

COMPETITIVE LANDSCAPE. We think Pfizer's size gives it important competitive advantages over peers, especially in terms of marketing prowess in managed care and Medicare markets. In our opinion, the company's size and financial resources also empower it with a greater ability to make acquisitions and form strategic alliances with smaller pharmaceutical and biotechnology companies. Pfizer's drug portfolio is unmatched in terms of breadth and depth in the global drug market, by our analysis. Foreign sales accounted for 52% of total revenues in 2007.

Principal cardiovasculars include Lipitor, the world's largest-selling cholesterol-lowering agent as well as the biggest drug in any therapeutic category in 2007 (sales of $12.7 billion in 2007), and antihypertensives such as off-patent Norvasc ($3.0 billion), and Caduet ($568 million), a combination of Lipitor and Norvasc. Infectious disease drugs consist of Zyvox ($944 million), a treatment for severe bacterial infections, and Vfend ($632 million), an antifungal. Key central nervous system medicines include Lyrica, a treatment for nerve pain and epileptic seizures ($1.8 billion); and Geodon, an antipsychotic ($854 million).

## Company Financials Fiscal Year Ended Dec. 31

| Per Share Data ($) | 2007 | 2006 | 2005 | 2004 | 2003 | 2002 | 2001 | 2000 | 1999 | 1998 |
|---|---|---|---|---|---|---|---|---|---|---|
| Tangible Book Value | 4.93 | 3.65 | 1.91 | 1.48 | 0.85 | 3.04 | 2.64 | 2.26 | 2.11 | 2.06 |
| Cash Flow | 1.93 | 2.24 | 1.84 | 2.16 | 0.78 | 1.64 | 1.39 | 0.74 | 0.96 | 0.63 |
| Earnings | 1.18 | 1.52 | 1.09 | 1.49 | 0.22 | 1.47 | 1.22 | 0.59 | 0.82 | 0.49 |
| S&P Core Earnings | 1.14 | 1.53 | 1.02 | 1.45 | 0.29 | 1.35 | 1.09 | NA | NA | NA |
| Dividends | 1.16 | 0.96 | 0.76 | 0.68 | 0.60 | 0.52 | 0.44 | 0.36 | 0.31 | 0.25 |
| Payout Ratio | 98% | 63% | 70% | 46% | 273% | 35% | 36% | 61% | 37% | 51% |
| Prices:High | 27.73 | 28.60 | 29.21 | 38.89 | 36.92 | 42.46 | 46.75 | 49.25 | 50.04 | 42.98 |
| Prices:Low | 22.24 | 22.16 | 20.27 | 21.99 | 27.90 | 25.13 | 34.00 | 30.00 | 31.54 | 23.69 |
| P/E Ratio:High | 23 | 19 | 27 | 26 | NM | 29 | 38 | 83 | 61 | 87 |
| P/E Ratio:Low | 19 | 15 | 19 | 15 | NM | 17 | 28 | 51 | 38 | 48 |

| Income Statement Analysis (Million $) | 2007 | 2006 | 2005 | 2004 | 2003 | 2002 | 2001 | 2000 | 1999 | 1998 |
|---|---|---|---|---|---|---|---|---|---|---|
| Revenue | 48,418 | 48,371 | 51,298 | 52,516 | 45,188 | 32,373 | 32,259 | 29,574 | 16,204 | 13,544 |
| Operating Income | 19,983 | 19,575 | 20,501 | 22,117 | 17,061 | 13,436 | 12,147 | 9,758 | 5,091 | 4,092 |
| Depreciation | 5,200 | 5,293 | 5,576 | 5,093 | 4,078 | 1,036 | 1,068 | 968 | 542 | 489 |
| Interest Expense | 440 | 488 | 488 | 359 | 290 | 279 | 432 | 401 | 236 | 143 |
| Pretax Income | 9,278 | 13,028 | 11,534 | 14,007 | 3,263 | 11,796 | 10,329 | 5,781 | 4,448 | 2,594 |
| Effective Tax Rate | 11.0% | 15.3% | 29.7% | 19.0% | 49.7% | 22.1% | 24.8% | 35.4% | 28.0% | 24.7% |
| Net Income | 8,213 | 11,024 | 8,094 | 11,332 | 1,639 | 9,181 | 7,752 | 3,718 | 3,199 | 1,950 |
| S&P Core Earnings | 7,963 | 11,048 | 7,588 | 11,030 | 2,147 | 8,441 | 6,862 | NA | NA | NA |

| Balance Sheet & Other Financial Data (Million $) | 2007 | 2006 | 2005 | 2004 | 2003 | 2002 | 2001 | 2000 | 1999 | 1998 |
|---|---|---|---|---|---|---|---|---|---|---|
| Cash | 25,475 | 1,827 | 2,247 | 1,808 | 1,520 | 1,878 | 1,036 | 1,099 | 739 | 1,552 |
| Current Assets | 46,849 | 46,949 | 41,896 | 39,694 | 29,741 | 24,781 | 18,450 | 17,187 | 11,191 | 9,931 |
| Total Assets | 115,268 | 114,837 | 117,565 | 123,684 | 116,775 | 46,356 | 39,153 | 33,510 | 20,574 | 18,302 |
| Current Liabilities | 21,835 | 21,389 | 28,448 | 26,458 | 23,657 | 18,555 | 13,640 | 11,981 | 9,185 | 7,192 |
| Long Term Debt | 7,314 | 5,546 | 6,347 | 7,279 | 5,755 | 3,140 | 2,609 | 1,123 | 525 | 527 |
| Common Equity | 64,917 | 71,217 | 65,458 | 68,085 | 65,158 | 19,950 | 18,293 | 16,076 | 8,887 | 8,810 |
| Total Capital | 80,134 | 84,919 | 82,214 | 88,189 | 84,370 | 23,454 | 21,354 | 17,579 | 9,713 | 9,534 |
| Capital Expenditures | 1,880 | 2,050 | 2,106 | 2,601 | 2,641 | 1,758 | 2,203 | 2,191 | 1,561 | 1,198 |
| Cash Flow | 13,409 | 16,317 | 13,661 | 16,417 | 5,710 | 10,217 | 8,820 | 4,686 | 3,741 | 2,484 |
| Current Ratio | 2.2 | 2.2 | 1.5 | 1.5 | 1.3 | 1.3 | 1.4 | 1.4 | 1.2 | 1.4 |
| % Long Term Debt of Capitalization | 9.1 | 6.5 | 7.7 | 8.3 | 6.8 | 13.4 | 12.2 | 6.4 | 5.4 | 5.5 |
| % Net Income of Revenue | 17.0 | 22.8 | 15.8 | 21.6 | 3.6 | 28.4 | 24.0 | 12.6 | 19.7 | 14.4 |
| % Return on Assets | 7.1 | 9.5 | 6.7 | 9.4 | 2.0 | 21.5 | 21.3 | 11.5 | 16.5 | 11.6 |
| % Return on Equity | 12.1 | 16.1 | 12.1 | 17.0 | 3.8 | 48.0 | 45.1 | 24.8 | 36.2 | 23.3 |

Data as orig reptd.; bef. results of disc opers/spec. items. Per share data adj. for stk. divs.; EPS diluted. E-Estimated. NA-Not Available. NM-Not Meaningful. NR-Not Ranked. UR-Under Review.

**Office:** 235 East 42nd Street, New York, NY 10017-5703.
**Telephone:** 212-573-2323.
**Website:** http://www.pfizer.com
**Chrmn & CEO:** J.B. Kindler

**SVP & CFO:** F. D'Amelio
**SVP & Secy:** M.M. Foran
**SVP & General Counsel:** A.W. Schulman
**Chief Acctg Officer & Cntlr:** L.V. Cangialosi

**Investor Contact:** J. Davis (212-733-0717)
**Board Members:** D. A. Ausiello, M. S. Brown, M. A. Burns, R. N. Burt, W. D. Cornwell, W. H. Gray, III, C. J. Horner, W. R. Howell, S. N. Johnson, J. M. Kilts, J. B. Kindler, G. A. Lorch, D. G. Mead, W. C. Steere, Jr.

**Founded:** 1849
**Domicile:** Delaware
**Employees:** 86,600

**STANDARD &POOR'S**

# PG&E Corp

| S&P Recommendation | HOLD ★★★☆☆ | Price $37.21 (as of Nov 14, 2008) | 12-Mo. Target Price $37.00 | Investment Style Large-Cap Blend |
|---|---|---|---|---|

**GICS Sector** Utilities
**Sub-Industry** Multi-Utilities

**Summary** This energy holding company is the parent of Pacific Gas & Electric Co., which emerged from a bankruptcy reorganization in April 2004.

## Key Stock Statistics (Source S&P, Vickers, company reports)

| | | | | | | | |
|---|---|---|---|---|---|---|---|
| 52-Wk Range | $47.61–26.67 | S&P Oper. EPS 2008E | 2.92 | Market Capitalization(B) | $13.432 | Beta | 0.84 |
| Trailing 12-Month EPS | $2.81 | S&P Oper. EPS 2009E | 3.20 | Yield (%) | 4.19 | S&P 3-Yr. Proj. EPS CAGR(%) | 6 |
| Trailing 12-Month P/E | 13.2 | P/E on S&P Oper. EPS 2008E | 12.7 | Dividend Rate/Share | $1.56 | S&P Credit Rating | NR |
| $10K Invested 5 Yrs Ago | $17,566 | Common Shares Outstg. (M) | 361.0 | Institutional Ownership (%) | 68 | | |

## Price Performance

30-Week Mov. Avg. · · · · 10-Week Mov. Avg. - - · — GAAP Earnings vs. Previous Year    Volume Above Avg. STARS

12-Mo. Target Price — Relative Strength    ▲ Up ▼ Down ► No Change    Below Avg.

Options: ASE, CBOE, P

Analysis prepared by **Justin McCann** on October 20, 2008, when the stock traded at **$ 33.01**.

### Highlights

➤ We expect 2008 operating EPS to rise about 5% from 2007 operating EPS of $2.78, which grew 8.2% from 2006 operating EPS of $2.57. In the first half of 2008, operating EPS declined about 2% to $1.42, reflecting expenses related to severe storms in January and a refueling outage at the Diablo Canyon nuclear facility.

➤ For 2009, we expect operating EPS to grow about 8% from anticipated results in 2008. We believe the increase will be primarily driven by higher electric revenues resulting from Pacific Gas & Electric's pre-approved rate base transmission and generation investments.

➤ In March 2007, the CPUC approved a multi-party settlement resolving the 2007 General Rate Case for Pacific Gas & Electric (PG&E). The decision authorized a $222 million increase (to about $2.9 billion) for PG&E's electric distribution business, a $21 million increase (to around $1 billion) for its natural gas distribution segment, and a decrease of $30 million (to approximately $1 billion) for its electric generation operations. The net 4.5% increase, to about $4.9 billion, was made retroactively effective to January 1, 2007, and the new rates will remain in effect through the end of 2010.

### Investment Rationale/Risk

➤ The stock is down more than 25% year to date, reflecting, in our view, concerns over the crisis in the credit markets and an economic slowdown, which have hurt both the broader market and the utility sector. Although the shares have underperformed over the past two years and have been trading at a more than 11% discount to the peer average P/E (based on our 2008 EPS estimate), we expect the stock to perform more in line with the company's electric and gas utility peers over the next 12 months.

➤ Risks to our recommendation and target price include a much worse than expected earnings performance, and/or a major decline in the average P/E multiple of the group as a whole.

➤ The decline in the shares has reduced the P/E from about 15.6X our EPS estimate for 2008 in early December to around 12.5X our forecast. Given this decline and the recent increase in the dividend, the yield from the dividend has grown from about 3.1% to approximately 5.1%. However, the spread with the recent peer yield (which increased from 3.5% to around 5.5%) has remained essentially the same. Our 12-month target price is $37, reflecting a discount-to-peers P/E of 11.6X our 2009 estimate.

## Qualitative Risk Assessment

| LOW | MEDIUM | HIGH |
|---|---|---|

Our risk assessment reflects our view of the company's: strong and steady cash flow from the regulated Pacific Gas & Electric subsidiary; a much improved balance sheet and credit profile; a healthy economy in its service territory; and a greatly improved regulatory environment.

## Quantitative Evaluations

**S&P Quality Ranking**　　　　　　**B**

| D | C | B- | B | B+ | A- | A | A+ |
|---|---|---|---|---|---|---|---|

**Relative Strength Rank**　　　　**STRONG**

93

LOWEST = 1　　　　　　　　　　HIGHEST = 99

## Revenue/Earnings Data

**Revenue (Million $)**

| | 1Q | 2Q | 3Q | 4Q | Year |
|---|---|---|---|---|---|
| 2008 | 3,733 | 3,578 | 3,674 | -- | -- |
| 2007 | 3,356 | 3,187 | 3,279 | 3,415 | 13,237 |
| 2006 | 3,148 | 3,017 | 3,168 | 3,206 | 12,539 |
| 2005 | 2,669 | 2,498 | 2,804 | 3,732 | 11,703 |
| 2004 | 2,722 | 2,749 | 2,623 | 2,986 | 11,080 |
| 2003 | 2,065 | 2,729 | 3,103 | 2,538 | 10,435 |

**Earnings Per Share (Can. $)**

| | 1Q | 2Q | 3Q | 4Q | Year |
|---|---|---|---|---|---|
| 2008 | 0.62 | 0.80 | 0.83 | E0.67 | E2.92 |
| 2007 | 0.71 | 0.74 | 0.77 | 0.56 | 2.78 |
| 2006 | 0.60 | 0.65 | 1.09 | 0.43 | 2.76 |
| 2005 | 0.54 | 0.70 | 0.62 | 0.49 | 2.34 |
| 2004 | 7.15 | 0.88 | 0.53 | 0.44 | 8.97 |
| 2003 | -0.21 | 0.81 | 1.24 | 0.09 | 1.96 |

Fiscal year ended Dec. 31. Next earnings report expected: NA. EPS Estimates based on S&P Operating Earnings; historical GAAP earnings are as reported.

## Dividend Data (Dates: mm/dd Payment Date: mm/dd/yy)

| Amount (Can. $) | Date Decl. | Ex-Div. Date | Stk. of Record | Payment Date |
|---|---|---|---|---|
| 0.360 | 12/19 | 12/27 | 12/31 | 01/15/08 |
| 0.390 | 02/22 | 03/27 | 03/31 | 04/15/08 |
| 0.390 | 06/18 | 06/26 | 06/30 | 07/15/08 |
| 0.390 | 09/17 | 09/26 | 09/30 | 10/15/08 |

Dividends have been paid since 2005. Source: Company reports.

# PG&E Corp

STANDARD
&POOR'S

## Business Summary October 20, 2008

CORPORATE OVERVIEW. PG&E Corporation (PCG) is an energy-based holding company that conducts its business through Pacific Gas and Electric Company, a public utility operating in northern and central California. The utility's business consists of four main operational units: electricity and natural gas distribution, electricity generation, gas transmission, and electricity transmission. The utility is primarily regulated by the California Public Utilities Commission (CPUC) and the Federal Energy Regulatory Commission (FERC).

CORPORATE STRATEGY. In order to support anticipated customer growth and the improvement of its existing services, Pacific Gas & Electric plans to make major capital additions to its infrastructure. During 2008, it expects to connect about 65,000 new electric customers and around 51,000 new gas customers. The utility is also devoting substantial resources to the building and expansion of its transmission lines, which has become the fastest growing part of its business. It has proposed constructing additional gas and electric transmission arteries so as to create access to new supplies of renewable energy and new sources of natural gas. In addition to maintaining its ongoing investment in its existing hydroelectric and nuclear, the company is planning to build three new state-of-the-art power plants that are scheduled to come on line between 2009 and 2010, and to generate enough power for around 950,000 homes.

MARKET PROFILE. PG&E's electricity and gas distribution network covers 70,000 square miles and 47 out of the 58 counties in California. The utility served approximately 5.1 electricity distribution customers and about 4.2 million natural gas distribution customers as of December 31, 2006. In 2006, residential customers accounted for 41.% of electric utility revenues; commercial, 40.8%; industrial, 11.9%; agricultural, 4.5%; and other, 1.3%. Residential customers accounted for 64.7% of natural gas revenues in 2006; commercial, 22.7%; and other, 12.6%. As of December 31, 2006, the company had $34.4 billion in total assets.

## Company Financials Fiscal Year Ended Dec. 31

| Per Share Data ($) | 2007 | 2006 | 2005 | 2004 | 2003 | 2002 | 2001 | 2000 | 1999 | 1998 |
|---|---|---|---|---|---|---|---|---|---|---|
| Tangible Book Value | 25.80 | 20.89 | 19.67 | 20.60 | 10.11 | 8.92 | 11.87 | 8.74 | 19.13 | 21.06 |
| Earnings | 2.78 | 2.76 | 2.34 | 8.97 | 1.96 | -0.15 | 2.99 | -9.18 | 0.04 | 1.88 |
| S&P Core Earnings | 2.53 | 2.64 | 2.45 | 9.00 | 2.05 | -1.08 | 1.59 | NA | NA | NA |
| Dividends | 1.44 | 1.32 | 1.23 | Nil | Nil | Nil | Nil | 1.20 | 1.20 | 1.20 |
| Payout Ratio | 52% | 48% | 53% | Nil | Nil | Nil | Nil | NM | NM | 64% |
| Prices:High | 52.17 | 48.17 | 40.10 | 34.46 | 27.98 | 23.75 | 20.94 | 31.81 | 34.00 | 35.06 |
| Prices:Low | 42.58 | 36.25 | 31.83 | 25.90 | 11.69 | 8.00 | 6.50 | 17.00 | 20.25 | 29.06 |
| P/E Ratio:High | 19 | 17 | 17 | 4 | 14 | NM | 7 | NM | NM | 19 |
| P/E Ratio:Low | 15 | 13 | 14 | 3 | 6 | NM | 2 | NM | NM | 15 |

| Income Statement Analysis (Million Can. $) | 2007 | 2006 | 2005 | 2004 | 2003 | 2002 | 2001 | 2000 | 1999 | 1998 |
|---|---|---|---|---|---|---|---|---|---|---|
| Revenue | 13,237 | 12,539 | 11,703 | 11,080 | 10,435 | 12,495 | 22,959 | 26,232 | 20,820 | 19,942 |
| Depreciation | 1,770 | 1,709 | 1,735 | 1,497 | 1,222 | 1,309 | 1,068 | 3,659 | 1,780 | 1,609 |
| Maintenance | NA | NA | NA | NA | NA | NA | NA | NA | NA | NA |
| Fixed Charges Coverage | 3.03 | 3.09 | 3.48 | 2.75 | 2.23 | 2.94 | 2.48 | 3.01 | 2.99 | 2.65 |
| Construction Credits | NA | NA | NA | NA | NA | NA | NA | NA | Nil | Nil |
| Effective Tax Rate | 34.9% | 35.9% | 37.6% | 39.2% | 36.7% | NM | 35.8% | NM | 95.0% | 44.2% |
| Net Income | 1,006 | 991 | 904 | 3,820 | 791 | -57.0 | 1,090 | -3,324 | 13.0 | 719 |
| S&P Core Earnings | 940 | 972 | 974 | 3,828 | 830 | -404 | 580 | NA | NA | NA |

| Balance Sheet & Other Financial Data (Million Can. $) | 2007 | 2006 | 2005 | 2004 | 2003 | 2002 | 2001 | 2000 | 1999 | 1998 |
|---|---|---|---|---|---|---|---|---|---|---|
| Gross Property | 36,584 | 34,214 | 32,030 | 30,509 | 29,222 | 31,179 | 33,012 | 28,469 | 28,067 | 29,844 |
| Capital Expenditures | 2,769 | 2,402 | 1,804 | 1,559 | 1,698 | 3,032 | 2,665 | 1,758 | 1,584 | 1,619 |
| Net Property | 23,656 | 21,785 | 19,955 | 18,989 | 18,107 | 16,928 | 19,167 | 16,591 | 16,776 | 17,633 |
| Capitalization:Long Term Debt | 10,005 | 8,885 | 9,794 | 8,311 | 9,924 | 11,590 | 9,527 | 5,516 | 9,484 | 10,523 |
| Capitalization:% Long Term Debt | 53.9 | 53.2 | 57.5 | 49.0 | 70.2 | 76.2 | 68.8 | 63.5 | 57.9 | 56.6 |
| Capitalization:Preferred | Nil | Nil | Nil | Nil | Nil | Nil | Nil | Nil | Nil | Nil |
| Capitalization:% Preferred | Nil | Nil | Nil | Nil | Nil | Nil | Nil | Nil | Nil | Nil |
| Capitalization:Common | 8,553 | 7,811 | 7,240 | 8,633 | 4,215 | 3,613 | 4,322 | 3,172 | 6,886 | 8,066 |
| Capitalization:% Common | 46.1 | 46.8 | 42.5 | 51.0 | 29.8 | 23.8 | 31.2 | 36.5 | 42.1 | 43.4 |
| Total Capital | 21,611 | 19,642 | 20,238 | 20,596 | 15,122 | 16,786 | 15,668 | 10,536 | 19,748 | 22,733 |
| % Operating Ratio | 88.1 | 87.6 | 87.8 | 102.2 | 80.4 | 67.2 | 90.3 | 84.1 | 90.9 | 92.8 |
| % Earned on Net Property | 9.3 | 10.1 | 10.1 | 38.4 | 14.6 | 31.2 | 15.0 | 34.7 | 5.1 | 5.0 |
| % Return on Revenue | 7.6 | 7.9 | 7.7 | 34.5 | 7.6 | NM | 4.7 | NM | 0.1 | 3.6 |
| % Return on Invested Capital | 8.6 | 8.7 | 7.3 | 15.6 | 13.9 | 22.8 | 16.7 | 29.1 | 9.7 | 6.4 |
| % Return on Common Equity | 12.3 | 13.2 | 11.4 | 59.5 | 20.2 | NM | 29.1 | NM | 0.2 | 8.5 |

Data as orig reptd.; bef. results of disc opers/spec. items. Per share data adj. for stk. divs.; EPS diluted. E-Estimated. NA-Not Available. NM-Not Meaningful. NR-Not Ranked. UR-Under Review.

**Office:** 1 Mkt Spear Tower St Ste 2400, San Francisco, CA 94105-1415.
**Telephone:** 415-267-7000.
**Email:** invrel@pg-corp.com
**Website:** http://www.pgecorp.com

**Chrmn, Pres & CEO:** P.A. Darbee
**SVP, CFO, Chief Acctg Officer & Treas:** C.P. Johns
**SVP & General Counsel:** H. Park
**Secy:** L.Y. Cheng

**Investor Contact:** L.Y. Cheng (415-267-7070)
**Board Members:** D. R. Andrews, C. L. Cox, P. A. Darbee, M. C. Herringer, R. A. Meserve, M. S. Metz, B. L. Rambo, B. L. Williams

**Founded:** 1995
**Domicile:** California
**Employees:** 20,050

# Philip Morris Intl

## STANDARD &POOR'S

| S&P Recommendation | BUY ★★★★☆ | Price $38.41 (as of Nov 14, 2008) | 12-Mo. Target Price $49.00 | Investment Style Large-Cap Blend |
| --- | --- | --- | --- | --- |

**GICS Sector** Consumer Staples
**Sub-Industry** Tobacco

**Summary** This company, comprising the international operations recently spun off by Altria, is the largest publicly traded manufacturer and marketer of tobacco products.

## Key Stock Statistics (Source S&P, Vickers, company reports)

| | | | | | | | |
| --- | --- | --- | --- | --- | --- | --- | --- |
| 52-Wk Range | $56.26– 33.30 | S&P Oper. EPS 2008**E** | 3.36 | Market Capitalization(B) | $77.705 | Beta | NA |
| Trailing 12-Month EPS | $3.33 | S&P Oper. EPS 2009**E** | 3.78 | Yield (%) | 5.62 | S&P 3-Yr. Proj. EPS CAGR(%) | 12 |
| Trailing 12-Month P/E | 11.5 | P/E on S&P Oper. EPS 2008**E** | 11.4 | Dividend Rate/Share | $2.16 | S&P Credit Rating | NA |
| $10K Invested 5 Yrs Ago | NA | Common Shares Outstg. (M) | 2,023.0 | Institutional Ownership (%) | 70 | | |

## Price Performance

30-Week Mov. Avg. · · · · 10-Week Mov. Avg. – – – **GAAP Earnings vs. Previous Year** Volume Above Avg. STARS
12-Mo. Target Price — Relative Strength — ▲ Up ▼ Down ► No Change Below Avg. ★

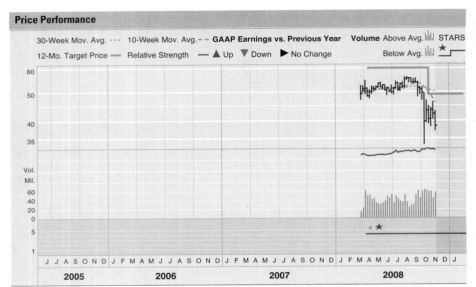

Options: ASE, CBOE, Ph

Analysis prepared by **Esther Y. Kwon, CFA** on October 23, 2008, when the stock traded at **$ 42.20**.

## Highlights

➤ In 2008, we project net revenue growth near 13% on flat to slightly lower volumes and positive foreign exchange and pricing. With growing health concerns, smoking bans and higher taxes, we look for a single digit percentage decline in consumption in Western Europe, offset by growth in emerging markets. We forecast over 7% net revenue growth in 2009.

➤ With its spin-off, PM embarked on an extensive three-year cost reduction program, which we calculate will widen operating margins on net savings of about $1 billion. Operations planning, procurement and supply chain initiatives, along with productivity savings through elimination of less profitable SKUs and streamlining of product specifications, should account for the majority of the savings, with the consolidation of common functions and back office operations accounting for the remainder. PM recently acquired Rothmans Inc., which we see being modestly accretive to 2009 EPS.

➤ On an effective tax rate of 29.5%, we project 2008 operating EPS of $3.36, up 20% from 2007's $2.79. For 2009, on a slightly lower tax rate, we estimate EPS of $3.78. Over two years, we look for share repurchases of at least $13 billion.

## Investment Rationale/Risk

➤ Separated from operations in the U.S. and the regulatory and litigation risk of that market, PM will, in our view, be better positioned to innovate, tailor offerings to higher growth emerging markets, achieve cost savings, and incentivize managers. We think PM's low penetration of markets with potentially high cigarette consumption, such as China, India and Vietnam, also provides attractive opportunities. In addition, the spin-off provided PM with currency for acquisitions. We believe its high cash flow generation is supportive of regular stock repurchases and its indicated dividend yield above 5%.

➤ Risks to our recommendation and target price include execution risk, higher than expected excise taxes or regulatory constraints, greater than expected price competition, and commodity cost inflation.

➤ Our 12-month target price of $49 is based on a blend of comparative and historical forward P/E and EV/EBITDA multiples. Considering PM's scale, growth prospects and brand equity, we believe a premium to its international tobacco peers, but a discount to global consumer products companies, is appropriate, and we assign about a 13X P/E to our 2009 EPS of $3.78.

## Qualitative Risk Assessment

| LOW | MEDIUM | HIGH |
| --- | --- | --- |

Our risk assessment reflects the geographic diversity of the company's operations and end-markets and its participation in a generally stable industry, producing ample free cash flow. Health concerns, excise tax increases, extensive regulation and, to some extent, litigation have limited the growth prospects for the industry, but have also kept barriers to entry high.

## Quantitative Evaluations

**S&P Quality Ranking**      NR

| D | C | B- | B | B+ | A- | A | A+ |
| --- | --- | --- | --- | --- | --- | --- | --- |

**Relative Strength Rank**      MODERATE

60

LOWEST = 1          HIGHEST = 99

## Revenue/Earnings Data

### Revenue (Million $)

| | 1Q | 2Q | 3Q | 4Q | Year |
| --- | --- | --- | --- | --- | --- |
| 2008 | 6,330 | 6,709 | 6,953 | -- | -- |
| 2007 | -- | -- | -- | -- | 22,798 |
| 2006 | -- | -- | -- | -- | -- |
| 2005 | -- | -- | -- | -- | -- |
| 2004 | -- | -- | -- | -- | -- |
| 2003 | -- | -- | -- | -- | -- |

### Earnings Per Share ($)

| | 1Q | 2Q | 3Q | 4Q | Year |
| --- | --- | --- | --- | --- | --- |
| 2008 | 0.89 | 0.80 | 1.01 | E0.68 | E3.36 |
| 2007 | -- | -- | -- | 9.15 | 40.17 |
| 2006 | -- | -- | -- | -- | -- |
| 2005 | -- | -- | -- | -- | -- |
| 2004 | -- | -- | -- | -- | -- |
| 2003 | -- | -- | -- | -- | -- |

Fiscal year ended Dec. 31. Next earnings report expected: NA. EPS Estimates based on S&P Operating Earnings; historical GAAP earnings are as reported.

## Dividend Data (Dates: mm/dd Payment Date: mm/dd/yy)

| Amount ($) | Date Decl. | Ex-Div. Date | Stk. of Record | Payment Date |
| --- | --- | --- | --- | --- |
| 0.460 | 06/18 | 06/26 | 06/30 | 07/10/08 |
| 0.540 | 08/29 | 09/11 | 09/15 | 10/10/08 |

Dividends have been paid since 2008. Source: Company reports.

---

**Please read the Required Disclosures and Analyst Certification on the last page of this report.**

The McGraw·Hill Companies

# Philip Morris Intl

STANDARD
&POOR'S

## Business Summary October 23, 2008

CORPORATE OVERVIEW. Philip Morris International is the world's largest publicly traded manufacturer and marketer of tobacco products, with a 15.6% share of 2007 international market volumes, according to Philip Morris estimates. PM sold 850 billion cigarettes in 2007, with the Marlboro brand contributing about 37% of total PM volume. Other brands include L&M, Parliament, Virginia Slims, Muratti and Chesterfield; low price brands such as Bond Street, Red & White and Next; and local brands such as Diana, Petra, f6, Assos and Delicados.

The geographic breakdown of 2007 revenue was as follows: European Union 48.5%; Eastern Europe, Middle East & Africa 22%; Asia 20%; and Latin America 9%. Adjusted operating margins (on revenues minus excise taxes) were highest in the European Union at 48.9%, followed by Eastern Europe, Middle East & Africa (38.4%), Asia (32.4%), and Latin America (27%)

CORPORATE STRATEGY. Philip Morris International's strategy for growth includes both organic growth and acquisition. Using its existing brands, PM plans to introduce new packaging, new blends and other line extensions across its portfolio and in existing and new markets. It sees four major markets -- China, India, Bangladesh and Vietnam -- where it has little or no presence and which account for approximately 40% of total international cigarette

consumption as opportunities. We estimate China alone accounts for about one-third of the total market. Additionally, PM plans on spending about half of its R&D budget to develop next generation products that meet consumer preferences and that could cause less harm than traditional tobacco products.

PM also plans to evaluate potential acquisitions and other business development opportunities. In September 2008, it acquired Rothmans Inc., Canada's second largest tobacco company, for C$2.0 billion.

Acquisitions in 2007 included the acquisition of an additional stake in a Pakistan cigarette manufacturer, Lakson Tobacco Company, and an additional stake in its Mexican tobacco business from Group Carso. In addition, PM reached an agreement with the China National Tobacco Corporation in 2005 for the licensed production of Marlboro in China and the establishment of an international joint venture to support the distribution of a portfolio of Chinese brands in international markets and explore other business development opportunities.

## Company Financials Fiscal Year Ended Dec. 31

| Per Share Data ($) | 2007 | 2006 | 2005 | 2004 | 2003 | 2002 | 2001 | 2000 | 1999 | 1998 |
|---|---|---|---|---|---|---|---|---|---|---|
| Tangible Book Value | 2.31 | NA | NA | NA | NA | NA | NA | NA | NA | NA |
| Cash Flow | 3.10 | NA | NA | NA | NA | NA | NA | NA | NA | NA |
| Earnings | 2.75 | 40.97 | 37.47 | 30.47 | NA | NA | NA | NA | NA | NA |
| S&P Core Earnings | 2.91 | 2.81 | NA | NA | NA | NA | NA | NA | NA | NA |
| Dividends | NA | NA | NA | NA | NA | NA | NA | NA | NA | NA |
| Payout Ratio | NA | NA | NA | NA | NA | NA | NA | NA | NA | NA |
| Prices:High | NA | NA | NA | NA | NA | NA | NA | NA | NA | NA |
| Prices:Low | NA | NA | NA | NA | NA | NA | NA | NA | NA | NA |
| P/E Ratio:High | NA | NA | NA | NA | NA | NA | NA | NA | NA | NA |
| P/E Ratio:Low | NA | NA | NA | NA | NA | NA | NA | NA | NA | NA |

| Income Statement Analysis (Million $) | 2007 | 2006 | 2005 | 2004 | 2003 | 2002 | 2001 | 2000 | 1999 | 1998 |
|---|---|---|---|---|---|---|---|---|---|---|
| Revenue | 55,096 | 20,794 | 20,013 | 17,583 | NA | NA | NA | NA | NA | NA |
| Operating Income | 9,685 | NA | NA | NA | NA | NA | NA | NA | NA | NA |
| Depreciation | 748 | 658 | 527 | 459 | NA | NA | NA | NA | NA | NA |
| Interest Expense | 209 | NA | NA | NA | NA | NA | NA | NA | NA | NA |
| Pretax Income | 8,572 | 8,226 | 7,641 | 6,478 | NA | NA | NA | NA | NA | NA |
| Effective Tax Rate | 28.9% | 22.2% | 24.0% | 27.2% | NA | NA | NA | NA | NA | NA |
| Net Income | 5,821 | 6,146 | 5,620 | 4,570 | NA | NA | NA | NA | NA | NA |
| S&P Core Earnings | 6,153 | 5,904 | NA | NA | NA | NA | NA | NA | NA | NA |

| Balance Sheet & Other Financial Data (Million $) | 2007 | 2006 | 2005 | 2004 | 2003 | 2002 | 2001 | 2000 | 1999 | 1998 |
|---|---|---|---|---|---|---|---|---|---|---|
| Cash | 1,284 | 1,676 | 1,209 | NA | NA | NA | NA | NA | NA | NA |
| Current Assets | 14,423 | NA | NA | NA | NA | NA | NA | NA | NA | NA |
| Total Assets | 31,414 | 26,120 | 23,135 | NA | NA | NA | NA | NA | NA | NA |
| Current Liabilities | 8,465 | NA | NA | NA | NA | NA | NA | NA | NA | NA |
| Long Term Debt | 5,578 | NA | NA | NA | NA | NA | NA | NA | NA | NA |
| Common Equity | 14,700 | 14,267 | 10,307 | NA | NA | NA | NA | NA | NA | NA |
| Total Capital | 21,481 | NA | NA | NA | NA | NA | NA | NA | NA | NA |
| Capital Expenditures | 1,072 | 886 | 736 | 711 | NA | NA | NA | NA | NA | NA |
| Cash Flow | 6,569 | NA | NA | NA | NA | NA | NA | NA | NA | NA |
| Current Ratio | 1.7 | 1.7 | 1.6 | NA | NA | NA | NA | NA | NA | NA |
| % Long Term Debt of Capitalization | 26.0 | 13.4 | 28.4 | Nil | NA | NA | NA | NA | NA | NA |
| % Net Income of Revenue | 10.6 | 29.6 | 28.1 | 26.0 | NA | NA | NA | NA | NA | NA |
| % Return on Assets | NA | 25.0 | NA | NA | NA | NA | NA | NA | NA | NA |
| % Return on Equity | NA | 50.0 | NA | NA | NA | NA | NA | NA | NA | NA |

Data as orig reptd.; bef. results of disc opers/spec. items. Per share data adj. for stk. divs.; EPS diluted. Data for 2007 are pro forma. E-Estimated. NA-Not Available. NM-Not Meaningful. NR-Not Ranked. UR-Under Review.

**Office:** 120 Park Avenue, New York, NY 10017.
**Telephone:** 917-663-2000.
**Website:** http://www.pmintl.com
**Chrmn & CEO:** L.C. Camilleri

**COO:** A. Calantzopoulos
**SVP & General Counsel:** M. Friedman
**CFO:** H. Waldemer
**Treas:** M. Kuepfer

**Board Members:** H. Brown, M. Cabiallavetta, L. C. Camilleri, J. D. Fishburn, C. S. Helu, G. Mackay, S. Marchionne, L. A. Noto, S. M. Wolf

**Founded:** 1987
**Domicile:** Virginia
**Employees:** 75,500

# Pinnacle West Capital Corp

**STANDARD &POOR'S**

| S&P Recommendation HOLD ★★★☆☆ | Price | 12-Mo. Target Price | Investment Style |
|---|---|---|---|
| | $29.23 (as of Nov 14, 2008) | $35.00 | Large-Cap Value |

**GICS Sector** Utilities
**Sub-Industry** Electric Utilities

**Summary** This utility holding company is the parent of Arizona Public Service (APS), Arizona's largest electric utility.

## Key Stock Statistics (Source S&P, Vickers, company reports)

| | | | | | | | |
|---|---|---|---|---|---|---|---|
| 52-Wk Range | $44.50– 26.27 | S&P Oper. EPS 2008**E** | 2.45 | Market Capitalization(B) | $2.947 | Beta | 0.63 |
| Trailing 12-Month EPS | $2.81 | S&P Oper. EPS 2009**E** | 2.52 | Yield (%) | 7.18 | S&P 3-Yr. Proj. EPS CAGR(%) | -4 |
| Trailing 12-Month P/E | 10.4 | P/E on S&P Oper. EPS 2008**E** | 11.9 | Dividend Rate/Share | $2.10 | S&P Credit Rating | BBB- |
| $10K Invested 5 Yrs Ago | $9,814 | Common Shares Outstg. (M) | 100.8 | Institutional Ownership (%) | 81 | | |

## Price Performance

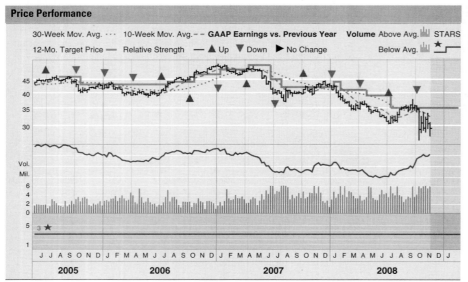

30-Week Mov. Avg. · · · 10-Week Mov. Avg. – – GAAP Earnings vs. Previous Year  Volume Above Avg. STARS
12-Mo. Target Price — Relative Strength  ▲ Up ▼ Down ► No Change  Below Avg.

Options: P

Analysis prepared by **Justin McCann** on September 18, 2008, when the stock traded at **$ 34.64**.

## Qualitative Risk Assessment

| LOW | MEDIUM | HIGH |
|---|---|---|

Our risk assessment reflects the steady cash flow that we project from the electric utility operations of Arizona Public Service, which has one of the fastest-growing service territories in the U.S. While the regulatory environment has often been difficult, we do not expect to see the general strength of the utility significantly impeded by regulatory rulings. This should help offset the less-predictable earnings stream from the real estate business and the power marketing and trading operations.

## Quantitative Evaluations

**S&P Quality Ranking**  B+

| D | C | B- | B | B+ | A- | A | A+ |
|---|---|---|---|---|---|---|---|

**Relative Strength Rank**  STRONG

74

LOWEST = 1    HIGHEST = 99

## Highlights

➤ We expect operating EPS in 2008 to decline about 18% from 2007 operating EPS of $3.05, reflecting our assumption of a return to normal weather at the Arizona Public Service utility (APS) after the abnormally hot summer in 2007. We expect that APS will account for nearly all of the earnings in 2008, with only a minimal contribution from the real estate business.

➤ For 2009, we expect operating EPS to increase about 3% from anticipated results in 2008. Our estimate assumes normal weather at APS and that a new rate increase will not be implemented until the fourth quarter. We also believe results will continue to be restricted by ongoing weakness in the real estate segment due to the slowdown in the regional market.

➤ On June 2, 2008, APS filed with the ACC an updated rate case request from its original filing of March 24, 2008. The new filing requested a net rate increase of $278.2 million (10.5%), up from $265.5 million (10.1%) in the original filing. Excluding the $53 million (2.0%) impact fee for new customers, the net increase for existing customers would be 8.5%, up from 8.1%. The new filing also extended the implementation date by three months, to October 1, 2009.

## Investment Rationale/Risk

➤ The shares are down about 18% year to date, partially due, in our view, to the uncertainty as to whether state regulators will authorize a rate increase that will enable APS to recover the rising costs of its infrastructure expansion. This follows a 16% decline in 2007, which we believe reflected the less-than-expected net retail rate increase for APS, problems at the Palo Verde nuclear facility, and weakness in the real estate business. We expect the stock to be partially supported by the well-above-peers yield (recently 6.1%) from the dividend, which has been lifted by the decline in the shares.

➤ Risks to our recommendation and target price include worse-than-expected earnings from the real estate business, and a sharp decline in the average P/E multiple of the group as a whole.

➤ With the December 2007 payment of a quarterly dividend of $0.525 a share, PNW discontinued its long-standing policy of increasing the annual dividend by $0.10 a year. We expect future decisions regarding the dividend will be dependent upon such factors as the company's free cash flow and payout ratio. Our 12-month target price is $35, reflecting a discount-to-peers P/E of about 13.6X our EPS estimate for 2009.

## Revenue/Earnings Data

**Revenue (Million $)**

| | 1Q | 2Q | 3Q | 4Q | Year |
|---|---|---|---|---|---|
| 2008 | 736.7 | 926.2 | 1,080 | -- | -- |
| 2007 | 695.1 | 863.4 | 1,206 | 759.1 | 3,524 |
| 2006 | 670.2 | 925.0 | 1,076 | 730.1 | 3,402 |
| 2005 | 585.4 | 755.3 | 955.6 | 691.7 | 2,988 |
| 2004 | 574.4 | 722.7 | 886.8 | 734.7 | 2,900 |
| 2003 | 552.6 | 683.3 | 847.7 | 734.2 | 2,818 |

**Earnings Per Share ($)**

| | | | | | |
|---|---|---|---|---|---|
| 2008 | -0.05 | 1.13 | 1.49 | E-0.04 | E2.45 |
| 2007 | 0.16 | 0.78 | 1.99 | -0.03 | 2.96 |
| 2006 | 0.12 | 1.11 | 1.84 | 0.10 | 3.17 |
| 2005 | 0.32 | 0.88 | 0.86 | 0.24 | 2.31 |
| 2004 | 0.33 | 0.78 | 1.14 | 0.32 | 2.57 |
| 2003 | 0.22 | 0.60 | 1.20 | 0.50 | 2.52 |

Fiscal year ended Dec. 31. Next earnings report expected: Late January. EPS Estimates based on S&P Operating Earnings; historical GAAP earnings are as reported.

## Dividend Data (Dates: mm/dd Payment Date: mm/dd/yy)

| Amount ($) | Date Decl. | Ex-Div. Date | Stk. of Record | Payment Date |
|---|---|---|---|---|
| 0.525 | 01/23 | 01/30 | 02/01 | 03/03/08 |
| 0.525 | 04/22 | 04/29 | 05/01 | 06/02/08 |
| 0.525 | 07/23 | 07/30 | 08/01 | 09/02/08 |
| 0.525 | 10/22 | 10/30 | 11/03 | 12/01/08 |

Dividends have been paid since 1993. Source: Company reports.

The **McGraw-Hill** Companies

# Pinnacle West Capital Corp

**STANDARD &POOR'S**

## Business Summary September 18, 2008

CORPORATE OVERVIEW. Pinnacle West Capital, formed in 1985, is the holding company for Arizona Public Service (APS), which, with about 1.1 million customers, is Arizona's largest electric utility. PNW's other major subsidiaries are APS Energy Services, which provides competitive energy services, including wholesale marketing and trading, and SunCor, which is engaged in real estate development and investment activities. In 2007, the regulated electricity segment accounted for 82.8% of PNW's consolidated revenues (compared to 77.4% in 2006); the marketing and trading segment, 9.7% (9.7%); the real estate segment, 6.1% (11.8%); and other, 1.4% (1.1%).

MARKET PROFILE. APS provides vertically integrated retail and wholesale service to the entire state of Arizona, with the exception of Tucson and about 50% of the Phoenix area. In 2007, residential customers accounted for 48.6% of the utility's regulated electric sales (48.2% in 2006); business customers, 46.4% (47.0%); and wholesale and other, 5.0% (4.7%). APS has a 29.1% owned or leased interest in the Palo Verde Nuclear Generating Station's Units 1 and 3, and a 17.0% interest in Unit 2. It has a 100% interest in Units 1, 2 and 3; a 15% interest in Units 4 and 5 of the coal-fueled Four Corners Steam Generating Station; and a 14.0% interest in Units 1, 2 and 3 of the coal-fueled Navajo Steam Generating Station (NGS). Consolidated fuel sources for APS in 2007

were: coal, 36.8% (31.2% in 2006); purchased power, 23.3% (35.0%); nuclear, 21.5% (16.5%); and gas, 18.4% (17.3%). With APS dependent on purchased power for so much of its fuel sources, we believe that it has been hurt by the sharp rise in natural gas prices and by the time lags involved in being authorized to recover the difference between its actual fuel costs and the rates the company is allowed to charge its customers.

SunCor develops residential, commercial and industrial real estate projects in Arizona, Idaho, New Mexico and Utah. The company, which had total assets of $607 million at the end of 2006, intends to continue its focus on the development of master-planned communities, mixed-use residential, commercial, office and industrial projects. In 2007, SunCor's operating revenues declined to approximately $215 million, from $400 million in 2006, and its net income was down by $37 million, to $24 million. While the decline has reflected the impact of the housing crisis in Arizona, we believe the business will be an important source of PNW's earnings and cash flow once the crisis has passed.

## Company Financials Fiscal Year Ended Dec. 31

| Per Share Data ($) | 2007 | 2006 | 2005 | 2004 | 2003 | 2002 | 2001 | 2000 | 1999 | 1998 |
|---|---|---|---|---|---|---|---|---|---|---|
| Tangible Book Value | 34.11 | 34.48 | 34.58 | 30.99 | 29.81 | 28.23 | 29.46 | 28.09 | 26.00 | 25.50 |
| Earnings | 2.96 | 3.17 | 2.31 | 2.57 | 2.52 | 2.53 | 3.85 | 3.56 | 1.97 | 2.85 |
| S&P Core Earnings | 2.71 | 3.00 | 2.00 | 2.15 | 2.43 | 1.65 | 3.00 | NA | NA | NA |
| Dividends | 2.10 | 2.03 | 1.93 | 1.83 | 1.73 | 1.63 | 1.53 | 1.43 | 1.33 | 1.23 |
| Payout Ratio | 71% | 64% | 83% | 71% | 68% | 64% | 40% | 40% | 67% | 43% |
| Prices:High | 51.67 | 51.00 | 46.68 | 45.84 | 40.48 | 46.68 | 50.70 | 52.69 | 43.38 | 49.25 |
| Prices:Low | 36.79 | 38.31 | 39.81 | 36.30 | 28.34 | 21.70 | 37.65 | 25.69 | 30.19 | 39.38 |
| P/E Ratio:High | 17 | 16 | 20 | 18 | 16 | 18 | 13 | 15 | 22 | 17 |
| P/E Ratio:Low | 12 | 12 | 17 | 14 | 11 | 9 | 10 | 7 | 15 | 14 |

| Income Statement Analysis (Million $) | 2007 | 2006 | 2005 | 2004 | 2003 | 2002 | 2001 | 2000 | 1999 | 1998 |
|---|---|---|---|---|---|---|---|---|---|---|
| Revenue | 3,524 | 3,402 | 2,988 | 2,900 | 2,818 | 2,637 | 4,551 | 3,690 | 2,423 | 2,131 |
| Depreciation | 373 | 359 | 348 | 401 | 438 | 425 | 428 | 394 | 386 | 380 |
| Maintenance | NA | NA | NA | NA | NA | NA | NA | NA | NA | NA |
| Fixed Charges Coverage | 3.37 | 3.23 | 2.77 | 2.75 | 2.43 | 2.64 | 3.80 | 3.95 | 3.61 | 3.17 |
| Construction Credits | 21.2 | 14.3 | 11.2 | 4.89 | 14.2 | NA | NA | NA | 11.7 | 18.6 |
| Effective Tax Rate | 33.6% | 33.0% | 36.2% | 35.4% | 31.4% | 39.1% | 39.5% | 42.5% | 38.4% | 40.4% |
| Net Income | 299 | 317 | 223 | 235 | 231 | 215 | 327 | 302 | 270 | 243 |
| S&P Core Earnings | 273 | 300 | 193 | 197 | 223 | 140 | 255 | NA | NA | NA |

| Balance Sheet & Other Financial Data (Million $) | 2007 | 2006 | 2005 | 2004 | 2003 | 2002 | 2001 | 2000 | 1999 | 1998 |
|---|---|---|---|---|---|---|---|---|---|---|
| Gross Property | 12,762 | 11,679 | 11,200 | 18,280 | 10,470 | 16,316 | 9,285 | 8,383 | 7,805 | 7,876 |
| Capital Expenditures | 919 | 738 | 634 | 538 | 693 | 896 | 1,041 | 659 | 343 | 319 |
| Net Property | 8,437 | 7,882 | 7,577 | 14,914 | 7,310 | 12,842 | 5,907 | 5,133 | 4,779 | 5,062 |
| Capitalization:Long Term Debt | 3,127 | 3,233 | 2,608 | 2,585 | 2,898 | 2,882 | 2,673 | 1,955 | 2,206 | 2,144 |
| Capitalization:% Long Term Debt | 47.0 | 48.4 | 43.2 | 46.7 | 50.6 | 51.8 | 51.7 | 45.1 | 50.0 | 49.8 |
| Capitalization:Preferred | Nil | Nil | Nil | Nil | Nil | Nil | Nil | Nil | Nil | Nil |
| Capitalization:% Preferred | Nil | Nil | Nil | Nil | Nil | Nil | Nil | Nil | Nil | Nil |
| Capitalization:Common | 3,532 | 3,446 | 3,425 | 2,950 | 2,830 | 2,686 | 2,499 | 2,383 | 2,206 | 2,163 |
| Capitalization:% Common | 53.0 | 51.6 | 56.8 | 53.3 | 49.4 | 48.2 | 48.3 | 54.9 | 50.0 | 50.2 |
| Total Capital | 7,902 | 7,905 | 7,259 | 6,763 | 7,057 | 6,777 | 6,237 | 5,481 | 5,599 | 5,678 |
| % Operating Ratio | 86.7 | 85.6 | 82.4 | 85.8 | 86.6 | 81.7 | 89.9 | 87.7 | 83.1 | 75.7 |
| % Earned on Net Property | 7.6 | 8.0 | 6.8 | 3.4 | 6.8 | 4.2 | 24.6 | 13.6 | 12.2 | 11.2 |
| % Return on Revenue | 8.5 | 9.3 | 7.5 | 8.1 | 8.2 | 8.2 | 7.2 | 8.2 | 11.1 | 11.4 |
| % Return on Invested Capital | 6.2 | 7.2 | 8.0 | 6.9 | 6.2 | 7.7 | 7.9 | 8.2 | 7.5 | 13.9 |
| % Return on Common Equity | 8.6 | 9.2 | 7.0 | 8.1 | 8.4 | 8.3 | 13.4 | 13.2 | 12.3 | 11.6 |

Data as orig reptd.; bef. results of disc opers/spec. items. Per share data adj. for stk. divs.; EPS diluted. E-Estimated. NA-Not Available. NM-Not Meaningful. NR-Not Ranked. UR-Under Review.

**Office:** 400 N 5th St Frnt, Phoenix, AZ 85004-3902.
**Telephone:** 602-250-1000.
**Website:** http://www.pinnaclewest.com
**Chrmn:** W.J. Post

**Pres, CEO & COO:** D.E. Brandt
**SVP & CFO:** J.R. Hatfield
**SVP, Secy & General Counsel:** N.C. Loftin
**Treas:** B.M. Gomez

**Investor Contact:** R. Hickman (602-250-5668)
**Board Members:** E. N. Basha, Jr., M. L. Gallagher, P. Grant, R. A. Herberger, Jr., W. S. Jamieson, Jr., H. S. Lopez, K. L. Munro, B. J. Nordstrom, W. D. Parker, W. J. Post, W. L. Stewart

**Founded:** 1920
**Domicile:** Arizona
**Employees:** 7,600

**The McGraw·Hill Companies**

# Pioneer Natural Resources Co

| S&P Recommendation HOLD ★★★☆☆ | Price $22.27 (as of Nov 14, 2008) | 12-Mo. Target Price $28.00 | Investment Style Large-Cap Blend |
|---|---|---|---|

**GICS Sector** Energy
**Sub-Industry** Oil & Gas Exploration & Production

**Summary** This company explores for and produces oil and natural gas in the U.S., Canada and Africa.

## Key Stock Statistics (Source S&P, Vickers, company reports)

| | | | | | | | |
|---|---|---|---|---|---|---|---|
| 52-Wk Range | $82.21– 20.59 | S&P Oper. EPS 2008**E** | 3.52 | Market Capitalization(B) | $2.665 | Beta | 1.19 |
| Trailing 12-Month EPS | $4.11 | S&P Oper. EPS 2009**E** | 3.06 | Yield (%) | 1.44 | S&P 3-Yr. Proj. EPS CAGR(%) | 26 |
| Trailing 12-Month P/E | 5.4 | P/E on S&P Oper. EPS 2008**E** | 6.3 | Dividend Rate/Share | $0.32 | S&P Credit Rating | BB+ |
| $10K Invested 5 Yrs Ago | $8,464 | Common Shares Outstg. (M) | 119.7 | Institutional Ownership (%) | 94 | | |

## Price Performance

30-Week Mov. Avg. · · · ·    10-Week Mov. Avg. – – **GAAP Earnings vs. Previous Year**   Volume Above Avg. STARS
12-Mo. Target Price —    Relative Strength —    ▲ Up   ▼ Down   ▶ No Change   Below Avg.   ★

Options: ASE, CBOE, P, Ph

Analysis prepared by **Michael Kay** on November 10, 2008, when the stock traded at **$ 24.87**.

## Qualitative Risk Assessment

| LOW | MEDIUM | HIGH |
|---|---|---|

Our risk assessment reflects what we see as PXD's aggressive financial risk profile in a volatile and capital-intensive segment of the energy industry. While its reserves are characterized by long production life, its lifting costs have been rising with the elimination of lower-cost Gulf of Mexico production.

## Quantitative Evaluations

**S&P Quality Ranking**      B

| D | C | B- | **B** | B+ | A- | A | A+ |
|---|---|---|---|---|---|---|---|

**Relative Strength Rank**      WEAK

19

LOWEST = 1      HIGHEST = 99

## Revenue/Earnings Data

**Revenue (Million $)**

| | 1Q | 2Q | 3Q | 4Q | Year |
|---|---|---|---|---|---|
| 2008 | 584.2 | 653.3 | 612.2 | -- | -- |
| 2007 | 367.3 | 444.7 | 490.4 | 530.9 | 1,833 |
| 2006 | 396.5 | 413.9 | 432.6 | 389.8 | 1,633 |
| 2005 | 550.9 | 592.6 | 568.2 | 622.2 | 2,216 |
| 2004 | 435.5 | 435.9 | 441.7 | 519.5 | 1,833 |
| 2003 | 281.2 | 340.0 | 332.5 | 352.7 | 1,299 |

**Earnings Per Share ($)**

| | 1Q | 2Q | 3Q | 4Q | Year |
|---|---|---|---|---|---|
| 2008 | 1.07 | 1.32 | -0.02 | E0.28 | E3.52 |
| 2007 | 0.25 | 0.29 | 0.77 | 0.71 | 1.99 |
| 2006 | -0.01 | 0.52 | 0.64 | 0.22 | 1.36 |
| 2005 | 0.58 | 0.72 | 0.74 | 1.07 | 3.02 |
| 2004 | 0.50 | 0.58 | 0.67 | 0.69 | 2.46 |
| 2003 | 0.58 | 0.65 | 1.62 | 0.48 | 3.33 |

Fiscal year ended Dec. 31. Next earnings report expected: Early February. EPS Estimates based on S&P Operating Earnings; historical GAAP earnings are as reported.

## Highlights

➤ After growth of 4% in 2007, we see oil and gas production rising 10% in both 2008 and 2009, respectively, driven by the Spraberry field, the Raton Basin, and the Edwards Trend. Our outlooks have recently been tempered by shut-ins from hurricanes and a lower budget for 2009. We see growth in Tunisia, where PXD has seen strong drilling results, discoveries, and initiated production last year. In October, PXD initiated production from its most prolific well at the South Coast Gas Project in Africa and drilled its first two wells in the Pierre Shale. During the second quarter of 2008, PXD commenced production at Oooguruk in Alaska's North Slope.

➤ PXD reported reserve replacement costs of $15.40 per BOE ($16.39 three-year average) and reserve replacement of 357% (206% three-year average) for 2007, reflecting acquisitions and successful drilling in Raton, Spraberry, Edwards Trend, and the Barnett Shale.

➤ We see 2008 EPS of $3.52, up from $2.17 in 2007. Despite higher production, we see lower prices negatively impacting our 2009 EPS estimate of $3.06. PXD's capital budget is $1.3 billion, down from $1.4 billion in 2007, and we see a capex cut of 30%-40% in 2009.

## Investment Rationale/Risk

➤ After a lengthy restructuring, we now view PXD as an onshore producer with strong production growth prospects and impending project start-ups. In the first nine months of 2008, we estimate PXD saw a combined 21% increase in production from its core Spraberry, Raton and Edwards fields. PXD reported limited hurricane damage to its own facilities, but saw minor shut-ins from a third-party facility that was damaged. We expect near-term asset sales at mature properties to reduce debt.

➤ Risks to our recommendation and target price include negative changes to economic, industrial and operating conditions, such as rising costs or increased geopolitical risk.

➤ A drop in oil and gas prices has caused a similar decline in exploration and production (E&P) shares. Due to weaker economic forecasts, we see the market discounting PXD's probable reserves and we now value companies based on proven reserve NAV estimates. We blend our proven reserve NAV of $37 with relative metrics to arrive at our 12-month target price of $28. We expect PXD to trade in line with peers, and our hold opinion reflects unusually high risk we see in the E&P sector and high relative debt levels.

## Dividend Data (Dates: mm/dd Payment Date: mm/dd/yy)

| Amount ($) | Date Decl. | Ex-Div. Date | Stk. of Record | Payment Date |
|---|---|---|---|---|
| 0.140 | 02/13 | 03/27 | 03/31 | 04/14/08 |
| 0.160 | 08/27 | 09/26 | 09/30 | 10/10/08 |

Dividends have been paid since 2004. Source: Company reports.

# Pioneer Natural Resources Co

STANDARD
&POOR'S

## Business Summary November 10, 2008

CORPORATE OVERVIEW. This independent oil and gas exploration and production company has an asset base anchored by the Spraberry oil field in West Texas, the Hugoton gas field in Kansas, the West Panhandle gas field in the Texas Panhandle, and the Raton gas field in southern Colorado. Complementing these areas, PXD has oil and gas exploration, development and production activities in the onshore Gulf Coast area, Alaska, South Africa and Tunisia. Given increasing capital costs and diminishing drilling success, PXD recently sold its deepwater Gulf of Mexico, Argentina and Canadian assets.

As of December 31, 2007, PXD had estimated proved reserves of 963.8 MM-BOE, of which 52% consisted of natural gas, and 48% crude oil and natural gas liquids. This compares to estimated proved reserves of 904.9 MMBOE, of which 54% was comprised of natural gas, 46% crude oil and natural gas liquids at year-end 2006. We estimate PXD's 2007 reserve life to be 23.3 years, compared to 25.2 years at the end of 2006.

MARKET PROFILE. PXD's addressable markets include onshore North American operations (98% of 2006 reserves), with some emerging fields in Africa. These assets are characterized by long reserve lives (generally reserve-

to-production ratios in excess of 10 years), with most production in the form of natural gas. Given these characteristics, PXD competes in a fragmented onshore natural gas market that has continued along a rationalization path over the past eight years, in our view. PXD competes with much larger onshore players. These producers increasingly employ unconventional drilling and production techniques to successfully boost production, in our opinion. Such unconventional resource plays include basin-centered tight gas formations, and fractured shale formations, which are characterized by a low proportion of exploration capital expenditures, resulting in relatively low risk resource acquisition capability. In our view, the main driver of value in these resource plays is the development of drilling techniques in a basin that are repeatable, increasing productivity organically and moving reserves characterized as probable and possible to the proven category.

## Company Financials Fiscal Year Ended Dec. 31

| Per Share Data ($) | 2007 | 2006 | 2005 | 2004 | 2003 | 2002 | 2001 | 2000 | 1999 | 1998 |
|---|---|---|---|---|---|---|---|---|---|---|
| Tangible Book Value | 24.38 | 22.01 | 14.82 | 19.55 | 14.75 | 11.73 | 12.37 | 9.19 | 7.72 | 7.87 |
| Cash Flow | 5.40 | 4.17 | 7.01 | 6.96 | 6.63 | 2.32 | 3.27 | 3.82 | 2.13 | -4.09 |
| Earnings | 1.99 | 1.36 | 3.02 | 2.46 | 3.33 | 0.43 | 1.04 | 1.65 | -0.22 | -7.46 |
| S&P Core Earnings | 1.57 | 1.34 | 2.00 | 2.41 | 3.26 | 0.32 | 0.93 | NA | NA | NA |
| Dividends | 0.27 | 0.25 | 0.22 | 0.20 | Nil | Nil | Nil | Nil | Nil | 0.10 |
| Payout Ratio | 14% | 18% | 7% | 8% | Nil | Nil | Nil | Nil | Nil | NM |
| Prices:High | 54.87 | 54.46 | 56.35 | 37.50 | 32.90 | 27.50 | 23.05 | 20.63 | 13.19 | 30.00 |
| Prices:Low | 35.51 | 36.43 | 32.91 | 29.27 | 22.76 | 16.10 | 12.62 | 6.75 | 5.00 | 7.75 |
| P/E Ratio:High | 28 | 40 | 19 | 15 | 10 | 64 | 22 | 12 | NM | NM |
| P/E Ratio:Low | 18 | 27 | 11 | 12 | 7 | 37 | 12 | 4 | NM | NM |

| Income Statement Analysis (Million $) | | | | | | | | | | |
|---|---|---|---|---|---|---|---|---|---|---|
| Revenue | 1,833 | 1,633 | 2,216 | 1,833 | 1,299 | 702 | 847 | 853 | 645 | 711 |
| Operating Income | 1,019 | 757 | 1,262 | 1,191 | 804 | 351 | 433 | 475 | 344 | 253 |
| Depreciation, Depletion and Amortization | 415 | 360 | 568 | 575 | 391 | 216 | 223 | 215 | 236 | 337 |
| Interest Expense | 168 | 107 | 128 | 103 | 91.4 | 95.8 | 132 | 162 | 170 | 164 |
| Pretax Income | 355 | 309 | 715 | 479 | 331 | 54.1 | 108 | 158 | -21.9 | -762 |
| Effective Tax Rate | 31.7% | 44.2% | 40.8% | 34.7% | NM | 9.35% | 3.73% | NM | NM | NM |
| Net Income | 242 | 172 | 424 | 313 | 395 | 49.1 | 104 | 164 | -22.5 | -746 |
| S&P Core Earnings | 192 | 170 | 280 | 307 | 386 | 36.4 | 92.2 | NA | NA | NA |

| Balance Sheet & Other Financial Data (Million $) | | | | | | | | | | |
|---|---|---|---|---|---|---|---|---|---|---|
| Cash | 12.2 | 7.03 | 18.8 | 7.26 | 19.3 | 8.49 | 14.3 | 26.2 | 34.8 | 59.2 |
| Current Assets | 765 | 537 | 624 | 312 | 205 | 147 | 256 | 191 | 183 | 202 |
| Total Assets | 8,617 | 7,355 | 7,329 | 6,647 | 3,952 | 3,455 | 3,271 | 2,954 | 2,929 | 3,481 |
| Current Liabilities | 994 | 887 | 1,033 | 544 | 430 | 275 | 228 | 217 | 197 | 527 |
| Long Term Debt | 2,755 | 1,497 | 2,058 | 2,569 | 1,604 | 1,669 | 1,577 | 1,579 | 1,745 | 1,869 |
| Common Equity | 3,043 | 2,985 | 2,217 | 2,832 | 1,760 | 1,375 | 1,285 | 905 | 775 | 789 |
| Total Capital | 7,028 | 5,654 | 4,276 | 5,927 | 3,376 | 3,052 | 2,876 | 2,512 | 2,563 | 5,823 |
| Capital Expenditures | 2,204 | 1,499 | 1,123 | 616 | 688 | 615 | 530 | 300 | 11.9 | 539 |
| Cash Flow | 657 | 532 | 992 | 888 | 786 | 265 | 326 | 379 | 214 | -409 |
| Current Ratio | 0.8 | 0.6 | 0.6 | 0.6 | 0.5 | 0.5 | 1.1 | 0.9 | 0.9 | 0.4 |
| % Long Term Debt of Capitalization | 39.2 | 26.5 | 48.1 | 43.3 | 47.5 | 54.7 | 54.8 | 62.8 | 68.1 | 68.7 |
| % Return on Assets | 3.0 | 2.3 | 6.0 | 5.9 | 10.7 | 1.5 | 3.3 | 5.6 | NM | NM |
| % Return on Equity | 8.0 | 6.6 | 16.8 | 13.6 | 25.2 | 3.7 | 9.5 | 19.6 | NM | NM |

Data as orig reptd.; bef. results of disc opers/spec. items. Per share data adj. for stk. divs.; EPS diluted. E-Estimated. NA-Not Available. NM-Not Meaningful. NR-Not Ranked. UR-Under Review.

Office: 5205 N O Connor Blvd Ste 200, Irving, TX 75039.
Telephone: 972-444-9001.
Email: ir@pxd.com
Website: http://www.pxd.com

Chrmn & CEO: S.D. Sheffield
Pres & COO: T.L. Dove
EVP & CFO: R.P. Dealy
EVP & General Counsel: M.S. Berg

Chief Admin Officer: L.N. Paulsen
Investor Contact: F.E. Hopkins (972-969-4065)
Board Members: J. R. Baroffio, E. Buchanan, R. H. Gardner, L. K. Lawson, A. D. Lundquist, C. E. Ramsey, Jr., F. A. Risch, M. S. Sexton, S. D. Sheffield, R. Solberg, J. A. Watson

Founded: 1997
Domicile: Delaware
Employees: 1,702

# Pitney Bowes Inc.

**STANDARD & POOR'S**

| S&P Recommendation | BUY ★★★★☆ | Price | 12-Mo. Target Price | Investment Style |
|---|---|---|---|---|
| | | $23.37 (as of Nov 14, 2008) | $32.00 | Large-Cap Growth |

**GICS Sector** Industrials
**Sub-Industry** Office Services & Supplies

**Summary** PBI, the world's largest maker of mailing systems, also provides production and document management equipment and facilities management services.

## Key Stock Statistics (Source S&P, Vickers, company reports)

| | | | | | | | | |
|---|---|---|---|---|---|---|---|---|
| 52-Wk Range | $39.98– 20.83 | S&P Oper. EPS 2008**E** | 2.82 | Market Capitalization(B) | $4.817 | Beta | | 0.60 |
| Trailing 12-Month EPS | $1.36 | S&P Oper. EPS 2009**E** | 2.95 | Yield (%) | 5.99 | S&P 3-Yr. Proj. EPS CAGR(%) | | 5 |
| Trailing 12-Month P/E | 17.2 | P/E on S&P Oper. EPS 2008**E** | 8.3 | Dividend Rate/Share | $1.40 | S&P Credit Rating | | A |
| $10K Invested 5 Yrs Ago | $6,620 | Common Shares Outstg. (M) | 206.1 | Institutional Ownership (%) | 84 | | | |

## Price Performance

30-Week Mov. Avg. ··· · 10-Week Mov. Avg. – – GAAP Earnings vs. Previous Year   Volume Above Avg. ▐▊▍▎ STARS
12-Mo. Target Price — Relative Strength — ▲ Up ▼ Down ► No Change   Below Avg. ▐▊▍▎ ★

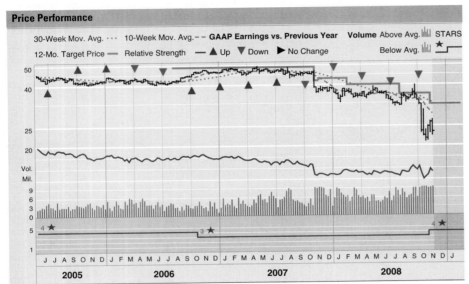

Options: CBOE, P, Ph

Analysis prepared by **Thomas W. Smith, CFA** on November 04, 2008, when the stock traded at **$ 25.00**.

## Highlights

► We look for revenues to rise 4% in 2008 and 3% in 2009. We see results being aided by postal regulatory changes and acquisitions, but hampered by moderating global economic growth and a slow migration to digital meters. We expect the mailstream services segment to ouperform the mailstream solutions segment. On November 15, 2007, PBI announced 1,500 job cuts, or about 4% of global staff, in a move to make product transitions and lower costs.

► We see gross margins dipping toward 52% in 2008 and 2009, from about 53.2% in 2007, as a less-favorable business mix outweighs the benefits of modest gains in volume. We expect operating margins to similarly dip in 2008, but then widen a bit in 2009 as cost savings from the restructuring plan are more fully realized. Results should continue to be favorably affected by share buybacks. The company repurchased about 1.7 million shares in the 2008 third quarter.

► We forecast 2008 EPS of $2.82, excluding restructuring and other special items. We expect EPS to improve to $2.95 in 2009.

## Investment Rationale/Risk

► PBI has a large recurring revenue stream, a growing international presence, and a leadership position within its market, in our view. We expect synergies from acquisitions, and from new product introductions focusing on digital technology, to aid future growth. PBI has been working on a restructuring plan since November 2007 that appears to be improving efficiency. Share price declines since September 2008 have made the valuation more attractive, in our view, and lifted the dividend yield above 5%.

► Risks to our recommendation and target price include increased competition in the document management outsourcing market, which would have an impact on pricing within PBI's Management Services division, which contributes close to 20% of revenues. Postal regulatory changes in key countries are also a risk factor.

► Our 12-month target price of $32 is based mainly on our P/E analysis. We apply a target P/E of 11X, toward the low end of a five-year historical range for PBI to reflect near-term revenue weakness we foresee, to our 12-month forward EPS estimate of $2.88.

## Qualitative Risk Assessment

| LOW | MEDIUM | HIGH |
|---|---|---|

Our risk assessment reflects our view of PBI's steady cash flow, recurring revenue streams, and history of a consistent dividend policy and share buyback programs. However, we think these factors are offset by a lackluster rate of revenue growth and integration risk associated with recent acquisitions.

## Quantitative Evaluations

**S&P Quality Ranking**  B+

| D | C | B- | B | B+ | A- | A | A+ |
|---|---|---|---|---|---|---|---|

**Relative Strength Rank**  MODERATE

58

LOWEST = 1          HIGHEST = 99

## Revenue/Earnings Data

**Revenue (Million $)**

| | 1Q | 2Q | 3Q | 4Q | Year |
|---|---|---|---|---|---|
| 2008 | 1,574 | 1,588 | 1,548 | -- | -- |
| 2007 | 1,414 | 1,543 | 1,508 | 1,664 | 6,130 |
| 2006 | 1,362 | 1,389 | 1,433 | 1,546 | 5,730 |
| 2005 | 1,318 | 1,360 | 1,356 | 1,458 | 5,492 |
| 2004 | 1,172 | 1,206 | 1,218 | 1,362 | 4,957 |
| 2003 | 1,091 | 1,134 | 1,137 | 1,215 | 4,577 |

**Earnings Per Share ($)**

| | | | | | |
|---|---|---|---|---|---|
| 2008 | 0.58 | 0.63 | 0.48 | E0.74 | E2.82 |
| 2007 | 0.66 | 0.69 | 0.59 | -0.32 | 1.63 |
| 2006 | 0.60 | 0.54 | 0.64 | 0.73 | 2.51 |
| 2005 | 0.64 | 0.60 | 0.62 | 0.41 | 2.27 |
| 2004 | 0.54 | 0.58 | 0.58 | 0.35 | 2.05 |
| 2003 | 0.48 | 0.50 | 0.50 | 0.61 | 2.10 |

Fiscal year ended Dec. 31. Next earnings report expected: Mid February. EPS Estimates based on S&P Operating Earnings; historical GAAP earnings are as reported.

## Dividend Data (Dates: mm/dd Payment Date: mm/dd/yy)

| Amount ($) | Date Decl. | Ex-Div. Date | Stk. of Record | Payment Date |
|---|---|---|---|---|
| 0.350 | 11/15 | 02/13 | 02/18 | 03/12/08 |
| 0.350 | 04/14 | 05/14 | 05/16 | 06/12/08 |
| 0.350 | 07/14 | 08/13 | 08/15 | 09/12/08 |
| 0.350 | 11/07 | 11/19 | 11/21 | 12/12/08 |

Dividends have been paid since 1934. Source: Company reports.

# Pitney Bowes Inc.

**STANDARD &POOR'S**

## Business Summary November 04, 2008

CORPORATE OVERVIEW. In business since 1920, Pitney Bowes is a major global provider of mail processing equipment and integrated mail solutions. The company's postage meters and other offerings help business customers optimize the flow of physical and electronic mail, documents and packages. The company operates seven business units within two business groups known as Mailstream Solutions and Mailstream Services.

The Mailstream Solutions segment, which accounted for 71% of 2007 revenue (72% in 2006), is comprised of four units. The first, U.S. Mailing, includes U.S. revenue and related expenses from the sale, rental and financing of mail finishing, mail creation, and shipping equipment and services. The second, International Mailing, includes non-U.S. revenue and related expenses from activities similar to those of the first unit. The third unit, Production Mail, includes the worldwide sales, service and financing of high-speed production mail systems and sorting equipment. The fourth unit, Software, includes the worldwide sales and support services of non-equipment-based mailing and customer communication and location intelligence software.

The Mailstream Services segment (29%, 28%) is made up of three units. The first, Management Services, includes worldwide facilities management services, secure mail services, reprographic, document management, litigation support, eDiscovery and other services. The second, Mail Services, offers presort mail services and cross-border mail services. The third, Marketing Services, focuses on direct marketing campaign services, web-tools for customization of promotional mail, and other marketing consulting services.

Reviewing revenue sources by product category, Business Services is the largest area, representing 29% of 2007 revenues, following by Equipment Sales 22%, Financing 13%, Support Services 12%, Rentals 12%, Supplies 6%, and Software 6%.

Revenue for 2007 was derived 72% (74% of 2006 revenues) from the U.S. and 28% (26%) from international regions. Profitability at the EBIT line came mostly from domestic operations, with about 86% of earnings before interest and taxes for 2007 sourced in the U.S.

## Company Financials Fiscal Year Ended Dec. 31

| Per Share Data ($) | 2007 | 2006 | 2005 | 2004 | 2003 | 2002 | 2001 | 2000 | 1999 | 1998 |
|---|---|---|---|---|---|---|---|---|---|---|
| Tangible Book Value | NM | NM | NM | NM | NM | 0.10 | 1.05 | 4.34 | 5.28 | 5.26 |
| Cash Flow | 3.37 | 4.21 | 3.70 | 3.36 | 3.32 | 2.98 | 3.44 | 3.55 | 4.05 | 3.31 |
| Earnings | 1.63 | 2.51 | 2.27 | 2.05 | 2.10 | 1.81 | 2.08 | 2.18 | 2.42 | 2.03 |
| S&P Core Earnings | 1.61 | 2.50 | 2.09 | 1.94 | 1.87 | 1.34 | 0.81 | NA | NA | NA |
| Dividends | 1.32 | 1.28 | 1.24 | 1.22 | 1.20 | 1.18 | 1.16 | 1.14 | 1.02 | 0.90 |
| Payout Ratio | 81% | 51% | 55% | 60% | 57% | 65% | 56% | 52% | 42% | 44% |
| Prices:High | 49.70 | 47.97 | 47.50 | 46.97 | 42.75 | 44.41 | 44.70 | 54.13 | 73.31 | 66.38 |
| Prices:Low | 36.40 | 40.18 | 40.34 | 38.88 | 29.45 | 28.55 | 32.00 | 24.00 | 40.88 | 42.22 |
| P/E Ratio:High | 30 | 19 | 21 | 23 | 20 | 25 | 21 | 25 | 30 | 33 |
| P/E Ratio:Low | 22 | 16 | 18 | 19 | 14 | 16 | 15 | 11 | 17 | 21 |

| Income Statement Analysis (Million $) | 2007 | 2006 | 2005 | 2004 | 2003 | 2002 | 2001 | 2000 | 1999 | 1998 |
|---|---|---|---|---|---|---|---|---|---|---|
| Revenue | 6,130 | 5,730 | 5,492 | 4,957 | 4,577 | 4,410 | 4,122 | 3,881 | 4,433 | 4,221 |
| Operating Income | 1,549 | 1,487 | 1,435 | 1,352 | 1,291 | 1,276 | 1,046 | 1,316 | 1,526 | 1,375 |
| Depreciation | 383 | 363 | 332 | 307 | 289 | 264 | 317 | 321 | 412 | 361 |
| Interest Expense | 251 | 228 | 214 | 172 | 168 | 185 | 193 | 201 | 184 | 169 |
| Pretax Income | 661 | 914 | 867 | 699 | 721 | 619 | 766 | 803 | 985 | 864 |
| Effective Tax Rate | 42.4% | 36.6% | 39.3% | 31.3% | 31.4% | 29.3% | 32.9% | 29.9% | 33.1% | 34.3% |
| Net Income | 361 | 566 | 527 | 481 | 495 | 438 | 514 | 563 | 659 | 568 |
| S&P Core Earnings | 357 | 564 | 485 | 456 | 440 | 324 | 199 | NA | NA | NA |

| Balance Sheet & Other Financial Data (Million $) | 2007 | 2006 | 2005 | 2004 | 2003 | 2002 | 2001 | 2000 | 1999 | 1998 |
|---|---|---|---|---|---|---|---|---|---|---|
| Cash | 440 | 239 | 244 | 316 | 294 | 315 | 232 | 198 | 254 | 129 |
| Current Assets | 3,320 | 2,919 | 2,742 | 2,693 | 2,513 | 2,553 | 2,557 | 2,627 | 3,343 | 2,509 |
| Total Assets | 9,550 | 8,480 | 10,621 | 9,821 | 8,891 | 8,732 | 8,318 | 7,901 | 8,223 | 7,661 |
| Current Liabilities | 3,556 | 2,747 | 2,911 | 3,294 | 2,647 | 3,350 | 3,083 | 2,882 | 2,873 | 2,722 |
| Long Term Debt | 3,802 | 4,232 | 3,850 | 3,109 | 3,151 | 2,317 | 2,419 | 2,192 | 2,308 | 2,023 |
| Common Equity | 642 | 698 | 1,301 | 1,289 | 1,086 | 852 | 890 | 1,283 | 1,624 | 1,734 |
| Total Capital | 5,302 | 5,287 | 7,074 | 4,399 | 5,898 | 4,706 | 4,584 | 4,704 | 5,015 | 4,680 |
| Capital Expenditures | 265 | 328 | 292 | 317 | 286 | 225 | 256 | 269 | 305 | 298 |
| Cash Flow | 744 | 929 | 858 | 787 | 784 | 702 | 832 | 884 | 1,071 | 929 |
| Current Ratio | 0.9 | 1.1 | 0.9 | 0.8 | 0.9 | 0.8 | 0.8 | 0.9 | 1.2 | 0.9 |
| % Long Term Debt of Capitalization | 71.7 | 80.0 | 54.4 | 70.7 | 53.4 | 49.2 | 52.8 | 46.6 | 46.0 | 43.2 |
| % Net Income of Revenue | 5.9 | 9.9 | 11.2 | 9.7 | 10.8 | 9.9 | 12.5 | 14.5 | 14.9 | 13.5 |
| % Return on Assets | 4.0 | 5.9 | 5.1 | 5.1 | 5.6 | 5.1 | 6.3 | 7.0 | 8.3 | 7.3 |
| % Return on Equity | 53.9 | 54.9 | 40.7 | 40.5 | 51.1 | 50.3 | 47.3 | 38.7 | 40.3 | 31.5 |

Data as orig reptd.; bef. results of disc opers/spec. items. Per share data adj. for stk. divs.; EPS diluted. E-Estimated. NA-Not Available. NM-Not Meaningful. NR-Not Ranked. UR-Under Review.

**Office:** 1 Elmcroft Rd, Stamford, CT 06926-0700.
**Telephone:** 203-351-6858.
**Email:** investorrelations@pb.com
**Website:** http://www.pb.com

**Chrmn:** M.J. Critelli
**Pres & CEO:** M.D. Martin
**EVP & CFO:** M. Monahan
**EVP & General Counsel:** V.A. O'Meara

**SVP & CTO:** J.E. Wall
**Investor Contact:** C.F. McBride (203-351-6349)
**Board Members:** R. C. Adkins, L. G. Alvarado, A. M. Busquet, M. J. Critelli, A. S. Fuchs, E. Green, J. H. Keyes, M. D. Martin, J. S. McFarlane, E. R. Menasce, M. I. Roth, D. L. Shedlarz, D. B. Snow, Jr., R. E. Weissman

**Founded:** 1920
**Domicile:** Delaware
**Employees:** 36,165

The McGraw·Hill Companies

# Plum Creek Timber Co Inc.

**STANDARD &POOR'S**

| S&P Recommendation **BUY** ★★★★☆ | Price $33.88 (as of Nov 14, 2008) | 12-Mo. Target Price $40.00 | Investment Style Large-Cap Blend |
|---|---|---|---|

**GICS Sector** Financials
**Sub-Industry** Specialized REITS

**Summary** Plum Creek Timber Co., a real estate investment trust (REIT), is the largest private timberland owner in the United States, with more than 7 million acres of timberlands in 18 states.

## Key Stock Statistics (Source S&P, Vickers, company reports)

| | | | | | | | |
|---|---|---|---|---|---|---|---|
| 52-Wk Range | $65.00–30.00 | S&P Oper. EPS 2008E | 1.50 | Market Capitalization(B) | $5.651 | Beta | 0.85 |
| Trailing 12-Month EPS | $1.49 | S&P Oper. EPS 2009E | 1.70 | Yield (%) | 4.96 | S&P 3-Yr. Proj. EPS CAGR(%) | 13 |
| Trailing 12-Month P/E | 22.7 | P/E on S&P Oper. EPS 2008E | 22.6 | Dividend Rate/Share | $1.68 | S&P Credit Rating | NA |
| $10K Invested 5 Yrs Ago | $15,905 | Common Shares Outstg. (M) | 166.8 | Institutional Ownership (%) | 69 | | |

## Price Performance

30-Week Mov. Avg. ···· 10-Week Mov. Avg. — **GAAP Earnings vs. Previous Year** Volume Above Avg. STARS
12-Mo. Target Price — Relative Strength — ▲ Up ▼ Down ► No Change Below Avg.

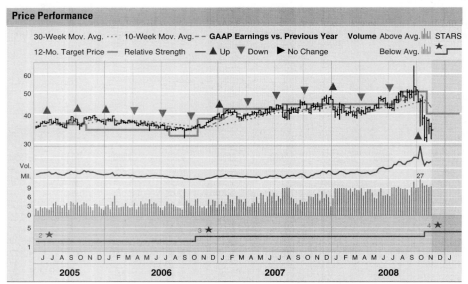

Options: CBOE, P, Ph

Analysis prepared by **Stuart J. Benway, CFA** on November 03, 2008, when the stock traded at **$ 37.13**.

## Highlights

➤ S&P projects that housing starts will decline 29% in 2008, to 953,000 units, and fall 2% further in 2009, to 934,000 units. We expect this to prevent any sustained rise in lumber and sawlog prices. However, we see pulpwood demand remaining steady. Overall, we forecast that harvest levels will decrease 5% in 2008. Rural land sales are expected to be up from last year, leading to an overall revenue gain of 1%. We look for sales to rise 5%-7% in 2009 due mainly to large land sales in Montana.

➤ We think that average wood product prices in 2008 will be about in line with 2007, as demand from the housing market continues to be weak. Overall, we expect margins to narrow in the timberland operations in 2008 before recovering slightly in 2009. We see PCL capturing improved prices for its higher and better use land sales, and believe this business will expand significantly over the long term.

➤ Our 2008 operating EPS estimate is $1.50, up nearly 10% from $1.37 earned in 2007. We note that the timing of real estate transactions could create some quarterly volatility. For 2009, we project EPS of $1.70.

## Investment Rationale/Risk

➤ We believe PCL has significant value in its land holdings, and we expect real estate to become a rising source of earnings in coming years. It plans to develop about 200,000 acres of land over the next 15 years, and we estimate that these properties can be sold at high margin levels. Over the next three years, PCL plans to sell 310,000 acres in Montana. In our view, this will allow PCL to pay a rising dividend. In the near term, however, log prices are likely to be hurt by what we see as weak residential construction activity.

➤ Risks to our recommendation and target price include renewed declines in log demand and prices due to weakness in the U.S. housing market, and lower-than-projected profits on sales of higher and better use land.

➤ Given the difficult conditions in the housing market in 2008, we do not see an increase in the payout this year. Our dividend discount model, which assumes a $1.72 dividend payout in 2009, a required rate of return of 9.8%, and constant dividend growth of 5.5%, indicates that the stock has an intrinsic value of $40, which is our 12-month target price.

## Qualitative Risk Assessment

| LOW | MEDIUM | HIGH |
|---|---|---|

Our risk assessment reflects that Plum Creek operates in a cyclical industry, with demand for its products tied to residential construction and paper manufacturing. It is subject to movements in interest rates, economic conditions and currency, and prices for its products have historically been volatile. However, it is a major landowner, and its debt levels are relatively low.

## Quantitative Evaluations

**S&P Quality Ranking**      **B**

| D | C | B- | B | B+ | A- | A | A+ |
|---|---|---|---|---|---|---|---|

**Relative Strength Rank**      **MODERATE**

59

LOWEST = 1      HIGHEST = 99

## Revenue/Earnings Data

**Revenue (Million $)**

| | 1Q | 2Q | 3Q | 4Q | Year |
|---|---|---|---|---|---|
| 2008 | 363.0 | 376.0 | 414.0 | -- | -- |
| 2007 | 369.0 | 395.0 | 407.0 | 504.0 | 1,675 |
| 2006 | 414.0 | 380.0 | 454.0 | 379.0 | 1,627 |
| 2005 | 400.0 | 358.0 | 427.0 | 391.0 | 1,576 |
| 2004 | 497.0 | 341.0 | 363.0 | 327.0 | 1,528 |
| 2003 | 273.0 | 318.0 | 290.0 | 315.0 | 1,196 |

**Earnings Per Share ($)**

| | 1Q | 2Q | 3Q | 4Q | Year |
|---|---|---|---|---|---|
| 2008 | 0.22 | 0.18 | 0.40 | E0.66 | E1.50 |
| 2007 | 0.25 | 0.33 | 0.34 | 0.68 | 1.60 |
| 2006 | 0.50 | 0.34 | 0.51 | 0.39 | 1.74 |
| 2005 | 0.56 | 0.37 | 0.52 | 0.34 | 1.79 |
| 2004 | 0.84 | 0.31 | 0.42 | 0.28 | 1.84 |
| 2003 | 0.18 | 0.31 | 0.25 | 0.30 | 1.04 |

Fiscal year ended Dec. 31. Next earnings report expected: Late January. EPS Estimates based on S&P Operating Earnings; historical GAAP earnings are as reported.

## Dividend Data (Dates: mm/dd Payment Date: mm/dd/yy)

| Amount ($) | Date Decl. | Ex-Div. Date | Stk. of Record | Payment Date |
|---|---|---|---|---|
| 0.420 | 02/05 | 02/12 | 02/14 | 02/29/08 |
| 0.420 | 05/06 | 05/14 | 05/16 | 05/30/08 |
| 0.420 | 08/05 | 08/13 | 08/15 | 08/29/08 |
| 0.420 | 11/05 | 11/13 | 11/17 | 11/28/08 |

Dividends have been paid since 1989. Source: Company reports.

---

**Please read the Required Disclosures and Analyst Certification on the last page of this report.**

The McGraw-Hill Companies

# Plum Creek Timber Co Inc.

**STANDARD &POOR'S**

## Business Summary November 03, 2008

CORPORATE OVERVIEW. Plum Creek Timber Co., a real estate investment trust (REIT), is the largest private timberland owner in the United States, with more than 7 million acres of timberlands in 18 states. In addition, the trust operates several wood products manufacturing facilities and is actively involved in land purchases and sales. The company conducts operations through four business segments: the timber operation accounted for 47% of 2007 revenues, manufacturing (28%), real estate (24%), and other (1%). The Northern Resources portion of the timber segment encompasses 3.8 million acres of timberlands, in Maine, Michigan, Montana, New Hampshire, Oregon, Washington, West Virginia, and Wisconsin. The Southern Resources portion of the timber segment consists of 4.2 million acres of timberlands primarily in Alabama, Arkansas, Florida, Georgia, Louisiana, Mississippi, North Carolina, Oklahoma, South Carolina, and Texas.

MARKET PROFILE. The timber industry provides raw materials and manages resources for the paper and forest products industry. Harvested logs are sold to third-party mills that produce lumber, plywood, oriented strand board, and pulp and paper products. There are five primary end markets for most of the timber harvested in the United States: new housing construction, home repair

and remodeling, products for industrial uses, raw material for the manufacture of pulp and paper, and logs for export.

The demand for timber is directly related to the underlying demand for pulp and paper products, lumber, panels, and other wood products. The demand for pulp and paper is largely driven by population growth, per-capita income levels, and industry capacity. The demand for lumber and manufactured wood products is primarily affected by the level of new residential construction activity and repair and remodeling activity, which, in turn, is affected by changes in general economic and demographic factors, including population growth and interest rates for home mortgages and construction loans. The market for wood fiber used in paper production and wood products manufacturing is very diverse, with many manufacturers of various sizes. We therefore believe that Plum Creek has only limited control over the prices that it can charge for timber and wood products.

## Company Financials Fiscal Year Ended Dec. 31

| Per Share Data ($) | 2007 | 2006 | 2005 | 2004 | 2003 | 2002 | 2001 | 2000 | 1999 | 1998 |
|---|---|---|---|---|---|---|---|---|---|---|
| Tangible Book Value | 12.06 | 11.80 | 12.62 | 12.19 | 11.57 | 12.04 | 12.21 | 7.46 | 7.70 | 8.78 |
| Cash Flow | 2.37 | 2.45 | 1.92 | 2.46 | 1.63 | 1.82 | 3.00 | 2.47 | 3.10 | 3.12 |
| Earnings | 1.60 | 1.74 | 1.79 | 1.84 | 1.04 | 1.26 | 2.58 | 1.91 | 1.72 | 0.90 |
| S&P Core Earnings | 1.61 | 1.67 | 1.78 | 1.82 | 1.04 | 1.24 | 2.57 | NA | NA | NA |
| Dividends | 1.68 | 1.60 | 1.52 | 1.42 | 1.40 | 1.49 | 2.85 | 2.28 | 2.28 | 2.26 |
| Payout Ratio | 105% | 92% | 85% | 77% | 135% | 118% | 110% | 119% | 133% | NM |
| Prices:High | 48.45 | 40.00 | 39.63 | 39.45 | 30.75 | 31.98 | 30.00 | 29.81 | 32.13 | 34.88 |
| Prices:Low | 37.13 | 31.21 | 33.40 | 27.30 | 20.88 | 18.92 | 23.30 | 21.50 | 23.13 | 23.44 |
| P/E Ratio:High | 30 | 23 | 22 | 21 | 30 | 25 | 12 | 16 | 19 | 39 |
| P/E Ratio:Low | 23 | 18 | 19 | 15 | 20 | 15 | 9 | 11 | 13 | 26 |
| **Income Statement Analysis (Million $)** | | | | | | | | | | |
| Revenue | 1,675 | 1,627 | 1,576 | 1,528 | 1,196 | 1,137 | 598 | 209 | 461 | 699 |
| Operating Income | 558 | 571 | 561 | 586 | 410 | 443 | 305 | 166 | 206 | 210 |
| Depreciation | 134 | 128 | 113 | 114 | 107 | 105 | 55.0 | 38.9 | 59.7 | 69.3 |
| Interest Expense | 147 | 133 | 109 | 111 | 117 | 103 | 54.0 | 46.8 | 63.5 | 60.6 |
| Pretax Income | 277 | 328 | 339 | 366 | 186 | 235 | 196 | 132 | 100 | 76.0 |
| Effective Tax Rate | NM | 3.90% | 2.30% | 7.40% | NM | 0.85% | NM | NM | NM | 0.68% |
| Net Income | 280 | 315 | 331 | 339 | 192 | 233 | 338 | 132 | 113 | 75.4 |
| S&P Core Earnings | 281 | 301 | 329 | 336 | 193 | 229 | 336 | NA | NA | NA |
| **Balance Sheet & Other Financial Data (Million $)** | | | | | | | | | | |
| Cash | 240 | 301 | 395 | 376 | 260 | 246 | 193 | 181 | 115 | 114 |
| Current Assets | 456 | 513 | 574 | 499 | 405 | 378 | 306 | 195 | 133 | 210 |
| Total Assets | 4,664 | 4,661 | 4,812 | 4,378 | 4,387 | 4,289 | 4,122 | 1,250 | 1,251 | 1,438 |
| Current Liabilities | 303 | 281 | 375 | 184 | 168 | 155 | 149 | 180 | 74.2 | 80.9 |
| Long Term Debt | 2,376 | 1,617 | 1,524 | 1,853 | 2,031 | 1,839 | 1,667 | 560 | 643 | 943 |
| Common Equity | 1,901 | 2,089 | 2,325 | 2,240 | 2,119 | 2,222 | 2,247 | 507 | 533 | 405 |
| Total Capital | 4,297 | 3,731 | 3,888 | 4,138 | 4,187 | 4,105 | 3,952 | 1,066 | 1,176 | 1,348 |
| Capital Expenditures | Nil | 86.0 | 89.0 | 70.0 | 246 | 231 | 59.0 | 21.7 | 25.6 | 54.9 |
| Cash Flow | 414 | 443 | 444 | 453 | 299 | 338 | 393 | 171 | 173 | 145 |
| Current Ratio | 1.5 | 1.8 | 1.5 | 2.7 | 2.4 | 2.4 | 2.1 | 1.1 | 1.8 | 2.6 |
| % Long Term Debt of Capitalization | 55.3 | 43.3 | 39.1 | 44.8 | 48.5 | 44.8 | 42.2 | 52.5 | 54.7 | 69.9 |
| % Net Income of Revenue | 16.7 | 19.3 | 21.0 | 22.2 | 16.1 | 20.5 | 56.5 | 63.1 | 24.6 | 10.8 |
| % Return on Assets | 6.0 | 6.6 | 7.2 | 7.7 | 4.4 | 5.5 | 11.8 | 10.5 | 8.4 | 5.5 |
| % Return on Equity | 14.0 | 14.2 | 14.5 | 15.6 | 8.8 | 10.4 | 28.3 | 25.4 | 24.2 | 17.2 |

Data as orig reptd.; bef. results of disc opers/spec. items. Per share data adj. for stk. divs.; EPS diluted. E-Estimated. NA-Not Available. NM-Not Meaningful. NR-Not Ranked. UR-Under Review.

**Office:** 999 3rd Ave Ste 4300, Seattle, WA 98104-4096.
**Telephone:** 206-467-3600.
**Email:** info@plumcreek.com
**Website:** http://www.plumcreek.com

**Chrmn:** I. Davidson
**Pres & CEO:** R.R. Holley
**COO:** T.M. Lindquist
**SVP & CFO:** D.W. Lambert

**SVP, Secy & General Counsel:** J.A. Kraft
**Investor Contact:** J. Hobbs (800-858-5347)
**Board Members:** I. Davidson, R. R. Holley, R. Josephs, J. G. McDonald, R. B. McLeod, J. F. Morgan, J. H. Scully, S. C. Tobias, M. A. White

**Founded:** 1989
**Domicile:** Delaware
**Employees:** 2,000

# PNC Financial Services Group Inc.

**STANDARD &POOR'S**

**S&P Recommendation**

| Price | 12-Mo. Target Price | Investment Style |
|---|---|---|
| $62.34 (as of Nov 14, 2008) | $73.00 | Large-Cap Value |

**GICS Sector** Financials
**Sub-Industry** Regional Banks

**Summary** This bank holding company conducts regional banking, wholesale banking and asset management businesses, primarily in Pennsylvania, Maryland and New Jersey.

## Key Stock Statistics (Source S&P, Vickers, company reports)

| | | | | | | | |
|---|---|---|---|---|---|---|---|
| 52-Wk Range | $87.99– 42.51 | S&P Oper. EPS 2008**E** | 4.84 | Market Capitalization(B) | $21.703 | Beta | 0.58 |
| Trailing 12-Month EPS | $3.76 | S&P Oper. EPS 2009**E** | 5.69 | Yield (%) | 4.23 | S&P 3-Yr. Proj. EPS CAGR(%) | 12 |
| Trailing 12-Month P/E | 16.6 | P/E on S&P Oper. EPS 2008**E** | 12.9 | Dividend Rate/Share | $2.64 | S&P Credit Rating | A+ |
| $10K Invested 5 Yrs Ago | $13,832 | Common Shares Outstg. (M) | 348.1 | Institutional Ownership (%) | 68 | | |

## Price Performance

- 30-Week Mov. Avg. · · · 10-Week Mov. Avg. – – **GAAP Earnings vs. Previous Year** **Volume** Above Avg. STARS
- 12-Mo. Target Price — Relative Strength — ▲ Up ▼ Down ► No Change Below Avg.

(chart: 2005 2006 2007 2008)

Options: ASE, CBOE, Ph

Analysis prepared by **Erik Oja** on October 10, 2008, when the stock traded at **$ 61.12**.

### Highlights

➤ We expect earning asset growth of 10% in 2008, and a net interest margin of 3.40%, up strongly from 3.00% in 2007, on a reduction in deposit costs. We expect PNC to increase its loan portfolio at a high-single digit rate in 2008, while restricting increases in deposits. In our estimation, this will lead to a gradual decrease in the deposit-to-loan ratio to 115% by the end of 2008, from approximately 121% at the end of 2007, a manageable development, in our view.

➤ Nonperforming loans, as a percentage of total loans, stood at 0.96% at the end of the second quarter, up from 0.34% a year earlier. By our calculation, the current level of nonperforming loans and the growth rate of nonperforming loans over the last year are still below peers and industry averages. While we are forecasting loan loss provisions of about $750 million for 2008, up from $315 million for 2007, we expect loan loss provisions to moderate in 2009, to a level of $260 million.

➤ We see 2008 operating EPS of $4.84. For 2009 and 2010, we expect EPS of $5.69 and $6.16, respectively.

### Investment Rationale/Risk

➤ We have a positive view of PNC's non-interest expense controls, ownership interest in Black-Rock, low exposure to CDO's (collateralized debt obligations) and SIV's (structured investment vehicles), relatively good capital levels (June 30 estimated Tier 1 of 8.1%, March 31 total risk based capital of 11.4%, and leverage ratio of 6.8%), and relatively high allowance for loan losses at quarter end (1.35% of total loans and 143% of nonperforming loans). However, the shares recently traded at 11.4X our forward four quarters EPS estimate of $5.34, a valuation that is ahead of peers, and that we think reflects PNC's solid second quarter results and 2008 outlook.

➤ Risks to our recommendation and target price include a flat or inverted yield curve, which could further increase the cost of deposits while keeping loan yields from increasing, and a further economic slowdown, which would adversely affect loan growth and credit quality.

➤ Our 12-month target price of $73 implies a P/E of 13.7X our forward four quarters EPS estimate of $5.34, above large regional banking peers. The shares recently yielded 3.9%.

### Qualitative Risk Assessment

| LOW | MEDIUM | HIGH |
|---|---|---|

Our risk assessment reflects our view of the company's large-cap valuation, strong loan portfolio credit quality, and history of profitability. In the last several years, PNC has produced relatively stable financial results.

### Quantitative Evaluations

**S&P Quality Ranking** B+

| D | C | B- | B | B+ | A- | A | A+ |
|---|---|---|---|---|---|---|---|

**Relative Strength Rank** STRONG

79

LOWEST = 1 HIGHEST = 99

### Revenue/Earnings Data

**Revenue (Million $)**

| | 1Q | 2Q | 3Q | 4Q | Year |
|---|---|---|---|---|---|
| 2008 | 2,586 | 2,639 | 2,228 | -- | -- |
| 2007 | 2,306 | 1,721 | 1,757 | 1,634 | 10,083 |
| 2006 | 2,251 | 2,356 | 4,146 | 2,186 | 10,939 |
| 2005 | 1,777 | 1,826 | 2,108 | 2,185 | 7,896 |
| 2004 | 1,577 | 1,395 | 1,523 | 1,413 | 6,315 |
| 2003 | 1,487 | 1,468 | 1,493 | 1,521 | 5,969 |

**Earnings Per Share ($)**

| | | | | | |
|---|---|---|---|---|---|
| 2008 | 1.09 | 1.45 | 0.71 | E1.32 | E4.84 |
| 2007 | 1.46 | 1.22 | 1.19 | 0.51 | 4.35 |
| 2006 | 1.19 | 1.28 | 5.01 | 1.27 | 8.73 |
| 2005 | 1.24 | 0.98 | 1.14 | 1.20 | 4.55 |
| 2004 | 1.15 | 1.07 | 0.91 | 1.08 | 4.21 |
| 2003 | 0.92 | 0.65 | 1.00 | 1.08 | 3.65 |

Fiscal year ended Dec. 31. Next earnings report expected: Mid January. EPS Estimates based on S&P Operating Earnings; historical GAAP earnings are as reported.

### Dividend Data (Dates: mm/dd Payment Date: mm/dd/yy)

| Amount ($) | Date Decl. | Ex-Div. Date | Stk. of Record | Payment Date |
|---|---|---|---|---|
| 0.630 | 01/03 | 01/09 | 01/11 | 01/24/08 |
| 0.660 | 04/04 | 04/10 | 04/14 | 04/24/08 |
| 0.660 | 07/03 | 07/09 | 07/11 | 07/24/08 |
| 0.660 | 10/02 | 10/09 | 10/13 | 10/24/08 |

Dividends have been paid since 1865. Source: Company reports.

Stock Report | November 15, 2008 | NYS Symbol: **PNC**

# PNC Financial Services Group Inc.

STANDARD
&POOR'S

## Business Summary October 10, 2008

CORPORATE OVERVIEW. PNC is a bank holding company that operates businesses engaged in retail banking, corporate and institutional banking, asset management, and global fund processing services. The company has four primary reportable business segments: Retail Banking, Corporate and Institutional Banking, BlackRock, and PFPC.

The Retail Banking and Corporate and Institutional Banking segments generate about 53% of total revenues. Retail Banking (36%) provides deposit, lending, brokerage, trust, investment management and cash management services to consumers and small businesses. Corporate and Institutional Banking (17%) offers lending, treasury management and capital markets products and services to mid-sized corporations, government entities and selectively to large corporations. The BlackRock segment (14%) includes the operations of 37%-owned BlackRock, Inc. (BLK: hold, $174). BLK, with $1.364 trillion in assets under management, provides diversified investment management services to institutional and individual investors worldwide through a variety of fixed income, cash management, equity and alternative investment products. PFPC (10%) provides mutual fund transfer agency and accounting and administration services.

MARKET PROFILE. As of June 30, 2007 (latest available FDIC branch-level data), PNC had 1,194 branches and $78.8 billion in deposits, including 231 branches and $13.4 billion in deposits acquired from Mercantile. According to Highline Data, 47.8% of deposits were concentrated in Pennsylvania, while 85.0% of deposits were in the three states of Pennsylvania, New Jersey and Maryland. In Pennsylvania, PNC had 409 branches, $37.7 billion in deposits, and a deposit market share of about 13.4%, ranking first, ahead of Wachovia (WB: sell, $15). In Maryland, PNC had 206 branches, including 187 from Mercantile, $11.0 billion in deposits, and a deposit market share of about 10.3%, ranking second, after Bank of America (BAC: strong sell, $23). In New Jersey, PNC had 329 branches, $18.3 billion in deposits, and a deposit market share of about 7.9%, ranking fourth. In the District of Columbia, PNC had 33 offices, deposits of $2.2 billion, and a deposit market share of 7.2%, ranking fourth. In addition, PNC had a total of 217 branches and $9.7 billion in deposits in Kentucky, Delaware, Virginia, Ohio, Indiana and Florida.

## Company Financials Fiscal Year Ended Dec. 31

| Per Share Data ($) | 2007 | 2006 | 2005 | 2004 | 2003 | 2002 | 2001 | 2000 | 1999 | 1998 |
|---|---|---|---|---|---|---|---|---|---|---|
| Tangible Book Value | 15.55 | 23.02 | 13.98 | 14.55 | 14.22 | 14.78 | 12.19 | 13.37 | 12.07 | 11.49 |
| Earnings | 4.35 | 8.73 | 4.55 | 4.21 | 3.65 | 4.20 | 1.26 | 4.09 | 4.15 | 3.60 |
| S&P Core Earnings | 4.47 | 8.63 | 4.43 | 4.00 | 3.53 | 3.83 | 0.92 | NA | NA | NA |
| Dividends | 2.44 | 2.15 | 2.00 | 2.00 | 1.94 | 1.92 | 1.92 | 1.83 | 1.68 | 1.58 |
| Payout Ratio | 56% | 25% | 44% | 48% | 53% | 46% | 152% | 45% | 40% | 44% |
| Prices:High | 76.41 | 75.15 | 65.66 | 59.79 | 55.55 | 62.80 | 75.81 | 75.00 | 62.00 | 66.75 |
| Prices:Low | 63.54 | 61.78 | 49.35 | 48.90 | 41.63 | 32.70 | 51.14 | 36.00 | 43.00 | 38.75 |
| P/E Ratio:High | 18 | 9 | 14 | 14 | 15 | 15 | 60 | 18 | 15 | 19 |
| P/E Ratio:Low | 15 | 7 | 11 | 12 | 11 | 8 | 41 | 9 | 10 | 11 |

| Income Statement Analysis (Million $) | 2007 | 2006 | 2005 | 2004 | 2003 | 2002 | 2001 | 2000 | 1999 | 1998 |
|---|---|---|---|---|---|---|---|---|---|---|
| Net Interest Income | 2,915 | 2,245 | 2,154 | 1,969 | 1,996 | 2,197 | 2,262 | 2,164 | 2,433 | 2,573 |
| Tax Equivalent Adjustment | 27.0 | 25.0 | 33.0 | NA | NA | NA | NA | 18.0 | 22.0 | 49.0 |
| Non Interest Income | 3,795 | 6,534 | 4,203 | 3,508 | 3,141 | 3,108 | 2,412 | 2,871 | 2,723 | 2,503 |
| Loan Loss Provision | 315 | 124 | 21.0 | 52.0 | 177 | 309 | 903 | 136 | 163 | 225 |
| % Expense/Operating Revenue | 64.0% | 50.5% | 48.6% | 68.2% | 67.7% | 60.8% | 71.4% | 60.8% | 60.3% | 63.6% |
| Pretax Income | 2,094 | 4,005 | 1,962 | 1,745 | 1,600 | 1,858 | 564 | 1,848 | 1,891 | 1,710 |
| Effective Tax Rate | 29.9% | 34.0% | 30.8% | 30.8% | 33.7% | 33.4% | 33.2% | 34.3% | 33.2% | 34.8% |
| Net Income | 1,467 | 2,595 | 1,325 | 1,197 | 1,029 | 1,200 | 377 | 1,214 | 1,264 | 1,115 |
| % Net Interest Margin | 3.00 | 2.92 | 3.00 | 3.22 | 3.64 | 3.99 | 3.84 | 3.64 | 3.68 | 3.85 |
| S&P Core Earnings | 1,503 | 2,565 | 1,294 | 1,134 | 993 | 1,093 | 270 | NA | NA | NA |

| Balance Sheet & Other Financial Data (Million $) | 2007 | 2006 | 2005 | 2004 | 2003 | 2002 | 2001 | 2000 | 1999 | 1998 |
|---|---|---|---|---|---|---|---|---|---|---|
| Money Market Assets | 2,729 | 1,763 | 350 | 1,635 | 50.0 | 3,658 | 1,335 | 1,151 | 1,148 | 1,014 |
| Investment Securities | 30,225 | 31,651 | 23,253 | 18,609 | 16,409 | 17,421 | 15,243 | 7,053 | 8,759 | 8,088 |
| Commercial Loans | 41,013 | 27,672 | 26,115 | 19,418 | 15,987 | 22,335 | 23,134 | 28,635 | 24,198 | 25,182 |
| Other Loans | 27,306 | 22,433 | 23,821 | 24,077 | 18,093 | 13,115 | 14,840 | 21,966 | 26,572 | 32,468 |
| Total Assets | 138,920 | 101,820 | 91,954 | 79,723 | 68,168 | 66,377 | 69,568 | 69,844 | 75,413 | 77,207 |
| Demand Deposits | 19,440 | 16,070 | 14,988 | 12,915 | 11,505 | 9,538 | 10,124 | 8,490 | 8,441 | 9,943 |
| Time Deposits | 63,256 | 50,231 | 45,287 | 40,354 | 33,736 | 35,444 | 37,180 | 39,174 | 38,227 | 37,553 |
| Long Term Debt | 21,157 | 10,266 | 6,797 | 8,684 | 7,667 | 9,112 | 8,922 | 7,266 | 9,395 | 10,994 |
| Common Equity | 14,854 | 10,788 | 8,563 | 7,548 | 6,735 | 6,943 | 5,822 | 6,649 | 5,939 | 6,036 |
| % Return on Assets | 1.2 | 2.7 | 1.5 | 1.6 | 1.5 | 1.8 | 0.5 | 1.7 | 1.7 | 1.5 |
| % Return on Equity | 11.4 | 26.8 | 16.5 | 16.8 | 15.0 | 18.7 | 5.9 | 19.0 | 20.8 | 19.2 |
| % Loan Loss Reserve | 1.2 | 1.1 | 1.2 | 1.3 | 1.8 | 1.8 | 1.5 | 1.3 | 1.2 | 1.3 |
| % Loans/Deposits | 79.5 | 79.1 | 123.7 | 84.8 | 78.4 | 82.4 | 89.1 | 109.6 | 119.7 | 121.4 |
| % Equity to Assets | 10.7 | 10.0 | 9.3 | 9.7 | 10.2 | 9.4 | 8.9 | 9.0 | 7.8 | 7.5 |

Data as orig reptd.; bef. results of disc opers/spec. items. Per share data adj. for stk. divs.; EPS diluted. E-Estimated. NA-Not Available. NM-Not Meaningful. NR-Not Ranked. UR-Under Review.

**Office:** 249 5th Ave, 1 PNC Plz, Pittsburgh, PA 15222-2707.
**Telephone:** 412-762-2000.
**Email:** corporate.communiations@pncbank.com
**Website:** http://www.pnc.com

**Chrmn & CEO:** J.E. Rohr
**Pres:** J.C. Guyaux
**EVP & Chief Admin Officer:** T.K. Whitford
**SVP, Chief Acctg Officer & Cntlr:** S.R. Patterson

**SVP & General Counsel:** H.P. Pudlin
**Investor Contact:** W. Callihan (800-843-2206)
**Board Members:** R. O. Berndt, C. E. Bunch, P. W. Chellgren, R. N. Clay, G. A. Davidson, Jr., K. C. James, R. B. Kelson, B. C. Lindsay, A. A. Massaro, J. G. Pepper, J. E. Rohr, D. J. Shepard, L. K. Steffes, D. F. Strigl, S. G. Thieke, T. J. Usher, G. H. Walls, Jr., H. H. Wehmeier

**Founded:** 1922
**Domicile:** Pennsylvania
**Employees:** 28,320

The McGraw-Hill Companies

# Polo Ralph Lauren Corp

STANDARD
&POOR'S

| S&P Recommendation | BUY ★★★★☆ | Price $42.15 (as of Nov 14, 2008) | 12-Mo. Target Price $60.00 | Investment Style Large-Cap Growth |
|---|---|---|---|---|

**GICS Sector** Consumer Discretionary
**Sub-Industry** Apparel, Accessories & Luxury Goods

**Summary** This company designs, markets and distributes men's and women's clothing and other premium lifestyle products.

## Key Stock Statistics (Source S&P, Vickers, company reports)

| | | | | | | | |
|---|---|---|---|---|---|---|---|
| 52-Wk Range | $82.02– 37.93 | S&P Oper. EPS 2009**E** | 4.00 | Market Capitalization(B) | $2.336 | Beta | 1.36 |
| Trailing 12-Month EPS | $4.58 | S&P Oper. EPS 2010**E** | 3.85 | Yield (%) | 0.47 | S&P 3-Yr. Proj. EPS CAGR(%) | 10 |
| Trailing 12-Month P/E | 9.2 | P/E on S&P Oper. EPS 2009**E** | 10.5 | Dividend Rate/Share | $0.20 | S&P Credit Rating | NA |
| $10K Invested 5 Yrs Ago | $15,093 | Common Shares Outstg. (M) | 98.7 | Institutional Ownership (%) | NM | | |

## Price Performance

30-Week Mov. Avg. ···  10-Week Mov. Avg. ━  **GAAP Earnings vs. Previous Year**  Volume Above Avg. STARS
12-Mo. Target Price ━  Relative Strength ━  ▲ Up  ▼ Down  ▶ No Change  Below Avg. ★

Options: ASE, CBOE, Ph

Analysis prepared by **Marie Driscoll, CFA** on October 16, 2008, when the stock traded at **$ 46.47**.

## Highlights

➤ Having successfully navigated a brand strategy over the past few years that included purchasing licenses, exiting tertiary doors, and decreasing exposure to the off-price channel, we see global expansion, the direct-to-consumer channel, new product categories and the moderate retail channel providing incremental growth opportunities for RL. We think the February 2008 exclusive launch of American Living at 600 JC Penney stores is a strong plus given weak traffic and sales trends at traditional department stores.

➤ We see FY 09 (Mar.) sales growth of 2%, to $5 billion, driven by a 5% gain in retail, flat wholesale revenues and an 8% gain in retail, offset by a 5% drop in licensing revenues.

➤ We see earnings before interest and taxes (EBIT) margins declining about 150 basis points, to 11.9% of sales in FY 09, reflecting investment in the European expansion and noncash goodwill charges (estimated at approximately $17 million). Long term, we see potential for margin improvement reflecting supply chain and sourcing initiatives.

## Investment Rationale/Risk

➤ Retail expansion, a more favorable merchandise mix and strong brand positioning provide RL with attractive long term growth opportunities in our view. Near term, we are concerned with a retrenching consumer, at both the affluent luxury level as well as at moderately priced department stores. We believe department stores are making reduced inventory investments and the strengthening U.S. dollar is expected to mitigate any benefit foreign exchange recently provided. Offsetting these negatives is RL's growing international business providing organic growth opportunities as RL extends its footprint over the next five years.

➤ Risks to our recommendation and target price include integration risk from recent licensee acquisitions. Regarding corporate governance, we are concerned that chairman, CEO and founder Ralph Lauren controls approximately 88% of the voting shares of the company.

➤ Our 12-month target price of $60 is about 16X our calendar 2009 EPS estimate of $3.66, about a 15% premium to peer luxury brands, which we believe is warranted by superior global growth opportunities we foresee.

## Qualitative Risk Assessment

| LOW | MEDIUM | HIGH |
|---|---|---|

Our risk assessment reflects our view of RL's strong balance sheet, offset by its exposure to the consolidating and contracting department store channel.

## Quantitative Evaluations

**S&P Quality Ranking** — NR

| D | C | B- | B | B+ | A- | A | A+ |
|---|---|---|---|---|---|---|---|

**Relative Strength Rank** — MODERATE

47

LOWEST = 1    HIGHEST = 99

## Revenue/Earnings Data

**Revenue (Million $)**

| | 1Q | 2Q | 3Q | 4Q | Year |
|---|---|---|---|---|---|
| 2009 | 1,114 | 1,429 | -- | -- | -- |
| 2008 | 1,070 | 1,299 | 1,270 | 1,241 | 4,880 |
| 2007 | 953.6 | 1,167 | 1,144 | 1,031 | 4,295 |
| 2006 | 751.9 | 964.8 | 995.5 | 971.6 | 3,746 |
| 2005 | 535.8 | 821.5 | 888.0 | 834.5 | 3,305 |
| 2004 | 477.7 | 707.8 | 645.4 | 818.8 | 2,650 |

**Earnings Per Share ($)**

| | | | | | |
|---|---|---|---|---|---|
| 2009 | 0.93 | 1.58 | E0.87 | E0.62 | E4.00 |
| 2008 | 0.82 | 1.09 | 1.08 | 1.00 | 3.99 |
| 2007 | 0.74 | 1.28 | 1.03 | 0.68 | 3.73 |
| 2006 | 0.48 | 0.97 | 0.84 | 0.58 | 2.87 |
| 2005 | 0.13 | 0.78 | 0.72 | 0.22 | 1.83 |
| 2004 | 0.05 | 0.54 | 0.35 | 0.75 | 1.69 |

Fiscal year ended Mar. 31. Next earnings report expected: Early February. EPS Estimates based on S&P Operating Earnings; historical GAAP earnings are as reported.

## Dividend Data (Dates: mm/dd Payment Date: mm/dd/yy)

| Amount ($) | Date Decl. | Ex-Div. Date | Stk. of Record | Payment Date |
|---|---|---|---|---|
| 0.050 | 12/17 | 12/26 | 12/28 | 01/11/08 |
| 0.050 | 03/17 | 03/26 | 03/28 | 04/11/08 |
| 0.050 | 06/17 | 06/25 | 06/27 | 07/11/08 |
| 0.050 | 09/16 | 09/24 | 09/26 | 10/10/08 |

Dividends have been paid since 2003. Source: Company reports.

---

**Please read the Required Disclosures and Analyst Certification on the last page of this report.**

The McGraw-Hill Companies

# Polo Ralph Lauren Corp

STANDARD
&POOR'S

## Business Summary October 16, 2008

CORPORATE OVERVIEW. Since its modest beginnings in men's ties more than 30 years ago, Polo Ralph Lauren has grown into one of America's leading lifestyle brands encompassing multiple permutations targeted at specific demographics, usage occasions and price points with merchandise available at approximately 10,800 locations throughout the world. Licensor relationships extend the brand to fragrance, eyewear, leather goods, jewelry and an extensive home merchandise offering. In total, we believe the Polo Ralph Lauren brand generates about $12 billion at retail worldwide.

MARKET PROFILE. The domestic men's, women's and children's apparel market represented an estimated $196 billion at retail in 2007, according to NPD Fashionworld consumer estimated data. The apparel market is fragmented, with national brands marketed by 20 companies accounting for about 30% of total apparel sales, and the remaining 70% comprised of smaller and/or private label "store" brands. The market is mature, in our view, with demand largely mirroring population growth and fashion trends accounting for a modicum of incremental volume. Deflationary pricing pressure is a function, we think, of channel competition and production steadily moving offshore to low-cost producers in India, Asia and China. S&P forecasts flat 2008 apparel sales, which compares with a 3% year-to-year advance in 2007, 5% in 2006, and 4% increments in both 2004 and 2005.

COMPETITIVE LANDSCAPE. By channel, specialty stores account for the largest share of apparel sales, at 31% in 2007, according to NPD. Mass merchants (Wal-Mart and Target) came in second, at 20%, and department stores, RL's primary channel, came in third, at 16%, and down 400 basis points since 2003. National chains (Sears and JC Penney) captured 15% of 2007 apparel sales, and off-price retailers (TJX and Ross Stores) 7%. The remaining 11% is divided among factory outlets and direct and e-mail pure plays. RL holds leading market shares in department stores, where it competes with Jones Apparel Group, Liz Claiborne, and VF Corp., as well as private label offerings, which garner about a third of total apparel purchases and are an important differentiator for retailers. RL also sells directly to consumers through 313 specialty retail locations spanning the luxury, mid-market and factory channels and at RalphLauren.com.

## Company Financials Fiscal Year Ended Mar. 31

| Per Share Data ($) | 2008 | 2007 | 2006 | 2005 | 2004 | 2003 | 2002 | 2001 | 2000 | 1999 |
|---|---|---|---|---|---|---|---|---|---|---|
| Tangible Book Value | 10.71 | 11.99 | 10.35 | 10.38 | 10.56 | 8.93 | 7.38 | 5.76 | 5.08 | 6.60 |
| Cash Flow | NA | 5.07 | 4.06 | 2.83 | 2.52 | 2.55 | 2.60 | 1.41 | 2.16 | 1.37 |
| Earnings | 3.99 | 3.73 | 2.87 | 1.83 | 1.69 | 1.76 | 1.75 | 0.61 | 1.49 | 0.91 |
| S&P Core Earnings | 3.99 | 3.75 | 2.80 | 2.32 | 1.53 | 1.55 | 1.54 | 0.44 | NA | NA |
| Dividends | 0.20 | 0.20 | 0.20 | 0.20 | Nil | Nil | Nil | Nil | Nil | Nil |
| Payout Ratio | 5% | 5% | 7% | 11% | Nil | Nil | Nil | Nil | Nil | Nil |
| Calendar Year | 2007 | 2006 | 2005 | 2004 | 2003 | 2002 | 2001 | 2000 | 1999 | 1998 |
| Prices:High | 102.58 | 83.15 | 56.84 | 42.83 | 31.52 | 30.82 | 31.34 | 23.25 | 25.38 | 31.38 |
| Prices:Low | 60.41 | 45.65 | 34.19 | 27.28 | 19.30 | 16.49 | 17.80 | 12.75 | 16.06 | 15.88 |
| P/E Ratio:High | 26 | 22 | 20 | 23 | 19 | 18 | 18 | 38 | 17 | 34 |
| P/E Ratio:Low | 15 | 12 | 12 | 15 | 11 | 9 | 10 | 21 | 11 | 17 |

| Income Statement Analysis (Million $) | 2008 | 2007 | 2006 | 2005 | 2004 | 2003 | 2002 | 2001 | 2000 | 1999 |
|---|---|---|---|---|---|---|---|---|---|---|
| Revenue | 4,880 | 4,295 | 3,746 | 3,305 | 2,650 | 2,439 | 2,364 | 2,226 | 1,956 | 1,713 |
| Operating Income | NA | 802 | 663 | 406 | 377 | 382 | 393 | 319 | 330 | 247 |
| Depreciation | 201 | 145 | 127 | 104 | 83.2 | 78.6 | 83.9 | 78.6 | 66.3 | 46.4 |
| Interest Expense | NA | 21.6 | 12.5 | 11.0 | 10.0 | 13.5 | 19.0 | 25.1 | 15.0 | 2.76 |
| Pretax Income | 644 | 659 | 516 | 298 | 266 | 274 | 276 | 98.0 | 249 | 153 |
| Effective Tax Rate | 34.5% | 36.8% | 37.7% | 36.0% | 35.7% | 36.5% | 37.5% | 39.5% | 40.8% | 40.7% |
| Net Income | 420 | 401 | 308 | 190 | 171 | 174 | 173 | 59.3 | 147 | 90.6 |
| S&P Core Earnings | 420 | 403 | 299 | 242 | 154 | 154 | 151 | 43.1 | NA | NA |

| Balance Sheet & Other Financial Data (Million $) | 2008 | 2007 | 2006 | 2005 | 2004 | 2003 | 2002 | 2001 | 2000 | 1999 |
|---|---|---|---|---|---|---|---|---|---|---|
| Cash | 626 | 564 | 286 | 350 | 343 | 344 | 239 | 102 | 165 | 88.7 |
| Current Assets | NA | 1,686 | 1,379 | 1,414 | 1,271 | 1,166 | 1,008 | 902 | 853 | 679 |
| Total Assets | 4,366 | 3,758 | 2,089 | 2,727 | 2,270 | 2,039 | 1,749 | 1,626 | 1,621 | 1,105 |
| Current Liabilities | NA | 640 | 844 | 622 | 501 | 500 | 392 | 440 | 406 | 348 |
| Long Term Debt | NA | 399 | Nil | 291 | 277 | 248 | 285 | 297 | 343 | 44.2 |
| Common Equity | 2,390 | 2,335 | 2,050 | 1,676 | 1,422 | 1,209 | 998 | 809 | 772 | 659 |
| Total Capital | NA | 2,734 | 2,070 | 1,967 | 1,699 | 1,457 | 1,284 | 1,106 | 1,115 | 703 |
| Capital Expenditures | 217 | 184 | 159 | 174 | 123 | 98.7 | 88.0 | 105 | 122 | 142 |
| Cash Flow | NA | 546 | 435 | 294 | 254 | 253 | 256 | 138 | 214 | 137 |
| Current Ratio | 2.1 | 2.6 | 1.6 | 2.3 | 2.5 | 2.3 | 2.6 | 2.1 | 2.1 | 2.0 |
| % Long Term Debt of Capitalization | 16.5 | 14.6 | Nil | 14.8 | 16.3 | 17.1 | 22.2 | 26.8 | 30.7 | 6.3 |
| % Net Income of Revenue | 8.6 | 9.3 | 8.2 | 5.8 | 6.5 | 7.1 | 7.3 | 2.7 | 7.5 | 5.3 |
| % Return on Assets | 10.3 | 11.7 | 12.8 | 7.6 | 7.9 | 9.2 | 10.2 | 3.7 | 10.8 | 9.4 |
| % Return on Equity | 17.8 | 18.3 | 16.5 | 12.3 | 13.0 | 15.8 | 19.1 | 7.5 | 20.6 | 14.6 |

Data as orig reptd.; bef. results of disc opers/spec. items. Per share data adj. for stk. divs.; EPS diluted. E-Estimated. NA-Not Available. NM-Not Meaningful. NR-Not Ranked. UR-Under Review.

**Office:** 650 Madison Ave, New York, NY 10022-1062.
**Telephone:** 212-318-7000.
**Website:** http://www.polo.com
**Chrmn & CEO:** R. Lauren

**Pres & COO:** R.N. Farah
**SVP, CFO & Chief Acctg Officer:** T.T. Travis
**SVP, Secy & General Counsel:** J.D. Drucker
**Investor Contact:** T.C. Travis (212-318-7000)

**Board Members:** J. R. Alchin, A. H. Aronson, F. A. Bennack, Jr., J. F. Brown, R. N. Farah, J. L. Fleishman, R. Lauren, J. A. McHale, S. P. Murphy, J. Nemerov, T. S. Semel, R. C. Wright

**Founded:** 1967
**Domicile:** Delaware
**Employees:** 15,000

# PPG Industries Inc.

**STANDARD &POOR'S**

**S&P Recommendation** BUY ★★★★☆

| Price | 12-Mo. Target Price | Investment Style |
|---|---|---|
| $45.38 (as of Nov 14, 2008) | $58.00 | Large-Cap Blend |

**GICS Sector** Materials
**Sub-Industry** Diversified Chemicals

**Summary** PPG is a leading manufacturer of coatings and resins, flat and fiber glass, and industrial and specialty chemicals.

## Key Stock Statistics (Source S&P, Vickers, company reports)

| | | | | | | | |
|---|---|---|---|---|---|---|---|
| 52-Wk Range | $72.21–43.00 | S&P Oper. EPS 2008E | 5.25 | Market Capitalization(B) | $7.452 | Beta | 0.90 |
| Trailing 12-Month EPS | $4.03 | S&P Oper. EPS 2009E | 5.75 | Yield (%) | 4.67 | S&P 3-Yr. Proj. EPS CAGR(%) | 8 |
| Trailing 12-Month P/E | 11.3 | P/E on S&P Oper. EPS 2008E | 8.6 | Dividend Rate/Share | $2.12 | S&P Credit Rating | A- |
| $10K Invested 5 Yrs Ago | $9,095 | Common Shares Outstg. (M) | 164.2 | Institutional Ownership (%) | 70 | | |

## Price Performance

30-Week Mov. Avg. ···· 10-Week Mov. Avg. ── **GAAP Earnings vs. Previous Year**  Volume Above Avg. ▮▮▮ STARS
12-Mo. Target Price ── Relative Strength ▲ Up ▼ Down ► No Change  Below Avg. ▮▮▮

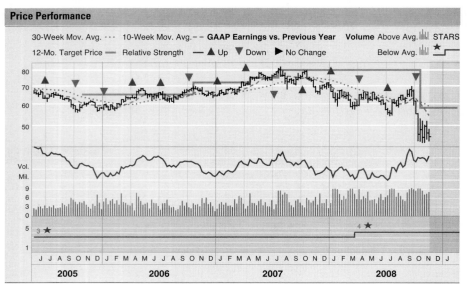

Options: ASE, CBOE, Ph

Analysis prepared by **Richard O'Reilly, CFA** on October 20, 2008, when the stock traded at **$ 49.44**.

## Highlights

➤ PPG in early 2008 acquired SigmaKalon, a Europe-based coatings producer with annual sales of about $3.0 billion, for $3.2 billion, and recently sold 60% of its auto glass businesses (annual sales of about $1.0 billion; reclassified as continuing operations in 2008). We forecast a modest rise in annual sales to around $16 billion for 2009. We think coatings and glass will continue to be limited by downturns in U.S. auto and construction markets.

➤ We forecast that margins for the coatings units will continue to be limited by increased raw materials and freight costs, largely offset by price increases. Optical products should continue to post good sales growth. We expect chlor-alkali profits to remain relatively strong into 2009 on sequential improvements in selling prices.

➤ We see the effective tax rate, before special items, to remain at about 31% in 2009. Our EPS estimate for 2008 excludes total special charges of about $1.21. The auto glass business had EPS of about $0.10 in 2008 through September.

## Investment Rationale/Risk

➤ We have a buy recommendation on the shares, based on valuation. The stock was recently trading at a P/E multiple of about 8.7X our recently reduced 2009 EPS estimate -- 25% below that of the S&P 500. The purchase of SigmaKalon greatly expanded PPG's coatings business, while the recent sale of a majority of the auto glass business significantly reduces its exposure to the domestic auto market. We believe that SigmaKalon will remain accretive for 2009 before special charges.

➤ Risks to our recommendation and target price include slower than projected industrial activity, unplanned production outages and interruptions, exposure to domestic auto makers, and unexpected weakness in selling prices for commodity chemicals.

➤ Our 12-month target price of $58 assumes that the stock's P/E multiple based on our 2009 operating EPS estimate will increase to a peer average 10X as a result of the expansion of the coatings businesses following the purchase of SigmaKalon. The dividend was recently increased for the 37th consecutive year, and the yield was well above that of the S&P 500.

## Qualitative Risk Assessment

| LOW | MEDIUM | HIGH |
|---|---|---|

Our risk assessment reflects the company's diversified business mix, large market shares in key products, and what we see as its healthy balance sheet, offset by the cyclical nature of the commodity chemicals business and the auto and construction-related end markets.

## Quantitative Evaluations

**S&P Quality Ranking**                     B+

| D | C | B- | B | B+ | A- | A | A+ |
|---|---|---|---|---|---|---|---|

**Relative Strength Rank**              MODERATE

63

LOWEST = 1                                    HIGHEST = 99

## Revenue/Earnings Data

**Revenue (Million $)**

| | 1Q | 2Q | 3Q | 4Q | Year |
|---|---|---|---|---|---|
| 2008 | 3,720 | 4,474 | 4,225 | -- | -- |
| 2007 | 2,917 | 3,173 | 2,823 | 2,874 | 11,206 |
| 2006 | 2,638 | 2,824 | 2,802 | 2,773 | 11,037 |
| 2005 | 2,493 | 2,656 | 2,547 | 2,505 | 10,201 |
| 2004 | 2,264 | 2,429 | 2,409 | 2,411 | 9,513 |
| 2003 | 2,071 | 2,304 | 2,206 | 2,175 | 8,756 |

**Earnings Per Share ($)**

| | | | | | |
|---|---|---|---|---|---|
| 2008 | 0.53 | 1.51 | 0.70 | E1.26 | E5.25 |
| 2007 | 1.17 | 1.50 | 1.29 | 1.17 | 4.91 |
| 2006 | 1.11 | 1.68 | 0.54 | 0.94 | 4.27 |
| 2005 | 0.55 | 1.34 | 0.92 | 0.68 | 3.49 |
| 2004 | 0.69 | 1.08 | 1.12 | 1.06 | 3.95 |
| 2003 | 0.49 | 0.89 | 0.83 | 0.71 | 2.92 |

Fiscal year ended Dec. 31. Next earnings report expected: Mid January. EPS Estimates based on S&P Operating Earnings; historical GAAP earnings are as reported.

## Dividend Data (Dates: mm/dd Payment Date: mm/dd/yy)

| Amount ($) | Date Decl. | Ex-Div. Date | Stk. of Record | Payment Date |
|---|---|---|---|---|
| 0.520 | 01/17 | 02/20 | 02/22 | 03/12/08 |
| 0.520 | 04/17 | 05/08 | 05/12 | 06/12/08 |
| 0.520 | 07/17 | 08/07 | 08/11 | 09/12/08 |
| 0.530 | 10/17 | 11/06 | 11/10 | 12/12/08 |

Dividends have been paid since 1899. Source: Company reports.

# PPG Industries Inc.

STANDARD
&POOR'S

## Business Summary October 20, 2008

CORPORATE OVERVIEW. PPG Industries is a diversified producer of coatings, chemicals and glass products. International operations contributed 44% of sales and 36% of operating profits in 2007.

PPG Industries is one of the world's leading producers of protective and decorative coatings. Industrial coatings (32% of sales in 2007 and 25% of operating profits) is comprised of original automotive and industrial coatings (used in appliance, industrial equipment and packaging markets). PPG also produces adhesives and sealants for the automotive industry and metal pretreatments.

Performance and applied coatings (34%, 37%) consists of automotive and industrial refinish coatings, aerospace coatings, and a major North American supplier of architectural coatings (Pittsburgh, Olympic, Porter and Lucite brands). The architectural finishes business at the end of 2007 operated 440 company-owned service centers in North America and 80 stores in Australia. The company is a global supplier of aircraft coatings, sealants, and transparencies to OEM, maintenance and aftermarket customers. PPG also makes marine and specialty industrial coatings. The coatings industry is highly competitive and consists of a few large firms with a global presence and many smaller firms serving local or regional markets.

PPG's commodity chemicals business (14%, 16%) is the fourth largest U.S. producer of chlorine and caustic soda (used in a wide variety of industrial applications), vinyl chloride monomer (for use in polyvinyl chloride resins), calcium hypochlorite, and chlorinated solvents. These commodity chemicals are highly cyclical; PPG volumes rose 9% in 2007 following two consecutive years of modest declines. The company's electrochemical unit (ECU) average prices declined in 2007 from a record level in 2006.

Optical and specialty materials (9%, 16%) consists of optical resins (Transitions photochromic lenses, sun lenses, and polarized film), silica compounds, and Teslin synthetic printing sheet. A fine chemicals business was sold in late 2007 (reported as discontinued operations). Aided by the introductions of new Transitions lenses, the optical products business has grown 14% annually since 1995. PPG introduced the newest version of the product in early 2008.

## Company Financials Fiscal Year Ended Dec. 31

| Per Share Data ($) | 2007 | 2006 | 2005 | 2004 | 2003 | 2002 | 2001 | 2000 | 1999 | 1998 |
|---|---|---|---|---|---|---|---|---|---|---|
| Tangible Book Value | 55.71 | 7.59 | 8.46 | 10.81 | 7.36 | 3.49 | 9.10 | 8.57 | 8.30 | 13.09 |
| Cash Flow | 7.20 | 6.61 | 5.66 | 6.19 | 5.23 | 1.99 | 4.93 | 6.20 | 12.99 | 6.69 |
| Earnings | 4.91 | 4.27 | 3.49 | 3.95 | 2.92 | -0.36 | 2.29 | 3.57 | 3.23 | 4.48 |
| S&P Core Earnings | 5.28 | 4.78 | 4.57 | 4.42 | 3.48 | 1.76 | 1.17 | NA | NA | NA |
| Dividends | 2.04 | 1.91 | 1.86 | 1.79 | 1.73 | 1.70 | 1.68 | 1.60 | 1.52 | 1.42 |
| Payout Ratio | 42% | 45% | 53% | 45% | 59% | NM | 73% | 45% | 47% | 32% |
| Prices:High | 82.42 | 69.80 | 74.73 | 68.79 | 64.42 | 62.86 | 59.75 | 65.06 | 70.75 | 76.63 |
| Prices:Low | 64.01 | 56.53 | 55.64 | 54.81 | 42.61 | 41.39 | 38.99 | 36.00 | 47.94 | 49.13 |
| P/E Ratio:High | 17 | 16 | 21 | 17 | 22 | NM | 26 | 18 | 22 | 17 |
| P/E Ratio:Low | 13 | 13 | 16 | 14 | 15 | NM | 17 | 10 | 15 | 11 |

| Income Statement Analysis (Million $) | | | | | | | | | | |
|---|---|---|---|---|---|---|---|---|---|---|
| Revenue | 11,254 | 11,037 | 10,201 | 9,513 | 8,756 | 8,067 | 8,169 | 8,629 | 7,757 | 7,510 |
| Operating Income | 1,698 | 1,703 | 1,648 | 1,496 | 1,367 | 1,309 | 1,371 | 1,649 | 1,528 | 1,659 |
| Depreciation | 380 | 380 | 372 | 388 | 394 | 398 | 447 | 447 | 419 | 383 |
| Interest Expense | 104 | 83.0 | 81.0 | 90.0 | 107 | 128 | 169 | 161 | 133 | 110 |
| Pretax Income | 1,243 | 1,060 | 947 | 1,063 | 843 | -28.0 | 666 | 1,017 | 973 | 1,294 |
| Effective Tax Rate | 28.6% | 26.2% | 29.8% | 30.3% | 34.8% | NM | 37.1% | 36.3% | 38.7% | 36.0% |
| Net Income | 815 | 711 | 596 | 683 | 500 | -60.0 | 387 | 620 | 568 | 801 |
| S&P Core Earnings | 877 | 797 | 780 | 765 | 597 | 300 | 197 | NA | NA | NA |

| Balance Sheet & Other Financial Data (Million $) | | | | | | | | | | |
|---|---|---|---|---|---|---|---|---|---|---|
| Cash | 2,232 | 455 | 466 | 709 | 499 | 117 | 108 | 111 | 158 | 128 |
| Current Assets | 7,136 | 4,592 | 4,019 | 4,054 | 3,537 | 2,945 | 2,703 | 3,093 | 3,062 | 2,660 |
| Total Assets | 12,629 | 10,021 | 8,681 | 8,932 | 8,424 | 7,863 | 8,452 | 9,125 | 8,914 | 7,387 |
| Current Liabilities | 4,661 | 2,787 | 2,349 | 2,221 | 2,139 | 1,920 | 1,955 | 2,543 | 2,384 | 1,912 |
| Long Term Debt | 1,201 | 1,155 | 1,169 | 1,184 | 1,339 | 1,699 | 1,699 | 1,810 | 1,836 | 1,081 |
| Common Equity | 4,151 | 3,234 | 3,053 | 3,572 | 2,911 | 2,150 | 3,080 | 3,097 | 3,106 | 2,880 |
| Total Capital | 5,649 | 4,673 | 4,420 | 4,997 | 4,475 | 4,044 | 5,453 | 5,578 | 5,560 | 4,488 |
| Capital Expenditures | 353 | 372 | 288 | 244 | 217 | 238 | 291 | 561 | 490 | 487 |
| Cash Flow | 1,195 | 1,091 | 968 | 1,071 | 894 | 338 | 834 | 1,067 | 987 | 1,184 |
| Current Ratio | 1.5 | 1.6 | 1.7 | 1.8 | 1.7 | 1.5 | 1.4 | 1.2 | 1.3 | 1.4 |
| % Long Term Debt of Capitalization | 21.3 | 24.7 | 26.4 | 23.7 | 29.9 | 42.0 | 31.2 | 32.4 | 33.0 | 24.0 |
| % Net Income of Revenue | 7.2 | 6.4 | 5.8 | 7.2 | 5.7 | NM | 4.7 | 7.2 | 7.3 | 10.7 |
| % Return on Assets | 7.2 | 7.6 | 6.8 | 7.9 | 6.1 | NM | 4.4 | 6.9 | 7.0 | 11.2 |
| % Return on Equity | 22.1 | 22.6 | 18.0 | 21.1 | 19.8 | NM | 12.5 | 20.0 | 19.0 | 29.7 |

Data as orig reptd.; bef. results of disc opers/spec. items. Per share data adj. for stk. divs.; EPS diluted. E-Estimated. NA-Not Available. NM-Not Meaningful. NR-Not Ranked. UR-Under Review.

**Office:** 1 PPG Place, Pittsburgh, PA 15272.
**Telephone:** 412-434-3131.
**Website:** http://www.ppg.com
**Chrmn & CEO:** C.E. Bunch

**Investor Contact:** W.H. Hernandez (412-434-3131)
**SVP, CFO & Chief Acctg Officer:** W.H. Hernandez
**SVP, Secy & General Counsel:** J.C. Diggs
**CTO:** J.A. Trainham

**Board Members:** J. G. Berges, C. E. Bunch, H. Grant, V. F. Haynes, M. J. Hooper, R. Mehrabian, M. H. Richenhagen, R. Ripp, T. J. Usher, D. R. Whitwam

**Founded:** 1883
**Domicile:** Pennsylvania
**Employees:** 34,900

# PPL Corp

**S&P Recommendation** HOLD ★★★☆☆

| Price | 12-Mo. Target Price | Investment Style |
|---|---|---|
| $32.62 (as of Nov 14, 2008) | $32.00 | Large-Cap Blend |

**GICS Sector** Utilities
**Sub-Industry** Electric Utilities

**Summary** This holding company for PPL Utilities also has holdings in the U.K.

## Key Stock Statistics (Source S&P, Vickers, company reports)

| | | | | | | | |
|---|---|---|---|---|---|---|---|
| 52-Wk Range | $55.23– 26.84 | S&P Oper. EPS 2008**E** | 2.05 | Market Capitalization(B) | $12.219 | Beta | 0.63 |
| Trailing 12-Month EPS | $2.84 | S&P Oper. EPS 2009**E** | 1.75 | Yield (%) | 4.11 | S&P 3-Yr. Proj. EPS CAGR(%) | 14 |
| Trailing 12-Month P/E | 11.5 | P/E on S&P Oper. EPS 2008**E** | 15.9 | Dividend Rate/Share | $1.34 | S&P Credit Rating | NA |
| $10K Invested 5 Yrs Ago | $18,699 | Common Shares Outstg. (M) | 374.6 | Institutional Ownership (%) | 63 | | |

## Price Performance

30-Week Mov. Avg. · · · 10-Week Mov. Avg. - - GAAP Earnings vs. Previous Year   Volume  Above Avg. STARS
12-Mo. Target Price — Relative Strength — ▲ Up ▼ Down ► No Change   Below Avg.

Options: CBOE, P, Ph

Analysis prepared by **Justin McCann** on November 05, 2008, when the stock traded at **$ 30.00**.

### Highlights

➤ We expect EPS in 2008 to decline more than 20% from 2007 operating EPS of $2.60. In the first nine months of 2008, EPS was down about 22% to $1.56, reflecting the absence of the divested Latin American operations, rising fuel costs, the loss of synfuel-related earnings, the absence of a one-time income tax benefit of $0.08, and a substantial third quarter drop in wholesale elecricity prices.

➤ For 2009, we expect EPS to decline nearly 15% from anticipated results in 2008. This would reflect significantly higher financing costs, the continued increase in coal commodity and transportation costs, the completion of the company's scrubber construction program, and the fall in sulfur dioxide allowance prices. However, we see a sharp rise in 2010 earnings as expired energy contracts are replaced by much higher-margin contracts.

➤ On August 7, 2008, Pennsylvania's Public Utility Commission approved PPL's rate stabilization plan that would enable residential and small-business customers to pay slightly higher bills for the remainder of 2008 and 2009 in order to minimize the very sharp increase expected in 2010 when the current rate cap expires.

### Investment Rationale/Risk

➤ We recently reduced our recommendation on the shares to hold, from buy. The stock has dropped nearly 45% year to date, hurt, in our view, by the crisis in the credit markets, the drop in wholesale power prices, and the sharply reduced earnings outlook for 2008 and 2009. However, we expect the stock to gradually recover once the market looks beyond the expected sharp EPS declines in 2008 and 2009, to the strong increase projected for 2010. The stock's dividend yield (recently 4.6%) remains below the peer average (5.2%), and the effective payout ratio (77% of our 2009 operating EPS estimate) is also well above that of peers (60%).

➤ Risks to our recommendation and target price include potentially unfavorable regulatory rulings, significantly lower results from the unregulated operations, and a major shift in the average P/E multiple of the peer group as a whole.

➤ Our 12-month target price is $32. Since we expect PPL's current weakness in its wholesale power business to dramatically recover in 2010, we expect the stock to trade at about 18.3X our 2009 EPS estimate, reflecting a more than 35% premium to the average projected peer P/E multiple, based on our EPS forecasts for 2009.

### Qualitative Risk Assessment

| LOW | MEDIUM | HIGH |
|---|---|---|

Our risk assessment reflects the steady cash flow we expect from the regulated Pennsylvania and U.K. distribution segments, which operate within supportive regulatory environments. This is offset by the highly profitable but less predictable earnings and cash flow from the power supply segment, as well as the currency risks related to the U.K. and Latin American businesses.

### Quantitative Evaluations

**S&P Quality Ranking** B+

| D | C | B- | B | B+ | A- | A | A+ |
|---|---|---|---|---|---|---|---|

**Relative Strength Rank** STRONG

77

LOWEST = 1    HIGHEST = 99

### Revenue/Earnings Data

**Revenue (Million $)**

| | 1Q | 2Q | 3Q | 4Q | Year |
|---|---|---|---|---|---|
| 2008 | 1,526 | 1,024 | 2,981 | -- | -- |
| 2007 | 1,638 | 1,613 | 1,763 | 1,606 | 6,498 |
| 2006 | 1,781 | 1,642 | 1,752 | 1,724 | 6,899 |
| 2005 | 1,602 | 1,476 | 1,643 | 1,498 | 6,219 |
| 2004 | 1,520 | 1,362 | 1,465 | 1,465 | 5,812 |
| 2003 | 1,487 | 1,338 | 1,456 | 1,296 | 5,587 |

**Earnings Per Share ($)**

| | | | | | |
|---|---|---|---|---|---|
| 2008 | 0.65 | 0.50 | 0.55 | E0.49 | E2.05 |
| 2007 | 0.58 | 0.63 | 0.72 | 0.57 | 2.63 |
| 2006 | 0.73 | 0.52 | 0.58 | 0.47 | 2.29 |
| 2005 | 0.44 | 0.47 | 0.51 | 0.50 | 1.92 |
| 2004 | 0.50 | 0.41 | 0.52 | 0.47 | 1.89 |
| 2003 | 0.53 | 0.34 | 0.49 | 0.72 | 2.08 |

Fiscal year ended Dec. 31. Next earnings report expected: Early February. EPS Estimates based on S&P Operating Earnings; historical GAAP earnings are as reported.

### Dividend Data (Dates: mm/dd Payment Date: mm/dd/yy)

| Amount ($) | Date Decl. | Ex-Div. Date | Stk. of Record | Payment Date |
|---|---|---|---|---|
| 0.305 | 11/15 | 12/06 | 12/10 | 01/01/08 |
| 0.335 | 02/22 | 03/06 | 03/10 | 04/01/08 |
| 0.335 | 05/21 | 06/06 | 06/10 | 07/01/08 |
| 0.335 | 08/22 | 09/08 | 09/10 | 10/01/08 |

Dividends have been paid since 1946. Source: Company reports.

---

**Please read the Required Disclosures and Analyst Certification on the last page of this report.**

The McGraw-Hill Companies

# PPL Corp

**STANDARD &POOR'S**

## Business Summary November 05, 2008

CORPORATE OVERVIEW. PPL Corporation (PPL) is an energy and utility holding company organized into three operating segments: the supply segment, the Pennsylvania delivery segment, and the international delivery segment. PPL's subsidiaries PPL Generation and PPL EnergyPlus comprise the supply segment. These units are involved in electricity generation and marketing of electricity and other power purchases to deregulated wholesale and retail markets. The Pennsylvania delivery segment operates through its PPL Electric subsidiary, which provides electric utility services in the regulated Pennsylvania market. On March 6, 2008, PPL announced an agreement to sell its natural gas distribution unit PPL Gas Utilities and its propane unit Penn Fuel Propane for $268 million in cash, subject to necessary approvals. After having completed the divestiture of its Latin American interests in 2007, the international delivery segment is now focused on an electricity distribution company in the U.K.

CORPORATE STRATEGY. The company's business strategy is to achieve stable growth in the regulated delivery business. It plans to earn long-term growth in delivery through efficient and low-cost operations while working to enhance strong customer and regulatory relations. In the unregulated supply business, PPL intends to reduce the volatility in both its cash flows and earnings and to ensure disciplined growth. The company's strategy for its electricity generation and marketing business is to build an effective risk manage-

ment framework to handle energy price risk and counterparty risk. It will work to reduce risk by entering into supply contracts of varying duration, which should reflect fluctuations in demand.

MARKET PROFILE. PPL provides electricity delivery service to 1.4 million customers in a 10,000-square-mile territory covering 29 counties of eastern and central Pennsylvania. In 2007, about 43% of electricity revenues were from residential customers, 37% from commercial customers, 19% from industrial customers, and 1% from other customer classes. In 2007, PPL's gas distribution and propane businesses (for which the company has announced an agreement to sell) provided gas and propane services to approximately 110,000 customers in Pennsylvania and parts of Maryland and Delaware. In addition, PPL Gas Utilities provided intra- and inter-state storage services from its storage fields in Pennsylvania. PPL Generation owned or controlled 11,418 megawatts (mw) of generating capacity at the end of 2007, with 9,076 mw at its plants in Pennsylvania and 1,287 mw in Montana. In the U.K., PPL operates two distribution companies that serve 2.6 million customers.

## Company Financials Fiscal Year Ended Dec. 31

| Per Share Data ($) | 2007 | 2006 | 2005 | 2004 | 2003 | 2002 | 2001 | 2000 | 1999 | 1998 |
|---|---|---|---|---|---|---|---|---|---|---|
| Tangible Book Value | 11.33 | 9.35 | 7.73 | 7.50 | 5.53 | 5.87 | 6.98 | 6.65 | 5.60 | 5.94 |
| Earnings | 2.63 | 2.29 | 1.92 | 1.89 | 2.08 | 1.17 | 0.58 | 1.68 | 1.57 | 1.15 |
| S&P Core Earnings | 2.61 | 2.33 | 1.87 | 1.74 | 1.95 | 0.79 | 0.90 | NA | NA | NA |
| Dividends | 1.22 | 1.10 | 1.21 | 0.82 | 0.77 | 0.68 | 0.53 | 0.53 | 0.50 | 0.67 |
| Payout Ratio | 47% | 48% | 63% | 43% | 37% | 57% | 92% | 32% | 32% | 59% |
| Prices:High | 54.58 | 37.34 | 33.68 | 27.08 | 22.17 | 19.98 | 31.18 | 23.06 | 16.00 | 14.47 |
| Prices:Low | 34.43 | 27.83 | 25.52 | 19.92 | 15.83 | 13.00 | 15.50 | 9.19 | 10.19 | 10.44 |
| P/E Ratio:High | 21 | 16 | 18 | 14 | 11 | 17 | 54 | 14 | 10 | 13 |
| P/E Ratio:Low | 13 | 12 | 13 | 11 | 8 | 11 | 27 | 5 | 6 | 9 |

| Income Statement Analysis (Million $) | 2007 | 2006 | 2005 | 2004 | 2003 | 2002 | 2001 | 2000 | 1999 | 1998 |
|---|---|---|---|---|---|---|---|---|---|---|
| Revenue | 6,498 | 6,899 | 6,219 | 5,812 | 5,587 | 5,429 | 5,725 | 5,683 | 4,590 | 3,786 |
| Depreciation | 756 | 446 | 420 | 412 | 380 | 367 | 254 | 261 | 257 | 338 |
| Maintenance | NA | NA | NA | NA | NA | 314 | 269 | 261 | 215 | 182 |
| Fixed Charges Coverage | 3.61 | 3.46 | 2.70 | 2.72 | 2.72 | 2.49 | 3.08 | 2.95 | 3.20 | 3.45 |
| Construction Credits | NA | NA | NA | NA | NA | NA | NA | NA | NA | Nil |
| Effective Tax Rate | 20.7% | 23.5% | 14.0% | 21.6% | 18.5% | 29.5% | 54.4% | 36.3% | 26.1% | 39.3% |
| Net Income | 1,013 | 885 | 737 | 700 | 748 | 425 | 221 | 513 | 478 | 379 |
| S&P Core Earnings | 1,007 | 897 | 716 | 645 | 674 | 240 | 262 | NA | NA | NA |

| Balance Sheet & Other Financial Data (Million $) | 2007 | 2006 | 2005 | 2004 | 2003 | 2002 | 2001 | 2000 | 1999 | 1998 |
|---|---|---|---|---|---|---|---|---|---|---|
| Gross Property | 20,377 | 20,079 | 18,615 | 18,692 | 17,775 | 16,406 | 12,477 | 11,418 | 10,717 | 10,489 |
| Capital Expenditures | 1,685 | 1,394 | 811 | 703 | 771 | 648 | 565 | 460 | 318 | 304 |
| Net Property | 12,605 | 12,069 | 10,916 | 11,209 | 10,446 | 9,566 | 6,135 | 5,948 | 5,644 | 4,363 |
| Capitalization:Long Term Debt | 6,890 | 6,728 | 6,044 | 6,881 | 8,145 | 6,562 | 5,906 | 4,717 | 4,103 | 3,092 |
| Capitalization:% Long Term Debt | 54.1 | 55.4 | 57.5 | 61.6 | 71.1 | 74.0 | 75.3 | 69.1 | 71.8 | 60.3 |
| Capitalization:Preferred | 301 | 301 | 51.0 | 51.0 | 51.0 | 82.0 | 82.0 | 97.0 | Nil | 347 |
| Capitalization:% Preferred | 2.40 | 2.50 | 0.50 | 0.46 | 0.45 | 0.92 | 1.05 | 1.42 | Nil | 6.70 |
| Capitalization:Common | 5,556 | 5,122 | 4,418 | 4,239 | 3,259 | 2,224 | 1,857 | 2,012 | 1,613 | 1,790 |
| Capitalization:% Common | 43.5 | 42.1 | 42.0 | 37.9 | 28.5 | 25.1 | 23.7 | 29.5 | 28.2 | 34.9 |
| Total Capital | 12,766 | 14,241 | 12,766 | 13,653 | 13,710 | 11,274 | 9,332 | 6,880 | 7,328 | 5,317 |
| % Operating Ratio | 78.3 | 80.8 | 80.3 | 79.5 | 78.9 | 76.8 | 81.1 | 84.0 | 84.8 | 79.8 |
| % Earned on Net Property | 13.6 | 13.9 | 12.2 | 12.7 | 13.4 | 17.5 | 14.2 | 28.6 | 22.3 | 10.3 |
| % Return on Revenue | 15.6 | 12.8 | 11.9 | 12.0 | 13.4 | 7.8 | 3.9 | 9.0 | 10.4 | 10.0 |
| % Return on Invested Capital | 12.1 | 10.3 | 9.5 | 9.0 | 10.0 | 12.6 | 12.4 | 14.3 | 11.3 | 13.1 |
| % Return on Common Equity | 19.0 | 18.6 | 17.0 | 18.6 | 26.2 | 17.5 | 8.7 | 28.3 | 28.1 | 16.5 |

Data as orig reptd.; bef. results of disc opers/spec. items. Per share data adj. for stk. divs.; EPS diluted. E-Estimated. NA-Not Available. NM-Not Meaningful. NR-Not Ranked. UR-Under Review.

**Office:** 2 N 9th St, Allentown, PA, USA 18101-1170.
**Telephone:** 610-774-5151.
**Email:** invrel@pplweb.com
**Website:** http://www.pplweb.com

**Chrmn, Pres & CEO:** J.H. Miller
**COO & EVP:** W.H. Spence
**EVP & CFO:** P.A. Farr
**SVP, Secy & General Counsel:** R.J. Grey

**Chief Acctg Officer & Cntlr:** J.M. Simmons, Jr.
**Investor Contact:** T.J. Paukovits (610-774-4124)
**Board Members:** F. Bernthal, J. W. Conway, E. A. Deaver, L. K. Goeser, S. E. Graham, S. Heydt, J. H. Miller, C. A. Rogerson, W. K. Smith, S. M. Stalnecker, K. H. Williamson

**Founded:** 1920
**Domicile:** Pennsylvania
**Employees:** 11,149

The McGraw-Hill Companies

# Praxair Inc.

STANDARD
&POOR'S

| S&P Recommendation | HOLD ★★★☆☆ | Price<br>$59.46 (as of Nov 14, 2008) | 12-Mo. Target Price<br>$65.00 | Investment Style<br>Large-Cap Growth |
|---|---|---|---|---|

**GICS Sector** Materials
**Sub-Industry** Industrial Gases

**Summary** This company is the largest producer of industrial gases in North and South America, and the second biggest worldwide. It also provides ceramic and metallic coatings.

## Key Stock Statistics (Source S&P, Vickers, company reports)

| | | | | | | | | |
|---|---|---|---|---|---|---|---|---|
| 52-Wk Range | $99.74–50.00 | S&P Oper. EPS 2008**E** | 4.24 | Market Capitalization(B) | $18.337 | Beta | 1.00 |
| Trailing 12-Month EPS | $4.13 | S&P Oper. EPS 2009**E** | 4.60 | Yield (%) | 2.52 | S&P 3-Yr. Proj. EPS CAGR(%) | 10 |
| Trailing 12-Month P/E | 14.4 | P/E on S&P Oper. EPS 2008**E** | 14.0 | Dividend Rate/Share | $1.50 | S&P Credit Rating | A |
| $10K Invested 5 Yrs Ago | $18,583 | Common Shares Outstg. (M) | 308.4 | Institutional Ownership (%) | 87 | | |

## Price Performance

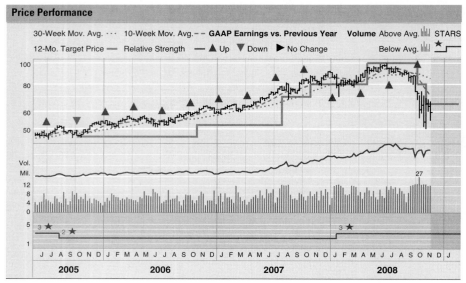

30-Week Mov. Avg. ···· 10-Week Mov. Avg. - - GAAP Earnings vs. Previous Year Volume Above Avg. STARS
12-Mo. Target Price — Relative Strength — ▲ Up ▼ Down ▶ No Change Below Avg.

Options: ASE, CBOE, Ph

Analysis prepared by **Richard O'Reilly, CFA** on October 30, 2008, when the stock traded at **$ 63.91**.

## Highlights

➤ We expect sales to rise only modestly in 2009 assuming unfavorable exchange rates and the pass-through of lower natural gas costs to customers. Underlying sales growth should be in the mid-to high single digits, down from about 12% for 2008, driven by the start-up of new projects and increased selling prices in most regions. We see North American and European gases volumes continuing to show low-single digit growth, due to the addition of new projects despite slower manufacturing sectors.

➤ We also see the South American region posting good sales gains, while Asian growth should continue in the double digits, driven by a large number of new projects and despite slowing electronics markets. We look for Surface Technologies' ongoing sales to expand close to 10% on stronger demand in coatings services for industrial equipment and OEM aircraft engines.

➤ We forecast that 2009 operating profit margins will recover from 2008's reduced level, reflecting the positive impact from the pass-through of lower natural gas costs. We look for an effective tax rate of 28%, while a more aggressive stock buyback program initiated in mid-2007 should help to boost EPS comparisons.

## Investment Rationale/Risk

➤ The shares are down about 30% year to date and were recently trading at 13.8X our 2009 EPS estimate of $4.60, a premium to the S&P 500. PX typically traded at a discount prior to 2004. We believe that the company's long-term fundamentals remain sound, and that it is concentrating on several less capital-intensive, faster-growing global markets such as energy, metals, and health care, as well as hydrogen for use by petroleum refiners.

➤ Risks to our recommendation and target price include an unexpected decline in industrial activity, especially energy and metals-related markets; higher-than-projected power and natural gas costs; and an inability to rapidly develop and successfully introduce new products and applications for industrial gases.

➤ Our 12-month target price of $65 assumes a widening of PX's P/E to about 14X, in line with its industrial gases peers in our coverage universe, applied to our 2009 EPS forecast. We expect the quarterly dividend to continue to be boosted over the long run.

## Qualitative Risk Assessment

| LOW | MEDIUM | HIGH |
|---|---|---|

Our risk assessment reflects the relatively stable growth and cash flow nature of the industrial gases industry versus commodity chemicals, and PX's high S&P Quality Ranking of A. This is offset by its exposure to volatile energy costs.

## Quantitative Evaluations

**S&P Quality Ranking**      A

| D | C | B- | B | B+ | A- | A | A+ |
|---|---|---|---|---|---|---|---|

**Relative Strength Rank**      MODERATE

61

LOWEST = 1          HIGHEST = 99

## Revenue/Earnings Data

**Revenue (Million $)**

| | 1Q | 2Q | 3Q | 4Q | Year |
|---|---|---|---|---|---|
| 2008 | 2,663 | 2,878 | 2,852 | -- | -- |
| 2007 | 2,175 | 2,332 | 2,372 | 2,523 | 9,402 |
| 2006 | 2,026 | 2,076 | 2,099 | 2,123 | 8,324 |
| 2005 | 1,827 | 1,919 | 1,890 | 2,020 | 7,656 |
| 2004 | 1,531 | 1,603 | 1,674 | 1,786 | 6,594 |
| 2003 | 1,337 | 1,401 | 1,414 | 1,461 | 5,613 |

**Earnings Per Share ($)**

| | | | | | |
|---|---|---|---|---|---|
| 2008 | 0.96 | 1.08 | 1.11 | E1.06 | E4.24 |
| 2007 | 0.81 | 0.89 | 0.94 | 0.98 | 3.62 |
| 2006 | 0.68 | 0.75 | 0.75 | 0.82 | 3.00 |
| 2005 | 0.59 | 0.63 | 0.33 | 0.67 | 2.22 |
| 2004 | 0.49 | 0.53 | 0.53 | 0.55 | 2.10 |
| 2003 | 0.40 | 0.46 | 0.46 | 0.47 | 1.77 |

Fiscal year ended Dec. 31. Next earnings report expected: Late January. EPS Estimates based on S&P Operating Earnings; historical GAAP earnings are as reported.

## Dividend Data (Dates: mm/dd Payment Date: mm/dd/yy)

| Amount<br>($) | Date<br>Decl. | Ex-Div.<br>Date | Stk. of<br>Record | Payment<br>Date |
|---|---|---|---|---|
| 0.375 | 01/23 | 03/05 | 03/07 | 03/17/08 |
| 0.375 | 04/22 | 06/04 | 06/06 | 06/16/08 |
| 0.375 | 07/23 | 09/03 | 09/05 | 09/15/08 |
| 0.375 | 10/29 | 12/03 | 12/05 | 12/15/08 |

Dividends have been paid since 1992. Source: Company reports.

---

**Please read the Required Disclosures and Analyst Certification on the last page of this report.**

The McGraw-Hill Companies

# Praxair Inc.

STANDARD
&POOR'S

## Business Summary October 30, 2008

CORPORATE OVERVIEW. Since its 1992 spin-off from Union Carbide Corp., PX, the largest producer of industrial gases in North and South America, has expanded its operations to 40 countries. Foreign sales accounted for 56% of the total in 2007, with Brazil alone providing 14%.

PX conducts its industrial gases business through four operating segments: North America (55% of sales and 53% of profits in 2007); South America (17%, 17%); Europe (14%,18%); and Asia (8%, 7%). The capital-intensive industrial gases business involves the production, distribution and sale of atmospheric gases (oxygen, nitrogen, argon and rare gases), carbon dioxide, hydrogen, helium, acetylene, and specialty and electronic gases. Atmospheric gases are produced through air separation processes, primarily cryogenic, while other gases are produced by various methods. PX also produces specialty products (sputtering targets, mechanical planarization slurries and polishing pads, and coatings) for use in semiconductor manufacturing. In addition, the business includes the construction and sale of equipment to produce industrial gases.

Industrial gases are supplied to customers through three basic methods: on-

site/pipeline (24% of total 2007 sales, sold under long-term contracts), merchant (30%, with three- to five-year contracts) and packaged (32%). At the end of 2007, the company had 260 major production facilities (air separation, hydrogen and carbon dioxide plants) in North America and five major pipeline complexes; 50 facilities and three pipeline complexes in Europe; more than 40 plants in South America, primarily in Brazil; and more than 25 plants in Asia, mainly in China, Korea and India. S.A. White Martins is the largest producer of industrial gases in South America.

The Surface Technologies business (6%, 5%) applies metallic and ceramic coatings and powders to parts and equipment provided by customers, including aircraft engine, printing, power generation and other industrial markets, and manufactures electric arc, plasma and oxygen fuel spray equipment. In July 2006, PX sold its aviation services business (annual sales of $80 million).

## Company Financials Fiscal Year Ended Dec. 31

| Per Share Data ($) | 2007 | 2006 | 2005 | 2004 | 2003 | 2002 | 2001 | 2000 | 1999 | 1998 |
|---|---|---|---|---|---|---|---|---|---|---|
| Tangible Book Value | 9.64 | 8.91 | 7.05 | 6.08 | 6.00 | 4.03 | 7.59 | 3.97 | 3.70 | 3.36 |
| Cash Flow | 6.01 | 5.12 | 4.23 | 3.85 | 3.33 | 3.12 | 2.84 | 2.59 | 2.73 | 2.73 |
| Earnings | 3.62 | 3.00 | 2.22 | 2.10 | 1.77 | 1.66 | 1.32 | 1.13 | 1.37 | 1.30 |
| S&P Core Earnings | 3.55 | 2.99 | 2.16 | 2.02 | 1.67 | 1.38 | 1.04 | NA | NA | NA |
| Dividends | 1.20 | 1.00 | 0.72 | 0.60 | 0.46 | 0.38 | 0.34 | 0.31 | 0.28 | 0.25 |
| Payout Ratio | 33% | 33% | 32% | 29% | 26% | 23% | 26% | 28% | 21% | 19% |
| Prices:High | 92.12 | 63.70 | 54.31 | 46.25 | 38.26 | 30.56 | 27.96 | 27.47 | 29.06 | 26.94 |
| Prices:Low | 57.97 | 50.36 | 41.06 | 34.52 | 25.02 | 22.28 | 18.25 | 15.16 | 16.00 | 15.34 |
| P/E Ratio:High | 25 | 21 | 24 | 22 | 22 | 18 | 21 | 24 | 21 | 21 |
| P/E Ratio:Low | 16 | 17 | 18 | 16 | 14 | 13 | 14 | 13 | 12 | 12 |

| Income Statement Analysis (Million $) | 2007 | 2006 | 2005 | 2004 | 2003 | 2002 | 2001 | 2000 | 1999 | 1998 |
|---|---|---|---|---|---|---|---|---|---|---|
| Revenue | 9,402 | 8,324 | 7,656 | 6,594 | 5,613 | 5,128 | 5,158 | 5,043 | 4,639 | 4,833 |
| Operating Income | 2,557 | 2,183 | 1,948 | 1,681 | 1,444 | 1,358 | 1,333 | 1,220 | 1,199 | 1,310 |
| Depreciation | 774 | 696 | 665 | 578 | 517 | 483 | 499 | 471 | 445 | 467 |
| Interest Expense | 208 | 155 | 163 | 155 | 151 | 206 | 224 | 224 | 204 | 260 |
| Pretax Income | 1,639 | 1,312 | 1,145 | 959 | 735 | 726 | 585 | 493 | 638 | 607 |
| Effective Tax Rate | 25.6% | 27.1% | 32.8% | 24.2% | 23.7% | 21.8% | 23.1% | 20.9% | 23.8% | 20.9% |
| Net Income | 1,177 | 988 | 732 | 697 | 585 | 548 | 432 | 363 | 441 | 425 |
| S&P Core Earnings | 1,154 | 983 | 711 | 671 | 552 | 454 | 343 | NA | NA | NA |

| Balance Sheet & Other Financial Data (Million $) | 2007 | 2006 | 2005 | 2004 | 2003 | 2002 | 2001 | 2000 | 1999 | 1998 |
|---|---|---|---|---|---|---|---|---|---|---|
| Cash | 17.0 | 36.0 | 173 | 25.0 | 50.0 | 39.0 | 39.0 | 31.0 | 76.0 | 34.0 |
| Current Assets | 2,408 | 2,059 | 2,133 | 1,744 | 1,449 | 1,286 | 1,276 | 1,361 | 1,335 | 1,394 |
| Total Assets | 13,382 | 11,102 | 10,491 | 9,878 | 8,305 | 7,401 | 7,715 | 7,762 | 7,722 | 8,096 |
| Current Liabilities | 2,650 | 1,758 | 2,001 | 1,875 | 1,117 | 1,100 | 1,194 | 1,439 | 1,725 | 1,289 |
| Long Term Debt | 3,364 | 2,981 | 2,926 | 2,876 | 2,661 | 2,510 | 2,725 | 2,641 | 2,111 | 2,895 |
| Common Equity | 5,142 | 4,554 | 3,902 | 3,608 | 3,088 | 2,340 | 2,477 | 2,357 | 2,290 | 2,332 |
| Total Capital | 8,506 | 7,757 | 6,828 | 6,709 | 5,944 | 5,014 | 5,363 | 5,156 | 4,835 | 5,789 |
| Capital Expenditures | 1,376 | 1,100 | 877 | 668 | 983 | 498 | 595 | 704 | 653 | 781 |
| Cash Flow | 1,951 | 1,684 | 1,397 | 1,275 | 1,102 | 1,031 | 931 | 834 | 886 | 892 |
| Current Ratio | 0.9 | 1.2 | 1.1 | 0.9 | 1.3 | 1.2 | 1.1 | 0.9 | 0.8 | 1.1 |
| % Long Term Debt of Capitalization | 39.5 | 38.4 | 42.9 | 42.9 | 44.8 | 50.1 | 50.8 | 51.2 | 43.7 | 50.0 |
| % Net Income of Revenue | 12.5 | 11.9 | 9.6 | 10.6 | 10.4 | 10.7 | 8.4 | 7.2 | 9.5 | 8.8 |
| % Return on Assets | 9.6 | 9.2 | 7.2 | 7.7 | 7.4 | 7.3 | 5.6 | 4.7 | 5.6 | 5.3 |
| % Return on Equity | 24.3 | 23.4 | 19.5 | 20.8 | 21.6 | 22.8 | 17.9 | 15.6 | 19.1 | 19.1 |

Data as orig reptd.; bef. results of disc opers/spec. items. Per share data adj. for stk. divs.; EPS diluted. E-Estimated. NA-Not Available. NM-Not Meaningful. NR-Not Ranked. UR-Under Review.

**Office:** 39 Old Ridgebury Rd, Danbury, CT 06810-5113.
**Telephone:** 203-837-2000.
**Website:** http://www.praxair.com
**Chrmn, Pres & CEO:** S.F. Angel

**EVP & CFO:** J.S. Sawyer
**SVP, Secy & General Counsel:** J.T. Breedlove
**Investor Contact:** E.T. Hirsch (203-837-2354)
**CTO:** R.P. Roberge

**Board Members:** S. F. Angel, N. Dicciani, E. G. Galante, C. W. Gargalli, I. D. Hall, R. W. LeBoeuf, L. D. McVay, W. T. Smith, H. M. Watson, Jr., R. L. Wood

**Founded:** 1988
**Domicile:** Delaware
**Employees:** 27,992

# Precision Castparts Corp.

**STANDARD &POOR'S**

---

**S&P Recommendation** BUY ★★★★☆

| Price | 12-Mo. Target Price | Investment Style |
|---|---|---|
| $55.04 (as of Nov 14, 2008) | $72.00 | Large-Cap Growth |

**GICS Sector** Industrials
**Sub-Industry** Aerospace & Defense

**Summary** This company is a provider of complex metal components used primarily in the manufacture of jet engines and industrial gas turbines, and in the oil and gas industry.

---

## Key Stock Statistics (Source S&P, Vickers, company reports)

| | | | | | | | | |
|---|---|---|---|---|---|---|---|---|
| 52-Wk Range | $154.50– 47.23 | S&P Oper. EPS 2009E | 7.33 | Market Capitalization(B) | $7.674 | Beta | 2.06 |
| Trailing 12-Month EPS | $7.61 | S&P Oper. EPS 2010E | 8.85 | Yield (%) | 0.22 | S&P 3-Yr. Proj. EPS CAGR(%) | 15 |
| Trailing 12-Month P/E | 7.2 | P/E on S&P Oper. EPS 2009E | 7.5 | Dividend Rate/Share | $0.12 | S&P Credit Rating | BBB+ |
| $10K Invested 5 Yrs Ago | $26,851 | Common Shares Outstg. (M) | 139.4 | Institutional Ownership (%) | 89 | | |

---

## Price Performance

30-Week Mov. Avg. ···   10-Week Mov. Avg. - -   **GAAP Earnings vs. Previous Year**   Volume Above Avg. STARS
12-Mo. Target Price —   Relative Strength —   ▲ Up  ▼ Down  ► No Change   Below Avg.

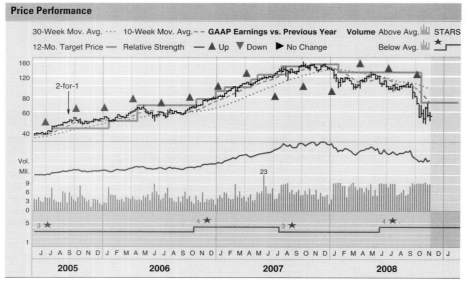

Options: ASE, CBOE, Ph

Analysis prepared by **Richard Tortoriello** on November 10, 2008, when the stock traded at **$ 55.31**.

## Qualitative Risk Assessment

LOW | MEDIUM | HIGH

Precision Castparts operates in a cyclical and capital-intensive industry and is subject to swings in commodity prices. However, due to PCP's large market share in most markets, we believe the company has significant pricing power for its products. We also consider its financial condition to be solid, including a relatively low debt level.

## Quantitative Evaluations

**S&P Quality Ranking**   B

| D | C | B- | **B** | B+ | A- | A | A+ |
|---|---|---|---|---|---|---|---|

**Relative Strength Rank**   MODERATE
45
LOWEST = 1                         HIGHEST = 99

## Revenue/Earnings Data

**Revenue (Million $)**

| | 1Q | 2Q | 3Q | 4Q | Year |
|---|---|---|---|---|---|
| 2009 | 1,835 | 1,820 | -- | -- | -- |
| 2008 | 1,660 | 1,727 | 1,697 | 1,791 | 6,852 |
| 2007 | 1,112 | 1,318 | 1,385 | 1,547 | 5,361 |
| 2006 | 854.6 | 874.9 | 864.4 | 952.6 | 3,546 |
| 2005 | 738.8 | 697.5 | 743.9 | 809.5 | 2,919 |
| 2004 | 475.7 | 476.3 | 517.6 | 705.1 | 2,175 |

**Earnings Per Share ($)**

| | 1Q | 2Q | 3Q | 4Q | Year |
|---|---|---|---|---|---|
| 2009 | 1.95 | 1.89 | E1.61 | E1.88 | E7.33 |
| 2008 | 1.61 | 1.67 | 1.73 | 1.88 | 6.89 |
| 2007 | 0.83 | 1.03 | 1.15 | 1.44 | 4.45 |
| 2006 | 0.58 | 0.60 | 0.67 | 0.74 | 2.57 |
| 2005 | 0.40 | 0.43 | 0.47 | 0.52 | 1.80 |
| 2004 | 0.33 | 0.27 | 0.26 | 0.32 | 1.18 |

Fiscal year ended Mar. 31. Next earnings report expected: Late January. EPS Estimates based on S&P Operating Earnings; historical GAAP earnings are as reported.

---

## Highlights

➤ We expect sales to rise 6% in FY 09 (Mar.), driven by demand in the Investment Cast Products and Fastener Products segments, reflecting our view of strong demand from aerospace OEMs for jet engine and other aerospace parts and from OEMs in the industrial gas turbine market, partially offset by the effects of a 57-day strike at Boeing. For FY 10, we project growth of about 14%. PCP has made several acquisitions over the past few years, and our sales projections do not include potential future acquisitions.

➤ We estimate an operating margin of 22.1% in FY 09, flat with FY 08 margins, as productivity programs are offset by inefficiencies due to the Boeing strike. We project significant margin improvement in FY 10, to 23.2%.

➤ We estimate EPS growth of about 6% in FY 09, to $7.33, and see about 21% growth in FY 10, to $8.85. We expect free cash flow per share in FY 09 to be about 80% of reported EPS.

## Investment Rationale/Risk

➤ We see PCP benefiting from a strong aerospace cycle, given our view of PCP's strong positions on both the Boeing 787 and the Airbus A380. We expect continued demand for industrial gas turbines (IGTs), used in power generation, particularly in international markets. Aerospace and IGT markets made up 79% of PCP's revenues in FY 08. We also expect PCP to continue to make judicious "bolt-on" acquisitions that have added to both revenue and earnings growth.

➤ Risks to our recommendation and target price include a slowdown in either aerospace or gas turbine demand or an inability to successfully integrate acquisitions, as well as other operational difficulties, resulting in slower-than-anticipated sales and earnings growth.

➤ Our 12-month target price of $72 is based on an enterprise value to estimated FY 09 EBITDA multiple of 6.0X, above 20-year lows for PCP of near 4.0X and below a 20-year average of 9.0X. We believe our view of strong near-term fundamentals, offset by risks associated with a global economic slowdown, warrant a below average multiple.

## Dividend Data (Dates: mm/dd Payment Date: mm/dd/yy)

| Amount ($) | Date Decl. | Ex-Div. Date | Stk. of Record | Payment Date |
|---|---|---|---|---|
| 0.030 | 02/13 | 03/05 | 03/07 | 03/31/08 |
| 0.030 | 05/22 | 06/04 | 06/06 | 06/30/08 |
| 0.030 | 08/13 | 09/03 | 09/05 | 09/29/08 |
| 0.030 | 11/14 | 12/03 | 12/05 | 12/29/08 |

Dividends have been paid since 1978. Source: Company reports.

---

**Please read the Required Disclosures and Analyst Certification on the last page of this report.**

The McGraw-Hill Companies

# Precision Castparts Corp.

**STANDARD &POOR'S**

## Business Summary November 10, 2008

COMPANY OVERVIEW. Precision Castparts, a manufacturer of jet engine and industrial gas turbine (IGT) engine components, conducts business through three operating units. The aerospace market accounted for 55% of FY 08 (Mar.) sales, power generation 24%, general industrial 16%, and automotive 5%. General Electric accounted for 12% of FY 08 sales.

PCP's Investment Cast Products segment (32% and 32% of FY 08 revenues and operating earnings, respectively) includes PCC Structurals, PCC Airfoils, and the Specialty Materials and Alloys Group (SMAG). These operations manufacture investment castings for aircraft engines, IGT engines, airframes, medical prostheses, armament and other industrial applications. Investment casting involves a technical, multi-step process that uses ceramic molds in the manufacture of metal components with more complex shapes, closer tolerances, and finer surface finishes than parts manufactured using other casting methods. PCP is the world's largest maker of jet engine structural castings (components made from molten metal poured into molds) used to strengthen sections of a jet engine. It also believes it is the leading supplier of investment casts for IGT engines. The company emphasizes low-cost, high quality products and timely delivery. SMAG principally provides alloys and waxes to the company's investment casting operations, as well as other companies with in-

vestment casting or other foundry operations.

The Forged Products segment (46% of sales and 44% of operating profits) is a large maker of forged components for the aerospace and power generation markets. Forged Products segment aerospace and IGT sales are primarily derived from the same large engine customers served by the Investment Cast segment, with additional aerospace sales to manufacturers of landing gear and airframes. In addition, Forged Products manufactures high performance nickel-based alloys used to produce forged components for aerospace and non-aerospace markets, which includes products for oil and gas, chemical processing, and pollution control applications. Forging involves heating high-temperature nickel alloys, titanium, or steel and then shaping them through pressing or extrusion, using hydraulic and mechanical presses. Through the May 2006 acquisition of Special Metals, PCP became the world's largest producer of high-performance, nickel-based alloys and superalloys, used in the forging process.

## Company Financials Fiscal Year Ended Mar. 31

| Per Share Data ($) | 2008 | 2007 | 2006 | 2005 | 2004 | 2003 | 2002 | 2001 | 2000 | 1999 |
|---|---|---|---|---|---|---|---|---|---|---|
| Tangible Book Value | 12.28 | 5.37 | 3.56 | 1.51 | 0.62 | 0.74 | NM | NM | NM | 1.75 |
| Cash Flow | NA | 5.27 | 3.30 | 2.53 | 1.73 | 2.28 | 1.37 | 2.23 | 1.62 | 1.61 |
| Earnings | 6.89 | 4.45 | 2.57 | 1.80 | 1.18 | 1.51 | 0.41 | 1.23 | 0.87 | 1.05 |
| S&P Core Earnings | 6.87 | 4.47 | 2.51 | 1.79 | 1.21 | 1.17 | 0.63 | 1.22 | NA | NA |
| Dividends | 0.12 | 0.11 | 0.06 | 0.06 | 0.06 | 0.06 | 0.06 | 0.06 | 0.06 | 0.06 |
| Payout Ratio | 2% | 2% | 2% | 3% | 5% | 4% | 15% | 5% | 7% | 6% |
| Calendar Year | 2007 | 2006 | 2005 | 2004 | 2003 | 2002 | 2001 | 2000 | 1999 | 1998 |
| Prices:High | 160.73 | 80.90 | 53.91 | 34.19 | 22.97 | 19.00 | 24.75 | 22.78 | 11.81 | 16.06 |
| Prices:Low | 77.51 | 48.80 | 31.15 | 20.68 | 10.61 | 8.43 | 9.00 | 5.92 | 5.86 | 8.16 |
| P/E Ratio:High | 23 | 18 | 21 | 19 | 19 | 13 | 61 | 19 | 14 | 15 |
| P/E Ratio:Low | 11 | 11 | 12 | 11 | 9 | 6 | 22 | 5 | 7 | 8 |

| Income Statement Analysis (Million $) | | | | | | | | | | |
|---|---|---|---|---|---|---|---|---|---|---|
| Revenue | 6,852 | 5,361 | 3,546 | 2,919 | 2,175 | 2,117 | 2,557 | 2,326 | 1,674 | 1,472 |
| Operating Income | NA | 1,086 | 656 | 517 | 380 | 390 | 448 | 401 | 267 | 246 |
| Depreciation | 130 | 113 | 99.2 | 97.0 | 88.2 | 82.5 | 101 | 102 | 74.2 | 54.1 |
| Interest Expense | NA | 52.2 | 41.4 | 56.6 | 54.1 | 56.4 | 66.2 | 81.0 | 47.1 | 27.6 |
| Pretax Income | 1,463 | 918 | 513 | 360 | 212 | 242 | 135 | 209 | 139 | 151 |
| Effective Tax Rate | 33.9% | 33.2% | 31.6% | 33.7% | 35.7% | 34.5% | 68.6% | 40.1% | 38.5% | 31.5% |
| Net Income | 966 | 615 | 349 | 240 | 136 | 159 | 42.4 | 125 | 85.3 | 103 |
| S&P Core Earnings | 963 | 618 | 341 | 237 | 140 | 123 | 65.4 | 124 | NA | NA |

| Balance Sheet & Other Financial Data (Million $) | | | | | | | | | | |
|---|---|---|---|---|---|---|---|---|---|---|
| Cash | 221 | 150 | 59.9 | 154 | 80.3 | 28.7 | 38.1 | 40.1 | 17.6 | 14.8 |
| Current Assets | NA | 2,037 | 1,234 | 1,213 | 1,188 | 786 | 878 | 863 | 752 | 557 |
| Total Assets | 6,050 | 5,259 | 3,751 | 3,625 | 3,756 | 2,467 | 2,565 | 2,573 | 2,416 | 1,450 |
| Current Liabilities | NA | 1,658 | 768 | 780 | 913 | 625 | 727 | 657 | 592 | 305 |
| Long Term Debt | NA | 319 | 600 | 799 | 823 | 532 | 697 | 838 | 884 | 370 |
| Common Equity | 4,045 | 2,836 | 2,244 | 1,780 | 1,715 | 1,062 | 952 | 902 | 774 | 697 |
| Total Capital | NA | 3,182 | 2,844 | 2,579 | 2,538 | 1,594 | 1,649 | 1,740 | 1,658 | 1,092 |
| Capital Expenditures | 226 | 222 | 99.2 | 61.7 | 65.5 | 70.5 | 125 | 90.2 | 49.3 | 74.8 |
| Cash Flow | NA | 727 | 448 | 337 | 224 | 242 | 143 | 227 | 160 | 157 |
| Current Ratio | 2.0 | 1.2 | 1.6 | 1.6 | 1.3 | 1.3 | 1.2 | 1.3 | 1.3 | 1.8 |
| % Long Term Debt of Capitalization | 7.6 | 10.0 | 21.1 | 31.0 | 32.4 | 33.4 | 42.3 | 48.2 | 53.3 | 33.8 |
| % Net Income of Revenue | 14.1 | 11.5 | 9.8 | 8.2 | 6.2 | 7.5 | 1.7 | 5.4 | 5.1 | 7.0 |
| % Return on Assets | 17.1 | 13.6 | 9.5 | 6.5 | 4.4 | 6.3 | 1.7 | 5.0 | 4.4 | 7.6 |
| % Return on Equity | 28.1 | 24.7 | 17.0 | 13.7 | 9.8 | 15.8 | 4.6 | 14.9 | 11.6 | 16.0 |

Data as orig reptd.; bef. results of disc opers/spec. items. Per share data adj. for stk. divs.; EPS diluted. E-Estimated. NA-Not Available. NM-Not Meaningful. NR-Not Ranked. UR-Under Review.

**Office:** 4650 SW Macadam Ave Ste 400, Portland, OR 97239-4262.
**Telephone:** 503-417-4850.
**Email:** info@precastcorp.com
**Website:** http://www.precast.com

**Chrmn, Pres & CEO:** M. Donegan
**SVP, CFO, Chief Acctg Officer & Cntlr:** S.R. Hagel
**Treas:** S.C. Blackmore
**Secy & General Counsel:** R.A. Cooke

**Investor Contact:** W.D. Larsson
**Board Members:** P. R. Bridenbaugh, M. Donegan, D. R. Graber, L. L. Lyles, D. Murphy, Jr., V. E. Oechsle, S. G. Rothmeier, U. Schmidt

**Founded:** 1949
**Domicile:** Oregon
**Employees:** 21,558

# Principal Financial Group Inc.

STANDARD &POOR'S

| S&P Recommendation | HOLD ★★★☆☆ | Price $16.83 (as of Nov 14, 2008) | 12-Mo. Target Price $30.00 | Investment Style Large-Cap Blend |
|---|---|---|---|---|

**GICS Sector** Financials
**Sub-Industry** Life & Health Insurance

**Summary** This company offers businesses, individuals and other clients various financial products and services, including insurance, retirement and investment services.

## Key Stock Statistics (Source S&P, Vickers, company reports)

| | | | | | | | | |
|---|---|---|---|---|---|---|---|---|
| 52-Wk Range | $70.85– 12.50 | S&P Oper. EPS 2008**E** | 3.59 | Market Capitalization(B) | $4.365 | Beta | 1.87 |
| Trailing 12-Month EPS | $1.78 | S&P Oper. EPS 2009**E** | 4.00 | Yield (%) | 2.67 | S&P 3-Yr. Proj. EPS CAGR(%) | 4 |
| Trailing 12-Month P/E | 9.5 | P/E on S&P Oper. EPS 2008**E** | 4.7 | Dividend Rate/Share | $0.45 | S&P Credit Rating | NA |
| $10K Invested 5 Yrs Ago | $5,773 | Common Shares Outstg. (M) | 259.3 | Institutional Ownership (%) | 56 | | |

## Price Performance

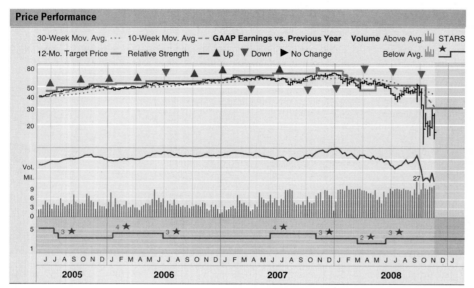

30-Week Mov. Avg. ···  10-Week Mov. Avg. - - **GAAP Earnings vs. Previous Year**  Volume Above Avg. STARS
12-Mo. Target Price — Relative Strength — ▲ Up ▼ Down ► No Change  Below Avg.

Options: CBOE

Analysis prepared by **Bret Howlett** on November 10, 2008, when the stock traded at **$ 24.48**.

## Highlights

➤ We expect operating earnings for the U.S. Asset Management and Accumulation (USAMA) segment to decline in 2008, on increased deferred acquisition cost (DAC) expenses, poor net flows, and lower AUMs as average account balances decline due to the weak equity markets. We have been impressed with the strong sales in Full Service Accumulation (FSA), despite the difficult market conditions and disruption with some distribution partners. However, we expect increased withdrawals to reduce net cash flow in this business.

➤ We believe earnings for Global Asset Management will be down this year due to lower AUMs and a decline in net investment income, a result of lower rates on escrows, and lower transaction and borrower fees, reflecting the weak real estate market. We expect earnings for the International Asset Management and Accumulation (IAMA) segment to experience double-digit growth based on higher AUMs, and improving pension operations in Hong Kong and Brazil. IAMA's earnings are less sensitive to the equity markets.

➤ We forecast 2008 operating EPS of $3.59. Our operating EPS estimate for 2009 is $4.00.

## Investment Rationale/Risk

➤ We believe the turmoil in the financial markets will weigh on PFG's profitability in 2008. Our hold recommendation is based on our belief that at current share price levels, a difficult operating environment has been discounted in the stock. In our view, PFG faces stiff headwinds, including lower earnings contributions from its fee-based businesses due to the decline in the equity markets. We also expect PFG to have difficulty reducing the volatility in its health insurance business due to its exposure to high-deductible health plans. Furthermore, we are concerned that further declines in credit market will pressure its investment portfolio, given its above-average exposure to mortgage-backed securities. We believe PFG's capital position is weak relative to its peers.

➤ Risks to our recommendation and target price include a significant decline in the equity markets, deteriorating margins in the company's health insurance business, outflows in its USAMA business, and weak credit and economic conditions.

➤ Our 12-month target price of $30 is 1.0X our 2009 year-end book value forecast (excluding SFAS 115), below historical multiples.

## Qualitative Risk Assessment

| LOW | MEDIUM | HIGH |
|---|---|---|

Our risk assessment reflects our view of PFG's significant exposure to the equity markets and potential for further investment losses. We believe PFG's capital position could come under strain if the economic environment and capital markets worsen.

## Quantitative Evaluations

**S&P Quality Ranking** NR

| D | C | B- | B | B+ | A- | A | A+ |
|---|---|---|---|---|---|---|---|

**Relative Strength Rank** WEAK

18

LOWEST = 1    HIGHEST = 99

## Revenue/Earnings Data

**Revenue (Million $)**

| | 1Q | 2Q | 3Q | 4Q | Year |
|---|---|---|---|---|---|
| 2008 | 2,501 | 2,658 | 2,498 | -- | -- |
| 2007 | 2,661 | 2,832 | 2,850 | 2,564 | 10,907 |
| 2006 | 2,402 | 2,460 | 2,450 | 2,559 | 9,871 |
| 2005 | 2,144 | 2,200 | 2,218 | 2,445 | 9,008 |
| 2004 | 1,997 | 1,980 | 2,089 | 2,239 | 8,304 |
| 2003 | 2,297 | 2,412 | 2,266 | 2,479 | 9,404 |

**Earnings Per Share ($)**

| | 1Q | 2Q | 3Q | 4Q | Year |
|---|---|---|---|---|---|
| 2008 | 0.67 | 0.64 | 0.35 | E0.90 | E3.59 |
| 2007 | 0.95 | 1.14 | 0.88 | 0.05 | 3.01 |
| 2006 | 1.01 | 0.76 | 0.92 | 0.93 | 3.63 |
| 2005 | 0.68 | 0.77 | 0.74 | 0.83 | 3.02 |
| 2004 | 0.62 | 0.40 | 0.62 | 0.71 | 2.23 |
| 2003 | 0.47 | 0.62 | 0.68 | 0.60 | 2.23 |

Fiscal year ended Dec. 31. Next earnings report expected: Early February. EPS Estimates based on S&P Operating Earnings; historical GAAP earnings are as reported.

## Dividend Data (Dates: mm/dd Payment Date: mm/dd/yy)

| Amount ($) | Date Decl. | Ex-Div. Date | Stk. of Record | Payment Date |
|---|---|---|---|---|
| 0.900 | 10/29 | 11/14 | 11/16 | 12/07/07 |
| 0.450 | 10/13 | 11/12 | 11/14 | 12/05/08 |

Dividends have been paid since 2002. Source: Company reports.

---

**Please read the Required Disclosures and Analyst Certification on the last page of this report.**

# Principal Financial Group Inc.

STANDARD
&POOR'S

## Business Summary November 10, 2008

CORPORATE OVERVIEW. The Principal Financial Group is a leading provider of retirement savings, investment and insurance products and services, with approximately $311.1 billion in assets under management at December 31, 2007. The focus of the company is to provide retirement and employment products and services, specifically 401(k) plans, to small and medium-sized businesses.

PFG's businesses are organized into five operating segments. The U.S. Asset Management and Accumulation segment (USAMA), which accounted for 45% of operating revenues excluding corporate and other in 2007, provides retirement savings and related investment products and services, and asset management operations, with a concentration on small and medium-sized businesses with fewer than 1,000 employees. At year-end 2007, USAMA account values totaled $178.1 billion.

The Global Asset Management segment includes Principal Global Investors and its affiliates and focuses on providing a range of asset management services. The segment accounted for 5.3% of operating revenues excluding cor-

porate and other in 2007.

The International Asset Management and Accumulation segment (IAMA) consists of Principal International and offers retirement products and services, annuities, mutual funds and life insurance through operations in Brazil, Chile, Mexico, China, Hong Kong and India. IAMA accounted for 7.0% of operating revenues from continuing operations in 2007.

The Life and Health Insurance segment, which accounted for 43% of operating revenues from continuing operations in 2007, offers individual and group life and disability insurance, as well as group health, dental and vision insurance. The Corporate and Other segment includes, among other things, intersegment eliminations, income on capital not allocated to other segments, and the company's financing activities.

## Company Financials Fiscal Year Ended Dec. 31

| Per Share Data ($) | 2007 | 2006 | 2005 | 2004 | 2003 | 2002 | 2001 | 2000 | 1999 | 1998 |
|---|---|---|---|---|---|---|---|---|---|---|
| Tangible Book Value | 22.35 | 22.24 | 24.14 | 23.67 | 22.12 | 19.32 | 10.59 | 14.89 | NA | NA |
| Operating Earnings | NA | NA | NA | NA | NA | 2.46 | 1.96 | NA | NA | NA |
| Earnings | 3.01 | 3.63 | 3.02 | 2.23 | 2.23 | 1.77 | 1.02 | 1.74 | NA | NA |
| S&P Core Earnings | 3.69 | 3.45 | 3.02 | 2.36 | 2.38 | 1.85 | 1.69 | NA | NA | NA |
| Dividends | 0.90 | 0.80 | 0.65 | 0.55 | 0.45 | 0.25 | Nil | NA | NA | NA |
| Payout Ratio | 30% | 22% | 22% | 25% | 20% | 14% | Nil | NA | NA | NA |
| Prices:High | 70.85 | 59.40 | 52.00 | 41.26 | 34.67 | 31.50 | 24.75 | NA | NA | NA |
| Prices:Low | 51.52 | 45.91 | 36.80 | 32.00 | 25.21 | 22.00 | 18.50 | NA | NA | NA |
| P/E Ratio:High | 24 | 16 | 17 | 19 | 16 | 18 | 24 | NA | NA | NA |
| P/E Ratio:Low | 17 | 13 | 12 | 14 | 11 | 12 | 18 | NA | NA | NA |

| Income Statement Analysis (Million $) | | | | | | | | | | |
|---|---|---|---|---|---|---|---|---|---|---|
| Life Insurance in Force | 243,119 | 218,947 | 197,690 | 180,344 | 136,530 | 137,794 | 62,309 | 60,389 | NA | NA |
| Premium Income:Life | 1,827 | 1,560 | 1,546 | 1,477 | 1,500 | 1,824 | 2,089 | 1,792 | NA | NA |
| Premium Income:A & H | 2,808 | 2,745 | 2,429 | 2,233 | 2,135 | 2,058 | 2,033 | 2,205 | NA | NA |
| Net Investment Income | 3,967 | 3,618 | 3,361 | 3,227 | 3,420 | 3,305 | 3,395 | 3,172 | NA | NA |
| Total Revenue | 10,907 | 9,871 | 9,008 | 8,304 | 9,404 | 9,223 | 8,818 | 8,885 | NA | NA |
| Pretax Income | 1,048 | 1,329 | 1,124 | 882 | 954 | 666 | 449 | 872 | NA | NA |
| Net Operating Income | NA | NA | NA | NA | NA | 864 | 711 | NA | NA | NA |
| Net Income | 840 | 1,034 | 892 | 702 | 728 | 620 | 370 | 627 | NA | NA |
| S&P Core Earnings | 991 | 951 | 871 | 742 | 778 | 647 | 608 | NA | NA | NA |

| Balance Sheet & Other Financial Data (Million $) | | | | | | | | | | |
|---|---|---|---|---|---|---|---|---|---|---|
| Cash & Equivalent | 2,119 | 2,314 | 2,324 | 1,131 | 2,344 | 1,685 | 1,218 | 940 | NA | NA |
| Premiums Due | 951 | 1,252 | 593 | 628 | 720 | 460 | 531 | 572 | NA | NA |
| Investment Assets:Bonds | 47,268 | 44,727 | 42,117 | 40,916 | 37,553 | 34,287 | 30,030 | 29,328 | NA | NA |
| Investment Assets:Stocks | 586 | 848 | 815 | 763 | 712 | 379 | 834 | 579 | NA | NA |
| Investment Assets:Loans | 13,522 | 12,515 | 12,312 | 12,529 | 14,312 | 11,900 | 11,898 | 12,359 | NA | NA |
| Investment Assets:Total | 64,365 | 60,367 | 57,583 | 57,012 | 55,578 | 48,996 | 44,773 | 44,403 | NA | NA |
| Deferred Policy Costs | 2,810 | 2,419 | 2,174 | 1,838 | 1,572 | 1,414 | 1,373 | 1,338 | NA | NA |
| Total Assets | 154,520 | 143,658 | 127,035 | 113,798 | 107,754 | 89,861 | 88,351 | 86,838 | NA | NA |
| Debt | 1,399 | 1,554 | 899 | 844 | 2,767 | 1,333 | 1,378 | 1,391 | NA | NA |
| Common Equity | 7,422 | 7,861 | 7,807 | 7,544 | 7,400 | 13,314 | 6,820 | 6,624 | NA | NA |
| % Return on Revenue | 7.7 | 10.5 | 9.9 | 8.5 | 7.7 | 7.0 | 4.2 | 7.1 | NA | NA |
| % Return on Assets | 0.6 | 0.8 | 0.7 | 0.6 | 0.7 | 0.7 | 0.4 | NA | NA | NA |
| % Return on Equity | 10.6 | 12.8 | 11.4 | 9.4 | 10.4 | 4.6 | 5.7 | NA | NA | NA |
| % Investment Yield | 6.4 | 6.1 | 5.9 | 5.8 | 6.5 | 7.0 | 7.8 | NA | NA | NA |

Data as orig reptd.; bef. results of disc opers/spec. items. Per share data adj. for stk. divs.; EPS diluted. E-Estimated. NA-Not Available. NM-Not Meaningful. NR-Not Ranked. UR-Under Review.

**Office:** 711 High Street, Des Moines, IA 50392-9992.
**Telephone:** 515-247-5111.
**Website:** http://www.principal.com
**Chrmn:** J.B. Griswell

**Pres & CEO:** L.D. Zimpleman
**EVP & General Counsel:** K.E. Shaff
**SVP & CFO:** T.J. Lillis
**SVP & Secy:** J.N. Hoffman

**Investor Contact:** T. Graf (515-235-9500)
**Board Members:** B. J. Bernard, J. Carter-Miller, G. E. Costley, M. T. Dan, C. Gelatt, Jr., J. B. Griswell, S. L. Helton, W. T. Kerr, R. L. Keyser, A. K. Mathrani, D. M. Stewart, E. E. Tallett, T. M. Vaughan, L. D. Zimpleman

**Founded:** 1998
**Domicile:** Delaware
**Employees:** 16,585

# Procter & Gamble Co (The)

STANDARD
&POOR'S

| S&P Recommendation | STRONG BUY ★★★★★ | Price | 12-Mo. Target Price | Investment Style |
|---|---|---|---|---|
| | | $63.11 (as of Nov 14, 2008) | $78.00 | Large-Cap Growth |

**GICS Sector** Consumer Staples
**Sub-Industry** Household Products

**Summary** This leading consumer products company markets household and personal care products in more than 180 countries.

## Key Stock Statistics (Source S&P, Vickers, company reports)

| | | | | | | | |
|---|---|---|---|---|---|---|---|
| 52-Wk Range | $75.18– 54.92 | S&P Oper. EPS 2009E | 3.73 | Market Capitalization(B) | $188.428 | Beta | 0.58 |
| Trailing 12-Month EPS | $3.75 | S&P Oper. EPS 2010E | NA | Yield (%) | 2.54 | S&P 3-Yr. Proj. EPS CAGR(%) | 12 |
| Trailing 12-Month P/E | 16.8 | P/E on S&P Oper. EPS 2009E | 16.9 | Dividend Rate/Share | $1.60 | S&P Credit Rating | AA- |
| $10K Invested 5 Yrs Ago | $14,629 | Common Shares Outstg. (M) | 2,985.7 | Institutional Ownership (%) | 59 | | |

## Price Performance

30-Week Mov. Avg. · · · 10-Week Mov. Avg. – – GAAP Earnings vs. Previous Year  Volume Above Avg. STARS
12-Mo. Target Price —  Relative Strength —  ▲ Up  ▼ Down  ► No Change  Below Avg.

Options: ASE, CBOE, P, Ph

Analysis prepared by **Loran Braverman, CFA** on October 29, 2008, when the stock traded at **$ 60.99.**

## Highlights

► For FY 09 (Jun.), we forecast growth of 2.3%, including a negative impact from foreign exchange of 1.5% and another 1.5% from divestitures. In June 2008, PG announced an agreement to merge its Folgers coffee business with The J.M. Smucker Company in a reverse Morris Trust transaction, subject to customary approvals and expected to be final by 2008 year end. We think PG is benefiting from its tiered portfolio, which offers products at different price points, from new products that command higher pricing through innovation, and from the company's broad geographic reach.

► We look for the operating margin to be slightly lower, with benefits from price increases, volume leveraging and cost saving programs more than offset by increases in commodity costs, "ongoing" restructuring charges and about $0.12 per share of "temporary" restructuring charges from programs designed to offset the earnings dilution from the loss of the Folgers business and related stranded overhead costs.

► We project an increase in EPS to $3.73 in FY 09, from $3.50 in FY 08, on an estimated 3% lower share count. Our forecast excludes an estimated $0.50 gain from the Folgers' transaction.

## Investment Rationale/Risk

► Our strong buy opinion reflects our confidence that PG will deliver consistent sales and earnings growth near the high end of its peer group over the next several years, benefits from the Gillette acquisition, and growth prospects in new markets and categories. We think PG is well positioned to benefit from demand growth for household and personal care products in developing countries, given its broad product portfolio and sizable distribution network.

► Risks to our recommendation and target price include heightened competition, unfavorable currency translation, greater commodity cost pressures, higher promotional spending, and low consumer acceptance of new products.

► Our 12-month target price of $78 is based on a blended valuation. Our historical P/E analysis uses a 21.8X multiple, close to the 10-year median, while our relative analysis, based on the company's strong track record of earnings growth and leading market positions, uses 15.5X, a premium to peers. These imply values based on our $3.98 calendar 2009 EPS estimate of $87 and $62, respectively. Our DCF model implies an $85 value, assuming a WACC of 7.7% and a 3% terminal growth rate.

## Qualitative Risk Assessment

| LOW | MEDIUM | HIGH |
|---|---|---|

Our risk assessment reflects that demand for household and personal care products is generally stable and not affected by changes in the economy or geopolitical factors, except for select categories such as fragrances.

## Quantitative Evaluations

**S&P Quality Ranking** A+

| D | C | B- | B | B+ | A- | A | A+ |
|---|---|---|---|---|---|---|---|

**Relative Strength Rank** STRONG

85

LOWEST = 1                     HIGHEST = 99

## Revenue/Earnings Data

**Revenue (Million $)**

| | 1Q | 2Q | 3Q | 4Q | Year |
|---|---|---|---|---|---|
| 2009 | 22,026 | -- | -- | -- | -- |
| 2008 | 20,199 | 21,575 | 20,463 | 21,266 | 83,503 |
| 2007 | 18,785 | 19,725 | 18,694 | 19,272 | 76,476 |
| 2006 | 14,793 | 18,337 | 17,250 | 17,842 | 68,222 |
| 2005 | 13,744 | 14,452 | 14,287 | 14,258 | 56,741 |
| 2004 | 12,195 | 13,221 | 13,029 | 12,962 | 51,407 |

**Earnings Per Share ($)**

| | | | | | |
|---|---|---|---|---|---|
| 2009 | 1.03 | E0.95 | E0.87 | E0.87 | E3.73 |
| 2008 | 0.92 | 0.98 | 0.82 | 0.92 | 3.64 |
| 2007 | 0.79 | 0.84 | 0.74 | 0.67 | 3.04 |
| 2006 | 0.77 | 0.72 | 0.63 | 0.55 | 2.64 |
| 2005 | 0.73 | 0.74 | 0.63 | 0.56 | 2.66 |
| 2004 | 0.63 | 0.65 | 0.55 | 0.50 | 2.32 |

Fiscal year ended Jun. 30. Next earnings report expected: Early February. EPS Estimates based on S&P Operating Earnings; historical GAAP earnings are as reported.

## Dividend Data (Dates: mm/dd Payment Date: mm/dd/yy)

| Amount ($) | Date Decl. | Ex-Div. Date | Stk. of Record | Payment Date |
|---|---|---|---|---|
| 0.350 | 01/08 | 01/16 | 01/18 | 02/15/08 |
| 0.400 | 04/08 | 04/16 | 04/18 | 05/15/08 |
| 0.400 | 07/08 | 07/16 | 07/18 | 08/15/08 |
| 0.400 | 10/14 | 10/22 | 10/24 | 11/14/08 |

Dividends have been paid since 1891. Source: Company reports.

---

**Please read the Required Disclosures and Analyst Certification on the last page of this report.**

# Procter & Gamble Co (The)

STANDARD &POOR'S

## Business Summary October 29, 2008

CORPORATE OVERVIEW. Procter & Gamble's business is focused on providing branded products of what it considers superior quality and value to improve the lives of the world's consumers. By doing so successfully, the company believes this will result in leadership sales, profits, and value creation for employees, shareholders and the communities in which it operates. PG markets in more than 180 countries. In FY 08 (Jun.), North America accounted for 44% of total sales, Western Europe 22%, Northeast Asia 4%, and developing markets 30%.

PG's customers include mass merchandisers, grocery stores, membership club stores, drug stores and high-frequency stores. Sales to Wal-Mart Stores, Inc. and its affiliates represented approximately 15% of total FY 08 revenue. The top 10 customers accounted for about 31% of total unit volume.

In FY 08, PG's business was structured in three Global Business Units (GBUs) and six reportable segments. The Beauty Unit consisted of the Beauty segment (23% of FY 08 sales and 22% of net earnings) and the Grooming segment

(10%, 13%); the Household Care Unit had the Fabric Care and Home Care segment (28%, 27%) and the Baby Care and Family Care Segment (16%, 14%); and the Health and Well-Being Unit had the Healtcare segment (17%, 20%) and the Snacks, Coffee and Pet Care segment (6%, 4%).

IMPACT OF MAJOR DEVELOPMENTS. On October 1, 2005, PG acquired The Gillette Company for approximately $54 billion. The Gillette Company is the world leader in the male and female grooming categories. Gillette also holds the number one position worldwide in alkaline batteries and toothbrushes. We expect the acquisition to add to shareholder value over time through cost synergies and sales growth opportunities. We estimate that the acquisition was neutral to slightly accretive to EPS in FY 08, following two years of dilution, and will be more accretive in FY 09.

## Company Financials Fiscal Year Ended Jun. 30

| Per Share Data ($) | 2008 | 2007 | 2006 | 2005 | 2004 | 2003 | 2002 | 2001 | 2000 | 1999 |
|---|---|---|---|---|---|---|---|---|---|---|
| Tangible Book Value | NM | NM | NM | NM | NM | 0.43 | NM | 0.78 | 0.68 | 1.31 |
| Cash Flow | NA | 4.30 | 3.56 | 3.30 | 2.90 | 2.41 | 2.11 | 1.85 | 2.01 | 2.00 |
| Earnings | 3.64 | 3.04 | 2.64 | 2.66 | 2.32 | 1.85 | 1.54 | 1.04 | 1.24 | 1.30 |
| S&P Core Earnings | 3.24 | 2.96 | 2.60 | 2.45 | 2.17 | 1.58 | 1.28 | 0.81 | NA | NA |
| Dividends | 1.45 | 1.28 | 1.15 | 1.03 | 0.93 | 0.82 | 0.76 | 0.70 | 0.64 | 0.57 |
| Payout Ratio | 40% | 42% | 44% | 39% | 40% | 44% | 49% | 68% | 52% | 44% |
| Prices:High | 73.81 | 75.18 | 64.73 | 59.70 | 57.40 | 49.97 | 47.38 | 40.86 | 59.19 | 57.81 |
| Prices:Low | 54.92 | 60.42 | 52.75 | 51.16 | 48.89 | 39.79 | 37.04 | 27.98 | 26.38 | 41.00 |
| P/E Ratio:High | 20 | 25 | 25 | 22 | 25 | 27 | 31 | 39 | 48 | 45 |
| P/E Ratio:Low | 15 | 20 | 20 | 19 | 21 | 22 | 24 | 27 | 21 | 32 |

### Income Statement Analysis (Million $)

| | 2008 | 2007 | 2006 | 2005 | 2004 | 2003 | 2002 | 2001 | 2000 | 1999 |
|---|---|---|---|---|---|---|---|---|---|---|
| Revenue | 83,503 | 76,476 | 68,222 | 56,741 | 51,407 | 43,377 | 40,238 | 39,244 | 39,951 | 38,125 |
| Operating Income | NA | 18,580 | 15,876 | 12,811 | 11,560 | 9,556 | 8,371 | 7,007 | 8,145 | 8,401 |
| Depreciation | 3,166 | 3,130 | 2,627 | 1,884 | 1,733 | 1,703 | 1,693 | 2,271 | 2,191 | 2,148 |
| Interest Expense | NA | 1,304 | 1,119 | 834 | 629 | 561 | 603 | 794 | 722 | 650 |
| Pretax Income | 16,078 | 14,710 | 12,413 | 10,439 | 9,350 | 7,530 | 6,383 | 4,616 | 5,536 | 5,838 |
| Effective Tax Rate | 24.9% | 29.7% | 30.0% | 30.5% | 30.7% | 31.1% | 31.8% | 36.7% | 36.0% | 35.5% |
| Net Income | 12,075 | 10,340 | 8,684 | 7,257 | 6,481 | 5,186 | 4,352 | 2,922 | 3,542 | 3,763 |
| S&P Core Earnings | 10,575 | 9,917 | 8,420 | 6,552 | 5,922 | 4,313 | 3,486 | 2,165 | NA | NA |

### Balance Sheet & Other Financial Data (Million $)

| | 2008 | 2007 | 2006 | 2005 | 2004 | 2003 | 2002 | 2001 | 2000 | 1999 |
|---|---|---|---|---|---|---|---|---|---|---|
| Cash | 3,541 | 5,354 | 6,693 | 6,389 | 5,469 | 5,912 | 3,427 | 2,306 | 1,415 | 2,294 |
| Current Assets | NA | 24,031 | 24,329 | 20,329 | 17,115 | 15,220 | 12,166 | 10,889 | 10,146 | 11,358 |
| Total Assets | 143,992 | 138,014 | 135,695 | 61,527 | 57,048 | 43,706 | 40,776 | 34,387 | 34,366 | 32,113 |
| Current Liabilities | NA | 30,717 | 19,985 | 25,039 | 22,147 | 12,358 | 12,704 | 9,846 | 10,141 | 10,761 |
| Long Term Debt | NA | 23,375 | 35,976 | 12,887 | 12,554 | 11,475 | 11,201 | 9,792 | 8,916 | 6,231 |
| Common Equity | 69,494 | 65,354 | 61,457 | 15,994 | 15,752 | 14,606 | 12,072 | 10,309 | 10,550 | 10,277 |
| Total Capital | NA | 102,150 | 111,238 | 33,258 | 32,093 | 29,057 | 25,984 | 22,696 | 21,828 | 18,651 |
| Capital Expenditures | 3,046 | 2,945 | 2,667 | 2,181 | 2,024 | 1,482 | 1,679 | 2,486 | 3,018 | 2,828 |
| Cash Flow | NA | 13,470 | 11,311 | 9,005 | 8,083 | 6,764 | 5,921 | 5,193 | 5,733 | 5,802 |
| Current Ratio | 0.8 | 0.8 | 1.2 | 0.8 | 0.8 | 1.2 | 1.0 | 1.1 | 1.0 | 1.1 |
| % Long Term Debt of Capitalization | 25.3 | 22.9 | 32.3 | 38.7 | 39.1 | 39.5 | 43.1 | 43.1 | 40.8 | 33.4 |
| % Net Income of Revenue | 14.5 | 13.5 | 12.7 | 12.8 | 12.6 | 12.0 | 10.8 | 7.4 | 8.9 | 9.9 |
| % Return on Assets | 8.6 | 7.6 | 8.8 | 12.2 | 12.9 | 12.3 | 11.6 | 8.5 | 10.7 | 11.9 |
| % Return on Equity | 17.9 | 16.3 | 22.1 | 45.7 | 41.8 | 37.9 | 37.8 | 28.0 | 34.0 | 35.3 |

Data as orig reptd.; bef. results of disc opers/spec. items. Per share data adj. for stk. divs.; EPS diluted. E-Estimated. NA-Not Available. NM-Not Meaningful. NR-Not Ranked. UR-Under Review.

**Office:** One Procter & Gamble Plaza, Cincinnati, OH 45202.
**Telephone:** 513-983-1100.
**Website:** http://www.pg.com
**Chrmn, Pres & CEO:** A. Lafley

**Vice Chrmn & CFO:** C.C. Daley, Jr.
**COO:** R.A. McDonald
**Chief Acctg Officer & Cntlr:** V.L. Sheppard
**Treas:** J.R. Moeller

**Investor Contact:** M. Erceg (800-742-6253)
**Board Members:** K. I. Chenault, S. D. Cook, C. C. Daley, Jr., R. K. Gupta, A. Lafley, C. R. Lee, L. Martin, W. J. McNerney, Jr., J. A. Rodgers, R. Snyderman, M. C. Whitman, P. A. Woertz, E. Zedillo

**Founded:** 1837
**Domicile:** Ohio
**Employees:** 138,000

# Progressive Corp (The)

**STANDARD &POOR'S**

| S&P Recommendation | HOLD ★★★☆☆ | Price $14.13 (as of Nov 14, 2008) | 12-Mo. Target Price $14.00 | Investment Style Large-Cap Growth |
|---|---|---|---|---|

**GICS Sector** Financials
**Sub-Industry** Property & Casualty Insurance

**Summary** This leading underwriter of nonstandard auto and other lines of coverage has expanded its product line and evolved into a full-service auto insurer.

## Key Stock Statistics (Source S&P, Vickers, company reports)

| | | | | | | | | |
|---|---|---|---|---|---|---|---|---|
| 52-Wk Range | $21.31– 10.29 | S&P Oper. EPS 2008**E** | 1.20 | Market Capitalization(B) | $9.546 | Beta | 0.57 |
| Trailing 12-Month EPS | $0.01 | S&P Oper. EPS 2009**E** | 1.30 | Yield (%) | 1.06 | S&P 3-Yr. Proj. EPS CAGR(%) | -1 |
| Trailing 12-Month P/E | NM | P/E on S&P Oper. EPS 2008**E** | 11.8 | Dividend Rate/Share | $0.15 | S&P Credit Rating | A+ |
| $10K Invested 5 Yrs Ago | $7,899 | Common Shares Outstg. (M) | 675.6 | Institutional Ownership (%) | 75 | | |

## Price Performance

30-Week Mov. Avg. · · · 10-Week Mov. Avg. – – **GAAP Earnings vs. Previous Year** Volume Above Avg. STARS
12-Mo. Target Price — Relative Strength — ▲ Up ▼ Down ► No Change Below Avg.

Options: ASE, CBOE, P, Ph

## Qualitative Risk Assessment

| LOW | MEDIUM | HIGH |
|---|---|---|

Our risk assessment reflects our view of PGR's position as a leading underwriter of personal lines coverage, combined with what we see as its superior financial strength. As primarily an auto insurer, PGR is less exposed to catastrophe losses than a number of peers. Nonetheless, exposure to catastrophe losses always exists.

## Quantitative Evaluations

**S&P Quality Ranking** B+

| D | C | B- | B | B+ | A- | A | A+ |
|---|---|---|---|---|---|---|---|

**Relative Strength Rank** STRONG

79

LOWEST = 1    HIGHEST = 99

## Revenue/Earnings Data

**Revenue (Million $)**

| | 1Q | 2Q | 3Q | 4Q | Year |
|---|---|---|---|---|---|
| 2008 | 3,586 | 3,537 | -- | -- | -- |
| 2007 | 3,687 | 3,671 | 3,710 | 3,615 | 14,687 |
| 2006 | 3,661 | 3,708 | 3,724 | 3,694 | 14,786 |
| 2005 | 3,492 | 3,590 | 3,623 | 3,599 | 14,303 |
| 2004 | 3,280 | 3,367 | 3,438 | 3,696 | 13,782 |
| 2003 | 2,720 | 2,921 | 3,081 | 3,170 | 11,892 |

**Earnings Per Share ($)**

| | | | | | |
|---|---|---|---|---|---|
| 2008 | 0.35 | 0.32 | E0.28 | E0.32 | E1.20 |
| 2007 | 0.49 | 0.39 | 0.42 | 0.34 | 1.65 |
| 2006 | 0.55 | 0.51 | 0.53 | 0.53 | 2.10 |
| 2005 | 0.51 | 0.49 | 0.39 | 0.36 | 1.75 |
| 2004 | 0.52 | 0.44 | 0.44 | 0.50 | 1.91 |
| 2003 | 0.33 | 0.32 | 0.36 | 0.41 | 1.42 |

Fiscal year ended Dec. 31. Next earnings report expected: Mid November. EPS Estimates based on S&P Operating Earnings; historical GAAP earnings are as reported.

## Highlights

► The 12-month target price for PGR has recently been changed to $14.00 from $15.00. The Highlights section of this Stock Report will be updated accordingly.

## Investment Rationale/Risk

► The Investment Rationale/Risk section of this Stock Report will be updated shortly. For the latest News story on PGR from MarketScope, see below.

► 11/12/08 04:52 pm ET ... S&P MAINTAINS HOLD RECOMMENDATION ON SHARES OF PRO-GRESSIVE CORP (PGR 12.18***): PGR released monthly underwriting results for October, which indicated to us it is still experiencing price competition in many lines. Earned and written premiums were flat year to year in October, but policy counts were up between 1% and 8%. We expect full year earned premiums to decline slightly in 2008 and expect investment results to remain challenging. At current levels, 2.1X October book value, we view PGR shares as fairly valued. Our target price, cut $1 today to $14, is 2X estimated '09 book, 11.7X our $1.20 '08 EPS estimate and 10.8X '09's, a premium to some peers. /C.Seifert

## Dividend Data (Dates: mm/dd Payment Date: mm/dd/yy)

| Amount ($) | Date Decl. | Ex-Div. Date | Stk. of Record | Payment Date |
|---|---|---|---|---|
| 0.145 | 12/14 | 01/17 | 12/31 | 01/31/08 |

Dividends have been paid since 1965. Source: Company reports.

Please read the **Required Disclosures and Analyst Certification** on the last page of this report.

*The McGraw-Hill Companies*

# Progressive Corp (The)

STANDARD
&POOR'S

## Business Summary October 16, 2008

CORPORATE OVERVIEW. Progressive underwrites an array of personal and commercial lines insurance. Net written premiums totaled $13.8 billion in 2007, of which personal lines accounted for 87% and commercial and other lines 13%.

PGR's core business (90% of 2007's $11.9 billion in personal lines net premiums written) is underwriting private passenger automobile insurance. Based on year-end 2006 industry net written premium data (latest available), the company was the third largest private U.S. passenger auto insurer, a position that PGR believes it retained in 2007. PGR's other lines of business include recreational vehicle, motorcycle and small commercial vehicle insurance, and, to a lesser degree, commercial indemnity insurance. PGR believes it is the market leader in providing coverage for watercraft vehicles and for motorcycles.

Personal lines products are distributed through a network of more than 30,000,

including independent agents, as well as brokers in New York and California, and strategic alliance business relationships with an array of financial institutions. During 2007, 63% of total net written premiums were distributed through the agency channel (64% in 2006). Distribution through direct channels, including a toll free telephone line and the Internet, accounted for 37% of net written premiums in 2007 (36% in 2006).

PGR conducts business in 49 states (all but Massachusetts) and in the District of Columbia. PGR expects to begin writing private passenger auto insurance in Massachusetts in the second quarter of 2008. In 2007, Florida accounted for 12% of net premiums written, Texas 8%, California 8%, and New York 6%.

## Company Financials Fiscal Year Ended Dec. 31

| Per Share Data ($) | 2007 | 2006 | 2005 | 2004 | 2003 | 2002 | 2001 | 2000 | 1999 | 1998 |
|---|---|---|---|---|---|---|---|---|---|---|
| Tangible Book Value | 7.26 | 9.15 | 7.74 | 6.43 | 5.85 | 4.32 | 3.69 | 3.25 | 3.14 | 2.94 |
| Operating Earnings | NA | NA | NA | NA | NA | 0.81 | 0.54 | 0.06 | 0.30 | 0.50 |
| Earnings | 1.65 | 2.10 | 1.75 | 1.91 | 1.42 | 0.75 | 0.46 | 0.05 | 0.33 | 0.51 |
| S&P Core Earnings | 1.55 | 2.11 | 1.77 | 1.85 | 1.40 | 0.79 | 0.52 | NA | NA | NA |
| Dividends | Nil | 0.06 | 0.03 | 0.04 | 0.03 | 0.02 | 0.02 | 0.02 | 0.02 | 0.02 |
| Payout Ratio | Nil | 3% | 2% | 2% | 2% | 3% | 5% | 44% | 7% | 4% |
| Prices:High | 25.16 | 30.09 | 31.23 | 24.32 | 21.17 | 15.12 | 12.65 | 9.25 | 14.52 | 14.33 |
| Prices:Low | 17.26 | 22.18 | 20.34 | 18.28 | 11.56 | 11.19 | 6.84 | 3.75 | 5.71 | 7.83 |
| P/E Ratio:High | 15 | 14 | 18 | 13 | 15 | 20 | 28 | NM | 44 | 28 |
| P/E Ratio:Low | 10 | 11 | 12 | 10 | 8 | 15 | 15 | NM | 17 | 15 |

| Income Statement Analysis (Million $) | 2007 | 2006 | 2005 | 2004 | 2003 | 2002 | 2001 | 2000 | 1999 | 1998 |
|---|---|---|---|---|---|---|---|---|---|---|
| Premium Income | 13,877 | 14,118 | 13,764 | 13,170 | 11,341 | 8,884 | 7,162 | 6,348 | 5,684 | 4,948 |
| Net Investment Income | 681 | 648 | 537 | 484 | 465 | 455 | 414 | 385 | 341 | 295 |
| Other Revenue | 116 | 20.7 | 539 | 612 | 54.5 | 34.3 | 24.7 | 37.4 | 99.0 | 49.6 |
| Total Revenue | 14,687 | 14,786 | 14,303 | 13,782 | 11,892 | 9,373 | 7,488 | 6,771 | 6,124 | 5,292 |
| Pretax Income | 1,693 | 2,433 | 2,059 | 2,451 | 1,860 | 981 | 588 | 31.8 | 412 | 661 |
| Net Operating Income | NA | NA | NA | NA | NA | 718 | 486 | 55.4 | 267 | 449 |
| Net Income | 1,183 | 1,648 | 1,394 | 1,649 | 1,255 | 667 | 411 | 46.1 | 295 | 457 |
| S&P Core Earnings | 1,113 | 1,654 | 1,415 | 1,591 | 1,234 | 702 | 469 | NA | NA | NA |

| Balance Sheet & Other Financial Data (Million $) | 2007 | 2006 | 2005 | 2004 | 2003 | 2002 | 2001 | 2000 | 1999 | 1998 |
|---|---|---|---|---|---|---|---|---|---|---|
| Cash & Equivalent | 148 | 140 | 139 | 124 | 110 | 94.8 | 86.4 | 73.1 | 68.2 | 71.7 |
| Premiums Due | 2,730 | 2,932 | 2,906 | 2,669 | 2,351 | 1,959 | 1,497 | 1,567 | 1,761 | 1,456 |
| Investment Assets:Bonds | 9,185 | 9,959 | 10,222 | 9,084 | 9,133 | 7,713 | 5,949 | 4,784 | 4,533 | 4,219 |
| Investment Assets:Stocks | 4,598 | 4,149 | 3,279 | 2,621 | 2,751 | 2,004 | 2,050 | 2,012 | 1,666 | 1,013 |
| Investment Assets:Loans | Nil | Nil | Nil | Nil | Nil | Nil | Nil | Nil | Nil | Nil |
| Investment Assets:Total | 14,165 | 14,689 | 14,275 | 13,082 | 12,532 | 10,284 | 8,226 | 6,983 | 6,428 | 5,674 |
| Deferred Policy Costs | 426 | 441 | 445 | 432 | 412 | 364 | 317 | 310 | 343 | 299 |
| Total Assets | 18,843 | 19,482 | 18,899 | 17,184 | 16,282 | 13,564 | 11,122 | 10,052 | 9,705 | 8,463 |
| Debt | 2,174 | 1,186 | 1,285 | 1,284 | 1,490 | 1,489 | 1,096 | 749 | 1,049 | 777 |
| Common Equity | 4,936 | 6,847 | 6,108 | 5,155 | 5,060 | 3,768 | 3,251 | 2,870 | 2,753 | 2,557 |
| Property & Casualty:Loss Ratio | 71.5 | 66.6 | 68.1 | 65.0 | 67.4 | 70.9 | 73.6 | 83.2 | 75.0 | 68.5 |
| Property & Casualty:Expense Ratio | 21.1 | 19.9 | 87.4 | 19.6 | 18.8 | 20.4 | 21.0 | 21.0 | 22.1 | 22.4 |
| Property & Casualty Combined Ratio | 92.6 | 86.5 | 19.3 | 84.6 | 86.2 | 91.3 | 94.7 | 104.2 | 97.1 | 90.9 |
| % Return on Revenue | 8.1 | 11.1 | 9.7 | 12.0 | 10.6 | 7.1 | 5.4 | 0.7 | 4.8 | 8.6 |
| % Return on Equity | 20.1 | 25.4 | 24.8 | 32.4 | 28.4 | 19.3 | 13.4 | 1.6 | 11.1 | 19.5 |

Data as orig reptd.; bef. results of disc opers/spec. items. Per share data adj. for stk. divs.; EPS diluted. E-Estimated. NA-Not Available. NM-Not Meaningful. NR-Not Ranked. UR-Under Review.

**Office:** 6300 Wilson Mills Road, Mayfield Village, OH 44143.
**Telephone:** 440-461-5000.
**Website:** http://www.progressive.com
**Chrmn:** P.B. Lewis

**Pres & CEO:** G.M. Renwick
**CFO:** B.C. Domeck
**Chief Acctg Officer:** J.W. Basch
**Treas:** T.A. King

**Investor Contact:** P. Brennan (440-395-2370)
**Board Members:** C. A. Davis, R. N. Farah, S. R. Hardis, B. P. Healy, J. D. Kelly, A. F. Kohnstamm, P. B. Lewis, N. S. Matthews, P. H. Nettles, G. M. Renwick, D. B. Shackelford, B. T. Sheares

**Founded:** 1965
**Domicile:** Ohio
**Employees:** 26,851

The McGraw-Hill Companies

# Progress Energy Inc.

## STANDARD &POOR'S

| S&P Recommendation | BUY ★★★★☆ | Price $38.84 (as of Nov 14, 2008) | 12-Mo. Target Price $45.00 | Investment Style Large-Cap Blend |
|---|---|---|---|---|

**GICS Sector** Utilities
**Sub-Industry** Electric Utilities

**Summary** This diversified energy company owns two electric utilities serving approximately 3.1 million customers in North Carolina, South Carolina and Florida.

## Key Stock Statistics (Source S&P, Vickers, company reports)

| | | | | | |
|---|---|---|---|---|---|
| 52-Wk Range | $50.25–32.60 | S&P Oper. EPS 2008**E** | 3.00 | Market Capitalization(B) | $10.218 | Beta | 0.54 |
| Trailing 12-Month EPS | $3.18 | S&P Oper. EPS 2009**E** | 3.14 | Yield (%) | 6.33 | S&P 3-Yr. Proj. EPS CAGR(%) | 7 |
| Trailing 12-Month P/E | 12.2 | P/E on S&P Oper. EPS 2008**E** | 12.9 | Dividend Rate/Share | $2.46 | S&P Credit Rating | BBB+ |
| $10K Invested 5 Yrs Ago | $11,744 | Common Shares Outstg. (M) | 263.1 | Institutional Ownership (%) | 58 | | |

## Price Performance

30-Week Mov. Avg. · · · 10-Week Mov. Avg. – · – **GAAP Earnings vs. Previous Year** Volume Above Avg. STARS
12-Mo. Target Price — Relative Strength — ▲ Up ▼ Down ▶ No Change Below Avg.

Options: ASE, CBOE, Ph

Analysis prepared by **Justin McCann** on November 05, 2008, when the stock traded at **$ 39.11**.

## Highlights

➤ We expect EPS from ongoing operations in 2008 to grow about 10% from 2007 EPS from ongoing operations of $2.72, aided by new plants added to the rate base and customer growth in the Carolinas. In the first nine months of 2008, operating EPS grew 8%, to $2.51, reflecting a strong second quarter and a flat third quarter, with both aided by increased retail sales in the Carolinas. EPS in the first nine months also benefited $0.20 from the regulatory allowance for funds used during construction.

➤ For 2009 operating EPS, we expect a mid-single digit increase from anticipated results for 2008. While we expect customer growth in the Carolinas to remain relatively strong, we believe it will remain weak in Florida. However, we think the weakness in the Florida economy will be partially offset by cost management efforts. Although PGN sold the remainder of its synthetic fuels business (for $94 million), it has carried forward, as of September 30, $803 million in deferred synfuel-related tax credits.

➤ An agreement with state utility regulators in Florida has provided rate certainty through 2009, and the utility may recover about 90% of its $252 million of storm-related costs.

## Investment Rationale/Risk

➤ With the shares down about 19% year to date, the yield from the dividend (recently at 6.3%) remains well above peers. We believe the stock has been hurt by the credit crisis and the weakness of the housing market and economy in Florida, but we expect it to recover once the situation improves. With the sale of remaining non-utility businesses, we believe the shares should benefit from PGN's increased focus on regulated operations. While the transactions related to PGN's exit from its merchant energy segment resulted in a 2007 loss of $1.24 a share from discontinued operations, that disposal is now behind it. We believe the shares are attractive for above-average total return.

➤ Risks to our recommendation and target price include the possibility of unfavorable regulatory rulings as well as a sharp decline in the average P/E of the group as a whole.

➤ Our 12-month target price of $47 represents a premium-to-peers P/E of approximately 14.3X our EPS estimate for 2009, and reflects the recent weakness in electric utility stocks and the contraction of the average peer P/E. We believe the stock will be supported by its well above peers dividend yield.

## Qualitative Risk Assessment

| LOW | MEDIUM | HIGH |
|---|---|---|

With the higher risk synthetic fuel business having been discontinued, our risk assessment for the company reflects the strong and steady cash flow that we expect from the regulated utilities in both the Carolinas and Florida, which we believe have well above average customer growth and operate within a generally supportive regulatory environment.

## Quantitative Evaluations

**S&P Quality Ranking** B

| D | C | B- | **B** | B+ | A- | A | A+ |
|---|---|---|---|---|---|---|---|

**Relative Strength Rank** STRONG

84

LOWEST = 1          HIGHEST = 99

## Revenue/Earnings Data

**Revenue (Million $)**

| | 1Q | 2Q | 3Q | 4Q | Year |
|---|---|---|---|---|---|
| 2008 | 2,066 | 2,244 | 2,696 | -- | -- |
| 2007 | 2,072 | 2,129 | 2,750 | 2,202 | 9,153 |
| 2006 | 2,433 | 2,499 | 2,913 | 2,273 | 9,570 |
| 2005 | 2,198 | 2,333 | 3,097 | 2,578 | 10,108 |
| 2004 | 2,234 | 2,430 | 2,775 | 2,358 | 9,772 |
| 2003 | 2,187 | 2,050 | 2,458 | 2,048 | 8,743 |

**Earnings Per Share ($)**

| | | | | | |
|---|---|---|---|---|---|
| 2008 | 0.58 | 0.77 | 1.18 | E0.49 | E3.00 |
| 2007 | 0.62 | 0.41 | 1.27 | 0.09 | 2.70 |
| 2006 | 0.19 | 0.06 | 0.97 | 0.51 | 2.05 |
| 2005 | 0.43 | 0.02 | 1.81 | 0.63 | 2.94 |
| 2004 | 0.45 | 0.63 | 1.24 | 0.78 | 3.10 |
| 2003 | 0.89 | 0.65 | 1.40 | 0.47 | 3.40 |

Fiscal year ended Dec. 31. Next earnings report expected: Mid February. EPS Estimates based on S&P Operating Earnings; historical GAAP earnings are as reported.

## Dividend Data (Dates: mm/dd Payment Date: mm/dd/yy)

| Amount ($) | Date Decl. | Ex-Div. Date | Stk. of Record | Payment Date |
|---|---|---|---|---|
| 0.615 | 12/12 | 01/08 | 01/10 | 02/01/08 |
| 0.615 | 03/19 | 04/08 | 04/10 | 05/01/08 |
| 0.615 | 05/14 | 07/08 | 07/10 | 08/01/08 |
| 0.615 | 09/19 | 10/08 | 10/10 | 11/03/08 |

Dividends have been paid since 1937. Source: Company reports.

---

**Please read the Required Disclosures and Analyst Certification on the last page of this report.**

The McGraw·Hill Companies

# Progress Energy Inc.

**STANDARD
&POOR'S**

## Business Summary November 05, 2008

CORPORATE OVERVIEW. Headquartered in Raleigh, NC, Progress Energy operates in retail utility markets in the southeastern U.S., and in competitive electricity, gas and other fuel markets in the eastern U.S. It is the holding company for the fully integrated regulated utilities Progress Energy Carolinas (PEC) and Progress Energy Florida (PEF), which together serve approximately 3.1 million retail electric customers. On October 12, 2007, the company permanently ceased production of synthetic fuels at its majority-owned facilities. In 2007, PEC contributed about 61% of utility income (58% in 2006), and PEF 39% (42%).

CORPORATE STRATEGY. As an integrated energy company, PGN has stated that its primary focus will be on the end-use and wholesale electricity markets in its service territory and region. It is intent on enhancing its operational excellence, strengthening its financial flexibility and growth, and preparing for

future power generating capacity. Over the past few years, the company had reduced its business risk by exiting the majority of its non-regulated operations, and upon the close of the agreed-to sale (announced on December 17, 2007) of its remaining non-regulated businesses, this process will have been completed. We believe the company made great progress in reducing its debt and related interest expense through selected asset sales. It had received proceeds of $1.65 billion through asset sales in 2006, and had reduced its debt by $1.7 billion by the end of 2006. PGN aims to achieve sustainable earnings growth from its regulated utilities and to continue its track record of having increased its dividend for 20 consecutive years.

## Company Financials Fiscal Year Ended Dec. 31

| Per Share Data ($) | 2007 | 2006 | 2005 | 2004 | 2003 | 2002 | 2001 | 2000 | 1999 | 1998 |
|---|---|---|---|---|---|---|---|---|---|---|
| Tangible Book Value | 18.33 | 18.09 | 15.94 | 14.48 | 13.78 | 12.43 | 10.58 | 7.48 | 19.43 | 19.20 |
| Earnings | 2.70 | 2.05 | 2.94 | 3.10 | 3.40 | 2.53 | 2.64 | 3.03 | 2.55 | 2.75 |
| S&P Core Earnings | 2.67 | 1.95 | 2.94 | 2.93 | 3.44 | 2.04 | 2.59 | NA | NA | NA |
| Dividends | 2.44 | 2.42 | 2.36 | 2.30 | 2.24 | 2.18 | 2.12 | 2.06 | 2.00 | 1.94 |
| Payout Ratio | 90% | 118% | 80% | 74% | 66% | 86% | 80% | 68% | 78% | 71% |
| Prices:High | 52.75 | 49.55 | 46.00 | 47.95 | 48.00 | 52.70 | 49.25 | 49.38 | 47.88 | 49.63 |
| Prices:Low | 43.12 | 40.27 | 40.19 | 40.09 | 37.45 | 32.84 | 38.78 | 28.25 | 29.25 | 39.19 |
| P/E Ratio:High | 20 | 24 | 16 | 15 | 14 | 21 | 19 | 16 | 19 | 18 |
| P/E Ratio:Low | 16 | 20 | 14 | 13 | 11 | 13 | 15 | 9 | 11 | 14 |
| **Income Statement Analysis** (Million $) | | | | | | | | | | |
| Revenue | 9,153 | 9,570 | 10,108 | 9,772 | 8,743 | 7,945 | 8,461 | 4,119 | 3,358 | 3,130 |
| Depreciation | 905 | 1,032 | 1,074 | 1,068 | 1,040 | 820 | 1,090 | 740 | 496 | 487 |
| Maintenance | NA | NA | NA | NA | NA | NA | NA | NA | NA | NA |
| Fixed Charges Coverage | 2.76 | 2.28 | 1.93 | 2.21 | 2.16 | 1.64 | 1.75 | 2.60 | 4.23 | 4.50 |
| Construction Credits | 17.0 | 7.00 | 13.0 | 6.00 | 7.00 | 8.13 | 18.0 | 20.7 | 11.5 | 6.82 |
| Effective Tax Rate | 32.2% | 28.1% | NM | 13.5% | NM | NM | NM | 29.8% | 40.3% | 39.2% |
| Net Income | 693 | 514 | 727 | 753 | 811 | 552 | 542 | 478 | 382 | 399 |
| S&P Core Earnings | 685 | 487 | 726 | 712 | 819 | 445 | 532 | NA | NA | NA |
| **Balance Sheet & Other Financial Data** (Million $) | | | | | | | | | | |
| Gross Property | 27,500 | 25,796 | 26,401 | 25,602 | 25,172 | 23,021 | 22,541 | 21,028 | 12,233 | 10,797 |
| Capital Expenditures | 2,201 | 1,423 | 1,286 | 998 | 1,018 | 2,109 | 1,216 | 950 | 765 | 527 |
| Net Property | 16,605 | 15,732 | 16,799 | 16,819 | 17,056 | 12,541 | 12,445 | 11,677 | 7,257 | 6,300 |
| Capitalization:Long Term Debt | 9,069 | 8,928 | 10,539 | 9,650 | 10,027 | 9,840 | 9,577 | 5,983 | 3,029 | 2,614 |
| Capitalization:% Long Term Debt | 51.8 | 51.9 | 56.7 | 55.8 | 57.4 | 59.6 | 61.5 | 52.4 | 46.6 | 46.5 |
| Capitalization:Preferred | Nil | Nil | Nil | Nil | Nil | Nil | Nil | Nil | 59.4 | 59.4 |
| Capitalization:% Preferred | Nil | Nil | Nil | Nil | Nil | Nil | Nil | Nil | 0.91 | 1.06 |
| Capitalization:Common | 8,422 | 8,286 | 8,038 | 7,633 | 7,444 | 6,677 | 6,004 | 5,424 | 3,413 | 2,949 |
| Capitalization:% Common | 48.2 | 48.1 | 43.3 | 44.2 | 42.6 | 40.4 | 38.5 | 47.6 | 52.5 | 52.4 |
| Total Capital | 17,575 | 17,681 | 19,061 | 18,058 | 18,398 | 17,656 | 17,241 | 13,476 | 8,337 | 7,514 |
| % Operating Ratio | 86.8 | 87.5 | 87.2 | 86.7 | 66.8 | 85.4 | 83.5 | 87.1 | 82.4 | 79.3 |
| % Earned on Net Property | 9.7 | 8.5 | 7.7 | 8.8 | 8.2 | 8.3 | 10.3 | 7.6 | 12.1 | 10.2 |
| % Return on Revenue | 7.6 | 5.4 | 7.2 | 7.7 | 9.3 | 6.9 | 6.4 | 11.6 | 11.4 | 12.8 |
| % Return on Invested Capital | 7.4 | 6.8 | 7.3 | 7.6 | 8.2 | 7.2 | 9.2 | 7.1 | 7.3 | 7.8 |
| % Return on Common Equity | 8.3 | 6.3 | 9.3 | 10.0 | 11.5 | 8.7 | 9.4 | 10.8 | 11.9 | 13.7 |

Data as orig reptd.; bef. results of disc opers/spec. items. Per share data adj. for stk. divs.; EPS diluted. E-Estimated. NA-Not Available. NM-Not Meaningful. NR-Not Ranked. UR-Under Review.

**Office:** 410 S Wilmington St, Raleigh, NC 27601-1849.
**Telephone:** 919-546-6111.
**Email:** shareholder.relations@progress-energy.com
**Website:** http://www.progress-energy.com

**Chrmn, Pres & CEO:** W.D. Johnson
**SVP & CFO:** M.F. Mulhern
**SVP & Secy:** J. McArthur
**CFO:** S.A. Allaire

**Chief Acctg Officer & Cntlr:** J.M. Stone
**Investor Contact:** B. Drennan (919-546-7474)
**Board Members:** J. E. Bostic, Jr., D. Burner, H. E. Deloach, Jr., J. B. Hyler, Jr., W. D. Johnson, R. W. Jones, W. S. Jones, E. M. McKee, J. H. Mullin, III, C. W. Pryor, Jr., C. A. Saladrigas, T. M. Stone, A. C. Tollison, Jr.

**Founded:** 1926
**Domicile:** North Carolina
**Employees:** 11,000

**The McGraw·Hill** Companies

# ProLogis

**STANDARD &POOR'S**

**S&P Recommendation** HOLD ★★★☆☆

**Price**
$5.08 (as of Nov 14, 2008)

**12-Mo. Target Price**
$8.00

**GICS Sector** Financials
**Sub-Industry** Industrial REITS

**Summary** This real estate investment trust (formerly ProLogis Trust) is the largest publicly held, U.S.-based owner and operator of distribution facilities, with operations in North America, Europe and Asia.

## Key Stock Statistics (Source S&P, Vickers, company reports)

| | | | | | | | |
|---|---|---|---|---|---|---|---|
| 52-Wk Range | $71.79– 3.62 | S&P FFO/Sh. 2008E | 3.58 | Market Capitalization(B) | $1.350 | Beta | 2.24 |
| Trailing 12-Month FFO/Share | NA | S&P FFO/Sh. 2009E | 2.56 | Yield (%) | 19.69 | S&P 3-Yr. FFO/Sh. Proj. CAGR(%) | -10 |
| Trailing 12-Month P/FFO | NA | P/FFO on S&P FFO/Sh. 2008E | 1.4 | Dividend Rate/Share | $1.00 | S&P Credit Rating | BBB+ |
| $10K Invested 5 Yrs Ago | $2,078 | Common Shares Outstg. (M) | 265.7 | Institutional Ownership (%) | NM | | |

## Price Performance

30-Week Mov. Avg. · · · 10-Week Mov. Avg. - - **GAAP Earnings vs. Previous Year** Volume Above Avg. STARS
12-Mo. Target Price — Relative Strength — ▲ Up ▼ Down ▶ No Change Below Avg.

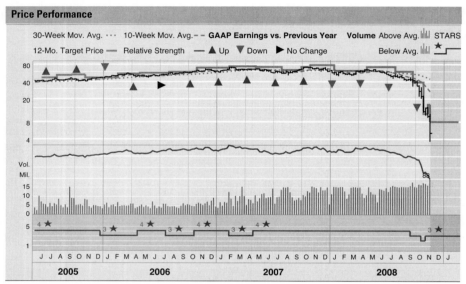

Options: ASE, CBOE, P, Ph

## Qualitative Risk Assessment

| LOW | MEDIUM | HIGH |
|---|---|---|

Our risk assessment reflects our view of PLD's position as one of the largest owners of industrial space in the world, its broad geographic and customer diversification, and what we see as its strong balance sheet.

## Quantitative Evaluations

**S&P Quality Ranking** A-

| D | C | B- | B | B+ | A- | A | A+ |
|---|---|---|---|---|---|---|---|

**Relative Strength Rank** WEAK

1

LOWEST = 1                          HIGHEST = 99

## Revenue/FFO Data

**Revenue (Million $)**

| | 1Q | 2Q | 3Q | 4Q | Year |
|---|---|---|---|---|---|
| 2008 | 1,637 | 1,515 | 1,122 | -- | -- |
| 2007 | 958.4 | 989.4 | 3,462 | 799.9 | 6,310 |
| 2006 | 571.1 | 687.4 | 580.5 | 624.9 | 2,464 |
| 2005 | 431.9 | 469.6 | 532.0 | 434.6 | 1,868 |
| 2004 | 151.0 | 150.1 | 148.8 | 150.0 | 598.1 |
| 2003 | 159.9 | 169.4 | 116.8 | 213.1 | 734.1 |

**FFO Per Share ($)**

| | 1Q | 2Q | 3Q | 4Q | Year |
|---|---|---|---|---|---|
| 2008 | 1.38 | 1.06 | E0.72 | E0.52 | E3.58 |
| 2007 | 1.25 | 1.16 | 1.41 | 0.79 | 4.61 |
| 2006 | 0.90 | 0.90 | 0.79 | 1.11 | 3.69 |
| 2005 | 0.90 | 0.90 | 0.79 | 0.58 | 2.51 |
| 2004 | 0.63 | 0.67 | 0.74 | 0.56 | 2.11 |
| 2003 | 0.55 | 0.54 | 0.30 | 0.80 | 2.17 |

Fiscal year ended Dec. 31. Next earnings report expected: Mid February. FFO Estimates based on S&P Funds From Operations Est..

## Highlights

➤ The 12-month target price for PLD has recently been changed to $8.00 from $16.00. The Highlights section of this Stock Report will be updated accordingly.

## Investment Rationale/Risk

➤ The Investment Rationale/Risk section of this Stock Report will be updated shortly. For the latest News story on PLD from MarketScope, see below.

➤ 11/12/08 10:22 am ET ... S&P REITERATES HOLD RECOMMENDATION ON SHARES OF PROLOGIS (PLD 5.76***): To conserve cash and enhance liquidity in a weak credit environment, PLD plans to cut its dividend from $2.07 in 2008 to $1.00 for 2009. It also intends to cut G&A expenses by 20%-25% and to curtail development activities. With nearly $1.5B in cash and credit availability, we believe PLD has sufficient liquidity to meet near-term debt obligations. At Q3-end, 93.4% of PLD's stabilized portfolio was leased, up from year-ago 92.2%, while same-property rent growth rose 2.7%. We keep our recently lowered '09 per-share funds from operations estimate at $2.56 and $8 target price. / R.McMillan

## Dividend Data (Dates: mm/dd Payment Date: mm/dd/yy)

| Amount ($) | Date Decl. | Ex-Div. Date | Stk. of Record | Payment Date |
|---|---|---|---|---|
| 0.518 | 02/01 | 02/13 | 02/15 | 02/29/08 |
| 0.518 | 05/01 | 05/13 | 05/15 | 05/30/08 |
| 0.518 | 08/01 | 08/13 | 08/15 | 08/29/08 |
| 0.518 | 11/03 | 11/07 | 11/12 | 11/26/08 |

Dividends have been paid since 1994. Source: Company reports.

# ProLogis

STANDARD &POOR'S

## Business Summary November 04, 2008

ProLogis (formerly ProLogis Trust, and prior to that Security Capital Industrial Trust) is a real estate investment trust that owns and operates industrial distribution and temperature-controlled distribution facilities in North America, Europe and Japan. The trust's investment strategy focuses on generic industrial distribution facilities in markets that PLD thinks offer attractive long-term growth prospects, and in which it believes it can achieve a strong market position by acquiring and developing flexible facilities for warehousing and light manufacturing uses.

PLD's business is organized into three main operating segments: property operations, fund management, and corporate distribution facilities services and other (CDFS). The property operations segment (about 43% of 2007 operating income) is involved in long-term ownership, management and leasing of industrial distribution facilities, usually adaptable for both distribution and light manufacturing or assembly uses. The trust earns income from rents and reimbursement of property operating expenses from unaffiliated customers, and management fees from entities in which it has an ownership interest. At December 31, 2007, PLD's property operations segment consisted of 1,409 operating properties aggregating 208.5 million square feet in North America, Eu-

rope and Asia. The properties are primarily distribution properties, although it owns 31 retail properties located in North America aggregating 1.2 million square feet.

The fund management segment (11% of 2007 operating income) is involved in the long-term investment management of unconsolidated property funds, and the properties they own, with the objective of generating a high level of returns for PLD and its fund partners. It allows PLD, as the manager of the property funds, to maintain the market presence and customer relationships that are the key drivers of the ProLogis Operating System, and it enables the trust to realize a portion of the development profits from its CDFS business activities by contributing its stabilized development properties to property funds. It also allows PLD to earn fees and incentives for providing services to the property funds and enables it to maintain a long-term ownership position in the properties.

## Company Financials Fiscal Year Ended Dec. 31

| Per Share Data ($) | 2007 | 2006 | 2005 | 2004 | 2003 | 2002 | 2001 | 2000 | 1999 | 1998 |
|---|---|---|---|---|---|---|---|---|---|---|
| Tangible Book Value | 25.44 | 23.09 | 21.08 | 14.82 | 14.35 | 13.96 | 12.94 | 13.53 | 13.86 | 12.83 |
| Earnings | 3.61 | 2.71 | 1.39 | 1.09 | 1.16 | 1.20 | 0.52 | 0.96 | 0.81 | 0.51 |
| S&P Core Earnings | 3.61 | 2.71 | 1.39 | 1.06 | 1.14 | 1.17 | 0.49 | NA | NA | NA |
| Dividends | 1.84 | 1.60 | 1.48 | 1.46 | 1.44 | 1.42 | 1.38 | 1.34 | 1.30 | 1.24 |
| Payout Ratio | 51% | 59% | 106% | 134% | 124% | 118% | NM | 140% | 160% | 267% |
| Prices:High | 73.35 | 67.52 | 47.62 | 43.33 | 32.62 | 26.00 | 23.30 | 24.69 | 22.19 | 26.50 |
| Prices:Low | 51.64 | 46.29 | 36.50 | 27.62 | 23.63 | 20.96 | 19.35 | 17.56 | 16.75 | 19.75 |
| P/E Ratio:High | 20 | 25 | 34 | 40 | 28 | 22 | 45 | 26 | 27 | 52 |
| P/E Ratio:Low | 14 | 17 | 26 | 25 | 20 | 17 | 37 | 18 | 20 | 39 |

| Income Statement Analysis (Million $) | | | | | | | | | | |
|---|---|---|---|---|---|---|---|---|---|---|
| Rental Income | 1,068 | 928 | 635 | 527 | Nil | 449 | 466 | 480 | 492 | 345 |
| Mortgage Income | Nil | Nil | Nil | Nil | Nil | Nil | Nil | Nil | Nil | Nil |
| Total Income | 6,205 | 2,464 | 1,868 | 598 | 734 | 675 | 574 | 644 | 567 | 368 |
| General Expenses | 4,760 | 1,403 | 1,210 | 224 | 210 | 91.0 | 83.0 | 78.0 | 76.7 | 58.1 |
| Interest Expense | 368 | 294 | 178 | 153 | 155 | 153 | 164 | 172 | 172 | 104 |
| Provision for Losses | Nil | Nil | Nil | Nil | Nil | Nil | Nil | Nil | Nil | Nil |
| Depreciation | 309 | 293 | 199 | 172 | 165 | 153 | 143 | 151 | 152 | 101 |
| Net Income | 987 | 718 | 318 | 234 | 251 | 249 | 128 | 214 | 182 | 111 |
| S&P Core Earnings | 962 | 692 | 292 | 199 | 208 | 210 | 86.8 | NA | NA | NA |

| Balance Sheet & Other Financial Data (Million $) | | | | | | | | | | |
|---|---|---|---|---|---|---|---|---|---|---|
| Cash | 419 | 1,775 | 1,241 | 1,145 | 1,009 | 111 | 28.0 | 57.9 | 69.3 | 63.1 |
| Total Assets | 19,724 | 15,904 | 13,114 | 7,098 | 6,369 | 5,924 | 5,604 | 5,946 | 5,848 | 4,331 |
| Real Estate Investment | 16,579 | 13,954 | 11,875 | 6,334 | 5,854 | 5,396 | 4,588 | 4,689 | 4,975 | 3,658 |
| Loss Reserve | Nil | Nil | Nil | Nil | Nil | Nil | Nil | Nil | Nil | Nil |
| Net Investment | 15,210 | 12,674 | 10,757 | 5,345 | 5,007 | 4,683 | 4,013 | 4,213 | 4,608 | 3,403 |
| Short Term Debt | Nil | Nil | Nil | Nil | Nil | 222 | 49.3 | 69.7 | 43.5 | 42.9 |
| Capitalization:Debt | 9,650 | 7,844 | 6,678 | 3,414 | 2,991 | 2,510 | 2,529 | 2,555 | 2,413 | 1,796 |
| Capitalization:Equity | 7,086 | 6,049 | 5,138 | 2,752 | 2,586 | 2,486 | 2,276 | 2,236 | 2,243 | 1,583 |
| Capitalization:Total | 17,165 | 14,295 | 12,225 | 6,583 | 6,089 | 5,439 | 5,251 | 5,574 | 5,428 | 4,104 |
| % Earnings & Depreciation/Assets | 7.3 | 4.7 | 5.1 | 6.0 | 6.8 | 7.0 | 4.7 | 6.2 | 6.6 | 5.7 |
| Price Times Book Value:High | 2.9 | 2.9 | 2.3 | 2.9 | 2.3 | 1.9 | 1.8 | 1.8 | 1.6 | 4.0 |
| Price Times Book Value:Low | 2.0 | 2.0 | 1.7 | 1.9 | 1.6 | 1.5 | 1.5 | 1.3 | 1.2 | 3.0 |

Data as orig reptd.; bef. results of disc opers/spec. items. Per share data adj. for stk. divs.; EPS diluted. E-Estimated. NA-Not Available. NM-Not Meaningful. NR-Not Ranked. UR-Under Review.

**Office:** 4545 Airport Way, Denver, CO 80239-5716.
**Telephone:** 303-567-5000.
**Email:** info@prologis.com
**Website:** http://www.prologis.com

**Chrmn:** S.L. Feinberg
**Pres:** T.R. Antenucci
**CEO:** W. Rakowich
**COO:** D.S. Paddison

**SVP & Chief Acctg Officer:** J.S. Finnin
**Investor Contact:** M. Marsden (303-567-5622)
**Trustees:** S. L. Feinberg, G. L. Fotiades, C. N. Garvey, L. V. Jackson, D. P. Jacobs, D. M. Steuert, W. D. Zollars, A. M. Zulberti, J. A. de Barros Teixeira

**Founded:** 1991
**Domicile:** Maryland
**Employees:** 1,535

# Prudential Financial Inc

STANDARD
&POOR'S

| S&P Recommendation BUY ★ ★ ★ ★ ☆ | Price<br>$25.24 (as of Nov 14, 2008) | 12-Mo. Target Price<br>$40.00 | Investment Style<br>Large-Cap Value |
|---|---|---|---|

**GICS Sector** Financials
**Sub-Industry** Life & Health Insurance

**Summary** Through its subsidiaries, Prudential Financial provides a wide range of insurance, investment management and other financial products and services to customers in the U.S. and overseas.

## Key Stock Statistics (Source S&P, Vickers, company reports)

| | | | | | | | | |
|---|---|---|---|---|---|---|---|---|
| 52-Wk Range | $98.31– 20.14 | S&P Oper. EPS 2008E | 6.40 | Market Capitalization(B) | $10.651 | Beta | 1.19 |
| Trailing 12-Month EPS | $3.11 | S&P Oper. EPS 2009E | 8.20 | Yield (%) | 2.30 | S&P 3-Yr. Proj. EPS CAGR(%) | 11 |
| Trailing 12-Month P/E | 8.1 | P/E on S&P Oper. EPS 2008E | 3.9 | Dividend Rate/Share | $0.58 | S&P Credit Rating | A+ |
| $10K Invested 5 Yrs Ago | $7,269 | Common Shares Outstg. (M) | 422.0 | Institutional Ownership (%) | 53 | | |

## Price Performance

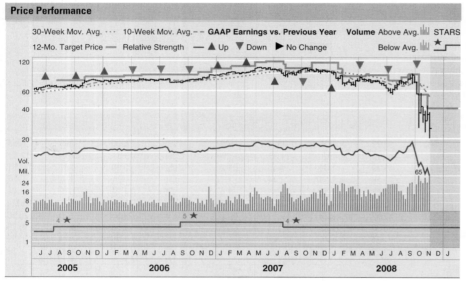

30-Week Mov. Avg. · · · ·  10-Week Mov. Avg. – –  ▬ GAAP Earnings vs. Previous Year  Volume Above Avg. ⅃⅃⅃ STARS
12-Mo. Target Price ▬  Relative Strength  — ▲ Up  ▼ Down  ► No Change  Below Avg. ⅃⅃⅃ ★

Options: ASE, CBOE, Ph

Analysis prepared by **Bret Howlett** on November 03, 2008, when the stock traded at **$ 32.95**.

## Highlights

➤ We expect operating income in the insurance division to decline in 2008 as a result of the difficult environment. We think the division will be hurt by unfavorable DAC unlocking and poor flows in annuities, partially offset by favorable mortality and improved group insurance results. We believe VA sales will decline as investors continue to fret about the turbulent equity markets. We forecast declining growth in operating income for the investment division, due to lackluster demand for retirement services and products, a slowdown in growth in the institutional business, and lower full service account values adversely affected by the market.

➤ We estimate that operating income for the international insurance and investments division will see mid-single digit growth in 2008, on strong sales of dollar-denominated products, improved margins, expanded distribution and strategic acquisitions, partially offset by higher expenses related to recruiting and client servicing. We expect strong growth to continue in Japan, particularly in Gibraltar Life operations.

➤ We forecast 2008 operating EPS of $6.40. Our operating EPS estimate for 2009 is $8.20.

## Investment Rationale/Risk

➤ Although we believe 2008 will prove to be a difficult year for PRU, our buy recommendation is based on the company's collection of high-growth businesses; also, at current price levels, we think the valuation is attractive. Over time, we believe PRU should expand earnings and return on equity (ROE). Despite the headwinds from the turbulent financial market, we believe PRU is adequately capitalized to weather the poor operating conditions and should benefit from its broad business mix, especially in its international division. We believe PRU's potential investment losses stemming from its exposure to the residential and commercial real estate markets are manageable, and it has a number of options to raise capital internally to absorb losses.

➤ Risks to our recommendation and target price include currency risk; reserving risks for new guaranteed minimum benefits; integration risks from acquisitions; credit risk; and exposure to a sharp decline in the equity markets.

➤ Our 12-month target price is $40, or 1.0X our 2008 book value estimate, below the historical multiple.

## Qualitative Risk Assessment

| LOW | MEDIUM | HIGH |
|---|---|---|

Our risk assessment reflects our view of PRU's varied product offerings, geographic diversification, disciplined capital management, prominent market position. However, our risk assessment also takes into account PRU's exposure to the equity markets and the risk for further asset impairments on its balance sheet.

## Quantitative Evaluations

**S&P Quality Ranking**  NR

| D | C | B- | B | B+ | A- | A | A+ |
|---|---|---|---|---|---|---|---|

**Relative Strength Rank**  WEAK

14

LOWEST = 1                                    HIGHEST = 99

## Revenue/Earnings Data

**Revenue (Million $)**

| | 1Q | 2Q | 3Q | 4Q | Year |
|---|---|---|---|---|---|
| 2008 | 7,564 | 7,709 | 7,036 | -- | -- |
| 2007 | 8,775 | 8,425 | 8,383 | 8,808 | 34,401 |
| 2006 | 7,850 | 7,373 | 8,408 | 8,857 | 32,488 |
| 2005 | 7,721 | 8,318 | 7,787 | 7,882 | 31,708 |
| 2004 | 6,743 | 6,904 | 7,346 | 7,355 | 28,348 |
| 2003 | 6,785 | 7,304 | 6,693 | 7,125 | 27,907 |

**Earnings Per Share ($)**

| | | | | | |
|---|---|---|---|---|---|
| 2008 | 0.20 | 1.35 | -0.24 | E1.95 | E6.40 |
| 2007 | 2.10 | 1.86 | 1.89 | 1.89 | 7.58 |
| 2006 | 1.39 | 0.92 | 2.24 | 1.85 | 6.37 |
| 2005 | 1.47 | 1.56 | 2.61 | 0.78 | 6.46 |
| 2004 | 0.72 | 0.98 | 1.09 | 0.64 | 3.45 |
| 2003 | 0.42 | 0.21 | 0.48 | 0.95 | 2.06 |

Fiscal year ended Dec. 31. Next earnings report expected: Early February. EPS Estimates based on S&P Operating Earnings; historical GAAP earnings are as reported.

## Dividend Data (Dates: mm/dd Payment Date: mm/dd/yy)

| Amount ($) | Date Decl. | Ex-Div. Date | Stk. of Record | Payment Date |
|---|---|---|---|---|
| 1.150 | 11/13 | 11/21 | 11/26 | 12/21/07 |
| 0.580 | 11/11 | 11/20 | 11/24 | 12/19/08 |

Dividends have been paid since 2002. Source: Company reports.

---

**Please read the Required Disclosures and Analyst Certification on the last page of this report.**

The McGraw-Hill Companies

# Prudential Financial Inc

STANDARD
&POOR'S

## Business Summary November 03, 2008

CORPORATE OVERVIEW. Prudential Financial is one of the largest U.S. financial services companies, with $648 billion in assets under management at year-end 2007, and customers in roughly 30 other countries.

The financial services business operates through four divisions: insurance (37% of 2007 operating revenues, 36% in 2006), investments (28%, 27%), international insurance and investments (33%, 34%), and corporate and other (2.0%, 2.6%). The insurance division consists of the individual life and annuities unit (51.5% of the division's 2007 operating revenues) and the group insurance unit (48.5%), which distributes group life, disability and related insurance products through employee and member benefit plans.

The asset management unit (31% of the division's 2007 operating revenues), the financial advisory unit (5.1%) and the retirement services unit (64%) comprise the investment division. International insurance and investments consists of insurance (91% of the division's 2007 operating revenues) and investments (8.6%).

The closed block businesses represent some insurance products no longer offered, including certain participating insurance and annuity policies. At De-

cember 31, 2006, PRU had reinsurance agreements covering about 90% of the closed block policies.

CORPORATE STRATEGY. We believe PRU is focused on two prime areas of growth: international businesses and domestic retirement and savings. To that end, Prudential has made strategic acquisitions to enhance these opportunities. In April 2004, the company acquired CIGNA's retirement business for $2.1 billion in cash.

At any time before July 1, 2008, PRU could have, subject to limitations, required Wachovia to purchase its interest in Wachovia Securities. The purchase price generally would have been $1 billion plus PRU's share of the joint venture's transition costs, adjusted for additional investments. On August 28, 2006, PRU announced a $600 million settlement with various regulatory agencies in connection with market timing activities at Prudential Securities.

## Company Financials Fiscal Year Ended Dec. 31

| Per Share Data ($) | 2007 | 2006 | 2005 | 2004 | 2003 | 2002 | 2001 | 2000 | 1999 | 1998 |
|---|---|---|---|---|---|---|---|---|---|---|
| Tangible Book Value | 52.43 | 46.32 | 45.53 | 42.40 | 39.65 | 37.89 | 34.90 | NA | NA | NA |
| Operating Earnings | NA | NA | NA | NA | NA | NA | NA | NA | NA | NA |
| Earnings | 7.58 | 6.37 | 6.46 | 3.45 | 2.06 | 1.36 | 0.07 | 0.82 | NA | NA |
| S&P Core Earnings | 6.18 | 5.41 | 4.96 | 1.91 | 1.79 | 1.13 | NA | NA | NA | NA |
| Dividends | 1.15 | 0.95 | 0.78 | 0.63 | 0.50 | 0.40 | Nil | NA | NA | NA |
| Payout Ratio | 15% | 15% | 12% | 18% | 24% | 29% | Nil | NA | NA | NA |
| Prices:High | 103.27 | 87.18 | 78.62 | 55.62 | 42.21 | 36.00 | 33.74 | NA | NA | NA |
| Prices:Low | 81.61 | 71.28 | 52.07 | 40.14 | 27.03 | 25.25 | 27.50 | NA | NA | NA |
| P/E Ratio:High | 14 | 14 | 12 | 16 | 20 | 26 | NM | NA | NA | NA |
| P/E Ratio:Low | 11 | 11 | 8 | 12 | 13 | 19 | NM | NA | NA | NA |

| Income Statement Analysis (Million $) | | | | | | | | | | |
|---|---|---|---|---|---|---|---|---|---|---|
| Life Insurance in Force | NA | NA | NA | NA | 1,928,650 | 1,800,788 | 1,768,038 | NA | NA | NA |
| Premium Income:Life | 14,351 | 13,908 | 13,685 | 12,580 | 10,972 | 10,897 | 10,078 | NA | NA | NA |
| Premium Income:A & H | NA | NA | NA | NA | 806 | 586 | 515 | NA | NA | NA |
| Net Investment Income | 12,017 | 11,354 | 10,560 | 9,079 | 8,681 | 8,832 | 9,151 | 9,467 | NA | NA |
| Total Revenue | 34,401 | 32,488 | 31,708 | 28,348 | 27,907 | 26,675 | 27,177 | 26,514 | NA | NA |
| Pretax Income | 4,932 | 4,611 | 4,471 | 3,287 | 1,958 | 64.0 | -227 | 525 | NA | NA |
| Net Operating Income | NA | NA | NA | NA | NA | NA | NA | NA | NA | NA |
| Net Income | 3,687 | 3,363 | 3,602 | 2,332 | 1,308 | 256 | -170 | 304 | NA | NA |
| S&P Core Earnings | 2,899 | 2,675 | 2,580 | 1,022 | 981 | 650 | -403 | NA | NA | NA |

| Balance Sheet & Other Financial Data (Million $) | | | | | | | | | | |
|---|---|---|---|---|---|---|---|---|---|---|
| Cash & Equivalent | 13,234 | 10,731 | 9,866 | 10,100 | 9,746 | 11,688 | 20,364 | 19,994 | NA | NA |
| Premiums Due | 2,119 | 1,958 | 3,548 | 32,790 | Nil | Nil | Nil | NA | NA | NA |
| Investment Assets:Bonds | 165,710 | 166,285 | 158,515 | 153,715 | 132,011 | 128,075 | 110,316 | NA | NA | NA |
| Investment Assets:Stocks | 26,216 | 24,574 | 18,792 | 4,283 | 6,703 | 2,807 | 2,272 | NA | NA | NA |
| Investment Assets:Loans | 39,384 | 34,626 | 32,811 | 32,761 | 27,621 | 22,094 | 28,299 | NA | NA | NA |
| Investment Assets:Total | 243,107 | 245,349 | 221,401 | 216,624 | 181,041 | 183,094 | 165,834 | 169,251 | NA | NA |
| Deferred Policy Costs | 12,339 | 10,863 | 9,438 | 8,847 | 7,826 | 7,031 | 6,868 | 6,751 | NA | NA |
| Total Assets | 485,814 | 454,266 | 417,776 | 401,058 | 321,274 | 292,746 | 293,030 | 298,414 | NA | NA |
| Debt | 14,101 | 11,423 | 8,270 | 7,627 | 5,610 | 4,757 | 5,304 | 14,812 | NA | NA |
| Common Equity | 23,457 | 22,892 | 22,763 | 22,344 | 21,292 | 21,330 | 20,453 | 20,692 | NA | NA |
| % Return on Revenue | 10.7 | 10.4 | 11.4 | 8.2 | 4.7 | 1.0 | NM | 1.1 | NA | NA |
| % Return on Assets | 0.8 | 0.8 | 0.9 | 0.6 | 0.4 | 0.1 | NM | NA | NA | NA |
| % Return on Equity | 15.9 | 14.7 | 16.0 | 10.7 | 6.1 | 1.2 | NM | NA | NA | NA |
| % Investment Yield | 5.0 | 4.8 | 4.8 | 4.6 | 4.8 | 5.1 | 5.8 | NA | NA | NA |

Data as orig reptd.; bef. results of disc opers/spec. items. Per share data adj. for stk. divs.; EPS diluted. E-Estimated. NA-Not Available. NM-Not Meaningful. NR-Not Ranked. UR-Under Review.

**Office:** 751 Broad St, Newark, NJ 07102.
**Telephone:** 973-802-6000.
**Email:** investor.relations@prudential.com
**Website:** http://www.investor.prudential.com

**Chrmn:** H. McGrath
**Pres & CEO:** J.R. Strangfeld, Jr.
**COO & SVP:** J.R. Leibowtiz
**EVP & CFO:** R.J. Carbone

**SVP, Chief Acctg Officer & Cntlr:** P.B. Sayre
**Board Members:** T. J. Baltimore, Jr., F. K. Becker, G. Bethune, G. Caperton, III, G. F. Casellas, J. G. Cullen, W. H. Gray, III, M. B. Grier, J. F. Hanson, C. J. Horner, K. J. Krapek, H. McGrath, C. A. Poon, J. R. Strangfeld, Jr., J. A. Unruh

**Founded:** 1875
**Domicile:** New Jersey
**Employees:** 40,703

# Public Storage

**STANDARD &POOR'S**

| S&P Recommendation **HOLD** ★★★☆☆ | Price $64.46 (as of Nov 14, 2008) | 12-Mo. Target Price $80.00 | Investment Style Large-Cap Blend |
|---|---|---|---|

**GICS Sector** Financials
**Sub-Industry** Specialized REITS

**Summary** This real estate investment trust invests primarily in self-service storage facilities (mini-warehouses), but also in commercial and industrial properties.

## Key Stock Statistics (Source S&P, Vickers, company reports)

| | | | | | | | |
|---|---|---|---|---|---|---|---|
| 52-Wk Range | $110.00– 63.76 | S&P FFO/Sh. 2008E | 4.70 | Market Capitalization(B) | $10.835 | Beta | 0.41 |
| Trailing 12-Month FFO/Share | NA | S&P FFO/Sh. 2009E | 5.18 | Yield (%) | 3.41 | S&P 3-Yr. FFO/Sh. Proj. CAGR(%) | 13 |
| Trailing 12-Month P/FFO | NA | P/FFO on S&P FFO/Sh. 2008E | 13.7 | Dividend Rate/Share | $2.20 | S&P Credit Rating | A- |
| $10K Invested 5 Yrs Ago | $16,917 | Common Shares Outstg. (M) | 168.1 | Institutional Ownership (%) | 68 | | |

## Price Performance

30-Week Mov. Avg. · · · · 10-Week Mov. Avg. – – **GAAP Earnings vs. Previous Year** Volume Above Avg. ▌▍▌ STARS
12-Mo. Target Price — Relative Strength — ▲ Up ▼ Down ► No Change Below Avg. ▌▍▌ ★

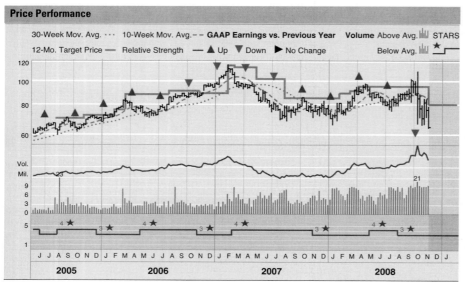

Options: ASE, Ph

Analysis prepared by **Robert McMillan** on November 07, 2008, when the stock traded at **$ 74.02**.

## Highlights

➤ Following revenue growth of about 34% in 2007, driven largely by contributions from the August 2006 acquisition of Shurgard Storage Centers, we look for revenues to fall about 5% in 2008, reflecting property dispositions and tepid growth in demand for storage space, before a rise of about 1% in 2009 on organic growth and contributions from acquisitions.

➤ Given our expectation of near-term economic softness in the U.S., we think a slowdown in moving and relocation activity in the U.S. may translate into slower growth. Same-store domestic occupancy inched up to 90.5% at the end of the third quarter, from 90.1% last year, while revenue per available square foot rose 2.3%. We look for strength in the U.S. dollar to contribute to near-term foreign exchange losses. Given the general economic weakness and PSA's healthy liquidity with no significant debt maturities until 2011, we look for PSA to make small property acquisitions.

➤ We look for per share funds from operations (FFO) of $4.70 in 2008 and $5.18 in 2009.

## Investment Rationale/Risk

➤ We believe that a moderately expanding economy will continue to generate moving activity. We see PSA benefiting from its ability to continue gaining share at the expense of smaller competitors by creating customer awareness in its markets and offering an array of customer services, such as container services, that many small competitors cannot provide.

➤ Risks to our recommendation and target price include slower-than-expected growth in rental rates and occupancy levels, a sharp drop in moving activity, and higher interest rates.

➤ The stock recently traded at about 15.1X trailing 12-month FFO per share. The shares and the valuation multiple have been volatile lately on concerns, in our view, on the state of the economy and housing market. Our 12-month target price of $80 is equal to about 16.5X our forward four-quarter FFO estimate of $4.88. We expect a widening of the valuation multiple to be driven by continued improvement in operating results.

## Qualitative Risk Assessment

| LOW | MEDIUM | HIGH |
|---|---|---|

Our risk assessment reflects PSA's position as one of the largest providers of self-storage space in a consolidating industry, as well as our view of its consistent growth and healthy balance sheet.

## Quantitative Evaluations

**S&P Quality Ranking** B+

| D | C | B- | B | B+ | A- | A | A+ |
|---|---|---|---|---|---|---|---|

**Relative Strength Rank** MODERATE

52

LOWEST = 1 HIGHEST = 99

## Revenue/FFO Data

**Revenue (Million $)**

| | 1Q | 2Q | 3Q | 4Q | Year |
|---|---|---|---|---|---|
| 2008 | 462.8 | 428.8 | 443.2 | -- | -- |
| 2007 | 434.4 | 449.2 | 469.0 | 464.4 | 1,829 |
| 2006 | 278.5 | 297.9 | 371.4 | 433.9 | 1,382 |
| 2005 | 243.8 | 254.3 | 264.9 | 273.6 | 1,061 |
| 2004 | 222.7 | 231.6 | 237.2 | 240.3 | 928.0 |
| 2003 | 206.9 | 217.1 | 228.0 | 223.1 | 875.1 |

**FFO Per Share ($)**

| | | | | | |
|---|---|---|---|---|---|
| 2008 | 1.39 | E1.27 | E1.29 | E1.12 | E4.70 |
| 2007 | 1.05 | 1.10 | 1.43 | 1.40 | 4.97 |
| 2006 | 0.94 | 0.99 | 0.77 | 0.89 | 3.57 |
| 2005 | 0.79 | 0.90 | 0.97 | 0.96 | 3.61 |
| 2004 | 0.58 | 0.77 | 0.76 | 0.82 | 2.93 |
| 2003 | 0.68 | 0.72 | 0.79 | 0.68 | 2.81 |

Fiscal year ended Dec. 31. Next earnings report expected: Early March. FFO Estimates based on S&P Funds From Operations Est..

## Dividend Data (Dates: mm/dd Payment Date: mm/dd/yy)

| Amount ($) | Date Decl. | Ex-Div. Date | Stk. of Record | Payment Date |
|---|---|---|---|---|
| 0.550 | 05/08 | 06/11 | 06/13 | 06/30/08 |
| 0.550 | 08/11 | 09/11 | 09/15 | 09/30/08 |
| 0.60 Spl. | 11/06 | 11/11 | 11/15 | 12/30/08 |
| 0.550 | 11/06 | 11/11 | 11/15 | 12/30/08 |

Dividends have been paid since 1981. Source: Company reports.

---

**Please read the Required Disclosures and Analyst Certification on the last page of this report.**

*The McGraw·Hill Companies*

# Public Storage

**STANDARD &POOR'S**

## Business Summary November 07, 2008

Public Storage is an equity real estate investment trust that was organized as a corporation under the laws of California on July 10, 1980. It is a fully integrated, self-administered and self-managed REIT that acquires, develops, owns and operates storage facilities.

PSA is the largest U.S. owner and operator of storage space, with direct and indirect equity investments in 2,012 self-storage facilities located in 38 states within the U.S. operating under the "Public Storage" name at the end of 2007. The facilities contain approximately 126 million net rentable square feet of space, and 174 self-storage facilities are located in seven Western European countries, which operate under the "Shurgard Storage Centers" name, containing approximately nine million net rentable square feet of space. The company also has direct and indirect equity interests in approximately 21 million net rentable square feet of commercial space located in 11 states in the U.S. operated under the "PS Business Parks" and Public Storage, Inc. brands.

PSA's growth strategies consist of improving the operating performance of stabilized existing traditional self-storage properties; acquiring additional interests in entities that own properties operated by the trust; purchasing interests in properties that are owned or operated by others; developing properties in selected markets; improving the operating performance of the containerized storage operations; and participating in the growth of PS Business Parks, Inc.

The trust's storage facilities are designed to offer accessible storage space for personal and business use at a relatively low cost. Individuals usually obtain this space for storage of furniture, household appliances, personal belongings, motor vehicles, boats, campers, motorcycles and other household goods. Businesses normally employ this space for storage of excess inventory, business records, seasonal goods, equipment and fixtures. A user rents a fully enclosed space that is for the user's exclusive use and that only the user has access to on an unrestricted basis during business hours. Some storage facilities also include rentable uncovered parking areas for vehicle storage, as well as space for portable storage containers. Leases for storage facility space may be on a long-term or short-term basis, although typically spaces are rented on a month-to-month basis. Rental rates vary according to the location of the property, the size of the storage space and the length of stay. PSA's self-storage facilities generally consist of three to seven buildings containing an aggregate of between 350 and 750 storage spaces, most of which have between 25 and 400 square feet and an interior height of approximately eight to 12 feet.

## Company Financials Fiscal Year Ended Dec. 31

| Per Share Data ($) | 2007 | 2006 | 2005 | 2004 | 2003 | 2002 | 2001 | 2000 | 1999 | 1998 |
|---|---|---|---|---|---|---|---|---|---|---|
| Tangible Book Value | NA | 28.16 | 16.72 | 16.69 | 17.03 | 16.16 | 28.37 | 18.24 | 21.43 | 16.65 |
| Earnings | 1.17 | 0.32 | 1.92 | 1.39 | 1.27 | 1.28 | 1.51 | 1.41 | 1.52 | 1.30 |
| S&P Core Earnings | 1.15 | 0.32 | 1.91 | 1.38 | 1.25 | 1.26 | 1.48 | NA | NA | NA |
| Dividends | 2.00 | 2.00 | 1.85 | 1.80 | 1.80 | 1.80 | 1.69 | 1.48 | 0.88 | 0.88 |
| Payout Ratio | 171% | NM | 97% | 129% | 142% | 1% | 112% | 105% | 58% | 68% |
| Prices:High | 117.16 | 98.05 | 72.02 | 57.64 | 45.81 | 39.29 | 35.15 | 26.93 | 29.38 | 33.63 |
| Prices:Low | 68.09 | 67.72 | 51.50 | 39.50 | 28.25 | 27.98 | 24.13 | 20.87 | 20.81 | 22.63 |
| P/E Ratio:High | NM | NM | 38 | 41 | 36 | 33 | 23 | 19 | 19 | 26 |
| P/E Ratio:Low | NM | NM | 27 | 28 | 22 | 24 | 16 | 15 | 14 | 17 |

| Income Statement Analysis (Million $) | | | | | | | | | | |
|---|---|---|---|---|---|---|---|---|---|---|
| Rental Income | NA | 1,240 | 980 | 894 | 844 | 813 | 782 | 703 | 628 | 536 |
| Mortgage Income | NA | Nil | Nil | Nil | Nil | Nil | Nil | Nil | Nil | Nil |
| Total Income | 1,829 | 1,382 | 1,061 | 928 | 875 | 841 | 835 | 757 | 677 | 582 |
| General Expenses | NA | 585 | 400 | 349 | 336 | 311 | 297 | 273 | 229 | 223 |
| Interest Expense | NA | 33.1 | 8.22 | 0.76 | 1.12 | 3.81 | 3.23 | 3.29 | 7.97 | 4.51 |
| Provision for Losses | NA | Nil | Nil | Nil | Nil | Nil | Nil | Nil | Nil | Nil |
| Depreciation | NA | 438 | 196 | 183 | 186 | 180 | 168 | 149 | 138 | 107 |
| Net Income | 458 | 312 | 450 | 367 | 335 | 319 | 324 | 297 | 288 | 227 |
| S&P Core Earnings | 197 | 44.7 | 247 | 179 | 157 | 156 | 183 | NA | NA | NA |

| Balance Sheet & Other Financial Data (Million $) | | | | | | | | | | |
|---|---|---|---|---|---|---|---|---|---|---|
| Cash | 245 | 857 | 329 | 708 | 205 | 103 | 49.3 | 89.5 | 55.1 | 51.2 |
| Total Assets | 10,643 | 11,198 | 5,552 | 5,205 | 4,968 | 4,844 | 4,626 | 4,514 | 4,214 | 3,404 |
| Real Estate Investment | NA | 11,262 | 6,314 | 5,908 | 5,544 | 5,424 | 5,062 | 4,822 | 4,421 | 3,496 |
| Loss Reserve | NA | Nil | Nil | Nil | Nil | Nil | Nil | Nil | Nil | Nil |
| Net Investment | NA | 9,507 | 4,814 | 4,588 | 4,391 | 4,436 | 4,242 | 4,154 | 3,887 | 3,085 |
| Short Term Debt | NA | Nil | Nil | Nil | Nil | 39.8 | Nil | Nil | Nil | Nil |
| Capitalization:Debt | NA | 1,848 | 134 | 130 | 76.0 | 76.1 | 144 | 156 | 167 | 81.4 |
| Capitalization:Equity | 5,236 | 5,353 | 2,319 | 2,328 | 2,353 | 2,342 | 2,369 | 2,569 | 2,534 | 2,250 |
| Capitalization:Total | NA | 8,785 | 5,205 | 4,989 | 4,722 | 4,675 | 4,508 | 4,413 | 4,043 | 3,340 |
| % Earnings & Depreciation/Assets | NA | 8.9 | 12.0 | 10.8 | 10.6 | 10.5 | 7.1 | 10.2 | 11.2 | 7.6 |
| Price Times Book Value:High | NA | 3.5 | 4.3 | 3.5 | 2.7 | 2.4 | 1.2 | 1.5 | 1.4 | 2.0 |
| Price Times Book Value:Low | NA | 2.4 | 3.1 | 2.4 | 1.7 | 1.7 | 0.9 | 1.1 | 1.0 | 1.4 |

Data as orig reptd.; bef. results of disc opers/spec. items. Per share data adj. for stk. divs.; EPS diluted. E-Estimated. NA-Not Available. NM-Not Meaningful. NR-Not Ranked. UR-Under Review.

**Office:** 701 Western Ave, Glendale, CA 91201-2349.
**Telephone:** 818-244-8080.
**Email:** investor@publicstorage.com
**Website:** http://www.publicstorage.com

**Chrmn:** B.W. Hughes
**Pres, Vice Chrmn & CEO:** R.L. Havner, Jr.
**COO & SVP:** M.C. Good
**Investor Contact:** J. Reyes (818-244-8080)

**SVP, CFO & Chief Acctg Officer:** J. Reyes
**Board Members:** D. V. Angeloff, W. C. Baker, J. T. Evans, U. P. Harkham, R. L. Havner, Jr., B. W. Hughes, B. W. Hughes, Jr., H. Lenkin, G. Pruitt, D. C. Staton

**Founded:** 1980
**Domicile:** California
**Employees:** 5,700

# Public Service Enterprise Group Inc

STANDARD &POOR'S

| S&P Recommendation **BUY** ★★★★☆ | Price $28.60 (as of Nov 14, 2008) | 12-Mo. Target Price $34.00 | Investment Style Large-Cap Blend |
|---|---|---|---|

**GICS Sector** Utilities
**Sub-Industry** Multi-Utilities

**Summary** PEG is the holding company for Public Service Electric and Gas (PSE&G), with a service area that encompasses 70% of New Jersey.

## Key Stock Statistics (Source S&P, Vickers, company reports)

| | | | | | | |
|---|---|---|---|---|---|---|
| 52-Wk Range | $52.30– 22.09 | S&P Oper. EPS 2008**E** | 2.90 | Market Capitalization(B) | $14.474 | Beta | 0.72 |
| Trailing 12-Month EPS | $2.31 | S&P Oper. EPS 2009**E** | 3.15 | Yield (%) | 4.51 | S&P 3-Yr. Proj. EPS CAGR(%) | 11 |
| Trailing 12-Month P/E | 12.4 | P/E on S&P Oper. EPS 2008**E** | 9.9 | Dividend Rate/Share | $1.29 | S&P Credit Rating | BBB |
| $10K Invested 5 Yrs Ago | $16,974 | Common Shares Outstg. (M) | 506.1 | Institutional Ownership (%) | 62 | | |

## Price Performance

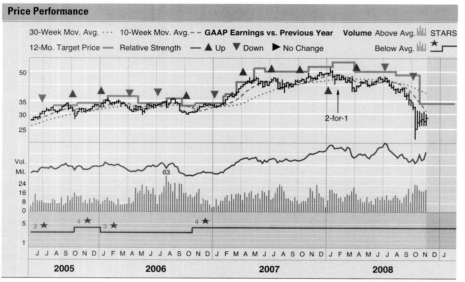

30-Week Mov. Avg. · · · 10-Week Mov. Avg. – – **GAAP Earnings vs. Previous Year** Volume Above Avg. STARS
12-Mo. Target Price — Relative Strength — ▲ Up ▼ Down ▶ No Change Below Avg. ★

2-for-1

2005  2006  2007  2008

Options: ASE, CBOE, Ph

Analysis prepared by **Justin McCann** on October 24, 2008, when the stock traded at **$ 28.88**.

## Highlights

➤ We expect operating EPS to increase about 16% in 2008 from 2007 operating EPS of $2.59. We see growth continuing to be driven by higher margins in PEG's power sector, which should more than offset higher financing and operating costs at the utility. Our estimate for 2008 excludes a one-time second quarter charge of $0.96 for certain leveraged leases. Per share data reflect a 2-for-1 stock split effective February 5, 2008.

➤ For 2009, we expect high single-digit operating EPS growth from anticipated results in 2008. In addition to the benefit of PEG's recently announced $750 million share repurchase program, we expect EPS to be driven by higher-priced renewal of expiring power contracts. We believe this trend will continue, and we expect PEG to realize high single-digit earnings growth for the next few years.

➤ On May 30, 2008, PSE&G filed for an approximate 20% increase in its residential gas bills. In its filing with the New Jersey Board of Public Utilities (BPU), the utility cited the sharp rise in wholesale supply prices as the reason for the increase.

## Investment Rationale/Risk

➤ With the shares down around 40% year to date (after a strong 48% gain in 2007), we believe the stock is attractive for above-average total return. In addition to the reduced EPS outlook for 2009, we think the stock has been hurt by the crisis in the credit markets. However, we expect the shares to outperform peers over the next 12 months, aided by the reduced, but still strong EPS growth that we forecast for the next three years.

➤ Risks to our recommendation and target price include a decline in the company's wholesale power margins, as well as weakness in the broader market and/or a reduction in the average P/E of the group as a whole.

➤ With the sharp year-to-date decline in the stock and the 10% increase in PEG's dividend (effective with the March payment), the dividend yield rose from 2.4% to 4.5%. While this is below the recent peer average of about 5.2%, it is slightly above yields of other growth-oriented utility holding companies, and we believe the stock will benefit from a projected growth rate well above peers. Our 12-month target price of $34 reflects a discount-to-peers P/E of 10.5X our EPS estimate for 2009.

## Qualitative Risk Assessment

| LOW | MEDIUM | HIGH |
|---|---|---|

Our risk assessment reflects our view of the strong and steady cash flows from the regulated electric and gas utility operations of PSE&G, as well as the strong albeit less predictable earnings and cash flows from the non-regulated power generating operations. It also reflects what we see as a lowering of the risk profile through the divestiture of its non-core international investments.

## Quantitative Evaluations

**S&P Quality Ranking** B+

| D | C | B- | B | B+ | A- | A | A+ |
|---|---|---|---|---|---|---|---|

**Relative Strength Rank** STRONG

71

LOWEST = 1          HIGHEST = 99

## Revenue/Earnings Data

**Revenue (Million $)**

| | 1Q | 2Q | 3Q | 4Q | Year |
|---|---|---|---|---|---|
| 2008 | 3,803 | 2,561 | 3,718 | -- | -- |
| 2007 | 3,508 | 2,718 | 3,356 | 3,271 | 12,853 |
| 2006 | 3,461 | 2,556 | 3,212 | 2,935 | 12,164 |
| 2005 | 3,310 | 2,442 | 3,376 | 3,472 | 12,430 |
| 2004 | 3,221 | 2,290 | 2,747 | 2,731 | 10,996 |
| 2003 | 3,364 | 2,419 | 2,805 | 2,586 | 11,116 |

**Earnings Per Share ($)**

| | | | | | |
|---|---|---|---|---|---|
| 2008 | 0.85 | -0.33 | 0.94 | E0.47 | E2.90 |
| 2007 | 0.64 | 0.56 | 0.96 | 0.44 | 2.59 |
| 2006 | 0.41 | Nil | 0.75 | 0.35 | 1.49 |
| 2005 | 0.59 | 0.21 | 0.53 | 0.45 | 1.76 |
| 2004 | 0.57 | 0.25 | 0.52 | 0.19 | 1.52 |
| 2003 | 0.71 | 0.33 | 0.47 | 0.35 | 1.86 |

Fiscal year ended Dec. 31. Next earnings report expected: Early February. EPS Estimates based on S&P Operating Earnings; historical GAAP earnings are as reported.

## Dividend Data (Dates: mm/dd Payment Date: mm/dd/yy)

| Amount ($) | Date Decl. | Ex-Div. Date | Stk. of Record | Payment Date |
|---|---|---|---|---|
| 2-for-1 | 01/15 | 02/05 | 01/25 | 02/04/08 |
| 0.323 | 01/15 | 03/06 | 03/10 | 03/31/08 |
| 0.323 | 04/15 | 06/05 | 06/09 | 06/30/08 |
| 0.323 | 07/15 | 09/04 | 09/08 | 09/30/08 |

Dividends have been paid since 1907. Source: Company reports.

---

# Public Service Enterprise Group Inc

STANDARD
&POOR'S

## Business Summary October 24, 2008

CORPORATE OVERVIEW. Headquartered in Newark, NJ, Public Service Enterprise Group has three primary operating units: Public Service Electric and Gas Co. - PSE&G ($380 million of net income in 2007), Power ($949 million), and Energy Holdings ($89 million). The parent company and intersegment eliminations accounted for a loss of $99 million. PEG has sought to minimize its earnings and cash flow volatility by entering into long-term contracts for most of its competitive wholesale power generation, and by reducing its exposure to international operations over time.

MARKET PROFILE. At the end of 2007, the company's New Jersey utility operations served approximately 2.1 million electric customers and 1.7 million natural gas customers. PSE&G earns income from the delivery of electricity and gas, with the cost of the gas passed through to ratepayers. In 2006, commercial customers accounted for 56% of total electric customers (36% of gas customers), residential 31% (60%), and industrial 13% (4%). As part of New Jer-

sey's utility deregulation, PSE&G transferred its power generating and gas supply operations to PEG's unregulated Power division in 2000 and 2002, respectively. Based on the proximity of its plants to PSE&G's customer base, Power has been able to win competitive bids for a significant portion of the utility's electricity supply obligations. Power's generating fleet, which had 13,314 megawatts of generating capacity as of December 31, 2007, is concentrated in the Pennsylvania, New Jersey and Maryland Interconnection (known as PJM), but it also has plants in Connecticut and New York. In addition to its electric business, Power provides PSE&G with all of the utility's gas supply needs under a contract that was extended from March 31, 2007, to March 31, 2012, and year to year thereafter.

## Company Financials Fiscal Year Ended Dec. 31

| Per Share Data ($) | 2007 | 2006 | 2005 | 2004 | 2003 | 2002 | 2001 | 2000 | 1999 | 1998 |
|---|---|---|---|---|---|---|---|---|---|---|
| Tangible Book Value | 14.23 | 12.23 | 10.79 | 10.71 | 10.42 | 7.39 | 8.47 | 9.60 | 9.25 | 10.93 |
| Earnings | 2.59 | 1.49 | 1.76 | 1.52 | 1.86 | 1.00 | 1.84 | 1.78 | 1.65 | 1.40 |
| S&P Core Earnings | 2.59 | 1.92 | 1.70 | 1.49 | 2.02 | 1.53 | 1.58 | NA | NA | NA |
| Dividends | 1.17 | 1.14 | 1.12 | 1.10 | 1.08 | 1.08 | 1.08 | 1.08 | 1.08 | 1.08 |
| Payout Ratio | 45% | 77% | 64% | 73% | 58% | 109% | 59% | 61% | 66% | 77% |
| Prices:High | 49.88 | 36.31 | 34.24 | 26.32 | 22.25 | 23.63 | 25.78 | 25.00 | 21.31 | 21.38 |
| Prices:Low | 32.16 | 29.50 | 24.66 | 19.05 | 16.05 | 10.00 | 18.44 | 12.84 | 16.00 | 15.16 |
| P/E Ratio:High | 19 | 24 | 20 | 17 | 12 | 24 | 14 | 14 | 13 | 15 |
| P/E Ratio:Low | 12 | 20 | 14 | 13 | 9 | 10 | 10 | 7 | 10 | 11 |

| Income Statement Analysis (Million $) | 2007 | 2006 | 2005 | 2004 | 2003 | 2002 | 2001 | 2000 | 1999 | 1998 |
|---|---|---|---|---|---|---|---|---|---|---|
| Revenue | 12,853 | 12,164 | 12,430 | 10,996 | 11,116 | 8,390 | 9,815 | 6,848 | 6,497 | 5,931 |
| Depreciation | 783 | 832 | 748 | 719 | 527 | 571 | 522 | 362 | 536 | 669 |
| Maintenance | NA | NA | NA | NA | NA | NA | NA | NA | NA | NA |
| Fixed Charges Coverage | 4.10 | 2.73 | 2.55 | 2.21 | 2.43 | 2.38 | 2.46 | 2.88 | 3.20 | 2.87 |
| Construction Credits | NA | NA | NA | NA | NA | NA | NA | NA | NA | 13.0 |
| Effective Tax Rate | 44.5% | NM | 38.7% | 38.2% | 35.3% | 37.3% | NM | 39.1% | 43.8% | 39.5% |
| Net Income | 1,319 | 752 | 858 | 721 | 852 | 416 | 763 | 764 | 723 | 644 |
| S&P Core Earnings | 1,316 | 967 | 834 | 708 | 925 | 638 | 656 | NA | NA | NA |

| Balance Sheet & Other Financial Data (Million $) | 2007 | 2006 | 2005 | 2004 | 2003 | 2002 | 2001 | 2000 | 1999 | 1998 |
|---|---|---|---|---|---|---|---|---|---|---|
| Gross Property | 19,310 | 18,851 | 18,896 | 19,121 | 17,406 | 16,562 | 14,886 | 11,968 | 11,156 | 18,386 |
| Capital Expenditures | 1,348 | 1,015 | 1,024 | 1,255 | 1,351 | 1,814 | 2,053 | 959 | 582 | 535 |
| Net Property | 13,275 | 13,002 | 13,336 | 13,750 | 12,422 | 11,449 | 10,064 | 7,702 | 7,078 | 11,026 |
| Capitalization:Long Term Debt | 8,742 | 10,450 | 11,359 | 13,005 | 13,025 | 12,391 | 11,061 | 6,505 | 5,783 | 4,813 |
| Capitalization:% Long Term Debt | 54.5 | 60.8 | 65.4 | 69.4 | 70.2 | 75.7 | 72.8 | 60.2 | 59.1 | 43.3 |
| Capitalization:Preferred | Nil | Nil | Nil | Nil | Nil | Nil | Nil | Nil | Nil | 1,208 |
| Capitalization:% Preferred | Nil | Nil | Nil | Nil | Nil | Nil | Nil | Nil | Nil | 10.9 |
| Capitalization:Common | 7,299 | 6,747 | 6,022 | 5,739 | 5,529 | 3,987 | 4,137 | 4,294 | 3,996 | 5,098 |
| Capitalization:% Common | 45.5 | 39.2 | 34.6 | 30.6 | 29.8 | 24.3 | 27.2 | 39.8 | 40.9 | 45.8 |
| Total Capital | 20,495 | 21,659 | 21,629 | 23,091 | 22,750 | 19,302 | 18,403 | 13,906 | 12,707 | 14,825 |
| % Operating Ratio | 85.0 | 78.7 | 88.6 | 87.5 | 86.5 | 78.8 | 76.9 | 79.6 | 80.4 | 80.0 |
| % Earned on Net Property | 23.3 | 15.1 | 15.9 | 14.9 | 17.3 | 14.3 | 21.3 | 18.9 | 20.4 | 10.7 |
| % Return on Revenue | 10.3 | 6.2 | 6.9 | 6.6 | 7.7 | 5.0 | 7.8 | 11.2 | 11.1 | 10.9 |
| % Return on Invested Capital | 9.3 | 9.3 | 7.6 | 6.9 | 8.1 | 9.3 | 9.6 | 10.8 | 9.5 | 8.1 |
| % Return on Common Equity | 18.8 | 11.8 | 14.6 | 12.8 | 18.1 | 10.2 | 18.8 | 18.4 | 15.9 | 12.5 |

Data as orig reptd.; bef. results of disc opers/spec. items. Per share data adj. for stk. divs.; EPS diluted. E-Estimated. NA-Not Available. NM-Not Meaningful. NR-Not Ranked. UR-Under Review.

**Office:** 80 Park Plaza, Newark, NJ 07102-4109.
**Telephone:** 973-430-7000.
**Email:** stkserv@pseg.com
**Website:** http://www.pseg.com

**Chrmn, Pres & CEO:** R. Izzo
**COO:** R. LaRossa
**EVP & CFO:** T.M. O'Flynn
**EVP & General Counsel:** R.E. Selover

**Chief Acctg Officer & Cntlr:** D.M. Dirisio
**Investor Contact:** K.A. Lally
**Board Members:** C. Dorsa, A. R. Gamper, Jr., C. K. Harper, W. V. Hickey, R. Izzo, S. A. Jackson, T. A. Renyi, H. C. Shin, R. J. Swift

**Founded:** 1985
**Domicile:** New Jersey
**Employees:** 8,767

The **McGraw-Hill** Companies

# Pulte Homes Inc.

**STANDARD &POOR'S**

| S&P Recommendation **BUY** ★★★★☆ | Price $9.08 (as of Nov 14, 2008) | 12-Mo. Target Price $13.00 | Investment Style Large-Cap Blend |
| --- | --- | --- | --- |

**GICS Sector** Consumer Discretionary
**Sub-Industry** Homebuilding

**Summary** This builder of a wide range of single-family homes and condominiums throughout the country is the leading U.S. developer of active adult communities, and has a mortgage banking unit.

## Key Stock Statistics (Source S&P, Vickers, company reports)

| | | | | | | | |
| --- | --- | --- | --- | --- | --- | --- | --- |
| 52-Wk Range | $23.24– 6.91 | S&P Oper. EPS 2008**E** | -5.00 | Market Capitalization(B) | $2.320 | Beta | 0.92 |
| Trailing 12-Month EPS | $-7.94 | S&P Oper. EPS 2009**E** | -1.00 | Yield (%) | 1.76 | S&P 3-Yr. Proj. EPS CAGR(%) | 3 |
| Trailing 12-Month P/E | NM | P/E on S&P Oper. EPS 2008**E** | NM | Dividend Rate/Share | $0.16 | S&P Credit Rating | BB |
| $10K Invested 5 Yrs Ago | $4,231 | Common Shares Outstg. (M) | 255.5 | Institutional Ownership (%) | 77 | | |

## Price Performance

30-Week Mov. Avg. ···· 10-Week Mov. Avg. – – **GAAP Earnings vs. Previous Year**    Volume Above Avg. ⅲⅲ STARS
12-Mo. Target Price — Relative Strength — ▲ Up ▼ Down ▶ No Change    Below Avg. ⅲⅲ ★

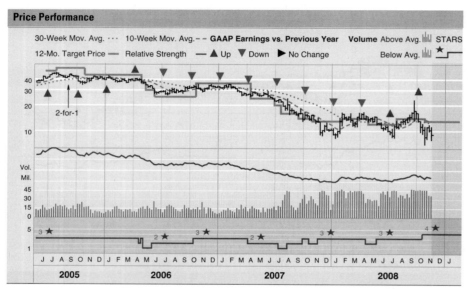

Options: ASE, CBOE, P, Ph

Analysis prepared by **Kenneth M. Leon, CPA** on October 23, 2008, when the stock traded at **$ 7.17.**

## Highlights

➤ After a 35% revenue drop in 2007, we forecast a similar decline in 2008, followed by a 24% decrease in 2009, as we think the homebuilding industry will head to its sales trough in the middle of 2009. Results for the third quarter show PHM's home settlement units down 28% from a year earlier, with a 12.7% drop in the average selling price per home, to $281,000. Net new orders decreased 38%, year to year, in the third quarter, a slight improvement from the 42% drop in the second quarter.

➤ Homebuilding gross margins were negative in 2007, and we estimate negative margins again in 2008 and positive 6% in 2009. We expect SG&A costs to remain in the 11% to 13% range in 2008 and 2009, compared to 11.6% in 2007.

➤ PHM booked $266 million in asset impairments in the third quarter; since the beginning of 2006, writedowns have totaled $4.3 billion. Our 2008 net loss forecast assumes no additional asset charges, although with weak market conditions, new charges are possible. We estimate losses per share of $5.00 for 2008 and $1.00 for 2009.

## Investment Rationale/Risk

➤ While the U.S. housing industry remains depressed, we think PHM, with $1.2 billion in cash on hand and plans to finish 2008 with $1.6 billion to $1.8 billion, can manage through the current downturn. Asset impairments eased in the first nine months of 2008 compared to the same period in 2007.

➤ Risks to our recommendation and target price include further weakening in housing demand, a deepening recession, tighter availability of mortgage lending, and future downward revaluations of PHM's land inventory. Asset impairment charges and contract cancellations may also be significantly higher in coming quarters.

➤ Despite a poor operating environment, PHM's relatively large size in the industry should enable the company to weather the housing downturn, in our opinion. Our 12-month target price of $13 is derived by applying a target price-to-book multiple of just over 1X -- toward the low end of the historical range for PHM, but near other large homebuilder peers -- to our forward book value per share estimate of $12.50.

## Qualitative Risk Assessment

| LOW | MEDIUM | **HIGH** |
| --- | --- | --- |

Our risk assessment reflects deteriorating market conditions, especially in California and Florida, which has led to a slowdown in completing communities. We believe PHM's cancellation rate of home closings will remain high until markets stabilize. The company is considering mothballing certain communities as well, as evident by its large asset impairment charges.

## Quantitative Evaluations

**S&P Quality Ranking**  A

| D | C | B- | B | B+ | A- | **A** | A+ |
| --- | --- | --- | --- | --- | --- | --- | --- |

**Relative Strength Rank**  MODERATE

49

LOWEST = 1                    HIGHEST = 99

## Revenue/Earnings Data

**Revenue (Million $)**

| | 1Q | 2Q | 3Q | 4Q | Year |
| --- | --- | --- | --- | --- | --- |
| 2008 | 1,442 | 1,619 | 1,565 | -- | -- |
| 2007 | 1,871 | 2,021 | 2,472 | 2,899 | 9,257 |
| 2006 | 2,963 | 3,359 | 3,564 | 4,389 | 14,274 |
| 2005 | 2,518 | 3,251 | 3,794 | 5,132 | 14,695 |
| 2004 | 2,032 | 2,515 | 2,960 | 4,205 | 11,711 |
| 2003 | 1,553 | 1,958 | 2,400 | 3,138 | 9,049 |

**Earnings Per Share ($)**

| | 1Q | 2Q | 3Q | 4Q | Year |
| --- | --- | --- | --- | --- | --- |
| 2008 | -2.75 | -0.62 | -1.11 | E-0.52 | E-5.00 |
| 2007 | -0.34 | -2.01 | -3.12 | -3.54 | -9.02 |
| 2006 | 1.01 | 0.94 | 0.74 | -0.03 | 2.67 |
| 2005 | 0.83 | 1.16 | 1.45 | 2.03 | 5.47 |
| 2004 | 0.51 | 0.73 | 1.00 | 1.60 | 3.84 |
| 2003 | 0.35 | 0.49 | 0.64 | 0.97 | 2.46 |

Fiscal year ended Dec. 31. Next earnings report expected: Late January. EPS Estimates based on S&P Operating Earnings; historical GAAP earnings are as reported.

## Dividend Data (Dates: mm/dd Payment Date: mm/dd/yy)

| Amount ($) | Date Decl. | Ex-Div. Date | Stk. of Record | Payment Date |
| --- | --- | --- | --- | --- |
| 0.040 | 12/06 | 12/17 | 12/19 | 01/03/08 |
| 0.040 | 02/07 | 03/14 | 03/18 | 04/01/08 |
| 0.040 | 05/15 | 06/17 | 06/19 | 07/01/08 |
| 0.040 | 09/11 | 09/22 | 09/24 | 10/01/08 |

Dividends have been paid since 1977. Source: Company reports.

---

**Please read the Required Disclosures and Analyst Certification on the last page of this report.**

The **McGraw·Hill** Companies

# Pulte Homes Inc.

STANDARD
&POOR'S

## Business Summary October 23, 2008

CORPORATE OVERVIEW. As of December 31, 2007, the company's homebuilding operations offered homes for sale in 636 communities. Sales prices of homes currently offered for sale in 72% of its communities fall within the range of $100,000 to $400,000 with a 2007 average unit selling price of $322,000, compared with $337,000 in 2006, $315,000 in 2005, $287,000 in 2004, and $259,000 in 2003. As of December 31, 2007, the homebuilding business operated in 51 markets spanning 26 states.

PHM targets buyers in nearly all home categories, but has recently concentrated its expansion efforts on affordable housing and on mature buyers (age 50 and over). In July 2001, it acquired Del Webb Corp., the leading U.S. builder of active adult communities, for a total of $1.9 billion in stock, cash, and the assumption of debt. Growth in this active adult segment and among first-time buyers, two groups that often prefer townhouses, condominiums or duplexes, helps to explain the decrease in single-family homes in PHM's product mix over the past five years.

CORPORATE STRATEGY. As of December 31, 2007, PHM controlled approximately 157,900 lots, of which 131,400 were owned and 26,500 were under op-

tion agreements. Land is generally purchased after it is properly zoned and developed or is ready for development. In addition, PHM will dispose of owned land not required in the business through sales to appropriate end users. Where the company develops land, its engages directly in many phases of the development process, including land and site planning, and obtaining environmental and other regulatory approvals, as well as constructing roads, sewers, water and drainage facilities, and other amenities.

To assist its home sales effort, PHM offers mortgage banking and title insurance services through Pulte Mortgage and other units mainly for the benefit of its domestic home buyers, but it also services the general public. In addition, it engages in the sale of loans and related servicing rights. Mortgage underwriting, processing and closing functions are centralized in Denver, CO, and Charlotte, NC, using a mortgage operations center concept.

## Company Financials Fiscal Year Ended Dec. 31

| Per Share Data ($) | 2007 | 2006 | 2005 | 2004 | 2003 | 2002 | 2001 | 2000 | 1999 | 1998 |
|---|---|---|---|---|---|---|---|---|---|---|
| Tangible Book Value | 16.35 | 23.82 | 21.49 | 15.95 | 12.13 | 9.41 | 7.64 | 7.51 | 6.32 | 5.34 |
| Cash Flow | -8.69 | 2.99 | 5.70 | 4.01 | 2.61 | 1.92 | 1.67 | 1.38 | 1.09 | 0.61 |
| Earnings | -9.02 | 2.67 | 5.47 | 3.84 | 2.46 | 1.80 | 1.50 | 1.30 | 1.02 | 0.58 |
| S&P Core Earnings | -7.69 | 2.59 | 5.46 | 3.82 | 2.45 | 1.76 | 1.43 | NA | NA | NA |
| Dividends | 0.16 | 0.16 | 0.09 | 0.10 | 0.04 | 0.04 | 0.04 | 0.04 | 0.04 | 0.04 |
| Payout Ratio | NM | 6% | 2% | 3% | 2% | 2% | 3% | 3% | 4% | 6% |
| Prices:High | 35.56 | 44.70 | 48.23 | 32.50 | 24.71 | 14.94 | 12.56 | 11.25 | 7.81 | 9.05 |
| Prices:Low | 8.78 | 26.02 | 30.01 | 20.00 | 11.36 | 9.05 | 6.53 | 3.81 | 4.19 | 4.98 |
| P/E Ratio:High | NM | 17 | 9 | 8 | 10 | 8 | 8 | 9 | 8 | 16 |
| P/E Ratio:Low | NM | 10 | 5 | 5 | 5 | 5 | 4 | 3 | 4 | 9 |

| Income Statement Analysis (Million $) | | | | | | | | | | |
|---|---|---|---|---|---|---|---|---|---|---|
| Revenue | 9,263 | 14,274 | 14,695 | 11,711 | 9,049 | 7,472 | 5,382 | 4,159 | 3,730 | 2,867 |
| Operating Income | -1,800 | 2,678 | 244 | 1,587 | 997 | 746 | 601 | 429 | 350 | 222 |
| Depreciation | 83.9 | 83.7 | 62.0 | 46.3 | 40.2 | 29.8 | 32.9 | 14.2 | 13.5 | 5.04 |
| Interest Expense | 260 | 256 | 43.3 | 56.4 | Nil | Nil | 81.6 | 65.1 | 56.8 | 51.1 |
| Pretax Income | -2,497 | 1,083 | 2,277 | 1,601 | 996 | 729 | 492 | 355 | 286 | 166 |
| Effective Tax Rate | NM | 36.3% | 36.8% | 37.6% | 38.0% | 39.0% | 38.5% | 38.5% | 37.8% | 39.0% |
| Net Income | -2,274 | 690 | 1,437 | 998 | 617 | 445 | 302 | 218 | 178 | 101 |
| S&P Core Earnings | -1,939 | 670 | 1,435 | 993 | 615 | 436 | 288 | NA | NA | NA |

| Balance Sheet & Other Financial Data (Million $) | | | | | | | | | | |
|---|---|---|---|---|---|---|---|---|---|---|
| Cash | 1,060 | 551 | 1,002 | 315 | 404 | 613 | 72.1 | 184 | 51.7 | 125 |
| Current Assets | NA | NA | NA | NA | NA | NA | NA | NA | NA | NA |
| Total Assets | 10,226 | 13,177 | 13,048 | 10,407 | 8,063 | 6,888 | 5,714 | 2,886 | 2,597 | 2,350 |
| Current Liabilities | NA | NA | NA | NA | NA | NA | NA | NA | NA | NA |
| Long Term Debt | 3,478 | 3,538 | 3,387 | 2,737 | 1,962 | 1,913 | 1,738 | 678 | 526 | 570 |
| Common Equity | 4,320 | 6,577 | 5,957 | 4,522 | 3,448 | 2,760 | 2,277 | 1,248 | 1,093 | 921 |
| Total Capital | 7,798 | 10,115 | 9,352 | 7,274 | 5,418 | 4,674 | 4,015 | 1,926 | 1,619 | 1,492 |
| Capital Expenditures | 70.1 | 98.6 | 88.9 | 75.2 | 39.1 | NA | NA | NA | NA | NA |
| Cash Flow | -2,191 | 773 | 1,499 | 1,044 | 657 | 474 | 335 | 233 | 192 | 106 |
| Current Ratio | 3.9 | 4.1 | 3.3 | 3.2 | 2.8 | 2.5 | 2.6 | 2.5 | 2.3 | 2.3 |
| % Long Term Debt of Capitalization | 44.6 | 35.0 | 36.2 | 37.6 | 36.2 | 40.9 | 43.3 | 35.2 | 32.5 | 38.2 |
| % Net Income of Revenue | NM | 4.8 | 9.7 | 8.5 | 6.8 | 6.0 | 5.6 | 5.3 | 4.8 | 3.5 |
| % Return on Assets | NM | 5.3 | 12.2 | 10.8 | 8.3 | 7.1 | 7.0 | 8.1 | 7.2 | 4.5 |
| % Return on Equity | NM | 11.0 | 27.4 | 25.0 | 19.9 | 17.7 | 17.2 | 18.7 | 17.7 | 11.7 |

Data as orig reptd.; bef. results of disc opers/spec. items. Per share data adj. for stk. divs.; EPS diluted. E-Estimated. NA-Not Available. NM-Not Meaningful. NR-Not Ranked. UR-Under Review.

**Office:** 100 Bloomfield Hills Pkwy Ste 300, Bloomfield Hills, MI 48304-2950.
**Telephone:** 248-647-2750.
**Website:** http://www.pulte.com
**Chrmn:** W.J. Pulte

**Pres & CEO:** R. Dugas, Jr.
**COO & EVP:** S.C. Petruska
**EVP & CFO:** R.A. Cregg
**Chief Acctg Officer & Cntlr:** V.J. Frees

**Investor Contact:** C. Boyd (248-647-2750)
**Board Members:** B. P. Anderson, D. K. Anderson, R. Dugas, Jr., C. W. Grise, D. J. Kelly-Ennis, D. N. McCammon, P. J. O'Leary, W. J. Pulte, B. W. Reznicek, A. E. Schwartz, F. J. Sehn, J. J. Shea, W. B. Smith, R. G. Wolford

**Founded:** 1969
**Domicile:** Michigan
**Employees:** 8,500

The McGraw-Hill Companies

# QLogic Corp

**STANDARD &POOR'S**

| S&P Recommendation | HOLD ★★★☆☆ | Price | 12-Mo. Target Price | Investment Style |
|---|---|---|---|---|
| | | $10.84 (as of Nov 14, 2008) | $15.00 | Large-Cap Growth |

**GICS Sector** Information Technology
**Sub-Industry** Computer Storage & Peripherals

**Summary** This company supplies storage networking and network infrastructure solutions primarily to original equipment manufacturers and distributors.

## Key Stock Statistics (Source S&P, Vickers, company reports)

| | | | | | | | |
|---|---|---|---|---|---|---|---|
| 52-Wk Range | $20.21–9.56 | S&P Oper. EPS 2009**E** | 1.20 | Market Capitalization(B) | $1.387 | Beta | 1.39 |
| Trailing 12-Month EPS | $0.84 | S&P Oper. EPS 2010**E** | 1.27 | Yield (%) | Nil | S&P 3-Yr. Proj. EPS CAGR(%) | 11 |
| Trailing 12-Month P/E | 12.9 | P/E on S&P Oper. EPS 2009**E** | 9.0 | Dividend Rate/Share | Nil | S&P Credit Rating | NA |
| $10K Invested 5 Yrs Ago | $3,920 | Common Shares Outstg. (M) | 127.9 | Institutional Ownership (%) | NM | | |

## Price Performance

- 30-Week Mov. Avg. · · · 10-Week Mov. Avg. - - **GAAP Earnings vs. Previous Year** Volume Above Avg. STARS
- 12-Mo. Target Price — Relative Strength — ▲ Up ▼ Down ► No Change Below Avg.

Options: ASE, CBOE, P, Ph

Analysis prepared by **Rafay Khalid** on October 23, 2008, when the stock traded at **$11.19**.

## Highlights

➤ Although we expect weak IT spending in the U.S. market, we forecast sales will rise 10% in FY 09 (Mar.) and 2% in FY 10. We foresee strength in Network and Silicon products, and modest growth in Host products. We continue to look for QLGC's Fibre Channel host bus adapters to drive performance, and we see revenue gains from these products during the rest of FY 09. In our view, QLGC continues to be a leader in the 4Gbps space, but as the migration approaches maturity, we think its leadership position will be challenged.

➤ We project that gross margins will remain flat at 66% in FY 09. Our outlook is based on what we see as a less favorable product mix, offset by our view of higher volumes and better manufacturing efficiencies. We expect the company will maintain a tight control over SG&A and R&D expenses in FY 09, compared to FY 08. As a result, we forecast operating margins will expand to 25% in FY 09, and remain at a similar level in FY 10.

➤ Our operating EPS estimates are $1.20 for FY 09 and $1.27 for FY 10. Our estimates assume a tax rate of 33% in FY 09 and FY 10.

## Investment Rationale/Risk

➤ We expect the continued economic malaise and credit crunch will cause softness in U.S. IT spending. In addition, we see challenges to QLGC's market leadership in the new upgrade cycle to 8Gbps technology. Still, we believe QLGC is financially well positioned to weather the economic slowdown, based on our projection that it will end FY 09 with $445 million in cash and investments ($3.44 per share) and generate $78 million in free cash flow.

➤ Risks to our recommendation and target price include a potential slowing of demand in storage networking products, a greater-than-expected decline in average selling prices, and substantial cost overruns for emerging technology developments.

➤ We use relative valuation analysis to arrive at our 12-month target price of $15. Our target price is based on a peer-group P/E of 13.9X and a peer-group P/E-to-growth ratio of 1.1X, using our next 12 months operating EPS estimate of $1.18 and an estimated three-year growth rate of 11%. We believe QLGC warrants a peer group multiple based on what we view as sales and earnings growth in line with the industry.

## Qualitative Risk Assessment

| LOW | MEDIUM | HIGH |
|---|---|---|

Our risk assessment reflects the volatile nature of the data storage industry and the rapid pace of technological change. Offsetting these factors is our view of the company's significant market share and strong financial position.

## Quantitative Evaluations

**S&P Quality Ranking**      B+

| D | C | B- | B | B+ | A- | A | A+ |
|---|---|---|---|---|---|---|---|

**Relative Strength Rank**      MODERATE

47

LOWEST = 1      HIGHEST = 99

## Revenue/Earnings Data

**Revenue (Million $)**

| | 1Q | 2Q | 3Q | 4Q | Year |
|---|---|---|---|---|---|
| 2009 | 168.4 | 171.2 | -- | -- | -- |
| 2008 | 139.8 | 140.3 | 158.0 | 159.7 | 597.9 |
| 2007 | 136.7 | 145.3 | 157.6 | 147.1 | 586.7 |
| 2006 | 158.8 | 119.0 | 129.2 | 130.5 | 494.1 |
| 2005 | 129.8 | 134.6 | 150.3 | 157.2 | 571.9 |
| 2004 | 126.2 | 132.3 | 137.1 | 128.3 | 523.9 |

**Earnings Per Share ($)**

| | 1Q | 2Q | 3Q | 4Q | Year |
|---|---|---|---|---|---|
| 2009 | 0.24 | 0.20 | E0.28 | E0.27 | E1.20 |
| 2008 | 0.12 | 0.16 | 0.23 | 0.17 | 0.67 |
| 2007 | 0.13 | 0.19 | 0.22 | 0.12 | 0.66 |
| 2006 | 0.23 | 0.17 | 0.20 | 0.19 | 0.70 |
| 2005 | 0.17 | 0.19 | 0.23 | 0.25 | 0.84 |
| 2004 | 0.17 | 0.18 | 0.18 | 0.17 | 0.70 |

Fiscal year ended Mar. 31. Next earnings report expected: Late January. EPS Estimates based on S&P Operating Earnings; historical GAAP earnings are as reported.

## Dividend Data

No cash dividends have been paid.

---

**Please read the Required Disclosures and Analyst Certification on the last page of this report.**

*The McGraw·Hill Companies*

# QLogic Corp

**STANDARD &POOR'S**

## Business Summary October 23, 2008

CORPORATE OVERVIEW. QLogic Corp. designs and develops storage networking infrastructure components sold to OEMs and distributors. QLGC produces host bus adapters (HBAs), fabric switches and management controller chips that provide the connectivity infrastructure for storage networks. The company serves customers with solutions based on various storage connectivity technologies, including Small Computer Systems Interface (SCSI), Internet SCSI (iSCSI), Fibre Channel and Infiniband.

International revenues accounted for 49% of net revenues in FY 08 (Mar.), up from 46% in FY 07. IBM, Hewlett-Packard and Sun Microsystems each accounted for over 10% of FY 08 sales. The 10 largest customers accounted for 80% of FY 07 revenues (latest available), up from 77% in FY 06. QLGC works closely with independent hardware and software vendors, as well as with developers and integrators who create, test and evaluate complementary storage networking products. Key alliance partners include Cisco Systems, Microsoft and Symantec.

MARKET PROFILE. According to research firm IDC, growing server virtualization is driving an increase in storage area network (SAN) connectivity levels,

more than offsetting moderating server growth rates through 2008. IDC predicts worldwide HBA port shipments will increase from 2.6 million to 5.3 million between 2006 and 2011, resulting in a compound annual growth rate (CAGR) of 15.2% for the period. IDC expects single-port and multiport Fiber Channel (FC) HBA unit shipments to grow somewhat slower (a 2006-2011 CAGR of 10%), with 2011 shipments reaching 3.4 million. IDC estimated that worldwide external disk storage systems factory revenues in the fourth quarter of 2007 grew 9.8% from a year ago to $5.3 billion, marking 20 consecutive quarters of year-over-year growth. For the 2007 fourth quarter, the total disk storage systems market increased to $26.3 billion, up 6.6% from the prior year's quarter. Total disk storage systems capacity shipped was 1,645 petabytes, growing 56.3% from the year-ago quarter. IDC projects that total capacity shipments will exceed 32,838 petabytes in 2011.

## Company Financials Fiscal Year Ended Mar. 31

| Per Share Data ($) | 2008 | 2007 | 2006 | 2005 | 2004 | 2003 | 2002 | 2001 | 2000 | 1999 |
|---|---|---|---|---|---|---|---|---|---|---|
| Tangible Book Value | 3.79 | 4.61 | 5.10 | 5.19 | 4.61 | 4.00 | 3.33 | 2.84 | 1.64 | 1.06 |
| Cash Flow | NA | 0.83 | 0.81 | 0.92 | 0.77 | 0.62 | 0.44 | 0.42 | 0.38 | 0.19 |
| Earnings | 0.67 | 0.66 | 0.70 | 0.84 | 0.70 | 0.55 | 0.37 | 0.36 | 0.35 | 0.17 |
| S&P Core Earnings | 0.70 | 0.70 | 0.49 | 0.67 | 0.52 | 0.35 | 0.22 | 0.16 | NA | NA |
| Dividends | Nil | Nil | Nil | Nil | Nil | Nil | Nil | Nil | Nil | Nil |
| Payout Ratio | Nil | Nil | Nil | Nil | Nil | Nil | Nil | Nil | Nil | Nil |
| Calendar Year | 2007 | 2006 | 2005 | 2004 | 2003 | 2002 | 2001 | 2000 | 1999 | 1998 |
| Prices:High | 22.46 | 22.94 | 21.83 | 26.57 | 29.36 | 28.55 | 49.56 | 101.63 | 41.88 | 8.41 |
| Prices:Low | 11.46 | 15.86 | 14.10 | 10.72 | 16.07 | 9.83 | 8.60 | 19.84 | 5.81 | 1.50 |
| P/E Ratio:High | 34 | 35 | 31 | 32 | 42 | 52 | NM | NM | NM | 49 |
| P/E Ratio:Low | 17 | 24 | 20 | 13 | 23 | 18 | NM | NM | NM | 9 |

| Income Statement Analysis (Million $) | | | | | | | | | | |
|---|---|---|---|---|---|---|---|---|---|---|
| Revenue | 598 | 587 | 494 | 572 | 524 | 441 | 344 | 358 | 203 | 117 |
| Operating Income | NA | 169 | 196 | 240 | 214 | 157 | 99.5 | 132 | 78.8 | 36.7 |
| Depreciation | 47.6 | 27.6 | 17.9 | 15.6 | 14.8 | 14.7 | 13.0 | 10.8 | 4.80 | 3.37 |
| Interest Expense | NA | Nil | Nil | Nil | Nil | Nil | Nil | Nil | 0.02 | 0.08 |
| Pretax Income | 148 | 155 | 200 | 242 | 216 | 159 | 106 | 117 | 81.7 | 38.9 |
| Effective Tax Rate | 34.9% | 31.9% | 39.2% | 35.0% | 38.0% | 35.0% | 33.0% | 41.2% | 34.0% | 34.0% |
| Net Income | 96.2 | 105 | 122 | 158 | 134 | 103 | 70.7 | 68.8 | 54.0 | 25.7 |
| S&P Core Earnings | 100 | 112 | 85.6 | 126 | 99.4 | 67.0 | 42.1 | 30.5 | NA | NA |

| Balance Sheet & Other Financial Data (Million $) | | | | | | | | | | |
|---|---|---|---|---|---|---|---|---|---|---|
| Cash | 321 | 544 | 125 | 166 | 157 | 138 | 76.1 | 128 | 64.1 | 43.2 |
| Current Assets | NA | 697 | 819 | 940 | 854 | 748 | 587 | 490 | 177 | 131 |
| Total Assets | 811 | 971 | 938 | 1,026 | 929 | 817 | 670 | 571 | 267 | 173 |
| Current Liabilities | NA | 94.5 | 78.4 | 68.8 | 60.8 | 66.7 | 51.0 | 47.8 | 24.2 | 20.2 |
| Long Term Debt | NA | Nil | Nil | Nil | Nil | Nil | Nil | Nil | Nil | Nil |
| Common Equity | 666 | 875 | 859 | 956 | 868 | 751 | 619 | 524 | 243 | 153 |
| Total Capital | NA | 877 | 859 | 958 | 868 | 751 | 619 | 524 | 243 | 153 |
| Capital Expenditures | 30.0 | 31.7 | 28.3 | 25.7 | 22.3 | 15.7 | 14.5 | 16.7 | 40.0 | 6.77 |
| Cash Flow | NA | 133 | 140 | 173 | 149 | 118 | 83.7 | 79.6 | 58.8 | 29.1 |
| Current Ratio | 5.4 | 7.4 | 10.5 | 13.7 | 14.0 | 11.2 | 11.5 | 10.3 | 7.3 | 6.5 |
| % Long Term Debt of Capitalization | Nil | Nil | Nil | Nil | Nil | Nil | Nil | Nil | Nil | Nil |
| % Net Income of Revenue | 16.1 | 18.0 | 24.7 | 27.6 | 25.5 | 23.5 | 20.5 | 19.2 | 26.6 | 21.9 |
| % Return on Assets | 10.8 | 11.0 | 12.4 | 16.1 | 15.3 | 13.9 | 11.4 | 14.2 | 24.5 | 16.6 |
| % Return on Equity | 12.5 | 12.2 | 13.4 | 17.3 | 16.5 | 15.1 | 12.4 | 15.6 | 27.3 | 19.0 |

Data as orig reptd.; bef. results of disc opers/spec. items. Per share data adj. for stk. divs.; EPS diluted. E-Estimated. NA-Not Available. NM-Not Meaningful. NR-Not Ranked. UR-Under Review.

**Office:** 26650 Aliso Viejo Pkwy, Aliso Viejo, CA 92656-2674.
**Telephone:** 949-389-6000.
**Website:** http://www.qlogic.com
**Chrmn & CEO:** H.K. Desai

**SVP & CFO:** S. Biddiscombe
**Secy & General Counsel:** M.L. Hawkins
**Investor Contact:** J.D. Herbert (949-389-6343)

**Board Members:** J. S. Birnbaum, L. R. Carter, H. K. Desai, J. R. Fiebiger, B. S. Iyer, K. B. Lewis, C. Miltner, G. Wells

**Founded:** 1992
**Domicile:** Delaware
**Employees:** 933

**STANDARD**
**&POOR'S**

# QUALCOMM Inc

| S&P Recommendation | SELL ★ ★ ★ ★ ★ | | Price | 12-Mo. Target Price | Investment Style |
|---|---|---|---|---|---|
| | | | $32.94 (as of Nov 14, 2008) | $28.00 | Large-Cap Growth |

**GICS Sector** Information Technology
**Sub-Industry** Communications Equipment

**Summary** This company focuses on developing products and services based on its advanced wireless broadband technology.

## Key Stock Statistics (Source S&P, Vickers, company reports)

| | | | | | | | |
|---|---|---|---|---|---|---|---|
| 52-Wk Range | $56.88– 20.63 | S&P Oper. EPS 2009E | 1.65 | Market Capitalization(B) | $54.531 | Beta | 1.47 |
| Trailing 12-Month EPS | $1.90 | S&P Oper. EPS 2010E | NA | Yield (%) | 1.94 | S&P 3-Yr. Proj. EPS CAGR(%) | 8 |
| Trailing 12-Month P/E | 17.3 | P/E on S&P Oper. EPS 2009E | 20.0 | Dividend Rate/Share | $0.64 | S&P Credit Rating | NA |
| $10K Invested 5 Yrs Ago | $14,611 | Common Shares Outstg. (M) | 1,655.5 | Institutional Ownership (%) | 78 | | |

## Price Performance

30-Week Mov. Avg. · · · 10-Week Mov. Avg. – – GAAP Earnings vs. Previous Year   Volume Above Avg. ▨▨▨ STARS
12-Mo. Target Price — Relative Strength  — ▲ Up ▼ Down ► No Change   Below Avg. ▨▨▨ ★

Options: ASE, CBOE, P, Ph

Analysis prepared by **Todd Rosenbluth** on November 10, 2008, when the stock traded at **$ 35.66**.

## Highlights

► We forecast a 3% revenue decline in FY 09 (Sep.) following a 26% rise in FY 08, inclusive of an unusually high royalty payment from Nokia in the fourth quarter. We see pressure on its chipset segment as customers reduce orders to deplete inventories amid the macroeconomic slowdown. While we see stronger growth for its royalty business aided by the return of business from Nokia, we see this also tempered by a dependence on growth in emerging markets with lower selling prices.

► Although we expect growth in the WCDMA handset market, which supports QCOM's high-margin royalty business, we see the rate being restricted as handset replacement rates slow. We look for gross margin to narrow to 68% in FY 09, from 69% in FY 08 as sales for chipsets decline.

► Even with lower legal costs, with an expected continued increase in R&D and reduced investment income we see net margins narrowing to 25% in FY 09 from 28% in FY 08. We estimate EPS declining to $1.65 in FY 09, inclusive of $0.39 of expenses for strategic investments and stock option.

## Investment Rationale/Risk

► Regarding our outlook for earnings, we no longer believe QCOM can weather the global economic slowdown as inventory levels at its handset maker and end user carrier customers are expected to rise. While we think QCOM's increased investments in R&D will support longer-term prospects, we contend this will further limit earnings over the next 12 months. That said, we believe QCOM has a strong balance sheet and will continue to generate sizable cash flow. But, based on the near-term challenges we see and inclusive of a premium valuation to peers, we recommend selling the stock.

► Risks to our recommendation and target price include stronger demand in the replacement rate expected for more advanced CDMA handsets; higher selling prices for handsets; a faster recovery in orders to replace low inventory level; and, share repurchases.

► Applying a P/E of 17X to our FY 09 EPS estimate -- a premium to peers, reflecting QCOM's above-average margins and cash flow generation -- we arrive at our 12-month target price of $28. We do not believe QCOM's dividend yield, recently about 2%, will provide support for its shares.

## Qualitative Risk Assessment

| LOW | MEDIUM | HIGH |
|---|---|---|

We believe QCOM's intellectual property rights and strong service provider relations give it a solid position in the industry. With our view of its healthy cash flow and no debt, we believe the company's cash balance can support potentially weaker demand from customers and litigation risks related to its CDMA patents.

## Quantitative Evaluations

**S&P Quality Ranking**          **B**

| D | C | B- | B | B+ | A- | A | A+ |
|---|---|---|---|---|---|---|---|

**Relative Strength Rank**          **MODERATE**

52

LOWEST = 1                    HIGHEST = 99

## Revenue/Earnings Data

**Revenue (Million $)**

| | 1Q | 2Q | 3Q | 4Q | Year |
|---|---|---|---|---|---|
| 2008 | 2,440 | 2,606 | 2,762 | 3,334 | 11,142 |
| 2007 | 2,019 | 2,221 | 2,325 | 2,306 | 8,871 |
| 2006 | 1,741 | 1,834 | 1,951 | 1,999 | 7,526 |
| 2005 | 1,390 | 1,365 | 1,358 | 1,560 | 5,673 |
| 2004 | 1,207 | 1,216 | 1,341 | 1,118 | 4,880 |
| 2003 | 1,097 | 1,043 | 921.6 | 908.8 | 3,971 |

**Earnings Per Share ($)**

| | | | | | |
|---|---|---|---|---|---|
| 2008 | 0.46 | 0.47 | 0.45 | 0.52 | 1.90 |
| 2007 | 0.38 | 0.43 | 0.47 | 0.67 | 1.95 |
| 2006 | 0.36 | 0.34 | 0.37 | 0.36 | 1.44 |
| 2005 | 0.30 | 0.31 | 0.33 | 0.32 | 1.26 |
| 2004 | 0.25 | 0.26 | 0.29 | 0.23 | 1.03 |
| 2003 | 0.15 | 0.07 | 0.12 | 0.18 | 0.51 |

Fiscal year ended Sep. 30. Next earnings report expected: NA. EPS Estimates based on S&P Operating Earnings; historical GAAP earnings are as reported.

## Dividend Data (Dates: mm/dd Payment Date: mm/dd/yy)

| Amount ($) | Date Decl. | Ex-Div. Date | Stk. of Record | Payment Date |
|---|---|---|---|---|
| 0.140 | 01/16 | 02/27 | 02/29 | 03/28/08 |
| 0.160 | 04/10 | 05/28 | 05/30 | 06/27/08 |
| 0.160 | 07/16 | 08/27 | 08/29 | 09/26/08 |
| 0.160 | 10/22 | 12/09 | 12/11 | 01/07/09 |

Dividends have been paid since 2003. Source: Company reports.

---

**Please read the Required Disclosures and Analyst Certification on the last page of this report.**

The McGraw-Hill Companies

# QUALCOMM Inc

**STANDARD &POOR'S**

## Business Summary November 10, 2008

CORPORATE OVERVIEW. The company is organized by these operating segments: CDMA technology (QCT), technology licensing (QTL), wireless and Internet (QWI), and strategic initiatives (QSI). The equipment and services segment, which is mostly from QCT, accounted for about 60% of total sales in FY 08 (Sep.) by providing integrated circuits and system software solutions to top wireless handset and infrastructure manufacturers. QCOM uses a fabless business model, employing several independent semiconductor foundries to manufacture its semiconductor products. Approximately 86 million model station modem (MSM) integrated circuits were sold during the fourth quarter of FY 08, compared to approximately 68 million a year earlier. QCOM expects a range of 60 million to 65 million MSM circuits to be sold in the first quarter of FY 09 due to slower end market device growth and a contraction in channel inventory during the first half of FY 09.

The license and royalty fee segment (QTL) accounted for about 33% of total sales, with 87% operating margins. QCOM holds a number of patents related to CDMA, and derives royalties from licensing its technology. Royalties are paid when manufacturers earn revenue from the sale of CDMA-based equipment, including CDMA and WCDMA handsets made by customers Samsung, LG Electronics, Motorola, and others. QCOM expects 25% growth in CDMA and WCDMA handsets in both calendar 2008 and 2009 with the majority from of the gains from WCDMA handsets. In October 2008, QCOM estimated that the average selling price of a handset was $219 in FY 08 and projects it to decline to $195 in FY 09, limiting the growth of its royalty revenues.

LEGAL/REGULATORY ISSUES. QCOM has been involved in various legal issues involving patents on its chipsets and on competitors' chipsets. The company's multiple disputes with Nokia included litigation over Nokia's obligation to pay royalties for the use of certain of QCOM's patents. Without a license contract with QCOM, Nokia had opted to cancel its CDMA-related handset division. However, in July 2008, QCOM and Nokia signed a new 15-year agreement covering various second, third and fourth-generation technology standards that we believe keeps QCOM's royalty pipeline active beyond supporting current handset offerings. In addition to lump-sum cash payment which helped boost fourth quarter FY 08 revenues by $580 million, Nokia returned to being a royalty customer of QCOM in late FY 08 that should help in FY 09.

## Company Financials Fiscal Year Ended Sep. 30

| Per Share Data ($) | 2008 | 2007 | 2006 | 2005 | 2004 | 2003 | 2002 | 2001 | 2000 | 1999 |
|---|---|---|---|---|---|---|---|---|---|---|
| Tangible Book Value | 8.05 | 8.82 | 7.37 | 6.43 | 5.69 | 4.54 | 2.77 | 2.82 | 3.14 | 2.22 |
| Cash Flow | NA | 2.18 | 1.60 | 1.38 | 1.13 | 0.62 | 0.47 | -0.14 | 0.57 | 0.28 |
| Earnings | 1.90 | 1.95 | 1.44 | 1.26 | 1.03 | 0.51 | 0.22 | -0.36 | 0.43 | 0.16 |
| S&P Core Earnings | 2.05 | 1.86 | 1.40 | 1.03 | 0.83 | 0.74 | 0.34 | -0.68 | NA | NA |
| Dividends | 0.60 | 0.54 | 0.42 | 0.32 | 0.19 | 0.09 | Nil | Nil | Nil | Nil |
| Payout Ratio | 32% | 28% | 29% | 25% | 18% | 17% | Nil | Nil | Nil | Nil |
| Prices:High | 56.88 | 47.72 | 53.01 | 46.60 | 44.99 | 27.43 | 26.67 | 44.69 | 100.00 | 92.52 |
| Prices:Low | 20.63 | 35.23 | 32.76 | 32.08 | 26.67 | 14.79 | 11.61 | 19.16 | 25.75 | 3.27 |
| P/E Ratio:High | 30 | 24 | 37 | 37 | 44 | 54 | NM | NM | NM | NM |
| P/E Ratio:Low | 11 | 18 | 23 | 25 | 26 | 29 | NM | NM | NM | 21 |

| Income Statement Analysis (Million $) | 2008 | 2007 | 2006 | 2005 | 2004 | 2003 | 2002 | 2001 | 2000 | 1999 |
|---|---|---|---|---|---|---|---|---|---|---|
| Revenue | 11,142 | 8,871 | 7,526 | 5,673 | 4,880 | 3,971 | 3,040 | 2,680 | 3,197 | 3,937 |
| Operating Income | NA | 3,266 | 2,962 | 2,586 | 2,266 | 1,684 | 1,068 | 877 | 1,105 | 564 |
| Depreciation | 456 | 383 | 272 | 200 | 163 | 180 | 394 | 320 | 244 | 158 |
| Interest Expense | NA | Nil | Nil | 3.00 | 2.00 | 30.7 | 25.7 | 10.2 | 4.92 | 14.7 |
| Pretax Income | 3,826 | 3,626 | 3,156 | 2,809 | 2,313 | 1,285 | 461 | -426 | 1,197 | 307 |
| Effective Tax Rate | 17.4% | 8.90% | 21.7% | 23.7% | 25.4% | 35.6% | 22.0% | NM | 44.0% | 34.5% |
| Net Income | 3,160 | 3,303 | 2,470 | 2,143 | 1,725 | 827 | 360 | -531 | 670 | 201 |
| S&P Core Earnings | 3,407 | 3,148 | 2,397 | 1,733 | 1,395 | 610 | 274 | -512 | NA | NA |

| Balance Sheet & Other Financial Data (Million $) | 2008 | 2007 | 2006 | 2005 | 2004 | 2003 | 2002 | 2001 | 2000 | 1999 |
|---|---|---|---|---|---|---|---|---|---|---|
| Cash | 6,411 | 6,581 | 5,721 | 6,548 | 5,982 | 4,561 | 2,795 | 2,283 | 1,772 | 660 |
| Current Assets | NA | 8,821 | 7,049 | 7,791 | 7,227 | 5,949 | 3,941 | 3,055 | 2,730 | 2,978 |
| Total Assets | 24,563 | 18,495 | 15,208 | 12,479 | 10,820 | 8,822 | 6,510 | 5,747 | 6,063 | 4,535 |
| Current Liabilities | NA | 2,258 | 1,422 | 1,070 | 894 | 808 | 675 | 521 | 472 | 876 |
| Long Term Debt | NA | Nil | Nil | Nil | Nil | 123 | 94.3 | Nil | Nil | 660 |
| Common Equity | 17,944 | 15,835 | 13,406 | 11,119 | 9,664 | 7,599 | 5,392 | 4,890 | 5,516 | 2,872 |
| Total Capital | NA | 15,835 | 13,406 | 11,119 | 9,664 | 7,722 | 5,530 | 4,896 | 5,563 | 3,584 |
| Capital Expenditures | 1,397 | 818 | 685 | 576 | 332 | 231 | 142 | 114 | 163 | 180 |
| Cash Flow | NA | 3,686 | 2,742 | 2,343 | 1,888 | 1,007 | 754 | -211 | 914 | 359 |
| Current Ratio | 5.1 | 3.9 | 5.0 | 7.3 | 8.1 | 7.4 | 5.8 | 5.9 | 5.8 | 3.4 |
| % Long Term Debt of Capitalization | Nil | Nil | Nil | Nil | Nil | 1.6 | 1.7 | Nil | Nil | 18.4 |
| % Net Income of Revenue | 28.4 | 37.2 | 32.8 | 37.8 | 35.3 | 20.8 | 11.8 | NM | 21.0 | 5.1 |
| % Return on Assets | 14.7 | 19.6 | 17.8 | 18.4 | 17.6 | 10.8 | 5.9 | NM | 12.6 | 5.7 |
| % Return on Equity | 18.7 | 22.5 | 20.1 | 20.6 | 20.0 | 12.7 | 7.1 | NM | 16.0 | 10.5 |

Data as orig reptd.; bef. results of disc opers/spec. items. Per share data adj. for stk. divs.; EPS diluted. E-Estimated. NA-Not Available. NM-Not Meaningful. NR-Not Ranked. UR-Under Review.

**Office:** 5775 Morehouse Drive, San Diego, CA 92121-1714.
**Telephone:** 858-587-1121.
**Email:** ir@qualcomm.com
**Website:** http://www.qualcomm.com

**Chrmn:** I.M. Jacobs
**Pres:** S.R. Altman
**CEO:** P.E. Jacobs
**COO:** L.J. Lauer

**EVP, CFO & Chief Acctg Officer:** W.E. Keitel
**Investor Contact:** J. Gilbert (858-658-4813)
**Board Members:** B. T. Alexander, S. M. Bennett, D. G. Cruickshank, R. V. Dittamore, I. M. Jacobs, P. E. Jacobs, R. E. Kahn, S. Lansing, D. A. Nelles, P. M. Sacerdote, B. Scowcroft, M. I. Stern

**Founded:** 1985
**Domicile:** Delaware
**Employees:** 15,400

# Questar Corp

STANDARD
&POOR'S

| S&P Recommendation BUY ★★★★☆ | Price $28.92 (as of Nov 14, 2008) | 12-Mo. Target Price $40.00 | Investment Style Large-Cap Growth |
|---|---|---|---|

**GICS Sector** Utilities
**Sub-Industry** Gas Utilities

**Summary** This integrated natural gas holding company is engaged in gas and oil exploration, energy marketing, gas gathering, transportation and storage, and retail gas distribution.

## Key Stock Statistics (Source S&P, Vickers, company reports)

| | | | | | | |
|---|---|---|---|---|---|---|
| 52-Wk Range | $74.87– 20.66 | S&P Oper. EPS 2008**E** | 3.75 | Market Capitalization(B) | $5.016 | Beta | 0.83 |
| Trailing 12-Month EPS | $3.94 | S&P Oper. EPS 2009**E** | 3.30 | Yield (%) | 1.73 | S&P 3-Yr. Proj. EPS CAGR(%) | 10 |
| Trailing 12-Month P/E | 7.3 | P/E on S&P Oper. EPS 2008**E** | 7.7 | Dividend Rate/Share | $0.50 | S&P Credit Rating | NR |
| $10K Invested 5 Yrs Ago | $18,649 | Common Shares Outstg. (M) | 173.4 | Institutional Ownership (%) | 77 | | |

## Price Performance

30-Week Mov. Avg. · · · · 10-Week Mov. Avg. - - GAAP Earnings vs. Previous Year Volume Above Avg. STARS
12-Mo. Target Price — Relative Strength — ▲ Up ▼ Down ▶ No Change Below Avg.

2-for-1

Options: ASE, CBOE, Ph

Analysis prepared by **Christopher B. Muir** on November 04, 2008, when the stock traded at **$ 33.88.**

## Highlights

➤ We forecast a 32% revenue increase in 2008 on higher prices and volumes. We expect STR's E&P segment to benefit from higher production volumes and prices in the Rockies. Our pipeline growth estimate reflects our expectations for continued strong gains in contract transportation as well as increased natural gas liquids volumes. We see the utility benefiting from continued customer growth. We see revenues falling 12% in 2009 due to falling commodity prices, partly offset by higher volumes.

➤ We project operating margins of 32.1% in 2008 and 31.3% in 2009, up from 31.1% in 2007. In 2008, we see higher per-revenue cost of sales and production taxes, partly offset by lower per revenue operations and maintenance expense. We see pretax profit margins rising to 29.7% in 2008, from 29.5%, as we expect higher interest expenses, partly offset by higher non-operating income. We see pretax margins returning to 29.5% in 2009.

➤ Assuming an effective tax rate of 36.9% and small share increases, we project operating EPS of $3.75 in 2008, up 30% from 2007's $2.88. Our 2009 EPS forecast is $3.30, down 12%, on lower commodity prices.

## Investment Rationale/Risk

➤ STR has posted steady production gains through an aggressive drilling program at its Rockies and Midcontinent assets. To date in 2008, production increased 20%, to 125.4 billion cubic feet equivalent (Bcfe), and we expect a 21% rise in 2008 to 168 Bcfe. Strong drilling activity by others in these regions should drive growth at STR's gas gathering and processing operations. We expect management to continue to focus on increasing fee-based gas gathering volumes from unaffiliated businesses. We like STR's strong hedging program, which we believe will significantly reduce exposure to oil and gas price changes.

➤ Risks to our recommendation and target price include a prolonged drop in natural gas and oil prices, unusually mild winter weather, weaker-than-expected economic growth, and sharply higher interest rates.

➤ The stock recently traded at about 10.3X our 2009 EPS estimate, a 23% discount to its gas utility peers. Our 12-month target price of $40 is 12.1X our 2009 EPS estimate, or a 10% discount to our peer target. We think this discount is warranted given our view of a higher risk level than at some peers.

## Qualitative Risk Assessment

| LOW | MEDIUM | HIGH |
|---|---|---|

Our risk assessment is based on our view that the company's higher risk exploration and production and energy marketing operations are balanced by its lower-risk regulated gas transmission and distribution businesses.

## Quantitative Evaluations

**S&P Quality Ranking** A

| D | C | B- | B | B+ | A- | A | A+ |
|---|---|---|---|---|---|---|---|

**Relative Strength Rank** MODERATE

47

LOWEST = 1          HIGHEST = 99

## Revenue/Earnings Data

### Revenue (Million $)

| | 1Q | 2Q | 3Q | 4Q | Year |
|---|---|---|---|---|---|
| 2008 | 1,045 | 825.8 | 760.0 | -- | -- |
| 2007 | 872.1 | 556.7 | 497.4 | 800.4 | 2,727 |
| 2006 | 911.4 | 596.2 | 555.1 | 772.9 | 2,836 |
| 2005 | 680.3 | 520.2 | 582.9 | 941.5 | 2,725 |
| 2004 | 563.6 | 369.5 | 360.2 | 608.1 | 1,901 |
| 2003 | 469.8 | 270.7 | 273.5 | 449.2 | 1,463 |

### Earnings Per Share ($)

| | 1Q | 2Q | 3Q | 4Q | Year |
|---|---|---|---|---|---|
| 2008 | 1.05 | 0.98 | 1.16 | E0.77 | E3.75 |
| 2007 | 0.86 | 0.64 | 0.64 | 0.74 | 2.89 |
| 2006 | 0.79 | 0.52 | 0.54 | 0.70 | 2.54 |
| 2005 | 0.55 | 0.35 | 0.38 | 0.60 | 1.87 |
| 2004 | 0.45 | 0.25 | 0.22 | 0.43 | 1.34 |
| 2003 | 0.42 | 0.12 | 0.17 | 0.36 | 1.07 |

Fiscal year ended Dec. 31. Next earnings report expected: Mid February. EPS Estimates based on S&P Operating Earnings; historical GAAP earnings are as reported.

## Dividend Data (Dates: mm/dd Payment Date: mm/dd/yy)

| Amount ($) | Date Decl. | Ex-Div. Date | Stk. of Record | Payment Date |
|---|---|---|---|---|
| 0.123 | 02/12 | 02/20 | 02/22 | 03/10/08 |
| 0.123 | 05/20 | 05/28 | 05/30 | 06/16/08 |
| 0.123 | 08/12 | 08/20 | 08/22 | 09/15/08 |
| 0.125 | 10/28 | 11/19 | 11/21 | 12/15/08 |

Dividends have been paid since 1935. Source: Company reports.

# Questar Corp

STANDARD
&POOR'S

## Business Summary November 04, 2008

CORPORATE OVERVIEW. Questar Corp. (STR) is a natural gas energy entity operating three divisions: Questar Market Resources (QMR), Questar Gas Company (QGC), and Questar Pipeline Company (QPC). QMR, which is engaged in natural gas and oil exploration and production (E&P), energy marketing, gas gathering and processing services, contributed 83% of net income in 2007; QGC, which distributes natural gas as a public utility in Utah, southwestern Wyoming and a small portion of southeastern Idaho, contributed 7%; and QPC, an interstate pipeline company that provides natural gas transportation and underground storage services in Utah, Wyoming and Colorado, contributed 9%.

CORPORATE STRATEGY. STR's integrated model spans the entire natural gas value chain. The unregulated QMR businesses are the primary growth drivers for STR. The company believes these businesses -- which include E&P, gas gathering, and processing services -- have the potential to offer higher returns than the regulated utility and pipeline operations. STR expects the share of unconventional reservoirs to total natural gas production to increase to 50% in the next decade, from the current 10%. STR's properties in the Rockies are expected to be a major contributor to this growth. The utility and pipeline

operations are less sensitive to commodity prices and help fund dividend payouts.

MARKET PROFILE. QMR operates E&P properties, primarily natural gas, in the Rockies region of Wyoming, Utah and Colorado, and the Midcontinent region of Oklahoma, Texas and Louisiana. It has reported an estimated 1,867 Bcfe of proved reserves, with 80% of the proved reserves in the Rockies and the remainder in the Midcontinent region. As of 2007, QMR had developed 61% of the proved reserves, with most of the undeveloped reserves in the Pinedale Anticline property. Wexpro, a division of QMR, develops certain properties owned by QGC, and had proved reserves of 642 Bcfe as of year-end 2007. Wexpro charges the utility for costs plus a specified return, which averaged 19.9% (after tax) during 2007. Gas Management owns 1,550 miles of gathering pipelines in Utah, Wyoming and Colorado. Energy Trading also owns an underground storage reservoir in Wyoming.

## Company Financials Fiscal Year Ended Dec. 31

| Per Share Data ($) | 2007 | 2006 | 2005 | 2004 | 2003 | 2002 | 2001 | 2000 | 1999 | 1998 |
|---|---|---|---|---|---|---|---|---|---|---|
| Tangible Book Value | 14.51 | 12.43 | 8.60 | 8.03 | 7.06 | 6.41 | 6.07 | 6.01 | 5.69 | 5.31 |
| Cash Flow | 5.05 | 4.34 | 3.34 | 2.66 | 3.41 | 2.21 | 1.90 | 1.85 | 1.43 | 1.43 |
| Earnings | 2.88 | 2.54 | 1.87 | 1.34 | 1.07 | 1.04 | 0.97 | 0.97 | 0.60 | 0.47 |
| S&P Core Earnings | 2.93 | 2.49 | 1.88 | 1.37 | 1.08 | 0.77 | 0.82 | NA | NA | NA |
| Dividends | 0.49 | 0.47 | 0.45 | 0.43 | 0.39 | 0.36 | 0.35 | 0.34 | 0.34 | 0.33 |
| Payout Ratio | 17% | 18% | 24% | 32% | 37% | 35% | 36% | 35% | 56% | 70% |
| Prices:High | 58.75 | 45.51 | 44.80 | 26.06 | 17.75 | 14.73 | 16.88 | 15.94 | 9.97 | 11.19 |
| Prices:Low | 37.98 | 33.69 | 23.37 | 16.91 | 13.02 | 9.01 | 9.29 | 6.78 | 7.38 | 7.91 |
| P/E Ratio:High | 20 | 18 | 24 | 20 | 17 | 14 | 17 | 16 | 17 | 24 |
| P/E Ratio:Low | 13 | 13 | 12 | 13 | 12 | 9 | 10 | 7 | 12 | 17 |

| Income Statement Analysis (Million $) | | | | | | | | | | |
|---|---|---|---|---|---|---|---|---|---|---|
| Revenue | 2,727 | 2,836 | 2,725 | 1,901 | 1,463 | 1,201 | 1,439 | 1,266 | 924 | 906 |
| Operating Income | 1,223 | 1,156 | 841 | 646 | 557 | 524 | 482 | 453 | 180 | 133 |
| Depreciation | 380 | 316 | 256 | 226 | 394 | 194 | 152 | 142 | 138 | 159 |
| Interest Expense | 80.2 | 73.6 | 69.3 | 68.4 | 70.7 | 81.1 | 64.8 | 63.5 | 53.9 | 48.0 |
| Pretax Income | 798 | 700 | 514 | 359 | 282 | 262 | 246 | 242 | 147 | 106 |
| Effective Tax Rate | 36.4% | 36.5% | 36.6% | 36.1% | 36.4% | 34.8% | 35.8% | 35.3% | 32.6% | 27.4% |
| Net Income | 507 | 444 | 326 | 229 | 179 | 171 | 158 | 157 | 98.8 | 76.9 |
| S&P Core Earnings | 516 | 438 | 327 | 234 | 182 | 125 | 132 | NA | NA | NA |

| Balance Sheet & Other Financial Data (Million $) | | | | | | | | | | |
|---|---|---|---|---|---|---|---|---|---|---|
| Cash | 14.2 | 24.6 | 13.4 | 3.68 | 13.9 | 21.6 | 11.3 | 14.8 | 45.0 | 17.5 |
| Current Assets | 659 | 753 | 756 | 480 | 345 | 280 | 344 | 427 | 239 | 247 |
| Total Assets | 5,944 | 5,065 | 4,357 | 3,647 | 3,309 | 3,068 | 3,236 | 2,539 | 2,238 | 2,161 |
| Current Liabilities | 999 | 679 | 874 | 544 | 483 | 301 | 781 | 535 | 324 | 437 |
| Long Term Debt | 1,021 | 1,022 | 983 | 933 | 950 | 1,145 | 997 | 715 | 735 | 616 |
| Common Equity | 2,578 | 2,206 | 1,550 | 1,440 | 1,261 | 1,139 | 1,081 | 991 | 926 | 878 |
| Total Capital | 4,542 | 3,992 | 3,157 | 2,906 | 2,666 | 2,676 | 2,422 | 1,971 | 1,878 | 1,697 |
| Capital Expenditures | 1,398 | 910 | 716 | 442 | 335 | 358 | 871 | 314 | 268 | 461 |
| Cash Flow | 888 | 760 | 581 | 455 | 573 | 365 | 310 | 299 | 237 | 236 |
| Current Ratio | 0.7 | 1.1 | 0.9 | 0.9 | 0.7 | 0.9 | 0.4 | 0.8 | 0.7 | 0.6 |
| % Long Term Debt of Capitalization | 22.5 | 25.6 | 31.1 | 32.1 | 35.6 | 42.8 | 41.2 | 36.3 | 39.1 | 36.3 |
| % Net Income of Revenue | 18.6 | 15.7 | 12.0 | 12.1 | 12.2 | 14.2 | 11.0 | 12.4 | 10.7 | 8.5 |
| % Return on Assets | 9.2 | 9.4 | 8.1 | 6.6 | 5.6 | 5.4 | 5.5 | 6.6 | 4.5 | 3.7 |
| % Return on Equity | 21.2 | 23.7 | 21.8 | 17.0 | 14.9 | 15.4 | 15.6 | 16.4 | 11.0 | 8.9 |

Data as orig reptd.; bef. results of disc opers/spec. items. Per share data adj. for stk. divs.; EPS diluted. E-Estimated. NA-Not Available. NM-Not Meaningful. NR-Not Ranked. UR-Under Review.

**Office:** 180 East 100th Street, Salt Lake City, UT 84139-1500.
**Telephone:** 801-324-5699.
**Website:** http://www.questar.com
**Chrmn, Pres & CEO:** K.O. Rattie

**COO & EVP:** C.B. Stanley
**SVP, CFO & Chief Acctg Officer:** S.E. Parks
**Treas:** M.H. Craven
**Secy:** A.L. Jones

**Investor Contact:** M. Craven (801-324-5077)
**Board Members:** P. S. Baker, Jr., T. Beck, R. D. Cash, L. R. Flury, J. A. Harmon, R. E. McKee, III, G. G. Michael, K. O. Rattie, M. W. Scoggins, H. H. Simmons, C. B. Stanley, B. A. Williamson

**Founded:** 1935
**Domicile:** Utah
**Employees:** 2,324

The McGraw·Hill Companies

# Quest Diagnostics Inc

STANDARD
&POOR'S

**S&P Recommendation** BUY ★★★★☆

| Price | 12-Mo. Target Price | Investment Style |
|---|---|---|
| $47.99 (as of Nov 14, 2008) | $64.00 | Large-Cap Growth |

**GICS Sector** Health Care
**Sub-Industry** Health Care Services

**Summary** This company provides diagnostic testing, information and services to physicians, hospitals, managed care organizations, employers and government agencies.

## Key Stock Statistics (Source S&P, Vickers, company reports)

| | | | | | | |
|---|---|---|---|---|---|---|
| 52-Wk Range | $59.95– 38.66 | S&P Oper. EPS 2008**E** | 3.22 | Market Capitalization(B) | $9.387 | Beta | 0.43 |
| Trailing 12-Month EPS | $2.07 | S&P Oper. EPS 2009**E** | 3.68 | Yield (%) | 0.83 | S&P 3-Yr. Proj. EPS CAGR(%) | 13 |
| Trailing 12-Month P/E | 23.2 | P/E on S&P Oper. EPS 2008**E** | 14.9 | Dividend Rate/Share | $0.40 | S&P Credit Rating | BBB+ |
| $10K Invested 5 Yrs Ago | $14,186 | Common Shares Outstg. (M) | 195.6 | Institutional Ownership (%) | 76 | | |

## Price Performance

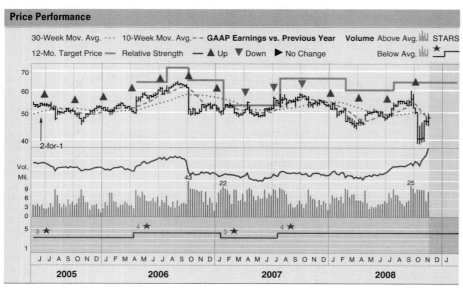

30-Week Mov. Avg. · · · · 10-Week Mov. Avg. - - GAAP Earnings vs. Previous Year Volume Above Avg. STARS
12-Mo. Target Price — Relative Strength ▲ Up ▼ Down ▶ No Change Below Avg. ★

Options: ASE, CBOE, Ph

Analysis prepared by **Jeffrey Loo, CFA** on October 30, 2008, when the stock traded at **$ 43.91**.

## Highlights

➤ We see 2008 sales increasing 8% to $7.27 billion, on mid-single digit organic growth and contributions from the May 2007 acquisition of AmeriPath. But AmeriPath had lower margins, and we believe DGX priced the Aetna contract aggressively, limiting margin expansion. We see 2008 operating margins rebounding 20 basis points (bps) following the 90 bps decline in 2007 due to loss of the UnitedHealthcare contract. We see operating margins being aided by aggressive cost cutting initiated in early 2007, partially offset by increased technology investments and costs associated with DGX's India start-up. In 2009, we see sales rising to $7.6 billion.

➤ DGX acquired AmeriPath for $2 billion in a deal financed with debt, significantly increasing interest costs. We do not expect DGX to pursue additional acquisitions over the next year due to its leverage, and as we believe it intends to pay down debt.

➤ Since May 2003, DGX has repurchased 43.4 million of its shares, aiding EPS. However, with a large increase in debt, we see DGX limiting buybacks until some debt is repaid. Our 2008 and 2009 EPS forecasts are $3.22 and $3.68.

## Investment Rationale/Risk

➤ We believe the sharp decline in share price is unwarranted. The shares are currently trading at 11.4X our 2009 EPS estimate, well below historical levels, and we believe the shares are undervalued. Although we have some concerns about economic challenges and significantly lower drug testing, we believe DGX should be able to maintain solid growth and margin expansion. Two important metrics, revenue per requisition and tests per requisition both increased in the first nine months of 2008, and we see this trend continuing into 2009. We also see better pricing stability as the majority of DGX's managed care contracts have been signed. But we see some challenges for DGX, including Ameripath's bad debt expense of 14% of revenue, although we believe DGX will continually improve on that rate.

➤ Risks to our recommendation and target price include the loss of more contracts and greater pricing pressure from third-party payors.

➤ Our 12-month target price of $64 is based on a P/E-to-growth ratio of about 1.3X applied to our 2009 EPS estimate and assuming a three-year EPS growth rate of 13%, in line with peers.

## Qualitative Risk Assessment

| LOW | MEDIUM | HIGH |
|---|---|---|

Our risk assessment reflects our view of DGX's leadership position in the large and mature diagnostic testing industry; the company's broad geographic service area; its diverse and balanced payor mix; and the growing recognition of the importance and significance of diagnostic testing.

## Quantitative Evaluations

**S&P Quality Ranking** B

| D | C | B- | B | B+ | A- | A | A+ |
|---|---|---|---|---|---|---|---|

**Relative Strength Rank** STRONG

93

LOWEST = 1 HIGHEST = 99

## Revenue/Earnings Data

**Revenue (Million $)**

| | 1Q | 2Q | 3Q | 4Q | Year |
|---|---|---|---|---|---|
| 2008 | 1,785 | 1,838 | 1,827 | -- | -- |
| 2007 | 1,526 | 1,641 | 1,767 | 1,770 | 6,705 |
| 2006 | 1,553 | 1,583 | 1,583 | 1,549 | 6,269 |
| 2005 | 1,319 | 1,378 | 1,372 | 1,435 | 5,504 |
| 2004 | 1,256 | 1,298 | 1,290 | 1,283 | 5,127 |
| 2003 | 1,093 | 1,220 | 1,221 | 1,204 | 4,738 |

**Earnings Per Share ($)**

| | | | | | |
|---|---|---|---|---|---|
| 2008 | 0.72 | 0.83 | 0.81 | E0.81 | E3.22 |
| 2007 | 0.55 | 0.73 | 0.77 | 0.79 | 2.84 |
| 2006 | 0.77 | 0.78 | 0.82 | 0.77 | 3.14 |
| 2005 | 0.64 | 0.72 | 0.66 | 0.64 | 2.66 |
| 2004 | 0.54 | 0.59 | 0.62 | 0.60 | 2.35 |
| 2003 | 0.43 | 0.56 | 0.56 | 0.51 | 2.06 |

Fiscal year ended Dec. 31. Next earnings report expected: Late February. EPS Estimates based on S&P Operating Earnings; historical GAAP earnings are as reported.

## Dividend Data (Dates: mm/dd Payment Date: mm/dd/yy)

| Amount ($) | Date Decl. | Ex-Div. Date | Stk. of Record | Payment Date |
|---|---|---|---|---|
| 0.100 | 12/18 | 01/07 | 01/09 | 01/23/08 |
| 0.100 | 02/14 | 04/02 | 04/04 | 04/18/08 |
| 0.100 | 05/21 | 07/01 | 07/03 | 07/18/08 |
| 0.100 | 08/05 | 10/01 | 10/03 | 10/20/08 |

Dividends have been paid since 2004. Source: Company reports.

# Quest Diagnostics Inc

STANDARD
&POOR'S

## Business Summary October 30, 2008

CORPORATE OVERVIEW. Quest Diagnostics is the largest independent U.S. clinical lab provider. The clinical lab market is estimated to be about a $45 billion market, with hospital-based labs accounting for about 60% of the market, independent commercial labs, such as DGX, accounting for 33%, and physician-office labs the rest. DGX offers a broad range of clinical laboratory testing services used by physicians in the detection, diagnosis, and treatment of diseases and other medical conditions. Tests range from routine (such as blood cholesterol tests) to highly complex esoteric (such as gene-based testing and molecular diagnostics testing). At the end of 2007, DGX had a network of 35 principal laboratories throughout the U.S., 150 smaller "rapid response" (STAT) laboratories, and over 2,100 patient service centers, along with facilities in Mexico, Puerto Rico, and England. In 2008, DGX has started construction of a laboratory in India.

DGX processes more than 145 million requisitions (order forms completed by physicians indicating tests to be performed) annually. Routine testing and anatomic pathology generated 73% of net sales in 2007 (75% in 2006), esoteric testing 18% (17% in 2006), clinical trials and risk assessment services from LabOne (acquired in November 2005) 9% (8%). Routine tests measure important health parameters such as the function of the kidney, heart, liver, thyroid and other organs. Esoteric tests are performed less frequently than routine tests, and/or require more sophisticated equipment and materials, professional hands-on attention, and more highly skilled personnel. As a result, they are generally priced substantially higher than routine tests.

## Company Financials Fiscal Year Ended Dec. 31

| Per Share Data ($) | 2007 | 2006 | 2005 | 2004 | 2003 | 2002 | 2001 | 2000 | 1999 | 1998 |
|---|---|---|---|---|---|---|---|---|---|---|
| Tangible Book Value | NM | NM | NM | NM | NM | NM | NM | NM | NM | 0.60 |
| Cash Flow | 4.06 | 4.24 | 3.51 | 3.12 | 2.79 | 2.31 | 1.70 | 1.27 | 0.64 | 0.79 |
| Earnings | 2.84 | 3.14 | 2.66 | 2.35 | 2.06 | 1.62 | 0.94 | 0.56 | -0.01 | 0.22 |
| S&P Core Earnings | 2.85 | 3.17 | 2.57 | 2.13 | 1.80 | 1.42 | 0.83 | NA | NA | NA |
| Dividends | 0.40 | 0.39 | 0.26 | 0.30 | Nil | Nil | Nil | Nil | Nil | Nil |
| Payout Ratio | 14% | 12% | 10% | 13% | Nil | Nil | Nil | Nil | Nil | Nil |
| Prices:High | 58.63 | 64.69 | 54.80 | 48.41 | 37.50 | 48.07 | 37.88 | 36.56 | 8.23 | 5.77 |
| Prices:Low | 47.98 | 48.59 | 44.32 | 35.94 | 23.68 | 24.55 | 18.30 | 7.28 | 4.44 | 3.63 |
| P/E Ratio:High | 21 | 21 | 21 | 21 | 18 | 30 | 40 | 66 | NM | 26 |
| P/E Ratio:Low | 17 | 15 | 17 | 15 | 11 | 15 | 19 | 13 | NM | 16 |

| Income Statement Analysis (Million $) | | | | | | | | | | |
|---|---|---|---|---|---|---|---|---|---|---|
| Revenue | 6,705 | 6,269 | 5,504 | 5,127 | 4,738 | 4,108 | 3,628 | 3,421 | 2,205 | 1,459 |
| Operating Income | 1,350 | 1,325 | 1,144 | 1,060 | 950 | 724 | 559 | 452 | 243 | 163 |
| Depreciation | 238 | 197 | 176 | 169 | 154 | 131 | 148 | 134 | 90.8 | 68.8 |
| Interest Expense | 186 | 96.5 | 61.4 | 57.9 | 59.8 | 53.7 | 70.5 | 120 | 69.8 | 44.0 |
| Pretax Income | 939 | 1,057 | 930 | 854 | 755 | 557 | 343 | 210 | 19.8 | 53.9 |
| Effective Tax Rate | 38.2% | 38.6% | 39.2% | 39.3% | 39.9% | 39.5% | 43.4% | 45.7% | NM | 50.1% |
| Net Income | 554 | 626 | 546 | 499 | 437 | 322 | 184 | 105 | -1.27 | 26.9 |
| S&P Core Earnings | 556 | 632 | 531 | 456 | 377 | 279 | 162 | NA | NA | NA |

| Balance Sheet & Other Financial Data (Million $) | | | | | | | | | | |
|---|---|---|---|---|---|---|---|---|---|---|
| Cash | 168 | 150 | 92.1 | 73.3 | 155 | 96.8 | 122 | 171 | 27.3 | 203 |
| Current Assets | 1,374 | 1,191 | 1,069 | 931 | 996 | 824 | 877 | 981 | 873 | 578 |
| Total Assets | 8,566 | 5,661 | 5,306 | 4,204 | 4,301 | 3,324 | 2,931 | 2,865 | 2,878 | 1,360 |
| Current Liabilities | 1,288 | 1,151 | 1,101 | 1,044 | 724 | 636 | 659 | 955 | 701 | 309 |
| Long Term Debt | 3,377 | 1,239 | 1,255 | 724 | 1,029 | 797 | 820 | 761 | 1,171 | 413 |
| Common Equity | 3,324 | 3,019 | 2,763 | 2,289 | 2,397 | 1,769 | 1,336 | 1,031 | 862 | 567 |
| Total Capital | 6,911 | 4,258 | 4,018 | 3,013 | 3,426 | 2,565 | 2,156 | 1,793 | 2,046 | 2,034 |
| Capital Expenditures | 219 | 193 | 224 | 176 | 175 | 155 | 149 | 116 | 76.0 | 39.6 |
| Cash Flow | 792 | 823 | 722 | 668 | 591 | 454 | 332 | 239 | 89.6 | 95.7 |
| Current Ratio | 1.1 | 1.0 | 1.0 | 0.9 | 1.4 | 1.3 | 1.3 | 1.0 | 1.2 | 1.9 |
| % Long Term Debt of Capitalization | 48.9 | 29.1 | 31.2 | 24.0 | 30.0 | 31.0 | 38.0 | 42.4 | 57.6 | 42.1 |
| % Net Income of Revenue | 8.3 | 10.0 | 9.9 | 9.7 | 9.2 | 7.8 | 5.1 | 3.1 | NM | 1.8 |
| % Return on Assets | 7.8 | 11.4 | 11.5 | 11.7 | 11.5 | 10.3 | 6.3 | 3.7 | NM | 1.9 |
| % Return on Equity | 17.5 | 21.6 | 21.6 | 21.3 | 20.9 | 20.8 | 15.5 | 11.1 | NM | 4.9 |

Data as orig reptd.; bef. results of disc opers/spec. items. Per share data adj. for stk. divs.; EPS diluted. E-Estimated. NA-Not Available. NM-Not Meaningful. NR-Not Ranked. UR-Under Review.

**Office:** 1290 Wall St W, Lyndhurst, NJ 07071-3683.
**Telephone:** 201-393-5000.
**Email:** investor@questdiagnostics.com
**Website:** http://www.questdiagnostics.com

**Chrmn, Pres & CEO:** S.N. Mohapatra
**COO:** W.R. Simmons
**SVP & CFO:** R.A. Hagemann
**SVP & General Counsel:** M.E. Prevoznik

**Chief Acctg Officer & Cntlr:** T.F. Bongiorno
**Investor Contact:** L. Park (973-520-2900)
**Board Members:** J. C. Baldwin, J. K. Britell, W. F. Buehler, R. Haggerty, S. N. Mohapatra, G. M. Pfeiffer, D. C. Stanzione, G. R. Wilensky, J. Ziegler

**Founded:** 1967
**Domicile:** Delaware
**Employees:** 43,500

The McGraw-Hill Companies

# Qwest Communications International Inc.

STANDARD
&POOR'S

| **S&P Recommendation** HOLD ★★★☆☆ | **Price** $2.86 (as of Nov 14, 2008) | **12-Mo. Target Price** $4.00 | **Investment Style** Large-Cap Blend |
|---|---|---|---|

**GICS Sector** Telecommunication Services
**Sub-Industry** Integrated Telecommunication Services

**Summary** This company provides wireline and wireless services, primarily serving customers in 14 western and midwestern U.S. states.

## Key Stock Statistics (Source S&P, Vickers, company reports)

| | | | | | | | | |
|---|---|---|---|---|---|---|---|---|
| 52-Wk Range | $7.41– 2.05 | S&P Oper. EPS 2008**E** | 0.39 | Market Capitalization(B) | $4.872 | Beta | | 1.41 |
| Trailing 12-Month EPS | $0.49 | S&P Oper. EPS 2009**E** | 0.35 | Yield (%) | 11.19 | S&P 3-Yr. Proj. EPS CAGR(%) | | 3 |
| Trailing 12-Month P/E | 5.8 | P/E on S&P Oper. EPS 2008**E** | 7.3 | Dividend Rate/Share | $0.32 | S&P Credit Rating | | BB |
| $10K Invested 5 Yrs Ago | $8,736 | Common Shares Outstg. (M) | 1,703.4 | Institutional Ownership (%) | 98 | | | |

## Price Performance

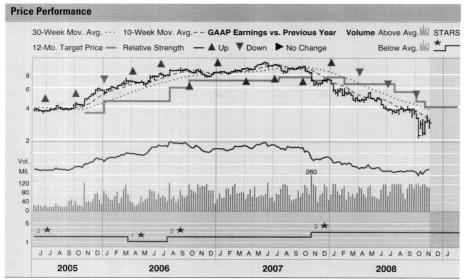

30-Week Mov. Avg. · · · 10-Week Mov. Avg. - - GAAP Earnings vs. Previous Year Volume Above Avg. STARS
12-Mo. Target Price — Relative Strength — ▲ Up ▼ Down ► No Change Below Avg. ★

Options: ASE, CBOE, P, Ph

Analysis prepared by **Todd Rosenbluth** on October 30, 2008, when the stock traded at **$ 2.67**.

## Highlights

➤ Following a projected 2.5% revenue decrease in 2008, we see a further 1.9% decline in 2009. We forecast pressure on voice services from access line losses, due to competition and slowing housing sales, and from wholesale weakness amid carrier customer consolidation. However, we expect broadband additions and gains in the enterprise segment from new contracts.

➤ We look for EBITDA margins to narrow slightly from a projected 32.8% in 2008 to 32.6% in 2009. We believe 2007 margins were helped by lower pension and facility costs. In our view, workforce savings efforts will be challenged by increased wages and a more aggressive broadband strategy. We see a modest decline in 2008 and 2009 offset by increased capital spending.

➤ We estimate operating EPS of $0.39 in 2008, reflecting a lower share count and including a $0.20 impact for recording taxes at a normal 37% rate after years of credits. We note that third-quarter 2007 results include a non-recurring $1.12 per share tax benefit and an $0.18 litigation-related charge. We see EPS of $0.35 in 2009.

## Investment Rationale/Risk

➤ We believe Q generates sufficient cash flow to support both its dividend policy and capital spending needs geared toward offsetting competition. However, the stock is down more than 60% in 2008 on what we view as macroeconomic concerns given the increased access line pressure thus far in 2008 and anticipated declines in EBITDA for 2009. We believe the discounted valuation reflects our forecast of limited earnings growth prospects, given competitive pressures and increased difficulty in finding cost savings.

➤ Risks to our recommendation and target price include greater-than-expected line losses, lower demand for Q's bundled services, which would hurt margins, and a dividend cut.

➤ With the operational challenges we foresee, we believe Q warrants a discounted valuation to peers. We apply a 4.7X peer group multiple to our 2009 EBITDA estimate and blend it with a P/E multiple of 11X, below our forecast for faster-growing peers, to arrive at our 12-month target price of $4.00. We believe Q's dividend yield, recently about 12%, adds support.

## Qualitative Risk Assessment

| LOW | MEDIUM | HIGH |
|---|---|---|

Our risk assessment reflects the highly competitive nature of the industry and our view of the above-average debt load that Q carries, offset by our view of steady operating cash flow that supports the dividend.

## Quantitative Evaluations

**S&P Quality Ranking** B-

| D | C | B- | B | B+ | A- | A | A+ |
|---|---|---|---|---|---|---|---|

**Relative Strength Rank** STRONG

73

LOWEST = 1 HIGHEST = 99

## Revenue/Earnings Data

**Revenue (Million $)**

| | 1Q | 2Q | 3Q | 4Q | Year |
|---|---|---|---|---|---|
| 2008 | 3,399 | 3,382 | 3,379 | -- | -- |
| 2007 | 3,446 | 3,463 | 3,434 | 3,435 | 13,778 |
| 2006 | 3,476 | 3,472 | 3,487 | 3,488 | 13,923 |
| 2005 | 3,449 | 3,470 | 3,504 | 3,480 | 13,903 |
| 2004 | 3,481 | 3,442 | 3,449 | 3,437 | 13,809 |
| 2003 | 3,624 | 3,596 | 3,570 | 3,498 | 14,288 |

**Earnings Per Share ($)**

| | | | | | |
|---|---|---|---|---|---|
| 2008 | 0.09 | 0.11 | 0.09 | E0.09 | E0.39 |
| 2007 | 0.12 | 0.13 | 1.08 | 0.20 | 1.52 |
| 2006 | 0.05 | 0.06 | 0.09 | 0.10 | 0.30 |
| 2005 | 0.03 | -0.09 | -0.08 | -0.27 | -0.41 |
| 2004 | -0.17 | -0.43 | -0.31 | -0.09 | -1.00 |
| 2003 | -0.07 | -0.07 | -0.39 | -0.22 | -0.76 |

Fiscal year ended Dec. 31. Next earnings report expected: Mid February. EPS Estimates based on S&P Operating Earnings; historical GAAP earnings are as reported.

## Dividend Data (Dates: mm/dd Payment Date: mm/dd/yy)

| Amount ($) | Date Decl. | Ex-Div. Date | Stk. of Record | Payment Date |
|---|---|---|---|---|
| 0.080 | 12/13 | 01/30 | 02/01 | 02/21/08 |
| 0.080 | 04/17 | 05/07 | 05/09 | 05/30/08 |
| 0.080 | 07/17 | 08/06 | 08/08 | 08/29/08 |
| 0.080 | 10/16 | 11/12 | 11/14 | 12/05/08 |

Dividends have been paid since 2008. Source: Company reports.

# Qwest Communications International Inc.

STANDARD
&POOR'S

## Business Summary October 30, 2008

CORPORATE OVERVIEW. Qwest Communications International (Q) provides telecommunications services in 14 midwestern and western states. As of September 2008, Q had 11.9 million local access lines for consumers and businesses and 2.8 million DSL broadband customers (up 11% from a year earlier), with approximately 80% of its access lines in its eight largest markets, including Denver, Portland and Seattle. In March 2004, Q began offering wireless services using Sprint's network but retained control of all marketing, customer service, pricing and promotional offerings. In May 2008, the company announced plans to switch to using Verizon Wireless and will migrate existing customers in early 2009. In 2007, 59% of Q's revenues were derived from a declining wireline voice services segment, a higher percentage than most peers, while 4% was derived from wireless service that was only used in Q's bundle. The remaining revenues were from data, Internet and video services. In 2007, Q's revenues were pressured in its wholesale segment (25% of overall revenues), but this was offset by gains in the enterprise segment (28%).

COMPETITIVE LANDSCAPE. We believe Q faces competitive challenges partly due to low barriers to entry and characteristics unique to the company. As of September 2008, Q's access line count was 8.9% lower than a year earlier, as wireless and cable telephony substitution was intense, and we believe fewer housing sales in core markets limited new customer additions. Q competes

with cable providers such as Cox Communications and Comcast that offer broadband services and telephony products that were aggressively marketed in the first half 2008. To offset possible customer migration to cable, Q is offering a triple-play package of voice, data and video services through a partnership with satellite provider Direct TV (766,000 customers); 12% of its primary mass markets lines are subscribing to the service. At the end of December 2007, 62% of its retail customers were receiving a bundle of two or more services from the company.

CORPORATE STRATEGY. During 2007 and 2008, Q was focused on reducing its operating expenses, aiming to improve its EBITDA margin. Q's headcount was reduced by 4% during 2007, and the company lowered its wireline facility costs. In addition, it was able to reduce its cost of sales due to adjustments to its pension accounting. In the first quarter of 2008, Q's voluntary retirement program resulted in a further workforce reduction and in the fourth quarter of 2008 Q plans to reduce an additional 3% of its staff.

## Company Financials Fiscal Year Ended Dec. 31

| Per Share Data ($) | 2007 | 2006 | 2005 | 2004 | 2003 | 2002 | 2001 | 2000 | 1999 | 1998 |
|---|---|---|---|---|---|---|---|---|---|---|
| Tangible Book Value | 0.32 | NM | NM | NM | NM | NM | 1.28 | 5.37 | 4.95 | 0.82 |
| Cash Flow | 2.80 | 1.51 | 1.26 | 0.74 | 1.07 | -7.65 | 0.83 | 2.56 | 1.13 | -1.15 |
| Earnings | 1.52 | 0.30 | -0.41 | -1.00 | -0.76 | -10.48 | -2.38 | -0.06 | 0.60 | -1.51 |
| S&P Core Earnings | 1.58 | 0.25 | -0.68 | -0.81 | -0.81 | -7.38 | -1.39 | NA | NA | NA |
| Dividends | Nil | Nil | Nil | Nil | Nil | Nil | 0.05 | Nil | Nil | Nil |
| Payout Ratio | Nil | Nil | Nil | Nil | Nil | Nil | NM | Nil | Nil | Nil |
| Prices:High | 10.45 | 9.22 | 5.95 | 5.00 | 6.15 | 15.19 | 48.19 | 66.00 | 52.38 | 25.66 |
| Prices:Low | 6.23 | 5.10 | 3.30 | 2.56 | 3.01 | 1.07 | 11.08 | 32.13 | 25.03 | 11.00 |
| P/E Ratio:High | 7 | 31 | NM | NM | NM | NM | NM | NM | 87 | NM |
| P/E Ratio:Low | 4 | 17 | NM | NM | NM | NM | NM | NM | 42 | NM |

| Income Statement Analysis (Million $) | 2007 | 2006 | 2005 | 2004 | 2003 | 2002 | 2001 | 2000 | 1999 | 1998 |
|---|---|---|---|---|---|---|---|---|---|---|
| Revenue | 13,778 | 13,923 | 13,903 | 13,809 | 14,288 | 15,385 | 19,695 | 16,610 | 3,928 | 2,243 |
| Depreciation | 2,459 | 2,381 | 3,065 | 3,123 | 3,167 | 3,847 | 5,335 | 3,342 | 404 | 202 |
| Maintenance | NA | NA | NA | NA | NA | NA | NA | NA | NA | NA |
| Construction Credits | NA | NA | NA | NA | NA | NA | NA | NA | NA | NA |
| Effective Tax Rate | NM | NM | NM | NM | NM | NM | NM | NM | 21.4% | NM |
| Net Income | 2,917 | 593 | -757 | -1,794 | -1,313 | -17,625 | -3,958 | -81.0 | 459 | -844 |
| S&P Core Earnings | 3,037 | 492 | -1,154 | -1,465 | -1,382 | -12,411 | -2,327 | NA | NA | NA |

| Balance Sheet & Other Financial Data (Million $) | 2007 | 2006 | 2005 | 2004 | 2003 | 2002 | 2001 | 2000 | 1999 | 1998 |
|---|---|---|---|---|---|---|---|---|---|---|
| Gross Property | 46,646 | 46,374 | 45,954 | 45,428 | 45,094 | 44,580 | 55,099 | 48,318 | 4,469 | 2,811 |
| Net Property | 13,671 | 14,579 | 15,568 | 16,853 | 18,149 | 18,995 | 29,977 | 25,583 | 4,109 | 2,655 |
| Capital Expenditures | 1,669 | 1,632 | 1,613 | 1,731 | 2,088 | 2,764 | 8,543 | 6,597 | 1,900 | 1,413 |
| Total Capital | 14,213 | 11,761 | 11,751 | 14,078 | 14,744 | 16,924 | 59,046 | 58,493 | 9,370 | 6,545 |
| Fixed Charges Coverage | 1.6 | 1.4 | 0.6 | NM | NM | 0.2 | 1.3 | 2.5 | 4.9 | 1.0 |
| Capitalization:Long Term Debt | 13,650 | 13,206 | 14,968 | 16,690 | 15,639 | 19,754 | 20,197 | 15,421 | 2,368 | 2,307 |
| Capitalization:Preferred | Nil | Nil | Nil | Nil | Nil | Nil | Nil | Nil | Nil | Nil |
| Capitalization:Common | 563 | -1,445 | -3,217 | -2,612 | -1,016 | -2,830 | 36,655 | 41,304 | 7,001 | 4,238 |
| % Return on Revenue | 21.2 | 4.3 | NM | NM | NM | NM | NM | NM | 11.7 | NM |
| % Return on Invested Capital | 31.0 | 15.0 | 8.1 | NM | NM | 12.4 | NM | 7.6 | 9.3 | 0.0 |
| % Return on Common Equity | NM | NM | NM | NM | NM | NM | NM | NM | 8.2 | NM |
| % Earned on Net Property | 12.4 | 10.3 | 5.3 | NM | 17.5 | 16.9 | 26.4 | 32.9 | 22.4 | 18.0 |
| % Long Term Debt of Capitalization | 96.0 | 112.3 | 127.4 | 118.6 | 106.9 | 116.7 | 34.2 | 27.2 | 25.3 | 35.2 |
| Capital % Preferred | Nil | Nil | Nil | Nil | Nil | Nil | Nil | Nil | Nil | Nil |
| Capitalization:% Common | 4.0 | -12.3 | -27.4 | -18.6 | -6.9 | -16.7 | 62.0 | 72.8 | 74.7 | 64.8 |

Data as orig reptd.; bef. results of disc opers/spec. items. Per share data adj. for stk. divs.; EPS diluted. E-Estimated. NA-Not Available. NM-Not Meaningful. NR-Not Ranked. UR-Under Review.

Office: 1801 California St, Denver, CO 80202-2658.
Telephone: 303-992-1400.
Email: investor.relations@qwest.com
Website: http://www.qwest.com

Chrmn & CEO: E.A. Mueller
COO: T.E. Richards
EVP & CFO: J.J. Euteneuer
EVP, Chief Admin Officer & General Counsel: R.N. Baer

SVP, Chief Acctg Officer & Cntlr: R.W. Johnston
Board Members: L. G. Alvarado, C. L. Biggs, K. D. Brooksher, P. S. Hellman, R. D. Hoover, P. J. Martin, C. S. Matthews, E. A. Mueller, W. W. Murdy, J. L. Murley, F. P. Popoff, J. A. Unruh, A. Welters

Founded: 1983
Domicile: Delaware
Employees: 37,000

# RadioShack Corp

**STANDARD & POOR'S**

| S&P Recommendation | HOLD ★★★☆☆ | Price | 12-Mo. Target Price | Investment Style |
|---|---|---|---|---|
| | | $9.65 (as of Nov 14, 2008) | $17.00 | Large-Cap Blend |

**GICS Sector** Consumer Discretionary
**Sub-Industry** Computer & Electronics Retail

**Summary** This consumer electronics retailer operates the RadioShack chain, which has about 7,000 outlets (including dealers/franchises).

## Key Stock Statistics (Source S&P, Vickers, company reports)

| | | | | | | | |
|---|---|---|---|---|---|---|---|
| 52-Wk Range | $20.34– 9.27 | S&P Oper. EPS 2008**E** | 1.77 | Market Capitalization(B) | $1.207 | Beta | 0.92 |
| Trailing 12-Month EPS | $1.77 | S&P Oper. EPS 2009**E** | 1.63 | Yield (%) | 2.59 | S&P 3-Yr. Proj. EPS CAGR(%) | 5 |
| Trailing 12-Month P/E | 5.5 | P/E on S&P Oper. EPS 2008**E** | 5.5 | Dividend Rate/Share | $0.25 | S&P Credit Rating | BB |
| $10K Invested 5 Yrs Ago | $3,221 | Common Shares Outstg. (M) | 125.1 | Institutional Ownership (%) | NM | | |

## Price Performance

30-Week Mov. Avg. · · · 10-Week Mov. Avg. – – **GAAP Earnings vs. Previous Year** Volume Above Avg. STARS
12-Mo. Target Price — Relative Strength — ▲ Up ▼ Down ► No Change Below Avg.

Options: ASE, CBOE, P

Analysis prepared by **Michael Souers** on October 27, 2008, when the stock traded at **$ 11.39.**

## Qualitative Risk Assessment

| LOW | MEDIUM | HIGH |
|---|---|---|

The company is the fifth largest player in a fragmented industry, with numerous suppliers and buyers, and a history of profitability. However, we view consumer electronics retailing as highly competitive, with numerous rivals and strong price competition.

## Quantitative Evaluations

**S&P Quality Ranking** B+

| D | C | B- | B | B+ | A- | A | A+ |
|---|---|---|---|---|---|---|---|

**Relative Strength Rank** MODERATE

31

LOWEST = 1 HIGHEST = 99

## Highlights

➤ We see sales declining 1.8% in 2009 following an expected 2.8% advance in 2008. We expect RSH to continue to focus on increasing profitability by opportunistically closing underperforming stores. We also look for the company to focus on lower-margin, faster-moving categories--such as MP3 players, video game equipment and digital cameras--to offset lost sales from continued weakness in wireless within RSH's core retail operations. We see comp-store sales declining in the low single-digits, driven by the challenging macroenvironment.

➤ We expect a slight narrowing in operating margins due to product mix shift and promotional selling, partially offset by continued cost-cutting efforts. We think that RSH will struggle to achieve historical gross margins due to increased competitive pressures and the company's focus on faster-moving, lower-margin categories.

➤ After taxes that we forecast at 38.0% and a slight decline in net interest expense, we project EPS of $1.63 in 2009, an 8% decrease from the $1.77 we project the company to earn in 2008, excluding one-time items.

## Investment Rationale/Risk

➤ We view the company in the middle stages of its turnaround plan, which is focused on increasing average unit volume, rationalizing its cost structure, and growing profitable square footage. While RSH's CEO has extensive retail experience with turnarounds, we think the longer-term outlook for the company is uncertain, due to the highly competitive environment for electronics products. Given our view of the company's lackluster longer-term sales outlook, we believe the risk/reward quotient for owning the shares is neutral, with the stock recently trading at about 7X our 2009 EPS estimate, a modest discount to peers.

➤ Risks to our recommendation and target price include an inability by management to rapidly execute its turnaround plan, and macroeconomic factors that could result in weaker than anticipated consumer spending levels.

➤ Our 12-month target price of $17, or about 10X our 2009 EPS estimate, is derived from our discounted cash flow analysis. Our DCF model assumes a weighted average cost of capital of 9.5% and a terminal growth rate of 3.0%.

## Revenue/Earnings Data

**Revenue (Million $)**

| | 1Q | 2Q | 3Q | 4Q | Year |
|---|---|---|---|---|---|
| 2008 | 949.0 | 994.9 | 1,022 | -- | -- |
| 2007 | 992.3 | 934.8 | 960.3 | 1,364 | 4,252 |
| 2006 | 1,160 | 1,100 | 1,060 | 1,458 | 4,778 |
| 2005 | 1,123 | 1,092 | 1,195 | 1,672 | 5,082 |
| 2004 | 1,093 | 1,054 | 1,102 | 1,593 | 4,841 |
| 2003 | 1,070 | 1,025 | 1,064 | 1,490 | 4,649 |

**Earnings Per Share ($)**

| | 1Q | 2Q | 3Q | 4Q | Year |
|---|---|---|---|---|---|
| 2008 | 0.30 | 0.32 | 0.39 | E0.76 | E1.77 |
| 2007 | 0.31 | 0.34 | 0.34 | 0.77 | 1.74 |
| 2006 | 0.06 | -0.02 | -0.12 | 0.62 | 0.54 |
| 2005 | 0.34 | 0.33 | 0.75 | 0.40 | 1.81 |
| 2004 | 0.41 | 0.42 | 0.43 | 0.81 | 2.08 |
| 2003 | 0.33 | 0.34 | 0.34 | 0.77 | 1.77 |

Fiscal year ended Dec. 31. Next earnings report expected: Late February. EPS Estimates based on S&P Operating Earnings; historical GAAP earnings are as reported.

## Dividend Data (Dates: mm/dd Payment Date: mm/dd/yy)

| Amount ($) | Date Decl. | Ex-Div. Date | Stk. of Record | Payment Date |
|---|---|---|---|---|
| 0.250 | 11/12 | 11/27 | 11/29 | 12/19/07 |
| 0.250 | 11/07 | 11/25 | 11/28 | 12/17/08 |

Dividends have been paid since 1987. Source: Company reports.

The McGraw-Hill Companies

# RadioShack Corp

STANDARD &POOR'S

## Business Summary October 27, 2008

CORPORATE OVERVIEW. As of December 31, 2007, this consumer electronics retailer had 4,447 company-operated stores located through the U.S., including Puerto Rico and the U.S. Virgin Islands. RSH also had a network of 1,484 dealer/franchise stores, including 36 located outside the U.S. At the end of 2007, RSH operated 739 non-RadioShack branded kiosks, which offer product lines such as wireless phones and associated accessories.

Each store carries an assortment of electronic parts, batteries and accessories; wireless and conventional phones; flat panel televisions; DVD players; direct-to-home (DTH) satellite systems; PCs; home entertainment, wireless and other computer accessories; wire, cable and connectivity products; digital cameras; and specialized products such as home air cleaners and unique toys. RSH also provides access to third-party services, such as cellular and PCS phone and DTH satellite activation, long-distance telephone service, prepaid wireless airtime, and extended service plans. We believe that RSH is focusing on revamping its product offerings in order to enhance its competitive position within the consumer electronics industry. In the second half of 2005, RSH began dedicating floor space to Apple's iPod and accessories, a rapidly growing consumer electronics category, and the company made a concerted push to sell video gaming products in 2007, another hot product category.

MARKET PROFILE. The domestic consumer electronics industry generated $148.1 billion in sales in 2006, according to the Consumer Electronics Association (CEA), a 13.7% increase from the $130.3 billion generated in 2005. Total industry sales are forecast to rise 8.2% in 2007, to $160.3 billion. For 2006, we estimate that RSH will have a market share of approximately 3%, trailing competitors such as Best Buy, Wal-Mart, Circuit City, and Dell. We expect pure-play electronics retailers to see increased competition from discounters and mass merchants as these companies have been ramping up their consumer electronics offerings to take advantage of what we view as a strong technology cycle. We believe that, historically, RSH has differentiated itself from big box competitors due to its heavy emphasis on high margin, smaller ticket items such as batteries and accessories. Along these lines, RSH's smaller store format does not afford the company the opportunity to capitalize on the strong demand for advanced televisions.

## Company Financials Fiscal Year Ended Dec. 31

| Per Share Data ($) | 2007 | 2006 | 2005 | 2004 | 2003 | 2002 | 2001 | 2000 | 1999 | 1998 |
|---|---|---|---|---|---|---|---|---|---|---|
| Tangible Book Value | 5.88 | 4.81 | 4.36 | 5.83 | 4.73 | 4.24 | 4.04 | 4.46 | 3.70 | 3.84 |
| Cash Flow | 2.57 | 1.48 | 2.65 | 2.70 | 2.31 | 1.97 | 1.41 | 2.38 | 1.87 | 0.73 |
| Earnings | 1.74 | 0.54 | 1.81 | 2.08 | 1.77 | 1.45 | 0.85 | 1.84 | 1.43 | 0.27 |
| S&P Core Earnings | 1.74 | 0.67 | 1.69 | 1.94 | 1.49 | 1.18 | 1.06 | NA | NA | NA |
| Dividends | 0.25 | 0.25 | 0.25 | 0.25 | 0.25 | 0.22 | 0.22 | 0.22 | 0.15 | 0.20 |
| Payout Ratio | 14% | 46% | 14% | 12% | 14% | 15% | 25% | 12% | 10% | 74% |
| Prices:High | 35.00 | 23.37 | 34.48 | 36.24 | 32.48 | 36.21 | 56.50 | 72.94 | 79.50 | 31.94 |
| Prices:Low | 16.69 | 13.73 | 20.55 | 26.04 | 18.74 | 16.99 | 20.10 | 35.06 | 20.59 | 15.19 |
| P/E Ratio:High | 20 | 43 | 19 | 17 | 18 | 25 | 66 | 40 | 56 | NM |
| P/E Ratio:Low | 10 | 25 | 11 | 13 | 11 | 12 | 24 | 19 | 14 | NM |

| Income Statement Analysis (Million $) | | | | | | | | | | |
|---|---|---|---|---|---|---|---|---|---|---|
| Revenue | 4,252 | 4,778 | 5,082 | 4,841 | 4,649 | 4,577 | 4,776 | 4,795 | 4,126 | 4,788 |
| Operating Income | 464 | 329 | 474 | 660 | 576 | 510 | 583 | 736 | 597 | 424 |
| Depreciation | 113 | 128 | 124 | 101 | 92.0 | 94.7 | 108 | 107 | 90.2 | 99.0 |
| Interest Expense | 38.8 | 44.3 | 44.5 | 29.6 | 35.7 | 43.4 | 50.8 | 53.9 | 37.2 | 45.4 |
| Pretax Income | 367 | 111 | 322 | 542 | 473 | 425 | 292 | 594 | 481 | 99.7 |
| Effective Tax Rate | 35.4% | 34.1% | 16.0% | 37.8% | 36.9% | 38.0% | 42.8% | 38.0% | 38.0% | 38.5% |
| Net Income | 237 | 73.4 | 270 | 337 | 299 | 263 | 167 | 368 | 298 | 61.3 |
| S&P Core Earnings | 236 | 92.3 | 251 | 315 | 252 | 211 | 200 | NA | NA | NA |

| Balance Sheet & Other Financial Data (Million $) | | | | | | | | | | |
|---|---|---|---|---|---|---|---|---|---|---|
| Cash | 510 | 472 | 224 | 438 | 635 | 447 | 401 | 131 | 165 | 64.5 |
| Current Assets | 1,567 | 1,600 | 1,627 | 1,775 | 1,667 | 1,707 | 1,714 | 1,818 | 1,403 | 1,299 |
| Total Assets | 1,990 | 2,070 | 2,205 | 2,517 | 2,244 | 1,707 | 2,245 | 2,577 | 2,142 | 1,994 |
| Current Liabilities | 748 | 984 | 986 | 957 | 858 | 829 | 826 | 1,232 | 925 | 880 |
| Long Term Debt | 348 | 346 | 495 | 507 | 541 | 591 | 565 | 303 | 319 | 235 |
| Common Equity | 770 | 654 | 589 | 922 | 769 | 729 | 714 | 812 | 758 | 748 |
| Total Capital | 1,118 | 1,000 | 1,084 | 1,429 | 1,311 | 1,320 | 1,344 | 1,284 | 1,150 | 1,083 |
| Capital Expenditures | 45.3 | 91.0 | 171 | 229 | 190 | 107 | 139 | 120 | 102 | 132 |
| Cash Flow | 350 | 202 | 394 | 439 | 391 | 354 | 270 | 470 | 383 | 155 |
| Current Ratio | 2.1 | 1.6 | 1.6 | 1.9 | 1.9 | 2.1 | 2.1 | 1.5 | 1.5 | 1.5 |
| % Long Term Debt of Capitalization | 31.1 | 34.6 | 45.7 | 35.5 | 41.3 | 44.8 | 42.1 | 23.6 | 27.8 | 21.7 |
| % Net Income of Revenue | 5.6 | 1.5 | 5.3 | 7.0 | 6.4 | 5.8 | 3.5 | 7.7 | 7.2 | 1.3 |
| % Return on Assets | 11.7 | 3.4 | 11.4 | 14.2 | 13.4 | 13.3 | 6.9 | 15.6 | 14.4 | 2.8 |
| % Return on Equity | 33.3 | 11.8 | 35.7 | 39.9 | 39.9 | 35.9 | 21.2 | 46.2 | 38.8 | 6.5 |

Data as orig reptd.; bef. results of disc opers/spec. items. Per share data adj. for stk. divs.; EPS diluted. E-Estimated. NA-Not Available. NM-Not Meaningful. NR-Not Ranked. UR-Under Review.

**Office:** 300 Radioshack Cir, Fort Worth, TX 76102-1964.
**Telephone:** 817-415-3011.
**Email:** investor.relations@radioshack.com
**Website:** http://www.radioshack.com

**Chrmn & CEO:** J.C. Day
**COO:** M. Carter
**EVP & CFO:** J.F. Gooch
**Chief Acctg Officer, Treas & Cntlr:** M.O. Moad

**Secy & General Counsel:** R.C. Donohoo
**Board Members:** F. J. Belatti, J. C. Day, R. S. Falcone, D. R. Feehan, R. J. Hernandez, H. E. Lockhart, J. L. Messman, T. G. Plaskett, E. D. Woodbury

**Founded:** 1899
**Domicile:** Delaware
**Employees:** 35,800

# Range Resources Corp.

**STANDARD &POOR'S**

| S&P Recommendation **BUY** ★★★★☆ | Price $40.62 (as of Nov 14, 2008) | 12-Mo. Target Price $39.00 | Investment Style Large-Cap Growth |

**GICS Sector** Energy
**Sub-Industry** Oil & Gas Exploration & Production

**Summary** This company explores, develops and acquires oil and gas properties, primarily in the Southwest, Appalachian and Gulf Coast regions of the U.S.

## Key Stock Statistics (Source S&P, Vickers, company reports)

| | | | | | | | | |
|---|---|---|---|---|---|---|---|---|
| 52-Wk Range | $76.81– 23.77 | S&P Oper. EPS 2008E | 2.01 | Market Capitalization(B) | $6.310 | Beta | 1.05 |
| Trailing 12-Month EPS | $1.85 | S&P Oper. EPS 2009E | 1.83 | Yield (%) | 0.39 | S&P 3-Yr. Proj. EPS CAGR(%) | 5 |
| Trailing 12-Month P/E | 22.0 | P/E on S&P Oper. EPS 2008E | 20.2 | Dividend Rate/Share | $0.16 | S&P Credit Rating | BB |
| $10K Invested 5 Yrs Ago | $77,643 | Common Shares Outstg. (M) | 155.3 | Institutional Ownership (%) | 91 | | |

## Price Performance

30-Week Mov. Avg. · · · 10-Week Mov. Avg. – – GAAP Earnings vs. Previous Year Volume Above Avg. STARS
12-Mo. Target Price — Relative Strength — ▲ Up ▼ Down ► No Change Below Avg.

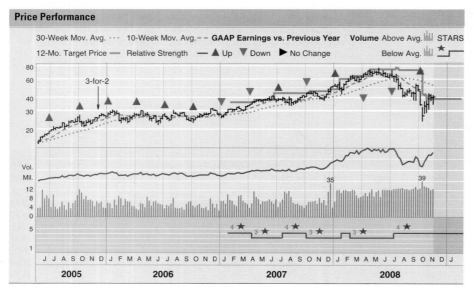

Options: ASE, CBOE, P, Ph

Analysis prepared by **Michael Kay** on October 29, 2008, when the stock traded at **$ 36.63**.

## Highlights

➤ We expect production boosts of 20% and 14% in 2008 and 2009, respectively, driven by the Devonian Shale play in the Nora field coal-bed methane (CBM) project in Virginia, excellent results in the Fort Worth Basin, an encouraging horizontal program at the Marcellus Shale play, and a significantly increased acreage position in the Barnett Shale. Despite some hurricane related curtailments, RRC exhibited strong third quarter growth through exceptional drilling results across its core regions.

➤ Cost controls remain encouraging, as lease operating expense (LOE) in 2007 was $1.28 per Mcfe, flat in a rising cost environment, and we see LOE up 13% and DD&A up 15% in 2008. We expect EBITDA growth of 73% in 2008 on production growth and strong oil and gas prices.

➤ With an expected boost in production and RRC's current hedge position -- about 69% of 2008 production at an average floor price of $8.84 per Mcf -- we see operating EPS of $2.01 in 2008, including $0.12 in non-cash derivative losses through nine months, and $1.83 in 2009 as we project lower oil and gas prices. RRC's 2008 capital budget is $1.27 billion, up from $850 million in 2007 and $612 million in 2006.

## Investment Rationale/Risk

➤ Through 2007, RRC posted a 3-year reserve CAGR of 17% with a reserve life of 17.7 years. Average 3-year reserve replacement of 459% (348% organic) and average 3-year finding and development costs of $1.86/Mcf demonstrate its ability to replace reserves at attractive prices, in our view. Most reserves are based in Appalachia, where economics appear attractive. With the acceleration of development in the Marcellus Shale, and a new processing facility, RRC estimates production from the play of 80-100 MMcfe/d by year-end 2009.

➤ Risks to our recommendation and target price include a sustained decline in oil and gas prices, an inability to replace reserves at reasonable costs, and production declines.

➤ A drop in oil and gas prices has caused a similar decline in exploration and production shares. On weakening economic forecasts, we see markets discounting probable reserve estimates, and we now value companies on our proven reserve NAV estimates. Our 12-month target price of $39 blends our proven NAV per share estimate, a target enterprise value to 2009 EBITDA ratio of 7X, and our DCF ($42; WACC 11.4%, terminal growth 3%).

## Qualitative Risk Assessment

| LOW | MEDIUM | **HIGH** |

Our risk assessment reflects the company's operations in a capital intensive industry that is cyclical and derives value from producing a commodity whose price is very volatile.

## Quantitative Evaluations

**S&P Quality Ranking** **B**

| D | C | B- | **B** | B+ | A- | A | A+ |

**Relative Strength Rank** **STRONG**

90

LOWEST = 1    HIGHEST = 99

## Revenue/Earnings Data

### Revenue (Million $)

| | 1Q | 2Q | 3Q | 4Q | Year |
|---|---|---|---|---|---|
| 2008 | 308.7 | 348.9 | 622.7 | -- | -- |
| 2007 | 152.8 | 243.5 | 242.4 | 223.4 | 868.9 |
| 2006 | 189.2 | 177.6 | 228.9 | 184.1 | 779.7 |
| 2005 | 108.0 | 119.7 | 141.9 | 166.5 | 536.0 |
| 2004 | 63.53 | 68.70 | 86.21 | 102.3 | 320.7 |
| 2003 | 56.97 | 54.72 | 76.16 | 61.35 | 249.2 |

### Earnings Per Share ($)

| | | | | | |
|---|---|---|---|---|---|
| 2008 | 0.01 | -0.23 | 1.81 | E0.43 | E2.01 |
| 2007 | 0.06 | 0.43 | 0.39 | 0.22 | 1.11 |
| 2006 | 0.41 | 0.37 | 0.46 | 0.19 | 1.42 |
| 2005 | 0.18 | 0.17 | 0.19 | 0.32 | 0.86 |
| 2004 | 0.07 | 0.08 | 0.11 | 0.11 | 0.38 |
| 2003 | 0.06 | 0.05 | 0.19 | 0.05 | 0.35 |

Fiscal year ended Dec. 31. Next earnings report expected: Late February. EPS Estimates based on S&P Operating Earnings; historical GAAP earnings are as reported.

## Dividend Data (Dates: mm/dd Payment Date: mm/dd/yy)

| Amount ($) | Date Decl. | Ex-Div. Date | Stk. of Record | Payment Date |
|---|---|---|---|---|
| 0.040 | 12/03 | 12/13 | 12/17 | 12/31/07 |
| 0.040 | 03/03 | 03/13 | 03/17 | 03/31/08 |
| 0.040 | 06/02 | 06/12 | 06/16 | 06/30/08 |
| 0.040 | 09/02 | 09/12 | 09/16 | 09/30/08 |

Dividends have been paid since 2004. Source: Company reports.

**Please read the Required Disclosures and Analyst Certification on the last page of this report.**

*The McGraw-Hill Companies*

# Range Resources Corp.

## Business Summary October 29, 2008

CORPORATE OVERVIEW. Range Resources Corp. is an independent oil and gas company primarily engaged in acquiring, developing, exploring and producing oil and gas properties. RRC has established three core operating areas in the Appalachian, Southwestern and Gulf Coast regions of the U.S. The Southwest business unit encompasses operations in East Texas, West Texas, New Mexico, and the Mid-continent region of Oklahoma and the Texas Panhandle.

As of December 31, 2007, RRC had estimated proved reserves of 2.23 Tcfe, of which 82% was natural gas and 64% was proved developed. This compares with estimated proved reserves of 1.76 Tcfe, 82% natural gas and 63% proved developed, at the end of 2006, a 27% increase. We forecast RRC's reserve life to be 17.7 years, compared to 17.4 years at the end of 2006.

RRC estimates that it replaced 537% (450% in 2006) of production in 2007, including 424% (377%) from drilling. We estimate finding and development costs (exclude acquisitions) in 2007 were $1.81 per Mcfe versus a three-year average of $1.87 per Mcfe. Total reserve replacement costs (including acquisitions) in 2007 were $1.83 per Mcfe, versus a three-year average of $1.84 per Mcfe.

CORPORATE STRATEGY. RRC pursues what we consider a balanced growth strategy that targets the exploitation of its inventory of development drilling locations, higher potential exploration projects, and acquisitions. RRC focuses on acquisition opportunities within its core operating areas to capitalize on regional expertise and drive down costs.

In June 2006, RRC completed the acquisition of Stroud Energy for $465.2 million, including $278 million in cash. RRC purchased 171 Bcfe of proved reserves located primarily in the Barnett Shale play of North Texas, the Cotton Valley play of East Texas and the Austin Chalk play of Central Texas. RRC has a goal of doubling production in this region over the next 12 months.

IMPACT OF MAJOR DEVELOPMENTS. In February 2007, RRC completed the sale of its Austin Chalk assets acquired in the Stroud Energy transaction in 2006 for $82 million. RRC originally stated its intention to sell the assets In late July 2006, just as natural gas prices fell into a fairly steep decline, and RRC had difficulty selling the assets.

## Company Financials Fiscal Year Ended Dec. 31

| Per Share Data ($) | 2007 | 2006 | 2005 | 2004 | 2003 | 2002 | 2001 | 2000 | 1999 | 1998 |
|---|---|---|---|---|---|---|---|---|---|---|
| Tangible Book Value | 11.57 | 9.04 | 5.36 | 4.65 | 3.24 | 2.50 | 3.11 | 2.43 | 1.73 | 1.94 |
| Cash Flow | 2.59 | 2.65 | 1.84 | 1.43 | 1.34 | 1.23 | 1.05 | 1.23 | 1.15 | -3.01 |
| Earnings | 1.11 | 1.42 | 0.86 | 0.38 | 0.35 | 0.29 | 0.07 | 0.38 | -0.23 | -4.55 |
| S&P Core Earnings | 1.11 | 1.42 | 0.82 | 0.29 | 0.33 | 0.29 | 0.18 | NA | NA | NA |
| Dividends | 0.13 | 0.09 | 0.07 | 0.03 | Nil | Nil | Nil | Nil | 0.02 | 0.08 |
| Payout Ratio | 12% | 6% | 8% | 9% | Nil | Nil | Nil | Nil | NM | NM |
| Prices:High | 51.88 | 31.77 | 28.37 | 14.43 | 6.57 | 3.97 | 4.75 | 4.67 | 4.75 | 11.67 |
| Prices:Low | 25.29 | 21.74 | 12.34 | 6.25 | 3.33 | 2.69 | 2.62 | 0.96 | 1.04 | 1.92 |
| P/E Ratio:High | 47 | 22 | 33 | 38 | 19 | 14 | 65 | 12 | NM | NM |
| P/E Ratio:Low | 23 | 15 | 14 | 16 | 9 | 9 | 36 | 3 | NM | NM |

| Income Statement Analysis (Million $) | | | | | | | | | | |
|---|---|---|---|---|---|---|---|---|---|---|
| Revenue | 857 | 780 | 536 | 321 | 230 | 195 | 219 | 188 | 161 | 142 |
| Operating Income | 560 | 549 | 344 | 193 | 140 | 119 | 152 | 132 | 102 | 74.8 |
| Depreciation, Depletion and Amortization | 221 | 170 | 128 | 103 | 86.5 | 76.8 | 77.8 | 72.2 | 76.4 | 60.2 |
| Interest Expense | 77.7 | 57.6 | 38.8 | 23.1 | 22.2 | 23.2 | 30.7 | 40.0 | 47.1 | 40.6 |
| Pretax Income | 266 | 321 | 177 | 66.8 | 49.4 | 19.3 | 4.99 | 18.6 | -8.62 | -230 |
| Effective Tax Rate | 37.2% | 38.5% | 37.4% | 36.8% | 37.4% | NM | NM | NM | NM | NM |
| Net Income | 167 | 198 | 111 | 42.2 | 30.9 | 23.8 | 5.05 | 20.2 | -10.2 | -175 |
| S&P Core Earnings | 167 | 198 | 105 | 27.9 | 27.3 | 23.5 | 14.1 | NA | NA | NA |

| Balance Sheet & Other Financial Data (Million $) | | | | | | | | | | |
|---|---|---|---|---|---|---|---|---|---|---|
| Cash | 4.02 | 2.38 | 4.75 | 18.4 | 0.63 | 1.33 | 3.25 | 2.48 | 15.1 | 14.2 |
| Current Assets | 262 | 320 | 208 | 136 | 66.1 | 37.4 | 78.6 | 62.1 | 72.9 | 107 |
| Total Assets | 4,017 | 3,188 | 2,019 | 1,595 | 830 | 658 | 692 | 689 | 752 | 922 |
| Current Liabilities | 305 | 232 | 322 | 177 | 107 | 67.2 | 44.0 | 45.9 | 53.6 | 116 |
| Long Term Debt | 1,151 | 1,049 | 616 | 621 | 358 | 368 | 392 | 458 | 572 | 672 |
| Common Equity | 1,728 | 1,346 | 770 | 566 | 224 | 206 | 246 | 185 | 126 | 132 |
| Total Capital | 3,470 | 2,864 | 1,561 | 1,305 | 643 | 574 | 648 | 643 | 699 | 805 |
| Capital Expenditures | 808 | 517 | 277 | 175 | 2.62 | 2.82 | 2.33 | 2.26 | 0.66 | 139 |
| Cash Flow | 388 | 367 | 239 | 140 | 117 | 101 | 82.9 | 91.0 | 63.9 | -117 |
| Current Ratio | 0.9 | 1.4 | 0.6 | 0.8 | 0.6 | 0.6 | 1.8 | 1.4 | 1.4 | 0.9 |
| % Long Term Debt of Capitalization | 33.1 | 36.6 | 39.5 | 47.6 | 55.7 | 64.1 | 60.6 | 71.2 | 81.8 | 83.5 |
| % Return on Assets | 4.7 | 7.6 | 6.1 | 3.5 | 4.2 | 3.5 | 0.7 | 2.8 | NM | NM |
| % Return on Equity | 10.9 | 18.7 | 16.1 | 9.4 | 14.0 | 10.8 | 2.3 | 12.1 | NM | NM |

Data as orig reptd.; bef. results of disc opers/spec. items. Per share data adj. for stk. divs.; EPS diluted. E-Estimated. NA-Not Available. NM-Not Meaningful. NR-Not Ranked. UR-Under Review.

**Office:** 100 Throckmorton St Ste 1200, Fort Worth, TX 76102-2842.
**Telephone:** 817-870-2601.
**Website:** http://www.rangeresources.com
**Chrmn & CEO:** J.H. Pinkerton

**Pres & COO:** J.L. Ventura
**EVP, CFO & Chief Acctg Officer:** R.S. Manny
**SVP, Secy & General Counsel:** D.P. Poole
**Investor Contact:** R.L. Waller (817-870-2601)

**Board Members:** C. L. Blackburn, A. V. Dub, V. R. Eales, A. Finkelson, J. S. Linker, K. S. McCarthy, J. H. Pinkerton, J. L. Ventura

**Founded:** 1976
**Domicile:** Delaware
**Employees:** 733

# Raytheon Co.

**STANDARD &POOR'S**

| S&P Recommendation | BUY ★★★★☆ | Price<br>$47.91 (as of Nov 14, 2008) | 12-Mo. Target Price<br>$57.00 | Investment Style<br>Large-Cap Value |
|---|---|---|---|---|

**GICS Sector** Industrials
**Sub-Industry** Aerospace & Defense

**Summary** Raytheon, the world's fifth largest military contractor, specializes in making high-tech missiles and electronics.

## Key Stock Statistics (Source S&P, Vickers, company reports)

| | | | | | | | |
|---|---|---|---|---|---|---|---|
| 52-Wk Range | $67.49– 41.81 | S&P Oper. EPS 2009**E** | 4.25 | Market Capitalization(B) | $19.838 | Beta | 0.60 |
| Trailing 12-Month EPS | $4.30 | S&P Oper. EPS 2010**E** | NA | Yield (%) | 2.34 | S&P 3-Yr. Proj. EPS CAGR(%) | 11 |
| Trailing 12-Month P/E | 11.1 | P/E on S&P Oper. EPS 2009**E** | 11.3 | Dividend Rate/Share | $1.12 | S&P Credit Rating | A- |
| $10K Invested 5 Yrs Ago | $19,187 | Common Shares Outstg. (M) | 414.1 | Institutional Ownership (%) | 80 | | |

## Price Performance

30-Week Mov. Avg. ···   10-Week Mov. Avg. --   **GAAP Earnings vs. Previous Year**   Volume Above Avg. ▮▮▮ STARS
12-Mo. Target Price —   Relative Strength —   ▲ Up  ▼ Down  ► No Change        Below Avg. ▮▮▮ ★

Options: ASE, CBOE, P

## Qualitative Risk Assessment

| LOW | MEDIUM | HIGH |
|---|---|---|

Our risk assessment reflects RTN's exposure to changes in defense spending and historically below-average earnings stability, offset by its relatively low long-term debt to capital ratio of 16%, as of December 2007, its leading defense contractor status, and its large project backlog.

## Quantitative Evaluations

**S&P Quality Ranking**      B

| D | C | B- | **B** | B+ | A- | A | A+ |
|---|---|---|---|---|---|---|---|

**Relative Strength Rank**      STRONG

77

LOWEST = 1      HIGHEST = 99

## Highlights

► The 12-month target price for RTN has recently been changed to $57.00 from $55.00. The Highlights section of this Stock Report will be updated accordingly.

## Investment Rationale/Risk

► The Investment Rationale/Risk section of this Stock Report will be updated shortly. For the latest News story on RTN from MarketScope, see below.

► 10/23/08 11:02 am ET ... S&P REITERATES BUY OPINION ON SHARES OF RAYTHEON (RTN 47.37****): Q3 EPS of $1.01 vs. $0.86 on 12% sales growth exceeds our $0.93 estimate. We are raising our '08 EPS forecast by $0.07 to $3.98 and '09's by $0.30 to $4.55, on a projected stronger performance in all business segments. Funded backlog rose 21%, year-to-year, to $21B. We are predicating our '09 estimate on about 6% sales growth, supported by moderate productivity improvement and a lower share count. We are also raising our 12-month target price by $2 to $57 on our increased estimates. We note that valuations on the shares remain low on several measures by historical standards. /R.Tortoriello

## Revenue/Earnings Data

### Revenue (Million $)

| | 1Q | 2Q | 3Q | 4Q | Year |
|---|---|---|---|---|---|
| 2008 | 5,354 | 5,870 | 5,864 | -- | -- |
| 2007 | 4,928 | 5,419 | 5,355 | 6,000 | 21,301 |
| 2006 | 4,660 | 4,973 | 4,936 | 5,722 | 20,291 |
| 2005 | 4,944 | 5,409 | 5,331 | 6,210 | 21,894 |
| 2004 | 4,676 | 4,929 | 4,936 | 5,704 | 20,245 |
| 2003 | 4,201 | 4,429 | 4,378 | 5,101 | 18,109 |

### Earnings Per Share ($)

| | 1Q | 2Q | 3Q | 4Q | Year |
|---|---|---|---|---|---|
| 2008 | 0.93 | 1.00 | 1.01 | E1.06 | E3.91 |
| 2007 | 0.69 | 0.79 | 0.69 | 1.45 | 3.80 |
| 2006 | 0.61 | 0.61 | 0.59 | 0.81 | 2.46 |
| 2005 | 0.43 | 0.51 | 0.51 | 0.63 | 2.08 |
| 2004 | 0.24 | -0.22 | 0.41 | 0.54 | 0.99 |
| 2003 | 0.27 | 0.45 | 0.05 | 0.52 | 1.29 |

Fiscal year ended Dec. 31. Next earnings report expected: Early February. EPS Estimates based on S&P Operating Earnings; historical GAAP earnings are as reported.

## Dividend Data (Dates: mm/dd Payment Date: mm/dd/yy)

| Amount<br>($) | Date<br>Decl. | Ex-Div.<br>Date | Stk. of<br>Record | Payment<br>Date |
|---|---|---|---|---|
| 0.255 | 12/12 | 12/31 | 01/03 | 01/31/08 |
| 0.280 | 03/26 | 03/28 | 04/01 | 04/29/08 |
| 0.280 | 06/27 | 07/08 | 07/10 | 08/07/08 |
| 0.280 | 09/25 | 10/03 | 10/07 | 11/04/08 |

Dividends have been paid since 1964. Source: Company reports.

---

**Please read the Required Disclosures and Analyst Certification on the last page of this report.**

# Raytheon Co.

**STANDARD**
**&POOR'S**

## Business Summary September 22, 2008

CORPORATE OVERVIEW. Raytheon, the world's fifth largest military contractor and a leading maker of missiles, conducts business through six business segments.

Integrated Defense Systems (20% of sales and 29% of operating profits in 2007) is a leading provider of integrated joint battlespace (e.g., space, air, surface, and subsurface) and homeland security solutions. Customers include the U.S. Missile Defense Agency (MDA), the U.S. Armed Forces, the Dept. of Homeland Security, as well as key international customers. Main product lines include seapower capability systems, focusing on the DDG-1000, the Navy's next-generation naval destroyer; national & theater security programs, including the X-band radars and missile defense systems; Patriot programs, principally the Patriot Air & Missile Defense System; global operations; and civil security and response programs.

Intelligence & Information Systems (12% of sales and 9% of profits) provides systems, subsystems, and software engineering services for national and tactical intelligence systems, as well as for homeland security and information technology (IT) solutions. Areas of concentration include signals and image processing, geospatial intelligence, air and space borne command & control, weather and environmental management, information technology, information

assurance, and homeland security.

Missile Systems (22% of sales and 19% of profits) makes and supports a broad range of leading-edge solutions and products for the armed forces of the U.S. and other countries. Business areas include naval weapon systems, which provides defensive missiles and guided projectiles to the navies of over 30 countries; strike, with products focused on ground-based targets, including the Tomahawk cruise missile; air-to-air missiles; land combat, which includes the Javelin anti-tank missile; and other programs.

Network Centric Systems (18% of sales and 18% of profits) makes mission solutions for networking, command and control, battle space awareness, and transportation management. Major programs include command and control systems, integrated communication systems, networked sensor systems and homeland security, as well as civil applications and components to create these systems. Major customers include the U.S. Armed Forces, the Federal Aviation Administration, and numerous international customers.

## Company Financials Fiscal Year Ended Dec. 31

| Per Share Data ($) | 2008 | 2007 | 2006 | 2005 | 2004 | 2003 | 2002 | 2001 | 2000 | 1999 |
|---|---|---|---|---|---|---|---|---|---|---|
| Tangible Book Value | NA | 2.15 | NM | NM | NM | NM | NM | NM | NM | NM |
| Cash Flow | NA | 4.63 | 3.28 | 3.19 | 1.93 | 2.22 | 2.74 | 2.03 | 3.50 | 3.46 |
| Earnings | 3.91 | 3.80 | 2.46 | 2.08 | 0.99 | 1.29 | 1.85 | 0.01 | 1.46 | 1.34 |
| S&P Core Earnings | NA | 4.15 | 3.10 | 2.61 | 1.96 | 1.11 | -0.25 | -2.68 | NA | NA |
| Dividends | 0.56 | 1.02 | 0.96 | 0.86 | 0.80 | 0.80 | 0.80 | 0.80 | 0.80 | 0.80 |
| Payout Ratio | 14% | 27% | 34% | 41% | 81% | 62% | 43% | NM | 55% | 60% |
| Prices:High | 67.49 | 65.94 | 54.17 | 40.57 | 41.89 | 33.97 | 45.70 | 37.44 | 35.81 | 76.56 |
| Prices:Low | 54.50 | 50.96 | 39.43 | 35.96 | 29.28 | 24.31 | 26.30 | 23.95 | 17.50 | 22.19 |
| P/E Ratio:High | 17 | 17 | 19 | 21 | 42 | 26 | 25 | NM | 25 | 57 |
| P/E Ratio:Low | 14 | 13 | 14 | 19 | 30 | 19 | 14 | NM | 12 | 17 |

| Income Statement Analysis (Million $) | | | | | | | | | | |
|---|---|---|---|---|---|---|---|---|---|---|
| Revenue | NA | 21,301 | 20,291 | 21,894 | 20,245 | 18,109 | 16,760 | 16,867 | 16,895 | 19,841 |
| Operating Income | NA | 2,700 | 2,213 | 2,131 | 1,822 | 1,709 | 2,118 | 1,488 | 2,319 | 2,251 |
| Depreciation | NA | 372 | 373 | 444 | 434 | 393 | 364 | 729 | 694 | 724 |
| Interest Expense | NA | 196 | 273 | 312 | 418 | 537 | 497 | 660 | 736 | 713 |
| Pretax Income | NA | 2,225 | 1,688 | 1,440 | 579 | 762 | 1,074 | 117 | 877 | 828 |
| Effective Tax Rate | NA | 23.9% | 34.4% | 34.6% | 24.2% | 29.8% | 29.7% | 95.7% | 43.2% | 44.8% |
| Net Income | NA | 1,693 | 1,107 | 942 | 439 | 535 | 755 | 5.00 | 498 | 457 |
| S&P Core Earnings | NA | 1,848 | 1,392 | 1,180 | 866 | 460 | -105 | -970 | NA | NA |

| Balance Sheet & Other Financial Data (Million $) | | | | | | | | | | |
|---|---|---|---|---|---|---|---|---|---|---|
| Cash | NA | 2,655 | 2,460 | 1,202 | 556 | 661 | 544 | 1,214 | 871 | 230 |
| Current Assets | NA | 7,616 | 9,517 | 7,567 | 7,124 | 6,585 | 7,190 | 8,362 | 8,013 | 8,931 |
| Total Assets | NA | 23,281 | 25,491 | 24,381 | 24,153 | 23,668 | 23,946 | 26,636 | 26,777 | 28,110 |
| Current Liabilities | NA | 4,788 | 6,715 | 5,900 | 5,644 | 3,849 | 5,107 | 5,753 | 4,865 | 7,886 |
| Long Term Debt | NA | 2,268 | 3,278 | 3,969 | 4,637 | 7,376 | 7,138 | 6,875 | 9,054 | 7,298 |
| Common Equity | NA | 12,542 | 11,101 | 10,798 | 10,611 | 9,162 | 8,870 | 11,290 | 10,823 | 10,959 |
| Total Capital | NA | 15,261 | 14,544 | 15,011 | 15,345 | 16,538 | 16,008 | 18,743 | 20,650 | 18,810 |
| Capital Expenditures | NA | 313 | 295 | 75.0 | 363 | 428 | 458 | 486 | 431 | 532 |
| Cash Flow | NA | 2,065 | 1,480 | 1,386 | 873 | 928 | 1,119 | 734 | 1,192 | 1,181 |
| Current Ratio | NA | 1.6 | 1.4 | 1.3 | 1.3 | 1.7 | 1.4 | 1.5 | 1.6 | 1.1 |
| % Long Term Debt of Capitalization | NA | 14.9 | 22.5 | 26.4 | 30.2 | 44.6 | 44.6 | 36.7 | 43.8 | 38.8 |
| % Net Income of Revenue | NA | 8.0 | 5.5 | 4.3 | 2.2 | 3.0 | 4.5 | 0.0 | 2.9 | 2.3 |
| % Return on Assets | NA | 19.8 | 4.4 | 3.9 | 1.8 | 2.2 | 3.0 | 0.0 | 1.8 | 1.6 |
| % Return on Equity | NA | 14.3 | 10.2 | 8.8 | 4.4 | 5.9 | 7.5 | 0.0 | 4.6 | 4.2 |

Data as orig reptd.; bef. results of disc opers/spec. items. Per share data adj. for stk. divs.; EPS diluted. E-Estimated. NA-Not Available. NM-Not Meaningful. NR-Not Ranked. UR-Under Review.

**Office:** 870 Winter St, Waltham, MA 02451-1449.
**Telephone:** 781-522-3000.
**Email:** invest@raytheon.com
**Website:** http://www.raytheon.com

**Chrmn & CEO:** W.H. Swanson
**Pres:** J.R. Harbison
**SVP & CFO:** D.C. Wajsgras
**SVP, Secy & General Counsel:** J.B. Stephens

**CFO:** D.E. Smith
**Investor Contact:** T. Rutledge (781-522-3000)
**Board Members:** V. E. Clark, J. M. Deutch, F. M. Poses, M. C. Ruettgers, R. L. Skates, W. R. Spivey, L. G. Stuntz, W. H. Swanson

**Founded:** 1928
**Domicile:** Delaware
**Employees:** 72,100

# Regions Financial Corp

STANDARD &POOR'S

| S&P Recommendation | HOLD ★★★☆☆ | Price | 12-Mo. Target Price | Investment Style |
|---|---|---|---|---|
| | | $9.67 (as of Nov 14, 2008) | $11.00 | Large-Cap Value |

**GICS Sector** Financials
**Sub-Industry** Regional Banks

**Summary** This major southeastern bank holding company, with over 1,900 offices in 16 Sunbelt states, completed a merger with AmSouth Corp. in 2006.

## Key Stock Statistics (Source S&P, Vickers, company reports)

| | | | | | | | |
|---|---|---|---|---|---|---|---|
| 52-Wk Range | $27.50–6.41 | S&P Oper. EPS 2008**E** | 1.32 | Market Capitalization(B) | $6.691 | Beta | 1.05 |
| Trailing 12-Month EPS | $1.00 | S&P Oper. EPS 2009**E** | 0.91 | Yield (%) | 4.14 | S&P 3-Yr. Proj. EPS CAGR(%) | -8 |
| Trailing 12-Month P/E | 9.7 | P/E on S&P Oper. EPS 2008**E** | 7.3 | Dividend Rate/Share | $0.40 | S&P Credit Rating | A |
| $10K Invested 5 Yrs Ago | $4,048 | Common Shares Outstg. (M) | 692.0 | Institutional Ownership (%) | 51 | | |

## Price Performance

30-Week Mov. Avg. · · · 10-Week Mov. Avg. - - Ṡ GAAP Earnings vs. Previous Year   Volume Above Avg. ‖‖ STARS
12-Mo. Target Price — Relative Strength — ▲ Up ▼ Down ▶ No Change   Below Avg. ‖‖ ★

Options: C, Ph

Analysis prepared by **Stuart Plesser** on October 24, 2008, when the stock traded at **$ 9.17**.

## Highlights

➤ Loan growth in the third quarter was 4.6%, year over year, as a slowdown in commercial lending was more than offset by a pickup in mortgage real estate lending. For 2008 and 2009, we forecast loan growth of 2.5% and 3.0%, respectively. Our net interest margin assumption for 2008 is 3.30%, which will likely decline to 3.25% in 2009, mostly due to a higher concentration of more costly deposits and an asset-sensitive balance sheet. We expect non-interest income to rise 3% in 2009, to 43.0% of revenues, about even with the 2008 ratio but up from 39.5% of revenues in 2007, reflecting an increase in brokerage income.

➤ We look for expenses to total 63.0% of revenue in 2008, declining to 62% in 2009, as RF will likely continue to look for cost reductions. We expect credit quality to continue to decline in 2009, largely due to RF's residential, construction and commercial loans, which should result in loan loss provisions of $1.7 billion in 2009, versus a projected $1.3 billion in 2008.

➤ We assume no share buybacks and estimate 2008 operating EPS of $1.32, down from 2007's $2.27. In 2009, we look for $0.91.

## Investment Rationale/Risk

➤ RF has two problems that we perceive. The first is credit quality, largely stemming from high chargeoff levels from its residential construction portfolio, particularly as it pertains to its Florida and Midwest exposure. We look for total chargeoffs to more than double in 2008, to 1.10% of average loans. At the same time, RF's net interest margin is being hurt by a shift to more costly deposits (CDs). Also, the company is facing capital restraints and has opted to put its share repurchase program on hold. On the positive side, the recently announced TARP program should enable RF to raise inexpensive capital. With the stock currently selling below tangible book value, we believe our concerns are already reflected in the share price.

➤ Risks to our recommendation and target price include a worsening of credit trends, a lower-than-expected net interest margin, and operational performance that falls short of our expectations.

➤ Our 12-month target price of $11 reflects a discount-to-peers multiple of 1.01X RF's tangible book value of $10.86.

## Qualitative Risk Assessment

| LOW | MEDIUM | HIGH |
|---|---|---|

Our risk assessment reflects our view of deteriorating credit quality of the company's loan portfolio coupled with the company's declining capital levels.

## Quantitative Evaluations

**S&P Quality Ranking**   B+

| D | C | B- | B | B+ | A- | A | A+ |
|---|---|---|---|---|---|---|---|

**Relative Strength Rank**   MODERATE

67

LOWEST = 1          HIGHEST = 99

## Revenue/Earnings Data

### Revenue (Million $)

| | 1Q | 2Q | 3Q | 4Q | Year |
|---|---|---|---|---|---|
| 2008 | 1,935 | 2,360 | 2,288 | -- | -- |
| 2007 | 2,797 | 2,724 | 2,742 | 2,667 | 10,925 |
| 2006 | 1,666 | 1,756 | 1,806 | 2,529 | 7,756 |
| 2005 | 1,423 | 1,565 | 1,564 | 1,572 | 6,124 |
| 2004 | 893.7 | 868.8 | 1,432 | 1,416 | 4,610 |
| 2003 | 917.6 | 940.1 | 888.6 | 871.7 | 3,618 |

### Earnings Per Share ($)

| | | | | | |
|---|---|---|---|---|---|
| 2008 | 0.48 | 0.30 | 0.13 | E0.23 | E1.32 |
| 2007 | 0.65 | 0.63 | 0.56 | 0.10 | 1.96 |
| 2006 | 0.64 | 0.75 | 0.77 | 0.56 | 2.67 |
| 2005 | 0.51 | 0.53 | 0.55 | 0.55 | 2.15 |
| 2004 | 0.61 | 0.58 | 0.55 | 0.50 | 2.19 |
| 2003 | 0.58 | 0.59 | 0.59 | 0.59 | 2.35 |

Fiscal year ended Dec. 31. Next earnings report expected: Late January. EPS Estimates based on S&P Operating Earnings; historical GAAP earnings are as reported.

## Dividend Data (Dates: mm/dd Payment Date: mm/dd/yy)

| Amount ($) | Date Decl. | Ex-Div. Date | Stk. of Record | Payment Date |
|---|---|---|---|---|
| 0.380 | 01/17 | 03/14 | 03/18 | 04/01/08 |
| 0.380 | 04/17 | 06/13 | 06/17 | 07/01/08 |
| 0.100 | 07/22 | 09/15 | 09/17 | 10/01/08 |
| 0.100 | 10/16 | 12/15 | 12/17 | 01/02/09 |

Dividends have been paid since 1968. Source: Company reports.

**Please read the Required Disclosures and Analyst Certification on the last page of this report.**

# Regions Financial Corp

STANDARD
&POOR'S

## Business Summary October 24, 2008

CORPORATE OVERVIEW. Regions Financial is a bank holding company that operates primarily in the southeastern U.S., with operations consisting of banking, brokerage and investment services, mortgage banking, insurance brokerage, credit life insurance, commercial accounts receivable factoring and specialty financing. RF conducts its banking operations through Regions Bank, an Alabama-chartered commercial bank that is a member of the Federal Reserve System.

Banking operations also include Regions Mortgage (RMI). RMI's primary business is the origination and servicing of mortgage loans for long-term investors. RMI generally provides services in the same states in which RF has banking operations. Financial services operations include Morgan Keegan, a regional full-service brokerage and investment bank, which was acquired in 2001.

Other subsidiaries include Regions Insurance Group, Inc., Regions Agency Inc., Regions Life Insurance Company, Regions Interstate Billings Service Inc., and Regions Equipment Finance Corporation, providing all lines of personal and commercial insurance, credit-related insurance products, and other financial services.

MARKET PROFILE. As of June 30, 2007, which is the latest available FDIC data, RF had 2,087 branches and $88.4 billion in deposits. About 60% of its deposits and 51% of branches were concentrated in the adjoining states of Tennessee, Alabama and Florida, by our calculations.

## Company Financials Fiscal Year Ended Dec. 31

| Per Share Data ($) | 2007 | 2006 | 2005 | 2004 | 2003 | 2002 | 2001 | 2000 | 1999 | 1998 |
|---|---|---|---|---|---|---|---|---|---|---|
| Tangible Book Value | 11.11 | 11.74 | 11.55 | 11.58 | 16.25 | 15.29 | 10.58 | 11.00 | 9.75 | 9.72 |
| Earnings | 1.96 | 2.67 | 2.15 | 2.19 | 2.35 | 2.20 | 1.81 | 1.93 | 1.90 | 1.52 |
| S&P Core Earnings | 1.97 | 2.67 | 2.11 | 2.17 | 2.32 | 2.11 | 1.63 | NA | NA | NA |
| Dividends | 1.46 | 2.11 | 1.36 | 0.93 | 1.00 | 0.94 | 0.91 | 0.87 | 0.79 | 0.72 |
| Payout Ratio | 74% | 79% | 63% | 43% | 43% | 43% | 50% | 45% | 42% | 47% |
| Prices:High | 38.17 | 39.15 | 35.54 | 35.97 | 30.70 | 31.10 | 26.72 | 22.68 | 33.72 | 36.96 |
| Prices:Low | 22.84 | 32.37 | 29.16 | 27.26 | 24.16 | 21.95 | 20.84 | 14.83 | 18.78 | 23.39 |
| P/E Ratio:High | 19 | 15 | 17 | 16 | 13 | 14 | 15 | 12 | 18 | 24 |
| P/E Ratio:Low | 12 | 12 | 14 | 12 | 10 | 10 | 11 | 8 | 10 | 15 |

| Income Statement Analysis (Million $) | | | | | | | | | | |
|---|---|---|---|---|---|---|---|---|---|---|
| Net Interest Income | 4,398 | 3,353 | 2,821 | 2,113 | 1,475 | 1,498 | 1,425 | 1,389 | 1,426 | 1,325 |
| Tax Equivalent Adjustment | 38.1 | NA | NA | NA | NA | NA | NA | NA | NA | NA |
| Non Interest Income | 2,864 | 2,054 | 1,832 | 1,591 | 1,373 | 1,207 | 950 | 641 | 537 | 468 |
| Loan Loss Provision | 555 | 143 | 165 | 129 | 122 | 128 | 165 | 127 | 114 | 60.5 |
| % Expense/Operating Revenue | 64.2% | 61.3% | 65.5% | 66.5% | 64.6% | 65.1% | 64.2% | 55.2% | 54.2% | 61.6% |
| Pretax Income | 2,039 | 1,959 | 1,422 | 1,176 | 912 | 869 | 718 | 742 | 785 | 635 |
| Effective Tax Rate | 31.7% | 30.9% | 29.6% | 29.9% | 28.5% | 28.7% | 29.1% | 28.9% | 33.1% | 33.6% |
| Net Income | 1,393 | 1,353 | 1,001 | 824 | 652 | 620 | 509 | 528 | 525 | 422 |
| % Net Interest Margin | 3.79 | 4.17 | 3.91 | 3.66 | 3.49 | 3.73 | 3.66 | 3.55 | 3.94 | 4.25 |
| S&P Core Earnings | 1,405 | 1,355 | 983 | 811 | 647 | 592 | 458 | NA | NA | NA |

| Balance Sheet & Other Financial Data (Million $) | | | | | | | | | | |
|---|---|---|---|---|---|---|---|---|---|---|
| Money Market Assets | 2,116 | 2,610 | 1,794 | 1,761 | 1,491 | 1,424 | 1,502 | 112 | 90.3 | 427 |
| Investment Securities | 17,369 | 18,562 | 11,979 | 12,617 | 9,088 | 8,995 | 7,847 | 8,994 | 10,913 | 7,969 |
| Commercial Loans | 20,907 | 24,145 | 14,728 | 15,180 | 9,914 | 10,842 | 9,912 | 9,070 | 8,230 | 7,144 |
| Other Loans | 74,472 | 70,360 | 43,677 | 42,556 | 22,501 | 20,144 | 21,225 | 22,402 | 19,992 | 17,286 |
| Total Assets | 141,042 | 143,369 | 84,786 | 84,106 | 48,598 | 47,939 | 45,383 | 43,688 | 42,714 | 36,832 |
| Demand Deposits | 18,417 | 20,709 | 13,699 | 11,424 | 5,718 | 5,148 | 5,085 | 4,513 | 4,420 | 4,577 |
| Time Deposits | 76,358 | 80,519 | 46,679 | 47,243 | 27,015 | 27,779 | 26,463 | 27,510 | 25,569 | 23,773 |
| Long Term Debt | 11,325 | 8,643 | 11,938 | 7,240 | 5,712 | 5,386 | 4,748 | 4,478 | 1,751 | 571 |
| Common Equity | 19,823 | 20,701 | 10,614 | 10,749 | 4,452 | 4,178 | 4,036 | 3,458 | 3,065 | 3,000 |
| % Return on Assets | 1.0 | 1.2 | 1.2 | 1.2 | 1.4 | 1.3 | 1.1 | 1.2 | 1.3 | 1.4 |
| % Return on Equity | 6.9 | 8.6 | 9.4 | 10.8 | 15.1 | 15.1 | 13.6 | 16.2 | 17.3 | 17.2 |
| % Loan Loss Reserve | 1.4 | 1.1 | 1.3 | 1.3 | 1.4 | 1.3 | 1.3 | 1.2 | 1.2 | 1.3 |
| % Loans/Deposits | 97.0 | 98.3 | 99.3 | 101.1 | 102.1 | 98.7 | 100.7 | 98.7 | 95.7 | 85.9 |
| % Equity to Assets | 14.3 | 13.7 | 12.6 | 11.5 | 8.9 | 8.8 | 8.4 | 7.5 | 7.6 | 8.2 |

Data as orig reptd.; bef. results of disc opers/spec. items. Per share data adj. for stk. divs.; EPS diluted. E-Estimated. NA-Not Available. NM-Not Meaningful. NR-Not Ranked. UR-Under Review.

**Office:** 1900 5th Ave N, Birmingham, AL 35203-2610.
**Telephone:** 205-944-1300.
**Email:** askus@regionsbank.com
**Website:** http://www.regions.com

**Chrmn, Pres & CEO:** C.D. Ritter
**Pres:** S.R. Story, III
**COO, EVP & CTO:** J. Owen
**EVP & CFO:** I. Esteves

**EVP, Chief Acctg Officer & Cntlr:** H.B. Kimbrough, Jr.
**Investor Contact:** M.G. Underwood, Jr. (205-244-2823)
**Board Members:** S. W. Bartholomew, Jr., G. W. Bryan, D. J. Cooper, D. DeFosset, Jr., E. W. Deavenport, Jr., J. R. Malone, S. W. Matlock, J. E. Maupin, Jr., C. D. McCrary, A. B. Morgan, Jr., C. B. Nielsen, C. D. Ritter, J. R. Roberts, L. J. Styslinger, III

**Founded:** 1970
**Domicile:** Delaware
**Employees:** 33,161

The McGraw-Hill Companies

# Reynolds American Inc

**STANDARD &POOR'S**

| S&P Recommendation | HOLD ★★★☆☆ | Price | 12-Mo. Target Price | Investment Style |
|---|---|---|---|---|
| | | $42.99 (as of Nov 14, 2008) | $49.00 | Large-Cap Value |

**GICS Sector** Consumer Staples
**Sub-Industry** Tobacco

**Summary** RAI, the second largest U.S. cigarette manufacturer, was formed via the mid-2004 merger of R.J. Reynolds and Brown & Williamson.

## Key Stock Statistics (Source S&P, Vickers, company reports)

| | | | | | | | |
|---|---|---|---|---|---|---|---|
| 52-Wk Range | $72.00–37.21 | S&P Oper. EPS 2008**E** | 4.72 | Market Capitalization(B) | $12.530 | Beta | 0.82 |
| Trailing 12-Month EPS | $4.68 | S&P Oper. EPS 2009**E** | 4.93 | Yield (%) | 7.91 | S&P 3-Yr. Proj. EPS CAGR(%) | 6 |
| Trailing 12-Month P/E | 9.2 | P/E on S&P Oper. EPS 2008**E** | 9.1 | Dividend Rate/Share | $3.40 | S&P Credit Rating | BBB- |
| $10K Invested 5 Yrs Ago | $20,949 | Common Shares Outstg. (M) | 291.5 | Institutional Ownership (%) | 49 | | |

## Price Performance

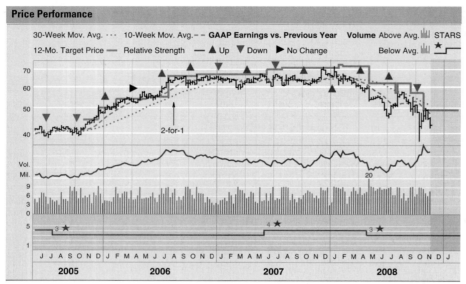

30-Week Mov. Avg. · · · ·   10-Week Mov. Avg. – –   **GAAP Earnings vs. Previous Year**   Volume Above Avg.   STARS
12-Mo. Target Price —   Relative Strength —   ▲ Up   ▼ Down   ▶ No Change   Below Avg.

2-for-1

Options: ASE, CBOE, P, Ph

Analysis prepared by **Esther Y. Kwon, CFA** on October 23, 2008, when the stock traded at **$ 45.16**.

## Highlights

➤ We expect RAI revenues to be down over 1% in 2008, with a favorable product mix shift, price increases (albeit at a lesser rate than in 2007), new product introductions and acquisitions offset by a shipment decline of over 5%. We see gains likely for growth brands Camel, Pall Mall and American Spirit, but anticipate large declines for other brands, as marketing efforts are reduced. We expect Conwood, which RAI acquired in mid-2006 for $3.5 billion, to continue gaining share in a growing smokeless tobacco industry.

➤ We see operating profits up slightly in 2008 as gross margins benefit from the rationalization of non-core brands and brand styles and higher pricing and lower promotions, while SG&A spending remains controlled. In September, RAI announced a restructuring, involving the elimination of 16% of its workforce.

➤ We forecast lower interest expense in 2008 following a refinancing of debt, and a higher effective tax rate of about 38% on the termination of the joint venture with Gallaher Group. We see EPS up slightly to $4.72, from 2007's $4.57, with fewer shares outstanding. In 2009, we expect EPS of $4.93.

## Investment Rationale/Risk

➤ Although we attribute part of the weakness in the company's first quarter results to an incorrect promotion strategy and timing as well as a one-time step-up in settlement payments, we think RAI's customer base is more sensitive to a deteriorating economic environment, which, combined with a declining industry, should continue to accelerate volume declines. We do not see brands in its lower-priced portfolio offsetting this impact, as RAI has chosen to de-emphasize its value brands. On slower profit growth, we believe RAI could be more open to consolidation opportunities.

➤ Risks to our recommendation and target price include additional regulation and taxation of tobacco products, in addition to near-term pressure on trading multiples due to ongoing litigation.

➤ Applying a forward P/E multiple of about 10X, a discount to peers, to our 2009 EPS estimate of $4.93, we arrive at a relative valuation of $49, which is our 12-month target price.

## Qualitative Risk Assessment

| LOW | MEDIUM | HIGH |
|---|---|---|

The domestic tobacco industry typically produces stable revenue streams and strong cash flow. While the industry is involved in significant litigation, recent rulings have led to an improvement in the litigation environment. However, we think RAI's "poison pill" anti-takeover provision is not in its shareholders' best interests.

## Quantitative Evaluations

**S&P Quality Ranking**      **B+**

| D | C | B- | B | B+ | A- | A | A+ |
|---|---|---|---|---|---|---|---|

**Relative Strength Rank**      **STRONG**

72

LOWEST = 1      HIGHEST = 99

## Revenue/Earnings Data

**Revenue (Million $)**

| | 1Q | 2Q | 3Q | 4Q | Year |
|---|---|---|---|---|---|
| 2008 | 2,057 | 1,839 | 2,272 | -- | -- |
| 2007 | 2,148 | 2,348 | 2,297 | 2,230 | 9,023 |
| 2006 | 1,960 | 2,291 | 2,190 | 2,069 | 8,510 |
| 2005 | 1,957 | 2,103 | 2,149 | 2,047 | 8,256 |
| 2004 | 1,218 | 1,352 | 1,866 | 2,001 | 6,437 |
| 2003 | 1,218 | 1,431 | 1,384 | 1,234 | 5,267 |

**Earnings Per Share ($)**

| | 1Q | 2Q | 3Q | 4Q | Year |
|---|---|---|---|---|---|
| 2008 | 1.71 | 1.24 | 0.72 | E1.21 | E4.72 |
| 2007 | 1.11 | 1.10 | 1.21 | 1.01 | 4.43 |
| 2006 | 0.95 | 1.24 | 1.05 | 0.61 | 3.85 |
| 2005 | 0.95 | 0.85 | 0.72 | 0.82 | 3.34 |
| 2004 | 0.72 | 0.88 | 1.14 | 0.22 | 2.81 |
| 2003 | 0.42 | 0.42 | -20.66 | -2.27 | -22.04 |

Fiscal year ended Dec. 31. Next earnings report expected: Early February. EPS Estimates based on S&P Operating Earnings; historical GAAP earnings are as reported.

## Dividend Data (Dates: mm/dd Payment Date: mm/dd/yy)

| Amount ($) | Date Decl. | Ex-Div. Date | Stk. of Record | Payment Date |
|---|---|---|---|---|
| 0.850 | 11/30 | 12/07 | 12/11 | 01/02/08 |
| 0.850 | 02/05 | 03/06 | 03/10 | 04/01/08 |
| 0.850 | 05/06 | 06/06 | 06/10 | 07/01/08 |
| 0.850 | 07/18 | 09/08 | 09/10 | 10/01/08 |

Dividends have been paid since 1999. Source: Company reports.

---

**Please read the Required Disclosures and Analyst Certification on the last page of this report.**

*The McGraw-Hill Companies*

# Reynolds American Inc

STANDARD &POOR'S

## Business Summary October 23, 2008

CORPORATE OVERVIEW. On July 30, 2004, R.J. Reynolds Tobacco Co. (RJRT) merged with Brown & Williamson (B&W), the U.S. operations of British American Tobacco (BTI), to form a new publicly traded company, Reynolds American, Inc. Combining RJRT and B&W, the second and third largest players, RAI is the second largest U.S. cigarette manufacturer, having a combined market share of approximately 30%.

RAI is the parent company of RJRT, Santa Fe Natural Tobacco, which RJRT acquired in 2002, and Lane Limited, which was purchased from BTI for $400 million as part of the merger. In 2003, prior to the merger, RJRT began a significant restructuring plan, targeting cost savings of $1 billion by the end of 2005 through a significant work force reduction, asset divestitures and associated exit activities. Full integration of RJRT and B&W was expected to be completed in 2006, but realization of cost savings continued into 2007. The business combination was expected to result in approximately $600 million in annualized savings, including headcount reductions and operations consolidation, when compared with a separate entity basis.

In May 2006, RAI completed the acquisition of Conwood, the second largest manufacturer of smokeless tobacco products in the U.S., for $3.5 billion. RAI combined Conwood with its Lane Limited subsidiary into an Other Tobacco Products division in 2007. RAI's reportable segments are RJRT and Conwood.

The company's leading products are its Camel and Salem brand cigarettes. The company's other brands include Winston, Pall Mall, Kool, Doral, Vantage, More, Eclipse, American Spirit, and Now. Eclipse, a cigarette that primarily heats rather than burns tobacco in an effort to reduce second-hand smoke, is offered in selected retail chain outlets.

CORPORATE STRATEGY. RAI's management has stated that its strategy is to generate sustainable earnings growth and strong cash flow in order to maximize shareholder value. To that end, RAI implemented a new portfolio strategy, designed to improve profitability, which established three categories for the combined brands of RJRT and B&W. The investment brand category, which includes Camel and Kool, receive the majority of resources to promote market share growth. The selective support brands, which includes Winston, Salem, Doral and Pall Mall, receive limited support to optimize profitability; and the remaining brands are called non-support brands, which are managed to maximize profitability.

## Company Financials Fiscal Year Ended Dec. 31

| Per Share Data ($) | 2007 | 2006 | 2005 | 2004 | 2003 | 2002 | 2001 | 2000 | 1999 | 1998 |
|---|---|---|---|---|---|---|---|---|---|---|
| Tangible Book Value | NM | NM | NM | NM | NM | NM | NM | NM | NM | NM |
| Cash Flow | 4.92 | 4.39 | 4.00 | 2.65 | -20.81 | 3.34 | 4.72 | 4.10 | 3.11 | NA |
| Earnings | 4.43 | 3.85 | 3.34 | 2.81 | -22.04 | 2.32 | 2.24 | 1.73 | 0.90 | -1.38 |
| S&P Core Earnings | 4.41 | 3.95 | 3.96 | 3.59 | 2.13 | 1.73 | 1.52 | NA | NA | NA |
| Dividends | 3.20 | 1.38 | 2.10 | 0.95 | 1.90 | 1.86 | 1.65 | 1.55 | 0.39 | NA |
| Payout Ratio | 72% | 36% | 63% | 34% | NM | 80% | 74% | 90% | 43% | NA |
| Prices:High | 71.72 | 67.09 | 51.19 | 40.27 | 30.07 | 35.95 | 31.35 | 25.13 | 17.00 | NA |
| Prices:Low | 58.55 | 47.48 | 38.24 | 26.69 | 13.76 | 17.42 | 22.09 | 7.88 | 8.00 | NA |
| P/E Ratio:High | 16 | 17 | 15 | 14 | NM | 15 | 14 | 15 | 19 | NA |
| P/E Ratio:Low | 13 | 12 | 11 | 9 | NM | 8 | 10 | 5 | 9 | NA |

| Income Statement Analysis (Million $) | | | | | | | | | | |
|---|---|---|---|---|---|---|---|---|---|---|
| Revenue | 9,023 | 8,510 | 8,256 | 6,437 | 5,267 | 6,211 | 8,585 | 8,167 | 7,567 | 5,716 |
| Operating Income | 2,496 | 2,183 | 1,880 | 1,239 | 873 | 1,200 | 1,409 | 1,399 | 1,368 | NA |
| Depreciation | 143 | 162 | 195 | 153 | 151 | 184 | 491 | 485 | 482 | NA |
| Interest Expense | 338 | 270 | 113 | 85.0 | 111 | 147 | 150 | 168 | 268 | 176 |
| Pretax Income | 2,073 | 1,809 | 1,416 | 829 | -3,918 | 683 | 892 | 748 | 510 | -340 |
| Effective Tax Rate | 37.0% | 37.2% | 30.4% | 24.4% | NM | 38.8% | 50.2% | 52.9% | 61.8% | NM |
| Net Income | 1,307 | 1,136 | 985 | 627 | -3,689 | 418 | 444 | 352 | 195 | -299 |
| S&P Core Earnings | 1,302 | 1,167 | 1,167 | 800 | 357 | 313 | 301 | NA | NA | NA |

| Balance Sheet & Other Financial Data (Million $) | | | | | | | | | | |
|---|---|---|---|---|---|---|---|---|---|---|
| Cash | 2,592 | 1,433 | 1,333 | 1,499 | 1,523 | 1,584 | 2,020 | 2,543 | 1,177 | 3,036 |
| Current Assets | 4,992 | 4,935 | 5,065 | 4,624 | 3,331 | 3,992 | 3,856 | 3,871 | 2,468 | 4,138 |
| Total Assets | 18,629 | 18,178 | 14,519 | 14,428 | 9,677 | 14,651 | 15,050 | 15,554 | 14,377 | 16,301 |
| Current Liabilities | 3,903 | 4,092 | 4,149 | 4,055 | 2,865 | 3,427 | 2,792 | 2,776 | 3,068 | 3,885 |
| Long Term Debt | 4,515 | 4,389 | 1,558 | 1,595 | 1,671 | 1,755 | 1,631 | 1,674 | 1,653 | 2,065 |
| Common Equity | 7,466 | 7,043 | 6,553 | 6,176 | 3,057 | 6,716 | 8,026 | 8,436 | 7,064 | 7,555 |
| Total Capital | 13,165 | 12,599 | 8,750 | 8,576 | 5,534 | 9,707 | 11,383 | 11,966 | 10,347 | 11,073 |
| Capital Expenditures | 142 | 136 | 105 | 92.0 | 70.0 | 111 | 74.0 | 60.0 | 55.0 | NA |
| Cash Flow | 1,450 | 1,298 | 1,180 | 780 | -3,538 | 602 | 935 | 837 | 677 | NA |
| Current Ratio | 1.3 | 1.2 | 1.2 | 1.1 | 1.2 | 1.2 | 1.4 | 1.4 | 0.8 | 1.1 |
| % Long Term Debt of Capitalization | 34.3 | 34.8 | 17.8 | 18.6 | 30.2 | 18.1 | 14.3 | 14.0 | 16.0 | 18.6 |
| % Net Income of Revenue | 14.5 | 13.3 | 11.9 | 9.7 | NM | 6.7 | 5.2 | 4.3 | 2.6 | NM |
| % Return on Assets | 7.1 | 6.9 | 6.8 | 5.2 | NM | 2.8 | 2.9 | 2.4 | 1.2 | NM |
| % Return on Equity | 18.0 | 16.7 | 15.5 | 13.6 | NM | 5.7 | 5.4 | 4.5 | 2.3 | NM |

Data as orig reptd.; bef. results of disc opers/spec. items. Per share data adj. for stk. divs.; EPS diluted. E-Estimated. NA-Not Available. NM-Not Meaningful. NR-Not Ranked. UR-Under Review.

**Office:** 401 North Main Street, Winston-Salem, NC 27102-2866.
**Telephone:** 336-741-2000.
**Email:** talktorjrt@rjrt.com
**Website:** http://www.reynoldsamerican.com

**Chrmn, Pres & CEO:** S.M. Ivey
**EVP & CFO:** T.R. Adams
**EVP & General Counsel:** E.J. Lambeth
**EVP & CIO:** D.I. Lamonds

**SVP & Chief Acctg Officer:** F.W. Smothers
**Board Members:** B. S. Atkins, N. Durante, M. Feinstein, S. M. Ivey, L. Jobin, H. K. Koeppel, N. Mensah, L. L. Nowell, III, H. G. Powell, J. P. Viviano, T. C. Wajnert, N. R. Withington, J. J. Zillmer, A. M. de Castro

**Auditor:** KPMG, Greensboro
**Founded:** 1875
**Domicile:** Delaware
**Employees:** 7,300

# Robert Half International Inc.

**STANDARD & POOR'S**

| S&P Recommendation | STRONG SELL ★☆☆☆☆ | Price $17.81 (as of Nov 14, 2008) | 12-Mo. Target Price $10.00 | Investment Style Large-Cap Blend |
| --- | --- | --- | --- | --- |

**GICS Sector** Industrials
**Sub-Industry** Human Resource & Employment Services

**Summary** This company is the world's largest specialized provider of temporary and permanent personnel in the fields of accounting and finance.

## Key Stock Statistics (Source S&P, Vickers, company reports)

| | | | | | | | |
| --- | --- | --- | --- | --- | --- | --- | --- |
| 52-Wk Range | $29.99– 14.31 | S&P Oper. EPS 2008**E** | 1.65 | Market Capitalization(B) | $2.762 | Beta | 0.77 |
| Trailing 12-Month EPS | $1.87 | S&P Oper. EPS 2009**E** | 0.85 | Yield (%) | 2.47 | S&P 3-Yr. Proj. EPS CAGR(%) | -18 |
| Trailing 12-Month P/E | 9.5 | P/E on S&P Oper. EPS 2008**E** | 10.8 | Dividend Rate/Share | $0.44 | S&P Credit Rating | NA |
| $10K Invested 5 Yrs Ago | $8,089 | Common Shares Outstg. (M) | 155.1 | Institutional Ownership (%) | 85 | | |

## Price Performance

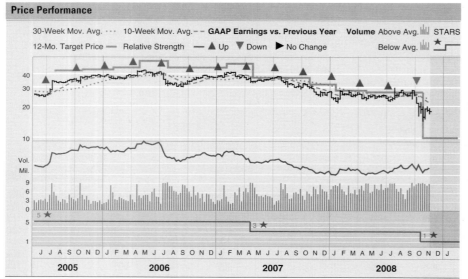

30-Week Mov. Avg. ···· 10-Week Mov. Avg. --- GAAP Earnings vs. Previous Year  Volume Above Avg. ▌▌▌ STARS
12-Mo. Target Price — Relative Strength — ▲ Up ▼ Down ▶ No Change  Below Avg. ▌▌▌ ★

2005  2006  2007  2008

Options: ASE, CBOE, Ph

Analysis prepared by **Michael W. Jaffe** on October 24, 2008, when the stock traded at **$ 15.94**.

## Highlights

➤ We expect a 14% revenue decline in 2009, as we see conditions remaining very challenging in the U.S. Also, although RHI's business has been solid in Europe, with particular strength in markets such as Germany, it started to see moderating conditions in most parts of Europe as 2008's third quarter progressed. We see that market weakening noticeably in coming periods. We also anticipate RHI being aided to an extent by its focus on the professional areas of accounting and finance, which we expect to be stronger than most non-professional areas over the coming year, but not enough in our view to allow RHI to record revenue growth.

➤ We forecast net margins to narrow considerably in 2009, on the negative impact that we see from for lower revenues. We also think RHI's margins will be hurt by the cost of investments at the Protiviti consulting unit, which we also see experiencing sluggish demand.

➤ We expect RHI's strongest results in coming periods to come from some ongoing strength in emerging markets such as Brazil and the Asia-Pacific area, whose labor markets seem likely to stay firm in coming periods.

## Investment Rationale/Risk

➤ We recently downgraded our opinion on the shares to strong sell, from hold. We expect RHI to record lower profits in coming periods, in light of the weak U.S. economy and our outlook for a significant downturn in labor markets in a number of the Western European markets served by the company. As such, we believe that RHI will be reporting negative earnings comparisons through at least the end of 2009. Based on these factors and valuation considerations, we think the shares are considerably overvalued.

➤ Risks to our recommendation and target price include a faster-than-expected revival of economies in the U.S. and Western Europe, and a greater-than-expected positive impact from business in emerging markets.

➤ The shares recently traded at about 19X our 2009 EPS forecast, which is in the bottom half of RHI's valuation for the past decade, but still well above its typical trough level. Based on our belief that RHI is in the midst of a significant business downturn through at least the next year, we think a valuation closer to its trough is merited. We have a 12-month target price of $10, or about 12X our 2009 EPS estimate.

## Qualitative Risk Assessment

| LOW | MEDIUM | HIGH |
| --- | --- | --- |

Our risk assessment reflects what we view as RHI's strong position in accounting and finance placements and a healthy balance sheet. This is offset by the highly cyclical nature of the company's business, which is largely dependent on the U.S. economy and the health of labor markets.

## Quantitative Evaluations

**S&P Quality Ranking**      **B**

| D | C | B- | B | B+ | A- | A | A+ |
| --- | --- | --- | --- | --- | --- | --- | --- |

**Relative Strength Rank**      **MODERATE**

63

LOWEST = 1      HIGHEST = 99

## Revenue/Earnings Data

**Revenue (Million $)**

| | 1Q | 2Q | 3Q | 4Q | Year |
| --- | --- | --- | --- | --- | --- |
| 2008 | 1,226 | 1,225 | 1,160 | -- | -- |
| 2007 | 1,097 | 1,149 | 1,179 | 1,220 | 4,646 |
| 2006 | 943.9 | 981.8 | 1,028 | 1,060 | 4,014 |
| 2005 | 770.0 | 816.7 | 867.0 | 884.8 | 3,338 |
| 2004 | 572.3 | 641.2 | 708.0 | 754.2 | 2,676 |
| 2003 | 473.2 | 483.0 | 501.1 | 517.7 | 1,975 |

**Earnings Per Share ($)**

| | 1Q | 2Q | 3Q | 4Q | Year |
| --- | --- | --- | --- | --- | --- |
| 2008 | 0.45 | 0.48 | 0.43 | E0.28 | E1.65 |
| 2007 | 0.42 | 0.44 | 0.46 | 0.50 | 1.81 |
| 2006 | 0.38 | 0.39 | 0.43 | 0.45 | 1.65 |
| 2005 | 0.29 | 0.33 | 0.37 | 0.37 | 1.36 |
| 2004 | 0.09 | 0.18 | 0.24 | 0.28 | 0.79 |
| 2003 | -0.02 | Nil | 0.03 | 0.03 | 0.04 |

Fiscal year ended Dec. 31. Next earnings report expected: Late January. EPS Estimates based on S&P Operating Earnings; historical GAAP earnings are as reported.

## Dividend Data (Dates: mm/dd Payment Date: mm/dd/yy)

| Amount ($) | Date Decl. | Ex-Div. Date | Stk. of Record | Payment Date |
| --- | --- | --- | --- | --- |
| 0.110 | 02/13 | 02/21 | 02/25 | 03/14/08 |
| 0.110 | 05/06 | 05/21 | 05/23 | 06/13/08 |
| 0.110 | 07/29 | 08/21 | 08/25 | 09/15/08 |
| 0.110 | 10/29 | 11/21 | 11/25 | 12/15/08 |

Dividends have been paid since 2004. Source: Company reports.

# Robert Half International Inc.

## Business Summary October 24, 2008

Robert Half International is the world's largest specialized staffing service in the fields of accounting and finance. In May 2002, RHI expanded its offerings to include risk consulting and internal audit services through its Protiviti unit. In 2007, the company derived 79% of its revenues from activities in temporary and consultant staffing, 10% from permanent placement staffing, and 12% from risk consulting and internal audit services. Foreign operations accounted for about one-quarter of RHI's revenues in 2007. As of 2007 year end, the company's staffing businesses had more than 360 offices in 42 states, the District of Columbia and 18 foreign countries, while Protiviti had 60 offices in 22 states and 14 foreign countries.

RHI's Accountemps temporary services division offers customers an economical means of dealing with uneven or peak work loads for accounting, tax and finance personnel. The temporary workers are employees of Accountemps, and are paid by Accountemps only when working on customer assignments. The customer pays a fixed rate for hours worked. If the client converts the temporary hire to a permanent worker, it typically pays a one-time fee for the conversion.

RHI offers permanent placement services through Robert Half Finance & Accounting, which specializes in accounting, financial, tax and banking personnel. Fees for successful permanent placements are paid only by the employer and are usually a percentage of the new employee's annual salary.

Since the early 1990s, the company has expanded into additional specialty fields. OfficeTeam, formed in 1991, provides skilled temporary and full-time administrative and office personnel. In 1992, RHI acquired Robert Half Legal (formerly The Affiliates), which places temporary and regular employees in attorney, paralegal, legal administrative and other legal support positions. In 1994, Robert Half Technology (formerly RHI Consulting) was created to concentrate on the placement of contract and full-time information technology consultants. In 1997, the company established Robert Half Management Resources (formerly RHI Management Resources) to provide senior level project professionals specializing in the accounting and finance fields. The Creative Group, which started up in 1999, provides project staffing in the advertising, marketing and Web design fields. In 2007, Accountemps provided 38% of revenues, OfficeTeam 19%, other placement businesses 32%, and Protiviti 12%.

## Company Financials Fiscal Year Ended Dec. 31

| Per Share Data ($) | 2007 | 2006 | 2005 | 2004 | 2003 | 2002 | 2001 | 2000 | 1999 | 1998 |
|---|---|---|---|---|---|---|---|---|---|---|
| Tangible Book Value | 4.99 | 5.15 | 4.72 | 4.30 | 3.65 | 3.41 | 3.69 | 3.13 | 2.28 | 1.89 |
| Cash Flow | 2.25 | 2.00 | 1.66 | 1.07 | 0.42 | 0.42 | 1.07 | 1.30 | 0.98 | 0.82 |
| Earnings | 1.81 | 1.65 | 1.36 | 0.79 | 0.04 | 0.01 | 0.67 | 1.00 | 0.77 | 0.70 |
| S&P Core Earnings | 1.81 | 1.65 | 1.29 | 0.71 | -0.11 | -0.17 | 0.51 | NA | NA | NA |
| Dividends | 0.40 | 0.32 | 0.28 | 0.18 | Nil | Nil | Nil | Nil | Nil | Nil |
| Payout Ratio | 22% | 19% | 21% | 23% | Nil | Nil | Nil | Nil | Nil | Nil |
| Prices:High | 42.21 | 43.94 | 39.86 | 30.98 | 25.18 | 30.90 | 30.90 | 38.63 | 24.19 | 30.13 |
| Prices:Low | 24.41 | 29.91 | 23.95 | 20.69 | 11.44 | 11.94 | 18.50 | 12.34 | 10.22 | 14.50 |
| P/E Ratio:High | 23 | 27 | 29 | 39 | NM | NM | 46 | 39 | 32 | 43 |
| P/E Ratio:Low | 13 | 18 | 18 | 26 | NM | NM | 28 | 12 | 13 | 21 |

| Income Statement Analysis (Million $) | | | | | | | | | | |
|---|---|---|---|---|---|---|---|---|---|---|
| Revenue | 4,646 | 4,014 | 3,338 | 2,676 | 1,975 | 1,905 | 2,453 | 2,699 | 2,081 | 1,793 |
| Operating Income | 549 | 511 | 433 | 280 | 75.0 | 71.2 | 261 | 348 | 268 | 240 |
| Depreciation | 71.4 | 61.1 | 51.3 | 49.1 | 65.9 | 72.3 | 73.1 | 56.6 | 39.1 | 24.6 |
| Interest Expense | 4.10 | Nil | Nil | Nil | Nil | Nil | Nil | Nil | Nil | Nil |
| Pretax Income | 490 | 466 | 392 | 235 | 11.7 | 3.50 | 196 | 302 | 235 | 221 |
| Effective Tax Rate | 39.6% | 39.3% | 39.3% | 40.1% | 45.5% | 38.0% | 38.3% | 38.3% | 39.7% | 40.5% |
| Net Income | 296 | 283 | 238 | 141 | 6.39 | 2.17 | 121 | 186 | 141 | 132 |
| S&P Core Earnings | 296 | 283 | 224 | 125 | -18.4 | -30.2 | 91.1 | NA | NA | NA |

| Balance Sheet & Other Financial Data (Million $) | | | | | | | | | | |
|---|---|---|---|---|---|---|---|---|---|---|
| Cash | 310 | 447 | 458 | 437 | 377 | 317 | 347 | 239 | 151 | 166 |
| Current Assets | 1,060 | 1,112 | 1,017 | 916 | 699 | 643 | 686 | 672 | 491 | 430 |
| Total Assets | 1,450 | 1,459 | 1,319 | 1,199 | 980 | 936 | 994 | 971 | 777 | 704 |
| Current Liabilities | 448 | 403 | 337 | 280 | 189 | 184 | 177 | 237 | 176 | 153 |
| Long Term Debt | 3.75 | 3.83 | 2.70 | 2.27 | 2.34 | 2.40 | 2.48 | 2.54 | 2.60 | 3.40 |
| Common Equity | 984 | 1,043 | 971 | 912 | 789 | 745 | 806 | 719 | 576 | 522 |
| Total Capital | 988 | 1,047 | 974 | 914 | 791 | 747 | 808 | 721 | 601 | 551 |
| Capital Expenditures | 83.8 | 80.4 | 61.8 | 32.9 | 36.5 | 48.3 | 84.7 | 74.0 | 52.6 | 67.2 |
| Cash Flow | 368 | 344 | 289 | 190 | 72.3 | 74.5 | 194 | 243 | 181 | 156 |
| Current Ratio | 2.4 | 2.8 | 3.0 | 3.3 | 3.7 | 3.5 | 3.9 | 2.8 | 2.8 | 2.8 |
| % Long Term Debt of Capitalization | 0.4 | 0.4 | 0.3 | 0.2 | 0.3 | 0.3 | 0.3 | 0.4 | 0.4 | 0.6 |
| % Net Income of Revenue | 6.4 | 7.1 | 7.1 | 5.3 | 0.3 | 0.1 | 4.9 | 6.9 | 6.8 | 7.3 |
| % Return on Assets | 20.4 | 20.4 | 18.9 | 12.9 | 0.7 | 0.2 | 12.3 | 21.3 | 19.1 | 20.8 |
| % Return on Equity | 29.2 | 28.1 | 25.3 | 16.5 | 0.8 | 0.3 | 15.9 | 28.7 | 25.7 | 28.0 |

Data as orig reptd.; bef. results of disc opers/spec. items. Per share data adj. for stk. divs.; EPS diluted. E-Estimated. NA-Not Available. NM-Not Meaningful. NR-Not Ranked. UR-Under Review.

**Office:** 2884 Sand Hill Rd, Menlo Park, CA 94025-7072.
**Telephone:** 650-234-6000.
**Website:** http://www.rhi.com
**Chrmn & CEO:** H.M. Messmer, Jr.

**Pres, Vice Chrmn & CFO:** M.K. Waddell
**EVP, Chief Admin Officer, Chief Acctg Officer & Treas:** M.C. Buckley
**SVP, Secy & General Counsel:** S. Karel
**CIO:** K. White

**Board Members:** A. S. Berwick, Jr., F. P. Furth, E. W. Gibbons, H. M. Messmer, Jr., F. A. Richman, T. J. Ryan, J. S. Schaub, M. K. Waddell

**Founded:** 1967
**Domicile:** Delaware
**Employees:** 272,300

# Rockwell Automation Inc.

| S&P Recommendation | HOLD ★★★☆☆ | Price $26.08 (as of Nov 14, 2008) | 12-Mo. Target Price $28.00 | Investment Style Large-Cap Blend |
|---|---|---|---|---|

**GICS Sector** Industrials
**Sub-Industry** Electrical Components & Equipment

**Summary** This former aerospace and defense contractor (formerly Rockwell International) now primarily manufactures automated industrial equipment and power generators.

## Key Stock Statistics (Source S&P, Vickers, company reports)

| | | | | | | | |
|---|---|---|---|---|---|---|---|
| 52-Wk Range | $72.53–21.51 | S&P Oper. EPS 2009E | 3.12 | Market Capitalization(B) | $3.797 | Beta | 1.60 |
| Trailing 12-Month EPS | $3.90 | S&P Oper. EPS 2010E | 4.15 | Yield (%) | 4.45 | S&P 3-Yr. Proj. EPS CAGR(%) | 6 |
| Trailing 12-Month P/E | 6.7 | P/E on S&P Oper. EPS 2009E | 8.4 | Dividend Rate/Share | $1.16 | S&P Credit Rating | A |
| $10K Invested 5 Yrs Ago | $9,075 | Common Shares Outstg. (M) | 145.6 | Institutional Ownership (%) | 66 | | |

## Price Performance

30-Week Mov. Avg. · · · ·  10-Week Mov. Avg. – – **GAAP Earnings vs. Previous Year**  Volume Above Avg. STARS

12-Mo. Target Price —  Relative Strength —  ▲ Up  ▼ Down  ▶ No Change  Below Avg. ★

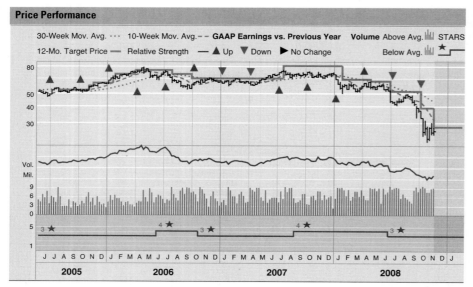

Options: ASE, CBOE, Ph

Analysis prepared by **Mathew Christy, CFA** on November 14, 2008, when the stock traded at **$ 27.67**.

## Highlights

➤ We expect revenues to fall more than 6% in FY 09 (Sep.), primarily reflecting reduced orders and the negative effect of foreign exchange, offset somewhat by the benefits of recent acquisitions, leading to lower sales results at both the Control Products and Architecture Software segments. Our forecast is based on a 5% drop in revenues at the Control Products segment and a 7% revenue decline in the Architecture Software unit. In FY 10, we forecast that revenue will rise somewhat more than 6%.

➤ In our opinion, operating margins are likely to decline in FY 09, despite recent restructuring efforts and ROK's focus on higher-margin products in the Architecture and Software segment, due to lower operating leverage, lower pricing, and product mix. In FY 10, we expect operating margins to rise somewhat on higher gross margins and lower operating costs as a percentage of sales.

➤ Assuming slightly higher effective tax rates, we project operating EPS of $3.12 in FY 09 and $4.15 in FY 09.

## Investment Rationale/Risk

➤ We believe that future results will be negatively affected by the slowing global economy and lower industrial production. Despite our view of declining revenue and earnings in FY 09, we believe that ROK's share price fairly discounts lower future results, as the shares recently traded at about 8X our FY 09 EPS estimate. In addition, we are positive on ROK's share repurchase program, and view its balance sheet as strong and its free cash flow and dividend yield as attractive.

➤ Risks to our recommendation and target price include weaker-than-expected global economic growth, rising raw material costs, and lower-than-forecast benefits from rationalization plans.

➤ Our 12-month price target of $28 represents a blend of two valuation metrics. Our DCF model, which assumes a 3% perpetual growth rate and an 11.7% discount rate, indicates an intrinsic value of $30. We also apply a target P/E multiple of 8X, in line with ROK's peers but lower than historical low P/E multiples, to our FY 09 EPS per share estimate, implying a value of $25.

## Qualitative Risk Assessment

| LOW | MEDIUM | HIGH |
|---|---|---|

Our risk assessment reflects the highly cyclical end-market demand for the company's products, offset by corporate governance practices that we view as favorable, an S&P Quality Ranking of B+, reflecting average stability in earnings and dividend growth, and low capital requirements.

## Quantitative Evaluations

**S&P Quality Ranking** B+

| D | C | B- | B | B+ | A- | A | A+ |
|---|---|---|---|---|---|---|---|

**Relative Strength Rank** MODERATE

50

LOWEST = 1    HIGHEST = 99

## Revenue/Earnings Data

**Revenue (Million $)**

| | 1Q | 2Q | 3Q | 4Q | Year |
|---|---|---|---|---|---|
| 2008 | 1,332 | 1,407 | 1,475 | 1,484 | 5,698 |
| 2007 | 1,146 | 1,207 | 1,281 | 1,371 | 5,004 |
| 2006 | 1,301 | 1,378 | 1,428 | 1,454 | 5,561 |
| 2005 | 1,185 | 1,218 | 1,265 | 1,335 | 5,003 |
| 2004 | 990.3 | 1,080 | 1,135 | 1,206 | 4,411 |
| 2003 | 984.0 | 1,029 | 1,033 | 1,058 | 4,104 |

**Earnings Per Share ($)**

| | | | | | |
|---|---|---|---|---|---|
| 2008 | 1.04 | 0.96 | 1.03 | 0.87 | 3.90 |
| 2007 | 0.76 | 0.65 | 1.07 | 1.07 | 3.53 |
| 2006 | 0.80 | 0.83 | 0.83 | 1.04 | 3.49 |
| 2005 | 0.65 | 0.75 | 0.68 | 0.69 | 2.77 |
| 2004 | 0.30 | 0.39 | 0.66 | 0.51 | 1.85 |
| 2003 | 0.22 | 0.26 | 0.67 | 0.33 | 1.49 |

Fiscal year ended Sep. 30. Next earnings report expected: Late January. EPS Estimates based on S&P Operating Earnings; historical GAAP earnings are as reported.

## Dividend Data (Dates: mm/dd Payment Date: mm/dd/yy)

| Amount ($) | Date Decl. | Ex-Div. Date | Stk. of Record | Payment Date |
|---|---|---|---|---|
| 0.290 | 02/06 | 02/14 | 02/19 | 03/10/08 |
| 0.290 | 04/02 | 05/08 | 05/12 | 06/02/08 |
| 0.290 | 05/30 | 08/07 | 08/11 | 09/02/08 |
| 0.290 | 11/05 | 11/13 | 11/17 | 12/08/08 |

Dividends have been paid since 1948. Source: Company reports.

# Rockwell Automation Inc.

STANDARD
&POOR'S

## Business Summary November 14, 2008

CORPORATE OVERVIEW. In the early 1990s, Rockwell Automation (formerly Rockwell International) operated a broad range of manufacturing businesses. Following a series of divestitures that included the 2001 spin-off of Rockwell Collins and the 2006 divestiture of Power Systems, it now operates two business segments: Control Products and Solutions and Architecture and Software.

The Control Products and Solutions (CS) segment accounted for 56% of FY 07 (Sep.) total revenues and 40% of total operating profits, with 14% profit margins. CS supplies industrial control products and services focused on helping customers control, monitor and improve manufacturing processes. Products include industrial controls, variable frequency drives, smart motor controls, electronic overload controls, power control and motor control centers, drive systems, custom OEM panels, information systems and systems integration. Major markets served include consumer products, food and beverage, trans-

portation, metals, mining, pulp and paper, and oil and gas. Competitors include Emerson Electric, GE, and Schneider Electric.

The Architecture and Software segment (A&S) generated 44% of FY 07 sales and 60% of operating profits, with 26% operating margins. The division offers control platforms and software as well as bundled automation products for enterprise business systems, distribution and supply chains. Offerings include controllers, motor control sensors, programmable logic controllers (PLCs), input/output devices, sensors and software, networks, packaged software and safety components.

## Company Financials Fiscal Year Ended Sep. 30

| Per Share Data ($) | 2008 | 2007 | 2006 | 2005 | 2004 | 2003 | 2002 | 2001 | 2000 | 1999 |
|---|---|---|---|---|---|---|---|---|---|---|
| Tangible Book Value | NA | 4.29 | 4.40 | 2.95 | 3.95 | 2.41 | 2.61 | 2.23 | 6.90 | 6.56 |
| Cash Flow | NA | 4.26 | 4.35 | 3.68 | 2.83 | 2.53 | 2.29 | 5.39 | 4.80 | 4.74 |
| Earnings | 3.90 | 3.53 | 3.49 | 2.77 | 1.85 | 1.49 | 1.20 | 0.68 | 3.35 | 3.01 |
| S&P Core Earnings | NA | 3.45 | 3.48 | 2.68 | 1.88 | 1.16 | 0.75 | -0.06 | NA | NA |
| Dividends | NA | 1.16 | 0.90 | 0.78 | 0.66 | 0.66 | 0.66 | 0.93 | 1.02 | 1.02 |
| Payout Ratio | NA | 33% | 26% | 28% | 36% | 44% | 55% | 137% | 30% | 34% |
| Prices:High | NA | 75.60 | 799.47 | 63.30 | 49.97 | 36.10 | 22.79 | 49.45 | 54.50 | 64.94 |
| Prices:Low | NA | 56.73 | 53.49 | 45.40 | 28.45 | 18.75 | 14.71 | 11.78 | 27.69 | 39.94 |
| P/E Ratio:High | NA | 21 | 23 | 23 | 27 | 24 | 19 | 73 | 16 | 22 |
| P/E Ratio:Low | NA | 16 | 15 | 16 | 15 | 13 | 12 | 17 | 8 | 13 |

| Income Statement Analysis (Million $) | 2008 | 2007 | 2006 | 2005 | 2004 | 2003 | 2002 | 2001 | 2000 | 1999 |
|---|---|---|---|---|---|---|---|---|---|---|
| Revenue | 5,698 | 5,004 | 5,561 | 5,003 | 4,411 | 4,104 | 3,909 | 4,279 | 7,151 | 7,043 |
| Operating Income | NA | 937 | 1,073 | 944 | 691 | 543 | 488 | 1,079 | 1,223 | 1,203 |
| Depreciation | 137 | 118 | 154 | 171 | 187 | 198 | 206 | 872 | 276 | 337 |
| Interest Expense | NA | 63.4 | 58.4 | 45.8 | 41.7 | 52.0 | 66.0 | 83.0 | 73.0 | 84.0 |
| Pretax Income | 809 | 789 | 365 | 737 | 438 | 299 | 233 | 168 | 943 | 890 |
| Effective Tax Rate | 28.6% | 27.8% | NM | 29.7% | 19.2% | 5.69% | 3.00% | 25.6% | 32.6% | 34.6% |
| Net Income | 578 | 569 | 628 | 518 | 354 | 282 | 226 | 125 | 636 | 582 |
| S&P Core Earnings | NA | 556 | 628 | 498 | 361 | 221 | 142 | -12.0 | NA | NA |

| Balance Sheet & Other Financial Data (Million $) | 2008 | 2007 | 2006 | 2005 | 2004 | 2003 | 2002 | 2001 | 2000 | 1999 |
|---|---|---|---|---|---|---|---|---|---|---|
| Cash | 582 | 624 | 415 | 464 | 474 | 226 | 289 | 121 | 190 | 356 |
| Current Assets | NA | 2,382 | 2,188 | 2,187 | 2,026 | 1,736 | 1,775 | 1,697 | 3,206 | 3,582 |
| Total Assets | 4,594 | 4,546 | 4,735 | 4,525 | 4,201 | 3,986 | 4,024 | 4,074 | 6,390 | 6,704 |
| Current Liabilities | NA | 1,745 | 1,293 | 941 | 864 | 820 | 966 | 867 | 1,820 | 2,108 |
| Long Term Debt | NA | 406 | 748 | 748 | 758 | 764 | 767 | 922 | 924 | 911 |
| Common Equity | 1,689 | 1,743 | 1,918 | 1,649 | 1,861 | 1,587 | 1,609 | 1,600 | 2,669 | 2,637 |
| Total Capital | NA | 2,149 | 2,822 | 2,397 | 2,708 | 2,388 | 2,534 | 2,693 | 3,593 | 3,548 |
| Capital Expenditures | 151 | 131 | 150 | 124 | 98.0 | 109 | 104 | 157 | 315 | 377 |
| Cash Flow | NA | 687 | 782 | 690 | 541 | 480 | 432 | 997 | 912 | 919 |
| Current Ratio | 3.9 | 1.4 | 1.7 | 2.3 | 2.3 | 2.1 | 1.8 | 2.0 | 1.8 | 1.7 |
| % Long Term Debt of Capitalization | 34.9 | 18.9 | 26.5 | 31.2 | 28.0 | 32.0 | 30.3 | 34.2 | 25.7 | 25.7 |
| % Net Income of Revenue | 10.1 | 11.4 | 11.3 | 10.4 | 8.0 | 6.9 | 5.8 | 2.9 | 8.9 | 8.3 |
| % Return on Assets | 12.6 | 12.3 | 13.6 | 11.9 | 8.7 | 7.1 | 5.6 | 2.7 | 9.8 | 8.4 |
| % Return on Equity | 33.7 | 31.1 | 35.2 | 29.5 | 20.5 | 17.6 | 14.1 | 5.9 | 24.4 | 19.8 |

Data as orig reptd.; bef. results of disc opers/spec. items. Per share data adj. for stk. divs.; EPS diluted. E-Estimated. NA-Not Available. NM-Not Meaningful. NR-Not Ranked. UR-Under Review.

**Office:** 1201 S 2nd St, Milwaukee, WI 53204-2498.
**Telephone:** 414-382-2000.
**Website:** http://www.rockwellautomation.com
**Chrmn, Pres & CEO:** K.D. Nosbusch

**COO:** M. Thomas
**SVP & CFO:** T.D. Crandall
**SVP & CTO:** S. Chand
**SVP, Secy & General Counsel:** D.M. Hagerman

**Board Members:** B. C. Alewine, V. G. Istock, B. C. Johnson, W. T. Mccormick, Jr., K. D. Nosbusch, D. R. Parfet, B. M. Rockwell, D. B. Speer, J. F. Toot, Jr.

**Founded:** 1928
**Domicile:** Delaware
**Employees:** 20,000

# Rockwell Collins Inc.

**STANDARD &POOR'S**

**S&P Recommendation** HOLD ★★★☆☆

| Price | 12-Mo. Target Price | Investment Style |
|---|---|---|
| $33.07 (as of Nov 14, 2008) | $48.00 | Large-Cap Growth |

**GICS Sector** Industrials
**Sub-Industry** Aerospace & Defense

**Summary** This company is one of the world's largest makers of military and commercial avionics and electronics, including cockpit controls, communications and navigation systems, and in-flight entertainment systems.

## Key Stock Statistics (Source S&P, Vickers, company reports)

| | | | | | | | |
|---|---|---|---|---|---|---|---|
| 52-Wk Range | $74.54–30.57 | S&P Oper. EPS 2009E | 4.20 | Market Capitalization(B) | $5.272 | Beta | 1.41 |
| Trailing 12-Month EPS | $4.16 | S&P Oper. EPS 2010E | NA | Yield (%) | 2.90 | S&P 3-Yr. Proj. EPS CAGR(%) | 12 |
| Trailing 12-Month P/E | 8.0 | P/E on S&P Oper. EPS 2009E | 7.9 | Dividend Rate/Share | $0.96 | S&P Credit Rating | NA |
| $10K Invested 5 Yrs Ago | $13,347 | Common Shares Outstg. (M) | 159.4 | Institutional Ownership (%) | 67 | | |

## Price Performance

30-Week Mov. Avg. · · · 10-Week Mov. Avg. – – GAAP Earnings vs. Previous Year    Volume Above Avg. STARS
12-Mo. Target Price — Relative Strength — ▲ Up ▼ Down ► No Change    Below Avg. ★

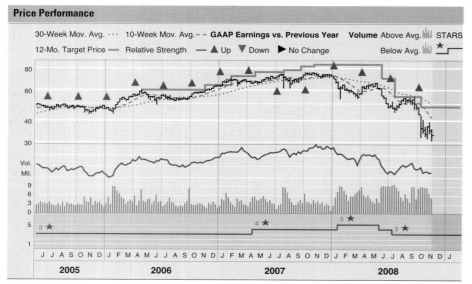

Options: ASE, CBOE, Ph

Analysis prepared by **Richard Tortoriello** on October 08, 2008, when the stock traded at **$ 40.38**.

## Qualitative Risk Assessment

| LOW | MEDIUM | HIGH |
|---|---|---|

Our risk assessment reflects the company's exposure to the airline industry, dependence on U.S. military procurement and R&D budgets, and high fixed-cost structure, offset by what we view as a solid balance sheet, strong returns, and corporate governance practices that we consider favorable versus peers.

## Quantitative Evaluations

**S&P Quality Ranking** NR

| D | C | B- | B | B+ | A- | A | A+ |
|---|---|---|---|---|---|---|---|

**Relative Strength Rank** MODERATE

52

LOWEST = 1    HIGHEST = 99

## Revenue/Earnings Data

### Revenue (Million $)

| | 1Q | 2Q | 3Q | 4Q | Year |
|---|---|---|---|---|---|
| 2008 | 1,112 | 1,186 | 1,194 | 1,277 | 4,769 |
| 2007 | 993.0 | 1,083 | 1,113 | 1,226 | 4,415 |
| 2006 | 881.0 | 957.0 | 964.0 | 1,061 | 3,863 |
| 2005 | 763.0 | 829.0 | 890.0 | 963.0 | 3,445 |
| 2004 | 628.0 | 719.0 | 744.0 | 839.0 | 2,930 |
| 2003 | 561.0 | 618.0 | 620.0 | 743.0 | 2,542 |

### Earnings Per Share ($)

| | | | | | |
|---|---|---|---|---|---|
| 2008 | 0.93 | 1.03 | 1.07 | 1.13 | 4.16 |
| 2007 | 0.84 | 0.82 | 0.86 | 0.93 | 3.45 |
| 2006 | 0.59 | 0.65 | 0.70 | 0.79 | 2.73 |
| 2005 | 0.50 | 0.52 | 0.56 | 0.62 | 2.20 |
| 2004 | 0.38 | 0.39 | 0.42 | 0.48 | 1.67 |
| 2003 | 0.27 | 0.33 | 0.43 | 0.40 | 1.43 |

Fiscal year ended Sep. 30. Next earnings report expected: Late January. EPS Estimates based on S&P Operating Earnings; historical GAAP earnings are as reported.

## Highlights

➤ We project that sales will rise about 7% in FY 08 (Sep.), driven by 8% growth in commercial-aerospace-related systems and 6% growth in government/military aircraft systems. We expect commercial systems growth to be driven by strong commercial aerospace and business jet OEM markets. We see slowing aftermarket parts and service growth, due to tough comparisons and high jet fuel prices and slowing air traffic growth, which are causing airlines to reduce fleet sizes. We also anticipate continued demand for military aircraft upgrade programs and defense communications. Due to our view of slowing aftermarket sales, we see sales growth of 6% in FY 09.

➤ We project a 120 basis point (bps) increase in segment operating margins in FY 08, to 22.1%, on volume growth and continued improvement in efficiency. We are modeling a slight decrease in operating margins in FY 09.

➤ We forecast EPS of $4.01 for FY 08, followed by a 5% increase, to $4.20, in FY 09. We project free cash flow (cash flow from operating activities less capital expenditures) of about 80% of net income in each year.

## Investment Rationale/Risk

➤ Although we see COL benefiting from what we view as a strong aerospace OEM market and favorable execution by management, we expect slowing commercial aftermarket demand to constrain earnings growth. COL's return on invested capital was 33% in FY 07, and we expect continued high ROIC in FY 08. We expect ROIC of at least 20% to 25% in FY 08, and see cash generation capability as remaining strong. We see COL conserving cash for attractive acquisitions, which we view as likely to favorably expand its market position.

➤ Risks to our recommendation and target price include a slowdown in global aerospace demand, failure to gain new contracts, and operational or other missteps.

➤ Our 12-month target price of $48 is based on an enterprise to 2008 estimated EBITDA multiple of 7X. Over its six-plus year operating history COL has recorded EV-to-EBITDA multiples ranging from 7X to 15X. We believe that economic and stock market conditions warrant a multiple at the low end of this range.

## Dividend Data (Dates: mm/dd Payment Date: mm/dd/yy)

| Amount ($) | Date Decl. | Ex-Div. Date | Stk. of Record | Payment Date |
|---|---|---|---|---|
| 0.160 | 01/29 | 02/07 | 02/11 | 03/03/08 |
| 0.240 | 04/16 | 05/08 | 05/12 | 06/02/08 |
| 0.240 | 07/28 | 08/07 | 08/11 | 09/02/08 |
| 0.240 | 10/27 | 11/13 | 11/17 | 12/08/08 |

Dividends have been paid since 2001. Source: Company reports.

---

**Please read the Required Disclosures and Analyst Certification on the last page of this report.**

The McGraw-Hill Companies

# Rockwell Collins Inc.

**STANDARD &POOR'S**

## Business Summary October 08, 2008

CORPORATE OVERVIEW. This global $4.5 billion revenue aircraft electronics (avionics) maker conducts its business through two segments: Commercial Systems (CS) and Government Systems (GS). CS (50% of revenues and 48% of segment operating earnings, and segment operating margins of 20% in FY 07 (Sep.)) primarily makes flight deck electronic systems and in-flight entertainment systems. CS also provides a range of repair and overhaul services. GS (50%; 52%; 22%) primarily makes communication radios and cockpit displays installed in military jets. GS also makes navigation equipment embedded in guided missiles.

Commercial Systems products include integrated avionics systems, which include liquid crystal flight displays, flight management, integrated flight control, automatic flight controls, engine indications, and crew alerts; cabin electronics, including passenger connectivity and entertainment, business support systems, networks, and environmental controls; communications products and systems; navigation products and systems; and situational awareness and surveillance products and systems, such as Heads-Up Guidance Systems, weather radar, and collision avoidance systems; flight deck systems, including liquid crystal, cathode ray tube, and heads-up displays; information management systems; simulation and training systems; and maintenance, repair, parts, and support services. Customers include large commercial airplane, regional jet, and business jet makers; commercial airlines; regional airlines; fractional jet operators; and business jet operators.

Government Systems products include communications systems and products; military data link products; navigation systems and products, including radio navigation systems, global positioning systems (GPS), handheld navigation systems, and multi-mode receivers; subsystems for the flight deck that combine flight operations with navigation and guidance functions; cockpit display systems, including flat panel, helmet-mounted and other displays for fighter/attack aircraft; simulation and training systems; and maintenance, repair, parts, and support services. Customers include the U.S. Department of Defense, other government agencies, civil agencies, defense contractors, and foreign ministries of defense. Products are used for airborne, ground, and shipboard applications.

In FY 07, U.S. Government sales accounted for 36% of total COL sales. Export sales and products made abroad accounted for 32% of total sales. About 89% of FY 07 sales were from fixed-price contracts, which allow benefits of cost savings but carry the burden of potential cost overruns.

## Company Financials Fiscal Year Ended Sep. 30

| Per Share Data ($) | 2008 | 2007 | 2006 | 2005 | 2004 | 2003 | 2002 | 2001 | 2000 | 1999 |
|---|---|---|---|---|---|---|---|---|---|---|
| Tangible Book Value | NA | 5.97 | 3.30 | 2.13 | 3.29 | 2.21 | 2.93 | 4.48 | NA | NA |
| Cash Flow | NA | 4.14 | 3.34 | 2.86 | 2.28 | 2.02 | 1.85 | 1.47 | 1.87 | NA |
| Earnings | 4.16 | 3.45 | 2.73 | 2.20 | 1.67 | 1.43 | 1.28 | 0.72 | 1.35 | NA |
| S&P Core Earnings | NA | 3.35 | 2.66 | 2.04 | 1.47 | 0.82 | 0.46 | NA | NA | NA |
| Dividends | NA | 0.64 | 0.56 | 0.48 | 0.39 | 0.36 | 0.36 | Nil | NA | NA |
| Payout Ratio | NA | 19% | 21% | 22% | 23% | 25% | 28% | Nil | NA | NA |
| Prices:High | NA | 76.00 | 64.31 | 49.80 | 40.94 | 30.10 | 28.00 | 27.12 | NA | NA |
| Prices:Low | NA | 61.25 | 43.49 | 37.22 | 29.16 | 17.20 | 18.50 | 11.80 | NA | NA |
| P/E Ratio:High | NA | 22 | 24 | 23 | 25 | 21 | 22 | 38 | NA | NA |
| P/E Ratio:Low | NA | 18 | 16 | 17 | 17 | 12 | 14 | 16 | NA | NA |

| Income Statement Analysis (Million $) | | | | | | | | | | |
|---|---|---|---|---|---|---|---|---|---|---|
| Revenue | 4,769 | 4,415 | 3,863 | 3,445 | 2,930 | 2,542 | 2,492 | 2,820 | 2,510 | 2,438 |
| Operating Income | NA | 959 | 776 | 660 | 539 | 440 | 427 | 492 | 492 | NA |
| Depreciation | 129 | 118 | 106 | 119 | 109 | 105 | 105 | 131 | 99.0 | 86.0 |
| Interest Expense | NA | 13.0 | 13.0 | 11.0 | 8.00 | 3.00 | 6.00 | 3.00 | 20.0 | NA |
| Pretax Income | 953 | 843 | 689 | 547 | 430 | 368 | 341 | 224 | 381 | 437 |
| Effective Tax Rate | 28.9% | 30.6% | 30.8% | 27.6% | 30.0% | 29.9% | 30.8% | 37.9% | 32.5% | 33.4% |
| Net Income | 678 | 585 | 477 | 396 | 301 | 258 | 236 | 139 | 257 | 291 |
| S&P Core Earnings | NA | 568 | 465 | 367 | 264 | 148 | 86.8 | 59.2 | NA | NA |

| Balance Sheet & Other Financial Data (Million $) | | | | | | | | | | |
|---|---|---|---|---|---|---|---|---|---|---|
| Cash | 175 | 231 | 144 | 145 | 196 | 66.0 | 49.0 | 60.0 | 20.0 | 20.0 |
| Current Assets | NA | 2,169 | 1,927 | 1,775 | 1,663 | 1,427 | 1,438 | 1,639 | 1,531 | NA |
| Total Assets | 4,144 | 3,750 | 3,278 | 3,140 | 2,874 | 2,591 | 2,560 | 2,628 | 2,628 | 2,033 |
| Current Liabilities | NA | 1,459 | 1,324 | 1,177 | 964 | 901 | 1,043 | 1,135 | 1,073 | NA |
| Long Term Debt | NA | 223 | 245 | 200 | 201 | Nil | Nil | Nil | Nil | NA |
| Common Equity | 1,408 | 1,573 | 1,206 | 939 | 1,133 | 833 | 987 | 1,110 | 1,086 | 695 |
| Total Capital | NA | 1,840 | 1,451 | 1,139 | 1,334 | 833 | 987 | 1,110 | 1,086 | NA |
| Capital Expenditures | 171 | 125 | 144 | 111 | 94.0 | 72.0 | 62.0 | 110 | NA | 127 |
| Cash Flow | NA | 703 | 583 | 515 | 410 | 363 | 341 | 270 | 356 | NA |
| Current Ratio | 1.3 | 1.5 | 1.5 | 1.5 | 1.7 | 1.6 | 1.4 | 1.4 | 1.4 | 1.5 |
| % Long Term Debt of Capitalization | 13.9 | 12.1 | 16.9 | 17.6 | 15.1 | Nil | Nil | Nil | Nil | Nil |
| % Net Income of Revenue | 14.2 | 13.3 | 12.3 | 11.5 | 10.3 | 10.1 | 9.5 | 4.9 | 10.2 | 11.9 |
| % Return on Assets | 17.2 | 16.7 | 14.8 | 13.2 | 11.0 | 10.0 | 9.1 | 5.9 | NA | NA |
| % Return on Equity | 45.5 | 42.1 | 44.5 | 38.2 | 30.6 | 28.4 | 22.5 | 13.8 | NA | NA |

Data as orig reptd.; bef. results of disc opers/spec. items. Per share data adj. for stk. divs.; EPS diluted. E-Estimated. NA-Not Available. NM-Not Meaningful. NR-Not Ranked. UR-Under Review.

**Office:** 400 Collins Rd NE, Cedar Rapids, IA 52498-0503.
**Telephone:** 319-295-1000.
**Email:** investorrelations@rockwellcollins.com
**Website:** http://www.rockwellcollins.com

**Chrmn, Pres & CEO:** C.M. Jones
**COO:** J.A. Moore
**SVP & CFO:** P.E. Allen
**SVP & CTO:** N. Mattai

**SVP, Secy & General Counsel:** G.R. Chadick
**Investor Contact:** D. Crookshank (319-295-7575)
**Board Members:** D. R. Beall, A. J. Carbone, C. A. Davis, M. Donegan, R. E. Eberhart, C. M. Jones, A. J. Policano, C. L. Shavers

**Employees:** 19,500

*The McGraw-Hill Companies*

# Rohm and Haas Co

**STANDARD &POOR'S**

| S&P Recommendation | HOLD ★★★★★ | Price $72.94 (as of Nov 14, 2008) | 12-Mo. Target Price $78.00 |
|---|---|---|---|

**GICS Sector** Materials
**Sub-Industry** Specialty Chemicals

**Summary** ROH, one of the world's largest producers of specialty chemicals and plastics, in July 2008 agreed to be acquired for $78 a share.

## Key Stock Statistics (Source S&P, Vickers, company reports)

| | | | | | | | |
|---|---|---|---|---|---|---|---|
| 52-Wk Range | $76.50–44.13 | S&P Oper. EPS 2008**E** | 3.35 | Market Capitalization(B) | $14.238 | Beta | 0.58 |
| Trailing 12-Month EPS | $3.20 | S&P Oper. EPS 2009**E** | 3.50 | Yield (%) | 2.25 | S&P 3-Yr. Proj. EPS CAGR(%) | 10 |
| Trailing 12-Month P/E | 22.8 | P/E on S&P Oper. EPS 2008**E** | 21.8 | Dividend Rate/Share | $1.64 | S&P Credit Rating | BBB |
| $10K Invested 5 Yrs Ago | $20,754 | Common Shares Outstg. (M) | 195.2 | Institutional Ownership (%) | 87 | | |

## Price Performance

30-Week Mov. Avg. · · · 10-Week Mov. Avg. – – **GAAP Earnings vs. Previous Year** Volume Above Avg. STARS
12-Mo. Target Price — Relative Strength — ▲ Up ▼ Down ► No Change Below Avg. ★

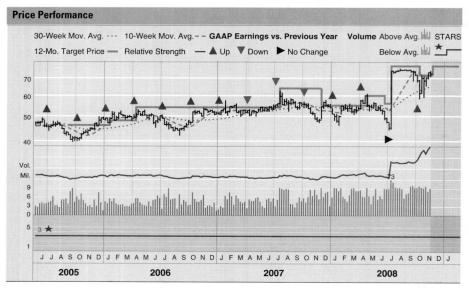

Options: ASE, CBOE, Ph

## Qualitative Risk Assessment

| LOW | MEDIUM | HIGH |
|---|---|---|

Our risk assessment reflects our view of the broad mix and cash flow generation ability of the company's business segments, offset by the cyclical nature of many of the product lines and exposure to volatile raw material and energy costs.

## Quantitative Evaluations

**S&P Quality Ranking** A-

| D | C | B- | B | B+ | A- | A | A+ |
|---|---|---|---|---|---|---|---|

**Relative Strength Rank** STRONG

95

LOWEST = 1    HIGHEST = 99

## Revenue/Earnings Data

**Revenue (Million $)**

| | 1Q | 2Q | 3Q | 4Q | Year |
|---|---|---|---|---|---|
| 2008 | 2,507 | 2,567 | 2,471 | -- | -- |
| 2007 | 2,160 | 2,190 | 2,204 | 2,343 | 8,897 |
| 2006 | 2,058 | 2,081 | 2,065 | 2,026 | 8,230 |
| 2005 | 2,022 | 2,007 | 1,953 | 2,012 | 7,994 |
| 2004 | 1,832 | 1,801 | 1,803 | 1,864 | 7,300 |
| 2003 | 1,613 | 1,570 | 1,591 | 1,647 | 6,421 |

**Earnings Per Share ($)**

| | | | | | |
|---|---|---|---|---|---|
| 2008 | 0.88 | 0.75 | 0.66 | E0.88 | E3.35 |
| 2007 | 0.86 | 0.75 | 0.61 | 0.91 | 3.13 |
| 2006 | 0.93 | 0.87 | 0.86 | 0.76 | 3.41 |
| 2005 | 0.70 | 0.80 | 0.76 | 0.59 | 2.86 |
| 2004 | 0.51 | 0.52 | 0.61 | 0.56 | 2.21 |
| 2003 | 0.37 | -0.02 | 0.45 | 0.49 | 1.30 |

Fiscal year ended Dec. 31. Next earnings report expected: Late January. EPS Estimates based on S&P Operating Earnings; historical GAAP earnings are as reported.

## Highlights

➤ The 12-month target price for ROH has recently been changed to $78.00 from $78.00. The Highlights section of this Stock Report will be updated accordingly.

## Investment Rationale/Risk

➤ The Investment Rationale/Risk section of this Stock Report will be updated shortly. For the latest News story on ROH from MarketScope, see below.

➤ 11/14/08 12:12 pm ET ... S&P MAINTAINS HOLD RECOMMENDATION ON SHARES OF ROHM & HAAS (ROH 72.56***): We are raising our target price by $6 to $78 to reflect our greater confidence that the planned buyout of ROH at $78 a share by Dow Chemical (DOW 21.95****) will be completed in early '09 as planned, subject to regulatory approvals. We note that a large portion of the nearly $19 billion price of the merger will come from the pending formation of a 50%-owned JV for $9.5B with Kuwait Petrochemical, involving DOW's global ethylene chain plastics, and a $4 billion investment in DOW from Kuwait Investment Authority and Berkshire Hathaway (BRK.A 100950***). /R. O'Reilly-CFA

## Dividend Data (Dates: mm/dd Payment Date: mm/dd/yy)

| Amount ($) | Date Decl. | Ex-Div. Date | Stk. of Record | Payment Date |
|---|---|---|---|---|
| 0.370 | 02/04 | 02/13 | 02/15 | 03/01/08 |
| 0.410 | 05/05 | 05/14 | 05/16 | 06/01/08 |
| 0.410 | 07/21 | 08/06 | 08/08 | 09/01/08 |
| 0.410 | 09/25 | 10/29 | 10/31 | 12/01/08 |

Dividends have been paid since 1927. Source: Company reports.

---

**Please read the Required Disclosures and Analyst Certification on the last page of this report.**

The **McGraw·Hill** Companies

# Rohm and Haas Co

## Business Summary October 08, 2008

CORPORATE OVERVIEW. Rohm & Haas, one of the world's largest specialty chemical companies, on July 10, 2008, agreed to be acquired for $78.00 a share by Dow Chemical Co. From the 1999 purchase of Morton International Inc., the company is now a leading global maker of chemicals used in coatings, adhesives, sealants, plastics, and electronic materials. International operations accounted for 56% of sales in 2007.

As a result of a reorganization in January 2007, the company reported six new segments beginning in 2007 (electronic materials and salt segments remain unchanged). Paint and coatings materials (21% of sales and 27% of income in 2007) includes polymers and resins (including opaque polymers, emulsions, rheology modifiers, binders, thickeners, dispersants) for use in architectural and industrial paints and coatings. Packaging and building materials (18%, 13%) consists of the plastic additives business (impact modifiers, processing aids, thermal stabilizers and lubricants); the former adhesives and sealants segment consisting of materials for use in pressure sensitive tapes and labels, laminated food packaging, graphic arts, and industrial products; and specialty polymers and coatings for use in leather, textile, graphic arts, paper, and packaging applications.

The primary materials segment (21%, 9%) consists of the former monomers business, which produces methyl methacrylate, acrylic acid and specialty monomers, as well as polyacrylic acid dispersants. ROH uses these products in many of its acrylic technologies in other segments, and they are also sold externally (47% in 2007) for use in superabsorbent polymers and acrylic resins and sheet.

The performance materials segment (12%, 11%) largely consists of process chemicals and biocides (63% of segment sales), including ion exchange and fluid process chemicals for water treatment and food and chemical processing; inorganic chemicals (sodium borohydride); and antimicrobials, water-soluble emulsions, dispersants, and scale inhibitors for cleaning and personal care products. The segment also includes powder coatings (28%) for automobile parts, building products, appliances, furniture and machinery; and other niche technologies such as the AgroFresh business. In October 2006, ROH sold its automotive liquids coatings business (excluding European operations) for $230 million (reported as discontinued operations in 2006; sales of $109 million in 2005). In June 2007, ROH sold its European automotive coatings business to Mader Group.

## Company Financials Fiscal Year Ended Dec. 31

| Per Share Data ($) | 2007 | 2006 | 2005 | 2004 | 2003 | 2002 | 2001 | 2000 | 1999 | 1998 |
|---|---|---|---|---|---|---|---|---|---|---|
| Tangible Book Value | NM | 4.58 | 3.14 | 1.37 | 0.13 | NM | NM | NM | NM | 8.77 |
| Cash Flow | 5.35 | 5.52 | 5.00 | 4.36 | 3.44 | 3.04 | 2.24 | 4.39 | 5.87 | 4.04 |
| Earnings | 3.12 | 3.41 | 2.86 | 2.21 | 1.30 | 0.98 | -0.31 | 1.61 | 1.27 | 2.52 |
| S&P Core Earnings | 3.45 | 3.45 | 2.81 | 1.98 | 0.90 | 0.23 | -0.91 | NA | NA | NA |
| Dividends | 1.81 | 1.28 | 1.12 | 0.97 | 0.86 | 0.82 | 0.80 | 0.78 | 0.74 | 0.69 |
| Payout Ratio | 58% | 38% | 39% | 44% | 66% | 84% | NM | 48% | 58% | 27% |
| Prices:High | 62.68 | 53.99 | 50.00 | 45.41 | 43.05 | 42.60 | 38.70 | 49.44 | 49.25 | 38.88 |
| Prices:Low | 47.05 | 41.92 | 39.47 | 35.90 | 26.26 | 30.19 | 24.90 | 24.38 | 28.13 | 26.00 |
| P/E Ratio:High | 20 | 16 | 17 | 21 | 33 | 43 | NM | 31 | 39 | 15 |
| P/E Ratio:Low | 15 | 12 | 14 | 16 | 20 | 31 | NM | 15 | 22 | 10 |

| Income Statement Analysis (Million $) | 2007 | 2006 | 2005 | 2004 | 2003 | 2002 | 2001 | 2000 | 1999 | 1998 |
|---|---|---|---|---|---|---|---|---|---|---|
| Revenue | 8,897 | 8,230 | 7,994 | 7,300 | 6,421 | 5,727 | 5,666 | 6,879 | 5,339 | 3,720 |
| Operating Income | 1,492 | 1,565 | 1,522 | 1,291 | 1,264 | 1,066 | 973 | 1,395 | 1,220 | 898 |
| Depreciation | 469 | 465 | 481 | 481 | 478 | 457 | 562 | 613 | 902 | 276 |
| Interest Expense | 132 | 94.0 | 117 | 133 | 126 | 132 | 182 | 241 | 159 | 34.0 |
| Pretax Income | 880 | 1,042 | 872 | 692 | 415 | 320 | -64.0 | 576 | 465 | 690 |
| Effective Tax Rate | 23.4% | 26.3% | 25.7% | 29.9% | 30.6% | 31.9% | NM | 39.4% | 46.2% | 34.1% |
| Net Income | 660 | 755 | 638 | 496 | 288 | 218 | -70.0 | 354 | 249 | 453 |
| S&P Core Earnings | 731 | 763 | 627 | 446 | 209 | 50.9 | -202 | NA | NA | NA |

| Balance Sheet & Other Financial Data (Million $) | 2007 | 2006 | 2005 | 2004 | 2003 | 2002 | 2001 | 2000 | 1999 | 1998 |
|---|---|---|---|---|---|---|---|---|---|---|
| Cash | 268 | 593 | 566 | 625 | 196 | 295 | 92.0 | 92.0 | 57.0 | 16.0 |
| Current Assets | 3,527 | 3,411 | 3,205 | 3,247 | 2,527 | 2,543 | 2,421 | 2,781 | 2,497 | 1,287 |
| Total Assets | 10,208 | 9,553 | 9,727 | 10,095 | 9,445 | 9,706 | 10,350 | 11,267 | 11,256 | 3,648 |
| Current Liabilities | 1,870 | 1,988 | 1,694 | 1,740 | 1,797 | 1,621 | 1,624 | 2,194 | 2,510 | 875 |
| Long Term Debt | 3,139 | 1,688 | 2,074 | 2,563 | 2,468 | 2,872 | 2,720 | 3,225 | 3,122 | 409 |
| Common Equity | 3,146 | 4,031 | 3,917 | 3,697 | 3,357 | 3,333 | 3,815 | 3,693 | 3,475 | 1,488 |
| Total Capital | 7,266 | 6,595 | 7,089 | 7,423 | 6,775 | 7,402 | 7,831 | 8,228 | 7,847 | 2,157 |
| Capital Expenditures | 417 | 404 | 333 | 5.00 | 339 | 407 | 401 | 391 | 323 | 229 |
| Cash Flow | 1,129 | 1,220 | 1,119 | 977 | 766 | 675 | 492 | 967 | 1,149 | 723 |
| Current Ratio | 1.9 | 1.7 | 1.9 | 1.9 | 1.4 | 1.6 | 1.5 | 1.3 | 1.0 | 1.5 |
| % Long Term Debt of Capitalization | 43.2 | 25.6 | 29.3 | 34.5 | 36.4 | 38.8 | 34.7 | 39.2 | 39.8 | 19.0 |
| % Net Income of Revenue | 7.4 | 9.2 | 8.0 | 6.8 | 4.5 | 3.8 | NM | 5.1 | 4.7 | 12.2 |
| % Return on Assets | 6.7 | 7.8 | 6.4 | 5.1 | 3.0 | 2.2 | NM | 3.1 | 3.3 | 12.0 |
| % Return on Equity | 18.4 | 19.0 | 16.8 | 14.1 | 8.9 | 5.9 | NM | 9.8 | 10.0 | 28.3 |

Data as orig reptd.; bef. results of disc opers/spec. items. Per share data adj. for stk. divs.; EPS diluted. E-Estimated. NA-Not Available. NM-Not Meaningful. NR-Not Ranked. UR-Under Review.

**Office:** 100 S Independence Mall W, Philadelphia, PA 19106.
**Telephone:** 215-592-3000.
**Website:** http://www.rohmhaas.com
**Chrmn & CEO:** R.L. Gupta

**Pres & COO:** P.R. Brondeau
**EVP & CFO:** J.M. Croisetiere
**EVP, Secy & General Counsel:** R.A. Lonergan
**EVP & CIO:** A.M. Wilms

**Investor Contact:** A.D. Sandifer (215-592-3312)
**Board Members:** W. J. Avery, R. L. Gupta, D. W. Haas, T. W. Haas, R. L. Keyser, R. J. Mills, S. O. Moose, G. S. Omenn, G. L. Rogers, R. Schmitz, G. M. Whitesides, M. C. Whittington

**Founded:** 1909
**Domicile:** Delaware
**Employees:** 15,710

# Rowan Companies Inc.

| S&P Recommendation HOLD ★★★☆☆ | Price $16.04 (as of Nov 14, 2008) | 12-Mo. Target Price $23.00 | Investment Style Large-Cap Value |
|---|---|---|---|

**GICS Sector** Energy
**Sub-Industry** Oil & Gas Drilling

**Summary** This company performs contract oil and natural gas drilling, and builds heavy equipment and offshore drilling rigs.

## Key Stock Statistics (Source S&P, Vickers, company reports)

| | | | | | | | |
|---|---|---|---|---|---|---|---|
| 52-Wk Range | $47.94–13.75 | S&P Oper. EPS 2008**E** | 4.02 | Market Capitalization(B) | $1.813 | Beta | 1.55 |
| Trailing 12-Month EPS | $4.17 | S&P Oper. EPS 2009**E** | 4.79 | Yield (%) | 2.49 | S&P 3-Yr. Proj. EPS CAGR(%) | 23 |
| Trailing 12-Month P/E | 3.9 | P/E on S&P Oper. EPS 2008**E** | 4.0 | Dividend Rate/Share | $0.40 | S&P Credit Rating | NR |
| $10K Invested 5 Yrs Ago | $7,068 | Common Shares Outstg. (M) | 113.0 | Institutional Ownership (%) | 92 | | |

## Price Performance

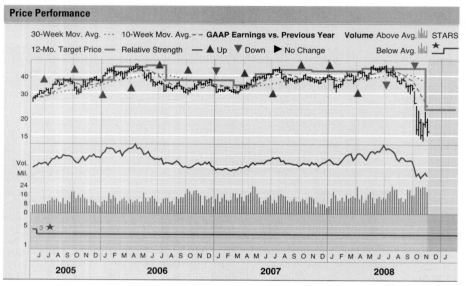

30-Week Mov. Avg. ···  10-Week Mov. Avg. - - GAAP Earnings vs. Previous Year  Volume Above Avg. STARS
12-Mo. Target Price — Relative Strength — ▲ Up ▼ Down ▶ No Change  Below Avg. ★

Options: ASE, CBOE, P

Analysis prepared by **Stewart Glickman, CFA** on November 05, 2008, when the stock traded at **$ 21.87**.

## Highlights

➤ In September, RDC lost its lowest-specification jackup rig, the Rowan Anchorage, during Hurricane Ike. However, as the rig was insured for more than book value, we expect RDC to incur a gain from the event, and we think the loss of the rig curtails 2009 EPS by perhaps $0.10 - $0.15 (roughly 2% to 3%). We expect U.S. Gulf of Mexico jackup dayrates to be weak (relative to international jackup dayrates) in 2009, and we would not be surprised to see RDC mobilize some of its existing eight domestic units to international waters for better pricing and longer-term deals; recent domestic jackup utilization was only around 70%.

➤ As of November 2008, RDC had nine premium jackups under construction, versus 20 active rigs, implying a more than 40% expansion to its rig count - well in excess of most peers. We do see some risk of delivery slippage, given the recent credit crisis and damage sustained to RDC's Houston facilities during the recent hurricanes. RDC said in October that plans to monetize its LTI manufacturing division were on hold, given the uncertain credit environment.

➤ We see operating EPS of $4.02 in 2008, rising to $4.79 in 2009.

## Investment Rationale/Risk

➤ We expect international jackup dayrates to remain strong in 2009. RDC has successfully diversified its fleet geographically, with 12 of 20 active rigs working in non-U.S. waters (versus just 3 of 19 rigs two years ago), and with a fleet of largely premium assets, we also believe further rig mobilizations away from the Gulf are possible. While global newbuild jackup deliveries loom on the horizon, mainly in 2009-2011, we believe the potential for delays in deliveries, natural rig attrition, and rising demand for rigs should mitigate some of this concern.

➤ Risks to our recommendation and target price include lower dayrates and utilization; reduced drilling activity in the Gulf of Mexico; and shipyard delays.

➤ Our net asset valuation model, assuming terminal growth of 3% per year and a weighted average cost of capital of 11.1%, indicates that the shares have an intrinsic value of $27. Assuming relative multiples of 3X estimated 2009 EBITDA and 4X projected 2009 earnings (a discount to peers, warranted, we think, by a below-peers ROIC), and blending with our NAV model, our 12-month target price is $23.

## Qualitative Risk Assessment

| LOW | MEDIUM | HIGH |
|---|---|---|

Our risk assessment reflects RDC's exposure to volatile crude oil and natural gas prices, capital spending decisions made by its oil and gas producing customers, and risks associated with operating in frontier regions. Offsetting these risks is the company's relatively higher specification jackup rig fleet than peers.

## Quantitative Evaluations

**S&P Quality Ranking**                                     B

| D | C | B- | B | B+ | A- | A | A+ |
|---|---|---|---|---|---|---|---|

**Relative Strength Rank**                             WEAK

27

LOWEST = 1                                      HIGHEST = 99

## Revenue/Earnings Data

**Revenue (Million $)**

| | 1Q | 2Q | 3Q | 4Q | Year |
|---|---|---|---|---|---|
| 2008 | 485.5 | 587.1 | 527.1 | -- | -- |
| 2007 | 465.3 | 507.0 | 502.2 | 623.6 | 2,095 |
| 2006 | 299.8 | 382.9 | 417.1 | 411.0 | 1,511 |
| 2005 | 222.4 | 244.6 | 284.4 | 317.4 | 1,069 |
| 2004 | 170.5 | 190.9 | 234.6 | 202.2 | 708.5 |
| 2003 | 131.4 | 158.1 | 193.9 | 195.8 | 679.1 |

**Earnings Per Share ($)**

| | | | | | |
|---|---|---|---|---|---|
| 2008 | 0.88 | 1.06 | 1.00 | E1.08 | E4.02 |
| 2007 | 0.77 | 1.14 | 1.16 | 1.23 | 4.31 |
| 2006 | 0.53 | 0.98 | 0.77 | 0.56 | 2.84 |
| 2005 | 0.28 | 0.39 | 0.67 | 0.63 | 1.97 |
| 2004 | -0.11 | -0.02 | 0.09 | 0.15 | 0.25 |
| 2003 | -0.18 | -0.07 | 0.12 | 0.05 | -0.08 |

Fiscal year ended Dec. 31. Next earnings report expected: Late February. EPS Estimates based on S&P Operating Earnings; historical GAAP earnings are as reported.

## Dividend Data (Dates: mm/dd Payment Date: mm/dd/yy)

| Amount ($) | Date Decl. | Ex-Div. Date | Stk. of Record | Payment Date |
|---|---|---|---|---|
| 0.100 | 01/31 | 02/12 | 02/14 | 02/29/08 |
| 0.100 | 05/15 | 05/28 | 05/30 | 06/13/08 |
| 0.100 | 08/01 | 08/12 | 08/14 | 08/29/08 |
| 0.100 | 10/31 | 11/12 | 11/14 | 11/28/08 |

Dividends have been paid since 2005. Source: Company reports.

---

## Business Summary November 05, 2008

CORPORATE OVERVIEW. Rowan Companies, a major provider of international and domestic contract drilling services, also operates a mini-steel mill, a manufacturing facility that produces heavy equipment, and a marine construction division. As of February 2008, RDC operated 21 jackup rigs (comprised of 17 cantilever jackups and four conventional jackups), and a fleet of 29 land rigs. Of the 21 active jackups in the fleet, nine were in the Middle East, eight were in the Gulf of Mexico (GOM), three were in the North Sea, and one was in Trinidad. The company's jackup rigs perform both exploratory and development drilling and, in certain areas, well workover operations. Its larger jackups can drill to depths of 20,000 ft. to 30,000 ft. in maximum water depths of 250 ft. to 490 ft. Of the 17 active cantilever jackup rigs, three are harsh environment Gorilla Class rigs, four are enhanced Super Gorilla Class rigs, and three are Tarzan Class rigs.

In 2007, the Drilling Services segment (which includes the offshore rigs and land rigs) contributed 66% of total revenues, and 90% of income from operations. RDC's Manufacturing operations, conducted by LeTourneau Technologies, Inc., comprise the remaining 34% and 10%, respectively, through two operating segments: Drilling Products and Systems (DPS; 24% and 6%), and Mining, Forestry and Steel Products (MFS; 10% and 4%).

IMPACT OF MAJOR DEVELOPMENTS. In March 2008, the company said it would explore strategic alternatives for its LeTourneau Technologies Inc. business, including a potential spin-off to RDC shareholders. From a strategic perspective, we think such a move could be beneficial to RDC, given that operating margins in its Manufacturing operations are typically lower than for its Drilling Services segment.

LEGAL PROCEEDINGS. The construction of RDC's fourth Tarzan-class rig, the JP Bussell, was originally subcontracted to an outside Gulf of Mexico shipyard, Signal International LLC (Signal), and slated for delivery in the third quarter of 2007, at a total cost of approximately $145 million. However, as a result of problems encountered in this project, RDC now expects the rig to be delayed at least one year behind its original schedule, with a final cost at least 20% above the original estimate. Consequently, RDC has declared breach of contract against Signal, initiated court proceedings to relocate the rig to one of RDC's own DPS facilities for completion, and to recover any costs incurred over and above the contract price.

## Company Financials Fiscal Year Ended Dec. 31

| Per Share Data ($) | 2007 | 2006 | 2005 | 2004 | 2003 | 2002 | 2001 | 2000 | 1999 | 1998 |
|---|---|---|---|---|---|---|---|---|---|---|
| Tangible Book Value | 20.99 | 16.97 | 14.75 | 12.97 | 11.95 | 12.09 | 11.84 | 11.17 | 8.69 | 8.77 |
| Cash Flow | 5.37 | 3.64 | 2.71 | 1.14 | 0.84 | 1.72 | 1.52 | 1.36 | 0.54 | 2.00 |
| Earnings | 4.31 | 2.84 | 1.97 | 0.25 | -0.08 | 0.90 | 0.80 | 0.74 | -0.12 | 1.43 |
| S&P Core Earnings | 4.10 | 2.76 | 1.63 | 0.28 | -0.05 | -0.31 | 0.65 | NA | NA | NA |
| Dividends | 0.40 | 0.30 | Nil | Nil | Nil | Nil | Nil | Nil | Nil | Nil |
| Payout Ratio | 9% | 11% | Nil | Nil | Nil | Nil | Nil | Nil | Nil | Nil |
| Prices:High | 46.16 | 48.15 | 39.50 | 27.26 | 26.72 | 27.03 | 33.89 | 34.25 | 21.69 | 32.50 |
| Prices:Low | 29.48 | 29.03 | 24.53 | 20.44 | 17.70 | 16.04 | 11.10 | 19.06 | 8.50 | 9.00 |
| P/E Ratio:High | 11 | 17 | 20 | NM | NM | 30 | 42 | 46 | NM | 23 |
| P/E Ratio:Low | 7 | 10 | 12 | NM | NM | 18 | 14 | 26 | NM | 6 |

| Income Statement Analysis (Million $) | | | | | | | | | | |
|---|---|---|---|---|---|---|---|---|---|---|
| Revenue | 2,095 | 1,511 | 1,069 | 709 | 679 | 617 | 731 | 646 | 461 | 706 |
| Operating Income | 812 | 555 | 355 | 152 | 89.0 | 65.1 | 193 | 170 | 45.1 | 232 |
| Depreciation, Depletion and Amortization | 119 | 90.0 | 81.3 | 95.7 | 86.9 | 78.1 | 68.5 | 58.9 | 54.7 | 49.7 |
| Interest Expense | 25.9 | 20.6 | 22.0 | 18.7 | 15.9 | 15.9 | 13.1 | 12.1 | 11.5 | 1.24 |
| Pretax Income | 739 | 493 | 345 | 42.8 | -12.0 | 133 | 120 | 111 | -14.5 | 194 |
| Effective Tax Rate | 34.5% | 35.8% | 36.9% | 38.4% | NM | 35.0% | 35.9% | 36.7% | NM | 35.7% |
| Net Income | 484 | 317 | 218 | 26.4 | -7.77 | 86.3 | 77.0 | 70.2 | -9.67 | 124 |
| S&P Core Earnings | 460 | 308 | 181 | 28.9 | -4.74 | -30.2 | 62.8 | NA | NA | NA |

| Balance Sheet & Other Financial Data (Million $) | | | | | | | | | | |
|---|---|---|---|---|---|---|---|---|---|---|
| Cash | 284 | 258 | 676 | 466 | 58.2 | 179 | 237 | 193 | 87.1 | 149 |
| Current Assets | 1,303 | 1,103 | 1,208 | 815 | 444 | 470 | 507 | 483 | 325 | 366 |
| Total Assets | 3,875 | 3,435 | 2,975 | 2,492 | 2,191 | 2,055 | 1,939 | 1,678 | 1,356 | 1,249 |
| Current Liabilities | 496 | 517 | 341 | 235 | 150 | 116 | 201 | 104 | 202 | 79.6 |
| Long Term Debt | 420 | 485 | 550 | 574 | 569 | 513 | 438 | 372 | 297 | 310 |
| Common Equity | 2,348 | 1,874 | 1,620 | 1,409 | 1,137 | 1,132 | 1,108 | 1,053 | 724 | 730 |
| Total Capital | 3,182 | 2,707 | 2,485 | 2,147 | 1,924 | 1,811 | 1,674 | 1,516 | 1,099 | 1,116 |
| Capital Expenditures | 463 | 479 | 200 | 137 | 250 | 243 | 305 | 216 | 205 | 248 |
| Cash Flow | 603 | 407 | 299 | 122 | 79.1 | 164 | 145 | 129 | 45.0 | 174 |
| Current Ratio | 2.6 | 2.1 | 3.5 | 3.5 | 3.0 | 4.1 | 2.5 | 4.6 | 1.6 | 4.6 |
| % Long Term Debt of Capitalization | 13.2 | 17.9 | 22.1 | 26.8 | 29.6 | 28.3 | 26.2 | 24.5 | 27.0 | 27.8 |
| % Return on Assets | 13.2 | 9.9 | 8.0 | 1.1 | NM | 4.3 | 4.3 | 4.6 | NM | 10.5 |
| % Return on Equity | 22.9 | 18.1 | 14.4 | 2.1 | NM | 7.7 | 7.1 | 7.9 | NM | 18.0 |

Data as orig reptd.; bef. results of disc opers/spec. items. Per share data adj. for stk. divs.; EPS diluted. E-Estimated. NA-Not Available. NM-Not Meaningful. NR-Not Ranked. UR-Under Review.

**Office:** 2800 Post Oak Blvd Ste 5450, Houston, TX 77056-6127.
**Telephone:** 713-621-7800.
**Email:** ir@rowancompanies.com
**Website:** http://www.rowancompanies.com

**Chrmn, Pres & CEO:** D. McNease
**CFO:** W.H. Wells
**Chief Acctg Officer & Cntlr:** G.M. Hatfield
**Secy:** M.M. Trent

**General Counsel:** J.L. Buvens
**Investor Contact:** W.C. Provine (713-960-7575)
**Board Members:** R. G. Croyle, W. T. Fox, III, G. Hearne, J. R. Huff, R. E. Kramek, F. R. Lausen, H. E. Lentz, Jr., D. McNease, C. B. Moynihan, P. D. Peacock

**Founded:** 1923
**Domicile:** Delaware
**Employees:** 5,704

# Ryder System Inc

**STANDARD & POOR'S**

**S&P Recommendation** HOLD ★★★☆☆

| Price | 12-Mo. Target Price | Investment Style |
|---|---|---|
| $36.91 (as of Nov 14, 2008) | $46.00 | Large-Cap Value |

**GICS Sector** Industrials
**Sub-Industry** Trucking

**Summary** This company provides truck leasing and rental, logistics, and supply chain management solutions worldwide.

## Key Stock Statistics (Source S&P, Vickers, company reports)

| | | | | | | | |
|---|---|---|---|---|---|---|---|
| 52-Wk Range | $76.64– 34.15 | S&P Oper. EPS 2008E | 4.48 | Market Capitalization(B) | $2.053 | Beta | 1.10 |
| Trailing 12-Month EPS | $4.55 | S&P Oper. EPS 2009E | 4.95 | Yield (%) | 2.49 | S&P 3-Yr. Proj. EPS CAGR(%) | 13 |
| Trailing 12-Month P/E | 8.1 | P/E on S&P Oper. EPS 2008E | 8.2 | Dividend Rate/Share | $0.92 | S&P Credit Rating | BBB+ |
| $10K Invested 5 Yrs Ago | $13,989 | Common Shares Outstg. (M) | 55.6 | Institutional Ownership (%) | NM | | |

## Price Performance

30-Week Mov. Avg. ···  10-Week Mov. Avg. – – **GAAP Earnings vs. Previous Year**  Volume Above Avg. STARS
12-Mo. Target Price — Relative Strength  ▲ Up  ▼ Down  ► No Change  Below Avg.

Options: ASE, CBOE, P

Analysis prepared by **Kevin Kirkeby** on October 22, 2008, when the stock traded at **$ 38.57.**

## Highlights

➤ We see revenues increasing almost 9% in 2008, with about 6% of that from fuel surcharges. For 2009, we see revenues, excluding the fuel surcharges, rising 8%. Within its largest segment, fleet management solutions, we see new client wins and acquisitions offsetting ongoing softness in commercial rental and auto-related volumes. Fleet size, which we forecast to be flat in 2009, is closely tied to customer demand in the commercial segment.

➤ We anticipate relatively flat margins in 2009, as cost-cutting measures and reductions in fleet size are offset by less favorable lease terms. We expect R to have some difficulty passing along higher funding costs to lease customers whose businesses are likely under pressure from the weakening economy. Following a right-sizing of the tractor fleet in 2008, we look for fewer gains from asset sales in 2009.

➤ We forecast 2009 EPS of $4.95, representing a 10% increase from the $4.48, excluding special items, expected for 2008. In October 2008, R announced plans to acquire two companies involved in logistics and warehousing, for undisclosed terms.

## Investment Rationale/Risk

➤ We expect the company to focus on a strategy of profitable revenue growth in the next few years. Its lease and supply chain segments have provided earnings support during the recent trucking sector slowdown. We believe the more economically sensitive segments, such as commercial rentals, will begin to improve in 2009 and contribute to faster earnings growth. However, with ongoing cuts in auto production, and valuations below their 10-year average, we consider the shares fairly valued.

➤ Risks to our recommendation and target price include weaker than expected economic growth; declining leasing demand and lease rates; increased competition from traditional truckload providers; higher interest rates, to which R is exposed in light of its financial leverage; and declining used vehicle prices.

➤ Our DCF model assumes a WACC of 7.5% and terminal growth of 3.5%, and calculates intrinsic value of $50. Applying an 8.5X multiple, near the bottom of its historical range, to our 12-month forward earnings per share estimate yields a $42 value. Blending these two metrics, we arrive at our 12-month target price of $46.

## Qualitative Risk Assessment

| LOW | MEDIUM | HIGH |
|---|---|---|

Our risk assessment reflects our view of the company's financial leverage, exposure to low-margin businesses, and heavy capital spending needs to maintain its rental fleet, offset by its strong market position in truck leasing and what we see as steady cash flow generated by multi-year lease contracts.

## Quantitative Evaluations

**S&P Quality Ranking**  B+

| D | C | B- | B | B+ | A- | A | A+ |
|---|---|---|---|---|---|---|---|

**Relative Strength Rank**  MODERATE

39

LOWEST = 1  HIGHEST = 99

## Revenue/Earnings Data

**Revenue (Million $)**

| | 1Q | 2Q | 3Q | 4Q | Year |
|---|---|---|---|---|---|
| 2008 | 1,452 | 1,660 | 1,626 | -- | -- |
| 2007 | 1,594 | 1,658 | 1,648 | 1,666 | 6,566 |
| 2006 | 1,496 | 1,596 | 1,621 | 1,594 | 6,307 |
| 2005 | 1,316 | 1,390 | 1,491 | 1,545 | 5,741 |
| 2004 | 1,212 | 1,269 | 1,306 | 1,363 | 5,150 |
| 2003 | 1,194 | 1,197 | 1,194 | 1,217 | 4,802 |

**Earnings Per Share ($)**

| | | | | | |
|---|---|---|---|---|---|
| 2008 | 0.96 | 1.10 | 1.25 | E1.08 | E4.48 |
| 2007 | 0.84 | 1.07 | 1.11 | 1.24 | 4.24 |
| 2006 | 0.77 | 1.13 | 1.06 | 1.08 | 4.04 |
| 2005 | 0.64 | 0.98 | 0.98 | 0.93 | 3.53 |
| 2004 | 0.53 | 0.97 | 0.83 | 0.96 | 3.28 |
| 2003 | 0.33 | 0.55 | 0.63 | 0.61 | 2.12 |

Fiscal year ended Dec. 31. Next earnings report expected: Early February. EPS Estimates based on S&P Operating Earnings; historical GAAP earnings are as reported.

## Dividend Data (Dates: mm/dd Payment Date: mm/dd/yy)

| Amount ($) | Date Decl. | Ex-Div. Date | Stk. of Record | Payment Date |
|---|---|---|---|---|
| 0.230 | 02/08 | 02/15 | 02/20 | 03/14/08 |
| 0.230 | 05/02 | 05/15 | 05/19 | 06/13/08 |
| 0.230 | 07/10 | 08/14 | 08/18 | 09/12/08 |
| 0.230 | 10/24 | 11/13 | 11/17 | 12/12/08 |

Dividends have been paid since 1976. Source: Company reports.

---

**Please read the Required Disclosures and Analyst Certification on the last page of this report.**

The McGraw-Hill Companies

# Ryder System Inc

## Business Summary October 22, 2008

CORPORATE OVERVIEW. Ryder System is primarily a provider of transportation services and equipment to third parties. In 2007, the company generated over 89% of revenues in the United States and Canada, with the remainder spread across Europe, Asia and Latin America. The company serves a broad array of industries, with clients in the automotive, electronics, paper and paper products, food and beverage and retailing industries, among others. For reporting purposes, operations are divided into three segments: Fleet Management Solutions(FMS), Supply Chain Solutions(SCS), and Dedicated Contract Carriage (DCC).

FMS (57% of revenues and 77% of operating profits before eliminations and unallocated costs in 2007) provides full-service truck leasing to customers worldwide. Under a typical full-service lease, R provides customers with vehicles, maintenance, supplies and related equipment necessary for operation, while customers furnish and supervise their own drivers, as well as dispatch and exercise control over the vehicles. R leased approximately 114,100 vehicles under full-service leases at December 31, 2007. FMS also services customer vehicles under maintenance contracts, and provides short-term truck rental to commercial customers that need to supplement their fleets during peak periods. Approximately 50% of Ryder's lease customers in 2006 (latest available) were also customers of the rental unit. About 14% of FMS revenue is generated through commercial rentals. At December 31, 2007, the commer-

cial rental fleet had about 34,100 units, down from about 38,400 at the end of 2005, since the company has been more focused on the longer-term, contractual portions of its business.

SCS (34%, 13%) provides logistics support and transportation along the entire supply chain for its customers. This includes managing inbound raw materials that are sourced far from the manufacturing facility all the way through to distribution of finished goods. Services include combinations of logistics systems and information technology design, the provision of vehicles and equipment (including maintenance and drivers), warehouse and transportation management, vehicle dispatch, and just-in-time delivery. General Motors was one of the unit's largest customers in 2007, accounting for 42% of segment revenues.

The DCC segment (9%, 10%) combines the equipment, maintenance and administrative services of a full-service lease with additional services, including driver hiring and training, routing and scheduling, fleet sizing, and other technical support.

## Company Financials Fiscal Year Ended Dec. 31

| Per Share Data ($) | 2007 | 2006 | 2005 | 2004 | 2003 | 2002 | 2001 | 2000 | 1999 | 1998 |
|---|---|---|---|---|---|---|---|---|---|---|
| Tangible Book Value | 29.32 | 25.48 | 21.81 | 20.65 | 18.09 | 14.97 | 17.51 | 17.43 | 16.87 | 11.51 |
| Cash Flow | 17.89 | 10.57 | 15.65 | 14.03 | 11.90 | 10.65 | 9.30 | 11.20 | 10.12 | 11.12 |
| Earnings | 4.24 | 4.04 | 3.53 | 3.28 | 2.12 | 1.80 | 0.31 | 1.49 | 1.06 | 2.16 |
| S&P Core Earnings | 3.43 | 3.72 | 3.09 | 2.80 | 2.26 | 0.84 | -0.76 | NA | NA | NA |
| Dividends | 0.84 | 0.72 | 0.64 | 0.60 | 0.60 | 0.60 | 0.60 | 0.60 | 0.60 | 0.60 |
| Payout Ratio | 20% | 18% | 18% | 18% | 28% | 33% | 194% | 40% | 57% | 28% |
| Prices:High | 57.70 | 59.93 | 47.82 | 55.55 | 34.65 | 31.09 | 23.19 | 25.13 | 28.75 | 40.56 |
| Prices:Low | 38.95 | 39.61 | 32.00 | 33.61 | 20.00 | 21.05 | 16.06 | 14.81 | 18.81 | 19.44 |
| P/E Ratio:High | 14 | 15 | 14 | 17 | 16 | 17 | 75 | 17 | 27 | 19 |
| P/E Ratio:Low | 9 | 10 | 9 | 10 | 9 | 12 | 52 | 10 | 18 | 9 |

| Income Statement Analysis (Million $) | | | | | | | | | | |
|---|---|---|---|---|---|---|---|---|---|---|
| Revenue | 6,566 | 6,307 | 5,741 | 5,150 | 4,802 | 4,776 | 5,006 | 5,337 | 4,952 | 5,189 |
| Operating Income | 1,336 | 1,218 | 1,165 | 1,076 | 905 | 854 | 798 | 906 | 997 | 1,115 |
| Depreciation | 817 | 743 | 740 | 706 | 625 | 552 | 545 | 580 | 623 | 665 |
| Interest Expense | 160 | 141 | 120 | 100 | 96.2 | 91.7 | 119 | 154 | 184 | 199 |
| Pretax Income | 405 | 786 | 357 | 331 | 212 | 176 | 30.7 | 141 | 117 | 258 |
| Effective Tax Rate | 37.4% | 18.3% | 36.3% | 34.9% | 36.2% | 36.0% | 39.2% | 37.0% | 37.9% | 38.4% |
| Net Income | 254 | 642 | 228 | 216 | 136 | 113 | 18.7 | 89.0 | 72.9 | 159 |
| S&P Core Earnings | 206 | 229 | 200 | 184 | 145 | 53.1 | -46.3 | NA | NA | NA |

| Balance Sheet & Other Financial Data (Million $) | | | | | | | | | | |
|---|---|---|---|---|---|---|---|---|---|---|
| Cash | 200 | 129 | 129 | 101 | 141 | 104 | 118 | 122 | 113 | 138 |
| Current Assets | 1,222 | 1,262 | 1,164 | 1,228 | 1,107 | 1,024 | 982 | 928 | 1,209 | 1,110 |
| Total Assets | 6,855 | 6,829 | 6,033 | 5,638 | 5,279 | 4,767 | 4,924 | 5,475 | 5,770 | 5,709 |
| Current Liabilities | 1,019 | 1,268 | 1,253 | 1,455 | 1,074 | 862 | 1,014 | 1,302 | 1,450 | 1,363 |
| Long Term Debt | 2,553 | 2,484 | 1,916 | 1,394 | 1,449 | 1,389 | 1,392 | 1,604 | 1,819 | 2,100 |
| Common Equity | 1,888 | 1,721 | 1,527 | 1,510 | 1,344 | 1,108 | 1,231 | 1,253 | 1,205 | 1,095 |
| Total Capital | 5,425 | 5,112 | 4,293 | 3,775 | 3,688 | 3,431 | 3,625 | 3,874 | 4,035 | 4,003 |
| Capital Expenditures | 1,317 | 1,695 | 1,399 | 1,092 | 725 | 600 | 657 | 1,289 | 1,734 | 1,369 |
| Cash Flow | 1,071 | 642 | 968 | 922 | 760 | 665 | 564 | 669 | 696 | 824 |
| Current Ratio | 1.2 | 1.0 | 0.9 | 0.8 | 1.0 | 1.2 | 1.0 | 0.7 | 0.8 | 0.8 |
| % Long Term Debt of Capitalization | 47.1 | 48.6 | 44.6 | 36.9 | 39.3 | 40.5 | 38.4 | 41.4 | 45.1 | 52.5 |
| % Net Income of Revenue | 3.9 | 10.2 | 4.0 | 4.2 | 2.8 | 2.4 | 0.4 | 1.7 | 1.5 | 3.1 |
| % Return on Assets | 3.7 | 10.0 | 3.9 | 3.9 | 2.7 | 2.3 | 0.4 | 1.6 | 1.3 | 2.8 |
| % Return on Equity | 14.1 | 39.5 | 15.0 | 15.1 | 11.1 | 9.6 | 1.5 | 7.2 | 1.1 | 14.7 |

Data as orig reptd.; bef. results of disc opers/spec. items. Per share data adj. for stk. divs.; EPS diluted. E-Estimated. NA-Not Available. NM-Not Meaningful. NR-Not Ranked. UR-Under Review.

**Office:** 11690 NW 105th St, Medley, FL 33178-1103.
**Telephone:** 305-593-3726.
**Email:** ryderforinvestor@ryder.com
**Website:** http://www.ryder.com

**Chrmn & CEO:** G.T. Swienton
**EVP & CFO:** R.E. Sanchez
**EVP, Secy & General Counsel:** R.D. Fatovic
**SVP, Chief Acctg Officer & Cntlr:** A.A. Garcia

**SVP & CIO:** K. Bott
**Investor Contact:** B. Brunn (305-500-4053)
**Board Members:** J. S. Beard, J. M. Berra, D. I. Fuente, J. A. Georges, L. P. Hassey, L. Martin, L. P. Nieto, Jr., E. A. Renna, A. J. Smith, E. F. Smith, G. T. Swienton, H. E. Tookes, II, C. Varney

**Founded:** 1955
**Domicile:** Florida
**Employees:** 28,800

# Safeway Inc

STANDARD
&POOR'S

| S&P Recommendation | BUY ★★★★☆ | | Price<br>$20.99 (as of Nov 14, 2008) | 12-Mo. Target Price<br>$26.00 | Investment Style<br>Large-Cap Blend |
|---|---|---|---|---|---|

**GICS Sector** Consumer Staples
**Sub-Industry** Food Retail

**Summary** This major food retailer operates about 1,750 stores in the U.S. and Canada.

## Key Stock Statistics (Source S&P, Vickers, company reports)

| | | | | | | | |
|---|---|---|---|---|---|---|---|
| 52-Wk Range | $36.00– 19.45 | S&P Oper. EPS 2008E | 2.25 | Market Capitalization(B) | $8.998 | Beta | 0.96 |
| Trailing 12-Month EPS | $2.11 | S&P Oper. EPS 2009E | 2.40 | Yield (%) | 1.58 | S&P 3-Yr. Proj. EPS CAGR(%) | 11 |
| Trailing 12-Month P/E | 10.0 | P/E on S&P Oper. EPS 2008E | 9.3 | Dividend Rate/Share | $0.33 | S&P Credit Rating | BBB |
| $10K Invested 5 Yrs Ago | $10,514 | Common Shares Outstg. (M) | 428.7 | Institutional Ownership (%) | 94 | | |

## Price Performance

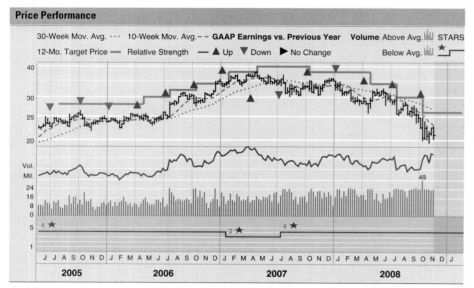

30-Week Mov. Avg. ···· 10-Week Mov. Avg. -- GAAP Earnings vs. Previous Year  Volume Above Avg. ▮▮▮ STARS
12-Mo. Target Price — Relative Strength — ▲ Up ▼ Down ► No Change  Below Avg. ▮▮▮ ★

Options: ASE, CBOE, P

Analysis prepared by **Joseph Agnese** on October 14, 2008, when the stock traded at **$ 23.31.**

## Highlights

➤ We expect sales to rise about 3% in 2009 to $45.4 billion, from our estimate of $44.0 billion in 2008, as benefits from the Lifestyle remodelings are anticipated to help fuel identical-store sales growth, excluding fuel, of around 1.0%. We project that square footage will increase about 1%, reflecting the completion of store remodelings and the opening of new stores.

➤ Gross margins in 2009 should narrow, excluding fuel, reflecting a more aggressive pricing strategy in an adverse economic environment, partially offset by reduced advertising expense and a shift in product mix. Although we expect a negative sales impact from consumers trading down to lower priced goods, we look for operating margins to widen slightly, as efficiency gains stemming from centralized marketing and procurement functions should offset increased operating expenses associated with the expansion of new store formats.

➤ Interest expense will likely be lower, in our opinion, as a reduction in debt levels offsets higher borrowing rates. We project 2009 operating EPS of $2.40, up 6.7% from our estimate of $2.25 in 2008.

## Investment Rationale/Risk

➤ We expect earnings growth to be maintained despite an adverse economic environment, reflecting rising industry demand as consumers trade down to retail food outlets from foodservice operators as well as improved merchandise presentation within the company's newly remodeled Lifestyle stores.

➤ Risks to our recommendation and target price include a more intense competitive environment than we anticipate. In addition, we have concerns with regard to corporate governance because the CEO and chairman of the board positions are not separate.

➤ The stock recently traded at about 9.7X our 2008 EPS estimate, below its five-year historical average forward P/E multiple of 15X. Due to our view of favorable sales trends and increased contributions from its Blackhawk gift card business, we project three-year annual EPS growth of 11%. Our 12-month target price of $26, equal to about 11X our 2009 EPS estimate of $2.40, is based on our assumption that the shares will trade closer to their historical forward 12-month P/E, as we expect favorable trends to continue despite an adverse economic environment.

## Qualitative Risk Assessment

| LOW | MEDIUM | HIGH |
|---|---|---|

Our risk assessment reflects our view of an improved shopping experience associated with new Lifestyle store remodelings as well as potential opportunities to gain market share following the consolidation of a major rival. This is offset by a continued intense competitive environment as new entrants enter the company's markets.

## Quantitative Evaluations

**S&P Quality Ranking**     **B**

| D | C | B- | B | B+ | A- | A | A+ |
|---|---|---|---|---|---|---|---|

**Relative Strength Rank**     **STRONG**

72

LOWEST = 1        HIGHEST = 99

## Revenue/Earnings Data

### Revenue (Million $)

| | 1Q | 2Q | 3Q | 4Q | Year |
|---|---|---|---|---|---|
| 2008 | 9,999 | 10,120 | 100,169 | -- | -- |
| 2007 | 9,322 | 9,823 | 9,785 | 13,356 | 42,286 |
| 2006 | 8,895 | 9,367 | 9,420 | 12,504 | 40,185 |
| 2005 | 8,621 | 8,803 | 8,946 | 12,046 | 38,416 |
| 2004 | 7,639 | 8,361 | 8,297 | 11,390 | 35,823 |
| 2003 | 8,043 | 8,248 | 8,277 | 10,985 | 35,553 |

### Earnings Per Share ($)

| | | | | | |
|---|---|---|---|---|---|
| 2008 | 0.44 | 0.53 | 0.46 | E0.81 | E2.25 |
| 2007 | 0.39 | 0.49 | 0.44 | 0.68 | 1.99 |
| 2006 | 0.32 | 0.55 | 0.39 | 0.69 | 1.94 |
| 2005 | 0.29 | 0.30 | 0.27 | 0.39 | 1.25 |
| 2004 | 0.10 | 0.35 | 0.35 | 0.45 | 1.25 |
| 2003 | 0.36 | 0.36 | 0.45 | -1.57 | -0.38 |

Fiscal year ended Dec. 31. Next earnings report expected: Late February. EPS Estimates based on S&P Operating Earnings; historical GAAP earnings are as reported.

## Dividend Data (Dates: mm/dd Payment Date: mm/dd/yy)

| Amount ($) | Date Decl. | Ex-Div. Date | Stk. of Record | Payment Date |
|---|---|---|---|---|
| 0.069 | 12/05 | 12/24 | 12/27 | 01/17/08 |
| 0.069 | 03/07 | 03/25 | 03/27 | 04/17/08 |
| 0.083 | 05/14 | 06/24 | 06/26 | 07/17/08 |
| 0.083 | 08/27 | 09/23 | 09/25 | 10/16/08 |

Dividends have been paid since 2005. Source: Company reports.

---

**Please read the Required Disclosures and Analyst Certification on the last page of this report.**

The McGraw-Hill Companies

# Safeway Inc

## Business Summary October 14, 2008

CORPORATE OVERVIEW. Safeway is one of the largest U.S. food and drug retailers, operating about 1,750 stores principally in California, Oregon, Washington, Alaska, Colorado, Arizona, Texas, the Chicago metropolitan area, and the Mid-Atlantic region in the U.S., and in British Columbia, Alberta and Manitoba/Saskatchewan in Canada. To support its store network, SWY has a network of distribution, manufacturing and food processing facilities. The company seeks to provide value to customers by maintaining high store standards and a wide selection of high-quality produce and meat at competitive prices. The company also provides third-party gift cards, prepaid cards and sports and entertainment cards to retailers for sales to customers in North America and the U.K. through its Blackhawk subsidiary.

MARKET PROFILE. The U.S. grocery industry was a $964 billion business in 2007, according to Progressive Grocer. Supermarkets generated $535 billion, or 56% of total grocery industry sales, followed by convenience stores ($307 billion, 32%) and warehouse clubs ($102 billion, 11%). When supermarkets are broken down by format, conventional supermarkets have the largest market share, holding 67% of the supermarket category, with $357 billion in sales. However, supercenters are quickly gaining market share, and generated a 26% market share in 2007 ($142 billion in sales).

With $42.3 billion in sales in 2007, Safeway held about an 8% market share within the supermarket category and 4.4% of total grocery sales. The average size of Safeway's stores (about 46,000 square feet) exceeded the industry average (33,300 square feet). Additionally, the company's sales per square foot ($527 per square foot) is higher than the supermarket average of $460 per square foot in 2007.

## Company Financials Fiscal Year Ended Dec. 31

| Per Share Data ($) | 2007 | 2006 | 2005 | 2004 | 2003 | 2002 | 2001 | 2000 | 1999 | 1998 |
|---|---|---|---|---|---|---|---|---|---|---|
| Tangible Book Value | 9.76 | 7.44 | 5.60 | 4.24 | 2.79 | 1.77 | 1.67 | 1.35 | NM | NM |
| Cash Flow | 4.40 | 4.16 | 3.32 | 3.24 | 1.57 | 2.91 | 4.29 | 3.77 | 3.24 | 2.63 |
| Earnings | 1.99 | 1.94 | 1.25 | 1.25 | -0.38 | 1.20 | 2.44 | 2.13 | 1.88 | 1.59 |
| S&P Core Earnings | 1.87 | 1.91 | 1.26 | 1.15 | 1.21 | 2.42 | 2.19 | NA | NA | NA |
| Dividends | 0.26 | 0.22 | 0.15 | Nil | Nil | Nil | Nil | Nil | Nil | Nil |
| Payout Ratio | 13% | 11% | 12% | Nil | Nil | Nil | Nil | Nil | Nil | Nil |
| Prices:High | 38.31 | 35.61 | 26.46 | 25.64 | 25.83 | 46.90 | 61.38 | 62.69 | 62.44 | 61.38 |
| Prices:Low | 30.10 | 22.23 | 17.85 | 17.26 | 16.20 | 18.45 | 37.44 | 30.75 | 29.31 | 30.50 |
| P/E Ratio:High | 19 | 18 | 21 | 21 | NM | 39 | 25 | 29 | 33 | 39 |
| P/E Ratio:Low | 15 | 11 | 14 | 14 | NM | 15 | 15 | 14 | 16 | 19 |

| Income Statement Analysis (Million $) | 2007 | 2006 | 2005 | 2004 | 2003 | 2002 | 2001 | 2000 | 1999 | 1998 |
|---|---|---|---|---|---|---|---|---|---|---|
| Revenue | 42,286 | 40,185 | 38,416 | 35,823 | 35,553 | 32,399 | 34,301 | 31,977 | 28,860 | 24,484 |
| Operating Income | 2,816 | 2,591 | 2,147 | 2,067 | 2,167 | 3,190 | 3,535 | 3,119 | 2,698 | 2,134 |
| Depreciation | 1,071 | 991 | 933 | 895 | 864 | 812 | 946 | 838 | 700 | 533 |
| Interest Expense | 405 | 396 | 403 | 411 | 442 | 369 | 447 | 457 | 362 | 244 |
| Pretax Income | 1,404 | 1,240 | 849 | 794 | 141 | 1,320 | 2,095 | 1,867 | 1,674 | 1,397 |
| Effective Tax Rate | 36.7% | 29.8% | 33.9% | 29.4% | NM | 56.9% | 40.1% | 41.5% | 42.0% | 42.2% |
| Net Income | 888 | 871 | 561 | 560 | -170 | 568 | 1,254 | 1,092 | 971 | 807 |
| S&P Core Earnings | 835 | 859 | 566 | 517 | 538 | 1,140 | 1,122 | NA | NA | NA |

| Balance Sheet & Other Financial Data (Million $) | 2007 | 2006 | 2005 | 2004 | 2003 | 2002 | 2001 | 2000 | 1999 | 1998 |
|---|---|---|---|---|---|---|---|---|---|---|
| Cash | 278 | 217 | 373 | 267 | 175 | 73.7 | 68.5 | 91.7 | 106 | 46.0 |
| Current Assets | 4,008 | 3,566 | 3,702 | 3,598 | 3,508 | 4,259 | 3,312 | 3,224 | 3,052 | 2,320 |
| Total Assets | 17,651 | 16,274 | 15,757 | 15,377 | 15,097 | 16,047 | 17,463 | 15,965 | 14,900 | 11,390 |
| Current Liabilities | 5,136 | 4,601 | 4,264 | 3,792 | 3,464 | 3,936 | 3,883 | 3,780 | 3,583 | 2,894 |
| Long Term Debt | 4,658 | 5,037 | 5,605 | 6,124 | 7,072 | 7,522 | 6,712 | 5,822 | 6,357 | 4,651 |
| Common Equity | 6,702 | 5,667 | 4,920 | 4,307 | 3,644 | 3,628 | 5,890 | 5,390 | 4,086 | 3,082 |
| Total Capital | 11,614 | 10,821 | 10,748 | 10,894 | 11,139 | 11,727 | 13,100 | 11,721 | 10,822 | 7,950 |
| Capital Expenditures | 1,769 | 1,674 | 1,384 | 1,213 | 936 | 1,371 | 1,793 | 1,573 | 1,334 | 1,075 |
| Cash Flow | 1,960 | 1,862 | 1,494 | 1,455 | 694 | 1,381 | 2,200 | 1,930 | 1,671 | 1,340 |
| Current Ratio | 0.8 | 0.8 | 0.9 | 0.9 | 1.0 | 1.1 | 0.9 | 0.9 | 0.9 | 0.8 |
| % Long Term Debt of Capitalization | 40.1 | 46.5 | 52.2 | 56.2 | 63.5 | 64.1 | 51.2 | 49.7 | 58.7 | 58.5 |
| % Net Income of Revenue | 2.1 | 2.2 | 1.5 | 1.6 | NM | 1.8 | 3.7 | 3.4 | 3.4 | 3.3 |
| % Return on Assets | 5.2 | 5.4 | 3.6 | 3.7 | NM | 3.4 | 7.5 | 7.1 | 7.4 | 8.1 |
| % Return on Equity | 14.4 | 16.4 | 12.2 | 14.1 | NM | 11.9 | 22.2 | 23.0 | 27.1 | 30.9 |

Data as orig reptd.; bef. results of disc opers/spec. items. Per share data adj. for stk. divs.; EPS diluted. E-Estimated. NA-Not Available. NM-Not Meaningful. NR-Not Ranked. UR-Under Review.

**Office:** 5918 Stoneridge Mall Road, Pleasanton, CA 94588-3229.
**Telephone:** 925-467-3000.
**Website:** http://www.safeway.com
**Chrmn, Pres & CEO:** S. Burd

**Co-Chrmn:** G. Charters
**EVP & CFO:** R.L. Edwards
**EVP & Chief Admin Officer:** L.M. Renda
**SVP & Chief Acctg Officer:** D.F. Bond

**Investor Contact:** M.C. Plaisance (925-467-3790)
**Board Members:** S. Burd, J. Grove, M. Gyani, P. M. Hazen, F. C. Herringer, R. I. MacDonnell, D. J. Mackenzie, K. W. Oder, R. Stirn, W. Tauscher, R. Viault

**Founded:** 1915
**Domicile:** Delaware
**Employees:** 201,000

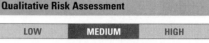

**STANDARD &POOR'S**

# St. Jude Medical Inc.

| S&P Recommendation | STRONG BUY ★★★★★ | Price $32.92 (as of Nov 14, 2008) | 12-Mo. Target Price $54.00 | Investment Style Large-Cap Growth |
|---|---|---|---|---|

**GICS Sector** Health Care
**Sub-Industry** Health Care Equipment

**Summary** St. Jude, the leading maker of mechanical heart valves, also produces pacemakers, defibrillators and other cardiac devices. In July 2008, STJ acquired EP Medsystems Inc. for $91 million in a deal that expanded its capabilities in the atrial fibrillation market.

## Key Stock Statistics (Source S&P, Vickers, company reports)

| | | | | | | | |
|---|---|---|---|---|---|---|---|
| 52-Wk Range | $48.49– 27.06 | S&P Oper. EPS 2008**E** | 2.30 | Market Capitalization(B) | $11.330 | Beta | 0.54 |
| Trailing 12-Month EPS | $1.99 | S&P Oper. EPS 2009**E** | 2.65 | Yield (%) | Nil | S&P 3-Yr. Proj. EPS CAGR(%) | 15 |
| Trailing 12-Month P/E | 16.5 | P/E on S&P Oper. EPS 2008**E** | 14.3 | Dividend Rate/Share | Nil | S&P Credit Rating | A- |
| $10K Invested 5 Yrs Ago | $10,995 | Common Shares Outstg. (M) | 344.2 | Institutional Ownership (%) | 84 | | |

## Price Performance

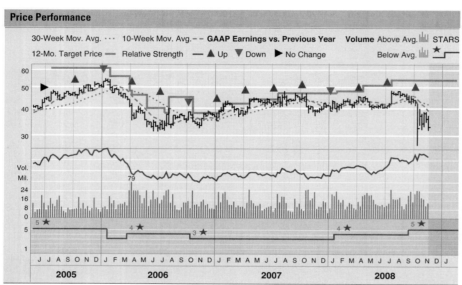

30-Week Mov. Avg. · · · · 10-Week Mov. Avg. – – GAAP Earnings vs. Previous Year  Volume Above Avg. STARS
12-Mo. Target Price — Relative Strength — ▲ Up ▼ Down ► No Change  Below Avg.

Options: ASE, CBOE

## Qualitative Risk Assessment

| LOW | MEDIUM | HIGH |

The company operates in a highly competitive industry characterized by relatively short product life cycles and volatile market share fluctuations. However, there are significant barriers to entry in the company's core markets, as products must obtain FDA approval prior to launch and they require a large investment in both research and development, and sales.

## Quantitative Evaluations

**S&P Quality Ranking**  B+

| D | C | B- | B | B+ | A- | A | A+ |

**Relative Strength Rank**  MODERATE

61

LOWEST = 1  HIGHEST = 99

Analysis prepared by **Robert M. Gold** on October 15, 2008, when the stock traded at **$ 37.70**.

### Highlights

➤ In our opinion, new product launches and enhancements to existing products will allow STJ to capture share in the global ICD market in 2008, and we think the cardiac rhythm management category will grow by about 7% as sluggishness in the U.S. is outweighed by rising demand overseas. Our 2008 revenue forecast of $4.4 billion assumes $2.8 billion of combined ICD and pacemaker revenues, atrial fibrillation of $526 million, neuromodulation of $240 million and cardiovascular of $850 million. Our 2009 revenue forecast stands at $4.8 billion.

➤ We expect that 2008 gross margins will approximate 74.6%, with SG&A expenses consuming 36.6% of sales and R&D outlays representing about 12.2% of sales. Interest expense is modeled at $10 million. We expect that the effective tax rate in 2008 will approximate 27.6%. We believe the 2008 diluted share count will approximate 350 million.

➤ Excluding in-process R&D charges, our 2008 EPS estimate is $2.30, up from operating EPS of $1.85 in 2007. We see 2009 EPS reaching $2.65.

### Investment Rationale/Risk

➤ We are concerned about the sluggishness that we see throughout ICD markets. However, we think the global ICD market can grow by about 7% in 2008, and we expect faster growth from St. Jude as it continues to gain market share. We believe revised Medicare reimbursement guidelines to hospitals for ICDs calling for an approximate 3% reimbursement reduction, versus an earlier proposal for a cut of up to 23%, is positive and could spur some incremental ICD implantations. Nevertheless, we think the market will be challenged to resume growth in excess of 10% in the foreseeable future. We also view the neuromodulation and atrial fibrillation categories as significant new growth drivers.

➤ Risks to our recommendation and target price include the failure to successfully commercialize new products, adverse changes to Medicare and private pay reimbursement rates, and negative patent litigation outcomes.

➤ Our 12-month target price of $54 applies a peer-average P/E to growth ratio of 1.4X to our 2009 EPS estimate. We see three-year EPS growth of 15%, in line with peers in our coverage.

## Revenue/Earnings Data

### Revenue (Million $)

| | 1Q | 2Q | 3Q | 4Q | Year |
|---|---|---|---|---|---|
| 2008 | 1,011 | 1,136 | 1,084 | -- | -- |
| 2007 | 887.0 | 947.3 | 926.8 | 1,018 | 3,779 |
| 2006 | 784.4 | 832.9 | 821.3 | 863.8 | 3,302 |
| 2005 | 663.9 | 723.7 | 737.8 | 789.9 | 2,915 |
| 2004 | 548.6 | 556.6 | 578.3 | 610.7 | 2,294 |
| 2003 | 441.4 | 495.1 | 477.5 | 518.6 | 1,933 |

### Earnings Per Share ($)

| | | | | | |
|---|---|---|---|---|---|
| 2008 | 0.53 | 0.58 | 0.55 | E0.62 | E2.30 |
| 2007 | 0.41 | 0.39 | 0.46 | 0.34 | 1.59 |
| 2006 | 0.36 | 0.38 | 0.32 | 0.42 | 1.47 |
| 2005 | 0.32 | 0.27 | 0.44 | 0.01 | 1.04 |
| 2004 | 0.26 | 0.27 | 0.25 | 0.33 | 1.10 |
| 2003 | 0.22 | 0.22 | 0.23 | 0.26 | 0.92 |

Fiscal year ended Dec. 31. Next earnings report expected: Late January. EPS Estimates based on S&P Operating Earnings; historical GAAP earnings are as reported.

## Dividend Data

No cash dividends have been paid since 1994.

*The McGraw-Hill Companies*

# St. Jude Medical Inc.

**STANDARD
&POOR'S**

## Business Summary October 15, 2008

CORPORATE OVERVIEW. St. Jude Medical sells medical devices in the cardiac rhythm management (CRM), cardiac surgery, atrial fibrillation, and pain management categories. Although the company has a diversified product line, the principal driver of growth in recent years has been the CRM segment, where it sells pacemakers and defibrillators.

CRM products (63% of 2007 sales) include implantable cardioverter defibrillators (ICDs) that are used to treat hearts that beat too fast (tachycardia) by monitoring the heartbeat and delivering high energy electrical impulses to terminate ventricular tachycardia and ventricular fibrillation. ICD products include the Atlas, Photon, and Contour lines, as well as the Epic HF and Atlas+ HF ICDs with the ventricle-to-ventricle (V-to-V) timing feature.

Also within the CRM division, pacemakers and related systems are sold to treat patients with hearts that beat too slowly (bradycardia). Current pacemakers include the Victory and Victory XL models, which offer automatic P-wave and R-wave measurements with trends, lead monitoring and automatic polarity switch, follow-up electrograms, and Ventricular Intrinsic Preference to reduce right ventricle pacing and a ventricular rate during an automatic mode switch histogram.

Other pacemakers offer features such as AF Suppression Pacing Algorithm and the beat-by-beat Autocapture pacing system that lets the pacemaker monitor each paced beat to verify heart stimulation, deliver a back-up pulse in the event of non-stimulation, continuously measure the threshold, and adjust energy output to match changing patient needs. The Identity pacemaker line expands the feature set to include a suite of arrhythmia diagnostics. Outside the U.S., STJ sells the Genesis System, a device-based ventricular resynchronization system designed to treat congestive heart failure and suppress atrial fibrillation.

The company also offers low voltage device-based ventricular resynchronization systems (bi-ventricular) designed to treat heart failure and suppress atrial fibrillation. In the U.S., the company's pacemakers are the only bi-ventricular pacing devices indicated for use in patients with chronic atrial fibrillation who have been treated with atrioventricular nodal ablation.

## Company Financials Fiscal Year Ended Dec. 31

| Per Share Data ($) | 2007 | 2006 | 2005 | 2004 | 2003 | 2002 | 2001 | 2000 | 1999 | 1998 |
|---|---|---|---|---|---|---|---|---|---|---|
| Tangible Book Value | 2.25 | 2.23 | 1.84 | 4.27 | 3.02 | 3.27 | 2.28 | 1.50 | 1.02 | 1.44 |
| Cash Flow | 2.08 | 1.92 | 1.38 | 1.34 | 1.12 | 0.96 | 0.74 | 0.65 | 0.32 | 0.57 |
| Earnings | 1.59 | 1.47 | 1.04 | 1.10 | 0.92 | 0.76 | 0.48 | 0.38 | 0.07 | 0.38 |
| S&P Core Earnings | 1.64 | 1.47 | 0.90 | 1.03 | 0.82 | 0.63 | 0.38 | NA | NA | NA |
| Dividends | Nil | Nil | Nil | Nil | Nil | Nil | Nil | Nil | Nil | Nil |
| Payout Ratio | Nil | Nil | Nil | Nil | Nil | Nil | Nil | Nil | Nil | Nil |
| Prices:High | 48.10 | 54.75 | 52.80 | 42.90 | 32.00 | 21.56 | 19.52 | 15.63 | 10.19 | 9.92 |
| Prices:Low | 34.90 | 31.20 | 34.48 | 29.90 | 19.38 | 15.26 | 11.11 | 5.91 | 5.73 | 4.80 |
| P/E Ratio:High | 30 | 37 | 51 | 39 | 35 | 29 | 41 | 41 | NM | 26 |
| P/E Ratio:Low | 22 | 21 | 33 | 27 | 21 | 20 | 23 | 16 | NM | 13 |

| Income Statement Analysis (Million $) | 2007 | 2006 | 2005 | 2004 | 2003 | 2002 | 2001 | 2000 | 1999 | 1998 |
|---|---|---|---|---|---|---|---|---|---|---|
| Revenue | 3,779 | 3,302 | 2,915 | 2,294 | 1,933 | 1,590 | 1,347 | 1,179 | 1,115 | 1,016 |
| Operating Income | 1,093 | 945 | 911 | 672 | 533 | 445 | 347 | 326 | 300 | 263 |
| Depreciation | 176 | 167 | 130 | 85.8 | 76.7 | 74.9 | 90.3 | 92.3 | 85.7 | 68.9 |
| Interest Expense | 38.2 | 33.9 | Nil | Nil | Nil | Nil | Nil | Nil | Nil | 23.7 |
| Pretax Income | 744 | 721 | 621 | 537 | 459 | 373 | 228 | 177 | 67.0 | 186 |
| Effective Tax Rate | 24.9% | 23.9% | 36.7% | 23.7% | 26.0% | 26.0% | 24.3% | 27.2% | 63.8% | 30.5% |
| Net Income | 559 | 548 | 393 | 410 | 339 | 276 | 173 | 129 | 24.2 | 129 |
| S&P Core Earnings | 576 | 548 | 341 | 377 | 302 | 231 | 136 | NA | NA | NA |

| Balance Sheet & Other Financial Data (Million $) | 2007 | 2006 | 2005 | 2004 | 2003 | 2002 | 2001 | 2000 | 1999 | 1998 |
|---|---|---|---|---|---|---|---|---|---|---|
| Cash | 389 | 79.9 | 535 | 688 | 461 | 402 | 148 | 108 | 88.9 | 88.0 |
| Current Assets | 2,128 | 1,690 | 1,941 | 1,863 | 1,492 | 1,114 | 798 | 705 | 690 | 682 |
| Total Assets | 5,329 | 4,790 | 4,845 | 3,231 | 2,556 | 1,951 | 1,629 | 1,533 | 1,554 | 1,385 |
| Current Liabilities | 1,849 | 676 | 1,534 | 605 | 510 | 375 | 322 | 297 | 283 | 203 |
| Long Term Debt | 182 | 859 | 177 | 235 | 352 | Nil | 123 | 295 | 477 | 375 |
| Common Equity | 2,928 | 2,969 | 2,883 | 2,334 | 1,604 | 1,577 | 1,184 | 941 | 794 | 806 |
| Total Capital | 3,217 | 3,992 | 3,217 | 2,625 | 2,046 | 1,577 | 1,307 | 1,235 | 1,272 | 1,181 |
| Capital Expenditures | 287 | 268 | 159 | 89.5 | 49.6 | 62.2 | 63.1 | 39.7 | 69.4 | 74.2 |
| Cash Flow | 735 | 715 | 524 | 496 | 416 | 351 | 263 | 221 | 110 | 198 |
| Current Ratio | 1.2 | 2.5 | 1.3 | 3.1 | 2.9 | 3.0 | 2.5 | 2.4 | 2.4 | 3.4 |
| % Long Term Debt of Capitalization | 5.7 | 21.5 | 5.5 | 8.9 | 17.2 | Nil | 9.4 | 23.8 | 37.6 | 31.7 |
| % Net Income of Revenue | 14.8 | 16.6 | 13.5 | 17.9 | 17.6 | 17.4 | 12.8 | 11.0 | 2.2 | 12.7 |
| % Return on Assets | 29.3 | 11.4 | 9.7 | 14.2 | 15.1 | 15.4 | 10.9 | 8.4 | 1.6 | 9.1 |
| % Return on Equity | 19.0 | 18.7 | 15.1 | 20.8 | 21.3 | 20.0 | 16.2 | 14.9 | 3.0 | 14.4 |

Data as orig reptd.; bef. results of disc opers/spec. items. Per share data adj. for stk. divs.; EPS diluted. E-Estimated. NA-Not Available. NM-Not Meaningful. NR-Not Ranked. UR-Under Review.

**Office:** One Lillehei Plaza, St. Paul, MN 55117.
**Telephone:** 651-483-2000.
**Website:** http://www.sjm.com
**Chrmn, Pres & CEO:** D.J. Starks

**EVP, CFO & Chief Acctg Officer:** J.C. Heinmiller
**Secy & General Counsel:** P.S. Krop
**Investor Contact:** A. Craig (651-481-7789)
**Cntlr:** D.J. Zurbay

**Board Members:** J. W. Brown, R. R. Devenuti, S. M. Essig, T. H. Garrett, III, B. B. Hill, M. A. Rocca, D. J. Starks, S. Widensohler, W. L. Yarno

**Founded:** 1976
**Domicile:** Minnesota
**Employees:** 12,000

# salesforce.com inc

| S&P Recommendation **BUY** ★★★★☆ | Price<br>$26.40 (as of Nov 14, 2008) | 12-Mo. Target Price<br>$43.00 | Investment Style<br>Large-Cap Growth |
|---|---|---|---|

**GICS Sector** Information Technology
**Sub-Industry** Application Software

**Summary** This San Francisco-based company is a leading provider of on-demand customer relationship management applications.

## Key Stock Statistics (Source S&P, Vickers, company reports)

| | | | | | | | |
|---|---|---|---|---|---|---|---|
| 52-Wk Range | **$75.21– 23.78** | S&P Oper. EPS 2009**E** | 0.30 | Market Capitalization(B) | **$3.194** | Beta | 2.55 |
| Trailing 12-Month EPS | **$0.27** | S&P Oper. EPS 2010**E** | 0.65 | Yield (%) | Nil | S&P 3-Yr. Proj. EPS CAGR(%) | NM |
| Trailing 12-Month P/E | 97.8 | P/E on S&P Oper. EPS 2009**E** | 88.0 | Dividend Rate/Share | Nil | S&P Credit Rating | NA |
| $10K Invested 5 Yrs Ago | NA | Common Shares Outstg. (M) | 121.0 | Institutional Ownership (%) | 91 | | |

## Price Performance

30-Week Mov. Avg. · · · · 10-Week Mov. Avg. - - - **GAAP Earnings vs. Previous Year** Volume Above Avg. 📊 STARS
12-Mo. Target Price — Relative Strength — ▲ Up ▼ Down ► No Change Below Avg. 📊 ★

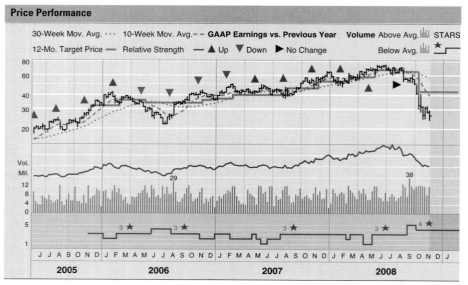

Options: CBOE, Ph

Analysis prepared by **Zaineb Bokhari** on October 13, 2008, when the stock traded at **$ 34.47**.

## Highlights

➤ We forecast 44% sales growth in FY 09 (Jan.) to $1.075 billion, driven by a 45% rise in subscription and support revenues. We think customer and subscriber growth remain drivers of subscription revenues, but they have become less reliable means of forecasting. CRM is providing less information on growth as it broadens its offerings and pricing tiers. We expect sales to rise 31% in FY 10, to $1.4 billion.

➤ We expect the gross margin in FY 09 to improve to about 80%, from 77% in FY 08, primarily due to wider professional services gross margins, but we still expect cost of revenues for professional services to slightly exceed revenues. We forecast increased operating margins of between 5%-6% in FY 09, from 2.7% in FY 08. Our outlook is affected by higher stock-based compensation expense, which we believe will rise to $80 million-$85 million in both FY 09 and FY 10, from $55 million in FY 08. We anticipate wider operating margins in FY 10.

➤ We forecast EPS of $0.30 in FY 09, up from $0.15 in FY 08. We expect some variability in CRM's quarterly tax rate, which we project at 48% in FY 09, down from approximately 51% in FY 08. We estimate EPS of $0.65 in FY 10.

## Investment Rationale/Risk

➤ We recently lowered our recommendation on CRM shares to buy, from strong buy, to reflect our conservatism about enterprise IT spending for the balance of 2008, after the recent deterioration in the global macro economy. We think this could have an impact on bookings, which are becoming more seasonal. We expect tougher comparisons in future periods, and we see revenue growth also slowing as a result. As CRM continues to add scale in its business, we expect profitability to improve; nevertheless, we think this will be partly offset by what we consider to be high levels of stock-based compensation expense. We continue to expect competitive offerings from traditional vendors in future periods, in an effort to capitalize on strong growth prospects for on-demand software delivery.

➤ Risks to our recommendation and target price include a deceleration in customer, revenue, or bookings growth from projected levels and increased competition.

➤ We derive our 12-month target price of $43 by applying a 3.5X enterprise value-to-sales multiple to our FY 10 revenue estimate of $1.4 billion, within CRM's 3.3X-7.5X historical range.

## Qualitative Risk Assessment

| LOW | MEDIUM | HIGH |
|---|---|---|

Our risk assessment reflects the company's short operating history and early dominance in an emerging area of the software market. We think that rising competition from traditional software vendors and increasingly difficult annual comparisons may result in lower future reported growth relative to historical rates.

## Quantitative Evaluations

**S&P Quality Ranking** NR

| D | C | B- | B | B+ | A- | A | A+ |
|---|---|---|---|---|---|---|---|

**Relative Strength Rank** WEAK

27

LOWEST = 1 HIGHEST = 99

## Revenue/Earnings Data

**Revenue (Million $)**

| | 1Q | 2Q | 3Q | 4Q | Year |
|---|---|---|---|---|---|
| 2009 | 247.6 | 263.1 | -- | -- | -- |
| 2008 | 162.4 | 176.6 | 192.8 | 216.9 | 748.7 |
| 2007 | 104.7 | 118.1 | 130.1 | 144.2 | 497.1 |
| 2006 | 64.18 | 71.94 | 82.67 | 91.06 | 309.9 |
| 2005 | 34.84 | 40.58 | 46.36 | 54.59 | 176.4 |
| 2004 | 18.91 | 21.62 | 25.43 | 30.05 | 96.02 |

**Earnings Per Share ($)**

| | | | | | |
|---|---|---|---|---|---|
| 2009 | 0.08 | 0.08 | E0.07 | E0.08 | E0.30 |
| 2008 | 0.01 | 0.08 | 0.05 | 0.06 | 0.15 |
| 2007 | Nil | Nil | Nil | Nil | Nil |
| 2006 | 0.04 | 0.04 | 0.11 | 0.05 | 0.24 |
| 2005 | Nil | 0.01 | 0.02 | 0.03 | 0.07 |
| 2004 | -- | -- | -- | -- | 0.04 |

Fiscal year ended Jan. 31. Next earnings report expected: Mid November. EPS Estimates based on S&P Operating Earnings; historical GAAP earnings are as reported.

## Dividend Data

No cash dividends have been paid.

# salesforce.com inc

**STANDARD &POOR'S**

## Business Summary October 13, 2008

CORPORATE OVERVIEW. Salesforce.com is a leading provider of "on-demand" customer relationship management software. On demand refers to the delivery of application services over the Internet as needed. Under this delivery model, customers access a software provider's applications via the Web, with minor implementation and customization and no on-premise installation or maintenance of software. Payment for this "service" is generally on a per-seat per-user basis over an agreed-upon term.

In our view, the delivery of software on demand offers unique benefits to customers, including lower upfront investment, increased vendor accountability and risk sharing, greater awareness of customer needs due to the constant feedback from customers, and flexible subscription pricing, which can be tailored to customer requirements. This model offers benefits to the software vendor, including improved visibility into customers' needs and potentially higher customer satisfaction and retention levels. Another benefit we see is lower development and support costs arising from the use of a single version of software across a vendor's installed base.

CRM experienced service outages in late December 2005 and in early 2006. We believe these service issues have been addressed, since they have not resurfaced. The company moved to increase transparency regarding the performance, uptime, and security of its system, in our view. Since the delivery of its service over the Web is a key point of differentiation, we expect the company to continue to invest in infrastructure in future quarters. The low upfront cost of CRM's products has significant appeal to small- and mid-sized businesses, in our view; we estimate that the average customer had 23 to 25 subscribers in FY 08 (Jan.), up from 18 to 20 subscribers we calculate for FY 06, and 20 to 23 in FY 07. CRM also continues to sign a number of large customers, including ADP, Cisco Systems, Merrill Lynch and Thomson Reuters, among others.

COMPANY STRATEGY. CRM's corporate strategy includes highlighting the benefits of its on-demand, or software-as-a-service method of delivery over traditional on-premise license deployments. CRM is also of the companies leading the charge to platform-as-a-service whereby it provides tools and encouragement for third-party developers to build applications on its platform. The company's other strategic focus includes the ongoing development of its core customer relationship management offering, including the development of modules that offer additional functionality for an additional fee. Expansion of customer base and geographic footprint are also strategic.

## Company Financials  Fiscal Year Ended Jan. 31

| Per Share Data ($) | 2008 | 2007 | 2006 | 2005 | 2004 | 2003 | 2002 | 2001 | 2000 | 1999 |
|---|---|---|---|---|---|---|---|---|---|---|
| Tangible Book Value | 3.71 | 2.40 | 1.78 | 1.38 | 1.13 | NA | NA | NA | NA | NA |
| Cash Flow | 0.29 | 0.11 | 0.29 | 0.09 | 0.06 | -0.27 | -1.25 | NA | NA | NA |
| Earnings | 0.15 | Nil | 0.24 | 0.07 | 0.04 | -0.37 | -1.36 | -2.38 | NA | NA |
| S&P Core Earnings | 0.14 | Nil | 0.07 | -0.04 | -0.02 | -0.43 | NA | NA | NA | NA |
| Dividends | Nil | Nil | Nil | Nil | NA | NA | NA | NA | NA | NA |
| Payout Ratio | Nil | Nil | Nil | Nil | NA | NA | NA | NA | NA | NA |
| Calendar Year | 2007 | 2006 | 2005 | 2004 | 2003 | 2002 | 2001 | 2000 | 1999 | 1998 |
| Prices:High | 65.52 | 44.58 | 36.19 | 22.70 | NA | NA | NA | NA | NA | NA |
| Prices:Low | 35.55 | 21.64 | 12.96 | 9.00 | NA | NA | NA | NA | NA | NA |
| P/E Ratio:High | NM | NM | NM | NM | NA | NA | NA | NA | NA | NA |
| P/E Ratio:Low | NM | NM | NM | NM | NA | NA | NA | NA | NA | NA |

### Income Statement Analysis (Million $)

| | 2008 | 2007 | 2006 | 2005 | 2004 | 2003 | 2002 | 2001 | 2000 | 1999 |
|---|---|---|---|---|---|---|---|---|---|---|
| Revenue | 749 | 497 | 310 | 176 | 96.0 | 51.0 | 22.4 | 5.43 | NA | NA |
| Operating Income | 37.1 | 8.91 | 25.8 | 9.67 | 2.86 | -7.84 | -19.5 | NA | NA | NA |
| Depreciation | 16.8 | 12.5 | 6.03 | 3.15 | 2.59 | 2.66 | 2.40 | 0.86 | NA | NA |
| Interest Expense | 0.05 | 0.19 | 0.07 | 0.04 | 0.02 | 0.08 | 0.27 | NA | NA | NA |
| Pretax Income | 46.2 | 12.5 | 28.2 | 9.15 | 4.24 | -10.0 | -29.0 | -31.9 | NA | NA |
| Effective Tax Rate | 50.6% | 78.4% | NM | 13.3% | 12.8% | Nil | Nil | NA | NA | NA |
| Net Income | 18.4 | 0.48 | 28.5 | 7.35 | 3.51 | -9.72 | -28.6 | -31.7 | NA | NA |
| S&P Core Earnings | 17.5 | 0.48 | 8.59 | -3.26 | -0.61 | -11.4 | NA | NA | NA | NA |

### Balance Sheet & Other Financial Data (Million $)

| | 2008 | 2007 | 2006 | 2005 | 2004 | 2003 | 2002 | 2001 | 2000 | 1999 |
|---|---|---|---|---|---|---|---|---|---|---|
| Cash | 451 | 252 | 208 | 119 | 142 | 16.0 | 11.7 | NA | NA | NA |
| Current Assets | 741 | 419 | 303 | 179 | NA | NA | NA | NA | NA | NA |
| Total Assets | 1,090 | 665 | 435 | 280 | 191 | 39.4 | 29.1 | NA | NA | NA |
| Current Liabilities | 606 | 377 | 235 | 132 | NA | NA | NA | NA | NA | NA |
| Long Term Debt | Nil | 0.01 | 0.18 | 0.72 | Nil | NA | NA | NA | NA | NA |
| Common Equity | 452 | 282 | 196 | 145 | 115 | -56.1 | -52.0 | NA | NA | NA |
| Total Capital | 461 | 286 | 199 | 147 | 115 | 115 | NA | NA | NA | NA |
| Capital Expenditures | 43.6 | 22.1 | 23.4 | 4.31 | NA | 2.37 | 0.71 | 5.87 | NA | NA |
| Cash Flow | 35.2 | 13.0 | 34.5 | 10.5 | 6.11 | -7.06 | -26.2 | NA | NA | NA |
| Current Ratio | 1.2 | 1.1 | 1.3 | 1.4 | NA | 1.1 | 1.5 | NA | NA | NA |
| % Long Term Debt of Capitalization | Nil | 0.0 | 0.1 | 0.5 | Nil | Nil | Nil | NA | NA | NA |
| % Net Income of Revenue | 2.5 | 0.1 | 9.2 | 4.2 | 3.7 | NM | NM | NM | NA | NA |
| % Return on Assets | 2.1 | 0.1 | 8.0 | 4.0 | NA | NM | NA | NA | NA | NA |
| % Return on Equity | 5.0 | 0.2 | 16.7 | 14.9 | NA | NM | NA | NA | NA | NA |

Data as orig reptd.; bef. results of disc opers/spec. items. Per share data adj. for stk. divs.; EPS diluted. E-Estimated. NA-Not Available. NM-Not Meaningful. NR-Not Ranked. UR-Under Review.

**Office:** The Landmark @ One Market, San Francisco, CA 94105.
**Telephone:** 415-901-7000.
**Website:** http://www.salesforce.com
**Chrmn & CEO:** M. Benioff

**Pres:** S.M. Cakebread
**EVP & CFO:** G. Smith
**SVP, Secy & General Counsel:** D. Schellhase
**CTO:** B. Pech

**Board Members:** M. Benioff, C. A. Conway, A. G. Hassenfeld, C. Ramsey, S. R. Robertson, S. Sclavos, L. J. Tomlinson, M. G. Webb, Jr., S. Young

**Founded:** 1999
**Domicile:** Delaware
**Employees:** 2,606

The **McGraw·Hill** Companies

**STANDARD &POOR'S**

# SanDisk Corp

| S&P Recommendation | HOLD ★★★☆☆ | Price | 12-Mo. Target Price | Investment Style |
|---|---|---|---|---|
| | | $7.15 (as of Nov 14, 2008) | $18.00 | Large-Cap Growth |

**GICS Sector** Information Technology
**Sub-Industry** Computer Storage & Peripherals

**Summary** This company designs, makes and markets flash memory storage products used in a wide variety of electronic systems.

## Key Stock Statistics (Source S&P, Vickers, company reports)

| | | | | | | | |
|---|---|---|---|---|---|---|---|
| 52-Wk Range | $39.63– 6.78 | S&P Oper. EPS 2008**E** | -1.53 | Market Capitalization(B) | $1.616 | Beta | 0.89 |
| Trailing 12-Month EPS | $-0.44 | S&P Oper. EPS 2009**E** | -0.43 | Yield (%) | Nil | S&P 3-Yr. Proj. EPS CAGR(%) | NM |
| Trailing 12-Month P/E | NM | P/E on S&P Oper. EPS 2008**E** | NM | Dividend Rate/Share | Nil | S&P Credit Rating | B |
| $10K Invested 5 Yrs Ago | $1,772 | Common Shares Outstg. (M) | 226.0 | Institutional Ownership (%) | 82 | | |

## Price Performance

30-Week Mov. Avg. ···· 10-Week Mov. Avg. - - **GAAP Earnings vs. Previous Year** Volume Above Avg. STARS
12-Mo. Target Price — Relative Strength — ▲ Up ▼ Down ▶ No Change  Below Avg. ★

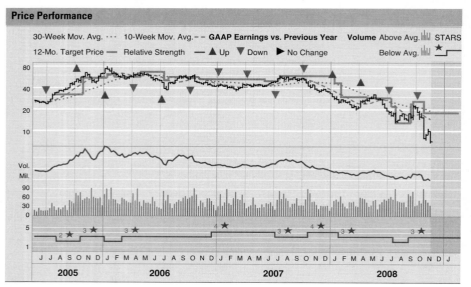

Options: ASE, CBOE, P, Ph

Analysis prepared by **Rafay Khalid** on October 21, 2008, when the stock traded at **$ 14.76**.

## Highlights

➤ We project that sales will decline 14% in 2008 and another 15% in 2009, reflecting above-average price deflation due to oversupplied industry conditions, partially offset by solid growth in megabytes. We foresee slowing consumer spending on flash memory, due to U.S. macroeconomic weakness more than outweighing what we see as increased market share gains in international markets based on aggressive price discounts. We expect license and royalty revenue to generate 14% growth in 2008, but decline 4% in 2009 on our projection for weak license sales.

➤ We forecast that the gross margin will contract to 13% in 2008, from 31% in 2007, as the company's products face aggressive pricing pressure from an industry oversupply in NAND flash. We estimate average selling prices per megabyte dropping about 60% in 2008, similar to the price decline in 2007. In our opinion, de-leveraging of SG&A and R&D expenses will contribute to a negative operating margin of 17% in 2008 and negative 7% in 2009, compared to a positive operating margin of 7% in 2007.

➤ Our GAAP earnings forecasts are for losses of $1.53 a share in 2008 and $0.43 in 2009.

## Investment Rationale/Risk

➤ Although SNDK rejected Samsung's proposal to be acquired for $26 per share in cash, subject to approvals, we believe a tie-up would strengthen the company's position in the NAND flash industry. However, we see antitrust concerns as a potential issue, since a combined company would have over 50% of the NAND market. In general, we believe the industry supply imbalance and weak demand amid the economic slowdown will pressure sales and earnings in the short term. Over the long term, we see SNDK's restructuring initiatives and lower capital expenditures aiding margins and free cash flow.

➤ Risks to our recommendation and target price include the potential for less aggressive price erosion than we forecast and an acceleration in end-market demand.

➤ Our 12-month target price of $18 is based on a blend of our enterprise value-to-sales and DCF analyses. Applying an enterprise value-to-sales ratio of 1.1X, in line with similar M&A transactions, to our 2009 revenue projection, we derive a $24 valuation. Our DCF model assumes a 13.7% weighted average cost of capital and 3% terminal growth rate, and yields a $12 intrinsic value.

## Qualitative Risk Assessment

| LOW | MEDIUM | HIGH |
|---|---|---|

Our risk assessment reflects the volatile nature of the flash memory space, an intensifying competitive environment, and what we deem to be significant price erosion within the industry.

## Quantitative Evaluations

**S&P Quality Ranking**   B

| D | C | B- | B | B+ | A- | A | A+ |
|---|---|---|---|---|---|---|---|

**Relative Strength Rank**   WEAK

14

LOWEST = 1                                    HIGHEST = 99

## Revenue/Earnings Data

**Revenue (Million $)**

| | 1Q | 2Q | 3Q | 4Q | Year |
|---|---|---|---|---|---|
| 2008 | 850.0 | 816.0 | 821.5 | -- | -- |
| 2007 | 786.1 | 827.0 | 1,037 | 1,246 | 3,896 |
| 2006 | 623.3 | 719.2 | 751.4 | 1,164 | 3,258 |
| 2005 | 451.0 | 514.9 | 589.6 | 750.6 | 2,306 |
| 2004 | 386.9 | 433.3 | 408.0 | 548.9 | 1,777 |
| 2003 | 174.5 | 234.6 | 281.4 | 389.3 | 1,080 |

**Earnings Per Share ($)**

| | | | | | |
|---|---|---|---|---|---|
| 2008 | 0.08 | -0.30 | -0.69 | E-0.63 | E-1.53 |
| 2007 | Nil | 0.12 | 0.36 | 0.45 | 0.93 |
| 2006 | 0.17 | 0.47 | 0.51 | -0.17 | 0.96 |
| 2005 | 0.39 | 0.37 | 0.55 | 0.68 | 2.00 |
| 2004 | 0.34 | 0.38 | 0.29 | 0.42 | 1.44 |
| 2003 | 0.17 | 0.26 | 0.09 | 0.47 | 1.02 |

Fiscal year ended Dec. 31. Next earnings report expected: Late January. EPS Estimates based on S&P Operating Earnings; historical GAAP earnings are as reported.

## Dividend Data

No cash dividends have been paid.

The McGraw-Hill Companies

# SanDisk Corp

## Business Summary October 21, 2008

CORPORATE OVERVIEW. SanDisk Corp. designs, makes and markets flash storage card products used in a wide variety of consumer electronics products such as digital cameras, mobile phones, Universal Serial Bus, or USB, drives, gaming devices and MP3 players. The company's strategy focuses on identifying and developing current and emerging mass consumer markets for flash storage products and -- through its vertical integration supply strategy -- selling all major card formats in high volumes.

CORPORATE STRATEGY. SNDK focuses primarily on four primary markets: consumer, mobile phones, digital audio and video players, computing. In the imaging market, the company makes cards used in all major brands of digital cameras. For mobile phones, SNDK's cards are experiencing increasing demand as multimedia features such as video and Internet access become more prevalent. Finally, SNDK offers a number of digital audio players, which allow consumers to download, store and play music.

Products are available to end users at approximately 222,000 retail storefronts around the globe and as data storage cards bundled with host products by SNDK's OEM customers. In 2007, the retail market accounted for 63% of product revenues, compared to 68% in 2006, while the OEM channel comprised 37% (32%). SNDK's top 10 customers and licensees in 2007 accounted for 46% of total revenues, down from 52% in 2006. No customer accounted for greater than 10% of revenues in 2007 or 2006. Product revenues from outside of North America made up 65% of the total in 2007, up from 57% in 2006 and 53% in 2005.

SNDK develops and owns leading-edge technology and patents for flash memory and data storage cards. The company has an extensive patent portfolio that has been licensed by several leading semiconductor companies. Over the past three years, on a cumulative basis, SNDK's license and royalty revenues exceeded $1 billion.

IMPACT OF MAJOR DEVELOPMENTS. The company is investing with Toshiba in high-volume state-of-the-art manufacturing facilities in Japan. Under terms of the agreement, SNDK is committed to purchasing 50% of the output of the ventures at manufacturing cost and sharing in the cost of SNDK-Toshiba joint research and development activities related to flash memory. In September 2004, SNDK and Toshiba formed the Flash Partners, Ltd. venture, and in July 2006, the companies created a new company, Flash Alliance, Ltd., in which SNDK owns 49.9% and is expected to invest $1.5 billion through the end of 2008.

## Company Financials Fiscal Year Ended Dec. 31

| Per Share Data ($) | 2007 | 2006 | 2005 | 2004 | 2003 | 2002 | 2001 | 2000 | 1999 | 1998 |
|---|---|---|---|---|---|---|---|---|---|---|
| Tangible Book Value | 16.94 | 15.31 | 13.41 | 10.78 | 9.32 | 4.54 | 4.93 | 6.40 | 4.38 | 1.95 |
| Cash Flow | 1.97 | 1.61 | 2.34 | 1.62 | 1.12 | 0.40 | -2.04 | 2.17 | 0.26 | 0.17 |
| Earnings | 0.93 | 0.96 | 2.00 | 1.44 | 1.02 | 0.26 | -2.19 | 2.06 | 0.22 | 0.11 |
| S&P Core Earnings | 0.96 | 0.94 | 1.76 | 1.29 | 0.89 | 0.18 | -1.05 | NA | NA | NA |
| Dividends | Nil | Nil | Nil | Nil | Nil | Nil | Nil | Nil | Nil | Nil |
| Payout Ratio | Nil | Nil | Nil | Nil | Nil | Nil | Nil | Nil | Nil | Nil |
| Prices:High | 59.75 | 79.80 | 65.49 | 36.35 | 43.15 | 14.60 | 24.34 | 84.81 | 25.16 | 6.56 |
| Prices:Low | 32.74 | 37.34 | 20.25 | 19.28 | 7.39 | 4.80 | 4.30 | 13.75 | 3.31 | 1.28 |
| P/E Ratio:High | 64 | 83 | 33 | 25 | 42 | 57 | NM | 41 | NM | 61 |
| P/E Ratio:Low | 35 | 39 | 10 | 13 | 7 | 19 | NM | 7 | NM | 12 |

| Income Statement Analysis (Million $) | | | | | | | | | | |
|---|---|---|---|---|---|---|---|---|---|---|
| Revenue | 3,896 | 3,258 | 2,306 | 1,777 | 1,080 | 541 | 366 | 602 | 247 | 136 |
| Operating Income | 536 | 688 | 642 | 457 | 280 | 79.5 | -124 | 141 | 37.2 | 18.6 |
| Depreciation | 246 | 136 | 65.8 | 38.9 | 23.0 | 21.3 | 20.5 | 15.9 | 7.15 | 5.84 |
| Interest Expense | 16.9 | Nil | 0.57 | 5.95 | 6.75 | 6.70 | Nil | Nil | Nil | Nil |
| Pretax Income | 398 | 431 | 613 | 423 | 242 | 40.0 | -442 | 492 | 39.6 | 18.5 |
| Effective Tax Rate | 43.9% | 53.4% | 37.0% | 37.0% | 30.2% | 9.35% | NM | 39.3% | 33.0% | 36.0% |
| Net Income | 218 | 199 | 386 | 267 | 169 | 36.2 | -298 | 299 | 26.6 | 11.8 |
| S&P Core Earnings | 225 | 195 | 339 | 239 | 149 | 25.7 | -144 | NA | NA | NA |

| Balance Sheet & Other Financial Data (Million $) | | | | | | | | | | |
|---|---|---|---|---|---|---|---|---|---|---|
| Cash | 1,835 | 1,581 | 762 | 464 | 734 | 267 | 254 | 106 | 146 | 15.4 |
| Current Assets | 3,300 | 4,242 | 2,576 | 1,880 | 1,725 | 757 | 542 | 697 | 568 | 186 |
| Total Assets | 7,235 | 6,968 | 3,120 | 2,320 | 2,024 | 976 | 932 | 1,108 | 658 | 256 |
| Current Liabilities | 914 | 896 | 571 | 353 | 347 | 173 | 127 | 171 | 85.6 | 47.9 |
| Long Term Debt | 1,225 | 1,225 | Nil | Nil | 150 | 150 | 125 | Nil | Nil | Nil |
| Common Equity | 4,960 | 4,768 | 2,524 | 1,940 | 1,501 | 628 | 675 | 863 | 572 | 208 |
| Total Capital | 6,200 | 5,999 | 2,524 | 1,940 | 1,651 | 778 | 800 | 863 | 572 | 208 |
| Capital Expenditures | 259 | 176 | 134 | 126 | 52.5 | 16.6 | 26.2 | 26.6 | 21.4 | 7.49 |
| Cash Flow | 464 | 334 | 452 | 305 | 192 | 57.6 | -277 | 315 | 33.7 | 17.7 |
| Current Ratio | 3.6 | 4.7 | 4.5 | 5.3 | 5.0 | 4.4 | 4.3 | 4.1 | 6.6 | 3.9 |
| % Long Term Debt of Capitalization | 19.8 | 20.4 | Nil | Nil | 9.1 | 19.3 | 15.6 | Nil | Nil | Nil |
| % Net Income of Revenue | 5.6 | 6.1 | 16.8 | 15.0 | 15.6 | 6.7 | NM | 49.6 | 10.7 | 8.7 |
| % Return on Assets | 3.1 | 3.9 | 14.2 | 12.2 | 11.3 | 3.8 | NM | 33.8 | 5.8 | 4.7 |
| % Return on Equity | 4.5 | 5.5 | 17.3 | 15.4 | 15.9 | 5.6 | NM | 41.6 | 6.8 | 5.9 |

Data as orig reptd.; bef. results of disc opers/spec. items. Per share data adj. for stk. divs.; EPS diluted. E-Estimated. NA-Not Available. NM-Not Meaningful. NR-Not Ranked. UR-Under Review.

**Office:** 601 McCarthy Blvd, Milpitas, CA 95035-7932.
**Telephone:** 408-801-1000.
**Email:** investor_relations@sandisk.com
**Website:** http://www.sandisk.com

**Chrmn & CEO:** E. Harari
**Pres & COO:** S. Mehrotra
**Vice Chrmn:** I. Federman
**SVP, Secy & General Counsel:** J. Brelsford

**Investor Contact:** J. Bruner
**Board Members:** I. Federman, S. Gomo, E. Harari, E. W. Hartenstein, C. P. Lego, M. E. Marks, J. D. Meindl

**Founded:** 1988
**Domicile:** Delaware
**Employees:** 3,172

# Sara Lee Corp

| S&P Recommendation HOLD ★★★☆☆ | Price<br>$9.47 (as of Nov 14, 2008) | 12-Mo. Target Price<br>$12.00 | Investment Style<br>Large-Cap Blend |
|---|---|---|---|

**GICS Sector** Consumer Staples
**Sub-Industry** Packaged Foods & Meats

**Summary** This diversified provider of branded food products (e.g., meats, fresh and frozen baked goods, and coffee) also sells household and body care products.

## Key Stock Statistics (Source S&P, Vickers, company reports)

| | | | | | | | |
|---|---|---|---|---|---|---|---|
| 52-Wk Range | $16.95– 9.01 | S&P Oper. EPS 2009E | 0.82 | Market Capitalization(B) | $6.694 | Beta | 0.89 |
| Trailing 12-Month EPS | $-0.07 | S&P Oper. EPS 2010E | 0.91 | Yield (%) | 4.65 | S&P 3-Yr. Proj. EPS CAGR(%) | 7 |
| Trailing 12-Month P/E | NM | P/E on S&P Oper. EPS 2009E | 11.5 | Dividend Rate/Share | $0.44 | S&P Credit Rating | BBB+ |
| $10K Invested 5 Yrs Ago | NA | Common Shares Outstg. (M) | 706.9 | Institutional Ownership (%) | 72 | | |

## Price Performance

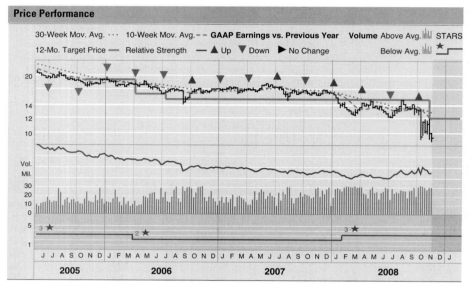

30-Week Mov. Avg. · · · · 10-Week Mov. Avg. - - GAAP Earnings vs. Previous Year Volume Above Avg. STARS
12-Mo. Target Price — Relative Strength — ▲ Up ▼ Down ► No Change Below Avg.

Options: ASE, CBOE, P

Analysis prepared by **Tom Graves, CFA** on November 10, 2008, when the stock traded at **$ 10.00**.

## Highlights

➤ The company is implementing a multi-year transformation plan, which has resulted in special charges. The plans included the divestiture of various businesses, including Hanesbrands apparel, European meats, direct selling, European branded apparel, U.K. apparel, U.S. retail coffee, European snacks & nuts, and U.S. meat snacks.

➤ In FY 09 (Jun.), we look for net sales to approximate the $13.2 billion reported for FY 08. If the value of the dollar is relatively strong relative to other currencies, we expect that currency translation could adversely affect reported sales, after a benefiting from weakness in the dollar in FY 08.

➤ Excluding special items, and including a benefit from a lower tax rate, we forecast FY 09 EPS of $0.82, down slightly from $0.83 in FY 08. We look for SLE's operating profit margin, before special items, to narrow somewhat from FY 08's 8.1%. Among the special items excluded from our estimate are a $0.21 a share benefit in FY 09's first quarter related to the sale of a European tobacco business. For FY 10, we estimate EPS of $0.91.

## Investment Rationale/Risk

➤ We believe the company has been significantly reshaped, and we see SLE making progress with its transformation plan. SLE's decline in total sales, from the $15.9 billion of sales reported for FY 06, was primarily due to the September 2006 spinoff of the Hanesbrands business, which is now being treated as a discontinued operation.

➤ Risks to our recommendation and target price include weaker than expected sales growth, and a failure to produce anticipated profit margin improvement.

➤ Our 12-month target price of $12 reflects our view that the stock should trade at a P/E discount to what we expect, on average, from a group of packaged food stocks. We expect that the stock has been hurt recently by concern about the impact that foreign currency fluctuation and economic weakness overseas may have on FY 09 results. In FY 08, 48% of SLE's sales came from outside the U.S. Following the Hanesbrands spinoff in 2006, SLE reduced its dividend by about 49%. However, with its current dividend rate, the stock recently had an indicated dividend yield of about 4.4%.

## Qualitative Risk Assessment

| LOW | MEDIUM | HIGH |
|---|---|---|

Our risk assessment for Sara Lee reflects the relatively stable nature of the company's end markets, strong cash flow, and corporate governance practices that we view as favorable relative to peers.

## Quantitative Evaluations

**S&P Quality Ranking** B

| D | C | B- | B | B+ | A- | A | A+ |
|---|---|---|---|---|---|---|---|

**Relative Strength Rank** MODERATE

54

LOWEST = 1     HIGHEST = 99

## Revenue/Earnings Data

**Revenue (Million $)**

| | 1Q | 2Q | 3Q | 4Q | Year |
|---|---|---|---|---|---|
| 2009 | 3,349 | -- | -- | -- | -- |
| 2008 | 3,054 | 3,408 | 3,243 | 3,507 | 13,212 |
| 2007 | 2,891 | 3,182 | 3,006 | 3,199 | 12,278 |
| 2006 | 3,900 | 2,974 | 3,789 | 4,100 | 15,944 |
| 2005 | 4,861 | 5,199 | 4,785 | 4,754 | 19,254 |
| 2004 | 4,666 | 5,017 | 4,745 | 5,138 | 19,566 |

**Earnings Per Share ($)**

| | 1Q | 2Q | 3Q | 4Q | Year |
|---|---|---|---|---|---|
| 2009 | 0.32 | E0.20 | E0.20 | E0.27 | E0.82 |
| 2008 | 0.28 | 0.25 | 0.33 | -0.96 | -0.06 |
| 2007 | 0.34 | -0.08 | 0.15 | 0.16 | 0.57 |
| 2006 | 0.25 | -0.06 | 0.18 | -0.15 | 0.53 |
| 2005 | 0.44 | 0.41 | 0.24 | -0.14 | 0.92 |
| 2004 | 0.29 | 0.39 | 0.47 | 0.44 | 1.59 |

Fiscal year ended Jun. 30. Next earnings report expected: Mid February. EPS Estimates based on S&P Operating Earnings; historical GAAP earnings are as reported.

## Dividend Data (Dates: mm/dd Payment Date: mm/dd/yy)

| Amount<br>($) | Date<br>Decl. | Ex-Div.<br>Date | Stk. of<br>Record | Payment<br>Date |
|---|---|---|---|---|
| 0.105 | 01/31 | 02/28 | 03/03 | 04/07/08 |
| 0.105 | 04/24 | 05/29 | 06/02 | 07/08/08 |
| 0.105 | 06/26 | 08/29 | 09/03 | 10/07/08 |
| 0.110 | 10/30 | 11/26 | 12/01 | 01/08/09 |

Dividends have been paid since 1946. Source: Company reports.

---

**Please read the Required Disclosures and Analyst Certification on the last page of this report.**

The McGraw-Hill Companies

# Sara Lee Corp

## Business Summary November 10, 2008

CORPORATE PROFILE. Sara Lee, best known for its baked goods, also has various other branded food and non-food businesses. In North America, this includes Jimmy Dean and Hillshire Farm meat products, while outside the U.S., it includes coffee and tea, and household and body care products. In North America, in addition to providing products to retailers, SLE provides coffee, meats and bakery products to foodservice operators.

At the beginning of FY 06 (Jun.), Sara Lee reorganized its businesses around distinct customers and geographic markets. In FY 08, North American Retail Meats represented 18% of total sales; North American Retail Bakery accounted for about 16%; Foodservice 17%; International Beverage 24%; International Bakery 7%; and Household and Body Care 17%. SLE's Branded Apparel business, which had sales of $4.5 billion in FY 06, was spun off in September 2006.

CORPORATE STRATEGY. In February 2005, the company announced a comprehensive restructuring program, involving a reorganization of business units and plans to dispose of various businesses. The key components of this plan were to transform the company's portfolio, reorganize continuing operations, improve operational efficiency, and consolidate the North American and Euro-

pean headquarters. We look for the transformation plan to be completed by 2010.

During FY 06, Sara Lee disposed of its direct selling European branded apparel, U.K. apparel, U.S. retail coffee, European snacks & nuts, and U.S. meat snacks businesses. In August 2006, Sara Lee completed the sale of its European meats business. Also, in September 2006, the company completed the spinoff of its branded apparel Americas/Asia business. This business was spun off as an independent company named Hanesbrands Inc.

We expect SLE spending on information technology initiatives to include the implementation of a standardized information technology platform in North American operations and continued consolidation of information processing in both the U.S. and Europe.

## Company Financials Fiscal Year Ended Jun. 30

| Per Share Data ($) | 2008 | 2007 | 2006 | 2005 | 2004 | 2003 | 2002 | 2001 | 2000 | 1999 |
|---|---|---|---|---|---|---|---|---|---|---|
| Tangible Book Value | NM | NM | NM | NM | NM | NM | NM | NM | NM | NM |
| Cash Flow | NA | 1.33 | 1.46 | 1.87 | 2.53 | 2.44 | 1.94 | 2.80 | 1.92 | 1.83 |
| Earnings | -0.06 | 0.57 | 0.53 | 0.92 | 1.59 | 1.50 | 1.23 | 1.87 | 1.27 | 1.26 |
| S&P Core Earnings | 0.69 | 0.50 | 0.44 | 0.86 | 1.67 | 1.30 | 1.00 | 0.92 | NA | NA |
| Dividends | 0.42 | 0.50 | 0.79 | 0.78 | 0.60 | 0.62 | 0.60 | 0.57 | 0.54 | 0.49 |
| Payout Ratio | NM | 88% | 149% | 85% | 38% | 41% | 48% | 30% | 43% | 39% |
| Prices:High | 16.08 | 18.15 | 19.64 | 25.00 | 24.49 | 23.13 | 23.84 | 24.75 | 25.31 | 28.75 |
| Prices:Low | 9.01 | 14.75 | 14.08 | 17.31 | 20.17 | 16.25 | 16.15 | 18.26 | 13.38 | 21.06 |
| P/E Ratio:High | NM | 32 | 37 | 27 | 15 | 15 | 19 | 13 | 20 | 23 |
| P/E Ratio:Low | NM | 26 | 27 | 19 | 13 | 11 | 13 | 10 | 11 | 17 |

| Income Statement Analysis (Million $) | | | | | | | | | | |
|---|---|---|---|---|---|---|---|---|---|---|
| Revenue | 13,212 | 12,278 | 15,944 | 19,254 | 19,566 | 18,291 | 17,628 | 17,747 | 17,511 | 20,012 |
| Operating Income | NA | 1,242 | 1,779 | 2,183 | 2,386 | 2,345 | 2,138 | 2,191 | 2,345 | 2,304 |
| Depreciation | 520 | 539 | 701 | 737 | 734 | 674 | 582 | 599 | 602 | 553 |
| Interest Expense | NA | 265 | 308 | 290 | 271 | 276 | 304 | 270 | 252 | 237 |
| Pretax Income | 137 | 419 | 683 | 934 | 1,542 | 1,484 | 1,185 | 1,851 | 1,567 | 1,671 |
| Effective Tax Rate | 146.7% | NM | 40.0% | 21.7% | 17.5% | 17.7% | 14.8% | 13.4% | 26.1% | 28.7% |
| Net Income | -64.0 | 426 | 410 | 731 | 1,272 | 1,221 | 1,010 | 1,603 | 1,158 | 1,191 |
| S&P Core Earnings | 501 | 385 | 339 | 684 | 1,336 | 1,047 | 806 | 768 | NA | NA |

| Balance Sheet & Other Financial Data (Million $) | | | | | | | | | | |
|---|---|---|---|---|---|---|---|---|---|---|
| Cash | 1,284 | 2,520 | 2,231 | 545 | 638 | 942 | 298 | 548 | 314 | 279 |
| Current Assets | NA | 5,643 | 6,774 | 5,811 | 5,746 | 5,953 | 4,986 | 5,083 | 5,974 | 4,987 |
| Total Assets | 10,830 | 12,190 | 14,522 | 14,412 | 14,883 | 15,084 | 13,753 | 10,167 | 11,611 | 10,521 |
| Current Liabilities | NA | 4,301 | 6,277 | 4,968 | 5,423 | 5,199 | 5,463 | 4,958 | 6,759 | 5,953 |
| Long Term Debt | NA | 2,803 | 3,807 | 4,115 | 4,171 | 5,157 | 4,326 | 2,640 | 2,248 | 1,892 |
| Common Equity | 2,811 | 2,615 | 2,449 | 2,938 | 2,948 | 1,870 | 1,534 | 899 | 1,007 | 1,034 |
| Total Capital | NA | 6,066 | 6,324 | 7,134 | 7,194 | 7,806 | 7,252 | 4,646 | 4,271 | 3,866 |
| Capital Expenditures | 454 | 529 | 625 | 538 | 530 | 746 | 669 | 532 | 647 | 535 |
| Cash Flow | NA | 965 | 1,111 | 1,468 | 2,006 | 1,895 | 1,592 | 2,191 | 1,748 | 1,732 |
| Current Ratio | 1.2 | 1.3 | 1.1 | 1.2 | 1.1 | 1.1 | 0.9 | 1.0 | 0.9 | 0.8 |
| % Long Term Debt of Capitalization | Nil | 46.2 | 60.2 | 57.6 | 58.0 | 66.1 | 59.7 | 56.8 | 52.6 | 48.9 |
| % Net Income of Revenue | NM | 3.5 | 2.6 | 3.8 | 6.5 | 6.7 | 5.7 | 9.0 | 6.6 | 6.0 |
| % Return on Assets | NA | 3.2 | 2.8 | 5.0 | 8.4 | 8.5 | 8.4 | 14.7 | 10.6 | 11.1 |
| % Return on Equity | NA | 16.8 | 15.2 | 24.7 | 52.8 | 71.7 | 83.0 | 167.1 | 112.3 | 90.9 |

Data as orig reptd.; bef. results of disc opers/spec. items. Per share data adj. for stk. divs.; EPS diluted. E-Estimated. NA-Not Available. NM-Not Meaningful. NR-Not Ranked. UR-Under Review.

**Office:** 3500 Lacey Rd, Downers Grove, IL 60515-5422.
**Telephone:** 630-598-6000.
**Website:** http://www.saralee.com
**Chrmn & CEO:** B.C. Barnes

**Investor Contact:** L.M. de Kool (630-598-8100)
**EVP, CFO & Chief Admin Officer:** L.M. de Kool
**EVP, Secy & General Counsel:** M.M. Foran
**SVP, Chief Acctg Officer & Cntlr:** T.S. Shilen

**Board Members:** B. C. Barnes, C. B. Begley, V. W. Colbert, J. S. Crown, L. T. Koellner, C. V. Lede, J. D. McAdam, I. Prosser, R. L. Ridgway, N. Sorensen, J. W. Ubben, J. Ward

**Founded:** 1941
**Domicile:** Maryland
**Employees:** 44,000

# Schering-Plough

STANDARD
&POOR'S

| S&P Recommendation | BUY ★★★★☆ | Price $15.76 (as of Nov 14, 2008) | 12-Mo. Target Price $20.00 | Investment Style Large-Cap Blend |
|---|---|---|---|---|

**GICS Sector** Health Care
**Sub-Industry** Pharmaceuticals

**Summary** This leading producer of prescription and OTC pharmaceuticals also has important interests in sun care, animal health and foot care products.

## Key Stock Statistics (Source S&P, Vickers, company reports)

| | | | | | | | |
|---|---|---|---|---|---|---|---|
| 52-Wk Range | $31.53– 11.97 | S&P Oper. EPS 2008**E** | 1.66 | Market Capitalization(B) | $25.629 | Beta | 1.32 |
| Trailing 12-Month EPS | $-1.37 | S&P Oper. EPS 2009**E** | 1.70 | Yield (%) | 1.65 | S&P 3-Yr. Proj. EPS CAGR(%) | 7 |
| Trailing 12-Month P/E | NM | P/E on S&P Oper. EPS 2008**E** | 9.5 | Dividend Rate/Share | $0.26 | S&P Credit Rating | A- |
| $10K Invested 5 Yrs Ago | $10,430 | Common Shares Outstg. (M) | 1,626.2 | Institutional Ownership (%) | 82 | | |

## Price Performance

30-Week Mov. Avg. ···· 10-Week Mov. Avg. --- **GAAP Earnings vs. Previous Year**   Volume Above Avg. ⅃⅃⅃⅃ STARS
12-Mo. Target Price — Relative Strength — ▲ Up ▼ Down ► No Change   Below Avg. ⅃⅃⅃⅃ ★

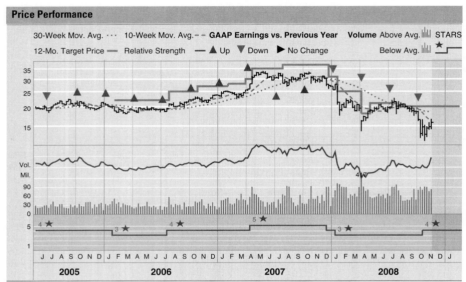

Options: ASE, CBOE, P, Ph

Analysis prepared by **Herman B. Saftlas** on October 27, 2008, when the stock traded at **$ 13.12**.

## Highlights

➤ We forecast 2009 revenue growth of about 5%, with the gain restricted by expected negative foreign exchange. Drugs poised for robust growth, in our opinion, include Remicade treatment for inflammatory diseases and Nasonex allergy drug. We also see contributions from new drugs such as sugammadex anesthesia product and golimumab oncology agent. We also see higher sales of consumer health care products, but expect declines in PEG-Intron and Claritin/Clarinex lines.

➤ SGP's gross margins are well below those of peer drugmakers because most of its earnings are derived from equity income. Nonetheless, we see overall profitability benefiting from cost-cutting measures. However, we project lower equity income from SGP's Vytorin/Zetia anti-cholesterol joint venture with Merck, reflecting ongoing fallout from the disappointing EN-HANCE and SEAS trial results.

➤ After a likely increase in the tax rate to about 16%, from an indicated 15% in 2008, we project operating EPS of $1.70 for 2009, up from an estimated $1.66 in 2008, excluding non-recurring items.

## Investment Rationale/Risk

➤ Faced with what we believe to be ongoing erosion in the Vytorin/Zetia cholesterol franchise, SGP has undertaken to offset that shortfall through a cost reduction program aimed at providing $1.5 billion of savings by 2012. Vytorin/Zetia has been severely impacted by a trial that showed Vytorin was no more effective than generic Zocor in blocking arterial plaque. On the plus side, we see significant promise in recently acquired Organon BioSciences, as well as from pipeline drugs, which include a novel anesthesia product, and treatments for cancer, psychosis and other diseases.

➤ Risks to our recommendation and target price include possibly larger-than-expected erosion in Vytorin and Zetia, worsening competitive pressures in other lines, and pipeline setbacks.

➤ Our 12-month target price of $20 applies a peer-level P/E of 11.8X to our 2009 EPS estimate. Our discounted cash flow model, which assumes steady free cash flow growth over 10 years, a weighted average cost of capital of 7.3%, and terminal growth of 2%, also indicates intrinsic value in the $20 area.

## Qualitative Risk Assessment

| LOW | MEDIUM | HIGH |
|---|---|---|

Our risk assessment incorporates our view that SGP's turnaround phase will continue for several more years. We also think the company is dependent on a relatively small number of drugs to support future growth.

## Quantitative Evaluations

**S&P Quality Ranking**   B+

| D | C | B- | B | B+ | A- | A | A+ |
|---|---|---|---|---|---|---|---|

**Relative Strength Rank**   STRONG

86

LOWEST = 1                    HIGHEST = 99

## Revenue/Earnings Data

**Revenue (Million $)**

| | 1Q | 2Q | 3Q | 4Q | Year |
|---|---|---|---|---|---|
| 2008 | 4,657 | 4,921 | 4,576 | -- | -- |
| 2007 | 2,975 | 3,178 | 2,812 | 3,724 | 12,690 |
| 2006 | 2,551 | 2,818 | 2,574 | 2,650 | 10,594 |
| 2005 | 2,369 | 2,532 | 2,284 | 2,324 | 9,508 |
| 2004 | 1,963 | 2,147 | 1,978 | 2,184 | 8,272 |
| 2003 | 2,082 | 2,338 | 1,998 | 1,948 | 8,334 |

**Earnings Per Share ($)**

| | 1Q | 2Q | 3Q | 4Q | Year |
|---|---|---|---|---|---|
| 2008 | 0.16 | 0.24 | 0.34 | E0.30 | E1.66 |
| 2007 | 0.36 | 0.34 | 0.45 | -2.11 | -1.04 |
| 2006 | 0.22 | 0.16 | 0.19 | 0.12 | 0.69 |
| 2005 | 0.07 | -0.05 | 0.03 | 0.07 | 0.12 |
| 2004 | -0.05 | -0.04 | 0.01 | -0.58 | -0.67 |
| 2003 | 0.12 | 0.12 | -0.18 | -0.12 | -0.06 |

Fiscal year ended Dec. 31. Next earnings report expected: Mid February. EPS Estimates based on S&P Operating Earnings; historical GAAP earnings are as reported.

## Dividend Data (Dates: mm/dd Payment Date: mm/dd/yy)

| Amount ($) | Date Decl. | Ex-Div. Date | Stk. of Record | Payment Date |
|---|---|---|---|---|
| 0.065 | 12/14 | 01/30 | 02/01 | 02/26/08 |
| 0.065 | 02/29 | 04/30 | 05/02 | 05/27/08 |
| 0.065 | 06/24 | 07/30 | 08/01 | 08/26/08 |
| 0.065 | 09/16 | 11/05 | 11/07 | 11/25/08 |

Dividends have been paid since 1952. Source: Company reports.

---

**Please read the Required Disclosures and Analyst Certification on the last page of this report.**

# Schering-Plough

**STANDARD &POOR'S**

## Business Summary October 27, 2008

CORPORATE PROFILE. Schering-Plough is a leading maker of niche-oriented prescription pharmaceuticals. It also has interests in animal health products, over-the-counter (OTC) medications, and consumer products. On November 19, 2007, SGP completed the acquisition of Organon BioSciences from Akzo Nobel N.V. for some $15 billion in cash. A maker of a broad line of human and animal health products, Organon BioSciences had annual sales of close to $5 billion in 2006.

Prescription pharmaceuticals accounted for about 80% of total sales in 2007, consumer health care products for 10%, and animal health items for 10%. Sales outside of the U.S. represented 64% of total sales in 2007.

Through a joint venture with Merck & Co., Schering-Plough shares in the profits of two cholesterol-lowering drugs. These are Zetia, a novel lipid-lowering agent that works by blocking the absorption of cholesterol in the intestines, and Vytorin, a combination of Zetia with Merck's Zocor statin cholesterol agent. SGP booked equity income of $2.0 billion from this venture in 2007, up from $1.5 billion in 2006. Sales of Zetia and Vytorin (not booked by SGP) totaled $5.1 billion in 2007, up from $3.8 billion in 2006, with U.S. sales up 26%, and international sales rising 70%. The joint venture plans to launch a combination of Zetia with generic Lipitor, after Pfizer's patent on Lipitor expires in 2010 or

2011.

SGP is a global leader in treatments for hepatitis C with its PEG-Intron (sales of $911 million in 2007), a once-weekly alpha interferon, combined with Rebetol antiviral agent ($211 million). In the anti-inflammatory area, SGP offers Remicade ($1.6 billion), a TNF-alpha treatment for rheumatoid arthritis and Crohn's disease. Other important products are Temodar ($861 million), a treatment for brain tumors; Integrilin ($332 million) for cardiovascular problems; Avelox ($384 million), a treatment for bacterial infections; Intron A for cancer and viral infections; Subutex for opiate dependence; Caelyx for skin cancer; Cipro, an antibiotic; and Elocon, for inflammatory skin conditions.

A long-time leader in the U.S. respiratory/allergy market, SGP's most important prescription drugs in that area are Nasonex corticosteroid nasal spray ($1.1 billion) and Clarinex/Aerius non-sedating antihistamine ($799 million). Other important allergy/respiratory drugs include Asmanex and Foradil.

## Company Financials Fiscal Year Ended Dec. 31

| Per Share Data ($) | 2007 | 2006 | 2005 | 2004 | 2003 | 2002 | 2001 | 2000 | 1999 | 1998 |
|---|---|---|---|---|---|---|---|---|---|---|
| Tangible Book Value | NM | 4.04 | 3.64 | 4.73 | 4.57 | 4.07 | 4.41 | 3.75 | 3.11 | 2.33 |
| Cash Flow | -0.70 | 1.08 | 0.45 | -0.36 | 0.22 | 1.28 | 1.54 | 1.84 | 1.60 | 0.44 |
| Earnings | -1.04 | 0.69 | 0.12 | -0.67 | -0.06 | 1.34 | 1.32 | 1.64 | 1.42 | 1.18 |
| S&P Core Earnings | -1.04 | 0.72 | 0.19 | -0.72 | 0.16 | 1.17 | 1.41 | NA | NA | NA |
| Dividends | 0.25 | 0.22 | 0.22 | 0.22 | 0.57 | 0.67 | 0.62 | 0.55 | 0.49 | 0.43 |
| Payout Ratio | NM | 32% | 183% | NM | NM | 50% | 47% | 33% | 34% | 36% |
| Prices:High | 33.81 | 24.07 | 22.53 | 21.37 | 23.75 | 36.25 | 57.25 | 60.00 | 60.81 | 57.75 |
| Prices:Low | 22.30 | 17.88 | 17.67 | 15.45 | 14.16 | 16.10 | 32.35 | 30.50 | 40.25 | 30.34 |
| P/E Ratio:High | NM | 35 | NM | NM | NM | 27 | 43 | 37 | 43 | 49 |
| P/E Ratio:Low | NM | 26 | NM | NM | NM | 12 | 25 | 19 | 28 | 26 |

### Income Statement Analysis (Million $)

| | 2007 | 2006 | 2005 | 2004 | 2003 | 2002 | 2001 | 2000 | 1999 | 1998 |
|---|---|---|---|---|---|---|---|---|---|---|
| Revenue | 12,690 | 10,594 | 9,508 | 8,272 | 8,334 | 10,180 | 9,802 | 9,815 | 9,176 | 8,077 |
| Operating Income | 728 | 559 | 409 | 237 | 975 | 2,941 | 3,248 | 3,394 | 3,015 | 2,566 |
| Depreciation | 511 | 568 | 486 | 453 | 417 | 372 | 320 | 299 | 264 | 238 |
| Interest Expense | 263 | Nil | Nil | Nil | 81.0 | Nil | Nil | 44.0 | 29.0 | 19.0 |
| Pretax Income | -1,215 | 1,483 | 497 | -168 | -46.0 | 2,563 | 2,523 | 3,188 | 2,795 | 2,326 |
| Effective Tax Rate | NM | 24.4% | 45.9% | NM | NM | 23.0% | 23.0% | 24.0% | 24.5% | 24.5% |
| Net Income | -1,473 | 1,121 | 269 | -947 | -92.0 | 1,974 | 1,943 | 2,423 | 2,110 | 1,756 |
| S&P Core Earnings | -1,581 | 1,077 | 279 | -1,052 | 247 | 1,717 | 2,070 | NA | NA | NA |

### Balance Sheet & Other Financial Data (Million $)

| | 2007 | 2006 | 2005 | 2004 | 2003 | 2002 | 2001 | 2000 | 1999 | 1998 |
|---|---|---|---|---|---|---|---|---|---|---|
| Cash | 2,311 | 2,666 | 4,767 | 4,984 | 4,218 | 3,521 | 2,716 | 2,397 | 1,876 | 1,259 |
| Current Assets | 10,846 | 10,423 | 9,732 | 10,003 | 9,147 | 8,272 | 6,519 | 5,720 | 4,909 | 3,958 |
| Total Assets | 29,156 | 16,071 | 15,469 | 15,911 | 15,102 | 14,136 | 12,174 | 10,805 | 9,375 | 7,840 |
| Current Liabilities | 6,043 | 4,162 | 4,659 | 5,208 | 4,609 | 4,729 | 3,917 | 3,645 | 3,209 | 3,032 |
| Long Term Debt | 9,019 | 2,414 | 2,399 | 2,392 | 2,410 | Nil | Nil | Nil | Nil | 4.00 |
| Common Equity | 7,885 | 6,470 | 16,825 | 6,118 | 7,337 | 8,142 | 7,125 | 6,119 | 5,165 | 4,002 |
| Total Capital | 21,105 | 10,444 | 20,779 | 10,059 | 9,981 | 8,500 | 7,427 | 6,333 | 5,449 | 4,297 |
| Capital Expenditures | 618 | 458 | 478 | 489 | 701 | 770 | 759 | 763 | 543 | 389 |
| Cash Flow | -1,080 | 1,603 | 669 | -528 | 325 | 2,346 | 2,263 | 2,722 | 2,374 | 1,994 |
| Current Ratio | 1.8 | 2.5 | 2.1 | 1.9 | 2.0 | 1.7 | 1.7 | 1.6 | 1.5 | 1.3 |
| % Long Term Debt of Capitalization | 42.7 | 23.1 | 11.5 | 23.8 | 24.1 | Nil | Nil | Nil | Nil | 0.1 |
| % Net Income of Revenue | NM | 10.6 | 2.8 | NM | NM | 19.4 | 19.8 | 24.7 | 23.0 | 21.7 |
| % Return on Assets | NM | 7.1 | 1.7 | NM | NM | 15.0 | 16.9 | 24.0 | 24.5 | 24.5 |
| % Return on Equity | NM | 16.7 | 1.1 | NM | NM | 25.9 | 29.3 | 42.9 | 46.0 | 51.5 |

Data as orig reptd.; bef. results of disc opers/spec. items. Per share data adj. for stk. divs.; EPS diluted. E-Estimated. NA-Not Available. NM-Not Meaningful. NR-Not Ranked. UR-Under Review.

**Office:** 2000 Galloping Hill Road, Kenilworth, NJ 07033.
**Telephone:** 908-298-4000.
**Website:** http://www.schering-plough.com
**Chrmn, Pres & CEO:** F. Hassan

**EVP & CFO:** R.J. Bertolini
**EVP & CTO:** C.D. Strader
**EVP & General Counsel:** T.J. Sabatino, Jr.
**SVP & CSO:** I. Kola

**Investor Contact:** E.K. Moore (908-298-4000)
**Board Members:** H. W. Becherer, T. J. Colligan, F. Hassan, C. R. Kidder, E. R. McGrath, C. E. Mundy, A. M. Perez, P. F. Russo, J. Stahl, C. B. Thompson, K. C. Turner, R. F. Van Oordt, A. Weinbach

**Founded:** 1970
**Domicile:** New Jersey
**Employees:** 55,000

# Schlumberger Ltd

## STANDARD &POOR'S

| S&P Recommendation | BUY ★★★★☆ | Price<br>$48.76 (as of Nov 14, 2008) | 12-Mo. Target Price<br>$68.00 | Investment Style<br>Large-Cap Blend |
|---|---|---|---|---|

**GICS Sector** Energy
**Sub-Industry** Oil & Gas Equipment & Services

**Summary** This leading oilfield services company provides equipment and technology to the oil and gas industry worldwide.

### Key Stock Statistics (Source S&P, Vickers, company reports)

| | | | | | | | |
|---|---|---|---|---|---|---|---|
| 52-Wk Range | $111.95– 42.01 | S&P Oper. EPS 2008**E** | 4.78 | Market Capitalization(B) | $58.325 | Beta | 1.12 |
| Trailing 12-Month EPS | $4.62 | S&P Oper. EPS 2009**E** | 5.62 | Yield (%) | 1.72 | S&P 3-Yr. Proj. EPS CAGR(%) | 23 |
| Trailing 12-Month P/E | 10.6 | P/E on S&P Oper. EPS 2008**E** | 10.2 | Dividend Rate/Share | $0.84 | S&P Credit Rating | A+ |
| $10K Invested 5 Yrs Ago | $21,530 | Common Shares Outstg. (M) | 1,196.2 | Institutional Ownership (%) | 78 | | |

### Price Performance

30-Week Mov. Avg. · · · ·  10-Week Mov. Avg. – – –  **GAAP Earnings vs. Previous Year**  Volume Above Avg. ᴵᴵᴵᴵ STARS
12-Mo. Target Price —  Relative Strength —  ▲ Up  ▼ Down  ▶ No Change  Below Avg. ᴵᴵᴵᴵ ★

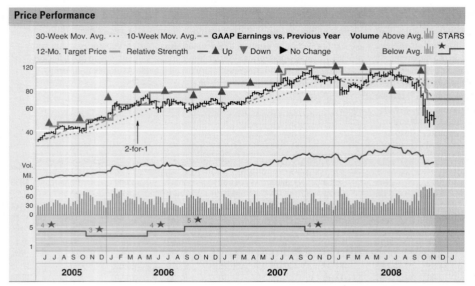

2-for-1

Options: ASE, CBOE, P, Ph

Analysis prepared by **Stewart Glickman, CFA** on October 17, 2008, when the stock traded at **$ 51.53**.

### Highlights

➤ In October, SLB noted that the rapid deterioration in credit markets would undoubtedly have an adverse impact on activity levels, though it expected the impact to be limited mainly to North America and exploration in some emerging markets overseas. Nonetheless, we are now less sanguine on expectations for non-North America revenue growth, and no longer anticipate revenue growth in these areas of 20%+ in 2009, as we expect SLB's upstream customers to pull back on capital spending in the face of high macroeconomic uncertainty.

➤ Across the equipment & services sub-industry, we now look at 2009 as a brief hiatus from the strong secular growth in oilfield services since 2004. We also note, however, that ultimately we expect demand to recover when credit markets recover, and to the extent that supply growth dissipates during a pullback, activity levels could rebound sharply. SLB's U.S. onshore region was strong in the third quarter, as was Canada, but weakness in the U.S. Gulf Coast due to the arrival of hurricanes Ike and Gustav shaved $0.04 off of third quarter results.

➤ We project EPS of $4.78 in 2008, rising to $5.62 in 2009.

### Investment Rationale/Risk

➤ Long term, we believe SLB is well positioned to benefit from an increasing trend toward new oil and gas development opportunities that require higher levels of technology content, especially in emerging markets, which we believe plays to the benefit of larger oilfield service providers. However, in the short term, we think that ongoing credit worries will weigh on customer demand and result in 2009 revenue growth being relatively modest, in the 10% range.

➤ Risks to our recommendation and target price include a decline in oil and gas exploration and production activity; reduced demand for integrated systems in oilfield services; and political risk in emerging markets.

➤ Our DCF model, assuming free cash flow growth of about 12% per year for 10 years and 3% thereafter, shows an intrinsic value of about $84 per share. We think the shares merit a premium to peers on the strength of SLB's leadership position. Applying an enterprise value of 7X to our 2009 EBITDA estimate, a multiple of 8X projected 2009 cash flow (both premiums to compressed peer averages), and blending with our DCF model, our 12-month target price is $68.

### Qualitative Risk Assessment

| LOW | MEDIUM | HIGH |
|---|---|---|

Our risk assessment reflects the company's exposure to volatile crude oil and natural gas prices; its dependence on capital spending decisions by its oil and gas producing customers; and political risk associated with operating in frontier regions around the world. This is offset by the company's leading industry position.

### Quantitative Evaluations

**S&P Quality Ranking**  NR

| D | C | B- | B | B+ | A- | A | A+ |
|---|---|---|---|---|---|---|---|

**Relative Strength Rank**  MODERATE

38

LOWEST = 1                                    HIGHEST = 99

### Revenue/Earnings Data

**Revenue (Million $)**

| | 1Q | 2Q | 3Q | 4Q | Year |
|---|---|---|---|---|---|
| 2008 | 6,290 | 6,746 | 7,259 | -- | -- |
| 2007 | 5,464 | 5,639 | 5,926 | 6,248 | 23,277 |
| 2006 | 4,239 | 4,687 | 4,955 | 5,350 | 19,230 |
| 2005 | 3,159 | 3,429 | 3,698 | 4,023 | 14,309 |
| 2004 | 2,673 | 2,833 | 2,906 | 3,068 | 11,480 |
| 2003 | 3,263 | 3,485 | 3,474 | 3,671 | 14,059 |

**Earnings Per Share ($)**

| | 1Q | 2Q | 3Q | 4Q | Year |
|---|---|---|---|---|---|
| 2008 | 1.06 | 1.16 | 1.25 | E1.31 | E4.78 |
| 2007 | 0.96 | 1.02 | 1.09 | 1.12 | 4.20 |
| 2006 | 0.59 | 0.69 | 0.81 | 0.92 | 3.01 |
| 2005 | 0.44 | 0.39 | 0.45 | 0.54 | 1.81 |
| 2004 | 0.09 | 0.22 | 0.25 | 0.29 | 0.85 |
| 2003 | 0.13 | 0.12 | -0.05 | 0.20 | 0.41 |

Fiscal year ended Dec. 31. Next earnings report expected: Late January. EPS Estimates based on S&P Operating Earnings; historical GAAP earnings are as reported.

### Dividend Data (Dates: mm/dd Payment Date: mm/dd/yy)

| Amount ($) | Date Decl. | Ex-Div. Date | Stk. of Record | Payment Date |
|---|---|---|---|---|
| 0.210 | 01/17 | 02/15 | 02/20 | 04/04/08 |
| 0.210 | 04/17 | 06/02 | 06/04 | 07/11/08 |
| 0.210 | 07/17 | 08/29 | 09/03 | 10/03/08 |
| 0.210 | 10/16 | 12/01 | 12/03 | 01/09/09 |

Dividends have been paid since 1957. Source: Company reports.

---

**Please read the Required Disclosures and Analyst Certification on the last page of this report.**

The McGraw-Hill Companies

# Schlumberger Ltd

## Business Summary October 17, 2008

CORPORATE OVERVIEW. As a global oilfield and information services company with major activity in the energy industry, Schlumberger operates in two primary business segments: Oilfield Services (87% of 2007 revenues; 85% of 2007 segment operating income), and WesternGeco (13%, 15%). Oilfield Services provides exploration and production services, solutions and technology to the petroleum industry. It is managed through four geographic areas (North America, South America, Europe/CIS/Africa, and the Middle East/Asia). The company is largely focused on international operations; North America generated only 26% of Oilfield Services' total revenues in 2007, and 26% of the segment's pretax operating income. The Middle East/Asia region generated the highest operating margins in 2007, at 35.1%, with North America second, at 28.8%. Operations within oilfield services are organized into six technology segments: wireline services, providing information technology to evaluate the reservoir, plan and monitor wells, and evaluate and monitor production; drilling and measurements, including directional drilling, measurement while drilling and logging while drilling services; well services, constructing mostly oil and gas wells; well completions and productivity; data and consulting services; and Schlumberger Information Solutions. Supporting these six technologies are 23 R&D centers.

In addition, SLB operates its WesternGeco seismic segment. WesternGeco provides worldwide comprehensive reservoir imaging, monitoring and development services, with seismic crews and data processing centers, as well as a large multiclient seismic library. Services include 3D and time-lapse (4D) seismic surveys, and multi-component surveys for delineating prospects and reservoir management. In January 2007, SLB announced that it would construct its eighth and ninth Q-marine seismic vessels for this segment, due in 2008 and 2009, respectively.

CORPORATE STRATEGY. SLB has made a strategic focus of improving its research and development of advanced oilfield technologies, with the goal of enhancing oilfield efficiency, reducing finding and development (F&D) costs, improving productivity, maximizing reserve recovery, and increasing asset values. We believe that advanced technology will become increasingly important, as existing oilfields mature and new oilfields are developed in harsh environments and challenging geological conditions. We anticipate that most new major oilfield developments are likely to be found in the Eastern Hemisphere, given relatively lower F&D costs and higher growth reservoir potential.

## Company Financials Fiscal Year Ended Dec. 31

| Per Share Data ($) | 2007 | 2006 | 2005 | 2004 | 2003 | 2002 | 2001 | 2000 | 1999 | 1998 |
|---|---|---|---|---|---|---|---|---|---|---|
| Tangible Book Value | 8.48 | 3.84 | 3.63 | 2.54 | 1.87 | 0.70 | 1.14 | 5.87 | 5.65 | 6.24 |
| Cash Flow | 5.41 | 4.24 | 2.89 | 1.89 | 1.74 | -0.75 | 2.08 | 1.73 | 1.20 | 1.91 |
| Earnings | 4.20 | 3.01 | 1.81 | 0.85 | 0.41 | -2.09 | 0.46 | 0.64 | 0.29 | 0.91 |
| Dividends | 0.70 | 0.50 | 0.42 | 0.38 | 0.38 | 0.38 | 0.38 | 0.38 | 0.38 | 0.38 |
| Payout Ratio | 17% | 17% | 23% | 44% | 93% | NM | 82% | 59% | 129% | 41% |
| Prices:High | 114.84 | 74.75 | 51.49 | 34.95 | 28.12 | 31.22 | 41.41 | 44.44 | 35.34 | 43.22 |
| Prices:Low | 55.68 | 49.20 | 31.57 | 26.27 | 17.81 | 16.70 | 20.42 | 26.75 | 22.72 | 20.03 |
| P/E Ratio:High | 27 | 25 | 28 | 41 | 69 | NM | 91 | 70 | NM | 48 |
| P/E Ratio:Low | 13 | 16 | 17 | 31 | 44 | NM | 45 | 42 | NM | 22 |

| Income Statement Analysis (Million $) | 2007 | 2006 | 2005 | 2004 | 2003 | 2002 | 2001 | 2000 | 1999 | 1998 |
|---|---|---|---|---|---|---|---|---|---|---|
| Revenue | 23,277 | 19,230 | 14,309 | 11,480 | 14,059 | 13,474 | 13,746 | 9,611 | 8,395 | 11,816 |
| Operating Income | 7,994 | 6,458 | 4,520 | 2,895 | 2,474 | -456 | 3,165 | 2,084 | 1,327 | 2,428 |
| Depreciation, Depletion and Amortization | 1,526 | 1,561 | 1,351 | 1,308 | 1,571 | 1,545 | 1,896 | 1,271 | 1,021 | 1,137 |
| Interest Expense | 275 | 235 | 197 | 272 | 334 | 368 | 385 | 276 | 193 | 150 |
| Pretax Income | 6,624 | 4,948 | 2,972 | 1,327 | 568 | -2,230 | 1,126 | 959 | 470 | 1,323 |
| Effective Tax Rate | 21.9% | 24.0% | 22.9% | 20.9% | 36.9% | NM | 51.1% | 23.8% | 29.9% | 23.4% |
| Net Income | 5,177 | 3,710 | 2,199 | 1,014 | 473 | -2,418 | 522 | 733 | 329 | 1,014 |

| Balance Sheet & Other Financial Data (Million $) | 2007 | 2006 | 2005 | 2004 | 2003 | 2002 | 2001 | 2000 | 1999 | 1998 |
|---|---|---|---|---|---|---|---|---|---|---|
| Cash | 3,169 | 166 | 191 | 224 | 234 | 168 | 178 | 3,040 | 4,390 | 3,957 |
| Current Assets | 11,055 | 9,186 | 8,554 | 7,060 | 10,369 | 7,185 | 7,705 | 7,493 | 8,606 | 8,805 |
| Total Assets | 27,853 | 22,832 | 18,077 | 16,001 | 20,041 | 19,435 | 22,326 | 17,173 | 15,081 | 16,078 |
| Current Liabilities | 7,505 | 6,455 | 5,515 | 4,701 | 6,795 | 6,451 | 6,218 | 3,991 | 3,474 | 3,919 |
| Long Term Debt | 3,794 | 4,664 | 3,591 | 3,944 | 6,097 | 6,029 | 6,216 | 3,573 | 3,183 | 3,285 |
| Common Equity | 14,876 | 10,420 | 7,592 | 6,117 | 5,881 | 5,606 | 8,378 | 8,295 | 7,721 | 8,119 |
| Total Capital | 18,732 | 15,084 | 11,688 | 10,477 | 12,376 | 12,188 | 15,231 | 12,474 | 10,904 | 11,404 |
| Capital Expenditures | 3,191 | 2,457 | 1,593 | 1,216 | 1,025 | 1,366 | 2,053 | 1,323 | 792 | 1,887 |
| Cash Flow | 6,703 | 5,271 | 3,550 | 2,322 | 2,044 | -872 | 2,418 | 2,003 | 1,350 | 2,151 |
| Current Ratio | 1.5 | 1.4 | 1.6 | 1.5 | 1.5 | 1.1 | 1.2 | 1.9 | 2.5 | 2.2 |
| % Long Term Debt of Capitalization | 20.3 | 30.9 | 30.7 | 37.6 | 49.3 | 49.5 | 40.8 | 28.6 | 29.2 | 28.8 |
| % Return on Assets | 20.4 | 18.1 | 12.9 | 5.6 | 2.4 | NM | 2.6 | 4.5 | 2.1 | 7.2 |
| % Return on Equity | 40.9 | 41.2 | 32.1 | 16.9 | 8.2 | NM | 6.3 | 9.1 | 4.2 | 13.7 |

Data as orig reptd.; bef. results of disc opers/spec. items. Per share data adj. for stk. divs.; EPS diluted. E-Estimated. NA-Not Available. NM-Not Meaningful. NR-Not Ranked. UR-Under Review.

**Office:** 5599 San Felipe St 17th Fl, Houston, TX 77056-2724.
**Telephone:** 713-513-2000.
**Email:** irsupport@slb.com
**Website:** http://www.slb.com

**Chrmn & CEO:** A. Gould
**EVP & CFO:** S. Ayat
**CTO:** A. Belani
**Chief Acctg Officer:** H. Guild

**Treas:** H.S. Oyinlola
**Investor Contact:** M. Theobald (713-375-3535)
**Board Members:** P. Camus, J. Gorelick, A. Gould, A. E. Isaac, N. Kudryavtsev, A. Lajous, M. E. Marks, L. R. Reif, R. C. Ross, T. Sandvold, N. Seydoux, L. G. Stuntz

**Founded:** 1956
**Domicile:** Netherlands Antilles
**Employees:** 80,000

# Schwab (Charles) Corp

**STANDARD &POOR'S**

| S&P Recommendation | BUY ★★★★☆ | Price<br>$16.61 (as of Nov 14, 2008) | 12-Mo. Target Price<br>$25.00 | Investment Style<br>Large-Cap Blend |
|---|---|---|---|---|

**GICS Sector** Financials
**Sub-Industry** Investment Banking & Brokerage

**Summary** This company's Charles Schwab & Co. subsidiary is among the largest brokerage companies in the U.S., primarily serving retail clients.

## Key Stock Statistics (Source S&P, Vickers, company reports)

| | | | | | | | |
|---|---|---|---|---|---|---|---|
| 52-Wk Range | $28.75– 14.83 | S&P Oper. EPS 2008**E** | 1.06 | Market Capitalization(B) | $19.188 | Beta | 1.39 |
| Trailing 12-Month EPS | $1.05 | S&P Oper. EPS 2009**E** | 1.20 | Yield (%) | 1.44 | S&P 3-Yr. Proj. EPS CAGR(%) | 12 |
| Trailing 12-Month P/E | 15.8 | P/E on S&P Oper. EPS 2008**E** | 15.7 | Dividend Rate/Share | $0.24 | S&P Credit Rating | A |
| $10K Invested 5 Yrs Ago | $14,859 | Common Shares Outstg. (M) | 1,155.2 | Institutional Ownership (%) | 67 | | |

## Price Performance

30-Week Mov. Avg. · · · · 10-Week Mov. Avg. ----- **GAAP Earnings vs. Previous Year** Volume Above Avg. STARS
12-Mo. Target Price —— Relative Strength —— ▲ Up ▼ Down ► No Change Below Avg. ★

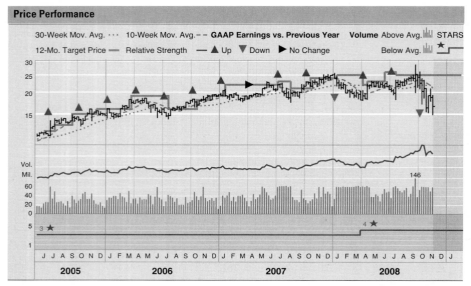

Options: ASE, CBOE, P, Ph

Analysis prepared by **Rikin Pandya** on October 28, 2008, when the stock traded at **$ 17.70**.

## Highlights

➤ We expect revenues to decline 4% to 6% in 2009, primarily reflecting lower fee-based client assets due to declining market values of equities, and lower volatility than in 2008, resulting in a 6% decline in daily average revenue trades (DARTs). At September 30, 2008, client assets totaled approximately $1.3 trillion, down 7% sequentially. Nevertheless, we view SCHW as an excellent asset gatherer, which we think will help the company stay afloat during this economic downturn and allow it to emerge even stronger once markets stabilize by virtue of the fact that most of its revenues are derived from fee income, which tends to provide a more stable revenue stream than commission-based revenues.

➤ We expect revenue compression to be partially offset by declines in expenses, led by our forecast of an 8% reduction in compensation costs in 2009. Overall, we expect operating costs to be cut by 4% in 2009.

➤ We expect SCHW to earn $1.06 in 2008 and $1.20 in 2009, aided by higher fees as a percentage of total client assets, well contained expense growth, and the impact of share buybacks.

## Investment Rationale/Risk

➤ We think the premium multiple afforded to the shares compared to peers is appropriate given the company's brand recognition, affluent client base, and high proportion of recurring asset-based fees. We see SCHW's success servicing the independent investment adviser channel as a positive, but we think the banking segment, although growing, merits a lower valuation. We view positively SCHW's ongoing push to diversify its revenue base while maintaining its core customer focus. While we have some concerns about slowing retail trading activity and lower client assets, particularly due to declining equity market values, we believe that SCHW's revenue streams are better diversified than other discount brokers.

➤ Risks to our recommendation and target price include reduced trading volumes, equity market declines, and a potentially more onerous regulatory environment.

➤ Our 12-month target price of $25 is 20.8X our 2009 EPS estimate, a premium to discount brokerage peers, warranted, we think, by SCHW's leading market position, strong client asset base and less volatile mix of business versus some peers.

## Qualitative Risk Assessment

| LOW | MEDIUM | HIGH |
|---|---|---|

Our risk assessment reflects our view of the company's strong competitive position, brand recognition and affluent client base, offset by industry cyclicality and our concerns about corporate governance.

## Quantitative Evaluations

**S&P Quality Ranking** B+

| D | C | B- | B | B+ | A- | A | A+ |
|---|---|---|---|---|---|---|---|

**Relative Strength Rank** MODERATE

56

LOWEST = 1    HIGHEST = 99

## Revenue/Earnings Data

**Revenue (Million $)**

| | 1Q | 2Q | 3Q | 4Q | Year |
|---|---|---|---|---|---|
| 2008 | 1,307 | 51.00 | 1,251 | -- | -- |
| 2007 | 1,153 | 1,205 | 1,291 | 1,345 | 623.0 |
| 2006 | 1,054 | 1,093 | 1,066 | 1,096 | 4,309 |
| 2005 | 1,059 | 1,087 | 1,138 | 1,180 | 4,464 |
| 2004 | 1,108 | 1,034 | 1,000 | 1,060 | 4,202 |
| 2003 | 900.0 | 1,018 | 1,051 | 1,118 | 4,087 |

**Earnings Per Share ($)**

| | 1Q | 2Q | 3Q | 4Q | Year |
|---|---|---|---|---|---|
| 2008 | 0.26 | 0.27 | 0.26 | E0.28 | E1.06 |
| 2007 | 0.19 | 0.23 | 0.27 | 0.26 | 0.92 |
| 2006 | 0.19 | 0.19 | 0.21 | 0.37 | 0.69 |
| 2005 | 0.11 | 0.14 | 0.16 | 0.14 | 0.56 |
| 2004 | 0.12 | 0.08 | -0.03 | 0.04 | 0.30 |
| 2003 | 0.05 | 0.09 | 0.09 | 0.11 | 0.35 |

Fiscal year ended Dec. 31. Next earnings report expected: NA. EPS Estimates based on S&P Operating Earnings; historical GAAP earnings are as reported.

## Dividend Data (Dates: mm/dd Payment Date: mm/dd/yy)

| Amount<br>($) | Date<br>Decl. | Ex-Div.<br>Date | Stk. of<br>Record | Payment<br>Date |
|---|---|---|---|---|
| 0.050 | 01/24 | 02/06 | 02/08 | 02/22/08 |
| 0.050 | 04/24 | 05/07 | 05/09 | 05/23/08 |
| 0.060 | 07/22 | 08/06 | 08/08 | 08/22/08 |
| 0.060 | 10/23 | 11/12 | 11/14 | 11/28/08 |

Dividends have been paid since 1989. Source: Company reports.

# Schwab (Charles) Corp

**STANDARD &POOR'S**

## Business Summary October 28, 2008

CORPORATE OVERVIEW. Charles Schwab Corp. (SCHW) is a financial holding company that provides securities brokerage and related financial services through three segments, Schwab Investor Services, Schwab Institutional and Schwab Corporate and Retirement Services. Another subsidiary, Charles Schwab Investment Management, is the investment adviser for Schwab's proprietary mutual funds. In December 2007, CyberTrader, Inc., formerly a subsidiary of SCHW, which provides electronic trading and brokerage services to highly active, online traders, was merged into Schwab.

Through the Schwab Investor Services segment (67% of 2007 net revenue), the company provides retail brokerage and banking services. Through various types of brokerage accounts, Schwab offers the purchase and sale of securities, including NASDAQ, exchange-listed and other equity securities, options, mutual funds, unit investment trusts, variable annuities and fixed-income investments. At the end of 2007, the company, through subsidiaries, served 8.5 million active client accounts, and held client assets of $1.4 trillion.

Through its Schwab Institutional segment (22%), SCHW provides custodial,

trade execution and support services to investment advisers, serves company 401(k) plan sponsors and third-party administrators, and supports company stock option plans. The company's Institutional segment had some $583.5 billion in assets under management as of December 31, 2007. The Schwab Advisor Network (launched in 2002) refers affluent investors to local investment advisers.

Through the Schwab Corporate & Retirement Services segment (10%), SCHW provides retirement plan services, plan administrator services, stock plan services, mutual fund clearing services, and supports the availability of Schwab proprietary mutual funds on third-party platforms. This division services all aspects of employer sponsored plans: equity compensation, defined contribution plans, defined benefit plans, and other investment related benefit plans. At year-end 2007, assets under management totalled more than $236.7 billion.

## Company Financials Fiscal Year Ended Dec. 31

| Per Share Data ($) | 2007 | 2006 | 2005 | 2004 | 2003 | 2002 | 2001 | 2000 | 1999 | 1998 |
|---|---|---|---|---|---|---|---|---|---|---|
| Tangible Book Value | 2.76 | 3.63 | 2.71 | 2.57 | 2.56 | 0.55 | 2.58 | 2.69 | 1.81 | 1.15 |
| Cash Flow | 1.04 | 0.81 | 0.72 | 0.47 | 0.35 | 0.30 | 0.30 | 0.70 | 0.59 | 0.39 |
| Earnings | 0.92 | 0.69 | 0.56 | 0.30 | 0.35 | 0.07 | 0.06 | 0.51 | 0.47 | 0.28 |
| S&P Core Earnings | 0.92 | 0.68 | 0.53 | 0.23 | 0.27 | -0.02 | -0.09 | NA | NA | NA |
| Dividends | 0.20 | 0.14 | 0.09 | 0.07 | 0.05 | 0.04 | 0.04 | 0.04 | 0.04 | 0.04 |
| Payout Ratio | 22% | 14% | 16% | 25% | 14% | 63% | 73% | 8% | 8% | 13% |
| Prices:High | 25.72 | 19.49 | 16.14 | 13.92 | 14.20 | 19.00 | 33.00 | 44.75 | 51.67 | 22.83 |
| Prices:Low | 17.41 | 14.00 | 9.65 | 8.25 | 6.25 | 7.22 | 8.13 | 22.46 | 16.96 | 6.17 |
| P/E Ratio:High | 28 | 21 | 29 | 46 | 41 | NM | NM | 88 | NM | 81 |
| P/E Ratio:Low | 19 | 15 | 17 | 28 | 18 | NM | NM | 44 | NM | 22 |

| Income Statement Analysis (Million $) | | | | | | | | | | |
|---|---|---|---|---|---|---|---|---|---|---|
| Commissions | 860 | 785 | 779 | 936 | 1,207 | 1,206 | 1,355 | 2,294 | 1,863 | 1,309 |
| Interest Income | 2,270 | 2,113 | 1,944 | 1,213 | 970 | 1,186 | 1,857 | 2,589 | 1,471 | 1,127 |
| Total Revenue | 5,617 | 4,988 | 5,151 | 4,479 | 4,328 | 4,480 | 5,281 | 7,139 | 4,713 | 3,388 |
| Interest Expense | 623 | 679 | 687 | 277 | 241 | 345 | 928 | 1,352 | 768 | 652 |
| Pretax Income | 1,853 | 1,476 | 1,185 | 645 | 710 | 168 | 135 | 1,231 | 971 | 577 |
| Effective Tax Rate | 39.6% | 39.6% | 38.4% | 35.8% | 33.5% | 42.3% | 42.2% | 41.7% | 39.4% | 39.6% |
| Net Income | 1,120 | 891 | 730 | 414 | 472 | 97.0 | 78.0 | 718 | 589 | 348 |
| S&P Core Earnings | 1,117 | 875 | 678 | 314 | 357 | -31.5 | -131 | NA | NA | NA |

| Balance Sheet & Other Financial Data (Million $) | | | | | | | | | | |
|---|---|---|---|---|---|---|---|---|---|---|
| Total Assets | 42,286 | 48,992 | 47,351 | 47,133 | 45,866 | 39,705 | 40,464 | 38,154 | 29,299 | 22,264 |
| Cash Items | 15,567 | 15,369 | 17,589 | 21,797 | 24,175 | 24,119 | 22,148 | 14,300 | 10,547 | 11,399 |
| Receivables | 16,482 | 11,577 | 11,600 | 10,323 | 9,137 | 7,067 | 10,066 | 16,680 | 17,543 | 9,980 |
| Securities Owned | 8,201 | 6,386 | 6,857 | 5,335 | 4,023 | 1,716 | 1,700 | 1,603 | 340 | 242 |
| Securities Borrowed | Nil | Nil | Nil | Nil | Nil | Nil | Nil | Nil | Nil | Nil |
| Due Brokers & Customers | 22,212 | 22,119 | 25,994 | 28,622 | 29,845 | 27,877 | 27,822 | 26,785 | 25,171 | 19,867 |
| Other Liabilities | 15,441 | 21,477 | NA | NA | NA | NA | NA | NA | NA | NA |
| Capitalization:Debt | 899 | 388 | 514 | 585 | 772 | 642 | 730 | 770 | 455 | 351 |
| Capitalization:Equity | 3,732 | 5,008 | 4,450 | 4,386 | 4,461 | 4,011 | 4,163 | 4,230 | 2,274 | 1,429 |
| Capitalization:Total | 4,631 | 5,396 | 4,964 | 4,971 | 5,233 | 4,653 | 4,893 | 5,000 | 2,729 | 1,780 |
| % Return on Revenue | 19.9 | 17.9 | 14.2 | 9.2 | 15.1 | 3.0 | 2.0 | 14.8 | 20.7 | 10.3 |
| % Return on Assets | 2.5 | 1.8 | 1.5 | 0.9 | 1.1 | 0.2 | 0.2 | 2.0 | 2.3 | 1.8 |
| % Return on Equity | 25.6 | 18.8 | 16.5 | 9.4 | 11.1 | 2.4 | 1.9 | 21.1 | 31.8 | 27.5 |

Data as orig reptd.; bef. results of disc opers/spec. items. Per share data adj. for stk. divs.; EPS diluted. Quarterly revs. excl. interest expense. E-Estimated. NA-Not Available. NM-Not Meaningful. NR-Not Ranked. UR-Under Review.

**Office:** 120 Kearny St, San Francisco, CA 94108-4899.
**Telephone:** 415-636-7000.
**Email:** investor.relations@schwab.com
**Website:** http://www.aboutschwab.com

**Chrmn:** C.R. Schwab, Jr.
**Pres & CEO:** W.W. Bettinger, II
**EVP, CFO & Chief Acctg Officer:** J.R. Martinetto
**EVP, Secy & General Counsel:** C.E. Dwyer

**EVP & CIO:** J. Hier-King
**Investor Contact:** R.G. Fowler (415-636-9869)
**Board Members:** W. F. Aldinger, III, N. H. Bechtle, W. W. Bettinger, II, C. P. Butcher, D. G. Fisher, F. C. Herringer, S. T. McLin, C. R. Schwab, Jr., P. A. Sneed, R. O. Walther, R. N. Wilson

**Founded:** 1971
**Domicile:** Delaware
**Employees:** 13,300

# Scripps Networks Interactive Inc

**STANDARD &POOR'S**

| S&P Recommendation | BUY ★ ★ ★ ★ ☆ | Price | 12-Mo. Target Price | Investment Style |
|---|---|---|---|---|
| | | $26.00 (as of Nov 14, 2008) | $33.00 | Large-Cap Value |

**GICS Sector** Consumer Discretionary
**Sub-Industry** Cable & Satellite

**Summary** SNI owns and operates lifestyle properties including HGTV, Food Network, Fine Living, DIY Network and GAC, in addition to online consumer search businesses.

## Key Stock Statistics (Source S&P, Vickers, company reports)

| | | | | | | | |
|---|---|---|---|---|---|---|---|
| 52-Wk Range | $44.98– 20.90 | S&P Oper. EPS 2008E | 1.82 | Market Capitalization(B) | $3.292 | Beta | NA |
| Trailing 12-Month EPS | $-0.74 | S&P Oper. EPS 2009E | 1.95 | Yield (%) | 1.15 | S&P 3-Yr. Proj. EPS CAGR(%) | NM |
| Trailing 12-Month P/E | NM | P/E on S&P Oper. EPS 2008E | 14.3 | Dividend Rate/Share | $0.30 | S&P Credit Rating | NA |
| $10K Invested 5 Yrs Ago | NA | Common Shares Outstg. (M) | 163.5 | Institutional Ownership (%) | 16 | | |

## Price Performance

30-Week Mov. Avg. · · ·   10-Week Mov. Avg. - -   **GAAP Earnings vs. Previous Year**   Volume Above Avg. ▏▍▏ STARS

12-Mo. Target Price —   Relative Strength —   ▲ Up   ▼ Down   ► No Change   Below Avg. ▏▍▏ ★

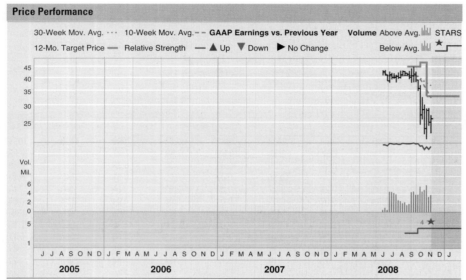

Options: Ph

## Qualitative Risk Assessment

| LOW | MEDIUM | HIGH |
|---|---|---|

Our risk assessment reflects SNI's leading TV properties and our view of the company's solid ratings and advertising revenue growth. This is offset by a soft advertising market and higher volatility in the interactive segment.

## Quantitative Evaluations

**S&P Quality Ranking**   NR

| D | C | B- | B | B+ | A- | A | A+ |
|---|---|---|---|---|---|---|---|

**Relative Strength Rank**   MODERATE

**55**

LOWEST = 1                                        HIGHEST = 99

## Revenue/Earnings Data

**Revenue (Million $)**

| | 1Q | 2Q | 3Q | 4Q | Year |
|---|---|---|---|---|---|
| 2008 | 388.3 | 416.1 | 374.7 | -- | -- |
| 2007 | -- | -- | -- | -- | 1,441 |
| 2006 | -- | -- | -- | -- | -- |
| 2005 | -- | -- | -- | -- | -- |
| 2004 | -- | -- | -- | -- | -- |
| 2003 | -- | -- | -- | -- | -- |

**Earnings Per Share ($)**

| | 1Q | 2Q | 3Q | 4Q | Year |
|---|---|---|---|---|---|
| 2008 | 0.40 | 0.33 | 0.35 | E0.52 | E1.82 |
| 2007 | -- | -- | -- | -- | -0.72 |
| 2006 | -- | -- | -- | -- | -- |
| 2005 | -- | -- | -- | -- | -- |
| 2004 | -- | -- | -- | -- | -- |
| 2003 | -- | -- | -- | -- | -- |

Fiscal year ended Dec. 31. Next earnings report expected: NA. EPS Estimates based on S&P Operating Earnings; historical GAAP earnings are as reported.

## Highlights

➤ The 12-month target price for SNI has recently been changed to $33.00 from $47.00. The Highlights section of this Stock Report will be updated accordingly.

## Investment Rationale/Risk

➤ The Investment Rationale/Risk section of this Stock Report will be updated shortly. For the latest News story on SNI from MarketScope, see below.

➤ 10/29/08 INTERACTIVE (SNI 25.97****): Q3 EPS of $0.35 for SNI is flat with '07 and below our $0.38 estimate, but includes $0.06 in spin-off charges. We have a favorable view of these results, as SNI generated an 8.9% revenue rise amid rather unfavorable ad conditions. A 14.7% interactive segment growth is better than we expected, and is encouraging, given recent uncertainties. That said, SNI is not immune to industry difficulties, and its Q4 guidance is slightly lower than our view. We lowering our '08 EPS estimate to $1.82 from $1.90, and our target price to $33 from $47 on updated relative analyses. /E.Kolb

## Dividend Data (Dates: mm/dd Payment Date: mm/dd/yy)

| Amount ($) | Date Decl. | Ex-Div. Date | Stk. of Record | Payment Date |
|---|---|---|---|---|
| 0.075 | 07/29 | 08/27 | 08/31 | 09/10/08 |
| 0.075 | 11/07 | 11/25 | 11/28 | 12/10/08 |

Dividends have been paid since 2008. Source: Company reports.

# Scripps Networks Interactive Inc

**STANDARD & POOR'S**

## Business Summary October 03, 2008

CORPORATE OVERVIEW. Scripps Networks Interactive is a lifestyle content and Internet search company with national television networks and interactive brands. SNI manages its operations through the Lifestyle Media (formerly Scripps Networks) and Interactive Services (formerly Interactive Media) segments. Lifestyle Media includes HGTV, Food Network, DIY, Fine Living, Great American Country, a minority interest in Fox-BRV South Sports Holdings, and Internet-based businesses, including RecipeZaar.com, HGTVPro.com, and FrontDoor.com. Interactive Media includes online comparison shopping and consumer information services, including Shopzilla, BizRate, uSwitch and Up-MyStreet.

The Lifestyle Media segment derives revenues principally from advertising sales, affiliate fees, and ancillary sales, including the sale and licensing of consumer products. Revenues from the Interactive Media segment are gener-

ated primarily from referral fees and commissions paid by merchants and service providers for online leads generated by its websites. Lifestyle Media and Interactive Services accounted for 83% and 17% of 2007 revenue, respectively, compared to 80% and 20% in 2006, and 90% and 10% in 2005.

In 2007, HGTV accounted for 12.6% of operating revenue, Food Network for 11.5%, DIY for 13.2%, Fine Living for 24.0%, and GAC for 25.1%. In 2007, the HGTV network reached 5.0% of homes, according to Nielsen; Food Network 5.2%; DIY 11.1%; Fine Living 17.7%; and GAC 14.9%.

## Company Financials Fiscal Year Ended Dec. 31

| Per Share Data ($) | 2007 | 2006 | 2005 | 2004 | 2003 | 2002 | 2001 | 2000 | 1999 | 1998 |
|---|---|---|---|---|---|---|---|---|---|---|
| Tangible Book Value | 2.25 | NA | NA | NA | NA | NA | NA | NA | NA | NA |
| Cash Flow | -0.19 | NA | NA | NA | NA | NA | NA | NA | NA | NA |
| Earnings | -0.72 | NA | NA | NA | NA | NA | NA | NA | NA | NA |
| S&P Core Earnings | 1.11 | 1.44 | NA | NA | NA | NA | NA | NA | NA | NA |
| Dividends | NA | NA | NA | NA | NA | NA | NA | NA | NA | NA |
| Payout Ratio | NA | NA | NA | NA | NA | NA | NA | NA | NA | NA |
| Prices:High | NA | NA | NA | NA | NA | NA | NA | NA | NA | NA |
| Prices:Low | NA | NA | NA | NA | NA | NA | NA | NA | NA | NA |
| P/E Ratio:High | NA | NA | NA | NA | NA | NA | NA | NA | NA | NA |
| P/E Ratio:Low | NA | NA | NA | NA | NA | NA | NA | NA | NA | NA |

| Income Statement Analysis (Million $) | 2007 | 2006 | 2005 | 2004 | 2003 | 2002 | 2001 | 2000 | 1999 | 1998 |
|---|---|---|---|---|---|---|---|---|---|---|
| Revenue | 1,441 | 1,323 | 1,002 | NA | NA | NA | NA | NA | NA | NA |
| Operating Income | 591 | NA | NA | NA | NA | NA | NA | NA | NA | NA |
| Depreciation | 86.7 | 101 | 67.0 | NA | NA | NA | NA | NA | NA | NA |
| Interest Expense | 15.2 | 54.0 | 37.0 | NA | NA | NA | NA | NA | NA | NA |
| Pretax Income | 98.7 | 427 | 343 | NA | NA | NA | NA | NA | NA | NA |
| Effective Tax Rate | NM | 28.3% | 32.8% | NA | NA | NA | NA | NA | NA | NA |
| Net Income | -118 | 234 | 176 | NA | NA | NA | NA | NA | NA | NA |
| S&P Core Earnings | 183 | 235 | NA | NA | NA | NA | NA | NA | NA | NA |

| Balance Sheet & Other Financial Data (Million $) | 2007 | 2006 | 2005 | 2004 | 2003 | 2002 | 2001 | 2000 | 1999 | 1998 |
|---|---|---|---|---|---|---|---|---|---|---|
| Cash | 44.2 | 19.0 | NA | NA | NA | NA | NA | NA | NA | NA |
| Current Assets | 658 | NA | NA | NA | NA | NA | NA | NA | NA | NA |
| Total Assets | 2,064 | 2,385 | NA | NA | NA | NA | NA | NA | NA | NA |
| Current Liabilities | 124 | NA | NA | NA | NA | NA | NA | NA | NA | NA |
| Long Term Debt | 450 | NA | NA | NA | NA | NA | NA | NA | NA | NA |
| Common Equity | 1,157 | 1,186 | NA | NA | NA | NA | NA | NA | NA | NA |
| Total Capital | 1,391 | NA | NA | NA | NA | NA | NA | NA | NA | NA |
| Capital Expenditures | NA | 40.4 | 29.0 | NA | NA | NA | NA | NA | NA | NA |
| Cash Flow | -31.0 | NA | NA | NA | NA | NA | NA | NA | NA | NA |
| Current Ratio | 5.3 | 3.5 | NA | NA | NA | NA | NA | NA | NA | NA |
| % Long Term Debt of Capitalization | 32.3 | 39.2 | Nil | NA | NA | NA | NA | NA | NA | NA |
| % Net Income of Revenue | NM | 17.7 | 17.5 | NA | NA | NA | NA | NA | NA | NA |
| % Return on Assets | NM | NA | NA | NA | NA | NA | NA | NA | NA | NA |
| % Return on Equity | NM | NA | NA | NA | NA | NA | NA | NA | NA | NA |

Data as orig reptd.; bef. results of disc opers/spec. items. Per share data adj. for stk. divs.; EPS diluted. Data for 2007 pro forma; bal. sheet & book val. as of March 31, 2008. E-Estimated. NA-Not Available. NM-Not Meaningful. NR-Not Ranked. UR-Under Review.

**Office:** 312 Walnut Street, Cincinnati, OH 45202.
**Telephone:** 513-977-3000.
**Website:**
http://www.scrippsnetworksinteractive.com
**Chrmn, Pres & CEO:** K.W. Lowe

**COO:** R. Boehne
**EVP & CFO:** J. Clayton
**EVP, Secy & General Counsel:** A.B. Cruz, III
**SVP & CTO:** M.S. Hale

**Board Members:** J. H. Burlingame, D. A. Galloway, K. W. Lowe, J. Mohn, N. B. Paumgarten, M. M. Peirce, D. Pond, J. Sagansky, N. E. Scagliotti, R. W. Tysoe
**Founded:** 2007
**Domicile:** Ohio

**STANDARD &POOR'S**

# Sealed Air Corp

| S&P Recommendation HOLD ★★★☆☆ | Price $15.99 (as of Nov 14, 2008) | 12-Mo. Target Price $19.00 | Investment Style Large-Cap Growth |
|---|---|---|---|

**GICS Sector** Materials
**Sub-Industry** Paper Packaging

**Summary** This company is a leading global manufacturer of a wide range of food and protective packaging materials and systems.

## Key Stock Statistics (Source S&P, Vickers, company reports)

| | | | | | | | |
|---|---|---|---|---|---|---|---|
| 52-Wk Range | $28.32– 14.71 | S&P Oper. EPS 2008**E** | 1.35 | Market Capitalization(B) | $2.528 | Beta | 1.10 |
| Trailing 12-Month EPS | $1.16 | S&P Oper. EPS 2009**E** | 1.55 | Yield (%) | 3.00 | S&P 3-Yr. Proj. EPS CAGR(%) | 10 |
| Trailing 12-Month P/E | 13.8 | P/E on S&P Oper. EPS 2008**E** | 11.8 | Dividend Rate/Share | $0.48 | S&P Credit Rating | BBB- |
| $10K Invested 5 Yrs Ago | $6,347 | Common Shares Outstg. (M) | 158.1 | Institutional Ownership (%) | 92 | | |

## Price Performance

30-Week Mov. Avg. ···· 10-Week Mov. Avg. --- **GAAP Earnings vs. Previous Year** Volume Above Avg. STARS
12-Mo. Target Price — Relative Strength — ▲ Up ▼ Down ► No Change Below Avg. ★

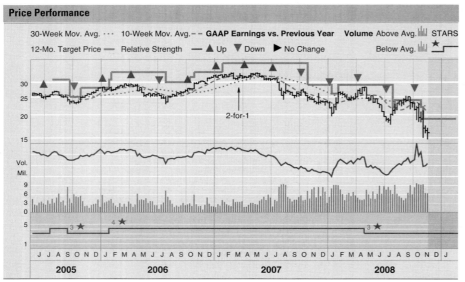

Options: CBOE, P, Ph

Analysis prepared by **Stewart Scharf** on October 30, 2008, when the stock traded at **$ 16.15**.

## Qualitative Risk Assessment

| LOW | MEDIUM | HIGH |
|---|---|---|

Our risk assessment reflects asbestos litigation, volatile energy prices, and food-related health issues that could lead to restrictions on imports and exports, and some corporate governance concerns. This is offset by our view of the company's sound balance sheet and cash flow generation.

## Quantitative Evaluations

**S&P Quality Ranking** B

| D | C | B- | B | B+ | A- | A | A+ |
|---|---|---|---|---|---|---|---|

**Relative Strength Rank** MODERATE

54

LOWEST = 1          HIGHEST = 99

## Revenue/Earnings Data

**Revenue (Million $)**

| | 1Q | 2Q | 3Q | 4Q | Year |
|---|---|---|---|---|---|
| 2008 | 1,177 | 1,279 | 1,219 | -- | -- |
| 2007 | 1,095 | 1,145 | 1,161 | 1,250 | 4,651 |
| 2006 | 1,019 | 1,082 | 1,081 | 1,146 | 4,328 |
| 2005 | 969.8 | 1,020 | 1,020 | 1,076 | 4,085 |
| 2004 | 913.1 | 923.7 | 944.2 | 1,017 | 3,798 |
| 2003 | 822.9 | 865.6 | 908.7 | 934.8 | 3,532 |

**Earnings Per Share ($)**

| | | | | | |
|---|---|---|---|---|---|
| 2008 | 0.33 | 0.34 | 0.05 | E0.34 | E1.35 |
| 2007 | 0.67 | 0.40 | 0.39 | 0.43 | 1.89 |
| 2006 | 0.30 | 0.31 | 0.41 | 0.45 | 1.47 |
| 2005 | 0.29 | 0.33 | 0.34 | 0.39 | 1.35 |
| 2004 | 0.31 | 0.32 | 0.35 | 0.17 | 1.13 |
| 2003 | 0.26 | 0.28 | 0.21 | 0.25 | 1.00 |

Fiscal year ended Dec. 31. Next earnings report expected: Late January. EPS Estimates based on S&P Operating Earnings; historical GAAP earnings are as reported.

## Highlights

➤ We project modest organic sales growth (before foreign exchange and acquisitions) through 2009, as weak unit volume, especially on the protective packaging side, in Europe and North America, offsets increased price/mix. We still see some favorable demand trends for new food packaging and solutions products in parts of Latin America and Asia/Pacific. However, in our view, total sales in 2009 will be limited by softening European markets and a strengthening U.S. dollar.

➤ We expect gross margins to narrow by more than 300 basis points in 2008, from 28% in 2007, before a gradual sequential rebound during 2009 on price hikes, a better product mix, improved supply chain efficiencies and stabilizing resin and energy costs. We expect EBITDA margins in 2008 to fall below 13%, from 16.2% in 2007, but $115 million in projected cost savings from lower resin costs, a better mix, a shift in production overseas and a 5% work force reduction should benefit margins in 2009.

➤ We estimate a tax rate of near 24% in 2008, and operating EPS of $1.35 (before about $0.38 of restructuring charges), advancing 15% in 2009 to $1.55.

## Investment Rationale/Risk

➤ Our hold opinion is based primarily on our view of challenging global market conditions. We expect cost savings from a global manufacturing strategy and a new consolidation plan, while SEE continues to develop technologies and innovative new products. Our valuation models also suggest the shares are fairly valued.

➤ Risks to our recommendation and target price include a severe and prolonged global economic downturn, another significant increase in resin costs, a stronger U.S. dollar, a new mad cow disease scare and a prolonged embargo on Brazilian beef. We have some concern regarding corporate governance issues, since at least one former CEO serves on the board of directors.

➤ Applying a P/E of less than 10X to our 2009 EPS estimate -- a discount to historical levels and slightly below the S&P Paper Packaging sub-industry group multiple -- we arrive at a value of $15. Our DCF model, which assumes a perpetual growth rate of 3.5% and a weighted average cost of capital of 9%, leads to an intrinsic value of $23. Our 12-month target price of $19 is a blend of these two metrics.

## Dividend Data (Dates: mm/dd Payment Date: mm/dd/yy)

| Amount ($) | Date Decl. | Ex-Div. Date | Stk. of Record | Payment Date |
|---|---|---|---|---|
| 0.120 | 02/19 | 03/05 | 03/07 | 03/21/08 |
| 0.120 | 04/10 | 06/04 | 06/06 | 06/20/08 |
| 0.120 | 07/23 | 09/03 | 09/05 | 09/19/08 |
| 0.120 | 10/23 | 12/03 | 12/05 | 12/19/08 |

Dividends have been paid since 2006. Source: Company reports.

---

**Please read the Required Disclosures and Analyst Certification on the last page of this report.**

*The McGraw-Hill Companies*

# Sealed Air Corp

**STANDARD**
**&POOR'S**

## Business Summary October 30, 2008

CORPORATE OVERVIEW. Sealed Air Corp., a leading protective and specialty packaging company, expects an increasing proportion of sales to come from outside the U.S. Foreign operations (excluding Canada, with about 3%) accounted for 52% of sales in 2007, with Europe accounting for 30% of total sales, Latin America 8.6%, and Asia Pacific 12.9%.

As of the second quarter of 2007, the company realigned its segment reporting to reflect its growth strategies in core markets and new business opportunities, as it focuses on long-term global trends, including higher living standards in emerging markets, conservation and energy efficiency, convenience and longevity. The food packaging segment (40% of net sales in 2007; $228 million of operating income) focuses on industrial products and new technologies that enable food processors to package and ship fresh and processed meats and cheeses through their supply chain. Food Solutions (20%; $86 million) targets advancements in food packaging technologies that provide consumers with fresh meals from food service outlets or expanding retail cases at grocery stores. Protective Packaging (32%; $209 million) includes core packaging technologies and solutions slated for traditional industrial applications while emphasizing consumer-oriented packaging solutions. Other sales accounted for 6.8% ($28 million).

Food packaging products primarily consist of flexible materials and related systems marketed mainly under the Cryovac trademark for a broad range of perishable food applications. The segment also manufactures polystyrene foam trays that are used by supermarkets and food processors to protect and display fresh meat, poultry and produce. The U.S. Department of Agriculture (USDA) projects increases in U.S. protein consumption. Case-ready packaging sales exceeded $450 million in 2007. The protective packaging products segment includes surface protection and other cushioning products such as air cellular packaging materials, and plastic sheets containing encapsulated air bubbles that protect products from damage during shipment, under the Bubble Wrap and Air Cap brand names. The new "Other" segment focuses on newer markets, including specialty materials for non-packaging applications such as insulation and products for value-added medical applications, as well as new ventures that include products sourced from renewable materials.

## Company Financials Fiscal Year Ended Dec. 31

| Per Share Data ($) | 2007 | 2006 | 2005 | 2004 | 2003 | 2002 | 2001 | 2000 | 1999 | 1998 |
|---|---|---|---|---|---|---|---|---|---|---|
| Tangible Book Value | NM | NM | NM | NM | NM | NM | NM | NM | NM | NM |
| Cash Flow | 2.62 | 2.30 | 2.64 | 1.99 | 1.95 | -1.17 | 1.92 | 2.16 | 1.70 | 1.22 |
| Earnings | 1.89 | 1.47 | 1.35 | 1.13 | 1.00 | -2.15 | 0.61 | 0.97 | 0.84 | 0.06 |
| S&P Core Earnings | 1.78 | 1.49 | 1.37 | 1.14 | 1.03 | 1.29 | 0.63 | NA | NA | NA |
| Dividends | 0.40 | 0.30 | Nil | Nil | Nil | Nil | Nil | Nil | Nil | Nil |
| Payout Ratio | 21% | 20% | Nil | Nil | Nil | Nil | Nil | Nil | Nil | Nil |
| Prices:High | 33.87 | 32.88 | 28.32 | 27.45 | 27.24 | 24.20 | 23.55 | 30.94 | 34.22 | 34.00 |
| Prices:Low | 22.41 | 22.81 | 22.78 | 22.03 | 17.50 | 6.35 | 14.40 | 13.19 | 22.25 | 13.69 |
| P/E Ratio:High | 18 | 22 | 21 | 24 | 27 | NM | 39 | 32 | 41 | NM |
| P/E Ratio:Low | 12 | 16 | 17 | 20 | 17 | NM | 24 | 14 | 26 | NM |

### Income Statement Analysis (Million $)

| | 2007 | 2006 | 2005 | 2004 | 2003 | 2002 | 2001 | 2000 | 1999 | 1998 |
|---|---|---|---|---|---|---|---|---|---|---|
| Revenue | 4,651 | 4,328 | 4,085 | 3,798 | 3,532 | 3,204 | 3,067 | 3,068 | 2,840 | 2,507 |
| Operating Income | 712 | 707 | 687 | 716 | 693 | 1,766 | 641 | 687 | 648 | 524 |
| Depreciation | 149 | 168 | 175 | 180 | 154 | 166 | 221 | 220 | 147 | 178 |
| Interest Expense | 150 | 148 | 150 | 154 | 134 | 65.3 | 76.4 | 64.5 | 58.1 | 53.6 |
| Pretax Income | 456 | 400 | 377 | 323 | 377 | -392 | 297 | 413 | 396 | 199 |
| Effective Tax Rate | 22.6% | 31.5% | 32.1% | 33.2% | 36.2% | NM | 47.3% | 45.5% | 46.6% | 63.3% |
| Net Income | 353 | 274 | 256 | 216 | 240 | -309 | 157 | 225 | 211 | 73.0 |
| S&P Core Earnings | 333 | 278 | 259 | 219 | 192 | 227 | 111 | NA | NA | NA |

### Balance Sheet & Other Financial Data (Million $)

| | 2007 | 2006 | 2005 | 2004 | 2003 | 2002 | 2001 | 2000 | 1999 | 1998 |
|---|---|---|---|---|---|---|---|---|---|---|
| Cash | 430 | 407 | 456 | 412 | 365 | 127 | 13.8 | 11.2 | 13.7 | 45.0 |
| Current Assets | 1,936 | 1,757 | 1,695 | 1,611 | 1,428 | 1,056 | 776 | 877 | 803 | 845 |
| Total Assets | 5,438 | 5,021 | 4,864 | 4,855 | 4,704 | 4,261 | 3,908 | 4,048 | 3,855 | 4,040 |
| Current Liabilities | 1,742 | 1,406 | 1,534 | 1,304 | 1,190 | 1,153 | 627 | 675 | 582 | 535 |
| Long Term Debt | 1,532 | 1,827 | 1,813 | 2,088 | 2,260 | 868 | 788 | 944 | 665 | 997 |
| Common Equity | 2,020 | 1,530 | 1,392 | 1,334 | 1,124 | 813 | 850 | 753 | 551 | 437 |
| Total Capital | 3,561 | 3,364 | 3,229 | 3,448 | 3,418 | 3,039 | 3,215 | 3,301 | 3,193 | 3,425 |
| Capital Expenditures | 211 | 168 | 96.9 | 103 | 124 | 91.6 | 146 | 114 | 75.1 | 82.4 |
| Cash Flow | 502 | 442 | 430 | 395 | 366 | -197 | 322 | 381 | 287 | 179 |
| Current Ratio | 1.1 | 1.2 | 1.1 | 1.2 | 1.2 | 0.9 | 1.2 | 1.3 | 1.4 | 1.6 |
| % Long Term Debt of Capitalization | 43.0 | 54.3 | 56.1 | 60.5 | 66.1 | 28.6 | 24.5 | 28.6 | 20.8 | 29.1 |
| % Net Income of Revenue | 7.6 | 6.3 | 6.3 | 5.7 | 6.8 | NM | 5.1 | 7.3 | 7.4 | 2.9 |
| % Return on Assets | 6.8 | 5.5 | 5.3 | 4.5 | 5.4 | NM | 3.9 | 5.7 | 5.3 | 1.9 |
| % Return on Equity | 19.2 | 19.9 | 18.8 | 17.5 | 21.9 | NM | 12.7 | 24.7 | 28.3 | 0.2 |

Data as orig reptd.; bef. results of disc opers/spec. items. Per share data adj. for stk. divs.; EPS diluted. E-Estimated. NA-Not Available. NM-Not Meaningful. NR-Not Ranked. UR-Under Review.

**Office:** 200 Riverfront Blvd, Elmwood Park, NJ 07407-1033.
**Telephone:** 201-791-7600.
**Website:** http://www.sealedair.com
**Pres & CEO:** W.V. Hickey

**SVP & CFO:** D.H. Kelsey
**Chief Acctg Officer & Cntlr:** J.S. Warren
**Treas:** T.S. Christie
**Secy & General Counsel:** H.K. White

**Investor Contact:** A. Butler (201-703-4210)
**Board Members:** H. Brown, M. Chu, L. R. Codey, D. T. Dunphy, C. F. Farrell, Jr., W. V. Hickey, J. Kosecoff, K. P. Manning, W. J. Marino

**Founded:** 1996
**Domicile:** Delaware
**Employees:** 17,700

# Sears Holdings Corp

STANDARD &POOR'S

| S&P Recommendation | SELL ★ ★ ☆ ☆ ☆ | Price | 12-Mo. Target Price | Investment Style |
|---|---|---|---|---|
| | | $38.27 (as of Nov 14, 2008) | $48.00 | Large-Cap Blend |

**GICS Sector** Consumer Discretionary
**Sub-Industry** Department Stores

**Summary** Through its wholly owned Sears and Kmart subsidiaries, Sears Holdings is the fourth largest broadline retailer in the U.S.

## Key Stock Statistics (Source S&P, Vickers, company reports)

| | | | | | | | |
|---|---|---|---|---|---|---|---|
| 52-Wk Range | $120.63– 38.09 | S&P Oper. EPS 2009**E** | 1.20 | Market Capitalization(B) | $4.838 | Beta | 0.53 |
| Trailing 12-Month EPS | $3.28 | S&P Oper. EPS 2010**E** | 0.75 | Yield (%) | Nil | S&P 3-Yr. Proj. EPS CAGR(%) | -46 |
| Trailing 12-Month P/E | 11.7 | P/E on S&P Oper. EPS 2009**E** | 31.9 | Dividend Rate/Share | Nil | S&P Credit Rating | BB |
| $10K Invested 5 Yrs Ago | $12,757 | Common Shares Outstg. (M) | 126.4 | Institutional Ownership (%) | NM | | |

## Price Performance

30-Week Mov. Avg. · · · ·   10-Week Mov. Avg. - - -   **GAAP Earnings vs. Previous Year**   Volume Above Avg. ▌▌▌ STARS
12-Mo. Target Price —   Relative Strength —   ▲ Up  ▼ Down  ▶ No Change   Below Avg. ▌▌▌ ★

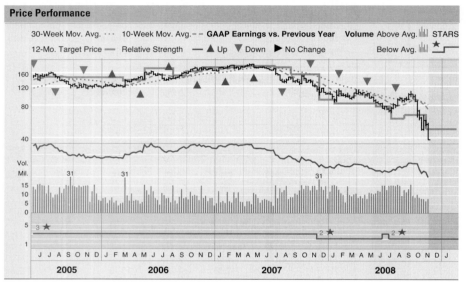

Options: ASE, CBOE, P, Ph

Analysis prepared by **Jason N. Asaeda** on November 04, 2008, when the stock traded at **$ 57.05**.

### Highlights

➤ We expect net sales of $47.64 billion in FY 09 (Jan.) and $45.85 billion in FY 10 on projected negative same-store sales at both the Sears and Kmart divisions, and closures of underperforming stores. We look for SHLD to maintain a measured pace of Kmart-to-Sears store conversions. We see continued sales weakness across most major merchandise categories at both Sears and Kmart, due to our view of limited success of remerchandising efforts over the past two years, and, in the case of tools and big ticket home appliances, a weaker U.S. housing market. We also think a projected slowdown in consumer spending further diminishes the company's chances of executing a turnaround.

➤ We look for SHLD, in response to weak sales, to take aggressive markdowns to improve inventory turns. While we anticipate tight cost controls, we do not think the company will be able to achieve expense leverage on consolidated same-store sales declines of 8% in FY 09 and 6% in FY 10 we foresee, leading to significant operating margin erosion.

➤ Factoring in likely share buybacks, we see operating EPS of $1.20 in FY 09 and $0.75 in FY 10.

### Investment Rationale/Risk

➤ While we believe Sears and Kmart remain viable businesses, we see a lack of prospects for a near-term material improvement in SHLD's sales and profits. We also anticipate market share losses for both chains over the next 12 months, as we perceive Wal-Mart Stores, Inc. (WMT: strong buy, $56) and Target Corp. (TGT: hold, $41) doing a better job in communicating a stronger value proposition to consumers than Kmart. In addition, we think Sears's merchandising lacks differentiation and newness relative to moderate-price department store peers such as J.C. Penney (JCP: hold, $23). Our corporate governance concerns include cash-only payments to directors and the non-disclosure of specific hurdle rates for performance-based equity awards.

➤ Risks to our recommendation and target price include better-than-expected sales due to an improvement in consumer confidence and more favorable customer response to SHLD's remerchandising and brand marketing efforts.

➤ Our 12-month target price of $48 is based on an EV/EBITDA multiple of 5.0X, the stock's five-year historical low, applied to our FY 10 EBITDA estimate of $1.45 billion.

## Qualitative Risk Assessment

| LOW | MEDIUM | HIGH |
|---|---|---|

Our risk assessment reflects what we consider Kmart's and Sears's long records of inconsistent sales and earnings. This is partially offset by our view of SHLD's opportunity to leverage the two units' best practices and brands to strengthen its competitive positioning.

## Quantitative Evaluations

**S&P Quality Ranking**    NR

| D | C | B- | B | B+ | A- | A | A+ |
|---|---|---|---|---|---|---|---|

**Relative Strength Rank**    WEAK

17

LOWEST = 1    HIGHEST = 99

## Revenue/Earnings Data

**Revenue (Million $)**

| | 1Q | 2Q | 3Q | 4Q | Year |
|---|---|---|---|---|---|
| 2009 | 11,068 | 11,762 | -- | -- | -- |
| 2008 | 11,702 | 12,239 | 11,548 | 1,507 | 50,703 |
| 2007 | 11,998 | 12,785 | 11,941 | 16,288 | 53,012 |
| 2006 | 7,626 | 13,192 | 12,202 | 16,086 | 49,124 |
| 2005 | 4,615 | 4,785 | 4,392 | 5,909 | 19,701 |
| 2004 | -- | 5,652 | 5,092 | 6,328 | 17,072 |

**Earnings Per Share ($)**

| | | | | | |
|---|---|---|---|---|---|
| 2009 | -0.42 | 0.50 | E-0.76 | E2.28 | E1.20 |
| 2008 | 1.40 | 0.51 | 0.01 | 3.21 | 5.70 |
| 2007 | 1.14 | 1.88 | 1.27 | 5.33 | 9.57 |
| 2006 | 0.65 | 0.98 | 0.35 | 4.03 | 6.17 |
| 2005 | 0.94 | 1.54 | 5.45 | 3.09 | 11.00 |
| 2004 | -- | -0.06 | -0.26 | 2.78 | 2.52 |

Fiscal year ended Jan. 31. Next earnings report expected: Late November. EPS Estimates based on S&P Operating Earnings; historical GAAP earnings are as reported.

## Dividend Data

No cash dividends have been paid.

---

**Please read the Required Disclosures and Analyst Certification on the last page of this report.**

The McGraw-Hill Companies

# Sears Holdings Corp

## Business Summary November 04, 2008

CORPORATE OVERVIEW. Through the March 2005 merger of Kmart Holding Corp. and Sears, Roebuck and Co., which continue to operate under their separate brand names, Sears Holdings has emerged as the fourth largest broadline retailer in the U.S. based on FY 08 (Jan.) reported revenues. As of May 3, 2008, the company operated 2,410 Sears-branded full line and specialty stores in the U.S. and Canada (operated by Sears Canada), and 1,388 Kmart-branded discount stores and supercenters across the U.S. SHLD completed the integration of the Sears and Kmart supply chain, IT, finance, legal, human resources, marketing, and merchandising functions during FY 06, and the combination of store operations in February 2006.

CORPORATE STRATEGY. SHLD believes it has an opportunity to leverage Kmart's off-mall locations to expand the distribution of Sears products and services at a more rapid pace and at a lower cost than Sears would have been able to accomplish on its own. The company also sees the potential for

Kmart to improve its value proposition and competitive positioning through the addition of Sears-owned brands and services (cross-selling).

In FY 06, SHLD introduced select Sears private label branded products, including Kenmore appliances and Craftsman tools, into about 100 Kmart stores. The company further completed a national roll-out of Sears credit card acceptance to all Kmart locations, and tested certain Sears customer services at select Kmart locations. In FY 07, SHLD completed a national roll-out of Craftsman tools to Kmart locations, and expanded the number of Kmart stores carrying home appliances to 180. SHLD continued to roll out Sears brand products into Kmart locations in FY 08.

## Company Financials Fiscal Year Ended Jan. 31

| Per Share Data ($) | 2008 | 2007 | 2006 | 2005 | 2004 | 2003 | 2002 | 2001 | 2000 | 1999 |
|---|---|---|---|---|---|---|---|---|---|---|
| Tangible Book Value | 42.64 | 49.25 | 41.80 | 50.21 | 24.36 | NA | NA | NA | NA | NA |
| Cash Flow | 12.95 | 16.90 | 12.24 | 11.59 | 2.81 | NA | NA | NA | NA | NA |
| Earnings | 5.70 | 9.58 | 6.17 | 11.00 | 2.52 | -5.47 | -5.24 | -0.48 | 1.22 | 1.01 |
| S&P Core Earnings | 4.44 | 9.24 | 4.53 | 4.51 | -4.53 | -6.80 | -5.74 | -0.55 | NA | NA |
| Dividends | Nil | Nil | Nil | Nil | Nil | Nil | NA | NA | NA | NA |
| Payout Ratio | Nil | Nil | Nil | Nil | Nil | Nil | NA | NA | NA | NA |
| Calendar Year | 2007 | 2006 | 2005 | 2004 | 2003 | 2002 | 2001 | 2000 | 1999 | 1998 |
| Prices:High | 195.18 | 182.38 | 163.50 | 119.69 | 34.55 | NA | NA | NA | NA | NA |
| Prices:Low | 98.25 | 114.90 | 84.51 | 22.41 | 12.00 | NA | NA | NA | NA | NA |
| P/E Ratio:High | 34 | 19 | 26 | 11 | 14 | NA | NA | NA | NA | NA |
| P/E Ratio:Low | 17 | 12 | 14 | 2 | 5 | NA | NA | NA | NA | NA |

| Income Statement Analysis (Million $) | | | | | | | | | | |
|---|---|---|---|---|---|---|---|---|---|---|
| Revenue | 50,703 | 53,012 | 49,124 | 19,701 | 17,072 | 30,762 | 36,151 | 37,028 | 35,925 | 33,674 |
| Operating Income | 2,542 | 3,611 | 2,901 | 944 | 442 | -1,303 | NA | NA | NA | NA |
| Depreciation | 1,049 | 1,142 | 932 | 69.0 | 31.0 | 737 | 824 | 777 | 770 | 671 |
| Interest Expense | 286 | 337 | 322 | 146 | 105 | 155 | NA | NA | NA | NA |
| Pretax Income | 1,452 | 2,464 | 1,965 | 1,775 | 400 | -3,286 | -2,702 | -378 | 970 | 748 |
| Effective Tax Rate | 37.9% | 37.7% | 36.4% | 37.7% | 38.0% | NM | 4.26% | 35.5% | 34.7% | 30.8% |
| Net Income | 826 | 1,490 | 948 | 1,106 | 248 | -3,262 | -2,587 | -244 | 633 | 518 |
| S&P Core Earnings | 645 | 1,439 | 696 | 448 | -405 | -3,439 | -2,840 | -260 | NA | NA |

| Balance Sheet & Other Financial Data (Million $) | | | | | | | | | | |
|---|---|---|---|---|---|---|---|---|---|---|
| Cash | 1,622 | 3,968 | 4,440 | 3,435 | 2,088 | 613 | 1,245 | 401 | 344 | 710 |
| Current Assets | 12,802 | 15,406 | 15,207 | 7,541 | 5,811 | 6,102 | NA | NA | NA | NA |
| Total Assets | 27,397 | 30,066 | 30,573 | 8,651 | 6,084 | 11,238 | 14,298 | 14,630 | 15,104 | 14,166 |
| Current Liabilities | 9,562 | 10,052 | 10,350 | 2,086 | 1,776 | 2,120 | NA | NA | NA | NA |
| Long Term Debt | 2,606 | 2,849 | 3,268 | 661 | 819 | 623 | NA | NA | NA | NA |
| Common Equity | 10,667 | 12,714 | 11,611 | 4,469 | 2,192 | -301 | 3,459 | 6,083 | 6,304 | 5,979 |
| Total Capital | 13,586 | 15,563 | 14,879 | 5,130 | 3,011 | 322 | NA | NA | NA | NA |
| Capital Expenditures | 570 | 513 | 546 | 230 | 108 | 252 | 1,456 | 1,087 | 1,277 | 981 |
| Cash Flow | 1,875 | 2,632 | 1,880 | 1,175 | 279 | -2,525 | NA | NA | NA | NA |
| Current Ratio | 1.3 | 1.5 | 1.5 | 3.6 | 3.3 | 2.9 | 12.6 | 2.0 | 2.0 | 2.1 |
| % Long Term Debt of Capitalization | 19.2 | 18.3 | 22.0 | 12.9 | 27.2 | NM | 56.9 | 32.6 | 30.1 | 29.4 |
| % Net Income of Revenue | 1.6 | 2.8 | 1.9 | 5.6 | 1.5 | NM | NM | NM | 1.8 | 1.5 |
| % Return on Assets | 2.9 | 4.9 | 4.8 | 15.0 | 3.9 | NM | NM | NM | 4.3 | 3.7 |
| % Return on Equity | 7.1 | 12.3 | 11.8 | 33.1 | 12.7 | NM | NM | NM | 10.3 | 9.1 |

Data as orig reptd.; bef. results of disc opers/spec. items. Per share data adj. for stk. divs.; EPS diluted. E-Estimated. NA-Not Available. NM-Not Meaningful. NR-Not Ranked. UR-Under Review.

**Office:** 3333 Beverly Rd, Hoffman Estates, IL 60179-0001.
**Telephone:** 847-286-2500.
**Website:** http://www.searsholdings.com
**Chrmn:** E.S. Lampert

**Pres & CEO:** W.B. Johnson
**EVP & CFO:** J.M. Reidy
**EVP & Chief Admin Officer:** W.C. Crowley
**EVP & CIO:** K.A. Austin

**Board Members:** W. C. Crowley, E. S. Lampert, S. T. Mnuchin, R. C. Perry, A. N. Reese, K. B. Rollins, E. Scott, T. J. Tisch

**Founded:** 1899
**Domicile:** Delaware
**Employees:** 337,000

# Sempra Energy

**STANDARD &POOR'S**

| S&P Recommendation | STRONG BUY ★★★★★ | Price | 12-Mo. Target Price | Investment Style |
|---|---|---|---|---|
| | | $42.09 (as of Nov 14, 2008) | $60.00 | Large-Cap Blend |

**GICS Sector** Utilities
**Sub-Industry** Multi-Utilities

**Summary** This gas and electric utility is also engaged in unregulated power, liquefied natural gas and international energy projects.

## Key Stock Statistics (Source S&P, Vickers, company reports)

| | | | | | | | |
|---|---|---|---|---|---|---|---|
| 52-Wk Range | $64.21– 34.29 | S&P Oper. EPS 2008**E** | 3.91 | Market Capitalization(B) | $10.370 | Beta | 0.79 |
| Trailing 12-Month EPS | $4.24 | S&P Oper. EPS 2009**E** | 4.53 | Yield (%) | 3.33 | S&P 3-Yr. Proj. EPS CAGR(%) | 8 |
| Trailing 12-Month P/E | 9.9 | P/E on S&P Oper. EPS 2008**E** | 10.8 | Dividend Rate/Share | $1.40 | S&P Credit Rating | BBB+ |
| $10K Invested 5 Yrs Ago | $17,428 | Common Shares Outstg. (M) | 246.4 | Institutional Ownership (%) | 71 | | |

## Price Performance

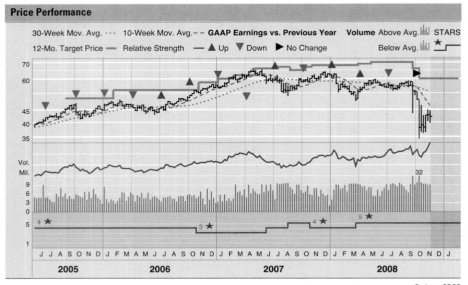

30-Week Mov. Avg. · · · 10-Week Mov. Avg. — **GAAP Earnings vs. Previous Year** Volume Above Avg. STARS
12-Mo. Target Price — Relative Strength — ▲ Up ▼ Down ▶ No Change Below Avg.

Options: CBOE

Analysis prepared by **Christopher B. Muir** on October 14, 2008, when the stock traded at **$ 41.99**.

## Highlights

➤ We see revenues rising 1.6% in 2008 and 7.0% in 2009. Growth should slow in 2008 due to the spin-off of the commodities trading business into a joint venture with Royal Bank of Scotland (RBS: buy, $1.71). However, SRE has one fully contracted LNG facility that opened in May and one scheduled to open in early 2009, which should help revenues. We also see higher revenues in the pipelines and storage and generation businesses.

➤ We expect operating margins to narrow to 10.7% in 2008 and 9.6% in 2009, from 14.6% in 2007, due mostly to the placement of SRE's higher-margin commodities business into a joint venture. We see pretax margins falling to 13.6% in 2008 and 12.8% in 2009, from 14.4% in 2007, a slower decline than seen for operating margins, as we expect earnings from the joint venture to more than offset higher interest expense and lower operating margins.

➤ Assuming an effective tax rate of 38.4% and a 5.6% decrease in average shares outstanding in 2008, we forecast operating EPS of $3.90 this year, down 4.6% from 2007's relatively strong $4.09. Our 2009 forecast is $4.51, a 16% increase.

## Investment Rationale/Risk

➤ We view the agreement that SRE has with RBS very favorably. We think the placement of its commodities business in a joint venture has substantially lowered SRE's risk profile, freed up about $1.0 billion in collateral payments, and still allows SRE to participate in the upside of the business. We also think the unique profit-sharing mechanism of the joint venture provides incentive for RBS to give its full support to the business. Separately, we expect two LNG projects, one under construction and one commencing operations, to add $0.40 to $0.45 per share to earnings starting in late 2009.

➤ Risks to our recommendation and target price include a failure to complete LNG projects, declining wholesale power margins, potential losses from energy and metals trading, and a weaker economy.

➤ The stock recently traded at a P/E of 8.8X our 2009 EPS estimate, an 8% discount to multi-utility peers. Our 12-month target price of $60 is 13.3X our 2009 EPS estimate, a slight premium to our peer P/E forecast, warranted, we believe, by SRE's prospects for stronger-than-peers EPS and dividend growth beyond 2008, and an anticipated large share repurchase program.

## Qualitative Risk Assessment

| LOW | MEDIUM | HIGH |
|---|---|---|

Our risk assessment reflects a balance between stable and steady earnings provided by SRE's regulated gas and electric utility operations and cyclical and volatile earnings from unregulated businesses, including power generation, energy marketing and trading, and international energy investments.

## Quantitative Evaluations

**S&P Quality Ranking**  B+

| D | C | B- | B | B+ | A- | A | A+ |
|---|---|---|---|---|---|---|---|

**Relative Strength Rank**  STRONG

74

LOWEST = 1                HIGHEST = 99

## Revenue/Earnings Data

**Revenue (Million $)**

| | 1Q | 2Q | 3Q | 4Q | Year |
|---|---|---|---|---|---|
| 2008 | 3,270 | 2,503 | 2,692 | -- | -- |
| 2007 | 3,004 | 2,661 | 2,663 | 3,110 | 11,438 |
| 2006 | 3,336 | 2,486 | 2,694 | 3,245 | 11,761 |
| 2005 | 2,697 | 2,276 | 2,770 | 3,994 | 11,737 |
| 2004 | 2,360 | 1,996 | 2,165 | 2,889 | 9,410 |
| 2003 | 1,923 | 1,840 | 2,058 | 2,066 | 7,887 |

**Earnings Per Share ($)**

| | | | | | |
|---|---|---|---|---|---|
| 2008 | 0.92 | 0.98 | 1.24 | E0.92 | E3.91 |
| 2007 | 0.86 | 1.06 | 1.24 | 1.10 | 4.26 |
| 2006 | 0.90 | 0.71 | 2.07 | 0.49 | 4.17 |
| 2005 | 0.92 | 0.49 | 0.86 | 1.40 | 3.69 |
| 2004 | 0.96 | 0.55 | 0.98 | 1.43 | 3.93 |
| 2003 | 0.56 | 0.56 | 1.00 | 1.11 | 3.24 |

Fiscal year ended Dec. 31. Next earnings report expected: Late February. EPS Estimates based on S&P Operating Earnings; historical GAAP earnings are as reported.

## Dividend Data (Dates: mm/dd Payment Date: mm/dd/yy)

| Amount ($) | Date Decl. | Ex-Div. Date | Stk. of Record | Payment Date |
|---|---|---|---|---|
| 0.310 | 12/04 | 12/18 | 12/20 | 01/15/08 |
| 0.320 | 02/13 | 03/18 | 03/20 | 04/15/08 |
| 0.350 | 05/22 | 06/17 | 06/19 | 07/15/08 |
| 0.350 | 09/09 | 09/23 | 09/25 | 10/15/08 |

Dividends have been paid since 1998. Source: Company reports.

---

**Please read the Required Disclosures and Analyst Certification on the last page of this report.**

**The McGraw-Hill Companies**

# Sempra Energy

STANDARD
&POOR'S

## Business Summary October 14, 2008

CORPORATE OVERVIEW. Sempra Energy is a holding company that operates five segments divided into California Utilities (CU--62% of 2007 revenue) and Sempra Global and parent (38%). The CU segment includes regulated public utilities Southern California Gas (SCG) and San Diego Gas & Electric (SDGE), which provide electricity and natural gas services in the Southern California. Sempra Global includes Sempra Generation, which develops and operates power plants and energy infrastructure; Sempra RBS Commodities, a joint venture that provides marketing and risk management services for energy products and base metals; Sempra LNG, which constructs and operates LNG receipt terminals in North America; and Sempra Pipelines & Storage, which operates in Mexico, the U.S. and South America.

CORPORATE STRATEGY. Sempra seeks to increase EPS through faster growth in its unregulated businesses through both acquisitions and organic growth. In the utility segment, the company focuses on managing regulatory risk as well as operating and capital expenditures. During 2003 to 2005, SRE focused on acquisitions as well as on new construction in generation, LNG, and pipelines and storage segments. Starting in 2006, the company changed course related to generation, selling ownership interests in some plants, but has focused recently on developing renewable generation initiatives. In 2008,

we believe the company reduced its risk profile and enhanced its growth prospects by placing its commodities trading business into a joint venture with a partner that has a stronger credit profile, which should allow for faster growth with less capital.

In July 2007, the company announced a deal with the Royal Bank of Scotland (RBS) that placed its commodity trading business in a joint venture. At closing, on April 1, 2008, SRE received about $1 billion in cash that had been used as collateral. Earnings from the joint venture will be divided into tranches so that each partner receives pretax 15% return on capital. SRE is to receive 70% of the first $500 million in pretax income above that threshold and then 30% of any pretax income above the latter level. We think this structure gives RBS a huge incentive to commit its substantial resources to growing the business. The company announced a dividend increase and share repurchase program as a result of the returned cash and increased growth expected at the company.

## Company Financials Fiscal Year Ended Dec. 31

| Per Share Data ($) | 2007 | 2006 | 2005 | 2004 | 2003 | 2002 | 2001 | 2000 | 1999 | 1998 |
|---|---|---|---|---|---|---|---|---|---|---|
| Tangible Book Value | 31.27 | 28.67 | 23.97 | 20.79 | 17.14 | 13.78 | 13.17 | 12.27 | 12.60 | 12.14 |
| Cash Flow | 6.86 | 6.70 | 6.25 | 6.59 | 6.12 | 5.68 | 5.35 | NA | NA | NA |
| Earnings | 4.26 | 4.17 | 3.69 | 3.93 | 3.24 | 2.79 | 2.52 | 2.06 | 1.66 | 1.24 |
| S&P Core Earnings | 4.26 | 4.19 | 3.44 | 3.65 | 3.29 | 2.16 | 1.76 | NA | NA | NA |
| Dividends | 1.24 | 1.20 | 1.16 | 1.00 | 1.00 | 1.00 | 1.00 | 1.00 | 1.56 | 1.56 |
| Payout Ratio | 29% | 29% | 31% | 25% | 31% | 36% | 40% | 49% | 94% | 126% |
| Prices:High | 66.38 | 57.35 | 47.86 | 37.93 | 30.90 | 26.25 | 28.61 | 24.88 | 26.00 | 29.31 |
| Prices:Low | 50.95 | 42.90 | 35.53 | 29.51 | 22.25 | 15.50 | 17.31 | 16.19 | 17.13 | 23.75 |
| P/E Ratio:High | 16 | 14 | 13 | 10 | 10 | 9 | 11 | 12 | 16 | 24 |
| P/E Ratio:Low | 12 | 10 | 10 | 8 | 7 | 6 | 7 | 8 | 10 | 19 |

| Income Statement Analysis (Million $) | | | | | | | | | | |
|---|---|---|---|---|---|---|---|---|---|---|
| Revenue | 11,438 | 11,761 | 11,737 | 9,410 | 7,887 | 6,020 | 8,029 | 7,143 | 5,360 | 5,481 |
| Operating Income | 2,365 | 1,785 | 1,111 | 1,272 | 939 | 987 | 993 | NA | 1,617 | 1,536 |
| Depreciation | 686 | 657 | 646 | 621 | 615 | 596 | 579 | 563 | 879 | 929 |
| Interest Expense | 381 | 361 | 321 | 332 | 327 | 323 | 352 | 301 | 229 | 207 |
| Pretax Income | 1,659 | 1,732 | 971 | 1,113 | 742 | 721 | 731 | 699 | 573 | 432 |
| Effective Tax Rate | 31.6% | 37.0% | 4.33% | 17.3% | 6.33% | 20.2% | 29.1% | 38.6% | 31.2% | 31.9% |
| Net Income | 1,135 | 1,091 | 929 | 920 | 695 | 575 | 518 | 429 | 394 | 294 |
| S&P Core Earnings | 1,124 | 1,096 | 866 | 855 | 708 | 445 | 362 | NA | NA | NA |

| Balance Sheet & Other Financial Data (Million $) | | | | | | | | | | |
|---|---|---|---|---|---|---|---|---|---|---|
| Cash | 669 | 920 | 772 | 419 | 432 | 455 | 605 | 637 | 487 | 424 |
| Current Assets | 11,338 | 12,016 | 13,318 | 8,776 | 7,886 | 7,010 | 4,808 | NA | NA | NA |
| Total Assets | 30,091 | 28,949 | 29,213 | 23,643 | 22,009 | 17,757 | 15,156 | 15,612 | 11,270 | 10,456 |
| Current Liabilities | 10,394 | 10,349 | 12,157 | 9,082 | 8,348 | 7,247 | 5,524 | NA | NA | NA |
| Long Term Debt | 4,655 | 4,704 | 5,002 | 4,371 | 4,199 | 4,487 | 3,840 | NA | NA | NA |
| Common Equity | 8,339 | 7,511 | 6,160 | 4,865 | 3,890 | 2,825 | 2,692 | 2,494 | 2,986 | 2,913 |
| Total Capital | 13,852 | 12,694 | 11,480 | 9,734 | 8,807 | 8,202 | 7,474 | 7,093 | 6,813 | 6,489 |
| Capital Expenditures | 2,011 | 1,907 | 1,404 | 1,083 | 1,049 | 1,214 | 1,068 | 759 | 589 | 438 |
| Cash Flow | 1,811 | 1,748 | 1,575 | 1,541 | 1,310 | 1,171 | 1,097 | NA | NA | NA |
| Current Ratio | 1.1 | 1.2 | 1.1 | 1.0 | 0.9 | 1.0 | 0.9 | 0.9 | 0.9 | 1.0 |
| % Long Term Debt of Capitalization | 33.6 | 37.1 | 43.6 | 44.9 | 47.7 | 54.7 | 51.4 | 54.8 | 48.0 | 46.3 |
| % Net Income of Revenue | 9.9 | 9.3 | 7.9 | 9.8 | 8.8 | 9.6 | 6.5 | 6.1 | 7.4 | 5.4 |
| % Return on Assets | 3.8 | 3.7 | 3.5 | 4.0 | 3.3 | 3.5 | 3.4 | NA | NA | NA |
| % Return on Equity | 14.2 | 16.0 | 16.9 | 21.0 | 20.7 | 20.8 | 20.0 | 15.7 | 13.4 | 13.1 |

Data as orig reptd.; bef. results of disc opers/spec. items. Per share data adj. for stk. divs.; EPS diluted. E-Estimated. NA-Not Available. NM-Not Meaningful. NR-Not Ranked. UR-Under Review.

**Office:** 101 Ash Street, San Diego, CA 92101-3017.
**Telephone:** 619-696-2034.
**Email:** investor@sempra.com
**Website:** http://www.sempra.com

**Chrmn & CEO:** D.E. Felsinger
**Pres & COO:** N.E. Schmale
**COO:** M.R. Niggli
**EVP & CFO:** M.A. Snell

**EVP & General Counsel:** J. Chaudhri
**Investor Contact:** J. Martin (619-696-2901)
**Board Members:** J. G. Brocksmith, Jr., R. A. Collato, D. E. Felsinger, W. D. Godbold, Jr., W. D. Jones, R. G. Newman, W. G. Ouchi, T. A. Page, W. C. Rusnack, W. P. Rutledge, C. R. Sacristan, L. Schenk, N. E. Schmale

**Founded:** 1998
**Domicile:** California
**Employees:** 13,500

# Sherwin-Williams Co (The)

**STANDARD & POOR'S**

| **S&P Recommendation** HOLD ★★★☆☆ | **Price** $54.50 (as of Nov 14, 2008) | **12-Mo. Target Price** $60.00 | **Investment Style** Large-Cap Growth |
|---|---|---|---|

**GICS Sector** Consumer Discretionary
**Sub-Industry** Home Improvement Retail

**Summary** This company, the largest U.S. producer of paints, is also a major seller of wallcoverings and related products.

## Key Stock Statistics (Source S&P, Vickers, company reports)

| | | | | | | | |
|---|---|---|---|---|---|---|---|
| 52-Wk Range | $65.00– 44.51 | S&P Oper. EPS 2008**E** | 4.25 | Market Capitalization(B) | $6.371 | Beta | 0.63 |
| Trailing 12-Month EPS | $4.35 | S&P Oper. EPS 2009**E** | 4.30 | Yield (%) | 2.57 | S&P 3-Yr. Proj. EPS CAGR(%) | 8 |
| Trailing 12-Month P/E | 12.5 | P/E on S&P Oper. EPS 2008**E** | 12.8 | Dividend Rate/Share | $1.40 | S&P Credit Rating | A- |
| $10K Invested 5 Yrs Ago | $18,436 | Common Shares Outstg. (M) | 116.9 | Institutional Ownership (%) | 78 | | |

## Price Performance

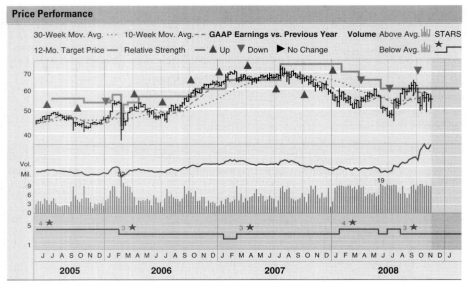

30-Week Mov. Avg. · · · · 10-Week Mov. Avg. - - GAAP Earnings vs. Previous Year Volume Above Avg. STARS
12-Mo. Target Price — Relative Strength — ▲ Up ▼ Down ▶ No Change Below Avg. ★

Options: CBOE

Analysis prepared by **Michael Souers** on October 22, 2008, when the stock traded at **$ 54.60**.

## Highlights

➤ We expect sales to increase 2.6% in 2009, following our projection of a 1.7% advance in 2008. We forecast continued softness in residential construction, which will likely negatively affect architectural sales, and we also foresee slowing demand in do-it-yourself (DIY) paint sales. Paint store segment sales will likely increase slightly, as we project the addition of approximately 20 net new stores being only partially offset by a low single-digit same-store-sales decline. We expect SHW to make several small acquisitions throughout the year.

➤ We project a slight decline in gross margins in 2009 as expected increases in raw material costs should offset improved pricing and product mix. Moreover, we anticipate a 30 basis point narrowing of operating margins, as expenses are de-leveraged due to expected weak same-store sales.

➤ With a projected 33.0% effective tax rate and a diluted share count that is seen about 2% lower, reflecting SHW's aggressive buyback program, we estimate 2009 EPS of $4.30, a 1% increase from the $4.25 we project the company to earn in 2008, excluding charges.

## Investment Rationale/Risk

➤ We continue to have a positive outlook with regard to the company's market niche, balance sheet and generation of free cash flow. In addition, we think the ruling by the Rhode Island Supreme Court, which overturned a negative verdict against SHW over the manufacturing and selling of lead paint, makes future negative rulings far less likely. However, we remain concerned that a slowing housing market will limit sales and earnings growth potential over the medium term. Following the recent increase in the share price, we think the shares are fairly valued at about 13X our 2009 EPS estimate.

➤ Risks to our recommendation and target price include a significant decrease in economic growth; an increase in interest rates, which could cause further weakness for the slowing housing market; and further rapid increases in raw material costs.

➤ At about 13X our 2009 EPS estimate, SHW recently traded at a modest premium to the S&P 500. Our 12-month target price of $60 is based on our DCF analysis, which assumes a weighted average cost of capital of 9.8% and a terminal growth rate of 3%.

## Qualitative Risk Assessment

| LOW | MEDIUM | HIGH |
|---|---|---|

Our risk assessment for Sherwin-Williams reflects the cyclical nature of the company's business, which is reliant on new housing starts and remodeling, and lead pigment litigation risk, offset by an S&P Quality Ranking of A.

## Quantitative Evaluations

**S&P Quality Ranking**     A

| D | C | B- | B | B+ | A- | A | A+ |
|---|---|---|---|---|---|---|---|

**Relative Strength Rank**     STRONG

88

LOWEST = 1       HIGHEST = 99

## Revenue/Earnings Data

**Revenue (Million $)**

| | 1Q | 2Q | 3Q | 4Q | Year |
|---|---|---|---|---|---|
| 2008 | 1,782 | 2,230 | 2,269 | -- | -- |
| 2007 | 1,756 | 2,198 | 2,197 | 1,854 | 8,005 |
| 2006 | 1,769 | 2,130 | 2,117 | 1,795 | 7,810 |
| 2005 | 1,539 | 1,965 | 1,977 | 1,710 | 7,191 |
| 2004 | 1,320 | 1,618 | 1,677 | 1,499 | 6,114 |
| 2003 | 1,148 | 1,472 | 1,503 | 1,285 | 5,408 |

**Earnings Per Share ($)**

| | 1Q | 2Q | 3Q | 4Q | Year |
|---|---|---|---|---|---|
| 2008 | 0.64 | 1.45 | 1.50 | E0.56 | E4.25 |
| 2007 | 0.83 | 1.52 | 1.55 | 0.80 | 4.70 |
| 2006 | 0.82 | 1.33 | 1.30 | 0.73 | 4.19 |
| 2005 | 0.58 | 1.08 | 1.07 | 0.54 | 3.28 |
| 2004 | 0.35 | 0.87 | 0.92 | 0.57 | 2.72 |
| 2003 | 0.21 | 0.75 | 0.82 | 0.48 | 2.26 |

Fiscal year ended Dec. 31. Next earnings report expected: Late January. EPS Estimates based on S&P Operating Earnings; historical GAAP earnings are as reported.

## Dividend Data (Dates: mm/dd Payment Date: mm/dd/yy)

| Amount ($) | Date Decl. | Ex-Div. Date | Stk. of Record | Payment Date |
|---|---|---|---|---|
| 0.350 | 02/20 | 02/27 | 02/29 | 03/14/08 |
| 0.350 | 04/16 | 05/14 | 05/16 | 06/06/08 |
| 0.350 | 07/16 | 08/20 | 08/22 | 09/12/08 |
| 0.350 | 10/15 | 11/12 | 11/14 | 12/05/08 |

Dividends have been paid since 1979. Source: Company reports.

---

**Please read the Required Disclosures and Analyst Certification on the last page of this report.**

The McGraw·Hill Companies

# Sherwin-Williams Co (The)

**STANDARD &POOR'S**

## Business Summary October 22, 2008

CORPORATE PROFILE. Sherwin-Williams manufactures, distributes and sells paints, coatings and related products to professional, industrial, commercial and retail customers primarily in North and South America. The company is structured into three reportable segments: Paint Stores, Consumer and Global.

The Paint Stores segment (62% of revenues in 2007) offers Sherwin-Williams branded architectural and industrial paints, stains and related products. Its diverse customer base includes architectural and industrial painting contractors, residential and commercial builders, property owners and managers, OEM product finishers and do-it-yourself (DIY) homeowners. In 2007, SHW acquired 172 stores and opened 107 net new stores, bringing the North America Paint Stores store count to 3,325.

The Consumer segment (16%) develops, manufactures and distributes architectural paints, stains, varnishes, industrial maintenance products, wood finishing products, paint applicators, corrosion inhibitors and paint-related products. Brands include Dutch Boy, Krylon, Minwax, Thompson's Water Seal,

Purdy and Pratt & Lambert, as well as private label brands.

The Global segment (22%) develops, licenses, manufactures, distributes and sells paints, stains, coatings, varnishes, industrial products, wood finishing products, applicators, aerosols, high performance interior and exterior coatings for the automotive, aviation, fleet and heavy truck markets, OEM product finishes and related products. SHW sells these products through 519 company-operated architectural, automotive, industrial and chemical coatings branches and other operations in the United States, Argentina, Brazil, Canada, Chile, China, France, India, Ireland, Italy, Mexico, Peru, United Kingdom and Uruguay. It also distributes these products to 16 other countries through wholly owned subsidiaries, joint ventures and licensees of technology, trademarks and tradenames.

## Company Financials Fiscal Year Ended Dec. 31

| Per Share Data ($) | 2007 | 2006 | 2005 | 2004 | 2003 | 2002 | 2001 | 2000 | 1999 | 1998 |
|---|---|---|---|---|---|---|---|---|---|---|
| Tangible Book Value | 23.99 | 2.67 | 3.83 | 3.12 | 2.95 | 4.05 | 3.69 | 3.18 | 2.32 | 1.76 |
| Cash Flow | 5.76 | 5.41 | 4.30 | 3.59 | 3.13 | 2.86 | 2.39 | 0.77 | 2.42 | 2.17 |
| Earnings | 4.70 | 4.19 | 3.28 | 2.72 | 2.26 | 2.04 | 1.68 | 0.10 | 1.80 | 1.57 |
| S&P Core Earnings | 4.59 | 4.11 | 3.24 | 2.60 | 2.15 | 1.81 | 1.62 | NA | NA | NA |
| Dividends | 1.58 | 1.00 | 0.82 | 0.68 | 0.62 | 0.60 | 0.58 | 0.54 | 0.48 | 0.45 |
| Payout Ratio | 34% | 24% | 25% | 25% | 27% | 29% | 35% | NM | 27% | 29% |
| Prices:High | 73.96 | 64.76 | 48.84 | 45.61 | 34.77 | 33.24 | 28.23 | 27.63 | 32.88 | 37.88 |
| Prices:Low | 56.75 | 37.40 | 40.47 | 32.95 | 24.42 | 21.75 | 19.73 | 17.13 | 18.75 | 19.44 |
| P/E Ratio:High | 16 | 15 | 15 | 17 | 15 | 16 | 17 | NM | 18 | 24 |
| P/E Ratio:Low | 12 | 9 | 12 | 12 | 11 | 11 | 12 | NM | 10 | 12 |

| Income Statement Analysis (Million $) | 2007 | 2006 | 2005 | 2004 | 2003 | 2002 | 2001 | 2000 | 1999 | 1998 |
|---|---|---|---|---|---|---|---|---|---|---|
| Revenue | 8,005 | 7,810 | 7,191 | 6,114 | 5,408 | 5,185 | 5,067 | 5,212 | 5,004 | 4,934 |
| Operating Income | 1,145 | 1,024 | 898 | 758 | 690 | 670 | 599 | 676 | 680 | 629 |
| Depreciation | 139 | 146 | 144 | 126 | 117 | 116 | 109 | 109 | 105 | 97.8 |
| Interest Expense | 71.6 | 67.2 | 49.6 | 39.9 | 38.7 | 40.5 | 54.6 | 62.0 | 61.2 | 72.0 |
| Pretax Income | 913 | 834 | 656 | 580 | 523 | 497 | 424 | 143 | 490 | 440 |
| Effective Tax Rate | 32.6% | 31.0% | 29.2% | 32.0% | 36.5% | 37.5% | 38.0% | 88.8% | 38.0% | 38.0% |
| Net Income | 616 | 576 | 463 | 393 | 332 | 311 | 263 | 16.0 | 304 | 273 |
| S&P Core Earnings | 602 | 564 | 458 | 376 | 317 | 276 | 254 | NA | NA | NA |

| Balance Sheet & Other Financial Data (Million $) | 2007 | 2006 | 2005 | 2004 | 2003 | 2002 | 2001 | 2000 | 1999 | 1998 |
|---|---|---|---|---|---|---|---|---|---|---|
| Cash | 27.3 | 469 | 36.0 | 45.9 | 303 | 164 | 119 | 2.90 | 18.6 | 19.1 |
| Current Assets | 2,070 | 2,450 | 1,891 | 1,782 | 1,715 | 1,506 | 1,507 | 1,552 | 1,597 | 1,547 |
| Total Assets | 4,855 | 4,995 | 4,369 | 4,274 | 3,683 | 3,432 | 3,628 | 3,751 | 4,052 | 4,065 |
| Current Liabilities | 2,141 | 2,075 | 1,554 | 1,520 | 1,154 | 1,083 | 1,141 | 1,115 | 1,190 | 1,112 |
| Long Term Debt | 293 | 292 | 487 | 488 | 503 | 507 | 504 | 624 | 624 | 730 |
| Common Equity | 1,461 | 1,559 | 1,696 | 1,475 | 1,174 | 1,300 | 1,319 | 1,472 | 1,699 | 1,716 |
| Total Capital | 2,079 | 2,284 | 2,218 | 2,139 | 1,962 | 1,849 | 1,991 | 2,095 | 2,323 | 2,446 |
| Capital Expenditures | 166 | 210 | 143 | 107 | 117 | 127 | 82.6 | 133 | 134 | 146 |
| Cash Flow | 755 | 722 | 607 | 519 | 449 | 426 | 372 | 125 | 409 | 371 |
| Current Ratio | 1.0 | 1.2 | 1.2 | 1.2 | 1.5 | 1.4 | 1.3 | 1.4 | 1.3 | 1.4 |
| % Long Term Debt of Capitalization | 14.0 | 12.8 | 22.0 | 22.8 | 25.6 | 27.4 | 25.3 | 29.8 | 26.9 | 29.9 |
| % Net Income of Revenue | 7.7 | 7.4 | 6.4 | 6.4 | 6.1 | 6.0 | 5.2 | 0.3 | 6.1 | 5.5 |
| % Return on Assets | 12.5 | 12.3 | 10.7 | 9.9 | 9.3 | 8.8 | 7.1 | 0.4 | 7.5 | 6.7 |
| % Return on Equity | 32.6 | 35.4 | 29.2 | 29.7 | 26.8 | 23.7 | 18.9 | 1.0 | 17.8 | 16.5 |

Data as orig reptd.; bef. results of disc opers/spec. items. Per share data adj. for stk. divs.; EPS diluted. E-Estimated. NA-Not Available. NM-Not Meaningful. NR-Not Ranked. UR-Under Review.

**Office:** 101 Prospect Avenue N.W., Cleveland, OH 44115-1075.
**Telephone:** 216-566-2000.
**Website:** http://www.sherwin.com
**Chrmn & CEO:** C.M. Connor

**Pres & COO:** J.G. Morikis
**SVP & CFO:** S.P. Hennessy
**Chief Admin Officer:** R.M. Weaver
**Chief Acctg Officer & Cntlr:** J.L. Ault

**Investor Contact:** R.J. Wells (216-566-2244)
**Board Members:** A. F. Anton, J. C. Boland, C. M. Connor, D. E. Evans, D. F. Hodnik, S. J. Kropf, R. W. Mahoney, G. E. McCullough, A. M. Mixon, III, C. E. Moll, R. K. Smucker

**Founded:** 1866
**Domicile:** Ohio
**Employees:** 31,572

The **McGraw·Hill** Companies

# Sigma Aldrich Corporation

| S&P Recommendation | **BUY** ★★★★☆ | Price<br>$40.84 (as of Nov 14, 2008) | 12-Mo. Target Price<br>$52.00 | Investment Style<br>Large-Cap Growth |
|---|---|---|---|---|

**GICS Sector** Materials
**Sub-Industry** Specialty Chemicals

**Summary** This company makes and sells a wide range of biochemicals, organic chemicals and chromatography products.

## Key Stock Statistics (Source S&P, Vickers, company reports)

| | | | | | | | |
|---|---|---|---|---|---|---|---|
| 52-Wk Range | $63.04– 34.42 | S&P Oper. EPS 2008**E** | 2.66 | Market Capitalization(B) | $5.120 | Beta | 0.56 |
| Trailing 12-Month EPS | $2.62 | S&P Oper. EPS 2009**E** | 2.90 | Yield (%) | 1.27 | S&P 3-Yr. Proj. EPS CAGR(%) | 12 |
| Trailing 12-Month P/E | 15.6 | P/E on S&P Oper. EPS 2008**E** | 15.4 | Dividend Rate/Share | $0.52 | S&P Credit Rating | NA |
| $10K Invested 5 Yrs Ago | $16,634 | Common Shares Outstg. (M) | 125.4 | Institutional Ownership (%) | 81 | | |

## Price Performance

30-Week Mov. Avg. · · · · 10-Week Mov. Avg. - - GAAP Earnings vs. Previous Year  Volume Above Avg. STARS
12-Mo. Target Price — Relative Strength ▲ Up ▼ Down ▶ No Change  Below Avg. ★

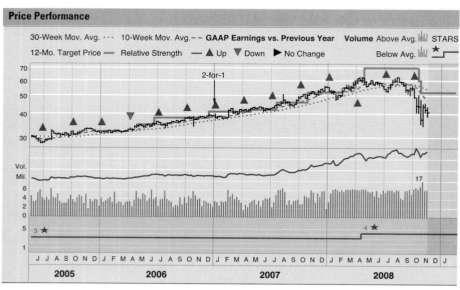

Options: ASE, CBOE

Analysis prepared by **Jeffrey Loo, CFA** on November 13, 2008, when the stock traded at **$ 39.23**.

## Highlights

➤ We expect a sales increase of 10% in 2008 to $2.2 billion, with 6% organic growth and 4% from foreign exchange translation. We see organic growth of 4% in Research Essentials, 7% in Research Specialities, 8% in Research Biotech, and 6% in SAFC, its Fine Chemicals unit, aided by strong sales of Hitech products but adversely affected by slowing pharmaceutical sales. We think SIAL's efforts to increase international sales are paying off, and we see robust growth in the low double digits in Canada, Asia Pacific, and Latin America. In 2009, we expect sales to rise 4% to $2.3 billion.

➤ We project gross margins to improve slightly due to SIAL's supply-chain initiative, partially offset by higher freight costs, and see operating margins improving about 60 basis points on leverage and increased Web-based ordering. Web-based sales now account for 51% of sales to U.S. customers and 43% worldwide.

➤ We see an effective tax rate of 31.0% for 2008, up from 28.9% in 2007, due to a higher net international tax level but aided by the reinstatement of the U.S. R&D tax credit. We think EPS should benefit from more share repurchases. We see 2008 EPS of $2.66 and 2009 EPS of $2.90.

## Investment Rationale/Risk

➤ We think SIAL can grow faster than the industry average and supplement organic growth with additional strategic acquisitions. However, we note that operating income and net income growth is projected to rise only slightly ahead of sales growth. We believe the company needs to improve efficiency and take advantage of leverage to improve its margins. In our view, SIAL's five-year supply chain initiative plan, which began in 2007, should significantly improve margins beginning in 2009. New marketing initiatives and an expanded sales force have increased operating expenses, but we think these initiatives should aid sales and begin to lift margins in 2009.

➤ Risks to our recommendation and target price include unexpected weakness in key markets such as pharmaceuticals and academia, greater price competition, adverse currency exchange movements, an inability to successfully introduce new products, and failure to successfully integrate future acquisitions.

➤ Our 12-month target price of $52 is based on an in-line-with-peers P/E-to-growth ratio of 1.5X based on our 2009 EPS estimate and assuming a three-year growth rate of 12%.

## Qualitative Risk Assessment

| LOW | MEDIUM | HIGH |
|---|---|---|

Our risk assessment reflects the stable nature of the company's laboratory chemicals business, its broad geographic sales mix, and our view of its strong balance sheet.

## Quantitative Evaluations

**S&P Quality Ranking**  A+

| D | C | B- | B | B+ | A- | A | A+ |
|---|---|---|---|---|---|---|---|

**Relative Strength Rank**  MODERATE

66

LOWEST = 1    HIGHEST = 99

## Revenue/Earnings Data

**Revenue (Million $)**

| | 1Q | 2Q | 3Q | 4Q | Year |
|---|---|---|---|---|---|
| 2008 | 569.6 | 580.7 | 540.6 | -- | -- |
| 2007 | 495.9 | 507.5 | 503.2 | 532.1 | 2,039 |
| 2006 | 443.1 | 448.5 | 441.4 | 464.5 | 1,798 |
| 2005 | 399.8 | 444.0 | 412.2 | 410.5 | 1,667 |
| 2004 | 368.1 | 348.6 | 340.6 | 351.9 | 1,409 |
| 2003 | 334.7 | 327.1 | 314.2 | 322.2 | 1,298 |

**Earnings Per Share ($)**

| | | | | | |
|---|---|---|---|---|---|
| 2008 | 0.64 | 0.70 | 0.64 | E0.68 | E2.66 |
| 2007 | 0.56 | 0.60 | 0.54 | 0.64 | 2.34 |
| 2006 | 0.49 | 0.52 | 0.51 | 0.53 | 2.05 |
| 2005 | 0.54 | 0.46 | 0.47 | 0.42 | 1.88 |
| 2004 | 0.45 | 0.43 | 0.41 | 0.40 | 1.67 |
| 2003 | 0.36 | 0.34 | 0.33 | 0.34 | 1.34 |

Fiscal year ended Dec. 31. Next earnings report expected: Mid February. EPS Estimates based on S&P Operating Earnings; historical GAAP earnings are as reported.

## Dividend Data (Dates: mm/dd Payment Date: mm/dd/yy)

| Amount ($) | Date Decl. | Ex-Div. Date | Stk. of Record | Payment Date |
|---|---|---|---|---|
| 0.130 | 02/12 | 02/27 | 02/29 | 03/14/08 |
| 0.130 | 05/06 | 05/28 | 05/30 | 06/13/08 |
| 0.130 | 08/12 | 08/28 | 09/02 | 09/15/08 |
| 0.130 | 11/11 | 11/26 | 12/01 | 12/15/08 |

Dividends have been paid since 1970. Source: Company reports.

# Sigma Aldrich Corporation

STANDARD &POOR'S

## Business Summary November 13, 2008

CORPORATE OVERVIEW. Sigma-Aldrich, well known for its extensive catalog business, is one of the world's largest providers of research chemicals, reagents, chromatography products, and related products.

Foreign sales accounted for 63% of the total in 2007.

SIAL distributes more than 100,000 chemical products, under the Sigma, Aldrich, Fluka and Supelco brands names, for use primarily in research and development, diagnosis of disease, and as specialty chemicals for manufacturing. About 75% of sales are to customers in the life sciences, with the remaining 25% used in high-technology applications. Customer sectors include pharmaceutical (40% of sales), academia and government (30%), chemical industry (20%), and hospitals and commercial laboratories (10%). The company itself produces about 46,000 products, accounting for 60% of 2007 net sales of chemical products. Remaining products are purchased from outside sources. The company also supplies 30,000 equipment products.

The Research Essentials unit (19% of sales in 2007) sells biological buffers, cell culture reagents, biochemicals, chemicals, solvents, and other reagents and kits. The Research Specialties unit (37%) sells organic chemicals, biochemicals, analytical reagents, chromatography consumables, reference materials and high-purity products. The Research Biotech unit (15%) supplies immunochemical, molecular biology, cell signaling and neuroscience biochemicals and kits used in biotechnology, genomic, proteomic and other life science research applications. Sigma-Genosys (acquired in 1998) is a major maker of custom synthetic DNA products, synthetic peptides and genes to the life science product categories. SIAL believes it is the leading supplier of products used in cell signaling and neuroscience. The SAFC (Fine Chemicals) unit (29%) is a top 10 supplier of large-scale organic chemicals and biochemicals used in development and production by pharmaceutical, biotechnology, industrial and diagnostic companies. The February 2007 purchase of Epichem Group (with annual sales of $40 million) greatly expanded SAFC's high technology sales.

SIAL also offers about 80,000 esoteric chemicals (less than 1% of total sales) as a special service to customers that screen them for potential applications.

## Company Financials Fiscal Year Ended Dec. 31

| Per Share Data ($) | 2007 | 2006 | 2005 | 2004 | 2003 | 2002 | 2001 | 2000 | 1999 | 1998 |
|---|---|---|---|---|---|---|---|---|---|---|
| Tangible Book Value | 8.19 | 7.00 | 5.71 | 7.67 | 6.42 | 5.45 | 3.38 | 3.67 | 5.79 | 5.48 |
| Cash Flow | 3.07 | 1.37 | 2.54 | 2.19 | 1.83 | 1.72 | 1.41 | 1.24 | 1.07 | 1.13 |
| Earnings | 2.34 | 2.05 | 1.88 | 1.67 | 1.34 | 0.89 | 0.94 | 0.83 | 0.74 | 0.82 |
| S&P Core Earnings | 2.34 | 2.05 | 1.81 | 1.58 | 1.28 | 1.05 | 0.88 | NA | NA | NA |
| Dividends | 0.46 | 0.42 | 0.38 | 0.34 | 0.25 | 0.17 | 0.17 | 0.16 | 0.15 | 0.14 |
| Payout Ratio | 20% | 20% | 20% | 20% | 19% | 19% | 18% | 19% | 20% | 17% |
| Prices:High | 56.59 | 39.68 | 33.55 | 30.81 | 28.96 | 26.40 | 25.75 | 20.44 | 17.63 | 21.38 |
| Prices:Low | 37.40 | 31.27 | 27.67 | 26.61 | 20.47 | 19.08 | 18.13 | 10.09 | 12.25 | 12.88 |
| P/E Ratio:High | 24 | 19 | 18 | 18 | 22 | 30 | 28 | 25 | 24 | 26 |
| P/E Ratio:Low | 16 | 15 | 15 | 16 | 15 | 21 | 19 | 12 | 17 | 16 |

| Income Statement Analysis (Million $) | 2007 | 2006 | 2005 | 2004 | 2003 | 2002 | 2001 | 2000 | 1999 | 1998 |
|---|---|---|---|---|---|---|---|---|---|---|
| Revenue | 2,039 | 1,798 | 1,667 | 1,409 | 1,298 | 1,207 | 1,179 | 1,096 | 1,038 | 1,194 |
| Operating Income | 557 | 494 | 452 | 392 | 353 | 323 | 291 | 284 | 275 | 305 |
| Depreciation | 97.8 | 90.9 | 90.1 | 73.4 | 69.3 | 66.3 | 71.4 | 67.6 | 66.9 | 61.8 |
| Interest Expense | 28.9 | 24.0 | 18.1 | 7.20 | 10.1 | 13.8 | 18.2 | 10.2 | Nil | 0.92 |
| Pretax Income | 438 | 379 | 343 | 312 | 273 | 272 | 202 | 203 | 204 | 243 |
| Effective Tax Rate | 28.9% | 26.9% | 24.8% | 25.3% | 30.2% | 31.4% | 30.2% | 31.5% | 27.1% | 31.4% |
| Net Income | 311 | 277 | 258 | 233 | 190 | 187 | 141 | 139 | 149 | 166 |
| S&P Core Earnings | 310 | 276 | 249 | 221 | 180 | 155 | 133 | NA | NA | NA |

| Balance Sheet & Other Financial Data (Million $) | 2007 | 2006 | 2005 | 2004 | 2003 | 2002 | 2001 | 2000 | 1999 | 1998 |
|---|---|---|---|---|---|---|---|---|---|---|
| Cash | 238 | 174 | 98.6 | 169 | 128 | 52.4 | 37.6 | 31.1 | 43.8 | 24.3 |
| Current Assets | 1,283 | 1,113 | 950 | 893 | 815 | 695 | 727 | 714 | 775 | 773 |
| Total Assets | 2,629 | 2,334 | 2,131 | 1,745 | 1,548 | 1,390 | 1,440 | 1,348 | 1,432 | 1,433 |
| Current Liabilities | 635 | 443 | 461 | 231 | 257 | 266 | 398 | 335 | 106 | 142 |
| Long Term Debt | 207 | 338 | 283 | 177 | 176 | 177 | 178 | 101 | 0.21 | 0.42 |
| Common Equity | 1,617 | 1,411 | 1,233 | 1,212 | 999 | 882 | 810 | 859 | 1,259 | 1,216 |
| Total Capital | 1,866 | 1,797 | 1,597 | 1,389 | 1,176 | 1,059 | 987 | 960 | 1,260 | 1,217 |
| Capital Expenditures | 79.7 | 74.5 | 92.2 | 70.3 | 57.7 | 60.7 | 110 | 69.2 | 91.8 | 130 |
| Cash Flow | 409 | 368 | 348 | 306 | 260 | 253 | 212 | 207 | 216 | 228 |
| Current Ratio | 2.0 | 2.5 | 2.1 | 3.9 | 3.2 | 2.6 | 1.8 | 2.1 | 7.3 | 5.4 |
| % Long Term Debt of Capitalization | 11.1 | 18.8 | 17.7 | 12.8 | 15.0 | 16.7 | 18.0 | 10.5 | 0.0 | 0.0 |
| % Net Income of Revenue | 15.3 | 15.4 | 15.5 | 16.5 | 14.7 | 15.5 | 11.9 | 12.7 | 14.3 | 13.9 |
| % Return on Assets | 12.5 | 12.4 | 13.3 | 14.1 | 12.7 | 13.2 | 10.1 | 10.0 | 10.4 | 12.4 |
| % Return on Equity | 20.6 | 20.9 | 21.1 | 21.1 | 20.2 | 22.1 | 16.9 | 13.1 | 12.0 | 14.5 |

Data as orig reptd.; bef. results of disc opers/spec. items. Per share data adj. for stk. divs.; EPS diluted. E-Estimated. NA-Not Available. NM-Not Meaningful. NR-Not Ranked. UR-Under Review.

**Office:** 3050 Spruce Street, St. Louis, MO 63103.
**Telephone:** 314-771-5765.
**Website:** http://www.sigma-aldrich.com
**Chrmn:** D.R. Harvey

**Pres:** J.P. Porwoll
**Pres & CEO:** J.P. Nagarkatti
**CFO & Chief Admin Officer:** M. Hogan
**Chief Acctg Officer & Cntlr:** K.J. Miller

**Investor Contact:** K.A. Richter (314-286-8004)
**Board Members:** R. M. Bergman, D. R. Harvey, W. L. McCollum, J. P. Nagarkatti, A. M. Nash, S. M. Paul, J. P. Reinhard, T. R. Sear, D. D. Spatz, B. Toan

**Founded:** 1951
**Domicile:** Delaware
**Employees:** 7,862

# Simon Property Group Inc.

**STANDARD &POOR'S**

| S&P Recommendation | STRONG BUY ★★★★★ | Price | 12-Mo. Target Price | Investment Style |
|---|---|---|---|---|
| | | $52.20 (as of Nov 14, 2008) | $86.00 | Large-Cap Blend |

**GICS Sector** Financials
**Sub-Industry** Retail REITS

**Summary** This real estate investment trust owns, develops and manages retail real estate, primarily regional malls, outlet centers and community/lifestyle centers, across the U.S.

## Key Stock Statistics (Source S&P, Vickers, company reports)

| | | | | | | | |
|---|---|---|---|---|---|---|---|
| 52-Wk Range | $106.43– 48.82 | S&P FFO/Sh. 2008E | 6.40 | Market Capitalization(B) | $11.787 | Beta | 1.30 |
| Trailing 12-Month FFO/Share | NA | S&P FFO/Sh. 2009E | 6.80 | Yield (%) | 6.90 | S&P 3-Yr. FFO/Sh. Proj. CAGR(%) | 9 |
| Trailing 12-Month P/FFO | NA | P/FFO on S&P FFO/Sh. 2008E | 8.2 | Dividend Rate/Share | $3.60 | S&P Credit Rating | A- |
| $10K Invested 5 Yrs Ago | $13,475 | Common Shares Outstg. (M) | 225.8 | Institutional Ownership (%) | NM | | |

## Price Performance

30-Week Mov. Avg. · · · 10-Week Mov. Avg. - - **GAAP Earnings vs. Previous Year**   Volume Above Avg. STARS
12-Mo. Target Price — Relative Strength — ▲ Up ▼ Down ▶ No Change   Below Avg. ★

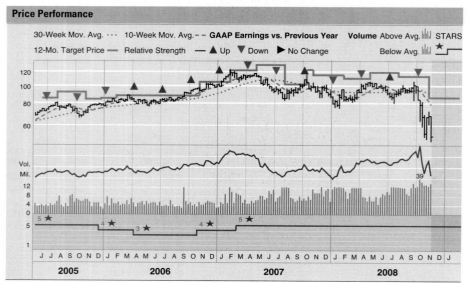

Analysis prepared by **Robert McMillan** on November 04, 2008, when the stock traded at **$ 69.45.**

## Highlights

➤ We expect the company to continue to benefit from what we view as a successful strategy of operating large and strategically located regional malls and shopping centers in major metropolitan markets.

➤ We look for total revenues, after increasing 9.6% in 2007, to advance about 5.3% in 2008 and 5.1% in 2009, reflecting expected higher rents and tenant reimbursements, and new domestic and international developments. In the third quarter, comparable sales per square foot rose fractionally, year to year, in SPG's regional mall portfolio, and 4.2% in its premium outlet center portfolio, while average rent per square foot rose 6.3% for the regional malls, 6.6% for the premium outlet centers, and 7.0% for the community and lifestyle centers despite a small downtick in occupancies on more store closures. We look for continued retailer expansion, albeit at a slower pace, and a drop in new construction activity, due to more stringent lending terms, to benefit SPG in the longer term.

➤ We see FFO per share of $6.40 in 2008 and $6.80 in 2009.

## Investment Rationale/Risk

➤ We think SPG's position as one of the largest owners and managers of shopping centers in the U.S. and its established relationships with numerous retailers will allow it to continue to generate robust growth. We also view the geographic, customer and format diversity of SPG's portfolio and management's acquisitions and developments in both the U.S. and overseas as positive factors in our valuation.

➤ Risks to our recommendation and target price include slower-than-expected growth in retailer expansion, higher-than-normal retailer bankruptcies, and a rise in interest rates.

➤ The shares recently traded at about 10.8X SPG's trailing 12-month FFO. We believe the stock and the valuation multiple have been volatile recently on concerns about the economy and the impact of a weak housing market on consumer spending. Our 12-month target price of $86 is equal to about 13.0X our forward 12-month FFO estimate of $6.64. We believe that the multiple will expand based on expected improvements in the company's operating performance, and on the continued easing of concerns about the impact of the housing market on SPG's retailer-dependent business.

## Qualitative Risk Assessment

| LOW | MEDIUM | HIGH |
|---|---|---|

Our risk assessment reflects SPG's position as one of the largest owners of shopping centers with a diverse tenant and geographic mix and a variety of shopping center formats. The majority of SPG's customers are under long-term leases, which helps lessen short-term volatility. The company also has a strong balance sheet, in our view.

## Quantitative Evaluations

**S&P Quality Ranking** B+

| D | C | B- | B | B+ | A- | A | A+ |
|---|---|---|---|---|---|---|---|

**Relative Strength Rank** MODERATE

33

LOWEST = 1   HIGHEST = 99

## Revenue/FFO Data

### Revenue (Million $)

| | 1Q | 2Q | 3Q | 4Q | Year |
|---|---|---|---|---|---|
| 2008 | 895.3 | 913.5 | 932.2 | -- | -- |
| 2007 | 852.1 | 855.9 | 907.2 | 1,036 | 3,632 |
| 2006 | 787.7 | 798.7 | 818.7 | 927.0 | 3,332 |
| 2005 | 756.9 | 756.3 | 786.8 | 889.8 | 3,167 |
| 2004 | 582.1 | 600.6 | 623.0 | 836.1 | 2,642 |
| 2003 | 547.8 | 566.3 | 566.6 | 659.9 | 2,314 |

### FFO Per Share ($)

| | 1Q | 2Q | 3Q | 4Q | Year |
|---|---|---|---|---|---|
| 2008 | 1.46 | 1.49 | 1.61 | E1.84 | E6.40 |
| 2007 | 1.37 | 1.31 | 1.46 | 1.76 | 5.90 |
| 2006 | 1.26 | 1.26 | 1.30 | 1.57 | 5.39 |
| 2005 | 1.12 | 1.18 | 1.19 | 1.47 | 4.96 |
| 2004 | 0.96 | 1.01 | 1.04 | 1.36 | 4.39 |
| 2003 | 0.89 | 0.96 | 0.93 | 1.26 | 4.04 |

Fiscal year ended Dec. 31. Next earnings report expected: Early February. FFO Estimates based on S&P Funds From Operations Est..

## Dividend Data (Dates: mm/dd Payment Date: mm/dd/yy)

| Amount ($) | Date Decl. | Ex-Div. Date | Stk. of Record | Payment Date |
|---|---|---|---|---|
| 0.900 | 02/01 | 02/13 | 02/15 | 02/29/08 |
| 0.900 | 04/29 | 05/14 | 05/16 | 05/30/08 |
| 0.900 | 07/28 | 08/13 | 08/15 | 08/29/08 |
| 0.900 | 11/03 | 11/12 | 11/14 | 11/28/08 |

Dividends have been paid since 1994. Source: Company reports.

Options: ASE, CBOE, Ph

# Simon Property Group Inc.

STANDARD &POOR'S

## Business Summary November 04, 2008

CORPORATE OVERVIEW. Simon Property Group is a real estate investment trust that owns, develops, manages, leases and acquires primarily regional malls and community shopping centers. It is one of the largest owners of shopping centers in the world. At December 31, 2007, SPG owned 320 income-producing properties in the U.S. SPG also had ownership interests in 51 European shopping centers and eight premium outlet centers in Japan, Mexico and South Korea. Also, through a joint venture arrangement, SPG has a 32.5% interest in five shopping centers under development in China.

SPG's regional malls typically contain at least one traditional department store anchor or a combination of anchors and big box retailers with a wide variety of smaller stores located in enclosed malls connecting the anchors. Additional freestanding stores are usually located along the perimeter of the parking area. SPG's 168 regional malls range in size from approximately 400,000 to 2.3 million square feet of gross leasable area (GLA) and contain more than 18,300 occupied stores, including approximately 675 anchors, which are mostly national retailers. The regional mall totals include certain lifestyle centers when the center contains a traditional department store anchor.

SPG's premium outlet centers contain a wide variety of retailers located in open-air manufacturers' outlet centers. The company's 38 premium outlet centers range in size from approximately 200,000 to 850,000 square feet of GLA and are generally located near metropolitan areas .

SPG's 67 community and lifestyle shopping centers are generally unenclosed and smaller than its regional malls. The community and lifestyle centers usually range in size from approximately 100,000 to 900,000 square feet of GLA and are designed to serve a larger trade area, and typically contain at least two anchors and other tenants that are usually national retailers among the leaders in their markets. These tenants generally occupy a significant portion of the GLA of the center. The company also owns traditional community shopping centers that focus primarily on value-oriented and convenience goods and services. These centers are usually anchored by a supermarket, discount retailer, or drugstore and are designed to service a neighborhood area. The trust also owns open-air centers adjacent to its regional malls designed to take advantage of the drawing power of the mall.

## Company Financials Fiscal Year Ended Dec. 31

| Per Share Data ($) | 2007 | 2006 | 2005 | 2004 | 2003 | 2002 | 2001 | 2000 | 1999 | 1998 |
|---|---|---|---|---|---|---|---|---|---|---|
| Tangible Book Value | 12.40 | 13.98 | 14.64 | 16.21 | 14.66 | 13.87 | 13.00 | 14.29 | 15.36 | 15.70 |
| Earnings | 2.08 | 2.19 | 1.27 | 1.44 | 1.53 | 1.93 | 0.87 | 1.13 | 1.00 | 1.01 |
| S&P Core Earnings | 2.20 | 2.19 | 1.12 | 1.44 | 1.55 | 2.07 | 0.97 | NA | NA | NA |
| Dividends | 3.36 | 3.04 | 2.80 | 2.60 | 2.40 | 2.18 | 2.08 | 2.02 | 2.02 | 2.02 |
| Payout Ratio | 162% | 139% | NM | 181% | 157% | 113% | NM | 179% | 202% | 200% |
| Prices:High | 123.96 | 104.08 | 80.97 | 65.87 | 48.59 | 36.95 | 30.97 | 27.13 | 30.94 | 34.88 |
| Prices:Low | 82.60 | 76.14 | 58.29 | 44.39 | 31.70 | 28.80 | 23.75 | 21.50 | 20.44 | 25.81 |
| P/E Ratio:High | 60 | 48 | 64 | 46 | 32 | 19 | 36 | 24 | 31 | 34 |
| P/E Ratio:Low | 40 | 35 | 46 | 31 | 21 | 15 | 27 | 19 | 20 | 26 |
| **Income Statement Analysis** (Million $) | | | | | | | | | | |
| Rental Income | NA | 3,063 | 2,920 | 2,411 | 1,423 | 1,386 | 1,320 | 1,284 | 1,207 | 900 |
| Mortgage Income | NA | Nil | Nil | Nil | Nil | Nil | Nil | Nil | Nil | Nil |
| Total Income | 3,651 | 3,332 | 3,167 | 2,642 | 2,314 | 2,186 | 2,045 | 2,013 | 1,895 | 1,405 |
| General Expenses | 1,210 | 856 | 820 | 675 | 611 | 788 | 712 | 674 | 655 | 495 |
| Interest Expense | 1,535 | 822 | 799 | 662 | 615 | 603 | 622 | 667 | 580 | 420 |
| Provision for Losses | 9.56 | 9.50 | 8.10 | 17.7 | Nil | 8.97 | 8.41 | 9.64 | 8.50 | 6.60 |
| Depreciation | 906 | 856 | 850 | 623 | 498 | 423 | 453 | 420 | 382 | 268 |
| Net Income | 519 | 563 | 457 | 450 | 339 | 1,109 | 201 | 242 | 210 | 160 |
| S&P Core Earnings | 491 | 486 | 247 | 301 | 288 | 371 | 169 | NA | NA | NA |
| **Balance Sheet & Other Financial Data** (Million $) | | | | | | | | | | |
| Cash | 502 | 929 | 929 | 520 | 536 | 397 | 255 | 214 | 155 | 130 |
| Total Assets | 23,606 | 22,084 | 21,131 | 22,070 | 15,685 | 14,905 | 13,794 | 13,911 | 14,199 | 13,277 |
| Real Estate Investment | 24,415 | 24,390 | 23,307 | 23,175 | 14,972 | 14,250 | 13,187 | 13,038 | 12,794 | 11,850 |
| Loss Reserve | Nil | Nil | Nil | Nil | Nil | 20.5 | 24.7 | 20.1 | 14.6 | 14.5 |
| Net Investment | 19,103 | 19,784 | 19,499 | 20,012 | 12,415 | 12,027 | 11,311 | 11,558 | 11,697 | 11,127 |
| Short Term Debt | 810 | NA | NA | NA | 1,481 | 940 | 665 | 1,164 | 1,162 | 1,030 |
| Capitalization:Debt | 16,409 | 13,711 | 14,106 | 13,044 | 8,786 | 8,606 | 8,176 | 7,904 | 9,109 | 7,973 |
| Capitalization:Equity | 2,817 | 3,095 | 3,227 | 3,580 | 2,971 | 2,653 | 2,327 | 2,515 | 3,246 | 3,409 |
| Capitalization:Total | 21,821 | 18,885 | 19,681 | 19,065 | 13,241 | 12,074 | 11,381 | 10,958 | 12,355 | 11,382 |
| % Earnings & Depreciation/Assets | 6.2 | 6.7 | 6.0 | 5.7 | 5.5 | 10.7 | 4.7 | 4.7 | 4.3 | 4.1 |
| Price Times Book Value:High | 10.0 | 7.4 | 5.5 | 4.1 | 3.3 | 2.7 | 2.4 | 1.9 | 2.0 | 2.2 |
| Price Times Book Value:Low | 6.7 | 5.4 | 4.0 | 2.7 | 2.2 | 2.1 | 1.8 | 1.5 | 1.3 | 1.6 |

Data as orig reptd.; bef. results of disc opers/spec. items. Per share data adj. for stk. divs.; EPS diluted. E-Estimated. NA-Not Available. NM-Not Meaningful. NR-Not Ranked. UR-Under Review.

**Office:** 225 W Washington St, Indianapolis, IN 46204-3438.
**Telephone:** 317-636-1600.
**Website:** http://www.simon.com
**Chrmn & CEO:** D.E. Simon

**Pres & COO:** R.S. Sokolov
**EVP & CFO:** S.E. Sterrett
**SVP & Chief Acctg Officer:** J. Dahl
**SVP & Treas:** A.A. Juster

**Investor Contact:** S.J. Doran (317-685-7330)
**Board Members:** B. Bayh, M. E. Bergstein, D. C. Bloom, L. W. Bynoe, K. N. Horn, R. S. Leibowitz, H. C. Mautner, F. W. Petri, D. E. Simon, H. Simon, M. J. Simon, J. A. Smith, Jr., R. S. Sokolov, M. D. York, P. S. van den Berg

**Founded:** 1993
**Domicile:** Delaware
**Employees:** 5,100

# SLM Corp

**STANDARD &POOR'S**

| S&P Recommendation | HOLD ★★★☆☆ | Price | 12-Mo. Target Price | Investment Style |
|---|---|---|---|---|
| | | $7.43 (as of Nov 14, 2008) | $11.00 | Large-Cap Growth |

**GICS Sector** Financials
**Sub-Industry** Consumer Finance

**Summary** This company (formerly USA Education) is a leading U.S. provider of post-secondary educational financial services.

## Key Stock Statistics (Source S&P, Vickers, company reports)

| | | | | | | | |
|---|---|---|---|---|---|---|---|
| 52-Wk Range | $39.05– 4.19 | S&P Oper. EPS 2008**E** | 1.20 | Market Capitalization(B) | $3.472 | Beta | 1.82 |
| Trailing 12-Month EPS | $-3.81 | S&P Oper. EPS 2009**E** | 1.64 | Yield (%) | Nil | S&P 3-Yr. Proj. EPS CAGR(%) | NM |
| Trailing 12-Month P/E | NM | P/E on S&P Oper. EPS 2008**E** | 6.2 | Dividend Rate/Share | Nil | S&P Credit Rating | BBB- |
| $10K Invested 5 Yrs Ago | $2,079 | Common Shares Outstg. (M) | 467.3 | Institutional Ownership (%) | NM | | |

## Price Performance

30-Week Mov. Avg. ···· 10-Week Mov. Avg. ── **GAAP Earnings vs. Previous Year** Volume Above Avg. ▏▊▎ STARS
12-Mo. Target Price ── Relative Strength ── ▲ Up ▼ Down ▶ No Change Below Avg. ▏▊▎ ★

Options: ASE, CBOE, P

Analysis prepared by **Kevin Cole, CFA** on October 23, 2008, when the stock traded at **$ 8.72**.

## Highlights

➤ We believe that private student loans will be slightly higher as a percentage of loans under management in 2008 due to the exit of many competitors from the business. Based on our expectations for declining student loan spreads and lower loan origination volumes, we see SLM's core net interest income decreasing roughly 5.3% in 2008. We believe loan loss provisions will decline slightly, reflecting SLM's voluntary pullback from originating loans from non-traditional schools, in which delinquencies and chargeoffs have run much higher than SLM's traditional school business.

➤ We project a 30% decrease in other income in 2008, mostly reflecting a decline in revenue from collection services and impairment charges related to declines in the fair value of assets in SLM's purchased paper subsidiary. We expect expenses to decrease slightly in 2008 versus the previous year, as cost-cutting efforts are mostly offset by restructuring charges.

➤ Assuming a 36.7% effective tax rate, we forecast operating EPS of $1.20 in 2008 and $1.64 in 2009. SLM reported operating EPS of $1.23 for 2007.

## Investment Rationale/Risk

➤ Our hold recommendation is based on our concerns resulting from SLM's financing issues, offset by a steep decline in SLM's stock price and the potential for further funding support from the government. In July, SLM was able to refinance its $30 billion credit facility, which should provide the company much-needed liquidity. However, SLM has only been able to retire $4 billion of the facility through the end of the third quarter, leaving $26 billion left coming due in February 2009. We are encouraged by the passing of legislation allowing the government to provide more liquidity to the student loan market by purchasing loans from lenders.

➤ Risks to our recommendation and target price include an extended downturn in the credit markets, worse-than-expected credit deterioration, and higher funding costs than expected.

➤ Our 12-month target price of $11 is roughly 6.7X our 2009 operating EPS forecast of $1.64, and a discount to the historical average, reflecting our view of a weaker job market's effect on student loan delinquencies and potential financing concerns.

## Qualitative Risk Assessment

| LOW | MEDIUM | HIGH |
|---|---|---|

Our risk assessment reflects the deteriorating credit quality of student loans, partly offset by SLM's leading position in education finance and its participation in the Federal Family Education Loan Program.

## Quantitative Evaluations

**S&P Quality Ranking** B

| D | C | B- | B | B+ | A- | A | A+ |
|---|---|---|---|---|---|---|---|

**Relative Strength Rank** WEAK

25

LOWEST = 1          HIGHEST = 99

## Revenue/Earnings Data

**Revenue (Million $)**

| | 1Q | 2Q | 3Q | 4Q | Year |
|---|---|---|---|---|---|
| 2008 | 1,963 | 2,331 | 1,697 | -- | -- |
| 2007 | 2,466 | 2,495 | 2,119 | 1,270 | 9,171 |
| 2006 | 1,766 | 2,695 | 2,252 | 2,038 | 8,751 |
| 2005 | 1,285 | 1,506 | 1,715 | 2,012 | 6,518 |
| 2004 | 915.1 | 1,509 | 1,047 | 1,525 | 4,997 |
| 2003 | 1,109 | 1,047 | 1,013 | 955.9 | 4,160 |

**Earnings Per Share ($)**

| | | | | | |
|---|---|---|---|---|---|
| 2008 | -0.28 | 0.50 | -0.40 | E0.23 | E1.20 |
| 2007 | 0.26 | 1.03 | -0.85 | -3.98 | -2.26 |
| 2006 | 0.34 | 1.52 | 0.60 | 0.02 | 2.63 |
| 2005 | 0.49 | 0.66 | 0.95 | 0.96 | 3.05 |
| 2004 | 0.64 | 1.36 | 0.80 | 1.40 | 4.04 |
| 2003 | 0.88 | 0.80 | 0.76 | 0.57 | 3.01 |

Fiscal year ended Dec. 31. Next earnings report expected: Late January. EPS Estimates based on S&P Operating Earnings; historical GAAP earnings are as reported.

## Dividend Data

Dividends were omitted in April 2007.

---

**Please read the Required Disclosures and Analyst Certification on the last page of this report.**

*The McGraw-Hill Companies*

# SLM Corp

**STANDARD &POOR'S**

## Business Summary October 23, 2008

CORPORATE OVERVIEW. SLM Corp., formerly USA Education Inc., is the largest U.S. private source of funding, delivery and service support for higher education loans, primarily through its participation in the Federal Family Education Loan Program (FFELP). The company's main business is to originate, acquire and hold student loans with the net interest income and gains on the sales of student loans in securitization, the primary source of earnings. The company funds its operation through student loan asset-backed securities and unsecured debt securities. SLM was chartered by an Act of Congress in 1972, but in 1996 it was rechartered as a private sector corporation and completed its privatization process in December 2004.

The company is divided into two business segments: Lending and Asset Performance Group (APG). According to the company, the SLM Lending segment manages the largest portfolio of FFELP and Private Education Loans in the student loan industry. As of December 31, 2007, the company served nearly 10 million borrowers, and managed $163.6 billion of student loans, of which 83%

were federally insured. In 2007, 63% of its student loan acquisitions were through its Preferred Channel. Its APG segment provides a wide range of accounts receivable and collections services.

PRIMARY BUSINESS DYNAMICS. There are two competing programs that divide student loans where the ultimate risk lies with the federal government: the FFELP and the Federal Direct Lending program (FDLP). FFELP loans are provided by private sector institutions, such as SLM, and are ultimately guaranteed by the U.S. Department of Education (ED). FDLP loans are funded by taxpayers and provided to borrowers directly by ED. Private Education Loans are originated by financial institutions where the lender assumes the credit risk of the borrower.

## Company Financials Fiscal Year Ended Dec. 31

| Per Share Data ($) | 2007 | 2006 | 2005 | 2004 | 2003 | 2002 | 2001 | 2000 | 1999 | 1998 |
|---|---|---|---|---|---|---|---|---|---|---|
| Tangible Book Value | 5.93 | 5.90 | 5.13 | 4.81 | 4.55 | 3.08 | 3.59 | 2.54 | 1.43 | 1.33 |
| Earnings | -2.26 | 2.63 | 3.05 | 4.04 | 3.01 | 1.64 | 0.76 | 0.92 | 1.02 | 0.98 |
| S&P Core Earnings | -2.24 | 2.62 | 2.98 | 3.95 | 2.75 | 1.40 | 0.53 | NA | NA | NA |
| Dividends | 0.25 | 0.97 | 0.85 | 0.74 | 0.59 | 0.28 | 0.24 | 0.22 | 0.20 | 0.19 |
| Payout Ratio | NM | 37% | 28% | 18% | 20% | 17% | 32% | 24% | 20% | 19% |
| Prices:High | 58.00 | 58.35 | 56.48 | 54.44 | 42.92 | 35.65 | 29.33 | 22.75 | 17.98 | 17.13 |
| Prices:Low | 18.68 | 44.65 | 45.56 | 36.43 | 33.73 | 25.67 | 18.63 | 9.27 | 13.17 | 9.17 |
| P/E Ratio:High | NM | 22 | 19 | 13 | 14 | 22 | 39 | 25 | 18 | 17 |
| P/E Ratio:Low | NM | 17 | 15 | 9 | 11 | 16 | 25 | 10 | 13 | 9 |

| Income Statement Analysis (Million $) | 2007 | 2006 | 2005 | 2004 | 2003 | 2002 | 2001 | 2000 | 1999 | 1998 |
|---|---|---|---|---|---|---|---|---|---|---|
| Interest on:Mortgages | 7,966 | 6,074 | 4,233 | 2,500 | 2,197 | 2,124 | 2,625 | 2,977 | 2,569 | 2,293 |
| Interest on:Investment | 708 | 503 | 277 | 233 | 151 | 87.9 | 373 | 501 | 240 | 295 |
| Interest Expense | 7,086 | 5,123 | 3,059 | 1,434 | 1,022 | 1,203 | 2,124 | 2,837 | 2,115 | 1,925 |
| Guaranty Fees | Nil | Nil | Nil | Nil | Nil | Nil | Nil | Nil | Nil | Nil |
| Loan Loss Provision | 1,015 | 287 | 203 | 111 | 147 | 117 | 66.0 | 32.1 | 34.4 | Nil |
| Administration Expenses | 1,552 | 1,346 | 1,138 | 895 | 808 | 690 | 708 | 586 | 359 | 361 |
| Pretax Income | -482 | 1,995 | 2,117 | 2,557 | 2,183 | 1,223 | 617 | 712 | 752 | 750 |
| Effective Tax Rate | NM | 41.8% | 34.4% | 25.1% | 35.7% | 35.3% | 36.2% | 33.1% | 31.9% | 31.7% |
| Net Income | -896 | 1,157 | 1,382 | 1,913 | 1,404 | 792 | 384 | 465 | 501 | 501 |
| S&P Core Earnings | -923 | 1,119 | 1,324 | 1,853 | 1,276 | 664 | 261 | NA | NA | NA |

| Balance Sheet & Other Financial Data (Million $) | 2007 | 2006 | 2005 | 2004 | 2003 | 2002 | 2001 | 2000 | 1999 | 1998 |
|---|---|---|---|---|---|---|---|---|---|---|
| Mortgages | 125,327 | 97,228 | 83,980 | 66,161 | 51,078 | 43,541 | 42,037 | 38,635 | 34,852 | 29,825 |
| Investment | 6,008 | 5,986 | 4,775 | 3,579 | 5,268 | 4,231 | 5,072 | 5,206 | 5,185 | 3,990 |
| Cash & Equivalent | 7,582 | 2,621 | 2,499 | 3,395 | 1,652 | 758 | 715 | 734 | 590 | 116 |
| Total Assets | 155,565 | 116,136 | 99,339 | 84,094 | 64,611 | 53,175 | 52,874 | 48,792 | 44,025 | 37,210 |
| Short Term Debt | 35.9 | 3.50 | 3,810 | 2,208 | 18,735 | 25,619 | 31,065 | 30,464 | 37,491 | 26,588 |
| Long Term Debt | 111,098 | 104,559 | 88,119 | 75,915 | 23,211 | 22,242 | 17,285 | 14,911 | 4,496 | 8,811 |
| Equity | 3,659 | 3,795 | 3,226 | 2,937 | 3,564 | 1,833 | 1,507 | 1,250 | 676 | 654 |
| % Return on Assets | NM | 1.1 | 1.5 | 2.6 | 2.4 | 1.5 | 0.8 | 1.0 | 1.2 | 1.3 |
| % Return on Equity | NM | 31.9 | 44.1 | 70.4 | 25.8 | 47.4 | 27.8 | 48.2 | 75.1 | 75.5 |
| Equity/Assets Ratio | 28.3 | 30.7 | 29.8 | 27.5 | 10.9 | 3.1 | 2.7 | 2.1 | 1.6 | 1.7 |
| Price Times Book Value:High | 9.8 | 9.9 | 11.0 | 11.3 | 9.4 | 11.6 | 8.2 | 8.9 | 12.6 | 12.9 |
| Price Times Book Value:Low | 3.2 | 7.6 | 8.9 | 7.6 | 7.4 | 8.3 | 5.2 | 3.6 | 9.2 | 6.9 |

Data as orig reptd.; bef. results of disc opers/spec. items. Per share data adj. for stk. divs.; EPS diluted. E-Estimated. NA-Not Available. NM-Not Meaningful. NR-Not Ranked. UR-Under Review.

**Office:** 12061 Bluemont Way, Reston, VA 20190-5684.
**Telephone:** 703-810-3000.
**Website:** http://www.salliemae.com
**Chrmn:** A.P. Terracciano

**Vice Chrmn & CEO:** A.L. Lord
**Vice Chrmn, CFO & Chief Acctg Officer:** J.F. Remondi
**COO:** R.S. Autor
**SVP & Secy:** M.F. Eure

**Investor Contact:** S. McGarry (703-810-7746)
**Board Members:** A. T. Bates, W. M. Diefenderfer, III, D. S. Gilleland, E. A. Goode, R. F. Hunt, A. L. Lord, M. E. Martin, B. Munitz, H. H. Newman, A. Porter, Jr., F. C. Puleo, J. F. Remondi, W. Schoellkopf, S. L. Shapiro, J. T. Strange, A. P. Terracciano, B. L. Williams

**Founded:** 1972
**Domicile:** Delaware
**Employees:** 11,000

*The McGraw-Hill Companies*

# Smith International Inc.

**STANDARD &POOR'S**

| S&P Recommendation | HOLD ★★★ ★ ★ | Price | 12-Mo. Target Price | Investment Style |
|---|---|---|---|---|
| | | $27.12 (as of Nov 14, 2008) | $38.00 | Large-Cap Growth |

**GICS Sector** Energy
**Sub-Industry** Oil & Gas Equipment & Services

**Summary** This company is an international supplier of products and services primarily used in drilling of oil and gas.

## Key Stock Statistics (Source S&P, Vickers, company reports)

| | | | | | | | |
|---|---|---|---|---|---|---|---|
| 52-Wk Range | $88.40– 25.57 | S&P Oper. EPS 2008**E** | 3.88 | Market Capitalization(B) | $5.876 | Beta | 1.05 |
| Trailing 12-Month EPS | $3.60 | S&P Oper. EPS 2009**E** | 4.54 | Yield (%) | 1.77 | S&P 3-Yr. Proj. EPS CAGR(%) | 22 |
| Trailing 12-Month P/E | 7.5 | P/E on S&P Oper. EPS 2008**E** | 7.0 | Dividend Rate/Share | $0.48 | S&P Credit Rating | BBB+ |
| $10K Invested 5 Yrs Ago | $14,276 | Common Shares Outstg. (M) | 216.7 | Institutional Ownership (%) | 85 | | |

## Price Performance

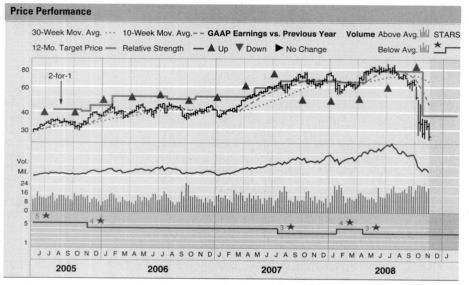

30-Week Mov. Avg. · · · · 10-Week Mov. Avg.- - - **GAAP Earnings vs. Previous Year** Volume Above Avg. STARS
12-Mo. Target Price — Relative Strength — ▲ Up ▼ Down ▶ No Change Below Avg.

Options: ASE, CBOE, P, Ph

Analysis prepared by **Stewart Glickman, CFA** on October 29, 2008, when the stock traded at **$ 29.76**.

## Highlights

➤ SII closed its acquisition of W-H Energy Services late in the third quarter, when quarterly results benefited from 37 days of activity from the acquired businesses. We see higher drilling activity in deepwater fields in the near term and expect SII to benefit, given a strong position in drilling fluids and drill bit technology. Typically, deepwater drilling and completion projects demand more advanced equipment, reflecting the relatively harsh environments found in such projects.

➤ We expect total revenues to increase about 18% in 2009, led by acquisition gains. Organically, we see advances in international regions outpacing domestic growth, and anticipate that a credit crisis-fueled slowdown is most likely to hurt North American land activity, and the shallow U.S. Gulf of Mexico, but expect deepwater Gulf activity to remain solid. Internationally, we see drilling activity accelerating as more newly-built rigs become operational, and the orderbook of deepwater-capable rigs should benefit SII in 2009.

➤ We estimate operating EPS of $3.88 in 2008, rising to $4.54 in 2009.

## Investment Rationale/Risk

➤ On a fundamental basis, we believe SII is well positioned to benefit from ongoing secular trends in oil and gas exploration and production towards deeper, more challenging plays. We also view the pending WHQ acquisition, if approved, as a strategic positive for SII, enabling it to compete in directional drilling, complementing SII's franchise in drill bits.

➤ Risks to our recommendation and target price include political risk in frontier regions; reduced demand for drilling fluids and drill bits; and increased competition from larger companies in the drilling fluids business.

➤ Our DCF model, assuming a weighted average cost of capital of 10.5% and 3% terminal growth, indicates intrinsic value of about $36. On a relative valuation basis, we think the shares should trade slightly below peers, as we project return on invested capital of 17% in 2009, below peers. Assuming a 5.5X multiple on projected 2009 EBITDA and a 9X multiple on estimated 2009 earnings (both below peers), and blending with our DCF model, we derive our 12-month target price of $38.

## Qualitative Risk Assessment

| LOW | MEDIUM | HIGH |
|---|---|---|

Our risk assessment reflects SII's exposure to volatile crude oil and natural gas prices, capital spending decisions made by its oil and gas producing customers, and political risk associated with operating in frontier regions. Offsetting these risks is SII's strong position in drill bits and drilling fluids.

## Quantitative Evaluations

**S&P Quality Ranking** B+

| D | C | B- | B | B+ | A- | A | A+ |
|---|---|---|---|---|---|---|---|

**Relative Strength Rank** WEAK

20

LOWEST = 1 HIGHEST = 99

## Revenue/Earnings Data

**Revenue (Million $)**

| | 1Q | 2Q | 3Q | 4Q | Year |
|---|---|---|---|---|---|
| 2008 | 2,371 | 2,494 | 2,849 | -- | -- |
| 2007 | 2,108 | 2,114 | 2,245 | 2,297 | 8,764 |
| 2006 | 1,682 | 1,738 | 1,914 | 1,999 | 7,334 |
| 2005 | 1,288 | 1,350 | 1,410 | 1,530 | 5,579 |
| 2004 | 1,018 | 1,064 | 1,119 | 1,218 | 4,419 |
| 2003 | 808.8 | 877.7 | 924.8 | 983.5 | 3,595 |

**Earnings Per Share ($)**

| | | | | | |
|---|---|---|---|---|---|
| 2008 | 0.87 | 0.91 | 1.00 | E1.11 | E3.88 |
| 2007 | 0.80 | 0.76 | 0.83 | 0.83 | 3.20 |
| 2006 | 0.53 | 0.59 | 0.66 | 0.71 | 2.49 |
| 2005 | 0.33 | 0.33 | 0.39 | 0.44 | 1.48 |
| 2004 | 0.22 | 0.14 | 0.26 | 0.29 | 0.89 |
| 2003 | 0.11 | 0.15 | 0.18 | 0.19 | 0.62 |

Fiscal year ended Dec. 31. Next earnings report expected: Late January. EPS Estimates based on S&P Operating Earnings; historical GAAP earnings are as reported.

## Dividend Data (Dates: mm/dd Payment Date: mm/dd/yy)

| Amount ($) | Date Decl. | Ex-Div. Date | Stk. of Record | Payment Date |
|---|---|---|---|---|
| 0.100 | 10/17 | 12/12 | 12/14 | 01/14/08 |
| 0.120 | 02/06 | 03/12 | 03/14 | 04/14/08 |
| 0.120 | 04/30 | 06/11 | 06/13 | 07/14/08 |
| 0.120 | 07/17 | 09/10 | 09/12 | 10/14/08 |

Dividends have been paid since 2005. Source: Company reports.

---

**Please read the Required Disclosures and Analyst Certification on the last page of this report.**

*The McGraw-Hill Companies*

# Smith International Inc.

STANDARD
&POOR'S

## Business Summary October 29, 2008

CORPORATE OVERVIEW. Driven by exploration and production activities worldwide, Smith International manufactures and markets technologically advanced products and services to the oil and gas industry. Approximately 55% of total 2007 revenues were derived from equipment sold or services provided to customers outside the United States (versus 54% in 2006). In 2007, top non-U.S. regions included Europe/Africa (24%), Canada (9%), Middle East/Asia (14%), and Latin America (8%). The Oilfield Products and Services segment (76% of 2007 revenues, and 90% of segment operating profits) consists of three businesses: M-I SWACO (50% of 2007 revenues); Smith Technologies (12%); and Smith Services (14%).

M-I SWACO provides drilling and completion fluid systems and services, solids control equipment and waste management services. Drilling fluid products and systems are used to cool and lubricate the bit during drilling, contain formation pressures, remove rock cuttings, and maintain the stability of the wellbore. Engineering services ensure that products are applied to optimize operations.

Smith Technologies is a worldwide leader in the design, manufacture and marketing of drilling bits primarily used in drilling oil and natural gas wells. In addition, Smith Technologies is the leading provider of downhole turbine products and services that enhance the operating performance of drillbits.

Smith Services manufactures and markets products used in the oil and gas industry for drilling, workover, well completion, and well re-entry. Drilling Optimization Solutions provides a broad range of downhole impact tools for drilling applications. Fishing and Remedial Solutions removes obstructions from the wellbore that may arise during drilling, completion or workover activities, and manufactures and markets hole openers and underreamers that create larger hole diameters in certain sections of the wellbore. Casing Exit and Multilateral Solutions manufactures proprietary casing exit tools. Completion Solutions specializes in providing fit-for-purpose liner hangers, liner cementing equipment, isolation packers, retrievable and permanent packers, packer products and multilateral completion equipment.

The Distribution segment (24% of total 2007 revenues, and 10% of total segment operating profits) consists of Wilson, a supply-chain management company that markets pipe, valves, fittings, and mill and safety products.

## Company Financials Fiscal Year Ended Dec. 31

| Per Share Data ($) | 2007 | 2006 | 2005 | 2004 | 2003 | 2002 | 2001 | 2000 | 1999 | 1998 |
|---|---|---|---|---|---|---|---|---|---|---|
| Tangible Book Value | 9.23 | 4.89 | 3.40 | 3.06 | 2.72 | 2.23 | 1.90 | 1.83 | 1.89 | 1.79 |
| Cash Flow | 4.00 | 3.23 | 2.05 | 1.41 | 1.12 | 0.91 | 1.22 | 0.76 | 0.67 | 0.54 |
| Earnings | 3.20 | 2.49 | 1.48 | 0.89 | 0.62 | 0.47 | 0.76 | 0.36 | 0.29 | 0.18 |
| S&P Core Earnings | 3.20 | 2.49 | 1.41 | 0.94 | 0.57 | 0.42 | 0.72 | NA | NA | NA |
| Dividends | 0.40 | 0.32 | 0.24 | Nil | Nil | Nil | Nil | Nil | Nil | Nil |
| Payout Ratio | 13% | 13% | 16% | Nil | Nil | Nil | Nil | Nil | Nil | Nil |
| Prices:High | 76.99 | 46.48 | 40.08 | 31.49 | 21.59 | 19.36 | 21.13 | 22.13 | 13.02 | 16.13 |
| Prices:Low | 36.13 | 34.87 | 25.80 | 20.03 | 14.75 | 11.60 | 8.08 | 11.25 | 5.89 | 4.31 |
| P/E Ratio:High | 24 | 19 | 27 | 35 | 35 | 42 | 28 | 61 | 45 | 92 |
| P/E Ratio:Low | 11 | 14 | 17 | 23 | 24 | 25 | 11 | 31 | 20 | 25 |

| Income Statement Analysis (Million $) | 2007 | 2006 | 2005 | 2004 | 2003 | 2002 | 2001 | 2000 | 1999 | 1998 |
|---|---|---|---|---|---|---|---|---|---|---|
| Revenue | 8,764 | 7,334 | 5,579 | 4,419 | 3,595 | 3,170 | 3,551 | 2,761 | 1,806 | 2,119 |
| Operating Income | 1,531 | 1,230 | 788 | 545 | 430 | 345 | 464 | 280 | 310 | 278 |
| Depreciation, Depletion and Amortization | 162 | 150 | 118 | 106 | 102 | 89.3 | 92.9 | 80.7 | 76.0 | 70.3 |
| Interest Expense | 70.0 | 63.0 | 44.4 | 38.8 | 41.0 | 40.9 | 45.4 | 36.8 | 40.8 | 46.0 |
| Pretax Income | 1,304 | 1,020 | 628 | 401 | 290 | 218 | 329 | 164 | 111 | 81.9 |
| Effective Tax Rate | 31.3% | 32.0% | 32.3% | 32.3% | 32.2% | 30.6% | 32.3% | 33.5% | 43.2% | 32.1% |
| Net Income | 647 | 502 | 302 | 182 | 125 | 93.2 | 152 | 72.8 | 56.7 | 34.1 |
| S&P Core Earnings | 646 | 503 | 290 | 192 | 115 | 84.6 | 145 | NA | NA | NA |

| Balance Sheet & Other Financial Data (Million $) | 2007 | 2006 | 2005 | 2004 | 2003 | 2002 | 2001 | 2000 | 1999 | 1998 |
|---|---|---|---|---|---|---|---|---|---|---|
| Cash | 158 | 80.4 | 62.5 | 53.6 | 51.3 | 86.8 | 44.7 | 36.5 | 24.1 | 22.7 |
| Current Assets | 3,728 | 3,271 | 2,437 | 2,020 | 1,680 | 1,427 | 1,523 | 1,310 | 1,055 | 997 |
| Total Assets | 6,062 | 5,335 | 4,060 | 3,507 | 3,097 | 2,750 | 2,736 | 2,295 | 1,895 | 1,759 |
| Current Liabilities | 1,173 | 1,379 | 933 | 887 | 631 | 595 | 666 | 643 | 457 | 693 |
| Long Term Debt | 846 | 801 | 611 | 388 | 489 | 442 | 539 | 375 | 347 | 369 |
| Common Equity | 2,595 | 1,987 | 1,365 | 1,401 | 1,236 | 1,064 | 949 | 817 | 720 | 634 |
| Total Capital | 4,732 | 3,710 | 2,827 | 2,537 | 2,392 | 2,087 | 2,019 | 1,615 | 1,422 | 1,012 |
| Capital Expenditures | 356 | 308 | 178 | 111 | 98.9 | 97.1 | 128 | 94.6 | 57.2 | 119 |
| Cash Flow | 809 | 652 | 420 | 289 | 226 | 183 | 245 | 153 | 133 | 104 |
| Current Ratio | 3.2 | 2.4 | 2.6 | 2.3 | 2.7 | 2.4 | 2.3 | 2.0 | 2.3 | 1.4 |
| % Long Term Debt of Capitalization | 17.9 | 21.6 | 21.6 | 15.3 | 20.4 | 21.2 | 26.7 | 23.2 | 24.4 | 36.4 |
| % Return on Assets | 11.4 | 10.7 | 8.0 | 5.5 | 4.3 | 3.4 | 6.0 | 3.5 | 3.1 | 2.2 |
| % Return on Equity | 28.2 | 28.2 | 21.9 | 13.8 | 10.8 | 9.3 | 17.2 | 9.5 | 8.4 | 6.2 |

Data as orig reptd.; bef. results of disc opers/spec. items. Per share data adj. for stk. divs.; EPS diluted. E-Estimated. NA-Not Available. NM-Not Meaningful. NR-Not Ranked. UR-Under Review.

**Office:** 16740 E Hardy Rd, Houston, TX 77032-1125.
**Telephone:** 281-443-3370.
**Website:** http://www.smith.com
**Chrmn, Pres, CEO & COO:** D.L. Rock

**SVP, CFO, Chief Acctg Officer & Treas:** M.K. Dorman
**SVP, Secy & General Counsel:** R.E. Chandler, Jr.
**Cntlr:** J.S. Rinando, III

**Board Members:** L. Carroll, D. A. Fraser, J. R. Gibbs, R. Kelley, L. R. Machado, D. L. Rock, J. Yearwood

**Founded:** 1937
**Domicile:** Delaware
**Employees:** 19,865

The McGraw-Hill Companies

# J.M. Smucker Co (The)

STANDARD &POOR'S

| S&P Recommendation | **STRONG BUY** ★★★★★ | Price<br>$39.00 (as of Nov 14, 2008) | 12-Mo. Target Price<br>$58.00 | Investment Style<br>Large-Cap Blend |
|---|---|---|---|---|

**GICS Sector** Consumer Staples
**Sub-Industry** Packaged Foods & Meats

**Summary** This company's products include fruit spreads, peanut butter, shortening and oils, ice cream toppings, health and natural foods, and beverages.

## Key Stock Statistics (Source S&P, Vickers, company reports)

| | | | | | | | |
|---|---|---|---|---|---|---|---|
| 52-Wk Range | $56.69– 37.51 | S&P Oper. EPS 2009**E** | 3.47 | Market Capitalization(B) | $2.138 | Beta | 0.79 |
| Trailing 12-Month EPS | $3.07 | S&P Oper. EPS 2010**E** | NA | Yield (%) | 3.28 | S&P 3-Yr. Proj. EPS CAGR(%) | 7 |
| Trailing 12-Month P/E | 12.7 | P/E on S&P Oper. EPS 2009**E** | 11.2 | Dividend Rate/Share | $1.28 | S&P Credit Rating | NA |
| $10K Invested 5 Yrs Ago | $10,601 | Common Shares Outstg. (M) | 54.8 | Institutional Ownership (%) | 54 | | |

## Price Performance

- 30-Week Mov. Avg. · · ·
- 10-Week Mov. Avg. - - -
- **GAAP Earnings vs. Previous Year**
- Volume Above Avg. STARS
- 12-Mo. Target Price —
- Relative Strength · · ·
- ▲ Up  ▼ Down  ▶ No Change
- Below Avg.  ★

Options: ASE, CBOE, Ph

Analysis prepared by **Tom Graves, CFA** on October 27, 2008, when the stock traded at **$ 43.50**.

## Highlights

- In June 2008, SJM signed a definitive agreement to acquire Procter & Gamble's (PG: strong buy, $59) Folgers coffee business. SJM plans to pay a one-time special dividend of $5 a share to SJM shareholders, after which PG shareholders would receive about 63 million SJM shares (about 53.5% of expected outstanding shares) in exchange for the Folgers business. Subject to approvals, we look for the Folgers acquisition to occur in early November 2008.

- On a pro forma basis, we look for the Folgers transaction to create a company with annual sales of about $4.7 billion. We expect the transaction to result in one-time costs of about $100 million between now and the end of 2010, but to enable annual synergy benefits of more than $80 million.

- Before special items, for SJM as currently constituted, we estimate FY 09 (Apr.) EPS of $3.47, compared to $3.15 in FY 08, which excludes some special items but includes $0.05 related to an insurance settlement. In FY 10, assuming completion of the Folgers acquisition and before special charges, we look for pro forma EPS of $3.64.

## Investment Rationale/Risk

- We have a generally favorable view of SJM's plan to acquire the Folgers coffee business, which should add diversification and economies of scale to SJM. From its existing business, we anticipate that SJM will face commodity cost pressure. However, we expect at least some of this to be offset by price increases and cost management. We look for sales to benefit from the introduction of new or reformulated products, including such items as Crisco olive oil, Jif-branded snack nuts, and reduced sugar products.

- Risks to our recommendation and target price include competitive pressures in SJM's businesses, commodity cost inflation, consumer acceptance of new product introductions, and the company's ability to fully integrate and realize expected cost savings from acquisitions.

- Our 12-month target price of $58 reflects a target P/E (based on estimated pro forma CY 2009 EPS for SJM) that is at a moderate discount to what we expect from a group of other packaged food stocks. Excluding the expected special dividend to stockholders of record on September 30, 2008, SJM shares recently had an indicated dividend yield of about 2.8%.

## Qualitative Risk Assessment

| LOW | MEDIUM | HIGH |
|---|---|---|

Our risk assessment reflects the relative stability of the company's end markets, our view of its strong balance sheet, and an S&P Quality Ranking of A, which reflects historical stability of earnings and dividends.

## Quantitative Evaluations

**S&P Quality Ranking**  A+

| D | C | B- | B | B+ | A- | A | **A+** |
|---|---|---|---|---|---|---|---|

**Relative Strength Rank**  MODERATE

60

LOWEST = 1    HIGHEST = 99

## Revenue/Earnings Data

**Revenue (Million $)**

| | 1Q | 2Q | 3Q | 4Q | Year |
|---|---|---|---|---|---|
| 2009 | 663.7 | -- | -- | -- | -- |
| 2008 | 561.5 | 707.9 | 665.4 | 590.0 | 2,525 |
| 2007 | 526.5 | 605.0 | 523.1 | 493.5 | 2,148 |
| 2006 | 510.3 | 606.3 | 536.5 | 501.7 | 2,155 |
| 2005 | 415.8 | 588.9 | 550.2 | 491.5 | 2,044 |
| 2004 | 350.3 | 374.2 | 355.3 | 325.4 | 1,417 |

**Earnings Per Share ($)**

| | 1Q | 2Q | 3Q | 4Q | Year |
|---|---|---|---|---|---|
| 2009 | 0.77 | E0.98 | E0.84 | E0.89 | E3.47 |
| 2008 | 0.77 | 0.87 | 0.75 | 0.67 | 3.00 |
| 2007 | 0.50 | 0.80 | 0.71 | 0.75 | 2.76 |
| 2006 | 0.51 | 0.79 | 0.54 | 0.62 | 2.45 |
| 2005 | 0.50 | 0.69 | 0.60 | 0.45 | 2.26 |
| 2004 | 0.51 | 0.64 | 0.65 | 0.44 | 2.21 |

Fiscal year ended Apr. 30. Next earnings report expected: Mid November. EPS Estimates based on S&P Operating Earnings; historical GAAP earnings are as reported.

## Dividend Data (Dates: mm/dd Payment Date: mm/dd/yy)

| Amount ($) | Date Decl. | Ex-Div. Date | Stk. of Record | Payment Date |
|---|---|---|---|---|
| 0.320 | 07/24 | 08/13 | 08/15 | 09/02/08 |
| 5.0 Spl. | 09/15 | 09/26 | 09/30 | 10/31/08 |
| 0.320 | 10/21 | 11/17 | 11/19 | 12/08/08 |

Dividends have been paid since 1949. Source: Company reports.

---

**Please read the Required Disclosures and Analyst Certification on the last page of this report.**

# J.M. Smucker Co (The)

STANDARD
&POOR'S

## Business Summary October 27, 2008

CORPORATE PROFILE. From its origins in 1897, when Jerome M. Smucker first pressed cider at a mill that he opened in that year, the J. M. Smucker Co. has become a leading U.S. producer of fruit spread products, health and natural foods, beverages, ice cream toppings, and natural peanut butter.

In June 2008, SJM signed a definitive agreement to acquire Procter & Gamble's (PG: strong buy, $59) Folgers coffee business. SJM plans to pay a one-time special dividend of $5 a share to SJM shareholders, after which PG shareholders would receive about 63 million SJM shares (about 53.5% of expected outstanding shares) in exchange for the Folgers business. Subject to approvals, we look for the Folgers acquistion to close in early November 2008.

SJM has two reported segments: U.S. retail market and special markets. The U.S. retail market segment includes the consumer foods and oils businesses and represented 74% of sales and 78% of segment operating profits in FY 08 (Apr.). The special markets segment (26% of sales, 22% of segment operating profit) includes foodservice, international, industrial and beverage business-es.

Principal product categories include peanut butter (19% of sales in FY 08), shortening and oils (14%), fruit spreads (13%), baking mixes and frostings (10%), canned milk (10%), flour and baking ingredients (8%), portion control (5%), juices and beverages (5%), Uncrustables frozen sandwiches (5%), toppings and syrups (4%), pickles and condiments (3%), and other (4%).

Trademarks utilized by SJM include Smucker's, Jif, Crisco, Eagle Brand, Mary Ellen, Dutch Girl, Martha White, LaPina, White Lily, Hungry Jack, Uncrustables, Simply Jif, Golden Temple, Softasilk, Dickinson's, Plate Scrapers, Bick's, Five Roses, Robin Hood, Carnation, Europe's Best, and R. W. Knudsen Family. Some trademarks utilized by SJM are used under license.

## Company Financials Fiscal Year Ended Apr. 30

| Per Share Data ($) | 2008 | 2007 | 2006 | 2005 | 2004 | 2003 | 2002 | 2001 | 2000 | 1999 |
|---|---|---|---|---|---|---|---|---|---|---|
| Tangible Book Value | 0.98 | 5.75 | 5.52 | 4.61 | 7.10 | 5.58 | 9.32 | 8.27 | 9.29 | 9.04 |
| Cash Flow | 4.11 | 3.81 | 3.77 | 3.19 | 3.01 | 2.81 | 2.39 | 2.40 | 1.83 | 2.09 |
| Earnings | 3.00 | 2.76 | 2.45 | 2.26 | 2.21 | 2.02 | 1.24 | 1.23 | 0.92 | 1.29 |
| S&P Core Earnings | 2.55 | 2.70 | 2.30 | 2.16 | 2.20 | 1.89 | 1.10 | 1.19 | NA | NA |
| Dividends | 1.12 | 1.08 | 1.00 | 0.92 | 0.76 | 0.76 | 0.64 | 0.60 | 0.59 | 0.55 |
| Payout Ratio | 37% | 39% | 41% | 41% | 34% | 38% | 52% | 49% | 64% | 43% |
| Calendar Year | 2007 | 2006 | 2005 | 2004 | 2003 | 2002 | 2001 | 2000 | 1999 | 1998 |
| Prices:High | 64.32 | 49.98 | 51.65 | 53.50 | 46.75 | 40.42 | 37.73 | 29.00 | 25.75 | 28.19 |
| Prices:Low | 46.57 | 37.15 | 43.64 | 40.80 | 33.00 | 28.71 | 22.61 | 15.00 | 18.38 | 20.63 |
| P/E Ratio:High | 21 | 18 | 21 | 24 | 21 | 20 | 30 | 24 | 28 | 22 |
| P/E Ratio:Low | 16 | 13 | 18 | 18 | 15 | 14 | 18 | 12 | 20 | 16 |

### Income Statement Analysis (Million $)

| | 2008 | 2007 | 2006 | 2005 | 2004 | 2003 | 2002 | 2001 | 2000 | 1999 |
|---|---|---|---|---|---|---|---|---|---|---|
| Revenue | 2,525 | 2,148 | 2,155 | 2,044 | 1,417 | 1,312 | 687 | 651 | 632 | 602 |
| Operating Income | 354 | 318 | 325 | 526 | 227 | 214 | 88.4 | 83.7 | 81.9 | 82.4 |
| Depreciation | 62.6 | 58.9 | 71.1 | 56.0 | 39.9 | 37.8 | 28.6 | 26.9 | 26.2 | 23.4 |
| Interest Expense | 42.1 | 23.4 | 24.0 | 22.6 | 6.37 | 8.75 | 9.21 | 0.78 | 3.11 | 0.18 |
| Pretax Income | 255 | 241 | 216 | 205 | 179 | 155 | 50.2 | 50.0 | 41.5 | 61.6 |
| Effective Tax Rate | 33.1% | 34.8% | 33.5% | 36.2% | 37.7% | 38.0% | 38.5% | 36.6% | 36.5% | 38.7% |
| Net Income | 170 | 157 | 143 | 130 | 111 | 96.3 | 30.9 | 31.7 | 26.4 | 37.8 |
| S&P Core Earnings | 144 | 154 | 134 | 126 | 111 | 90.5 | 25.9 | 28.9 | NA | NA |

### Balance Sheet & Other Financial Data (Million $)

| | 2008 | 2007 | 2006 | 2005 | 2004 | 2003 | 2002 | 2001 | 2000 | 1999 |
|---|---|---|---|---|---|---|---|---|---|---|
| Cash | 184 | 200 | 121 | 75.8 | 163 | 181 | 91.9 | 51.1 | 33.1 | 8.68 |
| Current Assets | 776 | 639 | 571 | 556 | 425 | 467 | 280 | 229 | 229 | 186 |
| Total Assets | 3,130 | 2,694 | 2,650 | 2,636 | 1,684 | 1,615 | 525 | 470 | 475 | 434 |
| Current Liabilities | 239 | 236 | 235 | 308 | 175 | 167 | 80.4 | 67.1 | 68.2 | 87.6 |
| Long Term Debt | 790 | 393 | 429 | 432 | 135 | 135 | 135 | 135 | 75.0 | Nil |
| Common Equity | 1,800 | 1,796 | 1,728 | 1,691 | 1,211 | 1,124 | 280 | 247 | 313 | 324 |
| Total Capital | 2,765 | 2,347 | 2,312 | 2,233 | 1,482 | 1,393 | 419 | 387 | 392 | 331 |
| Capital Expenditures | 76.4 | 57.0 | 63.2 | 87.6 | 100 | 49.5 | 23.5 | 29.4 | 32.2 | 38.7 |
| Cash Flow | 233 | 216 | 214 | 187 | 151 | 134 | 59.4 | 58.6 | 52.6 | 61.2 |
| Current Ratio | 3.2 | 2.7 | 2.4 | 1.8 | 2.4 | 2.8 | 3.5 | 3.4 | 3.4 | 2.1 |
| % Long Term Debt of Capitalization | 28.6 | 16.7 | 18.5 | 19.3 | 9.1 | 9.7 | 32.2 | 34.9 | 19.1 | Nil |
| % Net Income of Revenue | 6.8 | 7.3 | 6.7 | 6.4 | 7.9 | 7.3 | 4.5 | 4.9 | 4.2 | 6.3 |
| % Return on Assets | 5.9 | 5.9 | 5.4 | 6.0 | 6.7 | 9.0 | 6.1 | 6.8 | 5.8 | 9.0 |
| % Return on Equity | 9.5 | 8.9 | 8.4 | 9.0 | 9.5 | 13.7 | 11.6 | 11.3 | 8.3 | 12.1 |

Data as orig reptd.; bef. results of disc opers/spec. items. Per share data adj. for stk. divs.; EPS diluted. E-Estimated. NA-Not Available. NM-Not Meaningful. NR-Not Ranked. UR-Under Review.

**Office:** 1 Strawberry Ln, Orrville, OH 44667-0280.
**Telephone:** 330-682-3000.
**Email:** investor.relations@jmsmucker.com
**Website:** http://www.smuckers.com

**Co-Chrmn, Pres & Co-CEO:** R.K. Smucker
**Co-Chrmn & Co-CEO:** T.P. Smucker
**CFO & Treas:** M.R. Belgya
**Chief Acctg Officer & Cntlr:** J.W. Denman

**Secy & General Counsel:** M.A. Harlan
**Investor Contact:** S. Robinson (330-684-3440)
**Board Members:** V. C. Byrd, R. D. Cowan, K. W. Dindo, P. J. Dolan, N. L. Knight, E. V. Long, G. A. Oatey, R. K. Smucker, T. P. Smucker, W. H. Steinbrink

**Founded:** 1897
**Domicile:** Ohio
**Employees:** 3,250

**STANDARD &POOR'S**

# Snap-On Inc

| S&P Recommendation **BUY** ★★★★☆ | Price $32.33 (as of Nov 14, 2008) | 12-Mo. Target Price $55.00 | Investment Style Large-Cap Value |
|---|---|---|---|

**GICS Sector** Consumer Discretionary
**Sub-Industry** Household Appliances

**Summary** This company is the largest manufacturer and distributor of hand tools, storage units and diagnostic equipment for professional mechanics.

## Key Stock Statistics (Source S&P, Vickers, company reports)

| | | | | | | | |
|---|---|---|---|---|---|---|---|
| 52-Wk Range | $62.21–29.82 | S&P Oper. EPS 2008**E** | 4.05 | Market Capitalization(B) | $1.857 | Beta | 1.32 |
| Trailing 12-Month EPS | $4.05 | S&P Oper. EPS 2009**E** | 4.45 | Yield (%) | 3.71 | S&P 3-Yr. Proj. EPS CAGR(%) | 5 |
| Trailing 12-Month P/E | 8.0 | P/E on S&P Oper. EPS 2008**E** | 8.0 | Dividend Rate/Share | $1.20 | S&P Credit Rating | A- |
| $10K Invested 5 Yrs Ago | $12,515 | Common Shares Outstg. (M) | 57.4 | Institutional Ownership (%) | 96 | | |

## Price Performance

- 30-Week Mov. Avg. ····
- 10-Week Mov. Avg. - - -
- **GAAP Earnings vs. Previous Year**
- Volume Above Avg.
- STARS
- 12-Mo. Target Price —
- Relative Strength —
- ▲ Up ▼ Down ► No Change
- Below Avg.

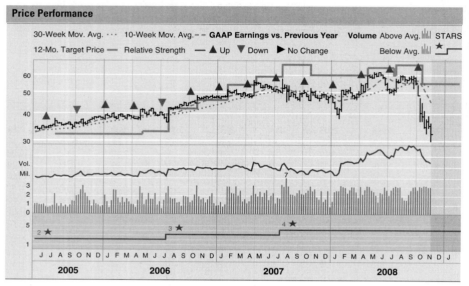

Options: ASE, Ph

Analysis prepared by **Kenneth M. Leon, CPA** on October 27, 2008, when the stock traded at **$ 34.98**.

## Highlights

➤ Following an estimated 2% sales decline in 2008, we expect sales to be flat to down slightly in 2009. SNA continues to focus on improving its dealer business, which we think will ultimately benefit future sales. We foresee 2009 contributions to growth from its Diagnostics and Information Group, flat growth in its Snap-On Tools Group, and eroding demand in its Commercial & Industrial Group.

➤ We think SNA has done a good job of improving its cost structure, particularly while facing external cost pressures. We believe investments to improve the Tools Group franchise system in 2006 contributed to wider gross margins of 44.4% in 2007. Despite economic headwinds, we forecast SNA to achieve 45% to 46% gross margins in 2008 and 2009 with cost controls, respectively.

➤ We expect that investment spending in its major businesses will improve operating efficiency and profitability when major economies recover. SNA's goal of at least low teens operating margins (versus 8% in 2006) was achieved with 11.2% for 2007, and we forecast 13.7% in 2008. We estimate operating EPS of $4.05 in 2008 and $4.45 in 2009.

## Investment Rationale/Risk

➤ We believe SNA is undergoing a transformation to become a leaner organization, with a high priority on bettering customer responsiveness and top-line growth. We expect these ongoing improvements to ultimately restore margins to prior levels when economies rebound. We believe the company's diversified products and customer base around the globe will smooth some of its exposure to a U.S. and European recession better than its peers.

➤ Risks to our recommendation and target price include weaker-than-expected results in SNA's major markets, failure to successfully introduce new products to the pipeline, an inability to achieve goals for revenue growth or productivity initiatives, and any negative effects from a deeper global recession.

➤ With the stock recently trading at about 9X our 2008 EPS estimate of $4.05, a discount to peers, we view the shares as attractively valued, despite our concerns about an economic downturn for the industry. Our 12-month target price of $55 is based on our historical P/E model, which applies a target P/E of about 12.3X to our 2009 operating EPS forecast.

## Qualitative Risk Assessment

| LOW | MEDIUM | HIGH |
|---|---|---|

Our risk assessment is based on our view of SNA's strong brand equity and healthy balance sheet, offset by intense competition and weaker economies in the U.S. and Europe. We believe an improved global supply chain and cost reduction initiatives may offset rising raw material costs and delivery costs.

## Quantitative Evaluations

**S&P Quality Ranking** B+

| D | C | B- | B | B+ | A- | A | A+ |
|---|---|---|---|---|---|---|---|

**Relative Strength Rank** MODERATE

39

LOWEST = 1    HIGHEST = 99

## Revenue/Earnings Data

**Revenue (Million $)**

| | 1Q | 2Q | 3Q | 4Q | Year |
|---|---|---|---|---|---|
| 2008 | 721.6 | 784.4 | 697.8 | -- | -- |
| 2007 | 709.7 | 711.9 | 680.7 | 742.9 | 2,904 |
| 2006 | 593.5 | 624.4 | 599.5 | 656.0 | 2,522 |
| 2005 | 612.8 | 608.6 | 567.2 | 573.6 | 2,362 |
| 2004 | 616.3 | 612.1 | 568.8 | 610.0 | 2,407 |
| 2003 | 543.1 | 565.2 | 525.6 | 599.3 | 2,233 |

**Earnings Per Share ($)**

| | | | | | |
|---|---|---|---|---|---|
| 2008 | 0.97 | 1.15 | 0.94 | E0.99 | E4.05 |
| 2007 | 0.66 | 0.90 | 0.70 | 0.99 | 3.23 |
| 2006 | 0.37 | 0.20 | 0.48 | 0.64 | 1.69 |
| 2005 | 0.31 | 0.46 | 0.36 | 0.47 | 1.59 |
| 2004 | 0.22 | 0.38 | 0.39 | 0.42 | 1.40 |
| 2003 | 0.37 | 0.38 | 0.30 | 0.30 | 1.35 |

Fiscal year ended Dec. 31. Next earnings report expected: Late January. EPS Estimates based on S&P Operating Earnings; historical GAAP earnings are as reported.

## Dividend Data (Dates: mm/dd Payment Date: mm/dd/yy)

| Amount ($) | Date Decl. | Ex-Div. Date | Stk. of Record | Payment Date |
|---|---|---|---|---|
| 0.300 | 02/13 | 02/21 | 02/25 | 03/10/08 |
| 0.300 | 04/24 | 05/15 | 05/19 | 06/09/08 |
| 0.300 | 08/07 | 08/14 | 08/18 | 09/08/08 |
| 0.300 | 11/06 | 11/13 | 11/17 | 12/08/08 |

Dividends have been paid since 1939. Source: Company reports.

*The McGraw-Hill Companies*

# Snap-On Inc

STANDARD
&POOR'S

## Business Summary October 27, 2008

CORPORATE OVERVIEW. Snap-On Inc. is a major global manufacturer and marketer of high-quality tool, diagnostic, service and equipment solutions for professional tool and equipment users under various brands and trade names. Product lines include a broad range of hand and power tools, tool storage, saws and cutting tools, pruning tools, vehicle service diagnostics equipment, vehicle service equipment, including wheel service, safety testing and collision repair equipment, vehicle service information, business management systems, equipment repair services, and other tool and equipment solutions. SNA's customers include automotive technicians, vehicle service centers, manufacturers, industrial tool and equipment users, and those involved in commercial applications such as construction, electrical and agriculture. SNA services these customers through three primary channels of distribution: the mobile dealer van channel, including the company's technical representatives; company direct sales; and distributors.

SNA has four reportable business segments. The Snap-on Tools Group, formerly the Dealer Group (35% of 2007 sales, 41% of 2006 sales) consists of SNA's business operations serving the worldwide franchised dealer van

channel. The Commercial and Industrial Group (43%, 42%) provides tools, equipment products and equipment repair services to industrial and commercial customers worldwide through direct, distributor and other non-franchised distribution channels. The Diagnostics and Information Group (21%, 16%) provides diagnostic equipment, vehicle service information, business management systems and other solutions for customers in the vehicle service and repair marketplace. Financial Services (1%, 2%) is a relatively new business segment, which was originated in 2004. It consists of Snap-on Credit LLC, a consolidated 50%-owned joint venture between SNA and The CIT Group, and SNA's wholly owned finance subsidiaries in international markets where SNA has dealer operations. In regard to global reach, more than 45% of total sales in the fourth quarter of 2007 were outside the U.S. market with margins widening in most of its operations overseas, in our opinion.

## Company Financials Fiscal Year Ended Dec. 31

| Per Share Data ($) | 2007 | 2006 | 2005 | 2004 | 2003 | 2002 | 2001 | 2000 | 1999 | 1998 |
|---|---|---|---|---|---|---|---|---|---|---|
| Tangible Book Value | 3.94 | 0.72 | 8.17 | 9.67 | 8.29 | 6.27 | 6.01 | 6.53 | 6.69 | 9.60 |
| Cash Flow | 4.52 | 2.57 | 2.48 | 2.45 | 2.38 | 2.65 | 1.54 | 3.23 | 3.10 | 0.68 |
| Earnings | 3.23 | 1.69 | 1.59 | 1.40 | 1.35 | 1.76 | 0.37 | 2.10 | 2.16 | -0.08 |
| S&P Core Earnings | 3.14 | 2.07 | 1.56 | 1.35 | 1.31 | 0.92 | 0.09 | NA | NA | NA |
| Dividends | 1.11 | 1.08 | 1.00 | 1.00 | 1.00 | 1.00 | 0.97 | 0.96 | 0.94 | 0.90 | 0.86 |
| Payout Ratio | 34% | 64% | 63% | 71% | 74% | 55% | NM | 45% | 42% | NM |
| Prices:High | 57.81 | 48.65 | 38.71 | 34.67 | 32.38 | 35.15 | 34.40 | 32.44 | 37.81 | 46.44 |
| Prices:Low | 44.58 | 36.38 | 30.57 | 27.15 | 22.60 | 20.71 | 21.15 | 20.88 | 26.44 | 25.50 |
| P/E Ratio:High | 18 | 29 | 24 | 25 | 24 | 20 | 93 | 15 | 18 | NM |
| P/E Ratio:Low | 14 | 22 | 19 | 19 | 17 | 12 | 57 | 10 | 12 | NM |

| Income Statement Analysis (Million $) | | | | | | | | | | |
|---|---|---|---|---|---|---|---|---|---|---|
| Revenue | 2,841 | 2,522 | 2,362 | 2,407 | 2,233 | 2,109 | 2,096 | 2,176 | 1,946 | 1,773 |
| Operating Income | 401 | 217 | 220 | 203 | 167 | 217 | 168 | 270 | 228 | 102 |
| Depreciation | 76.0 | 51.9 | 52.2 | 61.0 | 60.3 | 51.7 | 68.0 | 66.2 | 55.4 | 45.0 |
| Interest Expense | 46.0 | 20.6 | 21.7 | 23.0 | 24.4 | 28.7 | 35.5 | 40.7 | 27.4 | 21.3 |
| Pretax Income | 284 | 146 | 148 | 120 | 117 | 161 | 47.6 | 193 | 198 | 10.8 |
| Effective Tax Rate | 32.5% | 31.4% | 37.2% | 32.1% | 32.6% | 36.0% | 54.8% | 36.1% | 35.7% | NM |
| Net Income | 189 | 100 | 92.9 | 81.7 | 78.7 | 103 | 21.5 | 123 | 127 | -4.78 |
| S&P Core Earnings | 184 | 123 | 91.6 | 78.3 | 76.6 | 53.9 | 5.49 | NA | NA | NA |

| Balance Sheet & Other Financial Data (Million $) | | | | | | | | | | |
|---|---|---|---|---|---|---|---|---|---|---|
| Cash | 93.0 | 63.4 | 170 | 150 | 96.1 | 18.4 | 6.70 | 6.10 | 17.6 | 15.0 |
| Current Assets | 1,187 | 1,113 | 1,073 | 1,193 | 1,132 | 1,051 | 1,139 | 1,186 | 1,206 | 1,080 |
| Total Assets | 2,765 | 2,655 | 2,008 | 2,290 | 2,139 | 1,994 | 1,974 | 2,050 | 2,150 | 1,675 |
| Current Liabilities | 639 | 682 | 506 | 674 | 567 | 552 | 549 | 538 | 453 | 458 |
| Long Term Debt | 502 | 506 | 202 | 203 | 303 | 304 | 446 | 473 | 247 | 247 |
| Common Equity | 1,280 | 1,076 | 962 | 1,111 | 1,011 | 830 | 868 | 844 | 825 | 762 |
| Total Capital | 1,873 | 1,671 | 1,239 | 1,390 | 1,348 | 1,168 | 1,339 | 1,342 | 1,099 | 1,018 |
| Capital Expenditures | 62.0 | 50.5 | 40.1 | 38.7 | 29.4 | 45.8 | 53.6 | 57.6 | 35.4 | 46.8 |
| Cash Flow | 265 | 152 | 145 | 143 | 139 | 155 | 89.5 | 189 | 183 | 40.2 |
| Current Ratio | 1.9 | 1.6 | 2.1 | 1.8 | 2.0 | 1.9 | 2.1 | 2.2 | 2.7 | 2.4 |
| % Long Term Debt of Capitalization | 26.8 | 30.3 | 16.3 | 14.6 | 22.5 | 26.0 | 33.3 | 35.3 | 22.4 | 24.2 |
| % Net Income of Revenue | 6.6 | 4.0 | 3.9 | 3.4 | 3.5 | 4.9 | 1.0 | 5.7 | 6.5 | NM |
| % Return on Assets | 6.9 | 4.3 | 4.3 | 3.7 | 3.8 | 5.2 | 1.1 | 5.9 | 6.7 | NM |
| % Return on Equity | 16.0 | 9.8 | 9.0 | 7.7 | 8.5 | 12.9 | 2.4 | 14.7 | 16.0 | NM |

Data as orig reptd.; bef. results of disc opers/spec. items. Per share data adj. for stk. divs.; EPS diluted. E-Estimated. NA-Not Available. NM-Not Meaningful. NR-Not Ranked. UR-Under Review.

**Office:** 2801 80th St, Kenosha, WI 53143-5656.
**Telephone:** 262-656-5200.
**Website:** http://www.snapon.com
**Chrmn:** J.D. Michaels

**Pres & CEO:** N.T. Pinchuk
**Investor Contact:** M.M. Ellen (262-656-6462)
**SVP & CFO:** M.M. Ellen
**Chief Acctg Officer & Cntlr:** C.R. Johnsen

**Board Members:** B. S. Chelberg, K. L. Daniel, R. J. Decyk, J. F. Fiedler, J. P. Holden, N. J. Jones, A. L. Kelly, W. D. Lehman, J. D. Michaels, N. T. Pinchuk, E. H. Rensi, R. F. Teerlink

**Founded:** 1920
**Domicile:** Delaware
**Employees:** 11,600

# Southern Co (The)

STANDARD
&POOR'S

| S&P Recommendation | HOLD ★★★☆☆ | Price | 12-Mo. Target Price | Investment Style |
|---|---|---|---|---|
| | | $35.21 (as of Nov 14, 2008) | $37.00 | Large-Cap Value |

**GICS Sector** Utilities
**Sub-Industry** Electric Utilities

**Summary** This Atlanta-based energy holding company is one of the largest producers of electricity in the U.S.

## Key Stock Statistics (Source S&P, Vickers, company reports)

| | | | | | | | |
|---|---|---|---|---|---|---|---|
| 52-Wk Range | $40.60– 29.82 | S&P Oper. EPS 2008**E** | 2.36 | Market Capitalization(B) | $27.273 | Beta | 0.39 |
| Trailing 12-Month EPS | $2.28 | S&P Oper. EPS 2009**E** | 2.41 | Yield (%) | 4.77 | S&P 3-Yr. Proj. EPS CAGR(%) | 4 |
| Trailing 12-Month P/E | 15.4 | P/E on S&P Oper. EPS 2008**E** | 14.9 | Dividend Rate/Share | $1.68 | S&P Credit Rating | A |
| $10K Invested 5 Yrs Ago | $15,055 | Common Shares Outstg. (M) | 774.6 | Institutional Ownership (%) | 44 | | |

## Price Performance

30-Week Mov. Avg. ···   10-Week Mov. Avg. —   **GAAP Earnings vs. Previous Year**   Volume Above Avg. ▍▍  STARS
12-Mo. Target Price —   Relative Strength —   ▲ Up  ▼ Down  ► No Change   Below Avg. ▍▍  ★

Options: ASE, CBOE, P, Ph

Analysis prepared by **Justin McCann** on October 29, 2008, when the stock traded at **$ 35.56**.

## Highlights

► We expect operating EPS to increase more than 6% in 2008 from 2007 operating EPS of $2.21, which excludes $0.08 from synfuel-related tax credits. These credits expired at the end of 2007. SO is seeing an economic slowdown in its service territory, but it is less severe than in other areas of the country. While customer growth has slowed, EPS in 2008 should benefit from a rate increase at Georgia Power. This should be partially offset by higher interest and operation and maintenance expenses.

► Operating results in the first nine months of 2008 were aided by the recovery of infrastructure and environmental investments. For 2009, we expect EPS to grow about 2% from anticipated results in 2008. For the longer term, however, we expect SO to post average annual EPS growth of 4% to 6%, with the utilities returning to annual customer growth of approximately 1.7% and demand growth of around 2%.

► We expect the company to have total capital expenditures of about $14.4 billion in the 2008 through 2010 period, with $4.4 billion in 2008 (including $1.8 billion for SO's environmental construction program), $5.2 billion in 2009 ($1.5 billion), and $4.8 billion in 2010 ($600 million).

## Investment Rationale/Risk

► Although the shares are down about 7% year-to-date, this is far less than the decline seen in the electric utility sector as a whole. We believe this reflects the relatively milder decline in SO's regional housing market and economy. While the stock underperformed SO's peers in both 2007 and 2006, we believe it will perform in line with peers over the next 12 months. Despite the recent below-peers yield from the dividend, we expect SO's shares to trade at a premium to its peers, reflecting the relative predictability of the company's earnings and dividend stream.

► Risks to our recommendation and target price include a possible economic downturn in the company's service territory, and a significant decline in the average P/E of the electric utility group as a whole.

► We expect future dividends to increase at around a 4% annual rate. With the current dividend payout ratio at 71% of our EPS estimate for 2008, such an increase would fall within SO's targeted payout range of 70% to 75%. We see the shares trading at a premium-to-peers P/E of about 15.4X our EPS estimate for 2009. Our 12-month target price is $37.

## Qualitative Risk Assessment

| LOW | MEDIUM | HIGH |
|---|---|---|

Our risk assessment reflects our view of the company's strong and steady cash flow from the regulated electric utility operations, its solid balance sheet, a healthy economy in most of its service territories, and a generally supportive regulatory environment.

## Quantitative Evaluations

**S&P Quality Ranking**   A-

| D | C | B- | B | B+ | A- | A | A+ |
|---|---|---|---|---|---|---|---|

**Relative Strength Rank**   STRONG

89

LOWEST = 1   HIGHEST = 99

## Revenue/Earnings Data

**Revenue (Million $)**

| | 1Q | 2Q | 3Q | 4Q | Year |
|---|---|---|---|---|---|
| 2008 | 3,683 | 4,215 | 5,426 | -- | -- |
| 2007 | 3,409 | 3,772 | 4,832 | 3,340 | 15,353 |
| 2006 | 3,063 | 3,592 | 4,549 | 3,152 | 14,356 |
| 2005 | 2,864 | 3,144 | 4,378 | 3,287 | 13,554 |
| 2004 | 2,732 | 3,009 | 3,441 | 2,720 | 11,902 |
| 2003 | 2,553 | 2,859 | 3,319 | 2,564 | 11,251 |

**Earnings Per Share ($)**

| | | | | | |
|---|---|---|---|---|---|
| 2008 | 0.47 | 0.55 | 1.01 | E0.25 | E2.36 |
| 2007 | 0.45 | 0.57 | 1.00 | 0.27 | 2.28 |
| 2006 | 0.35 | 0.52 | 0.99 | 0.25 | 2.10 |
| 2005 | 0.43 | 0.52 | 0.97 | 0.21 | 2.14 |
| 2004 | 0.45 | 0.47 | 0.87 | 0.27 | 2.06 |
| 2003 | 0.41 | 0.59 | 0.84 | 0.17 | 2.02 |

Fiscal year ended Dec. 31. Next earnings report expected: Late January. EPS Estimates based on S&P Operating Earnings; historical GAAP earnings are as reported.

## Dividend Data (Dates: mm/dd Payment Date: mm/dd/yy)

| Amount ($) | Date Decl. | Ex-Div. Date | Stk. of Record | Payment Date |
|---|---|---|---|---|
| 0.403 | 01/18 | 01/31 | 02/04 | 03/06/08 |
| 0.420 | 04/21 | 05/01 | 05/05 | 06/06/08 |
| 0.420 | 07/21 | 07/31 | 08/04 | 09/06/08 |
| 0.420 | 10/20 | 10/30 | 11/03 | 12/06/08 |

Dividends have been paid since 1948. Source: Company reports.

# Southern Co (The)

STANDARD
&POOR'S

## Business Summary October 29, 2008

CORPORATE OVERVIEW. The Southern Company is one of the largest producers of electricity in the U.S. Based in Atlanta, GA, this utility holding company has approximately 41,785 megawatts of generating capacity and provides electricity to around 4.3 million customers in the Southeast through the following integrated utilities: Alabama Power, Georgia Power, Gulf Power (located in the northwestern portion of Florida), and Mississippi Power. Savannah Electric & Power was merged into Georgia Power on July 1, 2006.

MARKET PROFILE. Southern Power Company (SPC) was formed by SO in January 2001 to own, manage and finance wholesale generating assets in the Southeast. It serves both the utility units and the wholesale power market. Energy from SPC's assets, which included 6,896 megawatts of generating capacity at the end of 2007, was to be marketed to wholesale customers through the Southern Company Generation and Energy Marketing unit. SPC and the

utility units enter into contracts for power purchases, sales and exchanges among themselves, as well as with other utilities in the Southeast. Although Southern Power is not subject to the state regulation that the utilities are, it is subject to regulation by the Federal Energy Regulatory Commission.

SO is also the parent company for SouthernLINC Wireless, which provides digital, wireless communications services to SO's four utility units, as well as to non-affiliates within the Southeast. It also provides wholesale fiber optic solutions to telecommunication providers in the Southeast.

## Company Financials Fiscal Year Ended Dec. 31

| Per Share Data ($) | 2007 | 2006 | 2005 | 2004 | 2003 | 2002 | 2001 | 2000 | 1999 | 1998 |
|---|---|---|---|---|---|---|---|---|---|---|
| Tangible Book Value | 16.23 | 15.00 | 14.19 | 13.65 | 12.92 | 11.56 | 10.87 | 15.12 | 6.14 | 8.77 |
| Earnings | 2.28 | 2.10 | 2.14 | 2.06 | 2.02 | 1.85 | 1.61 | 1.52 | 1.86 | 1.40 |
| S&P Core Earnings | 2.26 | 2.06 | 2.04 | 1.93 | 1.85 | 1.35 | 1.12 | NA | NA | NA |
| Dividends | 1.60 | 1.54 | 1.48 | 1.77 | 1.39 | 1.36 | 1.34 | 1.34 | 1.34 | 1.34 |
| Payout Ratio | 70% | 72% | 69% | 86% | 69% | 74% | 83% | 88% | 72% | 96% |
| Prices:High | 39.35 | 37.40 | 36.47 | 33.96 | 32.00 | 31.14 | 35.72 | 35.00 | 29.63 | 31.56 |
| Prices:Low | 33.16 | 30.48 | 31.14 | 27.44 | 27.00 | 23.22 | 20.89 | 20.38 | 22.06 | 23.94 |
| P/E Ratio:High | 17 | 18 | 17 | 16 | 16 | 17 | 22 | 23 | 16 | 23 |
| P/E Ratio:Low | 15 | 14 | 15 | 13 | 13 | 13 | 13 | 13 | 12 | 17 |

| Income Statement Analysis (Million $) | 2007 | 2006 | 2005 | 2004 | 2003 | 2002 | 2001 | 2000 | 1999 | 1998 |
|---|---|---|---|---|---|---|---|---|---|---|
| Revenue | 15,353 | 14,356 | 13,554 | 11,902 | 11,251 | 10,549 | 10,155 | 10,066 | 11,585 | 11,403 |
| Depreciation | 1,245 | 1,200 | 1,176 | 955 | 1,027 | 1,047 | 1,173 | 1,171 | 1,307 | 1,539 |
| Maintenance | 1,175 | 1,096 | 1,116 | 1,027 | 937 | 961 | 909 | 852 | 945 | 887 |
| Fixed Charges Coverage | 3.73 | 3.73 | 3.90 | 4.11 | 4.21 | 3.80 | 3.25 | 2.87 | 2.71 | 2.63 |
| Construction Credits | 106 | 50.0 | 51.0 | 47.0 | 25.0 | 22.0 | NA | NA | NA | NA |
| Effective Tax Rate | 31.9% | 33.2% | 27.2% | 27.7% | 29.3% | 28.6% | 33.3% | 37.2% | 33.2% | 38.8% |
| Net Income | 1,734 | 1,574 | 1,591 | 1,532 | 1,474 | 1,318 | 1,119 | 994 | 1,276 | 977 |
| S&P Core Earnings | 1,720 | 1,551 | 1,532 | 1,436 | 1,351 | 964 | 776 | NA | NA | NA |

| Balance Sheet & Other Financial Data (Million $) | 2007 | 2006 | 2005 | 2004 | 2003 | 2002 | 2001 | 2000 | 1999 | 1998 |
|---|---|---|---|---|---|---|---|---|---|---|
| Gross Property | 53,094 | 50,167 | 47,580 | 45,585 | 43,722 | 41,764 | 38,104 | 35,972 | 38,620 | 37,363 |
| Capital Expenditures | 3,545 | 2,994 | 2,370 | 2,110 | 2,002 | 2,717 | 2,617 | 2,225 | 2,560 | 2,005 |
| Net Property | 35,681 | 33,585 | 31,853 | 30,634 | 29,418 | 26,315 | 23,084 | 21,622 | 24,544 | 24,124 |
| Capitalization:Long Term Debt | 15,223 | 13,247 | 13,442 | 13,010 | 10,587 | 8,956 | 10,941 | 10,457 | 14,443 | 13,020 |
| Capitalization:% Long Term Debt | 55.1 | 53.8 | 55.7 | 55.9 | 52.3 | 50.7 | 57.8 | 49.4 | 60.8 | 57.1 |
| Capitalization:Preferred | Nil | Nil | Nil | Nil | Nil | Nil | Nil | Nil | Nil | Nil |
| Capitalization:% Preferred | Nil | Nil | Nil | Nil | Nil | Nil | Nil | Nil | Nil | Nil |
| Capitalization:Common | 12,385 | 11,371 | 10,689 | 10,278 | 9,648 | 8,710 | 7,984 | 10,690 | 9,296 | 9,797 |
| Capitalization:% Common | 44.9 | 46.2 | 44.3 | 44.1 | 47.7 | 49.3 | 42.2 | 50.6 | 39.2 | 42.9 |
| Total Capital | 33,447 | 31,110 | 30,394 | 29,077 | 25,809 | 22,937 | 24,147 | 26,436 | 29,662 | 24,790 |
| % Operating Ratio | 83.8 | 83.0 | 82.5 | 81.2 | 79.7 | 80.5 | 81.9 | 82.0 | 81.7 | 82.6 |
| % Earned on Net Property | 9.6 | 9.9 | 9.5 | 9.4 | 10.0 | 10.1 | 10.7 | 11.4 | 8.5 | 7.3 |
| % Return on Revenue | 11.3 | 11.0 | 11.7 | 12.9 | 13.1 | 12.5 | 11.0 | 9.9 | 11.0 | 8.6 |
| % Return on Invested Capital | 8.3 | 8.0 | 8.0 | 7.9 | 8.9 | 8.5 | 7.4 | 7.3 | 9.6 | 13.8 |
| % Return on Common Equity | 14.6 | 14.3 | 15.2 | 15.4 | 16.1 | 15.8 | 12.0 | 10.0 | 13.4 | 10.0 |

Data as orig reptd.; bef. results of disc opers/spec. items. Per share data adj. for stk. divs.; EPS diluted. E-Estimated. NA-Not Available. NM-Not Meaningful. NR-Not Ranked. UR-Under Review.

**Office:** 30 Ivan Allen Jr Blvd NW, Atlanta, GA 30308-3003.
**Telephone:** 404-506-5000.
**Email:** investors@southerncompany.com
**Website:** http://www.southernco.com

**Chrmn, Pres & CEO:** D.M. Ratcliffe
**COO & EVP:** T. Fanning
**EVP & CFO:** W.P. Bowers
**EVP, Secy & General Counsel:** G.E. Holland, Jr.

**Chief Acctg Officer & Cntlr:** W.R. Hinson
**Investor Contact:** G. Kundert (404-506-5135)
**Board Members:** J. P. Baranco, F. S. Blake, J. A. Boscia, T. F. Chapman, H. W. Habermeyer, Jr., W. A. Hood, Jr., D. M. James, G. J. Pe', J. N. Purcell, D. M. Ratcliffe, W. G. Smith, Jr.

**Founded:** 1945
**Domicile:** Delaware
**Employees:** 26,742

The McGraw-Hill Companies

# Southwestern Energy Co

**STANDARD &POOR'S**

| S&P Recommendation | SELL ★★☆☆☆ | Price $30.26 (as of Nov 14, 2008) | 12-Mo. Target Price $26.00 | Investment Style Large-Cap Growth |
|---|---|---|---|---|

**GICS Sector** Energy
**Sub-Industry** Oil & Gas Exploration & Production

**Summary** SWN is engaged in natural gas and crude oil exploration and production in the Arkoma Basin, East Texas, the Permian Basin, and the onshore Gulf Coast. It also has natural gas gathering and marketing activities located in core market areas.

## Key Stock Statistics (Source S&P, Vickers, company reports)

| | | | | | | | | |
|---|---|---|---|---|---|---|---|---|
| 52-Wk Range | $52.69– 19.05 | S&P Oper. EPS 2008E | 1.68 | Market Capitalization(B) | $10.389 | Beta | 1.44 |
| Trailing 12-Month EPS | $1.54 | S&P Oper. EPS 2009E | 1.80 | Yield (%) | Nil | S&P 3-Yr. Proj. EPS CAGR(%) | 49 |
| Trailing 12-Month P/E | 19.7 | P/E on S&P Oper. EPS 2008E | 18.0 | Dividend Rate/Share | Nil | S&P Credit Rating | BB+ |
| $10K Invested 5 Yrs Ago | $123,636 | Common Shares Outstg. (M) | 343.3 | Institutional Ownership (%) | 89 | | |

## Price Performance

30-Week Mov. Avg. ···· 10-Week Mov. Avg. - - - GAAP Earnings vs. Previous Year  Volume Above Avg. ▌▌▌ STARS
12-Mo. Target Price — Relative Strength — ▲ Up ▼ Down ► No Change  Below Avg. ▌▌▌ ★

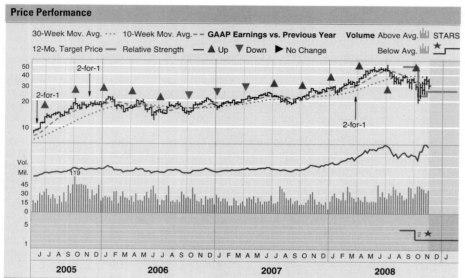

Options: ASE, CBOE, Ph

Analysis prepared by **Michael Kay** on November 12, 2008, when the stock traded at **$ 30.07.**

### Highlights

➤ Production of 137 Bcfe so far in 2008 is up 74% from a year earlier, reflecting 600 MMcfe/day from the Fayetteville Shale, up from about 260 MMcfe/d. SWN sees growth in the James Lime play in East Texas and at its Arkoma Basin properties. In 2008, SWN sold Fayetteville Shale assets for $518.3 million, properties in the Gulf Coast and Permian Basin for $250 million, and Arkansas Western Gas Co. (AWG) for $230 million. Proceeds from sales should exceed $1 billion and no more sales are planned.

➤ SWN is a low-cost producer, in our view, with average finding and development costs of $2.26 per Mcfe between 2004 and 2007. Lease operating expense (LOE) of $0.73 per Mcfe was up 11% in 2007, well below average, and is up 19% thus far in 2008, on higher service costs.

➤ On estimated production growth of 68% in 2008 and 23% in 2009, we see EBITDA rising 106% in 2008, helped by higher prices, and 14% in 2009, despite lower prices. We see 2008 EPS of $1.68, up from $0.65 in 2007, and rising to $1.80 in 2009. SWN's E&P exploration and development budget for 2008 stands at $1.7 billion, up 14%.

### Investment Rationale/Risk

➤ SWN plans to spend $1.3 billion in the Fayetteville Shale in 2008, 70% of its total budget, providing further production and reserve growth visibility. We maintain a positive view on SWN's growth prospects at Fayetteville and its low-cost operations and view SWN as well positioned to boost earnings and cash flow in coming years. However, we expect SWN to underperform peers as the shares trade above our proven reserve NAV assumption and we see markets discounting unbooked potential.

➤ Risks to our recommendation and target price include a sustained climb in oil and gas prices and an improvement in global economic conditions resulting in higher energy demand.

➤ A drop in oil and gas prices has caused a similar decline in exploration and production shares. Given weakening economic forecasts, we see markets discounting most probable and possible reserve estimates, in our view, and we now value companies on our proven reserve NAV estimates. We blend our proven NAV estimate of $26 with a target of 7X our 2009 EBITDA estimate, above peers on impressive growth rates, for a 12-month target price of $26.

## Qualitative Risk Assessment

| LOW | MEDIUM | HIGH |
|---|---|---|

Our risk assessment reflects SWN's operations in a capital-intensive industry that is competitive and cyclical and derives value from producing a commodity whose price is very volatile.

## Quantitative Evaluations

**S&P Quality Ranking**  B

| D | C | B- | B | B+ | A- | A | A+ |
|---|---|---|---|---|---|---|---|

**Relative Strength Rank**  STRONG

79

LOWEST = 1        HIGHEST = 99

## Revenue/Earnings Data

**Revenue (Million $)**

| | 1Q | 2Q | 3Q | 4Q | Year |
|---|---|---|---|---|---|
| 2008 | 524.1 | 604.5 | 683.0 | -- | -- |
| 2007 | 284.7 | 270.1 | 297.6 | 402.8 | 1,255 |
| 2006 | 226.7 | 154.0 | 168.4 | 214.0 | 763.1 |
| 2005 | 161.1 | 132.5 | 162.1 | 220.7 | 676.3 |
| 2004 | 119.8 | 96.43 | 111.4 | 149.5 | 477.1 |
| 2003 | 98.66 | 66.49 | 71.07 | 91.19 | 327.4 |

**Earnings Per Share ($)**

| | | | | | |
|---|---|---|---|---|---|
| 2008 | 0.31 | 0.39 | 0.63 | E0.45 | E1.68 |
| 2007 | 0.15 | 0.14 | 0.15 | 0.21 | 0.64 |
| 2006 | 0.17 | 0.11 | 0.10 | 0.10 | 0.48 |
| 2005 | 0.11 | 0.09 | 0.13 | 0.15 | 0.48 |
| 2004 | 0.08 | 0.07 | 0.09 | 0.11 | 0.35 |
| 2003 | 0.06 | 0.03 | 0.04 | 0.05 | 0.19 |

Fiscal year ended Dec. 31. Next earnings report expected: Late February. EPS Estimates based on S&P Operating Earnings; historical GAAP earnings are as reported.

## Dividend Data (Dates: mm/dd Payment Date: mm/dd/yy)

| Amount ($) | Date Decl. | Ex-Div. Date | Stk. of Record | Payment Date |
|---|---|---|---|---|
| 2-for-1 | 02/28 | 03/26 | 03/14 | 03/25/08 |

Source: Company reports.

---

**Please read the Required Disclosures and Analyst Certification on the last page of this report.**

The *McGraw-Hill* Companies

# Southwestern Energy Co

## Business Summary November 12, 2008

CORPORATE OVERVIEW. Southwestern Energy Company (SWN) is primarily focused on the exploration and production of natural gas. SWN is engaged in natural gas and crude oil exploration and production (E&P) in the Arkoma Basin, East Texas, the Permian Basin, and the onshore Gulf Coast. SWN also has natural gas gathering and marketing activities located in core market areas. With the recent sale of its wholly owned subsidiary, Arkansas Western Gas Company (AWG), for about $230 million, SWN exited the natural gas distribution business and now operates in two segments: Exploration & Production, and Midstream Services.

As of December 31, 2007, SWN had estimated proved reserves of 1.45 Tcfe, of which 96% was natural gas and 64% was proved developed. This compares with estimated proved reserves of 1.03 Tcfe, 95% natural gas and 65% proved developed, at the end of 2006, a 41% increase. We forecast SWN's reserve life to be 12.8 years.

We estimate that SWN replaced 474% of production in 2007 (386% in 2006). As of the end of 2007, SWN's three-year average reserve replacement ratio was 430%. During 2007, SWN invested a total of $1.38 billion in the E&P business and participated in drilling 653 wells, 439 of which were successful, 17 were dry and 197 were in progress at year end. Capital spending focused primarily

on active drilling programs in the Fayetteville Shale (70%), East Texas (15%), and the conventional Arkoma Basin (11%).

CORPORATE STRATEGY. SWN is focused on promoting long-term growth in the net asset value of its business. The key elements of SWN's E&P business strategy are to exploit and develop its existing asset base, control operations and costs, hedge production to stabilize cash flow, and achieve growth through new exploration and development activities.

SWN's primary business is natural gas and oil exploration, development and production, with operations primarily located in Arkansas, Oklahoma and Texas. These operations are conducted through its wholly owned subsidiaries, SEECO, Inc., and Southwestern Energy Production Company (SEPCO). Diamond M, also wholly owned, has interests in properties in the Permian Basin of Texas. DeSoto Drilling, Inc. (DDI), a wholly owned subsidiary of SEPCO, operates drilling rigs in the Fayetteville Shale play and in East Texas.

## Company Financials Fiscal Year Ended Dec. 31

| Per Share Data ($) | 2007 | 2006 | 2005 | 2004 | 2003 | 2002 | 2001 | 2000 | 1999 | 1998 |
|---|---|---|---|---|---|---|---|---|---|---|
| Tangible Book Value | 4.82 | 4.25 | 3.32 | 1.54 | 1.19 | 0.86 | 0.91 | 0.71 | 0.95 | 0.93 |
| Cash Flow | 1.49 | 0.92 | 0.78 | 0.60 | 0.39 | 0.33 | 0.43 | 0.00 | 0.26 | 0.08 |
| Earnings | 0.64 | 0.48 | 0.48 | 0.35 | 0.19 | 0.07 | 0.17 | -0.23 | 0.05 | -0.15 |
| S&P Core Earnings | 0.63 | 0.46 | 0.46 | 0.33 | 0.17 | 0.05 | 0.15 | NA | NA | NA |
| Dividends | Nil | Nil | Nil | Nil | Nil | Nil | Nil | 0.02 | 0.03 | 0.03 |
| Payout Ratio | Nil | Nil | Nil | Nil | Nil | Nil | Nil | NM | 60% | NM |
| Prices:High | 28.50 | 22.14 | 20.90 | 6.93 | 3.19 | 1.91 | 2.04 | 1.30 | 1.38 | 1.62 |
| Prices:Low | 15.57 | 11.83 | 5.51 | 2.42 | 1.36 | 1.19 | 1.10 | 0.68 | 0.65 | 0.69 |
| P/E Ratio:High | 45 | 47 | 44 | 20 | 17 | 28 | 12 | NM | 27 | NM |
| P/E Ratio:Low | 24 | 25 | 12 | 7 | 7 | 17 | 6 | NM | 13 | NM |

| Income Statement Analysis (Million $) | | | | | | | | | | |
|---|---|---|---|---|---|---|---|---|---|---|
| Revenue | 1,255 | 763 | 676 | 477 | 327 | 262 | 345 | 364 | 280 | 266 |
| Operating Income | 969 | 246 | 246 | 182 | 97.3 | 111 | 145 | 112 | 36.1 | -29.0 |
| Depreciation | 294 | 151 | 96.2 | 73.7 | 55.9 | 54.0 | 52.9 | 45.9 | 41.6 | 46.9 |
| Interest Expense | 37.7 | 12.4 | 21.0 | 19.8 | 19.1 | 21.5 | 24.0 | 23.2 | 17.4 | 17.2 |
| Pretax Income | 357 | 262 | 234 | 163 | 78.6 | 23.0 | 57.2 | -74.7 | 16.4 | -50.1 |
| Effective Tax Rate | 38.1% | 38.0% | 36.7% | 36.2% | 35.8% | 35.6% | 38.3% | NM | 39.3% | NM |
| Net Income | 221 | 163 | 148 | 104 | 49.8 | 14.3 | 35.3 | -45.8 | 9.90 | -30.6 |
| S&P Core Earnings | 217 | 157 | 143 | 98.6 | 46.6 | 10.3 | 30.8 | NA | NA | NA |

| Balance Sheet & Other Financial Data (Million $) | | | | | | | | | | |
|---|---|---|---|---|---|---|---|---|---|---|
| Cash | 0.73 | 43.0 | 224 | 1.20 | 1.30 | 1.69 | 3.64 | 2.39 | 1.20 | 1.62 |
| Current Assets | 363 | 324 | 461 | 131 | 100 | 76.1 | 93.2 | 113 | 70.2 | 72.3 |
| Total Assets | 3,623 | 2,379 | 1,869 | 1,146 | 891 | 740 | 743 | 705 | 671 | 648 |
| Current Liabilities | 431 | 379 | 302 | 134 | 95.1 | 74.6 | 71.5 | 240 | 56.3 | 54.8 |
| Long Term Debt | 978 | 136 | 100 | 325 | 279 | 342 | 350 | 225 | 295 | 282 |
| Common Equity | 1,647 | 1,434 | 1,110 | 448 | 342 | 177 | 183 | 141 | 190 | 186 |
| Total Capital | 103 | 1,953 | 1,477 | 989 | 780 | 649 | 668 | 464 | 612 | 589 |
| Capital Expenditures | 1,519 | 851 | 454 | 291 | 167 | 92.1 | 106 | 75.7 | 66.9 | 64.4 |
| Cash Flow | 515 | 314 | 244 | 177 | 106 | 68.3 | 88.2 | 0.07 | 56.6 | 16.3 |
| Current Ratio | 0.8 | 0.9 | 1.5 | 1.0 | 1.1 | 1.0 | 1.3 | 0.5 | 1.3 | 1.3 |
| % Long Term Debt of Capitalization | 31.5 | 6.9 | 6.7 | 32.9 | 35.7 | 52.8 | 52.4 | 48.5 | 48.1 | 47.8 |
| % Net Income of Revenue | 17.6 | 21.3 | 21.8 | 21.7 | 15.2 | 5.5 | 10.2 | NM | 3.5 | NM |
| % Return on Assets | 7.4 | 7.6 | 9.8 | 10.2 | 6.1 | 1.9 | 4.9 | NM | 1.5 | NM |
| % Return on Equity | 14.3 | 12.7 | 18.9 | 26.2 | 19.2 | 7.9 | 21.8 | NM | 5.2 | NM |

Data as orig reptd.; bef. results of disc opers/spec. items. Per share data adj. for stk. divs.; EPS diluted. E-Estimated. NA-Not Available. NM-Not Meaningful. NR-Not Ranked. UR-Under Review.

**Office:** 2350 N Sam Houston Pkwy E Ste 125, Houston , TX 77032-3132.
**Telephone:** 281-618-4700.
**Website:** http://www.swn.com
**Chrmn & CEO:** H.M. Korell

**Pres & COO:** S.L. Mueller
**EVP & CFO:** G.D. Kerley
**EVP, Secy & General Counsel:** M.K. Boling
**Chief Acctg Officer & Cntlr:** S.T. Wilson

**Investor Contact:** B.D. Sylvester (281-618-4897)
**Board Members:** L. E. Epley, Jr., R. L. Howard, H. M. Korell, V. A. Kuuskraa, K. R. Mourton, C. E. Scharlau

**Founded:** 1929
**Domicile:** Delaware
**Employees:** 1,521

# Southwest Airlines Co.

**STANDARD &POOR'S**

| S&P Recommendation | BUY ★★★★☆ | Price $10.16 (as of Nov 14, 2008) | 12-Mo. Target Price $20.00 |
|---|---|---|---|

**GICS Sector** Industrials
**Sub-Industry** Airlines

**Summary** LUV, the sixth largest U.S. airline, offers discounted fares, primarily for short-haul, point-to-point flights.

## Key Stock Statistics (Source S&P, Vickers, company reports)

| | | | | | | | |
|---|---|---|---|---|---|---|---|
| 52-Wk Range | $16.77– 9.57 | S&P Oper. EPS 2008**E** | 0.42 | Market Capitalization(B) | $7.516 | Beta | 0.12 |
| Trailing 12-Month EPS | $0.47 | S&P Oper. EPS 2009**E** | 0.55 | Yield (%) | 0.18 | S&P 3-Yr. Proj. EPS CAGR(%) | 5 |
| Trailing 12-Month P/E | 21.6 | P/E on S&P Oper. EPS 2008**E** | 24.2 | Dividend Rate/Share | $0.02 | S&P Credit Rating | BBB+ |
| $10K Invested 5 Yrs Ago | $5,469 | Common Shares Outstg. (M) | 739.7 | Institutional Ownership (%) | 86 | | |

## Price Performance

30-Week Mov. Avg. ··· 10-Week Mov. Avg. - - GAAP Earnings vs. Previous Year  Volume Above Avg. STARS
12-Mo. Target Price — Relative Strength — ▲ Up ▼ Down ► No Change  Below Avg.

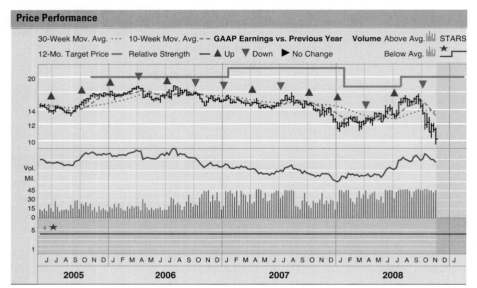

Options: ASE, CBOE, P, Ph

Analysis prepared by **Jim Corridore** on October 21, 2008, when the stock traded at **$ 12.64**.

## Qualitative Risk Assessment

| LOW | MEDIUM | HIGH |
|---|---|---|

Even though Southwest participates in the highly volatile airline industry, we think its conservative balance sheet, with low debt to total capitalization, its track record of 35 consecutive years of profitability, and the industry's leading fuel hedge position offset this risk.

## Quantitative Evaluations

**S&P Quality Ranking**  B+

| D | C | B- | B | B+ | A- | A | A+ |
|---|---|---|---|---|---|---|---|

**Relative Strength Rank**  MODERATE

51

LOWEST = 1                HIGHEST = 99

## Highlights

➤ We look for 2009 revenues to rise about 15%, following our forecast of a 13% rise in 2008. We expect 2009 revenues to benefit from sharply higher average fares as LUV gains traction with its new business fares, sale of assigned boarding slots, and as it continues to roll out a more sophisticated revenue management system. We also expect higher load factors as LUV slows its capacity growth, and as we see some capacity reductions by major airlines in some of its markets. We see 2% capacity growth in 2009 versus 4% growth we project for 2008.

➤ We see fuel costs up 20% in 2009. LUV has 75% of its estimated 2009 fuel needs hedged at an oil price of $73 a barrel, versus 2008's 70% of usage hedged at about $55 a barrel. We think LUV will be able to partly offset these cost pressures with improved productivity, higher revenue yields, and restrained costs in salaries and other operating expenses. We also expect a more profitable mix of passengers on average. We expect the number of employees per aircraft to continue to decline, and continuing a long-term trend.

➤ We estimate 2009 operating EPS of $0.55, versus our 2008 EPS estimate of $0.42.

## Investment Rationale/Risk

➤ We believe LUV is the financially strongest U.S. airline. It has posted 35 consecutive years and 70 consecutive quarters of profitable operations, and we see the quality of those earnings as high. In our view, LUV has ample cash, and its debt to total capitalization is significantly below peer levels. We think these measures warrant a premium valuation to peers and the S&P 500. We believe Southwest has the ability to participate in industry consolidation, should that occur, as the company has the ability to fund potential asset purchases.

➤ Risks to our recommendation and target price include a possible price war with one or more competitors, and substantial weakening of air travel demand. We are concerned about LUV's corporate governance relating to its use of affiliated outsiders on its board of directors' nominating and compensation committees.

➤ Our 12-month target price of $20 is equal to about 36X our 2009 EPS estimate of $0.55, near the higher end of LUV's five-year historical P/E range. We expect the shares to be volatile due to difficult industry conditions and fluctuating oil prices, but less so than peers.

## Revenue/Earnings Data

### Revenue (Million $)

| | 1Q | 2Q | 3Q | 4Q | Year |
|---|---|---|---|---|---|
| 2008 | 2,530 | 2,869 | 2,891 | -- | -- |
| 2007 | 2,198 | 2,583 | 2,588 | 2,492 | 9,861 |
| 2006 | 2,019 | 2,449 | 2,342 | 2,276 | 9,086 |
| 2005 | 1,663 | 1,944 | 1,989 | 1,987 | 7,584 |
| 2004 | 1,484 | 1,716 | 1,674 | 1,633 | 6,530 |
| 2003 | 1,351 | 1,515 | 1,553 | 1,517 | 5,937 |

### Earnings Per Share ($)

| | | | | | |
|---|---|---|---|---|---|
| 2008 | 0.05 | 0.44 | -0.16 | E0.09 | E0.42 |
| 2007 | 0.12 | 0.36 | 0.22 | 0.15 | 0.84 |
| 2006 | 0.07 | 0.40 | 0.06 | 0.07 | 0.61 |
| 2005 | 0.09 | 0.20 | 0.28 | 0.10 | 0.67 |
| 2004 | 0.03 | 0.14 | 0.15 | 0.07 | 0.38 |
| 2003 | 0.03 | 0.30 | 0.13 | 0.08 | 0.54 |

Fiscal year ended Dec. 31. Next earnings report expected: Late January. EPS Estimates based on S&P Operating Earnings; historical GAAP earnings are as reported.

## Dividend Data (Dates: mm/dd Payment Date: mm/dd/yy)

| Amount ($) | Date Decl. | Ex-Div. Date | Stk. of Record | Payment Date |
|---|---|---|---|---|
| 0.005 | 11/15 | 12/04 | 12/06 | 01/03/08 |
| 0.005 | 01/17 | 02/26 | 02/28 | 03/20/08 |
| 0.005 | 05/21 | 06/10 | 06/12 | 06/26/08 |
| 0.005 | 07/17 | 08/26 | 08/28 | 09/18/08 |

Dividends have been paid since 1976. Source: Company reports.

---

**Please read the Required Disclosures and Analyst Certification on the last page of this report.**

The McGraw-Hill Companies

# Southwest Airlines Co.

**STANDARD & POOR'S**

## Business Summary October 21, 2008

CORPORATE OVERVIEW. Southwest Airlines was the largest provider of scheduled domestic passenger air travel in the U.S. in 2007. Overall, the airline ranks as the sixth largest in U.S., based on total revenue passenger miles (RPMs). At December 31, 2007, it served 64 cities in 32 states. LUV specializes in low fare, point-to-point, short-haul, high-frequency service. Although 80% of its work force belongs to unions, the company believes that it has generally enjoyed harmonious labor relations. LUV began service to Philadelphia in May 2004, and started service to Pittsburgh in May 2005 and Ft. Myers, FL, in October 2005, Denver in January 2006, and Washington D.C. (Dulles) in October 2006.

MARKET PROFILE. The U.S. airline industry is a $164 billion market, according to 2006 data (latest available) from the U.S. Department of Transportation. With 2006 revenues of $9.1 billion (which grew 8%, to $9.9 billion, in 2007), LUV comprised around 5.5% of total industry revenues. Southwest also has an approximate 9.3% market share when measured by RPMs, as of August 2007. Southwest was profitable in 2007 for the 35th consecutive year and was profitable throughout the industry downturn that took place after 9/11/01. Over the same period (2001-2005), S&P believes the 10 largest U.S. airlines lost about

$58.6 billion. Over the same time period, LUV's net income totaled $2.1 billion.

COMPETITIVE LANDSCAPE. The industry consists of about 43 mainline commercial passenger airlines, of which about 11 are considered major airlines, defined as airlines with annual revenues in excess of $1.0 billion. Major competitors include AMR Corp.'s American Airlines (18% market share, as measured by RPMs, as of August 2007), UAL Corp.'s United Airlines (15%), Delta Air Lines (13%), Northwest Airlines (9%), Continental (10%), and JetBlue Airways (3%). US Airways Group, which merged in late 2005 with America West, has about an 8% market share. The U.S. airline industry is fragmented, and highly competitive. Barriers to entry are high, and there are highly entrenched competitors. Pricing is extremely competitive. Fuel costs, the second largest cost category for Southwest, have risen sharply over the past three years, although Southwest is partly protected by a fuel hedging position that we think is by far the best in the industry.

## Company Financials Fiscal Year Ended Dec. 31

| Per Share Data ($) | 2007 | 2006 | 2005 | 2004 | 2003 | 2002 | 2001 | 2000 | 1999 | 1998 |
|---|---|---|---|---|---|---|---|---|---|---|
| Tangible Book Value | 10.49 | 8.23 | 8.38 | 7.04 | 6.40 | 5.69 | 5.23 | 4.57 | 3.79 | 3.21 |
| Cash Flow | 1.56 | 1.23 | 1.25 | 0.91 | 1.00 | 0.74 | 1.03 | 1.14 | 0.90 | 0.83 |
| Earnings | 0.84 | 0.61 | 0.67 | 0.38 | 0.54 | 0.30 | 0.63 | 0.79 | 0.59 | 0.55 |
| S&P Core Earnings | 0.83 | 0.60 | 0.62 | 0.30 | 0.48 | 0.23 | 0.61 | NA | NA | NA |
| Dividends | 0.02 | 0.02 | 0.02 | 0.02 | 0.02 | 0.02 | 0.01 | 0.01 | 0.01 | 0.01 |
| Payout Ratio | 2% | 3% | 3% | 5% | 3% | 6% | 2% | 1% | 2% | 2% |
| Prices:High | 16.96 | 18.20 | 16.95 | 17.06 | 19.69 | 22.00 | 23.32 | 23.32 | 15.72 | 10.56 |
| Prices:Low | 12.12 | 14.61 | 13.05 | 12.88 | 11.72 | 10.90 | 11.25 | 10.00 | 9.58 | 6.81 |
| P/E Ratio:High | 20 | 30 | 25 | 45 | 36 | 73 | 37 | 30 | 26 | 19 |
| P/E Ratio:Low | 14 | 24 | 19 | 34 | 22 | 36 | 18 | 13 | 16 | 12 |
| **Income Statement Analysis (Million $)** | | | | | | | | | | |
| Revenue | 9,861 | 9,086 | 7,584 | 6,530 | 5,937 | 5,522 | 5,555 | 5,650 | 4,736 | 4,164 |
| Operating Income | 1,371 | 1,449 | 1,289 | 985 | 867 | 774 | 949 | 1,302 | 1,030 | 909 |
| Depreciation | 555 | 515 | 469 | 431 | 384 | 356 | 318 | 281 | 249 | 225 |
| Interest Expense | 119 | 77.0 | 83.0 | 49.0 | 58.0 | 89.3 | 49.3 | 42.3 | 22.9 | 30.7 |
| Pretax Income | 1,058 | 790 | 874 | 489 | 708 | 393 | 828 | 1,017 | 774 | 705 |
| Effective Tax Rate | 39.0% | 36.8% | 37.3% | 36.0% | 37.6% | 38.6% | 38.2% | 38.5% | 38.7% | 38.5% |
| Net Income | 645 | 499 | 548 | 313 | 442 | 241 | 511 | 625 | 474 | 433 |
| S&P Core Earnings | 635 | 489 | 504 | 236 | 385 | 188 | 486 | NA | NA | NA |
| **Balance Sheet & Other Financial Data (Million $)** | | | | | | | | | | |
| Cash | 2,779 | 1,390 | 2,280 | 1,305 | 1,865 | 1,815 | 2,280 | 523 | 419 | 379 |
| Current Assets | 4,443 | 2,601 | 3,620 | 2,172 | 2,313 | 2,232 | 2,520 | 832 | 631 | 574 |
| Total Assets | 16,772 | 13,460 | 14,218 | 11,337 | 9,878 | 8,954 | 8,997 | 6,670 | 5,652 | 4,716 |
| Current Liabilities | 4,838 | 2,887 | 3,848 | 2,142 | 172 | 1,434 | 2,239 | 1,298 | 960 | 851 |
| Long Term Debt | 2,050 | 1,567 | 1,394 | 1,700 | 1,332 | 1,553 | 1,327 | 761 | 872 | 623 |
| Common Equity | 6,941 | 6,449 | 6,675 | 5,524 | 5,052 | 4,422 | 4,014 | 3,451 | 2,836 | 2,398 |
| Total Capital | 11,526 | 10,120 | 9,965 | 8,834 | 7,804 | 7,202 | 6,399 | 5,065 | 4,400 | 3,570 |
| Capital Expenditures | 1,331 | 1,399 | 1,210 | 1,775 | 1,238 | 603 | 998 | 1,135 | 1,168 | 947 |
| Cash Flow | 1,200 | 1,014 | 1,017 | 744 | 826 | 597 | 829 | 906 | 723 | 659 |
| Current Ratio | 0.9 | 0.9 | 0.9 | 1.0 | 13.4 | 1.6 | 1.1 | 0.6 | 0.7 | 0.7 |
| % Long Term Debt of Capitalization | 17.8 | 15.5 | 14.0 | 19.2 | 17.1 | 21.6 | 20.7 | 15.0 | 19.8 | 17.5 |
| % Net Income of Revenue | 6.5 | 5.5 | 7.2 | 4.8 | 7.4 | 4.4 | 9.2 | 11.1 | 10.0 | 10.4 |
| % Return on Assets | 4.3 | 3.6 | 4.3 | 3.0 | 4.7 | 2.7 | 6.5 | 10.1 | 9.2 | 9.7 |
| % Return on Equity | 9.6 | 7.6 | 9.0 | 5.9 | 9.3 | 5.7 | 13.7 | 19.9 | 18.1 | 19.7 |

Data as orig reptd.; bef. results of disc opers/spec. items. Per share data adj. for stk. divs.; EPS diluted. E-Estimated. NA-Not Available. NM-Not Meaningful. NR-Not Ranked. UR-Under Review.

**Office:** P.O. Box 36611, Dallas, TX 75235-1611.
**Telephone:** 214-792-4000.
**Website:** http://www.southwest.com
**Chrmn, Pres & CEO:** G.C. Kelly

**COO & EVP:** M.G. Van De Ven
**EVP & Secy:** R. Ricks
**SVP, CFO & Chief Acctg Officer:** L.H. Wright
**SVP & Chief Admin Officer:** J. Lamb

**Investor Contact:** L. Wright (214-792-4415)
**Board Members:** D. W. Biegler, L. E. Caldera, C. W. Crockett, W. H. Cunningham, T. C. Johnson, G. C. Kelly, N. B. Loeffler, J. Montford

**Founded:** 1967
**Domicile:** Texas
**Employees:** 34,378

# Sovereign Bancorp Inc.

**STANDARD &POOR'S**

| S&P Recommendation | HOLD ★★★☆☆ | Price | 12-Mo. Target Price | Investment Style |
|---|---|---|---|---|
| | | $2.39 (as of Nov 14, 2008) | $5.00 | Large-Cap Blend |

**GICS Sector** Financials
**Sub-Industry** Thrifts & Mortgage Finance

**Summary** This $90 billion bank holding company has branches in Pennsylvania, New Jersey, Connecticut, New Hampshire, Rhode Island, Massachusetts, New York, Maryland, and Delaware. SOV has agreed to be acquired by Banco Santander.

## Key Stock Statistics (Source S&P, Vickers, company reports)

| | | | | | | | | |
|---|---|---|---|---|---|---|---|---|
| 52-Wk Range | $14.85– 2.02 | S&P Oper. EPS 2008**E** | -0.98 | Market Capitalization(B) | $1.584 | Beta | | 1.79 |
| Trailing 12-Month EPS | $-4.31 | S&P Oper. EPS 2009**E** | 0.75 | Yield (%) | Nil | S&P 3-Yr. Proj. EPS CAGR(%) | | NM |
| Trailing 12-Month P/E | NM | P/E on S&P Oper. EPS 2008**E** | NM | Dividend Rate/Share | Nil | S&P Credit Rating | | BBB |
| $10K Invested 5 Yrs Ago | $1,196 | Common Shares Outstg. (M) | 662.7 | Institutional Ownership (%) | 59 | | | |

## Price Performance

30-Week Mov. Avg. · · · · 10-Week Mov. Avg. - - - GAAP Earnings vs. Previous Year  Volume Above Avg. STARS
12-Mo. Target Price —  Relative Strength —  ▲ Up  ▼ Down  ▶ No Change  Below Avg.  ★

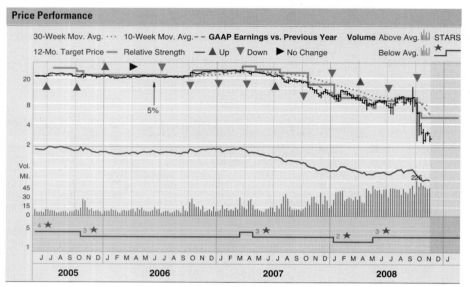

Options: ASE, CBOE, P, Ph

Analysis prepared by **Kevin Cole, CFA** on October 16, 2008, when the stock traded at **$ 3.06**.

## Highlights

➤ Absent any further asset write-downs, we believe SOV's total revenue will rise 18% in 2008, helped by a higher net interest margin. Our 2008 estimates include a net interest margin of 2.99% (up from 2.73% in 2007 due to lower funding costs and repositioning of the balance sheet), slightly lower earning assets reflecting a planned runoff of a portion of SOV's out of footprint auto portfolio, and a 68% increase in non-interest income due to the absence of large securities impairments seen in 2007.

➤ We look for SOV's expenses to decline to 59.1% of revenues in 2008, from 66.0% in 2007, due largely to revenue growth. Credit quality will likely deteriorate this year, and charge-offs should continue to rise, necessitating a high level of provisions. Specifically, we expect loan loss provisions of about $650 million in 2008, up from $408 million in 2007. Reserves look appropriate, by our analysis, at 165% of nonperforming loans.

➤ We estimate a 2008 operating loss of $0.98 per share, versus a loss of $2.52 in 2007. We see SOV returning to profitability in 2009 with EPS of $0.75.

## Investment Rationale/Risk

➤ Recently, SOV agreed to be acquired by Banco Santander (STD,12.78.****) in a stock-for-stock transaction. STD currently owns roughly 24% of SOV's outstanding common shares. SOV shareholders will receive 1 STD ADS for each 3.42 shares they own. Based on the closing stock price for STD's ADSs on October 14, 2008, the transaction values SOV shares at $4.24. The deal is subject to customary closing conditions, including regulatory approvals in the U.S. and Spain and approval by both companies' shareholders, and is expected to close in the first quarter of 2009.

➤ Risks to our recommendation and target price include credit quality concerns and loan deterioration issues that would impede SOV's acquisition by STD.

➤ Our 12-month target price of $5 is derived by applying a combination of the current deal value of $4.24, and our 12-month target price for STD ADSs.

## Qualitative Risk Assessment

| LOW | MEDIUM | HIGH |
|---|---|---|

Our risk assessment reflects concerns over the credit quality of SOV's loan portfolio, which has a high concentration of consumer and construction loans. We believe these loans may significantly deteriorate if housing prices continue to decline or unemployment rises substantially.

## Quantitative Evaluations

**S&P Quality Ranking**                                                      **B**

| D | C | B- | B | B+ | A- | A | A+ |
|---|---|---|---|---|---|---|---|

**Relative Strength Rank**                                              **WEAK**

12

LOWEST = 1                                                         HIGHEST = 99

## Revenue/Earnings Data

**Revenue (Million $)**

| | 1Q | 2Q | 3Q | 4Q | Year |
|---|---|---|---|---|---|
| 2008 | 1,248 | 1,209 | -35.91 | -- | -- |
| 2007 | 1,274 | 1,330 | 1,293 | 1,113 | 5,011 |
| 2006 | 973.9 | 829.0 | 1,442 | 1,367 | 4,612 |
| 2005 | 802.5 | 872.0 | 921.2 | 969.6 | 3,565 |
| 2004 | 627.6 | 639.7 | 714.1 | 726.0 | 2,706 |
| 2003 | 621.6 | 621.5 | 601.8 | 607.2 | 2,452 |

**Earnings Per Share ($)**

| | | | | | |
|---|---|---|---|---|---|
| 2008 | 0.20 | 0.22 | -1.48 | E0.08 | E-0.98 |
| 2007 | 0.09 | 0.29 | 0.11 | -3.34 | -2.85 |
| 2006 | 0.36 | -0.15 | 0.37 | -0.28 | 0.30 |
| 2005 | 0.36 | 0.45 | 0.46 | 0.42 | 1.69 |
| 2004 | 0.31 | 0.40 | 0.23 | 0.36 | 1.30 |
| 2003 | 0.26 | 0.35 | 0.35 | 0.36 | 1.31 |

Fiscal year ended Dec. 31. Next earnings report expected: Late January. EPS Estimates based on S&P Operating Earnings; historical GAAP earnings are as reported.

## Dividend Data (Dates: mm/dd Payment Date: mm/dd/yy)

| Amount ($) | Date Decl. | Ex-Div. Date | Stk. of Record | Payment Date |
|---|---|---|---|---|
| 0.080 | 10/18 | 10/30 | 11/01 | 11/15/07 |

Dividends have been paid since 1987. Source: Company reports.

---

**Please read the Required Disclosures and Analyst Certification on the last page of this report.**

*The McGraw-Hill Companies*

# Sovereign Bancorp Inc.

STANDARD &POOR'S

## Business Summary October 16, 2008

CORPORATE OVERVIEW. Sovereign Bancorp, once a small thrift, has grown into a large banking franchise, with nearly $85 billion in assets as of December 2007. The company has grown largely through acquisitions. From 1990 through December 2007, SOV acquired 28 financial institutions, branch networks and/or related businesses. From 1995, 18 of these acquisitions had assets totaling approximately $52 billion.

The company has nearly 750 community banking offices, and over 2,300 ATMs located principally in Pennsylvania, New Jersey, Connecticut, New Hampshire, Rhode Island, Massachusetts New York, and Maryland. SOV, which gathers substantially all of its deposits in these market areas, uses them, as well as other financing sources, to fund its loan and investment portfolios. SOV earns interest on its loan portfolio. In addition, the company generates non-interest income from a number of sources, including deposit and loan services, sales of residential loans and investment securities, capital markets products and bank-owned life insurance. SOV's principal non-interest expense includes employee compensation and benefits, occupancy and facility-related costs, technology and other administrative expenses.

PRIMARY BUSINESS DYNAMICS. SOV's financial results highly correlate with the economic environment, including interest rates, consumer and business confidence and spending, as well as competitive conditions. The company be-

lieves that its major strengths are: strong franchise value in terms of market share and demographics; a stable low-cost core deposit base; a diversified loan portfolio and products; a strong service culture; and the ability to cross-sell multiple product lines.

As of December 31, 2007, total loans of $57.7 billion were 23% residential real estate loans, 46% commercial loans, and 31% consumer loans (mostly home equity and auto loans). We look for residential loans to decline in 2008 as the company should de-emphasize its multi-family loan business. As of December 31, 2007, deposits totaling $49.9 billion consisted of 13% demand accounts, 57% core accounts, and 30% CDs. The company is attempting to attract more low-cost deposits by launching new products and services such as remote image capture, remote check clearing, and health savings accounts. We think this will help widen net margins. The allowance for loan losses at December 31, 2007 was $709.4 million (equal to 2.1X total non-performing assets), up from $471.0 million (2.0X) a year earlier. Net chargeoffs in 2007 totaled $143.8 million (0.25% of average loans), compared to $139.4 million (0.25%) in 2006.

## Company Financials Fiscal Year Ended Dec. 31

| Per Share Data ($) | 2007 | 2006 | 2005 | 2004 | 2003 | 2002 | 2001 | 2000 | 1999 | 1998 |
|---|---|---|---|---|---|---|---|---|---|---|
| Tangible Book Value | 5.80 | 5.75 | 7.60 | 7.11 | 6.30 | 5.02 | 3.24 | 2.04 | 5.74 | 4.51 |
| Earnings | -2.85 | 0.30 | 1.69 | 1.30 | 1.31 | 1.17 | 0.46 | -0.17 | 0.96 | 0.81 |
| S&P Core Earnings | 0.44 | 0.30 | 1.68 | 1.28 | 1.31 | 1.15 | 0.38 | NA | NA | NA |
| Dividends | 0.32 | 0.29 | 0.16 | 0.11 | 0.10 | 0.10 | 0.10 | 0.10 | 0.09 | 0.07 |
| Payout Ratio | NM | 98% | 10% | 8% | 7% | 8% | 21% | NM | 9% | 9% |
| Prices:High | 26.70 | 26.60 | 23.61 | 23.57 | 24.00 | 15.14 | 12.86 | 9.49 | 25.00 | 21.67 |
| Prices:Low | 9.92 | 19.47 | 19.10 | 18.39 | 12.00 | 10.67 | 6.82 | 5.95 | 6.67 | 8.33 |
| P/E Ratio:High | NM | 89 | 14 | 18 | 18 | 13 | 28 | NM | 26 | 27 |
| P/E Ratio:Low | NM | 65 | 11 | 14 | 9 | 9 | 15 | NM | 7 | 10 |

| Income Statement Analysis (Million $) | | | | | | | | | | |
|---|---|---|---|---|---|---|---|---|---|---|
| Net Interest Income | 1,864 | 1,822 | 1,588 | 1,405 | 1,206 | 1,160 | 1,054 | 855 | 615 | 494 |
| Loan Loss Provision | 408 | 484 | 90.0 | 127 | 162 | 147 | 97.1 | 56.5 | 30.0 | 28.0 |
| Non Interest Income | 531 | 598 | 635 | 468 | 456 | 381 | 411 | 230 | 130 | 106 |
| Non Interest Expenses | 3,220 | 1,547 | 2,319 | 2,100 | 968 | 979 | 1,175 | 1,013 | 446 | 360 |
| Pretax Income | -1,410 | 19.1 | 915 | 603 | 598 | 467 | 209 | -106 | 269 | 211 |
| Effective Tax Rate | NM | NM | 23.6% | 21.2% | 25.6% | 26.7% | 12.7% | NM | 33.3% | 35.4% |
| Net Income | -1,349 | 137 | 676 | 454 | 402 | 342 | 123 | -41.0 | 179 | 136 |
| % Net Interest Margin | 2.73 | 2.75 | 3.09 | 3.24 | 3.42 | 3.61 | 3.57 | 3.19 | 2.86 | 2.56 |
| S&P Core Earnings | 211 | 127 | 669 | 450 | 401 | 336 | 101 | NA | NA | NA |

| Balance Sheet & Other Financial Data (Million $) | | | | | | | | | | |
|---|---|---|---|---|---|---|---|---|---|---|
| Total Assets | 84,746 | 89,642 | 63,679 | 54,471 | 43,505 | 39,524 | 35,475 | 33,458 | 26,607 | 21,914 |
| Loans | 57,070 | 62,118 | 43,384 | 36,222 | 25,821 | 22,829 | 20,135 | 21,656 | 14,094 | 11,152 |
| Deposits | 49,916 | 52,385 | 37,978 | 32,556 | 27,344 | 26,785 | 23,298 | 24,499 | 11,720 | 12,323 |
| Capitalization:Debt | 6,227 | 9,181 | 9,330 | 9,642 | 12,124 | 6,240 | 6,869 | 5,367 | 316 | 4,108 |
| Capitalization:Equity | 6,797 | 8,449 | 5,811 | 4,988 | 3,260 | 2,764 | 2,202 | 1,949 | 1,821 | 1,204 |
| Capitalization:Total | 13,365 | 17,982 | 15,347 | 14,834 | 15,587 | 9,205 | 2,202 | 7,315 | 2,138 | 5,312 |
| % Return on Assets | NM | 0.2 | 1.1 | 0.9 | 1.0 | 0.9 | 0.4 | NM | 19.2 | 82.7 |
| % Return on Equity | NM | 1.9 | 12.5 | 11.0 | 13.3 | 13.8 | 5.9 | NM | 11.9 | 13.8 |
| % Loan Loss Reserve | 1.2 | 0.8 | 1.0 | 1.1 | 1.3 | 1.3 | 1.3 | 1.2 | -0.9 | 1.2 |
| % Risk Based Capital | 10.4 | 10.1 | 10.7 | 11.6 | 12.1 | 7.6 | 10.7 | 10.3 | 14.9 | 10.3 |
| Price Times Book Value:High | 4.6 | 4.6 | 3.1 | 3.3 | 3.8 | 3.0 | 2.9 | 4.6 | 4.4 | 4.8 |
| Price Times Book Value:Low | 1.7 | 3.4 | 2.5 | 2.6 | 1.9 | 2.1 | 1.8 | 2.9 | 1.2 | 1.9 |

Data as orig reptd.; bef. results of disc opers/spec. items. Per share data adj. for stk. divs.; EPS diluted. E-Estimated. NA-Not Available. NM-Not Meaningful. NR-Not Ranked. UR-Under Review.

**Office:** 1500 Market St, Philadelphia, PA 19102-2100.
**Telephone:** 067-256-8601.
**Email:** investor@sovereignbank.com
**Website:** http://www.sovereignbank.com

**Chrmn:** M.P. Soura
**Chrmn:** M.P. Ehlerman
**Pres, CEO, CFO & Chief Admin Officer:** K.W. Walters
**EVP & Chief Acctg Officer:** T.D. Cestare

**EVP & General Counsel:** D. Silverman
**Investor Contact:** S. Weikel (610-208-6112)
**Board Members:** J. P. Campanelli, M. P. Ehlerman, B. Hard, M. L. Heard, A. C. Hove, Jr., G. Jaramillo, W. J. Moran, M. F. Ramirez, C. C. Troilo, R. V. Whitworth, G. de Las Heras

**Founded:** 1984
**Domicile:** Pennsylvania
**Employees:** 11,976

# Spectra Energy Corp

STANDARD
&POOR'S

| S&P Recommendation | HOLD ★★★☆☆ | Price $16.73 (as of Nov 14, 2008) | 12-Mo. Target Price $21.00 | Investment Style Large-Cap Blend |
|---|---|---|---|---|

**GICS Sector** Energy
**Sub-Industry** Oil & Gas Storage & Transportation

**Summary** This integrated natural gas holding company is engaged in gas gathering and processing and gas transportation and storage in the U.S. and Canada, and retail gas distribution to 1.3 million customers in Ontario, Canada.

## Key Stock Statistics (Source S&P, Vickers, company reports)

| | | | | | | | | |
|---|---|---|---|---|---|---|---|---|
| 52-Wk Range | $29.18– 15.24 | S&P Oper. EPS 2008E | 1.99 | Market Capitalization(B) | $10.223 | Beta | NA |
| Trailing 12-Month EPS | $1.98 | S&P Oper. EPS 2009E | 2.05 | Yield (%) | 5.98 | S&P 3-Yr. Proj. EPS CAGR(%) | 12 |
| Trailing 12-Month P/E | 8.5 | P/E on S&P Oper. EPS 2008E | 8.4 | Dividend Rate/Share | $1.00 | S&P Credit Rating | NA |
| $10K Invested 5 Yrs Ago | NA | Common Shares Outstg. (M) | 611.0 | Institutional Ownership (%) | 66 | | |

## Price Performance

- 30-Week Mov. Avg. · · · 10-Week Mov. Avg. – – GAAP Earnings vs. Previous Year  Volume Above Avg. STARS
- 12-Mo. Target Price — Relative Strength — ▲ Up ▼ Down ▶ No Change  Below Avg.

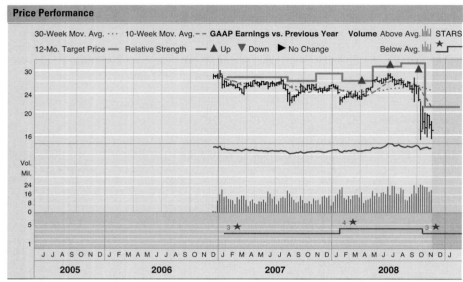

Options: ASE, CBOE, Ph

Analysis prepared by **Tanjila Shafi** on October 20, 2008, when the stock traded at **$ 18.92**.

## Highlights

➤ In 2007, its first year as a publicly traded entity, SE made major strides on a three-year capital expansion program and delivered solid growth on strong demand in the U.S. pipeline and storage segment and better-than-expected results from expansion projects. We expect revenues to experience high-single to low double-digit growth in 2008 and 2009, on higher throughput volumes and $1.6 billion in new pipeline, gas processing, storage and distribution projects coming on line in 2008.

➤ SE expects to spend about $3.0 billion on capital expenditures from 2008-2010, after spending $1.0 billion in 2007. Last year, expansion projects totaling $650 million were brought on line. This year the company plans to complete and bring into service $1.6 billion in new projects. Expansion projects include $1.5 billion in natural gas projects in the Northeast between 2007 and 2009.

➤ In 2007, SE posted EPS of $1.53. We forecast 2008 EPS of $1.92.

## Investment Rationale/Risk

➤ SE was formed on January 2, 2007, after Duke Energy spun off its natural gas businesses. SE operates a large and diverse portfolio of natural gas transportation and storage assets in the U.S. and Canada. In July 2007, SE spun off some assets into Spectra Energy Partners L.P. (SEP: NR $20) and received $345 million. In November 2007, SE announced plans to build the Bronco Pipeline, a new 650-mile gas pipeline stretching from the Rocky Mountains to Oregon, with initial capacity of over 1 Bcf/d, and an expected cost in excess of $3 billion. Bronco is expected to be in service in 2011 or 2012.

➤ Risks to our opinion and target price include a slowdown in natural gas production growth, declines in long-term natural gas prices, higher interest rates than expected, and warmer than normal winter weather.

➤ Our 12-month target price of $21 blends peer-average multiples of 15X our 2008 EPS estimate, 5.8X enterprise value-to-2008 EBITDA projections, and a target yield of 5% on projected dividends.

## Qualitative Risk Assessment

| LOW | MEDIUM | HIGH |
|---|---|---|

Our risk assessment reflects the company's large market capitalization and the lower risk inherent in its regulated gas transmission and distribution businesses, offset by its investments in higher-risk gas gathering and processing businesses.

## Quantitative Evaluations

**S&P Quality Ranking**  NR

| D | C | B- | B | B+ | A- | A | A+ |
|---|---|---|---|---|---|---|---|

**Relative Strength Rank**  MODERATE

53

LOWEST = 1   HIGHEST = 99

## Revenue/Earnings Data

**Revenue (Million $)**

| | 1Q | 2Q | 3Q | 4Q | Year |
|---|---|---|---|---|---|
| 2008 | 1,608 | 1,141 | 1,080 | -- | -- |
| 2007 | 1,401 | 985.0 | 959.0 | 1,397 | 4,742 |
| 2006 | NA | NA | NA | -- | 4,532 |
| 2005 | -- | -- | -- | -- | 4,132 |
| 2004 | -- | -- | -- | -- | -- |
| 2003 | -- | -- | -- | -- | -- |

**Earnings Per Share ($)**

| | 1Q | 2Q | 3Q | 4Q | Year |
|---|---|---|---|---|---|
| 2008 | 0.58 | 0.47 | 0.49 | E0.46 | E1.99 |
| 2007 | 0.37 | 0.29 | 0.38 | 0.45 | 1.49 |
| 2006 | NA | NA | NA | -- | NA |
| 2005 | -- | -- | -- | -- | 1.07 |
| 2004 | -- | -- | -- | -- | -- |
| 2003 | -- | -- | -- | -- | -- |

Fiscal year ended Dec. 31. Next earnings report expected: NA. EPS Estimates based on S&P Operating Earnings; historical GAAP earnings are as reported.

## Dividend Data (Dates: mm/dd Payment Date: mm/dd/yy)

| Amount ($) | Date Decl. | Ex-Div. Date | Stk. of Record | Payment Date |
|---|---|---|---|---|
| 0.230 | 01/04 | 02/13 | 02/15 | 03/17/08 |
| 0.230 | 04/04 | 05/14 | 05/16 | 06/16/08 |
| 0.250 | 07/03 | 08/13 | 08/15 | 09/15/08 |
| 0.250 | 10/28 | 11/12 | 11/14 | 12/15/08 |

Dividends have been paid since 2007. Source: Company reports.

# Spectra Energy Corp

STANDARD
&POOR'S

## Business Summary October 20, 2008

CORPORATE OVERVIEW. SE owns and operates a diversified portfolio of natural gas-related energy assets and is primarily a natural gas midstream company. The company operates in three areas of the natural gas industry: transmission and storage, distribution, and gathering and processing. SE also owns a natural gas distribution company, Union Gas, and participates in a 50%-owned joint venture, DCP Midstream.

MARKET PROFILE. The company manages its business in four segments: U.S. Transmission, Distribution, Western Canada Transmission and Processing, and Field Services.

The U.S. Transmission segment provides transportation and storage of natural gas for customers in the eastern and southeastern U.S. and the Maritime provinces of Canada. The segment has 12,915 miles of natural gas pipelines and 85 billion cubic feet (bcf) of storage capacity. The company's largest pipeline, Texas Eastern Transmission, is 9,040 miles, has a capacity of 6.2 billion cubic feet per day (bcf/d), and has 75.1 bcf of storage capacity. The pipeline connects Gulf Coast gas supply to demand centers in the Northeast, as well as to the East Tennessee Natural Gas and Algonquin Gas Transmission pipelines. The Algonquin pipeline can transport 1.9 bcf/d and connects to both the Texas Eastern and Maritimes and Northeast pipelines to provide gas

to areas between Boston, MA, and northern New Jersey. The East Tennessee pipeline brings gas from the Texas Eastern pipeline through eastern Tennessee as far as Roanoke, VA. The 50%-owned Gulfstream pipeline brings natural gas into the fast growing state of Florida. The Maritimes and Northeast pipeline provides Sable Island area Canadian natural gas down into the Boston area and helps to supply the Algonquin pipeline. The segment also operates other pipeline interconnection assets and storage assets.

The Distribution segment provides retail natural gas distribution in Ontario, Canada, as well as natural gas transportation and storage services to other utilities and energy market participants in Ontario, Quebec and the U.S. Union Gas is the company's regulated transmission and distribution subsidiary, serving 1.3 million customers in 400 communities throughout Ontario, Canada. Union Gas distributes its gas through 21,600 miles of distribution pipelines and owns 2,750 miles of transmission pipelines and 150 bcf of high deliverability storage.

## Company Financials Fiscal Year Ended Dec. 31

| Per Share Data ($) | 2007 | 2006 | 2005 | 2004 | 2003 | 2002 | 2001 | 2000 | 1999 | 1998 |
|---|---|---|---|---|---|---|---|---|---|---|
| Tangible Book Value | 4.60 | NM | NA | NA | NA | NA | NA | NA | NA | NA |
| Cash Flow | 2.31 | NA | 2.04 | NA | NA | NA | NA | NA | NA | NA |
| Earnings | 1.49 | NA | 1.07 | NA | NA | NA | NA | NA | NA | NA |
| S&P Core Earnings | 1.46 | NA | NA | NA | NA | NA | NA | NA | NA | NA |
| Dividends | 0.88 | Nil | Nil | NA | NA | NA | NA | NA | NA | NA |
| Payout Ratio | 59% | Nil | Nil | NA | NA | NA | NA | NA | NA | NA |
| Prices:High | 30.00 | 29.00 | NA | NA | NA | NA | NA | NA | NA | NA |
| Prices:Low | 21.24 | 27.50 | NA | NA | NA | NA | NA | NA | NA | NA |
| P/E Ratio:High | 20 | NA | NA | NA | NA | NA | NA | NA | NA | NA |
| P/E Ratio:Low | 14 | NA | NA | NA | NA | NA | NA | NA | NA | NA |

### Income Statement Analysis (Million $)

| | 2007 | 2006 | 2005 | 2004 | 2003 | 2002 | 2001 | 2000 | 1999 | 1998 |
|---|---|---|---|---|---|---|---|---|---|---|
| Revenue | 4,742 | 4,532 | 4,132 | 13,255 | 10,784 | NA | NA | NA | NA | NA |
| Operating Income | 1,967 | 1,804 | 1,697 | NA | NA | NA | NA | NA | NA | NA |
| Depreciation | 525 | 606 | 458 | NA | NA | NA | NA | NA | NA | NA |
| Interest Expense | 651 | 605 | 607 | 744 | 806 | NA | NA | NA | NA | NA |
| Pretax Income | 1,458 | 1,376 | 862 | 1,156 | 719 | NA | NA | NA | NA | NA |
| Effective Tax Rate | 30.4% | 28.7% | 41.7% | 123.8% | 29.2% | NA | NA | NA | NA | NA |
| Net Income | 944 | 936 | 502 | -489 | 404 | NA | NA | NA | NA | NA |
| S&P Core Earnings | 928 | 926 | NA | NA | NA | NA | NA | NA | NA | NA |

### Balance Sheet & Other Financial Data (Million $)

| | 2007 | 2006 | 2005 | 2004 | 2003 | 2002 | 2001 | 2000 | 1999 | 1998 |
|---|---|---|---|---|---|---|---|---|---|---|
| Cash | 94.0 | 299 | NA | NA | NA | NA | NA | NA | NA | NA |
| Current Assets | 1,379 | 1,625 | 18,601 | NA | NA | NA | NA | NA | NA | NA |
| Total Assets | 22,970 | 20,345 | 21,442 | NA | NA | NA | NA | NA | NA | NA |
| Current Liabilities | 2,422 | 2,358 | 2,052 | NA | NA | NA | NA | NA | NA | NA |
| Long Term Debt | 8,345 | 7,726 | 7,957 | NA | NA | NA | NA | NA | NA | NA |
| Common Equity | 6,857 | 5,639 | 5,225 | NA | NA | NA | NA | NA | NA | NA |
| Total Capital | 16,008 | 16,910 | 16,100 | NA | NA | NA | NA | NA | NA | NA |
| Capital Expenditures | 1,202 | 987 | NA | NA | NA | NA | NA | NA | NA | NA |
| Cash Flow | 1,469 | 1,542 | 960 | NA | NA | NA | NA | NA | NA | NA |
| Current Ratio | 0.6 | 0.7 | NA | NA | NA | NA | NA | NA | NA | NA |
| % Long Term Debt of Capitalization | 52.1 | 45.7 | Nil | Nil | Nil | NA | NA | NA | NA | NA |
| % Net Income of Revenue | 19.9 | 20.7 | 12.2 | NM | 3.8 | NA | NA | NA | NA | NA |
| % Return on Assets | 4.4 | 3.4 | NA | NA | NA | NA | NA | NA | NA | NA |
| % Return on Equity | 15.1 | 10.9 | NA | NA | NA | NA | NA | NA | NA | NA |

Data as orig reptd.; bef. results of disc opers/spec. items. Per share data adj. for stk. divs.; EPS diluted. E-Estimated. NA-Not Available. NM-Not Meaningful. NR-Not Ranked. UR-Under Review.

**Office:** 5400 Westheimer Court, Houston, TX 77056-5310.
**Telephone:** 713-627-5400 .
**Website:** http://www.spectraenergy.com
**Chrmn:** P.R. Anderson

**Pres & CEO:** F.J. Fowler
**COO:** A.N. Harris
**CFO:** G.L. Ebel
**Chief Admin Officer:** D. Ables

**Investor Contact:** J. Arensdorf (713-627-4600)
**Board Members:** A. A. Adams, P. R. Anderson, P. L. Carter, F. A. Comper, W. T. Esrey, F. J. Fowler, P. B. Hamilton, D. R. Hendrix, M. McShane, M. E. Phelps

**Founded:** 2006
**Domicile:** Delaware
**Employees:** 5,100

# Sprint Nextel Corp

## STANDARD &POOR'S

| S&P Recommendation | HOLD ★★★☆☆ | Price<br>$2.30 (as of Nov 14, 2008) | 12-Mo. Target Price<br>$5.00 | Investment Style<br>Large-Cap Value |
|---|---|---|---|---|

**GICS Sector** Telecommunication Services
**Sub-Industry** Wireless Telecommunication Services

**Summary** This leading provider of wireless and other telecommunications services was formed in August 2005 via the merger of Sprint Corp. and Nextel Communications, Inc.

## Key Stock Statistics (Source S&P, Vickers, company reports)

| | | | | | | | |
|---|---|---|---|---|---|---|---|
| 52-Wk Range | $15.92– 1.77 | S&P Oper. EPS 2008E | 0.08 | Market Capitalization(B) | $6.571 | Beta | 1.94 |
| Trailing 12-Month EPS | $-10.75 | S&P Oper. EPS 2009E | -0.12 | Yield (%) | Nil | S&P 3-Yr. Proj. EPS CAGR(%) | 6 |
| Trailing 12-Month P/E | NM | P/E on S&P Oper. EPS 2008E | 28.8 | Dividend Rate/Share | Nil | S&P Credit Rating | BB |
| $10K Invested 5 Yrs Ago | NA | Common Shares Outstg. (M) | 2,856.8 | Institutional Ownership (%) | 94 | | |

## Price Performance

30-Week Mov. Avg. · · · ·  10-Week Mov. Avg. - - -  **GAAP Earnings vs. Previous Year**  Volume Above Avg. STARS
12-Mo. Target Price —  Relative Strength —  ▲ Up  ▼ Down  ► No Change  Below Avg.  ★

Options: ASE, CBOE, P, Ph

Analysis prepared by **James Moorman, CFA** on November 10, 2008, when the stock traded at **$ 2.97**.

### Qualitative Risk Assessment

| LOW | MEDIUM | HIGH |
|---|---|---|

As S is one of the weakest national wireless carriers, its free cash flow could continue to be pressured in the near term, in our view. We believe this risk is offset by our view of the company's strong balance sheet and operating expense reductions.

### Quantitative Evaluations

**S&P Quality Ranking**    **B**

| D | C | B- | B | B+ | A- | A | A+ |
|---|---|---|---|---|---|---|---|

**Relative Strength Rank**    **WEAK**

10

LOWEST = 1      HIGHEST = 99

### Revenue/Earnings Data

**Revenue (Million $)**

| | 1Q | 2Q | 3Q | 4Q | Year |
|---|---|---|---|---|---|
| 2008 | 9,334 | 9,055 | 8,816 | -- | -- |
| 2007 | 10,092 | 10,163 | 10,044 | 9,847 | 40,146 |
| 2006 | 11,548 | 10,014 | 10,496 | 10,444 | 41,028 |
| 2005 | 6,936 | 7,113 | 9,335 | 11,296 | 34,680 |
| 2004 | 6,707 | 6,869 | 6,922 | 6,930 | 27,428 |
| 2003 | 3,581 | 3,530 | 3,538 | 3,536 | 14,185 |

**Earnings Per Share ($)**

| | | | | | |
|---|---|---|---|---|---|
| 2008 | -0.18 | -0.12 | -0.11 | E-0.03 | E0.08 |
| 2007 | -0.07 | 0.01 | 0.02 | -10.36 | -10.31 |
| 2006 | 0.14 | 0.10 | 0.08 | 0.09 | 0.34 |
| 2005 | 0.32 | 0.40 | 0.23 | 0.07 | 0.87 |
| 2004 | 0.16 | 0.16 | -1.32 | 0.29 | -0.71 |
| 2003 | 0.31 | 0.10 | -0.48 | 0.40 | 0.33 |

Fiscal year ended Dec. 31. Next earnings report expected: Late February. EPS Estimates based on S&P Operating Earnings; historical GAAP earnings are as reported.

### Highlights

➤ Following a decline in revenues of 2.2% in 2007, we expect revenues to decline 10.5% in 2008 and 8.2% in 2009, as S begins to reposition its wireless business (83% of projected revenues), which is expected to result in above-average customer churn. We believe the company will have difficulty retaining its customers as it migrates its subscriber base. In addition, we believe the focus on retaining subscribers could limit its ability to attract new subscribers. Within global markets, we see slight declines in revenues from competitive pressures.

➤ We estimate total EBITDA margins of 21.0% in 2008 and 19.8% in 2009, versus 25.8% in 2007, as we think S needs more time to realize cost savings from multiple acquisitions and the cost of slowly migrating its customer base to one network. The announced layoff of 4,000 employees and closure of 125 retail locations should help cut costs, but we see challenges as S looks to maintain its wireless market share. We believe margins will be somewhat supported by cost reductions in the global markets segment.

➤ We estimate operating EPS of $0.08 in 2008 and a loss of $0.12 in 2009.

### Investment Rationale/Risk

➤ In our opinion, the company is in a transition, trying to regain favor with customers as competitors take market share. We expect S to offer handset subsidies to stimulate subscriber growth, which, along with subscriber losses, should result in a sharp decline in EBITDA, despite the cost reduction efforts that are under way. We believe the new CEO is making the necessary changes, but this will be a long uphill struggle that we think will prevent the shares from appreciating significantly in the near term.

➤ Risks to our recommendation and target price include higher capital spending to deploy new services, liquidity issues relating to declining cash flow, the decision to focus on the iDEN network rather than sell it, and increased competition from nationwide peers that could lead to delayed growth in subscriber additions.

➤ Our 12-month target price of $5 assumes an enterprise value of 5.0X our 2009 EBITDA estimate, below larger-cap telecom peers, due to S's subscriber losses and below smaller pure-play wireless carriers that we think have stronger growth prospects.

### Dividend Data (Dates: mm/dd Payment Date: mm/dd/yy)

| Amount ($) | Date Decl. | Ex-Div. Date | Stk. of Record | Payment Date |
|---|---|---|---|---|
| 0.025 | 11/05 | 12/05 | 12/07 | 12/28/07 |

Dividends have been paid since 1939. Source: Company reports.

---

**Please read the Required Disclosures and Analyst Certification on the last page of this report.**

The McGraw-Hill Companies

# Sprint Nextel Corp

**STANDARD &POOR'S**

## Business Summary November 10, 2008

CORPORATE OVERVIEW. On August 15, 2005, the shares of Sprint Nextel Corp. began trading under the symbol S. The company has a balanced mix of consumer, business and government wireless services. S spun off to shareholders the local telephone business in May 2006. As of the end of the third quarter of 2008, S provided service to roughly 50.5 million wireless subscribers, with 75% of them direct post-paid customers, while 8% were prepaid (Boost Mobile), and 16% were wholesale customers (from Virgin Mobile and others). S also generates revenues from wireline voice and data communication services and services to the cable multiple systems operators that use S's network and back-office capabilities.

COMPETITIVE LANDSCAPE. In most major U.S. metropolitan markets, four national carriers offer competing wireless services to customers along with some regional carriers. Wireless carriers such as S have adjusted to potential substitutes by integrating the service features into the handsets. Until recently, S had a unique service with push-to-talk service through Nextel's iDEN network, but AT&T (formerly Cingular) has launched a competing nationwide service aimed at the consumer segment, in contrast to S's dominant position with small business and enterprise firms.

Wireless services are very price elastic. For the consumer market, service rate plans have taken on new features such as $9.99 for each family member added to the account. S realized 2.15% post-paid churn in the third quarter of 2008, above that of its larger peers, but generated $56 in average revenue per user (ARPU). Pre-paid customers had a 8.2% churn rate and generated $31 in ARPU. The company has simplified its pricing with plans that include a $100 plan with unlimited voice, data, text and others, as well as a $90 plan for unlimited voice and texting. We believe this translates to roughly $80 for unlimited voice and compares to recent offers by the other three major wireless companies of $100 for unlimited voice alone. We believe this is a good move that will help change S's image, but we do not expect the plans to drive big changes in customer growth.

## Company Financials Fiscal Year Ended Dec. 31

| Per Share Data ($) | 2007 | 2006 | 2005 | 2004 | 2003 | 2002 | 2001 | 2000 | 1999 | 1998 |
|---|---|---|---|---|---|---|---|---|---|---|
| Tangible Book Value | NM | NM | 0.88 | 3.85 | 14.40 | 11.45 | 11.41 | 13.95 | 10.42 | 10.45 |
| Cash Flow | -7.17 | 3.67 | 3.93 | 2.56 | 3.12 | 4.14 | 2.60 | 4.00 | -4.35 | 7.19 |
| Earnings | -10.31 | 0.34 | 0.87 | -0.71 | 0.33 | 1.18 | -0.16 | 1.45 | 1.97 | 1.78 |
| S&P Core Earnings | -0.05 | 0.30 | 0.86 | -0.72 | 1.20 | 1.26 | -0.12 | NA | NA | NA |
| Dividends | 0.10 | 0.13 | 0.30 | 0.50 | 0.50 | 0.50 | 0.50 | 0.50 | 0.50 | 0.50 |
| Payout Ratio | NM | 37% | 34% | NM | 152% | 42% | NM | 34% | 25% | 28% |
| Prices:High | 23.42 | 26.89 | 27.20 | 25.80 | 16.76 | 20.47 | 29.31 | 67.81 | 75.94 | 42.66 |
| Prices:Low | 12.96 | 15.92 | 21.57 | 15.74 | 10.22 | 6.65 | 18.50 | 19.63 | 36.88 | 27.63 |
| P/E Ratio:High | NM | 79 | 31 | NM | 51 | 17 | NM | 47 | 39 | 24 |
| P/E Ratio:Low | NM | 47 | 25 | NM | 31 | 6 | NM | 14 | 19 | 16 |

| Income Statement Analysis (Million $) | | | | | | | | | | |
|---|---|---|---|---|---|---|---|---|---|---|
| Revenue | 40,146 | 41,028 | 34,680 | 27,428 | 14,185 | 15,182 | 16,924 | 17,688 | 17,016 | 17,135 |
| Operating Income | 10,282 | 12,283 | 10,220 | 8,148 | 4,376 | 4,488 | 4,238 | 5,101 | -5,059 | 3,075 |
| Depreciation | 9,023 | 9,592 | 6,269 | 4,720 | 2,519 | 2,645 | 2,449 | 2,267 | 2,129 | 2,705 |
| Interest Expense | 1,433 | 1,533 | 1,351 | 1,248 | 236 | 295 | 57.0 | 76.0 | 182 | 895 |
| Pretax Income | -29,945 | 1,817 | 2,906 | -1,603 | 434 | 1,453 | -129 | 2,170 | -2,797 | 698 |
| Effective Tax Rate | NM | 26.9% | 38.0% | NM | 32.3% | 28.0% | NM | 40.5% | 37.9% | 56.2% |
| Net Income | -29,580 | 1,329 | 1,801 | -1,012 | 294 | 1,046 | -146 | 1,292 | -1,736 | 457 |
| S&P Core Earnings | -155 | 849 | 1,772 | -1,036 | 1,096 | 1,132 | -112 | NA | NA | NA |

| Balance Sheet & Other Financial Data (Million $) | | | | | | | | | | |
|---|---|---|---|---|---|---|---|---|---|---|
| Cash | 2,440 | 2,061 | 10,665 | 4,556 | 1,635 | 641 | 134 | 122 | 104 | 605 |
| Current Assets | 8,661 | 10,304 | 19,092 | 9,975 | 4,378 | 3,327 | 3,485 | 4,512 | 4,282 | 4,388 |
| Total Assets | 64,109 | 97,161 | 102,580 | 41,321 | 21,862 | 23,043 | 24,164 | 23,649 | 21,803 | 33,231 |
| Current Liabilities | 9,104 | 9,798 | 14,050 | 6,902 | 2,359 | 4,320 | 6,298 | 5,004 | 4,301 | 4,551 |
| Long Term Debt | 20,469 | 21,011 | Nil | 15,916 | 2,627 | 2,736 | 3,258 | 3,482 | 4,531 | 11,942 |
| Common Equity | 21,999 | 53,131 | 51,937 | 13,521 | 13,372 | 11,814 | 11,704 | 12,343 | 10,514 | 12,202 |
| Total Capital | 51,157 | 84,237 | 52,184 | 29,684 | 17,632 | 16,385 | 16,514 | 17,101 | 15,980 | 26,221 |
| Capital Expenditures | 6,322 | 7,556 | 5,057 | 3,980 | 1,674 | 2,181 | 5,295 | 4,105 | 3,534 | 42,311 |
| Cash Flow | -20,557 | 10,919 | 8,063 | 3,701 | 2,821 | 3,698 | 2,310 | 3,566 | -3,858 | 3,156 |
| Current Ratio | 1.0 | 1.1 | 1.4 | 1.4 | 1.9 | 0.8 | 0.6 | 0.9 | 1.0 | 1.0 |
| % Long Term Debt of Capitalization | 40.0 | 24.9 | Nil | 53.6 | 14.9 | 16.7 | 19.7 | 20.4 | 28.4 | 45.5 |
| % Net Income of Revenue | NM | 3.2 | 5.2 | NM | 2.1 | 6.9 | NM | 7.3 | 10.2 | 2.6 |
| % Return on Assets | NM | 1.3 | 2.5 | NM | 1.3 | 4.4 | NM | 5.7 | 8.5 | 1.8 |
| % Return on Equity | NM | 2.5 | 5.5 | NM | 2.3 | 8.8 | NM | 11.2 | 17.7 | 4.2 |

Data as orig reptd.; bef. results of disc opers/spec. items. Per share data adj. for stk. divs.; EPS diluted. E-Estimated. NA-Not Available. NM-Not Meaningful. NR-Not Ranked. UR-Under Review.

**Office:** 6200 Sprint Pkwy, Overland Park, KS 66251-6117.
**Telephone:** 800-829-0965.
**Email:** investorrelation.sprintcom@mail.sprint.com
**Website:** http://www.sprint.com

**Chrmn:** J.H. Hance, Jr.
**Chrmn:** P.H. Henson
**Pres & CEO:** D.R. Hesse
**SVP & Treas:** R.S. Lindahl

**CFO:** R.H. Brust
**Board Members:** W. Batts, R. R. Bennett, G. Bethune, L. C. Glasscock, J. H. Hance, Jr., D. R. Hesse, V. J. Hill, I. O. Hockaday, Jr., S. Nilsson, W. Nuti, R. O'Neal

**Founded:** 1925
**Domicile:** Kansas
**Employees:** 60,000

*The McGraw-Hill Companies*

# Stanley Works (The)

| S&P Recommendation | STRONG BUY ★★★★★ | Price | 12-Mo. Target Price | Investment Style |
|---|---|---|---|---|
| | | $31.12 (as of Nov 14, 2008) | $50.00 | Large-Cap Blend |

**GICS Sector** Consumer Discretionary
**Sub-Industry** Household Appliances

**Summary** This company is a worldwide producer of tools, hardware and specialty hardware for home improvement, consumer, industrial and professional use.

## Key Stock Statistics (Source S&P, Vickers, company reports)

| | | | | | | | |
|---|---|---|---|---|---|---|---|
| 52-Wk Range | $52.88– 28.18 | S&P Oper. EPS 2008**E** | 3.90 | Market Capitalization(B) | $2.452 | Beta | 1.24 |
| Trailing 12-Month EPS | $5.01 | S&P Oper. EPS 2009**E** | 4.00 | Yield (%) | 4.11 | S&P 3-Yr. Proj. EPS CAGR(%) | 5 |
| Trailing 12-Month P/E | 6.2 | P/E on S&P Oper. EPS 2008**E** | 8.0 | Dividend Rate/Share | $1.28 | S&P Credit Rating | A |
| $10K Invested 5 Yrs Ago | $10,584 | Common Shares Outstg. (M) | 78.8 | Institutional Ownership (%) | 78 | | |

## Price Performance

30-Week Mov. Avg. · · · 10-Week Mov. Avg. -- GAAP Earnings vs. Previous Year  Volume Above Avg. STARS
12-Mo. Target Price — Relative Strength — ▲ Up ▼ Down ▶ No Change  Below Avg.

Options: P

Analysis prepared by **Kenneth M. Leon, CPA** on October 22, 2008, when the stock traded at **$ 34.26.**

## Highlights

➤ We project that total sales will be flat to up slightly in 2009, following an estimated flat to 1% lower 2008 and a 12% increase in 2007, stemming from volume growth, price increases and acquisitions. Should the housing market rebound earlier than the middle of next year, we think the company would grow faster than our baseline sales forecast in 2009.

➤ We expect strong sales advances in the Security Solutions segment and flat sales in the Industrial Tools segment, while the Construction segment may lag as we think the consumer market will remain a challenge throughout 2009. Our sales outlook takes into account a very weak North American market and a weaker European market, partly offset by positive growth in emerging markets.

➤ With higher material costs, we look for operating margins to narrow to the 13% to 14% level in 2008 and 2009, from 2007's 14.1%. After taxes at an effective rate we see near 25% to 26%, versus the 25.4% rate of 2007, we project operating EPS of $3.90 this year, rising to $4.00 in 2009.

## Investment Rationale/Risk

➤ We are positive on SWK's ability to profitably grow its diversified businesses that are benefiting from growth markets in emerging countries and focused cost control efforts and synergies from acquisitions. Despite weakening economies in the U.S. and Europe, we believe SWK is well positioned to take advantage of higher growth in its security solutions markets and a potential rebound in the U.S. housing market in 2009.

➤ Risks to our recommendation and target price include the possibility of a more severe weakening in SWK's major markets, lower-than-projected synergies from recent acquisitions, an inability to achieve the Security Solutions segment's target margin, and intense competition.

➤ Our 12-month target price of $50 applies a P/E of 12.5X to our 12-month forward operating EPS estimate of $4.00. This is slightly above SWK's current peer group multiple but below its five-year historical average, a level that we think discounts what we view as SWK's strong management team, a mix of growth opportunities, and challenging macroeconomic factors.

## Qualitative Risk Assessment

| LOW | MEDIUM | HIGH |
|---|---|---|

Our risk assessment takes into account our positive view of SWK's strong brand name and solid competitive position, offset by our negative view of industry cyclicality. Weak consumer markets are partly offsets by positive growth from industrial and other non-consumer customer markets.

## Quantitative Evaluations

**S&P Quality Ranking**     B+

| D | C | B- | B | B+ | A- | A | A+ |
|---|---|---|---|---|---|---|---|

**Relative Strength Rank**     MODERATE

55

LOWEST = 1                                    HIGHEST = 99

## Revenue/Earnings Data

**Revenue (Million $)**

| | 1Q | 2Q | 3Q | 4Q | Year |
|---|---|---|---|---|---|
| 2008 | 1,097 | 1,154 | 1,120 | -- | -- |
| 2007 | 1,062 | 1,123 | 1,131 | 1,167 | 4,484 |
| 2006 | 968.7 | 1,018 | 1,013 | 1,019 | 4,019 |
| 2005 | 796.3 | 814.7 | 834.9 | 839.4 | 3,285 |
| 2004 | 734.8 | 753.9 | 751.8 | 802.9 | 3,043 |
| 2003 | 632.2 | 652.6 | 665.6 | 727.7 | 2,678 |

**Earnings Per Share ($)**

| | | | | | |
|---|---|---|---|---|---|
| 2008 | 0.85 | 0.95 | 0.98 | E0.95 | E3.90 |
| 2007 | 0.80 | 1.01 | 1.09 | 1.11 | 4.01 |
| 2006 | 0.45 | 0.90 | 1.09 | 1.04 | 3.47 |
| 2005 | 0.78 | 0.77 | 0.89 | 0.75 | 3.18 |
| 2004 | 0.66 | 0.70 | 0.73 | 0.77 | 2.85 |
| 2003 | 0.22 | 0.11 | 0.46 | 0.38 | 1.14 |

Fiscal year ended Dec. 31. Next earnings report expected: Late January. EPS Estimates based on S&P Operating Earnings; historical GAAP earnings are as reported.

## Dividend Data (Dates: mm/dd Payment Date: mm/dd/yy)

| Amount ($) | Date Decl. | Ex-Div. Date | Stk. of Record | Payment Date |
|---|---|---|---|---|
| 0.310 | 02/20 | 03/03 | 03/05 | 03/25/08 |
| 0.310 | 04/23 | 06/02 | 06/04 | 06/24/08 |
| 0.320 | 07/18 | 09/03 | 09/05 | 09/23/08 |
| 0.320 | 10/17 | 12/03 | 12/05 | 12/16/08 |

Dividends have been paid since 1877. Source: Company reports.

---

**Please read the Required Disclosures and Analyst Certification on the last page of this report.**

The **McGraw-Hill** Companies

# Stanley Works (The)

## Business Summary October 22, 2008

CORPORATE OVERVIEW. The Stanley Works is a worldwide supplier of industrial tools and security solutions for professional, industrial and consumer use. The company offers a broad line of hand tools and has many well known brands. SWK's operations are classified into three business segments: Consumer Products (40% of 2007 sales), Industrial Tools (28%), and Security Solutions (32%).

MARKET PROFILE. In Consumer Products, SWK manufactures and markets hand tools, consumer mechanics tools and storage units, and hardware. Products are distributed directly to retailers (including home centers, mass merchants, hardware stores, and retail lumber yards) as well as third-party distributors, and include measuring instruments, hammers, knives and blades, screwdrivers, sockets and tool boxes. Among the company's brands are Stanley, FatMax, Powerlock, IntelliTools, ZAG, and National.

The Industrial Tools segment manufactures and markets professional mechanics tools and storage systems, pneumatic tools and fasteners, hydraulic tools and accessories, assembly tools and systems, and electronic measuring tools. Products are distributed primarily through third-party distributors. Brands include Stanley, Proto, Facom, USAG, MAC, Jensen, Bostich, Virax,

David White, and Rolatape.

The Security Solutions segment is a provider of access and security solutions primarily for retailers, educational and healthcare institutions, government, financial institutions, and commercial and industrial customers. Products include security integration systems, software, related installation and maintenance services, automatic doors, and locking mechanisms, and are sold on a direct sales basis. Brands include Stanley, Blick, Frisco Bay, PAC, ISR, WanderGuard, StanVision, Sargent and Greenleaf, BEST and Xmark.

About 58.5% of 2007 sales were made in the U.S., 9% in Other Americas, 12% in France, 15% in Other Europe, and 5.5% in Asia. A large portion of SWK's products in the Consumer Products and Industrial Tools segments are sold through home centers and mass merchant distribution channels in the U.S. market.

## Company Financials Fiscal Year Ended Dec. 31

| Per Share Data ($) | 2007 | 2006 | 2005 | 2004 | 2003 | 2002 | 2001 | 2000 | 1999 | 1998 |
|---|---|---|---|---|---|---|---|---|---|---|
| Tangible Book Value | NM | NM | 4.59 | 3.56 | 2.65 | 5.05 | 7.05 | 6.59 | 6.18 | 5.33 |
| Cash Flow | 5.94 | 4.92 | 4.40 | 4.07 | 2.16 | 2.90 | 2.76 | 3.17 | 2.62 | 2.41 |
| Earnings | 4.00 | 3.47 | 3.18 | 2.85 | 1.14 | 2.10 | 1.81 | 2.22 | 1.67 | 1.53 |
| S&P Core Earnings | 4.08 | 3.57 | 3.16 | 2.49 | 1.12 | 1.43 | 1.30 | NA | NA | NA |
| Dividends | 1.22 | 1.18 | 1.14 | 1.08 | 1.03 | 0.99 | 0.94 | 0.90 | 0.87 | 0.83 |
| Payout Ratio | 30% | 34% | 36% | 38% | 90% | 47% | 52% | 41% | 52% | 54% |
| Prices:High | 64.25 | 54.59 | 51.75 | 49.33 | 37.87 | 52.00 | 46.97 | 31.88 | 35.00 | 57.25 |
| Prices:Low | 47.01 | 41.60 | 41.51 | 36.42 | 20.84 | 27.31 | 28.06 | 18.44 | 22.00 | 23.50 |
| P/E Ratio:High | 16 | 16 | 16 | 17 | 33 | 25 | 26 | 14 | 21 | 37 |
| P/E Ratio:Low | 12 | 12 | 13 | 13 | 18 | 13 | 16 | 8 | 13 | 15 |

| Income Statement Analysis (Million $) | | | | | | | | | | |
|---|---|---|---|---|---|---|---|---|---|---|
| Revenue | 4,484 | 4,019 | 3,285 | 3,043 | 2,678 | 2,594 | 2,624 | 2,749 | 2,752 | 2,729 |
| Operating Income | 800 | 567 | 493 | 513 | 342 | 360 | 412 | 424 | 321 | 331 |
| Depreciation | 162 | 121 | 96.5 | 95.0 | 86.5 | 71.2 | 82.9 | 83.3 | 86.0 | 79.7 |
| Interest Expense | 85.2 | 69.3 | 40.4 | 38.6 | 34.2 | 28.5 | 18.9 | 34.6 | 33.0 | 31.0 |
| Pretax Income | 451 | 367 | 358 | 329 | 133 | 273 | 237 | 294 | 231 | 215 |
| Effective Tax Rate | 25.4% | 20.8% | 24.1% | 27.0% | 27.3% | 32.1% | 33.1% | 33.8% | 35.1% | 36.0% |
| Net Income | 337 | 291 | 272 | 240 | 96.7 | 185 | 158 | 194 | 150 | 138 |
| S&P Core Earnings | 343 | 299 | 270 | 209 | 94.7 | 127 | 113 | NA | NA | NA |

| Balance Sheet & Other Financial Data (Million $) | | | | | | | | | | |
|---|---|---|---|---|---|---|---|---|---|---|
| Cash | 240 | 177 | 658 | 250 | 204 | 122 | 115 | 93.6 | 88.0 | 110 |
| Current Assets | 1,768 | 1,639 | 1,826 | 1,372 | 1,201 | 1,190 | 1,141 | 1,094 | 1,091 | 1,086 |
| Total Assets | 4,780 | 3,935 | 3,545 | 2,851 | 2,424 | 2,418 | 2,056 | 1,885 | 1,891 | 1,933 |
| Current Liabilities | 1,278 | 1,251 | 875 | 819 | 754 | 681 | 826 | 707 | 693 | 702 |
| Long Term Debt | 1,212 | 679 | 895 | 482 | 535 | 564 | 197 | 249 | 290 | 345 |
| Common Equity | 1,729 | 1,552 | 1,946 | 1,388 | 1,032 | 1,165 | 844 | 933 | 737 | 669 |
| Total Capital | 3,022 | 2,298 | 2,925 | 1,960 | 1,567 | 1,729 | 1,041 | 1,181 | 1,027 | 1,014 |
| Capital Expenditures | 65.5 | 59.6 | 53.3 | 47.6 | 31.4 | 37.2 | 55.7 | 59.8 | 78.0 | 56.9 |
| Cash Flow | 499 | 412 | 368 | 335 | 183 | 256 | 241 | 278 | 236 | 218 |
| Current Ratio | 1.4 | 1.3 | 2.1 | 1.7 | 1.6 | 1.7 | 1.4 | 1.5 | 1.6 | 1.5 |
| % Long Term Debt of Capitalization | 40.1 | 29.6 | 30.6 | 24.6 | 34.1 | 32.6 | 18.9 | 21.1 | 28.2 | 34.0 |
| % Net Income of Revenue | 7.5 | 7.2 | 8.3 | 7.9 | 3.6 | 7.1 | 6.0 | 7.1 | 5.5 | 5.0 |
| % Return on Assets | 7.7 | 7.8 | 8.5 | 9.1 | 4.0 | 8.3 | 8.0 | 10.3 | 7.8 | 7.5 |
| % Return on Equity | 20.5 | 19.4 | 14.4 | 19.8 | 8.8 | 16.9 | 20.0 | 20.8 | 20.8 | 21.6 |

Data as orig reptd.; bef. results of disc opers/spec. items. Per share data adj. for stk. divs.; EPS diluted. E-Estimated. NA-Not Available. NM-Not Meaningful. NR-Not Ranked. UR-Under Review.

**Office:** 1000 Stanley Dr, New Britain, CT 06053.
**Telephone:** 860-225-5111.
**Website:** http://www.stanleyworks.com
**Chrmn & CEO:** J.F. Lundgren

**COO:** J.H. Chen
**EVP & CFO:** J.M. Loree
**SVP & CIO:** H.W. Davis, Jr.
**CTO:** D.E. Bither

**Investor Contact:** G. Waybright (860-827-3544)
**Board Members:** J. G. Breen, P. D. Campbell, C. M. Cardoso, V. W. Colbert, R. B. Coutts, E. S. Kraus, J. F. Lundgren, M. M. Parrs, L. A. Zimmerman

**Founded:** 1843
**Domicile:** Connecticut
**Employees:** 20,000

# Staples Inc

**S&P Recommendation** BUY ★★★★☆

| Price | 12-Mo. Target Price | Investment Style |
|---|---|---|
| $17.09 (as of Nov 14, 2008) | $30.00 | Large-Cap Growth |

**GICS Sector** Consumer Discretionary
**Sub-Industry** Specialty Stores

**Summary** This leading operator of office products superstores has over 2,000 units in the U.S. and internationally.

## Key Stock Statistics (Source S&P, Vickers, company reports)

| | | | | | | | |
|---|---|---|---|---|---|---|---|
| 52-Wk Range | $26.57– 13.57 | S&P Oper. EPS 2009E | 1.42 | Market Capitalization(B) | $12.152 | Beta | 0.67 |
| Trailing 12-Month EPS | $1.36 | S&P Oper. EPS 2010E | 1.63 | Yield (%) | 1.93 | S&P 3-Yr. Proj. EPS CAGR(%) | 13 |
| Trailing 12-Month P/E | 12.6 | P/E on S&P Oper. EPS 2009E | 12.0 | Dividend Rate/Share | $0.33 | S&P Credit Rating | BBB |
| $10K Invested 5 Yrs Ago | $10,577 | Common Shares Outstg. (M) | 711.0 | Institutional Ownership (%) | 91 | | |

## Price Performance

30-Week Mov. Avg. · · · · 10-Week Mov. Avg. - - GAAP Earnings vs. Previous Year  Volume Above Avg. STARS
12-Mo. Target Price — Relative Strength — ▲ Up ▼ Down ► No Change  Below Avg. ★

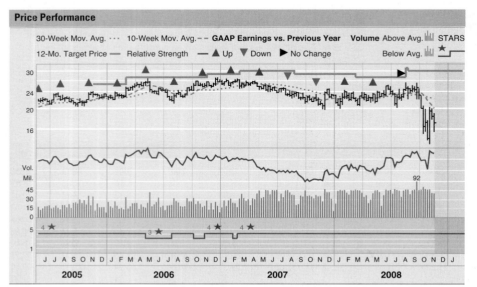

Options: ASE, CBOE, P, Ph

Analysis prepared by **Michael Souers** on September 03, 2008, when the stock traded at **$ 25.18**.

## Highlights

➤ We estimate sales growth of 30% in FY 09 (Jan.), following a 6.7% advance in FY 08. Sales growth should be achieved by the acquisition of Corporate Express, which closed in early July, continued international penetration, and about 100 net new store additions in North America. We expect same-store sales in North American Retail to decline 5%-6%, as customer traffic has weakened modestly -- a byproduct of the overall slowdown in consumer spending.

➤ We expect a modest narrowing of gross margins due to the acquisition of Corporate Express, which carries lower margins. We expect this to be partially offset by benefits from a growing private label business, supply chain initiatives, and lower sourcing costs. We also anticipate a significant decline in operating margins due to the acquisition and lackluster same-store sales results.

➤ We project a significant increase in net interest expense, an effective tax rate of 34.5%, and approximately 1% fewer shares outstanding. We estimate FY 09 operating EPS of $1.42, in line with the $1.42 the company earned in FY 08, excluding one-time items. We see FY 10 EPS of $1.63.

## Investment Rationale/Risk

➤ We believe the solid job market bodes well for SPLS, despite the slowdown in consumer spending. The North American Delivery division's recent performance has been stellar, in our opinion, and we anticipate continued strong results. Long term, we believe China and South America will provide SPLS with additional growth avenues. At about 15X our FY 09 EPS estimate, the shares recently traded at a slight discount to the S&P 500. We think a modest premium valuation is merited due to what we see as SPLS's strong balance sheet, long-term growth prospects and the significant cost synergies from the Corporate Express acquisition that should accrue over the next several years.

➤ Risks to our recommendation and target price include a sharp slowdown in economic growth and slower-than-expected capital spending and hiring by businesses. International risks include economic instability and unfavorable currency movements.

➤ Our 12-month target price of $30, about 18X our FY 10 EPS projection, is derived from our discounted cash flow model, which assumes a weighted average cost of capital of 9.9% and a terminal growth rate of 3.0%.

## Qualitative Risk Assessment

| LOW | MEDIUM | HIGH |
|---|---|---|

Our risk assessment reflects the rather cyclical nature of the company, which relies on consumer as well as business spending, and investments in emerging markets for future growth. This is offset by untapped growth areas in major domestic metro markets.

## Quantitative Evaluations

**S&P Quality Ranking**  B+

| D | C | B- | B | B+ | A- | A | A+ |
|---|---|---|---|---|---|---|---|

**Relative Strength Rank**  MODERATE

66

LOWEST = 1   HIGHEST = 99

## Revenue/Earnings Data

### Revenue (Million $)

| | 1Q | 2Q | 3Q | 4Q | Year |
|---|---|---|---|---|---|
| 2009 | 4,885 | 5,048 | -- | -- | -- |
| 2008 | 4,589 | 4,290 | 5,168 | 5,324 | 19,373 |
| 2007 | 4,238 | 3,881 | 4,757 | 5,286 | 18,161 |
| 2006 | 3,899 | 3,472 | 4,246 | 4,462 | 16,079 |
| 2005 | 3,452 | 3,089 | 3,830 | 4,077 | 14,448 |
| 2004 | 3,147 | 2,869 | 3,485 | 3,681 | 13,181 |

### Earnings Per Share ($)

| | 1Q | 2Q | 3Q | 4Q | Year |
|---|---|---|---|---|---|
| 2009 | 0.30 | 0.21 | E0.42 | E0.49 | E1.42 |
| 2008 | 0.29 | 0.21 | 0.38 | 0.47 | 1.38 |
| 2007 | 0.25 | 0.22 | 0.39 | 0.46 | 1.32 |
| 2006 | 0.20 | 0.20 | 0.32 | 0.39 | 1.12 |
| 2005 | 0.17 | 0.16 | 0.27 | 0.33 | 0.93 |
| 2004 | 0.03 | 0.12 | 0.22 | 0.28 | 0.66 |

Fiscal year ended Jan. 31. Next earnings report expected: Late November. EPS Estimates based on S&P Operating Earnings; historical GAAP earnings are as reported.

## Dividend Data (Dates: mm/dd Payment Date: mm/dd/yy)

| Amount ($) | Date Decl. | Ex-Div. Date | Stk. of Record | Payment Date |
|---|---|---|---|---|
| 0.330 | 03/04 | 03/26 | 03/28 | 04/17/08 |

Dividends have been paid since 2004. Source: Company reports.

---

**Please read the Required Disclosures and Analyst Certification on the last page of this report.**

# Staples Inc

## Business Summary September 03, 2008

CORPORATE OVERVIEW. Staples is the world's leading office products company, with net sales of nearly $19.4 billion in FY 08 (Jan.). Staples operates under three segments: North American Retail (52% of total revenues in FY 08); North American Delivery (34%); and International Operations (14%). Sales by product line were: office supplies and services 42%; business machines and related products 31%; computers and related products 20%; and office furniture 7%.

At February 2, 2008, SPLS operated 2,038 superstores, mostly in the United States (1,440 stores) and Canada (298 stores), but also in five European countries: the U.K. (134), Germany (58), the Netherlands (47), Portugal (25) and Belgium (4). In addition, Staples operates 32 retail stores in China (32).

SPLS has approximately 8,000 stock keeping units (SKUs) stocked in each of its typical North American retail stores and approximately 15,000 SKUs stocked in its North American Delivery fulfillment centers. On Staples.com, the company's Internet site, approximately 50,000 SKUs are available to customers.

CORPORATE STRATEGY. Staples seeks to maintain its leadership position in the office products industry by differentiating itself from the competition, delivering industry-best execution and expanding its market share. In FY 09, it plans to add over 100 new stores in North America, filling in existing markets along with expansion into untapped metro markets. Staples entered the Chicago, Miami and Denver markets in recent years, with initial results exceeding expectations, according to the company. We believe significant growth opportunities remain in other metropolitan markets where SPLS has yet to venture, and we expect the company to establish a strong Midwest presence over the next several years. SPLS also plans to open approximately 10 stores in Europe in FY 09.

## Company Financials Fiscal Year Ended Jan. 31

| Per Share Data ($) | 2008 | 2007 | 2006 | 2005 | 2004 | 2003 | 2002 | 2001 | 2000 | 1999 |
|---|---|---|---|---|---|---|---|---|---|---|
| Tangible Book Value | 5.28 | 4.64 | 3.84 | 3.45 | 3.01 | 1.74 | 2.63 | 2.19 | 1.99 | 2.18 |
| Cash Flow | NA | 1.78 | 1.56 | 1.33 | 1.03 | 1.01 | 0.73 | 0.42 | 0.67 | 0.69 |
| Earnings | 1.38 | 1.32 | 1.12 | 0.93 | 0.66 | 0.63 | 0.42 | 0.10 | 0.45 | 0.27 |
| S&P Core Earnings | 1.42 | 1.32 | 1.05 | 0.88 | 0.61 | 0.58 | 0.32 | 0.21 | NA | NA |
| Dividends | 0.22 | 0.17 | 0.17 | 0.13 | Nil | Nil | Nil | Nil | NA | NA |
| Payout Ratio | 16% | 13% | 15% | 14% | Nil | Nil | Nil | Nil | Nil | Nil |
| Calendar Year | 2007 | 2006 | 2005 | 2004 | 2003 | 2002 | 2001 | 2000 | 1999 | 1998 |
| Prices:High | 27.66 | 28.00 | 24.14 | 22.57 | 18.58 | 14.97 | 12.97 | 19.17 | 23.96 | 20.53 |
| Prices:Low | 19.69 | 21.08 | 18.64 | 15.79 | 10.49 | 7.79 | 7.35 | 6.83 | 10.96 | 7.06 |
| P/E Ratio:High | 20 | 21 | 22 | 24 | 28 | 24 | 31 | NM | 54 | 75 |
| P/E Ratio:Low | 14 | 16 | 17 | 17 | 16 | 12 | 17 | NM | 25 | 26 |

### Income Statement Analysis (Million $)

| | 2008 | 2007 | 2006 | 2005 | 2004 | 2003 | 2002 | 2001 | 2000 | 1999 |
|---|---|---|---|---|---|---|---|---|---|---|
| Revenue | 19,373 | 18,161 | 16,079 | 14,448 | 13,181 | 11,596 | 10,744 | 10,674 | 8,937 | 7,123 |
| Operating Income | NA | 1,802 | 1,617 | 1,405 | 1,081 | 950 | 768 | 719 | 708 | 514 |
| Depreciation | 389 | 339 | 304 | 279 | 283 | 267 | 249 | 231 | 174 | 99.2 |
| Interest Expense | NA | 47.8 | 56.8 | 39.9 | 20.2 | 20.6 | 27.2 | 45.2 | 17.1 | 17.4 |
| Pretax Income | 1,554 | 1,471 | 1,314 | 1,116 | 778 | 662 | 431 | 244 | 516 | 306 |
| Effective Tax Rate | 36.0% | 33.8% | 36.5% | 36.5% | 37.0% | 32.6% | 38.5% | 75.5% | 39.0% | 39.5% |
| Net Income | 996 | 974 | 834 | 708 | 490 | 446 | 265 | 59.7 | 315 | 185 |
| S&P Core Earnings | 1,020 | 974 | 784 | 667 | 450 | 413 | 221 | 147 | NA | NA |

### Balance Sheet & Other Financial Data (Million $)

| | 2008 | 2007 | 2006 | 2005 | 2004 | 2003 | 2002 | 2001 | 2000 | 1999 |
|---|---|---|---|---|---|---|---|---|---|---|
| Cash | 1,272 | 1,018 | 978 | 997 | 457 | 596 | 395 | 264 | 110 | 358 |
| Current Assets | NA | 4,431 | 4,145 | 3,782 | 3,479 | 2,717 | 2,403 | 2,356 | 2,192 | 2,064 |
| Total Assets | 9,036 | 8,397 | 7,677 | 7,071 | 6,503 | 5,721 | 4,093 | 3,989 | 3,814 | 3,179 |
| Current Liabilities | NA | 2,788 | 2,480 | 2,197 | 2,123 | 2,175 | 1,596 | 1,711 | 1,455 | 1,265 |
| Long Term Debt | NA | 569 | 528 | 558 | 567 | 732 | 350 | 441 | 501 | 205 |
| Common Equity | 5,718 | 5,022 | 4,425 | 4,115 | 3,663 | 2,659 | 2,054 | 1,764 | 1,829 | 1,657 |
| Total Capital | NA | 5,600 | 4,963 | 4,696 | 4,230 | 3,441 | 2,411 | 2,205 | 2,330 | 1,862 |
| Capital Expenditures | 470 | 528 | 456 | 335 | 278 | 265 | 340 | 450 | 355 | 322 |
| Cash Flow | NA | 1,313 | 1,138 | 987 | 773 | 713 | 514 | 291 | 489 | 285 |
| Current Ratio | 1.8 | 1.6 | 1.7 | 1.7 | 1.6 | 1.2 | 1.5 | 1.4 | 1.5 | 1.6 |
| % Long Term Debt of Capitalization | 5.6 | 10.2 | 10.6 | 11.9 | 13.4 | 21.3 | 14.5 | 20.0 | 21.5 | 11.0 |
| % Net Income of Revenue | 5.1 | 5.4 | 5.2 | 4.9 | 3.7 | 3.8 | 2.5 | 0.6 | 3.5 | 2.6 |
| % Return on Assets | 11.4 | 12.1 | 11.3 | 10.4 | 8.0 | 9.1 | 6.6 | 1.5 | 9.0 | 6.6 |
| % Return on Equity | 18.5 | 20.5 | 19.5 | 18.2 | 15.5 | 18.9 | 13.9 | 3.3 | 18.1 | 14.1 |

Data as orig reptd.; bef. results of disc opers/spec. items. Per share data adj. for stk. divs.; EPS diluted. E-Estimated. NA-Not Available. NM-Not Meaningful. NR-Not Ranked. UR-Under Review.

**Office:** Five Hundred Staples Dr, Framingham , MA 01702.
**Telephone:** 508-253-5000.
**Email:** investor@staples.com
**Website:** http://www.staples.com

**Chrmn & CEO:** R.L. Sargent
**Pres & COO:** M.A. Miles, Jr.
**Vice Chrmn & CFO:** J.J. Mahoney
**EVP & CIO:** B.T. Light

**SVP, Chief Acctg Officer & Cntlr:** C.T. Komola
**Investor Contact:** N. Hotchkin (800-468-7751)
**Board Members:** B. L. Anderson, A. M. Blank, M. E. Burton, J. M. King, J. J. Mahoney, C. Meyrowitz, R. T. Moriarty, R. C. Nakasone, R. L. Sargent, E. A. Smith, R. E. Sulentic, M. Trust, V. Vishwanath, P. F. Walsh

**Founded:** 1985
**Domicile:** Delaware
**Employees:** 75,588

# Starbucks Corp

| S&P Recommendation | STRONG BUY ★ ★ ★ ★ ★ | Price<br>$8.61 (as of Nov 14, 2008) | 12-Mo. Target Price<br>$19.00 | Investment Style<br>Large-Cap Growth |
|---|---|---|---|---|

**GICS Sector** Consumer Discretionary
**Sub-Industry** Restaurants

**Summary** Starbucks purchases and roasts high-quality whole bean coffees, which it sells -- together with rich-brewed coffees -- primarily through its more than 16,000 retail stores globally.

## Key Stock Statistics (Source S&P, Vickers, company reports)

| | | | | | | | |
|---|---|---|---|---|---|---|---|
| 52-Wk Range | $23.87– 8.08 | S&P Oper. EPS 2009E | 0.85 | Market Capitalization(B) | $6.290 | Beta | 1.09 |
| Trailing 12-Month EPS | $0.43 | S&P Oper. EPS 2010E | 1.05 | Yield (%) | Nil | S&P 3-Yr. Proj. EPS CAGR(%) | 7 |
| Trailing 12-Month P/E | 20.0 | P/E on S&P Oper. EPS 2009E | 10.1 | Dividend Rate/Share | Nil | S&P Credit Rating | BBB |
| $10K Invested 5 Yrs Ago | $5,370 | Common Shares Outstg. (M) | 730.6 | Institutional Ownership (%) | 66 | | |

## Price Performance

- 30-Week Mov. Avg. · · · · 10-Week Mov. Avg. - - - GAAP Earnings vs. Previous Year   Volume Above Avg. ⦙⦙⦙⦙ STARS
- 12-Mo. Target Price —   Relative Strength — ▲ Up ▼ Down ► No Change   Below Avg. ⦙⦙⦙⦙

Options: ASE, CBOE, P, Ph

## Highlights

▶ The 12-month target price for SBUX has recently been changed to $19.00 from $24.00. The Highlights section of this Stock Report will be updated accordingly.

## Investment Rationale/Risk

▶ The Investment Rationale/Risk section of this Stock Report will be updated shortly. For the latest News story on SBUX from MarketScope, see below.

▶ 11/11/08 10:56 am ET ... S&P REITERATES STRONG BUY RECOMMENDATION ON SHARES OF STARBUCKS CORP. (SBUX 9.9*****): Sep-Q operating EPS of $0.10 vs. $0.21 is below our $0.13 estimate. We think SBUX has largely completed initial steps in its transformation plan, which should enable it to boost profits at lower levels of comparable sales and be less reliant on company-financed growth. SBUX intends to reduce capex sizably in FY 09 (Sep.) and pay down short-term debt. We now see 4% lower global comp-store sales in FY 09 (Sep.), and lower our EPS estimate to $0.85 from $1.00. On higher assumed 12.3% weighted average cost of capital, vs. 11.7%, we lower our DCF-based target price by $5, to $19. /M.Basham

## Qualitative Risk Assessment

| LOW | MEDIUM | HIGH |
|---|---|---|

Our risk assessment reflects the early stage of plans to reinvigorate the Starbucks brand and improve profitability. We also see a threat from gourmet coffee offerings by competitors. Partly offsetting these concerns, we think the company has significant financial strength, affording it the capacity to continue on its growth trajectory.

## Quantitative Evaluations

**S&P Quality Ranking**                    B+

| D | C | B- | B | B+ | A- | A | A+ |
|---|---|---|---|---|---|---|---|

**Relative Strength Rank**                 MODERATE

32

LOWEST = 1                                 HIGHEST = 99

## Revenue/Earnings Data

**Revenue (Million $)**

| | 1Q | 2Q | 3Q | 4Q | Year |
|---|---|---|---|---|---|
| 2008 | 2,768 | 2,526 | 2,574 | 2,515 | 10,383 |
| 2007 | 2,356 | 2,256 | 2,359 | 2,441 | 9,411 |
| 2006 | 1,934 | 1,886 | 1,964 | 2,003 | 7,787 |
| 2005 | 1,590 | 1,519 | 1,602 | 1,659 | 6,369 |
| 2004 | 1,281 | 1,241 | 1,319 | 1,453 | 5,294 |
| 2003 | 1,004 | 954.2 | 1,037 | 1,081 | 4,076 |

**Earnings Per Share ($)**

| | | | | | |
|---|---|---|---|---|---|
| 2008 | 0.28 | 0.15 | -0.01 | 0.01 | 0.43 |
| 2007 | 0.26 | 0.19 | 0.21 | 0.21 | 0.87 |
| 2006 | 0.22 | 0.16 | 0.18 | 0.17 | 0.73 |
| 2005 | 0.17 | 0.12 | 0.16 | 0.16 | 0.61 |
| 2004 | 0.14 | 0.10 | 0.12 | 0.13 | 0.48 |
| 2003 | 0.10 | 0.07 | 0.09 | 0.09 | 0.34 |

Fiscal year ended Sep. 30. Next earnings report expected: Late January. EPS Estimates based on S&P Operating Earnings; historical GAAP earnings are as reported.

## Dividend Data

No cash dividends have been paid.

---

# Starbucks Corp

STANDARD &POOR'S

## Business Summary August 19, 2008

CORPORATE OVERVIEW. The Starbucks brand is nearly synonymous with specialty coffee. However, a slowing economy and overexpansion under prior management has led the company under returning CEO H. Schultz to slow down growth and evolve the brand beyond coffee.

The number of Starbucks retail stores grew to 16,548 at June 30, 2008, from 165 at the end of FY 92 (Sep.). Company-operated retail stores accounted for 85% of FY 07 net sales (85% in FY 06). Stores are typically clustered in high-traffic, high-visibility locations in each market. They are located in office buildings, downtown and suburban retail centers, and kiosks placed in building lobbies, airport terminals and supermarkets. In FY 07, the retail store sales mix by product type was 75% beverages, 17% food items, 3% whole bean coffees, and 5% coffee-related hardware items.

At June 30, 2008, SBUX owned and operated 7,375 of its stores in the U.S., and 1,932 stores in international markets. It opened a total of 1,342 company-owned stores in FY 07. There were also 4,195 licensed retail stores in the U.S. and 3,046 in international markets. Revenue from retail licensees was approximately 7% of total revenues in FY 07 (7% in FY 06). The Global Consumer Products Group accounted for 4% of total revenues in FY 07 (4% in FY 06). The company also has approximately 16,200 foodservice accounts. Foodservice revenues were 4% of total revenues in FY 07 (4% in FY 06).

KEY DEVELOPMENTS. At the time of the January 7 reappointment of Howard Schultz as CEO, the company outlined a five-point agenda: 1) improve the U.S. business by focusing on the customer experience and other factors affecting store operations; 2) slow the pace of U.S. expansion and close underperforming U.S. locations; 3) re-energize the Starbucks brand and create an emotional connection to the brand with customers and employees; 4) realign and streamline management and back-end functions to better support customer-focused initiatives; and 5) accelerate expansion outside the U.S. and drive profit margins higher at international operations.

New in-store programs to retain and attract customers announced under Schultz include implementation of the proprietary in-store Clover brewing system, resumption of grinding beans in stores, implementation of a new espresso system, and the launch of a first phase of a new customer loyalty rewards program that includes free refills while inside the store.

## Company Financials Fiscal Year Ended Sep. 30

| Per Share Data ($) | 2008 | 2007 | 2006 | 2005 | 2004 | 2003 | 2002 | 2001 | 2000 | 1999 |
|---|---|---|---|---|---|---|---|---|---|---|
| Tangible Book Value | NA | 2.74 | 2.68 | 2.56 | 3.00 | 2.52 | 2.20 | 1.78 | 1.50 | 1.29 |
| Cash Flow | NA | 1.51 | 1.25 | 1.06 | 0.85 | 0.66 | 0.55 | 0.45 | 0.48 | 0.28 |
| Earnings | 0.43 | 0.87 | 0.73 | 0.61 | 0.48 | 0.34 | 0.27 | 0.23 | 0.12 | 0.14 |
| S&P Core Earnings | NA | 0.87 | 0.73 | 0.53 | 0.42 | 0.29 | 0.23 | 0.18 | NA | NA |
| Dividends | NA | Nil | Nil | Nil | Nil | Nil | Nil | Nil | Nil | Nil |
| Payout Ratio | NA | Nil | Nil | Nil | Nil | Nil | Nil | Nil | Nil | Nil |
| Prices:High | NA | 36.61 | 40.01 | 32.46 | 32.13 | 16.72 | 12.85 | 12.83 | 12.70 | 10.25 |
| Prices:Low | NA | 19.89 | 28.72 | 22.29 | 16.45 | 9.81 | 9.22 | 6.73 | 5.78 | 4.97 |
| P/E Ratio:High | NA | 42 | 55 | 53 | 68 | 50 | 48 | 56 | NM | 76 |
| P/E Ratio:Low | NA | 23 | 39 | 37 | 35 | 29 | 34 | 29 | NM | 37 |

| Income Statement Analysis (Million $) | | | | | | | | | | |
|---|---|---|---|---|---|---|---|---|---|---|
| Revenue | 10,383 | 9,411 | 7,787 | 6,369 | 5,294 | 4,076 | 3,289 | 2,649 | 2,169 | 1,680 |
| Operating Income | NA | 1,437 | 1,213 | 1,071 | 854 | 646 | 504 | 430 | 334 | 264 |
| Depreciation | 604 | 491 | 413 | 367 | 305 | 259 | 221 | 177 | 142 | 108 |
| Interest Expense | NA | Nil | Nil | Nil | Nil | Nil | Nil | Nil | Nil | 1.36 |
| Pretax Income | 460 | 1,056 | 906 | 796 | 624 | 436 | 341 | 289 | 161 | 164 |
| Effective Tax Rate | 31.3% | 36.3% | 35.8% | 37.9% | 37.2% | 38.5% | 37.0% | 37.3% | 41.1% | 38.0% |
| Net Income | 316 | 673 | 581 | 494 | 392 | 268 | 215 | 181 | 94.6 | 102 |
| S&P Core Earnings | NA | 673 | 579 | 437 | 346 | 231 | 181 | 143 | NA | NA |

| Balance Sheet & Other Financial Data (Million $) | | | | | | | | | | |
|---|---|---|---|---|---|---|---|---|---|---|
| Cash | 322 | 281 | 313 | 174 | 299 | 201 | 175 | 113 | 70.8 | 66.4 |
| Current Assets | NA | 1,696 | 1,530 | 1,209 | 1,368 | 924 | 848 | 594 | 460 | 387 |
| Total Assets | 5,673 | 5,344 | 4,429 | 3,514 | 3,328 | 2,730 | 2,293 | 1,851 | 1,493 | 1,253 |
| Current Liabilities | NA | 2,156 | 1,936 | 1,227 | 783 | 609 | 537 | 445 | 313 | 252 |
| Long Term Debt | NA | 550 | 1.96 | 2.87 | 3.62 | 4.35 | 5.08 | 5.79 | 6.48 | 7.02 |
| Common Equity | 2,491 | 2,284 | 2,229 | 2,091 | 2,487 | 2,082 | 1,727 | 1,376 | 1,148 | 961 |
| Total Capital | NA | 2,834 | 2,230 | 2,094 | 2,537 | 2,120 | 1,754 | 1,406 | 1,180 | 1,001 |
| Capital Expenditures | 984 | 1,080 | 771 | 644 | 386 | 357 | 375 | 384 | 316 | 262 |
| Cash Flow | NA | 1,164 | 994 | 862 | 697 | 528 | 436 | 358 | 367 | 209 |
| Current Ratio | 0.8 | 0.8 | 0.8 | 1.0 | 1.7 | 1.5 | 1.6 | 1.3 | 1.5 | 1.5 |
| % Long Term Debt of Capitalization | 18.1 | 19.4 | 0.1 | 0.1 | 0.1 | 0.2 | 0.3 | 0.4 | 0.5 | 0.7 |
| % Net Income of Revenue | 3.0 | 7.1 | 7.5 | 7.8 | 7.4 | 6.6 | 6.5 | 6.8 | 4.4 | 6.1 |
| % Return on Assets | 5.7 | 13.8 | 14.6 | 14.3 | 12.9 | 10.9 | 10.4 | 10.8 | 6.9 | 9.1 |
| % Return on Equity | 13.2 | 29.8 | 26.9 | 21.7 | 17.1 | 14.1 | 13.9 | 14.4 | 9.0 | 11.6 |

Data as orig reptd.; bef. results of disc opers/spec. items. Per share data adj. for stk. divs.; EPS diluted. E-Estimated. NA-Not Available. NM-Not Meaningful. NR-Not Ranked. UR-Under Review.

**Office:** 2401 Utah Avenue South, Seattle, WA 98134.
**Telephone:** 206-447-1575.
**Email:** investorrelations@starbucks.com
**Website:** http://www.starbucks.com

**Chrmn, Pres & CEO:** H.D. Schultz
**EVP, CFO, Chief Admin Officer & Chief Acctg Officer:** P.J. Bocian
**EVP, Secy & General Counsel:** P.E. Boggs
**SVP & CIO:** S. Gillett

**Board Members:** B. Bass, H. Behar, W. W. Bradley, M. L. Hobson, O. C. Lee, H. D. Schultz, J. G. Shennan, Jr., J. G. Teruel, M. E. Ullman, III, C. E. Weatherup
**Founded:** 1985
**Domicile:** Washington
**Employees:** 172,000

# Starwood Hotels & Resorts Worldwide Inc.

STANDARD
&POOR'S

| S&P Recommendation HOLD ★★★☆☆ | Price $14.99 (as of Nov 14, 2008) | 12-Mo. Target Price $18.00 | Investment Style Large-Cap Blend |
|---|---|---|---|

**GICS Sector** Consumer Discretionary
**Sub-Industry** Hotels, Resorts & Cruise Lines

**Summary** Starwood is one of the world's largest lodging companies, with over 900 hotels in more than 100 countries operating under eight brands.

## Key Stock Statistics (Source S&P, Vickers, company reports)

| | | | | | | | |
|---|---|---|---|---|---|---|---|
| 52-Wk Range | $56.00–13.92 | S&P Oper. EPS 2008**E** | 1.86 | Market Capitalization(B) | $2.744 | Beta | 1.11 |
| Trailing 12-Month EPS | $2.09 | S&P Oper. EPS 2009**E** | 1.15 | Yield (%) | 6.00 | S&P 3-Yr. Proj. EPS CAGR(%) | -22 |
| Trailing 12-Month P/E | 7.2 | P/E on S&P Oper. EPS 2008**E** | 8.1 | Dividend Rate/Share | $0.90 | S&P Credit Rating | BBB- |
| $10K Invested 5 Yrs Ago | $5,783 | Common Shares Outstg. (M) | 183.0 | Institutional Ownership (%) | 90 | | |

## Price Performance

30-Week Mov. Avg. ···  10-Week Mov. Avg. - -  GAAP Earnings vs. Previous Year  Volume Above Avg. ▌▌▌ STARS
12-Mo. Target Price —  Relative Strength —  ▲ Up  ▼ Down  ► No Change  Below Avg. ▌▌▌ ★

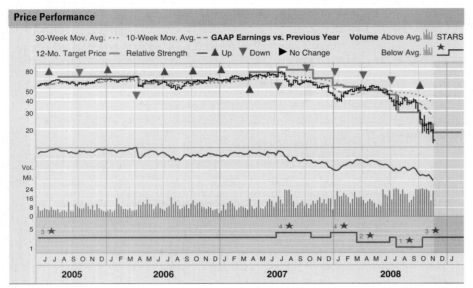

Options: CBOE, Ph

## Highlights

➤ The 12-month target price for HOT has recently been changed to $18.00 from $22.00. The Highlights section of this Stock Report will be updated accordingly.

## Investment Rationale/Risk

➤ The Investment Rationale/Risk section of this Stock Report will be updated shortly. For the latest News story on HOT from MarketScope, see below.

➤ 11/13/08 09:43 am ET … S&P MAINTAINS HOLD SHARES OF STARWOOD HOTELS & RESORTS (HOT 15.26***): Although mid-teen percentage declines in US hotel occupancy and revenue per available room for the first week in November, as reported by Smith Travel Research, may not continue at that level, we think fundamentals are clearly weakening. We now expect a 7%-10% decline in US RevPAR for 2009. Global conditions continue to weaken as well. With diverse operations across geographies and hotel classes, HOT is fully exposed to the slowdown. We lower our EPS estimates for '08 by $0.05 to $1.85 and '09 by $0.10 to $1.15. On 8.5X revised EV/EBITDA, we lower our target price by $4 to $18. /M.Basham

## Qualitative Risk Assessment

| LOW | MEDIUM | HIGH |
|---|---|---|

In our view, Starwood's ongoing divestiture of non-strategic hotels has moved the company's business mix more toward management and franchising of hotels, with less emphasis on real estate ownership, making it somewhat less sensitive, but not immune, to macroeconomic conditions. Despite our expectation that the company will likely generate significant free cash flow over the long term, conditions in the global lodging industry are likely to deteriorate, in our view, over the intermediate term.

## Quantitative Evaluations

**S&P Quality Ranking**                                    NR

| D | C | B- | B | B+ | A- | A | A+ |
|---|---|---|---|---|---|---|---|

**Relative Strength Rank**                              WEAK

19

LOWEST = 1                                      HIGHEST = 99

## Revenue/Earnings Data

**Revenue (Million $)**

| | 1Q | 2Q | 3Q | 4Q | Year |
|---|---|---|---|---|---|
| 2008 | 1,466 | 1,573 | 1,535 | -- | -- |
| 2007 | 1,431 | 1,572 | 1,540 | 1,610 | 6,153 |
| 2006 | 1,441 | 1,505 | 1,461 | 1,572 | 5,979 |
| 2005 | 1,406 | 1,559 | 1,496 | 1,516 | 5,977 |
| 2004 | 1,227 | 1,363 | 1,336 | 1,442 | 5,368 |
| 2003 | 1,073 | 1,220 | 1,140 | 1,197 | 4,630 |

**Earnings Per Share ($)**

| | 1Q | 2Q | 3Q | 4Q | Year |
|---|---|---|---|---|---|
| 2008 | 0.42 | 0.57 | 0.62 | E0.25 | E1.86 |
| 2007 | 0.56 | 0.67 | 0.61 | 0.74 | 2.57 |
| 2006 | 0.34 | 3.01 | 0.71 | 0.94 | 5.01 |
| 2005 | 0.36 | 0.65 | 0.18 | 0.72 | 1.88 |
| 2004 | 0.16 | 0.56 | 0.49 | 0.51 | 1.72 |
| 2003 | -0.58 | 0.42 | 0.23 | 0.42 | 0.51 |

Fiscal year ended Dec. 31. Next earnings report expected: Early February. EPS Estimates based on S&P Operating Earnings; historical GAAP earnings are as reported.

## Dividend Data (Dates: mm/dd Payment Date: mm/dd/yy)

| Amount ($) | Date Decl. | Ex-Div. Date | Stk. of Record | Payment Date |
|---|---|---|---|---|
| 0.900 | 11/08 | 12/29 | 12/31 | 01/09/09 |

Dividends have been paid since 1995. Source: Company reports.

# Starwood Hotels & Resorts Worldwide Inc.

STANDARD
&POOR'S

## Business Summary October 20, 2008

CORPORATE OVERVIEW. Starwood Hotels & Resorts (HOT) is one of the world's largest hotel companies, with owned, leased, managed or franchised hotels in approximately 100 countries. At June 30, 2008, the company's business included 908 hotels, with 277,069 rooms. In addition, HOT had 28 vacation ownership resorts in operation. Some of these resorts, plus some additional HOT-related resorts, were actively selling inventory.

HOT's business includes owned, managed and franchised properties. Its brands include St. Regis (luxury full-service hotels and resorts), The Luxury Collection (luxury full-service hotels and resorts), Westin (luxury and upscale full-service hotels and resorts), Sheraton (full-service hotels and resorts), W (boutique full-service urban hotels), and Four Points (moderately priced full-service hotels). At June 30, 2008, the company's hotel business included 404 Sheratons (141,227 rooms), 158 Westins (62,722 rooms), 70 properties (12,603 rooms) in the St. Regis and Luxury Collection groups, 130 Four Points (22,691 rooms), 22 hotels (6,608 rooms) in the W chain, 111 Le Meridien properties (28,627 rooms), four hotels with 402 rooms in HOT's new boutique hotel brand aloft, and 10 other hotels (2,189 rooms).

The company's top five domestic markets by percentage of total owned EBIT-

DA during 2007 were: New York (15.2%), Hawaii (8.0%), Phoenix (5.7%), Chicago (4.7%), and Atlanta (4.2%). The top six international markets were Italy (10.5%), Canada (7.9%), Mexico (7.6%), Australia (4.0%), and Argentina and United Kingdom (both 3.2%). Worldwide operating statistics for the 68 owned hotels operating in both 2006 and 2007 were: average daily rate of $222.03 in 2007, up 9.2% from $203.31 in 2006, and occupancy of 72.2% vs. 71.6%, which resulted in RevPAR of $160.38, up 10.2% from $145.57.

The company had 28 vacation ownership resorts as of June 30, 2008, including 19 in operations and 17 in active sales. Two of these were owned by unconsolidated joint ventures. There were 4,443 completed units, with 499 additional units under development. A potential additional 2,511 units were possible, based on land owned and average unit densities in existing markets. In total and assuming 52 intervals per unit, HOT had inventory of 387,556 vacation ownership intervals.

## Company Financials Fiscal Year Ended Dec. 31

| Per Share Data ($) | 2007 | 2006 | 2005 | 2004 | 2003 | 2002 | 2001 | 2000 | 1999 | 1998 |
|---|---|---|---|---|---|---|---|---|---|---|
| Tangible Book Value | NM | 3.31 | 13.59 | 10.73 | 4.55 | 3.57 | 2.35 | 2.50 | 2.16 | 1.43 |
| Cash Flow | 4.02 | 6.37 | 3.69 | 3.72 | 2.58 | 2.28 | 3.29 | 4.30 | -0.86 | 3.73 |
| Earnings | 2.57 | 5.01 | 1.88 | 1.72 | 0.51 | 1.20 | 0.73 | 1.96 | -3.41 | 0.67 |
| S&P Core Earnings | 2.69 | 4.87 | 1.66 | 1.37 | 0.12 | 0.77 | 0.52 | NA | NA | NA |
| Dividends | 0.90 | 0.84 | 0.84 | 0.84 | 0.84 | 0.84 | 0.80 | 0.69 | 0.60 | 2.04 |
| Payout Ratio | 35% | 17% | 45% | 49% | 165% | 70% | 110% | 35% | NM | NM |
| Prices:High | 75.45 | 68.87 | 65.22 | 59.50 | 37.60 | 39.94 | 40.89 | 37.50 | 37.75 | 57.88 |
| Prices:Low | 42.78 | 49.68 | 51.50 | 34.81 | 21.68 | 19.00 | 17.10 | 19.75 | 19.50 | 18.75 |
| P/E Ratio:High | 29 | 14 | 35 | 35 | 74 | 33 | 56 | 19 | NM | 86 |
| P/E Ratio:Low | 17 | 10 | 27 | 20 | 43 | 16 | 23 | 10 | NM | 28 |

| Income Statement Analysis (Million $) | 2007 | 2006 | 2005 | 2004 | 2003 | 2002 | 2001 | 2000 | 1999 | 1998 |
|---|---|---|---|---|---|---|---|---|---|---|
| Revenue | 6,153 | 5,979 | 5,977 | 5,368 | 4,630 | 4,659 | 3,967 | 4,345 | 3,862 | 4,710 |
| Operating Income | 1,217 | 1,145 | 1,242 | 1,047 | 1,698 | 1,856 | 1,191 | 1,509 | 1,329 | 1,361 |
| Depreciation | 306 | 306 | 407 | 431 | 429 | 222 | 526 | 481 | 476 | 556 |
| Interest Expense | 215 | 244 | 258 | 257 | 287 | 338 | 369 | 439 | 516 | 639 |
| Pretax Income | 733 | 682 | 642 | 412 | -5.00 | 252 | 200 | 610 | 533 | 43.0 |
| Effective Tax Rate | 25.8% | NM | 34.1% | 10.4% | NM | 1.59% | 23.0% | 33.0% | NM | NM |
| Net Income | 543 | 1,115 | 423 | 369 | 105 | 246 | 151 | 401 | -638 | 141 |
| S&P Core Earnings | 570 | 1,084 | 376 | 291 | 27.7 | 157 | 107 | NA | NA | NA |

| Balance Sheet & Other Financial Data (Million $) | 2007 | 2006 | 2005 | 2004 | 2003 | 2002 | 2001 | 2000 | 1999 | 1998 |
|---|---|---|---|---|---|---|---|---|---|---|
| Cash | 358 | 183 | 897 | 326 | 508 | 216 | 157 | 189 | 436 | 290 |
| Current Assets | 1,824 | 1,810 | 2,283 | 1,683 | 1,245 | 950 | 897 | 1,048 | 1,176 | 1,077 |
| Total Assets | 9,622 | 9,280 | 12,454 | 12,298 | 11,894 | 12,259 | 12,461 | 12,660 | 12,923 | 16,101 |
| Current Liabilities | 2,101 | 2,461 | 2,879 | 2,128 | 1,644 | 2,199 | 1,587 | 1,805 | 2,303 | 2,074 |
| Long Term Debt | 3,590 | 1,827 | 2,926 | 3,823 | 4,393 | 4,449 | 5,269 | 5,074 | 4,779 | 8,111 |
| Common Equity | 2,076 | 3,008 | 5,211 | 4,788 | 4,326 | 6,357 | 3,756 | 3,851 | 3,690 | 4,202 |
| Total Capital | 5,720 | 4,891 | 8,724 | 9,518 | 9,676 | 11,882 | 10,380 | 10,417 | 10,167 | 13,580 |
| Capital Expenditures | 384 | 371 | 464 | 333 | 307 | 82.0 | 477 | 544 | 521 | 832 |
| Cash Flow | 849 | 1,421 | 830 | 800 | 534 | 468 | 677 | 882 | -162 | 697 |
| Current Ratio | 0.9 | 0.7 | 0.8 | 0.8 | 0.8 | 0.4 | 0.6 | 0.6 | 0.5 | 0.5 |
| % Long Term Debt of Capitalization | 62.8 | 37.4 | 33.5 | 40.2 | 45.4 | 37.4 | 50.8 | 48.7 | 47.0 | 59.7 |
| % Net Income of Revenue | 8.8 | 18.6 | 7.1 | 6.9 | NM | 5.3 | 3.8 | 9.2 | NM | 3.0 |
| % Return on Assets | 5.8 | 10.2 | 3.4 | 3.1 | NM | 2.0 | 1.2 | 3.1 | NM | 1.2 |
| % Return on Equity | 21.4 | 27.1 | 8.5 | 8.1 | NM | 3.9 | 4.0 | 10.6 | NM | 4.1 |

Data as orig reptd.; bef. results of disc opers/spec. items. Per share data adj. for stk. divs.; EPS diluted. E-Estimated. NA-Not Available. NM-Not Meaningful. NR-Not Ranked. UR-Under Review.

**Office:** 1111 Westchester Avenue, White Plains, NY 10604.
**Telephone:** 914-640-8100.
**Website:** http://www.starwoodhotels.com
**Chrmn:** B.W. Duncan

**Pres & CEO:** F. van Paasschen
**Investor Contact:** V.M. Prabhu (914-640-8100)
**EVP & CFO:** V.M. Prabhu
**EVP, Chief Admin Officer, Secy & General Counsel:** K.S. Siegel

**Board Members:** A. M. Aron, C. Barshefsky, J. Chapus, T. E. Clarke, C. C. Daley, Jr., B. W. Duncan, L. Galbreath, E. C. Hippeau, S. R. Quazzo, T. O. Ryder, K. C. Youngblood, F. van Paasschen

**Founded:** 1969
**Domicile:** Maryland
**Employees:** 155,000

The McGraw-Hill Companies

# State Street Corp

**STANDARD &POOR'S**

| S&P Recommendation HOLD ★★★☆☆ | Price $38.89 (as of Nov 14, 2008) | 12-Mo. Target Price $50.00 | Investment Style Large-Cap Growth |
|---|---|---|---|

**GICS Sector** Financials
**Sub-Industry** Asset Management & Custody Banks

**Summary** This bank holding company, with about $11 trillion in assets under custody, is a leading servicer of financial assets worldwide.

## Key Stock Statistics (Source S&P, Vickers, company reports)

| | | | | | | | |
|---|---|---|---|---|---|---|---|
| 52-Wk Range | $86.55–29.09 | S&P Oper. EPS 2008**E** | 5.17 | Market Capitalization(B) | $16.799 | Beta | 1.10 |
| Trailing 12-Month EPS | $4.38 | S&P Oper. EPS 2009**E** | 4.83 | Yield (%) | 2.47 | S&P 3-Yr. Proj. EPS CAGR(%) | 4 |
| Trailing 12-Month P/E | 8.9 | P/E on S&P Oper. EPS 2008**E** | 7.5 | Dividend Rate/Share | $0.96 | S&P Credit Rating | AA- |
| $10K Invested 5 Yrs Ago | $8,205 | Common Shares Outstg. (M) | 432.0 | Institutional Ownership (%) | 83 | | |

## Price Performance

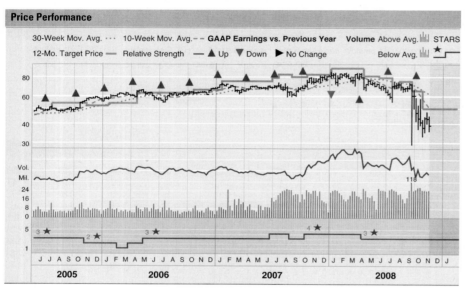

30-Week Mov. Avg. · · · 10-Week Mov. Avg. — — GAAP Earnings vs. Previous Year  Volume Above Avg. STARS
12-Mo. Target Price — Relative Strength — ▲ Up ▼ Down ► No Change  Below Avg.

Options: Ph

Analysis prepared by **Stuart Plesser** on October 21, 2008, when the stock traded at **$ 41.11**.

## Highlights

➤ We expect revenue growth of 2.4% for 2009, helped by the Investors Financial acquisition and STT's success in gaining new assets both in the U.S. and internationally, offset by a slowdown in securities finance service and trading revenues. A steepened yield curve should result in net interest income growth. We believe that long-term macro trends affecting STT remain intact, including the outsourcing of custody services, growth in worldwide pension systems, the development of more complex investment vehicles, consolidation among financial processing providers, and increasing pressure on public retirement systems.

➤ We remain confident in management's ability to better align operating expenses with its market-sensitive revenue model. We expect expenses of roughly 68% of revenue in line with our projections for 2008. We expect STT's pretax operating margin to total over 30% in 2009.

➤ We project operating EPS of $5.17 for 2008, assuming a roughly 14% increase in average dilutive shares. In 2009, we look for EPS of $4.83.

## Investment Rationale/Risk

➤ We have concerns regarding STT's exposure to asset-backed commercial paper, and the possibility of an increase in losses in its securities portfolio. Specifically, unrealized losses rose to $3.3 billion in the third quarter, up from $2.0 billion in the previous quarter. We also are concerned that STT may have to transfer its conduit facilities to its balance sheet putting a strain on capital. Separately, STT's main custody business is performing well, and should benefit from providing services for the U.S. government. With the shares recently trading at about 8X our 2009 EPS estimate, we think our concerns are already priced into the stock.

➤ Risks to our recommendation and target price include a significant slowdown in capital markets; further securities writedowns; the need for STT to transfer its conduit facilities onto its balance sheet; and, rising legal costs.

➤ Our 12-month target price is $50, or 10.4X our 2009 EPS estimate, a discount to peers and STT's historical average, which we view as justified by off balance sheet exposure and the possibility of having to realize further securities losses.

## Qualitative Risk Assessment

| LOW | MEDIUM | HIGH |
|---|---|---|

Our risk assessment reflects our view of solid fundamentals coupled with a strong customer base and good diversification. We believe STT has a well-established business and has maintained healthy earnings growth, offset by exposure to off balance sheet conduits.

## Quantitative Evaluations

**S&P Quality Ranking**    A

| D | C | B- | B | B+ | A- | A | A+ |
|---|---|---|---|---|---|---|---|

**Relative Strength Rank**    MODERATE

46

LOWEST = 1    HIGHEST = 99

## Revenue/Earnings Data

**Revenue (Million $)**

| | 1Q | 2Q | 3Q | 4Q | Year |
|---|---|---|---|---|---|
| 2008 | 2,577 | -- | 2,771 | -- | -- |
| 2007 | 1,696 | 2,740 | 3,165 | 2,479 | 11,818 |
| 2006 | 2,218 | 2,409 | 2,349 | 2,531 | 9,510 |
| 2005 | 1,699 | 1,837 | 1,925 | 2,035 | 7,496 |
| 2004 | 1,400 | 1,469 | 1,424 | 1,604 | 5,897 |
| 2003 | 1,213 | 1,290 | 1,287 | 1,673 | 5,463 |

**Earnings Per Share ($)**

| | 1Q | 2Q | 3Q | 4Q | Year |
|---|---|---|---|---|---|
| 2008 | 1.35 | 1.35 | 1.09 | E1.14 | E5.17 |
| 2007 | 0.93 | 1.07 | 0.91 | 0.57 | 3.45 |
| 2006 | 0.84 | 0.68 | 0.83 | 0.91 | 3.26 |
| 2005 | 0.67 | 0.66 | 0.75 | 0.74 | 2.82 |
| 2004 | 0.63 | 0.65 | 0.52 | 0.55 | 2.35 |
| 2003 | 0.29 | -0.07 | 0.60 | 1.33 | 2.15 |

Fiscal year ended Dec. 31. Next earnings report expected: NA. EPS Estimates based on S&P Operating Earnings; historical GAAP earnings are as reported.

## Dividend Data (Dates: mm/dd Payment Date: mm/dd/yy)

| Amount ($) | Date Decl. | Ex-Div. Date | Stk. of Record | Payment Date |
|---|---|---|---|---|
| 0.230 | 12/13 | 12/28 | 01/02 | 01/15/08 |
| 0.230 | 03/20 | 03/28 | 04/01 | 04/15/08 |
| 0.240 | 06/19 | 06/27 | 07/01 | 07/15/08 |
| 0.240 | 09/17 | 09/29 | 10/01 | 10/15/08 |

Dividends have been paid since 1910. Source: Company reports.

---

**Please read the Required Disclosures and Analyst Certification on the last page of this report.**

The McGraw-Hill Companies

# State Street Corp

STANDARD
&POOR'S

## Business Summary October 21, 2008

CORPORATE OVERVIEW. STT is a leading specialist in meeting the needs of institutional investors worldwide. Its customers include mutual funds and other collective investment funds, corporate and public pension funds, investment managers, and others. STT operates in the U.S., Australia, Austria, Belgium, Canada, the Cayman Islands, Chile, France, Germany, India, Ireland, Italy, Japan, Luxembourg, Mauritius, the Netherlands, New Zealand, China, Singapore, South Africa, South Korea, Switzerland, Taiwan, Thailand, the United Arab Emirates, and the United Kingdom.

STT reports two lines of business: Investment Servicing and Investment Management. Investment Servicing provides services for mutual funds and collective investment funds, corporate and public retirement plans, insurance companies, foundations, endowments, and other investment pools worldwide. Products include custody, product- and participant-level accounting, daily pricing and administration; master trust and master custody; record keeping; foreign exchange, brokerage and other trading services; securities finance; deposit and short-term investment facilities; loans and lease financing; investment manager and hedge fund manager operations outsourcing; and performance, risk and compliance analytics to support institutional investors.

Investment Management offers a broad array of services for managing financial assets, including investment management and investment research services, primarily for institutional investors worldwide. These services include passive and active U.S. and non-U.S. equity and fixed income strategies, and other related services, such as securities finance.

CORPORATE STRATEGY. STT maintains several goals in operating its business: generate positive operating leverage, increase non-U.S. revenue to 50% over time, actively manage its balance sheet, and continue to win new customers and penetrate existing customers. In 2007, STT achieved about 500 basis points of operating leverage. In 2007, STT's non-U.S. revenue was 41% of total revenue, compared to 43% in 2006 39% in 2005 and 37% in 2004. The 2007 percentage reflects revenue from the acquired Investors Financial business, which predominantly generates revenue in the U.S. We note that STT is taking advantage of faster-growing and less mature markets in Europe and the Asia/Pacific region.

## Company Financials Fiscal Year Ended Dec. 31

| Per Share Data ($) | 2007 | 2006 | 2005 | 2004 | 2003 | 2002 | 2001 | 2000 | 1999 | 1998 |
|---|---|---|---|---|---|---|---|---|---|---|
| Tangible Book Value | 12.67 | 16.37 | 13.73 | 12.49 | 11.66 | 12.92 | 11.87 | 10.13 | 8.31 | 7.19 |
| Earnings | 3.45 | 3.26 | 2.82 | 2.35 | 2.15 | 3.10 | 1.90 | 1.82 | 1.89 | 1.33 |
| S&P Core Earnings | 3.47 | 3.30 | 2.80 | 2.30 | 1.41 | 2.01 | 1.83 | NA | NA | NA |
| Dividends | 0.88 | 0.80 | 0.72 | 0.64 | 0.56 | 0.48 | 0.41 | 0.35 | 0.29 | 0.25 |
| Payout Ratio | 26% | 25% | 26% | 27% | 26% | 15% | 21% | 19% | 15% | 19% |
| Prices:High | 82.53 | 68.56 | 59.80 | 56.90 | 53.63 | 58.36 | 63.93 | 68.40 | 47.63 | 37.16 |
| Prices:Low | 59.13 | 54.39 | 40.62 | 39.91 | 30.37 | 32.11 | 36.25 | 31.22 | 27.75 | 23.94 |
| P/E Ratio:High | 24 | 21 | 21 | 24 | 25 | 19 | 34 | 38 | 25 | 28 |
| P/E Ratio:Low | 17 | 17 | 14 | 17 | 14 | 10 | 19 | 17 | 15 | 18 |

| Income Statement Analysis (Million $) | | | | | | | | | | |
|---|---|---|---|---|---|---|---|---|---|---|
| Net Interest Income | 1,730 | 1,110 | 907 | 859 | 810 | 979 | 1,025 | 894 | 781 | 745 |
| Tax Equivalent Adjustment | 58.0 | NA | 42.0 | 45.0 | 51.0 | 61.0 | 67.0 | 65.0 | 40.0 | 40.0 |
| Non Interest Income | 6,599 | 5,201 | 4,566 | 4,074 | 3,925 | 3,421 | 2,782 | 2,665 | 2,255 | 1,997 |
| Loan Loss Provision | Nil | Nil | Nil | -18.0 | Nil | 4.00 | 10.0 | 9.00 | 80.0 | 17.0 |
| % Expense/Operating Revenue | 77.2% | 71.9% | 73.8% | 76.2% | 76.5% | 64.6% | 75.3% | 74.3% | 76.9% | 75.4% |
| Pretax Income | 1,903 | 1,771 | 1,432 | 1,192 | 1,112 | 1,555 | 930 | 906 | 968 | 657 |
| Effective Tax Rate | 33.7% | 38.1% | 34.0% | 33.1% | 35.1% | 34.7% | 32.5% | 34.3% | 36.1% | 33.6% |
| Net Income | 1,261 | 1,096 | 945 | 798 | 722 | 1,015 | 628 | 595 | 619 | 436 |
| % Net Interest Margin | 1.71 | 1.25 | 1.08 | 1.08 | 1.17 | 1.42 | 1.66 | 1.66 | 1.66 | 1.90 |
| S&P Core Earnings | 1,269 | 1,107 | 939 | 782 | 473 | 658 | 604 | NA | NA | NA |

| Balance Sheet & Other Financial Data (Million $) | | | | | | | | | | |
|---|---|---|---|---|---|---|---|---|---|---|
| Money Market Assets | 29,841 | 20,699 | 12,039 | 26,829 | 31,694 | 46,342 | 37,991 | 44,083 | 35,616 | 26,399 |
| Investment Securities | 74,559 | 64,992 | 59,870 | 37,571 | 38,215 | 28,071 | 20,781 | 13,740 | 14,703 | 9,737 |
| Commercial Loans | 13,822 | 6,617 | 4,152 | 2,352 | 2,768 | 2,052 | 3,289 | 3,476 | 2,326 | 4,721 |
| Other Loans | 1,980 | 2,329 | 2,312 | 2,277 | 2,253 | 2,122 | 2,052 | 1,797 | 1,967 | 1,588 |
| Total Assets | 142,543 | 107,353 | 97,968 | 94,040 | 87,534 | 85,794 | 69,896 | 69,298 | 60,896 | 47,082 |
| Demand Deposits | 15,039 | 10,194 | 9,402 | 13,671 | 7,893 | 7,279 | 9,390 | 10,009 | 8,943 | 8,386 |
| Time Deposits | 80,750 | 55,452 | 50,244 | 41,458 | 39,623 | 38,189 | 29,169 | 27,928 | 25,202 | 19,153 |
| Long Term Debt | 3,636 | 2,616 | 2,659 | 2,458 | 2,222 | 1,270 | 1,217 | 1,219 | 921 | 922 |
| Common Equity | 11,299 | 7,252 | 6,367 | 6,159 | 5,747 | 4,787 | 3,845 | 3,262 | 2,652 | 2,311 |
| % Return on Assets | 1.0 | 1.1 | 1.0 | 0.9 | 0.8 | 1.3 | 0.9 | 0.9 | 1.1 | 1.0 |
| % Return on Equity | 13.6 | 16.1 | 15.1 | 13.4 | 13.7 | 23.5 | 17.7 | 20.1 | 24.9 | 20.3 |
| % Loan Loss Reserve | 0.1 | 0.2 | 0.3 | 0.4 | 1.2 | 1.5 | 1.1 | 1.1 | 1.1 | 1.3 |
| % Loans/Deposits | 15.3 | 13.6 | 10.9 | 8.4 | 10.6 | 9.2 | 13.9 | 13.9 | 12.6 | 22.9 |
| % Equity to Assets | 7.4 | 6.6 | 6.5 | 6.6 | 6.1 | 5.5 | 5.1 | 4.5 | 4.6 | 5.1 |

Data as orig reptd.; bef. results of disc opers/spec. items. Per share data adj. for stk. divs.; EPS diluted. E-Estimated. NA-Not Available. NM-Not Meaningful. NR-Not Ranked. UR-Under Review.

**Office:** 1 Lincoln St, Boston, MA 02111-2900.
**Telephone:** 617-786-3000.
**Email:** ir@statestreet.com
**Website:** http://www.statestreet.com

**Chrmn & CEO:** R.E. Logue
**Pres & COO:** J.L. Hooley
**EVP & CFO:** E.J. Resch
**EVP & Chief Admin Officer:** J.W. Chow

**EVP, Chief Acctg Officer & Cntlr:** J.J. Malerba
**Investor Contact:** S.K. MacDonald (617-786-3000)
**Board Members:** K. F. Burnes, P. Coym, N. F. Darehshori, A. Fawcett, D. P. Gruber, L. A. Hill, C. R. LaMantia, R. E. Logue, R. P. Sergel, R. L. Skates, G. L. Summe, R. E. Weissman

**Founded:** 1832
**Domicile:** Massachusetts
**Employees:** 27,110

The McGraw-Hill Companies

# Stryker Corp

**STANDARD &POOR'S**

**S&P Recommendation** BUY ★★★★☆

| Price | 12-Mo. Target Price | Investment Style |
|---|---|---|
| $44.59 (as of Nov 14, 2008) | $64.00 | Large-Cap Growth |

**GICS Sector** Health Care
**Sub-Industry** Health Care Equipment

**Summary** This company makes specialty surgical and medical products such as orthopedic implants, endoscopic items, and hospital beds. A division that operates outpatient physical therapy clinics was divested in June 2007.

## Key Stock Statistics (Source S&P, Vickers, company reports)

| | | | | | |
|---|---|---|---|---|---|
| 52-Wk Range | $76.89– 43.60 | S&P Oper. EPS 2008**E** | 2.88 | Market Capitalization(B) | $18.003 |
| Trailing 12-Month EPS | $2.75 | S&P Oper. EPS 2009**E** | 3.30 | Yield (%) | 0.74 |
| Trailing 12-Month P/E | 16.2 | P/E on S&P Oper. EPS 2008**E** | 15.5 | Dividend Rate/Share | $0.33 |
| $10K Invested 5 Yrs Ago | $11,127 | Common Shares Outstg. (M) | 403.7 | Institutional Ownership (%) | 54 |

| | |
|---|---|
| Beta | 0.97 |
| S&P 3-Yr. Proj. EPS CAGR(%) | 15 |
| S&P Credit Rating | A+ |

## Price Performance

30-Week Mov. Avg. ···  10-Week Mov. Avg. – –  **GAAP Earnings vs. Previous Year**   **Volume** Above Avg. STARS
12-Mo. Target Price —  Relative Strength —   ▲ Up  ▼ Down  ► No Change   Below Avg. ★

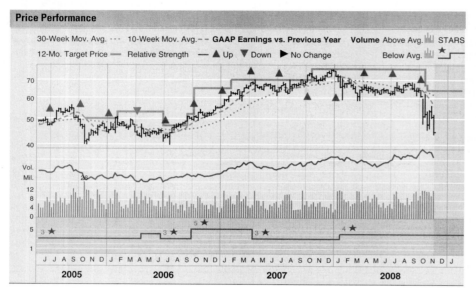

Options: ASE, CBOE, Ph

Analysis prepared by **Robert M. Gold** on October 20, 2008, when the stock traded at **$ 52.71**.

## Highlights

► We expect 2008 sales to approximate $6.8 billion, driven by growth of 11% to 12% in the orthopedic implant business and 13% in the medical/surgical division. We do not anticipate any contributions from the company's OP-1 bone growth compound prior to 2009, due to ongoing struggles in obtaining FDA approval, and believe the impact from a hip resurfacing product will be modest due to the extensive physician training required. We see 2009 sales rising about 10%, to $7.5 billion.

► We believe costs related to efforts to improve manufacturing quality controls, along with higher raw material costs, will continue to pressure margins in the fourth quarter of 2008. But we expect that these pressures will abate in 2009 and think gross margins in the 71% to 72% range are sustainable over the long term. We expect that SG&A costs will absorb about 37% of sales over the coming three years, and we see R&D costs consuming between 5% and 6% of sales. We project free cash flow of about $1.0 billion in 2008 and $1.2 billion in 2009.

► Our 2008 EPS estimate is $2.88, and we look for 2009 EPS to reach $3.30.

## Investment Rationale/Risk

► We think Stryker will generate EPS growth of about 15% during the three-year period 2008 through 2011, driven by new product launches, enhancements to existing products, and cost controls. We believe the company can meaningfully expand its implant segment operating margins, in particular, and we expect that it will generate sales and EPS growth at the high end of the orthopedic device peer group. We anticipate that the company will utilize its free cash flow and cash on hand to make strategic acquisitions and repurchase common stock. We believe the orthopedics group offers consistent unit growth of 10% to 11%, and that global pricing will be a modest benefit through 2009.

► Risks to our recommendation and target price include unfavorable patent litigation outcomes, Medicare reimbursement rate reductions, greater-than-expected impact from recent product recalls and unit price erosion in core markets.

► Our 12-month target price of $64 reflects a forward PEG ratio of about 1.3X, in line with large-cap device peers, using our 2009 EPS estimate and assuming three-year EPS growth of 15%.

## Qualitative Risk Assessment

| LOW | MEDIUM | HIGH |
|---|---|---|

Stryker operates in very competitive areas of the global medical device industry, characterized by rapid technological innovation and relatively high levels of market share volatility. However, we believe that demand for the company's orthopedic products is largely immune from economic cycles, and that long-term unit demand drivers are more closely related to an aging global population.

## Quantitative Evaluations

**S&P Quality Ranking**     A+

| D | C | B- | B | B+ | A- | A | A+ |
|---|---|---|---|---|---|---|---|

**Relative Strength Rank**     MODERATE

50

LOWEST = 1     HIGHEST = 99

## Revenue/Earnings Data

**Revenue (Million $)**

| | 1Q | 2Q | 3Q | 4Q | Year |
|---|---|---|---|---|---|
| 2008 | 1,634 | 1,713 | 1,653 | -- | -- |
| 2007 | 1,426 | 1,464 | 1,453 | 1,658 | 6,001 |
| 2006 | 1,321 | 1,328 | 1,294 | 1,463 | 5,406 |
| 2005 | 1,203 | 1,219 | 1,172 | 1,279 | 4,872 |
| 2004 | 1,035 | 1,043 | 1,029 | 1,156 | 4,262 |
| 2003 | 846.9 | 891.7 | 885.4 | 1,001 | 3,625 |

**Earnings Per Share ($)**

| | | | | | |
|---|---|---|---|---|---|
| 2008 | 0.70 | 0.73 | 0.66 | E0.77 | E2.88 |
| 2007 | 0.58 | 0.58 | 0.55 | 0.66 | 2.37 |
| 2006 | 0.36 | 0.52 | 0.46 | 0.55 | 1.89 |
| 2005 | 0.42 | 0.45 | 0.32 | 0.45 | 1.64 |
| 2004 | 0.33 | 0.37 | 0.04 | 0.40 | 1.14 |
| 2003 | 0.26 | 0.26 | 0.26 | 0.33 | 1.12 |

Fiscal year ended Dec. 31. Next earnings report expected: Late January. EPS Estimates based on S&P Operating Earnings; historical GAAP earnings are as reported.

## Dividend Data (Dates: mm/dd Payment Date: mm/dd/yy)

| Amount ($) | Date Decl. | Ex-Div. Date | Stk. of Record | Payment Date |
|---|---|---|---|---|
| 0.330 | 12/06 | 12/27 | 12/31 | 01/31/08 |

Dividends have been paid since 1992. Source: Company reports.

---

**Please read the Required Disclosures and Analyst Certification on the last page of this report.**

The McGraw·Hill Companies

# Stryker Corp

**STANDARD &POOR'S**

## Business Summary October 20, 2008

Stryker Corp. traces its origins to a business founded in 1941 by Dr. Homer H. Stryker, a leading orthopedic surgeon and the inventor of several orthopedic products. The company has significant exposure to the artificial hip, prosthetic knee and trauma product areas. International sales accounted for 36% of the total in 2007.

Orthopedic implants (60% of 2007 sales) consist of products such as hip, knee, shoulder and spinal implants, associated implant instrumentation, trauma-related products, and bone cement. Artificial joints are made of cobalt chromium, titanium alloys, ceramics, or ultra-high molecular weight polyethylene, and are implanted in patients whose natural joints have been damaged by arthritis, osteoporosis, other diseases, or injury. SYK also sells trauma-related products, used primarily in the fixation of fractures resulting from sudden injury, including internal fixation devices such as nails, plates and screws, and external fixation devices such as pins, wires and connection bars. In addition, the division sells Simplex bone cement, a material used to secure cemented implants to bone, and the OP-1 Bone Growth Device. Composed of recombinant human osteogenic protein-1 and a bioresorbable collagen matrix, the product induces the formation of new bone when implanted into existing bone, and is approved to treat long bone fractures in patients in whom use of autograft treatments has failed or is not a feasible option. Stryker continues to develop OP-1 for spinal indications, including spinal stenosis, and is working with the FDA to obtain U.S. marketing clearance. In 2006, SYK began the initial

launch of a hip resurfacing product in certain international markets.

During 2006, Stryker acquired Sightline Inc., a privately held developer of flexible endoscopes for gastrointestinal and other markets, with a technology that is believed to improve insertion and sterilization during colonoscopy procedures. In August 2004, Stryker bought SpineCore Inc., a developer of artificial lumbar and cervical spinal discs.

The medical and surgical equipment unit (40%) operates through four units. Stryker Instruments sells powered surgical drills, saws, fixation and reaming equipment, as well as other instruments used for drilling, burring, rasping or cutting bone, wiring or pinning bone fractures, and preparing hip or knee surfaces for the placement of artificial hip or knee joints. Stryker Endoscopy offers medical video cameras, light sources, arthroscopes, laparascopes, powered surgical instruments, and disposable suction/irrigation devices. Stryker Medical produces 30 types of specialty stretchers customized for acute care and specialty surgical facilities. Stryker Leibinger makes plate and screw systems for craniomaxillofacial surgery to repair small bones in the hands, face and head, and sells a proprietary bone substitute material, BoneSource.

## Company Financials Fiscal Year Ended Dec. 31

| Per Share Data ($) | 2007 | 2006 | 2005 | 2004 | 2003 | 2002 | 2001 | 2000 | 1999 | 1998 |
|---|---|---|---|---|---|---|---|---|---|---|
| Tangible Book Value | 10.84 | 7.98 | 5.75 | 4.44 | 2.98 | 1.42 | 0.65 | 0.04 | NM | NM |
| Cash Flow | 2.79 | 2.69 | 2.34 | 1.78 | 1.71 | 1.30 | 1.09 | 0.97 | 0.46 | 0.20 |
| Earnings | 2.37 | 1.89 | 1.64 | 1.14 | 1.12 | 0.85 | 0.67 | 0.55 | 0.05 | 0.10 |
| S&P Core Earnings | 2.37 | 1.89 | 1.57 | 1.08 | 1.08 | 0.80 | 0.63 | NA | NA | NA |
| Dividends | 0.33 | 0.22 | 0.11 | 0.09 | 0.07 | 0.06 | 0.05 | 0.03 | 0.03 | 0.03 |
| Payout Ratio | 14% | 12% | 7% | 8% | 6% | 7% | 7% | 5% | 60% | 27% |
| Prices:High | 76.89 | 55.92 | 56.32 | 57.66 | 42.68 | 33.74 | 31.60 | 28.88 | 18.31 | 13.94 |
| Prices:Low | 54.89 | 39.77 | 39.74 | 40.30 | 29.83 | 21.93 | 21.65 | 12.22 | 11.11 | 7.75 |
| P/E Ratio:High | 32 | 30 | 34 | 51 | 38 | 40 | 47 | 52 | NM | NM |
| P/E Ratio:Low | 23 | 21 | 24 | 35 | 27 | 26 | 32 | 22 | NM | NM |

| Income Statement Analysis (Million $) | 2007 | 2006 | 2005 | 2004 | 2003 | 2002 | 2001 | 2000 | 1999 | 1998 |
|---|---|---|---|---|---|---|---|---|---|---|
| Revenue | 6,001 | 5,406 | 4,872 | 4,262 | 3,625 | 3,012 | 2,602 | 2,289 | 2,104 | 1,103 |
| Operating Income | 1,506 | 1,459 | 1,305 | 1,092 | 901 | 751 | 645 | 600 | 329 | 226 |
| Depreciation | 179 | 332 | 290 | 251 | 230 | 186 | 172 | 169 | 163 | 37.6 |
| Interest Expense | 22.2 | Nil | 7.70 | 6.80 | 22.6 | 40.3 | 67.9 | 96.6 | 123 | 12.2 |
| Pretax Income | 1,370 | 1,104 | 1,003 | 717 | 652 | 507 | 406 | 335 | 29.8 | 60.0 |
| Effective Tax Rate | 28.0% | 29.5% | 32.7% | 35.0% | 30.5% | 31.8% | 33.0% | 34.0% | 34.9% | 34.0% |
| Net Income | 987 | 778 | 675 | 466 | 454 | 346 | 272 | 221 | 19.4 | 39.6 |
| S&P Core Earnings | 987 | 779 | 645 | 441 | 436 | 324 | 257 | NA | NA | NA |

| Balance Sheet & Other Financial Data (Million $) | 2007 | 2006 | 2005 | 2004 | 2003 | 2002 | 2001 | 2000 | 1999 | 1998 |
|---|---|---|---|---|---|---|---|---|---|---|
| Cash | 2,411 | 1,415 | 1,057 | 349 | 65.9 | 37.8 | 50.1 | 54.0 | 80.0 | 142 |
| Current Assets | 4,905 | 3,534 | 2,870 | 2,143 | 1,398 | 1,151 | 993 | 997 | 1,110 | 1,312 |
| Total Assets | 7,354 | 5,874 | 4,944 | 4,084 | 3,159 | 2,816 | 2,424 | 2,431 | 2,581 | 2,886 |
| Current Liabilities | 1,333 | 1,352 | 1,249 | 1,114 | 850 | 708 | 533 | 617 | 670 | 699 |
| Long Term Debt | Nil | Nil | 184 | 0.70 | 18.8 | 491 | 721 | 876 | 1,181 | 1,488 |
| Common Equity | 5,379 | 4,191 | 3,252 | 2,752 | 2,155 | 1,498 | 1,056 | 855 | 672 | 643 |
| Total Capital | 5,524 | 4,191 | 3,436 | 2,753 | 2,174 | 1,989 | 1,777 | 1,731 | 1,853 | 2,148 |
| Capital Expenditures | 188 | 218 | 272 | 188 | 145 | 139 | 162 | 80.7 | 76.2 | 51.2 |
| Cash Flow | 1,165 | 1,110 | 965 | 717 | 683 | 532 | 444 | 390 | 182 | 77.2 |
| Current Ratio | 3.7 | 2.6 | 2.3 | 1.9 | 1.6 | 1.6 | 1.9 | 1.6 | 1.7 | 1.9 |
| % Long Term Debt of Capitalization | Nil | Nil | 5.4 | 0.0 | 0.9 | 24.7 | 40.6 | 50.6 | 63.8 | 69.3 |
| % Net Income of Revenue | 16.4 | 14.4 | 13.9 | 10.9 | 12.5 | 11.5 | 10.4 | 9.7 | 0.9 | 3.6 |
| % Return on Assets | 14.9 | 14.3 | 15.0 | 12.9 | 15.2 | 13.2 | 11.2 | 8.8 | 0.7 | 2.0 |
| % Return on Equity | 20.6 | 20.8 | 22.5 | 19.0 | 24.8 | 27.1 | 28.4 | 29.0 | 2.9 | 6.1 |

Data as orig reptd.; bef. results of disc opers/spec. items. Per share data adj. for stk. divs.; EPS diluted. E-Estimated. NA-Not Available. NM-Not Meaningful. NR-Not Ranked. UR-Under Review.

**Office:** 2825 Airview Blvd, Portage, MI 49002-1802.
**Telephone:** 269-385-2600.
**Website:** http://www.stryker.com
**Chrmn:** J.W. Brown

**Pres & CEO:** S.P. MacMillan
**CFO:** D.H. Bergy
**Chief Acctg Officer:** T. McKinney
**Treas:** J. Blondia

**Investor Contact:** K.A. Owen (269-385-2600)
**Board Members:** J. W. Brown, H. E. Cox, Jr., D. M. Engelman, L. L. Francesconi, S. P. MacMillan, W. U. Parfet, R. E. Stryker

**Founded:** 1946
**Domicile:** Michigan
**Employees:** 16,026

# Sunoco Inc.

**STANDARD &POOR'S**

| S&P Recommendation HOLD ★★★☆☆ | Price $37.97 (as of Nov 14, 2008) | 12-Mo. Target Price $37.00 | Investment Style Large-Cap Blend |
|---|---|---|---|

**GICS Sector** Energy
**Sub-Industry** Oil & Gas Refining & Marketing

**Summary** One of the largest independent refiners in the U.S., this company has diversified operations in refining, marketing, chemicals, logistics and cokemaking.

## Key Stock Statistics (Source S&P, Vickers, company reports)

| | | | | | | | |
|---|---|---|---|---|---|---|---|
| 52-Wk Range | $73.68– 21.30 | S&P Oper. EPS 2008**E** | 5.84 | Market Capitalization(B) | $4.437 | Beta | 1.22 |
| Trailing 12-Month EPS | $4.80 | S&P Oper. EPS 2009**E** | 5.28 | Yield (%) | 3.16 | S&P 3-Yr. Proj. EPS CAGR(%) | -10 |
| Trailing 12-Month P/E | 7.9 | P/E on S&P Oper. EPS 2008**E** | 6.5 | Dividend Rate/Share | $1.20 | S&P Credit Rating | BBB |
| $10K Invested 5 Yrs Ago | $18,181 | Common Shares Outstg. (M) | 116.9 | Institutional Ownership (%) | 92 | | |

## Price Performance

30-Week Mov. Avg. · · · · 10-Week Mov. Avg. ‒ ‒ GAAP Earnings vs. Previous Year   Volume Above Avg. STARS
12-Mo. Target Price ‒ Relative Strength — ▲ Up ▼ Down ► No Change   Below Avg.

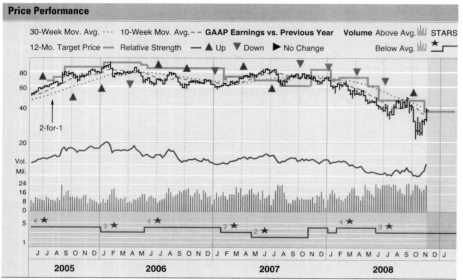

Options: CBOE, Ph

Analysis prepared by **Tina J. Vital** on November 06, 2008, when the stock traded at **$ 30.04**.

## Highlights

► Third quarter refining throughputs declined 6.2%, reflecting rate reductions due to a weak margin environment, but were above our expectations. We expect fourth quarter refining throughputs to rise from third quarter levels.

► U.S. refining margins industry wide have weakened as refined product prices failed to keep pace with the sharp increase in crude oil prices; we project these margins will narrow about 18% in 2008 and 2009. Coke earnings rose fourfold during the quarter on the start-up of a second cokemaking facility at Haverhill and the impact of higher coal prices.

► During the third quarter, SUN reduced the amount of Nigerian-sourced crude oil by more than 200,000 b/d from historical levels. We expect some margin improvement in the 2008 second half on SUN's increased use of lower-cost crude oil feedstocks; however, we expect run rates will remain reduced due to a challenging industry environment. After-tax operating earnings declined 15% in 2007, and we expect an 18% drop in 2008 and 10% in 2009.

## Investment Rationale/Risk

► While SUN's focus on light sweet crude oil feedstocks has limited its ability to lower crude costs and take advantage of the wider sour crude refining margins, it has permitted a relatively high volume of higher-grade products. We believe its strong East Coast and Midwest retail distribution provides long-term earnings stability, and its stake in Sunoco Logistics Partners L.P. provides a stable source of distribution. We see limited internal growth opportunities, and expect SUN to pursue acquisitions across all of its business lines.

► Risks to our recommendation and target price include changes in economic, industry and operating conditions that could lead to a narrowing of refining, chemical, coke or logistics margins, or overpaying for an acquisition.

► A blend of our discounted cash flow analysis ($38 per share, assuming a weighted average cost of capital of 10.7% and a terminal growth rate of 3%) and narrowed relative valuations leads to our 12-month target price of $37. This result represents an expected enterprise value of 4.1X our 2009 EBITDA estimate, a discount to U.S. peers.

## Qualitative Risk Assessment

| LOW | MEDIUM | HIGH |
|---|---|---|

Our risk assessment reflects the company's solid business profile in the volatile and competitive refining industry, and diversification into retail marketing, chemicals, logistics and cokemaking.

## Quantitative Evaluations

**S&P Quality Ranking**          A-

| D | C | B- | B | B+ | A- | A | A+ |
|---|---|---|---|---|---|---|---|

**Relative Strength Rank**          STRONG
98
LOWEST = 1          HIGHEST = 99

## Revenue/Earnings Data

**Revenue (Million $)**

| | 1Q | 2Q | 3Q | 4Q | Year |
|---|---|---|---|---|---|
| 2008 | 12,813 | 15,426 | 15,447 | -- | -- |
| 2007 | 9,305 | 10,764 | 11,497 | 13,162 | 44,728 |
| 2006 | 8,593 | 10,590 | 10,496 | 9,036 | 38,715 |
| 2005 | 7,209 | 7,990 | 9,295 | 9,270 | 33,764 |
| 2004 | 5,245 | 6,276 | 6,558 | 7,429 | 25,508 |
| 2003 | 4,570 | 4,189 | 4,594 | 4,576 | 17,929 |

**Earnings Per Share ($)**

| | | | | | |
|---|---|---|---|---|---|
| 2008 | -0.50 | 0.70 | 4.70 | E1.04 | E5.84 |
| 2007 | 1.44 | 4.20 | 1.81 | -0.08 | 7.43 |
| 2006 | 0.59 | 3.22 | 2.76 | 1.00 | 7.59 |
| 2005 | 0.84 | 1.75 | 2.39 | 2.12 | 7.08 |
| 2004 | 0.58 | 1.54 | 0.70 | 1.24 | 4.04 |
| 2003 | 0.56 | 0.52 | 0.70 | 0.24 | 2.02 |

Fiscal year ended Dec. 31. Next earnings report expected: Early February. EPS Estimates based on S&P Operating Earnings; historical GAAP earnings are as reported.

## Dividend Data (Dates: mm/dd Payment Date: mm/dd/yy)

| Amount ($) | Date Decl. | Ex-Div. Date | Stk. of Record | Payment Date |
|---|---|---|---|---|
| 0.275 | 01/03 | 02/06 | 02/08 | 03/10/08 |
| 0.300 | 02/07 | 05/07 | 05/09 | 06/10/08 |
| 0.300 | 07/03 | 08/07 | 08/11 | 09/10/08 |
| 0.300 | 10/02 | 11/06 | 11/10 | 12/10/08 |

Dividends have been paid since 1904. Source: Company reports.

# Sunoco Inc.

## Business Summary November 06, 2008

CORPORATE OVERVIEW. Sunoco Inc. (SUN) has been active in the petroleum industry since 1886, and conducts its business through five operating segments: Refining and Supply (49% of 2007 revenues; 83% of 2007 segment income); Retail Marketing (35%; 3%); Chemicals (7%; 8%); Logistics (8%; 2%); and Coke (1%; 4%).

Refining and Supply manufactures refined petroleum products and commodity petrochemicals. As of December 31, 2007, SUN owned and operated five refineries with a crude unit capacity of about 910,000 barrels per day (b/d), located in the Northeast (655,000 b/d; in Marcus Hook, PA, Philadelphia, PA, and "Eagle Point" in Westville, NJ), and the MidContinent (255,000 b/d; Toledo, OH, and Tulsa, OK). Total production rose 0.3%, to 949,400 b/d, in 2007 (gasoline 46%, middle distillates 33%, residual fuels 7%, petrochemicals 4%, lubricants 1%, and other 9%).

SUN meets all of its crude oil requirements through purchases from third parties. Approximately 63% of SUN's 2007 crude oil supply came from West Africa (40% from Nigeria), 15% from the U.S., 11% from Canada, 5% from Central Asia, 1% from the North Sea, 4% from South and Central America, and 1%

from lubes extracted from gasoil/naphtha intermediate feedstock. In the 2004 second half, the company began processing limited amounts of lower value high acid sweet crude oils in some of its Northeast refineries; during 2007, about 62,000 b/d of high acid crude oil was processed.

The Chemicals segment manufactures, distributes and markets commodity and intermediate petrochemicals, consisting of aromatic derivatives (cumene, phenol, acetone and bispenol-A) and polypropylene. At year-end 2007, chemical plant capacity totaled 8.443 billion pounds. During 2007, SUN permanently shut down a previously idled phenol production line at its Haverhill, OH, plant that had become uneconomic to restart, and recorded an $8 million after-tax provision to write off the affected production line. Also during 2007, SUN recorded a $7 million after-tax loss associated with the sale of its Neville Island, PA, terminal facility.

## Company Financials Fiscal Year Ended Dec. 31

| Per Share Data ($) | 2007 | 2006 | 2005 | 2004 | 2003 | 2002 | 2001 | 2000 | 1999 | 1998 |
|---|---|---|---|---|---|---|---|---|---|---|
| Tangible Book Value | NM | 17.01 | 15.42 | 11.65 | 10.23 | 9.05 | 10.88 | 10.03 | 8.37 | 8.41 |
| Cash Flow | 11.43 | 11.15 | 10.20 | 9.50 | 4.35 | 1.85 | 4.38 | 4.05 | 2.05 | 2.72 |
| Earnings | 7.43 | 7.59 | 7.08 | 4.04 | 2.02 | -0.31 | 2.43 | 2.35 | 0.54 | 1.48 |
| S&P Core Earnings | 6.74 | 7.63 | 7.56 | 4.19 | 2.13 | -0.70 | 1.88 | NA | NA | NA |
| Dividends | 1.08 | 0.95 | 0.75 | 0.58 | 0.51 | 0.50 | 0.50 | 0.50 | 0.50 | 0.50 |
| Payout Ratio | 14% | 13% | 11% | 14% | 25% | NM | 21% | 21% | 93% | 34% |
| Prices:High | 86.40 | 97.25 | 85.29 | 42.26 | 26.30 | 21.13 | 21.37 | 17.28 | 19.72 | 22.16 |
| Prices:Low | 56.68 | 57.50 | 38.10 | 25.26 | 14.84 | 13.51 | 14.56 | 10.97 | 11.44 | 14.75 |
| P/E Ratio:High | 12 | 13 | 12 | 10 | 13 | NM | 9 | 7 | 37 | 15 |
| P/E Ratio:Low | 8 | 8 | 5 | 6 | 7 | NM | 6 | 5 | 21 | 10 |

| Income Statement Analysis (Million $) | | | | | | | | | | |
|---|---|---|---|---|---|---|---|---|---|---|
| Revenue | 44,728 | 38,715 | 33,764 | 25,508 | 17,929 | 14,384 | 14,063 | 14,300 | 10,068 | 8,413 |
| Operating Income | 1,835 | 2,049 | 2,078 | 1,501 | 934 | 313 | 954 | 948 | 331 | 605 |
| Depreciation, Depletion and Amortization | 480 | 459 | 429 | 818 | 363 | 329 | 321 | 298 | 276 | 257 |
| Interest Expense | 127 | 89.0 | 69.0 | 97.0 | 111 | 108 | 103 | 78.0 | 82.0 | 71.0 |
| Pretax Income | 1,476 | 1,580 | 1,580 | 995 | 495 | -73.0 | 587 | 596 | 150 | 389 |
| Effective Tax Rate | 35.1% | 38.0% | 38.4% | 39.2% | 37.0% | NM | 32.2% | 31.0% | 35.3% | 28.0% |
| Net Income | 891 | 979 | 974 | 605 | 312 | -47.0 | 398 | 411 | 97.0 | 280 |
| S&P Core Earnings | 808 | 984 | 1,040 | 626 | 330 | -106 | 307 | NA | NA | NA |

| Balance Sheet & Other Financial Data (Million $) | | | | | | | | | | |
|---|---|---|---|---|---|---|---|---|---|---|
| Cash | 648 | 263 | 919 | 405 | 431 | 390 | 42.0 | 239 | 87.0 | 38.0 |
| Current Assets | 4,638 | 4,015 | 3,687 | 2,551 | 2,068 | 1,898 | 1,510 | 1,683 | 1,456 | 1,180 |
| Total Assets | 12,426 | 10,982 | 9,931 | 8,079 | 6,922 | 6,441 | 5,932 | 5,426 | 5,196 | 4,849 |
| Current Liabilities | 5,640 | 4,755 | 4,210 | 3,022 | 2,170 | 1,776 | 1,778 | 1,646 | 1,766 | 1,384 |
| Long Term Debt | 1,724 | 1,705 | 1,234 | 1,379 | 1,350 | 1,453 | 1,142 | 933 | 878 | 823 |
| Common Equity | 2,533 | 2,075 | 2,051 | 1,607 | 1,556 | 1,394 | 1,642 | 1,702 | 4,782 | 1,514 |
| Total Capital | 5,723 | 5,227 | 4,749 | 4,271 | 3,940 | 3,816 | 3,335 | 2,885 | 5,897 | 2,512 |
| Capital Expenditures | 1,179 | 1,019 | 970 | 832 | 425 | 385 | 331 | 465 | 374 | 457 |
| Cash Flow | 1,371 | 1,438 | 1,403 | 1,423 | 675 | 282 | 719 | 709 | 373 | 517 |
| Current Ratio | 0.8 | 0.8 | 0.9 | 0.8 | 1.0 | 1.1 | 0.8 | 1.0 | 0.8 | 0.9 |
| % Long Term Debt of Capitalization | 30.1 | 32.6 | 26.0 | 32.3 | 34.3 | 38.1 | 34.2 | 32.3 | 14.9 | 32.8 |
| % Return on Assets | 7.6 | 9.4 | 10.8 | 8.0 | 4.7 | NM | 7.0 | 7.7 | 1.9 | 5.9 |
| % Return on Equity | 38.7 | 47.5 | 53.3 | 38.3 | 21.2 | NM | 23.8 | 25.6 | 2.0 | 23.1 |

Data as orig reptd.; bef. results of disc opers/spec. items. Per share data adj. for stk. divs.; EPS diluted. E-Estimated. NA-Not Available. NM-Not Meaningful. NR-Not Ranked. UR-Under Review.

**Office:** 1735 Market St Ste LL, Philadelphia, PA 19103-7583.
**Telephone:** 215-977-3000.
**Email:** sunocoonline@sunocoinc.com
**Website:** http://www.sunocoinc.com

**Chrmn:** J.G. Drosdick
**Pres & CEO:** L.L. Elsenhans
**SVP & CFO:** T.W. Hofmann
**SVP & General Counsel:** M.S. Kuritzkes

**Chief Acctg Officer & Cntlr:** J.P. Krott
**Investor Contact:** T. Harr (215-977-6764)
**Investor Contact:** T.P. Delaney
**Board Members:** R. J. Darnall, J. G. Drosdick, G. W. Edwards, L. L. Elsenhans, U. F. Fairbairn, T. P. Gerrity, R. B. Greco, J. P. Jones, III, J. G. Kaiser, R. A. Pew, G. J. Ratcliffe, Jr., J. W. Rowe, J. K. Wulff

**Founded:** 1886
**Domicile:** Pennsylvania
**Employees:** 14,200

**STANDARD & POOR'S**

# Sun Microsystems Inc

| S&P Recommendation **SELL** ★★☆☆☆ | Price $4.12 (as of Nov 14, 2008) | 12-Mo. Target Price $3.00 | Investment Style Large-Cap Blend |
|---|---|---|---|

**GICS Sector** Information Technology
**Sub-Industry** Computer Hardware

**Summary** This company makes high-performance servers, workstations and operating system software, and invented the Java programming language.

## Key Stock Statistics (Source S&P, Vickers, company reports)

| | | | | | | | |
|---|---|---|---|---|---|---|---|
| 52-Wk Range | $21.55– 3.50 | S&P Oper. EPS 2009**E** | -0.25 | Market Capitalization(B) | $3.043 | Beta | 1.76 |
| Trailing 12-Month EPS | $-1.75 | S&P Oper. EPS 2010**E** | 0.25 | Yield (%) | Nil | S&P 3-Yr. Proj. EPS CAGR(%) | 1 |
| Trailing 12-Month P/E | NM | P/E on S&P Oper. EPS 2009**E** | NM | Dividend Rate/Share | Nil | S&P Credit Rating | BB+ |
| $10K Invested 5 Yrs Ago | $2,512 | Common Shares Outstg. (M) | 738.6 | Institutional Ownership (%) | 72 | | |

## Price Performance

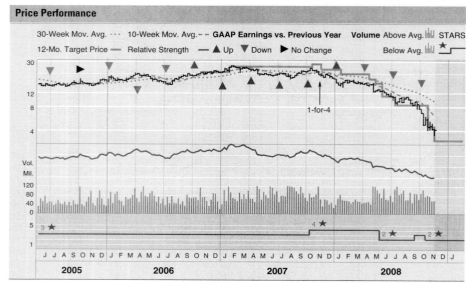

30-Week Mov. Avg. ···· 10-Week Mov. Avg. – – **GAAP Earnings vs. Previous Year** Volume Above Avg. STARS
12-Mo. Target Price — Relative Strength — ▲ Up ▼ Down ▶ No Change Below Avg. ★

Options: ASE, CBOE, P, Ph

Analysis prepared by **Thomas W. Smith, CFA** on November 13, 2008, when the stock traded at **$3.67**.

## Highlights

➤ We forecast a revenue decrease of 8% for FY 09 (Jun.), followed by a 3% increase in FY 10. We believe that the positive forces of partnerships and new products will be outweighed in FY 09 by weakness in enterprise IT spending. We see the potential for longer-term profitability being aided by lower costs from ongoing restructuring efforts. In the FY 09 first quarter, the company took a $1.445 billion non-cash charge for goodwill impairment.

➤ We look for strong pricing competition to be partly offset by manufacturing efficiencies from restructuring. As a result, we anticipate that the gross margin level will dip toward 41% in FY 09, from about 46.5% in FY 08. Absolute spending on R&D in the September quarter was lower than in any quarter in the past two fiscal years, which reduces costs but might hinder product development.

➤ We estimate per-share operating results, excluding restructuring and goodwill impairment charges, of a loss of $0.25 for FY 09, with improvement to EPS of $0.25 in FY 10. A $1 billion share repurchase plan announced July 31 could help per-share results.

## Investment Rationale/Risk

➤ We see a high overall risk profile resulting from intensifying competition in the low-end server market and a near-term slowdown in server demand. Work force reductions are under way, as is integration of the MySQL acquisition, which also clouds earnings visibility, in our opinion. Share buybacks should aid results, but they also contribute to our sense of a low quality of earnings.

➤ Risks to our recommendation and target price include the possibilities of a faster migration toward UNIX systems, shorter sales cycles, and server market share gains. In addition, the pace of customer spending on information technology equipment could prove faster than our projections.

➤ Our 12-month target price of $3.00 is based on applying a target price-to-book ratio of 1.1X, which is near the cycle-trough levels experienced by JAVA in prior industry slowdowns, to our tangible book value estimate of $2.75 a share. Although the company had recently returned to GAAP profitability, the goodwill writedown in the FY 09 first quarter indicates renewed challenges, in our view.

## Qualitative Risk Assessment

| LOW | MEDIUM | **HIGH** |
|---|---|---|

Our risk assessment reflects the spotty earnings record the company has compiled over the past several years, our view of its reliance on high-end systems sales, and the pricing pressures we see in the computer hardware industry.

## Quantitative Evaluations

**S&P Quality Ranking** C

| D | **C** | B- | B | B+ | A- | A | A+ |
|---|---|---|---|---|---|---|---|

**Relative Strength Rank** WEAK

26

LOWEST = 1    HIGHEST = 99

## Revenue/Earnings Data

**Revenue (Million $)**

| | 1Q | 2Q | 3Q | 4Q | Year |
|---|---|---|---|---|---|
| 2009 | 2,990 | -- | -- | -- | -- |
| 2008 | 3,219 | 3,615 | 3,266 | 3,780 | 13,880 |
| 2007 | 3,189 | 3,566 | 3,283 | 3,835 | 13,873 |
| 2006 | 2,726 | 3,337 | 3,177 | 3,828 | 13,068 |
| 2005 | 2,628 | 2,841 | 2,627 | 2,974 | 11,070 |
| 2004 | 2,536 | 2,888 | 2,651 | 3,110 | 11,185 |

**Earnings Per Share ($)**

| | | | | | |
|---|---|---|---|---|---|
| 2009 | -2.24 | E-0.03 | E-0.12 | E0.03 | E-0.25 |
| 2008 | 0.12 | 0.32 | -0.04 | 0.11 | 0.49 |
| 2007 | -0.08 | 0.16 | 0.08 | 0.36 | 0.52 |
| 2006 | -0.16 | -0.28 | -0.24 | -0.36 | -1.00 |
| 2005 | -0.16 | Nil | -0.04 | 0.04 | -0.12 |
| 2004 | -0.36 | -0.16 | -0.92 | 0.92 | -0.48 |

Fiscal year ended Jun. 30. Next earnings report expected: Late January. EPS Estimates based on S&P Operating Earnings; historical GAAP earnings are as reported.

## Dividend Data (Dates: mm/dd Payment Date: mm/dd/yy)

| Amount ($) | Date Decl. | Ex-Div. Date | Stk. of Record | Payment Date |
|---|---|---|---|---|
| 1-for-4 REV. | -- | 11/12 | -- | 11/12/07 |

Source: Company reports.

---

**The McGraw-Hill Companies**

# Sun Microsystems Inc

STANDARD
&POOR'S

## Business Summary November 13, 2008

CORPORATE OVERVIEW. Sun Microsystems (JAVA), founded in 1982, operates in over 100 countries and serves a variety of markets including financial services, government, manufacturing, retail and telecommunications, as it continues to focus on a single vision -- that the network is the computer.

Sun is a primary supplier of networked computing products, including workstations, servers and storage products -- which had primarily used the company's own Scaleable Processor Architecture (SPARC) microprocessors and its Solaris software -- but this has been expanded to include other chips and operating system software. Other core brands include the Java technology platform, the MySQL database management system, and Sun StorageTek storage. Computer systems accounted for 45% of net revenues in FY 08 (Jun.), storage 17%, support services 29%, and client solutions and educational services 9%. In FY 08, electronics distributor Avnet accounted for 11% of total revenue.

Sun generates the majority of its business from overseas markets. In FY 08,

63% of net revenues were from outside the U.S., up from 59% in FY 07. The main regions contributing to international sales in FY 08 included Canada and Latin America (7%); Europe Middle-East and Africa (38%); and Asia, Australia and New Zealand (18%).

CORPORATE STRATEGY. Sun's R&D programs are intended to sustain and enhance its competitive position by incorporating the latest advances in hardware, software, graphics, networking data communications and storage technologies. Over the past three fiscal years, Sun has averaged in excess of $1.9 billion per year of R&D. We believe this level of spending, combined with a number of U.S. and foreign patents, provides a significant barrier for new firms contemplating entry into the computer hardware industry.

## Company Financials Fiscal Year Ended Jun. 30

| Per Share Data ($) | 2008 | 2007 | 2006 | 2005 | 2004 | 2003 | 2002 | 2001 | 2000 | 1999 |
|---|---|---|---|---|---|---|---|---|---|---|
| Tangible Book Value | 2.40 | 4.56 | 3.20 | 7.20 | 7.08 | 7.52 | 9.28 | 10.52 | 8.90 | 6.19 |
| Cash Flow | NA | 1.45 | -0.34 | 0.67 | 0.42 | -3.15 | 0.47 | 2.59 | 3.11 | 2.04 |
| Earnings | 0.49 | 0.52 | -1.00 | -0.12 | -0.48 | -4.28 | -0.72 | 1.16 | 2.20 | 1.28 |
| S&P Core Earnings | 0.39 | 0.48 | -1.04 | -1.00 | -2.68 | -3.24 | -1.52 | 0.56 | NA | NA |
| Dividends | Nil | Nil | Nil | Nil | Nil | Nil | Nil | Nil | Nil | Nil |
| Payout Ratio | Nil | Nil | Nil | Nil | Nil | Nil | Nil | Nil | Nil | Nil |
| Prices:High | 18.14 | 27.12 | 23.52 | 21.04 | 23.72 | 22.56 | 57.64 | 140.50 | 258.63 | 166.03 |
| Prices:Low | 3.50 | 17.96 | 14.96 | 13.68 | 13.16 | 12.08 | 9.36 | 30.08 | 100.50 | 43.56 |
| P/E Ratio:High | 37 | 52 | NM | NM | NM | NM | NM | NM | NM | NM |
| P/E Ratio:Low | 7 | 35 | NM | NM | NM | NM | NM | 26 | 46 | 34 |

| Income Statement Analysis (Million $) | | | | | | | | | | |
|---|---|---|---|---|---|---|---|---|---|---|
| Revenue | 13,880 | 13,873 | 13,068 | 11,070 | 11,185 | 11,434 | 12,496 | 18,250 | 15,721 | 11,726 |
| Operating Income | NA | 1,236 | 119 | 556 | 3.00 | 694 | 239 | 2,617 | 3,181 | 2,269 |
| Depreciation | 786 | 830 | 575 | 671 | 730 | 918 | 970 | 1,229 | 776 | 627 |
| Interest Expense | NA | Nil | 55.0 | 49.0 | 37.0 | 43.0 | 58.0 | 100 | 84.0 | 0.68 |
| Pretax Income | 610 | 583 | -675 | -184 | 437 | -2,653 | -1,048 | 1,584 | 2,771 | 1,606 |
| Effective Tax Rate | 33.9% | 18.9% | NM | NM | NM | NM | NM | 38.1% | 33.1% | 35.8% |
| Net Income | 403 | 473 | -864 | -107 | -388 | -3,429 | -587 | 981 | 1,854 | 1,031 |
| S&P Core Earnings | 328 | 426 | -904 | -864 | -2,166 | -2,581 | -1,253 | 471 | NA | NA |

| Balance Sheet & Other Financial Data (Million $) | | | | | | | | | | |
|---|---|---|---|---|---|---|---|---|---|---|
| Cash | 2,701 | 4,582 | 4,065 | 3,396 | 3,601 | 3,062 | 2,885 | 1,472 | 1,849 | 1,089 |
| Current Assets | NA | 9,328 | 8,273 | 7,191 | 7,303 | 6,779 | 7,777 | 7,934 | 6,877 | 6,116 |
| Total Assets | 14,468 | 15,838 | 15,082 | 14,190 | 14,503 | 12,985 | 16,522 | 18,181 | 14,152 | 8,420 |
| Current Liabilities | NA | 5,451 | 6,165 | 4,766 | 5,113 | 4,129 | 5,057 | 5,146 | 4,759 | 3,227 |
| Long Term Debt | NA | 1,264 | 575 | 1,123 | 1,175 | 1,531 | 1,449 | 1,705 | 1,720 | Nil |
| Common Equity | 5,588 | 7,179 | 6,344 | 6,674 | 6,438 | 6,491 | 9,801 | 10,586 | 7,309 | 4,812 |
| Total Capital | NA | 8,443 | 6,919 | 7,797 | 7,613 | 8,022 | 11,250 | 13,035 | 9,393 | 4,812 |
| Capital Expenditures | 520 | 488 | 315 | 257 | 249 | 373 | 559 | 1,292 | 982 | 739 |
| Cash Flow | NA | 1,303 | -289 | 564 | 342 | -2,511 | 383 | 2,210 | 2,630 | 1,658 |
| Current Ratio | 1.4 | 1.7 | 1.3 | 1.5 | 1.4 | 1.6 | 1.5 | 1.5 | 1.4 | 1.9 |
| % Long Term Debt of Capitalization | 18.5 | 15.0 | 8.3 | 14.4 | 15.4 | 19.1 | 12.8 | 13.1 | 18.3 | Nil |
| % Net Income of Revenue | 2.9 | 3.4 | NM | NM | NM | NM | NM | 5.4 | 11.8 | 8.8 |
| % Return on Assets | 2.7 | 3.1 | NM | NM | NM | NM | NM | 6.1 | 16.4 | 14.6 |
| % Return on Equity | 6.3 | 7.0 | NM | NM | NM | NM | NM | 11.0 | 30.5 | 24.8 |

Data as orig reptd.; bef. results of disc opers/spec. items. Per share data adj. for stk. divs.; EPS diluted. E-Estimated. NA-Not Available. NM-Not Meaningful. NR-Not Ranked. UR-Under Review.

**Office:** 4150 Network Circle, Santa Clara, CA 95054.
**Telephone:** 650-960-1300.
**Email:** investor-relations@sun.com
**Website:** http://www.sun.com

**Chrmn:** S.G. McNealy
**Pres & CEO:** J.I. Schwartz
**COO:** C. Resse
**EVP & CFO:** M.E. Lehman

**EVP & CTO:** G.M. Papadopoulos
**Investor Contact:** P. Ziots
**Board Members:** J. L. Barksdale, S. M. Bennett, P. L. Currie, R. J. Finocchio, Jr., J. H. Greene, Jr., J. Marcus, M. E. Marks, S. G. McNealy, P. E. Mitchell, M. K. Oshman, P. A. Ridder, J. I. Schwartz, A. Spence

**Founded:** 1982
**Domicile:** Delaware
**Employees:** 34,900

The McGraw-Hill Companies

# SunTrust Banks Inc.

**STANDARD &POOR'S**

**S&P Recommendation** HOLD ★★★☆☆

| Price | 12-Mo. Target Price | Investment Style |
|---|---|---|
| $33.52 (as of Nov 14, 2008) | $40.00 | Large-Cap Blend |

**GICS Sector** Financials
**Sub-Industry** Regional Banks

**Summary** This bank holding company, which has about $177 billion in assets and nearly $120 billion in deposits, operates in 11 southeastern states and Washington, DC.

## Key Stock Statistics (Source S&P, Vickers, company reports)

| | | | | | | | |
|---|---|---|---|---|---|---|---|
| 52-Wk Range | $73.34– 25.60 | S&P Oper. EPS 2008E | 3.39 | Market Capitalization(B) | $11.870 | Beta | 0.70 |
| Trailing 12-Month EPS | $3.23 | S&P Oper. EPS 2009E | 3.39 | Yield (%) | 6.44 | S&P 3-Yr. Proj. EPS CAGR(%) | 8 |
| Trailing 12-Month P/E | 10.4 | P/E on S&P Oper. EPS 2008E | 9.9 | Dividend Rate/Share | $2.16 | S&P Credit Rating | A+ |
| $10K Invested 5 Yrs Ago | $5,760 | Common Shares Outstg. (M) | 354.1 | Institutional Ownership (%) | 67 | | |

## Price Performance

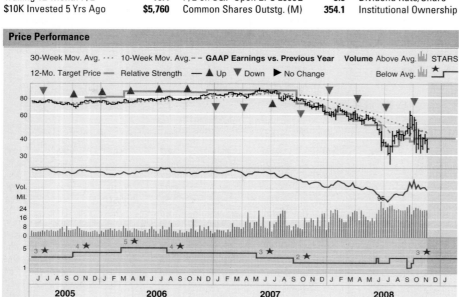

30-Week Mov. Avg. · · · · 10-Week Mov. Avg. - - GAAP Earnings vs. Previous Year   Volume Above Avg. STARS
12-Mo. Target Price — Relative Strength — ▲ Up ▼ Down ▶ No Change   Below Avg.

Options: CBOE, P, Ph

Analysis prepared by **Erik Oja** on October 10, 2008, when the stock traded at **$ 34.45**.

## Qualitative Risk Assessment

| LOW | MEDIUM | HIGH |
|---|---|---|

Our risk assessment reflects SunTrust's large-cap valuation and its history of profitability, offset by its exposure to possible further declines in residential and commercial lending credit quality.

## Quantitative Evaluations

**S&P Quality Ranking**  A

| D | C | B- | B | B+ | A- | A | A+ |
|---|---|---|---|---|---|---|---|

**Relative Strength Rank**  MODERATE
54
LOWEST = 1                    HIGHEST = 99

## Revenue/Earnings Data

**Revenue (Million $)**

| | 1Q | 2Q | 3Q | 4Q | Year |
|---|---|---|---|---|---|
| 2008 | 3,316 | 3,479 | 3,303 | -- | -- |
| 2007 | 3,407 | 3,698 | 3,334 | 3,025 | 13,313 |
| 2006 | 3,130 | 3,299 | 3,384 | 3,447 | 13,260 |
| 2005 | 2,470 | 2,614 | 2,829 | 2,973 | 10,886 |
| 2004 | 1,769 | 1,811 | 1,880 | 2,363 | 7,823 |
| 2003 | 1,766 | 1,771 | 1,752 | 1,783 | 7,072 |

**Earnings Per Share ($)**

| | 1Q | 2Q | 3Q | 4Q | Year |
|---|---|---|---|---|---|
| 2008 | 0.82 | 1.53 | 0.88 | E0.53 | E3.39 |
| 2007 | 1.44 | 1.89 | 1.18 | 0.01 | 4.55 |
| 2006 | 1.46 | 1.49 | 1.47 | 1.39 | 5.82 |
| 2005 | 1.36 | 1.28 | 1.40 | 1.43 | 5.47 |
| 2004 | 1.26 | 1.29 | 1.30 | 1.26 | 5.19 |
| 2003 | 1.17 | 1.17 | 1.18 | 1.21 | 4.73 |

Fiscal year ended Dec. 31. Next earnings report expected: Late January. EPS Estimates based on S&P Operating Earnings; historical GAAP earnings are as reported.

## Highlights

▶ During the second quarter, in response to several Fed rate cuts, STI's deposit rates fell faster than loan yields, the reverse of what happened in the prior two quarters. This produced a 6 basis point sequential increase in STI's second-quarter net interest margin, to 3.13%. STI's net interest margin was 3.11% for all of 2007, but we expect a small decrease for 2008, as we see STI's loan yields falling slightly. Quarterly fee income, excluding a large gain from the sale of Coca-Cola shares, was up only 1.0% from a year ago, as trust and investment management income lagged 2007 levels. For 2008, we expect a 4.3% increase in recurring fee income, on higher deposit service charge fees.

▶ STI's loan loss provisioning expense fell to $448 million in the second quarter, from $560 million in the first quarter, as additions beyond net chargeoffs declined to $125 million, from $262 million in the first quarter. We forecast $875 million of provisions for the last two quarters of 2008, a figure that includes $250 million of reserve building in excess of our net chargeoff forecast, for a 2008 total of nearly $1.9 billion.

▶ We project 2008 EPS of $3.51, and 2009 operating EPS of $3.64.

## Investment Rationale/Risk

▶ STI had nearly $2.79 billion of non-performing loans at June 30, up 91% from $1.46 billion at December 31, and up 265% from $764.6 million at June 30, 2007, while loan loss reserves were only $1.83 billion, or 66% of nonperforming loans. Unlike peers, which have seen deterioration mainly in residential construction loans, STI has also been affected by residential mortgages, nearly 4.2% of which were non-performing at June 30. In total, 2.2% of STI's loans at June 30 were non-performing, higher than all but two of its large regional banking peers. However, early-stage delinquencies were stable, suggesting to us that late-stage credit deterioration will slow in the remainder of 2008. We also see STI as having more tools at its disposal than its peers, including its ongoing program to raise Tier 1 capital by selling its large holdings of Coca-Cola Corp.

▶ Risks to our recommendation and target price include higher than expected loan chargeoffs, a slower than expected housing market recovery, and a reduction of the current dividend.

▶ Our 12-month target price of $40 is based on a P/E of 11.0X our 2009 EPS estimate of $3.64, a multiple slightly below regional banking peers.

## Dividend Data (Dates: mm/dd Payment Date: mm/dd/yy)

| Amount ($) | Date Decl. | Ex-Div. Date | Stk. of Record | Payment Date |
|---|---|---|---|---|
| 0.770 | 02/12 | 02/27 | 02/29 | 03/14/08 |
| 0.770 | 04/29 | 05/29 | 06/02 | 06/13/08 |
| 0.770 | 08/12 | 08/28 | 09/02 | 09/15/08 |
| 0.540 | 11/12 | 11/26 | 12/01 | 12/15/08 |

Dividends have been paid since 1985. Source: Company reports.

---

**Please read the Required Disclosures and Analyst Certification on the last page of this report.**

The McGraw·Hill Companies

# SunTrust Banks Inc.

**STANDARD &POOR'S**

## Business Summary October 10, 2008

CORPORATE OVERVIEW. SunTrust Banks Inc. (STI) owns SunTrust Bank, an organization aligned as follows by geographic region: the Carolinas Group (North and South Carolina), the Central Group (Georgia, Tennessee), the Florida Group, and the Mid-Atlantic Group (D.C., Maryland, Virginia and West Virginia). The company has five lines of business: Retail Banking, Commercial Banking, Corporate and Investment Banking, Mortgage Banking, and Wealth and Investment Management.

The Retail and Commercial Banking segments generate about 55% of total segment net income. Retail Banking (35%) provides lending and deposit gathering as well as other banking-related products and services to consumers and small businesses with sales up to $10 million. Commercial Banking (20%) offers financial products and services, including commercial lending, treasury management, financial risk management, and corporate bankcard services, to enterprises with sales up to $250 million.

The Corporate and Investment Banking segment (10%) houses the company's corporate banking, investment banking, capital markets, commercial leasing and merchant banking activities. This segment focuses on companies with sales in excess of $250 million, and concentrates on small-cap and mid-cap growth companies, raising public and private equity, and providing merger and acquisition advisory services for investment banking.

The Mortgage Banking segment (12%) offers residential mortgage products nationally through its retail, broker and correspondent channels. The Wealth and Investment Management segment (13%) provides wealth management products and professional services to individual and institutional clients. The remaining 10% of segment net income is allocated to corporate, other, treasury, and reconciling items.

The company has adopted an enterprise risk management model, which seeks to synthesize, assess, report and mitigate the full set of risks at the enterprise level and to provide management with an overall picture of the company's risk profile. The model incorporates an analysis of credit risk, organizational risk, market risk from trading activities, market risk from non-trading activities, and market liquidity risk.

## Company Financials Fiscal Year Ended Dec. 31

| Per Share Data ($) | 2007 | 2006 | 2005 | 2004 | 2003 | 2002 | 2001 | 2000 | 1999 | 1998 |
|---|---|---|---|---|---|---|---|---|---|---|
| Tangible Book Value | 28.41 | 26.04 | 24.67 | 23.13 | 29.73 | 25.46 | 26.67 | 25.07 | 22.13 | 22.99 |
| Earnings | 4.55 | 5.82 | 5.47 | 5.19 | 4.73 | 4.66 | 4.70 | 4.30 | 3.50 | 3.04 |
| S&P Core Earnings | 4.37 | 5.64 | 5.39 | 5.17 | 4.80 | 4.38 | 4.50 | NA | NA | NA |
| Dividends | 2.92 | 2.44 | 2.20 | 2.00 | 1.80 | 1.72 | 1.60 | 1.48 | 1.38 | 1.00 |
| Payout Ratio | 64% | 42% | 40% | 39% | 38% | 37% | 34% | 34% | 39% | 33% |
| Prices:High | 94.18 | 85.64 | 75.77 | 76.65 | 71.73 | 70.20 | 72.35 | 68.06 | 79.81 | 87.75 |
| Prices:Low | 60.02 | 69.68 | 65.32 | 61.27 | 51.44 | 51.48 | 57.29 | 41.63 | 60.44 | 54.00 |
| P/E Ratio:High | 21 | 15 | 14 | 15 | 15 | 15 | 15 | 16 | 23 | 26 |
| P/E Ratio:Low | 13 | 12 | 12 | 12 | 11 | 11 | 12 | 10 | 17 | 16 |

| Income Statement Analysis (Million $) | 2007 | 2006 | 2005 | 2004 | 2003 | 2002 | 2001 | 2000 | 1999 | 1998 |
|---|---|---|---|---|---|---|---|---|---|---|
| Net Interest Income | 4,720 | 4,660 | 4,579 | 3,685 | 3,320 | 3,244 | 3,253 | 3,108 | 3,145 | 2,929 |
| Tax Equivalent Adjustment | 103 | 87.9 | 75.5 | NA | 45.0 | 39.5 | 40.8 | 40.4 | 42.5 | 46.4 |
| Non Interest Income | 3,186 | 3,519 | 3,162 | 2,646 | 2,179 | 2,187 | 2,003 | 1,767 | 1,769 | 1,708 |
| Loan Loss Provision | 683 | 263 | 177 | 136 | 314 | 470 | 275 | 134 | 170 | 215 |
| % Expense/Operating Revenue | 66.2% | 59.0% | 60.6% | 67.3% | 68.4% | 61.5% | 59.2% | 58.0% | 59.3% | 62.8% |
| Pretax Income | 2,250 | 2,986 | 2,866 | 2,257 | 1,909 | 1,823 | 2,020 | 1,920 | 1,696 | 1,498 |
| Effective Tax Rate | 27.4% | 29.1% | 30.7% | 30.3% | 30.2% | 27.0% | 32.2% | 32.6% | 33.7% | 35.2% |
| Net Income | 1,634 | 2,117 | 1,987 | 1,573 | 1,332 | 1,332 | 1,369 | 1,294 | 1,124 | 971 |
| % Net Interest Margin | 3.11 | 3.00 | 3.16 | 3.15 | 3.08 | 3.41 | 3.58 | 3.55 | 3.88 | 3.97 |
| S&P Core Earnings | 1,542 | 2,045 | 1,957 | 1,570 | 1,351 | 1,253 | 1,310 | NA | NA | NA |

| Balance Sheet & Other Financial Data (Million $) | 2007 | 2006 | 2005 | 2004 | 2003 | 2002 | 2001 | 2000 | 1999 | 1998 |
|---|---|---|---|---|---|---|---|---|---|---|
| Money Market Assets | 11,890 | 3,849 | 4,457 | 3,796 | 3,243 | 2,820 | 3,025 | 2,223 | 1,869 | 2,027 |
| Investment Securities | 16,264 | 25,102 | 26,526 | 28,941 | 25,607 | 23,445 | 19,656 | 18,810 | 18,317 | 17,559 |
| Commercial Loans | 48,539 | 47,182 | 33,764 | 31,824 | 30,682 | 28,694 | 28,946 | 30,781 | 26,933 | 24,590 |
| Other Loans | 73,780 | 74,273 | 80,791 | 69,602 | 50,050 | 44,474 | 40,013 | 41,459 | 39,069 | 40,496 |
| Total Assets | 179,574 | 182,162 | 179,714 | 158,870 | 125,393 | 117,323 | 104,741 | 103,496 | 95,390 | 93,170 |
| Demand Deposits | 21,083 | 22,887 | 41,973 | 30,979 | 24,185 | 21,250 | 19,200 | 15,064 | 14,201 | 14,066 |
| Time Deposits | 80,787 | 101,134 | 80,081 | 72,382 | 57,004 | 58,456 | 48,337 | 54,469 | 45,900 | 44,968 |
| Long Term Debt | 22,957 | 18,993 | 20,779 | 22,127 | 15,314 | 11,880 | 12,661 | 8,945 | 6,017 | 5,808 |
| Common Equity | 17,553 | 17,314 | 16,887 | 15,987 | 9,731 | 16,030 | 15,064 | 14,536 | 13,691 | 8,179 |
| % Return on Assets | 0.9 | 1.2 | 1.2 | 1.1 | 1.1 | 1.2 | 1.3 | 1.3 | 1.2 | 1.3 |
| % Return on Equity | 9.2 | 12.3 | 12.1 | 12.2 | 14.4 | 8.6 | 9.3 | 9.2 | 8.0 | 14.5 |
| % Loan Loss Reserve | 1.0 | 0.8 | 0.5 | 1.0 | 1.1 | 1.1 | 1.2 | 1.2 | 1.3 | 1.5 |
| % Loans/Deposits | 100.4 | 107.4 | 171.3 | 104.5 | 106.3 | 101.5 | 108.5 | 106.4 | 112.4 | 110.3 |
| % Equity to Assets | 9.6 | 9.5 | 9.7 | 9.1 | 7.6 | 14.0 | 14.2 | 14.2 | 14.8 | 8.9 |

Data as orig reptd.; bef. results of disc opers/spec. items. Per share data adj. for stk. divs.; EPS diluted. E-Estimated. NA-Not Available. NM-Not Meaningful. NR-Not Ranked. UR-Under Review.

**Office:** 303 Peachtree St NE, Atlanta, GA 30308-3201.
**Telephone:** 404-588-7711.
**Website:** http://www.suntrust.com
**Chrmn, Pres & CEO:** J.M. Wells, III

**Investor Contact:** M.A. Chancy (800-568-3476)
**EVP & CFO:** M.A. Chancy
**EVP & Chief Admin Officer:** D.F. Dierker
**EVP, Secy & General Counsel:** R.D. Fortin

**Board Members:** R. Beall, II, A. D. Correll, J. C. Crowe, P. C. Frist, B. P. Garrett, Jr., D. H. Hughes, M. D. Ivester, J. H. Lanier, G. G. Minor, III, L. L. Prince, F. S. Royal, J. M. Wells, III, K. H. Williams, P. Wynn, Jr.

**Founded:** 1891
**Domicile:** Georgia
**Employees:** 32,323

*The McGraw-Hill Companies*

# SUPERVALU INC.

| S&P Recommendation | HOLD ★★★☆☆ | Price $11.92 (as of Nov 14, 2008) | 12-Mo. Target Price $21.00 | Investment Style Large-Cap Blend |
|---|---|---|---|---|

**GICS Sector** Consumer Staples
**Sub-Industry** Food Retail

**Summary** One of the largest U.S. food wholesalers, this company is also one of the biggest supermarket retailers in the U.S.

## Key Stock Statistics (Source S&P, Vickers, company reports)

| | | | | | | | |
|---|---|---|---|---|---|---|---|
| 52-Wk Range | $43.30–11.46 | S&P Oper. EPS 2009**E** | 2.85 | Market Capitalization(B) | $2.524 | Beta | 1.44 |
| Trailing 12-Month EPS | $2.75 | S&P Oper. EPS 2010**E** | 3.05 | Yield (%) | 5.79 | S&P 3-Yr. Proj. EPS CAGR(%) | 9 |
| Trailing 12-Month P/E | 4.3 | P/E on S&P Oper. EPS 2009**E** | 4.2 | Dividend Rate/Share | $0.69 | S&P Credit Rating | BB- |
| $10K Invested 5 Yrs Ago | $5,395 | Common Shares Outstg. (M) | 211.8 | Institutional Ownership (%) | 94 | | |

## Price Performance

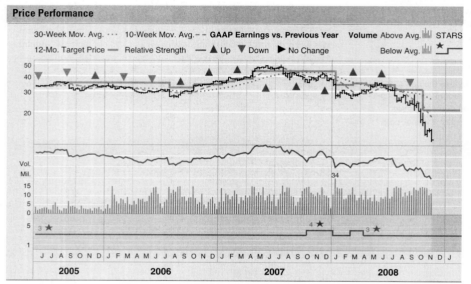

30-Week Mov. Avg. · · · · 10-Week Mov. Avg. - - **GAAP Earnings vs. Previous Year** Volume Above Avg. STARS
12-Mo. Target Price — Relative Strength — ▲ Up ▼ Down ▶ No Change Below Avg.

Options: CBOE, P, Ph

Analysis prepared by **Joseph Agnese** on October 16, 2008, when the stock traded at **$ 16.64**.

## Highlights

➤ We see FY 09 (Feb.) revenues increasing slightly, to about $45 billion, from $44 billion in FY 08, reflecting one extra sales week, flat identical store sales growth and about 2% new square footage growth, offset by store closures. In FY 09, the company plans to open 14 standard stores and 45 to 55 limited assortment stores, while completing 155 major remodels. We think food distribution sales will be hurt by the loss of a major customer contract in the second half of the year, despite new business wins.

➤ We project margins will narrow as an unfavorable change in product mix outweighs benefits from acquisition synergies due to leveraging its larger scale through better purchasing, the removal of duplicate administrative expenses and the rationalization of its current supply chain network. We expect interest expense to decline as the company pays off debt, which rose significantly as a result of the Albertson's acquisition.

➤ We look for FY 09 operating EPS of $2.85, down 4.0% from $2.97 in FY 08 (excluding $0.04 and $0.21 of one-time transaction costs due to acquisitions in the respective years).

## Investment Rationale/Risk

➤ Although we believe SVU is well positioned, with strong regional marketshares, we remain cautious as the company integrates acquisitions in an intensely competitive environment. We see significant benefits from synergies over the next three years as well as from an increased focus on improving the shopping experience at newly acquired stores.

➤ Risks to our recommendation and target price include difficulty integrating newly acquired stores, a sharp deterioration in the economic environment, and a slower than expected improvement in results due to increased competition.

➤ The shares traded recently at an enterprise value of around 4.3X our estimated FY 09 EBITDA of $2.7 billion, below its largest peers' average of 5.6X. Due to its weaker balance sheet and high risks associated with the integration of recently acquired stores, we believe the shares should trade below the peer average. Applying an enterprise vale to EBITDA multiple of 4.7X, at a 10% discount to its closest peer, to our FY 09 EBITDA estimate, we arrive at our 12-month target price of $21.

## Qualitative Risk Assessment

| LOW | MEDIUM | **HIGH** |
|---|---|---|

Our risk assessment reflects the intensely competitive environment in which the company operates, and threats of new entrants into its markets, partially offset by SVU's strong market share positions.

## Quantitative Evaluations

**S&P Quality Ranking** A-

| D | C | B- | B | B+ | **A-** | A | A+ |
|---|---|---|---|---|---|---|---|

**Relative Strength Rank** WEAK

25

LOWEST = 1                    HIGHEST = 99

## Revenue/Earnings Data

**Revenue (Million $)**

| | 1Q | 2Q | 3Q | 4Q | Year |
|---|---|---|---|---|---|
| 2009 | 13,347 | 10,226 | -- | -- | -- |
| 2008 | 13,292 | 10,159 | 10,211 | 10,386 | 44,048 |
| 2007 | 5,783 | 10,666 | 10,657 | 10,301 | 37,406 |
| 2006 | 5,972 | 4,556 | 4,695 | 4,640 | 19,864 |
| 2005 | 5,911 | 4,487 | 4,555 | 4,591 | 19,543 |
| 2004 | 5,836 | 4,591 | 4,739 | 5,044 | 20,210 |

**Earnings Per Share ($)**

| | | | | | |
|---|---|---|---|---|---|
| 2009 | 0.76 | 0.60 | E0.66 | E0.82 | E2.85 |
| 2008 | 0.69 | 0.69 | 0.66 | 0.73 | 2.76 |
| 2007 | 0.57 | 0.61 | 0.54 | 0.57 | 2.32 |
| 2006 | 0.64 | 0.24 | 0.53 | 0.04 | 1.46 |
| 2005 | 1.04 | 0.55 | 0.46 | 0.65 | 2.71 |
| 2004 | 0.55 | 0.46 | 0.36 | 0.70 | 2.07 |

Fiscal year ended Feb. 29. Next earnings report expected: Early January. EPS Estimates based on S&P Operating Earnings; historical GAAP earnings are as reported.

## Dividend Data (Dates: mm/dd Payment Date: mm/dd/yy)

| Amount ($) | Date Decl. | Ex-Div. Date | Stk. of Record | Payment Date |
|---|---|---|---|---|
| 0.170 | 02/06 | 02/28 | 03/03 | 03/17/08 |
| 0.170 | 05/28 | 05/29 | 06/02 | 06/18/08 |
| 0.173 | 08/06 | 08/28 | 09/02 | 09/15/08 |
| 0.173 | 10/02 | 11/26 | 12/01 | 12/15/08 |

Dividends have been paid since 1936. Source: Company reports.

**Please read the Required Disclosures and Analyst Certification on the last page of this report.**

# SUPERVALU INC.

STANDARD
&POOR'S

## Business Summary October 16, 2008

CORPORATE OVERVIEW. SUPERVALU, organized in 1925 as the successor to two wholesale grocery concerns established in the 1870s, has grown into the largest U.S. food distributor to supermarkets, and the second largest conventional food retailer in the U.S. Retail operations are conducted through limited assortment stores, food stores, and combination food and drug stores. As of February 2008, the company operated about 2,500 multi-format retail food stores and was the primary grocery supplier to approximately 2,200 stores in addition to its own retail operations.

CORPORATE STRATEGY. The company aims to leverage its retail food and supply chain services by benefiting from economies of scale and its low-cost supply chain network. The company operated 891 combination stores, 392 food stores, and 318 limited assortment food stores through 71.3 million square feet of space as of February 2008. Combination food store banners (bigg's, Sav-On and Jewel-Osco, for example) typically carry 50,000 items and average 60,000 square feet. Food store banners (Bristol Farms, Jewel, Hornbacher's, Acme Markets and Lucky) typically carry 40,000 items and average

approximately 40,000 square feet. Other major banners that operate both combination food store and food stores include Albertson's, Shaw's Supermarkets, Cub Foods, Shoppers Food & Pharmacy, Farm Fresh, Shop n' Save, and Star Market banners.

Limited assortment food stores include Save-A-Lot stores. The company licenses 873 Save-A-Lot stores to independent operators. Save-A-Lot food stores are typically 15,000 square feet and stock 1,400 high volume food items as well as a limited number of general merchandise items. The majority of food products offered for sale are private label products. The company positions itself to offer low prices by carrying a limited selection of the most frequently purchased goods. The majority of Save-A-Lot stores are found in small town/rural communities as opposed to urban and suburban locations.

## Company Financials Fiscal Year Ended Feb. 29

| Per Share Data ($) | 2008 | 2007 | 2006 | 2005 | 2004 | 2003 | 2002 | 2001 | 2000 | 1999 |
|---|---|---|---|---|---|---|---|---|---|---|
| Tangible Book Value | NM | NM | 7.37 | 6.52 | 4.84 | 3.24 | 2.54 | 1.43 | 1.40 | 6.10 |
| Cash Flow | 7.55 | 6.79 | 3.55 | 4.75 | 4.34 | 4.14 | 4.08 | 3.20 | 4.03 | 3.48 |
| Earnings | 2.76 | 2.32 | 1.46 | 2.71 | 2.07 | 1.91 | 1.53 | 0.62 | 1.87 | 1.57 |
| S&P Core Earnings | 2.42 | 2.45 | 1.90 | 2.21 | 2.03 | 1.61 | 1.24 | 0.39 | NA | NA |
| Dividends | 0.66 | 0.64 | 0.60 | 0.58 | 0.57 | 0.56 | 0.55 | 0.54 | 0.54 | 0.52 |
| Payout Ratio | 24% | 28% | 41% | 21% | 27% | 29% | 36% | 87% | 29% | 33% |
| Calendar Year | 2007 | 2006 | 2005 | 2004 | 2003 | 2002 | 2001 | 2000 | 1999 | 1998 |
| Prices:High | 49.78 | 36.59 | 35.88 | 35.15 | 28.84 | 30.81 | 24.10 | 22.88 | 28.88 | 28.94 |
| Prices:Low | 34.46 | 26.14 | 29.55 | 25.70 | 12.60 | 14.75 | 12.60 | 11.75 | 16.81 | 20.19 |
| P/E Ratio:High | 18 | 16 | 25 | 13 | 14 | 16 | 16 | 37 | 15 | 18 |
| P/E Ratio:Low | 12 | 11 | 20 | 9 | 6 | 8 | 8 | 19 | 9 | 13 |

### Income Statement Analysis (Million $)

| | 2008 | 2007 | 2006 | 2005 | 2004 | 2003 | 2002 | 2001 | 2000 | 1999 |
|---|---|---|---|---|---|---|---|---|---|---|
| Revenue | 44,048 | 37,406 | 19,864 | 19,543 | 20,210 | 19,160 | 20,909 | 23,194 | 20,339 | 17,421 |
| Operating Income | 2,788 | 2,058 | 750 | 936 | 919 | 870 | 904 | 860 | 800 | 652 |
| Depreciation | 1,030 | 879 | 311 | 303 | 302 | 297 | 341 | 344 | 277 | 234 |
| Interest Expense | 733 | 600 | 139 | 138 | 166 | 182 | 194 | 213 | 154 | 124 |
| Pretax Income | 977 | 747 | 329 | 601 | 455 | 408 | 344 | 154 | 448 | 316 |
| Effective Tax Rate | 39.3% | 39.5% | 37.4% | 35.8% | 38.4% | 37.0% | 40.1% | 46.8% | 45.8% | 39.6% |
| Net Income | 593 | 452 | 206 | 386 | 280 | 257 | 206 | 82.0 | 243 | 191 |
| S&P Core Earnings | 518 | 477 | 269 | 313 | 276 | 217 | 166 | 51.2 | NA | NA |

### Balance Sheet & Other Financial Data (Million $)

| | 2008 | 2007 | 2006 | 2005 | 2004 | 2003 | 2002 | 2001 | 2000 | 1999 |
|---|---|---|---|---|---|---|---|---|---|---|
| Cash | 243 | 285 | 686 | 464 | 292 | 29.2 | 12.0 | 11.0 | 11.0 | 8.00 |
| Current Assets | 4,147 | 4,460 | 2,168 | 2,127 | 2,037 | 1,647 | 1,604 | 2,092 | 2,178 | 1,583 |
| Total Assets | 21,062 | 21,702 | 6,038 | 6,278 | 6,153 | 5,896 | 5,825 | 6,407 | 6,495 | 4,266 |
| Current Liabilities | 4,607 | 4,705 | 1,507 | 1,632 | 1,872 | 1,525 | 1,701 | 2,341 | 2,510 | 1,522 |
| Long Term Debt | 8,502 | 9,192 | 1,406 | 1,579 | 1,634 | 2,020 | 1,875 | 2,008 | 1,954 | 1,246 |
| Common Equity | 5,953 | 5,306 | 2,619 | 2,511 | 2,210 | 2,009 | 1,918 | 1,793 | 1,821 | 1,300 |
| Total Capital | 14,455 | 15,006 | 4,079 | 4,240 | 3,986 | 4,146 | 3,873 | 3,831 | 3,778 | 2,606 |
| Capital Expenditures | 1,191 | 837 | 308 | 233 | 328 | 383 | 293 | 398 | 408 | 240 |
| Cash Flow | 1,623 | 1,331 | 517 | 689 | 582 | 554 | 547 | 426 | 520 | 425 |
| Current Ratio | 0.9 | 0.9 | 1.4 | 1.3 | 1.1 | 1.1 | 0.9 | 0.9 | 0.9 | 1.0 |
| % Long Term Debt of Capitalization | 58.8 | 61.3 | 34.5 | 37.2 | 41.0 | 48.7 | 48.4 | 52.4 | 51.7 | 47.8 |
| % Net Income of Revenue | 1.4 | 1.2 | 1.0 | 2.0 | 1.4 | 1.3 | 1.0 | 0.4 | 1.2 | 1.1 |
| % Return on Assets | 2.8 | 3.2 | 3.3 | 6.2 | 4.6 | 4.4 | 3.4 | 1.3 | 4.5 | 4.6 |
| % Return on Equity | 10.5 | 11.4 | 8.0 | 16.3 | 13.3 | 13.2 | 11.1 | 4.5 | 15.6 | 15.3 |

Data as orig reptd.; bef. results of disc opers/spec. items. Per share data adj. for stk. divs.; EPS diluted. E-Estimated. NA-Not Available. NM-Not Meaningful. NR-Not Ranked. UR-Under Review.

**Office:** 11840 Valley View Road, Eden Prairie, MN 55344.
**Telephone:** 952-828-4000.
**Website:** http://www.supervalu.com
**Chrmn & CEO:** J. Noddle

**Pres & COO:** M. Jackson
**EVP, CFO & Chief Acctg Officer:** P.K. Knous
**SVP & CIO:** P.L. Singer
**Treas:** J. Stoffel

**Investor Contact:** Y. Scharton (952-828-4540)
**Board Members:** A. G. Ames, I. Cohen, R. E. Daly, L. A. Del Santo, S. E. Engel, P. L. Francis, E. C. Gage, G. L. Keith, Jr., C. M. Lillis, J. Noddle, M. T. Peterson, S. S. Rogers, W. Sales, K. P. Seifert

**Founded:** 1871
**Domicile:** Delaware
**Employees:** 192,000

The *McGraw·Hill* Companies

# Symantec Corp

**S&P Recommendation** HOLD ★★★☆☆

| Price | 12-Mo. Target Price | Investment Style |
|---|---|---|
| $12.21 (as of Nov 14, 2008) | $15.00 | Large-Cap Blend |

**GICS Sector** Information Technology
**Sub-Industry** Systems Software

**Summary** This company provides software solutions that enable customers to protect their network infrastructure from potential threats and to store their data.

## Key Stock Statistics (Source S&P, Vickers, company reports)

| | | | | | | | |
|---|---|---|---|---|---|---|---|
| 52-Wk Range | $22.80–11.25 | S&P Oper. EPS 2009**E** | 0.73 | Market Capitalization(B) | $10.208 | Beta | 0.76 |
| Trailing 12-Month EPS | $0.75 | S&P Oper. EPS 2010**E** | 0.75 | Yield (%) | Nil | S&P 3-Yr. Proj. EPS CAGR(%) | 9 |
| Trailing 12-Month P/E | 16.3 | P/E on S&P Oper. EPS 2009**E** | 16.7 | Dividend Rate/Share | Nil | S&P Credit Rating | NR |
| $10K Invested 5 Yrs Ago | $7,479 | Common Shares Outstg. (M) | 836.0 | Institutional Ownership (%) | 93 | | |

## Price Performance

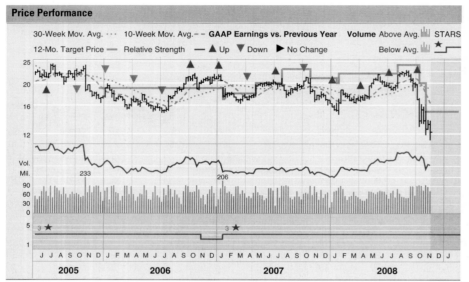

30-Week Mov. Avg. ···· 10-Week Mov. Avg. -- **GAAP Earnings vs. Previous Year** Volume Above Avg. STARS
12-Mo. Target Price — Relative Strength — ▲ Up ▼ Down ► No Change Below Avg.

Options: ASE, CBOE, P, Ph

Analysis prepared by **Jim Yin** on November 03, 2008, when the stock traded at **$ 13.49**.

## Qualitative Risk Assessment

| LOW | MEDIUM | HIGH |
|---|---|---|

Our risk assessment for Symantec reflects the highly competitive market in which the company operates and integration risks from recent acquisitions.

## Quantitative Evaluations

**S&P Quality Ranking** B

| D | C | B- | **B** | B+ | A- | A | A+ |
|---|---|---|---|---|---|---|---|

**Relative Strength Rank** MODERATE

43

LOWEST = 1 HIGHEST = 99

## Revenue/Earnings Data

### Revenue (Million $)

| | 1Q | 2Q | 3Q | 4Q | Year |
|---|---|---|---|---|---|
| 2009 | 1,650 | 1,518 | -- | -- | -- |
| 2008 | 1,400 | 1,419 | 1,515 | 1,540 | 5,874 |
| 2007 | 1,259 | 1,262 | 1,313 | 1,357 | 5,199 |
| 2006 | 699.9 | 1,056 | 1,149 | 1,239 | 4,143 |
| 2005 | 556.6 | 618.3 | 695.2 | 712.7 | 2,583 |
| 2004 | 391.1 | 428.7 | 493.9 | 556.4 | 1,870 |

### Earnings Per Share ($)

| | | | | | |
|---|---|---|---|---|---|
| 2009 | 0.22 | 0.16 | E0.15 | E0.18 | E0.73 |
| 2008 | 0.10 | 0.06 | 0.15 | 0.22 | 0.53 |
| 2007 | 0.09 | 0.12 | 0.12 | 0.07 | 0.41 |
| 2006 | 0.27 | -0.21 | 0.08 | 0.11 | 0.15 |
| 2005 | 0.16 | 0.19 | 0.22 | 0.16 | 0.74 |
| 2004 | 0.09 | 0.12 | 0.16 | 0.16 | 0.54 |

Fiscal year ended Mar. 31. Next earnings report expected: Late January. EPS Estimates based on S&P Operating Earnings; historical GAAP earnings are as reported.

## Dividend Data

No cash dividends have been paid.

## Highlights

➤ We see total revenues increasing 1.2% in FY 10 (Mar.), compared to our projected 4.9% rise in FY 09. The decelerating revenue growth we see in FY 10 reflects our view of a slowing global economy, lower than expected growth in endpoint management and increased competition in the data center management business. In addition, we forecast revenue declines for SYMC's consumer products amid weak consumer spending and a loss of market share to its main competitor, McAfee (MFE: hold, $32).

➤ We look for gross margins in FY 10 to remain at 80%, the same as in FY 09. We see operating expenses at 64% of revenues, down from 65% in FY 09, as a result of cost savings from a recently announced restructuring plan, including a head count reduction. We expect FY 10 operating margins to remain at 15%.

➤ Our FY 10 EPS estimate is $0.75, compared to the $0.73 we see in FY 09. The expected increase reflects slightly higher revenues and fewer shares outstanding. The number of shares has declined 6% in the past four quarters, reflecting SYMC's share buyback program.

## Investment Rationale/Risk

➤ Our hold recommendation reflects our view of a more challenging enterprise IT spending environment in 2009 due to a slowdown in the global economy, which we believe will last through the second half of 2009. In our view, the sales cycle will lengthen, as we believe larger-sized deals will be more difficult to close. Additionally, we believe earnings will be hurt by unfavorable foreign exchange due to the rising value of the U.S. dollar. However, we think the shares are fairly valued following a steep price decline.

➤ Risks to our recommendation and target price include intense competition in the Internet security software industry, a potential slowdown in corporate information technology spending, and integration risk associated with recent acquisitions.

➤ Our 12-month target price of $15 is based on a blend of our discounted cash flow (DCF) and P/E analyses. Our DCF model assumes a 12% WACC and 3% terminal growth, yielding an intrinsic value of $19. For our P/E analysis, we derive a value of $12 based on an industry P/E-to-growth ratio of 1.78X, or 16X our FY 10 EPS estimate of $0.75.

---

**Please read the Required Disclosures and Analyst Certification on the last page of this report.**

# Symantec Corp

**STANDARD &POOR'S**

## Business Summary November 03, 2008

CORPORATE OVERVIEW. SYMC is a provider of security, storage and systems management solutions that enable enterprises and consumers to protect their network infrastructure from potential threats and to archive and recover their data. Its products include virus protection, firewall, virtual private network, data protection, compliance, vulnerability management, intrusion detection, remote management technologies, and security services.

The company is organized into five operating segments:

Consumer Products -- focuses on Internet security. Key products include Norton 360 and Norton Internet Security, which protect against viruses, worms and other security risks; Norton AntiVirus, which removes viruses, Trojan horses and worms; and Norton SystemWorks, which enables users to maintain and optimize their computers. The Consumer Products segment accounted for 30% of total revenue in both FY 07 (Mar.) and FY 08.

Security and Compliance -- provides security throughout the network, including behind the gateway and at the client level including servers, desktop PCs, laptops and other mobile devices. Its Information Risk Management solutions enforce data security policies on email, storage systems, and archiving. The company's enterprise security solutions address the following areas: An-

tivirus, Antispam, Compliance, and Managed Security Services. The Security and Compliance segment accounted for 27% and 28% of total revenue in FY 07 and FY 08, respectively.

Storage and Server Management -- provides software solutions designed to protect, back up, archive and restore data across the enterprise. It also helps customers manage heterogeneous storage and server environments. This segment accounted for 37% and 36% of total revenue in FY 07 and FY 08, respectively.

Services -- assists SYMC's customers in implementing, supporting and maintaining their security, storage and infrastructure software solutions. Services accounted for 6% of total revenues in both FY 07 and FY 08, respectively.

The Other segment is comprised of products nearing the end of their life cycle. Revenues were insignificant during FY 07 and FY 08.

## Company Financials Fiscal Year Ended Mar. 31

| Per Share Data ($) | 2008 | 2007 | 2006 | 2005 | 2004 | 2003 | 2002 | 2001 | 2000 | 1999 |
|---|---|---|---|---|---|---|---|---|---|---|
| Tangible Book Value | NM | NM | 0.63 | 3.07 | 1.97 | 2.89 | 1.26 | 0.97 | 1.11 | 0.59 |
| Cash Flow | 1.46 | 1.24 | 0.48 | 0.86 | 0.62 | 0.45 | 0.37 | 0.18 | 0.43 | 0.16 |
| Earnings | 0.53 | 0.41 | 0.15 | 0.74 | 0.54 | 0.38 | -0.05 | 0.12 | 0.34 | 0.11 |
| S&P Core Earnings | 0.55 | 0.40 | -0.06 | 0.59 | 0.43 | 0.26 | -0.19 | 0.03 | NA | NA |
| Dividends | Nil | Nil | Nil | Nil | Nil | Nil | Nil | Nil | Nil | Nil |
| Payout Ratio | Nil | Nil | Nil | Nil | Nil | Nil | Nil | Nil | Nil | Nil |
| Calendar Year | 2007 | 2006 | 2005 | 2004 | 2003 | 2002 | 2001 | 2000 | 1999 | 1998 |
| Prices:High | 21.86 | 22.19 | 26.60 | 34.05 | 17.50 | 11.55 | 9.19 | 10.20 | 8.66 | 4.08 |
| Prices:Low | 15.97 | 14.78 | 16.32 | 17.27 | 9.09 | 6.80 | 3.90 | 3.42 | 1.56 | 1.09 |
| P/E Ratio:High | 41 | 54 | NM | 46 | 33 | 30 | 78 | NM | 25 | 38 |
| P/E Ratio:Low | 30 | 36 | NM | 23 | 17 | 18 | 33 | NM | 5 | 10 |

### Income Statement Analysis (Million $)

| | 2008 | 2007 | 2006 | 2005 | 2004 | 2003 | 2002 | 2001 | 2000 | 1999 |
|---|---|---|---|---|---|---|---|---|---|---|
| Revenue | 5,874 | 5,199 | 4,143 | 2,583 | 1,870 | 1,407 | 1,071 | 854 | 746 | 593 |
| Operating Income | 1,597 | 1,402 | 942 | 926 | 611 | 417 | 269 | 240 | 191 | 90.0 |
| Depreciation | 824 | 811 | 340 | 96.3 | 78.8 | 59.6 | 238 | 105 | 42.9 | 30.2 |
| Interest Expense | 29.5 | 27.2 | 18.0 | 12.3 | 21.2 | 21.2 | 9.17 | Nil | 0.02 | 1.80 |
| Pretax Income | 713 | 632 | 363 | 858 | 542 | 364 | 45.5 | 141 | 257 | 83.2 |
| Effective Tax Rate | 34.9% | 36.0% | 56.8% | 37.5% | 31.6% | 31.7% | NM | 54.6% | 33.9% | 39.6% |
| Net Income | 464 | 404 | 157 | 536 | 371 | 248 | -28.2 | 63.9 | 170 | 50.2 |
| S&P Core Earnings | 488 | 393 | -51.0 | 423 | 284 | 157 | -106 | 14.8 | NA | NA |

### Balance Sheet & Other Financial Data (Million $)

| | 2008 | 2007 | 2006 | 2005 | 2004 | 2003 | 2002 | 2001 | 2000 | 1999 |
|---|---|---|---|---|---|---|---|---|---|---|
| Cash | 2,427 | 2,559 | 2,316 | 1,091 | 2,410 | 1,706 | 1,375 | 557 | 432 | 193 |
| Current Assets | 3,730 | 4,071 | 3,908 | 3,688 | 2,842 | 1,988 | 1,563 | 782 | 546 | 316 |
| Total Assets | 18,092 | 17,751 | 17,913 | 5,614 | 4,456 | 3,266 | 2,503 | 1,792 | 846 | 563 |
| Current Liabilities | 3,800 | 3,318 | 3,478 | 1,701 | 1,287 | 895 | 579 | 413 | 227 | 217 |
| Long Term Debt | 2,100 | 2,100 | 24.9 | 4.41 | 606 | 607 | 604 | 2.36 | 1.55 | 1.50 |
| Common Equity | 10,973 | 11,602 | 13,668 | 3,705 | 2,426 | 1,764 | 1,320 | 1,377 | 618 | 345 |
| Total Capital | 13,293 | 14,045 | 14,187 | 3,798 | 3,077 | 2,371 | 1,924 | 1,379 | 620 | 347 |
| Capital Expenditures | 274 | 420 | 267 | 91.5 | 111 | 192 | 141 | 61.2 | 28.5 | 25.1 |
| Cash Flow | 1,288 | 1,216 | 497 | 633 | 453 | 308 | 210 | 95.9 | 213 | 74.2 |
| Current Ratio | 1.0 | 1.2 | 1.1 | 2.2 | 2.2 | 2.2 | 31.3 | 1.9 | 2.4 | 1.5 |
| % Long Term Debt of Capitalization | 15.8 | 15.0 | 0.2 | 0.1 | 19.7 | 25.6 | 0.3 | 0.2 | 0.3 | 2.1 |
| % Net Income of Revenue | 7.9 | 7.8 | 3.8 | 20.8 | 19.8 | 17.7 | NM | 7.5 | 22.8 | 8.5 |
| % Return on Assets | 2.6 | 2.3 | 1.3 | 10.6 | 9.6 | 8.6 | NM | 4.8 | 24.1 | 9.7 |
| % Return on Equity | 4.1 | 3.2 | 1.8 | 17.5 | 17.7 | 16.1 | NM | 6.4 | 35.3 | 15.2 |

Data as orig reptd.; bef. results of disc opers/spec. items. Per share data adj. for stk. divs.; EPS diluted. E-Estimated. NA-Not Available. NM-Not Meaningful. NR-Not Ranked. UR-Under Review.

**Office:** 20330 Stevens Creek Boulevard, Cupertino, CA 95014-2132.
**Telephone:** 408-517-8000.
**Email:** investor-relations@symantec.com
**Website:** http://www.symantec.com

**Chrmn & CEO:** J. Thompson
**COO:** E. Salem
**EVP & CFO:** J. Beer
**EVP & CTO:** M.F. Bregman

**EVP, Secy & General Counsel:** S.C. Taylor
**Investor Contact:** H. Corcos (408-517-8324)
**Board Members:** M. R. Brown, W. T. Coleman, III, F. Dangeard, G. B. Laybourne, D. Mahoney, R. S. Miller, Jr., G. Reyes, D. H. Schulman, J. Thompson, V. Unruh

**Founded:** 1983
**Domicile:** Delaware
**Employees:** 17,600

# Sysco Corp

| S&P Recommendation | HOLD ★★★☆☆ | Price | 12-Mo. Target Price | Investment Style |
|---|---|---|---|---|
| | | $22.68 (as of Nov 14, 2008) | $29.00 | Large-Cap Blend |

**GICS Sector** Consumer Staples
**Sub-Industry** Food Distributors

**Summary** This company is the largest U.S. marketer and distributor of foodservice products.

## Key Stock Statistics (Source S&P, Vickers, company reports)

| | | | | | | | |
|---|---|---|---|---|---|---|---|
| 52-Wk Range | $35.00– 21.77 | S&P Oper. EPS 2009**E** | 1.95 | Market Capitalization(B) | $13.588 | Beta | 0.91 |
| Trailing 12-Month EPS | $1.84 | S&P Oper. EPS 2010**E** | NA | Yield (%) | 3.88 | S&P 3-Yr. Proj. EPS CAGR(%) | 10 |
| Trailing 12-Month P/E | 12.3 | P/E on S&P Oper. EPS 2009**E** | 11.6 | Dividend Rate/Share | $0.88 | S&P Credit Rating | AA- |
| $10K Invested 5 Yrs Ago | $7,249 | Common Shares Outstg. (M) | 599.1 | Institutional Ownership (%) | 76 | | |

## Price Performance

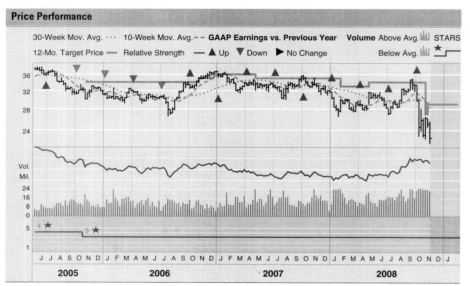

30-Week Mov. Avg. · · · ·  10-Week Mov. Avg. - - ·  **GAAP Earnings vs. Previous Year**  Volume Above Avg. STARS
12-Mo. Target Price —  Relative Strength —  ▲ Up  ▼ Down  ► No Change  Below Avg. ★

Options: ASE, CBOE, P

Analysis prepared by **Loran Braverman, CFA** on November 04, 2008, when the stock traded at **$ 25.31**.

## Highlights

➤ In FY 08 (Jun.), sales rose 7.1%. SYY estimated that it experienced inflation in its cost of goods sold of 6.0%, which would imply that it had modest "real" sales growth. With SYY's most important end market - restaurants - under pressure from rising costs and weak consumer discretionary spending, we forecast slower sales growth of 5.4% in FY 09. We think SYY gained market share in FY 08 and expect it to gain share again in FY 09.

➤ The operating margin improved slightly in FY 08, with good expense control and greater productivity helping to offset commodity cost pressures. Despite only modest sales growth expected, we look for a slightly higher margin in FY 09 due to great efficiency. Over time, we expect SYY's profitability to benefit from an increased amount of consolidated purchasing, the addition of regional distribution centers, improved management of freight costs, and better inventory management.

➤ Our FY 09 EPS estimate is $1.95, up from $1.81 in FY 08. We see capital expenditures in FY 09 rising to $675 million - $725 million, compared to $516 million in FY 08, as certain projects experienced delays in FY 08.

## Investment Rationale/Risk

➤ Longer term, we expect results of this leading U.S. food distributor to include both internal growth and additional acquisitions. We think that SYY is gaining market share during the current difficult period for restaurant sales, which we believe is being caused by the weak consumer discretionary environment. Restaurants accounted for 63% of SYY's FY 08 sales.

➤ Risks to our recommendation and target price include a slowing of growth rates given SYY's significant size and reach, sharp increases in gasoline prices, and a potential prolonged slowdown in restaurant sales.

➤ Our 12-month target price of $29 is a blend of our historical and relative analyses. Our historical analysis applies a 14.2X multiple, near the low end of the 10-year range, to our calendar 2009 EPS estimate of $2.05, implying a value of $29. We use a P/E near the low end due to what we see as the decreased likelihood of SYY consistently achieving its former sales growth rates, given its size, and also S&P's negative outlook for the restaurant industry. Our peer analysis applies a P/E of 14.1X, in line with the average of a small group of other food distributor stocks, also suggesting a value of $29.

## Qualitative Risk Assessment

| LOW | MEDIUM | HIGH |
|---|---|---|

Our risk assessment reflects that SYY operates in a relatively stable industry, in which we believe it has the largest market share.

## Quantitative Evaluations

**S&P Quality Ranking** — A+

| D | C | B- | B | B+ | A- | A | A+ |
|---|---|---|---|---|---|---|---|

**Relative Strength Rank** — MODERATE

58

LOWEST = 1          HIGHEST = 99

## Revenue/Earnings Data

**Revenue (Million $)**

| | 1Q | 2Q | 3Q | 4Q | Year |
|---|---|---|---|---|---|
| 2009 | 9,877 | -- | -- | -- | -- |
| 2008 | 9,406 | 9,240 | 9,147 | 9,730 | 37,522 |
| 2007 | 8,672 | 8,569 | 8,573 | 9,228 | 35,042 |
| 2006 | 8,010 | 7,971 | 8,138 | 8,509 | 32,628 |
| 2005 | 7,532 | 7,331 | 7,437 | 7,981 | 30,282 |
| 2004 | 7,134 | 7,037 | 7,026 | 8,139 | 29,335 |

**Earnings Per Share ($)**

| | | | | | |
|---|---|---|---|---|---|
| 2009 | 0.46 | E0.45 | E0.46 | E0.58 | E1.95 |
| 2008 | 0.43 | 0.43 | 0.40 | 0.55 | 1.81 |
| 2007 | 0.37 | 0.39 | 0.35 | 0.49 | 1.60 |
| 2006 | 0.31 | 0.33 | 0.30 | 0.41 | 1.35 |
| 2005 | 0.35 | 0.36 | 0.34 | 0.44 | 1.47 |
| 2004 | 0.32 | 0.34 | 0.30 | 0.43 | 1.37 |

Fiscal year ended Jun. 30. Next earnings report expected: Late January. EPS Estimates based on S&P Operating Earnings; historical GAAP earnings are as reported.

## Dividend Data (Dates: mm/dd Payment Date: mm/dd/yy)

| Amount ($) | Date Decl. | Ex-Div. Date | Stk. of Record | Payment Date |
|---|---|---|---|---|
| 0.220 | 11/09 | 01/02 | 01/04 | 01/25/08 |
| 0.220 | 02/22 | 04/02 | 04/04 | 04/25/08 |
| 0.220 | 05/14 | 07/01 | 07/03 | 07/25/08 |
| 0.220 | 09/12 | 10/01 | 10/03 | 10/24/08 |

Dividends have been paid since 1970. Source: Company reports.

Please read the **Required Disclosures and Analyst Certification on the last page of this report.**

The **McGraw·Hill** Companies

# Sysco Corp

## Business Summary November 04, 2008

CORPORATE OVERVIEW. Sysco is the largest distributor of foodservice products in the U.S. and Canada. As of June 2008, it operated 180 distribution facilities in the U.S. and Canada. The company provided products and services to over 400,000 customers, including restaurants (63% of FY 08 sales), hospitals and nursing homes (10%), schools and colleges (5%), hotels and motels (6%), and others (16%).

Sysco distributes food products, including frozen foods such as meats, fully prepared entrees, fruits, vegetables and desserts; canned and dry foods; fresh meats; imported specialties; and fresh produce. The company also distributes non-food products. These include paper products, tableware such as china and silverware, cookware, restaurant and kitchen equipment and supplies, and cleaning supplies. The company stresses prompt and accurate delivery of orders, and close contact with customers, and also provides customers with ancillary services, such as providing product usage reports, menu-planning advice, food safety training, and assistance in inventory control. No single customer accounted for more than 10% of sales in FY 08.

CORPORATE STRATEGY. SYY seeks to expand its business by gaining an increased share of products purchased by existing customers, the development of new customers, the use of foldouts (new facilities built in established markets), and an acquisition program. SYY distributes nationally branded merchandise, as well as products packaged under SYY private brands. We believe that Sysco-branded products typically carry wider profit margins than other branded products distributed by the company. From its inception through the end of FY 08, the company had acquired 145 companies or divisions of companies. At June 28, 2008, SYY's balance sheet included $1.413 billion of goodwill.

Over time, we look for SYY's profitability to benefit from an increased amount of consolidated purchasing, the addition of regional distribution centers, improved management of freight costs, and better inventory management. SYY's National Supply Group has three major supply chain initiatives. The first involves the construction of regional distribution centers (RDCs); SYY expects to build five to seven of these centers, with two already operational. The second initiative involves the capability to view and manage all of SYY's inbound freight, both to RDCs and the operating companies, as a network and not as individual locations. FY 08 was the first full year SYY operated under this initiative. The third initiative is the national implementation of demand planning and inventory management software. In FY 08, SYY continued to improve this software and implemented it at additional broadline companies.

## Company Financials Fiscal Year Ended Jun. 30

| Per Share Data ($) | 2008 | 2007 | 2006 | 2005 | 2004 | 2003 | 2002 | 2001 | 2000 | 1999 |
|---|---|---|---|---|---|---|---|---|---|---|
| Tangible Book Value | 3.17 | 2.99 | 2.67 | 2.35 | 2.11 | 1.68 | 1.85 | 2.07 | 1.90 | 1.71 |
| Cash Flow | NA | 2.23 | 1.89 | 1.96 | 1.80 | 1.59 | 1.47 | 1.27 | 1.02 | 0.84 |
| Earnings | 1.81 | 1.60 | 1.35 | 1.47 | 1.37 | 1.18 | 1.01 | 0.88 | 0.68 | 0.54 |
| S&P Core Earnings | 1.68 | 1.59 | 1.38 | 1.39 | 1.31 | 1.08 | 0.92 | 0.82 | NA | NA |
| Dividends | 0.82 | 0.72 | 0.64 | 0.56 | 0.48 | 0.40 | 0.32 | 0.23 | 0.22 | 0.19 |
| Payout Ratio | 45% | 45% | 47% | 38% | 35% | 34% | 32% | 26% | 32% | 35% |
| Prices:High | 35.00 | 36.74 | 37.04 | 38.04 | 41.27 | 37.57 | 32.58 | 30.12 | 30.44 | 20.56 |
| Prices:Low | 21.77 | 29.90 | 26.50 | 29.98 | 29.48 | 22.90 | 21.25 | 21.75 | 13.06 | 12.47 |
| P/E Ratio:High | 19 | 23 | 27 | 26 | 30 | 32 | 32 | 34 | 45 | 38 |
| P/E Ratio:Low | 12 | 19 | 20 | 20 | 22 | 19 | 21 | 25 | 19 | 23 |
| **Income Statement Analysis** (Million $) | | | | | | | | | | |
| Revenue | 37,522 | 35,042 | 32,628 | 30,282 | 29,335 | 26,140 | 23,351 | 21,784 | 19,303 | 17,423 |
| Operating Income | NA | 2,071 | 1,840 | 1,906 | 1,816 | 1,597 | 1,439 | 1,286 | 1,030 | 873 |
| Depreciation | 373 | 363 | 345 | 317 | 284 | 273 | 278 | 248 | 220 | 206 |
| Interest Expense | NA | 105 | 109 | 75.0 | 69.9 | 72.2 | 62.9 | 71.0 | 71.0 | 73.0 |
| Pretax Income | 1,791 | 1,621 | 1,395 | 1,525 | 1,475 | 1,260 | 1,101 | 967 | 738 | 594 |
| Effective Tax Rate | 38.3% | 38.3% | 39.3% | 37.0% | 38.5% | 38.3% | 38.3% | 38.3% | 38.5% | 39.1% |
| Net Income | 1,106 | 1,001 | 846 | 961 | 907 | 778 | 680 | 597 | 454 | 362 |
| S&P Core Earnings | 1,022 | 995 | 866 | 890 | 868 | 710 | 618 | 559 | NA | NA |
| **Balance Sheet & Other Financial Data** (Million $) | | | | | | | | | | |
| Cash | 552 | 208 | 202 | 192 | 200 | 421 | 230 | 136 | 159 | 149 |
| Current Assets | NA | 4,676 | 4,400 | 4,002 | 3,851 | 3,630 | 3,185 | 2,985 | 2,733 | 2,409 |
| Total Assets | 10,082 | 9,519 | 8,992 | 8,268 | 7,848 | 6,937 | 5,990 | 5,469 | 4,814 | 4,097 |
| Current Liabilities | NA | 3,415 | 3,226 | 3,458 | 3,127 | 2,701 | 2,239 | 2,090 | 1,783 | 1,428 |
| Long Term Debt | NA | 1,758 | 1,627 | 956 | 1,231 | 1,249 | 1,176 | 961 | 1,024 | 998 |
| Common Equity | 3,409 | 3,278 | 3,052 | 2,759 | 2,565 | 2,198 | 2,133 | 2,148 | 1,762 | 1,427 |
| Total Capital | NA | 5,037 | 5,403 | 4,440 | 4,483 | 3,945 | 3,750 | 3,379 | 3,032 | 2,669 |
| Capital Expenditures | 516 | 603 | 515 | 390 | 530 | 436 | 416 | 341 | 266 | 287 |
| Cash Flow | NA | 1,364 | 1,191 | 1,278 | 1,191 | 1,051 | 958 | 845 | 674 | 567 |
| Current Ratio | 1.5 | 1.4 | 1.4 | 1.2 | 1.2 | 1.3 | 1.4 | 1.4 | 1.5 | 1.7 |
| % Long Term Debt of Capitalization | 36.7 | 34.9 | 30.1 | 21.5 | 27.4 | 31.7 | 31.4 | 28.4 | 33.8 | 37.4 |
| % Net Income of Revenue | 3.0 | 2.9 | 2.6 | 3.2 | 3.1 | 3.0 | 2.9 | 2.7 | 2.4 | 2.1 |
| % Return on Assets | 11.3 | 10.8 | 9.8 | 11.9 | 12.3 | 12.0 | 12.0 | 11.6 | 10.2 | 9.2 |
| % Return on Equity | 33.1 | 31.6 | 29.1 | 36.1 | 38.1 | 35.9 | 32.1 | 30.5 | 28.5 | 26.0 |

Data as orig reptd.; bef. results of disc opers/spec. items. Per share data adj. for stk. divs.; EPS diluted. E-Estimated. NA-Not Available. NM-Not Meaningful. NR-Not Ranked. UR-Under Review.

**Office:** 1390 Enclave Parkway, Houston, TX, USA 77077-2099.
**Telephone:** 281-584-1390.
**Website:** http://www.sysco.com
**Chrmn:** P.J. Seipp

**Pres & COO:** K.F. Spitler
**CEO:** T.K. Hogan
**EVP & CFO:** W.J. DeLaney, III
**EVP & Chief Admin Officer:** K.J. Carrig

**Board Members:** J. M. Cassaday, J. L. Craven, M. A. Fernandez, J. Golden, J. A. Hafner, Jr., H. Koerber, R. G. Merrill, N. S. Newcomb, R. Schnieders, P. J. Seipp, P. S. Sewell, R. G. Tilghman, J. M. Ward

**Founded:** 1969
**Domicile:** Delaware
**Employees:** 50,000

# Target Corp

| S&P Recommendation | HOLD ★★★☆☆ | Price | 12-Mo. Target Price | Investment Style |
|---|---|---|---|---|
| | | $33.03 (as of Nov 14, 2008) | $53.00 | Large-Cap Growth |

**GICS Sector** Consumer Discretionary
**Sub-Industry** General Merchandise Stores

**Summary** This company operates about 1,400 Target and 230 SuperTarget general merchandise stores across the U.S.

## Key Stock Statistics (Source S&P, Vickers, company reports)

| | | | | | | | | |
|---|---|---|---|---|---|---|---|---|
| 52-Wk Range | $61.00– 30.45 | S&P Oper. EPS 2009**E** | 3.44 | Market Capitalization(B) | $24.926 | Beta | | 0.84 |
| Trailing 12-Month EPS | $3.35 | S&P Oper. EPS 2010**E** | 3.75 | Yield (%) | 1.94 | S&P 3-Yr. Proj. EPS CAGR(%) | | 8 |
| Trailing 12-Month P/E | 9.9 | P/E on S&P Oper. EPS 2009**E** | 9.6 | Dividend Rate/Share | $0.64 | S&P Credit Rating | | A+ |
| $10K Invested 5 Yrs Ago | $8,905 | Common Shares Outstg. (M) | 754.7 | Institutional Ownership (%) | 92 | | | |

## Price Performance

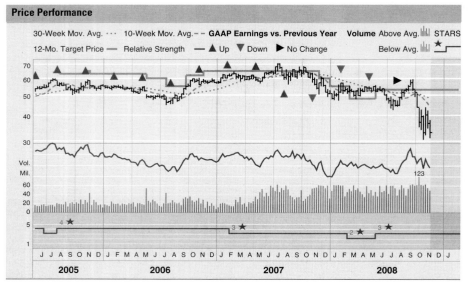

30-Week Mov. Avg. · · · · 10-Week Mov. Avg. - - - **GAAP Earnings vs. Previous Year** Volume Above Avg. STARS
12-Mo. Target Price — Relative Strength — ▲ Up ▼ Down ► No Change Below Avg.

Options: ASE, CBOE, Ph

Analysis prepared by **Jason N. Asaeda** on August 20, 2008, when the stock traded at **$ 50.02**.

## Highlights

➤ We look for revenues of $66.9 billion in FY 09 (Jan.) and $70.9 billion in FY 10, driven by expansion. Amid a weakening economy, we think TGT will benefit from some trading down by consumers for staples. However, we also see the company at risk of losing market share to main competitor Wal-Mart Stores (WMT: buy, $50). Despite TGT's marketing efforts to convey its "Expect More. Pay Less" brand message, we perceive WMT as communicating a stronger value proposition to consumers. Weighing these factors, we project same-store sales to be flat in FY 09 and up 1% in FY 10.

➤ We anticipate annual operating margin pressure from faster sales growth in lower-margin consumables/perishables, increased marketing spending, investments in store rebuilds, and higher bad debt expense, partly offset by higher merchandise markups, supported by direct imports and better inventory management, and cost controls.

➤ Factoring in higher net interest expense and expected share buybacks under the company's $10 billion share repurchase authorization, we see operating EPS of $3.44 in FY 09 and $3.75 in FY 10.

## Investment Rationale/Risk

➤ We believe food and other consumables remain less of a traffic driver for TGT than WMT. We also question TGT's ability to increase customer shopping frequency over the near term with its apparel and home assortments, which we view as lacking differentiation and newness relative to moderate-price department stores such as J.C. Penney (JCP: buy, $36). Given a tough retail environment, we look for the company to aggressively manage its flow of goods, which should help keep inventories in line with sales trends, and to control dollar expense growth as a means to limiting margin erosion. We also expect TGT to use proceeds from its recent sale of a 47% stake in its credit card receivables to JPMorgan Chase to fund share repurchases and capital investments--actions that should improve shareholder value.

➤ Risks to our recommendation and target price include sales shortfalls due to lackluster customer response to TGT's remerchandising and brand marketing efforts, and aggressive competition from peers.

➤ Our 12-month target price of $53 applies a peer-median forward P/E multiple of 14.1X to our FY 10 EPS estimate.

## Qualitative Risk Assessment

| LOW | MEDIUM | HIGH |
|---|---|---|

Our risk assessment reflects our view of TGT's fairly consistent earnings track record, and its healthy balance sheet and cash flow, offset by our concerns over potential loss of market share this year as a result of lackluster merchandising and aggressive pricing by competitors.

## Quantitative Evaluations

**S&P Quality Ranking** A+

| D | C | B- | B | B+ | A- | A | A+ |
|---|---|---|---|---|---|---|---|

**Relative Strength Rank** MODERATE

48

LOWEST = 1 HIGHEST = 99

## Revenue/Earnings Data

**Revenue (Million $)**

| | 1Q | 2Q | 3Q | 4Q | Year |
|---|---|---|---|---|---|
| 2009 | 14,302 | 15,472 | -- | -- | -- |
| 2008 | 14,041 | 14,620 | 14,835 | 19,872 | 63,367 |
| 2007 | 12,863 | 13,347 | 13,570 | 19,710 | 59,490 |
| 2006 | 11,477 | 11,990 | 12,206 | 16,947 | 52,620 |
| 2005 | 11,587 | 10,556 | 10,909 | 15,194 | 46,839 |
| 2004 | 10,322 | 10,984 | 11,286 | 15,571 | 48,163 |

**Earnings Per Share ($)**

| | | | | | |
|---|---|---|---|---|---|
| 2009 | 0.74 | 0.82 | E0.52 | E1.36 | E3.44 |
| 2008 | 0.75 | 0.82 | 0.56 | 1.23 | 3.33 |
| 2007 | 0.63 | 0.70 | 0.59 | 1.29 | 3.21 |
| 2006 | 0.55 | 0.61 | 0.49 | 1.06 | 2.71 |
| 2005 | 0.48 | 0.40 | 0.37 | 0.90 | 2.07 |
| 2004 | 0.38 | 0.39 | 0.33 | 0.91 | 2.01 |

Fiscal year ended Jan. 31. Next earnings report expected: Mid November. EPS Estimates based on S&P Operating Earnings; historical GAAP earnings are as reported.

## Dividend Data (Dates: mm/dd Payment Date: mm/dd/yy)

| Amount ($) | Date Decl. | Ex-Div. Date | Stk. of Record | Payment Date |
|---|---|---|---|---|
| 0.140 | 01/10 | 02/15 | 02/20 | 03/10/08 |
| 0.140 | 03/13 | 05/16 | 05/20 | 06/10/08 |
| 0.160 | 06/12 | 08/18 | 08/20 | 09/10/08 |
| 0.160 | 09/11 | 11/18 | 11/20 | 12/10/08 |

Dividends have been paid since 1965. Source: Company reports.

---

**Please read the Required Disclosures and Analyst Certification on the last page of this report.**

# Target Corp

## Business Summary August 20, 2008

CORPORATE PROFILE. In FY 05 (Jan.), TGT shed its non-core legacy department store operations, retaining only its eponymous chain of upscale general merchandise stores that cater to middle- and upper-income consumers. As of August 2, 2008, the company operated 1,417 Target locations, and 231 SuperTarget stores. SuperTarget stores combine a full line of groceries with fashion apparel, electronics, home furnishings and other general merchandise found in Target stores. TGT's Web site serves as both a sales driver and a marketing vehicle. Target.com offers a more extensive selection of merchandise than the company's physical stores, including exclusive online products. To support sales and earnings growth, TGT offers credit to qualified customers. In FY 08, its credit card operations contributed $1.3 billion of revenues in finance charges.

PRIMARY BUSINESS DYNAMICS. TGT's primary growth drivers are new store openings and same-store sales (sales results for stores open for over one year). From FY 03 through FY 08, the company increased its retail square footage at a compound annual growth rate (CAGR) of 6.8%, as its store count rose from 1,147 to 1,591. At the end of FY 08, only 13% of TGT's store base was comprised of SuperTargets (210 stores). As a result, we believe consumers still do not associate the term "supercenter" with the company. TGT added a net of 70 Target and 33 SuperTarget locations to its store base in FY 08.

From FY 03 through FY 08, same-store sales trended positive, averaging about a 4.5% increase annually. To drive same-store sales, TGT seeks to appeal to customers that are interested in sophisticated styles and quality by offering fashion newness, trusted brands, and exclusive designer names such as Isaac Mizrahi. Under the "Expect More. Pay Less." brand promise, the company believes it satisfies customer demand for value by matching Wal-Mart prices on identical and similar items in local markets, and by pricing its differentiated products at deep discounts. This is important for TGT, as it has historically drawn far less traffic from food than main competitive Wal-Mart, in our view. However, the company has also been steadily expanding food assortments in its Target stores since FY 05 as a means of driving shopping frequency and improving convenience for shoppers. In FY 07, TGT right-sized over 150 Target stores to incorporate an expanded offering of dry grocery and refrigerated and frozen foods. At SuperTarget locations, the company is also expanding self-service delis, and broadening assortments of organic and natural foods and locally grown produce.

## Company Financials Fiscal Year Ended Jan. 31

| Per Share Data ($) | 2008 | 2007 | 2006 | 2005 | 2004 | 2003 | 2002 | 2001 | 2000 | 1999 |
|---|---|---|---|---|---|---|---|---|---|---|
| Tangible Book Value | 18.44 | 18.17 | 16.25 | 14.63 | 12.14 | 10.38 | 8.68 | 7.27 | 6.43 | 5.71 |
| Cash Flow | 5.30 | 4.93 | 4.29 | 3.45 | 3.45 | 3.14 | 2.70 | 2.41 | 2.19 | 1.87 |
| Earnings | 3.33 | 3.21 | 2.71 | 2.07 | 2.01 | 1.81 | 1.51 | 1.38 | 1.27 | 1.02 |
| S&P Core Earnings | 3.32 | 3.21 | 2.68 | 2.06 | 1.95 | 1.70 | 1.42 | 1.37 | NA | NA |
| Dividends | 0.44 | 0.36 | 0.30 | 0.26 | 0.26 | 0.24 | 0.21 | 0.20 | 0.20 | 0.18 |
| Payout Ratio | 13% | 11% | 11% | 13% | 13% | 13% | 14% | 14% | 16% | 18% |
| Calendar Year | 2007 | 2006 | 2005 | 2004 | 2003 | 2002 | 2001 | 2000 | 1999 | 1998 |
| Prices:High | 70.75 | 60.34 | 60.00 | 54.14 | 41.80 | 46.15 | 41.74 | 39.19 | 38.50 | 27.13 |
| Prices:Low | 48.85 | 44.70 | 45.55 | 36.63 | 25.60 | 24.90 | 26.00 | 21.63 | 25.03 | 15.72 |
| P/E Ratio:High | 21 | 19 | 22 | 26 | 21 | 25 | 28 | 28 | 30 | 27 |
| P/E Ratio:Low | 15 | 14 | 17 | 18 | 13 | 14 | 17 | 16 | 20 | 15 |

**Income Statement Analysis (Million $)**

| | 2008 | 2007 | 2006 | 2005 | 2004 | 2003 | 2002 | 2001 | 2000 | 1999 |
|---|---|---|---|---|---|---|---|---|---|---|
| Revenue | 63,367 | 59,490 | 52,620 | 46,839 | 48,163 | 43,917 | 39,888 | 36,903 | 33,702 | 30,951 |
| Operating Income | 6,931 | 6,565 | 5,732 | 4,860 | 4,839 | 4,476 | 3,759 | 3,418 | 3,183 | 2,734 |
| Depreciation | 1,659 | 1,496 | 1,409 | 1,259 | 1,320 | 1,212 | 1,079 | 940 | 854 | 780 |
| Interest Expense | 747 | 597 | 532 | 674 | 559 | 588 | 464 | 425 | 393 | 398 |
| Pretax Income | 4,625 | 4,497 | 3,860 | 3,031 | 2,960 | 2,676 | 2,216 | 2,053 | 1,936 | 1,556 |
| Effective Tax Rate | 38.4% | 38.0% | 37.6% | 37.8% | 37.8% | 38.2% | 38.0% | 38.4% | 38.8% | 38.2% |
| Net Income | 2,849 | 2,787 | 2,408 | 1,885 | 1,841 | 1,654 | 1,374 | 1,264 | 1,185 | 962 |
| S&P Core Earnings | 2,841 | 2,784 | 2,383 | 1,876 | 1,791 | 1,553 | 1,289 | 1,247 | NA | NA |

**Balance Sheet & Other Financial Data (Million $)**

| | 2008 | 2007 | 2006 | 2005 | 2004 | 2003 | 2002 | 2001 | 2000 | 1999 |
|---|---|---|---|---|---|---|---|---|---|---|
| Cash | 2,450 | 813 | 1,648 | 2,245 | 716 | 758 | 499 | 356 | 220 | 255 |
| Current Assets | 18,906 | 14,706 | 14,405 | 13,922 | 12,928 | 11,935 | 9,648 | 7,304 | 6,483 | 6,005 |
| Total Assets | 44,560 | 37,349 | 34,995 | 32,293 | 31,392 | 28,603 | 24,154 | 19,490 | 17,143 | 15,666 |
| Current Liabilities | 11,782 | 11,117 | 9,588 | 8,220 | 8,314 | 7,523 | 7,054 | 6,301 | 5,850 | 5,057 |
| Long Term Debt | 15,126 | 8,675 | 9,119 | 9,034 | 10,217 | 10,186 | 8,088 | 5,634 | 4,521 | 4,452 |
| Common Equity | 15,307 | 15,633 | 14,205 | 13,029 | 11,065 | 9,443 | 7,860 | 6,519 | 5,862 | 5,043 |
| Total Capital | 30,903 | 24,885 | 24,175 | 23,036 | 21,282 | 21,080 | 15,948 | 12,153 | 10,383 | 10,585 |
| Capital Expenditures | 4,369 | 3,928 | 3,388 | 3,068 | 3,004 | 3,221 | 3,163 | 2,528 | 1,918 | 1,657 |
| Cash Flow | 4,508 | 4,283 | 3,817 | 3,144 | 3,161 | 2,866 | 2,453 | 2,204 | 2,039 | 1,742 |
| Current Ratio | 1.6 | 1.3 | 1.5 | 1.7 | 1.6 | 1.6 | 1.4 | 1.2 | 1.1 | 1.2 |
| % Long Term Debt of Capitalization | 49.0 | 34.9 | 37.7 | 39.2 | 48.0 | 48.3 | 50.7 | 46.4 | 43.5 | 42.1 |
| % Net Income of Revenue | 4.5 | 4.7 | 4.5 | 4.0 | 3.8 | 3.8 | 3.4 | 3.4 | 3.5 | 3.1 |
| % Return on Assets | 7.0 | 7.7 | 7.1 | 5.9 | 6.1 | 6.3 | 6.3 | 6.9 | 7.2 | 6.4 |
| % Return on Equity | 18.4 | 18.7 | 17.6 | 15.6 | 18.0 | 19.1 | 19.1 | 20.4 | 21.7 | 20.8 |

Data as orig reptd.; bef. results of disc opers/spec. items. Per share data adj. for stk. divs.; EPS diluted. E-Estimated. NA-Not Available. NM-Not Meaningful. NR-Not Ranked. UR-Under Review.

**Office:** 1000 Nicollet Mall, Minneapolis, MN 55403-2467.
**Telephone:** 612-304-6073.
**Website:** http://www.target.com
**Chrmn:** R.J. Ulrich

**Pres & CEO:** G.W. Steinhafel
**Investor Contact:** D.A. Scovanner
**EVP, CFO & Chief Acctg Officer:** D.A. Scovanner
**EVP, Secy & General Counsel:** T.R. Baer

**Board Members:** R. S. Austin, C. Darden, M. N. Dillon, J. A. Johnson, R. M. Kovacevich, M. E. Minnick, A. M. Mulcahy, D. W. Rice, S. W. Sanger, G. W. Steinhafel, G. W. Tamke, S. Trujillo, R. J. Ulrich
**Founded:** 1902
**Domicile:** Minnesota
**Employees:** 366,000

# TECO Energy Inc.

**STANDARD &POOR'S**

| S&P Recommendation  HOLD ★★★☆☆ | Price | 12-Mo. Target Price | Investment Style |
|---|---|---|---|
| | $12.08 (as of Nov 14, 2008) | $16.00 | Large-Cap Value |

**GICS Sector** Utilities
**Sub-Industry** Multi-Utilities

**Summary** This company owns Tampa Electric Co., which serves the Tampa Bay region in west central Florida and has significant diversified operations related to its core business.

## Key Stock Statistics (Source S&P, Vickers, company reports)

| | | | | | | |
|---|---|---|---|---|---|---|
| 52-Wk Range | $21.99–11.30 | S&P Oper. EPS 2008E | 0.87 | Market Capitalization(B) | $2.570 | Beta | 1.00 |
| Trailing 12-Month EPS | $1.49 | S&P Oper. EPS 2009E | 1.42 | Yield (%) | 6.62 | S&P 3-Yr. Proj. EPS CAGR(%) | 20 |
| Trailing 12-Month P/E | 8.1 | P/E on S&P Oper. EPS 2008E | 13.9 | Dividend Rate/Share | $0.80 | S&P Credit Rating | BBB- |
| $10K Invested 5 Yrs Ago | $11,985 | Common Shares Outstg. (M) | 212.8 | Institutional Ownership (%) | 60 | | |

## Price Performance

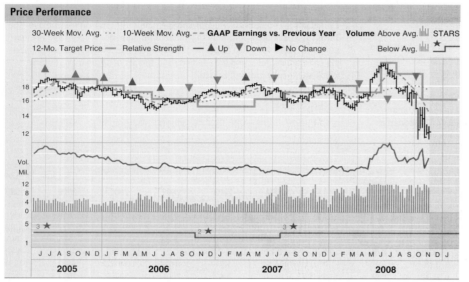

30-Week Mov. Avg. · · · 10-Week Mov. Avg. – – GAAP Earnings vs. Previous Year  Volume Above Avg. STARS
12-Mo. Target Price — Relative Strength — ▲ Up ▼ Down ▶ No Change  Below Avg.

Options: Ph

Analysis prepared by **Justin McCann** on October 24, 2008, when the stock traded at **$14.25**.

### Highlights

➤ We expect operating EPS in 2008 to decline about 9% from 2007 EPS from continuing operations of $0.96, due to rising production costs at the coal business and the impact on customer growth and energy sales for Tampa Electric and Peoples Gas from a weak Florida economy and housing market. We expect the absence of earnings from TECO Transport to be partly offset by reduced debt and interest expense.

➤ For 2009, we expect EPS to rise more than 60% from anticipated results in 2008. As we expect to see a deepening weakness in the economy and housing market, we project little improvement at the utilities. However, we see a sharp increase in earnings at TECO Coal, primarily reflecting the projected renewal of below-market contracts with contracts that should reflect the dramatic rise in coal prices, as well as a significant increase in international demand. However, this should be partially offset by rising production cost pressures.

➤ On December 5, 2007, TE completed the sale of its TECO Transport subsidiary for net proceeds of about $375 million, and an after-tax gain of $0.70 a share. TECO intended to use a large portion of the proceeds for debt reduction.

### Investment Rationale/Risk

➤ After having risen more than 20% earlier in the year, the shares are down approximately 17% year to date. We think the sharp rise reflected the much greater than previously projected increase in earnings from TECO Coal in 2009, while the subsequent decline has reflected the severe crisis in the credit markets, the rise in the coal operation's production costs and the weakness in the Florida economy and housing market. However, we think the shares will recover once these situations stabilize. The recent dividend yield of 5.6% was above the recent average yield (5.2%) of the company's electric and gas utility peers.

➤ Risks to our recommendation and target price include longer-than-expected weakness in the housing market, a sharp decrease in the average P/E of the Electric Utility group as a whole, and much lower-than-anticipated earnings from the non-regulated coal operations.

➤ TE's dividend represents 92% of our EPS estimate for 2008 (compared to the peer payout ratio average of 58%), but only 56% of our 2009 projection (versus a peer average of 52%). Our 12-month target price of $16, reflects a discount-to-peers P/E of 11.3X our 2009 forecast.

### Qualitative Risk Assessment

| LOW | MEDIUM | HIGH |

Our risk assessment reflects the steady cash flow that we expect from the regulated electric and gas utilities, which operate within a generally supportive regulatory environment, offset by our view of the much less predictable earnings and cash flow from the unregulated coal and transport operations, particularly given the uncertainties concerning the tax credits related to the synthetic fuel operations.

### Quantitative Evaluations

**S&P Quality Ranking**                          B

| D | C | B- | **B** | B+ | A- | A | A+ |

**Relative Strength Rank**                 MODERATE

58

LOWEST = 1                                      HIGHEST = 99

### Revenue/Earnings Data

**Revenue (Million $)**

| | 1Q | 2Q | 3Q | 4Q | Year |
|---|---|---|---|---|---|
| 2008 | 791.7 | 887.2 | 926.1 | -- | -- |
| 2007 | 821.3 | 866.5 | 990.0 | 858.3 | 3,536 |
| 2006 | 836.4 | 862.6 | 922.9 | 826.2 | 3,448 |
| 2005 | 684.7 | 719.0 | 836.4 | 770.0 | 3,010 |
| 2004 | 642.3 | 713.0 | 742.3 | 660.2 | 2,669 |
| 2003 | 651.8 | 695.3 | 759.1 | 633.8 | 2,740 |

**Earnings Per Share ($)**

| | 1Q | 2Q | 3Q | 4Q | Year |
|---|---|---|---|---|---|
| 2008 | 0.15 | 0.24 | 0.27 | E0.18 | E0.87 |
| 2007 | 0.35 | 0.28 | 0.44 | 0.83 | 1.90 |
| 2006 | 0.26 | 0.29 | 0.38 | 0.23 | 1.17 |
| 2005 | 0.25 | 0.04 | 0.45 | 0.24 | 1.00 |
| 2004 | 0.15 | -0.44 | 0.27 | -2.05 | -2.10 |
| 2003 | -0.12 | 0.03 | 0.03 | -0.02 | -0.08 |

Fiscal year ended Dec. 31. Next earnings report expected: Early February. EPS Estimates based on S&P Operating Earnings; historical GAAP earnings are as reported.

### Dividend Data (Dates: mm/dd Payment Date: mm/dd/yy)

| Amount ($) | Date Decl. | Ex-Div. Date | Stk. of Record | Payment Date |
|---|---|---|---|---|
| 0.195 | 01/30 | 02/13 | 02/15 | 02/28/08 |
| 0.200 | 04/30 | 05/13 | 05/15 | 05/28/08 |
| 0.200 | 07/30 | 08/13 | 08/15 | 08/28/08 |
| 0.200 | 10/29 | 11/12 | 11/14 | 11/28/08 |

Dividends have been paid since 1900. Source: Company reports.

---

**Please read the Required Disclosures and Analyst Certification on the last page of this report.**

*The McGraw-Hill Companies*

# TECO Energy Inc.

STANDARD
&POOR'S

## Business Summary October 24, 2008

CORPORATE OVERVIEW. TECO Energy (TE) is a holding company for a diverse set of energy companies including the regulated utility subsidiary Tampa Electric Company, which provides retail electric service in west central Florida. TE's other regulated utility is Peoples Gas System, which distributes natural gas in Florida's metropolitan areas. TE's unregulated businesses include TECO Coal, which has coal-mining operations; and TECO Guatemala, which participates in independent power projects and electric distribution in Guatemala. In December 2007, TE completed the sale of TECO Transport, which provided shipping and storage services for coal and other dry-bulk commodities. In 2007, Tampa Electric accounted for 60.3% of TE's consolidated revenues; Peoples Gas System 16.5%; TECO Coal 15.0%; TECO Transport 8.0%; and TECO Guatemala 0.2%.

CORPORATE STRATEGY. With the divestiture of its non-core operations completed in January 2006, TE eliminated its exposure to the merchant power sec-

tor. This enabled it to strengthen its balance sheet and to meet its goal of repaying all the debt that is maturing in 2007, in our opinion. This was, in our view, a major step in reducing the company's business risk, improving its cash flows, and eventually restoring its investment grade credit rating. On December 4, 2007, the company completed the sale of its TECO Transport subsidiary (announced on October 29, 2007) to an investment group for approximately $405 million. TE plans to use the $375 million in after-tax proceeds to further reduce its debt, and realize a portion of the capital that would be needed for the expansion of its generating capacity and the upgrading of its infrastructure. The company expected to record a pretax book gain of between $235 million and 245 million in the fourth quarter of 2007.

## Company Financials Fiscal Year Ended Dec. 31

| Per Share Data ($) | 2007 | 2006 | 2005 | 2004 | 2003 | 2002 | 2001 | 2000 | 1999 | 1998 |
|---|---|---|---|---|---|---|---|---|---|---|
| Tangible Book Value | 9.28 | 7.97 | 7.36 | 6.13 | 8.55 | 13.75 | 12.94 | 11.93 | 11.19 | 11.42 |
| Earnings | 1.90 | 1.17 | 1.00 | -2.10 | -0.08 | 1.95 | 2.24 | 1.97 | 1.53 | 1.52 |
| S&P Core Earnings | 1.25 | 1.19 | 1.00 | -1.58 | 0.24 | 1.75 | 2.04 | NA | NA | NA |
| Dividends | 0.78 | 0.76 | 0.76 | 0.76 | 0.93 | 1.41 | 1.37 | 1.33 | 1.29 | 1.23 |
| Payout Ratio | 41% | 65% | 76% | NM | NM | 72% | 61% | 68% | 84% | 81% |
| Prices:High | 18.58 | 17.73 | 19.30 | 15.49 | 17.00 | 29.05 | 32.97 | 33.19 | 28.00 | 30.63 |
| Prices:Low | 14.84 | 14.40 | 14.87 | 11.30 | 9.47 | 10.02 | 24.75 | 17.25 | 18.38 | 24.75 |
| P/E Ratio:High | 10 | 15 | 19 | NM | NM | 15 | 15 | 17 | 18 | 20 |
| P/E Ratio:Low | 8 | 12 | 15 | NM | NM | 5 | 11 | 9 | 12 | 16 |

| Income Statement Analysis (Million $) | 2007 | 2006 | 2005 | 2004 | 2003 | 2002 | 2001 | 2000 | 1999 | 1998 |
|---|---|---|---|---|---|---|---|---|---|---|
| Revenue | 3,536 | 3,448 | 3,010 | 2,669 | 2,740 | 2,676 | 2,649 | 2,295 | 1,983 | 1,958 |
| Depreciation | 264 | 282 | 282 | 282 | 326 | 303 | 298 | 268 | 232 | 228 |
| Maintenance | 184 | 183 | 168 | 141 | 152 | 162 | 151 | 140 | 125 | 129 |
| Fixed Charges Coverage | 2.06 | 1.42 | 1.25 | 1.26 | 2.30 | 2.43 | 2.51 | 2.59 | 3.30 | 3.95 |
| Construction Credits | 6.20 | 3.80 | Nil | 1.00 | 27.4 | 9.60 | 2.60 | 0.70 | 0.50 | Nil |
| Effective Tax Rate | 40.4% | 40.2% | 45.1% | NM | NM | NM | NM | 6.87% | 30.2% | 28.8% |
| Net Income | 399 | 246 | 211 | -404 | -14.7 | 298 | 304 | 251 | 201 | 200 |
| S&P Core Earnings | 260 | 248 | 212 | -306 | 44.4 | 267 | 277 | NA | NA | NA |

| Balance Sheet & Other Financial Data (Million $) | 2007 | 2006 | 2005 | 2004 | 2003 | 2002 | 2001 | 2000 | 1999 | 1998 |
|---|---|---|---|---|---|---|---|---|---|---|
| Gross Property | 6,894 | 7,084 | 6,755 | 6,723 | 8,040 | 8,215 | 7,544 | 6,560 | 8,501 | 5,601 |
| Capital Expenditures | 494 | 456 | 295 | 273 | 591 | 1,065 | 966 | 688 | 426 | 296 |
| Net Property | 4,888 | 4,767 | 4,567 | 4,658 | 5,679 | 5,464 | 4,838 | 3,970 | 6,064 | 3,308 |
| Capitalization:Long Term Debt | 3,158 | 3,213 | 3,709 | 3,880 | 4,393 | 3,973 | 2,043 | 1,575 | 1,208 | 1,280 |
| Capitalization:% Long Term Debt | 61.0 | 65.0 | 70.0 | 75.1 | 73.0 | 43.2 | 50.9 | 51.1 | 46.0 | 45.9 |
| Capitalization:Preferred | Nil | Nil | Nil | Nil | Nil | Nil | Nil | Nil | Nil | Nil |
| Capitalization:% Preferred | Nil | Nil | Nil | Nil | Nil | Nil | Nil | Nil | Nil | Nil |
| Capitalization:Common | 2,017 | 1,729 | 1,592 | 1,284 | 1,622 | 5,223 | 1,972 | 1,507 | 1,418 | 1,508 |
| Capitalization:% Common | 39.0 | 35.0 | 30.0 | 24.9 | 27.0 | 56.8 | 49.1 | 48.9 | 54.0 | 54.1 |
| Total Capital | 5,188 | 4,957 | 5,318 | 5,691 | 6,537 | 9,719 | 4,545 | 3,564 | 3,284 | 3,334 |
| % Operating Ratio | 94.3 | 91.9 | 91.4 | 80.2 | 83.7 | 84.0 | 83.7 | 82.8 | 83.0 | 82.6 |
| % Earned on Net Property | 8.6 | 9.0 | 7.7 | NA | 0.3 | 7.6 | 9.6 | 10.9 | 7.3 | 12.1 |
| % Return on Revenue | 11.3 | 7.1 | 7.0 | NM | NM | 11.1 | 11.5 | 10.9 | 10.1 | 10.2 |
| % Return on Invested Capital | 6.3 | 8.5 | 9.3 | 14.2 | 9.6 | 6.4 | 11.9 | 12.4 | 9.7 | 11.3 |
| % Return on Common Equity | 21.3 | 14.8 | 14.7 | NM | NM | 6.5 | 17.5 | 17.2 | 13.7 | 13.6 |

Data as orig reptd.; bef. results of disc opers/spec. items. Per share data adj. for stk. divs.; EPS diluted. E-Estimated. NA-Not Available. NM-Not Meaningful. NR-Not Ranked. UR-Under Review.

**Office:** 702 N Franklin St, Tampa, FL 33602.
**Telephone:** 813-228-1111.
**Website:** http://www.tecoenergy.com
**Chrmn & CEO:** S.W. Hudson

**Pres & COO:** J.B. Ramil
**EVP & CFO:** G.L. Gillette
**Chief Acctg Officer & Treas:** S.W. Callahan
**Secy:** D.E. Schwartz

**Investor Contact:** M.M. Kane (813-228-1772)
**Board Members:** D. Ausley, J. L. Ferman, Jr., L. Guinot, Jr., S. W. Hudson, J. P. Lacher, L. A. Penn, J. B. Ramil, T. L. Rankin, W. Rockford, J. T. Touchton, P. L. Whiting

**Founded:** 1899
**Domicile:** Florida
**Employees:** 4,300

# Tellabs Inc

STANDARD &POOR'S

**S&P Recommendation** SELL ★ ★ ☆ ☆ ☆

| Price | 12-Mo. Target Price |
|---|---|
| $3.68 (as of Nov 14, 2008) | $3.00 |

**GICS Sector** Information Technology
**Sub-Industry** Communications Equipment

**Summary** This company manufactures voice and data equipment used in public and private communications networks worldwide.

## Key Stock Statistics (Source S&P, Vickers, company reports)

| | | | | | | | |
|---|---|---|---|---|---|---|---|
| 52-Wk Range | $7.39– 3.10 | S&P Oper. EPS 2008**E** | 0.13 | Market Capitalization(B) | $1.465 | Beta | 1.39 |
| Trailing 12-Month EPS | $-2.29 | S&P Oper. EPS 2009**E** | 0.12 | Yield (%) | Nil | S&P 3-Yr. Proj. EPS CAGR(%) | 5 |
| Trailing 12-Month P/E | NM | P/E on S&P Oper. EPS 2008**E** | 28.3 | Dividend Rate/Share | Nil | S&P Credit Rating | NA |
| $10K Invested 5 Yrs Ago | $4,515 | Common Shares Outstg. (M) | 398.0 | Institutional Ownership (%) | 77 | | |

## Price Performance

30-Week Mov. Avg. ···   10-Week Mov. Avg. - -   **GAAP Earnings vs. Previous Year**   Volume Above Avg. STARS
12-Mo. Target Price —   Relative Strength —   ▲ Up ▼ Down ► No Change   Below Avg.

Options: ASE, CBOE, P, Ph

## Highlights

➤ The STARS recommendation for TLAB has recently been changed to 2 (sell) from 3 (hold) and the 12-month target price has recently been changed to $3.00 from $4.00. The Highlights section of this Stock Report will be updated accordingly.

## Investment Rationale/Risk

➤ The Investment Rationale/Risk section of this Stock Report will be updated shortly. For the latest News story on TLAB from MarketScope, see below.

➤ 11/14/08 12:18 pm ET ... S&P DOWNGRADES OPINION ON SHARES OF TELLABS TO SELL FROM HOLD (TLAB 3.72**): We expect results over the next several quarters to be hurt by poor access sales as telecom carriers delay equipment purchases amid a weakening macroeconomic environment. We see savings from cost-cutting initiatives and a lower share count from aggressive stock repurchases, but outweighed by declining sales, an unfavorable product mix, and lower interest income. We keep our '08 EPS estimate at $0.13, but cut '09's by $0.09 to $0.12. We lower our target price by $1 to $3, 1X cash, below peers, warranted, we think, by our view of deteriorating fundamentals and falling earnings. /A.Bensinger

## Qualitative Risk Assessment

| LOW | MEDIUM | HIGH |
|---|---|---|

Our risk assessment reflects the competitive pressure the company faces, and its dependence on a consolidating telecom industry.

## Quantitative Evaluations

**S&P Quality Ranking**     B-

| D | C | B- | B | B+ | A- | A | A+ |
|---|---|---|---|---|---|---|---|

**Relative Strength Rank**     MODERATE

70

LOWEST = 1     HIGHEST = 99

## Revenue/Earnings Data

**Revenue (Million $)**

| | 1Q | 2Q | 3Q | 4Q | Year |
|---|---|---|---|---|---|
| 2008 | 464.1 | 432.5 | 424.1 | -- | -- |
| 2007 | 451.9 | 534.5 | 457.9 | 469.1 | 1,913 |
| 2006 | 514.7 | 549.3 | 522.5 | 454.7 | 2,041 |
| 2005 | 435.6 | 462.5 | 463.9 | 521.4 | 1,883 |
| 2004 | 263.8 | 304.3 | 284.3 | 379.4 | 1,232 |
| 2003 | 222.5 | 234.1 | 244.5 | 279.3 | 980.4 |

**Earnings Per Share ($)**

| | | | | | |
|---|---|---|---|---|---|
| 2008 | 0.04 | -0.10 | -2.51 | E0.04 | E0.13 |
| 2007 | 0.06 | 0.07 | 0.01 | 0.02 | 0.15 |
| 2006 | 0.11 | 0.12 | 0.13 | 0.07 | 0.43 |
| 2005 | Nil | 0.09 | 0.09 | 0.20 | 0.39 |
| 2004 | 0.03 | 0.12 | 0.11 | -0.32 | -0.07 |
| 2003 | -0.10 | -0.27 | -0.16 | -0.06 | -0.58 |

Fiscal year ended Dec. 31. Next earnings report expected: Late January. EPS Estimates based on S&P Operating Earnings; historical GAAP earnings are as reported.

## Dividend Data

No cash dividends have been paid.

# Tellabs Inc

STANDARD &POOR'S

## Business Summary October 10, 2008

CORPORATE OVERVIEW. Tellabs designs, manufactures, markets and services optical networking, next-generation switching and broadband access solutions. The company's products enable the delivery of wireline and wireless voice, data and video services. Solutions are primarily focused on the last mile of the communications network, the part of the network that is closest to homes and businesses. Results are reported in three business segments; broadband, transport and services.

The broadband segment enables service providers to deliver bundled voice, video and high-speed Internet data services over copper or fiber networks. Broadband access products include digital loop carriers, digital subscriber line access multiplexers, fiber-to-the-premise (FTTP) optical line terminals for broadband passive optical networks, and voice gateways for voice over Internet protocol (VoIP). Managed access products include aggregation and transport products that deliver wireless and business services outside of the United States. Data products include next-generation packet-switched products that enable wireline and wireless carriers to deliver business services and next-generation wireless services to their customers.

The transport segment enables service providers to transport services and manage bandwidth by adding capacity when and where it is needed. Wireline and wireless providers use these to support wireless services, business services for enterprises, and triple-play voice, video and data services for consumers. Products include voice-quality enhancement products, digital cross-connect systems and optical transport systems.

The services segment delivers deployment, training, support services and professional consulting to customers. Services in the planning phase include network architecture and design, network and applications planning, network management design, migration planning and others. Building services include applications integration, program and project management, installation, testing, network integration, third-party systems integration and others.

## Company Financials Fiscal Year Ended Dec. 31

| Per Share Data ($) | 2007 | 2006 | 2005 | 2004 | 2003 | 2002 | 2001 | 2000 | 1999 | 1998 |
|---|---|---|---|---|---|---|---|---|---|---|
| Tangible Book Value | 4.14 | 3.97 | 3.53 | 3.34 | 3.76 | 4.45 | 5.55 | 6.26 | 4.85 | 3.40 |
| Cash Flow | 0.35 | 0.66 | 0.66 | 0.12 | -0.32 | -0.41 | -0.06 | 2.09 | 1.56 | 1.18 |
| Earnings | 0.15 | 0.43 | 0.39 | -0.07 | -0.58 | -0.76 | -0.44 | 1.82 | 1.36 | 1.03 |
| S&P Core Earnings | 0.16 | 0.44 | 0.38 | -0.14 | -0.71 | -1.03 | -0.68 | NA | NA | NA |
| Dividends | Nil | Nil | Nil | Nil | Nil | Nil | Nil | Nil | Nil | Nil |
| Payout Ratio | Nil | Nil | Nil | Nil | Nil | Nil | Nil | Nil | Nil | Nil |
| Prices:High | 13.67 | 17.28 | 11.49 | 11.37 | 9.73 | 17.47 | 67.13 | 76.94 | 77.25 | 46.56 |
| Prices:Low | 6.52 | 8.84 | 6.56 | 7.40 | 5.07 | 4.00 | 8.98 | 37.63 | 32.38 | 15.69 |
| P/E Ratio:High | 91 | 40 | 29 | NM | NM | NM | NM | 42 | 57 | 45 |
| P/E Ratio:Low | 43 | 21 | 17 | NM | NM | NM | NM | 21 | 24 | 15 |

**Income Statement Analysis** (Million $)

| | 2007 | 2006 | 2005 | 2004 | 2003 | 2002 | 2001 | 2000 | 1999 | 1998 |
|---|---|---|---|---|---|---|---|---|---|---|
| Revenue | 1,913 | 2,041 | 1,883 | 1,232 | 980 | 1,317 | 2,200 | 3,387 | 2,319 | 1,660 |
| Operating Income | 124 | 358 | 330 | 152 | -77.1 | -12.7 | 70.9 | 1,117 | 832 | 593 |
| Depreciation | 90.7 | 104 | 126 | 82.3 | 110 | 143 | 158 | 116 | 84.6 | 56.1 |
| Interest Expense | Nil | Nil | Nil | Nil | 0.70 | 0.90 | 0.51 | 0.63 | 0.58 | 0.29 |
| Pretax Income | 70.2 | 285 | 213 | -10.2 | -245 | -328 | -245 | 1,109 | 816 | 590 |
| Effective Tax Rate | 7.41% | 31.8% | 17.5% | NM | NM | NM | NM | 31.5% | 31.5% | 32.5% |
| Net Income | 65.0 | 194 | 176 | -29.8 | -242 | -313 | -182 | 760 | 559 | 398 |
| S&P Core Earnings | 68.7 | 198 | 171 | -58.9 | -295 | -427 | -277 | NA | NA | NA |

**Balance Sheet & Other Financial Data** (Million $)

| | 2007 | 2006 | 2005 | 2004 | 2003 | 2002 | 2001 | 2000 | 1999 | 1998 |
|---|---|---|---|---|---|---|---|---|---|---|
| Cash | 1,510 | 154 | 1,371 | 293 | 246 | 1,019 | 1,102 | 1,022 | 966 | 643 |
| Current Assets | 2,112 | 2,233 | 1,873 | 1,819 | 1,499 | 1,534 | 1,945 | 2,322 | 1,786 | 1,253 |
| Total Assets | 3,747 | 3,922 | 3,515 | 3,523 | 2,608 | 2,623 | 2,866 | 3,073 | 2,353 | 1,628 |
| Current Liabilities | 673 | 762 | 525 | 524 | 208 | 257 | 320 | 412 | 274 | 218 |
| Long Term Debt | Nil | Nil | Nil | Nil | Nil | Nil | 3.39 | 2.85 | 2.85 | 2.85 |
| Common Equity | 2,913 | 2,938 | 2,815 | 2,797 | 2,219 | 2,290 | 2,466 | 2,628 | 2,048 | 1,377 |
| Total Capital | 2,992 | 2,938 | 2,815 | 2,797 | 2,319 | 2,290 | 2,490 | 2,637 | 2,058 | 1,391 |
| Capital Expenditures | 57.7 | 67.2 | 61.8 | 41.4 | 9.50 | 34.1 | 208 | 208 | 98.9 | 75.9 |
| Cash Flow | 156 | 298 | 302 | 52.5 | -131 | -171 | -24.5 | 876 | 644 | 454 |
| Current Ratio | 3.1 | 2.9 | 3.6 | 3.5 | 7.2 | 6.0 | 6.1 | 5.6 | 6.5 | 5.7 |
| % Long Term Debt of Capitalization | Nil | Nil | Nil | Nil | Nil | Nil | 0.1 | 0.1 | 0.1 | 0.2 |
| % Net Income of Revenue | 3.4 | 9.5 | 9.3 | NM | NM | NM | NM | 22.4 | 24.1 | 24.0 |
| % Return on Assets | 1.7 | 5.2 | 5.0 | NM | NM | NM | NM | 28.0 | 28.0 | 28.3 |
| % Return on Equity | 2.2 | 6.7 | 6.3 | NM | NM | NM | NM | 32.5 | 32.5 | 34.5 |

Data as orig reptd.; bef. results of disc opers/spec. items. Per share data adj. for stk. divs.; EPS diluted. E-Estimated. NA-Not Available. NM-Not Meaningful. NR-Not Ranked. UR-Under Review.

**Office:** 1415 W Diehl Rd, Naperville, IL 60563-2349.
**Telephone:** 630-798-8800.
**Website:** http://www.tellabs.com
**Chrmn:** M.J. Birck

**Pres & CEO:** R.W. Pullen
**COO:** J.M. Brots
**Investor Contact:** T.J. Wiggins (630-798-3602)
**EVP & CFO:** T.J. Wiggins

**Board Members:** L. W. Beck, M. J. Birck, B. Hedfors, F. Ianna, F. A. Krehbiel, M. E. Lavin, S. P. Marshall, R. W. Pullen, J. Schofield, W. F. Souders, J. H. Suwinski
**Founded:** 1974
**Domicile:** Delaware
**Employees:** 3,716

# Tenet Healthcare Corp

STANDARD
&POOR'S

| S&P Recommendation | HOLD ★★★☆☆ | Price $1.95 (as of Nov 14, 2008) | 12-Mo. Target Price $3.50 | Investment Style Large-Cap Value |
|---|---|---|---|---|

**GICS Sector** Health Care
**Sub-Industry** Health Care Facilities

**Summary** This company is the second largest U.S. for-profit hospital manager.

## Key Stock Statistics (Source S&P, Vickers, company reports)

| | | | | | | | | |
|---|---|---|---|---|---|---|---|---|
| 52-Wk Range | $6.88– 1.82 | S&P Oper. EPS 2008**E** | -0.07 | Market Capitalization(B) | $0.930 | Beta | 0.43 |
| Trailing 12-Month EPS | $-0.04 | S&P Oper. EPS 2009**E** | -0.06 | Yield (%) | Nil | S&P 3-Yr. Proj. EPS CAGR(%) | NA |
| Trailing 12-Month P/E | NM | P/E on S&P Oper. EPS 2008**E** | NM | Dividend Rate/Share | Nil | S&P Credit Rating | B |
| $10K Invested 5 Yrs Ago | $1,472 | Common Shares Outstg. (M) | 477.2 | Institutional Ownership (%) | NM | | |

## Price Performance

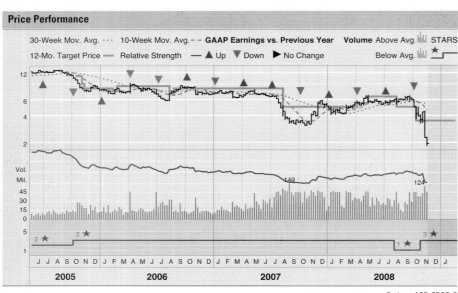

30-Week Mov. Avg. ····· 10-Week Mov. Avg. – – – **GAAP Earnings vs. Previous Year** Volume Above Avg. STARS
12-Mo. Target Price — Relative Strength — ▲ Up ▼ Down ► No Change Below Avg.

Options: ASE, CBOE, P

Analysis prepared by **Jeffrey Englander, CFA** on November 07, 2008, when the stock traded at **$ 2.32**.

## Highlights

➤ We forecast a modest decline in revenues in 2008, to about $8.8 billion, as THC continues to pursue its turnaround efforts amid a difficult market environment and continued challenges in its key California, Florida, and Texas markets. We expect revenue growth of about 4% in 2009 as management's efforts to improve quality and physician recruitment and expand managed care contracts should favorably begin to affect admissions growth.

➤ We see EBITDA margins widening dramatically in 2008, as declines in most operating expenses offset increases in bad debt, all as a percent of sales. While we expect THC's Targeted Growth Initiative to result in a greater focus on high-demand services and rationalization of under-performing facilities, we now think it may take until 2009 before meaningful results are seen. We expect an improvement in EBITDA margins in 2009 from continued declines in virtually all operating expense categories other than bad debt, where we see a modest uptick as a percentage of sales.

➤ We see an operating loss of $0.06 per share in 2008 and operating loss of $0.07 in 2009.

## Investment Rationale/Risk

➤ We view 2008 as a transitional year as THC struggles with inconsistent volume growth, which we see as the key to any turnaround. Although management is working to improve service quality as well as relationships with physicians and managed care payors, we expect that these initiatives will take time to help, leaving THC to serve lower-margin Medicare and Medicaid patients. In addition, we expect THC to fall short of its recently revised goal of approximately $925 million in adjusted EBITDA by year-end 2009.

➤ Risks to our recommendation and target price include a more favorable government or third-party reimbursement environment than expected, and more rapid physician recruitment than anticipated. In addition, lower self-pay volumes could positively impact bad debt expense compared to our expectations.

➤ Our $3.50 target price assumes an EV/EBITDA multiple of approximately 7.3X, based on our 2009 EBITDA estimate, a discount to THC's historical levels, given the risk we see to revenues from economic weakness in core THC markets.

## Qualitative Risk Assessment

| LOW | MEDIUM | HIGH |
|---|---|---|

Our risk assessment for THC reflects our view of stable demand for health care services and its generally favorable corporate governance practices. This is offset by our view of a high level of debt and the company's strong dependence on third-party reimbursements, including Medicare and Medicaid, which can be unpredictable.

## Quantitative Evaluations

**S&P Quality Ranking**     C

| D | C | B- | B | B+ | A- | A | A+ |
|---|---|---|---|---|---|---|---|

**Relative Strength Rank**     WEAK

10

LOWEST = 1      HIGHEST = 99

## Revenue/Earnings Data

**Revenue (Million $)**

| | 1Q | 2Q | 3Q | 4Q | Year |
|---|---|---|---|---|---|
| 2008 | 2,371 | 2,184 | 2,158 | -- | -- |
| 2007 | 2,218 | 2,171 | 2,212 | 2,251 | 8,852 |
| 2006 | 2,414 | 2,195 | 2,117 | 2,179 | 8,701 |
| 2005 | 2,501 | 2,420 | 2,394 | 2,299 | 9,614 |
| 2004 | 2,574 | 2,505 | 2,428 | 2,412 | 9,919 |
| 2003 | 3,417 | 3,346 | 3,268 | 3,181 | 13,212 |

**Earnings Per Share ($)**

| | | | | | |
|---|---|---|---|---|---|
| 2008 | -0.02 | -0.04 | -0.24 | E-0.01 | E-0.07 |
| 2007 | 0.20 | -0.06 | -0.07 | -0.18 | -0.10 |
| 2006 | -0.03 | -0.95 | -0.06 | -0.83 | -1.85 |
| 2005 | 0.04 | Nil | -0.82 | -0.54 | -1.32 |
| 2004 | -0.04 | -0.45 | -0.11 | -3.43 | -3.85 |
| 2003 | 0.03 | -0.28 | -0.50 | -2.34 | -3.01 |

Fiscal year ended Dec. 31. Next earnings report expected: Late February. EPS Estimates based on S&P Operating Earnings; historical GAAP earnings are as reported.

## Dividend Data

Dividends, initiated in 1973, were omitted beginning in 1993. A special dividend of $0.01 a share was paid in March 2000.

# Tenet Healthcare Corp

STANDARD &POOR'S

## Business Summary November 07, 2008

CORPORATE OVERVIEW. Tenet Healthcare ranks as the second largest U.S. for-profit hospital manager. At December 31, 2007, it owned or operated 57 hospitals (excluding 3 hospitals not yet divested but classified as discontinued operations), with 15,244 licensed beds. The largest concentrations of hospital beds were in California, Florida and Texas. THC also owns and operates a small number of rehabilitation hospitals, a specialty hospital, skilled nursing facilities, and medical office buildings located on or near the general hospital properties. In 2007, on a same-facility basis, admissions fell 1.0% and revenue per inpatient admission increased 4.1%. In 2006, on a same-facility basis, admissions were down 2.2% and revenue per inpatient admission increased 4.8%.

In January 2003, THC was sued by the U.S. Justice Department for allegedly submitting false claims to Medicare. In October 2003, the Justice Department served THC with a subpoena related to its investigation of Medicare outlier payments. In September 2003, the U.S. Senate launched an investigation into the company's corporate governance practices with respect to federal health care programs. In October 2004, additional investigations were announced into THC's medical directorship arrangements and physician relocation agreements.

In January 2006, THC reached an agreement to settle federal securities class action lawsuits as well as shareholder derivative litigation for $215 million in cash; insurance proceeds covered $75 million of the this amount. The lawsuits were filed against the company beginning in 2002 and were consolidated in January 2003. In June 2006, THC and the U.S. Department of Justice reached an agreement to settle the ongoing investigation into Medicare outlier billing. The company agreed to pay $725 million over a period of four years, plus interest, and to waive its right to collect $175 million in Medicare payments for past services. In order to fund the settlement, at that time THC announced it would sell 11 hospitals. The settlement does not involve the Securities and Exchange Commission, which is investigating THC's financial disclosures surrounding the Medicare outlier payments. In our view, the Justice Department settlement removes some risk in the stock, but we expect its valuation to continue to be driven by the company's underlying operating fundamentals.

## Company Financials Fiscal Year Ended Dec. 31

### Per Share Data ($)

| | 2007 | 2006 | 2005 | 2004 | 2003 | 2002 | 2001 | 2000 | 1999 | 1998 |
|---|---|---|---|---|---|---|---|---|---|---|
| Tangible Book Value | NM | NM | NM | 1.63 | 4.85 | 4.40 | 4.40 | 3.45 | 1.57 | 1.01 |
| Cash Flow | 0.59 | -1.12 | -0.51 | -3.02 | -2.00 | 1.54 | 3.24 | 2.51 | 1.85 | 1.71 |
| Earnings | -0.10 | -1.85 | -1.32 | -3.85 | -3.01 | 0.93 | 2.04 | 1.39 | 0.72 | 0.53 |
| S&P Core Earnings | -0.11 | -0.34 | -1.14 | -2.28 | 0.27 | 1.54 | 1.24 | NA | NA | NA |
| Dividends | Nil | Nil | Nil | Nil | Nil | Nil | Nil | Nil | 0.01 | Nil |
| Payout Ratio | Nil | Nil | Nil | Nil | Nil | Nil | Nil | Nil | 1% | Nil |
| Prices:High | 7.80 | 9.27 | 13.06 | 18.73 | 19.25 | 52.50 | 41.85 | 30.50 | 18.12 | 27.29 |
| Prices:Low | 3.06 | 5.77 | 7.27 | 9.15 | 11.32 | 13.70 | 24.67 | 11.29 | 10.25 | 15.83 |
| P/E Ratio:High | NM | NM | NM | NM | NM | 56 | 21 | 22 | 25 | 52 |
| P/E Ratio:Low | NM | NM | NM | NM | NM | 15 | 12 | 8 | 14 | 30 |

### Income Statement Analysis (Million $)

| | 2007 | 2006 | 2005 | 2004 | 2003 | 2002 | 2001 | 2000 | 1999 | 1998 |
|---|---|---|---|---|---|---|---|---|---|---|
| Revenue | 8,852 | 8,701 | 9,614 | 9,919 | 13,212 | 8,743 | 13,913 | 12,053 | 11,414 | 10,880 |
| Operating Income | 669 | 687 | 571 | 434 | 1,072 | 1,676 | 2,797 | 2,244 | 1,935 | 1,858 |
| Depreciation | 330 | 342 | 382 | 388 | 471 | 302 | 604 | 554 | 533 | 556 |
| Interest Expense | 430 | 409 | 405 | 333 | 296 | 147 | 327 | 456 | 479 | 485 |
| Pretax Income | -103 | -1,129 | -701 | -1,616 | -1,829 | 777 | 1,799 | 1,156 | 639 | 481 |
| Effective Tax Rate | 56.3% | NM | NM | NM | NM | 38.5% | 40.9% | 40.1% | 43.5% | 46.8% |
| Net Income | -49.0 | -871 | -621 | -1,797 | -1,404 | 459 | 1,025 | 678 | 340 | 249 |
| S&P Core Earnings | -52.3 | -159 | -561 | -1,061 | 123 | 760 | 607 | NA | NA | NA |

### Balance Sheet & Other Financial Data (Million $)

| | 2007 | 2006 | 2005 | 2004 | 2003 | 2002 | 2001 | 2000 | 1999 | 1998 |
|---|---|---|---|---|---|---|---|---|---|---|
| Cash | 592 | 784 | 1,373 | 654 | 619 | 210 | 38.0 | 62.0 | 135 | 29.0 |
| Current Assets | 2,560 | 3,025 | 3,508 | 3,992 | 4,248 | 3,792 | 3,394 | 3,226 | 3,594 | 3,962 |
| Total Assets | 8,393 | 8,539 | 9,812 | 10,078 | 12,298 | 13,780 | 13,814 | 12,995 | 13,161 | 13,771 |
| Current Liabilities | 2,048 | 1,925 | 2,292 | 2,130 | 2,394 | 2,381 | 2,584 | 2,166 | 1,912 | 2,022 |
| Long Term Debt | 4,771 | 4,760 | 4,784 | 4,395 | 4,039 | 3,872 | 3,919 | 4,202 | 5,668 | 6,391 |
| Common Equity | 54.0 | 995 | 1,760 | 2,460 | 4,361 | 5,723 | 5,619 | 5,079 | 4,066 | 3,870 |
| Total Capital | 4,944 | 5,862 | 6,756 | 7,166 | 8,404 | 10,121 | 10,227 | 9,835 | 10,225 | 10,701 |
| Capital Expenditures | 729 | 631 | 568 | 454 | 753 | 490 | 889 | 601 | 619 | 592 |
| Cash Flow | 281 | -529 | -239 | -1,409 | -933 | 761 | 1,629 | 1,232 | 873 | 805 |
| Current Ratio | 1.3 | 1.6 | 1.5 | 1.9 | 1.8 | 1.6 | 1.3 | 1.5 | 1.9 | 2.0 |
| % Long Term Debt of Capitalization | 96.5 | 81.2 | 70.8 | 61.3 | 48.1 | 38.3 | 38.3 | 42.7 | 55.4 | 59.7 |
| % Net Income of Revenue | NM | NM | NM | NM | NM | 5.2 | 7.4 | 5.6 | 3.0 | 2.3 |
| % Return on Assets | NM | NM | NM | NM | NM | NM | 7.6 | 5.2 | 2.5 | 1.9 |
| % Return on Equity | NM | NM | NM | NM | NM | 19.2 | 14.8 | 8.6 | 6.7 | |

Data as orig reptd.; bef. results of disc opers/spec. items. Per share data adj. for stk. divs.; EPS diluted. E-Estimated. NA-Not Available. NM-Not Meaningful. NR-Not Ranked. UR-Under Review.

**Office:** 13737 Noel Rd, Dallas, TX 75240-1331.
**Telephone:** 469-893-2200.
**Email:** feedback@tenethealth.com
**Website:** http://www.tenethealth.com

**Chrmn:** E. Kangas
**Pres & CEO:** T. Fetter
**COO:** S.L. Newman
**EVP & CIO:** S.F. Brown

**SVP & General Counsel:** G. Ruff
**Investor Contact:** T. Rice (469-893-2522)
**Board Members:** J. E. Bush, T. Fetter, B. J. Gaines, K. M. Garrison, E. Kangas, J. Kerrey, F. D. Loop, R. R. Pettingill, J. A. Unruh, J. M. Williams

**Founded:** 1967
**Domicile:** Nevada
**Employees:** 63,264

# Teradata Corp

**STANDARD &POOR'S**

**S&P Recommendation** BUY ★★★★☆

| | | |
|---|---|---|
| **Price** $12.01 (as of Nov 14, 2008) | **12-Mo. Target Price** $19.00 | **Investment Style** Large-Cap Blend |

**GICS Sector** Information Technology
**Sub-Industry** Computer Hardware

**Summary** This Ohio-based company has global operations focused on data warehousing and enterprise analytics. Teradata was spun off from NCR Corporation in 2007.

## Key Stock Statistics (Source S&P, Vickers, company reports)

| | | | | | | | |
|---|---|---|---|---|---|---|---|
| 52-Wk Range | $27.90– 11.80 | S&P Oper. EPS 2008**E** | 1.38 | Market Capitalization(B) | $2.158 | Beta | NA |
| Trailing 12-Month EPS | $1.38 | S&P Oper. EPS 2009**E** | 1.55 | Yield (%) | Nil | S&P 3-Yr. Proj. EPS CAGR(%) | 17 |
| Trailing 12-Month P/E | 8.7 | P/E on S&P Oper. EPS 2008**E** | 8.7 | Dividend Rate/Share | Nil | S&P Credit Rating | NA |
| $10K Invested 5 Yrs Ago | NA | Common Shares Outstg. (M) | 179.7 | Institutional Ownership (%) | 85 | | |

## Price Performance

30-Week Mov. Avg. · · · · 10-Week Mov. Avg. - - GAAP Earnings vs. Previous Year   Volume Above Avg. ⅢⅢ STARS

12-Mo. Target Price — Relative Strength — ▲ Up ▼ Down ► No Change   Below Avg. ⅢⅢ ★

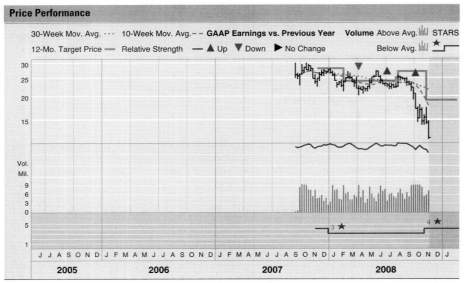

Options: CBOE, Ph

Analysis prepared by **Thomas W. Smith, CFA** on November 04, 2008, when the stock traded at **$ 16.72**.

## Highlights

➤ We project revenues will rise 3% in 2008 and 3% in 2009, reflecting moderating global economic growth. This compares with 10% revenue growth reported for 2007, which included a 2% boost from currency fluctuations. The company operated as the Data Warehousing segment of NCR Corporation (NCR: strong buy, $19) through September 2007. A primary force driving sales is rising interest among enterprises in using their transaction data to study and improve their patterns of operation.

➤ We anticipate gross margins will be steady near 54% in 2008 and then widen toward 55% in 2009. The company is seeking efficiencies as a stand-alone operation and, based on third-quarter 2008 results, is starting to find advantages on the gross margin line. A lack of long-term debt and the establishment of a $300 million credit facility indicates to us that currently negligible interest expense could rise.

➤ We estimate operating EPS of $1.38 for 2008 and $1.55 for 2009. A share repurchase plan should lend minor support to per-share results, in our view.

## Investment Rationale/Risk

➤ We recently upgraded our opinion on the shares to buy, from hold. We view Teradata as operating in a fairly steady, moderate-growth information technology business. It serves a global, broad base of enterprise customers and reports adding new customers so far in 2008. We believe TDC has the potential to do well as a stand-alone company based on its one-stop shopping approach to offering business intelligence hardware, software and consulting. We think being one of a small number of pure-play investments in the industry, with no debt, will add to investor interest. Based on our forward P/E analysis, we view TDC's valuation as attractive.

➤ Risks to our recommendation and target price include slowdowns in the general pace of spending on information technology for business, any failure to keep pace with rapidly evolving computer and analytical technology, competition on price and quality of products and services, and possible disruptions from the shift to being independent.

➤ Applying a peer-based P/E multiple of 13X, to our 12-month forward EPS estimate of $1.47, we arrive at our 12-month target price of $19.

## Qualitative Risk Assessment

| LOW | MEDIUM | HIGH |
|---|---|---|

The newly independent Teradata participates in a large and growing global market we see for storing, retrieving and analyzing data produced by businesses. While competition is lively for technology and pricing, we believe a stream of revenue from services, and a lack of debt, lends some stability.

## Quantitative Evaluations

**S&P Quality Ranking**   NR

| D | C | B- | B | B+ | A- | A | A+ |
|---|---|---|---|---|---|---|---|

**Relative Strength Rank**   MODERATE

30

LOWEST = 1                                    HIGHEST = 99

## Revenue/Earnings Data

**Revenue (Million $)**

| | 1Q | 2Q | 3Q | 4Q | Year |
|---|---|---|---|---|---|
| 2008 | 375.0 | 455.0 | 439.0 | -- | -- |
| 2007 | 367.0 | 430.0 | 439.0 | 466.0 | 1,702 |
| 2006 | 323.0 | 396.0 | 375.0 | 466.0 | 1,560 |
| 2005 | 347.0 | 357.0 | 358.0 | 405.0 | 1,467 |
| 2004 | -- | -- | -- | -- | 1,349 |
| 2003 | -- | -- | -- | -- | -- |

**Earnings Per Share ($)**

| | 1Q | 2Q | 3Q | 4Q | Year |
|---|---|---|---|---|---|
| 2008 | 0.23 | 0.38 | 0.33 | E0.40 | E1.38 |
| 2007 | 0.24 | 0.27 | 0.16 | 0.46 | 1.10 |
| 2006 | 0.20 | -- | -- | -- | 1.09 |
| 2005 | -- | -- | -- | -- | 1.14 |
| 2004 | -- | -- | -- | -- | 0.76 |
| 2003 | -- | -- | -- | -- | -- |

Fiscal year ended Dec. 31. Next earnings report expected: Mid February. EPS Estimates based on S&P Operating Earnings; historical GAAP earnings are as reported.

## Dividend Data

No cash dividends have been paid.

# Teradata Corp

## Business Summary November 04, 2008

CORPORATE OVERVIEW. Teradata Corporation aims to help its enterprise customers make smarter and faster use of their stored data to improve decision-making. It views itself as a global leader in data warehousing and analytic technologies. The company offers hardware and software, as well as services including consulting, customer support and training. In 2007, almost 52% of revenues were derived from products (52% for 2006), and 48% (48%) came from services.

Headquartered in Dayton, Ohio, the company has offices throughout the Americas and operates in 60 countries worldwide. Teradata has more than 850 customers and over 1,900 project implementations. The top 10 customers in 2007 represented 16% of sales. In 2007, revenue came 57% from the Americas, 25% from EMEA (Europe, Middle East, Africa), and 18% from APJ (Asia Pacific/Japan). Gross margins have typically been widest for the Americas region, near 58% compared to a company average of 54% in 2007.

Data warehousing is the process of capturing, storing and analyzing data to gain insight, according to the company. This activity can be a significant

source of intelligence for the enterprise and become a competitive advantage. Beyond mere storage of data, modern solutions allow for near real-time information access and analysis. Predictive analytics on customer or business activity may be run. Both long-term strategic and short-term tactical inquiries may be pursued.

In one example of active data warehousing, a business's call center could produce raw data on call attributes (e.g., number of calls, duration, agent, customer, dropped calls, results), which could be a starting point for mapping and analyzing overall interactions with customers, including Internet communications, which could then become the basis for a plan to improve customer satisfaction. The company serves many large clients in the communications industry, as well as in media and entertainment, financial services, government, health care, manufacturing, retail, and transportation.

## Company Financials Fiscal Year Ended Dec. 31

| Per Share Data ($) | 2007 | 2006 | 2005 | 2004 | 2003 | 2002 | 2001 | 2000 | 1999 | 1998 |
|---|---|---|---|---|---|---|---|---|---|---|
| Tangible Book Value | 2.91 | 2.15 | NA | NA | NA | NA | NA | NA | NA | NA |
| Cash Flow | 1.48 | 1.40 | 1.44 | 1.03 | NA | NA | NA | NA | NA | NA |
| Earnings | 1.10 | 1.09 | 1.14 | 0.76 | NA | NA | NA | NA | NA | NA |
| S&P Core Earnings | 1.18 | 1.09 | 1.10 | NA | NA | NA | NA | NA | NA | NA |
| Dividends | Nil | NA | NA | NA | NA | NA | NA | NA | NA | NA |
| Payout Ratio | Nil | NA | NA | NA | NA | NA | NA | NA | NA | NA |
| Prices:High | 30.08 | NA | NA | NA | NA | NA | NA | NA | NA | NA |
| Prices:Low | 22.35 | NA | NA | NA | NA | NA | NA | NA | NA | NA |
| P/E Ratio:High | 27 | NA | NA | NA | NA | NA | NA | NA | NA | NA |
| P/E Ratio:Low | 20 | NA | NA | NA | NA | NA | NA | NA | NA | NA |

| Income Statement Analysis (Million $) | 2007 | 2006 | 2005 | 2004 | 2003 | 2002 | 2001 | 2000 | 1999 | 1998 |
|---|---|---|---|---|---|---|---|---|---|---|
| Revenue | 1,702 | 1,560 | 1,467 | 1,349 | NA | NA | NA | NA | NA | NA |
| Operating Income | 405 | 367 | 339 | 247 | NA | NA | NA | NA | NA | NA |
| Depreciation | 68.0 | 55.0 | 55.0 | 48.0 | NA | NA | NA | NA | NA | NA |
| Interest Expense | Nil | Nil | Nil | Nil | NA | NA | NA | NA | NA | NA |
| Pretax Income | 322 | 312 | 284 | 199 | NA | NA | NA | NA | NA | NA |
| Effective Tax Rate | 37.9% | 36.5% | 27.5% | 30.7% | NA | NA | NA | NA | NA | NA |
| Net Income | 200 | 198 | 206 | 138 | NA | NA | NA | NA | NA | NA |
| S&P Core Earnings | 213 | 198 | 200 | NA | NA | NA | NA | NA | NA | NA |

| Balance Sheet & Other Financial Data (Million $) | 2007 | 2006 | 2005 | 2004 | 2003 | 2002 | 2001 | 2000 | 1999 | 1998 |
|---|---|---|---|---|---|---|---|---|---|---|
| Cash | 270 | 200 | NA | NA | NA | NA | NA | NA | NA | NA |
| Current Assets | 873 | 645 | NA | NA | NA | NA | NA | NA | NA | NA |
| Total Assets | 1,295 | 983 | 911 | NA | NA | NA | NA | NA | NA | NA |
| Current Liabilities | 572 | 428 | NA | NA | NA | NA | NA | NA | NA | NA |
| Long Term Debt | Nil | Nil | NA | NA | NA | NA | NA | NA | NA | NA |
| Common Equity | 631 | 477 | 517 | NA | NA | NA | NA | NA | NA | NA |
| Total Capital | 631 | 477 | NA | NA | NA | NA | NA | NA | NA | NA |
| Capital Expenditures | 50.0 | 20.0 | 18.0 | 14.0 | NA | NA | NA | NA | NA | NA |
| Cash Flow | 268 | 253 | 261 | 186 | NA | NA | NA | NA | NA | NA |
| Current Ratio | 1.5 | 1.5 | 1.2 | NA | NA | NA | NA | NA | NA | NA |
| % Long Term Debt of Capitalization | Nil | Nil | Nil | 10.2 | NA | NA | NA | NA | NA | NA |
| % Net Income of Revenue | 11.8 | 12.7 | 14.0 | 10.2 | NA | NA | NA | NA | NA | NA |
| % Return on Assets | 17.4 | NM | NM | NA | NA | NA | NA | NA | NA | NA |
| % Return on Equity | 32.6 | NM | NM | NA | NA | NA | NA | NA | NA | NA |

Data as orig reptd.; bef. results of disc opers/spec. items. Per share data adj. for stk. divs.; EPS diluted. E-Estimated. NA-Not Available. NM-Not Meaningful. NR-Not Ranked. UR-Under Review.

**Office:** 1700 S. Patterson Blvd., Dayton, OH 45479.
**Telephone:** 937-445-5000.
**Website:** http://www.teradata.com
**Chrmn:** J.M. Ringler

**Pres & CEO:** M.F. Koehler
**COO:** B.A. Langos
**EVP, CFO & Chief Acctg Officer:** S.M. Scheppmann
**Chief Admin Officer:** R.A. Young

**Investor Contact:** S. Scheppmann (888-261-6779)
**Board Members:** E. P. Boykin, P. L. Fiore, C. T. Fu, D. E. Kepler, II, M. F. Koehler, V. L. Lund, J. M. Ringler, W. S. Stavropoulos

**Auditor:** PricewaterhouseCoopers
**Founded:** 1979
**Domicile:** Delaware
**Employees:** 5,900

# Teradyne Inc.

STANDARD &POOR'S

**S&P Recommendation** HOLD ★★★☆☆

| | |
|---|---|
| **Price** | $4.05 (as of Nov 14, 2008) |
| **12-Mo. Target Price** | $6.00 |
| **Investment Style** | Large-Cap Blend |

**GICS Sector** Information Technology
**Sub-Industry** Semiconductor Equipment

**Summary** This company makes automatic test equipment (ATE) used primarily by the semiconductor and telecommunications industries.

## Key Stock Statistics (Source S&P, Vickers, company reports)

| | | | | | | | |
|---|---|---|---|---|---|---|---|
| 52-Wk Range | $14.50– 3.83 | S&P Oper. EPS 2008E | 0.25 | Market Capitalization(B) | $0.686 | Beta | 2.07 |
| Trailing 12-Month EPS | $0.04 | S&P Oper. EPS 2009E | -0.10 | Yield (%) | Nil | S&P 3-Yr. Proj. EPS CAGR(%) | 5 |
| Trailing 12-Month P/E | NM | P/E on S&P Oper. EPS 2008E | 16.2 | Dividend Rate/Share | Nil | S&P Credit Rating | NR |
| $10K Invested 5 Yrs Ago | $1,761 | Common Shares Outstg. (M) | 169.3 | Institutional Ownership (%) | 94 | | |

## Price Performance

30-Week Mov. Avg. · · · · 10-Week Mov. Avg. - - GAAP Earnings vs. Previous Year Volume Above Avg. STARS
12-Mo. Target Price — Relative Strength — ▲ Up ▼ Down ► No Change Below Avg.

Options: ASE, CBOE, P, Ph

Analysis prepared by **Angelo Zino** on October 23, 2008, when the stock traded at **$ 5.05**.

## Highlights

➤ Following our projection for a low single digit revenue increase in 2008, we expect revenues to decline 24% in 2009, reflecting declining sales in the system-on-chip (SOC) test equipment market and muted NAND flash memory test sales. Longer term, we expect TER to expand into higher growth adjacent markets, such as Dynamic Random Access Memory (DRAM). We believe TER can sustain its market share leading position in the highly competitive SOC test market over the next several years.

➤ We project gross margin of 44% for 2009, compared to 45% in 2008. We believe margins will be pressured by lower production volume and declining average selling prices. We see TER continuing initiatives to reduce costs through outsourcing more of the manufacturing processes to low-cost countries. We expect TER to lower its quarterly breakeven level by an additional $20 million in 2009 and see the effective tax rate increasing to a long-term rate of 28% in 2009.

➤ We view positively the planned acquisition of Eagle Test Systems (EGLT: $15), as EGLT's power management and analog test applications complement many of its SOC products.

## Investment Rationale/Risk

➤ We see potential for market share gains through new product introductions and think that TER's expansion into the flash memory test market will allow it to outperform the industry's historical 3%-5% growth rate over the next several years. TER's leadership position in the business, and what we view as its strong cash position, offset by the competitive and low-growth environment for testers, are incorporated into our opinion. Although TER had about $297 million remaining on its repurchase plan at the end of September 2008, we anticipate it will refrain from repurchasing shares until industry conditions begin to improve.

➤ Risks to our recommendation and target price include intensified pricing pressures, technological obsolescence, weakness in the global economy, and competitive threats.

➤ We derive our 12-month target price of $6 by applying a price-to-sales (P/S) multiple of 1.2X to our 2009 sales per share forecast of $5.10, near comparable back-end equipment manufacturers. The shares recently traded below TER's historical three- and five-year P/S averages of 2.1X and 2.4X, respectively.

## Qualitative Risk Assessment

| LOW | MEDIUM | HIGH |
|---|---|---|

Our risk assessment reflects the historical cyclicality of the semiconductor equipment industry, the lack of visibility in the medium term, and intense competition, which we think are only partially offset by Teradyne's market position and financial strength.

## Quantitative Evaluations

**S&P Quality Ranking** B-

| D | C | B- | B | B+ | A- | A | A+ |
|---|---|---|---|---|---|---|---|

**Relative Strength Rank** WEAK

22

LOWEST = 1     HIGHEST = 99

## Revenue/Earnings Data

**Revenue (Million $)**

| | 1Q | 2Q | 3Q | 4Q | Year |
|---|---|---|---|---|---|
| 2008 | 297.3 | 317.7 | 297.3 | -- | -- |
| 2007 | 258.1 | 288.7 | 299.5 | 260.4 | 1,102 |
| 2006 | 362.9 | 391.6 | 359.1 | 263.2 | 1,377 |
| 2005 | 210.4 | 226.2 | 293.6 | 345.2 | 1,075 |
| 2004 | 430.6 | 526.5 | 457.8 | 377.0 | 1,792 |
| 2003 | 334.6 | 331.5 | 329.2 | 357.6 | 1,353 |

**Earnings Per Share ($)**

| | | | | | |
|---|---|---|---|---|---|
| 2008 | 0.01 | 0.06 | -0.14 | E-0.14 | E0.25 |
| 2007 | -0.04 | 0.14 | 0.19 | 0.10 | 0.39 |
| 2006 | 0.23 | 0.40 | 0.33 | 0.06 | 1.03 |
| 2005 | -0.28 | -0.26 | -0.22 | 0.44 | -0.31 |
| 2004 | 0.20 | 0.39 | 0.21 | 0.02 | 0.84 |
| 2003 | -0.41 | -0.28 | -0.28 | -0.06 | -1.03 |

Fiscal year ended Dec. 31. Next earnings report expected: Late January. EPS Estimates based on S&P Operating Earnings; historical GAAP earnings are as reported.

## Dividend Data

No cash dividends have been paid.

The McGraw-Hill Companies

# Teradyne Inc.

**STANDARD &POOR'S**

## Business Summary October 23, 2008

CORPORATE OVERVIEW. Founded in 1960, Teradyne is a leading global supplier of automatic test equipment (ATE) for the electronics industry. As electronic systems have become more complex, the need for products to test the systems has grown dramatically. TER's product segments include Semiconductor Test (80% of 2007 revenue, 80% in 2006) and Systems Test Group (20%, 20%).

Semiconductor Test products test system on a chip (SOC) semiconductor devices during the manufacturing process. These systems are used for wafer level and device packaging testing and span a broad range of end users and functionality. TER's systems help customers improve and control quality, reduce time to market, increase production yields, and improve product performance. TER's FLEX Test platform is designed for scalability and allows for simultaneous parallel testing, reducing costs. The versatility of the FLEX system to handle a wide range of devices makes it attractive to subcontracting testhouses.

The J750 platform is designed to address the highest volume semiconductor devices such as microcontrollers, with a single circuit board providing up to 64 digital input/output channels. The J750 platform technology has been extended to create the IP 750 Image Sensor test system, which focuses on testing image sensor devices used in digital cameras and other imaging products.

TER released its J750Ex platform in 2007, with additional products to be released in 2008. The J750 platform has been expanded to include critical new devices that include high-end microcontroller, LCD drivers, and the latest generation of cameras.

The Systems Test Group segment is comprised of three segments: Commercial Board Test, Military/Aerospace Test, and Diagnostic Solutions. Commercial Board test systems are sold to electronic manufacturers of cell phones, servers, computers, Internet switches, automobiles and avionics systems. Products test and inspect printed circuit boards (PCBs), which are thin plates or cards on which semiconductor chips and other electronic components are placed. In-circuit test systems assess electrical interconnections, verify interoperation on PCBs, and are used both in prototype testing and high-volume board manufacturing. Imaging inspection systems, such as the Xstation MX, use a 3-dimensional X-ray system for higher-density double-sided boards where half of all solder connections are invisible to optical inspection systems.

## Company Financials Fiscal Year Ended Dec. 31

| Per Share Data ($) | 2007 | 2006 | 2005 | 2004 | 2003 | 2002 | 2001 | 2000 | 1999 | 1998 |
|---|---|---|---|---|---|---|---|---|---|---|
| Tangible Book Value | 6.70 | 6.84 | 5.75 | 5.00 | 4.33 | 4.97 | 8.69 | 9.89 | 6.77 | 6.13 |
| Cash Flow | 0.71 | 1.35 | 0.16 | 1.47 | -0.22 | -3.06 | -0.36 | 3.42 | 1.56 | 1.04 |
| Earnings | 0.39 | 1.03 | -0.31 | 0.84 | -1.03 | -3.93 | -1.15 | 2.86 | 1.07 | 0.60 |
| S&P Core Earnings | 0.37 | 0.92 | -0.80 | 0.37 | -1.44 | -4.25 | -1.65 | NA | NA | NA |
| Dividends | Nil | Nil | Nil | Nil | Nil | Nil | Nil | Nil | Nil | Nil |
| Payout Ratio | Nil | Nil | Nil | Nil | Nil | Nil | Nil | Nil | Nil | Nil |
| Prices:High | 18.53 | 18.08 | 17.33 | 30.70 | 26.31 | 40.20 | 47.21 | 115.44 | 66.00 | 24.22 |
| Prices:Low | 10.02 | 11.50 | 10.80 | 12.53 | 8.75 | 7.10 | 18.43 | 23.00 | 20.63 | 7.50 |
| P/E Ratio:High | 48 | 18 | NM | 37 | NM | NM | NM | 40 | 62 | 41 |
| P/E Ratio:Low | 26 | 11 | NM | 15 | NM | NM | NM | 8 | 19 | 13 |

| Income Statement Analysis (Million $) | 2007 | 2006 | 2005 | 2004 | 2003 | 2002 | 2001 | 2000 | 1999 | 1998 |
|---|---|---|---|---|---|---|---|---|---|---|
| Revenue | 1,102 | 1,377 | 1,075 | 1,792 | 1,353 | 1,222 | 1,441 | 3,044 | 1,791 | 1,489 |
| Operating Income | 117 | 236 | 27.1 | 318 | 47.3 | -192 | -1.54 | 813 | 345 | 210 |
| Depreciation | 59.4 | 73.5 | 91.2 | 124 | 152 | 160 | 139 | 102 | 86.4 | 76.3 |
| Interest Expense | 0.69 | 11.1 | 16.2 | 18.8 | 20.9 | 21.8 | 4.09 | 1.84 | 1.66 | 1.57 |
| Pretax Income | 79.2 | 230 | -80.1 | 188 | -186 | -561 | -326 | 740 | 274 | 146 |
| Effective Tax Rate | 9.29% | 12.0% | NM | 12.1% | NM | NM | NM | 30.0% | 30.0% | 30.0% |
| Net Income | 71.9 | 203 | -60.5 | 165 | -194 | -718 | -202 | 518 | 192 | 102 |
| S&P Core Earnings | 68.3 | 179 | -161 | 73.3 | -270 | -777 | -290 | NA | NA | NA |

| Balance Sheet & Other Financial Data (Million $) | 2007 | 2006 | 2005 | 2004 | 2003 | 2002 | 2001 | 2000 | 1999 | 1998 |
|---|---|---|---|---|---|---|---|---|---|---|
| Cash | 638 | 945 | 695 | 285 | 586 | 541 | 586 | 464 | 387 | 298 |
| Current Assets | 945 | 889 | 1,095 | 806 | 769 | 809 | 1,207 | 1,378 | 908 | 759 |
| Total Assets | 1,555 | 1,721 | 1,860 | 1,923 | 1,785 | 1,895 | 2,542 | 2,356 | 1,568 | 1,313 |
| Current Liabilities | 223 | 260 | 515 | 277 | 281 | 279 | 296 | 619 | 392 | 256 |
| Long Term Debt | Nil | Nil | 1.82 | 399 | 408 | 451 | 452 | 8.35 | 8.95 | 13.2 |
| Common Equity | 1,229 | 1,361 | 1,243 | 1,134 | 950 | 1,028 | 1,764 | 1,707 | 1,153 | 1,026 |
| Total Capital | 1,229 | 1,361 | 1,244 | 1,532 | 1,357 | 1,479 | 2,216 | 1,737 | 1,176 | 1,057 |
| Capital Expenditures | 86.1 | 110 | 113 | 165 | 30.8 | 46.4 | 198 | 235 | 120 | 119 |
| Cash Flow | 131 | 276 | 30.7 | 290 | -41.5 | -559 | -63.5 | 620 | 278 | 178 |
| Current Ratio | 4.2 | 3.4 | 2.1 | 2.9 | 2.7 | 2.9 | 4.1 | 2.2 | 2.3 | 3.0 |
| % Long Term Debt of Capitalization | Nil | Nil | 0.1 | 26.0 | 30.0 | 30.5 | 20.4 | 0.5 | 0.8 | 1.2 |
| % Net Income of Revenue | 6.5 | 14.7 | NM | 9.2 | NM | NM | NM | 17.0 | 10.7 | 6.9 |
| % Return on Assets | 4.4 | 11.3 | NM | 8.9 | NM | NM | NM | 26.4 | 13.3 | 8.0 |
| % Return on Equity | 5.6 | 15.6 | NM | 15.9 | NM | NM | NM | 36.2 | 17.6 | 10.4 |

Data as orig reptd.; bef. results of disc opers/spec. items. Per share data adj. for stk. divs.; EPS diluted. E-Estimated. NA-Not Available. NM-Not Meaningful. NR-Not Ranked. UR-Under Review.

**Office:** 600 Riverpark Dr, North Reading, MA 01864-2634.
**Telephone:** 978-370-2700.
**Email:** investorrelations@teradyne.com
**Website:** http://www.teradyne.com

**Chrmn:** P.S. Wolpert
**Pres & CEO:** M.A. Bradley
**CFO, Chief Acctg Officer & Treas:** G.R. Beecher
**Secy & General Counsel:** E. Casal

**Investor Contact:** J. Moore
**Board Members:** J. W. Bageley, M. A. Bradley, A. Carnesale, E. Gillis, V. M. O'Reilly, P. J. Tufano, R. Vallee, P. S. Wolpert

**Founded:** 1960
**Domicile:** Massachusetts
**Employees:** 3,600

**The McGraw-Hill Companies**

# Tesoro Corp

## STANDARD &POOR'S

| S&P Recommendation **HOLD** ★★★☆☆ | Price $10.25 (as of Nov 14, 2008) | 12-Mo. Target Price $14.00 | Investment Style Large-Cap Blend |
|---|---|---|---|

**GICS Sector** Energy
**Sub-Industry** Oil & Gas Refining & Marketing

**Summary** Tesoro is one of the largest independent refiners and marketers of petroleum products in the U.S., with operations focused on the West Coast.

### Key Stock Statistics (Source S&P, Vickers, company reports)

| | | | | | | |
|---|---|---|---|---|---|---|
| 52-Wk Range | $57.10– 7.61 | S&P Oper. EPS 2008**E** | 1.72 | Market Capitalization(B) | $1.419 | Beta | 2.05 |
| Trailing 12-Month EPS | $1.01 | S&P Oper. EPS 2009**E** | 2.62 | Yield (%) | 3.90 | S&P 3-Yr. Proj. EPS CAGR(%) | -46 |
| Trailing 12-Month P/E | 10.2 | P/E on S&P Oper. EPS 2008**E** | 6.0 | Dividend Rate/Share | $0.40 | S&P Credit Rating | BB+ |
| $10K Invested 5 Yrs Ago | $16,939 | Common Shares Outstg. (M) | 138.5 | Institutional Ownership (%) | 82 | | |

### Price Performance

30-Week Mov. Avg. · · · · 10-Week Mov. Avg. - - - GAAP Earnings vs. Previous Year   Volume Above Avg. STARS
12-Mo. Target Price — Relative Strength — ▲ Up ▼ Down ► No Change   Below Avg. ★

Options: ASE, CBOE, Ph

Analysis prepared by **Tina J. Vital** on November 06, 2008, when the stock traded at **$ 9.23**.

### Qualitative Risk Assessment

| LOW | MEDIUM | HIGH |
|---|---|---|

Our risk assessment reflects our view of TSO's solid business profile in a competitive and volatile refining industry. We believe the company has strong asset quality and solid liquidity.

### Quantitative Evaluations

**S&P Quality Ranking**      B

| D | C | B- | B | B+ | A- | A | A+ |
|---|---|---|---|---|---|---|---|

**Relative Strength Rank**      **MODERATE**

48

LOWEST = 1          HIGHEST = 99

### Revenue/Earnings Data

**Revenue (Million $)**

| | 1Q | 2Q | 3Q | 4Q | Year |
|---|---|---|---|---|---|
| 2008 | 6,531 | 8,754 | 8,698 | -- | -- |
| 2007 | 3,876 | 5,604 | 5,902 | 6,533 | 21,915 |
| 2006 | 3,877 | 4,929 | 5,278 | 4,020 | 18,104 |
| 2005 | 3,171 | 4,033 | 5,017 | 4,360 | 16,581 |
| 2004 | 2,430 | 3,155 | 3,289 | 3,389 | 12,262 |
| 2003 | 2,286 | 2,116 | 2,330 | 2,113 | 8,846 |

**Earnings Per Share ($)**

| | 1Q | 2Q | 3Q | 4Q | Year |
|---|---|---|---|---|---|
| 2008 | -0.60 | -0.03 | 1.86 | E0.58 | E1.72 |
| 2007 | 0.84 | 3.17 | 0.34 | -0.29 | 4.06 |
| 2006 | 0.31 | 2.33 | 1.96 | 1.14 | 5.73 |
| 2005 | 0.20 | 1.31 | 1.60 | 0.49 | 3.60 |
| 2004 | 0.38 | 1.56 | 0.47 | Nil | 2.38 |
| 2003 | 0.16 | -0.06 | 0.55 | -0.06 | 0.58 |

Fiscal year ended Dec. 31. Next earnings report expected: Early February. EPS Estimates based on S&P Operating Earnings; historical GAAP earnings are as reported.

### Highlights

- Third-quarter refining throughputs declined 4.9% from the same period last year, below our expectations as volumes were reduced to reflect lower product demand. Based on management guidance, we expect fourth-quarter throughputs will decline about 6% from third-quarter levels.

- Refined petroleum products prices have failed to keep pace with the sharp rise in oil prices, but third quarter margins widened compared to the second quarter, on improved product pricing and a decline in oil prices. We project U.S. industry-wide refining margins will narrow about 18% in both 2008 and 2009.

- Going forward, TSO expects to balance the supply of production and inventories around consumer demand and profitability of the last barrel produced. The company is managing inventory levels and working capital by shortening supply lines in both crude and products. We expect after-tax operating earnings will fall 61% in 2008 before rebounding 51% in 2009.

### Investment Rationale/Risk

- Reflecting refineries located on the U.S. West Coast, we believe TSO's exposure to high refining margin environments such those in California enhances its earnings potential. As a significant portion of TSO's refining capacity is of lower complexity, we expect the company to achieve greater operational efficiencies from recent upgrades at several of its refineries.

- Risks to our recommendation and target price include changes in economic, industry and operating conditions that could lead to narrowed refining margins or reduced refining volumes. About 57% of TSO's refining capacity is concentrated in three refineries (Martinez and Los Angeles, CA, and Anacortes, WA), which exposes the company to operational risk, in our view.

- A blend of our discounted cash flow (intrinsic value of $11 per share assuming a WACC of 11.5% and terminal growth of 3%) and narrowed relative valuations leads to our 12-month target price of $14 per share, representing an expected enterprise value of about 3.0X our 2009 EBITDA estimate, a discount to peers.

### Dividend Data (Dates: mm/dd Payment Date: mm/dd/yy)

| Amount ($) | Date Decl. | Ex-Div. Date | Stk. of Record | Payment Date |
|---|---|---|---|---|
| 0.100 | 01/31 | 02/28 | 03/03 | 03/17/08 |
| 0.100 | 05/06 | 05/29 | 06/02 | 06/16/08 |
| 0.100 | 07/30 | 08/28 | 09/02 | 09/16/08 |
| 0.100 | 10/29 | 11/26 | 12/01 | 12/15/08 |

Dividends have been paid since 2005. Source: Company reports.

---

**Please read the Required Disclosures and Analyst Certification on the last page of this report.**

The McGraw-Hill Companies

# Tesoro Corp

**STANDARD &POOR'S**

## Business Summary November 06, 2008

CORPORATE OVERVIEW. Tesoro Corp. (TSO; formerly Tesoro Petroleum Corp.) is one of the largest independent refiners and marketers of petroleum products in the U.S. The company operates in two business segments: Refining (87% of 2007 revenues; 92% of gross margin) and Retail (13%; 8%).

The Refining segment refines crude oil and other feedstocks at its seven refineries (total refining capacity 658,000 b/d, as of December 31, 2007) in the U.S. west and mid-continent: California ("Wilmington" in Los Angeles, CA, 100,000 b/d; "Golden Eagle" in Martinez, CA, 161,000 b/d), the Pacific Northwest (Anacortes, WA, 113,000 b/d; and Kenai, AK, 72,000 b/d), the Mid-Pacific (Kapolei, HI, 94,000 b/d) and the Mid-Continent (Mandan, ND, 58,000 b/d; and Salt Lake City, UT, 60,000 b/d). Total refining yield rose 13%, to 619,000 b/d, in 2007: gasoline 45%, jet fuel 12%, diesel fuel 20%, and heavy oils, residual products and other 23%.

The company purchases its crude oil and other feedstocks for its refineries from various domestic (about 52% of its 2007 crude oil, including about 16% from Alaska's North Slope) and foreign (around 48%, including about 14%

from Canada) sources through term agreements (40%), which are mainly short term, and in the spot market. About 23% of its total refining throughput was heavy oil (API specific gravity of 24 or less) in 2007, up from 18% in 2006.

MARKET PROFILE. TSO is one of the largest independent refiners in the U.S. The company operates the largest refineries in Hawaii and Utah, and the second largest refineries in northern California and Alaska.

Through its network of retail stations, TSO sells gasoline and diesel fuel in the western and mid-continental U.S. As of December 31, 2007, TSO's retail segment included 911 branded retail stations (under the Tesoro, Mirastar, Shell and USA Gasoline brands), comprising 449 company-operated retail gasoline stations and 462 jobber/dealer stations. Reflecting recent acquisitions, retail fuel sales climbed 153%, to 1.1 billion gallons.

## Company Financials Fiscal Year Ended Dec. 31

| Per Share Data ($) | 2007 | 2006 | 2005 | 2004 | 2003 | 2002 | 2001 | 2000 | 1999 | 1998 |
|---|---|---|---|---|---|---|---|---|---|---|
| Tangible Book Value | 20.73 | 17.09 | 12.12 | 8.31 | 5.70 | 5.00 | 6.75 | 7.17 | 8.57 | 8.65 |
| Cash Flow | 5.82 | 7.50 | 4.92 | 3.50 | 1.72 | 0.11 | 2.07 | 1.28 | 0.96 | 0.87 |
| Earnings | 4.06 | 5.73 | 3.60 | 2.38 | 0.58 | -0.97 | 1.05 | 0.88 | 0.31 | -0.36 |
| S&P Core Earnings | 4.12 | 5.73 | 3.65 | 2.42 | 0.78 | -0.97 | 1.00 | NA | NA | NA |
| Dividends | 0.35 | 0.20 | 0.10 | Nil | Nil | Nil | Nil | Nil | Nil | Nil |
| Payout Ratio | 9% | 3% | 3% | Nil | Nil | Nil | Nil | Nil | Nil | Nil |
| Prices:High | 65.98 | 38.40 | 35.91 | 17.33 | 7.56 | 7.65 | 8.25 | 6.50 | 9.41 | 10.69 |
| Prices:Low | 31.47 | 26.48 | 14.13 | 7.00 | 1.69 | 0.62 | 4.85 | 4.47 | 3.72 | 4.78 |
| P/E Ratio:High | 16 | 7 | 10 | 7 | 13 | NM | 8 | 7 | 30 | NM |
| P/E Ratio:Low | 8 | 5 | 4 | 3 | 3 | NM | 5 | 5 | 12 | NM |

| Income Statement Analysis (Million $) | | | | | | | | | | |
|---|---|---|---|---|---|---|---|---|---|---|
| Revenue | 21,915 | 18,104 | 16,581 | 12,262 | 8,846 | 7,119 | 5,218 | 5,104 | 3,000 | 1,469 |
| Operating Income | 1,473 | 1,614 | 1,232 | 881 | 638 | 120 | 290 | 205 | 140 | 144 |
| Depreciation, Depletion and Amortization | 246 | 247 | 186 | 154 | 148 | 131 | 91.2 | 45.5 | 42.9 | 66.0 |
| Interest Expense | 125 | 77.0 | 211 | 167 | 212 | 166 | 52.8 | 32.7 | 37.6 | 33.0 |
| Pretax Income | 905 | 1,286 | 831 | 547 | 123 | -181 | 147 | 124 | 51.2 | -15.5 |
| Effective Tax Rate | 37.5% | 37.7% | 39.0% | 40.0% | 38.2% | NM | 40.1% | 40.6% | 37.1% | NM |
| Net Income | 566 | 801 | 507 | 328 | 76.1 | -117 | 88.0 | 73.3 | 32.2 | -15.0 |
| S&P Core Earnings | 574 | 800 | 514 | 333 | 101 | -117 | 77.2 | NA | NA | NA |

| Balance Sheet & Other Financial Data (Million $) | | | | | | | | | | |
|---|---|---|---|---|---|---|---|---|---|---|
| Cash | 23.0 | 986 | 440 | 185 | 77.2 | 110 | 51.9 | 14.1 | 142 | 12.9 |
| Current Assets | 2,600 | 2,811 | 2,215 | 1,393 | 1,024 | 1,054 | 878 | 630 | 612 | 391 |
| Total Assets | 8,128 | 5,904 | 5,097 | 4,075 | 3,661 | 3,759 | 2,662 | 1,544 | 1,487 | 1,428 |
| Current Liabilities | 2,494 | 1,672 | 1,502 | 993 | 687 | 608 | 538 | 382 | 322 | 208 |
| Long Term Debt | 1,657 | 1,029 | 1,044 | 1,215 | 1,605 | 1,907 | 1,113 | 307 | 390 | 531 |
| Common Equity | 3,052 | 2,502 | 1,887 | 1,327 | 965 | 888 | 757 | 505 | 463 | 394 |
| Total Capital | 5,097 | 3,908 | 3,320 | 2,835 | 2,750 | 2,923 | 2,006 | 1,084 | 1,099 | 1,161 |
| Capital Expenditures | 747 | 436 | 258 | 179 | 101 | 204 | 210 | 94.0 | 84.7 | 185 |
| Cash Flow | 812 | 1,048 | 693 | 482 | 224 | 13.7 | 173 | 107 | 63.1 | 51.0 |
| Current Ratio | 1.0 | 1.7 | 1.5 | 1.4 | 1.5 | 1.7 | 1.6 | 1.6 | 1.9 | 1.9 |
| % Long Term Debt of Capitalization | 32.5 | 26.3 | 31.4 | 42.9 | 58.4 | 65.2 | 55.4 | 28.3 | 35.5 | 45.7 |
| % Return on Assets | 8.1 | 14.6 | 11.1 | 8.5 | 2.1 | NM | 4.2 | 4.8 | 2.2 | NM |
| % Return on Equity | 20.4 | 36.5 | 31.5 | 28.6 | 8.2 | NM | 13.0 | 12.7 | 4.7 | NM |

Data as orig reptd.; bef. results of disc opers/spec. items. Per share data adj. for stk. divs.; EPS diluted. E-Estimated. NA-Not Available. NM-Not Meaningful. NR-Not Ranked. UR-Under Review.

**Office:** 300 Concord Plaza Drive, San Antonio, TX 78216-6999 .
**Telephone:** 210-828-8484.
**Email:** investor_relations@tesoropetroleum.com
**Website:** http://www.tsocorp.com

**Chrmn, Pres & CEO:** B.A. Smith
**COO & EVP:** E.D. Lewis
**EVP & Chief Admin Officer:** G.A. Wright
**SVP, CFO & Treas:** O.C. Schwethelm

**SVP, Secy & General Counsel:** C.S. Parrish
**Investor Contact:** S. Phipps (210-283-2882)
**Board Members:** J. F. Bookout, III, R. F. Chase, R. W. Goldman, S. H. Grapstein, W. J. Johnson, J. W. Nokes, D. H. Schmude, B. A. Smith, M. E. Wiley

**Founded:** 1939
**Domicile:** Delaware
**Employees:** 5,500

# Texas Instruments Inc

STANDARD
&POOR'S

| S&P Recommendation | HOLD ★★★☆☆ | Price $16.11 (as of Nov 14, 2008) | 12-Mo. Target Price $20.00 | Investment Style Large-Cap Growth |
|---|---|---|---|---|

**GICS Sector** Information Technology
**Sub-Industry** Semiconductors

**Summary** One of the world's largest manufacturers of semiconductors, this company also produces handheld graphing calculator products.

## Key Stock Statistics (Source S&P, Vickers, company reports)

| | | | | | | |
|---|---|---|---|---|---|---|
| 52-Wk Range | $34.60– 15.60 | S&P Oper. EPS 2008**E** | 1.68 | Market Capitalization(B) | $20.885 | Beta | 1.70 |
| Trailing 12-Month EPS | $1.90 | S&P Oper. EPS 2009**E** | 1.31 | Yield (%) | 2.73 | S&P 3-Yr. Proj. EPS CAGR(%) | -8 |
| Trailing 12-Month P/E | 8.5 | P/E on S&P Oper. EPS 2008**E** | 9.6 | Dividend Rate/Share | $0.44 | S&P Credit Rating | A |
| $10K Invested 5 Yrs Ago | $5,802 | Common Shares Outstg. (M) | 1,296.4 | Institutional Ownership (%) | 78 | | |

## Price Performance

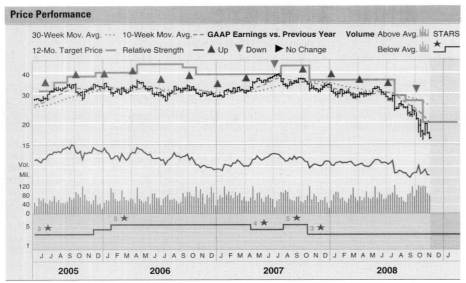

30-Week Mov. Avg. ···· 10-Week Mov. Avg. - - GAAP Earnings vs. Previous Year   Volume Above Avg. STARS
12-Mo. Target Price — Relative Strength — ▲ Up ▼ Down ► No Change   Below Avg.

Options: ASE, CBOE, P, Ph

Analysis prepared by **Clyde Montevirgen** on October 22, 2008, when the stock traded at **$ 17.01**.

### Highlights

➤ We expect sales to fall 9% in 2009, after an estimated decrease of around 7% in 2008, reflecting macroeconomic headwinds and market share loss. We think TXN will be able to extend its share leadership in a fragmented analog market, which we believe will grow faster than the broader semiconductor industry. But, we anticipate slowing global economic conditions to hurt orders over the near-term, and see TXN's sales slide exacerbated by share loss in its wireless segment as handset customers diversify supply bases. We also see 2009 revenues negatively impacted by the planned sale of its merchant baseband business.

➤ We expect gross margins to narrow to around 49% in 2009, below the 51% we see for 2008. We think TXN will reduce production to accommodate lower orders, which will reduce plant utilization rates and ultimately gross margins. We also see Non-GAAP operating margins falling to the 20% area in 2009 from an estimated 22% in 2008, reflecting lower sales and margins but balanced by restructuring efforts.

➤ We estimate operating EPS of $1.31 for 2009 from a projected $1.68 for 2008.

### Investment Rationale/Risk

➤ Our hold opinion reflects our view of weakening fundamentals balanced by valuations near recent historic lows. We think TXN is well positioned to take market share in the high-performance analog space over the longer-term, and we favorably view its decision to refocus on this fast-growing semiconductor segment. Although we think TXN has a broad product portfolio and a well-diversified customer base, we still see macroeconomic pressure and slowing orders hurting near-term results. We also expect slowing growth as its largest handset customers diversify their supplier bases.

➤ Risks to our recommendation and target price include a worse than expected downturn, competition, and faster-than-anticipated share loss in the wireless handset chip market.

➤ Our 12-month target price of $20 is based on relative metrics. We apply a P/E multiple of about 14X to our 2009 EPS estimate to derive a value of $18. We use a price-to-sales ratio of about 2.3X and our 12-month forward sales per share estimate to also arrive at a value of $21. Both multiples are below historical averages to account for expected slower growth.

### Qualitative Risk Assessment

| LOW | MEDIUM | HIGH |
|---|---|---|

Our risk assessment reflects the cyclicality of the industry in which TXN operates and the volatility of its shares, offset by the large number of company operations, TXN's diverse line of semiconductor products with exposure to many end markets and customers, our view of its low debt levels, and long corporate history.

### Quantitative Evaluations

**S&P Quality Ranking**                                    B+

| D | C | B- | B | B+ | A- | A | A+ |
|---|---|---|---|---|---|---|---|

**Relative Strength Rank**                          MODERATE

50

LOWEST = 1                                          HIGHEST = 99

### Revenue/Earnings Data

**Revenue (Million $)**

| | 1Q | 2Q | 3Q | 4Q | Year |
|---|---|---|---|---|---|
| 2008 | 3,272 | 3,351 | 3,387 | -- | -- |
| 2007 | 3,191 | 3,424 | 3,663 | 3,556 | 13,835 |
| 2006 | 3,334 | 3,697 | 3,761 | 3,463 | 14,255 |
| 2005 | 2,972 | 3,239 | 3,590 | 3,591 | 13,392 |
| 2004 | 2,936 | 3,241 | 3,250 | 3,153 | 12,580 |
| 2003 | 2,192 | 2,339 | 2,533 | 2,770 | 9,834 |

**Earnings Per Share ($)**

| | 1Q | 2Q | 3Q | 4Q | Year |
|---|---|---|---|---|---|
| 2008 | 0.49 | 0.44 | 0.43 | E0.32 | E1.68 |
| 2007 | 0.35 | 0.42 | 0.52 | 0.54 | 1.83 |
| 2006 | 0.33 | 0.47 | 0.45 | 0.45 | 1.69 |
| 2005 | 0.24 | 0.38 | 0.38 | 0.40 | 1.39 |
| 2004 | 0.21 | 0.25 | 0.32 | 0.28 | 1.05 |
| 2003 | 0.07 | 0.07 | 0.25 | 0.29 | 0.68 |

Fiscal year ended Dec. 31. Next earnings report expected: Late January. EPS Estimates based on S&P Operating Earnings; historical GAAP earnings are as reported.

### Dividend Data (Dates: mm/dd Payment Date: mm/dd/yy)

| Amount ($) | Date Decl. | Ex-Div. Date | Stk. of Record | Payment Date |
|---|---|---|---|---|
| 0.100 | 01/17 | 01/29 | 01/31 | 02/11/08 |
| 0.100 | 04/16 | 04/28 | 04/30 | 05/19/08 |
| 0.100 | 07/17 | 07/29 | 07/31 | 08/18/08 |
| 0.110 | 09/18 | 10/29 | 10/31 | 11/17/08 |

Dividends have been paid since 1962. Source: Company reports.

---

**Please read the Required Disclosures and Analyst Certification on the last page of this report.**

# Texas Instruments Inc

STANDARD
&POOR'S

## Business Summary October 22, 2008

CORPORATE OVERVIEW. Texas Instruments is the world's third largest semi-conductor company, in terms of 2005 revenues. It has design, sales or manufacturing operations in more than 25 countries. The company has increasingly concentrated on digital signal processors (DSPs), and on analog and mixed-signal integrated circuits. Semiconductors grew from less than 60% of revenues in 1996 to 87% in the boom year of 2000, and accounted for 96% in 2007 (96% in 2006). The Educational Technology segment represented 4% of 2007 sales (4%) and is a leading supplier of graphing calculators used in education, science and business.

End markets for TXN's chips in 2007 included communications, at 50% of Semiconductor sales, computing 25%, consumer electronics 10%, industrial 10%, and automotive 5%.

CORPORATE STRATEGY. The DSP market has recently been a fast-growing area of the semiconductor industry, driven by strong demand for devices such as wireless phones, modems, and computer networking gear. Increased use

of digital components in embedded systems in automobiles, appliances, and manufacturing equipment could also enhance market opportunities. DSPs accounted for 40% of Semiconductor segment revenues in 2007 (40% of sales in 2006); analog chips provided 40% (40%); and the remaining came from other semiconductor products such as digital light processing (DLP) products, reduced instruction-set computing (RISC) microprocessors, microcontrollers, standard logic devices, and royalties.

DSP and analog product lines are largely complementary. In the example of mobile phones, a market where TXN has a major presence, a voice signal is captured by analog chips in one mobile phone, processed into a digital format for better transmission and storage, and converted back into an audio signal for the listener at the receiving phone.

## Company Financials Fiscal Year Ended Dec. 31

| Per Share Data ($) | 2007 | 2006 | 2005 | 2004 | 2003 | 2002 | 2001 | 2000 | 1999 | 1998 |
|---|---|---|---|---|---|---|---|---|---|---|
| Tangible Book Value | 6.72 | 7.08 | 6.99 | 7.13 | 6.35 | 5.73 | 6.42 | 6.71 | 5.39 | 4.19 |
| Cash Flow | 2.57 | 2.37 | 2.32 | 1.93 | 1.54 | 0.78 | 0.94 | 2.49 | 1.47 | 0.97 |
| Earnings | 1.83 | 1.69 | 1.39 | 1.05 | 0.68 | -0.20 | -0.12 | 1.73 | 0.84 | 0.26 |
| S&P Core Earnings | 1.81 | 1.68 | 1.26 | 0.86 | 0.40 | -0.16 | -0.34 | NA | NA | NA |
| Dividends | 0.30 | 0.13 | 0.11 | 0.09 | 0.09 | 0.09 | 0.09 | 0.09 | 0.09 | 0.06 |
| Payout Ratio | 16% | 8% | 8% | 9% | 13% | NM | NM | 5% | 10% | 24% |
| Prices:High | 39.63 | 36.40 | 34.68 | 33.98 | 31.67 | 35.94 | 54.69 | 99.78 | 55.75 | 22.61 |
| Prices:Low | 28.24 | 26.77 | 20.70 | 18.06 | 13.90 | 13.10 | 20.10 | 35.00 | 21.50 | 10.06 |
| P/E Ratio:High | 22 | 22 | 25 | 32 | 47 | NM | NM | 58 | 66 | 89 |
| P/E Ratio:Low | 15 | 16 | 15 | 17 | 20 | NM | NM | 20 | 26 | 39 |

### Income Statement Analysis (Million $)

| | 2007 | 2006 | 2005 | 2004 | 2003 | 2002 | 2001 | 2000 | 1999 | 1998 |
|---|---|---|---|---|---|---|---|---|---|---|
| Revenue | 13,835 | 14,255 | 13,392 | 12,580 | 9,834 | 8,383 | 8,201 | 11,875 | 9,468 | 8,460 |
| Operating Income | 4,580 | 4,419 | 4,222 | 3,756 | 2,493 | 1,977 | 1,246 | 3,715 | 2,751 | 1,568 |
| Depreciation | 1,070 | 1,052 | 1,431 | 1,549 | 1,528 | 1,689 | 1,828 | 1,376 | 1,055 | 1,169 |
| Interest Expense | 1.00 | 7.00 | 9.00 | 21.0 | 39.0 | 57.0 | 61.0 | 75.0 | 75.0 | 75.0 |
| Pretax Income | 3,692 | 3,625 | 2,988 | 2,421 | 1,250 | -346 | -426 | 4,578 | 2,019 | 617 |
| Effective Tax Rate | 28.5% | 27.2% | 22.2% | 23.1% | 4.16% | NM | NM | 32.6% | 30.4% | 34.0% |
| Net Income | 2,641 | 2,638 | 2,324 | 1,861 | 1,198 | -344 | -201 | 3,087 | 1,406 | 407 |
| S&P Core Earnings | 2,609 | 2,614 | 2,110 | 1,516 | 701 | -275 | -587 | NA | NA | NA |

### Balance Sheet & Other Financial Data (Million $)

| | 2007 | 2006 | 2005 | 2004 | 2003 | 2002 | 2001 | 2000 | 1999 | 1998 |
|---|---|---|---|---|---|---|---|---|---|---|
| Cash | 2,924 | 1,183 | 1,219 | 2,668 | 1,818 | 949 | 431 | 745 | 662 | 540 |
| Current Assets | 6,918 | 7,854 | 9,185 | 10,190 | 7,709 | 6,126 | 5,775 | 8,115 | 6,055 | 4,846 |
| Total Assets | 12,667 | 13,930 | 15,063 | 16,299 | 15,510 | 14,679 | 15,779 | 17,720 | 15,028 | 11,250 |
| Current Liabilities | 2,025 | 2,078 | 2,346 | 1,925 | 2,200 | 1,934 | 1,580 | 2,813 | 2,628 | 2,196 |
| Long Term Debt | Nil | Nil | 360 | 368 | 395 | 833 | 1,211 | 1,216 | 1,097 | 1,027 |
| Common Equity | 9,975 | 11,711 | 11,937 | 13,063 | 11,864 | 10,734 | 11,879 | 12,588 | 9,255 | 6,527 |
| Total Capital | 10,024 | 11,734 | 12,320 | 13,471 | 12,318 | 11,696 | 13,421 | 14,273 | 11,346 | 7,935 |
| Capital Expenditures | 686 | 1,272 | 1,330 | 1,298 | 800 | 802 | 1,790 | 2,762 | 1,373 | 1,031 |
| Cash Flow | 3,711 | 3,690 | 3,882 | 3,410 | 2,726 | 1,345 | 1,627 | 4,463 | 2,461 | 1,551 |
| Current Ratio | 3.4 | 3.8 | 3.9 | 5.3 | 3.5 | 3.2 | 3.7 | 2.9 | 2.3 | 2.2 |
| % Long Term Debt of Capitalization | Nil | Nil | 2.9 | 2.7 | 3.2 | 7.1 | 9.0 | 8.5 | 9.7 | 12.9 |
| % Net Income of Revenue | 19.1 | 18.5 | 17.4 | 14.8 | 12.2 | NM | NM | 26.0 | 14.9 | 4.8 |
| % Return on Assets | 19.9 | 18.2 | 14.8 | 11.7 | 7.9 | NM | NM | 18.6 | 10.6 | 3.7 |
| % Return on Equity | 24.8 | 22.2 | 18.6 | 14.9 | 10.6 | NM | NM | 27.9 | 17.6 | 6.5 |

Data as orig reptd.; bef. results of disc opers/spec. items. Per share data adj. for stk. divs.; EPS diluted. E-Estimated. NA-Not Available. NM-Not Meaningful. NR-Not Ranked. UR-Under Review.

**Office:** PO Box 660199, Dallas, TX 75266-0199.
**Telephone:** 972-995-3773.
**Website:** http://www.ti.com
**Chrmn, Pres & CEO:** R.K. Templeton

**SVP, CFO & Chief Acctg Officer:** K.P. March
**SVP & CSO:** Y. Nishi
**SVP, Secy & General Counsel:** J.F. Hubach
**CTO:** H. Stork

**Investor Contact:** T.L. West
**Board Members:** J. R. Adams, D. L. Boren, D. A. Carp, C. S. Cox, D. Goode, S. P. MacMillan, P. H. Patsley, W. Sanders, R. J. Simmons, R. K. Templeton, C. T. Whitman

**Founded:** 1938
**Domicile:** Delaware
**Employees:** 30,175

# Textron Inc.

**STANDARD &POOR'S**

| S&P Recommendation | **BUY** ★★★★☆ | Price | 12-Mo. Target Price | Investment Style |
|---|---|---|---|---|
| | | $14.73 (as of Nov 14, 2008) | $23.00 | Large-Cap Value |

**GICS Sector** Industrials
**Sub-Industry** Industrial Conglomerates

**Summary** This aerospace and industrial conglomerate makes Cessna business jets, Bell helicopters, and industrial equipment and components. It also operates a diversified commercial finance company.

## Key Stock Statistics (Source S&P, Vickers, company reports)

| | | | | | | | |
|---|---|---|---|---|---|---|---|
| 52-Wk Range | $74.40– 10.09 | S&P Oper. EPS 2008**E** | 3.02 | Market Capitalization(B) | $3.551 | Beta | 2.08 |
| Trailing 12-Month EPS | $3.77 | S&P Oper. EPS 2009**E** | 3.40 | Yield (%) | 6.25 | S&P 3-Yr. Proj. EPS CAGR(%) | 6 |
| Trailing 12-Month P/E | 3.9 | P/E on S&P Oper. EPS 2008**E** | 4.9 | Dividend Rate/Share | $0.92 | S&P Credit Rating | A- |
| $10K Invested 5 Yrs Ago | $6,561 | Common Shares Outstg. (M) | 241.1 | Institutional Ownership (%) | 73 | | |

## Price Performance

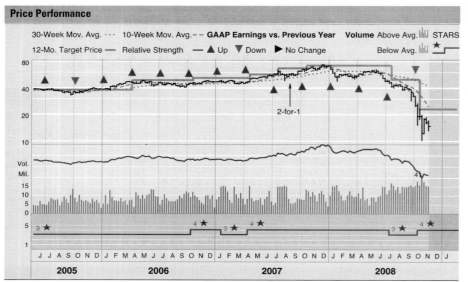

30-Week Mov. Avg. · · · 10-Week Mov. Avg. – – **GAAP Earnings vs. Previous Year** Volume Above Avg. STARS
12-Mo. Target Price — Relative Strength — ▲ Up ▼ Down ▶ No Change Below Avg.

2-for-1

2005 2006 2007 2008

Options: ASE, CBOE, P, Ph

Analysis prepared by **Richard Tortoriello** on November 10, 2008, when the stock traded at **$ 15.60.**

## Highlights

➤ We project sales growth of 11% in 2008 and 2009. Our 2008 and 2009 growth projections reflect expected strong gains at Cessna (19%), as it ramps up business jet production to work off a $16 billion backlog, moderately strong growth in the new Defense & Intelligence segment where TXT is making Armored Security Vehicles for the Army, 9% growth at Bell, offset by declines in the Industrial segment and in Finance.

➤ We forecast operating margins of 11.3% in 2008, down from 12.4% in 2007, on margin declines in all segments except Bell, with particularly strong margin declines in Finance, due to increased loan loss provisions and decreased financing profit margins. For 2009, we project a further narrowing in operating margins to 10.5%, due to projected continued loan loss provisions and a further deterioration in Industrial margins.

➤ We estimate EPS of $3.02 in 2008, down 14% from 2007, and see a 13% advance, to $3.40, in 2009. We project free cash flow per share about equal to EPS in 2008.

## Investment Rationale/Risk

➤ We recently raised our opinion on the shares to buy, from hold, as we believe that the sell-off in TXT shares was overdone. Although we expect to see significant loan losses in TXT's Finance portfolio, we believe our earnings estimates have factored in a relatively "high loss" scenario. We also expect continued production increases at Cessna, where the backlog of Citation jets is very high, and continued military demand at Bell and Defense & Intelligence. At the same time we see valuations on a variety of measures for TXT at historical lows.

➤ Risks to our recommendation and target price include a strong or prolonged global recession, continued problems with TXT's military helicopter programs, and operational difficulties in any of TXT's business segments.

➤ Our 12-month target price of $23 is based on a enterprise value to estimated 2008 EBITDA multiple of about 6.5X, just above a 20-year EV/ EBITDA low for TXT of about 6.0X. We believe that given a weak global economy and distressed global financial system, a below-average multiple is justified.

## Qualitative Risk Assessment

| LOW | **MEDIUM** | HIGH |
|---|---|---|

Our risk assessment reflects our view of TXT's cyclical earnings and the stock's above-average volatility, offset by a stable or rising dividend over the past 10 years.

## Quantitative Evaluations

**S&P Quality Ranking** B+

| D | C | B- | B | **B+** | A- | A | A+ |
|---|---|---|---|---|---|---|---|

**Relative Strength Rank** WEAK

20

LOWEST = 1 HIGHEST = 99

## Revenue/Earnings Data

**Revenue (Million $)**

| | 1Q | 2Q | 3Q | 4Q | Year |
|---|---|---|---|---|---|
| 2008 | 3,518 | 3,919 | 3,533 | -- | -- |
| 2007 | 2,964 | 3,235 | 3,263 | 3,763 | 13,225 |
| 2006 | 2,632 | 2,820 | 2,837 | 3,201 | 11,490 |
| 2005 | 2,791 | 3,188 | 2,862 | 2,701 | 10,043 |
| 2004 | 2,354 | 2,547 | 2,569 | 2,833 | 10,242 |
| 2003 | 2,399 | 2,530 | 2,231 | 2,699 | 9,859 |

**Earnings Per Share ($)**

| | 1Q | 2Q | 3Q | 4Q | Year |
|---|---|---|---|---|---|
| 2008 | 0.93 | 1.03 | 0.85 | E0.22 | E3.02 |
| 2007 | 0.78 | 0.85 | 0.95 | 1.02 | 3.59 |
| 2006 | 0.60 | 0.67 | 0.68 | 0.77 | 2.72 |
| 2005 | 0.29 | 0.47 | -0.63 | 0.63 | 1.89 |
| 2004 | 0.13 | 0.36 | 0.37 | 0.44 | 1.33 |
| 2003 | 0.25 | 0.31 | 0.17 | 0.30 | 1.03 |

Fiscal year ended Dec. 31. Next earnings report expected: Late January. EPS Estimates based on S&P Operating Earnings; historical GAAP earnings are as reported.

## Dividend Data (Dates: mm/dd Payment Date: mm/dd/yy)

| Amount ($) | Date Decl. | Ex-Div. Date | Stk. of Record | Payment Date |
|---|---|---|---|---|
| 0.230 | 02/27 | 03/12 | 03/14 | 04/01/08 |
| 0.230 | 04/23 | 06/11 | 06/13 | 07/01/08 |
| 0.230 | 07/23 | 09/10 | 09/12 | 10/01/08 |
| 0.230 | 10/22 | 12/10 | 12/12 | 01/01/09 |

Dividends have been paid since 1942. Source: Company reports.

# Textron Inc.

**STANDARD &POOR'S**

## Business Summary November 10, 2008

CORPORATE OVERVIEW. This $13 billion in revenue aerospace and industrial conglomerate conducts business through five operating segments.

Bell Helicopter (19% of 2007 sales and 9% of operating profits) is the third largest helicopter maker behind United Technologies' Sikorsky Unit and EADS's Eurocopter unit. Bell makes helicopters and tiltrotor aircraft (the V-22 Osprey) for both military and commercial applications, and provides spare parts and service. Bell supplies advanced military helicopters and support (including spare parts, support equipment, technical data, trainers, etc.) to the U.S. government and to military customers outside the U.S. Bell is also a leading supplier of commercially certified helicopters to corporate, offshore petroleum exploration and development, utility, charter, police, fire, rescue and emergency medical helicopter operators. The V-22 Osprey is a military tiltrotor aircraft built in conjunction with Boeing. Bell also makes the Marine Corps. H-1 helicopter (AH-1Z and UH-1Z), with a program of record that calls for 280 production units. Bell is also working on the development of the Armed Reconnaissance Helicopter (ARH) for the Army.

The Defense & Intelligence segment (10% of sales and 12% of profits) consists of the former Textron Systems sub-segment of Bell. D&I was broken out as a separate business segment in April 2008, due to growth in the business. D&I makes precision weapons, airborne and ground-based surveillance systems, sophisticated intelligence and situational awareness software, armored vehicles and turrets, reciprocating piston aircraft engines, and aircraft and missile control actuators, valves and related components. As of March 2008, D&I had produced about 900 armored security vehicles for the U.S. Army since 2005. The contract calls for more than 750 additional units through May 2009. D&I is also a tier-one supplier of unattended ground sensors and intelligent munition systems for the U.S. Army's Future Combat System program.

The Cessna segment (38% of sales and 53% of profits) primarily makes the Cessna brand aircraft. Business lines include Citation business jets, Caravan single engine turboprops, Cessna single-engine piston aircraft, and aftermarket services. Based on revenues, Cessna is the world's fourth largest corporate jet maker, behind Canada's Bombardier, General Dynamics' Gulfstream division, and France's Dassault aviation.

## Company Financials Fiscal Year Ended Dec. 31

### Per Share Data ($)

| | 2007 | 2006 | 2005 | 2004 | 2003 | 2002 | 2001 | 2000 | 1999 | 1998 |
|---|---|---|---|---|---|---|---|---|---|---|
| Tangible Book Value | 2.77 | 4.86 | 8.02 | 7.35 | 8.09 | 6.46 | 6.20 | 5.80 | 5.28 | 2.77 |
| Cash Flow | 4.91 | 3.95 | 3.15 | 2.69 | 2.32 | 2.61 | 2.38 | 2.64 | 3.45 | 2.43 |
| Earnings | 3.59 | 2.72 | 1.89 | 1.33 | 1.03 | 1.30 | 0.58 | 0.95 | 2.03 | 1.34 |
| S&P Core Earnings | 3.51 | 2.66 | 2.06 | 1.01 | 0.59 | 0.14 | -0.70 | NA | NA | NA |
| Dividends | 0.85 | 0.78 | 0.70 | 0.66 | 0.65 | 0.65 | 0.65 | 0.65 | 0.63 | 0.55 |
| Payout Ratio | 24% | 29% | 37% | 50% | 63% | 50% | NM | 68% | 9% | 41% |
| Prices:High | 74.40 | 49.48 | 40.36 | 37.46 | 29.00 | 26.80 | 30.24 | 38.75 | 49.00 | 40.47 |
| Prices:Low | 43.60 | 37.76 | 32.60 | 25.30 | 13.00 | 16.10 | 15.65 | 20.34 | 32.94 | 26.03 |
| P/E Ratio:High | 21 | 18 | 21 | 28 | 28 | 21 | 52 | 41 | 24 | 30 |
| P/E Ratio:Low | 12 | 14 | 17 | 19 | 13 | 12 | 27 | 21 | 16 | 19 |

### Income Statement Analysis (Million $)

| | 2007 | 2006 | 2005 | 2004 | 2003 | 2002 | 2001 | 2000 | 1999 | 1998 |
|---|---|---|---|---|---|---|---|---|---|---|
| Revenue | 13,225 | 11,490 | 10,043 | 10,242 | 9,859 | 10,658 | 12,321 | 13,090 | 11,579 | 9,683 |
| Operating Income | 2,120 | 1,703 | 1,450 | 1,260 | 1,171 | 1,285 | 1,461 | 2,074 | 1,702 | 1,439 |
| Depreciation | 336 | 290 | 303 | 353 | 356 | 368 | 514 | 494 | 440 | 361 |
| Interest Expense | 484 | 438 | 290 | 248 | 283 | 330 | 459 | 492 | 260 | 315 |
| Pretax Income | 1,300 | 437 | 739 | 528 | 388 | 464 | 393 | 585 | 1,004 | 737 |
| Effective Tax Rate | 29.6% | NM | 30.2% | 29.4% | 27.6% | 21.6% | 57.8% | 52.6% | 37.9% | 39.9% |
| Net Income | 915 | 706 | 516 | 373 | 281 | 364 | 166 | 277 | 623 | 443 |
| S&P Core Earnings | 895 | 690 | 565 | 282 | 161 | 38.6 | -202 | NA | NA | NA |

### Balance Sheet & Other Financial Data (Million $)

| | 2007 | 2006 | 2005 | 2004 | 2003 | 2002 | 2001 | 2000 | 1999 | 1998 |
|---|---|---|---|---|---|---|---|---|---|---|
| Cash | 531 | 780 | 796 | 732 | 843 | 307 | 260 | 289 | 209 | 53.0 |
| Current Assets | 4,846 | 4,287 | 4,975 | 4,168 | 3,592 | 3,887 | 4,017 | 3,914 | 3,735 | 4,355 |
| Total Assets | 19,956 | 17,550 | 16,499 | 15,875 | 15,090 | 15,505 | 16,052 | 16,370 | 16,393 | 13,721 |
| Current Liabilities | 7,248 | 2,994 | 3,147 | 2,975 | 2,256 | 2,239 | 3,075 | 3,263 | 3,256 | 3,919 |
| Long Term Debt | 6,384 | 6,150 | 7,079 | 6,141 | 6,144 | 7,038 | 5,962 | 6,648 | 6,142 | 4,192 |
| Common Equity | 3,505 | 2,639 | 3,266 | 3,642 | 3,680 | 3,395 | 3,923 | 3,982 | 4,365 | 2,984 |
| Total Capital | 10,363 | 8,799 | 10,816 | 10,246 | 10,224 | 10,842 | 10,253 | 10,957 | 10,826 | 7,511 |
| Capital Expenditures | 401 | 431 | 365 | 302 | 301 | 296 | 532 | 527 | 532 | 475 |
| Cash Flow | 1,251 | 996 | 819 | 726 | 637 | 732 | 680 | 771 | 1,062 | 803 |
| Current Ratio | 1.2 | 1.4 | 1.6 | 1.4 | 1.6 | 1.7 | 1.3 | 1.2 | 1.1 | 1.1 |
| % Long Term Debt of Capitalization | 61.6 | 69.9 | 65.4 | 59.9 | 60.1 | 64.9 | 58.1 | 60.7 | 56.7 | 55.8 |
| % Net Income of Revenue | 6.9 | 6.1 | 5.1 | 3.6 | 2.9 | 3.4 | 1.3 | 2.1 | 5.4 | 4.6 |
| % Return on Assets | 4.9 | 4.1 | 3.2 | 2.4 | 1.8 | 2.3 | 1.0 | 1.7 | 4.1 | 2.7 |
| % Return on Equity | 29.8 | 23.9 | 14.9 | 10.2 | 7.9 | 9.9 | 4.2 | 6.6 | 16.9 | 14.3 |

Data as orig reptd.; bef. results of disc opers/spec. items. Per share data adj. for stk. divs.; EPS diluted. E-Estimated. NA-Not Available. NM-Not Meaningful. NR-Not Ranked. UR-Under Review.

**Office:** 40 Westminster Street, Providence, RI 02903-2525.
**Telephone:** 401-421-2800.
**Website:** http://www.textron.com
**Chrmn, Pres & CEO:** L.B. Campbell

**COO & EVP:** S.C. Donnelly
**EVP & CFO:** T.R. French
**EVP & General Counsel:** T. O'Donnell
**SVP & Cntlr:** R.L. Yates

**Investor Contact:** D.R. Wilburne (401-457-2353)
**Board Members:** K. M. Bader, L. B. Campbell, R. K. Clark, I. J. Evans, L. K. Fish, J. T. Ford, P. E. Gagne, D. M. Hancock, C. D. Powell, L. G. Trotter, T. B. Wheeler, J. L. Ziemer

**Founded:** 1928
**Domicile:** Delaware
**Employees:** 44,000

The **McGraw·Hill** Companies

# Thermo Fisher Scientific Inc

STANDARD &POOR'S

| S&P Recommendation | STRONG BUY ★★★★★ | Price $34.04 (as of Nov 14, 2008) | 12-Mo. Target Price $68.00 | Investment Style Large-Cap Growth |
| --- | --- | --- | --- | --- |

**GICS Sector** Health Care
**Sub-Industry** Life Sciences Tools & Services

**Summary** Thermo Fisher Scientific was formed through the November 2006 merger of Thermo Electron and Fisher Scientific. TMO is a leading manufacturer and developer of analytical and laboratory instruments and supplies for life science, drug discovery and industrial applications.

## Key Stock Statistics (Source S&P, Vickers, company reports)

| | | | | | | | |
| --- | --- | --- | --- | --- | --- | --- | --- |
| 52-Wk Range | $62.77– 32.80 | S&P Oper. EPS 2008**E** | 3.17 | Market Capitalization(B) | $14.304 | Beta | 1.16 |
| Trailing 12-Month EPS | $2.15 | S&P Oper. EPS 2009**E** | 3.70 | Yield (%) | Nil | S&P 3-Yr. Proj. EPS CAGR(%) | 16 |
| Trailing 12-Month P/E | 15.8 | P/E on S&P Oper. EPS 2008**E** | 10.7 | Dividend Rate/Share | Nil | S&P Credit Rating | BBB+ |
| $10K Invested 5 Yrs Ago | $14,641 | Common Shares Outstg. (M) | 420.2 | Institutional Ownership (%) | 95 | | |

## Price Performance

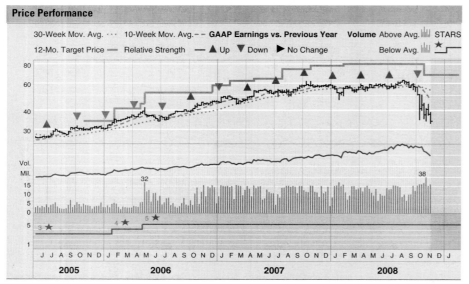

30-Week Mov. Avg. · · ·    10-Week Mov. Avg. — —    **GAAP Earnings vs. Previous Year**    Volume Above Avg. STARS
12-Mo. Target Price —    Relative Strength —    ▲ Up ▼ Down ▶ No Change    Below Avg. ★

Options: ASE, CBOE, Ph

Analysis prepared by **Jeffrey Loo, CFA** on October 29, 2008, when the stock traded at **$ 35.25**.

## Highlights

➤ We see sales growing 8% to $10.5 billion in 2008 and 6% to $11.1 billion in 2009, driven by new products, broad geographic coverage and diverse mix of products amid some uncertainty in various end-markets. We expect Lab Products and Services (LPS) to grow 6% to $6.2 billion and Analytical Technologies (AT) sales to grow 7% to $4.3 billion on moderating life science demand and robust industrial demand. We view this growth rate positively as AT's operating margins are significantly higher than LPS's. However, we think tight credit markets will have an adverse impact on equipment sales.

➤ We expect gross margins to rise 80 basis points on better pricing from sourcing initiative. We also believe TMO should benefit from operational improvements, driving operating margins up 120 basis points. We believe TMO's estimates of $150 million in cost savings and $50 million in revenue synergies within three years of the Fisher merger will prove conservative.

➤ We anticipate 2008 and 2009 operating EPS of $3.17 and $3.70, respectively, before amortization of acquisition-related intangible assets.

## Investment Rationale/Risk

➤ We believe the recent decline in share price is unwarranted. TMO is currently trading at 9.4X our 2009 EPS estimate and at a 0.6X P/E-to-growth ratio, both well below historical levels. We see continued solid revenue growth within each of TMO's end-markets and think TMO's comprehensive product offering drives sales and provides operating leverage and purchasing power to improve margins. We expect further margin expansion from better efficiency as we think the combined TMO and Fisher can use their extensive global sales and distribution network to drive cost and revenue synergies, enabling a potential operating margin expansion of over 300 basis points within three years.

➤ Risks to our recommendation and target price include a slowdown in pharmaceutical R&D spending; an inability to achieve expected costs and revenue synergies; and the potential for a negative foreign currency impact.

➤ Our 12-month target price of $68 assumes a P/E-to-growth (PEG) ratio of 1.15X, in line with peers, based on our 2009 EPS estimate of $3.70 and a three year growth rate of 16%.

## Qualitative Risk Assessment

| LOW | MEDIUM | HIGH |
| --- | --- | --- |

Our risk assessment reflects TMO's broad product lines and geographic coverage, spread across the life sciences, health care and industrial marketplaces, which we believe reduces risk. However, TMO has a proactive acquisition strategy that we believe raises its risk profile.

## Quantitative Evaluations

**S&P Quality Ranking**    B-

| D | C | B- | B | B+ | A- | A | A+ |
| --- | --- | --- | --- | --- | --- | --- | --- |

**Relative Strength Rank**    MODERATE

39

LOWEST = 1    HIGHEST = 99

## Revenue/Earnings Data

**Revenue (Million $)**

| | 1Q | 2Q | 3Q | 4Q | Year |
| --- | --- | --- | --- | --- | --- |
| 2008 | 2,554 | 2,710 | 2,588 | -- | -- |
| 2007 | 2,338 | 2,386 | 2,401 | 2,621 | 9,746 |
| 2006 | 684.3 | 713.5 | 725.0 | 1,669 | 3,792 |
| 2005 | 559.2 | 653.6 | 679.4 | 740.8 | 2,633 |
| 2004 | 525.0 | 525.3 | 542.3 | 613.3 | 2,206 |
| 2003 | 500.2 | 516.4 | 497.1 | 583.4 | 2,097 |

**Earnings Per Share ($)**

| | 1Q | 2Q | 3Q | 4Q | Year |
| --- | --- | --- | --- | --- | --- |
| 2008 | 0.54 | 0.56 | 0.50 | E0.87 | E3.17 |
| 2007 | 0.31 | 0.42 | 0.51 | 0.53 | 1.76 |
| 2006 | 0.26 | 0.30 | 0.30 | 0.08 | 0.82 |
| 2005 | 0.28 | 0.35 | 0.25 | 0.34 | 1.21 |
| 2004 | 0.24 | 0.30 | 0.26 | 0.52 | 1.31 |
| 2003 | 0.19 | 0.32 | 0.24 | 0.30 | 1.04 |

Fiscal year ended Dec. 31. Next earnings report expected: Early February. EPS Estimates based on S&P Operating Earnings; historical GAAP earnings are as reported.

## Dividend Data

No cash dividends have been paid.

# Thermo Fisher Scientific Inc

## Business Summary October 29, 2008

CORPORATE OVERVIEW. In November 2006, Thermo Electron Corp. and Fisher Scientific completed a stock-for-stock merger. The combined company was renamed Thermo Fisher Scientific (TMO) and is a leading provider of life science and laboratory analytical instruments, equipment, reagents and consumables, software and services for research, analysis, discovery and diagnosis. We expect annual revenues in excess of $9 billion, with over 30,000 employees in 38 countries providing services and sales in over 150 countries. Major end markets served include drug discovery, proteomics research, biopharma services, molecular diagnostics, immunohistochemistry, cell screening, environmental regulatory compliance, and food safety. TMO believes these markets represent a combined $70 billion to $80 billion annual marketplace. We believe TMO is the largest company within its marketplace, with the broadest product offering and geographic coverage.

The legacy Thermo Electron business focuses primarily on the development and manufacture of analytical systems, instruments and components and provides solutions to monitor, collect and analyze data. These instruments are used primarily in life science, drug discovery, clinical, environmental and industrial laboratory applications. The legacy Fisher Scientific business focuses on providing a broad range of over 600,000 scientific research, health care and safety-related products and services. Customers included pharmaceutical and biotechnology companies, colleges and universities, medical research institutions, hospitals and reference labs, and research and development labs.

The company now reports through two business segments: Analytical Technologies and Laboratory Products and Services. Analytical Technologies should account for about 40% of sales and focuses on scientific instruments, bioscience reagents, lab informatics and automation, diagnostics, environmental monitoring instruments and industrial process instruments. Analytical Technologies is comprised primarily of the legacy Thermo Electron business. Laboratory Products and Services, comprised primarily of legacy Fisher Scientific business should account for about 60% of sales and focuses on lab equipment and consumables and biopharma outsourcing services.

## Company Financials Fiscal Year Ended Dec. 31

| Per Share Data ($) | 2007 | 2006 | 2005 | 2004 | 2003 | 2002 | 2001 | 2000 | 1999 | 1998 |
|---|---|---|---|---|---|---|---|---|---|---|
| Tangible Book Value | NM | NM | 2.32 | 6.19 | 5.00 | 3.79 | 1.33 | 6.34 | 5.03 | 1.51 |
| Cash Flow | 3.46 | 2.00 | 1.95 | 1.70 | 1.35 | 1.35 | 0.81 | 0.94 | 0.63 | 1.90 |
| Earnings | 1.76 | 0.82 | 1.21 | 1.31 | 1.04 | 1.12 | 0.27 | 0.36 | -0.11 | 1.04 |
| S&P Core Earnings | 1.78 | 0.83 | 1.01 | 1.18 | 0.79 | 0.50 | 0.02 | NA | NA | NA |
| Dividends | Nil | Nil | Nil | Nil | Nil | Nil | Nil | Nil | Nil | Nil |
| Payout Ratio | Nil | Nil | Nil | Nil | Nil | Nil | Nil | Nil | Nil | Nil |
| Prices:High | 62.02 | 46.34 | 31.87 | 31.40 | 25.40 | 24.60 | 30.62 | 31.24 | 20.25 | 44.25 |
| Prices:Low | 43.60 | 29.95 | 23.94 | 24.00 | 16.89 | 14.33 | 16.55 | 14.00 | 12.50 | 13.56 |
| P/E Ratio:High | 35 | 57 | 26 | 24 | 24 | 22 | NM | 87 | NM | 43 |
| P/E Ratio:Low | 25 | 37 | 20 | 18 | 16 | 13 | NM | 39 | NM | 13 |

| Income Statement Analysis (Million $) | | | | | | | | | | |
|---|---|---|---|---|---|---|---|---|---|---|
| Revenue | 9,746 | 3,792 | 2,633 | 2,206 | 2,097 | 2,086 | 2,188 | 2,281 | 2,471 | 3,868 |
| Operating Income | 1,823 | 528 | 404 | 319 | 292 | 264 | 265 | 296 | 362 | 538 |
| Depreciation | 757 | 241 | 123 | 66.1 | 58.5 | 56.4 | 98.5 | 97.5 | 114 | 162 |
| Interest Expense | 140 | 51.9 | 26.7 | 11.0 | 18.7 | Nil | 71.8 | Nil | Nil | 104 |
| Pretax Income | 881 | 209 | 286 | 259 | 219 | 288 | 70.7 | 185 | 37.5 | 392 |
| Effective Tax Rate | 11.5% | 20.6% | 30.6% | 15.8% | 21.0% | 32.3% | 38.1% | 60.7% | NM | 43.6% |
| Net Income | 780 | 166 | 198 | 218 | 173 | 195 | 49.6 | 62.0 | -14.6 | 177 |
| S&P Core Earnings | 785 | 169 | 164 | 196 | 131 | 79.3 | 5.63 | NA | NA | NA |

| Balance Sheet & Other Financial Data (Million $) | | | | | | | | | | |
|---|---|---|---|---|---|---|---|---|---|---|
| Cash | 639 | 667 | 214 | 327 | 304 | 339 | 298 | 506 | 282 | 397 |
| Current Assets | 3,665 | 3,660 | 1,354 | 1,470 | 1,395 | 1,772 | 1,965 | 2,466 | 2,517 | 3,301 |
| Total Assets | 21,207 | 21,262 | 4,252 | 3,577 | 3,389 | 3,647 | 3,825 | 4,863 | 5,182 | 6,332 |
| Current Liabilities | 1,902 | 2,152 | 792 | 579 | 685 | 1,104 | 1,142 | 729 | 1,066 | 1,138 |
| Long Term Debt | 2,046 | 2,181 | 469 | 226 | 230 | 451 | 728 | 1,528 | 1,566 | 2,026 |
| Common Equity | 14,488 | 13,912 | 2,793 | 2,666 | 2,383 | 2,033 | 1,908 | 2,534 | 2,014 | 2,248 |
| Total Capital | 18,814 | 18,650 | 3,327 | 2,907 | 2,624 | 2,495 | 2,650 | 4,098 | 4,026 | 5,025 |
| Capital Expenditures | 176 | 76.8 | 43.5 | 50.0 | 46.1 | 51.2 | 84.8 | 74.0 | 87.2 | 148 |
| Cash Flow | 1,536 | 407 | 322 | 285 | 231 | 252 | 148 | 160 | 99.1 | 339 |
| Current Ratio | 1.9 | 1.7 | 1.7 | 2.5 | 2.0 | 1.6 | 1.7 | 3.4 | 2.4 | 2.9 |
| % Long Term Debt of Capitalization | 10.9 | 11.7 | 14.1 | 7.8 | 8.7 | 18.1 | 27.4 | 37.3 | 38.9 | 40.3 |
| % Net Income of Revenue | 8.0 | 4.4 | 7.5 | 9.9 | 8.2 | 9.4 | 2.3 | 2.7 | NM | 4.6 |
| % Return on Assets | 3.7 | 1.3 | 5.1 | 6.3 | 4.9 | 5.2 | 1.1 | 1.2 | NM | 2.9 |
| % Return on Equity | 5.5 | 2.0 | 7.3 | 8.7 | 7.8 | 9.9 | 2.2 | 2.7 | NM | 8.3 |

Data as orig reptd.; bef. results of disc opers/spec. items. Per share data adj. for stk. divs.; EPS diluted. E-Estimated. NA-Not Available. NM-Not Meaningful. NR-Not Ranked. UR-Under Review.

**Office:** 81 Wyman St PO Box 9046, Waltham, MA 02254-9046.
**Telephone:** 781-622-1000.
**Website:** http://www.fishersci.com
**Chrmn:** J.P. Manzi

**Pres & CEO:** M.E. Dekkers
**COO & EVP:** M.N. Casper
**SVP & CFO:** P.M. Wilver
**SVP, Secy & General Counsel:** S.H. Hoogasian

**Investor Contact:** K.J. Apicerno (781-622-1111)
**Board Members:** M. A. Bell, M. E. Dekkers, S. Kaufman, J. C. Lewent, P. J. Manning, J. P. Manzi, W. G. Parrett, M. E. Porter, S. M. Sperling, E. S. Ullian

**Founded:** 1956
**Domicile:** Delaware
**Employees:** 33,000

# 3M Co

STANDARD
&POOR'S

| S&P Recommendation | BUY ★★★★☆ | Price | 12-Mo. Target Price | Investment Style |
|---|---|---|---|---|
| | | $63.06 (as of Nov 14, 2008) | $67.00 | Large-Cap Growth |

**GICS Sector** Industrials
**Sub-Industry** Industrial Conglomerates

**Summary** This diversified global company has operations in electronics, health care, industrial, consumer and office, telecommunications, safety and security, and other markets.

## Key Stock Statistics (Source S&P, Vickers, company reports)

| | | | | | | | |
|---|---|---|---|---|---|---|---|
| 52-Wk Range | $88.70–50.01 | S&P Oper. EPS 2008E | 5.47 | Market Capitalization(B) | $43.698 | Beta | 0.81 |
| Trailing 12-Month EPS | $5.29 | S&P Oper. EPS 2009E | 5.70 | Yield (%) | 3.17 | S&P 3-Yr. Proj. EPS CAGR(%) | 6 |
| Trailing 12-Month P/E | 11.9 | P/E on S&P Oper. EPS 2008E | 11.5 | Dividend Rate/Share | $2.00 | S&P Credit Rating | AA |
| $10K Invested 5 Yrs Ago | $8,966 | Common Shares Outstg. (M) | 693.0 | Institutional Ownership (%) | 67 | | |

## Price Performance

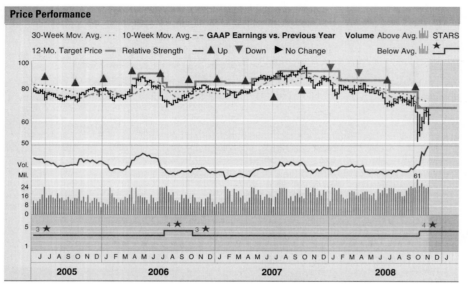

30-Week Mov. Avg. · · · 10-Week Mov. Avg. - - GAAP Earnings vs. Previous Year    Volume Above Avg. STARS
12-Mo. Target Price — Relative Strength — ▲ Up ▼ Down ► No Change    Below Avg. ★

Options: ASE, CBOE, P, Ph

Analysis prepared by **Mathew Christy, CFA** on October 27, 2008, when the stock traded at **$ 62.33**.

## Qualitative Risk Assessment

| LOW | MEDIUM | HIGH |
|---|---|---|

Our risk assessment reflects our view of the company's historical stability in earnings and dividends, its leading position in many of the end markets that it serves, a strong balance sheet with a relatively low amount of debt, and free cash flow that has averaged about 95% of net income over the past 10 years.

## Quantitative Evaluations

**S&P Quality Ranking**  A+

| D | C | B- | B | B+ | A- | A | A+ |
|---|---|---|---|---|---|---|---|

**Relative Strength Rank**  STRONG

86

LOWEST = 1    HIGHEST = 99

## Revenue/Earnings Data

**Revenue (Million $)**

| | 1Q | 2Q | 3Q | 4Q | Year |
|---|---|---|---|---|---|
| 2008 | 6,463 | 6,739 | 6,558 | -- | -- |
| 2007 | 5,937 | 6,142 | 6,177 | 6,206 | 24,462 |
| 2006 | 5,595 | 5,688 | 5,858 | 5,782 | 22,923 |
| 2005 | 5,166 | 5,294 | 5,382 | 5,325 | 21,167 |
| 2004 | 4,939 | 5,012 | 4,969 | 5,091 | 20,011 |
| 2003 | 4,318 | 4,580 | 4,616 | 4,718 | 18,232 |

**Earnings Per Share ($)**

| | | | | | |
|---|---|---|---|---|---|
| 2008 | 1.38 | 1.33 | 1.41 | E1.32 | E5.47 |
| 2007 | 1.85 | 1.25 | 1.32 | 1.17 | 5.60 |
| 2006 | 1.17 | 1.15 | 1.18 | 1.57 | 5.06 |
| 2005 | 1.03 | 1.00 | 1.10 | 1.04 | 4.16 |
| 2004 | 0.90 | 0.97 | 0.97 | 0.91 | 3.75 |
| 2003 | 0.63 | 0.78 | 0.83 | 0.77 | 3.02 |

Fiscal year ended Dec. 31. Next earnings report expected: Late January. EPS Estimates based on S&P Operating Earnings; historical GAAP earnings are as reported.

## Highlights

➤ We see revenues increasing nearly 6% in 2008 and 3% in 2009. We expect revenues this year and next to benefit from acquisitions, further penetration of the Asia-Pacific and Latin America regions, the development of adjacent market opportunities, and an expanding pipeline of new products, offset somewhat by weakness in the Optical unit and a slowing economy. We expect slightly positive organic revenue growth in 2008, but see contributions from acquisitions and currency leading to better results overall.

➤ We foresee a small decline in 2008 EBIT margins, as projected benefits from Six Sigma and higher volumes are offset by an expected decline in profitability in the Display and Graphics segment, R&D spending, and acquisitions. In 2009, we expect EBIT margins to remain relatively flat with 2008. Over the next few years, we believe that continued efforts to streamline this diverse company will enable MMM to maintain above-average profitability.

➤ Assuming a steady 32% effective tax rate, we forecast MMM's operating EPS for 2008 and 2009 will be $5.47 and $5.60, respectively.

## Investment Rationale/Risk

➤ We expect decelerating growth in MMM's industrial, transportation, consumer and office businesses due to the effects of the slowing economy. In addition, we see overall gains being pressured by continued declines in the Optical unit. However, we believe MMM's broad diversity will provide insulation against a downturn, as we expect continued strong growth in segments such as the Health Care and Security units, and we are positive on MMM's ability to generate returns on capital greater than 20% and strong cash flows.

➤ Risks to our recommendation and target price include slower global economic growth, lower than projected growth in the optical display business, and execution risk associated with acquisitions and/or cost saving initiatives.

➤ Our 12-month target price of $67 is based on a blend of valuations. Our DCF model, which assumes 3% growth in perpetuity and a 9.5% discount rate, indicates intrinsic value of about $70. In terms of relative valuation, we apply a P/E multiple of about 11X, ahead of peers and equal to historical low multiples, to our 2009 EPS estimate, suggesting a value of $64.

## Dividend Data (Dates: mm/dd Payment Date: mm/dd/yy)

| Amount ($) | Date Decl. | Ex-Div. Date | Stk. of Record | Payment Date |
|---|---|---|---|---|
| 0.500 | 02/11 | 02/20 | 02/22 | 03/12/08 |
| 0.500 | 05/13 | 05/21 | 05/23 | 06/12/08 |
| 0.500 | 08/11 | 08/20 | 08/22 | 09/12/08 |
| 0.500 | 11/10 | 11/19 | 11/21 | 12/12/08 |

Dividends have been paid since 1916. Source: Company reports.

---

# 3M Co

## Business Summary October 27, 2008

CORPORATE OVERVIEW. During the first quarter of 2006, 3M combined its Industrial and Transportation segments. The new reportable business units are Industrial and Transportation; Health Care; Display and Graphics; Consumer and Office; Electro and Communications; and Safety, Security and Protection Services.

The Industrial and Transportation segment (30% of 2007 revenues with a 21% operating margin) serves a broad range of markets, from appliances and electronics to paper and packaging, food and beverages, automotive, automotive aftermarket, aerospace and marine, and other transportation-related industries. Products include pressure-sensitive tapes, abrasives, adhesives, specialty materials, supply chain management software and solutions, insulation components, films, masking tapes, fasteners, adhesives and abrasives used in the repair and maintenance of automotive, marine, aircraft and other specialty vehicles.

The Health Care segment (16% and 28%) serves markets worldwide, including medical and surgical, pharmaceutical, dental, health information systems and personal care. Products provided include medical and surgical, infection pre-

vention, pharmaceuticals, drug delivery systems, dental products, health information systems, personal care and other products.

The Display and Graphics segment (16% and 31%) serves markets that include electronic display, touch screen, commercial graphics and traffic control materials. Optical products include Vikkuiti display enhancement films for electronic displays, lens systems for projection televisions, and 3M MicroTouch touch screens and touch monitors. Other products include 3M Scotchlite reflective sheeting for transportation safety and Scotchprint commercial graphics systems.

The Consumer and Office segment (14% and 20%) serves markets that include consumer, office, education, home improvement, building maintenance, food service and other markets. Offerings consist of office supplies, construction and home improvement products, protective materials, and visual systems.

## Company Financials Fiscal Year Ended Dec. 31

| Per Share Data ($) | 2007 | 2006 | 2005 | 2004 | 2003 | 2002 | 2001 | 2000 | 1999 | 1998 |
|---|---|---|---|---|---|---|---|---|---|---|
| Tangible Book Value | 13.40 | 7.04 | 8.13 | 9.62 | 6.62 | 4.91 | 6.23 | 7.17 | 7.06 | 7.39 |
| Cash Flow | 7.06 | 6.48 | 5.43 | 5.01 | 4.23 | 3.70 | 3.15 | 3.60 | 3.28 | 2.55 |
| Earnings | 5.60 | 5.06 | 4.16 | 3.75 | 3.02 | 2.49 | 1.79 | 2.32 | 2.17 | 1.49 |
| S&P Core Earnings | 4.68 | 4.26 | 4.13 | 3.66 | 2.91 | 1.71 | 0.94 | NA | NA | NA |
| Dividends | 1.92 | 1.84 | 1.68 | 1.44 | 1.32 | 1.24 | 1.20 | 1.16 | 1.12 | 1.10 |
| Payout Ratio | 34% | 36% | 40% | 38% | 44% | 50% | 67% | 50% | 52% | 74% |
| Prices:High | 97.00 | 88.35 | 87.45 | 90.29 | 85.40 | 65.78 | 63.50 | 61.47 | 51.69 | 48.94 |
| Prices:Low | 72.90 | 67.05 | 69.71 | 73.31 | 59.73 | 50.00 | 42.93 | 39.09 | 34.66 | 32.81 |
| P/E Ratio:High | 17 | 17 | 21 | 24 | 28 | 26 | 35 | 26 | 24 | 33 |
| P/E Ratio:Low | 13 | 13 | 17 | 20 | 20 | 20 | 24 | 17 | 16 | 22 |
| **Income Statement Analysis (Million $)** | | | | | | | | | | |
| Revenue | 24,462 | 22,923 | 21,167 | 20,011 | 18,232 | 16,332 | 16,079 | 16,724 | 15,659 | 15,021 |
| Operating Income | 6,584 | 6,252 | 5,995 | 5,577 | 4,677 | 4,000 | 3,274 | 3,898 | 3,828 | 3,398 |
| Depreciation | 1,072 | 1,079 | 986 | 999 | 964 | 954 | 1,089 | 1,025 | 900 | 866 |
| Interest Expense | 210 | 122 | 82.0 | 69.0 | 84.0 | 80.0 | 124 | 111 | 109 | 139 |
| Pretax Income | 6,115 | 5,625 | 4,983 | 4,555 | 3,657 | 3,005 | 2,186 | 2,974 | 2,880 | 1,952 |
| Effective Tax Rate | 32.1% | 30.6% | 34.0% | 33.0% | 32.9% | 32.1% | 32.1% | 34.5% | 35.8% | 35.1% |
| Net Income | 4,096 | 3,851 | 3,234 | 2,990 | 2,403 | 1,974 | 1,430 | 1,857 | 1,763 | 1,213 |
| S&P Core Earnings | 3,418 | 3,242 | 3,227 | 2,918 | 2,319 | 1,356 | 750 | NA | NA | NA |
| **Balance Sheet & Other Financial Data (Million $)** | | | | | | | | | | |
| Cash | 2,475 | 1,918 | 1,072 | 2,757 | 1,836 | 618 | 616 | 302 | 387 | 448 |
| Current Assets | 9,838 | 8,946 | 7,115 | 8,720 | 7,720 | 6,059 | 6,296 | 6,379 | 6,066 | 6,318 |
| Total Assets | 24,694 | 21,294 | 20,513 | 20,708 | 17,600 | 15,329 | 14,606 | 14,522 | 13,896 | 14,153 |
| Current Liabilities | 5,362 | 7,323 | 5,238 | 6,071 | 5,082 | 4,457 | 4,509 | 4,754 | 3,819 | 4,386 |
| Long Term Debt | 4,088 | 1,047 | 1,309 | 727 | 1,735 | 2,140 | 1,520 | 971 | 1,480 | 1,614 |
| Common Equity | 11,747 | 10,097 | 10,100 | 10,378 | 7,885 | 5,993 | 6,086 | 6,531 | 6,289 | 5,936 |
| Total Capital | 16,515 | 11,433 | 11,409 | 11,105 | 9,620 | 8,133 | 7,606 | 7,502 | 7,769 | 7,550 |
| Capital Expenditures | 1,422 | 1,168 | 943 | 937 | 677 | 763 | 980 | 1,115 | 1,039 | 1,430 |
| Cash Flow | 5,168 | 4,930 | 4,220 | 3,989 | 3,367 | 2,928 | 2,519 | 2,882 | 2,663 | 2,079 |
| Current Ratio | 1.8 | 1.2 | 1.4 | 1.4 | 1.5 | 1.4 | 1.4 | 1.3 | 1.6 | 1.4 |
| % Long Term Debt of Capitalization | 24.8 | 9.4 | 11.5 | 6.5 | 18.0 | 26.3 | 20.0 | 12.9 | 19.1 | 21.3 |
| % Net Income of Revenue | 16.7 | 16.8 | 15.3 | 14.9 | 13.2 | 12.1 | 8.9 | 11.1 | 11.3 | 8.1 |
| % Return on Assets | 17.8 | 18.4 | 15.7 | 15.6 | 14.6 | 13.2 | 9.8 | 13.1 | 12.6 | 8.9 |
| % Return on Equity | 37.7 | 37.3 | 31.6 | 32.7 | 34.6 | 32.7 | 22.7 | 29.0 | 28.8 | 20.5 |

Data as orig reptd.; bef. results of disc opers/spec. items. Per share data adj. for stk. divs.; EPS diluted. E-Estimated. NA-Not Available. NM-Not Meaningful. NR-Not Ranked. UR-Under Review.

**Office:** 3M Center, St. Paul, MN 55144-1000.
**Telephone:** 651-733-1110.
**Email:** innovation@mmm.com
**Website:** http://www.3m.com

**Chrmn, Pres & CEO:** G.W. Buckley
**COO:** I.G. Thulin
**EVP & CTO:** F.J. Palensky
**SVP & CFO:** P.D. Campbell

**SVP & General Counsel:** M.I. Smith
**Investor Contact:** M. Colin (651-733-8206)
**Board Members:** L. G. Alvarado, G. W. Buckley, V. D. Coffman, M. L. Eskew, W. Farrell, H. L. Henkel, E. M. Liddy, R. S. Morrison, A. L. Peters, R. J. Ulrich

**Founded:** 1902
**Domicile:** Delaware
**Employees:** 76,239

# Tiffany & Co.

**STANDARD &POOR'S**

| S&P Recommendation HOLD ★★★☆☆ | Price $20.31 (as of Nov 14, 2008) | 12-Mo. Target Price $30.00 | Investment Style Large-Cap Growth |
|---|---|---|---|

**GICS Sector** Consumer Discretionary
**Sub-Industry** Specialty Stores

**Summary** Tiffany is a leading international retailer, designer, manufacturer and distributor of fine jewelry and gift items.

## Key Stock Statistics (Source S&P, Vickers, company reports)

| | | | | | | | |
|---|---|---|---|---|---|---|---|
| 52-Wk Range | $51.13– 18.73 | S&P Oper. EPS 2009E | 2.80 | Market Capitalization(B) | $2.519 | Beta | 1.63 |
| Trailing 12-Month EPS | $2.68 | S&P Oper. EPS 2010E | 2.85 | Yield (%) | 3.35 | S&P 3-Yr. Proj. EPS CAGR(%) | 10 |
| Trailing 12-Month P/E | 7.6 | P/E on S&P Oper. EPS 2009E | 7.3 | Dividend Rate/Share | $0.68 | S&P Credit Rating | NR |
| $10K Invested 5 Yrs Ago | $4,924 | Common Shares Outstg. (M) | 124.0 | Institutional Ownership (%) | 100 | | |

## Price Performance

30-Week Mov. Avg. ···· 10-Week Mov. Avg. - - GAAP Earnings vs. Previous Year Volume Above Avg. STARS
12-Mo. Target Price — Relative Strength — ▲ Up ▼ Down ► No Change Below Avg.

Options: CBOE, P, Ph

Analysis prepared by **Marie Driscoll, CFA** on October 15, 2008, when the stock traded at **$ 26.27**.

## Qualitative Risk Assessment

| LOW | MEDIUM | HIGH |
|---|---|---|

Our risk assessment reflects TIF's favorable market position as a premier global luxury brand, as well as its improving profit margin trends, offset by the uncertain outlook for U.S. consumer discretionary spending.

## Quantitative Evaluations

**S&P Quality Ranking**      **A**

| D | C | B- | B | B+ | A- | A | A+ |
|---|---|---|---|---|---|---|---|

**Relative Strength Rank**     **WEAK**

29

LOWEST = 1      HIGHEST = 99

## Revenue/Earnings Data

**Revenue (Million $)**

| | 1Q | 2Q | 3Q | 4Q | Year |
|---|---|---|---|---|---|
| 2009 | 668.2 | 732.4 | -- | -- | -- |
| 2008 | 595.7 | 662.6 | 627.3 | 1,053 | 2,939 |
| 2007 | 539.2 | 574.9 | 547.8 | 986.4 | 2,648 |
| 2006 | 509.9 | 526.7 | 500.1 | 858.5 | 2,395 |
| 2005 | 457.0 | 476.6 | 461.2 | 810.1 | 2,205 |
| 2004 | 395.8 | 442.5 | 430.1 | 731.6 | 2,000 |

**Earnings Per Share ($)**

| | | | | | |
|---|---|---|---|---|---|
| 2009 | 0.50 | 0.63 | E0.42 | E1.25 | E2.80 |
| 2008 | 0.36 | 0.63 | 0.73 | 0.89 | 2.40 |
| 2007 | 0.30 | 0.29 | 0.21 | 1.02 | 1.80 |
| 2006 | 0.27 | 0.35 | 0.16 | 0.97 | 1.75 |
| 2005 | 0.25 | 0.22 | 0.12 | 1.48 | 2.05 |
| 2004 | 0.24 | 0.28 | 0.19 | 0.74 | 1.45 |

Fiscal year ended Jan. 31. Next earnings report expected: Early December. EPS Estimates based on S&P Operating Earnings; historical GAAP earnings are as reported.

## Highlights

➤ In FY 09 (Jan.), we expect to see a 13% increase in TIF's worldwide locations, equating to about 9% worldwide square footage growth, with expansion focused internationally. TIF is testing a smaller retail format in the U.S. which could boost its addressable market to 170 stores, from 100 if successful. On the product front, eyeglasses and watches were launched in January 2008 as the company embarked on a lifestyle branding strategy.

➤ We see about a 9% increase in TIF's FY 09 sales, to $3.2 billion. We see same store sales weakening globally, but remaining positive internationally and turning negative in the U.S. in the second half of FY 09. New store productivity should support the sales gain along with an estimated 5% lift in direct marketing sales. We expect weakness in Japan and the U.S. to be offset by strength in Asia/Pacific and Latin America. We look for sales growth to slow to 5% in FY 10.

➤ We project a flat operating margin in FY 09 at 18% of sales and look for about 100 bps contraction in FY 10 reflecting reduced store productivity and difficulties leveraging fixed expenses.

## Investment Rationale/Risk

➤ We see continued deterioration in economic fundamentals that impact discretionary spending along with negative investor sentiment towards the luxury goods sector which we believe is reflected in the current valuation. We see muted demand in tandem with recession-like economic trends in most developed nations. Long term, we think TIF has a strong global brand that is under-penetrated, with lucrative expansion opportunities in continental and eastern Europe.

➤ Risks to our recommendation and target price include better than expected sales, same store sales and earnings; a short shallow recession, stronger than expected global consumer demand for luxury goods and reduced competition from European luxury brands and independent high-end jewelers. Our corporate governance concerns include a lack of performance reviews of individual directors and the non-disclosure of specific hurdle rates for performance-based equity incentive awards.

➤ We derive our 12-month target price of $30 by applying a P/E of 10.5X to our FY 10 EPS estimate, a modest discount to global luxury goods peers.

## Dividend Data (Dates: mm/dd Payment Date: mm/dd/yy)

| Amount ($) | Date Decl. | Ex-Div. Date | Stk. of Record | Payment Date |
|---|---|---|---|---|
| 0.150 | 11/15 | 12/18 | 12/20 | 01/10/08 |
| 0.150 | 02/21 | 03/18 | 03/20 | 04/10/08 |
| 0.170 | 05/15 | 06/18 | 06/20 | 07/10/08 |
| 0.170 | 08/21 | 09/18 | 09/22 | 10/10/08 |

Dividends have been paid since 1988. Source: Company reports.

---

**Please read the Required Disclosures and Analyst Certification on the last page of this report.**

The McGraw-Hill Companies

# Tiffany & Co.

STANDARD
&POOR'S

## Business Summary October 15, 2008

CORPORATE OVERVIEW. Charles Lewis Tiffany founded Tiffany & Co. in 1837. Jewelry is the company's primary sales driver, accounting for 86% of FY 08 (Jan.) net sales. The Tiffany & Co. brand also encompasses timepieces, sterling silver merchandise, china, crystal, stationery, fragrances, and personal accessories. TIF additionally sells other brands of timepieces and tableware in its U.S. stores.

Products are sold via four distribution channels: U.S. retail, comprised of company-owned stores and non-Internet, business-to-business sales (50% of FY 08 net sales); international retail (41%), including both retail and wholesale sales and a limited amount of business-to-business and Internet sales; U.S. direct marketing (6%), consisting of Internet, direct mail catalog and business-to-business Internet sales; and other (3%), which reflects sales transacted under trademarks and trade names other than Tiffany & Co., as well as wholesale sales of diamonds that do not meet the company's quality standards.

CORPORATE STRATEGY. Diamonds are at the heart of TIF's merchandise offering, which also includes colored gemstones and silver and gold fashion jewelry. In FY 08, the company produced 59% of its jewelry merchandise,

based on cost, and purchased almost all non-jewelry merchandise from third-party vendors. To drive sales, TIF introduces new products annually. In FY 07 architect Frank Gehry was added to TIF's list of outside designers and his designs accounted for 2% of FY 07 and FY 08 sales. Other outside designers whose jewelry is licensed and sold exclusively under the Tiffany & Co. brand include Jean Schlumberger, Elsa Peretti (11% of FY 08 sales) and Paloma Picasso (3%).

TIF believes that its multi-channel distribution represents a competitive advantage in a large and fragmented industry. In recent years, the company has expanded its direct marketing business, with a focus on e-commerce. TIF offers over 3,500 products through its U.S. consumer Web site, www.tiffany.com, which was launched in FY 00. The company extended e-commerce purchase capabilities to the U.K. in FY 02 and to both Japan and Canada in FY 06, and launched an informational Web site for China in FY 07.

## Company Financials Fiscal Year Ended Jan. 31

| Per Share Data ($) | 2008 | 2007 | 2006 | 2005 | 2004 | 2003 | 2002 | 2001 | 2000 | 1999 |
|---|---|---|---|---|---|---|---|---|---|---|
| Tangible Book Value | 12.92 | 13.28 | 12.85 | 11.77 | 10.01 | 8.34 | 7.15 | 6.34 | 5.23 | 3.72 |
| Cash Flow | 3.28 | 2.64 | 2.50 | 2.79 | 2.06 | 1.80 | 1.58 | 1.56 | 1.25 | 0.83 |
| Earnings | 2.40 | 1.80 | 1.75 | 2.05 | 1.45 | 1.28 | 1.15 | 1.26 | 0.98 | 0.63 |
| S&P Core Earnings | 1.95 | 1.84 | 1.80 | 1.22 | 1.37 | 1.16 | 1.09 | 1.20 | NA | NA |
| Dividends | 0.38 | 0.38 | 0.30 | 0.23 | 0.19 | 0.16 | 0.16 | 0.15 | 0.11 | 0.09 |
| Payout Ratio | 16% | 16% | 17% | 11% | 13% | 13% | 14% | 12% | 11% | 14% |
| Calendar Year | 2007 | 2006 | 2005 | 2004 | 2003 | 2002 | 2001 | 2000 | 1999 | 1998 |
| Prices:High | 57.34 | 41.29 | 43.80 | 45.22 | 49.45 | 41.00 | 38.25 | 45.38 | 45.00 | 13.00 |
| Prices:Low | 38.17 | 29.63 | 28.60 | 27.00 | 21.60 | 19.40 | 19.90 | 27.09 | 12.63 | 6.75 |
| P/E Ratio:High | 24 | 23 | 25 | 22 | 34 | 32 | 33 | 36 | 46 | 21 |
| P/E Ratio:Low | 16 | 16 | 16 | 13 | 15 | 15 | 17 | 22 | 13 | 11 |

| Income Statement Analysis (Million $) | | | | | | | | | | |
|---|---|---|---|---|---|---|---|---|---|---|
| Revenue | 2,939 | 2,648 | 2,395 | 2,205 | 2,000 | 1,707 | 1,607 | 1,668 | 1,462 | 1,169 |
| Operating Income | NA | 533 | 492 | 403 | 446 | 397 | 375 | 374 | 298 | 191 |
| Depreciation | 122 | 118 | 109 | 108 | 90.4 | 78.0 | 64.6 | 46.7 | 41.5 | 29.7 |
| Interest Expense | NA | 26.1 | 23.1 | 22.0 | 14.9 | 15.1 | 19.8 | 16.2 | 15.0 | 9.33 |
| Pretax Income | 522 | 404 | 368 | 472 | 343 | 300 | 289 | 318 | 248 | 156 |
| Effective Tax Rate | 36.6% | 37.2% | 30.8% | 35.6% | 37.1% | 36.6% | 40.0% | 40.0% | 41.3% | 42.1% |
| Net Income | 331 | 254 | 255 | 304 | 216 | 190 | 174 | 191 | 146 | 90.1 |
| S&P Core Earnings | 269 | 260 | 261 | 181 | 204 | 173 | 164 | 181 | NA | NA |

| Balance Sheet & Other Financial Data (Million $) | | | | | | | | | | |
|---|---|---|---|---|---|---|---|---|---|---|
| Cash | 247 | 177 | 394 | 188 | 276 | 156 | 174 | 196 | 217 | 189 |
| Current Assets | NA | 1,707 | 1,699 | 1,608 | 1,348 | 1,070 | 954 | 1,005 | 892 | 816 |
| Total Assets | 2,922 | 2,846 | 2,777 | 2,666 | 2,391 | 1,924 | 1,630 | 1,568 | 1,344 | 1,057 |
| Current Liabilities | NA | 453 | 365 | 400 | 395 | 300 | 341 | 337 | 281 | 293 |
| Long Term Debt | NA | 406 | 427 | 398 | 393 | 297 | 179 | 242 | 250 | 194 |
| Common Equity | 1,637 | 1,805 | 1,831 | 1,701 | 1,468 | 1,208 | 1,037 | 925 | 757 | 516 |
| Total Capital | NA | 2,211 | 2,257 | 2,132 | 1,884 | 1,505 | 1,216 | 1,168 | 1,007 | 711 |
| Capital Expenditures | 186 | 182 | 157 | 142 | 273 | 220 | 171 | 108 | 171 | 62.8 |
| Cash Flow | NA | 372 | 364 | 412 | 306 | 268 | 238 | 237 | 187 | 120 |
| Current Ratio | 3.2 | 3.8 | 4.7 | 4.0 | 3.4 | 3.6 | 2.8 | 3.0 | 3.2 | 2.8 |
| % Long Term Debt of Capitalization | 16.8 | 18.4 | 18.9 | 18.7 | 20.9 | 19.7 | 14.7 | 20.7 | 24.8 | 27.3 |
| % Net Income of Revenue | 11.3 | 9.6 | 10.6 | 13.8 | 10.8 | 11.1 | 10.8 | 11.4 | 10.0 | 7.7 |
| % Return on Assets | 11.5 | 9.0 | 9.4 | 12.0 | 10.0 | 10.7 | 10.8 | 13.1 | 12.1 | 9.6 |
| % Return on Equity | 19.3 | 14.0 | 14.4 | 19.2 | 16.1 | 16.9 | 17.7 | 22.7 | 22.9 | 18.8 |

Data as orig reptd.; bef. results of disc opers/spec. items. Per share data adj. for stk. divs.; EPS diluted. E-Estimated. NA-Not Available. NM-Not Meaningful. NR-Not Ranked. UR-Under Review.

**Office:** 727 Fifth Avenue, New York, NY 10022.
**Telephone:** 212-755-8000.
**Website:** http://www.tiffany.com
**Chrmn & CEO:** M.J. Kowalski

**Pres:** J.E. Quinn
**COO:** J.S. Petterson
**EVP & CFO:** J.N. Fernandez
**SVP, Secy & General Counsel:** P.B. Dorsey

**Investor Contact:** M.L. Aaron (212-230-5301)
**Board Members:** R. M. Bravo, W. R. Chaney, G. E. Costley, L. K. Fish, A. F. Kohnstamm, M. J. Kowalski, C. K. Marquis, P. W. May, J. T. Presby, W. A. Shutzer

**Founded:** 1837
**Domicile:** Delaware
**Employees:** 8,800

# Time Warner Inc.

| S&P Recommendation HOLD ★★★☆☆ | Price $9.15 (as of Nov 14, 2008) | 12-Mo. Target Price $12.00 | Investment Style Large-Cap Blend |
|---|---|---|---|

**GICS Sector** Consumer Discretionary
**Sub-Industry** Movies & Entertainment

**Summary** The world's largest media company, TWX has diversified interests in web properties, filmed entertainment content, cable systems, television networks and publishing.

## Key Stock Statistics (Source S&P, Vickers, company reports)

| | | | | | | | |
|---|---|---|---|---|---|---|---|
| 52-Wk Range | $17.50– 8.01 | S&P Oper. EPS 2008**E** | 1.14 | Market Capitalization(B) | $32.825 | Beta | 1.28 |
| Trailing 12-Month EPS | $1.01 | S&P Oper. EPS 2009**E** | 1.24 | Yield (%) | 2.73 | S&P 3-Yr. Proj. EPS CAGR(%) | 12 |
| Trailing 12-Month P/E | 9.1 | P/E on S&P Oper. EPS 2008**E** | 8.0 | Dividend Rate/Share | $0.25 | S&P Credit Rating | BBB+ |
| $10K Invested 5 Yrs Ago | $6,042 | Common Shares Outstg. (M) | 3,587.4 | Institutional Ownership (%) | 81 | | |

## Price Performance

30-Week Mov. Avg. ··· 10-Week Mov. Avg. -- **GAAP Earnings vs. Previous Year** Volume Above Avg. STARS
12-Mo. Target Price — Relative Strength — ▲ Up ▼ Down ► No Change Below Avg.

Options: ASE, CBOE, P, Ph

## Qualitative Risk Assessment

| LOW | MEDIUM | HIGH |
|---|---|---|

Our risk assessment reflects our view of the company's leading content and distribution businesses and ample financial flexibility, offset by increased competition, cyclical advertising exposure, a volatile stock price, and a continued audience fragmentation for traditional media platforms.

## Quantitative Evaluations

**S&P Quality Ranking**     B

| D | C | B- | B | B+ | A- | A | A+ |
|---|---|---|---|---|---|---|---|

**Relative Strength Rank**     MODERATE

49

LOWEST = 1     HIGHEST = 99

## Revenue/Earnings Data

**Revenue (Million $)**

| | 1Q | 2Q | 3Q | 4Q | Year |
|---|---|---|---|---|---|
| 2008 | 11,417 | 11,555 | 11,706 | -- | -- |
| 2007 | 11,184 | 10,980 | 11,676 | 12,642 | 46,482 |
| 2006 | 10,327 | 10,519 | 10,912 | 12,466 | 44,224 |
| 2005 | 10,483 | 10,744 | 10,538 | 11,887 | 43,652 |
| 2004 | 10,178 | 10,858 | 9,936 | 11,109 | 42,081 |
| 2003 | -- | -- | -- | -- | 39,496 |

**Earnings Per Share ($)**

| | | | | | |
|---|---|---|---|---|---|
| 2008 | 0.21 | 0.22 | 0.30 | E0.37 | E1.14 |
| 2007 | 0.30 | 0.25 | 0.24 | 0.28 | 1.08 |
| 2006 | 0.26 | 0.20 | 0.33 | 0.43 | 1.21 |
| 2005 | 0.20 | -0.07 | 0.19 | 0.29 | 0.62 |
| 2004 | 0.15 | 0.19 | 0.11 | 0.24 | 0.69 |
| 2003 | 0.09 | 0.23 | 0.12 | 0.24 | 0.68 |

Fiscal year ended Dec. 31. Next earnings report expected: Mid February. EPS Estimates based on S&P Operating Earnings; historical GAAP earnings are as reported.

## Highlights

➤ The 12-month target price for TWX has recently been changed to $12.00 from $17.00. The Highlights section of this Stock Report will be updated accordingly.

## Investment Rationale/Risk

➤ The Investment Rationale/Risk section of this Stock Report will be updated shortly. For the latest News story on TWX from MarketScope, see below.

➤ 11/05/08 02:49 pm ET ... UPDATE - S&P KEEPS HOLD OPINION ON SHARES OF TIME WARNER (TWX 10.48***): TWX in its conference call sees some resistance to slowed economy from its diversified revenue base and compelling content. We see partial justification, as compared to large media peers. But early '09 separation of Time Warner Cable (TWC 20.56*****), upon which TWX today said it plans reverse split, should leave content-focused TWX with higher earnings volatility (film/TV, AOL, print). Beyond deeper cost cuts at Publishing and Film, we think Q3 further underscored urgent strategic challenges for AOL. We cut our target price by $5 to $12, on revised DCF and sum-of-the-parts. /T. Amobi - CPA, CFA

## Dividend Data (Dates: mm/dd Payment Date: mm/dd/yy)

| Amount ($) | Date Decl. | Ex-Div. Date | Stk. of Record | Payment Date |
|---|---|---|---|---|
| 0.063 | 01/31 | 02/27 | 02/29 | 03/15/08 |
| 0.063 | 04/24 | 05/28 | 05/31 | 06/15/08 |
| 0.063 | 07/31 | 08/27 | 08/31 | 09/15/08 |
| 0.063 | 10/30 | 11/25 | 11/30 | 12/15/08 |

Dividends have been paid since 2005. Source: Company reports.

# Time Warner Inc.

**STANDARD &POOR'S**

## Business Summary September 12, 2008

CORPORATE OVERVIEW. In January 2001, online access and content company America Online (AOL) merged with cable systems and media concern Time Warner, forming AOL Time Warner (later changed to Time Warner in October 2003), in a $106 billion transaction. Revenues consist of subscriptions (54% of 2007 revenues), content (25%), advertising (19%), and other (2%).

AOL had nearly 8.1 million subscribers in the U.S. at June 30, 2008. It owns the AOL, CompuServe and Netscape access brands, and the AOL.com, AIM and MapQuest portals and Websites. Time Warner Cable serves about 13.3 million basic subscribers, also offering high-speed data, digital video (including SVOD/VOD, DVRs, HDTV), and digital (VoIP) phone. In July 2006, Time Warner Cable closed on the Adelphia/Comcast transactions to consolidate its position as the second-largest U.S. cable multiple system operator (MSO).

Filmed Entertainment includes the Warner Bros. and New Line Cinema (independent) studios and home entertainment businesses, with key franchises such as Harry Potter, Lord of the Rings and Batman. The Networks segment includes cable networks CNN, HBO/Cinemax and Turner (TNT, TBS). In September 2006, TWX's WB broadcast network merged with CBS's UPN to create the CW network. Publishing includes Time Inc., with over 130 magazine titles worldwide, including Time, People, Sports Illustrated and Fortune.

CORPORATE STRATEGY. Upon assuming the CEO position in January 2008, Jeffrey Bewkes unveiled a three-pronged mission focused on efficient operations, optimal corporate structure and a strong financial position. TWX plans to complete a full structural separation (through a spin or split) of its 84%-owned Time Warner Cable (TWC: strong buy, $27) in the 2008 fourth quarter. Pursuant to an AOL turnaround plan leading up to a separation of its online division's access and ad businesses, the company also expects both units to operate independently starting in 2009. AOL has made a number of recent acquisitions, notably including Bebo, a social networking site purchased in May 2008 for $850 million in cash. In March 2006, Google invested $1 billion for a 5% stake in AOL.

## Company Financials Fiscal Year Ended Dec. 31

| Per Share Data ($) | 2007 | 2006 | 2005 | 2004 | 2003 | 2002 | 2001 | 2000 | 1999 | 1998 |
|---|---|---|---|---|---|---|---|---|---|---|
| Tangible Book Value | NM | NM | NM | NM | NM | NM | NM | 2.51 | 2.44 | 1.17 |
| Cash Flow | 3.86 | 2.86 | 2.06 | 2.13 | 2.00 | NA | NA | 0.62 | 0.61 | 0.42 |
| Earnings | 1.08 | 1.21 | 0.62 | 0.69 | 0.68 | -9.43 | -1.20 | 0.45 | 0.48 | 0.30 |
| S&P Core Earnings | 0.95 | 1.07 | 0.83 | 0.62 | 0.42 | -3.44 | -1.08 | NA | NA | NA |
| Dividends | 0.24 | 0.21 | 0.10 | Nil | Nil | Nil | Nil | Nil | Nil | Nil |
| Payout Ratio | 22% | 17% | 16% | Nil | Nil | Nil | Nil | Nil | Nil | Nil |
| Prices:High | 23.15 | 22.25 | 19.64 | 19.90 | 18.32 | 32.92 | 58.51 | 83.38 | 83.38 | 95.81 |
| Prices:Low | 16.17 | 15.70 | 16.10 | 15.41 | 9.90 | 8.70 | 27.40 | 32.75 | 32.75 | 32.50 |
| P/E Ratio:High | 21 | 18 | 32 | 29 | 27 | NM | NM | NM | NM | NM |
| P/E Ratio:Low | 15 | 13 | 26 | 22 | 15 | NM | NM | NM | NM | NM |

| Income Statement Analysis (Million $) | | | | | | | | | | |
|---|---|---|---|---|---|---|---|---|---|---|
| Revenue | 46,482 | 44,224 | 43,652 | 42,081 | 39,496 | 36,955 | 33,765 | 7,703 | 6,886 | 4,777 |
| Operating Income | 19,217 | 14,837 | 14,312 | 13,535 | 11,839 | NA | NA | 2,271 | 1,776 | 851 |
| Depreciation | 10,488 | 6,953 | 6,781 | 6,743 | 6,086 | NA | NA | 444 | 363 | 298 |
| Interest Expense | 2,509 | 1,971 | 1,622 | 1,754 | 1,926 | 1,900 | 1,576 | 55.0 | 40.0 | 20.0 |
| Pretax Income | 6,795 | 6,826 | 4,007 | 5,206 | 4,763 | -44,156 | -4,465 | 1,884 | 2,014 | 1,096 |
| Effective Tax Rate | 34.4% | 19.6% | 27.2% | 33.0% | 29.0% | NM | NM | 38.9% | 38.8% | 30.5% |
| Net Income | 4,051 | 5,114 | 2,921 | 3,239 | 3,164 | -42,003 | -5,313 | 1,152 | 1,232 | 762 |
| S&P Core Earnings | 3,579 | 4,551 | 3,929 | 2,938 | 1,999 | -15,240 | -4,771 | NA | NA | NA |

| Balance Sheet & Other Financial Data (Million $) | | | | | | | | | | |
|---|---|---|---|---|---|---|---|---|---|---|
| Cash | 1,516 | 1,549 | 4,220 | 6,139 | 3,040 | 1,730 | 771 | 2,610 | 2,490 | 887 |
| Current Assets | 12,451 | 10,851 | 13,463 | 14,639 | 12,268 | 11,155 | 10,274 | 4,671 | 4,428 | 1,979 |
| Total Assets | 133,830 | 131,669 | 122,745 | 123,149 | 121,748 | 115,508 | 209,429 | 10,827 | 10,673 | 5,348 |
| Current Liabilities | 12,193 | 12,780 | 12,608 | 14,673 | NA | NA | NA | 2,328 | 2,395 | 1,725 |
| Long Term Debt | 37,304 | 35,233 | 20,238 | 20,703 | 23,458 | 27,354 | 22,792 | 1,411 | 1,630 | 348 |
| Common Equity | 58,536 | 60,389 | 62,679 | 60,719 | 56,131 | 52,891 | 150,667 | 6,778 | 6,161 | 3,033 |
| Total Capital | 113,898 | 112,857 | 103,760 | 103,285 | NA | NA | NA | 8,189 | 7,791 | 3,381 |
| Capital Expenditures | 4,430 | 4,085 | 3,246 | 3,024 | 2,761 | 3,023 | 3,634 | 485 | 642 | 301 |
| Cash Flow | 14,539 | 12,067 | 9,702 | 9,982 | 9,250 | NA | NA | 1,596 | 1,595 | 1,060 |
| Current Ratio | 1.0 | 0.8 | 1.1 | 1.0 | 0.8 | 0.8 | 0.8 | 2.0 | 1.8 | 1.1 |
| % Long Term Debt of Capitalization | 32.8 | 31.2 | 19.5 | 20.0 | NA | NA | NA | 17.2 | 20.9 | 10.3 |
| % Net Income of Revenue | 8.7 | 11.6 | 6.7 | 7.7 | 8.0 | NM | NM | 15.0 | 17.9 | 16.0 |
| % Return on Assets | 3.1 | 4.0 | 2.4 | 2.6 | 2.7 | NM | NM | 10.9 | 15.3 | 18.5 |
| % Return on Equity | 6.8 | 8.2 | 4.7 | 5.5 | 5.8 | NM | NM | 17.6 | 26.6 | 37.8 |

Data as orig reptd.; bef. results of disc opers/spec. items. Per share data adj. for stk. divs.; EPS diluted. E-Estimated. NA-Not Available. NM-Not Meaningful. NR-Not Ranked. UR-Under Review.

**Office:** 1 Time Warner Ctr, New York, NY 10019-6038.
**Telephone:** 212-484-8000.
**Email:** aoltwir@aoltw.com
**Website:** http://www.timewarner.com

**Chrmn:** R.D. Parsons
**Pres:** D.M. Davis
**Pres & CEO:** J.L. Bewkes
**EVP & CFO:** J. Martin, Jr.

**EVP & General Counsel:** P.T. Cappuccio
**Investor Contact:** J.E. Burtson
**Board Members:** H. M. Allison, Jr., J. L. Barksdale, J. L. Bewkes, S. F. Bollenbach, F. J. Caufield, R. C. Clark, M. Dopfner, J. P. Einhorn, J. V. Kimsey, R. Mark, M. A. Miles, K. J. Novack, R. D. Parsons, D. C. Wright

**Founded:** 1985
**Domicile:** Delaware
**Employees:** 86,400

**The McGraw-Hill Companies**

# Titanium Metals Corp

STANDARD &POOR'S

| S&P Recommendation | HOLD ★★★★★ | Price | 12-Mo. Target Price | Investment Style |
|---|---|---|---|---|
| | | $7.67 (as of Nov 14, 2008) | $11.00 | Large-Cap Blend |

**GICS Sector** Materials
**Sub-Industry** Diversified Metals & Mining

**Summary** This company is a worldwide integrated producer of titanium metal products.

## Key Stock Statistics (Source S&P, Vickers, company reports)

| | | | | | | | | |
|---|---|---|---|---|---|---|---|---|
| 52-Wk Range | $30.25– 6.37 | S&P Oper. EPS 2008E | 0.87 | Market Capitalization(B) | $1.389 | Beta | 2.21 |
| Trailing 12-Month EPS | $1.03 | S&P Oper. EPS 2009E | 0.83 | Yield (%) | 3.91 | S&P 3-Yr. Proj. EPS CAGR(%) | -5 |
| Trailing 12-Month P/E | 7.5 | P/E on S&P Oper. EPS 2008E | 8.8 | Dividend Rate/Share | $0.30 | S&P Credit Rating | NR |
| $10K Invested 5 Yrs Ago | $75,062 | Common Shares Outstg. (M) | 181.1 | Institutional Ownership (%) | 39 | | |

## Price Performance

30-Week Mov. Avg. · · · · 10-Week Mov. Avg. - - - GAAP Earnings vs. Previous Year   Volume Above Avg. STARS
12-Mo. Target Price — Relative Strength — ▲ Up ▼ Down ▶ No Change   Below Avg.

Options: ASE, CBOE, Ph

Analysis prepared by **Leo J. Larkin** on November 05, 2008, when the stock traded at **$ 9.62.**

### Highlights

➤ Following an estimated sales decline of 12% in 2008, we look for a sales decrease of 5% in 2009, reflecting another drop in volume and another decrease in the average realized price of both melted and mill products. We see demand being adversely affected by the impact of the Boeing strike, high customer inventories and the lingering effect from the delay of Boeing's 787 airplane project. We also assume negative GDP growth of 0.1% in 2009, versus estimated GDP growth of 1.6% in 2008.

➤ Penalized by a combination of lower volume of shipments and reduced selling prices, we look for a contraction in margins and another decline in operating profit. Following minimal interest expense and a flat tax rate, we estimate a decline in EPS in 2009 to $0.83, from estimated EPS of $0.87 in 2008.

➤ Long term, we look for higher EPS on a continued upturn in the commercial aerospace industry, share repurchases, and increased use of titanium in other industrial applications and rising consumption in Asia.

### Investment Rationale/Risk

➤ We view TIE as a vehicle for participation in a continued upturn in construction of new planes for commercial aerospace, growing acceptance of titanium in other industrial markets, and rising Asian demand for titanium. In our view, demand for titanium in commercial aerospace will increase through 2010. According to the Airline Monitor, an industry trade publication, delivery of commercial aircraft will rise steadily through 2010. Higher deliveries along with increasing demand from other industrial sectors should provide a base for future growth of EPS and free cash flow. Other positive factors include TIE's low debt levels and a stock repurchase program. But, with the shares recently selling with just modest upside to our target price, we would not add to positions.

➤ Risks to our recommendation and target price include the possibility of additional delays in construction of commercial aircraft in 2009.

➤ We project that TIE's P/E on our 2009 estimate will reach 13.3X, which is below the mid-point of its historical range and at a premium to the P/E we project for its peers. On that basis, our 12-month target price is $11.

### Qualitative Risk Assessment

| LOW | MEDIUM | HIGH |
|---|---|---|

Our risk assessment reflects the company's low debt levels and its large share of the markets it serves. Partly offsetting this is its heavy reliance on aerospace industry demand and the volatility of its raw material costs.

### Quantitative Evaluations

**S&P Quality Ranking** B-

| D | C | B- | B | B+ | A- | A | A+ |
|---|---|---|---|---|---|---|---|

**Relative Strength Rank** MODERATE

47

LOWEST = 1          HIGHEST = 99

### Revenue/Earnings Data

**Revenue (Million $)**

| | 1Q | 2Q | 3Q | 4Q | Year |
|---|---|---|---|---|---|
| 2008 | 293.7 | 297.3 | 295.4 | -- | -- |
| 2007 | 341.7 | 341.2 | 297.3 | 298.6 | 1,279 |
| 2006 | 286.9 | 300.9 | 271.8 | 323.5 | 1,183 |
| 2005 | 155.2 | 183.8 | 190.0 | 220.8 | 749.8 |
| 2004 | 120.5 | 124.1 | 120.3 | 137.0 | 501.8 |
| 2003 | 99.30 | 101.8 | 83.64 | 100.6 | 385.3 |

**Earnings Per Share ($)**

| | | | | | |
|---|---|---|---|---|---|
| 2008 | 0.22 | 0.26 | 0.22 | E0.17 | E0.87 |
| 2007 | 0.41 | 0.42 | 0.29 | 0.61 | 1.46 |
| 2006 | 0.32 | 0.31 | 0.29 | 0.61 | 1.53 |
| 2005 | 0.23 | 0.21 | 0.20 | 0.23 | 0.86 |
| 2004 | -0.01 | 0.02 | 0.17 | 0.08 | 0.28 |
| 2003 | -0.11 | -0.05 | -0.02 | 0.08 | -0.11 |

Fiscal year ended Dec. 31. Next earnings report expected: Late February. EPS Estimates based on S&P Operating Earnings; historical GAAP earnings are as reported.

### Dividend Data (Dates: mm/dd Payment Date: mm/dd/yy)

| Amount ($) | Date Decl. | Ex-Div. Date | Stk. of Record | Payment Date |
|---|---|---|---|---|
| 0.075 | 02/21 | 03/07 | 03/11 | 03/25/08 |
| 0.075 | 05/22 | 06/06 | 06/10 | 06/24/08 |
| 0.075 | 08/14 | 09/08 | 09/10 | 09/24/08 |
| 0.075 | 10/30 | 12/08 | 12/10 | 12/24/08 |

Dividends have been paid since 2007. Source: Company reports.

---

# Titanium Metals Corp

STANDARD
&POOR'S

## Business Summary November 05, 2008

CORPORATE OVERVIEW. Titanium Metals Corp. is the one of the world's largest producers of titanium melted and mill products and the largest U.S. producer of titanium sponge (the raw material for titanium). The company estimates that it accounted for some 16% of global industry shipments of titanium mill products in 2007 and 6% of worldwide sponge production. Melted and mill products and sponge are sold principally to the commercial aerospace industry. Other sources of product demand include the military, industrial and emerging markets. As of March 31, 2008, 28.2% of TIE's common shares were held by Contran Corporation and its subsidiaries, and an additional 8.5% of TIE's shares were held by a trust sponsored by Contran.

Products include titanium sponge; melted products (ingot, electrodes and slab); mill products, including billet and bar, plate, strip and pipe; and fabricated products such as spools, pipe fittings, manifolds and vessels. In 2007, mill products accounted for 74% of sales, melted products 15%, and other products (titanium fabrications, titanium scrap and titanium tetrachloride), 11%.

Sales by market sector in 2007 were: aerospace, 55%; military, 19%; chemical products, oil and gas, consumer, sporting goods, automotive and power generation 16%; other 10%. In 2007, North American accounted for 58% of sales, Europe, 33% and other regions, 9%.

CORPORATE STRATEGY. The company's long-term strategy is to maximize the value of its core aerospace business while expanding its presence in non-aerospace markets. Additionally, the company seeks to develop new applications for its products.

## Company Financials  Fiscal Year Ended Dec. 31

### Per Share Data ($)

| | 2007 | 2006 | 2005 | 2004 | 2003 | 2002 | 2001 | 2000 | 1999 | 1998 |
|---|---|---|---|---|---|---|---|---|---|---|
| Tangible Book Value | 6.16 | 4.92 | 2.91 | 1.41 | 1.20 | 1.18 | 1.92 | 2.32 | 2.69 | 2.94 |
| Cash Flow | 1.65 | 1.68 | 0.96 | 0.47 | 0.19 | -0.24 | -0.01 | 0.03 | 0.08 | 0.53 |
| Earnings | 1.46 | 1.53 | 0.86 | 0.28 | -0.11 | -0.53 | -0.33 | -0.30 | -0.25 | 0.37 |
| S&P Core Earnings | 1.35 | 1.29 | 0.82 | 0.29 | -0.08 | -0.37 | -0.41 | NA | NA | NA |
| Dividends | 0.08 | Nil | Nil | Nil | Nil | Nil | Nil | Nil | 0.03 | 0.03 |
| Payout Ratio | 5% | Nil | Nil | Nil | Nil | Nil | Nil | Nil | 13% | 8% |
| Prices:High | 39.80 | 47.63 | 19.86 | 3.33 | 1.51 | 1.35 | 3.60 | 2.23 | 3.31 | 8.25 |
| Prices:Low | 25.26 | 15.96 | 2.91 | 1.06 | 0.39 | 0.23 | 0.59 | 0.78 | 0.89 | 1.78 |
| P/E Ratio:High | 27 | 31 | 23 | 12 | NM | NM | NM | NM | NM | 23 |
| P/E Ratio:Low | 17 | 10 | 3 | 4 | NM | NM | NM | NM | NM | 5 |

### Income Statement Analysis (Million $)

| | 2007 | 2006 | 2005 | 2004 | 2003 | 2002 | 2001 | 2000 | 1999 | 1998 |
|---|---|---|---|---|---|---|---|---|---|---|
| Revenue | 1,279 | 1,183 | 750 | 502 | 385 | 367 | 487 | 427 | 480 | 708 |
| Operating Income | 420 | 403 | 177 | 43.8 | 17.2 | -9.02 | 28.2 | 1.81 | 19.6 | 138 |
| Depreciation | 41.1 | 34.1 | 31.5 | 32.8 | 36.6 | 37.1 | 40.1 | 41.9 | 42.7 | 32.5 |
| Interest Expense | 2.60 | 3.43 | 3.96 | 12.5 | 16.4 | 3.38 | 4.06 | 7.70 | 7.09 | 2.92 |
| Pretax Income | 394 | 418 | 185 | 39.0 | -11.3 | -54.5 | 4.47 | -43.1 | -33.7 | 85.8 |
| Effective Tax Rate | 29.7% | 30.7% | 13.2% | NM | NM | NM | NM | NM | NM | 34.0% |
| Net Income | 268 | 281 | 156 | 39.9 | -12.9 | -67.2 | -41.8 | -38.0 | -31.4 | 45.8 |
| S&P Core Earnings | 243 | 230 | 136 | 37.9 | -9.92 | -46.4 | -51.7 | NA | NA | NA |

### Balance Sheet & Other Financial Data (Million $)

| | 2007 | 2006 | 2005 | 2004 | 2003 | 2002 | 2001 | 2000 | 1999 | 1998 |
|---|---|---|---|---|---|---|---|---|---|---|
| Cash | 90.0 | 86.2 | 17.6 | 54.4 | 35.0 | 6.21 | 24.5 | 9.80 | 20.7 | 95.5 |
| Current Assets | 898 | 758 | 550 | 344 | 276 | 263 | 309 | 248 | 343 | 396 |
| Total Assets | 1,420 | 1,217 | 907 | 666 | 567 | 564 | 699 | 759 | 883 | 953 |
| Current Liabilities | 178 | 211 | 167 | 162 | 78.5 | 92.6 | 122 | 116 | 194 | 137 |
| Long Term Debt | NA | Nil | 57.2 | 12.2 | 9.77 | 217 | 221 | 229 | 233 | 311 |
| Common Equity | 1,129 | 804 | 430 | 206 | 159 | 159 | 298 | 357 | 408 | 448 |
| Total Capital | 1,168 | 918 | 660 | 404 | 180 | 388 | 533 | 604 | 662 | 782 |
| Capital Expenditures | 101 | 101 | 61.1 | 23.6 | 12.5 | 7.77 | 16.1 | 11.2 | 24.8 | 115 |
| Cash Flow | 304 | 309 | 175 | 68.4 | 23.7 | -30.1 | -1.63 | 3.91 | 11.3 | 78.3 |
| Current Ratio | 5.1 | 3.6 | 3.3 | 2.1 | 3.5 | 2.8 | 2.5 | 2.1 | 1.8 | 2.9 |
| % Long Term Debt of Capitalization | Nil | Nil | 8.7 | 3.0 | 5.4 | 56.0 | 41.4 | 37.9 | 35.3 | 39.8 |
| % Net Income of Revenue | 21.0 | 23.8 | 20.8 | 8.0 | NM | NM | NM | NM | NM | 6.5 |
| % Return on Assets | 20.3 | 26.5 | 19.4 | 6.5 | NM | NM | NM | NM | NM | 5.2 |
| % Return on Equity | 27.2 | 44.5 | 43.4 | 19.5 | NM | NM | NM | NM | NM | 10.7 |

Data as orig reptd.; bef. results of disc opers/spec. items. Per share data adj. for stk. divs.; EPS diluted. E-Estimated. NA-Not Available. NM-Not Meaningful. NR-Not Ranked. UR-Under Review.

**Office:** 5430 Lbj Fwy Ste 1700, Dallas, TX 75240-2620.
**Telephone:** 972-233-1700.
**Website:** http://www.timet.com
**Chrmn:** H.C. Simmons

**Pres:** B.D. O'Brien
**Vice Chrmn & CEO:** S.L. Watson
**CFO:** J.W. Brown
**CTO:** M.W. Kearns

**Board Members:** K. R. Coogan, G. R. Simmons, H. C. Simmons, T. P. Stafford, S. L. Watson, T. N. Worrell, P. J. Zucconi

**Founded:** 1950
**Domicile:** Delaware
**Employees:** 2,530

# TJX Companies Inc. (The)

**STANDARD &POOR'S**

| S&P Recommendation | BUY ★★★★☆ | Price $21.32 (as of Nov 14, 2008) | 12-Mo. Target Price $28.00 | Investment Style Large-Cap Growth |
|---|---|---|---|---|

**GICS Sector** Consumer Discretionary
**Sub-Industry** Apparel Retail

**Summary** TJX operates seven chains of off-price apparel and home fashion specialty stores in the U.S., Canada, Germany, Ireland and the U.K.

## Key Stock Statistics (Source S&P, Vickers, company reports)

| | | | | | | |
|---|---|---|---|---|---|---|
| 52-Wk Range | $37.52– 20.17 | S&P Oper. EPS 2009**E** | 2.05 | Market Capitalization(B) | $8.942 | Beta | 0.55 |
| Trailing 12-Month EPS | $2.09 | S&P Oper. EPS 2010**E** | 2.20 | Yield (%) | 2.06 | S&P 3-Yr. Proj. EPS CAGR(%) | 10 |
| Trailing 12-Month P/E | 10.2 | P/E on S&P Oper. EPS 2009**E** | 10.4 | Dividend Rate/Share | $0.44 | S&P Credit Rating | A |
| $10K Invested 5 Yrs Ago | $10,105 | Common Shares Outstg. (M) | 419.4 | Institutional Ownership (%) | NM | | |

## Price Performance

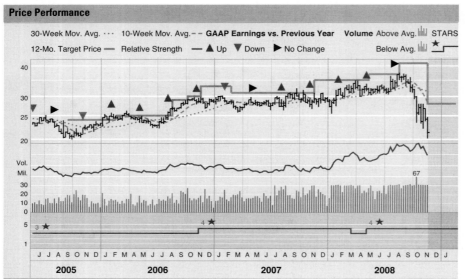

30-Week Mov. Avg. · · · 10-Week Mov. Avg. - - **GAAP Earnings vs. Previous Year** Volume Above Avg. STARS
12-Mo. Target Price — Relative Strength — ▲ Up ▼ Down ▶ No Change Below Avg. ★

Options: ASE, CBOE

## Qualitative Risk Assessment

| LOW | MEDIUM | HIGH |
|---|---|---|

Our risk assessment reflects our view of TJX's leadership position in off-price retail and promising new merchandising and productivity initiatives that could boost sales and profit margins. This is offset by what we see as an inconsistent earnings track record and an uncertain outlook for consumer discretionary spending.

## Quantitative Evaluations

**S&P Quality Ranking** A+

| D | C | B- | B | B+ | A- | A | A+ |
|---|---|---|---|---|---|---|---|

**Relative Strength Rank** MODERATE

43

LOWEST = 1    HIGHEST = 99

## Revenue/Earnings Data

**Revenue (Million $)**

| | 1Q | 2Q | 3Q | 4Q | Year |
|---|---|---|---|---|---|
| 2009 | 4,364 | 4,621 | -- | -- | -- |
| 2008 | 4,108 | 4,313 | 4,737 | 5,488 | 18,647 |
| 2007 | 3,871 | 3,964 | 4,473 | 5,097 | 17,405 |
| 2006 | 3,652 | 3,648 | 4,042 | 4,716 | 16,058 |
| 2005 | 3,353 | 3,414 | 3,817 | 4,329 | 14,913 |
| 2004 | 2,789 | 3,046 | 3,387 | 4,106 | 13,328 |

**Earnings Per Share ($)**

| | | | | | |
|---|---|---|---|---|---|
| 2009 | 0.43 | 0.45 | E0.57 | E0.60 | E2.05 |
| 2008 | 0.34 | 0.45 | 0.54 | 0.66 | 1.66 |
| 2007 | 0.34 | 0.29 | 0.48 | 0.51 | 1.63 |
| 2006 | 0.28 | 0.23 | 0.32 | 0.60 | 1.41 |
| 2005 | 0.32 | 0.23 | 0.40 | 0.35 | 1.30 |
| 2004 | 0.22 | 0.24 | 0.36 | 0.47 | 1.28 |

Fiscal year ended Jan. 31. Next earnings report expected: NA. EPS Estimates based on S&P Operating Earnings; historical GAAP earnings are as reported.

## Highlights

> The 12-month target price for TJX has recently been changed to $28.00 from $30.00. The Highlights section of this Stock Report will be updated accordingly.

## Investment Rationale/Risk

> The Investment Rationale/Risk section of this Stock Report will be updated shortly. For the latest News story on TJX from MarketScope, see below.

> 11/11/08 01:13 pm ET ... S&P REITERATES BUY OPINION ON SHARES OF TJX COMPANIES (TJX 23.01****): Oct-Q operating EPS of $0.57 vs. $0.54 meets our estimate. We think TJX is benefiting as consumers trade down from higher-price retailers for more affordable, brand-name apparel and accessories. We also see the company generating ample cash flow to fund growth initiatives and additional share buybacks. But with forex negatively impacting sales and earnings, we are trimming our FY 09 (Jan.) and FY 10 operating EPS estimates each by $0.15, to $2.05 and $2.20, respectively. We are also lowering our P/E-based 12-month target price by $2 to $28. /J.Asaeda

## Dividend Data (Dates: mm/dd Payment Date: mm/dd/yy)

| Amount ($) | Date Decl. | Ex-Div. Date | Stk. of Record | Payment Date |
|---|---|---|---|---|
| 0.090 | 12/04 | 02/05 | 02/07 | 02/28/08 |
| 0.110 | 04/01 | 05/06 | 05/08 | 05/29/08 |
| 0.110 | 06/03 | 08/05 | 08/07 | 08/28/08 |
| 0.110 | 09/09 | 11/04 | 11/06 | 11/26/08 |

Dividends have been paid since 1980. Source: Company reports.

The **McGraw·Hill** Companies

# TJX Companies Inc. (The)

**STANDARD &POOR'S**

## Business Summary November 10, 2008

COMPANY PROFILE. With over $18.6 billion in annual revenues, TJX is the largest U.S. off-price family apparel and home fashion retailer via its seven retail concepts. As of August 20, 2008, the company's core Marmaxx Group division operated 859 T.J. Maxx and 787 Marshalls stores. TJX also operated 132 A.J. Wright units and 297 HomeGoods stores in the U.S.; six HomeSense and 231 T.K. Maxx stores in Europe; and 73 HomeSense and 196 Winners stores in Canada. The company sold its 34-store Bob's Store chain to private equity firms Versa Capital Management and Crystal Capital in August 2008.

TJX believes it derives a competitive advantage by offering rapidly changing assortments of affordable, quality brand name and designer merchandise. Prices at T.J. Maxx and Marshalls are usually 20% to 60% below department and specialty store regular prices. With over 2,500 stores, the company has substantial buying power with more than 10,000 vendors worldwide. TJX purchases later in the buying cycle than department and specialty stores. Generally, purchases are for current selling seasons, with a limited quantity of packaway inventory intended for a future selling season. A combination of opportunistic buying, an expansive distribution infrastructure, and a low expense structure enable the company to offer everyday savings to its customers.

PRIMARY BUSINESS DYNAMICS. TJX's primary growth drivers are new store openings and same-store sales (sales results for stores open for all or a portion of two consecutive fiscal years). From FY 00 through FY 06 (Jan.), the company increased its consolidated store count from 1,493 to 2,381 at a compound annual growth rate (CAGR) of about 12%. TJX reported a 7.1% increase in FY 06, down from 7.8% in FY 05, and an 11% run rate from FY 00 through FY 04. Growth has slowed with the maturing of the core Marmaxx division. From FY 07 through FY 09, the company plans to further slow its new store growth to 4% to 5% annually as it implements changes at A.J. Wright and HomeGoods to improve store operations. Store expansion fell below plan in FY 07, with the consolidated store count rising only 3.6%, to 2,466, due to the closure of 34 underperforming A.J. Wright locations in January 2007. TJX's consolidated store count grew by 3.9% in FY 08, to 2,563.

## Company Financials Fiscal Year Ended Jan. 31

### Per Share Data ($)

| | 2008 | 2007 | 2006 | 2005 | 2004 | 2003 | 2002 | 2001 | 2000 | 1999 |
|---|---|---|---|---|---|---|---|---|---|---|
| Tangible Book Value | 4.55 | 4.65 | 3.71 | 3.06 | 2.74 | 2.36 | 2.14 | 1.85 | 1.55 | 1.59 |
| Cash Flow | 2.43 | 2.35 | 2.23 | 1.86 | 1.75 | 1.46 | 1.34 | 1.23 | 1.08 | 0.85 |
| Earnings | 1.66 | 1.63 | 1.41 | 1.30 | 1.28 | 1.08 | 0.97 | 0.93 | 0.83 | 0.65 |
| S&P Core Earnings | 1.63 | 1.64 | 1.40 | 1.22 | 1.21 | 1.01 | 0.91 | 0.90 | NA | NA |
| Dividends | 0.27 | 0.23 | 0.17 | 0.14 | 0.13 | 0.12 | 0.11 | 0.07 | 0.07 | 0.06 |
| Payout Ratio | 16% | 14% | 12% | 10% | 10% | 11% | 11% | 7% | 8% | 9% |
| Calendar Year | 2007 | 2006 | 2005 | 2004 | 2003 | 2002 | 2001 | 2000 | 1999 | 1998 |
| Prices:High | 32.46 | 29.84 | 25.96 | 26.82 | 23.70 | 22.45 | 20.30 | 15.75 | 18.50 | 15.00 |
| Prices:Low | 25.74 | 22.16 | 19.95 | 20.64 | 15.54 | 15.30 | 13.56 | 6.97 | 8.25 | 7.75 |
| P/E Ratio:High | 20 | 18 | 18 | 21 | 19 | 21 | 21 | 17 | 22 | 23 |
| P/E Ratio:Low | 16 | 14 | 14 | 16 | 12 | 14 | 14 | 7 | 10 | 12 |

### Income Statement Analysis (Million $)

| | 2008 | 2007 | 2006 | 2005 | 2004 | 2003 | 2002 | 2001 | 2000 | 1999 |
|---|---|---|---|---|---|---|---|---|---|---|
| Revenue | 18,647 | 17,405 | 16,058 | 14,913 | 13,328 | 11,981 | 10,709 | 9,579 | 8,795 | 7,949 |
| Operating Income | 1,811 | 1,616 | 1,444 | 1,394 | 1,334 | 1,171 | 1,104 | 1,064 | 1,022 | 842 |
| Depreciation | 365 | 353 | 405 | 288 | 238 | 208 | 204 | 176 | 160 | 137 |
| Interest Expense | 39.9 | 39.2 | 39.0 | 33.5 | 27.3 | 25.4 | 25.6 | 34.7 | 20.4 | 1.69 |
| Pretax Income | 1,243 | 1,247 | 1,009 | 1,080 | 1,068 | 938 | 874 | 865 | 854 | 704 |
| Effective Tax Rate | 37.9% | 37.7% | 31.6% | 38.5% | 38.4% | 38.3% | 38.2% | 37.8% | 38.3% | 38.5% |
| Net Income | 772 | 777 | 690 | 664 | 658 | 578 | 540 | 538 | 527 | 433 |
| S&P Core Earnings | 756 | 778 | 687 | 615 | 619 | 546 | 506 | 519 | NA | NA |

### Balance Sheet & Other Financial Data (Million $)

| | 2008 | 2007 | 2006 | 2005 | 2004 | 2003 | 2002 | 2001 | 2000 | 1999 |
|---|---|---|---|---|---|---|---|---|---|---|
| Cash | 733 | 857 | 466 | 307 | 246 | 492 | 493 | 133 | 372 | 461 |
| Current Assets | 3,992 | 3,749 | 3,140 | 2,905 | 2,452 | 2,241 | 2,116 | 1,722 | 1,701 | 1,743 |
| Total Assets | 6,600 | 6,086 | 5,496 | 5,075 | 4,397 | 3,940 | 3,596 | 2,932 | 2,805 | 2,748 |
| Current Liabilities | 2,761 | 2,383 | 2,252 | 2,204 | 1,691 | 1,566 | 1,315 | 1,229 | 1,366 | 1,307 |
| Long Term Debt | 853 | 808 | 807 | 599 | 692 | 694 | 702 | 319 | 319 | 220 |
| Common Equity | 2,131 | 2,290 | 1,893 | 1,653 | 1,552 | 1,409 | 1,341 | 1,219 | 1,119 | 1,221 |
| Total Capital | 3,028 | 3,120 | 2,700 | 2,405 | 2,369 | 2,145 | 2,043 | 1,538 | 1,439 | 1,441 |
| Capital Expenditures | 527 | 378 | 496 | 429 | 409 | 397 | 449 | 257 | 239 | 208 |
| Cash Flow | 1,137 | 1,130 | 1,096 | 953 | 897 | 786 | 744 | 714 | 687 | 566 |
| Current Ratio | 1.5 | 1.6 | 1.4 | 1.3 | 1.5 | 1.4 | 1.6 | 1.4 | 1.2 | 1.3 |
| % Long Term Debt of Capitalization | 28.2 | 25.9 | 29.9 | 24.9 | 29.2 | 32.3 | 34.4 | 20.8 | 22.2 | 15.3 |
| % Net Income of Revenue | 4.1 | 4.5 | 4.3 | 4.5 | 4.9 | 4.8 | 5.0 | 5.6 | 6.0 | 5.4 |
| % Return on Assets | 12.2 | 13.4 | 13.1 | 14.0 | 15.8 | 15.3 | 16.6 | 18.8 | 19.0 | 16.2 |
| % Return on Equity | 34.9 | 37.1 | 37.9 | 41.4 | 44.5 | 42.1 | 42.2 | 46.0 | 45.0 | 37.2 |

Data as orig reptd.; bef. results of disc opers/spec. items. Per share data adj. for stk. divs.; EPS diluted. E-Estimated. NA-Not Available. NM-Not Meaningful. NR-Not Ranked. UR-Under Review.

**Office:** 770 Cochituate Road, Framingham, MA 01701-4666.
**Telephone:** 508-390-1000.
**Website:** http://www.tjx.com
**Chrmn:** B. Cammarata

**Pres & CEO:** C. Meyrowitz
**EVP, CFO & Chief Acctg Officer:** N.K. Tripathy
**EVP & Chief Admin Officer:** J.G. Naylor
**EVP, Secy & General Counsel:** A. McCauley

**Investor Contact:** S. Lang (508-390-2323)
**Board Members:** J. B. Alvarez, A. Bennett, D. A. Brandon, B. Cammarata, D. T. Ching, M. F. Hines, A. B. Lane, C. Meyrowitz, J. F. O'Brien, R. F. Shapiro, W. B. Shire, F. H. Wiley

**Founded:** 1956
**Domicile:** Delaware
**Employees:** 129,000

The *McGraw-Hill* Companies

# Torchmark Corp

STANDARD
&POOR'S

| S&P Recommendation | HOLD ★★★☆☆ | Price | 12-Mo. Target Price | Investment Style |
|---|---|---|---|---|
| | | $38.47 (as of Nov 14, 2008) | $40.00 | Large-Cap Blend |

**GICS Sector** Financials
**Sub-Industry** Life & Health Insurance

**Summary** This financial services company derives most of its earnings from life and health insurance operations.

## Key Stock Statistics (Source S&P, Vickers, company reports)

| | | | | | | | | |
|---|---|---|---|---|---|---|---|---|
| 52-Wk Range | $66.00– 31.73 | S&P Oper. EPS 2008**E** | NA | Market Capitalization(B) | $3.271 | Beta | 0.65 |
| Trailing 12-Month EPS | $4.91 | S&P Oper. EPS 2009**E** | NA | Yield (%) | 1.46 | S&P 3-Yr. Proj. EPS CAGR(%) | 9 |
| Trailing 12-Month P/E | 7.8 | P/E on S&P Oper. EPS 2008**E** | null | Dividend Rate/Share | $0.56 | S&P Credit Rating | A |
| $10K Invested 5 Yrs Ago | $9,093 | Common Shares Outstg. (M) | 85.0 | Institutional Ownership (%) | 75 | | |

## Price Performance

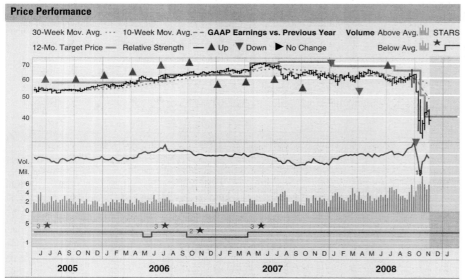

30-Week Mov. Avg. · · · · 10-Week Mov. Avg. - - **GAAP Earnings vs. Previous Year**   Volume Above Avg. STARS
12-Mo. Target Price — Relative Strength — ▲ Up ▼ Down ▶ No Change   Below Avg. ★

2005   2006   2007   2008

Options: ASE

Analysis prepared by **Bret Howlett** on October 28, 2008, when the stock traded at **$ 34.95**.

### Highlights

➤ We expect life underwriting margins to increase in the low single digits in 2008, based on our expectation of solid premium growth, partially offset by a decline in health underwriting margins. We expect new life sales to experience high single-digit growth in the second half of the year, due to improvements in the company's distribution channels, partially offset by weaker demand for its products. We view TMK's realignment and eventual plans to merge its struggling United American channel with the Liberty National channel positively, and think it will lead to overall better results from the combined unit. We anticipate the company's insert media circulation sales to weaken slightly in 2008 due to the slowing economy.

➤ We expect sales in TMK's health business to decline as the company focuses more on its life operations. Heath sales have struggled in 2008 in part from intense competition, and TMK believes its life products are significantly more profitable and have a higher persistency rate.

➤ We estimate 2008 operating EPS of $5.88, which would represent an 7.9% advance from 2007 operating EPS of $5.45. Our operating EPS estimate for 2009 is $6.20.

### Investment Rationale/Risk

➤ TMK trades at a premium to the life insurance group, we think on solid fundamentals of its life insurance segment and minimal exposure to equity markets. However, TMK has recently been impacted by significant investment losses, and we remained concerned about sizable exposure to below investment grade corporate debt, in particular, holdings of financial services credits. In addition, we expect lower health income to remain on a drag on earnings given that the decline in Medicare Part D enrollment sales has yet to stabilize. We view TMK's large exposure to traditional life insurance products positively and should preserve its earnings during this difficult operating environment.

➤ Risks to our recommendation and target price include material investment losses, increased competition for some products, a decline in recruitment of agents, higher loss ratios for TMK's Medicare Part D business, and, adverse mortality.

➤ Our 12-month target price of $40 is based on 1.0X our 2008 book value forecast (before SFAS 115), below historical multiples.

### Qualitative Risk Assessment

| LOW | MEDIUM | HIGH |
|---|---|---|

Our risk assessment reflects our view of its varied product lineup and diversified distribution network. TMK generates strong cash flow growth, in our opinion, and uses excess cash flow to repurchase shares and pay its dividend. However, we remained concerned about future investment losses in TMK's investment portfolio.

### Quantitative Evaluations

**S&P Quality Ranking**                                  A

| D | C | B- | B | B+ | A- | A | A+ |
|---|---|---|---|---|---|---|---|

**Relative Strength Rank**                        MODERATE

54

LOWEST = 1                                      HIGHEST = 99

### Revenue/Earnings Data

**Revenue (Million $)**

| | 1Q | 2Q | 3Q | 4Q | Year |
|---|---|---|---|---|---|
| 2008 | 872.4 | 860.5 | 753.4 | -- | -- |
| 2007 | 906.0 | 876.6 | 863.6 | 840.5 | 3,487 |
| 2006 | 857.0 | 869.1 | 837.9 | 857.1 | 3,421 |
| 2005 | 783.0 | 804.8 | 769.0 | 769.1 | 3,126 |
| 2004 | 772.5 | 764.0 | 774.2 | 760.8 | 3,072 |
| 2003 | 718.4 | 734.3 | 730.4 | 747.5 | 2,931 |

**Earnings Per Share ($)**

| | | | | | |
|---|---|---|---|---|---|
| 2008 | 1.29 | 1.47 | 0.72 | E1.50 | E5.88 |
| 2007 | 1.37 | 1.32 | 1.41 | 1.41 | 5.50 |
| 2006 | 1.16 | 1.26 | 1.28 | 1.43 | 5.13 |
| 2005 | 1.09 | 1.25 | 1.14 | 1.21 | 4.68 |
| 2004 | 1.05 | 1.04 | 1.12 | 1.05 | 4.25 |
| 2003 | 0.85 | 0.95 | 0.94 | 0.98 | 3.73 |

Fiscal year ended Dec. 31. Next earnings report expected: NA. EPS Estimates based on S&P Operating Earnings; historical GAAP earnings are as reported.

### Dividend Data (Dates: mm/dd Payment Date: mm/dd/yy)

| Amount ($) | Date Decl. | Ex-Div. Date | Stk. of Record | Payment Date |
|---|---|---|---|---|
| 0.140 | 02/27 | 04/02 | 04/04 | 05/01/08 |
| 0.140 | 04/25 | 07/02 | 07/07 | 08/01/08 |
| 0.140 | 07/18 | 10/01 | 10/03 | 10/31/08 |
| 0.140 | 10/31 | 12/30 | 01/02 | 01/30/09 |

Dividends have been paid since 1933. Source: Company reports.

---

**Please read the Required Disclosures and Analyst Certification on the last page of this report.**

The McGraw-Hill Companies

# Torchmark Corp

**STANDARD &POOR'S**

## Business Summary October 28, 2008

CORPORATE OVERVIEW. TMK's subsidiaries offer a full line of nonparticipating ordinary individual life products and health insurance, as well as fixed and variable annuities. Traditional whole life insurance constituted 58% of life insurance in force at the end of 2007 as measured by annualized premiums, interest-sensitive whole life 7.1%, term life 31%, and other life products 3.2%. Medicare supplemental insurance accounted for 42% of supplemental health insurance in force at the end of 2007, as measured by annualized premiums, limited-benefit plans 42%, and Medicare Part D 16%. The number of individual health policies in force (excluding Medicare Part D) was 1.56 million at December 31, 2007, versus 1.60 million at prior year-end. Medicare Part D enrollees to begin the 2007 plan year were 189,000 at December 31, 2006. Annuity separate account assets totaled $1.423 billion at December 31, 2007, down 5.0% from the year-earlier level.

Life segment premium revenue accounted for 56% of total premium revenue in 2007 (55% in 2006), the health segment 44% (44%), and the annuity segment 0.7% (0.8%).

CORPORATE STRATEGY. A key corporate strategy for TMK is to improve its

distribution system. Distribution is through direct solicitation, independent agents, and exclusive agents. The Liberty National exclusive agency markets products to middle-income families in the Southeastern U.S. through full-time sales representatives. The American Income exclusive agency focuses on members of labor unions, credit unions, and other associations in the U.S., Canada and New Zealand. The United Investors agency markets to middle-income Americans through independent agents. The military agency consists of a nationwide independent agency comprised of former commissioned and noncommissioned military officers who sell exclusively to military officers and their families. The United American independent agency focuses primarily on health insurance in the U.S. and Canada to individuals over the age of 50. The United American branch office agency also focuses on health insurance to over-age-50 individuals through exclusive producing agents.

## Company Financials Fiscal Year Ended Dec. 31

| Per Share Data ($) | 2009 | 2008 | 2007 | 2006 | 2005 | 2004 | 2003 | 2002 | 2001 | 2000 |
|---|---|---|---|---|---|---|---|---|---|---|
| Tangible Book Value | NA | NA | 31.74 | 31.39 | 29.49 | 28.16 | 25.39 | 20.91 | 17.24 | 14.34 |
| Operating Earnings | NA | NA | NA | NA | NA | NA | 3.87 | 3.51 | 3.12 | 2.85 |
| Earnings | 6.20 | NA | 5.50 | 5.13 | 4.68 | 4.25 | 3.73 | 3.18 | 3.11 | 2.82 |
| S&P Core Earnings | NA | NA | 5.35 | 5.07 | 4.29 | 4.03 | 3.68 | 3.39 | 2.73 | NA |
| Dividends | NA | NA | 0.52 | 0.48 | 0.44 | 0.44 | 0.38 | 0.36 | 0.36 | 0.36 |
| Payout Ratio | NA | NA | 9% | 9% | 9% | 10% | 10% | 11% | 12% | 13% |
| Prices:High | NA | NA | 70.54 | 64.59 | 57.50 | 57.57 | 45.75 | 42.17 | 43.25 | 41.19 |
| Prices:Low | NA | NA | 58.50 | 53.91 | 50.05 | 44.61 | 33.00 | 30.02 | 32.56 | 18.75 |
| P/E Ratio:High | NA | NA | 13 | 13 | 12 | 14 | 12 | 13 | 14 | 15 |
| P/E Ratio:Low | NA | NA | 11 | 11 | 11 | 10 | 9 | 9 | 10 | 7 |

| Income Statement Analysis (Million $) | | | | | | | | | | |
|---|---|---|---|---|---|---|---|---|---|---|
| Life Insurance in Force | NA | NA | 145,349 | 141,134 | 139,233 | 134,640 | 126,737 | 118,660 | 113,055 | 108,319 |
| Premium Income:Life | NA | NA | 1,570 | 1,524 | 1,468 | 1,396 | 1,246 | 1,221 | 1,144 | 1,082 |
| Premium Income:A & H | NA | NA | 1,237 | 1,238 | 1,015 | 1,049 | 1,034 | 1,019 | 1,011 | 911 |
| Net Investment Income | NA | NA | 649 | 629 | 603 | 577 | 557 | 519 | 492 | 472 |
| Total Revenue | NA | NA | 3,487 | 3,421 | 3,126 | 3,072 | 2,931 | 2,738 | 2,707 | 2,516 |
| Pretax Income | NA | NA | 797 | 774 | 732 | 721 | 655 | 580 | 597 | 553 |
| Net Operating Income | NA | NA | NA | NA | NA | NA | 446 | 424 | 393 | 365 |
| Net Income | NA | NA | 528 | 519 | 495 | 476 | 430 | 383 | 391 | 362 |
| S&P Core Earnings | NA | NA | 514 | 512 | 455 | 452 | 424 | 408 | 343 | NA |

| Balance Sheet & Other Financial Data (Million $) | | | | | | | | | | |
|---|---|---|---|---|---|---|---|---|---|---|
| Cash & Equivalent | NA | NA | 193 | 185 | 178 | 164 | 155 | 140 | 129 | 154 |
| Premiums Due | NA | NA | 86.7 | 78.8 | 67.3 | 73.4 | 80.7 | 70.4 | 67.5 | 75.0 |
| Investment Assets:Bonds | NA | NA | 9,226 | 9,127 | 8,837 | 8,715 | 8,103 | 7,194 | 6,526 | 5,950 |
| Investment Assets:Stocks | NA | NA | 21.3 | 41.2 | 48.0 | 36.9 | 57.4 | 24.5 | 0.57 | 0.54 |
| Investment Assets:Loans | NA | NA | 344 | 329 | 317 | 338 | 704 | 401 | 393 | 374 |
| Investment Assets:Total | NA | NA | 9,772 | 9,703 | 9,649 | 9,405 | 8,795 | 7,784 | 7,154 | 6,471 |
| Deferred Policy Costs | NA | NA | 3,159 | 2,956 | 2,768 | 2,506 | 2,330 | 2,184 | 2,066 | 1,942 |
| Total Assets | NA | NA | 15,241 | 14,980 | 14,769 | 14,252 | 13,461 | 12,361 | 12,428 | 12,963 |
| Debt | NA | NA | 598 | 598 | 353 | 540 | 693 | 552 | 681 | 366 |
| Common Equity | NA | NA | 3,325 | 3,459 | 3,433 | 6,840 | 3,240 | 2,851 | 2,497 | 2,202 |
| % Return on Revenue | NA | NA | 15.1 | 15.2 | 15.8 | 15.5 | 14.7 | 14.0 | 14.4 | 14.4 |
| % Return on Assets | NA | NA | 3.5 | 3.5 | 3.4 | 3.4 | 3.3 | 3.1 | 3.1 | 2.9 |
| % Return on Equity | NA | NA | 15.6 | 15.1 | 14.5 | 7.1 | 14.1 | 14.3 | 16.6 | 17.2 |
| % Investment Yield | NA | NA | 6.7 | 6.5 | 6.3 | 6.4 | 6.7 | 7.0 | 7.2 | 7.5 |

Data as orig reptd.; bef. results of disc opers/spec. items. Per share data adj. for stk. divs.; EPS diluted. E-Estimated. NA-Not Available. NM-Not Meaningful. NR-Not Ranked. UR-Under Review.

**Office:** 3700 S Stonebridge Dr, McKinney, TX 75070-5934.
**Telephone:** 972-569-4000.
**Website:** http://www.torchmarkcorp.com
**Chrmn & CEO:** M.S. McAndrew

**EVP & CFO:** G.L. Coleman
**EVP & Chief Admin Officer:** V.D. Herbel
**EVP & General Counsel:** L.M. Hutchison
**Chief Acctg Officer:** D.H. Almond

**Investor Contact:** J.L. Lane (972-569-3627)
**Board Members:** C. E. Adair, D. L. Boren, J. M. Buchan, R. W. Ingram, J. L. Lanier, Jr., M. S. McAndrew, L. W. Newton, S. R. Perry, L. Smith, P. J. Zucconi

**Founded:** 1900
**Domicile:** Delaware
**Employees:** 3,596

# Total System Services Inc.

**STANDARD &POOR'S**

| S&P Recommendation | HOLD ★★★☆☆ | Price | 12-Mo. Target Price | Investment Style |
|---|---|---|---|---|
| | | $12.16 (as of Nov 14, 2008) | $15.00 | Large-Cap Growth |

**GICS Sector** Information Technology
**Sub-Industry** Data Processing & Outsourced Services

**Summary** This company processes data, transactions and payments for domestic and international issuers of credit, debit, commercial, and private-label cards.

## Key Stock Statistics (Source S&P, Vickers, company reports)

| | | | | | | | |
|---|---|---|---|---|---|---|---|
| 52-Wk Range | $29.93–11.08 | S&P Oper. EPS 2008**E** | 1.28 | Market Capitalization(B) | $2.393 | Beta | 1.18 |
| Trailing 12-Month EPS | $1.16 | S&P Oper. EPS 2009**E** | 1.40 | Yield (%) | 2.30 | S&P 3-Yr. Proj. EPS CAGR(%) | 13 |
| Trailing 12-Month P/E | 10.5 | P/E on S&P Oper. EPS 2008**E** | 9.5 | Dividend Rate/Share | $0.28 | S&P Credit Rating | NA |
| $10K Invested 5 Yrs Ago | $4,923 | Common Shares Outstg. (M) | 196.8 | Institutional Ownership (%) | 55 | | |

## Price Performance

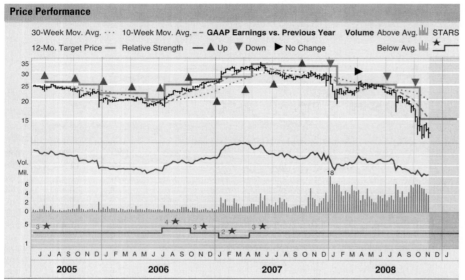

30-Week Mov. Avg. · · · 10-Week Mov. Avg. - - GAAP Earnings vs. Previous Year  Volume Above Avg. STARS
12-Mo. Target Price — Relative Strength — ▲ Up ▼ Down ▶ No Change  Below Avg. ★

Options: CBOE, Ph

Analysis prepared by **Zaineb Bokhari** on October 15, 2008, when the stock traded at **$ 13.91**.

### Highlights

➤ We expect operating revenues (before reimbursable items) to rise 5% in 2008 to $1.5 billion, driven largely by international growth. We see gains in operating revenues being impacted by slowing growth at TSS's domestic customers and some related price erosion, both attributable to the slowing domestic economy. We expect year-over-year growth comparisons to become easier in late 2008 due to the July 2007 termination of JPMorgan Chase's (JPM: strong buy, $41) processing agreement with TSS. We forecast 5% growth for operating revenues in 2009.

➤ We look for operating margins to widen modestly to 26% in 2008 from 25.6% in 2007, (excluding items) reflecting ongoing expense management measures, which the company is undertaking to offset anticipated shifts in its customer base, partly offset by expenses related to TSS's deconsolidation from Synovus. We expect 2008 operating margins to be helped by the shift of JPM to a license from an outsourcing customer. We anticipate modestly wider operating margins in 2009.

➤ We project 2008 GAAP EPS of $1.28, up from $1.20 in 2007. Our 2009 EPS estimate is $1.40.

### Investment Rationale/Risk

➤ We think TSS has managed itself well through a difficult period marked by sizable customer losses, particularly JPM's card portfolio of about 91 million accounts during the third quarter of 2007, which penalized revenue growth for that year. TSS has not recouped the lost accounts, and accounts on file numbered 355.4 million as of September 30, 2008, modestly below the year ago quarter. While TSS has lowered overhead, resulting in wider operating margins, we expect this migration to have a negative impact on account growth. We think TSS added flexibility to make acquisitions, pay dividends and buy back shares after its spin-off from Synovus Financial (SNV: hold, $10).

➤ Risks to our recommendation and target price include increased competition (particularly on price) from other payment processors, and an increased potential for business disruptions or loss due to ongoing industry consolidation. We expect the slowing U.S. economy to impact card growth.

➤ We derive our 12-month target price of $15 by applying a P/E of 11X to our 2009 estimate, below the recent average for peers of 12.6X, given our view of sales growth concerns.

### Qualitative Risk Assessment

| LOW | MEDIUM | HIGH |
|---|---|---|

Our risk assessment reflects our view that the company has managed itself well through a difficult period of sizable customer losses. We continue to view TSS as a leading low-cost provider of card processing services, but we expect ongoing business disruptions and price erosion in future quarters.

### Quantitative Evaluations

**S&P Quality Ranking**  A

| D | C | B- | B | B+ | A- | A | A+ |
|---|---|---|---|---|---|---|---|

**Relative Strength Rank**  MODERATE

49

LOWEST = 1  HIGHEST = 99

### Revenue/Earnings Data

**Revenue (Million $)**

| | 1Q | 2Q | 3Q | 4Q | Year |
|---|---|---|---|---|---|
| 2008 | 461.7 | 483.1 | 500.4 | -- | -- |
| 2007 | 429.6 | 460.2 | 457.6 | 458.5 | 1,806 |
| 2006 | 412.3 | 429.2 | 441.8 | 503.9 | 1,787 |
| 2005 | 350.0 | 410.2 | 422.0 | 420.7 | 1,603 |
| 2004 | 285.2 | 289.6 | 305.0 | 307.2 | 1,187 |
| 2003 | 251.4 | 257.7 | 266.1 | 278.3 | 1,053 |

**Earnings Per Share ($)**

| | | | | | |
|---|---|---|---|---|---|
| 2008 | 0.29 | 0.32 | 0.33 | E0.34 | E1.28 |
| 2007 | 0.29 | 0.33 | 0.35 | 0.23 | 1.20 |
| 2006 | 0.26 | 0.29 | 0.28 | 0.44 | 1.26 |
| 2005 | 0.23 | 0.26 | 0.24 | 0.25 | 0.99 |
| 2004 | 0.17 | 0.18 | 0.20 | 0.22 | 0.76 |
| 2003 | 0.16 | 0.17 | 0.18 | 0.20 | 0.71 |

Fiscal year ended Dec. 31. Next earnings report expected: Late January. EPS Estimates based on S&P Operating Earnings; historical GAAP earnings are as reported.

### Dividend Data (Dates: mm/dd Payment Date: mm/dd/yy)

| Amount ($) | Date Decl. | Ex-Div. Date | Stk. of Record | Payment Date |
|---|---|---|---|---|
| 0.070 | 11/30 | 12/19 | 12/17 | 01/02/08 |
| 0.070 | 03/10 | 03/18 | 03/20 | 04/01/08 |
| 0.070 | 06/09 | 06/17 | 06/19 | 07/01/08 |
| 0.070 | 09/05 | 09/16 | 09/18 | 10/01/08 |

Dividends have been paid since 1990. Source: Company reports.

---

**Please read the Required Disclosures and Analyst Certification on the last page of this report.**

*The McGraw-Hill Companies*

# Total System Services Inc.

## Business Summary October 15, 2008

CORPORATE PROFILE. Total System Services provides electronic payment processing and associated services to financial and non-financial institutions in the U.S., Canada, Mexico, Honduras, Puerto Rico and Europe. Electronic payment processing services (which accounted for 67% of operating revenue in 2007, versus 69% in 2006 and 67% in 2005) are generated primarily from charges based on the number of accounts on file, transactions and authorizations processed, statements mailed, and other processing services for cardholder accounts on file. As of December 2007, TSS had 375.5 million accounts on file, down from 461.4 million in 2006 and 437.9 million in 2005. Synovus Financial Corp. , which owned an 80.7% interest in TSS in October 2007, completed its spin-off of TSS in December 2007.

Services provided include processing for consumer, debit, commercial, stored value and retail cards, as well as for student loans. The company divides its services into three operating segments: domestic-based support services (70.5% of 2007 revenues, down from 74% in 2006, and 75% in 2005), international-based support services (13.8%, 10%, 9%), and merchant acquiring services (15.7%, 16%, 16%).

MARKET PROFILE. In 2007, TSS believed that its market share was 42% in U.S.

consumer card processing, up from 39% in 2006 and 2005 and 21% in 2004. The company's share of Visa and MasterCard U.S. commercial card processing grew to 87% in 2007 from 86% in 2006 and 84.6% in 2005, while its U.S. retail card processing share declined to 10% from 14% in 2006 and 14.4% in 2005.

CORPORATE STRATEGY. Acquisitions have played an important role in expanding the company's reach into complementary businesses and internationally. In July 2006, TSS acquired Card Tech, a private, London-based payment processing/merchant acquiring firm for $59.3 million. The acquisition expanded TSS's geographic reach into the Asia-Pacific and EMEA regions. In December 2005, TSYS, TSS's Vital Processing Services subsidiary, acquired a 34% equity stake in China UnionPay Data Co. (CUP Data), the data processing subsidiary of China UnionPay, China's largest bankcard processor, for $37 million. In August 2006, TSS raised its ownership interest in CUP Data to 44.56% for $15.6 million.

## Company Financials Fiscal Year Ended Dec. 31

| Per Share Data ($) | 2007 | 2006 | 2005 | 2004 | 2003 | 2002 | 2001 | 2000 | 1999 | 1998 |
|---|---|---|---|---|---|---|---|---|---|---|
| Tangible Book Value | 3.51 | 5.40 | 4.49 | 4.01 | 3.57 | 3.06 | 2.57 | 2.10 | 1.72 | 1.39 |
| Cash Flow | 1.44 | 2.20 | 1.75 | 1.31 | 1.21 | 1.01 | 0.82 | 0.70 | 0.61 | 0.47 |
| Earnings | 1.20 | 1.26 | 0.99 | 0.76 | 0.71 | 0.64 | 0.53 | 0.44 | 0.35 | 0.28 |
| S&P Core Earnings | 1.20 | 1.26 | 0.95 | 0.74 | 0.69 | 0.60 | 0.51 | NA | NA | NA |
| Dividends | 0.35 | 0.27 | 0.22 | 0.14 | 0.08 | 0.07 | 0.06 | 0.05 | 0.04 | 0.04 |
| Payout Ratio | 29% | 21% | 22% | 18% | 11% | 11% | 11% | 11% | 11% | 12% |
| Prices:High | 35.05 | 26.61 | 25.88 | 31.27 | 31.50 | 29.44 | 35.84 | 22.75 | 26.25 | 24.19 |
| Prices:Low | 24.35 | 17.87 | 17.76 | 19.47 | 13.25 | 11.01 | 18.91 | 14.88 | 14.13 | 14.44 |
| P/E Ratio:High | 29 | 21 | 26 | 41 | 44 | 46 | 68 | 52 | 75 | 86 |
| P/E Ratio:Low | 20 | 14 | 18 | 26 | 19 | 17 | 36 | 34 | 40 | 52 |

| Income Statement Analysis (Million $) | | | | | | | | | | |
|---|---|---|---|---|---|---|---|---|---|---|
| Revenue | 1,806 | 1,787 | 1,603 | 1,187 | 1,053 | 955 | 650 | 601 | 534 | 396 |
| Operating Income | 415 | 542 | 438 | 311 | 289 | 232 | 193 | 164 | 138 | 104 |
| Depreciation | 47.1 | 185 | 151 | 109 | 98.4 | 74.5 | 57.4 | 51.6 | 50.2 | 37.5 |
| Interest Expense | 3.13 | 0.57 | 0.37 | 0.94 | Nil | 1.10 | Nil | Nil | Nil | Nil |
| Pretax Income | 383 | 376 | 298 | 228 | 212 | 184 | 156 | 132 | 104 | 81.8 |
| Effective Tax Rate | 37.5% | 33.6% | 34.7% | 33.9% | 33.4% | 31.5% | 33.9% | 35.0% | 33.8% | 33.0% |
| Net Income | 237 | 249 | 195 | 151 | 141 | 126 | 103 | 85.6 | 68.6 | 54.8 |
| S&P Core Earnings | 237 | 249 | 188 | 145 | 136 | 119 | 99.5 | NA | NA | NA |

| Balance Sheet & Other Financial Data (Million $) | | | | | | | | | | |
|---|---|---|---|---|---|---|---|---|---|---|
| Cash | 240 | 389 | 238 | 232 | 123 | 113 | 56.0 | 80.1 | 54.9 | 9.56 |
| Current Assets | 587 | 745 | 512 | 448 | 274 | 266 | 206 | 211 | 180 | 120 |
| Total Assets | 1,479 | 1,634 | 1,411 | 1,282 | 1,001 | 783 | 652 | 604 | 457 | 349 |
| Current Liabilities | 274 | 296 | 277 | 278 | 147 | 114 | 103 | 147 | 103 | 59.3 |
| Long Term Debt | 257 | 3.63 | 3.56 | 4.51 | 29.7 | 0.07 | Nil | Nil | 0.16 | 0.21 |
| Common Equity | 844 | 1,217 | 1,013 | 865 | 733 | 602 | 501 | 409 | 334 | 270 |
| Total Capital | 1,177 | 1,296 | 1,106 | 1,004 | 854 | 668 | 550 | 446 | 354 | 290 |
| Capital Expenditures | 55.3 | 26.5 | 40.9 | 53.9 | 125 | 14.8 | 30.8 | 31.8 | 19.8 | 37.0 |
| Cash Flow | 285 | 434 | 346 | 259 | 239 | 200 | 160 | 137 | 119 | 92.3 |
| Current Ratio | 2.1 | 2.5 | 1.8 | 1.6 | 1.9 | 2.3 | 2.0 | 1.4 | 1.7 | 2.0 |
| % Long Term Debt of Capitalization | 21.8 | 0.3 | 0.3 | 0.4 | 3.5 | 0.0 | Nil | Nil | 0.0 | 0.1 |
| % Net Income of Revenue | 13.2 | 13.9 | 12.1 | 12.7 | 13.4 | 13.2 | 15.8 | 14.2 | 12.8 | 13.8 |
| % Return on Assets | 15.3 | 16.4 | 14.4 | 13.2 | 15.8 | 17.5 | 16.4 | 16.0 | 17.0 | 16.9 |
| % Return on Equity | 23.0 | 22.3 | 20.7 | 18.9 | 21.1 | 22.7 | 22.6 | 23.0 | 22.7 | 22.4 |

Data as orig reptd.; bef. results of disc opers/spec. items. Per share data adj. for stk. divs.; EPS diluted. E-Estimated. NA-Not Available. NM-Not Meaningful. NR-Not Ranked. UR-Under Review.

**Office:** 1600 First Avenue, Columbus, GA 31902.
**Telephone:** 706-649-2262.
**Email:** ir@tsys.com
**Website:** http://www.tsys.com

**Chrmn & CEO:** P.W. Tomlinson
**Pres & COO:** M.T. Woods
**EVP, CFO & Treas:** J.B. Lipham
**EVP & CTO:** S.W. Humber

**EVP, Chief Acctg Officer & Cntlr:** D.K. Weaver
**Investor Contact:** S. Roberts (706-644-6081)
**Board Members:** R. E. Anthony, J. H. Blanchard, R. Y. Bradley, K. Cloninger, III, W. W. Driver, Jr., G. W. Garrard, Jr., S. E. Harris, A. W. Jones, III, M. H. Lampton, W. W. Miller, Jr., H. L. Page, P. W. Tomlinson, J. T. Turner, R. W. Ussery, M. T. Woods, J. D. Yancey, R. K. Yarbrough

**Founded:** 1982
**Domicile:** Georgia
**Employees:** 6,921

# Transocean Inc

STANDARD &POOR'S

| S&P Recommendation | STRONG BUY ★ ★ ★ ★ ★ | Price | 12-Mo. Target Price | Investment Style |
|---|---|---|---|---|
| | | $70.89 (as of Nov 14, 2008) | $109.00 | Large-Cap Blend |

**GICS Sector** Energy
**Sub-Industry** Oil & Gas Drilling

**Summary** This leading provider of contract drilling services for the oil and gas industry operates the world's largest fleet of mobile offshore drilling units.

## Key Stock Statistics (Source S&P, Vickers, company reports)

| | | | | | | | |
|---|---|---|---|---|---|---|---|
| 52-Wk Range | $187.98–56.95 | S&P Oper. EPS 2008E | 14.58 | Market Capitalization(B) | $22.626 | Beta | 1.38 |
| Trailing 12-Month EPS | $14.64 | S&P Oper. EPS 2009E | 16.74 | Yield (%) | Nil | S&P 3-Yr. Proj. EPS CAGR(%) | 74 |
| Trailing 12-Month P/E | 4.8 | P/E on S&P Oper. EPS 2008E | 4.9 | Dividend Rate/Share | Nil | S&P Credit Rating | NA |
| $10K Invested 5 Yrs Ago | $25,485 | Common Shares Outstg. (M) | 319.2 | Institutional Ownership (%) | 87 | | |

## Price Performance

30-Week Mov. Avg. ···· 10-Week Mov. Avg. -- **GAAP Earnings vs. Previous Year** Volume Above Avg. STARS
12-Mo. Target Price — Relative Strength — ▲ Up ▼ Down ▶ No Change Below Avg.

0.6996-for

Options: ASE, CBOE, P, Ph

Analysis prepared by **Stewart Glickman, CFA** on November 07, 2008, when the stock traded at **$ 76.26**.

## Highlights

▸ In November, RIG said it had contracted a new-build drillship, to commence operations in the fourth quarter of 2010, for five years at a dayrate in the range of $640,000 to $650,000 per day. We think this underscores the strong demand for deepwater rigs and high visibility going forward. Third-quarter operating expenses were above our expectations, but we note that most of the sequential uptick was due to a single rig incident. We expect 2009 operating expenses to be up in the high single digits, below recent annualized cost inflation levels.

▸ We view the late 2007 Transocean-Global-SantaFe merger as a monetization of its then-combined $33 billion backlog; the total cash outlay of about $15 billion (to shareholders of both predecessor companies) is being financed via debt, and free cash flow over the first two years will be used to reduce that debt. As of October 2008, RIG's backlog had jumped to $41 billion. Although the recent credit crisis is a concern for the industry, we see RIG as able to pay off the debt in short order by virtue of its strong backlog and high earnings visibility.

▸ We estimate operating EPS of $14.58 in 2008, and $16.74 in 2009.

## Investment Rationale/Risk

▸ We view RIG as a solid deepwater play that, by virtue of its merger with the former Global-SantaFe, now has a strong presence in the premium jackup market. While RIG's active fleet is roughly a 50/50 split between floaters and jack-ups, we estimate floaters will generate about 68% of contract drilling revenues in 2008 and 71% in 2009. In July, RIG said that the market for high specification deepwater rigs was tightening for 2010. With most newbuild floaters already under contract, we expect deepwater dayrates to remain strong over at least the next 3-5 years.

▸ Risks to our recommendation and target price include lower crude oil and natural gas prices; lower utilization and dayrates; lower-than-expected operating cash flows with which to reduce the added debt burden of the merger; and higher-than-expected cost inflation.

▸ On improved growth expectations, we think RIG shares merit a premium to peers. Using a 7X multiple of our estimate of 2009 EPS and 5X projected 2009 EBITDA (both premiums to peers), and blending with our net asset valuation, our 12-month target price is $109.

## Qualitative Risk Assessment

| LOW | MEDIUM | HIGH |
|---|---|---|

Our risk assessment reflects RIG's exposure to volatile crude oil and natural gas prices, capital spending decisions by oil and gas producing customers, and risks associated with operating in frontier regions. Offsetting these risks is RIG's leadership position in deepwater drilling.

## Quantitative Evaluations

**S&P Quality Ranking** NR

| D | C | B- | B | B+ | A- | A | A+ |
|---|---|---|---|---|---|---|---|

**Relative Strength Rank** MODERATE

42

LOWEST = 1        HIGHEST = 99

## Revenue/Earnings Data

**Revenue (Million $)**

| | 1Q | 2Q | 3Q | 4Q | Year |
|---|---|---|---|---|---|
| 2008 | 3,110 | 3,102 | 3,192 | -- | -- |
| 2007 | 1,328 | 1,434 | 1,538 | 2,077 | 6,377 |
| 2006 | 817.0 | 854.0 | 1,025 | 1,186 | 3,882 |
| 2005 | 630.5 | 727.4 | 762.6 | 771.2 | 2,892 |
| 2004 | 652.0 | 633.2 | 651.8 | 676.9 | 2,614 |
| 2003 | 616.0 | 603.9 | 622.9 | 591.5 | 2,434 |

**Earnings Per Share ($)**

| | | | | | |
|---|---|---|---|---|---|
| 2008 | 3.70 | 3.45 | 3.45 | E3.99 | E14.58 |
| 2007 | 2.63 | 2.63 | 4.63 | 4.16 | 14.14 |
| 2006 | 0.87 | 1.07 | 1.37 | 2.93 | 6.12 |
| 2005 | 0.40 | 1.29 | 0.71 | 0.64 | 3.04 |
| 2004 | 0.10 | 0.21 | 0.69 | -0.33 | 0.67 |
| 2003 | 0.21 | -0.20 | 0.04 | 0.03 | 0.09 |

Fiscal year ended Dec. 31. Next earnings report expected: Late February. EPS Estimates based on S&P Operating Earnings; historical GAAP earnings are as reported.

## Dividend Data (Dates: mm/dd Payment Date: mm/dd/yy)

| Amount ($) | Date Decl. | Ex-Div. Date | Stk. of Record | Payment Date |
|---|---|---|---|---|
| 0.6996-for-1 REV. | -- | 11/27 | -- | 11/27/07 |

Source: Company reports.

---

The McGraw-Hill Companies

# Transocean Inc

**STANDARD &POOR'S**

## Business Summary November 07, 2008

CORPORATE OVERVIEW. Transocean (RIG; formerly Transocean Sedco Forex), the world's largest offshore drilling company, acquired R&B Falcon (FLC) on January 31, 2001. In May 2002, the company adopted its current name. In November 2007, Transocean and a former rival, GlobalSantaFe, merged. Transocean was the surviving entity and kept its name.

RIG historically has focused mainly on deepwater drilling activity, where RIG defines the deepwater sector as that which begins in water depths of 4,500 ft., and extending to practical maximum depth, which is currently at about 10,000 ft. of water. The mid-water market typically covers water depths of 400 ft. to 4,500 ft., while the shallow water jackup market covers water depths of up to 400 ft. By virtue of the GlobalSantaFe transaction, however, RIG now possesses a fleet of 136 active drilling rigs, comprised of 68 floaters, 66 jackups, and two drilling barges.

COMPETITIVE LANDSCAPE. RIG's addressable market for offshore drilling rigs is global in nature, given that rigs can be mobilized from region to region.

Active offshore drilling regions around the globe include the U.S. Gulf of Mexico, the North Sea, West Africa, Southeast Asia, the Mediterranean, the Caspian Sea, and the Middle East. With 136 actively marketed mobile offshore drilling rigs as of March 2008, RIG is the leading player in this market. Of the 136 rigs, 68 are floater rigs--semisubmersibles and drillships--of which 34 are rated for deepwater drilling. In addition, the company has eight other new-build floaters under construction, due for delivery between 2009 and 2011. The company has the vast majority of its drilling rigs located in seven regions: West Africa (28), Northwest Europe (24 rigs), the U.S. Gulf of Mexico (19), Egypt/the Middle East/ the Mediterranean (19), Asia Pacific (16), India (12), and Brazil (4).

## Company Financials Fiscal Year Ended Dec. 31

| Per Share Data ($) | 2007 | 2006 | 2005 | 2004 | 2003 | 2002 | 2001 | 2000 | 1999 | 1998 |
|---|---|---|---|---|---|---|---|---|---|---|
| Tangible Book Value | 13.70 | 22.71 | 25.41 | 22.86 | 22.23 | 22.04 | 19.93 | 20.13 | 26.60 | 18.52 |
| Cash Flow | 16.35 | 7.86 | 4.72 | 2.97 | 2.35 | -8.37 | 4.07 | 2.48 | 1.29 | 6.52 |
| Earnings | 14.14 | 6.12 | 3.04 | 0.67 | 0.09 | -10.61 | 1.23 | 0.71 | 0.76 | 4.87 |
| Dividends | Nil | Nil | Nil | Nil | Nil | 0.09 | 0.17 | 0.17 | 0.17 | 0.17 |
| Payout Ratio | Nil | Nil | Nil | Nil | Nil | NM | 14% | 24% | 23% | 4% |
| Prices:High | 187.98 | 128.87 | 101.39 | 61.82 | 37.02 | 56.18 | 82.46 | 93.62 | 52.17 | 85.67 |
| Prices:Low | 103.59 | 92.22 | 56.88 | 33.02 | 26.30 | 25.87 | 32.95 | 41.81 | 28.05 | 32.88 |
| P/E Ratio:High | 13 | 21 | 33 | 92 | NM | NM | 67 | NM | 69 | 18 |
| P/E Ratio:Low | 7 | 15 | 19 | 49 | NM | NM | 27 | NM | 37 | 7 |

| Income Statement Analysis (Million $) | 2007 | 2006 | 2005 | 2004 | 2003 | 2002 | 2001 | 2000 | 1999 | 1998 |
|---|---|---|---|---|---|---|---|---|---|---|
| Revenue | 6,377 | 3,882 | 2,892 | 2,614 | 2,434 | 2,674 | 2,820 | 1,230 | 648 | 1,090 |
| Operating Income | 3,536 | 1,637 | 1,096 | 821 | 759 | 1,114 | 1,159 | 375 | 181 | 577 |
| Depreciation, Depletion and Amortization | 499 | 401 | 406 | 525 | 508 | 500 | 625 | 259 | 132 | 117 |
| Interest Expense | 248 | 115 | 111 | 172 | 202 | 212 | 224 | 3.03 | 10.3 | 23.9 |
| Pretax Income | 3,384 | 1,607 | 802 | 240 | 21.6 | -2,489 | 361 | 144 | 48.8 | 487 |
| Effective Tax Rate | 7.48% | 13.8% | 10.8% | 38.0% | 13.9% | NM | 23.8% | 25.4% | NM | 29.5% |
| Net Income | 3,131 | 1,385 | 716 | 152 | 18.4 | -2,368 | 272 | 107 | 58.1 | 343 |

| Balance Sheet & Other Financial Data (Million $) | 2007 | 2006 | 2005 | 2004 | 2003 | 2002 | 2001 | 2000 | 1999 | 1998 |
|---|---|---|---|---|---|---|---|---|---|---|
| Cash | 1,241 | 467 | 445 | 451 | 474 | 1,214 | 853 | 34.5 | 166 | 69.5 |
| Current Assets | 4,296 | 1,656 | 1,279 | 1,109 | 1,179 | 1,912 | 1,737 | 448 | 559 | 362 |
| Total Assets | 34,364 | 11,476 | 10,457 | 10,758 | 11,663 | 12,665 | 17,020 | 6,359 | 6,140 | 3,251 |
| Current Liabilities | 7,902 | 1,039 | 924 | 430 | 511 | 1,504 | 1,144 | 495 | 529 | 192 |
| Long Term Debt | 11,085 | 3,200 | 1,197 | 2,462 | 3,612 | 3,630 | 4,539 | 1,430 | 1,188 | 814 |
| Common Equity | 12,566 | 6,836 | 7,982 | 7,393 | 7,193 | 7,141 | 10,910 | 4,004 | 3,910 | 1,979 |
| Total Capital | 24,337 | 10,094 | 9,247 | 9,983 | 10,848 | 10,879 | 15,767 | 5,794 | 5,482 | 3,023 |
| Capital Expenditures | 1,380 | 876 | 182 | 127 | 496 | 141 | 506 | 575 | 537 | 573 |
| Cash Flow | 3,630 | 1,786 | 1,121 | 677 | 527 | -1,868 | 897 | 367 | 190 | 460 |
| Current Ratio | 0.5 | 1.6 | 1.4 | 2.6 | 2.3 | 1.3 | 1.5 | 0.9 | 1.1 | 1.9 |
| % Long Term Debt of Capitalization | 45.6 | 31.7 | 12.9 | 24.7 | 33.3 | 33.4 | 28.7 | 24.7 | 21.7 | 26.9 |
| % Return on Assets | 13.7 | 12.6 | 6.7 | 1.4 | 0.2 | NM | 2.3 | 1.7 | 1.5 | 11.4 |
| % Return on Equity | 32.3 | 18.7 | 9.3 | 2.1 | 0.3 | NM | 3.6 | 2.7 | 2.6 | 19.1 |

Data as orig reptd.; bef. results of disc opers/spec. items. Per share data adj. for stk. divs.; EPS diluted. E-Estimated. NA-Not Available. NM-Not Meaningful. NR-Not Ranked. UR-Under Review.

**Office:** 4 Greenway Plaza, Houston, TX 77046.
**Telephone:** 713-232-7500.
**Email:** lmilner@mail.deepwater.com
**Website:** http://www.deepwater.com

**Chrmn:** R. Rose
**Pres & COO:** S.L. Newman
**CEO:** R.L. Long
**SVP & CFO:** G.L. Cauthen

**SVP & General Counsel:** E.B. Brown
**Investor Contact:** G.S. Panagos (713-232-7551)
**Board Members:** W. R. Anderson, T. W. Cason, R. L. George, V. E. Grijalva, R. L. Long, J. A. Marshall, M. B. McNamara, E. R. Muller, R. Rose, K. Siem, R. M. Sprague, I. C. Strachan, J. M. Talbert, J. L. Whitmire, III

**Founded:** 1953
**Domicile:** Cayman Islands
**Employees:** 21,100

**The McGraw-Hill Companies**

# Travelers Companies Inc (The)

**STANDARD &POOR'S**

| S&P Recommendation | STRONG BUY ★★★★★ | Price $41.88 (as of Nov 14, 2008) | 12-Mo. Target Price $50.00 | Investment Style Large-Cap Value |
|---|---|---|---|---|

**GICS Sector** Financials
**Sub-Industry** Property & Casualty Insurance

**Summary** Formed via the 2004 merger of Travelers Property Casualty Corp. and Saint Paul Cos., TRV is a leading provider of commercial property-liability and homeowners and auto insurance.

## Key Stock Statistics (Source S&P, Vickers, company reports)

| | | | | | | | |
|---|---|---|---|---|---|---|---|
| 52-Wk Range | $58.57– 28.91 | S&P Oper. EPS 2008**E** | 4.90 | Market Capitalization(B) | $24.480 | Beta | 0.92 |
| Trailing 12-Month EPS | $5.13 | S&P Oper. EPS 2009**E** | 5.75 | Yield (%) | 2.87 | S&P 3-Yr. Proj. EPS CAGR(%) | -1 |
| Trailing 12-Month P/E | 8.2 | P/E on S&P Oper. EPS 2008**E** | 8.5 | Dividend Rate/Share | $1.20 | S&P Credit Rating | A- |
| $10K Invested 5 Yrs Ago | $27,194 | Common Shares Outstg. (M) | 584.5 | Institutional Ownership (%) | 88 | | |

## Price Performance

30-Week Mov. Avg. · · · 10-Week Mov. Avg. - - **GAAP Earnings vs. Previous Year** Volume Above Avg. STARS
12-Mo. Target Price — Relative Strength — ▲ Up ▼ Down ▶ No Change Below Avg.

[Price Performance chart with years 2005, 2006, 2007, 2008 and monthly labels J J A S O N D]

Options: ASE, CBOE, Ph

Analysis prepared by **Cathy A. Seifert** on October 23, 2008, when the stock traded at **$38.00**.

## Highlights

➤ We expect earned premium growth from continuing operations of 1% to 2% to in 2008, versus earned premium growth of 3% reported for 2007. Earned premiums should rise slightly in 2009, as ongoing price competition is partly offset by new business opportunities. Our premium forecasts for TRV are ahead of what we expect for the property-casualty industry as a whole. We attribute this to TRV's mix of business, partly offset by some heightened price competition. Higher catastrophe claims are likely to be partly offset by continued favorable prior-year loss trends in certain casualty lines.

➤ We believe net investment income will decline 10% in 2008, reflecting a more challenging investment environment. Net investment income was up 7% in 2007. We think investment income will rise 4% to 6% in 2009.

➤ We estimate operating EPS of $4.90 in 2008 and $5.75 in 2009, versus operating EPS of $6.71 in 2007. Our estimates assume that both underwriting and investment results will deteriorate slightly from the unusually favorable results posted for 2007, but that TRV will not incur any significant reserve boosts.

## Investment Rationale/Risk

➤ Although our outlook remains tempered by concerns we have that both the underwriting and investment environments will remain challenging in 2008, we believe TRV's shares do not adequately reflect the actions the company has taken in recent years to improve its underwriting results and to better withstand what we see as heightened competitive pressures in the property-casualty insurance market.

➤ Risks to our recommendation and target price include a deterioration in asbestos and environmental claims and reserve development, an erosion in underwriting trends, a surge in catastrophe losses, and an erosion in the credit quality of TRV's investment portfolio.

➤ Our 12-month target price of $50 assumes a forward price/earnings multiple of 8.7X our 2009 operating earnings per share estimate. This target multiple assumes TRV shares will trade at the low end of their historical valuation range, but at a premium to some peers.

## Qualitative Risk Assessment

| LOW | MEDIUM | HIGH |
|---|---|---|

Our risk assessment reflects our view of TRV as a leading property-casualty underwriter with a diversified mix of business and sound capital management practices. Offsetting this is our view that TRV may have to add to loss reserves for certain "long tail" liability lines of coverage, and could see impairments to its fixed income investment portfolio.

## Quantitative Evaluations

**S&P Quality Ranking** NR

| D | C | B- | B | B+ | A- | A | A+ |
|---|---|---|---|---|---|---|---|

**Relative Strength Rank** STRONG

95

LOWEST = 1 HIGHEST = 99

## Revenue/Earnings Data

**Revenue (Million $)**

| | 1Q | 2Q | 3Q | 4Q | Year |
|---|---|---|---|---|---|
| 2008 | 6,232 | 6,295 | 6,145 | -- | -- |
| 2007 | 6,427 | 6,612 | 6,526 | 6,491 | 26,017 |
| 2006 | 6,050 | 6,255 | 6,316 | 6,469 | 25,090 |
| 2005 | 6,105 | 6,037 | 6,042 | 6,181 | 24,365 |
| 2004 | 4,128 | 6,181 | 6,261 | 6,365 | 22,934 |
| 2003 | 3,603 | 3,749 | 3,746 | 4,042 | 15,139 |

**Earnings Per Share ($)**

| | | | | | |
|---|---|---|---|---|---|
| 2008 | 1.54 | 1.54 | 0.36 | E1.21 | E4.90 |
| 2007 | 1.56 | 1.86 | 1.81 | 1.64 | 6.86 |
| 2006 | 1.41 | 1.36 | 1.47 | 1.68 | 5.91 |
| 2005 | 1.25 | 1.33 | 0.11 | 0.26 | 2.95 |
| 2004 | 1.34 | -0.42 | 0.50 | 0.44 | 1.53 |
| 2003 | 0.34 | 0.44 | 0.42 | 0.49 | 1.68 |

Fiscal year ended Dec. 31. Next earnings report expected: Late January. EPS Estimates based on S&P Operating Earnings; historical GAAP earnings are as reported.

## Dividend Data (Dates: mm/dd Payment Date: mm/dd/yy)

| Amount ($) | Date Decl. | Ex-Div. Date | Stk. of Record | Payment Date |
|---|---|---|---|---|
| 0.290 | 02/06 | 03/06 | 03/10 | 03/31/08 |
| 0.300 | 05/07 | 06/06 | 06/10 | 06/30/08 |
| 0.300 | 08/06 | 09/08 | 09/10 | 09/30/08 |
| 0.300 | 11/06 | 12/08 | 12/10 | 12/31/08 |

Dividends have been paid since 2003. Source: Company reports.

---

**Please read the Required Disclosures and Analyst Certification on the last page of this report.**

The McGraw-Hill Companies

# Travelers Companies Inc (The)

STANDARD
&POOR'S

## Business Summary October 23, 2008

CORPORATE OVERVIEW. The Travelers Companies (TRV) is a leading property-casualty underwriter. Net written premiums of $21.6 billion in 2007 were divided as follows: business insurance 52%; personal lines 32%; and financial, professional and international lines 16%.

The business insurance lines segment offers a broad array of coverages distributed through about 6,300 independent brokers and agencies in the U.S. Business insurance net written premiums of $11.3 billion in 2007 were divided as follows: commercial multi-peril 27%, workers' compensation 20%, commercial automobile 18%, commercial property 18%, and general liability and other 17%. This segment's underwriting results in 2007 improved amid a lower level of losses and some favorable reserve development. As such, the combined loss and expense ratio improved to 87.8% in 2007 from 90.9% in 2006.

The financial, professional and international segment underwrites a number of specialized lines of business, including lines of coverage related to the surety bond business, the construction industry, and certain types of professional and managerial liability. This unit operates throughout the U.S. and in the U.K., Canada and Ireland. Net written premiums of $3.5 billion in 2007 were

divided as follows: general liability 27%, fidelity and surety 33%, international 36%, and other 4%. Underwriting results in this segment improved in 2007, with a combined loss and expense ratio of 87.0%, versus 89.0% in 2006.

The personal lines segment underwrites an array of coverage for personal risks (primarily personal automobile and homeowners' coverage) via a network of independent agencies. Net premiums written of $6.8 billion in 2007 were divided as follows: personal auto 53% and homeowners' and other 47%. At year-end 2007, automobile policies in force increased slightly to about 2.48 million (from 2.45 million in 2006), while homeowners' and other policies in force rose to 4.68 million (from 4.54 million in 2006). Underwriting results in 2007 deteriorated slightly, reflecting higher catastrophe losses and a rise in loss costs (other than those associated with catastrophes) outweighing the impact of contained underwriting expense growth. As a result, the combined ratio ended 2007 at 88.8%, versus 83.1% at the end of 2006.

## Company Financials Fiscal Year Ended Dec. 31

| Per Share Data ($) | 2007 | 2006 | 2005 | 2004 | 2003 | 2002 | 2001 | 2000 | 1999 | 1998 |
|---|---|---|---|---|---|---|---|---|---|---|
| Tangible Book Value | 35.56 | 31.85 | 25.66 | 20.93 | 9.52 | 10.29 | 6.66 | NA | NA | NA |
| Operating Earnings | NA | NA | NA | NA | NA | NA | NA | NA | NA | NA |
| Earnings | 6.86 | 5.91 | 2.95 | 1.53 | 1.68 | 0.23 | 1.06 | 1.71 | 1.48 | NA |
| S&P Core Earnings | 6.67 | 5.87 | 2.87 | 1.50 | 3.71 | 0.14 | 2.42 | NA | NA | NA |
| Dividends | 1.13 | 1.01 | 0.91 | 0.74 | 0.28 | Nil | NA | NA | NA | NA |
| Payout Ratio | 16% | 17% | 31% | 48% | 17% | Nil | NA | NA | NA | NA |
| Prices:High | 56.99 | 55.00 | 46.97 | 43.31 | 17.42 | 19.50 | NA | NA | NA | NA |
| Prices:Low | 47.26 | 40.23 | 33.70 | 16.55 | 12.98 | 12.09 | NA | NA | NA | NA |
| P/E Ratio:High | 8 | 9 | 16 | 28 | 10 | 85 | NA | NA | NA | NA |
| P/E Ratio:Low | 7 | 7 | 11 | 11 | 8 | 53 | NA | NA | NA | NA |

| Income Statement Analysis (Million $) | 2007 | 2006 | 2005 | 2004 | 2003 | 2002 | 2001 | 2000 | 1999 | 1998 |
|---|---|---|---|---|---|---|---|---|---|---|
| Premium Income | 21,470 | 20,760 | 20,341 | 19,038 | 12,545 | 11,155 | 9,411 | NA | NA | NA |
| Net Investment Income | 3,761 | 3,517 | 3,165 | 2,663 | 1,869 | 1,881 | 2,034 | NA | NA | NA |
| Other Revenue | 825 | 813 | 859 | 20,271 | 725 | 1,234 | 786 | NA | NA | NA |
| Total Revenue | 26,017 | 25,090 | 24,365 | 22,934 | 15,139 | 14,270 | 12,231 | 11,071 | 10,573 | NA |
| Pretax Income | 6,216 | 5,725 | 2,671 | 1,128 | 2,229 | -260 | 1,389 | 1,864 | 1,839 | NA |
| Net Operating Income | NA | NA | NA | NA | NA | NA | NA | NA | NA | NA |
| Net Income | 4,601 | 4,208 | 2,061 | 955 | 1,696 | 216 | 1,062 | 1,312 | 1,136 | NA |
| S&P Core Earnings | 4,464 | 4,171 | 2,001 | 937 | 1,615 | 41.1 | 803 | NA | NA | NA |

| Balance Sheet & Other Financial Data (Million $) | 2007 | 2006 | 2005 | 2004 | 2003 | 2002 | 2001 | 2000 | 1999 | 1998 |
|---|---|---|---|---|---|---|---|---|---|---|
| Cash & Equivalent | 1,132 | 1,286 | 1,098 | 933 | 714 | 432 | 865 | 196 | NA | NA |
| Premiums Due | 6,142 | 6,181 | 6,124 | 6,201 | 4,090 | 3,861 | NA | NA | NA | NA |
| Investment Assets:Bonds | 64,920 | 62,666 | 58,983 | 54,256 | 33,046 | 30,003 | NA | NA | NA | NA |
| Investment Assets:Stocks | 488 | 476 | 579 | 791 | 733 | 852 | NA | NA | NA | NA |
| Investment Assets:Loans | Nil | Nil | 145 | 191 | 211 | 258 | 32,843 | NA | NA | NA |
| Investment Assets:Total | 74,818 | 72,268 | 68,287 | 64,710 | 38,652 | 38,425 | 32,619 | 30,754 | NA | NA |
| Deferred Policy Costs | 1,809 | 1,615 | 1,527 | 1,559 | 925 | 873 | NA | NA | NA | NA |
| Total Assets | 115,224 | 113,761 | 113,187 | 111,815 | 64,872 | 64,138 | 57,599 | 53,850 | NA | NA |
| Debt | 6,242 | 4,588 | 5,850 | 5,709 | 2,675 | 2,744 | 3,755 | NA | NA | NA |
| Common Equity | 26,504 | 25,006 | 33,077 | 32,323 | 11,987 | 10,137 | 9,729 | 9,214 | NA | NA |
| Property & Casualty:Loss Ratio | 56.6 | 57.5 | 71.9 | NA | NA | NA | 80.7 | NA | NA | NA |
| Property & Casualty:Expense Ratio | 30.8 | 30.6 | 29.4 | NA | NA | NA | 27.3 | NA | NA | NA |
| Property & Casualty Combined Ratio | 87.4 | 88.1 | 101.3 | 107.7 | 96.9 | 117.4 | 108.0 | NA | NA | NA |
| % Return on Revenue | 17.8 | 20.3 | 8.5 | 4.2 | 11.2 | 1.6 | 8.7 | 11.9 | 10.7 | NA |
| % Return on Equity | 17.9 | 17.8 | 6.3 | 3.7 | 15.3 | NA | 10.7 | NA | NA | NA |

Data as orig reptd.; bef. results of disc opers/spec. items. Per share data adj. for stk. divs.; EPS diluted. E-Estimated. NA-Not Available. NM-Not Meaningful. NR-Not Ranked. UR-Under Review.

**Office:** 385 Washington Street, Saint Paul, MN 55102.
**Telephone:** 651-310-7911.
**Website:** http://www.stpaultravelers.com
**Chrmn & CEO:** J.S. Fishman

**Pres & COO:** B.W. MacLean
**EVP & Chief Admin Officer:** A. Bessette
**SVP, Chief Acctg Officer, Treas & Cntlr:** D.K. Russell
**SVP & Secy:** B.A. Backberg

**Investor Contact:** M. Parr (860-277-0779)
**Board Members:** A. L. Beller, J. H. Dasburg, J. M. Dolan, K. M. Duberstein, J. S. Fishman, L. G. Graev, P. L. Higgins, T. R. Hodgson, C. L. Killingsworth, Jr., R. I. Lipp, B. J. McGarvie, G. D. Nelson

**Auditor:** KPMG
**Founded:** 1853
**Domicile:** Minnesota
**Employees:** 33,300

The McGraw-Hill Companies

**STANDARD
&POOR'S**

# T. Rowe Price Group Inc

| S&P Recommendation HOLD ★★★☆☆ | Price $31.51 (as of Nov 14, 2008) | 12-Mo. Target Price $36.00 | Investment Style Large-Cap Growth |
|---|---|---|---|

**GICS Sector** Financials
**Sub-Industry** Asset Management & Custody Banks

**Summary** This company (formerly T. Rowe Price Associates) operates one of the largest no-load mutual fund complexes in the United States.

## Key Stock Statistics (Source S&P, Vickers, company reports)

| | | | | | | | |
|---|---|---|---|---|---|---|---|
| 52-Wk Range | $70.20– 26.64 | S&P Oper. EPS 2008**E** | 2.19 | Market Capitalization(B) | $8.142 | Beta | 1.41 |
| Trailing 12-Month EPS | $2.40 | S&P Oper. EPS 2009**E** | 2.17 | Yield (%) | 3.05 | S&P 3-Yr. Proj. EPS CAGR(%) | -1 |
| Trailing 12-Month P/E | 13.1 | P/E on S&P Oper. EPS 2008**E** | 14.4 | Dividend Rate/Share | $0.96 | S&P Credit Rating | NA |
| $10K Invested 5 Yrs Ago | $15,998 | Common Shares Outstg. (M) | 258.4 | Institutional Ownership (%) | 71 | | |

## Price Performance

30-Week Mov. Avg. ···· 10-Week Mov. Avg. - - GAAP Earnings vs. Previous Year    Volume Above Avg. STARS
12-Mo. Target Price — Relative Strength — ▲ Up ▼ Down ▶ No Change    Below Avg.

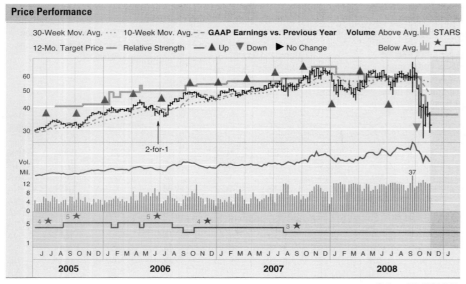

Options: ASE, CBOE, P, Ph

Analysis prepared by **Matthew Albrecht** on October 31, 2008, when the stock traded at **$ 38.76**.

## Highlights

➤ We expect relatively strong flows to TROW's target-date retirement funds and separate accounts to continue, but we also think equity market declines could push client assets under management down more than 15% this year. We think investors favor target-date retirement funds because of the increasing number of defined contribution sponsors opting for automatic enrollment that offer the option. Global and international funds may see a reversal of strong flows due to the underperformance of international markets. We also look for modest flows from customers domiciled outside the U.S., considering the disparity in savings rates and the low penetration of mutual funds. Equity market declines have resulted in an unfavorable asset mix, however, pressuring management fees.

➤ We expect a slight increase in compensation expenses this year as revenue growth slows but headcount additions continue, before a modest decline in 2009 to about 36.5% of net revenues. We see rising occupancy and advertising costs, as well as less investment income, pressuring margins.

➤ We see EPS of $2.19 in 2008 and $2.17 in 2009.

## Investment Rationale/Risk

➤ We believe that TROW's relative investment performance is strong and will continue to drive net client inflows into its mutual funds and separately managed accounts. We also view favorably the company's low debt levels, as well as its consistently growing dividend payout and recent increase in its share repurchase authorization. The stock outperformed peers in 2007, but we think that its strong fund performance and consistent flows are appropriately reflected in the current share price.

➤ Risks to our recommendation and target price include stock and bond market volatility. Regarding corporate governance, we view stock option grants as generous, especially given reductions at competitors, and we would like to see more independent directors on the board.

➤ The shares recently traded at 17.5X our 2008 EPS estimate. Our 12-month target price of $36 is equal to 16.6X our 2009 EPS estimate, which is a discount to TROW's five-year average P/E multiple, but a premium to falling peer multiples to reflect TROW's well capitalized balance sheet and strong fund performance.

## Qualitative Risk Assessment

| LOW | MEDIUM | HIGH |
|---|---|---|

Our risk assessment reflects the company's strong market share and our view of its consistent net client inflows and impressive relative investment performance, taking into account industry cyclicality.

## Quantitative Evaluations

### S&P Quality Ranking                                         A

| D | C | B- | B | B+ | A- | A | A+ |
|---|---|---|---|---|---|---|---|

### Relative Strength Rank                          MODERATE

34

LOWEST = 1                                           HIGHEST = 99

## Revenue/Earnings Data

### Revenue (Million $)

| | 1Q | 2Q | 3Q | 4Q | Year |
|---|---|---|---|---|---|
| 2008 | 560.4 | 587.7 | 554.8 | -- | -- |
| 2007 | 508.4 | 551.1 | 571.0 | 597.8 | 2,233 |
| 2006 | 429.3 | 446.0 | 450.6 | 489.1 | 1,819 |
| 2005 | 358.0 | 364.5 | 389.6 | 403.8 | 1,516 |
| 2004 | 306.5 | 310.5 | 317.0 | 346.4 | 1,280 |
| 2003 | 219.5 | 238.3 | 259.1 | 364.5 | 996.5 |

### Earnings Per Share ($)

| | | | | | |
|---|---|---|---|---|---|
| 2008 | 0.55 | 0.60 | 0.56 | E0.48 | E2.19 |
| 2007 | 0.51 | 0.58 | 0.63 | 0.68 | 2.40 |
| 2006 | 0.42 | 0.49 | 0.46 | 0.53 | 1.90 |
| 2005 | 0.35 | 0.38 | 0.43 | 0.43 | 1.58 |
| 2004 | 0.29 | 0.30 | 0.31 | 0.36 | 1.26 |
| 2003 | 0.16 | 0.21 | 0.26 | 0.26 | 0.89 |

Fiscal year ended Dec. 31. Next earnings report expected: Late January. EPS Estimates based on S&P Operating Earnings; historical GAAP earnings are as reported.

## Dividend Data (Dates: mm/dd Payment Date: mm/dd/yy)

| Amount ($) | Date Decl. | Ex-Div. Date | Stk. of Record | Payment Date |
|---|---|---|---|---|
| 0.240 | 02/14 | 03/12 | 03/14 | 03/28/08 |
| 0.240 | 06/05 | 06/12 | 06/16 | 06/27/08 |
| 0.240 | 09/04 | 09/11 | 09/15 | 09/29/08 |
| 0.240 | 10/20 | 12/16 | 12/18 | 12/30/08 |

Dividends have been paid since 1986. Source: Company reports.

---

**Please read the Required Disclosures and Analyst Certification on the last page of this report.**

The McGraw-Hill Companies

# T. Rowe Price Group Inc

**STANDARD &POOR'S**

## Business Summary October 31, 2008

CORPORATE OVERVIEW. T. Rowe Price Group (TROW) is the successor to an investment counseling business formed by the late Thomas Rowe Price, Jr. in 1937. It is now the investment adviser to the T. Rowe Price family of no-load mutual funds, and is one of the largest publicly held U.S. mutual fund complexes. At the end of 2007, TROW had about $400 billion in assets under management, up from $335 billion at the end of 2006. At the end of 2007, 80% of assets under management were invested in stock and blended asset portfolios, and 20% were invested in bond and money market portfolios.

T. Rowe Price offers mutual funds that employ a broad range of investment styles, including growth, value, sector-focused, tax-efficient, and quantitative index-oriented approaches. The company's investment approach is based upon a strong commitment to proprietary research, sophisticated risk-management processes, and a strict adherence to stated investment objectives. The company employs both fundamental and quantitative methods in performing security analyses, using internal equity and fixed income investment research capabilities. We believe T. Rowe Price's broad line of no-load mutual funds makes it easy for investors to reallocate assets among funds

(which is not the case at some smaller fund companies), contributing to increased client retention.

All of the company's funds are sold without a sales commission, known as no-load funds. TROW also manages private accounts for individuals and institutions. At the end of 2007, assets under management were sourced about 20%-30% from each of the following: individual U.S. investors, U.S. defined contribution retirement plans, third-party distributors, and institutional investors. Revenues primarily come from investment advisory fees for managing portfolios, which depend largely on the total value and composition of assets under management. At December 31, 2007, the six largest Price funds--Equity Income, Mid-Cap Growth, Growth Stock, Blue Chip Growth, Capital Appreciation and Equity Index 500---accounted for 25% of assets under management and nearly 28% of 2007 investment advisory revenues.

## Company Financials Fiscal Year Ended Dec. 31

| Per Share Data ($) | 2007 | 2006 | 2005 | 2004 | 2003 | 2002 | 2001 | 2000 | 1999 | 1998 |
|---|---|---|---|---|---|---|---|---|---|---|
| Tangible Book Value | 7.97 | 6.63 | 5.21 | 3.98 | 2.66 | 1.91 | 1.68 | 1.21 | 3.18 | 2.53 |
| Cash Flow | 2.60 | 2.07 | 1.80 | 1.48 | 1.11 | 0.96 | 20.71 | 1.33 | 1.13 | 0.80 |
| Earnings | 2.40 | 1.90 | 1.58 | 1.26 | 0.89 | 0.76 | 0.76 | 1.04 | 0.93 | 0.67 |
| S&P Core Earnings | 2.40 | 1.90 | 1.43 | 1.16 | 0.78 | 0.67 | 0.65 | NA | NA | NA |
| Dividends | 0.75 | 0.59 | 0.49 | 0.40 | 0.35 | 0.33 | 0.31 | 0.27 | 0.20 | 0.17 |
| Payout Ratio | 31% | 31% | 31% | 32% | 40% | 43% | 40% | 26% | 22% | 25% |
| Prices:High | 65.46 | 48.50 | 37.70 | 31.70 | 23.80 | 21.35 | 21.97 | 24.97 | 21.63 | 21.44 |
| Prices:Low | 44.59 | 34.87 | 27.10 | 21.92 | 19.19 | 10.63 | 11.72 | 15.03 | 12.94 | 10.44 |
| P/E Ratio:High | 27 | 26 | 24 | 25 | 27 | 28 | 29 | 24 | 23 | 32 |
| P/E Ratio:Low | 19 | 18 | 17 | 17 | 22 | 14 | 15 | 14 | 14 | 16 |

| Income Statement Analysis (Million $) | 2007 | 2006 | 2005 | 2004 | 2003 | 2002 | 2001 | 2000 | 1999 | 1998 |
|---|---|---|---|---|---|---|---|---|---|---|
| Income Interest | 5.90 | 5.40 | 4.28 | 3.78 | 3.91 | 3.06 | 32.8 | 59.1 | 37.5 | 28.5 |
| Income Other | 2,227 | 1,814 | 1,512 | 1,277 | 995 | 923 | 995 | 1,153 | 999 | 858 |
| Total Income | 2,233 | 1,819 | 1,516 | 1,280 | 999 | 926 | 1,028 | 1,212 | 1,036 | 886 |
| General Expenses | 1,179 | 982 | 814 | 638 | 585 | 552 | 603 | 690 | 589 | 540 |
| Interest Expense | 4.80 | 4.30 | 4.03 | 3.30 | 3.29 | 4.96 | 12.7 | 9.72 | Nil | Nil |
| Depreciation | 54.0 | 47.0 | 42.0 | 40.0 | 45.3 | 50.6 | 80.5 | 53.7 | 32.6 | 32.6 |
| Net Income | 671 | 530 | 431 | 337 | 227 | 194 | 196 | 269 | 239 | 174 |
| S&P Core Earnings | 671 | 530 | 391 | 309 | 198 | 169 | 167 | NA | NA | NA |

| Balance Sheet & Other Financial Data (Million $) | 2007 | 2006 | 2005 | 2004 | 2003 | 2002 | 2001 | 2000 | 1999 | 1998 |
|---|---|---|---|---|---|---|---|---|---|---|
| Cash | 785 | 773 | 804 | 500 | 237 | 111 | 79.7 | 80.5 | 358 | 284 |
| Receivables | 265 | 224 | 175 | 158 | 121 | 96.8 | 104 | 131 | 122 | 101 |
| Cost of Investments | 1,002 | 762 | 378 | 329 | 273 | 216 | 154 | 250 | 279 | 220 |
| Total Assets | 3,177 | 2,765 | 2,311 | 1,929 | 1,547 | 1,370 | 1,313 | 1,469 | 998 | 797 |
| Loss Reserve | Nil | Nil | Nil | Nil | Nil | Nil | Nil | Nil | Nil | Nil |
| Short Term Debt | Nil | Nil | Nil | Nil | Nil | Nil | Nil | Nil | Nil | Nil |
| Capitalization:Debt | Nil | Nil | Nil | Nil | Nil | Nil | 104 | 312 | 17.7 | Nil |
| Capitalization:Equity | 2,777 | 2,427 | 2,036 | 1,697 | 1,329 | 1,189 | 1,078 | 991 | 770 | 614 |
| Capitalization:Total | 2,777 | 2,427 | 2,036 | 1,697 | 1,329 | 1,189 | 1,181 | 1,304 | 848 | 667 |
| Price Times Book Value:High | 8.2 | 7.3 | 7.2 | 7.9 | 9.0 | 11.2 | 13.1 | 20.6 | 6.8 | 8.5 |
| Price Times Book Value:Low | 5.6 | 5.3 | 5.2 | 5.5 | 7.2 | 5.6 | 7.0 | 12.4 | 4.1 | 4.1 |
| Cash Flow | 725 | 577 | 473 | 377 | 273 | 245 | 276 | 323 | 272 | 207 |
| % Expense/Operating Revenue | 55.4 | 52.3 | 56.7 | 63.8 | 65.8 | 65.7 | 67.8 | 62.2 | 60.0 | 64.7 |
| % Earnings & Depreciation/Assets | 24.4 | 22.7 | 22.3 | 21.7 | 18.7 | 18.3 | 19.9 | 26.2 | 30.3 | 28.6 |

Data as orig reptd.; bef. results of disc opers/spec. items. Per share data adj. for stk. divs.; EPS diluted. E-Estimated. NA-Not Available. NM-Not Meaningful. NR-Not Ranked. UR-Under Review.

**Office:** 100 East Pratt Street, Baltimore, MD 21202.
**Telephone:** 410-345-2000.
**Email:** info@troweprice.com
**Website:** http://www.troweprice.com

**Chrmn:** B.C. Rogers
**Pres:** H. Stiles
**Pres & CEO:** J.A. Kennedy
**Vice Chrmn:** E.C. Bernard

**CFO:** K.V. Moreland
**Board Members:** E. C. Bernard, J. T. Brady, J. A. Broaddus, Jr., D. B. Hebb, Jr., J. A. Kennedy, B. C. Rogers, A. Sommer, D. S. Taylor, A. M. Whittemore

**Founded:** 1937
**Domicile:** Maryland
**Employees:** 5,081

The *McGraw-Hill* Companies

**STANDARD &POOR'S**

# Tyco Electronics Ltd

| S&P Recommendation HOLD ★★★☆☆ | Price $14.50 (as of Nov 14, 2008) | 12-Mo. Target Price $17.00 | Investment Style Large-Cap Blend |
|---|---|---|---|

**GICS Sector** Information Technology
**Sub-Industry** Electronic Manufacturing Services

**Summary** This company designs, manufactures and markets engineered electronic components, network solutions, and wireless systems for the automotive, appliances, aerospace and defense, telecommunications, computers and consumer electronics industries.

## Key Stock Statistics (Source S&P, Vickers, company reports)

| | | | | | | | |
|---|---|---|---|---|---|---|---|
| 52-Wk Range | $40.34– 12.95 | S&P Oper. EPS 2009E | 1.73 | Market Capitalization(B) | $6.849 | Beta | NA |
| Trailing 12-Month EPS | $3.67 | S&P Oper. EPS 2010E | 1.62 | Yield (%) | 4.41 | S&P 3-Yr. Proj. EPS CAGR(%) | -13 |
| Trailing 12-Month P/E | 4.0 | P/E on S&P Oper. EPS 2009E | 8.4 | Dividend Rate/Share | $0.64 | S&P Credit Rating | NA |
| $10K Invested 5 Yrs Ago | NA | Common Shares Outstg. (M) | 472.3 | Institutional Ownership (%) | 91 | | |

## Price Performance

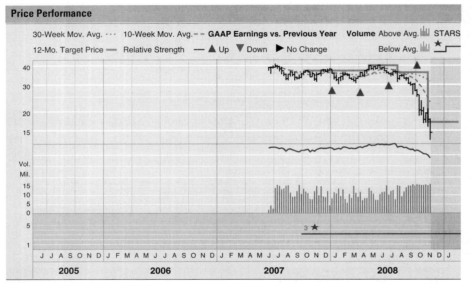

- 30-Week Mov. Avg. · · ·
- 10-Week Mov. Avg. - - -
- **GAAP Earnings vs. Previous Year**
- Volume Above Avg. STARS
- 12-Mo. Target Price —
- Relative Strength —
- ▲ Up ▼ Down ► No Change
- Below Avg.

Options: ASE, CBOE, P

Analysis prepared by **Rafay Khalid** on November 07, 2008, when the stock traded at **$ 17.70**.

## Highlights

- We see revenues declining 20% in FY 09 (Sep.) and another 5% in FY 10, reflecting our expectation for notably weak demand in the company's important automotive components business, which generated 30% of FY 08 sales. However, we believe that sales in the network solutions segment will be flat in FY 09, based on our outlook for strength in energy markets offset by our view of a slowdown in communications and building networks markets. In addition, we expect the wireless systems segment to be slightly positive.

- We project that gross margins will narrow to 24% in FY 09, from 25% in FY 08, on pricing pressure and lower volumes, partially offset by a decrease in material costs. Despite TEL's restructuring initiatives, we forecast SG&A costs as a percentage of sales will rise on the lower revenues that we foresee. As a result, we project adjusted operating margins will decline to 11% in FY 09 and remain at a similar level in FY 10, from 14% in FY 08.

- Our operating EPS estimates are $1.73 in FY 09 and $1.62 in FY 10, following $2.67 in FY 08.

## Investment Rationale/Risk

- We believe weakness in the auto market, especially in Europe, will significantly hurt sales and earnings in FY 09 and FY 10. However, we think moving to low-cost regions and exiting low-margin businesses, along with restructuring initiatives, will be beneficial in the long run. With a debt-to-capital ratio of 22%, we view TEL's balance sheet as solid, based on our projection that it will end FY 09 with $1.5 billion in cash and generate about $400 million in free cash flow.

- Risks to our recommendation and target price include delays in divesting non-strategic businesses and an inability to pass along higher material costs to customers.

- Our 12-month target price of $17 is based on a blend of P/E and DCF analyses. Applying a peer-discount P/E of 9.8X to our FY 09 operating EPS projection, we derive a $17 valuation. We believe TEL warrants a peer-discount based on our view of its lower earnings growth potential. Our DCF model assumes a 10.6% weighted average cost of capital and 2% terminal growth, resulting in intrinsic value of $17.

## Qualitative Risk Assessment

| LOW | MEDIUM | HIGH |
|---|---|---|

Our risk assessment is based on our view of the company's reliance on cyclical businesses that are largely affected by the North American macroeconomic environment, offset by its efforts to reorganize its operations and target greater profitability. We see TEL's major electronic component business continuing to effect overall mix and profitability.

## Quantitative Evaluations

**S&P Quality Ranking** NR

| D | C | B- | B | B+ | A- | A | A+ |
|---|---|---|---|---|---|---|---|

**Relative Strength Rank** WEAK

23

LOWEST = 1    HIGHEST = 99

## Revenue/Earnings Data

**Revenue (Million $)**

| | 1Q | 2Q | 3Q | 4Q | Year |
|---|---|---|---|---|---|
| 2008 | 3,675 | 3,662 | 3,908 | 3,706 | 14,834 |
| 2007 | 3,094 | 3,335 | 3,412 | 3,619 | 13,460 |
| 2006 | -- | -- | -- | -- | 12,812 |
| 2005 | -- | -- | -- | -- | -- |
| 2004 | -- | -- | -- | -- | -- |
| 2003 | -- | -- | -- | -- | -- |

**Earnings Per Share ($)**

| | | | | | |
|---|---|---|---|---|---|
| 2008 | 1.75 | 0.62 | 0.66 | 0.23 | 3.28 |
| 2007 | 0.48 | 0.15 | -0.17 | 0.16 | -0.29 |
| 2006 | -- | -- | -- | -- | 2.24 |
| 2005 | -- | -- | -- | -- | -- |
| 2004 | -- | -- | -- | -- | -- |
| 2003 | -- | -- | -- | -- | -- |

Fiscal year ended Sep. 30. Next earnings report expected: Early February. EPS Estimates based on S&P Operating Earnings; historical GAAP earnings are as reported.

## Dividend Data (Dates: mm/dd Payment Date: mm/dd/yy)

| Amount ($) | Date Decl. | Ex-Div. Date | Stk. of Record | Payment Date |
|---|---|---|---|---|
| 0.140 | 12/28 | 01/10 | 01/14 | 02/04/08 |
| 0.140 | 03/13 | 04/10 | 04/14 | 05/06/08 |
| 0.140 | 06/27 | 07/11 | 07/15 | 08/05/08 |
| 0.160 | 09/23 | 10/09 | 10/14 | 11/04/08 |

Dividends have been paid since 2007. Source: Company reports.

---

**Please read the Required Disclosures and Analyst Certification on the last page of this report.**

The McGraw-Hill Companies

# Tyco Electronics Ltd

STANDARD &POOR'S

## Business Summary November 07, 2008

CORPORATE OVERVIEW. Tyco Electronics (TEL) came into existence as a stand-alone entity following the January 13, 2006 decision by the company's former parent, Tyco International, to separate into three companies: Tyco Electronics, Tyco Healthcare, and Tyco International. Subsequently, Tyco Electronics separated from Tyco International on June 29, 2007, and began trading on the NYSE on July 2, 2007.

Tyco Electronics Ltd. designs, manufactures and markets engineered electronic components, network solutions, and wireless systems for customers in the automotive, appliances, aerospace and defense, telecommunications, computers and consumer electronics industries. TEL operates through four reporting segments: Electronic Components, Network Solutions, Wireless Systems, and Other.

Electronic Components supplies passive electronic components, including connectors and interconnect systems, relays, switches, circuit protection devices, touch screens, sensors, and wires and cable, primarily to the automotive, computer, consumer electronics, communication equipment, appliance, aerospace and defense, industrial machinery and instrumentation markets.

Network Solutions is a global supplier of infrastructure components for the telecommunications and energy markets. Its products include connectors, above- and below-ground enclosures, heat shrink tubing, cable accessories, surge arrestors, fiber optic cabling, copper cabling, and racks for copper and fiber networks.

Wireless Systems products include radio frequency and RFID components, radar sensors, microwave subsystems, and land mobile radio systems and networks sold primarily to the aerospace and defense, public safety, communication equipment and automotive markets.

Tyco Electronics also includes several other businesses, which manufacture, distribute, maintain and install power systems and undersea telecommunication systems. The Power Systems business is currently being treated as a discontinued operation.

## Company Financials Fiscal Year Ended Sep. 30

### Per Share Data ($)

| | 2008 | 2007 | 2006 | 2005 | 2004 | 2003 | 2002 | 2001 | 2000 | 1999 |
|---|---|---|---|---|---|---|---|---|---|---|
| Tangible Book Value | NA | 7.33 | NM | NA | NA | NA | NA | NA | NA | NA |
| Cash Flow | NA | 0.79 | 3.29 | NA | NA | NA | NA | NA | NA | NA |
| Earnings | 3.28 | -0.29 | 2.24 | NA | NA | NA | NA | NA | NA | NA |
| Dividends | NA | 0.14 | NA | NA | NA | NA | NA | NA | NA | NA |
| Payout Ratio | NA | NM | NA | NA | NA | NA | NA | NA | NA | NA |
| Prices:High | NA | 41.28 | NA | NA | NA | NA | NA | NA | NA | NA |
| Prices:Low | NA | 31.31 | NA | NA | NA | NA | NA | NA | NA | NA |
| P/E Ratio:High | NA | NM | NA | NA | NA | NA | NA | NA | NA | NA |
| P/E Ratio:Low | NA | NM | NA | NA | NA | NA | NA | NA | NA | NA |

### Income Statement Analysis (Million $)

| | 2008 | 2007 | 2006 | 2005 | 2004 | 2003 | 2002 | 2001 | 2000 | 1999 |
|---|---|---|---|---|---|---|---|---|---|---|
| Revenue | 14,834 | 13,460 | 12,812 | 11,890 | 11,099 | NA | NA | NA | NA | NA |
| Operating Income | NA | 2,319 | 2,269 | NA | NA | NA | NA | NA | NA | NA |
| Depreciation | 559 | 535 | 531 | 542 | 513 | NA | NA | NA | NA | NA |
| Interest Expense | NA | 231 | 256 | NA | NA | NA | NA | NA | NA | NA |
| Pretax Income | 2,157 | 356 | 1,201 | 1,355 | 1,206 | NA | NA | NA | NA | NA |
| Effective Tax Rate | 25.9% | NM | 2.66% | 26.6% | 33.6% | NA | NA | NA | NA | NA |
| Net Income | 1,594 | -144 | 1,163 | 990 | 791 | NA | NA | NA | NA | NA |

### Balance Sheet & Other Financial Data (Million $)

| | 2008 | 2007 | 2006 | 2005 | 2004 | 2003 | 2002 | 2001 | 2000 | 1999 |
|---|---|---|---|---|---|---|---|---|---|---|
| Cash | 1,086 | 936 | 470 | 284 | NA | NA | NA | NA | NA | NA |
| Current Assets | NA | 9,873 | 6,040 | NA | NA | NA | NA | NA | NA | NA |
| Total Assets | 21,600 | 23,688 | 19,091 | 18,473 | NA | NA | NA | NA | NA | NA |
| Current Liabilities | NA | 6,185 | 9,142 | NA | NA | NA | NA | NA | NA | NA |
| Long Term Debt | NA | 3,373 | 3,371 | NA | NA | NA | NA | NA | NA | NA |
| Common Equity | 11,073 | 11,377 | 11,160 | 9,842 | NA | NA | NA | NA | NA | NA |
| Total Capital | NA | 15,427 | 14,927 | NA | NA | NA | NA | NA | NA | NA |
| Capital Expenditures | 619 | 892 | 560 | 481 | 410 | NA | NA | NA | NA | NA |
| Cash Flow | NA | 391 | 1,694 | NA | NA | NA | NA | NA | NA | NA |
| Current Ratio | 2.1 | 1.6 | 1.0 | 1.7 | NA | NA | NA | NA | NA | NA |
| % Long Term Debt of Capitalization | 22.2 | 21.8 | 22.6 | 26.5 | Nil | NA | NA | NA | NA | NA |
| % Net Income of Revenue | 10.8 | NM | 9.1 | 8.3 | 7.1 | NA | NA | NA | NA | NA |
| % Return on Assets | 7.0 | NM | 6.2 | NA | NA | NA | NA | NA | NA | NA |
| % Return on Equity | 14.2 | NM | 11.1 | NA | NA | NA | NA | NA | NA | NA |

Data as orig reptd.; bef. results of disc opers/spec. items. Per share data adj. for stk. divs.; EPS diluted. E-Estimated. NA-Not Available. NM-Not Meaningful. NR-Not Ranked. UR-Under Review.

Office: 96 Pitts Bay Road, Pembroke, Bermuda HM 08.
Telephone: 441-294-0607.
Website: http://www.tycoelectronics.com
Chrmn: F.M. Poses

CEO: T.J. Lynch
COO: M. Robinson
EVP & CFO: T.R. Curtin
EVP & General Counsel: R.A. Scott

Investor Contact: M. Calastri (441-294-0600)
Board Members: P. R. Brondeau, R. Charan, J. W. Gromer, R. M. Hernandez, T. J. Lynch, D. J. Phelan, F. M. Poses, L. S. Smith, P. A. Sneed, D. P. Steiner, S. S. Wijnberg

Founded: 2000
Domicile: Bermuda
Employees: 94,000

# Tyco International Ltd

**STANDARD &POOR'S**

| S&P Recommendation HOLD ★★★☆☆ | Price $20.50 (as of Nov 14, 2008) | 12-Mo. Target Price $24.00 | Investment Style Large-Cap Blend |
|---|---|---|---|

**GICS Sector** Industrials
**Sub-Industry** Industrial Conglomerates

**Summary** Tyco split into three separate publicly traded companies in June 2007, with the company maintaining its former Fire & Security and Engineered Products divisions.

## Key Stock Statistics (Source S&P, Vickers, company reports)

| | | | | | | | |
|---|---|---|---|---|---|---|---|
| 52-Wk Range | $47.95– 18.77 | S&P Oper. EPS 2010**E** | 2.75 | Market Capitalization(B) | $9.734 | Beta | 1.55 |
| Trailing 12-Month EPS | $2.64 | S&P Oper. EPS 2011**E** | NA | Yield (%) | 3.90 | S&P 3-Yr. Proj. EPS CAGR(%) | 15 |
| Trailing 12-Month P/E | 7.8 | P/E on S&P Oper. EPS 2010**E** | 7.5 | Dividend Rate/Share | $0.80 | S&P Credit Rating | BBB |
| $10K Invested 5 Yrs Ago | NA | Common Shares Outstg. (M) | 474.8 | Institutional Ownership (%) | 91 | | |

## Price Performance

30-Week Mov. Avg. · · · · 10-Week Mov. Avg. - - **GAAP Earnings vs. Previous Year**    Volume Above Avg. ‖‖‖ STARS
12-Mo. Target Price —  Relative Strength —   ▲ Up  ▼ Down  ▶ No Change    Below Avg. ‖‖‖ ★

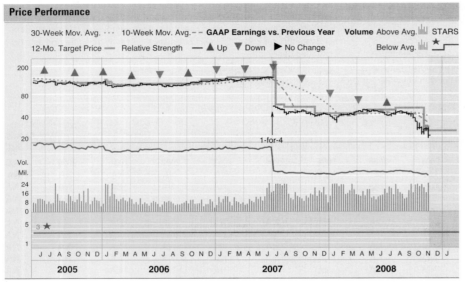

1-for-4

Options: ASE, CBOE, P, Ph

## Highlights

▸ The 12-month target price for TYC has recently been changed to $24.00 from $28.00. The Highlights section of this Stock Report will be updated accordingly.

## Investment Rationale/Risk

▸ The Investment Rationale/Risk section of this Stock Report will be updated shortly. For the latest News story on TYC from MarketScope, see below.

▸ 11/11/08 02:26 pm ET ... S&P REITERATES HOLD OPINION ON SHARES OF TYCO INTERNATIONAL (TYC 21.98***): Sep-Q EPS of $0.81 vs. $0.57, both before one-time items, is $0.19 above our forecast. TYC posts profit gains in all units except ADT Worldwide, with the strongest growth in Electrical and Metal Products, on better pricing for steel and copper products. But based on the likelihood of much lower pricing in Electrical and Metal in coming periods, and a negative impact from forex, we are cutting our FY 09 (Sep.) EPS estimate by $0.25 to $2.40, and see $2.75 in FY 10. We are also cutting our target price by $4 to $24, 9.8X our calendar '09 EPS estimate, about in line with S&P 500. /M.Jaffe

## Qualitative Risk Assessment

| LOW | MEDIUM | HIGH |
|---|---|---|

Our risk assessment reflects what we see as strong cash flow characteristics and high levels of recurring revenues in a number of Tyco's businesses. However, the company has also been in the process of trying to repair what we view as an inefficient operating model, which was put together by an executive team that was replaced more than five years ago.

## Quantitative Evaluations

**S&P Quality Ranking**    B

| D | C | B- | B | B+ | A- | A | A+ |
|---|---|---|---|---|---|---|---|

**Relative Strength Rank**    MODERATE

30

LOWEST = 1    HIGHEST = 99

## Revenue/Earnings Data

**Revenue (Million $)**

| | 1Q | 2Q | 3Q | 4Q | Year |
|---|---|---|---|---|---|
| 2008 | 4,870 | 4,866 | 5,215 | -- | -- |
| 2007 | 10,329 | 10,838 | 5,085 | 5,028 | 18,781 |
| 2006 | 9,603 | 10,093 | 10,504 | 10,760 | 40,960 |
| 2005 | 10,065 | 10,456 | 10,562 | 10,030 | 39,727 |
| 2004 | 9,665 | 9,821 | 10,225 | 10,442 | 40,153 |
| 2003 | 8,927 | 8,989 | 9,413 | 9,473 | 36,801 |

**Earnings Per Share ($)**

| | | | | | |
|---|---|---|---|---|---|
| 2008 | 0.74 | 0.56 | 0.41 | E0.62 | E2.90 |
| 2007 | 1.48 | 1.68 | -6.13 | 0.42 | -5.09 |
| 2006 | 1.56 | 2.08 | 1.72 | 2.52 | 7.88 |
| 2005 | 1.40 | 0.44 | 2.24 | 1.68 | 6.04 |
| 2004 | 1.36 | 1.36 | 1.72 | 1.08 | 5.64 |
| 2003 | 1.12 | 0.24 | 1.08 | -0.44 | 2.08 |

Fiscal year ended Sep. 30. Next earnings report expected: NA. EPS Estimates based on S&P Operating Earnings; historical GAAP earnings are as reported.

## Dividend Data (Dates: mm/dd Payment Date: mm/dd/yy)

| Amount ($) | Date Decl. | Ex-Div. Date | Stk. of Record | Payment Date |
|---|---|---|---|---|
| 0.150 | 12/06 | 12/31 | 01/03 | 02/01/08 |
| 0.200 | 03/13 | 09/29 | 10/01 | 11/03/08 |

Dividends have been paid since 1975. Source: Company reports.

# Tyco International Ltd

**STANDARD &POOR'S**

## Business Summary November 04, 2008

CORPORATE OVERVIEW. At the close of trading on June 29, 2007, Tyco International divided its portfolio of businesses into three separate publicly traded companies. TYC maintained the units that had been part of its Fire & Security and Engineered Products & Services divisions, and spun off its Healthcare (now Covidien; COV) and Electronics (trading as Tyco Electronics; TEL) units. The businesses retained by Tyco recorded pro forma revenues of $18.6 billion in FY 06 (Sep.). Tyco now divides its businesses into five separate segments, ADT Worldwide; Fire Protection Services; Flow Control; Safety Products; and Electrical and Metal Products. The company derived 53% of its revenues outside the U.S. in FY 07, with more than half of that total in Europe.

ADT Worldwide (41% of TYC's revenues in FY 07) sells, installs, services and monitors electronic security systems. The Fire Protection Services segment (19%) provides and services fire detection and fire suppression systems. Both ADT and Fire Protection serve commercial, industrial and government customers. Safety Products (9%) makes fire protection, security and life safety products, including fire suppression products, breathing apparatus, intrusion security, access control and video management systems.

The company's Flow Control division (20% of FY 07 revenues) manufactures and services valves, pipe fittings, valve automation and heat tracing products for the water and wastewater, oil, gas and other energy, and general process industries. The Electrical and Metal Products division (11%) makes steel tubing, pipe and cable products, used primarily by trade contractors in the construction and modernization of non-residential structures.

IMPACT OF MAJOR DEVELOPMENTS. TYC's business separation was accomplished through the payment of tax-free stock dividends to its shareholders. Under the separation, each TYC shareholder received one share of the Covidien health care business and one share of Tyco Electronics for each four TYC shares held as of June 18. In addition, every four shares of the reorganized Tyco were converted into one TYC share in a reverse stock split.

## Company Financials Fiscal Year Ended Sep. 30

| Per Share Data ($) | 2009 | 2008 | 2007 | 2006 | 2005 | 2004 | 2003 | 2002 | 2001 | 2000 |
|---|---|---|---|---|---|---|---|---|---|---|
| Tangible Book Value | NA | NA | 2.49 | 10.92 | 5.56 | NM | NM | NM | NM | 1.68 |
| Cash Flow | NA | NA | -2.76 | 11.79 | 9.78 | 9.35 | 5.01 | -2.09 | 14.88 | 14.39 |
| Earnings | 2.65 | 2.90 | -5.09 | 7.88 | 6.04 | 5.64 | 2.08 | -6.16 | 10.20 | 10.56 |
| Dividends | NA | 0.35 | 1.90 | 1.20 | 1.60 | 0.20 | 0.20 | 0.20 | 0.20 | 0.20 |
| Payout Ratio | NA | 12% | NM | 15% | 26% | 4% | 10% | NM | 2% | 2% |
| Prices:High | NA | 47.95 | 137.92 | 127.44 | 146.32 | 145.68 | 108.72 | 235.24 | 252.84 | 236.75 |
| Prices:Low | NA | 18.77 | 37.46 | 98.60 | 102.64 | 104.04 | 44.80 | 27.92 | 156.96 | 128.00 |
| P/E Ratio:High | NA | 17 | NM | 16 | 24 | 26 | 52 | NM | 25 | 22 |
| P/E Ratio:Low | NA | 6 | NM | 13 | 17 | 18 | 22 | NM | 15 | 12 |

**Income Statement Analysis (Million $)**

| | 2009 | 2008 | 2007 | 2006 | 2005 | 2004 | 2003 | 2002 | 2001 | 2000 |
|---|---|---|---|---|---|---|---|---|---|---|
| Revenue | NA | NA | 18,781 | 40,960 | 39,727 | 40,153 | 36,801 | 35,644 | 34,037 | 28,932 |
| Operating Income | NA | NA | 1,720 | 7,754 | 7,637 | 7,957 | 5,568 | 6,509 | 8,865 | 7,393 |
| Depreciation | NA | NA | 1,151 | 2,065 | 2,100 | 2,176 | 1,472 | 2,033 | 2,141 | 1,644 |
| Interest Expense | NA | NA | 313 | 713 | 815 | 963 | 1,148 | 1,077 | 776 | 845 |
| Pretax Income | NA | NA | -2,181 | 4,884 | 4,192 | 4,159 | 1,803 | -2,811 | 6,004 | 6,465 |
| Effective Tax Rate | NA | NA | NM | 16.4% | 23.5% | 27.4% | 42.4% | NM | 21.4% | 29.8% |
| Net Income | NA | NA | -2,519 | 4,075 | 3,199 | 3,005 | 1,035 | -3,070 | 4,671 | 4,520 |

**Balance Sheet & Other Financial Data (Million $)**

| | 2009 | 2008 | 2007 | 2006 | 2005 | 2004 | 2003 | 2002 | 2001 | 2000 |
|---|---|---|---|---|---|---|---|---|---|---|
| Cash | NA | NA | 1,894 | 2,926 | 3,196 | 4,467 | 4,329 | 6,383 | 2,587 | 1,265 |
| Current Assets | NA | NA | 12,345 | 18,785 | 18,537 | 18,545 | 17,240 | 19,765 | NA | 12,816 |
| Total Assets | NA | NA | 32,815 | 63,722 | 62,621 | 63,667 | 63,545 | 66,414 | 111,287 | 40,404 |
| Current Liabilities | NA | NA | 9,101 | 11,066 | 11,835 | 11,152 | 10,572 | 19,632 | NA | 11,679 |
| Long Term Debt | NA | NA | 4,076 | 9,365 | 10,600 | 14,617 | 18,251 | 16,487 | 38,503 | 9,462 |
| Common Equity | NA | NA | 15,624 | 35,419 | 32,450 | 30,292 | 26,369 | 24,791 | 31,737 | 17,033 |
| Total Capital | NA | NA | 19,767 | 44,838 | 43,111 | 44,977 | 44,733 | 41,320 | 70,542 | 27,630 |
| Capital Expenditures | NA | NA | 669 | 1,569 | 1,272 | 1,015 | 1,170 | 1,709 | 1,798 | 1,704 |
| Cash Flow | NA | NA | -1,368 | 6,140 | 5,299 | 5,181 | 2,507 | -1,037 | 6,812 | 6,165 |
| Current Ratio | NA | NA | 1.4 | 1.7 | 1.6 | 1.7 | 1.6 | 1.0 | 1.3 | 1.1 |
| % Long Term Debt of Capitalization | NA | NA | 20.6 | 20.9 | 24.6 | 32.5 | 40.8 | 39.9 | 54.6 | 34.2 |
| % Net Income of Revenue | NA | NA | NM | 9.9 | 8.1 | 7.5 | 2.8 | NM | 13.7 | 15.6 |
| % Return on Assets | NA | NA | NM | 6.4 | 5.1 | 4.7 | 1.6 | NM | 6.2 | 12.4 |
| % Return on Equity | NA | NA | NM | 12.0 | 10.2 | 10.6 | 4.1 | NM | 19.2 | 30.7 |

Data as orig reptd.; bef. results of disc opers/spec. items. Per share data adj. for stk. divs.; EPS diluted. E-Estimated. NA-Not Available. NM-Not Meaningful. NR-Not Ranked. UR-Under Review.

**Office:** 90 Pitts Bay Road, Pembroke, Bermuda HM 08.
**Telephone:** 441-292-8674.
**Email:** info@tyco.com
**Website:** http://www.tyco.com

**Chrmn & CEO:** E.D. Breen
**EVP & CFO:** C.J. Coughlin
**EVP & General Counsel:** J.A. Reinsdorf
**SVP, Chief Acctg Officer & Cntlr:** C.A. Davidson

**SVP & Treas:** A. Nayar
**Investor Contact:** E.C. Arditte (609-720-4621)
**Board Members:** D. C. Blair, E. D. Breen, T. M. Donahue, B. Duperreault, B. S. Gordon, R. L. Gupta, J. A. Krol, B. O'Neill, W. S. Stavropoulos, S. S. Wijnberg, J. B. York

**Founded:** 1960
**Domicile:** Bermuda
**Employees:** 118,000

# Tyson Foods Inc.

STANDARD &POOR'S

**S&P Recommendation** | HOLD ★★★☆☆

| Price | 12-Mo. Target Price | Investment Style |
|---|---|---|
| $4.90 (as of Nov 14, 2008) | $8.00 | Large-Cap Blend |

**GICS Sector** Consumer Staples
**Sub-Industry** Packaged Foods & Meats

**Summary** Tyson is the world's largest supplier of beef, chicken and pork products.

## Key Stock Statistics (Source S&P, Vickers, company reports)

| | | | | | | | |
|---|---|---|---|---|---|---|---|
| 52-Wk Range | $19.50–4.50 | S&P Oper. EPS 2009**E** | 0.60 | Market Capitalization(B) | $1.397 | Beta | 1.09 |
| Trailing 12-Month EPS | $0.24 | S&P Oper. EPS 2010**E** | NA | Yield (%) | 3.27 | S&P 3-Yr. Proj. EPS CAGR(%) | NA |
| Trailing 12-Month P/E | 20.4 | P/E on S&P Oper. EPS 2009**E** | 8.2 | Dividend Rate/Share | $0.16 | S&P Credit Rating | BB |
| $10K Invested 5 Yrs Ago | $3,638 | Common Shares Outstg. (M) | 355.1 | Institutional Ownership (%) | 89 | | |

## Price Performance

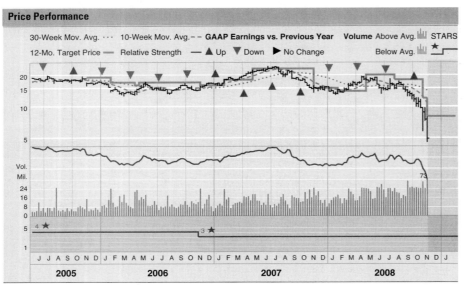

30-Week Mov. Avg. ···· 10-Week Mov. Avg. ─ ─ **GAAP Earnings vs. Previous Year**   Volume Above Avg. STARS
12-Mo. Target Price ─ Relative Strength ─ ▲ Up ▼ Down ► No Change   Below Avg. ★

Options: ASE, CBOE, P

Analysis prepared by **Joseph Agnese** on November 12, 2008, when the stock traded at **$ 4.81**.

## Highlights

➤ We expect sales to rise 4.3% to about $28.0 billion in FY 09 (Sep.) from $26.9 billion in FY 08, reflecting improved pricing power in beef and pork due to strong international demand, declining protein market supply levels and an increased need to raise end product pricing to cover rising raw material costs.

➤ We expect chicken results to be significantly lower in the first half of FY 09 as high industry production levels and increased raw material costs erode pricing power and negatively impact margins. We look for pricing power to return in the second half of the year after industry production cuts are implemented. In beef, we believe margins will widen amid strengthening demand from the re-opening of international markets and improved pricing power as protein market supply levels eventually return to more favorable levels, offsetting high raw material expenses. We think pork margins will be stable as international exports slow on strengthening U.S. currency. We believe prepared foods should experience increased pressure from higher protein market prices.

➤ We see FY 09 operating EPS of $0.60, up significantly from operating EPS of $0.09 in FY 08.

## Investment Rationale/Risk

➤ We believe intermediate term visibility is poor, reflecting uncertainty over the timing of the return of pricing power in the chicken industry. However, we believe TSN, as the largest protein supplier in the U.S., is better positioned than competitors to sustain a difficult environment. In the longer term, we think the company is well positioned to benefit from reduced commodity exposure due to a strategy focused on expansion in value-added prepared food products.

➤ Risks to our recommendation and target price include currency risks, decreased access to capital markets, and corporate governance concerns that we have related to board issues.

➤ We believe increased pricing power will drive a recovery in beef and, eventually, chicken margins. However, due to an adverse commodity market that we expect over the next six months, our P/E analysis assumes that the shares will trade at a multiple of 13X our FY 09 EPS estimate of $0.60, near the lower end of the company's historical trading range of 8X-22X but in line with consumer staples peers. This suggests a value of $8, which is our 12-month target price.

## Qualitative Risk Assessment

| LOW | MEDIUM | HIGH |
|---|---|---|

Our risk assessment reflects the company's cyclical operations, which are significantly affected by exposure to commodity crop and meat markets, and international trade restrictions.

## Quantitative Evaluations

**S&P Quality Ranking**   B-

| D | C | B- | B | B+ | A- | A | A+ |
|---|---|---|---|---|---|---|---|

**Relative Strength Rank**   WEAK

10

LOWEST = 1   HIGHEST = 99

## Revenue/Earnings Data

**Revenue (Million $)**

| | 1Q | 2Q | 3Q | 4Q | Year |
|---|---|---|---|---|---|
| 2008 | 6,766 | 6,612 | 6,849 | 7,201 | 26,862 |
| 2007 | 6,558 | 6,501 | 6,958 | 6,883 | 26,900 |
| 2006 | 6,454 | 6,251 | 6,383 | 6,471 | 25,559 |
| 2005 | 6,452 | 6,359 | 6,708 | 6,495 | 26,014 |
| 2004 | 6,505 | 6,153 | 6,634 | 7,149 | 26,441 |
| 2003 | 5,802 | 5,845 | 6,330 | 6,572 | 24,549 |

**Earnings Per Share ($)**

| | | | | | |
|---|---|---|---|---|---|
| 2008 | 0.10 | -0.01 | -0.01 | 0.13 | 0.24 |
| 2007 | 0.16 | 0.20 | 0.31 | 0.09 | 0.76 |
| 2006 | 0.11 | -0.37 | -0.15 | -0.15 | -0.56 |
| 2005 | 0.14 | 0.21 | 0.36 | 0.28 | 0.99 |
| 2004 | 0.16 | 0.33 | 0.45 | 0.19 | 1.13 |
| 2003 | 0.11 | 0.20 | 0.23 | 0.42 | 0.96 |

Fiscal year ended Sep. 30. Next earnings report expected: Late January. EPS Estimates based on S&P Operating Earnings; historical GAAP earnings are as reported.

## Dividend Data (Dates: mm/dd Payment Date: mm/dd/yy)

| Amount ($) | Date Decl. | Ex-Div. Date | Stk. of Record | Payment Date |
|---|---|---|---|---|
| 0.040 | 11/15 | 02/27 | 03/01 | 03/15/08 |
| 0.040 | 02/01 | 05/28 | 06/01 | 06/15/08 |
| 0.040 | 05/02 | 08/27 | 09/01 | 09/15/08 |
| 0.040 | 08/04 | 11/26 | 12/01 | 12/15/08 |

Dividends have been paid since 1976. Source: Company reports.

---

# Tyson Foods Inc.

**STANDARD &POOR'S**

## Business Summary November 12, 2008

CORPORATE OVERVIEW. Tyson Foods is the world's largest producer of beef and one of the largest chicken and pork producers in the world. The company holds about 25% of the U.S. beef market, 24% of the chicken market, and 17% of the pork market. Its goal is to become the primary protein provider for its customers. The company exports to more than 80 countries including Canada, China, Europe, Japan, Mexico, Russia and South Korea.

CORPORATE STRATEGY. The company's strategy is to discover and sell market leading products and services to grow the Tyson Foods brand. It opened a discovery center in early 2007 in which it operates 19 test kitchens. These kitchens are used to develop new products for direct shipment to stores for testing. As of February 2008, 41 new products and concepts are either in testing or have been launched. The company utilizes its scale and diversified product mix as a competitive advantage to gain additional market share in each of the product categories in which it operates. Its major operational segments include beef, chicken, pork and prepared foods.

The beef segment (43% of FY 08 (Sep.) revenues) includes the slaughter of live cattle and fabrication into primal and sub-primal meat cuts and case-ready products. Operations reduce live cattle to dressed carcasses and allied prod-

ucts for sales to further processors. The company markets its products to food retailers, distributors, wholesalers, restaurants and hotel chains, and other food processors. Allied products are marketed to manufacturers of pharmaceuticals and animal feeds. The company's primary supply of live cattle is purchased on a daily basis.

The chicken segment (33%) includes fresh, frozen and value-added chicken products sold through domestic foodservice, domestic retail markets for at-home consumption, wholesale club markets targeted to small food service operations, and individuals and distributors that deliver to restaurants, schools and international markets throughout the world. Also included in this segment are sales from allied products and TSN's chicken breeding stock subsidiary. The segment's primary raw material is live chickens that are raised by independent contractors. Profitability is partially dependent on corn and soybean meal, which represents about 40% of the cost of growing a chicken.

## Company Financials Fiscal Year Ended Sep. 30

| Per Share Data ($) | 2008 | 2007 | 2006 | 2005 | 2004 | 2003 | 2002 | 2001 | 2000 | 1999 |
|---|---|---|---|---|---|---|---|---|---|---|
| Tangible Book Value | NA | 5.96 | 5.05 | 5.66 | 4.49 | 3.17 | 2.92 | 1.71 | NM | 5.09 |
| Cash Flow | NA | 2.20 | 1.31 | 2.39 | 2.50 | 2.26 | 2.39 | 1.91 | -1.97 | 2.26 |
| Earnings | 0.24 | 0.75 | -0.56 | 0.99 | 1.13 | 0.96 | 1.08 | 0.40 | 0.68 | 1.00 |
| S&P Core Earnings | NA | 0.64 | -0.56 | 1.06 | 1.10 | 0.64 | 1.02 | 0.39 | NA | NA |
| Dividends | NA | 0.16 | 0.16 | 0.16 | 0.16 | 0.16 | 0.16 | 0.16 | 0.16 | 0.13 |
| Payout Ratio | NA | 21% | NM | 16% | 14% | 17% | 15% | 40% | 24% | 13% |
| Prices:High | NA | 24.32 | 17.33 | 19.91 | 21.28 | 15.10 | 15.71 | 14.20 | 17.38 | 23.75 |
| Prices:Low | NA | 13.50 | 12.57 | 12.50 | 12.97 | 7.25 | 9.27 | 8.10 | 8.50 | 14.88 |
| P/E Ratio:High | NA | 32 | NM | 20 | 19 | 16 | 15 | 35 | 26 | 24 |
| P/E Ratio:Low | NA | 18 | NM | 13 | 11 | 8 | 9 | 20 | 13 | 15 |

### Income Statement Analysis (Million $)

| | 2008 | 2007 | 2006 | 2005 | 2004 | 2003 | 2002 | 2001 | 2000 | 1999 |
|---|---|---|---|---|---|---|---|---|---|---|
| Revenue | 26,862 | 26,900 | 25,559 | 26,014 | 26,441 | 24,549 | 23,367 | 10,751 | 7,268 | 7,363 |
| Operating Income | NA | 1,130 | 510 | 1,266 | 1,415 | 837 | 1,407 | 650 | 643 | 854 |
| Depreciation | 493 | 514 | 517 | 501 | 490 | 458 | 467 | 335 | 294 | 291 |
| Interest Expense | NA | 232 | 268 | 227 | 275 | 592 | 305 | 144 | 116 | 124 |
| Pretax Income | 154 | 410 | -293 | 528 | 635 | 523 | 593 | 165 | 234 | 371 |
| Effective Tax Rate | 44.2% | 34.6% | NM | 33.1% | 36.5% | 35.6% | 35.4% | 35.2% | 35.5% | 34.9% |
| Net Income | 86.0 | 268 | -191 | 353 | 403 | 337 | 383 | 88.0 | 151 | 230 |
| S&P Core Earnings | NA | 228 | -190 | 379 | 392 | 224 | 365 | 87.5 | NA | NA |

### Balance Sheet & Other Financial Data (Million $)

| | 2008 | 2007 | 2006 | 2005 | 2004 | 2003 | 2002 | 2001 | 2000 | 1999 |
|---|---|---|---|---|---|---|---|---|---|---|
| Cash | 250 | 42.0 | 28.0 | 40.0 | 33.0 | 25.0 | 51.0 | 70.0 | 43.0 | 30.0 |
| Current Assets | NA | 3,596 | 4,187 | 3,485 | 3,532 | 3,371 | 3,144 | 3,290 | 1,576 | 1,727 |
| Total Assets | 10,850 | 10,227 | 11,121 | 10,504 | 10,464 | 10,486 | 10,372 | 10,632 | 4,854 | 5,083 |
| Current Liabilities | NA | 2,115 | 2,846 | 2,157 | 2,293 | 2,475 | 2,093 | 2,416 | 886 | 987 |
| Long Term Debt | NA | 2,642 | 2,987 | 2,869 | 3,024 | 3,114 | 3,733 | 4,016 | 1,357 | 1,515 |
| Common Equity | 5,014 | 4,731 | 4,900 | 4,615 | 4,912 | 3,954 | 3,662 | 3,354 | 2,175 | 2,128 |
| Total Capital | NA | 7,740 | 8,382 | 8,141 | 8,631 | 7,790 | 8,038 | 7,979 | 3,917 | 4,041 |
| Capital Expenditures | 425 | 285 | 531 | 571 | 486 | 402 | 433 | 261 | 196 | 363 |
| Cash Flow | NA | 782 | 326 | 854 | 893 | 795 | 850 | 423 | 445 | 521 |
| Current Ratio | 2.1 | 1.7 | 1.5 | 1.6 | 1.5 | 1.4 | 1.5 | 1.4 | 1.8 | 1.7 |
| % Long Term Debt of Capitalization | 36.5 | 34.1 | 35.6 | 35.2 | 35.0 | 40.0 | 46.4 | 50.3 | 34.6 | 37.5 |
| % Net Income of Revenue | 0.3 | 1.0 | NM | 1.4 | 1.5 | 1.4 | 1.6 | 0.8 | 2.1 | 3.1 |
| % Return on Assets | 0.8 | 2.5 | NM | 3.4 | 3.8 | 3.2 | 3.6 | 1.1 | 3.0 | 4.5 |
| % Return on Equity | 1.8 | 5.6 | NM | 7.9 | 8.5 | 8.8 | 10.9 | 3.2 | 7.0 | 11.2 |

Data as orig reptd.; bef. results of disc opers/spec. items. Per share data adj. for stk. divs.; EPS diluted. E-Estimated. NA-Not Available. NM-Not Meaningful. NR-Not Ranked. UR-Under Review.

**Office:** 2210 West Oaklawn Drive, Springdale, AR 72762-6999.
**Telephone:** 479-290-4000.
**Email:** tysonir@tyson.com
**Website:** http://www.tyson.com

**Chrmn:** J.H. Tyson
**Pres & CEO:** R.L. Bond
**EVP & CFO:** D. Leatherby
**EVP & General Counsel:** D.L. Van Bebber

**SVP, Chief Acctg Officer & Cntlr:** C.J. Hart
**Investor Contact:** R.A. Wisener (479-290-4235)
**Board Members:** R. L. Bond, L. V. Hackley, J. D. Kever, K. M. McNamara, B. T. Sauer, J. A. Smith, B. A. Tyson, D. Tyson, J. H. Tyson, A. C. Zapanta

**Founded:** 1935
**Domicile:** Delaware
**Employees:** 104,000

*The McGraw-Hill Companies*

**STANDARD &POOR'S**

# Union Pacific Corp

| S&P Recommendation | HOLD ★★★☆☆ | Price | 12-Mo. Target Price | Investment Style |
|---|---|---|---|---|
| | | $57.27 (as of Nov 14, 2008) | $65.00 | Large-Cap Blend |

**GICS Sector** Industrials
**Sub-Industry** Railroads

**Summary** Union Pacific operates the largest U.S. railroad, with over 32,200 miles of rail serving the western two-thirds of the country.

## Key Stock Statistics (Source S&P, Vickers, company reports)

| | | | | | | | |
|---|---|---|---|---|---|---|---|
| 52-Wk Range | $85.80–51.24 | S&P Oper. EPS 2008E | 4.44 | Market Capitalization(B) | $29.003 | Beta | 1.33 |
| Trailing 12-Month EPS | $4.17 | S&P Oper. EPS 2009E | 5.16 | Yield (%) | 1.89 | S&P 3-Yr. Proj. EPS CAGR(%) | 15 |
| Trailing 12-Month P/E | 13.7 | P/E on S&P Oper. EPS 2008E | 12.9 | Dividend Rate/Share | $1.08 | S&P Credit Rating | BBB |
| $10K Invested 5 Yrs Ago | $19,279 | Common Shares Outstg. (M) | 506.4 | Institutional Ownership (%) | 88 | | |

## Price Performance

30-Week Mov. Avg. · · · · 10-Week Mov. Avg. - - **GAAP Earnings vs. Previous Year** Volume Above Avg. STARS
12-Mo. Target Price — Relative Strength — ▲ Up ▼ Down ► No Change Below Avg.

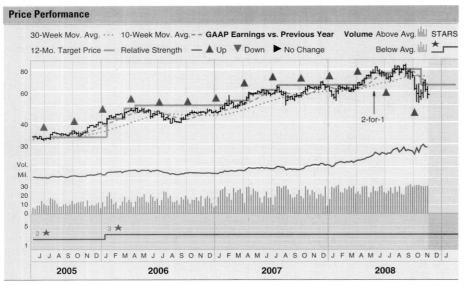

Options: CBOE, Ph

Analysis prepared by **Kevin Kirkeby** on October 23, 2008, when the stock traded at **$58.25**.

## Highlights

► After an expected 13% rise in 2008, we anticipate that UNP will achieve revenue growth of 5% in 2009. We see pricing holding firm during the year and believe carloadings will be relatively flat. Fuel surcharges, which are largely a cost pass through, should begin to stabilize, in our view. We see ongoing strength in its coal segment largely offsetting further weakness in intermodal and automotive volumes. We believe investments in the company's Powder River Basin infrastructure and interest in coal sourced from other Western fields will support the volumes we forecast for 2009.

► We see a further widening of margins in 2009, coming from pricing initiatives and improved productivity. Fuel costs are likely to remain elevated, but UNP's efforts to incorporate newer locomotives into the fleet should reduce fuel consumption. Opportunities for additional contract repricings, in our view, are limited, with about 2% of contracts up for renewal in 2009.

► We forecast 2009 operating EPS of $5.16, up about 16% from the $4.44, excluding one-time items, in EPS we expect in 2008. This includes an estimated 2% reduction in share count from September 2008 levels.

## Investment Rationale/Risk

► For the period 2008-2012, we forecast compound annual growth in revenue of 12%. We think some of the revenue drivers include expanding international trade with Asia and NAFTA, and a shifting of long-haul volumes from trucks to railroads. However, as we see pricing gains slowing, valuations slightly below their 10-year average, and an increasing proportion of EPS growth coming from share buybacks, we view current valuations as fair.

► Risks to our recommendation and target price include sharply weaker-than-expected economic growth, shifts in shipping volumes away from UNP served ports, unusually severe weather, rapid fluctuations in fuel prices, and rising regulatory scrutiny of its pricing policies.

► Our relative valuation model suggests a forward enterprise value to EBITDA multiple of about 7.7X, which is the 5-year historical average, and a value of $73. Our discounted cash flow model, which assumes a 9.8% weighted average cost of capital and a 3.5% terminal growth rate, estimates an intrinsic value of $57. Blending these models, we arrive at our 12-month target price of $65.

## Qualitative Risk Assessment

| LOW | MEDIUM | HIGH |
|---|---|---|

Our risk assessment reflects UNP's exposure to economic cycles, regulations, and labor and fuel costs, coupled with significant capital expenditure requirements, and challenges in maintaining system fluidity, offset by our view of the company's historically positive cash flow generation and moderate financial leverage.

## Quantitative Evaluations

**S&P Quality Ranking** A

| D | C | B- | B | B+ | A- | A | A+ |
|---|---|---|---|---|---|---|---|

**Relative Strength Rank** MODERATE

66

LOWEST = 1        HIGHEST = 99

## Revenue/Earnings Data

**Revenue (Million $)**

| | 1Q | 2Q | 3Q | 4Q | Year |
|---|---|---|---|---|---|
| 2008 | 4,270 | 4,568 | 4,846 | -- | -- |
| 2007 | 3,849 | 4,046 | 4,191 | 4,197 | 16,283 |
| 2006 | 3,710 | 3,923 | 3,983 | 3,962 | 15,578 |
| 2005 | 3,152 | 3,344 | 3,461 | 3,621 | 13,578 |
| 2004 | 2,893 | 3,029 | 3,076 | 3,217 | 12,215 |
| 2003 | 2,736 | 2,894 | 2,956 | 2,965 | 11,551 |

**Earnings Per Share ($)**

| | | | | | |
|---|---|---|---|---|---|
| 2008 | 0.85 | 1.02 | 1.38 | E1.26 | E4.44 |
| 2007 | 0.71 | 0.83 | 1.00 | 0.93 | 3.46 |
| 2006 | 0.58 | 0.72 | 0.77 | 0.89 | 2.96 |
| 2005 | 0.24 | 0.44 | 0.69 | 0.55 | 1.93 |
| 2004 | 0.32 | 0.30 | 0.39 | 0.15 | 1.15 |
| 2003 | 0.30 | 0.55 | 0.61 | 0.64 | 2.04 |

Fiscal year ended Dec. 31. Next earnings report expected: Late January. EPS Estimates based on S&P Operating Earnings; historical GAAP earnings are as reported.

## Dividend Data (Dates: mm/dd Payment Date: mm/dd/yy)

| Amount ($) | Date Decl. | Ex-Div. Date | Stk. of Record | Payment Date |
|---|---|---|---|---|
| 0.440 | 02/28 | 03/10 | 03/12 | 04/01/08 |
| 2-for-1 | 05/01 | 05/29 | 05/12 | 05/28/08 |
| 0.220 | 05/01 | 06/04 | 06/06 | 07/01/08 |
| 0.270 | 07/31 | 08/27 | 08/29 | 10/01/08 |

Dividends have been paid since 1900. Source: Company reports.

---

**Please read the Required Disclosures and Analyst Certification on the last page of this report.**

*The McGraw-Hill Companies*

# Union Pacific Corp

STANDARD &POOR'S

## Business Summary October 23, 2008

CORPORATE OVERVIEW. We believe that Union Pacific, operating the largest U.S. railroad, will focus on improving service levels, system fluidity, and re-moving bottlenecks--challenges that we believe hampered its results in 2004 and 2005. UNP's system spans about 32,200 miles, linking Pacific Coast and Gulf Coast ports to midwestern and eastern gateways, and schedules are co-ordinated with other carriers.

MARKET PROFILE. We believe UNP's intermodal business, representing 19% of 2007 freight revenue, will be UNP's fastest-growing segment longer term, driven by rising international trade and the outsourcing of manufacturing to Asia. However, the weakening economy, and homebuilding sector weakness in particular, slowed revenue growth for the segment to a low single-digit rate in 2007, following double-digit gains in both 2005 and 2006. Industrial products, sensitive to GDP trends, provided 20% of freight revenues in 2007, and includ-ed building products, metals and minerals. Energy accounted for 20% of 2007 freight revenues. UNP is a major transporter of low-sulfur coal, with about 67% of its energy traffic consisting of coal originating in the Powder River Basin of Wyoming and Montana, primarily delivered to power utilities. We be-lieve chemicals, agricultural products, and automotive, representing 15%, 17%, and 9% of 2007 freight revenues, respectively, all face low long-term vol-ume growth prospects.

COMPETITIVE LANDSCAPE. The U.S. rail industry has an oligopoly-like struc-ture, with over 80% of revenues generated by the four largest railroads: UNP and Burlington Northern Santa Fe Corp. (BNI, hold, $96) operating on the West Coast, and CSX Corp. (CSX: buy, $56) and Norfolk Southern Corp. (NSC: buy, $66) operating on the East Coast. Railroads simultaneously compete for cus-tomers while cooperating by sharing assets, interfacing systems, and com-pleting customer movements. Key suppliers include locomotive and rail equip-ment manufacturers, fuel suppliers, and labor. UNP's employees, about 85% of whom are unionized, enjoy above national average compensation due to their significant bargaining power.

## Company Financials Fiscal Year Ended Dec. 31

| Per Share Data ($) | 2007 | 2006 | 2005 | 2004 | 2003 | 2002 | 2001 | 2000 | 1999 | 1998 |
|---|---|---|---|---|---|---|---|---|---|---|
| Tangible Book Value | 31.73 | 28.34 | 25.58 | 24.25 | 23.93 | 21.00 | 19.15 | 17.54 | 16.15 | 14.97 |
| Cash Flow | 5.92 | 5.23 | 4.13 | 3.27 | 3.96 | 4.60 | 3.93 | 3.67 | 3.46 | 0.89 |
| Earnings | 3.46 | 2.96 | 1.93 | 1.15 | 2.04 | 2.53 | 1.89 | 1.67 | 1.56 | -1.29 |
| S&P Core Earnings | 3.37 | 2.86 | 1.66 | 1.05 | 1.88 | 1.92 | 1.41 | NA | NA | NA |
| Dividends | 0.75 | 0.60 | 0.60 | 0.60 | 0.50 | 0.42 | 0.40 | 0.40 | 0.40 | 0.52 |
| Payout Ratio | 22% | 20% | 31% | 52% | 24% | 16% | 21% | 24% | 26% | NM |
| Prices:High | 68.78 | 48.75 | 40.63 | 34.78 | 34.75 | 32.58 | 30.35 | 26.41 | 33.94 | 31.88 |
| Prices:Low | 44.79 | 38.81 | 29.09 | 27.40 | 25.45 | 26.50 | 21.88 | 17.13 | 19.50 | 18.66 |
| P/E Ratio:High | 20 | 16 | 21 | 30 | 17 | 13 | 16 | 16 | 22 | NM |
| P/E Ratio:Low | 13 | 13 | 15 | 24 | 13 | 10 | 12 | 10 | 13 | NM |

| Income Statement Analysis (Million $) | | | | | | | | | | |
|---|---|---|---|---|---|---|---|---|---|---|
| Revenue | 16,283 | 15,578 | 13,578 | 12,215 | 11,551 | 12,491 | 11,973 | 11,878 | 11,273 | 10,553 |
| Operating Income | 4,696 | 4,121 | 2,970 | 2,406 | 3,200 | 3,530 | 2,072 | 2,043 | 2,887 | 1,446 |
| Depreciation | 1,321 | 1,237 | 1,175 | 1,111 | 1,067 | 1,206 | 1,174 | 1,140 | 1,083 | 1,070 |
| Interest Expense | 482 | 477 | 504 | 527 | 574 | 633 | 701 | 723 | 733 | 714 |
| Pretax Income | 3,009 | 2,525 | 1,436 | 856 | 1,637 | 2,016 | 1,533 | 1,310 | 1,202 | -696 |
| Effective Tax Rate | 38.4% | 36.4% | 28.6% | 29.4% | 35.5% | 33.5% | 37.0% | 35.7% | 34.9% | NM |
| Net Income | 1,855 | 1,606 | 1,026 | 604 | 1,056 | 1,341 | 966 | 842 | 783 | -633 |
| S&P Core Earnings | 1,808 | 1,553 | 886 | 551 | 972 | 1,003 | 708 | NA | NA | NA |

| Balance Sheet & Other Financial Data (Million $) | | | | | | | | | | |
|---|---|---|---|---|---|---|---|---|---|---|
| Cash | 878 | 827 | 773 | 977 | 527 | 369 | 113 | 105 | 175 | 176 |
| Current Assets | 2,594 | 2,411 | 2,325 | 2,290 | 2,089 | 2,152 | 1,542 | 1,285 | 1,314 | 1,502 |
| Total Assets | 38,033 | 36,515 | 35,620 | 34,589 | 33,460 | 32,764 | 31,551 | 30,499 | 29,888 | 29,374 |
| Current Liabilities | 3,041 | 3,539 | 3,384 | 2,516 | 2,456 | 2,701 | 2,692 | 2,962 | 2,885 | 2,932 |
| Long Term Debt | 7,543 | 6,000 | 6,760 | 7,981 | 7,822 | 8,928 | 9,386 | 9,644 | 9,926 | 10,011 |
| Common Equity | 15,585 | 15,312 | 13,707 | 12,655 | 12,354 | 10,651 | 9,575 | 8,662 | 8,001 | 7,393 |
| Total Capital | 33,178 | 31,008 | 29,949 | 29,816 | 29,345 | 28,057 | 26,843 | 25,449 | 24,642 | 23,712 |
| Capital Expenditures | 2,496 | 2,242 | 2,169 | 1,876 | 1,752 | 1,887 | 1,736 | 1,783 | 1,834 | 2,111 |
| Cash Flow | 3,176 | 2,843 | 2,201 | 1,715 | 2,123 | 2,547 | 2,140 | 1,982 | 1,866 | 437 |
| Current Ratio | 0.9 | 0.7 | 0.7 | 0.9 | 0.9 | 0.8 | 0.6 | 0.4 | 0.5 | 0.5 |
| % Long Term Debt of Capitalization | 22.7 | 19.3 | 22.6 | 26.8 | 26.7 | 31.8 | 35.0 | 37.9 | 40.3 | 42.2 |
| % Net Income of Revenue | 11.4 | 10.3 | 7.6 | 4.9 | 9.1 | 10.7 | 8.1 | 7.1 | 6.9 | NM |
| % Return on Assets | 5.0 | 4.5 | 2.9 | 1.8 | 3.2 | 4.2 | 3.1 | 2.8 | 2.6 | NM |
| % Return on Equity | 12.0 | 11.1 | 7.8 | 4.8 | 9.2 | 13.3 | 10.6 | 10.1 | 10.2 | NM |

Data as orig reptd.; bef. results of disc opers/spec. items. Per share data adj. for stk. divs.; EPS diluted. E-Estimated. NA-Not Available. NM-Not Meaningful. NR-Not Ranked. UR-Under Review.

**Office:** 1400 Douglas St, Omaha, NE 68179-0002.
**Telephone:** 402-544-5000.
**Website:** http://www.up.com
**Chrmn, Pres & CEO:** J.R. Young

**EVP & CFO:** R.M. Knight, Jr.
**SVP & Secy:** B.W. Schaefer
**SVP & General Counsel:** J.M. Hemmer
**SVP & CIO:** L.L. Tennison

**Investor Contact:** M.S. Jones (402-544-6111)
**Board Members:** A. H. Card, Jr., E. B. Davis, Jr., T. J. Donohue, Jr., A. Dunham, J. R. Hope, C. C. Krulak, M. R. McCarthy, M. W. McConnell, T. F. McLarty, III, S. R. Rogel, J. R. Young

**Founded:** 1862
**Domicile:** Utah
**Employees:** 50,089

# UnitedHealth Group Inc

STANDARD
&POOR'S

**S&P Recommendation** HOLD ★★★☆☆

| Price | 12-Mo. Target Price | Investment Style |
|---|---|---|
| $20.02 (as of Nov 14, 2008) | $26.00 | Large-Cap Growth |

**GICS Sector** Health Care
**Sub-Industry** Managed Health Care

**Summary** This leading health care services company provided health benefit services to more than 31 million individuals across the U.S. as of December 31, 2007.

## Key Stock Statistics (Source S&P, Vickers, company reports)

| | | | | | | | | |
|---|---|---|---|---|---|---|---|---|
| 52-Wk Range | $59.46– 14.51 | S&P Oper. EPS 2008E | 3.03 | Market Capitalization(B) | $24.180 | Beta | 1.17 |
| Trailing 12-Month EPS | $2.74 | S&P Oper. EPS 2009E | 3.00 | Yield (%) | 0.15 | S&P 3-Yr. Proj. EPS CAGR(%) | NM |
| Trailing 12-Month P/E | 7.3 | P/E on S&P Oper. EPS 2008E | 6.6 | Dividend Rate/Share | $0.03 | S&P Credit Rating | A- |
| $10K Invested 5 Yrs Ago | $8,082 | Common Shares Outstg. (M) | 1,207.8 | Institutional Ownership (%) | 84 | | |

## Price Performance

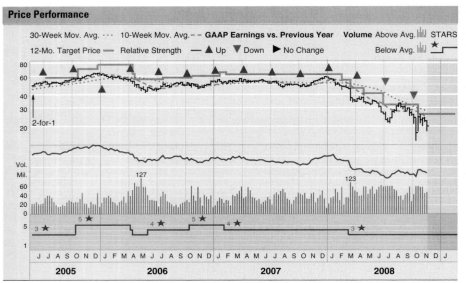

30-Week Mov. Avg. · · · 10-Week Mov. Avg. – – GAAP Earnings vs. Previous Year   Volume Above Avg. STARS
12-Mo. Target Price — Relative Strength ▲ Up ▼ Down ► No Change   Below Avg.

Options: ASE, CBOE, P

Analysis prepared by **Phillip M. Seligman** on October 20, 2008, when the stock traded at **$ 25.25**.

## Highlights

➤ We look for operating revenues to grow by over 2% to about $82 billion in 2009, from the approximately $80 billion we see in 2008. Drivers should include higher premium pricing, healthy Medicare and Medicaid enrollment growth, the full-year benefit of the June 2008 acquisition of Unison, and non-health plan business growth. We estimate 650,000 fewer risk-based commercial members and about 100,000 fewer members through attrition in the fee-based commercial accounts, mainly due to the soft economy. Sierra Health Plans' and Fiserv's (FISV: buy, $37) health businesses were acquired early in 2008, so we expect only a modest benefit from them on full-year 2009 revenue growth.

➤ We forecast that the consolidated medical loss ratio (MLR) will grow by up to 70 basis points (bps) to about 83% after the 170 bps rise we project for 2008, as Medicare and Medicaid enrollment increases and risk-based commercial enrollment declines. We expect the SG&A cost ratio to decline, on cost control initiatives, but investment income to be lower.

➤ We estimate operating EPS of $3.03 in 2008, versus 2007's $3.50, and $3.00 in 2009, aided by share buybacks.

## Investment Rationale/Risk

➤ We are encouraged by UNH's indication that it is applying more disciplined underwriting and better product positioning to help strengthen its operating performance. While we believe these moves will make it harder for UNH to retain and attract risk-based commercial members amid competition and our view of rising unemployment, we expect the profitability of its commercial risk business to improve. Meanwhile, its Medicaid business is performing well, and we see UNH in a healthy financial position - the company appears to us to be adequately capitalized and it wrote down only $0.02 per share in 2008's third quarter for troubled assets. We are also encouraged by its $5 billion operating cash flow target for 2008, excluding stock option lawsuit settlement costs.

➤ Risks to our recommendation and target price include a sharp rise in medical costs and unfavorable rulings in government probes of UNH's past stock option grants and California's probe of its claims handling practices.

➤ Our 12-month target price of $26 assumes a P/E of 8.7X our 2009 EPS estimate, reflecting peer-wide valuation contraction and our forecast of slower long-term EPS growth.

## Qualitative Risk Assessment

| LOW | MEDIUM | HIGH |
|---|---|---|

Our risk assessment reflects UNH's leadership in the highly fragmented managed care market and its wide geographic, market and product diversity, which we believe permits stable operational performance even during periods of economic downturn. However, we see commercial enrollment growth slowing from an expanding base and as a result of intensifying competition.

## Quantitative Evaluations

**S&P Quality Ranking**   A+

| D | C | B- | B | B+ | A- | A | A+ |
|---|---|---|---|---|---|---|---|

**Relative Strength Rank**   MODERATE

58

LOWEST = 1   HIGHEST = 99

## Revenue/Earnings Data

**Revenue (Million $)**

| | 1Q | 2Q | 3Q | 4Q | Year |
|---|---|---|---|---|---|
| 2008 | 20,304 | 20,272 | 20,156 | -- | -- |
| 2007 | 19,047 | 18,926 | 18,679 | 18,705 | 75,431 |
| 2006 | 17,581 | 17,863 | 17,970 | 18,128 | 71,542 |
| 2005 | 10,887 | 11,111 | 11,322 | 12,045 | 45,365 |
| 2004 | 8,144 | 8,704 | 9,859 | 10,511 | 37,218 |
| 2003 | 6,975 | 7,087 | 7,238 | 7,523 | 28,823 |

**Earnings Per Share ($)**

| | | | | | |
|---|---|---|---|---|---|
| 2008 | 0.78 | 0.27 | 0.75 | E0.80 | E3.03 |
| 2007 | 0.66 | 0.87 | 0.95 | 0.92 | 3.42 |
| 2006 | 0.63 | 0.70 | 0.80 | 0.84 | 2.97 |
| 2005 | 0.58 | 0.61 | 0.64 | 0.65 | 2.48 |
| 2004 | 0.44 | 0.47 | 0.52 | 0.55 | 1.97 |
| 2003 | 0.33 | 0.36 | 0.39 | 0.42 | 1.48 |

Fiscal year ended Dec. 31. Next earnings report expected: Late January. EPS Estimates based on S&P Operating Earnings; historical GAAP earnings are as reported.

## Dividend Data (Dates: mm/dd Payment Date: mm/dd/yy)

| Amount ($) | Date Decl. | Ex-Div. Date | Stk. of Record | Payment Date |
|---|---|---|---|---|
| 0.030 | 02/21 | 03/31 | 04/02 | 04/16/08 |

Dividends have been paid since 1990. Source: Company reports.

---

**Please read the Required Disclosures and Analyst Certification on the last page of this report.**

The McGraw-Hill Companies

# UnitedHealth Group Inc

**STANDARD &POOR'S**

## Business Summary October 20, 2008

CORPORATE OVERVIEW. UnitedHealth Group, a U.S. leader in health care management, provides a broad range of health care products and services, including health maintenance organizations (HMOs), point of service (POS) plans, preferred provider organizations (PPOs), and managed fee for service programs.

The company reports results in four business segments, organized by product basis:

The Health Care Services segment (79% of 2007 revenues and 82% of operating earnings before eliminations) consists of the following business units: UnitedHealthcare coordinates network-based health and well-being services on behalf of multistate mid-sized and local employers and for individuals. Uniprise provides these services to large, self-insured accounts in return for administrative fees; it generally assumes no responsibility for health care costs. AmeriChoice facilitates and manages health care services for state Medicaid programs and their beneficiaries. Ovations delivers health and well-being services to Americans over the age of 50. At September 30, 2008, risk and fee-based Health Care Services enrollment totaled 32,800,000, versus 31,005,000 at December 31, 2007, including risk-based commercial (10,495,000 versus 10,805,000), fee-based commercial (15,975,000 versus 14,720,000),

Medicare Advantage (1,480,000 versus 1,370,000), Medicaid (2,340,000 versus 1,710,000), and Standardized Medicare Supplement (2,510,000 versus 2,400,000).

OptumHealth (5% and 11%) provides specialized benefits such as behavioral, dental and vision offerings, and financial services (Exante).

Ingenix (1% and 3%) is a leader in the field of health care data, analysis and application, serving pharmaceutical companies, health insurers and other payers, physicians and other health care providers, large employers and governments. We view Ingenix as key to the other segments' competitive strengths.

Prescription Solutions (15% and 4%) offers pharmacy benefit management and specialty pharmacy management services to employer groups, union trusts, seniors -- through Medicare prescription drug plans, and commercial health plans.

## Company Financials Fiscal Year Ended Dec. 31

| Per Share Data ($) | 2007 | 2006 | 2005 | 2004 | 2003 | 2002 | 2001 | 2000 | 1999 | 1998 |
|---|---|---|---|---|---|---|---|---|---|---|
| Tangible Book Value | 1.18 | 1.55 | NM | 0.04 | 1.24 | 0.79 | 0.88 | 0.61 | 0.75 | 1.03 |
| Cash Flow | 4.00 | 3.44 | 2.82 | 2.26 | 1.72 | 1.26 | 0.90 | 0.73 | 0.56 | -0.01 |
| Earnings | 3.42 | 2.97 | 2.48 | 1.97 | 1.48 | 1.07 | 0.70 | 0.55 | 0.40 | -0.14 |
| S&P Core Earnings | 3.40 | 2.94 | 2.36 | 1.86 | 1.37 | 0.99 | 0.62 | NA | NA | NA |
| Dividends | 0.03 | 0.03 | 0.02 | 0.02 | 0.01 | 0.01 | 0.01 | 0.00 | 0.00 | 0.00 |
| Payout Ratio | 1% | 1% | 1% | 1% | 1% | 1% | 1% | 1% | 1% | NM |
| Prices:High | 59.46 | 62.93 | 64.61 | 44.38 | 29.34 | 25.25 | 18.20 | 15.86 | 8.75 | 9.24 |
| Prices:Low | 45.82 | 41.44 | 42.63 | 27.73 | 19.60 | 16.96 | 12.63 | 5.80 | 4.92 | 3.70 |
| P/E Ratio:High | 17 | 21 | 26 | 23 | 20 | 24 | 26 | 29 | 22 | NM |
| P/E Ratio:Low | 13 | 14 | 17 | 14 | 13 | 16 | 18 | 11 | 12 | NM |

| Income Statement Analysis (Million $) | 2007 | 2006 | 2005 | 2004 | 2003 | 2002 | 2001 | 2000 | 1999 | 1998 |
|---|---|---|---|---|---|---|---|---|---|---|
| Revenue | 75,431 | 71,542 | 45,365 | 37,218 | 28,823 | 25,020 | 23,454 | 21,122 | 19,343 | 17,106 |
| Operating Income | 8,821 | 6,783 | 5,826 | 4,475 | 3,234 | 2,441 | 1,831 | 1,215 | 957 | 619 |
| Depreciation | 796 | 670 | 453 | 374 | 299 | 255 | 265 | 247 | 233 | 185 |
| Interest Expense | 544 | 456 | 241 | 128 | 95.0 | 90.0 | 94.0 | 72.0 | 49.0 | 4.00 |
| Pretax Income | 7,305 | 6,528 | 5,132 | 3,973 | 2,840 | 2,096 | 1,472 | 1,155 | 894 | -46.0 |
| Effective Tax Rate | 36.3% | 36.3% | 35.7% | 34.9% | 35.7% | 35.5% | 38.0% | 36.3% | 36.5% | NM |
| Net Income | 4,654 | 4,159 | 3,300 | 2,587 | 1,825 | 1,352 | 913 | 736 | 568 | -166 |
| S&P Core Earnings | 4,629 | 4,108 | 3,137 | 2,443 | 1,689 | 1,260 | 812 | NA | NA | NA |

| Balance Sheet & Other Financial Data (Million $) | 2007 | 2006 | 2005 | 2004 | 2003 | 2002 | 2001 | 2000 | 1999 | 1998 |
|---|---|---|---|---|---|---|---|---|---|---|
| Cash | 9,619 | 10,940 | 5,421 | 3,991 | 2,262 | 1,130 | 1,540 | 1,419 | 1,605 | 1,644 |
| Current Assets | 15,544 | 16,044 | 10,640 | 8,241 | 6,120 | 5,174 | 4,946 | 4,405 | 4,568 | 4,280 |
| Total Assets | 50,899 | 48,320 | 41,374 | 27,879 | 17,634 | 14,164 | 12,486 | 11,053 | 10,273 | 9,701 |
| Current Liabilities | 18,492 | 18,497 | 16,644 | 11,329 | 8,768 | 8,379 | 7,491 | 6,570 | 5,892 | 5,342 |
| Long Term Debt | 9,063 | 5,973 | 3,850 | 3,350 | 1,750 | 950 | 900 | 650 | 400 | 249 |
| Common Equity | 20,063 | 20,810 | 17,733 | 10,717 | 5,128 | 4,428 | 3,891 | 3,688 | 3,863 | 4,038 |
| Total Capital | 29,126 | 26,783 | 21,583 | 14,067 | 6,878 | 5,378 | 4,791 | 4,338 | 4,263 | 4,287 |
| Capital Expenditures | 871 | 728 | 5,876 | 350 | 352 | 419 | 425 | 245 | 196 | 210 |
| Cash Flow | 5,450 | 4,829 | 3,753 | 2,961 | 2,124 | 1,607 | 1,178 | 983 | 801 | -9.00 |
| Current Ratio | 0.8 | 0.9 | 0.6 | 0.7 | 0.7 | 0.6 | 0.7 | 0.7 | 0.8 | 0.8 |
| % Long Term Debt of Capitalization | 31.1 | 22.3 | 17.8 | 23.8 | 25.4 | 17.7 | 18.8 | 15.0 | 9.4 | 5.8 |
| % Net Income of Revenue | 6.2 | 5.9 | 7.3 | 7.0 | 6.3 | 5.4 | 3.9 | 3.5 | 2.9 | NM |
| % Return on Assets | 9.4 | 9.3 | 9.5 | 11.4 | 11.5 | 10.1 | 7.8 | 6.9 | 5.7 | NM |
| % Return on Equity | 22.8 | 21.5 | 23.2 | 32.7 | 38.2 | 32.5 | 24.1 | 19.5 | 14.4 | NM |

Data as orig reptd.; bef. results of disc opers/spec. items. Per share data adj. for stk. divs.; EPS diluted. E-Estimated. NA-Not Available. NM-Not Meaningful. NR-Not Ranked. UR-Under Review.

**Office:** 9900 Bren Rd E, Minnetonka, MN 55343.
**Telephone:** 952-936-1300.
**Website:** http://www.unitedhealthgroup.com
**Chrmn:** R.T. Burke

**Pres & CEO:** S.J. Hemsley
**COO & EVP:** D.S. Wichmann
**EVP & CFO:** G.L. Mikan, III
**EVP & General Counsel:** T.L. Strickland

**Board Members:** W. C. Ballard, Jr., R. T. Burke, R. J. Darretta, S. J. Hemsley, M. J. Hooper, D. W. Leatherdale, G. M. Renwick, G. R. Wilensky

**Founded:** 1974
**Domicile:** Minnesota
**Employees:** 67,000

The McGraw-Hill Companies

# United Parcel Service Inc.

**STANDARD &POOR'S**

| S&P Recommendation | HOLD ★★★★★ | Price $53.14 (as of Nov 14, 2008) | 12-Mo. Target Price $50.00 | Investment Style Large-Cap Growth |
|---|---|---|---|---|

**GICS Sector** Industrials
**Sub-Industry** Air Freight & Logistics

**Summary** UPS is the world's largest express delivery company, and has established itself as a facilitator of e-commerce.

## Key Stock Statistics (Source S&P, Vickers, company reports)

| | | | | | | | |
|---|---|---|---|---|---|---|---|
| 52-Wk Range | $75.82– 43.32 | S&P Oper. EPS 2008**E** | 3.55 | Market Capitalization(B) | $36.003 | Beta | 0.75 |
| Trailing 12-Month EPS | $0.10 | S&P Oper. EPS 2009**E** | 3.60 | Yield (%) | 3.39 | S&P 3-Yr. Proj. EPS CAGR(%) | 10 |
| Trailing 12-Month P/E | NM | P/E on S&P Oper. EPS 2008**E** | 15.0 | Dividend Rate/Share | $1.80 | S&P Credit Rating | AA- |
| $10K Invested 5 Yrs Ago | $8,162 | Common Shares Outstg. (M) | 995.2 | Institutional Ownership (%) | 68 | | |

## Price Performance

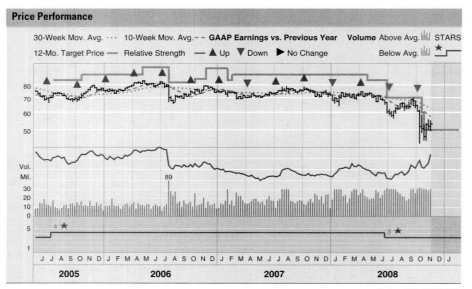

30-Week Mov. Avg. ···· 10-Week Mov. Avg. ─ ─ **GAAP Earnings vs. Previous Year**    Volume Above Avg. | STARS
12-Mo. Target Price ── Relative Strength ── ▲ Up ▼ Down ► No Change    Below Avg. | ★ ─

Options: ASE, CBOE, P, Ph

Analysis prepared by **Jim Corridore** on November 07, 2008, when the stock traded at **$ 49.87.**

### Highlights

➤ We expect 2009 revenues to rise about 2%, based on recently announced 5.9% ground and 4.9% air express rate increases. These increases along with the weak economy will likely spur an increase in less profitable delivery methods like second and third day services. We see overall domestic volumes declining about 5% and see international volumes up about 5%. Customers may become more willing to absorb rate increases as fuel surcharges come down due to the large recent downswing in oil prices. We foresee 6% growth in supply chain and freight revenues in 2009.

➤ We see operating margins being hurt by a weaker package mix. We also think productivity gains from new technology could be offset by inefficiencies created by pushing a lower volume of packages through the network. UPS's implementation of its package flow technology is targeted to save the company $600 million annually. The company is also restructuring its supply chain business, aimed at saving $100 million annually.

➤ We estimate 2009 EPS of $3.60 up 1.4% over our 2008 EPS estimate of $3.55. Both these estimates are below 2007 adjusted EPS of $4.17.

### Investment Rationale/Risk

➤ We think the stock deserves to trade near the low end of its historical valuation due to worries about the overall weak U.S. economy. Given our view that a U.S. economic recovery is likely to be pushed out until late 2009, we do not expect increased investor interest in the stock during the remainder of this year. Partly offsetting this, we expect increased share repurchases to be accretive to earnings and provide support for the stock. By our analysis, UPS's valuation on a P/E basis is near a trough, which should provide some downside protection despite the risks we see.

➤ Risks to our recommendation and target price include a more severe economic slowdown and a possible price war with competitors. Regarding corporate governance, we are concerned that Class A shareholders have 10 votes per share on many matters.

➤ Our 12-month target price of $50 values the stock at 14X our 2009 EPS estimate, the low end of UPS's five-year historical P/E range, due to the economic risks we foresee. We view positively return on assets and cash flow from operations.

### Qualitative Risk Assessment

| LOW | MEDIUM | HIGH |
|---|---|---|

Our risk assessment reflects what we see as UPS's geographically diversified and increasing revenue base, a strong balance sheet with ample cash and low debt relative to total capitalization, and a track record of earnings and cash flow growth.

### Quantitative Evaluations

**S&P Quality Ranking**                    B+

| D | C | B- | B | B+ | A- | A | A+ |
|---|---|---|---|---|---|---|---|

**Relative Strength Rank**                STRONG

79

LOWEST = 1                                HIGHEST = 99

### Revenue/Earnings Data

**Revenue (Million $)**

| | 1Q | 2Q | 3Q | 4Q | Year |
|---|---|---|---|---|---|
| 2008 | 12,675 | 13,001 | 13,113 | -- | -- |
| 2007 | 11,906 | 12,189 | 12,205 | 13,392 | 49,692 |
| 2006 | 11,521 | 11,736 | 11,662 | 12,628 | 47,547 |
| 2005 | 9,886 | 10,191 | 10,550 | 11,954 | 42,581 |
| 2004 | 8,919 | 8,871 | 8,952 | 9,840 | 36,582 |
| 2003 | 8,015 | 8,226 | 8,312 | 8,932 | 33,485 |

**Earnings Per Share ($)**

| | | | | | |
|---|---|---|---|---|---|
| 2008 | 0.87 | 0.85 | 0.96 | E0.87 | E3.55 |
| 2007 | 0.78 | 1.04 | 1.02 | -2.52 | 0.36 |
| 2006 | 0.89 | 0.97 | 0.96 | 1.04 | 3.86 |
| 2005 | 0.78 | 0.88 | 0.86 | 0.95 | 3.47 |
| 2004 | 0.67 | 0.72 | 0.78 | 0.76 | 2.93 |
| 2003 | 0.54 | 0.61 | 0.65 | 0.75 | 2.55 |

Fiscal year ended Dec. 31. Next earnings report expected: Late January. EPS Estimates based on S&P Operating Earnings; historical GAAP earnings are as reported.

### Dividend Data (Dates: mm/dd Payment Date: mm/dd/yy)

| Amount ($) | Date Decl. | Ex-Div. Date | Stk. of Record | Payment Date |
|---|---|---|---|---|
| 0.450 | 01/31 | 02/07 | 02/11 | 03/04/08 |
| 0.450 | 05/08 | 05/15 | 05/19 | 06/03/08 |
| 0.450 | 08/14 | 08/21 | 08/25 | 09/09/08 |
| 0.450 | 11/06 | 11/13 | 11/17 | 12/03/08 |

Dividends have been paid since 2000. Source: Company reports.

---

**Please read the Required Disclosures and Analyst Certification on the last page of this report.**

The McGraw-Hill Companies

# United Parcel Service Inc.

**STANDARD &POOR'S**

## Business Summary November 07, 2008

United Parcel Service is the world's largest express and package delivery company. It is also a leading commerce facilitator, offering various logistics and financial services. The company, which was privately held since its founding in 1907, had its IPO of Class B stock in November 1999.

The company seeks to position itself as the primary coordinator of the flow of goods, information and funds throughout the entire supply chain (the movement from the raw materials and parts stage through final consumption of the finished product).

Domestic package delivery services accounted for 62% of revenues in 2007, down from 64% in 2006. About 84% of the 13.9 million daily domestic shipments handled by the company in 2007 were moved by its ground delivery service, which is available to every address in the 48 contiguous states in the U.S. Domestic air delivery is provided throughout the U.S., including next-day air, which is guaranteed by 10:30 a.m. to more than 75% of the U.S. population, and by noon to an additional 15% of the population.

UPS entered the international arena in 1975. In 2007, it handled 1.9 million international shipments per day. Its international package delivery service (21% of total revenues in 2007) is growing faster than its domestic business. UPS delivers international shipments to more than 200 countries and territories worldwide and provides delivery within one to two business days to the world's major business centers. Services include export (packages that cross national borders) and domestic (packages that stay within a single country's boundaries). UPS has a portfolio of domestic services in 20 major countries. Transborder services within the European Union are expected to continue to be a growth engine for the company. Asia continues to be an area in which UPS is investing in infrastructure and technology.

## Company Financials Fiscal Year Ended Dec. 31

| Per Share Data ($) | 2007 | 2006 | 2005 | 2004 | 2003 | 2002 | 2001 | 2000 | 1999 | 1998 |
|---|---|---|---|---|---|---|---|---|---|---|
| Tangible Book Value | 9.04 | 11.46 | 12.44 | 12.84 | 12.03 | 11.09 | 9.14 | 8.58 | 10.31 | 13.10 |
| Cash Flow | 2.00 | 5.46 | 4.94 | 4.33 | 3.91 | 4.20 | 3.41 | 3.50 | 1.77 | 5.15 |
| Earnings | 0.36 | 3.86 | 3.47 | 2.93 | 2.55 | 2.87 | 2.12 | 2.50 | 0.77 | 1.57 |
| S&P Core Earnings | 0.20 | 3.78 | 3.40 | 2.87 | 2.46 | 2.48 | 1.70 | NA | NA | NA |
| Dividends | 1.68 | 1.52 | 1.32 | 1.12 | 0.92 | 0.76 | 0.76 | 0.81 | Nil | NA |
| Payout Ratio | NM | 39% | 38% | 38% | 36% | 26% | 36% | 32% | Nil | NA |
| Prices:High | 78.99 | 83.99 | 85.84 | 89.11 | 74.87 | 67.10 | 62.50 | 69.75 | 76.94 | NA |
| Prices:Low | 68.66 | 65.50 | 66.10 | 67.51 | 53.00 | 54.25 | 46.15 | 49.50 | 50.00 | NA |
| P/E Ratio:High | NM | 22 | 25 | 30 | 29 | 23 | 29 | 28 | NM | NA |
| P/E Ratio:Low | NM | 17 | 19 | 23 | 21 | 19 | 22 | 20 | NM | NA |

| Income Statement Analysis (Million $) | 2007 | 2006 | 2005 | 2004 | 2003 | 2002 | 2001 | 2000 | 1999 | 1998 |
|---|---|---|---|---|---|---|---|---|---|---|
| Revenue | 49,692 | 47,547 | 42,581 | 36,582 | 33,485 | 31,272 | 30,646 | 29,771 | 27,052 | 24,788 |
| Operating Income | 8,758 | 8,383 | 7,787 | 6,532 | 5,994 | 5,560 | 5,358 | 5,685 | 5,127 | 4,202 |
| Depreciation | 1,745 | 1,748 | 1,644 | 1,543 | 1,549 | 1,464 | 1,396 | 1,173 | 1,139 | 1,112 |
| Interest Expense | 313 | 211 | 172 | 149 | 121 | 173 | 184 | 205 | 228 | 227 |
| Pretax Income | 431 | 6,510 | 6,075 | 4,922 | 4,370 | 5,009 | 3,937 | 4,834 | 2,088 | 2,902 |
| Effective Tax Rate | 11.4% | 35.5% | 36.3% | 32.3% | 33.7% | 35.0% | 38.4% | 39.3% | 57.7% | 40.0% |
| Net Income | 382 | 4,202 | 3,870 | 3,333 | 2,898 | 3,254 | 2,425 | 2,934 | 883 | 1,741 |
| S&P Core Earnings | 212 | 4,109 | 3,784 | 3,261 | 2,790 | 2,820 | 1,948 | NA | NA | NA |

| Balance Sheet & Other Financial Data (Million $) | 2007 | 2006 | 2005 | 2004 | 2003 | 2002 | 2001 | 2000 | 1999 | 1998 |
|---|---|---|---|---|---|---|---|---|---|---|
| Cash | 2,604 | 794 | 1,369 | 5,197 | 2,951 | 2,211 | 1,616 | 1,952 | 6,278 | 1,629 |
| Current Assets | 11,760 | 9,377 | 11,003 | 12,605 | 9,853 | 8,738 | 7,597 | 7,124 | 11,138 | 5,425 |
| Total Assets | 39,042 | 33,210 | 35,222 | 33,026 | 28,909 | 26,357 | 24,636 | 21,662 | 23,043 | 17,067 |
| Current Liabilities | 9,840 | 6,719 | 6,793 | 6,483 | 5,518 | 5,555 | 4,629 | 4,501 | 4,198 | 3,717 |
| Long Term Debt | 7,506 | 3,133 | 3,159 | 3,261 | 3,149 | 3,495 | 4,648 | 2,981 | 1,912 | 2,191 |
| Common Equity | 12,183 | 15,482 | 16,884 | 16,384 | 14,852 | 12,455 | 10,248 | 9,735 | 12,474 | 7,598 |
| Total Capital | 22,309 | 21,144 | 20,043 | 25,027 | 18,001 | 15,950 | 14,896 | 12,716 | 14,386 | 9,789 |
| Capital Expenditures | 2,820 | 3,085 | 2,187 | 2,127 | 1,947 | 1,658 | 2,372 | 2,147 | 1,476 | 1,645 |
| Cash Flow | 2,127 | 5,950 | 5,514 | 4,876 | 4,447 | 4,718 | 3,821 | 4,107 | 2,022 | 2,853 |
| Current Ratio | 1.2 | 1.4 | 1.6 | 1.9 | 1.8 | 1.6 | 1.6 | 1.6 | 2.7 | 1.5 |
| % Long Term Debt of Capitalization | 33.7 | 14.8 | 15.8 | 13.0 | 17.5 | 21.9 | 31.2 | 23.4 | 13.3 | 22.4 |
| % Net Income of Revenue | 0.8 | 8.8 | 9.1 | 9.1 | 8.7 | 10.4 | 7.9 | 9.9 | 3.3 | 7.0 |
| % Return on Assets | 1.1 | 12.3 | 11.3 | 10.6 | 10.5 | 12.8 | 10.5 | 13.1 | 4.4 | 10.6 |
| % Return on Equity | 2.8 | 26.0 | 23.3 | 21.3 | 21.2 | 28.7 | 24.3 | 26.4 | 8.8 | 25.4 |

Data as orig reptd.; bef. results of disc opers/spec. items. Per share data adj. for stk. divs.; EPS diluted. E-Estimated. NA-Not Available. NM-Not Meaningful. NR-Not Ranked. UR-Under Review.

**Office:** 55 Glenlake Parkway N.E., Atlanta, GA 30328.
**Telephone:** 404-828-6000.
**Website:** http://www.shareholder.com/ups
**Chrmn & CEO:** D.S. Davis

**COO & SVP:** D.P. Abney
**SVP, CFO, Chief Acctg Officer & Treas:** K. Kuehn
**SVP, Secy & General Counsel:** T.P. McClure
**SVP & CIO:** D. Barnes

**Investor Contact:** M. Vale (404-828-6703)
**Board Members:** F. D. Ackerman, M. J. Burns, D. S. Davis, S. E. Eizenstat, M. L. Eskew, A. M. Livermore, R. Markham, J. Thompson, C. B. Tome, B. Verwaayen

**Founded:** 1907
**Domicile:** Delaware
**Employees:** 425,300

# U.S. Bancorp

**STANDARD &POOR'S**

| S&P Recommendation | HOLD ★★★☆☆ | Price $26.30 (as of Nov 14, 2008) | 12-Mo. Target Price $32.00 | Investment Style Large-Cap Blend |
|---|---|---|---|---|

**GICS Sector** Financials
**Sub-Industry** Diversified Banks

**Summary** This bank holding company was formed through the February 2001 merger of Minneapolis-based U.S. Bancorp and Milwaukee-based Firstar Corp.

## Key Stock Statistics (Source S&P, Vickers, company reports)

| | | | | | | | |
|---|---|---|---|---|---|---|---|
| 52-Wk Range | $42.23– 20.57 | S&P Oper. EPS 2008**E** | 1.95 | Market Capitalization(B) | $46.145 | Beta | 0.52 |
| Trailing 12-Month EPS | $1.99 | S&P Oper. EPS 2009**E** | 2.22 | Yield (%) | 6.46 | S&P 3-Yr. Proj. EPS CAGR(%) | 3 |
| Trailing 12-Month P/E | 13.2 | P/E on S&P Oper. EPS 2008**E** | 13.5 | Dividend Rate/Share | $1.70 | S&P Credit Rating | AA |
| $10K Invested 5 Yrs Ago | $12,141 | Common Shares Outstg. (M) | 1,754.6 | Institutional Ownership (%) | 61 | | |

## Price Performance

30-Week Mov. Avg. · · · 10-Week Mov. Avg. - - **GAAP Earnings vs. Previous Year** Volume Above Avg. STARS
12-Mo. Target Price — Relative Strength — ▲ Up ▼ Down ► No Change Below Avg. ★

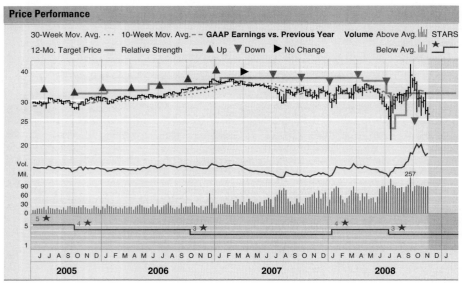

Options: ASE, CBOE, Ph

Analysis prepared by **Stuart Plesser** on October 23, 2008, when the stock traded at **$ 27.99.**

## Qualitative Risk Assessment

| LOW | MEDIUM | HIGH |
|---|---|---|

Our risk assessment for U.S. Bancorp reflects our view of the company's solid fundamentals, along with good geographic and product diversification. We think USB is positioned to weather a downturn in the U.S. economy better than many peers.

## Quantitative Evaluations

**S&P Quality Ranking**      A-

| D | C | B- | B | B+ | A- | A | A+ |
|---|---|---|---|---|---|---|---|

**Relative Strength Rank**     MODERATE

65

LOWEST = 1      HIGHEST = 99

## Highlights

➤ USB remains one of the most profitable large-cap banks in our coverage universe in terms of returns on equity and assets, which highlights the company's focus on revenue growth and cost controls, and what we see as its attractive mix of high-margin fee businesses. We look for revenues and earnings to increase steadily in 2009, in line with the higher middle-market and corporate commercial loan growth that we expect, partially offset by a challenging real estate market and more stringent loan prerequisites.

➤ We forecast a net interest margin of around 3.60% in 2009, in line with our 2008 projection, assuming the yield curve remains steep. Although USB is well reserved for its non-performing loans, we believe chargeoffs will continue to increase in 2009, causing the need for higher provisions. Notably, USB is one of the best capitalized banks in our coverage universe, with a Tier 1 capital ratio of 8.5%; possible participation in the TARP program would augment capital levels further.

➤ We expect operating EPS of $1.95 in 2008, on minimal share repurchases. For 2009, we forecast EPS of $2.22.

## Investment Rationale/Risk

➤ We believe that the company's diversified revenue model, focus on its fee-based revenues in its payment services and wealth management businesses, and strong focus on expense management will generate above industry average profitability. However, we forecast deteriorating credit quality and higher mortgage-related and credit card net charge-offs in 2009, and we believe USB will focus on loan quality over loan growth. We are particularly concerned about credit deterioration spilling over from its riskier assets to some of its more stable assets.

➤ Risks to our recommendation and target price include a severe economic downturn, a further tightening of the credit markets, a marked decline in consumer spending, a significant deterioration in credit quality, legal and regulatory risks, and any serious event that could hurt U.S. equity markets.

➤ Our 12-month target price of $32 is based on our dividend discount model, which assumes an 8.8% discount rate and a terminal growth rate of 4%. We believe this valuation methodology is warranted given USB's strong capital position.

## Revenue/Earnings Data

**Revenue (Million $)**

| | 1Q | 2Q | 3Q | 4Q | Year |
|---|---|---|---|---|---|
| 2008 | 5,249 | 4,907 | 4,469 | -- | -- |
| 2007 | 4,883 | 5,091 | 5,178 | 5,156 | 20,308 |
| 2006 | 4,505 | 4,773 | 4,897 | 4,934 | 19,109 |
| 2005 | 3,817 | 4,106 | 4,294 | 4,379 | 16,596 |
| 2004 | 3,576 | 3,478 | 3,827 | 3,825 | 14,706 |
| 2003 | 3,697 | 3,801 | 3,489 | 3,584 | 14,571 |

**Earnings Per Share ($)**

| | | | | | |
|---|---|---|---|---|---|
| 2008 | 0.62 | 0.53 | 0.32 | E0.48 | E1.95 |
| 2007 | 0.63 | 0.65 | 0.62 | 0.53 | 2.43 |
| 2006 | 0.63 | 0.66 | 0.66 | 0.66 | 2.61 |
| 2005 | 0.57 | 0.60 | 0.62 | 0.62 | 2.42 |
| 2004 | 0.52 | 0.54 | 0.56 | 0.56 | 2.18 |
| 2003 | 0.46 | 0.48 | 0.49 | 0.50 | 1.92 |

Fiscal year ended Dec. 31. Next earnings report expected: NA. EPS Estimates based on S&P Operating Earnings; historical GAAP earnings are as reported.

## Dividend Data (Dates: mm/dd Payment Date: mm/dd/yy)

| Amount ($) | Date Decl. | Ex-Div. Date | Stk. of Record | Payment Date |
|---|---|---|---|---|
| 0.425 | 12/11 | 12/27 | 12/31 | 01/15/08 |
| 0.425 | 03/18 | 03/27 | 03/31 | 04/15/08 |
| 0.425 | 06/17 | 06/26 | 06/30 | 07/15/08 |
| 0.425 | 09/16 | 09/26 | 09/30 | 10/15/08 |

Dividends have been paid since 1863. Source: Company reports.

---

**Please read the Required Disclosures and Analyst Certification on the last page of this report.**

*The McGraw-Hill Companies*

# U.S. Bancorp

**STANDARD &POOR'S**

## Business Summary October 23, 2008

CORPORATE OVERVIEW. USB consists of several major lines of business, which include wholesale banking, consumer banking, wealth management & securities services, payment services, and treasury and corporate support. Wholesale banking offers lending, depository, treasury management and other financial services to middle-market, large corporate and public sector clients. Consumer banking delivers products and services through banking offices, telephone servicing and sales, online services, direct mail and ATMs. It encompasses community banking, metropolitan banking, in-store banking, small business banking, including lending guaranteed by the Small Business Administration, small-ticket leasing, consumer lending, mortgage banking, consumer finance, workplace banking, student banking, 24-hour banking, and investment product and insurance sales.

Wealth management & securities services provides trust, custody, private banking, financial advisory, investment management, retail brokerage services, insurance, custody and mutual fund servicing through five businesses:

wealth management, corporate trust, FAF Advisors, institutional trust and custody, and fund services. Payment services includes consumer and business credit cards, stored-value cards, debit cards, corporate and purchasing card services, consumer lines of credit, ATM processing and merchant processing.

CORPORATE STRATEGY. USB has several goals in order to achieve long-term success, including: 10% plus EPS growth, a 20% plus ROE, reducing credit and earnings volatility, providing high-quality customer service, investing in future growth, and targeting an 80% return on earnings to shareholders. In banking, USB is maintaining what we view as its low-cost, highly efficient model and plans to grow organically and through smaller, fill-in acquisitions in higher-growth markets.

## Company Financials Fiscal Year Ended Dec. 31

| Per Share Data ($) | 2007 | 2006 | 2005 | 2004 | 2003 | 2002 | 2001 | 2000 | 1999 | 1998 |
|---|---|---|---|---|---|---|---|---|---|---|
| Tangible Book Value | 6.31 | 5.34 | 5.62 | 5.87 | 5.77 | 4.93 | 4.64 | 7.11 | 4.66 | 5.38 |
| Earnings | 2.43 | 2.61 | 2.42 | 2.18 | 1.92 | 1.73 | 0.88 | 1.32 | 0.87 | 0.65 |
| S&P Core Earnings | 2.54 | 2.59 | 2.41 | 2.16 | 1.89 | 1.59 | 0.66 | NA | NA | NA |
| Dividends | 1.63 | 1.39 | 1.23 | 1.02 | 0.86 | 0.78 | 0.75 | 0.65 | 0.40 | Nil |
| Payout Ratio | 67% | 53% | 51% | 47% | 45% | 45% | 85% | 49% | 46% | Nil |
| Prices:High | 36.84 | 36.85 | 31.36 | 31.65 | 30.00 | 24.50 | 26.06 | 28.00 | 35.33 | 31.31 |
| Prices:Low | 29.09 | 28.99 | 26.80 | 24.89 | 18.56 | 16.05 | 16.50 | 15.38 | 19.56 | 23.50 |
| P/E Ratio:High | 15 | 14 | 13 | 15 | 16 | 14 | 30 | 21 | 41 | 48 |
| P/E Ratio:Low | 12 | 11 | 11 | 11 | 10 | 9 | 19 | 12 | 22 | 36 |

| Income Statement Analysis (Million $) | | | | | | | | | | |
|---|---|---|---|---|---|---|---|---|---|---|
| Net Interest Income | 6,689 | 6,741 | 7,055 | 7,111 | 7,189 | 6,840 | 6,409 | 2,699 | 2,643 | 1,413 |
| Tax Equivalent Adjustment | 75.0 | 49.0 | 33.0 | 28.6 | 28.2 | 36.6 | 55.9 | 45.1 | 54.3 | 43.3 |
| Non Interest Income | 7,157 | 6,832 | 6,151 | 5,624 | 5,068 | 5,569 | 5,030 | 1,505 | 1,388 | 859 |
| Loan Loss Provision | 792 | 544 | 666 | 670 | 1,254 | 1,349 | 2,529 | 222 | 187 | 114 |
| % Expense/Operating Revenue | 49.6% | 45.4% | 44.3% | 45.3% | 45.7% | 83.7% | 57.5% | 55.0% | 59.9% | 65.7% |
| Pretax Income | 6,207 | 6,863 | 6,571 | 6,176 | 5,651 | 5,103 | 2,634 | 1,927 | 1,413 | 638 |
| Effective Tax Rate | 30.3% | 30.8% | 31.7% | 32.5% | 34.4% | 34.8% | 35.2% | 31.4% | 38.0% | 32.6% |
| Net Income | 4,324 | 4,751 | 4,489 | 4,167 | 3,710 | 3,326 | 1,707 | 1,284 | 875 | 430 |
| % Net Interest Margin | 3.47 | 3.65 | 3.97 | 4.25 | 4.49 | 4.61 | 4.45 | 4.73 | 4.83 | 4.46 |
| S&P Core Earnings | 4,470 | 4,674 | 4,470 | 4,135 | 3,655 | 3,062 | 1,280 | NA | NA | NA |

| Balance Sheet & Other Financial Data (Million $) | | | | | | | | | | |
|---|---|---|---|---|---|---|---|---|---|---|
| Money Market Assets | Nil | Nil | Nil | Nil | Nil | 1,332 | 1,607 | 200 | 897 | 2.75 |
| Investment Securities | 43,116 | 40,117 | 39,768 | 41,481 | 43,334 | 28,488 | 26,608 | 13,866 | 13,114 | 6,432 |
| Commercial Loans | 80,281 | 74,835 | 71,405 | 67,758 | 65,768 | 68,811 | 71,703 | 28,498 | 26,198 | 15,241 |
| Other Loans | 73,546 | 68,762 | 66,401 | 58,557 | 52,467 | 47,440 | 42,702 | 25,208 | 24,428 | 10,627 |
| Total Assets | 237,615 | 219,232 | 209,465 | 195,104 | 189,286 | 180,027 | 171,390 | 77,585 | 72,788 | 38,476 |
| Demand Deposits | 33,334 | 32,128 | 32,214 | 30,756 | 32,470 | 35,106 | 31,212 | 10,980 | 10,300 | 10,498 |
| Time Deposits | 98,111 | 92,754 | 92,495 | 89,985 | 86,582 | 80,428 | 74,007 | 45,298 | 41,586 | 18,353 |
| Long Term Debt | 43,440 | 37,602 | 37,069 | 22,807 | 33,816 | 31,582 | 28,542 | 3,877 | 5,038 | 1,709 |
| Common Equity | 20,046 | 20,197 | 20,086 | 19,539 | 19,242 | 18,101 | 16,461 | 6,528 | 6,309 | 3,530 |
| % Return on Assets | 1.9 | 2.2 | 2.2 | 2.2 | 2.0 | 1.9 | 1.0 | 1.7 | 1.2 | 1.2 |
| % Return on Equity | 21.2 | 23.6 | 22.7 | 21.5 | 19.7 | 19.2 | 10.8 | 20.0 | 13.6 | 13.7 |
| % Loan Loss Reserve | 1.3 | 1.4 | 1.5 | 1.6 | 2.0 | 2.0 | 2.1 | 1.3 | 1.4 | 1.5 |
| % Loans/Deposits | 118.1 | 117.6 | 111.9 | 105.8 | 100.5 | 100.6 | 111.4 | 95.4 | 98.8 | 89.7 |
| % Equity to Assets | 8.8 | 9.4 | 9.8 | 10.1 | 10.2 | 9.8 | 9.4 | 8.5 | 8.8 | 8.8 |

Data as orig reptd.; bef. results of disc opers/spec. items. Per share data adj. for stk. divs.; EPS diluted. E-Estimated. NA-Not Available. NM-Not Meaningful. NR-Not Ranked. UR-Under Review.

**Office:** 800 Nicollet Mall, Minneapolis, MN 55402-7000.
**Telephone:** 651-466-3000.
**Website:** http://www.usbank.com
**Chrmn:** T.H. Jacobsen

**Chrmn, Pres & CEO:** R. Davis
**Vice Chrmn:** M.C. Wheeler, Jr.
**EVP, Chief Acctg Officer & Cntlr:** T.R. Dolan
**EVP & Treas:** K.D. Nelson

**Investor Contact:** J.T. Murphy (612-303-0783)
**Board Members:** D. M. Baker, Jr., G. B. Cameron, A. D. Collins, Jr., R. Davis, D. Garvin, V. B. Gluckman, J. F. Hladky, T. H. Jacobsen, J. W. Johnson, O. F. Kirtley, J. W. Levin, S. B. Lubar, F. Lyon, Jr., D. F. McKeithan, Jr., D. B. O'Maley, O. M. Owens, R. G. Reiten, C. D. Schnuck, P. T. Stokes, M. C. Wheeler, Jr., W. W. Wirtz

**Founded:** 1929
**Domicile:** Delaware
**Employees:** 52,277

# United States Steel Corp

STANDARD &POOR'S

| S&P Recommendation | STRONG BUY ★ ★ ★ ★ ★ | Price $29.75 (as of Nov 14, 2008) | 12-Mo. Target Price $46.00 | Investment Style Large-Cap Value |
|---|---|---|---|---|

**GICS Sector** Materials
**Sub-Industry** Steel

**Summary** This company manufactures and sells a wide variety of steel sheet, plate, tubular and tin products, coke, and taconite pellets.

## Key Stock Statistics (Source S&P, Vickers, company reports)

| | | | | | | | |
|---|---|---|---|---|---|---|---|
| 52-Wk Range | $196.00– 26.60 | S&P Oper. EPS 2008**E** | 17.61 | Market Capitalization(B) | $3.459 | Beta | 3.06 |
| Trailing 12-Month EPS | $15.71 | S&P Oper. EPS 2009**E** | 7.38 | Yield (%) | 4.03 | S&P 3-Yr. Proj. EPS CAGR(%) | 4 |
| Trailing 12-Month P/E | 1.9 | P/E on S&P Oper. EPS 2008**E** | 1.7 | Dividend Rate/Share | $1.20 | S&P Credit Rating | BB+ |
| $10K Invested 5 Yrs Ago | $13,443 | Common Shares Outstg. (M) | 116.3 | Institutional Ownership (%) | 91 | | |

## Price Performance

30-Week Mov. Avg. ···   10-Week Mov. Avg. - -   **GAAP Earnings vs. Previous Year**   Volume Above Avg.▐▌ STARS
12-Mo. Target Price —   Relative Strength —   ▲ Up   ▼ Down   ► No Change   Below Avg.▐▌ ★

Options: ASE, CBOE

Analysis prepared by **Leo J. Larkin** on October 28, 2008, when the stock traded at **$ 30.10**.

## Highlights

► Following a projected sales gain of 70% for 2008, we look for a 21% sales decline for 2009, on a projected decline in both tons shipped and the average realized price per ton. Our expectation for lower volume and prices rests on several assumptions. First, S&P forecasts negative GDP growth of 0.1% in 2009, versus GDP growth of 1.6% in 2008. We see the lower GDP leading to reduced demand for durable goods. Second, we think demand for oil country tubular goods will decline from 2008's high levels. Third, we see distributors cutting inventory through at least the first half of 2009. Fourth, after declining in 2007 and 2008, we believe that imports will rise in 2009. Finally, we expect that demand for durable goods in Europe will decline from 2008's levels and thereby depress sales in that operation.

► Penalized by higher unit costs stemming from lower volume along with reduced revenue per ton, we estimate EPS of $7.38 in 2009, versus estimated EPS of $17.61 in 2008.

► We think EPS over the longer term will benefit from industry consolidation, rising demand for oil country tubular goods, and a gradual decline in costs for employee pensions and health care.

## Investment Rationale/Risk

► In our view, sharply higher costs for raw materials will prompt moves to internally produce raw materials and/or further merger activity in the global steel industry. Also, we believe consolidation will help the industry regain some pricing power. Over the longer term, we see earnings rising on a gradual decline in pension and health care costs, further acquisitions, well controlled raw material costs in domestic operations, and a secular increase in demand for oil country tubular goods used for oil and gas exploration. Recently trading at about 4.1X our 2009 EPS estimate, we think X shares are very attractively valued. On that basis, our recommendation is strong buy.

► Risks to our recommendation and target price include a decrease in shipment volume and average realized price per ton in 2009 in excess of what we currently project.

► We look for X to trade at about 6.2X our 2009 EPS estimate, which is toward the low end of the historical range. In our view, in the context of negative GDP in 2009 and falling EPS compared with 2008, we think that X deserves to trade at a low P/E. On that basis, our 12-month target price is $46.

## Qualitative Risk Assessment

| LOW | MEDIUM | HIGH |
|---|---|---|

Our risk assessment reflects the company's exposure to highly cyclical industries such as autos and construction. While X has reduced debt and improved free cash flow in recent years, its unfunded health care liabilities totaled $2.9 billion at the end of 2007.

## Quantitative Evaluations

**S&P Quality Ranking**          B-

| D | C | B- | B | B+ | A- | A | A+ |
|---|---|---|---|---|---|---|---|

**Relative Strength Rank**          WEAK

9

LOWEST = 1          HIGHEST = 99

## Revenue/Earnings Data

**Revenue (Million $)**

| | 1Q | 2Q | 3Q | 4Q | Year |
|---|---|---|---|---|---|
| 2008 | 5,196 | 6,744 | 7,312 | -- | -- |
| 2007 | 3,756 | 4,228 | 4,354 | 4,535 | 16,873 |
| 2006 | 3,728 | 4,107 | 4,106 | 3,774 | 15,715 |
| 2005 | 3,787 | 3,582 | 3,200 | 3,470 | 14,039 |
| 2004 | 2,963 | 3,466 | 3,729 | 3,932 | 14,108 |
| 2003 | 1,907 | 2,362 | 2,508 | 2,681 | 9,458 |

**Earnings Per Share ($)**

| | | | | | |
|---|---|---|---|---|---|
| 2008 | 1.99 | 5.65 | 7.79 | E2.18 | E17.61 |
| 2007 | 2.30 | 2.54 | 2.27 | 0.30 | 7.40 |
| 2006 | 2.04 | 3.22 | 3.42 | 2.50 | 11.18 |
| 2005 | 3.51 | 1.91 | 0.71 | 0.85 | 7.00 |
| 2004 | 0.36 | 1.62 | 2.72 | 3.59 | 8.37 |
| 2003 | -0.35 | -0.01 | -3.47 | -0.26 | -4.09 |

Fiscal year ended Dec. 31. Next earnings report expected: Late January. EPS Estimates based on S&P Operating Earnings; historical GAAP earnings are as reported.

## Dividend Data (Dates: mm/dd Payment Date: mm/dd/yy)

| Amount ($) | Date Decl. | Ex-Div. Date | Stk. of Record | Payment Date |
|---|---|---|---|---|
| 0.250 | 01/29 | 02/11 | 02/13 | 03/10/08 |
| 0.250 | 04/29 | 05/12 | 05/14 | 06/10/08 |
| 0.300 | 07/29 | 08/11 | 08/13 | 09/10/08 |
| 0.300 | 10/28 | 11/07 | 11/12 | 12/10/08 |

Dividends have been paid since 1991. Source: Company reports.

---

**Please read the Required Disclosures and Analyst Certification on the last page of this report.**

# United States Steel Corp

STANDARD
&POOR'S

## Business Summary October 28, 2008

CORPORATE OVERVIEW. Following its acquisition of Stelco Inc. and Lone Star Technologies in 2007, U.S. Steel is the fifth largest steel producer in the world, the largest integrated steel producer headquartered in North America, and one of the largest integrated flat-rolled producers in Central Europe. X ended 2007 with raw steelmaking capacity of 31.7 million tons, up from 24.3 million tons at 2006 year end. In 2007, X produced 16.8 million tons of steel in the U.S. and 6.8 million tons in Europe.

The company's other business activities include the production of coke in both North America and Central Europe; and the production of iron ore pellets from taconite, transportation services (railroad and barge operations), real estate operations, and engineering and consulting services in North America.

CORPORATE STRATEGY. The company seeks to boost its revenues and earnings by expanding its value-added product mix, becoming a prime supplier of steel to growing European markets, strengthening its balance sheet, and becoming more cost competitive.

MARKET PROFILE. The primary factor affecting demand for steel products is economic growth in general, and growth in demand for durable goods in par-

ticular. The two largest end markets for steel products in the U.S. are autos and construction, which together accounted for 29.5% of shipments in 2007. Other end markets include appliances, containers, machinery, and oil and gas. Distributors, also known as service centers, accounted for 20.4% of industry shipments in the U.S. in 2007. Distributors are the largest single market for the steel industry in the U.S. Because distributors sell to a wide variety of OEMs, it is impossible to trace the final destination of much of the industry's shipments. Consequently, consumption of steel by the auto, construction and other industries may be higher than the shipment data would suggest. U.S. production was 108.2 million tons in 2007, and X's market share was 15.5%. X's largest end markets in 2007 were distributors (20% of revenues), appliances (7%), converters (23%), construction (13%), automotive (14%), containers (8%), oil and gas (7%), and other (8%). U.S. consumption increased at a compound annual growth rate (CAGR) of 1.4% from 1997 through 2006. Global steel consumption rose at a CAGR of 5.2% from 1997 through 2006.

## Company Financials Fiscal Year Ended Dec. 31

| Per Share Data ($) | 2007 | 2006 | 2005 | 2004 | 2003 | 2002 | 2001 | 2000 | 1999 | 1998 |
|---|---|---|---|---|---|---|---|---|---|---|
| Tangible Book Value | 28.81 | 36.82 | 25.63 | 32.30 | 7.98 | 15.81 | 28.16 | 21.54 | 23.22 | 22.22 |
| Cash Flow | 11.66 | 14.69 | 11.54 | 11.17 | -0.57 | 4.24 | 1.42 | 3.72 | 3.93 | 6.72 |
| Earnings | 7.40 | 11.18 | 7.00 | 8.37 | -4.09 | 0.62 | -2.45 | -0.33 | 0.48 | 3.92 |
| S&P Core Earnings | 7.42 | 11.76 | 6.64 | 8.74 | -1.06 | -4.10 | -8.47 | NA | NA | NA |
| Dividends | 0.60 | 0.25 | 0.28 | 0.20 | 0.20 | 0.20 | 0.55 | 1.00 | 1.00 | 1.00 |
| Payout Ratio | 8% | 2% | 4% | 2% | NM | 32% | NM | NM | NM | 26% |
| Prices:High | 127.26 | 79.01 | 63.90 | 54.06 | 37.05 | 22.00 | 22.00 | 32.94 | 34.25 | 43.06 |
| Prices:Low | 68.83 | 48.05 | 33.59 | 25.22 | 9.61 | 10.66 | 13.00 | 12.69 | 21.75 | 20.44 |
| P/E Ratio:High | 17 | 7 | 9 | 6 | NM | 35 | NM | NM | 71 | 11 |
| P/E Ratio:Low | 9 | 4 | 5 | 3 | NM | 17 | NM | NM | 45 | 5 |

| Income Statement Analysis (Million $) | 2007 | 2006 | 2005 | 2004 | 2003 | 2002 | 2001 | 2000 | 1999 | 1998 |
|---|---|---|---|---|---|---|---|---|---|---|
| Revenue | 16,873 | 15,715 | 14,039 | 14,108 | 9,458 | 7,054 | 6,375 | 6,090 | 5,380 | 6,189 |
| Operating Income | 1,804 | 2,143 | 1,740 | 1,964 | 316 | 478 | -61.0 | 422 | 520 | 763 |
| Depreciation | 506 | 441 | 366 | 382 | 363 | 350 | 344 | 360 | 304 | 283 |
| Interest Expense | 163 | Nil | 107 | 138 | 148 | 136 | 153 | 115 | 75.0 | 53.0 |
| Pretax Income | 1,108 | 1,723 | 1,312 | 1,461 | -860 | 13.0 | -546 | -1.00 | 76.0 | 537 |
| Effective Tax Rate | 19.7% | 18.8% | 27.8% | 24.0% | NM | NM | NM | NM | 32.9% | 32.2% |
| Net Income | 879 | 1,374 | 910 | 1,077 | -406 | 61.0 | -218 | -21.0 | 51.0 | 364 |
| S&P Core Earnings | 882 | 1,438 | 847 | 1,104 | -109 | -398 | -755 | NA | NA | NA |

| Balance Sheet & Other Financial Data (Million $) | 2007 | 2006 | 2005 | 2004 | 2003 | 2002 | 2001 | 2000 | 1999 | 1998 |
|---|---|---|---|---|---|---|---|---|---|---|
| Cash | 401 | 1,422 | 1,479 | 1,037 | 316 | 243 | 147 | 219 | 22.0 | 9.00 |
| Current Assets | 4,959 | 5,196 | 4,831 | 4,243 | 3,107 | 2,440 | 2,073 | 2,717 | 1,981 | 1,275 |
| Total Assets | 15,632 | 10,586 | 9,822 | 10,956 | 7,838 | 7,977 | 8,337 | 8,711 | 7,525 | 6,693 |
| Current Liabilities | 3,003 | 2,702 | 2,749 | 2,531 | 2,130 | 1,372 | 1,259 | 1,391 | 1,266 | 1,016 |
| Long Term Debt | 3,147 | 943 | 1,363 | 1,363 | 1,890 | 1,408 | 1,434 | 2,485 | 1,151 | 712 |
| Common Equity | 5,531 | 4,365 | 3,108 | 3,754 | 867 | 2,027 | 2,506 | 1,917 | 2,053 | 2,090 |
| Total Capital | 8,736 | 5,346 | 4,719 | 5,959 | 2,989 | 3,658 | 4,672 | 5,070 | 3,555 | 2,805 |
| Capital Expenditures | 692 | 612 | 741 | 579 | 316 | 258 | 287 | 244 | 287 | 310 |
| Cash Flow | 1,385 | 1,807 | 1,258 | 1,441 | -59.0 | 411 | 126 | 331 | 346 | 638 |
| Current Ratio | 1.7 | 1.9 | 1.8 | 1.7 | 1.5 | 1.8 | 1.6 | 2.0 | 1.6 | 1.3 |
| % Long Term Debt of Capitalization | 36.0 | 17.6 | 28.9 | 22.9 | 63.2 | 38.5 | 30.7 | 49.0 | 32.4 | 25.4 |
| % Net Income of Revenue | 5.2 | 8.7 | 6.5 | 7.8 | NM | 0.9 | NM | NM | 0.9 | 5.9 |
| % Return on Assets | 6.7 | 13.5 | 8.7 | 11.5 | NM | 0.7 | NM | NM | 0.7 | 5.4 |
| % Return on Equity | 17.8 | 36.6 | 25.6 | 45.8 | NM | 2.7 | NM | NM | 2.0 | 18.4 |

Data as orig reptd.; bef. results of disc opers/spec. items. Per share data adj. for stk. divs.; EPS diluted. E-Estimated. NA-Not Available. NM-Not Meaningful. NR-Not Ranked. UR-Under Review.

**Office:** 600 Grant Street, Pittsburgh, PA 15219-2702.
**Telephone:** 412-433-1121.
**Email:** shareholderservices@uss.com
**Website:** http://www.ussteel.com

**Chrmn & CEO:** J. Surma, Jr.
**COO & EVP:** J.H. Goodish
**EVP & CFO:** G.R. Haggerty
**SVP & General Counsel:** J.D. Garraux

**SVP & Cntlr:** L.G. Schultz
**Investor Contact:** N. Harper (412-433-1184)
**Board Members:** R. J. Darnall, J. G. Drosdick, R. A. Gephardt, C. R. Lee, J. M. Lipton, F. J. Lucchino, G. G. McNeal, S. E. Schofield, G. B. Spanier, J. Surma, Jr., D. S. Sutherland, P. A. Tracey

**Founded:** 2001
**Domicile:** Delaware
**Employees:** 49,000

The McGraw-Hill Companies

# United Technologies Corp

STANDARD &POOR'S

| S&P Recommendation | STRONG BUY ★ ★ ★ ★ ★ | Price $50.23 (as of Nov 14, 2008) | 12-Mo. Target Price $70.00 | Investment Style Large-Cap Growth |
|---|---|---|---|---|

**GICS Sector** Industrials
**Sub-Industry** Aerospace & Defense

**Summary** This aerospace-industrial conglomerate's portfolio includes Pratt & Whitney jet engines, Sikorsky helicopters, Otis elevators and Carrier air conditioners, among other products.

## Key Stock Statistics (Source S&P, Vickers, company reports)

| | | | | | | | |
|---|---|---|---|---|---|---|---|
| 52-Wk Range | $79.30–43.28 | S&P Oper. EPS 2008E | 4.93 | Market Capitalization(B) | $47.749 | Beta | 0.81 |
| Trailing 12-Month EPS | $4.75 | S&P Oper. EPS 2009E | 5.20 | Yield (%) | 3.07 | S&P 3-Yr. Proj. EPS CAGR(%) | 9 |
| Trailing 12-Month P/E | 10.6 | P/E on S&P Oper. EPS 2008E | 10.2 | Dividend Rate/Share | $1.54 | S&P Credit Rating | A |
| $10K Invested 5 Yrs Ago | $12,744 | Common Shares Outstg. (M) | 950.6 | Institutional Ownership (%) | 81 | | |

## Price Performance

30-Week Mov. Avg. · · · 10-Week Mov. Avg. - - GAAP Earnings vs. Previous Year  Volume Above Avg. STARS
12-Mo. Target Price — Relative Strength — ▲ Up ▼ Down ▶ No Change  Below Avg.

2-for-1

Options: ASE, CBOE, P, Ph

Analysis prepared by **Richard Tortoriello** on November 04, 2008, when the stock traded at **$ 57.25**.

## Qualitative Risk Assessment

| LOW | MEDIUM | HIGH |
|---|---|---|

Our risk assessment is based on our view of UTX's history of steady growth in both earnings and dividends over the past 10 years, as reflected in an S&P Quality Ranking of A+. We also consider UTX's balance sheet strong, with long-term debt at 27% of total capital and cash of 6.4% of assets as of September 2008.

## Quantitative Evaluations

**S&P Quality Ranking**  A+

| D | C | B- | B | B+ | A- | A | A+ |
|---|---|---|---|---|---|---|---|

**Relative Strength Rank**  STRONG

72

LOWEST = 1   HIGHEST = 99

## Highlights

➤ We project sales growth of about 10% in 2008 and 6% in 2009. Organic sales growth was 9% in 2007, and has been about 5.7% through the first nine months of 2008, which we attribute to a slowing economy. We see sales growth led by Otis, UTC Fire & Security, Hamilton Sundstrand and Sikorsky, with more moderate growth at Pratt & Whitney and Carrier, the latter of which is suffering from a slowdown in the U.S. housing market.

➤ We project a 2008 operating profit margin of 13.2%, up from 12.9% in 2007, on improvement in all business segments, driven by increased productivity, pricing and volume. For 2009, we expect operating margins to remain flat. We project an EPS increase of 15%, to $4.93, in 2008, and we see 5.5% growth, to $5.20, in 2009.

➤ We estimate free cash flow of over $5 billion this year, and expect about the same level in 2009, versus estimated dividends of $1.2 billion in 2008 and $1.4 billion in 2009, leaving ample cash flow, in our view, to continue UTC's large share repurchase plan, which we estimate to be $3 billion in 2008.

## Investment Rationale/Risk

➤ We see the following trends positively affecting UTC's business: very large backlogs of commercial aircraft at both Airbus and Boeing, which we view as providing sustainable production through 2010; continued moderate demand for global infrastructure, particularly in emerging economies; and strong demand for military helicopters. We see these positives offset in 2009 by a stronger U.S. dollar versus 2008, a weak residential housing market, and slowing global growth. However, we think recent valuations make UTX a compelling purchase.

➤ Risks to our recommendation and target price include a severe recession in the global economy, operational issues within UTX's operating segments, and a continued rise in the dollar.

➤ Our 12-month target price of $70 is based on an enterprise value to estimated 2008 EBITDA multiple of 8.0X, a valuation not seen on the shares since late 2003. We note that UTX recently sold at historic lows on a P/E, price to cash flow and price to book basis, as well as highs on a dividend yield basis.

## Revenue/Earnings Data

**Revenue (Million $)**

| | 1Q | 2Q | 3Q | 4Q | Year |
|---|---|---|---|---|---|
| 2008 | 13,701 | 15,667 | 14,814 | -- | -- |
| 2007 | 12,278 | 13,904 | 13,863 | 14,714 | 54,759 |
| 2006 | 10,446 | 12,046 | 11,972 | 12,654 | 47,829 |
| 2005 | 9,309 | 10,974 | 10,832 | 11,172 | 42,725 |
| 2004 | 8,646 | 9,622 | 9,339 | 8,938 | 37,445 |
| 2003 | 6,702 | 7,790 | 7,954 | 8,588 | 31,034 |

**Earnings Per Share ($)**

| | | | | | |
|---|---|---|---|---|---|
| 2008 | 1.03 | 1.32 | 1.33 | E1.25 | E4.93 |
| 2007 | 0.82 | 1.16 | 1.21 | 1.08 | 4.27 |
| 2006 | 0.76 | 1.09 | 0.99 | 0.87 | 3.71 |
| 2005 | 0.64 | 0.95 | 0.81 | 0.71 | 3.12 |
| 2004 | 0.57 | 0.83 | 0.72 | 0.65 | 2.76 |
| 2003 | 0.50 | 0.63 | 0.64 | 0.58 | 2.35 |

Fiscal year ended Dec. 31. Next earnings report expected: Late January. EPS Estimates based on S&P Operating Earnings; historical GAAP earnings are as reported.

## Dividend Data (Dates: mm/dd Payment Date: mm/dd/yy)

| Amount ($) | Date Decl. | Ex-Div. Date | Stk. of Record | Payment Date |
|---|---|---|---|---|
| 0.320 | 02/04 | 02/13 | 02/15 | 03/10/08 |
| 0.320 | 04/09 | 05/14 | 05/16 | 06/10/08 |
| 0.320 | 06/11 | 08/13 | 08/15 | 09/10/08 |
| 0.385 | 10/08 | 11/12 | 11/14 | 12/10/08 |

Dividends have been paid since 1936. Source: Company reports.

---

# United Technologies Corp

**STANDARD &POOR'S**

## Business Summary November 04, 2008

CORPORATE OVERVIEW. United Technologies is a multi-industry holding company that conducts business through six business segments: Carrier, Otis, Pratt & Whitney, UTC Fire & Security, Hamilton Sundstrand, and Sikorsky.

Carrier (25% of sales and 14% of operating profits in 2007) is the world's largest maker of heating, ventilating and air-conditioning (HVAC) and refrigeration systems. It offers HVAC, refrigeration systems and food service equipment, and related controls for residential, commercial, industrial and transportation applications. In addition, Carrier provides installation, retrofit, and parts and services for its products, as well as those of other HVAC and refrigeration makers. International sales, including U.S. export sales, accounted for 59% of segment sales in 2007.

Otis (23% and 34%) is the world's largest maker of elevators and escalators. Otis designs, manufactures, sells, installs, maintains and modernizes a wide range of passenger and freight elevators for low-, medium- and high-speed applications, as well as a broad line of escalators and moving walkways. International revenues were 81% of total segment revenues in 2007.

Pratt & Whitney (22% and 26%) is a major supplier of jet engines for commercial, general aviation and military aircraft. P&W also sells engines for auxiliary power units, industrial gas turbines (for industrial power generation) and space propulsion systems. P&W's Global Service Partners provides maintenance, repair and overhaul services. Boeing and Airbus accounted for 6% and 10%, respectively, of segment sales in 2007, and the U.S. government accounted for 30%. International revenues were 56% of total segment revenues in 2007.

UTC Fire & Security (11% and 7%) is a global provider of security and fire safety products and services, including fire and special hazard detection and supression systems; fire fighting equipment; electronic security, monitoring and rapid response systems; and service and security personnel services. International sales accounted for 82% of total segment sales in 2007.

## Company Financials Fiscal Year Ended Dec. 31

| Per Share Data ($) | 2007 | 2006 | 2005 | 2004 | 2003 | 2002 | 2001 | 2000 | 1999 | 1998 |
|---|---|---|---|---|---|---|---|---|---|---|
| Tangible Book Value | 2.45 | NM | 0.91 | 1.84 | 2.32 | 1.46 | 1.66 | 0.95 | 0.80 | 2.92 |
| Cash Flow | 5.38 | 4.74 | 4.09 | 3.73 | 3.14 | 2.93 | 2.81 | 2.63 | 1.66 | 2.13 |
| Earnings | 4.27 | 3.71 | 3.12 | 2.76 | 2.35 | 2.21 | 1.92 | 1.78 | 0.83 | 1.26 |
| S&P Core Earnings | 4.17 | 3.64 | 3.05 | 2.59 | 2.16 | 1.32 | 1.14 | NA | NA | NA |
| Dividends | 1.17 | 1.02 | 0.88 | 0.70 | 0.57 | 0.49 | 0.45 | 0.41 | 0.38 | 0.35 |
| Payout Ratio | 27% | 27% | 28% | 25% | 24% | 22% | 23% | 23% | 46% | 28% |
| Prices:High | 82.50 | 67.47 | 58.89 | 53.14 | 48.38 | 38.88 | 43.75 | 39.88 | 37.98 | 28.13 |
| Prices:Low | 61.85 | 54.20 | 48.43 | 40.34 | 26.76 | 24.42 | 20.05 | 23.25 | 25.81 | 16.75 |
| P/E Ratio:High | 19 | 18 | 19 | 19 | 21 | 18 | 23 | 22 | 46 | 22 |
| P/E Ratio:Low | 14 | 15 | 16 | 15 | 11 | 11 | 10 | 13 | 31 | 13 |

| Income Statement Analysis (Million $) | | | | | | | | | | |
|---|---|---|---|---|---|---|---|---|---|---|
| Revenue | 54,759 | 47,829 | 42,725 | 37,445 | 31,034 | 28,212 | 27,897 | 26,583 | 23,844 | 25,687 |
| Operating Income | 8,223 | 7,131 | 6,166 | 5,448 | 4,644 | 4,384 | 4,138 | 3,999 | 2,361 | 2,993 |
| Depreciation | 1,173 | 1,033 | 984 | 978 | 799 | 727 | 905 | 859 | 844 | 854 |
| Interest Expense | 666 | 606 | 498 | 363 | 375 | 381 | 426 | 382 | 260 | 204 |
| Pretax Income | 6,384 | 5,492 | 4,684 | 4,107 | 3,470 | 3,276 | 2,807 | 2,758 | 1,257 | 1,963 |
| Effective Tax Rate | 28.8% | 27.2% | 26.8% | 26.4% | 27.1% | 27.1% | 26.9% | 30.9% | 25.9% | 31.7% |
| Net Income | 4,224 | 3,732 | 3,164 | 2,788 | 2,361 | 2,236 | 1,938 | 1,808 | 841 | 1,255 |
| S&P Core Earnings | 4,125 | 3,653 | 3,089 | 2,619 | 2,147 | 1,298 | 1,113 | NA | NA | NA |

| Balance Sheet & Other Financial Data (Million $) | | | | | | | | | | |
|---|---|---|---|---|---|---|---|---|---|---|
| Cash | 2,904 | 2,546 | 2,247 | 2,265 | 1,623 | 2,080 | 1,558 | 748 | 957 | 550 |
| Current Assets | 22,071 | 18,844 | 17,206 | 15,522 | 12,364 | 11,751 | 11,263 | 10,662 | 10,627 | 9,355 |
| Total Assets | 54,575 | 47,141 | 45,925 | 40,035 | 34,648 | 29,090 | 26,969 | 25,364 | 24,366 | 18,375 |
| Current Liabilities | 17,469 | 15,208 | 15,345 | 12,947 | 10,295 | 7,903 | 8,371 | 9,344 | 9,215 | 7,735 |
| Long Term Debt | 8,015 | 7,037 | 5,935 | 4,231 | 4,257 | 4,632 | 4,237 | 3,476 | 3,086 | 1,575 |
| Common Equity | 21,355 | 17,297 | 16,991 | 14,008 | 11,707 | 10,506 | 8,369 | 7,662 | 7,117 | 3,998 |
| Total Capital | 30,282 | 25,170 | 23,704 | 19,149 | 16,673 | 16,445 | 13,899 | 12,514 | 11,664 | 6,994 |
| Capital Expenditures | 1,153 | 954 | 929 | 795 | 530 | 586 | 793 | 937 | 762 | 866 |
| Cash Flow | 5,319 | 4,765 | 4,148 | 3,766 | 3,160 | 2,963 | 2,843 | 2,667 | 1,685 | 2,109 |
| Current Ratio | 1.3 | 1.2 | 1.1 | 1.2 | 1.2 | 1.5 | 1.3 | 1.1 | 1.2 | 1.2 |
| % Long Term Debt of Capitalization | 26.5 | 28.0 | 25.0 | 22.1 | 25.5 | 28.2 | 30.5 | 27.8 | 26.5 | 22.5 |
| % Net Income of Revenue | 7.7 | 7.8 | 7.4 | 7.4 | 7.6 | 7.9 | 6.9 | 6.8 | 3.5 | 4.9 |
| % Return on Assets | 8.3 | 8.0 | 7.3 | 7.4 | 7.4 | 8.0 | 7.4 | 7.3 | 4.0 | 7.2 |
| % Return on Equity | 21.9 | 21.8 | 20.2 | 21.7 | 23.9 | 23.0 | 24.2 | 24.5 | 14.6 | 32.8 |

Data as orig reptd.; bef. results of disc opers/spec. items. Per share data adj. for stk. divs.; EPS diluted. E-Estimated. NA-Not Available. NM-Not Meaningful. NR-Not Ranked. UR-Under Review.

**Office:** 1 Financial Plz, Hartford, CT 06103.
**Telephone:** 860-728-7000.
**Email:** invrelations@corphq.utc.com
**Website:** http://www.utc.com

**Chrmn:** G. David
**Pres, CEO & COO:** L. Chenevert
**SVP & CFO:** G.J. Hayes
**SVP & General Counsel:** C.D. Gill

**CFO:** G.A. Renaud
**Investor Contact:** J. Moran (860-728-7062)
**Board Members:** L. Chenevert, G. David, J. V. Faraci, J. Garnier, J. Gorelick, C. R. Lee, R. D. McCormick, H. McGraw, III, R. B. Myers, H. P. Swygert, A. F. Villeneuve, C. T. Whitman

**Founded:** 1934
**Domicile:** Delaware
**Employees:** 225,600

*The McGraw·Hill Companies*

# Unum Group

**STANDARD &POOR'S**

| S&P Recommendation | **HOLD** ★★★☆☆ | Price $15.04 (as of Nov 14, 2008) | 12-Mo. Target Price $20.00 | Investment Style Large-Cap Value |
|---|---|---|---|---|

**GICS Sector** Financials
**Sub-Industry** Life & Health Insurance

**Summary** This leading provider of individual and group disability coverage was formed through the June 1999 merger of Provident Cos. and UNUM Corp.

## Key Stock Statistics (Source S&P, Vickers, company reports)

| | | | | | | | |
|---|---|---|---|---|---|---|---|
| 52-Wk Range | $27.50–12.43 | S&P Oper. EPS 2008E | 2.48 | Market Capitalization(B) | $4.980 | Beta | 1.03 |
| Trailing 12-Month EPS | $1.93 | S&P Oper. EPS 2009E | 2.70 | Yield (%) | 1.99 | S&P 3-Yr. Proj. EPS CAGR(%) | 15 |
| Trailing 12-Month P/E | 7.8 | P/E on S&P Oper. EPS 2008E | 6.1 | Dividend Rate/Share | $0.30 | S&P Credit Rating | BBB- |
| $10K Invested 5 Yrs Ago | $11,290 | Common Shares Outstg. (M) | 331.1 | Institutional Ownership (%) | 94 | | |

## Price Performance

30-Week Mov. Avg. ···   10-Week Mov. Avg. - - -   **GAAP Earnings vs. Previous Year**   Volume Above Avg. STARS
12-Mo. Target Price —   Relative Strength —   ▲ Up ▼ Down ► No Change   Below Avg.

Options: ASE, CBOE, P

Analysis prepared by **Bret Howlett** on November 03, 2008, when the stock traded at **$ 16.48.**

## Highlights

➤ We expect 2008 pretax operating earnings for the Unum US segment to increase, as the group income protection sub-segment benefits from an improving benefit ratio, partially offset by lower net investment income. We expect solid core group and voluntary benefit sales, although we believe sales in the large case market will decline due to increased competition. We see operating earnings growth for the Unum UK segment increasing in the single digits in 2008, reflecting an improvement in the benefit ratio, partially offset by slower premium growth, and the decline the value of the British pound.

➤ We look for operating earnings for the Colonial segment to rise slightly in 2008, based on its improved distribution efforts and diversified products. However, we expect sales in the segment to grow more slowly than UNM forecasted. For the run-off closed block individual income protection segment, we estimate lower pretax operating earnings in 2008, owing to lower net investment income and continued run-off.

➤ Our forecast for 2008 EPS from continuing operations is $2.48. We estimate 2009 EPS from continuing operations of $2.70.

## Investment Rationale/Risk

➤ We expect that the group income protection sub-segment will achieve its stated goal of an 88% to 89% benefit ratio by early 2009, reflecting solid risk results, changes in sales mix, underwriting discipline, and operational improvements. However, we believe UNM will continue to have difficulty increasing sales in the large case market due to intense competition, and as a result, has shifted its focus to serving the smaller and medium case market. UNM has not been exposed to the magnitude of investment losses that have affected other life insurers, and we anticipate its risk-based capital (RBC) ratio will end 2008 in the range of 315%-325%. We believe UNM's low leverage and ample liquidity are positives in this environment.

➤ Risks to our recommendation and target price include worse-than-expected client retention and sales following income protection product price increases; unfavorable claims handling in the group income protection area; higher-than-forecast costs for reassessed claims; and investment losses.

➤ Our 12-month target price of $20 is 7.4X our estimate of 2009 operating EPS ,below UNM's historical multiples.

## Qualitative Risk Assessment

| LOW | MEDIUM | **HIGH** |
|---|---|---|

Our risk assessment for UNM reflects regulatory scrutiny surrounding certain claims practices. Although the largest suits have been settled, UNM faces the possibility of additional suits and increased reserving for benefit costs in its claims reassessment. In addition, our risk assessment reflects the unfavorable operating environment for life insurers.

## Quantitative Evaluations

**S&P Quality Ranking** B

| D | C | B- | **B** | B+ | A- | A | A+ |
|---|---|---|---|---|---|---|---|

**Relative Strength Rank** **MODERATE**

46

LOWEST = 1      HIGHEST = 99

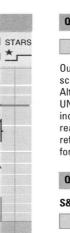

## Revenue/Earnings Data

**Revenue (Million $)**

| | 1Q | 2Q | 3Q | 4Q | Year |
|---|---|---|---|---|---|
| 2008 | 2,541 | 2,675 | 2,443 | -- | -- |
| 2007 | 2,601 | 2,666 | 2,610 | 2,644 | 10,520 |
| 2006 | 2,600 | 2,622 | 2,617 | 2,696 | 10,535 |
| 2005 | 2,572 | 2,657 | 2,544 | 2,665 | 10,437 |
| 2004 | 2,624 | 2,509 | 2,655 | 2,677 | 10,465 |
| 2003 | 2,395 | 2,529 | 2,556 | 2,511 | 9,992 |

**Earnings Per Share ($)**

| | 1Q | 2Q | 3Q | 4Q | Year |
|---|---|---|---|---|---|
| 2008 | 0.46 | 0.69 | 0.32 | E0.63 | E2.48 |
| 2007 | 0.49 | 0.43 | 0.52 | 0.45 | 1.89 |
| 2006 | 0.23 | 0.37 | -0.19 | 0.79 | 1.21 |
| 2005 | 0.49 | 0.55 | 0.17 | 0.43 | 1.64 |
| 2004 | -1.93 | 0.25 | 0.55 | 0.45 | -0.65 |
| 2003 | -1.02 | 0.36 | 0.36 | -0.71 | -0.96 |

Fiscal year ended Dec. 31. Next earnings report expected: Late January. EPS Estimates based on S&P Operating Earnings; historical GAAP earnings are as reported.

## Dividend Data (Dates: mm/dd Payment Date: mm/dd/yy)

| Amount ($) | Date Decl. | Ex-Div. Date | Stk. of Record | Payment Date |
|---|---|---|---|---|
| 0.075 | 01/14 | 01/24 | 01/28 | 02/15/08 |
| 0.075 | 04/17 | 04/24 | 04/28 | 05/16/08 |
| 0.075 | 07/15 | 07/24 | 07/28 | 08/15/08 |
| 0.075 | 10/08 | 10/23 | 10/27 | 11/21/08 |

Dividends have been paid since 1925. Source: Company reports.

---

**Please read the Required Disclosures and Analyst Certification on the last page of this report.**

# Unum Group

**STANDARD &POOR'S**

## Business Summary November 03, 2008

CORPORATE OVERVIEW. UNM provides group and individual income protection insurance in North America and the U.K. through its subsidiaries. The company offers other products, including long-term care insurance, life insurance, group benefits, and related services.

The company has six operating segments: Unum US, Unum UK, Colonial, individual income protection - closed block, other, and corporate. Unum US accounted for 59% of operating revenue in 2007, Unum UK 11%, Colonial 9.5%, individual income protection - closed block 18%, other 1.3%, and corporate 0.4%. In 2007, premium income for Unum US declined 3.5%, Unum UK premium income rose almost 15%, and Colonial premium income increased 7.7%.

The Unum US segment includes group income protection insurance, group life and accidental death and dismemberment products, and supplemental and voluntary lines of business. The Unum UK segment includes group long-term income protection insurance, group life products, and individual income protection products issued by Unum Limited and sold primarily in the U.K. through field sales personnel and independent brokers and consultants. The Colonial segment includes a broad line of products sold mainly to employees at their workplaces, including income protection, life, and cancer and critical illness products. The other segment includes products that are no longer actively marketed, with the exception of the closed block business, including individual life and corporate-owned life insurance, reinsurance pools and management operations, group pension, health insurance, and individual annuities. The corporate segment includes investment income on unallocated corporate assets, interest expense, and certain unallocated corporate income and expense items.

The individual income protection - closed block segment mainly includes individual income protection insurance written on a noncancelable basis with a fixed annual premium. Generally, the policies are individual disability insurance policies designed to be distributed to individuals in a non-workplace setting and written prior to UNM's restructuring of its individual disability business, where the focus was changed to workplace distribution.

## Company Financials Fiscal Year Ended Dec. 31

| Per Share Data ($) | 2007 | 2006 | 2005 | 2004 | 2003 | 2002 | 2001 | 2000 | 1999 | 1998 |
|---|---|---|---|---|---|---|---|---|---|---|
| Tangible Book Value | 21.72 | 21.93 | 23.76 | 23.45 | 22.94 | 25.58 | 21.74 | 20.29 | 17.82 | 20.05 |
| Operating Earnings | NA | NA | NA | NA | NA | 2.52 | 2.44 | 2.37 | -1.00 | 2.14 |
| Earnings | 1.89 | 1.21 | 1.64 | -0.65 | -0.96 | 1.68 | 2.39 | 2.33 | -0.77 | 1.82 |
| S&P Core Earnings | 2.10 | 1.29 | 1.81 | -0.26 | -0.54 | 2.35 | 2.30 | NA | NA | NA |
| Dividends | 0.30 | 0.30 | 0.30 | 0.30 | 0.37 | 0.59 | 0.59 | 0.59 | 0.35 | 0.40 |
| Payout Ratio | 16% | 25% | 18% | NM | NM | 35% | 25% | 25% | NM | 22% |
| Prices:High | 28.20 | 24.44 | 22.90 | 18.25 | 19.54 | 29.70 | 33.75 | 31.94 | 56.88 | 42.44 |
| Prices:Low | 19.79 | 16.15 | 15.50 | 11.41 | 5.91 | 16.30 | 22.25 | 11.94 | 26.00 | 26.13 |
| P/E Ratio:High | 15 | 20 | 14 | NM | NM | 18 | 14 | 14 | NM | 23 |
| P/E Ratio:Low | 10 | 13 | 9 | NM | NM | 10 | 9 | 5 | NM | 14 |

| Income Statement Analysis (Million $) | | | | | | | | | | |
|---|---|---|---|---|---|---|---|---|---|---|
| Life Insurance in Force | 692,012 | 773,070 | 833,363 | 908,034 | 787,199 | 712,826 | 642,988 | 583,848 | 567,215 | 158,317 |
| Premium Income:Life | 1,641 | 1,761 | 7,816 | 5,985 | 1,800 | 1,683 | 1,554 | 1,448 | 1,452 | 503 |
| Premium Income:A & H | 6,261 | 6,187 | 1,787 | 1,855 | 5,816 | 5,770 | 5,524 | 5,608 | 5,391 | 1,845 |
| Net Investment Income | 2,410 | 2,321 | 2,188 | 2,159 | 2,158 | 2,086 | 2,003 | 2,060 | 2,060 | 1,374 |
| Total Revenue | 10,520 | 10,535 | 10,437 | 10,465 | 9,992 | 9,613 | 9,395 | 9,432 | 9,330 | 3,938 |
| Pretax Income | 997 | 465 | 710 | -260 | -435 | 1,019 | 825 | 866 | -166 | 403 |
| Net Operating Income | NA | NA | NA | NA | NA | 614 | 593 | NA | NA | 368 |
| Net Income | 672 | 404 | 514 | -192 | -265 | 817 | 582 | 564 | -183 | 254 |
| S&P Core Earnings | 748 | 428 | 570 | -77.1 | -150 | 568 | 564 | NA | NA | NA |

| Balance Sheet & Other Financial Data (Million $) | | | | | | | | | | |
|---|---|---|---|---|---|---|---|---|---|---|
| Cash & Equivalent | 791 | 768 | 688 | 719 | 663 | 734 | 2,515 | NA | 836 | 366 |
| Premiums Due | 1,915 | 2,057 | NA | NA | NA | NA | NA | NA | NA | NA |
| Investment Assets:Bonds | 35,655 | 35,002 | 34,857 | 32,488 | 31,187 | 27,486 | 24,393 | 22,589 | 22,357 | 15,142 |
| Investment Assets:Stocks | Nil | Nil | 13.6 | 12.9 | 39.1 | 27.9 | 10.9 | 24.5 | 38.0 | 2.10 |
| Investment Assets:Loans | 3,705 | 944 | 3,941 | 3,572 | 3,353 | 3,344 | 3,510 | 3,679 | 3,595 | 2,107 |
| Investment Assets:Total | 40,951 | 40,163 | 39,357 | 36,588 | 35,028 | 31,152 | 28,324 | 26,604 | 26,549 | 17,333 |
| Deferred Policy Costs | 2,381 | 2,983 | 2,913 | 2,883 | 3,052 | 2,982 | 2,675 | 2,424 | 2,391 | 465 |
| Total Assets | 52,433 | 52,823 | 51,867 | 50,832 | 49,718 | 45,260 | 42,443 | 40,364 | 38,448 | 23,088 |
| Debt | NA | 2,660 | 3,262 | 2,862 | 2,789 | 1,914 | 2,304 | 1,915 | 1,467 | 900 |
| Common Equity | 8,040 | 7,719 | 7,364 | 7,224 | 7,271 | 9,398 | 5,940 | 5,576 | 4,983 | 3,409 |
| % Return on Revenue | 6.4 | 3.9 | 4.9 | NM | NM | 8.5 | 6.2 | 6.0 | NM | 6.5 |
| % Return on Assets | 1.3 | 0.8 | 1.0 | NM | NM | 1.9 | 1.4 | 1.4 | NM | 1.1 |
| % Return on Equity | 8.5 | 5.4 | 7.0 | NM | NM | 9.1 | 10.1 | 10.7 | NM | 7.7 |
| % Investment Yield | 5.9 | 5.8 | 5.8 | 6.0 | 6.5 | 7.0 | 7.3 | 7.8 | NM | 7.9 |

Data as orig reptd.; bef. results of disc opers/spec. items. Per share data adj. for stk. divs.; EPS diluted. E-Estimated. NA-Not Available. NM-Not Meaningful. NR-Not Ranked. UR-Under Review.

**Office:** 1 Fountain Square, Chattanooga, TN 37402-1307.
**Telephone:** 423-294-1011.
**Website:** http://www.unum.com
**Chrmn:** J.S. Fossel

**Pres & CEO:** S. Hall
**Pres & CEO:** T.R. Watjen
**EVP, CFO & Chief Acctg Officer:** R.C. Greving
**EVP & General Counsel:** E.L. Bishop, III

**Board Members:** E. M. Caulfield, J. S. Fossel, P. H. Godwin, R. E. Goldsberry, K. T. Kabat, T. A. Kinser, G. C. Larson, A. MacMillan, Jr., E. J. Muhl, M. J. Passarella, W. J. Ryan, T. R. Watjen

**Founded:** 1887
**Domicile:** Delaware
**Employees:** 9,700

# UST Inc.

STANDARD
&POOR'S

| S&P Recommendation | HOLD ★★★☆☆ | Price $68.74 (as of Nov 14, 2008) | 12-Mo. Target Price $70.00 | Investment Style Large-Cap Blend |
|---|---|---|---|---|

**GICS Sector** Consumer Staples
**Sub-Industry** Tobacco

**Summary** UST is a leading producer of moist smokeless tobacco products, marketed under leading brand names such as Copenhagen and Skoal. It also produces and imports wines.

## Key Stock Statistics (Source S&P, Vickers, company reports)

| | | | | | | | |
|---|---|---|---|---|---|---|---|
| 52-Wk Range | $69.14– 49.28 | S&P Oper. EPS 2008**E** | 3.64 | Market Capitalization(B) | $10.198 | Beta | -0.40 |
| Trailing 12-Month EPS | $3.51 | S&P Oper. EPS 2009**E** | 3.80 | Yield (%) | 3.67 | S&P 3-Yr. Proj. EPS CAGR(%) | 7 |
| Trailing 12-Month P/E | 19.6 | P/E on S&P Oper. EPS 2008**E** | 18.9 | Dividend Rate/Share | $2.52 | S&P Credit Rating | A |
| $10K Invested 5 Yrs Ago | $24,698 | Common Shares Outstg. (M) | 148.4 | Institutional Ownership (%) | 83 | | |

## Price Performance

30-Week Mov. Avg. · · · 10-Week Mov. Avg. - - GAAP Earnings vs. Previous Year  Volume Above Avg. STARS
12-Mo. Target Price — Relative Strength — ▲ Up ▼ Down ► No Change  Below Avg.

Options: ASE, CBOE, P

Analysis prepared by **Esther Y. Kwon, CFA** on September 08, 2008, when the stock traded at **$ 68.62**.

## Qualitative Risk Assessment

| LOW | MEDIUM | **HIGH** |
|---|---|---|

Our risk assessment reflects that the tobacco industry is typified by relatively stable revenue streams, while tobacco company stocks typically have below-average betas. Although the smokeless tobacco industry is not subject to as much litigation as cigarette manufacturers, there is a risk, in our opinion, that future litigation could affect cash flow. Also, due to its large market share, UST has been subject to antitrust actions.

## Quantitative Evaluations

**S&P Quality Ranking**          B+

| D | C | B- | B | **B+** | A- | A | A+ |
|---|---|---|---|---|---|---|---|

**Relative Strength Rank**          STRONG

97

LOWEST = 1          HIGHEST = 99

## Highlights

➤ We see a net sales increase of about 4% in 2008, reflecting improving moist smokeless tobacco (MST) volume trends and growth in the wine segment. With planned marketing increases, we foresee volume trends improving for higher-margin premium MST brands, although we expect continued pricing pressure as UST focuses on shoring up market share. We look for price-value segment volume to continue to expand and accelerate as its Husky brand gains more traction with better distribution. We see new line extensions, pouches, and other product innovations contributing to sales growth longer term.

➤ We look for a stabilizing of tobacco gross margins, as increased promotional activity offsets possible volume growth in the price-value category. However, we see momentum in wine volume building and pressuring overall corporate gross margins, offset slightly by cost savings from UST's Project Momentum initiative.

➤ After stock repurchases anticipated to be approximately $300 million, we estimate 2008 operating EPS of $3.65, up from 2007's $3.46. In 2009, we see EPS advancing to $3.95.

## Investment Rationale/Risk

➤ We recently reduced our opinion to hold from buy as the shares exceeded our price target on reports that Altria Group was in discussions to acquire the company. In September, Altria Group agreed to acquire UST for $69.50 per share in cash, pending approvals.

➤ Risks to our recommendation and target price include failure to consummate the planned deal.

➤ Our 12-month target price of $70 is based on Altria's offer price. At more than 17X forward 2009 EPS, Altria's offer of $69.50 is a significant premium to peer and historical averages but about in line with other transacations in the tobacco sector on a EV/EBITDA basis.

## Revenue/Earnings Data

**Revenue (Million $)**

| | 1Q | 2Q | 3Q | 4Q | Year |
|---|---|---|---|---|---|
| 2008 | 472.7 | 506.2 | 484.6 | -- | -- |
| 2007 | 447.0 | 491.3 | 479.6 | 532.9 | 1,951 |
| 2006 | 433.6 | 472.9 | 458.7 | 485.7 | 1,851 |
| 2005 | 440.5 | 480.1 | 456.8 | 474.4 | 1,852 |
| 2004 | 433.3 | 464.7 | 462.0 | 478.3 | 1,838 |
| 2003 | 420.0 | 438.9 | 437.6 | 446.2 | 1,743 |

**Earnings Per Share ($)**

| | | | | | |
|---|---|---|---|---|---|
| 2008 | 0.83 | 0.94 | 0.84 | E0.94 | E3.64 |
| 2007 | 0.67 | 0.87 | 0.84 | 0.89 | 3.27 |
| 2006 | 0.71 | 0.83 | 0.71 | 0.85 | 3.10 |
| 2005 | 0.73 | 0.82 | 0.80 | 0.88 | 3.23 |
| 2004 | 0.73 | 0.92 | 0.80 | 0.77 | 3.23 |
| 2003 | 0.66 | 0.77 | 0.74 | -0.27 | 1.90 |

Fiscal year ended Dec. 31. Next earnings report expected: Late January. EPS Estimates based on S&P Operating Earnings; historical GAAP earnings are as reported.

## Dividend Data (Dates: mm/dd Payment Date: mm/dd/yy)

| Amount ($) | Date Decl. | Ex-Div. Date | Stk. of Record | Payment Date |
|---|---|---|---|---|
| 0.630 | 02/21 | 03/12 | 03/14 | 03/31/08 |
| 0.630 | 05/06 | 06/12 | 06/16 | 06/30/08 |
| 0.630 | 08/07 | 09/11 | 09/15 | 09/30/08 |
| 0.630 | 11/06 | 12/11 | 12/15 | 12/30/08 |

Dividends have been paid since 1912. Source: Company reports.

# UST Inc.

**STANDARD &POOR'S**

## Business Summary September 08, 2008

CORPORATE OVERVIEW. UST is the holding company for United States Smokeless Tobacco Company, which was formed in 1911. The company's three segments include Smokeless Tobacco Products, Wine, and Other operations including international tobacco.

The company's moist smokeless tobacco products include Copenhagen and Skoal, the world's two best-selling brands of moist smokeless tobacco. Moist brands also include Skoal Long Cut, Skoal Bandits, Copenhagen Long Cut, Rooster, and Husky. Dry tobacco products carry the names Bruton, CC, and Red Seal. The company's tobacco products (79% of 2007 revenues) are sold throughout the U.S., principally to chain stores and tobacco and grocery wholesalers.

In addition to its smokeless tobacco offerings, UST is also a significant importer and producer of wines, and has other operations. Wines (18% of 2007 revenues) consist of premium varietal and blended wines dominated by Washington State-produced Chateau Ste. Michelle and Columbia Crest, and Villa Mt. Eden, a premium-quality California wine. In the third quarter of 2006, the company acquired the Erath label, an Oregon wine.

Other businesses (3% of 2007 revenues) include UST's international operation, which markets moist smokeless tobacco, and formerly included the manufacture and marketing of premium cigars (Don Tomas, Astral, and Hellix). In March 2004, UST paid $200 million and transferred its cigar operations to Swedish Match North America, to dismiss a case brought by that company.

CORPORATE STRATEGY. UST's objective in the Smokeless Tobacco segment is to continue to grow the moist smokeless tobacco category by building awareness and social acceptability of smokeless tobacco products among adult smokers, and by being competitive in every moist smokeless tobacco category segment. The company believes its future growth and profitability is in attracting growing numbers of adult consumers, primarily smokers, as approximately every 1% of adult smokers who convert to moist smokeless tobacco represents a 7% to 8% increase in the segment's adult consumer base. In addition to advertising initiatives, in 2004 and 2005, UST began a direct mail program to over 1 million adult smokers and began an advertising campaign to promote the convenience of smokeless tobacco relative to cigarettes. UST believes category growth has accelerated from these initiatives and is expecting category growth of 5% to 6% in 2008.

## Company Financials Fiscal Year Ended Dec. 31

| Per Share Data ($) | 2007 | 2006 | 2005 | 2004 | 2003 | 2002 | 2001 | 2000 | 1999 | 1998 |
|---|---|---|---|---|---|---|---|---|---|---|
| Tangible Book Value | NM | 0.40 | 0.46 | 0.06 | NM | NM | 3.47 | 1.66 | 1.20 | 2.57 |
| Cash Flow | 3.55 | 3.38 | 3.51 | 3.52 | 2.15 | -1.31 | 3.23 | 2.94 | 2.89 | 2.61 |
| Earnings | 3.27 | 3.10 | 3.23 | 3.23 | 1.90 | -1.61 | 2.97 | 2.70 | 2.68 | 2.44 |
| S&P Core Earnings | 2.86 | 3.14 | 3.20 | 3.24 | 1.93 | 3.13 | 2.84 | NA | NA | NA |
| Dividends | 2.40 | 2.28 | 2.20 | 2.08 | 2.00 | 1.92 | 1.84 | 1.76 | 1.68 | 1.62 |
| Payout Ratio | 73% | 74% | 68% | 64% | 105% | NM | 62% | 65% | 63% | 66% |
| Prices:High | 61.17 | 59.49 | 56.90 | 48.97 | 37.79 | 41.35 | 36.00 | 28.88 | 34.94 | 36.88 |
| Prices:Low | 47.40 | 37.96 | 37.59 | 34.00 | 26.73 | 25.30 | 23.38 | 13.88 | 24.06 | 24.56 |
| P/E Ratio:High | 19 | 19 | 18 | 15 | 20 | NM | 12 | 11 | 13 | 15 |
| P/E Ratio:Low | 14 | 12 | 12 | 11 | 14 | NM | 8 | 5 | 9 | 10 |

| Income Statement Analysis (Million $) | 2007 | 2006 | 2005 | 2004 | 2003 | 2002 | 2001 | 2000 | 1999 | 1998 |
|---|---|---|---|---|---|---|---|---|---|---|
| Revenue | 1,951 | 1,851 | 1,852 | 1,838 | 1,743 | 1,683 | 1,670 | 1,548 | 1,512 | 1,423 |
| Operating Income | 942 | 905 | 936 | 960 | 958 | 912 | 876 | 792 | 813 | 764 |
| Depreciation | 45.6 | 45.8 | 46.4 | 47.6 | 41.6 | 49.7 | 43.2 | 39.6 | 37.0 | 31.7 |
| Interest Expense | 58.0 | 57.1 | 50.6 | 75.0 | 76.9 | 46.1 | 66.2 | 47.4 | 13.5 | 4.42 |
| Pretax Income | 813 | 793 | 828 | 838 | 515 | -444 | 799 | 718 | 763 | 734 |
| Effective Tax Rate | 36.0% | 36.7% | 35.4% | 35.8% | 38.1% | NM | 38.5% | 38.5% | 38.5% | 38.0% |
| Net Income | 520 | 502 | 534 | 538 | 319 | -271 | 492 | 442 | 469 | 455 |
| S&P Core Earnings | 455 | 509 | 529 | 540 | 323 | 528 | 470 | NA | NA | NA |

| Balance Sheet & Other Financial Data (Million $) | 2007 | 2006 | 2005 | 2004 | 2003 | 2002 | 2001 | 2000 | 1999 | 1998 |
|---|---|---|---|---|---|---|---|---|---|---|
| Cash | 73.7 | 254 | 202 | 510 | 438 | 382 | 272 | 96.0 | 75.0 | 33.2 |
| Current Assets | 846 | 998 | 890 | 1,173 | 1,248 | 2,291 | 892 | 691 | 580 | 507 |
| Total Assets | 1,487 | 1,440 | 1,367 | 1,659 | 1,726 | 2,765 | 2,012 | 1,646 | 1,016 | 913 |
| Current Liabilities | 400 | 300 | 259 | 619 | 521 | 1,462 | 222 | 170 | 261 | 197 |
| Long Term Debt | 1,090 | 840 | 840 | 840 | 1,140 | 1,140 | 863 | 869 | 411 | 100 |
| Common Equity | -320 | 3,373 | 75.1 | 9.66 | -115 | -47.0 | 581 | 271 | 201 | 468 |
| Total Capital | 798 | 4,213 | 927 | 859 | -47.0 | 1,093 | 1,627 | 1,326 | 612 | 568 |
| Capital Expenditures | 88.4 | 37.0 | 89.9 | 70.3 | 45.1 | 57.2 | 47.2 | 51.1 | 59.3 | 56.3 |
| Cash Flow | 566 | 548 | 581 | 586 | 360 | -222 | 535 | 481 | 506 | 487 |
| Current Ratio | 2.1 | 3.3 | 3.4 | 1.9 | 2.4 | 1.6 | 4.0 | 4.1 | 2.2 | 2.6 |
| % Long Term Debt of Capitalization | 136.6 | 19.9 | 90.6 | 97.8 | 110.8 | 104.3 | 53.0 | 65.5 | 67.2 | 17.6 |
| % Net Income of Revenue | 26.7 | 27.1 | 28.9 | 29.3 | 18.3 | NM | 29.4 | 28.6 | 31.0 | 32.0 |
| % Return on Assets | 35.5 | 35.8 | 35.3 | 31.8 | 14.2 | NM | 26.9 | 33.2 | 48.7 | 52.3 |
| % Return on Equity | NM | 15.8 | 12.6 | NM | NM | NM | 115.4 | 187.5 | 19.3 | 100.5 |

Data as orig reptd.; bef. results of disc opers/spec. items. Per share data adj. for stk. divs.; EPS diluted. E-Estimated. NA-Not Available. NM-Not Meaningful. NR-Not Ranked. UR-Under Review.

**Office:** 6 High Ridge Park Bldg A, Stamford, CT 06905-1323.
**Telephone:** 203-817-3000.
**Website:** http://www.ustinc.com
**Chrmn, Pres, CEO & COO:** M.S. Kessler

**EVP & Secy:** R.A. Kohlberger
**SVP & CFO:** R.P. Silcock
**Chief Acctg Officer & Cntlr:** J.D. Patracuolla
**Treas:** K.N. Tamaro

**Investor Contact:** R.D. Silcock (203-817-3520)
**Board Members:** J. D. Barr, J. P. Clancey, P. D. Dennis, J. E. Heid, M. S. Kessler, P. J. Neff, A. Parsons, R. J. Rossi, L. J. Ruisi

**Founded:** 1911
**Domicile:** Delaware
**Employees:** 4,610

The McGraw-Hill Companies

# Valero Energy Corp

**STANDARD &POOR'S**

| S&P Recommendation **BUY** ★★★★☆ | Price | 12-Mo. Target Price | Investment Style |
|---|---|---|---|
| | $19.51 (as of Nov 14, 2008) | $25.00 | Large-Cap Blend |

**GICS Sector** Energy
**Sub-Industry** Oil & Gas Refining & Marketing

**Summary** Valero is the largest oil refiner in North America, one of the largest independent U.S. refined petroleum products retailers, and operates refineries that can process sour and acidic crude oils.

## Key Stock Statistics (Source S&P, Vickers, company reports)

| | | | | | | | |
|---|---|---|---|---|---|---|---|
| 52-Wk Range | $71.25– 14.59 | S&P Oper. EPS 2009**E** | 4.02 | Market Capitalization(B) | $10.067 | Beta | 1.63 |
| Trailing 12-Month EPS | $5.03 | S&P Oper. EPS 2010**E** | 3.84 | Yield (%) | 3.08 | S&P 3-Yr. Proj. EPS CAGR(%) | -21 |
| Trailing 12-Month P/E | 3.9 | P/E on S&P Oper. EPS 2009**E** | 4.9 | Dividend Rate/Share | $0.60 | S&P Credit Rating | BBB |
| $10K Invested 5 Yrs Ago | $18,365 | Common Shares Outstg. (M) | 516.0 | Institutional Ownership (%) | 74 | | |

## Price Performance

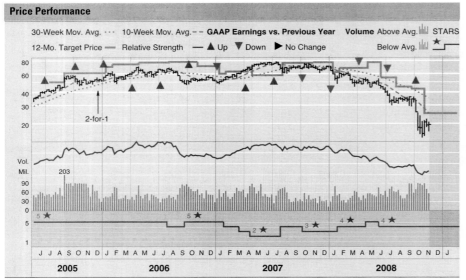

| 30-Week Mov. Avg. ···· | 10-Week Mov. Avg. - - - | GAAP Earnings vs. Previous Year | Volume Above Avg. ᴵᴵᴵᴵ | STARS |
|---|---|---|---|---|
| 12-Mo. Target Price — | Relative Strength — | ▲ Up ▼ Down ▶ No Change | Below Avg. ᴵᴵᴵᴵ | ★ |

2-for-1

Vol. Mil.    203

2005   2006   2007   2008

Options: ASE, CBOE, P, Ph

Analysis prepared by **Tina J. Vital** on October 28, 2008, when the stock traded at **$ 16.81**.

### Highlights

➤ As oil prices have climbed this year, U.S. refining margins narrowed as refiners were unable to pass along higher costs to customers. However, the recent fall in oil prices should boost U.S. refining margins, particularly those for distillates. Not all refiners are the same, and we like VLO's flexible, high conversion facilities, which offer cost advantages and enhanced product yields.

➤ Third-quarter refining throughputs declined 9%, below our expectations, reflecting asset sales and Gulf hurricane impacts. Based on management guidance, we expect refining throughputs to rise about 4% from the third to the fourth quarter. We expect planned turnarounds will be mild in the fourth quarter, with a pickup in 2009.

➤ A weak U.S. economy and high oil prices have resulted in reduced U.S. fuel demand, and we expect U.S. industry-wide refining margins to narrow by about 18% in 2008 and 2009. After-tax operating earnings decreased 12% in 2007, we expect a 51% drop in 2008 and 6% in 2009.

### Investment Rationale/Risk

➤ As VLO is the largest refiner in North America, we believe its size and ability to refine heavy sour crude feedstocks offer strategic and economic advantages. With the majority of refining costs focused on feedstocks, we think the company's ability to refine lower-quality crudes (over half of feedstocks are heavy, sour or acidic) is a competitive advantage. We estimate that VLO holds an above-average level of conversion capacity, and a major $1.4 billion expansion is underway at its St. Charles refinery.

➤ Risks to our recommendation and target price include weakened economic, industry and operating conditions that lead to a narrowing of margins or decrease in production.

➤ A blend of our discounted cash flow ($34 per share; assuming a weighted average cost of capital of 11.3% and terminal growth of 3%) and narrowed relative valuations leads to our 12-month target price of $25 per share. This result represents an expected enterprise value of about 3.3X our 2009 EBITDA estimate, in line with peers.

## Qualitative Risk Assessment

| LOW | MEDIUM | HIGH |
|---|---|---|

Our risk assessment reflects our view of VLO's strong business profile in the volatile and competitive oil refining industry. The company is the largest oil refiner in the U.S. and possesses above-average refining complexity, which allows it to process a large amount of lower-cost heavy and sour crudes.

## Quantitative Evaluations

**S&P Quality Ranking**    B+

| D | C | B- | B | B+ | A- | A | A+ |
|---|---|---|---|---|---|---|---|

**Relative Strength Rank**    MODERATE

48

LOWEST = 1                                    HIGHEST = 99

## Revenue/Earnings Data

### Revenue (Million $)

| | 1Q | 2Q | 3Q | 4Q | Year |
|---|---|---|---|---|---|
| 2008 | 27,945 | 36,436 | 35,753 | -- | -- |
| 2007 | 19,698 | 23,999 | 23,699 | 28,671 | 94,527 |
| 2006 | 20,941 | 26,781 | 24,319 | 19,792 | 91,833 |
| 2005 | 14,943 | 18,032 | 23,283 | 25,894 | 82,162 |
| 2004 | 11,082 | 13,808 | 14,339 | 15,390 | 54,619 |
| 2003 | 9,693 | 8,844 | 9,922 | 9,509 | 37,969 |

### Earnings Per Share ($)

| | | | | | |
|---|---|---|---|---|---|
| 2008 | 0.48 | 1.38 | 2.18 | E0.65 | E4.24 |
| 2007 | 1.86 | 3.57 | 1.34 | 1.02 | 7.72 |
| 2006 | 1.32 | 2.98 | 2.55 | 1.80 | 8.64 |
| 2005 | 0.96 | 1.53 | 1.47 | 2.06 | 6.10 |
| 2004 | 0.46 | 1.14 | 0.79 | 0.88 | 3.27 |
| 2003 | 0.38 | 0.27 | 0.38 | 0.25 | 1.27 |

Fiscal year ended Dec. 31. Next earnings report expected: Late January. EPS Estimates based on S&P Operating Earnings; historical GAAP earnings are as reported.

## Dividend Data (Dates: mm/dd Payment Date: mm/dd/yy)

| Amount ($) | Date Decl. | Ex-Div. Date | Stk. of Record | Payment Date |
|---|---|---|---|---|
| 0.120 | 01/17 | 02/11 | 02/13 | 03/12/08 |
| 0.150 | 05/01 | 05/23 | 05/28 | 06/18/08 |
| 0.150 | 07/09 | 08/04 | 08/06 | 09/10/08 |
| 0.150 | 10/16 | 11/07 | 11/12 | 12/10/08 |

Dividends have been paid since 1997. Source: Company reports.

---

**Please read the Required Disclosures and Analyst Certification on the last page of this report.**

The McGraw·Hill Companies

# Valero Energy Corp

**STANDARD &POOR'S**

## Business Summary October 28, 2008

CORPORATE OVERVIEW. Incorporated in 1981 under the name Valero Refining and Marketing Co., the company changed its name to Valero Energy Co. (VLO) in 1997. In 2001, VLO merged with Ultramar Diamond Shamrock, and in September 2005 with Premcor Inc., creating the largest refiner in North America, based on atmospheric distillation capacity.

The company operates in two business segments: Refining (91% of 2007 revenues, 97% of 2007 operating income), and Retail (9%, 3%). VLO serves customers in the U.S. (86% of 2007 revenues), Canada (9%), and other countries (5%); no single customer accounted for over 10% of consolidated operating revenues.

The Refining segment includes refining operations, wholesale marketing, product supply and distribution, and transportation operations. As of year-end 2007, the company owned and operated 17 refineries in the U.S., Canada, and Aruba, with a combined throughput capacity of 3.1 million barrels per day (b/d). These capacities by region include: Gulf Coast (nine refineries, 55% of 2007 throughput capacity), the Mid-Continent (three, 15%), the West Coast (two, 10%), and the Northeast (three, 20%).

During 2007, sour crude oils, acidic sweet crude oils, and residuals represented 57% of VLO's throughput volumes; sweet crude oil 26%, and blendstocks and other feedstocks 17%. About 65% of VLO's current crude oil feedstock requirements were purchased through term contracts, with the remainder generally purchased on the spot market. About 80% of these 2007 crude oil feedstocks are imported from foreign sources, and around 20% were domestic.

VLO is one of the largest independent retailers of refined products in the central and southwest U.S. and eastern Canada. Its retail operations are segregated geographically into two groups: Retail-U.S. System (sales of 113,500 b/d in 2007) and Retail-Canada (77,000 b/d).

## Company Financials Fiscal Year Ended Dec. 31

| Per Share Data ($) | 2008 | 2007 | 2006 | 2005 | 2004 | 2003 | 2002 | 2001 | 2000 | 1999 |
|---|---|---|---|---|---|---|---|---|---|---|
| Tangible Book Value | NA | 31.75 | 23.33 | 15.82 | 9.55 | 5.86 | 3.24 | 3.90 | 6.28 | 4.84 |
| Cash Flow | NA | 9.55 | 10.47 | 7.57 | 3.24 | 2.31 | 1.23 | 2.75 | 1.86 | 0.47 |
| Earnings | 3.50 | 7.72 | 8.64 | 6.10 | 3.27 | 1.27 | 0.21 | 2.21 | 1.40 | 0.06 |
| S&P Core Earnings | NA | 7.73 | 8.32 | 6.02 | 3.25 | 1.25 | 0.14 | 2.14 | NA | NA |
| Dividends | 0.42 | 0.48 | 0.30 | 0.19 | 0.15 | 0.15 | 0.10 | 0.09 | 0.08 | 0.08 |
| Payout Ratio | 12% | 6% | 3% | 3% | 4% | 11% | 48% | 4% | 6% | 128% |
| Prices:High | 71.12 | 78.68 | 70.75 | 58.63 | 23.91 | 11.77 | 12.49 | 13.15 | 9.66 | 6.33 |
| Prices:Low | 29.32 | 47.66 | 46.84 | 21.01 | 11.43 | 8.05 | 5.79 | 7.88 | 4.63 | 4.17 |
| P/E Ratio:High | 20 | 10 | 8 | 10 | 7 | 9 | 60 | 6 | 7 | NM |
| P/E Ratio:Low | 8 | 6 | 5 | 3 | 3 | 6 | 28 | 4 | 3 | NM |

### Income Statement Analysis (Million $)

| | 2008 | 2007 | 2006 | 2005 | 2004 | 2003 | 2002 | 2001 | 2000 | 1999 |
|---|---|---|---|---|---|---|---|---|---|---|
| Revenue | NA | 95,327 | 91,833 | 82,162 | 54,619 | 37,969 | 26,976 | 14,988 | 14,671 | 7,961 |
| Operating Income | NA | 8,278 | 9,165 | 6,334 | 2,979 | 1,733 | 920 | 1,139 | 723 | 162 |
| Depreciation, Depletion and Amortization | NA | 1,360 | 1,155 | 875 | NA | 511 | 449 | 138 | 112 | 92.4 |
| Interest Expense | NA | 466 | 210 | 266 | 260 | 278 | 256 | 102 | 83.0 | 55.4 |
| Pretax Income | NA | 6,726 | 8,196 | 5,287 | 2,710 | 989 | 164 | 895 | 528 | 20.2 |
| Effective Tax Rate | NA | 32.1% | 33.3% | 32.1% | 33.4% | 36.9% | 35.5% | 37.0% | 35.8% | 29.2% |
| Net Income | NA | 4,565 | 5,463 | 3,590 | 1,804 | 622 | 91.5 | 564 | 339 | 14.3 |
| S&P Core Earnings | NA | 4,572 | 5,258 | 3,534 | 1,785 | 604 | 60.0 | 547 | NA | NA |

### Balance Sheet & Other Financial Data (Million $)

| | 2008 | 2007 | 2006 | 2005 | 2004 | 2003 | 2002 | 2001 | 2000 | 1999 |
|---|---|---|---|---|---|---|---|---|---|---|
| Cash | NA | 2,495 | 1,590 | 436 | 864 | 369 | 409 | 346 | 14.6 | 60.1 |
| Current Assets | NA | 14,792 | 10,760 | 8,276 | 5,264 | 3,817 | 3,536 | 4,113 | 1,285 | 829 |
| Total Assets | NA | 42,722 | 37,753 | 32,728 | 19,392 | 15,664 | 14,465 | 14,337 | 4,308 | 2,979 |
| Current Liabilities | NA | 11,914 | 8,822 | 7,305 | 4,534 | 3,064 | 3,007 | 4,730 | 1,039 | 719 |
| Long Term Debt | NA | 6,470 | 4,657 | 5,156 | 3,901 | 4,245 | 4,867 | 2,805 | 1,042 | 785 |
| Common Equity | NA | 18,507 | 18,605 | 14,982 | 7,590 | 5,535 | 4,308 | 4,203 | 1,527 | 1,085 |
| Total Capital | NA | 28,998 | 27,309 | 20,206 | 13,710 | 11,585 | 10,592 | 8,884 | 3,149 | 2,146 |
| Capital Expenditures | NA | 2,260 | 3,187 | 2,133 | 1,292 | 976 | 628 | 394 | 195 | 101 |
| Cash Flow | NA | 5,529 | 6,616 | 4,452 | 1,791 | 1,128 | 541 | 701 | 451 | 107 |
| Current Ratio | NA | 1.2 | 1.2 | 1.1 | 1.2 | 1.2 | 1.2 | 0.9 | 1.2 | 1.2 |
| % Long Term Debt of Capitalization | NA | 22.3 | 17.1 | 25.5 | 28.5 | 36.6 | 45.9 | 31.6 | 33.0 | 36.5 |
| % Return on Assets | NA | 11.4 | 15.5 | 13.8 | 10.3 | 4.1 | 0.6 | 6.0 | 9.3 | 0.5 |
| % Return on Equity | NA | 24.6 | 32.5 | 31.7 | 27.3 | 12.5 | 2.2 | 19.7 | 26.0 | 1.3 |

Data as orig reptd.; bef. results of disc opers/spec. items. Per share data adj. for stk. divs.; EPS diluted. E-Estimated. NA-Not Available. NM-Not Meaningful. NR-Not Ranked. UR-Under Review.

**Office:** 1 Valero Way, San Antonio, TX 78249-1616.
**Telephone:** 210-345-2000.
**Email:** investorrelations@valero.com
**Website:** http://www.valero.com

**Chrmn, Pres & CEO:** W.R. Klesse
**COO & EVP:** R.J. Marcogliese
**Investor Contact:** M.S. Ciskowski (210-345-2000)
**EVP, CFO & Chief Acctg Officer:** M.S. Ciskowski

**SVP & Secy:** J.D. Browning
**Board Members:** W. E. Bradford, R. K. Calgaard, J. D. Choate, I. F. Engelhardt, R. M. Escobedo, W. R. Klesse, B. Marbut, D. L. Nickles, R. Profusek, S. K. Purcell, S. M. Waters

**Founded:** 1955
**Domicile:** Delaware
**Employees:** 21,651

# Varian Medical Systems Inc

**STANDARD &POOR'S**

**S&P Recommendation** BUY ★★★★☆

| Price | 12-Mo. Target Price | Investment Style |
|---|---|---|
| $40.69 (as of Nov 14, 2008) | $50.00 | Large-Cap Growth |

**GICS Sector** Health Care
**Sub-Industry** Health Care Equipment

**Summary** This leading maker of radiotherapy cancer systems also supplies X-ray tubes and flat-panel digital subsystems for imaging in medical, scientific and industrial applications.

## Key Stock Statistics (Source S&P, Vickers, company reports)

| | | | | | | |
|---|---|---|---|---|---|---|
| 52-Wk Range | $65.84– 37.34 | S&P Oper. EPS 2009**E** | 2.50 | Market Capitalization(B) | $5.080 | Beta | 0.61 |
| Trailing 12-Month EPS | $2.19 | S&P Oper. EPS 2010**E** | 2.80 | Yield (%) | Nil | S&P 3-Yr. Proj. EPS CAGR(%) | 12 |
| Trailing 12-Month P/E | 18.6 | P/E on S&P Oper. EPS 2009**E** | 16.3 | Dividend Rate/Share | Nil | S&P Credit Rating | NA |
| $10K Invested 5 Yrs Ago | $12,098 | Common Shares Outstg. (M) | 124.8 | Institutional Ownership (%) | 93 | | |

## Price Performance

30-Week Mov. Avg. ··· 10-Week Mov. Avg. - - **GAAP Earnings vs. Previous Year**  Volume Above Avg. STARS
12-Mo. Target Price — Relative Strength — ▲ Up ▼ Down ► No Change  Below Avg.

Options: ASE

Analysis prepared by **Robert M. Gold** on October 24, 2008, when the stock traded at **$ 41.44**.

## Highlights

➤ We expect that revenues in FY 09 (Sep.) will approximate $2.25 billion, on rising Intensity Modulated Radiation Therapy sales, upgrades to image-guided radiation therapy technology, and accelerating growth for X-ray and brachytherapy products. We believe that efforts by the U.S. government to deploy automated cargo screening systems capable of detecting nuclear materials will help drive increased linear accelerator sales in the coming years. Our FY 10 revenue estimate is $2.45 billion.

➤ We see gross margins benefiting from a higher proportion of software revenues and rising contributions from the sale of flat panel displays, but negatively affected by higher raw material costs and some expected unit pricing pressures; our FY 09 gross margin estimate is 41.0%, down from 41.8% in FY 08. We expect to see some leverage on the SG&A line into FY 09, and believe R&D spending will continue to absorb 6.0%-6.5% of sales in FY 09.

➤ Including expected common share buybacks, our FY 09 EPS forecast is $2.50, and we see FY 10 EPS reaching $2.80. Over the coming three years, we think EPS growth will average 12%.

## Investment Rationale/Risk

➤ We believe high single digit revenue growth will reflect clinical adoption of IMRT and IGRT upgrades, along with clinical adoption of RapidArc, which was launched in early 2008. We also believe that the recent acquisition of an independent distributor of medical X-ray tubes in China could potentially spur increased sales in China. We do have concern, however, over slowing hospital capital equipment spending amid tight credit market conditions and a recessionary economic backdrop, and believe a stronger U.S. dollar could negatively affect revenues in coming quarters.

➤ Risks to our recommendation and target price include unfavorable changes in Medicare reimbursements, equipment pricing pressures, the potential for lost equipment sales overseas with a stronger U.S. dollar, and stagnation in the global oncology equipment order backlog.

➤ Our 12-month target price of $50 is 20X our FY 09 EPS estimate and 2.8X our estimate of FY 09 revenues per share, and reflects a PEG ratio of 1.7X. These are premiums to mid-cap device peers that we think are warranted by what we view as Varian's favorable long-term demand drivers.

## Qualitative Risk Assessment

| LOW | MEDIUM | HIGH |
|---|---|---|

Our risk assessment reflects that while Varian offers some of the more technologically advanced products in the oncology equipment industry, the company operates in a competitive industry characterized by technological innovation and new product entrants. In addition, although we believe radiation therapy will continue to be an integral component of global cancer treatment protocols, the continued development of drug-based oncology treatments represents a substantial threat to the company's radiation therapy equipment business. In our view, tightening credit market conditions globally could also negatively affect capital expenditure decisions by Varian's customers.

## Quantitative Evaluations

**S&P Quality Ranking** B+

| D | C | B- | B | B+ | A- | A | A+ |
|---|---|---|---|---|---|---|---|

**Relative Strength Rank** MODERATE

57

LOWEST = 1    HIGHEST = 99

## Revenue/Earnings Data

**Revenue (Million $)**

| | 1Q | 2Q | 3Q | 4Q | Year |
|---|---|---|---|---|---|
| 2008 | 458.5 | 527.5 | 512.8 | 592.7 | 2,070 |
| 2007 | 387.9 | 442.6 | 423.7 | 522.4 | 1,777 |
| 2006 | 334.2 | 413.9 | 395.7 | 454.0 | 1,598 |
| 2005 | 299.0 | 350.8 | 346.5 | 386.2 | 1,383 |
| 2004 | 267.0 | 320.6 | 303.1 | 344.8 | 1,236 |
| 2003 | 206.7 | 266.2 | 265.5 | 303.3 | 1,042 |

**Earnings Per Share ($)**

| | | | | | |
|---|---|---|---|---|---|
| 2008 | 0.43 | 0.56 | 0.58 | 0.68 | 2.31 |
| 2007 | 0.37 | 0.46 | 0.39 | 0.61 | 1.83 |
| 2006 | 0.30 | 0.41 | 0.49 | 0.61 | 1.80 |
| 2005 | 0.29 | 0.39 | 0.37 | 0.45 | 1.50 |
| 2004 | 0.21 | 0.30 | 0.30 | 0.37 | 1.18 |
| 2003 | 0.15 | 0.24 | 0.23 | 0.31 | 0.92 |

Fiscal year ended Sep. 30. Next earnings report expected: Late January. EPS Estimates based on S&P Operating Earnings; historical GAAP earnings are as reported.

## Dividend Data

Cash dividends were last paid in 1999.

# Varian Medical Systems Inc

**STANDARD &POOR'S**

## Business Summary October 24, 2008

CORPORATE OVERVIEW. Varian is one of the largest manufacturers of oncology diagnostic products, X-ray tubes, and imaging subsystems. The company is focused primarily on capturing share in the global oncology radiation therapy markets. Cancer rates are expected to increase 50% by 2020.

MARKET PROFILE. Driven by an aging global population and improved diagnostic methods, the number of newly diagnosed cancer cases continues to increase. According to estimates published in February 2005 by the Annals of Oncology, nearly 2.9 million new cancer cases were diagnosed during 2004, and the U.S. National Cancer Institute estimates that cancer diagnoses will rise 1.6 million per year by 2010, a 23% increase from the 1.3 million cancers per year seen in 2000. Radiation therapy is commonly used in the treatment of cancer, alone or in combination with surgery or chemotherapy. The most common type of radiotherapy uses X-rays delivered by external beams, and is administered using linear accelerators. In addition to external radiation, radioactive seeds, wires or ribbons are sometimes inserted into a tumor or into a body cavity (brachytherapy), a modality that does not require radiation to pass through healthy tissues.

Varian's oncology systems group (81% of FY 08 (Sep.) revenues) designs, mar-

kets and services hardware and software products for cancer radiation treatment, including linear accelerators, treatment simulators and verification products, and software systems for planning cancer treatment and managing information and images for radiation oncology. Products focus on enabling a new therapy that delivers high doses of radiation to tumors while reducing risk to surrounding tissues. This three-dimensional conformal radiation therapy, called Intensity Modulation Radiation Therapy (IMRT), links treatment planning, information management and driver software to the treatment delivery device, the linear accelerator. This is designed to allow clinicians to determine and deliver a clinically optimized plan of radiation for each patient. IMRT is used to treat head and neck, breast, prostate, pancreatic, lung, liver, gynecological and central nervous system cancers. VAR has also developed image-guided radiation therapy (IGRT), which improves radiation therapy precision by using technologies that compensate for tumor changes and movements during and between treatments.

## Company Financials Fiscal Year Ended Sep. 30

| Per Share Data ($) | 2008 | 2007 | 2006 | 2005 | 2004 | 2003 | 2002 | 2001 | 2000 | 1999 |
|---|---|---|---|---|---|---|---|---|---|---|
| Tangible Book Value | NA | 4.92 | 5.21 | 4.11 | 3.74 | 3.71 | 3.05 | 2.93 | 2.13 | 1.51 |
| Cash Flow | NA | 2.08 | 2.02 | 1.70 | 1.32 | 1.06 | 0.81 | 0.64 | 0.55 | 0.38 |
| Earnings | 2.31 | 1.83 | 1.80 | 1.50 | 1.18 | 0.92 | 0.66 | 0.50 | 0.41 | 0.07 |
| S&P Core Earnings | NA | 1.83 | 1.80 | 1.34 | 1.04 | 0.78 | 0.54 | 0.40 | NA | NA |
| Dividends | NA | Nil | Nil | Nil | Nil | Nil | Nil | Nil | Nil | 0.03 |
| Payout Ratio | NA | Nil | Nil | Nil | Nil | Nil | Nil | Nil | Nil | 37% |
| Prices:High | NA | 53.22 | 61.70 | 52.92 | 46.49 | 35.65 | 25.66 | 19.31 | 17.75 | 10.75 |
| Prices:Low | NA | 37.30 | 41.10 | 31.65 | 29.63 | 23.70 | 15.80 | 13.50 | 6.88 | 4.06 |
| P/E Ratio:High | NA | 29 | 34 | 35 | 39 | 39 | 39 | 39 | 43 | NM |
| P/E Ratio:Low | NA | 20 | 23 | 21 | 25 | 26 | 24 | 27 | 17 | NM |

| Income Statement Analysis (Million $) | | | | | | | | | | |
|---|---|---|---|---|---|---|---|---|---|---|
| Revenue | 2,070 | 1,777 | 1,598 | 1,383 | 1,236 | 1,042 | 873 | 774 | 690 | 590 |
| Operating Income | NA | 367 | 339 | 332 | 277 | 219 | 165 | 129 | 108 | 91.4 |
| Depreciation | NA | 32.2 | 29.6 | 27.1 | 20.8 | 20.3 | 20.4 | 19.3 | 17.8 | 37.4 |
| Interest Expense | NA | 4.79 | 4.65 | 4.70 | 4.67 | 4.38 | 4.49 | 4.13 | 5.16 | 10.0 |
| Pretax Income | 426 | 343 | 319 | 308 | 257 | 201 | 146 | 107 | 84.9 | 18.2 |
| Effective Tax Rate | 30.7% | 30.1% | 23.6% | 33.0% | 35.0% | 35.0% | 36.0% | 36.5% | 37.5% | 55.0% |
| Net Income | 295 | 239 | 244 | 207 | 167 | 131 | 93.6 | 68.0 | 53.0 | 8.20 |
| S&P Core Earnings | NA | 240 | 245 | 184 | 148 | 111 | 75.9 | 54.2 | NA | NA |

| Balance Sheet & Other Financial Data (Million $) | | | | | | | | | | |
|---|---|---|---|---|---|---|---|---|---|---|
| Cash | 397 | 263 | 366 | 378 | 352 | 323 | 299 | 219 | 83.3 | 25.1 |
| Current Assets | NA | 1,160 | 1,156 | 1,017 | 885 | 806 | 651 | 620 | 451 | 382 |
| Total Assets | 1,976 | 1,684 | 1,512 | 1,317 | 1,170 | 1,053 | 910 | 759 | 603 | 539 |
| Current Liabilities | NA | 782 | 644 | 544 | 461 | 409 | 358 | 285 | 250 | 270 |
| Long Term Debt | NA | 40.4 | 49.4 | 57.3 | 53.3 | 58.5 | 58.5 | 58.5 | 58.5 | 58.5 |
| Common Equity | 1,027 | 821 | 797 | 659 | 614 | 564 | 504 | 418 | 270 | 185 |
| Total Capital | NA | 862 | 847 | 716 | 667 | 622 | 562 | 477 | 329 | 244 |
| Capital Expenditures | NA | 64.1 | 41.4 | 43.9 | 24.2 | 18.9 | 25.9 | 16.5 | 19.2 | 39.4 |
| Cash Flow | NA | 272 | 273 | 234 | 188 | 151 | 114 | 87.3 | 70.8 | 45.6 |
| Current Ratio | 1.8 | 1.5 | 1.8 | 1.9 | 1.9 | 2.0 | 1.8 | 2.2 | 1.8 | 1.4 |
| % Long Term Debt of Capitalization | 3.0 | 4.7 | 5.8 | 8.0 | 8.0 | 9.4 | 10.4 | 12.3 | 17.8 | 24.0 |
| % Net Income of Revenue | 14.3 | 13.5 | 15.2 | 14.9 | 13.5 | 12.6 | 10.7 | 8.8 | 7.7 | 1.4 |
| % Return on Assets | 16.1 | 15.0 | 17.2 | 16.5 | 15.0 | 13.3 | 11.2 | 10.0 | 9.3 | 0.1 |
| % Return on Equity | 32.0 | 29.6 | 33.4 | 32.2 | 28.4 | 25.3 | 20.3 | 19.2 | 23.3 | 2.2 |

Data as orig reptd.; bef. results of disc opers/spec. items. Per share data adj. for stk. divs.; EPS diluted. E-Estimated. NA-Not Available. NM-Not Meaningful. NR-Not Ranked. UR-Under Review.

**Office:** 3100 Hansen Way, Palo Alto, CA 94304-1030.
**Telephone:** 650-493-4000.
**Website:** http://www.varian.com
**Chrmn:** R.M. Levy

**Pres & CEO:** T.E. Guertin
**SVP & CFO:** E.W. Finney
**CTO:** G.A. Zdasiuk
**Chief Acctg Officer & Cntlr:** T. Chen

**Investor Contact:** S. Sias (650-424-5782)
**Board Members:** S. L. Bostrom, J. S. Brown, R. A. Eckert, T. E. Guertin, M. R. Laret, R. M. Levy, D. W. Martin, Jr., R. Naumann-Etienne, K. J. Thiry

**Founded:** 1976
**Domicile:** Delaware
**Employees:** 4,500

**STANDARD &POOR'S**

# VeriSign Inc

| S&P Recommendation HOLD ★★★☆☆ | Price<br>$18.64 (as of Nov 14, 2008) | 12-Mo. Target Price<br>$24.00 | Investment Style<br>Large-Cap Blend |
|---|---|---|---|

**GICS Sector** Information Technology
**Sub-Industry** Internet Software & Services

**Summary** This company is a leading provider of infrastructure services that enable secure digital communications and commerce. VRSN is in the process of selling many of its businesses by 2009, in order to focus on core operations.

## Key Stock Statistics (Source S&P, Vickers, company reports)

| | | | | | | | |
|---|---|---|---|---|---|---|---|
| 52-Wk Range | $42.50– 17.07 | S&P Oper. EPS 2008**E** | 0.90 | Market Capitalization(B) | $3.617 | Beta | 1.62 |
| Trailing 12-Month EPS | $-2.37 | S&P Oper. EPS 2009**E** | 1.25 | Yield (%) | Nil | S&P 3-Yr. Proj. EPS CAGR(%) | 23 |
| Trailing 12-Month P/E | NM | P/E on S&P Oper. EPS 2008**E** | 20.7 | Dividend Rate/Share | Nil | S&P Credit Rating | NA |
| $10K Invested 5 Yrs Ago | $11,549 | Common Shares Outstg. (M) | 194.0 | Institutional Ownership (%) | NM | | |

## Price Performance

30-Week Mov. Avg. ···· 10-Week Mov. Avg. --- GAAP Earnings vs. Previous Year    Volume Above Avg. STARS
12-Mo. Target Price — Relative Strength — ▲ Up ▼ Down ▶ No Change    Below Avg.

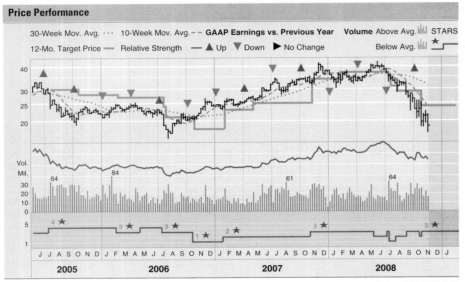

Options: ASE, CBOE, P, Ph

Analysis prepared by **Scott H. Kessler** on November 13, 2008.

## Highlights

➤ We project that revenues from continuing operations will rise 13% in 2008 and 11% in 2009, owing in part to higher domain-name prices. This forecast excludes substantial telecommunications-related businesses that we expect to be divested by the end of 2009.

➤ In August 2007, VRSN issued $1.25 billion in convertible notes, and had been aggressively repurchasing shares with this and other capital. In February 2008, VRSN announced a new $800 million buyback plan, and in August 2008, announced it had $1 billion authorized for repurchases (adding $680 million).

➤ VRSN has pursued notable divestitures in recent years (including the October 2008-announced sale of a joint-venture stake for some $200 million), and has plans for considerable additional activity, constituting what accounted for roughly half of VRSN's revenues in 2007. In August 2008, VRSN indicated that issues related to macroeconomic and credit challenges could contribute to some material divestiture activity being pushed out into 2009.

## Investment Rationale/Risk

➤ We believe VRSN became too dispersed following transactional efforts from mid-2004 to mid-2006. A largely new management team was installed in late 2006 and 2007, and was focused on realigning and repositioning the company, promoting better sales practices and divesting a number of businesses. Four high level executives left VRSN in 2008, including former CEO and board member Bill Roper. We see the stock as appropriately valued.

➤ Risks to our opinion and target price include more weakness then we expect in domain name registrations and e-commerce activity, and less successful actions intended to generate shareholder value than we foresee.

➤ VRSN's forward 12-month P/E and P/E-to-growth (PEG) ratios were recently higher than the S&P 500 Internet Software & Services sub-industry's. We believe VRSN's business model warrants premiums, and our related P/E analysis yields a value of $22. Similar PEG considerations result in a valuation of about $26. Our blended 12-month target price is $24.

## Qualitative Risk Assessment

| LOW | MEDIUM | HIGH |
|---|---|---|

Our risk assessment reflects what we consider the emerging nature of, and notable competition in, many of the company's businesses, substantial corporate transactional activity since 2004, and numerous one-time items appearing in the company's recent financials.

## Quantitative Evaluations

**S&P Quality Ranking**                  B-

| D | C | B- | B | B+ | A- | A | A+ |
|---|---|---|---|---|---|---|---|

**Relative Strength Rank**          MODERATE

44

LOWEST = 1                    HIGHEST = 99

## Revenue/Earnings Data

**Revenue (Million $)**

| | 1Q | 2Q | 3Q | 4Q | Year |
|---|---|---|---|---|---|
| 2008 | 354.3 | 303.2 | 246.1 | -- | -- |
| 2007 | 373.1 | 363.2 | 373.6 | 386.4 | 1,496 |
| 2006 | 372.8 | 390.7 | 399.5 | 412.2 | 1,575 |
| 2005 | 401.0 | 444.8 | 414.8 | 392.1 | 1,609 |
| 2004 | 229.1 | 256.1 | 325.3 | 356.0 | 1,166 |
| 2003 | 269.8 | 265.3 | 268.1 | 251.6 | 1,055 |

**Earnings Per Share ($)**

| | | | | | |
|---|---|---|---|---|---|
| 2008 | 0.06 | -0.35 | 0.22 | E0.32 | E0.90 |
| 2007 | 0.24 | -0.02 | 0.07 | -0.88 | -0.61 |
| 2006 | 0.06 | 1.52 | 0.06 | -0.12 | 1.53 |
| 2005 | 0.17 | 0.14 | 0.17 | 0.07 | 0.53 |
| 2004 | 0.04 | 0.09 | 0.16 | 0.43 | 0.72 |
| 2003 | -0.22 | -0.60 | -0.13 | -0.13 | -1.08 |

Fiscal year ended Dec. 31. Next earnings report expected: Early February. EPS Estimates based on S&P Operating Earnings; historical GAAP earnings are as reported.

## Dividend Data

No cash dividends have been paid.

The **McGraw·Hill** Companies

# VeriSign Inc

STANDARD
&POOR'S

## Business Summary November 13, 2008

CORPORATE OVERVIEW. VeriSign provides infrastructure services intended to enable secure digital content, communications and commerce. Core offerings include information and security services, naming and directory services, and telecommunications services. VRSN has two primary operating units: the Internet Services Group (61% and 49% of revenues in 2007 and 2006, respectively), and the Communications Services Group (39%, 51%).

The Internet Services Group consists of two businesses: Information and Security Services, and Naming Services. Information and Security Services include network and applications security services (including managed security and global security consulting services), authentication services, commerce site services, and digital certificate services. Naming Services (largely associated with VRSN being the exclusive registry of the .com and .net domain names) includes domain name registry services (VRSN owns and maintains the shared registration system for second-level domains), intelligent supply chain services, real-time publisher services, and digital brand management services.

The Communications Services Group provides communications services to wireline, broadband and mobile operators, and enterprise customers. They include network connectivity and interoperability services, intelligent database

services, content and application services, messaging services, clearing and settlement services, and billing and payment services. VRSN intends to divest all business lines within Communications Services.

CORPORATE STRATEGY. We believe VRSN has diversified itself with multiple primary businesses. Although we see its business segments as largely independent of one another, they offer unusual potential for cross-selling and shared research and development efforts, in our view. With its areas of focus established, VRSN expanded via regular acquisitions. The companies that VRSN purchased generally had proprietary offerings and technology that VRSN leveraged with its expansive geographic footprint, customer base, and corporate alliances. We believe this was a good strategy, particularly because many of the applications and areas that VRSN had been emphasizing were significantly fragmented, by our analysis. The company's challenge was to purchase the best companies at attractive valuations, and to integrate them successfully.

## Company Financials Fiscal Year Ended Dec. 31

### Per Share Data ($)

| | 2007 | 2006 | 2005 | 2004 | 2003 | 2002 | 2001 | 2000 | 1999 | 1998 |
|---|---|---|---|---|---|---|---|---|---|---|
| Tangible Book Value | 2.17 | 2.44 | 2.98 | 2.92 | 3.16 | 1.89 | 3.50 | 4.15 | 2.88 | 0.88 |
| Cash Flow | 0.36 | 2.47 | 1.25 | 1.05 | -0.61 | 0.16 | 1.63 | 0.64 | 0.08 | -0.38 |
| Earnings | -0.61 | 1.53 | 0.53 | 0.72 | -1.08 | -20.97 | -65.64 | -19.57 | 0.03 | -0.24 |
| S&P Core Earnings | -0.30 | 1.45 | NA | 0.01 | -1.75 | -8.79 | -35.05 | NA | NA | NA |
| Dividends | Nil | Nil | Nil | Nil | Nil | Nil | Nil | Nil | Nil | Nil |
| Payout Ratio | Nil | Nil | Nil | Nil | Nil | Nil | Nil | Nil | Nil | Nil |
| Prices:High | 41.96 | 26.77 | 33.67 | 36.09 | 17.55 | 39.23 | 97.75 | 258.50 | 212.00 | 19.38 |
| Prices:Low | 22.92 | 15.95 | 19.01 | 14.94 | 6.55 | 3.92 | 26.25 | 65.38 | 13.50 | 3.50 |
| P/E Ratio:High | NM | 17 | 64 | 50 | NM | NM | NM | NM | NM | NM |
| P/E Ratio:Low | NM | 10 | 36 | 21 | NM | NM | NM | NM | NM | NM |

### Income Statement Analysis (Million $)

| | 2007 | 2006 | 2005 | 2004 | 2003 | 2002 | 2001 | 2000 | 1999 | 1998 |
|---|---|---|---|---|---|---|---|---|---|---|
| Revenue | 1,496 | 1,575 | 1,609 | 1,166 | 1,055 | 1,222 | 984 | 475 | 84.8 | 38.9 |
| Operating Income | 309 | 340 | 416 | 242 | 304 | 287 | 277 | 70.0 | 2.09 | -15.6 |
| Depreciation | 231 | 232 | 191 | 85.6 | 114 | 5,000 | 13,687 | 3,217 | 5.40 | 3.95 |
| Interest Expense | 18.3 | Nil | Nil | Nil | Nil | 149 | 20.7 | Nil | Nil | Nil |
| Pretax Income | -130 | 140 | 248 | 214 | -237 | -4,951 | -13,433 | -3,114 | 3.12 | -21.0 |
| Effective Tax Rate | NM | NM | 42.2% | 12.9% | NM | NM | NM | NM | NM | NM |
| Net Income | -145 | 378 | 139 | 186 | -260 | -4,961 | -13,356 | -3,115 | 3.96 | -19.7 |
| S&P Core Earnings | -72.0 | 359 | -1.39 | 2.76 | -421 | -2,080 | -7,134 | NA | NA | NA |

### Balance Sheet & Other Financial Data (Million $)

| | 2007 | 2006 | 2005 | 2004 | 2003 | 2002 | 2001 | 2000 | 1999 | 1998 |
|---|---|---|---|---|---|---|---|---|---|---|
| Cash | 1,378 | 501 | 477 | 331 | 394 | 282 | 306 | 460 | 70.4 | 22.8 |
| Current Assets | 1,750 | 1,332 | 1,228 | 1,006 | 880 | 604 | 1,091 | 1,186 | 183 | 53.7 |
| Total Assets | 4,023 | 3,974 | 3,173 | 2,593 | 2,100 | 2,391 | 7,538 | 19,195 | 341 | 64.3 |
| Current Liabilities | 946 | 1,359 | 938 | 700 | 555 | 665 | 834 | 665 | 42.7 | 22.6 |
| Long Term Debt | 1,265 | Nil | Nil | Nil | Nil | Nil | Nil | Nil | Nil | Nil |
| Common Equity | 1,528 | 2,377 | 2,032 | 1,692 | 1,414 | 1,579 | 6,506 | 18,471 | 299 | 40.7 |
| Total Capital | 2,851 | 2,449 | 2,092 | 1,728 | 1,443 | 1,579 | 6,533 | 18,471 | 299 | 41.7 |
| Capital Expenditures | 152 | 182 | 140 | 92.5 | 108 | 176 | 380 | 58.8 | 6.02 | 4.41 |
| Cash Flow | 85.9 | 609 | 330 | 272 | -145 | 38.9 | 331 | 101 | 9.36 | -15.8 |
| Current Ratio | 1.9 | 1.0 | 1.3 | 1.4 | 1.6 | 0.9 | 1.3 | 1.8 | 4.3 | 2.4 |
| % Long Term Debt of Capitalization | 44.4 | Nil | Nil | Nil | Nil | Nil | Nil | Nil | Nil | Nil |
| % Net Income of Revenue | NM | 24.0 | 8.6 | 16.0 | NM | NM | NM | NM | 4.7 | NM |
| % Return on Assets | NM | 10.6 | 4.8 | 7.9 | NM | NM | NM | NM | 2.0 | NM |
| % Return on Equity | NM | 17.1 | 7.4 | 12.1 | NM | NM | NM | NM | 2.3 | NM |

Data as orig reptd.; bef. results of disc opers/spec. items. Per share data adj. for stk. divs.; EPS diluted. E-Estimated. NA-Not Available. NM-Not Meaningful. NR-Not Ranked. UR-Under Review.

**Office:** 487 East Middlefield Road, Mountain View, CA 94043.
**Telephone:** 650-961-7500.
**Website:** http://www.verisign.com
**Chrmn, Pres & CEO:** D.J. Bidzos

**SVP & CFO:** B.G. Robins
**SVP & Chief Admin Officer:** G.L. Clark
**SVP & CTO:** K. Silva
**SVP, Chief Acctg Officer & Cntlr:** R.D. Sisco

**Investor Contact:** K. Bond (650-426-3744)
**Board Members:** D. J. Bidzos, B. Chenevich, K. A. Cote, R. H. Moore, J. D. Roach, L. A. Simpson, T. Tomlinson

**Founded:** 1995
**Domicile:** Delaware
**Employees:** 4,251

# Verizon Communications Inc

**STANDARD &POOR'S**

**S&P Recommendation** BUY ★★★★☆

| Price | 12-Mo. Target Price | Investment Style |
|---|---|---|
| $30.00 (as of Nov 14, 2008) | $35.00 | Large-Cap Value |

**GICS Sector** Telecommunication Services
**Sub-Industry** Integrated Telecommunication Services

**Summary** VZ offers wireline, wireless and broadband services primarily in the northeastern United States. VZ acquired MCI Inc in 2006 and has since sold or spun off non-core assets. The company announced a wireless deal in June 2008, subject to necessary approvals.

## Key Stock Statistics (Source S&P, Vickers, company reports)

| | | | | | | | |
|---|---|---|---|---|---|---|---|
| 52-Wk Range | $45.71– 23.07 | S&P Oper. EPS 2008E | NA | Market Capitalization(B) | $85.215 | Beta | 0.81 |
| Trailing 12-Month EPS | $2.19 | S&P Oper. EPS 2009E | NA | Yield (%) | 6.13 | S&P 3-Yr. Proj. EPS CAGR(%) | 6 |
| Trailing 12-Month P/E | 13.7 | P/E on S&P Oper. EPS 2008E | null | Dividend Rate/Share | $1.84 | S&P Credit Rating | NR |
| $10K Invested 5 Yrs Ago | NA | Common Shares Outstg. (M) | 2,840.5 | Institutional Ownership (%) | 63 | | |

## Price Performance

30-Week Mov. Avg. ···· 10-Week Mov. Avg. - - GAAP Earnings vs. Previous Year   Volume Above Avg. STARS
12-Mo. Target Price — Relative Strength — ▲ Up ▼ Down ► No Change   Below Avg.

Options: ASE, CBOE, P, Ph

Analysis prepared by **Todd Rosenbluth** on October 28, 2008, when the stock traded at **$ 29.76**.

## Highlights

➤ We see total revenues of $97.6 billion in 2008 and $100.8 billion in 2009, up from $93 billion in 2007, following the exclusion of discontinued non-core assets. Strong 9% wireless revenue growth in 2009, driven by data services, and the penetration of FiOS services should outweigh a decline in the domestic telecom unit's voice revenues, by our analysis. We expect the marketing of FiOS to result in fewer DSL additions. We believe the enterprise segment will improve as a result of contract signings.

➤ We project EBITDA margin expansion to nearly 34% in 2008 and holding steady in 2009, versus 33% in 2007. We forecast operational expense savings in wireline from the integration of back office functions, despite new product rollouts. We believe profitability at the wireless unit will be strong, though somewhat restricted by handset subsidies. Depreciation charges should be higher in 2009.

➤ We see net income being helped by what we expect to be a low tax rate in 2008 and modest share repurchases. Our operating EPS estimates are $2.58 for 2008 and $2.69 for 2009.

## Investment Rationale/Risk

➤ We think VZ's results and its recently announced dividend hike indicate that the economic slowdown has had a limited impact on its business. On the wireless side, following a strong third quarter, we believe customer additions will remain ahead of peers and see the proposed acquisition of Alltel, subject to necessary approvals, as providing both benefits and risks. While consumer wireline appears to us to be weakening, we see fiber promotions as a partial offset. We believe VZ's dividend is secure.

➤ Risks to our recommendation and target price include a greater impact of a slowing economy, pricing pressures, enterprise customer migration, a weaker balance sheet, and the cost of and level of success of fiber-based services.

➤ Our blended 12-month target price of $35 is based on a P/E multiple of 12.5X, and an enterprise value/EBITDA multiple of 5X, our 2009 estimates, slight premiums to peers based on stronger growth. VZ's 6% dividend yield adds support to the shares, in our view. At a P/E of 11X, VZ recently traded at the low end of its historical range.

## Qualitative Risk Assessment

| LOW | MEDIUM | HIGH |
|---|---|---|

Our risk assessment reflects our view of VZ's strong cash flow generation and the pricing power it has over its suppliers, offset by the competitive landscape it faces offering telecom services.

## Quantitative Evaluations

**S&P Quality Ranking**   B

| D | C | B- | B | B+ | A- | A | A+ |
|---|---|---|---|---|---|---|---|

**Relative Strength Rank**   STRONG   85

LOWEST = 1   HIGHEST = 99

## Revenue/Earnings Data

**Revenue (Million $)**

| | 1Q | 2Q | 3Q | 4Q | Year |
|---|---|---|---|---|---|
| 2008 | 23,833 | 24,124 | 24,752 | -- | -- |
| 2007 | 22,584 | 23,273 | 23,772 | 23,840 | 93,469 |
| 2006 | 21,221 | 21,876 | 22,449 | 22,598 | 88,144 |
| 2005 | 18,179 | 18,569 | 19,038 | 19,326 | 75,112 |
| 2004 | 17,056 | 17,758 | 18,206 | 18,263 | 71,283 |
| 2003 | 16,490 | 16,829 | 17,155 | 17,278 | 67,752 |

**Earnings Per Share ($)**

| | | | | | |
|---|---|---|---|---|---|
| 2008 | 0.57 | 0.65 | 0.59 | E0.65 | E2.58 |
| 2007 | 0.51 | 0.58 | 0.44 | 0.37 | 1.90 |
| 2006 | 0.57 | 0.43 | 0.53 | 0.48 | 1.87 |
| 2005 | 0.63 | 0.75 | 0.67 | 0.59 | 2.65 |
| 2004 | 0.42 | 0.64 | 0.64 | 0.90 | 2.59 |
| 2003 | 0.63 | 0.46 | 0.64 | -0.53 | 1.27 |

Fiscal year ended Dec. 31. Next earnings report expected: Late January. EPS Estimates based on S&P Operating Earnings; historical GAAP earnings are as reported.

## Dividend Data (Dates: mm/dd Payment Date: mm/dd/yy)

| Amount ($) | Date Decl. | Ex-Div. Date | Stk. of Record | Payment Date |
|---|---|---|---|---|
| Stk. | 02/27 | 04/01 | 03/07 | 03/31/08 |
| 0.430 | 03/17 | 04/08 | 04/10 | 05/01/08 |
| 0.430 | 06/05 | 07/08 | 07/10 | 08/01/08 |
| 0.460 | 09/04 | 10/08 | 10/10 | 11/03/08 |

Dividends have been paid since 1984. Source: Company reports.

# Verizon Communications Inc

## Business Summary October 28, 2008

CORPORATE OVERVIEW. As of September 2008, Verizon Communications (VZ) provided wireline service to 37 million access lines (down 9% from a year earlier), and, through its joint venture with the Vodafone Group, was the second-largest wireless carrier, with 70.8 million wireless customers (up 11%). In 2006, VZ completed its $8.5 billion acquisition of MCI Inc., adding consumer long distance operations and telecom services targeted to government and medium and large enterprise customers. In late 2006, Verizon spun off its directory operations and sold its Dominican Republic operations. At the end of March 2008, VZ completed the spin-off of 1.4 million access lines in New England, which were subsequently merged with Fairpoint Communications (FRP). The New England operations generated $1.2 billion in revenues during 2007. During the third quarter of 2008, Verizon Wireless acquired Rural Cellular Corp.

In June 2008, Verizon Wireless announced plans to acquire privately held Alltel for $28 billion ($22 billion debt), subject to necessary approvals that it expects by the end of 2008. Alltel had 13 million CDMA subscribers and generated nearly $8 billion in 2007 service revenues (39% EBITDA margin). VZ believes the deal will generate $1 billion in operating and capital expense synergies in 2009, which we think could prove conservative, but we see financing risks due to a tight credit market.

MARKET PROFILE. In the first nine months of 2008, Verizon Wireless added 5 million net subscribers (including 650,000 from acquisitions) and, together with peer AT&T, continued to capture market share. Strong wireless rivalry has raised the level of competition, in our view, with new service plans and data services. As of September 2008, Verizon Wireless had a better-than-average 1.3% monthly churn rate, and more than 41 million customers were utilizing its data services. Wireless data average revenue per user rose 43% in the third quarter of 2008 and comprised 26% of service revenues. First nine months 2008 EBITDA service margin of 45% for Verizon Wireless was the best in the industry.

Similar to its telecom peers, Verizon serves the Internet market through its broadband offerings (8.5 million connections) and has lowered prices and increased the speed of its connectivity in what we view as an effort to upgrade dial-up customers. However, thus far in 2008, traditional DSL customer growth has slowed.

## Company Financials Fiscal Year Ended Dec. 31

| Per Share Data ($) | 2009 | 2008 | 2007 | 2006 | 2005 | 2004 | 2003 | 2002 | 2001 | 2000 |
|---|---|---|---|---|---|---|---|---|---|---|
| Tangible Book Value | NA | NA | NM | NM | NM | NM | NM | NM | NM | 12.79 |
| Cash Flow | NA | NA | 6.85 | 1.87 | 7.61 | 7.67 | 6.14 | 6.56 | 5.22 | 8.43 |
| Earnings | 2.69 | NA | 1.90 | 1.87 | 2.65 | 2.59 | 1.27 | 1.67 | 0.22 | 3.95 |
| S&P Core Earnings | NA | NA | 1.85 | 1.87 | 2.42 | 2.76 | 1.76 | 1.91 | 0.58 | NA |
| Dividends | NA | NA | 1.65 | 1.62 | 1.60 | 1.54 | 1.54 | 1.54 | 1.54 | 1.54 |
| Payout Ratio | NA | NA | 88% | 86% | 60% | 60% | 121% | 92% | NM | 39% |
| Prices:High | NA | NA | 46.24 | 38.95 | 41.06 | 42.27 | 44.31 | 51.09 | 57.40 | 66.00 |
| Prices:Low | NA | NA | 35.60 | 30.04 | 29.13 | 34.13 | 31.10 | 26.01 | 43.80 | 39.06 |
| P/E Ratio:High | NA | NA | 25 | 21 | 15 | 16 | 35 | 31 | NM | 17 |
| P/E Ratio:Low | NA | NA | 19 | 16 | 11 | 13 | 24 | 16 | NM | 10 |

| Income Statement Analysis (Million $) | | | | | | | | | | |
|---|---|---|---|---|---|---|---|---|---|---|
| Revenue | NA | NA | 93,469 | 88,144 | 75,112 | 71,283 | 67,752 | 67,625 | 67,190 | 64,707 |
| Depreciation | NA | NA | 14,377 | 14,545 | 14,047 | 13,910 | 13,617 | 13,423 | 13,657 | 12,261 |
| Maintenance | NA | NA | NA | NA | NA | NA | NA | NA | NA | NA |
| Construction Credits | NA | NA | NA | NA | NA | NA | NA | NA | NA | NA |
| Effective Tax Rate | NA | NA | 27.4% | 21.9% | 23.5% | 22.8% | 19.7% | 21.7% | 64.2% | 38.9% |
| Net Income | NA | NA | 5,510 | 5,480 | 7,397 | 7,261 | 3,509 | 4,584 | 590 | 10,810 |
| S&P Core Earnings | NA | NA | 5,370 | 5,467 | 6,774 | 7,724 | 4,859 | 5,250 | 1,557 | NA |

| Balance Sheet & Other Financial Data (Million $) | | | | | | | | | | |
|---|---|---|---|---|---|---|---|---|---|---|
| Gross Property | NA | NA | 213,994 | 204,109 | 193,610 | 185,522 | 180,975 | 178,028 | 169,586 | 158,957 |
| Net Property | NA | NA | 85,294 | 82,356 | 75,305 | 74,124 | 75,316 | 74,496 | 74,419 | 69,504 |
| Capital Expenditures | NA | NA | 17,538 | 17,101 | 15,324 | 13,259 | 11,884 | 11,984 | 17,371 | 17,633 |
| Total Capital | NA | NA | 125,856 | 121,788 | 120,714 | 120,819 | 118,935 | 122,120 | 116,888 | 115,923 |
| Fixed Charges Coverage | NA | NA | 8.6 | 5.9 | 6.7 | 5.1 | 2.5 | 5.5 | 3.6 | 3.7 |
| Capitalization:Long Term Debt | NA | NA | 28,203 | 28,646 | 31,869 | 35,674 | 39,413 | 44,791 | 45,657 | 42,491 |
| Capitalization:Preferred | NA | NA | Nil | Nil | Nil | Nil | Nil | Nil | Nil | Nil |
| Capitalization:Common | NA | NA | 50,581 | 48,535 | 39,680 | 37,560 | 33,466 | 33,720 | 32,539 | 36,342 |
| % Return on Revenue | NA | NA | 5.9 | 6.2 | 9.8 | 10.2 | 5.2 | 6.8 | 0.9 | 16.7 |
| % Return on Invested Capital | NA | NA | 9.5 | 9.8 | 10.5 | 8.6 | 5.1 | 7.6 | 4.0 | 15.4 |
| % Return on Common Equity | NA | NA | 11.1 | 12.4 | 19.2 | 20.4 | 10.6 | 13.5 | 1.8 | 33.5 |
| % Earned on Net Property | NA | NA | 18.6 | 17.2 | 37.9 | 36.2 | 28.1 | 34.5 | 50.5 | 38.3 |
| % Long Term Debt of Capitalization | NA | NA | 35.8 | 37.1 | 44.5 | 48.7 | 54.1 | 36.6 | 58.4 | 53.9 |
| Capital % Preferred | NA | NA | Nil | Nil | Nil | Nil | Nil | Nil | Nil | Nil |
| Capitalization:% Common | NA | NA | 64.2 | 62.9 | 55.5 | 51.3 | 45.9 | 42.9 | 41.6 | 46.1 |

Data as orig reptd.; bef. results of disc opers/spec. items. Per share data adj. for stk. divs.; EPS diluted. E-Estimated. NA-Not Available. NM-Not Meaningful. NR-Not Ranked. UR-Under Review.

Office: 1095 Avenue of the Americas, New York, NY 10036.
Telephone: 212-395-2121.
Website: http://www.verizon.com
Chrmn & CEO: I.G. Seidenberg

Pres: W.E. Huyard
Pres & COO: D.F. Strigl
EVP & CFO: D.A. Toben
EVP & CTO: R.J. Lynch

Investor Contact: C. Webster (212-395-1000)
Board Members: R. Carrion, M. F. Keeth, R. W. Lane, S. O. Moose, J. Neubauer, D. Nicolaisen, T. H. O'Brien, Jr., C. Otis, Jr., H. B. Price, I. G. Seidenberg, J. W. Snow, J. R. Stafford

Founded: 1983
Domicile: Delaware
Employees: 234,971

# V.F. Corp

**STANDARD &POOR'S**

| S&P Recommendation | BUY ★★★★☆ | Price $47.20 (as of Nov 14, 2008) | 12-Mo. Target Price $82.00 | Investment Style Large-Cap Blend |
|---|---|---|---|---|

**GICS Sector** Consumer Discretionary
**Sub-Industry** Apparel, Accessories & Luxury Goods

**Summary** This global apparel company with leading shares in denim and daypacks is transforming into a designer and marketer of lifestyle apparel brands.

## Key Stock Statistics (Source S&P, Vickers, company reports)

| | | | | | | | | |
|---|---|---|---|---|---|---|---|---|
| 52-Wk Range | $84.60– 44.25 | S&P Oper. EPS 2008E | 5.85 | Market Capitalization(B) | $5.196 | Beta | 0.65 |
| Trailing 12-Month EPS | $5.83 | S&P Oper. EPS 2009E | 5.95 | Yield (%) | 5.00 | S&P 3-Yr. Proj. EPS CAGR(%) | 8 |
| Trailing 12-Month P/E | 8.1 | P/E on S&P Oper. EPS 2008E | 8.1 | Dividend Rate/Share | $2.36 | S&P Credit Rating | A- |
| $10K Invested 5 Yrs Ago | $12,764 | Common Shares Outstg. (M) | 110.1 | Institutional Ownership (%) | 92 | | |

## Price Performance

30-Week Mov. Avg. ···· 10-Week Mov. Avg. ── GAAP Earnings vs. Previous Year  Volume Above Avg. STARS
12-Mo. Target Price ── Relative Strength ── ▲ Up ▼ Down ▶ No Change  Below Avg.

Options: CBOE

Analysis prepared by **Marie Driscoll, CFA** on November 03, 2008, when the stock traded at **$ 54.85**.

## Highlights

➤ We look for about 8% consolidated sales growth in 2008, a combination of organic growth and recent acquisitions. We see double digit gains in VFC's lifestyle brands and low single digit increases in its denim, sportswear and imagewear businesses. 7 for All Mankind and lucy activewear (part of the newly created Contemporary Brands coalition) are projected to generate $400+ million in 2008 as VFC executes on brand extensions and store expansion. We believe increased market penetration will benefit VFC's international jeanswear and Vans businesses. We look for sales growth to slow to a 4% pace in 2009 reflecting global economic weakness.

➤ We project a flat EBIT margin in 2008 and 2009, at 13.5%. We see a more favorable sales mix, sourcing benefits and accretive 2007 acquisitions offset by increases in marketing spending to support VFC's lifestyle brands.

➤ We estimate EPS of $5.85 and $5.95 in 2008 and 2009, respectively.

## Investment Rationale/Risk

➤ We believe that a number of VFC's recent acquisitions have superior growth potential, as does further penetration of the international market. Given our view of VFC's executive acumen, we anticipate market share gains and improving profitability and regard its long-term goals of $11 billion in sales and a 15% operating margin in 2012 as achievable. VFC continues to seek lifestyle brand acquisitions to add to its portfolio. Despite its maturity, we think that VFC's denim business provides steady low single digit growth while generating substantial cash flow and profits that VFC can employ at faster-growing lifestyle brands with superior ROI opportunities. VFC ended 2007 in what we view as strong financial condition: $322 million in cash and a debt-to-total capital ratio of 26%.

➤ Risks to our recommendation and target price include fashion and inventory risk, and integration risk from recent acquisitions.

➤ Our 12-month target price of $82 is about 14X our 2009 EPS estimate of $5.95, a modest premium to the 12X forward multiple of VFC's apparel and footwear peers. The dividend has more than doubled since 2005, and recently yielded about 4.3%.

## Qualitative Risk Assessment

| LOW | MEDIUM | HIGH |
|---|---|---|

Our risk assessment reflects our view of VFC's strong cash flow, offset by integration risk as VFC pursues growth via acquisitions.

## Quantitative Evaluations

**S&P Quality Ranking**   A-

| D | C | B- | B | B+ | A- | A | A+ |
|---|---|---|---|---|---|---|---|

**Relative Strength Rank**   MODERATE
42
LOWEST = 1          HIGHEST = 99

## Revenue/Earnings Data

**Revenue (Million $)**

| | 1Q | 2Q | 3Q | 4Q | Year |
|---|---|---|---|---|---|
| 2008 | 1,846 | 1,677 | 2,207 | -- | -- |
| 2007 | 1,674 | 1,517 | 2,073 | 1,955 | 7,219 |
| 2006 | 1,456 | 1,351 | 1,810 | 1,599 | 6,216 |
| 2005 | 1,582 | 1,452 | 1,822 | 1,646 | 6,502 |
| 2004 | 1,433 | 1,270 | 1,793 | 1,560 | 6,055 |
| 2003 | 1,250 | 1,135 | 1,435 | 1,387 | 5,207 |

**Earnings Per Share ($)**

| | 1Q | 2Q | 3Q | 4Q | Year |
|---|---|---|---|---|---|
| 2008 | 1.33 | 0.94 | 2.10 | E1.55 | E5.85 |
| 2007 | 1.17 | 0.93 | 1.86 | 1.46 | 5.41 |
| 2006 | 1.05 | 0.80 | 1.64 | 1.24 | 4.73 |
| 2005 | 1.00 | 0.85 | 1.57 | 1.13 | 4.54 |
| 2004 | 0.93 | 0.80 | 1.38 | 1.10 | 4.21 |
| 2003 | 0.83 | 0.68 | 1.14 | 0.96 | 3.61 |

Fiscal year ended Dec. 31. Next earnings report expected: Early February. EPS Estimates based on S&P Operating Earnings; historical GAAP earnings are as reported.

## Dividend Data (Dates: mm/dd Payment Date: mm/dd/yy)

| Amount ($) | Date Decl. | Ex-Div. Date | Stk. of Record | Payment Date |
|---|---|---|---|---|
| 0.580 | 02/05 | 03/06 | 03/10 | 03/20/08 |
| 0.580 | 04/22 | 06/06 | 06/10 | 06/20/08 |
| 0.580 | 07/15 | 09/05 | 09/09 | 09/19/08 |
| 0.590 | 10/17 | 12/05 | 12/09 | 12/19/08 |

Dividends have been paid since 1941. Source: Company reports.

# V.F. Corp

**STANDARD &POOR'S**

## Business Summary November 03, 2008

CORPORATE OVERVIEW. VF Corp. is the world's largest apparel manufacturer, and holds the leading position in several market categories, including jean-swear, workwear and daypacks. In early 2004, VFC developed a growth plan to support its long-term sales growth target of 8% annually, its 14% operating margin goal, and a 17% return on invested capital goal. The growth strategy consists of six drivers: building new, growing lifestyle brands; expanding share with successful retailers; growing internationally; leveraging supply chain and information technology; identifying, developing and recruiting qualified leaders; and expanding its direct to consumer business.

MARKET PROFILE. VFC participates in the broad apparel market, spanning product categories from women's activewear to denim, as well as the outdoor market for apparel and accessories via its lifestyle brands. Apparel is a mature market, with demand mirroring population growth and a modicum related to fashion; it is fragmented, with national brands marketed by 20 companies accounting for about 30% of total apparel sales and the remaining 70% comprised of smaller and/or private label "store" brands. Deflationary pricing pressure is, we think, a function of channel competition and production steadily moving offshore to low-cost producers in Asia, especially India and China. S&P forecasts a low single digit increase in 2008 apparel sales, generally in line with GDP growth. In 2007, apparel sales rose 3%, and the category expanded at a 4% annual pace in the 2004-2006 period.

The SGMA (Sporting Goods Manufacturers Association) estimates sports apparel equipment and sportswear wholesale revenues of $69.6 billion in 2008, up 1.5%, after rising 3% in 2007. Apparel represents about 43% of the mix, footwear 19%, and equipment 38%. Sports apparel and footwear brands more frequently serve a fashion market than a true athletic or active sports market; generally only a third of sports apparel and footwear is purchased with the intent that it will be used in an active sport, according to the NPD Group.

## Company Financials  Fiscal Year Ended Dec. 31

### Per Share Data ($)

| | 2007 | 2006 | 2005 | 2004 | 2003 | 2002 | 2001 | 2000 | 1999 | 1998 |
|---|---|---|---|---|---|---|---|---|---|---|
| Tangible Book Value | 7.86 | 13.18 | 8.78 | 7.56 | 8.61 | 10.91 | 9.97 | 9.71 | 10.08 | 9.36 |
| Cash Flow | 6.48 | 5.74 | 5.56 | 5.53 | 4.64 | 4.35 | 0.00 | 3.73 | 5.71 | 4.39 |
| Earnings | 5.41 | 4.73 | 4.54 | 4.21 | 3.61 | 3.24 | 1.19 | 2.27 | 2.99 | 3.10 |
| S&P Core Earnings | 5.31 | 4.82 | 4.67 | 4.36 | 3.70 | 2.75 | 0.77 | NA | NA | NA |
| Dividends | 2.23 | 1.94 | 1.10 | 1.05 | 1.01 | 0.97 | 0.93 | 0.89 | 0.85 | 0.81 |
| Payout Ratio | 41% | 41% | 24% | 25% | 28% | 30% | 78% | 39% | 28% | 26% |
| Prices:High | 96.20 | 83.10 | 61.61 | 55.61 | 44.08 | 45.64 | 42.70 | 36.90 | 55.00 | 54.69 |
| Prices:Low | 68.15 | 53.25 | 50.44 | 42.06 | 32.62 | 31.50 | 28.15 | 20.94 | 27.44 | 33.44 |
| P/E Ratio:High | 18 | 18 | 14 | 13 | 12 | 14 | 36 | 16 | 18 | 18 |
| P/E Ratio:Low | 13 | 11 | 11 | 10 | 9 | 10 | 24 | 9 | 9 | 11 |

### Income Statement Analysis (Million $)

| | 2007 | 2006 | 2005 | 2004 | 2003 | 2002 | 2001 | 2000 | 1999 | 1998 |
|---|---|---|---|---|---|---|---|---|---|---|
| Revenue | 7,219 | 6,216 | 6,502 | 6,055 | 5,207 | 5,084 | 5,519 | 5,748 | 5,552 | 5,479 |
| Operating Income | 1,081 | 935 | 944 | 874 | 718 | 729 | 516 | 683 | 820 | 845 |
| Depreciation | 122 | 108 | 116 | 141 | 104 | 107 | 169 | 173 | 335 | 161 |
| Interest Expense | 72.1 | 57.3 | 70.6 | 76.1 | 61.4 | 71.3 | 93.4 | 88.7 | 71.4 | 62.0 |
| Pretax Income | 906 | 777 | 771 | 712 | 599 | 562 | 263 | 432 | 596 | 631 |
| Effective Tax Rate | 32.3% | 31.2% | 32.7% | 33.3% | 33.5% | 35.1% | 47.6% | 38.1% | 38.5% | 38.5% |
| Net Income | 613 | 535 | 519 | 475 | 398 | 364 | 138 | 267 | 366 | 388 |
| S&P Core Earnings | 602 | 544 | 532 | 490 | 406 | 303 | 84.6 | NA | NA | NA |

### Balance Sheet & Other Financial Data (Million $)

| | 2007 | 2006 | 2005 | 2004 | 2003 | 2002 | 2001 | 2000 | 1999 | 1998 |
|---|---|---|---|---|---|---|---|---|---|---|
| Cash | 322 | 343 | 297 | 486 | 515 | 496 | 332 | 119 | 79.9 | 63.0 |
| Current Assets | 2,645 | 2,578 | 2,365 | 2,379 | 2,209 | 2,075 | 2,031 | 2,110 | 1,877 | 1,848 |
| Total Assets | 6,447 | 5,466 | 5,171 | 5,004 | 4,246 | 3,503 | 4,103 | 4,358 | 4,027 | 3,837 |
| Current Liabilities | 1,134 | 1,015 | 1,152 | 1,372 | 872 | 875 | 814 | 1,006 | 1,113 | 1,033 |
| Long Term Debt | 1,145 | 635 | 648 | 557 | 956 | 602 | 904 | 905 | 518 | 522 |
| Common Equity | 3,577 | 3,265 | 2,808 | 2,513 | 1,951 | 1,658 | 2,113 | 2,192 | 2,164 | 2,046 |
| Total Capital | 4,722 | 3,901 | 3,479 | 3,096 | 2,938 | 2,297 | 3,062 | 3,145 | 2,733 | 2,622 |
| Capital Expenditures | 114 | 127 | 110 | 81.4 | 86.6 | 64.5 | 81.6 | 125 | 150 | 189 |
| Cash Flow | 735 | 643 | 635 | 615 | 502 | 472 | 304 | 437 | 698 | 549 |
| Current Ratio | 2.3 | 2.5 | 2.1 | 1.7 | 2.5 | 2.4 | 2.5 | 2.1 | 1.7 | 1.8 |
| % Long Term Debt of Capitalization | 24.2 | 16.3 | 18.6 | 18.0 | 32.6 | 26.2 | 29.5 | 28.8 | 18.9 | 19.9 |
| % Net Income of Revenue | 8.5 | 8.6 | 7.9 | 7.8 | 7.6 | 7.2 | 2.5 | 4.6 | 6.6 | 7.1 |
| % Return on Assets | 10.3 | 10.1 | 10.2 | 10.3 | 10.3 | 9.6 | 3.3 | 6.4 | 9.3 | 10.8 |
| % Return on Equity | 17.9 | 17.6 | 19.5 | 21.3 | 22.1 | 19.3 | 6.3 | 12.1 | 17.1 | 20.0 |

Data as orig reptd.; bef. results of disc opers/spec. items. Per share data adj. for stk. divs.; EPS diluted. E-Estimated. NA-Not Available. NM-Not Meaningful. NR-Not Ranked. UR-Under Review.

**Office:** 105 Corporate Center Boulevard , Greensboro, NC 27408.
**Telephone:** 336-424-6000.
**Email:** irrequest@vfc.com
**Website:** http://www.vfc.com

**Chrmn, Pres & CEO:** E.C. Wiseman
**SVP & CFO:** R.K. Shearer
**Chief Admin Officer, Secy & General Counsel:** C.S. Cummings
**Chief Acctg Officer & Cntlr:** B.W. Batten

**Treas:** F.C. Pickard, III
**Investor Contact:** C. Knoebel (336-424-6189)
**Board Members:** C. V. Bergh, E. E. Crutchfield, U. F. Fairbairn, B. S. Feigin, G. Fellows, R. J. Hurst, W. A. McCollough, C. Otis, Jr., M. R. Sharp, R. Viault, E. C. Wiseman, J. E. de Bedout

**Founded:** 1899
**Domicile:** Pennsylvania
**Employees:** 54,200

**STANDARD &POOR'S**

# Viacom Inc

| S&P Recommendation | STRONG SELL ★☆☆☆☆ | Price $16.78 (as of Nov 14, 2008) | 12-Mo. Target Price $12.00 | Investment Style Large-Cap Blend |
|---|---|---|---|---|

**GICS Sector** Consumer Discretionary
**Sub-Industry** Movies & Entertainment

**Summary** Among the key brands of this entertainment content provider, one of the two companies that emerged after the January 2006 split of "old" Viacom into two companies, are MTV Networks and Paramount Pictures (which acquired DreamWorks studios).

## Key Stock Statistics (Source S&P, Vickers, company reports)

| | | | | | | | |
|---|---|---|---|---|---|---|---|
| 52-Wk Range | $45.40– 14.51 | S&P Oper. EPS 2008**E** | 2.51 | Market Capitalization(B) | $9.332 | Beta | 1.25 |
| Trailing 12-Month EPS | $2.58 | S&P Oper. EPS 2009**E** | 2.85 | Yield (%) | Nil | S&P 3-Yr. Proj. EPS CAGR(%) | 12 |
| Trailing 12-Month P/E | 6.5 | P/E on S&P Oper. EPS 2008**E** | 6.7 | Dividend Rate/Share | Nil | S&P Credit Rating | NA |
| $10K Invested 5 Yrs Ago | NA | Common Shares Outstg. (M) | 613.5 | Institutional Ownership (%) | 83 | | |

## Price Performance

30-Week Mov. Avg. · · · 10-Week Mov. Avg. – – **GAAP Earnings vs. Previous Year** Volume Above Avg. STARS
12-Mo. Target Price — Relative Strength — ▲ Up ▼ Down ► No Change Below Avg. ★

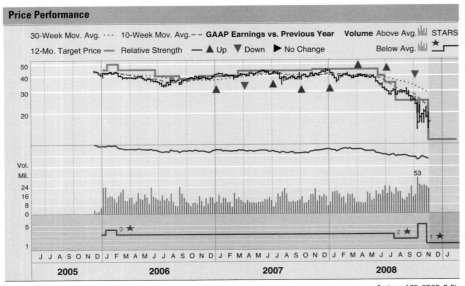

Options: ASE, CBOE, P, Ph

## Highlights

► The STARS recommendation for VIA.B has recently been changed to 1 (strong sell) from 5 (strong buy) and the 12-month target price has recently been changed to $12.00 from $25.00. The Highlights section of this Stock Report will be updated accordingly.

## Investment Rationale/Risk

► The Investment Rationale/Risk section of this Stock Report will be updated shortly. For the latest News story on VIA.B from MarketScope, see below.

► 11/12/08 03:03 pm ET ... S&P REDUCES OPINION ON VIACOM CLASS B SHARES TO STRONG SELL FROM STRONG BUY (VIA.B 15.49*): While Chairman Sumner Redstone recently ruled out further sales of VIA.B shares amid talks on debt refi by National Amusements, his controlling vehicle, we see overhang exacerbated by VIA.B price action, potentially complicated by resignation of daughter, Shari Redstone, as Chairman of NAI-affiliated Midway Games (MWY 0.24, NR). We see near-term selling pressure, given uncertain outcome of debt talks, potentially including further sales by Redstone, and key asset divestitures at possible fire-sale valuations. With ad picture weak, we cut PEG-based target price by $13 to $12. /T. Amobi - CPA, CFA

## Qualitative Risk Assessment

| LOW | MEDIUM | HIGH |
|---|---|---|

Our risk assessment of this pure content player reflects what we view as its leading demographically targeted brands, relatively strong growth prospects and ample financial flexibility, offset by exposure to cyclical advertising and a highly volatile filmed entertainment business.

## Quantitative Evaluations

**S&P Quality Ranking** NR

| D | C | B- | B | B+ | A- | A | A+ |
|---|---|---|---|---|---|---|---|

**Relative Strength Rank** MODERATE

42

LOWEST = 1     HIGHEST = 99

## Revenue/Earnings Data

**Revenue (Million $)**

| | 1Q | 2Q | 3Q | 4Q | Year |
|---|---|---|---|---|---|
| 2008 | 3,117 | 3,857 | 3,408 | -- | -- |
| 2007 | 2,746 | 3,186 | 3,271 | 4,248 | 13,423 |
| 2006 | 2,368 | 2,847 | 2,660 | 3,593 | 11,467 |
| 2005 | 2,107 | 2,302 | 2,478 | 2,724 | 9,610 |
| 2004 | -- | -- | -- | -- | 8,132 |
| 2003 | -- | -- | -- | -- | -- |

**Earnings Per Share ($)**

| | | | | | |
|---|---|---|---|---|---|
| 2008 | 0.42 | 0.64 | 0.62 | E0.89 | E2.51 |
| 2007 | 0.29 | 0.63 | 0.67 | 0.84 | 2.41 |
| 2006 | 0.43 | 0.58 | 0.50 | 0.69 | 2.19 |
| 2005 | -- | -- | -- | 0.29 | 1.73 |
| 2004 | -- | -- | -- | -- | 1.48 |
| 2003 | -- | -- | -- | -- | -- |

Fiscal year ended Dec. 31. Next earnings report expected: Early March. EPS Estimates based on S&P Operating Earnings; historical GAAP earnings are as reported.

## Dividend Data

No cash dividends have been paid.

# Viacom Inc

**STANDARD &POOR'S**

## Business Summary November 04, 2008

CORPORATE OVERVIEW. In its present form, the "new" Viacom is one of the two public companies created after the January 2006 separation of the "old" Viacom into two independent public entities (the "old" Viacom was renamed CBS Corp.). Each Class A and B shareholder of the "old" Viacom received 0.5 of a share of the corresponding A or B stock of each of the new entities. We believe that the company is the faster growing of the two companies resulting from the separation, and is specifically targeted to growth-oriented investors.

The company's media networks segment (60% of 2007 revenues) is mainly comprised of MTV Networks (including MTV, Nickelodeon, VH1, Comedy Central, Country Music Television, Spike TV, TV Land, Logo, Neopets, Xfire and VIVA) and BET Networks. The entertainment segment (37%) includes Paramount Pictures film studio (and home entertainment) and Famous Music (publishing). About 35% of 2007 revenues were derived from ad sales, 27% from affiliate fees, 29% from feature films, and 9% from other ancillary sources (including merchandise licensing).

CORPORATE STRATEGY. We see various digital initiatives, aided by partnerships with Internet and technology companies, such as pacts with Microsoft, Yahoo, Comcast/Fancast, AOL, Bebo, Dailymotion, Veoh, GoFish, and MeeVee. Since the start of 2006, the company has made selective digital acquisitions (mostly in online gaming and films), including Xfire, Y2M, Atom Entertainment, Harmonic Music and Quizilla. The company's global footprint traverses Europe and emerging markets (India and China), with nearly 130 channels (including MTV channels) across 169 territories in 28 languages, reaching nearly 450 million homes. The company recently had about 300 web sites, and launched a social networking site called Flux.

## Company Financials Fiscal Year Ended Dec. 31

| Per Share Data ($) | 2007 | 2006 | 2005 | 2004 | 2003 | 2002 | 2001 | 2000 | 1999 | 1998 |
|---|---|---|---|---|---|---|---|---|---|---|
| Tangible Book Value | NM | NM | NM | NM | NA | NA | NA | NA | NA | NA |
| Cash Flow | 2.99 | 2.70 | 2.08 | 1.78 | NA | NA | NA | NA | NA | NA |
| Earnings | 2.41 | 2.19 | 1.73 | 1.48 | NA | NA | NA | NA | NA | NA |
| S&P Core Earnings | 2.34 | 2.22 | 1.46 | 1.47 | NA | NA | NA | NA | NA | NA |
| Dividends | Nil | Nil | Nil | NA | NA | NA | NA | NA | NA | NA |
| Payout Ratio | Nil | Nil | Nil | NA | NA | NA | NA | NA | NA | NA |
| Prices:High | 45.40 | 43.90 | 44.95 | NA | NA | NA | NA | NA | NA | NA |
| Prices:Low | 33.74 | 32.42 | 39.78 | NA | NA | NA | NA | NA | NA | NA |
| P/E Ratio:High | 19 | 20 | 26 | NA | NA | NA | NA | NA | NA | NA |
| P/E Ratio:Low | 14 | 15 | 23 | NA | NA | NA | NA | NA | NA | NA |

### Income Statement Analysis (Million $)

| | 2007 | 2006 | 2005 | 2004 | 2003 | 2002 | 2001 | 2000 | 1999 | 1998 |
|---|---|---|---|---|---|---|---|---|---|---|
| Revenue | 13,423 | 11,467 | 9,610 | 8,132 | 7,304 | 6,051 | NA | NA | NA | NA |
| Operating Income | 3,404 | 3,137 | 2,625 | 2,534 | NA | NA | NA | NA | NA | NA |
| Depreciation | 393 | 366 | 259 | 2,522 | 198 | 195 | NA | NA | NA | NA |
| Interest Expense | 487 | 472 | 23.0 | 20.0 | NA | NA | NA | NA | NA | NA |
| Pretax Income | 2,579 | 2,322 | 2,328 | 2,017 | 1,938 | 1,641 | NA | NA | NA | NA |
| Effective Tax Rate | 36.0% | 31.8% | 43.8% | 36.4% | 40.6% | 39.3% | NA | NA | NA | NA |
| Net Income | 1,630 | 1,570 | 1,304 | 1,281 | 1,147 | 994 | NA | NA | NA | NA |
| S&P Core Earnings | 1,588 | 1,592 | 1,165 | 1,282 | NA | NA | NA | NA | NA | NA |

### Balance Sheet & Other Financial Data (Million $)

| | 2007 | 2006 | 2005 | 2004 | 2003 | 2002 | 2001 | 2000 | 1999 | 1998 |
|---|---|---|---|---|---|---|---|---|---|---|
| Cash | 920 | 706 | 361 | 99.2 | 58.3 | NA | NA | NA | NA | NA |
| Current Assets | 4,833 | 4,211 | 3,513 | 2,384 | NA | NA | NA | NA | NA | NA |
| Total Assets | 22,904 | 21,797 | 19,116 | 18,400 | 22,304 | NA | NA | NA | NA | NA |
| Current Liabilities | 5,273 | 4,617 | 3,269 | 2,617 | NA | NA | NA | NA | NA | NA |
| Long Term Debt | 8,060 | 7,584 | 5,702 | 3,718 | NA | NA | NA | NA | NA | NA |
| Common Equity | 7,111 | 7,166 | 7,788 | 9,905 | 15,816 | NA | NA | NA | NA | NA |
| Total Capital | 15,312 | 14,932 | 13,534 | 13,623 | NA | NA | NA | NA | NA | NA |
| Capital Expenditures | 237 | 210 | 193 | NA | 114 | 122 | NA | NA | NA | NA |
| Cash Flow | 2,023 | 1,936 | 1,563 | 1,533 | NA | NA | NA | NA | NA | NA |
| Current Ratio | 0.9 | 0.9 | 1.1 | 0.9 | 0.9 | NA | NA | NA | NA | NA |
| % Long Term Debt of Capitalization | 52.6 | 50.8 | 42.1 | 27.3 | Nil | Nil | NA | NA | NA | NA |
| % Net Income of Revenue | 12.2 | 13.7 | 13.6 | 15.8 | 15.7 | 16.4 | NA | NA | NA | NA |
| % Return on Assets | 7.3 | 7.7 | 6.9 | NA | NA | NA | NA | NA | NA | NA |
| % Return on Equity | 22.8 | 21.0 | 12.3 | NA | NA | NA | NA | NA | NA | NA |

Data as orig reptd.; bef. results of disc opers/spec. items. Per share data adj. for stk. divs.; EPS diluted. E-Estimated. NA-Not Available. NM-Not Meaningful. NR-Not Ranked. UR-Under Review.

**Office:** 1515 Broadway, New York, NY 10036-5794.
**Telephone:** 212-258-6000.
**Website:** http://www.viacom.com
**Chrmn:** S.M. Redstone

**Pres & CEO:** P.P. Dauman
**Vice Chrmn:** S.E. Redstone
**COO & EVP:** R.M. Bakish
**EVP, CFO & Chief Admin Officer:** T. Dooley

**Investor Contact:** J. Bombassei (212-258-6700)
**Board Members:** G. S. Abrams, P. P. Dauman, T. Dooley, A. C. Greenberg, A. C. Greenberg, R. K. Kraft, B. J. McGarvie, C. E. Phillips, Jr., S. E. Redstone, S. M. Redstone, F. V. Salerno, W. Schwartz

**Founded:** 2005
**Domicile:** Delaware
**Employees:** 10,800

**STANDARD & POOR'S**

# Vornado Realty Trust

| S&P Recommendation | HOLD ★★★☆☆ | Price | 12-Mo. Target Price | Investment Style |
|---|---|---|---|---|
| | | $56.28 (as of Nov 14, 2008) | $75.00 | Large-Cap Blend |

**GICS Sector** Financials
**Sub-Industry** Diversified REITS

**Summary** This real estate investment trust owns a diverse group of properties, including Northeast retail properties, New York City office buildings, and other interests.

## Key Stock Statistics (Source S&P, Vickers, company reports)

| | | | | | | | | |
|---|---|---|---|---|---|---|---|---|
| 52-Wk Range | $108.15–53.35 | S&P FFO/Sh. 2008E | 5.50 | Market Capitalization(B) | $8.687 | Beta | | 1.24 |
| Trailing 12-Month FFO/Share | NA | S&P FFO/Sh. 2009E | 6.00 | Yield (%) | 6.75 | S&P 3-Yr. FFO/Sh. Proj. CAGR(%) | | 8 |
| Trailing 12-Month P/FFO | NA | P/FFO on S&P FFO/Sh. 2008E | 10.2 | Dividend Rate/Share | $3.80 | S&P Credit Rating | | BBB+ |
| $10K Invested 5 Yrs Ago | $13,094 | Common Shares Outstg. (M) | 154.4 | Institutional Ownership (%) | 90 | | | |

## Price Performance

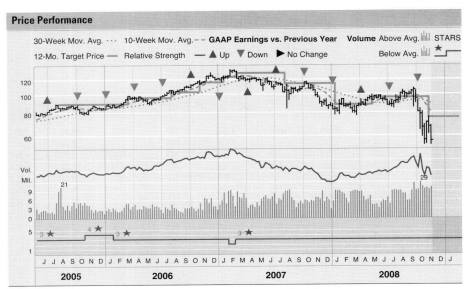

30-Week Mov. Avg. · · · · 10-Week Mov. Avg. – – **GAAP Earnings vs. Previous Year** Volume Above Avg. STARS
12-Mo. Target Price — Relative Strength — ▲ Up ▼ Down ► No Change Below Avg.

Analysis prepared by **Royal F. Shepard, CFA** on November 11, 2008, when the stock traded at **$ 61.55**.

### Highlights

> We think VNO's NYC portfolio is benefiting from embedded rent increases as leases renew for its office and retail properties. The trust has also increased occupancy levels in its Washington, DC, office portfolio. However, due to a challenging economic environment, we think it may become more difficult in 2009 to sign tenants to long-term leases in the core financial services and government sectors.

> Tight credit markets, in our view, may also delay VNO's pipeline of development projects. We think several retail renovations will be completed in 2008 and begin to make a moderate contribution to earnings by year end. We believe that $4 billion in 2007 acquisitions, such as the Manhattan Mall and the Filene's property in Boston, will take longer to pay off.

> Our 2008 FFO estimate of $5.50 is adjusted to exclude all non-recurring investment items, including gains on the recent sale of investments in Americold Realty and GMH Realty Trust. This would match comparable FFO in 2007, reflecting higher same-property income from existing real estate holdings, offset by properties placed under development and the sale of its interest in Americold Realty.

### Investment Rationale/Risk

> We think VNO has the financial resources to expand a strong portfolio of office and retail assets in supply-limited markets. Its pipeline of development opportunities in New York City is particularly attractive, in our view. However, these projects could be delayed by a more challenging economic environment. Recent turmoil in the credit markets may also defer the trust's ability to unlock capital gains on existing assets. We think the shares, recently selling at a substantial premium to diversified peers based on price to estimated 2009 FFO, fairly reflect long term growth prospects.

> Risks to our opinion and target price include rising interest rates, and economic declines in New York and/or Washington, DC. We also have corporate governance concerns related to anti-takeover defenses, including a classified board and blank check preferred stock.

> Our 12-month target price of $75 represents a multiple of 12.5X our 2009 FFO forecast, a premium to peers. We arrive at a similar valuation using our dividend discount model, which assumes a 10.1% discount rate and a terminal growth rate of 4%.

## Qualitative Risk Assessment

| LOW | MEDIUM | HIGH |
|---|---|---|

Our risk assessment of VNO reflects its large market capitalization, and what we see as its financial strength, diversified asset portfolio and low stock volatility.

## Quantitative Evaluations

**S&P Quality Ranking** A-

| D | C | B- | B | B+ | A- | A | A+ |
|---|---|---|---|---|---|---|---|

**Relative Strength Rank** MODERATE

39

LOWEST = 1    HIGHEST = 99

## Revenue/FFO Data

### Revenue (Million $)

| | 1Q | 2Q | 3Q | 4Q | Year |
|---|---|---|---|---|---|
| 2008 | 652.5 | 674.4 | 657.6 | -- | -- |
| 2007 | 737.1 | 793.5 | 851.7 | 888.5 | 3,333 |
| 2006 | 647.3 | 663.0 | 678.5 | 723.3 | 2,712 |
| 2005 | 598.7 | 594.8 | 657.0 | 697.2 | 2,548 |
| 2004 | 391.4 | 397.8 | 413.4 | 504.7 | 1,707 |
| 2003 | 365.0 | 371.1 | 380.2 | 386.8 | 1,503 |

### FFO Per Share ($)

| | 1Q | 2Q | 3Q | 4Q | Year |
|---|---|---|---|---|---|
| 2008 | 3.27 | 1.27 | E1.26 | E1.25 | E5.50 |
| 2007 | 1.65 | 1.72 | 1.35 | 1.18 | 5.89 |
| 2006 | 1.37 | 1.49 | 1.31 | 1.34 | 5.51 |
| 2005 | 1.84 | 1.51 | 0.65 | 1.26 | 5.21 |
| 2004 | 1.01 | 1.22 | 1.18 | 2.22 | 5.63 |
| 2003 | 1.15 | 1.14 | 1.04 | 1.08 | 4.38 |

Fiscal year ended Dec. 31. Next earnings report expected: Late February. FFO Estimates based on S&P Funds From Operations Est..

## Dividend Data (Dates: mm/dd Payment Date: mm/dd/yy)

| Amount ($) | Date Decl. | Ex-Div. Date | Stk. of Record | Payment Date |
|---|---|---|---|---|
| 0.900 | 01/16 | 01/28 | 01/30 | 02/20/08 |
| 0.900 | 05/01 | 05/08 | 05/12 | 05/22/08 |
| 0.900 | 07/31 | 08/07 | 08/11 | 08/22/08 |
| 0.950 | 10/31 | 11/07 | 11/12 | 11/21/08 |

Dividends have been paid since 1990. Source: Company reports.

**Please read the Required Disclosures and Analyst Certification on the last page of this report.**

The McGraw-Hill Companies

# Vornado Realty Trust

STANDARD
&POOR'S

## Business Summary November 11, 2008

CORPORATE OVERVIEW. Vornado Realty Trust is a diversified REIT that has interests in a wide range of properties, including office buildings, retail properties, refrigerated warehouses, a hotel, and dry warehouses, among others, primarily in the Northeast. The company conducts its business through, was the sole general partner of, and, as of December 31, 2007, owned 90.1% of the limited partnership interests, in Vornado Realty L.P.

MARKET PROFILE. During 2007, VNO derived 46% of operating segment EBITDA from office properties. The market for office leases is inherently cyclical. The U.S. office market tends to track the overall economy on a lagged basis. At year-end 2007, we believe the national vacancy rate was about 12.5%, reflecting improvement since cyclical lows in 2002-2003.

Local economic conditions, particularly the employment level, play an important role in determining competitive dynamics. In our opinion, VNO's principal target markets, the New York City metropolitan area and Washington DC, have among the lowest vacancy rates in the nation at less than 10%. In addition, unlike many markets, rates on new or renewed leases are often at higher rates than those previously in place. At December 31, 2007, VNO owned or had an interest in 112 office properties totaling 35.4 million sq. ft. The New York portfolio was 97.6% occupied at December 31, 2007; the Washington, DC, portfolio was 93.2% occupied.

In 2007, VNO derived about 16% of EBITDA from its retail segment. As of December 31, 2007, the retail portfolio included about 21.7 million sq. ft. in 21 states, Washington DC, and Puerto Rico. For VNO, as well as other retail oriented REITs, location and the financial health and growth of its retail tenants are among the most important factors affecting the success of its portfolio. Further, the companies in this industry enjoy relatively high barriers to entry, since developing new shopping centers requires large amounts of capital as well as time-consuming regulatory approvals which have been difficult to obtain in the recent past amid concerns about traffic and pollution. We expect VNO to focus on the re-development of recently acquired properties, including the Manhattan Mall, in New York City, and 15 shopping centers acquired in Northern New Jersey and Long Island, New York.

## Company Financials Fiscal Year Ended Dec. 31

| Per Share Data ($) | 2007 | 2006 | 2005 | 2004 | 2003 | 2002 | 2001 | 2000 | 1999 | 1998 |
|---|---|---|---|---|---|---|---|---|---|---|
| Tangible Book Value | 34.57 | 35.22 | 31.38 | 26.86 | 24.15 | 21.68 | 21.15 | 18.31 | 18.14 | 17.55 |
| Earnings | 2.86 | 3.13 | 3.27 | 3.75 | 2.29 | 2.18 | 2.50 | 2.21 | 1.94 | 1.59 |
| S&P Core Earnings | 2.69 | 2.62 | 3.09 | 3.62 | 3.63 | 2.15 | 2.58 | NA | NA | NA |
| Dividends | 3.45 | 3.25 | 3.85 | 2.89 | 2.91 | 2.97 | 2.31 | 1.97 | 1.81 | 1.64 |
| Payout Ratio | 107% | 104% | 118% | 77% | 127% | 136% | 92% | 89% | 93% | 103% |
| Prices:High | 136.55 | 131.35 | 89.70 | 76.99 | 55.84 | 47.20 | 42.03 | 40.75 | 40.00 | 49.81 |
| Prices:Low | 82.82 | 83.28 | 68.25 | 47.00 | 33.25 | 33.20 | 34.47 | 29.87 | 29.69 | 26.00 |
| P/E Ratio:High | 42 | 42 | 27 | 21 | 24 | 22 | 17 | 18 | 21 | 31 |
| P/E Ratio:Low | 26 | 27 | 21 | 13 | 15 | 15 | 14 | 14 | 15 | 16 |

### Income Statement Analysis (Million $)

| | 2007 | 2006 | 2005 | 2004 | 2003 | 2002 | 2001 | 2000 | 1999 | 1998 |
|---|---|---|---|---|---|---|---|---|---|---|
| Rental Income | 1,989 | 1,568 | 1,397 | 1,345 | 1,261 | 1,249 | 842 | 695 | 591 | 426 |
| Mortgage Income | Nil | Nil | Nil | Nil | Nil | Nil | Nil | Nil | Nil | Nil |
| Total Income | 3,271 | 2,712 | 2,548 | 1,707 | 1,503 | 1,435 | 986 | 827 | 697 | 510 |
| General Expenses | 2,935 | 1,588 | 1,488 | 825 | 706 | 668 | 472 | 366 | 322 | 295 |
| Interest Expense | 635 | 478 | 341 | 242 | 230 | 240 | 173 | 170 | 142 | 115 |
| Provision for Losses | Nil | Nil | Nil | Nil | Nil | Nil | Nil | Nil | Nil | Nil |
| Depreciation | 530 | 397 | 335 | 243 | 215 | 206 | 124 | 99.8 | 83.6 | 59.2 |
| Net Income | 510 | 607 | 507 | 514 | 285 | 263 | 267 | 235 | 203 | 153 |
| S&P Core Earnings | 426 | 393 | 435 | 476 | 421 | 236 | 238 | NA | NA | NA |

### Balance Sheet & Other Financial Data (Million $)

| | 2007 | 2006 | 2005 | 2004 | 2003 | 2002 | 2001 | 2000 | 1999 | 1998 |
|---|---|---|---|---|---|---|---|---|---|---|
| Cash | 1,858 | 2,690 | 763 | NA | NA | NA | NA | NA | NA | NA |
| Total Assets | 22,479 | 17,954 | 13,637 | 11,581 | 9,519 | 9,018 | 6,777 | 6,370 | 5,479 | 4,426 |
| Real Estate Investment | 18,972 | 13,553 | 11,449 | 9,757 | 7,748 | 7,560 | 4,690 | 4,295 | 3,922 | 3,316 |
| Loss Reserve | Nil | Nil | Nil | Nil | Nil | Nil | Nil | Nil | Nil | Nil |
| Net Investment | 16,565 | 11,585 | 9,776 | 8,349 | 6,879 | 6,822 | 4,184 | 3,901 | 3,613 | 3,089 |
| Short Term Debt | 527 | 778 | 398 | Nil | Nil | Nil | Nil | 425 | 681 | 268 |
| Capitalization:Debt | 12,426 | 9,056 | 5,857 | 4,937 | 3,768 | 3,622 | 1,643 | 2,232 | 1,368 | 1,783 |
| Capitalization:Equity | 5,293 | 5,322 | 4,260 | 3,301 | 2,827 | 2,362 | 2,101 | 1,597 | 1,577 | 1,782 |
| Capitalization:Total | 20,038 | 16,335 | 12,208 | 8,238 | 8,767 | 8,287 | 5,693 | 5,767 | 4,645 | 2,216 |
| % Earnings & Depreciation/Assets | 5.1 | 6.3 | 6.6 | 7.1 | 5.4 | 5.9 | 5.9 | 5.6 | 5.8 | 6.1 |
| Price Times Book Value:High | 3.9 | 3.7 | 2.9 | 2.9 | 2.3 | 2.2 | 2.0 | 2.2 | 2.2 | 2.8 |
| Price Times Book Value:Low | 2.4 | 2.4 | 2.2 | 1.7 | 1.4 | 1.5 | 1.6 | 1.6 | 1.6 | 1.5 |

Data as orig reptd.; bef. results of disc opers/spec. items. Per share data adj. for stk. divs.; EPS diluted. E-Estimated. NA-Not Available. NM-Not Meaningful. NR-Not Ranked. UR-Under Review.

The McGraw·Hill Companies

# Vulcan Materials Co

**STANDARD &POOR'S**

**S&P Recommendation** SELL ★ ★ ☆ ☆ ☆

| | | |
|---|---|---|
| **Price** $53.25 (as of Nov 14, 2008) | **12-Mo. Target Price** $48.00 | **Investment Style** Large-Cap Growth |

**GICS Sector** Materials
**Sub-Industry** Construction Materials

**Summary** This company is a major producer of aggregates and concrete used in road construction and the building of commercial, residential and public buildings and infrastructure.

## Key Stock Statistics (Source S&P, Vickers, company reports)

| | | | | | | | |
|---|---|---|---|---|---|---|---|
| 52-Wk Range | $100.25–41.56 | S&P Oper. EPS 2008**E** | 2.15 | Market Capitalization(B) | $5.865 | Beta | 1.25 |
| Trailing 12-Month EPS | $2.74 | S&P Oper. EPS 2009**E** | 2.25 | Yield (%) | 3.68 | S&P 3-Yr. Proj. EPS CAGR(%) | -14 |
| Trailing 12-Month P/E | 19.4 | P/E on S&P Oper. EPS 2008**E** | 24.8 | Dividend Rate/Share | $1.96 | S&P Credit Rating | BBB+ |
| $10K Invested 5 Yrs Ago | $13,273 | Common Shares Outstg. (M) | 110.1 | Institutional Ownership (%) | 93 | | |

## Price Performance

- 30-Week Mov. Avg. ···· 10-Week Mov. Avg. – – **GAAP Earnings vs. Previous Year** Volume Above Avg. STARS
- 12-Mo. Target Price — Relative Strength ▲ Up ▼ Down ▶ No Change Below Avg.

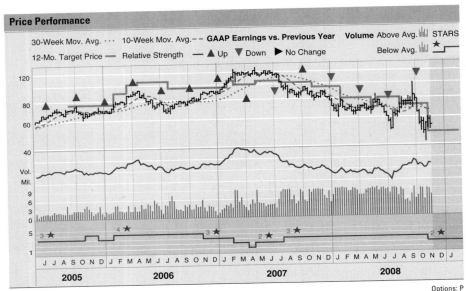

Options: P

Analysis prepared by **Stuart J. Benway, CFA** on November 10, 2008, when the stock traded at **$ 59.01**.

## Highlights

➤ We expect revenues to increase 20% in 2008, due to the acquisition in late 2007 of Florida Rock Industries. Demand for construction aggregates is likely to be weak this year, as we expect housing starts to decline 29%. However, spending on highways and other public infrastructure is expected to increase. We forecast sales in 2009 to decline slightly as continued weak demand is unlikely to be offset by additional price increases.

➤ Operating margins are expected to decline significantly in 2008. The higher cost base of acquired operations and integration costs hurt profitability early on, and as the year progressed lower shipments have led to underutilized capacity. Higher energy and raw material costs have also penalized margins. In 2009, we forecast input costs to decline significantly, while prices are expected to be higher. However, capacity is still likely to be underutilized.

➤ We project operating EPS of $2.15 in 2008, following EPS of $4.85 in 2007. This would mark the first earnings decline at VMC since 2002. For 2009, we project a slight rebound to $2.25.

## Investment Rationale/Risk

➤ We recently lowered our opinion on the shares to sell, from hold. We expect conditions in most of Vulcan's markets to remain very weak over the next several quarters. Our forecast is for a further decline in new home starts and a significant drop in commercial construction in 2009. Industrial markets should provide some stability as they are more long term in nature.

➤ Risks to our recommendation and target price include the chance that demand is greater than we project due to higher commercial construction activity and that public infrastructure spending is helped by a government-sponsored economic stimulus plan.

➤ A peer group of construction materials stocks was recently trading at 18.6X our 2009 EPS estimates. Applying a slight discount to this forward P/E due to VMC's stronger presence in the residential sector, we derive a value of $38. Our DCF model, which assumes a 9.6% weighted average cost of capital, 7% free cash flow grow over the next five years, and 3% cash flow growth in perpetuity, indicates intrinsic value of $55. Our 12-month target price of $48 is a weighted blend of these metrics.

## Qualitative Risk Assessment

| LOW | MEDIUM | HIGH |
|---|---|---|

Our risk assessment reflects that while VMC's earnings are exposed to the construction industry, about 44% of the aggregates volume comes from public construction, which is more stable than commercial construction. In addition, we view VMC's balance sheet and free cash flow generation as strong.

## Quantitative Evaluations

**S&P Quality Ranking** A-

| D | C | B- | B | B+ | A- | A | A+ |
|---|---|---|---|---|---|---|---|

**Relative Strength Rank** MODERATE

68

LOWEST = 1 HIGHEST = 99

## Revenue/Earnings Data

**Revenue (Million $)**

| | 1Q | 2Q | 3Q | 4Q | Year |
|---|---|---|---|---|---|
| 2008 | 817.3 | 1,022 | 1,013 | -- | -- |
| 2007 | 687.2 | 878.8 | 904.9 | 856.9 | 3,328 |
| 2006 | 708.7 | 888.2 | 929.3 | 816.3 | 3,342 |
| 2005 | 528.6 | 782.1 | 830.0 | 754.6 | 2,895 |
| 2004 | 617.5 | 816.3 | 891.2 | 608.7 | 2,454 |
| 2003 | 566.7 | 766.8 | 829.9 | 728.7 | 2,892 |

**Earnings Per Share ($)**

| | 1Q | 2Q | 3Q | 4Q | Year |
|---|---|---|---|---|---|
| 2008 | 0.13 | 1.27 | 0.54 | E0.54 | E2.15 |
| 2007 | 0.91 | 1.46 | 1.47 | 0.83 | 4.66 |
| 2006 | 0.70 | 1.47 | 1.45 | 1.19 | 4.79 |
| 2005 | 0.21 | 0.98 | 1.23 | 0.89 | 3.30 |
| 2004 | 0.14 | 0.85 | 0.96 | 0.62 | 2.52 |
| 2003 | 0.01 | 0.65 | 0.91 | 0.59 | 2.18 |

Fiscal year ended Dec. 31. Next earnings report expected: Mid February. EPS Estimates based on S&P Operating Earnings; historical GAAP earnings are as reported.

## Dividend Data (Dates: mm/dd Payment Date: mm/dd/yy)

| Amount ($) | Date Decl. | Ex-Div. Date | Stk. of Record | Payment Date |
|---|---|---|---|---|
| 0.490 | 02/08 | 02/21 | 02/25 | 03/10/08 |
| 0.490 | 05/09 | 05/22 | 05/27 | 06/10/08 |
| 0.490 | 07/11 | 08/25 | 08/27 | 09/10/08 |
| 0.490 | 10/10 | 11/24 | 11/26 | 12/10/08 |

Dividends have been paid since 1934. Source: Company reports.

# Vulcan Materials Co

## Business Summary November 10, 2008

CORPORATE OVERVIEW. Vulcan Materials is the largest U.S. producer of construction aggregates, a major producer of asphalt and concrete, and a leading producer of cement in Florida. Proven and probable reserves of aggregates were estimated at 12.7 billion tons at the end of 2007, representing a reserve life of 43 years based on current production rates. Vulcan shipped 231 million tons of aggregates in 2007 to 22 states, the District of Columbia, Mexico, and the Bahamas from 334 production facilities and distribution points. Construction aggregates were 75% of sales in 2007, asphalt mix and concrete 24.8%, and cement was 0.2% (Florida Rock was only included for about six weeks of the year). VMC estimates that 47% of its aggregates shipments in 2007 went to publicly funded construction projects, 31% was used for nonresidential construction, 19% went to the private residential construction market, and 3% was used as railroad ballast and in non-construction uses including agriculture and various industrial applications.

CORPORATE STRATEGY. VMC's main strategies are to grow through focused acquisitions, to concentrate on geographic markets that are growing at above average rates, to secure ample reserves to serve its markets, and to weight its business mix heavily toward infrastructure projects and nonresidential construction.

MARKET PROFILE. Construction aggregates include crushed stone, sand and

gravel, rock asphalt and recrushed asphalt and concrete. According to the U.S. Geological Survey (USGS), aggregates production in the U.S. in 2007 totaled 2.56 billion metric tons. Aggregates are employed in virtually all types of construction, including highway construction and maintenance, and in the production of asphaltic and portland cement concrete mixes. VMC's main competitors in the aggregates business are La Farge North America, Martin Marietta Materials, and Texas Industries. VMC estimates that the 10 largest aggregates producers in the nation supply approximately 35%-40% of the total national market, resulting in highly fragmented markets in some areas. Because of the relatively high transportation costs inherent in the business, competition generally is limited to areas in proximity to production facilities. Barriers to enter the aggregates industry are high. Zoning and permitting regulations have made it increasingly difficult for the construction aggregates industry to expand existing quarries or to develop new quarries in some markets. Consequently, aggregates prices are less price constrained, particularly in markets where there are limited reserves.

## Company Financials  Fiscal Year Ended Dec. 31

### Per Share Data ($)

| | 2007 | 2006 | 2005 | 2004 | 2003 | 2002 | 2001 | 2000 | 1999 | 1998 |
|---|---|---|---|---|---|---|---|---|---|---|
| Tangible Book Value | NM | 14.60 | 15.05 | 13.77 | 12.01 | 11.04 | 10.02 | 9.00 | 8.63 | 11.47 |
| Cash Flow | 7.33 | 7.04 | 5.43 | 4.88 | 4.87 | 4.47 | 4.89 | 4.43 | 4.37 | 3.86 |
| Earnings | 4.66 | 4.79 | 3.30 | 2.52 | 2.18 | 1.86 | 2.17 | 2.29 | 2.35 | 2.50 |
| S&P Core Earnings | 4.22 | 4.53 | 3.17 | 2.29 | 1.89 | 1.51 | 1.81 | NA | NA | NA |
| Dividends | 1.84 | 1.48 | 1.16 | 1.04 | 0.97 | 0.94 | 0.90 | 0.84 | 0.78 | 0.69 |
| Payout Ratio | 39% | 31% | 35% | 41% | 44% | 51% | 41% | 37% | 33% | 28% |
| Prices:High | 128.62 | 93.85 | 76.31 | 55.53 | 48.60 | 49.95 | 55.30 | 48.88 | 51.25 | 44.67 |
| Prices:Low | 77.04 | 65.85 | 52.36 | 41.94 | 28.75 | 32.35 | 37.50 | 36.50 | 34.31 | 31.33 |
| P/E Ratio:High | 28 | 20 | 23 | 22 | 22 | 27 | 25 | 21 | 22 | 18 |
| P/E Ratio:Low | 17 | 14 | 16 | 17 | 13 | 17 | 17 | 16 | 15 | 13 |

### Income Statement Analysis (Million $)

| | 2007 | 2006 | 2005 | 2004 | 2003 | 2002 | 2001 | 2000 | 1999 | 1998 |
|---|---|---|---|---|---|---|---|---|---|---|
| Revenue | 3,328 | 3,342 | 2,895 | 2,454 | 2,892 | 2,797 | 3,020 | 2,492 | 2,356 | 1,776 |
| Operating Income | 954 | 914 | 690 | 623 | 618 | 560 | 649 | 573 | 565 | 481 |
| Depreciation | 266 | 225 | 221 | 245 | 277 | 268 | 278 | 232 | 207 | 138 |
| Interest Expense | 53.4 | 26.3 | 37.1 | 40.3 | 54.1 | 55.0 | 61.3 | 48.1 | 48.6 | 7.23 |
| Pretax Income | 668 | 703 | 480 | 376 | 311 | 260 | 324 | 312 | 352 | 375 |
| Effective Tax Rate | 30.6% | 32.1% | 28.4% | 30.4% | 28.3% | 25.8% | 31.3% | 29.6% | 31.8% | 31.7% |
| Net Income | 463 | 477 | 344 | 261 | 223 | 190 | 223 | 220 | 240 | 256 |
| S&P Core Earnings | 419 | 452 | 328 | 236 | 194 | 155 | 186 | NA | NA | NA |

### Balance Sheet & Other Financial Data (Million $)

| | 2007 | 2006 | 2005 | 2004 | 2003 | 2002 | 2001 | 2000 | 1999 | 1998 |
|---|---|---|---|---|---|---|---|---|---|---|
| Cash | 34.9 | 55.2 | 275 | 271 | 417 | 171 | 101 | 55.3 | 52.8 | 181 |
| Current Assets | 1,157 | 731 | 1,165 | 1,418 | 1,050 | 790 | 730 | 695 | 625 | 576 |
| Total Assets | 8,936 | 3,424 | 3,589 | 3,665 | 3,637 | 3,448 | 3,398 | 3,229 | 2,839 | 1,659 |
| Current Liabilities | 2,528 | 494 | 579 | 427 | 543 | 298 | 344 | 572 | 387 | 211 |
| Long Term Debt | 1,530 | 322 | 323 | 605 | 339 | 858 | 906 | 685 | 699 | 76.5 |
| Common Equity | 3,760 | 2,001 | 2,127 | 2,014 | 1,803 | 1,697 | 1,604 | 1,471 | 1,324 | 1,154 |
| Total Capital | 5,961 | 2,611 | 2,725 | 2,967 | 2,573 | 2,993 | 2,829 | 2,426 | 2,273 | 1,329 |
| Capital Expenditures | 483 | 435 | 216 | 204 | 194 | 249 | 287 | 340 | 315 | 203 |
| Cash Flow | 729 | 702 | 565 | 506 | 501 | 458 | 501 | 452 | 447 | 394 |
| Current Ratio | 0.5 | 1.5 | 2.0 | 3.3 | 1.9 | 2.7 | 2.1 | 1.2 | 1.6 | 2.7 |
| % Long Term Debt of Capitalization | 25.7 | 12.3 | 11.9 | 20.4 | 13.2 | 28.7 | 32.0 | 28.3 | 30.7 | 5.8 |
| % Net Income of Revenue | 13.9 | 14.3 | 11.9 | 10.6 | 7.7 | 6.8 | 7.4 | 8.8 | 10.2 | 14.4 |
| % Return on Assets | 7.5 | 13.6 | 9.5 | 7.2 | 6.3 | 5.6 | 6.7 | 7.2 | 10.7 | 16.5 |
| % Return on Equity | 16.1 | 23.1 | 16.6 | 13.7 | 12.8 | 11.5 | 14.5 | 15.7 | 19.4 | 23.5 |

Data as orig reptd.; bef. results of disc opers/spec. items. Per share data adj. for stk. divs.; EPS diluted. E-Estimated. NA-Not Available. NM-Not Meaningful. NR-Not Ranked. UR-Under Review.

**Office:** 1200 Urban Center Drive, Birmingham, AL 35242.
**Telephone:** 205-298-3000.
**Email:** ir@vmcmail.com
**Website:** http://www.vulcanmaterials.com

**Chrmn & CEO:** D.M. James
**SVP & CFO:** D.F. Sansone
**SVP & General Counsel:** R.A. Wason, IV
**Chief Acctg Officer, Cntlr & CIO:** E.A. Khan

**Treas:** J.P. Alford
**Investor Contact:** M. Warren (205-298-3220)
**Board Members:** J. D. Baker, II, P. Carroll, Jr., P. W. Farmer, H. A. Franklin, D. M. James, A. M. Korologos, D. J. McGregor, J. V. Napier, R. T. O'Brien, D. B. Rice, O. R. Smith, V. J. Trosino

**Founded:** 1910
**Domicile:** New Jersey
**Employees:** 10,522

**STANDARD &POOR'S**

# Wachovia Corp

| S&P Recommendation **HOLD** ★★★☆☆ | Price $5.49 (as of Nov 14, 2008) | 12-Mo. Target Price $6.00 | Investment Style Large-Cap Value |

**GICS Sector** Financials
**Sub-Industry** Diversified Banks

**Summary** This bank holding company, the fourth largest in the U.S., operates banking offices in 21 states and Washington, DC. WB is in the midst of a merger dispute between Citigroup and Wells Fargo for control of the company.

## Key Stock Statistics (Source S&P, Vickers, company reports)

| | | | | | | | |
|---|---|---|---|---|---|---|---|
| 52-Wk Range | $45.43– 0.75 | S&P Oper. EPS 2008**E** | -16.46 | Market Capitalization(B) | $11.732 | Beta | 2.59 |
| Trailing 12-Month EPS | $-16.48 | S&P Oper. EPS 2009**E** | -1.46 | Yield (%) | 3.64 | S&P 3-Yr. Proj. EPS CAGR(%) | -9 |
| Trailing 12-Month P/E | NM | P/E on S&P Oper. EPS 2008**E** | NM | Dividend Rate/Share | $0.20 | S&P Credit Rating | A+ |
| $10K Invested 5 Yrs Ago | $1,505 | Common Shares Outstg. (M) | 2,137.0 | Institutional Ownership (%) | 73 | | |

### Price Performance

30-Week Mov. Avg. · · · ·  10-Week Mov. Avg. —  **GAAP Earnings vs. Previous Year**  Volume Above Avg. ▭▭ STARS ★
12-Mo. Target Price —  Relative Strength —  ▲ Up  ▼ Down  ▶ No Change  Below Avg. ▭▭

Analysis prepared by **Stuart Plesser** on October 27, 2008, when the stock traded at **$ 5.88.**

Options: ASE, CBOE, P, Ph

## Highlights

➤ WB has agreed to merge with Wells Fargo (WFC: buy, $32), pending necessary approvals. WB will receive 0.1991 WFC shares for each WB share. Given the fact that WFC does not plan to split up WB, and the relatively higher valuation to Citigroup's offer (C: hold $12), we look favorably upon the deal.

➤ Excluding the sale of WB, we look for revenue growth of roughly 22.0% in 2009, helped by a widening net interest margin, and assuming only moderate securities write-downs versus 2008. WB took writedowns in its securities portfolio of $940 million in the thrid quarter versus $565 million the previous quarter. We look for writedowns to decline in coming quarters, assuming spreads narrow in the secondary markets. We look for provisions of about $18.8 billion in 2008, declining to roughly $16.5 billion in 2009. Although provisions are well ahead of chargeoff levels, we think chargeoffs will pick up significantly due to the magnitude of WB's Option Arm portfolio.

➤ We estimate an operating loss of $16.46 a share in 2008 which includes goodwill impairment. In 2009, we look for a loss of $1.46.

## Investment Rationale/Risk

➤ Our recommendation is hold. WB's merger agreement, pending necessary approvals, calls for a fixed exchange ratio of 0.1991 WFC shares for each WB share. Based on WFC's current price, we value the deal at roughly $6.00 per share. Currently, the shares are selling at a slight discount to the purchase price. Based on the higher price of WFC's offer versus C's, and the government's interest in having WB's riskier assets in a more stable bank's portfolio, we think the deal will go through, and is fair, given WB's risky portfolio. Also, we think broker and client attrition will be minimal.

➤ Risks to our recommendation and target price include failure of the purchase by WFC to go through, a severe economic downturn, and client and broker attrition.

➤ Our 12-month target price of $6.00 is based on a slight discount to WFC's $6.25 a share offer. We think a discount is warranted due to the chance that a deal may not get consummated.

## Qualitative Risk Assessment

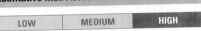

Our risk assessment reflects our view of Wachovia's high exposure to the California mortgage market from the Golden West acquisition, its concentration of Option Arm loans, and declining capital levels. Partly offsetting this is what we see as its solid fundamentals coupled with a diversity in business lines and geography.

## Quantitative Evaluations

### S&P Quality Ranking                    B+

| D | C | B- | B | B+ | A- | A | A+ |

### Relative Strength Rank                    WEAK

23

LOWEST = 1                                    HIGHEST = 99

## Revenue/Earnings Data

### Revenue (Million $)

| | 1Q | 2Q | 3Q | 4Q | Year |
|---|---|---|---|---|---|
| 2008 | 7,896 | 11,811 | 10,133 | -- | -- |
| 2007 | 13,889 | 14,595 | 13,592 | 13,436 | 54,807 |
| 2006 | 10,224 | 10,987 | 11,249 | 14,350 | 46,810 |
| 2005 | 8,448 | 8,679 | 9,302 | 9,479 | 35,908 |
| 2004 | 6,766 | 6,626 | 6,902 | 7,773 | 28,067 |
| 2003 | 5,776 | 5,841 | 6,315 | 6,542 | 24,474 |

### Earnings Per Share ($)

| | 1Q | 2Q | 3Q | 4Q | Year |
|---|---|---|---|---|---|
| 2008 | -0.36 | -4.31 | -11.18 | E-0.84 | E-16.46 |
| 2007 | 1.20 | 1.24 | 0.89 | 0.03 | 3.26 |
| 2006 | 1.09 | 1.17 | 1.17 | 1.18 | 4.61 |
| 2005 | 1.01 | 1.04 | 1.06 | 0.95 | 4.05 |
| 2004 | 0.94 | 0.95 | 0.96 | 0.95 | 3.81 |
| 2003 | 0.76 | 0.77 | 0.82 | 0.83 | 3.17 |

Fiscal year ended Dec. 31. Next earnings report expected: Late January. EPS Estimates based on S&P Operating Earnings; historical GAAP earnings are as reported.

## Dividend Data (Dates: mm/dd Payment Date: mm/dd/yy)

| Amount ($) | Date Decl. | Ex-Div. Date | Stk. of Record | Payment Date |
|---|---|---|---|---|
| 0.640 | 02/19 | 02/27 | 02/29 | 03/17/08 |
| 0.375 | 04/14 | 05/28 | 05/30 | 06/16/08 |
| 0.050 | 07/22 | 08/27 | 08/29 | 09/15/08 |
| 0.050 | 10/21 | 11/25 | 01/28 | 12/15/08 |

Dividends have been paid since 1914. Source: Company reports.

---

**Please read the Required Disclosures and Analyst Certification on the last page of this report.**

# Wachovia Corp

**STANDARD**
**&POOR'S**

## Business Summary October 27, 2008

CORPORATE OVERVIEW. WB consists of several reporting segments: general bank (GB); capital management (CM); wealth management (WM); corporate and investment bank (CIB); and parent. GB provides a broad range of banking products and services to individuals, small businesses, commercial enterprises and governmental institutions in 21 states and Washington, DC. It focuses on small business customers with annual revenues of up to $3 million; business banking customers with annual revenues between $3 million and $15 million; and commercial customers with revenues between $15 million and $250 million. CM leverages its multi-channel distribution to provide a full line of proprietary and nonproprietary investment and retirement products and services to retail and institutional clients. With the addition of A.G. Edwards, retail brokerage services are offered through 14,600 financial advisors in 3,700 offices of Wachovia Securities nationwide. Evergreen Investments, a large and diversified asset management company, manages investments for a broad range of retail and institutional investors.

WM provides private banking, trust and investment management and financial

planning services to high-net-worth individuals, their families and businesses. Wachovia Insurance Services offers commercial insurance brokerage and risk management services, employee benefits, life insurance, executive benefits and personal insurance services to businesses and individuals. The CIB division serves domestic and global corporate and institutional clients typically with revenues in excess of $250 million, and primarily in these key industry sectors: health care; media and communications; technology and services; finance; real estate; consumer and retail; industrial growth; defense and aerospace; and energy and power. CIB includes corporate lending, investment banking, and treasury and international trade finance lines of business. CIB also serves an institutional client base of money managers, hedge funds, insurance companies, pension funds, banks and broker dealers.

## Company Financials Fiscal Year Ended Dec. 31

| Per Share Data ($) | 2007 | 2006 | 2005 | 2004 | 2003 | 2002 | 2001 | 2000 | 1999 | 1998 |
|---|---|---|---|---|---|---|---|---|---|---|
| Tangible Book Value | 14.97 | 15.60 | 15.76 | 15.25 | 15.27 | 14.48 | 11.50 | 11.92 | 11.22 | 12.36 |
| Earnings | 3.26 | 4.61 | 4.05 | 3.81 | 3.17 | 2.60 | 1.45 | 0.12 | 3.33 | 2.95 |
| S&P Core Earnings | 3.22 | 4.61 | 4.02 | 3.75 | 3.09 | 2.32 | 1.14 | NA | NA | NA |
| Dividends | 2.40 | 2.14 | 1.94 | 1.66 | 1.25 | 1.00 | 0.96 | 1.92 | 1.88 | 1.58 |
| Payout Ratio | 74% | 46% | 48% | 44% | 39% | 38% | 66% | NM | 56% | 54% |
| Prices:High | 58.80 | 60.04 | 56.28 | 55.01 | 46.74 | 39.88 | 36.60 | 38.88 | 65.75 | 65.94 |
| Prices:Low | 36.69 | 50.85 | 46.30 | 43.05 | 32.12 | 28.57 | 25.22 | 23.50 | 32.00 | 40.94 |
| P/E Ratio:High | 18 | 13 | 14 | 14 | 15 | 15 | 25 | NM | 20 | 22 |
| P/E Ratio:Low | 11 | 11 | 11 | 11 | 10 | 11 | 17 | NM | 10 | 14 |

| Income Statement Analysis (Million $) | 2007 | 2006 | 2005 | 2004 | 2003 | 2002 | 2001 | 2000 | 1999 | 1998 |
|---|---|---|---|---|---|---|---|---|---|---|
| Net Interest Income | 18,130 | 15,249 | 13,681 | 11,961 | 10,607 | 9,823 | 7,775 | 7,277 | 7,452 | 7,277 |
| Tax Equivalent Adjustment | 152 | 155 | 219 | 250 | 256 | 218 | 159 | 117 | 118 | 117 |
| Non Interest Income | 13,565 | 14,545 | 12,130 | 10,789 | 9,309 | 7,836 | 7,003 | 5,682 | 6,995 | 6,198 |
| Loan Loss Provision | 2,261 | 434 | 249 | 257 | 586 | 1,479 | 1,947 | 691 | 692 | 691 |
| % Expense/Operating Revenue | 62.5% | 60.5% | 60.9% | 63.8% | 65.4% | 65.3% | 65.8% | 89.6% | 60.8% | 67.5% |
| Pretax Income | 9,344 | 11,470 | 9,804 | 7,633 | 6,080 | 4,667 | 2,293 | 703 | 4,831 | 3,965 |
| Effective Tax Rate | 26.3% | 31.3% | 30.9% | 31.7% | 30.1% | 23.3% | 29.4% | 80.4% | 33.3% | 27.1% |
| Net Income | 6,312 | 7,745 | 6,429 | 5,214 | 4,247 | 3,579 | 1,619 | 138 | 3,223 | 2,891 |
| % Net Interest Margin | 2.94 | 3.12 | 3.24 | 3.41 | 3.72 | 3.92 | 3.57 | 3.81 | 3.79 | 3.81 |
| S&P Core Earnings | 6,239 | 7,740 | 6,386 | 5,141 | 4,144 | 3,187 | 1,255 | NA | NA | NA |

| Balance Sheet & Other Financial Data (Million $) | 2007 | 2006 | 2005 | 2004 | 2003 | 2002 | 2001 | 2000 | 1999 | 1998 |
|---|---|---|---|---|---|---|---|---|---|---|
| Money Market Assets | 74,388 | 62,452 | 65,257 | 72,809 | 61,747 | 45,827 | 46,180 | 36,109 | 27,542 | 12,675 |
| Investment Securities | 115,037 | 108,619 | 114,889 | 110,597 | 100,445 | 75,804 | 58,467 | 49,246 | 53,035 | 53,988 |
| Commercial Loans | 136,422 | 121,626 | 112,695 | 141,226 | 107,466 | 109,097 | 61,258 | 87,447 | 80,619 | 79,689 |
| Other Loans | 325,532 | 298,532 | 146,320 | 82,614 | 58,105 | 54,000 | 102,543 | 36,313 | 54,947 | 59,720 |
| Total Assets | 782,896 | 707,121 | 520,755 | 493,324 | 401,032 | 341,839 | 330,452 | 254,170 | 253,024 | 237,363 |
| Demand Deposits | 60,893 | 66,572 | 67,587 | 64,197 | 48,683 | 44,640 | 43,464 | 30,315 | 31,375 | 35,614 |
| Time Deposits | 388,236 | 340,886 | 257,407 | 230,856 | 172,542 | 146,878 | 143,989 | 112,353 | 109,672 | 106,853 |
| Long Term Debt | 161,007 | 138,594 | 48,971 | 46,759 | 36,730 | 39,662 | 41,733 | 35,809 | 31,975 | 22,949 |
| Common Equity | 74,572 | 69,716 | 47,561 | 47,317 | 32,428 | 32,078 | 28,438 | 15,347 | 16,709 | 17,173 |
| % Return on Assets | 0.9 | 1.2 | 1.3 | 1.2 | 1.1 | 1.1 | 0.6 | 0.1 | 1.3 | 1.5 |
| % Return on Equity | 8.8 | 13.2 | 13.6 | 13.1 | 13.2 | 11.8 | 7.4 | 0.9 | 19.2 | 19.8 |
| % Loan Loss Reserve | 1.0 | 1.0 | 1.0 | 1.2 | 1.5 | 1.7 | -1.8 | 1.4 | 1.3 | 1.3 |
| % Loans/Deposits | 103.0 | 102.2 | 81.7 | 80.3 | 74.8 | 85.2 | 87.4 | 86.7 | 96.1 | 97.7 |
| % Equity to Assets | 9.7 | 10.5 | 9.4 | 8.9 | 8.7 | 9.0 | 7.5 | 6.3 | 6.9 | 7.4 |

Data as orig reptd.; bef. results of disc opers/spec. items. Per share data adj. for stk. divs.; EPS diluted. E-Estimated. NA-Not Available. NM-Not Meaningful. NR-Not Ranked. UR-Under Review.

**Office:** One Wachovia Center, Charlotte, NC 28288-0013.
**Telephone:** 704-374-6565.
**Website:** http://www.wachovia.com
**Chrmn & CEO:** L.L. Smith

**Pres & CEO:** R.K. Steel
**EVP & CTO:** G.A. Enos, Jr.
**EVP, Secy & General Counsel:** J.C. Sherburne
**SVP, Chief Acctg Officer & Cntlr:** P.M. Carlson

**Investor Contact:** A. Lehman (704-374-6782)
**Board Members:** J. D. Baker, II, P. C. Browning, J. T. Casteen, III, R. W. Galea, J. A. Gitt, W. H. Goodwin, Jr., M. C. Herringer, R. A. Ingram, D. M. James, M. J. Mcdonald, J. Neubauer, T. D. Proctor, E. S. Rady, V. Richey, R. G. Shaw, L. L. Smith, R. K. Steel, D. D. Young

**Auditor:** KPMG
**Founded:** 1879
**Domicile:** North Carolina
**Employees:** 121,890

*The McGraw-Hill Companies*

# Walgreen Co

**STANDARD &POOR'S**

| S&P Recommendation | HOLD ★★★☆☆ | Price | 12-Mo. Target Price | Investment Style |
|---|---|---|---|---|
| | | $23.43 (as of Nov 14, 2008) | $35.00 | Large-Cap Growth |

**GICS Sector** Consumer Staples
**Sub-Industry** Drug Retail

**Summary** The largest U.S. retail drug chain in terms of revenues, this company operates about 6,500 drug stores throughout the U.S. and Puerto Rico.

## Key Stock Statistics (Source S&P, Vickers, company reports)

| | | | | | | | |
|---|---|---|---|---|---|---|---|
| 52-Wk Range | $40.04– 21.28 | S&P Oper. EPS 2009**E** | 2.30 | Market Capitalization(B) | $23.181 | Beta | 0.70 |
| Trailing 12-Month EPS | $2.17 | S&P Oper. EPS 2010**E** | NA | Yield (%) | 1.92 | S&P 3-Yr. Proj. EPS CAGR(%) | 11 |
| Trailing 12-Month P/E | 10.8 | P/E on S&P Oper. EPS 2009**E** | 10.2 | Dividend Rate/Share | $0.45 | S&P Credit Rating | A+ |
| $10K Invested 5 Yrs Ago | $6,783 | Common Shares Outstg. (M) | 989.4 | Institutional Ownership (%) | 66 | | |

## Price Performance

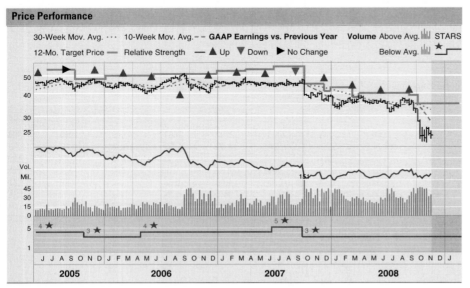

30-Week Mov. Avg. · · · 10-Week Mov. Avg. — **GAAP Earnings vs. Previous Year** Volume Above Avg. ▯▮▯ STARS
12-Mo. Target Price — Relative Strength — ▲ Up ▼ Down ▶ No Change  Below Avg. ▯▯▯ ★

Options: ASE, CBOE, P

Analysis prepared by **Joseph Agnese** on October 02, 2008, when the stock traded at **$ 29.49**.

## Highlights

➤ We see sales advancing about 9% in FY 09 (Aug.), to roughly $64 billion, from $59 billion in FY 08, fueled by the expected opening of about 495 net new stores, a pharmacy same-store sales gain of about 3%, and front-end same-store sales growth of about 3%. We see front-end growth benefiting from improved traffic trends and better convenience levels as the company expands store operating hours and the number of freestanding locations while improving the product assortment.

➤ We expect margins to narrow as benefits from increased sales of wider margin generic drugs, improved sales leverage from new stores and well controlled store salaries are offset by a shift in the mix as the pharmacy segment becomes a larger portion of the product mix, increased promotional spending and expansion costs. We think WAG's investment in in-store digital photo finishing labs will continue to benefit sales and gross margins by increasing traffic flow, despite increased operating costs.

➤ We look for operating EPS to increase 6.0%, to $2.30, in FY 09, from $2.17 in FY 08.

## Investment Rationale/Risk

➤ We believe the company is well positioned to benefit in the long term from favorable demographics, improved non-pharmacy merchandising, increased generic drug sales, and new store growth, despite decreased demand we see in the near term due to an adverse economic environment .

➤ Risks to our recommendation and target price include a weaker than expected economy, increased competition from peers and other retail formats, and legislative changes that may affect drug reimbursements.

➤ Our 12-month target price of $35 is based on our forward P/E analysis. The stock recently traded at about 13.8X FY 08 operating EPS of $2.17, around 1.3X our projected three-year EPS growth rate of 11%, and in line with the shares of other drug chain peers we cover. We believe the shares should trade at 15X our FY 09 EPS estimate, in line with its 5% premium to the S&P 500, based on its defensive position within the retail drug store industry and what we see as WAG's long history of stable earnings growth and its strong balance sheet. Applying a P/E of 15X to our FY 09 EPS estimate of $2.30 results in a value of $35.

## Qualitative Risk Assessment

| LOW | **MEDIUM** | HIGH |
|---|---|---|

Our risk assessment reflects the company's strong market share positions in the relatively stable U.S. retail drug industry, offset by growth of non-traditional competitors and potential legislation changes.

## Quantitative Evaluations

**S&P Quality Ranking**  A+

| D | C | B- | B | B+ | A- | A | **A+** |
|---|---|---|---|---|---|---|---|

**Relative Strength Rank**  MODERATE

**61**

LOWEST = 1   HIGHEST = 99

## Revenue/Earnings Data

**Revenue (Million $)**

| | 1Q | 2Q | 3Q | 4Q | Year |
|---|---|---|---|---|---|
| 2008 | 14,028 | 15,394 | 15,016 | 14,597 | 59,034 |
| 2007 | 12,709 | 13,934 | 13,698 | 13,422 | 53,762 |
| 2006 | 10,900 | 12,163 | 12,175 | 12,170 | 47,409 |
| 2005 | 9,889 | 10,987 | 10,831 | 10,495 | 42,202 |
| 2004 | 8,721 | 9,782 | 9,579 | 9,427 | 37,508 |
| 2003 | 7,485 | 8,446 | 8,328 | 8,246 | 32,505 |

**Earnings Per Share ($)**

| | | | | | |
|---|---|---|---|---|---|
| 2008 | 0.46 | 0.69 | 0.58 | 0.45 | 2.17 |
| 2007 | 0.43 | 0.65 | 0.56 | 0.40 | 2.03 |
| 2006 | 0.34 | 0.51 | 0.46 | 0.41 | 1.72 |
| 2005 | 0.32 | 0.48 | 0.40 | 0.32 | 1.52 |
| 2004 | 0.25 | 0.42 | 0.33 | 0.32 | 1.32 |
| 2003 | 0.22 | 0.36 | 0.29 | 0.27 | 1.14 |

Fiscal year ended Aug. 31. Next earnings report expected: Late December. EPS Estimates based on S&P Operating Earnings; historical GAAP earnings are as reported.

## Dividend Data (Dates: mm/dd Payment Date: mm/dd/yy)

| Amount ($) | Date Decl. | Ex-Div. Date | Stk. of Record | Payment Date |
|---|---|---|---|---|
| 0.095 | 01/09 | 02/14 | 02/19 | 03/12/08 |
| 0.095 | 04/09 | 05/19 | 05/21 | 06/12/08 |
| 0.113 | 07/09 | 08/18 | 08/20 | 09/12/08 |
| 0.113 | 10/08 | 11/13 | 11/17 | 12/12/08 |

Dividends have been paid since 1933. Source: Company reports.

---

**Please read the Required Disclosures and Analyst Certification on the last page of this report.**

*The McGraw·Hill Companies*

# Walgreen Co

STANDARD &POOR'S

## Business Summary October 02, 2008

CORPORATE OVERVIEW. Walgreen Co. is one of the largest drug store chains in the U.S., based on sales and store count. In 1909, the company's founder, Charles Rudolph Walgreen Sr., purchased one of the busiest drug stores on Chicago's South Side, and transformed it by constructing an ice cream fountain that featured his own brand of ice cream. The ice cream fountain was the forerunner of the famous Walgreen's soda fountain, which became the main attraction for customers from the 1920s through the 1950s. People lined up to buy a product that WAG invented in the early 1920s: the milkshake. The company continued to be innovative by pioneering computerized pharmacies connected by satellite in 1981, completing chain wide point-of-sale scanning in 1991, and introducing freestanding stores with drive-thru pharmacies in 1992. It also operates worksite health centers, home care facilities and specialty, institutional and mail service pharmacies. Its Take Care Health Systems subsidiary manages 247 convenient care clinics at Walgreens drug stores.

MARKET PROFILE. Walgreen operates the largest U.S. drugstore chain based on sales, generating $59.0 billion in sales in FY 08 (Aug.). According to our

analysis, the company filled 583 million prescriptions in FY 07, accounting for about 17% of the U.S. retail market. The company experienced a 5.7% growth rate in prescription volume in FY 07, outpacing our estimate of a low single digit growth rate for the industry. On a dollar basis, WAG pharmacy sales rose 15% in FY 07, to $35 billion, versus our estimate of an upper single digit growth rate for the total industry, on comparable prescription sales growth of 9.5%. Sales of non-pharmacy items outperformed competitors, with the company increasing market share in 59 out of its top 60 core categories versus drug store, grocery and mass merchant competition. Based on store count, Walgreen is the second largest chain store operator in the U.S. As of September 30, 2008, the company operated 6,479 drug stores (out of a total of 6,971 locations) throughout the U.S. and Puerto Rico.

## Company Financials Fiscal Year Ended Aug. 31

| Per Share Data ($) | 2008 | 2007 | 2006 | 2005 | 2004 | 2003 | 2002 | 2001 | 2000 | 1999 |
|---|---|---|---|---|---|---|---|---|---|---|
| Tangible Book Value | 11.56 | 10.13 | 9.61 | 8.69 | 8.04 | 7.02 | 6.08 | 5.11 | 4.19 | 3.47 |
| Cash Flow | NA | 2.70 | 2.28 | 1.99 | 1.71 | 1.47 | 1.29 | 1.12 | 0.99 | 0.82 |
| Earnings | 2.17 | 2.03 | 1.72 | 1.52 | 1.32 | 1.14 | 0.99 | 0.86 | 0.76 | 0.62 |
| S&P Core Earnings | 2.17 | 2.03 | 1.71 | 1.44 | 1.27 | 1.07 | 0.93 | 0.80 | NA | NA |
| Dividends | NA | 0.33 | 0.27 | 0.22 | 0.18 | 0.16 | 0.15 | 0.14 | 0.14 | 0.13 |
| Payout Ratio | NA | 16% | 16% | 15% | 14% | 14% | 15% | 16% | 18% | 21% |
| Prices:High | NA | 49.10 | 51.60 | 49.01 | 39.51 | 37.42 | 40.70 | 45.29 | 45.75 | 33.94 |
| Prices:Low | NA | 35.80 | 39.55 | 39.66 | 32.00 | 26.90 | 27.70 | 28.70 | 22.06 | 22.69 |
| P/E Ratio:High | NA | 24 | 30 | 32 | 30 | 33 | 41 | 53 | 60 | 55 |
| P/E Ratio:Low | NA | 18 | 23 | 26 | 24 | 24 | 28 | 33 | 29 | 37 |

| Income Statement Analysis (Million $) | | | | | | | | | | |
|---|---|---|---|---|---|---|---|---|---|---|
| Revenue | 59,034 | 53,762 | 47,409 | 42,202 | 37,508 | 32,505 | 28,681 | 24,623 | 21,207 | 17,839 |
| Operating Income | NA | 3,827 | 3,274 | 2,906 | 2,546 | 2,194 | 1,932 | 1,668 | 1,454 | 1,226 |
| Depreciation | 840 | 676 | 572 | 482 | 403 | 346 | 307 | 269 | 230 | 210 |
| Interest Expense | NA | Nil | Nil | Nil | Nil | Nil | Nil | 3.10 | 0.40 | 0.40 |
| Pretax Income | 3,430 | 3,189 | 2,754 | 2,456 | 2,176 | 1,889 | 1,637 | 1,423 | 1,263 | 1,027 |
| Effective Tax Rate | 37.1% | 36.0% | 36.4% | 36.5% | 37.5% | 37.8% | 37.8% | 37.8% | 38.5% | 39.2% |
| Net Income | 2,157 | 2,041 | 1,751 | 1,560 | 1,360 | 1,176 | 1,019 | 886 | 777 | 624 |
| S&P Core Earnings | 2,158 | 2,042 | 1,754 | 1,478 | 1,302 | 1,104 | 955 | 820 | NA | NA |

| Balance Sheet & Other Financial Data (Million $) | | | | | | | | | | |
|---|---|---|---|---|---|---|---|---|---|---|
| Cash | 443 | 255 | 920 | 577 | 1,696 | 1,017 | 450 | 16.9 | 12.8 | 142 |
| Current Assets | NA | 9,511 | 9,705 | 8,317 | 7,764 | 6,358 | 5,167 | 4,394 | 3,550 | 3,222 |
| Total Assets | 22,410 | 19,314 | 17,131 | 14,609 | 13,342 | 11,406 | 9,879 | 8,834 | 7,104 | 5,907 |
| Current Liabilities | NA | 6,744 | 5,755 | 4,481 | 4,078 | 3,421 | 2,955 | 3,012 | 2,304 | 1,924 |
| Long Term Debt | NA | Nil | Nil | Nil | Nil | Nil | Nil | Nil | Nil | Nil |
| Common Equity | 12,869 | 11,104 | 10,116 | 8,890 | 8,228 | 7,196 | 6,230 | 5,207 | 4,234 | 3,484 |
| Total Capital | NA | 11,263 | 10,257 | 9,130 | 8,556 | 7,424 | 6,407 | 5,344 | 4,336 | 3,559 |
| Capital Expenditures | 2,225 | 1,785 | 1,338 | 1,238 | 940 | 795 | 934 | 1,237 | 1,119 | 696 |
| Cash Flow | NA | 2,717 | 2,323 | 2,042 | 1,763 | 1,522 | 1,327 | 1,155 | 1,007 | 834 |
| Current Ratio | 1.6 | 1.4 | 1.7 | 1.9 | 1.9 | 1.9 | 1.7 | 1.5 | 1.5 | 1.7 |
| % Long Term Debt of Capitalization | 9.4 | Nil | Nil | Nil | Nil | Nil | Nil | Nil | Nil | Nil |
| % Net Income of Revenue | 3.7 | 3.8 | 3.7 | 3.7 | 3.6 | 3.6 | 3.6 | 3.6 | 3.7 | 3.5 |
| % Return on Assets | 10.3 | 11.2 | 11.0 | 11.2 | 10.9 | 11.0 | 10.9 | 11.1 | 11.9 | 11.5 |
| % Return on Equity | 18.0 | 19.2 | 18.4 | 18.3 | 17.6 | 17.5 | 17.8 | 18.8 | 20.1 | 19.7 |

Data as orig reptd.; bef. results of disc opers/spec. items. Per share data adj. for stk. divs.; EPS diluted. E-Estimated. NA-Not Available. NM-Not Meaningful. NR-Not Ranked. UR-Under Review.

**Office:** 200 Wilmot Road, Deerfield, IL 60015.
**Telephone:** 847-940-2500.
**Email:** investor.relations@walgreens.com
**Website:** http://www.walgreens.com

**Chrmn & CEO:** A.G. McNally
**Pres & COO:** G.D. Wasson
**SVP & CFO:** W.D. Miquelon
**SVP, Secy & General Counsel:** D.I. Green

**Chief Acctg Officer & Cntlr:** M.M. Scholz
**Investor Contact:** R.J. Hans (847-940-2500)
**Board Members:** W. C. Foote, A. G. McNally, C. Reed, N. M. Schlichting, D. Y. Schwartz, A. Silva, J. A. Skinner, M. M. Von Ferstel, C. R. Walgreen, III

**Founded:** 1901
**Domicile:** Illinois
**Employees:** 237,000

The McGraw-Hill Companies

# Wal-Mart Stores Inc

**STANDARD &POOR'S**

| S&P Recommendation | STRONG BUY ★★★★★ | Price $52.71 (as of Nov 14, 2008) | 12-Mo. Target Price $61.00 | Investment Style Large-Cap Blend |
| --- | --- | --- | --- | --- |

**GICS Sector** Consumer Staples
**Sub-Industry** Hypermarkets & Super Centers

**Summary** WMT, the largest retailer in North America, operates a chain of discount department stores, wholesale clubs, and combination discount stores and supermarkets.

## Key Stock Statistics (Source S&P, Vickers, company reports)

| | | | | | | | |
| --- | --- | --- | --- | --- | --- | --- | --- |
| 52-Wk Range | $63.85– 43.11 | S&P Oper. EPS 2009**E** | 3.44 | Market Capitalization(B) | $207.360 | Beta | 0.05 |
| Trailing 12-Month EPS | $3.36 | S&P Oper. EPS 2010**E** | 3.68 | Yield (%) | 1.80 | S&P 3-Yr. Proj. EPS CAGR(%) | 10 |
| Trailing 12-Month P/E | 15.7 | P/E on S&P Oper. EPS 2009**E** | 15.3 | Dividend Rate/Share | $0.95 | S&P Credit Rating | AA |
| $10K Invested 5 Yrs Ago | $10,280 | Common Shares Outstg. (M) | 3,934.0 | Institutional Ownership (%) | 40 | | |

## Price Performance

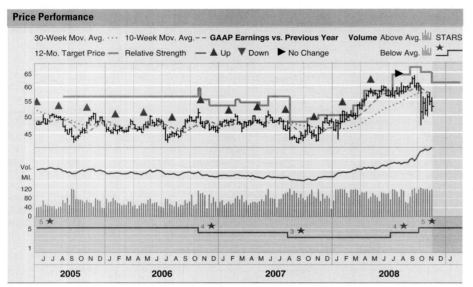

- 30-Week Mov. Avg. · · · 10-Week Mov. Avg. – – **GAAP Earnings vs. Previous Year**  **Volume** Above Avg. STARS
- 12-Mo. Target Price — Relative Strength — ▲ Up ▼ Down ► No Change  Below Avg.

Options: ASE, CBOE, P, Ph

Analysis prepared by **Joseph Agnese** on November 13, 2008, when the stock traded at **$ 51.93**.

## Qualitative Risk Assessment

| LOW | MEDIUM | HIGH |
| --- | --- | --- |

Our risk assessment of Wal-Mart Stores reflects our view of the company's high quality earnings, as reflected in its S&P Quality Ranking of A+, its dominant market share positions, continued price leadership and strong cash flow generation.

## Quantitative Evaluations

**S&P Quality Ranking** A+

| D | C | B- | B | B+ | A- | A | A+ |
| --- | --- | --- | --- | --- | --- | --- | --- |

**Relative Strength Rank** STRONG

81

LOWEST = 1 HIGHEST = 99

## Revenue/Earnings Data

**Revenue (Million $)**

| | 1Q | 2Q | 3Q | 4Q | Year |
| --- | --- | --- | --- | --- | --- |
| 2009 | 95,303 | 102,667 | -- | -- | -- |
| 2008 | 85,387 | 91,990 | 90,880 | 106,269 | 378,799 |
| 2007 | 79,613 | 85,430 | 84,467 | 99,078 | 344,992 |
| 2006 | 71,680 | 76,811 | 75,436 | 89,273 | 312,427 |
| 2005 | 64,763 | 69,722 | 68,520 | 82,216 | 285,222 |
| 2004 | 56,718 | 62,637 | 62,480 | 74,494 | 256,329 |

**Earnings Per Share ($)**

| | | | | | |
| --- | --- | --- | --- | --- | --- |
| 2009 | 0.76 | 0.86 | E0.74 | E1.06 | E3.44 |
| 2008 | 0.68 | 0.86 | 0.70 | 1.03 | 3.16 |
| 2007 | 0.64 | 0.72 | 0.62 | 0.95 | 2.92 |
| 2006 | 0.58 | 0.67 | 0.57 | 0.86 | 2.68 |
| 2005 | 0.50 | 0.62 | 0.54 | 0.75 | 2.41 |
| 2004 | 0.41 | 0.52 | 0.46 | 0.63 | 2.03 |

Fiscal year ended Jan. 31. Next earnings report expected: NA. EPS Estimates based on S&P Operating Earnings; historical GAAP earnings are as reported.

## Highlights

➤ We expect net sales to increase 6.7% in FY 10 (Jan.) to $438 billion, from our estimate of $410 billion in FY 09, driven by 2% growth in same-store sales and the addition of around 5% square footage of new retail space, with square footage growth shifting toward international markets (19-20 million square feet) from domestic expansion (15-17 million square feet).

➤ We estimate that EBITDA margins will be flat as increased sales leverage and well controlled inventory levels are offset by unfavorable foreign exchange rates and a shift in the product mix, reflecting higher sales of food and pharmacy products and sluggish sales in discretionary categories such as apparel and home departments. We believe an increased focus on low-to mid-price point merchandise and private label offerings should help offset weaker demand in the home and apparel categories beginning in late FY 09. Additionally, we see benefits from improved labor productivity due to the rollout of new scheduling software.

➤ We project operating EPS of $3.68 for FY 10, up 7.0% from our estimate of $3.44 in FY 09.

## Investment Rationale/Risk

➤ We believe the company is well positioned to gain market share in an adverse economic environment, as we think consumers will continue to trade down from higher cost competitors and take advantage of its one-stop shopping convenience.

➤ Risks to our recommendation and target price include economic pressures such as rising unemployment or lower consumer confidence, which we think would negatively affect WMT's core customers and the company's results.

➤ Our 12-month target price of $61 reflects a blend of our analysis of relative P/E ratios and our discounted cash flow (DCF) model. Our DCF model suggests an intrinsic value of $63 per share, assuming a weighted average cost of capital of 9% and a terminal growth rate of 3%. We believe the company is well positioned, as a low-price retailer, to gain market share in an adverse economic environment. Applying a P/E multiple of 16.4X, in line with the three-year historical forward 12-month average, to our FY 10 EPS estimate of $3.68 implies a value of $60.

## Dividend Data (Dates: mm/dd Payment Date: mm/dd/yy)

| Amount ($) | Date Decl. | Ex-Div. Date | Stk. of Record | Payment Date |
| --- | --- | --- | --- | --- |
| 0.238 | 03/06 | 03/12 | 03/14 | 04/07/08 |
| 0.238 | 03/06 | 05/14 | 05/16 | 06/02/08 |
| 0.238 | 03/06 | 08/13 | 08/15 | 09/02/08 |
| 0.238 | 03/06 | 12/11 | 12/15 | 01/02/09 |

Dividends have been paid since 1973. Source: Company reports.

---

**Please read the Required Disclosures and Analyst Certification on the last page of this report.**

*The McGraw-Hill Companies*

# Wal-Mart Stores Inc

**STANDARD
&POOR'S**

## Business Summary November 13, 2008

CORPORATE OVERVIEW. Wal-Mart, the largest retailer in North America, has set its sights on other parts of the world. The company's operations are divided into three divisions: Wal-Mart, Sam's Club, and International. In FY 08 (Jan.), the Wal-Mart segment, comprised of discount stores, Supercenters and Neighborhood Markets, had sales of $239.5 billion, up 5.8% from the level of FY 07. Sam's Club sales totaled $44.4 billion, up 6.7%. In international markets, in which WMT operates a variety of formats, some via joint ventures, sales rose 17.5%, to $90.6 billion. Internationally, WMT operated 21 units in Argentina, 313 in Brazil, 305 in Canada, 202 in China (through joint ventures), 457 in Central America, 394 in Japan, 1,023 in Mexico, 54 in Puerto Rico, and 352 in the U.K.

MARKET PROFILE. With over 138 million people walking into Wal-Mart stores every week, the company is a dominant player in many of the markets in

which it competes. With FY 08 sales of about $134 billion within supermarket-related categories (grocery, health and beauty aids, and health and wellness), the Wal-Mart division is the largest supermarket operator in the U.S., commanding over 20% market share of the $500+ billion supermarket industry. Other major product categories within the Wal-Mart division include entertainment, electronics & toys ($34 billion in estimated sales in FY 08), seasonal & hardlines ($29 billion), apparel, shoes & jewelry ($29 billion), and home ($14 billion). Sam's Club is the second largest warehouse club in the U.S., with sales of $44.4 billion in FY 08. About 65% of Sam's Club sales were generated from sundries and food categories.

## Company Financials Fiscal Year Ended Jan. 31

| Per Share Data ($) | 2008 | 2007 | 2006 | 2005 | 2004 | 2003 | 2002 | 2001 | 2000 | 1999 |
|---|---|---|---|---|---|---|---|---|---|---|
| Tangible Book Value | 12.22 | 11.57 | 9.84 | 9.12 | 7.83 | 6.78 | 5.95 | 4.99 | 3.69 | 4.75 |
| Cash Flow | NA | 4.23 | 3.81 | 3.44 | 2.91 | 2.58 | 2.22 | 2.04 | 1.78 | 1.41 |
| Earnings | 3.16 | 2.92 | 2.68 | 2.41 | 2.03 | 1.81 | 1.50 | 1.40 | 1.25 | 0.99 |
| S&P Core Earnings | 3.16 | 2.92 | 2.66 | 2.41 | 2.03 | 1.79 | 1.47 | 1.39 | NA | NA |
| Dividends | 0.67 | 0.67 | 0.60 | 0.52 | 0.36 | 0.30 | 0.28 | 0.24 | 0.20 | 0.16 |
| Payout Ratio | 21% | 23% | 22% | 22% | 18% | 17% | 19% | 17% | 16% | 16% |
| Calendar Year | 2007 | 2006 | 2005 | 2004 | 2003 | 2002 | 2001 | 2000 | 1999 | 1998 |
| Prices:High | 51.44 | 52.15 | 54.60 | 61.31 | 60.20 | 63.94 | 58.75 | 69.00 | 70.25 | 41.38 |
| Prices:Low | 42.09 | 42.31 | 42.31 | 51.08 | 46.25 | 43.72 | 42.00 | 41.44 | 38.68 | 18.78 |
| P/E Ratio:High | 16 | 18 | 20 | 25 | 30 | 35 | 39 | 49 | 56 | 42 |
| P/E Ratio:Low | 13 | 14 | 16 | 21 | 23 | 24 | 28 | 30 | 31 | 19 |

### Income Statement Analysis (Million $)

| | 2008 | 2007 | 2006 | 2005 | 2004 | 2003 | 2002 | 2001 | 2000 | 1999 |
|---|---|---|---|---|---|---|---|---|---|---|
| Revenue | 378,799 | 348,650 | 312,427 | 285,222 | 256,329 | 244,524 | 217,799 | 191,329 | 165,013 | 137,634 |
| Operating Income | NA | 22,298 | 23,247 | 18,729 | 16,525 | 15,075 | 15,367 | 12,392 | 10,684 | 8,418 |
| Depreciation | 6,317 | 5,459 | 4,717 | 4,405 | 3,852 | 3,432 | 3,290 | 2,868 | 2,375 | 1,872 |
| Interest Expense | NA | 1,809 | 1,420 | 1,187 | 996 | 1,063 | 1,326 | 1,374 | 1,022 | 797 |
| Pretax Income | 20,198 | 18,968 | 17,358 | 16,105 | 14,193 | 12,719 | 10,751 | 10,116 | 9,083 | 7,323 |
| Effective Tax Rate | 34.2% | 33.6% | 33.4% | 34.7% | 36.1% | 35.3% | 36.2% | 36.5% | 36.8% | 37.4% |
| Net Income | 12,884 | 12,178 | 11,231 | 10,267 | 8,861 | 8,039 | 6,671 | 6,295 | 5,575 | 4,430 |
| S&P Core Earnings | 12,880 | 12,178 | 11,134 | 10,267 | 8,861 | 7,955 | 6,592 | 6,235 | NA | NA |

### Balance Sheet & Other Financial Data (Million $)

| | 2008 | 2007 | 2006 | 2005 | 2004 | 2003 | 2002 | 2001 | 2000 | 1999 |
|---|---|---|---|---|---|---|---|---|---|---|
| Cash | 5,569 | 7,373 | 6,414 | 5,488 | 5,199 | 2,758 | 2,161 | 2,054 | 1,856 | 1,879 |
| Current Assets | NA | 46,588 | 43,824 | 38,491 | 34,421 | 30,483 | 28,246 | 26,555 | 24,356 | 21,132 |
| Total Assets | 163,514 | 151,193 | 138,187 | 120,223 | 104,912 | 94,685 | 83,451 | 78,130 | 70,349 | 49,996 |
| Current Liabilities | NA | 51,754 | 48,826 | 42,888 | 37,418 | 32,617 | 27,282 | 28,949 | 25,803 | 16,762 |
| Long Term Debt | NA | 30,735 | 30,171 | 23,669 | 20,099 | 19,608 | 18,732 | 15,655 | 16,674 | 9,607 |
| Common Equity | 64,608 | 61,573 | 53,171 | 49,396 | 43,623 | 39,337 | 35,102 | 31,343 | 25,834 | 21,112 |
| Total Capital | NA | 94,468 | 84,809 | 74,388 | 65,206 | 60,307 | 55,041 | 48,138 | 43,987 | 32,518 |
| Capital Expenditures | 14,937 | 15,666 | 14,563 | 12,893 | 10,308 | 9,355 | 8,383 | 8,042 | 6,183 | 3,734 |
| Cash Flow | NA | 17,637 | 15,948 | 14,672 | 12,713 | 11,471 | 9,961 | 9,163 | 7,950 | 6,302 |
| Current Ratio | 0.8 | 0.9 | 0.9 | 0.9 | 0.9 | 0.9 | 1.0 | 0.9 | 0.9 | 1.3 |
| % Long Term Debt of Capitalization | 29.1 | 32.5 | 35.6 | 31.8 | 30.8 | 32.5 | 34.0 | 32.5 | 38.0 | 29.5 |
| % Net Income of Revenue | 3.4 | 3.5 | 3.5 | 3.6 | 3.5 | 3.3 | 3.1 | 3.3 | 3.4 | 3.2 |
| % Return on Assets | 8.2 | 8.4 | 8.7 | 9.1 | 8.9 | 9.0 | 8.3 | 3.3 | 9.3 | 9.3 |
| % Return on Equity | 20.4 | 21.2 | 21.9 | 22.1 | 21.3 | 21.6 | 20.1 | 22.0 | 23.8 | 22.4 |

Data as orig reptd.; bef. results of disc opers/spec. items. Per share data adj. for stk. divs.; EPS diluted. E-Estimated. NA-Not Available. NM-Not Meaningful. NR-Not Ranked. UR-Under Review.

**Office:** 702 S.W. 8th Street, Bentonville, AR 72716.
**Telephone:** 479-273-4000.
**Website:** http://www.walmartstores.com
**Chrmn:** S.R. Walton

**Pres & CEO:** H.L. Scott, Jr.
**Vice Chrmn:** M.T. Duke
**EVP & CFO:** T.M. Schoewe
**EVP & Treas:** C.M. Holley, Jr.

**Investor Contact:** M. Beckstead (479-277-9558)
**Board Members:** A. M. Alvarez, J. W. Breyer, M. M. Burns, J. I. Cash, Jr., R. C. Corbett, D. Daft, M. T. Duke, D. D. Glass, G. B. Penner, A. I. Questrom, H. L. Scott, Jr., A. M. Sorenson, J. Walton, S. R. Walton, C. J. Williams, L. S. Wolf

**Founded:** 1945
**Domicile:** Delaware
**Employees:** 2,100,000

*The McGraw-Hill Companies*

# Washington Post Co (The)

STANDARD
&POOR'S

| S&P Recommendation | HOLD ★★★☆☆ | Price<br>$393.00 (as of Nov 14, 2008) | 12-Mo. Target Price<br>$450.00 | Investment Style<br>Large-Cap Growth |
|---|---|---|---|---|

**GICS Sector** Consumer Discretionary
**Sub-Industry** Publishing

**Summary** WPO publishes The Washington Post newspaper and Newsweek magazine, operates TV stations and cable systems, and provides education and database services.

## Key Stock Statistics (Source S&P, Vickers, company reports)

| | | | | | | | |
|---|---|---|---|---|---|---|---|
| 52-Wk Range | $823.25– 322.41 | S&P Oper. EPS 2008**E** | 27.10 | Market Capitalization(B) | $3.173 | Beta | 0.85 |
| Trailing 12-Month EPS | $13.60 | S&P Oper. EPS 2009**E** | 25.10 | Yield (%) | 2.19 | S&P 3-Yr. Proj. EPS CAGR(%) | -1 |
| Trailing 12-Month P/E | 28.9 | P/E on S&P Oper. EPS 2008**E** | 14.5 | Dividend Rate/Share | $8.60 | S&P Credit Rating | A+ |
| $10K Invested 5 Yrs Ago | $5,452 | Common Shares Outstg. (M) | 9.4 | Institutional Ownership (%) | 81 | | |

## Price Performance

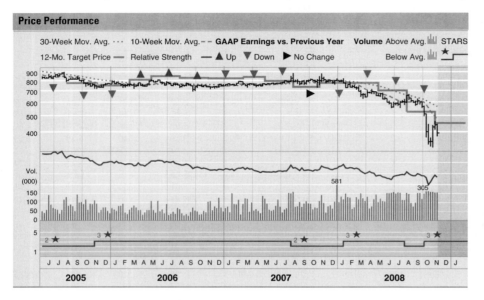

30-Week Mov. Avg. ···· 10-Week Mov. Avg.–-– **GAAP Earnings vs. Previous Year** Volume Above Avg. STARS
12-Mo. Target Price — Relative Strength —— ▲ Up ▼ Down ▶ No Change Below Avg.

Analysis prepared by **Jason N. Asaeda** on November 04, 2008, when the stock traded at **$ 446.93**.

### Highlights

➤ We look for revenues to rise 8.1% in 2008, to $4.51 billion. We see continued growth in the education segment, driven by a mix of organic gains and acquisitions. We forecast double-digit percentage cable revenue growth as WPO continues to add cable modem customers, and from recent subscriber rate increases. We expect television revenues to be about flat, with anticipated second half gains from Olympic and political advertising offsetting first half declines. We project double-digit declines in the company's magazine and newspaper segments due to cyclical and secular challenges we see persisting for print media. We see growth in the education and cable segments supporting a 5.0% revenue increase in 2009, to $4.73 billion.

➤ We expect operating margin contraction to 8.8% in 2009, down from our forecast for 10.0% in 2008. We see declines in profitability in WPO's publishing businesses and revenue growth in the company's low-margin education unit outweighing margin improvement we forecast in the cable division.

➤ Factoring in likely share buybacks, we see operating EPS of $27.10 in 2008 and $25.10 in 2009.

### Investment Rationale/Risk

➤ Our hold recommendation is based on valuation. WPO's education segment has grown revenues steadily through numerous acquisitions and has helped the company diversify away from traditional media businesses. But despite some recent modest improvement due mostly to lower option expense, segment profitability has consistently declined over the past few years, and we expect this to remain a low margin business for the foreseeable future. We also see a sluggish U.S. economy hurting revenues and profitability for WPO's publishing operations.

➤ Risks to our recommendation and target price include weaker than expected revenue growth in WPO's education and cable operations. Regarding corporate governance, 29 holders of non-publicly traded Class A shares have the right to elect a majority of the directors, which we believe may not be in the best interests of common (Class B) stockholders.

➤ Our 12-month target price of $450 is based on a peer-median EV/EBITDA multiple of 6.2X our 2009 EBITDA estimate of $693 million.

## Qualitative Risk Assessment

| LOW | MEDIUM | HIGH |
|---|---|---|

Our risk assessment incorporates our view of a highly competitive environment for advertising among publishers and other media, offset by the recurring nature of a significant portion of company revenues, and the company's low beta.

## Quantitative Evaluations

**S&P Quality Ranking** B+

| D | C | B- | B | B+ | A- | A | A+ |
|---|---|---|---|---|---|---|---|

**Relative Strength Rank** MODERATE

58

LOWEST = 1     HIGHEST = 99

## Revenue/Earnings Data

**Revenue (Million $)**

| | 1Q | 2Q | 3Q | 4Q | Year |
|---|---|---|---|---|---|
| 2008 | 1,063 | 1,106 | 1,129 | -- | -- |
| 2007 | 985.6 | 1,047 | 1,023 | 1,126 | 4,180 |
| 2006 | 948.3 | 969.0 | 946.9 | 1,041 | 3,905 |
| 2005 | 833.9 | 897.6 | 873.7 | 948.7 | 3,554 |
| 2004 | 759.0 | 818.4 | 820.0 | 902.7 | 3,300 |
| 2003 | 640.4 | 706.9 | 706.1 | 785.5 | 2,839 |

**Earnings Per Share ($)**

| | 1Q | 2Q | 3Q | 4Q | Year |
|---|---|---|---|---|---|
| 2008 | 4.08 | -0.31 | 1.08 | E9.31 | E27.10 |
| 2007 | 6.70 | 7.19 | 7.60 | 8.72 | 30.19 |
| 2006 | 8.48 | 8.17 | 7.60 | 9.97 | 34.21 |
| 2005 | 6.87 | 8.16 | 6.89 | 10.65 | 32.59 |
| 2004 | 6.15 | 8.82 | 8.57 | 11.03 | 34.59 |
| 2003 | 7.59 | 6.32 | 2.06 | 9.15 | 25.12 |

Fiscal year ended Dec. 31. Next earnings report expected: Late February. EPS Estimates based on S&P Operating Earnings; historical GAAP earnings are as reported.

## Dividend Data (Dates: mm/dd Payment Date: mm/dd/yy)

| Amount ($) | Date Decl. | Ex-Div. Date | Stk. of Record | Payment Date |
|---|---|---|---|---|
| 2.150 | 01/17 | 01/24 | 01/28 | 02/08/08 |
| 2.150 | 02/26 | 04/24 | 04/28 | 05/09/08 |
| 2.150 | 06/26 | 07/24 | 07/28 | 08/08/08 |
| 2.150 | 09/11 | 10/23 | 10/27 | 11/07/08 |

Dividends have been paid since 1956. Source: Company reports.

# Washington Post Co (The)

**STANDARD &POOR'S**

## Business Summary November 04, 2008

CORPORATE OVERVIEW. The Washington Post operates principally in four areas of the media business: newspaper publishing, television broadcasting, magazine publishing, and cable television. Through its subsidiary Kaplan, Inc., the company also provides educational services for individuals, schools and businesses. In 2007, about 88% of the company's revenues were derived from the United States, down from 91% and 93% in 2006 and 2005, respectively.

The company divides Kaplan's various educational businesses (49% of 2007 revenues) into three categories: higher education (50% of segment revenues), test preparation and admissions (28%), and professional (22%). Higher education includes Kaplan's domestic and international post-secondary education businesses, including fixed facility colleges and online post-secondary and career programs. We note that approximately 73% of Kaplan's higher education revenues came from Title IV (federal financial aid) programs in 2007, and thus we believe the segment is vulnerable to budget cuts for education spending. Test prep includes standardized test prep and English-language courses, as well as the K12 and Score! businesses. Professional includes the domestic and overseas professional businesses, including study programs for the CFA and CPA exams. Part of the company's strategy in the education business is to grow through acquisition; along those lines, Kaplan made nine acquisitions in 2007 and eleven in 2006.

The Newspaper division (21%) includes The Washington Post, The Washington Post National Weekly Edition, Express (a free weekly tabloid), Washingtonpost.Newsweek Interactive (WPNI), and other publications. WPNI holds a 16.5% interest in Classified Ventures, a company that provides online classified advertising databases for cars, apartment rentals and residential real estate. Newspaper segment online revenues grew about 11% to $114 million in 2007, well below industry online advertising growth of about 25% as estimated by the Interactive Advertising Bureau.

## Company Financials  Fiscal Year Ended Dec. 31

### Per Share Data ($)

| | 2007 | 2006 | 2005 | 2004 | 2003 | 2002 | 2001 | 2000 | 1999 | 1998 |
|---|---|---|---|---|---|---|---|---|---|---|
| Tangible Book Value | NM | 143.64 | 103.66 | 92.76 | 64.70 | 59.82 | 50.31 | 50.03 | 51.03 | 69.84 |
| Cash Flow | 55.26 | 57.76 | 53.26 | 54.04 | 43.38 | 40.93 | 38.62 | 26.79 | 38.45 | 54.84 |
| Earnings | 30.19 | 34.21 | 32.59 | 34.59 | 25.12 | 22.61 | 24.06 | 14.32 | 22.30 | 41.10 |
| S&P Core Earnings | 25.02 | 30.53 | 26.50 | 29.88 | 15.68 | 12.98 | -1.24 | NA | NA | NA |
| Dividends | 8.20 | 7.80 | 7.40 | 7.00 | 5.80 | 5.60 | 5.60 | 5.40 | 5.20 | 5.00 |
| Payout Ratio | 27% | 23% | 23% | 20% | 23% | 25% | 23% | 38% | 23% | 12% |
| Prices:High | 885.23 | 815.00 | 982.03 | 999.50 | 819.50 | 743.00 | 651.50 | 628.75 | 594.50 | 605.50 |
| Prices:Low | 726.93 | 690.00 | 716.00 | 790.21 | 650.03 | 516.00 | 470.00 | 467.25 | 490.13 | 462.00 |
| P/E Ratio:High | 29 | 24 | 30 | 29 | 33 | 33 | 27 | 44 | 27 | 15 |
| P/E Ratio:Low | 24 | 20 | 22 | 23 | 26 | 23 | 20 | 33 | 22 | 11 |

### Income Statement Analysis (Million $)

| | 2007 | 2006 | 2005 | 2004 | 2003 | 2002 | 2001 | 2000 | 1999 | 1998 |
|---|---|---|---|---|---|---|---|---|---|---|
| Revenue | 4,180 | 3,905 | 3,554 | 3,300 | 2,839 | 2,584 | 2,417 | 2,412 | 2,216 | 2,110 |
| Operating Income | 716 | 682 | 713 | 748 | 497 | 549 | 358 | 458 | 551 | 518 |
| Depreciation | 239 | 222 | 198 | 185 | 174 | 172 | 138 | 118 | 163 | 139 |
| Interest Expense | 24.1 | 25.3 | 26.8 | 28.0 | 27.8 | 33.8 | 49.6 | 54.7 | 26.8 | 11.5 |
| Pretax Income | 481 | 519 | 500 | 542 | 383 | 354 | 388 | 230 | 375 | 668 |
| Effective Tax Rate | 40.0% | 36.5% | 37.1% | 38.7% | 37.0% | 38.8% | 40.7% | 40.6% | 39.9% | 37.5% |
| Net Income | 289 | 330 | 314 | 333 | 241 | 216 | 230 | 136 | 226 | 417 |
| S&P Core Earnings | 238 | 293 | 255 | 287 | 150 | 124 | -13.4 | NA | NA | NA |

### Balance Sheet & Other Financial Data (Million $)

| | 2007 | 2006 | 2005 | 2004 | 2003 | 2002 | 2001 | 2000 | 1999 | 1998 |
|---|---|---|---|---|---|---|---|---|---|---|
| Cash | 373 | 348 | 216 | 119 | 87.4 | 28.8 | 31.5 | 20.3 | 75.5 | 15.2 |
| Current Assets | 995 | 935 | 818 | 754 | 496 | 383 | 397 | 405 | 476 | 405 |
| Total Assets | 6,005 | 5,381 | 4,585 | 4,317 | 3,902 | 3,584 | 3,559 | 3,201 | 2,987 | 2,730 |
| Current Liabilities | 1,013 | 803 | 695 | 688 | 712 | 736 | 434 | 409 | 823 | 389 |
| Long Term Debt | 401 | 402 | 404 | 426 | 422 | 406 | 1,862 | 873 | 398 | 395 |
| Common Equity | 3,461 | 3,160 | 2,638 | 2,412 | 2,075 | 1,837 | 1,683 | 1,481 | 1,368 | 1,588 |
| Total Capital | 4,583 | 4,173 | 3,477 | 3,254 | 2,814 | 2,517 | 3,781 | 2,485 | 1,891 | 2,079 |
| Capital Expenditures | 290 | 284 | 238 | 205 | 126 | 153 | 224 | 130 | 130 | 244 |
| Cash Flow | 526 | 551 | 511 | 518 | 414 | 387 | 367 | 253 | 388 | 555 |
| Current Ratio | 1.0 | 1.2 | 1.2 | 1.1 | 0.7 | 0.5 | 0.9 | 1.0 | 0.6 | 1.0 |
| % Long Term Debt of Capitalization | 8.7 | 9.6 | 11.6 | 13.1 | 15.0 | 16.1 | 49.3 | 35.1 | 21.0 | 19.0 |
| % Net Income of Revenue | 6.9 | 8.4 | 8.8 | 10.1 | 8.5 | 8.4 | 9.5 | 5.7 | 10.2 | 19.8 |
| % Return on Assets | 5.1 | 6.6 | 7.1 | 8.0 | 6.4 | 6.1 | 6.8 | 4.4 | 7.9 | 17.4 |
| % Return on Equity | 8.7 | 11.3 | 12.4 | 14.9 | 12.3 | 12.2 | 14.4 | 9.5 | 15.2 | 30.0 |

Data as orig reptd.; bef. results of disc opers/spec. items. Per share data adj. for stk. divs.; EPS diluted. E-Estimated. NA-Not Available. NM-Not Meaningful. NR-Not Ranked. UR-Under Review.

**Office:** 1150 15th Street N.W., Washington, DC 20071-0002.
**Telephone:** 202-334-6000.
**Website:** http://www.washpostco.com
**Chrmn & CEO:** D. Graham

**Investor Contact:** J.B. Morse, Jr. (202-334-6662)
**SVP & CFO:** J.B. Morse, Jr.
**SVP, Secy & General Counsel:** V. Dillon
**CTO:** R.S. Terkowitz

**Board Members:** L. C. Bollinger, W. Buffett, C. C. Davis, B. Diller, J. L. Dotson, Jr., M. F. Gates, T. S. Gayner, D. Graham, A. M. Mulcahy, R. L. Olson

**Founded:** 1947
**Domicile:** Delaware
**Employees:** 19,000

**The McGraw-Hill Companies**

# Waste Management Inc.

**STANDARD &POOR'S**

| S&P Recommendation **BUY** ★★★☆ | Price $31.20 (as of Nov 14, 2008) | 12-Mo. Target Price $35.00 | Investment Style Large-Cap Blend |
| --- | --- | --- | --- |

**GICS Sector** Industrials
**Sub-Industry** Environmental & Facilities Services

**Summary** This Houston-based company is the largest U.S. trash hauling/disposal concern.

## Key Stock Statistics (Source S&P, Vickers, company reports)

| | | | | | | | |
| --- | --- | --- | --- | --- | --- | --- | --- |
| 52-Wk Range | $39.25– 24.51 | S&P Oper. EPS 2008**E** | 2.20 | Market Capitalization(B) | $15.306 | Beta | 0.74 |
| Trailing 12-Month EPS | $2.36 | S&P Oper. EPS 2009**E** | 2.45 | Yield (%) | 3.46 | S&P 3-Yr. Proj. EPS CAGR(%) | 9 |
| Trailing 12-Month P/E | 13.2 | P/E on S&P Oper. EPS 2008**E** | 14.2 | Dividend Rate/Share | $1.08 | S&P Credit Rating | BBB |
| $10K Invested 5 Yrs Ago | $12,535 | Common Shares Outstg. (M) | 490.6 | Institutional Ownership (%) | 84 | | |

## Price Performance

30-Week Mov. Avg. ··· 10-Week Mov. Avg. — **GAAP Earnings vs. Previous Year** Volume Above Avg. STARS
12-Mo. Target Price — Relative Strength — ▲ Up ▼ Down ▶ No Change Below Avg.

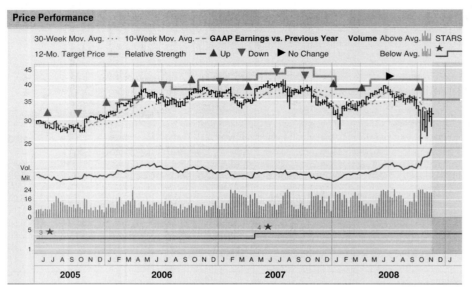

Options: ASE, CBOE, P, Ph

Analysis prepared by **Stewart Scharf** on November 11, 2008, when the stock traded at **$ 30.50**.

### Highlights

➤ We project slightly lower core internal revenue growth for 2008, with a modest recovery seen for 2009 as volume declines stabilize. In our view, core price hikes of 3% (before recycling commodity prices and fuel surcharges) should offset soft collection volume resulting from the weak economy and residential housing market. We still see WMI sacrificing market share in favor of price.

➤ In our view, gross margins (before D&A) will expand fractionally in 2008 from 36.8% in 2007, with further improvement likely in 2009, given cost savings from routing initiatives, and further price hikes in the collection business, as well as on the disposal side. We see the EBITDA margin widening in 2009 from our projection of near 26% for 2008 (26% in 2007), as WMI focuses on pricing, accretive acquisitions, improving productivity, and reducing maintenance and safety costs. SG&A expenses should remain well controlled at about 10.5%.

➤ We estimate a higher effective tax rate of 40% for 2008, as energy-related tax credits expired in 2007, and we see operating EPS of $2.20, advancing 11% to $2.45 in 2009.

### Investment Rationale/Risk

➤ Our buy recommendation is based on our valuation metrics, and WMI's pricing and divestiture strategy. The company recently withdrew its buyout offer for Republic Services (RSG: buy, $24) in light of tight credit markets. Earlier, RSG had rejected WMI's sweetened bid.

➤ Risks to our opinion and target price include a significant rise in fuel costs, a prolonged downturn in the U.S. economy, further labor disputes, a steep decline in the customer retention rate, and a potential inability to raise prices enough to meet return on invested capital (ROIC) goals.

➤ We view the stock's recent dividend yield of 3.5%, above the 2.9% yield of the S&P 500, as attractive. Correlating various relative metrics, including WMI's historical five-year average P/E, we believe WMI should trade at an above-peers average P/E of 14.7X our EPS estimate for 2009, or $36. Based on our discounted cash flow model, assuming an 8.5% weighted average cost of capital and 3% terminal growth, our intrinsic value estimate is $34. Blending these metrics, we derive our 12-month target price of $35.

### Qualitative Risk Assessment

| LOW | MEDIUM | HIGH |
| --- | --- | --- |

Our risk assessment reflects broad-based pricing initiatives and fuel surcharges geared to reducing volatile fuel costs, a favorable interest rate environment, and what we view as a strong balance sheet with declining debt levels and solid return on equity. In addition, we view WMI's corporate governance practices as sound.

### Quantitative Evaluations

**S&P Quality Ranking** B+

| D | C | B- | B | B+ | A- | A | A+ |
| --- | --- | --- | --- | --- | --- | --- | --- |

**Relative Strength Rank** STRONG

88

LOWEST = 1        HIGHEST = 99

### Revenue/Earnings Data

**Revenue (Million $)**

| | 1Q | 2Q | 3Q | 4Q | Year |
| --- | --- | --- | --- | --- | --- |
| 2008 | 3,266 | 3,489 | 3,525 | -- | -- |
| 2007 | 3,188 | 3,358 | 3,403 | 3,361 | 13,310 |
| 2006 | 3,229 | 3,410 | 3,441 | 3,283 | 13,363 |
| 2005 | 3,038 | 3,289 | 3,375 | 3,372 | 13,074 |
| 2004 | 2,896 | 3,138 | 3,274 | 3,208 | 12,516 |
| 2003 | 2,716 | 2,915 | 2,975 | 2,968 | 11,574 |

**Earnings Per Share ($)**

| | 1Q | 2Q | 3Q | 4Q | Year |
| --- | --- | --- | --- | --- | --- |
| 2008 | 0.48 | 0.64 | 0.63 | E0.47 | E2.20 |
| 2007 | 0.42 | 0.64 | 0.54 | 0.61 | 2.23 |
| 2006 | 0.34 | 0.76 | 0.55 | 0.46 | 2.10 |
| 2005 | 0.26 | 0.92 | 0.38 | 0.52 | 2.09 |
| 2004 | 0.25 | 0.37 | 0.52 | 0.47 | 1.60 |
| 2003 | 0.18 | 0.30 | 0.35 | 0.39 | 1.21 |

Fiscal year ended Dec. 31. Next earnings report expected: Mid February. EPS Estimates based on S&P Operating Earnings; historical GAAP earnings are as reported.

### Dividend Data (Dates: mm/dd Payment Date: mm/dd/yy)

| Amount ($) | Date Decl. | Ex-Div. Date | Stk. of Record | Payment Date |
| --- | --- | --- | --- | --- |
| 0.270 | 02/27 | 03/06 | 03/10 | 03/21/08 |
| 0.270 | 05/09 | 05/29 | 06/02 | 06/20/08 |
| 0.270 | 08/25 | 08/28 | 09/02 | 09/19/08 |
| 0.270 | 11/12 | 11/26 | 12/01 | 12/19/08 |

Dividends have been paid since 1998. Source: Company reports.

# Waste Management Inc.

## Business Summary November 11, 2008

CORPORATE OVERVIEW. Waste Management, the largest waste disposal company in North America, provides collection, transfer, recycling and re-source recovery, as well as disposal services. It also owns U.S. waste-to-energy facilities. As of December 31, 2007, it served nearly 20 million cus-tomers through 354 collection operations, 341 transfer stations, 277 owned or operated landfills (six hazardous waste landfills), 16 waste-to-energy plants, 105 recycling plants, and 108 beneficial-use landfill gas projects. In 2007, rev-enues from the North American solid waste (NASW) business were: 56% col-lection; 20% landfill; 5.6% waste-to-energy (Wheelabrator Technologies unit); 11% transfer; and 8.3% recycling and other. WMI's average remaining landfill life was recently about 30 years when considering remaining permitted ca-pacity and projected annual disposal volume. It is seeking expansion permits at 54 landfills. WMI's internalization rate was 67.5% at September 30, 2008, up from 66.5% a year earlier.

We project free cash flow of about $1.4 billion for 2008 ($1.2 billion through first nine months). WMI bought back $1.42 billion of stock (nearly 40 million shares) in 2007. It spent $410 million for nearly 12.7 million shares in the first nine months of 2008. We expect WMI to invest in landfill gas-to-energy, med-ical waste projects and other initiatives. In October 2008, WMI said capital spending for 2008 would be somewhat lower than its earlier forecast of $1.45 billion, due to cutbacks in landfill construction spending and other areas that

have been impacted by lower volume. It plans to maintain its fleet invest-ments. Additionally, the company noted that even though for every 1% price increase it can lose 3% to 5% of volume, it can still boost profit.

CORPORATE STRATEGY. WMI plans to divest underperforming collection op-erations, transfer stations, and glass and plastic recycling plants, targeting a total of over $900 million in annual revenues. Proceeds from divestitures in 2007 were $278 million. Three major divestitures accounted for $230 million in annual revenues. We think the company will benefit from its intention to sim-plify its organizational structure by placing more emphasis on the day-to-day decision making at its regional operations, and by reducing costs at its group and corporate offices. In October 2007, the company announced an environ-mental initiative, under which it plans to invest in waste-based energy pro-duction, recycling and new waste technologies, including up to $500 million a year for 10 years to increase fuel efficiency of its fleet. We view this as a posi-tive long-term environmental strategy as more methane in landfills is convert-ed into energy.

## Company Financials Fiscal Year Ended Dec. 31

| Per Share Data ($) | 2007 | 2006 | 2005 | 2004 | 2003 | 2002 | 2001 | 2000 | 1999 | 1998 |
|---|---|---|---|---|---|---|---|---|---|---|
| Tangible Book Value | 0.52 | 1.52 | 1.10 | 0.91 | 0.24 | 0.21 | 0.43 | NM | NM | NM |
| Cash Flow | 4.64 | 4.66 | 4.50 | 3.90 | 3.44 | 5.29 | 2.97 | 2.14 | 1.99 | 1.25 |
| Earnings | 2.23 | 2.10 | 2.09 | 1.60 | 1.21 | 1.33 | 0.80 | -0.16 | -0.64 | -1.31 |
| S&P Core Earnings | 2.18 | 2.05 | 1.90 | 1.48 | 1.09 | 1.17 | 1.04 | NA | NA | NA |
| Dividends | 0.96 | 0.88 | 0.80 | 0.75 | 0.01 | 0.01 | 0.01 | 0.01 | 0.02 | 0.02 |
| Payout Ratio | 43% | 42% | 38% | 47% | 1% | 1% | 1% | NM | NM | NM |
| Prices:High | 41.19 | 38.64 | 31.03 | 31.42 | 29.72 | 31.25 | 32.50 | 28.31 | 60.00 | 58.19 |
| Prices:Low | 32.40 | 30.08 | 26.80 | 25.67 | 19.39 | 20.20 | 22.51 | 13.00 | 14.00 | 34.44 |
| P/E Ratio:High | 18 | 18 | 15 | 20 | 25 | 23 | 41 | NM | NM | NM |
| P/E Ratio:Low | 15 | 14 | 13 | 16 | 16 | 15 | 28 | NM | NM | NM |

| Income Statement Analysis (Million $) | | | | | | | | | | |
|---|---|---|---|---|---|---|---|---|---|---|
| Revenue | 13,310 | 13,363 | 13,074 | 12,516 | 11,574 | 11,142 | 11,322 | 12,492 | 13,127 | 12,703 |
| Operating Income | 3,746 | 3,388 | 3,167 | 3,021 | 2,841 | 2,870 | 3,034 | 3,216 | 2,154 | 4,010 |
| Depreciation | 1,259 | 1,334 | 1,361 | 1,336 | 1,265 | 2,444 | 1,371 | 1,429 | 1,614 | 1,499 |
| Interest Expense | 521 | 545 | 496 | 455 | 439 | 462 | 541 | 748 | 770 | 681 |
| Pretax Income | 1,784 | 1,518 | 1,140 | 1,214 | 1,129 | 1,240 | 792 | 344 | -139 | -676 |
| Effective Tax Rate | 30.2% | 21.4% | NM | 20.3% | 35.8% | 34.2% | 35.9% | NM | NM | NM |
| Net Income | 1,163 | 1,149 | 1,182 | 931 | 719 | 823 | 503 | -97.0 | -395 | -767 |
| S&P Core Earnings | 1,133 | 1,121 | 1,072 | 864 | 643 | 725 | 653 | NA | NA | NA |

| Balance Sheet & Other Financial Data (Million $) | | | | | | | | | | |
|---|---|---|---|---|---|---|---|---|---|---|
| Cash | 348 | 614 | 666 | 443 | 135 | 264 | 730 | 94.0 | 181 | 88.7 |
| Current Assets | 2,480 | 3,182 | 3,451 | 2,819 | 2,588 | 2,700 | 3,124 | 2,457 | 6,221 | 3,881 |
| Total Assets | 20,175 | 20,600 | 21,135 | 20,905 | 20,656 | 19,631 | 19,490 | 18,565 | 22,681 | 22,715 |
| Current Liabilities | 2,598 | 3,268 | 3,257 | 3,205 | 3,332 | 3,173 | 3,721 | 2,937 | 7,489 | 4,294 |
| Long Term Debt | 8,008 | 7,495 | 8,165 | 8,182 | 7,997 | 8,062 | 7,709 | 8,372 | 8,399 | 11,114 |
| Common Equity | 5,792 | 6,222 | 6,121 | 5,971 | 5,563 | 5,308 | 5,392 | 4,801 | 4,403 | 4,372 |
| Total Capital | 15,521 | 15,357 | 15,931 | 14,435 | 15,473 | 13,389 | 14,241 | 14,067 | 13,540 | 16,069 |
| Capital Expenditures | 1,211 | 1,329 | 1,180 | 1,258 | 1,200 | 1,287 | 1,328 | 1,313 | 1,327 | 1,651 |
| Cash Flow | 2,422 | 2,483 | 2,543 | 2,267 | 1,984 | 3,267 | 1,874 | 1,332 | 1,219 | 732 |
| Current Ratio | 1.0 | 1.0 | 1.1 | 0.9 | 0.8 | 0.9 | 0.8 | 0.8 | 0.8 | 0.9 |
| % Long Term Debt of Capitalization | 51.5 | 48.8 | 51.3 | 56.7 | 51.7 | 60.2 | 54.1 | 59.5 | 62.0 | 69.2 |
| % Net Income of Revenue | 8.7 | 8.6 | 9.0 | 7.4 | 6.2 | 7.4 | 4.4 | NM | NM | NM |
| % Return on Assets | 5.7 | 5.5 | 5.6 | 4.5 | 3.5 | 4.2 | 2.6 | NM | NM | NM |
| % Return on Equity | 19.3 | 18.6 | 19.6 | 16.1 | 13.2 | 15.4 | 9.9 | NM | NM | NM |

Data as orig reptd.; bef. results of disc opers/spec. items. Per share data adj. for stk. divs.; EPS diluted. E-Estimated. NA-Not Available. NM-Not Meaningful. NR-Not Ranked. UR-Under Review.

**Office:** 1001 Fannin Street, Houston, TX 77002.
**Telephone:** 713-512-6200.
**Website:** http://www.wm.com
**Chrmn:** J.C. Pope

**Pres & COO:** L. O'Donnell, III
**CEO:** D.P. Steiner
**SVP & CFO:** R.G. Simpson
**SVP & General Counsel:** R.L. Wittenbraker

**Investor Contact:** J. Alderson (713-394-2281)
**Board Members:** P. S. Cafferty, F. M. Clark, Jr., P. W. Gross, J. C. Pope, W. R. Reum, S. G. Rothmeier, D. P. Steiner, T. H. Weidemeyer

**Founded:** 1894
**Domicile:** Delaware
**Employees:** 47,400

The McGraw-Hill Companies

# Waters Corp

STANDARD &POOR'S

| S&P Recommendation | HOLD ★★★☆☆ | Price $39.14 (as of Nov 14, 2008) | 12-Mo. Target Price $62.00 | Investment Style Large-Cap Growth |
|---|---|---|---|---|

**GICS Sector** Health Care
**Sub-Industry** Life Sciences Tools & Services

**Summary** This company manufactures scientific and industrial analytical equipment such as liquid chromatography, thermal analysis and mass spectrometry products.

## Key Stock Statistics (Source S&P, Vickers, company reports)

| | | | | | |
|---|---|---|---|---|---|
| 52-Wk Range | $81.84–37.00 | S&P Oper. EPS 2008**E** | 3.34 | Market Capitalization(B) | $3.848 | Beta | 1.54 |
| Trailing 12-Month EPS | $3.17 | S&P Oper. EPS 2009**E** | 3.72 | Yield (%) | Nil | S&P 3-Yr. Proj. EPS CAGR(%) | 13 |
| Trailing 12-Month P/E | 12.4 | P/E on S&P Oper. EPS 2008**E** | 11.7 | Dividend Rate/Share | Nil | S&P Credit Rating | NA |
| $10K Invested 5 Yrs Ago | $12,774 | Common Shares Outstg. (M) | 98.3 | Institutional Ownership (%) | 93 | | |

## Price Performance

30-Week Mov. Avg. · · · 10-Week Mov. Avg. - - **GAAP Earnings vs. Previous Year** Volume Above Avg. STARS
12-Mo. Target Price — Relative Strength — ▲ Up ▼ Down ► No Change    Below Avg.

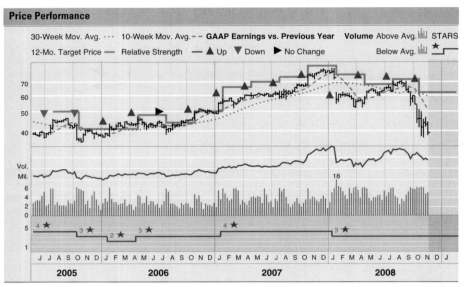

Options: ASE, CBOE, Ph

Analysis prepared by **Jeffrey Loo, CFA** on October 24, 2008, when the stock traded at **$ 40.01.**

## Highlights

➤ We see sales rising 10% in 2008 to $1.62 billion but increasing only 6% in 2009 to $1.71 billion as we believe foreign exchange will adversely affect sales beginning in the fourth quarter of 2008. We also believe softness in the large pharmaceutical end-user market will continue through the first half of 2009. However, we expect increased consumable and chemistry sales on a larger installed instrument base. Consumable and service sales now account for over 50% of WAT's sales and are growing at about 10% annually. We anticipate solid growth in the Thermal Analysis unit, albeit at a slower rate than in recent years, and also see robust growth in food safety-related instruments.

➤ We project gross margins will rebound 110 basis points (bps) on improved production efficiencies, following an 80 bps decline in 2007. We see operating leverage lifting operating margins 170 bps in 2008.

➤ We estimate 2008 and 2009 operating EPS at $3.34 and $3.72, respectively, aided by a lower share count due to stock buybacks. However, we believe WAT's buyback program leverages the company as it finances the program with debt as well as free cash flow.

## Investment Rationale/Risk

➤ We see uncertainty in several of WAT's key markets amid tight credit markets, including the large pharmaceutical end-user market in the U.S. and Europe, and think the nominal increase in the NIH budget will adversely affect sales growth. But we are encouraged by efforts to expand consumable and service-related sales, aided by a higher installed instrument base. That said, we think instrument sales growth will moderate in 2008 and 2009 after a robust 2007, despite our favorable view of WAT's systems integration approach and new products such as the Synapt High Definition MS and tandem quadrupole devices. We also anticipate continued strength in industrial end markets and food safety applications.

➤ Risks to our recommendation and target price include soft equipment sales if pharmaceutical and research firms limit capital spending, and a softening in industrial end markets following several years of robust growth.

➤ Based on our P/E-to-growth (PEG) analysis, using our 2009 EPS forecast, a PEG ratio of 1.3X, in line with peers, and a 13% projected three-year growth rate, our 12-month target price is $62.

## Qualitative Risk Assessment

| LOW | MEDIUM | HIGH |
|---|---|---|

Our risk assessment reflects WAT's strong market share in the liquid chromatography and mass spectrometry markets, offset by a highly competitive marketplace and a reliance on customer demand for expensive instruments.

## Quantitative Evaluations

**S&P Quality Ranking**                      B+

| D | C | B- | B | B+ | A- | A | A+ |
|---|---|---|---|---|---|---|---|

**Relative Strength Rank**                  MODERATE

46

LOWEST = 1                                HIGHEST = 99

## Revenue/Earnings Data

**Revenue (Million $)**

| | 1Q | 2Q | 3Q | 4Q | Year |
|---|---|---|---|---|---|
| 2008 | 371.7 | 398.8 | 386.3 | -- | -- |
| 2007 | 330.8 | 352.6 | 352.6 | 437.0 | 1,473 |
| 2006 | 290.2 | 301.9 | 301.2 | 386.9 | 1,280 |
| 2005 | 268.3 | 284.6 | 273.0 | 332.3 | 1,158 |
| 2004 | 255.1 | 260.5 | 264.8 | 324.2 | 1,105 |
| 2003 | 221.0 | 231.8 | 230.4 | 275.1 | 958.2 |

**Earnings Per Share ($)**

| | | | | | |
|---|---|---|---|---|---|
| 2008 | 0.67 | 0.82 | 0.71 | E1.10 | E3.34 |
| 2007 | 0.54 | 0.59 | 0.52 | 0.96 | 2.62 |
| 2006 | 0.42 | 0.46 | 0.49 | 0.78 | 2.13 |
| 2005 | 0.38 | 0.46 | 0.22 | 0.71 | 1.74 |
| 2004 | 0.33 | 0.49 | 0.42 | 0.58 | 1.82 |
| 2003 | 0.26 | 0.33 | 0.29 | 0.47 | 1.34 |

Fiscal year ended Dec. 31. Next earnings report expected: Late January. EPS Estimates based on S&P Operating Earnings; historical GAAP earnings are as reported.

## Dividend Data

No cash dividends have been paid.

# Waters Corp

**STANDARD
&POOR'S**

## Business Summary October 24, 2008

CORPORATE OVERVIEW. Waters manufactures, distributes, and services analytical instruments to the pharmaceutical, life sciences, biochemical, industrial, academic, and government end markets. Analytical instruments and components manufactured include high-performance liquid chromatography (HPLC) instruments, columns and other consumables, mass spectrometry (MS) instruments that can be integrated with other analytical instruments, and thermal analysis (TA) and rheology instruments. HPLC is the standard technique to identify and analyze constituent components of various chemicals and materials. Its unique performance capabilities let it separate and identify 80% of known chemicals and materials. HPLC is used to analyze substances in a variety of industries for R&D, quality control, and process engineering applications. Pharmaceutical and life science industries use HPLC primarily to identify new drugs.

In March 2004, WAT introduced a novel technology that it describes as Ultra Performance Chromatography, the Acquity UPLC. WAT believes the Acquity UPLC provides more comprehensive chemical separation and faster analysis times compared to the HPLC. MS is an analytical technique used to identify unknown compounds, quantify known materials, and elucidate the structural and chemical properties of molecules by measuring the masses of individual molecules that have been converted into ions. These products serve diverse markets, including pharmaceutical and environmental industries. The TA In-

struments division makes and services thermal analysis and rheology instruments used for the physical characterization of polymers and related materials. Thermal analysis measures physical characteristics of materials as a function of temperature. Changes in temperature affect several characteristics of materials, such as their physical state, weight, dimension and mechanical and electrical properties, which may be measured using thermal analysis techniques. As a result, thermal analysis is widely used to develop, produce, and characterize materials in industries such as plastics, chemicals, and pharmaceuticals.

WAT has supplemented its internal growth with various strategic acquisitions. In March 2004, it acquired NuGenesis Technologies Corp. for about $43 million. NuGenesis and Creon Lab formed the company's new Lab Informatics market segment. In March 2006, WAT acquired VICAM, a provider of bioseparation and rapid detection instruments for food safety. In August 2006, WAT acquired Thermometric AB, and in November 2006, it acquired Environmental Resource Associates, a provider of environmental testing and services. In 2007 WAT acquired Calorimetry Sciences Corporation.

## Company Financials Fiscal Year Ended Dec. 31

| Per Share Data ($) | 2007 | 2006 | 2005 | 2004 | 2003 | 2002 | 2001 | 2000 | 1999 | 1998 |
|---|---|---|---|---|---|---|---|---|---|---|
| Tangible Book Value | 5.71 | NM | NM | 3.05 | 2.67 | NM | 3.19 | 2.21 | 0.98 | NM |
| Cash Flow | 2.88 | 2.57 | 2.12 | 2.16 | 1.60 | 1.40 | 1.08 | 1.36 | 1.14 | 0.78 |
| Earnings | 2.62 | 2.13 | 1.74 | 1.82 | 1.34 | 1.12 | 0.84 | 1.14 | 0.92 | 0.57 |
| S&P Core Earnings | 2.62 | 2.18 | 1.57 | 1.45 | 1.18 | 0.99 | 1.07 | NA | NA | NA |
| Dividends | Nil | Nil | Nil | Nil | Nil | Nil | Nil | Nil | Nil | Nil |
| Payout Ratio | Nil | Nil | Nil | Nil | Nil | Nil | Nil | Nil | Nil | Nil |
| Prices:High | 81.53 | 51.64 | 51.57 | 49.80 | 33.42 | 39.25 | 85.38 | 90.94 | 33.84 | 21.88 |
| Prices:Low | 48.55 | 37.06 | 33.99 | 33.10 | 19.79 | 17.86 | 22.33 | 21.97 | 18.13 | 9.13 |
| P/E Ratio:High | 31 | 24 | 30 | 27 | 25 | 35 | NM | 80 | 37 | 39 |
| P/E Ratio:Low | 19 | 17 | 20 | 18 | 15 | 16 | NM | 19 | 20 | 16 |

| Income Statement Analysis (Million $) | | | | | | | | | | |
|---|---|---|---|---|---|---|---|---|---|---|
| Revenue | 1,473 | 1,280 | 1,158 | 1,105 | 958 | 890 | 859 | 795 | 704 | 619 |
| Operating Income | 389 | 355 | 330 | 321 | 271 | 251 | 258 | 240 | 205 | 164 |
| Depreciation | 27.5 | 46.2 | 43.7 | 41.9 | 33.8 | 37.2 | 34.0 | 29.4 | 28.9 | 27.2 |
| Interest Expense | 56.5 | 51.7 | 24.7 | 10.1 | 2.37 | 2.48 | 1.26 | Nil | 8.95 | 18.3 |
| Pretax Income | 323 | 263 | 275 | 286 | 224 | 195 | 147 | 211 | 168 | 102 |
| Effective Tax Rate | 17.1% | 15.5% | 26.4% | 21.6% | 23.6% | 22.1% | 22.3% | 26.0% | 27.0% | 26.7% |
| Net Income | 268 | 222 | 202 | 224 | 171 | 152 | 115 | 156 | 122 | 74.4 |
| S&P Core Earnings | 268 | 227 | 183 | 179 | 150 | 134 | 147 | NA | NA | NA |

| Balance Sheet & Other Financial Data (Million $) | | | | | | | | | | |
|---|---|---|---|---|---|---|---|---|---|---|
| Cash | 693 | 514 | 494 | 539 | 357 | 313 | 227 | 75.5 | 3.80 | 5.50 |
| Current Assets | 1,237 | 1,000 | 913 | 974 | 715 | 636 | 523 | 344 | 247 | 252 |
| Total Assets | 1,881 | 1,617 | 1,429 | 1,460 | 1,131 | 1,011 | 887 | 692 | 584 | 578 |
| Current Liabilities | 658 | 686 | 604 | 493 | 379 | 320 | 281 | 221 | 198 | 186 |
| Long Term Debt | 500 | 500 | 500 | 250 | 125 | Nil | Nil | Nil | 81.1 | 218 |
| Common Equity | 586 | 362 | 284 | 679 | 590 | 665 | 582 | 452 | 292 | 150 |
| Total Capital | 1,086 | 862 | 784 | 929 | 715 | 665 | 582 | 452 | 373 | 377 |
| Capital Expenditures | 60.3 | 51.4 | 51.0 | 66.2 | 34.6 | 37.9 | 42.4 | 35.4 | 19.4 | 15.0 |
| Cash Flow | 296 | 268 | 246 | 266 | 205 | 189 | 148 | 186 | 151 | 101 |
| Current Ratio | 1.9 | 1.5 | 1.5 | 2.0 | 1.9 | 2.0 | 1.9 | 1.6 | 1.3 | 1.4 |
| % Long Term Debt of Capitalization | 46.0 | 58.0 | 63.8 | 26.9 | 17.5 | Nil | Nil | Nil | 21.7 | 57.8 |
| % Net Income of Revenue | 18.2 | 17.4 | 17.4 | 20.3 | 17.8 | 17.1 | 13.3 | 19.6 | 17.4 | 12.0 |
| % Return on Assets | 15.3 | 14.6 | 14.0 | 17.3 | 15.9 | 16.0 | 14.5 | 24.4 | 21.1 | 13.2 |
| % Return on Equity | 56.5 | 68.8 | 42.0 | 35.3 | 27.2 | 24.3 | 22.2 | 42.0 | 55.3 | 69.1 |

Data as orig reptd.; bef. results of disc opers/spec. items. Per share data adj. for stk. divs.; EPS diluted. E-Estimated. NA-Not Available. NM-Not Meaningful. NR-Not Ranked. UR-Under Review.

**Office:** 34 Maple Street, Milford, MA 01757-3696.
**Telephone:** 508-478-2000.
**Email:** info@waters.com
**Website:** http://www.waters.com

**Chrmn, Pres & CEO:** D.A. Berthiaume
**CFO, Chief Admin Officer & Chief Acctg Officer:** J.A. Ornell
**Secy & General Counsel:** M.T. Beaudouin
**Cntlr:** W. Curry

**Board Members:** J. Bekenstein, M. J. Berendt, D. A. Berthiaume, E. W. Conard, L. H. Glimcher, C. A. Kuebler, W. J. Miller, J. A. Reed, T. P. Salice

**Founded:** 1991
**Domicile:** Delaware
**Employees:** 4,956

*The McGraw-Hill Companies*

# Watson Pharmaceuticals Inc.

**STANDARD &POOR'S**

| S&P Recommendation **BUY** ★★★★☆ | Price $23.61 (as of Nov 14, 2008) | 12-Mo. Target Price $30.00 | Investment Style Large-Cap Blend |
|---|---|---|---|

**GICS Sector** Health Care
**Sub-Industry** Pharmaceuticals

**Summary** This company produces generic and branded drugs. In November 2006, Watson acquired rival generic drugmaker Andrx Corp. for $1.9 billion in cash.

## Key Stock Statistics (Source S&P, Vickers, company reports)

| | | | | | | | |
|---|---|---|---|---|---|---|---|
| 52-Wk Range | $32.70– 20.17 | S&P Oper. EPS 2008**E** | 2.00 | Market Capitalization(B) | $2.470 | Beta | 0.85 |
| Trailing 12-Month EPS | $1.94 | S&P Oper. EPS 2009**E** | 2.17 | Yield (%) | Nil | S&P 3-Yr. Proj. EPS CAGR(%) | 8 |
| Trailing 12-Month P/E | 12.2 | P/E on S&P Oper. EPS 2008**E** | 11.8 | Dividend Rate/Share | Nil | S&P Credit Rating | BBB- |
| $10K Invested 5 Yrs Ago | $5,256 | Common Shares Outstg. (M) | 104.6 | Institutional Ownership (%) | 98 | | |

## Price Performance

30-Week Mov. Avg. ···   10-Week Mov. Avg. - -   **GAAP Earnings vs. Previous Year**   Volume Above Avg. STARS

12-Mo. Target Price —   Relative Strength —   ▲ Up   ▼ Down   ▶ No Change   Below Avg. ★

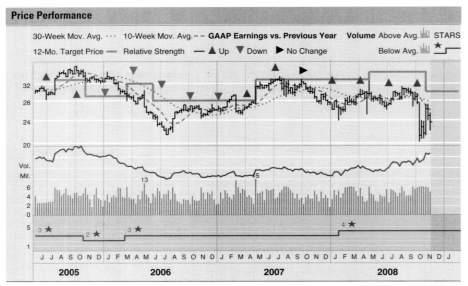

Options: ASE, CBOE, Ph

Analysis prepared by **Herman B. Saftlas** on November 05, 2008, when the stock traded at **$ 26.50**.

## Qualitative Risk Assessment

| LOW | **MEDIUM** | HIGH |
|---|---|---|

Our risk assessment reflects risks common to the generic pharmaceutical business, which include the ability to successfully develop generic products, obtain regulatory approvals and legally challenge branded patents. However, we believe these risks are offset by the company's wide and diverse generic portfolio and the balance afforded by WPI's branded drug business.

## Quantitative Evaluations

**S&P Quality Ranking**     **B-**

| D | C | **B-** | B | B+ | A- | A | A+ |
|---|---|---|---|---|---|---|---|

**Relative Strength Rank**     **STRONG**

75

LOWEST = 1      HIGHEST = 99

## Highlights

► We project revenues to rise about 6% in 2009. Generic drug sales should be augmented by new products such as generic versions of Prilosec, Toprol XL, Wellbutrin XL, Flonase, Concerta and Lovenox. In total, Watson has about 60 ANDAs pending at the FDA. New product flow should also benefit from the new Davie, FL plant, which recently obtained FDA clearance. On the branded side of the business, we see growth driven by Trelstar for prostate cancer, and new products such as Rapaflow for enlarged prostates, and Oxytrol gel for incontinence. We also see higher sales for distributed products.

► We expect gross margins to widen somewhat in 2009, helped by savings accruing from the closings of excess manufacturing capacity, and other supply chain improvements. We see SG&A and R&D spending rising in line with revenues, but amortization charges and interest expense are expected to decline sharply.

► After taxes of about 37.5% (similar to the indicated 2008 rate), we project EPS of $2.17 for 2009, up from an estimated $2.00 in 2008, before nonrecurring charges.

## Investment Rationale/Risk

► We believe that the company's diversified business platform, which comprises growing positions in generics, branded drugs and drug distribution, coupled with ongoing cost streamlining measures, will provide the underpinnings for respectable earnings growth over the coming years. We see Watson's new top management as well positioned to complete the task of integrating the acquisition of Andrx Corp. and expanding the depth and geographic reach of WPI's drug businesses. We are also encouraged by recent FDA clearance of the Davie, FL plant, which we expect to begin producing new generics this year.

► Risks to our recommendation and target price include sooner than expected loss of exclusive marketing rights to Ferrlecit, stronger-than-expected competitive pressures, and possible pipeline disappointments.

► Our 12-month target price of $30 is based on a modest premium-to-peers P/E of 13.8X our 2009 EPS estimate. This is supported by our DCF model, which assumes decelerating cash flow growth over the next 10 years, a WACC of 7%, and perpetuity growth of 1%, indicating intrinsic value of $30.

## Revenue/Earnings Data

**Revenue (Million $)**

| | 1Q | 2Q | 3Q | 4Q | Year |
|---|---|---|---|---|---|
| 2008 | 627.0 | 622.6 | 640.7 | -- | -- |
| 2007 | 671.6 | 603.0 | 594.7 | 627.3 | 2,497 |
| 2006 | 407.2 | 510.4 | 440.5 | 621.2 | 1,979 |
| 2005 | 400.8 | 416.3 | 410.3 | 418.8 | 1,646 |
| 2004 | 409.7 | 399.4 | 408.0 | 423.5 | 1,641 |
| 2003 | 336.9 | 355.9 | 358.8 | 406.2 | 1,458 |

**Earnings Per Share ($)**

| | 1Q | 2Q | 3Q | 4Q | Year |
|---|---|---|---|---|---|
| 2008 | 0.45 | 0.53 | 0.62 | E0.53 | E2.00 |
| 2007 | 0.29 | 0.33 | 0.31 | 0.34 | 1.27 |
| 2006 | 0.23 | -0.15 | 0.31 | -4.80 | -4.37 |
| 2005 | 0.32 | 0.35 | 0.35 | 0.19 | 1.21 |
| 2004 | 0.39 | 0.29 | 0.13 | 0.46 | 1.27 |
| 2003 | 0.44 | 0.47 | 0.47 | 0.48 | 1.86 |

Fiscal year ended Dec. 31. Next earnings report expected: Late February. EPS Estimates based on S&P Operating Earnings; historical GAAP earnings are as reported.

## Dividend Data

No cash dividends have been paid.

---

*The McGraw-Hill Companies*

# Watson Pharmaceuticals Inc.

STANDARD &POOR'S

## Business Summary November 05, 2008

CORPORATE PROFILE. Watson Pharmaceuticals is a leading maker of generic pharmaceuticals. WPI targets difficult to produce niche off-patent drugs. WPI significantly expanded its generic business with the acquisition of Andrx Corp. Watson also offers a line of specialty branded pharmaceuticals, largely in the areas of urology and nephrology.

Many WPI pharmaceuticals incorporate the company's novel proprietary drug delivery systems, such as transmucosal, vaginal and transdermal systems that allow for defined rates of drug release. Total revenues in 2007 were 60% from generic drugs, 17% from branded drugs, and 23% from distributed products. Drugs produced by third-party manufacturers represented about 57% of WPI's revenues in 2007.

WPI markets over 150 generic drug products, which comprise a broad cross section of therapeutic categories. Key segments include oral contraceptives, analgesics, antihypertensives, diuretics, antiulcers, antipsychotics, anti-inflammatories, analgesics, hormone replacements, antispasmodics and antidiarrheals.

During 2007, WPI launched 16 new generic products. Key launches in 2007 included generic versions of Wellbutrin XL antidepressant; Duragesic, a trans-

dermal fentanyl analgesic; Proventil, a bronchodilator; and Tilia Fe, an oral contraceptive. Also, beginning in July 2007, WPI began to earn royalties on Sandoz's sales of metoprolol succinate extended release tablets.

Branded pharmaceuticals comprise specialty drugs and nephrology products. Specialty drugs includes urology; antihypertensive, psychiatry, pain management and dermatology products; and a genital warts treatment. Key products include Trelstar, a treatment for prostate cancer; Oxytrol, an oxybutynin transdermal patch to treat urinary incontinence; and Androderm, a testosterone transdermal patch.

The nephrology product line consists of products used to treat iron deficiency anemia. The primary product is Ferrlecit, which is indicated for patients undergoing hemodialysis in conjunction with erythropoietin therapy. Ferrlecit accounted for about 5% of revenues and 12% of gross profits in 2007. Branded products are marketed to urologists, primary care physicians, endocrinologists, obstetricians and gynecologists.

## Company Financials Fiscal Year Ended Dec. 31

| Per Share Data ($) | 2007 | 2006 | 2005 | 2004 | 2003 | 2002 | 2001 | 2000 | 1999 | 1998 |
|---|---|---|---|---|---|---|---|---|---|---|
| Tangible Book Value | 3.56 | 0.09 | 8.81 | 7.97 | 5.54 | 4.33 | 3.79 | 0.98 | 5.00 | 3.08 |
| Cash Flow | 3.37 | -2.23 | 2.87 | 2.07 | 2.78 | 2.45 | 2.01 | 2.34 | 2.28 | 1.66 |
| Earnings | 1.27 | -4.37 | 1.21 | 1.27 | 1.86 | 1.64 | 1.07 | 1.65 | 1.83 | 1.32 |
| S&P Core Earnings | 1.24 | -4.32 | 1.09 | 1.16 | 1.64 | 1.36 | 0.52 | NA | NA | NA |
| Dividends | Nil | Nil | Nil | Nil | Nil | Nil | Nil | Nil | Nil | Nil |
| Payout Ratio | Nil | Nil | Nil | Nil | Nil | Nil | Nil | Nil | Nil | Nil |
| Prices:High | 33.91 | 35.27 | 36.93 | 49.19 | 50.12 | 33.25 | 66.39 | 71.50 | 62.94 | 63.00 |
| Prices:Low | 25.02 | 21.35 | 27.99 | 24.50 | 26.90 | 17.95 | 26.50 | 33.69 | 26.50 | 30.50 |
| P/E Ratio:High | 27 | NM | 31 | 39 | 27 | 20 | 62 | 43 | 34 | 48 |
| P/E Ratio:Low | 20 | NM | 23 | 19 | 14 | 11 | 25 | 20 | 14 | 23 |

**Income Statement Analysis** (Million $)

| | 2007 | 2006 | 2005 | 2004 | 2003 | 2002 | 2001 | 2000 | 1999 | 1998 |
|---|---|---|---|---|---|---|---|---|---|---|
| Revenue | 2,497 | 1,979 | 1,646 | 1,641 | 1,458 | 1,223 | 1,161 | 812 | 689 | 556 |
| Operating Income | 515 | 364 | 450 | 419 | 439 | 386 | 404 | 227 | 281 | 237 |
| Depreciation | 254 | 218 | 207 | 107 | 100 | 86.6 | 101 | 71.4 | 44.0 | 31.3 |
| Interest Expense | 44.5 | 22.1 | 14.5 | 13.3 | 25.8 | 22.1 | 27.8 | 24.3 | 11.1 | 7.06 |
| Pretax Income | 224 | -411 | 219 | 237 | 318 | 279 | 199 | 355 | 273 | 199 |
| Effective Tax Rate | 37.1% | NM | 37.0% | 36.1% | 36.2% | 37.0% | 41.5% | 52.0% | 34.4% | 39.3% |
| Net Income | 141 | -445 | 138 | 151 | 203 | 176 | 116 | 171 | 179 | 121 |
| S&P Core Earnings | 138 | -441 | 123 | 137 | 178 | 146 | 56.3 | NA | NA | NA |

**Balance Sheet & Other Financial Data** (Million $)

| | 2007 | 2006 | 2005 | 2004 | 2003 | 2002 | 2001 | 2000 | 1999 | 1998 |
|---|---|---|---|---|---|---|---|---|---|---|
| Cash | 216 | 161 | 630 | 680 | 574 | 273 | 329 | 238 | 116 | 72.7 |
| Current Assets | 1,174 | 1,262 | 1,360 | 1,370 | 1,323 | 921 | 890 | 831 | 435 | 293 |
| Total Assets | 3,472 | 3,761 | 3,080 | 3,244 | 3,283 | 2,663 | 2,528 | 2,580 | 1,439 | 1,070 |
| Current Liabilities | 445 | 690 | 246 | 256 | 339 | 375 | 245 | 280 | 129 | 94.8 |
| Long Term Debt | 899 | 1,124 | 588 | 588 | 723 | 332 | 416 | 438 | 150 | 150 |
| Common Equity | 1,849 | 1,680 | 2,104 | 2,243 | 2,057 | 1,798 | 1,672 | 1,548 | 1,055 | 750 |
| Total Capital | 2,928 | 3,008 | 2,692 | 2,831 | 2,924 | 2,282 | 2,274 | 2,242 | 1,292 | 955 |
| Capital Expenditures | 75.1 | 44.4 | 78.8 | 69.2 | 151 | 87.5 | 62.0 | 34.3 | 26.8 | 26.5 |
| Cash Flow | 395 | -227 | 345 | 258 | 303 | 262 | 218 | 242 | 223 | 152 |
| Current Ratio | 2.6 | 1.8 | 5.5 | 5.4 | 3.9 | 2.5 | 3.6 | 3.0 | 3.4 | 3.1 |
| % Long Term Debt of Capitalization | 30.7 | 37.4 | 21.8 | 20.8 | 24.7 | 14.5 | 18.3 | 19.6 | 11.6 | 15.7 |
| % Net Income of Revenue | 5.7 | NM | 8.4 | 9.2 | 13.9 | 14.4 | 10.0 | 21.0 | 26.0 | 21.7 |
| % Return on Assets | 3.9 | NM | 4.4 | 4.6 | 6.8 | 6.8 | 4.6 | 8.4 | 13.9 | 13.2 |
| % Return on Equity | 8.0 | NM | 6.4 | 7.0 | 10.5 | 10.1 | 7.2 | 13.1 | 19.3 | 18.4 |

Data as orig reptd.; bef. results of disc opers/spec. items. Per share data adj. for stk. divs.; EPS diluted. E-Estimated. NA-Not Available. NM-Not Meaningful. NR-Not Ranked. UR-Under Review.

**Office:** 311 Bonnie Circle, Corona, CA 92880-2882.
**Telephone:** 951-493-5300.
**Website:** http://www.watson.com
**Chrmn:** A.L. Turner

**Pres & CEO:** P.M. Bisaro
**SVP & CFO:** M.W. Durand
**SVP, Secy & General Counsel:** D.A. Buchen
**SVP & CIO:** T.R. Giordano

**Investor Contact:** P. Eisenhaur (951-493-5611)
**Board Members:** P. M. Bisaro, M. Fedida, M. J. Feldman, A. F. Hummel, C. M. Klema, J. Michelson, R. Taylor, A. L. Turner, F. G. Weiss

**Founded:** 1983
**Domicile:** Nevada
**Employees:** 5,640

# Weatherford International Ltd.

| S&P Recommendation **BUY** ★★★★☆ | Price $12.80 (as of Nov 14, 2008) | 12-Mo. Target Price $24.00 | Investment Style Large-Cap Growth |
|---|---|---|---|

**GICS Sector** Energy
**Sub-Industry** Oil & Gas Equipment & Services

**Summary** This company is one of the leading global providers of equipment and services used for the drilling, completion and production of oil and natural gas wells.

## Key Stock Statistics (Source S&P, Vickers, company reports)

| | | | | | | |
|---|---|---|---|---|---|---|
| 52-Wk Range | $49.98– 11.04 | S&P Oper. EPS 2008**E** | 2.05 | Market Capitalization(B) | $8.718 | Beta | 1.31 |
| Trailing 12-Month EPS | $1.91 | S&P Oper. EPS 2009**E** | 2.58 | Yield (%) | Nil | S&P 3-Yr. Proj. EPS CAGR(%) | 26 |
| Trailing 12-Month P/E | 6.7 | P/E on S&P Oper. EPS 2008**E** | 6.2 | Dividend Rate/Share | Nil | S&P Credit Rating | BBB+ |
| $10K Invested 5 Yrs Ago | $15,468 | Common Shares Outstg. (M) | 681.1 | Institutional Ownership (%) | 98 | | |

## Price Performance

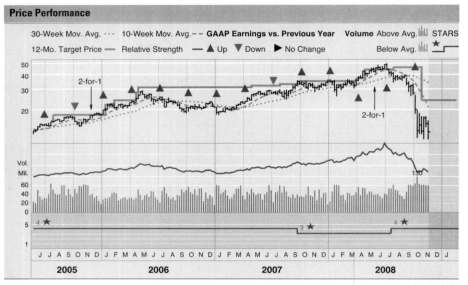

30-Week Mov. Avg. · · · · 10-Week Mov. Avg. – – **GAAP Earnings vs. Previous Year** Volume Above Avg. STARS
12-Mo. Target Price — Relative Strength — ▲ Up ▼ Down ► No Change Below Avg.

Options: CBOE

Analysis prepared by **Stewart Glickman, CFA** on October 22, 2008, when the stock traded at **$ 14.45**.

### Highlights

➤ In October, WFT said that its eight integrated drilling projects in the Eastern Hemisphere, and one such project in Mexico, would ramp up through the first quarter of 2009, and remained on schedule. WFT said in July that the Mexico project is of strategic importance to PEMEX, and we believe that successful execution by WFT could yield significant follow-on work beyond the initial $900 million commitment. For the other eight projects, we estimate revenue impact to WFT at approximately $3.3 billion over three years.

➤ Also in October, WFT said that results from all product lines improved in the third quarter, with standout performance from wireline, directional and underbalanced drilling, and artificial lift. WFT said further that while incremental margins in North America should narrow in the near term, such margins should widen in International markets, as absorption of fixed costs from prior international investments should improve.

➤ For 2008, we see total revenue growth of 22%, and an EPS gain of 29%, to a split-adjusted $2.05. For 2009, we project revenue growth of 20% and EPS of $2.58.

### Investment Rationale/Risk

➤ We think WFT's long-time focus on international growth has been well-timed, as we expect the brunt of the scaling back of upstream capital spending in 2009 to affect North America (albeit with more modest reductions elsewhere). While WFT said in October that it may reduce 2009 capital spending to $1.5 billion - $2.0 billion (versus a planned $2.2 billion for 2008), we think that any such cut, should it occur, would more likely affect 2010 results. WFT also noted that lead times for equipment have shrunk recently, and WFT has made improvements to its supply chain, which we think affords an opportunity to respond more nimbly to changes in market conditions.

➤ Risks to our recommendation and target price include reduced upstream capital spending; sharply lower oil and natural gas prices; and labor and raw material cost inflation.

➤ Our DCF model, assuming free cash flow growth of 14% per year for 10 years, and terminal growth of 3%, indicates intrinsic value of $25. Based on a 7X multiple on our 2009 EBITDA estimate, a 10X multiple on our 2009 EPS estimate (in line with peers), and our DCF model, our 12-month target price is $24.

### Qualitative Risk Assessment

| LOW | MEDIUM | HIGH |
|---|---|---|

Our risk assessment reflects the company's exposure to crude oil and natural gas prices and capital spending decisions by oil and gas producers, and geographic risk associated with operating in frontier regions around the globe. This is offset by our view of its leading-edge technology and its commitment to technological innovation in oilfield services.

### Quantitative Evaluations

**S&P Quality Ranking** NR

| D | C | B- | B | B+ | A- | A | A+ |
|---|---|---|---|---|---|---|---|

**Relative Strength Rank** WEAK

20

LOWEST = 1          HIGHEST = 99

### Revenue/Earnings Data

**Revenue (Million $)**

| | 1Q | 2Q | 3Q | 4Q | Year |
|---|---|---|---|---|---|
| 2008 | 2,196 | 2,229 | 2,541 | -- | -- |
| 2007 | 1,852 | 1,816 | 1,972 | 2,192 | 7,832 |
| 2006 | 1,536 | 1,539 | 1,697 | 1,808 | 6,579 |
| 2005 | 857.7 | 937.3 | 1,077 | 1,461 | 4,333 |
| 2004 | 712.6 | 742.2 | 794.3 | 882.6 | 3,132 |
| 2003 | 589.3 | 617.7 | 660.5 | 723.9 | 2,591 |

**Earnings Per Share ($)**

| | | | | | |
|---|---|---|---|---|---|
| 2008 | 0.41 | 0.52 | 0.53 | E0.57 | E2.05 |
| 2007 | 0.41 | 0.26 | 0.43 | 0.49 | 1.57 |
| 2006 | 0.29 | 0.26 | 0.33 | 0.39 | 1.27 |
| 2005 | 0.14 | 0.16 | 0.08 | 0.35 | 0.74 |
| 2004 | 0.10 | 0.14 | 0.12 | 0.23 | 0.59 |
| 2003 | 0.07 | 0.06 | 0.06 | 0.09 | 0.28 |

Fiscal year ended Dec. 31. Next earnings report expected: Late January. EPS Estimates based on S&P Operating Earnings; historical GAAP earnings are as reported.

### Dividend Data (Dates: mm/dd Payment Date: mm/dd/yy)

| Amount ($) | Date Decl. | Ex-Div. Date | Stk. of Record | Payment Date |
|---|---|---|---|---|
| 2-for-1 | -- | 05/27 | 05/09 | 05/23/08 |

Source: Company reports.

---

**Please read the Required Disclosures and Analyst Certification on the last page of this report.**

# Weatherford International Ltd.

**STANDARD &POOR'S**

## Business Summary October 22, 2008

CORPORATE OVERVIEW. Weatherford International is one of the world's leading providers of equipment and services for the drilling, completion and production of oil and natural gas wells. As of December 31, 2007, it had more than 800 manufacturing and service locations in over 100 countries. North America contributed 50% of 2007 revenues, while International operations contributed 50%. Internationally, the Middle East, North Africa and Asia region accounted for 23% of total revenues; Europe/CIS/West Africa 15%; and Latin America 11%.

CORPORATE STRATEGY. WFT has focused its long-term strategy on the geographic expansion of its products and services to the Eastern Hemisphere (Europe, Africa, the Middle East, Russia and Asia), as well as to Latin America, and on product and service expansion that assists in the drilling of new oilfields or efficiently producing oil and gas from existing oilfields. We view this strategy as consistent with ongoing secular trends in the energy industry, as oil and gas producers -- including supermajors, large independents and nationalized oil companies -- seek low-cost, high-growth opportunities. Frequently, such opportunities tend to be located in such frontier regions, and/or are found in challenging geological conditions that demand improved technologies.

IMPACT OF MAJOR DEVELOPMENTS. Following the April 2000 spin-off of the

Grant Prideco Drilling Products division and the February 2001 merger of the Compression Services division into a subsidiary of Universal Compression Holdings, Inc., WFT's business was divided into three principal operating divisions: Drilling and Intervention Services; Completion Systems; and Artificial Lift Systems. In April 2003, the company restructured its reporting divisions, and reported results in two segments: Drilling Services and Production Systems. In August 2005, WFT completed the acquisition of Precision Energy Services (PES) and Precision Drilling International (PDI). Following these acquisitions, the company reorganized into three operating segments: Evaluation, Drilling & Intervention Services; Completion & Production Services; and Other Operations. In the first quarter of 2007, the company reorganized again into four geographically based operating segments: North America, Latin America, Europe/West Africa/CIS, and Middle East/North Africa/Asia. Also in 2007, the company approved a plan to sell its oil and gas development and production business; a portion of this business was sold in 2007, and WFT expects to complete the remainder of the sale in the first half of 2008.

## Company Financials Fiscal Year Ended Dec. 31

| Per Share Data ($) | 2007 | 2006 | 2005 | 2004 | 2003 | 2002 | 2001 | 2000 | 1999 | 1998 |
|---|---|---|---|---|---|---|---|---|---|---|
| Tangible Book Value | 5.49 | 3.78 | 3.23 | 2.47 | 1.55 | 0.45 | 0.97 | 0.59 | 1.95 | 1.75 |
| Cash Flow | 2.44 | 1.94 | 1.24 | 1.00 | 0.71 | 0.44 | 0.79 | 0.37 | 0.44 | 0.60 |
| Earnings | 1.57 | 1.27 | 0.74 | 0.59 | 0.27 | -0.01 | 0.44 | -0.10 | 0.04 | 0.17 |
| Dividends | Nil | Nil | Nil | Nil | Nil | Nil | Nil | Nil | Nil | Nil |
| Payout Ratio | Nil | Nil | Nil | Nil | Nil | Nil | Nil | Nil | Nil | Nil |
| Prices:High | 36.11 | 29.37 | 18.97 | 13.81 | 11.93 | 13.56 | 15.09 | 15.50 | 10.53 | 14.61 |
| Prices:Low | 17.95 | 18.25 | 11.91 | 8.96 | 7.83 | 8.14 | 5.68 | 7.94 | 4.19 | 3.75 |
| P/E Ratio:High | 23 | 23 | 26 | 24 | 44 | NM | 34 | NM | NM | 89 |
| P/E Ratio:Low | 11 | 14 | 16 | 15 | 29 | NM | 13 | NM | NM | 23 |
| **Income Statement Analysis** (Million $) | | | | | | | | | | |
| Revenue | 7,832 | 6,579 | 4,333 | 3,132 | 2,591 | 2,329 | 2,329 | 1,814 | 1,240 | 2,011 |
| Operating Income | 2,261 | 1,817 | 977 | 649 | 499 | 488 | 596 | 372 | 231 | 461 |
| Depreciation, Depletion and Amortization | 606 | 483 | 334 | 256 | 233 | 215 | 208 | 199 | 167 | 171 |
| Interest Expense | 183 | 110 | 80.3 | 63.6 | 76.7 | 85.5 | 74.0 | 59.3 | 44.9 | 54.5 |
| Pretax Income | 1,444 | 1,224 | 626 | 431 | 195 | -9.84 | 339 | 71.3 | 28.4 | 99.4 |
| Effective Tax Rate | 23.0% | 25.9% | 25.4% | 21.5% | 26.0% | NM | 36.3% | NM | 29.9% | 34.8% |
| Net Income | 1,092 | 896 | 466 | 337 | 143 | -6.03 | 215 | -38.9 | 16.2 | 64.8 |
| **Balance Sheet & Other Financial Data** (Million $) | | | | | | | | | | |
| Cash | 171 | 126 | 134 | 317 | 56.1 | 48.8 | 88.8 | 154 | 44.4 | 40.2 |
| Current Assets | 4,472 | 3,360 | 2,639 | 1,943 | 1,436 | 1,259 | 1,231 | 1,242 | 869 | 1,082 |
| Total Assets | 13,191 | 10,139 | 8,580 | 5,543 | 5,000 | 4,495 | 4,296 | 3,462 | 3,514 | 2,832 |
| Current Liabilities | 2,202 | 2,043 | 1,998 | 660 | 782 | 877 | 760 | 463 | 666 | 557 |
| Long Term Debt | 3,066 | 1,565 | 632 | 1,404 | 1,380 | 1,514 | 1,500 | 1,133 | 629 | 632 |
| Common Equity | 7,407 | 6,175 | 5,667 | 3,313 | 2,708 | 1,974 | 1,838 | 1,338 | 1,833 | 1,494 |
| Total Capital | 10,671 | 7,876 | 6,387 | 4,748 | 4,107 | 3,523 | 3,437 | 2,834 | 2,661 | 2,126 |
| Capital Expenditures | 1,635 | 1,071 | 527 | 311 | 303 | 269 | 339 | 267 | 174 | 206 |
| Cash Flow | 1,698 | 1,379 | 801 | 593 | 376 | 209 | 423 | 160 | 183 | 236 |
| Current Ratio | 2.0 | 1.6 | 1.3 | 2.9 | 1.8 | 1.4 | 1.6 | 2.7 | 1.3 | 1.9 |
| % Long Term Debt of Capitalization | 28.7 | 19.9 | 9.9 | 29.6 | 33.6 | 43.0 | 43.6 | 40.0 | 23.6 | 29.7 |
| % Return on Assets | 9.4 | 9.6 | 6.6 | 6.4 | 3.0 | NM | 5.5 | NM | 0.5 | 3.1 |
| % Return on Equity | 16.1 | 15.1 | 10.4 | 11.2 | 6.1 | NM | 13.5 | NM | 1.0 | 6.4 |

Data as orig reptd.; bef. results of disc opers/spec. items. Per share data adj. for stk. divs.; EPS diluted. E-Estimated. NA-Not Available. NM-Not Meaningful. NR-Not Ranked. UR-Under Review.

**Office:** 515 Post Oak Boulevard, Houston, TX 77027-3415.
**Telephone:** 713-693-4000.
**Email:** investor.relations@weatherford.com
**Website:** http://www.weatherford.com

**Chrmn, Pres & CEO:** B.J. Duroc-Danner
**Vice Chrmn:** D.J. Butters
**COO & SVP:** K.R. Morley
**Investor Contact:** A.P. Becnel (713-693-4136)

**SVP & CFO:** A.P. Becnel
**Board Members:** N. F. Brady, D. J. Butters, B. J. Duroc-Danner, W. E. Macaulay, R. B. Millard, R. K. Moses, Jr., R. A. Rayne

**Founded:** 1972
**Domicile:** Bermuda
**Employees:** 38,000

**The McGraw·Hill Companies**

# WellPoint Inc

**STANDARD & POOR'S**

| S&P Recommendation | HOLD ★★★☆☆ | Price | 12-Mo. Target Price | Investment Style |
|---|---|---|---|---|
| | | $35.24 (as of Nov 14, 2008) | $48.00 | Large-Cap Growth |

**GICS Sector** Health Care
**Sub-Industry** Managed Health Care

**Summary** This managed health organization is the largest in the U.S., serving 35 million members mainly under the Blue Cross and/or Blue Shield license in 14 states.

## Key Stock Statistics (Source S&P, Vickers, company reports)

| | | | | | | | |
|---|---|---|---|---|---|---|---|
| 52-Wk Range | $90.00– 32.71 | S&P Oper. EPS 2008**E** | 5.51 | Market Capitalization(B) | $17.939 | Beta | 1.09 |
| Trailing 12-Month EPS | $5.61 | S&P Oper. EPS 2009**E** | 5.85 | Yield (%) | Nil | S&P 3-Yr. Proj. EPS CAGR(%) | 5 |
| Trailing 12-Month P/E | 6.3 | P/E on S&P Oper. EPS 2008**E** | 6.4 | Dividend Rate/Share | Nil | S&P Credit Rating | A- |
| $10K Invested 5 Yrs Ago | $10,256 | Common Shares Outstg. (M) | 509.0 | Institutional Ownership (%) | 85 | | |

## Price Performance

30-Week Mov. Avg. · · · · 10-Week Mov. Avg. - - - **GAAP Earnings vs. Previous Year** Volume Above Avg. STARS
12-Mo. Target Price ── Relative Strength ── ▲ Up ▼ Down ► No Change Below Avg. ★

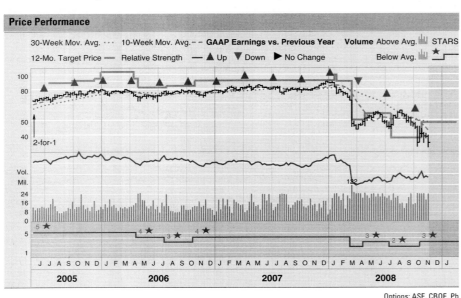

Options: ASE, CBOE, Ph

Analysis prepared by **Phillip M. Seligman** on October 28, 2008, when the stock traded at **$39.20**.

## Highlights

► We look for 2009 operating revenues to rise to about $62.6 billion, from $61.6 billion we see in 2008. Drivers we see include higher premiums, partly offset by 1% to 2% lower enrollment. WLP recently cited 400,000 net new national account members gained so far for 2009, but we see attrition from existing national, local group and individual accounts, given the soft economy. We also project 50,000 fewer Medicare Advantage members, on WLP's planned elimination of a poorly designed private fee-for-service plan, and 253,000 fewer Medicaid members, on two state program exits.

► We forecast that the firmwide medical loss ratio (MLR) will decline 50 basis points (bps) in 2009 on higher prices and assuming there are no medical cost spikes, after rising an estimated 120 bps in 2008, mainly on higher medical cost trends. While we expect the MLR to benefit from fewer Medicare and Medicaid members, we assume that benefit will be offset by fewer more-profitable individual and small-group members. We also estimate a modestly lower SG&A cost ratio, on revenue leverage.

► We look for operating EPS of $5.51 in 2008, versus 2007's $5.56, and see $5.85 in 2009.

## Investment Rationale/Risk

► We are encouraged by WLP's moves to fix its problems. The company is exiting underperforming Medicaid markets, and instituted account retention and broker incentive programs and launched new products to help turn around commercial risk enrollment. It also began pricing actions and provider contracting initiatives to help mitigate the impact of higher medical cost trends. Nonetheless, we are concerned that competition and our view of a rising unemployment rate will lead to more member attrition. Elsewhere, despite what we saw as a high level of investment losses in the third quarter, we believe WLP remains well capitalized. We continue to view its operating cash flow as healthy, providing financial flexibility.

► Risks to our recommendation and target price include enrollment losses above our expectations, higher medical costs, and unfavorable regulatory changes.

► Our 12-month target price of $48 reflects a peer-level forward P/E of about 8X applied to our 2009 EPS estimate. This P/E is at the midpoint of the target 7X to 9X peer range we see, following what we view as groupwide valuation compression.

## Qualitative Risk Assessment

| LOW | MEDIUM | HIGH |
|---|---|---|

Our risk assessment reflects WLP's leadership in the highly fragmented managed care market. We believe that its geographic, market and product diversity and its Blue Cross/Blue Shield tie are competitive strengths. However, we think that enrollment growth going forward will be limited by heightened competition that we see following consolidation in the managed care industry and by the difficult economic environment.

## Quantitative Evaluations

**S&P Quality Ranking** NR

| D | C | B- | B | B+ | A- | A | A+ |
|---|---|---|---|---|---|---|---|

**Relative Strength Rank** MODERATE

57

LOWEST = 1    HIGHEST = 99

## Revenue/Earnings Data

**Revenue (Million $)**

| | 1Q | 2Q | 3Q | 4Q | Year |
|---|---|---|---|---|---|
| 2008 | 15,554 | 15,667 | 14,961 | -- | -- |
| 2007 | 15,079 | 15,260 | 15,234 | 15,561 | 61,134 |
| 2006 | 13,820 | 14,152 | 14,426 | 14,556 | 56,953 |
| 2005 | 11,100 | 11,299 | 11,305 | 11,432 | 45,136 |
| 2004 | 4,574 | 4,608 | 4,807 | 6,826 | 20,815 |
| 2003 | 4,100 | 4,114 | 4,262 | 4,295 | 16,771 |

**Earnings Per Share ($)**

| | | | | | |
|---|---|---|---|---|---|
| 2008 | 1.07 | 1.44 | 1.60 | E1.42 | E5.51 |
| 2007 | 1.26 | 1.35 | 1.45 | 1.51 | 5.56 |
| 2006 | 1.09 | 1.17 | 1.29 | 1.28 | 4.82 |
| 2005 | 0.98 | 0.90 | 1.02 | 1.04 | 3.94 |
| 2004 | 1.04 | 0.83 | 0.85 | 0.46 | 3.05 |
| 2003 | 0.68 | 0.63 | 0.69 | 0.74 | 2.73 |

Fiscal year ended Dec. 31. Next earnings report expected: NA. EPS Estimates based on S&P Operating Earnings; historical GAAP earnings are as reported.

## Dividend Data

No cash dividends have been paid.

---

**Please read the Required Disclosures and Analyst Certification on the last page of this report.**

The McGraw-Hill Companies

# WellPoint Inc

STANDARD &POOR'S

## Business Summary October 28, 2008

CORPORATE OVERVIEW. WellPoint, Inc. was formed by the merger consummated on November 30, 2004, between publicly traded managed care giants Anthem, Inc. and WellPoint Health Networks Inc. (WHN). Consequently, all historical data in this report are for Anthem. WLP is the largest publicly traded commercial health benefits company in the U.S., serving slightly over 35.3 million members as of September 30, 2008 (versus 34.8 million at December 31, 2007), and an independent licensee of the Blue Cross and Blue Shield Association. It serves members as the Blue Cross licensee for California and the Blue Cross or Blue Cross and Blue Shield (BCBS) licensee in all or parts of 13 other states. WLP also serves members in various parts of the U.S. as UniCare and conducts insurance operations in all 50 states and Puerto Rico through an affiliate.

WLP's network-based managed care plans include preferred provider organizations (PPOs), health maintenance organizations (HMOs), point-of-service plans (POS), traditional indemnity plans and other hybrid plans, including consumer-driven health plans (CDHPs), hospital only, and limited benefit products. It also provides managed care services to self-funded customers. In addition, WLP provides specialty and other products and services, including

pharmacy benefit management, group life and disability insurance, dental, vision, behavioral health, workers compensation and long-term care insurance. Approximately 93% of 2007 operating revenue was derived from premium income and 7% from administrative services and other revenues.

The customer base includes local groups (16,683,000 members as of September 30, 2008, versus 16,663,000 as of December 31, 2007); individuals under age 65 (2,341,000 versus 2,390,000); National Accounts (multi-state employers primarily headquartered in WLP's service area with 1,000 or more eligible employees, with 5% or more located outside headquarters state, 6,808,000 versus 6,389,000); BlueCard (enrollees of non-owned BCBS plans who receive benefits in WLP's BCBS markets, 4,785,000 versus 4,563,000); Senior (1,308,000 versus 1,250,000); State Sponsored (2,022,000 versus 2,174,000); and Federal Employee Program (1,390,000 versus 1,380,000).

## Company Financials Fiscal Year Ended Dec. 31

| Per Share Data ($) | 2007 | 2006 | 2005 | 2004 | 2003 | 2002 | 2001 | 2000 | 1999 | 1998 |
|---|---|---|---|---|---|---|---|---|---|---|
| Tangible Book Value | 0.60 | 2.92 | 2.78 | 2.03 | 8.44 | 5.76 | 7.71 | 7.66 | NA | NA |
| Cash Flow | 6.24 | 4.82 | 3.94 | 2.05 | 3.59 | 2.90 | 2.23 | 1.55 | NA | NA |
| Earnings | 5.56 | 4.82 | 3.94 | 3.05 | 2.73 | 2.26 | 1.65 | 1.05 | NA | NA |
| S&P Core Earnings | 5.50 | 4.79 | 3.82 | 2.69 | 2.49 | 1.93 | 1.16 | NA | NA | NA |
| Dividends | Nil | Nil | Nil | Nil | Nil | Nil | Nil | NA | NA | NA |
| Payout Ratio | Nil | Nil | Nil | Nil | Nil | Nil | Nil | NA | NA | NA |
| Prices:High | 89.95 | 80.37 | 80.40 | 58.88 | 41.45 | 37.75 | 25.95 | NA | NA | NA |
| Prices:Low | 72.90 | 65.50 | 54.58 | 36.10 | 26.50 | 23.20 | 18.00 | NA | NA | NA |
| P/E Ratio:High | 16 | 17 | 20 | 19 | 15 | 17 | 16 | NA | NA | NA |
| P/E Ratio:Low | 13 | 14 | 14 | 12 | 10 | 10 | 11 | NA | NA | NA |

| Income Statement Analysis (Million $) | 2007 | 2006 | 2005 | 2004 | 2003 | 2002 | 2001 | 2000 | 1999 | 1998 |
|---|---|---|---|---|---|---|---|---|---|---|
| Revenue | 61,134 | 56,953 | 45,136 | 20,815 | 16,771 | 13,282 | 10,445 | 8,771 | 6,270 | 5,682 |
| Operating Income | 6,117 | 5,748 | 4,750 | 2,072 | 1,595 | 1,093 | 733 | 487 | NA | NA |
| Depreciation | 411 | 430 | 634 | 279 | 245 | 157 | 121 | 102 | NA | NA |
| Interest Expense | 448 | 404 | 226 | 142 | 131 | 98.5 | 60.2 | 69.6 | NA | NA |
| Pretax Income | 5,258 | 4,914 | 3,890 | 1,443 | 1,219 | 808 | 525 | 315 | 60.8 | 288 |
| Effective Tax Rate | 36.4% | 37.0% | 36.7% | 33.5% | 36.1% | 31.6% | 35.0% | 30.8% | 16.8% | 38.5% |
| Net Income | 3,345 | 3,095 | 2,464 | 960 | 774 | 549 | 342 | 216 | 50.9 | 178 |
| S&P Core Earnings | 3,308 | 3,077 | 2,402 | 842 | 708 | 467 | 240 | NA | NA | NA |

| Balance Sheet & Other Financial Data (Million $) | 2007 | 2006 | 2005 | 2004 | 2003 | 2002 | 2001 | 2000 | 1999 | 1998 |
|---|---|---|---|---|---|---|---|---|---|---|
| Cash | 6,535 | 2,602 | 2,897 | 1,457 | 523 | 744 | 406 | 421 | 204 | NA |
| Current Assets | 13,032 | 11,807 | 25,945 | 19,358 | 8,865 | 7,877 | 5,300 | 5,025 | NA | NA |
| Total Assets | 52,060 | 51,760 | 51,405 | 39,738 | 13,439 | 12,293 | 6,277 | 6,021 | 4,816 | NA |
| Current Liabilities | 14,388 | 15,323 | 14,857 | 11,571 | 4,772 | 4,449 | 2,963 | 2,784 | NA | NA |
| Long Term Debt | 9,024 | 6,493 | 6,325 | 4,277 | 1,663 | 1,659 | 818 | 789 | NA | NA |
| Common Equity | 22,990 | 25,299 | 25,755 | 20,331 | 6,000 | 5,362 | 2,060 | 2,055 | 1,661 | NA |
| Total Capital | 35,018 | 35,142 | 35,386 | 27,204 | 8,188 | 7,412 | 2,878 | 2,844 | NA | NA |
| Capital Expenditures | 322 | 194 | 162 | 137 | 111 | 123 | 70.4 | NA | NA | NA |
| Cash Flow | 3,756 | 3,095 | 2,464 | 1,239 | 1,019 | 706 | 463 | 318 | NA | NA |
| Current Ratio | 0.9 | 0.8 | 1.7 | 1.7 | 1.9 | 1.8 | 1.8 | 1.8 | 1.7 | NA |
| % Long Term Debt of Capitalization | 25.8 | 18.5 | 17.9 | 15.7 | 20.3 | 22.4 | 28.4 | 27.7 | 23.9 | Nil |
| % Net Income of Revenue | 5.5 | 62.1 | 5.5 | 4.7 | 4.6 | 50.8 | 35.6 | 2.5 | 0.8 | 3.1 |
| % Return on Assets | 6.5 | 6.0 | 5.4 | 3.6 | 6.0 | 5.9 | 5.7 | NA | NA | NA |
| % Return on Equity | 14.1 | 12.1 | 10.7 | 7.2 | 13.6 | 14.8 | 17.2 | 12.6 | NA | NA |

Data as orig reptd.; bef. results of disc opers/spec. items. Per share data adj. for stk. divs.; EPS diluted. E-Estimated. NA-Not Available. NM-Not Meaningful. NR-Not Ranked. UR-Under Review.

**Office:** 120 Monument Circle, Indianapolis, IN 46204-4903.
**Telephone:** 317-488-6000.
**Email:** anthem.corporate.communications@anthem.com
**Website:** http://www.wellpoint.com

**Chrmn:** L.C. Glasscock
**Pres & CEO:** A.F. Braly
**Investor Contact:** W.S. Deveydt (317-488-6390)
**EVP & CFO:** W.S. Deveydt

**EVP & General Counsel:** J. Cannon, III
**Board Members:** L. D. Baker, Jr., S. B. Bayh, A. F. Braly, S. P. Burke, W. H. Bush, L. C. Glasscock, J. A. Hill, W. Y. Jobe, V. S. Liss, W. G. Mays, R. Peru, J. G. Pisano, D. W. Riegle, Jr., W. J. Ryan, G. A. Schaefer, Jr., J. M. Ward, J. E. Zuccotti

**Founded:** 1944
**Domicile:** Indiana
**Employees:** 41,700

# Wells Fargo & Co

## STANDARD &POOR'S

| S&P Recommendation | BUY ★★★★☆ | Price $28.73 (as of Nov 14, 2008) | 12-Mo. Target Price $35.00 | Investment Style Large-Cap Blend |
|---|---|---|---|---|

**GICS Sector** Financials
**Sub-Industry** Diversified Banks

**Summary** This bank holding company provides banking, insurance, investment, mortgage and consumer finance services throughout North America.

## Key Stock Statistics (Source S&P, Vickers, company reports)

| | | | | | | | |
|---|---|---|---|---|---|---|---|
| 52-Wk Range | $44.69–20.46 | S&P Oper. EPS 2008E | 2.05 | Market Capitalization(B) | $95.534 | Beta | 0.17 |
| Trailing 12-Month EPS | $2.03 | S&P Oper. EPS 2009E | 2.04 | Yield (%) | 4.73 | S&P 3-Yr. Proj. EPS CAGR(%) | 10 |
| Trailing 12-Month P/E | 14.2 | P/E on S&P Oper. EPS 2008E | 14.0 | Dividend Rate/Share | $1.36 | S&P Credit Rating | AA+ |
| $10K Invested 5 Yrs Ago | $12,085 | Common Shares Outstg. (M) | 3,325.2 | Institutional Ownership (%) | 74 | | |

## Price Performance

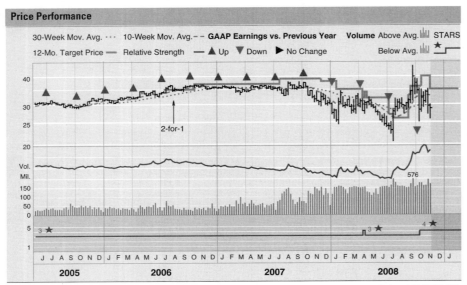

30-Week Mov. Avg. · · · 10-Week Mov. Avg. - - GAAP Earnings vs. Previous Year Volume Above Avg. STARS
12-Mo. Target Price — Relative Strength ▲ Up ▼ Down ► No Change Below Avg. ★

Options: ASE, CBOE, P, Ph

Analysis prepared by **Stuart Plesser** on November 07, 2008, when the stock traded at **$28.14**.

## Qualitative Risk Assessment

| LOW | MEDIUM | HIGH |
|---|---|---|

Our risk assessment reflects what we see as solid business fundamentals and a strong customer base. We view WFC as well diversified with a strong capital base.

## Quantitative Evaluations

**S&P Quality Ranking**     A

| D | C | B- | B | B+ | A- | A | A+ |
|---|---|---|---|---|---|---|---|

**Relative Strength Rank**    STRONG
76
LOWEST = 1       HIGHEST = 99

## Revenue/Earnings Data

**Revenue (Million $)**

| | 1Q | 2Q | 3Q | 4Q | Year |
|---|---|---|---|---|---|
| 2008 | 13,652 | 13,728 | 12,772 | -- | -- |
| 2007 | 12,570 | 13,268 | 13,796 | 13,959 | 53,596 |
| 2006 | 11,217 | 11,882 | 12,286 | 12,594 | 47,979 |
| 2005 | 9,509 | 9,529 | 10,427 | 10,897 | 40,407 |
| 2004 | 7,955 | 8,269 | 8,305 | 9,347 | 33,876 |
| 2003 | 7,561 | 7,637 | 8,170 | 8,257 | 31,800 |

**Earnings Per Share ($)**

| | 1Q | 2Q | 3Q | 4Q | Year |
|---|---|---|---|---|---|
| 2008 | 0.60 | 0.53 | 0.49 | E0.43 | E2.05 |
| 2007 | 0.66 | 0.67 | 0.68 | 0.37 | 2.38 |
| 2006 | 0.60 | 0.61 | 0.64 | 0.64 | 2.49 |
| 2005 | 0.54 | 0.56 | 0.58 | 0.57 | 2.25 |
| 2004 | 0.52 | 0.50 | 0.51 | 0.52 | 2.05 |
| 2003 | 0.44 | 0.45 | 0.46 | 0.48 | 1.83 |

Fiscal year ended Dec. 31. Next earnings report expected: NA. EPS Estimates based on S&P Operating Earnings; historical GAAP earnings are as reported.

## Highlights

► WFC is taking advantage of the exit of weaker players, and will likely continue to grow its loan book by gaining market share, in our view. Notably, average earning assets rose roughly 15% in the third quarter, while core deposits were up 10%. It should also continue to benefit from a low interest rate environment, with the net interest margin likely to remain above 4.80%, by our analysis. We look for non-interest income to be up about 9.0% in 2009, due to higher mortgage banking, insurance revenue and fee business. We expect revenue growth of roughly 10.5% in 2009, driven by double-digit loan growth, and net interest margin expansion.

► Based on cost initiatives, we see expenses totaling 49.0% of revenue in 2009, versus a projected 52.0% in 2008. We expect continued deterioration in WFC's home equity loan portfolio due to falling housing prices, and also project credit deterioration in WFC's other loan portfolios, but not as severe. As a result, we look for 2008 provisions to more than double from 2007 levels and for provisions to remain elevated throughout 2009.

► We project EPS of $2.05 in 2008, versus $3.30 in 2007. In 2009, we look for $2.04.

## Investment Rationale/Risk

► With Citigroup (C: hold, $12) withdrawing from negotiations, WFC will purchase Wachovia (WB: hold, $5.50), pending the necessary approvals. We think WB fits nicely with WFC, and adds significantly to WFC's footprint, particularly in the Northeast. WFC's proposed writedown of WB's book through purchase accounting is conservative, in our view. This aside, WFC's credit book has held up well through a difficult credit environment, which we think is a result of conservative underwriting that largely took place in its retail outlets. We believe WFC should be able to continue to gain market share and post solid loan growth.

► Risks to our recommendation and target price include a severe economic downturn; a worse-than-expected decline in housing prices; and litigation and regulatory risks.

► Our 12-month target price of $35 is 17.2X our 2009 EPS estimate of $2.04, above its historical average and a premium to peers. We think the multiple is justified due to WFC's strong credit quality and our belief that it will benefit from synergies from the pending WB acquisition.

## Dividend Data (Dates: mm/dd Payment Date: mm/dd/yy)

| Amount ($) | Date Decl. | Ex-Div. Date | Stk. of Record | Payment Date |
|---|---|---|---|---|
| 0.310 | 01/22 | 02/06 | 02/08 | 03/01/08 |
| 0.310 | 04/29 | 05/07 | 05/09 | 06/01/08 |
| 0.340 | 07/16 | 08/06 | 08/08 | 09/01/08 |
| 0.340 | 10/22 | 11/05 | 11/07 | 12/01/08 |

Dividends have been paid since 1939. Source: Company reports.

# Wells Fargo & Co

STANDARD
&POOR'S

## Business Summary November 07, 2008

CORPORATE OVERVIEW. Wells Fargo & Co. (WFC) has three lines of business for management reporting: community banking, wholesale banking, and Wells Fargo Financial. The community banking group offers a complete line of banking and diversified financial products and services to consumers and small businesses with annual sales generally up to $20 million, in which the owner generally is the financial decision maker. Community banking also offers investment management and other services to retail customers and high-net-worth individuals, insurance, securities brokerage through affiliates and venture capital financing.

Community banking serves customers through a wide range of channels, which include traditional banking stores, in-store banking centers, business centers and ATMs. In addition, Phone Bank centers and the National Business Banking Center provide 24-hour telephone service.

The wholesale banking group serves businesses across the U.S. with annual sales generally in excess of $10 million. Wholesale banking provides a complete line of commercial, corporate and real estate banking products and ser-

vices. These include traditional commercial loans and lines of credit, letters of credit, asset-based lending, equipment leasing, mezzanine financing, high-yield debt, international trade facilities, foreign exchange services, treasury management, investment management, institutional fixed income and equity sales, interest rate, commodity and equity risk management, online/electronic products, insurance brokerage services and investment banking services.

Wholesale banking manages and administers institutional investments, employee benefit trusts and mutual funds, including the Wells Fargo Advantage Funds. Wholesale banking includes the majority ownership interest in the Wells Fargo HSBC Trade Bank, which provides trade financing, letters of credit, and collection services, and is sometimes supported by the Export-Import Bank of the United States.

## Company Financials Fiscal Year Ended Dec. 31

| Per Share Data ($) | 2007 | 2006 | 2005 | 2004 | 2003 | 2002 | 2001 | 2000 | 1999 | 1998 |
|---|---|---|---|---|---|---|---|---|---|---|
| Tangible Book Value | 5.55 | 10.13 | 8.76 | 7.95 | 7.04 | 6.11 | 4.90 | 4.59 | 3.96 | 3.39 |
| Earnings | 2.38 | 2.49 | 2.25 | 2.05 | 1.83 | 1.66 | 0.99 | 1.17 | 1.12 | 0.58 |
| S&P Core Earnings | 2.39 | 2.47 | 2.18 | 1.96 | 1.78 | 1.57 | 0.84 | NA | NA | NA |
| Dividends | 1.18 | 1.08 | 1.00 | 0.93 | 0.75 | 0.55 | 0.50 | 0.45 | 0.39 | 0.35 |
| Payout Ratio | 50% | 43% | 44% | 45% | 41% | 33% | 51% | 39% | 35% | 60% |
| Prices:High | 37.99 | 36.99 | 32.35 | 32.02 | 29.59 | 26.72 | 27.41 | 28.19 | 24.97 | 21.94 |
| Prices:Low | 29.29 | 30.31 | 28.81 | 27.16 | 21.64 | 21.65 | 19.13 | 15.69 | 16.09 | 13.75 |
| P/E Ratio:High | 16 | 15 | 14 | 16 | 16 | 16 | 28 | 24 | 22 | 37 |
| P/E Ratio:Low | 12 | 12 | 13 | 13 | 12 | 13 | 19 | 13 | 14 | 24 |

| Income Statement Analysis (Million $) | 2007 | 2006 | 2005 | 2004 | 2003 | 2002 | 2001 | 2000 | 1999 | 1998 |
|---|---|---|---|---|---|---|---|---|---|---|
| Net Interest Income | 20,974 | 19,951 | 18,504 | 17,150 | 16,007 | 14,855 | 12,460 | 10,865 | 9,355 | 8,990 |
| Tax Equivalent Adjustment | 146 | 116 | 110 | 104 | NA | NA | NA | 65.0 | 64.0 | 59.0 |
| Non Interest Income | 17,473 | 15,021 | 14,054 | 12,530 | 12,323 | 9,348 | 7,227 | 9,565 | 6,653 | 6,427 |
| Loan Loss Provision | 4,939 | 2,204 | 2,383 | 1,717 | 1,722 | 1,733 | 1,780 | 1,329 | 1,045 | 1,545 |
| % Expense/Operating Revenue | 59.4% | 59.3% | 58.2% | 64.8% | 60.7% | 52.2% | 65.5% | 57.7% | 60.9% | 68.4% |
| Pretax Income | 11,627 | 12,745 | 11,548 | 10,769 | 9,477 | 8,854 | 5,479 | 6,549 | 5,948 | 3,293 |
| Effective Tax Rate | 30.7% | 33.4% | 33.6% | 34.9% | 34.6% | 35.5% | 37.5% | 38.5% | 37.0% | 40.8% |
| Net Income | 8,057 | 8,482 | 7,671 | 7,014 | 6,202 | 5,710 | 3,423 | 4,026 | 3,747 | 1,950 |
| % Net Interest Margin | 4.74 | 4.83 | 4.86 | 4.89 | 5.08 | 5.57 | 5.36 | 5.35 | 5.66 | 5.79 |
| S&P Core Earnings | 8,099 | 8,401 | 7,423 | 6,722 | 6,055 | 5,374 | 2,894 | NA | NA | NA |

| Balance Sheet & Other Financial Data (Million $) | 2007 | 2006 | 2005 | 2004 | 2003 | 2002 | 2001 | 2000 | 1999 | 1998 |
|---|---|---|---|---|---|---|---|---|---|---|
| Money Market Assets | 10,481 | 11,685 | 16,211 | 14,020 | 2,745 | 3,174 | 2,530 | 1,598 | 1,554 | 1,517 |
| Investment Securities | 72,951 | 42,629 | 41,834 | 33,717 | 32,953 | 27,947 | 40,308 | 38,655 | 38,518 | 31,997 |
| Commercial Loans | 152,841 | 122,065 | 108,903 | 98,515 | 48,729 | 47,292 | 47,547 | 60,541 | 46,538 | 41,830 |
| Other Loans | 229,354 | 273,069 | 201,934 | 189,071 | 204,344 | 149,342 | 124,952 | 10,583 | 72,926 | 66,164 |
| Total Assets | 575,442 | 481,996 | 481,741 | 427,849 | 387,798 | 349,259 | 307,569 | 272,426 | 218,102 | 202,475 |
| Demand Deposits | 84,348 | 89,119 | 87,712 | 81,082 | 74,387 | 74,094 | 65,362 | 55,096 | 42,916 | 43,732 |
| Time Deposits | 260,112 | 221,124 | 226,738 | 193,776 | 173,140 | 142,822 | 121,904 | 114,463 | 89,792 | 90,056 |
| Long Term Debt | 99,393 | 72,404 | 79,668 | 73,580 | 63,642 | 50,205 | 38,530 | 32,981 | 24,160 | 19,709 |
| Common Equity | 47,660 | 45,492 | 40,335 | 37,596 | 34,255 | 30,107 | 26,996 | 26,103 | 21,860 | 20,296 |
| % Return on Assets | 1.5 | 1.8 | 1.7 | 1.7 | 1.7 | 1.7 | 1.2 | 1.6 | 1.8 | 1.0 |
| % Return on Equity | 17.2 | 19.8 | 19.7 | 19.5 | 19.3 | 20.0 | 12.8 | 16.2 | 17.6 | 14.2 |
| % Loan Loss Reserve | 1.4 | 1.1 | 1.1 | 1.2 | 1.3 | 1.5 | 1.8 | 2.1 | 2.5 | 2.9 |
| % Loans/Deposits | 107.1 | 113.8 | 111.9 | 118.6 | 117.0 | 117.3 | 110.9 | 104.7 | 93.8 | 79.0 |
| % Equity to Assets | 8.9 | 8.9 | 8.6 | 8.8 | 8.7 | 8.7 | 9.2 | 9.7 | 10.0 | 10.2 |

Data as orig reptd.; bef. results of disc opers/spec. items. Per share data adj. for stk. divs.; EPS diluted. E-Estimated. NA-Not Available. NM-Not Meaningful. NR-Not Ranked. UR-Under Review.

**Office:** 420 Montgomery St, San Francisco, CA 94163.
**Telephone:** 1-866-878-5865.
**Website:** http://www.wellsfargo.com
**Chrmn:** R.M. Kovacevich

**Pres & CEO:** J.G. Stumpf
**EVP & CFO:** H.I. Atkins
**EVP, Chief Acctg Officer & Cntlr:** R.D. Levy
**EVP & General Counsel:** J.M. Strother

**Board Members:** J. S. Chen, L. H. Dean, S. E. Engel, E. Hernandez, Jr., R. L. Joss, R. M. Kovacevich, R. D. McCormick, C. Milligan, N. G. Moore, P. J. Quigley, D. B. Rice, J. M. Runstad, S. W. Sanger, J. G. Stumpf, S. G. Swenson, M. W. Wright

**Founded:** 1929
**Domicile:** Delaware
**Employees:** 159,800

# Western Union Co

**STANDARD &POOR'S**

| S&P Recommendation | HOLD ★★★☆☆ | Price $13.49 (as of Nov 14, 2008) | 12-Mo. Target Price $19.00 | Investment Style Large-Cap Blend |
|---|---|---|---|---|

**GICS Sector** Information Technology
**Sub-Industry** Data Processing & Outsourced Services

**Summary** Spun off from First Data Corp. in September 2006, Western Union is a leading independent provider of consumer money transfer services.

## Key Stock Statistics (Source S&P, Vickers, company reports)

| | | | | | | | | |
|---|---|---|---|---|---|---|---|---|
| 52-Wk Range | $28.62–12.28 | S&P Oper. EPS 2008E | 1.30 | Market Capitalization(B) | $9.653 | Beta | NA |
| Trailing 12-Month EPS | $1.23 | S&P Oper. EPS 2009E | 1.47 | Yield (%) | 0.30 | S&P 3-Yr. Proj. EPS CAGR(%) | 14 |
| Trailing 12-Month P/E | 11.0 | P/E on S&P Oper. EPS 2008E | 10.4 | Dividend Rate/Share | $0.04 | S&P Credit Rating | NA |
| $10K Invested 5 Yrs Ago | NA | Common Shares Outstg. (M) | 715.6 | Institutional Ownership (%) | 90 | | |

## Price Performance

- 30-Week Mov. Avg. · · · ·  10-Week Mov. Avg. - -  GAAP Earnings vs. Previous Year  Volume Above Avg. STARS
- 12-Mo. Target Price —  Relative Strength —  ▲ Up  ▼ Down  ► No Change  Below Avg.

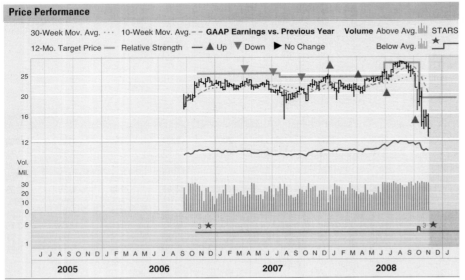

Options: ASE, CBOE, P, Ph

Analysis prepared by **Zaineb Bokhari** on October 28, 2008, when the stock traded at **$ 15.05.**

### Highlights

► We forecast a 10% rise in revenues in 2008, reflecting an 8% increase in transaction fees and 20% higher foreign exchange revenues. WU's domestic business remains challenged by the weak macro-economy; we note that the slowdown seems to be spreading quickly to global markets and will impact growth. While many of WU's transactions are non-discretionary in nature, the worsening economic outlook has resulted in a decline in the amount of principal sent per transaction, impacting growth in transaction fees. We forecast 8% revenue growth in 2009.

► We expect gross margins to narrow modestly reflecting our outlook for a competitive pricing environment for WU's core money transfer business, although some stability has been reported in recent quarters. We expect operating margins (before charges) to remain at 27%, as an ongoing shift in mix from higher-margin U.S.-originated money transfers to lower-margin international business is offset by internal expense management. We see modestly wider operating margins in 2009.

► We estimate operating EPS of $1.30 in 2008, rising to $1.47 in 2009.

### Investment Rationale/Risk

► We expect the deterioration in the global economy to have a negative impact on transaction volumes, fees and foreign exchange revenues per transaction. Despite this, we think WU will be able to expand operating margins as it benefits from a recent restructuring. With over $1.1 billion in cash and equivalents on its balance sheet at and $1.2 billion in projected cash from operations in 2008, we think WU has adequate near-term liquidity, though we look for somewhat more conservative share buybacks given the tighter credit markets and the upcoming maturity of $500 million in floating rate notes. WU recently withdrew long-term sales and EPS growth objectives, which has raised concerns about 2009 prospects.

► Risks to our recommendation and target price include accelerating consumer adoption of digital alternatives to WU's money transfer offerings, and competition from traditional financial institutions and money transfer peers.

► We derive our 12-month target price of $19 by applying a 13X P/E to our 2009 EPS estimate, above the recent 12X mean for data processing and outsourced services peers, but near historic lows for WU shares.

## Qualitative Risk Assessment

| LOW | MEDIUM | HIGH |
|---|---|---|

Our risk assessment reflects what we see as relatively high barriers to entry in WU's businesses and potential for operating margin expansion, offset by risks related to the recent deterioration in the global macro economy which we expect will impact transaction volumes.

## Quantitative Evaluations

**S&P Quality Ranking** NR

| D | C | B- | B | B+ | A- | A | A+ |
|---|---|---|---|---|---|---|---|

**Relative Strength Rank** MODERATE

32

LOWEST = 1    HIGHEST = 99

## Revenue/Earnings Data

**Revenue (Million $)**

| | 1Q | 2Q | 3Q | 4Q | Year |
|---|---|---|---|---|---|
| 2008 | 1,266 | 1,347 | 1,377 | -- | -- |
| 2007 | 1,131 | 1,203 | 1,257 | 1,309 | 4,900 |
| 2006 | 1,043 | 1,114 | 1,140 | 1,173 | 4,470 |
| 2005 | 919.6 | 980.8 | 1,019 | 1,068 | 3,988 |
| 2004 | -- | -- | -- | -- | -- |
| 2003 | -- | -- | -- | -- | -- |

**Earnings Per Share ($)**

| | 1Q | 2Q | 3Q | 4Q | Year |
|---|---|---|---|---|---|
| 2008 | 0.27 | 0.31 | 0.33 | E0.35 | E1.30 |
| 2007 | 0.25 | 0.26 | 0.28 | 0.32 | 1.11 |
| 2006 | 0.29 | 0.29 | 0.34 | 0.28 | 1.19 |
| 2005 | -- | -- | -- | -- | 0.96 |
| 2004 | -- | -- | -- | -- | -- |
| 2003 | -- | -- | -- | -- | -- |

Fiscal year ended Dec. 31. Next earnings report expected: Early February. EPS Estimates based on S&P Operating Earnings; historical GAAP earnings are as reported.

## Dividend Data (Dates: mm/dd Payment Date: mm/dd/yy)

| Amount ($) | Date Decl. | Ex-Div. Date | Stk. of Record | Payment Date |
|---|---|---|---|---|
| 0.040 | 12/04 | 12/12 | 12/14 | 12/28/07 |

Dividends have been paid since 2006. Source: Company reports.

---

**Please read the Required Disclosures and Analyst Certification on the last page of this report.**

**The McGraw-Hill Companies**

# Western Union Co

STANDARD
&POOR'S

## Business Summary October 28, 2008

CORPORATE OVERVIEW. Spun off from First Data Corp. in September 2006, Western Union is a leading independent provider of consumer money transfer services. WU offers its services through a network of over 355,000 agent locations (at June 30, 2008) spanning more than 200 countries and territories. The company provides its services globally, mainly under the Western Union brand name and also under the Orlandi Valuta and Vigo brands. WU derives the majority of revenues from fees that consumers pay when they send money. The company's main segments include consumer-to-consumer (C2C; 83% of 2007 revenues) and consumer-to-business (C2B; 15%).

WU's core C2C services allow customers to transfer money to other individuals. The majority of these transfers are originated in cash at Western Union agent locations, although consumers can also send money via the Internet, telephone, credit or debit card and, in some cases, through bank debits. In 2007, C2C transactions increased 14%, to 167.7 million, while C2C transaction fees rose about 7%.

Through its C2B segment, consumers can make payments to businesses electronically, over the telephone, via the Internet, or at one of WU's agent locations. The company has long-standing relationships with billers such as utilities, auto finance companies, mortgage servicers, financial service providers and government agencies who accept such payments. In 2007, WU's C2B

transactions increased 62%, to 404.5 million, while C2B transaction fees rose about 12%.

CORPORATE STRATEGY. The pursuit of growth through international expansion is a key tenet of Western Union's growth strategy. The company believes that a majority of its C2C transactions involve at least one non-U.S. location. Domestic transactions accounted for 11% of 2007 consolidated revenues while Mexico accounted for 7%. Outside of these two countries, WU's revenue base is well-diversified geographically. Building on and maintaining its well-recognized consumer brand is another key element to the company's strategy. WU has spent approximately 7% of revenues on marketing, advertising and developing customer loyalty programs in each of 2004, 2005 and 2006. In 2007, the company spent 6%. The company has also invested about 3% of annual revenues in selective price reductions on its C2C services in individual markets depending on the dynamics within those markets. We think the difference in growth between transaction fees and transaction volumes is evidence of this strategy.

## Company Financials Fiscal Year Ended Dec. 31

| Per Share Data ($) | 2007 | 2006 | 2005 | 2004 | 2003 | 2002 | 2001 | 2000 | 1999 | 1998 |
|---|---|---|---|---|---|---|---|---|---|---|
| Tangible Book Value | NM | NM | NM | NA | NA | NA | NA | NA | NA | NA |
| Cash Flow | 1.17 | 1.32 | NA | NA | NA | NA | NA | NA | NA | NA |
| Earnings | 1.11 | 1.19 | 0.96 | NA | NA | NA | NA | NA | NA | NA |
| S&P Core Earnings | 1.11 | 1.18 | 1.10 | 0.95 | NA | NA | NA | NA | NA | NA |
| Dividends | 0.04 | 0.01 | NA | NA | NA | NA | NA | NA | NA | NA |
| Payout Ratio | 4% | 1% | NA | NA | NA | NA | NA | NA | NA | NA |
| Prices:High | 24.83 | 24.14 | NA | NA | NA | NA | NA | NA | NA | NA |
| Prices:Low | 15.00 | 16.85 | NA | NA | NA | NA | NA | NA | NA | NA |
| P/E Ratio:High | 22 | 20 | NA | NA | NA | NA | NA | NA | NA | NA |
| P/E Ratio:Low | 14 | 14 | NA | NA | NA | NA | NA | NA | NA | NA |

| Income Statement Analysis (Million $) | 2007 | 2006 | 2005 | 2004 | 2003 | 2002 | 2001 | 2000 | 1999 | 1998 |
|---|---|---|---|---|---|---|---|---|---|---|
| Revenue | 4,900 | 4,470 | 3,988 | 3,524 | 3,121 | NA | NA | NA | NA | NA |
| Operating Income | 1,393 | 1,415 | NA | NA | NA | NA | NA | NA | NA | NA |
| Depreciation | 49.1 | 104 | NA | 79.2 | 78.4 | NA | NA | NA | NA | NA |
| Interest Expense | 189 | 53.0 | 202 | NA | NA | NA | NA | NA | NA | NA |
| Pretax Income | 1,222 | 1,335 | 1,063 | 1,098 | 970 | NA | NA | NA | NA | NA |
| Effective Tax Rate | 29.9% | 31.5% | 29.5% | 31.5% | 34.1% | NA | NA | NA | NA | NA |
| Net Income | 857 | 914 | 749 | 752 | 639 | NA | NA | NA | NA | NA |
| S&P Core Earnings | 857 | 913 | 859 | 734 | NA | NA | NA | NA | NA | NA |

| Balance Sheet & Other Financial Data (Million $) | 2007 | 2006 | 2005 | 2004 | 2003 | 2002 | 2001 | 2000 | 1999 | 1998 |
|---|---|---|---|---|---|---|---|---|---|---|
| Cash | 2,030 | 1,422 | 1,186 | 470 | NA | NA | NA | NA | NA | NA |
| Current Assets | NA | NA | NA | NA | NA | NA | NA | NA | NA | NA |
| Total Assets | 5,784 | 5,321 | 4,659 | 3,307 | NA | NA | NA | NA | NA | NA |
| Current Liabilities | NA | NA | NA | NA | NA | NA | NA | NA | NA | NA |
| Long Term Debt | 2,500 | 2,996 | 3,500 | NA | NA | NA | NA | NA | NA | NA |
| Common Equity | 50.7 | -315 | -687 | 1,909 | NA | NA | NA | NA | NA | NA |
| Total Capital | 2,814 | 2,681 | 2,183 | NA | NA | NA | NA | NA | NA | NA |
| Capital Expenditures | 83.5 | 64.0 | NA | 26.5 | 23.6 | NA | NA | NA | NA | NA |
| Cash Flow | 906 | 1,018 | NA | NA | NA | NA | NA | NA | NA | NA |
| Current Ratio | 1.3 | 1.9 | NA | 7.0 | NA | NA | NA | NA | NA | NA |
| % Long Term Debt of Capitalization | 88.8 | 112.0 | 160.3 | 0.5 | Nil | NA | NA | NA | NA | NA |
| % Net Income of Revenue | 17.5 | 20.4 | 18.8 | 21.3 | 20.5 | NA | NA | NA | NA | NA |
| % Return on Assets | 15.4 | 18.3 | NA | NA | NA | NA | NA | NA | NA | NA |
| % Return on Equity | NM | NM | NA | NA | NA | NA | NA | NA | NA | NA |

Data as orig reptd.; bef. results of disc opers/spec. items. Per share data adj. for stk. divs.; EPS diluted. Pro forma data in 2005, balance sheet and book value as of Jun. 30, 2006. E-Estimated. NA-Not Available. NM-Not Meaningful. NR-Not Ranked. UR-Under Review.

**Office:** 12500 East Belford Avenue, Englewood, CO 80112.
**Telephone:** 866-405-5012.
**Website:** http://www.westernunion.com
**Chrmn:** J.M. Greenberg

**Pres & CEO:** C.A. Gold
**EVP & CFO:** S.T. Scheirman
**EVP, Secy & General Counsel:** D.L. Schlapbach
**SVP, Chief Acctg Officer & Cntlr:** A.T. Schenkel

**Investor Contact:** G. Kohn (720-332-8276)
**Board Members:** D. S. Devitre, C. A. Gold, J. M. Greenberg, B. D. Holden, A. J. Lacy, L. F. Levinson, R. G. Mendoza, M. A. Miles, Jr., D. Stevenson

**Founded:** 1851
**Domicile:** Delaware
**Employees:** 6,100

# Weyerhaeuser Co

**STANDARD &POOR'S**

| S&P Recommendation | HOLD ★★★☆☆ | Price $32.78 (as of Nov 14, 2008) | 12-Mo. Target Price $38.00 | Investment Style Large-Cap Blend |
|---|---|---|---|---|

**GICS Sector** Materials
**Sub-Industry** Forest Products

**Summary** One of the world's largest integrated forest products companies, WY grows timber; makes and sells forest products, and pulp; and engages in real estate construction and development.

## Key Stock Statistics (Source S&P, Vickers, company reports)

| | | | | | | | |
|---|---|---|---|---|---|---|---|
| 52-Wk Range | $78.00– 29.53 | S&P Oper. EPS 2008E | -0.50 | Market Capitalization(B) | $6.926 | Beta | 1.41 |
| Trailing 12-Month EPS | $-0.13 | S&P Oper. EPS 2009E | -0.50 | Yield (%) | 7.32 | S&P 3-Yr. Proj. EPS CAGR(%) | -15 |
| Trailing 12-Month P/E | NM | P/E on S&P Oper. EPS 2008E | NM | Dividend Rate/Share | $2.40 | S&P Credit Rating | BBB |
| $10K Invested 5 Yrs Ago | $7,007 | Common Shares Outstg. (M) | 211.3 | Institutional Ownership (%) | 85 | | |

## Price Performance

30-Week Mov. Avg. · · · 10-Week Mov. Avg.– – GAAP Earnings vs. Previous Year   Volume Above Avg. STARS
12-Mo. Target Price — Relative Strength — ▲ Up ▼ Down ► No Change   Below Avg.

Options: CBOE, P

Analysis prepared by **Stuart J. Benway, CFA** on November 07, 2008, when the stock traded at **$ 32.05.**

## Highlights

➤ We look for a 15%-20% drop in revenues in 2008. S&P expects housing starts to plunge 29% in 2008 and fall an additional 2% in 2009. We believe this projected downturn will prevent a significant recovery in prices for lumber and panels and lead to lower closings and sale prices in the homebuilding segment. However, we expect the pulp business to post modest top-line gains. In 2009, we project a 5%-10% sales decline due to continued economic weakness.

➤ We believe cost reductions will be more than offset by higher raw material and energy costs. In addition, an expected continuation of the housing market downturn is likely to lead to further losses at the wood products and homebuilding businesses. However, higher prices and volume in fibers should be a partial offsetting factor. We estimate that operating margins will fall 400 basis points in 2008, and do not foresee any recovery in 2009.

➤ For 2008, we see an operating loss of $0.50 per share, compared to the $1.65 earned in 2007. We look for little change in 2009, with another loss of $0.50 per share.

## Investment Rationale/Risk

➤ WY has divested major assets to focus on its timber, wood products, real estate, and fiber businesses. Although these sales generated significant proceeds, its lumber and homebuilding businesses have been hurt badly by the downturn in the residential real estate market. We think a reduction in the dividend is possible given expected losses. However, WY is considering adopting the REIT form of corporate structure, which would likely result in a large distribution.

➤ Risks to our recommendation and target price include a further drop in wood product prices, continued contraction of the credit markets, and a lack of recovery in the housing market.

➤ Given the company's recent and potential corporate repositioning moves, we believe it is appropriate to value WY shares on a sum-of-the-parts basis. Our model recognizes the cyclical characteristics of the wood products and real estate businesses, the relative stability of the fibers unit, and what we view as the significant value of the timberlands. Considering these factors, we value the shares at $38, which is our 12-month target price.

## Qualitative Risk Assessment

| LOW | MEDIUM | HIGH |
|---|---|---|

Our risk assessment reflects that Weyerhaeuser operates in a cyclical industry, with large capital requirements and significant variability in both costs and prices. However, the company is one of the largest companies in the industry, and we believe it has a major base of assets and modest debt levels.

## Quantitative Evaluations

**S&P Quality Ranking**     B

| D | C | B- | B | B+ | A- | A | A+ |
|---|---|---|---|---|---|---|---|

**Relative Strength Rank**     MODERATE

39

LOWEST = 1      HIGHEST = 99

## Revenue/Earnings Data

**Revenue (Million $)**

| | 1Q | 2Q | 3Q | 4Q | Year |
|---|---|---|---|---|---|
| 2008 | 2,096 | 2,174 | 2,107 | -- | -- |
| 2007 | 3,891 | 4,334 | 4,146 | 3,937 | 16,308 |
| 2006 | 5,256 | 5,657 | 5,328 | 5,655 | 21,896 |
| 2005 | 5,404 | 5,838 | 5,604 | 5,868 | 22,629 |
| 2004 | 5,037 | 5,893 | 5,849 | 5,886 | 22,665 |
| 2003 | 4,614 | 4,930 | 5,184 | 5,145 | 19,873 |

**Earnings Per Share ($)**

| | 1Q | 2Q | 3Q | 4Q | Year |
|---|---|---|---|---|---|
| 2008 | -1.08 | -0.98 | -0.95 | E-0.24 | E-0.50 |
| 2007 | -0.07 | 0.17 | 0.34 | -0.21 | 0.23 |
| 2006 | -2.36 | 1.20 | 0.75 | 1.67 | 1.44 |
| 2005 | 0.98 | 1.22 | 1.16 | -1.00 | 2.36 |
| 2004 | 0.54 | 1.57 | 2.45 | 0.82 | 5.43 |
| 2003 | -0.19 | 0.71 | 0.37 | 0.41 | 1.30 |

Fiscal year ended Dec. 31. Next earnings report expected: Mid February. EPS Estimates based on S&P Operating Earnings; historical GAAP earnings are as reported.

## Dividend Data (Dates: mm/dd Payment Date: mm/dd/yy)

| Amount ($) | Date Decl. | Ex-Div. Date | Stk. of Record | Payment Date |
|---|---|---|---|---|
| 0.600 | 01/10 | 01/30 | 02/01 | 02/25/08 |
| 0.600 | 04/17 | 04/30 | 05/02 | 05/27/08 |
| 0.600 | 06/25 | 07/30 | 08/01 | 08/25/08 |
| 0.600 | 10/16 | 11/05 | 11/07 | 12/01/08 |

Dividends have been paid since 1933. Source: Company reports.

# Weyerhaeuser Co

## Business Summary November 07, 2008

CORPORATE OVERVIEW. Weyerhaeuser, one of the world's largest integrated forest products companies, is primarily engaged in growing and harvesting timber; the production, distribution and sale of wood and paper products; and real estate development. Through its timberlands segment (6% of 2007 sales), WY manages 5.7 million acres of company-owned timberlands and leases 700,000 acres of timberlands in eight states. The wood products businesses (35%) produce and sell softwood and hardwood lumber, plywood and veneer, composite panels, oriented strand board, and engineered lumber. Products made by the pulp and paper unit (14%) include paper grade, absorbent, dissolving and specialty pulp grades. Paper products include coated papers, which are used in the printing and publishing industries. The containerboard, packaging and recycling segment (31%) manufactures corrugating medium, linerboard and kraft paper (this business was sold in August 2008). Through Weyerhaeuser Real Estate Company (14%), the company is involved in the development of single-family housing and residential lots, including the development of master-planned communities.

MARKET PROFILE. Weyerhaeuser operates in a highly cyclical and capital-intensive industry. Demand for the company's products is dependent on a number of factors, including industrial non-durable goods production, consumer spending, white collar employment levels, domestic and Japanese new home construction and repair and remodeling activity, and movements in currency exchange rates. Historical prices for paper and wood products have been volatile, and, despite its size, WY has had only a limited direct influence over the timing and extent of price changes for its products. Pricing is significantly affected by the relationship between supply and demand, and supply is influenced primarily by fluctuations in available manufacturing capacity.

## Company Financials Fiscal Year Ended Dec. 31

| Per Share Data ($) | 2007 | 2006 | 2005 | 2004 | 2003 | 2002 | 2001 | 2000 | 1999 | 1998 |
|---|---|---|---|---|---|---|---|---|---|---|
| Tangible Book Value | 27.35 | 28.92 | 27.81 | 24.84 | 17.44 | 15.80 | 25.45 | 25.95 | 27.15 | 22.74 |
| Cash Flow | 4.43 | 6.88 | 7.80 | 10.76 | 7.23 | 6.63 | 5.94 | 7.52 | 6.07 | 4.55 |
| Earnings | 0.23 | 1.44 | 2.36 | 5.43 | 1.30 | 1.09 | 1.61 | 3.72 | 2.98 | 1.47 |
| S&P Core Earnings | -0.25 | 2.97 | 1.79 | 4.37 | 0.70 | -0.75 | NA | NA | NA | NA |
| Dividends | 2.40 | 2.20 | 1.90 | 1.60 | 1.60 | 1.60 | 1.60 | 1.60 | 1.60 | 1.60 |
| Payout Ratio | NM | 182% | 81% | 29% | 123% | 147% | 99% | 43% | 54% | 109% |
| Prices:High | 87.09 | 75.50 | 71.85 | 68.59 | 64.70 | 68.09 | 63.50 | 74.50 | 73.94 | 62.00 |
| Prices:Low | 59.67 | 54.25 | 60.62 | 55.06 | 45.40 | 37.35 | 42.77 | 36.06 | 49.56 | 36.75 |
| P/E Ratio:High | NM | 62 | 30 | 13 | 50 | 62 | 39 | 20 | 25 | 42 |
| P/E Ratio:Low | NM | 45 | 26 | 10 | 35 | 34 | 27 | 10 | 17 | 25 |

| Income Statement Analysis (Million $) | 2007 | 2006 | 2005 | 2004 | 2003 | 2002 | 2001 | 2000 | 1999 | 1998 |
|---|---|---|---|---|---|---|---|---|---|---|
| Revenue | 16,308 | 21,896 | 22,629 | 22,665 | 19,873 | 18,521 | 14,545 | 15,980 | 12,262 | 10,766 |
| Operating Income | 1,628 | 2,914 | 3,443 | 4,028 | 2,716 | 2,455 | 1,689 | 2,536 | 1,902 | 1,385 |
| Depreciation | 925 | 1,283 | 1,337 | 1,322 | 1,318 | 1,225 | 876 | 859 | 640 | 616 |
| Interest Expense | 586 | 531 | 730 | 829 | 796 | 771 | 344 | 351 | 277 | 273 |
| Pretax Income | 59.0 | 826 | 906 | 1,945 | 436 | 371 | 516 | 1,323 | 970 | 463 |
| Effective Tax Rate | 13.6% | 57.0% | 35.8% | 34.0% | 33.9% | 35.0% | 31.4% | 36.5% | 36.5% | 36.5% |
| Net Income | 51.0 | 355 | 582 | 1,283 | 288 | 241 | 354 | 840 | 616 | 294 |
| S&P Core Earnings | -53.0 | 728 | 444 | 1,029 | 156 | -168 | 2.35 | NA | NA | NA |

| Balance Sheet & Other Financial Data (Million $) | 2007 | 2006 | 2005 | 2004 | 2003 | 2002 | 2001 | 2000 | 1999 | 1998 |
|---|---|---|---|---|---|---|---|---|---|---|
| Cash | 114 | 243 | 1,104 | 1,197 | 202 | 122 | 204 | 123 | 1,643 | 35.0 |
| Current Assets | NA | 4,121 | 4,876 | 5,293 | 4,021 | 3,888 | 3,061 | 3,288 | 4,543 | 2,170 |
| Total Assets | 23,806 | 26,862 | 28,229 | 29,954 | 28,109 | 28,219 | 18,293 | 18,195 | 18,339 | 12,834 |
| Current Liabilities | NA | 3,129 | 3,255 | 3,149 | 2,525 | 2,994 | 1,863 | 2,704 | 2,934 | 1,499 |
| Long Term Debt | 6,522 | 7,675 | 8,262 | 10,144 | 12,397 | 12,721 | 5,715 | 5,114 | 4,453 | 4,662 |
| Common Equity | 7,981 | 9,095 | 9,800 | 9,255 | 7,109 | 6,623 | 6,695 | 6,832 | 7,173 | 4,526 |
| Total Capital | 17,830 | 20,461 | 22,097 | 23,932 | 23,800 | 23,400 | 14,787 | 14,323 | 13,611 | 10,592 |
| Capital Expenditures | 880 | 837 | 861 | 492 | 608 | 930 | 660 | 848 | 487 | 615 |
| Cash Flow | 976 | 1,638 | 1,919 | 2,605 | 1,606 | 1,466 | 1,230 | 1,699 | 1,256 | 910 |
| Current Ratio | 2.1 | 1.3 | 1.5 | 1.7 | 1.6 | 1.3 | 1.6 | 1.2 | 1.5 | 1.4 |
| % Long Term Debt of Capitalization | 36.6 | 37.5 | 37.4 | 42.4 | 52.1 | 54.4 | 38.6 | 35.7 | 32.7 | 44.0 |
| % Net Income of Revenue | 0.3 | 1.6 | 2.6 | 5.7 | 1.4 | 1.3 | 2.4 | 5.3 | 5.0 | 2.7 |
| % Return on Assets | 0.2 | 1.3 | 2.0 | 4.4 | 1.0 | 1.0 | 1.9 | 4.6 | 4.0 | 2.3 |
| % Return on Equity | 0.6 | 3.8 | 6.1 | 15.7 | 4.2 | 3.6 | 5.2 | 12.0 | 10.5 | 6.4 |

Data as orig reptd.; bef. results of disc opers/spec. items. Per share data adj. for stk. divs.; EPS diluted. E-Estimated. NA-Not Available. NM-Not Meaningful. NR-Not Ranked. UR-Under Review.

**Office:** 33663 Weyerhaeuser Way South, Federal Way, WA 98003.
**Telephone:** 253-924-2345.
**Email:** invrelations@weyerhaeuser.com
**Website:** http://www.weyerhaeuser.com

**Chrmn:** S.R. Rogel
**Pres & CEO:** D.S. Fulton
**EVP & CFO:** P.M. Bedient
**SVP & CTO:** M.P. Drake

**SVP & General Counsel:** S.D. McDade
**Investor Contact:** K.F. McAuley (253-924-2058)
**Board Members:** D. A. Cafaro, M. A. Emmert, D. S. Fulton, J. I. Kieckhefer, A. G. Langbo, D. Mazankowski, N. Piasecki, S. R. Rogel, R. H. Sinkfield, D. M. Steuert, J. N. Sullivan, K. Williams, C. R. Williamson

**Founded:** 1900
**Domicile:** Washington
**Employees:** 37,857

# Whirlpool Corp

**STANDARD &POOR'S**

**S&P Recommendation** SELL ★★☆☆☆

| Price | 12-Mo. Target Price | Investment Style |
|---|---|---|
| $39.09 (as of Nov 14, 2008) | $35.00 | Large-Cap Blend |

**GICS Sector** Consumer Discretionary
**Sub-Industry** Household Appliances

**Summary** Whirlpool, which acquired Maytag in 2006, is the world's largest manufacturer of home appliances. Sears, Roebuck is its biggest customer.

## Key Stock Statistics (Source S&P, Vickers, company reports)

| | | | | | | | |
|---|---|---|---|---|---|---|---|
| 52-Wk Range | $98.00– 36.95 | S&P Oper. EPS 2008E | 5.80 | Market Capitalization(B) | $2.873 | Beta | 1.40 |
| Trailing 12-Month EPS | $7.30 | S&P Oper. EPS 2009E | 4.25 | Yield (%) | 4.40 | S&P 3-Yr. Proj. EPS CAGR(%) | 3 |
| Trailing 12-Month P/E | 5.4 | P/E on S&P Oper. EPS 2008E | 6.7 | Dividend Rate/Share | $1.72 | S&P Credit Rating | BBB |
| $10K Invested 5 Yrs Ago | $6,571 | Common Shares Outstg. (M) | 73.5 | Institutional Ownership (%) | NM | | |

## Price Performance

30-Week Mov. Avg. · · · 10-Week Mov. Avg. — GAAP Earnings vs. Previous Year   Volume Above Avg. STARS
12-Mo. Target Price — Relative Strength — ▲ Up ▼ Down ▶ No Change   Below Avg.

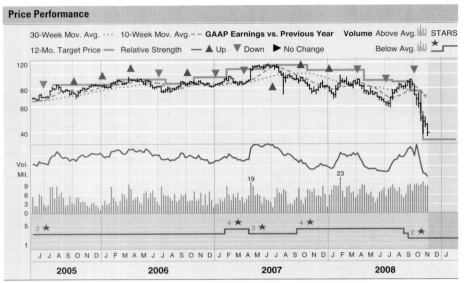

Options: CBOE, P

Analysis prepared by **Kenneth M. Leon, CPA** on October 28, 2008, when the stock traded at **$ 44.35**.

## Qualitative Risk Assessment

| LOW | MEDIUM | HIGH |
|---|---|---|

Our risk assessment reflects WHR's leading market share across many brands, offset by intense industry rivalry and heightened competition from foreign companies. While WHR benefits from its scale advantages, sales may weaken with a global recession negatively impacting household appliance demand.

## Quantitative Evaluations

**S&P Quality Ranking**   B+

| D | C | B- | B | B+ | A- | A | A+ |
|---|---|---|---|---|---|---|---|

**Relative Strength Rank**   WEAK

25

LOWEST = 1   HIGHEST = 99

## Highlights

▶ Following a sales increase of 7.3% in 2007, we forecast flat to low-single digit growth in 2008 and a 10% sales decline in 2009, as weakening economies in Europe and North America may spread to Latin America. In 2008, the company sees industry unit shipments increasing 5% to 8% in emerging markets, compared to a 3% to 4% unit decline in Europe and a 10% unit decrease in the U.S. market.

▶ We believe WHR's addressable markets for appliances may prove to be materially weaker in 2009 than current conditions, triggered by a global recession, in our opinion. Despite improved cost control initiatives in manufacturing and distribution, we think that higher raw material costs will pressure gross margins and cause them to narrow to 14% in 2008 and 2009 from 2007's 14.5%.

▶ WHR's operating margin widened to 5.8% in 2007, from 5.0% in 2006, but we see a narrowing to 4.2% in 2008, followed by 4.1% in 2009. Long term, we believe that WHR will benefit from its larger scale and purchasing power, when customer markets recover. Including tax benefits, we see operating EPS of $5.80 in 2008, decreasing to $4.25 in 2009.

## Investment Rationale/Risk

▶ The prospect of weaker demand for WHR's products remains a concern, as the industry association for appliances reported that major appliance shipments were down 10.6%, year to year, in December 2007 and continue to post weak results in 2008. With a global recession anticipated into 2009, we forecast declining sales for WHR in Europe and the Americas, with Asia showing growth but it is not material to total sales.

▶ Risks to our opinion and target price include favorable changes in business conditions or growth prospects in WHR's major markets, particularly in the Americas and Europe, less competition and/or gains in market share, further declines in raw material prices, and acceleration of cost savings from the Maytag merger.

▶ Reflecting our negative outlook for the appliance sub-industry, our 12-month target price of $35 is based on a target P/E of about 8.2X, near the lowest end of the five-year historical range for WHR and peers, applied to our 2009 EPS projection of $4.25. Our EPS estimates include favorable tax benefits, which should boost weak operating results for 2008 and 2009.

## Revenue/Earnings Data

**Revenue (Million $)**

| | 1Q | 2Q | 3Q | 4Q | Year |
|---|---|---|---|---|---|
| 2008 | 4,614 | 5,076 | 4,902 | -- | -- |
| 2007 | 4,389 | 4,854 | 4,840 | 5,325 | 19,408 |
| 2006 | 3,536 | 4,747 | 4,843 | 4,954 | 18,080 |
| 2005 | 3,208 | 3,556 | 3,599 | 3,954 | 14,317 |
| 2004 | 3,007 | 3,264 | 3,318 | 3,632 | 13,220 |
| 2003 | 2,716 | 2,988 | 3,113 | 3,359 | 12,176 |

**Earnings Per Share ($)**

| | | | | | |
|---|---|---|---|---|---|
| 2008 | 1.22 | 1.53 | 2.15 | E0.52 | E5.80 |
| 2007 | 1.55 | 2.00 | 2.20 | 2.39 | 8.10 |
| 2006 | 1.70 | 1.26 | 1.68 | 1.67 | 6.35 |
| 2005 | 1.26 | 1.42 | 1.66 | 1.83 | 6.19 |
| 2004 | 1.43 | 1.53 | 1.50 | 1.44 | 5.90 |
| 2003 | 1.32 | 1.35 | 1.48 | 1.76 | 5.91 |

Fiscal year ended Dec. 31. Next earnings report expected: Early February. EPS Estimates based on S&P Operating Earnings; historical GAAP earnings are as reported.

## Dividend Data (Dates: mm/dd Payment Date: mm/dd/yy)

| Amount ($) | Date Decl. | Ex-Div. Date | Stk. of Record | Payment Date |
|---|---|---|---|---|
| 0.430 | 02/19 | 02/22 | 02/26 | 03/15/08 |
| 0.430 | 04/15 | 05/21 | 05/23 | 06/15/08 |
| 0.430 | 08/19 | 08/27 | 08/29 | 09/15/08 |
| 0.430 | 10/21 | 11/12 | 11/14 | 12/15/08 |

Dividends have been paid since 1929. Source: Company reports.

**Please read the Required Disclosures and Analyst Certification on the last page of this report.**

The **McGraw·Hill** Companies

# Whirlpool Corp

## Business Summary October 28, 2008

CORPORATE OVERVIEW. Whirlpool Corp. (WHR) manufactures and markets a full line of major appliances and related products, primarily for home use. Products are manufactured in 12 countries and marketed worldwide under 13 main brand names. The company's growth strategy over the past several years has been to introduce innovative new products, strengthen customer loyalty, expand its global footprint, enhance distribution channels, and make strategic acquisitions where appropriate.

MARKET PROFILE. WHR's total sales in 2007 were 60% from North America. As the market leader, its major product brands in the U.S. include Whirlpool, Maytag, KitchenAid, Jenn-Air, Roper, Estate, Admiral, Magic Chef, Amana, and Inglis. In Europe, which generated 20% of sales, products are marketed under the Whirlpool, Maytag, Amana, Bauknecht, Ignis, Laden, Polar and KitchenAid brand names. Markets also include Latin America and Asia. About 18% of total sales in 2007 were from Latin America, where WHR distributes its major home appliances under the Whirlpool, Brastemp, Consul and Eslabon de Lugo brand names. About 2% of sales were from Asia.

COMPETITIVE LANDSCAPE. The company has been able to retain a number

one position in brand and market share in most global regions. Combined with high reliability, WHR has developed strong customer loyalty. Competitors in the appliance industry include long-time incumbents Electrolux and General Electric, as well as expanding foreign operations such as LG Electronics, Bosch Siemens, Samsung, Fisher & Paykel, and Haier.

Net sales in 2007 increased 7.3% compared to 2006 due to strong international sales, higher global average unit prices and the sales contribution from the Maytag acquisition. Excluding currency fluctuations and the impact of the acquisition of Maytag, sales were essentially equal to the prior year. WHR's international businesses experienced strong performance in 2007 driven by an 8.8% increase in units sold. It experienced a 6.4% decrease in unit sales during 2007 in North America, primarily resulting from a decline in appliance industry demand, lower original equipment manufacturer sales and lower share within the value and Maytag brands.

## Company Financials Fiscal Year Ended Dec. 31

| Per Share Data ($) | 2007 | 2006 | 2005 | 2004 | 2003 | 2002 | 2001 | 2000 | 1999 | 1998 |
|---|---|---|---|---|---|---|---|---|---|---|
| Tangible Book Value | 6.06 | NM | 21.49 | 19.85 | 15.23 | 5.82 | 11.10 | 13.97 | 14.29 | 14.01 |
| Cash Flow | 15.52 | 13.54 | 12.65 | 12.35 | 12.00 | 9.62 | 6.32 | 10.39 | 9.64 | 9.71 |
| Earnings | 8.10 | 6.35 | 6.19 | 5.90 | 5.91 | 3.78 | 0.50 | 5.20 | 4.56 | 4.06 |
| S&P Core Earnings | 7.33 | 6.33 | 5.99 | 5.58 | 5.71 | 2.12 | -1.91 | NA | NA | NA |
| Dividends | 1.72 | 2.15 | 1.72 | 1.72 | 1.36 | 1.36 | 1.02 | 1.36 | 1.36 | 1.36 |
| Payout Ratio | 21% | 34% | 28% | 29% | 23% | 36% | NM | 26% | 30% | 33% |
| Prices:High | 118.00 | 96.00 | 86.52 | 80.00 | 73.35 | 79.80 | 74.20 | 68.31 | 78.25 | 75.25 |
| Prices:Low | 72.10 | 74.07 | 60.78 | 54.53 | 42.80 | 39.23 | 45.88 | 31.50 | 40.94 | 43.69 |
| P/E Ratio:High | 15 | 15 | 14 | 14 | 12 | 21 | NM | 13 | 17 | 19 |
| P/E Ratio:Low | 9 | 12 | 10 | 9 | 7 | 10 | NM | 6 | 9 | 11 |

### Income Statement Analysis (Million $)

| | 2007 | 2006 | 2005 | 2004 | 2003 | 2002 | 2001 | 2000 | 1999 | 1998 |
|---|---|---|---|---|---|---|---|---|---|---|
| Revenue | 19,408 | 18,080 | 14,317 | 13,220 | 12,176 | 11,016 | 10,343 | 10,325 | 10,511 | 10,323 |
| Operating Income | 1,717 | 1,428 | 1,291 | 1,218 | 1,219 | 1,207 | 1,147 | 1,178 | 1,261 | 1,126 |
| Depreciation | 593 | 550 | 442 | 445 | 427 | 405 | 396 | 371 | 386 | 438 |
| Interest Expense | 203 | 202 | 130 | 128 | 137 | 143 | 162 | 180 | 166 | 260 |
| Pretax Income | 786 | 620 | 598 | 615 | 652 | 468 | 89.0 | 580 | 510 | 565 |
| Effective Tax Rate | 14.9% | 20.3% | 28.6% | 34.0% | 35.0% | 41.2% | 48.3% | 34.5% | 38.6% | 37.0% |
| Net Income | 647 | 486 | 422 | 406 | 414 | 262 | 34.0 | 367 | 347 | 310 |
| S&P Core Earnings | 587 | 484 | 408 | 384 | 401 | 147 | -130 | NA | NA | NA |

### Balance Sheet & Other Financial Data (Million $)

| | 2007 | 2006 | 2005 | 2004 | 2003 | 2002 | 2001 | 2000 | 1999 | 1998 |
|---|---|---|---|---|---|---|---|---|---|---|
| Cash | 201 | 262 | 524 | 243 | 249 | 192 | 316 | 114 | 261 | 636 |
| Current Assets | 6,555 | 6,476 | 4,710 | 4,514 | 3,865 | 3,327 | 3,311 | 3,237 | 3,177 | 3,882 |
| Total Assets | 14,009 | 13,878 | 8,248 | 8,181 | 7,361 | 6,631 | 6,967 | 6,902 | 6,826 | 7,935 |
| Current Liabilities | 5,893 | 6,002 | 4,301 | 3,985 | 3,589 | 3,505 | 3,082 | 3,303 | 2,892 | 3,267 |
| Long Term Debt | 1,668 | 1,798 | 745 | 1,160 | 1,134 | 1,092 | 1,295 | 795 | 714 | 1,087 |
| Common Equity | 3,911 | 3,283 | 1,745 | 1,606 | 1,301 | 796 | 2,126 | 1,684 | 1,867 | 2,001 |
| Total Capital | 5,648 | 5,481 | 2,749 | 3,074 | 2,734 | 2,083 | 3,725 | 2,801 | 2,738 | 3,854 |
| Capital Expenditures | 536 | 576 | 484 | 511 | 423 | 430 | 378 | 375 | 437 | 523 |
| Cash Flow | 1,240 | 1,036 | 864 | 851 | 841 | 667 | 430 | 738 | 733 | 748 |
| Current Ratio | 1.1 | 1.1 | 1.1 | 1.1 | 1.1 | 0.9 | 1.1 | 1.0 | 1.1 | 1.2 |
| % Long Term Debt of Capitalization | 29.5 | 32.8 | 27.1 | 37.8 | 41.5 | 52.4 | 34.8 | 28.4 | 26.1 | 28.2 |
| % Net Income of Revenue | 3.3 | 2.7 | 2.9 | 3.1 | 3.4 | 2.4 | 0.3 | 3.6 | 3.3 | 3.0 |
| % Return on Assets | 4.6 | 4.4 | 5.1 | 5.2 | 5.9 | 3.9 | 0.5 | 5.3 | 4.7 | 3.8 |
| % Return on Equity | 18.0 | 19.3 | 25.2 | 27.9 | 40.6 | 22.8 | 1.5 | 20.7 | 17.9 | 16.4 |

Data as orig reptd.; bef. results of disc opers/spec. items. Per share data adj. for stk. divs.; EPS diluted. E-Estimated. NA-Not Available. NM-Not Meaningful. NR-Not Ranked. UR-Under Review.

Office: 2000 N M 63, Benton Harbor, MI 49022-2692. Telephone: 269-923-5000. Email: info@whirlpool.com Website: http://www.whirlpool.com

Chrmn & CEO: J.M. Fettig EVP & CFO: R.W. Templin SVP, Secy & General Counsel: D.F. Hopp Chief Acctg Officer & Cntlr: A.B. Petitt

Investor Contact: G. Fritz (269-923-2641) Board Members: H. Cain, G. T. Dicamillo, J. M. Fettig, K. J. Hempel, M. F. Johnston, W. T. Kerr, A. G. Langbo, M. L. Marsh, P. G. Stern, J. D. Stoney, M. A. Todman, M. D. White

Founded: 1906 Domicile: Delaware Employees: 73,682

# Whole Foods Market Inc

**STANDARD &POOR'S**

| S&P Recommendation HOLD ★★★☆☆ | Price $9.38 (as of Nov 14, 2008) | 12-Mo. Target Price $14.00 | Investment Style Large-Cap Blend |
|---|---|---|---|

**GICS Sector** Consumer Staples
**Sub-Industry** Food Retail

**Summary** This company owns and operates the largest U.S. chain of natural and organic foods supermarkets.

## Key Stock Statistics (Source S&P, Vickers, company reports)

| | | | | | | | |
|---|---|---|---|---|---|---|---|
| 52-Wk Range | $45.09– 8.52 | S&P Oper. EPS 2009**E** | 0.90 | Market Capitalization(B) | $1.316 | Beta | 0.99 |
| Trailing 12-Month EPS | $0.82 | S&P Oper. EPS 2010**E** | NA | Yield (%) | Nil | S&P 3-Yr. Proj. EPS CAGR(%) | -3 |
| Trailing 12-Month P/E | 11.4 | P/E on S&P Oper. EPS 2009**E** | 10.4 | Dividend Rate/Share | Nil | S&P Credit Rating | BB- |
| $10K Invested 5 Yrs Ago | $3,216 | Common Shares Outstg. (M) | 140.3 | Institutional Ownership (%) | NM | | |

## Price Performance

- 30-Week Mov. Avg.
- 10-Week Mov. Avg.
- GAAP Earnings vs. Previous Year
- 12-Mo. Target Price
- Relative Strength
- ▲ Up  ▼ Down  ▶ No Change
- Volume  Above Avg.  STARS
- Below Avg.

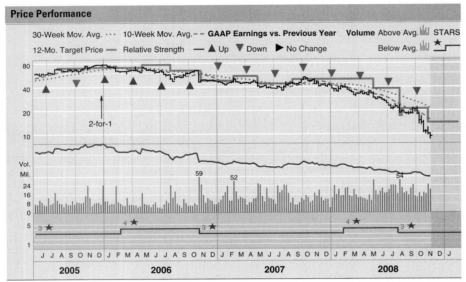

Options: ASE

Analysis prepared by **Joseph Agnese** on November 12, 2008, when the stock traded at **$ 9.20**.

## Highlights

► We expect FY 09 (Sep.) sales to grow to about $8.2 billion, up 2.5% from $8.0 billion in FY 08. We see growth driven by the integration of Wild Oats Markets, about 2% square footage growth reflecting eight net new store openings, and projected comparable-store sales declines of 2.0%.

► We believe margins will expand as the company cuts costs in a weak economic environment and completes the integration of acquired Wild Oats Markets stores, as recently opened stores mature, and on an improved product mix. We believe margin benefits will be partially offset as the company competitively prices branded products in an effort to improve store traffic. We estimate that pre-opening and relocation expenses will decline significantly as a percentage of sales as square footage growth slows and Wild Oats becomes fully integrated. The company expects net interest expense to rise to $35 million to $40 million, from $30 million in FY 08.

► We project that FY 09 operating EPS will increase 9.7%, to $0.90 (excluding our estimate of $0.19 from potential issuance of preferred shares), from $0.82 in FY 08.

## Investment Rationale/Risk

► We see earnings growth slowing significantly in FY 09 as an adverse economic environment results in customers trading down to lower priced products within stores and as customers trade down to lower priced competitors. We view potential issuance of preferred shares as beneficial in helping strengthen the company's balance sheet in an environment where earnings growth is slowing and access to credit markets has become more difficult.

► Risks to our recommendation and target price include slower than expected comparable store sales growth as customers trade down to lower priced products within stores and to competitors.

► Although we see near-term earnings weakness as consumers trade down to lower-priced food retailers, we believe the shares should trade at a premium to the S&P 500 and peers given our expectation that the company will grow faster than peers in the long term. Assuming the shares trade at a multiple of 15.5X (versus peers at 13.5X) our FY 09 EPS estimate of $0.90, our target price is $14.

## Qualitative Risk Assessment

| LOW | MEDIUM | HIGH |
|---|---|---|

Our risk assessment reflects the intensely competitive environment in the retail food industry, partly offset by our view of WFMI's strong balance sheet and growing natural and organic food industry sales momentum.

## Quantitative Evaluations

**S&P Quality Ranking** B

| D | C | B- | B | B+ | A- | A | A+ |
|---|---|---|---|---|---|---|---|

**Relative Strength Rank** WEAK

24

LOWEST = 1     HIGHEST = 99

## Revenue/Earnings Data

### Revenue (Million $)

| | 1Q | 2Q | 3Q | 4Q | Year |
|---|---|---|---|---|---|
| 2008 | 2,457 | 1,866 | 1,841 | 1,789 | 7,954 |
| 2007 | 1,871 | 1,463 | 1,514 | 1,743 | 6,592 |
| 2006 | 1,667 | 1,312 | 1,338 | 1,291 | 5,607 |
| 2005 | 1,368 | 1,085 | 1,133 | 1,115 | 4,701 |
| 2004 | 1,118 | 902.1 | 917.4 | 927.3 | 3,865 |
| 2003 | 923.8 | 725.1 | 749.0 | 750.7 | 3,149 |

### Earnings Per Share ($)

| | | | | | |
|---|---|---|---|---|---|
| 2008 | 0.28 | 0.29 | 0.24 | 0.01 | 0.82 |
| 2007 | 0.38 | 0.32 | 0.35 | 0.24 | 1.29 |
| 2006 | 0.40 | 0.36 | 0.37 | 0.28 | 1.41 |
| 2005 | 0.35 | 0.29 | 0.29 | 0.07 | 0.99 |
| 2004 | 0.30 | 0.27 | 0.25 | 0.23 | 1.05 |
| 2003 | 0.21 | 0.21 | 0.23 | 0.19 | 0.83 |

Fiscal year ended Sep. 30. Next earnings report expected: Late February. EPS Estimates based on S&P Operating Earnings; historical GAAP earnings are as reported.

## Dividend Data (Dates: mm/dd Payment Date: mm/dd/yy)

| Amount ($) | Date Decl. | Ex-Div. Date | Stk. of Record | Payment Date |
|---|---|---|---|---|
| 0.200 | 11/20 | 01/09 | 01/11 | 01/22/08 |
| 0.200 | 03/18 | 04/09 | 04/11 | 04/22/08 |
| 0.200 | 06/11 | 07/09 | 07/11 | 07/22/08 |

Dividends have been paid since 2004. Source: Company reports.

*The McGraw-Hill Companies*

# Whole Foods Market Inc

## Business Summary November 12, 2008

CORPORATE OVERVIEW. Whole Foods Market, established in 1980, has grown into the largest U.S. retailer of natural and organic foods, with $8.0 billion in sales in FY 08 (Sep.). Reflecting a series of store openings and acquisitions, the company has expanded from a single Austin, TX, store in 1980 to a chain of more than 275 stores in 37 states plus Washington, DC; six stores in Canada; and five stores in the United Kingdom. The company strives to differentiate its stores from those of its competitors by tailoring its product mix, customer service attitude and store environment to appeal to health conscious and gourmet customers.

CORPORATE STRATEGY. The company opens or acquires stores in existing regions, and in metropolitan areas in which it believes it can become the leading natural foods supermarket retailer. In developing new stores, WFMI seeks to open large format units of 35,000 sq. ft. to 50,000 sq. ft., located on premium sites, often in urban, highly populated areas. Although approximately 32% of its store base consists of acquired stores, the company expects more of its future growth to come from developing new stores. As of November 2008, WFMI had signed leases for 66 stores averaging approximately 49,100 square feet in size, which is about 135% larger than its existing store base average. It oper-

ated about 10 million square feet of retail space, with about 3.3 million square feet (33% of existing sq. ft.) of retail space that were under development at that time.

Stores average about 38,200 sq. ft., and offer a selection of some 30,000 food and non-food products. Each store contributes an average of almost $37 million in annual sales and average about 7.3 years old. Products sold include natural and organic foods and beverages; dietary supplements; natural personal care products; natural household goods; and educational products. Natural foods can be defined as foods that are minimally processed, largely or completely free of artificial ingredients, preservatives and other non-naturally occurring chemicals, and as near as possible to their whole, natural state. Organic foods are based on the minimal use of off-farm inputs and on management practices that restore, maintain and enhance the ecology.

## Company Financials Fiscal Year Ended Sep. 30

| Per Share Data ($) | 2008 | 2007 | 2006 | 2005 | 2004 | 2003 | 2002 | 2001 | 2000 | 1999 |
|---|---|---|---|---|---|---|---|---|---|---|
| Tangible Book Value | NA | 4.97 | 9.00 | 9.06 | 6.82 | 5.57 | 4.21 | 2.98 | 2.11 | 2.35 |
| Cash Flow | NA | 2.60 | 2.48 | 1.93 | 1.84 | 1.54 | 1.34 | 1.16 | 0.85 | 0.87 |
| Earnings | 0.82 | 1.29 | 1.41 | 0.99 | 1.05 | 0.83 | 0.70 | 0.61 | 0.26 | 0.39 |
| S&P Core Earnings | NA | 1.29 | 1.40 | -0.21 | 0.85 | 0.70 | 0.58 | 0.38 | NA | NA |
| Dividends | NA | 0.69 | 0.88 | 0.42 | 0.23 | Nil | Nil | Nil | Nil | Nil |
| Payout Ratio | NA | 53% | 62% | 42% | 22% | Nil | Nil | Nil | Nil | Nil |
| Prices:High | NA | 53.65 | 78.27 | 79.90 | 48.74 | 33.81 | 27.30 | 23.25 | 15.94 | 12.41 |
| Prices:Low | NA | 36.00 | 45.56 | 44.14 | 32.96 | 22.39 | 17.74 | 9.73 | 8.59 | 7.06 |
| P/E Ratio:High | NA | 42 | 56 | 81 | 47 | 41 | 39 | 38 | 60 | 32 |
| P/E Ratio:Low | NA | 28 | 32 | 45 | 32 | 27 | 25 | 16 | 32 | 18 |

| Income Statement Analysis (Million $) | 2008 | 2007 | 2006 | 2005 | 2004 | 2003 | 2002 | 2001 | 2000 | 1999 |
|---|---|---|---|---|---|---|---|---|---|---|
| Revenue | 7,954 | 6,592 | 5,607 | 4,701 | 3,865 | 3,149 | 2,690 | 2,272 | 1,839 | 1,568 |
| Operating Income | NA | 484 | 475 | 363 | 341 | 285 | 248 | 209 | 181 | 144 |
| Depreciation | 249 | 186 | 156 | 134 | 112 | 98.0 | 85.9 | 78.8 | 63.9 | 53.3 |
| Interest Expense | NA | 4.21 | 0.03 | 2.22 | 7.25 | 8.11 | 10.4 | 17.9 | 15.1 | 8.25 |
| Pretax Income | 207 | 305 | 340 | 237 | 229 | 173 | 141 | 89.8 | 63.5 | 69.1 |
| Effective Tax Rate | 44.6% | 40.0% | 40.0% | 42.5% | 40.0% | 40.0% | 40.0% | 42.5% | 54.5% | 39.0% |
| Net Income | 115 | 183 | 204 | 136 | 137 | 104 | 84.5 | 51.6 | 28.9 | 42.2 |
| S&P Core Earnings | NA | 183 | 202 | -28.0 | 109 | 85.0 | 70.4 | 43.0 | NA | NA |

| Balance Sheet & Other Financial Data (Million $) | 2008 | 2007 | 2006 | 2005 | 2004 | 2003 | 2002 | 2001 | 2000 | 1999 |
|---|---|---|---|---|---|---|---|---|---|---|
| Cash | 30.5 | Nil | 2.25 | 309 | 198 | 166 | 12.6 | 1.84 | 0.40 | 9.02 |
| Current Assets | NA | 668 | 624 | 673 | 485 | 364 | 172 | 145 | 152 | 141 |
| Total Assets | 3,381 | 3,213 | 2,043 | 1,889 | 1,520 | 1,197 | 943 | 829 | 760 | 660 |
| Current Liabilities | NA | 785 | 510 | 418 | 331 | 240 | 176 | 156 | 143 | 121 |
| Long Term Debt | NA | 736 | 8.61 | 12.9 | 165 | 163 | 162 | 251 | 298 | 209 |
| Common Equity | 1,506 | 1,459 | 1,404 | 1,366 | 988 | 776 | 589 | 409 | 307 | 311 |
| Total Capital | NA | 2,195 | 1,413 | 1,379 | 1,173 | 942 | 751 | 660 | 605 | 525 |
| Capital Expenditures | 522 | 140 | 132 | 116 | 110 | 84.1 | 61.4 | 49.0 | 111 | 75.0 |
| Cash Flow | NA | 369 | 360 | 270 | 249 | 202 | 170 | 130 | 92.8 | 95.5 |
| Current Ratio | 0.9 | 0.9 | 1.2 | 1.6 | 1.5 | 1.5 | 1.0 | 0.9 | 1.1 | 1.2 |
| % Long Term Debt of Capitalization | 38.1 | 33.5 | 0.6 | 0.9 | 14.0 | 17.3 | 21.6 | 38.0 | 49.2 | 39.8 |
| % Net Income of Revenue | 1.4 | 2.8 | 3.6 | 2.9 | 3.5 | 3.3 | 3.1 | 2.3 | 1.6 | 2.7 |
| % Return on Assets | 3.5 | 7.0 | 10.4 | 8.0 | 10.1 | 9.7 | 9.5 | 6.5 | 4.1 | 7.0 |
| % Return on Equity | 7.7 | 12.8 | 14.7 | 11.8 | 15.5 | 15.2 | 16.9 | 14.4 | 9.4 | 14.3 |

Data as orig reptd.; bef. results of disc opers/spec. items. Per share data adj. for stk. divs.; EPS diluted. E-Estimated. NA-Not Available. NM-Not Meaningful. NR-Not Ranked. UR-Under Review.

**Office:** 550 Bowie St, Austin, TX 78703-4644.
**Telephone:** 512-477-4455.
**Website:** http://www.wholefoods.com
**Chrmn & CEO:** J.P. Mackey

**COO & Co-Pres:** W. Robb
**COO & Co-Pres:** A.C. Gallo
**EVP, CFO, Chief Acctg Officer & Secy:** G. Chamberlain
**General Counsel:** R. Lang

**Investor Contact:** C. McCann (512-477-4455)
**Board Members:** J. B. Elstrott, G. E. Greene, S. M. Hassan, J. P. Mackey, J. A. Seiffer, M. Siegel, J. D. Sokoloff, R. Sorenson

**Founded:** 1978
**Domicile:** Texas
**Employees:** 52,600

**STANDARD &POOR'S**

# Williams Cos Inc. (The)

| S&P Recommendation | HOLD ★★★☆☆ | Price $16.45 (as of Nov 14, 2008) | 12-Mo. Target Price $20.00 | Investment Style Large-Cap Blend |
|---|---|---|---|---|

**GICS Sector** Energy
**Sub-Industry** Oil & Gas Storage & Transportation

**Summary** This Oklahoma-based company, which primarily finds, produces, gathers, processes and transports natural gas, also manages a wholesale power business.

## Key Stock Statistics (Source S&P, Vickers, company reports)

| | | | | | | | | |
|---|---|---|---|---|---|---|---|---|
| 52-Wk Range | $40.75– 12.38 | S&P Oper. EPS 2008E | 2.27 | Market Capitalization(B) | $9.519 | Beta | | 1.20 |
| Trailing 12-Month EPS | $2.56 | S&P Oper. EPS 2009E | 2.02 | Yield (%) | 2.67 | S&P 3-Yr. Proj. EPS CAGR(%) | | 9 |
| Trailing 12-Month P/E | 6.4 | P/E on S&P Oper. EPS 2008E | 7.2 | Dividend Rate/Share | $0.44 | S&P Credit Rating | | BBB- |
| $10K Invested 5 Yrs Ago | $19,157 | Common Shares Outstg. (M) | 578.7 | Institutional Ownership (%) | 77 | | | |

## Price Performance

30-Week Mov. Avg. ···· 10-Week Mov. Avg. – – **GAAP Earnings vs. Previous Year** Volume Above Avg. |||| STARS
12-Mo. Target Price — Relative Strength ▲ Up ▼ Down ▶ No Change Below Avg. |||| ★

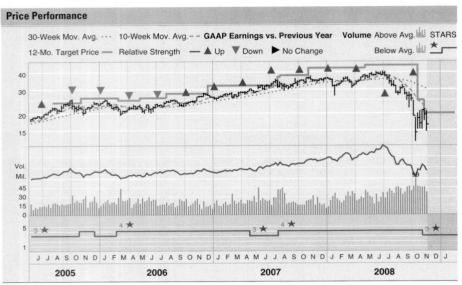

Options: ASE, CBOE, P

Analysis prepared by **Michael Kay** on November 11, 2008, when the stock traded at **$ 18.28**.

## Highlights

➤ We see natural gas volume growth of 15%-20% per annum over the next three years, and pipeline and midstream operations as key earnings drivers. Pipelines are seeing higher returns from the Transco system and Rockies capacity expansions. We expect E&P to benefit from the development of drilling prospects, especially in the Piceance and Powder River basins, but see lower prices impeding segment profits in 2009. WMB sees hurricane damage negatively impacting fourth quarter profit by $10-$20 million, mainly from damage at midstream facilities.

➤ Given volatile markets, we expect WMB to limit asset dropdowns into master limited partnerships Williams Partners (WPZ: $18) and Williams Pipeline Partners (WMZ: $15). WMB's capital budget stands at $3.375-$3.575 billion for 2008 and $2.8-$3.1 billion for 2009. WMB is spending about $2 billion in E&P, which we see coming down some in 2009.

➤ We see 2008 EPS of $2.27, up 34%, on higher natural gas prices and NGL margins. We see lower NGL margins and natural gas prices leading to an 11% drop in 2009 EPS, to $2.02. In July 2008, WMB completed a $1 billion stock repurchase program.

## Investment Rationale/Risk

➤ We expect WMB to expand drilling in the highly active Piceance Basin and the Barnett Shale, a significant inventory of acreage that, if developed, could boost proven reserves by well over 50%. We view positively WMB's stable fee-based business and regulated assets, rising oil and gas reserves and what we view as its stable liquidity position. The company is evaluating structural changes to enhance shareholder value, and should have a specific plan early in 2009. WMB stated the potential of splitting one or more of its primary business units.

➤ Risks to our recommendation and target price include sharply higher interest rates, slower than projected economic growth, a sustained decline in natural gas prices, and lower rates for FERC regulated pipelines.

➤ Lower oil and gas prices have caused a similar decline in energy stocks. Given declining economic forecasts, and the ongoing credit crisis, we expect the market to discount unproven reserve potential and we now value WMB on proven reserves. Our 12-month target price of $20 reflects an enterprise value to projected 2009 EBITDA multiple of 3.5X and our NAV based on WMB's proved reserves only of $23.

## Qualitative Risk Assessment

| LOW | MEDIUM | HIGH |
|---|---|---|

Our risk assessment reflects our belief that although WMB has an E&P segment that can be very volatile, its business portfolio is overweighted in regulated industries with largely fixed returns.

## Quantitative Evaluations

**S&P Quality Ranking**      B

| D | C | B- | B | B+ | A- | A | A+ |
|---|---|---|---|---|---|---|---|

**Relative Strength Rank**     MODERATE

41

LOWEST = 1      HIGHEST = 99

## Revenue/Earnings Data

**Revenue (Million $)**

| | 1Q | 2Q | 3Q | 4Q | Year |
|---|---|---|---|---|---|
| 2008 | 3,224 | 3,729 | 3,267 | -- | -- |
| 2007 | 2,368 | 2,824 | 2,860 | 2,506 | 10,558 |
| 2006 | 3,028 | 2,715 | 3,300 | 2,770 | 11,813 |
| 2005 | 2,954 | 2,871 | 3,082 | 3,676 | 12,584 |
| 2004 | 3,070 | 3,052 | 3,375 | 2,964 | 12,461 |
| 2003 | 4,833 | 3,657 | 4,795 | 3,549 | 16,834 |

**Earnings Per Share ($)**

| | | | | | |
|---|---|---|---|---|---|
| 2008 | 0.70 | 0.70 | 0.63 | E0.45 | E2.27 |
| 2007 | 0.28 | 0.40 | 0.38 | 0.34 | 1.39 |
| 2006 | 0.22 | -0.11 | 0.19 | 0.25 | 0.55 |
| 2005 | 0.34 | 0.07 | 0.01 | 0.12 | 0.53 |
| 2004 | Nil | -0.03 | 0.03 | 0.17 | 0.18 |
| 2003 | -0.09 | 0.17 | 0.04 | -0.16 | -0.03 |

Fiscal year ended Dec. 31. Next earnings report expected: Late February. EPS Estimates based on S&P Operating Earnings; historical GAAP earnings are as reported.

## Dividend Data (Dates: mm/dd Payment Date: mm/dd/yy)

| Amount ($) | Date Decl. | Ex-Div. Date | Stk. of Record | Payment Date |
|---|---|---|---|---|
| 0.100 | 11/15 | 12/12 | 12/14 | 12/31/07 |
| 0.100 | 01/25 | 03/12 | 03/14 | 03/31/08 |
| 0.110 | 05/15 | 06/11 | 06/13 | 06/30/08 |
| 0.110 | 07/17 | 08/20 | 08/22 | 09/08/08 |

Dividends have been paid since 1974. Source: Company reports.

---

**Please read the Required Disclosures and Analyst Certification on the last page of this report.**

*The McGraw·Hill Companies*

# Williams Cos Inc. (The)

STANDARD
&POOR'S

## Business Summary November 11, 2008

CORPORATE OVERVIEW. WMB primarily finds, produces, gathers, and processes and transports natural gas. Operations are concentrated in the Pacific Northwest, Rocky Mountains, Gulf Coast, Southern California and Eastern Seaboard.

In February 2003, WMB announced a business strategy focused on migrating to an integrated natural gas business comprised of a smaller portfolio of natural gas businesses, reducing debt and increasing liquidity via asset sales, strategic levels of financing, and reductions in operating costs.

CORPORATE STRATEGY. WMB has transitioned its corporate strategy toward aggressively focusing on the market in the segments in which it perceives a sustainable competitive advantage, primarily its exploration and production (E&P) segment and its midstream segment. WMB has about 4.14 Tcfe of proved reserves (99% natural gas, 54% proved developed), with natural gas produced from tight sands formations and coal bed methane reserves in the Piceance (69% of total reserves at December 31, 2007), San Juan (14%), Powder River (10%), Midcontinent and other basins (7%).

The midstream division provides natural gas gathering, processing and treating, and natural gas liquid fractionation, storage and marketing, with primary service areas concentrated in the western states of Wyoming, Colorado and

New Mexico, and the onshore and offshore shelf and deepwater areas in and around the Gulf Coast states of Texas, Louisiana, Mississippi and Alabama. Geographically, midstream natural gas assets are positioned to maximize commercial and operational synergies with other WMB assets (e.g., offshore gathering and processing assets attach and process or condition natural gas supplies delivered to the Transco pipeline; WMB gathering and processing facilities in the San Juan basin handle about 80% of the group's wellhead production in the basin).

The gas pipeline division has 14,200 miles of pipeline, with total annual throughput of 2,700 trillion BTUs, including the Transcontinental Gas Pipeline (Transco) and the Northwest Pipeline. Each pipeline system operates under Federal Energy Regulatory Commission (FERC) approved tariffs that establish rates, cost recovery mechanisms, and service terms and conditions. The established rates are a function of WMB's cost of providing services, including a "reasonable" return on invested capital (ROIC).

## Company Financials Fiscal Year Ended Dec. 31

| Per Share Data ($) | 2007 | 2006 | 2005 | 2004 | 2003 | 2002 | 2001 | 2000 | 1999 | 1998 |
|---|---|---|---|---|---|---|---|---|---|---|
| Tangible Book Value | 9.51 | 8.48 | 7.70 | 7.06 | 5.96 | 7.15 | 9.43 | 13.26 | 11.69 | 8.34 |
| Cash Flow | 3.16 | 1.97 | 1.75 | 1.37 | 1.27 | 0.53 | 3.17 | 3.80 | 2.04 | 1.82 |
| Earnings | 1.39 | 0.55 | 0.53 | 0.18 | -0.03 | -1.14 | 1.67 | 1.95 | 0.36 | 0.32 |
| S&P Core Earnings | 1.41 | 0.78 | 0.64 | 0.05 | -0.26 | -1.34 | 1.40 | NA | NA | NA |
| Dividends | 0.39 | 0.35 | 0.25 | 0.08 | 0.04 | 0.42 | 0.68 | 0.60 | 0.60 | 0.60 |
| Payout Ratio | 28% | 63% | 47% | 44% | NM | NM | 41% | 31% | 167% | 171% |
| Prices:High | 37.74 | 28.32 | 25.72 | 17.18 | 10.73 | 26.35 | 46.44 | 49.75 | 53.75 | 36.94 |
| Prices:Low | 25.17 | 19.35 | 15.18 | 8.49 | 2.51 | 0.78 | 20.80 | 29.50 | 28.00 | 20.00 |
| P/E Ratio:High | 27 | 51 | 49 | 95 | NM | NM | 28 | 26 | NM | NM |
| P/E Ratio:Low | 18 | 35 | 29 | 47 | NM | NM | 12 | 15 | NM | NM |

| Income Statement Analysis (Million $) | | | | | | | | | | |
|---|---|---|---|---|---|---|---|---|---|---|
| Revenue | 10,558 | 11,813 | 12,584 | 12,461 | 16,834 | 5,608 | 11,035 | 10,398 | 8,593 | 7,658 |
| Operating Income | 2,938 | 2,124 | 1,972 | 1,903 | 1,849 | 1,566 | 3,389 | 2,602 | 1,591 | 1,372 |
| Depreciation | 1,082 | 866 | 740 | 668 | 671 | 775 | 798 | 832 | 742 | 646 |
| Interest Expense | 685 | 659 | 664 | 833 | 1,241 | 1,325 | 747 | 1,010 | 668 | 515 |
| Pretax Income | 1,461 | 579 | 557 | 246 | 71.0 | -617 | 1,533 | 1,415 | 316 | 247 |
| Effective Tax Rate | 35.9% | 35.6% | 38.4% | 53.4% | 51.3% | NM | 41.1% | 39.1% | 51.0% | 44.6% |
| Net Income | 847 | 333 | 317 | 93.2 | 15.2 | -502 | 835 | 873 | 162 | 147 |
| S&P Core Earnings | 852 | 480 | 388 | 27.3 | -144 | -699 | 703 | NA | NA | NA |

| Balance Sheet & Other Financial Data (Million $) | | | | | | | | | | |
|---|---|---|---|---|---|---|---|---|---|---|
| Cash | 1,699 | 2,269 | 1,597 | 930 | 2,316 | 2,019 | 1,301 | 1,211 | 1,092 | 503 |
| Current Assets | 5,538 | 6,322 | 9,697 | 6,044 | 8,795 | 12,886 | 12,938 | 15,477 | 6,517 | 3,532 |
| Total Assets | 25,061 | 25,402 | 29,443 | 23,993 | 27,022 | 34,989 | 38,906 | 40,197 | 25,289 | 18,647 |
| Current Liabilities | 4,431 | 4,694 | 8,450 | 5,146 | 6,270 | 11,309 | 13,495 | 16,804 | 5,772 | 4,439 |
| Long Term Debt | 7,757 | 7,622 | 7,591 | 7,712 | 11,040 | 11,896 | 10,621 | 10,532 | 9,746 | 6,366 |
| Common Equity | 6,375 | 6,073 | 5,428 | 4,956 | 4,102 | 4,778 | 6,044 | 5,892 | 5,585 | 4,155 |
| Total Capital | 18,558 | 17,656 | 15,741 | 15,238 | 17,595 | 20,723 | 21,532 | 20,693 | 18,475 | 13,193 |
| Capital Expenditures | 2,816 | -2,509 | 1,299 | 787 | 957 | 1,824 | 1,922 | 4,904 | 3,513 | 1,708 |
| Cash Flow | 1,929 | 1,198 | 1,057 | 762 | 657 | 274 | 1,633 | 1,705 | 901 | 786 |
| Current Ratio | 1.3 | 1.3 | 1.1 | 1.2 | 1.4 | 1.1 | 1.0 | 0.9 | 1.1 | 0.8 |
| % Long Term Debt of Capitalization | 41.8 | 43.2 | 48.2 | 50.6 | 62.7 | 57.4 | 49.3 | 50.9 | 52.8 | 48.3 |
| % Net Income of Revenue | 8.0 | 2.8 | 2.5 | 0.7 | 0.1 | NM | 7.6 | 8.4 | 1.9 | 1.9 |
| % Return on Assets | 3.4 | 1.2 | 1.2 | 0.4 | 0.0 | NM | 2.3 | 2.7 | 0.7 | 0.9 |
| % Return on Equity | 13.6 | 5.8 | 6.1 | 2.1 | 0.0 | NM | 14.0 | 15.2 | 3.3 | 3.7 |

Data as orig reptd.; bef. results of disc opers/spec. items. Per share data adj. for stk. divs.; EPS diluted. E-Estimated. NA-Not Available. NM-Not Meaningful. NR-Not Ranked. UR-Under Review.

**Office:** 1 Williams Ctr, Tulsa, OK 74172-0140.
**Telephone:** 918-573-2000.
**Website:** http://www.williams.com
**Chrmn, Pres & CEO:** S.J. Malcolm

**Pres:** J.C. Bumgarner, Jr.
**SVP & CFO:** D.R. Chappel
**SVP & General Counsel:** J.J. Bender
**Chief Admin Officer:** R. Ewing

**Board Members:** J. R. Cleveland, K. B. Cooper, I. F. Engelhardt, W. R. Granberry, W. E. Green, J. H. Hinshaw, W. R. Howell, C. M. Lillis, G. A. Lorch, W. G. Lowrie, F. T. MacInnis, S. J. Malcolm, J. D. Stoney

**Founded:** 1908
**Domicile:** Delaware
**Employees:** 4,319

**STANDARD &POOR'S**

# Windstream Corp

| S&P Recommendation | BUY ★★★★☆ | Price $8.43 (as of Nov 14, 2008) | 12-Mo. Target Price $11.00 | Investment Style Large-Cap Value |
|---|---|---|---|---|

**GICS Sector** Telecommunication Services
**Sub-Industry** Integrated Telecommunication Services

**Summary** This company was formed through the combination of former Alltel wireline assets and Valor Communications in July 2006. It provides telephone service to more than 3 million lines in rural markets.

## Key Stock Statistics (Source S&P, Vickers, company reports)

| | | | | | | | |
|---|---|---|---|---|---|---|---|
| 52-Wk Range | $14.10–6.37 | S&P Oper. EPS 2008**E** | 1.06 | Market Capitalization(B) | $3.704 | Beta | 0.93 |
| Trailing 12-Month EPS | $2.04 | S&P Oper. EPS 2009**E** | 1.02 | Yield (%) | 11.86 | S&P 3-Yr. Proj. EPS CAGR(%) | 3 |
| Trailing 12-Month P/E | 4.1 | P/E on S&P Oper. EPS 2008**E** | 8.0 | Dividend Rate/Share | $1.00 | S&P Credit Rating | NA |
| $10K Invested 5 Yrs Ago | NA | Common Shares Outstg. (M) | 439.4 | Institutional Ownership (%) | 73 | | |

## Price Performance

- 30-Week Mov. Avg. ···· 10-Week Mov. Avg. - - GAAP Earnings vs. Previous Year Volume Above Avg. ▏▎▍ STARS
- 12-Mo. Target Price — Relative Strength — ▲ Up ▼ Down ▶ No Change Below Avg. ▏▎▍ ★

Options: CBOE, Ph

Analysis prepared by **Todd Rosenbluth** on November 10, 2008, when the stock traded at **$ 8.30**.

### Highlights

➤ We project revenues of $3.2 billion in 2008 and $3.1 billion in 2009, down slightly from 2007, which included an acquisition but excluded directory operations. We see broadband customer additions nearly offsetting the impact of increasing access line losses, although growth will likely slow due to an above-average penetration rate and greater competition. Our estimates do not reflect any regulatory changes that may be approved.

➤ We expect WIN to generate $1.64 billion of EBITDA in 2008 and $1.59 billion in 2009, with EBITDA margins narrowing slightly to 51% on increased sales and marketing costs to grow the broadband business. We see benefits from the integration of customer service and network service costs increasing in 2009.

➤ We forecast operating EPS of $1.06 in 2008 and $1.02 in 2009, with a slowdown in share repurchases in 2009. We see results aided by lower depreciation and a decline in interest costs following the directory asset sale in late 2007, which resulted in a one-time gain of $1.00 per share.

### Investment Rationale/Risk

➤ WIN shares fell sharply in October. We believe the decline reflected the potentially negative impact from proposed FCC rule changes that could lead to reduced universal service funding (USF) and intercarrier compensation. We think the stock more than reflects these risks, and we believe that less than 10% of revenues are exposed to changes, which we see as being phased in over time. We believe WIN will generate strong cash flow into 2009, which should support the company's dividend, due to an expansion of its customer base for DSL and video offerings and cost synergies from acquisitions.

➤ Risks to our recommendation and target price include increased cable telephony competition, regulatory changes that pressure cash flow, and a free cash flow dilutive acquisition.

➤ Our 12-month target price is $11, representing a P/E of 11X our 2009 EPS estimate and an enterprise value/EBITDA multiple of 6X, in line with rural telecom peers. At our target price, WIN's dividend yield would be an above average 9%.

## Qualitative Risk Assessment

| LOW | MEDIUM | HIGH |
|---|---|---|

Our risk assessment reflects the stable rural markets that WIN serves and our view of its lower-than-peers debt leverage, offset by the risks we see in integrating acquisitions.

## Quantitative Evaluations

**S&P Quality Ranking** NR

| D | C | B- | B | B+ | A- | A | A+ |
|---|---|---|---|---|---|---|---|

**Relative Strength Rank** MODERATE

66

LOWEST = 1       HIGHEST = 99

## Revenue/Earnings Data

### Revenue (Million $)

| | 1Q | 2Q | 3Q | 4Q | Year |
|---|---|---|---|---|---|
| 2008 | 811.7 | 799.9 | 794.1 | -- | -- |
| 2007 | 783.7 | 826.7 | 822.6 | 827.8 | 3,261 |
| 2006 | -- | 125.5 | 771.4 | 827.6 | 3,033 |
| 2005 | -- | -- | -- | -- | 3,414 |
| 2004 | -- | -- | -- | -- | -- |
| 2003 | -- | -- | -- | -- | -- |

### Earnings Per Share ($)

| | | | | | |
|---|---|---|---|---|---|
| 2008 | 0.28 | 0.27 | 0.24 | E0.26 | E1.06 |
| 2007 | 0.21 | 0.24 | 0.25 | 1.25 | 1.94 |
| 2006 | -- | 0.22 | 0.21 | 0.25 | 1.02 |
| 2005 | -- | -- | -- | -- | 0.83 |
| 2004 | -- | -- | -- | -- | -- |
| 2003 | -- | -- | -- | -- | -- |

Fiscal year ended Dec. 31. Next earnings report expected: Mid February. EPS Estimates based on S&P Operating Earnings; historical GAAP earnings are as reported.

## Dividend Data (Dates: mm/dd Payment Date: mm/dd/yy)

| Amount ($) | Date Decl. | Ex-Div. Date | Stk. of Record | Payment Date |
|---|---|---|---|---|
| 0.250 | 02/07 | 03/27 | 03/31 | 04/15/08 |
| 0.250 | 05/08 | 06/26 | 06/30 | 07/15/08 |
| 0.250 | 08/07 | 09/26 | 09/30 | 10/15/08 |
| 0.250 | 11/06 | 12/29 | 12/31 | 01/15/09 |

Dividends have been paid since 2006. Source: Company reports.

*The McGraw-Hill Companies*

# Windstream Corp

## Business Summary November 10, 2008

CORPORATE OVERVIEW. In July 2006, Alltel Corp spun off its wireline operations into a separate entity. Immediately after the consummation of the tax free spin-off, the entity merged with Valor Communications, and the resulting company was renamed Windstream Corporation. As of September 2008, WIN had 3.08 million access lines, including more than 100,000 lines that were previously part of CT Communications, which was acquired in August 2007. The company also had 2 million long distance customers and 963,000 broadband customers (31% of total access lines and more than 44% of primarily residential lines), up 16% from a year earlier. WIN operates primarily in rural markets in the southern U.S., such as Lexington, KY, and Lincoln, NE, with an average of only 25 access lines per square mile. The company's offerings include local and long distance voice and data services, both for mostly residential customers.

In addition, during most of 2007, WIN operated a directory publication business. In November 2007, it completed the sale of its directory operations to a private equity firm for $525 million in a tax-free transaction that led to $210 million in debt retirement. We believe 2007 revenues were boosted by network asset sales to Alltel previously considered part of internal operations.

CORPORATE STRATEGY. In the first half of 2008, WIN consolidated call centers and IT systems and launched a new brand. The company is looking to grow by offering broadband and digital TV (through a wholesale satellite product with Echostar with 251,000 customers) to retain its wireline customers and improve revenue per customer. In 2008, WIN has had success in upgrading existing DSL customers with higher-speed offerings and was offering 12 Mbps of broadband service, 10 times the speed of traditional DSL service, in certain markets. As of September 2008, WIN's average monthly revenue per household was $83, up fractionally from a year earlier. In our view, this is a different approach than some rural telecom providers that initially featured a wholesale wireless offering. In 2008, WIN was targeting customers who did not have a wireline phone and recommending its broadband product.

In August 2007, WIN completed its acquisition of CT Communications (CTCI), a telecom service provider in North Carolina, for $31.50 a share, or $585 million. CTCI had $179 million of revenue and $57 million of EBITDA in the 12 months ended March 2007. As part of keeping its spin-off from Alltel tax-free, Windstream was limited in the number of shares it could issue to raise capital. That lock-up ended in mid-July 2008 and in our view could allow WIN to focus on additional acquisitions.

## Company Financials Fiscal Year Ended Dec. 31

| Per Share Data ($) | 2007 | 2006 | 2005 | 2004 | 2003 | 2002 | 2001 | 2000 | 1999 | 1998 |
|---|---|---|---|---|---|---|---|---|---|---|
| Tangible Book Value | NM | NM | NM | NA | NA | NA | NA | NA | NA | NA |
| Cash Flow | 3.08 | 1.88 | 2.08 | NA | NA | NA | NA | NA | NA | NA |
| Earnings | 1.94 | 1.02 | 0.83 | 0.96 | NA | NA | NA | NA | NA | NA |
| S&P Core Earnings | 1.00 | 0.95 | 0.80 | 0.80 | NA | NA | NA | NA | NA | NA |
| Dividends | 1.00 | 0.38 | NA | NA | NA | NA | NA | NA | NA | NA |
| Payout Ratio | 52% | 37% | NA | NA | NA | NA | NA | NA | NA | NA |
| Prices:High | 15.63 | 14.43 | NA | NA | NA | NA | NA | NA | NA | NA |
| Prices:Low | 12.38 | 11.13 | NA | NA | NA | NA | NA | NA | NA | NA |
| P/E Ratio:High | 8 | 14 | NA | NA | NA | NA | NA | NA | NA | NA |
| P/E Ratio:Low | 6 | 11 | NA | NA | NA | NA | NA | NA | NA | NA |

| Income Statement Analysis (Million $) | | | | | | | | | | |
|---|---|---|---|---|---|---|---|---|---|---|
| Revenue | 3,261 | 3,033 | 3,414 | 2,934 | NA | NA | NA | NA | NA | NA |
| Operating Income | 1,705 | 1,398 | 1,617 | NA | NA | NA | NA | NA | NA | NA |
| Depreciation | 540 | 450 | 593 | 509 | NA | NA | NA | NA | NA | NA |
| Interest Expense | 443 | 210 | 391 | 35.6 | NA | NA | NA | NA | NA | NA |
| Pretax Income | 1,169 | 722 | 662 | 646 | NA | NA | NA | NA | NA | NA |
| Effective Tax Rate | 21.6% | 38.3% | 40.5% | 40.2% | NA | NA | NA | NA | NA | NA |
| Net Income | 917 | 446 | 394 | 386 | NA | NA | NA | NA | NA | NA |
| S&P Core Earnings | 471 | 451 | 382 | 382 | NA | NA | NA | NA | NA | NA |

| Balance Sheet & Other Financial Data (Million $) | | | | | | | | | | |
|---|---|---|---|---|---|---|---|---|---|---|
| Cash | 72.0 | 387 | 119 | NA | NA | NA | NA | NA | NA | NA |
| Current Assets | 498 | 877 | 533 | NA | NA | NA | NA | NA | NA | NA |
| Total Assets | 8,211 | 8,031 | 7,751 | NA | NA | NA | NA | NA | NA | NA |
| Current Liabilities | 641 | 685 | 459 | NA | NA | NA | NA | NA | NA | NA |
| Long Term Debt | 5,331 | 5,456 | 5,525 | NA | NA | NA | NA | NA | NA | NA |
| Common Equity | 700 | 470 | 533 | NA | NA | NA | NA | NA | NA | NA |
| Total Capital | 7,137 | 6,917 | 7,064 | NA | NA | NA | NA | NA | NA | NA |
| Capital Expenditures | 366 | 374 | NA | 338 | NA | NA | NA | NA | NA | NA |
| Cash Flow | 1,457 | 895 | 987 | NA | NA | NA | NA | NA | NA | NA |
| Current Ratio | 0.8 | 1.3 | 1.2 | NA | NA | NA | NA | NA | NA | NA |
| % Long Term Debt of Capitalization | 74.7 | 78.9 | 78.2 | Nil | NA | NA | NA | NA | NA | NA |
| % Net Income of Revenue | 28.1 | 14.7 | 11.5 | 13.2 | NA | NA | NA | NA | NA | NA |
| % Return on Assets | 11.3 | 6.9 | NA | NA | NA | NA | NA | NA | NA | NA |
| % Return on Equity | 156.8 | 22.5 | NA | NA | NA | NA | NA | NA | NA | NA |

Data as orig reptd.; bef. results of disc opers/spec. items. Per share data adj. for stk. divs.; EPS diluted. E-Estimated. NA-Not Available. NM-Not Meaningful. NR-Not Ranked. UR-Under Review.

**Office:** 4001 N Rodney Parham Rd, Little Rock, AR 72212-2442.
**Telephone:** 501-748-7000.
**Website:** http://www.windstream.com
**Chrmn:** F.X. Frantz

**Pres, CEO & COO:** J. Gardner
**EVP & CFO:** B.K. Whittington
**EVP, Secy & General Counsel:** J.P. Fletcher
**Chief Acctg Officer & Cntlr:** A.W. Thomas

**Investor Contact:** M. Michaels (501-748-7578)
**Board Members:** C. Armitage, S. E. Beall, III, D. E. Foster, F. X. Frantz, J. Gardner, J. T. Hinson, J. K. Jones, J. K. Jones, W. A. Montgomery, F. E. Reed

**Founded:** 2000
**Domicile:** Delaware
**Employees:** 7,570

# Wisconsin Energy Corp

## STANDARD &POOR'S

| S&P Recommendation HOLD ★★★☆☆ | Price $42.17 (as of Nov 14, 2008) | 12-Mo. Target Price $49.00 | Investment Style Large-Cap Blend |

**GICS Sector** Utilities
**Sub-Industry** Multi-Utilities

**Summary** This energy company serves more than 1.1 million electric customers in Wisconsin and Michigan's Upper Peninsula, and more than 1 million natural gas customers in Wisconsin.

## Key Stock Statistics (Source S&P, Vickers, company reports)

| | | | | | | | | |
|---|---|---|---|---|---|---|---|---|
| 52-Wk Range | $50.48– 34.89 | S&P Oper. EPS 2008E | 2.95 | Market Capitalization(B) | $4.930 | Beta | | 0.48 |
| Trailing 12-Month EPS | $2.99 | S&P Oper. EPS 2009E | 3.25 | Yield (%) | 2.56 | S&P 3-Yr. Proj. EPS CAGR(%) | | 7 |
| Trailing 12-Month P/E | 14.1 | P/E on S&P Oper. EPS 2008E | 14.3 | Dividend Rate/Share | $1.08 | S&P Credit Rating | | BBB+ |
| $10K Invested 5 Yrs Ago | $14,719 | Common Shares Outstg. (M) | 116.9 | Institutional Ownership (%) | 70 | | | |

## Price Performance

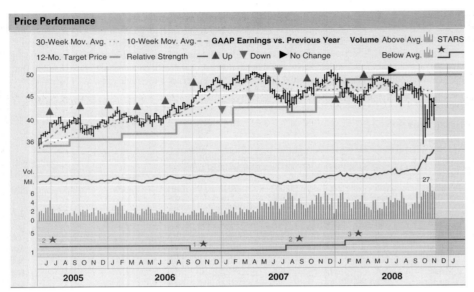

30-Week Mov. Avg. · · · · 10-Week Mov. Avg. - - GAAP Earnings vs. Previous Year Volume Above Avg. STARS
12-Mo. Target Price — Relative Strength ▲ Up ▼ Down ▶ No Change Below Avg. ★

Analysis prepared by **Justin McCann** on September 26, 2008, when the stock traded at **$ 45.01**.

## Qualitative Risk Assessment

| LOW | MEDIUM | HIGH |

Our risk assessment reflects our view of the company's strong and steady cash flow from the regulated electric and gas utility operations, and a regulatory environment that has historically been supportive. We believe this is partially offset by the higher risk profile of the company's non-regulated power generating subsidiary, as well as by the high level of capital expenditures the company expects to incur over the next five years.

## Quantitative Evaluations

**S&P Quality Ranking** B

| D | C | B- | B | B+ | A- | A | A+ |

**Relative Strength Rank** STRONG

89

LOWEST = 1 HIGHEST = 99

## Highlights

➤ We expect EPS from continuing operations in 2008 to increase about 2% from 2007 EPS from continuing operations of $2.84, which rose 10% from 2006 EPS from continuing operations of $2.58. The modest increase reflects the projected impact of a reduced rate base due to the sale of the Point Beach nuclear plant and the inability of the regulated utilities to fully recover their higher fuel and purchased power costs. This should be largely offset by the amortization of the gain related to the sale of the plant.

➤ In 2009, we expect operating EPS to grow approximately 10% from anticipated results in 2008. We expect results to benefit from a full year of the Port Washington generating unit and the Blue Sky wind farm, each of which went into operation in May 2008.

➤ WEC plans capital expenditures of about $1.2 billion in 2008, $816 million in 2009, and $800 million in 2010. It has targeted $660 million for the utilities in 2008, $592 million in 2009, and $753 million in 2010, with the remainder for non-regulated We Power operations. A new power plant came on line in May 2008, and we expect two more to come on line in 2009 and 2010.

## Investment Rationale/Risk

➤ The stock is down more than 6% year to date (after only a 2.6% increase in 2007), and we expect it to perform in line with the company's electric and gas utility peers over the next 12 months. While WEC's recent dividend yield (2.4%) and dividend payout ratio (37% of our 2008 operating EPS estimate) are well below peers (4.3% and 59%, respectively), the company has indicated it might consider a significant increase in its dividend in 2009. We would hold the shares for their total return potential.

➤ Risks to our recommendation and target price include significant delays in bringing the new power plants into operation (which could result in sharply higher costs), unfavorable regulatory rulings, and a decrease in the average P/E of the group as a whole.

➤ WEC increased its dividend about 8% with the March 2008 payment, and is considering a policy under which it would raise the annual dividend at a rate of about half that of its EPS growth. We expect the stock to trade at a discount-to-peers P/E of 15.2X our EPS estimate for 2009, which leads to our 12-month target price of $49.

## Revenue/Earnings Data

**Revenue (Million $)**

| | 1Q | 2Q | 3Q | 4Q | Year |
|---|---|---|---|---|---|
| 2008 | 1,432 | 946.1 | 852.5 | -- | -- |
| 2007 | 1,301 | 906.5 | 881.5 | 1,149 | 4,238 |
| 2006 | 1,247 | 814.4 | 839.8 | 1,095 | 3,996 |
| 2005 | 1,095 | 788.5 | 797.3 | 1,135 | 3,816 |
| 2004 | 1,066 | 716.4 | 696.6 | 952.0 | 3,431 |
| 2003 | 1,229 | 914.3 | 878.5 | 1,032 | 4,054 |

**Earnings Per Share ($)**

| | | | | | |
|---|---|---|---|---|---|
| 2008 | 1.04 | 0.49 | 0.65 | E0.77 | E2.95 |
| 2007 | 0.85 | 0.49 | 0.70 | 0.80 | 2.84 |
| 2006 | 0.88 | 0.50 | 0.60 | 0.65 | 2.64 |
| 2005 | 0.76 | 0.48 | 0.56 | 0.77 | 2.56 |
| 2004 | 0.69 | 0.17 | -0.56 | 0.73 | 1.03 |
| 2003 | 0.79 | 0.42 | 0.26 | 0.60 | 2.06 |

Fiscal year ended Dec. 31. Next earnings report expected: Early February. EPS Estimates based on S&P Operating Earnings; historical GAAP earnings are as reported.

## Dividend Data (Dates: mm/dd Payment Date: mm/dd/yy)

| Amount ($) | Date Decl. | Ex-Div. Date | Stk. of Record | Payment Date |
|---|---|---|---|---|
| 0.270 | 01/17 | 02/12 | 02/14 | 03/01/08 |
| 0.270 | 04/24 | 05/12 | 05/14 | 06/01/08 |
| 0.270 | 07/24 | 08/12 | 08/14 | 09/01/08 |
| 0.270 | 10/16 | 11/12 | 11/14 | 12/01/08 |

Dividends have been paid since 1939. Source: Company reports.

**Please read the Required Disclosures and Analyst Certification on the last page of this report.**

The *McGraw-Hill* Companies

# Wisconsin Energy Corp

STANDARD
&POOR'S

## Business Summary September 26, 2008

CORPORATE OVERVIEW. Wisconsin Energy Corporation (WEC) is a holding company that primarily operates in two segments: utility energy and non-utility energy. The principal utilities are: We Energies (the trade name for Wisconsin Electric Power Company and Wisconsin Gas LLC) and Edison Sault Electric Company. The company's non-regulated segment consists primarily of We Power, which was formed to design, construct, own and lease to Wisconsin Electric the new generating capacity included in the company's Power the Future strategy. In 2007, utility operations contributed 99.7% of total operating revenues and 93.2% of consolidated operating income.

CORPORATE STRATEGY. WEC's goal is to strengthen its utility business through the development of a reliable power supply and the upgrade of its infrastructure, and to continue the divestiture of its non-energy and real estate operations. The company has initiated its "Power the Future" strategy, which is expected to significantly improve the supply and reliability of power. The company is investing in four new electric generation facilities (three of them currently being constructed by We Power) and is also upgrading the existing ones. The strategy also includes an upgrade of existing distribution facilities. WEC is working to achieve operational synergies by integrating the businesses of Wisconsin Electric and Wisconsin Gas, which it believes will result in improved customer satisfaction.

MARKET PROFILE. In 2007, We Energies served more than 1.13 million electric customers in Wisconsin and (through its Edison Sault unit) the Upper Peninsula of Michigan, about 1.05 million gas customers in Wisconsin, around 3,040 water customers in Milwaukee, and about 470 steam customers in Milwaukee. The Edison Sault unit served 22,900 electric customers in the Upper Peninsula of Michigan. Over the next five years, WEC estimates that the utility energy segment in the service territories will grow at an annual rate of 1.0% to 1.5%; annual electric demand is projected to grow at a rate of 2.0% to 3.0%. In 2007, residential customers accounted for 34.4% of electric utility revenues; small commercial/industrial customers 31.8%; large commercial and industrial users 25.0%; other retail 0.7%; other wholesale 3.5%; resale-utilities 3.0%; and other 1.5%. Residential customers accounted for 63.1% of gas utility revenues in 2007; commercial/industrial customers, 32.8%; transported gas, 3.3%; and other, 0.9%. In 2007, coal accounted for 54.1% of total fuel sources, nuclear 17.3%; purchased power 21.3%; natural gas 6.2%; and hydroelectric 1.1%.

## Company Financials Fiscal Year Ended Dec. 31

| Per Share Data ($) | 2007 | 2006 | 2005 | 2004 | 2003 | 2002 | 2001 | 2000 | 1999 | 1998 |
|---|---|---|---|---|---|---|---|---|---|---|
| Tangible Book Value | 22.72 | 20.92 | 0.71 | 17.53 | 12.86 | 11.26 | 10.61 | 10.03 | 16.89 | 16.46 |
| Earnings | 2.84 | 2.64 | 2.56 | 1.03 | 2.06 | 1.44 | 1.77 | 1.27 | 1.79 | 1.65 |
| S&P Core Earnings | 2.70 | 2.70 | 2.55 | 0.84 | 1.97 | 0.93 | 1.19 | NA | NA | NA |
| Dividends | 1.00 | 0.92 | 0.88 | 0.83 | 0.80 | 0.80 | 0.80 | 1.37 | 1.56 | 1.56 |
| Payout Ratio | 35% | 35% | 34% | 81% | 39% | 56% | 45% | 108% | 87% | 94% |
| Prices:High | 50.48 | 48.70 | 40.83 | 34.60 | 33.68 | 26.48 | 24.62 | 23.56 | 31.56 | 34.00 |
| Prices:Low | 41.06 | 38.16 | 33.35 | 29.50 | 22.56 | 20.17 | 19.13 | 16.81 | 19.06 | 27.00 |
| P/E Ratio:High | 18 | 18 | 16 | 34 | 16 | 18 | 14 | 19 | 18 | 21 |
| P/E Ratio:Low | 14 | 14 | 13 | 29 | 11 | 14 | 11 | 13 | 11 | 16 |
| **Income Statement Analysis** (Million $) | | | | | | | | | | |
| Revenue | 4,238 | 3,996 | 3,816 | 3,431 | 4,054 | 3,736 | 3,929 | 3,355 | 2,273 | 1,980 |
| Depreciation | 328 | 326 | 332 | 327 | 332 | 321 | 342 | 336 | 270 | 243 |
| Maintenance | NA | NA | NA | NA | NA | NA | NA | NA | NA | 169 |
| Fixed Charges Coverage | 4.00 | 3.60 | 3.61 | 2.64 | 2.68 | 2.03 | 2.17 | 1.64 | 2.68 | 3.18 |
| Construction Credits | NA | NA | NA | 2.80 | 18.6 | 11.2 | 15.2 | 16.2 | 13.3 | 10.8 |
| Effective Tax Rate | 39.1% | 35.9% | 33.0% | 39.7% | 35.6% | 38.8% | 41.9% | 44.9% | 34.7% | 34.1% |
| Net Income | 337 | 313 | 304 | 122 | 244 | 167 | 209 | 154 | 209 | 188 |
| S&P Core Earnings | 320 | 319 | 302 | 98.5 | 233 | 108 | 142 | NA | NA | NA |
| **Balance Sheet & Other Financial Data** (Million $) | | | | | | | | | | |
| Gross Property | 10,805 | 10,476 | 9,651 | 9,025 | 9,017 | 8,406 | 8,014 | 8,065 | 6,969 | 6,651 |
| Capital Expenditures | 1,212 | 929 | 745 | 637 | 659 | 557 | 672 | 611 | 518 | 399 |
| Net Property | 7,681 | 7,053 | 6,363 | 5,903 | 5,926 | 4,399 | 4,188 | 4,152 | 3,719 | 3,643 |
| Capitalization:Long Term Debt | 3,203 | 3,104 | 3,061 | 3,270 | 3,605 | 3,261 | 3,468 | 2,933 | 2,365 | 1,779 |
| Capitalization:% Long Term Debt | 50.8 | 51.8 | 50.9 | 55.3 | 60.1 | 60.4 | 62.8 | 59.3 | 54.1 | 48.3 |
| Capitalization:Preferred | Nil | Nil | Nil | Nil | Nil | Nil | Nil | Nil | Nil | Nil |
| Capitalization:% Preferred | Nil | Nil | Nil | Nil | Nil | Nil | Nil | Nil | Nil | Nil |
| Capitalization:Common | 3,099 | 2,889 | 2,955 | 2,645 | 2,393 | 2,139 | 2,056 | 2,017 | 2,008 | 1,903 |
| Capitalization:% Common | 49.2 | 48.2 | 49.1 | 44.7 | 39.9 | 39.6 | 37.2 | 40.7 | 45.9 | 51.7 |
| Total Capital | 6,854 | 6,618 | 6,666 | 6,507 | 6,712 | 6,039 | 6,147 | 5,617 | 5,078 | 4,338 |
| % Operating Ratio | 90.4 | 90.2 | 89.2 | 86.9 | 88.6 | 86.8 | 88.4 | 90.5 | 84.8 | 86.2 |
| % Earned on Net Property | 8.4 | 8.5 | 9.2 | 6.5 | 9.6 | 10.7 | 14.5 | 11.1 | 9.7 | 7.8 |
| % Return on Revenue | 7.9 | 7.8 | 8.0 | 3.6 | 6.0 | 4.5 | 5.3 | 4.6 | 9.2 | 9.5 |
| % Return on Invested Capital | 6.8 | 7.5 | 7.2 | 7.1 | 8.1 | 13.6 | 8.0 | 7.9 | 7.9 | 10.2 |
| % Return on Common Equity | 11.2 | 11.2 | 10.8 | 4.9 | 10.5 | 8.0 | 10.2 | 7.7 | 10.7 | 10.0 |

Data as orig reptd.; bef. results of disc opers/spec. items. Per share data adj. for stk. divs.; EPS diluted. E-Estimated. NA-Not Available. NM-Not Meaningful. NR-Not Ranked. UR-Under Review.

**Office:** 231 West Michigan Street, Milwaukee, WI 53201.
**Telephone:** 414-221-2345.
**Website:** http://www.wisconsinenergy.com
**Chrmn, Pres & CEO:** G.E. Klappa

**EVP & CFO:** A.L. Leverett
**EVP & General Counsel:** J. Fleming
**SVP & Chief Admin Officer:** K.A. Rappe
**Chief Acctg Officer & Cntlr:** S.P. Dickson

**Investor Contact:** C.F. Henderson (414-221-2592)
**Board Members:** J. F. Bergstrom, B. L. Bowles, P. W. Chadwick, R. A. Cornog, C. S. Culver, T. Fischer, G. E. Klappa, U. Payne, Jr., C. P. Stratton, Jr.

**Founded:** 1981
**Domicile:** Wisconsin
**Employees:** 4,985

The McGraw-Hill Companies

# Wyeth

**STANDARD &POOR'S**

| S&P Recommendation HOLD ★★★☆☆ | Price $34.14 (as of Nov 14, 2008) | 12-Mo. Target Price $40.00 | Investment Style Large-Cap Growth |
|---|---|---|---|

**GICS Sector** Health Care
**Sub-Industry** Pharmaceuticals

**Summary** Wyeth is a leading maker of prescription drugs and OTC medications.

## Key Stock Statistics (Source S&P, Vickers, company reports)

| | | | | | | | |
|---|---|---|---|---|---|---|---|
| 52-Wk Range | $49.80– 28.06 | S&P Oper. EPS 2008**E** | 3.55 | Market Capitalization(B) | $45.457 | Beta | 0.71 |
| Trailing 12-Month EPS | $3.31 | S&P Oper. EPS 2009**E** | 3.70 | Yield (%) | 3.51 | S&P 3-Yr. Proj. EPS CAGR(%) | 6 |
| Trailing 12-Month P/E | 10.3 | P/E on S&P Oper. EPS 2008**E** | 9.6 | Dividend Rate/Share | $1.20 | S&P Credit Rating | A+ |
| $10K Invested 5 Yrs Ago | $9,320 | Common Shares Outstg. (M) | 1,331.5 | Institutional Ownership (%) | 81 | | |

## Price Performance

30-Week Mov. Avg. · · · 10-Week Mov. Avg. - - **GAAP Earnings vs. Previous Year** Volume Above Avg. STARS
12-Mo. Target Price — Relative Strength — ▲ Up ▼ Down ► No Change Below Avg. ★

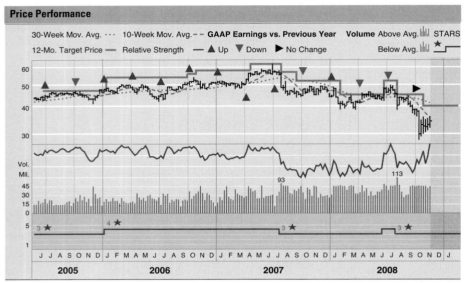

Options: ASE, CBOE, P, Ph

Analysis prepared by **Herman B. Saftlas** on October 28, 2008, when the stock traded at **$ 31.55**.

## Highlights

➤ We expect 2009 revenues to roughly approximate the $23.4 billion that we estimate for 2008, with sales likely to be impacted by unfavorable foreign currency exchange. We project lower sales of Effexor antidepressant, Protonix gastrointestinal, and Zosyn penicillin, due to generic erosion. On the plus side, we see robust growth for Prevnar vaccines, supported by line extensions and expanded geographic reach. Sales of Enbrel anti-inflammatory agent should also rise sharply. In addition, we expect volume to be augmented by higher sales of new drugs such as Tygacil antibiotic, Torisel anticancer agent and Pristiq antidepressant.

➤ We project gross margins in 2009 to be comparable with an indicated 73% in 2008, helped by manufacturing efficiencies. Benefiting from cost controls, we expect SG&A and R&D spending to decline slightly. We also expect other income to be somewhat higher.

➤ Helped by an expected lower tax rate, and by reduced shares outstanding, we project 2009 operating EPS of $3.70, up from an estimated $3.55 in 2008.

## Investment Rationale/Risk

➤ Although Wyeth is presently grappling with widening generic competition in three key products (Protonix, Effexor and Zosyn), we believe the company should still be able to show EPS growth over the next few years, buoyed by growth in other lines, new drugs, and cost streamlining measures. Key new drug launches, in our opinion, include Tygacil, Torisel and Pristiq. WYE also initiated a major cost reduction program designed to generate annual cost savings of $1.0 billion to $1.5 billion. While we like WYE's overall pipeline, we think the company faces a major challenge with its key bapineuzimab Alzheimer's compound, which has shown mixed clinical results.

➤ Risks to our recommendation and target price include possible future pipeline setbacks, as well as earlier-than-expected losses of patent protection on key products.

➤ Our 12-month target price of $40 applies a peer-level P/E of 11.3X to our 2008 EPS estimate. Our DCF model, which assumes decelerated cash flow growth over the next 10 years, a WACC of 8.2%, and terminal growth of 2%, also indicates intrinsic value of $40.

## Qualitative Risk Assessment

| LOW | MEDIUM | HIGH |
|---|---|---|

Our risk assessment reflects Wyeth's exposure to the risks inherent in the pharmaceuticals business, which include generic threats to branded drugs, as well as pipeline and regulatory risks. However, although the company still has significant potential diet drug liability risk, we believe it has made meaningful progress in resolving diet drug litigation, with planned agreements to settle most of its remaining outstanding cases.

## Quantitative Evaluations

**S&P Quality Ranking** B

| D | C | B- | B | B+ | A- | A | A+ |
|---|---|---|---|---|---|---|---|

**Relative Strength Rank** STRONG

81

LOWEST = 1     HIGHEST = 99

## Revenue/Earnings Data

**Revenue (Million $)**

| | 1Q | 2Q | 3Q | 4Q | Year |
|---|---|---|---|---|---|
| 2008 | 5,711 | 5,945 | 5,830 | -- | -- |
| 2007 | 5,369 | 5,648 | 5,620 | 5,764 | 22,400 |
| 2006 | 4,838 | 5,157 | 5,136 | 5,220 | 20,351 |
| 2005 | 4,579 | 4,714 | 4,716 | 4,747 | 18,756 |
| 2004 | 4,015 | 4,223 | 4,472 | 4,648 | 17,358 |
| 2003 | 3,689 | 3,747 | 4,082 | 4,333 | 15,851 |

**Earnings Per Share ($)**

| | | | | | |
|---|---|---|---|---|---|
| 2008 | 0.89 | 0.83 | 0.84 | E0.82 | E3.55 |
| 2007 | 0.92 | 0.87 | 0.84 | 0.75 | 3.38 |
| 2006 | 0.82 | 0.78 | 0.85 | 0.63 | 3.08 |
| 2005 | 0.80 | 0.72 | 0.64 | 0.54 | 2.70 |
| 2004 | 0.56 | 0.62 | 1.06 | -1.32 | 0.91 |
| 2003 | 0.96 | 0.65 | -0.32 | 0.25 | 1.54 |

Fiscal year ended Dec. 31. Next earnings report expected: Early February. EPS Estimates based on S&P Operating Earnings; historical GAAP earnings are as reported.

## Dividend Data (Dates: mm/dd Payment Date: mm/dd/yy)

| Amount ($) | Date Decl. | Ex-Div. Date | Stk. of Record | Payment Date |
|---|---|---|---|---|
| 0.280 | 01/25 | 02/11 | 02/13 | 03/03/08 |
| 0.280 | 04/24 | 05/09 | 05/13 | 06/02/08 |
| 0.280 | 06/26 | 08/11 | 08/13 | 09/02/08 |
| 0.300 | 09/25 | 11/10 | 11/13 | 12/01/08 |

Dividends have been paid since 1919. Source: Company reports.

**Please read the Required Disclosures and Analyst Certification on the last page of this report.**

The *McGraw-Hill* Companies

# Wyeth

STANDARD
&POOR'S

## Business Summary October 28, 2008

CORPORATE OVERVIEW. Wyeth (formerly American Home Products) is a leading producer of prescription pharmaceuticals, as well as consumer medications and animal health products. WYE's corporate strategy in recent years has focused on higher-margin products, while divesting less profitable businesses. Human prescription pharmaceuticals accounted for 83% of total sales in 2007, consumer health care products 12%, and animal health products 5%. Foreign operations are significant, accounting for 49% of sales in 2007.

WYE's largest selling product is Effexor (sales of $3.8 billion in 2007), an antidepressant that works on both serotonin and norepinephrine. Other key products include Protonix ($1.9 billion), a treatment for heartburn caused by gastroesophageal erosive reflux disease; Prevnar ($2.4 billion), a broad-based pediatric vaccine; Enbrel ($2.0 billion), a treatment for rheumatoid arthritis that is marketed in conjunction with Amgen, Inc.; and Zosyn/Tazocin ($1.1 billion), an injectable penicillin antibiotic. The company also offers Cordarone, Veralan and Ziac cardiovasculars; Lodine, Oruvail and Naprelan antiarthritics; Suprax and Minocin anti-infectives; and Refacto, a factor VIII treatment for hemophilia A.

WYE remains a leader in women's drugs, with its line of Premarin estrogen and PremPro/Premphase estrogen/progestin hormone replacement therapy (HRT) products (sales of $1.1 billion in 2007), and oral contraceptives ($433 million) such as Triphasil, Lo/Ovral and Alesse. The HRT business was negatively affected by clinical studies released in mid-2002 that highlighted cardiovascular and cancer risks with HRT products.

A full line of pediatric and adult nutritional products (sales of $1.4 billion) is offered, including infant formulas and adult supplements. The Whitehall and A.H. Robins divisions offer a broad range of OTC medications such as Advil and Anacin analgesics, Dimetapp and Robitussin for coughs and colds, Primatene for asthma, Preparation H for hemorrhoids, and Centrum and Solgar vitamins.

## Company Financials Fiscal Year Ended Dec. 31

| Per Share Data ($) | 2007 | 2006 | 2005 | 2004 | 2003 | 2002 | 2001 | 2000 | 1999 | 1998 |
|---|---|---|---|---|---|---|---|---|---|---|
| Tangible Book Value | 10.93 | 7.71 | 6.23 | 4.33 | 4.01 | 3.22 | 0.17 | NM | NM | 1.23 |
| Cash Flow | 4.03 | 3.72 | 3.26 | 1.37 | 1.94 | 3.72 | 2.17 | -0.28 | -0.42 | 2.35 |
| Earnings | 3.38 | 3.08 | 2.70 | 0.91 | 1.54 | 3.33 | 1.72 | -0.69 | -0.94 | 1.85 |
| S&P Core Earnings | 3.37 | 3.11 | 2.49 | 2.62 | 1.78 | 1.73 | 1.92 | NA | NA | NA |
| Dividends | 1.06 | 1.01 | 0.94 | 0.92 | 0.92 | 0.92 | 0.92 | 0.92 | 0.91 | 0.87 |
| Payout Ratio | 31% | 33% | 35% | 101% | 60% | 28% | 53% | NM | NM | 47% |
| Prices:High | 62.20 | 54.13 | 47.88 | 44.70 | 49.95 | 66.51 | 63.80 | 65.25 | 70.25 | 58.75 |
| Prices:Low | 43.65 | 41.91 | 38.48 | 33.50 | 32.75 | 28.25 | 52.00 | 39.38 | 36.50 | 37.75 |
| P/E Ratio:High | 18 | 18 | 18 | 49 | 32 | 20 | 37 | NM | NM | 32 |
| P/E Ratio:Low | 13 | 14 | 14 | 37 | 21 | 8 | 30 | NM | NM | 20 |

| Income Statement Analysis (Million $) | | | | | | | | | | |
|---|---|---|---|---|---|---|---|---|---|---|
| Revenue | 22,400 | 20,351 | 18,756 | 17,358 | 15,851 | 14,584 | 14,129 | 13,263 | 13,550 | 13,463 |
| Operating Income | 7,268 | 5,955 | 5,244 | 4,773 | 4,450 | 4,060 | 4,299 | 3,808 | 3,759 | 3,931 |
| Depreciation | 919 | 803 | 787 | 622 | 538 | 485 | 608 | 534 | 682 | 665 |
| Interest Expense | 697 | 499 | 357 | 110 | 103 | 202 | 146 | 239 | 343 | 323 |
| Pretax Income | 6,457 | 5,430 | 4,781 | -130 | 2,362 | 6,097 | 2,869 | -1,101 | -1,926 | 3,585 |
| Effective Tax Rate | 28.5% | 22.7% | 23.5% | NM | 13.1% | 27.1% | 20.3% | NM | NM | 31.0% |
| Net Income | 4,616 | 4,197 | 3,656 | 1,234 | 2,051 | 4,447 | 2,285 | -901 | -1,227 | 2,474 |
| S&P Core Earnings | 4,599 | 4,228 | 3,372 | 3,542 | 2,379 | 2,313 | 2,551 | NA | NA | NA |

| Balance Sheet & Other Financial Data (Million $) | | | | | | | | | | |
|---|---|---|---|---|---|---|---|---|---|---|
| Cash | 14,038 | 8,727 | 8,235 | 6,489 | 7,180 | 3,947 | 3,027 | 2,985 | 2,413 | 1,301 |
| Current Assets | 22,984 | 17,514 | 18,045 | 14,438 | 14,962 | 11,596 | 9,767 | 10,181 | 9,738 | 7,956 |
| Total Assets | 42,717 | 36,479 | 35,841 | 33,630 | 31,032 | 25,995 | 22,968 | 21,092 | 23,906 | 21,079 |
| Current Liabilities | 7,324 | 7,222 | 9,948 | 8,536 | 8,430 | 5,476 | 7,257 | 9,742 | 7,110 | 4,211 |
| Long Term Debt | 11,493 | 9,097 | 9,231 | 7,792 | 8,076 | 7,546 | 7,357 | 2,395 | 3,669 | 3,859 |
| Common Equity | 18,211 | 14,653 | 11,994 | 9,848 | 9,294 | 8,156 | 4,073 | 2,818 | 6,216 | 9,615 |
| Total Capital | 29,862 | 23,749 | 21,226 | 17,640 | 17,371 | 15,702 | 11,430 | 5,213 | 9,885 | 13,695 |
| Capital Expenditures | 1,391 | 1,290 | 1,081 | 1,255 | 1,909 | 1,932 | 1,924 | 1,682 | 1,000 | 810 |
| Cash Flow | 5,535 | 5,000 | 4,443 | 1,856 | 2,589 | 4,932 | 2,893 | -367 | -545 | 3,139 |
| Current Ratio | 3.1 | 2.4 | 1.8 | 1.7 | 1.8 | 2.1 | 1.3 | 1.0 | 1.4 | 1.9 |
| % Long Term Debt of Capitalization | 38.5 | 38.3 | 43.5 | 44.2 | 46.5 | 48.1 | 64.4 | 45.9 | 37.1 | 28.2 |
| % Net Income of Revenue | 20.6 | 20.6 | 19.5 | NM | 12.9 | 30.5 | 16.2 | NM | NM | 18.4 |
| % Return on Assets | 11.7 | 11.6 | 10.5 | NM | 7.2 | 18.2 | 10.4 | NM | NM | 11.8 |
| % Return on Equity | 28.1 | 31.5 | 33.5 | NM | 23.5 | 72.7 | 66.3 | NM | NM | 27.8 |

Data as orig reptd.; bef. results of disc opers/spec. items. Per share data adj. for stk. divs.; EPS diluted. E-Estimated. NA-Not Available. NM-Not Meaningful. NR-Not Ranked. UR-Under Review.

**Office:** 5 Giralda Farms, Madison, NJ 07940-1021.
**Telephone:** 973-660-5000.
**Website:** http://www.wyeth.com
**Chrmn, Pres & CEO:** B. Poussot

**SVP & CFO:** G. Norden
**SVP & General Counsel:** L.V. Stein
**Treas:** R.E. Landry, Jr.
**Secy:** E.M. Lach

**Investor Contact:** J.R. Victoria (973-660-5000)
**Board Members:** R. M. Amen, M. J. Critelli, F. D. Fergusson, V. F. Ganzi, R. S. Langer, J. P. Mascotte, R. J. McGuire, M. L. Polan, B. Poussot, G. L. Rogers, J. R. Torell, III

**Founded:** 1926
**Domicile:** Delaware
**Employees:** 50,527

# Wyndham Worldwide Corp

**STANDARD &POOR'S**

**S&P Recommendation** BUY ★★★★☆

| Price | 12-Mo. Target Price | Investment Style |
|---|---|---|
| $5.63 (as of Nov 14, 2008) | $8.00 | Large-Cap Blend |

**GICS Sector** Consumer Discretionary
**Sub-Industry** Hotels, Resorts & Cruise Lines

**Summary** This company's operations include the sale of interests in vacation ownership resorts; facilitating the exchange and rental of access to vacation properties; and the franchising of hotels.

## Key Stock Statistics (Source S&P, Vickers, company reports)

| | | | | | | | |
|---|---|---|---|---|---|---|---|
| 52-Wk Range | $30.85– 4.85 | S&P Oper. EPS 2008**E** | 1.88 | Market Capitalization(B) | $0.999 | Beta | 1.40 |
| Trailing 12-Month EPS | $2.17 | S&P Oper. EPS 2009**E** | 1.50 | Yield (%) | 2.84 | S&P 3-Yr. Proj. EPS CAGR(%) | -7 |
| Trailing 12-Month P/E | 2.6 | P/E on S&P Oper. EPS 2008**E** | 3.0 | Dividend Rate/Share | $0.16 | S&P Credit Rating | BBB- |
| $10K Invested 5 Yrs Ago | NA | Common Shares Outstg. (M) | 177.5 | Institutional Ownership (%) | 93 | | |

## Price Performance

30-Week Mov. Avg. · · · 10-Week Mov. Avg. - - - **GAAP Earnings vs. Previous Year** Volume Above Avg. STARS
12-Mo. Target Price — Relative Strength — ▲ Up ▼ Down ▶ No Change Below Avg.

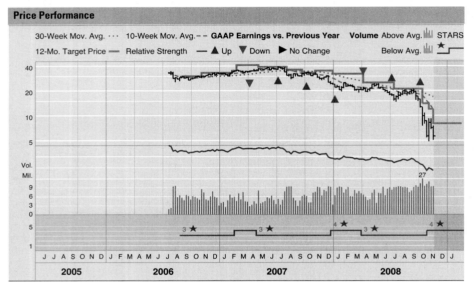

Options: CBOE, Ph

## Qualitative Risk Assessment

| LOW | MEDIUM | HIGH |
|---|---|---|

Our risk assessment reflects our view that the company's business is likely to be sensitive to changes in consumer confidence and hotel room demand, as well as the receptivity of credit markets to its securitized vacation ownership receivables.

## Quantitative Evaluations

**S&P Quality Ranking** NR

| D | C | B- | B | B+ | A- | A | A+ |
|---|---|---|---|---|---|---|---|

**Relative Strength Rank** WEAK

12

LOWEST = 1    HIGHEST = 99

## Revenue/Earnings Data

**Revenue (Million $)**

| | 1Q | 2Q | 3Q | 4Q | Year |
|---|---|---|---|---|---|
| 2008 | 1,012 | 1,132 | 1,226 | -- | -- |
| 2007 | 1,012 | 1,100 | 1,216 | 1,032 | 4,360 |
| 2006 | 870.0 | 955.0 | 1,047 | 970.0 | 3,842 |
| 2005 | -- | -- | -- | -- | 3,471 |
| 2004 | -- | -- | -- | -- | -- |
| 2003 | -- | -- | -- | -- | -- |

**Earnings Per Share ($)**

| | 1Q | 2Q | 3Q | 4Q | Year |
|---|---|---|---|---|---|
| 2008 | 0.24 | 0.55 | 0.80 | E0.29 | E1.88 |
| 2007 | 0.45 | 0.52 | 0.65 | 0.59 | 2.20 |
| 2006 | 0.46 | 0.37 | 0.45 | 0.48 | 1.77 |
| 2005 | -- | -- | -- | -- | 1.73 |
| 2004 | -- | -- | -- | -- | -- |
| 2003 | -- | -- | -- | -- | -- |

Fiscal year ended Dec. 31. Next earnings report expected: Mid February. EPS Estimates based on S&P Operating Earnings; historical GAAP earnings are as reported.

## Highlights

▶ The 12-month target price for WYN has recently been changed to $8.00 from $12.00. The Highlights section of this Stock Report will be updated accordingly.

## Investment Rationale/Risk

▶ The Investment Rationale/Risk section of this Stock Report will be updated shortly. For the latest News story on WYN from MarketScope, see below.

▶ 11/13/08 09:34 am ET ... S&P MAINTAINS BUY OPINION ON SHARES OF WYNDHAM WORLDWIDE (WYN 5.41****): We believe WYN's earlier decision to reduce the size of and cut costs in its timeshare business is the appropriate course of action for the current downturn. Also, WYN's completion of a new $943 million vacation ownership receivables conduit facility this past Monday gives us greater confidence that the business will continue to operate normally. That said, operating conditions remain weak. We are cutting our EPS estimate for '08 by $0.02 to $1.88 and for '09 by $0.15 to $1.50. On revised enterprise value/EBITDA valuation, we lower our 12-month target price by $4 to $8. / M.Basham

## Dividend Data (Dates: mm/dd Payment Date: mm/dd/yy)

| Amount ($) | Date Decl. | Ex-Div. Date | Stk. of Record | Payment Date |
|---|---|---|---|---|
| 0.040 | 02/29 | 03/04 | 03/06 | 03/13/08 |
| 0.040 | 04/24 | 05/27 | 05/29 | 06/12/08 |
| 0.040 | 07/24 | 08/26 | 08/28 | 09/11/08 |
| 0.040 | 10/23 | 11/24 | 11/26 | 12/11/08 |

Dividends have been paid since 2007. Source: Company reports.

# Wyndham Worldwide Corp

**STANDARD &POOR'S**

## Business Summary November 10, 2008

CORPORATE OVERVIEW. Wyndham Worldwide (WYN) operates lodging, vacation exchange and rental and vacation ownership businesses. The company became an independent entity on July 31, 2006, when former parent Cendant Corp. distributed one share of WYN common stock for every five shares of Cendant common stock.

The Wyndham Hotel Group franchises hotels in various segments of the lodging industry under brands such as Super 8, Days Inn, Ramada, Travelodge, and Wyndham Hotels. As of September 30, 2008, WYN's lodging business had about 7,000 franchised hotels with more than 583,000 rooms in operation. As of September 30, 2008, there were also about 990 hotels with about 111,000 rooms in the development pipeline, of which 51% represented new construction, as opposed to conversion from other property brands, and 41% were in international markets.

WYN's Group RCI provides vacation exchange products and services to developers, managers and owners of intervals of vacation ownership interests, and markets vacation rental properties. WYN's vacation exchange and rental business has access for specified periods, often on an exclusive basis, to over 67,000 vacation properties located in 100 countries. Membership as of September 30, 2008, was nearly 3.7 million.

WYN's vacation ownership segment includes marketing and sales of vacation ownership interests, consumer financing in connection with the purchase by individuals of vacation ownership interests, property management services for property owners' associations, and development and acquisition of vacation ownership resorts. WYN's vacation ownership business is now affiliated with the Wyndham brand in a de-emphasis of the Fairfield and Trendwest brands. WYN has developed or acquired about 145 vacation ownership resorts in North America, the Caribbean and the South Pacific that serve more than 800,000 owners of vacation ownership and other real estate interests.

CORPORATE STRATEGY. We expect WYN's growth strategy to include efforts to add more properties to its hotel systems, especially outside of North America and in the middle and upscale segments of the North American market; to add more vacation rental properties in North America; and to leverage the Wyndham name in the higher-end vacation ownership market.

## Company Financials Fiscal Year Ended Dec. 31

| Per Share Data ($) | 2007 | 2006 | 2005 | 2004 | 2003 | 2002 | 2001 | 2000 | 1999 | 1998 |
|---|---|---|---|---|---|---|---|---|---|---|
| Tangible Book Value | NM | NM | NM | NA | NA | NA | NA | NA | NA | NA |
| Cash Flow | 2.96 | 2.63 | 2.37 | NA | NA | NA | NA | NA | NA | NA |
| Earnings | 2.20 | 1.77 | 1.73 | NA | NA | NA | NA | NA | NA | NA |
| S&P Core Earnings | 2.20 | 1.75 | 1.97 | NA | NA | NA | NA | NA | NA | NA |
| Dividends | 0.08 | Nil | Nil | NA | NA | NA | NA | NA | NA | NA |
| Payout Ratio | 4% | Nil | Nil | NA | NA | NA | NA | NA | NA | NA |
| Prices:High | 39.40 | 34.87 | NA | NA | NA | NA | NA | NA | NA | NA |
| Prices:Low | 23.28 | 25.48 | NA | NA | NA | NA | NA | NA | NA | NA |
| P/E Ratio:High | 18 | 20 | NA | NA | NA | NA | NA | NA | NA | NA |
| P/E Ratio:Low | 11 | 14 | NA | NA | NA | NA | NA | NA | NA | NA |

| Income Statement Analysis (Million $) | 2007 | 2006 | 2005 | 2004 | 2003 | 2002 | 2001 | 2000 | 1999 | 1998 |
|---|---|---|---|---|---|---|---|---|---|---|
| Revenue | 4,360 | 3,842 | 3,471 | 3,014 | 2,652 | NA | NA | NA | NA | NA |
| Operating Income | 821 | 824 | 699 | NA | NA | NA | NA | NA | NA | NA |
| Depreciation | 139 | 148 | 135 | 119 | 107 | NA | NA | NA | NA | NA |
| Interest Expense | 96.0 | 67.0 | 41.0 | NA | NA | NA | NA | NA | NA | NA |
| Pretax Income | 655 | 542 | 523 | 587 | 500 | NA | NA | NA | NA | NA |
| Effective Tax Rate | 38.5% | 35.1% | 29.8% | 39.9% | 37.2% | NA | NA | NA | NA | NA |
| Net Income | 403 | 352 | 367 | 349 | 299 | NA | NA | NA | NA | NA |
| S&P Core Earnings | 404 | 352 | 419 | NA | NA | NA | NA | NA | NA | NA |

| Balance Sheet & Other Financial Data (Million $) | 2007 | 2006 | 2005 | 2004 | 2003 | 2002 | 2001 | 2000 | 1999 | 1998 |
|---|---|---|---|---|---|---|---|---|---|---|
| Cash | 276 | 269 | 106 | 94.0 | NA | NA | NA | NA | NA | NA |
| Current Assets | 2,056 | 2,052 | 1,874 | NA | NA | NA | NA | NA | NA | NA |
| Total Assets | 10,459 | 9,520 | 8,590 | 8,343 | NA | NA | NA | NA | NA | NA |
| Current Liabilities | 2,180 | 1,977 | 2,212 | NA | NA | NA | NA | NA | NA | NA |
| Long Term Debt | 3,195 | 1,322 | 1,733 | NA | NA | NA | NA | NA | NA | NA |
| Common Equity | 3,516 | 3,559 | 3,464 | 4,679 | NA | NA | NA | NA | NA | NA |
| Total Capital | 7,638 | 5,663 | 5,987 | NA | NA | NA | NA | NA | NA | NA |
| Capital Expenditures | 194 | 191 | 134 | 116 | 102 | NA | NA | NA | NA | NA |
| Cash Flow | 542 | 500 | 502 | NA | NA | NA | NA | NA | NA | NA |
| Current Ratio | 0.9 | 1.0 | 0.9 | 1.8 | NA | NA | NA | NA | NA | NA |
| % Long Term Debt of Capitalization | 41.8 | 23.3 | 28.9 | 22.9 | Nil | NA | NA | NA | NA | NA |
| % Net Income of Revenue | 9.2 | 9.2 | 10.5 | 11.6 | 11.3 | NA | NA | NA | NA | NA |
| % Return on Assets | 4.0 | 3.8 | NA | NA | NA | NA | NA | NA | NA | NA |
| % Return on Equity | 11.4 | 8.2 | NA | NA | NA | NA | NA | NA | NA | NA |

Data as orig reptd.; bef. results of disc opers/spec. items. Per share data adj. for stk. divs.; EPS diluted. E-Estimated. NA-Not Available. NM-Not Meaningful. NR-Not Ranked. UR-Under Review.

**Office:** Seven Sylvan Way, Parsippany, NJ 07054.
**Telephone:** 973-753-6000.
**Website:** http://www.wyndhamworldwide.com
**Chrmn & CEO:** S.P. Holmes

**EVP & CFO:** V.M. Wilson
**EVP & General Counsel:** S.G. McLester
**SVP & Chief Acctg Officer:** N. Rossi
**SVP & Secy:** L.A. Feldman

**Investor Contact:** M. Happer (973-753-5500)
**Board Members:** M. J. Biblowit, J. E. Buckman, G. Herrera, S. P. Holmes, B. Mulroney, P. Richards, M. H. Wargotz

**Founded:** 2003
**Domicile:** Delaware
**Employees:** 33,200

The McGraw-Hill Companies

# Wynn Resorts Ltd

STANDARD &POOR'S

| S&P Recommendation | SELL ★★☆☆☆ | Price | 12-Mo. Target Price | Investment Style |
|---|---|---|---|---|
| | | $43.00 (as of Nov 14, 2008) | $46.00 | Large-Cap Growth |

**GICS Sector** Consumer Discretionary
**Sub-Industry** Casinos & Gaming

**Summary** This company is involved in the design, development, financing and construction of gaming projects in Las Vegas and Macau.

## Key Stock Statistics (Source S&P, Vickers, company reports)

| | | | | | | | |
|---|---|---|---|---|---|---|---|
| 52-Wk Range | $137.93– 28.06 | S&P Oper. EPS 2008E | 2.94 | Market Capitalization(B) | $4.473 | Beta | 2.23 |
| Trailing 12-Month EPS | $3.91 | S&P Oper. EPS 2009E | 2.42 | Yield (%) | Nil | S&P 3-Yr. Proj. EPS CAGR(%) | NM |
| Trailing 12-Month P/E | 11.0 | P/E on S&P Oper. EPS 2008E | 14.6 | Dividend Rate/Share | Nil | S&P Credit Rating | BB |
| $10K Invested 5 Yrs Ago | $23,978 | Common Shares Outstg. (M) | 104.0 | Institutional Ownership (%) | 66 | | |

## Price Performance

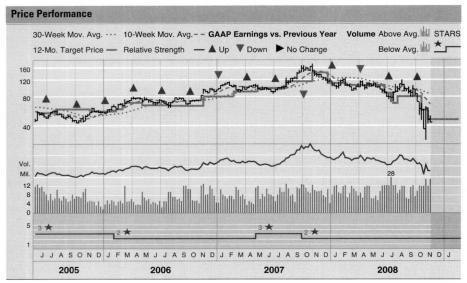

30-Week Mov. Avg. · · · · 10-Week Mov. Avg. - - GAAP Earnings vs. Previous Year    Volume Above Avg. STARS
12-Mo. Target Price — Relative Strength — ▲ Up ▼ Down ► No Change    Below Avg.

Options: ASE, CBOE, P, Ph

Analysis prepared by **Esther Y. Kwon, CFA** on October 31, 2008, when the stock traded at **$ 49.99**.

## Qualitative Risk Assessment

| LOW | MEDIUM | HIGH |
|---|---|---|

In our view, there is likely to be an opportunity for additional expansion by WYNN in Macau; however, we see uncertainty surrounding the regulatory environment there and the extent to which demand in that market will develop, adding to risk. Also, in our opinion, the stock's premium valuation creates the prospect of above-average vulnerability to disappointing news.

## Quantitative Evaluations

**S&P Quality Ranking** NR

| D | C | B- | B | B+ | A- | A | A+ |
|---|---|---|---|---|---|---|---|

**Relative Strength Rank** WEAK

29

LOWEST = 1    HIGHEST = 99

## Highlights

➤ We look for net revenue in 2008 to be up approximately 17% from the $2.7 billion reported for 2007, including an expansion to WYNN's casino and retail operations in Macau in late 2007 and early 2008. Domestically, we project revenues to be down on weaker trends, while we still forecast healthy growth in Macau. Longer term, we see expansion projects bolstering the top line through 2009.

➤ The initial phase of the Wynn Macau casino/hotel project included about 600 hotel rooms or suites, and about 110,000 sq. ft. of gaming space. The second phase included the addition of 85 tables and 552 new slot machines and an expanded retail promenade with 11 new stores. In addition, WYNN is developing plans for Wynn Diamond Suites, which would be a second resort hotel at Wynn Macau. The company is also developing a Las Vegas project, known as Encore at Wynn Las Vegas, which is expected to open in late 2008.

➤ Before special items and with fewer shares outstanding, we see 2008 EPS of $2.94. In 2009, we look for EPS to decline to $2.42 on higher depreciation and interest expense, and softer results in Las Vegas.

## Investment Rationale/Risk

➤ Our sell opinion is based on valuation. We still look for Las Vegas to be a challenging market in 2009 but forecast lower gains at Wynn Macau than we had previously expected due to further potential tightening of visa restrictions and increased competitive dislocation as junket commissions have been recently capped by the government.

➤ Risks to our opinion and target price include the possibility that expected profit contributions from Macau will be more favorable than we anticipate, or that Las Vegas properties will experience a sustained rise in room revenue or gaming handle.

➤ Our 12-month target price of $46 is based on an EV/EBITDA multiple of 10X, below WYNN's recent average, on our 2009 EBITDA estimate, compared to a peer average of about 8X. We believe WYNN is an above-average operator with a clear, focused strategy, and with high development potential in Macau. While we think the shares deserve a premium to peers, given reduced capital market activity and the slowdown in Las Vegas, we view the shares as overvalued; private equity transactions peaked at about 17X forward EV/EBITDA.

## Revenue/Earnings Data

### Revenue (Million $)

| | 1Q | 2Q | 3Q | 4Q | Year |
|---|---|---|---|---|---|
| 2008 | 778.7 | 825.2 | 769.2 | -- | -- |
| 2007 | 635.3 | 687.5 | 653.4 | 711.3 | 2,688 |
| 2006 | 277.2 | 273.4 | 318.1 | 563.6 | 1,432 |
| 2005 | Nil | 201.1 | 251.4 | 269.4 | 722.0 |
| 2004 | 0.14 | 0.06 | Nil | Nil | 0.20 |
| 2003 | 0.19 | 0.28 | 0.26 | 0.28 | 1.02 |

### Earnings Per Share ($)

| | | | | | |
|---|---|---|---|---|---|
| 2008 | 0.41 | 2.42 | 0.49 | E0.53 | E2.94 |
| 2007 | 0.54 | 0.82 | 0.41 | 0.57 | 2.34 |
| 2006 | -0.12 | -0.20 | 6.43 | -0.51 | 6.24 |
| 2005 | -0.30 | -0.43 | -0.09 | -0.10 | -0.92 |
| 2004 | -0.16 | -0.49 | -0.26 | -1.31 | -2.37 |
| 2003 | -0.12 | -0.16 | -0.18 | -0.15 | -0.62 |

Fiscal year ended Dec. 31. Next earnings report expected: Mid February. EPS Estimates based on S&P Operating Earnings; historical GAAP earnings are as reported.

## Dividend Data (Dates: mm/dd Payment Date: mm/dd/yy)

| Amount ($) | Date Decl. | Ex-Div. Date | Stk. of Record | Payment Date |
|---|---|---|---|---|
| 6.0 Spl. | 11/20 | 11/28 | 11/30 | 12/10/07 |

Dividends have been paid since 2006. Source: Company reports.

---

**Please read the Required Disclosures and Analyst Certification on the last page of this report.**

# Wynn Resorts Ltd

STANDARD &POOR'S

## Business Summary October 31, 2008

CORPORATE OVERVIEW. Wynn Resorts is involved in the design, development, financing and construction of gaming projects in Las Vegas and Macau. The company's first such project, Wynn Las Vegas, opened in April 2005. We believe that the cost of this project was about $2.7 billion.

Wynn Las Vegas, which occupies about 215 acres of land, includes about 2,716 guest rooms and suites, an approximate 111,000 sq. ft. casino, 22 food and beverage outlets, an 18-hole golf course, about 223,000 sq. ft. of meeting space, a Ferrari and Maserati dealership, and about 76,000 sq. ft. of retail space.

The company is also developing a Las Vegas project, known as Encore at Wynn Las Vegas, which is expected to include about 2,034 guest rooms, suites or villas, plus additional gaming, entertainment and other facilities. In February 2007, WYNN said that the Encore project had an estimated cost of about $2.1 billion.

In China, the company is operating Wynn Macau under a 20-year concession agreement with the government of Macau. The initial stage of Wynn Macau opened in September 2006, and included about 600 hotel rooms or suites, about 100,000 sq. ft. of gaming space, seven restaurants, and additional facilities. A second phase included additional casino space and other facilities. We believe that Wynn Macau, including the second phase, had a project budget of about $1.2 billion. This excludes Wynn Diamond Suites, a resort hotel for which WYNN is developing plans, which is expected to be a further expansion of Wynn Macau. Also, the company has submitted an application for a land concession on 52 acres in Macau's Cotai Strip area, where we expect additional WYNN-related development could occur. There are a limited number of companies with casino operating rights in Macau.

## Company Financials Fiscal Year Ended Dec. 31

| Per Share Data ($) | 2007 | 2006 | 2005 | 2004 | 2003 | 2002 | 2001 | 2000 | 1999 | 1998 |
|---|---|---|---|---|---|---|---|---|---|---|
| Tangible Book Value | 16.79 | 14.75 | 14.16 | 15.64 | 11.38 | 11.70 | 12.92 | NA | NA | NA |
| Cash Flow | 4.24 | 7.20 | 0.13 | -2.29 | -0.54 | -0.49 | -0.25 | NA | NA | NA |
| Earnings | 2.34 | 6.24 | -0.92 | -2.37 | -0.62 | -0.68 | -0.45 | -79.62 | NA | NA |
| S&P Core Earnings | 2.29 | 1.00 | -1.00 | -2.41 | -0.64 | -0.69 | -84.35 | NA | NA | NA |
| Dividends | 6.00 | 6.00 | Nil | Nil | Nil | Nil | NA | NA | NA | NA |
| Payout Ratio | 256% | 96% | Nil | Nil | Nil | Nil | NA | NA | NA | NA |
| Prices:High | 176.14 | 98.45 | 76.45 | 72.99 | 28.61 | 14.39 | NA | NA | NA | NA |
| Prices:Low | 85.53 | 52.44 | 42.06 | 27.50 | 12.76 | 10.76 | NA | NA | NA | NA |
| P/E Ratio:High | 75 | 16 | NM | NM | NM | NM | NA | NA | NA | NA |
| P/E Ratio:Low | 37 | 8 | NM | NM | NM | NM | NA | NA | NA | NA |

| Income Statement Analysis (Million $) | | | | | | | | | | |
|---|---|---|---|---|---|---|---|---|---|---|
| Revenue | 2,688 | 1,432 | 722 | 0.20 | 1.02 | 1.16 | 1.16 | 0.13 | NA | NA |
| Operating Income | 708 | 249 | 77.5 | -81.5 | -46.9 | -24.8 | 0.73 | NA | NA | NA |
| Depreciation | 220 | 175 | 103 | 6.98 | 5.74 | 8.93 | 8.16 | 6.07 | NA | NA |
| Interest Expense | 188 | 206 | 103 | 2.69 | 9.03 | 1.90 | NA | NA | NA | NA |
| Pretax Income | 327 | 799 | -90.8 | -207 | -45.8 | -30.8 | -17.7 | -15.9 | NA | NA |
| Effective Tax Rate | 21.1% | 21.3% | NM | NM | NM | NM | NM | NA | NA | NA |
| Net Income | 258 | 629 | -90.8 | -206 | -48.9 | -31.7 | -17.7 | -15.9 | NA | NA |
| S&P Core Earnings | 252 | 44.1 | -98.6 | -210 | -50.9 | -32.0 | -17.3 | NA | NA | NA |

| Balance Sheet & Other Financial Data (Million $) | | | | | | | | | | |
|---|---|---|---|---|---|---|---|---|---|---|
| Cash | 1,275 | 789 | 434 | 330 | 342 | 110 | 39.3 | 54.4 | NA | NA |
| Current Assets | 1,582 | 1,096 | 685 | 451 | 402 | 112 | NA | NA | NA | NA |
| Total Assets | 6,299 | 4,660 | 3,945 | 3,464 | 1,733 | 1,399 | 389 | 387 | NA | NA |
| Current Liabilities | 585 | 511 | 270 | 170 | 71.2 | 20.7 | NA | NA | NA | NA |
| Long Term Debt | 3,539 | 2,381 | 2,091 | 1,628 | 730 | 382 | 1,501 | NA | NA | NA |
| Common Equity | 1,948 | 1,646 | 1,563 | 1,644 | 1,002 | 992 | 972 | 382 | NA | NA |
| Total Capital | 5,640 | 4,123 | 3,654 | 3,272 | 1,733 | 1,378 | 2,473 | NA | NA | NA |
| Capital Expenditures | 1,007 | 643 | 877 | 1,008 | 415 | 66.3 | 29.1 | 85.7 | NA | NA |
| Cash Flow | 478 | 804 | 12.5 | -199 | -43.1 | -22.8 | -9.56 | NA | NA | NA |
| Current Ratio | 2.7 | 2.1 | 2.5 | 2.7 | 5.7 | 5.4 | 10.4 | 11.8 | NA | NA |
| % Long Term Debt of Capitalization | 62.8 | 57.7 | 57.2 | 49.8 | 42.1 | 27.7 | 0.1 | 0.1 | NA | NA |
| % Net Income of Revenue | 9.6 | 43.9 | NM | NM | NM | NM | NM | NM | NA | NA |
| % Return on Assets | 4.7 | 14.6 | NM | NM | NM | NM | NM | NM | NA | NA |
| % Return on Equity | 14.4 | 39.2 | NM | NM | NM | NM | NM | NA | NA | NA |

Data as orig reptd.; bef. results of disc opers/spec. items. Per share data adj. for stk. divs.; EPS diluted. E-Estimated. NA-Not Available. NM-Not Meaningful. NR-Not Ranked. UR-Under Review.

**Office:** 3131 Las Vegas Blvd S, Las Vegas, NV 89109.
**Telephone:** 702-733-4444.
**Email:** investorrelations@wynnresorts.com
**Website:** http://www.wynnresorts.com

**Chrmn & CEO:** S.A. Wynn
**Vice Chrmn:** K. Okada
**COO:** M.D. Schorr
**Investor Contact:** J. Strzemp (702-770-7555)

**EVP & Chief Admin Officer:** J. Strzemp
**Board Members:** L. Chen, R. Goldsmith, R. R. Irani, R. J. Miller, J. A. Moran, K. Okada, A. V. Shoemaker, D. B. Wayson, E. P. Wynn, S. A. Wynn, A. Zeman

**Founded:** 2002
**Domicile:** Nevada
**Employees:** 16,500

# Xcel Energy Inc.

STANDARD &POOR'S

**S&P Recommendation** BUY ★★★★☆

| Price | 12-Mo. Target Price | Investment Style |
|---|---|---|
| $17.98 (as of Nov 14, 2008) | $20.00 | Large-Cap Value |

**GICS Sector** Utilities
**Sub-Industry** Multi-Utilities

**Summary** This energy holding company was created through the August 2000 merger of Minneapolis-based Northern States Power and Denver-based New Century Energies.

## Key Stock Statistics (Source S&P, Vickers, company reports)

| | | | | | | | | |
|---|---|---|---|---|---|---|---|---|
| 52-Wk Range | $23.50– 15.32 | S&P Oper. EPS 2008E | 1.45 | Market Capitalization(B) | $8.074 | Beta | | 0.62 |
| Trailing 12-Month EPS | $1.41 | S&P Oper. EPS 2009E | 1.47 | Yield (%) | 5.28 | S&P 3-Yr. Proj. EPS CAGR(%) | | 4 |
| Trailing 12-Month P/E | 12.8 | P/E on S&P Oper. EPS 2008E | 12.4 | Dividend Rate/Share | $0.95 | S&P Credit Rating | | BBB+ |
| $10K Invested 5 Yrs Ago | $13,696 | Common Shares Outstg. (M) | 449.0 | Institutional Ownership (%) | 56 | | | |

## Price Performance

30-Week Mov. Avg. · · · · 10-Week Mov. Avg. - - - **GAAP Earnings vs. Previous Year** Volume Above Avg. ılıll STARS
12-Mo. Target Price — Relative Strength — ▲ Up ▼ Down ▶ No Change Below Avg. ılıll

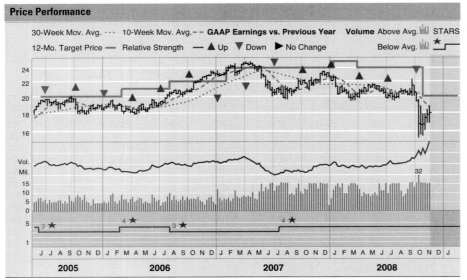

Options: ASE, CBOE

Analysis prepared by **Justin McCann** on October 27, 2008, when the stock traded at **$ 16.71**.

## Highlights

➤ We expect 2008 operating EPS to realize only a low single-digit increase from 2007 EPS from continuing operations of $1.43. While results in 2008 are expected to benefit from electric and gas rate increases in Wisconsin, as well as a full year of gas rate hikes in Colorado, Minnesota and North Dakota, we believe this will be largely offset by sharply higher fuel, purchased power, and natural gas costs. In December 2007, the Public Service Commission of Wisconsin authorized an approximate 8.4% increase in electric rates and a 3.3% increase in gas rates, effective January 2008.

➤ For 2009, we expect operating EPS to remain relatively flat with anticipated results in 2008. Despite a full year of electric rate increases implemented in 2008 and an expected increase in Texas in early 2009, we see earnings being restricted by flat electric sales, higher operating expenses and increased uncollected accounts.

➤ On August 27, 2008, XEL reached an agreement with the Attorney General of New York state in which it would provide in its annual 10-K filings more detailed analyses of the potential legal or financial impact that climate-change legislation or related suits could have on its operations.

## Investment Rationale/Risk

➤ Although the shares are down more than 25% year to date, we expect them to gradually recover a portion of their decline over the next 12 months and to perform more in line with XEL's electric and gas utility peers. The sharp decline has, in our view, largely reflected the crisis in the credit markets and its potential impact on the overall economy. As of October 21, 2008, XEL had available credit lines of $1.59 billion and cash of $311 million. We believe this $1.9 billion of total liquidity is more than adequate for XEL's near term requirements.

➤ Risks to our recommendation and target price include the possibility of a severe economic downturn in the company's service territory, unfavorable legislative or regulatory decisions, and a major decline in the average P/E of the electric and gas utility sectors.

➤ With an above-peer yield from its dividend, recently at 5.7% (versus an average peer yield of 5.3%) we believe the stock remains attractive for total return potential. We expect the dividend to be increased at a rate of 2% to 4% a year. Our 12-month target price is $20, which reflects an approximate peer P/E of 13.6X our operating EPS estimate for 2009.

## Qualitative Risk Assessment

| LOW | MEDIUM | HIGH |
|---|---|---|

Our risk assessment reflects the steady cash flow that we expect from the regulated electric and gas utility operations, which have a relatively low-cost power supply, our view of a generally healthy economy in most of the company's service territories, and a relatively supportive regulatory environment.

## Quantitative Evaluations

**S&P Quality Ranking** B

| D | C | B- | B | B+ | A- | A | A+ |
|---|---|---|---|---|---|---|---|

**Relative Strength Rank** STRONG

85

LOWEST = 1 HIGHEST = 99

## Revenue/Earnings Data

**Revenue (Million $)**

| | 1Q | 2Q | 3Q | 4Q | Year |
|---|---|---|---|---|---|
| 2008 | 3,028 | 2,616 | 2,852 | -- | -- |
| 2007 | 2,764 | 2,267 | 2,400 | 2,603 | 10,034 |
| 2006 | 2,888 | 2,074 | 2,412 | 2,467 | 9,840 |
| 2005 | 2,381 | 2,074 | 2,289 | 2,882 | 9,625 |
| 2004 | 2,280 | 1,797 | 2,009 | 2,259 | 8,345 |
| 2003 | 2,086 | 1,722 | 2,020 | 2,110 | 7,938 |

**Earnings Per Share ($)**

| | | | | | |
|---|---|---|---|---|---|
| 2008 | 0.35 | 0.24 | 0.51 | E0.35 | E1.45 |
| 2007 | 0.28 | 0.16 | 0.59 | 0.31 | 1.34 |
| 2006 | 0.36 | 0.24 | 0.53 | 0.23 | 1.35 |
| 2005 | 0.31 | 0.18 | 0.47 | 0.24 | 1.20 |
| 2004 | 0.35 | 0.21 | 0.40 | 0.30 | 1.27 |
| 2003 | 0.31 | 0.14 | 0.43 | 0.36 | 1.23 |

Fiscal year ended Dec. 31. Next earnings report expected: Early December. EPS Estimates based on S&P Operating Earnings; historical GAAP earnings are as reported.

## Dividend Data (Dates: mm/dd Payment Date: mm/dd/yy)

| Amount ($) | Date Decl. | Ex-Div. Date | Stk. of Record | Payment Date |
|---|---|---|---|---|
| 0.230 | 12/12 | 12/24 | 12/27 | 01/20/08 |
| 0.230 | 02/20 | 03/25 | 03/27 | 04/20/08 |
| 0.238 | 05/21 | 06/24 | 06/26 | 07/20/08 |
| 0.238 | 08/12 | 09/23 | 09/25 | 10/20/08 |

Dividends have been paid since 1910. Source: Company reports.

---

**Please read the Required Disclosures and Analyst Certification on the last page of this report.**

The McGraw-Hill Companies

# Xcel Energy Inc.

STANDARD
&POOR'S

## Business Summary October 27, 2008

CORPORATE OVERVIEW. Xcel Energy Inc. (XEL) is a holding company with a diverse portfolio of regulated and nonregulated subsidiaries. The company's utility subsidiaries are Northern States Power Company of Minnesota and Wisconsin (NSPM and NSPW, respectively), Public Service Company of Colorado (PSCo), and Southwestern Public Service Co. (SPS), which provide electric and gas services in eight western and Midwestern states, and West-Gas Interstate Inc. (WGI), an interstate natural gas pipeline. XEL's nonregulated subsidiaries include Eloigne Co., which operates rental housing projects. The electric utility operations accounted for 78.2% of operating revenues in 2007; the natural gas utility operations for 21.1%; and non-regulated and other for 0.7%.

CORPORATE STRATEGY. XEL's strategy is to continue investing in the core utility business and to earn the authorized returns, and to divest those businesses not linked to the electric and natural gas operations. In its most significant transaction, the company divested its ownership interest in NRG Energy, which was involved in independent power projects in the U.S. and internation-

ally, in December 2003. XEL had divested its ownership interest in nearly all of its non-utility subsidiaries as of December 31, 2005. XEL's other remaining non-utility businesses are WGI, a small interstate national gas pipeline company, and Eloigne, which invests in projects qualifying for low income housing tax credits. In 2007, XEL filed resource plans in Minnesota and Colorado that would, if approved, increase the company's overall system wind capacity from around 2,800 megawatts at the end of 2007 to approximately 6,000 megawatts by 2020. The company also has a strong focus on system reliability and continues to invest in transmission and distribution systems. To recover the cost without the delay caused by the filing of rate cases, XEL gets regulatory approval for rate riders. This ensures fair returns on the company's investment.

## Company Financials Fiscal Year Ended Dec. 31

| Per Share Data ($) | 2007 | 2006 | 2005 | 2004 | 2003 | 2002 | 2001 | 2000 | 1999 | 1998 |
|---|---|---|---|---|---|---|---|---|---|---|
| Tangible Book Value | 14.70 | 14.28 | 13.11 | 12.99 | 12.95 | 11.44 | 17.91 | 15.79 | 15.67 | 15.58 |
| Earnings | 1.34 | 1.35 | 1.20 | 1.27 | 1.23 | -4.36 | 2.27 | 1.54 | 1.43 | 1.84 |
| S&P Core Earnings | 1.31 | 1.35 | 1.15 | 1.21 | 1.03 | -4.57 | 1.68 | NA | NA | NA |
| Dividends | 0.91 | 0.88 | 0.85 | 0.81 | 0.75 | 1.13 | 1.50 | 1.47 | 1.44 | 1.42 |
| Payout Ratio | 68% | 65% | 71% | 64% | 61% | NM | 66% | 96% | 101% | 77% |
| Prices:High | 25.03 | 23.63 | 20.19 | 18.78 | 17.40 | 28.49 | 31.85 | 30.00 | 27.94 | 30.81 |
| Prices:Low | 19.59 | 17.80 | 16.50 | 15.48 | 10.40 | 5.12 | 24.19 | 16.13 | 19.31 | 25.69 |
| P/E Ratio:High | 19 | 18 | 17 | 15 | 14 | NM | 14 | 19 | 20 | 17 |
| P/E Ratio:Low | 15 | 13 | 14 | 12 | 8 | NM | 11 | 10 | 14 | 14 |

| Income Statement Analysis (Million $) | | | | | | | | | | |
|---|---|---|---|---|---|---|---|---|---|---|
| Revenue | 10,034 | 9,840 | 9,625 | 8,345 | 7,938 | 9,524 | 15,028 | 11,592 | 2,869 | 2,819 |
| Depreciation | 827 | 822 | 782 | 708 | 756 | 1,037 | 949 | 792 | 356 | 338 |
| Maintenance | NA | NA | NA | NA | NA | NA | NA | NA | 179 | 181 |
| Fixed Charges Coverage | 2.62 | 2.43 | 2.43 | 2.36 | 2.50 | 1.54 | 2.37 | 2.54 | 1.86 | 2.64 |
| Construction Credits | 71.8 | 56.0 | 0.88 | 33.6 | NA | NA | NA | NA | 7.00 | 15.8 |
| Effective Tax Rate | 33.8% | 24.2% | 25.8% | 23.2% | 23.7% | NM | 28.2% | 34.2% | 22.8% | 27.1% |
| Net Income | 576 | 569 | 499 | 527 | 510 | -1,661 | 785 | 546 | 224 | 282 |
| S&P Core Earnings | 554 | 566 | 472 | 498 | 417 | -1,745 | 579 | NA | NA | NA |

| Balance Sheet & Other Financial Data (Million $) | | | | | | | | | | |
|---|---|---|---|---|---|---|---|---|---|---|
| Gross Property | 26,726 | 25,219 | 24,054 | 23,160 | 22,371 | 29,119 | 31,770 | 25,000 | 13,478 | 11,049 |
| Capital Expenditures | 2,096 | 1,626 | 1,304 | 1,274 | 951 | 1,503 | 5,366 | 2,196 | 462 | 411 |
| Net Property | 16,676 | 15,549 | 14,696 | 14,096 | 13,667 | 18,816 | 21,165 | 15,273 | 8,146 | 6,020 |
| Capitalization:Long Term Debt | 6,342 | 6,450 | 5,898 | 6,493 | 6,519 | 7,044 | 12,612 | 8,060 | 3,653 | 2,051 |
| Capitalization:% Long Term Debt | 49.8 | 52.1 | 51.3 | 55.0 | 55.0 | 59.6 | 66.7 | 58.7 | 57.8 | 44.2 |
| Capitalization:Preferred | 105 | 105 | 105 | 105 | 105 | 105 | 105 | 105 | 104 | 105 |
| Capitalization:% Preferred | 0.80 | 0.85 | 0.91 | 0.89 | 0.89 | 0.89 | 0.56 | 0.76 | 1.65 | 2.26 |
| Capitalization:Common | 6,301 | 5,817 | 5,484 | 5,203 | 5,222 | 4,665 | 6,194 | 5,562 | 2,558 | 2,482 |
| Capitalization:% Common | 49.4 | 47.0 | 47.7 | 44.1 | 44.1 | 39.5 | 32.8 | 40.5 | 40.5 | 53.5 |
| Total Capital | 15,302 | 14,751 | 13,813 | 14,019 | 14,017 | 13,303 | 22,040 | 15,996 | 7,246 | 5,581 |
| % Operating Ratio | 89.5 | 89.9 | 98.6 | 88.8 | 88.1 | 78.0 | 87.1 | 87.0 | 85.9 | 85.6 |
| % Earned on Net Property | 8.4 | 7.8 | 13.0 | 7.8 | 8.0 | 13.0 | 10.7 | 11.2 | 4.8 | 6.2 |
| % Return on Revenue | 5.7 | 5.8 | 5.2 | 6.3 | 6.4 | NM | 5.2 | 4.7 | 7.8 | 10.0 |
| % Return on Invested Capital | 7.4 | 7.4 | 6.9 | 7.0 | 7.3 | 12.4 | 10.9 | 10.3 | 7.5 | 11.5 |
| % Return on Common Equity | 9.4 | 10.1 | 9.2 | 10.1 | 10.1 | NM | 13.5 | 10.0 | 8.7 | 11.4 |

Data as orig reptd.; bef. results of disc opers/spec. items. Per share data adj. for stk. divs.; EPS diluted. E-Estimated. NA-Not Available. NM-Not Meaningful. NR-Not Ranked. UR-Under Review.

**Office:** 414 Nicollet Mall, Minneapolis, MN 55401-1993.
**Telephone:** 612-330-5500.
**Website:** http://www.xcelenergy.com
**Chrmn, Pres & CEO:** R.C. Kelly

**CFO:** B.G. Fowke, III
**Chief Admin Officer:** R.E. Gogel
**Chief Acctg Officer & Cntlr:** T.S. Madden
**Treas:** G.E. Tyson, II

**Investor Contact:** P. Johnson (612-215-4535)
**Board Members:** C. C. Burgess, F. W. Corrigan, R. Davis, R. R. Hemminghaus, A. B. Hirschfeld, R. C. Kelly, D. W. Leatherdale, A. F. Moreno, M. R. Preska, A. P. Sampson, R. H. Truly, D. A. Westerlund, T. V. Wolf

**Founded:** 1909
**Domicile:** Minnesota
**Employees:** 10,917

# Xerox Corp

**STANDARD &POOR'S**

| S&P Recommendation | SELL ★★☆☆☆ | Price | 12-Mo. Target Price | Investment Style |
|---|---|---|---|---|
| | | $6.36 (as of Nov 14, 2008) | $6.00 | Large-Cap Blend |

**GICS Sector** Information Technology
**Sub-Industry** Office Electronics

**Summary** This company serves the worldwide document processing market, offering a complete line of copiers, electronic printers, and other office and computer equipment.

## Key Stock Statistics (Source S&P, Vickers, company reports)

| | | | | | | | |
|---|---|---|---|---|---|---|---|
| 52-Wk Range | $17.68– 6.04 | S&P Oper. EPS 2008E | 1.11 | Market Capitalization(B) | $5.505 | Beta | 1.04 |
| Trailing 12-Month EPS | $0.67 | S&P Oper. EPS 2009E | 1.00 | Yield (%) | 2.67 | S&P 3-Yr. Proj. EPS CAGR(%) | 1 |
| Trailing 12-Month P/E | 9.5 | P/E on S&P Oper. EPS 2008E | 5.7 | Dividend Rate/Share | $0.17 | S&P Credit Rating | BBB |
| $10K Invested 5 Yrs Ago | $6,102 | Common Shares Outstg. (M) | 865.6 | Institutional Ownership (%) | 86 | | |

## Price Performance

30-Week Mov. Avg. · · · · 10-Week Mov. Avg. - - GAAP Earnings vs. Previous Year    Volume Above Avg. STARS
12-Mo. Target Price — Relative Strength — ▲ Up ▼ Down ► No Change    Below Avg.

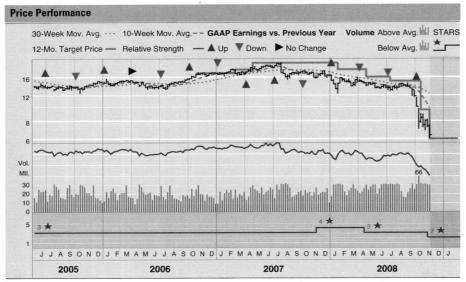

Options: ASE, CBOE, P, Ph

Analysis prepared by **Thomas W. Smith, CFA** on November 13, 2008, when the stock traded at **$ 6.58**.

## Qualitative Risk Assessment

| LOW | MEDIUM | HIGH |
|---|---|---|

Our risk assessment reflects our view of XRX's efforts to spur growth and improve profitability, offset by what we see as lackluster organic revenue growth.

## Quantitative Evaluations

**S&P Quality Ranking**    B

| D | C | B- | B | B+ | A- | A | A+ |
|---|---|---|---|---|---|---|---|

**Relative Strength Rank**    WEAK

28

LOWEST = 1    HIGHEST = 99

## Revenue/Earnings Data

**Revenue (Million $)**

| | 1Q | 2Q | 3Q | 4Q | Year |
|---|---|---|---|---|---|
| 2008 | 4,335 | 4,533 | 4,370 | -- | -- |
| 2007 | 3,836 | 4,208 | 4,302 | 4,882 | 17,228 |
| 2006 | 3,695 | 3,977 | 3,844 | 4,379 | 15,895 |
| 2005 | 3,771 | 3,921 | 3,759 | 4,250 | 15,701 |
| 2004 | 3,827 | 3,853 | 3,716 | 4,326 | 15,722 |
| 2003 | 3,757 | 3,920 | 3,732 | 4,292 | 15,701 |

**Earnings Per Share ($)**

| | | | | | |
|---|---|---|---|---|---|
| 2008 | -0.27 | 0.24 | 0.29 | E0.32 | E1.11 |
| 2007 | 0.24 | 0.28 | 0.27 | 0.41 | 1.19 |
| 2006 | 0.20 | 0.26 | 0.54 | 0.22 | 1.22 |
| 2005 | 0.20 | 0.35 | 0.06 | 0.27 | 0.90 |
| 2004 | 0.17 | 0.21 | 0.17 | 0.24 | 0.78 |
| 2003 | -0.10 | 0.09 | 0.17 | 0.22 | 0.36 |

Fiscal year ended Dec. 31. Next earnings report expected: Late January. EPS Estimates based on S&P Operating Earnings; historical GAAP earnings are as reported.

## Highlights

➤ We expect revenues to rise 4% in 2008 and decrease 3% in 2009. Prime drivers we see include many new digital and color offerings, plus continuing expansion in international markets, outweighed in 2009 by a weak economy. Also tempering growth is the maturity of the U.S. market. In May 2007, XRX acquired Global Imaging Systems in a debt-financed transaction valued at $1.5 billion, which enhanced distribution into small- and medium-sized business markets.

➤ We see gross margins narrowing to about 41% for fourth quarter 2008, excluding the effects of restructuring charges of about $400 million the company plans for the fourth quarter, and holding steady near 41% for 2009, as the negative effects of lower volumes are roughly matched by the benefits of new products and efficiencies from cost control initiatives. We believe a challenging pricing environment will restrain margin progress over the long term.

➤ Excluding charges for litigation expense of $0.54 a share in the first quarter, and restructuring charges, we estimate operating EPS of $1.11 for 2008, and $1.00 for 2009. EPS should be aided by an active stock buyback program.

## Investment Rationale/Risk

➤ We believe XRX will suffer near term from lower demand for printers, in line with moderation we foresee in the pace of global technology spending. Despite earlier efficiency campaigns, management saw a need for another round of restructuring in the fourth quarter. We view the valuation as unattractive based on our P/E and price-to-book analyses.

➤ Risks to our recommendation and target price include a less aggressive pricing environment, shorter sales cycles, and faster deployment of new products than we project. The company's significant percentage of recurring revenues could contribute to higher earnings levels than we estimate.

➤ We apply a target P/E multiple of 7X, toward the low end of an historical average for XRX to reflect economic headwinds we foresee, to our 2009 operating EPS estimate of $1.00, to obtain a value of $7.00. We similarly apply a target price-to-book ratio of 1.3X, near the low end of an historical range, to our forward estimate of tangible book value per share of $4.00, to obtain a value of $5.20. Blending our theoretical values, our 12-month target price is $6.00.

## Dividend Data (Dates: mm/dd Payment Date: mm/dd/yy)

| Amount ($) | Date Decl. | Ex-Div. Date | Stk. of Record | Payment Date |
|---|---|---|---|---|
| 0.043 | 02/19 | 03/27 | 03/31 | 04/30/08 |
| 0.043 | 05/22 | 06/26 | 06/30 | 07/31/08 |
| 0.043 | 07/10 | 09/26 | 09/30 | 10/31/08 |
| 0.043 | 10/08 | 12/29 | 12/31 | 01/31/09 |

Dividends have been paid since 2008. Source: Company reports.

---

**Please read the Required Disclosures and Analyst Certification on the last page of this report.**

*The McGraw·Hill Companies*

# Xerox Corp

STANDARD
&POOR'S

## Business Summary November 13, 2008

CORPORATE OVERVIEW: Xerox is a global manufacturer of document equipment such as document equipment printing and publishing systems; digital copiers; laser and solid ink printers; fax machines; and digital multifunctional devices, which can print, copy, scan and fax. Equipment sales represented 28% of sales in 2007 and in 2006, with the remaining 72% in each year coming from post-sale operations including maintenance, services, supplies, and financing.

Since early 2008, the company reports in three operating segments, which are grouped according to the type of customer they serve. Production represented 31% of 2007 revenues (32% of 2006 revenues), Office 55% (55%), and Other 14% (13%). Production provides large enterprises, and companies in the graphic communications industry with high-end devices that enable digital on-demand printing, digital full-color printing and enterprise printing. Office serves global, national and small- to medium-size commercial customers with a lineup of digital printers, and copiers. Lastly, Other includes revenue from

paper sales, value-added services, wide-format systems and GIS network integration solutions and electronic presentations systems. In 2007 and earlier, the company also reported a segment known as Developing Market Operations (DMO), which described businesses that have matured sufficiently for the company to fold the results into the other main segments.

The company operates in over 160 countries and derived 53% of revenues in 2007 (53% of 2006 revenues) from the U.S., 34% (34%) from Europe, and 13% (13%) from Other Areas. The company's manufacturing operations include plants in Rochester, NY, Wilsonville, OR, and Dunwalk, Ireland. The company also outsources some manufacturing operations, and in 2007 entered a multi-year master supply agreement with Flextronics.

## Company Financials Fiscal Year Ended Dec. 31

| Per Share Data ($) | 2007 | 2006 | 2005 | 2004 | 2003 | 2002 | 2001 | 2000 | 1999 | 1998 |
|---|---|---|---|---|---|---|---|---|---|---|
| Tangible Book Value | 4.93 | 5.04 | 4.68 | 4.29 | 1.57 | NM | 0.52 | 2.86 | 4.79 | 4.76 |
| Cash Flow | 1.88 | 1.95 | 1.62 | 1.45 | 1.25 | 1.38 | 1.72 | 0.96 | 3.13 | 2.00 |
| Earnings | 1.19 | 1.22 | 0.90 | 0.78 | 0.36 | 0.10 | -0.17 | -0.44 | 1.96 | 0.80 |
| S&P Core Earnings | 1.16 | 1.27 | 0.88 | 0.75 | 0.53 | -0.17 | -1.33 | NA | NA | NA |
| Dividends | 0.04 | Nil | Nil | Nil | Nil | Nil | 0.05 | 0.65 | 0.78 | 0.70 |
| Payout Ratio | 4% | Nil | Nil | Nil | Nil | Nil | NM | NM | 40% | 87% |
| Prices:High | 20.18 | 17.31 | 17.02 | 17.24 | 13.89 | 11.45 | 11.35 | 29.31 | 63.94 | 60.81 |
| Prices:Low | 15.26 | 13.16 | 12.40 | 12.55 | 7.90 | 4.20 | 4.69 | 3.75 | 19.00 | 33.09 |
| P/E Ratio:High | 17 | 14 | 19 | 22 | 39 | NM | NM | NM | 33 | 76 |
| P/E Ratio:Low | 13 | 11 | 14 | 16 | 22 | NM | NM | NM | 10 | 41 |

| Income Statement Analysis (Million $) | 2007 | 2006 | 2005 | 2004 | 2003 | 2002 | 2001 | 2000 | 1999 | 1998 |
|---|---|---|---|---|---|---|---|---|---|---|
| Revenue | 17,228 | 15,895 | 15,701 | 15,722 | 15,701 | 15,849 | 17,008 | 18,701 | 19,228 | 19,449 |
| Operating Income | 2,699 | 2,165 | 2,159 | 2,451 | 2,585 | 2,803 | 3,011 | 1,946 | 3,815 | 3,685 |
| Depreciation | 656 | 636 | 637 | 686 | 748 | 1,035 | 1,332 | 948 | 935 | 821 |
| Interest Expense | 316 | 305 | 231 | 708 | 362 | 401 | 457 | 605 | 547 | 570 |
| Pretax Income | 1,535 | 922 | 928 | 1,116 | 494 | 306 | 418 | -323 | 2,104 | 837 |
| Effective Tax Rate | 26.0% | NM | NM | 30.5% | 27.1% | 19.6% | NM | NM | 30.0% | 24.7% |
| Net Income | 1,135 | 1,210 | 933 | 776 | 360 | 154 | -109 | -257 | 1,424 | 585 |
| S&P Core Earnings | 1,101 | 1,235 | 862 | 666 | 434 | -128 | -931 | NA | NA | NA |

| Balance Sheet & Other Financial Data (Million $) | 2007 | 2006 | 2005 | 2004 | 2003 | 2002 | 2001 | 2000 | 1999 | 1998 |
|---|---|---|---|---|---|---|---|---|---|---|
| Cash | 1,099 | 1,399 | 1,322 | 3,218 | 2,477 | 2,887 | 3,990 | 1,741 | 126 | 79.0 |
| Current Assets | 8,540 | 8,754 | 8,736 | 10,928 | 10,335 | 11,019 | 12,600 | 13,022 | 11,985 | 12,475 |
| Total Assets | 23,543 | 21,709 | 21,953 | 24,884 | 24,591 | 25,458 | 27,689 | 29,475 | 28,814 | 30,024 |
| Current Liabilities | 4,077 | 4,698 | 4,346 | 6,300 | 7,569 | 7,787 | 10,260 | 6,268 | 7,950 | 8,507 |
| Long Term Debt | 7,571 | 6,284 | 6,765 | 7,767 | 8,739 | 11,485 | 11,815 | 16,042 | 11,632 | 11,505 |
| Common Equity | 8,588 | 7,080 | 6,319 | 6,244 | 3,291 | 1,893 | 1,820 | 3,493 | 4,911 | 4,857 |
| Total Capital | 16,159 | 13,364 | 13,973 | 14,900 | 13,418 | 14,001 | 14,313 | 20,323 | 17,339 | 17,173 |
| Capital Expenditures | 236 | 215 | 181 | 204 | 197 | 146 | 219 | 452 | 594 | 566 |
| Cash Flow | 1,791 | 1,846 | 1,512 | 1,389 | 1,037 | 1,116 | 1,209 | 638 | 2,305 | 1,350 |
| Current Ratio | 2.1 | 1.9 | 2.0 | 1.7 | 1.4 | 1.4 | 1.2 | 2.1 | 1.5 | 1.5 |
| % Long Term Debt of Capitalization | 46.8 | 47.0 | 48.4 | 52.1 | 65.1 | 82.0 | 82.5 | 78.9 | 67.1 | 67.0 |
| % Net Income of Revenue | 6.5 | 7.6 | 5.9 | 4.9 | 2.3 | 1.0 | NM | NM | 7.4 | 3.0 |
| % Return on Assets | 5.0 | 5.5 | 4.0 | 3.1 | 1.4 | 0.6 | NM | NM | 4.8 | 2.0 |
| % Return on Equity | 14.4 | 18.1 | 13.9 | 14.7 | 11.1 | 4.4 | NM | NM | 28.1 | 10.7 |

Data as orig reptd.; bef. results of disc opers/spec. items. Per share data adj. for stk. divs.; EPS diluted. E-Estimated. NA-Not Available. NM-Not Meaningful. NR-Not Ranked. UR-Under Review.

**Office:** 45 Glover Ave, Norwalk, CT 06850-1203.
**Telephone:** 203-968-3000.
**Website:** http://www.xerox.com
**Chrmn & CEO:** A.M. Mulcahy

**Pres:** U.M. Burns
**EVP & CFO:** L.A. Zimmerman
**SVP, Secy & General Counsel:** D.H. Liu
**CTO:** S.V. Vanderbroek

**Investor Contact:** J.H. Lesko (800-828-6396)
**Board Members:** G. A. Britt, U. M. Burns, R. J. Harrington, W. C. Hunter, V. E. Jordan, Jr., R. A. McDonald, A. M. Mulcahy, N. J. Nicholas, Jr., C. Prince, III, A. N. Reese, M. Wilderotter

**Founded:** 1906
**Domicile:** New York
**Employees:** 57,400

# Xilinx Inc

**STANDARD &POOR'S**

| S&P Recommendation | HOLD ★★★☆☆ | Price $15.95 (as of Nov 14, 2008) | 12-Mo. Target Price $26.00 | Investment Style Large-Cap Growth |
|---|---|---|---|---|

**GICS Sector** Information Technology
**Sub-Industry** Semiconductors

**Summary** This California-based company is the world's largest supplier of programmable logic chips and related development system software.

## Key Stock Statistics (Source S&P, Vickers, company reports)

| | | | | | | | |
|---|---|---|---|---|---|---|---|
| 52-Wk Range | $28.21– 15.15 | S&P Oper. EPS 2009E | 1.60 | Market Capitalization(B) | $4.369 | Beta | 1.31 |
| Trailing 12-Month EPS | $1.28 | S&P Oper. EPS 2010E | NA | Yield (%) | 3.51 | S&P 3-Yr. Proj. EPS CAGR(%) | 13 |
| Trailing 12-Month P/E | 12.5 | P/E on S&P Oper. EPS 2009E | 10.0 | Dividend Rate/Share | $0.56 | S&P Credit Rating | NA |
| $10K Invested 5 Yrs Ago | $4,940 | Common Shares Outstg. (M) | 273.9 | Institutional Ownership (%) | NM | | |

## Price Performance

30-Week Mov. Avg. · · · · 10-Week Mov. Avg. – – GAAP Earnings vs. Previous Year   Volume Above Avg. STARS
12-Mo. Target Price — Relative Strength — ▲ Up ▼ Down ► No Change   Below Avg.

Options: ASE, CBOE, P

Analysis prepared by **Clyde Montevirgen** on October 20, 2008, when the stock traded at **$ 20.94**.

## Highlights

➤ We project revenues will increase 6% in FY 09 (Mar.), compared to essentially flat sales in FY 08, reflecting our view of relatively easy annual growth comparisons. We think that XLNX's communications business will improve, and believe that its focus on producing technologically leading-edge products will help its competitive position. However, we believe that competitor Altera's (ALTR: hold, $17) latest competitive offerings have had strong design win momentum, preventing XLNX's overall share gains. We are also modeling slower sales to the industrial and consumer markets, given our view of economic risks.

➤ We see gross margins of about 63% in FY 09, similar to FY 08 results. We think XLNX will be able to maintain fairly steady gross margins in the low 60% area due to what we view as its cost effective manufacturing partnerships with chip foundries and its product portfolio of higher-margin programmable devices. We look for adjusted operating margins of about 27% in FY 09, wider than 23% in FY 08, reflecting restructuring actions.

➤ We forecast non-GAAP EPS of $1.60 for FY 09, compared to $1.33 in FY 08.

## Investment Rationale/Risk

➤ XLNX is the share leader in the programmable chips market, which we expect to expand faster than the overall semiconductor industry next year. We think the company has a formidable product pipeline that should lead to healthy growth ahead. However, we see competitor Altera continuing to take market share in the near term with its latest product offerings, and also believe its next-generation products will pose problems for XLNX in higher-end markets. XLNX has effectively cut costs to improve profitability, by our analysis, but we think valuation multiples will be subdued until it exhibits better top-line growth.

➤ Risks to our recommendation and target price include industry cyclicality, dependence on chip foundry partners for production, fluctuation in chip inventories, and possible negative impact from macroeconomic headwinds.

➤ Our 12-month target price of $26 is based on our price-to-earnings analysis. We apply a P/E multiple of around 16X, slightly below our target multiple for faster-growing competitor Altera, to our FY 09 EPS estimate.

## Qualitative Risk Assessment

| LOW | MEDIUM | HIGH |
|---|---|---|

Our risk assessment reflects the cyclicality of the semiconductor industry, offset by the company's position as the largest competitor in a fast-growing niche, our view of its debt-free position, its diverse end markets, and its sharing of factory operations risk with chip foundry partners.

## Quantitative Evaluations

**S&P Quality Ranking**          **B**

| D | C | B- | B | B+ | A- | A | A+ |
|---|---|---|---|---|---|---|---|

**Relative Strength Rank**        **MODERATE**

47

LOWEST = 1        HIGHEST = 99

## Revenue/Earnings Data

**Revenue (Million $)**

| | 1Q | 2Q | 3Q | 4Q | Year |
|---|---|---|---|---|---|
| 2009 | 488.3 | 483.5 | -- | -- | -- |
| 2008 | 445.9 | 444.9 | 474.8 | 475.8 | 1,841 |
| 2007 | 481.4 | 467.2 | 450.7 | 443.5 | 1,843 |
| 2006 | 405.4 | 398.9 | 449.6 | 472.3 | 1,726 |
| 2005 | 423.6 | 403.3 | 355.4 | 391.0 | 1,573 |
| 2004 | 313.3 | 315.6 | 365.6 | 403.4 | 1,398 |

**Earnings Per Share ($)**

| | | | | | |
|---|---|---|---|---|---|
| 2009 | 0.30 | 0.29 | E0.38 | E0.40 | E1.60 |
| 2008 | 0.28 | 0.30 | 0.35 | 0.34 | 1.25 |
| 2007 | 0.24 | 0.27 | 0.26 | 0.27 | 1.02 |
| 2006 | 0.21 | 0.24 | 0.23 | 0.32 | 1.00 |
| 2005 | 0.26 | 0.24 | 0.18 | 0.19 | 0.87 |
| 2004 | 0.13 | 0.16 | 0.19 | 0.36 | 0.85 |

Fiscal year ended Mar. 31. Next earnings report expected: Mid January. EPS Estimates based on S&P Operating Earnings; historical GAAP earnings are as reported.

## Dividend Data (Dates: mm/dd Payment Date: mm/dd/yy)

| Amount ($) | Date Decl. | Ex-Div. Date | Stk. of Record | Payment Date |
|---|---|---|---|---|
| 0.120 | 01/17 | 02/04 | 02/06 | 02/27/08 |
| 0.140 | 02/25 | 05/05 | 05/07 | 05/28/08 |
| 0.140 | 07/16 | 08/04 | 08/06 | 08/27/08 |
| 0.140 | 10/15 | 11/03 | 11/05 | 11/25/08 |

Dividends have been paid since 2004. Source: Company reports.

---

**Please read the Required Disclosures and Analyst Certification on the last page of this report.**

The McGraw-Hill Companies

# Xilinx Inc

**STANDARD &POOR'S**

## Business Summary October 20, 2008

CORPORATE OVERVIEW. Founded in 1984, Xilinx is the world's leading supplier of programmable logic devices (PLDs) based on market share. These devices include field programmable gate arrays (FPGAs) and complex programmable logic devices (CPLDs). They are standard integrated circuits (ICs) that are programmed by customers to perform desired logic operations. The company believes it provides high levels of integration and creates significant time and cost savings for electronic equipment manufacturers in the telecommunications, networking, computing and industrial markets.

Xilinx's FPGAs are proprietary ICs designed by the company; they provide a combination of the high logic density usually associated with custom gate arrays, the time-to-market advantages of programmable logic, and the availability of a standard product. The company has several product families, including the XC4000, Coolrunner, Spartan and Virtex lines. The Virtex-II Pro product line, introduced in March 2002, is a platform for programmable systems, enabling very high-bandwidth system-on-a-chip designs with the flexibility and low development cost of programmable logic. FPGAs account for the vast majority of sales, but the company also derives revenue from development and system software tools, and field engineering support.

Products are classified as new, mainstream, base and support. New products accounted for 23% of FY 07 (Mar.) sales (12% in FY 06), mainstream products 54% (61%), base products 17% (21%), and support products 6% (6%). Revenue by end market in FY 07 broke down as follows: 45% (49% in FY 06) communications, 45% (40%) consumer, automotive, industrial and other, and 10% (11%) data processing.

Xilinx sells its products globally to OEMs and to electronic components distributors who resell these products. Avnet distributes the majority of the company's products worldwide. Following the 2005 merger of Avnet and Memec, another of the company's distributors, the combined entity accounted for 86% of total FY 07 revenues. No end customer accounted for more than 10% of Xilinx's revenues.

## Company Financials Fiscal Year Ended Mar. 31

### Per Share Data ($)

| | 2008 | 2007 | 2006 | 2005 | 2004 | 2003 | 2002 | 2001 | 2000 | 1999 |
|---|---|---|---|---|---|---|---|---|---|---|
| Tangible Book Value | 5.45 | 5.54 | 7.53 | 7.24 | 6.79 | 5.44 | 5.26 | 5.82 | 5.68 | 2.82 |
| Cash Flow | NA | 1.24 | 1.19 | 1.05 | 1.05 | 0.57 | -0.02 | 0.36 | 2.03 | 0.52 |
| Earnings | 1.25 | 1.02 | 1.00 | 0.87 | 0.85 | 0.36 | -0.34 | 0.10 | 1.90 | 0.42 |
| S&P Core Earnings | 1.28 | 1.01 | 0.78 | 0.58 | 0.57 | 0.05 | -0.31 | 0.35 | NA | NA |
| Dividends | 0.36 | 0.36 | 0.28 | 0.20 | Nil | Nil | Nil | Nil | Nil | Nil |
| Payout Ratio | 29% | 35% | 28% | 23% | Nil | Nil | Nil | Nil | Nil | Nil |
| Calendar Year | 2007 | 2006 | 2005 | 2004 | 2003 | 2002 | 2001 | 2000 | 1999 | 1998 |
| Prices:High | 30.50 | 29.98 | 32.30 | 45.40 | 39.20 | 47.15 | 59.25 | 98.31 | 48.56 | 16.75 |
| Prices:Low | 21.14 | 18.35 | 21.25 | 25.21 | 18.50 | 13.50 | 19.52 | 35.25 | 15.31 | 7.44 |
| P/E Ratio:High | 24 | 29 | 32 | 47 | 46 | NM | NM | NM | 26 | 40 |
| P/E Ratio:Low | 17 | 18 | 21 | 26 | 22 | NM | NM | NM | 8 | 18 |

### Income Statement Analysis (Million $)

| | 2008 | 2007 | 2006 | 2005 | 2004 | 2003 | 2002 | 2001 | 2000 | 1999 |
|---|---|---|---|---|---|---|---|---|---|---|
| Revenue | 1,841 | 1,843 | 1,726 | 1,573 | 1,398 | 1,156 | 1,016 | 1,659 | 1,021 | 662 |
| Operating Income | NA | 424 | 489 | 442 | 412 | 283 | 87.3 | 568 | 371 | 214 |
| Depreciation | 72.0 | 73.9 | 69.5 | 63.1 | 67.9 | 72.5 | 106 | 93.5 | 44.2 | 32.1 |
| Interest Expense | NA | Nil | Nil | Nil | Nil | Nil | 0.06 | 0.17 | Nil | 11.9 |
| Pretax Income | 474 | 431 | 457 | 401 | 351 | 170 | -193 | 61.1 | 1,030 | 184 |
| Effective Tax Rate | 21.1% | 18.7% | 22.4% | 21.9% | 13.6% | 26.0% | NM | 42.3% | 36.7% | 29.8% |
| Net Income | 374 | 351 | 354 | 313 | 303 | 126 | -114 | 35.3 | 652 | 129 |
| S&P Core Earnings | 382 | 348 | 277 | 205 | 204 | 18.1 | -103 | 132 | NA | NA |

### Balance Sheet & Other Financial Data (Million $)

| | 2008 | 2007 | 2006 | 2005 | 2004 | 2003 | 2002 | 2001 | 2000 | 1999 |
|---|---|---|---|---|---|---|---|---|---|---|
| Cash | 1,296 | 636 | 783 | 449 | 337 | 214 | 230 | 209 | 85.5 | 53.6 |
| Current Assets | NA | 1,700 | 1,648 | 1,466 | 1,302 | 1,175 | 999 | 1,102 | 1,041 | 658 |
| Total Assets | 3,137 | 3,179 | 3,174 | 3,039 | 2,937 | 2,422 | 2,335 | 2,502 | 2,349 | 1,070 |
| Current Liabilities | NA | 303 | 345 | 298 | 381 | 314 | 196 | 350 | 245 | 167 |
| Long Term Debt | NA | 1,000 | Nil | Nil | Nil | Nil | Nil | Nil | Nil | Nil |
| Common Equity | 1,672 | 1,773 | 2,729 | 2,674 | 2,483 | 1,951 | 1,904 | 1,918 | 1,777 | 879 |
| Total Capital | NA | 2,875 | 2,821 | 2,741 | 2,556 | 2,108 | 2,140 | 2,152 | 2,104 | 903 |
| Capital Expenditures | 45.6 | 111 | 67.0 | 61.4 | 41.0 | 46.0 | 94.9 | 223 | 144 | 40.9 |
| Cash Flow | NA | 425 | 424 | 376 | 371 | 198 | -7.51 | 129 | 697 | 161 |
| Current Ratio | 5.3 | 5.6 | 4.8 | 4.9 | 3.4 | 3.7 | 5.1 | 3.1 | 4.3 | 3.9 |
| % Long Term Debt of Capitalization | 37.4 | 34.8 | Nil | Nil | Nil | Nil | Nil | Nil | Nil | Nil |
| % Net Income of Revenue | 20.3 | 19.0 | 20.5 | 19.8 | 21.7 | 10.9 | NM | 2.1 | 63.9 | 19.5 |
| % Return on Assets | 11.8 | 11.0 | 11.4 | 10.5 | 11.3 | 5.3 | NM | 1.5 | 38.2 | 12.9 |
| % Return on Equity | 21.7 | 15.6 | 13.1 | 12.1 | 13.7 | 6.5 | NM | 1.9 | 49.1 | 18.1 |

Data as orig reptd.; bef. results of disc opers/spec. items. Per share data adj. for stk. divs.; EPS diluted. E-Estimated. NA-Not Available. NM-Not Meaningful. NR-Not Ranked. UR-Under Review.

**Office:** 2100 Logic Drive, San Jose, CA, USA 95124-3400.
**Telephone:** 408-559-7778.
**Email:** ir@xilinx.com
**Website:** http://www.xilinx.com

**Chrmn:** W.P. Roelandts
**Pres & CEO:** M.N. Gavrielov
**COO:** B.C. Ooi
**Investor Contact:** J.A. Olson (408-559-7778)

**SVP, CFO & Chief Acctg Officer:** J.A. Olson
**Board Members:** J. L. Doyle, J. G. Fishman, M. N. Gavrielov, P. T. Gianos, W. G. Howard, Jr., J. M. Patterson, W. P. Roelandts, M. Turner, Jr., E. W. Vanderslice

**Founded:** 1984
**Domicile:** Delaware
**Employees:** 3,415

# XL Capital Ltd

**STANDARD &POOR'S**

| S&P Recommendation **BUY** ★★★★☆ | Price $6.14 (as of Nov 14, 2008) | 12-Mo. Target Price $14.00 | Investment Style Large-Cap Blend |
|---|---|---|---|

**GICS Sector** Financials
**Sub-Industry** Property & Casualty Insurance

**Summary** Bermuda-based XL, which originally provided excess liability coverage, has expanded into providing a broad array of commercial lines insurance, reinsurance and other risk management services.

## Key Stock Statistics (Source S&P, Vickers, company reports)

| | | | | | | | |
|---|---|---|---|---|---|---|---|
| 52-Wk Range | $63.67– 3.45 | S&P Oper. EPS 2008E | 4.50 | Market Capitalization(B) | $2.031 | Beta | 1.94 |
| Trailing 12-Month EPS | $-12.04 | S&P Oper. EPS 2009E | 3.80 | Yield (%) | 24.76 | S&P 3-Yr. Proj. EPS CAGR(%) | -20 |
| Trailing 12-Month P/E | NM | P/E on S&P Oper. EPS 2008E | 1.4 | Dividend Rate/Share | $1.52 | S&P Credit Rating | NA |
| $10K Invested 5 Yrs Ago | $946 | Common Shares Outstg. (M) | 330.8 | Institutional Ownership (%) | NM | | |

## Price Performance

30-Week Mov. Avg. · · · 10-Week Mov. Avg. - - GAAP Earnings vs. Previous Year Volume Above Avg. STARS
12-Mo. Target Price — Relative Strength — ▲ Up ▼ Down ▶ No Change Below Avg.

Options: CBOE, P, Ph

Analysis prepared by **Cathy A. Seifert** on October 17, 2008, when the stock traded at **$ 10.12**.

## Highlights

➤ We expect earned premiums to decline 5% to 7% in 2008, versus a decrease of 4.8% in 2007, amid a more competitive pricing environment and the disruptive effects of XL's exposure to beleaguered bond insurer SCA. We see underwriting margins contracting in 2008, as favorable prior-year loss developments on certain casualty lines are offset by the impact of higher property loss costs.

➤ Net investment income in 2008 will likely decline more than 10% from 2007 levels, reflecting a more challenging investment environment.

➤ We estimate operating EPS of $4.50 for 2008 and $3.80 for 2009, versus $9.72 in 2007. These estimates exclude net realized investment gains and/or losses. XL expects to report a third quarter 2008 net loss of between $6.08 and $6.17, due mainly to a $1.4 billion charge taken to (among other things) terminate a reinsurance agreement with Syncora Holdings (formerly Security Capital Assurance/SCA: hold, $1.00). XL reported net income of $2.01 a share for 2007, after a $7.71 a share realized investment loss on its investment in SCA, and write downs on other investments.

## Investment Rationale/Risk

➤ We upgraded our opinion on the shares to buy from hold in mid-October after XL pre-announced its third quarter results. At current levels, the shares were trading at approximately 53% of estimated year end 2008 book value. This represents a discount to most peers, reflecting concerns over the quality of XL's balance and its exposure to troubled bond insurer Syncora Holdings. We believe XL has significantly reduced its exposure to SCA.

➤ Risks to our recommendation and target price include a greater-than-anticipated decline in premium rates and underwriting margins; more significant deterioration in the credit quality of XL's investment portfolio; and a greater-than-anticipated negative financial impact stemming from XL's relationship with SCA.

➤ Our 12-month target price of $14 assumes that the shares will trade at approximately 0.7 X our estimate of year end 2008 book value, 3.1 X our 2008 operating EPS estimate of $4.50, and 3.7X our 2009 operating EPS estimate of $3.80. This still represents a significant discount to most peers, over 50%.

## Qualitative Risk Assessment

| LOW | MEDIUM | HIGH |
|---|---|---|

Our risk assessment reflects our concerns about XL's exposure to catastrophe losses and financial guarantee reinsurance claim related costs, the adequacy of its loss reserves in certain liability lines of business, and our view that XL could face write-downs of its fixed income investment portfolio and certain other investments. This is only partially offset by our view of XL as an opportunistic underwriter seeking to leverage opportunities for growth.

## Quantitative Evaluations

**S&P Quality Ranking** B-

| D | C | B- | B | B+ | A- | A | A+ |
|---|---|---|---|---|---|---|---|

**Relative Strength Rank** WEAK

11

LOWEST = 1    HIGHEST = 99

## Revenue/Earnings Data

**Revenue (Million $)**

| | 1Q | 2Q | 3Q | 4Q | Year |
|---|---|---|---|---|---|
| 2008 | 2,174 | 2,125 | 1,744 | -- | -- |
| 2007 | 2,483 | 2,597 | 2,153 | 1,902 | 9,136 |
| 2006 | 2,473 | 2,499 | 2,364 | 2,496 | 9,833 |
| 2005 | 2,401 | 4,108 | 2,296 | 2,479 | 11,285 |
| 2004 | 2,157 | 3,179 | 2,370 | 2,390 | 10,028 |
| 2003 | 1,792 | 1,892 | 1,969 | 2,363 | 8,017 |

**Earnings Per Share ($)**

| | 1Q | 2Q | 3Q | 4Q | Year |
|---|---|---|---|---|---|
| 2008 | 1.20 | 1.34 | -6.09 | -- | E4.50 |
| 2007 | 3.06 | 3.00 | 1.82 | -6.88 | 1.15 |
| 2006 | 2.56 | 2.10 | 2.32 | 2.62 | 9.60 |
| 2005 | 3.18 | 0.97 | -7.53 | -5.51 | -9.14 |
| 2004 | 3.25 | 2.62 | 0.16 | 2.07 | 8.13 |
| 2003 | 1.74 | 2.51 | 2.51 | -2.29 | 2.69 |

Fiscal year ended Dec. 31. Next earnings report expected: Early February. EPS Estimates based on S&P Operating Earnings; historical GAAP earnings are as reported.

## Dividend Data (Dates: mm/dd Payment Date: mm/dd/yy)

| Amount ($) | Date Decl. | Ex-Div. Date | Stk. of Record | Payment Date |
|---|---|---|---|---|
| 0.380 | 01/25 | 03/12 | 03/14 | 03/31/08 |
| 0.380 | 04/25 | 06/11 | 06/13 | 06/30/08 |
| 0.190 | 07/28 | 09/10 | 09/12 | 09/30/08 |
| 0.190 | 10/31 | 12/05 | 12/09 | 12/30/08 |

Dividends have been paid since 1992. Source: Company reports.

---

**Please read the Required Disclosures and Analyst Certification on the last page of this report.**

*The McGraw-Hill Companies*

# XL Capital Ltd

**STANDARD &POOR'S**

## Business Summary October 17, 2008

CORPORATE OVERVIEW. Bermuda-based XL was formed in 1986 by a consortium of Fortune 500 companies to provide excess liability coverage. Since then, XL has expanded (mostly via acquisitions) to include insurance, reinsurance, and other financial services. Gross written premiums of nearly $9.0 billion in 2007 (down 8.2% from $9.8 billion in 2006) were divided: insurance 60%, reinsurance 30%, life operations 8%, and other 2%.

Insurance business written includes general liability, as well as other specialized types of liability coverage, such as directors' and officers' liability and professional and employment practices liability coverage. An array of property coverage, as well as marine and aviation coverage, is also offered. Insurance net written premiums of $4.19 billion in 2007 were divided: professional liability 33%, casualty 20%, property 16%, marine/energy/aviation/satellite 15%, other specialty lines 14%, and property catastrophe and other lines of coverage 2%.

Reinsurance business written includes treaty and facultative reinsurance to primary insurers of casualty risk. Reinsurance net written premiums totaled $2.1 billion in 2007 and were divided: property 32%, casualty 25%, property catastrophe 14%, professional lines 12%, marine, energy aviation and satellite 6%, and other lines (which include political risk, surety, warranty, accident/health and structured indemnity) 11%.

Life operations include reinsurance written from other life insurers, principally

to help in managing mortality, morbidity, survivorship, investment, and lapse risks. Net written premiums totaled $698.7 million in 2007 and were divided: annuity risks 39%, life insurance 61%. The "other lines" segment is comprised of the guaranteed investment contract (GIC) and funding agreement (FA) business. At year-end 2007, XL had approximately $4 billion of deposit liabilities associated with this business, for which there were correspondingly matched invested assets. In the wake of certain financial strength ratings downgrades XL and certain of its subsidiaries have received, the company anticipates that these obligations will be settled by late March 2008.

In July 2001, the company acquired Winterthur International, for about $330.2 million in cash (as adjusted). As part of the transaction, XL received certain post-closing arrangements protecting it against (among other things) certain types of adverse loss development. XL valued the post-closing payment at $1.45 billion, and Winterthur Swiss Insurance Co. (the seller) believed the post-closing payment was $541 million. In December 2005, an independent actuarial review concluded that Winterthur's estimate was closer than the estimate submitted by XL. As a result of this difference, XL recorded a fourth-quarter 2005 after-tax charge of $834.2 million.

## Company Financials Fiscal Year Ended Dec. 31

| Per Share Data ($) | 2007 | 2006 | 2005 | 2004 | 2003 | 2002 | 2001 | 2000 | 1999 | 1998 |
|---|---|---|---|---|---|---|---|---|---|---|
| Tangible Book Value | 39.95 | 45.93 | 37.08 | 42.55 | 37.07 | 36.13 | 28.35 | 31.86 | 30.91 | 29.67 |
| Operating Earnings | NA | NA | NA | NA | NA | 5.10 | -3.67 | 4.52 | 3.63 | 4.36 |
| Earnings | 1.15 | 9.60 | -9.14 | 8.13 | 2.69 | 2.88 | -4.55 | 4.03 | 3.62 | 6.20 |
| Dividends | 1.52 | 1.52 | 2.00 | 1.96 | 1.92 | 1.88 | 1.84 | 1.80 | 1.76 | 1.64 |
| Payout Ratio | 76% | 16% | NM | 24% | 71% | 65% | NM | 45% | 49% | 26% |
| Prices:High | 85.67 | 72.90 | 79.80 | 82.00 | 88.87 | 98.48 | 96.50 | 89.25 | 75.75 | 84.00 |
| Prices:Low | 48.16 | 59.82 | 60.03 | 66.70 | 63.49 | 58.45 | 61.50 | 39.00 | 41.94 | 59.13 |
| P/E Ratio:High | 43 | 8 | NM | 10 | 33 | 34 | NM | 22 | 21 | 14 |
| P/E Ratio:Low | 24 | 6 | NM | 8 | 24 | 20 | NM | 10 | 12 | 10 |

| Income Statement Analysis (Million $) | | | | | | | | | | |
|---|---|---|---|---|---|---|---|---|---|---|
| Premium Income | 7,205 | 7,570 | 2,238 | 1,406 | 6,969 | 5,990 | 3,476 | 2,035 | 1,750 | 685 |
| Net Investment Income | 2,249 | 1,978 | 1,475 | 995 | 780 | 735 | 563 | 542 | 525 | 279 |
| Other Revenue | -318 | 8,904 | 8,864 | 7,426 | 268 | -147 | 18.0 | 140 | 236 | 253 |
| Total Revenue | 9,136 | 9,833 | 11,285 | 10,028 | 8,017 | 6,578 | 4,057 | 2,717 | 2,511 | 1,218 |
| Pretax Income | 534 | 2,007 | -1,194 | 1,260 | 451 | 442 | -764 | 451 | 431 | 594 |
| Net Operating Income | NA | NA | NA | NA | NA | 701 | -465 | NA | NA | NA |
| Net Income | 276 | 1,763 | -1,252 | 1,167 | 412 | 406 | -576 | 506 | 471 | 588 |

| Balance Sheet & Other Financial Data (Million $) | | | | | | | | | | |
|---|---|---|---|---|---|---|---|---|---|---|
| Cash & Equivalent | 4,328 | 2,656 | 4,085 | 2,631 | 2,698 | 3,785 | 2,044 | 1,074 | 669 | 503 |
| Premiums Due | 4,455 | 4,698 | 4,842 | 4,934 | 4,847 | 4,833 | 2,182 | 1,120 | 1,126 | 690 |
| Investment Assets:Bonds | 33,608 | 36,121 | 32,310 | 25,100 | 19,494 | 14,483 | 10,832 | 8,605 | 7,581 | 5,213 |
| Investment Assets:Stocks | 855 | 891 | 869 | 963 | 583 | 575 | 548 | 557 | 1,136 | 1,129 |
| Investment Assets:Loans | Nil | Nil | Nil | Nil | Nil | Nil | Nil | Nil | Nil | Nil |
| Investment Assets:Total | 39,585 | 42,137 | 38,171 | 30,066 | 22,821 | 17,956 | 13,741 | 10,472 | 9,768 | 6,616 |
| Deferred Policy Costs | 755 | 870 | 866 | 845 | 778 | 688 | 394 | 309 | 276 | 98.0 |
| Total Assets | 57,762 | 59,309 | 58,455 | 49,015 | 40,764 | 35,647 | 27,963 | 16,942 | 15,091 | 10,109 |
| Debt | 2,869 | 3,368 | 3,413 | 2,721 | 1,905 | 1,878 | 1,605 | 450 | 411 | Nil |
| Common Equity | 9,948 | 16,422 | 14,078 | 12,286 | 10,171 | 6,569 | 5,437 | 5,574 | 5,577 | 4,818 |
| Property & Casualty:Loss Ratio | 59.8 | 60.7 | 107.1 | 68.6 | 75.3 | 68.0 | 105.0 | 70.4 | 69.1 | 57.0 |
| Property & Casualty:Expense Ratio | 29.0 | 27.8 | 25.8 | 27.4 | 27.3 | 29.0 | 34.9 | 36.4 | 34.3 | 26.3 |
| Property & Casualty Combined Ratio | 88.8 | 88.5 | 132.9 | 96.0 | 102.6 | 97.0 | 139.9 | 106.8 | 103.4 | 83.3 |
| % Return on Revenue | 3.0 | 18.6 | NM | 11.9 | 5.2 | 6.0 | NM | 18.6 | 19.9 | 48.3 |
| % Return on Equity | 2.1 | 11.3 | NM | 10.0 | 3.9 | 6.6 | NM | 9.1 | 8.4 | 16.1 |

Data as orig reptd.; bef. results of disc opers/spec. items. Per share data adj. for stk. divs.; EPS diluted. E-Estimated. NA-Not Available. NM-Not Meaningful. NR-Not Ranked. UR-Under Review.

**Office:** XL House, 1 Bermudiana Rd, Hamilton, Bermuda HM 11.
**Telephone:** 441-292-8515.
**Website:** http://www.xlcapital.com
**Chrmn:** B.M. O'Hara

**CEO:** M.S. McGavick
**EVP & CFO:** B.W. Nocco
**EVP, Secy & General Counsel:** K.R. Gould
**SVP & Treas:** F. Muldoon

**Investor Contact:** D.R. Radulski (441-292-8515)
**Board Members:** D. R. Comey, R. R. Glauber, H. N. Haag, J. Mauriello, M. S. McGavick, E. McQuade, B. M. O'Hara, R. Parker, R. S. Parker, A. Z. Senter, J. T. Thornton, E. E. Thrower, J. M. Vereker

**Founded:** 1986
**Domicile:** Cayman Islands
**Employees:** 4,011

*The McGraw-Hill Companies*

# XTO Energy Inc.

| S&P Recommendation BUY ★★★★☆ | Price $33.54 (as of Nov 14, 2008) | 12-Mo. Target Price $45.00 | Investment Style Large-Cap Growth |
|---|---|---|---|

**GICS Sector** Energy
**Sub-Industry** Oil & Gas Exploration & Production

**Summary** This independent oil and gas producer is highly leveraged to unconventional natural gas resources (such as tight gas, shale gas and coal bed methane) in the U.S.

## Key Stock Statistics (Source S&P, Vickers, company reports)

| | | | | | | | |
|---|---|---|---|---|---|---|---|
| 52-Wk Range | $73.74– 23.80 | S&P Oper. EPS 2008E | 3.77 | Market Capitalization(B) | $19.346 | Beta | 0.71 |
| Trailing 12-Month EPS | $3.93 | S&P Oper. EPS 2009E | 3.65 | Yield (%) | 1.43 | S&P 3-Yr. Proj. EPS CAGR(%) | 3 |
| Trailing 12-Month P/E | 8.5 | P/E on S&P Oper. EPS 2008E | 8.9 | Dividend Rate/Share | $0.48 | S&P Credit Rating | BBB |
| $10K Invested 5 Yrs Ago | NA | Common Shares Outstg. (M) | 576.8 | Institutional Ownership (%) | 80 | | |

## Price Performance

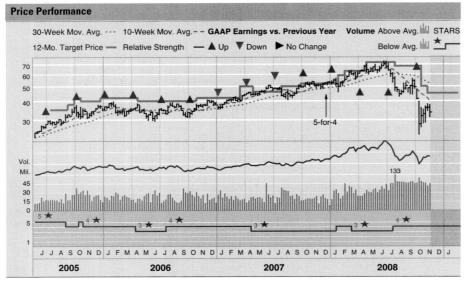

30-Week Mov. Avg. · · · ·  10-Week Mov. Avg. - - -  **GAAP Earnings vs. Previous Year**  Volume Above Avg.  STARS
12-Mo. Target Price —  Relative Strength —  ▲ Up  ▼ Down  ► No Change  Below Avg.

5-for-4

133

Options: ASE, CBOE, P, Ph

Analysis prepared by **Michael Kay** on November 07, 2008, when the stock traded at **$ 35.17**.

## Qualitative Risk Assessment

| LOW | MEDIUM | **HIGH** |
|---|---|---|

Our risk assessment for XTO reflects our view of its position as a large independent exploration and production company focused on unconventional natural gas resources with sizable acreage positions in low-risk drilling opportunities in the U.S. This is offset by our view of XTO's relatively high debt leverage, reflecting its aggressive growth through acquisition strategy.

## Quantitative Evaluations

**S&P Quality Ranking** B+

| D | C | B- | B | **B+** | A- | A | A+ |
|---|---|---|---|---|---|---|---|

**Relative Strength Rank** MODERATE

59

LOWEST = 1        HIGHEST = 99

## Revenue/Earnings Data

**Revenue (Million $)**

| | 1Q | 2Q | 3Q | 4Q | Year |
|---|---|---|---|---|---|
| 2008 | 1,673 | 1,936 | 2,125 | -- | -- |
| 2007 | 1,169 | 1,329 | 1,421 | 1,594 | 5,513 |
| 2006 | 1,215 | 1,066 | 1,096 | 1,199 | 4,576 |
| 2005 | 628.9 | 748.7 | 964.2 | 1,177 | 3,519 |
| 2004 | 394.8 | 444.8 | 507.4 | 600.7 | 1,948 |
| 2003 | 253.5 | 282.2 | 322.1 | 331.9 | 1,190 |

**Earnings Per Share ($)**

| | | | | | |
|---|---|---|---|---|---|
| 2008 | 0.92 | 1.11 | 0.94 | E0.75 | E3.77 |
| 2007 | 0.82 | 0.91 | 0.84 | 0.95 | 3.53 |
| 2006 | 1.01 | 1.30 | 0.79 | 0.93 | 4.02 |
| 2005 | 0.38 | 0.48 | 0.68 | 0.98 | 2.52 |
| 2004 | 0.24 | 0.24 | 0.32 | 0.40 | 1.21 |
| 2003 | 0.18 | 0.15 | 0.26 | 0.16 | 0.76 |

Fiscal year ended Dec. 31. Next earnings report expected: Mid February. EPS Estimates based on S&P Operating Earnings; historical GAAP earnings are as reported.

## Highlights

➤ Oil and gas production climbed 28% through the first nine months of 2008, slightly above expectations, and we project growth of 29% and 23% in 2008 and 2009 on the development of projects in the East Texas Freestone Trend, Barnett Shale, Permian Basin, San Juan Region, Woodford and Fayetteville Shale plays. XTO's third quarter production was negatively impacted by 4 Bcfe, due to hurricane shut-ins, and it sees some effects persisting into the fourth quarter, for an impact of about 4 to 4.5 Bcfe.

➤ XTO continues to pursue 'bolt-on' acquisitions for its best development fields, as evidenced by the $800 million July 2008 Barnett Shale acquisition of 300 Bcfe of proved reserves. Also, we view the acquisition of Hunt Petroleum positively, complementing existing acreage positions, mainly in East Texas/Louisiana and the Bakken Shale in North Dakota, while also adding Gulf Coast and North Sea acreage.

➤ After-tax operating earnings rose 5.8% in 2007, and we expect growth of over 17% in 2008 on production gains partly offset by lower pricing. XTO's capital budget stands at $3.5 billion and we are forecasting about $3 billion in 2009.

## Investment Rationale/Risk

➤ We believe XTO will continue to seek production growth through developments, but we expect XTO to become more conservative with respect to acquisitions given the ongoing credit crunch and XTO's above-peer debt levels. In May 2008, XTO entered the Bakken Shale with its agreement to pay $1.85 billion for 352,000 net acres from Headington Oil Co. In September, XTO closed on the purchase of privately held Hunt Petroleum for $4.2 billion in cash and stock. In 2008, XTO has raised $3.3 billion in stock and debt offerings to fund acquisitions.

➤ Risks to our recommendation and target price include changes in economic, industrial and operating conditions, such as rising operating costs, difficulties in replacing reserves, aggressively priced and financed acquisitions, and sustained declines in oil and gas prices.

➤ A drop in oil and gas prices has caused a similar decline in E&P shares. Due to weaker economic forecasts, we see the market discounting probable reserves, and we now value XTO on proved reserve NAV estimates. We blend our NAV of $52 with our DCF (WACC 9.4%, terminal growth 3%) and relative valuations to get our 12-month target price of $45.

## Dividend Data (Dates: mm/dd Payment Date: mm/dd/yy)

| Amount ($) | Date Decl. | Ex-Div. Date | Stk. of Record | Payment Date |
|---|---|---|---|---|
| 0.120 | 11/14 | 12/27 | 12/31 | 01/15/08 |
| 0.120 | 02/19 | 03/27 | 03/31 | 04/15/08 |
| 0.120 | 05/20 | 06/26 | 06/30 | 07/15/08 |
| 0.120 | 08/19 | 09/26 | 09/30 | 10/15/08 |

Dividends have been paid since 1993. Source: Company reports.

---

**Please read the Required Disclosures and Analyst Certification on the last page of this report.**

# XTO Energy Inc.

## Business Summary November 07, 2008

CORPORATE OVERVIEW. XTO Energy Inc. (formerly Cross Timbers Oil Co.) is engaged in the acquisition, development, exploitation and exploration of producing oil and gas properties, and in the production, processing and marketing and transportation of oil and natural gas. The company operates in the U.S. and is focused on the following areas: Eastern Region (East Texas Basin, northwestern Louisiana and Mississippi); North Texas Region (including the Barnett Shale); San Juan Region; Permian and South Texas Region; and the Mid-Continent and Rocky Mountain Region (including the Fayetteville and Woodford Shales).

Proved oil and gas reserves rose 32% to 11.289 trillion cubic feet equivalent (Tcfe; 66% developed, 84% natural gas) in 2007. Oil and gas production rose 19% to 1.821 Bcfe per day in 2006 (80% natural gas). We estimate XTO's 2007 organic reserve replacement at 309%. Using data from John S. Herold, we estimate XTO's three-year (2004-06) reserve replacement at 429%, slightly above the peer average; its three-year proved acquisition costs at $10 per boe, in line with peers; and its three-year finding & development costs at $8.25 per boe, below the peer average. In February 2008, XTO estimated it had replaced 513% of its 2007 reserves (308% through developments).

COMPETITIVE LANDSCAPE. XTO's operations are highly leveraged to unconventional natural gas plays, and it has build sizable acreage positions in tight

gas, shale gas and coalbed methane (CBM) basins in the U.S. As a result of its large acreage position, XTO has a solid inventory of low-risk drilling opportunities, by our analysis. Although these basins can be technically challenging and entail complex drilling and fracturing techniques, we believe XTO has proved itself a competent operator. Over the years, we believe XTO has built a solid track record of finding, developing and producing reserves in a generally consistent and cost efficient manner.

In February 2008, XTO announced a strategic goal of increasing production 20% over 2007 levels and to increase proved reserves by 15 Tcfe by year-end 2009. To achieve these targets, XTO plans to drill 1,160 (980 net) development wells and perform approximately 750 (600 net) workovers and recompletions in 2008.

IMPACT OF MAJOR DEVELOPMENTS. Acquisitions have played a key role in XTO's growth strategy. In 2007, the company was particularly active, and acquired proved and unproved reserves for a total of $4.03 billion.

## Company Financials Fiscal Year Ended Dec. 31

| Per Share Data ($) | 2007 | 2006 | 2005 | 2004 | 2003 | 2002 | 2001 | 2000 | 1999 | 1998 |
|---|---|---|---|---|---|---|---|---|---|---|
| Tangible Book Value | 15.92 | 12.20 | 8.81 | 4.49 | 3.76 | 2.57 | 2.39 | 1.45 | 0.82 | 0.53 |
| Cash Flow | 6.01 | 6.00 | 4.03 | 1.65 | 1.52 | 1.12 | 1.32 | 1.26 | 0.51 | 0.04 |
| Earnings | 3.53 | 4.02 | 2.52 | 1.21 | 0.76 | 0.53 | 0.85 | 0.37 | 0.15 | -0.26 |
| S&P Core Earnings | 3.53 | 3.38 | 2.41 | 1.13 | 0.73 | 0.52 | 0.72 | NA | NA | NA |
| Dividends | 0.41 | 0.25 | 0.19 | 0.07 | 0.02 | 0.01 | 0.01 | 0.01 | 0.01 | 0.01 |
| Payout Ratio | 12% | 6% | 8% | 6% | 3% | 3% | 2% | 2% | 7% | NM |
| Prices:High | 53.99 | 40.99 | 38.09 | 22.13 | 14.06 | 9.50 | 7.82 | 6.96 | 2.42 | 3.38 |
| Prices:Low | 35.09 | 29.21 | 19.09 | 12.28 | 8.17 | 5.29 | 4.43 | 1.21 | 0.73 | 0.81 |
| P/E Ratio:High | 15 | 10 | 15 | 18 | 19 | 18 | 9 | 19 | 16 | NM |
| P/E Ratio:Low | 10 | 7 | 8 | 10 | 11 | 10 | 5 | 3 | 5 | NM |

| Income Statement Analysis (Million $) | 2007 | 2006 | 2005 | 2004 | 2003 | 2002 | 2001 | 2000 | 1999 | 1998 |
|---|---|---|---|---|---|---|---|---|---|---|
| Revenue | 5,513 | 4,576 | 3,519 | 1,948 | 1,190 | 810 | 839 | 601 | 341 | 249 |
| Operating Income | 4,068 | 3,445 | 2,198 | 1,338 | 801 | 550 | 611 | 398 | 208 | 124 |
| Depreciation, Depletion and Amortization | 1,187 | 875 | 655 | 407 | 284 | 204 | 154 | 260 | 112 | 83.6 |
| Interest Expense | 297 | 180 | 153 | 93.7 | 63.8 | 53.6 | 55.6 | 78.9 | 64.2 | 52.1 |
| Pretax Income | 2,642 | 2,961 | 1,810 | 826 | 445 | 287 | 455 | 176 | 70.6 | -106 |
| Effective Tax Rate | 36.0% | 37.2% | 36.4% | 38.5% | 35.5% | 35.1% | 35.6% | 33.7% | 33.9% | NM |
| Net Income | 1,691 | 1,860 | 1,152 | 508 | 287 | 186 | 293 | 117 | 46.7 | -69.8 |
| S&P Core Earnings | 1,691 | 1,565 | 1,098 | 476 | 275 | 183 | 249 | NA | NA | NA |

| Balance Sheet & Other Financial Data (Million $) | 2007 | 2006 | 2005 | 2004 | 2003 | 2002 | 2001 | 2000 | 1999 | 1998 |
|---|---|---|---|---|---|---|---|---|---|---|
| Cash | Nil | 5.00 | 2.00 | 9.70 | 7.00 | 15.0 | 6.81 | 7.44 | 5.73 | 12.3 |
| Current Assets | 1,287 | 1,585 | 943 | 437 | 261 | 245 | 239 | 193 | 113 | 138 |
| Total Assets | 18,922 | 12,885 | 9,857 | 6,110 | 3,611 | 2,648 | 2,132 | 1,592 | 1,477 | 1,208 |
| Current Liabilities | 1,537 | 1,240 | 884 | 501 | 321 | 286 | 202 | 219 | 74.2 | 99.6 |
| Long Term Debt | 6,320 | 3,451 | 3,109 | 2,043 | 1,252 | 1,118 | 856 | 769 | 991 | 921 |
| Common Equity | 7,941 | 5,865 | 4,209 | 2,599 | 1,466 | 908 | 821 | 470 | 249 | 149 |
| Total Capital | 16,871 | 11,294 | 7,318 | 5,398 | 3,144 | 2,312 | 1,876 | 1,349 | 1,395 | 1,105 |
| Capital Expenditures | 7,346 | 616 | 1,621 | 1,905 | 654 | 358 | 225 | 45.6 | 270 | 296 |
| Cash Flow | 2,878 | 2,735 | 1,807 | 915 | 571 | 390 | 448 | 375 | 157 | 12.0 |
| Current Ratio | 0.8 | 1.3 | 1.1 | 0.9 | 0.8 | 0.9 | 1.2 | 0.9 | 1.5 | 1.4 |
| % Long Term Debt of Capitalization | 37.5 | 30.6 | 42.5 | 37.8 | 39.8 | 48.4 | 45.6 | 57.0 | 71.1 | 83.3 |
| % Return on Assets | 10.6 | 16.4 | 14.4 | 10.4 | 9.2 | 7.8 | 15.8 | 7.6 | 3.5 | NM |
| % Return on Equity | 24.5 | 36.9 | 33.8 | 25.0 | 24.1 | 21.5 | 45.4 | 32.0 | 21.3 | NM |

Data as orig reptd.; bef. results of disc opers/spec. items. Per share data adj. for stk. divs.; EPS diluted. E-Estimated. NA-Not Available. NM-Not Meaningful. NR-Not Ranked. UR-Under Review.

**Office:** 810 Houston St, Fort Worth, TX 76102.
**Telephone:** 817-870-2800.
**Email:** investor_relations@xtoenergy.com
**Website:** http://www.xtoenergy.com

**Chrmn & CEO:** B.R. Simpson
**Pres:** K.A. Hutton
**EVP & CFO:** L.G. Baldwin
**SVP, Chief Acctg Officer & Cntlr:** B.G. Kniffen

**SVP & Treas:** B.W. Clum
**Investor Contact:** G.D. Simpson (817-870-2800)
**Board Members:** W. H. Adams, III, M. Arntzen, L. G. Baldwin, L. G. Collins, K. A. Hutton, P. R. Kevil, T. L. Petrus, J. P. Randall, S. Sherman, H. D. Simons, B. R. Simpson, G. D. Simpson, V. O. Vennerberg, II

**Founded:** 1986
**Domicile:** Delaware
**Employees:** 2,361

# Yahoo! Inc

**STANDARD &POOR'S**

| S&P Recommendation **BUY** ★★★★☆ | Price $10.82 (as of Nov 14, 2008) | 12-Mo. Target Price $20.00 | Investment Style Large-Cap Growth |
|---|---|---|---|

**GICS Sector** Information Technology
**Sub-Industry** Internet Software & Services

**Summary** This company is one of the world's largest providers of online content and services.

## Key Stock Statistics (Source S&P, Vickers, company reports)

| | | | | | | | |
|---|---|---|---|---|---|---|---|
| 52-Wk Range | $30.25–9.76 | S&P Oper. EPS 2008**E** | 0.40 | Market Capitalization(B) | $15.015 | Beta | 1.22 |
| Trailing 12-Month EPS | $0.66 | S&P Oper. EPS 2009**E** | 0.50 | Yield (%) | Nil | S&P 3-Yr. Proj. EPS CAGR(%) | 17 |
| Trailing 12-Month P/E | 16.4 | P/E on S&P Oper. EPS 2008**E** | 27.1 | Dividend Rate/Share | Nil | S&P Credit Rating | NR |
| $10K Invested 5 Yrs Ago | $5,198 | Common Shares Outstg. (M) | 1,387.7 | Institutional Ownership (%) | 70 | | |

## Price Performance

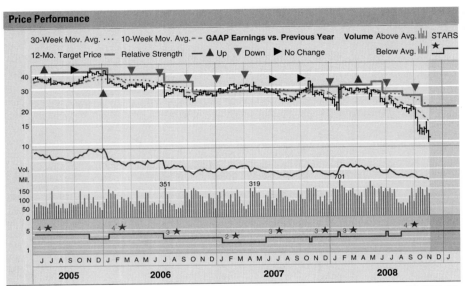

30-Week Mov. Avg. · · · · 10-Week Mov. Avg. – – GAAP Earnings vs. Previous Year    Volume Above Avg. STARS
12-Mo. Target Price — Relative Strength ▲ Up ▼ Down ► No Change    Below Avg. ★

Options: ASE, CBOE, P, Ph

Analysis prepared by **Scott H. Kessler** on October 23, 2008, when the stock traded at **$ 12.34**.

## Highlights

➤ We see revenues excluding traffic acquisition costs rising 6% in 2008, reflecting the impact of new advertising technology systems, and offset by a global economic slowdown, the sale of Overture Japan, and revised broadband relationships. We expect that YHOO will increasingly focus on providing more holistic advertising solutions, initially through its "apt" offering.

➤ We expect that revenues will continue to benefit from secular growth in online advertising. We think operating margins will bottom in 2008, reflecting changed broadband partnerships and aggressive investment in new initiatives.

➤ In February 2008, Microsoft (MSFT: buy, $22) announced a bid to purchase YHOO in a deal worth $31 a share. In May, an unconfirmed report in the Wall Street Journal indicated that MSFT raised the value of its offer to as much as $33. In June, the companies announced an acquisition would not occur, and YHOO announced a new search agreement with Google (GOOG: buy, $356) that is undergoing regulatory review. In August 2008, YHOO announced that activist Carl Icahn and two of his allies joined the company's newly constituted 11-person board of directors.

## Investment Rationale/Risk

➤ We think an increasing percentage of advertising budgets is being spent online, and YHOO's global reach has appeal. However, we have concerns about YHOO's large display advertising business. Nonetheless, despite considerable challenges, we see YHOO as undervalued.

➤ Risks to our recommendation and target price include the potential worsening of the global economic downturn, increasing competition, and the value of YHOO's Alibaba investments appreciating less significantly than we expect.

➤ After excluding the value of YHOO's Asia-based equity investments and cash/equivalents, comparing its P/E to those of its peers yields a value of $7, and similar P/E-to-growth considerations lead to a value of $8. Our DCF analysis, with assumptions including a WACC of 12.4%, projected annual FCF growth of 14% from 2008 to 2012, and a perpetuity growth rate of 3%, results in a value of $20. We calculate the value of YHOO's Asian investments at $6 and cash/investments at $2. Weighing these peer and intrinsic assessments, and adding the value of the investments and cash/equivalents, leads to our 12-month target price of $20.

## Qualitative Risk Assessment

| LOW | MEDIUM | **HIGH** |
|---|---|---|

The company is a large and well-capitalized leader in a number of areas related to Internet content and services. However, in our view, the markets in which it participates change rapidly and have relatively low barriers to entry, which have contributed to the notable competition and inconsistent financial execution that we have observed.

## Quantitative Evaluations

**S&P Quality Ranking**    **B**

| D | C | B- | **B** | B+ | A- | A | A+ |
|---|---|---|---|---|---|---|---|

**Relative Strength Rank**    **MODERATE**

35

LOWEST = 1    HIGHEST = 99

## Revenue/Earnings Data

**Revenue (Million $)**

| | 1Q | 2Q | 3Q | 4Q | Year |
|---|---|---|---|---|---|
| 2008 | 1,818 | 1,798 | 1,786 | -- | -- |
| 2007 | 1,672 | 1,698 | 1,768 | 1,832 | 6,969 |
| 2006 | 1,567 | 1,576 | 1,580 | 1,702 | 6,426 |
| 2005 | 1,174 | 1,253 | 1,330 | 1,501 | 5,258 |
| 2004 | 757.8 | 832.3 | 906.7 | 1,078 | 3,575 |
| 2003 | 283.0 | 321.4 | 356.8 | 663.9 | 1,625 |

**Earnings Per Share ($)**

| | 1Q | 2Q | 3Q | 4Q | Year |
|---|---|---|---|---|---|
| 2008 | 0.37 | 0.09 | 0.04 | E0.10 | E0.40 |
| 2007 | 0.10 | 0.11 | 0.11 | 0.15 | 0.47 |
| 2006 | 0.11 | 0.11 | 0.11 | 0.19 | 0.52 |
| 2005 | 0.14 | 0.51 | 0.17 | 0.46 | 1.28 |
| 2004 | 0.07 | 0.08 | 0.17 | 0.25 | 0.58 |
| 2003 | 0.04 | 0.04 | 0.05 | 0.06 | 0.19 |

Fiscal year ended Dec. 31. Next earnings report expected: Late January. EPS Estimates based on S&P Operating Earnings; historical GAAP earnings are as reported.

## Dividend Data

No cash dividends have been paid.

# Yahoo! Inc

STANDARD &POOR'S

## Business Summary October 23, 2008

CORPORATE OVERVIEW. Yahoo! is one of the world's largest Internet companies. Primary categories for its properties and services are Front Doors (including the Yahoo front page, My Yahoo and the Yahoo Toolbar), Search (consisting of offerings related to search, yellow pages, maps, local, shopping, travel, and personals, and Yahoo Answers), Communications and Communities (including mail and messaging offerings, and Yahoo Groups, Yahoo 360 and Flickr), Media (consisting of information/entertainment offerings related to news, finance, sports (including Rivals.com), music, movies, television, games, autos, real estate, food, consumer technology, kids and health), and Connected Life (including Yahoo Mobile, Yahoo Digital Home, and Yahoo Desktop). We estimate that YHOO has more than 500 million worldwide registered users (excluding the 33% stake in Yahoo! Japan, 41% interest in Alibaba Group, 30% holding in Alibaba.com, and 10% share of Gmarket as of mid-2008).

Blake Jorgensen became CFO in June 2007. Soon thereafter, co-founder Jerry Yang replaced Terry Semel as CEO, and long-time CFO Sue Decker became President and COO. One-time COO Dan Rosensweig, CTO and Technology Group leader Farzad Nazem, and Chief Sales Officer Wenda Millard left the company in the first half of 2007. Many other important executives have also left the company since early 2007, and the pace and magnitude of these departures increased around mid-2008, in our view.

CORPORATE STRATEGY. In mid-2007, YHOO unveiled a new strategy intended in part to help the company deliver better financial performance. The company will be emphasizing three main areas of differentiation to strengthen and grow its ecosystem -- offering unique insights to its constituencies, promoting significant solution openness through its websites and platforms, and providing the most compelling options for partners. We believe these are reasonable priorities, and will enable the company to more effectively innovate and execute.

More importantly, in our view, YHOO also has set three primary multi-year objectives. First, the company wants to be the starting point for the most Internet consumers. Second, it wants to be a "must buy" for the most advertisers. Third, it wants to deliver industry-leading platforms that attract the most developers. We think this set of goals will enable the company to better streamline its operations and focus its investment. In January 2008, YHOO announced it would "realign" 1,000 employees. In June 2008, the company announced a streamlined operating structure. In October 2008, YHOO announced a plan to reduce $400 million in costs/expenses and 10% of its workforce.

## Company Financials Fiscal Year Ended Dec. 31

### Per Share Data ($)

| | 2007 | 2006 | 2005 | 2004 | 2003 | 2002 | 2001 | 2000 | 1999 | 1998 |
|---|---|---|---|---|---|---|---|---|---|---|
| Tangible Book Value | 3.70 | 4.25 | 3.59 | 2.94 | 1.64 | 1.47 | 1.52 | 1.69 | 1.11 | 0.62 |
| Cash Flow | 0.94 | 0.89 | 1.54 | 0.79 | 0.31 | 0.18 | 0.03 | 0.11 | 0.09 | 0.04 |
| Earnings | 0.47 | 0.52 | 1.28 | 0.58 | 0.19 | 0.09 | -0.08 | 0.06 | 0.05 | 0.03 |
| S&P Core Earnings | 0.46 | 0.51 | 0.56 | 0.24 | 0.03 | -0.32 | -0.85 | NA | NA | NA |
| Dividends | Nil | Nil | Nil | Nil | Nil | Nil | Nil | Nil | Nil | Nil |
| Payout Ratio | Nil | Nil | Nil | Nil | Nil | Nil | Nil | Nil | Nil | Nil |
| Prices:High | 34.08 | 43.66 | 43.45 | 39.79 | 22.74 | 10.68 | 21.69 | 125.03 | 112.00 | 35.75 |
| Prices:Low | 22.27 | 22.65 | 30.30 | 20.57 | 8.25 | 4.47 | 4.01 | 12.53 | 27.50 | 3.60 |
| P/E Ratio:High | 73 | 84 | 34 | 69 | NM | NM | NM | NM | NM | NM |
| P/E Ratio:Low | 47 | 44 | 24 | 35 | NM | NM | NM | NM | NM | NM |

### Income Statement Analysis (Million $)

| | 2007 | 2006 | 2005 | 2004 | 2003 | 2002 | 2001 | 2000 | 1999 | 1998 |
|---|---|---|---|---|---|---|---|---|---|---|
| Revenue | 6,969 | 6,426 | 5,258 | 3,575 | 1,625 | 953 | 717 | 1,110 | 589 | 203 |
| Operating Income | 1,355 | 1,481 | 1,505 | 1,000 | 455 | 198 | 34.5 | 390 | 197 | 58.4 |
| Depreciation | 659 | 540 | 397 | 311 | 160 | 109 | 131 | 69.1 | 42.3 | 10.2 |
| Interest Expense | Nil | Nil | Nil | Nil | Nil | Nil | Nil | Nil | Nil | Nil |
| Pretax Income | 1,000 | 293 | 2,672 | 1,280 | 391 | 180 | -81.1 | 264 | 104 | 43.3 |
| Effective Tax Rate | 33.7% | NM | 28.7% | 34.2% | 37.6% | 39.7% | NM | 71.2% | 39.0% | 41.1% |
| Net Income | 660 | 751 | 1,896 | 840 | 238 | 107 | -92.8 | 70.8 | 61.1 | 25.6 |
| S&P Core Earnings | 651 | 744 | 840 | 353 | 35.5 | -377 | -966 | NA | NA | NA |

### Balance Sheet & Other Financial Data (Million $)

| | 2007 | 2006 | 2005 | 2004 | 2003 | 2002 | 2001 | 2000 | 1999 | 1998 |
|---|---|---|---|---|---|---|---|---|---|---|
| Cash | 2,001 | 2,601 | 2,561 | 3,512 | 1,310 | 774 | 926 | 1,120 | 872 | 433 |
| Current Assets | 3,238 | 3,750 | 3,450 | 4,090 | 1,722 | 970 | 1,052 | 1,291 | 946 | 467 |
| Total Assets | 12,230 | 11,514 | 10,832 | 9,178 | 5,932 | 2,790 | 2,379 | 2,270 | 1,470 | 622 |
| Current Liabilities | 2,300 | 1,474 | 1,204 | 1,181 | 708 | 412 | 359 | 311 | 192 | 80.0 |
| Long Term Debt | Nil | 750 | 750 | 750 | 750 | Nil | Nil | Nil | Nil | Nil |
| Common Equity | 9,533 | 9,161 | 8,566 | 7,101 | 4,363 | 2,262 | 1,967 | 1,897 | 1,261 | 536 |
| Total Capital | 9,545 | 9,919 | 9,316 | 7,896 | 5,151 | 2,294 | 1,997 | 1,926 | 1,265 | 540 |
| Capital Expenditures | 602 | 689 | 409 | 246 | 117 | 51.6 | 86.2 | 94.4 | 49.5 | 11.9 |
| Cash Flow | 1,319 | 1,291 | 2,293 | 1,151 | 398 | 216 | 37.8 | 140 | 103 | 35.8 |
| Current Ratio | 1.4 | 2.5 | 2.9 | 3.5 | 2.4 | 2.4 | 2.9 | 4.1 | 4.9 | 5.8 |
| % Long Term Debt of Capitalization | Nil | 7.6 | 8.0 | 9.5 | 14.6 | Nil | Nil | Nil | Nil | Nil |
| % Net Income of Revenue | 9.5 | 11.7 | 36.0 | 23.5 | 14.6 | 11.2 | NM | 6.4 | 10.3 | 12.6 |
| % Return on Assets | 5.6 | 6.7 | 18.9 | 11.1 | 5.5 | 4.1 | NM | 3.7 | 5.4 | 6.7 |
| % Return on Equity | 7.1 | 8.5 | 24.2 | 14.6 | 7.2 | 5.1 | NM | 4.5 | 6.3 | 7.8 |

Data as orig reptd.; bef. results of disc opers/spec. items. Per share data adj. for stk. divs.; EPS diluted. E-Estimated. NA-Not Available. NM-Not Meaningful. NR-Not Ranked. UR-Under Review.

**Office:** 701 First Avenue, Sunnyvale, CA 94089.
**Telephone:** 408-349-3300.
**Email:** investor_relations@yahoo-inc.com
**Website:** http://www.yahoo.com

**Chrmn:** R.J. Bostock
**Pres:** S. Decker
**CEO:** J. Yang
**COO:** J.E. Marcom, Jr.

**EVP, Secy & General Counsel:** M.J. Callahan
**Board Members:** F. J. Biondi, Jr., R. J. Bostock, R. W. Burkle, J. H. Chapple, E. C. Hippeau, C. C. Icahn, V. Joshi, A. Kern, M. Wilderotter, G. L. Wilson, J. Yang

**Founded:** 1995
**Domicile:** Delaware
**Employees:** 14,300

**STANDARD &POOR'S**

# YUM! Brands Inc.

| S&P Recommendation | HOLD ★★★☆☆ | Price $24.98 (as of Nov 14, 2008) | 12-Mo. Target Price $30.00 | Investment Style Large-Cap Growth |
|---|---|---|---|---|

**GICS Sector** Consumer Discretionary
**Sub-Industry** Restaurants

**Summary** This company operates, franchises, has interests in, or licenses the largest number of fast food restaurants in the world, with approximately 35,800 units, including the KFC, Pizza Hut and Taco Bell chains.

## Key Stock Statistics (Source S&P, Vickers, company reports)

| | | | | | |
|---|---|---|---|---|---|
| 52-Wk Range | $41.73– 22.50 | S&P Oper. EPS 2008**E** | 1.91 | Market Capitalization(B) | $11.555 |
| Trailing 12-Month EPS | $1.97 | S&P Oper. EPS 2009**E** | 2.00 | Yield (%) | 3.04 |
| Trailing 12-Month P/E | 12.7 | P/E on S&P Oper. EPS 2008**E** | 13.1 | Dividend Rate/Share | $0.76 |
| $10K Invested 5 Yrs Ago | $15,397 | Common Shares Outstg. (M) | 462.6 | Institutional Ownership (%) | 83 |

| | |
|---|---|
| Beta | 1.01 |
| S&P 3-Yr. Proj. EPS CAGR(%) | 9 |
| S&P Credit Rating | BBB- |

## Price Performance

30-Week Mov. Avg. · · · 10-Week Mov. Avg. - - GAAP Earnings vs. Previous Year   Volume Above Avg. | STARS
12-Mo. Target Price —  Relative Strength —  ▲ Up ▼ Down ► No Change   Below Avg. | ★

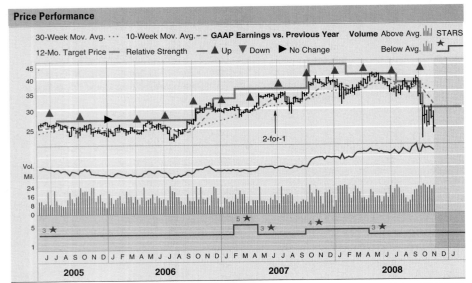

2-for-1

Options: ASE, CBOE, Ph

Analysis prepared by **Mark S. Basham** on October 21, 2008, when the stock traded at **$ 28.93**.

## Highlights

➤ YUM is focused on international expansion. For 2008, we see at least 550 net new restaurants in the China division, approximately 750 net new units in Yum Restaurants International (YRI), and a net reduction of about 150-200 units in the U.S.

➤ In 2008, margins are likely to be hurt by rising commodity costs. In the U.S., we expect operating profit to decline about 7%, despite comparisons to 2007 when lost sales and additional costs were incurred from negative publicity surrounding two food safety incidents. We project operating profit growth of 29% for the China division, somewhat less than the 45% sales growth that we see. We estimate profit growth of 15% for YRI, as results benefit from the weak dollar.

➤ We project 2008 EPS of $1.91, including $0.06 in the first quarter from the sale of YUM's minority interest in KFC Japan, up 14% from the $1.68 earned in 2007. We expect 2009 to be a more difficult year for YUM, with moderating growth in the China, and tough conditions in the U.S. and YRI divisions. We estimate 2009 EPS of $2.00, aided by share repurchases.

## Investment Rationale/Risk

➤ Our hold recommendation is indicative of our view that the shares are appropriately valued at recent levels. We see heightened risks to growth in 2009 in China, and the likelihood of weak conditions in the U.S. and YRI divisions, as the credit crisis unfolds. Our lowered financial projections for 2009 represent a departure from our prior outlook that YUM would increase earnings per share on average by about 10% annually over the 2008-2011 period.

➤ Risks to our recommendation and target price include potentially greater-than-expected increases in food and labor costs, currency exchange rate risk, and other political and operating risks associated with international expansion. Tight credit may make it more difficult for YUM and its franchisees to expand.

➤ Our 12-month target price of $30 is based on our discounted cash flow analysis, which assumes a weighted average cost of capital of 10.1%, and free cash flow increases averaging 6% to 8% annually for the next five years, then gradually slowing to a terminal rate of 2%.

## Qualitative Risk Assessment

| LOW | MEDIUM | HIGH |
|---|---|---|

YUM competes in the relatively stable fast food industry, in which its concepts possess a very strong brand name presence. However, operating margins can vary widely due to fluctuations in food costs. Furthermore, YUM's profits can be affected by changing currency exchange rates due to its large and fast-growing international business.

## Quantitative Evaluations

**S&P Quality Ranking**  B+

| D | C | B- | B | B+ | A- | A | A+ |
|---|---|---|---|---|---|---|---|

**Relative Strength Rank**   MODERATE

55

LOWEST = 1   HIGHEST = 99

## Revenue/Earnings Data

**Revenue (Million $)**

| | 1Q | 2Q | 3Q | 4Q | Year |
|---|---|---|---|---|---|
| 2008 | 2,408 | 2,653 | 2,835 | -- | -- |
| 2007 | 2,223 | 2,367 | 2,564 | 3,262 | 10,416 |
| 2006 | 2,085 | 2,182 | 2,278 | 3,016 | 9,561 |
| 2005 | 2,054 | 2,153 | 2,243 | 2,899 | 9,349 |
| 2004 | 1,970 | 2,077 | 2,179 | 2,785 | 9,011 |
| 2003 | 1,802 | 1,936 | 1,989 | 2,653 | 8,380 |

**Earnings Per Share ($)**

| | 1Q | 2Q | 3Q | 4Q | Year |
|---|---|---|---|---|---|
| 2008 | 0.50 | 0.45 | 0.58 | E0.38 | E1.91 |
| 2007 | 0.35 | 0.39 | 0.50 | 0.44 | 1.68 |
| 2006 | 0.29 | 0.34 | 0.42 | 0.42 | 1.46 |
| 2005 | 0.25 | 0.29 | 0.35 | 0.39 | 1.28 |
| 2004 | 0.24 | 0.29 | 0.31 | 0.39 | 1.21 |
| 2003 | 0.20 | 0.20 | 0.26 | 0.35 | 1.01 |

Fiscal year ended Dec. 31. Next earnings report expected: Early February. EPS Estimates based on S&P Operating Earnings; historical GAAP earnings are as reported.

## Dividend Data (Dates: mm/dd Payment Date: mm/dd/yy)

| Amount ($) | Date Decl. | Ex-Div. Date | Stk. of Record | Payment Date |
|---|---|---|---|---|
| 0.150 | 11/16 | 01/09 | 01/11 | 02/01/08 |
| 0.150 | 03/14 | 04/09 | 04/11 | 05/02/08 |
| 0.190 | 05/06 | 07/09 | 07/11 | 08/01/08 |
| 0.190 | 09/10 | 10/15 | 10/17 | 11/07/08 |

Dividends have been paid since 2004. Source: Company reports.

---

**Please read the Required Disclosures and Analyst Certification on the last page of this report.**

The *McGraw-Hill* Companies

# YUM! Brands Inc.

**STANDARD &POOR'S**

## Business Summary October 21, 2008

CORPORATE PROFILE. Yum! Brands has the world's largest quick service restaurant (QSR) system, with approximately 35,800 restaurants, including licensee units, in more than 100 countries and territories. The company operates and franchises restaurants under the KFC, Pizza Hut, Taco Bell, Long John Silver's and A&W All American Food concepts. In 2007, the company's brands generated $33.5 billion in systemwide sales and $10.4 billion in worldwide revenues, up 8.9% from 2006.

KFC (originally Kentucky Fried Chicken) is the leader in the U.S. chicken QSR segment, with about a 45% market share during 2007 (46% in 2006), according to NPD Group CREST. Systemwide sales totaled approximately $5.3 billion in the U.S. and $16.1 billion worldwide in 2007. At the end of 2007, there were 5,358 units in the U.S. and 9,534 units internationally.

Pizza Hut is the world's largest restaurant chain specializing in ready-to-eat pizza products. In 2007, it led the U.S. pizza QSR segment with about a 15% market share (15%). Systemwide sales totaled $5.4 billion in the U.S. and $10.0 billion worldwide in 2007. As of December 2007, there were 7,515 units in the U.S. and 5,362 units internationally.

Taco Bell is the leader in the U.S. Mexican food QSR segment, with about a

54% market share (58%). Systemwide sales totaled $6.1 billion in the U.S. and $6.3 billion worldwide in 2007. At the end of 2007, it had 5,580 units in the U.S. and 238 units internationally.

In each concept, units are operated by the company as well as by independent franchisees, licensees, or unconsolidated affiliates. The company intends to refranchise restaurants as part of a long range plan to reduce company ownership of U.S. restaurants to below 10% of the total by 2010. During 2008, it expects to reduce company ownership in the U.S. to about 17% from 22% at the end of 2007. During 2007, 304 company-owned U.S. restaurants were sold to franchisees.

In 2007, international operations accounted for 50% of total revenues, up from 41% in 2006. At the end of 2007, the company had 15,440 units (including licensees) in operation outside the U.S, compared to 14,534 at the end of 2006. The company's largest international markets include China, Japan, Great Britain, Canada, Australia, and Korea.

## Company Financials Fiscal Year Ended Dec. 31

### Per Share Data ($)

| | 2007 | 2006 | 2005 | 2004 | 2003 | 2002 | 2001 | 2000 | 1999 | 1998 |
|---|---|---|---|---|---|---|---|---|---|---|
| Tangible Book Value | 0.27 | 0.81 | 1.04 | 1.20 | 0.42 | NM | NM | NM | NM | NM |
| Cash Flow | 2.67 | 2.46 | 2.07 | 1.95 | 1.67 | 1.54 | 1.39 | 1.29 | 1.58 | 1.38 |
| Earnings | 1.68 | 1.46 | 1.28 | 1.21 | 1.01 | 0.94 | 0.81 | 0.69 | 0.98 | 0.71 |
| S&P Core Earnings | 1.69 | 1.51 | 1.26 | 1.15 | 1.04 | 0.80 | 0.68 | NA | NA | NA |
| Dividends | 0.52 | 0.26 | 0.22 | 0.10 | Nil | Nil | Nil | Nil | Nil | Nil |
| Payout Ratio | 31% | 18% | 17% | 8% | Nil | Nil | Nil | Nil | Nil | Nil |
| Prices:High | 40.60 | 31.84 | 26.90 | 23.74 | 17.71 | 16.58 | 13.33 | 9.64 | 18.47 | 12.72 |
| Prices:Low | 27.51 | 22.11 | 22.37 | 16.07 | 10.77 | 10.18 | 7.89 | 5.89 | 8.75 | 6.27 |
| P/E Ratio:High | 24 | 22 | 21 | 20 | 18 | 18 | 16 | 14 | 19 | 18 |
| P/E Ratio:Low | 16 | 15 | 18 | 13 | 11 | 11 | 10 | 9 | 9 | 9 |

### Income Statement Analysis (Million $)

| | 2007 | 2006 | 2005 | 2004 | 2003 | 2002 | 2001 | 2000 | 1999 | 1998 |
|---|---|---|---|---|---|---|---|---|---|---|
| Revenue | 10,416 | 9,561 | 9,349 | 9,011 | 8,380 | 7,757 | 6,953 | 7,093 | 7,822 | 8,468 |
| Operating Income | 1,808 | 1,724 | 1,538 | 1,518 | 1,471 | 1,375 | 1,220 | 1,217 | 1,280 | 1,185 |
| Depreciation | 533 | 479 | 469 | 448 | 401 | 370 | 354 | 354 | 386 | 417 |
| Interest Expense | 199 | 154 | 127 | 129 | 173 | 172 | 158 | 176 | 202 | 272 |
| Pretax Income | 1,191 | 1,108 | 1,026 | 1,026 | 886 | 858 | 733 | 684 | 1,038 | 756 |
| Effective Tax Rate | 23.7% | 25.6% | 25.7% | 27.9% | 30.2% | 32.1% | 32.9% | 39.6% | 39.6% | 41.1% |
| Net Income | 909 | 824 | 762 | 740 | 618 | 583 | 492 | 413 | 627 | 445 |
| S&P Core Earnings | 913 | 849 | 754 | 704 | 635 | 494 | 416 | NA | NA | NA |

### Balance Sheet & Other Financial Data (Million $)

| | 2007 | 2006 | 2005 | 2004 | 2003 | 2002 | 2001 | 2000 | 1999 | 1998 |
|---|---|---|---|---|---|---|---|---|---|---|
| Cash | 789 | 319 | 158 | 62.0 | 192 | 130 | 110 | 133 | 89.0 | 121 |
| Current Assets | 1,481 | 901 | 837 | 747 | 806 | 730 | 547 | 688 | 486 | 625 |
| Total Assets | 7,242 | 6,353 | 5,698 | 5,696 | 5,620 | 5,400 | 4,388 | 4,149 | 3,961 | 4,531 |
| Current Liabilities | 2,062 | 1,724 | 1,605 | 1,376 | 1,461 | 1,520 | 1,805 | 1,216 | 1,298 | 1,473 |
| Long Term Debt | 2,924 | 2,045 | 1,649 | 1,731 | 2,056 | 2,299 | 1,552 | 2,397 | 2,391 | 3,436 |
| Common Equity | 1,139 | 1,437 | 1,449 | 1,595 | 1,120 | 594 | 104 | -322 | -560 | -1,163 |
| Total Capital | 4,063 | 3,482 | 3,098 | 3,326 | 3,176 | 2,893 | 1,656 | 2,085 | 1,838 | 2,338 |
| Capital Expenditures | 742 | 614 | 609 | 645 | 663 | 760 | 636 | 572 | 470 | 460 |
| Cash Flow | 1,442 | 1,303 | 1,231 | 1,188 | 1,019 | 953 | 846 | 767 | 1,013 | 862 |
| Current Ratio | 0.7 | 0.5 | 0.5 | 0.5 | 0.6 | 0.5 | 0.3 | 0.6 | 0.4 | 0.4 |
| % Long Term Debt of Capitalization | 71.9 | 58.7 | 53.2 | 52.0 | 64.7 | 79.5 | 93.7 | 115.0 | 130.1 | 147.0 |
| % Net Income of Revenue | 8.7 | 8.6 | 8.2 | 8.2 | 7.4 | 7.5 | 7.1 | 5.8 | 8.0 | 5.3 |
| % Return on Assets | 13.4 | 13.6 | 13.4 | 13.1 | 11.2 | 11.9 | 11.5 | 10.2 | 14.8 | 9.2 |
| % Return on Equity | 70.6 | 57.1 | 50.1 | 54.5 | 72.1 | 167.0 | NM | NM | NM | NM |

Data as orig reptd.; bef. results of disc opers/spec. items. Per share data adj. for stk. divs.; EPS diluted. E-Estimated. NA-Not Available. NM-Not Meaningful. NR-Not Ranked. UR-Under Review.

**Office:** 1441 Gardiner Lane, Louisville, KY 40213.
**Telephone:** 502-874-8300.
**Email:** yum.investors@yum.com
**Website:** http://www.yum.com

**Chrmn, Pres & CEO:** D.C. Novak
**Vice Chrmn:** J.S. Su
**COO:** E.J. Brolick
**SVP, Chief Acctg Officer & Cntlr:** T.F. Knopf

**SVP & General Counsel:** C.L. Campbell
**Investor Contact:** B. Bishop (502-874-8905)
**Board Members:** D. W. Dorman, M. Ferragamo, J. Grissom, B. Hill, R. Holland, Jr., K. G. Langone, J. S. Linen, T. C. Nelson, D. C. Novak, T. M. Ryan, J. S. Su, J. Trujillo, R. D. Walter

**Founded:** 1997
**Domicile:** North Carolina
**Employees:** 301,000

# Zimmer Holdings Inc.

STANDARD &POOR'S

**S&P Recommendation** HOLD ★★★☆☆

| | | |
|---|---|---|
| **Price** $42.00 (as of Nov 14, 2008) | **12-Mo. Target Price** $52.00 | **Investment Style** Large-Cap Growth |

**GICS Sector** Health Care
**Sub-Industry** Health Care Equipment

**Summary** This company, spun off by Bristol-Myers Squibb in August 2001, manufactures orthopedic reconstructive implants, fracture management products and dental implants.

## Key Stock Statistics (Source S&P, Vickers, company reports)

| | | | | | | | | |
|---|---|---|---|---|---|---|---|---|
| 52-Wk Range | $80.92–37.19 | S&P Oper. EPS 2008E | 3.97 | Market Capitalization(B) | $9.432 | Beta | 0.78 |
| Trailing 12-Month EPS | $4.09 | S&P Oper. EPS 2009E | 4.35 | Yield (%) | Nil | S&P 3-Yr. Proj. EPS CAGR(%) | 10 |
| Trailing 12-Month P/E | 10.3 | P/E on S&P Oper. EPS 2008E | 10.6 | Dividend Rate/Share | Nil | S&P Credit Rating | A- |
| $10K Invested 5 Yrs Ago | $6,583 | Common Shares Outstg. (M) | 224.6 | Institutional Ownership (%) | 76 | | |

## Price Performance

30-Week Mov. Avg. ···   10-Week Mov. Avg. – –   GAAP Earnings vs. Previous Year   Volume Above Avg.  STARS
12-Mo. Target Price —   Relative Strength —   ▲ Up  ▼ Down  ▶ No Change   Below Avg.

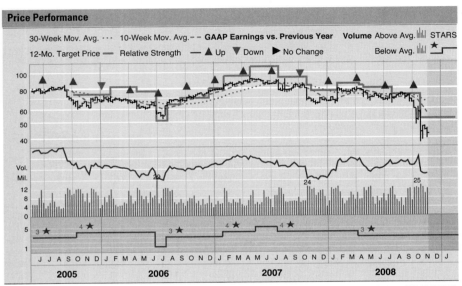

Options: ASE, CBOE, P, Ph

Analysis prepared by **Robert M. Gold** on October 24, 2008, when the stock traded at **$ 39.81**.

## Qualitative Risk Assessment

| LOW | MEDIUM | HIGH |
|---|---|---|

Our risk assessment reflects that Zimmer operates in a highly competitive industry characterized by relatively short product life cycles, thereby requiring a significant number of new product introductions to maintain market share and sustain gross profit margins. Many of the company's customers are reimbursed by the federal government through Medicare, and a more restrictive budgetary environment could, in our view, result in lower prices paid to medical device suppliers such as Zimmer. However, this is offset as we believe the company stands among the dominant manufacturers in the orthopedic device industry, with substantial global salesforce capabilities and an expansive product line.

## Quantitative Evaluations

**S&P Quality Ranking**  NR

| D | C | B- | B | B+ | A- | A | A+ |
|---|---|---|---|---|---|---|---|

**Relative Strength Rank**  MODERATE

43

LOWEST = 1        HIGHEST = 99

## Highlights

➤ We see 2008 revenues of $4.1 billion, up from $3.9 billion in 2007, which assumes reconstructive implant sales of about $3.6 billion, fracture management of $200 million, spine of $190 million and other sales of $170 million. We believe global pricing across the implant space will rise by about 1% in 2008, but think a stronger U.S. dollar, broad economic weakness globally and the loss of some physician customers as the company continues to implement revised consulting practices will lead to lost share in the orthopedic implant markets into 2009. Our 2009 revenue estimate is $4.3 billion.

➤ We believe competition in the hip business will impact unit pricing, and anticipate some margin pressures on international manufacturing expansion, product recalls/suspensions, and related excess manufacturing capacity. We think operating margins in 2008 will be hurt by higher SG&A spending and costs associated with the settlement of a Department of Justice investigation.

➤ Including the dilutive impact of the recently acquired spine unit of Abbott Labs, we see operating EPS of $3.97 for 2008 and $4.35 in 2009.

## Investment Rationale/Risk

➤ Although we anticipate that the company will face challenges generating double digit sales and earnings growth in 2009, we think the long term demand drivers for its orthopedic implants remain intact. In our view, the pace of new product rollouts in 2007 and 2008 was disappointing, especially in the hip and knee areas, but we think the pipeline remains among the best in our orthopedic device coverage universe.

➤ Risks to our recommendation and target price include unfavorable Medicare reimbursement changes and greater than expected device reimbursement cuts in key overseas markets, particularly Japan.

➤ Our 12-month target price is $52, or about 12X our 2009 EPS estimate and 1.2X on a forward P/E-to-growth basis, below peers. In our opinion, competitive pressures, higher R&D spending, costs tied to the DoJ settlement and a higher effective tax rate will continue to impact net margins, and although we expect the operating environment will likely improve by mid-2009, we have concerns regarding the recessionary environment and the company's execution in the implant markets.

## Revenue/Earnings Data

**Revenue (Million $)**

| | 1Q | 2Q | 3Q | 4Q | Year |
|---|---|---|---|---|---|
| 2008 | 1,059 | 1,080 | 952.2 | -- | -- |
| 2007 | 950.2 | 970.6 | 903.2 | 1,074 | 3,898 |
| 2006 | 860.4 | 881.6 | 819.8 | 933.6 | 3,495 |
| 2005 | 828.5 | 846.8 | 762.5 | 848.3 | 3,286 |
| 2004 | 742.2 | 737.4 | 700.2 | 801.1 | 2,981 |
| 2003 | 390.1 | 411.1 | 398.2 | 701.6 | 1,901 |

**Earnings Per Share ($)**

| | 1Q | 2Q | 3Q | 4Q | Year |
|---|---|---|---|---|---|
| 2008 | 1.02 | 0.99 | 0.95 | E1.07 | E3.97 |
| 2007 | 0.98 | 0.97 | 0.19 | 1.12 | 3.26 |
| 2006 | 0.82 | 0.81 | 0.76 | 1.02 | 3.40 |
| 2005 | 0.70 | 0.76 | 0.67 | 0.80 | 2.93 |
| 2004 | 0.40 | 0.47 | 0.52 | 0.81 | 2.19 |
| 2003 | 0.41 | 0.45 | 0.43 | 0.15 | 1.38 |

Fiscal year ended Dec. 31. Next earnings report expected: Late January. EPS Estimates based on S&P Operating Earnings; historical GAAP earnings are as reported.

## Dividend Data

No cash dividends have been paid.

---

# Zimmer Holdings Inc.

STANDARD &POOR'S

## Business Summary October 24, 2008

CORPORATE OVERVIEW. Zimmer Holdings primarily designs, develops, manufactures and markets orthopedic reconstructive implants and fracture management products. The former division of Bristol-Myers Squibb was spun off to BMY shareholders in August 2001.

Zimmer's reconstructive implants (84% of 2007 sales) are used to restore function lost due to disease or trauma in joints such as knees, hips, shoulders and elbows. The company offers a wide range of products for specialized knee procedures, including The NexGen Complete Knee Solution, NexGen Legacy, NexGen Revision Knee, Innex Total Knee System, M/G Unicompartmental Knee System, and Prolong Highly Crosslinked Polyethylene Articular Surface material. Hip replacement products include the VerSys Hip System, the ZMR Hip System, the Trilogy Acetabular System and a line of specialty hip products. The company also continues to develop a portfolio of minimally invasive hip replacement procedures. ZMH sells the Coonrad/Morrey product line of elbow replacement implant products, along with a line of restorative dental products.

In the spine/trauma area (10%), the company sells devices used to reattach or stabilize damaged bone and tissue to support the body's natural healing process. The most common stabilization of bone fractures concerns the internal fixation of bone fragments, which can involve the use of an assortment of plates, screws, rods, wires and pins. ZMH offers a line of products designed for use in fracture fixation. In October 2008, the company acquired the spinal business of Abbott Labs for $360 million in cash.

ZMH makes and markets other orthopedic surgical products (6%) used by surgeons for orthopedic as well as non-orthopedic procedures. Products include tourniquets, blood management systems, wound debridgement products, powered surgical instruments, pain management devices, and orthopedic soft goods that provide support and/or heat retention and compression for trauma of the knee, ankle, back and upper extremities, including the shoulder, elbow, neck and wrist.

## Company Financials Fiscal Year Ended Dec. 31

| Per Share Data ($) | 2007 | 2006 | 2005 | 2004 | 2003 | 2002 | 2001 | 2000 | 1999 | 1998 |
|---|---|---|---|---|---|---|---|---|---|---|
| Tangible Book Value | 9.76 | 7.15 | 7.94 | 2.52 | 0.38 | 1.88 | 0.41 | NM | NA | NA |
| Cash Flow | 4.22 | 4.21 | 3.68 | 2.92 | 1.87 | 1.43 | 0.89 | 0.92 | NA | NA |
| Earnings | 3.26 | 3.40 | 2.93 | 2.19 | 1.38 | 1.31 | 0.77 | 0.81 | 0.78 | NA |
| S&P Core Earnings | 3.94 | 3.36 | 2.73 | 2.08 | 1.31 | 1.24 | 0.70 | NA | NA | NA |
| Dividends | Nil | Nil | Nil | Nil | Nil | Nil | Nil | NA | NA | NA |
| Payout Ratio | Nil | Nil | Nil | Nil | Nil | Nil | Nil | NA | NA | NA |
| Prices:High | 94.38 | 79.11 | 89.10 | 89.44 | 71.85 | 43.00 | 33.30 | NA | NA | NA |
| Prices:Low | 63.00 | 52.20 | 60.19 | 64.40 | 38.02 | 28.00 | 24.70 | NA | NA | NA |
| P/E Ratio:High | 29 | 23 | 30 | 41 | 52 | 33 | 43 | NA | NA | NA |
| P/E Ratio:Low | 19 | 15 | 21 | 29 | 28 | 21 | 32 | NA | NA | NA |

| Income Statement Analysis (Million $) | | | | | | | | | | |
|---|---|---|---|---|---|---|---|---|---|---|
| Revenue | 3,898 | 3,495 | 3,286 | 2,981 | 1,901 | 1,372 | 1,179 | 1,041 | 939 | 861 |
| Operating Income | 1,553 | 1,369 | 1,297 | 1,026 | 633 | 426 | 272 | 291 | NA | NA |
| Depreciation | 230 | 197 | 186 | 181 | 103 | 25.0 | 23.4 | 23.0 | 22.0 | 26.0 |
| Interest Expense | Nil | 4.00 | 14.0 | 32.0 | 13.0 | 12.0 | 7.40 | 29.0 | NA | NA |
| Pretax Income | 1,132 | 1,169 | 1,040 | 732 | 438 | 389 | 241 | 239 | 231 | 211 |
| Effective Tax Rate | 31.6% | 28.5% | 29.5% | 25.9% | 33.6% | 33.7% | 37.8% | 34.3% | 35.1% | 31.3% |
| Net Income | 773 | 835 | 733 | 542 | 291 | 258 | 150 | 157 | 150 | 145 |
| S&P Core Earnings | 936 | 823 | 682 | 515 | 277 | 244 | 137 | NA | NA | NA |

| Balance Sheet & Other Financial Data (Million $) | | | | | | | | | | |
|---|---|---|---|---|---|---|---|---|---|---|
| Cash | 466 | 266 | 233 | 155 | 78.0 | 16.0 | 18.4 | 50.0 | NA | NA |
| Current Assets | 2,083 | 1,746 | 1,576 | 1,561 | 1,339 | 612 | 509 | 487 | NA | NA |
| Total Assets | 6,634 | 5,974 | 5,722 | 5,696 | 5,156 | 859 | 745 | 669 | 606 | NA |
| Current Liabilities | 749 | 628 | 607 | 701 | 645 | 401 | 373 | 217 | NA | NA |
| Long Term Debt | 104 | 100 | 82.0 | 624 | 1,008 | Nil | 214 | 500 | NA | NA |
| Common Equity | 5,450 | 4,921 | 4,683 | 3,943 | 3,143 | 366 | 78.7 | -48.0 | 391 | NA |
| Total Capital | 5,554 | 5,024 | 4,767 | 4,574 | 4,158 | 366 | 293 | 452 | NA | NA |
| Capital Expenditures | 331 | 142 | 105 | 101 | 45.0 | 34.0 | 54.7 | NA | 33.0 | 20.0 |
| Cash Flow | 1,003 | 1,032 | 919 | 723 | 394 | 283 | 173 | 180 | NA | NA |
| Current Ratio | 2.8 | 2.8 | 2.6 | 2.2 | 2.1 | 1.5 | 1.4 | 2.2 | 2.0 | NA |
| % Long Term Debt of Capitalization | 1.8 | 1.9 | 1.7 | 13.6 | 24.2 | Nil | 73.0 | 110.6 | Nil | Nil |
| % Net Income of Revenue | 19.8 | 23.8 | 22.3 | 18.1 | 15.3 | 18.9 | 12.7 | 15.1 | 16.0 | 16.8 |
| % Return on Assets | 12.3 | 14.2 | 12.8 | 9.9 | 9.7 | 32.1 | 22.4 | NA | NA | NA |
| % Return on Equity | 14.9 | 17.3 | 16.9 | 15.2 | 10.6 | 115.0 | NM | NA | NA | NA |

Data as orig reptd.; bef. results of disc opers/spec. items. Per share data adj. for stk. divs.; EPS diluted. E-Estimated. NA-Not Available. NM-Not Meaningful. NR-Not Ranked. UR-Under Review.

**Office:** 345 East Main Street, Warsaw, IN 46580.
**Telephone:** 574-267-6131.
**Email:** zimmer.infoperson@zimmer.com
**Website:** http://www.zimmer.com

**Chrmn:** J.L. McGoldrick
**Pres & CEO:** D.C. Dvorak
**COO:** R.C. Stair
**EVP & CFO:** J.T. Crines

**SVP & CSO:** C.R. Blanchard
**Investor Contact:** P.G. Blair (574-267-6131)
**Board Members:** D. C. Dvorak, L. C. Glasscock, R. A. Hagemann, A. J. Higgins, J. L. McGoldrick, C. B. Pickett, A. A. White, III

**Founded:** 1927
**Domicile:** Delaware
**Employees:** 7,600

STANDARD &POOR'S

# Zions BanCorp

**S&P Recommendation** HOLD ★★★☆☆

**Price**
$32.69 (as of Nov 14, 2008)

**12-Mo. Target Price**
$35.00

**Investment Style**
Large-Cap Blend

**GICS Sector** Financials
**Sub-Industry** Regional Banks

**Summary** ZION has more than 500 full-service banking offices in 10 western states. At December 31, 2007, it had assets of $52.9 billion and deposits of $36.9 billion.

## Key Stock Statistics (Source S&P, Vickers, company reports)

| | | | | | | | |
|---|---|---|---|---|---|---|---|
| 52-Wk Range | **$107.59– 17.53** | S&P Oper. EPS 2008**E** | **2.21** | Market Capitalization(B) | **$3.771** | Beta | **-0.20** |
| Trailing 12-Month EPS | **$2.33** | S&P Oper. EPS 2009**E** | **2.84** | Yield (%) | **3.92** | S&P 3-Yr. Proj. EPS CAGR(%) | **NM** |
| Trailing 12-Month P/E | **14.0** | P/E on S&P Oper. EPS 2008**E** | **14.8** | Dividend Rate/Share | **$1.28** | S&P Credit Rating | **BBB+** |
| $10K Invested 5 Yrs Ago | **$5,813** | Common Shares Outstg. (M) | **115.3** | Institutional Ownership (%) | **86** | | |

## Price Performance

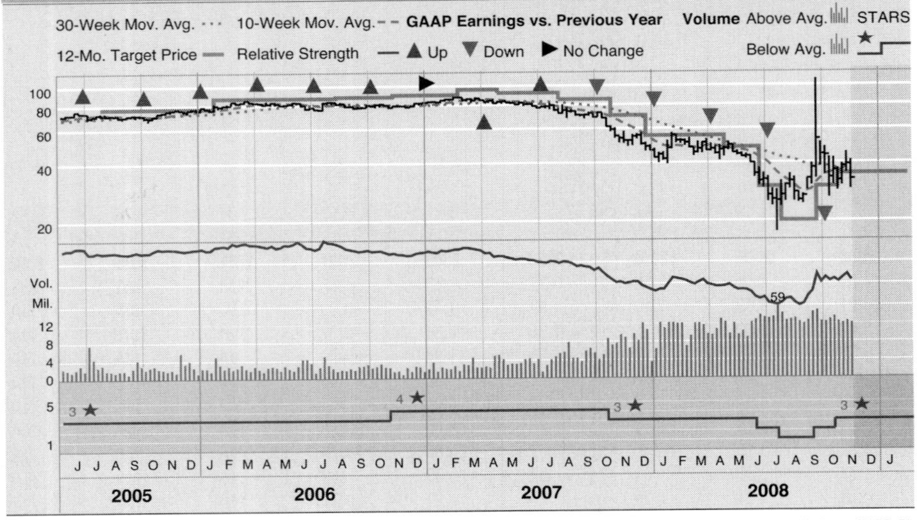


Options: CBOE, Ph

Analysis prepared by **Kevin Cole, CFA** on October 22, 2008, when the stock traded at **$ 32.11**.

## Highlights

- Our 2008 forecasts for ZION are: loan growth of about 6.1%; a 26 basis point reduction in the net interest margin (NIM), to 4.17%; and net interest income growth of 1.7%. We expect revenues to decline slightly due to lower loan rates and the effect of securities impairments on noninterest income.
- Until the third quarter of 2007, ZION's credit quality was among the best in the regional banking industry in our coverage. With the increase in nonperforming loans to 1.83% of total loans at September 30, 2008, from 1.36% at June 30, 2008, we think ZION is under-reserved with the ratio of reserves to nonperforming loans dropping to 80% from roughly 100%. (Ideally, we like to see companies with increasing nonperformers reserving at well over 100% of nonperformers.) We see provisions of roughly $475 million in 2008 and $550 million in 2009, up from $152 million in 2007.
- We project EPS of $2.21 in 2008, down 59% from 2007's EPS of $5.39. We forecast 2009 EPS of $2.84. We do not expect any share repurchases in 2008.

## Investment Rationale/Risk

- We recently upgraded the shares to hold, from sell, based on the potential impact of the Treasury's Troubled Asset Relief Program (TARP) on the company's ability to make acquisitions and grow its loan portfolio. ZION plans to apply for between $500 million and $1.5 billion in TARP funds. As a relatively large, profitable bank with a strong footprint in the troubled Southwest region, ZION is a good candidate to receive funds, in our view. In addition, ZION recently raised $250.0 million in common equity in a tough capital raising environment, and received the deposits of a failed bank in Nevada. However, we still expect commercial loans to weaken throughout 2008 and 2009, leading ZION to take significantly higher provisions.
- Risks to our recommendation and target price include the Treasury declining ZION's request for TARP funds, and larger-than-expected securities write-downs.
- Our 12-month target price of $35 is based on a forward P/E multiple of about 12.3X our 2009 EPS estimate of $2.84, above the multiple at which we estimate ZION's mid-cap regional banking peers currently trade, reflecting ZION's relatively strong capital position.

## Qualitative Risk Assessment

| LOW | MEDIUM | **HIGH** |
|---|---|---|

Our risk assessment reflects the company's credit exposure to housing and commercial real estate in California, Arizona and Nevada, and recent capital raising difficulties.

## Quantitative Evaluations

**S&P Quality Ranking** **A**

| D | C | B- | B | B+ | A- | **A** | A+ |
|---|---|---|---|---|---|---|---|

**Relative Strength Rank** **STRONG**

75

LOWEST = 1 HIGHEST = 99

## Revenue/Earnings Data

**Revenue (Million $)**

| | 1Q | 2Q | 3Q | 4Q | Year |
|---|---|---|---|---|---|
| 2008 | 901.1 | 795.3 | 825.3 | -- | -- |
| 2007 | 915.9 | 931.0 | 963.6 | 807.3 | 3,776 |
| 2006 | 767.1 | 824.1 | 876.9 | 901.2 | 3,369 |
| 2005 | 525.8 | 562.3 | 594.5 | 666.5 | 2,349 |
| 2004 | 457.4 | 469.8 | 492.6 | 503.3 | 1,923 |
| 2003 | 445.7 | 454.3 | 539.6 | 449.8 | 1,889 |

**Earnings Per Share ($)**

| | 1Q | 2Q | 3Q | 4Q | Year |
|---|---|---|---|---|---|
| 2008 | 0.98 | 0.65 | 0.31 | **E**0.27 | **E**2.21 |
| 2007 | 1.36 | 1.43 | 1.22 | 0.40 | 4.42 |
| 2006 | 1.28 | 1.35 | 1.42 | 1.32 | 5.36 |
| 2005 | 1.20 | 1.30 | 1.34 | 1.32 | 5.16 |
| 2004 | 1.10 | 1.09 | 1.13 | 1.15 | 4.47 |
| 2003 | 0.96 | 1.02 | 0.71 | 1.05 | 3.74 |

Fiscal year ended Dec. 31. Next earnings report expected: Late January. EPS Estimates based on S&P Operating Earnings; historical GAAP earnings are as reported.

## Dividend Data (Dates: mm/dd Payment Date: mm/dd/yy)

| Amount ($) | Date Decl. | Ex-Div. Date | Stk. of Record | Payment Date |
|---|---|---|---|---|
| 0.430 | 01/24 | 02/04 | 02/06 | 02/20/08 |
| 0.430 | 04/24 | 05/05 | 05/07 | 05/21/08 |
| 0.430 | 07/18 | 08/04 | 08/06 | 08/20/08 |
| 0.320 | 10/28 | 11/03 | 11/05 | 11/19/08 |

Dividends have been paid since 1966. Source: Company reports.

**Please read the Required Disclosures and Analyst Certification on the last page of this report.**

# Zions BanCorp

STANDARD
&POOR'S

## Business Summary October 22, 2008

CORPORATE OVERVIEW. ZION is a financial holding company that operates eight different banks in 10 western states, with each bank operating as an individual segment under a different name and management. In addition, the company's Other segment contains the parent company operations, certain nonbank subsidiaries and operating units, The Commerce Bank of Oregon, and eliminations of transactions between segments.

The company's largest bank, Zions First National Bank, serves Utah and Idaho and accounted for 34% of loans and 32% of deposits at year-end 2007. ZFNB also houses the company's capital markets and wealth management operations. California Bank & Trust (20% of loans and 21% of deposits) serves California and has loan production offices in Arizona, Colorado, Florida, Georgia, Illinois, Michigan, Missouri, Nevada, Ohio, Oregon and Washington. Amegy Corporation (20% of loans and 22% of deposits), acquired in December 2005, serves Houston and Dallas, Texas. National Bank of Arizona (12% of loans and

10% of deposits) serves the Phoenix and Tucson metropolitan areas. Nevada State Bank (8% of loans and 8% of deposits) serves the state of Nevada. Vectra Bank Colorado (5% of loans and 5% of deposits) serves Colorado. The Commerce Bank of Washington (1% of loans and 2% of deposits) has one office in the Seattle area serving businesses, executives, and professionals.

The company tries to control risks by maintaining formal loan policies and procedures, independent compliance examinations of adherence to the policies and procedures, performing portfolio risk analysis, using financial instruments to reduce interest rate risk, and by pursuing a loan portfolio diversification strategy.

## Company Financials Fiscal Year Ended Dec. 31

| Per Share Data ($) | 2007 | 2006 | 2005 | 2004 | 2003 | 2002 | 2001 | 2000 | 1999 | 1998 |
|---|---|---|---|---|---|---|---|---|---|---|
| Tangible Book Value | 27.02 | 25.15 | 20.45 | 23.29 | 20.96 | 17.21 | 15.19 | 13.06 | 11.61 | 9.44 |
| Earnings | 4.42 | 5.36 | 5.16 | 4.47 | 3.74 | 3.44 | 3.15 | 1.86 | 2.26 | 1.91 |
| S&P Core Earnings | 4.46 | 5.36 | 5.04 | 4.33 | 4.42 | 3.17 | 2.42 | NA | NA | NA |
| Dividends | 1.68 | 1.47 | 1.44 | 1.26 | 1.02 | 0.80 | 0.80 | 0.89 | 0.86 | 0.52 |
| Payout Ratio | 38% | 27% | 28% | 28% | 27% | 23% | 25% | 48% | 38% | 27% |
| Prices:High | 88.56 | 85.25 | 77.67 | 69.29 | 63.86 | 59.65 | 64.00 | 62.88 | 75.88 | 62.50 |
| Prices:Low | 45.70 | 75.13 | 63.33 | 54.08 | 39.31 | 34.14 | 42.30 | 32.00 | 48.25 | 37.88 |
| P/E Ratio:High | 20 | 16 | 15 | 16 | 17 | 17 | 20 | 34 | 34 | 33 |
| P/E Ratio:Low | 10 | 14 | 12 | 12 | 11 | 10 | 13 | 17 | 21 | 20 |

| Income Statement Analysis (Million $) | | | | | | | | | | |
|---|---|---|---|---|---|---|---|---|---|---|
| Net Interest Income | 1,882 | 1,765 | 1,361 | 1,174 | 1,095 | 1,035 | 950 | 803 | 741 | 544 |
| Tax Equivalent Adjustment | 26.1 | 24.3 | 21.1 | NA | NA | NA | NA | NA | 16.2 | 8.84 |
| Non Interest Income | 395 | 527 | 439 | 425 | 426 | 402 | 388 | 274 | 270 | 199 |
| Loan Loss Provision | 152 | 72.6 | 43.0 | 44.1 | 69.9 | 71.9 | 73.2 | 31.8 | 18.0 | 12.2 |
| % Expense/Operating Revenue | 61.7% | 57.4% | 56.4% | 57.8% | 63.7% | 59.8% | 63.9% | 75.9% | 66.4% | 68.3% |
| Pretax Income | 738 | 913 | 742 | 624 | 546 | 481 | 440 | 243 | 309 | 218 |
| Effective Tax Rate | 32.0% | 34.8% | 35.5% | 35.3% | 39.1% | 34.9% | 35.8% | 32.8% | 35.5% | 32.5% |
| Net Income | 494 | 583 | 480 | 406 | 340 | 317 | 290 | 162 | 194 | 147 |
| % Net Interest Margin | 4.43 | 4.63 | 4.58 | 4.32 | 4.45 | 4.56 | 4.64 | 4.27 | 4.31 | 4.60 |
| S&P Core Earnings | 483 | 579 | 469 | 394 | 402 | 292 | 223 | NA | NA | NA |

| Balance Sheet & Other Financial Data (Million $) | | | | | | | | | | |
|---|---|---|---|---|---|---|---|---|---|---|
| Money Market Assets | 1,500 | 369 | 667 | 593 | 569 | 543 | 280 | 528 | 525 | 804 |
| Investment Securities | 6,895 | 6,790 | 6,996 | 5,786 | 5,402 | 4,238 | 3,463 | 4,188 | 4,437 | 3,488 |
| Commercial Loans | 31,508 | 27,559 | 23,122 | 16,337 | 10,404 | 13,648 | 4,110 | 3,615 | 3,311 | 2,905 |
| Other Loans | 7,744 | 7,260 | 7,131 | 6,395 | 9,613 | 5,195 | 13,304 | 10,843 | 9,133 | 7,777 |
| Total Assets | 52,947 | 46,970 | 42,780 | 31,470 | 28,558 | 26,566 | 24,304 | 21,939 | 20,281 | 16,649 |
| Demand Deposits | 24,430 | 25,869 | 9,954 | 6,822 | 5,883 | 5,117 | 4,481 | 3,586 | 3,277 | 3,170 |
| Time Deposits | 12,492 | 9,113 | 22,689 | 16,471 | 15,014 | 15,015 | 13,361 | 11,484 | 10,786 | 8,622 |
| Long Term Debt | 2,815 | 2,495 | 2,746 | 1,919 | 1,843 | 1,310 | 781 | 420 | 453 | 511 |
| Common Equity | 5,053 | 4,747 | 4,237 | 2,790 | 2,540 | 2,374 | 2,281 | 1,779 | 1,660 | 1,014 |
| % Return on Assets | 1.0 | 1.3 | 1.3 | 2.0 | 1.2 | 1.2 | 1.3 | 0.8 | 1.0 | 1.1 |
| % Return on Equity | 9.8 | 12.9 | 13.7 | 15.2 | 13.8 | 13.6 | 14.3 | 9.4 | 12.5 | 17.6 |
| % Loan Loss Reserve | 1.2 | 1.1 | 1.1 | 1.2 | 0.9 | 1.4 | 1.5 | 1.3 | 1.6 | 1.9 |
| % Loans/Deposits | 103.1 | 99.1 | 92.3 | 97.1 | 142.6 | 96.0 | 97.0 | 96.6 | 91.0 | 79.8 |
| % Equity to Assets | 9.8 | 10.0 | 9.5 | 13.3 | 8.9 | 9.2 | 8.8 | 8.1 | 8.1 | 6.4 |

Data as orig reptd.; bef. results of disc opers/spec. items. Per share data adj. for stk. divs.; EPS diluted. E-Estimated. NA-Not Available. NM-Not Meaningful. NR-Not Ranked. UR-Under Review.

Office: 1 S Main St 15th Fl, Salt Lake City, UT, USA 84111-1904.
Telephone: 801-524-4787.
Website: http://www.zionsbancorporation.com
Chrmn, Pres & CEO: H.H. Simmons

EVP & CFO: D. Arnold
EVP, Secy & General Counsel: T.E. Laursen
EVP & CIO: J.T. Itokazu
SVP, Chief Acctg Officer & Cntlr: N.X. Bellon

Investor Contact: C.B. Hinckley (801-524-4787)
Board Members: J. C. Atkin, R. D. Cash, P. Frobes, J. D. Heaney, R. B. Porter, S. D. Quinn, H. H. Simmons, L. E. Simmons, S. Wheelwright, S. T. Williams

Founded: 1961
Domicile: Utah
Employees: 10,933

The McGraw-Hill Companies